Schedule
on hot Regents
Days pupils
4-5:00

The Longman Anthology
of British Literature

Compact Edition

Literature
course

Electives
History of Cinema
Women's Literature

PSS
If they
have room
on their
program...

Art Courses
Interiors   Oral Comment
Cartooning -
Art - photo - reg
Painting
Fashion - How to Design
2-3
Writing workshop 221 - Miscellaneous
Course -

THE MIDDLE AGES
Christopher Baswell   Anne Howland Schotter
Barnard College   *Wagner College*

THE EARLY MODERN PERIOD
Constance Jordan   Clare Carroll
Claremont Graduate University   *Queens College, CUNY*

THE RESTORATION AND THE 18TH CENTURY
Stuart Sherman
Fordham University

THE ROMANTICS AND THEIR CONTEMPORARIES
Susan Wolfson   Peter Manning
Princeton University   *University of Southern California*

THE VICTORIAN AGE
Heather Henderson   William Sharpe
Mount Holyoke College   *Barnard College*

THE TWENTIETH CENTURY
Kevin Dettmar   Jennifer Wicke
Southern Illinois University   *University of Virginia*

The Longman Anthology of British Literature

Compact Edition

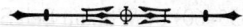

David Damrosch
Columbia University

General Editor

LONGMAN

An imprint of Addison Wesley Longman, Inc.

New York • Reading, Massachusetts • Menlo Park, California • Harlow, England
Don Mills, Ontario • Sydney • Mexico City • Madrid • Amsterdam

Editorial Director: *Richard Wohl*
Development Editor: *Mark Getlein*
Senior Marketing Manager: *Melanie Goulet*
Supplements Editor: *Donna Campion*
Senior Production Manager: *Valerie Zaborski*
Project Coordination: *Dora Rizzuto*
Electronic Page Makeup: *Sarah Johnson* and *Heather A. Peres*
Senior Cover Design Manager: *Nancy Danahy*
Cover Designer: *Kay Petronio*
On the Cover: *Iron and Coal* (c. 1855–60) by William Bell Scott, The National Trust,
    Trevelyan Collection, Wallington Hall, Morpeth, U. K.
Photo Researcher: *Julie Tesser*
Publishing Services Manager: *Al Dorsey*
Senior Print Buyer: *Hugh Crawford*
Printer and Binder: *World Color Book Services*
Cover Printer: *The Lehigh Press, Inc.*

For permission to use copyrighted material, grateful acknowledgment is made to the copyright
holders on pages pages 2667–2670, which are hereby made part of this copyright page.

Library of Congress Cataloging-in-Publication Data

The Longman anthology of British literature: compact edition / David Damrosch, general
    editor.
        p.   cm.
    Includes bibliographical references and indexes.
    Contents: v. A. The Middle Ages / Christopher Baswell and Anne Howland
Schotter. The early modern period / Constance Jordan and Clare
Carroll. The Restoration and the 18th century / Stuart Sherman —
v. B. The romantics and their contemporaries / Susan Wolfson and Peter
Manning. The Victorian age / Heather Henderson and William Sharpe.
The twentieth century / Kevin Dettmar and Jennifer Wicke.
    1. English literature.   2. Great Britain—Literary collections.
I. Damrosch, David.

ISBN 0-321-07670-2 (Single Volume Edition)
ISBN 0-321-07672-9 (Volume A)
ISBN 0-321-07673-7 (Volume B)

1 2 3 4 5 6 7 8 9 0–WC–02010099

CONTENTS

The Early Modern Period   361

The Restoration and the Eighteenth Century   905

The Romantics and Their Contemporaries   1313

The Victorian Age   1783

The Twentieth Century   2165

THOMAS HARDY   2254

PERSPECTIVES: THE GREAT WAR: CONFRONTING THE MODERN   2264

SPEECHES ON IRISH INDEPENDENCE   2312

PREFACE

This is an exciting time to be reading British literature. Literary studies are experiencing a time of transformation, involving lively debate about the nature of literature itself, its relations to the wider culture, and the best ways to read and understand it. These questions have been sharpened by the "culture wars" of recent years, in which traditionalists have debated advocates of fundamental reform, close readers have come up against cultural theorists who may seem more interested in politics than in aesthetic questions, and lovers of canonical texts have found themselves sharing the stage with multiculturalists who typically focus on ethnic and minority literatures, usually contemporary and often popular in nature, rather than on earlier and more elite literary productions.

The goal of this anthology is to present the wealth of British literature, old and new, classic and newly current, in ways that will respond creatively to these debates. We have constructed this anthology in the firm belief that it is important to attend both to aesthetic and to cultural questions as we study literature, and to continue to read the great classics even as we discover or rediscover new or neglected works. Admittedly, it is difficult to do all this at once, especially within the pages of a single anthology or the time constraints of a survey course. To work toward these goals, it has been necessary to rethink the very form of an anthology. This preface can serve as a kind of road map to the many pages that follow.

A NEW LITERARY GEOGRAPHY

Let us begin by defining our basic terms: What is "British" literature? What is literature itself? And just what is the function of an anthology at the present time? The term "British" can mean many things, some of them contradictory, some of them even offensive to people on whom the name has been imposed. If the term has no ultimate essence, it does have a history. The first British were Celtic people who inhabited the British Isles and the northern coast of France (still called Brittany), before various Germanic tribes of Angles and Saxons moved onto the islands in the fifth and sixth centuries. Gradually the Angles and Saxons amalgamated into the Anglo-Saxon culture that became dominant in the southern and eastern regions of Britain and then spread outward; the old British people were pushed west, toward what became known as Cornwall, Wales, and Ireland, which remained independent kingdoms for centuries, as did Celtic Scotland to the north. By an ironic twist of linguistic fate, the Anglo-Saxons began to appropriate the term British from the Britons they had displaced, and they took as a national hero the legendary Welsh King Arthur. By the seventeenth century, English monarchs had extended their sway over Wales, Ireland, and Scotland, and they began to refer to their holdings as "Great Britain." Today, Great Britain includes England, Wales, Scotland, and Northern Ireland, but does not include the Republic of Ireland, which has been independent from England since 1922.

This anthology uses "British" in a broad sense, as a geographical term encompassing the whole of the British Isles. For all its fraught history, it seems a more satisfactory term than to speak simply of "English" literature, for two reasons. First: most speakers of English live in countries that are not the focus of this anthology; second, while the English language and its literature have long been dominant in the British Isles, other cultures in the region have always used other languages and have produced great literature in these languages. Important works by Irish, Welsh, and Scots writers appear regularly in the body of this anthology, some of them written directly in their languages and presented here in translation, others written in an English inflected by the rhythms, habits of thought, and modes of expression characteristic of these other languages and the people who use them. Important works, moreover, have often been written in the British Isles by recent arrivals, from Marie de France in the twelfth century to T. S. Eliot and Salman Rushdie in the twentieth; in a very real sense, their writings too are part of British literary production.

We use the term "literature" itself in a similarly capacious sense, to refer to a range of artistically shaped works written in a charged language, appealing to the imagination at least as much as to discursive reasoning. It is only relatively recently that creative writers have been able to make a living composing poems, plays, and novels purely "for art's sake," and only in the past hundred years or so have "belles lettres" or works of high literary art been thought of as sharply separate from other sorts of writing that the same authors would regularly produce. Sometimes, Romantic poets wrote sonnets to explore the deepest mysteries of individual perception and memory; at other times, they wrote sonnets the way a person might now write an Op-Ed piece, and such a sonnet would be published and read along with parliamentary debates and letters to the editor on the most pressing contemporary issues.

Great literature is double in nature: it is deeply rooted in its cultural moment, and yet it transcends this moment as well, speaking to new readers in distant times and places, long after the immediate circumstances of its production have been forgotten. The challenge today is to restore our awareness of cultural contexts without trapping our texts within them. Great writers create imaginative worlds that have their own compelling internal logic, built around the stories they tell using formal patterns of genre, literary reference, imagery, and style. At the same time, as Virginia Woolf says in *A Room of One's Own,* the gossamer threads of the artist's web are joined to reality "with bands of steel." To understand where a writer is taking us imaginatively, it is helpful to know where we are supposed to be starting from in reality: any writer assumes a common body of current knowledge, which this anthology attempts to fill in by means of detailed period introductions, full introductions to the individual authors, and notes and glosses to each text. Many of the greatest works of literature, moreover, have been written in response to the most sharply contested issues of the authors' own times. This anthology presents and groups selections in such a way as to suggest the literary and cultural contexts in which, and for which, they were created.

WOMEN'S WRITING, AND MEN'S

Literary culture has always involved an interplay between central and marginal regions, groups, and individuals. At a given time, some will seem dominant; in retrospect, some will remain so and others will be eclipsed, for a time or permanently, while formerly neglected writers may achieve a new currency. A major emphasis in literary study in recent years has been the recovery of writing by a range of women writers, some of them little read until recently, others major figures in their time and now again fascinating to read. Attending to the voices of such compelling writers as Katherine Philips, Aphra Behn, Mary Wollstonecraft, and Elizabeth Bowen often involves a shift in our understanding of the literary landscape, giving a new and live-ly perspective on much-read works. On a larger scale, the first third of the nine-teenth century can be defined more broadly than as a "Romantic Age" dominated by six male poets; looking closely at women's writing as well as men's, and at prose writing as well as poetry, we can deepen our understanding of the period as a whole—including the specific achievements of Blake, William Wordsworth, Coleridge, Keats, Percy Shelley, and Byron, all of whom continue to have a major presence in these pages as most of them did during the nineteenth century.

HISTORICAL PERIODS IN PERSPECTIVE

Overall, we have sought to give a varied presentation of the major periods of liter-ary history, as customarily construed by scholars today: the Middle Ages (punctuat-ed by the Norman Conquest in 1066); the early modern period or Renaissance; the Restoration and the eighteenth century; the era of the Romantics and their con-temporaries; the Victorian age; and the twentieth century. These names mix chronology, politics, and literary movements: each period is of course a mixture of all of these elements and many others. Further, the boundaries of all these periods are fluid. Milton, for instance, should be thought of in the context of Restoration politics as well as of early modern humanism. In general, one of the great pleasures of a survey of centuries of British literary production is the opportunity to see the ways texts speak to one another both across periods and within them, and indeed several layers of time may coexist within a single era: many writers consciously or unconsciously hearken back to earlier values (there were medievalists in the nineteenth century), while other writers cast "shadows of futurity" before them, in Percy Shelley's phrase.

Within periods, we have sought a variety of means to suggest the many linkages that make up a rich literary culture, which is something more than a sequence of individual writers all producing their separate bodies of work. In this anthology, each period includes several groupings called "Perspectives," with texts that address an important literary or social issue of the time. These Perspective sections typically illuminate underlying issues in a variety of the major works of their time, as with a section on Arthurian myth that relates broadly to Marie de France, to *Gawain and the Green Knight*, and to Malory's *Morte Darthur*. Most of the writers included in Per-spective sections are important period figures, less well known today, who might be neglected if they were listed on their own with just a few pages each; grouping them together should be useful pedagogically as well as intellectually. Perspective sections may also include writing by a major author whose primary listing appears elsewhere in the period (Wordsworth on slavery, Dickens on industry), so as to give a rounded presentation of the issues in ways that can inform the reading of those authors in their individual sections.

WORKS IN CONTEXT

Periodically throughout the anthology we also present major works "In Context," to show the terms of a specific debate to which an author is responding. Thus Sir Philip Sidney's great *Apology for Poetry* is accompanied by a context section to show the controversy that was raging at the time concerning the nature and value of poetry. Additionally, we include "Companion Readings" to present specific prior texts to which a work is responding: when Sir Thomas Wyatt creates a beautiful poem, *The Long Love, That in My Thought Doth Harbor*, by making a free translation of a Petrarch sonnet, we include Petrarch's original (and a more literal translation) as a companion reading. For Conrad's *Heart of Darkness*, companion texts include Conrad's diary of the Congo journey on which he based his novella, and a bizarre lecture by Sir Henry Morton Stanley, the explorer-adventurer whose travel writings Conrad parodies.

ILLUSTRATING VISUAL CULTURE

Literature has always been a product of cultures that are visual as well as verbal. We include many illustrations in the body of the anthology, presenting artistic and cultural images that figured importantly for literary creation. Sometimes, a poem refers to a specific painting, or more generally emulates qualities of a school of visual art. At other times, photographs, advertisements, or political cartoons can set the stage for literary works. In some cases, visual and literary creation have merged, as in Hogarth's series *A Rake's Progress*, or Blake's engravings of his *Songs of Innocence and Experience*.

Our cover illustration, *Iron and Coal*, by the Scottish painter William Bell Scott, is an excellent instance of a beautiful image that illustrates both the artistic and the social culture of its times. Scott (1811–1890) was a poet as well as a painter, a lifelong friend of the poet-painter Dante Gabriel Rossetti and a member of the Pre-Raphaelite circle. In 1857 he was asked by Sir Walter and Lady Pauline Trevelyan to create a cycle of paintings for the central hall of Wallington House, their home in Northumberland, in the north of England. Depicting scenes from Northumberland history, the cycle begins with *The Building of the Roman Wall* and culminates with *Iron and Coal*, one of the earliest artistic celebrations of the new commercial world made possible through scientific and industrial progress. The view from the factory— a picture within a picture—portrays a bustling port with a train passing overhead. Inside, heroically proportioned "strikers" emphasize the immense human labor that underlies industrial work. Caught in mid-swing, they could almost be one striker in a multiple-exposure photograph, a kind of image that would soon be produced in the astonishing photographs of motion by the Victorian photographer Eadweard Muybridge. The pose also suggests that the men themselves are merging with the machinery that underlies England's future prosperity. One of the strikers is in fact a portrait of an heir to Wallington House. The actual owner of the factory is represented in turn by his own children. The boy surveys the world he will literally inherit. The girl is reading a book, but she pauses, looking out from her world into ours.

AIDS TO UNDERSTANDING

We have tried to contextualize our selections in a suggestive rather than an exhaustive way, wishing to enhance rather than overwhelm the experience of reading the texts themselves. Our introductions to periods and authors are intended to open up ways of reading rather than dictating a particular interpretation, and the suggestions presented here should always be seen as points of departure rather than definitive pronouncements. We have striven for clarity and ease of use in our editorial matter. Thus, when difficult or archaic words need defining in poems, we use glosses in the margins, in all periods, so as to disrupt the reader's eye as little as possible; footnotes are intended to be concise and informative, rather than massive or interpretive. Spelling and punctuation are modernized through the eighteenth century, except when older forms are important for meter or rhyme, and with general exceptions for certain major writers, like Chaucer and Spenser, whose specific usages are crucial to their understanding. Important literary and social terms are defined when they are used. For further reading, carefully selected bibliographies for each period and for each author can be found at the end of the volume.

VARIETIES OF LITERARY EXPERIENCE

Above all, we have striven to give as full a presentation as possible within the boundaries of a compact edition to the varieties of great literature produced over the centuries in the British Isles, by women as well as by men, in outlying regions as well as in the metropolitan center of London, and in prose, drama, and verse alike. In making our selections for this compact edition from the six thousand pages of the full *Longman Anthology*, we have chosen the best-loved and most often taught works of the classic major authors, together with a range of the most compelling newly-recovered writing we know. We have striven to show the wealth and the variety of the literary culture of the British Isles over the centuries, from medieval works like *Beowulf* and the lyrics of the trenchantly witty Dafydd ap Gwilym to the powerful contemporary voices of Philip Larkin, Seamus Heaney, Nuala Ní Dhomhnaill, and Derek Walcott— himself a product of colonial British education, heir of Shakespeare and James Joyce, who closes the anthology with poems about Englishness abroad and foreignness in Britain.

As topical as these contemporary writers are, we hope that this anthology will show that the great works of earlier centuries can also speak to us compellingly today, their value only increased by the resistance they offer to our views of ourselves and our world. To read and reread the full sweep of this literature is to be struck anew by the degree to which the most radically new works are rooted in centuries of prior innovation. Even this preface can close in no better way than by quoting the words written eighteen hundred years ago by Apuleius—both a consummate artist and a kind of anthologist of extraordinary tales—when he concluded the prologue to his masterpiece *The Golden Ass:* Attend, reader, and pleasure is yours.

David Damrosch

ACKNOWLEDGMENTS

In preparing this new version of our anthology, the editors have benefited enormously from advice and support of many kinds. Our first debt is to Rich Wohl, Editorial Director at Longman's College Division, who has given the project unfailing and indeed ebullient support, seconded by that of Roth Wilkofsky, the head of the division. Our editors Janice Wiggins Clarke, at the start of the process, and Laura McKenna more recently, have helped us refine our work, and as with the original anthology, we benefited greatly from the advice, and the art-historical knowledge, of our developmental editor, Mark Getlein. Melanie Goulet and her associates have been working creatively and effectively to bring both versions of the anthology to our audience.

In producing the volume, Stephanie Argeros-Magean oversaw copyediting with her characteristic lucidity and good judgment. Val Zaborski, Dora Rizzuto, and their associates handled thousands of pages of marked-up text, and a very challenging production schedule, with sunny good humor and exceptional care. Robert Ravas and his associates cleared our hundreds of permissions requests, and Julie Tesser secured our illustrations.

In deciding which works to select for this compact edition, we were guided by the thoughtful advice of colleagues both in the United States and in Canada, who often took time to give us very detailed responses to our draft table of contents. We owe hearty thanks to Rosemary Allen (Georgetown College), Matthew C. Brennen (Indiana State University), Gregory Chaplin (University of Texas, Austin), Robert Christopher (Ramapo University), Michael Delahoyde (Washington State University), Laura Fascik (Moorhead State University), Joan Haahr (Yeshiva University), Tony Harrison (North Carolina State University), Nelson Hilton (University of Georgia, Athens), Glenn Hopp (Howard Payne University), Stewart Justman (University of Montana, Missoula), Maurine Magliocco (Western Illinois University), Jean LeDre Metcalfe (Wilfrid Laurier University), Doris Miller (McMurry University), Lanier R. Parks, Jr. (Radford University), Elizabeth Sauer (Brock University), Daniel R. Schwarz (Cornell University), Richard C. Taylor (East Carolina University), Rob Watson (Grand Valley State University), and Carlson Yost (Shawnee State University).

The present volume continues to bear the mark of the excellent advice we received from many colleagues as we prepared the full anthology from which this edition is drawn. We wish to express our ongoing gratitude to Lucien Agosta (California State University, Sacramento), Anne W. Astell (Purdue University), Derek Attridge (Rutgers University), Linda Austin (Oklahoma State University), Joseph Bartolomeo (University of Massachusetts, Amherst), Todd Bender (University of Wisconsin, Madison), Bruce Boehrer (Florida State University), Joel J. Brattin (Worcester Polytechnic Institute), James Campbell (University of Central Florida), J. Douglas Canfield (University of Arizona), Paul A. Cantor (University of Virginia), George Allan Cate (University of Maryland, College Park), Eugene R. Cunnar (New Mexico State University), Earl Dachslager (University of Houston), Elizabeth Davis (University of California, Davis), Andrew Elfenbein (University of Minnesota),

Margaret Ferguson (University of California, Davis), Sandra K. Fisher (State University of New York, Albany), Allen J. Frantzen (Loyola University, Chicago), Kate Garder Frost (University of Texas), Leon Gottfried (Purdue University), Mark L. Greenberg (Drexel University), James Hala (Drew University), Wayne Hall (University of Cincinnati), Wendell Harris (Pennsylvania State University), Richard H. Haswell (Washington State University), Susan Sage Heinzelman (University of Texas, Austin), Standish Henning (University of Wisconsin, Madison), Jack W. Herring (Baylor University), Maurice Hunt (Baylor University), Colleen Juarretche (University of California, Los Angeles), R. B. Kershner (University of Florida), Lisa Klein (Ohio State University), Rita S. Kranidis (Radford University), Elizabeth B. Loizeaux (University of Maryland), John J. Manning (University of Connecticut), Michael B. McDonald (Iowa State University), Celia Millward (Boston University), Thomas C. Moser, Jr. (University of Maryland), Jude V. Nixon (Baylor University), Violet O'Valle (Tarrant County Junior College, Texas), Richard Pearce (Wheaton College), Renée Pigeon (California State University, San Bernardino), Tadeusz Pioro (Southern Methodist University), Deborah Preston (Dekalb College), Elizabeth Robertson (University of Colorado), Deborah Rogers (University of Maine), Brian Rosenberg (Allegheny College), Charles Ross (Purdue University), Harry Rusche (Emory University), Kenneth D. Shields (Southern Methodist University), Clare A. Simmons (Ohio State University), Sally Slocum (University of Akron), Phillip Snyder (Brigham Young University), Isabel Bonnyman Stanley (East Tennessee University), Margaret Sullivan (University of California, Los Angeles), Herbert Sussmann (Northeastern University), Ronald R. Thomas (Trinity College), Theresa Tinkle (University of Michigan), William A. Ulmer (University of Alabama), Jennifer A. Wagner (University of Memphis), Anne D. Wallace (University of Southern Mississippi), Jackie Walsh (McNeese State University, Louisiana), John Watkins (University of Minnesota), Martin Wechselblatt (University of Cincinnati), Arthur Weitzman (Northeastern University), Bonnie Wheeler (Southern Methodist University), Dennis L. Williams (Central Texas College), and Paula Woods (Baylor University).

Other colleages brought our developing book into the classroom, teaching from portions of the work-in-progress while it was still in page proof. Our thanks for classroom testing to Lisa Abney (Northwestern State University), Charles Lynn Batten (University of California, Los Angeles), Brenda Riffe Brown (College of the Mainland, Texas), John Brugaletta (California State University, Fullerton), Dan Butcher (Southeastern Louisiana University), Lynn Byrd (Southern University at New Orleans), David Cowles (Brigham Young University), Sheila Drain (John Carroll University), Lawrence Frank (University of Oklahoma), Leigh Garrison (Virginia Polytechnic Institute), David Griffin (New York University), Rita Harkness (Virginia Commonwealth University), Linda Kissler (Westmoreland County Community College, Pennsylvania), Brenda Lewis (Motlow State Community College, Tennessee), Paul Lizotte (River College), Wayne Luckman (Green River Community College, Washington), Arnold Markely (Pennsylvania State University, Delaware County), James McKusick (University of Maryland, Baltimore), Eva McManus (Ohio Northern University), Manuel Moyrao (Old Dominion University), Kate Palguta (Shawnee State University, Ohio), Paul Puccio (University of Central Florida), Sarah Polito (Cape Cod Community College), Meredith Poole (Virginia West-

The Middle Ages

At the present time, there are five languages in Britain, just as the divine law is written in five books, all devoted to seeking out and setting forth one and the same kind of wisdom, namely the knowledge of sublime truth and of true sublimity. These are the English, British, Irish, Pictish, as well as the Latin languages; through the study of the scriptures, Latin is in general use among them all.

Bede, *Ecclesiastical History of the English People*

The Venerable Bede's famous and enormously influential *Ecclesiastical History of the English People,* written in the early 700s, reflects a double triumph. First, its very title acknowledges the dominance by Bede's day of the Anglo-Saxons, who, centuries earlier, had established themselves on an island already inhabited by Celtic Britons and by Picts. Second, the Latin of Bede's text and his own life as a monk point to the presence of ancient Mediterranean influences in the British Isles, earlier through Rome's military colonization of ancient Britain and later through the conversion of Bede's people to Roman Christianity.

In this first chapter of his first book, Bede shows a complex awareness of the several populations still active in Britain and often resisting or encroaching on Anglo-Saxon rule, and much of his *History* narrates the successive waves of invaders and missionaries who had brought their languages, governments, cultures, and beliefs to his island. This initial emphasis on peoples and languages should not be taken as early medieval multiculturalism, however: Bede's brief comparison to the single truth embodied in the five books of divine law also shows us his eagerness to draw his fragmented world into a coherent and transcendent system of Latin-based Christianity.

It is useful today, however, to think about medieval Britain, before and long after Bede, as a multilingual and multicultural setting, densely layered with influences and communities that divide, in quite different ways, along lines of geography, language, and ethnicity, as well as religion, gender, and class. These elements produced extraordinary cultures and artistic works, whose richness and diversity challenge the modern imagination. The medieval British Isles were a meeting place, but also a point of resistance, for wave after wave of cultural and political influences. Awareness of these multiple origins, moreover, persisted. Six hundred years after Bede we encounter a historian like Sir Thomas Gray complaining that recent disorders were "characteristic of a medley of different races. Wherefore some people are of the opinion that the diversity of spirit among the English is the cause of their revolutions" (*Scalacronica,* c. 1363).

This complex mixture sometimes resulted from systematic conquest, as with the Romans and, three centuries after Bede, the famous Norman Conquest of 1066; sometimes it was from slower, less unified movements of ethnic groups, such as the Celts, Anglo-Saxons, the Irish in Scotland, and the Vikings. Other important influences arrived more subtly: various forms of Christianity, classical Latin literature and learning, continental French culture in the thirteenth century, and an imported Italian humanism toward the close of the British Middle Ages.

Map of England, from Matthew Paris's *Historia Major*. Mid-13th century. A monk of Saint Albans, Matthew Paris wrote a monumental *History of England,* of which two illustrated copies in his own hand survive. Matthew's richly detailed map of England, including counties and major towns, illustrates the geographical knowledge of his day. It further suggests how alert he was to the ethnic divisions that still crossed his island and to the settlements and invasions, both mythic and actual, that had given rise to them. His inscription near the depiction of Hadrian's Wall, for example, informs us that the wall "once divided the English and the Picts." Recalling the claim that the original Britons were Trojan refugees, he writes about Wales (left center): "The people of this region are descended from the followers of Brutus." The story of Arthur's conception may have led Paris to identify Tintagel (*Tintaiol,* lower left). Matthew also links geography and racial character, as in his comment on northern Scotland (top center): "A mountainous, woody region producing an uncivilized people."

Our understanding of this long period and our very name for it also reflect a long history of multiple influences and cultural and political orders. The term "medieval" began as a condescending and monolithic label, first applied by Renaissance humanists who were eager to distinguish their revived classical scholarship from what they interpreted as a "barbarous" past. They and later readers often dismissed the Middle Ages as rigidly hierarchical, feudal, and Church-dominated. Others embraced the period for equally tendentious reasons, rosily picturing "feudal" England and Europe as a harmonious society of contented peasants, chivalrous nobles, and holy clerics. It is true that those who exercised political and religious control during the Middle Ages—the Roman church and the Anglo-Norman and then the English monarchy— sought to impose hierarchy on their world and created explicit ideologies to justify doing so. They were not unopposed, however; those who had been pushed aside continued to resist—and to contribute to Britain's multiple and dynamic literatures.

The period that we call "the Middle Ages" is vast and ungainly, spanning eight hundred years by some accounts. Scholars traditionally divide medieval English literature into the Old English period, from about 700 to 1066 (the date of the Norman Conquest), and the Middle English period, from 1066 to about 1500. Given the very different state of the English language during the two periods and given the huge impact of the Norman Conquest, this division is reasonable. There were substantial continuities, nevertheless, before and after the Conquest, especially in the Celtic areas beyond the Normans' immediate control.

THE CELTS

It is with the Celts, in fact, that the recorded history of Britain begins, and their literatures continue to the present day in Ireland and Wales. The Celts first migrated to Britain about 400 B.C., after spreading over most of Europe in the two preceding centuries. In England these "Brittonic" Celts absorbed some elements of Roman culture and social order during Rome's partial occupation of the island from the first to the fifth centuries A.D. After the conversion of the Roman emperor Constantine in the fourth century and the establishment of Christianity as the official imperial religion, many British Celts adopted Christianity. The language of these "British" to whom Bede refers gave rise to Welsh. The Celts maintained contact with their people on the Continent, who were already being squeezed toward what is now Brittany, in the west of France. The culture of the Brittonic Celts was thus not exclusively insular, and their myths and legends came to incorporate these cross-Channel memories, especially in the stories of King Arthur.

Celts also arrived in Ireland; and as one group, the "Goidelic" Celts, achieved linguistic and social dominance there, their language split off from that of the Britons. Some of these Irish Celts later established themselves in Argyll and the western isles of Scotland, "either by friendly treaty or by the sword," says Bede, and from them the Scottish branch of the Celtic languages developed. Bede mentions this language as the "Irish" that is spoken in Britain. The Irish converted to Christianity early but slowly, without the pressure of a Christianized colonizer. When the great Irish monasteries flourished in the sixth century, their extraordinary Latin scholarship seems to have developed alongside the traditional learning preserved by the rigorous schools of vernacular poetry. If anything, Irish monastic study was stimulated by these surviving institutions of a more poetic and priestly class. The Irish monasteries in turn became the impetus behind Irish and Anglo-Saxon missionaries who carried Christianity to the northern and eastern reaches of Europe. Both as missionaries and as scholars, insular Christians had great impact on continental Europe, especially in the eighth and ninth centuries.

By 597 when Pope Gregory the Great sent Augustine (later of Canterbury) to expand the Christian presence in England, there was already a flourishing Christian Celtic society, especially in Ireland. Ensuing disagreements over Celtic versus Roman ways of worship were ultimately resolved in favor of the Roman liturgy and calendar, but the cultural impact of Celts on British Christianity remained enormous. The Irish Book of Kells, shown on the facing page, and the Lindisfarne Gospels, produced in England, are enlivened by the swirls, interlace, and stylized animals long evident in the work of pagan Celtic craftsmen on the continent. The monks who illuminated such magnificent gospel books also copied classical Latin texts, notably Virgil's *Aeneid* and works by Cicero and Seneca, thereby helping keep ancient Roman literature alive when much of continental Europe fell into near chaos during the Germanic invasions that led to the fall of Rome.

THE GERMANIC MIGRATIONS

While Celtic culture flourished in Ireland, the British Celts and their faith suffered a series of disastrous reversals after the withdrawal of the Romans and the aggressive incursions of the pagan Angles, Saxons, and Jutes from the continent. The Picts and Scots in the north, never Romanized, had begun to harass the Britons, who responded by inviting allies from among the Germanic tribes on the continent in the mid-fifth century. These protectors soon became predators, demanding land and establishing small kingdoms of their own in roughly the eastern half of modern-day England. Uneasy and temporary settlements followed. The Britons retained a presence in the northwest, in the kingdoms of Rheged and of the Strathclyde Welsh; others were slowly pressed toward present-day Wales in the southwest.

The Angles, Saxons, and Jutes were not themselves a monolithic force, though. Divided into often warring states, they faced resistance, however diminishing, from the Britons and still had to battle the aggressive Picts and Scots, who were the original reason for their arrival. Their own culture was further changed as they converted to Christianity. The piecemeal Anglo-Saxon colonization of England in the sixth and seventh centuries and the island's conversion and later reconversion to Christianity present a complex picture, then—one that could be retold very differently depending on the perspectives of later historians. As the Angles and Saxons settled in and extended their control, the emerging "English" culture drew on new interpretations of the region's history. The most influential account of all was Bede's *Ecclesiastical History*, completed in 731. Our most reliable and eloquent source for early British history, Bede nonetheless wrote as an Anglo-Saxon. He presented his people's history from a providential perspective, seeing their role in Britain and their conversion to Christianity as a crucial part of a divine plan. King Alfred extended this world view when, in the late ninth century, he wrote of his people's struggle against the invading pagan Vikings.

Bede thus adopts an approach to history that reflects his own devout Christian faith and the disciplined religious practices of his monastic brethren in Northumberland. Nevertheless, Bede lived in a wider culture still deeply imbued with the tribal values of its Germanic and pagan past, a culture that maintained at least a nostalgic regard for the kind of individual heroic glory that rarely looks beyond this world.

Saint John, from the
Book of Kells. Late 8th
century.

Even in Bede's day, most kings died young and on the battlefield. And natural disasters such as those in 664 (a plague, and the deaths of a king and an archbishop occurring on the day of an eclipse) could send the Anglo-Saxons back to pagan worship. The two worlds, one with its roots in Mediterranean Christianity and the other in Germanic paganism, overlapped and interpenetrated for generations.

The pagan culture that is the setting for the epic *Beowulf* still strongly resembled that of the Germanic "barbarians" described by the Roman historian Tacitus in the first century. The heroic code of the Germanic warrior bands—what Tacitus called the *"comitatus"*—valued courage in battle above all, followed by loyalty to the tribal leader and the warband. These formed the core of heroic identity. A warrior whose leader fell in battle was obliged to seek vengeance at any cost; it was an indelible shame to survive an unavenged leader. Family links were also profound, however, and a persistent tragic theme in Germanic and Anglo-Saxon heroic narrative pits the claims of vengeance against those of family loyalty.

Early warrior culture in the British Isles, as elsewhere, was fraught with violence, as fragile truces between warring tribes and clans were continually broken. The tone of Old English poetry (as of much of Old Irish heroic narrative) is consequently somber, often suffused with a sense of doom. Even moments of high festivity are darkened by allusions to later disasters. Humor often occurs through a kind of ironic understatement: a poet may state that a warrior strode less swiftly into battle, for example, when the warrior in fact is dead. Similarly Cet, an Irish warrior, claims that if his brother were in the house, he would overcome his opponent, Conall. Conall replies, "But he is in the house," and almost casually flings the brother's head at Cet. A lighter tone is found mostly in shorter forms, such as the playful Anglo-Saxon riddles and in some Old Irish poetry.

The Angles and Saxons had come to England as military opportunists, and they in turn faced attacks and settlement from across the Channel. Their increasingly ordered political world and their thriving monastic establishments, such as Bede's monastery of Jarrow, were plundered by Vikings in swift attacks by boat as early as the end of the eighth century. This continued for a hundred years, and eventually resulted in widespread Scandinavian settlements north of the Thames, in areas called the Danelaw. By the 890s Christian Viking kings reigned at York and in East Anglia, extending a history of independence from the southern kingdoms. The period of raids and looting was largely over by 900, but even King Alfred (d. 899) faced Viking incursions in Wessex and consciously depicted himself as a Christian hero holding the line against pagan invaders. Only his kingdom, in fact, resisted their attacks with complete success. Vikings also intermarried with Anglo-Saxons and expanded their influence by political means. Profiting from English dynastic disorder around the turn of the eleventh century, aristocrats in the Danelaw became brokers of royal power. From 1016 to 1035 the Danish Cnut (Canute) was king of both England and Denmark, briefly uniting the two in a maritime empire. The Scandinavian presence was not exclusively combative, however. They sent peaceful traders to the British Isles and also left their mark on literature and language, as in the early Middle English romance *Havelock the Dane*, which contains many words borrowed from Old Norse.

PAGAN AND CHRISTIAN: TENSION AND CONVERGENCE

Given that writing in the Roman alphabet was introduced to pre-Conquest England by churchmen, it is not surprising that most texts from the period are written in Latin on Christian subjects. Most writing even in the Old English language was also religious. In Anglo-Saxon England and in the Celtic cultures, vernacular literature tended at first to be orally composed and performed. The body of written vernacular Anglo-Saxon poetry that survives is thus very small indeed, although there are plenty of prose religious works. It is something of a miracle that *Beowulf*, which celebrates the exploits of a pagan hero, was deemed worthy of being copied by scribes who were almost certainly clerics. (In fact, almost all the greatest Anglo-Saxon poetry survives in only a single copy—so tenuous is our link to that past.) Yet the copying of *Beowulf* also hints at the complex interaction of the pagan and Christian traditions in Anglo-Saxon culture.

The conflict between the two traditions was characterized (and perhaps exaggerated) by Christian writers and readers as a struggle between pagan violence and Christian values of forgiveness. The old, deep-seated respect for treasure as a sign of power and achievement seemed to conflict with Christian contempt for worldly goods. In fact, however, pagan Germanic and Christian values were alike in many respects and coexisted with various degrees of mutual influence.

Old English poets explored the tensions as well as the overlap between the two sets of values in two primary poetic modes—the heroic and the elegiac. The heroic mode, of which *Beowulf* is the supreme example, celebrates the values of bravery, loyalty, vengeance, and desire for treasure. The elegiac mode, by contrast, calls the value of these things into question, as at best transient and at worst a worldly distraction from spiritual life. The elegiac speaker, usually an exile, laments the loss of earthly goods—his lord, his comrades, the joys of the mead hall—and, in the case of the short poem known as *The Wanderer*, turns his thoughts to heaven. *Beowulf*, composed most likely by a Christian poet looking back at the deeds of his pagan Scandinavian ancestors, uses elements of both the heroic and the elegiac to focus on the overlap of pagan and Christian virtues.

The goals of earthly glory and heavenly salvation that concern Old English poetry are presented primarily as they affect men. Recent scholarship, however, reveals the active roles played in society by Anglo-Saxon women, particularly aristocratic ones. One of these is Aethelflaed, daughter of King Alfred, who co-ruled the kingdom of Mercia with her brother Edward at the turn of the tenth century, taking an active military role in fighting off the Danes. Better known today is Abbess Hilda, who founded and ran the great monastery at Whitby from 657 until her death in 680; five Whitby monks became bishops across England during her rule. Nevertheless, women generally take a marginal role in Old English poetry. In secular works marriages are portrayed as being arranged to strengthen military alliances, in efforts (often doomed) to heal bloody rifts between clans. Women thus function primarily as "peace weavers," a term referring occasionally to their active diplomacy in settling disputes but more often to their passive role in marriage exchanges. This latter role was fraught with danger, for if a truce were broken between the warring groups, the woman would face tragically conflicting loyalties to husband and male kin.

The effect of the Germanic heroic code on women is explored in two tantalizingly short poems that invest the elegiac mode with women's voices: *Wulf and Eadwacer* and *The Wife's Lament*. In both, a woman speaker laments her separation from her lord, whether husband or lover, through some shadowy events of heroic warfare. More indicative of the actual power of aristocratic and religious women in Anglo-Saxon society, perhaps, is the Old English poem *Judith*, a biblical narrative which uses heroic diction reminiscent of that in *Beowulf* to celebrate the heroine's military triumph over the pagan Holofernes.

ORAL POETRY, WRITTEN MANUSCRIPTS

For all their deep linguistic differences and territorial conflicts, the Celts and Anglo-Saxons had affinities in the heroic themes and oral settings of their greatest surviving narratives and in the echoes of a pre-Christian culture that endure there. Indeed, these can be compared to conditions of authorship in oral cultures worldwide, from Homer's Greece to parts of contemporary Africa. In a culture with little or no writing, the singer of tales has an enormously important role as the conservator of the past. In *Beowulf*, for instance, the traditional content and verbal formulas of the poetry of praise are swiftly reworked to celebrate the hero's killing of the monster Grendel:

> And now and then one of Hrothgar's thanes
> who brimmed with poetry, and remembered lays,

a man acquainted with ancient traditions
of every kind, composed a new song
in correct metre. Most skilfully that man
began to sing of Beowulf's feat,
to weave words together, and fluently
to tell a fitting tale.

A poet of this kind (in Anglo-Saxon, a *scop* or "shaper") does not just enhance the great warrior's prestige by praising his hero's ancestors and accomplishments. He also recalls and performs the shared history and beliefs of the entire people, in great feats of memory that make the poet virtually the encyclopedia of his culture. A poet from the oral tradition might also become a singer of the new Christian cosmology, like the illiterate herdsman Caedmon, whom Bede describes as having been called to monastic vows by the Abbess Hilda, in honor of his Christian poems composed in the vernacular oral mode.

In Celtic areas, oral poets had even greater status. The ancient class of learned Irish poets were honored servants of noblemen and kings; they remained as a powerful if reduced presence after the establishment of Christianity. The legal status of such a poet (a *fili*) was similar to that of a bishop, and indeed the *fili* carried out some functions of spells and divination inherited from the pagan priestly class, the druids. The ongoing influence of these poets in Irish politics and culture is reflected in the body of surviving secular literature from medieval Ireland, which is considerably larger than that from Anglo-Saxon England. A comparable situation prevailed in Wales. Even in the quite late Welsh *Tale of Taliesin*, the poet Taliesin appears as a public performer before the king as well as a possessor of arcane wisdom, magic, and prophecy.

In a culture in which a poet has such a wide and weighty role, ranging from entertainer to purveyor of the deepest reaches of religious belief, possession of the word bestows tremendous, even magical power. In a text that describes the wonders of the Irish epic the *Táin*, we hear about the promise of "a year's protection to him to whom it is recited." Even when these tales were copied into manuscripts, their written versions were essentially scripts for later performance, or for memorization. In a twelfth-century Irish manuscript, the copyist wishes "A blessing on everyone who will memorize the *Táin* with fidelity in this form and will not put any other form on it."

This attitude of awe toward the word as used by the oral poet was only enhanced by the arrival of Christianity, a faith that attributes creation itself to an act of divine speech. Throughout the Middle Ages and long after orally composed poetry had retreated from many centers of high culture, the power of the word also inhered in its written form, as encountered in certain prized books. Chief among these were the Bible and other books of religious story, especially by such church fathers as Saints Augustine and Jerome, and books of the liturgy. Since these texts bore the authority of divine revelation, the manuscripts that contained them shared in their charisma.

The power of these manuscripts was both reflected and aided by their visual grandeur. Among the highest expressions of the fervor and discipline of early insular monasticism is its production of beautifully copied and exquisitely decorated books of the Bible. The extreme elaboration of their production and the great labor and expense lavished on them suggest their almost holy status. Figures holding a book in the Book of Kells, or writing in the Lindisfarne Gospels, indicate this importance; a fascination with the new technology is suggested by Old English riddles whose answers are "a hand writing," "a book worm," or "a bookcase."

The cost and effort of making manuscript books and their very scarcity contributed to their aura. Parchment was produced from animal skins, stretched and scraped. The training and discipline involved in copying texts, especially sacred texts, were great. The decoration of the most ambitious manuscripts involved rare colors, gold leaf, and often supreme artistry. Thus these magnificent manuscripts could become almost magical icons: Bede, for example, tells of scrapings from Irish manuscripts which mixed with water cured the bites of poisonous snakes.

Manuscripts slowly became more widely available. By the twelfth century we hear more of manuscripts in private hands and the beginning of production outside ecclesiastical settings. By the fourteenth century merchants and private scholars were buying books from shops that resembled modern booksellers. The glamour and prestige of beautiful manuscripts remained, though, even if the sense of their magic faded to a degree. Great families would donate psalters and gospels to religious foundations, with the donor carefully represented in the decoration presenting the book to the Virgin Mary or the Christ child. Spectacular books of private devotion were at once a medium for spiritual meditation and proof of great wealth. Stories of epic conquest like the *Aeneid* would sometimes feature their aristocratic owners' coat of arms.

THE NORMAN CONQUEST

By the time of these developments in book production, though, a gigantic change had occurred. In a single year, 1066, England witnessed the death of the Anglo-Saxon King Edward and the coronation of his disputed successor King Harold, the invasion and triumph of the foreigner William of Normandy, and his own coronation as King William. The Normans conquered, with relative ease, an Anglo-Saxon kingdom disordered by civil strife. The monastic movement had lost much of its earlier fervor and discipline, despite reform in the tenth century. Baronial interests had weakened severely the reign of the late King Edward "the Confessor." On an island that already perceived itself as repeatedly colonized, 1066 nonetheless represented a climactic change, experienced and registered at virtually all levels of social, religious, and cultural experience.

One sign of how great a breach had been opened in England, paradoxically, is the multifaceted effort put forth by conquerors and conquered to maintain—or invent—continuity with the pre-Conquest past. In religious institutions, in dynastic genealogies, in the intersection of history and racial myth, in the forms and records of social institutions, the generations after 1066 sought to absorb a radically changed world yet to ground their world in an increasingly mythicized Anglo-Saxon or Briton antiquity. The Normans and their dynastic successors the Angevins eagerly took up and adapted to their own preoccupations ancient Briton political myths such as that of King Arthur and his court, and the stories of such saintly Anglo-Saxon kings as Oswald and Edward the Confessor.

They promoted narratives of their ancestors, like Wace's *Roman de Rou*, the story of the Normans' founder Rollo, commissioned by Henry II. Geoffrey of Monmouth dedicated his *History of the Kings of England* partly to Henry II's uncle, Robert Duke of

Anne, Duchess of Bedford, kneeling before the Virgin Mary and Saint Anne, from the *Bedford Hours*. Early 15th century. A book of hours was a prayerbook used by laypersons for private devotion. The *Bedford Hours* was produced in a Paris workshop for the Duke of Bedford, a brother of King Henry V, and his wife, Anne of Burgundy. Here, Saint Anne is shown teaching her daughter, the Virgin Mary, to read; another book lies open on a lectern in front of the kneeling Anne of Burgundy.

Gloucester. In that work Geoffrey links the ⟨Arthur and his fol-⟩
lowers to an equally ancient myth that England wa⟨s... the Middle Ages ...the sur-⟩
vivors of Troy; he makes his combined, largely fictive ⟨...healing work⟩
available to a Norman audience by writing it in Latin. Geo⟨ffrey's... on retold⟩
in "romance," the French from which vernacular texts took the⟨ir name... Angevin⟩
court also supported the "romances of antiquity," poems in French tha⟨t... sto-⟩
ry of Troy (the *Roman de Troie*), its background (*Roman de Thèbes*), and ⟨th⟩
(*Roman d'Eneas*), thus creating a model in the antique past for the Normans a⟨nd th⟩
westward conquest of England. And the *Song of Roland*, the great crusading narrati⟨ve⟩,
celebrating the heroic death of Charlemagne's nephew as he protected Christendom
from the Spanish Moslems, was probably written in the milieu of Henry II's court.

The Normans brought with them a new system of government, a freshly renovated Latin culture, and most important a new language. Anglo-Saxon sank into relative insignificance at the level of high culture and central government. Norman
French became the language of the courts of law, of literature, and of most of the
nobility. By the time English rose again to widespread cultural significance, about
250 years later, it was a hybrid that combined Romance and Germanic elements.

Latin offered a lifeline of communication at some social levels of this initially
fractured society. The European clerics who arrived under the immigrant archbishops
Lanfranc and Anselm brought a new and different learning, and often new and
deeply unwelcome religious practices: a celibate priesthood, skepticism about local
saints, and newly disciplined monasticism. Yet despite these differences and the tensions that accompanied them, clerics of European or British origin were linked by a
common liturgy, a considerable body of shared reading, and most of all a common
learned language. Secular as well as religious society were coming to be based more
and more on the practical use of the written word: the letter, the charter, the documentary record, and the written book. Whereas Anglo-Saxon England had been governed by the word enacted and performed—a law of oral witness and a culture of oral
poets—Norman England increasingly became a land of documents and books.

SOCIAL AND RELIGIOUS ORDER

The famed Domesday Book is a first instance of many of these developments. The
Domesday survey was a gigantic undertaking, carried out with a speed that still astonishes between Christmas 1085 and William the Conqueror's death in September
1087. A county-by-county survey of the lands of King William and those held by his
tenants-in-chief and subtenants, Domesday also records the obligations of landholders and thus reflects a new feudal system by which, increasingly, land was held in
post-Conquest England.

Under the Normans a nobleman held land from the king as a fief, in exchange
for which he owed the king certain military and judicial services, including the provision of armed knights. These knights in turn held land from their lord, to whom
they also owed military service and other duties. Some of this land they might keep
for their own farming and profit, and the rest they divided among serfs (who were
obliged, in theory, to stay on the land to which they were born) and free peasantry.
Both groups owed their knight or lord labor and either a portion of their agricultural
produce or rents in cash. This system of land tenure was surely more complex and
irregular in practice than in the theoretical model called feudalism. For instance, services at all levels were sometimes (and increasingly) commuted to cash payment, and

The *[text obscured]* ally held only by an individual for a lifetime, increasingly *...* that they would be inherited. Royal power gradually grew while *fief...* and fourteenth centuries, yet the local basis of landholding and there *w...ys* acted as a counterbalance, even a block, to royal ambition. during *...nesday* Book was only one piece of the multifaceted effort by which the *soci...d* later kings sought to extend and centralize royal power in their territories. *...m* and his successors established a system of royal justices who traveled throughout *...* realm and reported ultimately to the king, and an organized royal bureaucracy began to appear. The most powerful and learned of these Anglo-Norman kings was William the Conqueror's great-grandson, Henry II, who ruled from 1154 to 1177. Under Henry, royal justice, bureaucracy, and record-keeping made great advances; the production of documents was centralized and took on more standardized forms, and copies of these documents (called "pipe rolls") began to be produced for later reference and proof.

Along with a stronger royal government, the Normans brought a clergy invigorated both by new learning and by the spirituality of recent monastic reforms. Saint Anselm, the second of the Norman archbishops of Canterbury, was a great prelate and the writer of beautiful and widely influential texts and prayers of private devotion. The Victorines and the Cistercians (inspired in part by Saint Bernard of Clairvaux) also brought a strong mystical streak to English monasticism. All these would bear fruit once again in the fourteenth century in a group of mystics writing in Latin and in English.

On the other hand, the Norman prelates, like their kings, brought an urge toward centralized order in the church and a belief that the church and its public justice (the "canon law") should be independent of secular power. This created frequent conflict with kings and aristocrats, who wanted to extend their judicial power and expected to wield considerable influence in the appointment of church officials.

The most explosive moment in this ongoing controversy occurred in the disagreements between Henry II and Thomas Becket, who was Henry's Chancellor and then Archbishop of Canterbury. Becket's increasingly public refusal to accommodate the king, either in the judicial sphere or the matter of clerical appointments, finally led to his murder by Henry's henchmen in 1170 at the altar of Can-

The Murder of Thomas Becket, from Matthew Paris's *Historia Major.* Mid-13th century.

terbury Cathedral and his canonization very soon thereafter. A large body of hagiography (narratives of his martyrdom and posthumous miracles) swiftly developed, adding to an already rich tradition of writing about the lives of English saints. As Saint Thomas, Becket became a powerful focus for ecclesiastical ambition, popular devotion and pilgrimage, and religious and secular narrative. In fact, the characters of Chaucer's *Canterbury Tales* tell their stories while making a pilgrimage to his shrine.

At least in theory, feudal tenure involved an obligation of personal loyalty between lord and vassal that was symbolically enacted in the rituals of enfeoffment, in which the lord would bestow a fief on his vassal. This belief was elaborated in a large body of secular literature in the twelfth century and after. Yet feudal loyalty was always fragile and ideologically charged. Vassals regularly resisted the wills of their lord or king when their interests collided, sometimes to the extent of officially withdrawing from the feudal bond. Connected to feudal relations was the notion of a chivalric code among the knightly class (those who fought on horses, *chevaliers*), which involved not just loyalty to the lord but also honorable behavior within the class, even among enemies. Chivalric literature is thus full of stories of captured opponents being treated with the utmost politeness, as indeed happened when Henry II's son Richard was held hostage for years in Germany, awaiting ransom.

Similarly, although medieval theories of social order had some basis in fact, they exercised shifting influence within a much more complex social reality. For instance, medieval society was often analyzed by the model of the "three estates"—those who fought (secular aristocrats), those who prayed (the clergy), and those who worked the land (the free and servile peasantry). This model appears more or less explicitly in Chaucer's poetry. Such a system, though, did not allow for the gradual increase in manufacturing (weaving, pottery, metalwork, even the copying of books) or for the urban merchants who traded in such products. As society became more complex, a model of the "mystical social body" gained popularity, especially in the fourteenth century. Here a wider range of classes and jobs was compared to limbs and other body parts. Even this more flexible image was strictly hierarchical, though. Peasants and laborers were the feet, knights (on the right) and merchants (on the left) were hands, and townspeople were the heart, but the head was made up of kings, princes, and prelates of the church.

CONTINENTAL AND INSULAR CULTURES

The arrival of the Normans, and especially the learned clerics who came then and after, opened England to influences from a great intellectual current that was stirring on the continent, the "renaissance of the twelfth century," which was to have a significant impact in the centuries that followed. A period of comparative political stability and economic growth made travel easier, and students and teachers were on the move, seeking new learning in Paris and the Loire valley, in northern Italy, and in Toledo with its Arab and Jewish cultures. Schools were expanding beyond the monasteries and into the precincts of urban cathedrals and other religious foundations. Along with offering traditional biblical and theological study, these schools sparked a revived interest in elegant Latin writing, Neoplatonic philosophy, and science deriving from Aristotle.

Because the Normans and Angevins ruled large territories on the Continent, movement across the Channel was frequent; by the mid-twelfth century learned English culture was urbane and international. English clerics like John of Salisbury studied at Chartres and Paris, and texts by eminent speculative and scientific writers like William of Conches and Bernard Silvestris came to England. As these foreign works entered England, education became more ambitious and widely available, and its products show growing contact with the works of classical Latin writers such as Horace, Virgil, Terence, Cicero, Seneca, and Ovid in his erotic as much as in his mythological poetry.

The renewed attention to these works went along with a revival of interest in the *trivium*, the traditional division of the arts of eloquence: grammar, rhetoric, and dialectic. The most aggressive of these was dialectic, a form of logic developed by the Greeks and then rediscovered by Christian Europe from Arab scholars who had preserved and pursued Greek learning. John of Salisbury, who promoted dialectic in his *Metalogicon*, described it with metaphors of military prowess, as though it were an extension of knightly jousting. "Since dialectic is carried on between two persons," he writes, Aristotle's *Topics* "teaches the matched contestants whom it trains and provides with reasons and topics, to handle their proper weapons and engage in verbal, rather than physical conflict." Rhetoric was elaborately codified in technical manuals of poetry. Though in one sense it was merely ornamental, teaching how to flesh out a description or incident with figures of speech, rhetoric could be as coercive as dialectic, though, since it specified strategies of persuasion in a tradition deriving from ancient oratory. Rhetorical texts also instructed the student in letter-writing, increasingly important as an administrative skill and as a form of elevated composition.

The study of the *trivium* generated many Latin school texts and helped foster a high level of Latinity and a self-consciously sophisticated, classicizing literature in the second half of the twelfth century. Some school texts had great influence on vernacular literature, such as the *Poetria Nova* by Geoffrey of Vinsauf, a rhetorical handbook filled with vivid poetic examples. More intriguing is *Pamphilus*, a short Ovidian poem about a seduction, aided by Venus, which turns into a rape. It is thought to have been an exercise in *disputatio*, the oral form that dialectic assumed in the classroom. The poem was immensely popular in the next few centuries and was translated into many vernacular languages. *Pamphilus* was a conduit at once for Ovidian eroticism and for the language of debate on love. Chaucer mentions it as a model of passionate love and seems to have adapted some of its plot devices in his *Troilus and Criseyde*.

While classical Latin literature was often read with a frank interest in pagan ideas and practices, commentators also offered allegorical interpretations that drew pagan stories into the spiritual and cosmological preoccupations of medieval Christianity. Ovid's *Metamorphoses* were thus interpreted in a French poem, the *Ovide Moralisé*, that was clearly known to Chaucer, and in Latin commentaries such as the *Ovidius moralizatus* of Pierre Bersuire. For instance, Ovid describes Jupiter, in the form of a bull, carrying the Tyrian princess Europa into the sea to rape her. Bersuire interprets this as Christ taking on human flesh in order to take up the human soul he loves. Alternatively, he offers an explicitly misogynist allegory, casting Europa as young women who like to see handsome young men—bulls: "They are drawn through the stormy sea of evil temptations and are raped." Neither text is often very subtle in the extraction of Christian or moral analogies from Ovid's stories, yet both were popular and influential, if only because they also tell Ovid's tales before allegorizing them.

The allegorization of ancient secular literature was only one facet of allegorical reading, which was even more persistently applied to the Bible. Allegory became a complex and fruitful area of the medieval imagination and had profound implications for artistic production as well as reading. In its simplest sense, an allegorical text takes a metaphor and extends it into narrative, often personifying a quality as a character. Yet this practice takes a wealth of forms, often drawing from the interpretive practice of typology, which sees Old Testament events (such as Abraham's willingness to sacrifice his son Isaac) as literally true but also symbolically predictive of and fulfilled by events in the New Testament. Typology so deeply colored the medieval reader's perceptions that we can see it operating in approaches to secular history and texts as well; we will encounter an instance of this in Geoffrey of Monmouth's *History of the Kings of Britain*.

The continent provided not only Latin but also significant vernacular influences: French was the international language of aristocratic culture and an important literary language in England, and continental French literature was crucial in the rise of courtly literature in Middle English. Many English Arthurian works, including *Sir Gawain and the Green Knight* and Sir Thomas Malory's *Morte Darthur*, are less indebted to English sources than to French romances, whether written on the continent or in England by authors such as Marie de France and Thomas of Britain. Chaucer translated into English the enormously popular allegorical dream vision the *Roman de la Rose* by Guillaume de Lorris and Jean de Meun. He also borrowed the conventions and imagery of Guillaume de Machaut and Eustache Deschamps; even the meter of his earlier poetry derives from their French octosyllabic couplet. Italian influences can be seen in Chaucer's use of Dante's *Divine Comedy* and his extensive borrowing from Petrarch and Boccaccio. Such continental vernacular literatures infiltrated even the Celtic cultures, as seen in the witty mix of Welsh and European traditions in the poems of Dafydd ap Gwilym.

If such writers and records reflect the higher achievements of education in England of the twelfth century and later, literacy was also diffusing in wider circles and new venues. In a society like England's that continued to produce considerable oral and public literature, indeed, the divide between literacy and illiteracy was always unstable and permeable. A secular aristocrat might have a clerk read to him or her; an urbanite could attend and absorb parts of public rituals that involved poems and orations; even a peasant would be able to pick up Latin tags from sermons or the liturgy. Thus a fourteenth-century writer like William Langland could expect his wide and mixed audience to recognize at least some of the Latin phrases he used along with English; and Chaucer could imagine a character like the Wife of Bath who, at best semi-literate, could still quote bits of the Latin liturgy. Access to texts and the self-awareness fostered by private reading may have helped promote the social ambitions and disruptions within the mercantile and even peasant classes during the later Middle Ages.

WOMEN, COURTLINESS, AND COURTLY LOVE

Access to books also increased the self-awareness of women. Possession of books that encouraged prayer and private devotion, such as psalters and Books of Hours, appears to have facilitated early language training in the home. The many images in manuscripts of women reading—especially the Virgin Mary and her mother, Saint Anne—have interesting implications for our understanding of women's literacy and cultural roles. A number of aristocratic Norman and Angevin women received good educa-

Grotesques and a Courtly Scene, from the *Ormesby Psalter.* c. 1310–1325.

tions at convents. Women in the holy life possessed at least some literacy, though this often may have been minimal indeed. Even well-educated women were more likely to read English or French than Latin, with the exception of liturgical books.

The roles of women in the society and cultural imagination of post-Conquest England are complex and contradictory. No Anglo-Norman woman held ecclesiastical prestige like the Anglo-Saxon abbess Hilda or other Anglo-Saxon holy women. Women's power seems to have declined in the long term, both in worldly affairs and in the church, as the Normans consolidated their hold on England and imposed their order on society. Nevertheless, ambitious women could have great influence, especially when they seized upon moments of disruption. In civil strife over the succession to King Henry I, the Empress Matilda organized an army, issued royal writs, and in the end guaranteed the accession of her son Henry II. If Henry II's wife, Eleanor of Aquitaine, spent the latter decades of her husband's reign under virtual house arrest, it was largely because she had conspired with her sons to raise an army against her own husband.

Despite the limitations of their actual power, women were the focus, often the worshiped focus, of much of the best imaginative literature of the twelfth and thirteenth centuries; and women were central to the social rituals we associate with courtliness and the idea of courtly love. Despite her later imprisonment, Eleanor of Aquitaine was a crucial influence in the diffusion of courtly ideas from the continent, especially the south of France; and among the great writers of the century was Marie de France, who was probably related to Henry II. Scholars continue to debate whether the observances of "courtly love" were in fact widely practiced and whether its worship of women was empowering or restrictive: the image of the distant, adored lady implies immobility and even silence on her part. Certainly lyrics and narratives that embody courtly values are widespread, even if they often question what they celebrate; and the ideals of courtliness may have had as great an impact through these imaginative channels as through actual enactment.

The ideas and rituals of courtliness reach back to Greek and Roman models of controlled and stylized behavior in the presence of great power. In the Middle Ages, values of discretion and modesty also may have filtered into the secular world from

A Knight, rubbing from a funerary brass. Early 14th century. This funerary brass depicts a knight as he presented himself to eternity, sheathed in chain mail and fully armed but with his hands joined in prayer. The dog at his feet is a symbol of fidelity.

the rigidly disciplined setting of the monasteries. As the society of western Europe took on a certain degree of order in the eleventh and twelfth centuries, courtly attainments began to converge and even compete with simple martial prowess in the achievement of worldly power. The presence of large numbers of armed and ambitious men at the great courts provided at once an opportunity for courtly behavior and the threat of its disruption.

Whatever its historical reality, courtly love as a literary concept had an immense influence. In this it adopted the vocabulary of two distinct traditions: the veneration of the Virgin Mary and the love poetry of Ovid and his heirs. Mariolatry, which has a particularly rich tradition in England, celebrates the perfection of Mary as a woman and mother, who undid the sins of Eve and now intercedes for fallen mankind. Ovid, with his celebration of sensuality and cynical instructions for achieving the lover's desire, provided medieval Europe with a whole catalog of love psychology and erotic persuasion.

The self-conscious command of fine manners, whether the proper way of hunting, dressing, addressing a superior, or wooing a lady, became a key mark of an aristocrat. Great reputations grew around courtly attainment, as in the legends that circulated about Richard I. Centuries later, the hero of *Sir Gawain and the Green Knight* is tested as much through his courtly behavior as through his martial bravery. A literature of etiquette emerged as early as the reign of Henry I in England and continued through the thirteenth century. In the court of Henry II, Daniel of Beccles wrote *Urbanus Magnus*, a verse treatise in Latin on courtesy. In this poem he offers detailed advice in many arenas of specific behavior at court: avoiding frivolity, giving brief counsel, and especially comporting oneself among the wealthy:

> Eating at the table of the rich, speak little
> Lest you be called a chatterbox among the diners.
> Be modest, make reverence your companion.

In a mildly misogynist passage, Daniel especially warns against becoming involved with the lord's wife, even if she makes an overture, as occurs in Marie de France's *Lanval*. Should this happen, Daniel offers polite evasive strategies, skills we see demonstrated in *Sir Gawain and the Green Knight*.

ROMANCE

Courtliness was expressed both in lyric poetry and in a wide range of vernacular narratives that we now loosely call "romances"—referring both to their genre and to the romance language in which they were first written. The Arthurian tradition, featured in this anthology, is only one of many romance traditions; others include the legends of Tristan and Isolde, Alexander, and Havelock the Dane. In romances that focus on courtly love, the hero's devotion to an unapproachable lady tends to elevate his character. Although many courtly romances conclude in a happy and acceptable marriage of hero and heroine, others such as Marie's *Lanval* warn of the dangers of transgressive love to the hero and his society. To the extent that they portray women as disruptive agents of erotic desire, some romances take on elements of the misogynist tradition that persisted in clerical thought alongside the adoration of the Virgin. Near the end of *Sir Gawain and the Green Knight*, even the courtly Gawain explodes in a virulent diatribe against women.

Love was not the only subject of romance, however. Stories of love and war typically lead the protagonists into encounters with the uncanny, the marvelous, the taboo. This is not so surprising when we recall the practices of medieval Christianity that brought the believer into daily contact with such miracles as the Eucharist; even chronicles of saints' lives regularly showed the divine will breaking miraculously into everyday life. We may say today that romance looses the hero and heroine onto the landscape of the private or social subconscious; a medieval writer might have stressed that nature itself is imbued with mystery both by God and by other, more shadowy, spiritual forces.

In romances, the line between the mundane and the extraordinary is often high-ly permeable: an episode may move swiftly from a simple ride to a meeting with a magical lady or malevolent dwarf, as often occurs in Thomas Malory. Romance also seems to be a form of imaginative literature in which medieval society could acknowledge the transgressions of its own ordering principles: adultery, incest, unmotivated martial violence. And it often revisits areas of belief and imagination that official culture long had put aside: *Sir Gawain and the Green Knight,* for instance, features a magical knight who can survive having his head cut off and a powerful aged woman who is called a goddess. Both characters reach back, however indirectly, to pre-Christian figures encountered in early Irish and Welsh stories.

THE RETURN OF ENGLISH

The romances are another of the dense points of contact among the many languages and ethnicities of the medieval British Isles. These powerful and evocative narratives often feature figures of Celtic origin like the British King Arthur and his court who came to French- and English-language culture through the Latin *History* of Geoffrey of Monmouth. Such transmission is typical of the linguistic mix in post-Conquest England. The language of the aristocracy was French, used in government and law as well as in the nascent vernacular literature. A few conservative monasteries contin-ued the famed Anglo-Saxon Chronicle in its original language after the Conquest. But increasingly English or an evolving form of Anglo-Saxon was the working lan-guage of the peasantry. Mixed-language households must have appeared as provincial Anglo-Saxon gentry began, quite quickly, to intermarry with the Normans and their descendants. The twelfth-century satirist Nigel of Canterbury (or "Wireker"), author of the *Mirror of Fools*, came from just such a mixed family.

Few writings in Middle English survive from the late twelfth century, and very little of value besides the extraordinary *Brut* of Layamon, which retranslates much of Geoffrey of Monmouth's *History* from a French version. A manuscript containing the earliest English lyric in this collection, the thirteenth-century *sumer is ycumen in*, can suggest the linguistic complexity of the era: it contains lyrics in English and French, and instructions for performance in Latin.

English began to reenter the world of official discourse in the thirteenth century. Communications between the church and the laity took place increasingly in Eng-lish, and by the late 1250s, Archbishop Sewal of York tended to reject papal candi-dates for bishoprics if they did not have good English. In 1258 King Henry III issued a proclamation in Latin, French, and English, though the circumstances were unusu-al. Teaching glossaries include a growing number of English words, as well as the French traditionally used to explain difficult Latin.

The fourteenth century inaugurated a distinct change in the status of English, how-ever, as it became the language of parliament and a growing number of governmental activities. We hear of Latin being taught in the 1340s through English rather than French. In 1362 a statute tried (but failed) to switch the language of law courts from French to English, and in 1363 Parliament was opened in English. The period also wit-nesses tremendous activity in translating a wide range of works into English, including Chaucer's version of Boethius' *Consolation of Philosophy* and the Wycliffite translations of the Bible, completed by 1396. Finally, at the close of the century, the Rolls of Parliament record in Latin the overthrow of Richard II, but they feature Henry IV (in what was probably a self-consciously symbolic gesture) claiming the throne in a brief, grave speech in English and promising to uphold "the gude lawes and custumes of the Rewme."

The reemergence of English allowed an extraordinary flowering of vernacular literature, most notably the achievements of Chaucer, Langland, and the anonymous genius who wrote *Sir Gawain and the Green Knight*. It would be more accurate, nevertheless, to speak of the reemergence of "Englishes" in the second half of the fourteenth century. The language scholars now call Middle English divides into four quite distinct major dialects in different regions of the island. These dialects were in many ways mutually unintelligible, so that Chaucer, who was from London in the Southeast Midlands, might have been hard-pressed to understand *Sir Gawain and the Green Knight*, written in the West Midlands near Lancashire. (Certainly Chaucer was aware of dialects and mimics some northern vocabulary in his *Canterbury Tales*.) London was the center of government and commerce in this era and later the place of early book printing, which served to stabilize the language. Thus Chaucer's dialect ultimately dominated and developed into modern English. Therefore English-speaking students today can read Chaucer in the original without much difficulty, whereas Langland's *Piers Plowman* is very challenging and *Sir Gawain* may seem virtually a foreign tongue. As a result, the latter work is offered in translation in this anthology. (For a practical guide to Chaucer's Middle English, also helpful in reading lyrics and *The Second Play of the Shepherds*, see pages 218–220.)

Not only is *Sir Gawain* written in a dialect different from that of Chaucer's London, it also employs a quite distinct poetic style which descends from the alliterative meter of Old English poetry, based on repetitions of key consonants and on general patterns of stress. By contrast, the rhymed syllabic style used by poets like Chaucer developed under the influence of medieval French poetry and its many lyric forms. Fourteenth-century alliterative poetry was part of a revival that occurred in the North and West of the country, at a time when the form would have seemed old fashioned to many readers in the South. In the next two centuries, in a region even more distant from London, alliterative poetry or its echoes persisted in the Middle Scots poetry of William Dunbar, Robert Henryson, and Gavin Douglas.

POLITICS AND SOCIETY IN THE FOURTEENTH CENTURY

The fourteenth-century authors wrote in a time of enormous ferment, culturally and politically as well as linguistically. During the second half of the fourteenth century, new social and theological movements shook past certainties about the divine right of kings, the division of society among three estates, the authority of the church, and the role of women. An optimistic backward view can see in that time the struggle of the peasantry for greater freedom, the growing power of the Commons in Parliament, and the rise of a mercantile middle class. These changes often appeared far darker at the time, though, with threatening, even apocalyptic implications.

The forces of nature also cast a shadow across the century. In a time that never produced large agricultural surpluses, poor harvests led to famine in the second and third decades of the century, and an accompanying deflation drove people off the land. In 1348 the Black Death arrived in England, killing at least 35 percent of the population by 1350. Plague struck violently three more times before 1375, emptying whole villages. Overall, as much as half the population may have died.

The kingship was already in trouble. After the consolidation of royal power under Henry II and the Angevins in the twelfth century, the regional barons began to reassert their power. In a climactic confrontation in 1215, they forced King John to sign the Magna Carta, guaranteeing (in theory at least) their traditional rights and privileges as well as due process in law and judgment by peers. In the fourteenth century the monarchy came under considerable new pressures. Edward II (1307–1327) was deposed by one of his barons, Roger de Mortimer, and with the connivance of his own queen, Isabella. His son Edward III had a long and initially brilliant reign, marked by great military triumphs in a war against France, but the conflict dragged on so long that it became known as the Hundred Years' War. Edward III's reign was marked at home by famine, deflation, and then, most horribly, plague. His later years were marked by premature senility and control by a court circle. These years were further darkened by the death of that paragon of chivalry, Edward's son and heir-apparent, Edward "The Black Prince." Edward's successor, the Black Prince's son Richard II, launched a major peace initiative in the Hundred Years' War and became a great patron of the arts, but he was also capable of great tyranny. In 1399 like his great-grandfather, he was deposed. An ancient and largely creaky royal bureaucracy had difficulty running a growing mercantile economy, and when royal justice failed to control crime in the provinces, it was increasingly replaced by local powers.

   The aristocracy too experienced pressures from the increased economic power of the urban merchants and from the peasants' efforts to exploit labor shortages and win better control over their land. The aristocrats responded with fierce, though only partly successful, efforts to limit wages and with stricter and more articulate divisions within society, even between the peerage and gentry. It is not clear, however, that fourteenth-century aristocrats perceived themselves as a threatened order. If anything, events may have pressed them toward a greater class cohesion, a more self-conscious pursuit of chivalric culture and values. The reign of Edward III saw the foundation of the royal Order of the Garter, a select group of nobles honored for their chivalric accomplishments as much as their power (the order is almost certainly evoked at the close of *Sir Gawain and the Green Knight*). Edward further exploited the Arthurian myth in public rituals such as tournaments and Round Tables. The ancient basis of the feudal tie, land tenure, began to give way to contract and payment in the growing, hierarchicalized retinues of the period. These were still lifelong relationships between lord and retainer, nevertheless, and contemporary historians of aristocratic sympathies like Jean Froissart idealize an ongoing community of chivalric conduct that could reach even across combating nations.

   The second estate, the church, was also troubled—in part, paradoxically, because of the growing and active piety of the laity. Encouraged by the annual confession that had been required since the Fourth Lateran Council of 1215, laymen increasingly took control of their own spiritual lives. But the new emphasis on confession also led to clerical corruption. Mendicant (begging) friars, armed with manuals of penance, spread across the countryside to confess penitents in their own homes and sometimes accepted money for absolving them. Whether or not these abuses were truly widespread, they inspired much anticlerical satire—as is reflected in the works of Chaucer and Langland—and the Church's authority diminished in the process. The traditional priesthood, if better educated, was also more worldly than in the past, increasingly pulled from parish service into governmental bureaucracy; it too faced widespread literary satire. Well aware of clerical venality, the church nevertheless fearfully resisted the criticisms and innovations of "reforming clerics" like John Wycliffe and his supporters among the gentry, the "Lollard knights." The church's control over religious experience was further complicated and perhaps undermined by the rise of popular mysticism, among both the clergy and the laity, which was difficult to contain within the traditional ecclesiastical hierarchy. Mystical writing by people as varied as Richard Rolle, Julian of Norwich, the anonymous author of *The Cloud of Unknowing*, and the emotive Margery Kempe all promulgate the notion of an individual's direct experience of the divine. Finally, and on a much broader scale, all of Christian Europe was rocked by the Great Schism of 1378, when believers faced the disconcerting spectacle of two popes ruling simultaneously.

The third estate, the commoners, was the most problematic and rapidly evolving of the three in the fourteenth century. The traditional division of medieval society into three estates had no place for the rising mercantile bourgeoisie and grouped them with the peasants who worked the land. In fact the new urban wealthy formed a class quite of their own. Patrons and consumers of culture, they also served in the royal bureaucracy under Edward III, as is illustrated by the career of Geoffrey Chaucer who came from just such a background. Yet only the wealthiest married into the landed gentry, and poor health conditions in the cities made long mercantile dynasties uncommon. Cities in anything like a modern sense were few and retained rural features. Houses often had gardens, even orchards, and pigs (and pig dung) filled the narrow, muddy streets. Only magnates built in stone; only they and ecclesiastical institutions had the luxury of space and privacy. Otherwise, cities were crowded and dirty—the suburbs especially disreputable—and venues for communicable disease.

The peasants too had a new sense of class cohesion. Events had already loosened the traditional bond of serfs to the land on which they were born, and the plagues further shifted the relative economic power of landowning and labor. As peasants found they could demand better pay, fiercely repressive laws were passed to stop them. These and other discontents, like the arrival of foreign labor and technologies, led to the Rising of 1381 (also known as the Peasants' Revolt). Led by literate peasants and renegade priests, the rebels attacked aristocrats, foreigners, and some priests. They were swiftly and violently put down, but the event was nevertheless a watershed and haunted the minds of the English.

When one leader of the revolt, the priest John Ball, cited Langland's fictional character Piers Plowman with approval, Langland reacted with dismay and revised his poem to emphasize the proper place of peasants. Even more conservative, Chaucer's friend John Gower wrote a horrified Latin allegory on the revolt, *Vox Clamantis* (*The Voice of One Crying*), where he compared the rebels to beasts. By contrast, Chaucer virtually ignored the revolt, aside from a brief comic reference in the *Nun's Priest's Tale*; it remains unclear, though, whether Chaucer's silence reflects comfortable bourgeois indifference or stems from deep anxiety and discomfort. At the same time, these disruptions introduced a period of cultural ferment, and the mercantile middle class also provided a creative force, appearing (though not without some nervous condescension) in some of Chaucer's most enduring characters like the *Canterbury Tales*' Merchant, the Wife of Bath, and the Miller.

It is both from this new middle class and from the established upper class that wider choices in the lives of women emerged in the later Middle Ages. Their social and political power had been curtailed both by clerical antifeminism and by the increasingly centralized government during the twelfth and thirteenth centuries. Starting in the fourteenth century, however, women began to regain an increased voice and presence. Among the aristocracy, Edward II's wife Isabella was an important player in events that brought about the king's deposition. And at the end of the century, Edward III's mistress Alice Perrers was widely criticized for her avarice and her influence on the aging king (for instance by William Langland who refers to her in the allegorical figure Lady Meed).

Women were also important in the spread of lay literacy among the middle class. In France, Christine de Pizan reexamined whole areas of her culture, especially ancient and biblical narrative, from a feminist perspective; her work was known and translated in England. Important autobiographical works were composed in Middle English by Julian of Norwich and Margery Kempe. Julian was an anchoress, living a cloistered religious life but able to speak to visitors such as Margery herself; Margery was an illiterate but prosperous townswoman, daughter of a mayor, who dictated to scribes her experiences of wifehood and rebellion against it, of travel to holy places, and of spiritual growth. Still, for the representation of women's voices in this period we are largely dependent on the fictional creations of men. Chaucer's famous Wife of Bath, for instance, strikes many modern readers as an articulate voice opposing women's repression and expressing their ambitions, but for all her critique of the antifeminist stereotypes of the church, she is in many ways their supreme embodiment. And in a number of Middle English lyrics, probably by men, the woman's voice may evoke scorn rather than pity as she laments her seduction and abandonment by a smooth-talking man, usually a cleric.

THE SPREAD OF BOOK CULTURE IN THE FIFTEENTH CENTURY

Geoffrey Chaucer died in 1400, a convenient date for those who like their eras to end with round numbers. Certainly literary historians have often closed off the English Middle Ages with Chaucer and left the fifteenth century as a sort of drab and undefined waiting period before the dawn of the Renaissance. Yet parts of fifteenth-century England are sites of vital and burgeoning literary culture. Book ownership spread more and more widely. Already in the late fourteenth century, Chaucer had imagined a fictional Clerk of Oxford with a solid collection of university texts despite his relative poverty. More of the urban bourgeoisie bought books and even had appealing collections assembled for them. When printing came to England in the later fifteenth century, books became even more available, though still not cheap.

Whether in manuscript or print, a swiftly growing proportion of these books was in English. The campaigns of Henry V in the second decade of the fifteenth century and his death in 1422 mark England's last great effort to reclaim the old Norman and Angevin territories on the continent. With the loss of all but a scrap of this land and the decline of French as a language of influence, these decades consolidate a notion of cultural and nationalistic Englishness. The Lancastrian kings, Henry the Fourth, Fifth, and Sixth, seem to have adopted English as the medium for official culture and patronized translators like Lydgate. Later in the period William Caxton made a great body of French and English texts available to aristocratic and middle-class readers, both by translating and by diffusing them in the new medium of print.

Ancient aristocratic narratives continued to evolve, as in Thomas Malory's retelling of the Arthurian story in his *Morte Darthur*, one of the books printed by Caxton. Malory works mostly from French prose versions but trims back much of the exploration of love and the uncanny; the result is a recharged tale of chivalric battle and familial and political intrigue. Other continental and local traditions are revived in another courtly setting by a group of Scots poets including William Dunbar.

As more and more commoners had educational and financial access to books, they also participated in a lively public literary culture in towns and cities. The fifteenth century sees the flowering of the great dramatic "mystery cycles," sets of plays on religious themes produced and in part performed by craft guilds of larger towns in the Midlands and North. Included here is a brilliant sample, *The Second Play of the Shepherds* from the Wakefield Plays. Probably written by clerics, these plays are nonetheless dense with the preoccupations of contemporary working people and enriched by implicit analogies between the lives of their actors and the biblical events they portray. Lyrics and political poems continue to flourish. Sermons remain a popular and widespread form of religious instruction and literary production. And highly literary public rituals, such as Henry V's triumphal civic entries as he returned from his French campaigns, are part of Lancastrian royal propaganda.

By the time Caxton was editing and printing Malory in 1485 with an eye to sales and profit, over eight hundred years had passed since Caedmon is said to have composed his first Christian hymn under angelic direction. The idea of the poet had moved from a version of magician and priest to something more like a modern author; and the dominant model of literary transmission was shifting from listening to an oral performance to reading a book privately. Chaucer, that most bookish of poets, is a case in point. Many of his early poems refer to the pleasures of reading, not only for instruction but even as a mere pastime, often to avoid insomnia. He opens the dream vision *The Parliament of Fowls* with the poet reading a classical Latin text, Cicero's *Dream of Scipio*. Chaucer, of course, read his books and disseminated his own work in handwritten manuscript; in his humorous lyric *To His Scribe Adam* he expresses his frustration with copyists who might mistranscribe his words.

Despite such private bookishness, however, a more public and oral literary culture never disappeared from medieval Britain. Considerable interdependence between oral and literate modes of communication remained; poetry was both silently read and orally performed. In the *Canterbury Tales*, for instance, when the pilgrim Chaucer apologizes for the bawdiness of *The Miller's Tale*, he suggests that if the listener/reader doesn't like what he *hears*, he should simply turn the *page* and choose another tale. At the same time, literate clerics practiced what we might call learned orality, through lectures or disputations at Oxford and Cambridge or from the pulpit in a more popular setting. Chaucer uses the sermon form in the *Wife of Bath's Prologue*, *Pardoner's Tale*, and *Parson's Tale*. The popular orality of minstrel performance, harking back however distantly to the world of the Anglo-Saxon *scop* and the Irish *fili*, was also exploited with great self-consciousness by literate poets. *Sir Gawain and the Green Knight* presents itself as an oral performance, based on a tale that the narrator has heard recited. By contrast, Chaucer gently twits minstrels in his marvelous parody of popular romance, *Sir Thopas*. Chaucer remains a learned poet whose greatest achievement, paradoxically, was the presentation of fictional oral performances—the tale-telling of the Canterbury pilgrims.

The speed with which communication technologies are changing in our own era has heightened our awareness of such changes in the past. We are now closing the era of the book and moving into the era of the endlessly malleable electronic text. In many ways the means by which we have come to receive and transmit information—television, radio, CD-ROM, Internet—mix orality and literacy in a fashion wholly new yet also intriguingly reminiscent of the later Middle Ages. In contrast to the seeming fixity of texts in the intervening centuries, contemporary literary culture may be recovering the sense of textual and cultural fluidity that brought such dynamism to literary creation in the Middle Ages.

Beowulf

Beowulf has come down to us as if by chance, for it is preserved only in a single manuscript, Cotton Vitellius A.XV, which almost perished in a fire in 1731. An anonymous poem transcribed in the West Saxon dialect of Old English at the end of the tenth century, it was most likely composed two centuries earlier. Although it was studied by a few antiquarians during the Renaissance, the poem remained virtually unknown until its first printing in 1815; only in this century has it achieved a place in the canon, not just as a cultural artifact or a good adventure story but as a philosophical epic of great complexity and power.

Several features of *Beowulf* make its genre a challenge for modern readers: the vivid accounts of battles with monsters link it to the folktale, and the recurring tone of sorrow for the passing of worldly things marks it as elegiac. Nevertheless, the poem is best approached as an epic. Like the *Iliad* and the *Odyssey*, it is a "primary epic," originating in oral tradition and recounting the legendary wars and exploits of great heroes from a lost heroic age.

The values of Germanic tribal society are central to *Beowulf*. A member of the *comitatus*—the band of warriors following a tribal lord—was expected to follow a code of heroic behavior stressing bravery, loyalty, and willingness to avenge his comrades and his lord at any cost. His lord rewarded him with treasure that symbolized this obligation, and he would suffer the shame of exile if he should survive his lord in battle. The values of the Germanic heroic code are invoked at the end of the poem, when Wiglaf, the hero's only loyal retainer, upbraids his comrades for having abandoned Beowulf to the dragon. He says that their prince wasted his war gear when he gave it to them at the mead hall and predicts the demise of their people, the Geats, once their ancient enemies, the Swedes, hear that Beowulf is dead.

Beowulf offers an extraordinarily double perspective, however. First, for all its acceptance of the values of pagan heroic code, it also refers to Christian concepts which in many cases conflict with them. While all characters in the poem—Danes, Swedes, and Geats, as well as the monsters—are pagan, the monster Grendel is described as descended from Cain and going to hell. Furthermore, while violence in the service of revenge is presented as the proper way for Beowulf to respond to inhuman assailants such as Grendel's mother, the narrator expresses a pacifist view, perhaps influenced by Christianity, of the unending chain of violence engaged in by feuding tribes. And although the Danish king Hrothgar uses wealth as a kind of social sacrament when he lavishly rewards Beowulf for his military aid, he simultaneously invokes God in a "sermon" warning him against excessive pride in his youthful strength. This rich division of emotional loyalty probably arises from a poet and audience of Christians who look back at their pagan Scandinavian ancestors with both pride and grief, stressing the intersection of pagan and Christian values in an effort to reconcile the two. By restricting Biblical references to events in the Old Testament, the poet shows the Germanic revenge ethic as consistent with the Old Law of retribution and plays down the New Testament injunction to forgive one's enemies.

Beowulf's style is simultaneously a challenge and a reward to the modern reader. Some of its features, such as the variation of an idea in different words—which would have been welcomed by a listening, and often illiterate, audience—can seem repetitious to a literate audience. Other features equally indebted to the poem's oral origin are admired today. For instance, like other Old English poems, *Beowulf* uses alliteration as a structural principle, beginning the first three of four stressed words in a line with the same letter, as in "wæs se grimma gæst Grendel hāten" ("this gruesome creature was called Grendel"). Such alliterative formulas—collocations of words—were an aid to a Germanic poet reliant on memory for composing poems. The *Beowulf* poet also loves to use compound words. While these are common in Germanic languages, including modern English (e.g., "mankind," "homesick"), this poet uses them with unusual inventiveness and force. Examples in the passage below include the terms "fifelcynnes" ("of monsterkind"), "mearcstapa" ("borderland-prowler"), and "wonsaeli" ("unhappy," "cursed"). A specific type of compound that is used for powerful stylistic effects is the "kenning," a kind of compressed metaphor, as in "swan's way" for "ocean." The kennings resemble the Old English riddles in their teasing, riddling quality.

On a larger narrative level is another feature, also traceable to the poem's oral origin: the tendency to digress into stories tangential to the action of the main plot. The poet's digressions, however, actually contribute to his artistry of broad contrasts—youth and age, joy and sorrow, good and bad kingship. For instance, Hrothgar, while urging humility and generosity on the victorious Beowulf, tells the story of the proud and stingy King Heremod. Similarly, when Beowulf returns home in glory to the kingdom of the Geats, the poet praises his uncle Hygelac's young Queen Hygd by contrasting her with the bad Queen Thryth, who lost her temper and sent her suitors to death.

The poet uses digression in a subtler way to foreshadow events to come. To celebrate Beowulf's victory over Grendel, the Scop at Hrothgar's hall sings of events generations earlier, in which a feud caused the deaths of a Danish princess's brother and son. Although this story has nothing to do with the main plot of the poem, there is an implied parallel a few lines later: the original audience would have known that after Hrothgar's death, his queen would lose her own son in comparable circumstances. The poet thus applies his broad principle of comparison and contrast to complex narrative situations as well as to simpler concepts such as good and bad kings. It is the often tragic tenor of these digressions that evokes much of the dark mood that suffuses *Beowulf*, even in its moments of heroic triumph.

The following passage of *Beowulf*, describing the monster's genealogy and menacing behavior, illustrates some of the stylistic features discussed above; included is a literal translation which makes these points more clearly than the more elegant one used in this anthology.*

	Swā ðā drihtguman drēamum lifdon,
100	ēadiglice, oð ðæt ān ongan
	fyrene fre(m)man fēond on helle;
	wæs se grimma gæst Grendel hāten,
	mǣre mearcstapa, sē þe mōras hēold,
	fen ond fæsten; fifelcynnes eard
105	wonsǣeliwer weardode hwile,
	siþðan him Scyppend forscrifen haefde
	in Cāines cynne— þone cwealm gewraec
	ēce Drihten, þaes þe hē Abel slōg;
	ne gefeah hē þǣre fǣð, ac hē hine feor forwraec,
110	Metod for þȳ māne mancynne fram.

* The passage is taken from *Beowulf and the Fight at Finnsburg*, ed. Frederick Klaeber, 3d ed. (Boston: D. C. Heath, 1950). The translation is by Anne Schotter.

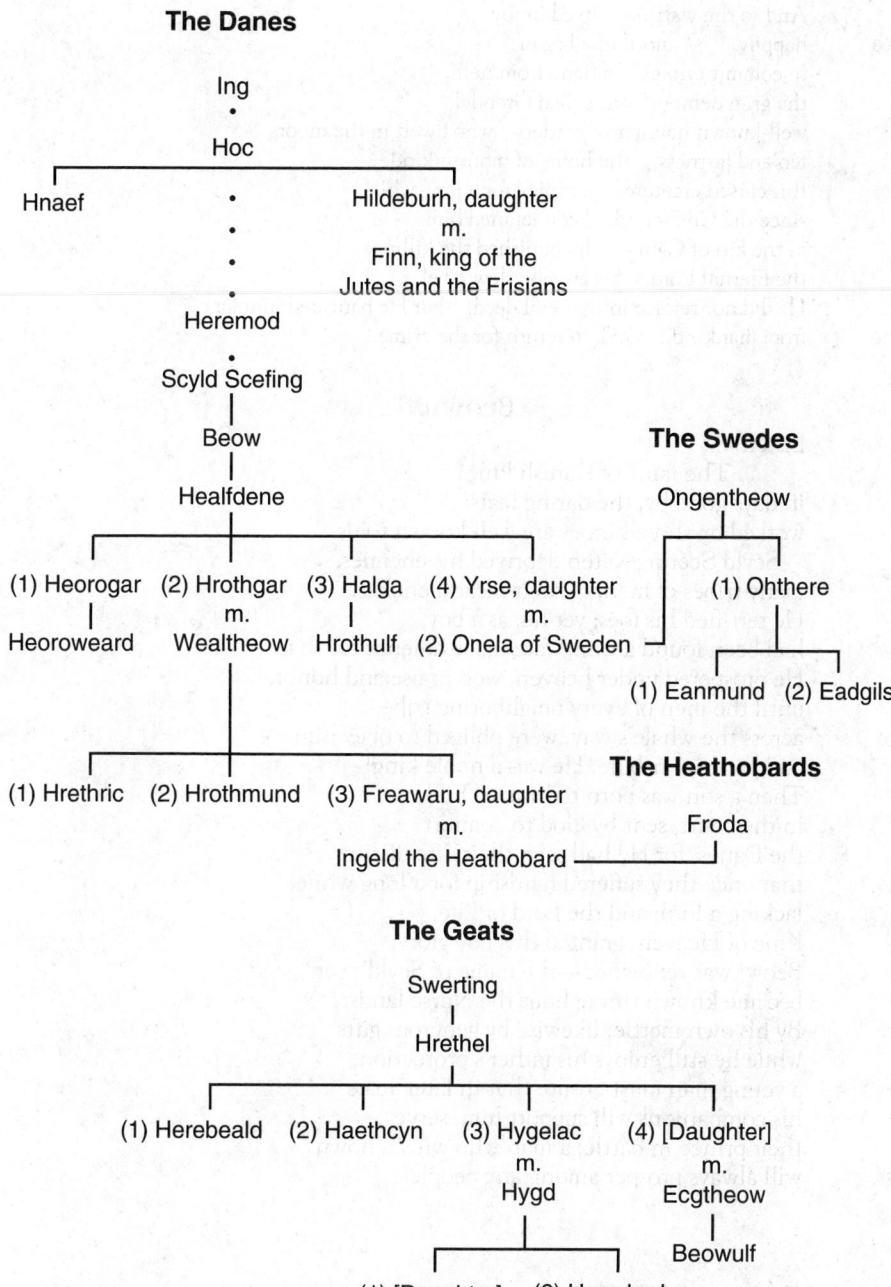

The Danes

Ing
•
Hoc

Hnaef   •   Hildeburh, daughter
         •   m.
         •   Finn, king of the
         •   Jutes and the Frisians

Heremod
•
Scyld Scefing

Beow

Healfdene   **The Swedes**

                                       Ongentheow

(1) Heorogar (2) Hrothgar (3) Halga (4) Yrse, daughter   (1) Ohthere
              m.   m.
Heoroweard   Wealtheow   Hrothulf   (2) Onela of Sweden

                                                      (1) Eanmund   (2) Eadgils

(1) Hrethric (2) Hrothmund (3) Freawaru, daughter   **The Heathobards**
                             m.   Froda
                Ingeld the Heathobard

The Geats

Swerting

Hrethel

(1) Herebeald   (2) Haethcyn   (3) Hygelac   (4) [Daughter]
                               m.   m.
                               Hygd   Ecgtheow

                                             Beowulf

                   (1) [Daughter]   (2) Heardred
                   m.
                   Eofor

Royal genealogies of the Northern European tribes according to the *Beowulf* text.

And so the warriors   lived in joy
100   happily   until one began
to commit crimes,   a fiend from hell
the grim demon   was called Grendel,
well-known haunter of borders   who dwelt in the moors
fen and fastness;   the home of monsterkind
105   this cursed creature   occupied for a long while
since the Creator   had condemned him
as the kin of Cain—   he punished the killing,
the Eternal Lord,   because he slew Abel;
He did not rejoice in that evil deed,   but He banished him far
110   from mankind,   God, in return for the crime.

Beowulf[1]

Listen!
         The fame of Danish kings
in days gone by, the daring feats
worked by those heroes are well known to us.
         Scyld Scefing[2] often deprived his enemies,
5   many tribes of men, of their mead-benches.
He terrified his foes; yet he, as a boy,
had been found a waif;[3] fate made amends for that.
He prospered under heaven, won praise and honor,
until the men of every neighboring tribe,
10   across the whale's way, were obliged to obey him
and pay him tribute. He was a noble king!
Then a son was born to him, a child
in the court, sent by God to comfort
the Danes; for He had seen their dire distress,
15   that once they suffered hardship for a long while,
lacking a lord; and the Lord of Life,
King of Heaven, granted this boy glory;
Beow[4] was renowned—the name of Scyld's son
became known throughout the Norse lands.
20   By his own mettle, likewise by generous gifts
while he still enjoys his father's protection,
a young man must ensure that in later years
his companions will support him, serve
their prince in battle; a man who wins renown
25   will always prosper among any people.

1. The modern English translation is by Kevin Crossley-Holland (1968).
2. The traditional founder of the Danish royal house. His name means "shield" or "protection" of the "sheaf," suggesting an earlier association in Norse mythology with the god of vegetation. The Danes are known afterwards as "Scyldings," descendants of Scyld.
3. Scyld Scefing arrives among the Danes as a foundling, a dangerous position in both Norse and Anglo-Saxon cultures. Solitaries and outcasts were generally regarded with suspicion; it is a tribute to Scyld Scefing that he surmounted these obstacles to become the leader and organizer of the Danish people.
4. The manuscript reads "Beowulf" here, the copyist's mind having skipped ahead to the story's protagonist.

Then Scyld departed at the destined hour,
that powerful man sought the Lord's protection.
His own close companions carried him
down to the sea, as he, lord of the Danes,
30   had asked while he could still speak.
That well-loved man had ruled his land for many years.
There in harbor stood the ring-prowed ship,
the prince's vessel, icy, eager to sail;
and then they laid their dear lord,
35   the giver of rings, deep within the ship
by the mast in majesty; many treasures
and adornments from far and wide were gathered there.
I have never heard of a ship equipped
more handsomely with weapons and war-gear,
40   swords and corslets; on his breast
lay countless treasures that were to travel far
with him into the waves' domain.
They gave him great ornaments, gifts
no less magnificent than those men had given him
45   who long before had sent him alone,
child as he was, across the stretch of the seas.
Then high above his head they placed
a golden banner and let the waves bear him,
bequeathed him to the sea; their hearts were grieving,
50   their minds mourning. Mighty men
beneath the heavens, rulers in the hall,
cannot say who received that cargo.
    When his royal father had traveled from the earth,
Beow of Denmark, a beloved king,
55   ruled long in the stronghold, famed
amongst men; in the time Healfdene the brave
was born to him; who, so long as he lived,
gray-haired and redoubtable, ruled the noble Danes.
Beow's son Healfdene, leader of men,
60   was favored by fortune with four children:
Heorogar and Hrothgar and Halga the good;
Yrse, the fourth, was Onela's queen,
the beloved wife of that warlike Swedish king.
    Hrothgar[5] won honor in war,
65   glory in battle, and so ensured
his followers' support—young men
whose number multiplied into a mighty troop.
And he resolved to build a hall,
a large and noble feasting-hall
70   of whose splendors men would always speak,

---

5. Significantly, Hrothgar is not the first-born of his generation. Leadership of the tribe was customarily conferred by acclamation upon the royal candidate who showed the greatest promise and ability.

and there to distribute as gifts to old and young
all the things that God had given him—
but not men's lives or the public land.
Then I heard that tribes without number, even
75 to the ends of the earth, were given orders
to decorate the hall. And in due course
(before very long) this greatest of halls
was completed. Hrothgar, whose very word was counted
far and wide as a command, called it Heorot.[6]
80 He kept his promise, gave presents of rings
and treasure at the feasting. The hall towered high,
lofty and wide-gabled—fierce tongues of loathsome fire
had not yet attacked it, nor was the time yet near
when a mortal feud should flare between father-
85 and son-in-law, sparked off by deeds of deadly enmity.[7]
        Then the brutish demon who lived in darkness
impatiently endured a time of frustration:
day after day he heard the din of merry-making
inside the hall, and the sound of the harp
90 and the bard's clear song. He who could tell
of the origin of men from far-off times lifted his voice,
sang that the Almighty made the earth,
this radiant plain encompassed by oceans;
and that God, all powerful, ordained
95 sun and moon to shine for mankind,
adorned all regions of the world
with trees and leaves; and sang that He gave life
to every kind of creature that walks about earth.
So those warrior Danes lived joyful lives,
100 in complete harmony, until the hellish fiend
began to perpetrate base crimes.
This gruesome creature was called Grendel,
notorious prowler of the borderland, ranger of the moors,
the fen and the fastness; this cursed creature
105 lived in a monster's lair for a time
after the Creator had condemned him
as one of the seed of Cain—the Everlasting Lord
avenged Abel's murder. Cain had
no satisfaction from that feud, but the Creator
110 sent him into exile, far from mankind,
because of his crime.[8] He could no longer
approach the throne of grace, that precious place
in God's presence, nor did he feel God's love.
In him all evil-doers find their origin,

6. The name of Hrothgar's hall in Anglo-Saxon literally
means "hart" or "stag," a male deer. The epithet "adorned
with horns," which is applied to Heorot later, may further
suggest its function as a hunting lodge.
7. The peace concluded between the Danes and the

Heathobards through intermarriage is already doomed
before it has taken place. The events foreshadowed here
will occur long after the time of the poem.
8. See Genesis 4.3–16.

115   monsters and elves and spiteful spirits of the dead,
        also the giants who grappled with God
        for a long while; the Lord gave them their deserts.
             Then, under cover of night, Grendel came
        to Hrothgar's lofty hall to see how the Ring-Danes[9]
120   were disposed after drinking ale all evening;
        and he found there a band of brave warriors,
        well-feasted, fast asleep, dead to worldly sorrow,
        man's sad destiny. At once that hellish monster,
        grim and greedy, brutally cruel,
125   started forward and seized thirty thanes
        even as they slept; and then, gloating
        over his plunder, he hurried from the hall,
        made for his lair with all those slain warriors.
        Then at dawn, as day first broke,
130   Grendel's power was at once revealed;
        a great lament was lifted, after the feast
        an anguished cry at that daylight discovery.
        The famous prince, best of all men, sat apart in mourning;
        when he saw Grendel's gruesome footprints,
135   that great man grieved for his retainers.
        This enmity was utterly one-sided, too repulsive,
        too long-lasting. Nor were the Danes allowed respite,
        but the very next day Grendel committed
        violent assault, murders more atrocious than before,
140   and he had no qualms about it. He was caught up in his crimes.
        Then it was not difficult to find the man
        who preferred a more distant resting-place,
        a bed in the outbuildings, for the hatred
        of the hall-warden was quite unmistakable.
145   He who had escaped the clutches of the fiend
        kept further off, at a safe distance.
             Thus Grendel ruled, resisted justice,
        one against all, until the best of halls
        stood deserted. And so it remained:
150   for twelve long winters the lord of the Danes
        was sorely afflicted with sorrows and cares;
        then men were reminded in mournful songs
        that the monster Grendel fought with Hrothgar
        for a long time, fought with fierce hatred
155   committing crime and atrocity day after day
        in continual strife. He had no wish for peace
        with any of the Danes, would not desist
        from his deadly malice or pay *wergild*.[1]
        No! None of the counselors could hold out hope
160   Of handsome compensation at that slayer's hands.

---

9. "Ring-Danes" refers to the Danes' practice of giving gifts in exchange for military services.
1. A cash payment for someone's death. *Wergild* was

regarded as an advance over violent revenge, and Grendel is marked as uncivilized because he refuses to acknowledge this practice.

But the cruel monster constantly terrified
young and old, the dark death-shadow
lurked in ambush; he prowled the misty moors
at the dead of night; men do not know
165   where such hell-whisperers shrithe in their wanderings.
Such were the many and outrageous injuries
that the fearful solitary, foe of all men,
endlessly inflicted; he occupied Heorot,
that hall adorned with treasures, on cloudless nights.
170   This caused the lord of the Danes deep,
heart-breaking grief. Strong men often sat
in consultation, trying in vain to devise
a good plan as to how best valiant men
could safeguard themselves against sudden attack.
175   At times they offered sacrifices to the idols
in their pagan tabernacles, and prayed aloud
to the soul-slayer[2] that he would assist them
in their dire distress. Such was the custom
and comfort of the heathen; they brooded in their hearts
180   on hellish things—for the Creator, Almighty God,
the judge of all actions, was neglected by them;
truly they did not know how to praise the Protector of Heaven,
the glorious Ruler. Woe to the man who,
in his wickedness, commits his soul to the fire's embrace;
185   he must expect neither comfort nor change.
He will be damned forever. Joy shall be his
who, when he dies, may stand before the Lord,
seek peace in the embrace of our Father.
    Thus Healfdene's son endlessly brooded
190   over the afflictions of this time; that wise warrior
was altogether helpless, for the hardship upon them—
violent visitations, evil events in the night—
was too overwhelming, loathsome, and long-lasting.
    One of Hygelac's thanes,[3] Beowulf by name,
195   renowned among the Geats[4] for his great bravery,
heard in his own country of Grendel's crimes;
he was the strongest man alive,
princely and powerful. He gave orders
that a good ship should be prepared, said he would sail
200   over the sea to assist the famous leader,
the warrior king, since he needed hardy men.
Wise men admired his spirit of adventure.
Dear to them though he was, they encouraged
the warrior and consulted the omens.
205   Beowulf searched out the bravest of the Geats,

---

2. In their fear, the Danes resume heathen practices. In Christian belief, the pagan gods were transformed into devils.
3. One of the king's principal retainers, chief among these being the earls.
4. A Germanic tribe who lived along the southwestern coast of what is now Sweden.

asked them to go with him; that seasoned sailor
led fourteen thanes to the ship at the shore.
    Days went by; the boat was on the water,
moored under the cliff. The warriors, all prepared,
210   stepped onto the prow—the water streams eddied,
stirred up sand; the men stowed
gleaming armor, noble war-gear
deep within the ship; then those warriors launched
the well-built boat and so began their journey.
215   Foaming at the prow and most like a sea-bird,
the boat sped over the waves, urged on by the wind;
until next day, at the expected time,
so far had the curved prow come
that the travelers sighted land,
220   shining cliffs, steep hills,
broad headlands. So did they cross the sea;
their journey was at its end. Then the Geats
disembarked, lost no time in tying up
the boat—their corslets clanked;
225   the warriors gave thanks to God
for their safe passage over the sea.
    Then, on the cliff-top, the Danish watchman
(whose duty it was to stand guard by the shore)
saw that the Geats carried flashing shields
230   and gleaming war-gear down the gangway,
and his mind was riddled with curiosity.
Then Hrothgar's thane leapt onto his horse
and, brandishing a spear, galloped
down to the shore; there, he asked at once:
235   "Warriors! Who are you, in your coats of mail,
who have steered your tall ship over the sea-lanes
to these shores? I've been a coastguard here
for many years, kept watch by the sea,
so that no enemy band should encroach
240   upon this Danish land and do us injury.
Never have warriors, carrying their shields,
come to this country in a more open manner.
Nor were you assured of my leaders' approval,
my kinsmen's consent. I've never set eyes
245   on a more noble man, a warrior in armor,
than one among your band; he's no mere retainer,
so ennobled by his weapons. May his looks never belie him,
and his lordly bearing. But now, before you step
one foot further on Danish land
250   like faithless spies, I must know
your lineage. Bold seafarers,
strangers from afar, mark my words
carefully: you would be best advised
quickly to tell me the cause of your coming."
255   The man of highest standing, leader of that troop,

unlocked his hoard of words, answered him:
"We are all Geats, hearth-companions of Hygelac;
my father was famed far and wide,
a noble lord, Ecgtheow by name—
260   he endured many winters before he,
in great old age, went on his way; every wise man
in this world readily recalls him.
We have sailed across the sea to seek your lord,
Healfdene's son, protector of the people,
265   with most honorable intentions; give us your guidance!
We have come on an errand of importance
to the great Danish prince; nor, I imagine, will the cause
of our coming long remain secret. You will know
whether it is true—as we have heard tell—
270   that here among the Danes a certain evil-doer,
a fearful solitary, on dark nights commits deeds
of unspeakable malice—damage
and slaughter. In all good conscience
I can counsel Hrothgar, that wise and good man,
275   how he shall overcome the fiend,
and how his anguish shall be assuaged—
if indeed his fate ordains that these foul deeds
should ever end, and be avenged;
he will suffer endless hardship otherwise,
280   dire distress, as long as Heorot, best of dwellings,
stands unshaken in its lofty place."
        Still mounted, the coastguard,
a courageous thane, gave him this reply:
"The discriminating warrior—one whose mind is keen—
285   must perceive the difference between words and deeds.
But I see you are a company well disposed
towards the Danish prince. Proceed, and bring
your weapons and armor! I shall direct you.
And I will command my companions, moreover,
290   to guard your ship with honor
against any foe—your beached vessel,
caulked so recently—until the day that timbered craft
with its curved prow shall carry back
the beloved man across the sea currents
295   to the shores of the storm-loving Geats:
he who dares deeds with such audacity and valor
shall be granted safety in the squall of battle."
        Then they hurried on. The ship lay still;
securely anchored, the spacious vessel
300   rode on its hawser. The boar crest, brightly gleaming,
stood over their helmets: superbly tempered,
plated with glowing gold, it guarded the lives
of those grim warriors. The thanes made haste,
marched along together until they could discern
305   the glorious, timbered hall, adorned with gold;

they saw there the best-known building
under heaven. The ruler lived in it;
its brilliance carried across countless lands.
Then the fearless watchman pointed out the path

310 leading to Heorot, bright home of brave men,
so that they should not miss the way;
that bold warrior turned his horse, then said:
"I must leave you here. May the Almighty Father,
of His grace, guard you in your enterprise.

315 I will go back to the sea again,
and there stand watch against marauding bands."
      The road was paved; it showed those warriors
the way. Their corslets were gleaming,
the strong links of shining chain-mail

320 clinked together. When the sea-stained travelers
had reached the hall itself in their fearsome armor,
they placed their broad shields
(worked so skillfully) against Heorot's wall.
Then they sat on a bench; the brave men's

325 armor sang. The seafarers' gear
stood all together, a gray-tipped forest
of ash spears; that armed troop was well equipped
with weapons.
                  Then Wulfgar, a proud warrior,
asked the Geats about their ancestry:

330 "Where have you come from with these gold-plated shields,
these gray coats of mail, these visored helmets,

Boar, from a bas-relief carving on Saint Nicholas Church, Ipswich, England, 12th century.
Although this large and vigorous boar dates from the 12th century, it retains stylistic elements of
earlier Anglo-Saxon and Viking art. An ancient totem of power, boars were often depicted on
early medieval weapons and helmets.

and this pile of spears? I am Hrothgar's
messenger, his herald. I have never seen
so large a band of strangers of such bold bearing.
335   You must have come to Hrothgar's court
not as exiles, but from audacity and high ambition."
Then he who feared no man, the proud leader
of the Geats, stern-faced beneath his helmet,
gave him this reply: "We are Hygelac's
340   companions at the bench: my name is Beowulf.
I wish to explain to Healfdene's son,
the famous prince, your lord,
why we have come if he, in his goodness,
will give us leave to speak with him."
345   Wulfgar replied—a prince of the Vandals,
his mettle, his wisdom and prowess in battle
were widely recognized: "I will ask
the lord of the Danes, ruler of the Scyldings,
renowned prince and ring-giver,
350   just as you request, regarding your journey,
and bring back to you at once whatever answer
that gracious man thinks fit to give me."
      Then Wulfgar hurried to the place where Hrothgar sat,
grizzled and old, surrounded by his thanes;
355   the brave man moved forward until he stood
immediately before the Danish lord;
he well knew the customs of warriors.
Wulfgar addressed his friend and leader:
"Geatish men have traveled to this land,
360   come from far, across the stretch of the seas.
These warriors call their leader Beowulf;
they ask, my lord, that they should be allowed
to speak with you. Gracious Hrothgar,
do not give them *no* for answer.
365   They, in their armor, seem altogether worthy
of the highest esteem. I have no doubt of their leader's
might, he who has brought these brave men to Heorot."
Hrothgar, defender of the Danes, answered:
"I knew him when he was a boy;
370   his illustrious father was called Ecgtheow;
Hrethel the Geat gave him his only daughter
in marriage; now his son, with daring spirit,
has voyaged here to visit a loyal friend.
And moreover, I have heard seafarers say—
375   men who have carried rich gifts to the Geats
as a mark of my esteem—that in the grasp
of his hand that man renowned in battle
has the might of thirty men. I am convinced
that Holy God, of His great mercy,
380   has directed him to us West-Danes[5]

5. Hrothgar is, in fact, king of all the Danes: North, South, East, and West. The different terms merely conform to the
Anglo-Saxon alliterative pattern established in each line.

and that he means to come to grips with Grendel.
I will reward this brave man with treasures.
Hurry! Tell them to come in and meet
our band of kinsmen; and make it clear, too,
385   that they are most welcome to the Danes!"
Then Wulfgar went to the hall door with Hrothgar's reply:
"My conquering lord, the leader of the East-Danes
commands me to tell you that he knows your lineage
and that you, so bold in mind, are welcome
390   to these shores from over the rolling sea.
You may see Hrothgar in your armor,
under your helmets, just as you are;
but leave your shields out here, and your deadly ashen spears,
let them await the outcome of your words."
395   Then noble Beowulf rose from the bench,
flanked by his fearless followers; some stayed behind
at the brave man's bidding, to stand guard over their armor.
Guided by Wulfgar, the rest hurried into Heorot
together; there went that hardy man, stern-faced
400   beneath his helmet, until he was standing under Heorot's roof.
Beowulf spoke—his corslet, cunningly linked
by the smith, was shining: "Greetings, Hrothgar!
I am Hygelac's kinsman and retainer. In my youth
I achieved many daring exploits. Word of Grendel's deeds
405   has come to me in my own country;
seafarers say that this hall Heorot,
best of all buildings, stands empty and useless
as soon as the evening light is hidden under the sky.
So, Lord Hrothgar, men known by my people
410   to be noble and wise advised me to visit you
because they knew of my great strength:
they saw me themselves when, stained by my enemies' blood,
I returned from the fight when I destroyed five,
a family of giants, and by night slew monsters
415   on the waves; I suffered great hardship,
avenged the affliction of the Storm-Geats and crushed
their fierce foes—they were asking for trouble.
And now, I shall crush the giant Grendel
in single combat. Lord of the mighty Danes,
420   guardian of the Scyldings, I ask one favor:
protector of warriors, lord beloved of your people,
now that I have sailed here from so far,
do not refuse my request—that I alone, with my band
of brave retainers, may cleanse Heorot.
425   I have also heard men say this monster
is so reckless he spurns the use of weapons.
Therefore (so that Hygelac, my lord,
may rest content over my conduct) I deny myself
the use of a sword and a broad yellow shield
430   in battle; but I shall grapple with this fiend
hand to hand; we shall fight for our lives,
foe against foe; and he whom death takes off

must resign himself to the judgment of God.
I know that Grendel, should he overcome me,
435   will without dread devour many Geats,
matchless warriors, in the battle-hall,
as he has often devoured Danes before. If death claims me
you will not have to cover my head,
for he already will have done so—
440   with a sheet of shining blood; he will carry off
the blood-stained corpse, meaning to savor it;
the solitary one will eat without sorrow
and stain his lair; no longer then
will you have to worry about burying my body.
445   But if battle should claim me, send this most excellent
coat of mail to Hygelac, this best of corslets
that protects my breast; it once belonged to Hrethel,
the work of Weland.[6] Fate goes ever as it must!"
    Hrothgar, protector of the Scyldings, replied:
450   "Beowulf, my friend! So you have come here,
because of past favors, to fight on our behalf!
Your father Ecgtheow, by striking a blow,
began the greatest of feuds. He slew Heatholaf of the Wylfings
with his own hand; after that, the Geats
455   dared not harbor him for fear of war.
So he sailed here, over the rolling waves,
to this land of the South-Danes, the honored Scyldings;
I was young then, had just begun to reign
over the Danes in this glorious kingdom,
460   this treasure-stronghold of heroes; my elder brother,
Heorogar, Healfdene's son, had died
not long before; he was a better man than I!
I settled your father's feud by payment;
I sent ancient treasures to the Wylfings
465   over the water's back; and Ecgtheow swore oaths to me.
It fills me with anguish to admit to all the evil
that Grendel, goaded on by his hatred,
has wreaked in Heorot with his sudden attacks
and infliction of injuries; my hall-troop is depleted,
470   my band of warriors; fate has swept them
into Grendel's ghastly clutches. Yet God can easily
prevent this reckless ravager from committing such crimes.
After quaffing beer, brave warriors of mine
have often boasted over the ale-cup
475   that they would wait in Heorot
and fight against Grendel with their fearsome swords.
Then, the next morning, when day dawned,
men could see that this great mead-hall was stained
by blood, that the floor by the benches
480   was spattered with gore; I had fewer followers,
dear warriors, for death had taken them off.

6. Legendary blacksmith of the Norse gods.

But first, sit down at our feast, and in due course,
as your inclination takes you, tell how warriors
have achieved greatness."
                                        Then, in the feasting-hall,
485   a bench was cleared for the Geats all together,
and there those brave men went and sat,
delighting in their strength; a thane did his duty—
held between his hands the adorned ale-cup,
poured out gleaming liquor; now and then the poet sang,
490   raised his clear voice in Heorot; the warriors caroused,
no small company of Scyldings and Geats.
Ecglaf's son, Unferth,[7] who sat at the feet
of the lord of the Scyldings, unlocked his thoughts
with these unfriendly words—for the journey of Beowulf,
495   the brave seafarer, much displeased him
in that he was unwilling for any man
in this wide world to gain more glory than himself:
"Are you the Beowulf who competed with Breca,
vied with him at swimming in the open sea
500   when, swollen with vanity, you both braved
the waves, risked your lives on deep waters
because of a foolish boast? No one,
neither friend nor foe, could keep you
from your sad journey, when you swam out to sea,
505   clasped in your arms the water-streams,
passed over the sea-paths, swiftly moved your hands
and sped over the ocean. The sea heaved,
the winter flood; for seven nights
you both toiled in the water; but Breca outstayed you,
510   he was the stronger; and then, on the eighth morning,
the sea washed him up on the shores of the Heathoreams.
From there he sought his own country,
the land of the Brondings who loved him well;
he went to his fair stronghold where he had a hall
515   and followers and treasures. In truth, Beanstan's son
fulfilled his boast that he could swim better than you.
So I am sure you will pay a heavy price—
although you have survived countless battle storms,
savage sword-play—if you dare
520   ambush Grendel in the watches of the night."
Beowulf, the son of Ecgtheow, replied:
"Truly, Unferth my friend, all this beer
has made you talkative: you have told us much
about Breca and his exploits. But I maintain
525   I showed the greater stamina, endured
hardship without equal in the heaving water.
Some years ago when we were young men,
still in our youth, Breca and I made a boast,

---

7. Hrothgar's spokesman or court jester; his rude behavior toward Beowulf is consistent with other figures in epics and romances who taunt the hero before he undertakes his exploits. "Unferth" may mean "strife."

a solemn vow, to venture our lives
530   on the open sea; and we kept our word.
When we swam through the water, we each held
a naked sword with which to ward off
whales; by no means could Breca
swim faster than I, pull away from me
535   through the press of the waves—
I had no wish to be separated from him.
So for five nights we stayed together in the sea,
until the tides tore us apart,
the foaming water, the freezing cold,
540   day darkening into night—until the north wind,
that savage warrior, rounded against us.
Rough were the waves; fishes in the sea
were roused to great anger. Then my coat of mail,
hard and hand-linked, guarded me against my enemies;
545   the woven war-garment, adorned with gold,
covered my breast. A cruel ravager
dragged me down to the sea-bed, a fierce monster
held me tightly in its grasp; but it was given to me
to bury my sword, my battle weapon,
550   in its breast; the mighty sea-beast
was slain by my blow in the storm of battle.
In this manner, and many times, loathsome monsters
harassed me fiercely; with my fine sword
I served them fittingly.
555   I did not allow those evil destroyers to enjoy
a feast, to eat me limb by limb
seated at a banquet on the sea-bottom;
but the next morning they lay in the sand
along the shore, wounded by sword strokes,
560   slain by battle-blades, and from that day on
they could not hinder seafarers from sailing
over deep waters. Light came from the east,
God's bright beacon; the swell subsided,
and I saw then great headlands,
565   cliffs swept by the wind. Fate will often spare
an undoomed man, if his courage is good.
As it was I slew nine sea-beasts
with my sword. I have never heard
of a fiercer fight by night under heaven's vault
570   nor of a man who endured more on the ocean streams.
But I escaped with my life from the enemies' clutches,
worn out by my venture. Then the swift current,
the surging water, carried me
to the land of the Lapps. I have not heard tell
575   that you have taken part in any such contests,
in the peril of sword-play. Neither you nor Breca
have yet dared such a deed with shining sword
in battle—I do not boast because of this—
though of course it is true you slew your own brothers,

580   your own close kinsmen. For that deed, however clever
you may be, you will suffer damnation in hell.
I tell you truly, son of Ecglaf,
that if you were in fact as unflinching
as you claim, the fearsome monster Grendel
585   would never have committed so many crimes
against your lord, nor created such havoc in Heorot;
but he has found he need not fear unduly
your people's enmity, fearsome assault
with swords by the victorious Scyldings.
590   So he spares none but takes his toll
of the Danish people, does as he will,
kills and destroys, expects no fight
from the Spear-Danes. But soon, quite soon,
I shall show him the strength, the spirit and skill
595   of the Geats. And thereafter, when day dawns,
when the radiant sun shines from the south
over the sons of men, he who so wishes
may enter the mead-hall without terror."
        Then the grizzled warrior, giver of gold,
600   was filled with joy; the lord of the Danes,
shepherd of his people, listened to Beowulf's
brave resolution and relied on his help.
The warriors laughed, there was a hum
of contentment. Wealhtheow came forward,[8]
605   mindful of ceremonial—she was Hrothgar's queen;
adorned with gold, that proud woman
greeted the men in the hall, then offered the cup
to the Danish king first of all.
She begged him, beloved of his people,
610   to enjoy the feast; the king, famed
for victory, ate and drank in happiness.
Then the lady of the Helmings walked about the hall,
offering the precious, ornamented cup
to old and young alike, until at last
615   the queen, excellent in mind, adorned with rings,
moved with the mead-cup towards Beowulf.
She welcomed the Geatish prince and with wise words
thanked God that her wish was granted
that she might depend on some warrior for help
620   against such attacks. The courageous warrior
took the cup from Wealhtheow's hands
and, eager for battle, made a speech:
Beowulf, the son of Ecgtheow, said:
"When I put to sea, sailed
625   through the breakers with my band of men,
I resolved to fulfill the desire

---

8. "Wealhtheow" means "foreign slave," and she may be British or Celtic in origin. Even after her marriage to Hrothgar, she continues to maintain her identity as the "lady of the Helmings," an epithet recalling her father Helm.

of your people, or suffer the pangs of death,
caught fast in Grendel's clutches.
Here, in Heorot, I shall either work a deed
630   of great daring, or lay down my life."
Beowulf's brave boast delighted Wealhtheow:
adorned with gold, the noble Danish queen
went to sit beside her lord.
      Then again, as of old, fine words were spoken
635   in the hall, the company rejoiced,
a conquering people, until in due course
the son of Healfdene wanted to retire
and take his rest. He realized the monster
meant to attack Heorot after the blue hour,
640   when black night has settled over all—
when shadowy shapes come shrithing
dark beneath the clouds. All the company rose.
Then the heroes Hrothgar and Beowulf saluted
one another; Hrothgar wished him luck
645   and control of Heorot, and confessed:
"Never since I could lift hand and shield,
have I entrusted this glorious Danish hall
to any man as I do now to you.
Take and guard this greatest of halls.
650   Make known your strength, remember your might,
stand watch against your enemy. You shall have
all you desire if you survive this enterprise."
      Then Hrothgar, defender of the Danes,
withdrew from the hall with his band of warriors.
655   The warlike leader wanted to sleep with Wealhtheow,
his queen. It was said the mighty king
had appointed a hall-guard—a man who undertook
a dangerous duty for the Danish king,
elected to stand watch against the monster.
660   Truly, the leader of the Geats fervently trusted
in his own great strength and in God's grace.
Then he took off his helmet and his corslet
of iron, and gave them to his servant,
with his superb, adorned sword,
665   telling him to guard them carefully.
And then, before he went to his bed,
the brave Geat, Beowulf, made his boast:
"I count myself no less active in battle,
no less brave than Grendel himself:
670   thus, I will not send him to sleep with my sword,
so deprive him of life, though certainly I could.
Despite his fame for deadly deeds,
he is ignorant of these noble arts, that he might strike
at me, and hew my shield; but we, this night,
675   shall forgo the use of weapons, if he dares fight
without them; and then may wise God,
the holy Lord, give glory in battle

to whichever of us He should think fitting."
Then the brave prince leaned back, put his head
680   on the pillow while, around him,
many a proud seafarer lay back on his bed.
Not one of them believed he would see
day dawn, or ever return to his family
and friends, and the place where he was born;
685   they well knew that in recent days
far too many Danish men had come to bloody ends
in that hall. But the Lord wove the webs of destiny,
gave the Geats success in their struggle,
help and support, in such a way
690   that all were enabled to overcome their enemy
through the strength of one man. We cannot doubt
that mighty God has always ruled
over mankind.[9]
          Then the night prowler
came shrithing through the shadows. All the Geats
695   guarding Heorot had fallen asleep—
all except one. Men well knew that the evil enemy
could not drag them down into the shadows
when it was against the Creator's wishes,
but Beowulf, watching grimly for his adversary Grendel,
700   awaited the ordeal with increasing anger.
Then, under night's shroud, Grendel walked down
from the moors; he shouldered God's anger.
The evil plunderer intended to ensnare
one of the race of men in the high hall.
705   He strode under the skies, until he stood
before the feasting-hall, in front of the gift-building
gleaming with gold. And this night was not the first
on which he had so honored Hrothgar's home.
But never in his life did he find hall-wardens
710   more greatly to his detriment. Then the joyless warrior
journeyed to Heorot. The outer door, bolted
with iron bands, burst open at a touch from his hands:
with evil in his mind, and overriding anger,
Grendel swung open the hall's mouth itself. At once,
715   seething with fury, the fiend stepped onto
the tessellated floor; a horrible light,
like a lurid flame, flickered in his eyes.
He saw many men, a group of warriors,
a knot of kinsmen, sleeping in the hall.
720   His spirits leapt, his heart laughed;
the savage monster planned to sever,
before daybreak, the life of every warrior
from his body—he fully expected to eat

---

9. This interpolation of Christian belief into what is essentially a pagan tradition has been taken as evidence of a conscious rewriting of much earlier material. The narrative assures its reader that Christian beliefs were still valid, regardless of what the characters in the story may have believed.

920 had no longer believed that my afflictions
would ever end: this finest of buildings
stood stained with battle blood,
a source of sorrow to my counselors;
they all despaired of regaining this hall

925 for many years to come, of guarding it from foes,
from devils and demons. Yet now one warrior
alone, through the Almighty's power, has succeeded
where we failed for all our fine plans.
Indeed, if she is still alive,

930 that woman (whoever she was) who gave birth
to such a son, to be one of humankind,
may claim that the Creator was gracious to her
in her childbearing. Now, Beowulf,
best of men, I will love you in my heart

935 like a son; keep to our new kinship
from this day on. You shall lack
no earthly riches I can offer you.
Most often I have honored a man for less,
given treasure to a poorer warrior,

940 more sluggish in the fight. Through your deeds
you have ensured that your glorious name
will endure forever. May the Almighty grant you
good fortune, as He has always done before!"
Beowulf, the son of Ecgtheow, answered:

945 "We performed that dangerous deed
with good will; at peril we pitted ourselves
against the unknown. I wish so much
that you could have seen him for yourself,
that fiend in his trappings, in the throes of death.

950 I meant to throttle him on that bed of slaughter
as swiftly as possible, with savage grips,
to hear death rattle in his throat
because of my grasp, unless he should escape me.
But I could not detain him, the Lord

955 did not ordain it—I did not hold my deadly enemy
firm enough for that; the fiend jerked free
with immense power. Yet, so as to save
his life, he left behind his hand,
his arm and shoulder; but the wretched monster

960 has bought himself scant respite;
the evil marauder, tortured by his sins,
will not live the longer, but agony
embraces him in its deadly bonds,
squeezes life out of his lungs; and now this creature,

965 stained with crime, must await the day of judgment
and his just deserts from the glorious Creator."
After this, the son of Ecglaf [3] boasted less
about his prowess in battle—when all the warriors,

---

3. Unferth is referred to by his father's name. This may be ironic, since Unferth has killed members of his own family.

through Beowulf's might, had been enabled
970 to examine that hand, the fiend's fingers,
nailed up on the gables. Seen from in front,
each nail, each claw of that warlike,
heathen monster looked like steel—
a terrifying spike. Everyone said
975 that no weapon whatsoever, no proven sword
could possibly harm it, could damage
that battle-hardened, blood-stained hand.

    Then orders were quickly given for the inside of Heorot
to be decorated; many servants, both men and women,
980 bustled about that wine-hall, adorned that building
of retainers. Tapestries, worked in gold,
glittered on the walls, many a fine sight
for those who have eyes to see such things.
That beautiful building, braced within
985 by iron bands, was badly damaged;
the door's hinges were wrenched; when the monster,
damned by all his crimes, turned in flight,
despairing of his life, the hall roof only
remained untouched. Death is not easy
990 to escape, let him who will attempt it.
Man must go to the grave that awaits him—
fate has ordained this for all who have souls,
children of men, earth's inhabitants—
and his body, rigid on its clay bed,
995 will sleep there after the banquet.
                               Then it was time
for Healfdene's son to proceed to the hall,
the king himself was eager to attend the feast.
I have never heard of a greater band of kinsmen
gathered with such dignity around their ring-giver.
1000 Then the glorious warriors sat on the benches,
rejoicing in the feast. Courteously
their kinsmen, Hrothgar and Hrothulf,
quaffed many a mead-cup, confident warriors
in the high hall. Heorot was packed
1005 with feasters who were friends; the time was not yet come
when the Scyldings practiced wrongful deeds.[4]
Then Hrothgar gave Beowulf Healfdene's sword,
and a battle banner, woven with gold,
and a helmet and a corslet, as rewards for victory;
1010 many men watched while the priceless, renowned sword
was presented to the hero. Beowulf emptied
the ale-cup in the hall; he had no cause
to be ashamed at those precious gifts.
There are few men, as far as I have heard,
1015 who have given four such treasures, gleaming with gold,
to another on the mead-bench with equal generosity.
A jutting ridge, wound about with metal wires,

4. Possibly an allusion to the later usurpation of the Danish throne by Hrothgar's nephew Hrothulf.

ran over the helmet's crown, protecting the skull,
so that well-ground swords, proven in battle,
1020 could not injure the well-shielded warrior
when he advanced against his foes.
Then the guardian of thanes ordered
that eight horses with gold-plated bridles
be led into the courtyard; onto one was strapped
1025 a saddle, inlaid with jewels, skillfully made.
That was the war-seat of the great king,
Healfdene's son, whenever he wanted
to join in the sword-play. That famous man
never lacked bravery at the front in battle,
1030 when men about him were cut down like corn.
Then the king of the Danes, Ing's[5] descendants,
presented the horses and weapons to Beowulf,
bade him use them well and enjoy them.
Thus the renowned prince, the retainers' gold-warden,
1035 rewarded those fierce sallies in full measure,
with horses and treasure, so that no man
would ever find reason to reproach him fairly.
Furthermore, the guardian of warriors gave
a treasure, an heirloom at the mead-bench,
1040 to each of those men who had crossed the sea
with Beowulf; and he ordered that gold
be paid for that warrior Grendel slew
so wickedly—as he would have slain many another,
had not foreseeing God and the warrior's courage
1045 together forestalled him. The Creator ruled over
all humankind, even as He does today.
Wherefore a wise man will value forethought
and understanding. Whoever lives long
on earth, endures the unrest of these times,
1050 will be involved in much good and much evil.
      Then Hrothgar, leader in battle, was entertained
with music—harp and voice in harmony.
The strings were plucked, many a song rehearsed,
when it was the turn of Hrothgar's poet
1055 to please men at the mead-bench, perform in the hall.
He sang of Finn's troop,[6] victims of surprise attack,
and of how that Danish hero, Hnaef of the Scyldings,
was destined to die among the Frisian slain.
      Hildeburh, indeed, could hardly recommend
1060 the honor of the Jutes; that innocent woman
lost her loved ones, son and brother,
in the shield-play; they fell, as fate ordained,

---

5. Another, earlier king of the Danes.
6. The following episode is one of the most obscure in
Beowulf. It seems that Hnaef and Hildeburh are both
children of an earlier Danish king named Hoc and that
Hildeburh has been sent to marry Finn, the son of Folcwalda and king of the Jutes and Frisians, in order to
conclude a marriage alliance and thus settle a prior

blood feud between the two tribes. Upon going to visit
his sister and her husband, Hnaef is treacherously
ambushed and killed by Finn's men; Hildeburh's son by
Finn is also killed. In her role as peace-weaver, Hildeburh, is torn by conflicting allegiances, foreshadowing
the fate of Hrothgar's own daughter Freawaru in her
marriage to Ingeld.

stricken by spears; and she was stricken with grief.
Not without cause did Hoc's daughter
1065 mourn the shaft of fate, for in the light of morning
she saw that her kin lay slain under the sky,
the men who had been her endless pride
and joy. That encounter laid claim
to all but a few of Finn's thanes,
1070 and he was unable to finish that fight
with Hnaef's retainer, with Hengest in the hall,
unable to dislodge the miserable survivors;
indeed, terms for a truce were agreed:
that Finn should give up to them another hall,
1075 with its high seat, in its entirety,
which the Danes should own in common with the Jutes;
and that at the treasure-giving the son of Folcwalda
should honor the Danes day by day,
should distribute rings and gold-adorned gifts
1080 to Hengest's band and his own people in equal measure.
Both sides pledged themselves to this peaceful
settlement. Finn swore Hengest solemn oaths
that he would respect the sad survivors
as his counselors ordained, and that no man there
1085 must violate the covenant with word or deed,
or complain about it, although they
would be serving the slayer of their lord
(as fate had forced those lordless men to do);
and he warned the Frisians that if, in provocation,
1090 they should mention the murderous feud,
the sword's edge should settle things.
The funeral fire was prepared, glorious gold
was brought up from the hoard: the best of Scyldings,
that race of warriors, lay ready on the pyre.
1095 Blood-stained corslets, and images of boars
(cast in iron and covered in gold)
were plentiful on that pyre, and likewise the bodies
of many retainers, ravaged by wounds;
renowned men fell in that slaughter.
1100 Then Hildeburh asked that her own son
be committed to the flames at her brother's funeral,
that his body be consumed on Hnaef's pyre.
That grief-stricken woman keened over his corpse,
sang doleful dirges. The warriors' voices
1105 soared towards heaven. And so did the smoke
from the great funeral fire that roared
before the barrow; heads sizzled,
wounds split open, blood burst out
from battle scars. The ravenous flames
1110 swallowed those men whole, made no distinction
between Frisians and Danes; the finest men departed.
Then those warriors, their friends lost to them,
went to view their homes, revisit the stronghold
and survey the Frisian land. But Hengest

1115 stayed with Finn, in utter dejection, all through
      that blood-stained winter. And he dreamed
      of his own country, but he was unable to steer
      his ship homeward, for the storm-beaten sea
      wrestled with the wind; winter sheathed the waves
1120 in ice—until once again spring made its sign
      (as still it does) among the houses of men:
      clear days, warm weather, in accordance as always
      with the law of the seasons. Then winter was over,
      the face of the earth was fair; the exile
1125 was anxious to leave that foreign people
      and the Frisian land. And yet he brooded
      more about vengeance than about a voyage,
      and wondered whether he could bring about a clash
      so as to repay the sons of the Jutes.
1130 Thus Hengest did not shrink from the duty of vengeance
      after Hunlafing had placed the flashing sword,
      finest of all weapons, on his lap;
      this sword's edges had scarred many Jutes.
      And so it was that cruel death by the sword later
1135 cut down the brave warrior Finn in his own hall,
      after Guthlaf and Oslaf, arrived from a sea-journey,
      had fiercely complained of that first attack,
      condemned the Frisians on many scores:
      the Scyldings' restless spirits could no longer
1140 be restrained. Then the hall ran red with the blood
      of the enemy—Finn himself was slain,
      the king with his troop, and Hildeburh was taken.
      The Scylding warriors carried that king's
      heirlooms down to their ship,
1145 all the jewels and necklaces they discovered
      at Finn's hall. They sailed over the sea-paths,
      brought that noble lady back to Denmark
      and her own people.
                          Thus was the lay sung,
      the song of the poet. The hall echoed with joy,
1150 waves of noise broke out along the benches;
      cup-bearers carried wine in glorious vessels.
      Then Wealhtheow, wearing her golden collar, walked
      to where Hrothgar and Hrothulf were sitting side by side,
      uncle and nephew, still friends together, true to one another.
1155 And the spokesman Unferth sat at the feet
      of the Danish lord; all men admired
      his spirit and audacity, although he had deceived
      his own kinsmen in a feud. Then the lady of the Scyldings
      spoke these words: "Accept this cup, my loved lord,
1160 treasure-giver; O gold-friend of men,
      learn the meaning of joy again, and speak words
      of gratitude to the Geats, for so one ought to do.
      And be generous to them too, mindful of gifts
      which you have now amassed from far and wide.
1165 I am told you intend to adopt this warrior,

take him for your son. This resplendent ring-hall,
Heorot, has been cleansed; give many rewards
while you may, but leave this land and the Danish people
to your own descendants when the day comes
1170   for you to die. I am convinced
that gracious Hrothulf will guard our children
justly, should he outlive you, lord of the Scyldings,
in this world; I believe he will repay our sons
most generously if he remembers all we did
1175   for his benefit and enjoyment when he was a boy."
Then Wealhtheow walked to the bench where her sons,
Hrethric and Hrothmund, sat with the sons of thanes,
fledgling warriors; where also that brave man,
Beowulf of the Geats, sat beside the brothers.
1180   To him she carried the cup, and asked in gracious words
if he would care to drink; and to him she presented
twisted gold with courtly ceremonial—
two armlets, a corslet and many rings,
and the most handsome collar in the world.
1185   I have never heard that any hero had a jewel
to equal that, not since Hama made off
for his fortress with the Brosings' necklace,[7] that pendant
in its precious setting; he fled from the enmity
of underhand Eormenric, he chose long-lasting gain.
1190   Hygelac the Geat, grandson of Swerting,
wore that necklace on his last raid
when he fought beneath his banner to defend his treasure,
his battle spoils; fate claimed him then,
when he, foolhardy, courted disaster,
1195   a feud with the Frisians. On that occasion the famous prince
had carried the treasure, the priceless stones,
over the cup of the waves; he crumpled under his shield.
Then the king's body fell into the hands of Franks,
his coat of mail and the collar also;
1200   after that battle, weaker warriors picked at
and plundered the slain; many a Geat lay dead, guarding
that place of corpses.
              Applause echoed in the hall.
Wealhtheow spoke these words before the company:
"May you, Beowulf, beloved youth, enjoy
1205   with all good fortune this necklace and corslet,
treasures of the people; may you always prosper;
win renown through courage, and be kind in your counsel
to these boys; for that, I will reward you further.
You have ensured that men will always sing
1210   your praises, even to the ends of the world,
as far as oceans still surround cliffs,
home of the winds. May you thrive, O prince,

---

7. The narrative jumps ahead beyond Beowulf's return home to the Geats. His uncle, Hygelac, the king, will not only receive the necklace from Beowulf but will die with it in battle among the Frisians. The necklace thus connects different events at different times.

afflicts the Danish people. Yrmenlaf's
elder brother, Aeschere, is dead,
my closest counselor and my comrade,
my shoulder-companion when we shielded
1315   our heads in the fight, when soldiers clashed on foot,
slashed at boar-crests. Aeschere was all
that a noble man, a warrior should be.
The wandering, murderous monster slew him
in Heorot; and I do not know where that ghoul,
1320   drooling at her feast of flesh and blood,
made off afterwards. She has avenged her son
whom you savaged yesterday with vicelike holds
because he had impoverished and killed my people
for many long years. He fell in mortal combat,
1325   forfeit of his life; and now another mighty
evil ravager has come to avenge her kinsman;
and many a thane, mournful in his mind
for his treasure-giver, may feel she has avenged
that feud already, indeed more than amply;
1330   now that hand lies still which once sustained you.
    "I have heard my people say,
men of this country, counselors in the hall,
that they have seen *two* such beings,
equally monstrous, rangers of the fell-country,
1335   rulers of the moors; and these men assert
that so far as they can see one bears
a likeness to a woman; grotesque though he was,
the other who trod the paths of exile looked like a man,
though greater in height and build than a goliath;
1340   he was christened *Grendel* by my people
many years ago; men do not know if he
had a father, a fiend once begotten
by mysterious spirits. These two live
in a little-known country, wolf-slopes, windswept headlands,
1345   perilous paths across the boggy moors, where a mountain stream
plunges under the mist-covered cliffs,
rushes through a fissure. It is not far from here,
if measured in miles, that the lake stands
shadowed by trees stiff with hoar-frost.
1350   A wood, firmly-rooted, frowns over the water.
There, night after night, a fearful wonder may be seen—
fire on the water; no man alive
is so wise as to know the nature of its depths.
Although the moor-stalker, the stag with strong horns,
1355   when harried by hounds will make for the wood,
pursued from afar, he will succumb
to the hounds on the brink, rather than plunge in
and save his head. That is not a pleasant place.
When the wind arouses the wrath of the storm,
1360   whipped waves rear up black from the lake,
reach for the skies, until the air becomes misty,

the heavens weep. Now, once again, help may be had
from you alone. As yet, you have not seen the haunt,
the perilous place where you may meet this most evil monster
1365   face to face. Do you dare set eyes on it?
If you return unscathed, I will reward you
for your audacity, as I did before,
with ancient treasures and twisted gold."
        Beowulf, the son of Ecgtheow, answered:
1370   "Do not grieve, wise Hrothgar! Better each man
should avenge his friend than deeply mourn.
The days on earth for every one of us
are numbered; he who may should win renown
before his death; that is a warrior's
1375   best memorial when he has departed from this world.
Come, O guardian of the kingdom, let us lose
no time but track down Grendel's kinswoman.
I promise you that wherever she turns—
to honeycomb caves, to mountain woods,
1380   to the bottom of the lake she shall find no refuge.
Shoulder your sorrows with patience
this day; this is what I expect of you."
        Then the old king leapt up, poured out his gratitude
to God Almighty for the Geat's words.
1385   Hrothgar's horse, his stallion with plaited mane,
was saddled and bridled; the wise ruler
set out in full array; his troop of shield-bearers
fell into step. They followed the tracks
along forest paths and over open hill-country
1390   for mile after mile; the monster had made
for the dark moors directly, carrying the corpse
of the foremost thane of all those
who, with Hrothgar, had guarded the hall.
Then the man of noble lineage left Heorot far behind,
1395   followed narrow tracks, string-thin paths
over steep, rocky slopes—remote parts
with beetling crags and many lakes
where water-demons lived. He went ahead
with a handful of scouts to explore the place;
1400   all at once he came upon a dismal wood,
mountain trees standing on the edge
of a gray precipice; the lake lay beneath,
blood-stained and turbulent. The Danish retainers
were utterly appalled when they came upon
1405   the severed head of their comrade Aeschere
on the steep slope leading down to the lake;
all the thanes were deeply distressed.
        The water boiled with blood, with hot gore;
the warriors gaped at it. At times the horn sang
1410   an eager battle-song. The brave men all sat down;
then they saw many serpents in the water,
strange sea-dragons swimming in the lake,

and also water-demons, lying on cliff-ledges,
monsters and serpents of the same kind
1415 as often, in the morning, molest ships
on the sail-road. They plunged to the lake bottom,
bitter and resentful, rather than listen
to the song of the horn. The leader of the Geats
1420 picked off one with his bow and arrow,
ended its life; the metal tip
stuck in its vitals; it swam more sluggishly
after that, as the life-blood ebbed from its body;
in no time this strange sea-dragon
1425 bristled with barbed boar-spears, was subdued
and drawn up onto the cliff; men examined
that disgusting enemy.
                Beowulf donned
his coat of mail, did not fear for his own life.
His massive corslet, linked by hand
1430 and skillfully adorned, was to essay the lake—
it knew how to guard the body, the bone-chamber,
so that his foe's grasp, in its malicious fury,
could not crush his chest, squeeze out his life;
and his head was guarded by the gleaming helmet
1435 which was to explore the churning waters,
stir their very depths; gold decorated it,
and it was hung with chain-mail, as the weapon smith
had wrought it long before, wondrously shaped it
and beset it with boar-images, so that
1440 afterwards no battle-blade could do it damage.
Not least among his mighty aids was Hrunting,
the long-hilted sword Unferth lent him in his need;
it was one of the finest of heirlooms; the iron blade
was engraved with deadly, twiglike patterning,
1445 tempered with battle blood. It had not failed
any of those men who had held it in their hands,
risked themselves on hazardous exploits,
pitted themselves against foes. That was not
the first time it had to do a hard day's work.
1450 Truly, when Ecglaf's son, himself so strong,
lent that weapon to his better as a swordsman,
he had forgotten all those taunts he flung
when tipsy with wine; he dared not chance
his own arm under the breakers, dared not
1455 risk his life; at the lake he lost
his renown for bravery. It was not so with Beowulf
once he had armed himself for battle.
    The Geat, son of Ecgtheow, spoke:
"Great son of Healfdene, gracious ruler,
1460 gold-friend of men, remember now—
for I am now ready to go—
what we agreed if I, fighting on your behalf,
should fail to return: that you would always

be like a father to me after I had gone.
1465   Guard my followers, my dear friends,
if I die in battle; and, beloved Hrothgar,
send to Hygelac the treasures you gave me.
When the lord of the Geats, Hrethel's son,
sees those gifts of gold, he will know
1470   that I found a noble giver of rings
and enjoyed his favor for as long as I lived.
And, O Hrothgar, let renowned Unferth
have the ancient treasure, the razor sharp
ornamented sword; and I will make my name
1475   with Hrunting, or death will destroy me."
　　After these words the leader of the Geats
dived bravely from the bank, did not even
wait for an answer; the seething water
received the warrior. A full day elapsed
1480   before he could perceive the bottom of the lake.
　　She who had guarded the lake's length and breadth
for fifty years, vindictive, fiercely ravenous for blood,
soon realized that one of the race of men
was looking down into the monsters' lair.
1485   Then she grasped him, clutched the Geat
in her ghastly claws; and yet she did not
so much as scratch his skin; his coat of mail
protected him; she could not penetrate
the linked metal rings with her loathsome fingers.
1490   Then the sea-wolf dived to the bottom-most depths,
swept the prince to the place where she lived,
so that he, for all his courage, could not
wield a weapon; too many wondrous creatures
harassed him as he swam; many sea-serpents
1495   with savage tusks tried to bore through his corslet,
the monsters molested him. Then the hero saw
that he had entered some loathsome hall
in which there was no water to impede him,
a vaulted chamber where the floodrush
1500   could not touch him. A light caught his eye,
a lurid flame flickering brightly.
　　Then the brave man saw the sea-monster,
fearsome, infernal; he whirled his blade,
swung his arm with all his strength,
1505   and the ring-hilted sword sang a greedy war-song
on the monster's head. Then that guest realized
that his gleaming blade could not bite into her flesh,
break open her bone-chamber; its edge failed Beowulf
when he needed it; yet it had endured
1510   many a combat, sheared often through the helmet,
split the corslet of a fated man; for the first time
that precious sword failed to live up to its name.
　　Then, resolute, Hygelac's kinsman took his courage
in both hands, trusted in his own strength.

1515 Angrily the warrior hurled Hrunting away,
      the damascened sword with serpent patterns on its hilt;
      tempered and steel-edged, it lay useless on the earth.
      Beowulf trusted in his own strength,
      the might of his hand. So must any man
1520 who hopes to gain long-lasting fame
      in battle; he must risk his life, regardless.
      Then the prince of the Geats seized the shoulder
      of Grendel's mother—he did not mourn their feud;
      when they grappled, that brave man in his fury
1525 flung his mortal foe to the ground.
      Quickly she came back at him, locked him
      in clinches and clutched at him fearsomely.
      Then the greatest of warriors stumbled and fell.
      She dropped on her hall-guest, drew her dagger,
1530 broad and gleaming; she wanted to avenge her son,
      her only offspring. The woven corslet
      that covered his shoulders saved Beowulf's life,
      denied access to both point and edge.
      Then Ecgtheow's son, leader of the Geats,
1535 would have died far under the wide earth
      had not his corslet, his mighty chain-mail,
      guarded him, and had not holy God
      granted him victory; the wise Lord,
      Ruler of the Heavens, settled the issue
1540 easily after the hero had scrambled to his feet.
         Then Beowulf saw among weapons an invincible sword
      wrought by the giants, massive and double-edged,
      the joy of many warriors; that sword was matchless,
      well-tempered and adorned, forged in a finer age,
1545 only it was so huge that no man but Beowulf
      could hope to handle it in the quick of combat.
      Ferocious in battle, the defender of the Scyldings
      grasped the ringed hilt, swung the ornamented sword
      despairing of his life—he struck such a savage blow
1550 that the sharp blade slashed through her neck,
      smashed the vertebrae; it severed her head
      from the fated body; she fell at his feet.
      The sword was bloodstained; Beowulf rejoiced.
         A light gleamed; the chamber was illumined
1555 as if the sky's bright candle were shining
      from heaven. Hygelac's thane inspected
      the vaulted room, then walked round the walls,
      fierce and resolute, holding the weapon firmly
      by the hilt. The sword was not too large
1560 for the hero's grasp, but he was eager to avenge
      at once all Grendel's atrocities,
      all the many visits the monster had inflicted
      on the West-Danes—which began with the time
      he slew Hrothgar's sleeping hearth-companions,
1565 devoured fifteen of the Danish warriors

even as they slept, and carried off as many more,
a monstrous prize. But the resolute warrior
had already repaid him to such a degree
that he now saw Grendel lying on his death-bed,
his life's-blood drained because of the wound
he had sustained in battle at Heorot. Then Grendel's corpse
received a savage blow at the hero's hands,
his body burst open: Beowulf lopped off his head.
        At once the wise men, anxiously gazing at
the lake with Hrothgar, saw that the water
had begun to chop and churn, that the waves
were stained with blood. The gray-haired Scyldings
discussed that bold man's fate, agreed
there was no hope of seeing that brave thane again—
no chance that he would come, rejoicing in victory,
before their renowned king; it seemed certain
to all but a few that the sea-wolf had destroyed him.
        Then the ninth hour came. The noble Scyldings
left the headland; the gold-friend of men
returned to Heorot; the Geats, sick at heart,
sat down and stared at the lake.
Hopeless, they yet hoped to set eyes
on their dear lord.
                        Then the battle-sword
began to melt like a gory icicle
because of the monster's blood. Indeed,
it was a miracle to see it thaw entirely,
as does ice when the Father (He who ordains
all times and seasons) breaks the bonds of frost,
unwinds the flood fetters; He is the true Lord.
The leader of the Geats took none of the treasures
away from the chamber—though he saw many there—
except the monster's head and the gold-adorned
sword-hilt; the blade itself had melted,
the patterned sword had burned, so hot was that blood,
so poisonous the monster who had died in the cave.
He who had survived the onslaught of his enemies
was soon on his way, swimming up through the water;
when the evil monster ended his days on earth,
left this transitory life, the troubled water
and all the lake's expanse was purged of its impurity.
        Then the fearless leader of the seafarers
swam to the shore, exulting in his plunder,
the heavy burdens he had brought with him.
The intrepid band of thanes hurried towards him,
giving thanks to God, rejoicing
to see their lord safe and sound of limb.
The brave man was quickly relieved of his helmet
and corslet.
                The angry water under the clouds,
the lake stained with battle-blood, at last became calm.

1570

1575

1580

1585

1590

1595

1600

1605

1610

to visit the court of the Geatish king,
he will be warmly welcomed. Strong men
1820 should seek fame in far-off lands."
      Hrothgar replied: "The wise Lord put these words
into your mind; I have never heard a warrior
speak more sagely while still so young.
You are very strong and very shrewd,
1825 you speak with discerning. If your leader,
Hrethel's son, guardian of the people,
were to lose his life by illness or by iron,
by spear or grim swordplay, and if you survived him,
it seems to me that the Geats could not choose
1830 a better man for king, should you wish to rule
the land of your kinsmen. Beloved Beowulf,
the longer I know you, the more I like your spirit.
Because of your exploit, your act of friendship,
there will be an end to the gross outrages,
1835 the old enmity between Geats and Danes;
they will learn to live in peace.
For as long as I rule this spacious land,
heirlooms will be exchanged; many men
will greet their friends with gifts, send them
1840 over the seas where gannets swoop and rise;
the ring-prowed ship will take tokens of esteem,
treasures across the waters. I know the Geats
are honorable to friend and foe alike,
always faithful to their ancient code."
1845 Then Healfdene's son, guardian of thanes,
gave him twelve treasures in the hall,
told him to go safely with those gifts
to his own dear kinsmen, and to come back soon.
That king, descendant of kings,
1850 leader of the Scyldings, kissed and embraced
the best of thanes; tears streamed down
the old man's face. The more that warrior thought,
wise and old, the more it seemed
improbable that they would meet again,
1855 brave men in council. He so loved Beowulf
that he could not conceal his sense of loss;
but in his heart and in his head,
in his very blood, a deep love burned
for that dear man.   Then Beowulf the warrior,
1860 proudly adorned with gold, crossed the plain,
exulting in his treasure. The ship
rode at anchor, waiting for its owner.
Then, as they walked, they often praised
Hrothgar's generosity. He was an altogether
1865 faultless king, until old age deprived him
of his strength, as it does most men.
      Then that troop of brave young retainers
came to the water's edge; they wore ring-mail,

for that fated man; he was the first to fall;
2060 Grendel tore that famous young retainer to bits
between his teeth, and swallowed the whole body
of that dear man, that girded warrior.
And even then that murderer, mindful of evil,
his mouth caked with blood, was not content
2065 to leave the gold-hall empty-handed
but, famed for his strength, he tackled me,
gripped me with his outstretched hand.
A huge unearthly glove swung at his side,
firmly secured with subtle straps;
2070 it had been made with great ingenuity,
with devils' craft and dragons' skins.
Innocent as I was, the demon monster
meant to shove me in it, and many another
innocent besides; that was beyond him
2075 after I leapt up, filled with fury.
It would take too long to tell you how I repaid
that enemy of men for all his outrages;
but there, my prince, I ennobled your people
with my deeds. Grendel escaped,
2080 and lived a little longer; but he left
behind at Heorot his right hand; and, in utter
wretchedness, sank to the bottom of the lake.
      "The sun rose; we sat down together
to feast, then the leader of the Scyldings
2085 paid a good price for the bloody battle,
gave me many a gold-plated treasure.
There was talk and song; the gray-haired Scylding
opened his immense hoard of memories;
now and then a happy warrior touched
2090 the wooden harp, reciting some story,
mournful and true; at times the generous king
recalled in proper detail some strange incident;
and as the shadows lengthened, an aged thane,
cramped and rheumatic, raised his voice
2095 time and again, lamenting his lost youth,
his prowess in battle; worn with winters,
his heart quickened to the call of the past.
      "In these ways we relaxed agreeably
throughout the long day until darkness closed in,
2100 another night for men. Then, in her grief,
bent on vengeance, Grendel's mother
hastened to the hall where death had lain
in wait for her son—the battle-hatred
of the Geats. The horrible harridan avenged
2105 her offspring, slew a warrior brazenly.
Aeschere, the wise old counselor, lost
his life. And when morning came,
the Danes were unable to cremate him,
to place the body of that dear man

2110 on the funeral pyre; for Grendel's mother
had carried it off in her gruesome grasp,
taken it under the mountain lake.
Of all the grievous sorrows Hrothgar
long sustained, none was more terrible.
2115 Then the king in his anger called upon your name
and entreated me to risk my life,
to accomplish deeds of utmost daring
in the tumult of waves; he promised me rewards.
And so, as men now know all over the earth,
2120 I found the grim guardian of the lake-bottom.
For a while we grappled; the water boiled
with blood; then in that battle-hall,
I lopped off Grendel's mother's head
with the mighty sword. I barely escaped
2125 with my life; but I was not fated.
"And afterwards the guardian of thanes,
Healfdene's son, gave me many treasures.
Thus the king observed excellent tradition:
in no wise did I feel unrewarded
2130 for all my efforts, but Healfdene's son
offered me gifts of my own choosing;
gifts, O noble king, I wish now
to give to you in friendship. I still depend
entirely on your favors; I have few
2135 close kinsmen but you, O Hygelac!"
Then Beowulf caused to be brought in
a standard bearing the image of a boar,
together with a helmet towering in battle,
a gray corslet, and a noble sword; he said:
2140 "Hrothgar, the wise king, gave me
these trappings and purposely asked me
to tell you their history: he said that Heorogar,
lord of the Scyldings, long owned them.
Yet he has not endowed his own brave son,
2145 Heoroweard, with this armor, much as
he loves him. Make good use of everything!"
I heard that four bays, apple-brown,
were brought into the hall after the armor—
swift as the wind, identical. Beowulf gave them
2150 as he gave the treasures. So should a kinsman do,
and never weave nets with underhand subtlety
to ensnare others, never have designs
on a close comrade's life. His nephew,
brave in battle, was loyal to Hygelac;
2155 each man was mindful of the other's pleasure.
I heard that he gave Hygd the collar,
the wondrous ornament with which Wealhtheow,
daughter of the prince, had presented him,
and gave her three horses also, graceful creatures
2160 with brightly-colored saddles; Hygd

wore that collar, her breast was adorned.

    Thus Ecgtheow's son, feared in combat,
confirmed his courage with noble deeds;
he lived a life of honor, he never slew

2165   companions at the feast; savagery was
alien to him, but he, so brave in battle,
made the best use of those ample talents
with which God endowed him.

                       He had been despised
for a long while, for the Geats saw no spark

2170   of bravery in him, nor did their king deem him
worthy of much attention on the mead-bench;
people thought that he was a sluggard,
a feeble princeling. How fate changed,
changed completely for that glorious man!

2175   Then the guardian of thanes, the famous king,
ordered that Hrethel's gold-adorned heirloom
be brought in; no sword was so treasured
in all Geatland; he laid it in Beowulf's lap,
and gave him seven thousand hides of land,

2180   a hall and princely throne. Both men
had inherited land and possessions
in that country; but the more spacious kingdom
had fallen to Hygelac, who was of higher rank.

    In later days, after much turmoil,

2185   things happened in this way: when Hygelac lay dead
and murderous battle-blades had beaten down
the shield of his son Heardred,
and when the warlike Swedes, savage warriors,
had hunted him down among his glorious people,

2190   attacked Hereric's nephew with hatred,
the great kingdom of the Geats passed
into Beowulf's hands. He had ruled it well
for fifty winters—he was a wise king,
a grizzled guardian of the land—when, on dark nights,

2195   a dragon began to terrify the Geats:
he lived on a cliff, kept watch over a hoard
in a high stone barrow; below, there was
a secret path; a man strayed
into this barrow by chance, seized

2200   some of the pagan treasures, stole drinking vessels.
At first the sleeping dragon was deceived
by the thief's skill, but afterwards he avenged
this theft of gleaming gold; people far and wide
bands of retainers, became aware of his wrath.

2205   That man did not intrude upon the hoard
deliberately, he who robbed the dragon;
but it was some slave, a wanderer in distress
escaping from men's anger who entered there,
seeking refuge. He stood guilty of some sin.

2210 As soon as he peered in, the outsider
stiffened with horror. Unhappy as he was,
he stole the vessel, the precious cup.
There were countless heirlooms in that earth-cave,
the enormous legacy of a noble people,
2215 ancient treasures which some man or other
had cautiously concealed there many years
before. Death laid claim to all that people
in days long past, and then that retainer
who outlived the rest, a gold-guardian
2220 mourning his friends, expected the same fate—
thought he would enjoy those assembled heirlooms
a little while only. A newly built barrow
stood ready on a headland which overlooked
the sea, protected by the hazards of access.
2225 To this barrow the protector of rings brought the heirlooms,
the plated gold, all that part of the precious treasure
worthy of hoarding; then he spoke a few words:
"Hold now, O earth, since heroes could not,
these treasures owned by nobles! Indeed, strong men
2230 first quarried them from you. Death in battle,
ghastly carnage, has claimed all my people—
men who once made merry in the hall
have laid down their lives; I have no one
to carry the sword, to polish the plated vessel,
2235 this precious drinking-cup; all the retainers
have hurried elsewhere. The iron helmet
adorned with gold shall lose its ornaments;
men who should polish battle-masks are sleeping;
the coat of mail, too, that once withstood
2240 the bite of swords in battle, after shields were shattered,
decays like the warriors; the linked mail may no longer
range far and wide with the warrior,
stand side by side with heroes. Gone is the pleasure
of plucking the harp, no fierce hawk
2245 swoops about the hall, nor does the swift stallion
strike sparks in the courtyard. Cruel death
has claimed hundreds of this human race."
    Thus the last survivor mourned time passing,
and roamed about by day and night,
2250 sad and aimless, until death's lightning
struck at his heart.
                    The aged dragon of darkness
discovered that glorious hoard unguarded,
he who sought out barrows, smooth-scaled
and evil, and flew by night, breathing
2255 fire; the Geats feared him greatly.
He was destined to find the hoard
in that cave and, old in winters, guard
the heathen gold; much good it did him!
    Thus the huge serpent who harassed men

2260   guarded that great stronghold under the earth
       for three hundred winters, until
       a man enraged him; the wanderer carried
       the inlaid vessel to his lord, and begged him
       for a bond of peace. Then the hoard was raided
2265   and plundered, and that unhappy man
       was granted his prayer. His lord examined
       the ancient work of smiths for the first time.
           There was conflict once more after the dragon
       awoke; intrepid, he slid swiftly
2270   along by the rock, and found the footprints
       of the intruder; that man had skillfully
       picked his way right past the dragon's head.
       Thus he who is undoomed will easily survive
       anguish and exile provided he enjoys
2275   the grace of God. The warden of the hoard
       prowled up and down, anxious to find
       the man who had pillaged it while he slept.
       Breathing fire and filled with fury,
       he circled the outside of the earth mound
2280   again and again; but there was no one
       in that barren place; yet he exulted at the thought
       of battle, bloody conflict; at times he wheeled back
       into the barrow, hunting for the priceless heirloom.
       He realized at once that one of the race of men
2285   had discovered the gold, the glorious treasure.
       Restlessly the dragon waited for darkness;
       the guardian of the hoard was bursting with rage,
       he meant to avenge the vessel's theft
       with fire.
                       Then daylight failed
2290   as the dragon desired; he could no longer
       confine himself to the cave but flew in a ball
       of flame, burning for vengeance. The Geats
       were filled with dread as he began his flight;
       it swiftly ended in disaster for their lord.
2295   Then the dragon began to breathe forth fire,
       to burn fine buildings; flame tongues flickered,
       terrifying men; the loathsome winged creature
       meant to leave the whole place lifeless.
       Everywhere the violence of the dragon, the venom
2300   of that hostile one, was clearly to be seen—
       how he had wrought havoc, hated and humiliated
       the Geatish people. Then, before dawn he rushed back
       to his hidden lair and the treasure hoard.
       He had girdled the Geats with fire,
2305   with ravening flames; he relied on his own strength,
       and on the barrow and the cliff; his trust played him false.
           Then news of that terror was quickly brought
       to Beowulf, that flames enveloped
       his own hall, best of buildings,

2310   and the gift-throne of the Geats. That good man
         was choked with intolerable grief.
         Wise that he was, he imagined
         he must have angered God, the Lord Eternal,
         by ignoring some ancient law; he was seldom
2315   dispirited, but now his heart was like lead.
             The fire dragon had destroyed the fortified hall,
         the people's stronghold, and laid waste with flames
         the land by the sea. The warlike king,
         prince of the Geats, planned to avenge this.
2320   The protector of warriors, leader of men,
         instructed the smith to forge a curious shield
         made entirely of iron; he well knew
         that a linden shield would not last long
         against the flames. The eminent prince
2325   was doomed to reach the end of his days on earth,
         his life in this world. So too was the dragon,
         though he had guarded the hoard for generations.
             Then the giver of gold disdained
         to track the dragon with a troop
2330   of warlike men; he did not shrink
         from single combat, nor did he set much store
         by the fearless dragon's power, for had he not before
         experienced danger, again and again
         survived the storm of battle, beginning with that time
2335   when, blessed with success, he cleansed
         Hrothgar's hall, and crushed in battle
         the monster and his vile mother?
                                 That grim combat
         in which Hygelac was slain—Hrethel's son,
         leader of the Geats, dear lord of his people,
2340   struck down by swords in the bloodbath
         in Frisia—was far from the least
         of his encounters. Beowulf escaped
         because of his skill and stamina at swimming;
         he waded into the water, bearing no fewer
2345   than thirty corslets, a deadweight on his arms.
         But the Frankish warriors who shouldered
         their shields against him had no cause to boast
         about that combat; a handful only
         eluded that hero and returned home.
2350   Then the son of Ecgtheow, saddened and alone,
         rode with the white horses to his own people.
         Hygd offered him heirlooms there, and even
         the kingdom, the ancestral throne itself; for she feared
         that her son would be unable to defend it
2355   from foreign invaders now that Hygelac was gone.
         But the Geats, for all their anguish, failed
         to prevail upon the prince—he declined
         absolutely to become Heardred's lord,
         or to taste the pleasures of royal power.

2360 But he stood at his right hand,
ready with advice, always friendly,
and respectful, until the boy came of age
and could rule the Geats himself.
                                    Two exiles,
Ohthere's sons, sailed to Heardred's court;
2365 they had rebelled against the ruler of the Swedes,
a renowned man, the best of sea-kings,
gold-givers in Sweden. By receiving them,
Heardred rationed the days of his life;
in return for his hospitality, Hygelac's son
2370 was mortally wounded, slashed by swords.
Once Heardred lay lifeless in the dust,
Onela, son of Ongentheow, sailed home again;
he allowed Beowulf to inherit the throne
and rule the Geats; he was a noble king!
2375 But Beowulf did not fail with help
after the death of the prince, although years passed;
he befriended unhappy Eadgils, Ohthere's son,
and supplied him with weapons and warriors
beyond the wide seas. Eadgils afterwards
2380 avenged Eanmund, he ravaged and savaged
the Swedes, and killed the king, Onela himself.
     Thus the son of Ecgtheow had survived
these feuds, these fearful battles, these acts
of single combat, up to that day
2385 when he was destined to fight against the dragon.
Then in fury the leader of the Geats set out
with eleven to search for the winged serpent.
By then Beowulf knew the cause of the feud,
bane of men; the famous cup
2390 had come to him through the hands of its finder.
The unfortunate slave who first brought about
such strife made the thirteenth man
in that company—cowed and disconsolate,
he had to be their guide. Much against his will,
2395 he conducted them to the entrance of the cave,
an earth-hall full of filigree work
and fine adornments close by the sea,
the fretting waters. The vile guardian,
the serpent who had long lived under the earth,
2400 watched over the gold, alert; he who hoped
to gain it bargained with his own life.
     Then the brave king sat on the headland,
the gold-friend of the Geats wished success
to his retainers. His mind was most mournful,
2405 angry, eager for slaughter; fate hovered
over him, so soon to fall on that old man,
to seek out his hidden spirit, to split
life and body; flesh was to confine
the soul of the king only a little longer.

2410 Beowulf, the son of Ecgtheow, spoke:
      "Often and often in my youth I plunged
      into the battle maelstrom; how well I remember it.
      I was seven winters old when the treasure guardian,
      ruler of men, received me from my father.[3]
2415 King Hrethel took me into his ward, reared me,
      fed me, gave me gold, mindful of our kinship;
      for as long as he lived, he loved me no less
      than his own three sons, warriors with me
      in the citadel, Herebeald, Haethcyn, and my dear Hygelac.
2420 A death-bed for the firstborn was unrolled
      most undeservedly by the action of his kinsman—
      Haethcyn drew his horn-tipped bow
      and killed his lord-to-be; he missed his mark,
      his arrow was stained with his brother's blood.
2425 That deed was a dark sin, sickening
      to think of, not to be settled by payment of *wergild*;
      yet Herebeald's death could not be requited.
         "Thus the old king, Hrethel, is agonized
      to see his son, so young, swing
2430 from the gallows.[4] He sings a dirge, a song
      dark with sorrow, while his son hangs,
      raven's carrion, and he cannot help him
      in any way, wise and old as he is.
      He wakes each dawn to the ache
2435 of his son's death; he has no desire
      for a second son, to be his heir
      in the stronghold, now that his firstborn
      has finished his days and deeds on earth.
      Grieving, he wanders through his son's dwelling,
2440 sees the wine-hall now deserted, joyless,
      home of the winds; the riders, the warriors,
      sleep in their graves. No longer is the harp
      plucked, no longer is there happiness in that place.
      Then Hrethel takes to his bed, and intones
2445 dirges for his dead son, Herebeald;
      his house and his lands seem empty now,
      and far too large. Thus the lord of the Geats
      endured in his heart the ebb and flow
      of sorrow for his firstborn; but he could not
2450 avenge that feud on the slayer—his own son;
      although Hrethel had no love for Haethcyn,
      he could no more readily requite death
      with death. Such was his sorrow that he lost
      all joy in life, chose the light of God;
2455 he bequeathed to his sons, as a wealthy man does,
      his citadel and land, when he left this life.

---

3. It was customary for nephews to be brought up in the house of their maternal uncles as foster-children.
4. Even in cases of involuntary manslaughter, punish-ment was required to avenge the dead. In this instance, it seems that a ritual, sacrificial hanging was performed to spare Haethcyn for murdering his brother Herebeald.

"Then there was strife, savage conflict
between Swedes and Geats; after Hrethel's death
the feud we shared, the fierce hatred
2460   flared up across the wide water.
The sons of Ongentheow, Onela and Ohthere,
were brave and battle-hungry; they had no wish
for peace over the sea but several times,
and wantonly, butchered the people of the Geats
2465   on the slopes of Slaughter Hill. As is well known,
my kinsmen requited that hatred, those crimes;
but one of them paid with his own life—
a bitter bargain; that fight was fatal
to Haethcyn, ruler of the Geats.
2470   Then I heard that in the morning
one kinsman avenged another, repaid
Haethcyn's slayer with the battle-blade,
when Ongentheow attacked the Geat Eofor;
the helmet split, the old Swede fell,
2475   pale in death; Eofor remembered
that feud well enough, his hand and sword
spared nothing in their death-swing.
    "I repaid Hygelac for his gifts of heirlooms
with my gleaming blade, repaid him in battle,
2480   as was granted to me; he gave me land
and property, a happy home. He had
no need to hunt out and hire mercenaries—
inferior warriors from the Gepidae,
from the Spear-Danes or from tribes in Sweden;
2485   but I was always at the head of his host,
alone in the van; and I shall still fight
for as long as I live and this sword lasts,
that has often served me early and late
since I became the daring slayer
2490   of Daeghrefn, champion of the Franks.
He was unable to bring adornments,
breast-decorations to the Frisian king,
but fell in the fight bearing the standard,
a brave warrior; it was my battle-grip,
2495   not the sharp blade, that shattered his bones,
silenced his heartbeat. Now the shining edge,
hand and tempered sword, shall engage in battle
for the treasure hoard. I fought many battles
when I was young; yet I will fight again,
2500   the old guardian of my people, and achieve
a mighty exploit if the evil dragon dares
confront me, dares come out of the earth-cave!"
    Then he addressed each of the warriors,
the brave heroes, his dear companions,
2505   a last time: "I would not wield a sword
against the dragon if I could grasp this hideous being
with my hands (and thus make good my boast),

as once I grasped the monster Grendel;
but I anticipate blistering battle-fire,
2510   venomous breath; therefore I have with me
my shield and corslet. I will not give an inch
to the guardian of the mound, but at that barrow
it will befall us both as fate ordains,
every man's master. My spirit is bold,
2515   I will not boast further against the fierce flier.
Watch from the barrow, warriors in armor,
guarded by corslets, which of us will better
weather his wounds after the combat.
This is not your undertaking, nor is it
2520   possible for any man but me alone
to pit his strength against the gruesome one,
and perform great deeds. I will gain the gold
by daring, or else battle, dread destroyer
of life, will lay claim to your lord."
2525   Then the bold warrior, stern-faced beneath his helmet,
stood up with his shield; sure of his own strength,
he walked in his corslet towards the cliff;
the way of the coward is not thus!
Then that man endowed with noble qualities,
2530   he who had braved countless battles, weathered
the thunder when warrior troops clashed together,
saw a stone arch set in the cliff
through which a stream spurted; steam rose
from the boiling water; he could not stay long
2535   in the hollow near the hoard for fear
of being scorched by the dragon's flames.
Then, such was his fury, the leader of the Geats
threw out his chest and gave a great roar,
the brave man bellowed; his voice, renowned
2540   in battle, hammered the gray rock's anvil.
The guardian of the hoard knew the voice for human;
violent hatred stirred within him. Now no time
remained to entreat for peace. At once
the monster's breath, burning battle vapor,
2545   issued from the barrow; the earth itself snarled.
The lord of the Geats, standing under the cliff,
raised his shield against the fearsome stranger;
then that sinuous creature spoiled
for the fight. The brave and warlike king
2550   had already drawn his keen-edged sword,
(it was an ancient heirloom); a terror of each other
lurked in the hearts of the two antagonists.
While the winged creature coiled himself up,
the friend and lord of men stood unflinching
2555   by his shield; Beowulf waited ready armed.
        Then, fiery and twisted, the dragon swiftly
shrithed towards its fate. The shield protected
the life and body of the famous prince
for far less time than he had looked for.

2560 It was the first occasion in all his life
      that fate did not decree triumph for him
      in battle. The lord of the Geats raised
      his arm, and struck the mottled monster
      with his vast ancestral sword; but the bright blade's
2565 edge was blunted by the bone, bit
      less keenly than the desperate king required.
      The defender of the barrow bristled with anger
      at the blow, spouted murderous fire, so that flames
      leapt through the air. The gold-friend of the Geats
2570 did not boast of famous victories; his proven sword,
      the blade bared in battle, had failed him
      as it ought not to have done. That great Ecgtheow's
      greater son had to journey on from this world
      was no pleasant matter; much against his will,
2575 he was obliged to make his dwelling
      elsewhere—sooner or later every man must leave
      this transitory life. It was not long
      before the fearsome ones closed again.
      The guardian of the hoard was filled with fresh hope,
2580 his breast was heaving; he who had ruled a nation
      suffered agony, surrounded by flame.
      And Beowulf's companions, sons of nobles—
      so far from protecting him in a troop together,
      unflinching in the fright—shrank back into the forest
2585 scared for their own lives. One man alone
      obeyed his conscience. The claims of kinship
      can never be ignored by a right-minded man.
        His name was Wiglaf, a noble warrior,
      Weohstan's son, kinsman of Aelfhere,
2590 a leader of the Swedes; he saw that his lord,
      helmeted, was tormented by the intense heat.
      Then he recalled the honors Beowulf had bestowed
      on him—the wealthy citadel of the Waegmundings,
      the rights to land his father owned before him.
2595 He could not hold back then; he grasped the round,
      yellow shield; he drew his ancient sword,
      reputed to be the legacy of Eanmund,
      Ohthere's son.
                  Weohstan had slain him
      in a skirmish while Eanmund was a wanderer,
2600 a friendless man, and then had carried off
      to his own kinsmen the gleaming helmet,
      the linked corslet, the ancient sword
      forged by giants. It was Onela,
      Eanmund's uncle, who gave him that armor,
2605 ready for use; but Onela did not refer to the feud,
      though Weohstan had slain his brother's son.
      For many years Weohstan owned that war-gear,
      sword and corslet, until his son was old enough
      to achieve great feats as he himself had done.
2610 Then, when Weohstan journeyed on from the earth,

an old man, he left Wiglaf—who was
with the Geats—a great legacy of armor
of every kind.
                    This was the first time
the young warrior had weathered the battle storm,
2615   standing at the shoulder of his lord.
His courage did not melt, nor did his kinsman's sword
fail him in the fight. The dragon found that out
when they met in mortal combat.
         Wiglaf spoke, constantly reminding
2620   his companions of their duty—he was mournful.
"I think of that evening we emptied the mead-cup
in the feasting-hall, partook and pledged our lord,
who presented us with rings, that we would repay him
for his gifts of armor, helmets and hard swords,
2625   if ever the need, need such as this, arose.
For this very reason he asked us
to join with him in this journey, deemed us
worthy of renown, and gave me these treasures;
he looked on us as loyal warriors,
2630   brave in battle; even so, our lord,
guardian of the Geats, intended to perform
this feat alone, because of all men
he had achieved the greatest exploits,
daring deeds. Now the day has come
2635   when our lord needs support, the might
of strong men; let us hurry forward
and help our leader as long as fire remains,
fearsome, searing flames. God knows
I would rather that fire embraced my body
2640   beside the charred body of my gold-giver;
it seems wrong to me that we should shoulder
our shields, carry them home afterwards,
unless we can first kill the venomous foe,
guard the prince of the Geats. I know
2645   in my heart his feats of old were such
that he should not now be the only Geat to suffer
and fall in combat; in common we shall share
sword, helmet, corslet, the trappings of war."
         Then that man fought his way through the fumes,
2650   went helmeted to help his lord. He shouted out:
"Brave Beowulf, may success attend you—
for in the days when you were young, you swore
that so long as you lived you would never allow
your fame to decay; now, O resolute king,
2655   renowned for your exploits, you must guard your life
with all your skill. I shall assist you."
         At this the seething dragon attacked a second time;
shimmering with fire the venomous visitor fell on his foes,
the men he loathed. With waves of flame, he burned
2660   the shield right up to its boss; Wiglaf's
corslet afforded him no protection whatsoever.

But the young warrior still fought bravely, sheltered
behind his kinsman's shield after his own
was consumed by flames. Still the battle-king
2665 set his mind on deeds of glory; with prodigious strength
he struck a blow so violent that his sword stuck
in the dragon's skull. But Naegling snapped!
Beowulf's old gray-hued sword
failed him in the fight. Fate did not ordain
2670 that the iron edge should assist him
in that struggle; Beowulf's hand was too strong.
Indeed I have been told that he overtaxed
each and every weapon, hardened by blood, that he bore
into battle; his own great strength betrayed him.
2675 Then the dangerous dragon, scourge of the Geats,
was intent a third time upon attack; he rushed
at the renowned man when he saw an opening:
fiery, battle-grim, he gripped the hero's neck
between his sharp teeth; Beowulf was bathed
2680 in blood; it spurted out in streams.
Then, I have heard, the loyal thane
alongside the Geatish king displayed great courage,
strength and daring, as was his nature.
To assist his kinsman, that man in mail
2685 aimed not for the head but lunged at the belly
of their vile enemy (in so doing his hand
was badly burned); his sword, gleaming and adorned,
sank in up to the hilt and at once the flames
began to abate. The king still had control then
2690 over his senses; he drew the deadly knife,
keen-edged in battle, that he wore on his corslet;
then the lord of the Geats dispatched the dragon.
Thus they had killed their enemy—their courage
enabled them—the brave kinsmen together
2695 had destroyed him. Such should a man,
a thane, be in time of necessity!
        That was the last
of all the king's achievements, his last
exploit in the world. Then the wound
the earth-dragon had inflicted with his teeth
2700 began to burn and swell; very soon he
was suffering intolerable pain as the poison
boiled within him. Then the wise leader
tottered forward and slumped on a seat
by the barrow; he gazed at the work of giants,
2705 saw how the ancient earthwork contained
stone arches supported by columns.
Then, with his own hands, the best of thanes
refreshed the renowned prince with water,
washed his friend and lord, blood-stained
2710 and battle-weary, and unfastened his helmet.
  Beowulf began to speak, he defied
his mortal injury; he was well aware

that his life's course, with all its delights,
had come to an end; his days on earth
2715   were exhausted, death drew very close:
"It would have made me happy, at this time,
to pass on war-gear to my son, had I
been granted an heir to succeed me,
sprung of my seed. I have ruled the Geats
2720   for fifty winters; no king of any
neighboring tribe has dared to attack me
with swords, or sought to cow and subdue me.
But in my own home I have awaited
my destiny, cared well for my dependents,
2725   and I have not sought trouble, or sworn
any oaths unjustly. Because of all these things
I can rejoice, drained now by death-wounds;
for the Ruler of Men will have no cause to blame me
after I have died on the count that I deprived
2730   other kinsmen of their lives. Now hurry,
dear Wiglaf; rummage the hoard
under the gray rock, for the dragon sleeps,
riddled with wounds, robbed of his treasure.
Be as quick as you can so that I may see
2735   the age-old golden treasure, and examine
all the priceless, shimmering stones; once I
have set eyes on such a store, it will be
more easy for me to die, to abandon
the life and land that have so long been mine."
2740   Then, I have been told, as soon as he heard
the words of his lord, wounded in battle,
Wiglaf hastened into the earth-cavern,
still wearing his corslet, his woven coat of mail.
After the fierce warrior, flushed with victory,
2745   had walked past a dais, he came upon
the hoard—a hillock of precious stones,
and gold treasure glowing on the ground;
he saw wondrous wall-hangings; the lair
of the serpent, the aged twilight-flier;
2750   and the stoups and vessels of a people
long dead, now lacking a polisher,
deprived of adornments. There were many old,
rusty helmets, and many an armlet
cunningly wrought. A treasure hoard,
2755   gold in the ground, will survive its owner
easily, whosoever hides it!
And he saw also hanging high
over the hoard a standard fashioned with gold strands,
a miracle of handiwork; a light shone from it,
2760   by which he was able to distinguish the earth
and look at the adornments. There was no sign
of the serpent, the sword had savaged and slain him.
Then I heard that Wiglaf rifled the hoard
in the barrow, the antique work of giants—

2765   he chose and carried off as many cups and salvers
         as he could; and he also took the standard,
         the incomparable banner; Beowulf's sword,
         iron-edged, had injured
         the guardian of the hoard, he who had held it
2770   through the ages and fought to defend it
         with flames—terrifying, blistering,
         ravening at midnight—until he was slain.
         Wiglaf hurried on his errand, eager to return,
         spurred on by the treasures; in his heart he was troubled
2775   whether he would find the prince of the Geats,
         so grievously wounded, still alive
         in the place where he had left him.
         Then at last he came, carrying the treasures,
         to the renowned king; his lord's life-blood
2780   was ebbing; once more he splashed him
         with water, until Beowulf revived a little,
         began to frame his thoughts.
                         Gazing at the gold,
         the warrior, the sorrowing king, said:
         "With these words I thank
2785   the King of Glory, the Eternal Lord,
         the Ruler, for all the treasures here before me,
         that in my lifetime I have been able
         to gain them for the Geats.
         And now that I have bartered my old life
2790   for this treasure hoard, you must serve
         and inspire our people. I will not long be with you.
         Command the battle-warriors, after the funeral fire,
         to build a fine barrow overlooking the sea;
         let it tower high on Whaleness
2795   as a reminder to my people.
         And let it be known as *Beowulf's barrow*
         to all seafarers, to men who steer their ships
         from far over the swell and the saltspray."
         Then the prince, bold of mind, detached
2800   his golden collar and gave it to Wiglaf,
         the young spear-warrior, and also his helmet
         adorned with gold, his ring and his corslet,
         and enjoined him to use them well;
         "You are the last survivor of our family,
2805   the Waegmundings; fate has swept
         all my kinsmen, those courageous warriors,
         to their doom. I must follow them."
         Those were the warrior's last words
         before he succumbed to the raging flames
2810   on the pyre; his soul migrated from his breast
         to meet the judgment of righteous men.
         Then it was harrowing for the young hero
         that he should have to see that beloved man
         lying on the earth at his life's end,
2815   wracked by pain. His slayer lay

there too, himself slain, the terrible
cave-dragon. That serpent, coiled evilly,
could no longer guard the gold-hoard,
but blades of iron, beaten and tempered
2820   by smiths, notched in battle, had taken him off;
his wings were clipped now, he lay
mortally wounded, motionless on the earth
at the mound's entrance. No more did he fly
through the night sky, or spread his wings,
2825   proud of his possessions; but he lay prostrate
because of the power of Beowulf, their leader.
Truly, I have heard that no hero of the Geats,
no fire-eater, however daring, could quell
the scorching blast of that venomous one
2830   and lay his hands on the hoard in the lair,
should he find its sentinel waiting there,
watching over the barrow. Beowulf paid
the price of death for that mighty hoard;
both he and the dragon had traveled to the end
2835   of this transitory life.
                              Not long after that
the lily-livered ones slunk out of the wood;
ten cowardly oath-breakers, who had lacked
the courage to let fly with their spears
as their lord so needed, came forward together;
2840   overcome with shame, they carried their shields
and weapons to where their leader lay;
they gazed at Wiglaf. That warrior, bone-weary,
knelt beside the shoulders of his lord; he tried
to rouse him with water; it was all in vain.
2845   For all his efforts, his longing, he could not
detain the life of his leader on earth,
or alter anything the Ruler ordained.
God in His wisdom governed the deeds
of all men, as He does now.
2850   Then the young warrior was not at a loss
for well-earned, angry words for those cowards.
Wiglaf, Weohstan's son, sick at heart,
eyed those faithless men and said:
"He who does not wish to disguise the truth
2855   can indeed say that—when it was a question
not of words but war—our lord completely wasted
the treasures he gave you, the same war-gear
you stand in over there, helmets and corslets
the prince presented often to his thanes on the ale-bench
2860   in the feasting-hall, the very finest weapons
he could secure from far and wide.
The king of the Geats had no need to bother
with boasts about his battle-companions;
yet God, Giver of victories, granted
2865   that he should avenge himself with his sword
single-handed, when all his courage was called for.

I could hardly begin to guard his life
in the fight; but all the same I attempted
to help my kinsman beyond my power.
2870   Each time I slashed at that deadly enemy,
he was a little weaker, the flames leaped
less fiercely from his jaws. Too few defenders
rallied round our prince when he was most pressed.
Now you and your dependents can no longer delight
2875   in gifts of swords, or take pleasure in property,
a happy home; but, after thanes from far and wide
have heard of your flight, your shameful cowardice,
each of your male kinsmen will be condemned
to become a wanderer, an exile deprived
2880   of the land he owns. For every warrior
death is better than dark days of disgrace."
    Then Wiglaf ordered that Beowulf's great feat
be proclaimed in the stronghold, up along the cliff-edge,
where a troop of shield-warriors had waited all morning,
2885   wondering sadly if their dear lord was dead,
or if he would return.
                The man who galloped
to the headland gave them the news at once;
he kept back nothing but called out:
"The lord of the Geats, he who gave joy
2890   to all our people, lies rigid on his death-bed;
slaughtered by the dragon, he now sleeps;
and his deadly enemy, slashed by the knife,
sleeps beside him; he was quite unable
to wound the serpent with a sword. Wiglaf,
2895   son of Weohstan, sits by Beowulf,
the quick and the dead—both brave men—
side by side; weary in his heart
he watches over friend and foe alike.
    "Now the Geats must make ready for a time
2900   of war, for the Franks and the Frisians,
in far-off regions, will hear soon
of the king's death. Our feud with the Franks
grew worse when Hygelac sailed with his fleet
to the shores of Frisia. Frankish warriors
2905   attacked him there, and outfought him,
bravely forced the king in his corslet
to give ground; he fell, surrounded
by his retainers; that prince presented
not one ornament to his followers. Since then,
2910   the king of the Franks has been no friend of ours.
    "Nor would I in the least rely on peace
or honesty from the Swedish people; everyone
remembers how Ongentheow slew Haethcyn,
Hrethel's son, in battle near Ravenswood
2915   when, rashly, the Geats first attacked the Swedes.
At once Ongentheow, Ohthere's father,
old but formidable, retaliated; he killed

Haethcyn, and released his wife from captivity,
set free the mother of Onela and Ohthere,
2920 an aged woman bereft of all her ornaments;
and then he pursued his mortal enemies
until, lordless, with utmost difficulty,
they reached and found refuge in Ravenswood.
Then Ongentheow, with a huge army, penned in
2925 those warriors, exhausted by wounds,
who had escaped the sword; all night long
he shouted fearsome threats at those shivering thanes,
swore that in the morning he and his men would let
their blood in streams with sharp-edged swords,
2930 and string some up on gallows-trees
as sport for birds. Just as day dawned
those despairing men were afforded relief;
they heard the joyful song of Hygelac's
horn and trumpet as that hero came,
2935 hurrying to their rescue with a band of retainers.
after that savage, running battle, the soil
was blood-stained, scuffled—a sign of how
the Swedes and the Geats fomented their feud.
Then Ongentheow, old and heavy-hearted,
2940 headed for his stronghold with his retainers,
that resolute man retreated; he realized
how spirit and skill combined in the person
of proud Hygelac; he had no confidence
about the outcome of an open fight with the seafarers,
2945 the Geatish warriors, in defense of his hoard,
his wife and children; the old man thus withdrew
behind an earth-wall. Then the Swedes were pursued,
Hygelac's banner was hoisted over that earth-work
after the Geats, sons of Hrethel, had stormed
2950 the stronghold. Then gray-haired Ongentheow
was cornered by swords, the king of the Swedes
was constrained to face and suffer his fate
as Eofor willed it. Wulf, the son
of Wonred, slashed angrily at Ongentheow
2955 with his sword, so that blood spurted
from the veins under his hair. The old Swede,
king of his people, was not afraid
but as soon as he had regained his balance
repaid that murderous blow with interest.
2960 Then Wonred's daring son could no longer
lift his hand against the aged warrior
but, with that stroke, Ongentheow had sheared
right through his helmet so that Wulf, blood-stained,
was thrown to the ground; he was not yet doomed to die
2965 but later recovered from that grievous wound.
When Wulf collapsed, his brother Eofor,
Hygelac's brave thane, swung his broad sword,
made by giants, shattered the massive helmet
above the raised shield; Ongentheow fell,

2970   the guardian of the people was fatally wounded.
    Then many warriors quickly rescued Wulf,
    and bandaged his wounds, once they had won control
    (as fate decreed) of that field of corpses.
    Meanwhile Eofor stripped Ongentheow's body
2975   of its iron corslet, wrenched the helmet
    from his head, the mighty sword from his hands;
    he carried the old man's armor to Hygelac.
    He received those battle adornments, honorably
    promised to reward Eofor above other men;
2980   he kept his word; the king of the Geats,
    Hrethel's son, repaid Eofor and Wulf
    for all they had accomplished with outstanding gifts
    when he had returned home; he gave each of them
    land and interlocked rings to the value
2985   of a hundred thousand pence—no man on earth
    had cause to blame the brothers for accepting
    such wealth, they had earned it by sheer audacity.
    Then, as a pledge of friendship, Hygelac gave
    Eofor his only daughter to grace his home.
2990   "That is the history of hatred and feud
    and deadly enmity; and because of it,
    I expect the Swedes to attack us
    as soon as they hear our lord is lifeless—
    he who in earlier days defended a land
2995   and its treasure against two monstrous enemies
    after the death of its heroes, daring Scyldings,
    he who protected the people, and achieved feats
    all but impossible.
                "Let us lose no time now
    but go and gaze there upon our king
3000   and carry him, who gave us rings,
    to the funeral pyre. And let us not grudge gold
    to melt with that bold man, for we have a mighty hoard,
    a mint of precious metal, bought with pain;
    and now, from this last exploit, a harvest
3005   he paid for with his own life; these the fire
    shall devour, the ravening flames embrace.
    No thane shall wear or carry these treasures
    in his memory, no fair maiden shall hang
    an ornament of interlinked rings at her throat,
3010   but often and again, desolate, deprived of gold,
    they must tread the paths of exile,
    now that their lord has laid aside laughter,
    festivity, happiness. Henceforth, fingers must grasp,
    hands must hold, many a spear
3015   chill with the cold of morning; no sound of the harp
    shall rouse the warriors but, craving for carrion,
    the dark raven shall have its say
    and tell the eagle how it fared at the feast
    when, competing with the wolf, it laid bare the bones of corpses."
3020   Thus the brave messenger told of and foretold

harrowing times; and he was not far wrong.
Those events were fated. Every man in the troop
stood up, stained with tears, and set out
for Eagleness to see that strange spectacle.
3025   There they found him lifeless on the sand,
the soft bed where he slept, who often before
had given them rings; that good man's days
on earth were ended; the warrior-king,
lord of the Geats, had died a wondrous death.
3030   But first they saw a strange creature
there, a loathsome serpent lying
nearby; the fire-dragon, fierce
and mottled, was scorched by its own flames.
It measured fifty paces from head to tail;
3035   sometimes it had soared at night
through the cool air, then dived
to its dark lair; now it lay rigid in death,
no longer to haunt caverns under the earth.
Goblets and vessels stood by it,
3040   salvers and valuable swords, eaten through
by rust, as if they had lain
for a thousand winters in the earth's embrace.
That mighty legacy, gold of men long dead,
lay under a curse; it was enchanted
3045   so that no human might enter
the cavern save him to whom God,
the true Giver of Victories, Guardian of Men,
granted permission to plunder the hoard—
whichever warrior seemed worthy to Him.
3050   Then it was clear that, whoever devised it,
the evil scheme of hiding the hoard under the rock
had come to nothing; the guardian had killed
a brave and famous man; that feud
was violently avenged. The day that a warrior,
3055   renowned for his courage, will reach the end
(as fate ordains) of his life on earth,
that hour when a man may feast in the hall
with his friends no longer, is always unpredictable.
It was thus with Beowulf when he tracked down
3060   and attacked the barrow's guardian; he himself
was not aware how he would leave this world.
The glorious princes who first placed that gold there
had solemnly pronounced that until domesday
any man attempting to plunder the hoard
3065   should be guilty of wickedness, confined,
tormented and tortured by the devil himself.
Never before had Beowulf been granted
such a wealth of gold by the gracious Lord.
      Wiglaf, the son of Weohstan, said:
3070   "Many thanes must often suffer
because of the will of one, as we do now.
We could not dissuade the king we loved,

or in any way restrain the lord of our land
from drawing his sword against the gold-warden,
3075   from letting him lie where he had long lain
and remain in his lair until the world's end;
but he fulfilled his high destiny. The hoard,
so grimly gained, is now easy of access;
our king was driven there by too harsh a fate.
3080   I took the path under the earth-wall,
entered the hall and examined all
the treasures after the dragon deserted it;
I was hardly invited there. Hurriedly
I grasped as many treasures as I could,
3085   a huge burden, and carried them here
to my king; he was still alive then,
conscious and aware of this world around him.
He found words for his thronging thoughts,
born of sorrow, asked me to salute you,
3090   said that as a monument to your lord's exploits
you should build a great and glorious barrow
over his pyre, for he of all men
was the most famous warrior on the wide earth
for as long as he lived, happy in his stronghold.
3095   Now let us hurry once more together
and see the hoard of priceless stones,
that wonder under the wall; I will lead you
so that you will come sufficiently close
to the rings, the solid gold. After we
3100   get back, let us quickly build the bier,
and then let us carry our king,
the man we loved, to where he must
long remain in the Lord's protection."
    Then the brave warrior, Weohstan's son,
3105   directed that orders be given to many men
(to all who owned houses, elders of the people)
to fetch wood from far to place beneath
their prince on the funeral pyre:
              "Now flames,
the blazing fire, must devour the lord of warriors
3110   who often endured the iron-tipped arrow-shower,
when the dark cloud loosed by bow strings
broke above the shield-wall, quivering;
when the eager shaft, with its feather garb,
discharged its duty to the barb."
3115   I have heard that Weohstan's wise son
summoned from Beowulf's band his seven
best thanes, and went with those warriors
into the evil grotto; the man leading
the way grasped a brand. Then those retainers
3120   were not hesitant about rifling the hoard
as soon as they set eyes on any part of it,
lying unguarded, gradually rusting,
in that rock cavern; no man was conscience-stricken

about carrying out those priceless treasures
3125 as quickly as he could. Also, they pushed the dragon,
the serpent over the precipice; they let the waves take him,
the dark waters embrace the warden of the hoard.
Then the wagon was laden with twisted gold,
with treasures of every kind, and the king,
3130 the old battle-warrior, was borne to Whaleness.
    Then, on the headland, the Geats prepared a mighty pyre
for Beowulf, hung round with helmets and shields
and shining mail, in accordance with his wishes;
and then the mourning warriors laid
3135 their dear lord, the famous prince, upon it.
    And there on Whaleness, the heroes kindled
the most mighty of pyres; the dark wood-smoke
soared over the fire, the roaring flames
mingled with weeping—the winds' tumult subsided—
3140 until the body became ash, consumed even
to its core. The heart's cup overflowed;
they mourned their loss, the death of their lord.
And, likewise, a maiden of the Geats,
with her tresses swept up, intoned
3145 a dirge for Beowulf time after time,
declared she lived in dread of days to come
dark with carnage and keening, terror of the enemy,
humiliation and captivity.
                                    Heaven swallowed the smoke.
    Then the Geats built a barrow on the headland—
3150 it was high and broad, visible from far
to all seafarers; in ten days they built the beacon
for that courageous man; and they constructed
as noble an enclosure as wise men
could devise, to enshrine the ashes.
3155 They buried rings and brooches in the barrow,
all those adornments that brave men
had brought out from the hoard after Beowulf died.
They bequeathed the gleaming gold, treasure of men,
to the earth, and there it still remains
3160 as useless to men as it was before.
    Then twelve brave warriors, sons of heroes,
rode round the barrow, sorrowing;
they mourned their king, chanted
an elegy, spoke about that great man:
3165 they exalted his heroic life, lauded
his daring deeds; it is fitting for a man,
when his lord and friend must leave this life,
to mouth words in his praise
and to cherish his memory.
3170 Thus the Geats, his hearth-companions,
grieved over the death of their lord;
they said that of all kings on earth
he was the kindest, the most gentle,
the most just to his people, the most eager for fame.

—•—❦—•—

Judith

The Old English poem *Judith*, concerning the legendary beheader of the Assyrian general Holofernes, has been seen most often as a heroic poem, like *Beowulf*, which it immediately follows in the same unique manuscript. It expresses the same fierce love of battle, and uses the same heroic poetic conventions—archaic diction, formulas, and themes. *Judith* achieves ironic effects, however, by placing these conventions in unexpected contexts, for instance calling Holofernes a "brave man" as he hides behind a net to spy on his retainers. Similarly, it presents his raucous feast as an antifeast—a symbol of misrule rather than of social harmony—and his henchmen as a parody of the traditional band of loyal retainers, as they flee in terror to save their lives.

In addition to *Beowulf*, *Judith* has affinities with Old English poems based on the Old Testament, like *Exodus* and *Daniel*, whose heroes devote their military zeal to the glory of God. Like them, it assumes the timeless perspective of Christian salvation history, so that the apparent anachronisms of Judith's praying to the Trinity or Christ's abhorring Holofernes are entirely appropriate. Based on the Book of Judith in the Latin Bible, which the Anglo-Saxons considered canonical, this poem, like many others in Old English, exists only in fragmentary form. The original audience would have known that Holofernes had entered Judea to besiege the Hebrew city of Bethulia. At the point where the Old English poem begins, the "wickedly promiscuous" general, after his drunken feast, orders the beautiful Hebrew maiden Judith to be brought to his bed. Finding him stretched out in a drunken stupor, she first prays for help and then decapitates him. She thereupon returns to her camp, brandishing the head and exhorting the Hebrews to battle with a stirring speech, which inspires them to victory over the leaderless Assyrians.

The poem does not simply express the timeless Christian theme of the struggle of God's people against the pagans, but also comments on the immediate social and historical context of its time. It seems to reflect the resistance of the Christian Anglo-Saxons against the pagan Danes during the ninth-century invasions, perhaps exaggerating the Assyrians' drunkenness in order to comment on the notorious Danish drinking habits. Furthermore, Holofernes' plan to rape Judith may evoke the rape of Anglo-Saxon women by Danish soldiers in the presence of their husbands and fathers.

Judith's identity as a woman warrior also puts the poem in the social context of the time. The poem's emphasis on her power, in contrast to the biblical source's emphasis on God's power to operate through the hand of a mere woman, reflects the relatively strong role of aristocratic women in England before the Norman Conquest. (Other Old English poems that reflect this strength include *Juliana*, a typical saint's legend whose heroine is martyred while resisting a Roman general's advances, and *Elene*, whose heroine—Constantine's mother Saint Helen—was believed to have discovered the true cross.) Finally, Judith's heroic action has been seen as an inversion of the rape which Holofernes himself intends to commit upon her, as, seeing him unconscious on his bed, she "took the heathen man by the hair, dragged him ignominiously towards her with her hands, and carefully laid out the debauched and odious man."

Judith[1]

. . . She was suspicious of gifts in this wide world. So she readily met with a helping hand from the glorious Prince when she had most need of the supreme Judge's support and that he, the Prime Mover, should protect her against this supreme danger.

1. Translated by S. A. J. Bradley.

The illustrious Father in the skies granted her request in this because she always had firm faith in the Almighty.

I have heard, then, that Holofernes cordially issued invitations to a banquet and had dishes splendidly prepared with all sorts of wonderful things, and to it this lord over men summoned all the most senior functionaries. With great alacrity those shield-wielders complied and came wending to the puissant prince, the nation's chief person. That was on the fourth day after Judith, shrewd of purpose, the woman of elfin beauty first visited him.

So they went and settled down to the feasting, insolent men to the wine-drinking, all those brash armored warriors, his confederates in evil. Deep bowls were borne continually along the benches there and brimming goblets and pitchers as well to the hall-guests. They drank it down as doomed men, those celebrated shield-wielders—though the great man, the awesome lord over evils, did not foresee it. Then Holofernes, the bountiful lord of his men, grew merry with tippling. He laughed and bawled and roared and made a racket so that the children of men could hear from far away how the stern-minded man bellowed and yelled, insolent and flown with mead, and frequently exhorted the guests on the benches to enjoy themselves well. So the whole day long the villain, the stern-minded dispenser of treasure, plied his retainers with wine until they lay unconscious, the whole of his retinue drunk as though they had been struck dead, drained of every faculty.

Thus the men's elder commanded the hall-guests to be ministered to until the dark night closed in on the children of men. Then, being wickedly promiscuous, he commanded the blessed virgin, decked with bracelets and adorned with rings, to be fetched in a hurry to his bed. The attendants promptly did as their master, the ruler of armored warriors, required them. They went upon the instant to the guest-hall where they found the astute Judith, and then the shield-wielding warriors speedily conducted the noble virgin to the lofty pavilion where the great man always rested of a night, Holofernes, abhorrent to the Savior.

There was an elegant all-golden fly-net there, hung about the commandant's bed so that the debauched hero of his soldiers could spy through on every one of the sons of men who came in there, but no one of humankind on him, unless, brave man, he summoned one of his evilly renowned soldiers to go nearer to him for a confidential talk.

Hastily, then, they brought the shrewd lady to bed. Then they went, stout-hearted heroes, to inform their master that the holy woman had been brought to his pavilion. The man of mark, lord over cities, then grew jovial of mood: he meant to defile the noble lady with filth and with pollution. To that heaven's Judge, Shepherd of the celestial multitude, would not consent but rather he, the Lord, Ruler of the hosts, prevented him from the act.

So this species of fiend, licentious, debauched, went with a crowd of his men to seek his bed—where he was to lose his life, swiftly, within the one night: he had then come to his violent end upon earth, such as he had previously deserved, the stern-minded prince over men, while he lived in this world under the roof of the skies.

Then the great man collapsed in the midst of his bed, so drunk with wine that he was oblivious in mind of any of his designs. The soldiers stepped out of his quarters with great alacrity, wine-glutted men who had put the perjurer, the odious persecutor, to bed for the last time.

Then the glorious handmaid of the Savior was sorely preoccupied as to how she might most easily deprive the monster of his life before the sordid fellow, full of corruption, awoke. Then the ringletted girl, the Maker's maiden, grasped a sharp sword, hardy in the storms of battle, and drew it from its sheath with her right hand. Then she called by name upon the Guardian of heaven, the Savior of all the world's inhabitants, and spoke these words:

"God of beginnings, Spirit of comfort, Son of the universal Ruler, I desire to entreat you for your grace upon me in my need, Majesty of the Trinity. My heart is now sorely anguished and my mind troubled and much afflicted with anxieties. Give me, Lord of heaven, victory and true faith so that with this sword I may hew down this dispenser of violent death. Grant me my safe deliverance, stern-minded Prince over men. Never have I had greater need of your grace. Avenge now, mighty Lord, illustrious Dispenser of glory, that which is so bitter to my mind, so burning in my breast."

Then the supreme Judge at once inspired her with courage—as he does every single man dwelling here who looks to him for help with resolve and with true faith. So hope was abundantly renewed in the holy woman's heart. She then took the heathen man firmly by his hair, dragged him ignominiously towards her with her hands and carefully laid out the debauched and odious man so as she could most easily manage the wretch efficiently. Then the ringletted woman struck the malignant-minded enemy with the gleaming sword so that she sliced through half his neck, so that he lay unconscious, drunk and mutilated.

He was not then yet dead, not quite lifeless. In earnest then the courageous woman struck the heathen dog a second time so that his head flew off on to the floor. His foul carcass lay behind, dead; his spirit departed elsewhere beneath the deep ground and was there prostrated and chained in torment ever after, coiled about by snakes, trussed up in tortures and cruelly prisoned in hellfire after his going hence. Never would he have cause to hope, engulfed in darkness, that he might get out of that snake-infested prison, but there he shall remain forever to eternity henceforth without end in that murky abode, deprived of the joys of hope.

Judith then had won outstanding glory in the struggle according as God the Lord of heaven, who gave her the victory, granted her. Then the clever woman swiftly put the harrier's head, all bloody, into the bag in which her attendant, a pale-cheeked woman, one proved excellent in her ways, had brought food for them both; and then Judith put it, all gory, into her hands for her discreet servant to carry home. From there the two women then proceeded onwards, emboldened by courage, until they had escaped, brave, triumphant virgins, from among the army, so that they could clearly see the walls of the beautiful city, Bethulia, shining. Then the ring-adorned women hurried forward on their way until, cheered at heart, they had reached the rampart gate.

There were soldiers, vigilant men, sitting and keeping watch in the fortress just as Judith the artful-minded virgin had enjoined the despondent folk when she set out on her mission, courageous lady. Now she had returned, their darling, to her people, and quickly then the shrewd woman summoned one of the men to come out from the spacious city to meet her and speedily to let them in through the gate of the rampart; and to the victorious people she spoke these words:

"I can tell you something worthy of thanksgiving: that you need no longer grieve in spirit. The ordaining Lord, the Glory of kings, is gracious to you. It has been revealed abroad through the world that dazzling and glorious success is impending for you and triumph is granted you over those injuries which you long have suffered."

Then the citizens were merry when they heard how the saintly woman spoke across the high rampart. The army was in ecstasies and the people rushed towards the fortress gate, men and women together, in flocks and droves; in throngs and troops they surged forward and ran towards the handmaid of the Lord, both old and young in their thousands. The heart of each person in that city of mead-halls was exhilarated when they realized that Judith had returned home; and then with humility they hastily let her in.

Then the clever woman ornamented with gold directed her attentive servant-girl to unwrap the harrier's head and to display the bloody object to the citizens as proof of how she had fared in the struggle. The noble lady then spoke to the whole populace:

"Victorious heroes, leaders of the people; here you may openly gaze upon the head of that most odious heathen warrior, the dead Holofernes, who perpetrated upon us the utmost number of violent killings of men and painful miseries, and who intended to add to it even further, but God did not grant him longer life so that he might plague us with afflictions. I took his life, with God's help. Now I want to urge each man among these citizens, each shield-wielding soldier, that you immediately get yourselves ready for battle. Once the God of beginnings, the steadfastly gracious King, has sent the radiant light from the east, go forth bearing shields, bucklers in front of your breasts and mail-coats and shining helmets into the ravagers' midst; cut down the commanders, the doomed leaders, with gleaming swords. Your enemies are sentenced to death and you shall have honor and glory in the fight according as the mighty Lord has signified to you by my hand."

Then an army of brave and keen men was quickly got ready for the battle. Renowned nobles and their companions advanced; they carried victory-banners; beneath their helms the heroes issued forth straight into battle from out of the holy city upon the very dawning of the day. Shields clattered, loudly resonated. At that, the lean wolf in the wood rejoiced, and that bird greedy for carrion, the black raven. Both knew that the men of that nation meant to procure them their fill among those doomed to die; but in their wake flew the eagle, eager for food, speckled-winged; the dark-feathered, hook-beaked bird sang a battle-chant.

On marched the soldiers, warriors to the warfare, protected by their shields, hollowed linden bucklers, they who a while previously had been suffering the abuse of aliens, the blasphemy of heathens. This was strictly repaid to all the Assyrians in the spear-fight once the Israelites under their battle-ensigns had reached the camp. Firmly entrenched, they vigorously let fly from the curved bow showers of darts, arrows, the serpents of battle. Loudly the fierce fighting-men roared and sent spears into their cruel enemies' midst. The heroes, the in-dwellers of the land, were enraged against the odious race. Stern of mood they advanced; hardened of heart they roughly roused their drink-stupefied enemies of old. With their hands, retainers unsheathed from scabbards bright-ornamented swords, proved of edge, and set about the Assyrian warriors in earnest, intending to smite them. Of that army they spared not one of the men alive, neither the lowly nor the mighty, whom they could overpower.

Thus in the hour of morn those comrades in arms the whole time harried the aliens until those who were their adversaries, the chief sentries of the army, acknowledged that the Hebrew people were showing them very intensive sword-play. They went to inform the most senior officers of this by word of mouth and they roused those warriors and fearfully announced to them in their drunken stupor the dreadful news, the terror of the morning, the frightful sword-encounter.

Then, I have heard, those death-doomed heroes quickly shook off their sleep and thronged in flocks, demoralized men, to the pavilion of the debauched Holofernes. They meant to give their lord warning of battle at once, before the terror and the force of the Hebrews descended upon him; all supposed that the men's leader and that beautiful woman were together in the handsome tent, the noble Judith and the lecher, fearsome and ferocious. Yet there was not one of the nobles who dared awaken the warrior to inquire how it had turned out for the soldier with the holy virgin, the woman of the Lord.

The might of the Hebrews, their army, was drawing closer; vehemently they fought with tough and bloody weapons and violently they indemnified with gleaming swords their former quarrels and old insults: in that day's work the Assyrians' repute was withered, their arrogance abased. The men stood around their lord's tent, extremely agitated and growing gloomier in spirit. Then all together they began to cough and loudly make noises and, having no success, to chew the grist with their teeth, suffering agonies. The time of their glory, good fortune and valorous doings was at an end. The nobles thought to awaken their lord and friend; they succeeded not at all.

Then one of the soldiers belatedly and tardily grew so bold that he ventured pluckily into the pavilion as necessity compelled him. Then he found his lord lying pallid on the bed, deprived of his spirit, dispossessed of life. Straightway then he fell chilled to the ground, and distraught in mind he began to tear his hair and his clothing alike and he uttered these words to the soldiers who were waiting there miserably outside:

"Here is made manifest our own perdition, and here it is imminently signalled that the time is drawn near, along with its tribulations, when we must perish and be destroyed together in the strife. Here, hacked by the sword, decapitated, lies our lord."

Then distraught in mind they threw down their weapons; demoralized they went scurrying away in flight. The nation magnified in strength attacked them in the rear until the greatest part of the army lay on the field of victory levelled by battle, hacked by swords, as a treat for the wolves and a joy to the carrion-greedy birds. Those who survived fled from the linden spears of their foes. In their wake advanced the troop of Hebrews, honoured with the victory and glorified in the judgment: the Lord God, the almighty Lord, had come handsomely to their aid. Swiftly then with their gleaming swords those valiant heroes made an inroad through the thick of their foes; they hacked at targes and sheared through the shield-wall. The Hebrew spear-throwers were wrought up to the fray; the soldiers lusted mightily after a spear-contest on that occasion. There in the dust fell the main part of the muster-roll of the Assyrian nobility, of that odious race. Few survivors reached their native land.

The soldiers of royal renown turned back in retirement amidst carnage and reeking corpses. That was the opportunity for the land's in-dwellers to seize from those most odious foes, their old dead enemies, bloodied booty, resplendent accoutrements, shield and broad sword, burnished helmets, costly treasures. The guardians of their homeland had honorably conquered their enemies on the battlefield and destroyed with swords their old persecutors. In their trail lay dead those who of living peoples had been most inimical to their existence.

Then the whole nation, most famous of races, proud, curled-locked, for the duration of one month were carrying and conveying into the beautiful city, Bethulia, helmets and hip-swords, gray mail-coats, and men's battle-dress ornamented with gold, more glorious treasures than any man among ingenious men can tell. All that the people splendidly gained, brave beneath their banners in the fray, through the shrewd advice of Judith, the courageous woman. As a reward the celebrated spearmen brought back for her from the expedition the sword and the bloodied helmet of Holofernes as well as his huge mail-coat adorned with red gold; and everything the ruthless lord of the warriors owned of riches or personal wealth, of rings and of beautiful treasures, they gave it to that beautiful and resourceful lady.

For all this Judith gave glory to the Lord of hosts who granted her esteem and renown in the realm of earth and likewise too a reward in heaven, the prize of victory in the glory of the sky because she always had true faith in the Almighty. Certainly at the end she did not doubt the reward for which she long had yearned.

For this be glory into eternity to the dear Lord who created the wind and the clouds, the skies and the spacious plains and likewise the cruel seas and the joys of heaven, through his peculiar mercy.

Taliesin

The name of Taliesin resonated through Welsh literary imagination for more than a millennium, from the late sixth century until the end of the Middle Ages. Only a small cluster of about a dozen poems can be securely identified with him, all of them praise poems and elegies for contemporary kings. These must have circulated for generations in oral form. They appear in their earliest surviving manuscript, the late thirteenth-century Book of Taliesin, already embedded within a nimbus of intriguing legends and falsely attributed works that had been attached to the prestige of his name across the centuries.

Despite this central role, Taliesin was not a poet of "Wales" in anything like its modern geography. In the later sixth century when he was active, Welsh-speaking kingdoms survived in the north and west of Britain and into modern Scotland. They were embattled, pressured by the expanding Anglo-Saxon kingdoms to the east and south, by Picts in the north, and by Irish Celts in the kingdom of Dalriada to the far northwest. Among these unstable Welsh kingdoms, especially Rheged around the Solway Firth, Taliesin became an important court poet.

The warrior kings in the Welsh north, such as Taliesin's chief patrons Urien king of Rheged and his son Owain, were extolled in a poetic culture that celebrated treasure and heroic violence, yet did so in forms of considerable intricacy and language of dramatic spareness. Taliesin's poems use ambitious meters and stanzas involving internal rhyme, end rhyme, and alliteration. They do not merely glory in armed bloodshed but also explore the boasts and emotions leading up to battle; they often display a haunting visual sense of its grisly aftermath. Taliesin further celebrates the generosity and gaiety of the triumphant court: in ways reminiscent of the Anglo-Saxon *Wanderer*, one poem here registers the poet's terror at the thought of losing his patron and protector. In an elegy for Owain ap Urien, Taliesin combines all these elements, yet brackets them with a suddenly broadened and suggestively discordant perspective, a Christian plea for the needs of Owain's soul.

Urien Yrechwydd[1]

Urien of Yrechwydd   most generous of Christian men,
much do you give   to the people of your land;
as you gather   so also you scatter,
the poets of Christendom   rejoice while you stand.
5   More is the gaiety   and more is the glory
that Urien and his heirs   are for riches renowned,
and he is the chieftain,   the paramount ruler,
the far-flung refuge,   first of fighters found.
The Lloegrians[2] know it   when they count their numbers,
10   death have they suffered   and many a shame,
their homesteads a-burning,   stripped their bedding,
and many a loss   and many a blame,
and never a respite   from Urien of Rheged.
Rheged's defender,   famed lord, your land's anchor,
15   all that is told of you   has my acclaim.
Intense is your spear-play   when you hear ploy of battle,
when to battle you come   'tis a killing you can,
fire in their houses ere day   in the lord of Yrechwydd's way,
Yrechwydd the beautiful   and its generous clan.
20   The Angles are succorless.   Around the fierce king
are his fierce offspring.   Of those dead, of those living,
of those yet to come,   you head the column.
To gaze upon him   is a widespread fear;
Gaiety clothes him,   the ribald ruler,
25   gaiety clothes him   and riches abounding,
gold king of the Northland   and of kings king.

The Battle of Argoed Llwyfain[1]

There was a great battle Saturday morning
From when the sun rose until it grew dark.
The fourfold hosts of Fflamddwyn[2] invaded,
Goddau and Rheged gathered in arms,
5   Summoned from Argoed as far as Arfynydd[3]—
They might not delay by as much as a day.

With a great blustering din, Fflamddwyn shouted,
"Have these the hostages come? Are they ready?"[4]
To him then Owain, scourge of the eastlands,
10   "They've not come, no! they're not, nor shall they be ready."
And a whelp of Coel would indeed be afflicted
Did he have to give any man as a hostage!

---

1. "I-*rech*-ooeed" (guttural "ch"), or Rheged. Like many Anglo-Saxon poems, this poem uses a break (caesura) in mid-line. Translated by Saunders Lewis.
2. The Angles and Saxons.
1. "Ar-*goid* Lloo-*ee*-vine, the Welsh "ll" rather like "tl" pronounced quickly as a single sound. Translated by Anthony Conran.

2. "Flom-*thoo*-een," the Flame-bearer, identity uncertain.
3. "Goddau ("*Go*-thy,") and Arfynydd ("Ar-*vi*-nith") British territories.
4. Fflamddwyn arrogantly demands hostages, guarantees of submission, before the battle. The use of direct quotation is unique among Taliesin's poems.

And Urien, lord of Erechwydd, shouted,
"If they would meet us now for a treaty,
15   High on the hilltop let's raise our ramparts,
Carry our faces over the shield rims,
Raise up our spears, men, over our heads
And set upon Fflamddwyn in the midst of his hosts
And slaughter him, ay, and all that go with him!"

20   There was many a corpse beside Argoed Llwyfain;
From warriors ravens grew red
And with their leader a host attacked.
For a whole year I shall sing to their triumph.

The War-Band's Return[1]

Through a single year
This man has poured out
Wine, bragget, and mead,
Reward for valor.
5   A host of singers,
A swarm about spits,
Their torques round their heads,
Their places splendid.
Each went on campaign,
10   Eager in combat,
His steed beneath him,
Set to raid Manaw
For the sake of wealth,
Profit in plenty,
15   Eight herds alike
Of calves and cattle,
Milch cows and oxen,
And each one worthy.

I could have no joy
20   Should Urien be slain,
So loved before he left,
Brandishing his lance,
And his white hair soaked,
And a bier his fate,
25   And gory his cheek
With the stain of blood,
A strong, steadfast man,
His wife made a widow,
My faithful king,
30   My faithful trust,
My bulwark, my chief,
Before savage pain.

1. Translated by Joseph P. Clancy.

Go, lad, to the door:
What is that clamor?
35   Is the earth shaking?
Is the sea in flood?
The chant grows stronger
From marching men!

Were a foe in hill,
40   Urien will stab him;
Were a foe in dale,
Urien has pierced him;
Were foe in mountain,
Urien conquers him;
45   Were foe on hillside,
Urien will wound him;
Were foe on rampart,
Urien will smite him:
Foe on path, foe on peak,
50   Foe at every bend,
Not one sneeze or two
He permits before death.
No famine can come,
Plunder about him.
55   Like death his spear
Piercing a foeman.
And until I die, old,
By death's strict demand,
I shall not be joyful
60   Unless I praise Urien.

Lament for Owain Son of Urien[1]

God, consider the soul's need
    Of Owain son of Urien!
Rheged's prince, secret in loam:
    No shallow work to praise him.

5   A straight° grave, a man much praised,   *narrow*
    His whetted spear the wings of dawn:
That lord of bright Llwyfenydd,
    Where is his peer?

Reaper of enemies; strong of grip;
10   One kind with his fathers;
Owain, to slay Fflamddwyn,
    Thought it no more than sleep.

Sleepeth the wide host of England
    With light in their eyes,

1. Translated by Saunders Lewis.

15   And those that had not fled
          Were braver than were wise.

      Owain dealt them doom
          As the wolves devour sheep;
      That warrior, bright of harness,
20   Gave stallions for the bard.

      Though he hoarded wealth like a miser
          For his soul's sake he gave it.
      God, consider the soul's need
          Of Owain son of Urien!

⊷ ⊰◈⊱ ⊶

The Wanderer

In the Exeter Book, a manuscript copied about 975 and donated to the Bishop of Exeter, are preserved some of the greatest short poems in Old English, including a number of poems referred to as elegies—laments which contrast past happiness with present sorrow and remark on how fleeting is the former. Along with *The Wanderer*, the elegies include its companion piece *The Seafarer*; *The Ruin*; *The Husband's Message*; *The Wife's Lament*; and *Wulf and Eadwacer*. While the last two are exceptional in dealing with female experience, elegies for the most part focus on male bonds and companionship, particularly the joys of the mead hall. Old English poetry as a whole is almost entirely devoid of interest in romantic love between men and women and focuses instead on the bond between lord and retainer; elegiac poems such as *The Wanderer* have in fact been called "the love poetry of a heroic society."

    The Wanderer opens with an appeal to a Christian concept, as the third-person narrator speaks of the wanderer's request for God's mercy. The body of the poem, however—primarily a first-person account in the wanderer's voice—reflects more pagan values in its regret for the loss of earthly joys. Though the poem's structure is somewhat confusing, one can discern two major parts. In the first, the wanderer laments his personal situation: he was once a member of a warrior band, but his lord—his beloved "gold-friend"—has died, leaving him a homeless exile. He dreams that he "clasps and kisses" his lord, but he then wakes to see only the dark waves, the snow, and the sea birds.

    The second part of the poem turns from personal narrative to a more general statement of the transitoriness of all earthly things. The speaker (possibly someone other than the wanderer at this point), looking at the ruin of ancient buildings, is moved to express the ancient Roman motif known as *"ubi sunt"* (Latin for "where are"): "Where has the horse gone? Where the man? Where the giver of gold? / Where is the feasting place? And where the pleasures of the hall?" In the concluding five lines, the reader is urged to seek comfort in heaven.

    There has been much debate about the degrees of Christianity and paganism in this tenth-century poem. The positions range from the view that the Christian opening and closing are totally extraneous to the poem and have been tacked on by a monkish copyist, to the view that the poem is a Christian allegory about a soul exiled from his heavenly home, longing for his lord Jesus Christ. It is now generally held that the poem is authentically Christian, in a literal rather than an allegorical way, but that the values of pagan society still exert a powerful pull in it.

The Wanderer[1]

Often the wanderer pleads for pity
and mercy from the Lord; but for a long time,
sad in mind, he must dip his oars
into icy waters, the lanes of the sea;
5   he must follow the paths of exile: fate is inflexible.

Mindful of hardships, grievous slaughter,
the ruin of kinsmen, the wanderer said:
"Time and again at the day's dawning
I must mourn all my afflictions alone.
10   There is no one still living to whom I dare open
the doors of my heart. I have no doubt
that it is a noble habit for a man
to bind fast all his heart's feelings,
guard his thoughts, whatever he is thinking.
15   The weary in spirit cannot withstand fate,
a troubled mind finds no relief:
wherefore those eager for glory often
hold some ache imprisoned in their hearts.
Thus I had to bind my feelings in fetters,
20   often sad at heart, cut off from my country,
far from my kinsmen, after, long ago,
dark clods of earth covered my gold-friend;
I left that place in wretchedness,
plowed the icy waves with winter in my heart;
25   in sadness I sought far and wide
for a treasure-giver, for a man
who would welcome me into his mead-hall,
give me good cheer (for I boasted no friends),
entertain me with delights. He who has experienced it
30   knows how cruel a comrade sorrow can be
to any man who has few loyal friends:
for him are the ways of exile, in no wise twisted gold;
for him is a frozen body, in no wise the fruits of the earth.
He remembers hall-retainers and treasure
35   and how, in his youth, his gold-friend
entertained him. Those joys have all vanished.
A man who lacks advice for a long while
from his loved lord understands this,
that when sorrow and sleep together
40   hold the wretched wanderer in their grip,
it seems that he clasps and kisses
his lord, and lays hands and head
upon his lord's knee as he had sometimes done
when he enjoyed the gift-throne in earlier days.
45   Then the friendless man wakes again
and sees the dark waves surging around him,

1. Translated by Kevin Crossley-Holland.

Though scholars agree that *Wulf and Eadwacer* is "heart-rending" and "haunting," they cannot agree on the dramatic situation—each translation is an act of interpretation. The present translator, Kevin Crossley-Holland, sees the poem as involving the female speaker; her husband (Eadwacer); her lover (Wulf), from whom she is separated; and her child (a "cub"). Although what transpired before is unclear, she wistfully concludes, "men easily savage what was never secure, our song together." The dramatic setting of *The Wife's Lament* is similary ambiguous; it is not clear whether the woman's anger is directed toward her husband or to a third person who plotted to separate them.

Wulf and Eadwacer

Prey, it's as if my people have been handed prey.
They'll tear him to pieces if he comes with a troop.

O, we are apart.

Wulf is on one island, I on another,
5   a fastness that island, a fen-prison.
Fierce men roam there, on that island;
they'll tear him to pieces if he comes with a troop.

O, we are apart.

How I have grieved for my Wulf's wide wanderings.
10   When rain slapped the earth and I sat apart weeping,
when the bold warrior wrapped his arms about me,
I seethed with desire and yet with such hatred.
Wulf, my Wulf, my yearning for you
and your seldom coming have caused my sickness,
15   my mourning heart, not mere starvation.
Can you heart, Eadwacer? Wulf will spirit
our pitiful whelp to the woods.
Men easily savage what was never secure,
our song together.

The Wife's Lament[1]

I draw these words from my deep sadness,
my sorrowful lot. I can say that,
since I grew up, I have not suffered
such hardships as now, old or new.
5   I am tortured by the anguish of exile.

First my lord forsook his family
for the tossing waves; I fretted at dawn
as to where in the world my lord might be.
In my sorrow I set out then,
10   a friendless wanderer, to search for my man.
But that man's kinsmen laid secret plans
to part us, so that we should live
most wretchedly, far from each other
in this wide world; I was seized with longings.

---

1. Translated by Kevin Crossley-Holland.

15   My lord asked me to live with him here;
      I had few loved ones, loyal friends
      in this country; that is reason for grief.
      Then I found my own husband was ill-starred,
      sad at heart, pretending, plotting
20   murder behind a smiling face. How often
      we swore that nothing but death should ever
      divide us; that is all changed now;
      our friendship is as if it had never been.
      Early and late, I must undergo hardship
25   because of the feud of my own dearest loved one.
      Men forced me to live in a forest grove,
      under an oak tree in the earth-cave.
      This cavern is age-old; I am choked with longings.
      Gloomy are the valleys, too high the hills,
30   harsh strongholds overgrown with briars:
      a joyless abode. The journey of my lord so often
      cruelly seizes me. There are lovers on earth,
      lovers alive who lie in bed,
      when I pass through this earth-cave alone
35   and out under the oak tree at dawn;
      there I must sit through the long summer's day
      and there I mourn my miseries,
      my many hardships; for I am never able
      to quiet the cares of my sorrowful mind,
40   all the longings that are my life's lot.

      Young men must always be serious in mind
      and stout-hearted; they must hide
      their heartaches, that host of constant sorrows,
      behind a smiling face.
                 Whether he is master
45   of his own fate or is exiled in a far-off land—
      sitting under rocky storm-cliffs, chilled
      with hoar-frost, weary in mind,
      surrounded by the sea in some sad place—
      my husband is caught in the clutches of anguish;
      over and again he recalls a happier home.
50   Grief goes side by side with those
      who suffer longing for a loved one.

PERSPECTIVES

Arthurian Myth in the History of Britain

Almost since it first appeared, the story of King Arthur has occupied a contested zone between myth and history. Far from diminishing the Arthurian tradition, though, this ambiguity has lent it a tremendous and protean impact on the political and cultural imagination of Europe, from the Middle Ages to the present. Probably no other body of medieval legend remains today as widely known and as often revisited as the Arthurian story.

One measure of Arthur's undiminished importance is the eager debate, eight centuries old and going strong, about his historical status. Whether or not a specific "Arthur" ever existed, legends and attributes gathered around his name from a very early date, mostly in texts of Welsh background. Around 600 a Welsh poem refers briefly to Arthur's armed might, and by about 1000, the story *Culhwch and Olwen*, from the Mabinogion, assumes knowledge of Arthur as a royal warlord. Other early Welsh texts begin to give him more-than-mortal attributes, associating Arthur with such marvels as an underworld quest and a mysterious tomb. In the ninth century, the Latin *History of the Britons* by the Welshman Nennius confidently speaks of Arthur as a great leader and lists his twelve victories ending with that at Mount Badon.

Some of this at least fits with better-documented history and with less-shadowy commanders who might have been models for an Arthurian figure, even if they were not "Arthur." When the Romans withdrew in 410, the romanized Britons soon faced territorial aggression from the Saxons and Picts. In the decades after midcentury, the Britons mounted a successful defense, led in part by Aurelius Ambrosius and culminating, it appears, with the battle of Badon in roughly 500, after which Saxon incursions paused for a time. In those same years of territorial threat, some Britons had emigrated to what is now Brittany, and in the 460s or 470s a warlord named Riothamus led an army, probably from Britain, and fought successfully in Gaul in alliance with local rulers sympathetic to Rome. His name was latinized from a British title meaning "supreme king." Both Riothamus and Aurelius Ambrosius correspond to parts of the later narratives of Arthur: his role as high king, his triumphs against the Saxons, his links to Rome (both friendly and hostile), and his campaigns on the continent.

Whether the origins of Arthur's story lie in fact or in an urge among the Welsh to imagine a great leader who once restored their power against the ever-expanding Anglo-Saxons, he was clearly an established figure in Welsh oral and written literature by the ninth century. Arthur, however, also held a broader appeal for other peoples of England. The British Isles were felt to lie at the outer edge of world geography, but the story of Arthur and his ancestor Brutus served to create a Britain with other kinds of centrality. The legend of Brutus made Britain the end point of an inexorable westward movement of Trojan imperial power, the *translatio imperii*, and Arthur's forebears became linked to Roman imperial dynasties. Finally, the general movement of Arthur's continental campaigns neatly reversed the patterns of Roman and then Norman colonization.

In the later Middle Ages and after, Arthur and his court are most often encountered in works that lay little claim to historical accuracy. Rather, they exploit the very uncertainty of Arthurian narrative to explore the highest (if sometimes self-deceiving) yearnings of private emotion and social order. These Arthurian romances also probe, often in tragic terms, the limits and taboos that both define and subvert such ideals, including the mutual threats posed by private emotion and social order.

Nevertheless, the Arthurian tradition has also been pulled persistently into the realm of the real. It was presented as serious historical writing from the twelfth century through the end of the Middle Ages. Political agents have used Arthur's kingship as a model or precedent for their own aspirations, as seen in the Kennedy administration's portrayal as a version of Camelot. Even elements of the Christian church wrote their doctrines into Arthurian narrative or claimed Arthur as a patron.

The texts in this section present three illuminating moments of Arthur's emergence into history and politics. Geoffrey of Monmouth's *History of the Kings of Britain*, finished around 1138, was the fullest version yet of Arthur's origin and career. Geoffrey was the first to make Arthur such a central figure in British history, and it was largely through Geoffrey's Latin "history" that Arthur became so widespread a feature of cultural imagination in the Middle Ages and beyond. Writing at the close of the twelfth century, Gerald of Wales narrates an occasion, possibly orchestrated by Henry II, in which Arthurian tradition was slightly altered and folded into emergent Norman versions of British antiquity.

The section ends with two politically charged versions of national origin, English and Scottish, proposed in 1301 as part of Edward I's efforts to influence royal succession in Scotland.

✦ ✤ ✦

Geoffrey of Monmouth
c. 1100–1155

From the perspective of surviving British peoples in Wales and Cornwall, the Norman Conquest of 1066 was only the last among successive waves of invasion by Romans, Picts, Anglo-Saxons, and Vikings. The Celtic Britons had long been pushed into the far south-west by the time the Normans arrived, where they continued to resist colonization. The Welsh maintained a vital language, culture, and ethnic mythology, including a memory of their fellow Celts in Brittany and a divided nostalgia for the long-departed Romans. Thus a whole Celtic linguistic and political world offered an alternative to the languages and legends of the Normans, much of which derived ultimately from Mediterranean antiquity. Arthur, king of the Britons, emerged as a key figure as these peoples and cultures began to articulate the complex new forms of political and private identity precipitated by the Conquest.

No one was more important in this process than Geoffrey of Monmouth. He was prior of the Abbey of Monmouth in Wales and later was named bishop of Saint Asaph, though civil disorder prevented his taking the post. Yet he was also active in the emerging schools of Oxford, he was patronized by Norman nobles and bishops, and he wrote in Latin. Geoffrey's learning reflects this double allegiance. Well schooled in the Latin curriculum that embraced ancient Roman and Christian literature, he was also deeply versed in the oral and written culture of Wales. As a creative negotiater between Welsh and Anglo-Norman legends and languages, his influence was without parallel.

Both of Geoffrey's surviving prose works, the *Prophecies of Merlin* (finished around 1135) and the *History of the Kings of Britain* (about 1138) present themselves as translations of ancient texts from Wales or Brittany. Geoffrey also wrote a *Life of Merlin* in Latin verse. He probably synthesized a number of sources and added material of his own in his "translations." It was a pointed gesture, nevertheless, to posit a Celtic text whose authority rivaled the Latin culture and legends that had underwritten later Anglo-Saxon and then Norman power in England. Geoffrey daringly inverted the general hierarchy of Latin and vernaculars in his time; instead, he offered "British" as the ancient tongue that he wanted to make more broadly accessible for Latin-reading newcomers.

Geoffrey's central heroes are Brutus, the exiled Trojan descendant who colonized and named Britain, and Arthur, who reunified England after Saxon and Pictish attacks, and repulsed Roman efforts to re-establish power there. Geoffrey's own purposes in the *History* were complex but he was responding in part to contemporary events. The 1130s were a decade of civil strife in England, as nobles shifted their allegiances between King Stephen and the other claimant to the throne, the future Henry II. Welsh nobles took advantage of this disorder to rebel and set up their own principalities. Scholars remain divided as to whether Geoffrey was more interested in a return to strong and unified rule in Norman England, or wanted rather to encourage the Welsh princes with the story of a great predecessor who might one day return.

Geoffrey's narrative carefully presents itself as history, in a century of great historical writing. He uses the typical armature of documentary and other written records, archeological evidence, and claims to well-founded witness. Casting the story of Arthur into this respected form allows Geoffrey to employ but also to counter the dominant master-narrative of Christian history in England, which was Bede's. Rather than a story of Anglo-Saxon arrival and conversion, Geoffrey offers a story of an earlier foundation and a prior conversion; he thus creates imaginative space for a convergence between Norman power and the culture and ambitions of people and languages at its edges. Moreover, the *History* generates an exterior (if now conveniently absent) common enemy in the imperial Romans. Geoffrey pulls in yet more ancient models by frequently echoing Virgil's *Aeneid* and its story of exile and refoundation, and by placing his story within biblical, Trojan, and Roman chronologies. And he points forward to his own time by inserting the earlier *Prophecies of Merlin* in the midst of the *History*.

The continued influence of Geoffrey's *History* on later literature is testimony to the powerful themes he folded into his story. Much that is developed in later romance explorations of the Arthurian world is already here: the tragedy of a people bravely battling its own decline; the danger and overwhelming attraction of illicit sexual desire; the ambivalent position of Mordred as cousin or nephew; the Arthurian realm brought down, ultimately, by the treachery of the king's own kin and by a transgression of the marriage bed that echoes Arthur's own conception.

The following selections from Geoffrey's *History* feature the Trojan background of Britain and the birth and early kingship of Arthur. Other texts in this section and following trace later episodes in his evolving legend: the development of Arthur's court, the celebration and tragedy of romantic desire, and the death of the king.

from **History of the Kings of Britain**[1]
Dedication

Whenever I have chanced to think about the history of the kings of Britain, on those occasions when I have been turning over a great many such matters in my mind, it has seemed a remarkable thing to me that, apart from such mention of them as Gildas and Bede had each made in a brilliant book on the subject, I have not been able to discover anything at all on the kings who lived here before the Incarnation of Christ, or indeed about Arthur and all the others who followed on after the Incarnation. Yet the deeds of these men were such that they deserve to be praised for all time. What is more, these deeds were handed joyfully down in oral tradition, just as if they had been committed to writing, by many peoples who had only their memory to rely on.

At a time when I was giving a good deal of attention to such matters, Walter, Archdeacon of Oxford, a man skilled in the art of public speaking and well-informed about the history of foreign countries, presented me with a certain very ancient book written in the British language.[2] This book, attractively composed to form a consecutive and orderly narrative, set out all the deeds of these men, from Brutus, the first King of the Britons, down to Cadwallader, the son of Cadwallo.[3] At Walter's request I have taken the trouble to translate the book into Latin, although, indeed, I have been content with my own expressions and my own homely style and I have gathered no gaudy flowers of speech in other men's gardens. If I had adorned my page with high-flown rhetorical figures, I should have bored my readers, for they would have been forced to spend more time in discovering the meaning of my words than in following the story.

1. Translated by Lewis Thorpe (1966).
2. Walter and Geoffrey were both associated with an early Oxford college, and their names appear together on several legal documents. In two of these, Geoffrey calls himself a *magister*, a teacher at an advanced level.
3. Bede's *Ecclesiastical History of the English People* was the source most used by 12th-century historians, but it has little to say about England before the coming of the Angles and Saxons. Geoffrey offers a (perhaps fictive) source for a more ancient history of the people who preceded the Saxons.

I ask you, Robert, Earl of Gloucester,[4] to do my little book this favor. Let it be so emended by your knowledge and your advice that it must no longer be considered as the product of Geoffrey of Monmouth's small talent. Rather, with the support of your wit and wisdom, let it be accepted as the work of one descended from Henry, the famous King of the English; of one whom learning has nurtured in the liberal arts and whom his innate talent in military affairs has put in charge of our soldiers, with the result that now, in our own lifetime, our island of Britain hails you with heartfelt affection, as if it had been granted a second Henry.

You too, Waleran, Count of Mellent, second pillar of our kingdom, give me your support, so that, with the guidance provided by the two of you, my work may appear all the more attractive when it is offered to its public.[5] For indeed, sprung as you are from the race of the most renowned King Charles, Mother Philosophy has taken you to her bosom, and to you she has taught the subtlety of her sciences. What is more, so that you might become famous in the military affairs of our army, she has led you to the camp of kings, and there, having surpassed your fellow-warriors in bravery, you have learned, under your father's guidance, to be a terror to your enemies and a protection to your own folk. Faithful defender as you are of those dependent on you, accept under your patronage this book which is published for your pleasure. Accept me, too, as your writer, so that, reclining in the shade of a tree which spreads so wide, and sheltered from envious and malicious enemies, I may be able in peaceful harmony to make music on the reed-pipe of a muse who really belongs to you.

[TROY, AENEAS, BRUTUS' EXILE][6]

After the Trojan war, Aeneas fled from the ruined city with his son Ascanius and came by boat to Italy. He was honorably received there by King Latinus, but Turnus, King of the Rutuli, became jealous of him and attacked him. In the battle between them Aeneas was victorious. Turnus was killed and Aeneas seized both the kingdom of Italy and the person of Lavinia, who was the daughter of Latinus.[7]

When Aeneas' last day came, Ascanius was elected King. He founded the town of Alba on the bank of the Tiber and became the father of a son called Silvius. This Silvius was involved in a secret love-affair with a certain niece of Lavinia's; he married her and made her pregnant. When this came to the knowledge of his father Ascanius, the latter ordered his soothsayers to discover the sex of the child which the girl had conceived. As soon as they had made sure of the truth of the matter, the soothsayers said that she would give birth to a boy, who would cause the death of both his father and his mother; and that after he had wandered in exile through many lands this boy would eventually rise to the highest honor.

The soothsayers were not wrong in their forecast. When the day came for her to have her child, the mother bore a son and died in childbirth. The boy was handed over to the midwife and was given the name Brutus. At last, when fifteen years had passed, the young man killed his father by an unlucky shot with an arrow, when they were out hunting together. Their beaters drove some stags into their path and Brutus, who was under the impression that he was aiming his weapon at these stags, hit his

---

4. An illegitimate son of King Henry I. He had a hand in the education of the future Henry II, his nephew.
5. Waleran de Beaumont, Count of Meulan (1104–1166) moved in the same circles as the Earl of Gloucester, and was patron of the Norman Abbey of Bec, a great center of learning. Geoffrey's fulsome tone is typical of dedications

to great magnates in the period.
6. From book 1, ch. 3.
7. This summarizes the political narrative of Virgil's *Aeneid,* a text Geoffrey knew well and echoed frequently throughout his *History.*

own father below the breast. As the result of this death Brutus was expelled from Italy by his relations, who were angry with him for having committed such a crime. He went in exile to certain parts of Greece; and there he discovered the descendants of Helenus, Priam's son, who were held captive in the power of Pandrasus, King of the Greeks. After the fall of Troy, Pyrrhus, the son of Achilles, had dragged this man Helenus off with him in chains, and a number of other Trojans, too. He had ordered them to be kept in slavery, so that he might take vengeance on them for the death of his father.

When Brutus realized that these people were of the same race as his ancestors, he stayed some time with them. However, he soon gained such fame for his military skill and prowess that he was esteemed by the kings and princes more than any young man in the country.

[THE NAMING OF BRITAIN][8]

[Brutus conquers the Greek king (reversing the Greek conquest of his ancestral Troy), marries the king's daughter Ignoge, and leads the Trojan descendants off to seek a new land. They pass through continental Europe, where they do battle with the Gauls.]

In their pursuit the Trojans continued to slaughter the Gauls, and they did not abandon the bloodshed until they had gained victory.

Although this signal triumph brought him great joy, Brutus was nevertheless filled with anxiety, for the number of his men became smaller every day, while that of the Gauls was constantly increasing. Brutus was in doubt as to whether he could oppose the Gauls any longer; and he finally chose to return to his ships in the full glory of his victory while the greater part of his comrades were still safe, and then to seek out the island which divine prophecy had promised would be his. Nothing else was done. With the approval of his men Brutus returned to his fleet. He loaded his ships with all the riches which he had acquired and then went on board. So, with the winds behind him, he sought the promised island, and came ashore at Totnes.

At this time the island of Britain was called Albion. It was uninhabited except for a few giants. It was, however, most attractive, because of the delightful situation of its various regions, its forests and the great number of its rivers, which teemed with fish; and it filled Brutus and his comrades with a great desire to live there. When they had explored the different districts, they drove the giants whom they had discovered into the caves in the mountains. With the approval of their leader they divided the land among themselves. They began to cultivate the fields and to build houses, so that in a short time you would have thought that the land had always been inhabited.

Brutus then called the island Britain from his own name, and his companions he called Britons. His intention was that his memory should be perpetuated by the derivation of the name. A little later the language of the people, which had up to then been known as Trojan or Crooked Greek, was called British, for the same reason.[9]

[BRUTUS BUILDS NEW TROY]

Once he had divided up his kingdom, Brutus decided to build a capital. In pursuit of this plan, he visited every part of the land in search of a suitable spot. He came at length to the River Thames, walked up and down its banks and so chose a site suited

8. From book 1, ch. 15–18 and book 2, ch. 1.
9. With this detail, Geoffrey creates a linguistic history in

which early Welsh is as ancient as classical Latin, and more purely "Trojan."

to his purpose. There then he built his city and called it Troia Nova. It was known by this name for long ages after, but finally by a corruption of the word it came to be called Trinovantum. * * *

When the above-named leader Brutus had built the city about which I have told you, he presented it to the citizens by right of inheritance, and gave them a code of laws by which they might live peacefully together. At that time the priest Eli was ruling in Judea and the Ark of the Covenant was captured by the Philistines. The sons of Hector reigned in Troy, for the descendants of Antenor had been driven out. In Italy reigned Aeneas Silvius, son of Aeneas and uncle of Brutus, the third of the Latin Kings. * * *[1]

In the meantime Brutus had consummated his marriage with his wife Ignoge. By her he had three sons called Locrinus, Kamber and Albanactus, all of whom were to become famous. When their father finally died, in the twenty-third year after his landing, these three sons buried him inside the walls of the town which he had founded. They divided the kingdom of Britain between them in such a way that each succeeded to Brutus in one particular district. Locrinus, who was the first-born, inherited the part of the island which was afterwards called Loegria after him. Kamber received the region which is on the further bank of the River Severn, the part which is now known as Wales but which was for a long time after his death called Kambria from his name. As a result the people of that country still call themselves Kambri today in the Welsh tongue. Albanactus, the youngest, took the region which is nowadays called Scotland in our language. He called it Albany, after his own name.

[MERLIN AND THE FIRST CONQUEST OF IRELAND][2]

[*The descendants of Brutus' three sons include Leir (Shakespeare's King Lear), the brothers Brennius and Belinus who conquer Rome, and Lud who rebuilds New Troy and names it Kaerlud after himself (whence "London"). In the reign of Lud's brother, Julius Caesar invades England; generations of Britons resist, until King Coel makes peace with the Roman legate Constantius. The latter succeeds Coel, marries Coel's daughter, and sires Constantine who becomes emperor of Rome. The Romans tire of defending Britain against invaders and withdraw from the island. Vortigern usurps the throne from the Briton line, then holds it in alliance with the Saxons Hengist and Horsa. The Saxons become aggressors, and Vortigern flees them but is overcome by the brothers Aurelius Ambrosius and Utherpendragon, who restore the Briton royal line and drive the Saxons into the north. Aurelius reigns, restoring churches and the rule of law; he wants to commemorate the Britons who died fighting off the Saxons.*]

Aurelius collected carpenters and stone-masons together from every region and ordered them to use their skill to contrive some novel building which would stand forever in memory of such distinguished men. The whole band racked their brains and then confessed themselves beaten. Then Tremorinus, Archbishop of the City of the Legions,[3] went to the King and said: "If there is anyone anywhere who has the ability to execute your plan, then Merlin, the prophet of Vortigern, is the man to do it.[4] In my opinion, there is no one else in your kingdom who has greater

---

1. Medieval historians often made such parallels between biblical and secular chronologies.
2. From book 8, ch. 10–13.
3. Also called Caerusk or Caerleon; Geoffrey mentions it often and may have had some connection with it.

4. Merlin, son of a Briton princess and a demonic spirit, has already appeared; he triumphed over Vortigern's magicians and uttered a series of prophecies. Merlin's roles as a royal advisor, a prophet, and even a shape-shifter can be compared to those of poets in early Celtic cultures.

skill, either in the foretelling of the future or in mechanical contrivances. Order Merlin to come and use his ability, so that the monument for which you are asking can be put up."

Aurelius asked many questions about Merlin; then he sent a number of messengers through the various regions of the country to find him and fetch him. They traveled through the provinces and finally located Merlin in the territory of the Gewissei, at the Galabes Springs, where he often went. They explained to him what they wanted of him and then conducted him to the King. The King received Merlin gaily and ordered him to prophesy the future, for he wanted to hear some marvels from him. "Mysteries of that sort cannot be revealed," answered Merlin, "except where there is the most urgent need for them. If I were to utter them as an entertainment, or where there was no need at all, then the spirit which controls me would forsake me in the moment of need."

He gave the same refusal to everyone present. The King had no wish to press him about the future, but he spoke to him about the monument which he was planning. "If you want to grace the burial-place of these men with some lasting monument," replied Merlin, "send for the Giants' Ring which is on Mount Killaraus in Ireland. In that place there is a stone construction which no man of this period could ever erect, unless he combined great skill and artistry. The stones are enormous and there is no one alive strong enough to move them. If they are placed in position round this site, in the way in which they are erected over there, they will stand forever."

At these words of Merlin's Aurelius burst out laughing. "How can such large stones be moved from so far-distant a country?" he asked. "It is hardly as if Britain itself is lacking in stones big enough for the job!" "Try not to laugh in a foolish way, your Majesty," answered Merlin. "What I am suggesting has nothing ludicrous about it. These stones are connected with certain secret religious rites and they have various properties which are medicinally important. Many years ago the Giants transported them from the remotest confines of Africa and set them up in Ireland at a time when they inhabited that country. Their plan was that, whenever they felt ill, baths should be prepared at the foot of the stones; for they used to pour water over them and to run this water into baths in which their sick were cured. What is more, they mixed the water with herbal concoctions and so healed their wounds. There is not a single stone among them which hasn't some medicinal virtue."

When the Britons heard all this, they made up their minds to send for the stones and to make war on the people of Ireland if they tried to hold them back. In the end the King's brother, Utherpendragon, and fifteen thousand men, were chosen to carry out the task. Merlin, too, was co-opted, so that all the problems which had to be met could have the benefit of his knowledge and advice. They made ready their ships and they put to sea. The winds were favorable and they arrived in Ireland.

At that time there reigned in Ireland a young man of remarkable valor called Gillomanius. As soon as he heard that the Britons had landed in the country, he collected a huge army together and hurried to meet them. When he learned the reason of their coming, Gillomanius laughed out loud at those standing round him. "I am not surprised that a race of cowards has been able to devastate the island of the Britons," said he, "for the Britons are dolts and fools. Who ever heard of such folly? Surely the stones of Ireland aren't so much better than those of Britain that our realm has to be invaded for their sake! Arm yourselves, men, and defend your fatherland, for as long as life remains in my body they shall not steal from us the minutest fragment of the Ring."

When he saw that the Irish were spoiling for a fight, Uther hurriedly drew up his own line of battle and charged at them. The Britons were successful almost immediately. The Irish were either mangled or killed outright, and Gillomanius was forced to flee. Having won the day, the Britons made their way to Mount Killaraus. When they came to the stone structure, they were filled with joy and wonder. Merlin came up to them as they stood round in a group. "Try your strength, young men," said he, "and see whether skill can do more than brute strength, or strength more than skill, when it comes to dismantling these stones!"

At his bidding they all set to with every conceivable kind of mechanism and strove their hardest to take the Ring down. They rigged up hawsers and ropes and they propped up scaling-ladders, each preparing what he thought most useful, but none of these things advanced them an inch. When he saw what a mess they were making of it, Merlin burst out laughing. He placed in position all the gear which he considered necessary and dismantled the stones more easily than you could ever believe. Once he had pulled them down, he had them carried to the ships and stored on board, and they all set sail once more for Britain with joy in their hearts.

The winds were fair. They came to the shore and then set off with the stones for the spot where the heroes had been buried. The moment that this was reported to him, Aurelius dispatched messengers to all the different regions of Britain, ordering the clergy and the people to assemble and, as they gathered, to converge on Mount Ambrius, where they were with due ceremony and rejoicing to re-dedicate the burial-place which I have described. At the summons from Aurelius the bishops and abbots duly assembled with men from every rank and file under the King's command. All came together on the appointed day. Aurelius placed the crown on his head and celebrated the feast of Whitsun in right royal fashion, devoting the next three days to one long festival. ✱ ✱ ✱

Once he had settled these matters, and others of a similar nature, Aurelius ordered Merlin to erect round the burial-place the stones which he had brought from Ireland. Merlin obeyed the King's orders and put the stones up in a circle round the sepulchre, in exactly the same way as they had been arranged on Mount Killaraus in Ireland, thus proving that his artistry was worth more than any brute strength.

[UTHERPENDRAGON SIRES ARTHUR][5]

[Vortigern's son attacks Aurelius Ambrosius and Utherpendragon. They drive him off, though Aurelius is poisoned through Saxon treachery. A miraculous star appears, which Merlin interprets as a sign of Uther's destined kingship, the coming of Arthur, and the rule of Uther's dynasty. At the same time, however, Merlin prophesies the decline of the Britons. As king, Uther fights off more Saxon incursions.]

The next Eastertide Uther told the nobles of his kingdom to assemble in that same town of London, so that he could wear his crown and celebrate so important a feast-day with proper ceremony. They all obeyed, traveling in from their various cities and assembling on the eve of the feast. The King was thus able to celebrate the feast as he had intended and to enjoy himself in the company of his leaders. They, too, were all happy, seeing that he had received them with such affability. A great

5. From book 8, ch. 19–24.

many nobles had gathered there, men worthy of taking part in such a gay festivity, together with their wives and daughters.

Among the others there was present Gorlois, Duke of Cornwall, with his wife Ygerna, who was the most beautiful woman in Britain. When the King saw her there among the other women, he was immediately filled with desire for her, with the result that he took no notice of anything else, but devoted all his attention to her. To her and to no one else he kept ordering plates of food to be passed and to her, too, he kept sending his own personal attendants with golden goblets of wine. He kept smiling at her and engaging her in sprightly conversation. When Ygerna's husband saw what was happening, he was so annoyed that he withdrew from the court without taking leave. No one present could persuade him to return, for he was afraid of losing the one object that he loved better than anything else. Uther lost his temper and ordered Gorlois to come back to court, so that he, the King, could seek satisfaction for the way in which he had been insulted. Gorlois refused to obey. The King was furious and swore an oath that he would ravage Gorlois' lands, unless the latter gave him immediate satisfaction.

Without more ado, while the bad blood remained between the two of them, the King collected a huge army together and hurried off to the Duchy of Cornwall, where he set fire to towns and castles. Gorlois' army was the smaller of the two and he did not dare to meet the King in battle. He preferred instead to garrison his castles and to bide his time until he could receive help from Ireland. As he was more worried about his wife than he was about himself, he left her in the castle of Tintagel,[6] on the sea-coast, which he thought was the safest place under his control. He himself took refuge in a fortified camp called Dimilioc,[7] so that, if disaster overtook them, they should not both be endangered together. When the King heard of this, he went to the encampment where Gorlois was, besieged it and cut off every line of approach.

Finally, after a week had gone by, the King's passion for Ygerna became more than he could bear. He called to him Ulfin of Ridcaradoch, one of his soldiers and a familiar friend, and told him what was on his mind. "I am desperately in love with Ygerna," said Uther, "and if I cannot have her I am convinced that I shall suffer a physical breakdown. You must tell me how I can satisfy my desire for her, for otherwise I shall die of the passion which is consuming me." "Who can possibly give you useful advice," answered Ulfin, "when no power on earth can enable us to come to her where she is inside the fortress of Tintagel? The castle is built high above the sea, which surrounds it on all sides, and there is no other way in except that offered by a narrow isthmus of rock. Three armed soldiers could hold it against you, even if you stood there with the whole kingdom of Britain at your side. If only the prophet Merlin would give his mind to the problem, then with his help I think you might be able to obtain what you want." The King believed Ulfin and ordered Merlin to be sent for, for he, too, had come to the siege.

Merlin was summoned immediately. When he appeared in the King's presence, he was ordered to suggest how the King could have his way with Ygerna. When Merlin saw the torment which the King was suffering because of this woman, he was amazed at the strength of his passion. "If you are to have your wish," he said, "you must make use of methods which are quite new and until

6. Tin-*ta*-jel, on the rocky northwestern coast of Cornwall.

7. Di-*mi*-li-oc, perhaps a site roughly five miles from Tintagel.

now unheard-of in your day. By my drugs I know how to give you the precise appearance of Gorlois, so that you will resemble him in every respect. If you do what I say, I will make you exactly like him, and Ulfin exactly like Gorlois' companion, Jordan of Tintagel. I will change my own appearance, too, and come with you. In this way you will be able to go safely to Ygerna in her castle and be admitted."

The King agreed and listened carefully to what he had to do. In the end he handed the siege over to his subordinates, took Merlin's drugs, and was changed into the likeness of Gorlois. Ulfin was changed into Jordan and Merlin into a man called Britaelis, so that no one could tell what they had previously looked like. They then set off for Tintagel and came to the Castle in the twilight. The moment the guard was told that his leader was approaching, he opened the gates and the men were let in. Who, indeed, could possibly have suspected anything, once it was thought that Gorlois himself had come? The King spent that night with Ygerna and satisfied his desire by making love with her. He had deceived her by the disguise which he had taken. He had deceived her, too, by the lying things that he said to her, things which he planned with great skill. He said that he had come out secretly from his besieged encampment so that he might make sure that all was well with her, whom he loved so dearly, and with his castle, too. She naturally believed all that he said and refused him nothing that he asked. That night she conceived Arthur, the most famous of men, who subsequently won great renown by his outstanding bravery.

Meanwhile, when it was discovered at the siege of Dimilioc that the King was no longer present, his army, acting without his instructions, tried to breach the walls and challenge the beleaguered Duke to battle. The Duke, equally illadvisedly, sallied forth with his men, imagining apparently that he could resist such a host of armed men with his own tiny band. As the struggle between them swayed this way and that, Gorlois was among the first to be killed. His men were scattered and the besieged camp was captured. The treasure which had been deposited there was shared out in the most inequitable way, for each man seized in his greedy fist whatever good luck and his own brute strength threw in his way.[8]

Not until the outrages which followed this daring act had finally subsided did messengers come to Ygerna to announce the death of the Duke and the end of the siege. When they saw the King sitting beside Ygerna in the likeness of their leader, they blushed red with astonishment to see that the man whom they had left behind dead in the siege had in effect arrived there safely before them. Of course, they did not know of the drugs prepared by Merlin. The King put his arms round the Duchess and laughed aloud to hear these reports. "I am not dead," he said. "Indeed, as you see, I am very much alive! However, the destruction of my camp saddens me very much and so does the slaughter of my comrades. What is more, there is great danger that the King may come this way and capture us in this castle. I will go out to meet him and make peace with him, lest even worse should befall us."

The King set out and made his way towards his own army, abandoning his disguise as Gorlois and becoming Utherpendragon once more. When he learned all

---

8. Geoffrey emphasizes the destructive potential of private greed, private ambition, and brute force, even in the rule of a strong king like Uther. This becomes a dominant theme in Geoffrey and later Arthurian narratives.

that had happened, he mourned for the death of Gorlois; but he was happy, all the same, that Ygerna was freed from her marital obligations. He returned to Tintagel Castle, captured it and seized Ygerna at the same time, she being what he really wanted. From that day on they lived together as equals, united by their great love for each other; and they had a son and a daughter. The boy was called Arthur and the girl Anna.

[ANGLO-SAXON INVASION]

As the days passed and lengthened into years, the King fell ill with a malady which affected him for a long time. Meanwhile the prison warders who guarded Octa and Eosa,[9] as I have explained above, led a weary life. In the end they escaped with their prisoners to Germany and in doing so terrified the kingdom: for rumor had it that they had already stirred up Germany, and had fitted out a huge fleet in order to return to the island and destroy it. This, indeed, actually happened. They came back with an immense fleet and more men than could ever be counted. They invaded certain parts of Albany[1] and busied themselves in burning the cities there and the citizens inside them. The British army was put under the command of Loth of Lodonesia, with orders that he should keep the enemy at a distance. This man was one of the leaders, a valiant soldier, mature both in wisdom and age. As a reward for his prowess, the King had given him his daughter Anna and put him in charge of the kingdom while he himself was ill. When Loth moved forward against the enemy he was frequently driven back again by them, so that he had to take refuge inside the cities. On other occasions he routed and dispersed them, forcing them to fly either into the forests or to their ships. Between the two sides the outcome of each battle was always in doubt, it being hard to tell which of them was victorious. Their own arrogance was a handicap to the Britons, for they were unwilling to obey the orders of their leaders. This undermined their strength and they were unable to beat the enemy in the field.

Almost all the island was laid waste. When this was made known to the King, he fell into a greater rage than he could really bear in his weakened state. He told all his leaders to appear before him, so that he could rebuke them for their overweening pride and their feebleness. As soon as he saw them all assembled in his presence, he reproached them bitterly and swore that he himself would lead them against the enemy. He ordered a litter to be built, so that he could be carried in it; for his weakness made any other form of progress impossible. Then he instructed them all to be in a state of preparedness, so that they could advance against the enemy as soon as the opportunity offered. The litter was constructed immediately, the men were made ready to start and the opportunity duly came.

They put the King in his litter and set out for Saint Albans, where the Saxons I have told you about were maltreating all the local population ∗ ∗ ∗

[Despite his illness, Uther prevails. Octa and Eosa are killed.]

Once the Saxons had been defeated, as I have explained above, they did not for that reason abandon their evil behavior. On the contrary, they went off to the northern provinces and preyed relentlessly upon the people there. King Uther was

---

9. A son and a kinsman of the Saxon Hengist; Uther had imprisoned them in London. Geoffrey closely connects the resurgence of the Saxon invaders with Uther's adul-

tery and the disorder within his own army.
1. That is, Scotland, named for Brutus' son Albanactus.

keen to pursue them, as he had proposed, but his princes dissuaded him from it, for after his victory his illness had taken an even more serious turn. As a result the enemy became bolder still in their enterprises, striving by every means in their power to take complete control of the realm. Having recourse, as usual, to treachery, they plotted to see how they could destroy the King by cunning. When every other approach failed, they made up their minds to kill him with poison. This they did: for while Uther lay ill in the town of St. Albans, they sent spies disguised as beggars, who were to discover how things stood at court. When the spies had obtained all the information that they wanted, they discovered one additional fact which they chose to use as a means of betraying Uther. Near the royal residence there was a spring of very limpid water which the King used to drink when he could not keep down any other liquids because of his illness. These evil traitors went to the spring and polluted it completely with poison, so that all the water which welled up was infected. When the King drank some of it, he died immediately. Some hundred men died after him, until the villainy was finally discovered. Then they filled the well in with earth. As soon as the death of the King was made known, the bishops of the land came with their clergy and bore his body to the monastery of Ambrius and buried it with royal honors at the side of Aurelius Ambrosius, inside the Giants' Ring.

[ARTHUR OF BRITAIN][2]

After the death of Utherpendragon, the leaders of the Britons assembled from their various provinces in the town of Silchester and there suggested to Dubricius, the Archbishop of the City of the Legions, that as their King he should crown Arthur, the son of Uther. Necessity urged them on, for as soon as the Saxons heard of the death of King Uther, they invited their own countrymen over from Germany, appointed Colgrin as their leader and began to do their utmost to exterminate the Britons. They had already over-run all that section of the island which stretches from the River Humber to the sea named Caithness.[3]

Dubricius lamented the sad state of his country. He called the other bishops to him and bestowed the crown of the kingdom upon Arthur. Arthur was a young man only fifteen years old; but he was of outstanding courage and generosity, and his inborn goodness gave him such grace that he was loved by almost all the people. Once he had been invested with the royal insignia, he observed the normal custom of giving gifts freely to everyone. Such a great crown of soldiers flocked to him that he came to an end of what he had to distribute. However, the man to whom openhandedness and bravery both come naturally may indeed find himself momentarily in need, but poverty will never harass him for long. In Arthur courage was closely linked with generosity, and he made up his mind to harry the Saxons, so that with their wealth he might reward the retainers who served his own household. The justness of his cause encouraged him, for he had a claim by rightful inheritance to the kingship of the whole island. He therefore called together all the young men whom I have just mentioned and marched on York. * * * [4]

2. From book 9, ch. 1–11.
3. That is, Northumberland and Scotland.
4. Geoffrey links the ancient practice of a king's largesse to his warrior band together with the claim of dynastic genealogy. Arthur will again use the latter claim when he decides to invade Gaul and then march toward Rome.

[Arthur and his followers attack Colgrin and ultimately subdue the Saxons; then they repel armies of Scots, Picts, and Irish. Arthur restores Briton dynasties throughout England, marries Guinevere, and establishes a stable peace.]

Arthur then began to increase his personal entourage by inviting very distinguished men from far-distant kingdoms to join it. In this way he developed such a code of courtliness in his household that he inspired peoples living far away to imitate him. The result was that even the man of noblest birth, once he was roused to rivalry, thought nothing at all of himself unless he wore his arms and dressed in the same way as Arthur's knights. At last the fame of Arthur's generosity and bravery spread to the very ends of the earth; and the kings of countries far across the sea trembled at the thought that they might be attacked and invaded by him, and so lose control of the lands under their dominion. They were so harassed by these tormenting anxieties that they rebuilt their towns and the towers in their towns, and then went so far as to construct castles on carefully chosen sites, so that, if invasion should bring Arthur against them, they might have a refuge in their time of need.

All this was reported to Arthur. The fact that he was dreaded by all encouraged him to conceive the idea of conquering the whole of Europe.

＋—❧—＋

Gerald of Wales
c. 1146–1222

Geoffrey of Monmouth's *History of the Kings of Britain* was soon translated into French, early Middle English, and Welsh, and it reappears in other languages for centuries. Contemporary historians, especially those interested in pre-Saxon history, were enthusiastic about this new story. Others were skeptical. Nevertheless, Geoffrey's narrative was soon accepted widely as fact, adopted, and revised to serve the interests of the Angevin dynasty.

The discovery of Arthur's bones at Glastonbury Abbey in 1191, as reported by the prolific writer Gerald of Wales, is a particularly rich instance of this habit, benefiting both the status of Henry II and the prestige of the abbey. Glastonbury faced a crisis common among Anglo-Saxon monastic foundations after the Norman Conquest. It was, in fact, probably the earliest Christian community in Britain; nonetheless, the oral tradition of its antiquity was weakened as the Normans took power, bringing with them a new insistence on written documentation. Glastonbury had little proof of its claims to ancient privilege, either by way of charters (and those mostly spurious) or the related prestige of holy relics. At the same time, Henry II was interested in ancient narratives that might legitimize his imperial aims.

Gerald's version of events both suggests Henry's almost wondrous wisdom in identifying the very spot of Arthur's burial and implies the existence of early written records at Glastonbury. To have Arthur as a patron, authenticated by King Henry himself, greatly substantiated the abbey's other claims. At the same time, Henry's knowledge mysteriously linked him to Arthur, and the corpse itself neatly altered Arthurian tradition, certifying Arthur's actual death and perhaps damping Welsh hopes for a messianic return.

from The Instruction of Princes[1]

The memory of Arthur, that most renowned King of the Britons, will endure forever. In his own day he was a munificent patron of the famous Abbey at Glastonbury, giving many donations to the monks and always supporting them strongly, and he is

---

1. Translated by Lewis Thorpe. Gerald reports the same events again in a later text, the *Speculum Ecclesiae*.

highly praised in their records. More than any other place of worship in his kingdom he loved the church of the Blessed Mary, Mother of God, in Glastonbury, and he fostered its interests with much greater loving care than that of any of the others. When he went out to fight, he had a full-length portrait of the Blessed Virgin painted on the front of his shield, so that in the heat of battle he could always gaze upon her; and whenever he was about to make contact with the enemy he would kiss her feet with great devoutness.

In our lifetime Arthur's body was discovered at Glastonbury, although the legends had always encouraged us to believe that there was something otherworldly about his ending, that he had resisted death and had been spirited away to some far-distant spot.[2] The body was hidden deep in the earth in a hollowed-out oak-bole and between two stone pyramids which had been set up long ago in the churchyard there. They carried it into the church with every mark of honor and buried it decently there in a marble tomb. It had been provided with most unusual indications which were, indeed, little short of miraculous, for beneath it—and not on top, as would be the custom nowadays—there was a stone slab, with a leaden cross attached to its underside. I have seen this cross myself and I have traced the lettering which was cut into it on the side turned towards the stone, instead of being on the outer side and immediately visible. The inscription read as follows: HERE IN THE ISLE OF AVALON LIES BURIED THE RENOWNED KING ARTHUR, WITH GUINEVERE, HIS SECOND WIFE.

There are many remarkable deductions to be made from this discovery. Arthur obviously had two wives, and the second one was buried with him. Her bones were found with those of her husband, but they were separate from his. Two-thirds of the coffin, the part towards the top end, held the husband's bones, and the other section, at his feet, contained those of his wife. A tress of woman's hair, blond, and still fresh and bright in color, was found in the coffin. One of the monks snatched it up and it immediately disintegrated into dust. There had been some indications in the Abbey records that the body would be discovered on this spot, and another clue was provided by lettering carved on the pyramids, but this had been almost completely erased by the passage of the years. The holy monks and other religious had seen visions and revelations. However, it was Henry II, King of England, who had told the monks that, according to a story which he had heard from some old British soothsayer,[3] they would find Arthur's body buried at least sixteen feet in the ground, not in a stone coffin but in a hollowed-out oak-bole. It had been sunk as deep as that, and carefully concealed, so that it could never be discovered by the Saxons, whom Arthur had attacked relentlessly as long as he lived and whom, indeed, he had almost wiped out, but who occupied the island [of Britain] after his death. That was why the inscription, which was eventually to reveal the truth, had been cut into the inside of the cross and turned inwards towards the stone. For many a long year this inscription was to keep the secret of what the coffin contained, but eventually, when time and circumstance were both opportune, the lettering revealed what it had so long concealed.

What is now known as Glastonbury used in ancient times to be called the Isle of Avalon. It is virtually an island, for it is completely surrounded by marshlands. In Welsh it is called "Ynys Avallon," which means the Island of Apples. "Aval" is the

2. In his other version (the *Speculum Ecclesiae*) Gerald is more nervously dismissive: "In their stupidity the British people maintain that he is still alive. . . . According to them, once he has recovered from his wounds this strong and all-powerful King will return to rule over the Britons in the normal way" (page 285).

3. In the *Speculum Ecclesiae*, Gerald says that Henry learned this "from the historical accounts of the Britons and from their bards" (page 286).

Welsh word for apple, and this fruit used to grow there in great abundance.[4] After the Battle of Camlann,[5] a noblewoman called Morgan, who was the ruler and patroness of these parts as well as being a close blood-relation of King Arthur, carried him off to the island now known as Glastonbury, so that his wounds could be cared for. Years ago the district had also been called "Ynys Gutrin" in Welsh, that is the Island of Glass, and from these words the invading Saxons later coined the place-name "Glastingebury." The word "glass" in their language means "vitrum" in Latin, and "bury" means "castrum" [camp] or "civitas" [city].

You must know that the bones of Arthur's body which were discovered there were so big that in them the poet's words seem to be fulfilled:

> All men will exclaim at the size of the bones they've exhumed.[6]

The Abbot showed me one of the shin-bones. He held it upright on the ground against the foot of the tallest man he could find, and it stretched a good three inches above the man's knee. The skull was so large and capacious that it seemed a veritable prodigy of nature, for the space between the eyebrows and the eye-sockets was as broad as the palm of a man's hand. Ten or more wounds could clearly be seen, but they had all mended except one. This was larger than the others and it had made an immense gash. Apparently it was this wound which had caused Arthur's death.

1193

◂━━◆◢◣◆━━▸

Edward I
1239–1307

Beginning in 1291, King Edward I of England revived an ancient claim to be feudal over-lord of Scotland and thereby sought to control a disputed succession to its throne. By 1293 the Scottish king John Balliol had become Edward's vassal, but rebelled and was forced to abdicate in 1296. The military and diplomatic struggle (later called the "Great Cause") stretched across the decade. By the turn of the fourteenth century, in an extraordinary move, both the English and Scots had turned to the court of Pope Boniface VIII for a legal decision. In pursuing Edward's claim, his agents ransacked chronicles—including Geoffrey of Monmouth's *History*—as well as ancient charters, to compile a dossier of historical and legal precedents. Despite his own bureaucratic reforms requiring documentary proof for most legal claims, Edward was ready to invoke common memory and ancient legends to support his position regarding Scotland. Knowing that such chronicle material would have no status in court, in May of 1301 Edward resorted to the following letter before Pope Boniface ruled in the matter.

The written letter was a highly developed and self-conscious genre during the Middle Ages. Letters were often meant to be public and could carry the force of law. Indeed, the form of many legal documents had developed from royal letters. Letter writing became an area for textbooks and school study, the *ars dictaminis*. Elaborate formulas of salutation and closing, and other rhetorical figures, were taught and used for important correspondence as a way of establishing the sender's learning and prestige. The papal curia employed a particularly challenging system of prose rhythm called the *cursus*, which was imitated in some royal chanceries and is found in the Latin of Edward's letter.

---

4. Citing and explaining words from the various British vernaculars is a widespread habit in Latin historical writing as early as Bede.

5. Arthur's last battle, fought against the rebel army of his

kinsman Mordred. Arthur kills Mordred but is himself mortally wounded.

6. Virgil, *Georgics*, 1.497.

King Edward I
Letter sent to the Papal Court of Rome concerning the king's rights in the realm of Scotland.[1]

To the most Holy Father in Christ lord Boniface, by divine providence the supreme pontiff of the Holy Roman and Universal Church, Edward, by grace of the same providence king of England, lord of Ireland, and duke of Aquitaine offers his humblest devotion to the blessed saints.[2] What follows we send to you not to be treated in the form or manner of a legal plea, but altogether extrajudicially, in order to set the mind of your Holiness at rest. The All-Highest, to whom all hearts are open, will testify how it is graven upon the tablets of our memory with an indelible mark, that our predecessors and progenitors, the kings of England, by right of lordship and dominion, possessed, from the most ancient times, the suzerainty of the realm of Scotland and its kings in temporal matters, and the things annexed thereto, and that they received from the self-same kings, and from such magnates of the realm as they so desired, liege homage and oaths of fealty. We, continuing in the possession of that very right and dominion, have received the same acknowledgments in our time, both from the king of Scotland, and from the magnates of that realm; and indeed such prerogatives of right and dominion did the kings of England enjoy over the realm of Scotland and its kings, that they have even granted to their faithful folk the realm itself, removed its kings for just causes, and constituted others to rule in their place under themselves. Beyond doubt these matters have been familiar from times long past and still are, though perchance it has been suggested otherwise to your Holiness' ears by foes of peace and sons of rebellion, whose elaborate and empty fabrications your wisdom, we trust, will treat with contempt.

Thus, in the days of Eli and of Samuel the prophet, after the destruction of the city of Troy, a certain valiant and illustrious man of the Trojan race called Brutus, landed with many noble Trojans, upon a certain island called, at that time, Albion.[3] It was then inhabited by giants, and after he had defeated and slain them, by his might and that of his followers, he called it, after his own name, Britain, and his people Britons, and built a city which he called Trinovant, now known as London. Afterwards he divided his realm among his three sons, that is he gave to his first born, Locrine, that part of Britain now called England, to the second, Albanact, that part then known as Albany, after the name of Albanact, but now as Scotland, and to Camber, his youngest son, the part then known by his son's name as Cambria and now called Wales, the royal dignity being reserved for Locrine, the eldest. Two years after the death of Brutus there landed in Albany a certain king of the Huns, called Humber, and he slew Albanact, the brother of Locrine. Hearing this, Locrine, the king of the Britons, pursued him, and he fled and was drowned in the river which from his name is called Humber, and thus Albany reverted to Locrine. ∗ ∗ ∗ Again, Arthur, king of the Britons, a prince most renowned, subjected to himself a rebellious Scotland, destroyed almost the whole nation, and afterwards installed as king of Scotland one Angusel by name. Afterwards, when King Arthur held a most famous feast at Caerleon, there were present there all the kings subject to him, and among

1. Translated by E. L. G. Stones (1965). Although sent in the name of the king, a Latin letter of such formality would have been written by notaries in his chancery. A French draft also survives, which might have been used by Edward himself.
2. A flowery opening formula was typical of formal letters between persons of power; it also provided a place for Edward to make ambitious (and in the case of Aquitaine, highly optimistic) territorial claims.
3. Here the letter borrows closely from Geoffrey of Monmouth's foundation narrative; see page 114.

them Angusel, king of Scotland, who manifested the service due for the realm of Scotland by bearing the sword of King Arthur before him; and in succession all the kings of Scotland have been subject to all the kings of the Britons. Succeeding kings of England enjoyed both monarchy and dominion in the island, and subsequently Edward, known as the elder, son of Alfred, king of England, had subject and subordinate to him, as lord superior, the kings of the Scots, the Cumbrians, and the Strathclyde Welsh. * * *

Since, indeed, from what has been said already, and from other evidence, it is perfectly clear and well-known that the realm of Scotland belongs to us of full right, by reason of property and of possession, and that we have not done and have not dared to do anything, as indeed we could not do, in writing or in action, by which any prejudice may be implied to our right or possession, we humbly beseech your Holiness to weigh all this with careful meditation, and to condescend to keep it all in mind when making your decision, setting no store, if you please, by the adverse assertions which come to you on this subject from our enemies, but, on the contrary, retaining our welfare and our royal rights, if it so please you, in your fatherly regard. May the Most High preserve you, to rule his Holy Church through many years of prosperity.

Kempsey, 7 May 1301, the twenty-ninth year of our reign.

COMPANION READING

A Report to Edward I[1]

Sir, seeing that you have lately sent a statement to the pope concerning your right to Scotland, the Scots are making efforts to nullify that statement by certain objections which are given below. * * * They say that in that letter you ground your right on old chronicles, which contain various falsehoods and lies, and are abrogated and made void by the subsequent contrary actions of your predecessors and of yourself, which vitiate all the remaining part of your letter, and therefore one should give no credence to such a document. And they say further, that with only this unworthy and feeble case to rely upon, you are striving to evade the cognizance of your true judge, and to suppress the truth, and unlawfully, by force of arms, to repel your weaker neighbors, and to prevent the pope from pursuing the examination of this case. * * *

Again, they say that the old chronicles that you use as evidence of your right could not assist you, even if they were authenticated, as is not the case, they say, because it is notorious that these same old chronicles are utterly made naught and of no avail by other subsequent documents of greater significance, by contrary agreements and actions, and by papal privileges. * * * Then, sir, in order that credence be not given to the documents, histories, and deeds described in your statement, they say that allegations like those recounted in your narrative are put out of court by the true facts, and they endeavor to demonstrate their assertion by chronicles and narratives of a contrary purport. Brutus divided between his three sons the island once

1. The Scots learned about Edward's letter and made their own response to the pope; this report to Edward, written in the French he would actually have used with his counselors, specifies the Scots' rebuttal. The Scots carefully assert the superior force of later charters and other legal instruments, and dismiss Edward's reliance on unauthenticated legends. In case Edward's story should carry weight with Boniface, however, they also provide a counternarrative of their own national foundation by Scota, daughter of the Pharaoh, and how she expelled British influence from her land. The English and Scots diplomats thus tell opposing prehistories that underwrite their current claims. Just as important, though, they are negotiating around an unusually articulate moment in the contest between different forms of textuality—legendary and chronicle tradition versus legal documents—in the creation of contemporary political power.

of the man who could love her so,
she granted him her love and her body.
Now Lanval was on the right road!
135   Afterward, she gave him a gift:
he would never again want anything,
he would receive as he desired;
however generously he might give and spend,
she would provide what he needed.
140   Now Lanval is well cared for.
The more lavishly he spends,
the more gold and silver he will have.
"Love," she said, "I admonish you now,
I command and beg you,
145   do not let any man know about this.
I shall tell you why:
you would lose me for good
if this love were known;
you would never see me again
150   or possess my body."
He answered that he would do
exactly as she commanded.
He lay beside her on the bed;
now Lanval is well cared for.
155   He remained with her
that afternoon, until evening
and would have stayed longer, if he could,
and if his love had consented.
"Love," she said, "get up.
160   You cannot stay any longer.
Go away now; I shall remain
but I will tell you one thing:
when you want to talk to me
there is no place you can think of
165   where a man might have his mistress
without reproach or shame,
that I shall not be there with you
to satisfy all your desires.
No man but you will see me
170   or hear my words."
When he heard her, he was very happy,
he kissed her, and then got up.
The girls who had brought him to the tent
dressed him in rich clothes;
175   when he was dressed anew,
there wasn't a more handsome youth in all the world;
he was no fool, no boor.
They gave him water for his hands
and a towel to dry them,
180   and they brought him food.
He took supper with his love;
it was not to be refused.

He was served with great courtesy,
he received it with great joy.
185   There was an entremet°   *side dish*
that vastly pleased the knight
for he kissed his lady often
and held her close.
When they finished dinner,
190   his horse was brought to him.
The horse had been well saddled;
Lanval was very richly served.
The knight took his leave, mounted,
and rode toward the city,
195   often looking behind him.
Lanval was very disturbed;
he wondered about his adventure
and was doubtful in his heart;
he was amazed, not knowing what to believe;
200   he didn't expect ever to see her again.
He came to his lodging
and found his men well dressed.
That night, his accommodations were rich
but no one knew where it came from.
205   There was no knight in the city
who really needed a place to stay
whom he didn't invite to join him
to be well and richly served.
Lanval gave rich gifts,
210   Lanval released prisoners,
Lanval dressed jongleurs,°   *performers*
Lanval offered great honors.
There was no stranger or friend
to whom Lanval didn't give.
215   Lanval's joy and pleasure were intense;
in the daytime or at night,
he could see his love often;
she was completely at his command.

In that same year, it seems to me,
220   after the feast of Saint John,
about thirty knights
were amusing themselves
in an orchard beneath the tower
where the queen was staying.
225   Gawain was with them
and his cousin, the handsome Yvain;[7]
Gawain, the noble, the brave,
who was so loved by all, said:
"By God, my lords, we wronged

---

7. Gawain and Yvain serve to place Marie's hero in the context of more famous Arthurian episodes. Gawain, nephew of Arthur and distinguished both for bravery and courtesy, increasingly acts as Lanval's sponsor in the rest of the *lai*.

230   our companion Lanval,
     who is so generous and courtly,
     and whose father is a rich king,
     when we didn't bring him with us."
     They immediately turned back,
235   went to his lodging
     and prevailed on Lanval to come along with them.
     At a sculpted window
     the queen was looking out;
     she had three ladies with her.
240   She saw the king's retinue,
     recognized Lanval and looked at him.
     Then she told one of her ladies
     to send for her maidens,
     the loveliest and the most refined;
245   together they went to amuse themselves
     in the orchard where the others were.
     She brought thirty or more with her;
     they descended the steps.
     The knights came to meet them,
250   because they were delighted to see them.
     The knights took them by the hand;
     their conversation was in no way vulgar.
     Lanval went off to one side,
     far from the others; he was impatient
255   to hold his love,
     to kiss and embrace and touch her;
     he thought little of others' joys
     if he could not have his pleasure.
     When the queen saw him alone,
260   she went straight to the knight.
     She sat beside him and spoke,
     revealing her whole heart:
     "Lanval, I have shown you much honor,
     I have cherished you, and loved you.
265   You may have all my love;
     just tell me your desire.
     I promise you my affection.
     You should be very happy with me."
     "My lady," he said, "let me be!
270   I have no desire to love you.
     I've served the king a long time;
     I don't want to betray my faith to him.
     Never, for you or for your love,
     will I do anything to harm my lord."
275   The queen got angry;
     in her wrath, she insulted him:
     "Lanval," she said, "I am sure
     you don't care for such pleasure;
     people have often told me
280   that you have no interest in women.

You have fine-looking boys
with whom you enjoy yourself.
Base coward, lousy cripple,
my lord made a bad mistake
285   when he let you stay with him.
For all I know, he'll lose God because of it."
When Lanval heard her, he was quite disturbed;
he was not slow to answer.
He said something out of spite
290   that he would later regret.
"Lady," he said, "of that activity
I know nothing,
but I love and I am loved
by one who should have the prize
295   over all the women I know.
And I shall tell you one thing;
you might as well know all:
any one of those who serve her,
the poorest girl of all,
300   is better than you, my lady queen,
in body, face, and beauty,
in breeding and in goodness."
The queen left him
and went, weeping, to her chamber.
305   She was upset and angry
because he had insulted her.
She went to bed sick;
never, she said, would she get up
unless the king gave her satisfaction
310   for the offense against her.
The king returned from the woods,
he'd had a very good day.
He entered the queen's chambers.
When she saw him, she began to complain.
315   She fell at his feet, asked his mercy,
saying that Lanval had dishonored her;
he had asked for her love,
and because she refused him
he insulted and offended her:
320   he boasted of a love
who was so refined and noble and proud
that her chambermaid,
the poorest one who served her,
was better than the queen.
325   The king got very angry;
he swore an oath:
if Lanval could not defend himself in court
he would have him burned or hanged.
The king left her chamber
330   and called for three of his barons;
he sent them for Lanval

who was feeling great sorrow and distress.
He had come back to his dwelling,
knowing very well
335 that he'd lost his love,
he had betrayed their affair.
He was all alone in a room,
disturbed and troubled;
he called on his love, again and again,
340 but it did him no good.
He complained and sighed,
from time to time he fainted;
then he cried a hundred times for her to have mercy
and speak to her love.
345 He cursed his heart and his mouth;
it's a wonder he didn't kill himself.
No matter how much he cried and shouted,
ranted and raged,
she would not have mercy on him,
350 not even let him see her.
How will he ever contain himself?
The men the king sent
arrived and told him
to appear in court without delay:
355 the king had summoned him
because the queen had accused him.
Lanval went with his great sorrow;
they could have killed him, for all he cared.
He came before the king;
360 he was very sad, thoughtful, silent;
his face revealed great suffering.
In anger the king told him:
"Vassal, you have done me a great wrong!
This was a base undertaking,
365 to shame and disgrace me
and to insult the queen.
You have made a foolish boast:
your love is much too noble
if her maid is more beautiful,
370 more worthy, than the queen."
Lanval denied that he'd dishonored
or shamed his lord,
word for word, as the king spoke:
he had not made advances to the queen;
375 but of what he had said,
he acknowledged the truth,
about the love he had boasted of,
that now made him sad because he'd lost her.
About that he said he would do
380 whatever the court decided.
The king was very angry with him;
he sent for all his men

to determine exactly what he ought to do
so that no one could find fault with his decision.
385   They did as he commanded,
whether they liked it or not.
They assembled,
judged, and decided,
that Lanval should have his day;
390   but he must find pledges for his lord
to guarantee that he would await the judgment,
return, and be present at it.[8]
Then the court would be increased,
for now there were none but the king's household.
395   The barons came back to the king
and announced their decision.
The king demanded pledges.
Lanval was alone and forlorn,
he had no relative, no friend.
400   Gawain went and pledged himself for him,
and all his companions followed.
The king addressed them: "I release him to you
on forfeit of whatever you hold from me,
lands and fiefs, each one for himself."
405   When Lanval was pledged, there was nothing else to do.
He returned to his lodging.
The knights accompanied him,
they reproached and admonished him
that he give up his great sorrow;
410   they cursed his foolish love.
Each day they went to see him,
because they wanted to know
whether he was drinking and eating;
they were afraid that he'd kill himself.
415   On the day that they had named,
the barons assembled.
The king and the queen were there
and the pledges brought Lanval back.
They were all very sad for him:
420   I think there were a hundred
who would have done all they could
to set him free without a trial
where he would be wrongly accused.
The king demanded a verdict
425   according to the charge and rebuttal.
Now it all fell to the barons.
They went to the judgment,
worried and distressed
for the noble man from another land
430   who'd gotten into such trouble in their midst.

---

8. Marie introduces judicial procedures that may have recalled those in Henry's reign: summons and accusation, setting a day for judgment, the rise of royal jurisdiction, the possibility of a champion, and trial by battle.

Many wanted to condemn him
in order to satisfy their lord.
The Duke of Cornwall said:
"No one can blame us;
435   whether it makes you weep or sing
justice must be carried out.
The king spoke against his vassal
whom I have heard named Lanval;
he accused him of felony,
440   charged him with a misdeed—
a love that he had boasted of,
which made the queen angry.
No one but the king accused him:
by the faith I owe you,
445   if one were to speak the truth,
there should have been no need for defense,
except that a man owes his lord honor
in every circumstance.
He will be bound by his oath,
450   and the king will forgive us our pledges
if he can produce proof;
if his love would come forward,
if what he said,
what upset the queen, is true,
455   then he will be acquitted,
because he did not say it out of malice.
But if he cannot get his proof,
we must make it clear to him
that he will forfeit his service to the king;
460   he must take his leave."
They sent to the knight,
told and announced to him
that he should have his love come
to defend and stand surety for him.
465   He told them that he could not do it:
he would never receive help from her.
They went back to the judges,
not expecting any help from Lanval.
The king pressed them hard
470   because of the queen who was waiting.
When they were ready to give their verdict
they saw two girls approaching,
riding handsome palfreys.
They were very attractive,
475   dressed in purple taffeta,
over their bare skin.
The men looked at them with pleasure.
Gawain, taking three knights with him,
went to Lanval and told him;
480   he pointed out the two girls.
Gawain was extremely happy, and begged him

to tell if his love were one of them.
Lanval said he didn't know who they were,
where they came from or where they were going.

485   The girls proceeded
still on horseback;
they dismounted before the high table
at which Arthur, the king, sat.
They were of great beauty,
490   and spoke in a courtly manner:
"King, clear your chambers,
have them hung with silk
where my lady may dismount;
she wishes to take shelter with you."
495   He promised it willingly
and called two knights
to guide them up to the chambers.
On that subject no more was said.
The king asked his barons
500   for their judgment and decision;
he said they had angered him very much
with their long delay.
"Sire," they said, "we have decided.
Because of the ladies we have just seen
505   we have made no judgment.
Let us reconvene the trial."
Then they assembled, everyone was worried;
there was much noise and strife.
While they were in that confusion,
510   two girls in noble array,
dressed in Phrygian silks
and riding Spanish mules,
were seen coming down the street.
This gave the vassals great joy;
515   to each other they said that now
Lanval, the brave and bold, was saved.
Gawain went up to him,
bringing his companions along.
"Sire," he said, "take heart.
520   For the love of God, speak to us.
Here come two maidens,
well adorned and very beautiful;
one must certainly be your love."
Lanval answered quickly
525   that he did not recognize them,
he didn't know them or love them.
Meanwhile they'd arrived,
and dismounted before the king.
Most of those who saw them praised them
530   for their bodies, their faces, their coloring;
each was more impressive
than the queen had ever been.

The older one was courtly and wise,
she spoke her message fittingly:
535 "King, have chambers prepared for us
to lodge my lady according to her need;
she is coming here to speak with you."
He ordered them to be taken
to the others who had preceded them.
540 There was no problem with the mules.
When he had seen to the girls,
he summoned all his barons
to render their judgment;
it had already dragged out too much.
545 The queen was getting angry
because she had fasted so long.
They were about to give their judgment
when through the city came riding
a girl on horseback:
550 there was none more beautiful in the world.
She rode a white palfrey,
who carried her handsomely and smoothly:
he was well apportioned in the neck and head,
no finer beast in the world.
555 The palfrey's trappings were rich;
under heaven there was no count or king
who could have afforded them all
without selling or mortgaging lands.
She was dressed in this fashion:
560 in a white linen shift
that revealed both her sides
since the lacing was along the side.
Her body was elegant, her hips slim,
her neck whiter than snow on a branch,
565 her eyes bright, her face white,
a beautiful mouth, a well-set nose,
dark eyebrows and an elegant forehead,
her hair curly and rather blond;
golden wire does not shine
570 like her hair in the light.
Her cloak, which she had wrapped around her,
was dark purple.
On her wrist she held a sparrow hawk,
a greyhound followed her.
575 In the town, no one, small or big,
old man or child,
failed to come look.
As they watched her pass,
there was no joking about her beauty.
580 She proceeded at a slow pace.
The judges who saw her
marveled at the sight;
no one who looked at her

was not warmed with joy.
585   Those who loved the knight
came to him and told him
of the girl who was approaching,
if God pleased, to rescue him.
"Sir companion, here comes one
590   neither tawny nor dark;
this is, of all who exist,
the most beautiful woman in the world."
Lanval heard them and lifted his head;
he recognized her and sighed.
595   The blood rose to his face;
he was quick to speak.
"By my faith," he said, "that is my love.
Now I don't care if I am killed,
if only she forgives me.
600   For I am restored, now that I see her."
The lady entered the palace;
no one so beautiful had ever been there.
She dismounted before the king
so that she was well seen by all.
605   And she let her cloak fall
so they could see her better.
The king, who was well bred,
rose and went to meet her;
all the others honored her
610   and offered to serve her.
When they had looked at her well,
when they had greatly praised her beauty,
she spoke in this way,
she didn't want to wait:
615   "I have loved one of your vassals:
you see him before you—Lanval.
He has been accused in your court—
I don't want him to suffer
for what he said; you should know
620   that the queen was in the wrong.
He never made advances to her.
And for the boast that he made,
if he can be acquitted through me,
let him be set free by your barons."
625   Whatever the barons judged by law
the king promised would prevail.
To the last man they agreed
that Lanval had successfully answered the charge.
He was set free by their decision
630   and the girl departed.
The king could not detain her,
though there were enough people to serve her.
Outside the hall stood
a great stone of dark marble

635   where heavy men mounted
        when they left the king's court;
        Lanval climbed on it.
        When the girl came through the gate
        Lanval leapt, in one bound,
640   onto the palfrey, behind her.
        With her he went to Avalun,[9]
        so the Bretons tell us,
        to a very beautiful island;
        there the youth was carried off.
645   No man heard of him again,
        and I have no more to tell.

Sir Gawain and the Green Knight

As a subject of literary romance, Arthurian tradition never had the centrality in later medieval England it had gained in France. It was only one of a wide range of popular topics like Havelok the Dane, King Horn, and the Troy story. Nevertheless Arthur and his court played an ongoing role in English society, written into histories and emulated by aristocrats and kings. And in the later fourteenth or early fifteenth century, several very distinguished Arthurian poems appeared, such as the alliterative *Morte Arthure* and the *Awntyrs* (Adventures) *off Arthure*.

Sir Gawain and the Green Knight is the greatest of the Arthurian romances produced in England. The poem embraces the highest aspirations of the late medieval aristocratic world, both courtly and religious, even while it eloquently admits the human failings that threaten those values. A knight's troth and word, a Christian's election and covenant, the breaking point of a person's or a society's virtues, all come in for celebration and painful scrutiny during Gawain's adventure.

Like *Beowulf*, *Sir Gawain and the Green Knight* comes down to us by the thread of a single copy. Its manuscript contains a group of poems (*Sir Gawain*, *Pearl*, *Purity*, and *Patience*) that mark their anonymous author as a poet whose range approaches that of his contemporary Chaucer, and whose formal craft is in some ways more ambitious than Chaucer's.

Gawain is the work of a highly sophisticated provincial court poet (likely in the northwest Midlands), working in a form and narrative tradition that is conservative in comparison with Chaucer's. The poet uses the alliterative long line, a meter with its roots in Anglo-Saxon poetry; the unrhymed alliterative stanzas, of irregular length, each end with five shorter rhymed lines often called a "bob-and-wheel" stanza. Within these traditional constraints, however, the poem achieves an apex of medieval courtly literature, as a superlatively crafted and stylized version of quest romance.

The romance never aims to detach itself from society or history, though. It opens and closes by referring to Troy, the ancient, fallen empire whose survivors were legendary founders of Britain, a connection well known through Geoffrey of Monmouth. Arthur, their ultimate heir, went on later in his myth to pursue imperial ambitions that, like those of Troy, were foiled by adulterous desire and political infidelity. *Sir Gawain* also echoes its contemporary

---

9. Avalon is the mysterious island to which Arthur is also carried, mortally wounded, after his final battle. Marie's contemporary Gerald of Wales expresses far older associations of Avalon with powerful women (see page 123).

world in the technical language of architecture, crafts, and arms. This helps draw in the kind of conservative, aristocratic court for which the poem seems to have been written, probably in Cheshire or Lancashire, a somewhat backward region whose nobles remained loyal to Richard II. Along with the pleasure it takes in fine armor and courtly ritual, the poem seems to enfold anxieties about the economic pressures of maintaining chivalric display in a period of costly new technology, inflation, and declining income from land.

By the time this poem was written, toward the close of the fourteenth century, Gawain was a famous Arthurian hero. His reputation was ambiguous, though; he was both Arthur's faithful retainer and nephew, but also a suave seducer. Which side of Gawain would dominate in this particular poem? Would he stand for a civilization of Christian chivalry or one of cynical sophistication?

The test that begins to answer this question occurs during Arthur's ritual celebrations of Christmas and the New Year, and within the civilized practices of Eucharist and secular feast. A gigantic green knight interrupts Arthur's banquet to offer a deadly game of exchanged axblows, to be resolved in one year's time. Although the Green Knight, with his ball of holly leaves, seems at first to come from the tradition of the Wild Man—a giant force of nature itself—he is also a sophisticated knight, gorgeously attired. He knows, too, just how to taunt a young king without quite overstepping the bounds of courtly behavior. Gawain takes up the challenge, but a still greater marvel ensues.

As the term of the agreement approaches, Gawain rides off, elaborately armed, to find the Green Knight and fulfill his obligation, even if that means his death. What Gawain encounters first, though, are temptations of character and sexuality even trickier and more crucial than they at first seem.

Sir Gawain and the Green Knight is remarkable not only for the intricacy of its plot but also for the virtuosity of its descriptions, such as the almost elegiac review of the passing seasons ("And so the year moves on in yesterdays many"). The poem rejoices in the masterful exercise of skill as the mark of civilization. Beautifully crafted knots appear everywhere, and we encounter artisanal craft as well in narrative elements like the Green Knight's dress (a dazzling mixture of leafy green and jeweler's gold), Gawain's decorated shield and arms, and the expertise of the master of the hunt who carves up the prey of Gawain's host with ritual precision. Even Gawain's exquisite courtly manners appear as a civilizing artifice.

The ambition of the poem's own craft is equally evident in its extraordinary range of formal devices. Preeminent among these is the symbolic register of number. The poem can be seen as a single unit, circling back to the Trojan scene with which it begins. It has a double structure, too, as it shifts between the courts of Arthur and Gawain's mysterious host. In the manuscript it is divided into four parts ("fits") that respond to the seasonal description at the opening of Part 2. The narrative proper ends by echoing the very start of the poem, at line 2525, itself a multiple of fives that recalls the pentangle on Gawain's shield symbolizing his virtues. The final rhyming stanza, with its formula of grace and salvation, brings the line total to 2530, whose individual digits add up to ten, a number associated with the divine in medieval numerology.

This symbolic structure can seem sometimes overdetermined. A range of elements, however, invites the reader to come at the poem from other perspectives. The poem's very circularity, narrative and formal, allows it to be viewed from beginning or ending. From the front it is a poem of male accomplishment, largely celebrating *men's* courts and *men's* virtues (even men's horses). At the other end, however, it focuses on a court presided over by an old woman (later called a goddess), a court whose irruption into the Arthurian world is explained as the playing out of an old and mysterious rivalry between two queens. Male, even patriarchal from one direction, the poem seems matriarchal, almost pagan, from the other. For all its formal cohesion and celebration of craft, the poem also pulls the reader back and keeps its mysteries intact by leaving many narrative loose ends and unanswered questions.

Unresolvable ambiguities reside most clearly in the pentangle on Gawain's shield and in the "green girdle" whose true owner remains uncertain. For all their differences, both are figures that insist on repetition, end where they begin, and possess a geometry that can be traced forward or backward. Yet the static perfection of the pentangle is subtly set against the protean green girdle, which passes through so many hands, alters its shape (being untied and retied repeatedly), and connects with so many issues in the poem: mortality, women's power, Gawain's fault and the acceptance of that fault by the whole Arthurian court. The girdle becomes an image both of flaw and triumph and of all the loose ends in this early episode of the Arthurian myth.

The girdle also serves to link *Sir Gawain* to political and social issues of the poet's own time, particularly efforts to revalidate a declining system of chivalry. After the last line in the manuscript, a later medieval hand has added "Hony Soyt Qui Mal Pence" ("shamed be he who thinks ill thereof"), the motto of the royal Order of the Garter, founded by Edward III in 1349 to promote a revival of knighthood. The Arthurian myth had already been redeployed to buttress royal power when Edward III refounded a Round Table in 1344. King Arthur's wisdom at the close of Gawain's adventure lies in transforming Gawain's shame, rage, and humiliated sense of sin into an emblem at once of mortal humanity and aristocratic cohesion. This is the place—back with the king and ritually connected with the Order of the Garter—where the closed circle of the poem opens to the social, historical world of empire, court, and kingship.

Sir Gawain and the Green Knight[1]
Part 1

Since the siege and the assault was ceased at Troy,
The walls breached and burnt down to brands and ashes,
The knight that had knotted the nets of deceit
Was impeached for his perfidy, proven most true.
5   It was high-born Aeneas[2] and his haughty race
That since prevailed over provinces, and proudly reigned
Over well-nigh all the wealth of the West Isles.[3]
Great Romulus to Rome repairs in haste;
With boast and with bravery builds he that city
10   And names it with his own name, that it now bears.
Ticius to Tuscany,[4] and towers raises,
Langobard[5] in Lombardy lays out homes,
And far over the French Sea, Felix Brutus[6]
On many broad hills and high Britain he sets,
15   most fair.
                Where war and wrack and wonder
                By shifts have sojourned there,
                And bliss by turns with blunder
                In that land's lot had share.

20   And since this Britain was built by this baron great,
Bold boys bred there, in broils delighting,
That did in their day many a deed most dire.

---

1. This translation, remarkably faithful to the original alliterative meter and stanza form, is by Marie Borroff (1967).
2. Aeneas led the survivors of Troy to Italy, after a series of ambiguous omens and misadventures. In medieval tradition, he was also said to have plotted to betray his own city. "The knight" in line 3, though, may refer to the Trojan Antenor, also said to have betrayed Troy.

3. Perhaps Europe, or just the British Isles. Many royal houses traced their ancestry to Rome and Troy.
4. Possibly Titus Tatius, ancient king of the Sabines.
5. Ancestor of the Lombards, and a nephew of Brutus.
6. According to Geoffrey of Monmouth and others, a great-grandson of Aeneas, exiled after accidentally killing his father and later the founder of Britain.

More marvels have happened in this merry land
Than in any other I know, since that olden time,
25   But of those that here built, of British kings,
King Arthur was counted most courteous of all,
Wherefore an adventure I aim to unfold,
That a marvel of might some men think it,
And one unmatched among Arthur's wonders.
30   If you will listen to my lay but a little while,
As I heard it in hall, I shall hasten to tell
anew.
As it was fashioned featly
In tale of derring-do,
35   And linked in measures meetly
By letters tried and true.

This king lay at Camelot[7] at Christmastide;
Many good knights and gay his guests were there,
Arrayed of the Round Table[8] rightful brothers,
40   With feasting and fellowship and carefree mirth.
There true men contended in tournaments many,
Joined there in jousting these gentle knights,
Then came to the court for carol-dancing,
For the feast was in force full fifteen days,
45   With all the meat and the mirth that men could devise,
Such gaiety and glee, glorious to hear,
Brave din by day, dancing by night.
High were their hearts in halls and chambers,
These lords and these ladies, for life was sweet.
50   In peerless pleasures passed they their days,
The most noble knights known under Christ,
And the loveliest ladies that lived on earth ever,
And he the comeliest king, that that court holds,
For all this fair folk in their first age[9]
55   were still.
Happiest of mortal kind,
King noblest famed of will;
You would now go far to find
So hardy a host on hill.

60   While the New Year was new, but yesternight come,
This fair folk at feast two-fold was served,
When the king and his company were come in together,
The chanting in chapel achieved and ended.
Clerics and all the court acclaimed the glad season,
65   Cried Noel anew, good news to men;
Then gallants gather gaily, hand-gifts to make,

---

7. Arthur's capital; its location is uncertain, probably in Wales, and perhaps it is to be connected with Caerleon-on-Usk where Arthur had been crowned. Knights were expected to gather at his court, in celebration and homage, on the five liturgical holidays on which Arthur wore his crown: Easter, Ascension, Pentecost, All Saints'

Day, and Christmas.
8. Its shape symbolized the unity of Arthur's knights but also avoided disputes over precedence.
9. Arthur is emphatically a young king here, even "boyish." The phrase may also recall the Golden Age, an era of uncorrupted happiness.

Called them out clearly, claimed them by hand,
Bickered long and busily about those gifts.
Ladies laughed aloud, though losers they were,
70　And he that won was not angered, as well you will know.[1]
All this mirth they made until meat was served;
When they had washed them worthily, they went to their seats,
The best seated above, as best it beseemed,
Guenevere the goodly queen gay in the midst
75　On a dais[2] well-decked and duly arrayed
With costly silk curtains, a canopy over,
Of Toulouse and Turkestan tapestries rich,
All broidered and bordered with the best gems
Ever brought into Britain, with bright pennies
80　　　　　　　　　　　to pay.
　　　　　　Fair queen, without a flaw,
　　　　　　She glanced with eyes of gray.
　　　　　　A seemlier that once he saw,
　　　　　　In truth, no man could say.

85　But Arthur would not eat till all were served;
So light was his lordly heart, and a little boyish;
His life he liked lively—the less he cared
To be lying for long, or long to sit,
So busy his young blood, his brain so wild.
90　And also a point of pride pricked him in heart,
For he nobly had willed, he would never eat
On so high a holiday, till he had heard first
Of some fair feat or fray some far-borne tale,
Of some marvel of might, that he might trust,
95　By champions of chivalry achieved in arms,
Or some suppliant came seeking some single knight
To join with him in jousting, in jeopardy each
To lay life for life, and leave it to fortune
To afford him on field fair hap or other.
100　Such is the king's custom, when his court he holds
At each far-famed feast amid his fair host
　　　　　　　　　so dear.
　　　　　　The stout king stands in state
　　　　　　Till a wonder shall appear;
105　　　　　He leads, with heart elate,
　　　　　　High mirth in the New Year.

So he stands there in state, the stout young king,
Talking before the high table of trifles fair.
There Gawain the good knight by Guenevere sits,
110　With Agravain à la dure main on her other side,
Both knights of renown, and nephews of the king.
Bishop Baldwin above begins the table,

---

1. The distribution of gifts at New Year, displayed the king's wealth and power; it was also the occasion here of some courtly game of exchange, in which the loser per-

haps gave up a kiss.
2. A medieval nobleman's hall typically had a raised platform at one end, on which the "high table" stood.

That is goodliest in green when groves are bare,
And an ax in his other, a huge and immense,
A wicked piece of work in words to expound:
210   The head on its haft was an ell long;
The spike of green steel, resplendent with gold;
The blade burnished bright, with a broad edge,
As well shaped to shear as a sharp razor;
Stout was the stave in the strong man's gripe,
215   That was wound all with iron to the weapon's end,
With engravings in green of goodliest work.
A lace lightly about, that led to a knot,
Was looped in by lengths along the fair haft,
And tassels thereto attached in a row,
220   With buttons of bright green, brave to behold.
This horseman hurtles in, and the hall enters;
Riding to the high dais, recked he no danger;
Not a greeting he gave as the guests he o'erlooked,
Nor wasted his words, but "Where is," he said,
225   "The captain of this crowd? Keenly I wish
To see that sire with sight, and to himself say
                    my say."
              He swaggered all about
              To scan the host so gay;
230   He halted, as if in doubt
              Who in that hall held sway.

There were stares on all sides as the stranger spoke,
For much did they marvel what it might mean
That a horseman and a horse should have such a hue,
235   Grow green as the grass, and greener, it seemed,
Than green fused on gold more glorious by far.
All the onlookers eyed him, and edged nearer,
And awaited in wonder what he would do,
For many sights had they seen, but such a one never,
240   So that phantom and faerie the folk there deemed it,
Therefore chary of answer was many a champion bold,
And stunned at his strong words stone-still they sat
In a swooning silence in the stately hall.
As all were slipped into sleep, so slackened their speech
245   apace.
              Not all, I think, for dread,
              But some of courteous grace
              Let him who was their head
              Be spokesman in that place.

250   Then Arthur before the high dais that entrance beholds,
And hailed him, as behooved, for he had no fear,
And said "Fellow, in faith you have found fair welcome;
The head of this hostelry Arthur am I;
Leap lightly down, and linger, I pray,
255   And the tale of your intent you shall tell us after."
"Nay, so help me," said the other, "He that on high sits,

To tarry here any time, 'twas not mine errand;
But as the praise of you, prince, is puffed up so high,
And your court and your company are counted the best,
260   Stoutest under steel-gear on steeds to ride,
Worthiest of their works the wide world over,
And peerless to prove in passages of arms,
And courtesy here is carried to its height,
And so at this season I have sought you out.
265   You may be certain by the branch that I bear in hand
That I pass here in peace,[7] and would part friends,
For had I come to this court on combat bent,
I have a hauberk at home, and a helm beside,
A shield and a sharp spear, shining bright,
270   And other weapons to wield, I ween well, to boot,
But as I willed no war, I wore no metal.
But if you be so bold as all men believe,
You will graciously grant the game that I ask
            by right."
275   Arthur answer gave
          And said, "Sir courteous knight,
          If contest here you crave,
          You shall not fail to fight."

"Nay, to fight, in good faith, is far from my thought;
280   There are about on these benches but beardless children,
Were I here in full arms on a haughty steed,
For measured against mine, their might is puny.
And so I call in this court for a Christmas game,
For 'tis Yule and New Year, and many young bloods about;
285   If any in this house such hardihood claims,
Be so bold in his blood, his brain so wild,
As stoutly to strike one stroke for another,
I shall give him as my gift this gisarme[8] noble,
This ax, that is heavy enough, to handle as he likes,
290   And I shall bide the first blow, as bare as I sit.
If there be one so willful my words to assay,
Let him leap hither lightly, lay hold of this weapon;
I quitclaim it forever, keep it as his own,
And I shall stand him a stroke, steady on this floor,
295   So you grant me the guerdon to give him another,
            sans blame.
          In a twelvemonth and a day
          He shall have of me the same;
          Now be it seen straightway
300   Who dares take up the game."

If he astonished them at first, stiller were then
All that household in hall, the high and the low;

---

7. A holly branch could symbolize peace and was used in   8. A long-handled ax with a spike at the end.
games of the Christmas season.

The stranger on his green steed stirred in the saddle,
And roisterously his red eyes he rolled all about,
305   Bent his bristling brows, that were bright green,
Wagged his beard as he watched who would arise.
When the court kept its counsel he coughed aloud,
And cleared his throat coolly, the clearer to speak:
"What, is this Arthur's house," said that horseman then,
310   "Whose fame is so fair in far realms and wide?
Where is now your arrogance and your awesome deeds,
Your valor and your victories and your vaunting words?
Now are the revel and renown of the Round Table
Overwhelmed with a word of one man's speech,
315   For all cower and quake, and no cut felt!"
With this he laughs so loud that the lord grieved;
The blood for sheer shame shot to his face,
                    and pride.
        With rage his face flushed red,
320   And so did all beside.
        Then the king as bold man bred
        Toward the stranger took a stride.

And said "Sir, now we see you will say but folly,
Which whoso has sought, it suits that he find.
325   No guest here is aghast of your great words.
Give to me your gisarme, in God's own name,
And the boon you have begged shall straight be granted."
He leaps to him lightly, lays hold of his weapon;
The green fellow on foot fiercely alights.
330   Now has Arthur his ax, and the haft grips,
And sternly stirs it about, on striking bent.
The stranger before him stood there erect,
Higher than any in the house by a head and more;
With stern look as he stood, he stroked his beard,
335   And with undaunted countenance drew down his coat,
No more moved nor dismayed for his mighty dints
Than any bold man on bench had brought him a drink
                    of wine.
        Gawain by Guenevere
340   Toward the king doth now incline:
        "I beseech, before all here,
        That this melee may be mine."

"Would you grant me the grace," said Gawain to the king,
"To be gone from this bench and stand by you there,
345   If I without discourtesy might quit this board,
And if my liege lady misliked it not,
I would come to your counsel before your court noble.
For I find it not fit, as in faith it is known,
When such a boon is begged before all these knights,
350   Though you be tempted thereto, to take it on yourself
While so bold men about upon benches sit,
That no host under heaven is hardier of will,

Nor better brothers-in-arms where battle is joined;
I am the weakest, well I know, and of wit feeblest;
355 And the loss of my life would be least of any;
That I have you for uncle is my only praise;
My body, but for your blood, is barren of worth;
And for that this folly befits not a king,
And 'tis I that have asked it, it ought to be mine,
360 And if my claim be not comely let all this court judge,
in sight."
The court assays the claim,
And in counsel all unite
To give Gawain the game
365 And release the king outright.

Then the king called the knight to come to his side,
And he rose up readily, and reached him with speed,
Bows low to his lord, lays hold of the weapon,
And he releases it lightly, and lifts up his hand,
370 And gives him God's blessing, and graciously prays
That his heart and his hand may be hardy both.
"Keep, cousin," said the king, "what you cut with this day,
And if you rule it aright, then readily, I know,
You shall stand the stroke it will strike after."
375 Gawain goes to the guest with gisarme in hand,
And boldly he bides there, abashed not a whit.
Then hails he Sir Gawain, the horseman in green:
"Recount we our contract, ere you come further.
First I ask and adjure you, how you are called
380 That you tell me true, so that trust it I may."
"In good faith," said the good knight, "Gawain am I
Whose buffet befalls you, whate'er betide after,
And at this time twelvemonth take from you another
With what weapon you will, and with no man else
385 alive."
The other nods assent:
"Sir Gawain, as I may thrive,
I am wondrous well content
That you this dint shall drive."

390 "Sir Gawain," said the Green Knight, "By God, I rejoice
That your fist shall fetch this favor I seek,
And you have readily rehearsed, and in right terms,
Each clause of my covenant with the king your lord,
Save that you shall assure me, sir, upon oath,
395 That you shall seek me yourself, wheresoever you deem
My lodgings may lie, and look for such wages
As you have offered me here before all this host."
"What is the way there?" said Gawain, "Where do you dwell?
I heard never of your house, by Him that made me,
400 Nor I know you not, knight, your name nor your court.
But tell me truly thereof, and teach me your name,
And I shall fare forth to find you, so far as I may,

And this I say in good certain, and swear upon oath."
"That is enough in New Year, you need say no more,"
405 Said the knight in the green to Gawain the noble,
"If I tell you true, when I have taken your knock,
And if you handily have hit, you shall hear straightway
Of my house and my home and my own name;
Then follow in my footsteps by faithful accord.
410 And if I spend no speech, you shall speed the better:
You can feast with your friends, nor further trace
                    my tracks.
            Now hold your grim tool steady
            And show us how it hacks."
415   "Gladly, sir; all ready,"
            Says Gawain; he strokes the ax.

The Green Knight upon ground girds him with care:
Bows a bit with his head, and bares his flesh:
His long lovely locks he laid over his crown,
420 Let the naked nape for the need be shown.
Gawain grips to his ax and gathers it aloft—
The left foot on the floor before him he set—
Brought it down deftly upon the bare neck,
That the shock of the sharp blow shivered the bones
425 And cut the flesh cleanly and clove it in twain,
That the blade of bright steel bit into the ground.
The head was hewn off and fell to the floor;
Many found it at their feet, as forth it rolled;
The blood gushed from the body, bright on the green,
430 Yet fell not the fellow, nor faltered a whit,
But stoutly he starts forth upon stiff shanks,
And as all stood staring he stretched forth his hand,
Laid hold of his head and heaved it aloft,
Then goes to the green steed, grasps the bridle,
435 Steps into the stirrup, bestrides his mount,
And his head by the hair in his hand holds,
And as steady he sits in the stately saddle
As he had met with no mishap, nor missing were
                    his head.
440   His bulk about he haled,
            That fearsome body that bled;
            There were many in the court that quailed
            Before all his say was said.

For the head in his hand he holds right up;
445 Toward the first on the dais directs he the face,
And it lifted up its lids, and looked with wide eyes,
And said as much with its mouth as now you may hear:
"Sir Gawain, forget not to go as agreed,
And cease not to seek till me, sir, you find,
450 As you promised in the presence of these proud knights.
To the Green Chapel come, I charge you, to take
Such a dint as you have dealt—you have well deserved

That your neck should have a knock on New Year's morn.
The Knight of the Green Chapel I am well-known to many,
455 Wherefore you cannot fail to find me at last;
Therefore come, or be counted a recreant knight."
With a roisterous rush he flings round the reins,
Hurtles out at the hall-door, his head in his hand,
That the flint-fire flew from the flashing hooves.
460 Which way he went, not one of them knew
Nor whence he was come in the wide world
                                            so fair.
              The king and Gawain gay
              Make game of the Green Knight there,
465   Yet all who saw it say
              'Twas a wonder past compare.

Though high-born Arthur at heart had wonder,
He let no sign be seen, but said aloud
To the comely queen, with courteous speech,
470 "Dear dame, on this day dismay you no whit;
Such crafts are becoming at Christmastide,
Laughing at interludes,[9] light songs and mirth,
Amid dancing of damsels with doughty knights.
Nevertheless of my meat now let me partake,
475 For I have met with a marvel, I may not deny."
He glanced at Sir Gawain, and gaily he said,
"Now, sir, hang up your ax,[1] that has hewn enough,"
And over the high dais it was hung on the wall
That men in amazement might on it look,
480 And tell in true terms the tale of the wonder.
Then they turned toward the table, these two together,
The good king and Gawain, and made great feast,
With all dainties double, dishes rare,
With all manner of meat and minstrelsy both,
485 Such happiness wholly had they that day
                                            in hold.
              Now take care, Sir Gawain,
              That your courage wax not cold
              When you must turn again
490   To your enterprise foretold.

Part 2

This adventure had Arthur of handsels[2] first
When young was the year, for he yearned to hear tales;
Though they wanted for words when they went to sup,
Now are fierce deeds to follow, their fists stuffed full.
495 Gawain was glad to begin those games in hall,
But if the end be harsher, hold it no wonder,
For though men are merry in mind after much drink,

9. Brief performances between the courses of the banquet.
1. A literal suggestion, but also an invitation to put the
matter aside.
2. New Year's gifts.

590 When he had on his arms, his harness was rich,
     The least latchet or loop laden with gold;
     So armored as he was, he heard a mass,
     Honored God humbly at the high altar.
     Then he comes to the king and his comrades-in-arms,
595 Takes his leave at last of lords and ladies,
     And they clasped and kissed him, commending him to Christ.
     By then Gringolet was girt with a great saddle
     That was gaily agleam with fine gilt fringe,
     New-furbished for the need with nail-heads bright;
600 The bridle and the bars bedecked all with gold;
     The breast-plate, the saddlebow, the side-panels both,
     The caparison and the crupper accorded in hue,
     And all ranged on the red the resplendent studs
     That glittered and glowed like the glorious sun.
605 His helm now he holds up and hastily kisses,
     Well-closed with iron clinches, and cushioned within;
     It was high on his head, with a hasp behind,
     And a covering of cloth to encase the visor,
     All bound and embroidered[8] with the best gems
610 On broad bands of silk, and bordered with birds,
     Parrots and popinjays preening their wings,
     Lovebirds and love-knots as lavishly wrought
     As many women had worked seven winters thereon,
                          entire.
615   The diadem costlier yet
               That crowned that comely sire,
                 With diamonds richly set,
               That flashed as if on fire.

     Then they showed forth the shield, that shone all red,
620 With the pentangle portrayed in purest gold.
     About his broad neck by the baldric he casts it,
     That was meet for the man, and matched him well.
     And why the pentangle[9] is proper to that peerless prince
     I intend now to tell, though detain me it must.
625 It is a sign by Solomon sagely devised
     To be a token of truth, by its title of old,
     For it is a figure formed of five points,
     And each line is linked and locked with the next
     For ever and ever, and hence it is called
630 In all England, as I hear, the endless knot.
     And well may he wear it on his worthy arms,
     For ever faithful five-fold in five-fold fashion
     Was Gawain in good works, as gold unalloyed,
     Devoid of all villainy, with virtues adorned
635   in sight.

8. The preceding technical language of armor is now
joined by an equally technical description of needlework,
for which English women were famous.
9. A five-pointed star and symbol of perfection and eter-

nity, since it can be drawn with an uninterrupted line
ending at the point of the star where it begins. Inscribed
within a circle, it was called Solomon's seal.

On shield and coat in view
He bore that emblem bright,
As to his word most true
And in speech most courteous knight.

640   And first, he was faultless in his five senses,
Nor found ever to fail in his five fingers,
And all his fealty was fixed upon the five wounds
That Christ got on the cross, as the creed tells;
And wherever this man in melee took part,
645   His one thought was of this, past all things else,
That all his force was founded on the five joys
That the high Queen of heaven had in her child.[1]
And therefore, as I find, he fittingly had
On the inner part of his shield her image portrayed,
650   That when his look on it lighted, he never lost heart.
The fifth of the five fives followed by this knight
Were beneficence boundless and brotherly love
And pure mind and manners, that none might impeach,
And compassion most precious—these peerless five
655   Were forged and made fast in him, foremost of men.
Now all these five fives were confirmed in this knight,
And each linked in other, that end there was none,
And fixed to five points, whose force never failed,
Nor assembled all on a side, nor asunder either,
660   Nor anywhere at an end, but whole and entire
However the pattern proceeded or played out its course.
And so on his shining shield shaped was the knot
Royally in red gold against red gules,
That is the peerless pentangle, prized of old
665   in lore.
Now armed is Gawain gay,
And bears his lance before,
And soberly said good day,
He thought forevermore.

670   He struck his steed with the spurs and sped on his way
So fast that the flint-fire flashed from the stones.
When they saw him set forth they were sore aggrieved,
And all sighed softly, and said to each other,
Fearing for their fellow, "Ill fortune it is
675   That you, man, must be marred, that most are worthy!
His equal on this earth can hardly be found;
To have dealt more discreetly had done less harm,
And have dubbed him a duke, with all due honor.
A great leader of lords he was like to become,
680   And better so to have been than battered to bits,
Beheaded by an elf-man, for empty pride!
Who would credit that a king could be counseled so,

---

1. Poems and meditations on the Virgin's joys and sorrows were widespread. Her five joys were the Annunciation, Nativity, Resurrection, Ascension, and Assumption.

And caught in a cavil in a Christmas game?"
Many were the warm tears they wept from their eyes
685   When goodly Sir Gawain was gone from the court
                    that day.
            No longer he abode,
            But speedily went his way
            Over many a wandering road,
690   As I heard my author say.

Now he rides in his array through the realm of Logres,[2]
Sir Gawain, God knows, though it gave him small joy!
All alone must he lodge through many a long night
Where the food that he fancied was far from his plate;
695   He had no mate but his mount, over mountain and plain,
Nor man to say his mind to but almighty God,
Till he had wandered well-nigh into North Wales.
All the islands of Anglesey he holds on his left,
And follows, as he fares, the fords by the coast,
700   Comes over at Holy Head, and enters next
The Wilderness of Wirral—few were within
That had great good will toward God or man.
And earnestly he asked of each mortal he met
If he had ever heard aught of a knight all green,
705   Or of a Green Chapel, on ground thereabouts,
And all said the same, and solemnly swore
They saw no such knight all solely green
                    in hue.
            Over country wild and strange
710   The knight sets off anew;
            Often his course must change
            Ere the Chapel comes in view.

Many a cliff must he climb in country wild;
Far off from all his friends, forlorn must he ride;
715   At each strand or stream where the stalwart passed
'Twere a marvel if he met not some monstrous foe,
And that so fierce and forbidding that fight he must.
So many were the wonders he wandered among
That to tell but the tenth part would tax my wits.
720   Now with serpents he wars, now with savage wolves,
Now with wild men of the woods, that watched from the rocks,
Both with bulls and with bears, and with boars besides,
And giants that came gibbering from the jagged steeps.
Had he not borne himself bravely, and been on God's side,
725   He had met with many mishaps and mortal harms.
And if the wars were unwelcome, the winter was worse,
When the cold clear rains rushed from the clouds
And froze before they could fall to the frosty earth.

2. Identified with England in Geoffrey of Monmouth, elsewhere a vaguer term for Arthur's kingdom. Here, Gawain is heading northward through Wales, then along the coast of the Irish Sea and into the forest of Wirral in Cheshire—a wild area and resort of outlaws in the 14th century. Gawain thus moves into the area around Chester, where the poem may well have been written.

Near slain by the sleet he sleeps in his irons
730   More nights than enough, among naked rocks,
Where clattering from the crest the cold stream ran
And hung in hard icicles high overhead.
Thus in peril and pain and predicaments dire
He rides across country till Christmas Eve,
735   our knight.
         And at that holy tide
         He prays with all his might
         That Mary may be his guide
         Till a dwelling comes in sight.

740   By a mountain next morning he makes his way
Into a forest fastness, fearsome and wild;
High hills on either hand, with hoar woods below,
Oaks old and huge by the hundred together.
The hazel and the hawthorn were all intertwined
745   With rough raveled moss, that raggedly hung,
With many birds unblithe upon bare twigs
That peeped most piteously for pain of the cold.
The good knight on Gringolet glides thereunder
Through many a marsh and mire, a man all alone;
750   He feared for his default, should he fail to see
The service of that Sire that on that same night
Was born of a bright maid, to bring us His peace.
And therefore sighing he said, "I beseech of Thee, Lord,
And Mary, thou mildest mother so dear,
755   Some harborage where haply I might hear mass
And Thy matins[3] tomorrow—meekly I ask it,
And thereto proffer and pray my pater and ave
                              and creed."[4]
         He said his prayer with sighs,
760   Lamenting his misdeed;
         He crosses himself, and cries
         On Christ in his great need.

No sooner had Sir Gawain signed himself thrice
Than he was ware, in the wood, of a wondrous dwelling,
765   Within a moat, on a mound, bright amid boughs
Of many a tree great of girth that grew by the water—
A castle as comely as a knight could own,
On grounds fair and green, in a goodly park
With a palisade of palings planted about
770   For two miles and more, round many a fair tree.
The stout knight stared at that stronghold great
As it shimmered and shone amid shining leaves,
Then with helmet in hand he offers his thanks
To Jesus and Saint Julian,[5] that are gentle both,

---

3. First of the canonical hours of prayer and praise in monastic tradition, observed between midnight and dawn.
4. The Paternoster ("Our Father . . ."), Ave Maria ("Hail Mary . . ."), and Creed (the articles of the Christian faith).
5. Patron saint of hospitality.

775   That in courteous accord had inclined to his prayer;
        "Now fair harbor," said he, "I humbly beseech!"
        Then he pricks his proud steed with the plated spurs,
        And by chance he has chosen the chief path
        That brought the bold knight to the bridge's end
780   in haste.
            The bridge hung high in air;
            The gates were bolted fast;
            The walls well-framed to bear
            The fury of the blast.

785   The man on his mount remained on the bank
        Of the deep double moat that defended the place.
        The wall went in the water wondrous deep,
        And a long way aloft it loomed overhead.
        It was built of stone blocks to the battlements' height,
790   With corbels under cornices in comeliest style;
        Watch-towers trusty protected the gate,
        With many a lean loophole, to look from within:
        A better-made barbican the knight beheld never.[6]
        And behind it there hoved a great hall and fair:
795   Turrets rising in tiers, with tines[7] at their tops,
        Spires set beside them, splendidly long,
        With finials well-fashioned, as filigree fine.
        Chalk-white chimneys over chambers high
        Gleamed in gay array upon gables and roofs;
800   The pinnacles in panoply, pointing in air,
        So vied there for his view that verily it seemed
        A castle cut of paper for a king's feast.[8]
        The good knight on Gringolet thought it great luck
        If he could but contrive to come there within
805   To keep the Christmas feast in that castle fair
                 and bright.
            There answered to his call
            A porter most polite;
            From his station on the wall
810   He greets the errant knight.

        "Good sir," said Gawain, "Wouldst go to inquire
        If your lord would allow me to lodge here a space?"
        "Peter!"[9] said the porter, "For my part, I think
        So noble a knight will not want for a welcome!"
815   Then he bustles off briskly, and comes back straight,
        And many servants beside, to receive him the better.
        They let down the drawbridge and duly went forth
        And kneeled down on their knees on the naked earth
        To welcome this warrior as best they were able.

---

6. The poet again revels in technical vocabulary, here architectural; this is a fashionable (if exaggerated) building of the 14th century.
7. Pinnacles.

8. Models in cut paper sometimes decorated elaborate feasts such as that at the beginning of the poem.
9. Swearing by Saint Peter, keeper of the keys to heaven.

820   They proffered him passage—the portals stood wide—
    And he beckoned them to rise, and rode over the bridge.
    Men steadied his saddle as he stepped to the ground,
    And there stabled his steed many stalwart folk.
    Now come the knights and the noble squires
825   To bring him with bliss into the bright hall.
    When his high helm was off, there hied forth a throng
    Of attendants to take it, and see to its care;
    They bore away his brand and his blazoned shield;
    Then graciously he greeted those gallants each one,
830   And many a noble drew near, to do the knight honor.
    All in his armor into hall he was led,
    Where fire on a fair hearth fiercely blazed.
    And soon the lord himself descends from his chamber
    To meet with good manners the man on his floor.
835   He said, "To this house you are heartily welcome:
    What is here is wholly yours, to have in your power
            and sway."
        "Many thanks," said Sir Gawain;
        "May Christ your pains repay!"
840   The two embrace amain
          As men well met that day.

    Gawain gazed on the host that greeted him there,
    And a lusty fellow he looked, the lord of that place:
    A man of massive mold, and of middle age;
845   Broad, bright was his beard, of a beaver's hue,
    Strong, steady his stance, upon stalwart shanks,
    His face fierce as fire, fair-spoken withal,
    And well-suited he seemed in Sir Gawain's sight
    To be a master of men in a mighty keep.
850   They pass into a parlor, where promptly the host
    Has a servant assigned him to see to his needs,
    And there came upon his call many courteous folk
    That brought him to a bower where bedding was noble,
    With heavy silk hangings hemmed all in gold,
855   Coverlets and counterpanes curiously wrought,
    A canopy over the couch, clad all with fur,
    Curtains running on cords, caught to gold rings,
    Woven rugs on the walls of eastern work,
    And the floor, under foot, well-furnished with the same.
860   With light talk and laughter they loosed from him then
    His war-dress of weight and his worthy clothes.
    Robes richly wrought they brought him right soon,
    To change there in chamber and choose what he would.
    When he had found one he fancied, and flung it about,
865   Well-fashioned for his frame, with flowing skirts,
    His face fair and fresh as the flowers of spring,
    All the good folk agreed, that gazed on him then,
    His limbs arrayed royally in radiant hues,
    That so comely a mortal never Christ made
870   as he.

Whatever his place of birth,
It seemed he well might be
Without a peer on earth
In martial rivalry.

875 A couch before the fire, where fresh coals burned,
They spread for Sir Gawain splendidly now
With quilts quaintly stitched, and cushions beside,
And then a costly cloak they cast on his shoulders
Of bright silk, embroidered on borders and hems,
880 With furs of the finest well-furnished within,
And bound about with ermine, both mantle and hood;
And he sat at that fireside in sumptuous estate
And warmed himself well, and soon he waxed merry.
Then attendants set a table upon trestles¹ broad,
885 And lustrous white linen they laid thereupon,
A saltcellar of silver, spoons of the same.
He washed himself well and went to his place,
Men set his fare before him in fashion most fit.
There were soups of all sorts, seasoned with skill,
890 Double-sized servings, and sundry fish,
Some baked, some breaded, some broiled on the coals,
Some simmered, some in stews, steaming with spice,
And with sauces to sup that suited his taste.
He confesses it a feast with free words and fair;
895 They requite him as kindly with courteous jests,
                                          well-sped.
          "Tonight you fast and pray;
          Tomorrow we'll see you fed."²
          The knight grows wondrous gay
900   As the wine goes to his head.

Then at times and by turns, as at table he sat,
They questioned him quietly, with queries discreet,
And he courteously confessed that he comes from the court,
And owns him of the brotherhood of high-famed Arthur,
905 The right royal ruler of the Round Table,
And the guest by their fireside is Gawain himself,
Who has happened on their house at that holy feast.
When the name of the knight was made known to the lord,
Then loudly he laughed, so elated he was,
910 And the men in that household made haste with joy
To appear in his presence promptly that day,
That of courage ever-constant, and customs pure,
Is pattern and paragon, and praised without end:
Of all knights on earth most honored is he.
915 Each said solemnly aside to his brother,
          "Now displays of deportment shall dazzle our eyes
          And the polished pearls of impeccable speech;

---

1. A castle's great hall had many uses; tables were set up for dining and then put aside or hung.
2. An exchange of graceful courtesies. Gawain has polite-ly praised the many fish dishes; his hosts demur, remind him that Christmas Eve is a fast day, and promise him better meals later.

The high art of eloquence is ours to pursue
Since the father of fine manners is found in our midst.
920 Great is God's grace, and goodly indeed,
That a guest such as Gawain he guides to us here
When men sit and sing of their Savior's birth
                    in view.
                With command of manners pure
925   He shall each heart imbue;
                Who shares his converse, sure,
                Shall learn love's language true."[3]

When the knight had done dining and duly arose,
The dark was drawing on; the day nigh ended.
930 Chaplains in chapels and churches about
Rang the bells aright, reminding all men
Of the holy evensong of the high feast.
The lord attends alone; his fair lady sits
In a comely closet, secluded from sight.
935 Gawain in gay attire goes thither soon;
The lord catches his coat, and calls him by name,
And has him sit beside him, and says in good faith
No guest on God's earth would be gladlier greet.
For that Gawain thanked him; the two then embraced
940 And sat together soberly the service through.
Then the lady, that longed to look on the knight,
Came forth from her closet with her comely maids.
The fair hues of her flesh, her face and her hair
And her body and her bearing were beyond praise,
945 And excelled the queen herself, as Sir Gawain thought.
He goes forth to greet her with gracious intent;
Another lady led her by the left hand
That was older than she—an ancient, it seemed,
And held in high honor by all men about.
950 But unlike to look upon, those ladies were,
For if the one was fresh, the other was faded:
Bedecked in bright red was the body of one;
Flesh hung in folds on the face of the other;
On one a high headdress, hung all with pearls;
955 Her bright throat and bosom fair to behold,
Fresh as the first snow fallen upon hills;
A wimple the other one wore round her throat;
Her swart chin well swaddled, swathed all in white,
Her forehead enfolded in flounces of silk
960 That framed a fair fillet, of fashion ornate,
And nothing bare beneath save the black brows,
The two eyes and the nose, the naked lips,
And they unsightly to see, and sorrily bleared.
A beldame, by God, she may well be deemed,
965   of pride!

3. Though Gawain is engaged on a serious quest, his reputation as a graceful courtier and master in the arts of love has preceded him.

She was short and thick of waist,
Her buttocks round and wide;
More toothsome, to his taste,
Was the beauty by her side.

970 When Gawain had gazed on that gay lady,
With leave of her lord, he politely approached;
To the elder in homage he humbly bows;
The lovelier he salutes with a light embrace.
He claims a comely kiss, and courteously he speaks;
975 They welcome him warmly, and straightway he asks
To be received as their servant, if they so desire.
They take him between them; with talking they bring him
Beside a bright fire; bade then that spices
Be freely fetched forth, to refresh them the better,
980 And the good wine therewith, to warm their hearts.
The lord leaps about in light-hearted mood;
Contrives entertainments and timely sports;
Takes his hood from his head and hangs it on a spear,
And offers him openly the honor thereof
985 Who should promote the most mirth at that Christmas feast;
"And I shall try for it, trust me—contend with the best,
Ere I go without my headgear by grace of my friends!"
Thus with light talk and laughter the lord makes merry
To gladden the guest he had greeted in hall
990   that day.
At the last he called for light
The company to convey;
Gawain says goodnight
And retires to bed straightway.

995 On the morn when each man is mindful in heart
That God's son was sent down to suffer our death,
No household but is blithe for His blessed sake;
So was it there on that day, with many delights.
Both at larger meals and less they were lavishly served
1000 By doughty lads on dais, with delicate fare;
The old ancient lady, highest she sits;
The lord at her left hand leaned, as I hear;
Sir Gawain in the center, beside the gay lady,
Where the food was brought first to that festive board,
1005 And thence throughout the hall, as they held most fit,
To each man was offered in order of rank.
There was meat, there was mirth, there was much joy,
That to tell all the tale would tax my wits,
Though I pained me, perchance, to paint it with care;
1010 But yet I know that our knight and the noble lady
Were accorded so closely in company there,
With the seemly solace of their secret words,
With speeches well-sped, spotless and pure,
That each prince's pastime their pleasures far
1015   outshone.

> Sweet pipes beguile their cares,
> And the trumpet of martial tone;
> Each tends his affairs
> And those two tend their own.

1020   That day and all the next, their disport was noble,
And the third day, I think, pleased them no less;
The joys of Saint John's Day[4] were justly praised,
And were the last of their like for those lords and ladies;
Then guests were to go in the gray morning,
1025   Wherefore they whiled the night away with wine and with mirth,
Moved to the measures of many a blithe carol;[5]
At last, when it was late, took leave of each other,
Each one of those worthies, to wend his way.
Gawain bids goodbye to his goodly host
1030   Who brings him to his chamber, the chimney beside,
And detains him in talk, and tenders his thanks
And holds it an honor to him and his people
That he has harbored in his house at that holy time
And embellished his abode with his inborn grace.
1035   "As long as I may live, my luck is the better
That Gawain was my guest at God's own feast!"
"Noble sir," said the knight, "I cannot but think
All the honor is your own—may heaven requite it!
And your man to command I account myself here
1040   As I am bound and beholden, and shall be, come
> > what may."
> > The lord with all his might
> > Entreats his guest to stay;
> > Brief answer makes the knight:
1045   > > Next morning he must away.

Then the lord of that land politely inquired
What dire affair had forced him, at that festive time,
So far from the king's court to fare forth alone
Ere the holidays wholly had ended in hall.
1050   "In good faith," said Gawain, "you have guessed the truth:
On a high errand and urgent I hastened away,
For I am summoned by myself to seek for a place—
I would I knew whither, or where it might be!
Far rather would I find it before the New Year
1055   Than own the land of Logres, so help me our Lord!
Wherefore, sir, in friendship this favor I ask,
That you say in sober earnest, if something you know
Of the Green Chapel, on ground far or near,
Or the lone knight that lives there, of like hue of green.
1060   A certain day was set by assent of us both
To meet at that landmark, if I might last,
And from now to the New Year is nothing too long,

---

4. December 27, traditionally given over to drinking and
celebration.
5. A ring dance.

And I would greet the Green Knight there, would God but allow,
More gladly, by God's son, than gain the world's wealth!
1065   And I must set forth to search, as soon as I may;
To be about the business I have but three days
And would as soon sink down dead as desist from my errand."
Then smiling said the lord, "Your search, sir, is done,
For we shall see you to that site by the set time.
1070   Let Gawain grieve no more over the Green Chapel;
You shall be in your own bed, in blissful ease,
All the forenoon, and fare forth the first of the year,
And make the goal by midmorn, to mind your affairs,
no fear!
1075   Tarry till the fourth day
             And ride on the first of the year.
             We shall set you on your way;
             It is not two miles from here."

Then Gawain was glad, and gleefully he laughed:
1080   "Now I thank you for this, past all things else!
Now my goal is here at hand! With a glad heart I shall
Both tarry, and undertake any task you devise."
Then the host seized his arm and seated him there;
Let the ladies be brought, to delight him the better,
1085   And in fellowship fair by the fireside they sit;
So gay waxed the good host, so giddy his words,
All waited in wonder what next he would say.
Then he stares on the stout knight, and sternly he speaks:
"You have bound yourself boldly my bidding to do—
1090   Will you stand by that boast, and obey me this once?"
"I shall do so indeed," said the doughty knight;
While I lie in your lodging, your laws will I follow."
"As you have had," said the host, "many hardships abroad
And little sleep of late, you are lacking, I judge,
1095   Both in nourishment needful and nightly rest;
You shall lie abed late in your lofty chamber
Tomorrow until mass, and meet then to dine
When you will, with my wife, who will sit by your side
And talk with you at table, the better to cheer
1100   our guest.
             A-hunting I will go
             While you lie late and rest."
             The knight, inclining low,
             Assents to each behest.

1105   "And Gawain," said the good host, "agree now to this:
Whatever I win in the woods I will give you at eve,
And all you have earned you must offer to me;
Swear now, sweet friend, to swap as I say,
Whether hands, in the end, be empty or better."
1110   "By God," said Sir Gawain, "I grant it forthwith!
If you find the game good, I shall gladly take part."

"Let the bright wine be brought, and our bargain is done,"
Said the lord of that land—the two laughed together.
Then they drank and they dallied and doffed all constraint,
1115   These lords and these ladies, as late as they chose,
And then with gaiety and gallantries and graceful adieux
They talked in low tones, and tarried at parting.
With compliments comely they kiss at the last;
There were brisk lads about with blazing torches
1120   To see them safe to bed, for soft repose
                long due.
         Their covenants, yet awhile,
         They repeat, and pledge anew;
         That lord could well beguile
1125   Men's hearts, with mirth in view.

Part 3

Long before daylight they left their beds;
Guests that wished to go gave word to their grooms,
And they set about briskly to bind on saddles,
Tend to their tackle, tie up trunks.
1130   The proud lords appear, appareled to ride,
Leap lightly astride, lay hold of their bridles,
Each one on his way to his worthy house.
The liege lord of the land was not the last
Arrayed there to ride, with retainers many;
1135   He had a bite to eat when he had heard mass;
With horn to the hills he hastens amain.[6]
By the dawn of that day over the dim earth,
Master and men were mounted and ready.
Then they harnessed in couples the keen-scented hounds,
1140   Cast wide the kennel-door and called them forth,
Blew upon their bugles bold blasts three;
The dogs began to bay with a deafening din,
And they quieted them quickly and called them to heel,
A hundred brave huntsmen, as I have heard tell,
1145   together.
         Men at stations meet;
         From the hounds they slip the tether;
         The echoing horns repeat,
         Clear in the merry weather.

1150   At the clamor of the quest, the quarry trembled;
Deer dashed through the dale, dazed with dread;
Hastened to the high ground, only to be
Turned back by the beaters, who boldly shouted.
They harmed not the harts, with their high heads,

---

6. The hunts that follow, for all their violent energy, are as ritualized in their procedure as the earlier feasts and games. The poet delights in describing still another area of knightly lore. A number of contemporary treatises on hunting survive.

Courtly Women Hunting and Dancing, from the *Taymouth Hours*. 14th century. Above, women in courtly dress dismember a stag, usually the work of aristocratic men. On the opposite page, women reenact another famous male moment, tying an inverted Christ to a cross.

1155   Let the bucks go by, with their broad antlers,
        For it was counted a crime, in the close season,
        If a man of that demesne should molest the male deer.
        The hinds were headed up, with "Hey!" and "Ware!"
        The does with great din were driven to the valleys.
1160   Then you were ware, as they went, of the whistling of arrows;
        At each bend under boughs the bright shafts flew
        That tore the tawny hide with their tapered heads.
        Ah! they bray and they bleed, on banks they die,
        And ever the pack pell-mell comes panting behind;
1165   Hunters with shrill horns hot on their heels—
        Like the cracking of cliffs their cries resounded.
        What game got away from the gallant archers
        Was promptly picked off at the posts below
        When they were harried on the heights and herded to the streams:
1170   The watchers were so wary at the waiting-stations,
        And the greyhounds so huge, that eagerly snatched,
        And finished them off as fast as folk could see
                    with sight.
            The lord, now here, now there,
1175   Spurs forth in sheer delight.
            And drives, with pleasures rare,
            The day to the dark night.

So the lord in the linden-wood leads the hunt
And Gawain the good knight in gay bed lies,
1180   Lingered late alone, till daylight gleamed,
Under coverlet costly, curtained about.
And as he slips into slumber, slyly there comes
A little din at his door, and the latch lifted,
And he holds up his heavy head out of the clothes;
1185   A corner of the curtain he caught back a little
And waited there warily, to see what befell.
Lo! it was the lady, loveliest to behold,
That drew the door behind her deftly and still
And was bound for his bed—abashed was the knight,
1190   And laid his head low again in likeness of sleep;
And she stepped stealthily, and stole to his bed,
Cast aside the curtain and came within,
And set herself softly on the bedside there,
And lingered at her leisure, to look on his waking.
1195   The fair knight lay feigning for a long while,
Conning in his conscience what his case might
Mean or amount to—a marvel he thought it.
But yet he said within himself, "More seemly it were
To try her intent by talking a little."
1200   So he started and stretched, as startled from sleep,

Lifts wide his lids in likeness of wonder,
And signs himself swiftly, as safer to be,
                              with art.
                    Sweetly does she speak
1205   And kindling glances dart,
                    Blent white and red on cheek
                    And laughing lips apart.

"Good morning, Sir Gawain," said that gay lady,
"A slack sleeper you are, to let one slip in!
1210 Now you are taken in a trice—a truce we must make,
Or I shall bind you in your bed, of that be assured."
Thus laughing lightly that lady jested.
"Good morning, good lady," said Gawain the blithe,
"Be it with me as you will; I am well content!
1215 For I surrender myself, and sue for your grace,
And that is best, I believe, and behooves me now."
Thus jested in answer that gentle knight.
"But if, lovely lady, you misliked it not,
And were pleased to permit your prisoner to rise,
1220 I should quit this couch and accoutre me better,
And be clad in more comfort for converse here."
"Nay, not so, sweet sir," said the smiling lady;
"You shall not rise from your bed; I direct you better:
I shall hem and hold you on either hand,
1225 And keep company awhile with my captive knight.
For as certain as I sit here, Sir Gawain you are,
Whom all the world worships, whereso you ride;
Your honor, your courtesy are highest acclaimed
By lords and by ladies, by all living men;
1230 And lo! we are alone here, and left to ourselves:
My lord and his liegemen are long departed,
The household asleep, my handmaids too,
The door drawn, and held by a well-driven bolt,
And since I have in this house him whom all love,
1235 I shall while the time away with mirthful speech
                              at will.
                    My body is here at hand,
                    Your each wish to fulfill;
                    Your servant to command
1240   I am, and shall be still."

"In good faith," said Gawain, "my gain is the greater,
Though I am not he of whom you have heard;
To arrive at such reverence as you recount here
I am one all unworthy, and well do I know it.
1245 By heaven, I would hold me the happiest of men
If by word or by work I once might aspire
To the prize of your praise—'twere a pure joy!"
"In good faith, Sir Gawain," said that gay lady,
"The well-proven prowess that pleases all others,
1250 Did I scant or scout it, 'twere scarce becoming.

But there are ladies, believe me, that had liefer far
Have thee here in their hold, as I have today,
To pass an hour in pastime with pleasant words,
Assuage all their sorrows and solace their hearts,
1255   Than much of the goodly gems and gold they possess.
But laud be to the Lord of the lofty skies,
For here in my hands all hearts' desire
                            doth lie."
                    Great welcome got he there
1260   From the lady who sat him by;
                    With fitting speech and fair
                    The good knight makes reply.

"Madame," said the merry man, "Mary reward you!
For in good faith, I find your beneficence noble.
1265   And the fame of fair deeds runs far and wide,
But the praise you report pertains not to me,
But comes of your courtesy and kindness of heart."
"By the high Queen of heaven" (said she) "I count it not so,
For were I worth all the women in this world alive,
1270   And all wealth and all worship were in my hands,
And I should hunt high and low, a husband to take,
For the nurture I have noted in thee, knight, here,
The comeliness and courtesies and courtly mirth—
And so I had ever heard, and now hold it true—
1275   No other on this earth should have me for wife."
"You are bound to a better man," the bold knight said,
"Yet I prize the praise you have proffered me here,
And soberly your servant, my sovereign I hold you,
And acknowledge me your knight, in the name of Christ."
1280   So they talked of this and that until 'twas nigh noon,
And ever the lady languishing in likeness of love.
With feat words and fair he framed his defense,
For were she never so winsome, the warrior had
The less will to woo, for the wound that his bane
1285   must be.
                    He must bear the blinding blow,
                    For such is fate's decree;
                    The lady asks leave to go;
                    He grants it full and free.

1290   Then she gaily said goodbye, and glanced at him, laughing,
And as she stood, she astonished him with a stern speech:
"Now may the Giver of all good words these glad hours repay!
But our guest is not Gawain—forgot is that thought."
"How so?" said the other, and asks in some haste,
1295   For he feared he had been at fault in the forms of his speech.
But she held up her hand, and made answer thus:
"So good a knight as Gawain is given out to be,
And the model of fair demeanor and manners pure,
Had he lain so long at a lady's side,
1300   Would have claimed a kiss, by his courtesy,

Through some touch or trick of phrase at some tale's end."
Said Gawain, "Good lady, I grant it at once!
I shall kiss at your command, as becomes a knight,
And more, lest you mislike, so let be, I pray."
1305 With that she turns toward him, takes him in her arms,
Leans down her lovely head, and lo! he is kissed.
They commend each other to Christ with comely words,
He sees her forth safely, in silence they part,
And then he lies no later in his lofty bed,
1310 But calls to his chamberlain, chooses his clothes,
Goes in those garments gladly to mass,
Then takes his way to table, where attendants wait,
And made merry all day, till the moon rose
                              in view
1315   Was never knight beset
                    'Twixt worthier ladies two:
                    The crone and the coquette;
                    Fair pastimes they pursue.

And the lord of the land rides late and long,
1320 Hunting the barren hind over the broad heath.
He had slain such a sum, when the sun sank low,
Of does and other deer, as would dizzy one's wits.
Then they trooped in together in triumph at last,
And the count of the quarry quickly they take.
1325 The lords lent a hand with their liegemen many,
Picked out the plumpest and put them together
And duly dressed the deer, as the deed requires.
Some were assigned the assay of the fat:
Two fingers'-width fully they found on the leanest.
1330 Then they slit the slot open and searched out the paunch,
Trimmed it with trencher-knives and tied it up tight.
They flayed the fair hide from the legs and trunk,
Then broke open the belly and laid bare the bowels,
Deftly detaching and drawing them forth.
1335 And next at the neck they neatly parted
The weasand[7] from the windpipe, and cast away the guts.
At the shoulders with sharp blades they showed their skill,
Boning them from beneath, lest the sides be marred;
They breached the broad breast and broke it in twain,
1340 And again at the gullet they begin with their knives,
Cleave down the carcass clear to the breach;
Two tender morsels they take from the throat,
Then round the inner ribs they rid off a layer
And carve out the kidney-fat, close to the spine,
1345 Hewing down to the haunch, that all hung together,
And held it up whole, and hacked it free,
And this they named the numbles,[8] that knew such terms
                              of art.

---

7. The esophagus.   8. Internal organs such as heart, liver, lungs.

They divide the crotch in two,
1350   And straightway then they start
To cut the backbone through
And cleave the trunk apart.

With hard strokes they hewed off the head and the neck,
Then swiftly from the sides they severed the chine,
1355   And the corbie's bone[9] they cast on a branch.
Then they pierced the plump sides, impaled either one
With the hock of the hind foot, and hung it aloft,
To each person his portion most proper and fit.
On a hide of a hind the hounds they fed
1360   With the liver and the lights,[1] the leathery paunches,
And bread soaked in blood well blended therewith.
High horns and shrill set hounds a-baying,
Then merrily with their meat they make their way home,
Blowing on their bugles many a brave blast.
1365   Ere dark had descended, that doughty band
Was come within the walls where Gawain waits
         at leisure.
         Bliss and hearth-fire bright
         Await the master's pleasure;
1370   When the two men met that night,
         Joy surpassed all measure.

Then the host in the hall his household assembles,
With the dames of high degree and their damsels fair.
In the presence of the people, a party he sends
1375   To convey him his venison in view of the knight.
And in high good-humor he hails him then,
Counts over the kill, the cuts on the tallies,
Holds high the hewn ribs, heavy with fat.
"What think you, sir, of this? Have I thriven well?
1380   Have I won with my woodcraft a worthy prize?"
"In good earnest," said Gawain, "this game is the finest
I have seen in seven years in the season of winter."
"And I give it to you, Gawain," said the goodly host,
"For according to our covenant, you claim it as your own."
1385   "That is so," said Sir Gawain, "the same say I:
What I worthily have won within these fair walls,
Herewith I as willingly award it to you."
He embraces his broad neck with both his arms,
And confers on him a kiss in the comeliest style.
1390   "Have here my profit, it proved no better;
Ungrudging do I grant it, were it greater far."
"Such a gift," said the good host, "I gladly accept—
Yet it might be all the better, would you but say
Where you won this same award, by your wits alone."

---

9. The gristle at the end of the breastbone was left for the   1. Lungs.
ravens ("corbies"), still another of the prescribed rituals
of the hunt.

1395   "That was no part of the pact; press me no further,
       For you have had what behooves; all other claims
                              forbear."
                   With jest and compliment
                   They conversed, and cast off care;
1400   To the table soon they went;
                   Fresh dainties wait them there.

       And then by the chimney-side they chat at their ease;
       The best wine was brought them, and bounteously served;
       And after in their jesting they jointly accord
1405   To do on the second day the deeds of the first:
       That the two men should trade, betide as it may,
       What each had taken in, at eve when they met.
       They seal the pact solemnly in sight of the court;
       Their cups were filled afresh to confirm the jest;
1410   Then at last they took their leave, for late was the hour,
       Each to his own bed hastening away.
       Before the barnyard cock had crowed but thrice
       The lord had leapt from his rest, his liegemen as well.
       Both of mass and their meal they made short work:
1415   By the dim light of dawn they were deep in the woods
                              away.
                   With huntsmen and with horns
                   Over plains they pass that day;
                   They release, amid the thorns,
1420   Swift hounds that run and bay.

       Soon some were on a scent by the side of a marsh;
       When the hounds opened cry, the head of the hunt
       Rallied them with rough words, raised a great noise.
       The hounds that had heard it came hurrying straight
1425   And followed along with their fellows, forty together.
       Then such a clamor and cry of coursing hounds
       Arose, that the rocks resounded again.
       Hunters exhorted them with horn and with voice;
       Then all in a body bore off together
1430   Between a mere in the marsh and a menacing crag,
       To a rise where the rock stood rugged and steep,
       And boulders lay about, that blocked their approach.
       Then the company in consort closed on their prey:
       They surrounded the rise and the rocks both,
1435   For well they were aware that it waited within,
       The beast that the bloodhounds boldly proclaimed.
       Then they beat on the bushes and bade him appear,
       And he made a murderous rush in the midst of them all;
       The best of all boars broke from his cover,
1440   That had ranged long unrivaled, a renegade old,
       For of tough-brawned boars he was biggest far,
       Most grim when he grunted—then grieved were many,
       For three at the first thrust he threw to the earth,
       And dashed away at once without more damage.

1445   With "Hi!" "Hi!" and "Hey!" "Hey!" the others followed,
        Had horns at their lips, blew high and clear.
        Merry was the music of men and of hounds
        That were bound after this boar, his bloodthirsty heart
                            to quell.
1450   Often he stands at bay,
                Then scatters the pack pell-mell;
                He hurts the hounds, and they
                Most dolefully yowl and yell.

        Men then with mighty bows moved in to shoot,
1455   Aimed at him with their arrows and often hit,
        But the points had no power to pierce through his hide,
        And the barbs were brushed aside by his bristly brow;
        Though the shank of the shaft shivered in pieces,
        The head hopped away, wheresoever it struck.
1460   But when their stubborn strokes had stung him at last,
        Then, foaming in his frenzy, fiercely he charges,
        Hies at them headlong that hindered his flight,
        And many feared for their lives, and fell back a little.
        But the lord on a lively horse leads the chase;
1465   As a high-mettled huntsman his horn he blows;
        He sounds the assembly and sweeps through the brush,
        Pursuing this wild swine till the sunlight slanted.
        All day with this deed they drive forth the time
        While our lone knight so lovesome lies in his bed
1470   Sir Gawain safe at home, in silken bower
                            so gay.
                The lady, with guile in heart,
                Came early where he lay;
                She was at him with all her art
1475   To turn his mind her way.

        She comes to the curtain and coyly peeps in;
        Gawain thought it good to greet her at once,
        And she richly repays him with her ready words,
        Settles softly at his side, and suddenly she laughs,
1480   And with a gracious glance, she begins on him thus:
        "Sir, if you be Gawain, it seems a great wonder—
        A man so well-meaning, and mannerly disposed,
        And cannot act in company as courtesy bids,
        And if one takes the trouble to teach him, 'tis all in vain.
1485   That lesson learned lately is lightly forgot,
        Though I painted it as plain as my poor wit allowed."
        "What lesson, dear lady?" he asked all alarmed;
        "I have been much to blame, if your story be true."
        "Yet my counsel was of kissing," came her answer then,
1490   "Where favor has been found, freely to claim
        As accords with the conduct of courteous knights."
        "My dear," said the doughty man, "dismiss that thought;
        Such freedom, I fear, might offend you much;
        It were rude to request if the right were denied."

1495   "But none can deny you," said the noble dame,
     "You are stout enough to constrain with strength, if you choose,
     Were any so ungracious as to grudge you aught."
     "By heaven," said he, "you have answered well,
     But threats never throve among those of my land,
1500   Nor any gift not freely given, good though it be.
     I am yours to command, to kiss when you please;
     You may lay on as you like, and leave off at will."
                      With this,
          The lady lightly bends
1505   And graciously gives him a kiss;
          The two converse as friends
          Of true love's trials and bliss.

     "I should like, by your leave," said the lovely lady,
     "If it did not annoy you, to know for what cause
1510   So brisk and so bold a young blood as you,
     And acclaimed for all courtesies becoming a knight—
     And name what knight you will, they are noblest esteemed
     For loyal faith in love, in life as in story;[2]
     For to tell the tribulations of these true hearts,
1515   Why, 'tis the very title and text of their deeds,
     How bold knights for beauty have braved many a foe,
     Suffered heavy sorrows out of secret love,
     And then valorously avenged them on villainous churls
     And made happy ever after the hearts of their ladies.
1520   And you are the noblest knight known in your time;
     No household under heaven but has heard of your fame,
     And here by your side I have sat for two days
     Yet never has a fair phrase fallen from your lips
     Of the language of love, not one little word!
1525   And you, that with sweet vows sway women's hearts,
     Should show your winsome ways, and woo a young thing,
     And teach by some tokens the craft of true love.
     How! are you artless, whom all men praise?
     Or do you deem me so dull, or deaf to such words?
1530   Fie! Fie!
          In hope of pastimes new
          I have come where none can spy;
          Instruct me a little, do,
          While my husband is not nearby."

1535   "God love you, gracious lady!" said Gawain then;
     "It is a pleasure surpassing, and a peerless joy,
     That one so worthy as you would willingly come
     And take the time and trouble to talk with your knight
     And content you with his company—it comforts my heart.
1540   But to take to myself the task of telling of love,

2. The lady compares Gawain's behavior to descriptions of courtly love in romances; the poem is mirrored within itself.

And touch upon its texts, and treat of its themes
To one that, I know well, wields more power
In that art, by a half, than a hundred such
As I am where I live, or am like to become,
1545   It were folly, fair dame, in the first degree!
In all that I am able, my aim is to please,
As in honor behooves me, and am evermore
Your servant heart and soul, so save me our Lord!"
Thus she tested his temper and tried many a time,
1550   Whatever her true intent, to entice him to sin,
But so fair was his defense that no fault appeared,
Nor evil on either hand, but only bliss
                they knew.
        They linger and laugh awhile;
1555   She kisses the knight so true,
        Takes leave in comeliest style
        And departs without more ado.

Then he rose from his rest and made ready for mass,
And then a meal was set and served, in sumptuous style;
1560   He dallied at home all day with the dear ladies,
But the lord lingered late at his lusty sport;
Pursued his sorry swine, that swerved as he fled,
And bit asunder the backs of the best of his hounds
When they brought him to bay, till the bowmen appeared
1565   And soon forced him forth, though he fought for dear life,
So sharp were the shafts they shot at him there.
But yet the boldest drew back from his battering head,
Till at last he was so tired he could travel no more,
But in as much haste as he might, he makes his retreat
1570   To a rise on rocky ground, by a rushing stream.
With the bank at his back he scrapes the bare earth,
The froth foams at his jaws, frightful to see.
He whets his white tusks—then weary were all
Those hunters so hardy that hoved round about
1575   Of aiming from afar, but ever they mistrust
                his mood.
        He had hurt so many by then
        That none had hardihood
        To be torn by his tusks again,
1580   That was brainsick, and out for blood.

Till the lord came at last on his lofty steed,
Beheld him there at bay before all his folk;
Lightly he leaps down, leaves his courser,
Bares his bright sword, and boldly advances;
1585   Straight into the stream he strides towards his foe.
The wild thing was wary of weapon and man;
His hackles rose high; so hotly he snorts
That many watched with alarm, lest the worst befall.
The boar makes for the man with a mighty bound
1590   So that he and his hunter came headlong together

Where the water ran wildest—the worse for the beast,
For the man, when they first met, marked him with care,
Sights well the slot, slips in the blade,
Shoves it home to the hilt, and the heart shattered,
1595   And he falls in his fury and floats down the water,
                              ill-sped.
                    Hounds hasten by the score
                    To maul him, hide and head;
                    Men drag him in to shore
1600   And dogs pronounce him dead.

With many a brave blast they boast of their prize,
All hallooed in high glee, that had their wind;
The hounds bayed their best, as the bold men bade
That were charged with chief rank in that chase of renown.
1605   Then one wise in woodcraft, and worthily skilled,
Began to dress the boar in becoming style:
He severs the savage head and sets it aloft,
Then rends the body roughly right down the spine;
Takes the bowels from the belly, broils them on coals,
1610   Blends them well with bread to bestow on the hounds.
Then he breaks out the brawn in fair broad flitches,
And the innards to be eaten in order he takes.
The two sides, attached to each other all whole,
He suspended from a spar that was springy and tough;
1615   And so with this swine they set out for home;
The boar's head was borne before the same man
That had stabbed him in the stream with his strong arm,
                              right through.
                    He thought it long indeed
1620   Till he had the knight in view;
                    At his call, he comes with speed
                    To claim his payment due.

The lord laughed aloud, with many a light word,
When he greeted Sir Gawain—with good cheer he speaks.
1625   They fetch the fair dames and the folk of the house;
He brings forth the brawn, and begins the tale
Of the great length and girth, the grim rage as well,
Of the battle of the boar they beset in the wood.
The other man meetly commended his deeds
1630   And praised well the prize of his princely sport,
For the brawn of that boar, the bold knight said,
And the sides of that swine surpassed all others.
Then they handled the huge head; he owns it a wonder,
And eyes it with abhorrence, to heighten his praise.
1635   "Now, Gawain," said the good man, "this game becomes yours
By those fair terms we fixed, as you know full well."
"That is true," returned the knight, "and trust me, fair friend,
All my gains, as agreed, I shall give you forthwith."
He clasps him and kisses him in courteous style,

1640   Then serves him with the same fare a second time.
        "Now we are even," said he, "at this evening feast,
        And clear is every claim incurred here to date,
                            and debt."
                "By Saint Giles!"[3] the host replies,
1645   "You're the best I ever met!
                If your profits are all this size,
                We'll see you wealthy yet!"

        Then attendants set tables on trestles about,
        And laid them with linen; light shone forth,
1650   Wakened along the walls in waxen torches.
        The service was set and the supper brought;
        Royal were the revels that rose then in hall
        At that feast by the fire, with many fair sports:
        Amid the meal and after, melody sweet,
1655   Carol-dances comely and Christmas songs,
        With all the mannerly mirth my tongue may describe.
        And ever our gallant knight beside the gay lady;
        So uncommonly kind and complaisant was she,
        With sweet stolen glances, that stirred his stout heart,
1660   That he was at his wits' end, and wondrous vexed;
        But he could not in conscience her courtship repay,
        Yet took pains to please her, though the plan might
                            go wrong.
                When they to heart's delight
1665   Had reveled there in throng,
                To his chamber he calls the knight,
                And thither they go along.

        And there they dallied and drank, and deemed it good sport
        To enact their play anew on New Year's Eve,
1670   But Gawain asked again to go on the morrow,
        For the time until his tryst was not two days.
        The host hindered that, and urged him to stay,
        And said, "On my honor, my oath here I take
        That you shall get to the Green Chapel to begin your chores
1675   By dawn on New Year's Day, if you so desire.
        Wherefore lie at your leisure in your lofty bed,
        And I shall hunt hereabouts, and hold to our terms,
        And we shall trade winnings when once more we meet,
        For I have tested you twice, and true have I found you;
1680   Now think this tomorrow: the third pays for all;
        Be we merry while we may, and mindful of joy,
        For heaviness of heart can be had for the asking."
        This is gravely agreed on and Gawain will stay.
        They drink a last draught and with torches depart
1685   to rest.

---

3. A hermit and patron saint of woodlands.

> To bed Sir Gawain went;
> His sleep was of the best;
> The lord, on his craft intent,
> Was early up and dressed.

1690   After mass, with his men, a morsel he takes;
        Clear and crisp the morning; he calls for his mount;
        The folk that were to follow him afield that day
        Were high astride their horses before the hall gates.
        Wondrous fair were the fields, for the frost was light;
1695   The sun rises red amid radiant clouds,
        Sails into the sky, and sends forth his beams.
        They let loose the hounds by a leafy wood;
        The rocks all around re-echo to their horns;
        Soon some have set off in pursuit of the fox,
1700   Cast about with craft for a clearer scent;
        A young dog yaps, and is yelled at in turn;
        His fellows fall to sniffing, and follow his lead,
        Running in a rabble on the right track,
        And he scampers all before; they discover him soon,
1705   And when they see him with sight they pursue him the faster,
        Railing at him rudely with a wrathful din.
        Often he reverses over rough terrain,
        Or loops back to listen in the lee of a hedge;
        At last, by a little ditch, he leaps over the brush,
1710   Comes into a clearing at a cautious pace,
        Then he thought through his wiles to have thrown off the hounds
        Till he was ware, as he went, of a waiting-station
        Where three athwart his path threatened him at once,
                        all gray.
1715   Quick as a flash he wheels
                    And darts off in dismay;
                    With hard luck at his heels
                    He is off to the wood away.

        Then it was heaven on earth to hark to the hounds
1720   When they had come on their quarry, coursing together!
        Such harsh cries and howls they hurled at his head
        As all the cliffs with a crash had come down at once.
        Here he was hailed, when huntsmen met him;
        Yonder they yelled at him, yapping and snarling;
1725   There they cried "Thief!" and threatened his life,
        And ever the harriers at his heels, that he had no rest.
        Often he was menaced when he made for the open,
        And often rushed in again, for Reynard was wily;
        And so he leads them a merry chase, the lord and his men,
1730   In this manner on the mountains, till midday or near,
        While our hero lies at home in wholesome sleep
        Within the comely curtains on the cold morning.
        But the lady, as love would allow her no rest,
        And pursuing ever the purpose that pricked her heart,
1735   Was awake with the dawn, and went to his chamber

In a fair flowing mantle that fell to the earth,
All edged and embellished with ermines fine;
No hood on her head, but heavy with gems
Were her fillet and the fret[4] that confined her tresses;
1740   Her face and her fair throat freely displayed;
Her bosom all but bare, and her back as well.
She comes in at the chamber-door, and closes it with care,
Throws wide a window—then waits no longer,
But hails him thus airily with her artful words,
1745   with cheer:
            "Ah, man, how can you sleep?
            The morning is so clear!"
            Though dreams have drowned him deep,
            He cannot choose but hear.

1750   Deep in his dreams he darkly mutters
As a man may that mourns, with many grim thoughts
Of that day when destiny shall deal him his doom
When he greets his grim host at the Green Chapel
And must bow to his buffet, bating all strife.
1755   But when he sees her at his side he summons his wits,
Breaks from the black dreams, and blithely answers.
That lovely lady comes laughing sweet,
Sinks down at his side, and salutes him with a kiss.
He accords her fair welcome in courtliest style;
1760   He sees her so glorious, so gaily attired,
So faultless her features, so fair and so bright,
His heart swelled swiftly with surging joys.
They melt into mirth with many a fond smile,
And there was bliss beyond telling between those two,
1765   at height.
            Good were their words of greeting;
            Each joyed in other's sight;
            Great peril attends that meeting
            Should Mary forget her knight.

1770   For that high-born beauty so hemmed him about,
Made so plain her meaning, the man must needs
Either take her tendered love or distastefully refuse.
His courtesy concerned him, lest crass he appear,
But more his soul's mischief, should he commit sin
1775   And belie his loyal oath to the lord of that house.
"God forbid!" said the bold knight, "That shall not befall!"
With a little fond laughter he lightly let pass
All the words of special weight that were sped his way;
"I find you much at fault," the fair one said,
1780   "Who can be cold toward a creature so close by your side,
Of all women in this world most wounded in heart,
Unless you have a sweetheart, one you hold dearer,
And allegiance to that lady so loyally knit

---

4. Ornamental hairnet.

That you will never love another, as now I believe.
1785   And, sir, if it be so, then say it, I beg you;
By all your heart holds dear, hide it no longer
                    with guile."
            "Lady, by Saint John,"
            He answers with a smile,
1790   "Lover have I none,
            Nor will have, yet awhile."

"Those words," said the woman, "are the worst of all,
But I have had my answer, and hard do I find it!
Kiss me now kindly; I can but go hence
1795   To lament my life long like a maid lovelorn."
She inclines her head quickly and kisses the knight,
Then straightens with a sigh, and says as she stands,
"Now, dear, ere I depart, do me this pleasure:
Give me some little gift, your glove or the like,
1800   That I may think on you, man, and mourn the less."
"Now by heaven," said he, "I wish I had here
My most precious possession, to put it in your hands,
For your deeds, beyond doubt, have often deserved
A repayment far passing my power to bestow.
1805   But a love-token, lady, were of little avail;
It is not to your honor to have at this time
A glove as a guerdon from Gawain's hand,
And I am here on an errand in unknown realms
And have no bearers with baggage with becoming gifts,
1810   Which distresses me, madame, for your dear sake.
A man must keep within his compass: account it neither grief
                    nor slight."
            "Nay, noblest knight alive,"
            Said that beauty of body white,
1815   "Though you be loath to give,
            Yet you shall take, by right."

She reached out a rich ring, wrought all of gold,
With a splendid stone displayed on the band
That flashed before his eyes like a fiery sun;
1820   It was worth a king's wealth, you may well believe.
But he waved it away with these ready words:
"Before God, good lady, I forgo all gifts;
None have I to offer, nor any will I take."
And she urged it on him eagerly, and ever he refused,
1825   And vowed in very earnest, prevail she would not.
And she sad to find it so, and said to him then,
"If my ring is refused for its rich cost—
You would not be my debtor for so dear a thing—
I shall give you my girdle; you gain less thereby."
1830   She released a knot lightly, and loosened a belt
That was caught about her kirtle, the bright cloak beneath,
Of a gay green silk, with gold overwrought,
And the borders all bound with embroidery fine,

And this she presses upon him, and pleads with a smile,
1835   Unworthy though it were, that it would not be scorned.
But the man still maintains that he means to accept
Neither gold nor any gift, till by God's grace
The fate that lay before him was fully achieved.
"And be not offended, fair lady, I beg,
1840   And give over your offer, for ever I must
                decline.
        I am grateful for favor shown
        Past all deserts of mine,
        And ever shall be your own
1845   True servant, rain or shine."

"Now does my present displease you," she promptly inquired,
"Because it seems in your sight so simple a thing?
And belike, as it is little, it is less to praise,
But if the virtue that invests it were verily known,
1850   It would be held, I hope, in higher esteem.
For the man that possesses this piece of silk,
If he bore it on his body, belted about,
There is no hand under heaven that could hew him down,
For he could not be killed by any craft on earth."
1855   Then the man began to muse, and mainly he thought
It was a pearl for his plight, the peril to come
When he gains the Green Chapel to get his reward:
Could he escape unscathed, the scheme were noble!
Then he bore with her words and withstood them no more,
1860   And she repeated her petition and pleaded anew,
And he granted it, and gladly she gave him the belt,
And besought him for her sake to conceal it well,
Lest the noble lord should know—and the knight agrees
That not a soul save themselves shall see it thenceforth
1865   with sight.
        He thanked her with fervent heart,
        As often as ever he might;
        Three times, before they part,
        She has kissed the stalwart knight.

1870   Then the lady took her leave, and left him there,
For more mirth with that man she might not have.
When she was gone, Sir Gawain got from his bed,
Arose and arrayed him in his rich attire;
Tucked away the token the temptress had left,
1875   Laid it reliably where he looked for it after.
And then with good cheer to the chapel he goes,
Approached a priest in private, and prayed to be taught
To lead a better life and lift up his mind,
Lest he be among the lost when he must leave this world.
1880   And shamefaced at shrift he showed his misdeeds
From the largest to the least, and asked the Lord's mercy,
And called on his confessor to cleanse his soul,
And he absolved him of his sins as safe and as clean

As if the dread Day of Judgment should dawn on the morrow.[5]
1885 And then he made merry amid the fine ladies
With deft-footed dances and dalliance light,
As never until now, while the afternoon wore
                    away.
            He delighted all around him,
1890   And all agreed, that day,
            They never before had found him
            So gracious and so gay.

Now peaceful be his pasture, and love play him fair!
The host is on horseback, hunting afield;
1895 He has finished off this fox that he followed so long:
As he leapt a low hedge to look for the villain
Where he heard all the hounds in hot pursuit,
Reynard comes racing out of a rough thicket,
And all the rabble in a rush, right at his heels.
1900 The man beholds the beast, and bides his time,
And bares his bright sword, and brings it down hard,
And he blenches from the blade, and backward he starts;
A hound hurries up and hinders that move,
And before the horse's feet they fell on him at once
1905 And ripped the rascal's throat with a wrathful din.
The lord soon alighted and lifted him free,
Swiftly snatched him up from the snapping jaws,
Holds him over his head, halloos with a will,
And the dogs bayed the dirge, that had done him to death.
1910 Hunters hastened thither with horns at their lips,
Sounding the assembly till they saw him at last.
When that comely company was come in together,
All that bore bugles blew them at once,
And the others all hallooed, that had no horns.
1915 It was the merriest medley that ever a man heard,
The racket that they raised for Sir Reynard's soul
                    that died.
            Their hounds they praised and fed,
            Fondling their heads with pride,
1920   And they took Reynard the Red
            And stripped away his hide.

And then they headed homeward, for evening had come,
Blowing many a blast on their bugles bright.
The lord at long last alights at his house,
1925 Finds fire on the hearth where the fair knight waits,
Sir Gawain the good, that was glad in heart.
With the ladies, that loved him, he lingered at ease;
He wore a rich robe of blue, that reached to the earth
And a surcoat lined softly with sumptuous furs;
1930 A hood of the same hue hung on his shoulders;

5. Gawain's confession and absolution are problematic, since he has just accepted the green girdle and resolved to break the covenant of exchange with his host.

With bands of bright ermine embellished were both.
He comes to meet the man amid all the folk,
And greets him good-humoredly, and gaily he says,
"I shall follow forthwith the form of our pledge
1935 That we framed to good effect amid fresh-filled cups."
He clasps him accordingly and kisses him thrice,
As amiably and as earnestly as ever he could.
"By heaven," said the host, "you have had some luck
Since you took up this trade, if the terms were good."
1940 "Never trouble about the terms," he returned at once,
"Since all that I owe here is openly paid."
"Marry!" said the other man, "mine is much less,
For I have hunted all day, and nought have I got
But this foul fox pelt, the fiend take the goods!
1945 Which but poorly repays those precious things
That you have cordially conferred, those kisses three
     so good."
    "Enough!" said Sir Gawain;
    "I thank you, by the rood!"
1950   And how the fox was slain
    He told him, as they stood.

With minstrelsy and mirth, with all manner of meats,
They made as much merriment as any men might
(Amid laughing of ladies and light-hearted girls,
1955 So gay grew Sir Gawain and the goodly host)
Unless they had been besotted, or brainless fools.
The knight joined in jesting with that joyous folk,
Until at last it was late; ere long they must part,
And be off to their beds, as behooved them each one.
1960 Then politely his leave of the lord of the house
Our noble knight takes, and renews his thanks:[6]
"The courtesies countless accorded me here,
Your kindness at this Christmas, may heaven's King repay!
Henceforth, if you will have me, I hold you my liege,
1965 And so, as I have said, I must set forth tomorrow,
If I may take some trusty man to teach, as you promised,
The way to the Green Chapel, that as God allows
I shall see my fate fulfilled on the first of the year."
"In good faith," said the good man, "with a good will
1970 Every promise on my part shall be fully performed."
He assigns him a servant to set him on the path,
To see him safe and sound over the snowy hills,
To follow the fastest way through forest green
     and grove.
1975   Gawain thanks him again,
    So kind his favors prove,
    And of the ladies then
    He takes his leave, with love.

---

6. Gawain's highly stylized leave-taking is typical of courtly romance and again emphasizes his command of fine manners.

Courteously he kissed them, with care in his heart,
1980   And often wished them well, with warmest thanks,
Which they for their part were prompt to repay.
They commend him to Christ with disconsolate sighs;
And then in that hall with the household he parts—
Each man that he met, he remembered to thank
1985   For his deeds of devotion and diligent pains,
And the trouble he had taken to tend to his needs;
And each one as woeful, that watched him depart,
As he had lived with him loyally all his life long.
By lads bearing lights he was led to his chamber
1990   And blithely brought to his bed, to be at his rest.
How soundly he slept, I presume not to say,
For there were matters of moment his thoughts might well
                                pursue.
              Let him lie and wait;
1995   He has little more to do,
              Then listen, while I relate
              How they kept their rendezvous.

Part 4

Now the New Year draws near, and the night passes,
The day dispels the dark, by the Lord's decree;
2000   But wild weather awoke in the world without:
The clouds in the cold sky cast down their snow
With great gusts from the north, grievous to bear.
Sleet showered aslant upon shivering beasts;
The wind warbled wild as it whipped from aloft,
2005   And drove the drifts deep in the dales below.
Long and well he listens, that lies in his bed;
Though he lifts not his eyelids, little he sleeps;
Each crow of the cock he counts without fail.
Readily from his rest he rose before dawn,
2010   For a lamp had been left him, that lighted his chamber.
He called to his chamberlain, who quickly appeared,
And bade him get him his gear, and gird his good steed,
And he sets about briskly to bring in his arms,
And makes ready his master in manner most fit.
2015   First he clad him in his clothes, to keep out the cold,
And then his other harness, made handsome anew,
His plate-armor of proof, polished with pains,
The rings of his rich mail rid of their rust,
And all was fresh as at first, and for this he gave thanks
2020   indeed.
              With pride he wears each piece,
              New-furbished for his need:
              No gayer from here to Greece;
              He bids them bring his steed.

2025   In his richest raiment he robed himself then:
His crested coat-armor, close-stitched with craft,

With stones of strange virtue on silk velvet set;
All bound with embroidery on borders and seams
And lined warmly and well with furs of the best.
2030   Yet he left not his love-gift, the lady's girdle;
Gawain, for his own good, forgot not that:
When the bright sword was belted and bound on his haunches,
Then twice with that token he twined him about.
Sweetly did he swathe him in that swatch of silk,
2035   That girdle of green so goodly to see,
That against the gay red showed gorgeous bright.
Yet he wore not for its wealth that wondrous girdle,
Nor pride in its pendants, though polished they were,
Though glittering gold gleamed at the tips,
2040   But to keep himself safe when consent he must
To endure a deadly dint, and all defense
                              denied.
            And now the bold knight came
            Into the courtyard wide;
2045   That folk of worthy fame
            He thanks on every side.

Then was Gringolet girt, that was great and huge,
And had sojourned safe and sound, and savored his fare;
He pawed the earth in his pride, that princely steed.
2050   The good knight draws near him and notes well his look,
And says sagely to himself, and soberly swears,
"Here is a household in hall that upholds the right!
The man that maintains it, may happiness be his!
Likewise the dear lady, may love betide her!
2055   If thus they in charity cherish a guest
That are honored here on earth, may they have His reward
That reigns high in heaven—and also you all;
And were I to live in this land but a little while,
I should willingly reward you, and well, if I might."
2060   Then he steps into the stirrup and bestrides his mount;
His shield is shown forth; on his shoulder he casts it;
Strikes the side of his steed with his steel spurs,
And he starts across the stones, nor stands any longer
                              to prance.
2065   On horseback was the swain
            That bore his spear and lance;
            "May Christ this house maintain
            And guard it from mischance!"

The bridge was brought down, and the broad gates
2070   Unbarred and carried back upon both sides;
He commended him to Christ, and crossed over the planks;
Praised the noble porter, who prayed on his knees
That God save Sir Gawain, and bade him good day,
And went on his way alone with the man
2075   That was to lead him ere long to that luckless place
Where the dolorous dint must be dealt him at last.

Under bare boughs they ride, where steep banks rise,[7]
Over high cliffs they climb, where cold snow clings;
The heavens held aloof, but heavy thereunder
2080   Mist mantled the moors, moved on the slopes.
Each hill had a hat, a huge cape of cloud;
Brooks bubbled and broke over broken rocks,
Flashing in freshets that waterfalls fed.
Roundabout was the road that ran through the wood
2085   Till the sun at that season was soon to rise,
                    that day.
           They were on a hilltop high;
           The white snow round them lay;
           The man that rode nearby
2090   Now bade his master stay.

"For I have seen you here safe at the set time,
And now you are not far from that notable place
That you have sought for so long with such special pains.
But this I say for certain, since I know you, sir knight,
2095   And have your good at heart, and hold you dear—
Would you heed well my words, it were worth your while—
You are rushing into risks that you reck not of:
There is a villain in yon valley, the veriest on earth,
For he is rugged and rude, and ready with his fists,
2100   And most immense in his mold of mortals alive,
And his body bigger than the best four
That are in Arthur's house, Hector[8] or any.
He gets his grim way at the Green Chapel;
None passes by that place so proud in his arms
2105   That he does not dash him down with his deadly blows,
For he is heartless wholly, and heedless of right,
For be it chaplain or churl that by the Chapel rides,
Monk or mass-priest or any man else,
He would as soon strike him dead as stand on two feet.
2110   Wherefore I say, just as certain as you sit there astride,
You cannot but be killed, if his counsel holds,
For he would trounce you in a trice, had you twenty lives
                    for sale.
           He has lived long in this land
2115   And dealt out deadly bale;
           Against his heavy hand
           Your power cannot prevail.

"And so, good Sir Gawain, let the grim man be;
Go off by some other road, in God's own name!
2120   Leave by some other land, for the love of Christ,
And I shall get me home again, and give you my word
That I shall swear by God's self and the saints above,

---

7. The grimness of this landscape, reminiscent of waste-lands in Anglo-Saxon poetry, swiftly returns the poem from the courtly world to the elemental challenge Gawain now faces.

8. Chief hero among the defenders of Troy and, like Arthur, one of the "Nine Worthies" celebrated for their heroic valor; or perhaps Arthur's knight Hector De Maris.

By heaven and by my halidom[9] and other oaths more,
To conceal this day's deed, nor say to a soul
2125 That ever you fled for fear from any that I knew."
"Many thanks!" said the other man—and demurring he speaks—
"Fair fortune befall you for your friendly words!
And conceal this day's deed I doubt not you would,
But though you never told the tale, if I turned back now,
2130 Forsook this place for fear, and fled, as you say,
I were a caitiff coward; I could not be excused.
But I must to the Chapel to chance my luck
And say to that same man such words as I please,
Befall what may befall through Fortune's will
2135   or whim.
                    Though he be a quarrelsome knave
                    With a cudgel great and grim,
                    The Lord is strong to save:
                    His servants trust in Him."

2140 "Marry," said the man, "since you tell me so much,
And I see you are set to seek your own harm,
If you crave a quick death, let me keep you no longer!
Put your helm on your head, your hand on your lance,
And ride the narrow road down yon rocky slope
2145 Till it brings you to the bottom of the broad valley.
Then look a little ahead, on your left hand,
And you will soon see before you that self-same Chapel,
And the man of great might that is master there.
Now goodbye in God's name, Gawain the noble!
2150 For all the world's wealth I would not stay here,
Or go with you in this wood one footstep further!"
He tarried no more to talk, but turned his bridle,
Hit his horse with his heels as hard as he might,
Leaves the knight alone, and off like the wind
2155   goes leaping.
                    "By God," said Gawain then,
                    "I shall not give way to weeping;
                    God's will be done, amen!
                    I commend me to His keeping."

2160 He puts his heels to his horse, and picks up the path;
Goes in beside a grove where the ground is steep,
Rides down the rough slope right to the valley;
And then he looked a little about him—the landscape was wild,
And not a soul to be seen, nor sign of a dwelling,
2165 But high banks on either hand hemmed it about,
With many a ragged rock and rough-hewn crag;
The skies seemed scored by the scowling peaks.
Then he halted his horse, and hoved there a space,
And sought on every side for a sight of the Chapel,
2170 But no such place appeared, which puzzled him sore,

9. "By my holy relics."

Yet he saw some way off what seemed like a mound,[1]
A hillock high and broad, hard by the water,
Where the stream fell in foam down the face of the steep
And bubbled as if it boiled on its bed below.

2175   The knight urges his horse, and heads for the knoll;
Leaps lightly to earth; loops well the rein
Of his steed to a stout branch, and stations him there.
He strides straight to the mound, and strolls all about,
Much wondering what it was, but no whit the wiser;

2180   It had a hole at one end, and on either side,
And was covered with coarse grass in clumps all without,
And hollow all within, like some old cave,
Or a crevice of an old crag—he could not discern
            aright.

2185   "Can this be the Chapel Green?
            Alack!" said the man, "Here might
            The devil himself be seen
            Saying matins at black midnight!"

"Now by heaven," said he, "it is bleak hereabouts;

2190   This prayer-house is hideous, half-covered with grass!
Well may the grim man mantled in green
Hold here his orisons, in hell's own style!
Now I feel it is the Fiend, in my five wits,
That has tempted me to this tryst, to take my life;

2195   This is a Chapel of mischance, may the mischief take it!
As accursed a country church as I came upon ever!"
With his helm on his head, his lance in his hand,
He stalks toward the steep wall of that strange house.
Then he heard, on the hill, behind a hard rock,

2200   Beyond the brook, from the bank, a most barbarous din:
Lord! it clattered in the cliff fit to cleave it in two,
As one upon a grindstone ground a great scythe!
Lord! it whirred like a mill-wheel whirling about!
Lord! it echoed loud and long, lamentable to hear!

2205   Then "By heaven," said the bold knight, "That business up there
Is arranged for my arrival, or else I am much
            misled.
            Let God work! Ah me!
            All hope of help has fled!

2210   Forfeit my life may be
            But noise I do not dread."

Then he listened no longer, but loudly he called,
"Who has power in this place, high parley to hold?
For none greets Sir Gawain, or gives him good day;

2215   If any would a word with him, let him walk forth
And speak now or never, to speed his affairs."
"Abide," said one on the bank above over his head,
"And what I promised you once shall straightway be given."

---

1. The barrow, perhaps a burial mound, seems to link the moment to ancient, probably pagan, inhabitants.

Yet he stayed not his grindstone, nor stinted its noise,
2220 But worked awhile at his whetting before he would rest,
And then he comes around a crag, from a cave in the rocks,
Hurtling out of hiding with a hateful weapon,
A Danish ax[2] devised for that day's deed,
With a broad blade and bright, bent in a curve,
2225 Filed to a fine edge—four feet it measured
By the length of the lace that was looped round the haft.
And in form as at first, the fellow all green,
His lordly face and his legs, his locks and his beard,
Save that firm upon two feet forward he strides,
2230 Sets a hand on the ax-head, the haft to the earth;
When he came to the cold stream, and cared not to wade,
He vaults over on his ax, and advances amain
On a broad bank of snow, overbearing and brisk
            of mood.
2235   Little did the knight incline
            When face to face they stood;
            Said the other man, "Friend mine,
            It seems your word holds good!"

"God love you, Sir Gawain!" said the Green Knight then,
2240 "And well met this morning, man, at my place!
And you have followed me faithfully and found me betimes,
And on the business between us we both are agreed:
Twelve months ago today you took what was yours,
And you at this New Year must yield me the same.
2245 And we have met in these mountains, remote from all eyes:
There is none here to halt us or hinder our sport;
Unhasp your high helm, and have here your wages;
Make no more demur than I did myself
When you hacked off my head with one hard blow."
2250 "No, by God," said Sir Gawain, "that granted me life,
I shall grudge not the guerdon, grim though it prove;
Bestow but one stroke, and I shall stand still,
And you may lay on as you like till the last of my part
            be paid.
2255   He proffered, with good grace,
            His bare neck to the blade,
            And feigned a cheerful face:
            He scorned to seem afraid.

Then the grim man in green gathers his strength,
2260 Heaves high the heavy ax to hit him the blow.
With all the force in his frame he fetches it aloft,
With a grimace as grim as he would grind him to bits;
Had the blow he bestowed been as big as he threatened,
A good knight and gallant had gone to his grave.
2265 But Gawain at the great ax glanced up aside
As down it descended with death-dealing force,

2. A long-bladed ax, associated with Viking raiders.

And his shoulders shrank a little from the sharp iron.
Abruptly the brawny man breaks off the stroke,
And then reproved with proud words that prince among knights.
2270 "You are not Gawain the glorious," the green man said,
"That never fell back on field in the face of the foe,
And now you flee for fear, and have felt no harm:
Such news of that knight I never heard yet!
I moved not a muscle when you made to strike,
2275 Nor caviled at the cut in King Arthur's house;
My head fell to my feet, yet steadfast I stood,
And you, all unharmed, are wholly dismayed—
Wherefore the better man I, by all odds,
                    must be."
2280   Said Gawain, "Strike once more;
               I shall neither flinch nor flee;
               But if my head falls to the floor
               There is no mending me!"

"But go on, man, in God's name, and get to the point!
2285 Deliver me my destiny, and do it out of hand,
For I shall stand to the stroke and stir not an inch
Till your ax has hit home—on my honor I swear it!"
"Have at thee then!" said the other, and heaves it aloft,
And glares down as grimly as he had gone mad.
2290 He made a mighty feint, but marred not his hide;
Withdrew the ax adroitly before it did damage.
Gawain gave no ground, nor glanced up aside,
But stood still as a stone, or else a stout stump
That is held in hard earth by a hundred roots.
2295 Then merrily does he mock him, the man all in green:
"So now you have your nerve again, I needs must strike;
Uphold the high knighthood that Arthur bestowed,
And keep your neck-bone clear, if this cut allows!"
Then was Gawain gripped with rage, and grimly he said,
2300 "Why, thrash away, tyrant, I tire of your threats;
You make such a scene, you must frighten yourself."
Said the green fellow, "In faith, so fiercely you speak
That I shall finish this affair, nor further grace
                    allow."
2305   He stands prepared to strike
               And scowls with both lip and brow;
               No marvel if the man mislike
               Who can hope no rescue now.

He gathered up the grim ax and guided it well:
2310 Let the barb at the blade's end brush the bare throat;
He hammered down hard, yet harmed him no whit
Save a scratch on one side, that severed the skin;
The end of the hooked edge entered the flesh,
And a little blood lightly leapt to the earth.
2315 And when the man beheld his own blood bright on the snow,

He sprang a spear's length with feet spread wide,
Seized his high helm, and set it on his head,
Shoved before his shoulders the shield at his back,[3]
Bares his trusty blade, and boldly he speaks—
2320   Not since he was a babe born of his mother
Was he once in this world one-half so blithe—
"Have done with your hacking—harry me no more!
I have borne, as behooved, one blow in this place;
If you make another move I shall meet it midway
2325   And promptly, I promise you, pay back each blow
                with brand.
      One stroke acquits me here;
      So did our covenant stand
      In Arthur's court last year—
2330   Wherefore, sir, hold your hand!"

He lowers the long ax and leans on it there,
Sets his arms on the head, the haft on the earth,
And beholds the bold knight that bides there afoot,
How he faces him fearless, fierce in full arms,
2335   And plies him with proud words—it pleases him well.
Then once again gaily to Gawain he calls,
And in a loud voice and lusty, delivers these words:
"Bold fellow, on this field your anger forbear!
No man has made demands here in manner uncouth,
2340   Nor done, save as duly determined at court.
I owed you a hit and you have it; be happy therewith!
The rest of my rights here I freely resign.
Had I been a bit busier, a buffet, perhaps,
I could have dealt more directly, and done you some harm.
2345   First I flourished with a feint, in frolicsome mood,
And left your hide unhurt—and here I did well
By the fair terms we fixed on the first night;
And fully and faithfully you followed accord:
Gave over all your gains as a good man should.
2350   A second feint, sir, I assigned for the morning
You kissed my comely wife—each kiss you restored.
For both of these there behooved but two feigned blows
                by right.
      True men pay what they owe;
2355   No danger then in sight.
      You failed at the third throw,
      So take my tap, sir knight.

"For that is my belt about you, that same braided girdle,
My wife it was that wore it; I know well the tale,
2360   And the count of your kisses and your conduct too,
And the wooing of my wife—it was all my scheme!

3. Gawain, who has displayed so much courtly refinement and religious emotion, now shows himself a practiced fighter, swiftly pulling his armor into place.

She made trial of a man most faultless by far
Of all that ever walked over the wide earth;
As pearls to white peas, more precious and prized,
2365   So is Gawain, in good faith, to other gay knights.
Yet you lacked, sir, a little in loyalty there,
But the cause was not cunning, nor courtship either,
But that you loved your own life; the less, then, to blame."
The other stout knight in a study stood a long while,
2370   So gripped with grim rage that his great heart shook.
All the blood of his body burned in his face
As he shrank back in shame from the man's sharp speech.
The first words that fell from the fair knight's lips:
"Accursed be a cowardly and covetous heart!
2375   In you is villainy and vice, and virtue laid low!"
Then he grasps the green girdle and lets go the knot,
Hands it over in haste, and hotly he says:
"Behold there my falsehood, ill hap betide it!
Your cut taught me cowardice, care for my life,
2380   And coveting came after, contrary both
To largesse and loyalty belonging to knights.
Now am I faulty and false, that fearful was ever
Of disloyalty and lies, bad luck to them both!
                    and greed.
2385   I confess, knight, in this place,
                Most dire is my misdeed;
                Let me gain back your good grace,
                And thereafter I shall take heed."

Then the other laughed aloud, and lightly he said,
2390   "Such harm as I have had, I hold it quite healed.
You are so fully confessed, your failings made known,
And bear the plain penance of the point of my blade,
I hold you polished as a pearl, as pure and as bright
As you had lived free of fault since first you were born.
2395   And I give you, sir, this girdle that is gold-hemmed
And green as my garments, that, Gawain, you may
Be mindful of this meeting when you mingle in throng
With nobles of renown—and known by this token
How it chanced at the Green Chapel, to chivalrous knights.
2400   And you shall in this New Year come yet again
And we shall finish out our feast in my fair hall,
                    with cheer."
                He urged the knight to stay,
                And said, "With my wife so dear
2405   We shall see you friends this day,
                Whose enmity touched you near."

"Indeed," said the doughty knight, and doffed his high helm,
And held it in his hands as he offered his thanks,
"I have lingered long enough—may good luck be yours,
2410   And He reward you well that all worship bestows!

And commend me to that comely one, your courteous wife,
Both herself and that other, my honored ladies,
That have trapped their true knight in their trammels so quaint.
But if a dullard should dote, deem it no wonder,

2415   And through the wiles of a woman be wooed into sorrow,
For so was Adam by one, when the world began,
And Solomon by many more, and Samson the mighty—
Delilah was his doom, and David thereafter
Was beguiled by Bathsheba, and bore much distress;[4]

2420   Now these were vexed by their devices—'twere a very joy
Could one but learn to love, and believe them not.
For these were proud princes, most prosperous of old,
Past all lovers lucky, that languished under heaven,
                                    bemused.

2425   And one and all fell prey
                   To women that they had used;
                   If I be led astray,
                   Methinks I may be excused.

"But your girdle, God love you! I gladly shall take

2430   And be pleased to possess, not for the pure gold,
Nor the bright belt itself, nor the beauteous pendants,
Nor for wealth, nor worldly state, nor workmanship fine,
But a sign of excess it shall seem oftentimes
When I ride in renown, and remember with shame

2435   The faults and the frailty of the flesh perverse,
How its tenderness entices the foul taint of sin;
And so when praise and high prowess have pleased my heart,
A look at this love-lace will lower my pride,
But one thing would I learn, if you were not loath,

2440   Since you are lord of yonder land where I have long sojourned
With honor in your house—may you have His reward
That upholds all the heavens, highest on throne!
How runs your right name?—and let the rest go."
"That shall I give you gladly," said the Green Knight then;

2445   "Bercilak de Hautdesert this barony I hold,
Through the might of Morgan le Fay,[5] that lodges at my house,
By subtleties of science and sorcerers' arts,
The mistress of Merlin, she has caught many a man,
For sweet love in secret she shared sometime

2450   With that wizard, that knows well each one of your knights
                                    and you.
                   Morgan the Goddess, she,
                   So styled by title true;
                   None holds so high degree

2455   That her arts cannot subdue.

---

4. Gawain suddenly erupts in a brief but fierce diatribe, including this list of treacherous women recognizable from contemporary misogynist texts.
5. Morgan is Arthur's half-sister and ruler of the mysterious Avalon; she learned magical arts from Merlin. Her presence can bode good or ill. In some stories she holds a deep grudge against Guinevere, yet she carries off the wounded Arthur after his final battle, perhaps to heal him. The earlier Celtic Morrigan, possibly related, is queen of demons, sower of discord, and goddess of war.

"She guided me in this guise to your glorious hall,
To assay, if such it were, the surfeit of pride
That is rumored of the retinue of the Round Table.
She put this shape upon me to puzzle your wits,
2460 To afflict the fair queen, and frighten her to death
With awe of that elvish man that eerily spoke
With his head in his hand before the high table.
She was with my wife at home, that old withered lady,
Your own aunt is she, Arthur's half-sister,
2465 The Duchess' daughter of Tintagel, that dear King Uther
Got Arthur on after, that honored is now.[6]
And therefore, good friend, come feast with your aunt;
Make merry in my house; my men hold you dear,
And I wish you as well, sir, with all my heart,
2470 As any mortal man, for your matchless faith."
But the knight said him nay, that he might by no means.
They clasped then and kissed, and commended each other
To the Prince of Paradise, and parted with one
                                        assent.
2475   Gawain sets out anew;
              Toward the court his course is bent;
              And the knight all green in hue,
              Wheresoever he wished, he went.

Wild ways in the world our worthy knight rides
2480 On Gringolet, that by grace had been granted his life.
He harbored often in houses, and often abroad,
And with many valiant adventures verily he met
That I shall not take time to tell in this story.
The hurt was whole that he had had in his neck,
2485 And the bright green belt on his body he bore,
Oblique, like a baldric, bound at his side,
Below his left shoulder, laced in a knot,
In betokening of the blame he had borne for his fault;
And so to court in due course he comes safe and sound.
2490 Bliss abounded in hall when the high-born heard
That good Gawain was come, glad tidings they thought it.
The king kisses the knight, and the queen as well,
And many a comrade came to clasp him in arms,
And eagerly they asked, and awesomely he told,
2495 Confessed all his cares and discomfitures many,
How it chanced at the Chapel, what cheer made the knight,
The love of the lady, the green lace at last.
The nick on his neck he naked displayed
That he got in his disgrace at the Green Knight's hands,
2500   alone.

6. The poem now recalls an earlier transgression of guest–host obligations, when Uther began to lust for Ygerne while her husband, Gorlois, was at his court; he later killed Gorlois and married Ygerne. See Geoffrey of Monmouth, pages 117–120.

With rage in heart he speaks,
And grieves with many a groan;
The blood burns in his cheeks
For shame at what must be shown.

2505 "Behold, sir," said he, and handles the belt,
"This is the blazon of the blemish that I bear on my neck;
This is the sign of sore loss that I have suffered there
For the cowardice and coveting that I came to there;
This is the badge of false faith that I was found in there,
2510 And I must bear it on my body till I breathe my last.
For one may keep a deed dark, but undo it no whit,
For where a fault is made fast, it is fixed evermore."
The king comforts the knight, and the court all together
Agree with gay laughter and gracious intent
2515 That the lords and the ladies belonging to the Table,
Each brother of that band, a baldric should have,
A belt oblique, of a bright green,
To be worn with one accord for that worthy's sake.
So that was taken as a token by the Table Round,
2520 And he honored that had it, evermore after,
As the best book of knighthood bids it be known.
In the old days of Arthur this happening befell;
The books of Brutus' deeds bear witness thereto
Since Brutus, the bold knight, embarked for this land
2525 After the siege ceased at Troy and the city fared
        amiss.
      Many such, ere we were born,
      Have befallen here, ere this.
      May He that was crowned with thorn
2530   Bring all men to His bliss! Amen.

             Hony Soyt Qui Mal Pence

Sir Thomas Malory
c. 1410–1471

The full identity of Sir Thomas Malory shimmers just beyond our grasp. In several of his colophons—those closing formulas to texts—the author of the *Morte Darthur* says he is "a knyght presoner, sir Thomas Malleorré," and prays that "God sende hym good delyveraunce sone and hastely." Scholars have traced a number of such names in the era, among whom two seem particularly likely: Sir Thomas Malory of Newbold Revell, and Thomas Malory of Papworth. The former Thomas Malory had a scabrous criminal record and was long kept prisoner awaiting trial, while the latter had links to a rich collection of Arthurian books.

    Another colophon provides the more useful information that "the hoole book of kyng Arthur and of his noble knyghtes of the Rounde Table" was completed in the ninth year of

King Edward IV, that is 1469 or 1470. So whichever Malory wrote the *Morte Darthur*, he was certainly working in the unsettled years of the War of the Roses, in which the great ducal families of York and Lancaster battled for control of the English throne. As one family gained dominance, adherents of the other were often jailed on flimsy charges. The spectacle of a nation threatening to crumble into clan warfare provides much of the thematic weight of the *Morte Darthur*, while the declining chivalric order of the later fifteenth century underlies Malory's increasingly elegiac tone.

Whether he gained his remarkable knowledge of French and English Arthurian tradition in or out of jail, Malory infused his version of these stories with a darkening perspective very much his own. Malory sensed the high aspirations, especially the bonds of honor and fellowship in battle, that held together Arthur's realm. Yet he was also bleakly aware of how tenuous those bonds were and how easily undone by tragically competing pressures. These include the centuries-old Arthurian preoccupation with transgressive love, but Malory is more concerned with the conflicting claims of loyalty to clan or king, the urge to avenge the death of a fellow knight, and the resulting alienation even among the best of knights. Still more unnerving, agents of a virtually unmotivated or unexplained malice have ever more impact as the *Morte Darthur* progresses.

For all his initial energy and control, Malory's Arthur is increasingly a king forced to suppress knightly grievances, to deplore religious quest, even to overlook the adultery of his wife and his greatest knight, all in the interest of his fading hopes for chivalric honor and unity. Arthur's commitment to courtesy finally undoes his honor in the eyes of his own knights. As the Round Table is broken (an image Malory uses repeatedly) Arthur is put in the agonizing position of acting as judge in his wife's trial, making war on his early companion Lancelot, and finally engaging in single combat with his own treacherous son Mordred.

Malory would have found many of these themes in his sources. Twelfth-century Arthurian romances in French verse had explored the elevation and danger of courtly eroticism, and the theme was extended in the enormous French prose versions of the thirteenth century that Malory had read in great detail. In these prose romances, too, religious and chivalric themes converged around the story of the Grail. Malory also knew the alliterative *Morte Arthur* poems of fourteenth-century England, with their emphases on conquest, treachery, and the military details of Arthur's final battles.

Malory regularly acknowledges these sources, but his powers of synthesis and the stamp of his style make his *Morte Darthur* unique. While he occasionally writes a complex, reflective sentence, Malory's prose is typically composed of simple, idiomatic narrative statements, and speeches so brief as to be almost gnomic. On hearing of his brother's death, Gawain faints, then rises and says only "Alas!" Yet the grief of his cry resonates across the closing episodes of the work. Malory's imagery is similarly resonant. He tends to strip it of the explanations that had become frequent in the French prose works, and he concentrates its impact by an almost obsessive repetition. The later episodes of the work become almost an incantation of breakage and dispersal, blood and wounds, each image cluster reaching alternately toward religious experience or secular destruction.

These versions of chivalric ambition, sacred or secular, do not divide easily in the *Morte Darthur*. The saintly Galahad and the scheming Mordred may represent extremes of contrary ambition, but Malory is more preoccupied by the sadly mixed motives of Lancelot or Arthur himself. In the late episodes offered below, the reader is drawn into the perspective of lesser knights like Bors and Bedivere, who witness great moments while affecting them only marginally. They bring back to the world of lesser men stories of uncanny experience and oversee their conversion from verbal rumor to written form, whether in books or on tombs. Much of Malory's power and his continuing appeal come from his unresolved doubleness of perspective. Whether by way of his characters or his style, resonant and mysterious elements emerge from a narrative of gritty realism.

from **MORTE DARTHUR**
from **The Poisoned Apple**[1]

So after the quest of the Sankgreall was fulfilled, and all knights that
were left on live were come home again unto the Table Round, as
The Book of the Sankgreall maketh mention, then was there great joy
in the court, and in especial King Arthur and Queen Guinevere
made great joy of the remnant that were come home. And passing
glad was the king and the queen of Sir Lancelot and of Sir Bors, for
they had been passing long away in the quest of the Sankgreall.

    Then, as the book saith, Sir Lancelot began to resort unto
Queen Guinevere again and forgat the promise and the perfection°   *of perfection*
that he made in the quest; for, as the book saith, had not Sir
Lancelot been in his privy° thoughts and in his mind so set inward-   *secret*
ly to the queen as he was in seeming outward to God, there had no
knight passed him in the quest of the Sankgreall. But ever his
thoughts privily were on the queen, and so they loved together
more hotter than they did to forehand, and had many such privy
draughts° together that many in the court spake of it, and in espe-   *meetings*
cial Sir Agravain, Sir Gawain's brother, for he was ever open-
mouthed.

    So it befell that Sir Lancelot had many resorts of° ladies and   *entreaties from*
damsels which daily resorted unto him, that besought him to be
their champion. In all such matters of right Sir Lancelot applied him
daily to do for the pleasure of Our Lord Jesu Christ, and ever as
much as he might he withdrew him from the company of Queen
Guinevere for to eschew the slander and noise.° Wherefore the   *rumor*
queen waxed wroth with Sir Lancelot.

    So on a day she called him unto her chamber and said thus:

    "Sir Lancelot, I see and feel daily that your love beginneth to
slake,° for ye have no joy to be in my presence, but ever ye are out of   *cool*
this court, and quarrels and matters ye have nowadays for ladies,
maidens and gentlewomen, more than ever ye were wont to have
beforehand."

    "Ah, madam," said Sir Lancelot, "in this ye must hold me
excused for divers causes. One is, I was but late in the quest of the
Sankgreall, and I thank God of His great mercy, and never of my
deserving, that I saw in that my quest as much as ever saw any sinful
man living, and so was it told me. And if that I had not had my privy
thoughts to return to your love again as I do, I had° seen as great mys-   *should have*
teries as ever saw my son, Sir Galahad, Perceval, other Sir Bors. And
therefore, madam, I was but late in that quest, and wit you well,
madam, it may not be yet lightly forgotten, the high service in whom
I did my diligent labour.

    "Also, madam, wit you well that there be many men speaketh of
our love in this court, and have you and me greatly in await,° as this   *suspicion*

---

1. From the section titled *The Book of Sir Launcelot and Queen Guinevere*, in *King Arthur and His
Knights*, ed. Eugène Vinaver (1975).

Sir Agravain and Sir Mordred.[2] And, madam, wit you well I dread them more for your sake than for any fear I have of them myself, for I may happen to escape and rid myself in a great need where, madam, ye must abide all that will be said unto you. And then, if that ye fall in any distress throughout° wilful folly, then is there none other help but by me and my blood.°

through
kinsmen

"And wit you well, madam, the boldness of you and me will bring us to shame and slander; and that were me loath to see you dishonoured. And that is the cause I take upon me more for to do for damsels and maidens than ever I did toforn:° that men should understand my joy and my delight is my pleasure to have ado for damsels and maidens."

before

All this while the queen stood still and let Sir Lancelot say what he would; and when he had all said she brast out of weeping, and so she sobbed and wept a great while. And when she might speak she said,

"Sir Lancelot, now I well understand that thou art a false, recreant° knight and a common lecher, and lovest and holdest other ladies, and of me thou hast disdain and scorn. For wit thou well, now I understand thy falsehood I shall never love thee more, and look thou be never so hardy° to come in my sight. And right here I discharge thee this court, that thou never come within it, and I forfend° thee my fellowship, and upon pain° of thy head that thou see me nevermore!"

cowardly

bold

forbid/at the risk

Right so Sir Lancelot departed with great heaviness that unneth° he might sustain himself for great dole-making.

scarcely

Then he called Sir Bors, Ector de Maris and Sir Lionel, and told them how the queen had forfended him the court, and so he was in will to depart into his own country.

"Fair sir," said Bors de Ganis, "ye shall not depart out of this land by mine advice, for ye must remember you what ye are, and renowned the most noblest knight of the world, and many great matters ye have in hand. And women in their hastiness will do oftentimes that after them sore repenteth. And therefore, by mine advice, ye shall take your horse and ride to the good hermit here beside Windsor, that sometime was a good knight; his name is Sir Brastias. And there shall ye abide till that I send you word of better tidings." * * *

[Queen Guinevere holds a feast at which one knight poisons another with a poisoned apple, to avenge an earlier slaying. The queen is accused of the murder. King Arthur believes in her innocence, but cannot defend her himself as he must judge the case. With Lancelot away, no one is willing to serve as her champion. Finally Arthur persuades Sir Bors to defend Guinevere's honor in battle against her accuser, Sir Mador.]

And thus it passed on till the morn, and so the king and the queen and all manner of knights that were there at that time drew° them

gathered

2. Mordred was Arthur's illegitimate son, by an incestuous encounter with his half-sister Morgause (or in some versions, Morgan le Fay).

unto the meadow beside Winchester where the battle should be. And
so when the king was come with the queen and many knights of the
Table Round, so the queen was then put in the constable's award,° and   *custody*
a great fire made about an iron stake, that an Sir Mador de le Porte had
the better, she should there be brent; for such custom was used in those
days: for favour, love, nother affinity° there should be none other but   *kinship*
righteous judgment, as well upon a king as upon a knight, and as well
upon a queen as upon another° poor lady.   *any*

So this meanwhile came in Sir Mador de la Porte, and took his
oath before the king, how that the queen did this treason until° his   *toward*
cousin Sir Patrise, "and unto mine oath I will prove it with my body,
hand for hand, who that will say the contrary."

Right so came in Sir Bors de Ganis and said that as for Queen
Guinevere, "she is in the right, and that will I make good that she is
not culpable of this treason that is put upon her."

"Then make thee ready," said Sir Mador, "and we shall prove
whether thou be in the right or I."

"Sir Mador," said Sir Bors, "wit you well, I know you for a good
knight. Notforthen° I shall not fear you so greatly but I trust to God   *nevertheless*
I shall be able to withstand your malice. But thus much have I
promised my lord Arthur and my lady the queen, that I shall do battle for her in this cause to the utterest, unless that there come a better knight than I am and discharge° me."   *release*

"Is that all?" said Sir Mador. "Other come thou off and do battle
with me, other else say nay!"

"Take your horse," said Sir Bors, "and, as I suppose, I shall not
tarry long but ye shall be answered."

Then either departed to their tents and made them ready to
horseback° as they thought best. And anon Sir Mador came into the   *to mount*
field with his shield on his shoulder and his spear in his hand, and so
rode about the place crying unto King Arthur,

"Bid your champion come forth an he dare!"

Then was Sir Bors ashamed, and took his horse and came to the   *jousting field's/*
lists'° end. And then was he ware° where came from a wood there   *noticed*
fast by a knight all armed upon a white horse with a strange shield of
strange arms, and he came driving all that° his horse might run. And   *as fast as*
so he came to Sir Bors and said thus:

"Fair knight, I pray you be not displeased, for here must a better
knight than ye are have this battle. Therefore I pray you withdraw
you, for wit you well I have had this day a right great journey and
this battle ought to be mine. And so I promised you when I spake
with you last, and with all my heart I thank you of your good will."

Then Sir Bors rode unto King Arthur and told him how there
was a knight come that would have the battle to fight for the queen.

"What knight is he?" said the king.

"I wot not," said Sir Bors, "but such covenant he made with me to
be here this day. Now, my lord," said Sir Bors, "here I am discharged."

Then the king called to that knight, and asked him if he would
fight for the queen. Then he answered and said,

"Sir, therefore come I hither. And therefore, sir king, tarry° me   *delay*
no longer, for anon as I have finished this battle I must depart hence,
for I have to do many battles elsewhere. For wit you well," said the
knight, "this is dishonour to you and to all knights of the Round
Table to see and know so noble a lady and so courteous as Queen
Guinevere is, thus to be rebuked and shamed amongst you."

Then they all marvelled what knight that might be that so took
the battle upon him, for there was not one that knew him but if it
were Sir Bors. Then said Sir Mador de la Porte unto the king:
"Now let me wit with whom I shall have ado."

And then they rode to the lists' end, and there they couched°   *lowered*
their spears and ran together with all their mights. And anon Sir
Mador's spear brake all to pieces, but the other's spear held and bare
Sir Mador's horse and all backwards to the earth a great fall. But
mightily and deliverly he avoided his horse from him and put his
shield before him and drew his sword and bade the other knight
alight and do battle with him on foot.

Then that knight descended down from his horse and put his
shield before him and drew his sword. And so they came eagerly
unto battle, and either gave other many sad° strokes, tracing and tra-   *grievous*
versing and foining° together with their swords as it were wild boars,   *thrusting*
thus fighting nigh an hour; for this Sir Mador was a strong knight,
and mightily proved in many strong battles. But at the last this
knight smote Sir Mador grovelling upon the earth, and the knight
stepped near him to have pulled Sir Mador flatling° upon the   *at full length*
ground; and therewith Sir Mador arose, and in his rising he smote
that knight through the thick of the thighs, that the blood brast out
fiercely.

And when he felt himself so wounded and saw his blood, he let
him arise upon his feet, and then he gave him such a buffet upon the
helm that he fell to the earth flatling. And therewith he strode to
him to have pulled off his helm off his head. And so Sir Mador
prayed that knight to save his life. And so he yielded him as overcome, and released the queen of his quarrel.°   *accusation*

"I will not grant thee thy life," said the knight, "only that° thou   *unless*
freely release the queen forever, and that no mention be made upon
Sir Patrise's tomb that ever Queen Guinevere consented to that
treason."

"All this shall be done," said Sir Mador, "I clearly discharge my
quarrel forever."

Then the knights parters° of the lists took up Sir Mador and led   *stewards*
him till his tent. And the other knight went straight to the stairfoot
where sat King Arthur. And by that time was the queen came to the
king, and either kissed other heartily.

And when the king saw that knight he stooped down to him and
thanked him, and in like wise did the queen. And the king prayed
him put off his helmet and to repose him and to take a sop of wine.

And then he put off his helm to drink, and then every knight
knew him that it was Sir Lancelot. And anon as the king wist

that, he took the queen in his hand and yode unto Sir Lancelot
and said,

"Sir, gramercy of your great travail° that ye have had this day for   *labor*
me and for my queen."

"My lord," said Sir Lancelot, "wit you well I ought of right ever
to be in your quarrel,° and my lady the queen's quarrel, to do battle;   *on your side*
for ye are the man that gave me the high Order of Knighthood, and
that day my lady, your queen, did me worship.° And else I had been   *honor*
shamed, for that same day that ye made me knight through my hastiness I lost my sword, and my lady, your queen, found it, and lapped°   *wrapped*
it in her train, and gave me my sword when I had need thereto; and
else had I been shamed among all knights. And therefore, my lord
Arthur, I promised her at that day ever to be her knight in right other in wrong."

"Gramercy," said the king, "for this journey. And wit you well,"
said the king, "I shall acquit° your goodness."   *reward*

And evermore the queen beheld Sir Lancelot and wept so
tenderly that she sank almost to the ground for sorrow, that he
had done to her so great kindness where she showed him great
unkindness. Then the knights of his blood drew unto him, and
there either of them made great joy of other. And so came all the
knights of the Table Round that were there at that time and welcomed him.

And then Sir Mador was healed of his leechcraft,° and Sir   *by surgery*
Lancelot was healed of his play.° And so there was made great joy   *wound*
and many mirths there was made in that court.

And so it befell that the Damsel of the Lake that hight Ninive,
which wedded the good knight Sir Pelleas, and so she came to the
court, for ever she did great goodness unto King Arthur and to all his
knights through her sorcery and enchantments. And so when she
heard how the queen was grieved° for the death of Sir Patrise, then   *blamed*
she told it openly that she was never guilty, and there she disclosed
by whom it was done, and named him Sir Pinel, and for what cause
he did it. There it was openly known and disclosed, and so the queen
was excused. And this knight Sir Pinel fled into his country, and was
openly known that he enpoisoned the apples at that feast to that
intent to have destroyed Sir Gawain, because Sir Gawain and his
breathren destroyed Sir Lamorak de Galis which Sir Pinel was cousin
unto.

Then was Sir Patrise buried in the church of Westminster in a
tomb, and thereupon was written: "Here lieth Sir Patrise of Ireland,
slain by Sir Pinel le Savage, that enpoisoned apples to have slain Sir
Gawain, and by misfortune Sir Patrise ate one of the apples, and
then suddenly he brast." Also there was written upon the tomb that
Queen Guinevere was appealed° of treason of° the death of Sir   *accused/for*
Patrise by Sir Mador de la Porte, and there was made the mention
how Sir Lancelot fought with him for Queen Guinevere and overcame him in plain battle. All this was written upon the tomb of Sir
Patrise in excusing of the queen.

And then Sir Mador sued daily and long to have the queen's good grace, and so by the means of Sir Lancelot he caused him to stand in the queen's good grace, and all was forgiven.

[In intervening episodes, Agravain and Mordred, nursing long-held grudges, connive to expose the adultery of Lancelot and Guinevere. Their brother, Gawain, reluctantly joins their plot. Mordred traps Lancelot at night in Guinevere's chamber, and in escaping Lancelot kills Agravain. Rescuing Guinevere as she is about to be burned at the stake, Lancelot kills another of Gawain's brothers, Gareth, thereby earning Gawain's implacable enmity. Arthur must now make war on Lancelot and, pressed by Gawain, repeats his siege even after Guinevere is returned to him. Arthur thus besieges Lancelot in his French domain, leaving Mordred as regent.]

The Day of Destiny[1]

As Sir Mordred was ruler of all England, he let make° letters as   *commissioned* though that they had come from beyond the sea, and the letters specified that King Arthur was slain in battle with Sir Lancelot. Wherefore Sir Mordred made a parliament, and called the lords together, and there he made them to choose him king. And so was he crowned at Canterbury, and held a feast there fifteen days.

And afterward he drew him unto Winchester, and there he took Queen Guinevere, and said plainly that he would wed her (which was his uncle's wife and his father's wife). And so he made ready for the feast, and a day prefixed that they should be wedded; wherefore Queen Guinevere was passing heavy,° but spake fair, and agreed to   *sad* Sir Mordred's will.

And anon she desired of Sir Mordred to go to London to buy all manner things that longed to the bridal. And because of her fair speech Sir Mordred trusted her and gave her leave; and so when she came to London she took the Tower of London and suddenly in all haste possible she stuffed it with all manner of victual, and well garnished° it with men, and so kept it.   *garrisoned*

And when Sir Mordred wist this he was passing wroth out of measure. And short tale to make, he laid a mighty siege about the Tower and made many assaults, and threw engines° unto them, and   *siege machines* shot great guns. But all might not prevail, for Queen Guinevere would never, for fair speech neither for foul, never to trust unto Sir Mordred to come in his hands again.

Then came the Bishop of Canterbury, which was a noble clerk and an holy man, and thus he said unto Sir Mordred:

"Sir, what will ye do? Will you first displease God and sithen°   *then* shame yourself and all knighthood? For is not King Arthur your uncle, and no farther but your mother's brother, and upon her he himself begat you, upon his own sister? Therefore how may you wed

---

1. From the section titled *The Most Piteous Tale of the Morte Arthur Saunz Guerdon,* in *King Arthur and His Knights,* ed. Eugène Vinaver (1975).

your own father's wife? And therefore, sir," said the Bishop, "leave this opinion,° other else I shall curse you with book, bell and candle." *intention*

"Do thou thy worst," said Sir Mordred, "and I defy thee!"

"Sir," said the Bishop, "and wit you well I shall not fear me to do that me ought to do. And also ye noise° that my lord Arthur is slain, *spread rumors* and that is not so, and therefore ye will make a foul work in this land!"

"Peace, thou false priest!" said Sir Mordred, "for an thou chafe° *anger* me any more, I shall strike off thy head."

So the Bishop departed, and did the cursing in the most orgulust° *defiant* wise that might be done. And then Sir Mordred sought the Bishop of Canterbury for to have slain him. Then the Bishop fled, and took part of his goods with him, and went nigh unto Glastonbury. And there he was a priest-hermit in a chapel, and lived in poverty and in holy prayers; for well he understood that mischievous war was at hand.

Then Sir Mordred sought upon Queen Guinevere by letters and sonds,° and by fair means and foul means, to have her to come out of *messengers* the Tower of London; but all this availed nought, for she answered him shortly, openly and privily,[2] that she had liefer° slay herself than *rather* be married with him.

Then came there word unto Sir Mordred that King Arthur had araised the siege from Sir Lancelot and was coming homeward with a great host to be avenged upon Sir Mordred; wherefore Sir Mordred made write writs° unto all the barony of this land, and much people *summonses* drew unto him. For then was the common voice among them that with King Arthur was never other life but war and strife, and with Sir Mordred was great joy and bliss. Thus was King Arthur depraved° and evil said of; and many there were that King Arthur *disparaged* had brought up of nought, and given them lands, that might not then say him a good word.

Lo ye Englishmen, see ye not what a mischief° here was? For he *evil* that was the most kind and noblest knight of the world, and most loved the fellowship of noble knights, and by him they all were upholden, and yet might not these Englishmen hold them content with him. Lo thus was the old custom and the usages of this land, and men say that we of this land have not yet lost that custom. Alas! this is a great default of us Englishmen, for there may no thing us please no term.° *length of time*

And so fared the people at that time: they were better pleased with Sir Mordred than they were with the noble King Arthur, and much people drew unto Sir Mordred and said they would abide with him for better and for worse. And so Sir Mordred drew with a great host to Dover, for there he heard say that King Arthur would arrive, and so he thought to beat his own father from his own lands. And the most party of all England held with Sir Mordred, for the people were so new-fangle.° *fond of new things*

And so as Sir Mordred was at Dover with his host, so came King Arthur with a great navy of ships and galleys and carracks, and there

2. At once, publicly and privately.

was Sir Mordred ready awaiting upon his landing, to let° his own   *stop*
father to land° upon the land that he was king over.   *from landing*

Then there was launching of great boats and small, and full of
noble men of arms; and there was much slaughter of gentle knights,
and many a full bold baron was laid full low, on both parties. But
King Arthur was so courageous that there might no manner of
knight let him to land, and his knights fiercely followed him. And so
they landed maugre° Sir Mordred's head° and all his power, and put   *against/will*
Sir Mordred aback, that he fled and all his people.

So when this battle was done King Arthur let search his people[3]
that were hurt and dead. And then was noble Sir Gawain found in a
great boat, lying more than half dead. When King Arthur knew that
he was laid so low he went unto him and so found him. And there
the king made great sorrow out of measure, and took Sir Gawain in
his arms, and thrice he there swooned. And then when he was
waked, King Arthur said,

"Alas! Sir Gawain, my sister son, here now thou liest, the man
in the world that I loved most. And now is my joy gone! For now,
my nephew, Sir Gawain, I will discover me unto° you, that in your   *disclose*
person and in Sir Lancelot I most had my joy and my affiance.° And   *trust*
now have I lost my joy of you both, wherefore all mine earthly joy is
gone from me!"

"Ah, mine uncle," said Sir Gawain, "now I will that ye wit that
my death-days be come! And all I may wite° mine own hastiness°   *blame/rashness*
and my wilfulness, for through my wilfulness I was causer of mine
own death; for I was this day hurt and smitten upon mine old wound
that Sir Lancelot gave me, and I feel myself that I must needs be
dead by the hour of noon. And through me and my pride ye have all
this shame and disease,° for had that noble knight, Sir Lancelot,   *sorrow*
been with you, as he was and would have been, this unhappy war
had never been begun; for he, through his noble knighthood and his
noble blood, held all your cankered° enemies in subjection and dan-   *malignant*
ger.° And now," said Sir Gawain, "ye shall miss Sir Lancelot. But   *control*
alas that I would not accord° with him! And therefore, fair uncle, I   *make peace*
pray you that I may have paper, pen and ink, that I may write unto
Sir Lancelot a letter written with mine own hand."

So when paper, pen and ink was brought, then Sir Gawain was set
up weakly° by King Arthur, for he was shriven a little afore. And then   *gently*
he took his pen and wrote thus, as the French book maketh mention:

"Unto thee, Sir Lancelot, flower of all noble knights that ever I
heard of or saw by my days, I, Sir Gawain, King Lot's son of Orkney,
and sister's son unto the noble King Arthur, send thee greeting, letting thee to have knowledge that the tenth day of May I was smitten upon the old wound that thou gave me afore the city of Ben-
wick, and through that wound I am come to my death-day. And I
will that all the world wit that I, Sir Gawain, knight of the Table

---

3. Had his people searched for.

Round, sought my death, and not through thy deserving, but mine own seeking. Wherefore I beseech thee, Sir Lancelot, to return again unto this realm and see my tomb and pray some prayer more other less for my soul. And this same day that I wrote the same cedle° I was hurt to the death, which wound was first given of thine hand, Sir Lancelot; for of a more nobler man might I not be slain.

letter

"Also, Sir Lancelot, for all the love that ever was betwixt us, make no tarrying, but come over the sea in all the goodly haste that ye may, with your noble knights, and rescue that noble king that made thee knight, for he is full straitly bestead with° a false traitor which is my half-brother, Sir Mordred. For he hath crowned himself king and would have wedded my lady, Queen Guinevere; and so had he done, had she not kept the Tower of London with strong hand. And so the tenth day of May last past my lord King Arthur and we all landed upon them at Dover, and there he put that false traitor, Sir Mordred, to flight. And so it misfortuned me to be smitten upon the stroke that ye gave me of old.

hard pressed by

"And the date of this letter was written but two hours and a half before my death, written with mine own hand and subscribed with part of my heart blood. And therefore I require thee, most famous knight of the world, that thou wilt see my tomb."

And then he wept and King Arthur both, and swooned. And when they were awaked both, the king made Sir Gawain to receive his sacrament, and then Sir Gawain prayed the king for to send for Sir Lancelot and to cherish him above all other knights.

And so at the hour of noon Sir Gawain yielded up the ghost. And then the king let inter him° in a chapel within Dover Castle. And there yet all men may see the skull of him, and the same wound is seen that Sir Lancelot gave in battle.

had him buried

Then was it told the king that Sir Mordred had pight a new field upon Barham Down.[4] And so upon the morn King Arthur rode thither to him, and there was a great battle betwixt them, and much people were slain on both parties. But at the last King Arthur's party stood best, and Sir Mordred and his party fled unto Canterbury.

And there the king let search all the downs for his knights that were slain and interred them; and salved them with soft salves° that full sore were wounded. Then much people drew unto King Arthur, and then they said that Sir Mordred warred upon King Arthur with wrong.

ointments

And anon King Arthur drew him with his host down by the sea-side westward, toward Salisbury. And there was a day assigned betwixt King Arthur and Sir Mordred, that they should meet upon a down beside Salisbury, and not far from the seaside. And this day was assigned on Monday after Trinity Sunday, whereof King Arthur was passing glad that he might be avenged upon Sir Mordred.

Then Sir Mordred araised much people about London, for they of Kent, Sussex and Surrey, Essex, Suffolk and Norfolk held the most party with Sir Mordred. And many a full noble knight drew unto

4. Set up a new battleground at Barham Down (southeast of Canterbury).

him and also to the king; but they that loved Sir Lancelot drew unto Sir Mordred.

So upon Trinity Sunday at night King Arthur dreamed a wonderful dream, and in his dream him seemed that he saw upon a chafflet° a chair, and the chair was fast to a wheel, and there- *platform* upon sat King Arthur in the richest cloth of gold that might be made. And the king thought there was under him, far from him, an hideous deep black water, and therein was all manner of ser- pents and worms° and wild beasts, foul and horrible. And sudden- *dragons* ly the king thought that the wheel turned up-so-down, and he fell among the serpents, and every beast took him by a limb. And then the king cried as he lay in his bed, "Help! help!"

And then knights, squires and yeomen awaked the king, and then he was so amazed that he wist not where he was. And then so he awaked until it was nigh day, and then he fell on slumbering again, not sleeping nor thoroughly waking. So° the king seemed ver- *to* ily that there came Sir Gawain unto him with a number of fair ladies with him. So when King Arthur saw him he said,

"Welcome, my sister's son, I weened° ye had been dead. And *thought* now I see thee on live, much am I beholden unto Almighty Jesu. Ah, fair nephew, what been these ladies that hither be come with you?"

"Sir," said Sir Gawain, "all these be ladies for whom I have foughten for, when I was man living. And all these are those that I did battle for in righteous quarrels, and God hath given them that grace at their great prayer, because I did battle for them for their right, that they should bring me hither unto you. Thus much hath given me leave God for to warn you of your death: for an ye fight as to-morn with Sir Mordred, as ye both have assigned, doubt ye not ye shall be slain, and the most party of your people on both parties. And for the great grace and goodness that Almighty Jesu hath unto you, and for pity of you and many more other good men there shall be slain, God hath sent me to you of His especial grace to give you warning that in no wise ye do battle as to-morn, but that ye take a treatise for a month-day.[5] And proffer you largely,° so that to-morn *generously* ye put in a delay. For within a month shall come Sir Lancelot with all his noble knights, and rescue you worshipfully, and slay Sir Mor- dred and all that ever will hold with him."

Then Sir Gawain and all the ladies vanished, and anon the king called upon his knights, squires, and yeomen, and charged° them *ordered* mightly to fetch his noble lords and wise bishops unto him. And when they were come the king told them of his avision: that Sir Gawain had told him and warned him that an he fought on the morn he should be slain. Then the king commanded Sir Lucan the Butler and his brother Sir Bedivere the Bold, with two bishops with them, and charged them in any wise to take a treatise for a month- day with Sir Mordred:

5. Make a compact for a month from today.

"And spare not, proffer him lands and goods as much as you think reasonable."

So then they departed and came to Sir Mordred where he had a grim° host of an hundred thousand. And there they entreated Sir Mordred long time, and at the last Sir Mordred was agreed for to have Cornwall and Kent by° King Arthur's days;° and after that all England, after the days of King Arthur. Then were they condescended° that King Arthur and Sir Mordred should meet betwixt both their hosts, and every each of them should bring fourteen persons. And so they came with this word unto Arthur. Then said he,

"I am glad that this is done," and so he went into the field.

And when King Arthur should depart he warned all his host that an they see any sword drawn, "look ye come on fiercely and slay that traitor, Sir Mordred, for I in no wise trust him." In like wise Sir Mordred warned his host that "an ye see any manner of sword drawn look that ye come on fiercely and so slay all that ever before you standeth, for in no wise I will not trust for this treatise." And in the same wise said Sir Mordred unto his host: "for I know well my father will be avenged upon me."

And so they met as their pointment was, and were agreed and accorded thoroughly. And wine was fette,° and they drank together. Right so came out an adder of a little heath-bush, and it stang a knight in the foot. And so when the knight felt him so stung, he looked down and saw the adder; and anon he drew his sword to slay the adder, and thought none other harm. And when the host on both parties saw that sword drawn, then they blew beams,° trumpets, and horns, and shouted grimly, and so both hosts dressed them together.° And King Arthur took his horse and said, "Alas, this unhappy day!" And so rode to his party, and Sir Mordred in like wise.

And never since was there seen a more dolefuller battle in no Christian land, for there was but rushing and riding, foining° and striking, and many a grim word was there spoken of either to other, and many a deadly stroke. But ever King Arthur rode throughout the battle° of Sir Mordred many times and did full nobly, as a noble king should do, and at all times he fainted never. And Sir Mordred did his devour° that day and put himself in great peril.

And thus they fought all the long day, and never stinted° till the noble knights were laid to the cold earth. And ever they fought still till it was near night, and by then was there an hundred thousand laid dead upon the earth. Then was King Arthur wood wroth° out of measure, when he saw his people so slain from him.

And so he looked about him and could see no mo° of all his host, and good knights left no mo on live but two knights: the tone° was Sir Lucan de Butler and his brother, Sir Bedivere; and yet they were full sore wounded.

"Jesu mercy!" said the king, "where are all my noble knights become? Alas, that ever I should see this doleful day! For now," said

---

fierce

during / lifetime

agreed

fetched

bugles

confronted each other

thrusting

battle formation

utmost effort

ceased

wild with rage

more

one

King Arthur, "I am come to mine end. But would to God," said he, "that I wist now where were that traitor Sir Mordred that hath caused all this mischief."°   *evil*

Then King Arthur looked about and was ware where stood Sir Mordred leaning upon his sword among a great heap of dead men.

"Now, give me my spear," said King Arthur unto Sir Lucan, "for yonder I have espied the traitor that all this woe hath wrought."

"Sir, let him be," said Sir Lucan, "for he is unhappy.° And if ye   *unlucky* pass this unhappy day ye shall be right well revenged. And, good lord, remember ye of your night's dream and what the spirit of Sir Gawain told you to-night, and yet God of His great goodness hath preserved you hitherto. And for God's sake, my lord, leave off this, for, blessed be God, ye have won the field: for yet we been here three on live, and with Sir Mordred is not one of live. And therefore if ye leave off now, this wicked day of Destiny is past!"

"Now tide° me death, tide me life," said the king, "now I see   *befall* him yonder alone, he shall never escape mine hands! For at a better avail° shall I never have him."   *advantage*

"God speed you well!" said Sir Bedivere.

Then the king gat his spear in both his hands, and ran toward Sir Mordred, crying and saying,

"Traitor, now is thy death-day come!"

And when Sir Mordred saw King Arthur he ran until° him   *toward* with his sword drawn in his hand, and there King Arthur smote Sir Mordred under the shield with a foin° of his spear throughout the   *thrust* body more than a fathom. And when Sir Mordred felt that he had his death wound he thrust himself with the might that he had up to the burr° of King Arthur's spear, and right so he smote his father,   *hand guard* King Arthur, with his sword holding in both his hands, upon the side of the head, that the sword pierced the helmet and the tay° of   *lining* the brain. And therewith Mordred dashed down stark dead to the earth.

And noble King Arthur fell in a swough to the earth, and there he swooned oftentimes, and Sir Lucan and Sir Bedivere oftentimes hove° him up. And so weakly° betwixt them they led him to a little   *lifted/gently* chapel not far from the sea, and when the king was there, him thought him reasonably eased.

Then heard they people cry in the field.

"Now go thou, Sir Lucan," said the king, "and do me to wit°   *let me know* what betokens that noise in the field."

So Sir Lucan departed, for he was grievously wounded in many places; and so as he rode he saw and harkened by the moonlight how that pillers° and robbers were come into the field to pille and to rob   *plunderers* many a full noble knight of brooches and bees° and of many a good ring   *bracelets* and many a rich jewel. And who that were not dead all out, there they slew them for their harness° and their riches.   *armor*

When Sir Lucan understood his work he came to the king as soon as he might, and told him all what he had heard and seen.

"Therefore by my rede,"° said Sir Lucan, "it is best that we bring you to some town." *advice*

"I would it were so," said the king, "but I may not stand, my head works° so. . . . Ah, Sir Lancelot!" said King Arthur, "this day have I sore missed thee! And alas, that ever I was against thee! For now have I my death, whereof Sir Gawain me warned in my dream." *aches*

Then Sir Lucan took up the king the tone party° and Sir Bedivere the other party, and in the lifting up the king swooned, and in the lifting Sir Lucan fell in a swoon, that part of his guts fell out of his body; and therewith the noble knight his heart brast. And when the king awoke he beheld Sir Lucan, how he lay foaming at the mouth and part of his guts lay at his feet. *on one side*

"Alas," said the king, "this is to me a full heavy sight, to see this noble duke so die for my sake, for he would have holpen° me that had more need of help than I! Alas, that he would not complain him, for his heart was so set to help me. Now Jesu have mercy upon his soul!" *helped*

Then Sir Bedivere wept for the death of his brother.

"Now leave this mourning and weeping, gentle knight," said the king, "for all this will not avail° me. For wit thou well an I might live myself, the death of Sir Lucan would grieve me evermore. But my time passeth on fast," said the king. "Therefore," said King Arthur unto Sir Bedivere, "take thou here Excalibur, my good sword, and go with it to yonder water's side; and when thou comest there, I charge thee throw my sword in that water, and come again and tell me what thou seest there." *aid*

"My lord," said Sir Bedivere, "your commandment shall be done, and lightly° bring you word again." *I will quickly*

So Sir Bedivere departed. And by the way he beheld that noble sword, and the pomell° and the haft° was all precious stones. And then he said to himself, "If I throw this rich sword in the water, thereof shall never come good, but harm and loss." And then Sir Bedivere hid Excalibur under a tree, and so soon as he might he came again unto the king and said he had been at the water and thrown the sword into the water. *hand guard/ handle*

"What saw thou there?" said the king.

"Sir," he said, "I saw nothing but waves and winds."

"That is untruly said of thee," said the king. "And therefore go thou lightly again, and do my commandment as thou art to me lief° and dear: spare not but throw it in." *beloved*

Then Sir Bedivere returned again and took the sword in his hand; and yet him thought sin and shame to throw away that noble sword. And so eft° he hid the sword and returned again and told the king that he had been at the water and done his commandment. *again*

"What sawest thou there?" said the king.

"Sir," he said, "I saw nothing but waters wap° and waves wan."° *lapping/dark*

"Ah, traitor unto me and untrue," said King Arthur, "now hast thou betrayed me twice! Who would ween° that thou who has been to me so lief and dear, and also named so noble a knight, that thou *believe* would betray me for the riches of this sword? But now go again lightly; for thy long tarrying putteth me in great jeopardy of my life, for I have taken cold. And but if° thou do now as I bid thee, if ever I may see thee, I shall slay thee mine own hands, for thou wouldest for my rich sword see me dead." *unless*

Then Sir Bedivere departed and went to the sword and lightly took it up, and so he went unto the water's side. And there he bound the girdle about the hilt, and threw the sword as far into the water as he might. And there came an arm and an hand above the water, and took it and cleight° it, and shook it thrice and brandished, and then vanished with the sword into the water. *clutched*

So Sir Bedivere came again to the king and told him what he saw.

"Alas!" said the king, "help me hence, for I dread me I have tarried over long."

Then Sir Bedivere took the king upon his back and so went with him to the water's side. And when they were there, even fast by° the bank hoved° a little barge with many fair ladies in it, and among them all was a queen, and all they had black hoods. And all they wept and shrieked when they saw King Arthur. *next to/floated*

"Now put me into that barge," said the king.

And so he did softly, and there received him three ladies with great mourning. And so they set him down, and in one of their laps King Arthur laid his head. And then the queen said,

"Ah, my dear brother!⁶ Why have you tarried so long from me? Alas, this wound on your head hath caught overmuch cold!"

And anon they rowed fromward° the land, and Sir Bedivere beheld all those ladies go fromward him. Then Sir Bedivere cried and said, *away from*

"Ah, my lord Arthur, what shall become of me, now ye go from me and leave me here alone among mine enemies?"

"Comfort thyself," said the king, "and do as well as thou mayst, for in me is no trust for to trust in. For I must into the vale of Avalon to heal me of my grievous wound. And if thou hear nevermore of me, pray for my soul!"

But ever the queen and ladies wept and shrieked, that it was pity to hear. And as soon as Sir Bedivere had lost sight of the barge he wept and wailed, and so took° the forest and went all that night. *went into*

And in the morning he was ware, betwixt two holts hoar°, of a chapel and an hermitage. Then was Sir Bedivere fain°, and thither he went, and when he came into the chapel he saw where lay an hermit grovelling° on all fours, fast thereby a tomb was new graven.° When the hermit saw Sir Bedivere he knew him well, for he was but little tofore Bishop of Canterbury, that Sir Mordred fleamed.° *gray woods* *glad* *face down/ freshly dug* *put to flight*

"Sir," said Sir Bedivere, "what man is there here interred that you pray so fast° for?" *intently*

"Fair son," said the hermit, "I wot not verily but by deeming.° But this same night, at midnight, here came a number of ladies and *guessing*

6. The queen is thus revealed as Morgan le Fay, in whose story magical healing powers mixed with inveterate hostility to Guinevere and sometimes to Arthur himself.

brought here a dead corse and prayed me to inter him. And here they offered an hundred tapers, and gave me a thousand besants."°   *gold coins*

"Alas," said Sir Bedivere, "that was my lord King Arthur, which lieth here graven° in this chapel."   *buried*

Then Sir Bedivere swooned, and when he awoke he prayed the hermit that he might abide with him still, there to live with fasting and prayers:

"For from hence will I never go," said Sir Bedivere, "by my will, but all the days of my life here to pray for my lord Arthur."

"Sir, ye are welcome to me," said the hermit, "for I know you better than ye ween that I do: for ye are Sir Bedivere the Bold, and the full noble duke Sir Lucan de Butler was your brother."

Then Sir Bedivere told the hermit all as you have heard tofore, and so he beleft° with the hermit that was beforehand   *remained*
Bishop of Canterbury. And there Sir Bedivere put upon him poor clothes, and served the hermit full lowly in fasting and in prayers.

Thus of Arthur I find no more written in books that been authorised, neither more of the very certainty of his death heard I never read, but thus was he led away in a ship wherein were three queens; that one was King Arthur's sister, Queen Morgan le Fay, the tother was the Queen of North Galis, and the third was the Queen of the Waste Lands.

Now more of the death of King Arthur could I never find, but that these ladies brought him to his grave, and such one was interred there which the hermit bare witness that sometime° Bishop of Can-   *was once*
terbury. But yet the hermit knew not in certain that he was verily the body of King Arthur; for this tale Sir Bedivere, a knight of the Table Round, made it to be written.

Yet some men say in many parts of England that King Arthur is not dead, but had° by the will of our Lord Jesu into another place;   *was carried*
and men say that he shall come again, and he shall win the Holy Cross. Yet I will not say that it shall be so, but rather I would say: here in this world he changed his life. And many men say that there is written upon the tomb this:

HIC IACET ARTHURUS REX QUONDAM REXQUE FUTURUS[7]

And thus leave I here Sir Bedivere with the hermit that dwelled that time in a chapel beside Glastonbury, and there was his hermitage. And so they lived in prayers and fastings and great abstinence.

And when Queen Guinevere understood that King Arthur was dead and all the noble knights, Sir Mordred and all the remnant, then she stole away with five ladies with her, and so she went to Amesbury. And there she let make herself° a nun, and weared white   *became*
clothes and black, and great penance she took upon her, as ever did sinful woman in this land. And never creature could make her merry, but ever she lived in fasting, prayers and alms-deeds, that all manner of people marvelled how virtuously she was changed.

---

7. Here lies Arthur, once and future king.

Geoffrey Chaucer

c. 1340–1400

On Easter weekend 1300, the Italian poet Dante Alighieri had a vision in which he descended to hell, climbed painfully through purgatory, and then attained a transcendent experience of paradise. He tells his tale in his visionary, passionately judgmental *Divine Comedy*. One hundred years later, on 25 October 1400, Geoffrey Chaucer—the least judgmental of poets—died quietly in his house at the outskirts of London. By a nice accident of history, these two great writers bracket the last great century of the Middle Ages.

Of Chaucer's own life our information is abundant but often frustrating. Many documents record the important and sensitive posts he held in government, but there are only faint hints of his career as a poet. During his lifetime, he was frequently in France and made at least two trips to Italy, which proved crucial for his own growth as a writer and indeed for the history of English literature. He also served under three kings: the aging Edward III, his brilliant and sometimes tyrannical grandson Richard II, and—at the very end of his life—Richard's usurper Henry IV.

Chaucer was born into a rising mercantile family, part of the growing bourgeois class that brought so much wealth to England even while it challenged medieval theories of social order. Chaucer's family fit nowhere easily in the old model of the three estates: those who pray (the clergy), those who fight (the aristocracy), and those who work the land (the peasants). Yet like many of their class, they aspired to a role among the aristocracy, and in fact Chaucer's parents succeeded in holding minor court positions. Chaucer himself became a major player in the cultural and bureaucratic life of the court, and Thomas Chaucer (who was very probably his son) was ultimately knighted.

Geoffrey was superbly but typically educated. He probably went to one of London's fine grammar schools, and as a young man he very likely followed a gentlemanly study of law at one of the Inns of Court. He shows signs of knowing and appreciating the topics debated in the university life of his time. His poems reflect a vast reading in classical Latin, French, and Italian (of which he was among the earliest English readers). *The Parliament of Fowls*, for instance, reveals the influence not only of French court poetry but also of Dante's *Divine Comedy;* and the frame-story structure of *The Canterbury Tales* may have been inspired by Boccaccio's *Decameron*.

By 1366 Chaucer had married Philippa de Roet, a minor Flemish noblewoman, and a considerable step up the social hierarchy. Her sister later became the mistress and ultimately the wife of Chaucer's great patron, John of Gaunt. Thus, when John's son Henry Bolingbroke seized the throne from Richard II, the elderly Geoffrey Chaucer found himself a distant in-law of his king. Chaucer had been associated with Richard II and suffered reverses when Richard's power was restricted by the magnates. But he was enough of a cultural figure that Henry IV continued (perhaps with some prompting) the old man's earlier annuities. Whatever western literature owes to Chaucer (and its debts are profound), in his own life his writing made a place in the world for him and his heirs.

Despite his lifelong productivity as a writer, and despite the slightly obtuse narrative voice he consistently uses, Geoffrey Chaucer was a canny and ambitious player in the world of his time. He was a soldier, courtier, diplomat, and government official in a wide range of jobs. These included controller of the customs on wool and other animal products, a lucrative post, and later controller of the Petty Custom that taxed wine and other goods. Chaucer's frequent work overseas extended his contacts with French and particularly Italian literature. He was ward of estates for several minors, a job that also benefited the guardian. Chaucer began to accumulate property in Kent, where he served as justice of the peace (an important judicial post) and then Member of Parliament in the mid-1380s.

Despite the comfortable worldly progress suggested by such activities, these were troubled years in the nation and in Chaucer's private life. Chaucer's personal fortunes were affected by the frequent struggles between King Richard and his magnates over control of the government. From another direction, the Peasants' Revolt exploded in 1381, rocking all of English society. The year before that, Chaucer had been accused of *raptus* by Cecilia Chaumpaigne, daughter of a baker in London. A great deal of nervous scholarship has been exercised over this case, but it becomes increasingly clear that in legal language *raptus* meant some form of rape. The case was settled, and there are signs of efforts to hush it up at quite high levels of government. The somewhat bland and bumbling quality of Chaucer's narrative persona would probably have seemed more artificially constructed and more ironic to Chaucer's contemporaries than it does at first glance today.

Chaucer was a Janus-faced poet, truly innovative at the levels of language and theme yet deeply involved with literary and intellectual styles that stretched back to Latin antiquity and twelfth- and thirteenth-century France. His early poems—the dream visions such as *The Parliament of Fowls* and the great romance *Troilus and Criseyde*—derive from essentially medieval genres and continental traditions: the French poets Deschamps and Machaut and the Italians Dante, Boccaccio, and Petrarch. Yet in his reliance on the English vernacular, Chaucer was in a vanguard generation along with the *Gawain* poet and William Langland. English was indeed gaining importance in other parts of this world, such as in Parliament, some areas of education, and in the "Wycliffite" translations of the Bible. Chaucer's own exclusive use of English was particularly ambitious, though, for a poet whose patronage came from the court of the francophile Richard II.

The major work of Chaucer's maturity, *The Canterbury Tales*, founds an indisputably English tradition. While he still uses the craft and allusions he learned from his continental

Portrait of Geoffrey the Canterbury Pilgrim, from an early 15th-century manuscript.

masters, he also experiments with the subject matter of everyday English life and the vocabularies of the newly valorized English vernacular. Moreover, starting with traditional forms and largely traditional models of society and the cosmos, Chaucer found spaces for new and sometimes disruptive perspectives, especially those of women and the rising mercantile class into which he had been born. Though always a court poet, Chaucer increasingly wrote in ways that reflected both the richness and the uncertainties of his entire social world. The *Tales* include a Knight who could have stepped from a twelfth-century *chanson de geste;* yet they also offer the spectacle of the Knight's caste being aped, almost parodied, and virtually shouted down by a sword-carrying peasant, the Miller. And the entire notion of old writings as sources of authoritative wisdom is powerfully challenged by the illiterate or only minimally literate Wife of Bath.

The *Canterbury Tales* also differ from the work of many of Chaucer's continental predecessors in their deep hesitation to cast straightforward judgment, either socially or spiritually. Here we may return to Chaucer's connection with Dante. His *Divine Comedy* presented mortal life as a pilgrimage and an overt test in stable dogma, a journey along a dangerous road toward certain damnation or the reward of the heavenly Jerusalem. *The Canterbury Tales* are literally about a pilgrimage, and Chaucer presents the road as beautiful and fascinating in its own right. The greatness of the poem lies in its exploration of the variousness of the journey and that journey's reflection of a world pressured by spiritual and moral fractures. In depicting a mixed company of English men and women traveling England's most famous pilgrimage route and telling one another stories, Chaucer shows us not only the spiritual meaning of humankind's earthly pilgrimage, but also its overflowing beauties and attractions as well as the evils and temptations that lie along the way. The vision of the serious future, the day of judgment, is constantly attended in *The Canterbury Tales* by the troubling yet hilarious and distracting present.

Unlike Dante, Chaucer almost never takes it upon himself to judge, at least not openly. He records his characters with dizzying immediacy, but he never tells his reader quite what to think of them, leaving the gaps for us as readers to fill. He does end the *Tales* with a kind of sermon, the Parson's long prose treatise on the Christian vices and virtues. That coda by no means erases the humor and seriousness, sentiment and ribaldry, high spiritual love and unmasked carnal desire, profound religious belief and squalid clerical corruption that have been encountered along the way. Indeed, Chaucer's genius is to transmute the disorder of his world almost into an aesthetic of plenitude: "foyson" in Middle English. His poem overflows constantly with rich detail, from exquisite visions to squabbling pilgrims. His language overflows with its multiple vocabularies, Anglo-Saxon, Latin, and French. And finally, the tales themselves are notable for the range of genres used by the pilgrims: the Miller's bawdy fabliau, the Wife of Bath's romance, the Nun's Priest's beast fable, the Pardoner's hypocritical cautionary tale, as well as the Parson's sermon. *The Canterbury Tales* are an anthology embracing almost every important literary type of Chaucer's day.

None of this celebratory richness, however, fully masks the unresolved social and spiritual tensions that underlie the *Tales*. The notion of spiritual pilgrimage is deeply challenged by the very density of characterization and worldly detail that so enlivens the work. And the model of a competitive game, which provides the fictional pretext for the tales themselves, is only one version of what the critic Peggy Knapp has called Chaucer's "social contest" in the work as a whole. The traditional estates such as knight and peasant openly clash during the pilgrimage, and the estate of the clergy is more widely represented by its corrupt than by its virtuous members. Women, merchants, common landowners, and others from outside the traditional three estates bulk large in the tales. And their stories cast doubt upon such fundamental religious institutions as penance and such social institutions as marriage. For all their pleasures, *The Canterbury Tales* have survived, in part, because they are so riven by challenge and doubt.

CHAUCER'S MIDDLE ENGLISH
Grammar

The English of Chaucer's London, and particularly the English of government bureaucracy, became the source for the more standardized vernacular that emerged in the era of print at the close of the Middle Ages. As a result, Chaucer's English is easier to understand today than the dialect of many of his great contemporaries such as the *Gawain* poet, who worked far to the north. The text that follows preserves Chaucer's language, with some spellings slightly modernized and regularized by its editor, E. Talbot Donaldson.

The marginal glosses in the readings are intended to help the nonspecialist reader through Chaucer's language without elaborate prior study. It will be helpful, though, to explain a few key differences from Modern English.

Nouns: The possessive is sometimes formed without a final -*s*.

Pronouns: Readers will recognize the archaic *thou, thine, thee* of second-person singular, and *ye* of the plural. Occasional confusion can arise from the form *hir*, which can mean "her" or "their." *Hem* is Chaucer's spelling for "them," and *tho* for "those." Chaucer uses *who* to mean "whoever."

Adverbs: Formed, as today, with -*ly*, but also with -*liche*. Sometimes an adverb is unchanged from its adjective form: *fairly, fairliche, faire* can all be adverbs.

Verbs: Second-person singular is formed with -*est* (*thou lovest*, past tense *thou lovedest*); third-person singular often with -*eth* (*he loveth*); plurals often with -*n* (*we loven*); and infinitive with -*n* (*loven*).

Strong verbs/impersonal verbs: Middle English has many "strong verbs," which form the past and perfect by changing a vowel in their stem; these are usually recognizable by analogy with surviving forms in Modern English (*go, went, gone; sing, sang, sung;* etc.). Middle English also often uses "impersonal verbs" (*liketh*, "it pleases"; *as me thinketh*, "as I think"), in which case sometimes no obvious subject noun or pronoun occurs.

Pronunciation

A few guidelines will help approximate the sound of Chaucer's English and the richness of his versification. For fuller discussion, consult sources listed in the bibliography.

Pronounce all consonants: *knight* is "k/neecht" with a guttural *ch*, not "nite"; *gnaw* is "g/naw." Middle English consonants preserve many of the sounds of the language's Germanic roots: guttural *gh*; sounded *l* and *w* in words like *folk* or *write*. (Exceptions occur in some words that derive from French, like *honour* whose *h* is silent.)

Final -*e* was sounded in early Middle English. Such pronunciation was becoming archaic by Chaucer's time, but was available to aid meter in the stylized context of poetry.

The distinction between short and long vowels was greater in Middle English than today. Middle English short vowels have mostly remained short in Modern English, with some shift in pronunciation: short *a* sounds like the *o* in *hot*, short *o* like a quick version of the *aw* in *law*, short *u* like the *u* in *full*.

Long vowels in Middle English are close to long vowels in modern Romance languages. The chart shows some differences in Middle English long vowels.

Middle English	pronounced as in	Modern English
a (as in *name*)		*father*
open *e* (*deel*)		*swear, bread*
close *e* (*sweet*)		*fame*
i (*whit*)		*feet*
open *o* (*holy*)		*law*
close *o* (*roote*)		*note*
u (as in *town, aboute*)		*root*
u (*Vertu*)		*few*

Open and close long vowels are a challenge for modern readers. Generally, open long *e* in Middle English (*deel*) has become Modern English spelling with *ea* (*deal*); close long *e* (*sweet*) has become Modern English spelling with *ee* (*sweet*). Open long *o* in Middle English has come to be pronounced as in *note*; close long *o* in Middle English has come to be pronounced *root*. This latter case illustrates the idea of "vowel shift," in which some long vowels have moved forward in the throat and palate across the centuries.

Versification

All of Chaucer's poetry presented here is in a loosely iambic pentameter line, which Chaucer was greatly responsible for bringing into prominence in England. He is a fluid versifier, though, and often shifts stress, producing metrical effects that have come to be called trochees and spondees. Final *-e* is often pronounced within lines to provide an unstressed syllable and is typically pronounced at the end of each line. Yet final *-e* may also elide with a following word that begins with a vowel. The following lines from *The Nun's Priest's Tale* have a proposed scansion, but the reader will see that alternate scansions are possible at several places.

> "Avoi," quod she, "fy on you, hertelees!
> Allas," quod she, "for by that God above,
> Now han ye lost myn herte and al my love!
> I can nat love a coward, by my faith.
> For certes, what so any womman saith,
> We alle desiren, if it mighte be,
> To han housbondes hardy, wise, and free,
> And secree, and no nigard, ne no fool,
> Ne him that is agast of every tool,
> Ne noon avauntour. By that God above,
> How dorste ye sayn for shame unto youre love
> That any thing mighte make you aferd?
> Have ye no mannes herte and han a beerd?

FROM THE CANTERBURY TALES
The General Prologue

The twenty-nine "sondry folke" of the Canterbury company gather at the Tabard Inn, ostensibly with the pious intent of making a pilgrimage to England's holiest shrine, the tomb of Saint Thomas Becket at Canterbury. From the start in the raffish and worldly London suburb of Southwerk, though, the pilgrims' attentions and energy veer wildly between the sacred and the profane. The mild story-telling competition proposed by the Host also slides swiftly into a contest among social classes. Set in Chaucer's own time and place, *The Canterbury Tales* reflect both the dynamism and the uncertainties of a society still nostalgic for archaic models of church and state, yet riven by such crises as plague, economic disruption, and the new claims of peasants and mercantile bourgeois—claims expressed and repressed most violently in the recent Rising, or "Peasants' Revolt," of 1381.

    Chaucer's *Prologue* has roots in the genre known as "estates satire." Such writings criticized the failure of the members of the three traditional "estates" of medieval society—the aristocracy, the clergy, and the commons—to fulfill their ordained function of fighting, praying, and working the land, respectively. From the beginning the pilgrims' portraits are couched in language fraught with class connotations. The Knight, the idealized (if archaic) representative of the aristocracy, is called *gentil* (that is, "noble, aristocratic") and is said never to have uttered any *vileynye*—speech characteristic of peasants or *villeyns*. Many of the pilgrims in the other two estates display aristocratic manners, among the clergy notably the Prioress, with her "cheere of court," and the Monk, who lives like a country gentleman, hunting with greyhounds and a stable full of fine horses. Both pilgrims contrast with the ideal of their estate, the Parson, who, though "*povre*" is "rich" in holy works.

The commons are traditionally the last of the "three estates," yet they bulk largest in the Canterbury company and fit least well in that model of social order. There are old-fashioned laborers on the pilgrimage, but many more characters from the emerging and disruptive world of small industry and commerce. They are commoners, but have ambitions that lead them both to envy and to mock the powers held by their aristocratic and clerical companions.

Among the group that traditionally comprised the commons, the peasants, Chaucer singles out one ideal, the Plowman, who is, significantly, the Parson's brother. He is characterized as a diligent *swynkere* (worker), in implicit contrast to the lazy peasants castigated in estates satire. Most of the rest of the commons, however, such as the Miller and the Cook, are presented as "churlish," and their tales have a coarse vigor that Chaucer clearly relishes even as he disassociates himself from their vulgarity.

In theory, women were treated as a separate category, defined by their sexual nature and marital role rather than by their class. Nevertheless, the Prioress and the Wife of Bath are both satirized as much for their social ambition as for the failings of their gender. The Prioress prides herself on her courtesy, and the commoner Wife of Bath aspires to the same social recognition as the guildsmen's upwardly mobile wives. Her portrait is complex, however, for she is simultaneously satirized and admired for challenging the expected roles of women at the time, with her economic independence (as a rich widow and a cloth-maker) and her resultant freedom to travel. The narrator's suggestion that she goes on many pilgrimages in order to find a sixth husband bears out the stereotype of unbridled female sexuality familiar from estates satire, as her fondness of talking and laughing bears out the stereotype of female garrulousness.

Chaucer's satire is pointed but also exceptionally subtle, largely because of the irony achieved through his use of the narrator, seemingly naive and a little dense. His deadpan narration leaves the readers themselves to supply the judgment.

FROM THE CANTERBURY TALES
The General Prologue

	Whan that April with his showres soote°	*sweet*
	The droughte of March hath perced to the roote,	
	And bathed every veine in swich licour,°	*such liquid*
	Of which vertu° engendred is the flowr;	*by whose strength*
5	Whan Zephyrus[1] eek° with his sweete breeth	*also*
	Inspired hath in every holt and heeth°	*wood and field*
	The tendre croppes, and the yonge sonne	
	Hath in the Ram° his halve cours yronne,	*the zodiac sign Aries*
	And smale fowles maken melodye	
10	That sleepen al the night with open yë°—	*eye*
	So priketh hem Nature in hir corages°—	*hearts, spirits*
	Thanne longen folk to goon on pilgrimages,	
	And palmeres[2] for to seeken straunge strondes°	*shores*
	To ferne halwes,° couthe° in sondry londes;	*far-off shrines / known*

1. In Roman mythology Zephyrus was the demigod of the west wind, herald of warmer weather.   2. Pilgrims who had traveled to the Holy Land.

15   And specially from every shires ende
     Of Engelond to Canterbury they wende,
     The holy blisful martyr[3] for to seeke
     That hem hath holpen° whan that they were seke.°   helped/sick
     Bifel that in that seson on a day,
20   In Southwerk[4] at the Tabard as I lay,
     Redy to wenden on my pilgrimage
     To Canterbury with ful devout corage,
     At night was come into that hostelrye
     Wel nine and twenty in a compaignye
25   Of sondry folk, by aventure yfalle
     In felaweshipe, and pilgrimes were they alle
     That toward Canterbury wolden ride.
     The chambres° and the stables weren wide,   guestrooms
     And wel we weren esed° at the beste.   accommodated
30   And shortly, whan the sonne was to reste,
     So hadde I spoken with hem everichoon
     That I was of hir felaweshipe anoon,
     And made forward° erly for to rise,   agreed
     To take oure way ther as I you devise.°   relate
35   But nathelees, whil I have time and space,°   opportunity
     Er that I ferther in this tale pace,°   proceed
     Me thinketh it accordant to resoun
     To telle you al the condicioun°   circumstances
     Of eech of hem, so as it seemed me,
40   And whiche they were, and of what degree,°   social status
     And eek in what array that they were inne:
     And at a knight thanne wol I first biginne.
        A Knight ther was, and that a worthy man,
     That fro the time that he first bigan
45   To riden out, he loved chivalrye,
     Trouthe and honour, freedom and curteisye.[5]
     Ful worthy was he in his lordes werre,°   war
     And therto hadde he riden, no man ferre,°   farther
     As wel in Cristendom as hethenesse,°   heathen lands
50   And evere honoured for his worthinesse.
        At Alisandre[6] he was whan it was wonne;
     Ful ofte time he hadde the boord bigonne[7]
     Aboven alle nacions in Pruce;
     In Lettou had he reised,° and in Ruce,   campaigned
55   No Cristen man so ofte of his degree;
     In Gernade at the sege eek hadde he be

3. St. Thomas Becket, murdered in Canterbury Cathedral in 1170.
4. Southwark, a suburb of London south of the Thames and the traditional starting point for the pilgrimage to Canterbury in Kent, was notorious as a center of gambling and prostitution. The Tabard Inn was an actual public house at the time, named for the shape of its sign which resembled the coarse, sleeveless outergarment worn by members of the lower classes, monks, and foot-soldiers alike.
5. Fidelity and good reputation, generosity and courtliness.

6. The place-names Chaucer lists over the next 15 lines were primarily associated with 14th-century Crusades against both Moslems and Eastern Orthodox Christians. Alisandre: Alexandria in Egypt; Pruce: Prussia; Lettou: Lithuania; Ruce: Russia; Gernade and Algezir: Granada and Algeciras in Spain; Belmarye: Ben-Marin near Morocco; Lyeis: Ayash in Turkey; Satalye: Atalia in Turkey; Grete See: Mediterranean; Tramissene: Tlemcen near Morocco; Palatye: Balat in Turkey.
7. Held the place of honor at feasts.

Of Algezir, and riden in Belmarye;

At Lyeis was he, and at Satalye,

Whan they were wonne; and in the Grete See

60 At many a noble arivee° hadde he be.   *military landing*

        At mortal batailes[8] hadde he been fifteene,

And foughten for oure faith at Tramissene

In listes° thries, and ay° slain his fo.   *duels/always*

        This ilke° worthy Knight hadde been also   *same*

65 Somtime with the lord of Palatye

Again° another hethen in Turkye;   *against*

And everemore he hadde a soverein pris.°   *reputation*

And though that he were worthy, he was wis,

And of his port° as meeke as is a maide.   *bearing*

70 He nevere yit no vilainye° ne saide   *rudeness*

In al his lif unto no manere wight:

He was a verray,° parfit,° gentil° knight.   *true/perfect/noble*

But for to tellen you of his array,°   *equipment*

His hors were goode, but he was nat gay.°   *gaily attired*

75 Of fustian° he wered a gipoun°   *coarse cloth/tunic*

Al bismotered with his haubergeoun,[9]

For he was late come from his viage,°   *expedition*

And wente for to doon his pilgrimage.

        With him ther was his sone, a yong Squier,

80 A lovere and a lusty bacheler,[1]

With lokkes crulle° as they were laid in presse.   *curled*

Of twenty yeer of age he was, I gesse.

Of his stature he was of evene° lengthe,   *average*

And wonderly delivere,° and of greet strengthe.   *agile*

85 And he hadde been som time in chivachye°   *cavalry expedition*

In Flandres, in Artois, and Picardye,[2]

And born him wel as of so litel space,°   *time*

In hope to stonden in his lady grace.°   *lady's favor*

Embrouded° was he as it were a mede,°   *embroidered/meadow*

90 Al ful of fresshe flowres, white and rede;

Singing he was, or floiting,° al the day: *playing the flute*

He was as fressh as is the month of May.

Short was his gowne, with sleeves longe and wide.

Wel coude he sitte on hors, and faire ride;

95 He coude songes make, and wel endite,°   *compose*

Juste° and eek daunce, and wel portraye° and write.   *joust/draw*

So hote he loved that by nightertale°   *nighttime*

He slepte namore than dooth a nightingale.

Curteis he was, lowely,° and servisable,°   *humble/attentive*

100 And carf° biforn his fader at the table   *carved*

        A Yeman[3] hadde he° and servants namo   *(the Knight)*

At that time, for him liste° ride so;   *he liked*

And he was clad in cote and hood of greene.

---

8. Tournaments waged to the death.

9. Rust-stained from his coat of mail.

1. An unmarried and unpropertied younger knight.

2. Regions in the north of France and in what is now Belgium, where the English and the French were fighting out

the Hundred Years' War.

3. A yeoman was a freeborn servant (not a peasant), who
looked after the affairs of the gentry. This particular yeoman was a forester and gamekeeper for the Knight.

	A sheef of pecok arwes,° bright and keene,	*peacock arrows*
105	Under his belt he bar ful thriftily;	
	Wel coude he dresse° his takel° yemanly:	*arrange/gear*
	His arwes drouped nought with fetheres lowe.	
	And in his hand he bar a mighty bowe.	
	A not-heed° hadde he with a brown visage.°	*short haircut/face*
110	Of wodecraft° wel coude he al the usage.	*forestry*
	Upon his arm he bar a gay bracer,°	*archer's armguard*
	And by his side a swerd and a bokeler,°	*small shield*
	And on that other side a gay daggere,	
	Harneised wel and sharp as point of spere;	
115	A Cristophre[4] on his brest of silver sheene;	
	An horn he bar, the baudrik° was of greene.	*shoulder strap*
	A forster° was he soothly, as I gesse.	*gamekeeper*
	Ther was also a Nonne, a Prioresse,	
	That of hir smiling was ful simple and coy.°	*quiet, shy*
120	Hir gretteste ooth was but by Sainte Loy![5]	
	And she was cleped° Madame Eglantine.°	*called/Briar-rose*
	Ful wel she soong the service divine,	
	Entuned in hir nose ful semely;	
	And Frenssh she spak ful faire and fetisly,°	*elegantly*
125	After the scole of Stratford at the Bowe[6]—	
	For Frenssh of Paris was to hire unknowe.	
	At mete° wel ytaught was she withalle:	*meals*
	She leet no morsel from hir lippes falle,	
	Ne wette hir fingres in hir sauce deepe;	
130	Wel coude she carye a morsel, and wel keepe°	*safeguard*
	That no drope ne fille upon hir brest.	
	In curteisye was set ful muchel hir lest.°	*her great pleasure*
	Hir over-lippe° wiped she so clene	*upper lip*
	That in hir coppe ther was no ferthing[7] seene	
135	Of grece,° whan she dronken hadde hir draughte;	*grease*
	Ful semely after hir mete she raughte.°	*reached for her food*
	And sikerly° she was of greet disport,°	*certainly/good cheer*
	And ful plesant, and amiable of port,	
	And pained hire to countrefete cheere°	*appearance*
140	Of court, and to been estatlich° of manere,	*stately*
	And to been holden digne° of reverence.	*worthy*
	But, for to speken of hir conscience,	
	She was so charitable and so pitous	
	She wolde weepe if that she saw a mous	
145	Caught in a trappe, if it were deed or bledde.	
	Of smale houndes hadde she that she fedde	
	With rosted flessh,° or milk and wastelbreed;[8]	*meat*
	But sore wepte she if oon of hem were deed,	
	Or if men smoot° it with a yerde° smerte;°	*hit/rod/painfully*
150	And al was conscience and tendre herte.	

---

4. Medal of St. Christopher, patron saint of travelers.
5. St. Eligius, patron saint of metalworkers, believed never to have sworn an oath in his life.
6. From the school (i.e., after the manner) of Stratford, a suburb of London where the prosperous convent of St.

Leonard's was located; her French is Anglo-Norman as opposed to the French spoken on the Continent.
7. Spot the size of a farthing.
8. Bread of the finest quality.

Ful semely hir wimpel[9] pinched was,
Hir nose tretis,° hir yën greye as glas,   *shapely*
Hir mouth ful smal, and therto softe and reed—
But sikerly she hadde a fair forheed:
155 It was almost a spanne[1] brood, I trowe,°   *believe*
For hardily,° she was nat undergrowe.°   *assuredly/short*
Ful fetis° was hir cloke, as I was war;   *elegant*
Of smal coral aboute hir arm she bar
A paire of bedes, gauded al with greene,[2]
160 And theron heeng a brooch of gold ful sheene,
On which ther was first writen a crowned A.[3]
And after, *Amor vincit omnia.*[4]
     Another Nonne with hire hadde she
That was hir chapelaine,° and preestes three.   *secretary*
165   A Monk ther was, a fair for the maistrye,°   *very good-looking*
An outridere[5] that loved venerye,°   *hunting*
A manly° man, to been an abbot able.   *courageous*
Ful many a daintee° hors hadde he in stable,   *fine*
And whan he rood, men mighte his bridel heere
170 Ginglen° in a whistling wind as clere   *jingling*
And eek as loude as dooth the chapel belle
Ther as this lord was kepere of the celle.[6]
The rule of Saint Maure or of Saint Beneit,[7]
By cause that it was old and somdeel strait°—   *somewhat strict*
175 This ilke Monk leet olde thinges pace,
And heeld after the newe world the space.°   *the times (customs)*
He yaf nought of that text° a pulled° hen   *regulation/plucked*
That saith that hunteres been nought holy men,
Ne that a monk, whan he is recchelees,°   *careless*
180 Is likned til a fissh that is waterlees—
This is to sayn, a monk out of his cloistre;
But thilke° text heeld he nat worth an oystre.   *that same*
And I saide his opinion was good:
What sholde he studye and make himselven wood°   *crazy*
185 Upon a book in cloistre alway to poure,
Or swinke° with his handes and laboure,   *work*
As Austin[8] bit?° How shal the world be served?   *orders*
Lat Austin have his swink to him reserved!
Therfore he was a prikasour° aright.   *hunter on horseback*
190 Grehoundes he hadde as swift as fowl in flight.
Of priking and of hunting for the hare
Was al his lust,° for no cost wolde he spare.   *pleasure*
I sawgh his sleeves purfiled° at the hand   *fur-lined*

9. A pleated headdress covering all but the face, such as nuns and married women wore.
1. A hand's width, 7 to 9 inches.
2. A set of rosary beads, marked off by larger beads (gauds) to indicate where the Paternosters should be said.
3. The letter "A" with a crown on top.
4. Love conquers all (Virgil, *Eclogues,* 10.69). Though pagan and secular in origin, the phrase was often used to refer to divine love as well.

5. A monk who worked outside the confines of the monastery.
6. Supervisor of the outlying cell of the monastery.
7. St. Benedict (Beneit) was the founder of Western monasticism, and his Rule prohibited monks from leaving the grounds of the monastery without special permission. St. Maurus introduced the Benedictine order into France.
8. St. Augustine recommended that monks perform manual labor.

With gris,° and that the fineste of a land;   *gray fur*
195   And for to festne his hood under his chin
He hadde of gold wrought a ful curious° pin: *elaborate*
A love-knotte[9] in the grettere° ende ther was.   *larger*
His heed was balled,° that shoon as any glas,   *bald*
And eek his face, as he hadde been anoint:
200   He was a lord ful fat and in good point;°   *in good shape*
His yën steepe,° and rolling in his heed,   *bright*
That stemed as a furnais of a leed;[1]
His bootes souple,° his hors in greet estat[2]—   *supple*
Now certainly he was a fair prelat.[3]
205   He was nat pale as a forpined° gost: *tormented*
A fat swan loved he best of any rost.
His palfrey° was as brown as is a berye.   *saddle horse*
      A Frere° ther was, a wantoune[4] and a merye,   *Friar*
A limitour,[5] a ful solempne man.
210   In alle the ordres foure[6] is noon that can°   *knows*
So muche of daliaunce° and fair langage: *flirtation*
He hadde maad ful many a mariage
Of yonge wommen at his owene cost;
Unto his ordre he was a noble post.°   *pillar*
215   Ful wel biloved and familier was he
With frankelains[7] over al in his contree,
And with worthy wommen of the town—
For he hadde power of confessioun,
As saide himself, more than a curat,°   *parish priest*
220   For of his ordre he was licenciat.[8]
Ful swetely herde he confessioun,
And plesant was his absolucioun.
He was an esy man to yive penaunce
Ther as he wiste to have a good pitaunce;[9]
225   For unto a poore ordre for to yive
Is signe that a man is wel yshrive;°   *absolved*
For if he yaf, he dorste make avaunt°   *boast*
He wiste that a man was repentaunt;
For many a man so hard is of his herte
230   He may nat weepe though him sore smerte:°   *hurts*
Therfore, in stede of weeping and prayeres,
Men mote yive silver to the poore freres.
      His tipet° was ay farsed° ful of knives   *scarf/packed*
And pinnes, for to yiven faire wives;
235   And certainly he hadde a merye note;
Wel coude he singe and playen on a rote;°   *fiddle*
Of yeddinges° he bar outrely the pris.[1]   *singing ballads*
His nekke whit was as the flowr-de-lis;[2]

9. An elaborate knot.
1. Glowed like a furnace under a cauldron.
2. Excellent condition.
3. Prelate, important churchman.
4. Jovial, pleasure-seeking.
5. Friar licensed by his order to beg for alms within a given district.

6. The four orders of friars were the Carmelites, Augustinians, Dominicans, and Franciscans.
7. Franklins, important property holders.
8. Licensed by the Church to hear confessions.
9. Where he knew he would get a good donation.
1. Utterly took the prize.
2. Lily, emblem of the royal house of France.

Therto he strong was as a champioun.

240 He knew the tavernes wel in every town,

And every hostiler and tappestere,°   *innkeeper and barmaid*

Bet than a lazar or a beggestere.°   *a leper or a beggar*

For unto swich a worthy man as he

Accorded nat, as by his facultee,°[3]   *official position*

245 To have with sike lazars aquaintaunce:

It is nat honeste,° it may nought avaunce,° *dignified/profit*

For to delen with no swich poraile,°   *poor people*

But al with riche, and selleres of vitaile;° *food*

And over al ther as profit sholde arise,

250 Curteis he was, and lowely° of servise.   *humble*

Ther was no man nowher so vertuous:°   *capable*

He was the beste beggere in his hous.

And yaf a certain ferme for the graunt:[4]

Noon of his brethren cam ther in his haunt.° *territory*

255 For though a widwe hadde nought a sho,

So plesant was his *In principio*[5]

Yit wolde he have a ferthing er he wente;

His purchas° was wel bettre than his rente.° *income/expense*

And rage° he coude as it were right a whelpe;° *flirt/puppy*

260 In love-dayes[6] ther coude he muchel helpe,

For ther he was nat lik a cloisterer,

With a thredbare cope, as is a poore scoler,

But he was lik a maister° or a pope.   *professor*

Of double worstede was his semicope,°[7]   *short cloak*

265 And rounded as a belle out of the presse.° *bell-mold*

Somwhat he lipsed for his wantounesse

To make his Englissh sweete upon his tonge;

And in his harping, whan that he hadde songe,

His yën twinkled in his heed aright

270 As doon the sterres in the frosty night.

This worthy limitour was cleped Huberd.

A Marchant was ther with a forked beerd,

In motlee,° and hye on hors he sat,   *multicolored fabric*

Upon his heed a Flandrissh° bevere hat,   *Flemish*

275 His bootes clasped faire and fetisly.°   *elegantly*

His resons° he spak ful solempnely,   *opinions*

Souning° alway th'encrees of his winning.   *announcing*

He wolde the see were kept for any thing°   *protected at all costs*

Bitwixen Middelburgh and Orewelle.[8]

280 Wel coude he in eschaunge sheeldes[9] selle.

This worthy man ful wel his wit bisette:°   *employed*

Ther wiste° no wight that he was in dette,   *knew*

So estatly° was he of his governaunce,°   *dignified/management*

With his bargaines, and with his chevissaunce.° *borrowing*

---

3. It was unbecoming to his official post.

4. And gave a certain fee for the license to beg.

5. "In the beginning," the opening line in Genesis and the Gospel of John, popular for devotions.

6. Holidays for settling disputes out of court.

7. His short cloak was made of thick woolen cloth.

8. Middleburgh in the Netherlands and Orwell in Suffolk were major ports for the wool trade.

9. Unit of exchange, a credit instrument for foreign merchants.

285   Forsoothe he was a worthy man withalle;
       But, sooth to sayn, I noot° how men him calle.   *do not know*
          A Clerk ther was of Oxenforde also
       That unto logik hadde longe ygo.
       As lene was his hors as is a rake,
290   And he was nought right fat, I undertake,
       But looked holwe, and therto sobrely.
       Ful thredbare was his overeste courtepy,°   *outer cloak*
       For he hadde geten him yit no benefice,°   *church income*
       Ne was so worldly for to have office.°   *secular employment*
295   For him was levere° have at his beddes heed   *rather*
       Twenty bookes, clad in blak or reed,
       Of Aristotle and his philosophye,
       Than robes riche, or fithele,° or gay sautrye.°   *fiddle / harp*
       But al be that he was a philosophre[1]
300   Yit hadde he but litel gold in cofre;
       But al that he mighte of his freendes hente,°   *get*
       On bookes and on lerning he it spente,
       And bisily gan for the soules praye
       Of hem that yaf him wherwith to scoleye.°   *study*
305   Of studye took he most cure° and most heede.   *care*
       Nought oo° word spak he more than was neede,   *one*
       And that was said in forme° and reverence,   *formally*
       And short and quik, and ful of heigh sentence:°   *lofty meaning*
       Souning in° moral vertu was his speeche,   *consonant with*
310   And gladly wolde he lerne, and gladly teche.
          A Sergeant of the Lawe,[2] war and wis,
       That often hadde been at the Parvis[3]
       Ther was also, ful riche of excellence.
       Discreet he was, and of greet reverence—
315   He seemed swich, his wordes weren so wise.
       Justice he was ful often in assise[4]
       By patente and by plein commissioun.[5]
       For his science° and for his heigh renown   *knowledge*
       Of fees and robes hadde he many oon.
320   So greet a purchasour° was nowher noon;   *buyer of land*
       Al was fee simple[6] to him in effect—
       His purchasing mighte nat been infect.°   *invalidated*
       Nowher so bisy a man as he ther nas;
       And yit he seemed bisier than he was.
325   In termes hadde he caas and doomes° alle   *lawsuits and judgments*
       That from the time of King William[7] were falle.
       Therto he coude endite and make a thing,[8]
       Ther coude no wight° pinchen° at his writing;   *person / find fault with*
       And every statut coude he plein by rote.[9]

---

1. A philosopher could be a scientist or alchemist.
2. A lawyer of the highest rank.
3. The porch of St. Paul's Cathedral, a meeting place for lawyers.
4. He was often judge in the court of assizes (civil court).
5. By letter of appointment from the king and by full jurisdiction.
6. Owned outright with no legal impediments.
7. Since the introduction of Norman law in England under William the Conqueror.
8. Compose and draw up a deed.
9. He knew entirely from memory.

330	He rood but hoomly° in a medlee° cote,	*simply / multicolored*
	Girt with a ceint° of silk, with barres° smale.	*belt / stripes*
	Of his array telle I no lenger tale.	
	A Frankelain[1] was in his compaignye:	
	Whit was his beerd as is the dayesye;°	*daisy*
335	Of his complexion he was sanguin.[2]	
	Wel loved he by the morwe a sop in win.[3]	
	To liven in delit° was evere his wone,°	*pleasure / custom*
	For he was Epicurus owene sone,	
	That heeld opinion that plein° delit	*complete*
340	Was verray felicitee parfit.[4]	
	An housholdere and that a greet was he:	
	Saint Julian[5] he was in his contree.	
	His breed, his ale, was always after oon;°	*just as good*
	A bettre envined° man was nevere noon.	*stocked with wine*
345	Withouten bake mete was nevere his hous,	
	Of fissh and flessh, and that so plentevous°	*plentiful*
	It snewed° in his hous of mete and drinke,	*snowed*
	Of alle daintees that men coude thinke.	
	After the sondry sesons of the yeer	
350	So chaunged he his mete and his soper.[6]	
	Ful many a fat partrich° hadde he in mewe,°	*partridge / cage*
	And many a breem,° and many a luce° in stewe.°	*carp / pike / pond*
	Wo was his cook but if his sauce were	
	Poinant° and sharp, and redy al his gere.	*pungent*
355	His table dormant[7] in his halle alway	
	Stood redy covered al the longe day.	
	At sessions[8] ther was he lord and sire.	
	Ful ofte time he was Knight of the Shire.[9]	
	An anlaas° and a gipser° al of silk	*dagger / purse*
360	Heeng at his girdel, whit as morne milk.	
	A shirreve hadde he been, and countour.[1]	
	Was nowher swich a worthy vavasour.[2]	
	An Haberdasshere° and a Carpenter,	*hat-maker*
	A Webbe, a Dyere, and a Tapicer[3]—	
365	And they were clothed alle in oo liveree°	*in the same uniform*
	Of a solempne and a greet fraternitee.°	*parish guild*
	Ful fresshe and newe hir gere apiked was;[4]	
	Hir knives were chaped° nought with bras,	*mounted*
	But al with silver; wrought ful clene and weel	
370	Hir girdles and hir pouches everydeel.	
	Wel seemed eech of hem a fair burgeis°	*townsperson*
	To sitten in a yeldehalle° on a dais.	*guildhall*

1. A large landholder, freeborn but not belonging to the nobility.
2. In temperament he was sanguine (optimistic, governed by blood as his chief humor).
3. In the morning a sop of bread soaked in wine.
4. True and perfect happiness.
5. Patron saint of hospitality.
6. For health he changed his diet according to the different seasons.
7. Left standing rather than dismantled between meals.
8. Meetings of the justices of the peace.
9. A representative of the district at Parliament.
1. He had been sheriff and auditor of the county finances.
2. Lower member of the feudal elite.
3. A weaver, dyer, and tapestry-maker, all members of the same commercial guild.
4. Their gear was decorated.

	Everich, for the wisdom that he can,°	knows
	Was shaply° for to been an alderman.°	fit/mayor
375	For catel° hadde they ynough and rente,°	property/income
	And eek hir wives wolde it wel assente—	
	And elles certain were they to blame:	
	It is ful fair to been ycleped° "Madame,"	called
	And goon to vigilies⁵ al bifore,	
380	And have a mantel royalliche ybore.	
	A Cook they hadde with hem for the nones,°	for the occasion
	To boile the chiknes with the marybones,°	marrowbones
	And powdre-marchant tart and galingale.°	aromatic spices
	Wel coude he knowe a draughte of London ale.	
385	He coude roste, and seethe,° and broile, and frye,	boil
	Maken mortreux,° and wel bake a pie.	stews
	But greet harm was it, as it thoughte me,	
	That on his shine a mormal° hadde he.	ulcer
	For blankmanger,° that made he with the beste.	thick stew
390	A Shipman was ther, woning° fer by weste—	dwelling
	For ought I woot, he was of Dertemouthe.⁶	
	He rood upon a rouncy° as he couthe,	nag
	In a gowne of falding° to the knee.	coarse brown cloth
	A daggere hanging on a laas° hadde he	strap
395	Aboute his nekke, under his arm adown.	
	The hote somer hadde maad his hewe al brown;	
	And certainly he was a good felawe.	
	Ful many a draughte of win hadde he drawe	
	Fro Burdeuxward, whil that the chapman° sleep⁷:	merchant
400	Of nice° conscience took he no keep;	scrupulous
	If that he faught and hadde the hyer hand,	
	By water he sente hem hoom to every land.	
	But of his craft, to rekene wel his tides,	
	His stremes° and his daungers° him bisides,	currents/hazards
405	His herberwe° and his moone, his lodemenage,°	harboring/navigation
	Ther was noon swich from Hulle to Cartage.⁸	
	Hardy he was and wis to undertake;	
	With many a tempest hadde his beerd been shake;	
	He knew alle the havenes as they were	
410	Fro Gotlond to the Cape of Finistere,⁹	
	And every crike° in Britaine° and in Spaine.	inlet/Brittany
	His barge ycleped was the Maudelaine.	
	With us ther was a Doctour of Physik:°	Medicine
	In al this world ne was ther noon him lik	
415	To speken of physik and of surgerye.	
	For he was grounded in astronomye,°	astrology
	He kepte his pacient a ful greet deel	
	In houres° by his magik naturel.	astronomical hours

5. Feasts held the night before a holy day.
6. Dartmouth, a port on the southwestern coast.
7. On the trip back from Bordeaux while the merchant slept.
8. Hull, on the northeastern coast in Yorkshire; Cartage:

Carthage in North Africa or Cartagena on the Mediterranean coast of Spain.
9. Gotland in the Baltic Sea; Finistere: Land's End in western Spain.

Wel coude he fortunen the ascendent[1]
420 Of his images° for his pacient.   *talismans*
He knew the cause of every maladye,
Were it of hoot or cold or moiste or drye,[2]
And where engendred° and of what humour:[3]   *originated*
He was a verray parfit praktisour.°   *practitioner*
425 The cause yknowe, and of his harm the roote,
Anoon he yaf the sike man his boote.°   *remedy*
     Ful redy hadde he his apothecaries
To senden him drogges and his letuaries,°   *medicines*
For eech of hem made other for to winne:
430 Hir frendshipe was nought newe to biginne.
Wel knew he the olde Esculapius,[4]
And Deiscorides and eek Rufus,
Olde Ipocras, Hali, and Galien,
Serapion, Razis, and Avicen,
435 Averrois, Damascien, and Constantin,
Bernard, and Gatesden, and Gilbertin.
Of his diete mesurable° was he,   *moderate*
For it was of no superfluitee,
But of greet norissing and digestible.
440 His studye was but litel on the Bible.
In sanguin° and in pers° he clad was al,   *red/Persian blue*
Lined with taffata and with sendal;°   *silks*
And yit he was but esy of dispence;°   *thrifty*
He kepte that he wan in pestilence.
445 For gold in physik is a cordial,°   *tonic*
Therfore he loved gold in special.
     A good Wif was ther of biside Bathe,
But she was somdeel deef, and that was scathe.°   *a pity*
Of cloth-making she hadde swich an haunt,°   *practice*
450 She passed hem of Ypres and of Gaunt.[5]
In al the parissh wif ne was ther noon
That to the offring[6] bifore hire sholde goon,
And if ther dide, certain so wroth° was she   *angry*
That she was out of alle charitee.
455 Hir coverchiefs ful fine were of ground[7]—
I dorste swere they weyeden° ten pound   *weighed*
That on a Sonday weren upon hir heed.
Hir hosen° weren of fin scarlet reed,   *stockings*
Ful straite yteyd,° and shoes ful moiste° and newe.   *tightly laced/supple*
460 Bold was hir face and fair and reed of hewe.

1. Calculate the ascendent (propitious moment).
2. The qualities of the four natural elements, corresponding to the humors of the body and the composition of the universe, needed to be kept in perfect balance.
3. Bodily fluids, or "humors," thought to govern moods (blood, phlegm, black bile, yellow bile).
4. The Physician is acquainted with a full range of medical authorities from among the ancient Greeks (Aesculapius, Dioscorides, Rufus, Hippocrates, Galen, and Serapion), the Persians (Hali and Rhazes), the Arabs (Avicenna and Averroes), the Mediterranean transmitters of Eastern science to the West (John of Damascus, Constantine the African), and later medical school professors (Bernard of Gordon, who taught at Montpellier; John of Gaddesden, who taught at Merton College; and Gilbertus Anglicus, an early contemporary of Chaucer's).
5. Centers of Flemish cloth-making.
6. The collection of gifts at the consecration of the Mass.
7. Her linen kerchiefs were fine in texture.

She was a worthy womman al hir live:
Housbondes at chirche dore she hadde five,
Withouten other compaignye in youthe—
But therof needeth nought to speke as nouthe.°   *for now*
465   And thries hadde she been at Jerusalem;
She hadde passed many a straunge streem;
At Rome she hadde been, and at Boloigne,[8]
In Galice at Saint Jame, and at Coloigne:
She coude° muchel of wandring by the waye.   *knew*
470   Gat-toothed° was she, soothly for to saye.   *gap-toothed*
Upon an amblere[9] esily she sat,
Ywimpled[1] wel, and on hir heed an hat
As brood as is a bokeler or a targe,°   *small shields*
A foot-mantel° aboute hir hipes large,   *riding skirt*
475   And on hir feet a paire of spores° sharpe.   *spurs*
In felaweshipe wel coude she laughe and carpe:
Of remedies of love she knew parchaunce,[2]
For she coude of that art the olde daunce.°   *tricks*
    A good man was ther of religioun,
480   And was a poore Person° of a town,   *parson*
But riche he was of holy thought and werk.
He was also a lerned man, a clerk,
That Cristes gospel trewely wolde preche;
His parisshens° devoutly wolde he teche.   *parishioners*
485   Benigne he was, and wonder diligent,
And in adversitee ful pacient,
And swich he was preved ofte sithes.
Ful loth were him to cursen for his tithes,[3]
But rather wolde he yiven, out of doute,
490   Unto his poore parisshens aboute
Of his offring and eek of his substaunce:°   *possessions*
He coude in litel thing have suffisaunce.
Wid was his parissh, and houses fer asonder,
But he ne lafte nought for rain ne thonder,
495   In siknesse nor in meschief, to visite
The ferreste in his parissh, muche and lite,[4]
Upon his feet, and in his hand a staf.
This noble ensample° to his sheep he yaf   *example*
That first he wroughte,° and afterward he taughte.   *did*
500   Out of the Gospel he tho wordes caughte,
And this figure° he added eek therto: *saying*
That if gold ruste, what shal iren do?
For if a preest be foul, on whom we truste,
No wonder is a lewed° man to ruste.   *uneducated*
505   And shame it is, if a preest take keep,°   *is concerned*
A shiten° shepherde and a clene sheep.   *shit-covered*

8. Rome, Boulogne, Santiago Compostela, and Cologne were major European pilgrimage sites.
9. A horse with a gentle pace.
1. Wearing a large headdress that covers all but the face.
2. She knew cures for lovesickness, as it happened.

3. And so was he shown to be many times. / He was most unwilling to curse parishioners (with excommunication) if they failed to pay his tithes (a tenth of their income due to the Church).
4. The furthest away in his parish, great and small.

Wel oughte a preest ensample for to yive
By his clennesse how that his sheep sholde live.
He sette nought his benefice to hire[5]
510 And leet his sheep encombred in the mire
And ran to London, unto Sainte Poules,
To seeken him a chaunterye for soules,
Or with a bretherhede to been withholde,
But dwelte at hoom and kepte wel his folde,
515 So that the wolf ne made it nought miscarye:
He was a shepherde and nought a mercenarye.
And though he holy were and vertuous,
He was to sinful men nought despitous,°   scornful
Ne of his speeche daungerous ne digne,°   haughty
520 But in his teching discreet and benigne,
To drawen folk to hevene by fairnesse
By good ensample—this was his bisinesse.
But it were any persone obstinat,
What so he were, of heigh or lowe estat,
525 Him wolde he snibben° sharply for the nones:°   rebuke/on the spot
A bettre preest I trowe° ther nowher noon is.   believe
He waited after° no pompe and reverence,   expected
Ne maked him a spiced° conscience,   overly critical
But Cristes lore° and his Apostles twelve   teaching
530 He taughte, but first he folwed it himselve.
      With him ther was a Plowman, was his brother,
That hadde ylad of dong ful many a fother.[6]
A trewe swinkere° and a good was he,   worker
Living in pees° and parfit charitee.   peace
535 God loved he best with al his hoole herte
At alle times, though him gamed or smerte,[7]
And thanne his neighebor right as himselve.
He wolde thresshe, and therto dike and delve,°   make ditches and dig
For Cristes sake, for every poore wight,
540 Withouten hire,° if it laye in his might.   pay
His tithes payed he ful faire and wel,
Bothe of his propre swink[8] and his catel.°   possessions
In a tabard°rood upon a mere.°   smock/mare
      Ther was also a Reeve° and a Millere,   estate manager
545 A Somnour, and a Pardoner[9] also,
A Manciple,° and myself—ther were namo.   Steward
      The Millere was a stout carl° for the nones. fellow
Ful big he was of brawn and eek of bones—
That preved wel, for overal ther he cam
550 At wrastling he wolde have alway the ram.[1]
He was short-shuldred, brood, a thikke knarre.°   bully
Ther was no dore that he nolde heve of harre,°   off its hinges

5. The priest did not rent out his parish to another in
order to take a more profitable position saying masses for
the dead at the chantries of St. Paul's in London or to
serve as chaplain to a wealthy guild (bretherhede).
6. That had carried many a cartload of manure.

7. Enjoyed himself or suffered pain.
8. Money earned from his own work.
9. A Summoner, a server of summonses for the ecclesiastical courts; Pardoner: a seller of indulgences.
1. Awarded as a prize for wrestling.

Or breke it at a renning with his heed.
His beerd as any sowe or fox was reed,
555 And therto brood, as though it were a spade;
Upon the cop° right of his nose he hade   *tip*
A werte, and theron stood a tuft of heres,
Rede as the bristles of a sowes eres;
His nosethirles° blake were and wide.   *nostrils*
560 A swerd and a bokeler bar he by his side.
His mouth as greet was as a greet furnais.
He was a janglere and a Goliardais,[2]
And that was most of sinne and harlotries.°   *obscenities*
Wel coude he stelen corn and tollen thries[3]—
565 And yit he hadde a thombe of gold,[4] pardee.
A whit cote and a blew hood wered he.
A baggepipe wel coude he blowe and soune,
And therwithal he broughte us out of towne.
    A gentil Manciple was ther of a temple,°   *law school*
570 Of which achatours° mighte take exemple   *buyers*
For to been wise in bying of vitaile;°   *food*
For wheither that he paide or took by taile,°   *on credit*
Algate he waited so in his achat[5]
That he was ay biforn° and in good stat.°   *ahead/well off*
575 Now is nat that of God a ful fair grace°   *blessing*
That swich a lewed° mannes wit shal pace°   *uneducated/surpass*
The wisdom of an heep of lerned men?
Of maistres hadde he mo than thries ten
That weren of lawe expert and curious,°   *skillful*
580 Of whiche ther were a dozeine in that house
Worthy to been stiwardes of rente° and lond   *managers of revenues*
Of any lord that is in Engelond,
To make him live by his propre good°   *own wealth*
In honour dettelees but if he were wood,°   *unless he were crazy*
585 Or live as scarsly° as him list° desire,   *thriftily/pleases*
And able for to helpen al a shire
In any caas° that mighte falle° or happe,   *event/befall*
And yit this Manciple sette hir aller cappe!°   *made fools of them all*
    The Reeve was a sclendre° colerik° man;   *lean/ill-tempered*
590 His beerd was shave as neigh° as evere he can;   *close*
His heer was by his eres ful round yshorn;
His top was dokked° lik a preest biforn;°   *clipped/in front*
Ful longe were his legges and ful lene,
Ylik a staf, ther was no calf yseene.
595 Wel coude he keepe a gerner° a binne—   *granary*
Ther was noon auditour coude on him winne.[6]
Wel wiste he by the droughte and by the rain
The yeelding of his seed and of his grain.

2. He was a teller of dirty stories and a reveller.
3. Collect three times as much tax as was due.
4. It was proverbial that millers were dishonest and that an honest miller was as rare as one who had a golden thumb. The statement is meant ironically.
5. He was always so watchful for his opportunities to purchase.
6. Gain anything (by catching him out).

His lordes sheep, his neet,° his dayerye,°   *cattle/dairy cattle*
600 His swim, his hors, his stoor,° and his pultrye   *livestock*
Was hoolly in this Reeves governinge,
And by his covenant° yaf the rekeninge,°   *contract/gave account*
Sin that his lord was twenty yeer of age.
Ther coude no man bringe him in arrerage.°   *financial arrears*
605 Ther nas baillif, hierde, nor other hine,[7]
That he ne knew his sleighte° and his covine°—   *tricks/plotting*
They were adrad of him as of the deeth.
His woning° was ful faire upon an heeth;°   *dwelling/meadow*
With greene trees shadwed was his place.
610 He coude bettre than his lord purchace.°   *buy property*
Ful riche he was astored prively.°   *stocked in secret*
His lord wel coude he plesen subtilly,
To yive and lene° him of his owene good,°   *lend/possessions*
And have a thank, and yit a cote and hood.
615 In youthe he hadde lerned a good mister:°   *profession*
He was a wel good wrighte, a carpenter.
This Reeve sat upon a ful good stot°   *stallion*
That was a pomely° grey and highte° Scot.   *dappled/named*
A long surcote° of pers° upon he hade,   *overcoat/blue*
620 And by his side he bar a rusty blade.
Of Northfolk[8] was this Reeve of which I telle,
Biside a town men clepen Baldeswelle.
Tukked[9] he was as is a frere aboute,
And evere he rood the hindreste° of oure route.°   *hindmost/group*
625   A Somnour was ther with us in that place
That hadde a fir-reed° cherubinnes° face,   *fire-red/cherub's*
For saucefleem° he was, with yën narwe,   *pimply*
And hoot he was, and lecherous as a sparwe,°   *sparrow*
With scaled° browes blake and piled[1] beerd: *scabby*
630 Of his visage children were aferd.°   *frightened*
Ther nas quiksilver, litarge, ne brimstoon,
Boras, ceruce, ne oile of tartre noon,[2]
Ne oinement that wolde clense and bite,
That him mighte helpen of his whelkes° white,   *blotches*
635 Nor of the knobbes° sitting on his cheekes.   *lumps*
Wel loved he garlek, oinons, and eek leekes,
And for to drinke strong win reed as blood.
Thanne wolde he speke and crye as he were wood;°   *crazy*
And whan that he wel dronken hadde the win,
640 Thanne wolde he speke no word but Latin:
A fewe termes hadde he, two or three,
That he hadde lerned out of som decree;
No wonder is—he herde it al the day,

---

7. There was no foreman, herdsman, or other farm-hand.
8. Norfolk in the north of England. The Reeve is notable for his northern dialect and regionalisms.
9. He wore his clothes tucked up with a cinch as friars did.

1. With hair falling out.
2. There was not mercury, lead ointment, or sulphur, / Borax, white lead, nor any oil of tartar that could clean him.

And eek ye knowe wel how that a jay°   *parrot*
645   Can clepen "Watte"° as wel as can the Pope—   *call "Walter"*
But whoso coude in other thing him grope,°   *examine*
Thanne hadde he spent all his philosophye;
Ay *Questio quid juris*[3] wolde he crye.
        He was a gentil harlot° and a kinde;   *rascal*
650   A bettre felawe sholde men nought finde:
He wolde suffre,° for a quart of win,   *allow*
A good felawe to have his concubin°   *mistress*
A twelfmonth, and excusen him at the fulle;
Ful prively a finch eek coude he pulle.[4]
655   And if he foond owher° a good felawe   *anywhere*
He wolde techen him to have noon awe
In swich caas of the Ercedekenes curs,[5]
But if a mannes soule were in his purs,°   *wallet*
For in his purs he sholde ypunisshed be.
660   "Purs is the Ercedekenes helle," saide he.
        But wel I woot he lied right in deede:
Of cursing° oughte eech gilty man him drede,°   *excommunication/fear*
For curs wol slee right as assoiling° savith—   *absolving*
And also war him of a *significavit*.[6]
665   In daunger hadde he at his owene gise[7]
The yonge girles of the diocise,
And knew hir conseil,° and was al hir reed.°   *secrets/advice*
A gerland hadde he set upon his heed
As greet as it were for an ale-stake;°   *tavern sign*
670   A bokeler hadde he maad him of a cake.°   *loaf of bread*
        With him ther rood a gentil Pardoner
Of Rouncival,[8] his freend and his compeer,°   *companion*
That straight was comen fro the Court of Rome.
Ful loude he soong, "Com hider, love, to me."[9]
675   This Somnour bar to him a stif burdoun:°   *a strong baritone*
Was nevere trompe° of half so greet a soun.   *trumpet*
        This Pardoner hadde heer as yelow as wex,
But smoothe it heeng as dooth a strike of flex;°   *clump of flax*
By ounces° heenge his lokkes that he hadde,   *thin strands*
680   And therwith he his shuldres overspradde,
But thinne it lay, by colpons,° oon by oon;   *strands*
But hood for jolitee° wered he noon,   *fanciness*
For it was trussed up in his walet:°   *pack*
Him thoughte he rood al of the newe jet.°   *fashion*
685   Dischevelee° save his cappe he rood al bare.   *loose-haired*
Swiche glaring yën hadde he as an hare.
A vernicle[1] hadde he sowed upon his cappe,
His walet biforn him in his lappe,

---

3. "The question as to what point of law (applies)"; often
used in ecclesiastical courts.
4. And secretly he also knew how to fool around.
5. In case of excommunication by the archdeacon.
6. Order of transfer from ecclesiastical to secular courts.

7. Under his control he had at his disposal.
8. A hospital at Charing Cross in London.
9. A popular ballad.
1. A pilgrim badge, reproducing St. Veronica's veil bearing the imprint of Christ's face.

	Bretful of pardon,[2] comen from Rome al hoot.	
690	A vois he hadde as smal° as hath a goot;°	*high-pitched/goat*
	No beerd hadde he, ne nevere sholde have;	
	As smoothe it was as it were late yshave:	
	I trowe he were a gelding or a mare.[3]	
	But of his craft,° fro Berwik into Ware,[4]	*skill*
695	Ne was ther swich another pardoner;	
	For in his male° he hadde a pilwe-beer°	*bag/pillowcase*
	Which that he saide was Oure Lady veil;	
	He saide he hadde a gobet° of the sail	*chunk*
	That Sainte Peter hadde whan that he wente	
700	Upon the see, til Jesu Crist him hente.°	*grabbed*
	He hadde a crois of laton,° ful of stones,	*brass cross*
	And in a glas he hadde pigges bones,	
	But with thise relikes whan that he foond	
	A poore person° dwelling upon lond,	*parson*
705	Upon a day he gat him more moneye	
	Than that the person gat in monthes twaye;	
	And thus with feined flaterye and japes°	*tricks*
	He made the person and the peple his apes.°	*dupes*
	But trewely to tellen at the laste,	
710	He was in chirche a noble ecclesiaste;	
	Wel coude he rede a lesson and a storye,°	*liturgical texts*
	But alderbest° he soong an offertorye,	*best of all*
	For wel he wiste whan that song was songe,	
	He moste preche and wel affile° his tonge	*sharpen*
715	To winne silver, as he ful wel coude—	
	Therfore he soong the merierly and loude.	
	Now have I told you soothly in a clause°	*briefly*
	Th'estaat, th'array, the nombre, and eek the cause	
	Why that assembled was this compaignye	
720	In Southwerk at this gentil hostelrye	
	That highte the Tabard, faste by the Belle;[5]	
	But now is time to you for to telle	
	How that we baren us that ilke° night	*same*
	Whan we were in that hostelrye alight;	
725	And after wol I telle of oure viage,°	*trip*
	And al the remenant of oure pilgrimage.	
	But first I praye you of youre curteisye	
	That ye n'arette° it nought my vilainye°	*consider/rudeness*
	Though that I plainly speke in this matere	
730	To telle you hir wordes and hir cheere,°	*comportment*
	Ne though I speke hir wordes proprely;°	*accurately*
	For this ye knowen also wel as I:	
	Who so shal telle a tale after a man	
	He moot reherce,° as neigh as evere he can,	*must repeat*

---

2. Full to the brim with indulgences.
3. I believe he was a gelding (eunuch) or a mare (perhaps a passive homosexual).
4. Towns north and south of London.
5. Another tavern in Southwark.

735   Everich a word, if it be in his charge,
       Al speke he nevere so rudeliche° and large,°   crudely/freely
       Or elles he moot telle his tale untrewe,
       Or feine° thing, or finde wordes newe;   invent, falsify
       He may nought spare although he were his brother:
740   He moot as wel saye oo word as another.
       Crist spak himself ful brode° in Holy Writ,   plainly
       And wel ye woot no vilainye is it;
       Eek Plato saith, who so can him rede,
       The wordes mote be cosin° to the deede.   closely related
745   Also I praye you to foryive it me
       Al° have I nat set folk in hir degree°   although/rank
       Here in this tale as that they sholde stonde:
       My wit is short, ye may wel understonde.
           Greet cheere made oure Host us everichoon,
750   And to the soper sette he us anoon.
       He served us with vitaile at the beste.
       Strong was the win, and wel to drinke us leste.°   it pleased
       A semely man oure Hoste was withalle
       For to been a marchal° in an halle;   master of ceremonies
755   A large man he was, with yën steepe;
       A fairer burgeis was ther noon in Chepe°—   Cheapside (in London)
       Bold of his speeche, and wis, and wel ytaught,
       And of manhood him lakkede right naught.
       Eek therto he was right a merye man,
760   And after soper playen he bigan,
       And spak of mirthe amonges othere thinges—
       Whan that we hadde maad oure rekeninges°—   paid the bill
       And saide thus, "Now, lordinges, trewely,
       Ye been to me right welcome, hertely.
765   For by my trouthe, if that I shal nat lie,
       I sawgh nat this yeer so merye a compaignye
       At ones in this herberwe° as is now.   inn
       Fain wolde I doon you mirthe, wiste I how.
       And of a mirthe I am right now bithought,
770   To doon you ese, and it shal coste nought.
           Ye goon to Canterbury—God you speede;
       The blisful martyr quite° you youre meede.°   repay/reward
       And wel I woot as ye goon by the waye
       Ye shapen° you to talen° and to playe,   intend/tell tales
775   For trewely, confort ne mirthe is noon
       To ride by the waye domb as stoon;
       And therfore wol I maken you disport
       As I saide erst,° and doon you som confort;   before
       And if you liketh alle, by oon assent,
780   For to stonden at my juggement,
       And for to werken as I shal you saye,
       Tomorwe whan ye riden by the waye—
       Now by my fader soule that is deed,
       But° ye be merye I wol yive you myn heed!   unless
785   Holde up youre handes withouten more speeche."

Oure conseil was nat longe for to seeche;°   seek
Us thoughte it was nat worth to make it wis,°   deliberate
And graunted him withouten more avis,°   opinions
And bade him saye his voirdit° as him leste.   verdict

790   "Lordinges," quod he, "now herkneth for the beste;
But taketh it nought, I praye you, in desdain.
This is the point, to speken short and plain,
That eech of you, to shorte with oure waye
In this viage, shal tellen tales twaye°—   two

795   To Canterburyward, I mene it so,
And hoomward he shal tellen othere two,
Of aventures that whilom° have bifalle;   long ago
And which of you that bereth him best of alle—
That is to sayn, that telleth in this cas

800   Tales of best sentence° and most solas°—   substance / pleasure
Shal have a soper at oure aller cost,
Here in this place, sitting by this post,
Whan that we come again fro Canterbury.
And for to make you the more mury

805   I wol myself goodly° with you ride—   gladly
Right at myn owene cost—and be youre gide.
And who so wol my juggement withsaye°   contradict
Shal paye al that we spende by the waye.
And if ye vouche sauf° that it be so,   grant

810   Telle me anoon, withouten wordes mo,
And I wol erly shape° me therfore."   prepare
This thing was graunted and oure othes swore
With ful glad herte, and prayden him also
That he wolde vouche sauf for to do so,

815   And that he wolde been oure governour,
And of oure tales juge° and reportour,°   judge / recordkeeper
And sette a soper at a certain pris,°   price
And we wol ruled been at his devis,°   plan
In heigh and lowe; and thus by oon assent

820   We been accorded to his juggement.
And therupon the win was fet° anoon;   fetched
We dronken and to reste wente eechoon
Withouten any lenger taryinge.
Amorwe° whan that day bigan to springe   next morning

825   Up roos oure Host and was oure aller cok,°   cock, wake-up call
And gadred us togidres in a flok,
And forth we riden, a litel more than pas,°   slow walk
Unto the watering of Saint Thomas;[6]
And ther oure Host bigan his hors arreste,°   stop

830   And saide, "Lordes, herkneth if you leste:
"Ye woot youre forward° and it you recorde:°   agreement / remember
If evensong and morwesong accorde,
Lat see now who shal telle the firste tale.
As evere mote I drinken win or ale,

6. A brook two miles from London.

835   Who so be rebel to my juggement
       Shal paye for al that by the way is spent.
       Now draweth cut° er that we ferrer twinne:°   *lots/separate furthur*
       He which that hath the shorteste shal biginne.
          "Sire Knight," quod he, "my maister and my lord,
840   Now draweth cut, for that is myn accord.°   *wish*
       Cometh neer," quod he, "my lady Prioresse,
       And ye, sire Clerk, lat be youre shamefastnesse°—   *modesty*
       Ne studieth nought. Lay hand to, every man!"
          Anoon to drawen every wight bigan,
845   And shortly for to tellen as it was,
       Were it by aventure, or sort, or cas,°   *luck, fate or chance*
       The soothe is this, the cut fil° to the Knight;   *fell*
       Of which ful blithe° and glad was every wight,   *happy*
       And telle he moste his tale, as was resoun,
850   By forward and by composicioun,°   *agreement*
       As ye han herd. What needeth wordes mo?
       And whan this goode man sawgh that it was so,
       As he that wis was and obedient
       To keepe his forward by his free assent,
855   He saide, "Sin I shal biginne the game,
       What, welcome be the cut, in Goddes name!
       Now lat us ride, and herkneth what I saye."
       And with that word we riden forth oure waye,
       And he bigan with right a merye cheere°   *expression*
860   His tale anoon, and saide as ye may heere.

The Miller's Tale

The Miller's Tale both answers and parodies *The Knight's Tale*, a long aristocratic romance about two knights in rivalry for the hand of a lady. While the Miller tells a neatly analogous story of erotic competition, his tale is radically shorter and explicitly sexual. Such brevity and physicality fit his tale's genre—a fabliau, or short comic tale, usually bawdy and often involving a clerk, a wife, and a cuckolded husband. Following the convention (if not the reality) that romances were written by and for the nobility and fabliaux by and for the commons, Chaucer suits *The Miller's Tale* to its teller as aptly as he does the Knight's. Slyly disclaiming responsibility for the tale, he explains its bawdiness by the Miller's class status: "the Millere is a cherle" and like his peer the Reeve who follows and "requites" him, tells "harlotrye."

The drunken Miller's insistence on telling his tale to requite the Knight's tale has been called a "literary peasants' revolt." Although the Miller, a free man, was not actually a peasant, yeomen of his status were active in the Rising of 1381, and millers in particular played a symbolic role in it. In fact, this tale is highly literate, with its echoes of the Song of Songs and its parody of the language of courtly love: an actual miller would have had neither the education nor the social sophistication to tell it. Yet a parody implies some degree of attachment to the very model being ridiculed, and *The Miller's Tale* is as much as claim upon the Knight's world as a repudiation of it. The Miller wants to "quiten" the Knight's tale, he says, using a word that can mean to repay or avenge, but also to fulfill. The tale's several plots converge brilliantly upon a single cry: "Water!" The tale's impact derives as well from its plenitude of pleasures (sexual, comic, even religious) after the austere and rigid desires of *The Knight's Tale*.

The Miller's Tale
The Introduction

Whan that the Knight hadde thus his tale ytold,
In al the route° nas ther yong ne old   *group*
That he ne saide it was a noble storye,
And worthy for to drawen° to memorye,   *recall*
5   And namely the gentils° everichoon.   *upper class*
Oure Hoste lough° and swoor, "So mote I goon,[1]   *laughed*
This gooth aright: unbokeled is the male.[2]
Lat see now who shal telle another tale.
For trewely the game is wel bigonne.
10   Now telleth ye, sire Monk, if that ye conne,°   *know*
Somwhat to quite° with the Knightes tale."   *repay*
The Millere, that for dronken was al pale,
So that unnethe° upon his hors he sat,   *barely*
He nolde avalen° neither hood ne hat,   *remove*
15   Ne abiden no man for his curteisye,
But in Pilates[3] vois he gan to crye,
And swoor, "By armes and by blood and bones,°   *(of Christ)*
I can° a noble tale for the nones,   *know*
With which I wol now quite the Knightes tale."
20   Oure Hoste sawgh that he was dronke of ale,
And saide, "Abide,° Robin, leve° brother,   *wait/dear*
Som bettre man shal telle us first another.
Abide, and lat us werken thriftily."°   *properly*
"By Goddes soule," quod he, "that wol nat I,
25   For I wol speke or elles go my way."
Oure Host answerde, "Tel on, a devele way!°   *in the devil's name*
Thou art a fool; thy wit is overcome."
"Now herkneth," quod the Millere, "alle and some.°   *one and all*
But first I make a protestacioun
30   That I am dronke: I knowe it by my soun.°   *sound*
And therfore if that I mis speke or saye,
Wite it° the ale of Southwerk, I you praye;   *blame it on*
For I wol telle a legende and a lif[4]
Bothe of a carpenter and of his wif,
35   How that a clerk hath set the wrightes cappe."[5]
The Reeve answerde and saide, "Stint thy clappe!°   *hold your tongue*
Lat be thy lewed° dronken harlotrye.°   *unlearned/obscenity*
It is a sinne and eek a greet folye
To apairen° any man or him defame,   *injure*
40   And eek to bringen wives in swich fame.
Thou maist ynough of othere thinges sayn."
This dronken Millere spak ful soone again,
And saide, "Leve brother Osewold,
Who hath no wif, he is no cokewold.°   *cuckold*

---

1. Thus I may proceed.
2. The bag is opened (i.e., the games are begun).
3. The role of Pilate was traditionally played in a loud

and raucous voice in the mystery plays.
4. The story of a saint's life.
5. Made a fool of the carpenter.

45   But I saye nat therfore that thou art oon.
     Ther ben ful goode wives many oon,
     And evere a thousand goode ayains oon badde.
     That knowestou wel thyself but if thou madde.°   *go insane*
     Why artou angry with my tale now?
50   I have a wif, pardee,° as wel as thou,   *by God*
     Yet nolde I, for the oxen in my plough,[6]
     Take upon me more than ynough
     As deemen° of myself that I were oon:°   *judge / one (a cuckold)*
     I wol bileve wel that I am noon.
55   An housbonde shal nought been inquisitif
     Of Goddes privetee,° nor of his wif.   *secrets*
     So he may finde Goddes foison° there,   *plenty*
     Of the remenant needeth nought enquere."
          What sholde I more sayn but this Millere
60   He nolde his wordes for no man forbere,
     But tolde his cherles° tale in his manere.   *commoner's*
     M'athinketh° that I shal reherce° it here,   *I regret / repeat*
     And therfore every gentil wight I praye,
     Deemeth nought, for Goddes love, that I saye
65   Of yvel entente, but for° I moot reherse   *because*
     Hir tales alle, be they bet or werse,
     Or elles falsen som of my matere.
     And therfore, whoso list it nought yheere
     Turne over the leef,° and chese° another tale,   *page / choose*
70   For he shal finde ynowe,° grete and smale,   *enough*
     Of storial° thing that toucheth gentilesse,° *historical / nobility*
     And eek moralitee and holinesse:
     Blameth nought me if that ye chese amis.
     The Millere is a cherl, ye knowe wel this,
75   So was the Reeve eek, and othere mo,
     And harlotrye they tolden bothe two.
     Aviseth you,° and putte me out of blame: *be warned*
     And eek men shal nought maken ernest of game.° *treat jokes seriously*

The Tale

     Whilom° ther was dwelling at Oxenforde   *long ago*
80   A riche gnof° that gestes heeld to boorde,° *fool / took in boarders*
     And of his craft he was a carpenter.
     With him ther was dwelling a poore scoler,
     Hadde lerned art,[7] but al his fantasye°   *fancy*
     Was turned for to lere° astrologye,   *learn*
85   And coude a certain of conclusiouns,°   *predictions*
     To deemen by interrogaciouns,[8]
     If that men axed° him in certain houres   *asked*
     Whan that men sholde have droughte or elles showres,
     Or if men axed him what shal bifalle

6. Yet I wouldn't, not even (in wager) for the oxen in my plough.

7. The arts curriculum (trivium).
8. To estimate by consulting (the stars).

90   Of every thing—I may nat rekene hem alle.

This clerk was cleped° hende[9] Nicholas.   *called*

Of derne° love he coude, and of solas,[1]   *secret*

And therto he was sly and ful privee,°   *secretive*

And lik a maide meeke for to see.

95   A chambre hadde he in that hostelrye°   *inn*

Allone, withouten any compaignye,

Ful fetisly ydight with herbes swoote,[2]

And he himself as sweete as is the roote

Of licoris or any setewale.[3]

100   His Almageste[4] and bookes grete and smale,

His astrelabye,[5] longing for° his art,   *belonging to*

His augrim stones,° layen faire apart   *abacus beads*

On shelves couched° at his beddes heed;   *arranged*

His presse° ycovered with a falding° reed;   *dresser/coarse cloth*

105   And al above ther lay a gay sautrye,°   *harp*

On which he made a-nightes melodye

So swetely that al the chambre roong,

And *Angelus ad Virginem*[6] he soong,

And after that he soong the *Kinges Note*:[7]

110   Ful often blessed was his merye throte.

And thus this sweete clerk his time spente

After his freendes finding and his rente.[8]

    This carpenter hadde wedded newe a wif

Which that he loved more than his lif.

115   Of eighteteene yeer she was of age;

Jalous he was, and heeld hire narwe in cage,

For she was wilde and yong, and he was old,

And deemed himself been lik a cokewold.

He knew nat Caton,[9] for his wit was rude,

120   That bad men sholde wedde his similitude:°   *equal in age*

Men sholde wedden after hir estat,°   *station in life*

For youthe and elde is often at debat.

But sith that he was fallen in the snare,

He moste endure, as other folk, his care.

125   Fair was this yonge wif, and therwithal

As any wesele hir body gent and smal.[1]

A ceint° she wered, barred° al of silk;   *belt/striped*

A barmcloth° as whit as morne milk   *apron*

Upon hir lendes,° ful of many a gore;°   *loins/flounce*

130   Whit was hir smok,° and broiden° al bifore   *slip/embroidered*

And eek bihinde, on hir coler aboute,°   *around her collar*

Of col-blak silk, withinne and eek withoute;

The tapes° of hir white voluper°   *ribbons/cap*

---

9. Handsome, courteous, handy.

1. Pleasure, (sexual) comforts.

2. Elegantly decked out with sweet herbs.

3. Setwall, a gingerlike spice used as a stimulant.

4. An astrological treatise by Ptolemy.

5. Astrolabe, an astrological instrument.

6. A prayer commemorating the Annunciation.

7. A popular song.

8. According to what his friends gave him and his income.

9. Cato, Latin author of a book of maxims used in elementary education.

1. Her body as delicate and slender as any weasel.

	Were of the same suite° of hir coler;	*pattern*
135	Hir filet° brood° of silk and set ful hye;	*headband/broad*
	And sikerly she hadde a likerous yë;[2]	
	Ful smale ypulled° were hir browes two,	*plucked*
	And tho were bent, and blake as any slo.°	*plum*
	She was ful more blisful on to see	
140	Than is the newe perejonette° tree,	*pear*
	And softer than the wolle is of a wether;°	*ram*
	And by hir girdel° heeng a purs of lether,	*belt*
	Tasseled with silk and perled° with latoun.°	*decorated/brass*
	In al this world, to seeken up and down,	
145	Ther nis no man so wis that coude thenche°	*imagine*
	So gay a popelote° or swich a wenche.[3]	*doll*
	Ful brighter was the shining of hir hewe	
	Than in the Towr the noble° yforged newe.[4]	*gold coin*
	But of hir song, it was as loud and yerne°	*lively*
150	As any swalwe sitting on a berne.	
	Therto she coude skippe and make game	
	As any kide or calf folwing his dame.°	*mother*
	Hir mouth was sweete as bragot or the meeth,°	*honey drinks*
	Or hoord of apples laid in hay or heeth.°	*heather*
155	Winsing° she was as is a joly° colt,	*skittish/spirited*
	Long as a mast, and upright° as a bolt.°	*strait/arrow*
	A brooch she bar upon hir lowe coler	
	As brood as is the boos° of a bokeler;°	*boss/shield*
	Hir shoes were laced on hir legges hye.	
160	She was a primerole,° a piggesnye,[5]	*primrose*
	For any lord to leggen in his bedde,	
	Or yet for any good yeman to wedde.	
	Now sire, and eft° sire, so bifel the cas	*again*
	That on a day this hende Nicholas	
165	Fil with this yonge wif to rage° and playe,	*sport*
	Whil that hir housbonde was at Oseneye°	*Osney, near Oxford*
	(As clerkes been ful subtil and ful quainte),°	*clever*
	And prively he caughte hire by the queinte,[6]	
	And saide, "Ywis,° but if ich have my wille,	*certainly*
170	For derne° love of thee, lemman,° I spille,"°	*secret/sweetheart/die*
	And heeld hire harde by the haunche-bones,	
	And saide, "Lemman, love me al atones,°	*at once*
	Or I wol dien, also° God me save."	*so*
	And she sproong as a colt dooth in a trave,[7]	
175	And with hir heed she wried° faste away;	*twisted*
	She saide, "I wol nat kisse thee, by my fay.°	*faith*
	Why, lat be," quod she, "lat be, Nicholas!	
	Or I wol crye "Out, harrow, and allas!'	
	Do way youre handes, for your curteisye!"	

---

2. And certainly she had a wanton eye.
3. Woman of the working class.
4. Than the new-forged gold coin in the Tower (of London, the royal mint).

5. Pig's eye, a flower.
6. Literally "dainty part," slang for the female genitals.
7. A restraint for horses when they are being shod.

180	This Nicholas gan mercy for to crye,	
	And spak so faire, and profred him° so faste,	*pressed his case*
	That she hir love him graunted atte laste,	
	And swoor hir ooth by Saint Thomas of Kent	
	That she wolde been at his comandement,	
185	Whan that she may hir leiser° wel espye.	*opportunity*
	"Myn housbonde is so ful of jalousye	
	That but ye waite wel and been privee,⁸	
	I woot right wel I nam but deed," quod she.	
	"Ye moste been ful derne as in this cas."	
190	"Nay, therof care thee nought," quod Nicholas.	
	"A clerk hadde litherly biset his while,°	*wasted his time*
	But if he coude a carpenter bigile."	
	And thus they been accorded and ysworn	
	To waite a time, as I have told biforn.	
195	Whan Nicholas hadde doon this everydeel,	
	And thakked° hire upon the lendes° weel,	*patted/loins*
	He kiste hire sweete, and taketh his sautrye,	
	And playeth faste, and maketh melodye.	
	Thanne fil it thus, that to the parissh chirche,	
200	Cristes owene werkes for to wirche,	
	This goode wif wente on an haliday:°	*holy day*
	Hir forheed shoon as bright as any day,	
	So was it wasshen whan she leet° hir werk.	*left off*
	Now was ther of that chirche a parissh clerk,	
205	The which that was ycleped° Absolon:	*called*
	Crul° was his heer, and as the gold it shoon,	*curly*
	And strouted as a fanne⁹ large and brode;	
	Ful straight and evene lay his joly shode.°	*part in his hair*
	His rode° was reed, his y'n greye as goos.	*complexion*
210	With Poules window¹ corven° on his shoos,	*carved*
	In hoses rede he wente fetisly.°	*elegantly*
	Yclad he was ful smale° and proprely,	*fine*
	Al in a kirtel° of a light waget°—	*tunic/blue*
	Ful faire and thikke been the pointes° set—	*laces*
215	And therupon he hadde a gay surplis,°	*clerical robe*
	As whit as is the blosme upon the ris.°	*twig*
	A merye child° he was, so God me save.	*lad*
	Wel coude he laten blood,² and clippe,° and shave,	*cut hair*
	And maken a chartre of land, or acquitaunce;°	*legal release*
220	In twenty manere coude he trippe and daunce	
	After the scole of Oxenforde tho,	
	And with his legges casten to and fro,	
	And playen songes on a smal rubible;°	*fiddle*
	Therto he soong somtime a loud quinible,°	*high treble*
225	And as wel coude he playe on a giterne:°	*guitar*
	In al the town nas brewhous ne taverne	

---

8. That unless you're very cautious and discreet.
9. And spread out like a winnowing fan (for separating wheat from chaff).

1. The windows of St. Paul's Chapel were intricately patterned.
2. Let blood (a medical treatment performed by barbers).

That he ne visited with his solas,[3]
Ther any gailard tappestere° was.   *saucy barmaid*
But sooth to sayn, he was somdeel squaimous°   *somewhat squeamish*
230   Of farting, and of speeche daungerous.°   *haughty*
      This Absolon, that joly was and gay,
Gooth with a cencer° on the haliday,   *incense bowl*
Cencing the wives of the parissh faste,
And many a lovely look on hem he caste,
235   And namely on this carpenteres wif:
To looke on hire him thoughte a merye lif.
She was so propre and sweete and likerous,
I dar wel sayn, if she hadde been a mous,
And he a cat, he wolde hire hente° anoon.   *catch*
240   This parissh clerk, this joly Absolon,
Hath in his herte swich a love-longinge
That of no wif ne took he noon offringe—
For curteisye he saide he wolde noon.
The moone, whan it was night, ful brighte shoon,
245   And Absolon his giterne hath ytake—
For paramours he thoughte for to wake—[4]
And forth he gooth, jolif° and amorous,   *pretty*
Til he cam to the carpenteres hous,
A litel after cokkes hadde ycrowe,
250   And dressed° him up by a shot-windowe°   *placed/hinged window*
That was upon the carpenteres wal.
He singeth in his vois gentil and smal,°   *high*
"Now dere lady, if thy wille be,
I praye you that ye wol rewe° on me,"   *take pity*
255   Ful wel accordant° to his giterninge.   *harmonizing*
This carpenter awook and herde him singe,
And spak unto his wif, and saide anoon,
"What, Alison, heerestou nought Absolon
That chaunteth thus under oure bowres° wal?"   *bedroom's*
260   And she answerde hir housbonde therwithal,
"Yis, God woot, John, I heere it everydeel."°   *every bit*
      This passeth forth. What wol ye bet than weel?[5]
Fro day to day this joly Absolon
So woweth° hire that him is wo-bigoon: *woos*
265   He waketh al the night and al the day;
He kembed° his lokkes brode° and made him gay;   *combed/wide-spreading*
He woweth hire by menes and brocage,[6]
And swoor he wolde been hir owene page;°   *attendant*
He singeth, brokking° as a nightingale;   *trilling*
270   He sente hire piment,° meeth,° and spiced ale, *spiced wine/mead*
And wafres° piping hoot out of the gleede;°   *pastries/coals*
And for she was of towne, he profred meede°—   *bribes*
For som folk wol be wonnen for richesse,
And som for strokes,° and som for gentilesse.   *by force*

3. Entertainment (also with sexual connotations).
4. For the sake of love he thought to keep a vigil.
5. What more would you want?
6. He woos her with go-betweens and mediation.

275	Somtime to shewe his lightnesse° and maistrye,°	*agility/skill*
	He playeth Herodes[7] upon a scaffold° hye.	*platform*
	But what availeth him as in this cas?	
	She loveth so this hende Nicholas	
	That Absolon may blowe the bukkes horn;[8]	
280	He ne hadde for his labour but a scorn.	
	And thus she maketh Absolon hir ape,°	*fool*
	And al his ernest turneth til a jape.°	*joke*
	Ful sooth is this proverbe, it is no lie;	
	Men saith right thus: "Alway the nye slye°	*sly one nearby*
285	Maketh the ferre leve to be loth."[9]	
	For though that Absolon be wood° or wroth,	*crazy*
	By cause that he fer was from hir sighte,	
	This nye Nicholas stood in his lighte.°	*in the way*
	Now beer thee wel, thou hende Nicholas,	
290	For Absolon may waile and singe allas.	
	And so bifel it on a Saterday	
	This carpenter was goon til Oseney,	
	And hende Nicholas and Alisoun	
	Accorded been to this conclusioun,	
295	That Nicholas shal shapen hem a wile°	*devise them a trick*
	This sely° jalous housbonde to bigile,	*innocent*
	And if so be this game wente aright,	
	She sholden sleepen in his arm al night—	
	For this was his desir and hire also.	
300	And right anoon, withouten wordes mo,	
	This Nicholas no lenger wolde tarye,	
	But dooth ful softe unto his chambre carye	
	Bothe mete and drinke for a day or twaye,	
	And to hir housbonde bad hire for to saye,	
305	If that he axed after Nicholas,	
	She sholde saye she niste° wher he was—	*did not know*
	Of al that day she sawgh him nought with yë:	
	She trowed° that he was in maladye,	*believed*
	For for no cry hir maide coude him calle,	
310	He nolde answere for no thing that mighte falle.°	*happen*
	This passeth forth al thilke Saterday	
	That Nicholas stille in his chambre lay,	
	And eet, and sleep, or dide what him leste,°	*he liked*
	Til Sonday that the sonne gooth to reste.	
315	This sely carpenter hath greet mervaile	
	Of Nicholas, or what thing mighte him aile,	
	And saide, "I am adrad,° by Saint Thomas,	*afraid*
	It stondeth nat aright with Nicholas.	
	God shilde° that he deide sodeinly!	*forbid*
320	This world is now ful tikel,° sikerly:	*changeable*
	I sawgh today a corps yborn to chirche	
	That now a Monday last I sawgh him wirche.°	*working*

---

7. In the English mystery plays, Herod was often portrayed as a bully.

8. Undertake a useless endeavor.

9. Makes the distant beloved seem hateful.

Go up," quod he unto his knave° anoon,   *manservant*
"Clepe° at his dore or knokke with a stoon.   *call*
325   Looke how it is and tel me boldely."
          This knave gooth him up ful sturdily,
And at the chambre dore whil that he stood
He cride and knokked as that he were wood,
"What? How? What do ye, maister Nicholay?
330   How may ye sleepen al the longe day?".
But al for nought: he herde nat a word.
An hole he foond ful lowe upon a boord,
Ther as the cat was wont in for to creepe,
And at that hole he looked in ful deepe,
335   And atte laste he hadde of him a sighte.
          This Nicholas sat evere caping° uprighte   *staring*
As he hadde kiked° on the newe moone.   *gazed*
Adown he gooth and tolde his maister soone
In what array° he saw this ilke man.   *condition*
340   This carpenter to blessen him[1] bigan,
And saide, "Help us, Sainte Frideswide![2]
A man woot litel what him shal bitide.
This man is falle, with his astromye,
In som woodnesse or in som agonye.°   *fit*
345   I thoughte ay wel how that it sholde be:
Men sholde nought knowe of Goddes privetee.
Ye, blessed be alway a lewed° man   *unlearned*
That nought but only his bileve can.°   *knows his creed*
So ferde° another clerk with astromye: *fared*
350   He walked in the feeldes for to prye°   *gaze*
Upon the sterres, what ther sholde bifalle,
Til he was in a marle-pit° yfalle—   *clay-pit*
He saw nat that. But yet, by Saint Thomas,
Me reweth sore° for hende Nicholas.   *feel sorry*
355   He shal be rated° of his studying,   *scolded*
If that I may, by Jesus, hevene king!
Get me a staf that I may underspore,°   *pry upward*
Whil that thou, Robin, hevest up the dore.
He shal out of his studying, as I gesse."
360   And to the chambre dore he gan him dresse.°   *placed himself*
His knave was a strong carl° for the nones,°   *fellow/purpose*
And by the haspe° he haaf° it up atones: *hinge/heaved*
Into the floor the dore fil anoon.
This Nicholas sat ay as stille as stoon,
365   And evere caped up into the air.
This carpenter wende° he were in despair,   *thought*
And hente° him by the shuldres mightily,   *grabbed*
And shook him harde, and cride spitously,°   *vigorously*
"What, Nicholay, what, how! What! Looke adown!
370   Awaak and thenk on Cristes passioun![3]

---

1. Bless himself (with the sign of the cross).   3. Thinking about Christ's death and resurrection was
2. A saint venerated for her healing powers.   supposed to ward off evil spells.

I crouche° thee from elves and fro wightes."°   *bless/evil spirits*
Therwith the nightspel° saide he anoonrightes   *charm*
On foure halves° of the hous aboute,   *sides*
And on the threshfold on the dore withoute:
375 "Jesu Crist and Sainte Benedight,[4]
Blesse this hous from every wikked wight!
For nightes nerye° the White Pater Noster.[5]   *protect*
Where wentestou, thou Sainte Petres soster?"°   *sister*
And at the laste this hende Nicholas
380 Gan for to sike° sore, and saide, "Allas,   *sigh*
Shal al the world be lost eftsoones° now?"   *immediately*
 This carpenter answerde, "What saistou?
What, thenk on God as we doon, men that swinke."°   *work*
 This Nicholas answerde, "Fecche me drinke,
385 And after wol I speke in privetee
Of certain thing that toucheth me and thee.
I wol telle it noon other man, certain."
 This carpenter gooth down and comth again,
And broughte of mighty ale a large quart,
390 And whan that eech of hem hadde dronke his part,
This Nicholas his dore faste shette,°   *shut*
And down the carpenter by him he sette,
And saide, "John, myn hoste lief° and dere,   *beloved*
Thou shalt upon thy trouthe° swere me here   *word of honor*
395 That to no wight thou shalt this conseil° wraye;°   *advice/disclose*
For it is Cristes conseil that I saye,
And if thou telle it man, thou art forlore,°   *lost*
For this vengeance thou shalt have therfore,
That if thou wraye me, thou shalt be wood."
400 "Nay, Crist forbede it, for his holy blood,"
Quod tho this sely man. "I nam no labbe,°   *blabbermouth*
And though I saye, I nam nat lief to gabbe.
Say what thou wilt, I shal it nevere telle
To child ne wif, by him that harwed helle."[6]
405 "Now John," quod Nicholas, "I wol nought lie.
I have yfounde in myn astrologye,
As I have looked in the moone bright,
That now a Monday next, at quarter night,°   *near dawn*
Shal falle a rain, and that so wilde and wood,°   *furious*
410 That half so greet was nevere Noees° flood.   *Noah's*
This world," he saide, "in lasse than an hour
Shal al be dreint,° so hidous is the showr.   *drowned*
Thus shal mankinde drenche° and lese hir lif."°   *drown / lose their lives*
 This carpenter answerde, "Allas, my wif!
415 And shal she drenche? Allas, myn Alisoun!"
For sorwe of this he fil almost adown,
And saide, "Is there no remedye in this cas?"
 "Why yis, for Gode," quod hende Nicholas,

---

4. St. Benedict, founder of western monasticism.
5. The Lord's Prayer, used as a charm.

6. Christ, who harrowed hell upon his resurrection, releasing captive souls.

"If thou wolt werken° after lore° and reed°—   *act/learning/advice*
420   Thou maist nought werken after thyn owene heed;
For thus saith Salomon that was ful trewe,
'Werk al by conseil and thou shalt nought rewe.'°   *regret*
And if thou werken wolt by good conseil,
I undertake, withouten mast or sail,
425   Yet shal I save hire and thee and me.
Hastou nat herd how saved was Noee
Whan that Oure Lord hadde warned him biforn
That al the world with water sholde be lorn?"°   *lost*
"Yis," quod this carpenter, "ful yore ago."
430   "Hastou nat herd," quod Nicholas, "also
The sorwe° of Noee with his felaweshipe?°   *sorrow/companions*
Er that he mighte gete his wif to shipe,
Him hadde levere,° I dar wel undertake,   *would have preferred*
At thilke time than alle his wetheres° blake   *rams*
435   That she hadde had a ship hirself allone.[7]
And therfore woostou° what is best to doone?   *do you know*
This axeth haste, and of an hastif° thing   *urgent*
Men may nought preche or maken tarying.
Anoon go gete us faste into this in°   *inn*
440   A kneeding trough or elles a kimelin°   *brewing trough*
For eech of us, but looke that they be large,
In whiche we mowen swimme as in a barge,
And han therinne vitaile suffisaunt°   *enough food*
But for a day—fy on the remenaunt!
445   The water shal aslake° and goon away   *recede*
Aboute prime° upon the nexte day.   *6 a.m.*
But Robin may nat wite° of this, thy knave,   *know*
Ne eek thy maide Gille I may nat save.
Axe nought why, for though thou axe me,
450   I wol nought tellen Goddes privetee.
Suffiseth thee, but if thy wittes madde,°   *go mad*
To han° as greet a grace as Noee hadde.   *have*
Thy wif shal I wel saven, out of doute.
Go now thy way, and speed thee heraboute.
455   But whan thou hast for hire and thee and me
Ygeten° us thise kneeding-tubbes three,   *gotten*
Thanne shaltou hangen hem in the roof ful hye,
That no man of oure purveyance° espye.   *preparations*
And whan thou thus hast doon as I have said,
460   And hast oure vitaile faire in hem ylaid,
And eek an ax to smite the corde atwo,
Whan that the water comth that we may go,
And broke an hole an heigh° upon the gable   *on high*
Unto the gardinward,° over the stable,   *toward the garden*
465   That we may freely passen forth oure way,
Whan that the grete showr is goon away,
Thanne shaltou swimme as merye, I undertake,

---

7. Noah's wife was traditionally portrayed in the mystery plays as a complaining wife who resisted boarding the ark.

As dooth the white doke° after hir drake.   *female duck*
Thanne wol I clepe, 'How, Alison? How, John?
470   Be merye, for the flood wol passe anoon.'
And thou wolt sayn, 'Hail, maister Nicholay!
Good morwe, I see thee wel, for it is day!'
And thanne shal we be lordes al oure lif
Of al the world, as Noee and his wif.
475   But of oo thing I warne thee ful right:
Be wel avised on that ilke night
That we been entred into shippes boord
That noon of us ne speke nought a word,
Ne clepe, ne crye, but been in his prayere,
480   For it is Goddes owene heeste° dere.   *commandment*
Thy wif and thou mote hange fer atwinne,°   *apart*
For that bitwixe you shal be no sinne—
Namore in looking than ther shal in deede.
This ordinance is said: go, God thee speede.
485   Tomorwe at night whan men been alle asleepe,
Into oure kneeding-tubbes wol we creepe,
And sitten there, abiding Goddes grace.
Go now thy way, I have no lenger space°   *time*
To make of this no lenger sermoning.
490   Men sayn thus: 'Send the wise and say no thing.'
Thou art so wis it needeth thee nat teche:
Go save oure lif, and that I thee biseeche."
    This sely carpenter gooth forth his way:
Ful ofte he saide allas and wailaway,
495   And to his wif he tolde his privetee,
And she was war,° and knew it bet° than he,   *aware / better*
What al this quainte cast° was for to saye.°   *clever trick / mean*
But nathelees she ferde° as she wolde deye,   *acted*
And saide, "Allas, go forth thy way anoon.
500   Help us to scape,° or we been dede eechoon.   *escape*
I am thy trewe verray wedded wif:
Go, dere spouse, and help to save oure lif."
    Lo, which a greet thing is affeccioun!°   *emotion*
Men may dien° of imaginacioun,°   *die / fantasy*
505   So deepe may impression be take.
This sely carpenter biginneth quake;
Him thinketh verrailiche° that he may see   *truly*
Noees flood come walwing° as the see   *rolling in*
To drenchen Alison, his hony dere.
510   He weepeth, waileth, maketh sory cheere;°   *expression*
He siketh° with ful many a sory swough,°   *sighs / breath*
And gooth and geteth him a kneeding-trough,
And after a tubbe and a kimelin,
And prively he sente hem to his in,
515   And heeng hem in the roof in privetee;
His owene hand he made laddres three,
To climben by the ronges and the stalkes°   *uprights*
Unto the tubbes hanging in the balkes,°   *rafters*

And hem vitailed, bothe trough and tubbe,
520 With breed and cheese and good ale in a jubbe,°   *jug*
Suffising right ynough as for a day.
But er that he hadde maad al this array,
He sente his knave, and eek his wenche also,
Upon his neede° to London for to go.   *errand*
525 And on the Monday whan it drow to nighte,
He shette his dore withouten candel-lighte,
And dressed° alle thing as it sholde be,   *arranged*
And shortly up they clomben alle three.
They seten stille wel a furlong way.[8]
530   "Now, Pater Noster, clum,"[9] saide Nicholay,
And "Clum" quod John, and "Clum" saide Alisoun.
This carpenter saide his devocioun,
And stille he sit and biddeth his prayere,
Awaiting on the rain, if he it heere.
535   The dede sleep, for wery bisinesse,
Fil on this carpenter right as I gesse
Aboute corfew time,° or litel more.   *dusk*
For travailing of his gost° he groneth sore,   *spirit*
And eft he routeth,° for his heed mislay.   *snores*
540   Down of the laddre stalketh Nicholay,
And Alison ful softe adown she spedde:
Withouten wordes mo they goon to bedde
Ther as the carpenter is wont to lie.
Ther was the revel and the melodye,
545 And thus lith Alison and Nicholas
In bisinesse of mirthe and of solas,
Til that the belle of Laudes[1] gan to ringe,
And freres° in the chauncel° gonne singe.   *friars/chapel*
      This parissh clerk, this amorous Absolon,
550 That is for love alway so wo-bigoon,
Upon the Monday was at Oseneye,
With compaignye him to disporte and playe,
And axed upon caas° a cloisterer[2]   *by chance*
Ful prively after John the carpenter;
555 And he drow him apart out of the chirche,
And saide, "I noot:° I sawgh him here nought wirche°   *don't know/working*
Sith Saterday. I trowe that he be went
For timber ther oure abbot hath him sent.
For he is wont for timber for to go,
560 And dwellen atte grange° a day or two.   *outlying farm*
Or elles he is at his hous, certain.
Where that he be I can nought soothly sayn."
      This Absolon ful jolif was and light,°   *amorous and happy*
And thoughte, "Now is time to wake al night,
565 For sikerly,° I sawgh him nought stiringe   *surely*
Aboute his dore sin day bigan to springe.
So mote I thrive,° I shal at cokkes crowe   *may I prosper*

Ful prively knokken at his windowe
That stant ful lowe upon his bowres° wal.   *bedroom's*
570 To Alison now wol I tellen al
My love-longing, for yet I shal nat misse
That at the leeste way I shal hire kisse.
Som manere confort shal I have, parfay.°   *indeed*
My mouth hath icched° al this longe day: *itched*
575 That is a signe of kissing at the leeste.
Al night me mette° eek I was at a feeste.   *dreamed*
Therfore I wol go sleepe an hour or twaye,
And al the night thanne wol I wake and playe."
      Whan that the firste cok hath crowe, anoon
580 Up rist this joly lovere Absolon,
And him arrayeth gay at point devis.°   *fastidiously*
But first he cheweth grain³ and licoris,
To smellen sweete, er he hadde kembd his heer.
Under his tonge a trewe-love⁴ he beer,
585 For therby wende° he to be gracious.°   *supposed/attractive*
He rometh to the carpenteres hous,
And stille he stant under the shot-windowe—
Unto his brest it raughte,° it was so lowe—   *reached*
And ofte he cougheth with a semisoun.°   *soft noise*
590 "What do ye, hony-comb, sweete Alisoun,
My faire brid,° my sweete cinamome?   *bird or bride*
Awaketh, lemman° myn, and speketh to me.   *sweetheart*
Wel litel thinken ye upon my wo
That for your love I swete° ther I go.   *dissolve*
595 No wonder is though that I swelte and swete:
I moorne as dooth a lamb after the tete.
Ywis,° lemman, I have swich love-longinge,   *certainly*
That lik a turtle° trewe is my moorninge: *turtle-dove*
I may nat ete namore than a maide."
600   "Go fro the windowe, Jakke fool," she saide.
"As help me God, it wol nat be com-pa-me.°   *come kiss me*
I love another, and elles I were to blame,
Wel bet than thee, by Jesu, Absolon.
Go forth thy way or I wol caste a stoon,
605 And lat me sleepe, a twenty devele way."⁵
      "Allas," quod Absolon, "and wailaway,
That trewe love was evere so yvele biset.°   *badly done to*
Thanne kis me, sin that it may be no bet,
For Jesus love and for the love of me."
610   "Woltou thanne go thy way therwith?" quod she.
"Ye, certes, lemman," quod this Absolon.
"Thanne maak thee redy," quod she. "I come anoon."
And unto Nicholas she said stille,
"Now hust,° and thou shalt laughen al thy fille."   *hush*
615   This Absolon down sette him on his knees,
And saide, "I am a lord at alle degrees,°   *in every way*

3. Grain of paradise, an aromatic spice.   5. In the name of twenty devils.
4. Four-leafed herb in the shape of a love knot.

For after this I hope ther cometh more.
Lemman, thy grace, and sweete brid, thyn ore!"°   *mercy*
   The windowe she undooth, and that in haste.
620   "Have do," quod she, "com of and speed thee faste,
Lest that oure neighebores thee espye."
   This Absolon gan wipe his mouth ful drye:
Derk was the night as pich or as the cole,
And at the windowe out she putte hir hole,
625   And Absolon, him fil no bet ne wers,
But with his mouth he kiste hir naked ers,
Ful savourly,° er he were war of this.   *enthusiastically*
Abak he sterte, and thoughte it was amis,
For wel he wiste a womman hath no beerd.
630   He felte a thing al rough and longe yherd,°   *haird*
And saide, "Fy, allas, what have I do?"
   "Teehee," quod she, and clapte the windowe to.
And Absolon gooth forth a sory pas.°   *with downcast step*
   "A beerd, a beerd!" quod hende Nicholas,
635   "By Goddes corpus,° this gooth faire and weel."   *body*
   This sely Absolon herde everydeel,
And on his lippe he gan for anger bite,
And to himself he saide, "I shal thee quite."°   *repay*
   Who rubbeth now, who froteth now his lippes
640   With dust, with sond, with straw, with cloth, with chippes,
But Absolon, that saith ful ofte allas?
"My soule bitake° I unto Satanas,   *hand over*
But me were levere than[6] all this town," quod he,
"Of this despit° awroken° for to be.   *insult/avenged*
645   Allas," quod he, "allas I ne hadde ybleint!"°   *turned aside*
His hote love was cold and al yqueint,°   *quenched*
For fro that time that he hadde kist hir ers
Of paramours he sette nought a kers,[7]
For he was heled of his maladye.
650   Ful ofte paramours he gan defye,°   *renounce*
And weep as dooth a child that is ybete.°   *beaten*
A softe paas he wente over the streete
Until a smith men clepen daun° Gervais,   *Sir*
That in his forge smithed plough harneis:°   *equipment*
655   He sharpeth shaar° and cultour° bisily.   *plowshare/plough-blade*
This Absolon knokketh al esily,°   *softly*
And saide, "Undo,° Gervais, and that anoon."   *open up*
   "What, who artou?" "It am I, Absolon."
   "What, Absolon? What, Cristes sweete tree!
660   Why rise ye so rathe?° Ey, benedicite,°   *early/bless me*
What aileth you? Som gay girl, God it woot,
Hath brought you thus upon the viritoot.°   *on the prowl*
By Sainte Note,[8] ye woot wel what I mene."
   This Absolon ne roughte nat a bene°   *did not care a bean*

665 Of al his play. No word again he yaf:
     He hadde more tow on his distaf[9]
     Than Gervais knew, and saide, "Freend so dere,
     This hote cultour in the chimenee° here,   fireplace
     As lene it me:[1] I have therwith to doone.
670 I wol bringe it thee again ful soone."
         Gervais answerde, "Certes, were it gold,
     Or in a poke nobles alle untold,[2]
     Thou sholdest have, as I am trewe smith.
     Ey, Cristes fo,[3] what wol ye do therwith?"
675   "Therof," quod Absolon, "be as be may.
     I shal wel telle it thee another day,"
     And caughte the cultour by the colde stele.°   handle
     Ful softe out at the dore he gan to stele,
     And wente unto the carpenteres wal:
680 He cougheth first and knokketh therwithal
     Upon the windowe, right as he dide er.°   before
         This Alison answerde, "Who is ther
     That knokketh so? I warante° it a thief."   bet
         "Why, nay," quod he, "God woot, my sweete lief,°   dear
685 I am thyn Absolon, my dereling.
     Of gold," quod he, "I have thee brought a ring—
     My moder yaf it me, so God me save;
     Ful fin it is and therto wel ygrave:°   engraved
     This wol I yiven thee if thou me kisse."
690   This Nicholas was risen for to pisse,
     And thoughte he wolde amenden al the jape:[4]
     He sholde kisse his ers er that he scape.
     And up the windowe dide he hastily,
     And out his ers he putteth prively,
695 Over the buttok to the haunche-boon.°   thigh
         And therwith spak this clerk, this Absolon,
     "Speek, sweete brid, I noot nought wher thou art."
     This Nicholas anoon leet flee° a fart   let fly
     As greet as it hadde been a thonder-dent°   thunderbolt
700 That with the strook he was almost yblent,°   blinded
     And he was redy with his iren hoot,
     And Nicholas amiddle the ers he smoot:
     Of gooth the skin an hande-brede° aboute;   hand's width
     The hote cultour brende so his toute°   backside
705 That for the smert° he wende° for to die;   pain/thought
     As he were wood for wo he gan to crye,
     "Help! Water! Water! Help, for Goddes herte!"
         This carpenter out of his slomber sterte,
     And herde oon cryen "Water!" as he were wood,
710 And thoughte, "Allas, now cometh Noweles° flood!"   Noah's
     He sette him up withoute wordes mo,
     And with his ax he smooth the corde atwo,

---

9. Flax on his distaff (i.e., cares on his mind).   3. By Christ's foe (i.e., the Devil).
1. Be so good as to lend it to me.   4. Make the joke even better.
2. Or in a pouch of uncounted gold coins.

And down gooth al: he foond neither to selle
Ne breed ne ale til he cam to the celle,[5]
715   Upon the floor, and ther aswoune° he lay.   *stunned*
    Up sterte hire Alison and Nicholay,
And criden "Out" and "Harrow" in the streete.
The neighebores, bothe smale and grete,[6]
In ronnen for to gauren° on this man   *stare*
720   That aswoune lay bothe pale and wan,
For with the fal he brosten° hadde his arm;   *broken*
But stonde he moste unto his owene harm,
For whan he spak he was anoon bore down°   *restrained*
With° hende Nicholas and Alisoun: *by*
725   They tolden every man that he was wood—
He was agast° so of Noweles flood,   *afraid*
Thurgh fantasye, that of his vanitee°   *folly*
He hadde ybought him kneeding-tubbes three,
And hadde hem hanged in the roof above,
730   And that he prayed hem, for Goddes love,
To sitten in the roof, *par compaignye.°*   *for fellowship*
    The folk gan laughen at his fantasye.
Into the roof they kiken° and they cape,°   *peer/gape*
And turned al his harm unto a jape,
735   For what so that this carpenter answerde,
It was for nought: no man his reson herde;
With othes grete he was so sworn adown,°   *refuted by oaths*
That he was holden wood in al the town,
For every clerk anoonright heeld with other:
740   They saide, "The man was wood, my leve brother,"
And every wight gan laughen at this strif.
Thus swived° was the carpenteres wif   *screwed*
For al his keeping and his jalousye,
And Absolon hath kist hir nether° yë,   *lower*
745   And Nicholas is scalded in the toute:
This tale is doon, and God save al the route!

The Wife of Bath's Prologue and Tale

Dame Alison, the Wife of Bath, is Chaucer's greatest contribution to the stock characters of western culture. She has a long literary ancestry, most immediately in the Duenna of the thirteenth-century French poem, *The Romance of the Rose*, and stretching back to the Roman poet Ovid. Dame Alison stands out in bold relief, even among the vivid Canterbury pilgrims, partly because Chaucer gives her so rebellious and explicitly self-created a biography. She has outlived five husbands, accumulated wealth from the first three, and made herself rich in the growing textile industry of her time. At once a great companion and greatly unnerving, Alison lives in constant battle with a secular and religious world mostly controlled by men and yet has a keen appetite both for the men and for the battle.

    The Wife of Bath's *Prologue* and *Tale* seem only the current installments of a multifaceted struggle in which she has long been engaged, at first through her body and social role and now,

---

5. He found no time to sell either bread or ale until he reached the floor (i.e., he fell to the ground too quickly to be aware of what was happening).
6. Lower- and upper-class people alike.

in the face of advancing years, through the remaining agency of retrospective storytelling. Dame Alison battles a society in which many young women are almost chattels in a marital market, as was the twelve-year-old version of herself who first was married off to a wealthier, much older man. She battles him and later husbands for power within the marriage, and her ambition to social dominance, as the *General Prologue* reports, extends to life in her urban parish.

By the moment of the Canterbury pilgrimage, though, the Wife's adversaries are more daunting, less easily conquered. The Wife's *Prologue*, for all its autobiographical energy, is primarily a debate with the clergy and with "auctoritee"—the whole armature of learning and literacy by which the clergy (like her clerically educated fifth husband, Jankyn) seeks to silence her.

The Wife of Bath's Tale, too, can be seen as an angry riposte to the secular fantasies of Arthurian chivalry and genetic nobility. The Wife's well-born Arthurian knight is a common rapist, who finds himself at the mercy of a queen and then in the arms of a crone. The tale turns Arthurian conventions on their head, lays sexual violence in the open, and puts legal and magical power in the hands of women. It is explicitly a fantasy, but a powerful one.

Alison's final enemy, mortality itself, is what makes her both most desperate and most sympathetic. The husbands are gone. Even the fondly recalled Jankyn slips into a rosy glow and the past tense; so does her own best friend and "gossip," the odd mirror-double "Alisoun." The Wife of Bath keeps addressing other "wives" in her *Prologue*, but there are no others on the pilgrimage. Her very argument with the institutionalized church distances her from its comforts, and she is deeply aware that time is stealing her beauty as it has taken away the companions who made up her earlier life. If Alison's *Tale* closes with a delicious fantasy of restored youth, it is only a pendant to the much longer *Prologue* and its cheerful yet poignant acceptance of age.

The Wife of Bath's Prologue

	Experience, though noon auctoritee[1]	
	Were in this world, is right ynough for me	
	To speke of wo that is in mariage:	
	For lordinges,° sith I twelf yeer was of age—	*gentlemen*
5	Thanked be God that is eterne on live—	
	Housbondes at chirche dore I have had five	
	(If I so ofte mighte han wedded be),	
	And alle were worthy men in hir° degree.	*their*
	But me was told, certain, nat longe agoon is,	
10	That sith that Crist ne wente nevere but ones°	*once*
	To wedding in the Cane of Galilee,[2]	
	That by the same ensample taughte he me	
	That I ne sholde wedded be but ones.	
	Herke eek, lo, which a sharp word for the nones,°	*for the purpose*
15	Biside a welle, Jesus, God and man,	
	Spak in repreve° of the Samaritan:[3]	*reproof*
	"Thou hast yhad five housbondes," quod he,	
	"And that ilke° man that now hath thee	*same*
	Is nat thyn housbonde." Thus saide he certain.	
20	What that he mente therby I can nat sayn,	
	But that I axe why that the fifthe man	
	Was noon housbonde to the Samaritan?	

1. Even if no authority, textual precedent.
2. Cana, where Jesus performed his first miracle at a wedding feast (John 2.1).

3. The story of Jesus and the Samaritan woman is related in John 4.6ff.

How manye mighte she han in mariage?
Yit herde I nevere tellen in myn age
25   Upon this nombre diffinicioun.
Men may divine° and glosen° up and down,   *guess/interpret*
But wel I woot,° expres,° withouten lie,   *know/manifestly*
God bad us for to wexe° and multiplye: *increase*
That gentil text can I wel understonde.
30   Eek wel I woot he saide that myn housbonde
Sholde lete° fader and moder and take to me,   *leave*
But of no nombre mencion made he—
Of bigamye or of octogamye:
Why sholde men thanne speke of it vilainye?°   *as churlish*
35   Lo, here the wise king daun° Salomon: *Lord*
I trowe° he hadde wives many oon,   *believe*
As wolde God it leveful° were to me   *lawful*
To be refresshed half so ofte as he.
Which yifte° of God hadde he for alle his wives!   *what a gift*
40   No man hath swich that in this world alive is.
God woot this noble king, as to my wit,°   *understanding*
The firste night hadde many a merye fit
With eech of hem, so wel was him on live.
Blessed be God that I have wedded five,
45   Of whiche I have piked° out the beste,   *picked*
Bothe of hir nether purs and of hir cheste.[4]
Diverse° scoles maken parfit° clerkes,   *different/accomplished*
And diverse practikes in sondry werkes
Maken the werkman° parfit sikerly: *craftsman*
50   Of five housbondes scoleying° am I.   *studying*
Welcome the sixte whan that evere he shal!
For sith I wol nat keepe me chast in al,
Whan myn housbonde is fro the world agoon,
Som Cristen man shal wedde me anoon.
55   For thanne th'Apostle[5] saith that I am free
To wedde, a Goddes half,[6] where it liketh° me.   *please*
He said that to be wedded is no sinne:
Bet° is to be wedded than to brinne.°   *better/burn (in hell)*
What rekketh° me though folk saye vilainye   *do I care*
60   Of shrewed° Lamech[7] and his bigamye?   *cursed*
I woot wel Abraham was an holy man,
And Jacob eek, as fer as evere I can,°   *know*
And eech of hem hadde wives mo than two,
And many another holy man also.
65   Where can ye saye in any manere age
That hye God defended° mariage   *prohibited*
By expres word? I praye you, telleth me.
Or where comanded he virginitee?
I woot as wel as ye, it is no drede,°   *doubt*
70   Th'Apostle, whan he speketh of maidenhede,°   *virginity*

4. Money chest, with a pun on body parts.
5. St. Paul, in Romans 7.2.
6. From God's perspective.
7. The earliest bigamist in the Bible (Genesis 4.19).

He saide that precept therof hadde he noon:
Men may conseile a womman to be oon,°   single
But conseiling nis no comandement.
He putte it in oure owene juggement.
75   For hadde God comanded maidenhede,
Thanne hadde he dampned° wedding with the deede;   condemned
And certes, if ther were no seed ysowe,
Virginitee, thanne wherof sholde it growe?
Paul dorste nat comanden at the leeste
80   A thing of which his maister yaf no heeste.°   commandment
The dart° is set up for virginitee: prize
Cacche whoso may, who renneth° best lat see.   runs
But this word is nought take° of every wight,   required
But ther as God list° yive it of his might.   pleases
85   I woot wel that th'Apostle was a maide,°   virgin
But nathelees, though that he wroot or saide
He wolde that every wight were swich as he,
Al nis but° conseil to virginitee;   it is only
And for to been a wif he yaf me leve
90   Of indulgence; so nis it no repreve
To wedde me if that my make° die,   mate
Withouten excepcion° of bigamye—   legal objection
Al were it good no womman for to touche
(He mente as in his bed or in his couche,
95   For peril is bothe fir and tow t'assemble[8]—
Ye knowe what this ensample may resemble).
This al and som,° he heeld virginitee   all told
More parfit than wedding in freletee.°   due to weakness
(Freletee clepe° I but if° that he and she   call/except
100   Wolde leden al hir lif in chastitee).
I graunte it wel, I have noon envye
Though maidenhede preferre° bigamye: surpasses
It liketh hem to be clene in body and gost.°   soul
Of myn estaat° ne wol I make no boost;   condition
105   For wel ye knowe, a lord in his houshold
Ne hath nat every vessel al of gold:
Some been of tree,° and doon hir lord servise.   wood
God clepeth folk to him in sondry wise,
And everich hath of God a propre yifte,
110   Som this, som that, as him liketh shifte.[9]
Virginitee is greet perfeccioun,
And continence eek with devocioun,
But Crist, that of perfeccion is welle,°   source
Bad nat every wight he sholde go selle
115   Al that he hadde and yive it to the poore,
And in swich wise folwe him and his fore:°   footsteps
He spak to hem that wolde live parfitly°—   perfectly
And lordinges, by youre leve, that am nat I.
I wol bistowe the flour of al myn age

---

8. To bring together fire and flax.   9. As it pleases him to provide.

120   In th'actes and in fruit of mariage.
         Telle me also, to what conclusioun°   *end*
       Were membres maad of generacioun
       And of so parfit wis a wrighte ywrought?[1]
       Trusteth right wel, they were nat maad for nought.
125   Glose whoso wol, and saye bothe up and down
       That they were maked for purgacioun
       Of urine, and oure bothe thinges smale
       Was eek to knowe a femele from a male,
       And for noon other cause—saye ye no?
130   Th'experience woot wel it is nought so.
       So that the clerkes be nat with me wrothe,
       I saye this, that they maked been for bothe—
       That is to sayn, for office° and for ese°   *use/pleasure*
       Of engendrure,° ther we nat God displese.   *procreation*
135   Why sholde men elles in hir bookes sette
       That man shal yeelde° to his wif hir dette?°   *pay/marriage debt*
       Now wherwith sholde he make his payement
       If he ne used his sely° instrument?   *innocent*
       Thanne were they maad upon a creature
140   To purge urine, and eek for engendrure.
         But I saye nought that every wight is holde,°   *bound*
       That hath swich harneis° as I to you tolde,   *equipment*
       To goon and usen hem in engendrure:
       Thanne sholde men take of chastitee no cure.°   *heed*
145   Crist was a maide and shapen as a man,
       And many a saint sith that the world bigan,
       Yit lived they evere in parfit chastitee.
       I nil envye no virginitee:
       Lat hem be breed° of pured° whete seed,   *bread/refined*
150   And lat us wives hote° barly breed—   *be called*
       And yit with barly breed, Mark telle can,
       Oure Lord Jesu refresshed many a man.
       In swich estaat as God hath cleped us
       I wol persevere: I nam nat precious.°   *fussy*
155   In wifhood wol I use myn instrument
       As freely° as my Makere hath it sent.   *generously*
       If I be daungerous,° God yive me sorwe: *withholding*
       Myn housbonde shal it han both eve and morwe,°   *morning*
       Whan that him list come forth and paye his dette.
160   An housbonde wol I have, I wol nat lette,°   *forgo*
       Which shal be bothe my dettour and my thral,°   *slave*
       And have his tribulacion withal
       Upon his flessh whil that I am his wif.
       I have the power during al my lif
165   Upon his propre° body, and nat he: *own*
       Right thus th'Apostle tolde it unto me,
       And bad oure housbondes for to love us weel.
       Al this sentence° me liketh everydeel.   *interpretation*

---

1. And created by so perfectly wise a Creator?

An Interlude

	Up sterte° the Pardoner and that anoon:	*started*
170	"Now dame," quod he, "by God and by Saint John,	
	Ye been a noble prechour° in this cas.	*preacher*
	I was aboute to wedde a wif: allas,	
	What° sholde I bye° it on my flessh so dere?	*why/buy*
	Yit hadde I levere° wedde no wif toyere."°	*rather/this year*
175	"Abid," quod she, "my tale is nat bigonne.	
	Nay, thou shalt drinken of another tonne,°	*barrel*
	Er that I go, shal savoure wors than ale.	
	And whan that I have told thee forth my tale	
	Of tribulacion in mariage,	
180	Of which I am expert in al myn age—	
	This is to saye, myself hath been the whippe—	
	Thanne maistou chese° wheither thou wolt sippe	*may you choose*
	Of thilke tonne that I shal abroche:°	*open*
	Be war of it, er thou too neigh approche,	
185	For I shal telle ensamples mo than ten.	
	'Whoso that nile° be war by othere men,	*will not*
	By him shal othere men corrected be.'	
	Thise same wordes writeth Ptolomee:[2]	
	Rede in his Almageste and take it there."	
190	"Dame, I wolde praye you if youre wil it were,"	
	Saide this Pardoner, "as ye bigan,	
	Telle forth youre tale; spareth for no man,	
	And teche us yonge men of youre practike."	
	"Gladly," quod she, "sith it may you like;	
195	But that I praye to al this compaignye,	
	If that I speke after my fantasye,°	*fancy*
	As taketh nat agrief° of that I saye,	*amiss*
	For myn entente nis but for to playe."	

The Wife Continues

	Now sire, thanne wol I telle you forth my tale.	
200	As evere mote I drinke win or ale,	
	I shal saye sooth: tho housbondes that I hadde,	
	As three of hem were goode, and two were badde.	
	The three men were goode, and riche, and olde;	
	Unnethe° mighte they the statut holde	*scarcely*
205	In which they were bounden unto me—	
	Ye woot wel what I mene of this, pardee.	
	As help me God, I laughe whan I thinke	
	How pitously anight I made hem swinke;°	*work*
	And by my fay, I tolde of it no stoor:°	*gave it no heed*
210	They hadde me yiven hir land and hir tresor;	
	Me needed nat do lenger diligence	
	To winne hir love or doon hem reverence.	
	They loved me so wel, by God above,	

2. Ptolemy, ancient Greek astronomer and author of the *Almageste*.

That I ne tolde no daintee° of hir love.   *set no value on*
215 A wis womman wol bisye hire evere in oon°   *constantly*
To gete hire love, ye, ther as she hath noon.
But sith I hadde hem hoolly in myn hand,
And sith that they hadde yiven me al hir land,
What sholde I take keep° hem for to plese,   *care*
220 But it were for my profit and myn ese?
I sette hem so awerke, by my fay,°   *faith*
That many a night they songen wailaway.
The bacon was nat fet° for hem, I trowe,   *collected*
That some men han in Essexe at Dunmowe.[3]
225 I governed hem so wel after my lawe
That eech of hem ful blisful was and fawe°   *glad*
To bringe me gaye thinges fro the faire;
They were ful glade whan I spak to hem faire,
For God it woot, I chidde° hem spitously.°   *scolded/cruelly*
230   Now herkneth how I bar me proprely:
Ye wise wives, that conne understonde,
Thus sholde ye speke and bere him wrong on honde°—   *wrongly accuse*
For half so boldely can ther no man
Swere and lie as a woman can.
235 I saye nat this by wives that been wise,
But if it be whan they hem misavise.°   *err*
A wis wif, if that she can hir good,[4]
Shal bere him on hande the cow is wood,[5]
And take witnesse of hir owene maide
240 Of hir assent.° But herkneth how I saide: *as her accomplice*
"Sire olde cainard,° is this thyn array?   *dotard*
Why is my neighebores wif so gay?
She is honoured overal ther she gooth:
I sitte at hoom; I have no thrifty° cloth.   *decent*
245 What doostou at my neighebores hous?
Is she so fair? Artou so amorous?
What roune° ye with oure maide, benedicite?°   *whisper/bless us*
Sire olde lechour, lat thy japes° be.   *tricks*
And if I have a gossib° or a freend,   *confidante*
250 Withouten gilt ye chiden as a feend,
If that I walke or playe unto his hous.
Thou comest hoom as dronken as a mous,
And prechest on thy bench, with yvel preef.°   *bad luck to you*
Thou saist to me, it is a greet meschief
255 To wedde a poore womman for costage.°   *expense*
And if that she be riche, of heigh parage,°   *breeding*
Thanne saistou that it is a tormentrye
To suffre hir pride and hir malencolye.
And if that she be fair, thou verray knave,
260 Thou saist that every holour° wol hire have: *whoremonger*
She may no while in chastitee abide

3. At Dunmowe, spouses who had spent a year without quarrelling were awarded a side of bacon.
4. Knows what's good for her.
5. Shall convince him the chough is mad. The chough, a crow-like bird, was fabled to reveal wives' infidelities.

That is assailed upon eech a side.
   "Thou saist som folk desiren us for richesse,
Som for oure shap, and som for oure fairnesse,
265   And som for she can outher° singe or daunce,   *either*
And som for gentilesse and daliaunce,°   *conversation*
Som for hir handes and hir armes smale—
Thus gooth al to the devel by thy tale!⁶
Thou saist men may nat keepe a castel wal,
270   It may so longe assailed been overal.
And if that she be foul, thou saist that she
Coveiteth° every man that she may see;   *desires*
For as a spaniel she wol on him lepe,
Til that she finde som man hire to chepe.°   *take*
275   Ne noon so grey goos gooth ther in the lake,
As, saistou, wol be withoute make;
And saist it is an hard thing for to weelde°   *control*
A thing that no man wol, his thankes,° heelde.°   *willingly/hold*
Thus saistou, lorel,° whan thou goost to bedde,   *scoundrel*
280   And that no wis man needeth for to wedde,
Ne no man that entendeth° unto hevene—   *expects (to go)*
With wilde thonder-dint° and firy levene° *thunderclap/lightning*
Mote° thy welked° nekke be tobroke!° *may/withered/broken*
Thou saist that dropping° houses and eek smoke   *leaking*
285   And chiding wives maken men to flee
Out of hir owene houses: a, benedicite,
What aileth swich an old man for to chide?
Thou saist we wives wil oure vices hide
Til we be fast,° and thanne we wol hem shewe— *bound (in marriage)*
290   Wel may that be a proverbe of a shrewe!°   *scoundrel*
Thou saist that oxen, asses, hors, and houndes,
They been assayed at diverse stoundes;
Bacins, lavours, er that men hem bye,
Spoones, stooles, and al swich housbondrye,
295   And so be pottes, clothes, and array—
But folk of wives maken noon assay
Til they be wedded—olde dotard shrewe!
And thanne, saistou, we wil oure vices shewe.
Thou saist also that it displeseth me
300   But if that thou wolt praise my beautee,
And but thou poure alway upon my face,
And clepe me 'Faire Dame' in every place,
And but thou make a feeste on thilke day
That I was born, and make me fressh and gay,
305   And but thou do to my norice° honour,   *nurse*
And to my chamberere° within my bowr,° *chambermaid/bedroom*
And to my fadres folk, and his allies°—   *kinsmen*
Thus saistou, olde barel-ful of lies.
And yit of our apprentice Janekin,
310   For his crispe heer,° shining as gold so fin,   *curly hair*

6. According to what you say.

And for he squiereth° me bothe up and down,   *chaperones*
Yit hastou caught a fals suspecioun;
I wil° him nat though thou were deed tomorwe.   *desire*
    "But tel me this, why hidestou with sorwe
315 The keyes of thy cheste away fro me?
It is my good as wel as thyn, pardee.
What, weenestou° make an idiot of oure dame?   *do you suppose*
Now by that lord that called is Saint Jame,[7]
Thou shalt nought bothe, though that thou were wood,°   *enraged*
320 Be maister of my body and of my good:
That oon thou shalt forgo, maugree thine yën.[8]
    "What helpeth it of me enquere and spyen?
I trowe thou woldest loke° me in thy cheste.   *lock*
Thou sholdest saye, 'Wif, go wher thee leste.
325 Taak youre disport. I nil leve° no tales: *believe*
I knowe you for a trewe wif, dame Alis.'
We love no man that taketh keep° or charge   *notice*
Wher that we goon: we wol been at oure large.°   *liberty*
Of alle men yblessed mote he be
330 The wise astrologen daun Ptolomee,
That saith this proverbe in his Almageste:
'Of alle men his wisdom is the hyeste
That rekketh° nat who hath the world in honde.'   *cares*
By this proverbe thou shalt understonde,
335 Have thou ynough, what thar° thee rekke or care   *need*
How merily that othere folkes fare?
For certes, olde dotard, by youre leve,
Ye shal han queinte° right ynough at eve: *sex*
He is too greet a nigard that wil werne°   *refuse*
340 A man to lighte a candle at his lanterne;
He shal han nevere the lasse lighte, pardee.°   *by God*
Have thou ynough, thee thar nat plaine thee.°   *complain*
    "Thou saist also that if we make us gay
With clothing and with precious array,
345 That it is peril of oure chastitee,
And yit with sorwe thou moste enforce thee,[9]
And saye thise wordes in th'Apostles name:
'In habit° maad with chastitee and shame   *clothing*
Ye wommen shal apparaile you,' quod he,
350 'And nat in tressed heer° and gay perree,°   *styled hair/jewels*
As perles ne with gold ne clothes riche.'
After thy text, ne after thy rubriche,[1]
I wol nat werke as muchel as a gnat.
Thou saidest this, that I was lik a cat:
355 For whoso wolde senge° a cattes skin,   *singe*
Thanne wolde the cat wel dwellen in his in;°   *inn*
And if the cattes skin be slik° and gay,   *sleek*

7. Santiago de Compostela, whose shrine in Spain the   9. Reinforce (your position).
Wife of Bath has already made a pilgrimage to visit.   1. Rubric, interpretive heading on a text.
8. In spite of your eyes (an oath).

She wol nat dwelle in house half a day,
But forth she wol, er any day be dawed,°   *dawned*
360 To shewe her skin and goon a-caterwawed.°   *caterwauling*
This is to saye, if I be gay, sire shrewe,
I wol renne out, my borel° for to shewe.   *coarse cloth*
Sire olde fool, what helpeth thee t'espyen?
Though thou praye Argus² with his hundred yën
365 To be my wardecors,° as he can best,   *bodyguard*
In faith, he shal nat keepe me but me lest:
Yit coude I make his beerd,³ so mote I thee.°   *so may I prosper*
       "Thou saidest eek that ther been thinges three,
The whiche thinges troublen al this erthe,
370 And that no wight may endure the ferthe.°   *fourth*
O leve sire shrewe, Jesu shorte thy lif!
Yit prechestou and saist an hateful wif
Yrekened° is for oon of thise meschaunces.   *accounted*
Been ther nat none othere resemblaunces
375 That ye may likne youre parables to,
But if a sely° wif be oon of tho?   *innocent*
       "Thou liknest eek wommanes love to helle,
To bareine land ther water may nat dwelle;
Thou liknest it also to wilde fir—
380 The more it brenneth,° the more it hath desir   *burns*
To consumen every thing that brent wol be;
Thou saist right as wormes shende° a tree,   *destroy*
Right so a wif destroyeth hir housbonde—
This knowen they that been to wives bonde."
385   Lordinges, right thus, as ye han understonde,
Bar I stifly° mine olde housbondes on honde°   *firmly/swore*
That thus they saiden in hir dronkenesse—
And al was fals, but that I took witnesse
On Janekin and on my nece° also.   *kinswoman*
390 O Lord, the paine I dide hem and the wo,
Ful giltelees, by Goddes sweete pine!°   *suffering*
For as an hors I coude bite and whine;
I coude plaine and° I was in the gilt,°   *when/wrong*
Or elles often time I hadde been spilt.°   *ruined*
395 Whoso that first to mille comth first grint.°   *grinds*
I plained first: so was oure werre° stint.°   *war/stopped*
They were ful glad to excusen hem ful blive°   *quickly*
Of thing of which they nevere agilte° hir live.   *offended (in)*
Of wenches wolde I beren hem on honde,
400 Whan that for sik they mighte unnethe° stonde,   *barely*
Yit tikled I his herte for that he
Wende° I hadde had of him so greet cheertee.°   *supposed/fondness*
I swoor that al my walking out by nighte
Was for to espye wenches that he dighte.°   *had sex with*
405 Under that colour° hadde I many a mirthe.   *pretense*

---

2. Mythical hundred-eyed monster employed by Juno to
guard over Io, one of Jove's many lovers, whom the goddess turned into a cow.
3. Deceive him.

For al swich wit is yiven us in oure birthe:
Deceite, weeping, spinning God hath yive
To wommen kindely° whil they may live.   *by nature*
And thus of oo thing I avaunte° me: *boast*

410   At ende I hadde the bet in eech degree,
By sleighte° or force, or by som manere thing,   *deception*
As by continuel murmur° or grucching;°   *complaining/grumbling*
Namely abedde° hadden they meschaunce:°   *in bed/misfortune*
Ther wolde I chide and do hem no plesaunce;

415   I wolde no lenger in the bed abide
If that I felte his arm over my side,
Til he hadde maad his raunson° unto me;   *amends*
Thanne wolde I suffre him do his nicetee.°   *lust*
And therfore every man this tale I telle:

420   Winne whoso may, for al is for to selle;
With empty hand men may no hawkes lure.
For winning° wolde I al his lust endure,   *profit*
And make me a feined appetit—
And yit in bacon° hadde I nevere delit.   *old meat*

425   That made me that evere I wolde hem chide;
For though the Pope hadde seten° hem biside,   *sat*
I wolde nought spare hem at hir owene boord.°   *table*
For by my trouthe, I quitte° hem word for word.   *repaid*
As help me verray God omnipotent,

430   Though I right now sholde make my testament,
I ne owe hem nat a word that it nis quit.
I broughte it so aboute by my wit
That they moste yive it up as for the beste,
Or elles hadde we nevere been in reste;

435   For though he looked as a wood leoun,
Yit sholde he faile of his conclusion.°   *purpose*
    Thanne wolde I saye, "Goodelief,° taak keep,   *Sweetheart*
How mekely looketh Wilekin, oure sheep!
Com neer my spouse, lat me ba° thy cheeke—   *kiss*

440   Ye sholden be al pacient and meeke,
And han a sweete-spiced conscience,
Sith ye so preche of Jobes⁴ pacience;
Suffreth alway, sin ye so wel can preche;
And but ye do, certain, we shal you teche

445   That it is fair to han a wif in pees.
Oon of us two moste bowen, doutelees,
And sith a man is more resonable
Than womman is, ye mosten been suffrable.°   *patient*
What aileth you to grucche thus and grone?

450   Is it for ye wolde have my queinte allone?
Why, taak it al—lo, have it everydeel.
Peter,° I shrewe° you but ye love it weel.   *by St. Peter/curse*
For if I wolde selle my bele chose,⁵

---

4. The Biblical Job, who suffers patiently the trials   5. "Beautiful thing," a euphemism for female genitals.
imposed by God.

I coude walke as fressh as is a rose;

455 But I wol keepe it for youre owene tooth.° *taste*
Ye be to blame. By God, I saye you sooth!"
Swiche manere wordes hadde we on honde.
Now wol I speke of my ferthe housbonde.
      My ferthe housbonde was a revelour—

460 This is to sayn, he hadde a paramour°— *lover*
And I was yong and ful of ragerye,° *wantonness*
Stibourne° and strong and joly as a pie:° *stubborn/magpie*
How coude I daunce to an harpe smale,° *gracefully*
And singe, ywis, as any nightingale,

465 Whan I hadde dronke a draughte of sweete win.
Metellius,[6] the foule cherl,° the swin, *ruffian*
That with a staf birafte his wif hir lif
For she drank win, though I hadde been his wif,
Ne sholde nat han daunted me fro drinke;

470 And after win on Venus moste I thinke,
For also siker° as cold engendreth hail, *certainly*
A likerous° mouth moste han a likerous° tail: *gluttonous/lecherous*
In womman vinolent° is no defence— *drunken*
This knowen lechours by experience.

475   But Lord Crist, whan that it remembreth me
Upon my youthe and on my jolitee,
It tikleth me aboute myn herte roote°— *bottom of my heart*
Unto this day it dooth myn herte boote° *good*
That I have had my world as in my time.

480 But age, allas, that al wol envenime,° *poison*
Hath me birafte my beautee and my pith°— *vigor*
Lat go, farewel, the devel go therwith!
The flour is goon, ther is namore to telle:
The bren° as I best can now moste I selle; *bran*

485 But yit to be right merye wol I fonde.° *try*
Now wol I tellen of my ferthe housbonde.
      I saye I hadde in herte greet despit
That he of any other hadde delit,
But he was quit,° by God and by Saint Joce:° *repaid/St. Judocus*

490 I made him of the same wode a croce°— *cross*
Nat of my body in no foul manere—
But, certainly, I made folk swich cheere
That in his owene grece° I made him frye, *grease*
For angre and for verray jalousye.

495 By God, in erthe I was his purgatorye,
For which I hope his soule be in glorye.
For God it woot, he sat ful ofte and soong
Whan that his sho° ful bitterly him wroong.° *shoe/pinched*
Ther was no wight save God and he that wiste

500 In many wise how sore I him twiste.
He deide whan I cam fro Jerusalem,
And lith ygrave° under the roode-beem,° *buried/crossbeam*

6. Egnatius Metellius, whose actions are described in Valerius Maximus' *Facta et dicta memorabilia*, 6.3.

Al is his tombe nought so curious°   *carefully made*
As was the sepulcre of him Darius,[7]
505   Which that Appelles wroughte subtilly:
It nis but wast to burye him preciously.°   *expensively*
Lat him fare wel, God yive his soule reste;
He is now in his grave and in his cheste.
    Now of my fifthe housbonde wol I telle—
510   God lete his soule nevere come in helle—
And yit he was to me the moste shrewe:
That feele I on my ribbes al by rewe,°   *in a row*
And evere shal unto myn ending day.
But in oure bed he was so fressh and gay,
515   And therwithal so wel coude he me glose°   *flatter*
Whan that he wolde han my bele chose,
That though he hadde me bet° on every boon,°   *beaten/bone*
He coude winne again my love anoon.
I trowe I loved him best for that he
520   Was of his love daungerous° to me.   *hard to get*
We wommen han, if that I shal nat lie,
In this matere a quainte fantasye:
Waite° what thing we may nat lightly° have,   *note that/easily*
Therafter wol we crye al day and crave;
525   Forbede us thing, and that desiren we;
Presse on us faste, and thanne wol we flee.
With daunger oute we al oure chaffare:[8]
Greet prees° at market maketh dere ware,°   *crowd/costly goods*
And too greet chepe° is holden at litel pris.   *bargain*
530   This knoweth every womman that is wis.
    My fifthe housbonde—God his soule blesse!—
Which that I took for love and no richesse,
He somtime was a clerk of Oxenforde,
And hadde laft scole and wente at hoom to boorde
535   With my gossib,° dwelling in oure town—   *close friend*
God have hir soule!—hir name was Alisoun;
She knew myn herte and eek my privetee°   *secrets*
Bet than oure parissh preest, as mote I thee.
To hire biwrayed° I my conseil° al,   *revealed/thoughts*
540   For hadde myn housbonde pissed on a wal,
Or doon a thing that sholde han cost his lif,
To hire, and to another worthy wif,
And to my nece which that I loved weel,
I wolde han told his conseil everydeel;
545   And so I dide ful often, God it woot,
That made his face often reed° and hoot°   *red/hot*
For verray shame, and blamed himself for he
Hadde told to me so greet a privetee.
    And so bifel that ones in a Lente—
550   So often times I to my gossib wente,

7. Persian Emperor defeated by Alexander the Great, whose tomb was elaborately designed by the Jewish craftsman Apelles.
8. With coyness we spread out all our merchandise.

For evere yit I loved to be gay,
And for to walke in March, Averil, and May,
From hous to hous, to heere sondry tales—
That Janekin clerk and my gossib dame Alis

555 And I myself into the feeldes wente.
Myn housbonde was at London al that Lente:
I hadde the better leiser° for to playe,   opportunity
And for to see, and eek for to be seye°   seen
Of lusty° folk—what wiste I wher my grace°   merry/luck

560 Was shapen° for to be, or in what place?   destined
Therfore I made my visitaciouns
To vigilies⁹ and to processiouns,
To preching eek, and to thise pilgrimages,
To playes of miracles and to mariages,

565 And wered upon my gaye scarlet gites°—   robes
Thise wormes ne thise motthes ne thise mites,
Upon my peril, frete° hem neveradeel: devoured
And woostou why? For they were used weel.
    Now wol I tellen forth what happed me.

570 I saye that in the feeldes walked we,
Til trewely we hadde swich daliaunce,°   flirtation
This clerk and I, that of my purveyaunce°   providence
I spak to him and saide him how that he,
If I were widwe, sholde wedde me.

575 For certainly, I saye for no bobaunce°   boast
Yit was I nevere withouten purveyaunce
Of mariage n'of othere thinges eek:
I holde a mouses herte nought worth a leek
That hath but oon hole for to sterte° to,   flee

580 And if that faile thanne is al ydo.
I bar him on hand he hadde enchaunted me
(My dame taughte me that subtiltee);
And eek I saide I mette° of him al night: dreamed
He wolde han slain me as I lay upright,°   facing up

585 And al my bed was ful of verray blood—
"But yit I hope that ye shul do me good;
For blood bitokeneth gold, as me was taught."
And al was fals, I dremed of it right naught,
But as I folwed ay my dames lore°   teaching

590 As wel of that as of othere thinges more.
But now sire—lat me see, what shal I sayn?
Aha, by God, I have my tale again.
    Whan that my ferthe housbonde was on beere,°   funeral bier
I weep algate,° and made sory cheere,   constantly

595 As wives moten, for it is usage,°   custom
And with my coverchief covered my visage;
But for that I was purveyed° of a make,°   provided/mate
I wepte but smale, and that I undertake.°   vouch
    To chirche was myn housbonde born amorwe°   next morning

9. Services on the eve of holy days.

600   With neighebores that for him maden sorwe,
       And Janekin oure clerk was oon of tho.
       As help me God, whan that I saw him go
       After the beere, me thoughte he hadde a paire
       Of legges and of feet so clene and faire,
605   That al myn herte I yaf unto his hold.°   *possession*
       He was, I trowe, twenty winter old,
       And I was fourty, if I shal saye sooth—
       But yit I hadde alway a coltes tooth:°   *youthful tastes*
       Gat-toothed° was I, and that bicam me weel;   *gap-toothed*
610   I hadde the prente° of Sainte Venus seel.°   *imprint/beauty mark*
       As help me God, I was a lusty oon,
       And fair and riche and yong and wel-bigoon,°   *well situated*
       And trewely, as mine housbondes tolde me,
       I hadde the beste quoniam° mighte be.   *you-know-what*
615   For certes I am al Venerien[1]
       In feeling, and myn herte is Marcien:°   *governed by Mars*
       Venus me yaf my lust, my likerousnesse,
       And Mars yaf me my sturdy hardinesse.
       Myn ascendent° was Taur° and Mars therinne—   *zodiac sign/Taurus*
620   Allas, allas, that evere love was sinne!
       I folwed ay my inclinacioun
       By vertu of my constellacioun;
       That made me I coude nought withdrawe°   *withhold*
       My chambre of Venus from a good felawe.
625   Yit have I Martes° merk upon my face,   *Mars's*
       And also in another privee place.
       For God so wis° be my savacioun,°   *surely/salvation*
       I loved nevere by no discrecioun,
       But evere folwede myn appetit,
630   Al were he short or long or blak or whit;
       I took no keep, so that he liked° me,   *pleased*
       How poore he was, ne eek of what degree.
            What sholde I saye but at the monthes ende
       This joly clerk Janekin that was so hende°   *courteous*
635   Hath wedded me with greet solempnitee,
       And to him yaf I al the land and fee°   *property*
       That evere was me yiven therbifore—
       But afterward repented me ful sore:
       He nolde suffre no thing of my list.°   *pleasure*
640   By God, he smoot° me ones on the list°   *struck/ear*
       For that I rente° out of his book a leef,°   *tore/page*
       That of the strook myn ere weex° al deef.   *grew, became*
       Stiborne I was as is a leonesse,
       And of my tonge a verray jangleresse,°   *chatterbox*
645   And walke I wolde, as I hadde doon biforn,
       From hous to hous, although he hadde it sworn;°   *prohibited*
       For which he often times wolde preche,
       And me of olde Romain geestes° teche,   *Latin stories*

1. Governed by Venus, the planet.

How he Simplicius Gallus[2] lafte his wif,
650 And hire forsook for terme of al his lif,
Nought but for open-heveded° he hire sey°   *bare-headed/saw*
Looking out at his dore upon a day.
    Another Romain[3] tolde he me by name
That, for his wif was at a someres° game   *summer's*
655 Withouten his witing,° he forsook hire eke;   *knowledge*
And thanne wolde he upon his Bible seeke
That ilke proverbe of Ecclesiaste[4]
Where he comandeth and forbedeth faste
Man shal nat suffre his wif go roule° aboute;   *roam*
660 Thanne wolde he saye right thus withouten doute:
"Whoso that buildeth his hous al of salwes,°   *willow branches*
And priketh° his blinde hors over the falwes,°   *rides/open fields*
And suffreth his wif to go seeken halwes,°   *shrines*
Is worthy to be hanged on the galwes."
665 But al for nought—I sette nought an hawe[5]
Of his proverbes n'of his olde sawe;
N'I wolde nat of him corrected be:
I hate him that my vices telleth me,
And so doon mo, God woot, of us than I.
670 This made him with me wood al outrely:°   *utterly*
I nolde nought forbere° him in no cas.   *submit*
    Now wol I saye you sooth, by Saint Thomas,
Why that I rente out of his book a leef,
For which he smoot me so that I was deef.
675 He hadde a book that gladly night and day
For his disport° he wolde rede alway.   *amusement*
He cleped° it Valerie and Theofraste,[6]   *called*
At which book he lough° alway ful faste;   *laughed*
And eek ther was somtime a clerk at Rome,
680 A cardinal, that highte Saint Jerome,
That made a book again Jovinian;
In which book eek ther was Tertulan,
Crysippus, Trotula, and Helouis,
That was abbesse nat fer fro Paris;
685 And eek the Parables of Salomon,
Ovides Art, and bookes many oon—
And alle thise were bounden in oo volume.
And every night and day was his custume,°   *custom*
Whan he hadde leiser and vacacioun
690 From other worldly occupacioun,

2. Narrated in Valerius Maximus' *Facta et dicta memorabilia*, 6.3.
3. P. Sempronius Sophus, as related in Valerius Maximus' *Facta*, 6.3.
4. Ecclesiasticus 25.25.
5. Hawthorn berry (i.e., little value).
6. Janekin's book is a collection of different works, nearly all of which are directed against women: Walter Map's fictitious letter entitled Valerius' *Dissuasion of Rufinus from Marrying* (Valerius); Theophrastus' *Golden Book on Marriage* (Theofraste); Saint Jerome's *Against Jovinian*; Tertullian's misogynist tracts on sexual continence (Tertulan); Crysippus' writings, mentioned by Jerome but otherwise unknown; *The Sufferings of Women*, an 11th-century book on gynecology by Trotula di Ruggiero, a female physician from Sicily (Trotula); the letters of the abbess Heloise to her lover Abelard (Helouis); the biblical Book of Proverbs (Parables of Salomon), and Ovid's *Art of Love*.

To reden in this book of wikked wives.
He knew of hem mo legendes and lives
Than been of goode wives in the Bible.
For trusteth wel, it is an impossible°   *impossibility*
695   That any clerk wol speke good of wives,
But if it be of holy saintes lives,
N'of noon other womman nevere the mo—
Who painted the leon, tel me who?[7]
By God, if wommen hadden writen stories,
700   As clerkes han within hir oratories,
They wolde han writen of men more wikkednesse
Than al the merk of° Adam may redresse.   *mark, sex*
The children of Mercurye and Venus[8]
Been in hir werking° ful contrarious:°   *deeds/contradictory*
705   Mercurye loveth wisdom and science,
And Venus loveth riot° and dispence;°   *celebration/expense*
And for hir diverse disposicioun
Each falleth in otheres exaltacioun,[9]
And thus, God woot, Mercurye is desolat°   *powerless*
710   In Pisces wher Venus is exaltat,
And Venus falleth ther Mercurye is raised:
Therfore no womman of no clerk is praised.
The clerk, whan he is old and may nought do
Of Venus werkes worth his olde sho,°   *shoe*
715   Thanne sit he down and writ in his dotage
That wommen can nat keepe hir mariage.
     But now to purpos why I tolde thee
That I was beten for a book, pardee:
Upon a night Janekin, that was oure sire,°   *master of our house*
720   Redde on his book as he sat by the fire
Of Eva[1] first, that for hir wikkednesse
Was al mankinde brought to wrecchednesse,
For which that Jesu Crist himself was slain
That boughte° us with his herte blood again—   *redeemed*
725   Lo, heer expres of wommen may ye finde
That womman was the los° of al mankinde.   *ruin*
     Tho redde he me how Sampson loste his heres:
Sleeping his lemman° kitte° it with hir sheres,   *lover/cut*
Thurgh which treson loste he both his yën.
730   Tho redde he me, if that I shal nat lien,
Of Ercules and of his Dianire,[2]
That caused him to sette himself afire.
     No thing forgat he the sorwe and wo
That Socrates hadde with his wives two—

7. In one of Aesop's fables, a lion asked this question
when confronted by a painting of a man killing a lion,
indicating that if a lion had painted the picture, the
scene would have been very different.
8. Followers of Mercury, the god of rhetoric (scholars,
poets, orators); followers of Venus (lovers).
9. Astrologically, one planet diminishes in influence as

the other ascends.
1. Eve's temptation by the serpent was blamed for
humanity's fall from grace and thus required Christ's
incarnation to redeem the world.
2. Deianira gave her husband, Hercules, a robe which she
believed was charmed with a love potion, but once he put
it on, it burned his flesh so badly that he died.

735 How Xantippa³ caste pisse upon his heed:
    This sely man sat stille as he were deed;
    He wiped his heed, namore dorste he sayn
    But "Er° that thonder stinte,° comth a rain."   *before/stops*
        Of Phasipha⁴ that was the queene of Crete—
740 For shrewednesse° him thoughte the tale sweete—   *wickedness*
    Fy, speek namore, it is a grisly thing
    Of hir horrible lust and hir liking.
        Of Clytermistra⁵ for hir lecherye
    That falsly made hir housbonde for to die,
745 He redde it with ful good devocioun.
        He tolde me eek for what occasioun
    Amphiorax⁶ at Thebes loste his lif:
    Myn housbonde hadde a legende of his wif
    Eriphylem, that for an ouche° of gold   *trinket*
750 Hath prively unto the Greekes told
    Wher that hir housbonde hidde him in a place,
    For which he hadde at Thebes sory grace.
        Of Livia⁷ tolde he me and of Lucie:
    They bothe made hir housbondes for to die,
755 That oon for love, that other was for hate;
    Livia hir housbonde on an even late
    Empoisoned hath for that she was his fo;
    Lucia likerous loved hir housbonde so
    That for he sholde alway upon hire thinke,
760 She yaf him swich a manere love-drinke
    That he was deed er it were by the morwe.
    And thus algates° housbondes han sorwe.   *continually*
        Thanne tolde he me how oon Latumius
    Complained unto his felawe Arrius
765 That in his gardin growed swich a tree,
    On which he saide how that his wives three
    Hanged hemself for herte despitous.°   *cruel*
        "O leve brother," quod this Arrius,
    "Yif me a plante of thilke blessed tree,
770 And in my gardin planted shal it be."
        Of latter date of wives hath he red
    That some han slain hir housbondes in hir bed
    And lete hir lechour dighte° hire al the night,   *screw*
    Whan that the cors° lay in the floor upright;°   *corpse/face up*
775 And some han driven nailes in hir brain
    Whil that they sleepe, and thus they han hem slain;
    Some han hem yiven poison in hir drinke.
    He spak more harm than herte may bithinke,
    And therwithal he knew of mo proverbes

---

3. Xanthippe was famous for nagging her husband, the philosopher Socrates.
4. Pasiphae, wife of Minos, became enamored of a bull, engendering the Minotaur.
5. Clytemnestra, queen of Mycenae, slew her husband Agamemnon when he returned from the Trojan War.

6. Amphiaraus died at the Siege of Thebes after listening to the advice of his wife, Eriphyle.
7. Livia poisoned her husband, Drusus, to satisfy her lover Sejanus; Lucia unwittingly poisoned her husband, the poet Lucretius, with a potion meant to keep him faithful.

780   Than in this world ther growen gras or herbes:
"Bet is," quod he, "thyn habitacioun
Be with a leon or a foul dragoun
Than with a wommman using° for to chide."   *accustomed*
"Bet is," quod he, "hye in the roof abide
785   Than with an angry wif down in the hous:
They been so wikked and contrarious,
They haten that hir housbondes loveth ay."
He saide, "A womman cast hir shame away
Whan she cast of hir smok,"° and ferthermo,   *slip*
790   "A fair womman, but she be chast also,
Is lik a gold ring in a sowes nose."
Who wolde weene, or who wolde suppose
The wo that in myn herte was and pine?
     And whan I sawgh he wolde nevere fine°   *end*
795   To reden on this cursed book al night,
Al sodeinly three leves have I plight°   *plucked*
Out of his book right as he redde, and eke
I with my fist so took° him on the cheeke   *struck*
That in oure fir he fil bakward adown.
800   And up he sterte as dooth a wood° leoun,   *enraged*
And with his fist he smoot me on the heed
That in the floor I lay as I were deed.
And whan he sawgh how stille that I lay,
He was agast,° and wolde have fled his way,   *afraid*
805   Til atte laste out of my swough° I braide:°   *faint/arose*
"O hastou slain me, false thief?" I saide,
"And for my land thus hastou mordred me?
Er I be deed yit wol I kisse thee."
     And neer he cam and kneeled faire adown,
810   And saide, "Dere suster Alisoun,
As help me God, I shal thee nevere smite.
That I have doon, it is thyself to wite.°   *blame*
Foryif it me, and that I thee biseeke."
And yit eftsoones° I hitte him on the cheeke,   *immediately*
815   And saide, "Thief, thus muchel am I wreke.°   *avenged*
Now wol I die: I may no lenger speke."
     But at the laste with muchel care and wo
We fille accorded by us selven two.
He yaf me al the bridel° in myn hand,   *bridle, control*
820   To han the governance of hous and land,
And of his tonge and his hand also;
And made him brenne his book anoonright tho.
And whan that I hadde geten unto me
By maistrye° al the sovereinetee,°   *skill/dominance*
825   And that he saide, "Myn owene trewe wif,
Do as thee lust° the terme of al thy lif,   *please*
Keep thyn honour, and keep eek myn estat,"
After that day we hadde nevere debat.
God help me so, I was to him as kinde
830   As any wif from Denmark unto Inde,

And also trewe, and so was he to me.
I praye to God that sit in majestee,
So blesse his soule for his mercy dere.
Now wol I saye my tale if ye wol heere.

Another Interruption

835 The Frere lough whan he hadde herd al this:
"Now dame," quod he, "so have I joye or blis,
This is a long preamble of a tale."
And whan the Somnour herde the Frere gale,°   *exclaim*
"Lo," quod the Somnour, "Goddes armes two,
840 A frere wol entremette him° everemo!   *interfere*
Lo, goode men, a flye and eek a frere
Wol falle in every dissh and eek matere.
What spekestou of preambulacioun?
What, amble or trotte or pisse or go sitte down!
845 Thou lettest oure disport in this manere."
    "Ye, woltou so, sire Somnour?" quod the Frere.
"Now by my faith, I shal er that I go
Telle of a somnour swich a tale or two
That al the folk shal laughen in this place."
850   "Now elles, Frere, I wol bishrewe thy face,"
Quod this Somnour, "and I bishrewe me,
But if I telle tales two or three
Of freres, er I come to Sidingborne,[8]
That I shal make thyn herte for to moorne—
855 For wel I woot thy pacience is goon."
    Oure Hoste cride, "Pees, and that anoon!"
And saide, "Lat the womman telle hir tale:
Ye fare as folk that dronken been of ale.
Do, dame, tel forth youre tale, and that is best."
860   "Al redy, sire," quod she, "right as you lest—
If I have licence of this worthy Frere."
"Yis, dame," quod he, "tel forth and I wol heere."

The Wife of Bath's Tale

In th'olde dayes of the King Arthour,
Of which that Britouns° speken greet honour,   *Bretons*
865 Al was this land fulfild° of faïrye: *filled*
The elf-queene° with hir joly compaignye   *fairy queen*
Daunced ful ofte in many a greene mede°—   *meadow*
This was the olde opinion as I rede;
I speke of many hundred yeres ago.
870 But now can no man see none elves mo,
For now the grete charitee and prayeres
Of limitours,[9] and othere holy freres,
That serchen every land and every streem,
As thikke as motes° in the sonne-beem,   *dust particles*

---

8. Sittingbourne, a town about 40 miles from London.   9. Friars licensed to beg within set districts.

875	Blessing halles, chambres, kichenes, bowres,°	*bedrooms*
	Citees, burghes,° castels, hye towres,	*boroughs*
	Thropes,° bernes,° shipnes,° dayeries—	*villages/barns/stables*
	This maketh that ther been no faïries.	
	For ther as wont° to walken was an elf	*where there used*
880	Ther walketh now the limitour himself,	
	In undermeles° and in morweninges,°	*afternoons/mornings*
	And saith his Matins° and his holy thinges,	*morning prayers*
	As he gooth in his limitacioun.°	*prescribed district*
	Wommen may go saufly° up and down:	*safely*
885	In every bussh or under every tree	
	Ther is noon other incubus[2] but he,	
	And he ne wol doon hem but dishonour.	
	And so bifel it that this King Arthour	
	Hadde in his hous a lusty bacheler,°	*young knight*
890	That on a day cam riding fro river,°	*hunting waterfowl*
	And happed that, allone as he was born,	
	He sawgh a maide walking him biforn;	
	Of which maide anoon, maugree hir heed,°	*against her will*
	By verray force he rafte° hir maidenheed;	*stole*
895	For which oppression was swich clamour,	
	And swich pursuite° unto the King Arthour,	*petitioning*
	That dampned° was this knight for to be deed	*condemned*
	By cours of lawe, and sholde han lost his heed—	
	Paraventure° swich was the statut tho°—	*as it happens/then*
900	But that the queene and othere ladies mo	
	So longe prayeden the king of grace,	
	Til he his lif him graunted in the place,	
	And yaf him to the queene, al at hir wille,	
	To chese° wheither she wolde him save or spille.°	*decide/destroy*
905	The queene thanked the king with al hir might,	
	And after this thus spak she to the knight,	
	Whan that she saw hir time upon a day:	
	"Thou standest yit," quod she, "in swich array°	*situation*
	That of thy lif yit hastou no suretee.°	*guarantee*
910	I graunte thee lif if thou canst tellen me	
	What thing it is that wommen most desiren:	
	Be war and keep thy nekke boon° from iren.°	*bone/iron*
	And if thou canst nat tellen me anoon,	
	Yit wol I yive thee leve for to goon	
	915	A twelfmonth and a day to seeche° and lere°	*seek out/learn*
	An answere suffisant° in this matere,	*satisfactory*
	And suretee° wol I han er that thou pace,°	*pledge/pass*
	Thy body for to yeelden° in this place."	*surrender*
	Wo was this knight, and sorwefully he siketh.°	*sighs*
920	But what, he may nat doon al as him liketh,	
	And atte laste he chees him° for to wende,°	*decided/travel*
	And come again right at the yeres ende,	
	With swich answere as God wolde him purveye,°	*provide*

1. Demon who fornicates with women.

	And taketh his leve and wendeth forth his waye.	
925	He seeketh every hous and every place	
	Wher as he hopeth for to finde grace,	
	To lerne what thing wommen love most.	
	But he ne coude arriven in no coost°	country
	Wher as he mighte finde in this matere	
930	Two creatures according in fere.°	agreeing together
	Some saiden wommen loven best richesse;	
	Some saide honour, some saide jolinesse;°	pleasure
	Some riche array, some saiden lust abedde,	
	And ofte time to be widwe and wedde.	
935	Some saide that oure herte is most esed	
	Whan that we been yflatered and yplesed—	
	He gooth ful neigh the soothe,° I wol nat lie:	near the truth
	A man shal winne us best with flaterye,	
	And with attendance and with bisinesse°	attentive service
940	Been we ylimed,° bothe more and lesse.	ensnared
	And some sayen that we loven best	
	For to be free, and do right as us lest,°	pleases
	And that no man repreve° us of oure vice,	scold
	But saye that we be wise and no thing nice.°	foolish
945	For trewely, ther is noon of us alle,	
	If any wight wol clawe us on the galle,°	rub a sore spot
	That we nil kike for he saith us sooth:	
	Assaye° and he shal finde it that so dooth.	try
	For be we nevere so vicious withinne,	
950	We wol be holden° wise and clene of sinne.	considered
	And some sayn that greet delit han we	
	For to be holden stable° and eek secree,°	constant/discreet
	And in oo purpos stedefastly to dwelle,	
	And nat biwraye° thing that men us telle—	reveal
955	But that tale is nat worth a rake-stele.°	rake handle
	Pardee, we wommen conne no thing hele:°	conceal
	Witnesse on Mida.² Wol ye heere the tale?	
	Ovide, amonges othere thinges smale,	
	Saide Mida hadde under his longe heres,	
960	Growing upon his heed, two asses eres,	
	The whiche vice° he hidde as he best mighte	fault
	Ful subtilly from every mannes sighte,	
	That save his wif ther wiste of it namo.°	no one else know
	He loved hire most and trusted hire also.	
965	He prayed hire that to no creature	
	She sholde tellen of his disfigure.°	deformity
	She swoor him nay, for al this world to winne,	
	She nolde° do that vilainye or sinne	would not
	To make hir housbonde han so foul a name:	
970	She nolde nat telle it for hir owene shame.	
	But nathelees, hir thoughte that she dyde°	would die
	That she so longe sholde a conseil° hide;	secret

2. Midas' story is recounted in Ovid's *Metamorphoses*, 9.

Hire thoughte it swal so sore aboute hir herte
That nedely° som word hire moste asterte,°   *surely/come out*
975   And sith she dorste nat telle it to no man,
Down to a mareis° faste° by she ran—   *marsh/close*
Til she cam there hir herte was afire—
And as a bitore° bombleth° in the mire,   *heron/squawks*
She laide hir mouth unto the water down:
980   "Biwray° me nat, thou water, with thy soun,"°   *betray/sound*
Quod she. "To thee I telle it and namo:
Myn housbonde hath longe asses eres two.
Now is myn herte al hool, now is it oute.
I mighte no lenger keepe it, out of doute."
985   Here may ye see, though we a time abide,
Yit oute it moot:° we can no conseil hide.   *must*
The remenant of the tale if ye wol heere,
Redeth Ovide, and ther ye may it lere.°   *learn*
    This knight of which my tale is specially,
990   Whan that he sawgh he mighte nat come therby—
This is to saye what wommen loven most—
Within his brest ful sorweful was his gost,°   *spirit*
But hoom he gooth, he mighte nat sojurne:°   *linger*
The day was come that hoomward moste he turne.
995   And in his way it happed him to ride
In al this care under a forest side,
Wher as he sawgh upon a daunce go
Of ladies foure and twenty and yit mo;
Toward the whiche daunce he drow° ful yerne,°   *drew/gladly*
1000 In hope that som wisdom sholde he lerne.
But certainly, er he cam fully there,
Vanisshed was this daunce, he niste° where.   *did not know*
No creature sawgh he that bar lif,
Save on the greene he sawgh sitting a wif—
1005 A fouler wight ther may no man devise.°   *imagine*
Again the knight this olde wif gan rise,
And saide, "Sire knight, heer forth lith no way.°   *road*
Telle me what ye seeken, by youre fay.°   *faith*
Paraventure it may the better be:
1010 Thise olde folk conne° muchel thing," quod she.   *know*
    "My leve moder," quod this knight, "certain,
I nam but deed but if that I can sayn
What thing it is that wommen most desire.
Coude ye me wisse,° I wolde wel quite youre hire."°   *inform/repay you*
1015 "Plight° me thy trouthe° here in myn hand," quod she,   *pledge/promise*
"The nexte thing that I require thee,
Thou shalt it do, if it lie in thy might,
And I wol telle it you er it be night."
    "Have heer my trouthe," quod the knight. "I graunte."
1020 "Thanne," quod she, "I dar me wel avaunte°   *brag*
Thy lif is sauf, for I wol stande therby.
Upon my lif the queene wol saye as I.
Lat see which is the pruddeste° of hem alle   *proudest*

That wereth on a coverchief or a calle°   *headdress*
1025 That dar saye nay of that I shal thee teche.
Lat us go forth withouten lenger speeche."
Tho rouned° she a pistel° in his ere,   *whispered/message*
And bad him to be glad and have no fere.
Whan they be comen to the court, this knight
1030 Saide he hadde holde his day as he hadde hight,° *promised*
And redy was his answere, as he saide.
Ful many a noble wif, and many a maide,
And many a widwe—for that they been wise—
The queene hirself sitting as justise,°   *judge*
1035 Assembled been this answere for to heere,
And afterward this knight was bode appere.
To every wight comanded was silence,
And that the knight sholde telle in audience
What thing that worldly wommen loven best.
1040 This knight ne stood nat stille° as dooth a best,° *silent/beast*
But to his question anoon answerde
With manly vois that al the court it herde.
"My lige° lady, generally," quod he,   *liege*
"Wommen desire to have sovereinetee
1045 As wel over hir housbonde as hir love,
And for to been in maistrye him above.
This is youre moste desir though ye me kille.
Dooth as you list: I am here at youre wille."
In al the court ne was ther wif ne maide
1050 Ne widwe that contraried that he saide,
But saiden he was worthy han his lif.
And with that word up sterte that olde wif,
Which that the knight sawgh sitting on the greene;
"Mercy," quod she, "my soverein lady queene,
1055 Er that youre court departe, do me right.
I taughte this answere unto the knight,
For which he plighte me his trouthe there
The firste thing I wolde him requere
He wolde it do, if it laye in his might.
1060 Bifore the court thanne praye I thee, sire knight,"
Quod she, "that thou me take unto thy wif,
For wel thou woost° that I have kept° thy lif. *know/saved*
If I saye fals, say nay, upon thy fay."
This knight answerde, "Allas and wailaway,
1065 I woot right wel that swich was my biheeste.° *promise*
For Goddes love, as chees° a newe requeste: *choose*
Taak al my good and lat my body go."
"Nay thanne," quod she, "I shrewe° us bothe two. *curse*
For though that I be foul and old and poore,
1070 I nolde for al the metal ne for ore
That under erthe is grave° or lith above,   *buried*
But if thy wif I were and eek thy love."
"My love," quod he. "Nay, my dampnacioun!
Allas, that any of my nacioun°   *lineage*

1075	Sholde evere so foule disparaged° be."	*degraded*
	But al for nought, th'ende is this, that he	
	Constrained was: he needes moste hire wedde,	
	And taketh his olde wif and gooth to bedde.	
	Now wolden some men saye, paraventure,	
1080	That for my necligence I do no cure	
	To tellen you the joy and al th'array	
	That at the feeste was that ilke day.	
	To which thing shortly answere I shal:	
	I saye ther nas no joye ne feeste at al;	
1085	Ther nas but hevinesse and muche sorwe.	
	For prively he wedded hire on morwe,	
	And al day after hidde him as an owle,	
	So wo was him, his wif looked so foule.	
	Greet was the wo the knight hadde in his thought:	
1090	Whan he was with his wif abedde brought,	
	He walweth° and he turneth to and fro.	*rolls over*
	His olde wif lay smiling everemo,	
	And saide, "O dere housbonde, benedicite,°	*bless us*
	Fareth° every knight thus with his wif as ye?	*behaves*
1095	Is this the lawe of King Arthures hous?	
	Is every knight of his thus daungerous?°	*reserved*
	I am youre owene love and youre wif;	
	I am she which that saved hath youre lif;	
	And certes yit ne dide I you nevere unright.°	*injustice*
1100	Why fare ye thus with me this firste night?	
	Ye faren like a man hadde lost his wit.	
	What is my gilt? For Goddes love, telle it,	
	And it shal been amended if I may."	
	"Amended!" quod this knight. "Allas, nay, nay,	
1105	It wol nat been amended neveremo.	
	Thou art so lothly° and so old also,	*loathsome*
	And therto comen of so lowe a kinde,°	*breeding*
	That litel wonder is though I walwe and winde.°	*turn*
	So wolde God myn herte wolde breste!"°	*burst*
1110	"Is this," quod she, "the cause of youre unreste?"	
	"Ye, certainly," quod he. "No wonder is."	
	"Now sire," quod she, "I coude amende al this,	
	If that me liste, er it were dayes three,	
	So° wel ye mighte bere you° unto me.	*provided that / behave*
1115	"But for ye speken of swich gentilesse°	*nobility*
	As is descended out of old richesse—	
	That therfore sholden ye be gentilmen—	
	Swich arrogance is nat worth an hen.	
	Looke who that is most vertuous alway,	
1120	Privee and apert,° and most entendeth ay	*privately and publicly*
	To do the gentil deedes that he can,	
	Taak him for the gretteste gentilman.	
	Crist wol° we claime of him oure gentilesse,	*wishes*
	Nat of oure eldres for hir 'old richesse.'	
1125	For though they yive us al hir heritage,	

For which we claime to been of heigh parage,°   *noble lineage*
Yit may they nat biquethe for no thing
To noon of us hir vertuous living,
That made hem gentilmen ycalled be,
1130   And bad us folwen hem in swich degree.
     "Wel can the wise poete of Florence,
That highte° Dant,³ speken in this sentence;°   *was called /opinion*
Lo, in swich manere rym is Dantes tale:
'Ful selde° up riseth by his braunches⁴ smale   *seldom*
1135   Prowesse° of man, for God of his prowesse   *excellence*
Wol that of him we claime oure gentilesse.'
For of oure eldres may we no thing claime
But temporel thing that man may hurte and maime.
Eek every wight woot this as wel as I,
1140   If gentilesse were planted natureelly
Unto a certain linage down the line,
Privee and apert, thanne wolde they nevere fine°   *end*
To doon of gentilesse the faire office°—   *duty*
They mighte do no vilainye or vice.
1145   "Taak fir and beer° it in the derkeste hous   *bring*
Bitwixe this and the Mount of Caucasus,
And lat men shette° the dores and go thenne,°   *shut /thence*
Yit wol the fir as faire lie and brenne
As twenty thousand men mighte it biholde:
1150   His° office natureel ay wol it holde,   *its*
Up peril of my lif, til that it die.
Heer may ye see wel how that genterye°   *gentility*
Is nat annexed° to possessioun,   *connected*
Sith folk ne doon hir operacioun
1155   Alway, as dooth the fir, lo, in his kinde.°   *nature*
For God it woot, men may wel often finde
A lordes sone do shame and vilainye;
And he that wol han pris° of his gentrye,°   *esteem /noble birth*
For he was boren of a gentil hous,
1160   And hadde his eldres noble and vertuous,
And nil° himselven do no gentil deedes,   *will not*
Ne folwen his gentil auncestre that deed is,
He nis nat gentil, be he duc or erl—
For vilaines sinful deedes maken a cherl.°   *ruffian*
1165   Thy gentilesse nis but renomee°   *reputation*
Of thine auncestres for hir heigh bountee,°   *generosity*
Which is a straunge° thing for thy persone.   *foreign*
For gentilesse cometh fro God allone.
Thanne comth oure verray gentilesse of grace:
1170   It was no thing biquethe us with oure place.
Thenketh how noble, as saith Valerius,⁵

---

3. Dante Alighieri, the 13th-century Italian poet, expressed similar views in his *Convivio*.
4. Branches (of his family tree).

5. The Roman historian Valerius Maximus, in his *Facta et dicta memorabilia*, 3.4.

Was thilke Tullius Hostilius[6]
That out of poverte roos to heigh noblesse.
Redeth Senek,[7] and redeth eek Boece:

1175   Ther shul ye seen expres that no drede° is   *doubt*
That he is gentil that dooth gentil deedes.
And therfore, leve housbonde, I thus conclude:
Al were it that mine auncestres weren rude,°   *low born*
Yit may the hye God—and so hope I—

1180   Graunte me grace to liven vertuously.
Thanne am I gentil whan that I biginne
To liven vertuously and waive° sinne.   *avoid*
    "And ther as ye of poverte me repreve,
The hye God, on whom that we bileve,

1185   In wilful poverte chees to live his lif;
And certes every man, maiden, or wif
May understonde that Jesus, hevene king,
Ne wolde nat chese a vicious living.
Glad poverte is an honeste° thing, certain;   *honorable*

1190   This wol Senek and othere clerkes sayn.
Whoso that halt him paid of his poverte,[8]
I holde him riche al° hadde he nat a sherte.° *although/shirt*
He that coveiteth is a poore wight,
For he wolde han that is nat in his might;

1195   But he that nought hath, ne coveiteth have,
Is riche, although we holde him but a knave.°   *servant*
Verray poverte it singeth proprely.
Juvenal[9] saith of poverte, 'Merily
The poore man, whan he gooth by the waye,

1200   Biforn the theves he may singe and playe.'
Poverte is hateful good, and as I gesse,
A ful greet bringere out of bisinesse;°   *wordly cares*
A greet amendere eek of sapience°   *wisdom*
To him that taketh it in pacience;

1205   Poverte is thing, although it seeme elenge,°   *miserable*
Possession that no wight wol chalenge;
Poverte ful often, whan a man is lowe,
Maketh his God and eek himself to knowe;
Poverte a spectacle° is, as thinketh me,   *eyeglass*

1210   Thurgh which he may his verray freendes see.
And therfore, sire, sin that I nought you greve,
Of my poverte namore ye me repreve.
    "Now sire, of elde° ye repreve me: *old age*
And certes sire, though noon auctoritee

1215   Were in no book, ye gentils of honour
Sayn that men sholde an old wight doon favour,
And clepe him fader for youre gentilesse—
And auctours° shal I finden, as I gesse.   *authorities*
    "Now ther ye saye that I am foul and old:

---

6. The legendary third king of Rome who started as a shepherd.
7. Seneca, the Stoic author, in his *Epistle* 44; Boece:
Boethius in his *Consolation of Philosophy*.
8. Whoever is satisfied with poverty.
9. The misogynist Roman poet in his *Satires* 10.21, 22.

1220	Thanne drede you nought to been a cokewold,°	*cuckold*
	For filthe and elde, also mote I thee,	
	Been grete wardeins° upon chastitee.	*guardians*
	But nathelees, sin I knowe your delit,	
	I shal fulfille youre worldly appetit.	
1225	"Chees now," quod she, "oon of thise thinges twaye:	
	To han me foul and old til that I deye	
	And be to you a trewe humble wif,	
	And nevere you displese in al my lif,	
	Or elles ye wol han me yong and fair,	
1230	And take youre aventure° of the repair°	*chances/visits*
	That shal be to youre hous by cause of me—	
	Or in som other place, wel may be.	
	Now chees youreselven wheither° that you liketh."	*whichever*
	This knight aviseth him° and sore siketh;°	*considers/sighs*
1335	But atte laste he saide in this manere:	
	"My lady and my love, and wif so dere,	
	I putte me in youre wise governaunce:	
	Cheseth yourself which may be most plesaunce	
	And most honour to you and me also.	
1240	I do no fors° the wheither of the two,	*do not care*
	For as you liketh it suffiseth° me."	*satisfies*
	"Thanne have I gete of you maistrye," quod she,	
	"Sin I may chese and governe as me lest?"	
	"Ye, certes, wif," quod he. "I holde it best."	
1245	"Kisse me," quod she. "We be no lenger wrothe.°	*opposed*
	For by my trouthe, I wol be to you bothe—	
	This is to sayn, ye, bothe fair and good.	
	I praye to God that I mote sterven wood,°	*die mad*
	But I to you be al so good and trewe	
1250	As evere was wif sin that the world was newe.	
	And but I be tomorn° as fair to seene	*in the morning*
	As any lady, emperisse, or queene,	
	That is bitwixe the eest and eek the west,	
	Do with my lif and deeth right as you lest:	
1255	Caste up the curtin, looke how that it is."	
	And whan the knight sawgh verraily al this,	
	That she so fair was and so yong therto,	
	For joye he hente° hire in his armes two;	*seized*
	His herte bathed in a bath of blisse;	
1260	A thousand time arewe° he gan hire kisse,	*in a row*
	And she obeyed him in every thing	
	That mighte do him plesance or liking.	
	And thus they live unto hir lives ende	
	In parfit joye. And Jesu Crist us sende	
1265	Housbondes meeke, yonge, and fresshe abedde—	
	And grace t'overbide° hem that we wedde.	*outlive*
	And eek I praye Jesu shorte hir lives	
	That nought wol be governed by hir wives,	
	And olde and angry nigardes of dispence°—	*misers in spending*
1270	God sende hem soone a verray pestilence!	

The Pardoner's Prologue and Tale

There is something in Chaucer's Pardoner to unnerve practically everyone. The Pardoner's physiology blurs gender itself, his apparent homosexuality challenges the dominant heterosexual ordering of medieval society, his *Prologue* subverts the notion that the intent and effect of words are connected, and his willingness to convert religious discourse into cash undermines the very bases of faith. He initiates a sequence of moments in the later tales that threaten to puncture or tear the social fabric of the Canterbury company.

The Pardoner and "his freend and his compeer," the Summoner, are the last two pilgrims described in *The General Prologue*, reflecting the distaste with which such marginal clergy were often regarded in the period. Summoners were the policing branch of the ecclesiastical courts, paid to bring in transgressors against the canon law. Pardoners had the job, criticized even within the church, of exchanging indulgences for cash. The sufferings of Christ and saintly martyrs, it was thought, had left the church with a legacy of goodness. This could be transferred to sinners, freeing them from a period in Purgatory, if they proved their penitence (among other ways) by gifts to support good works such as the hospital for which the Pardoner worked.

The Pardoner has turned this part of the structure of penitence into a profit center. In his own *Prologue*, the Pardoner is boastfully explicit about this:

> For myn entente is nat but for to winne,
> And no thing for correccion of sinne . . .

This merciless equation of his verbal power with cash profit deeply subverts the logic of Christian language and the priestly role in salvation. These are replaced by language working in a strange self-consuming circle: the Pardoner brilliantly achieves the very sin his sermon most vituperates.

The Pardoner's physiology—he has either lost his testicles or never had them—may emblematize this exploitation of language emptied of spiritual intention. His uncertain or incomplete gender, though, also challenges the fundamental distinctions of the body within the medieval social economy, as does his apparent homosexuality. The Pardoner's theatrical self-presentation, abetted by rhetorical techniques he lovingly describes, draws the fascinated if queasy attention of his audience and seems to provide him a monstrous though (as it turns out) fragile power.

The Pardoner's tale of three rioters and their encounter with death is actually folded into his Prologue as an exemplum, an illustrative story, in the sermon against cupidity he proposes to offer as a sample of his skills. Yet the Pardoner's obsession with bodies in extremity, seeking or denying death, skeletal or gorged, pulls against his tale as a parable of greed. The tale draws toward its close in a scene of rage, exposure, and angry silence, which threatens to undo the pilgrim society, rather as the Pardoner and his discourse have threatened so much of the broader social contract. The Knight steps in, though, and almost bullies the Host and the Pardoner into a kiss of peace. This ritual gesture, nearly as empty of real goodwill as any of the Pardoner's most cynical words, does allow the shaken group to continue on their way, even as it hints at the emptiness that may hide in other, less openly challenged systems of value in the tales and their world.

The Pardoner's Prologue
The Introduction

Oure Hoste gan to swere as he were wood;°   *mad*
"Harrow," quod he, "by nailes[1] and by blood,

---

1. Nails (of Christ's cross).

This was a fals cherl° and a fals justice.°[2]   *villain/judge*
    As shameful deeth as herte may devise
5   Come to thise juges and hir advocats.°   *lawyers*
    Algate° this sely° maide is slain, allas!   *anyway/innocent*
    Allas, too dere boughte she beautee!
    Wherfore I saye alday° that men may see   *always*
    The yiftes of Fortune and of Nature
10 Been cause of deeth to many a creature.
    As bothe yiftes that I speke of now,
    Men han ful ofte more for harm than prow.°   *profit*
      "But trewely, myn owene maister dere,
    This is a pitous tale for to heere.
15 But nathelees, passe over, is no fors:°   *concern*
    I praye to God so save thy gentil° cors,°   *noble/body*
    And eek thine urinals[3] and thy jurdones,°   *chamberpots*
    Thyn ipocras and eek thy galiones,[4]
    And every boiste° ful of thy letuarye°—   *box/medicine*
20 God blesse hem, and oure lady Sainte Marye.
    So mote I theen,° thou art a propre man,   *so may I prosper*
    And lik a prelat,° by Saint Ronian![5]   *Church officer*
    Saide I nat wel? I can nat speke in terme.°   *jargon*
    But wel I woot, thou doost myn herte to erme°   *grieve*
25 That I almost have caught a cardinacle.°   *heart condition*
    By corpus bones,[6] but if I have triacle,°   *medicine*
    Or elles a draughte of moiste° and corny° ale,   *fresh/malted*
    Or but I heere anoon a merye tale,
    Myn herte is lost for pitee of this maide.
30   "Thou bel ami,[7] thou Pardoner," he saide,
    "Tel us som mirthe or japes° right anoon."   *joke*
      "It shal be doon," quod he, "by Saint Ronian.
    But first," quod he, "here at this ale-stake°   *tavern marker*
    I wol bothe drinke and eten of a cake."°   *loaf of bread*
35   And right anoon thise gentils gan to crye,
    "Nay, lat him telle us of no ribaudye.°   *obscenity*
    Tel us som moral thing that we may lere,°   *learn*
    Som wit, and thanne wol we gladly heere."
      "I graunte, ywis," quod he, "but I moot thinke
40 Upon som honeste° thing whil that I drinke."   *honorable*

The Prologue

    Lordinges—quod he—in chirches whan I preche,
    I paine me to han an hautein° speeche,   *loud*
    And ringe it out as round as gooth a belle,
    For I can al by rote° that I telle.   *know it all by heart*
45 My theme is alway oon,° and evere was: *the same*

---

2. Harry Baily, the host, is responding to *The Physician's Tale* and the story of a young woman named Virginia whose father kills her rather than surrender her to a wicked judge and his accomplice.
3. Physician's vessels for analyzing urine samples.
4. Medicines named after the ancient Greek physicians Hypocrates and Galen.
5. Saint Ronan, a Scottish saint, with a possible pun on "runnions," the male sexual organs.
6. A confused oath mixing God's body and God's bones.
7. Fair friend (French, affected).

Radix malorum est cupiditas.[8]
First I pronounce whennes that I come,
And thanne my bulles° shewe I alle and some: *indulgences*
Oure lige lordes seel[9] on my patente,°   *license*
50   That shewe I first, my body to warente,°   *safeguard*
That no man be so bold, ne preest ne clerk,
Me to destourbe of Cristes holy werk.
And after that thanne telle I forth my tales—
Bulles of popes and of cardinales,
55   Of patriarkes and bisshopes I shewe,
And in Latin I speke a wordes fewe,
To saffron° with my predicacioun,°   *season/preaching*
And for to stire hem to devocioun.
        Thanne shewe I forth my longe crystal stones,°   *jars*
60   Ycrammed ful of cloutes° and of bones—   *rags*
Relikes been they, as weenen° they eechoon.   *suppose*
Thanne have I in laton° a shulder-boon   *brazened*
Which that was of an holy Jewes sheep.
"Goode men," I saye, "take of my wordes keep:°   *notice*
65   If that this boon be wasshe in any welle,
If cow, or calf, or sheep, or oxe swelle,
That any worm° hath ete or worm ystonge,   *snake*
Take water of that welle and wassh his tonge,
And it is hool° anoon. And ferthermoor,   *healthy*
70   Of pokkes° and of scabbe and every soor   *pox*
Shal every sheep be hool that of this welle
Drinketh a draughte. Take keep eek that I telle:
If that the goode man that the beestes oweth°   *owns*
Wol every wike,° er that the cok him croweth,   *week*
75   Fasting drinken of this welle a draughte—
As thilke holy Jew oure eldres taughte—
His beestes and his stoor° shal multiplye.   *stock*
        "And sire, also it heleth jalousye:
For though a man be falle in jalous rage,
80   Lat maken with this water his potage,°   *soup*
And nevere shal he more his wif mistriste,
Though he the soothe° of hir defaute wiste,°   *truth/knows*
Al hadde she taken preestes two or three.
        "Here is a mitein° eek that ye may see: *mitten*
85   He that his hand wol putte in this mitein
He shal have multiplying of his grain,
Whan he hath sowen, be it whete or otes—
So that he offre pens° or elles grotes.°   *pennies/silver coins*
        "Goode men and wommen, oo thing warne I you:
90   If any wight° be in this chirche now   *person*
That hath doon sinne horrible, that he
Dar nat for shame of it yshriven° be,   *confessed*
Or any womman, be she yong or old,
That hath ymaked hir housbonde cokewold,°   *cuckold*

---

8. Greed is the root of all evil.   9. Seal of our liege lord (i.e., the Pope).

95	Swich folk shal have no power ne no grace	
	To offren to my relikes in this place;	
	And whoso findeth him out of swich blame,	
	He wol come up and offre in Goddes name,	
	And I assoile° him by the auctoritee	absolve
100	Which that by bulle ygraunted was to me."	
	By this gaude° have I wonne, yeer by yeer,	trick
	An hundred mark[1] sith I was pardoner.	
	I stonde lik a clerk in my pulpet,	
	And whan the lewed° peple is down yset,	ignorant
105	I preche so as ye han herd bifore,	
	And telle an hundred false japes° more.	tricks
	Thanne paine I me to strecche forth the nekke,	
	And eest and west upon the peple I bekke°	nod
	As dooth a douve,° sitting on a berne;°	dove/barn
110	Mine handes and my tonge goon so yerne°	fast
	That it is joye to see my bisinesse.	
	Of avarice and of swich cursednesse	
	Is al my preching, for to make hem free°	generous
	To yiven hir pens, and namely unto me,	
115	For myn entente is nat but for to winne,°	profit
	And no thing for correccion of sinne:	
	I rekke° nevere whan that they been beried°	care/buried
	Though that hir soules goon a-blakeberied.[2]	
	For certes, many a predicacioun	
120	Comth ofte time of yvel entencioun:	
	Som for plesance of folk and flaterye,	
	To been avaunced by ypocrisye,	
	And som for vaine glorye, and som for hate;	
	For whan I dar noon otherways debate,	
125	Thanne wol I stinge him with my tonge smerte°	hurting
	In preching, so that he shal nat asterte°	escape
	To been defamed falsly, if that he	
	Hath trespassed to my bretheren or to me.	
	For though I telle nought his propre name,	
130	Men shal wel knowe that it is the same	
	By signes and by othere circumstaunces.	
	Thus quite° I folk that doon us displesaunces;°	repay/trouble
	Thus spete I out my venim under hewe°	color
	Of holinesse, to seeme holy and trewe.	
135	But shortly myn entente I wol devise:°	describe
	I preche of no thing but for coveitise;°	greed
	Therfore my theme is yit and evere was	
	Radix malorum est cupiditas.	
	Thus can I preche again that same vice	
140	Which that I use, and that is avarice.	
	But though myself be gilty in that sinne,	
	Yit can I make other folk to twinne°	separate
	From avarice, and sore to repente—	

---

1. About 66 pounds.   2. Looking for blackberries.

But that is nat my principal entente:
145 I preche no thing but for coveitise.
Of this matere it oughte ynough suffise.
    Thanne telle I hem ensamples° many oon   *exemplary tales*
Of olde stories longe time agoon,
For lewed peple loven tales olde—
150 Swiche thinges can they wel reporte° and holde.°   *repeat/remember*
What, trowe° ye that whiles I may preche,   *believe*
And winne gold and silver for I teche,
That I wol live in poverte wilfully?
Nay, nay, I thoughte it nevere, trewely,
155 For I wol preche and begge in sondry landes;
I wol nat do no labour with mine handes,
Ne make baskettes and live therby,
By cause I wol nat beggen idelly.°   *in vain*
I wol none of the Apostles countrefete:°   *imitate*
160 I wol have moneye, wolle,° cheese, and whete,   *wool*
Al were it yiven of the pooreste page,°   *servant*
Or of the pooreste widwe in a village—
Al sholde hir children sterve° for famine.   *die*
Nay, I wol drinke licour of the vine
165 And have a joly wenche in every town.
But herkneth, lordinges, in conclusioun,
Youre liking is that I shal telle a tale:
Now have I dronke a draughte of corny ale,
By God, I hope I shal you telle a thing
170 That shal by reson been at youre liking;
For though myself be a ful vicious man,
A moral tale yit I you telle can,
Which I am wont to preche for to winne.
Now holde youre pees, my tale I wol biginne.

The Pardoner's Tale

175 In Flandres whilom° was a compaignye   *once*
Of yonge folk that haunteden° folye—   *practiced*
As riot, hasard, stewes,[1] and tavernes,
Wher as with harpes, lutes, and giternes°   *guitars*
They daunce and playen at dees° bothe day and night,   *dice*
180 And ete also and drinke over hir might,
Thurgh which they doon the devel sacrifise
Withinne that develes temple in cursed wise
By superfluitee° abhominable.   *overindulgence*
Hir othes been so grete and so dampnable
185 That it is grisly for to heere hem swere:
Oure blessed Lordes body they totere°—   *rip apart*
Hem thoughte that Jewes rente° him nought ynough.   *tore*
And eech of hem at otheres sinne lough.°   *laughed*
And right anoon thanne comen tombesteres,°   *dancing girls*
190 Fetis° and smale,° and yonge frutesteres,[2]   *elegant/slender*

---

1. Such as carousing, gambling, brothels.   2. Girls selling fruit.

Singeres with harpes, bawdes, wafereres°—   *cake sellers*
Whiche been the verray develes officeres,
To kindle and blowe the fir of lecherye
That is annexed° unto glotonye:°   *connected/gluttony*
195   The Holy Writ take I to my witnesse
That luxure° is in win and dronkenesse.   *lechery*
Lo, how that dronken Lot³ unkindely°   *against nature*
Lay by his doughtres two unwitingly:
So dronke he was he niste what he wroughte.°   *knew not what he did*
200   Herodes,⁴ who so wel the stories soughte,
Whan he of win was repleet at his feeste,
Right at his owene table he yaf his heeste°   *command*
To sleen° the Baptist John, ful giltelees.   *slay*
    Senek⁵ saith a good word douteless:
205   He saith he can no difference finde
Bitwixe a man that is out of his minde
And a man which that is dronkelewe,°   *drunk*
But that woodnesse, yfallen in a shrewe,⁶
Persevereth lenger than dooth dronkenesse.
210   O glotonye, ful of cursednesse!
O cause first of oure confusioun!°   *ruin*
O original of oure dampnacioun,
Til Crist hadde bought° us with his blood again!   *redeemed*
Lo, how dere, shortly for to sayn,
215   Abought was thilke cursed vilainye;
Corrupt was al this world for glotonye:
Adam oure fader and his wif also
Fro Paradis to labour and to wo
Were driven for that vice, it is no drede.°   *doubt*
220   For whil that Adam fasted, as I rede,
He was in Paradis; and whan that he
Eet of the fruit defended° on a tree,   *forbidden*
Anoon he was out cast to wo and paine.
O glotonye, on thee wel oughte us plaine!°   *lament*
225   O, wiste a man how manye maladies
Folwen of excesse and of glotonies,
He wolde been the more mesurable°   *moderate*
Of his diete, sitting at his table.
Allas, the shorte throte, the tendre mouth,
230   Maketh that eest and west and north and south,
In erthe, in air, in water, men to swinke,°   *labor*
To gete a gloton daintee mete and drinke.
Of this matere, O Paul, wel canstou trete:°   *discuss*
"Mete unto wombe, and wombe° eek unto mete,   *belly*
235   Shal God destroyen bothe," as Paulus saith.⁷
    Allas, a foul thing is it, by my faith,
To saye this word, and fouler is the deede

---

3. Lot, the nephew of Abraham, whose story is told in Genesis 19.30–38.
4. King Herod, who was enticed by Salome into bringing her the head of John the Baptist (Mark 6.17–29,

Matthew 14.1–12).
5. The stoic author Seneca in his *Epistle* 83.18. 493–97.
6. Madness, occurring in a wicked person.
7. St. Paul in 1 Corinthians 6.13.

Whan man so drinketh of the white and rede°   *white and red wines*
That of his throte he maketh his privee°   *toilet*
240   Thurgh thilke cursed superfluitee.
        The Apostle[8] weeping saith ful pitously,
"Ther walken manye of which you told have I—
I saye it now weeping with pitous vois—
They been enemies of Cristes crois,°   *cross*
245   Of whiche the ende is deeth—wombe is hir god!"
O wombe, O bely, O stinking cod,°   *bag*
Fulfilled of dong and of corrupcioun!
At either ende of thee foul is the soun.°   *sound*
How greet labour and cost is thee to finde!°   *provide for*
250   Thise cookes, how they stampe and straine and grinde,
And turnen substance into accident[9]
To fulfillen al thy likerous talent!°   *greedy desire*
Out of the harde bones knokke they
The mary,° for they caste nought away   *marrow*
255   That may go thurgh the golet° softe and soote.°   *gullet/sweet*
Of spicerye of leef and bark and roote
Shal been his sauce ymaked by delit,
To make him yit a newer appetit.
But certes, he that haunteth swiche delices°   *delicacies*
260   Is deed whil that he liveth in tho vices.
        A lecherous thing is win, and dronkenesse
Is ful of striving° and of wrecchednesse.   *quarreling*
O dronke man, disfigured is thy face!
Sour is thy breeth, foul artou to embrace!
265   And thurgh thy dronke nose seemeth the soun
As though thou saidest ay "Sampsoun, Sampsoun."
And yit, God woot, Sampson drank nevere win.
Thou fallest as it were a stiked swin;°   *stuck pig*
Thy tonge is lost, and al thyn honeste cure,°   *care for honor*
270   For dronkenesse is verray sepulture°   *grave*
Of mannes wit and his discrecioun.
In whom that drinke hath dominacioun
He can no conseil keepe, it is no drede.
Now keepe you fro the white and fro the rede—
275   And namely fro the white win of Lepe[1]
That is to selle in Fisshstreete or in Chepe:[2]
The win of Spaine creepeth subtilly[3]
In othere wines growing faste° by,   *close*
Of which ther riseth swich fumositee°   *vapors*
280   That whan a man hath dronken draughtes three
And weeneth that he be at hoom in Chepe,
He is in Spaine, right at the town of Lepe,
Nat at The Rochele ne at Burdeux town;

---

8. St. Paul, in Philippians 3.18–19.
9. A philosophical joke playing on the transubstantiation
of bread and wine into the holy Eucharist, according to
Catholic doctrine, where matter (substance) is transformed in its qualities (accident).
1. Wine-growing region in Spain.

2. Commercial districts in London.
3. Chaucer is referring to the illegal practice of using
cheap wine (here, Spanish wine from Lepe) to dilute
more-expensive wines (from the neighoring French
provinces of La Rochelle and Bourdeaux).

And thanne wol he sayn "Sampsoun, Sampsoun."
285   But herkneth, lordinges, oo word I you praye,
That alle the soverein actes,° dar I saye,   *excellent deeds*
Of victories in the Olde Testament,
Thurgh verray God that is omnipotent,
Were doon in abstinence and in prayere:
290 Looketh the Bible and ther ye may it lere.°   *learn*
    Looke Attilla, the grete conquerour,[4]
Deide in his sleep with shame and dishonour,
Bleeding at his nose in dronkenesse:
A capitain sholde live in sobrenesse.
295   And overal this, aviseth you right wel
What was comanded unto Lamuel[5]—
Nat Samuel, but Lamuel, saye I—
Redeth the Bible and finde it expresly,
Of win-yiving° to hem that han° justise: *wine-serving/dispense*
300 Namore of this, for it may wel suffise.
    And now that I have spoken of glotonye,
Now wol I you defende hasardrye:°   *gambling*
Hasard is verray moder of lesinges,°   *lies*
And of deceite and cursed forsweringes,
305 Blaspheme of Crist, manslaughtre, and wast° also   *waste*
Of catel° and of time; and ferthermo,   *property*
It is repreve° and contrarye of honour   *reprobate*
For to been holden a commune hasardour,
And evere the hyer he is of estat
310 The more is he holden desolat.°   *dissolute*
If that a prince useth hasardrye,
In alle governance and policye
He is, as by commune opinioun,
Yholde the lasse in reputacioun.
315   Stilbon,[6] that was a wis embassadour,
Was sent to Corinthe in ful greet honour
Fro Lacedomye° to make hir alliaunce,   *Sparta*
And whan he cam him happede parchaunce
That alle the gretteste that were of that lond
320 Playing at the hasard he hem foond,
For which as soone as it mighte be
He stal him hoom again to his contree,
And saide, "Ther wol I nat lese my name,
N'I wol nat take on me so greet defame
325 You to allye unto none hasardours:
Sendeth othere wise embassadours,
For by my trouthe, me were levere° die   *I would rather*
Than I you sholde to hasardours allye.
For ye that been so glorious in honours
330 Shal nat allye you with hasardours
As by my wil, ne as by my tretee."

---

4. Attila the Hun died on his wedding night from excessive drinking.
5. Biblical king of Massa, warned against drinking in

Proverbs 31.4.
6. Possibly referring to the Greek philosopher Stilbo or Chilon.

This wise philosophre, thus saide he.
   Looke eek that to the king Demetrius
The King of Parthes,[7] as the book saith us,
335   Sente him a paire of dees of gold in scorn,
For he hadde used hasard therbiforn,
For which he heeld his glorye or his renown
At no value or reputacioun.
Lordes may finden other manere play
340   Honeste ynough to drive the day away.
   Now wol I speke of othes false and grete
A word or two, as olde bookes trete:
   Greet swering is a thing abhominable,
And fals swering is yit more reprevable.°   *reprehensible*
345   The hye God forbad swering at al—
Witnesse on Mathew. But in special
Of swering saith the holy Jeremie,[8]
"Thou shalt swere sooth thine othes and nat lie,
And swere in doom° and eek in rightwisnesse,"   *judgment*
350   But idel swering is a cursednesse."
   Biholde and see that in the firste Table°   *tablet*
Of hye Goddes heestes° honorable   *commandments*
How that the seconde heeste of him is this:
"Take nat my name in idel or amis."
355   Lo, rather° he forbedeth swich swering   *sooner*
Than homicide, or many a cursed thing.
I saye that as by ordre thus it stondeth—
This knoweth that° his heestes understondeth   *he who*
How that the seconde heeste of God is that.
360   And fertherover, I wol thee telle al plat°   *flatly*
That vengeance shal nat parten from his hous
That of his othes is too outrageous.
"By Goddes precious herte!" and "By his nailes!"
And "By the blood of Crist that is in Hailes,[9]
365   Sevene is my chaunce, and thyn is cink and traye!"°   *five and three*
"By Goddes armes, if thou falsly playe
This daggere shal thurghout thyn herte go!"
This fruit cometh of the bicche bones° two—   *cursed dice*
Forswering, ire, falsnesse, homicide.
370   Now for the love of Crist that for us dyde,
Lete° youre othes bothe grete and smale.   *leave off*
But sires, now wol I telle forth my tale.
   Thise riotoures° three of whiche I telle,   *revelers*
Longe erst er° prime° ronge of any belle,   *before/6 a.m.*
375   Were set hem in a taverne to drinke,
And as they sat they herde a belle clinke
Biforn a cors° was caried to his grave.   *corpse*
That oon of hem gan callen to his knave:°   *servant*
"Go bet,"° quod he, "and axe redily   *quickly*
380   What cors is this that passeth heer forby,

---

7. Parthia in northern Persia.
8. The prophet Jeremiah (4.2).

9. Hales Abbey in Gloucestershire owned a relic of Christ's blood.

And looke that thou reporte his name weel."
  "Sire," quod this boy, "it needeth neveradeel:[1]
It was me told er ye cam heer two houres.
He was, pardee, an old felawe of youres,

385   And sodeinly he was yslain tonight,
Fordronke° as he sat on his bench upright;   *very drunk*
Ther cam a privee° thief men clepeth° Deeth,   *stealthy/call*
That in this contree al the peple sleeth,
And with his spere he smoot his herte atwo,

390   And wente his way withouten wordes mo.
He hath a thousand slain this pestilence.°   *during this plague*
And maister, er ye come in his presence,
Me thinketh that it were necessarye
For to be war of swich an adversarye;

395   Beeth redy for to meete him everemore:
Thus taughte me my dame.° I saye namore."   *mother*
  "By Sainte Marye," saide this taverner,
"The child saith sooth, for he hath slain this yeer,
Henne° over a mile, within a greet village,   *from here*

400   Bothe man and womman, child and hine° and page.° *farmhand/servant*
I trowe his habitacion be there.
To been avised° greet wisdom it were   *warned*
Er that he dide a man a dishonour."
  "Ye, Goddes armes," quod this riotour,

405   "Is it swich peril with him for to meete?
I shal him seeke by way and eek by streete,
I make avow to Goddes digne° bones.   *worthy*
Herkneth, felawes, we three been alle ones:
Lat eech of us holde up his hand to other

410   And eech of us bicome otheres brother,
And we wol sleen this false traitour Deeth.
He shal be slain, he that so manye sleeth,
By Goddess dignitee, er it be night."
  Togidres han thise three hir trouthes° plight° *words of honor/pledged*

415   To live and dien eech of hem with other,
As though he were his owene ybore° brother.   *born*
And up they sterte, al dronken in this rage,
And forth they goon towardes that village
Of which the taverner hadde spoke biforn.

420   And many a grisly ooth thanne han they sworn,
And Cristes blessed body they torente:°   *tore apart*
Deeth shal be deed if that they may him hente.°   *capture*
  Whan they han goon nat fully half a mile,
Right as they wolde han treden° over a stile,   *stepped*

425   An old man and a poore with hem mette;
This olde man ful mekely hem grette,°   *greeted*
And saide thus, "Now lordes, God you see."°   *look after*
  The pruddeste° of thise riotoures three   *proudest*
Answerde again, "What, carl with sory grace,°   *unlucky fellow*

---

1. Is not necessary in the least.

430	Why artou al forwrapped° save thy face?	*bundled up*
	Why livestou so longe in so greet age?"	
	This olde man gan looke in his visage,	
	And saide thus, "For I ne can nat finde	
	A man, though that I walked into Inde,	
435	Neither in citee ne in no village,	
	That wolde chaunge his youthe for myn age;	
	And therfore moot I han myn age stille,	
	As longe time as it is Goddes wille.	
	"Ne Deeth, allas, ne wol nat have my lif.	
440	Thus walke I lik a restelees caitif,°	*wretch*
	And on the ground which is my modres° gate	*mother's*
	I knokke with my staf bothe erly and late,	
	And saye, 'Leve° moder, leet me in:	*dear*
	Lo, how I vanisshe, flessh and blood and skin.	
445	Allas, whan shal my bones been at reste?	
	Moder, with you wolde I chaunge° my cheste°	*exchange/strongbox*
	That in my chambre longe time hath be,	
	Ye, for an haire-clout° to wrappe me.'	*winding sheet*
	But yit to me she wol nat do that grace,	
450	For which ful pale and welked° is my face.	*withered*
	But sires, to you it is no curteisye	
	To speken to an old man vilainye,°	*discourtesy*
	But he trespasse in word or elles in deede.	
	In Holy Writ ye may yourself wel rede,	
455	'Agains an old man, hoor upon his heed,	
	Ye shal arise.' Wherfore I yive you reed,°	*advice*
	Ne dooth unto an old man noon harm now,	
	Namore than that ye wolde men dide to you	
	In age, if that ye so longe abide.	
460	And God be with you wher ye go or ride:	
	I moot go thider as I have to go."	
	"Nay, olde cherl, by God thou shalt nat so,"	
	Saide this other hasardour anoon.	
	"Thou partest nat so lightly,° by Saint John!	*easily*
465	Thou speke right now of thilke traitour Deeth,	
	That in this contree alle oure freendes sleeth:	
	Have here my trouthe, as thou art his espye,	
	Tel wher he is, or thou shalt it abye,°	*pay for*
	By God and by the holy sacrament!	
470	For soothly thou art oon of his assent°	*in league with him*
	To sleen us yonge folk, thou false thief."	
	"Now sires," quod he, "if that ye be so lief°	*eager*
	To finde Deeth, turne up this crooked way,	
	For in that grove I lafte him, by my fay,	
475	Under a tree, and ther he wol abide:	
	Nat for youre boost he wol him no thing hide.	
	See ye that ook?° Right ther ye shal him finde.	*oak*
	God save you, that boughte again° mankinde,	*redeemed*
	And you amende." Thus saide this olde man.	
480	And everich of thise riotoures ran	

Til he cam to that tree, and ther they founde
Of florins° fine of gold ycoined rounde   *gold coins*
Wel neigh an eighte busshels as hem thoughte—
Ne lenger thanne after Deeth they soughte,
485   But eech of hem so glad was of the sighte,
For that the florins been so faire and brighte,
That down they sette hem by this precious hoord.
The worste of hem he spak the firste word:
    "Bretheren," quod he, "take keep what that I saye:
490   My wit is greet though that I bourde° and playe.   *joke*
This tresor hath Fortune unto us yiven
In mirthe and jolitee oure lif to liven,
And lightly as it cometh so wol we spende.
Ey, Goddes precious dignitee, who wende°   *would suppose*
495   Today that we sholde han so fair a grace?
But mighte this gold be caried fro this place
Hoom to myn hous—or elles unto youres—
For wel ye woot that al this gold is oures—
Thanne were we in heigh felicitee.
500   But trewely, by daye it mighte nat be:
Men wolde sayn that we were theves stronge,°   *flagrant*
And for oure owene tresor doon us honge.°   *have us hanged*
This tresor moste ycaried be by nighte,
As wisely and as slyly as it mighte.
505   Therfore I rede that cut° amonges us alle   *lots*
Be drawe, and lat see wher the cut wol falle;
And he that hath the cut with herte blithe°   *happy*
Shal renne to the town, and that ful swithe,°   *swiftly*
And bringe us breed and win ful prively;
510   And two of us shal keepen subtilly
This tresor wel, and if he wol nat tarye,
Whan it is night we wol this tresor carye
By oon assent wher as us thinketh best."
That oon of hem the cut broughte in his fest°   *fist*
515   And bad hem drawe and looke wher it wol falle;
And it fil on the yongeste of hem alle,
And forth toward the town he wente anoon.
And also soone as that he was agoon,
That oon of hem spak thus unto that other:
520   "Thou knowest wel thou art my sworen brother;
Thy profit wol I telle thee anoon:
Thou woost wel that oure felawe is agoon,
And here is gold, and that ful greet plentee,
That shal departed° been among us three.   *divided*
525   But natheleles, if I can shape° it so   *arrange*
That it departed were among us two,
Hadde I nat doon a freendes turn to thee?"
    That other answerde, "I noot° how that may be: *do not know*
He woot that the gold is with us twaye.
530   What shal we doon? What shal we to him saye?"
    "Shal it be conseil?"° saide the firste shrewe.°   *secret/villain*

"And I shal telle in a wordes fewe
What we shul doon, and bringe it wel aboute."
　　"I graunte," quod that other, "out of doute,
535 That by my trouthe I wol thee nat biwraye."°   *betray*
　　"Now," quod the firste, "thou woost wel we be twaye,
And two of us shal strenger be than oon:
Looke whan that he is set that right anoon
Aris as though thou woldest with him playe,
540 And I shal rive° him thurgh the sides twaye,   *stab*
Whil that thou strugelest with him as in game,
And with thy daggere looke thou do the same;
And thanne shal al this gold departed be,
My dere freend, bitwixe thee and me.
545 Thanne we may bothe oure lustes° al fulfille,   *desires*
And playe at dees right at oure owene wille."
And thus accorded been thise shrewes twaye
To sleen the thridde, as ye han herd me saye.
　　This yongeste, which that wente to the town,
550 Ful ofte in herte he rolleth up and down
The beautee of thise florins newe and brighte.
"O Lord," quod he, "if so were that I mighte
Have al this tresor to myself allone,
Ther is no man that liveth under the trone°   *throne*
555 Of God that sholde live so merye as I."
And at the laste the feend oure enemy
Putte in his thought that he sholde poison beye,°   *buy*
With which he mighte sleen his felawes twaye—
Forwhy° the feend foond him in swich livinge   *wherefore*
560 That he hadde leve° him to sorwe bringe: *permission*
For this was outrely his fulle entente,
To sleen hem bothe, and nevere to repente.
　　And forth he gooth—no lenger wolde he tarye—
Into the town unto a pothecarye,°   *druggist*
565 And prayed him that he him wolde selle
Som poison that he mighte his rattes quelle,°   *kill*
And eek ther was a polcat° in his hawe°   *weasel/yard*
That, as he saide, his capons° hadde yslawe,°   *chickens/slain*
And fain° he wolde wreke° him if he mighte   *gladly/avenge*
570 On vermin that destroyed him by nighte.
　　The pothecarye answerde, "And thou shalt have
A thing that, also° God my soule save,   *so*
In al this world ther is no creature
That ete or dronke hath of this confiture°—   *concoction*
575 Nat but the mountance° of a corn° of whete—   *amount/grain*
That he ne shal his lif anoon forlete.°   *lose*
Ye, sterve° he shal, and that in lasse while   *die*
Than thou wolt goon a paas° nat but a mile,   *walking*
The poison is so strong and violent."
580 This cursed man hath in his hand yhent°   *taken*
This poison in a box and sith he ran
Into the nexte streete unto a man

And borwed of him large botels three,
And in the two his poison poured he—
585   The thridde he kepte clene for his drinke,
For al the night he shoop° him for to swinke°   *prepared/work*
In carying of the gold out of that place.
And whan this riotour with sory grace
Hadde filled with win his grete botels three,
590   To his felawes again repaireth he.
      What needeth it to sermone of it more?
For right as they had cast his deeth bifore,
Right so they han him slain, and that anoon.
And whan that this was doon, thus spak that oon:
595   "Now lat us sitte and drinke and make us merye,
And afterward we wol his body berye."
And with that word it happed him par cas°   *by chance*
To take the botel ther the poison was,
And drank, and yaf his felawe drinke also,
600   For which anoon they storven bothe two.
      But certes I suppose that Avicen[2]
Wroot nevere in no canon ne in no *fen*
Mo wonder signes of empoisoning
Than hadde thise wrecches two er hir ending:
605   Thus ended been thise homicides two,
And eek the false empoisonere also.
      O cursed sinne of alle cursednesse!
O traitours homicide, O wikkednesse!
O glotonye, luxure,° and hasardrye!   *lechery*
610   Thou balsphemour of Crist with vilainye
And othes grete of usage° and of pride!   *habit*
Allas, mankinde, how may it bitide
That to thy Creatour which that thee wroughte,
And with his precious herte blood thee boughte,
615   Thou art so fals and so unkinde,° allas?   *unnatural*
      Now goode men, God foryive you youre trespas,
And ware° you fro the sinne of avarice: *guard*
Myn holy pardon may you alle warice°—   *save*
So that ye offre nobles or sterlinges,°   *gold or silver coins*
620   Or elles silver brooches, spoones, ringes.
Boweth your heed under this holy bulle!
Cometh up, ye wives, offreth of youre wolle!°   *wool*
Youre name I entre here in my rolle: anoon
Into the blisse of hevene shul ye goon.
625   I you assoile° by myn heigh power—   *absolve*
Ye that wol offre—as clene and eek as cleer°   *pure*
As ye were born.—And lo, sires, thus I preche.
And Jesu Crist that is oure soules leeche°   *physician*
So graunte you his pardon to receive,
630   For that is best—I wol you nat deceive.

---

2. The 12th-century Arab philosopher Avicenna composed a *Canon of Medicine*, divided into sections called fens.

The Epilogue

"But sires, oo word forgat I in my tale:
I have relikes and pardon in my male°   *bag*
As faire as any man in Engelond,
Whiche were me yiven by the Popes hond.

635 If any of you wol of devocioun
Offren and han myn absolucioun,
Come forth anoon, and kneeleth here adown,
And mekely receiveth my pardoun,
Or elles taketh pardon as ye wende,

640 Al newe and fressh at every miles ende—
So that ye offre alway newe and newe°   *over and over*
Nobles or pens whiche that be goode and trewe.
It is an honour to everich that is heer
That ye mowe have a suffisant° pardoner   *competent*

645 T'assoile you in contrees as ye ride,
For aventures whiche that may bitide:
Paraventure ther may falle oon or two
Down of his hors and breke his nekke atwo;
Looke which a suretee° is it to you alle   *safeguard*

650 That I am in youre felaweshipe yfalle
That may assoile you, bothe more and lasse,
Whan that the soule shal fro the body passe.
I rede° that oure Hoste shal biginne,   *advise*
For he is most envoluped in sinne.

655 Com forth, sire Host, and offre first anoon,
And thou shalt kisse the relikes everichoon,
Ye, for a grote:° unbokele anoon thy purs."   *fourpence coin*
       "Nay, nay," quod he, "thanne have I Cristes curs!
Lat be," quod he, "it shal nat be, so theech!°   *may I prosper*

660 Thou woldest make me kisse thyn olde breech
And swere it were a relik of a saint,
Though it were with thy fundament° depeint.°   *bowels/stained*
But, by the crois° which that Sainte Elaine[3] foond,   *cross*
I wolde I hadde thy coilons° in myn hond,   *testicles*

665 In stede of relikes or of saintuarye.°   *container of relics*
Lat cutte hem of: I wol thee helpe hem carye.
They shal be shrined in an hogges tord."°   *turd*
       This Pardoner answerde nat a word:
So wroth he was no word ne wolde he saye.

670   "Now," quod oure Host, "I wol no lenger playe
With thee, ne with noon other angry man."
       But right anoon the worthy Knight bigan,
Whan that he sawgh that al the peple lough,
"Namore of this, for it is right ynough.

675 Sire Pardoner, be glad and merye of cheere,
And ye, sire Host that been to me so dere,
I praye you that ye kisse the Pardoner,

3. St. Helen, who was said to have found the True Cross on which Jesus was crucified.

And Pardoner, I praye thee, draw thee neer,
And as we diden lat us laughe and playe."
680   Anoon they kiste and riden forth hir waye.

The Nun's Priest's Tale

Of all his varied and ambitious output, *The Nun's Priest's Tale* may be Chaucer's most impressive tour de force. At its core is a wonderful animal fable, free of the conventionality and sometimes easy moralities this ancient form had taken on by the fourteenth century. The fable of Chauntecleer and Pertelote achieves quite extraordinary density, further, because of the multiple frames—structural and thematic—that surround it.

As part of the Canterbury tale-telling competition, the priest's fable plays a role in that broadest contest of classes and literary genres. More locally, it is one of many moments in which the Host, Harry Bailey, demands a tale from a male pilgrim in a style that also suggests a sexual challenge, and then adjusts his estimate of the teller's virility (even his social position) to suit. The fable itself is surrounded by an intimate portrait of Chauntecleer's peasant owner and her simple life, content with "hertes suffisaunce," a marked contrast to courtly values.

The central story of Chauntecleer's dream, danger, and escape works within a subtle and funny exploration of relations between the sexes. This is conditioned by courtly love conventions, literacy and education, and even the vocabulary of Pertelote's mostly Saxon diction and Chauntecleer's love of French. This linguistic competition has its high point when Chauntecleer condescendingly mistranslates a misogynist Latin tag. Linguistic vanity, though, is exactly what puts Chauntecleer most in jeopardy. It is not the destiny Chauntecleer thinks he glimpses in his dream that almost costs his life, but rather another verbal competition, and an almost Oedipal challenge to his father.

Much of the story's energy, however, derives not from its frames but from the explosion of those frames—literary, spatial, even social—enacted and recalled at the heart of the tale. The chickens are simultaneously, and hilariously, both courtly lovers and very realistic fowl. When Chauntecleer is carried off, the whole world of the tale—widow, daughters, dogs, even bees—bursts outward in pursuit. In the midst of mock-epic and mock-romance comparisons to this joyful disorder, Chaucer even inserts one of his very few direct references to the greatest disorder of his time, the Rising of 1381.

The Nun's Priest's Tale is a comedy as well as a fable, reversing a lugubrious series of tragedies in the preceding *Monk's Tale*. In the end, it is a story of canniness, acquired self-knowledge, and self-salvation. Woven into the priest's humor are a gentle satire and a quiet assertion that free will is the final resource of any agent, avian or human.

The Nun's Priest's Tale
The Introduction

"Ho!" quod the Knight, "good sire, namore of this:
That ye han said is right ynough, ywis,°   *indeed*
And muchel more, for litel hevinesse
Is right ynough to muche folk° I gesse:[1]   *for most folks*
5   I saye for me it is a greet disese,
Wher as men han been in greet welthe and ese,

---

1. The Monk has just told a series of stark and repetitive "tragedies"—the falls of men both ancient and modern.

To heeren of hir sodein° fal, allas;   *sudden*
And the contrarye is joye and greet solas,°   *comfort*
As whan a man hath been in poore estat,
10   And climbeth up and wexeth° fortunat,   *becomes*
And there abideth in prosperitee:
Swich thing is gladsom, as it thinketh° me,   *seems to*
And of swich thing were goodly for to telle."
    "Ye," quod oure Host, "by Sainte Poules° belle,   *Paul's*
15   Ye saye right sooth: this Monk he clappeth° loude.   *chatters*
He spak how Fortune covered with a cloude—
I noot nevere what.° And als of a tragedye   *I don't know what*
Right now ye herde, and pardee,° no remedye   *by God*
It is for to biwaile ne complaine
20   That that is doon, and als° it is a paine,   *also*
As ye han said, to heere of hevinesse.
    "Sire Monk, namore of this, so God you blesse:
Youre tale anoyeth al this compaignye;
Swich talking is nat worth a boterflye,
25   For therinne is ther no disport ne game.
Wherfore, sire Monk, or daun° Piers by youre name,   *Master*
I praye you hertely telle us somwhat elles:
For sikerly, nere clinking of youre belles,[2]
That on youre bridel hange on every side,
30   By hevene king that for us alle dyde,
I sholde er this have fallen down for sleep,
Although the slough° hadde nevere been so deep.   *mud*
Thanne hadde youre tale al be told in vain;
For certainly, as that thise clerkes sayn,
35   Wher as a man may have noon audience,
Nought helpeth it to tellen his sentence;°   *statement*
And wel I woot the substance is in me,
If any thing shal wel reported be.
Sire, saye somwhat of hunting, I you praye."
40   "Nay," quod this Monk, "I have no lust° to playe.   *wish*
Now lat another telle, as I have told."
    Thanne spak oure Host with rude speeche and bold,
And saide unto the Nonnes Preest anoon,
"Com neer, thou Preest,[3] com hider, thou sire John:
45   Tel us swich thing as may oure hertes glade.°   *gladden our hearts*
Be blithe,° though thou ride upon a jade!°   *happy/nag*
What though thyn hors be bothe foul and lene?
If he wol serve thee, rekke nat a bene.°   *don't care a bean*
Looke that thyn herte be merye everemo."
50   "Yis, sire," quod he, "yis, Host, so mote I go,
But I be merye, ywis, I wol be blamed."
And right anoon his tale he hath attamed,°   *begun*
And thus he saide unto us everichoon,
This sweete Preest, this goodly man sire John.

---

2. For truly, were it not for the jingling of your bells.   3. The Host uses the familiar, somewhat condescending "thou," then contemptuously calls the priest "Sir John."

The Tale

55	A poore widwe somdeel stape° in age
	Was whilom° dwelling in a narwe cotage,
	Biside a grove, stonding in a dale:
	This widwe of which I telle you my tale,
	Sin° thilke° day that she was last a wif,
60	In pacience ladde a ful simple lif.
	For litel was hir catel° and hir rente,°
	By housbondrye° of swich as God hire sente
	She foond° hirself and eek hir doughtren two.
	Three large sowes hadde she and namo,
65	Three kin,° and eek a sheep that highte° Malle.
	Ful sooty was hir bowr° and eek hir halle,
	In which she eet ful many a sclendre meel;
	Of poinant° sauce hire needed neveradeel:
	No daintee morsel passed thurgh hir throte—
70	Hir diete was accordant to hir cote.°
	Repleccioun° ne made hire nevere sik:
	Attempre° diete was al hir physik,
	And exercise and hertes suffisaunce.
	The goute lette hire nothing for to daunce,[4]
75	N'apoplexye shente° nat hir heed.
	No win ne drank she, neither whit ne reed:
	Hir boord° was served most with whit and blak,
	Milk and brown breed, in which she foond no lak;°
	Seind° bacon, and somtime an ey° or twaye,°
80	For she was as it were a manere daye.°
	A yeerd° she hadde, enclosed al withoute
	With stikkes, and a drye dich aboute,
	In which she hadde a cok heet° Chauntecleer:
	In al the land of crowing nas his peer.
85	His vois was merier than the merye orgon
	On massedayes that in the chirche goon;°
	Wel sikerer° was his crowing in his logge°
	Than is a clok or an abbeye orlogge;°
	By nature he knew eech ascensioun
90	Of th'equinoxial[5] in thilke town:
	For whan degrees fifteene were ascended,
	Thanne crew he that it mighte nat been amended.°
	His comb was redder than the fin coral,
	And batailed° as it were a castel wal;
95	His bile° was blak, and as the jeet it shoon;
	Like asure° were his legges and his toon;°
	His nailes whitter than the lilye flowr,
	And lik the burned° gold was his colour.
	This gentil cok hadde in his governaunce
100	Sevene hennes for to doon al his plesaunce,
	Whiche were his sustres and his paramours,°

Right-margin glosses:

- well along
- once upon a time
- since / that
- property / income
- management
- provided for
- cows / was named
- bedroom
- pungent
- cottage
- gluttony
- moderate
- hurt
- table
- fault
- singed / egg / two
- dairy maid
- yard
- called
- is played
- surer / dwelling
- timepiece
- surpassed
- crenellated
- beak
- azure / toes
- burnished
- lovers

---

4. Did not keep her from dancing.   5. The points marking the celestial hours.

And wonder like to him as of colours;
Of whiche the faireste hewed° on hir throte   *colored*
Was cleped° faire damoisele Pertelote: *called*
105   Curteis she was, discreet, and debonaire,°   *gracious*
And compaignable,° and bar hirself so faire,   *sociable*
Sin thilke day that she was seven night old,
That trewely she hath the herte in hold
Of Chauntecleer, loken in every lith.[6]
110   He loved hire so that wel was him therwith.
But swich a joye was it to heere hem singe,
Whan that the brighte sonne gan to springe,
In sweete accord "My Lief is Faren in Londe"[7]—
For thilke time, as I have understonde,
115   Beestes and briddes couden speke and singe.
    And so bifel that in a daweninge,
As Chauntecleer among his wives alle
Sat on his perche that was in the halle,
And next him sat this faire Pertelote,
120   This Chauntecleer gan gronen in his throte,
As man that in his dreem is drecched° sore.   *disturbed*
    And whan that Pertelote thus herde him rore,
She was agast, and saide, "Herte dere,
What aileth you to grone in this manere?
125   Ye been a verray° slepere, fy, for shame!"   *true*
    And he answerde and saide thus, "Madame,
I praye you that ye take it nat agrief.°   *amiss*
By God, me mette° I was in swich meschief   *I dreamed*
Right now, that yit myn herte is sore afright.
130   Now God," quod he, "my swevene recche aright,[8]
And keepe my body out of foul prisoun!
Me mette how that I romed up and down
Within oure yeerd, wher as I sawgh a beest,
Was lik an hound and wolde han maad arrest°   *taken captive*
135   Upon my body, and han had me deed.
His colour was bitwixe yelow and reed,
And tipped was his tail and bothe his eres
With blak, unlik the remenant of his heres;°   *the rest of his hair*
His snoute smal, with glowing yën twaye.
140   Yit of his look for fere almost I deye:
This caused me my groning, doutelees."
    "Avoi,"° quod she, "fy on you, hertelees!°   *Have done!/coward*
Allas," quod she, "for by that God above,
Now han ye lost myn herte and al my love!
145   I can nat love a coward, by my faith.
For certes, what so any womman saith,
We alle desiren, if it mighte be,
To han housbondes hardy, wise, and free,°   *generous*

6. Locked in every limb (i.e., thoroughly).   8. Intepret my dream correctly.
7. A popular ballad, "My Love Has Gone to the Country."

	And secree,° and no nigard, ne no fool,	*discreet*
150	Ne him that is agast° of every tool,°	*afraid/weapon*
	Ne noon avauntour.° By that God above,	*braggart*
	How dorste ye sayn for shame unto youre love	
	That any thing mighte make you aferd?	
	Have ye no mannes herte and han a beerd?	
155	Allas, and conne ye been agast of swevenes?	
	No thing, God woot, but vanitee° in swevene is!	*illusion*
	Swevenes engendren of replexiouns,	
	And ofte of fume° and of complexiouns,°	*gas/bodily humors*
	Whan humours been too habundant in a wight.°	*creature*
160	Certes, this dreem which ye han met tonight	
	Comth of the grete superfluitee	
	Of youre rede colera,⁹ pardee,°	*by God*
	Which causeth folk to dreden in hir dremes	
	Of arwes,° and of fir with rede lemes,°	*arrows/flames*
165	Of rede beestes, that they wol hem bite,	
	Of contek,° and of whelpes° grete and lite—	*strife/dogs*
	Right as the humour of malencolye¹	
	Causeth ful many a man in sleep to crye	
	For fere of blake beres or boles° blake,	*bulls*
170	Or elles blake develes wol hem take.	
	Of othere humours coude I telle also	
	That werken many a man in sleep ful wo,	
	But I wol passe as lightly as I can.	
	Lo, Caton,² which that was so wis a man,	
175	Saide he nat thus? 'Ne do no fors° of dremes.'	*pay no attention to*
	Now, sire," quod she, "whan we flee° fro the bemes,°	*fly/rafters*
	For Goddes love, as take som laxatif.	
	Up° peril of my soule and of my lif,	*upon*
	I conseile you the beste, I wol nat lie,	
180	That bothe of colere and of malencolye	
	Ye purge you; and for ye shal nat tarye,	
	Though in this town is noon apothecarye,	
	I shal myself to herbes techen you,	
	That shal been for youre hele° and for youre prow,°	*health/profit*
185	And in oure yeerd tho° herbes shal I finde,	*then*
	The whiche han of hir propretee by kinde°	*nature*
	To purge you binethe and eek above.	
	Foryet nat this, for Goddes owene love.	
	Ye been ful colerik of complexioun;	
190	Ware° the sonne in his ascencioun	*beware lest*
	Ne finde you nat repleet° of humours hote;°	*full/hot*
	And if it do, I dar wel laye³ a grote°	*fourpence*
	That ye shul have a fevere terciane,⁴	
	Or an agu° that may be youre bane.°	*fever/death*

---

9. Coleric bile, thought to overheat the body.
1. Black bile, thought to produce dark thoughts.
2. Marcus Porcius Cato, ancient author of a book of

proverbs used by school children.
3. Bet (with a pun on egg-laying).
4. Recurring fever.

195   A day or two ye shul han digestives
      Of wormes, er ye take youre laxatives
      Of lauriol, centaure, and fumetere,[5]
      Or elles of ellebor that groweth there,
      Of catapuce, or of gaitres beries,
200   Of herbe-ive growing in oure yeerd ther merye is.°   *where it is pleasant*
      Pekke hem right up as they growe and ete hem in.
      Be merye, housbonde, for youre fader kin!
      Dredeth no dreem: I can saye you namore."
      "Madame," quod he, "graunt mercy of youre lore.°   *learning*
205   But nathelees, as touching daun Catoun,
      That hath of wisdom swich a greet renown,
      Though that he bad no dremes for to drede,
      By God, men may in olde bookes rede
      Of many a man more of auctoritee
210   Than evere Caton was, so mote I thee,°   *so may I prosper*
      That al the revers sayn of his sentence,°   *opinion*
      And han wel founden by experience
      That dremes been significaciouns
      As wel of joye as tribulaciouns
215   That folk enduren in this lif present.
      Ther needeth make of this noon argument:
      The verray preve° sheweth it in deede.   *proof*
        "Oon of the gretteste auctour that men rede
      Saith thus, that whilom two felawes wente
220   On pilgrimage in a ful good entente,
      And happed so they comen in a town,
      Wher as ther was swich congregacioun
      Of peple, and eek so strait of herbergage,°   *short of lodging*
      That they ne founde as muche as oo° cotage   *one*
225   In which they bothe mighte ylogged be;
      Wherfore they mosten of necessitee
      As for that night departe compaignye.
      And eech of hem gooth to his hostelrye,
      And took his logging as it wolde falle.
230   That oon of hem was logged in a stalle,
      Fer in a yeerd, with oxen of the plough;
      That other man was logged wel ynough,
      As was his aventure or his fortune,
      That us governeth alle as in commune.
235   And so bifel that longe er it were day,
      This man mette in his bed, ther as he lay,
      How that his felawe gan upon him calle,
      And saide, 'Allas, for in an oxes stalle
      This night I shal be mordred° ther I lie!   *murdered*
240   Now help me, dere brother, or I die!
      In alle haste com to me,' he saide.
        "This man out of his sleep for fere abraide,°   *bolted up*

---

5. These and the following are bitter herbs that produce hot and dry sensations and lead to purging.

But whan that he was wakened of his sleep,
He turned him and took of this no keep:°   heed
245   Him thoughte his dreem nas° but a vanitee.   was not
Thus twies in his sleeping dremed he,
And atte thridde time yit his felawe
Cam, as him thoughte, and saide, 'I am now slawe:°   slain
Bihold my bloody woundes deepe and wide.
250   Aris up erly in the morwe tide°   morning time
And atte west gate of the town,' quod he,
'A carte ful of dong° ther shaltou see,   dung
In which my body is hid ful prively:
Do thilke carte arresten° boldely.   have seized
255   My gold caused my mordre, sooth° to sayn'—   truth
And tolde him every point how he was slain,
With a ful pitous face, pale of hewe.
And truste wel, his dreem he foond ful trewe,
For on the morwe as soone as it was day,
260   To his felawes in he took the way,
And whan that he cam to this oxes stalle,
After his felawe he bigan to calle.
       "The hostiler° answerde him anoon,   innkeeper
And saide, 'Sire, youre felawe is agoon:
265   As soone as day he wente out of the town.'
       "This man gan fallen in suspicioun,
Remembring on his dremes that he mette;
And forth he gooth, no lenger wolde he lette,°   delay
Unto the west gate of the town, and foond
270   A dong carte, wente as it were to donge° lond,   spread manure on
That was arrayed in that same wise
As ye han herd the dede man devise;
And with an hardy herte he gan to crye,
'Vengeance and justice of this felonye!
275   My felawe mordred is this same night,
And in this carte he lith gaping upright!°   facing up
I crye out on the ministres,'° quod he,   magistrates
'That sholde keepe and rulen this citee.
Harrow, allas, here lith my felawe slain!'
280   What sholde I more unto this tale sayn?
The peple up sterte and caste the carte to grounde,
And in the middel of the dong they founde
The dede man that mordred was al newe.°   just recently
       "O blisful God that art so just and trewe,
285   Lo, how that thou biwrayest° mordre alway!   reveal
Mordre wol out, that see we day by day:
Mordre is so wlatsom° and abhominable   loathsome
To God that is so just and resonable,
That he ne wol nat suffre it heled° be,   concealed
290   Though it abide a yeer or two or three.
Mordre wol out: this my conclusioun.
And right anoon ministres of that town
Han hent° the cartere and so sore him pined,°   seized/tortured

And eek the hostiler so sore engined,

295 That they biknewe° hir wikkednesse anoon,   *confessed*

And were anhanged by the nekke boon.

Here may men seen that dremes been to drede.

  "And certes, in the same book I rede—

Right in the nexte chapitre after this—

300 I gabbe° nat, so have I joye or blis—   *lie*

Two men that wolde han passed over see

For certain cause into a fer contree,

If that the wind ne hadde been contrarye

That made hem in a citee for to tarye,

305 That stood ful merye upon an haven° side—   *harbor*

But on a day again° the even tide   *toward*

The wind gan chaunge, and blewe right as hem leste:° *they wanted*

Jolif° and glad they wenten unto reste,   *merry*

And casten hem° ful erly for to saile.   *decided*

310 "But to that oo man fil a greet mervaile;

That oon of hem, in sleeping as he lay,

Him mette a wonder dreem again the day:

Him thoughte a man stood by his beddes side,

And him comanded that he sholde abide,

315 And saide him thus, 'If thou tomorwe wende,°   *travel*

Thou shalt be dreint:° my tale is at an ende.'   *drowned*

  "He wook and tolde his felawe what he mette,

And prayed him his viage to lette;°   *put off his journey*

As for that day he prayed him to bide.

320 "His felawe that lay by his beddes side

Gan for to laughe, and scorned him ful faste.

'No dreem,' quod he, 'may so myn herte agaste

That I wol lette for to do my thinges.°   *business*

I sette nat a straw by thy dreminges,

325 For swevenes been but vanitees and japes:°   *tricks*

Men dreme alday° of owles or of apes,   *constantly*

And of many a maze° therwithal—   *delusion*

Men dreme of thing that nevere was ne shal.

But sith° I see that thou wolt here abide,   *since*

330 And thus forsleuthen° wilfully thy tide, *waste due to sloth*

Good woot, it reweth me; and have good day.'

And thus he took his leve and wente his way.

But er that he hadde half his cours ysailed—

Noot° I nat why ne what meschaunce it ailed°— *know/went wrong*

335 But casuelly° the shippes botme rente,° *by accident/split apart*

And ship and man under the water wente,

In sighte of othere shippes it biside,

That with hem sailed at the same tide.

And therfore, faire Pertelote so dere,

340 By swiche ensamples olde maistou lere° *may you learn*

That no man sholde been too recchelees°   *careless*

Of dremes, for I saye thee doutelees

That many a dreem ful sore is for to drede.

"Lo, in the lif of Saint Kenelm[6] I rede—

345 That was Kenulphus sone, the noble king
Of Mercenrike—how Kenelm mette a thing
A lite er he was mordred on a day.
His mordre in his avision° he sey.° *dream/saw*
His norice° him expounded everydeel *nurse*

350 His swevene, and bad him for to keepe him° weel *guard against*
For traison, but he nas but seven yeer old,
And therfore litel tale hath he told° *he cared little for*
Of any dreem, so holy was his herte.
By God, I hadde levere than my sherte° *would give my shirt*

355 That ye hadde rad his legende as have I.
      "Dame Pertelote, I saye you trewely,
Macrobeus,[7] that writ the Avisioun
In Affrike of the worthy Scipioun,
Affermeth° dremes, and saith that they been *confirms*

360 Warning of thinges that men after seen.
      "And ferthermore, I praye you looketh wel
In the Olde Testament of Daniel,
If he heeld dremes any vanitee.[8]
      "Rede eek of Joseph and ther shul ye see

365 Wher° dremes be somtime—I saye nat alle— *whether*
Warning of thinges that shul after falle.
      "Looke of Egypte the king daun Pharao,
His bakere and his botelere° also, *butler*
Wher they ne felte noon effect in dremes.[9]

370 Whoso wol seeke actes of sondry remes° *various kingdoms*
May rede of dremes many a wonder thing.
      "Lo Cresus, which that was of Lyde° king, *Lydia*
Mette he nat that he sat upon a tree,
Which signified he sholde anhanged be?

375   "Lo here Andromacha, Ectores° wif, *Hector of Troy*
That day that Ector sholde lese° his lif, *lose*
She dremed on the same night biforn
How that the lif of Ector sholde be lorn,
If thilke day he wente into bataile;

380 She warned him, but it mighte nat availe:
He wente for to fighte nathelees,
But he was slain anoon of Achilles.
But thilke tale is al too long to telle,
And eek it is neigh day, I may nat dwelle.

385 Shortly I saye, as for conclusioun,
That I shal han of this avisioun
Adversitee, and I saye ferthermoor
That I ne telle of laxatives no stoor,° *hold no regard for*
For they been venimes,° I woot it weel: *poisons*

---

6. St. Cenhelm, son of Cenwulf, a 9th-century child-king in Mercia who was murdered at his sister's orders.
7. Macrobius, a 4th-century author, wrote an extensive commentary on Cicero's *Dream of Scipio*.
8. Daniel interprets the pagan King Nebuchadnezzar's dream, which foretells his downfall (Daniel 4).
9. Joseph interpreted dreams for the pharaoh's chief baker and butler (Genesis 40–41).

390   I hem defye, I love hem neveradeel.
       "Now lat us speke of mirthe and stinte° al this.   *stop*
    Madame Pertelote, so have I blis,
    Of oo thing God hath sente me large grace:
    For whan I see the beautee of youre face—
395   Ye been so scarlet reed aboute youre yën—
    It maketh al my drede for to dien.
    For also siker° as *In principio*,[1]   *certain*
    Mulier est hominis confusio.[2]
    Madame, the sentence° of this Latin is,   *meaning*
400   'Womman is mannes joye and al his blis.'
    For whan I feele anight youre softe side—
    Al be it that I may nat on you ride,
    For that oure perche is maad so narwe, allas—
    I am so ful of joye and of solas°   *delight*
405   That I defye bothe swevene and dreem."
    And with that word he fleigh down fro the beem,
    For it was day, and eek° his hennes alle,   *also*
    And with a "chuk" he gan hem for to calle,
    For he hadde founde a corn lay in the yeerd.
410   Real° he was, he was namore aferd:°   *regal/afraid*
    He fethered Pertelote twenty time,
    And trad° hire as ofte er it was prime.[3]   *mounted*
    He looketh as it were a grim leoun,°   *lion*
    And on his toes he rometh up and down:
415   Him deined nat to sette his foot to grounde.
    He chukketh whan he hath a corn yfounde,
    And to him rennen thanne his wives alle.
    Thus royal, as a prince is in his halle,
    Leve I this Chauntecleer in his pasture,
420   And after wol I telle his aventure.
       Whan that the month in which the world bigan,
    That highte March, whan God first maked man,
    Was compleet, and passed were also,
    Sin March biran,° thritty days and two,[4]   *finished*
425   Bifel that Chauntecleer in al his pride,
    His sevene wives walking him biside,
    Caste up his yën to the brighte sonne,
    That in the signe of Taurus hadde yronne
    Twenty degrees and oon and somwhat more,
430   And knew by kinde,° and by noon other lore,   *nature*
    That it was prime, and crew with blisful stevene.°   *voice*
    "The sonne," he saide, "is clomben up on hevene
    Fourty degrees and oon and more, ywis.
    Madame Pertelote, my worldes blis,
435   Herkneth thise blisful briddes° how they singe,   *birds*
    And see the fresshe flowres how they springe:
    Ful is myn herte of revel and solas."

---

1. "In the beginning," the opening verse of the Book of
Genesis and the Gospel of John.
2. "Woman is the ruination of mankind."

3. First hour of the day.
4. The date is thus May 3.

But sodeinly him fil a sorweful cas,°   *event*
For evere the latter ende of joye is wo—
440   God woot that worldly joye is soone ago,
And if a rethor° coude faire endite,°   *rhetorician/compose*
He in a cronicle saufly° mighte it write,   *safely*
As for a soverein notabilitee.
Now every wis man lat him herkne me:
445   This storye is also° trewe, I undertake,   *as*
As is the book of Launcelot de Lake,[5]
That wommen holde in ful greet reverence.
Now wol I turne again to my sentence.
    A colfox° ful of sly iniquitee,   *black fox*
450   That in the grove° hadde woned° yeres three,   *woods/lived*
By heigh imaginacion forncast,[6]
The same night thurghout the hegges brast
Into the yeerd ther Chauntecleer the faire
Was wont, and eek his wives, to repaire;
455   And in a bed of wortes° stille he lay   *cabbages*
Til it was passed undren° of the day,   *midmorning*
Waiting his time on Chauntecleer to falle,
As gladly doon thise homicides alle,
That in await liggen to mordre men.
460   O false mordrour, lurking in thy den!
O newe Scariot! Newe Geniloun![7]
False dissimilour!° O Greek Sinoun,[8]   *dissembler*
That broughtest Troye al outrely° to sorwe!   *entirely*
O Chauntecleer, accursed be that morwe
465   That thou into the yeerd flaugh fro the bemes!
Thou were ful wel ywarned by thy dremes
That thilke day was perilous to thee;
But what that God forwoot° moot needes be,   *foreknows*
After the opinion of certain clerkes:
470   Witnesse on him that any parfit° clerk is   *accomplished*
That in scole is greet altercacioun
In this matere, and greet disputisoun,
And hath been of an hundred thousand men.
But I ne can nat bulte it to the bren,[9]
475   As can the holy doctour Augustin,
Or Boece, or the bisshop Bradwardin[1]—
Wheither that Goddes worthy forwiting°   *foreknowledge*
Straineth° me nedely for to doon a thing   *compels*
("Nedely" clepe I simple necessitee),
480   Or elles if free chois be graunted me
To do that same thing or do it nought,
Though God forwoot it er that I was wrought;°   *made*

---

5. The adventures of the Arthurian knight.
6. Predicted (in Chauntecleer's dream).
7. Judas Iscariot, who handed Jesus over to the Roman authorities for execution; Ganelon, a medieval traitor who betrayed the hero Roland to his Saracen enemies.
8. The Greek who tricked the Trojans into accepting the

Trojan horse behind the city walls.
9. Sift it from the husks (i.e., discriminate).
1. St. Augustine, the ancient writer Boethius, and the 14th-century Archbishop of Canterbury Thomas Bradwardine attempted to explain how God's predestination of events still allowed for humans to have free will.

Or if his witing straineth neveradeel,
But by necessitee condicionel[2]—

485 I wol nat han to do of swich matere:
My tale is of a cok, as ye may heere,
That took his conseil of his wif with sorwe,
To walken in the yeerd upon that morwe
That he hadde met the dreem that I you tolde.

490 Wommenes conseils been ful ofte colde,°   *disastrous*
Wommanes conseil broughte us first to wo,
And made Adam fro Paradis to go,
Ther as he was ful merye and wel at ese.
But for I noot° to whom it mighte displese   *do not know*

495 If I conseil of wommen wolde blame,
Passe over, for I saide it in my game—
Rede auctours where they trete of swich matere,
And what they sayn of wommen ye may heere—
Thise been the cokkes wordes and nat mine:

500 I can noon harm of no womman divine.°   *guess at*
    Faire in the sond° to bathe hire merily   *sand*
Lith° Pertelote, and alle hir sustres by,   *lies*
Again the sonne, and Chauntecleer so free
Soong merier than the mermaide in the see—

505 For Physiologus[3] saith sikerly
How that they singen wel and merily.
    And so bifel that as he caste his yë
Among the wortes on a boterflye,°   *butterfly*
He was war of this fox that lay ful lowe.

510 No thing ne liste him° thanne for to crowe,   *he wanted*
But cride anoon "Cok cok!" and up he sterte,
As man that was affrayed in his herte—
For naturelly a beest desireth flee
Fro his contrarye° if he may it see,   *natural enemy*

515 Though he nevere erst° hadde seen it with his yë.   *before*
This Chauntecleer, whan he gan him espye,
He wolde han fled, but that the fox anoon
Saide, "Gentil sire, allas, wher wol ye goon?
Be ye afraid of me that am youre freend?

520 Now certes, I were worse than a feend°   *devil*
If I to you wolde harm or vilainye.
I am nat come youre conseil for t'espye,
But trewely the cause of my cominge
Was only for to herkne how that ye singe:

525 For trewely, ye han as merye a stevene°   *voice*
As any angel hath that is in hevene.
Therwith ye han in musik more feelinge
Than hadde Boece,[4] or any that can singe.
My lord your fader—God his soule blesse!—

530 And eek youre moder, of hir gentilesse,°   *gentility*

---

2. Boethius argued only for conditional necessity, which still permitted for much exercise of free will.
3. Said to have written a bestiary.

4. In addition to theology, Boethius also wrote a music textbook.

Han in myn hous ybeen, to my grete ese.

And certes sire, ful fain° wolde I you plese.   *gladly*

But for men speke of singing, I wol saye,

So mote I brouke° wel mine yën twaye,   *use*

535   Save ye, I herde nevere man so singe

As dide youre fader in the morweninge.

Certes, it was of herte° al that he soong.   *heartfelt*

And for to make his vois the more strong,

He wolde so paine him that with bothe his yën

540   He moste winke,° so loude wolde he cryen;   *shut his eyes*

And stonden on his tiptoon therwithal,

And strecche forth his nekke long and smal;

And eek he was of swich discrecioun

That ther nas no man in no regioun

545   That him in song or wisdom mighte passe.°   *surpass*

I have wel rad in Daun Burnel the Asse[5]

Among his vers how that ther was a cok,

For° a preestes sone yaf him a knok   *because*

Upon his leg whil he was yong and nice,°   *foolish*

550   He made him for to lese his benefice.[6]

But certain, ther nis no comparisoun

Bitwixe the wisdom and discrecioun

Of youre fader and of his subtiltee.

Now singeth, sire, for sainte° charitee!   *holy*

555   Lat see, conne ye youre fader countrefete?"°   *imitate*

This Chauntecleer his winges gan to bete,

As man that coude his traison nat espye,

So was he ravisshed with his flaterye.

Allas, ye lordes, many a fals flatour

560   Is in youre court, and many a losengeour,°   *deceiver*

That plesen you wel more, by my faith,

Than he that soothfastnesse° unto you saith!   *truth*

Redeth Ecclesiaste[7] of flaterye.

Beeth war, ye lordes, of hir trecherye.

565   This Chauntecleer stood hye upon his toos,

Strecching his nekke, and heeld his yën cloos,

And gan to crowe loude for the nones;°   *for the purpose*

And daun Russel the fox sterte up atones,

And by the gargat° hente° Chauntecleer,   *throat/seized*

570   And on his bak toward the wode him beer,

For yit ne was ther no man that him sued.

O destinee that maist nat been eschued!°   *avoided*

Allas that Chauntecleer fleigh fro the bemes!

Allas his wif ne roughte° nat of dremes!   *cared*

575   And on a Friday[8] fil al this meschaunce!

O Venus that art goddesse of plesaunce,

Sin that thy servant was this Chauntecleer,

And in thy service dide al his power—

---

5. The hero of a 12th-century satirical poem, *Speculum Stultorum*, by Nigel Wirecker, Brunellus was a donkey who traveled around Europe trying to educate himself.

6. Lose his commission (because he overslept).

7. The Book of Ecclesiasticus.

8. Venus' day, but also an ominous day of the week.

	More for delit than world° to multiplye—	population
580	Why woldestou suffre him on thy day to die?	
	O Gaufred,[9] dere maister soverein,	
	That, whan thy worthy king Richard was slain	
	With shot,° complainedest his deeth so sore,	(of an arrow)
	Why ne hadde I now thy sentence and thy lore,	
585	The Friday for to chide as diden ye?	
	For on a Friday soothly slain was he.	
	Thanne wolde I shewe you how that I coude plaine°	lament
	For Chauntecleres drede and for his paine.	
	Certes, swich cry ne lamentacioun	
590	Was nevere of ladies maad whan Ilioun°	Troy
	Was wonne, and Pyrrus[1] with his straite° swerd,	drawn
	Whan he hadde hent King Priam by the beerd	
	And slain him, as saith us Eneidos,°	Virgil's Aeneid
	As maden alle the hennes in the cloos,°	yard
595	Whan they hadde seen of Chauntecleer the sighte.	
	But sovereinly Dame Pertelote shrighte°	shrieked
	Ful louder than dide Hasdrubales wif[2]	
	Whan that hir housbonde hadde lost his lif,	
	And that the Romains hadden brend Cartage:	
600	She was so ful of torment and of rage	
	That wilfully unto the fir she sterte,	
	And brende hirselven with a stedefast herte.	
	O woful hennes, right so criden ye	
	As, whan that Nero[3] brende the citee	
605	Of Rome, criden senatoures wives	
	For that hir housbondes losten alle hir lives:	
	Withouten gilt this Nero hath hem slain.	
	Now wol I turne to my tale again.	
	The sely° widwe and eek hir doughtres two	innocent
610	Herden thise hennes crye and maken wo,	
	And out at dores sterten they anoon,	
	And sien° the fox toward the grove goon,	saw
	And bar upon his bak the cok away,	
	And criden, "Out, harrow, and wailaway,	
615	Ha, ha, the fox," and after him they ran,	
	And eek with staves many another man;	
	Ran Colle oure dogge, and Talbot and Gerland,[4]	
	And Malkin with a distaf in hir hand,	
	Ran cow and calf, and eek the verray hogges,	
620	Sore aferd for berking of the dogges	
	And shouting of the men and wommen eke.	
	They ronne so hem thoughte hir herte breke;	
	They yelleden as feendes doon in helle;	
	The dokes criden as men wolde hem quelle;°	kill

---

9. Geoffrey of Vinsauf, who wrote a poem when King Richard the Lion-Hearted died, cursing the day of the week on which he died, a Friday.

1. Pyrrhus, the son of Achilles, who slew Troy's king Priam.

2. Hasdrubal was king of Carthage when it was defeated by the Romans during the Punic Wars.

3. The Emperor Nero set fire to Rome, killing many of his senators.

4. Common names for dogs.

625 The gees for fere flowen over the trees;
     Out of the hive cam the swarm of bees;
     So hidous was the noise, a, benedicite,
     Certes, he Jakke Straw⁵ and his meinee
     Ne made nevere shoutes half so shrille
630 Whan that they wolden any Fleming kille,
     As thilke day was maad upon the fox:
     Of bras they broughten bemes° and of box,°   *trumpets/boxwood*
     Of horn, of boon, in whiche they blewe and pouped,°   *puffed*
     And therwithal they skriked and they houped—
635 It seemed as that hevene sholde falle.
         Now goode men, I praye you herkneth alle:
     Lo, how Fortune turneth sodeinly
     The hope and pride eek of hir enemy.
     This cok that lay upon the foxes bak,
640 In al his drede unto the fox he spak,
     And saide, "Sire, if that I were as ye,
     Yit sholde I sayn, as wis° God helpe me,   *certainly*
     'Turneth ayain, ye proude cherles° alle!   *ruffians*
     A verray pestilence upon you falle!
645 Now am I come unto this wodes side,
     Maugree° your heed,° the cok shal here abide.   *despite/planning*
     I wol him ete, in faith, and that anoon.'"
         The fox answerde, "In faith, it shal be doon."
     And as he spak that word, al sodeinly
650 The cok brak from his mouth deliverly,°   *nimbly*
     And hye upon a tree he fleigh anoon.
         And whan the fox sawgh that he was agoon,
     "Allas," quod he, "O Chauntecleer, allas!
     I have to you," quod he, "ydoon trespas,
655 In as muche as I maked you aferd
     Whan I you hente and broughte out of the yeerd.
     But sire, I dide it in no wikke° entente: *wicked*
     Come down, and I shal telle you what I mente.
     I shal saye sooth to you, God help me so."
660   "Nay thanne," quod he, "I shrewe° us bothe two: *curse*
     But first I shrewe myself, bothe blood and bones,
     If thou bigile me ofter than ones;
     Thou shalt namore thurgh thy flaterye
     Do° me to singe and winken with myn yë.   *make*
665 For he that winketh whan he sholde see,
     Al wilfully, God lat him nevere thee."°   *prosper*
         "Nay," quod the fox, "but God yive him meschaunce
     That is so undiscreet of governaunce
     That jangleth° whan he sholde holde his pees."   *chatters*
670   Lo, swich it is for to be recchelees°   *careless*
     And necligent and truste on flaterye.
     But ye that holden this tale a folye
     As of a fox, or of a cok and hen,

5. Jack Straw was one of the leaders of the Peasants' Revolt of 1381, which was directed in part against the Flemish traders in London.

Taketh the moralitee, goode men.

675 For Saint Paul saith that al that writen is

To oure doctrine° it is ywrit, ywis: *instruction*

Taketh the fruit, and lat the chaf be stille.

Now goode God, if that it be thy wille,

As saith my lord, so make us alle goode men,

680 And bringe us to his hye blisse. Amen.

The Epilogue

"Sire Nonnes Preest," oure Hoste saide anoon,

"Yblessed be thy breech° and every stoon:°   *buttocks/testicle*

This was a merye tale of Chauntecleer.

But by my trouthe, if thou were seculer°   *a layman*

685 Thou woldest been a tredefowl° aright: *a cock*

For if thou have corage° as thou hast might   *desire*

Thee were neede of hennes, as I weene,°   *suppose*

Ye, mo than sevene times seventeene.

See whiche brawnes° hath this gentil preest—   *muscles*

690 So greet a nekke and swich a large breest.

He looketh as a sperhawk° with his yën;   *sparrowhawk*

Him needeth nat his colour for to dyen

With brasil ne with grain of Portingale.[6]

Now sire, faire falle you for youre tale."

695 And after that he with ful merye cheere

Saide unto another as ye shul heere.

The Parson's Tale

Although *The Canterbury Tales* remain unfinished and even the order of the tales is unclear, we know that Chaucer's plan was to end them with *The Parson's Tale*, just as it was to begin them with the pilgrimage to Canterbury in *The General Prologue*. Thus, when the Parson responds to the Host's request for a final tale by praying Jesus to show the way to the "glorious pilgrimage" called "Jerusalem celestial," there is a sense of closure in his return to an idea that has been obscured during the tale-telling. His shift of the destination from Canterbury to the heavenly city, however, gives us pause. The view that life on earth is a pilgrimage to heaven was a Christian commonplace, but was it Chaucer's view? The three parts of *The Parson's Tale* included here raise questions about how Chaucer's religious beliefs relate to his art. What is his final judgment of the artful, but often sinful, tales he has been telling?

In the introduction, the Parson rejects the idea of poetry entirely, scornfully refusing to tell a "fable" or to adorn his tale with alliteration or rhyme; instead, he will tell what he refers to as a "merye tale in prose," which turns out to be a forty-page treatise on penitence. Thus Chaucer specifically attributes to him an ascetic view of art which is hard to reconcile with his own extraordinary poetry. Does the Parson speak for Chaucer? Although he has a measure of authority as the only exemplary member of the clergy on the pilgrimage, he is nevertheless a fictional character. Since, however, Chaucer is thought to have written the introduction to this tale as well as the *Retraction* at the end of his life, perhaps he could have come to share the Parson's aesthetic views.

The Parson begins his tale proper with a second reference to celestial Jerusalem, stating that the route to it is through penitence. The tale, which Chaucer had translated at an earlier period, belongs to a common type of manuals of confession for either clergy or laity. Included in it is an analysis of the seven deadly sins—pride, envy, anger, sloth, avarice, gluttony, and

---

6. Two types of red dye, the latter from Portugal.

lechery—in an order that suggests that Chaucer, like Dante, considered the last to be the least serious, although still worthy of damnation. The passage on lechery excerpted here offers an opportunity to measure *The Parson's Tale* against the tales that have gone before, particularly such "sinful" works as *The Miller's Tale* and *The Wife of Bath's Prologue*.

Whatever conclusion we draw about the relevance of *The Parson's Tale* to the tales preceding, the *Retraction* appended to it is troubling yet intriguing. In it Chaucer repudiates much of the work for which he is most loved and admired, such "worldly vanitees" as *Troilus and Criseyde, The Parliament of Fowls,* and those *Canterbury Tales* that "sounen [lead] into sinne." On the other hand, he thanks God for his works of "moralitee," including his translation of Boethius and his saints' legends, works that are seldom read today. He himself is engaged in penance—repentance, confession, and satisfaction—thus connecting his own spiritual experience with the manual he has translated. However disappointing it is to read this rejection of his most artistically satisfying tales, we must remember that a concept of art for art's sake would have been historically unavailable to him. Perhaps his last tale was indeed his last word.

from The Parson's Tale
The Introduction

	By that° the Manciple hadde his tale al ended,	*by that time*
	The sonne fro the south line[1] was descended	
	So lowe, that he nas nat to my sighte	
	Degrees nine and twenty as in highte.	
5	Four of the clokke it was, so as I gesse,	
	For elevene foot, or litel more or lesse,	
	My shadwe was at thilke time as there,	
	Of swich feet as my lengthe parted were	
	In sixe feet equal of proporcioun.	
10	Therwith the moones exaltacioun°—	*dominant influence*
	I mene Libra[2]—alway gan ascende,	
	As we were entring at a thropes ende.°	*village boundary*
	For which oure Host, as he was wont to gie°	*lead*
	As in this caas oure joly compaignye,	
15	Saide in this wise, "Lordinges everichoon,	
	Now lakketh us no tales mo than oon:	
	Fulfild is my sentence° and my decree;	*design*
	I trowe° that we han herd of eech degree;	*believe*
	Almost fulfild is al myn ordinaunce.	
20	I praye to God, so yive him right good chaunce	
	That telleth this tale to us lustily.	
	Sire preest," quod he, "artou a vicary,°	*vicar*
	Or arte a Person?° Say sooth, by thy fay.°	*parish priest/faith*
	Be what thou be, ne breek thou nat oure play,	
25	For every man save thou hath told his tale.	
	Unbokele and shew us what is in thy male!°	*bag*
	For trewely, me thinketh by thy cheere°	*expression*
	Thou sholdest knitte up wel a greet matere.	
	Tel us a fable anoon, for cokkes bones!"[3]	
30	This Person answerde al atones,	
	"Thou getest fable noon ytold for me,	
	For Paul, that writeth unto Timothee,[4]	

1. Astronomical marking parallel to the celestial equator.
2. Seventh sign in the Zodiac, the Scales.
3. Cock's bones, a euphemism for God's bones.
4. St. Paul's Epistle to Timothy.

Repreveth hem that waiven soothfastnesse,°   *truth*
And tellen fables and swich wrecchednesse.

35   Why sholde I sowen draf° out of my fest,°   *chaff/fist*
Whan I may sowen whete if that me lest?
For which I saye that if you list to heere
Moralitee and vertuous matere,
And thanne that ye wol yive me audience,

40   I wol ful fain,° at Cristes reverence,   *gladly*
Do you plesance leveful° as I can.   *lawfully*
But trusteth wel, I am a southren man:[5]
I can nat geeste° Rum-Ram-Ruf by lettre—   *tell stories*
Ne, God woot, rym holde° I but litel bettre.   *appreciate*

45   And therfore, if you list, I wol nat glose;°   *adorn my speech*
I wol you telle a merye tale in prose,
To knitte up al this feeste and make an ende.
And Jesu for his grace wit me sende
To shewe you the way in this viage°   *journey*

50   Of thilke parfit glorious pilgrimage
That highte Jerusalem celestial.
And if ye vouche sauf, anoon I shal
Biginne upon my tale, for which I praye
Telle youre avis:° I can no bettre saye.   *opinion*

55   But nathelees, this meditacioun
I putte it ay under correccioun
Of clerkes, for I am nat textuel:°   *a literalist*
I take but the sentence,° trusteth wel.   *sense*
Therfore I make protestacioun

60   That I wol stonde to correccioun."
    Upon this word we han assented soone,
For, as it seemed, it was for to doone
To enden in som vertuous sentence,
And for to yive him space° and audience;   *time*

65   And bede oure Host he sholde to him saye
That alle we to telle his tale him praye.
    Oure Hoste hadde the wordes for us alle:
"Sire preest," quod he, "now faire you bifalle:
Telleth," quod he, "youre meditacioun.

70   But hasteth you, the sonne wol adown.
Beeth fructuous, and that in litel space,
And to do wel God sende you his grace.
Saye what you list, and we wol gladly heere."
And with that word he saide in this manere.

from *The Tale*

Oure sweete Lord God of Hevene, that no man wol perisse[1] but wol
that we comen alle to the knowliche of him and to the blisful lif that is
perdurable,° amonesteth° us by the prophete Jeremie[2] that saith in   *enduring/warns*
this wise: "Stondeth upon the wayes and seeth and axeth of olde

5. The parson, like Chaucer himself, comes from the   north. Rum-Ram-Raf is an example of alliteration.
south of England and so is not accustomed to telling sto-   1. Who wishes no man to perish.
ries in the alliterative meter used traditionally in the   2. Jeremiah 6.16.

pathes (that is to sayn, of olde sentences)° which is the goode way, and   *opinions*
walketh in that way, and ye shul finde refresshing for youre soules."

Manye been the wayes espirituels that leden folk to oure Lord
Jesu Crist and to the regne of glorye: of whiche wayes ther is a ful
noble way and a ful covenable° which may nat faile to man ne to   *suitable*
womman that thurgh sinne hath misgoon fro the righte way of
Jerusalem celestial; and this way is cleped° Penitence. * * *   *called*

THE REMEDY FOR THE SIN OF LECHERY

Now cometh the remedye agains Lecherye, and that is generally
Chastitee and Continence that restraineth alle the desordainee
mevinges° that comen of flesshly talents.° And evere the gretter   *impulses/desires*
merite shal he han that most restraineth the wikkede eschaufinges°   *inflammations*
of the ardure of this sinne. And this is in two maneres: that is to
sayn, chastitee in mariage and chastitee of widwehood.

Now shaltou understonde that matrimoine is leeful° assembling   *lawful*
of man and of womman that receiven by vertu of the sacrement the
bond thurgh which they may nat be departed in al hir life—that is to
sayn, whil that they liven bothe. This, as saith the book, is a ful greet
sacrement: God maked it, as I have said, in Paradis, and wolde himself be born in mariage. And for to halwen° mariage, he was at a wed-   *bless*
ding where as he turned water into win, which was the firste miracle
that he wroughte in erthe biforn his disciples. Trewe effect of
mariage clenseth fornicacion and replenisseth Holy Chirche of good
linage° (for that is the ende of mariage), and it chaungeth deedly   *offspring*
sinne[3] into venial sinne bitwixe hem that been ywedded, and maketh
the hertes al oon° of hem that been ywedded, as wel as the bodies.   *united*

This is verray mariage that was establissed by God er that sinne
bigan, whan naturel lawe was in his right point° in Paradis; and it was   *order*
ordained that oo man sholde have but oo womman, and oo womman
but oo man (as saith Saint Augustine) by manye resons: First, for
mariage is figured° bitwixe Crist and Holy Chirche; and that other is for   *represented*
a man is heved° of a womman—algate,° by ordinance it sholde be so.   *head/at least*
For if a womman hadde mo men than oon, thanne sholde she have mo
hevedes than oon, and that were an horrible thing biforn God; and eek
a womman ne mighte nat plese to many folk at ones. And also ther ne
sholde nevere be pees ne reste amonges hem, for everich wolde axen his
owene thing. And fortherover, no man sholde knowe his owene engendrure,° ne who sholde have his heritage, and the womman sholde been   *offspring*
the lesse biloved fro the time that she were conjoint to manye men.

Now cometh how that a man sholde bere him with his wif, and
namely in two thinges, that is to sayn, in suffrance° and in rever-   *obedience*
ence, as shewed Crist whan he made first womman. For he ne made
hire nat of the heved of Adam for she sholde nat claime too greet
lorshipe: for ther as womman hath the maistrye she maketh too greet
desray° (ther needen none ensamples of this: the experience of day   *disorder*
by day oughte suffise). Also, certes, God ne made nat womman of
the foot of Adam, for she ne sholde nat be holden too lowe, for she

---

3. Sex remains a minor sin even within marriage, but it is a more serious sin outside of marriage.

can nat paciently suffre. But God made womman of the rib of Adam for womman sholde be felawe unto man. Man sholde bere him to his wif in faith, in trouthe, and in love, as saith Sainte Paul, that a man sholde loven his wif as Crist loved Holy Chirche, that loved it so wel that he deide for it. So sholde a man for his wif, if it were neede.

Now how that a womman sholde be subjet to hir housbonde, that telleth Sainte Peter: First, in obedience. And eek, as saith the decree, a womman that is a wif, as longe as she is a wif, she hath noon auctoritee to swere ne to bere witnesse withoute leve of hir housbonde that is hir lord—algate, he sholde be so by reson. She sholde eek serven him in alle honestee, and been attempree° of hir array; I woot wel that *moderate* they sholde setten hir entente° to plesen hir housbondes, but nat by *purpose* hir quaintise of array:° Saint Jerome saith that wives that been appa- *flamboyant attire* railed in silk and in precious purpre ne mowe nat clothen hem in Jesu Crist. What saith Saint John eek in this matere? Saint Gregorye eek saith that no wight seeketh precious array but only for vaine glorye to been honoured the more biforn the peple. It is a greet folye a womman to have a fair array outward and in hireself be foul inward. A wif sholde eek be mesurable° in looking and in bering and in laughing, *modest* and discreet in alle hir wordes and hir deedes. And aboven alle world-ly thinges she sholde loven hir housbonde with al hir herte, and to him be trewe of hir body (so sholde an housbonde eek be to his wif): for sith that° al the body is the housbondes, so sholde hir herte been, *since* or elles ther is bitwixe hem two as in that no parfit mariage.

Thanne shul men understonde that for three thinges a man and his wif flesshly mowen° assemble. The firste is in entente of engen- *may* drure of children to the service of God: for certes, that is the cause final of matrimoine. Another cause is to yeelden everich° of hem to *each* other the dette of hir bodies, for neither of hem hath power of his owene body. The thridde is for to eschewe lecherye and vilainye. The ferthe is, for soothe, deedly sinne. As to the firste, it is meritorye; the seconde also, for, as saith the decree, that she hath merite of chastitee that yeeldeth to hir housbonde the dette of hir body, ye, though it be again hir liking and the lust of hir herte. The thridde manere is venial sinne—and, trewely, scarsly may any of thise be withoute venial sinne, for the corrupcion and for the delit. The ferthe manere is for to under-stonde if they assemble only for amorous love and for noon of the for-saide causes, but for to accomplice thilke brenning delit—they rekke° *care* nevere how ofte—soothly, it is deedly sinne. And yit with sorwe some folk wol painen hem° more to doon than to hir appetit suffiseth. * * * *trouble them-*

Another remedye agains lecherye is specially to withdrawen *selves* swiche thinges as yive occasion to thilke vilainye, as ese,° eting, and *leisure* drinking: for certes, whan the pot boileth strongly, the beste remedye is to withdrawe the fir. Sleeping longe in greet quiete is eek a greet norice° to lecherye. Another remedye agains lecherye is that a man or *nurse* a womman eschewe the compaignye of hem by whiche he douteth° to *suspects* be tempted: for al be it so that the deede be withstonden, yit is ther greet temptacion. Soothly, a whit wal,° although it ne brenne nought *wall* fully by stiking of a candele, yit is the wal blak of the leit.° Ful ofte *from the flame* time I rede that no man truste in his owene perfeccion but he be stronger than Sampson, holier than David, and wiser than Salomon.

Chaucer's Retraction
HERE TAKETH THE MAKERE OF THIS BOOK HIS LEVE

Now praye I to hem alle that herkne this litel tretis° or rede,° that if ther be any thing in it that liketh° hem, that therof they thanken oure Lord Jesu Crist, of whom proceedeth al wit and al goodnesse. And if ther be any thing that displese hem, I praye hem also that they arrette° it to the defaute of myn unconning,° and nat to my wil, that wolde ful fain have said bettre if I hadde had conning. For oure book saith, "Al that is writen is writen for oure doctrine," and that is myn entente. Wherfore I biseeke you mekely, for the mercy of God, that ye praye for me that Crist have mercy on me and foryive me my giltes,° and namely of my translacions and enditinges° of worldly vanitees, the whiche I revoke in my retraccions:⁴ as is the book of Troilus; the book also of Fame; the book of the five and twenty Ladies; the book of the Duchesse; the book of Saint Valentines Day of the Parlement of Briddes; the tales of Canterbury, thilke that sounen° into sinne; the book of the Leon; and many another book, if they were in my remembrance, and many a song and many a leccherous lay: that Crist for his grete mercy foryive me the sinne. But of the translacion of Boece *de Consolatione,* and othere bookes of legendes of saintes, and omelies, and moralitee, and devocion, that thanke I oure Lord Jesu Crist and his blisful Moder and alle the saintes of hevene, biseeking hem that they from hennes forth unto my lives ende sende me grace to biwaile° my giltes and to studye to the salvacion of my soule, and graunte me grace of verray penitence, confession, and satisfaccion to doon in this present lif, thurgh the benigne grace of him that is king of kinges and preest over alle preestes, that boughte° us with the precious blood of his herte, so that I may been oon of hem at the day of doom that shulle be saved. *Qui cum patre et Spiritu Sancto vivis et regnas Deus per omnia saecula. Amen.*⁵

*treatise/advice
pleases*

*attribute
inability*

*sins
writings*

lead

repent

redeemed

To His Scribe Adam¹
Adam scrivain,° if evere it thee bifalle
Boece² or Troilus for to writen newe,

copyist

4. Here Chaucer repents having written most of his major works: *Troilus and Criseyde, The Book* (or *House*) *of Fame, The Legend of Good Women, The Book of the Duchess, The Parliament of Fowls,* and various of *The Canterbury Tales. The Book of the Lion* has not been preserved. Chaucer's translation of Boethius' *Consolation of Philosophy* is excepted.
5. You who live with the Father and the Holy Spirit and reign as God through all the centuries. Amen.
1. Given his position at court, Chaucer was asked to write many lyrics and occasional poems, such as this poem and the one that follows. In both, he wittily bemoans the conditions of authorship under which he was forced to work, depending on scribes to reproduce his poetry and on patrons to support it. In *To His Scribe Adam,* he strikes a

pose of affectionate raillery toward his scribe, whose occupation writers widely scorned. Perhaps he sees it as fitting to curse Adam with a skin disease which will make him scratch his scalp, just as Chaucer has had to scratch out the errors from his manuscripts. However, the poem has a serious undertone too. In fearing that Adam will miscopy his great romance, *Troilus and Criseyde,* he echoes a concern for the accurate reproduction of his work, which he voiced at the end of *Troilus* itself: he prays God that, in view of the great dialectal "diversitee/ in Englissh, and in writing of oure tonge," no one "miswrite" his book (5.1793–94).
2. Chaucer's translation of Boethius' *Consolation of Philosophy.*

Under thy longe lokkes thou moste have° the scalle,°   *may you get/mange*
But after my making thou write more trewe,[3]
So ofte a day I moot° thy werk renewe,   *must*
It to correcte, and eek to rubbe and scrape:
And al is thurgh thy necligence and rape.°   *haste*

Complaint to His Purse[1]

To you, my purs, and to noon other wight,°   *creature*
Complaine I, for ye be my lady dere.
I am so sory, now that ye be light,°   *empty, wanton*
For certes, but if° ye make me hevy cheere,[2]   *unless*
5   Me were as lief° be laid upon my beere;°   *I would prefer/bier*
For which unto youre mercy thus I crye:
Beeth hevy again, or elles moot° I die.   *must*

Now voucheth sauf this day er it be night
That I of you the blisful soun may heere,
10   Or see youre colour, lik the sonne bright,
That of yelownesse hadde nevere peere.
Ye be my lif, ye be myn hertes steere,°   *guide*
Queene of confort and of good compaignye:
Beeth hevy again, or elles moot I die.

15   Ye purs, that been to me my lives light
And saviour, as in this world down here,
Out of this tonne° helpe me thurgh your might,   *dark situation*
Sith that ye wol nat be my tresorere;
For I am shave as neigh° as any frere.[3]   *close*
20   But yit I praye unto youre curteisye:
Beeth hevy again, or elles moot I die.

Envoy to Henry IV[4]

O conquerour of Brutus Albioun,[5]
Which that by line° and free eleccioun   *inheritance*
Been verray king, this song to you I sende:
25   And ye, that mowen° alle oure harmes amende,   *may*
Have minde upon my supplicacioun.

---

3. Unless you make a more reliable copy of what I have composed.
1. This is a traditional "begging" poem, based on French models. The request for money is presented humorously, as a parody of a courtly love complaint to a cruel mistress. The parallel takes on ironic force when one recalls Chaucer's presentation of himself, in such early poems as *The Parliament of Fowls*, as a failed lover. This is one of Chaucer's last poems, written a year before his death. It was addressed to Henry IV when he took the throne in 1399, to request a renewal of the annuity Chaucer had received from the deposed Richard II. The flattering "envoy" to Henry at the end alludes to the tradition dating from Geoffrey of Monmouth that Britain was founded by Brutus, the grandson of Aeneas, the exiled prince of Troy and founder of Rome.
2. Serious expression (in a person); full weight (in a purse).
3. Friar (with a bald tonsure).
4. The "envoy" is the traditional close of a ballade, usually directed to its addressee.
5. According to legend, Brutus conquered the kingdom of Albion and renamed it "Britain," after himself.

The Second Play of the Shepherds

Medieval drama is marvelously entertaining, but it was meant to instruct as well. It developed not from classical drama, which virtually died out in the Middle Ages, but from the church liturgy. Although it originated on the Continent, its greatest flowering was in England, in the plays of the Corpus Christi cycle performed from the end of the fourteenth to the end of the sixteenth century. So called because they were put on at the feast of Corpus Christi in midsummer, these plays portray the entire cycle of sacred history from Creation to the Last Judgment, including such events as the Fall of Lucifer, Noah's flood, the Nativity, and Christ's Passion and Resurrection. The plays are given coherence by a pattern of typology whereby Satan's deception and Adam's sin are redeemed by Christ's sacrifice. Old Testament events and characters predict and are fulfilled by New Testament ones: Isaac and Moses are types of Christ, and Cain, Pharaoh, and Herod, usually played as comic tyrants, are types of Satan.

The Corpus Christi plays exist in four nearly complete versions, primarily from the north of England: the Chester, N-Town, York, and Wakefield (or Towneley) cycles. They were generally performed outdoors, in partnership with the Church, by craft guilds—associations of tradesmen who made up a newly prosperous mercantile class. Often these guilds sponsored plays whose subject matter was specifically appropriate to their craft—for instance, the Butchers putting on the killing of Abel, and the Water-drawers the story of Noah.

The popularity of the plays—as well as their function as a surrogate Bible for the poor—can be seen in Chaucer's *Miller's Tale*. The Miller himself insists on telling his tale out of turn, speaking in "Pilate's voice," the ranting manner of Pontius Pilate in the passion plays, and the foppish Absolon woos his beloved Alison by playing the role of the tyrant Herod on a scaffold. More importantly, the chief trick of this fabliau—the clerk Nicholas's arranging to be alone with Alison by frightening her husband with the threat of a second flood—relies on the old man's dim memory of the play of Noah.

Nicholas's invocation of a sacred story to pursue a profane goal walks a thin line between comedy and blasphemy. So too did many of the Corpus Christi plays, but for a more obviously sacred purpose. The Wakefield Annunciation, for instance, presents Joseph in fabliau fashion as an old man fearing that he has been cuckolded when he discovers that Mary, his young bride-to-be, is pregnant. Only at the end does he come to understand the divine purpose at work.

Nowhere are the sacred and profane paired as brilliantly as in the nativity play known as *The Second Play of the Shepherds*, one of the Wakefield plays, named after the prosperous Yorkshire town in which they were performed. It was written or revised by an artist of great imagination and skill, no doubt a cleric, known as the Wakefield master. His great achievement is his ability to relate biblical stories to fifteenth-century England in such a way that daily life takes on typological significance: a stolen sheep, hidden in swaddling clothes in a cradle, prefigures the newborn Christ child whom the shepherds visit at the end of the play. The shepherds show mercy to the thief by tossing him in a blanket rather than delivering him to be hanged, prefiguring the mercy that the Christ child will bring into the world.

No matter how neatly the typological scheme works, however, the author does not present the birth of Christ as entirely nullifying the dissatisfactions of the characters in the play. The thief Mak may be a type of the devil, with his guileful assault on the sheep fold and his concealment of a "horned lad" swaddled in a cradle, but his complaints of poverty (he stole the sheep to feed his rapidly expanding family) are real. So too are the lengthy opening complaints of the shepherds against taxes, lords and their condescending servants, and wives who produce too many mouths to feed. Their frustration reflects actual social and economic conditions stemming from the wool and cloth trade that enriched landowners but impoverished laborers in the fourteenth and fifteenth centuries, and thus cannot be dismissed as the grumbling of fallen men who fail to understand their need for divine grace. Similarly, the complaints of Mak's wife Gill about the burden of women's work should not be seen as simply setting her up as a foil to the Virgin Mary: the play gives vivid expression to pressing daily concerns.

The Second Play of the Shepherds

[Scene: Field near Bethlehem.]

I PASTOR Lord, what these weathers are cold! And I am ill happed.[1]

	I am near hand dold,° so long have I napped;	*almost numb*
	My legs they fold, my fingers are chapped.	
	It is not as I would, for I am all lapped°	*tied up*
5	In sorrow.	
	In storms and tempest,	
	Now in the east, now in the west,	
	Woe is him has never rest	
	Mid-day nor morrow!	
10	But we sely° shepherds that walks on the moor,	*poor*
	In faith we are near hands out of the door.	
	No wonder, as it stands, if we be poor,	
	For the tilthe of our lands lies fallow as the floor,	
	As ye ken.°	*know*
15	We are so hamed,°	*hamstrung*
	For-taxed° and ramed,°	*overburdened/oppressed*
	We are made hand tamed	
	With these gentlery men.°	*gentry, aristocrats*
	Thus they reave° us our rest, our Lady them wary!°	*rob/curse*
20	These men that are lord-fest,[2] they cause the plow tarry.	
	That men say is for the best, we find it contrary.	
	Thus are husbandys° opprest, in point to miscarry	*farmhands*
	On live.	
	Thus hold they us hunder;°	*under*
25	Thus they bring us in blonder;°	*trouble*
	It were great wonder	
	And ever should we thrive.	
	For may he get a paint slefe° or a broche now on days,	*painted sleeve*
	Woe is him that him grefe° or once again says!	*troubles*
30	Dare noman him reprefe,° what mastry° he mays,	*reprove/power*
	And yet may noman lefe° one word that he says,	*believe*
	No letter.	
	He can make purveance°	*provision*
	With boast and bragance,	
35	And all is through maintenance	
	Of men that are greater.	
	There shall come a swane as proud as a po,[3]	
	He must borrow my wane,° my plow also,	*wagon*
	Then I am full fane° to grant or he go.	*pleased*

---

1. Clothed.
2. Bound to their lords.

3. A servant as proud as a peacock.

40   Thus live we in pain,   anger, and woe,
     By night and day.
     He must have if he langed,°   *desired*
     If I should forgang° it;   *forgo*
     I were better be hanged
45   Then once say him nay.

     It does me good, as I walk   thus by mine one,
     Of this world for to talk   in manner of moan.
     To my sheep will I stalk,   and hearken anone,°   *awhile*
     There abide on a balk,°   or sit on a stone,   *ridge*
50   Full soon.
     For I trowe,° perde,°   *believe/by God*
     True men if they be,
     We get more company
     Or° it be noon.   *before*

     [The Second Shepherd enters without noticing the First.]
II PASTOR Benste and Dominus!⁴   What may this bemean?
     Why fares this world thus?   Oft have we not seen?
     Lord, these weathers are spytus,°   and the winds full keen,   *spiteful*
     And the frosts so hideous   they water my eyes—
     No lie.
60   Now in dry, now in wete,
     Now in snow, now in sleet;
     When my shoen° freeze to my feet,   *shoes*
     It is not all easy.

     But as far as I ken,   or yet as I go,
65   We sely wedmen   dre mekyll woe;⁵
     We have sorrow then and then: it falls oft so.
     Sely Copple,⁶ our hen,   both to and fro
     She cackles;
     But begin she to croak,
70   To groan or to cluck,
     Woe is him is of our cock,
     For he is in the shackels.

     These men that are wed   have not all their will;
     When they are full hard sted,°   they sigh full still;   *placed*
75   God wayte° they are led   full hard and full ill;   *knows*
     In bower° nor in bed   they say nought there till,°   *bedroom/thereto*
     This tide.°   *time*
     My part have I fun;°   *found*
     I know my lesson.
80   Woe is him that is bun,°   *bound in marriage*
     For he must abide.

     But now late in our lives   a marvel to me,
     That I think my heart rives°   such wonders to see.   *breaks*
     What that destiny drives   it should so be;
85   Some men will have two wives   and some men three,

---

4. Corruption of a Latin blessing, *Benedicite ad Dominum*.   6. A copple is the crest on a bird's head.
5. We poor, innocent married men suffer much.

In store;
Some are woe that has any,
But so far can I,
Woe is him that has many,
90   For he felys° sore.   *suffers*

But young men of a-wooing,   for God that you bought,°   *redeemed*
Be well ware of wedding,   and think in your thought,
"Had I wist"° is a thing   it serves of nought;   *known*
Mekyll° still° mourning   has wedding home brought,   *much/constant*
95   And griefs,
With many a sharp shower;
For thou may catch in an hour
That shall savour fulle sour
As long as thou lives.

100   For, as ever read I pistill[7]   I have one to my fere,°   *mate*
As sharp as a thistle,   as rough as a brere;
She is browed like a bristle   with a sour-loten cheer;[8]
Had she once wet her whistle   she could sing full clear
Her *Paternoster*.°   *Lord's Prayer*
105   She is as great as a whale;
She has a gallon of gall.
By him that died for us all,
I would I had run to° I had lost her.   *until*

I PASTOR God look over the raw![9]   Full deafly ye stand.
II PASTOR Yea, the devil in thy maw,°   so tariand.°   *mouth/slow*
Saw thou awre° of Daw?[1]   *anywhere*
I PASTOR   Yea, on a ley land°   *fallow ground*
Hard I him blaw.[2]   He comes here at hand,
Not far.
Stand still.
II PASTOR   Why?
I PASTOR For he comes, hope I.
II PASTOR He will make us both a lie
But if° we beware.   *unless*

[Enter Third Shepherd.]

III PASTOR Christ's cross me speed,   and Saint Nicholas!
There of had I need;   it is worse than it was.
120   Whoso could take heed   and let the world pass,
It is ever in dread   and brekill° as glass,   *brittle*
And slithes.°   *slides away*
This world fowre° never so,   *fared*
With marvels mo and mo,
125   Now in weal, now in woe,
And all thing writhes.°   *turns about*

---

7. [St.Paul's] Epistle.
8. Sour-looking face.
9. Let God pay attention to his audience (row), i.e., God

attend me.
1. The Third Shepherd.
2. I just blew by him.

Was never sin° Noah's flood   such floods seen;   *since*
Winds and rains so rude,   and storms so keen;
Some stammerd, some stood   in doubt,° as I ween;   *fear*
130   Now God turn all to good!   I say as I mean,
For° ponder.   *to*
These floods so they drown,
Both fields and in town,
And bears all down,
135   And that is a wonder.

We that walk on the nights,   our cattle to keep,
We see sudden sights   when other men sleep.
Yet me think my heart lights;   I see shrews peep;[3]
Ye are two ill wights.   I will give my sheep
140   A turn.
But full ill have I meant;
As I walk on this bent,
I may lightly repent,
My toes if I spurn.

145   Ah, sir, God you save,   and master mine!
A drink fain would I have,   and somewhat to dine.
I PASTOR Christ's curse, my knave,   thou art a leder hine!°   *lazy servant*
II PASTOR What, the boy list rave!   Abide unto sine;[4]
We have made it.[5]
150   Ill thrift on thy pate!
Though the shrew came late,
Yet is he in state
To dine, if he had it.

III PASTOR Such servants as I,   that sweats and swinks,°   *works*
155   Eats our bread full dry,   and that me forthinks;°   *upsets*
We are oft wet and weary   when master-men winks;°   *sleeps*
Yet comes full lately   both diners and drinks,
But nately.°   *thoroughly*
Both our dame and our sire,
160   When we have run in the mire,
They can nip° at our hire,°   *trim/wages*
And pay us full lately.

But here my troth, master: for the fare that ye make,
I shall do therafter,   work as I take;
165   I shall do a little, sir,   and emang ever lake,[6]
For yet lay my supper   never on my stomach
In fields.
Whereto should I threpe?°   *wrangle*
With my staff can I leap,
170   And men say "Light cheap°   *little cost*
Letherly for-yields."°   *poorly yields*

I PASTOR Thou were an ill lad   to ride a-wooing
With a man that had   but little of spending.

---

3. I see villains peeping out.   5. We have already eaten.
4. The boy is crazy; wait a while.   6. Keep playing besides.

II PASTOR Peace, boy, I bade.   No more jangling,°   *chattering*
175   Or I shall make there full rad,°   by the heavens king!   *quickly*
            With thy gauds°—   *tricks*
            Where are our sheep, boy?—we scorn.°   *despise*
III PASTOR Sir, this same day at morn
            I them left in the corn,
180   When they rang lauds.[7]

            They have pasture good,   they cannot go wrong.
I PASTOR That is right, by the roode![8]   these nights are long,
            Yet I would, or we yode,°   one gave us a song.   *went*
II PASTOR So I thought as I stood,   to mirth us among.
III PASTOR I grant.
I PASTOR Let me sing the tenory.
II PASTOR And I treble so hee.
III PASTOR Then the meyne° falls to me: *middle*
            Let see how ye chant.
        [*They sing.*]
        Tunc intrat Mak in clamide se super togam vestitus.[9]

MAK   Now, Lord, for thy names vii,[1]   that made both moon and starns°   *stars*
            Well mo then can I neven°   thy will, Lord, of me tharns;[2]   *say*
            I am all uneven,   that moves oft my harness.
            Now would God I were in heaven,   for there weep no barnes°   *babies*
            So still.
I PASTOR Who is that pipes so poor?
MAK   Would God ye wist how I foor!°   *fared*
            Lo, a man that walks on the moor,
            And has not all his will!

II PASTOR Mak, where has thou gone?   Tell us tiding.
III PASTOR Is he comme? Then ylkon°   take heed to his thing.   *everyone*
        Et accipit clamidem ab ipso.[3]
MAK   What! Ich be a yoman,[4]   I tell you, of the king;
            The self and the same,   sond° from a great lording,   *messenger*
            And sich.°   *such like*
            Fy on you! Goeth hence
205   Out of my presence!
            I must have reverence;
            Why, who be ich?
I PASTOR Why make ye it so quaint?[5]   Mak, ye do wrang.
II PASTOR But, Mak, list ye saint?   I trow that ye lang.[6]
III PASTOR I trow the shrew can paint,   the devill might him hang!
MAK   Ich shall make complaint, and make you all to thwang[7]
            At a word,
            And tell even how ye doth.

---

7. Lauds; first church service of the day.
8. Cross: The humor here, as with the other oaths, is based on the anachronism that Jesus has not yet been born, much less crucified.
9. Then Mak enters, wearing a cloak over his garment.
1. Seven (written by the copyist as the roman numeral).

2. Is lacking.
3. And he takes his cloak from him.
4. Free-born property-holder.
5. Why act so elegant?
6. Do you want to be a saint? I think you long to be.
7. Be beaten.

I PASTOR But, Mak, is that sooth?
215   Now take out that southren tooth,°   *accent*
       And set in a turd!

II PASTOR Mak, the devil in your eye!   A stroke would I lean° you.   *lend*
III PASTOR Mak, know ye not me?   By God, I could teen° you.   *rage at*
MAK   God look you all three!   Me thought I had seen you;
220   Ye are a fair company.
I PASTOR   Can ye now mean you?
II PASTOR Shrew, pepe![8]
       Thus late as thou goes,
       What will men suppose?
       And thou has an ill nose°   *reputation*
225   Of steeling of sheep.

MAK   And I am true as steel,   all men waytt,°   *know*
       But a sickness I feel   that holds me full haytt;°   *hot*
       My belly fares not weel;   it is out of estate.
III PASTOR Seldom lies the devil   dead by the gate.[9]
MAK   Therfore
       Full sore am I and ill,
       If I stand stone still;
       I eat not an nedill°   *scrap*
       This month and more.

I PASTOR How fares thy wife? By my hood,   how fares sho?°   *she*
MAK   Lies waltering,° by the rood,   by the fire, lo!   *collapsed*
       And a house full of brood.°   She drinks well, too;   *children*
       Ill spede° other good   that she will do!   *success*
       But sho
240   Eats as fast as she can,
       And ilk° year that comes to man   *each*
       She brings forth a lakan,°   *baby*
       And some years two.

       But were I not more gracious   and richer by far;
245   I were eaten out of house   and of harbar;°   *home*
       Yet is she a foul dowse,°   if ye come nar;   *wench*
       There is none that trowse°   nor knows a war°   *imagines*/*worse*
       Than ken I.
       Now will ye see what I proffer,
250   To give all in my coffer
       To morn at next to offer
       Her hed mas-penny.[1]

II PASTOR I wote so forwaked°   is none in this shire: *sleepless*
       I would sleep if I taked   less to my hire.
III PASTOR I am cold and naked,   and would have a fire.
I PASTOR I am weary, for-rakyd,°   and run in the mire.   *exhausted*
       Wake thou!

---

8. Villain, look around!.
9. Proverbial: The devil seldom lies dead by the wayside;

i.e., the devil is not often an innocent victim.
1. Penny offering for a mass for the dead.

II PASTOR Nay, I will lyg° down by,   *lie*
    For I must sleep truly.
III PASTOR As good a man's son was I
    As any of you.

    But, Mak, come hither! Between   shall thou lyg down.
[*Mak lies down with the Shepherds.*]
MAK   Then might I let you bedene   of that ye would rowne,[2]
    No drede.
265   From my top to my toe,
    Manus tuas commendo,
    Poncio Pilato;[3]
    Christ cross me speed!
Tunc surgit, pastoribus dormientibus, et dicit[4]

    Now were time for a man   that lacks what he would
270   To stalk privily than   unto a fold,
    And nimbly to work than,   and be not too bold,
    For he might aby the bargain,   if it were told
    At the ending.
    Now were time for to reyll;°   *revel*
275   But he needs good counsel
    That fain would fare well,
    And has but little spending.

    But about you a circle,   as round as a moon,
    Too I have done that I will,   till° that it be noon,[5]   *until*
280   That ye lyg stone still   to that I have done,
    And I shall say theretill   of good words a foyne.°   *a few*
    "On hight
    Over your heads my hand I lift;
    Out go your eyes! Fordo° your sight!"   *ruin*
285   But yet I must make better shift,
    And it be right.

    Lord, what they sleep hard!   That may ye all here;
    Was I never a shepherd,   but now will I lere.°   *learn*
    If the flock be scared,   yet shall I nip near.
290   How, drawes° hitherward!   Now mends our cheer   *come*
    From sorrow:
    A fat sheep, I dare say,
    A good fleece, dare I lay,
    Eft-whyte when I may,[6]
295   But this will I borrow.
[*Mak goes home to his wife.*]

2. That way I can readily prevent you from whispering together.
3. An amusing corruption of two Bible verses: "Into your hands I commend my soul" and "I wash my hands of this man."
4. Then Mak arises, while the shepherds are sleeping, and speaks.
5. Mak is casting a spell on the shepherds in the form of a fairy circle to keep them from waking.
6. I will pay it back when I can.

	How, GIll, art thou in? Get us some light.	
UXOR EIUS[7]	Who makes such din this time of the night?	
	I am set for to spin; I hope not[8] I might	
	Rise a penny to win,° I shrew° them on height!	*gain/curse*
300	So fares	
	A housewife that has been	
	To be raised° thus between:	*disturbed*
	Here may no note° be seen	*scrap*
	For such small chares.°	*chores*
MAK	Good wife, open the hek!° Sees thou not what I bring?	*inner door*
UXOR	I may thole the dray the snek.[9] Ah, come in, my sweeting!	
MAK	Yea, thou thar not rek° of my long standing.	*care*
UXOR	By the naked neck art thou like for to hing.	
MAK	Do way:	
310	I am worthy my meat,°	*supper*
	For in a strait° can I get	*tight spot*
	More than they that swink° and sweat	*work*
	All the long day.	
	Thus it fell to my lot, Gill, I had such grace.	
UXOR	It were a foul blot to be hanged for the case.	
MAK	I have skaped, Jelot,[1] oft as hard a glase.°	*blow*
UXOR	But so long goes the pot to the water, men says,	
	At last	
	Comes it home broken.	
MAK	Well know I the token,	
	But let it never be spoken;	
	But come and help fast.	
	I would he were flayn;° I lyst° well eat:	*skinned/wish*
	This twelvemonth was I not so fain of one sheep mete.	
UXOR	Come they or° he be slain, and hear the sheep bleat—	*before*
MAK	Then might I be tane.° That were a cold sweat!	*taken*
	Go spar°	*lock*
	The gate-door.	
UXOR	Yes, Mak,	
	For and° they come at thy back—	*if*
MAK	Then might I buy, for all the pack,[2]	
	The devil of the war.	
UXOR	A good bowrde° have I spied, sin thou can none.	*trick*
	Here shall we him hide to° they be gone;	*until*
335	In my cradle abide. Let me alone,	
	And I shall lyg beside in childbed, and groan.	
MAK	Thou red;°	*get ready*
	And I shall say thou was light°	*delivered*

7. His wife.
8. I don't expect that.
9. I will let you draw the latch.

1. Affectionate nickname for "Gill."
2. Then I may have the worse, for there are such a pack of them.

<table>
<tr><td></td><td>Of a knave child this night.</td><td></td></tr>
</table>

	Of a knave child this night.	
UXOR	Now well is me day bright,	
340	That ever was I bred.	
	This is a good gise° and a far cast;	way
	Yet a woman avise helps at the last.	
	I wote° never who spies, agane° go thou fast.	know/back
MAK	But I come or they rise, else blows a cold blast!	
345	I will go sleep.	

[*Mak returns to the Shepherds and lies down.*]

	Yet sleeps all this meneye,°	household
	And I shall go stalk privily	
	As it had never been I	
	That carried there sheep.	

I PASTOR	*Resurrex a mortruis!*[3] Have hold my hand.	
	Iudas carnas dominus![4] I may not well stand:	
	My foot sleeps, by Jesus, and I water fastand.[5]	
	I thought that we had laid us full near England.	

II PASTOR	Ah ye!	
355	Lord, what I have slept well;	
	As fresh as an eel,	
	As light I me feel	
	As leaf on a tree.	

III PASTOR	Benste° be here in! So my heart quakes,	a blessing
360	My heart is out of skin,° what so it makes.	(body)
	Who makes all this din? So my brows blakes°	darkens
	To the door will I win. Hark, fellows, wakes!	
	We were four:	
	See ye awre° of Mak now?	anywhere

I PASTOR	We were up or thou.	
II PASTOR	Man, I give God a vow,	
	Yet yede° he nawre.°	went/nowhere

III PASTOR	Me thought he was lapt,° in a wolf skin.	clothed
I PASTOR	So are many hapt° now namely within.	covered
II PASTOR	When we had long napped, me thought with a gyn°	trap
	A fat sheep he trapped, but he made no din.	
III PASTOR	Be still:	
	Thy dream makes thee woode:°	mad
	It is but phantom, by the roode.°	cross
I PASTOR	Now God turn all to good,	
	If it be his will.	

II PASTOR	Rise, Mak, for shame! Thou lies right long.	
MAK	Now Christ's holy name be us among!	
	What is this? For Saint Jame, I may not well gang!	

3. Corruption from the Latin Bible of "He rose from the dead."

4. A corruption into Latin gibberish, "Judas lord of the flesh."
5. Stagger from lack of food.

380	I trow I be the same. Ah, my neck has lain wrong
Enough.
Mekill,° thanks syn° yister even,	*many/since*
Now, by Saint Steven,
I was flayd° with a sweven,°	*frightened/dream*
385	My heart out of slough.°	*skin*
I thought Gill began to croak and travail° full sad,	*struggle*
Welner° at the first cock, of a young lad	*nearly*
For to mend our flock.   Then be I never glad;
I have tow° on my rock° more then ever I had.	*flax/distaff*
390	Ah, my head!
A house full of young tharms;°	*children*
The devil knock out their harns!°	*brains*
Woe is him has many barns,
And thereto little bread!
395	I must go home, by your leave, to Gill, as I thought.
I pray you looke,° my sleeve that I steal nought:	*inspect*
I am loath you to grieve, or from you take ought.
III PASTOR	Go forth, ill might thou chefe!° Now would I we sought,	*fare*
This morn,
400	That we had all our store.
I PASTOR	But I will go before;
Let us meet.
II PASTOR | Whore? |
III PASTOR | At the crooked thorn. |

[*The Shepherds leave. Mak knocks at his door.*]

MAK	Undo this door! Who is here? How long shall I stand?
UXOR EIUS	Who makes such a bere?° Now walk in the wenyand.[6]	*noise*
MAK	Ah Gill, what cheer? It is I, Mak, your husband.
UXOR	Then may we be here the devil in a band,
Sir Gyle:[7]
Lo, he comes with a lote°	*noise*
410	As he were holden° in the throat.	*held*
I may not sit at my note,°	*work*
A hand-lang° while.	*little*
MAK	Will ye hear what fare she makes to get her a glose?[8]
And does nought but lakes° and claws her toes.	*plays*
UXOR	Why, who wanders, who wakes? Who commes, who goes?
Who brews, who bakes? What makes me thus hose?°	*hoarse*
And than,
It is rewthe° to behold,	*pitiful*
Now in hot, now in cold,
420	Full woeful is the household
That wants a woman.

But what end has thou made   with the herds, Mak?

MAK   The last word that thay said   when I turned my back,
They would look that they had   their sheep, all the pack.

425   I hope⁹ they will not be well paid   when they their sheep lack,
Perde!
But how so the game goes,
To me they will suppose,
And make a foul noise,

430   And cry out upon me.

But thou must do as thou hight.°   said

UXOR   I accord me there till.
I shall swaddle him right   in my cradle;
If it were a greater sleight,°   yet could I help till.   trick
I will lyg down straight.   Come hap me.

MAK   I will.

UXOR   Behind!
Come Coll¹ and his maroo,°   mate
They will nyp° us full naroo.°   pinch/hard

MAK   But I may cry out "Haroo!"
The sheep if they find.

UXOR   Harken ay when they call;   they will come onone.°   soon
Come and make ready all   and sing by thine one;
Sing "lullay" thou shall,   for I must groan,
And cry out by the wall   on Mary and John,
For sore.

445   Sing "lullay" on fast
When thou hears at the last;
And but I play a false cast,°   trick
Trust me no more.

[At the crooked thorn.]

III PASTOR   Ah, Coll, good morn.   Why sleeps thou not?

I PASTOR   Alas, that ever was I born!   We have a foul blot.
A fat wether° have we lorne.°   ram/lost

III PASTOR   Mary, God's forbot!

II PASTOR   Who should do us that scorn?°   That were a foul spot.   harm

I PASTOR   Some shrewe.°   villain
I have sought with my dogs

455   All Horbury² shrogs,°   hedges
And of xv° hogs   fifteen
Found I but one ewe.

III PASTOR   Now trow me, if ye will,   by Saint Thomas of Kent,
Either Mak or Gill   was at that assent.°   affair

I PASTOR   Peace, man, be still!   I saw when he went;
Thou slanders him ill;   thou ought to repent,

9. Expect.   2. A town south of Wakefield.
1. The First Shepherd.

Good speed.

II PASTOR Now as ever might I the,°   *thrive*
　　　If I should even here die,
465　　I would say it were he,
　　　That did that same deed.

III PASTOR Go we thither, I read,   and run on our feet.
　　　Shall I never eat bread   the sothe to I wytt.[3]
I PASTOR Nor drink in my head   with him till I meet.
II PASTOR I will rest in no stead   till that I him greet,
　　　My brother.
　　　One I will hight:°   *promise*
　　　Till I see him in sight
　　　Shall I never sleep one night
475　　There I do another.

　　　[They approach Mak's house.]
III PASTOR Will ye hear how they hack?[4]   Our sire list croon.
I PASTOR Heard I never none crack   so clear out of toon;
　　　Call on him.
II PASTOR　　　　　Mak,   undo your door soon.
MAK　Who is that spake,   as it were noon
480　On loft?
　　　Who is that, I say?
III PASTOR Good felows, were it day.
MAK　As far as ye may,
　　　Good, speaks soft,

485　Over a sick woman's head   that is at malaise;
　　　I had lever° be dead   or she had any disease.   *rather*
UXOR Go to another stead!   I may not well qweasse.°   *breathe*
　　　Each foot that ye tread   goes through my nese,°   *nose*
　　　So hee!°   *loudly*
I PASTOR Tell us, Mak, if ye may,
　　　How fare ye, I say?
MAK　But are ye in this town to-day?
　　　Now how fare ye?

　　　Ye have run in the mire,   and are wet yit:
495　I shall make you a fire,   if you will sit.
　　　A nurse would I hire.   Think ye on yit,
　　　Well quit is my hire—[5]   my dream this is it—
　　　A season.
　　　I have barns, if ye knew,
500　Well mo then enewe,
　　　But we must drink as we brew,
　　　And that is but reason.

　　　I would ye dined or ye yode.[6]   Me think that ye sweat.

---

3. Until I know the truth.
4. Sing (badly).

5. My wages are paid; i.e., his dream has been fulfilled.
6. I would like you to eat before you go.

II PASTOR Nay, neither mends our mood   drink nor meat.

MAK   Why, sir, ails you ought but good?

III PASTOR   Yea, our sheep that we get,
       Are stolen as they yode.   Our loss is great.

MAK   Sirs, drinks!
       Had I been there,
       Some should have bought it full sore.

I PASTOR Mary, some men trowes° that ye wore,   believes
       And that us forthinks.°   disturbs

II PASTOR Mak, some men trowys   that it should be ye.

III PASTOR Either ye or your spouse,   so say we.

MAK   Now if ye have suspowse° to Gill or to me,   suspicion
515   Come and ripe° our house,   and then may ye see   search
       Who had her;
       If I any sheep fot,°   took
       Either cow or stot;°   heifer
       And Gill, my wife, rose not
520   Here sin she laid her.

       As I am true and leal,°   to God here I pray,   loyal
       That this be the first meal   that I shall eat this day.

I PASTOR Mak, as have I ceyll,°   advise thee, I say;   heaven
       He learned timely to steal   that could not say nay.

UXOR   I swelt!°   die
       Out, thieves, from my wonys!°   home
       Ye come to rob us for the nonys.°   for the purpose

MAK   Here ye not how she groans?
       Your hearts should melt.

UXOR   Out, thieves, from my barn!   Nigh him not thor!°   there

MAK   Wist ye how she had farn,°   your hearts would be sore. fared
       Ye do wrong, I you warn,   that thus comes before
       To a woman that has farn—   but I say no more.

UXOR   Ah, my medill!°   middle
535   I pray to God so mild,
       If ever I you beguiled,
       That I eat this child
       That lies in this cradle.

MAK   Peace, woman, for God's pain,   and cry not so:
540   Thou spills thy brain,   and makes me full woe.

II PASTOR I trow our sheep be slain.   What find ye two?

III PASTOR All work we in vain;   as well may we go.
       But hatters,°   (an oath)
       I can find no flesh,
545   Hard nor nesh,°   soft
       Salt nor fresh,
       But two tome° platters.   empty

       Whik° cattle but this,   tame nor wild,   living
       None, as have I bliss,   as loud as he smiled.°   smelled

UXOR   No, so God me bliss,   and give me joy of my child!

I PASTOR We have marked amiss;   I hold us beguiled.
II PASTOR Sir, don,°   *it is done*
      Sir, our Lady him save,
      Is your child a knave?[7]
MAK   Any lord might him have
      This child to his son.

      When he wakens he kips,°   that joy is to see.   *snatches*
III PASTOR In good time to his hips,   and in cele.°   *heaven*
      But who was his gossips°,   so soon rede?°   *godparents/ready*
MAK   So fair fall their lips!
I PASTOR   Hark now, a le.°   *lie*
MAK   So God them thank,
      Parkin, and Gibon Waller, I say,
      And gentle John Horne,[8] in good fay,
      He made all the garray,°   *noise*
565   With the great shank.°   *leg*

II PASTOR Mak, friends will we be,   for we are all one.
MAK   We? Now I hold for me,   for mends° get I none.   *profit*
      Farewell all three!   All glad were ye gone.
    [The Shepherds depart.]
III PASTOR Fair words may there be,   but love is there none
570   This year.
I PASTOR Gave ye the child anything?
II PASTOR I trow not one farthing.
III PASTOR Fast again will I fling,°   *hurry*
      Abide ye me there.
    [Returns to the house.]
575   Mak, take it to no grief   if I come to thy barn.°   *baby*
MAK   Nay, thou does me great reproof,   and foul has thou farn.°   *done*
III PASTOR The child will it not grief,   that little daystarn.[9]
      Mak, with your leaf,   let me give your barn
      But vi° pence.   *six*
MAK   Nay, do way: he sleeps.
III PASTOR Me think he peeps.
MAK   When he wakens he weeps.
      I pray you go hence.
    [The other Shepherds return.]

III PASTOR Give me leave him to kiss,   and lift up the clout.°   *cloth*
585   What the devil is this?   He has a long snout.
I PASTOR He is marked amiss.   We wat° ill about.   *watch*
II PASTOR Ill-spun weft, iwys,   ay comes foul out.[1]
      Aye, so!
      He is like to our sheep!
III PASTOR How, Gyb,°   may I peep?   *the Second Shepherd*

---

7. Boy-child (of the serving-class).
8. Parkin, Gibon Waller, and John Horne are the names of the shepherds in the First Play of the Shepherds, possibly referring to actual townspeople.

9. Little day star; a term also used of the Christ child later in the play, indicating a parallel with Mak's baby.
1. Badly spun thread always makes poor cloth.

I PASTOR I trow kind° will creep   *Nature*
          Where it may not go.°   *walk*

II PASTOR This was a quaint gawde,°   and a far cast.   *clever trick*
           It was a high fraud.

III PASTOR   Yea, sirs, was't.
595   Let bren° this bawd,   and bind her fast.   *burn*
          A false skawd°   hang at the last;   *scold*
          So shall thou.
          Will ye see how they swaddle
          His four feet in the middle?
600   Saw I never in a cradle
          A horned lad² or° now.   *before*

MAK   Peace bid I. What,   let be youre fare;
          I am he that him gat,°   and yond woman him bare.   *begat*

I PASTOR What devil shall he hat,°   Mak? Lo, God, Mak's heir.   *be called*

II PASTOR Let be all that.   Now God give him care,
          I sagh.°   *saw*

UXOR   A pretty child is he
          As sits on a woman's knee;
          A dillydown,° perde,   *darling*
610   To gar° a man laugh.   *make*

III PASTOR I know him by the earn mark: that is a good token.

MAK   I tell you, sirs, hark!—   his nose was broken.
          Sithen° told me a clerk   that he was forspoken.°   *since/bewitched*

I PASTOR This is a false work;   I would fain be wroken.°   *avenged*
615   Get wepyn.

UXOR   He was taken with° an elf;   *by*
          I saw it myself.
          When the clock struck twelve
          Was he forshapen.°   *changed*

II PASTOR Ye two are well feft°   sam° in a stead.   *endowed/together*

III PASTOR Sin they maintain their theft,   let do them to dead.

MAK   If I trespass eft,°   gird° off my head.   *again/cut*
          With you will I be left.

I PASTOR   Sirs, do my read.°   *advice*
          For this trespass,
625   We will neither ban ne flite,°   *curse nor quarrel*
          Fight nor chite,°   *chide*
          But have done as tite,°   *quickly*
          And cast him in canvas.

          [*They toss Mak in a sheet.*]
          Lord, what I am sore,   in point for to brist.
630   In faith I may no more;   therefore will I rist.

II PASTOR As a sheep of vii score³   he weighed in my fist.
          For to sleep ay-whore°   me think that I list.   *anywhere*

III PASTOR Now I pray you,
          Lyg down on this green.

2. A horned child (devil).   3. Seven score pounds (140 lbs).

I PASTOR On these thieves yet I mene.°   *speak*
III PASTOR Whereto should ye tene?°   *be angry*
       Do as I say you.
       [*The Shepherds sleep.*]
       Angelus cantat "Gloria in excelsis"; postea dicat[4]

ANGELUS Rise, herd-men heynd!   For now is he born
       That shall take fro the fiend   that Adam had lorn;°   *lost*
640   That warloo° to shend,°   this night is he born.   *devil/destroy*
       God is made your friend   now at this morn.
       He behestys°   *orders*
       At Bedlem° go see: *Bethlehem*
       There lies that fre°   *lord*
645   In a crib full poorly,
       Betwyx two bestys.

I PASTOR This was a quaint steven°   that ever yet I heard.   *voice*
       It is a marvel to neven,°   thus to be scared.   *mention*
II PASTOR Of God's son of heaven   he spake upward.°   *on high*
650   All the wood on a leven   me thought that he gard
       Appear.[5]
III PASTOR He spake of a barn
       In Bedlem, I you warn.
I PASTOR That betokens yond starn.°   *star*
655   Let us seek him there.

II PASTOR Say, what was his song?   Heard ye not how he cracked° it?   *roared*
       Three breves to a long.[6]
III PASTOR   Yea, marry, he hakt° it.   *sang*
       Was no crochett° wrong,   nor nothing that lacked it.   *note*
I PASTOR For to sing us among   right as he knacked° it,   *sang*
660   I can.
II PASTOR Let se how ye croon.
       Can ye bark at the moon?
III PASTOR Hold your tongues, have done!
I PASTOR Hark after than.
       [*Sings.*]

II PASTOR To Bedlem he bade   that we should gang:
       I am full fard°   that we tarry too lang.   *afraid*
III PASTOR Be merry and not sad;   of mirth is our sang;
       Ever-lasting glad   to mede° may we fang,°   *reward/get*
       Without noise.
I PASTOR Hie we thither for-thy;°   *therefore*
       If we be wet and weary,
       To that child and that lady,
       We have it not to lose.

II PASTOR We find by the prophecy—   let be your din—
675   Of David and Isay,[7]   and mo than I min,

---

4. The Angel sings "Glory to God in the highest," and
afterwards says.
5. I thought he lit up the woods like lightning.

6. Three short notes to one long.
7. The prophet Isaiah.

The Magi with Shepherds, from the *Luttrel Psalter.* Early 14th century.

	They prophesied by clergy that in a virgin	
	Should he light and lie, to sloken° our sin	*remove*
	And slake it,	
	Our kynd° from woe;	*humankind*
680	For Isay said so,	
	Ecce virgo	
	Concipiet[8] a child that is naked.	

III PASTOR Full glad may we be,   and abide that day
That lovely to see,   that all mights may.
685 Lord, well were me,   for once and for ay,
Might I kneel on my knee,   some word for to say
To that child.
But the angel said
In a crib was he laid;
690 He was poorly arrayed,   *poor*
Both mener° and milde.

I PASTOR Patriarchs that has been,   and prophets beforn,
They desired to have seen   this child that is born.
They are gone full clean,°   that have they lorn.°   *entirely/lost*
695 We shall see him, I ween,   or it be morn,
To token.°   *as proof*
When I see him and feel,
Then wot I full weel
It is true as steel
700 That prophets have spoken:

To so poore as we are   that he would appear,
First find, and declare   by his messenger.

II PASTOR Go we now, let us fare;   the place is us near.

III PASTOR I am ready and yare;°   go we in fere°   *prepared/together*
705 To that bright.
Lord, if thy wills be,
We are lewde° all three,   *unschooled*
Thou grant us somkyns glee°   *some kind of joy*
To comfort thy wight.°   *creature*
[*They enter the stable.*]

8. Behold, a virgin conceives (Isaiah 7.14).

I PASTOR Hail, comely and clean!   Hail, young child!
    Hail, maker, as I mean,   of a maiden so mild!
    Thou has waryd,° I ween,   the warlo° so wild;   *cursed/devil*
    The false gyler° of teen°   now goes he beguiled.   *deceiver/anger*
    Lo, he merries!
715   Lo, he laughs, my sweeting!
    A well fair meeting!
    I have holden my heting;°   *kept my promise*
    Have a bob° of cherries.   *bunch*

II PASTOR Hail, sovereign saviour,   for thou has us sought!
720   Hail, freely food and flour,[9]   that all thing has wrought!
    Hail, full of favour,   that made all of nought!
    Hail! I kneel and I cower.   A bird have I brought
    To my barn.
    Hail, little tyne mop!°   *tiny baby*
725   Of our creed thou art crop:°   *fruit, fulfillment*
    I would drink on thy cop,°   *cup*
    Little day starn.°   *star*

III PASTOR Hail, darling dear,   full of Godhede!
    I pray thee be near   when that I have need.
730   Hail, sweet is thy cheer!   My heart would bleed
    To see thee sit here   in so poor weed,°   *clothing*
    With no pennies.
    Hail, put forth thy dall!°   *hand*
    I bring thee but a ball:
735   Have and play thee with all,
    And go to the tenys.°   *tennis*

MARIA The Father of heaven,   God omnipotent,
    That set all on seven,[1]   his son has he sent.
    My name could he neven,°   and light or he went.   *name*
740   I conceived him full even   through might, as he ment,°   *intended*
    And now is he born.
    He keep you from woe!
    I shall pray him so.
    Tell forth as ye go,
745   And myn° on this morn.   *remember*

I PASTOR Farewell, lady,   so fair to behold,
    With thy child on thy knee.
II PASTOR   But he lies full cold.
    Lord, well is me!   Now we go, thou behold.
III PASTOR Forsooth already   it seems to be told
750   Full oft.
I PASTOR What grace we have fun!°   *found*
II PASTOR Come forth: now are we won.
III PASTOR To sing are we bun:°   *bound*
    Let take on loft![2]
    [*They go out singing.*]

Explicit pagina Pastorum.[3]

9. Noble child and flower.
1. Made everything in seven days.
2. Let us sing on high
3. The play of the Shepherds is finished.

Medieval Lyrics

━━◆━

Middle English Lyrics

Although many Middle English lyrics have a beguilingly fresh and unselfconscious tone, they owe much to learned and sophisticated continental sources—the medieval Latin lyrics of the "Goliard poets" and the Provençal and French lyrics of the Troubadours and Trouvères. Most authors were clerics, aware of the similarities between earthly and divine love, and fond of punning in Latin or English.

The anonymity of the Middle English lyrics prevents us from seeing them as part of a single poet's *oeuvre,* as we can, for instance, with the poems of Chaucer, Dunbar, and Dafydd ap Gwilym. Rather, we must rely on more general contexts, such as genre, to establish relationships among poems. One of the most popular genres among the secular lyrics was the *reverdie,* or poem celebrating the return of spring. The early thirteenth-century *Cuckoo Song* ("Sumer is icumen in") joyfully invokes the bird's song, and revels in the blossoming of the countryside and the calls of the animals to their young. More typical examples of the *reverdie* are *Alisoun* and *Spring,* whose male speakers ruefully contrast the burgeoning of nature with the stinginess of their beloveds; in *Spring,* flowers bloom, birds sing, animals mate—but one woman remains unmoved. In the genre of the love complaint, *My Lief Is Faren in a Lond* and *Fowls in the Frith* express erotic loss and frustration with great succinctness.

Frustration was not the only attitude in Middle English love lyrics, however. A stance more boasting than adoring or despairing is taken in the witty lyric *I Have a Noble Cock.* Furthermore, clerical misogyny is expressed in *Abuse of Women,* which ostensibly praises women by absolving them of the vices—gossip, infidelity, shrewishness—typically attributed to them in satires against women; yet the refrain first praises women as the best of creatures but then undercuts this claim in Latin, which few women would have been able to understand. Although most of the Middle English lyrics are in the male voice, there are a few "women's songs"—most likely written by men—which convey female experience. Occasionally these songs are invitations (for instance, the enigmatic *Irish Dancer*), but more often they are laments by an abandoned, and often pregnant, woman.

The majority of Middle English lyrics were not secular but religious. Songs in praise of the Virgin Mary or Christ, however, employ the same erotic language as the secular lyrics, often in conjunction with typological figures linking events in the Old Testament to those in the New. In *Adam Lay Ibounden,* for instance, the poet follows a statement of the "fortunate Fall"—that Adam's sin was necessary to permit Christ's redemption—with a courtly compliment to the Virgin Mary. Similarly, *I Sing of a Maiden* draws on the typological significance of Gideon's fleece in Judges 6 (the soaking of the fleece by dew figuring Mary's impregnation by the Holy Spirit) while also employing the courtly imagery of a poet "singing of a maiden" who "chooses" Christ as her son, as if he were a lover.

Occasionally the Middle English religious lyric uses secular motifs and genres in a way that approaches parody. For instance, the second stanza of the Nativity poem *Mary Is with Child* resembles a pregnancy lament by a young girl. Mary, however, explains that her condition will be a source of joy rather than shame, when she will sing a lullaby to her "darling." This Middle English poet, far from blaspheming, was trying to humanize the mystery of the Nativity and relate it to daily life. Other religious poems either celebrate Christ or reject the world, and some poets used erotic language in poems to Christ as well as those to Mary, as in *Jesus, My Sweet Lover.* Such poems show the connection of sacred and secular concerns that is

This page contains the words and music to one of the earliest and best loved of Middle English lyrics, *The Cuckoo Song* ("Summer is icumen in"). The lyric is a *reverdie,* or spring song, but its joyful description of nature's rebirth is given a more sober allegorical interpretation by the interlinear Latin gloss, apparently to be sung to the same tune. The gloss parallels the lyric's celebration of the reawakening landscape with an account of the "heavenly farmer" (*celicus agricola*) whom "rot on the vine" (*vitis vicio*) leads to sacrifice his Son. The fact that the manuscript was copied at a monastery reminds us that this song, like much other early English secular poetry, survives only because it was seen to have religious relevance.

widely found in the Middle Ages. All these poems reflect as well the pleasure that poets and audiences alike took in the creative reworking of traditional motifs.

The Cuckoo Song

	Sumer is icumen in,°	*spring has come in*
	Lhude° sing, cuccu!°	*loudly/cuckoo*
	Groweth sed° and bloweth° med°	*seed/blooms/meadow*
	And springth° the wude° nu.°	*grows/forest/now*
5	Sing, cuccu!	
	Awe° bleteth after lomb,	*ewe*
	Lhouth° after calve° cu,°	*lows/calf/cow*
	Bulluc sterteth,° bucke ferteth.°	*leaps/farts*
	Murie° sing, cuccu!	*merrily*
10	Cuccu, cuccu,	
	Wel singes thu, cuccu.	
	Ne swik° thu naver° nu!	*cease/never*
	Sing cuccu nu, sing cuccu!	
	Sing cuccu, sing cuccu nu!	

Spring

Lenten° is come with love to toune,°   *spring/town*
With blosmen° and with briddes° roune,°   *flowers/birds'/song*
   That all this blisse bringeth.
Dayeseyes° in this° dales,   *daisies/these*
5 Notes swete of nightegales—
   Uch° foul° song singeth.   *each/bird*
The threstelcok him threteth o;[1]
Away is here° winter wo their   *their*
When woderove° springeth.°   *woodruff/grows*
10 This foules° singeth ferly fele,°   *birds/wonderfully much*
And wliteth on here winne wele,[2]
   That all the wode ringeth.

The rose raileth hire rode,°   *puts on her rosy hue*
The leves on the lighte° wode   *bright*
15   Waxen° all with wille.°   *grow/pleasure*
The mone mandeth hire bleo,[3]
The lilie is lossom° to seo,°   *lovely/see*
   The fenil° and the fille.°   *fennel/chervil*
Wowes° this° wilde drakes;   *woo/these*
20 Miles murgeth here makes,[4]
   Ase strem that striketh° stille.°   *flows/softly*
Mody meneth, so doth mo;[5]
Ichot° ich° am one of tho,°   *I know/I/those*
   For love that likes° ille.   *pleases*

25 The mone mandeth hire light;
So doth the semly,° sonne bright,   *lovely*
   When briddes singeth breme.°   *loudly*
Deawes donketh the dounes;[6]
Deores with here derne rounes,[7]
30   Domes for to deme;[8]
Wormes woweth under cloude,°   *the soil*
Wimmen waxeth° wounder° proude,   *become/wondrously*
   So well it wol hem° seme.°   *to them/appear*
If me shall wonte wille of on,[9]
35 This wunne weole° I wole forgon   *wealth of joys*
   And wight° in wode be fleme.°   *quickly/exile*

Alisoun

Bitwene Mersh° and Averil°   *March/April*
When spray° biginneth to springe,°   *twig/grow*
The lutel° fowl° hath hire° will   *little/bird/her*
On° hire lud° to singe.   *in/language*
5 Ich° libbe° in love-longinge   *I/live*

---

1. The song thrush contends always.
2. And chirp their wealth of joys.
3. The moon sends forth her light.
4. Beasts gladden their mates.
5. The high-spirited man mourns, so do others.
6. Dew moistens the downs (hills).
7. Animals with their secret whispers.
8. Speak their opinions.
9. If I shall lack the pleasure of one.

For semlokest° of alle thinge: *fairest*
He° may me blisse bringe;   *she*
Ich° am in hire baundoun.°   *I/power*
   An hendy hap ich habbe ihent![1]
10   Ichot° from hevene it is me sent;   *I know*
   From alle wimmen my love is lent,°,   *taken away*
   And light° on Alisoun.[2]   *settled*

On hew° hire her° is fair inogh,   *color/hair*
Hire browe browne, hire eye blake;
15 With lossum chere he on me logh,[3]
With middel° small and well imake.°   *waist/made*
Bote° he me wolle° to hire take   *unless/will*
For to ben hire° owen° make,°   *her/own/mate*
Longe to liven ichulle° forsake,°   *I will/refuse*
20 And feye° fallen adoun.   *doomed*
   An hendy hap ich habbe ihent!
   Ichot from hevene it is me sent;
   From alle wimmen my love is lent,
   And light on Alisoun.

25 Nightes° when I wende° and wake—   *at night/turn*
Forthy min wonges waxeth won[4]—
Levedy,° all for thine sake   *lady*
Longinge is ilent° me on.   *come*
In world nis non so witer° mon   *wise*
30 That all hire° bounte° telle con: *her/excellence*
Hire swire° is whittore° then the swon,   *neck/whiter*
And feirest may° in toune.   *maiden*
   An hendy hap ich habbe ihent!
   Ichot from hevene it is me sent;
35   From alle wimmen my love is lent,
   And light on Alisoun.

Ich am for wowing all forwake,[5]
Wery so water in wore[6]
Lest eny reve° me my make°   *steal/mate*
40 Ich habbe iyerned yore.[7]
Betere is tholien while sore[8]
Then mournen evermore.
Geynest° under gore,°   *kindest/petticoat*
Herkne to my roun!°   *song*
45   An hendy hap ich habbe ihent!
   Ichot from hevene it is me sent;
   From alle wimmen my love is lent,
   And light on Alisoun.

---

1. A fair destiny I have received.
2. Alison is a stock name for a country woman, shared by the wife in Chaucer's *Miller's Tale* and by his Wife of Bath.
3. With lovely manner she laughed at me.
4. Therefore my cheeks become pale.
5. I am for wooing all sleepless.
6. Weary as water in a troubled pool.
7. (For whom) I have long yearned.
8. It is better to suffer sorely for a time.

I Have a Noble Cock

I have a gentil° cok,   noble
    Croweth° me day;   who crows
He doth° me risen erly,   makes
    My matins for to say.

5   I have a gentil cok,
    Comen he is of gret;°   a great family
His comb is of red corel,
    His tayel is of jet.

    I have a gentil cok,
10   Comen he is of kinde;°   good lineage
His comb is of red corel,
    His tail is of inde.°   indigo

His legges ben of asor,°   azure
    So gentil and so smale;
15 His spores° arn of silver white,   spurs
    Into the worte-wale.°   root of cock's spur

His eynen° arn of cristal,   eyes
    Loken° all in aumber;   set
And every night he percheth him
20 In min ladyes chaumber.

My Lefe Is Faren in a Lond[9]

My lefe is faren in a lond[1]—
Alas! why is she so?
And I am so sore bound
I may nat com her to.
She hath my hert in hold,°   imprisoned
Where-ever she ride or go,
With trew love a thousandfold.

Fowls in the Frith

Foweles° in the frith,°   birds/wood
The fisses° in the flod,°   fishes/river
And I mon° waxe° wod.°   must/become/mad
Mulch° sorw° I walke with   much/sorrow
For beste[2] of bon° and blod.°   bone/blood

Abuse of Women

Of all creatures women be best:
Cuius contrarium verum est.[3]

In every place ye may well see
That women be trewe as tirtil° on tree,   turtle-dove

---

9. Chaucer alludes to this poem in the *Nun's Priest's Tale*,
line 112.
1. My beloved has gone away.

2. Either "beast" or "best."
3. Latin for "The opposite of this is true."

5   Not liberal° in langage, but ever in secree,°   *licentious / secrecy*
    And gret joye amonge them is for to be.

       Of all creatures women be best:
       Cuius contrarium verum est.

    The stedfastnes of women will never be don,
10   So jentil, so curtes they be everychon,[4]
    Meke as a lambe, still as a stone,
    Croked° nor crabbed find ye none!   *perverse*

       Of all creatures women be best:
       Cuius contrarium verum est.

15   Men be more cumbers° a thousand fold,   *troublesome*
    And I mervail how they dare be so bold
    Against women for to hold,
    Seeing them so pacient, softe, and cold.

       Of all creatures women be best:
20   *Cuius contrarium verum est.*

    For tell a woman all your counsaile,
    And she can kepe it wonderly well;
    She had lever go quik° to hell,   *alive*
    Than to her neighbour she wold it tell!

25   *Of all creatures women be best:*
       Cuius contrarium verum est.

    For by women men be reconsiled,
    For by women was never man begiled,
    For they be of the condicion of curtes Grisell,[5]
30   For they be so meke and milde.

       Of all creatures women be best:
       Cuius contrarium verum est.

    Now say well by° women or elles be still,   *about*
    For they never displesed man by ther will;
35   To be angry or wroth they can° no skill,   *have*
    For I dare say they think non ill.

       Of all creatures women be best:
       Cuius contrarium verum est.

    Trow° ye that women list° to smater,°   *think / like / chatter*
40   Or against ther husbondes for to clater?
    Nay, they had lever° fast bred and water,   *rather*
    Then for to dele in suche a mater.

       Of all creatures women be best:
       Cuius contrarium verum est.

---

4. So well-bred, so courteous is each one.
5. Griselda, the long-suffering wife of Chaucer's *Clerk's*

Tale; the tale ends with the observation that there are no more Griseldas left.

45   Though all the paciens in the world were drownd,
        And non were lefte here on the ground,
        Again in a woman it might be found,
        Suche vertu in them dothe abound!

50   *Of all creatures women be best:*
           Cuius contrarium verum est.

        To the tavern they will not go,
        Nor to the alehous never the mo,°   *more*
        For, God wot,° ther hartes wold be wo, *knows*   *knows*
        To spende ther husbondes money so.

55   *Of all creatures women be best:*
           Cuius contrarium verum est.

        If here were a woman or a maid,
        That list for to go freshely arayed,
        Or with fine kirchers° to go displayed,   *kerchiefs*
60   Ye wold say, "They be proude": it is ill said.

        Of all creatures women be best:
           Cuius contrarium verum est.

The Irish Dancer

        Ich° am of Irlaunde,   *I*
        And of the holy londe
        Of Irlande.
        Gode° sire, pray ich thee,   *good*
        For of sainte° *charitee,*°   *holy/charity*
        Come and daunce wit me
        In Irlaunde.

Adam Lay Ibounden

        Adam lay ibounden,°   *bound*
        Bounden in a bond;
        Foure thousand winter
        Thowt° he not too long.   *thought*
5   And all was for an appil,
        An appil that he took,
        As clerkes finden wreten
        In here° book.   *their*

        Ne° hadde the appil take° ben,   *if not/taken*
10   The appil taken ben,
        Ne° hadde never our lady   *not*
        A ben hevene quen.[6]
        Blissed be the time
        That appil take was!
15   Therfore we moun° singen   *may*
        "Deo gracias!"°   *Thanks be to God!*

---

6. Have been heaven's queen.

I Sing of a Maiden

I sing of a maiden
That is makeles,[7]
King of alle kinges
To° here° sone she ches.°   *for/her/chose*

5 He cam also° stille°   *as/quietly*
Ther° his moder was   *where*
As dew in Aprille
That falleth on the gras.

He cam also stille
10 To his moderes bowr
As dew in Aprille
That falleth on the flour.

He cam also stille
Ther his moder lay
15 As dew in Aprille
That falleth on the spray.°   *twigs*

Moder and maiden
Was never non but she:
Well may swich° a lady   *such*
20 Godes moder be.

Mary Is with Child

Nowel! nowel! nowel!
Sing we with mirth!
Christ is come well
With us to dwell,
5 *By his most noble birth.*

Under a tree
In sporting me,
Alone by a wod-side,°   *side of a wood*
I hard° a maid[8]   *heard*
10 That swetly said,
"I am with child this tide.°   *time*

"Graciously
Conceived have I
The Son of God so swete:
15 His gracious will
I put me till,
As moder him to kepe.

"Both night and day
I will him pray,
20 And her° his lawes taught,   *hear*

7. Spotless, matchless, and mateless.
8. A poem that opens with the speaker in the countryside overhearing a woman's lament raises expectations that we will hear a *chanson d'aventure*, with erotic connotations.

And every dell°   *in every way*
His trewe gospell
In his apostles fraught.°   *carried*

"This ghostly° case°   *spiritual/act*
25 Doth me embrace,
Without despite or mock;
With my derling,
'Lullay,'° to sing,   *lullabye*
And lovely him to rock.

30 "Without distress
In grete lightness
I am both night and day.
This hevenly fod°   *child*
In his childhod
35 Shall daily with me play.

"Soone must I sing
With rejoicing,
For the time is all ronne°   *run out*
That I shall child,°   *give birth to*
40 All undefil'd,
The King of Heven's Sonne."

Jesus, My Sweet Lover

Jesu Christ, my lemmon° swete,   *lover*
That diyedest on the Rode° Tree,   *Cross*
With all my might I thee beseche,
For thy woundes two and three,
That also° faste mot° thy love   *as/may*
Into mine herte fitched° be   *fixed*
As was the spere into thine herte,
Whon thou soffredest deth for me.

—◦—✠—◦—

Dafydd ap Gwilym

Widely regarded as the greatest Welsh poet, Dafydd ap Gwilym flourished in the fourteenth century, during a period of relative peace between two failed rebellions—that of Llywelyn, the last native prince of Wales, in 1282, and that of Owain Glyn Dwr (Owen Glendower), in 1400. A member of an upper-class family whose ancestors had served the English king, he wrote for a sophisticated audience of poets and patrons.

Dafydd drew inspiration from both continental and Welsh poetry but not, significantly, from English. (Influence, if any, went the other way, for the Middle English Harley lyrics, composed near the Welsh border, may owe their intricate rhyme scheme and ornamental alliteration to Welsh poetry; see *Spring* and *Alisoun*, pages 342–343). Among continental poets, the Roman Ovid is the greatest influence, whether directly or through twelfth-century Latin adaptations. He is the only foreign poet whom Dafydd mentions by name (*One Saving Place,* line 40). Dafydd is also indebted to medieval French and Provençal lyric genres—the *aubade* (dawn song), and the *reverdie* (spring song)—as well as to the *fabliau.*

Much of Dafydd's charm comes from his undercutting and transforming inherited poetic conventions through his personal revelations. His most endearing device, the self-deprecating persona, has been compared to that of his younger contemporary, Geoffrey Chaucer. There is an important difference, however, for while Chaucer in early love poems like *The Parliament of Fowls* presents himself as a failed lover, Dafydd often boasts of his success. Although he gives comic accounts of romantic failures in such anecdotal poems as *The Girls of Llanbadarn* (in which the women he ogles in church scornfully dismiss him) and the *Tale of a Wayside Inn* (in which a tryst ends in disaster when he goes to the wrong room), these are as often due to external obstacles as to his own inadequacy. In fact, Dafydd's persona is much more akin to Ovid's than to Chaucer's, with *The Hateful Husband* echoing the exasperated and scheming lover of *Amores* 1.4 and 1.6. In *The Ruin,* Dafydd gives an erotic twist to the ascetic Christian motif of the impermanence of worldly pleasures (as in the Old English *Wanderer,* page 105) by recalling that he once made love in a cottage that is now abandoned. He concludes his complaint *The Winter* with the observation that he would not venture out in such snowy weather for the sake of any girl.

Dafydd's poetry owes an equal debt to the rich poetic tradition of Wales. He shows familiarity with characters from the Arthurian tradition, which was originally Celtic although transformed by French adaptations by the time it reached him. In the poems included here, he often emphasizes the local Welsh setting. In *One Saving Place,* for instance, he lists all the locales where he sought his beloved Morvith, or she refused him—places with names like Meirch, Eleirch, Rhiw, and Cwcwll hollow. In *The Winter,* it is specifically in north Wales that he is assailed by snow.

Dafydd's work is also distinguished by the poetic techniques of Welsh poetry, which are extraordinarily complex. His *cywyddau* (lyric poems) are written in the traditional lines of seven syllables, which rhyme in couplets, with the rhyming syllables alternately stressed and unstressed. He applies further ornamentation with a technique called *cynghanned*—internal alliteration or rhyme, which he sometimes extends over many lines. Although such an intricate style is impossible to capture in English, Rolfe Humphries has tried to approximate it in the translations given here. Easier to reproduce are Daffyd's *dyfalu*— strings of fanciful comparisons, such as the metaphors for snow used in *The Winter:*

> The snowflakes wander,
> A swarm of white bees.
> Over the woods
> A cold veil lies.
> A load of chalk
> Bows down the trees,
> * * *
> Will someone tell me
> What angels lift
> Planks in the flour-loft
> Floor of heaven
> Shaking down dust?
> An angel's cloak
> Is cold quicksilver.

In extending the virtuoso techniques of the native tradition, Dafydd set the standard for Welsh poets for the next two centuries.

One Saving Place

What wooer ever walked through frost and snow,
Through rain and wind, as I in sorrow?
My two feet took me to a tryst in Meirch[1]
No luck; I swam and waded the Eleirch,
5   No golden loveliness, no glimpse of her;
Night or day, I came no nearer
Except in Bleddyn's arbors, where I sighed
When she refused me, as she did beside
Maesalga's murmuring water-tide.
10   I crossed the river, Bergul, and went on
Beyond its threatening voices; I have gone
Through the mountain-pass of Meibion,
Came to Camallt, dark in my despair,
For one vision of her golden hair.
15   All for nothing. I've looked down from Rhiw,
All for nothing but a valley view,
Kept on going, on my journey through
Cyfylfaen's gorge, with rock and boulder,
Where I had thought to ermine-cloak her shoulder.
20   Never; not here, there, thither, thence,
Could I ever find her presence.
Eagerly on summer days I'd go
Brushing my way through Cwcwll hollow,
Never stopped, continued, skirting
25   Gastell Gwrgan and its ring
Where the red-winged blackbirds sing,
Tramped across fields where goslings feed
Below the cat-tail and the reed.
I have limped my way, a weary hound,
30   In shadow of the walls that bound
Adail Heilyn's broken ground.
I have hidden, like a friar,
In Ifor's Court, among the choir,
Sought to seek my sweet one there,
·35   But there was no sign of her.
On both sides of Nant-y-glo
There's no vale, no valley, no
Stick or stump where I failed to go,
Only Gwynn of the Mist for guide,
40   Without Ovid[2] at my side.

Gwenn-y-Talwrn!—there I found
My hand close on hers, on ground
Where no grass was ever green,
Where not even a shrub was seen,
45   There at last I made the bed
For my Morvith,[3] my moon-maid,

1. This and other Welsh place names are listed by Dafydd in his account of his search for his beloved, Morvith.
2. See introduction for Dafydd's indebtedness to the Roman love poet.
3. The lady most frequently mentioned in Dafydd's love poems, apparently married.

Underneath the dark leaf-cloak
Woven by saplings of an oak.
Bitter, if a man must move
50   On his journeys without love.
Bitter, if soul's pilgrimage
Must be like the body's rage,
Must go down the desolate road
Midway through the darkling wood.

The Hateful Husband

'Tis sorrow and pain,
'Tis endless chagrin
For Dafydd to gain
His dark-haired girl.
5   Her house is a jail,
Her turnkey a vile,
Sour, yellow-eyed, pale,
Odious churl.

She cannot go out
10   Unless he's about,
The blackguard, the lout,
The stingy boor.
The look in her eye
Of fondness for me—
15   God bless her bounty!—
He can't endure.

I know he hates play:
The greenwood in May,
The birds' roundelay
20   Are not for him.
The cuckoo, I know,
He'd never allow
To sing on his bough,
Light on his limb

25   The flash of the wing,
The swell of the song,
Harp-music playing
Draw his black looks.
The hounds in full cry,
30   A race-horse of bay,
He cannot enjoy
More than the pox.

My heart would be glad
At seeing him laid
35   All gray in his shroud;
How could I grieve?
Should he die this year,
I'd give him with cheer

40   Good oak for his bier,
      Sods for his grave.

      O starling, O swift,
      Go soaring aloft,
      Come down to the croft
      By Dovekie's home.
45   This message give her,
      Tell her I love her,
      And I will have her,
      All in good time.

The Winter

      Across North Wales
      The snowflakes wander,
      A swarm of white bees.
      Over the woods
5   A cold veil lies.
      A load of chalk
      Bows down the trees.

      No undergrowth
      Without its wool,
10   No field unsheeted;
      No path is left
      Through any field;
      On every stump
      White flour is milled.

15   Will someone tell me
      What angels lift
      Planks in the flour-loft
      Floor of heaven
      Shaking down dust?
20   An angel's cloak
      Is cold quicksilver.

      And here below
      The big drifts blow,
      Blow and billow
25   Across the heather
      Like swollen bellies.
      The frozen foam
      Falls in fleeces.

      Out of my house
30   I will not stir
      For any girl
      To have my coat
      Look like a miller's
      Or stuck with feathers
35   Of eider down.

What a great fall
Lies on my country!
A wide wall, stretching
One sea to the other,
40   Greater and graver
Than the sea's graveyard.
When will rain come?

The Ruin

Nothing but a hovel now
Between moorland and meadow,
Once the owners saw in you
A comely cottage, bright, new,
5   Now roof, rafters, ridge-pole, all
Broken down by a broken wall.

A day of delight was once there
For me, long ago, no care
When I had a glimpse of her
10   Fair in an ingle-corner.
Beside each other we lay
In the delight of that day.

Her forearm, snowflake-lovely,
Softly white, pillowing me,
15   proferred a pleasant pattern
For me to give in my turn,
And that was our blessing for
The new-cut lintel and door.

"Now the wild wind, wailing by,
20   Crashes with curse and with cry
Against my stones, a tempest
Born and bred in the East,
Or south ram-batterers break
The shelter that folk forsake."

25   Life is illusion and grief;
A tile whirls off, as a leaf
Or a lath goes sailing, high
In the keening of kite-kill cry.
Could it be, our couch once stood
30   Sturdily under that wood?

"Pillar and post, it would seem
Now you are less than a dream.
Are you that, or only the lost
Wreck of a riddle, rune-ghost?"

35   "Dafydd, the cross on their graves
Marks what little it saves,
Says, *They did well in their lives*."

William Dunbar

In the late fifteenth and early sixteenth centuries, Scotland enjoyed a brief flowering of poetry centered in a sophisticated court society. Relations with England were fraught with irony, marked, on the one hand, by royal alliance (James IV married Margaret Tudor, daughter of England's Henry VII in 1503) and on the other by disastrous warfare (James IV also, in alliance with France, invaded England and perished with most of the Scottish nobility at the Battle of Flodden in 1513). The poets of this period have been variously known as the "Scottish Chaucerians," the "Middle Scots Poets," and the "Makars"—each term privileging a significant, though only partial, aspect of their work. The first conveys the debt that William Dunbar, Robert Henryson, and Gavin Douglas (to name the three most famous) owed to Chaucer's subject matter, rhetorical style, and techniques of parody. The second suggests their equal debt to a native Scottish tradition, which includes such overtly nationalist works as Barbour's *Bruce* and Blind Harry's *Wallace*. The best term to describe these poets is perhaps the one used by Dunbar himself—"Makars" (makers)—for it suggests their powerful and self-conscious artistry.

Of all the Makars, Dunbar is the greatest virtuoso, intoxicated with language, whether it be the elevated vocabulary borrowed from Latin, or the Germanic diction of alliterative poetry, whose tradition was kept alive in Scotland a century after it had died out in England. He was versatile in his choice of genres, writing occasional poems (such an an allegory in celebration of the marriage of James IV and Princess Margaret), divine poems, and parodies such as *The Tretis of Two Mariit Wemen and the Wedo*, a bawdy satire on the morals of court ladies written in the traditional alliterative long line. Included here are a meditation on death (*Lament for the Makars*) and a parody of the courtly genre of the *chanson d'aventure* (*In Secreit Place This Hyndir Nycht*).

Lament for the Makars[1]

I that in heill° wes° and gladnes	*health/was*
Am trublit now with gret seiknes	
And feblit with infermite:	
Timor mortis conturbat me.[2]	

5   Our plesance heir is all vane glory,
    This fals warld is bot transitory,
    The flesche is brukle,° the Fend° is sle:°   *frail/Devil/sly*
        Timor mortis conturbat me.

    The stait of man dois change and vary,
10   Now sound, now seik, now blith, now sary,
    Now dansand mery, now like to dee:°   *die*
        Timor mortis conturbat me.

    No stait in erd° heir standis sickir;°   *on earth/secure*
    As with the wynd wavis the wickir,
15   Wavis this warldis vanite:
        Timor mortis conturbat me.

1. This poem reflects the late medieval fascination with death. The speaker wistfully observes that beautiful ladies, brave knights, and wise clerks have had their lives cut short but gives most of his attention to poets. He lists 23 of these—three English (Chaucer, Gower, and Lydgate) and 20 Scots, only half of whom modern scholars can identify. Since Death has taken all his "brothers," he regards himself as next and resolves to prepare himself for the next world. The poem was printed in 1508 by Walter Chepman and Andrew Myllar, who introduced the printing press to Scotland.

2. Fear of death shakes me (from the liturgical Office of the Dead).

On to the ded gois all estatis,
Princis, prelotis,° and potestatis,°   *prelates/rulers*
Baith riche and pur of al degre:
20   *Timor mortis conturbat me.*

He takis the knychtis° in to feild,°   *knights/the field*
Anarmit° under helme and scheild; armed   *armed*
Victour he is at all mellie:°.   *battles*
         Timor mortis conturbat me.

25   That strang unmercifull tyrand
Takis, on the moderis° breist sowkand,°   *mother's/sucking*
The bab full of benignite:
         Timor mortis conturbat me.

He takis the campion° in the stour,°   *champion/conflict*
30   The capitane closit in the tour,
The lady in bour° full of bewte: *bower*
         Timor mortis conturbat me.

He sparis no lord for his piscence,°   *power*
Na clerk for his intelligence;
35   His awfull strak° may no man fle: *stroke*
         Timor mortis conturbat me.

Art magicianis and astrologgis,
Rethoris,° logicianis and theologgis,   *rhetoricians*
Thame helpis no conclusionis sle:°   *clever*
40   *Timor mortis conturbat me.*

In medicyne the most practicianis,
Lechis,° surrigianis,° and phisicianis,   *doctors/surgeons*
Thame self fra ded° may not supple:°   *death/deliver*
         Timor mortis conturbat me.

45   I se that makaris° amang the laif°   *poets/remainder*
Playis heir ther pageant, syne gois to graif;°   *grave*
Sparit° is nocht ther faculte: *spared*
         Timor mortis conturbat me.

He hes done petuously devour
50   The noble Chaucer of makaris flour,°   *flower of poets*
The Monk of Bery,[3] and Gower, all thre:
         Timor mortis conturbat me.

The gude Syr Hew of Eglintoun,[4]
And eik Heryot, and Wyntoun,[5]
55   He hes tane out of this cuntre:
         Timor mortis conturbat me.

---

3. John Lydgate, monk of Bury St. Edmunds, a minor poet who was an imitator of Chaucer. He also used the "*timor mortis*" refrain in a poem on the same subject.
4. Brother-in-law of Robert II and not otherwise known as a poet.
5. Andrew of Wyntoun, author of the *Oryginale Chronykil of Scotland*.

That scorpion fell° hes done infek°   *fierce/infect*
Maister Johne Clerk and James Afflek[6]
Fra ballat making and tragidie:
60   *Timor mortis conturbat me.*

Holland and Barbour[7] he hes berevit;
Allace,° that he nocht with us levit   *alas*
Schir Mungo Lokert of the Le:[8]
      Timor mortis conturbat me.

65   Clerk of Tranent eik he hes tane,
That maid the Anteris° of Gawane;   *adventures*
Schir Gilbert Hay endit hes he:[9]
      Timor mortis conturbat me.

He hes Blind Hary and Sandy Traill
70   Slaine with his schour° of mortall haill,   *shower*
Quhilk Patrik Johnestoun[1] myght nocht fle:
      Timor mortis conturbat me.

He hes reft° Merseir his endite°   *taken from/talent*
That did in luf so lifly° write,   *in a lively manner*
75   So schort, so quyk, of sentence hie:
      Timor mortis conturbat me.

He hes tane Roull of Aberdene
And gentill Roull of Corstorphin;
Two bettir fallowis did no man se:
80   *Timor mortis conturbat me.*

In Dunfermelyne he hes done roune°   *held conversation*
With Maister Robert Henrisoun.[2]
Schir Johne the Ros enbrast° hes he: *embraced*
      Timor mortis conturbat me.

85   And he hes now tane last of aw
Gud gentill Stobo and Quintyne Schaw,[3]
Of quham all wichtis hes pete:[4]
      Timor mortis conturbat me.

Gud Maister Walter Kennedy[5]
90   In° poynt of dede° lyis veraly;°   *on/death/truly*
Gret reuth° it wer that so suld be: *pity*
      Timor mortis conturbat me.

---

6. These two are unknown, as are the other poets in this list not identified.
7. Sir Richard Holland, author of the allegorical *Buke of the Howlat* (c. 1450), and John Barbour, author of the patriotic *Actes and Life . . . of Robert Bruce* (1376).
8. This Scotsman (d. 1489?) is not otherwise known as a poet.
9. The "clerk of Tranent" is unknown, but Arthurian romances focusing on Gawain were popular in Scotland; Sir Gilbert Hay (d. 1456) translated the poem *The Buik of Alexander* from French.

1. Blind Harry is credited with writing the Scots epic *Wallace* (c. 1475); Patrick Johnstoune was a producer of stage entertainments at court in the late 1400s.
2. Henryson was a major Middle Scots poet.
3. John Reid, known as Stobo, was priest and secretary to James II, James III, and James IV; Schaw was a minor Scots poet.
4. On whom all people have pity.
5. Known for his *Flyting* (poem of ritual insult) with Dunbar.

Sen he hes all my brether tane
He will nocht lat me lif alane;

95 On forse° I man his nyxt pray be: *of necessity*
   Timor mortis conturbat me.

Sen for the deid remeid° is none,   *remedy*
Best is that we for dede dispone°   *prepare*
Eftir our deid that lif may we:
Timor mortis conturbat me.

In Secreit Place This Hyndir Nycht[1]

In secreit place this hyndir° nycht   *last*
I hard ane beyrne° say till ane bricht,°   *man/fair lady*
"My huny, my hart, my hoip, my heill,[2]
I have bene lang° your luifar° leill°   *long/lover/loyal*
5 And can of yow get confort nane:°   *none*
How lang will ye with danger deill?[3]
Ye brek my hart, my bony ane."°   *pretty one*

His bony beird was kemmit and croppit,[4]
Bot all with cale° it was bedroppit,°   *soup/smeared*
10 And he wes townysche, peirt and gukit.[5]
He clappit fast, he kist and chukkit[6]
As with the glaikis° he wer ouirgane;°   *lust/overcome*
Yit be his feirris° he wald have fukkit: *manner*
"Ye brek my hart, my bony ane."

15 Quod he, "My hairt, sweit° as the hunye,   *sweet*
Sen that I borne wes of my mynnye°   *mother*
I never wowit° weycht° bot yow;   *wooed/creature*
My wambe° is of your luif sa fow°   *belly/full*
That as ane gaist° I glour° and grane,°   *ghost/glower/groan*
20 I trymble° sa, ye will not trow:°   *tremble/believe*
Ye brek my hart, my bony ane."

"Tehe,"° quod scho, and gaif ane gawfe;°   *Teehee/guffaw*
"Be still my tuchan[7] and my calfe,
My new spanit howffing fra the sowk,[8]
25 And all the blythnes° of my bowk;°   *joy/body*
My sweit swanking,° saif yow allane   *fine fellow*
Na leid° I luiffit° all this owk:°   *no man/loved/week*
Full leifis° me° your graceles gane."°   *dear/to me/face*

Quod he, "My claver° and my curldodie,°   *clover/a plant*
30 My huny soppis, my sweit possodie,°   *sheep's head broth*

---

1. This comic account of the wooing of a kitchen maid by a boorish man parodies the *chanson d'aventure*, a genre in which the speaker overhears a dialogue between two lovers. Dunbar undercuts the poem's courtly language, which he has used seriously elsewhere, with overtly sexual references. In addition to words familiar to modern readers, the poem features terms of endearment from colloquial Scots which have long since been lost.
2. My honey, my heart, my hope, my salvation.

3. Ladies were expected to be "dangerous" (reluctant) in a courtship situation.
4. His handsome beard was combed and trimmed.
5. And he was townish (uncourtly), pert, and foolish.
6. He fondled fast, kissed and chucked her under the chin.
7. Calf skin stuffed with straw, to encourage a cow to give milk.
8. My clumsy fellow newly weaned from nursing.

	Be not oure bosteous° to your billie,°	rough/sweetheart
	Be warme hairtit° and not evill willie;°	hearted/ill-willed
	Your heylis quhyt as quhalis bane,⁹	
	Garris ryis° on loft my quhillelillie:°	makes rise/penis
35	Ye brek my hart, my bony ane."	

Quod scho, "My clype, my unspaynit gyane¹
With moderis° mylk yit in your mychane,°   *mother's/mouth*
My belly huddrun,° my swete hurle bawsy,²   *big-bellied glutton*
My huny gukkis,° my slawsy gawsy,   *sweet fool*
40   Your musing waild perse° ane hart of stane: *would pierce*
Tak gud confort, my grit heidit° slawsy,   *great-headed*
Full leifis me your graceles gane."
Quod he, "My kid, my capirculyoun,°   *woodgrouse*
My bony baib° with the ruch° brylyoun,   *babe/rough*
45   My tendir gyrle, my wallie gowdye,°   *pretty goldfinch*
My tyrlie myrlie, my crowdie mowdie,°   *milky porridge*
Quhone° that oure mouthis dois meit° at ane   *when/do meet*
My stang dois storkyn with your towdie:³
Ye brek my hairt, my bony ane."

50   Quod scho, "Now tak me be the hand,
Welcum, my golk° of Marie° land,   *cuckoo/fairy*
My chirrie and my maikles munyoun,⁴
My sowklar° sweit as ony unyoun,°   *suckling/any onion*
My strumill stirk yit new to spane,⁵
55   I am applyit° to your opunyoun:°   *inclined/opinion*
I luif rycht weill° your graceles gane."   *love right well*

He gaiff to hir ane apill rubye;°   *apple red*
Quod scho, "Gramercye,° my sweit cowhubye.°"   *thanks/fool*
And thai tway to ane play began
60   Quhilk° men dois call the dery dan,⁶   *which*
Quhill° that thair myrthis° met baythe in ane: *while/pleasure*
"Wo is me," quod scho, "Quhair will ye,° man?   *where will you go*
Best now I luif° that graceles gane."   *love*

---

9. Your neck white as whale's bone; a common alliterative phrase in the conventional love poetry.
1. Said she, "My big soft fellow, my unweaned giant."
2. An obscure term of endearment, as are several other phrases in the following lines.
3. My pole does stiffen by your thing.
4. My cherry and my matchless darling.
5. My stumbling bullock still newly weaned.
6. A dance (i.e., copulation).

Frontispiece from Saxton's *Atlas*. 1579.

The Early Modern Period

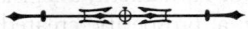

We see the past through lenses that show us something of the world we are living in. How we mark periods in history depends less on an objective evaluation of evidence than on our sense of its relation to our own present. The centuries between 1500 and 1700 have been termed the "Renaissance" and, more recently, "the early modern period." What do these two names mean and what do they tell us about our understanding of this single and continuous stretch of time?

However we describe these centuries, they encompassed events that changed profoundly the way people lived and thought. In 1500, the English church was part of a united Western Christendom led by the Pope, and people around the country prayed according to a common liturgy. It was understood that the earth was the center of the universe; that the human body was a balance of the four elements—earth, air, fire, and water; and that nature, read like a book, could reveal a moral order. English men and women had a deep respect for law, which they assumed would protect them from tyranny as well as anarchy. These beliefs had been challenged in the preceding century and a half by the natural calamities of plague and famine, by the political upheaval of the Rising of 1381, and more generally by the growth of towns, trade, and a degree of social mobility. Yet for most people in 1500 the old beliefs held fast, as did the traditional way of life that sustained them. And outside the growing merchant class, a person's place tended to be fixed at birth; the majority of folk lived in country villages, worked the land, and traded in regional markets.

By the end of the seventeenth century, much of this way of life had vanished. England had broken away from Roman religious authority; in addition to the Church of England and the Presbyterian churches of Scotland, Protestantism had created a variety of sects: Anabaptists, Puritans, and Quakers. Worship was conducted in English, not in the Latin that had been used for centuries. Catholics, suspected of subversive intentions, were barely tolerated. A natural philosophy based on experimental methods had begun to reshape the disciplines of physics, medicine, and biology; such ancient authorities as Aristotle, Galen, and Pliny were no longer unquestioned. Sketched in principle by Sir Francis Bacon in his treatise on scientific inquiry, *Novum Organum* (literally, "the new instrument"), published in 1620, a systematic investigation of nature had not begun before the restoration of the Stuart monarchy in 1660. But the world view it would help to confirm was already evident early in the seventeenth century: the work of the Italian physicist Galileo Galilei on gravitational force had demonstrated that the most elementary laws of nature were mathematical; the German astronomer Johannes Kepler had confirmed that the universe was heliocentric; and in England, William Harvey had established that the body was energized not by the eccentric flow of "humors" but by a circulation of blood to and from the heart. Scientists would consolidate their status as intellectuals by forming the Royal Society for the Advancement of Science in 1660—a foundation that was vigorously supported by the new Stuart king, Charles II.

Political life had taken a new direction as well. A civil war, interrupting the peace of over a century, had created a new kind of monarchy. The war had been fought over social and economic issues but also over a matter of principle: England was to be governed by a monarch whose authority and power were not absolute but limited by law and the actions of Parliament, a legislative assembly representing his subjects. The cities, enjoying a prosperity created by international commerce, became crowded even as they expanded with new streets, marketplaces, and buildings for private as well as public use. Country folk flocked to these burgeoning urban centers. Succumbing to diseases spread by filth and overcrowding, they often died younger than did their rural relatives. But England was becoming a nation of city dwellers, and everyone knew of "citizens" who had gained wealth and station in these exciting, if also terrifying, cities.

THE HUMANIST RENAISSANCE AND EARLY MODERN SOCIETY

The tumultuous character of the age has been described as a "renaissance"—literally a "rebirth." Nineteenth-century historians attributed the intellectual and social energy that initiated the reform of the medieval world to a revival of interest in the classical past. By 1400, Italian scholars had begun to reread the works of Greek and Roman authors—Plato and Aristotle, Virgil, Ovid, and Horace—and to look with fresh eyes at the physical monuments of the ancient world that were still so prominent in their landscapes. Their movement traveled north and west to France, the Low Countries, Germany, the Iberian peninsula, and eventually England. What was "reborn" as a result was a sense of the meanings to be discovered in the here and now, in the social, political and economic everyday world. Writing about the intellectual vitality of the age, the French humanist François Rabelais had his amiable giant Gargantua confess that his own education had been "darksome, obscured with clouds of ignorance." Gargantua knows, however, that his son will be taught differently:

> Good literature has been restored unto its former light and dignity, and with such amendment and increase of knowledge, that now hardly should I be admitted unto the first form of the little grammar-school boys . . . I see robbers, hangmen, freebooters, tapsters, ostlers, and such like, of the very rubbish of the people, more learned now than the doctors and preachers were in my time.

These comically overstated remarks nevertheless convey the spirit of the Renaissance: learning was no longer only to be devoted to securing salvation, but should address the conditions of ordinary life as well. The pre-Christian cultures of the ancient Mediterranean had introduced Europeans to philosophies that valued human society and its future generations; studying classical texts afresh, thinkers began to attend in new ways to the world around them. The writers and scholars responsible for the rebirth of a secular culture have been known as "humanists," because they read "humane" as well as "sacred" letters; and their intellectual and artistic practices have been termed "humanism."

The humanists cultivated certain habits of thought that became widely adopted by early modern thinkers of all kinds: skill in using language analytically, attentiveness to public and political affairs as well as private and moral ones, and an acute appreciation for differences between peoples, regions, and times. It was, after all, the humanists who began to realize that the classical past required *understanding;* they recognized the past as unfamiliar, neither Christian nor European, and they knew, therefore, that it had to be studied, interpreted, and, in a sense, reborn.

At the same time, changes were occurring for which there were no precedents. During these years, the modern world was born as much as an older world was reborn, and for this reason the sixteenth and seventeenth centuries have also been called the "early modern period." Its modernity was registered in many ways. Instruments for measuring time and space provided a knowledge of physical nature, a mapping of land, sea, and even the sky that began to permit global travel. Means had to be designed to compute the wealth that was being created by manufacture and trade, and new methods were employed by a people keen to exploit all kinds of resources, including the labor of individuals. Money was used in new and complex ways, its flow managed through such innovations as double-entry bookkeeping and letters of exchange that registered debt and credit in interregional markets. The capital that accumulated as a result of these kinds of transactions fueled merchant banks, joint-stock companies, and—notably in England—trading companies that sponsored colonies abroad. In England especially, wealth was increasingly based on money, not land, and the change encouraged a social mobility that reflected but also exploited the old hierarchy. Riches could and did make it possible for an artisan's son to purchase a coat of arms and become a gentleman, as William Shakespeare did. More important, moneyed wealth supported the artistic and scholarly institutions that allowed the stepson of a bricklayer to go to the best school in London, to profit from the business of the theater, and to compose literary works of sufficient brilliance to make him poet laureate, as Ben Jonson did. "Ambition is like choler," warned Francis Bacon; it makes men "active, earnest, full of alacrity and stirring." But if ambition "be stopped and cannot have his way, it becommeth adust, and thereby maligne and venomous." Early modern society was certainly both active and stirring; but the very energy that gave it momentum could also lead to hardship, distress, and personal tragedy.

Urban life flourished in conditions that were increasingly hospitable to commerce; rural existence became precarious as small farms failed. During the fifteenth century the nobility had begun to enlarge their estates by the incorporation or "enclosing" of what had formerly been public or common land. They sought to profit from a new activity: sheep farming. Thousands of men and women who had worked the land on modest estates lost their livelihoods as a result. Many came to the cities, particularly London; others traveled through the country, looking for odd work, begging, and thieving. The situation got worse when Henry VIII broke England's tie to the Catholic Church, for Henry added to the property of the very rich by giving them the land he had confiscated from the church. On the other hand, the great centers of commerce—Bristol, Norwich, and London—sustained not only trade but also many kinds of manufacture. One of the most important was printing. The invention of movable type in 1436 by a German printer, Johann Gutenberg, revolutionized the dissemination of texts. A single illuminated manuscript took years to produce and provided what was often a unique version of a text, an item that might cost as much as a small farm; a printing press could quickly produce multiple copies of identical versions of a text for as little as a few shillings.

Both the mentality of the "Renaissance" and the more comprehensive culture of the early modern period are illustrated by the history of the most frequently disseminated and contested text of these centuries: the Bible. It was the work of humanists to establish what that text was (after centuries of corrupted versions) and then to translate it into the vernacular languages. Desiderius Erasmus provided accurate Hebrew and Greek texts and translated them into Latin. Printed English translations

Hans Holbein. *The Ambassadors*. 1533. National Portrait Gallery, London.

begin with William Tyndale's New Testament, introduced to England in the 1520s. Later versions included the Geneva Bible with its Calvinist commentary; the Bishops' Bible, repudiating much of that commentary; and the King James Bible, or "Authorized Version," a work by forty-seven translators that was published in 1611. Protestant doctrine emphasized the importance of reading Scripture as a means to spiritual enlightenment, and the preface to the King James Bible insists that for this purpose a translation is as good as the original: "No cause why the word translated should be denied to be the word." But the importance of the Bible went beyond its status as the basis for religious belief.

People from various walks of life, not only humanists, found the Bible a source of inspiration for social reform, a means to link together religious conviction and political practice. Drawing on the Bible to justify their ideas of government, writers as different as the radical Bishop of Winchester, John Ponet, and the scholarly King James VI of Scotland, eventually James I of England, presented arguments for distinctive kinds of monarchy. Ponet insisted that a monarch was obliged to obey the law of the land and thus to adhere to a "constitution"; James thought that a monarch should respect only divine law and be considered "absolute." Other writers, inspired by their

SCVLPTVRA IN ÆS.

Sculptor noua arte, bracteata in lamina   Scalpit figuras, atque prælis imprimit.

Hans Collaert, after Jan van der Straet, called Stradanus. *The Printmaker's Workshop* (detail).

own understanding of God's word, forged new concepts of the state, the subject, and sovereignty that would continue to shape political philosophy to the American War of Independence.

The Bible and the attitudes it prompted were also factors in the establishment of an English church. The English people had been forced to break formally and definitively from the Catholic Church because their king, Henry VIII, wished to be independent of the papacy and its government in Rome. His reasons were many and complex. Certainly responsive to the demand for changes in church government, doctrine, and liturgy, Henry was motivated by personal and political interests as well. In love with a lady of the court, Anne Boleyn, he was persuaded that his marriage to Catherine of Aragon, the widow of his older brother, Prince Arthur, violated divine law. Catherine, mother of the girl who would become Mary I, had failed to give Henry a son, and he saw in his frustrated hopes for the dynastic stability that would come from having a male heir a sign that God was displeased with his marriage. He sought a divorce from the Pope and was refused. In 1533, however, his pliable Archbishop of Canterbury, Thomas Cranmer, defying the Pope out of loyalty to his king, pronounced Henry's marriage to Catherine invalid. The following year, Parliament passed the Act of Supremacy; besides making the monarch of England head of an English church, it made Henry immediately free from the Pope's jurisdiction. English clergy who had promoted the idea of a reformation began to institute the changes they had envisaged. But the socially destabilizing effects of the English reformation, far from abating, grew more profound as time went on.

Huge numbers of the faithful would suffer, Protestants as well as Catholics. The creation of an English church not only separated England from most of the continent, it disturbed the religious peace that had prevailed for centuries. The story is a grim one: Catholics in the north of England unsuccessfully resisted Henry's imposition of Protestantism in their Pilgrimage of Grace in 1536; Protestants were in turn persecuted by Mary I throughout her reign; Catholics were suppressed by Elizabeth I; and sectarians of various denominations were required to adhere to Anglican forms of worship and obey episcopal power under the Stuarts.

The prodigiously revolutionary changes in early modern England were vividly reflected in its profuse and varied literature. Topics and issues that for centuries had been considered by relatively small numbers of literate people were now registered in general debate. New and evolving conditions of religious, intellectual, and political life provided writers with a vast subject matter, and their work shed light on the world that they saw unfolding before them. They showed its potential for prosperous development through all kinds of human activity; they represented its long and varied history as proof of providential direction; and they praised its myriad forms as the expression of a divine and beneficent artificer.

As late twentieth-century readers, we come to the literature of this period with our own perspectives on what is modern and what we understand as postmodern. Many features of early modern culture are again in transition today: the printed book, which once superseded the manuscript, is now being challenged by computer-generated hypertext; the nation-state, which once eclipsed the feudal domain and divided "Christendom," is now qualified by an international economy; and the belief in human progress, which was once applauded as an advance over the medieval faith in divine providence, is now subject to criticism, in large part because of such kinds of injustice and inequity as slavery, colonialism, and the exploitation of wage labor—all factors in the growth of early modern England and of other states in Europe. As modern and postmodern readers, we have a special affinity with our early modern counterparts. Like them, we study change.

HISTORY AND EPIC

The political life of the sixteenth century was dominated by the genius of a single dynasty: the Tudors. Its founder was Owen Tudor, a squire of an ancient Welsh family who was employed at the court of Henry V and eventually married his widow, Catherine of Valois. Its first monarch was Owen Tudor's grandson, Henry, Earl of Richmond, who defeated Richard III at Bosworth Field in 1485 to become Henry VII. He married Elizabeth, daughter of Edward IV, whom Richard III had succeeded—a fortunate event for the people of England, as it united the two parties by whom the crown had been disputed for many decades. Once Henry, who represented the House of Lancaster (whose emblem was a white rose), was joined to Elizabeth, a member of the House of York (signified by a red rose), the "Wars of the Roses" were at an end. Henry VII's bureaucratic skills then settled the kingdom in ways that allowed it to grow and become identified as a single nation, however much it also comprised different peoples: the midlands and the north were distinguished from the more populous south by dialectal forms of speech; and to the west, in Cornwall and Wales, many English subjects still spoke Gaelic. More thoroughly Gaelic were Scotland to the north and Ireland across the sea to the west. Although the Anglo-Normans had invaded Ireland in the twelfth century, it was not until the reign of Elizabeth that the English pursued the subjugation of Ireland by establishing colonizing plantations and conducting a brutal military campaign that produced famine, massacres, and the forced relocation of people. But this supposed English fiefdom remained rebellious and effectively unconquered for Elizabeth's entire reign. Its resistance to English rule was crushed only in 1603, an event that marked the end of an independent Ireland for three hundred years. Scotland, to the far north, was a separate and generally unfriendly kingdom with strong ties to France until James VI of Scotland became James I of England. His accession to the English throne in 1603 began a process that would end with the complete union of the two kingdoms in 1707. There were also more remote regions to consider: England's colonization of the Americas began under Elizabeth I, progressed under James I, and allowed the English to think of themselves as an imperial power.

Writing history offered a way to reinforce the developing sense of nationhood, a project that was all the more appealing after the creation of an English church and the beginnings of a British empire. Medieval historians had concentrated on the actions of ambitious men and women whose lives reflected their good or bad qualities; early modern historians wrote about events and their manifold causes. William Camden's *Britannia* and Raphael Holinshed's *Chronicles of England, Scotland, and Ireland* (the source for many of Shakespeare's plays) celebrate the deeds and the character of the early peoples of the British Isles, including the ancient origins of the English kingdom, its exemplars of heroism and villainy, its struggle for unity realized under the Tudors, and the sturdy resistance of its subjects to absolute monarchic power. The land itself became the subject of comment: William Harrison wrote a description of the English counties (included in Holinshed), and John Stow surveyed the neighborhoods of London; Michael Drayton, a Stuart poet, wrote a mythopoetic account of England's towns and countryside entitled *Poly-Olbion;* and Richard Hakluyt's collection of travel histories, *The Principal Navigations, Voyages and Discoveries of the English Nation*, reported in magnificent detail the exploration of the New World. Accounts of this wild and fruitful land fired the imaginations of English readers, who, it was hoped, would decide to promote and even participate in the laborious task of colonization. Describing landfall on the coast of Virginia, Arthur Barlow wrote:

> we found shoal water, where we smelled so sweet and so strong a smell as if we had been in the midst of some delicate garden abounding with all kind of odoriferous flowers. . . . I think in all the world the like abundance is not to be found. And my selfe having seen those parts of Europe that most abound, find such difference as were incredible to be written.

All these works comprising history, the description of various regions, and reports of travel have been loosely described as *epic*, but none of them conforms to the genre as contemporary poetics represented it—expressing heroic grandeur not only in action but also in the musical verse form and elevated language of the epic tradition.

The masterpieces of the early modern English epic are Edmund Spenser's *The Faerie Queene* and John Milton's *Paradise Lost*. Spenser imitated continental models to create an English Protestant epic-romance, an optimistic projection of Elizabethan culture. The realities of Elizabeth I's reign, though far from the poet's vision of things, were nonetheless very impressive. England's cities had grown to be centers of commerce, her navy controlled the principal routes of trade, and her people pursued lucrative interests in Europe and the Americas, successfully resisting Spanish efforts to dominate world settlement and trade. The defeat of the Spanish Armada in 1588 and the bold explorations of such men as Sir Francis Drake and Sir Walter Raleigh testified to the nation's seafaring power. In the figures of his poem, Spenser embodied the energies producing this expansive growth. His virtuous knights overcome monstrous threats to order, peace, and tranquillity. Aspects of the queen's own genius are

reflected in his heroines. Like the warrior maiden Britomart, Elizabeth I assumed a
martial character when England was in danger from abroad; like his Queen Mercilla,
she could be gracious to her enemies; like the virgin Una, she stood for what the poet
and most of his readers believed was the one true faith: Protestantism. And like
Spenser's enigmatic and distant Queen Gloriana, the Faerie Queene of the title, Elizabeth exercised her authority and power in unpredictable ways: secrecy and dissimulation were her stock in trade. To her subjects, her majesty was awful and sometimes
terrifying. But she was also mortal, and at her death, few could have foreseen the new
and divided nation that came into being with the accession of James I. The new king
was greeted with mixed feelings: on the one hand, his claim to the throne was not
disputed; on the other hand, he came from Scotland, long an enemy of England and
always the source of anxiety to those who sought dominion over the British Isles as a
whole. Although he was educated by the humanist George Buchanan, whose treatises praising republican government were widely known and read, James favored
absolute rule and believed that a monarch should be *lex loquens,* the living spirit of
the law, beyond the control of Parliament and indifferent to the rights of his subjects.
His personal conduct appeared to be dubious: his critics represented him as frequently unkempt and claimed that he preferred to hunt deer rather than to take charge of
matters of state. Disputes with the House of Commons over money to support the
Crown's activities were frequent. Reports of intrigue with Catholic Spain shattered
the nation's sense of security; an attempt in 1605 to blow up the Houses of Parliament, revealed as the Gunpowder Plot, caused a near panic. These and other kinds of
unrest grew more intense when James's heir, Charles I, proved to be even more autocratic than his father. Charles's queen, Henrietta Maria, the daughter of Henry IV of
France, was a Catholic, and it was rumored that she was treacherous. Religious controversy raged throughout the British Isles, and the struggle over the authority and
power of the monarch culminated in a series of bloody civil wars. Across England and
Scotland, forces loyal the king fought the army of Parliament, led by Oliver
Cromwell, a Puritan Member of the Commons. The war, which lasted from 1642 to
1651, ended with the defeat of the royalists.

In 1649, Charles I was captured and executed by order of Parliament, and England began to be governed as a republic. She was no longer a kingdom but a Commonwealth, and this period in her history is known as the Interregnum, the period
between kingdoms. The long-advocated change, now a reality, could hardly have
begun in a more shocking way. The monarchy had always been regarded as a sacred
office and institution, as Shakespeare's Richard II had said:

> Not all the water in the rough rude sea
> Can wash the balm off from an anointed king;
> The breath of worldly men cannot depose
> The deputy elected by the Lord.

But in the course of half a century, the people had proved themselves to be a sovereign power, and it was politically irrelevant that Charles, on the block, exemplified
regal self-control. As the Parliamentarian poet Andrew Marvell later wrote of the
king's execution:

> He nothing common did or mean
> Upon that memorable scene,
>   But with his keener eye
>   The ax's edge did try,

Nor called the gods with vulgar spite
To vindicate his helpless right;
    But bowed his comely head
    Down as upon a bed.

The conflict itself, its causes, and its outcome have been variously interpreted. As a revolution in government, it was defined by common lawyers, energized by Puritan enthusiasm, and motivated by widespread hatred of Stuart autocracy. As a religious and cultural struggle, it has been described as the War of Three Kingdoms, comprising the resistance of Scots Presbyterians and Irish Catholics to the centralizing control of the English church and government. But whatever its historical character, the Civil War marked England's transition to a society in which the absolute rule of a monarch was no longer a possibility. The people themselves had acquired a political voice. To some extent, this was a religious voice: Puritans who professed a belief in congregational church government were generally proponents of republican rule. Their dedication to the ideal of a society of equals under the law was shared by men and women of other sects: the Levellers, led by John Lilburne, who argued for a written constitution, universal manhood suffrage, and religious toleration; the Diggers, led by Gerrard Winstanley, who proposed to institute a communistic society in the wastelands they were ploughing and cultivating; the Quakers, led by George Fox, who rejected all forms of church order in deference to the inner light of an individual conscience and, insisting on social equality, refused to take off their hats before gentry or nobility; and the Ranters, who denied the authority of Scripture and saw God everywhere in nature. Without widespread acceptance of the egalitarian concept that had initiated the Protestant reformation—all believers are members of a real though invisible priesthood—it is hard to see how the move from a monarchy to a representative and republican government could have taken place.

The most comprehensive contemporary history of the Civil War, *The True Historical Narrative of the Rebellion and Civil Wars in England*, by Edward Hyde, Earl of Clarendon, was not published before 1704, but the troubled period found an oblique commentary in what is arguably England's greatest and certainly most humanistic epic poem: Milton's *Paradise Lost*, in print by 1667. Milton's career was inextricably bound up with the fate of the Commonwealth. Educated at Cambridge and with his reputation as a poet well established, Milton had begun to contribute to a defense of Puritanism and the creation of a republican government by 1649. Despite worsening eyesight, he published *The Tenure of Kings and Magistrates*, a sustained and eloquent apology for tyrannicide, after the execution of Charles I; and in his *Eikonoklastes* ("image-breaker"), written after he was made Latin secretary to the new executive, the Council of State, Milton derided attempts by royalists to celebrate Charles I in their pamphlet *Eikon Basilike* ("image of a king"). In 1660, disturbed by the proposed restoration of Charles Stuart, soon to be Charles II, Milton—now completely blind—published his last political treatise, *The Ready and Easy Way to Establish a Commonwealth*. It represented the case for a republicanism that had already lost most of its popularity: the government of the Commonwealth had adopted measures that resembled the autocratic rule of the monarchy it had overthrown. Meanwhile, the composition of *Paradise Lost* was underway. Indebted to many of Spenser's themes in *The Faerie Queene*, Milton infused his subject—the fall of the rebellious angels and the exile from paradise of the disobedient Adam and Eve—with the spirit of the account in Genesis. His poem is the product of a doubly dark vision of life. Sightless and suffering again what he felt were the constraints of a monarchy, Milton shaped his story of exile from Paradise to speak of his own and England's loss of innocence and painful acquisition of the knowledge of good and evil during the Civil War, the Interregnum, and the Restoration. His *Paradise Lost* and its sequel, *Paradise Regained*, are poems that express the most provocative ambiguities of contemporary English culture; they were—and still are—praised as rivaling the epics of Homer, Virgil, and Dante in their power and scope.

DRAMA AND SOCIAL SATIRE

Drama provided another perspective on English life. While epic depicted the grander aspirations of the nation, its human character was expressed in stage plays, masques or speaking pageants, and dramatic processions. These forms exploited the material of chronicle so that it illustrated not only the virtues of heroes, but also their foibles and limitations; history's villains warned viewers that evil was punished, if not by civil authority then by providence. Writing tragedy based on history and legend, Christopher Marlowe and Shakespeare complicated the direct moralism of medieval drama. Rather than portraying characters who became victims of their own misdoings, rising to power only to fall to disgrace, the early modern stage showed virtue and vice as intertwined—a hero's tragic error could also be at the heart of his greatness. The origins of evil were seen to be mysterious, even obscure. Some sense of this moral ambiguity can be traced to the tragedies of the Roman philosopher Seneca, which were translated into English and published in 1581. English drama reproduced many of their features: the five-act structure; rapid-fire dialogue punctuated by pithy maxims; and images of tyranny, revenge, and fate illustrated by haunting dreams and echoing curses. Shakespeare's *Richard III*, the most frequently performed of his plays in his own time, and Elizabeth Cary's *Tragedy of Mariam*, the first tragedy in English by a woman, powerfully exemplify the qualities of early modern tragedy.

If tragedy turned away from straightforward piety, so did comedy. The medieval drama of Christian salvation, in which the hero's struggle against sin was ended by his acknowledgment of grace, was replaced with plays about the wars between the sexes and between parents and children. Much of this material was modeled on the comedies of Plautus, a Roman playwright, and on the tales or *novellas* of contemporary Italian writers. Playwrights such as Ben Jonson also found a wealth of material in the improvisatory Italian *commedia dell'arte*, with its stock characters of the old dotard, the cuckolded husband, the damsel in distress, and the mountebank or quack. An even more topical form of comedy combined some of these continental traditions with themes and figures specifically drawn from London life: Thomas Dekker and Thomas Middleton's *The Roaring Girl* dramatizes the urban culture of guildsmen, shopkeepers, city wives, and coney-catchers (con artists) as they encounter the city gentry and their servants. The social critique implicit in these plays was, of course, one reason why they were so popular; their pointed criticisms of various kinds of behaviors, including religious practices, appeared in various genres from city presses, and their popularity showed just how ready audiences were to imagine a reform of their society. The end of the century saw a brilliant example of satire in a series of pamphlets secretly published by an anonymous author, known as Martin Marprelate, who disparaged all aspects of the episcopacy and promoted in its place a frankly Presbyterian church, in which authority would reside in Scripture and in congregations rather than in a church hierarchy. These expressions of a new kind of self-consciousness revealed an understanding of the whole social order that appeared anarchic to some, particularly moralists opposed to stage plays. As Stephen Gosson wrote in *Plays Confuted in Five Actions*:

> If private men be suffered to forsake their calling because they desire to talk gentlemen-like in satin & velvet, with a buckler at their heels, proportion is so broken, unity dissolved, harmony confounded, that the whole body must be dismembered, and the prince or head cannot choose but sicken.

The fear was not only that the tricksters of drama would be the objects of emulation rather than scorn, but also that the actors' masquerade of identities would spur social instability in the public theater's audience from the "groundlings of the pit" (crowded in front of the stage) to the gentry in the higher-priced seats. Only in 1633 did Parliament repeal the strict sumptuary laws that determined which styles and fabrics were allowed to nobility but denied to everyone else. Although some, like the playwright Thomas Heywood, praised plays as a form of instruction of the unschooled, others, like the Puritan pamphleteer Philip Stubbes, asserted that plays "maintain bawdry, insinuate foolery, and revive the remembrance of heathen idolatry."

Londoners enjoyed two kinds of theater: public and private. The public theaters were open to all audiences for a fee and were generally immune from oversight because they were located outside the City of London in an area referred to as the Liberties, notorious for prostitution and the sport of bearbaiting. London's two biggest theaters were located there: the Fortune and the more famous Globe, home to Shakespeare's company. Private theaters—open only to invited guests—were located in the large houses of the gentry, the Inns of Court (the schools of common law), and the guildhalls; the best-known, Blackfriars, was housed in an old monastery. Their performances were acted almost exclusively by boy actors. The popularity of these companies was short-lived; James I, annoyed by the send-up of the Scots court in *Eastward Ho!*, a play that Ben Jonson had a part in writing, dissolved his queen's own company, known as the Queen's Revels Children. The most private and prestigious stage of all remained the royal court. Shakespeare's *Othello* was first acted at James's court in 1604. Of exclusive interest to this audience was the masque, a speaking pageant accompanied by music and dancing, staged with elaborate sets and costumes, and acted by members of the court, including the Queens Anne (wife of James I) and Henrietta Maria (wife of Charles I). But in 1649 a Puritan Parliament, disgusted by what it considered the immorality of the drama, banned all stage plays, and the theaters remained closed until the Restoration in 1660.

LYRIC POETRY AND ROMANCE

In early modern England, epic narratives, stage plays, and satire in all forms were genres designed for audiences and readers the writer did not know, a general public with varied tastes and background. Lyric poetry, prose romances, and tales were more often written for a closed circle of friends. Circulated in manuscript, works in these genres allowed a writer's wit to play on personal or coterie matters. Here writers could speak of the pain of love or the thrill of ambition, and both reveal and, in a sense, create their own identities in and through language. By imitating and at the same time changing the conventions of lyric, particularly as they were illustrated by the Italian poet Francesco Petrarch, English poets were able to represent a persona or fictive self that became, in turn, a model for others. Unlike Petrarch, who saw his

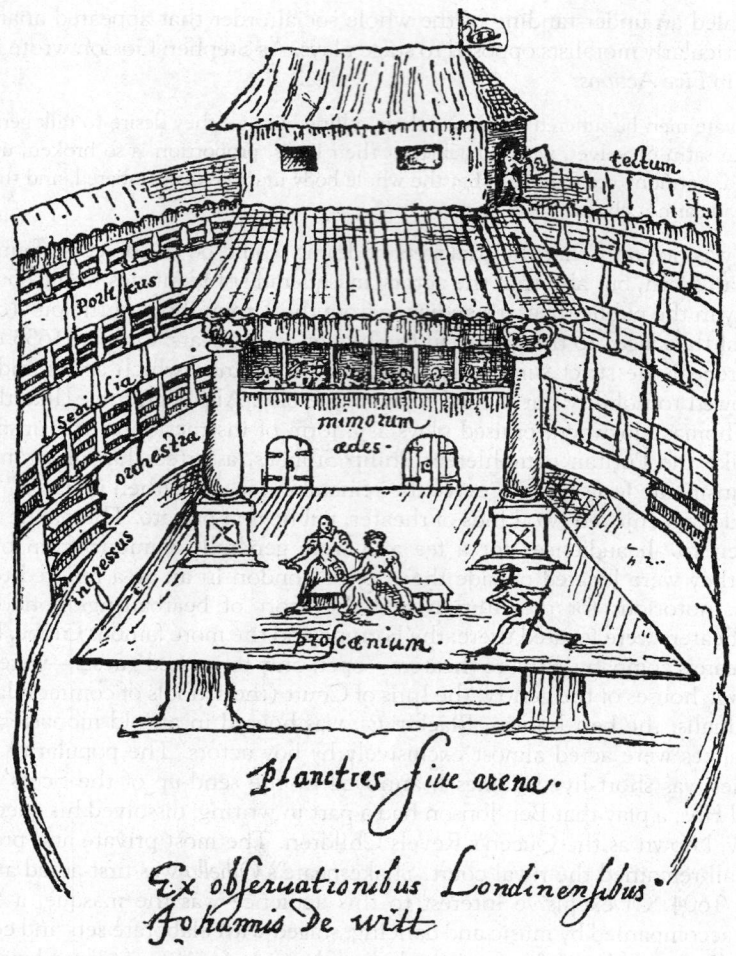

Arend von Buchell. The Swan Theater, after Johannes de Witt. c. 1596. The only extant drawing of a public theater in 1590s London, this sketch shows what Shakespeare's Globe must have looked like. The round playhouse centered on the curtainless platform of the stage (*proscenium*), which project- ed into the yard (*planities sive arena*). Raised above the stage by two pillars, the roof (*tectum*) stored machinery. At the back of the stage, the tiring house (*mimorum aedes*), where the actors dressed, contained two doors for entrances and exit. There were no stage sets and only moveable props such as thrones, tables, beds, and benches, like the one shown here. Other documents on the early modern stage are the contract of the Fortune Theatre, where *The Roaring Girl* was performed, and stage directions in the plays themselves. Modelled on The Globe, although square in shape, The Fortune featured a stage forty-three feet broad and twenty-seven and a half feet deep. Stage direc- tions include further clues: sometimes a curtained booth made "discovery" scenes possible; trap- doors allowed descents; and a space "aloft," such as the gallery above the stage doors, represented a room above the street. Eyewitness accounts fill out the picture. In the yard stood the groundlings who paid a penny for standing room, exposed to the sky, which provided natural lighting. For those willing to pay a penny or two more, three galleries (*orchestra, sedilia, and porticulus*) provided seats—the most expensive of which were cushioned. Spectators could buy food and drink during the performance. The early modern theater held an audience of roughly eight hundred standing in the yard, and fifteen hundred more seated in the galleries. According to Thomas Platter, who had seen Shakespeare's *Julius Caesar* in 1599, "everyone has a good view."

lady as imbued with numinous power before which he could only submit, such poets as Sir Thomas Wyatt, Sir Philip Sidney, Shakespeare, Ben Jonson, John Donne, and Andrew Marvell imagined love in social and very human terms; in the struggle to gain affection and power, their subjectivity took strength from their conquests as well as their resistance to defeat. Women poets, such as Mary Herbert, Amelia Lanyer, Lady Mary Wroth, and Katherine Philips reworked the conventions of love lyric to encompass a feminine perspective on passion and, equally important, on friendship. Sonnet sequences were popular and, reflecting a taste for narrative romance, often dramatized a conflict between lovers. Shakespeare wrote the best-known sonnets of the period; his cast of characters, including the poet as principal speaker, his beloved male friend, a rival poet, and a fickle lady, appear as protagonists in a drama of love, betrayal, devotion, and despair. Some poets embedded their love poetry in prose narratives that told a story, as the Italian poet Dante Alighieri had in his sequence of songs and sonnets to the lady Beatrice, entitled *The New Life*. A brilliant tale of seduction frames George Gascoigne's lyrics in his *Adventures of Master F.J.*, and Sidney's eclogues or pastoral poems punctuate the long and complicated narrative of his romance *Arcadia*.

Prose romances also provided images of new kinds of identity. Stories of marvels surrounded the lives of the powerful and exotic—such as Robert Greene's *Pandosto* (the source for Shakespeare's *The Winter's Tale*) and Thomas Lodge's *Rosalind*—while the tales of lower-class artisan-adventurers illustrate the enthusiasm with which early modern writers and readers embraced a freedom to reinvent themselves. The romantic notion of the "marvelous" gained a new meaning in the tales of tricksters as well as of sturdy entrepreneurs who survived against all odds—they illustrated the creative energies possessed by plain folk. The short fiction of Thomas Nashe, Thomas Deloney, and the hilarious (and anonymous) *Life and Pranks of Long Meg of Westminster* conclusively broke with the delicate sentimentality of pure romance and, appealing to a taste for the ordinarily wonderful, pointed the way for such later novelists as Daniel Defoe, Henry Fielding, and Charles Dickens. Finally, the spirit of romance infused narratives of travel, many of which made little distinction between fact and fantasy.

Sir John Mandeville's fifteenth-century *Travels*, in print throughout the sixteenth century, responded to Europeans' growing curiosity about the wonders of nature in distant lands, which harbored whole peoples who were pictured as utterly different from anything known at home. The wonders reported in popular collections of travel narratives—such as Richard Hakluyt's *Principal Navigations, Voyages, and Discoveries of the English Nation* (1589) and Samuel Purchas's *Purchas his Pilgrimage, or Relations of the World and the Religions observed in all Ages* (1613)—were designed to attract not repel readers, but a horror of "the other" was nevertheless implied in many of these accounts. Shakespeare's Othello both embodies foreignness himself and shares the European love of the exotic: confusing fact with fantasy, he tells the Venetian senate that parts of the globe are inhabited by "Cannibals that each other eat, / The Anthropophagi," as well as "men whose heads / Do grow beneath their shoulders." But the lure of distant lands could also attract the social critic who sought to devise images of an ideal world in order to better the real world. Sir Thomas More's *Utopia* projects a fantasy of a communal state that does double duty by pointing to both the inequities of English society and the absurdities of reforms that assume men and women can be consistently reasonable. Literally describing a *utopia*, or a "nowhere," More's treatise is effectively also a "dystopia," or a work describing a "bad place." Neither Sir Francis Bacon's *New Atlantis* (1627) nor James Harrington's *Commonwealth of Oceana* (1656)—true utopias suggesting a radical reform of political and intellectual life—emulates More's embrace of both utopian and dystopian perspectives. But the dystopias of later writers, such as Jonathan Swift's *Gulliver's Travels* (1726), Samuel Butler's *Erewhon,* an anagram for "nowhere" (1872), and George Orwell's *Nineteen-Eighty-Four* (1949) impressively illustrate the hazards of idealistic and visionary social thought.

The situation for women was somewhat different. Ancient philosophy and medieval theology had insisted that womankind was essentially and naturally different from *man*kind, distinguished by physical weakness, intellectual passivity, and an aptitude for housework, childcare, and the minor decorative arts. The fact that women had distinguished themselves in occupations traditionally reserved for men was understood to signal an exception, and in general social doctrine imposed rigid codes of behavior on men and women. But early modern life was changing in this respect, too. Contemporary treatises devoted to pro-woman argument or the defense of womankind drew on evidence that supported a revolution in ideas of sex and gender. The Bible, they pointed out, stated that woman, like man, was made in the image of God and therefore had the same degree of reason as man; history, they insisted, revealed that women had undertaken all kinds of activity and therefore had same range of talents as man. In short, they maintained that the absolute difference between man and woman was not naturally part of things, but rather was conventional and subject to modification. Social practice reflected and substantiated some of this argument. Early modern women who were classified as legally independent or *femes soles* (literally, women alone) could own and manage property and businesses as men did; educated women, such as Mary Herbert, Aemilia Lanyer, and Katherine Philips, contributed to all the literary genres and got their work published; and during the Civil War, sectarian women registered political protest in public places, including the House of Commons.

These novel ways of understanding women found corresponding changes in attitudes toward men. Departing from medieval social norms, humanists had stressed that men should be educated in the arts as well as arms, and writers such as Sir Philip Sidney, illustrating the sensitivity of men to emotional life, devised characters whose masculinity was amplified by attributes that were conventionally associated with women: passion, sympathy, and an aptitude for creative deception. The central figure in Sidney's *Arcadia* is the prince Pyrocles who appears as an Amazonian warrior through most of the narrative; as the androgynous Cleophila, he is always referred to as "she." Flexibility with respect to categories of gender is also a feature of much lyric poetry; the male poet's beloved is sometimes another man. Shakespeare's sonnets include striking examples of homoerotic verse in this period, and homoerotic innuendo, often suggested as a feature of a love triangle, is common in all genres of writing. In Marlowe's poem *Hero and Leander* the youth Leander loves the girl Hero, and Leander attracts the sexual attentions of the sea-god Neptune.

Ideas as well as social forms and practices were also changing. The repeated shifts in religious practice, from medieval Catholicism to Henrician Protestantism back to the Catholicism dictated by Queen Mary I and then on to the Anglican Church of Queen Elizabeth I, revealed that divine worship could alter its form without bringing on the apocalypse. More subtly, the emerging capitalist economy produced a conceptual model for cultural exchange. Just as material goods flowed through regional and national markets, entering a particular locale to move elsewhere, sometimes great distances, so might ideas, styles, and artistic sensibilities. Drama especially conveyed how fluid were the customs, codes, and practices that gave society its sense of identity. The enthusiasm for stage plays was motivated, in part, by an interest in role-playing: If an actor who in real life might have been born a servant could perform the part of a king in a play, then might he not also perform the part of a king indeed? Was there more to being than performing? This mutability was both liberating and dangerous, as Shakespeare showed by dramatizing the protean powers of Othello's false friend, Iago, who chillingly boasts: "I am not what I am."

THE BUSINESS OF LITERATURE

It was the business of early modern literature to ask these questions. The idea that social convention was established on a natural order of things was no longer accepted. As Shakespeare's bastard Edmund declares, rejecting the customary inferiority of a person who is born out of wedlock, "Why bastard, Wherefore base? / When my dimensions are as well compact . . . As honest madam's issue." Writers were certainly supposed to educate their readers in virtuous ways. Spenser intended that his epic would "fashion a gentleman or noble person in vertuous and gentle discipline." And Sidney believed that poetry, at its finest, could "take naughtiness away and plant goodness even in the secretest cabinet of our souls." But literature also questioned matters of being and identity because writers themselves were in the forefront of a class that was in the process of changing its way of life and its means of support.

During the early modern period an educated man who sought employment as a writer was the object of patronage by the gentry or nobility, often functioning as a tutor or secretary in a prosperous household. The poet John Skelton taught the future Henry VIII; John Donne accompanied his patron Sir William Drury on his European journeys and dedicated his *Anniversaries* to Drury's deceased daughter Elizabeth; and Andrew Marvell educated Lord Fairfax's daughter Mary. Men who were employed in other ways—in diplomacy, law, or some aspect of commerce—might be rewarded for their writing by stipends from the rich. Elizabeth I gave Spenser, one of her administrators in Ireland, a single grant of fifty pounds for *The Faerie Queene*; and Ben Jonson, thanks to the generosity of James I, was able to make a successful career for himself as a poet. As a young man, Milton was patronized by the noble Egerton family, for whom he wrote a masque called *Comus*. But as the seventeeth century progressed, writers discovered that they could be supported by a broader public; after the Restoration the talented playwright Aphra Behn gained a living by selling her literary work to producers and printers. Increasingly, the forces of the market had moved to include the business of printing and thus to both liberate and captivate the energies of the nation's writers.

It was obvious to those in power and authority that the printing press was an agent of change; the question they had to answer was how to control it. Under Elizabeth I, all printing was regulated (in effect, subject to censorship) by the Stationer's Company, which had the exclusive right to print and sell literary work. The theater was also controlled. From 1574, all plays had to be licensed by the Master of Revels, a servant and appointee of the monarch, before they could be produced. These conditions bound writers to observe royal and ecclesiastical policy, at least in their direct statements. Some resorted to coded critique; others openly defied custom. In 1579 John Stubbs wrote a pamphlet against the Queen's proposed marriage to the French king's brother, the Duke of Alençon, entitled *The Discoverie of a Gaping Gulf wherein-to England is like to be Swallowed;* he was arrested and had his hand cut off as punishment. This situation, in which publication was officially regulated, was altered early in the seventeenth century by the development of a new institution: journalism.

By the middle of James I's reign, there was a market for a periodical news pamphlet known as a "coranto," or current of news, which contained foreign intelligence taken from foreign papers: the first was actually printed in Amsterdam and shipped to England. Within a short time, English printers were publishing their own news in the form of sixteen-page "newsbooks" or Diurnalls, and by 1646, Londoners could read fourteen different papers in English. The rapid growth of the news industry promoted a public readership increasingly informed of political affairs. Parliament grew alarmed and discussed imposing stringent forms of licensing; in 1649 it approved the publication of only two newspapers, both dedicated to printing official news. Underground presses continued to publish on current affairs, however; some of them took a royalist point of view and others endorsed Parliament's position. Their writers enjoyed a risky freedom, but it was still a freedom. The boldest of them was Marchamont Nedham, a supporter of Parliament and the chief author of the *Mercurius Britanicus* (still an important source of information about the Civil War and the Interregnum); he had to flee to Holland at the Restoration, although he subsequently was pardoned and returned to England. But journalism did more than provide news; it also created a basis for the freedom of writers in general. The most eloquent attack on a state-controlled press was by Milton, whose *Areopagitica* protested the practice of licensing books before their publication—that is, before readers had a chance to make up their minds about what these books contained. Milton drew on ideas of democracy from ancient Athens and on the Puritan notion that good emerges only in contact with evil: "I cannot praise a fugitive and cloistered virtue," he announced; no true virtue is untested, unchallenged, unexamined—it is valid only when it has deliberately and consciously rejected what is false. The journalistic enterprise of this period fostered the right to free speech and a free press that is now the bedrock of modern democracies.

THE LANGUAGES OF LITERATURE: THE NEW SCIENCE AND THE OLD NATURE

Changing ideas of identity, both personal and political, were reflected in changes in the English language, which responded to popular as well as learned culture. An accomplished classicist, Ben Jonson closely modeled his verses on Latin poems and their syntax; at the same time the language of his poetry and plays often echoes the cadences of the English spoken by ordinary folk. Authors of popular comic pamphlets, such as Thomas Dekker and Robert Greene, conveyed the lively language of London rogues and vagabonds, combining local slang with parodic Latin. The writing of English prose was further changed by the study of Latin grammar and rhetoric in the humanist curriculum that was inspired by the pedagogical reforms of Erasmus and his English followers, John Colet, Roger Ascham (tutor to Elizabeth I), and Richard Mulcaster. Many words of Latin origin were introduced into English vocabulary; many writers experimented with analytic prose by adapting Latin syntax, which allowed them to show relations of cause and effect by resorting to clauses beginning with "if," "when," "because," and so forth. The first Latin-English dictionary on humanist principles was compiled by Sir Thomas Elyot; and one of the most important English grammars, Ascham's *The Schoolmaster* (1570), instructed readers in the merits of an eloquent style.

This enrichment of language from various sources inevitably caused debate. Prose composition was especially affected. Proponents of the so-called Ciceronian style (after the Roman orator Cicero) liked long sentences of many clauses exhibiting variation and restatement. Practitioners of the Senecan style favored short, direct, and uncomplicated sentences. Francis Bacon in particular criticized Ciceronian rhetoric for its emphasis on decorative "tropes and figures" rather than descriptive substance or "weight of matter"; he argued for a language that would accurately denote what he considered "scientific" data: the measures of the physical world. Bacon's reforms influenced English pedagogy and were further realized in the enterprise of the Royal Academy of Science, founded in 1660 by Charles II, who was determined to give his monarchy a new look and a new purpose. The terse, clear, pointed language of Bacon's *Essays* (1597) resembles more what we might think of as modern than does, for example, the florid style that Robert Burton used a quarter of a century later for his mythological-historical, medical discourse *The Anatomy of Melancholy*.

Language and style were changing notions of the world and God's design in creating it. Habits of thought that had prevailed during the medieval period now seemed to be incompatible with knowledge that derived from experience of nature. Europeans had inherited from classical philosophy an idea of creation as a vast aggregate of layered systems or spheres, supposedly centered on the densest matter at the earth's core, that emanated out and up to end, finally, in the sphere of pure spirit or the ethereal presence of divinity. The entities in these layered spheres had assigned places that determined their natures both within their particular sphere and in relation to other spheres. Thus gold, the most precious metal, was superior to silver, but it was at the same time analogous to a lion, a king, and the sun, each also representing the peak of perfection within its particular class of beings. Human nature was also systematized, the body and personality alike being regulated by a balanced set of "humors," each of which consisted of a primary element. The earth, water, air, and fire that made up the great world, or macrocosm, of nature also composed the small universe, or microcosm, of the individual man or woman, whose personality was ideally balanced between impulses that were melancholic (caused by a kind of bile), phlegmatic (brought on by a watery substance), sanguine or bloody, and choleric or hot-tempered. Excessive learning, the contemplation of death, the darkness of night, and isolation were all associated with melancholia, a diseased condition that in more or less severe form is represented in such disparate texts as Marlowe's *Dr. Faustus*, Milton's *Il Penseroso*, and Sir Thomas Browne's *Religio Medici* (literally, "the religion of a doctor").

This view of creation was important for artists and writers because it gave them a symbolic language of correspondences by which they could refer to creatures in widely differing settings and conditions. In a sense, it made nature hospitable to poetry by seeing creation as a divine work of art, designed to inspire awe but also a kind of familiarity. Things were the likenesses of other things. In the poetry of Donne, Herbert, Henry Vaughan, and Marvell, human emotional experience is compared to the realms of astronomy, geography, medicine, Neoplatonic philosophy, and Christian theology. These correspondences are created through strikingly unusual metaphors, which some have called metaphysical conceits, from the Italian *concetto* ("concept"). The result is a pervasive sense of a universal harmony in all human experience.

Such analogies were not always respected, however; increasingly, they were questioned by proponents of a kind of vision that depended on a quantitative or denotative sense of identity or difference. Poetic metaphor might not be able to account for creation in all its complexity; instead, nature had to be understood through the abstractions of science. By the seventeenth century it was becoming difficult to regard creation as a single and comprehensive whole; natural philosophers and scientists in the making wanted to analyze it piece by individual piece. As John Donne wrote of the phenomenon of uniqueness in his elegy for Elizabeth Drury, *The First Anniversary:*

> The element of fire is quite put out;
> The Sun is lost, and th' earth, and no man's wit
> Can well direct him, where to look for it.
> And freely men confess, that this world's spent,
> When in the Planets, and the Firmament
> They seek so many new; they see that this
> Is crumbled out again to his Atomies.
> Tis all in pieces, all coherence gone;
> All just supply, and all Relation:
> Prince, Subject, Father, Son, are things forgot,
> For every man alone thinks he has got
> To be a Phoenix, and that there can be
> None of that kind, of which he is, but he.

The earth had been decentered by the insights of the astronomer Nicholas Copernicus, who in the 1520s deduced that the earth orbits the sun. This "Copernican revolution" was confirmed by the calculations of Tycho Brahe and Johannes Kepler, and our solar system itself was revealed as one among many. With traditional understandings of the natural order profoundly shaken, many thinkers feared for the survival of the human capacity to order and understand society as well. Ironically, Donne complains of radical individualism by invoking the emblem of the phoenix, the very sort of traditional metaphor that constituted the coherence that he claims has "gone." But whereas the symbol in a devotional book would carry with it the myth of the bird's Christlike death and rebirth, the image of the rare bird takes on a newly skeptical and even satirical meaning in *The Anniversary:* it becomes the sign of a dangerous fragmentation within nature's order. Donne's audience would have been familiar with such symbols from emblem books, which presented images along with poems and mottoes, as well as in interior decoration, clothing, coats of arms, and the printers' marks on title pages of books. They were also featured on the standards or flags carried in the Civil War—antique signs in a decidedly modern conflict.

THE CIVIL WAR AND THE MODERN ORDER OF THINGS

The Civil War, or the War of Three Kingdoms, ended with the restoration of the Stuart monarchy, but the society to which Charles II was heir in 1660 was very different from the one his grandfather, James I, had come from Scotland to rule in 1603. The terms of modern life were formulated during this period, even though they were only partially and inconsistently realized. They helped to shape these essentially modern institutions: a representative government under law, a market economy fueled by concentrations of capital, and a class system determined by wealth and the power it conferred. They supported a culture in which extreme and opposing points of view were usual. Milton's republican *Tenure of Kings and Magistrates* (1649) was followed by Thomas Hobbes's defense of absolute rule, *The Leviathan, or the Matter, Form, and Power of a Commonwealth, Ecclesiastical and Civil* (1651). Hobbes rejected

The Souldiers in their passage to York turn unto reformers pull down Popish pictures, break down rayles, turn altars into Tables.

Wenceslaus Hollar. *Parliamentarian soldiers in Yorkshire destroying "Popish" paintings, etc.* Illustration to *Sight of the Transactions of these latter yeares,* by John Vicars. 1646.

the assumption that had determined all previous political thought—based on Aristotle's idea that man was naturally sociable—by characterizing the natural condition of human life as "solitary, poor, nasty, brutish and short." A civil state, said Hobbes, depended on the willingness of each and every citizen to relinquish all his or her rights to the sovereign, which is the Commonwealth. The vigorous language of Puritan sermons, preached and published during the 1640s and 1650s, underlay such topical writing as Oliver Cromwell's letters from his campaign to subdue Ireland on behalf of Parliament, the Leveller John Lilburne's pamphlets supporting the common man (for God, he wrote, "doth not choose many rich, nor many wise"), and the corantoes, newsbooks, and Diurnalls of the period. These new forms would eventually lead to the sophisticated commentary of eighteenth-century journalism. Nationalism, however problematic, was registered in history and epic, as well as in attempts to colonize the Americas and to subdue the Gaelic peoples to the west and the north. Irish poems supporting the Stuarts and lamenting the losses of the Cromwellian wars would become rallying cries in the late seventeenth- and eighteenth-century nationalist risings against English control, eventually to result in Ireland's inclusion in the 1801 Union of Great Britain.

Intellectual thought, mental attitudes, religious practices, and the customs of the people fostered new relations to the past and a new sense of self. While Milton was perhaps the greatest humanist of his time, able to read and write Hebrew, Greek, Latin, Italian, and French, his contemporaries witnessed the disappearance of the culture of Petrarch, Erasmus, and More—humanists who had fashioned the disciplines of humanism. Much seventeenth-century literature reflected personal experience; the diary of Ralph Josselin, a prosperous country squire, and the printed testimony of the trial of Anna Trapnel, a Quaker woman accused of witchcraft, convey the details of social life with an immediacy that avoids the studied figures of earlier

Renaissance prose. Such personal reckonings are comparable to the spiritual interiority revealed in John Bunyan's allegorical novel about his conversion to faith in God, *The Pilgrim's Progress*, and the first-person narrative of Daniel Defoe's *Robinson Crusoe*, the story of a sailor shipwrecked on an island somewhere off the coast of South America, which was actually modeled on the history of a Scotsman, Alexander Selkirk, who was similarly marooned.

As more particularized portraits of individual life emerged, new philosophical trends promoted abstract figurations of the world. The modern organization of Europe was based on new modes of representation, such as schematic outlines of arguments, the grids sectioning the world maps of Gerardus Mercator (facilitating the circumnavigation of the globe), and the discourses of political economy characterized by an interest in quantitative analysis. Shortly after the Restoration of Charles II, the Royal Academy of Science would form "a committee for improving the English language," an attempt to design a universal grammar and an ideal philosophical language. This project, inspired by the intellectual reforms of Francis Bacon, would have been uncongenial to the skeptical casts of mind exhibited by Erasmus and More. The abstract rationalism of the new science, the growth of an empire overseas, a burgeoning industry and commerce at home, and a print culture spreading news throughout Europe and across the Atlantic would continue to be features of life in the British Isles through the eighteenth century.

Sir Thomas Wyatt
1503–1542

A gifted poet and diplomat, Sir Thomas Wyatt exemplified the ambitious mixture of social and artistic skills that later ages would see as the ideal of the "Renaissance man." Having entered the household of King Henry VIII immediately after his education at Cambridge, Wyatt promoted English interests on missions to France, Venice, Rome, Spain, and the Low Countries. His career was to prove more precarious at home, where he became involved in court politics. He was deeply attached to the Lady Anne Boleyn, who, by 1527, was the object of Henry's affections and a probable pretext for the King's divorce from Catherine of Aragon and England's break from the Roman Catholic Church. Made Henry's queen in 1533 but out of favor by 1536, Anne implicated by association those who were supposed to have been her lovers. Wyatt was lucky to suffer no more than imprisonment; the Queen's other favorites were executed. Wyatt subsequently regained political status both at home and abroad, although not without periods of disappointment: his verse letter *Mine Own John Poyns* praises the security of a country life away from London and its intrigues. Wyatt's most protracted mission was from 1537 to 1539, as the King's ambassador to the court of the Holy Roman Emperor in Spain. Despite the execution of his powerful patron Sir Thomas Cromwell and a second prison term in 1541 for suspected treason, Wyatt obtained Henry's goodwill at the end of his short life. He died from a fever at the age of thirty-nine while on a diplomatic mission for the king.

By any poetic reckoning, Wyatt is to be valued as a pioneer of English verse. Although many of his poems exhibit irregular meters, they have been praised for their remarkable texture and sense of surprise. His translations of Francesco Petrarch's sonnets established the principal forms of English lyric, the rhyming sonnet with its pentameter line and the more loosely configured song derived from the Italian *canzone*. Wyatt's own poems change the spirit of their Petrarchan themes by giving erotic subjects a satirical and even bitter twist, and political topics an inward and personal reference. In one of his best-known sonnets, *Whoso List to Hunt*, he writes of vainly pursuing a "hind" or "deer" (a dear or beloved lady) belonging to "Caesar" (King Henry VIII). Long understood to be a reference to Anne Boleyn, Wyatt's "deer" is quite a different figure than the "deer" in his source, Petrarch's sonnet to a "white doe," who represents his lady, Laura, whom he met in 1327 and loved from a distance until her death in 1350. While Petrarch's lady is imagined as chastely devoted to a heavenly Caesar or God, and therefore as inspiring a religious awe, Wyatt's beloved is the possession of an earthly Caesar, King Henry VIII, and thus the cause of his immediate frustration.

Wyatt's verse was circulated in manuscript during his lifetime and probably read only by his friends and his acquaintances at court. A few poems were published in 1540, in a collection entitled *The Court of Venus*, but the majority—ninety-seven poems in all—appeared in 1557, in a massive anthology called *Songs and Sonnets*, published by the printer Richard Tottel. This volume, which includes poems by Henry Howard, Earl of Surrey and others, was a milestone in the history of literature. Unlike the earlier sixteenth-century poetry of the British Isles, which remained relatively simple in its genres and diction, *Tottel's Miscellany* (as it has come to be known), exhibited a range of new forms and meters: the sonnet, the song (or *canzone*), the epigram, and rhyming and blank verse. Familiar to writers and readers of Italian and French, these forms allowed poets (now writing a recognizably modern English) to develop a stylistic flexibility and thematic richness previously achieved only by the Middle English poet Geoffrey Chaucer. Before presenting his anthology to the public, however, Tottel did some fairly drastic editing: smoothing out metrical irregularities by adding, subtracting, or changing words, he obviously sought to impress readers with what he judged to be the elegant and up-to-date styles represented by the works in his collection. The poems reprinted here are based not on the *Songs and Sonnets* but on Wyatt's original texts.

The Long Love, That in My Thought Doth Harbor

The long love, that in my thought doth harbor
And in mine heart doth keep his residence,
Into my face presseth with bold pretence,
And therein campeth, spreading his banner.
5   She that me learneth° to love and suffer,   *teaches*
And will that my trust and lust's negligence
Be reined by reason, shame and reverence,
With his hardiness° taketh displeasure.   *boldness*
Wherewithal, unto the heart's forest he fleeth,
10   Leaving his enterprise with pain and cry,
And there him hideth and not appeareth.
What may I do when my master feareth
But in the field with him to live and die?
For good is the life, ending faithfully.

COMPANION READING

Petrarch, Sonnet 140[1]

Amor, che nel penser mio vive et regna
e 'l suo seggio maggior nel mio cor tene,
talor armato ne la fronte vene;
ivi si loca et ivi pon sua insegna.
5   Quella ch' amare et sofferir ne 'nsegna
e vol che 'l gran desio, l'accesa spene
ragion, vergogna, et reverenza affrene,
di nostro ardir fra se stessa si sdegna.
Onde Amor paventoso fugge al core,
10   lasciando ogni sua impresa, et piange et trema;
ivi s'asconde et non appar più fore.
Che poss' io far, temendo il mio signore,
se non star seco infin a l'ora estrema?
ché bel fin fa chi ben amando more.

Petrarch, Sonnet 140: A Translation

Love, who lives and reigns in my thought and keeps his principal seat in my heart,
sometimes comes forth all in armor into my forehead, there camps, and there sets up
his banner.

She who teaches us to love and to be patient, and wishes my great desire, my
kindled hope, to be reined in by reason, shame, and reverence, at our boldness is
angry within herself.

Wherefore Love flees terrified to my heart, abandoning his every enterprise, and
weeps and trembles; there he hides and no more appears outside.

---

1. Petrarch (1304–1374), known to his fellow Italians as
Francesco Petrarca, was the virtual inventor of modern
lyric poetry. Comprising sonnets, songs (*canzone*), and
odes, his *Rime sparse* or "various poems"—widely circulated during and after his lifetime—were translated and imitated by poets throughout Europe. Petrarch's verse
demonstrated to his early modern readers that a lyric poet
could invest subjects with a spirituality and a seriousness
previously attributed to the epic, the ode, and to philosophical poems. Translation by Robert M. Durling.

What can I do, when my lord is afraid, except stay with him until the last hour?
For he makes a good end who dies loving well.

Whoso List to Hunt

Who so list° to hunt, I know where is an hind,°   *wishes/doe*
But as for me, helas, I may no more:
The vain travail° hath wearied me so sore.   *idle labor*
I am of them that farthest cometh behind.
5 Yet may I by no means my wearied mind
Draw from° the deer: but as she fleeth afore,   *forget*
Fainting I follow. I leave off therefore,
Since in a net I seek to hold the wind.
Who list her hunt I put him out of doubt,
10 As well as I may spend his time in vain:
And, graven° with diamonds, in letters plain   *engraved*
There is written her fair neck round about:
Noli me tangere,[1] for Caesar's I am,
And wild for to hold though I seem tame.

They Flee from Me

They flee from me that sometime did me seek
With naked foot stalking in my chamber.
I have seen them gentle tame and meek
That now are wild and do not remember
5 That sometime they put themself in danger
To take bread at my hand; and now they range
Busily seeking with a continual change.
Thanked be fortune, it hath been otherwise
Twenty times better; but once in special,
10 In thine array after a pleasant guise,°   *manner*
When her loose gown from her shoulders did fall,
And she me caught in her arms long and small;
Therewithal sweetly did me kiss,
And softly said, "dear heart, how like you this?"
15 It was no dream: I lay broad waking.
But all is turned through my gentleness
Into a strange fashion of forsaking;
And I have leave to go of her goodness,
And she also to use new fangledness.
20 But since that I so kindly am served,
I would fain° know what she hath deserved.   *wish to*

---

1. "Touch me not," the words the resurrected but not yet risen Christ spoke to Mary Magdalene before his tomb (John 20.17). The "deer" of the poem has often been identified with Anne Boleyn and "Caesar" with Henry VIII.

My Lute, Awake!

My lute, awake! perform the last
Labor that thou and I shall waste
  And end that I have now begun,
For when this song is sung and past,
5   My lute be still, for I have done.

As to be heard where ere is none,°   *there is no one*
As lead to grave in marble stone,
  My song may pierce her heart as sone;°   *soon*
Should we then sigh, or sing, or moan?
10   No, no, my lute, for I have done.

The rocks do not so cruelly
Repulse the waves continually,
  As she my suit and affection,
So that I am past remedy,
15   Whereby my lute and I have done.

Proud of the spoil that thou hast got
Of simple hearts through love's shot,
  By whom, unkind, thou has them won,
Think not he hath his bow forgot,
20   Although my lute and I have done.

Vengeance shall fall on thy disdain,
That makest but game on earnest pain;
  Think not alone under the sun
Unquit° to cause thy lover's plain,°   *freely/lament*
25   Although my lute and I have done.

Perchance thee lie weathered and old,
The winter nights that are so cold,
  Plaining in vain unto the mone;°   *moon*
Thy wishes then dare not be told,
30   Care then who list,° for I have done.   *wishes*

And then may chance thee to repent
The time that thou hast lost and spent
  To cause thy lover's sigh and swoon;
Then shalt thou know beauty but lent
35   And wish and want as I have done.

Now cease, my lute, this is the last
Labor that thou and I shall wast,°   *waste*
  And ended is that we begun;
Now is this song both sung and past,
40   My lute be still, for I have done.

Blame Not My Lute

Blame not my lute for he must sound
  Of this or that as liketh me,
For lack of wit the lute is bound
  To give such tunes as pleaseth me:

5   Though my songs be somewhat strange,
        And speaks such words as touch thy change,[1]
          Blame not my lute.

      My lute, alas, doth not offend,
        Though that perforce he must agree
10   To sound such tunes as I intend
        To sing to them that heareth me;
      Then though my songs be somewhat plain,
        And toucheth some that used to fain,[2]
          Blame not my lute.

15   My lute and strings may not deny,
        But as I strike they must obey;
      Break not them then so wrongfully,
        But wreak° thyself some wiser way: *revenge*
      And though the songs which I endite°   *write*
20   Do quit° thy change with rightful spite,   *discharge, answer*
          Blame not my lute.

      Spite asketh spite and changing change,
        And falsed° faith must needs be known;   *betrayed*
      The fault so great, the case so strange,
25   Of right it must abroad be blown:
      Then since that by thine own desart°   *desert*
      My songs do tell how true thou art,
          Blame not my lute.

      Blame but the self that hast misdone
30   And well deserved to have blame;
      Change thou thy way, so evil begun,
        And then my lute shall sound that same:
      But if till then my fingers play
        By thy desart their wonted way,
35   Blame not my lute.

      Farewell, unknown, for though thou break
        My strings in spite with great disdain,
      Yet have I found out for thy sake
        Strings for to string my lute again;
40   And if perchance this folys° rhyme   *foolish*
      Do make thee blush at any time,
          Blame not my lute.

Stand Whoso List

      Stand whoso list° upon the slipper° top   *wishes/slippery*
      Of courts' estates, and let me here rejoice;
      And use me° quiet without let° or stop,   *my/hindrance*
      Unknown in court, that hath such brackish joys:
5   In hidden place, so let my days forth pass,

---

1. I.e., the lady's change of heart, probably also to be signified by a change of tone in the music to which this lyric
was supposedly set.
2. Who used to be desirous or who used to feign desire.

That when my years be done, withouten noise,
I may die aged after the common trace.[1]
For him death greep' the° right hard by the crop°   grips / throat
That is much known of other; and of himself alas,
10   Doth die unknown, dazed with dreadful face.

━━━═◆═━━━

Henry Howard, Earl of Surrey
1517?–1545

To belong to a rich and powerful family was no guarantee of a secure and prosperous life. Henry Howard, son of the Duke of Norfolk, was one of the most gifted young men in the court of King Henry VIII, yet he was embroiled in factionalism from a very early age. As a boy, he was the companion of Henry Fitzroy, Duke of Richmond, the king's illegitimate son. They spent a year together as guests of the King of France and, after their return to England, continued their friendship at Windsor Castle. After Richmond's death in 1536, Surrey apparently ran afoul of the law and found himself again at Windsor Castle, this time the king's prisoner. Playing up the irony of his situation in *So Cruel Prison,* he memorializes Windsor, formerly a "place of bliss" but now the site of his sorrow at the loss of his freedom and the greater loss of his friend. Surrey was imprisoned again five years later in London, ostensibly for breaking windows. At twenty-seven, Surrey took part in the war against the French, was wounded, and, a year later, was made commander of Boulogne. But he fell from favor when he opposed his sister's marriage to the brother of his rival, Edward Seymour, Lord Hertford, and denounced Seymour as guardian of Prince Edward, Henry's heir. Angered beyond all reconciliation, Henry had Surrey tried and executed for treason in 1545.

As a poet, Surrey is often coupled with Wyatt, who was actually a generation older. Many of his poems (like Wyatt's) emulated Petrarchan forms, themes, and imagery, and were published initially by Richard Tottel in 1557 in a volume entitled *Songs and Sonnets.* But Surrey's own accomplishments were unique. He perfected English blank or unrhymed verse, characterized by the pentameter or five-stress line, and he was the likely inventor of the form that became the standard for the English sonnet: three quatrains followed by a couplet, rhyming *ababcdcdefefgg.* Some of his poems on social subjects adopt a satirical tone and convey his vigorous rejection of contemporary manners and morals.

Love That Doth Reign and Live within My Thought

Love that doth reign and live within my thought,
And built his seat within my captive breast,
Clad in the arms wherein with me he fought
Oft in my face he doth his banner rest.
5   But she that taught me love and suffer pain,
My doubtful hope and eke° my hot desire   also
With shamefast° cloak to shadow and refrain,   ashamed
Her smiling grace converteth straight to ire.

---

1. In the common or usual manner; from age and sickness rather than murder. Wyatt alludes to the perilous existence of a man in public life.

10 And coward love then to the heart apace

Taketh his flight, where he doth lurk and plain°   *complain*

His purpose lost, and dare not show his face.

For my lord's guilt thus faultless bide° I pain;   *suffer*

Yet from my lord shall not foot remove:

Sweet is the death that taketh end by love.

Alas, So All Things Now Do Hold Their Peace

Alas, so all things now do hold their peace.

Heaven and earth disturbed in nothing:

The beasts, the air, the birds their song do cease:

The night's chair° the stars about doth bring: *Ursa Major*

5   Calm is the sea, the waves work less and less:

So am not I, whom love alas doth wring,

Bringing before my face the great increase

Of my desires, whereat I weep and sing

In joy and woe as in a doubtful ease.

10 For my sweet thoughts sometime do pleasure bring:

But by and by the cause of my disease

Gives me a pang, that inwardly doth sting,

When that I think what grief it is again,

To live and lack the thing should rid my pain.

COMPANION READING

Petrarch, Sonnet 164

Or che 'l ciel et la terra e 'l vento tace

et le fere e gli augelli il sonno affrena,

notte il carro stellato in giro mena

et nel suo letto il mar senz' onda giace,

5   vegghio, penso, ardo, piango; et chi mi sface

sempre m'è inanzi per mia dolce pena:

guerra è 'l mio stato, d'ira e di duol piena,

et sol di lei pensando ò qualche pace.

Così sol d'una chiara fonte viva

10 move 'l dolce et l'amaro ond' io mi pasco,

una man sola mi risana et punge;

et perché 'l mio martir non giunga a riva,

mille volte il dì moro et mille nasco,

tanto da la salute mia son lunge.

Petrarch, Sonnet 164: A Translation[1]

Now that the heavens and the earth and the wind are silent, and sleep reins in the beasts and the birds, Night drives her starry car about, and in its bed the sea lies without a wave,

1. For Petrarch, see the introductory footnote to the Wyatt companion reading, page 382. This translation is also by Durling.

I am awake, I think, I burn, I weep; and she who destroys me is always before me, to my sweet pain: war is my state, full of sorrow and suffering, and only thinking of her do I have any peace.

Thus from one clear living fountain alone spring the sweet and the bitter on which I feed; one hand alone heals me and pierces me.

And that my suffering may not reach an end, a thousand times a day I die and a thousand am born, so distant am I from health.

So Cruel Prison

So cruel prison, how could betide,° alas,   *it happen*
As proud Windsor,[1] where I in lust and joy
With a king's son my childish years did pass,
In greater feast than Priam's sons of Troy;[2]

5   Where° each sweet place returns a taste full sour.   *that*
The large green courts, where we were wont to hove,° *accustomed to linger*
With eyes cast up unto the maidens' tower,
And easy sighs, such as folk draw in love.

The stately sales,° the ladies bright of hue,   *halls*
10   The dances short, long tales of great delight,
With words and looks that tigers could but rue,
Where each of us did plead the other's right.

The palm play,[3] where, despoiled for the game,
With dazed eyes oft we by gleams of love
15   Have missed the ball and got sight of our dame
To bait her eyes which kept the leads° above.   *roofs*

The graveled ground,° with sleeves tied on the helm,[4] *jousting arena*
On foaming horse, with swords and friendly hearts,
With cheer,° as° though the one should overwhelm, *joyfully/even*
20   Where we have fought and chased oft with darts.

With silver drops the meads yet spread for ruth,°   *pity*
In active games of nimbleness and strength
Where we did strain, trailed by swarms of youth,
Our tender limbs, that yet shot up in length.

25   The secret groves, which oft we made resound
Of pleasant plaint° and of our ladies' praise,   *complaint*
Recording soft what grace each one had found,
What hope of speed, what dread of long delays.

---

1. Surrey was imprisoned in Windsor Castle in 1537; in this poem his distress at his imprisonment is augmented by his memories of Henry Fitzroy, the Earl of Richmond and bastard son of Henry VIII, with whom he spent time at Windsor when they were young. Richmond married Surrey's sister in 1533; he died in 1536.
2. Priam, King of Troy, was defeated by the Greeks in the Trojan War.

3. Surrey refers to court tennis, a game resembling modern tennis but played against the walls of a court; he remembers that as players, he and Fitzroy watched the ladies who followed the game from the "leads," sheets of metal used to cover roofs.
4. When jousting, a man would tie the sleeve of a lady's garment to his helmet as a sign of her favor.

The wild forest, the clothed holts° with green,   *woods*
30 With reins avaled° and swift ybreathed° horse,   *slackened/panting*
     With cry of hounds and merry blasts between,
     Where we did chase the fearful hart a force.°   *ran it down*

     The void° walls eke, that harbored us each night;   *empty*
     Wherewith, alas, revive within my breast
35 The sweet accord, such sleeps as yet delight,
     The pleasant dreams, the quiet bed of rest,

     The secret thoughts imparted with such trust,
     The wanton talk, the divers change of play,
     The friendship sworn, each promise kept so just,
40 Wherewith we passed the winter nights away.

     And with this thought the blood forsakes my face,
     The tears berain my cheeks of deadly hue;
     The which, as soon as sobbing sighs, alas,
     Upsupped° have, thus I my plaint renew: *absorbed*

45 O place of bliss! renewer of my woes!
     Give me accompt where is my noble fere,°   *companion*
     Whom in thy walls thou didst each night enclose,
     To other lief,° but unto me most dear.   *dear*

     Each wall, alas, that doth my sorrow rue,
50 Returns thereto a hollow sound of plaint.
     Thus I, alone, where all my freedom grew,
     In prison pine with bondage and restraint,

     And with remembrance of the greater grief,
     To banish the less, I find my chief relief.

—— ✦ ——

Edmund Spenser
1552?–1599

A man whose poetry has come to be known as a monument to Queen Elizabeth's England began life modestly enough. Attending Cambridge as a "sizar," or "poor scholar," he worked as a servant to pay for his fees. Allegiance to the English church was expected of all subjects, and Spenser showed his support of the faith while still a student by contributing anti-Catholic verses to the first emblem book published in England. The genre, consisting of emblems or symbolic scenes explained by clever captions, acquainted the aspiring poet with elements of the mode he was later to master: allegory. Literally a writing that conveys "other" (from the Greek *allos*, "other") than literal meanings, the allegory that Spenser would eventually perfect for his epic poem *The Faerie Queene* produced narrative verse of great flexibility and verve. Building on powerful images, his verse allegories of education in a "virtuous" chivalry convey the challenges he saw attending the creation of a civil society in early modern England.

Shortly after leaving Cambridge in 1576, Spenser found employment as a secretary in the London household of the rich and influential Earl of Leicester, a favorite courtier of Queen Elizabeth and an ardent defender of international Protestantism. There he met Leicester's already famous nephew, Sir Philip Sidney, to whom Spenser dedicated his first work, the deliberately archaic, neo-Chaucerian *The Shepheardes Calendar*, a sequence of twelve eclogues or poems on pastoral subjects, one for each month of the year. A work of a paradoxically innovative style, *The Shepheardes Calendar* demonstrated a range of metrical forms that had yet to be seen in English poetry; probably more compelling to the general reader was Spenser's use of pastoral motifs and settings to represent opinions on love, poetry, and social order. Sidney's response to the poem was, nevertheless, somewhat ambivalent. While recognizing that Spenser's eclogues had "much poetry" in them, he stated that he disliked verse composed in an "old rustic language"; among earlier and model poets of pastoral, "neither Theocritus in Greek, Virgil in Latin, nor Sannazaro in Italian did affect it." But precisely because this "old rustic language" could be recognized as purely English and independent of European traditions, Spenser would use a modified form of it in *The Faerie Queene*; in this way he hoped to demonstrate that English literature had as rich a past as any in Europe. He probably began the poem while in Leicester's service; the seventeenth-century biographer John Aubrey reported the discovery of "an abundance of cards, with stanzas of the *Faerie Queene* written on them" in the wainscoting of Spenser's London lodging.

From 1580 to the end of his life, Spenser lived in Ireland, serving as secretary to the Lord Deputy of Ireland, Arthur Grey. At such a distance from Queen Elizabeth's court, Spenser could not have secured royal favor. He was rescued from obscurity in 1589 by Sir Walter Raleigh, who, impressed with the first three books of *The Faerie Queene*, invited Spenser to present his poem to the queen. Beside the gallant and charismatic Raleigh, the poet—said to have been a "little man, who wore short hair, little bands (collars) and little cuffs"—must have cut a poor figure. But the queen liked the poem that illustrated her majesty in so many ways, "desired at timely hours to hear" it, and rewarded Spenser with a life pension of £50 a year. When Spenser returned to Ireland in 1590, he met and fell in love with Elizabeth Boyle, a woman much his junior. They were married in 1594, and Spenser celebrated their courtship and wedding in the *Amoretti*, a sonnet sequence describing the poet's quest for his "deer" or dear, and *Epithalamion*, a hymn to each of the twenty-four hours of their wedding day. The second three books of *The Faerie Queene*, published in 1596, proved as popular with readers as the first three, although James VI of Scotland (later James I of England) thought slanderous its portrait of the evil queen Duessa, whom he identified as his mother, Mary, Queen of Scots. He demanded that Spenser be "duly tried and punished"; fortunately, however, Spenser's friends at court intervened, and nothing came of the king's displeasure.

The last years of the poet's life were full of grief and bitter disappointment. In 1598 the Irish in the province of Munster, rebelling against the English colonial authorities, burned the castle in which Spenser lived. The poet and his wife fled; their newborn child was reported to have perished in the flames. In December of that year, Spenser went to London to deliver letters to the queen from the Governor of Ireland concerning the uprising. He included a note describing his own assessment of the situation—a note that may have included material in a treatise entitled *A View of the Present State of Ireland*, supporting a militaristic policy to colonize the people of Ireland, which he is supposed to have written. He died a month after arriving in London in January of 1599 and was buried in Westminster Abbey near Geoffrey Chaucer, whose poetry had meant so much to him. The monument placed on his grave is inscribed with these words: "Prince of poets in his time, whose Divine Spirit needs no other witness than the works which he left behind."

Consciously aspiring both to Chaucer's humane dignity and to his vividly colloquial style, Spenser saw himself as fashioning and refashioning a tradition of English and possibly British poetry. As he made a point of using older terms and spelling, his poems are presented here unmodernized. Spenser's choice of language parallels his use of the motifs of knightly romance: turning to the past, he sought a vital perspective on the present. John Milton would later describe him as a "sage and serious" poet, who, in *The Faerie Queene*, wrote of the struggle of good against evil and the triumph of faith over falsehood. The subject, treated by weaving different story lines together to form a vast tapestry, interested not only Milton, who was clearly inspired by Spenser's complex understanding of human psychology, but also the next generation of poets in England, especially Ben Jonson, John Donne, and George Herbert, who turned to Spenser for a poetry of satirical vigor and spiritual insight. Yet other readers have been moved by Spenser's lyrics. His shorter poems and occasional verse show his skillful use of repetitive sounds or verbal echoes and reveal his unerring sense of language as a musical medium.

The Shepheardes Calender

The genre of pastoral, which originated with Greek and Latin poets, especially Virgil, was popular with early modern writers of lyric verse. Because the genre represents its subjects from the idealized perspectives of rural life, it gave writers who were critical of the more sophisticated manners of the city a chance to praise the virtues of simplicity and artlessness. In fact, Spenser's eclogues are rhetorically complex. Composed as dialogues, they exhibit a consciously archaic diction and a demanding rhyme scheme. *October* is "eclogue the tenth" (*aegloga decima*) in a series of twelve eclogues or pastoral poems, published in 1579. Each eclogue was composed for a month of the year and as a whole they formed a "calendar." The subject of *October* is the poet's craft; it presents an argument between Cuddie, a shepherd and also a piper who wants to renounce his art as unremunerative, and Piers, a shepherd who tells Cuddie that the purpose of his music is to lead its listeners in better ways.

from The Shepheardes Calender
October
AEGLOGA DECIMA
Argument[1]

In Cuddie is set out the perfecte paterne of a Poete, whiche finding no maintenaunce of his state and studies, complayneth of the contempte of Poetrie, and the causes thereof: Specially having bene in all ages, and even amongst the most barbarous alwayes of singular accounpt and honor, and being indede so worthy and commendable an arte: or rather no arte, but a divine gift and heavenly instinct not to bee gotten by laboure and learning, but adorned with both: and poured into the witte by a certaine ἐνθουσιασμὸς [enthusiasm] and celestiall inspiration, as the Author hereof els where at large discourseth, in his booke called the English Poete, which booke being lately come to my hands, I mynde also by Gods grace upon further advisement to publish.

> PIERS
> Cuddie, for shame hold up thy heavye head,
> And let us cast with what delight to chace,
> And weary thys long lingring Phoebus race.[2]

---

1. This "Argument" is a prose synopsis of the following dialogue and was written by "E.K.," thought to be Edward Kirke, a friend of Spenser.

2. The race of Apollo, god of the sun, through the day.

Whilome° thou wont the shepheards laddes to leade,   *formerly*
5   In rymes, in ridles, and in bydding base:°   *simple requests*
Now they in thee, and thou in sleepe art dead.

CUDDIE

Piers, I have pyped erst° so long with payne,   *first*
That all mine Oten reedes° bene rent and wore: *shepherd's pipe*
And my poore Muse hath spent her spared store,
10   Yet little good hath got, and much lesse gayne.
Such pleasaunce makes the Grashopper so poore,
And ligge so layd,[3] when Winter doth her straine:

The dapper ditties, that I wont devise,
To feede youthes fancie, and the flocking fry,°   *children*
15   Delighten much: what I the bett for thy?[4]
They han the pleasure, I a sclender prise.
I beate the bush, the byrds to them doe flye:[5]
What good thereof to Cuddie can arise?

PIERS

Cuddie, the prayse is better, then the price,°   *prize*
20   The glory eke° much greater then the gayne: *also*
O what an honor is it, to restraine
The lust of lawlesse youth with good advice:
Or pricke them forth with pleasaunce of thy vaine,°   *poetic vein*
Whereto thou list° their trayned willes entice.[6]   *wish*

25   Soone as thou gynst to sette thy notes in frame,
O how the rurall routes° to thee doe cleave: *crowds*
Seemeth thou dost their soule of sence bereave,
All as the shepheard, that did fetch his dame
From Plutoes balefull bowre withouten leave:
30   His musicks might the hellish hound did tame.[7]

CUDDIE

So praysen babes the Peacoks spotted traine,
And wondren at bright Argus[8] blazing eye:
But who rewards him ere° the more for thy?°   *ever/this*
Or feedes him once the fuller by a graine?
35   Sike° prayse is smoke, that sheddeth in the skye,   *such*
Sike words bene wynd, and wasten soone in vayne.

PIERS

Abandon then the base and viler clowne,°   *bumpkin*
Lyft up thy selfe out of the lowly dust:
And sing of bloody Mars,° of wars, of giusts,°   *god of war/jousts*
40   Turne thee to those, that weld° the awful crowne.   *wield*
To doubted° Knights, whose woundlesse armour rusts,   *undefeated*
And helmes unbruzed wexen° dayly browne.   *grow*

---

3. Having sung all summer, the grasshopper lies in poverty when winter comes.
4. What am I the better for this?
5. I rouse game that flies to others.
6. Piers advises Cuddie that a poet must entice the educated wills of his readers by the pleasure his subject matter gives them.
7. Orpheus, mythic father of poetry, rescued his wife from hell, kingdom of the underworld god Pluto, using his music to charm Pluto's savage guard dog Cerberus.
8. Mythical herdsman who had eyes all over his body.

There may thy Muse display her fluttryng wing,
And stretch her selfe at large from East to West:
45 Whither thou list in fayre Elisa⁹ rest,
Or if thee please in bigger notes to sing,
Advaunce the worthy whome shee loveth best,
That first the white beare to the stake did bring.¹

	And when the stubborne stroke of stronger stounds,°	*times*
50	Has somewhat slackt the tenor of thy string:	
	Of love and lustihead tho° mayst thou sing,	*then*
	And carrol lowde, and leade the Myllers rownde,	
	All° were Elisa one of thilke° same ring.	*although / that*
	So mought° our Cuddies name to Heaven sownde.	*might*

CUDDIE

55 Indeede the Romish Tityrus, I heare,
Through his Mecoenas left his Oaten reede,²
Whereon he earst had taught his flocks to feede,
And laboured lands to yield the timely eare,
And eft° did sing of warres and deadly drede,   *often*
60 So as the Heavens did quake his verse to here.

But ah Mecoenas is yclad in claye,
And great Augustus long ygoe is dead:
And all the worthies liggen° wrapt in leade,   *lie*
That matter made for Poets on to play:
65 For ever, who in derring doe° were dreade,°   *bold action / feared*
The loftie verse of hem° was loved aye.°   *about them / ever*

But after vertue gan for age to stoupe,
And mighty manhode brought a bedde of ease:
The vaunting Poets found nought worth a pease,
70 To put in preace° among the learned troupe.   *public*
Tho gan the streames of flowing wittes to cease,
And sonnebright honour pend in shamefull coupe.°   *pen*

And if that any buddes of Poesie,
Yet of the old stocke gan to shoote agayne:
75 Or it° mens follies mote be forst to fayne,°   *poetry / represent*
And rolle with rest in rymes of rybaudrye:
Or as it sprong, it wither must agayne:
Tom Piper makes us better melodie.³

PIERS

O pierlesse Poesye, where is then thy place?
80 If nor° in Princes pallace thou doe sitt: *neither*

9. Queen Elizabeth. Piers suggests that Cuddie may wish to take the queen for his poetic subject.
1. "He meaneth (as I guesse) the most honorable and renowned the Erle of Leycester" (E.K.). Leicester's emblem was a bear and staff.
2. Cuddie explains that when Tityrus (the name the poet Virgil assumes in his *Eclogues*) was patronized by Mecoenas, or Maecenas, a liberal patron of letters during the reign of the Roman Emperor Augustus, he could afford to write epic, that is, a long verse narrative that describes a heroic action.
3. Cuddie states that because the present age has no virtuous subjects, such poetry as epic is no longer written. To be revived, it must either represent the folly of the present time or wither again for lack of a subject; for the present, a "Tom Piper" or popular singer will produce better songs than poets can.

(And yet is Princes pallace the most fitt)
Ne° brest of baser birth doth thee embrace.   *nor*
Then make thee winges of thine aspyring wit,
And, whence thou camst, flye backe to heaven apace.

CUDDIE

85   Ah Percy it is all to weake and wanne,
So high to sore, and make so large a flight:
Her peeced pyneons bene not so in plight,[4]
For Colin[5] fittes° such famous flight to scanne: *it suits*
He, were he not with love so ill bedight,°   *afflicted*
90   Would mount as high, and sing as soote° as Swanne.   *sweet*

PIERS

Ah fon,° for love does teach him climbe so hie,   *fool*
And lyftes him up out of the loathsome myre:
Such immortall mirrhor, as he doth admire,
Would rayse ones mynd above the starry skie.
95   And cause a caytive° corage to aspire,   *cowardly*
For lofty love doth loath a lowly eye.

CUDDIE

All otherwise the state of Poet stands,
For lordly love is such a Tyranne fell:°   *terrible*
That where he rules, all power he doth expell.
100   The vaunted verse a vacant head demaundes,
Ne wont° with crabbed care the Muses dwell.   *used*
Unwisely weaves, that takes two webbes in hand.

Who ever casts to compasse° weightye prise,   *gain*
And thinks to throwe out thondring words of threate:
105   Let powre in lavish cups and thriftie° bitts of meate,   *good*
For Bacchus° fruite is frend to Phoebus wise.   *god of wine*
And when with Wine the braine begins to sweate,
The nombers flowe as fast as spring doth ryse.

Thou kenst not Percie howe the ryme should rage.
110   O if my temples were distaind with wine,
And girt in girlonds of wild Yvie twine,
How I could reare the Muse on stately stage,
And teache her tread aloft in bus-kin° fine,   *high boots*
With queint Bellona° in her equipage.   *gooddess of war*

115   But ah my corage cooles ere it be warme,
For thy,° content us in thys humble shade: *now*
Where no such troublous tydes han us assayde,°   *tried*
Here we our slender pipes may safely charme.

PIERS

And when my Gates° shall han their bellies layd:°   *she-goats/borne kids*
120   Cuddie shall have a Kidde to store° his farme.   *enrich*

Cuddies Embleme

Agitante calescimus illo &c.[6]

4. I.e., the mended wings of Poetry are not in such a condition.
5. Another of the shepherds who participate in the eclogues' dialogues.

6. "When he stirs, we glow, etc." From Ovid's *Fasti* 6.5, referring to "Deus in nobis," (the god [of poetry] within us).

THE FAERIE QUEENE

In 1583 Spenser told guests at a dinner he was attending that he proposed to write a poem in which he would "represent all the moral virtues, assigning to every virtue a knight in whose actions and chivalry the operations of that virtue are to be expressed, and the vices and unruly appetites that oppose themselves to be beaten down." The project, obviously ambitious, recalls the great epics of classical antiquity: the twenty-four books of Homer's *Iliad*, the twelve books of Virgil's *Aeneid*. Spenser must have believed he was prepared for such an undertaking; like Virgil, he had served his apprenticeship by writing pastoral poetry, with the composition of *The Shepheardes Calendar*. But whatever his intention, he realized his great work only in part. He depicted the first six virtues in the "legends" of Holiness, Temperance, Chastity, Friendship, Justice, and Courtesy, in which each virtue is perfected by the trials of a particular knight fighting the evil that most threatens his character. He published the first three books in 1590, adding the next three in a second edition in 1596. His plan for a second set of six books resulted in only two cantos—on the virtue of Constancy.

Spenser's moral chivalry is sponsored and sustained by the court of Gloriana, the Faerie Queene, in whom is reflected the imposing figure of Queen Elizabeth. Gloriana's story is illustrated by the actions of a character called Prince Arthur, who intervenes at crucial moments to assist Gloriana's knights and is otherwise bent on seeking out Gloriana herself, the bride he has chosen in a dream. In the mythical genealogy of the Tudors, King Arthur (known to Spenser's readers through Sir Thomas Malory's *Morte Darthur*) was identified as the dynasty's progenitor; thus, in the allegorical schema of the poem, the prospective marriage of the Faerie Queene and Prince Arthur, also the champion of Magnificence, signifies the perfect union of monarch and state.

Book 1 relates the adventures of the knight of Holiness, known as the Redcrosse Knight from the sign on his shield and identified as Saint George, England's patron saint. His mission is to overcome the machinations of spiritual error menacing the English church and to deliver the parents of Una, his lady, who is the Truth, from the demons of false faith. The foes of the Redcrosse Knight are many: the fiendish wizard Archimago, who stands for corrupt doctrine; the cunning queen Duessa, who, as the embodiment of duplicity, is never what she seems; the bloated giant Orgoglio, or Pride; and the loathsome many-headed dragon who is supposed to wield the institutional power of the Catholic Church. The Redcrosse Knight kills Pride and the dragon but, although he at last understands that they are thoroughly sinister, fails to capture Duessa and Archimago. They return in later books to trouble Gloriana's other knights.

Book 2 tells of the adventures of the knight of Temperance, Sir Guyon, who must destroy a garden of surpassing beauty, known as the Bower of Bliss, presided over by a brilliantly seductive witch called Acrasia. He is accompanied on his quest by the Palmer, who as the embodiment of reason, informs and guides him in achieving the perfection of his virtue. In Canto 12, perhaps the best-known canto in the entire poem, Guyon sails to Acrasia's island garden in the company of the Palmer, is tempted by the illusionistic pleasures Acrasia provides her suitors, but finally rejects her in a massive act of defiance, tearing down all the beguiling structures of her island in a salutary rage.

The verse form of *The Faerie Queene* is virtually unique to Spenser. It features a sequence of stanzas each (known to later readers as "Spenserian") comprising nine lines, of which the first eight contain five feet or accented syllables and the last contains six feet. They are rhymed in a pattern—*ababbcbcc*—particularly difficult for poets writing in English. Unlike the Romance languages (French, Italian, and Spanish), English has relatively few words ending in vowel sounds, which are easily rhymed. Spenser's ear for the sound of English allowed him to compose verse of a musicality comparable to what was possible in the Romance languages, itself an extraordinary accomplishment. The narrative units of Spenser's epic poem achieve a dramatic coherence by his constructive use of imagery in particular story lines that continuously develop new contexts for their subjects. In other words, a character signifying a special quality in one canto will not signify precisely that quality in another canto: Spenser will change his or her role with the setting the story demands. This gives the reader an active role in the poem's interpretation; in a sense, the reader finds the meaning of the poem in the process of reading it.

FROM THE FAERIE QUEENE

FROM The First Booke of the Faerie Queene
Contayning The Legende of the Knight of the Red Crosse,
or
Of Holinesse.

1

Lo I the man, whose Muse whilome° did maske,[1]   *formerly*
  As time her taught, in lowly Shepheards weeds,°   *clothing*
  Am now enforst a far unfitter taske,
  For trumpets sterne to chaunge mine Oaten reeds,
5 And sing of Knights and Ladies gentle deeds;
  Whose prayses having slept in silence long,
  Me, all too meane,° the sacred Muse areeds°   *lowly/commands*
  To blazon broad° emongst her learned throng: *proclaim abroad*
Fierce warres and faithfull loves shall moralize my song.

2

10 Helpe then, O holy Virgin chiefe of nine,[2]
  Thy weaker Novice to performe thy will,
  Lay forth out of thine everlasting scryne°   *treasure chest*
  The antique rolles,° which there lye hidden still,   *scrolls*
  Of Faerie knights and fairest Tanaquill,
15 Whom that most noble Briton Prince° so long   *Arthur*
  Sought through the world, and suffered so much ill,
  That I must rue° his undeserved wrong: *regret*
O helpe thou my weake wit, and sharpen my dull tong.

3

And thou most dreaded impe° of highest Jove,[3]   *child*
20 Faire Venus sonne,° that with thy cruell dart   *Cupid, god of love*
  At that good knight° so cunningly didst rove,°   *Arthur*
  That glorious fire it kindled in his hart,
  Lay now thy deadly Heben° bow apart,   *ebony*
  And with thy mother milde come to mine ayde:[4]
25 Come both, and with you bring triumphant Mart,°   *Mars*
  In loves and gentle jollities arrayd,
  After his murdrous spoiles and bloudy rage allayd.°   *quelled*

1. In this stanza and in the rest of the Proem (introduction), Spenser is announcing his intention to write an epic poem. His earlier *Shepheardes Calender* had been written in the more modest pastoral style, characterized by the "oaten reed" of the shepherd's pipe. Here, he casts off the guise of the shepherd to undertake the lofty subject of *The Faerie Queene.*
2. Spenser calls on a muse to inspire him; he may be referring to Clio, the muse of history, or to Calliope, the muse of epic poetry. Tanaquill was a Roman woman famous for her chaste and noble character; here Spenser establishes a symbolic relation between Tanaquill, the Faerie Queene

(whom Arthur seeks in the poem), and Queen Elizabeth I, much as he will later refer to other characters—most prominently, Britomart, Gloriana, and Mercilla—as figuring aspects of the queen, her power and attributes.
3. The king of the pagan gods. Like all the poets of the period who were not writing religious verse, Spenser refers to the classical pantheon as a way of alluding to God and to his various expressions of power.
4. Spenser also invokes Cupid, who combines the loving nature of Venus and the warlike spirit of Mars, to illustrate the mood of his poem.

4

And with them eke, O Goddesse heavenly bright,[5]
   Mirrour of grace and Majestie divine,
30   Great Lady of the greatest Isle, whose light
   Like Phoebus lampe throughout the world doth shine,
   Shed thy faire beames into my feeble eyne,
   And raise my thoughts too humble and too vile,
   To thinke of that true glorious type° of thine,   *the Faerie Queene*
35   The argument of mine afflicted stile:
As one for knightly The which to heare, vouchsafe,° O dearest dread° a-while.   *grant/power*

Canto 1

    The Patron of true Holinesse,
      Foule Errour doth defeate:
      Hypocrisie him to entrapp;
      Doth to his home entreate.

1

A Gentle Knight[6] was pricking° on the plaine,   *riding*
   Y cladd in mightie armes and silver shielde,
   Wherein old dints of deepe wounds did remaine,
   The cruell markes of many a bloudy fielde;
5   Yet armes till that time did he never wield:
   His angry steede did chide his foming bitt,
   As much disdayning to the curbe to yield:
   Full jolly knight he seemd, and faire did sitt,
As one for knightly giusts° and fierce encounters fitt.   *joust*

2

10 But on his brest a bloudie Crosse[7] he bore,
   The deare remembrance of his dying Lord,
   For whose sweete sake that glorious badge he wore,
   And dead as living ever him ador'd:
   Upon his shield the like was also scor'd,°   *represented*
15   For soveraine hope, which in his° helpe he had: *his Lord's*
   Right faithfull true he was in deede and word,
   But of his cheere° did seeme too solemne sad;   *demeanor*
Yet nothing did he dread,° but ever was ydrad.°   *fear/feared*

3

Upon a great adventure he was bond,
20   That greatest Gloriana[8] to him gave,
   That greatest Glorious Queene of Faerie lond,
   To winne him worship, and her grace to have,
   Which of all earthly things he most did crave;

---

5. Spenser celebrates the nature of Elizabeth I in grandiose terms: She is a "goddess" whose eyes, like the lamp of Phoebus Apollo (the sun), shine throughout the world and must now illuminate the poet's mind.
6. This gentle or well-born knight, soon to be identified as the Redcrosse Knight from the sign on his shield, wears the armor of Christianity. The armor itself has been worn by many who fought for the faith, but the Redcrosse Knight is new to the spiritual battlefield and will have to prove himself.

7. The red cross is Spenser's figure for the salvation offered by Christ to humankind through his death on the cross, the sacrifice of his blood, and his resurrection. It was also the badge traditionally worn by St. George, the patron saint of England, with whom the Redcrosse Knight will later be identified.
8. The character Spenser most frequently invokes when he alludes to Elizabeth I. Gloriana presides over the action of the poem, although she does not take part in it herself.

And ever as he rode, his hart did earne
25   To prove his puissance° in battell brave   *power*
Upon his foe, and his new force to learne;
Upon his foe, a Dragon horrible and stearne.

4

A lovely Ladie⁹ rode him faire beside,
Upon a lowly Asse more white then snow,
30   Yet she much whiter, but the same did hide
Under a vele, that wimpled° was full low,   *gathered*
And over all a blacke stole she did throw,
As one that inly mournd: so was she sad,
And heavie sat upon her palfrey¹ slow:
35   Seemed in heart some hidden care she had,
And by her in a line a milke white lambe she lad.

5

So pure an innocent, as that same lambe,
She was in life and every vertuous lore,
And by descent from Royall lynage came
40   Of ancient Kings and Queenes, that had of yore
Their scepters stretcht from East to Westerne shore,
And all the world in their subjection held;²
Till that infernall feend with foule uprore
Forwasted all their land, and them expeld:
45   Whom to avenge, she had this Knight from far compeld.

6

Behind her farre away a Dwarfe³ did lag,
That lasie seemd in being ever last,
Or wearied with bearing of her bag
Of needments at his backe. Thus as they past,
50   The day with cloudes was suddeine overcast,
And angry Jove an hideous storme of raine
Did poure into his Lemans⁴ lap so fast,
That every wight to shrowd° it did constrain,°   *shelter/impel*
And this faire couple eke° to shroud themselves were fain.° *also/desirous*

7

55   Enforst to seeke some covert° nigh at hand,   *hiding place*
A shadie grove not far away they spide,
That promist ayde the tempest to withstand:
Whose loftie trees yclad with sommers pride,
Did spred so broad, that heavens light did hide,
60   Not perceable with power of any starre:

9. Later revealed to be Una or ("one"). The undivided truth (as opposed to "two," that is, doubleness or duplicity), she is associated with the one true Church. The snow-white ass she rides signifies Christ's humility; her veil is emblematic of the veil that stands between Truth and fallen humanity; and the lamb symbolizes innocence and Christian sacrifice. The mourning garb she wears suggests her sorrow over the captivity of her parents, later understood to be Adam and Eve, trapped by the dragon that embodies the forces of evil that have conspired to corrupt the true Church.

1. A horse suitable for a woman.
2. The Lady traces her lineage to Adam and Eve, who held dominion over Eden before the Fall. The "infernall feend," or Satan, is represented as the destroyer of their realm, which stretched from East to West and was therefore truly universal, unlike the regions dominated by Rome or by the Catholic Church. By designating the Knight as the avenger of Adam and Eve, Spenser identifies him with Christ.
3. The servant who serves the Lady, a source of prudence, common sense, and wariness.
4. I.e., his lady love's, or the earth's.

And all within were pathes and alleies wide,
With footing worne, and leading inward farre:
Faire harbour that them seemes; so in they entred arre.

8

And foorth they passe, with pleasure forward led,
65   Joying to heare the birdes sweete harmony,
Which therein shrouded from the tempest dred,
Seemd in their song to scorne the cruell sky.
Much can they prayse the trees so straight and hy,
The sayling° Pine, the Cedar proud and tall,   *soaring*
70   The vine-prop Elme, the Poplar never dry,
The builder Oake, sole king of forrests all,
The Aspine good for staves,° the Cypresse funerall.   *poles*

9

The Laurell, meed° of mightie Conquerours   *reward*
And Poets sage, the Firre that weepeth still,
75   The Willow worne of forlorne Paramours,°   *forsaken lovers*
The Eugh obedient to the benders will,
The Birch for shaftes, the Sallow° for the mill,   *willow*
The Mirrhe sweete bleeding in the bitter wound,
The warlike Beech, the Ash for nothing ill,
80   The fruitfull Olive, and the Platane° round,   *sycamore*
The carver Holme,° the Maple seeldom inward sound.   *holly*

10

Led with delight, they thus beguile° the way,   *make pleasant*
Untill the blustring storme is overblowne;
When weening° to returne, whence they did stray,   *thinking*
85   They cannot finde that path, which first was showne,
But wander too and fro in wayes unknowne,
Furthest from end then, when they neerest weene,
That makes them doubt, their wits be not their owne:
So many pathes, so many turnings seene,
90   That which of them to take, in diverse doubt they been.

11

At last resolving forward still to fare,
Till that some end° they finde or° in or out,   *way/either*
That path they take, that beaten seemd most bare,
And like to lead the labyrinth about;
95   Which when by tract they hunted had throughout,
At length it brought them to a hollow cave,
Amid the thickest woods. The Champion stout
Eftsoones dismounted from his courser brave,
And to the Dwarfe a while his needlesse spere he gave.

12

100   Be well aware, quoth then that Ladie milde,
Least suddaine mischiefe ye too rash provoke:
The danger hid, the place unknowne and wilde,
Breedes dreadful doubts: Oft fire is without smoke,
And perill without show: therefore your stroke
105   Sir knight with-hold, till further triall made.

Ah Ladie (said he) shame were to revoke
   The forward footing for an hidden shade:
Vertue gives her selfe light, through darkenesse for to wade.[5]

13

110   Yea but (quoth she) the perill of this place
   I better wot° then you, though now too late   *know*
   To wish you backe returne with foule disgrace,
   Yet wisedome warnes, whilest foot is in the gate,
   To stay° the steppe, ere forced to retrate.°   *halt / retreat*
   This is the wandring wood, this Errours den,
115   A monster vile, whom God and man does hate:
   Therefore I read beware. Fly fly (quoth then
The fearefull Dwarfe:) this is no place for living men.

14

But full of fire and greedy hardiment,
   The youthfull knight could not for ought° be staide,   *anything*
120   But forth unto the darksome hole he went,
   And looked in: his glistring armor made
   A litle glooming light, much like a shade,
   By which he saw the ugly monster plaine,
   Halfe like a serpent horribly displaide,
125   But th'other halfe did womans shape retaine,[6]
Most lothsom, filthie, foule, and full of vile disdaine.

15

And as she lay upon the durtie ground,
   Her huge long taile her den all overspred,
   Yet was in knots and many boughtes° upwound,   *coils*
130   Pointed with mortall sting. Of her there bred
   A thousand yong ones, which she dayly fed,
   Sucking upon her poisonous dugs, eachone
   Of sundry shapes, yet all ill favored:
   Soone as that uncouth° light upon them shone,   *strange*
135   Into her mouth they crept, and suddain all were gone.

16

Their dam upstart, out of her den effraide,
   And rushed forth, hurling her hideous taile
   About her cursed head, whose folds displaid
   Were stretcht now forth at length without entraile.°   *coiling*
140   She lookt about, and seeing one in mayle°   *armor*
   Armed to point, sought backe to turne againe;
   For light she hated as the deadly bale,°   *injury*
   Ay wont° in desert darknesse to remaine,   *ever used*
Where plaine° none might her see, nor she see any plaine.   *plainly*

17

145   Which when the valiant Elfe° perceiv'd, he lept   *Redcrosse Knight*
   As Lyon fierce upon the flying pray,

---

5. Lacking humility and overly confident of his own virtue, the Redcrosse Knight believes he is strong enough to withstand the dangers of the wood. In fact, as we learn in the next stanza, he has stepped into the den of a mon-ster who personifies Error, one of Satan's many manifestations in the poem.

6. Spenser follows traditional treatments of Error in giving her a woman's face and a serpent's body.

And with his trenchand blade her boldly kept
From turning backe, and forced her to stay:
Therewith enrag'd she loudly gan to bray,
150   And turning fierce, her speckled taile advaunst,
Threatning her angry sting, him to dismay:
Who nought aghast, his mightie hand enhaunst:°   raised up
The stroke down from her head unto her shoulder glaunst.

                        18
Much daunted with that dint, her sence was dazd,
155   Yet kindling rage, her selfe she gathered round,
And all attonce her beastly body raizd
With doubled forces high above the ground:
Tho wrapping up her wrethed sterne° arownd,   tail
Lept fierce upon his shield, and her huge traine°   tail
160   All suddenly about his body wound,
That hand or foot to stirre he strove in vaine:
God helpe the man so wrapt in Errours endlesse traine.

                        19
His Lady sad to see his sore constraint,°   predicament
Cride out, Now now Sir knight, shew what ye bee,
165   Add faith unto your force, and be not faint:
Strangle her, else she sure will strangle thee.
That when he heard, in great perplexitie,
His gall did grate° for griefe and high disdaine,   anger was aroused
And knitting all his force got one hand free,
170   Wherewith he grypt her gorge with so great paine,
That soone to loose her wicked bands did her constraine.

                        20
Therewith she spewd out of her filthy maw°   stomach
A floud of poyson horrible and blacke,
Full of great lumpes of flesh and gobbets raw,
175   Which stunck so vildly, that it forst him slacke
His grasping hold, and from her turne him backe:
Her vomit full of bookes and papers was,[7]
With loathly frogs and toades, which eyes did lacke,
And creeping sought way in the weedy gras:
180   Her filthy parbreake° all the place defiled has.   vomit

                        21
As when old father Nilus° gins to swell   the river Nile
With timely pride aboue the Aegyptian vale,
His fattie° waves do fertile slime outwell,°   fertile / pour forth
And overflow each plaine and lowly dale:
185   But when his later spring° gins to avale,°   last waters / subside
Huge heapes of mudd he leaves, wherein there breed
Ten thousand kindes of creatures, partly male
And partly female of his fruitfull seed;
Such ugly monstrous shapes elswhere may no man reed.°   know

7. Error's vomit is a figurative depiction of the falsehoods that corrupt religion. The vehicles of such lies are both the spoken and written word; hence the material issuing from Error's mouth includes books as well as other poisonous things.

22

190   The same so sore annoyed has the knight,
        That welnigh choked with the deadly stinke,
        His forces faile, ne can no longer fight.
        Whose corage when the feend perceiv'd to shrinke,
        She poured forth out of her hellish sinke°   *womb*
195   Her fruitfull cursed spawne° of serpents small,   *offspring*
        Deformed monsters, fowle, and blacke as inke,
        Which swarming all about his legs did crall,
    And him encombred sore, but could not hurt at all.

23

    As gentle Shepheard in sweete even-tide,
200   When ruddy Phoebus gins to welke° in west,   *sink*
        High on an hill, his flocke to vewen wide,
        Markes which do byte their hasty supper best;
        A cloud of combrous gnattes do him molest,
        All striving to infixe their feeble stings,
205   That from their noyance he no where can rest,
        But with his clownish hands their tender wings
    He brusheth oft, and oft doth mar their murmurings.

24

    Thus ill bestedd,° and fearefull more of shame,   *situated*
        Then of the certaine perill he stood in,
210   Halfe furious unto his foe he came,
        Resolv'd in minde all suddenly to win,
        Or soone to lose, before he once would lin;°   *surrender*
        And strooke at her with more then manly force,
        That from her body full of filthie sin
215   He raft° her hatefull head without remorse;   *cut off*
    A streame of cole black bloud forth gushed from her corse.

25

    Her scattred brood, soone as their Parent deare
        They saw so rudely° falling to the ground,   *violently*
        Groning full deadly, all with troublous feare,
220   Gathred themselves about her body round,
        Weening their wonted entrance to have found
        At her wide mouth: but being there withstood
        They flocked all about her bleeding wound,
        And sucked up their dying mothers blood,
225   Making her death their life, and eke her hurt their good.

26

    That detestable sight him much amazde,
        To see th'unkindly Impes° of heaven accurst,   *unnatural offspring*
        Devoure their dam; on whom while so he gazd,
        Having all satisfide their bloudy thurst,
230   Their bellies swolne he saw with fulnesse burst,
        And bowels gushing forth: well worthy end
        Of such as drunke her life, the which them nurst;
        Now needeth him no lenger labour spend,
    His foes have slaine themselves, with whom he should contend.

27

235   His Ladie seeing all, that chaunst, from farre
      Approcht in hast to greet his victorie,
      And said, Faire knight, borne under happy starre,
      Who see your vanquisht foes before you lye:
      Well worthy be you of that Armorie,[8]
240   Wherein ye have great glory wonne this day,
      And proov'd your strength on a strong enimie,
      Your first adventure: many such I pray,
    And henceforth ever wish, that like succeed it may.

28

    Then mounted he upon his Steede againe,
245   And with the Lady backward sought to wend;
      That path he kept, which beaten was most plaine,
      Ne ever would to any by-way bend,
      But still did follow one unto the end,
      The which at last out of the wood them brought.
250   So forward on his way (with God to frend)
      He passed forth, and new adventure sought;
      Long way he travelled, before he heard of ought.

29

    At length they chaunst to meet upon the way
      An aged Sire, in long blacke weedes yclad,
255   His feete all bare, his beard all hoarie gray,
      And by his belt his booke he hanging had;
      Sober he seemde, and very sagely sad,
      And to the ground his eyes were lowly bent,
      Simple in shew, and voyde of malice bad,
260   And all the way he prayed, as he went,
    And often knockt his brest, as one that did repent.

30

    He faire the knight saluted, louting° low,   *bowing*
      Who faire him quited,° as that courteous was: *answered*
      And after asked him, if he did know
265   Of straunge adventures, which abroad did pas.
      Ah my deare Sonne (quoth he) how should, alas,
      Silly° old man, that lives in hidden cell,   *simple*
      Bidding° his beades all day for his trespas,   *telling*
      Tydings of warre and worldly trouble tell?
270   With holy father sits not with such things to mell.°   *meddle*

31

    But if of daunger which hereby doth dwell,
      And homebred evill ye desire to heare,
      Of a straunge man I can you tidings tell,
      That wasteth° all this countrey farre and neare.   *destroys*
275   Of such (said he)° I chiefly do inquere,   *Redcrosse Knight*
      And shall you well reward to shew the place,

---

8. The Lady is proclaiming that by conquering Error, the Redcrosse Knight has become worthy to wear the armor of Christ; the episode foreshadows the knight's final triumph over the many-headed dragon that represents false faith.

In which that wicked wight his dayes doth weare°:   *spend*
   For to all knighthood it is foule disgrace,
That such a cursed creature lives so long a space.

32

280 Far hence (quoth he)° in wastfull wildernesse   *the aged Sire*
   His dwelling is, by which no living wight
   May ever passe, but thorough° great distresse.   *through*
   Now (sayd the Lady) draweth toward night,
   And well I wote,° that of your later fight   *know*
285   Ye all forwearied° be: for what so strong,   *exhausted*
   But wanting rest will also want of might?
   The Sunne that measures heaven all day long,
At night doth baite° his steedes the Ocean waves emong.   *nourish*

33

Then with the Sunne take Sir, your timely rest,
290   And with new day new worke at once begin:
   Untroubled night they say gives counsell best.
   Right well Sir knight ye have advised bin,
   (Quoth then that aged man;) the way to win
   Is wisely to advise: now day is spent;
295   Therefore with me ye may take up your In
   For this same night. The knight was well content:
So with that godly father to his home they went.

34

A little lowly Hermitage it was,[9]
   Downe in a dale, hard by° a forests side,   *next to*
300   Far from resort of people, that did pas
   In travell to and froe: a little wyde
   There was an holy Chappell edifyde,°   *built*
   Wherein the Hermite dewly wont to say
   His holy things each morne and eventyde:
305   Thereby a Christall streame did gently play,
Which from a sacred fountaine welled forth alway.

35

Arrived there, the little house they fill,
   Ne looke for entertainement, where none was:
   Rest is their feast, and all things at their will;
310   The noblest mind the best contentment has.
   With faire discourse the evening so they pas:
   For that old man of pleasing wordes had store,
   And well could file his tongue as smooth as glas;
   He told of Saintes and Popes, and evermore
315 He strowd° an Ave-Mary after and before.[1]   *recited*

---

9. This stanza illustrates the use of symbol in allegory; taken as a whole, its imagery suggests that the Redcrosse Knight has met the hermit because he suffers from a failing that the hermit will exploit. The hermitage is down in a dale, or valley, because the knight has begun to descend into a false faith; it is isolated because he is traveling in a strange and unusual direction; and it is by a fountain that appears to be sacred but that will be revealed as the antithesis of the Well of Life that will later restore him.

1. Despite his pious demeanor, the old man's discourse of saints and popes and his recital of Ave Marias indicate his affiliation with Catholicism; they are therefore intended to signal his corrupt and duplicitous character. The Redcrosse Knight is intended to represent English Protestantism and the true Church; by contrast, Spenser rejects Catholicism as a corruption of that Church.

36

The drouping Night thus creepeth on them fast,
 And the sad humour° loading their eye liddes,   *moisture*
 As messenger of Morpheus° on them cast   *god of sleep*
 Sweet slombring deaw, the which to sleepe them biddes.
320 Unto their lodgings then his guestes he° riddes: *the aged Sire*
 Where when all drownd in deadly sleepe he findes,
 He to his study goes, and there amiddes
 His Magick bookes and artes of sundry kindes,
He seekes out mighty charmes, to trouble sleepy mindes.

37

325 Then choosing out few wordes most horrible,
 (Let none them read) thereof did verses frame,°   *compose*
 With which and other spelles like terrible,
 He bad awake blacke Plutoes griesly Dame,[2]
 And cursed heaven, and spake reprochfull shame
330 Of highest God, the Lord of life and light;
 A bold bad man, that dar'd to call by name
 Great Gorgon,[3] Prince of darknesse and dead night,
At which Cocytus quakes, and Styx is put to flight.[4]

38

And forth he cald out of deepe darknesse dred
335 Legions of Sprights,° the which like little flyes   *spirits*
 Fluttring about his ever damned hed,
 A-waite whereto their service he applyes,
 To aide his friends, or fray° his enimies: *frighten*
 Of those he chose out two, the falsest twoo,
340 And fittest for to forge true-seeming lyes;
 The one of them he gave a message too,
The other by him selfe staide other worke to doo.

39

He making speedy way through spersed° ayre,   *empty*
 And through the world of waters wide and deepe,
345 To Morpheus[5] house doth hastily repaire.
 Amid the bowels of the earth full steepe,
 And low, where dawning day doth never peepe,
 His dwelling is; there Tethys his wet bed
 Doth ever wash, and Cynthia still doth steepe
350 In silver deaw his ever-drouping hed,
Whiles sad Night over him her mantle black doth spred.

40

Whose double gates he findeth locked fast,
 The one faire fram'd of burnisht Yvory,
 The other all with silver overcast;
355 And wakefull dogges before them farre do lye,
 Watching to banish Care their enimy,

---

2. Persephone, Pluto's wife and sometimes goddess of the underworld.
3. One of a family of monsters, daughters of the primitive gods of antiquity; Spenser, making her male, identifies the Gorgon with Pluto and also Satan.

4. The Cocytus and the Styx were rivers in the classical underworld.
5. God of sleep, who lives in the depths of the dark earth: Tethus or the sea washes him; Cynthia or the moon bedews him, and Night covers him.

Who oft is wont to trouble gentle Sleepe.
By them the Sprite doth passe in quietly,
And unto Morpheus comes, whom drowned deepe
360   In drowsie fit° he findes: of nothing he takes keepe.°   *stupor/notice*

41

And more, to lulle him in his slumber soft,
A trickling streame from high rocke tumbling downe
And ever-drizling raine upon the loft,
Mixt with a murmuring winde, much like the sowne
365   Of swarming Bees, did cast him in a swowne°:   *faint*
No other noyse, nor peoples troublous cryes,
As still are wont t'annoy the walled towne,
Might there be heard: but carelesse Quiet lyes,
Wrapt in eternall silence farre from enemyes.

42

370   The messenger approching to him spake,
But his wast wordes returnd to him in vaine:
So sound he° slept, that nought mought him awake.   *Morpheus*
Then rudely he him thrust, and pusht with paine,
Whereat he gan to stretch: but he againe
375   Shooke him so hard, that forced him to speake.
As one then in a dreame, whose dryer braine
Is tost with troubled sights and fancies weake,
He mumbled soft, but would not all his silence breake.

43

The Sprite then gan more boldly him to wake,
380   And threatned unto him the dreaded name
Of Hecate:[6] whereat he gan to quake,
And lifting up his lumpish head, with blame
Halfe angry asked him, for what he came.
Hither (quoth he) me Archimago[7] sent,
385   He that the stubborne Sprites can wisely tame,
He bids thee to him send for his intent
A fit false dreame, that can delude the sleepers sent.°   *senses*

44

The God obayde, and calling forth straight way
A diverse dreame out of his prison darke,
390   Delivered it to him, and downe did lay
His heavie head, devoide of carefull carke,°   *sorrowful anxiety*
Whose sences all were straight benumbd and starke.°   *paralyzed*
He backe returning by the Yvorie dore,
Remounted up as light as chearefull Larke,
395   And on his litle winges the dreame he bore
In hast unto his Lord, where he him left afore.

45

Who all this while with charmes and hidden artes,
Had made a Lady of that other Spright,

---

6. The dark aspect of Cynthia, the moon, and thus also of Diana; Hecate figures the underworld, death, and darkness.
7. The sage Sire is named Archimago, an "arch (or chief) magus (or magician)" and hence a forger or architect of images rather than real things. Because these images are clever and deceptive imitations of reality, Archimago is associated with hypocrisy and magic, an art that Christians were forbidden to practice.

And fram'd of liquid ayre her tender partes
400 So lively, and so like in all mens sight,
That weaker sence it° could have ravisht quight: *the spright*
The maker selfe for all his wondrous witt,
Was nigh beguiled with so goodly sight:
Her all in white he clad, and over it
405 Cast a blacke stole, most like to seeme for Una[8] fit.

46

Now when that ydle dreame was to him brought,
Unto that Elfin knight he° bad him° fly,   *Archimago/the spright*
Where he slept soundly void of evill thought,
And with false shewes abuse his fantasy,
410 In sort as he him schooled privily:
And that new creature borne without her dew,°   *unnaturally*
Full of the makers guile, with usage sly
He taught to imitate that Lady trew,
Whose semblance she did carrie under feigned hew.

47

415 Thus well instructed, to their worke they hast,
And comming where the knight in slomber lay,
The one upon his hardy head him plast,
And made him dreame of loves and lustfull play,
That nigh his manly hart did melt away,
420 Bathed in wanton blis and wicked joy:
Then seemed him his Lady by him lay,
And to him playnd, how that false winged boy°   *Cupid*
Her chast hart had subdewd, to learne Dame pleasures toy.

48

And she her selfe of beautie soveraigne Queene,
425 Faire Venus seemde unto his bed to bring
Her,[9] whom he waking evermore did weene
To be the chastest flowre, that ay did spring
On earthly braunch, the daughter of a king,
Now a loose Leman to vile service bound:
430 And eke the Graces seemed all to sing,
Hymen iō Hymen,[1] dauncing all around,
Whilst freshest Flora her with Yvie girlond crownd.

49

In this great passion of unwonted lust,
Or wonted feare of doing ought amis,
435 He° started up, as seeming to mistrust   *Redcrosse Knight*
Some secret ill, or hidden foe of his:
Lo there before his face his Lady is,

---

8. Here the Lady is named Una; she is to symbolize the ideal unity of Truth and the Church whose faith the Redcrosse Knight defends. She is named only when her false double appears.
9. I.e., she, impersonating Una, seemed also a Venus; this composite queen of beauty appears to the Redcrosse Knight to have come unto his bed.
1. A Roman chant praising Hymen, the god of marriage, sung here by the Graces, handmaids of Venus, who personify the arts of courtesy and courtship. The union they celebrate in this case is not, however, a lawful Christian marriage but rather one provoked by lust and sexuality. In Roman mythology, Flora is the goddess of flowers, but early modern poets often gave her the role of a harlot. This entire scene uses the imagery of the Roman Bacchanalia (celebration of the god Bacchus) to suggest the mood of an orgy.

Under blake stole hyding her bayted hooke,
And as halfe blushing offred him to kis,
440   With gentle blandishment and lovely looke,
Most like that virgin true, which for her knight him took.

50

All cleane° dismayd to see so uncouth sight,   *fully*
And halfe enraged at her shamelesse guise,
He thought have slaine her in his fierce despight:°   *indignation*
445   But hasty heat tempring with sufferance° wise,   *patience*
He stayde his hand, and gan himselfe advise
To prove his sense,° and tempt° her faigned truth.[2]   *what he saw/test*
Wringing her hands in wemens pitteous wise,
Tho° can she weepe, to stirre up gentle ruth,   *then*
450   Both for her noble bloud, and for her tender youth.

51

And said, Ah Sir, my liege Lord and my love,
Shall I accuse the hidden cruell fate,
And mightie causes wrought in heaven above,
Or the blind God, that doth me thus amate,°   *dismay*
455   For hoped love to winne me certaine hate?
Yet thus perforce he bids me do, or die.
Die is my dew:° yet rew° my wretched state   *due/pity*
You, whom my hard avenging destinie
Hath made judge of my life or death indifferently.

52

460   Your owne deare sake forst me at first to leave
My Fathers kingdome, There she stopt with teares;
Her swollen hart her speach seemd to bereave,
And then againe begun, My weaker yeares
Captiv'd to fortune and frayle worldly feares,
465   Fly to your faith for succour and sure ayde:
Let me not dye in languor and long teares.
Why Dame (quoth he) what hath ye thus dismayd?
What frayes° ye, that were wont to comfort me affrayd?   *frightens*

53

Love of your selfe, she said, and deare° constraint°   *dire/danger*
470   Lets me not sleepe, but wast the wearie night
In secret anguish and unpittied plaint,
Whiles you in carelesse sleepe are drowned quight.
Her doubtfull words made that redoubted knight
Suspect her truth: yet since no'untruth he knew,
475   Her fawning love with foule disdainefull spight
He would not shend,° but said, Deare dame I rew,   *reproach*
That for my sake unknowne such griefe unto you grew.

54

Assure your selfe, it fell not all to ground;
For all so deare as life is to my hart,
480   I deeme your love, and hold me to you bound;

2. The Redcrosse Knight unwisely tests his senses rather than his faith. In doing so, he succumbs to the sensuality of the false Una and thus proves himself false to the true Una. The episode illustrates the danger inherent in powerful illusion; in such cases the false and the true may be indistinguishable.

Ne let vaine feares procure your needlesse smart,°   *pain*
Where cause is none, but to your rest depart.
Not all content, yet seemd she to appease
Her mournefull plaintes, beguiled of her art,
485   And fed with words, that could not chuse but please,
So slyding softly forth, she turnd as to her ease.

55

Long after lay he musing at her mood,
Much griev'd to thinke that gentle Dame so light,
For whose defence he was to shed his blood.
490   At last dull wearinesse of former fight
Having yrockt a sleepe his irkesome spright,
That troublous dreame gan freshly tosse his braine,
With bowres, and beds, and Ladies deare delight:
But when he saw his labour all was vaine,
495   With that misformed spright he backe returnd againe.

[By the end of Book 1, we see the Redcrosse Knight as victor over the forces representing the falsehood of the world. Neither Archimago, nor his ally the queen Duessa (her name suggests the doubleness of deceit), nor the vast and empty Orgolio the giant of Pride, remain to plague him with erroneous or counterfeit images of the truth. Knowing the truth and engaged to Una, he exemplifies Holiness, to Spenser the first and most important of all virtues. But there are other virtues that the poet wants to portray in his romance. While the Redcrosse Knight has seen through the worldy manifestations of falsehood, he has not destroyed them. To his ally Guyon, the Knight of Temperance and the hero of Book 2, Spenser assigns this task: to rid the world of pure illusion, works (sometimes of excellent artistry) that point to no truths and so distract the viewer from his life's work. Guyon's virtue causes him to reject such pleasing shows; he cannot be lulled into a passive enjoyment of idle pleasures. His greatest accomplishment, the destruction of the ravishing but quite lifeless Bower of Bliss, a garden created by the superbly gifted witch Acrasia, concludes Book 2.]

from **The Second Booke of the Faerie Queene**
Contayning The Legend of Sir Guyon
or
Temperaunce

from *Canto 12*

Guyon, by Palmers governance,
passing through perils great,
Doth overthrow the Bowre of blisse,
and Acrasie defeat.

1

Now gins° this goodly frame of Temperance   *begins*
Fairely to rise, and her adorned hed
To pricke of highest praise forth to advance,
Formerly° grounded, and fast setteled   *previously*
5   On firme foundation of true bountihed;[1]
And this brave knight, that for that vertue fights,

1. The spirit of temperance begins to be inspired to celebrate and highly praise temperance, now that this virtue is established on goodness ("bountihed").

Now comes to point of that same perilous sted,°   *dangerous place*
Where Pleasure dwelles in sensuall delights,
Mongst thousand dangers, and ten thousand magick mights.°   *powers*

* * *

42

370   Thence passing forth, they shortly do arrive,
Whereas the Bowre of Blisse was situate;
A place pickt out by choice of best alive,
That natures worke by art can imitate
In which what ever in this worldly state
375   Is sweet, and pleasing unto living sense,
Or that may dayntiest fantasie aggrate,°   *please*
Was poured forth with plentifull dispence,°   *abundance*
And made there to abound with lavish affluence.°   *extravagance*

43

Goodly it was enclosed round about,
380   Aswell their entred° guestes to keepe within,   *entered*
As those unruly beasts to hold without;°   *keep out*
Yet was the fence thereof but weake and thin;
Nought° feard their force, that fortilage° to win,   *nothing / fortress*
But wisedomes powre, and temperaunces might,
385   By which the mightiest things efforced bin:[2]
And eke the gate was wrought of substaunce light,
Rather for pleasure, then for battery° or fight.   *physical assault*

44

Yt framed was of precious yvory,
That seemd a worke of admirable wit;°   *skill*
390   And therein all the famous history
Of Jason and Medaea[3] was ywrit;
Her mighty charmes, her furious loving fit,
His goodly conquest of the golden fleece,
His falsed° faith, and love too lightly flit,°   *violated / fickle*
395   The wondred Argo, which in venturous peece°   *adventurous ship*
First through the Euxine seas bore all the flowr of Greece.

45

Ye might have seene the frothy billowes fry
Under the ship,° as thorough them she went,   *the Argo*
That seemd the waves were into yvory,
400   Or yvory into the waves were sent;
And other where° the snowy substaunce sprent°   *elsewhere / sprinkled*
With vermell, like the boyes bloud therein shed,[4]
A piteous spectacle did represent,
And otherwhiles° with gold besprinkeled;   *elsewhere*
405   Yt seemd th'enchaunted flame, which did Creüsa[5] wed.

---

2. Acrasia did not fear beasts but only the power of wisdom and temperance, which can control the mightiest things.
3. Jason sailed in the Argo, the first oceangoing ship, to capture the golden fleece, a Greek treasure, which belonged to King Aeetes of Colchis. The king's daughter, Medea, assisted Jason with her magical powers. When Jason abandoned her, betraying the fidelity he had promised her, Medea took revenge. Medea was said to have inherited her magical powers from Circe, her aunt.
4. A reference to Medea's murder of her brother, whose body she threw into the sea to distract her father as she and Jason fled from Colchis with the golden fleece.
5. The woman for whom Jason abandoned Medea. In revenge, Medea sent Creüsa an enchanted dress, which burned her to death with its own fire; hence Creüsa could be said to have wed a flame.

46

All this, and more might in that goodly gate
  Be red;° that ever open stood to all,   *seen*
  Which thither came: but in the Porch there sate
  A comely personage of stature tall,
410   And semblaunce pleasing, more then naturall,
  That travellers to him seemd to entize;°   *entice*
  His looser garment to the ground did fall,
  And flew about his heeles in wanton wize,°   *manner*
Not fit for speedy pace, or manly exercize.

47

415   They in that place him Genius[6] did call:
  Not that celestiall powre, to whom the care
  Of life, and generation of all
  That lives, pertaines in charge particulare,°   *as a special charge*
  Who wondrous things concerning our welfare,
420   And straunge phantomes° doth let us oft forsee,   *images*
  And oft of secret ill bids us beware:
  That is our Selfe, whom though we do not see,
Yet each doth in him selfe it well perceive to bee.

48

Therefore a God him sage Antiquity
425   Did wisely make, and good Agdistes call:
  But this same was to that quite contrary,
  The foe of life, that good envyes to all,
  That secretly doth us procure° to fall,   *cause*
  Through guilefull semblaunts,° which he makes us see.   *deceitful images*
430   He of this Gardin had the governall,°   *management*
  And Pleasures porter was devizd° to bee,   *appointed*
Holding a staffe in hand for more formalitee.

49

With diverse flowres he daintily was deekt,
  And strowed° round about, and by his side   *strewn*
435   A mighty Mazer° bowle of wine was set,   *maple*
  As if it had to him bene sacrifide;[7]
  Wherewith all new-come guests he gratifide:
  So did he eke Sir Guyon passing by:
  But he his idle curtesie defide,
440   And overthrew his bowle disdainfully;
And broke his staffe, with which he charmed semblants sly.

50

Thus being entred, they behold around
  A large and spacious plaine, on every side
  Strowed with pleasauns,° whose faire grassy ground   *small parks*
445   Mantled° with greene, and goodly beautifide   *cloaked*
  With all the ornaments of Floraes° pride,   *goddess of flowers*

---

6. Not what he is traditionally, that is, the spirit, associated with heavenly power, who has a specific duty to care for each individual man or woman. Identified as a "self" or ego, genius also has the force of a moral consciousness.

Although we do not see this genius, each of us has a sense of it. Spenser specifies that genius is called Agdistes. However, the figure at Acrasia's gate is his diabolical double.
7. As if it were a sacrificial offering.

Wherewith her mother Art, as halfe in scorne
Of niggard Nature, like a pompous bride
Did decke her, and too lavishly adorne,[8]
450   When forth from virgin bowre she comes in th'early morne.

51

There to the Heavens alwayes Joviall,°   *joyful*
Lookt on them lovely, still° in stedfast° state,   *always/constant*
Ne suffred° storme nor frost on them to fall,   *allowed*
Their tender buds or leaves to violate,
455   Nor scorching heat, nor cold intemperate
T'afflict the creatures, which therein did dwell,
But the milde aire with season moderate
Gently attempred,° and disposd so well,   *temperate*
That still it breathed forth sweet spirit and holesome smell.

52

460   More sweet and holesome, then the pleasaunt hill
Of Rhodope,[9] on which the Nimphe, that bore
A gyaunt babe, her selfe for griefe did kill;
Or the Thessalian Tempe, where of yore
Faire Daphne Phoebus hart with love did gore;
465   Or Ida, where the Gods lov'd to repaire,°   *retire*
When ever they their heavenly bowres forlore;
Or sweet Parnasse, the haunt of Muses faire;
Or Eden selfe, if ought° with Eden mote compaire.   *anything*

53

Much wondred Guyon at the faire aspect°   *appearance*
470   Of that sweet place, yet suffred° no delight   *allowed*
To sincke into his sence, nor mind affect,
But passed forth, and lookt still forward right,°   *straight ahead*
Bridling his will, and maistering his might:
Till that he came unto another gate;
475   No gate, but like one, being goodly dight°   *decorated*
With boughes and braunches, which did broad dilate°   *extend*
Their clasping armes, in wanton wreathings intricate.

54

So fashioned a Porch[1] with rare device,°   *design*
Archt over head with an embracing vine,
480   Whose bounches° hanging downe, seemed to entice   *bunches*
All passers by, to tast their lushious wine,
And did themselves into their hands incline,°   *hang*
As freely offering to be gathered:
Some deepe empurpled as the Hyacint,[2]
485   Some as the Rubine,° laughing sweetly red,   *ruby*
Some like faire Emeraudes,° not yet well ripened.   *emeralds*

---

8. Flora's mother, Art, scorns the simplicity of Nature
and dresses Flora in showy clothing.
9. Spenser compares the Bower of Bliss with five Greek
landscapes, all of which (except for Parnassus) were also
the scenes of montrosity and tragedy. Rhodope was the
hill where Orpheus sang and was torn to pieces by the
Maenads, also the name of a nymph who gave birth to a
giant child whose father was Neptune. Daphne was the

first love of Phoebus or Apollo, who could be said to have
wounded his heart by her disdain of him; Mount Ida was
the site of the beauty contest between Hera (Juno),
Aphrodite (Venus), and Athena (Minerva) that led to
the Trojan War.
1. The branches created a sort of porch.
2. Hyacinth or jacinth, a blue stone.

55

And them° amongst, some were of burnisht gold,   *the grapes*
   So made by art, to beautifie the rest,
   Which did themselves emongst the leaves enfold,
490   As lurking from the vew of covetous° guest,   *greedy*
   That the weake bowes,° with so rich load opprest,   *boughs*
   Did bow adowne, as over-burdened.
   Under that Porch a comely dame did rest,
   Clad in faire weedes, but fowle disordered,°   *sloppy*
495 And garments loose, that seemd unmeet for womanhed.[3]

56

In her left hand a Cup of gold she held,
   And with her right the riper fruit did reach,
   Whose sappy liquor, that with fulnesse sweld,
   Into her cup she scruzd,° with daintie breach°   *squeezed/crushing*
500   Of her fine fingers, without fowle empeach,[4]
   That so faire wine-presse made the wine more sweet:
   Thereof she usd to give to drinke to each,
   Whom passing by she happened to meet:
It was her guise, all Straungers goodly so to greet.

57

505 So she to Guyon offred it to tast;
   Who taking it out of her tender hond,
   The cup to ground did violently cast,
   That all in peeces it was broken fond,
   And with the liquor stained all the lond:
510   Whereat Excesse[5] exceedingly was wroth,
   Yet no'te° the same amend, ne yet withstond,°   *could not/prevent*
   But suffered him to passe, all were she loth;°   *reluctant*
Who nought regarding her displeasure forward goth.

58

There the most daintie Paradise on ground,
515   It selfe doth offer to his sober eye,
   In which all pleasures plenteously abound,
   And none does others happinesse envye:
   The painted flowres, the trees upshooting hye,
   The dales for shade, the hilles for breathing space,
520   The trembling groves, the Christall running by;
   And that, which all faire workes doth most aggrace,°   *add grace to*
The art, which all that wrought, appeared in no place.[6]

59

One would have thought, (so cunningly, the rude,
   And scorned parts were mingled with the fine,)
525   That nature had for wantonesse ensude°   *imitated*
   Art, and that Art at nature did repine;°   *fret*
   So striving each th'other to undermine,
   Each did the others worke more beautifie;
So diff'ring both in willes, agreed in fine:

---

3. Unsuitable for womanhood.
4. She used her own fingers to squeeze the grapes without soiling her fingers or ruining the grapes.

5. The lady at the Porch.
6. The scene appears natural, and the art that created it is invisible.

530   So all agreed through sweete diversitie,°   *disagreement*
       This Gardin to adorne with all varietie.
                        60
       And in the midst of all, a fountaine stood,
           Of richest substaunce, that on earth might bee,
           So pure and shiny, that the silver flood
535   Through every channell running one might see;
           Most goodly it with curious imageree
           Was over-wrought, and shapes of naked boyes,
           Of which some seemd with lively jollitee,
           To fly about, playing their wanton toyes,
540   Whilest others did them selves embay° in liquid joyes.   *bathe*
                        61
       And over all, of purest gold was spred,
           A trayle° of yvie in his native hew: *vine*
           For the rich mettall was so coloured,
           That wight, who did not well avis'd° it vew,   *carefully*
545   Would surely deeme it to be yvie trew:
           Low his° lascivious armes adown did creepe,   *the ivy's*
           That themselves dipping in the silver dew,
           Their fleecy flowres they tenderly did steepe,
       Which drops of Christall seemd for wantones to weepe.
                        62
550   Infinit streames continually did well
           Out of this fountaine, sweet and faire to see,
           The which into an ample laver° fell,   *basin*
           And shortly grew to so great quantitie,
           That like a little lake it seemd to bee;
555   Whose depth exceeded not three cubits° hight,   *about four feet*
           That through the waves one might the bottom see,
           All pav'd beneath with Jaspar° shining bright,   *green stone*
       That seemd the fountaine in that sea did sayle upright.[7]
                        63
       And all the margent° round about was set,   *edge*
560   With shady Laurell trees, thence to defend
           The sunny beames, which on the billowes bet,°   *beat*
           And those which therein bathed, mote offend.[8]
           As Guyon hapned by the same to wend,
           Two naked Damzelles he therein espyde,
565   Which therein bathing, seemed to contend,
           And wrestle wantonly,° ne car'd to hyde,   *lewdly*
       Their dainty parts from vew of any, which them eyde.
                        64
       Sometimes the one would lift the other quight
           Above the waters, and then downe againe
570   Her plong,° as over maistered by might,   *plunge*
           Where both awhile would covered remaine,
           And each the other from to rise restraine;

7. The jet of water rose up in the fountain so that it   8. The beams of the sun might bother bathers.
resembled a ship sailing on the sea.

   The whiles their snowy limbes, as through a vele,
   So through the Christall waves appeared plaine:
575 Then suddeinly both would themselves unhele,°   *release*
 And th'amarous sweet spoiles to greedy eyes revele.

65

  As that faire Starre, the messenger of morne,
   His deawy face out of the sea doth reare:
   Or as the Cyprian goddesse, newly borne
580 Of th'Oceans fruitfull froth, did first appeare:[9]
   Such seemed they, and so their yellow heare
   Christalline humour° dropped downe apace. *water of the fountain*
   Whom such when Guyon saw, he drew him neare,
   And somewhat gan relent his earnest° pace,   *brisk*
585 His stubborn brest gan secret pleasaunce° to embrace. *pleasure*

66

  The wanton Maidens him espying, stood
   Gazing a while at his unwonted° guise;° *unfamiliar/manner*
   Then th'one her selfe low ducked in the flood,
   Abasht, that her a straunger did a vise:°   *view*
590 But th'other rather higher did arise,
   And her two lilly paps° aloft displayd,   *breasts*
   And all, that might his melting hart entise
   To her delights, she unto him bewrayd:°   *revealed*
 The rest hid underneath, him more desirous made.

67

595 With that, the other likewise up arose,
   And her faire lockes,° which formerly were bownd *hair*
   Up in one knot, she low adowne did lose:
   Which flowing long and thick, her cloth'd arownd,
   And th'yvorie in golden mantle gownd:°   *draped*
600 So that faire spectacle from him was reft,°   *taken*
   Yet that, which reft it, no lesse faire was fownd:
   So hid in lockes and waves from lookers theft,
 Nought but her lovely face she for his looking left.

68

  Withall she laughed, and she blusht withall,
605 That blushing to her laughter gave more grace,
   And laughter to her blushing, as did fall:
   Now when they spide the knight to slacke his pace,
   Them to behold, and in his sparkling face
   The secret signes of kindled lust appeare,
610 Their wanton meriments they did encreace,
   And to him beckned, to approch more neare,
 And shewd him many sights, that courage cold could reare.[1]

69

  On which when gazing him the Palmer saw,
   He much rebukt those wandring eyes of his,
615 And counseld well, him forward thence did draw.° *move*

---

9. Both star and the Cyprian goddess signify Venus.   1. They showed Guyon many things that could arouse his
                            lust.

Now are they come nigh to the Bowre of blis
Of° her° fond favorites so nam'd amis:°   *by/Acrasia's/wrongly*
When thus° the Palmer; Now Sir, well avise;   *thus spoke*
For here the end of all our travell is:
620   Here wonnes° Acrasia,[2] whom we must surprise,   *dwells*
Else she will slip away, and all our drift° despise.   *purpose*

70

Eftsoones they heard a most melodious sound,
Of all° that mote delight a daintie eare,   *everything*
Such as attonce might not on living ground,
625   Save in this Paradise, be heard elswhere:
Right hard it was, for wight, which did it heare,
To read,° what manner musicke that mote bee: *understand*
For all that pleasing is to living eare,
Was there consorted° in one harmonee,   *joined*
630   Birdes, voyces, instruments, windes, waters, all agree.

71

The joyous birdes shrouded° in chearefull shade,   *hidden*
Their notes unto the voyce° attempred° sweet,   *harmony/attuned*
Th'Angelicall soft trembling voyces made
To th'instruments° divine respondence° meet: *of the Bower/answer*
635   The silver sounding instruments did meet
With the base murmure of the waters fall:
The waters fall with difference discreet,
Now soft, now loud, unto the wind did call:
The gentle warbling wind low answered to all.

72

640   There, whence that Musick seemed heard to bee,
Was the faire Witch her selfe now solacing,°   *relaxing*
With a new Lover, whom through sorceree
And witchcraft, she from farre did thither bring:
There she had him now layd a slombering,
645   In secret shade, after long wanton joyes:
Whilst round about them pleasauntly did sing
Many faire Ladies, and lascivious boyes,
That ever mixt their song with light licentious toyes.° *pastimes*

73

And all that while, right over him she hong,
650   With her false eyes fast fixed in his sight,
As seeking medicine, whence she was stong,
Or greedily depasturing° delight: *grazing on*
And oft inclining downe with kisses light,
For feare of waking him, his lips bedewd,°   *wet*
655   And through his humid eyes did sucke his spright,
Quite molten° into lust and pleasure lewd;   *melted*
Wherewith she sighed soft, as if his case she rewd.

74

The whiles some one did chaunt° this lovely lay;°   *sing/song*
Ah see, who so faire thing doest faine° to see,   *wish*

2. Ill-temper, incontinence, impotence (medieval Latin).

660   In springing flowre the image of thy day;°   *life*
        Ah see the Virgin Rose, how sweetly shee
        Doth first peepe forth with bashfull modestee,
        That fairer seemes, the lesse ye see her may;[3]
        Lo see soone after, how more bold and free
665   Her bared bosome she doth broad° display;   *openly*
Loe see soone after, how she fades, and falles away.

75

So passeth,° in the passing of a day,   *passes*
    Of mortall life the leafe, the bud, the flowre,
    Ne more doth flourish after first decay,°   *withering*
670   That earst was sought to decke° both bed and bowre,   *adorn*
    Of many a Ladie, and many a Paramowre:°   *lover*
    Gather therefore the Rose, whilest yet is prime,[4]
    For soone comes age, that will her pride deflowre:
    Gather the Rose of love, whilest yet is time,
675   Whilest loving thou mayst loved be with equall crime.

76

He ceast, and then gan all the quire° of birdes   *choir*
    Their diverse notes t'attune unto his lay,
    As in approvance° of his pleasing words.   *as if approving*
    The constant paire heard all, that he did say,
680   Yet swarved,° but kept their forward way,   *turned*
    Through many covert groves, and thickets close,
    In which they creeping did at last display°   *discover*
    That wanton Ladie, with her lover lose,
Whose sleepie head she in her lap did soft dispose.°   *lay*

77

685   Upon a bed of Roses she was layd,
    As faint through heat, or dight to° pleasant sin,   *prepared for*
    And was arayd, or rather disarayd,
    All in a vele of silke and silver thin,
    That hid no whit her alablaster° skin,   *white*
690   But rather shewd more white, if more might bee:
    More subtile web Arachne[5] cannot spin,
    Nor the fine nets, which oft we woven see
Of scorched° deaw, do not in th'aire more lightly flee.°   *dried/float*

78

Her snowy brest was bare to readie spoyle°   *easy view*
695   Of hungry eies, which n'ote° therewith be fild,   *could not*
    And yet through languour° of her late sweet toyle,   *weariness*
    Few drops, more cleare then Nectar, forth distild,°   *gathered*
    That like pure Orient perles adowne it trild,°   *trickled*
    And her faire eyes sweet smyling in delight,
700   Moystened their fierie beames, with which she thrild°   *pierced*

---

3. The less you see of her, the fairer she seems.
4. A figure common in love lyrics; the woman is compared to a flower that is to be picked just as it is about to bloom—an argument against moderation and temperance and for gratification and pleasure. Spenser concludes his version of the figure uncharacteristically, with a reminder that in the life of a temperate man or woman this kind of passion is a "crime."
5. A princess whose skill in the art of weaving surpassed that of the goddess Athena, who became jealous and transformed Arachne into a spider.

Fraile harts, yet quenched not; like starry light
Which sparckling on the silent waves, does seeme more bright.

79

The young man sleeping by her, seemd to bee
  Some goodly swayne of honorable place,
705   That certes it great pittie was to see
  Him his nobilitie so foule deface;°   *horribly disgrace*
  A sweet regard, and amiable grace,
  Mixed with manly sternnesse did appeare
  Yet sleeping, in his well proportiond face,
710   And on his tender lips the downy heare°   *hair*
Did now but freshly spring, and silken blossomes beare.

80

His warlike armes,° the idle instruments   *armor*
  Of sleeping praise, were hong upon a tree,
  And his brave shield, full of old moniments,° *marks of battle*
715   Was fowly ra'st,° that none the signes might see; *erased*
  Ne for them, ne for honour cared hee,
  Ne ought, that did to his advauncement tend,
  But in lewd loves, and wastfull luxuree,
  His dayes, his goods, his bodie he did spend:
720 O horrible enchantment, that him so did blend.° *blind*

81

The noble Elfe, and carefull Palmer drew
  So nigh them, minding nought, but lustfull game,° *pleasures*
  That suddein° forth they on them rusht, and threw *suddenly*
  A subtile net, which onely for the same
725   The skilfull Palmer formally° did frame. *especially*
  So held them under fast, the whiles the rest[6]
  Fled all away for feare of fowler° shame. *fouler*
  The faire Enchauntresse, so unwares opprest,
Tryde all her arts, and all her sleights, thence out to wrest.° *escape*

82

730 And eke her lover strove: but all in vaine;
  For that same net so cunningly was wound,° *woven*
  That neither guile, nor force might it distraine.° *destroy*
  They tooke them both, and both them strongly bound
  In captive bandes, which there they readie found:
735   But her in chaines of adamant° he tyde; *hard stone*
  For nothing else might keepe her safe and sound;
  But Verdant[7] (so he hight) he soone untyde,
And counsell sage in steed° thereof to him applyde. *stead*

83

But all those pleasant bowres and Pallace brave,
740   Guyon broke downe, with rigour° pittilesse; *violence*
  Ne ought their goodly workmanship might save
  Them from the tempest of his wrathfulnesse,
  But that their blisse he turn'd to balefulnesse:° *misery*

---

6. The Bower's other inhabitants.   7. Greening, growing green; here, one who is young and
at the beginning of his maturity.

Their groves he feld, their gardins did deface,
745   Their arbers spoyle, their Cabinets° suppresse,   *bowers*
Their banket° houses burne, their buildings race,°   *banquet/raze*
And of the fairest late, now made the fowlest place.

84

Then led they her away, and eke that knight
They with them led, both sorrowfull and sad:
750   The way they came, the same retourn'd they right,
Till they arrived, where they lately had
Charm'd those wild-beasts, that rag'd with furie mad.
Which now awaking, fierce at them gan fly,
As in their mistresse reskew, whom they lad;[8]
755   But them the Palmer soone did pacify.
Then Guyon askt, what meant those beastes, which there did ly.

85

Said he, These seeming beasts are men indeed,
Whom this Enchauntresse hath transformed thus,
Whylome° her lovers, which her lusts did feed,   *formerly*
760   Now turned into figures hideous,
According to their mindes like monstruous.
Sad end (quoth he) of life intemperate,
And mournefull meed of joyes delicious:
But Palmer, if it mote thee so aggrate,°   *please*
765   Let them returned be unto their former state.

86

Streight way he with his vertuous staffe them strooke,
And streight of beasts they comely men became;
Yet being men they did unmanly looke,
And stared ghastly, some for inward shame,
770   And some for wrath, to see their captive Dame:
But one above the rest in speciall,
That had an hog beene late, hight Grille[9] by name,
Repined° greatly, and did him miscall,°   *raged/insult*
That had from hoggish forme him brought to naturall.

87

775   Said Guyon, See the mind of beastly man,
That hath so soone forgot the excellence
Of his creation, when he life began,
That now he chooseth, with vile difference,
To be a beast, and lacke intelligence.
780   To whom the Palmer thus, The donghill kind
Delights in filth and foule incontinence:
Let Grill be Grill, and have his hoggish mind,
But let us hence depart, whilest wether serves and wind.[1]

---

8. The beasts attack Guyon and the Palmer as if to rescue their mistress, whom Guyon and the Palmer are leading.
9. Hog (Greek). Here Spenser follows the Odyssey: Grille is one of Ulysses's men whom Circe had transformed into a hog; he later refused to be returned to his human state.
1. While the weather and the wind are in our favor.

from **Amoretti**[1]

1

Happy ye leaves° when as those lilly hands,   *of the book*
Which hold my life in their dead doing° might,   *death-dealing*
Shall handle you and hold in loves soft bands,°   *bonds*
Lyke captives trembling at the victors sight.
5   And happy lines, on which with starry light,
Those lamping° eyes will deigne sometimes to look   *flashing*
And reade the sorrowes of my dying spright,°   *spirit*
Written with teares in harts close bleeding book.
And happy rymes bath'd in the sacred brooke,[2]
10   Of Helicon whence she derived is,
When ye behold that Angels blessed looke,
My soules long lacked foode, my heavens blis.
Leaves, lines, and rymes, seeke her to please alone,
Whom if ye please, I care for other none.

22

This holy season fit to fast and pray,[3]
Men to devotion ought to be inclynd:
Therefore, I lykewise on so holy day,
For my sweet Saynt some service fit will find.
5   Her temple fayre is built within my mind,
In which her glorious ymage placed is,
On which my thoughts doo day and night attend
Lyke sacred priests that never thinke amisse.
There I to her as th'author of my blisse,
10   Will builde an altar to appease her yre:°   *anger*
And on the same my hart will sacrifise,
Burning in flames of pure and chast desyre:
The which vouchsafe O goddesse to accept,
Amongst thy deerest relicks to be kept.

62

The weary yeare his race now having run,
The new[4] begins his compast° course anew: *encompassed*
With shew of morning mylde he hath begun,
Betokening peace and plenty to ensew.

---

1. "Little loves," a sonnet sequence apparently written for Elizabeth Boyle, whom Spenser married in 1594, though he may have written some of the sonnets much earlier and for another woman. The *Amoretti* were published in 1595 together with the *Epithalamion*, Spenser's marriage hymn upon his wedding. Both the sonnets and the hymn, each referring to regular moments in the passage of time, can be read as one continuous narrative.
2. Aganippe, which rises (or is "derived") from Helicon, a

mountain that is home to the Muses, goddesses of all the arts but known especially for their inspiration of poets.
3. The holy season is Lent; the holy day is Ash Wednesday. The sonnet celebrates the poet's admission that his love has a spiritual dimension; complimenting his heart's desire is the worship he gives to his lady's image in the temple of his mind.
4. The Christian new year, the Feast of the Annunciation.

5   So let us, which this chaunge of weather vew,
Chaunge eeke° our mynds and former lives amend,   *also*
The old yeares sinnes forepast° let us eschew,°   *gone by/avoid*
And fly the faults with which we did offend.
Then shall the new yeares joy forth freshly send,
10   Into the glooming° world his gladsome ray: *gloomy*
And all these stormes which now his beauty blend,°   *dim*
Shall turne to caulmes and tymely cleare away.
So likewise love cheare you your heavy spright,
And chaunge old yeares annoy° to new delight.   *grief*

68

Most glorious Lord of lyfe that on this day,[5]
Didst make thy triumph over death and sin:
And having harrowd hell, didst bring away
Captivity thence captive us to win.[6]
5   This joyous day, deare Lord, with joy begin,
And grant that we for whom thou diddest dye
Being with thy deare blood clene washt from sin,
May live for ever in felicity.
And that thy love we weighing worthily,
10   May likewise love thee for the same againe:
And for thy sake that all lyke deare° didst buy,   *at the same cost*
With love may one another entertayne.
So let us love, deare love, lyke as we ought,
Love is the lesson which the Lord us taught.

75

One day I wrote her name upon the strand,°   *beach*
But came the waves and washed it away:
Agayne I wrote it with a second hand,
But came the tyde, and made my paynes his pray.
5   Vayne man, sayd she, that doest in vaine assay,°   *attempt*
A mortall thing so to immortalize.
For I my selve shall lyke to this decay,
And eek my name bee wyped out lykewize.
Not so, (quod I) let baser things devize,°   *consent*
10   To dy in dust, but you shall live by fame:
My verse your vertues rare shall eternize,°   *make eternal*
And in the hevens wryte your glorious name:
Where whenas death shall all the world subdew,
Our love shall live, and later life renew.

---

5. The sonnet addresses the "dear Lord" of the Passion on Easter Day to harmonize the poet's love for his lady and his obligation to follow the lesson of Christ.
6. Christians believed that after his Resurrection, Christ descended into hell to rescue Adam and Eve and the patriarchs and prophets of the Hebrew Bible. The event is often described as the harrowing of hell.

Epithalamion[1]

Ye learned sisters[2] which have oftentimes
Beene to me ayding, others to adorne:
Whom ye thought worthy of your gracefull rymes,
That even the greatest did not greatly scorne
5   To heare theyr names sung in your simple layes,°   *verses*
But joyed° in theyr prayse.   *took pleasure*
And when ye list° your owne mishaps to mourne,   *wish*
Which death, or love, or fortunes wreck did rayse,
Your string could soone to sadder tenor turne,
10   And teach the woods and waters to lament
Your dolefull dreriment.°   *misfortune*
Now lay those sorrowfull complaints aside,
And having all your heads with girland° crownd,   *garlands*
Helpe me mine owne loves prayses to resound,
15   Ne let the same of any be envide:
So Orpheus[3] did for his owne bride,
So I unto my selfe alone will sing,
The woods shall to me answer and my Eccho ring.

Early before the worlds light giving lampe,
20   His golden beame upon the hils doth spred,
Having disperst the nights unchearefull dampe,
Doe ye awake and with fresh lusty hed,°   *merriment*
Go to the bowre of my beloved love,
My truest turtle dove
25   Bid her awake; for Hymen° is awake,   *god of marriage*
And long since ready forth his maske° to move,   *masque*
With his bright Tead° that flames with many a flake,   *torch*
And many a bachelor to waite on him,
In theyr fresh garments trim.
30   Bid her awake therefore and soone her dight,°   *dress*
For lo the wished day is come at last,
That shall for al the paynes and sorrowes past,
Pay to her usury of long delight,
And whylest she doth her dight,
35   Doe ye to her joy and solace sing,
That all the woods may answer and your eccho ring.

Bring with you all the Nymphes[4] that you can heare°   *here*
Both of the rivers and the forrests greene:
And of the sea that neighbours to her neare,

40   Al with gay girlands goodly wel beseene.°   *appearing*
     And let them also with them bring in hand,
     Another gay girland
     For my fayre love of lillyes and of roses,
     Bound truelove wize with a blew silke riband.

45   And let them make great store of bridale poses,°   *posies*
     And let them eeke bring store of other flowers
     To deck the bridale bowers.
     And let the ground whereas her foot shall tread,
     For feare the stones her tender foot should wrong

50   Be strewed with fragrant flowers all along,
     And diapred lyke the discolored mead.[5]
     Which done, doe at her chamber dore awayt,
     For she will waken strayt,°   *immediately*
     The whiles doe ye this song unto her sing,

55   The woods shall to you answer and your Eccho ring.

     Ye Nymphes of Mulla[6] which with carefull heed,°   *attention*
     The silver scaly trouts doe tend full well,
     And greedy pikes which use therein to feed,
     (Those trouts and pikes all others doo excell)

60   And ye likewise which keepe the rushy lake,
     Where none doo fishes take,
     Bynd up the locks° the which hang scatterd light,   *of the nymphs*
     And in his waters which your mirror make,
     Behold your faces as the christall bright,

65   That when you come whereas my love doth lie,
     No blemish she may spie.
     And eke ye lightfoot mayds which keepe the deere,
     That on the hoary mountayne use to towre,°   *soar*
     And the wylde wolves which seeke them to devoure,

70   With your steele darts doo chace from comming neer
     Be also present heere,
     To helpe to decke her and to help to sing,
     That all the woods may answer and your eccho ring.

     Wake now my love, awake; for it is time,

75   The Rosy Morne long since left Tithones[7] bed,
     All ready to her silver coche° to clyme,   *coach*
     And Phoebus[8] gins to shew his glorious hed.
     Hark how the cheerefull birds do chaunt° theyr laies°   *sing/songs*
     And carroll of loves praise.

80   The merry Larke hir mattins sings aloft,
     The thrush replyes, the Mavis° descant° playes,   *thrush/accompaniment*
     The Ouzell° shrills, the Ruddock° warbles soft,   *blackbird/redbreast*
     So goodly all agree with sweet consent,
     To this dayes merriment.

85   Ah my deere love why doe ye sleepe thus long,

---

5. Variegated like the many-colored fields.
6. Spenser's name for the Awbeg, a river in the county of
Munster in Ireland, where he was serving as a deputy for the

English crown at the time of his marriage to Elizabeth Boyle.
7. The mythical lover of the goddess of the dawn.
8. Apollo, the god of the sun.

When meeter° were that ye should now awake,   *more fitting*
T'awayt the comming of your joyous make,°   *mate*
And hearken to the birds lovelearned song,
The deawy leaves among.
90   For they of joy and pleasance to you sing,
That all the woods them answer and theyr eccho ring.

My love is now awake out of her dreame,
And her fayre eyes like stars that dimmed were
With darksome cloud, now shew theyr goodly beams
95   More bright then Hesperus[9] his head doth rere.
Come now ye damzels, daughters of delight,
Helpe quickly her to dight,
But first come ye fayre houres which were begot
In loves sweet paradice, of Day and Night,
100   Which doe the seasons of the yeare allot,
And al that ever in this world is fayre
Doe make and still° repayre.[1]   *forever*
And ye three handmayds of the Cyprian Queene,[2]
The which doe still adorne her beauties pride,
105   Helpe to addorne my beautifullest bride.
And as ye her array, still throw betweene
Some graces to be seene,
And as ye use to Venus, to her sing,
The whiles the woods shal answer and your eccho ring.

110   Now is my love all ready forth to come,
Let all the virgins therefore well awayt,
And ye fresh boyes that tend upon her groome
Prepare your selves; for he is comming strayt.
Set all your things in seemely good aray
115   Fit for so joyfull day,
The joyfulst day that ever sunne did see.
Faire Sun, shew forth thy favourable ray,
And let thy lifull° heat not fervent be   *full of life*
For feare of burning her sunshyny face,
120   Her beauty to disgrace.
O fayrest Phoebus,[3] father of the Muse,
If ever I did honour thee aright,
Or sing the thing, that mote° thy mind delight,   *could*
Doe not thy servants simple boone° refuse,   *favor*
125   But let this day let this one day be myne,
Let all the rest be thine.
Then I thy soverayne prayses loud wil sing,
That all the woods shal answer and theyr eccho ring.

Harke how the Minstrels gin to shrill aloud
130   Their merry Musick that resounds from far,

9. Venus, the evening or morning star.
1. The hours or time both create and recreate everything
in the world.
2. Venus, whose handmaids are the Graces, attributes of

courtesy and artistic expression.
3. Apollo, god of the sun and music, hence the father of
the Muses and the muse of lyric poetry.

The pipe, the tabor, and the trembling Croud,°   *violin*
That well agree withouten breach° or jar.   *discord*
But most of all the Damzels doe delite,
When they their tymbrels° smyte,   *tambourines*
135   And thereunto doe daunce and carrol sweet,
That all the sences they doe ravish quite,
The whyles the boyes run up and downe the street,
Crying aloud with strong confused noyce,
As if it were one voyce.
140   Hymen[4] io Hymen, Hymen they do shout,
That even to the heavens theyr shouting shrill
Doth reach, and all the firmament doth fill,
To which the people standing all about,
As in approvance° doe thereto applaud   *approval*
145   And loud advance her laud,°   *praise*
And evermore they Hymen Hymen sing,
That al the woods them answer and theyr eccho ring.

Loe where she comes along with portly° pace,   *dignified*
Lyke Phoebe[5] from her chamber of the East,
150   Arysing forth to run her mighty race,
Clad all in white, that seemes a virgin best.
So well it her beseemes° that ye would weene°   *befits / think*
Some angell she had beene.
Her long loose yellow locks lyke golden wyre,
155   Sprinckled with perle, and perling° flowres a tweene,°   *rippling / between*
Doe lyke a golden mantle her attyre,
And being crowned with a girland greene,
Seeme lyke some mayden Queene.
Her modest eyes abashed to behold
160   So many gazers, as on her do stare,
Upon the lowly ground affixed are.
Ne dare lift up her countenance too bold,
But blush to heare her prayses sung so loud,
So farre from being proud.
165   Nathlesse° doe ye still loud her prayses sing,   *nevertheless*
That all the woods may answer and your eccho ring.

Tell me ye merchants daughters did ye see
So fayre a creature in your towne before,
So sweet, so lovely, and so mild as she,
170   Adornd with beautyes grace and vertues store,
Her goodly eyes lyke Saphyres shining bright,
Her forehead yvory white,
Her cheekes lyke apples which the sun hath rudded,°   *reddened*
Her lips lyke cherryes charming men to byte,
175   Her brest like to a bowle of creame uncrudded,°   *uncurdled*
Her paps lyke lyllies budded,
Her snowie necke lyke to a marble towre,

---

4. The god of marriage who was invoked as part of the   5. Diana, goddess of the moon.
marriage ceremony.

And all her body like a pallace fayre,
Ascending uppe with many a stately stayre,
180   To honors seat and chastities sweet bowre.
Why stand ye still ye virgins in amaze,
Upon her so to gaze,
Whiles ye forget your former lay to sing,
To which the woods did answer and your eccho ring.

185   But if ye saw that which no eyes can see,
The inward beauty of her lively spright,
Garnisht with heavenly guifts of high degree,
Much more then would ye wonder at that sight,
And stand astonisht lyke to those which red°   *looked at*
190   Medusaes[6] mazeful hed.
There dwels sweet love and constant chastity,
Unspotted fayth and comely womanhood,
Regard of honour and mild modesty,
There vertue raynes as Queene in royal throne,
195   And giveth lawes alone.
The which the base affections doe obay,
And yeeld theyr services unto her will,
Ne thought of thing uncomely° ever may   *improper*
Thereto approch to tempt her mind to ill.
200   Had ye once seene these her celestial threasures,
And unrevealed pleasures,
Then would ye wonder and her prayses sing,
That al the woods should answer and your echo ring.

Open the temple gates unto my love,
205   Open them wide that she may enter in,
And all the postes adorne as doth behove,
And all the pillours deck with girlands trim,
For to recyve° this Saynt with honour dew,   *receive*
That commeth in to you.
210   With trembling steps and humble reverence,
She commeth in, before th'almighties vew,
Of her ye virgins learne obedience,
When so ye come into those holy places,
To humble your proud faces:
215   Bring her up to th'high altar that she may,
The sacred ceremonies there partake,
The which do endlesse matrimony make,
And let the roring Organs loudly play;
The praises of the Lord in lively notes,
220   The whiles with hollow throates
The Choristers the joyous Antheme sing,
That al the woods may answere and their eccho ring.

Behold whiles she before the altar stands
Hearing the holy priest that to her speakes

6. One of three mythological monstrous women, the Gorgons; Medusa, whose hair consisted of snakes (hence her head is "mazeful"), turned anyone who looked at her to stone.

225 And blesseth her with his two happy hands,
How the red roses flush up in her cheekes,
And the pure snow with goodly vermill° stayne,   *vermilion*
Like crimsin dyde in grayne,°   *fast dyed*
That even th'Angels which continually,
230 About the sacred Altare doe remaine,
Forget their service and about her fly,
Ofte peeping in her face that seemes more fayre,
The more they on it stare.
But her sad eyes still fastened on the ground,
235 Are governed with goodly modesty,
That suffers not one looke to glaunce awry,
Which may let in a little thought unsownd.°   *suspicions*
Why blush ye love to give to me your hand,
The pledge of all our band?
240 Sing ye sweet Angels, Alleluya sing,
That all the woods may answere and your eccho ring.

Now al is done; bring home the bride againe,
Bring home the triumph of our victory,
Bring home with you the glory of her gaine,
245 With joyance bring her and with jollity.°   *merriment*
Never had man more joyfull day then this,
Whom heaven would heape with blis.
Make feast therefore now all this live long day,
This day for ever to me holy is,
250 Poure out the wine without restraint or stay,
Poure not by cups, but by the belly full,
Poure out to all that wull,°   *will*
And sprinkle all the postes and wals with wine,
That they may sweat, and drunken be withall.
255 Crowne ye God Bacchus⁷ with a coronall,°   *garland*
And Hymen also crowne with wreathes of vine,
And let the Graces daunce unto the rest;
For they can doo it best:
The whiles the maydens doe theyr carroll sing,
260 To which the woods shal answer and theyr eccho ring.

Ring ye the bels, ye yong men of the towne,
And leave your wonted labors for this day:
This day is holy; doe ye write it downe,
That ye for ever it remember may.
265 This day the sunne is in his chiefest hight,
With Barnaby the bright,⁸
From whence declining daily by degrees,
He somewhat loseth of his heat and light,
When once the Crab⁹ behind his back he sees.
270 But for this time it ill ordained was,

---

7. The god of wine.
8. Spenser's wedding took place on St. Barnabas day, June 11, the solstice or longest day of the year in the Eliz- abethan calendar.
9. The constellation Cancer, through which the sun passes in late July.

To chose the longest day in all the yeare,
And shortest night, when longest fitter weare:°   *were*
Yet never day so long, but late would passe.
Ring ye the bels, to make it weare away,
275   And bonefiers° make all day,   *bonfires*
And daunce about them, and about them sing:
That all the woods may answer, and your eccho ring.

Ah when will this long weary day have end,
And lende me leave to come unto my love?
280   How slowly do the houres theyr numbers spend?
How slowly does sad Time his feathers° move?   *wings*
Hast thee O fayrest Planet[1] to thy home
Within the Westerne fome:°   *the sea*
Thy tyred steedes long since have need of rest.
285   Long though it be, at last I see it gloome,
And the bright evening star with golden creast
Appeare out of the East.
Fayre childe of beauty, glorious lampe of love
That all the host of heaven in rankes doost lead,
290   And guydest lovers through the nightes dread,
How chearefully thou lookest from above,
And seemst to laugh atweene° thy twinkling light   *between*
As joying in the sight
Of these glad many which for joy doe sing,
295   That all the woods them answer and their echo ring.

Now ceasse ye damsels your delights forepast;
Enough is it, that all the lay was youres:
Now day is doen, and night is nighing° fast: *approaching*
Now bring the Bryde into the brydall boures.°   *chambers*
300   Now night is come, now soone her disaray,°   *undress*
And in her bed her lay;
Lay her in lillies and in violets,
And silken courteins over her display,
And odourd sheetes, and Arras[2] coverlets.
305   Behold how goodly my faire love does ly
In proud humility;
Like unto Maia,[3] when as Jove her tooke,
In Tempe, lying on the flowry gras,
Twixt sleepe and wake, after she weary was,
310   With bathing in the Acidalian brooke.
Now it is night, ye damsels may be gon,
And leave my love alone,
And leave likewise your former lay to sing:
The woods no more shal answere, nor your echo ring.

315   Now welcome night, thou night so long expected,
That long daies labour doest at last defray,°   *repay*

1. The sun, according to Ptolomaic astronomy.
2. A town in France, famous for its textiles.

3. The daughter of Atlas and the mother of Mercury by Jupiter, i.e., Jove.

And all my cares, which cruell love collected,
Hast sumd in one, and cancelled for aye:°   *ever*
Spread thy broad wing over my love and me,

320   That no man may us see,
And in thy sable mantle us enwrap,
From feare of perrill and foule horror free.
Let no false treason seeke us to entrap,
Nor any dread disquiet once annoy

325   The safety of our joy:
But let the night be calme and quietsome,
Without tempestuous storms or sad afray:
Lyke as when Jove with fayre Alcmena[4] lay,
When he begot the great Tirynthian groome:

330   Or lyke as when he with thy selfe did lie,
And begot Majesty.
And let the mayds and yongmen cease to sing:
Ne let the woods them answer, nor theyr eccho ring.

Let no lamenting cryes, nor dolefull teares,
335   Be heard all night within nor yet without:
Ne let false whispers breeding hidden feares,
Breake gentle sleepe with misconceived dout.
Let no deluding dreames, nor dreadful sights
Make sudden sad affrights;

340   Ne let housefyres, nor lightnings helpelesse harmes,
Ne let the Pouke,° nor other evill sprights,   *a house fairy*
Ne let mischivous witches with theyr charmes,
Ne let hob Goblins, names whose sence we see not,
Fray° us with things that be not.   *frighten*

345   Let not the shriech Oule,° nor the Storke be heard: *screech owl*
Nor the night Raven that still deadly yels,
Nor damned ghosts cald up with mighty spels,
Nor griesly vultures make us once affeard:
Ne let th'unpleasant Quyre° of Frogs still croking   *choir*

350   Make us to wish theyr choking.
Let none of these theyr drery accents sing;
Ne let the woods them answer, nor theyr eccho ring.

But let stil Silence trew night watches keepe,
That sacred peace may in assurance rayne,
355   And tymely sleep, when it is tyme to sleepe,
May poure his limbs forth on your pleasant playne,°   *complaint of love*
The whiles an hundred little winged loves,
Like divers° fethered doves,   *many*
Shall fly and flutter round about your bed,

360   And in the secret darke, that none reproves,
Their prety stealthes shal worke, and snares shal spread
To filch away sweet snatches of delight,

4. The mother of Hercules, the "Tirynthian groom," who was supposed to have taken three nights to beget.

Conceald through covert night.
Ye sonnes of Venus, play your sports at will,
365   For greedy pleasure, carelesse of your toyes,
Thinks more upon her paradise of joyes,
Then what ye do, albe it good or ill.
All night therefore attend your merry play,
For it will soone be day:
370   Now none doth hinder you, that say or sing,
Ne will the woods now answer, nor your Eccho ring.

Who is the same, which at my window peepes?
Or whose is that faire face, that shines so bright,
Is it not Cinthia,° she that never sleepes,   *the moon*
375   But walkes about high heaven al the night?
O fayrest goddesse, do thou not envy
My love with me to spy:
For thou likewise didst love, though now unthought,
And for a fleece of woll, which privily,
380   The Latmian shephard[5] once unto thee brought,
His pleasures with thee wrought.
Therefore to us be favorable now;
And sith of wemens labours thou hast charge,
And generation goodly dost enlarge,
385   Encline thy will t'effect our wishfull vow,
And the chast wombe informe° with timely seed,   *implant*
That may our comfort breed:
Till which we cease our hopefull hap° to sing,   *condition*
Ne let the woods us answere, nor our Eccho ring.

390   And thou great Juno,[6] which with awful might
The lawes of wedlock still dost patronize,
And the religion of the faith first plight
With sacred rites hast taught to solemnize:
And eeke for comfort often called art
395   Of women in their smart,
Eternally bind thou this lovely band,
And all thy blessings unto us impart.
And thou glad Genius,[7] in whose gentle hand,
The bridale bowre and geniall° bed remaine,   *generative*
400   Without blemish or staine,
And the sweet pleasures of theyr loves delight
With secret ayde doest succour and supply,
Till they bring forth the fruitfull progeny,
Send us the timely fruit of this same night.
405   And thou fayre Hebe,[8] and thou Hymen free,
Grant that it may so be.
Til which we cease your further prayse to sing,
Ne any woods shal answer, nor your Eccho ring.

5. Endymion, beloved of Diana, goddess of the moon,   7. In Roman religion, the spirit of paternity who protect-
chastity, and childbirth, also known as Cynthia.   ed the family.
6. Wife of Jupiter, goddess of marriage.   8. Handmaid to the gods, daughter of Jupiter and Juno.

410 And ye high heavens, the temple of the gods,
In which a thousand torches flaming bright
Doe burne, that to us wretched earthly clods:
In dreadful darknesse lend desired light;
And all ye powers which in the same remayne,
More than we men can fayne,° *represent*
415 Poure out your blessing on us plentiously,
And happy influence upon us raine,
That we may raise a large posterity,
Which from the earth, which they may long possesse,
With lasting happinesse,
420 Up to your haughty° pallaces may mount, *high*
And for the guerdon° of theyr glorious merit *reward*
May heavenly tabernacles there inherit,
Of blessed Saints for to increase the count.
So let us rest, sweet love, in hope of this,
425 And cease till then our tymely joyes to sing,
The woods no more us answer, nor our eccho ring.

Song made in lieu of many ornaments,
With which my love should duly have bene dect,° *bedecked*
Which cutting off through hasty accidents,
430 Ye would not stay your dew time to expect,
But promist both to recompens,
Be unto her a goodly ornament,
And for short time an endlesse moniment.

Sir Philip Sidney
1554–1586

Reality is often stranger but hardly ever more perfect than fiction. As Sir Philip Sidney tells us, the poets bring forth a "golden world." Exempt from judgments about its truth or falsehood, "poetry" (by which Sidney meant fiction) should construct forms of the ideal to mitigate our suffering and move us to good action. Sidney's own work comments brilliantly on contemporary moral and political issues: his sonnet sequence *Astrophil and Stella* illustrates the lover's paradox (love may require chastity); his prose romance *The Arcadia* describes the politics of love and sexuality; and his *Apology for Poetry* defends poetic and dramatic art from critics who would dismiss it in favor of philosophy and history. Yet to his countrymen, Sidney's most important achievement may have been a life dedicated to a public heroism and shaped by a sense of personal honor.

History has portrayed him as a prodigy. As his friend Fulke Greville wrote, "though I knew him from a child, yet I never knew him other than a man, . . . his very play tending to enrich his mind, so that even his teachers found something in him to observe and learn above that which they had usually read or taught." Play—understood in the Renaissance manner as "serious play"—took up much of Sidney's early career. Leaving Oxford at the age of seventeen but without a degree, Sidney embarked on what in later centuries was known as the Grand Tour. He visited Europe's major cities, seeking men and women who were fashioning the political goals and aesthetic sensibilities of the age. They included the philosopher Hubert Languet, whose Protestantism was linked to a fiercely antityrannical politics; the artists Tintoretto and Paolo Veronese, whose luminous realism was to determine painterly style for more than a generation; and, finally, Henry of Navarre (later King Henry IV of France) and his wife, Margaret of Valois, whose reign would see the worst of the religious wars in Europe. Back in England by 1575, Sidney espoused a politics that challenged authority. Siding with his father, Henry Sidney, Queen Elizabeth's Lord Deputy Governor of Ireland, he argued for imposing a land tax on the Anglo-Irish nobility, citing their "unreasonable and arrogant pretensions" as a cause of civil unrest. And in 1580, seeking to protect the monarchy from foreign influences, he wrote to the Queen cautioning her against a match with Francis, Duke of Alençon and brother to the French king, Henry III. She was furious at his temerity and ordered him to the country, where he was to remain out of touch with court affairs. By 1584 she had relented, sending Sidney to the Netherlands to assess the Protestant resistance to Spanish rule. There, in 1586, fighting for the Queen's interest and the Protestant cause she championed, he died of an abscessed bullet wound in his thigh.

Sidney's first literary work was a brief pastoral masque entitled *The Lady of May*, composed in honor of the Queen in 1578. His subsequent exile from court provided him with extensive time to write. He was often at Wilton, the estate of his sister, Mary Herbert, Countess of Pembroke; it was there that he wrote the first two of his major works, in all likelihood with his sister and her circle as his first readers and critics. *The Apology for Poetry*, a work defending what Sidney called his "unelected vocation," answers attacks on art, poetry, and the theater by such censorious writers as Stephen Gosson. But its argument exceeds the limits of antitheatrical debate to embrace questions about the uses of history and the effectiveness of philosophy—a subject that bears comparison with the poetics of Aristotle and Horace. Readers have remembered most its insistence that "poetry" goes beyond nature to fashion an ideal; it works "not only to make a Cyrus, which had been but a particular excellency as nature might have done, but to bestow a Cyrus upon the world to make many Cyruses." Poetry's creatures—whether heroes, heroines, or villains—cannot misrepresent fact because they exist only in the imagination of readers and listeners: "for the poet," Sidney declared, "he nothing affirms, and therefore never lieth."

Sidney's last work, *Astrophil and Stella,* has often been understood as self-satire. Its principal character, the young Astrophil, is frustrated by the marriage of his beloved Stella to a man who is characterized as "rich," an apparent reference to Sidney's disappointment when Penelope Devereux, whom he had courted for several years, married Lord Rich. Sidney mocks the young lover's passionate complaints while at the same time transforming the courtly figure of the distant yet beloved lady to reveal a paradox: as "absent," Stella may be present to Astrophil in spirit; as "present," she can only deny him her intimate friendship. The sequence is a marvelously witty reconceptualization of the principal themes of English Petrarchanism, a style that by the 1580s had become rather trite. Addressing his Stella, Sidney's Astrophil ends a sonnet with these lines:

> And not content to be Perfection's heir
> Thyself, doest strive all minds that way to move:
> Who mark in thee what is in thee most fair.
> So while thy beauty draws the heart to love,
> As fast thy virtue bends that love to good:
> But ah, Desire still cries, give me some food.

Conventionally Petrarchan in his depiction of the lady as a model and inspiration to a moral virtue that would seem to rule out any physical expressions of love, Sidney is at last very unconventional: he refuses to renounce "Desire" and its "food," or sexual gratification. A more imitative poet would not have so rejected Petrarch's idealistic asceticism. But just as Sidney had challenged the authority of church and state to promote better government (as he saw it), so did he exploit the process of "invention," the discovery of new meaning in old matter, to revitalize literary forms and expression.

from **Astrophil and Stella**[1]

1

Loving in truth, and fain° in verse my love to show,   *wishing*
That she (dear she) might take some pleasure of my pain:
Pleasure might cause her read, reading might make her know,
Knowledge might pity win, and pity grace obtain,
5   I sought fit words to paint the blackest face of woe,
Studying inventions[2] fine, her wits to entertain:
Oft turning others' leaves, to see if thence would flow
Some fresh and fruitfull showers upon my sun-burned brain.
But words came halting forth, wanting Invention's stay,°   *support*
10   Invention Nature's child, fled step-dame Study's blows,
And others' feet still seemed but strangers in my way.
Thus great with child to speak, and helpless in my throes,°   *agonies*
Biting my trewand° pen, beating my self for spite,   *truant*
Fool, said my Muse to me, look in thy heart and write.

31

With how sad steps, O Moon, thou climb'st the skies,
How silently, and with how wan° a face,   *pale*
What may it be, that even in heavenly place
That busy archer° his sharp arrows tries?   *Cupid*
5   Sure if° that long with Love acquainted eyes   *surely if those*
Can judge of Love, thou feel'st a lover's case;
I read it in thy looks, thy languished grace
To me that feel the like, thy state descries.°   *reveals*
Then ev'n of fellowship, O Moon, tell me
10   Is constant Love deemed there but want of wit?
Are Beauties there as proud as here they be?
Do they above love to be loved, and yet
Those lovers scorn whom that Love doth possess?
Do they call Virtue there ungratefulness?

39

Come sleep, O sleep, the certain knot of peace,
The baiting° place of wit, the balm of woe,   *resting*
The poor man's wealth, the prisoner's release,
Th'indifferent judge between the high and low;
5   With shield of proof° shield me from out the prease°   *proven shield/throng*
Of those fierce darts, despair at me doth throw:
O make in me those civil wars to cease;
I will good tribute pay if thou do so.
Take thou of me smooth pillows, sweetest bed,
10   A chamber deaf to noise, and blind to light:
A rosy garland, and a weary head:
And if these things, as being thine by right,
Move not thy heavy grace, thou shalt in me
Livelier then elsewhere Stella's image see.

1. This sonnet sequence was composed in 1582, published in 1591.
2. "Invention" was the term early modern rhetoricians used to designate the choice of a literary subject and its development as an argument, in contrast to the forms of expression, figures of thought and speech, and imagery by which that subject was conveyed. As Sidney suggests, "invention" depended on the writer's imaginative intelligence, not on his literary education.

71

Who will in fairest book of Nature[3] know,
How Virtue may best lodged in beauty be,
Let him but learn of Love to read in thee
Stella, those fair lines, which true goodness show.
5   There shall he find all vices overthrow,°   *overthrown*
Not by rude force, but sweetest sovereignty
Of reason, from whose light those night-birds fly;
That inward sun in thine eyes shineth so.
And not content to be Perfection's heir
10   Thyself, doest strive all minds that way to move:
Who mark in thee what is in thee most fair.
So while thy beauty draws the heart to love,
As fast thy Virtue bends that love to good:
But ah, Desire still cries, give me some food.

106

O absent presence, Stella is not here;
False flattering hope, that with so fair a face,
Bare° me in hand, that in this orphan place,   *took*
Stella, I say my Stella, should appear.
5   What sayest thou now, where is that dainty cheer,°   *food*
Thou toldst mine eyes should help their famist° case?   *famished*
But thou art gone now that self felt disgrace,
Doth make me most to wish thy comfort near.[4]
But here I do store of fair ladies meet,
10   Who may with charm of conversation sweet,
Make in my heavy mold new thoughts to grow:
Sure they prevail as much with me, as he
That bad his friend but then new maimed,° to be   *wounded*
Merry with him, and not think of his woe.

108

When sorrow (using mine own fire's might)
Melts down his lead into my boiling breast,
Through that dark furnace to heart oppressed,
There shines a joy from thee my only light;
5   But soon as thought of thee breeds my delight,
And my young soul flutters to thee his nest,
Most rude despair my daily unbidden guest,
Clips straight my wings, straight wraps me in his night,
And makes me then bow down my head, and say,
10   Ah what doth Phoebus' gold that wretch avail,
Whom iron doors do keep from use of day?
So strangely (alas) thy works[5] in me prevail,
That in my woes for thee thou art my joy,
And in my joys for thee my only annoy.

---

3. All of creation, in effect the second "book" of God and a
supplement to the Bible. It was a philosophical commonplace that Nature was the repository of natural law, which
all human beings could discover through reason, just as the
Bible held divine law, which was revealed to the faithful

through grace.
4. I.e., you are gone now that that self (my own self) has felt
the disgrace of rejection; this makes me wish you here.
5. I.e., "your works," what you have done and meant,
affect me strangely.

from **The Apology for Poetry**

When the right virtuous Edward Wotton[1] and I were at the Emperor's court together, we gave ourselves to learn horsemanship of John Pietro Pugliano, one that with great commendation had the place of an esquire in his stable. And he, according to the fertileness of the Italian wit, did not only afford us the demonstration of his practice, but sought to enrich our minds with the contemplations therein, which he thought most precious. But with none I remember mine ears were at that time more laden, than when (either angered with slow payment, or moved with our learner-like admiration) he exercised his speech in the praise of his faculty. He said soldiers were the noblest estate of mankind, and horsemen the noblest of soldiers. He said they were the masters of war and ornaments of peace, speedy goers and strong abiders, triumphers both in camps and courts. Nay, to so unbelieved a point he proceeded as that no earthly thing bred such wonder to a prince as to be a good horseman—skill of government was but a *pedanteria* [pedantry] in comparison. Then would he add certain praises, by telling what a peerless beast the horse was, the only serviceable courtier without flattery, the beast of most beauty, faithfulness, courage, and such more, that if I had not been a piece of a logician before I came to him, I think he would have persuaded me to have wished myself a horse. But thus much at least with his no few words he drave into me, that self-love is better than any gilding to make that seem gorgeous wherein ourselves be parties. Wherein, if Pugliano's strong affection and weak arguments will not satisfy you, I will give you a nearer example of myself, who (I know not by what mischance) in these my not old years and idlest times having slipped into the title of a poet, am provoked to say something unto you in the defense of that my unelected vocation,[2] which if I handle with more good will than good reasons, bear with me, since the scholar is to be pardoned that followeth the steps of his master. And yet I must say that, as I have more just cause to make a pitiful defense of poor poetry, which from almost the highest estimation of learning is fallen to be the laughingstock of children, so have I need to bring some more available proofs: since the former is by no man barred of his deserved credit, the silly latter hath had even the names of philosophers used to the defacing of it, with great danger of civil war among the Muses.[3]

And first, truly, to all them that, professing learning, inveigh against poetry may justly be objected that they go very near to ungratefulness, to seek to deface that which, in the noblest nations and languages that are known, hath been the first light-giver to ignorance, and first nurse, whose milk by little and little enabled them to feed afterwards of tougher knowledges. And will they now play the hedgehog that, being received into the den, drive out his host? Or rather the vipers, that with their birth kill their parents?

Let learned Greece in any of his manifold sciences be able to show me one book before Musaeus, Homer, and Hesiod, all three nothing else but poets.[4] Nay, let any history be brought that can say any writers were there before them, if they were not

1. Edward Wotton (1548–1626), half-brother of Henry Wotton who saw diplomatic service under James I. Edward Wotton and Sidney undertook a mission to the court of the Emperor Maximilian at Vienna in 1574–1575.

2. Sidney refers to writing poetry as his "unelected vocation" because he would have readers believe that he undertook it only after Elizabeth I had exiled him from court.

3. Mythological figures who were thought to inspire the liberal arts.

4. Musaeus was in fact a poet of the 5th century A.D., reported to be a pupil of the mythical Orpheus, the first musician. Homer was the legendary author of the *Iliad*, an epic poem telling of the seige of Troy by the army of the Greeks led by the hero, Achilles; and of the *Odyssey*, recounting the return of the hero, Odysseus, from Troy to his homeland in Ithaka. Hesiod is known as the poet of the *Theogony*, which tells the story of the gods in Greece; and of *Works and Days*, which describes the rituals and practices of the agricultural year. Both Homer and Hesiod lived in the 8th century B.C.

men of the same skill, as Orpheus, Linus,[5] and some other are named, who, having been the first of that country that made pens deliverers of their knowledge to the posterity, may justly challenge to be called their fathers in learning: for not only in time they had this priority (although in itself antiquity be venerable) but went before them, as causes to draw with their charming sweetness the wild untamed wits to an admiration of knowledge. So, as Amphion[6] was said to move stones with his poetry to build Thebes, and Orpheus to be listened to by beasts—indeed stony and beastly people—so among the Romans were Livius Andronicus and Ennius. So in the Italian language the first that made it aspire to be a treasure-house of science were the poets Dante, Boccaccio, and Petrarch. So in our English were Gower and Chaucer, after whom, encouraged and delighted with their excellent fore-going,[7] others have followed, to beautify our mother tongue, as well in the same kind as in other arts.

This did so notably show itself, that the philosophers of Greece durst not a long time appear to the world but under the masks of poets. So Thales, Empedocles, and Parmenides[8] sang their natural philosophy in verses; so did Pythagoras and Phocylides their moral counsels; so did Tyrtaeus in war matters, and Solon in matters of policy: or rather they, being poets, did exercise their delightful vein in those points of highest knowledge, which before them lay hid to the world. For that wise Solon was directly a poet it is manifest, having written in verse the notable fable of the Atlantic Island, which was continued by Plato. And truly even Plato[9] whosoever well considereth shall find that in the body of his work, though the inside and strength were philosophy, the skin, as it were, and beauty depended most of[1] poetry: for all standeth upon dialogues, wherein he feigneth many honest burgesses of Athens to speak of such matters, that, if they had been set on the rack, they would never have confessed them, besides his poetical describing the circumstances of their meetings, as the well ordering of a banquet,[2] the delicacy of a walk, with interlacing mere tales, as Gyges' ring and others, which who knoweth not to be flowers of poetry did never walk into Apollo's garden.[3]

And even historiographers (although their lips sound of things done, and verity[4] be written in their foreheads) have been glad to borrow both fashion and, perchance, weight of the poets. So Herodotus entitled his History by the name of the nine Muses;[5] and both he and all the rest that followed him either stale[6] or usurped of poetry

---

5. Supposed to have been the teacher of Orpheus.

6. Sidney lists historical and legendary poets to illustrate his claim that they were the founders of civilization and culture. Amphion was supposed to have moved stones by playing his music and thus to have built the walls of Troy; Livius Andronicus (c. 284–204 B.C.) was believed to have been the first Latin poet; Ennius (c. 239–169 B.C.) was traditionally regarded as the greatest of the early Latin poets. Dante, Boccaccio, and Petrarch were the first of the great Italian poets of the early Renaissance; Chaucer and Gower were the most important of the late medieval poets who wrote in English.

7. Example.

8. Sidney lists the best-known of the Greek philosophers before Plato: Thales, a geometrician; Empedocles, who studied the concepts of change and permanence; Parmeneides, who investigated the nature of being; Pythagoras, a mathematician and astronomer; Phocylides, a moralist; and Tyrtaeus, a poet. Solon (c. 640–558 B.C.) was an Athenian statesman, poet, and constitutional reformer. No trace remains of a poem by Solon telling of Atlantis, an island beyond the pillars of

Hercules that vanishes beneath the sea; Sidney recalls Plato's dialogue (Timaeus, 21–24), in which Critias tells Socrates that the story of Atlantis originates in an unfinished poem of Solon.

9. Author of many works of philosophy in dialogue form, notably The Republic, on the construction of an ideal state, and The Symposium, on the nature of love and its association with beauty and truth. He was a key influence on Renaissance thinkers.

1. On.

2. A banquet is the setting of The Symposium; speakers take a walk in the The Phaedrus; and the story of Gyges' ring is told in The Republic.

3. Apollo was the god of poetry.

4. Truth.

5. Herodotus, a Greek historian (480–425) B.C.), wrote about the struggle between Asia and Greece; later classical editors divided his work, which he entitled simply History, into nine books named after the nine Muses: Calliope, Clio, Euterpe, Melpomene, Terpsichore, Erato, Polyhymnia, Urania, and Thalia.

6. Stole.

their passionate describing of passions, the many particularities of battles, which no man could affirm; or, if that be denied me, long orations put in the mouths of great kings and captains, which it is certain they never pronounced.

So that truly neither philosopher nor historiographer could at the first have entered into the gates of popular judgments, if they had not taken a great passport of poetry, which in all nations at this day where learning flourisheth not, is plain to be seen; in all which they have some feeling of poetry.

In Turkey, besides their law-giving divines, they have no other writers but poets. In our neighbor country Ireland, where truly learning goeth very bare, yet are their poets held in a devout reverence. Even among the most barbarous and simple Indians where no writing is, yet have they their poets who make and sing songs, which they call areytos,[7] both of their ancestors' deeds and praises of their gods: a sufficient probability that, if ever learning come among them, it must be by having their hard dull wits softened and sharpened with the sweet delights of poetry—for until they find a pleasure in the exercises of the mind, great promises of much knowledge will little persuade them that know not the fruits of knowledge. In Wales, the true remnant of the ancient Britons, as there are good authorities to show the long time they had poets, which they called bards, so through all the conquests of Romans, Saxons, Danes, and Normans, some of whom did seek to ruin all memory of learning from among them, yet do their poets even to this day last; so as it is not more notable in soon beginning than in long continuing.

But since the authors of most of our sciences[8] were the Romans, and before them the Greeks, let us a little stand upon their authorities, but even so far as to see what names they have given unto this now scorned skill.

Among the Romans a poet was called vates, which is as much as a diviner, foreseer, or prophet, as by his conjoined words vaticinium [prediction] and vaticinari [to foretell] is manifest: so heavenly a title did that excellent people bestow upon this heart-ravishing knowledge. And so far were they carried into the admiration thereof, that they thought in the chanceable hitting upon any such verses great foretokens of their following fortunes were placed. Whereupon grew the word of Sortes Virgilianae,[9] when by sudden opening Virgil's book they lighted upon any verse of his making, whereof the histories of the emperors' lives are full: as of Albinus, the governor of our island, who in his childhood met with this verse

> Arma amens capio nec sat rationis in armis[1]

and in his age performed it. Which, although it were a very vain and godless superstition, as also it was to think spirits were commanded by such verses—whereupon this word charms, derived of carmina [songs], cometh—so yet serveth it to show the great reverence those wits were held in; and altogether not without ground, since both the oracles of Delphos and Sibylla's prophecies were wholly delivered in verses.[2] For that same exquisite observing of number and measure[3] in the words, and that high flying liberty of conceit proper to the poet, did seem to have some divine force in it.

---

7. A West Indian dance, recorded by José de Acosta in his Natural and Moral History of the West Indies (translated into English in 1604).
8. Any body of knowledge, typically natural philosophy and also including ethics and politics.
9. The Virgilian lots, or fortune as it is implied in lines from the Aeneid, which the reader chose at random and then subjects to interpretation.

1. "I seize arms madly, nor is there reason in arming" (2.314).
2. The shrine of Apollo at Delphi was presided over by a priestess who was believed to know the god's thoughts about the future; the Sibyls were supposed to be ancient prophetesses whose words were collected in the Sibylline Books.
3. Meter and rhythm.

And may not I presume a little further, to show the reasonableness of this word *vates*, and say that the holy David's Psalms are a divine poem? If I do, I shall not do it without the testimony of great learned men, both ancient and modern. But even the name of Psalms will speak for me, which being interpreted, is nothing but songs; then that it is fully written in meter, as all learned Hebricians agree, although the rules be not yet fully found; lastly and principally, his handling his prophecy, which is merely poetical: for what else is the awaking his musical instruments, the often and free changing of persons, his notable *prosopopoeias* [personifications], when he maketh you, as it were, see God coming in His majesty, his telling of the beasts' joyfulness and hills leaping,[4] but a heavenly poesy, wherein almost he showeth himself a passionate lover of that unspeakable and everlasting beauty to be seen by the eyes of the mind, only cleared by faith? But truly now having named him, I fear me I seem to profane that holy name, applying it to poetry, which is among us thrown down to so ridiculous an estimation. But they that with quiet judgments will look a little deeper into it, shall find the end and working of it such as, being rightly applied, deserveth not to be scourged out of the Church of God.

But now let us see how the Greeks named it, and how they deemed of it. The Greeks called him a "poet," which name hath, as the most excellent, gone through other languages. It cometh of this word ποιεῖν, which is, to make: wherein, I know not whether by luck or wisdom, we Englishmen have met with the Greeks in calling him a maker: which name, how high and incomparable a title it is, I had rather were known by marking the scope of other sciences than by any partial allegation.

There is no art delivered to mankind that hath not the works of nature for his principal object, without which they could not consist, and on which they so depend, as they become actors and players, as it were, of what nature will have set forth. So doth the astronomer look upon the stars, and, by that he seeth, set down what order nature hath taken therein. So doth the geometrician and arithmetician in their diverse sorts of quantities. So doth the musicians in time tell you which by nature agree, which not. The natural philosopher thereon hath his name, and the moral philosopher standeth upon the natural virtues, vices, or passions of man; and follow nature (saith he) therein, and thou shalt not err. The lawyer saith what men have determined; the historian what men have done. The grammarian speaketh only of the rules of speech; and the rhetorician and logician, considering what in nature will soonest prove and persuade, thereon give artificial rules, which still are compassed within the circle of a question according to the proposed matter. The physician weigheth the nature of man's body, and the nature of things helpful or hurtful unto it. And the metaphysic,[5] though it be in the second and abstract notions, and therefore be counted supernatural, yet doth he indeed build upon the depth of nature. Only the poet, disdaining to be tied to any such subjection, lifted up with the vigor of his own invention, doth grow in effect another nature, in making things either better than nature bringeth forth, or, quite anew, forms such as never were in nature, as the Heroes, Demigods, Cyclops, Chimeras, Furies,[6] and such like: so as he

---

4. Psalm 29.
5. A philosopher who considered abstractions and aspects of mental and spiritual life entertained in a state of contemplation rather than of action.
6. Furies: supernatural forces figured as mad goddesses pursuing revenge; demigods: male offspring of a god and a mortal, having some divine powers; cyclops: a one-eyed giant; chimeras: imaginary monsters made up of grotesquely disparate parts.

goeth hand in hand with nature, not enclosed within the narrow warrant[7] of her gifts, but freely ranging only within the zodiac of his own wit. Nature never set forth the earth in so rich tapestry as divers poets have done; neither with so pleasant rivers, fruitful trees, sweet-smelling flowers, nor whatsoever else may make the too much loved earth more lovely. Her world is brazen, the poets only deliver a golden.

But let those things alone, and go to man—for whom as the other things are, so it seemeth in him her uttermost cunning is employed—and know whether she have brought forth so true a lover as Theagenes, so constant a friend as Pylades, so valiant a man as Orlando, so right a prince as Xenophon's Cyrus, so excellent a man every way as Virgil's Aeneas.[8] Neither let this be jestingly conceived, because the works of the one be essential, the other in imitation or fiction; for any understanding knoweth the skill of each artificer standeth in that *idea* or fore-conceit[9] of the work, and not in the work itself. And that the poet hath that *idea* is manifest, by delivering them forth in such excellency as he had imagined them. Which delivering forth also is not wholly imaginative, as we are wont to say by them that build castles in the air; but so far substantially it worketh, not only to make a Cyrus, which had been but a particular excellency as nature might have done, but to bestow a Cyrus upon the world to make many Cyruses, if they will learn aright why and how that maker made him.

Neither let it be deemed too saucy a comparison to balance the highest point of man's wit with the efficacy of nature; but rather give right honor to the heavenly Maker of that maker, who having made man to His own likeness, set him beyond and over all the works of that second nature: which in nothing he showeth so much as in poetry, when with the force of a divine breath he bringeth things forth surpassing her doings—with no small arguments to the credulous of that first accursed fall of Adam, since our erected wit maketh us know what perfection is, and yet our infected will keepeth us from reaching unto it. But these arguments will by few be understood, and by fewer granted. This much (I hope) will be given me, that the Greeks with some probability of reason gave him the name above all names of learning.

* * * [Now let us show] the poet's nobleness, by setting him before his other competitors. Among whom as principal challengers step forth the moral philosophers, whom, me thinketh, I see coming towards me with a sullen gravity, as though they could not abide vice by daylight, rudely clothed for to witness outwardly their contempt of outward things, with books in their hands against glory, whereto they set their names, sophistically speaking against subtlety, and angry with any man in whom they see the foul fault of anger. These men casting largess as they go, of definitions, divisions, and distinctions, with a scornful interrogative do soberly ask whether it be possible to find any path so ready to lead a man to virtue as that which teacheth what virtue is; and teach it not only by delivering forth his very being, his causes and

---

7. Authority.

8. Sidney cites men recognized for their virtues. Theagenes exemplifies the true lover in Heliodorus's romance, the *Aethiopica*; Pylades, who helped Orestes avenge his father Agamemnon's murder, was cited by Renaissance commentators as a perfect friend; Orlando (modeled on Roland, the knight who fought for Charlemagne against the Basques at the battle of Roncesvalles, A.D. 778) was the hero of Ariosto's *Orlando Furioso* and illustrated the Renaissance idea of valor. The *Anabasis* of Xenophon (himself a general in Cyrus's army) relates how Cyrus the Younger, a Persian

prince, helped the Peloponnesians resist the army of Athens and then died in an attempt to take the Persian throne from his brother Artaxerxes in the fifth century B.C. Aeneas, the hero of Virgil's *Aeneid* and the mythical founder of the Roman Empire, was generally considered to be the epitome of the statesman.

9. The element of the literary work that determines how and to what end its subject is conveyed. Sidney later states that an *Idea* works "substantially" because it makes readers want to imitate the virtuous characters represented in a literary work.

effects, but also by making known his enemy, vice, which must be destroyed, and his cumbersome servant, passion, which must be mastered; by showing the generalities that containeth it, and the specialities that are derived from it; lastly, by plain setting down how it extendeth itself out of the limits of a man's own little world to the government of families and maintaining of public societies.

The historian scarcely giveth leisure to the moralist to say so much, but that he, laden with old mouse-eaten records, authorizing himself (for the most part) upon other histories, whose greatest authorities are built upon the notable foundation of hearsay; having much ado to accord differing writers and to pick truth out of their partiality; better acquainted with a thousand years ago than with the present age, and yet better knowing how this world goeth than how his own wit runneth; curious for antiquities and inquisitive of novelties; a wonder to young folks and a tyrant in table talk, denieth, in a great chafe,[1] that any man for teaching of virtue, and virtuous actions is comparable to him. "I am *testis temporum, lux veritatis, vita memoriae, magistra vitae, nuntia vetustatis*.[2] The philosopher," saith he, "teacheth a disputative virtue, but I do an active. His virtue is excellent in the dangerless Academy of Plato,[3] but mine showeth forth her honorable face in the battles of Marathon, Pharsalia, Poitiers, and Agincourt.[4] He teacheth virtue by certain abstract considerations, but I only bid you follow the footing of them that have gone before you. Old-aged experience goeth beyond the fine-witted philosopher, but I give the experience of many ages. Lastly, if he make the songbook, I put the learner's hand to the lute; and if he be the guide, I am the light." Then would he allege you innumerable examples, confirming story by stories, how much the wisest senators and princes have been directed by the credit of history, as Brutus, Alphonsus of Aragon,[5] and who not, if need be? At length the long line of their disputation maketh a point in this, that the one giveth the precept, and the other the example.

Now whom shall we find (since the question standeth for the highest form in the school of learning) to be moderator? Truly, as me seemeth, the poet; and if not a moderator, even the man that ought to carry the title from them both, and much more from all other serving sciences. Therefore compare we the poet with the historian and with the moral philosopher; and if he go beyond them both, no other human skill can match him. For as for the divine, with all reverence it is ever to be excepted, not only for having his scope as far beyond any of these as eternity exceedeth a moment, but even for passing each of these in themselves. And for the lawyer, though *Ius* [Right] be the daughter of Justice, and justice the chief of virtues, yet because he seeketh to make men good rather *formidine poenae* than *virtutis amore*;[6] or, to say righter, doth not endeavor to make men good, but that their evil hurt not others; having no care, so he be a good citizen, how bad a man he be: therefore as our wickedness maketh him necessary, and necessity maketh

---

1. Heat, fury.

2. Sidney quotes Cicero in his *De Oratore* (*Concerning the Orator*): "I am the witness of time, the light of truth, the life of memory, the governess of life, the herald of antiquity."

3. The olive grove near Athens, where Plato and his successors taught philosophy.

4. Sidney mentions some memorable battles: The Athenians defeated the invading Persians at Marathon in 490 B.C.; Caesar defeated Pompey at Pharsalus in 48 B.C.; the Franks, under Charles Martel, defeated the Moors, led by Spanish emir Abd al-Rahman Ghafiqi in 732; the English, under Edward, the Black Prince, overcame the

French army and captured their king, John II in 1356, each time at Poitiers; finally, Henry V defeated the French in 1415 at Agincourt.

5. Brutus: Roman statesman, one of Caesar's assassins, who is said to have spent the night before the battle of Pharsalus reading history; Alphonsus: King of Aragon and Sicily who encouraged his soldiers to seize the libraries of those they conquered and to bring their books to him.

6. I.e., rather "from fear of punishment" than "from love of virtue" (Horace, *Epistles* 1.2.62). Sidney distinguishes between staying within the law and moral behavior.

him honorable, so is he not in the deepest truth to stand in rank with these who all endeavor to take naughtiness away and plant goodness even in the secretest cabinet of our souls. And these four are all that any way deal in that consideration of men's manners, which being the supreme knowledge, they that best breed it deserve the best commendation.

The philosopher, therefore, and the historian are they which would win the goal, the one by precept, the other by example. But both, not having both, do both halt.[7] For the philosopher, setting down with thorny arguments the bare rule, is so hard of utterance and so misty to be conceived, that one that hath no other guide but him shall wade in him till he be old before he shall find sufficient cause to be honest. For his knowledge standeth so upon the abstract and general, that happy is that man who may understand him, and more happy that can apply what he doth understand. On the other side, the historian, wanting the precept, is so tied, not to what should be but to what is, to the particular truth of things and not to the general reason of things, that his example draweth no necessary consequence, and therefore a less fruitful doctrine.

Now doth the peerless poet perform both: for whatsoever the philosopher saith should be done, he giveth a perfect picture of it in someone by whom he presupposeth it was done, so as he coupleth the general notion with the particular example. A perfect picture I say, for he yieldeth to the powers of the mind an image of that whereof the philosopher bestoweth but a wordish description, which doth neither strike, pierce, nor possess the sight of the soul so much as that other doth. For as in outward things, to a man that had never seen an elephant or a rhinoceros, who should tell him most exquisitely all their shapes, color, bigness, and particular marks, or of a gorgeous palace, an *architector* [architect], with declaring the full beauties, might well make the hearer able to repeat, as it were by rote, all he had heard, yet should never satisfy his inward conceit[8] with being witness to itself of a true lively knowledge; but the same man, as soon as he might see those beasts well painted, or the house well in model, should straightways grow, without need of any description, to a judicial comprehending of them: so no doubt the philosopher with his learned definitions—be it of virtue, vices, matters of public policy or private government— replenisheth the memory with many infallible grounds of wisdom, which, notwithstanding, lie dark before the imaginative and judging power, if they be not illuminated or figured forth by the speaking picture of poesy.

* * * [O]f all writers under the sun the poet is the least liar, and, though he would, as a poet can scarcely be a liar. The astronomer, with his cousin the geometrician, can hardly escape, when they take upon them to measure the height of the stars. How often, think you, do the physicians lie, when they aver things good for sicknesses, which afterwards send Charon[9] a great number of souls drowned in a potion before they come to his ferry? And no less of the rest, which take upon them to affirm. Now, for the poet, he nothing affirms, and therefore never lieth. For, as I take it, to lie is to affirm that to be true which is false. So as the other artists, and especially the historian, affirming many things, can, in the cloudy knowledge of mankind, hardly escape from many lies. But the poet (as I said before) never affirmeth. The poet never maketh any circles about your imagination, to conjure you to believe for true what he writes. He citeth not authorities of other histories, but

---

7. Limp.
8. The listener's mental picture or image.

9. According to Greek myth, Charon ferries souls across the River Styx to the underworld.

even for his entry calleth the sweet Muses to inspire into him a good invention; in truth, not laboring to tell you what is or is not, but what should or should not be. And therefore, though he recount things not true, yet because he telleth them not for true, he lieth not—without we will say that Nathan lied in his speech before-alleged to David; which as a wicked man durst scarce say, so think I none so simple would say that Aesop lied in the tales of his beasts; for who thinks that Aesop wrote it for actually true were well worthy to have his name chronicled among the beasts he writeth of. What child is there, that, coming to a play, and seeing *Thebes* written in great letters upon an old door, doth believe that it is Thebes? If then a man can arrive to that child's age to know that the poets' persons and doings are but pictures what should be, and not stories what have been, they will never give the lie to things not affirmatively but allegorically and figuratively written. And therefore, as in history, looking for truth, they may go away full fraught with falsehood, so in poesy, looking but for fiction, they shall use the narration but as an imaginative ground-plot of a profitable invention. But hereto is replied, that the poets give names to men they write of, which argueth a conceit of an actual truth, and so, not being true, proves a falsehood. And doth the lawyer lie then, when under the names of *John-a-stiles* and *John-a-nokes*[1] he puts his case? But that is easily answered. Their naming of men is but to make their picture the more lively, and not to build any history: painting men, they cannot leave men nameless. We see we cannot play at chess but that we must give names to our chessmen; and yet, methinks, he were a very partial champion of truth that would say we lied for giving a piece of wood the reverend title of a bishop. The poet nameth Cyrus or Aeneas no other way than to show what men of their fames, fortunes, and estates should do.

* * * So that since the ever-praiseworthy Poesy is full of virtue-breeding delightfulness, and void of no gift that ought to be in the noble name of learning; since the blames laid against it are either false or feeble; since the cause why it is not esteemed in England is the fault of poet-apes, not poets; since, lastly, our tongue is most fit to honor poesy, and to be honored by poesy; I conjure you all that have had the evil luck to read this ink-wasting toy of mine, even in the name of the nine Muses, no more to scorn the sacred mysteries of poesy; no more to laugh at the name of poets, as though they were next inheritors to fools; no more to jest at the reverent title of a rhymer; but to believe, with Aristotle, that they were the ancient treasurers of the Grecians' divinity; to believe, with Bembus, that they were first bringers-in of all civility; to believe, with Scaliger, that no philosopher's precepts can sooner make you an honest man than the reading of Virgil; to believe, with Clauserus,[2] the translator of Cornutus, that it pleased the heavenly Deity, by Hesiod and Homer, under the veil of fables, to give us all knowledge, logic, rhetoric, philosophy natural and moral, and *quid non?* [what not]; to believe, with me, that there are many mysteries contained in poetry, which of purpose were written darkly, lest by profane wits it should be abused; to believe, with Landino,[3] that they are so beloved of the gods that whatsoever they write proceeds of a divine fury; lastly, to believe themselves, when they tell you they will make you immortal by their verses. Thus doing, your name shall flourish in the printers' shops; thus doing, you shall be of kin to many a poetical preface; thus doing,

---

1. I.e., John Doe, or John Roe of ancient law courts.
2. Conrad Clauser, a 16th-century German scholar who translated the works of Lucius Annaeus Cornutus, a first-century Greek slave who wrote commentaries on Aristo-

tle and Virgil.
3. Cristofor Landino (1424–1504), an Italian humanist who wrote moral dialogues.

you shall be most fair, most rich, most wise, most all, you shall dwell upon superlatives; thus doing, though you be *libertino patre natus* [son of freed slave], you shall suddenly grow *Herculea proles* [a descendant of Hercules],

> *Si quid mea carmina possunt;*[4]

thus doing, your soul shall be placed with Dante's Beatrice, or Virgil's Anchises. But if (fie of such a but) you be born so near the dull-making cataract of Nilus[5] that you cannot hear the planet-like music of poetry; if you have so earth-creeping a mind that it cannot lift itself up to look to the sky of poetry, or rather, by a certain rustical disdain, will become such a mome as to be a Momus[6] of poetry; then, though I will not wish unto you the ass's ears of Midas, nor to be driven by a poet's verses, as Bubonax[7] was, to hang himself, nor to be rhymed to death, as is said to be done in Ireland; yet thus much curse I must send you, in the behalf of all poets, that while you live, you live in love, and never get favor for lacking skill of a sonnet; and, when you die, your memory die from the earth for want of an epitaph.

1579–80   1595

THE APOLOGY IN CONTEXT
The Art of Poetry

After the spread of Reformation doctrine on the importance of moral discipline, English readers often encountered denunciations of poetry and especially drama. The issues that Sidney took up when he defended poetry were the subject of sharp dispute. Stephen Gosson represented the opinions of many of poetry's detractors. As he declares in *The School of Abuse*, published shortly before Sidney wrote his *Apology*, poetry provides frivolous distraction from the serious business of life and, what is worse, temptations to godlessness. But others, like Sidney, took a more optimistic view of the subject. In *The Art of English Poesy*, George Puttenham states that poets were the first lawgivers (as Sidney had) and focuses particularly on epic poetry, which, he says, give readers images of a truth beyond history as well as consistently inspiring models of action to imitate. His popular treatise contains a wealth of practical advice for aspiring writers and even today remains a useful sourcebook for information on rhetorical figures of thought and speech.

In addition to the challenge posed by moralists such as Gosson, defenders of English poetry also had to confront purely practical problems. Unlike the Romance languages—Italian, French, and Spanish—sixteenth-century English had lost almost all its feminine endings, the accented vowel sounds that made rhyming fairly easy. English was also a language in which words of one syllable were quite common, and poets had trouble creating the metrical harmonies usual in poetry written in languages rich in polysyllables. George Gascoigne's brief treatise *Certain Notes of Instruction concerning the making of verse or rhyme in English* deals with these conditions directly. He warns against trying to achieve euphony or a musical quality by "rolling in pleasant words," as in the sequence "Rim, Ram, Ruff," and he insists that the "truer Englishman" uses words of one syllable. Critics could differ in what

---

4. "If my songs can do anything" (*Aeneid*, 9.446).
5. Cicero claimed that hearing the sound of the cataracts of the Nile river in Egypt caused deafness; the Neoplatonists thought the movement of the planets produced heavenly music, the music of the spheres.
6. Momus personified the faultfinder in Greek literature; a mome is a blockhead. Apollo changed Midas's ears to

those of an ass to signal his stupidity after Midas judged Pan's flute playing to be superior to Apollo's (Ovid, *Metamorphosis* 11.146).
7. Sidney conflates Hipponax, a Greek poet, with Bupalus, a sculptor. The latter had made an unflattering portrait of the former, who took revenge with deadly verses. Irish poets claimed their verses could kill man or beast.

they valued, of course; in *A Defence of Rhyme,* Samuel Daniel justified rhyme as "pleasing to nature," which desires form and closures, not chaos and infinity. More important, he defended English writers against the claim that they could never match their classical precursors. He reminded readers that imputations of barbarism and ignorance are based on relative, not absolute, judgments.

Stephen Gosson
from *The School of Abuse*[1]

The Syracusans used such variety of dishes in their banquets that when they were set and their boards furnished,[2] they were many times in doubt which they should touch first or taste last. And in my opinion the world giveth every writer so large a field to walk in that before he set pen to the book, he shall find himself feasted at Syracuse, uncertain where to begin or when to end. This caused Pindarus[3] to question with his Muse whether he were better with his art to decipher the life of Nimpe Melia, or Cadmus's encounter with the dragon, or the wars of Hercules at the walls of Thebes, or Bacchus's cups, or Venus's juggling? He saw so many turnings laid open to his feet, that he knew not which way to bend his pace.

Therefore, as I cannot but commend his wisdom which in banqueting feeds most upon that that doth nourish best, so must I dispraise his method in writing which, following the course of amorous poets, dwelleth longest on those points that profit least, and like a wanton whelp,[4] leaveth the game[5] to run riot. The scarab flies over many a sweet flower and lights in a cowsherd.[6] It is the custom of the fly to leave the sound places of the horse and suck at the botch,[7] the nature of colloquintida[8] to draw the worst humors to itself, the manner of swine to forsake the fair fields and wallow in the mire, and the whole practice of poets, either with fables to show their abuses or with plain terms to unfold their mischief, discover their shame, discredit themselves, and disperse their poison through the world. Virgil sweats in describing his gnat, Ovid bestirreth him to paint out his flea; the one shows his art in the lust of Dido, the other his cunning in the incest of Myrrha and that trumpet of bawdry, the craft of love.[9]

I must confess that poets are the whetstones of wit, notwithstanding that wit is dearly bought. Where honey and gall are mixed, it will be hard to sever the one from the other. The deceitful physician giveth sweet syrups to make his poison go down the smoother, the juggler casteth a mist to work the closer, the siren's song is the sailor's wrack,[1] the fowler's whistle the bird's death, the wholesome bait the fish's

---

1. Stephen Gosson was a playwright who turned against the stage, and then wrote Puritanical critiques of what he considered its immorality. His *School of Abuse* was published in 1579.
2. Tables set.
3. Pindar, the most difficult and obscure of Greek poets, famous for his odes. The story of Cadmus's encounter with the dragon is a fragment of a cycle of legends about the city of Thebes; the legendary hero Hercules delivered the city of Thebes from the burden of paying tribute to the foreign king Orchomenus; Bacchus was the Roman god of wine; and Venus's "juggling" refers to her erotic escapades.
4. Unruly puppy.
5. Hunt.

6. Cow dung.
7. Ulcer.
8. A wild cucumber, used as an herbal medicine.
9. Dido, Queen of Carthage, with whom the legendary Trojan hero Aeneas stayed on his way to founding Rome; Virgil's *Aeneid* provides the best-known account of this episode. According to legend, Myrrha was the mother of the Greek god of vegetation, Adonis, by her father, King Cinyras, who, when he learned of his incest, changed her into a myrtle; the story is told by Ovid in his *Metamorphoses,* a poem describing erotic transformations. Gosson condemns Ovid's poem *Ars Amatoria,* or "the craft (or art) of love," as an immoral work ("bawdry" is licentiousness).
1. The mermaid's song is the sailor's shipwreck.

bane. The Harpies[2] have virgin faces, and the vultures, talents; Hyena speaks like a friend and devours like a foe; the calmest seas hide dangerous rocks; the wolf jets in wether's fells.[3] Many good sentences are spoken by David to shadow his knavery,[4] and written by poets as ornaments to beautify their works and set their trumpery to sale without suspect.

But if you look well to Epaeus's horse,[5] you shall find in his bowels the destruction of Troy; open the sepulchre of Semiramis,[6] whose title promiseth such wealth to the kings of Persia, you shall see nothing but dead bones; rip up the golden ball that Nero consecrated to Jupiter Capitolinus,[7] you shall [find] it stuffed with the shavings of his beard; pull off the visor that poets mask in, you shall disclose their reproach, bewray[8] their vanity, loathe their wantonness, lament their folly, and perceive their sharp sayings to be placed as pearls in dunghills, fresh pictures on rotten walls, chaste matrons' apparel on common courtesans. These are the cups of Circe,[9] that turn reasonable creatures into brute beasts; the balls of Hippomenes,[1] that hinder the course of Atalanta; and the blocks of the Devil, that are cast in our ways to cut off the race of toward wits. No marvel though Plato shut them out of his school and banished them quite from his commonwealth as effeminate writers,[2] unprofitable members, and utter enemies to virtue.

George Puttenham
from *The Art of English Poesie*[1]

How Poets were the first Philosophers, the first Astronomers and Historiographers, and Orators and Musicians of the world.[2]

Utterance also and language is given by nature to man for persuasion of others and aid of themselves, I mean the first ability to speak. For speech itself is artificial and made by man, and the more pleasing it is, the more it prevaileth to such purpose as it is intended for. But speech by meter is a kind of utterance more cleanly couched and more delicate to the ear than prose is, because it is more current and slipper upon the tongue and withal tunable and melodious as a kind of music and therefore may be termed a musical speech or utterance which cannot but please the hearer very well. Another cause is for that[3] is briefer and more compendious and easier to bear away and be retained in memory than that which is contained in multitude of words and

---

2. Monstrous and filthy birds whom Aeneas and his companions encounter.
3. The wolf strolls in sheep's clothing.
4. King of the ancient Israelites and poet of the psalms, David was guilty of adulterous love for Bathsheba, whose husband he murdered.
5. The Trojan horse.
6. Mythical queen of Assyria, who is supposed to have built the city of Babylon.
7. The Emperor Nero is said to have consecrated a golden ball to Jupiter in his temple on the Capitoline Hill in Rome.
8. Expose.
9. In Homer's *Odyssey*, the goddess who transformed the companions of Odysseus into swine.
1. The legendary suitor of Atalanta, who refused to marry anyone she could defeat in a footrace. Hippomenes won the race by dropping golden apples on the race track.

Atalanta could not resist stopping to pick them up, and her delay allowed Hippomenes victory.
2. Plato exiles poets from his ideal republic (see *The Republic* 3, 398A).
1. George Puttenham has always been assumed to be the author of *The Art of English Poesy*, a critical treatise that appeared in 1589. Dividing his work into three books: *Of Poets and Poesy*, *Of Proportion*, and *Of Ornament*, Puttenham discusses the works of English poets, poetic forms and genres, and figures of speech and thought respectively. The work as a whole is a compendium of contemporary ideas and practices illustrating the proper way to compose and appreciate poetry.
2. In his *Apology for Poetry*, Sidney also claims that poets were the first human beings to express feeling, thought, and a sense of the higher purposes of life.
3. I.e., poetry.

full of tedious ambage and long periods.[4] It is beside a manner of utterance more eloquent and rhetorical than the ordinary proof which we use in our daily talk, because it is decked and set out with all manner of fresh colors and figures, which maketh that it sooner inveigleth[5] the judgment of man and carryeth his opinion this way and that, whither soever the heart by impression of the ear shall be most affectionately bent and directed. The utterance in prose is not of so great efficacy because not only it is daily used, and by that occasion the care is over-glutted with it, but is also not so voluble and slipper on the tongue, being wide and loose, and nothing numerous nor contrived into measures and founded with so gallant and harmonical accents, nor in fine allowed that figurative conveyance[6] nor so great license in choice of words and phrases as meter is. So as the poets were also from the beginning the best persuaders and their eloquence the first rhetoric of the world, even so it became[7] that the high mysteries of the gods should be revealed and taught by a manner of utterance and language of extraordinary phrase and brief and compendious and above all others sweet and civil as the metrical is. The same also was meetest to register the lives and noble gifts of princes, and of the great monarchs of the world and all other memorable accidents of time, so as the poet was also the first historiographer. Then forasmuch as they were the first observers of all natural causes and effects in the things generable and corruptable, and from thence mounted up to search after the celestial courses and influences and yet penetrated further to know the divine essences and substances separate,[8] as is said before, they were the first astronomers and philosophists and metaphysics. Finally, because they did altogether endeavor themselves to reduce[9] the life of man to a certain method of good manners, and made the first differences between virtue and vice, and then tempered all these knowledges and skills with the exercise of a delectable music by melodious instruments, which withall served them to delight their hearers and to call the people together by admiration to a plausible and virtuous conversation, therefore were they the first philosophers ethic[1] and the first artificial musicians of the world. Such was Linus, Orpheus, Amphion, and Musaeus,[2] the most ancient poets and philosophers, of whom there is left any memory by the profane writers. King David also and Solomon his son and many other of the holy prophets wrote in meters and used to sing them to the harp,[3] although to many of us ignorant of the Hebrew language and phrase and not observing it, the same seem but a prose. It cannot be therefore that any scorn or indignity should justly be offered to so noble, profitable, ancient, and divine a science as Poesie is. * * *

Of historical poesie,[4] by which the famous acts of Princes and the virtuous and worthy lives of our forefathers were reported.

There is nothing in man of all the potential parts of his mind (reason and will excepted) more noble or more necessary to the active life than memory. Because it

4. Dull indirection and long sentences.
5. Appeals to.
6. Expression.
7. Was appropriate.
8. I.e., to know the divine essences and the particular objects present in the heavens.
9. Abstract.
1. I.e., philosophers who consider ethics.
2. Puttenham names legendary figures who were thought to be among the first poets: Linus, a poet and the teacher

of Hercules, who later killed him with his own lyre; Orpheus, commonly considered the first poet, whose music charmed even the animals; Amphion, the poet whose music moved stones to build Thebes; and Musaeus, said to have been a pupil of Orpheus.
3. Scripture provides accounts of King David, supposed to be the author of the psalms, and Solomon, to whom the Song of Songs is attributed.
4. Epic poetry.

maketh[5] most to a sound judgment and perfect worldly wisdom, examining and comparing the times past with the present and by them both considering the time to come, [it] concludeth with a steadfast resolution what is the best course to be taken in all his actions and advices in this world. It came upon this reason: experience [is] to be so highly commended in all consultations of importance and preferred before any learning or science, and yet experience is no more than a mass of memories assembled, that is, such trials as man hath made in time before. Right so, no kind of argument in all the oratory craft doth better persuade and more universally satisfy than example, which is but the representation of old memories and like successes [that have] happened in times past. For these regards, the poesie historical is of all other, next[6] the divine, most honorable and worthy, as well for the common benefit as for the special comfort every man receiveth by it. No one thing in the world with more delectation [is] reviving our spirits than to behold, as it were in a glass, the lively image of our dear forefathers, their noble and virtuous manner of life, with other things authentic, which because we are not able otherwise to attain to the knowledge of by any of our fences,[7] we apprehend them by memory, whereas the present time and things so swiftly pass away [so] as they give us no leisure almost to look into them and much less to know and consider of them thoroughly. The things future, being also events very uncertain, and such as cannot possibly be known because they be not yet, cannot be used for example nor for delight otherwise than by hope, though many promise the contrary, by vain and deceitful arts taking upon them to reveal the truth of accidents to come, which if it were so as they surmise, are yet but sciences merely conjectural and not of any benefit to man or to the commonwealth where they be used or professed. Therefore the good and exemplary things and actions of the former ages were reserved only to the historical reports of wise and grave men; those of the present time [were] left to the fruition and judgment of our senses; the future as hazards and uncertain events [were] utterly neglected and laid aside for magicians and mockers to get their livings by, such manner of men as by negligence of magistrates and remisses of laws every country breedeth great store of. These historical men nevertheless used not the matter so precisely to wish that all they wrote should be accounted true,[8] for that was not needful nor expedient to the purpose, namely to be used either for example or for the pleasure, considering that many times it is seen a feigned matter or altogether fabulous, besides that it maketh more mirth than any other, works no less good conclusions for example than the most true and veritable, but oftentimes more, because the poet hath the handling of them[9] to fashion at his pleasure, but not so of the other[1] which must go according to their verity and none otherwise without the writers' great blame. Again as ye know, more and more excellent examples may be feigned in one day by a good wit than many ages through man's frailty are able to put in ure,[2] which made the learned and witty men of those times to devise many historical matters of no verity at all, but with purpose to do good and no hurt, as using them for a manner of discipline and precedent of commendable life. Such was the commonwealth of Plato, and Sir Thomas More's *Utopia*, resting all in device,[3] but never [to be] put in execution and easier wished

5. Benefits.
6. After.
7. Ways of arguing.
8. Puttenham identifies epic poets as historical, in that they represent the past, but not as historians, in that they do not represent it entirely truthfully.

9. His poetic subjects.
1. I.e., the historian who must try to discover the factual truth of the past.
2. Use.
3. Conception.

than to be performed. And you shall perceive that histories were of three sorts, wholly true and wholly false, and a third holding part of either, but for honest recreation and good example they were all of them.[4]

George Gascoigne
from *Certain Notes of Instruction*[1]

The first and most necessary point that ever I found meet to be considered in making of a delectable poem is this, to ground it upon some fine invention.[2] For it is not enough to roll in pleasant words, nor yet to thunder in Rim, Ram, Ruff, by letter (quoth my master Chaucer) nor yet to abound in apt vocables or epithets, unless the invention have in it also *aliquid salis* [something salty]. By this *aliquid salis* I mean some good and fine device, showing the quick capacity of a writer, and where I say some good and fine invention, I mean that I would have it both fine and good. For many inventions are so superfine that they are *Vix* [scarcely] good. And again many inventions are good, and yet not finely handled. And for a general forewarning: what theme soever you do take in hand, if you do handle it but *tanquam in oratione perpetua* [as a perpetual sermon], and never study for some depth of device in your invention and some figures also in the handling thereof, it will appear to the skillful reader but a tale of a tub. To deliver unto you general examples it were almost impossible, since the occasions of inventions are (as it were) infinite. Nevertheless, take in worth mine opinion and perceive my further meaning in these few points. If I should undertake to write in praise of a gentlewoman, I would neither praise her crystal eye nor her cherry lip, etc., for these things are *trita et obvia* [trite and obvious]. But I would either find some supernatural cause whereby my pen might walk in superlative degree, or else I would undertake to answer for any imperfection that she hath, and thereupon raise the praise of her commendation.[3] Likewise, if I should disclose my pretense in[4] love, I would either make a strange discourse of some intolerable passion, or find occasion to plead by the example of some history, or discover[5] my disquiet in shadows *per allegoriam* [through allegory], or use the covertest mean that I could to avoid the uncomely customs of common writers. Thus much I adventure to deliver unto you (my friend) upon [the] rule of invention, which of all other rules is most to be marked and hardest to be prescribed in certain and infallible rules. Nevertheless, to conclude therein, I would have you stand most upon the excellency of your invention and stick[6] not to study deeply for some fine device. For that being found, pleasant words will follow well enough and fast enough.

Your invention being once devised, take heed that neither pleasure of rhyme nor variety of device do carry you from it. For as to use obscure and dark phrases in a pleasant[7] sonnet is nothing delectable, so to intermingle merry jests in a serious matter is an indecorum.[8]

---

4. I.e., they were all equally good for recreation and good moral example.
1. George Gascoigne's *Certain Notes* was published in 1575 as part of his second work, containing both poetry and prose, entitled *The Posies of George Gascoigne.*
2. In early modern treatises on the art of writing poetry, "invention" meant the discovery and development of "matter," the topics and ideas that the poet will then represent. After "invention," he draws on a knowledge of

rhetoric, the techniques by which "matter" is made interesting and memorable.
3. My compliment to her.
4. Profession of.
5. Reveal.
6. Hesitate.
7. Lighthearted.
8. Improper act.

I will next advise you that you hold the just measure wherewith you begin your verse. I will not deny but this may seem a preposterous order, but because I covet rather to satisfy you particularly than to undertake a general tradition, I will not so much stand upon the manner as the matter of my precepts. I say then, remember to hold the same measure wherewith you begin, whether it be in a verse of six syllables, eight, ten, twelve, etc., and though this precept might seem ridiculous unto you, since every young scholar can conceive that he ought to continue in the same measure wherewith he beginneth, yet do I see and read many men's poems nowadays which beginning with the measure of twelve in the first line and fourteen in the second (which is the common kind of verse), they will yet (by that time they have passed over a few verses) fall into fourteen and fourteen and *sic de similibus* [so on], the which is either forgetfulness or carelessness. * * *

I think it not amiss to forewarn you that you thrust as few words of many syllables into your verse as may be, and hereunto I might allege many reasons. First, the most ancient English words are of one syllable, so that the more monosyllables that you use, the truer Englishman you shall seem, and the less you shall smell of the inkhorn.[9] Also, words of many syllables do cloy a verse and make it unpleasant, whereas words of one syllable will more easily fall to be short or long as occasion requireth, or will be adapted to become circumflex[1] or of an indifferent[2] sound.

I would exhort you also to beware of rhyme without reason. My meaning is hereby that your rhyme lead you not from your first invention, for many writers when they have laid the platform of their invention are yet drawn sometimes (by rhyme) to forget it or at least to alter it, as when they cannot readily find out a word which may rhyme to the first (and yet continue their determinate invention) they do then either botch it up with a word that will rhyme (how small reason soever it carry with it) or else they alter their first word and so perhaps decline or trouble their former invention. But do you always hold your first determined invention, and do rather search the bottom of your brains for apt words than change good reason for rumbling rhyme. * * *

Also as much as may be, eschew strange words or *obsoleta et inusitata* [obsolete and rare], unless the theme do give just occasion. Marry, in some places a strange word doth draw attentive reading, but yet I would have you therein to use discretion.

And as much as you may, frame your style to perspicuity and to be sensible, for the haughty obscure verse doth not much delight and the verse that is too easy is like a tale of a rusted[3] horse. But let your poem be such as may both delight and draw attentive reading and therewithal may deliver such matter as be worth the marking.

Samuel Daniel
from *A Defense of Rhyme*[1]

Such affliction doth laborsome curiosity[2] still lay upon our best delights (which ever must be made strange and variable) as if art were ordained to afflict nature and that

---

9. Inkpot.
1. Accentuated.
2. Soft.
3. Restless.
1. Samuel Daniel, a poet and playwright, published a variety of works throughout his long career, notably: a collection of sonnets, *Delia* (1592); two tragedies, *Cleopa-*

tra (1594) and *Philotas* (1604); an epic poem of the Wars of the Roses, *Civil Wars* (1595, 1609); and several masques. His essay on poetry, *A Defence of Rhyme*, was published in 1603.
2. Daniel's criticism of "laborsome curiosity" is comparable to Gascoigne's criticism of an "inkhorn" style: both poets reject pedantry.

we could not go but in fetters. Every science, every profession, must be so wrapped up in unnecessary intrications, as if it were not to fashion but to confound the understanding, which makes me much to distrust man and fear that our presumption goes beyond our ability and our curiosity is more than our judgment, laboring ever to seem to be more than we are or laying greater burdens upon our minds than they are well able to bear, because we would not appear like other men.

And indeed I have wished there were not that multiplicity of rhymes as is used by many in sonnets, which yet we see in some so happily to succeed and hath been so far from hindering their inventions as it hath begot conceit[3] beyond expectation and comparable to the best inventions of the world. For sure in an eminent spirit whom nature hath fitted for that mystery, rhyme is no impediment to his conceit, but rather gives him wings to mount and carries him, not out of his course, but as it were beyond his power to a far happier flight. All excellencies being sold us at the hard price of labor, it follows, where we bestow most thereof, we buy the best success, and rhyme being far more laborious than loose measures (whatsoever is objected), must needs, meeting with wit and industry, breed greater and worthier effects in our language. So that if our labors have wrought out a manumission[4] from bondage and that we go at liberty, notwithstanding these ties, we are no longer the slaves of rhyme but we make it a most excellent instrument to serve us. Nor is this certain limit observed in sonnets any tyrannical bounding of the conceit,[5] but rather a reducing it in *girum* [in bounds], and a just form, neither too long for the shortest project nor too short for the longest, being but only employed for a present passion. For the body of our imagination, being as an unformed chaos without fashion, without day, if by the divine power of the spirit it be wrought into an orb of order and form, is it not more pleasing to nature that desires a certainty and comports not with that which is infinite, to have these closes[6] rather than not to know where to end or how far to go, especially seeing our passions are often without measure. And we find in the best of the Latins many times either not concluding or else otherwise in the end than they began. Besides, is it not most delightful to see much excellently ordered in a small room, or little gallantly disposed and made to fill up a space of like capacity, in such sort that the one would not appear so beautiful in a larger circuit nor the other do well in a less, which often we find to be so, according to the powers of nature, in the workman. And these limited proportions and rests of stanzas, consisting of six, seven, or eight lines, are of that happiness, both for the disposition of the matter, the apt planting the sentence where it may best stand to hit, the certain close of delight with the full body of a just period well-carried,[7] is such as neither the Greeks or Latins ever attained unto. For their boundless running on often so confounds the reader that having once lost himself must either give off unsatisfied or certainly cast back to retrieve the escaped sense and to find way again into his matter.

Methinks we should not so soon yield our consents captive to the authority of antiquity unless we saw more reason. All our understandings are not to be built by the square of Greece and Italy. We are the children of nature as well as they, we are not so placed out of the way of judgment but that the same sun of discretion shineth upon us, we have our portion of the same virtues as well as of the same vices. * * *

---

3. Created conceptions.
4. Release.
5. I.e., the conception informing the poem.

6. Endings, as in rhyme.
7. A well-constructed sentence.

It is not the observing of trochaics nor their iambics[8] that will make our writings aught the wiser. All their poesie, all their philosophy is nothing unless we bring the discerning light of conceit[9] with us to apply it to use. It is not books, but only that great book of the world and the all-overspreading grace of heaven that makes men truly judicial.[1] Nor can it be but a touch of arrogant ignorance to hold this or that nation barbarous, these or those times gross, considering how this manifold creature man, wheresoever he stand in the world, hath always some disposition of worth, entertains the order of society, affects that which is most in use, and is eminent in some one thing or other that fits his humor and the times. The Grecians held all other nations barbarous but themselves, yet Pyrrhus when he saw the well-ordered marching of the Romans, which made them see their presumptuous error, could say it was no barbarous manner of preceding. The Goths, Vandals, and Longobards,[2] whose coming down like an innundation overwhelmed, as they say, all the glory of learning in Europe, have yet left us still their laws and customs as the originals of most of the provincial constitutions of Christendom, which well-considered with their other course of government may serve to clear them from this imputation of ignorance. And though the vanquished never yet spoke well of the conqueror,[3] yet even through the unsound coverings of malediction appear those monuments of truth as argue well their worth and proves them not without judgment, though without Greek and Latin.

⇥✦⇤

Isabella Whitney
fl. 1567–1573

Little is known about the life of Isabella Whitney. Biographers agree that she was the sister of Geoffrey Whitney, the author of the first emblem book in England, and that, like him, she was born in Cheshire. The rest is to be deduced from her poetry, which points to an author with little formal education, a sharp eye for the details of urban life, and some knowledge of classical mythology. The modesty of Whitney's literary background sets her off from such later and accomplished poets as Mary Herbert and Aemilia Lanyer, and her poems on the challenges of love, friendship, and survival in a large city distinguish her from women who wrote devotional verse. Her poems follow the form and conventions of broadside ballads, a feature that may have made them popular with readers who were drawn to stories that gave advice on affairs of the heart and matters of the purse. Of "the middling sort," Whitney probably came to London for employment and diversion, but she seems to have had difficulty supporting herself. In any case, after publishing two collections of verse, *The Copy of a Letter* (c. 1567) and *A Sweet Nosegay* (1573), she left the city, having lived out the dreams as well as the disappointments of many English villagers who went to London to find work.

---

8. Meters used in classical poetry.
9. Imagination.
1. Discriminating.
2. Lombards.
3. Daniels refers to the culture of conquered peoples

without specifying which conquests or peoples he has in mind. But he acknowledges that even in the curses of these peoples, as they complain about their conquerors, there are "monuments of truth" that reveal worth and judgment.

I.W. To Her Unconstant Lover

As close° as you your wedding[1] kept   *quiet*
    yet now the truth I hear,
Which you (ere now) might me have told
    what need you nay to swear?

5   You know I always wished you well,
    so will I during life,
But since you shall a husband be,
    God send you a good wife.

And this (whereso you shall become)
10   full boldly may you boast:
That once you had as true a love
    as dwelt in any coast.

Whose constantness had never quailed
    if you had not begun,
15   And yet it is not so far past,
    but might again be won.

If you so would; yea and not change
    so long as life should last,
But if that needs you marry must?
20   then farewell, hope is past.

And if you cannot be content
    to lead a single life?
(Although the same right quiet be)
    then take me to your wife.

25   So shall the promises be kept,
    that you so firmly made;
Now choose whether ye will be true,
    or be of Sinon's trade.[2]

Whose trade if that you long shall use,
30   it shall your kindred stain;
Example take by many a one
    whose falsehood now is plain.

As by Aeneas[3] first of all,
    who did poor Dido leave,
35   Causing the Queen by his untruth
    with sword her heart to cleave.

---

1. The formal announcement of an impending marriage; he is not yet actually married.
2. Posing as a deserter from the Greek army, Sinon persuaded the beseiged Trojans to open the city gates to him and a large wooden horse that he pretended was a gift from Athena but in fact hid Greek warriors in its belly.
3. Whitney lists unfaithful lovers recorded in myth: Aeneas, the Trojan hero and founder of Rome, who

deserted Dido, queen of Carthage, after expressing love for her; Theseus, the hero and king of Athens, who left Ariadne, the daughter of Minos, king of Crete, on a island in the sea, even though she had saved him from the monster, Minotaur; Jason, the leader of the Argonauts who captured the golden fleece—a Greek treasure—with the help of Medea, and then abandoned her in favor of Glauce, daughter of Creon, king of Corinth.

Also I find that Theseus did
    his faithful love forsake,
Stealing away within the night,
40   before she did awake.

Jason that came of noble race
    two ladies did beguile;
I muse how he durst show his face
    to them that knew his wile.°   *cunning*

45 For when he by Medea's art
    had got the fleece of gold
And also had of her that time
    all kind of things he would,

He took his ship and fled away
50   regarding not the vows,
That he did make so faithfully
    unto his loving spouse.

How durst he trust the surging seas
    knowing himself forsworn?
55 Why did he scape safe to the land
    before the ship was torn?

I think King Aeolus° stayed the winds   *god of the winds*
    and Neptune° ruled the sea;   *god of the sea*
Then might he boldly pass the waves
60   no perils could him slay.

But if his falsehood had to them
    been manifest before,
They would have rent the ship as soon
    as he had gone from shore.

65 Now may you hear how falseness is
    made manifest in time,
Although they that commit the same
    think it a venial crime.

For they, for their unfaithfulness,
70   did get perpetual fame.
Fame? Wherefore did I term it so?
    I should have called it shame.

Let Theseus be, let Jason pass,
    let Paris[4] also 'scape,°   *escape*
75 That brought destruction unto Troy
    all through the Grecian rape,

And unto me a Troilus[5] be,
    if not you may compare,

4. Son of Priam, king of Troy; he stole Helen, the wife of
King Menelaus of Sparta, a theft that brought about the
invasion of Troy by Menelaus and the Greeks.
5. Son of Priam, king of Troy; his fidelity to Cressida,
who deserted him in favor of Diomedes, a Greek warrior,
is recounted in a 4th century addition to the stories of the
Trojan War.

80   With any of these persons that
        above expressed are.

But if I cannot please your mind,
    for wants that rest in me,
Wed whom you list,° I am content,   *wish*
    your refuse for to be.

85   It shall suffice me simple soul
        of thee to be forsaken,
And it may chance, although not yet,
    you wish you had me taken.

But rather than you should have cause
90   to wish this through° your wife,   *because of*
I wish to her, ere her you have,
    no more but loss of life.

For she that shall so happy be,
    of thee to be elect,
95   I wish her virtues to be such,
        she need not be suspect.

I rather wish her Helen's face,
    than one of Helen's trade,
With chasteness of Penelope[6]
100   the which did never fade.

A Lucrece for her constancy,
    and Thisby for her truth;
If such thou have, then Peto[7] be,
    not Paris, that were ruth.

105   Perchance, ye will think this thing rare
        in one woman to find;
Save Helen's beauty, all the rest
    the gods have me assigned.

These words I do not speak, thinking
110   from thy new love to turn thee.
Thou knowest by proof what I deserve;
    I need not to inform thee.

But let that pass. Would God I had
    Cassandra's gift[8] me lent;
115   Then either thy ill chance or mine
        my foresight might prevent.

But all in vain for this I seek,
    wishes may not attain it;

---

6. Whitney alludes to women who exemplify fidelity: Penelope, who waited for the return of Odysseus from the Trojan War; Lucrece or Lucretia, who killed herself after confessing to her husband that she had been raped; and Thisby or Thisbe, who killed herself when she saw her dying lover, Pyramus.
7. The source of this name is unknown.
8. Daughter of Priam, king of Troy; she had prophetic powers, though her prophecies of the city's fall were not believed.

Therefore may hap° to me what shall,   *happen*
120   and I cannot refrain it.

Wherefore I pray God be my guide
    and also thee defend;
No worser than I wish myself,
    until thy life shall end.

125   Which life I pray God may again
    King Nestor's[9] life renew,
And after that your soul may rest
    amongst the heavenly crew.

Thereto I wish King Xerxes'[1] wealth,
130   or else King Croesus's gold,
With as much rest and quietness
    as man may have on mold.°   *in the world*

And when you shall this letter have
    let it be kept in store.
135   For she that sent the same hath sworn
    as yet to send no more.

And now farewell, for why at large
    my mind is here expressed?
The which you may perceive, if that
140   you do peruse the rest.

Finis.

A Careful Complaint by the Unfortunate Author

Good Dido[1] stint thy tears,
    and sorrows all resign
To me that born was to augment
    misfortune's luckless line.
5   Or using still the same,
    good Dido do thy best,
In helping to bewail the hap
    that furthereth mine unrest.
For though thy Troyan mate,
10   that Lord Aeneas hight,
Requiting all thy steadfast love,
    from Carthage took his flight,
And foully broke his oath,
    and promise made before,
15   Whose falsehood finished thy delight,
    before thy hairs were hoar.

9. King of Pylos and wise counselor to all the Greeks during their seige of Troy.
1. Whitney names men of legendary wealth: Xerxes, king of the Persians, who, with enormous resources gathered from all Asia Minor, attacked Athens and was defeated there by Themistocles; and Croesus, king of Lydia, who was defeated by Cyrus, king of the Persians.
1. Queen of Carthage, seduced and then abandoned by Aeneas on his way from Troy to Italy.

Yet greater cause of grief
   compels me to complain,
For Fortune fell° converted hath   *evil*
20   my health to heaps of pain.
And that she[2] swears my death,
   too plain it is (alas),
Whose end let malice still attempt
   to bring the same to pass.
25 O Dido, thou hadst lived
   a happy woman still,
If fickle fancy had not thralled°   *enslaved*
   thy wits to reckless will.
For as the man by whom
30   thy deadly dolors bred,
Without regard of plighted troth
   from Carthage city fled,
So might thy cares in time
   be banished out of thought,
35 His absence might well salve the sore
   that erst° his presence wrought.   *first*
For fire no longer burns
   than faggots° feed the flame,   *except when sticks*
The want of things that breed annoy
40   may soon redress the same.[3]
But I, unhappy most,
   and gripped with endless griefs,
Despair (alas) amid my hope,
   and hope without relief.
45 And as the swelt'ring heat
   consumes the war away,
So do the heaps of deadly harms
   still threaten my decay.
O death delay not long
50   thy duty to declare.
Ye Sisters three[4] dispatch my days
   and finish all my care.

Mary Herbert, Countess of Pembroke
1561–1621

Mary Herbert was like many women of her time in having two phases to her life: a period of service to men, followed by a phase of independent activity. Deeply attached to her brother, Sir Philip Sidney, she spent much of her young adulthood in his company. The estate she presided over as wife to Henry Herbert, Earl of Pembroke, was Sidney's place of refuge

2. I.e., Fortune, whose end or purpose, Whitney's death, malice will bring to pass.
3. I.e., "want," which breeds annoyance, will also end

annoyance, as it will eventually result in death.
4. I.e., the three Fates, who determine the length of life and the time of death.

after Queen Elizabeth had exiled him from court. At Wilton House and in his sister's company he wrote *The Apology for Poetry* and the first version of his prose romance, *The Arcadia*. Mary Herbert was an interested party in yet another project, his translation of the psalms, and when he died in 1586, she resolved to finish the project. Picking up where he had left off, at Psalm 43, she completed the cycle. Her work was encouraged by the circle of friends that gathered frequently at Wilton House and included such writers and musicians as Francis Mere, Edmund Spenser, Samuel Daniel, Nicholas Breton, Fulke Greville, and Abraham Fraunce. The seventeenth-century biographer John Aubrey spoke of the group as a "college."

Translations of the psalms were popular among Protestant writers of the period; they fulfilled the obligation to know both the Word and the indwelling spirit of God. Poets of religious lyric in the next century, especially George Herbert, would seek and represent a similar knowledge. Mary Herbert dedicated her work to Queen Elizabeth in a poem entitled *Even Now That Care*, which was followed by an elegy for her brother Philip, *To Thee Pure Sprite*. Although riddled with ellipses or words that have been deliberately omitted, they convey the spiritual intensity that characterizes her translations. Some critics think that she did not write a second elegy (here attributed to her), *The Doleful Lay of Clorinda;* it is, however, what we might expect a woman of her station and training to have written about the death of a beloved friend. Milton would later give a profoundly political and religious dimension to the genre in his *Lycidas*, an elegy that is as much for an age and its temperament as it is for a person.

Even Now That Care[1]

Even now that care which on thy crown attends,
And with thy happy greatness daily grows,
Tells me, thrice sacred Queen, my Muse offends,
And of respect to thee the line outgoes.[2]

5 One instant will, or willing can she° lose   *Queen Elizabeth*
I say not reading, but receiving rhymes,
On whom in chief dependeth to dispose
What Europe acts in these most active times?[3]

Yet dare I so, as humbleness may dare
10 Cherish some hope they shall acceptance find;
Not weighing less thy state, lighter thy care,
But knowing more thy grace, abler thy mind.
What heavenly powers thee highest throne assigned,
Assigned thee goodness suiting that degree,
15 And by thy strength thy burden so defined;
To others' toil, is exercise to thee.[4]

Cares though still great, cannot be greatest still;
Business must ebb, though leisure never flow.
Then these the posts of duty and goodwill
20 Shall press to offer what their senders owe,
Which once in two, now in one subject go,[5]
The poorer left, the richer reft away,

1. This poem prefaces Mary Herbert's translation of the psalms, dedicated to Queen Elizabeth.
2. I.e., my Muse oversteps the boundary of respect that your status demands.
3. I.e., will she or can she lose an instant receiving rhymes—she, who is governing Europe?

4. I.e., thy burden, defined by thy strength, is to others toil, to thee exercise.
5. I.e., Herbert and Sidney; the latter is the richer of the two subjects, the one who could better have offered the queen duty and good will.

Who better might (O might! Ah, word of woe)
Have given for me what I for him defray.°   *pay*

25   How can I name whom sighing sighs extend,°   *wordlessly amplify*
And not unstop my tears' eternal spring?
But he did warp, I weaved this web to end.[6]
The stuff not ours, our work no curious thing,
Wherein yet well we thought the psalmist king,
30   Now English denizened though Hebrew born,
Would to thy music undispleased sing,
Oft having worse, without repining worn.[7]

And I the cloth in both our names present,
A livery robe to be bestowed by° thee,   *on*
35   Small parcel of that undischarged rent,
From which nor pains, nor payments can us free.
And yet enough to cause our neighbors see
We will our best, though scanted° in our will;   *deficient*
And those nigh fields where sown thy favors be
40   Unwealthy do, not else unworthy till.[8]

For in our work what bring we but thine own?
What English is, by many names is thine.
There humble laurels in thy shadows grown
To garland others' world, themselves repine.°   *are sorrowful*
45   Thy breast the cabinet, thy seat the shrine,
Where Muses hang their vowed memories,
Where wit, where art, where all that is divine
Conceived best, and best defended lies.

Which if men did not (as they do) confess,
50   And wronging worlds would otherwise consent,[9]
Yet here° who minds° so meet a patroness   *in England / finds*
For author's state or writing's argument?
A king° should only to a queen be sent.   *King David*
God's loved choice unto his chosen love,
55   Devotion to devotion's president;°   *chief object*
What all applaud, to her whom none reprove.

And who sees aught,° but sees how justly square°   *anything / suitable*
His° haughty ditties to thy glorious days?   *King David's*
How well beseeming thee his triumphs are?
60   His hope, his zeal, his prayer, plaint,° and praise,   *complaint*
Needless thy person to their height to raise,
Less need to bend them down to thy degree;
These holy garments each good soul assays,°   *tries on*
Some sorting° all, all sort to none but thee.   *fitting*

65   For ev'n thy rule is painted° in his reign,   *illustrated*
Both clear in right, both nigh° by wrong oppressed.   *closely*

---

6. I.e., he laid the warp of this web (placed its threads
lengthwise); I wove it to completion (after his death).
7. I.e., you often had worse stuff than our web to wear (or our
poems to listen to), which you did without complaining.
8. I.e., those near fields where thy favors are sown (as

seed) we, not wealthy but not unworthy, cultivate. Herbert thanks the queen for her support.
9. I.e., if men did not confess that your breast is the shrine
of the Muses, even unfair worlds would otherwise agree
that this was the case.

And each at length (man crossing God in vain)
Possessed of place,° and each in peace possessed.   *office, rule*
Proud Philistines did interrupt his rest,
70   The foes of heav'n no less have been thy foes;
He with great conquest, thou with greater blessed;
Thou sure to win, and he secure to lose.°   *secure against loss*

Thus hand in hand with him thy glories walk,
But who can trace them where alone they go?
75   Of thee two hemispheres on honor talk,
And hands and seas thy trophies jointly show.
The very winds did on thy party° blow,   *ally*
And rocks in arms thy foemen eft defy;[1]
But soft my muse, thy pitch is earthly low,
80   Forbear this heaven, where only eagles fly.

Kings on a queen enforced their states to lay,
Mainlands for empire waiting on an isle;
Men drawn by worth a woman to obey,
One moving all, herself unmoved the while.[2]
85   Truth's restitution, vanity's exile,
Wealth sprung of want, war held without annoy;
Let subject be of some inspired style,
Till then the object of her subject's joy.[3]

Thy utmost can but offer to her sight
90   Her handmaid's task, which most her will endears,
And pray unto thy pains life from that light
Which lively light some court and kingdom cheers.
What[4] wish she° may (far past her living peers   *the Queen*
And rival still to Judah's faithful king,
95   In more than he and more triumphant years),
Sing what God doth, and do what men may sing.

        c. 1590

To Thee Pure Sprite[1]

To thee pure sprite,° to thee alone's addressed   *spirit*
   this coupled work, by double interest thine:
   first raised by thy blessed hand, and what is mine
Inspired by thee, thy secret power impressed.°   *informed by*
5   so dared my Muse with thine itself combine,
   as mortal stuff with that which is divine.
Thy lightening beams give lustre to the rest,

That heaven's king may deign his own transformed
   in substance no, but superficial tire°   *attire*

---

1. I.e., winds blew to help your allies; rocks defied your
enemies who were up in arms. Herbert then protests that
the level of her poetic skill is low; it must not aspire to a
height that only "eagles," or poets of great power, attain.
2. I.e., kings are forced to place their "states" (authority
and power) on a queen; mainlands anticipating empire
are forced to lay their "states" (conditions, resources) on
an island, i.e., England.

3. Herbert defines the subjects of an inspired style of
poetry: the restitution of truth, the exile of vanity, a
"wealth" created by necessity (i.e., moral virtue), war
without harm.
4. I.e., court and kingdom.
1. Herbert's elegy is for her brother, Sir Philip Sidney. In
it she acknowledges his part in the translations.

10   by thee° put on to praise,[2] not to aspire   *Sidney*
To those high tones so in themselves adorned,
     which angels sing in their celestial choir,
     and all of tongues with soul and voice admire.
These sacred hymns thy kingly prophet formed.

15   Oh, had that soul which honor brought to rest
          too soon not left, and reft the world of all
          what man could show, which we perfection call,
     This half-maimed piece had sorted with° the best.   *matched*
          deep wounds enlarged, long festered in their gall,
20   fresh bleeding smart; not eye- but heart-tears fall.
     Ah memory, what needs this new arrest?°   *delay*

     Yet here behold, (oh, wert thou to behold!)
          this[3] finished now, thy matchless Muse begun,
          the rest but pieced, as left by thee undone.
25   Pardon (oh, blessed soul) presumption too too bold,
          if love and zeal such error ill-become,
          'tis zealous love, love which hath never done,
     Nor can enough in world of words unfold.

     And since it hath no further scope to go,
30   nor other purpose but to honor thee,
          thee in thy works, where all the Graces[4] be
     As little streams with all their all do flow
          to their great sea, due tribute's grateful fee;[5]
          so press my thoughts, my burdened thoughts, in me,
35   To pay the debt of infinites I owe

     To thy great worth. Exceeding nature's store,
          wonder of men, sole° born perfection's kind,   *alone*
          phoenix[6] thou wert. So rare thy fairest mind,
     Heav'nly adorned, Earth justly might adore,
40   where truthful praise in highest glory shined,
          for there alone was praise to truth confined;
     And where but there, to live for ever more?

     Oh! When to this account, this cast up sum,
          this reckoning made, this audit of my woe,
45   I call my thoughts, whence so strange passions flow,
     How works my heart, my senses stricken dumb?
          that° would thee more than ever heart could show,   *my thoughts*
          and all too short,° who knew thee best doth know,   *inadequate*
     There lives no wit that may thy praise become.°   *express*

2. I.e., your intelligence informs this verse not so that the
king of heaven will consider his own light transformed
substantially; rather it is that your own attire, clothing, is
put over that light to praise him. Herbert returns to the
idea, expressed earlier in her dedicatory poem to Elizabeth, that the psalms are a web or woven cloth.
3. I.e., the translation.

4. Personifications of the elements of courtesy and courteous expression; typically, they are attributes of poetic
and artistic work.
5. I.e., the streams are a tribute to the sea.
6. A mythical bird, unique in the world, which is miraculously reborn from the ashes of its own funeral pyre.

50   Truth I invoke (who scorn elsewhere to move
       or here in aught my blood should partialize),⁷
       Truth, sacred Truth, thee sole to solemnize.
    Those precious rights well known best mind's approve;
       and who but doth, hath wisdom's open eyes,

55   not owly° blind the fairest light still° flies,   *owl-like / always*
    Confirm no less?⁸ At least 'tis sealed above.

    Where thou art fixed among my fellow lights,
       my day put out, my life in darkness cast,
       thy angel's soul, with highest angels placed,

60   There blessed sings enjoying heaven, delights°   *delights in*
       thy maker's praise, as far from earthly taste
       as here thy works so worthily embraced
    By all of worth, where never envy bites.

    As goodly buildings to some glorious end

65   cut off by fate, before the Graces had
       each wond'rous part in all their beauties clad,
    Yet so much done, as art would not amend;
       so thy rare works to which no wit can add,
       in all men's eyes, which are not blindly mad,

70   Beyond compare, above all praise extend.

    Immortal monuments of thy fair fame,
       though not complete, nor in the reach of thought,
       how on that passing peacetime would have wrought
    Had Heav'n so spared the life of life to frame

75   the rest?⁹ But ah, such loss! Hath this world aught
       can equal it? Or which like grievance brought?
    Yet there will live thy ever-praised name.

    To which these dearest offerings of my heart,
       dissolved to ink, while pen's impressions move

80   the bleeding veins of never dying love,
    I render here; these wounding lines of smart,
       sad characters indeed of simple love,
       not art nor skill which abler wits do prove,
    Of my full soul receive the meanest part.

85   Receive these hymns, these obsequies receive,
       if any mark of thy sweet sprite appear,
       well are they born,¹ no title else shall bear.
    I can no more. Dear soul, I take my leave;
       sorrow still strives, would mount thy highest sphere

90   presuming so just cause might meet thee there.²
    Oh happy change! Could so I take my leave.

c. 1590

---

7. I.e., I scorn that my blood (passion, temperament) should favor anything in a partial or prejudicial way.
8. I.e., who that has wisdom's open eyes and is not
9. I.e., had Heaven so spared your life so that you could frame the life of the rest of mankind.

1. I.e, the hymns are of good parentage.
2. I.e., my sorrow would climb to your sphere in heaven, presuming that so just a cause would allow my sorrow to be there.

Psalm 121: Levavi Oculos

Unto the hills, I now will bend
    And list° with joy my hopeful sight;   *incline*
To him who me doth comfort send,
    My gracious God, the Lord of might.
5   Even he (who ever blessed be he named)
            Who Heaven and Earth and all therein hath framed.

By him thy foot, from slip shall stay,°   *prevent*
    Nor will he sleep who thee sustains;
Israel's great God by night or day
10   To sleep or slumber aye° disdains.   *always*
            For he is still thy guard forever waking,
            On thy right hand thy safety undertaking.

So undertakes that neither sun
    By day with heat shall thee molest,
15   Nor moon by night, when day is done,
    Offend thee, or disturb thy rest.
            Yea, from all evil thou still in his protection
            Shalt safely dwell from harm or ill infection.

This Lord (who never fails his flock)
20   Shall thee in all thy ways attend
At home, abroad, thy fort, thy rock
    From all annoy shall thee defend.
            Yea, from this time from age to age for ever
            Will be thy God, and thee forsaking never.

c. 1590

The Doleful Lay° of Clorinda   *ballad*

Ay me, to whom shall I my case complain
That may compassion° my impatient grief?   *sympathize with*
Or where shall I unfold my inward pain,
That my enriven° ear may find relief?   *dismayed*
5   Shall I unto the heavenly powers it show?
    Or unto earthly men that dwell below?

To heavens? Ah they, alas, the authors were
And workers of my unremedied woe;
For they foresee what to us happens here,
10 And they foresaw, yet suffered this be so.
    From them comes good, from them comes also ill;
    That which they made, who can them warn to spill.°   *destroy*

To men? Ah they, alas, like wretched be
And subject to the heavens' ordinance;
15 Bound to abide whatever they decree,
    Their best redress is their best sufferance.[1]

---

1. I.e., the best recourse for men subject to heaven is to tolerate its decrees.

How then can they, like wretched, comfort me,
The which no less, need comforted to be?[2]

20 Then to myself will I my sorrow mourn,
Since none alive like sorrowful remains;
And to myself my plaints shall back return,
To pay their usury with doubled pains.
    The woods, the hills, the rivers shall resound
    The mournful accent of my sorrow's ground.°   *cause*

25 Wood, hills, and rivers now are desolate,
Since he is gone the which them all did grace;
And all the fields do wail their widow state,
Since death their fairest flower did late deface.
    The fairest flower in field that ever grew,
30   Was Astrophel;[3] that was, we all may rue.

What cruel hand of cursed fate unknown,
Hath cropped the stalk which bore so fair a flower?
Untimely cropped, before it were well grown,
And clean defaced in untimely hour.
35   Great loss to all that ever him did see,
    Great loss to all, but greatest loss to me.

Break now your garlands, O ye shepherds' lasses,
Since the fair flower which them adorned is gone;
The flower which them adorned is gone to ashes,
40 Never again let lass put garland on.
    Instead of garland, wear sad cypress now,
    And bitter elder, broken from the bow.

Nor ever sing the love-lays which he made,
Who ever made such lays of love as he?
45 Nor ever read the riddles which he said
Unto yourselves to make you merry glee.
    Your merry glee is now laid all abed,
    Your merry maker now, alas, is dead.

Death, the devourer of all world's delight,
50 Hath robbed you and reft from me my joy;
Both you and me and all the world he quite
Hath robbed of joyance and left sad annoy.
    Joy of the world, and shepherds' pride was he,
    Shepherds' hope, never like again to see.

55 Oh death, that hast us of such riches reft,
Tell us at least, what hast thou with it done?
What is become of him whose flower here left
Is but the shadow of his likeness gone,

2. I.e., how can they comfort me, wretched as I am, who
themselves need to be comforted?
3. Astrophel or Astrophil: the principal speaker and the

lover of "Stella," the figure representing the beloved
woman, in Sir Philip Sidney's sonnet sequence *Astrophil
and Stella.*

Scarce like the shadow of that which he was,
60 Naught° like, but that he like a shade did pass?   *nothing*

But that immortal spirit, which was decked
With all the dowries of celestial grace,
By sovereign choice from the heavenly choirs select,
And lineally derived from angel's race,
65   O what is now of it become, aread—°   *tell*
    Ay me, can so divine a thing be dead?

Ah no, it is not dead, nor can it die,
But lives for aye° in blissful paradise,   *ever*
Where like a newborn babe it soft doth lie,
70   In bed of lilies wrapped in tender wise.°   *manner*
        And compassed all about with roses sweet,
        And dainty violets from head to feet.

There thousand birds all of celestial brood,
To him do sweetly carol day and night,
75 And with strange notes, or him well understood,
Lull him asleep in angel-like delight,
        While in sweet dream to him presented be
        Immortal beauties which no eye may see.

But he them sees and takes exceeding pleasure
80 Of their divine aspects, appearing plain,
And kindling love in him above all measure,
Sweet love still joyous, never feeling pain.
        For what so goodly form he there doth see,
        He may enjoy from jealous rancor free.

85 There liveth he in everlasting bliss,
Sweet spirit never fearing more to die,
Nor dreading harm from any foes of his,
Nor fearing salvage° beasts more cruelty.   *savage*
        While we here, wretches, wail his private lack,
90   And with vain vows do often call him back.

But live thou there still happy, happy spirit,
And give us leave thee here thus to lament.
Not thee that dost thy heaven's joy inherit,
But our own selves that here in dole are drent.°   *drenched*
95   Thus do we weep and wail and wear our eyes,
        Mourning others, our own miseries.

⇥✠⇤

Aemilia Lanyer
1569–1645

Aemilia Lanyer was born Aemilia Bassano, the daughter of Queen Elizabeth's court musician, Baptista Bassano. Acquaintance with the nobility surrounding the Queen allowed her an education that was typically reserved for women of high station. At eighteen, shortly after her mother's death, she became the mistress of Henry Cary Hunsdon, the Lord Chancellor. Her position increased her presence at court until, at twenty-three, she became pregnant and was forced to marry a court musician. Their son, conspicuously named Henry, was born three months after the wedding. The first years of her married life were not auspicious. Alfonso Lanyer was a spendthrift, and the money Aemilia had acquired as Hunsdon's mistress was soon exhausted. Desperate for reassurance, she visited the astrologer Simon Forman to learn whether the stars indicated that Alfonso would gain a knighthood. The disreputable Forman appears to have had other ideas. His casebook records that on one occasion, he "went and supped with her and stayed all night, and she was familiar and friendly to him in all things. But only she would not halek [have intercourse] . . . he never obtained his purpose and she was a whore and dealt evil with him."

Lanyer's character is more accurately represented in the record of her long friendship with Margaret Clifford, Countess of Cumberland, and her daughter Anne. In 1610, partly in tribute to the loyal support of her patroness, Lanyer published a volume of poetry entitled *Salve Deus Rex Judaeorum*; this included a verse defense of women and a poem to Cookham, a country house leased by Margaret Clifford's brother, William Russell, and visited frequently by Lanyer until 1605. She particularly records two critical transformations in her sense of herself: a spiritual awakening, inspired by the piety of the Countess, and a confirmation of herself as a poet. Her impressions of Cookham express a unity among aesthetic elements that are usually opposed and antithetical: pagan culture and Christian vision, temporal experience and spiritual knowledge, and the erotic pleasure in the discipline of chastity.

The Description of Cookham

Farewell (sweet Cookham) where I first obtained
Grace from that Grace where perfit° grace remained;   *perfect*
And where the Muses[1] gave their full consent,
I should have power the virtuous to content;
5   Where princely Palace willed me to indite,°   *write*
The sacred story[2] of the soul's delight.
Farewell (sweet place) where virtue then did rest,
And all delights did harbor in her breast;
Never shall my said eyes again behold
10 Those pleasures which my thoughts did then unfold:
Yet you (great Lady),[3] Mistress of that place,
From whose desires did spring this work of grace;
Vouchsafe° to think upon those pleasures past,   *agree*
As fleeting worldly joys that could not last,
15 Or, as dim shadows of celestial pleasures,
Which are desired above all earthly treasures.
Oh how (me thought) against you thither came,[4]
Each part did seem some new delight to frame!
The house received all ornaments to grace it,
20 And would endure no foulness to deface it.
The walks put on their summer liveries,°   *uniforms*
And all things else did hold like similies:°   *comparisons*
The trees with leaves, with fruits, with flowers clad,
Embraced each other, seeming to be glad,

---

1. Divinities who presided over the arts and courtesy.
2. Possibly the story of the Passion, recounted in the poem *Salve Deus Rex Judaeorum*.

3. Margaret Clifford, the Countess of Cumberland.
4. In preparation for your arrival.

25 Turning themselves to beauteous canopies,
    To shade the bright sun from your brighter eyes.
    The crystal streams with silver spangles graced,
    While by the glorious sun they were embraced,
    The little birds in chirping notes did sing,
30 To entertain both you and that sweet spring.
    And Philomela[5] with her sundry lays,°   songs
    Both you and that delightful place did praise.
    Oh, how me thought each plant, each flower, each tree
    Set forth their beauties then to welcome thee:
35 The very hills right humbly did descend,
    When you to tread upon them did intend.
    And as you set your feet, they still did rise,
    Glad that they could receive so rich a prize.
    The gentle winds did take delight to be
40 Among those woods that were so graced by thee.
    And in sad° murmur uttered pleasing sound,   deep
    That pleasure in that place might more abound:
    The swelling banks delivered all their pride,
    When such a Phoenix[6] once they had espied.
45 Each arbor, bank, each seat, each stately tree,
    Thought themselves honored in supporting thee.
    The pretty birds would oft come to attend thee,
    Yet fly away for fear they should offend thee:
    The little creatures in the burrow by°   nearby
50 Would come abroad to sport them in your eye;
    Yet fearful of the bow in your fair hand,
    Would run away when you did make a stand.
    Now let me come unto that stately tree,
    Wherein such goodly prospects you did see;
55 That oak that did in height his fellows pass,
    As much as lofty trees, low growing grass
    Much like a comely cedar straight and tall,
    Whose beauteous stature far exceeded all.
    How often did you visit this fair tree,
60 Which seeming joyful in receiving thee,
    Would like a palm tree spread his arms abroad,
    Desirous that you there should make abode:
    Whose fair green leaves much like a comely veil,
    Defended Phoebus when he would assail:[7]
65 Whose pleasing boughs did yield a cool fresh air,
    Joying his happiness when you were there.
    Where being seated, you might plainly see,
    Hills, vales, and woods, as if on bended knee
    They had appeared, your honor to salute,
70 Or to prefer some strange unlooked for suit:
    All interlaced with brooks and crystal springs,
    A prospect fit to please the eyes of kings:

5. In Greek mythology a woman who was transformed into a swallow; in Latin versions of her story she becomes a nightingale.
6. A mythical bird, always unique on earth, that regener-
ates itself in its own funeral pyre and therefore signifies eternity; here it figures the Countess.
7. The leaves of the palm tree protected the Countess from Phoebus, the god of the sun.

And thirteen shires appeared all in your sight,
Europe could not afford much more delight.
75 What was there then but gave you all content,
While you the time in meditation spent,
Of their Creator's power, which there you saw,
In all his creatures held a perfit law;
And in their beauties did you plain descry,°   *discern*
80 His beauty, wisdom, grace, love, majesty.
In these sweet woods how often did you walk,
With Christ and his apostles there to talk;
Placing his holy writ in some fair tree,
To meditate what you therein did see:
85 With Moses you did mount his holy hill,[8]
To know his pleasure, and perform his will.
With lovely David[9] you did often sing
His holy hymns to heaven's eternal king.
And in sweet music did your soul delight,
90 To sound his praises, morning, noon, and night.
With blessed Joseph you did often feed
Your pined° brethren, when they stood in need.[1]   *poor*
And that sweet lady sprung from Clifford's race,[2]
Of noble Bedford's blood, fair steam of grace,
95 To honorable Dorset now espoused,
In whose fair breast true virtue then was housed.
Oh, what delight did my weak spirits find
In those pure parts of her well framed mind,
And yet it grieves me that I cannot be
100 Near unto her, whose virtues did agree
With those fair ornaments of outward beauty,
Which did enforce from all both love and duty.
Unconstant Fortune, thou art most to blame,
Who casts us down into so low a frame,
105 Where our great friends we cannot daily see,
So great a diffrence is there in degree.
Many are placed in those orbs of state,
Parters° in honor, so ordained by Fate;   *participants*
Nearer in show, yet farther off in love,
110 In which, the lowest always are above.[3]
But whither am I carried in conceit?°   *imagination*
My wit too weak to conster of° the great.   *understand*
Why not? although we are but born of earth,
We may behold the heavens, despising death;
115 And loving heaven that is so far above,
May in the end vouchsafe us entire love.
Therefore sweet memory do thou retain

8. Moses climbed Mount Sinai to receive the law of God (Exodus 24, 25).
9. King David the psalmist.
1. Sold by his jealous brothers into slavery, Joseph became Pharoah's right-hand man and granted these same brothers food and money during a famine many years later (Genesis 42.1–28).

2. The Lady is the Countess's daughter Anne, descended from Margaret Russell of Bedford and her father George Clifford, Duke of Cumberland. Anne married the Earl of Dorset in 1609 and is thus referred to as Dorset.
3. I.e., persons of low station or rank love more than those who are of the gentry or nobility.

Those pleasures past, which will not turn again;
Remember beauteous Dorset's former sports,
120 So far from being touched by ill reports;
Wherein myself did always bear a part,
While reverend Love presented my true heart.
Those recreations let me bear in mind,
Which her sweet youth and noble thoughts did find,
125 Whereof deprived, I evermore must grieve,
Hating blind Fortune, careless to relieve.
And you sweet Cookham, whom these ladies leave,
I now must tell the grief you did conceive
At their departure; when they went away,
130 How everything retained a sad dismay;
Nay long before, when once an inkling came,
Methought each thing did unto sorrow frame:
The trees that were so glorious in our view,
Forsook both flowers and fruit, when once they knew
135 Of your depart,° their very leaves did wither,   departure
Changing their colors as they grew together.
But when they saw this had no power to stay you,
They often wept, though speechless, could not pray⁴ you;
Letting their tears in your fair bosoms fall,
140 As if they said, "Why will ye leave us all?"
This being vain, they cast their leaves away,
Hoping that pity would have made you stay,
Their frozen tops like age's hoary hairs,
Shows their disasters, languishing in fears;
145 A swarthy riveled rine° all overspread,   bark
Their dying bodies half alive, half dead.
But your occasions called you so away,
That nothing there had power to make you stay:
Yet did I see a noble grateful mind,
150 Requiting each according to their kind,
Forgetting not to turn and take your leave
Of these sad creatures, powerless to receive
Your favor when with grief you did depart,
Placing their former pleasures in your heart;
155 Giving great charge to noble memory,
There to preserve their love continually:
But specially the love of that fair tree,
That first and last you did vouchsafe to see:
In which it pleased you oft to take the air,
160 With noble Dorset, then a virgin fair:
Where many a learned book was read and scanned
To this fair tree, taking me by the hand,
You did repeat the pleasures which had passed,
Seeming to grieve they could no longer last.
165 And with a chaste, yet loving kiss took leave,
Of which sweet kiss I did it soon bereave:⁵
Scorning a senseless creature should possess

4. Beg.   5. I.e., I took their kiss from the tree on which they had put it.

So rare a favor, so great happiness.
No other kiss it could receive from me,
170 For fear to give back what it took of thee:
So I ungrateful creature did deceive it,
Of that which you vouchsafed in love to leave it.
And though it oft° had given me much content,   *often*
Yet this great wrong I never could repent:
175 But of the happiest made it most forlorn,
To show that nothing's free from Fortune's scorn,
While all the rest with this most beauteous tree,
Made their sad consort° sorrow's harmony.   *music*
The flowers that on the banks and walks did grow,
180 Crept in the ground, the grass did weep for woe.
The winds and waters seemed to chide together,
Because you went away they know not whither:
And those sweet brooks that ran so fair and clear,
With grief and trouble wrinkled did appear.
185 Those pretty birds that wonted° were to sing,   *accustomed*
Now neither sing, nor chirp, nor use their wing;
But with their tender feet on some bare spray,
Warble forth sorrow, and their own dismay.
Fair Philomela leaves her mournful ditty,
190 Drowned in dead sleep, yet can procure no pity:
Each arbor, bank, each seat, each stately tree,
Looks bare and desolate now for want of thee;
Turning green tresses into frosty gray,
While in cold grief they wither all away.
195 The sun grew weak, his beams no comfort gave,
While all green things did make the earth their grave;
Each briar, each bramble, when you went away,
Caught fast your clothes, thinking to make you stay;
Delightful Echo[6] wonted° to reply   *used*
200 To our last words, did now for sorrow die:
The house cast off each garment that might grace it,
Putting on dust and cobwebs to deface it.
All desolation then there did appear,
When you were going whom they held so dear.
205 This last farewell to Cookham here I give,
When I am dead thy name in this may live,
Wherein I have performed her noble hest,°   *request*
Whose virtues lodge in my unworthy breast,
And ever shall, so long as life remains,
210 Tying my heart to her by those rich chains.

from Salve Deus Rex Judaeorum
To the Doubtful Reader

Gentle reader, if thou desire to be resolved, why I give this title, *Salve Deus Rex Judaeorum*, know for certain; that it was delivered unto me in sleep many years before I had any intent to write in this manner, and was quite out of my memory, until I had

---

6. A nymph who can only repeat what she has heard; in the absence of voices she dies.

written the Passion of Christ, when immediately it came into my remembrance, what I had dreamed long before; and thinking it a significant token, that I was appointed to perform this work, I gave the very same words I received in sleep as the fittest title I could devise for this book.

To the Virtuous Reader[1]

Often have I heard, that it is the property of some women, not only to emulate the virtues and perfections of the rest, but also by all their powers of ill speaking, to eclipse the brightness of their deserved fame. Now contrary to this custom, which men I hope unjustly lay to their charge, I have written this small volume, or little book, for the general use of all virtuous ladies and gentlewomen of this kingdom; and in commendation of some particular persons of our own sex, such as for the most part are so well known to myself, and others, that I dare undertake fame dares not to call any better. And this have I done, to make known to the world that all women deserve not to be blamed, though some—forgetting they are women themselves and in danger to be condemned by the words of their own mouths—fall into so great an error as to speak unadvisedly against the rest of their sex; which if it be true, I am persuaded they can show their own imperfection in nothing more: and therefore could wish (for their own ease, modesties, and credit) they would refer[2] such points of folly to be practiced by evil disposed men, who forgetting they were born of women, nourished of women, and that if it were not by the means of women, they would be quite extinguished out of the world and a final end of them all, do like vipers deface the wombs wherein they were bred, only to give way and utterance to their want of discretion and goodness. Such as these, were they that dishonored Christ his apostles and prophets, putting them to shameful deaths. Therefore we are not to regard any imputations, that they undeservedly lay upon us, no[3] otherwise than to make use of them to our own benefits as spurs to virtue, making us fly all occasions that may color their unjust speeches to pass current,[4] especially considering that they have tempted even the patience of God himself, who gave power to wise and virtuous women, to bring down their pride and arrogance: As was cruel *Caesar* by the discreet counsel of noble *Deborah*,[5] judge and prophetess of Israel; and resolution of *Jael*, wife of *Heber* the Kenite; wicked *Haman*, by the divine prayers and prudent proceedings of beautiful *Hester*; blasphemous *Holofernes*, by the invincible courage, rare wisdom, and confident carriage of *Judith*; and the unjust judges, by the innocence of chaste *Susanna*; with infinite others, which for brevity's sake I will omit. As also in respect it pleased our Lord and Savior Jesus Christ, without the assistance of man, being free from original and all other sins from the time of his conception till the hour of his death, to be begotten of a woman, born of a woman, nourished of a woman, obedient to a woman; and that he healed woman,[6] pardoned women, comforted women; yea, even when he was in his greatest agony and bloody sweat, going to be crucified, and also in the last hour of his death, took care to dispose of a woman;[7] after his resurrection, appeared first to a

---

1. This preface is Lanyer's general introduction to her poem *Salve Deus Rex Judaeorum* (Hail, Lord God, King of the Jews). An excerpt follows: Pilate's wife's apology for Eve.
2. Assign.
3. Not.
4. To avoid occasions in which their unjust speeches might appear to have some truth.
5. Lanyer lists virtuous women who benefited their people: Deborah, a wise judge and prophet of Israel, who urged the warrior Barak to attack their enemy, Sisera [Cesarus]; Jael, who killed Sisera with a blow to the head (both figures from

Judges 4); Hester [Esther], the queen of the Israelites, who hanged Haman (Esther 5–7); the Jewish heroine Judith, who saved her town by killing King Nebuchadnezzar's general Holofernes (the Apocryphal Book of Judith 8–12); and Susanna, whose chastity was proved by the prophet Daniel (the Apocryphal History of Daniel and Susanna).
6. Womankind.
7. Jesus, from the cross, ordered a disciple (traditionally understood to be John) to care for his mother (John 19.25–27).

woman, sent a woman to declare his most glorious resurrection to the rest of his disciples.[8] Many other examples I could allege of divers faithful and virtuous women, who have in all ages, not only been confessors, but also endured most cruel martyrdom for their faith in Jesus Christ. All which is sufficient to enforce all good Christians and honorable-minded men to speak reverently of our sex, and especially of all virtuous and good women. To the modest censures of both which, I refer these my imperfect endeavors, knowing that according to their own excellent dispositions, they will rather, cherish, nourish, and increase the least spark of virtue where they find it, by their favorable and best interpretations, than quench it by wrong constructions. To whom I wish all increase of virtue, and desire their best opinions.

[PILATE'S WIFE APOLOGIZES FOR EVE]

745	Now *Pontius Pilate*[9] is to judge the cause
	Of faultless *Jesus,* who before him stands;
	Who neither hath offended prince, nor laws,
	Although he now be brought in woeful bands:°
	"O noble governor, make thou you a pause,
750	Do not in innocent blood imbrue° thy hands;
	But hear the words of thy most worthy wife,
	Who sends to thee, to beg her Saviour's life.

bonds

stain

745 Now *Pontius Pilate*[9] is to judge the cause
Of faultless *Jesus,* who before him stands;
Who neither hath offended prince, nor laws,
Although he now be brought in woeful bands:°   *bonds*
"O noble governor, make thou you a pause,
750 Do not in innocent blood imbrue° thy hands;   *stain*
    But hear the words of thy most worthy wife,
    Who sends to thee, to beg her Saviour's life.

Let barbarous cruelty far depart from thee,
And in true justice take affliction's part;
755 Open thine eyes, that thou the truth mayest see;
Do not the thing that goes against thy heart,
Condemn not him that must thy Saviour be;
But view his holy life, his good desert.
    Let not us women glory in men's fall,
760   Who had power given to overrule us all.

Till now your indiscretion sets us free,
And makes our former fault much less appear;[1]
Our Mother *Eve,* who tasted of the tree,
Giving to *Adam* what she held most dear,
765 Was simply good, and had no power to see,
The after-coming harm did not appear:[2]
    The subtle serpent that our sex betrayed,
    Before our fall so sure a plot had laid.

That undiscerning ignorance° perceived   *i.e., of Eve*
770 No guile, or craft that was by him intended;
For had she known, of what we were bereaved,
To his request she had not condescended.
But she (poor soul) by cunning was deceived,

---

8. After his resurrection, Jesus appeared first to Mary Magdalene and "the other Mary," who then told the other disciples of this event (Matthew 28.8–10).
9. The Roman governor of Jerusalem, A.D. 26–36. He was the judge at the trial of Jesus, who was accused of violating the laws of Rome. His wife warned him against condemning Jesus, saying, "Have thou nothing to do with that just man: for I have suffered many things this day in a dream because of him" (Matthew 27.19).

1. Lanyer recapitulates points raised by many writers who denied that Eve should have all the blame for the loss of Eden and paradise. Lanyer stresses Eve's innocence, and emphasizes that Adam should have exercised authority over Eve. This latter point is central to Milton's representation of Adam's sin in *Paradise Lost,* exonerating Eve while also making her Adam's subordinate.
2. She could not foresee the harm that would follow her disobedience.

No hurt therein her harmless heart intended:
775   For she alleged God's word, which he denies,
            That they should die, but even as gods, be wise.

        But surely *Adam* cannot be excused,
        Her fault though great, yet he was most to blame;
        What weakness offered, strength might have refused,
780   Being Lord of all, greater was his shame:
        Although the serpent's craft had her abused,
        God's holy word ought all his actions frame,
            For he was lord and king of all the earth,
            Before poor *Eve* had either life or breath.

785   Who being framed by God's eternal hand,
        The perfectest man that ever breathed on earth;
        And from God's mouth received that strait° command,   *stern*
        The breach whereof he knew was present death:
        Yea, having power to rule both sea and land,
790   Yet with one apple won to lose that breath
            Which god had breathed in his beauteous face,
            Bringing us all in danger and disgrace.

        And then to lay the fault on Patience° back,   *Patience's*
        That we (poor women) must endure it all;
795   We know right well he did discretion lack,
        Being not persuaded thereunto at all;
        If *Eve* did err, it was for knowledge sake,
        The fruit being fair, persuaded him to fall:
            No subtle serpent's falsehood did betray him,
800   If he would eat it, who had power to stay him?

        Not *Eve*, whose fault was only too much love,
        Which made her give this present to her dear,
        That what she tasted, he likewise might prove,
        Whereby his knowledge might become more clear;
805   He never sought her weakness to reprove,
        With those sharp words, which he of God did hear:
            Yet men will boast of knowledge, which he took
            From *Eve's* fair hand, as from a learned book.

        If any evil did in her remain,
810   Being made of him, he was the ground of all;
        If one of many worlds³ could lay a stain
        Upon our sex, and work so great a fall
        To wretched man, by Satan's subtle train;
        What will so foul a fault amongst you all?
815   Her weakness did the serpent's words obey;
            But you in malice God's dear Son betray.

        Whom, if unjustly you condemn to die,
        Her sin was small, to what you do commit;

3. I.e., Adam who, as the father of all humankind, was of many people.

820

All mortal sins that do for vengeance cry,
Are not to be compared unto it:
If many worlds would altogether try,
By all their sins the wrath of God to get;
   This sin of yours, surmounts them all as far
   As doth the sun, another little star.

825

Then let us have our liberty again,
And challenge° to your selves no sovereignty;[4]   *attribute*
You came not in the world without our pain:
Make that a bar against your cruelty;
Your fault being greater, why should you disdain

830

Our being your equals, free from tyranny?
   If one weak woman simply did offend,
   This sin of yours, hath no excuse, nor end.

To which (poor souls) we never gave consent,
Witness thy wife (O *Pilate*) speaks for all,

835

Who did but dream, and yet a message sent,
That thou should'st have nothing to do at all
With that just man; which, if thy heart relent,
Why wilt thou be a reprobate° with *Saul?*   *sinner*
   To seek the death of him that is so good,

840

   For thy soul's health to shed his dearest blood.

⸺ ⸎ ⸺

Elizabeth I
1533–1603

No British monarch has left posterity a more dazzling record of accomplishments than Elizabeth Tudor, second daughter of Henry VIII. In the course of her reign, England became a nation to rival France and Spain; England's cities became centers of commerce, her navy controlled the principal routes of trade, and her people pursued lucrative interests in Europe and the New World. Having ruled England for almost half a century, Elizabeth has lived on as a figure of compelling power in the history of her people. What Shakespeare said of his character Cleopatra—"Age cannot wither her, nor custom stale her infinite variety"—conveys something of the fascination the memory of this extraordinary woman has had for the English people as well as for others around the globe. Age did, of course, eventually touch her being; doubtless, too, the brilliant strategies by which she governed subjects who were ever jealous of her royal prerogative must finally have become predictable. But Elizabeth was brought up in the atmosphere of a volatile politics, given to shifts in the winds of chance, susceptible to the heat of violent controversy and even to the flames of rebellion. She did what she had to do to remain on the throne; her father's example, if nothing else, taught her how fragile was the rule

---

4. Because men are afflicted with the weakness of Adam, they forfeit their original sovereignty over creation; their rule over woman is therefore a tyranny.

Robert Peake (attr.). *Queen Elizabeth Going in Procession to Blackfriars in 1600. This splendid painting is linked to no particular event. Its arrangement of figures suggests a Roman imperial triumph, and evokes the success of the queen's monarchy. She appears to be in a litter, but is actually in a chair on wheels pushed by attendants, and protected by a canopy held by courtiers. She is preceded by a knight, perhaps Gilbert Talbot, Earl of Shrewsbury, who carries the sword of state. Though Elizabeth was sixty-eight when this painting was made in 1601, she is shown as a much younger woman. Her wish to be recognized as always desirable and ever the object of courtly devotion is well illustrated by her pale, unlined face, her highly dressed hair and her stylized body, clothed in a bejeweled dress whose puffed sleeves and intricate lace ruff suggest an etherial and even divine creature. She is attended by six Knights of the Garter; the knight standing directly beside her (with a bald head and stiff grey beard) has been identified as her current favorite, Edward Somerset, Earl of Worcester; his two principal castles, Raglan and Chepstow, are probably those in the background of the painting.*

of a monarch who depended much more on the loyalty of subjects than on the authority of office or the power of the law.

Elizabeth's birth was itself a disappointment, at least to Henry VIII, who had hoped for a son. Her mother was the king's second wife, the charming Anne Boleyn, whom he married after divorcing Catherine of Aragon, the mother of his first daughter, Mary Tudor. The divorce precipitated the king's break with the Catholic Church, made Mary Tudor illegitimate, and effectively defined Anne's politics as unequivocally Protestant. But the new queen's influence was short-lived. Supporters of Catholicism, those who remained faithful to the memory of Catherine and respected the claims of Mary Tudor, may have been responsible for convincing the king that Anne had been unfaithful to him; in any case he ordered her execution. Ten days later, he married Jane Seymour, declared Elizabeth illegitimate, and again waited for the birth of a son. Elizabeth's half-brother, the future Edward VI, was born in 1537, when Elizabeth was four years old. Fortunately, at the age of ten, Elizabeth at last acquired a loving stepmother: Henry's sixth wife, Catherine

Parr, looked after her interests and education. An excellent student, fluent in Latin, French, and Italian and versed in history, Elizabeth was raised to be the subject of her brother, who became king after Henry's death in 1547. When he died in 1553, she became a pawn in a long and vicious struggle for the crown. Imprisoned in the Tower and then in Woodstock Castle in Oxfordshire by the Catholic supporters of her sister's claim to the throne, Elizabeth wrote lyrics that testify to both her fears and her faith during this dangerous time.

In 1558, Queen Mary died, and Elizabeth was crowned with much rejoicing; in the historian William Camden's words: "neither did the people ever embrace any other Prince with more willing and constant mind." Once on the throne, Elizabeth pursued a policy of exemplary discretion; she rewarded those who were loyal to her and punished those who showed signs of disobedience. In 1568, when her cousin Mary, Queen of Scots, abdicated the throne of Scotland in favor of her son, James VI, Elizabeth granted Mary refuge in England. Yet evidence later suggested that Mary, an ardent Catholic, had plotted to kill Elizabeth and restore Catholicism in England, and in 1587, Elizabeth ordered her execution with great regret. Reflecting on this action, also the subject of a speech to Parliament, the queen declared: "This death will wring my heart as long as I live."

A woman and reigning monarch, Elizabeth's position was anomalous. As a woman, she retained an important kind of social power only as long as she was an object of desire, to be courted and won; as a reigning monarch, she was expected not only to govern but also to secure the succession. In her speech to Parliament on the subject of marriage early in her reign, Elizabeth provided reasons why she would delay taking a husband. She probably never intended to take one. Continuing the fiction of courtship well past the age at which she could be expected to have a child, she saw to it that she remained at once attractive and unavailable. Most important, she succeeded in commanding the attention of her subjects by transforming her court into a center of literary and artistic activity. Late in life, she met her most serious suitor, the Duke of Alençon, brother to the French king, Henry III. A dwarf whose face was disfigured by smallpox, he was her "little frog," a man she is said to have loved dearly. The problem of succession required another kind of temporizing. She refused to name James VI of Scotland as the next king of England until shortly before she died—a silence that she maintained was necessary to preserve the peace.

Throughout her long reign she cultivated two personas. As a monarch, she could speak courageously (as she did to her soldiers at Tilbury on the Devon coast while they waited for the Spanish to invade); as a woman, she could convey understanding (as she did to her critics in her so-called Golden Speech curtailing her prerogative to create monopolies). Her government remained a conscientious one to its very end. She cultivated a habit of mind that must have helped to ensure its stability: when she was sixty years old, she translated Boethius's *Consolation of Philosophy*, and she never allowed herself to forget the vicissitudes of fortune and her own mortality.

Written with a Diamond on Her Window at Woodstock[1]

Much suspected by° me,   *to have been done by*
Nothing proved can be,
Quoth Elizabeth prisoner.

---

1. Elizabeth was imprisoned at Woodstock Castle, near Oxford, from May 23, 1554, to sometime late in April 1555. The queen, Mary I, Elizabeth's half-sister, suspected her of treason. This and the following poem are thought to have been written at this time.

Written on a Wall at Woodstock

Oh fortune, thy wresting wavering state
Hath fraught with cares my troubled wit,
Whose witness this present prison late
Could bear, where once was joy's loan quit.[1]
5   Thou causedst the guilty to be loosed
From bands° where innocents were inclosed,   *bonds*
And caused the guiltless to be reserved,°   *bound*
And freed those that death had well deserved.
But all herein° can be nothing wrought,   *in prison*
10   So God send to my foes all they have thought.[2]

The Doubt of Future Foes

The doubt° of future foes exiles my present joy,   *fear*
And wit me warns to shun such snares as threaten mine annoy;[1]
For falsehood now doth flow, and subjects' faith doth ebb,
Which should not be if reason ruled or wisdom weaved the web.
5   But clouds of joys untried° do cloak aspiring minds,   *untested*
Which turn to rain of late repent by changed course of winds.[2]
The top of hope supposed the root upreared shall be,
And fruitless all their grafted guile, as shortly ye shall see.[3]
The dazzled eyes with pride, which great ambition blinds,
10   Shall be unsealed by worthy wights[4] whose foresight falsehood finds.
The daughter of debate that discord aye° doth sow   *ever*
Shall reap no gain where former rule[5] still peace hath taught to know.
No foreign banished wight[6] shall anchor in this port;
Our realm brooks not seditious sects, let them elsewhere resort.
15   My rusty sword through rest shall first his edge employ
To poll their tops[7] that seek such change or gape[8] for future joy.

On Monsieur's Departure[1]

I grieve and dare not show my discontent,
I love and yet am forced to seem to hate,
I do, yet dare not say I ever meant,
I seem stark mute but inwardly do prate.
5   I am and not,° I freeze and yet am burned,   *am not*
Since from myself another self I turned.

My care is like my shadow in the sun,
Follows me flying, flies when I pursue it,

---

1. I.e., this prison could bear witness recently to fortune's wavering state, where once it did not have to borrow joy [as it does now].
2. I.e., nothing can be done by one who is in prison, so may God send to my foes what they have suspected me of planning.
1. My harm.
2. I.e., because of a change of wind, my enemies' clouds of joy can turn to the rain of repentance.
3. I.e., at their most hopeful, my enemies supposed that the tree of my monarchy would be uprooted, but their grafted limbs of guile will bear no fruit.

4. Men.
5. The rule of Elizabeth's father, Henry VIII, and brother, Edward VI, both Protestants.
6. Any supporter of Philip II, king of Spain and consort of Mary I.
7. Cut their heads off.
8. Smile.
1. The poem expresses Elizabeth's regret at the departure of the Duke d'Alençon, who had sought her hand in marriage. After four years of visits and inconclusive negotiations, the courtship ended in 1583.

Stands and lies by me, doth what I have done.
10   His too familiar care doth make me rue° it.   *regret*
No means I find to rid him from my breast,
Till by the end of things° it be supprest.   *death*

Some gentler passion slide into my mind,
For I am soft and made of melting snow;
15   Or be more cruel, love, and so be kind.
Let me or° float or sink, be high or low.   *either*
Or let me live with some more sweet content,
Or die and so forget what love ere meant.

SPEECHES

The speeches of Elizabeth I exemplify early modern public oratory at its most effective. But they are also marked by features uniquely derived from her sense of herself as a monarch who wished (and probably needed) to convince her subjects that their welfare was more important to her than her own. In the excerpts that follow, Elizabeth emphasizes that although nature made her a woman and therefore of the weaker sex, divine right has made her a "prince," a person endowed with a masculine persona whose function it is to command not obey. She further emphasizes that her principal care is for her subjects, who are her charges and in some sense her children. In her public dealings throughout her reign, she played the gender card for all it was worth; in so doing, she transformed the fact that she was a woman, potentially a liability, into an instrument of policy.

On Marriage[1]

I may say unto you that from my years of understanding, sith[2] I first had consideration of myself to be born a servitor of Almighty God, I happily chose this kind of life in which I yet live, which I assure you for mine own part hath hitherto best contented myself and I trust hath been most acceptable to God. From the which, if either ambition of high estate offered to me in marriage by the pleasure and appointment of my prince[3]— whereof I have some records in this presence, as you our Lord Treasurer[4] well know; or if the eschewing of the danger of mine enemies or the avoiding of the period of death, whose messenger or rather continual watchman, the prince's indignation, was not little time daily before mine eyes—by whose means, although I know or justly may suspect, yet I will not now utter; or if the whole cause were in my sister herself, I will not now burthen her therewith, because I will not charge the dead: if any of these I say, I had not now remained in this estate wherein you see me. But so constant have I always continued in this determination—although my youth and words may seem to some hardly to agree together—yet is it most true that at this day I stand free from any other meaning that either I have had in times past or have at this present. With which trade of life I am so thoroughly acquainted that I trust God, who hath hitherto therein preserved and led me by the hand, will not now of His goodness suffer me to go alone. * * *

1. In 1559, a year after she had acceded to the throne at the age of twenty-five, Elizabeth addressed Parliament on the subject of marriage. Because the monarchy passed on by inheritance, it was expected that a monarch would marry and have children. In this speech, Elizabeth hints that she will never marry and also that she trusts God to provide for her successor who, she guesses, may be more "beneficial" to the kingdom than any child of her own would be. She probably intended to convey to her subjects that she would never abandon the kingdom either to the rule of a foreign prince (as Mary I had) or to a succession crisis.
2. Since.
3. The "prince" Elizabeth refers to is probably not Philip II, the consort of Mary I, but rather Mary herself, who in her official capacity as queen regnant might have offered her sister's hand in marriage to a suitable consort. Elizabeth can refer to Mary as her "sister" when she alludes to a "cause" that had no implications for the state but is rather personal, "in my sister herself."
4. The Marquis of Winchester.

Nevertheless—if any of you be in suspect—whensoever it may please God to incline my heart to another kind of life, ye may well assure yourselves my meaning is not to do or determine anything wherewith the realm may or shall have just cause to be discontented. And therefore put that clean out of your heads.[5] For I assure you—what credit my assurance may have with you I cannot tell, but what credit it shall deserve to have the sequence shall declare—I will never in that matter conclude anything that shall be prejudicial to the realm, for the weal, good, and safety whereof I will never shun to spend my life. And whomsoever my chance shall be to light upon, I trust he shall be as careful for the realm and you—I will not say as myself, because I cannot so certainly determine of any other; but at the least ways, by my good will and desire he shall be such as shall be as careful for the preservation of the realm and you as myself.

And albeit it might please Almightly God to continue me still in this mind to live out of the state of marriage, yet it is not to be feared but He will so work in my heart and in your wisdoms as good provision by His help may be made in convenient time, whereby the realm shall not remain destitute of an heir that may be a fit governor, and peradventure more beneficial to the realm than such offspring as may come of me. For, although I be never so careful of your well doings and mind ever so to be, yet may my issue grow out of kind and become perhaps ungracious. And in the end, this shall be for me sufficient, that a marble stone shall declare that a Queen, having reigned such a time, lived and died a virgin.

On Mary, Queen of Scots[1]

The bottomless graces and immeasurable benefits bestowed upon me by the Almighty are and have been such, as I must not only acknowledge them but admire them, accounting them as well miracles as benefits; not so much in respect of His Divine Majesty—with whom nothing is more common than to do things rare and singular—as in regard of our weakness, who cannot sufficiently set forth His wonderful works and graces, which to me have been so many, so diversely folded and embroidered one upon another, as in no sort am I able to express them.

And although there liveth not any that may more justly acknowledge themselves infinitely bound unto God than I, whose life He hath miraculously preserved at sundry times (beyond my merit) from a multitude of perils and dangers, yet is not that the cause for which I count myself the deepliest bound to give Him my humblest thanks, or to yield Him greatest recognition; but this which I shall tell you hereafter, which will deserve the name of wonder, if rare things and seldom seen be worthy of account. Even this it is: that as I came to the crown with the willing hearts of subjects, so do I now, after twenty-eight years' reign, perceive in you no diminution of good wills, which, if haply I should want, well might I breathe but never think I lived.

And now, albeit I find my life hath been full dangerously sought, and death contrived by such as no desert procured it, yet am I thereof so clear from malice—which hath the property to make men glad at the falls and faults of their foes, and make

5. Elizabeth emphasizes that her subjects and their representatives in Parliament have no authority to force her into marriage, however desirable they may think marriage is for the future of the kingdom.
1. The text is Elizabeth's answer to a petition from Parliament to execute Mary, Queen of Scots, who was reported to have conspired to depose her cousin Elizabeth and who had been a prisoner of the English queen for ten years. In

August 1586, evidence of a new plot came to light, and the conspirators, led by Sir Thomas Babington, were executed. On the evidence in letters to Babington, Mary was then formally tried and convicted of treason by a special court of peers, counsellors, and judges. Elizabeth answered Parliament in October by asking for delay and divine enlightenment.

them seem to do for other causes, when rancor is the ground—as I protest it is and hath been my grievous thought that one, not different in sex, of like estate, and my near kin, should be fallen into so great a crime. Yea, I had so little purpose to pursue her with any color of malice, that as it is not unknown to some of my Lords here—for now I will play the blab—I secretly wrote her a letter upon the discovery of sundry treasons, that if she would confess them, and privately acknowledge them by her letters unto myself, she never should need be called for them into so public question. Neither did I it of mind to circumvent her, for then I knew as much as she could confess; and so did I write.

And if, even yet, now the matter is made but too apparent, I thought she truly would repent—as perhaps she would easily appear in outward show to do—and that for her none other would take the matter upon them; or that we were but as two milk-maids, with pails upon our arms; or that there were no more dependency upon us, but mine own life were only in danger, and not the whole estate of your religion and well doings; I protest—wherein you may believe me, for although I may have many vices, I hope I have not accustomed my tongue to be an instrument of untruth—I would most willingly pardon and remit this offence. Or if by my death other nations and kingdoms might truly say that this realm had attained an ever prosperous and flourishing estate, I would (I assure you) not desire to live, but gladly give my life, to the end my death might procure you a better prince. And for your sakes it is that I desire to live: to keep you from a worse. For, as for me, I assure you I find no great cause I should be fond to live. I take no such pleasure in it that I should much wish it, nor conceive such terror in death that I should greatly fear it. And yet I say not but, if the stroke were coming, perchance flesh and blood would be moved with it, and seek to shun it.

I have had good experience and trial of this world. I know what it is to be a subject, what to be a sovereign, what to have good neighbors, and sometime meet evil-willers. I have found treason in trust, seen great benefits little regarded, and instead of gratefulness, courses[2] of purpose to cross. These former remembrances, present feeling, and future expectation of evils, (I say), have made me think an evil is much the better the less while it dureth,[3] and so them happiest that are soonest hence;[4] and taught me to bear with a better mind these treasons, than is common to my sex—yea, with a better heart perhaps than is in some men. Which I hope you will not merely impute to my simplicity or want of understanding, but rather that I thus conceived—that had their purposes taken effect, I should not have found the blow, before I had felt it; nor, though my peril should have been great, my pain should have been but small and short. Wherein, as I would be loath to die so bloody a death, so doubt I not but God would have given me grace to be prepared for such an event; which, when it shall chance, I refer to His good pleasure.

And now, as touching their treasons and conspiracies, together with the contriver of them. I will not so prejudicate myself and this my realm as to say or think that I might not, without the last statute, by the ancient laws of this land have proceeded against her; which[5] was not made particularly to prejudice her, though perhaps it might then be suspected in respect of the disposition of such as depend that way. It was so far from being intended to entrap her, that it was rather an admonition to warn

---

2. Plans.
3. Lasts.
4. I.e., out of this world.

5. I.e., the Parliamentary statute of 1584–85, known as the Act for the Queen's Surety, which provided for the trial of Mary, Queen of Scots, should she be accused of treason.

the danger thereof. But sith it is made, and in the force of a law, I thought good, in that which might concern her, to proceed according thereunto rather than by course of common law. Wherein, if you the judges have not deceived me, or that the books you brought me were not false—which God forbid—I might as justly have tried her by the ancient laws of the land.

But you lawyers are so nice and so precise in sifting and scanning every word and letter, that many times you stand more upon form than matter, upon syllables than the sense of the law. For, in this strictness and exact following of common form, she must have been indicted in Staffordshire, been arraigned at the bar, holden up her hand, and then been tried by a jury: a proper course, forsooth, to deal in that manner with one of her estate! I thought it better, therefore, for avoiding of these and more absurdities, to commit the cause to the inquisition of a good number of the greatest and most noble personages of this realm, of the judges and others of good account, whose sentence I must approve.[6]

And all little enough: for we Princes, I tell you, are set on stages, in the sight and view of all the world duly observed. The eyes of many behold our actions; a spot is soon spied in our garments, a blemish quickly noted in our doings. It behoveth us, therefore, to be careful that our proceedings be just and honorable.

But I must tell you one thing more: that in this late Act of Parliament you have laid an hard hand on me—that I must give direction for her death, which cannot be but most grievous, and an irksome burden to me. And lest you might mistake mine absence from this Parliament—which I had almost forgotten: although there be no cause why I should willingly come amongst multitudes (for that amongst many, some may be evil), yet hath it not been the doubt of any such danger or occasion that kept me from thence, but only the great grief to hear this cause spoken of, especially that such one of state and kin should need so open a declaration, and that this nation should be so spotted with blots of disloyalty. Wherein, the less is my grief for that I hope the better part is mine; and those of the worse not much to be accounted of, for that in seeking my destruction they might have spoiled their own souls.

And even now could I tell you that which would make you sorry. It is a secret; and yet I will tell it you (although it be known I have the property to keep counsel but too well, often times to mine own peril). It is not long since mine eyes did see it written that an oath was taken within few days either to kill me or to be hanged themselves; and that to be performed ere one month were ended. Hereby I see your danger in me, and neither can or will be so unthankful or careless of your consciences as to take no care for your safety.

I am not unmindful of your oath made in the Association,[7] manifesting your great good wills and affections, taken and entered into upon good conscience and true knowledge of the guilt, for safeguard of my person; done (I protest to God) before I ever heard it, or ever thought of such a matter, till a thousand hands, with many obligations, were showed me at Hampton Court, signed and subscribed with the names and seals of the greatest of this land. Which, as I do acknowledge as a perfect argument of your true hearts and great zeal to my safety, so shall my bond be stronger tied to greater care for all your good.

---

6. Elizabeth claims that Mary could have been tried as a criminal in a common law court but that this would have been an improper way to proceed as Mary remained a Queen of Scotland and therefore was not liable under English law.

7. The Oath (or Bond) of Association was taken by the Queen's Council in October 1582. It provided for Mary's arrest and execution without a trial; in essence, it sanctioned a lynching.

But, for that this matter is rare, weighty and of great consequence, and I think you do not look for any present resolution—the rather for that, as it is not my manner in matters of far less moment to give speedy answer without due consideration, so in this of such importance—I think it very requisite with earnest prayer to beseech His Divine Majesty so to illuminate mine understanding and inspire me with His grace, as I may do and determine that which shall serve to the establishment of His Church, preservation of your estates, and prosperity of this Commonwealth under my charge. Wherein, for that I know delay is dangerous, you shall have with all conveniency our resolution delivered by our message. And what ever any prince may merit of their subjects, for their approved testimony of their unfeigned sincerity, either by governing justly, void of all partiality, or sufferance of any injuries done (even to the poorest), that do I assuredly promise inviolably to perform, for requital of your so many deserts.

On Mary's Execution[1]

Full grievous is the way whose going on and end breeds cumber[2] for the hire of a laborious journey. I have strived more this day than ever in my life whether I should speak or use silence. If I speak and not complain, I shall dissemble; if I hold my peace, your labor taken were full vain.

For me to make my moan were strange and rare, for I suppose you shall find few that, for their own particular, will cumber you with such a care. Yet such, I protest, hath been my greedy desire and hungry will that of your consultation might have fallen out some other means to work my safety, joined with your assurance, than that for which you are become so earnest suitors, as I protest I must needs use complaint[3]—though not of you, but unto you, and of the cause; for that I do perceive, by your advices, prayers, and desires, there falleth out this accident, that only my injurer's bane must be my life's surety.

But if any there live so wicked of nature to suppose that I prolonged this time only pro forma, to the intent to make a show of clemency, thereby to set my praises to the wire-drawers[4] to lengthen them the more, they do me so great a wrong as they can hardly recompense. Or if any person there be that think or imagine that the least vainglorious thought hath drawn me further herein, they do me as open injury as ever was done to any living creature—as He that is the maker of all thoughts knoweth best to be true. Or if there be any that think that the Lords, appointed in commission, durst do no other, as fearing thereby to displease or to be suspected to be of a contrary opinion to my safety, they do but heap upon me injurious conceits. For, either those put in trust by me to supply my place have not performed their duty towards me, or else they have signified unto you all that my desire was that every one should do according to his conscience, and in the course of these proceedings should enjoy both freedom of voice and liberty of opinion, and what they would not openly, they might privately to myself declare. It was of a willing mind and great desire I had, that some other means might be found out, wherein I should have taken more comfort than in any other thing under the sun.

---

1. Parliament had determined that Elizabeth's safety and the future of Protestantism in England could be secured only by Mary's execution; it sent a delegation to Elizabeth asking for her approval. Again Elizabeth demurred. It was only in February 1587, after a new conspiracy was discovered, that Elizabeth signed Mary's death warrant.
2. Distress.
3. Express regret.
4. One who draws metal into wire.

And since now it is resolved that my surety cannot be established without a princess's head, I have just cause to complain that I, who have in my time pardoned so many rebels, winked at so many treasons, and either not produced[5] them or altogether slipped them over with silence, should now be forced to this proceeding, against such a person. I have besides, during my reign, seen and heard many opprobrious books and pamphlets against me, my realm and state, accusing me to be a tyrant. I thank them for their alms. I believe therein their meaning was to tell me news: and news it is to me indeed. I would it were as strange to hear of their impiety. What will they not now say, when it shall be spread that for the safety of her life a maiden queen could be content to spill the blood even of her own kinswoman? I may therefore full well complain that any man should think me given to cruelty; whereof I am so guiltless and innocent as I should slander God if I should say He gave me so vile a mind. Yea, I protest, I am so far from it that for mine own life I would not touch her. Neither hath my care been so much bent how to prolong mine, as how to preserve both: which I am right sorry is made so hard, yea so impossible.

I am not so void of judgment as not to see mine own peril; nor yet so ignorant as not to know it were in nature a foolish course to cherish a sword to cut mine own throat; nor so careless as not to weigh that my life daily is in hazard. But this I do consider, that many a man would put his life in danger for the safeguard of a king. I do not say that so will I; but I pray you think that I have thought upon it.

But sith so many hath both written and spoken against me, I pray you give me leave to say somewhat for myself, and, before you return to your countries, let you know for what a one you have passed so careful thoughts. And, as I think myself infinitely beholding unto you all that seek to preserve my life by all the means you may, so I protest that there liveth no prince—nor ever shall be—more mindful to requite so good deserts. Wherein, as I perceive you have kept your old wont[6] in a general seeking the lengthening of my days, so am I sure that never shall I requite it, unless I had as many lives as you all; but for ever I will acknowledge it while there is any breath left me. Although I may not justify, but may justly condemn, my sundry faults and sins to God, yet for my care in this government let me acquaint you with my intents.

When first I took the sceptre, my title made me not forget the giver, and therefore [I] began as it became me, with such religion as both I was born in, bred in, and, I trust, shall die in; although I was not so simple as not to know what danger and peril so great an alteration might procure me—how many great princes of the contrary opinion would attempt all they might against me, and generally what enmity I should thereby breed unto myself. Which all I regarded not, knowing that He, for whose sake I did it, might and would defend me. Rather marvel that I am, than muse that I should not be if it were not God's holy hand that continueth me beyond all other expectation.

I was not simply trained up, nor in my youth spent my time altogether idly; and yet, when I came to the crown, then entered I first into the school of experience, bethinking myself of those things that best fitted a king—justice, temper, magnanimity, judgment. As for the two latter, I will not boast. But for the two first, this may I truly say: among my subjects I never knew a difference of person, where right was one;[7]

---

5. Acted upon.
6. Desire.

7. I.e., my justice was impartial; it did not regard rank, occupation, or property as factors in determining what was right.

nor never to my knowledge preferred for favor what I thought not fit for worth; nor bent mine ears to credit a tale that first was told me; nor was so rash to corrupt my judgment with my censure, ere I heard the cause. I will not say but many reports might fortune[8] be brought me by such as must hear the matter, whose partiality might mar the right; for we princes cannot hear all causes ourselves. But this dare I boldly affirm: my verdict went with the truth of my knowledge.

But full well wished Alcibiades[9] his friend, that he should not give any answer till he had recited the letters of the alphabet. So have I not used over-sudden resolutions in matters that have touched me full near: you will say that with me, I think. And therefore, as touching your counsels and consultations, I conceive them to be wise, honest, and conscionable; so provident and careful for the safety of my life (which I wish no longer than may be for your good), that though I never can yield you of recompense your due, yet shall I endeavor myself to give you cause to think your good will not ill bestowed, and strive to make myself worthy for such subjects. And as for your petition: your judgment I condemn not, neither do I mistake your reasons, but pray you to accept my thankfulness, excuse my doubtfulness, and take in good part my answer-answerless. Wherein I attribute not so much to my own judgment, but that I think many particular persons may go before me, though by my degree I go before them. Therefore, if I should say, I would not do what you request, it might peradventure be more than I thought; and to say I would do it, might perhaps breed peril of that you labor to preserve, being more than in your own wisdoms and discretions would seem convenient,[1] circumstances of place and time being duly considered.

To the English Troops at Tilbury, Facing the Spanish Armada[1]

My loving people, we have been persuaded by some that are careful of our safety, to take heed how we commit ourselves to armed multitudes, for fear of treachery. But I assure you, I do not desire to live to distrust my faithful and loving people. Let tyrants fear. I have always so behaved myself that, under God, I have placed my chiefest strength and safeguard in the loyal hearts and good will of my subjects; and therefore I am come amongst you, as you see, at this time, not for my recreation and disport,[2] but being at this time resolved, in the midst and heat of the battle, to live or die amongst you all, to lay down for my God, and for my kingdom, and for my people, my honor and my blood, even in the dust. I know I have the body of a weak and feeble woman, but I have the heart and stomach of a king, and of a king of England too, and think foul scorn[3] that Parma or Spain, or any prince of Europe should dare to invade the border of my realm; to which rather than any dishonor shall grow[4] by me, I myself will take up arms, I myself will be your general, judge, and rewarder of every one of your virtues in the field. I know,

---

8. By chance.
9. An Athenian statesman who took part in the Peloponnesian War; changed sides to support Athen's enemy, Sparta; and was finally assassinated by Persians with whom he sought an alliance. The source of Elizabeth's reference is unknown.
1. Elizabeth equivocates nicely. She refuses to disagree with Parliament, lest she not respect her own misgivings; she refuses to agree with Parliament, lest its policy not be

in her own interest.
1. In 1588, with the Spanish fleet threatening the south coast of England, Elizabeth went to Tilbury, in Dorset, to speak to the troops who were guarding England against an invasion.
2. Amusement.
3. Shameful.
4. Be caused.

already for your forwardness[5] you have deserved rewards and crowns;[6] and we do assure you, in the word of a prince, they shall be duly paid you.

The Golden Speech[1]

Mr. Speaker, we have heard your declaration and perceive your care of our estate, by falling into a consideration of a grateful acknowledgment of such benefits as you have received; and that your coming is to present thanks to us, which I accept with no less joy than your loves can have desire to offer such a present.

I do assure you there is no prince that loves his subjects better, or whose love can countervail our love. There is no jewel, be it of never so rich a price, which I set before this jewel: I mean your love. For I do esteem it more than any treasure or riches; for that we know how to prize, but love and thanks I count unvaluable. And, though God hath raised me high, yet this I count the glory of my crown, that I have reigned with your loves. This makes me that I do not so much rejoice that God hath made me to be a queen, as to be a queen over so thankful a people. Therefore, I have cause to wish nothing more than to content the subject; and that is a duty which I owe. Neither do I desire to live longer days than I may see your prosperity; and that is my only desire. And as I am that person that still yet under God hath delivered you, so I trust, by the almighty power of God, that I shall be His instrument to preserve you from every peril, dishonor, shame, tyranny and oppression; partly by means of your intended helps which we take very acceptably, because it manifesteth the largeness of your good loves and loyalties unto your sovereign.

Of myself I must say this: I never was any greedy, scraping grasper, nor a strait, fast-holding prince, nor yet a waster. My heart was never set on any worldly goods, but only for my subjects' good. What you bestow on me, I will not hoard it up, but receive it to bestow on you again. Yea, mine own properties I account yours, to be expended for your good; and your eyes shall see the bestowing of all for your good. Therefore, render unto them, I beseech you, Mr. Speaker, such thanks as you imagine my heart yieldeth, but my tongue cannot express.

Since I was queen, yet did I never put my pen to any grant but that, upon pretext and semblance made unto me, it was both good and beneficial to the subject in general, though a private profit to some of my ancient servants who had deserved well at my hands. But the contrary being found by experience, I am exceedingly beholding to such subjects as would move the same at the first. And I am not so simple to suppose, but that there be some of the Lower House whom these grievances never touched: and for them, I think they spake out of zeal to their countries,[2] and not out of spleen or malevolent affection as being parties grieved; and I take it exceeding gratefully from them, because it gives us to know that no respects or interest had moved them, other than the minds they have to suffer no diminution of our honor and our subjects' love unto us. The zeal of which affection, tending to ease my people and knit their hearts unto me, I embrace with a princely care, for above all earthly treasure I esteem my people's love, more than which I desire not to merit.

5. Courage.
6. Recompense.
1. The queen had the prerogative or absolute power to grant favored subjects a patent for an exclusive manufacture. But the monopolies so created were disliked by those who would otherwise have competed for business, and a move to limit them was begun in Parliament. In response, in 1601, Elizabeth met with a committee of the House of Commons, led by the Speaker, thanked them for the subsidies recently granted the crown by the Commons, and promised to reform her practice.
2. I.e., those members who protested monopolies in behalf of their constituents, or "countries," and not on their own account.

That my grants should be grievous to my people and oppressions privileged under color of our patents, our kingly dignity shall not suffer[3] it. Yea, when I heard it, I could give no rest unto my thoughts until I had reformed it. Shall they, think you, escape unpunished that have thus oppressed you, and have been respectless of their duty, and regardless of our honor?[4] No, I assure you, Mr. Speaker, were it not more for conscience' sake than for any glory or increase of love that I desire, these errors, troubles, vexations and oppressions, done by these varlets and lewd persons, not worthy the name of subjects, should not escape without condign punishment. But I perceive they dealt with me like physicians who, ministering a drug, make it more acceptable by giving it a good aromatical savor, or when they give pills do gild them all over.[5]

I have ever used to set the Last-Judgment Day before mine eyes, and so to rule as I shall be judged to answer before a higher Judge, to whose judgment seat I do appeal, that never thought was cherished in my heart that tended not unto my people's good. And now, if my kingly bounties have been abused, and my grants turned to the hurt of my people, contrary to my will and meaning, and if any in authority under me have neglected or perverted what I have committed to them, I hope God will not lay their culps[6] and offences to my charge; who, though there were danger in repealing our grants, yet what danger would I not rather incur for your good, than I would suffer them still to continue?

I know the title of a king is a glorious title; but assure yourself that the shining glory of princely authority hath not so dazzled the eyes of our understanding, but that we well know and remember that we also are to yield an account of our actions before the great Judge. To be a king and wear a crown is a thing more glorious to them that see it, than it is pleasant to them that bear it. For myself, I was never so much enticed with the glorious name of a king or royal authority of a queen, as delighted that God hath made me His instrument to maintain His truth and glory, and to defend this kingdom (as I said) from peril, dishonor, tyranny and oppression.

There will never queen sit in my seat with more zeal to my country, care for my subjects, and that will sooner with willingness venture her life for your good and safety, than myself. For it is my desire to live nor reign no longer than my life and reign shall be for your good. And though you have had and may have many princes more mighty and wise sitting in this seat, yet you never had nor shall have any that will be more careful and loving.

Shall I ascribe anything to myself and my sexly weakness? I were not worthy to live then; and, of all, most unworthy of the mercies I have had from God, who hath given me a heart that yet never feared any foreign or home enemy. And I speak it to give God the praise, as a testimony before you, and not to attribute anything to myself. For I, oh Lord! what am I, whom practices and perils past should not fear? Or what can I do? That I should speak for any glory, God forbid.

This, Mr. Speaker, I pray you deliver unto the House, to whom heartily recommend me. And so I commit you all to your best fortunes and further counsels. And I pray you, Mr. Comptroller,[7] Mr. Secretary,[8] and you of my Council, that before these gentlemen go into their countries, you bring them all to kiss my hand.

3. Allow.
4. I.e., those who benefited from a monopoly without regard to the welfare of the general public.
5. Elizabeth compares unscrupulous patentees to physicians who coat bitter pills with sugar; in this case she is the patient who did not realize what was being given to her.
6. Sins.
7. Sir William Knollys.
8. Sir Robert Cecil.

Sir Walter Raleigh

c. 1554–1618

Born in South Devon, a region in which ports and shipyards testified to the importance of England's world trade and colonies abroad, Sir Walter Raleigh spent a considerable part of his life outside his native land. As a boy, he fought with Huguenot armies in France; at twenty-four he led an expedition to the West Indies with his half-brother, Sir Humphrey Gilbert; and two years later, he commanded a contingent of English troops in Ireland. He is reported to have been a great favorite of Elizabeth, at least until in 1592, when he secretly married one of her ladies-in-waiting, Elizabeth Throckmorton; the queen, furious that she had had no say in the match, imprisoned Raleigh in the Tower of London for a period that summer.

Raleigh was famous for his travels. His most challenging expedition was intended to locate the legendary gold mines of El Dorado in South America. In 1595 he set out for the Spanish colony of Guiana, penetrating the interior of that land by venturing up the Orinoco. He described his trip in the brilliantly detailed *Discovery of the Large, Rich and Beautiful Empire of Guiana,* and although he returned to England without the gold he had gone for, his leadership of an expedition to sack the harbor of Cadiz in 1596 was enough to restore him to royal favor. But Raleigh was to encounter real trouble with the accession of James I. His enemies at court convinced the king that Raleigh had committed treason, and in 1603 he was tried, convicted, and once again confined to the Tower of London, this time with his wife and family. He remained there for thirteen years. His release was finally granted on the condition that he lead another expedition to Guiana. He had informed the king that on his earlier trip he had discovered an actual gold mine, and he now claimed that his new adventure would be successful. In fact, it was a disaster. Not only did he find no gold; the mine to whose existence he had sworn was revealed to be a fabrication. On this occasion the grounds for proving treason were stronger than they had been in 1603. Raleigh was executed in 1618.

During his long imprisonment, Raleigh began to write a complete history of the world, managing only to cover events in ancient history to 168 B.C. Entitled *The History of the World* and published in 1614, the work is primarily remembered for the stunning reflection on death that appears on its last page: "O eloquent, just and mighty Death! Whom none could advise, thou hast persuaded; what none hath dared, thou hast done; and whom all the world hath flattered, thou only hast cast out of the world and despised; thou hast drawn together all the far stretched greatness, all the pride, cruelty, and ambition of man, and covered it all over with those two narrow words, *Hic iacet.*"

Much of Raleigh's poetry is occasional, written to address the circumstances and the moment in which he found himself. It possesses the quality Castiglione celebrated in his treatise on court life: a brilliance of self-expression that contemporary Italians termed *sprezzatura,* created by the supposedly artless use of artifice showing not the courtier's education, but rather his native wit and talent. Raleigh exploits images of common life but with an unusual intensity, adding sensuous detail to expressions of affection and reminders of mortality to celebrations of love. His longest and greatest poem, *The 21st and Last Book of the Ocean to Cynthia,* remained fragmentary at the time of his death. Occasioned when Queen Elizabeth imprisoned him for his marriage, the poem illustrates Raleigh's fury at the queen's inconsistent treatment of her "Ocean" or "Water," as Raleigh pronounced his first name. It ends in an equivocation: Raleigh professes his devotion to Elizabeth, instancing his good will that "knit up by faith shall ever last"; but he also concludes that despite this, they will not be reconciled: "Her love hath end; my woe must ever last."

To the Queen[1]

Our passions are most like to floods and streams,
The shallow murmur, but the deep are dumb.
So when affections yield discourse, it seems
The bottom is but shallow whence they come.
    They that are rich in words must needs discover
    That they are poor in that which makes a lover.

Wrong not, dear empress of my heart,
    The merit of true passion,
With thinking that he feels no smart,
    That sues for no compassion.
Since, if my plaints serve not to prove
    The conquest of your beauty,
It comes not from defect of love,
    But from excess of duty.

For knowing that I sue to serve
    A saint of such perfection,
As all desire, but none deserve,
    A place in her affection;
I rather choose to want relief
    Than venture the revealing,
When glory recommends the grief,
    Despair distrusts the healing.

Thus those desires that aim too high
    For any mortal lover,
When reason cannot make them die,
    Discretion will them cover.
Yet when discretion doth bereave
    The plaints that they should utter,
Then your discretion may perceive
    That silence is a suitor.

Silence in love bewrays more woe
    Than words, though ne'er so witty,
A beggar that is dumb, you know,
    Deserveth double pity.
Then misconceive not (dearest heart)
    My true, though secret passion,
He smarteth most that hides his smart,
    And sues for no compassion.

c. 1590

On the Life of Man

What is our life? A play of passion,
Our mirth the music of division,

---

1. This elaborate compliment is typical of the courtly expressions of devotion Elizabeth I often inspired. Its respectful complaint can be compared to the bitter regret in Raleigh's later poem *The Book of the Ocean to Cynthia.*

Our mothers' wombs the tiring houses be,
Where we are dressed for this short comedy,
Heaven the judicious sharp spectator is,
That sits and marks still who doth act amiss,
Our graves that hide us from the searching sun,
Are like drawn curtains when the play is done;
Thus march we playing to our latest rest,
Only we die in earnest, that's no jest.

1612

The Author's Epitaph, Made by Himself

Even such is time, which takes in trust
Our youth, our joys, and all we have,
And pays us but with age and dust,
Who in the dark and silent grave,
When we have wandered all our days,
Shuts up the story of our days;
And from which earth, and grave, and dust,
The Lord shall raise me up, I trust.

from The 21st and Last Book of the Ocean to Cynthia[1]

Sufficeth to you, my joys interred,
In simple words that I my woes complain;
You that then died when first my fancy erred—[2]
Joys under dust that never live again.

5   If to the living were my muse addressed,
Or did my mind her own spirit still inhold,
Were not my living passion so repressed
As to the dead° the dead did these unfold,   *i.e., joys*

Some sweeter words, some more becoming verse
10 Should witness my mishap in higher kind;
But my love's wounds, my fancy in the hearse,
The idea but resting of a wasted mind,

The blossoms fallen, the sap gone from the tree,
The broken monuments of my great desires—

1. This lyric complaint, a fragment of what was projected as a much longer work, is the most important of Raleigh's poems. It tells of his despair at losing the Queen's favor and reproaches her for indifference to his devoted service. Adopting the conventions of pastoral, Raleigh styles himself "The Shepherd of the Ocean," perhaps to draw attention to his first name, which he pronounced "Water." "Cynthia" is, of course, Elizabeth, figured here (as she was so often) as the moon, ever changeful, as well as Diana, the goddess of the moon and of chastity. Characterizing Cynthia as the moving force in his life,

Raleigh's verse illustrates how conventions of courtly love could acquire a political reference: both Elizabeth and her courtiers were accustomed to conveying their hopes and desires in the coded language of erotic compliment. Spenser's poem *Colin Clout's Come Home Again* (1591) notes that the subject of Raleigh's "Cynthia" is "the great unkindness" and "usage hard" of the "Lady of the Sea," who has "from her presence faultless him (i.e., the Shepherd) debarred."

2. The poet complains to his own "joys" that are now dead and buried.

15 From these so lost what may the affections° be?   *passions*
    What heat in cinders of extinguished fires?

    Lost in the mud of those high-flowing streams,
    Which through more fairer fields their courses bend,
    Slain with self-thoughts, amazed in fearful dreams,
20 Woes without date, discomforts without end.

    From fruitless trees I gather withered leaves,
    And glean° the broken ears° with miser's hand,   *harvest / of grain*
    Who sometime did enjoy the weighty sheaves;
    I seek fair flowers amid the brinish° sand.   *salty*

25 All in the shade, even in the fair sun days,
    Under those healthless trees I sit alone,
    Where joyful birds sing neither lovely lays,
    Nor Philomen° recounts her direful moan.   *the nightingale*

    No feeding flocks, no shepherd's company,
30 That might renew my dolorous conceit,°   *imagination*
    While happy then, while love and fantasy
    Confined my thoughts on that fair flock to wait;

    No pleasing streams fast to the ocean wending,
    The messengers sometimes of my great woe;
35 But all on earth, as from the cold storms bending,
    Shrink from my thoughts in high heavens or below.

    Oh, hopeful love, my object and invention,
    Oh, true desire, the spur of my conceit,
    Oh, worthiest spirit, my mind's impulsion,°   *force*
40 Oh, eyes transpersant,° my affection's bait,   *that penetrate*

    Oh princely form, my fancy's adamant,°   *magnet*
    Divine conceit,° my pains' acceptance,   *image*
    Oh, all in one! Oh, heaven on earth transparent!
    The seat of joys and love's abundance!

45 Out of that mass of miracles, my muse
    Gathered those flowers, to her pure senses pleasing;
    Out of her eyes, the store of joys, did choose
    Equal delights, my sorrow's counterpoising.

    Her regal looks my vigorous sighs suppressed,
50 Small drops of joys sweetened great worlds of woes,
    One gladsome day a thousand cares redressed—
    Whom love defends, what fortune overthrows?

    When she did well, what did there else amiss?
    When she did ill, what empires would have pleased?
55 No other power affecting woe or bliss,
    She gave, she took, she wounded, she appeased.

    The honor of her love, love still devising,
    Wounding my mind with contrary conceit,

Transferred itself sometime to her aspiring,
60   Sometime the trumpet of her thought's retreat.³

To seek new worlds for gold, for praise, for glory,
To try° desire, to try love severed far,   *test*
When I was gone, she sent her memory,
More strong than were ten thousand ships of war,

65   To call me back; to leave great honor's thought;
To leave my friends, my fortune, my attempt;
To leave the purpose⁴ I so long had sought,
And hold both cares and comforts in contempt.

Such heat in ice, such fire in frost remained,
70   Such trust in doubt, such comfort in despair,
Which, like the gentle lamb, though lately weaned,
Plays with the dug, though finds no comfort there.

But as a body, violently slain,
Retaineth warmth although the spirit be gone,
75   And by a power in nature moves again
Till it be laid below the fatal stone;

Or as the earth, even in cold winter days,
Left for a time by her life-giving sun,
Doth by the power remaining of his rays
80   Produce some green, though not as it hath done;

Or as a wheel, forced by the falling stream,
Although the course be turned some other way,
Doth for a time go round upon the beam,
Till, wanting strength to move, it stands at stay;

85   So my forsaken heart, my withered mind—
Widow of all the joys it once possessed,
My hopes clean out of sight with forced wind—
To kingdoms strange, to lands far off, addressed,

Alone, forsaken, friendless, on the shore
90   With many wounds, with death's cold pangs embraced,
Writes in the dust, as one that could no more,
Whom love, and time, and fortune, had defaced,

Of things so great, so long, so manifold,
With means so weak, the soul even then depicting
95   The weal, the woe, the passages of old,
And worlds of thoughts descried° by one last sighing.   *discerned*

---

3. The honor of being loved by her creating love (in me), wounding me with a contrary (twofold) conception, sometimes aspiring to (please) her, sometimes heralding the withdrawal of her attention. In other words, the poet is constantly aware that his love makes him have a conflicted conception of how to approach Cynthia: some-times he pleases her, sometimes what he does causes her disdain.

4. Raleigh's "purpose" was to find gold for England in the wilderness of the New World; he continued to hope for success in this venture until 1617, when his last voyage to Guiana ended in nothing.

As if, when after Phoebus° is descended,   *the sun*
And leaves a light much like the past day's dawning,
And every toil and labor wholly ended,
100   Each living creature draweth to his resting,

We should begin by such a parting light
To write the story of all ages past,
And end the same before approaching night.

Such is again the labor of my mind,
105   Whose shroud, by sorrow woven now to end,
Hath seen that ever shining sun declined,
So many years that so could not descend,

But that the eyes of my mind held her beams
In every part transferred by love's swift thought,
110   Far off or near, in waking or in dreams,
Imagination strong in lustre brought.

Such force her angelic appearance had
To master distance, time, or cruelty,
Such art to grieve, and after to make glad,
115   Such fear in love, such love in majesty.

My weary lines her memory embalmed;
My darkest ways her eyes make clear as day.
What storms so great but Cynthia's beams appeased?
What rage so fierce, that love could not allay?

120   Twelve years entire I wasted in this war,[5]
Twelve years of my most happy younger days;
But I in them, and they now wasted are,
"Of all which past, the sorrow only stays."

. . .

Yet as the air in deep caves underground
125   Is strongly drawn when violent heat hath vent
Great clefts therein, till moisture do abound,
And then the same, imprisioned and up-pent,°   *pent up*

Breaks out in earthquakes, tearing all asunder,
So in the center of my cloven heart—
130   My heart, to whom her beauties were such wonder—
Lies the sharp, poisoned head of that love's dart

Which, till all break and dissolve to dust,
Thence drawn it cannot be, or therein known,
There, mixed with my heart-blood, the fretting rust
135   The better part hath eaten and outgrown.

But what of those or these? Or what of aught
Of that which was, or that which is, to treat?

---

5. The 12 years of service to Elizabeth began with his command of troops in Ireland in 1580 and ended, in the terms the poem supplies, with his marriage and imprisonment in 1592. Raleigh was only 36 at the time.

What I possess is but the same I sought;
My love was false, my labors were deceit.

140   Nor less than such they are esteemed to be,
A fraud bought at the price of many woes,
A guile, whereof the profits unto me—
Could it be thought premediate° for those?   *plead*

Witness those withered leaves left on the tree,
145   The sorrow-worn face, the pensive mind,
The external shows, what may the internal be;
Cold care hath bitten both the root and rind.

But stay, my thoughts, make end, give fortune way;
Harsh is the voice of woe and sorrow's sound;
150   Complaints cure not, and tears do but allay
Griefs for a time, which after more abound.

To seek for moisture in the Arabian sand
Is but a loss of labor and of rest,
The links which time did break of hearty bands
155   Words cannot knit, or wailings make anew,
Seek not the sun in clouds when it is set. . . .
On highest mountains, where those cedars⁶ grew,
Against whose banks the troubled ocean beat,

And were the marks to find thy hoped port,
160   Into a soil far off themselves remove.
On Sestos' shore, Leander's late resort,
Hero hath left no lamp to guide her love.⁷

Thou lookest for light in vain, and storms arise,
She sleeps thy death, that erst thy danger sighed,
165   Strive then no more, bow down thy weary eyes—
Eyes which to all these woes thy heart have guided.

She is gone, she is lost, she is found, she is ever fair;
Sorrow draws weakly where love draws not too,
Woe's cries sound nothing, but only in love's ear.
170   Do then by dying what life cannot do.

Unfold thy flocks and leave them to the fields,
To feed on hills or dales, where likes them best,
Of what the summer or the springtime yields,
For love and time hath given thee leave to rest.

175   Thy heart which was their fold, now in decay
By often storms and winter's many blasts,
All torn and rent, becomes misfortune's prey,
False hope, my shepherd's staff, now age hath brast.°   *broken*

My pipe, which love's own hand gave my desire
180   To sing her praises and my woe upon—

---

6. The cedar was identified as a tree of royalty; so Raleigh can speak of the ocean beating against banks over which the cedar presides.
7. Leander and Hero were two lovers who lived on oppo-site shores of the Hellespont. When Leander swam at night from Abydos to visit Hero in Sestos, she hung out a lantern to guide him.

Despair hath often threatened to the fire,
As vain to keep now all the rest are gone.

Thus home I draw, as death's long night draws on,
Yet every foot, old thoughts turn back mine eyes;
185   Constraint me guides, as old age draws a stone
Against a hill, which over-weighty lies

For feeble arms or wasted strength to move.
My steps are backward, gazing on my loss,
My mind's affection and my soul's sole love,
190   Not mixed with fancy's chaff or fortune's dross.

To God I leave it,° who first gave it me,   *my soul*
And I her gave, and she returned again,
As it was hers; so let His mercies be
Of my last comforts the essential mean.°   *factor*
195   But be it so or not, the effects are past;
Her love hath end, my woes must ever last.

from The Discovery of the Large, Rich and Beautiful Empire of Guiana[1]

from *Epistle Dedicatory*

To the Right Honorable my singular good lord and kinsman, Charles Howard,[2] Knight of the Garter, Baron, and Chancellor, and of the Admirals of England the most reknowned, and to the Right Honorable Sir Robert Cecil, Knight, Counselor in Her Highness's Privy Councils.[3]

For your Honors' many honorable and friendly parts, I have hitherto only returned promises, and now for answer of both your adventures, I have sent you a bundle of papers which I have divided between your Lordship and Sir Robert Cecil in these two respects chiefly. First, for it is reasonable that wasteful factors,[4] when they have consumed such stocks as they had in trust, do yield some color for the same in their account; secondly, for that I am assured that whatsoever shall be done or written by me shall need a double protection and defense. The trial that I had of both your loves, when I was left of all but of malice and revenge, makes me still presume that you will be pleased (knowing what little power I had to perform aught, and the great advantage of forewarned enemies) to answer that out of knowledge which others shall but object out of malice.[5] In my more happy times as I did especially honor you both, so I found that your loves sought me out in the darkest shadow of adversity, and the same affection which accompanied my better

1. A region in Venezuela. The full title of Raleigh's report is *The Discovery of the Large, Rich and Beautiful Empire of Guiana, with a relation of the Great and Golden City of Manoa (which the Spaniards call El Dorado) and the provinces of Emeria, Arromaia, Amapaia and other Countries, with their rivers, adjoining.* It was written and published in London in 1596, a year after Raleigh undertook his expedition.
2. Charles Howard (1536–1624) was Baron Howard of Effingham and Earl of Nottingham, commander of the Queen's navy at the defeat of the Armada and the capture of Cadiz.

3. Sir Robert Cecil was the first Earl of Salisbury, son of a principal advisor to Elizabeth I. Robert Cecil became Elizabeth's secretary of state in 1589 and was a key figure in the administration of James I, in which he eventually held the office of Lord Treasurer.
4. Raleigh refers to himself as a "factor," an agent who is commissioned to perform a certain function. Factors who exhausted the resources at their disposal had to account for their expenditures.
5. Raleigh presumes that Howard and Cecil will be able to answer his detractors (who speak from malice) with knowledge gained from this account of his travels to Guiana.

fortune, soared not away from me in my many miseries. All which, though I cannot requite, yet I shall ever acknowledge, and the great debt which I have no power to pay, I can do no more for a time but confess to be due. It is true that as my errors were great, so they have yielded very grievous effects, and if aught might have been deserved in former times to have counterpoised any part of offenses, the fruit thereof (as it seemeth) was long before fallen from the tree and the dead stock[6] only remained.[7] I did therefore even in the winter of my life undertake these travels, fitter for boys less blasted with misfortunes, for men of greater ability, and for minds of better encouragement, that thereby if it were possible I might recover but the moderation of excess and the least taste of the greatest plenty formerly possessed. If I had known other way to win, if I had imagined how greater adventures might have regained, if I could conceive what further means I might yet use but even to appease so powerful displeasure, I would not doubt but for one year more to hold fast my soul in my teeth til it were performed. Of that little remain I had, I have wasted in effect all therein,[8] I have undergone many constructions,[9] I have been accompanied with many sorrows, with labor, hunger, heat, sickness, and peril. * * * Many years since, I had knowledge by relation of that mighty, rich and beautiful Empire of Guiana and of that great and golden city which the Spaniards call El Dorado, and the naturals,[1] Manoa, which city was conquered, re-edified, and enlarged by a younger son of Guainacapa, Emperor of Peru, at such time as Francisco Pizarro[2] and others conquered the said empire from his two elder brethren, Guascar and Atabalipa, both then contending for the same, the one being favored by the Oreiones of Cuzco, the other by the people of Caximalca. I sent my servant Jacob Whiddon the year before to get knowledge of the passages, and I had some light from Captain Parker, sometime my servant and now attending on your Lordship, that such a place there was to the southward of the great bay of Charuas, or Guanipa, but I found that it was six hundred miles farther off than they supposed, and many other impediments to them unknown and unheard. After I had displanted[3] Don Antonio de Berreo, who was upon the same enterprise, leaving my ships at Trinidad, at the port called Curiapan, I wandered four hundred miles into the said country by land and river, the particulars I will leave to the following discourse.[4] The country hath more quantity of gold by manifold than the best parts of the Indies or Peru; all the most of the kings of the borders are already become Her Majesty's vassals and seem to desire nothing more than Her Majesty's protection and the return of the English nation.

6. Trunk.
7. Raleigh admits that he has made errors and that the successes he had earlier in his career, which might have compensated for these errors, can no longer serve this purpose.
8. I.e., of what was left of my resources, I have effectually wasted everything.
9. Trials.
1. Indigenous people.
2. Pizarro (1475–1541) conquered Peru by capturing the Incan king Atahualpa, whom Raleigh refers to as Atabalipa. Atahualpa was the son of Guainacapa and the brother of Guascar, whom he killed to get the throne. This passage suggests that Guianacapa had three sons;

Raleigh later states that he had only two sons. Pizarro captured Cuzco, the principal city of the Incas, in 1533. The Oreiones were the native people of Cuzco; Caximalca or Casimarca was another large city in Peru.
3. Dislodged.
4. Here Raleigh claims that a Captain Parker told him that El Dorado was south of the bay of Guanipa (which opens onto the Gulf of Paria and has no connection with the Orinoco), but he discovered that it was 600 miles in the interior of the country and away from the shore. Don Antonio de Berreo was the Spanish Governor of Trinidad and Guiana; Trinidad is an island just off the Venezuelan coast. Presumably, Raleigh marched from that coast 400 miles inland.

[THE AMAZONS]

I made inquiry amongst the most ancient and best traveled of the Orenoqueponi, and I had knowledge of all the rivers between Orenoque and [the river of the] Amazons, and was very desirous to understand the truth of those warlike women, because of some it is believed, of others not.[1] And though I digress from my purpose, yet I will set down what hath been delivered me for truth of those women, and I spake with a Casique or Lord of people that told me he had been in the river, and beyond it also. The nations of these women are on the south side of the river in the provinces of Topago, and their chiefest strengths and retreats are in the Islands situated on the south side of the entrance, some 60 leagues within the mouth of the said river. The memories of the like women are very ancient as well in Africa as in Asia. In Africa those that had Medusa[2] for Queen: others in Scithia near the rivers of Tanais and Thermadon: we find also that Lampedo and Marthesia[3] were Queens of the Amazons: in many histories they are verified to have been, and in diverse ages and provinces. But they which are not far from Guiana do accompany with men but once a year, and for the time of one month, which I gather by their relation to be in April. At that time all the kings of the borders assemble, and the queens of the Amazons, and after the queens have chosen, the rest cast lots for their Valentines. This one month, they feast, dance, and drink of their wines in abundance, and the moon being done, they all depart to their own provinces. If they conceive, and be delivered of a son, they return him to the father, if of a daughter they nourish it, and retain it, and as many as have daughters send unto the begetters a present, all being desirous to increase their own sex and kind, but that they cut off the right dug of the breast I do not find to be true. It was further told me, that if in the wars they took any prisoners that they used to accompany with those also at what time soever, but in the end for certain they put them to death: for they are said to be very cruel and bloodthirsty, especially to such as offer to invade their territories.

[THE ORINOCO]

The great river of Orenoque or Baraquan hath nine branches which fall out on the north side of his own main mouth. On the south side it hath seven other fallings into the sea, so it disemboqueth[1] by sixteen arms in all, between islands and broken ground, but the islands are very great, many of them as big as the Isle of Wight[2] and bigger, and many less. From the first branch on the north to the last of the south it is at least one hundred leagues, so as the river's mouth is no less than three hundred miles wide at his entrance into the sea, which I take to be far bigger than that of [the] Amazons. All those that inhabit in the mouth of this river upon the several north branches are these Tiuitiuas,[3] of which there are two chief lords which have continual wars one with the other. The islands which lie on the right hand are called Pallamos,

---

1. Raleigh takes his account of the Amazons from a native of Guiana. He associates this race of women, whose presence has never been verified, with a comparable people described in Greek mythology who are also warlike and consort with men only to conceive children.
2. A mythical monstrous woman, one of the Gorgons, who turned to stone whoever looked at her.

3. The legendary queen of the Amazons who fought in the Trojan war.
1. Discharges.
2. Island off the southern coast of England.
3. The Waraus, an indigenous people who live on the delta of the Orinoco and adjoining coasts. Spanish historians refer to them as the Guaraunos or Guaraunu.

and the land on the left, Hororotomaka, and the river by which John Douglas returned within the land from Amana to Capuri, they call Macuri.

These Tiuitiuas are a very goodly people and very valiant, and have the most manly speech and most deliberate that ever I heard of, what nation so ever. In the summer they have houses on the ground as in other places, where they build very artificial towns and villages, as it is written in the Spanish story of the West Indies, that those people do in the low lands near the gulf of Uraba. For between May and September, the river of Orenoque riseth thirty foot upright, and then those islands overflow twenty foot high above the level of the ground, saving some few raised grounds in the middle of them, and for this cause they are enforced to live in this manner. They never eat of anything that is set or sown, and as at home they use neither planting nor other manurance, so when they come abroad they refuse to feed of aught but of that which nature without labor bringeth forth.[4] They use the tops of *palmitos* [palm trees] for bread and kill deer, fish, and porks for the rest of their sustenance; they also have many sorts of fruits that grow in the woods and a great variety of birds and fowl.

And if to speak of them were not tedious and vulgar, surely we saw in those passages of very rare colors and forms not elsewhere to be found, for as much as I have either seen or read. Of these poeple, those that dwell upon the branches of the Orenoque called Capuri and Macureo are for the most part carpenters of *canoas* [canoes], for they make the most and fairest houses and sell them into Guiana for gold, and into Trinidad for tobacco, in the excessive taking whereof they exceed all nations, and notwithstanding the moistness of the air in which they live, the hardness of their diet, and the great labors they suffer to hunt, fish, and fowl for their living, in all my life either in the Indies or in Europe did I never behold a more goodly or better-favored people, or a more manly. They were wont to make war upon all nations and especially on the Cannibals, so as none durst without a good strength trade by those rivers; but of late they are at peace with their neighbors, all holding the Spaniards for a common enemy.[5] When their commanders die, they use great lamentation, and when they think the flesh of their bodies is putrified and fallen from the bones, then they take up the carcass again and hang it in the Casique's house that died, and deck his skull with feathers of all colors and hang all his gold plates about the bones of his arms, thighs, and legs. Those nations which are called Arwacas,[6] which dwell on the south of Orenoque (of which place and nation our Indian pilot was), are dispersed in many other places and do use to beat the bones of their lords into powder, and their wives and friends drink it all in their several sorts of drinks.

[THE NEW WORLD OF GUIANA]

To conclude, Guiana is a country that hath yet her maidenhead, never sacked, turned, nor wrought; the face of the earth hath not been torn, nor the virtue and salt of the soil spent by manurance, the graves have not been opened for gold, the mines not broken with sledges, nor their images pulled down out of their temples. It hath never been entered by any army of strength and never conquered or possessed by any

---

4. As people that do not farm, the Tiuitiuas would have been categorized by many Europeans as having no conception of property and therefore incapable of being dispossessed.
5. Here and throughout the narrative, Raleigh portrays the people of the region as desiring the protection of the Eng-

lish against the Spanish, whose mistreatment of the natives of the Americas was well publicized. Raleigh could claim that by making these natives vassals of the English monarch, England could acquire an empire to rival Spain's.
6. Known today as Arawaks, these people were neighbors of the Tiuitiuas.

Christian prince. It is besides so defensible that if two forts be builded in one of the provinces which I have seen, the flood setteth in so near the bank where the channel also lieth that no ship can pass but within a pike's length of the artillery, first of the one and afterwards of the other. Which two forts will be a sufficient guard both to the empire of *Inga* [Inca] and to an hundred other several kingdoms lying within the said river, even to the city of Quito in Peru.

There is therefore a great difference between the easiness of the conquest of Guiana and the defense of it being conquered, and the West or East Indies. Guiana hath but one entrance by the sea (if it have that) for any vessels of burden, so as whosoever shall first possess it, it shall be found inaccessible for any enemy except he come in wherries, barges, or *canoas*, or else in flat-bottomed boats; and if he do offer to enter it in that manner, the woods are so thick two hundred miles together upon the rivers of such entrance as a mouse cannot sit in a boat unhit from the bank. By land it is more impossible to approach, for it hath the strongest situation of any region under the sun, and is so environed with impassable mountains on every side as it is impossible to victual any company in the passage, which hath been well-proved by the Spanish nation, who, since the conquest of Peru have never left five years free from attempting this empire or discovering some way into it, and yet of twenty-three several gentlemen, knights, and noblemen, there was never any that knew which way to lead an army by land or to conduct ships by sea anything near the said country. Oreliano, of which the river of the Amazons taketh name, was the first, and Don Anthonio de Berreo (whom we displanted), the last; and I doubt much whether he himself or any of his yet know the best way into the said empire. It can therefore hardly be regained if any strength be formerly set down but in one or two places, and but two or three crumsters or galleys built and furnished upon the river within. The West Indies hath many ports, watering places, and landings, and nearer than three hundred miles to Guiana no man can harbor a ship, except he know one only place which is not learned in haste, and which I will undertake there is not any one of my companies that knoweth, whosoever hearkened after it.

Besides by keeping one good fort or building one town of strength, the whole empire is guarded, and whatsoever companies shall be afterwards planted within the land, although in twenty several provinces, those shall be able all to reunite themselves upon any occasion either by the way of one river or be able to march by land without either wood, bog, or mountain; whereas in the West Indies there are few towns or provinces that can succour or relieve one the other, either by land or sea. By land the countries are either desert, mountainous, or strong enemies. By sea, if any man invade to the eastward, those to the west cannot in many months turn against the breeze and east wind, besides the Spaniards are therein so dispersed as they are nowhere strong but in *Nueva Hispania* [New Spain] only. The sharp mountains, the thorns, the poisoned prickles, the sandy and deep ways in the valleys, the smothering heat and air, and want of water in other places are their only and best defense, which (because those nations that invade them are not victualled or provided to stay, neither have any place to friend adjoining) do serve them instead of good arms and great multitudes.

The West Indies were first offered Her Majesty's grandfather by Columbus,[1] a stranger in whom there might be doubt of deceit, and besides it was then thought

---

1. The brother of Christopher Columbus, Bartholomew Columbus, who invited Henry VII, King of England and grandfather of Elizabeth I, to accept his brother's services in his effort to find a continent west of England. Henry is reported to have accepted this offer but not before Christopher Columbus had contracted his services to Queen Isabella of Spain. Therefore the West Indies were not ever offered to Henry VII; they were and remained Spanish through the 19th century.

incredible that there were such and so many lands and regions never written of before. This empire is made known to Her Majesty by her own vassal, and by him that oweth to her more duty than an ordinary subject, so that it shall ill sort with the many graces and benefits which I have received to abuse Her Highness either with fables or imaginations. The country is already discovered,[2] many nations won to Her Majesty's love and obedience, and those Spaniards which have latest and longest labored about the conquest, beaten out, discouraged and disgraced, which among these nations were thought invincible. Her Majesty may in this enterprise employ all those soldiers and gentlemen that are younger brethren, and all captains and chieftains that want employment, and the charge will be only the first setting out in victualling and arming them, for after the first or second year I doubt not but to see in London a contratation house of more receipt for Guiana than there is now in Seville for the West Indies.[3]

And I am resolved that if there were but a small army afoot in Guiana, marching towards Manoa, the chief city of *Inga,* he would yield Her Majesty by composition so many hundred thousand pounds yearly as should both defend all enemies abroad and defray all expenses at home and that he would besides pay a garrison of three or four thousand soldiers very royally to defend him against other nations. For he cannot but know how his predecessors, yea, how his own great uncles Guascar and Atibalipa, sons to Guanacapa, Emperor of Peru, were (while they contended for the empire) beaten out by the Spaniards and that both of late years and ever since the said conquest, the Spaniards have sought the passages and entry of his country; and of their cruelties used to the borderers he cannot be ignorant. In which respects no doubt but he will be brought to tribute with great gladness, if not, he hath neither shot nor iron weapon in all his empire and therefore may be easily conquered.

And I further remember that Berreo confessed to me and others (which I protest before the majesty of God to be true) that there was found among the prophecies of Peru (at such time as the empire was reduced to Spanish obedience) in their chiefest temples, among diverse others, which foreshadowed the loss of the said empire, that from *Inglatierra* [England] those *Ingas* should be again in time to come restored and delivered from the servitude of the said conquerors. And I hope, as we with these few hands have displanted the first garrison and driven them out of the said country, so Her Majesty will give order for the rest and either defend it and hold it as tributary, or conquer and keep it as Empress of the same. For whatsoever Prince shall possess it shall be greatest, and if the king of Spain enjoy it, he will become unresistable. Her Majesty hereby shall confirm and strengthen the opinions of all nations as touching her great and princely actions. And where the south border of Guiana reacheth to the dominion and empire of the Amazons, those women shall hereby hear the name of a virgin which is not only able to defend her own territories and her neighbors, but also to invade and conquer so great empires so far removed.[4]

To speak more at this time I fear would be but troublesome. I trust in God, this being true will suffice, and that he which is King of all Kings and Lord of all Lords will put it into her heart which is Lady of Ladies to possess it, if not, I will judge those men worthy to be kings thereof that by her grace and leave will undertake of it themselves.

2. The continent of which Guiana is a part.
3. Raleigh states that there will be a trading house or mercantile exchange for investors in Guiana that will exceed in its volume of business the comparable institu-

tion for the West Indian trade in Seville.
4. This reference to the Amazons allows Raleigh to pay tribute to Elizabeth I, who represented herself as a powerful virgin queen.

Christopher Marlowe

1564–1593

When Christopher Marlowe began his career as a dramatist, the Elizabethan stage was at the height of its popularity and sophistication. Marlowe's plays were an immediate success, fascinating audiences with dazzling characters, exotic settings, and controversial subjects. Throughout his career—and even after his sudden death at the age of twenty-nine—Marlowe was Shakespeare's principal commercial and artistic rival.

A shoemaker's son, Marlowe went to Cambridge on a scholarship that was intended to prepare him for holy orders. His interests proved to be literary rather than religious, however, and he left Cambridge for London. As a student, he had composed a number of poems, notably the brilliant but unfinished *Hero and Leander*, a narrative of heterosexual and homosexual passion, but public recognition came with the production of his first play, *Tamburlaine the Great*, in 1587. This was followed by *The Second Part of Tamburlaine the Great, The Jew of Malta, Edward II, Dr. Faustus, Dido, Queen of Carthage*, and finally *The Massacre at Paris*, all composed within a period of six years. Marlowe's bold and inventive language captivated audiences; his blank verse, in which the sense of a sentence is not interrupted at the end of each line by the constraints of rhyme, brought the rhythms of natural speech to the language of theater. His characterizations of heroes were equally astonishing: driven by an incandescent desire that no conquest could satisfy, they revealed the torment and tragedy that were occasioned by pride.

Marlowe himself may have been employed in subversive activities. While still at Cambridge, he became a spy for Queen Elizabeth's secret service, dedicated to the infiltration and exposure of Catholic groups in England and abroad. How much activity he was responsible for remains guesswork. At the very least, the manner in which he died suggests his involvement in clandestine politics. In May 1593, the Queen's Privy Council issued a warrant for his arrest. The charge against him—blasphemy—seems to have come from Thomas Kyd, a fellow playwright with whom Marlowe shared lodgings. While in London waiting for a hearing, Marlowe, who was drinking in an alehouse, got into a fight with three men (all government spies), one of whom was Ingram Friser. Marlowe raised a dagger to stab Friser, but Friser, warding off the blow, managed to turn the dagger against Marlowe. It pierced his eye "in such sort that his brains coming out at the dagger point, he shortly after died." The affair did not end there; two days after Marlowe's death, Richard Baines (himself a former spy) accused him before the Privy Council of atheism, treason, and the opinion "that they that love not tobacco and boys were fools." Whether or not these accusations held any truth, they referred to views that were not unusual in the circles Marlowe traveled in; they indicate a skepticism in matters of religion and an indifference to social decorum that authorities responsible for political order would have considered dangerous. Some scholars think that Marlowe was murdered by government command. Although the mystery surrounding his death may never be solved, the mercurial brilliance of his work remains undisputed.

With the exception of the two parts of *Tamburlaine*, published in 1590, Marlowe's works were published after his death: *Edward II* and *Dido, Queen of Carthage* in 1594; *Hero and Leander* in 1598; *Dr. Faustus* in 1604; and *The Jew of Malta* in 1633. The celebrated lyric entitled *The Passionate Shepherd to His Love* first appeared in 1599 in an unauthorized collection of verse called *The Passionate Pilgrim* published by William Jaggard.

The Passionate Shepherd to His Love

Come live with me, and be my love,
And we will all the pleasures prove,
That valleys, groves, hills, and fields,
Woods, or steepy mountain yields.

5   And we will sit upon the rocks,
       Seeing the shepherds feed their flocks,
       By shallow rivers, to whose falls,
       Melodious birds sing madrigals.

       And I will make thee beds of roses,
10   And a thousand fragrant poesies,
       A cap of flowers, and a kirtle,
       Embroidered all with leaves of myrtle.

       A gown made of the finest wool,
       Which from our pretty lambs we pull,
15   Fair lined slippers for the cold,
       With buckles of the purest gold.

       A belt of straw, and ivy buds,
       With coral clasps and amber studs,
       And if these pleasures may thee move,
20   Come live with me, and be my love.

       The shepherd swains shall dance and sing,
       For thy delight each May morning,
       If these delights thy mind may move,
       Then live with me and be my love.

COMPANION READING

Sir Walter Raleigh: The Nymph's Reply to the Shepherd[1]

       If all the world and love were young,
       And truth in every shepherd's tongue,
       These pretty pleasures might me move,
       To live with thee, and be thy love.

5   Time drives the flocks from field to fold,
       When rivers rage, and rocks grow cold,
       And Philomel° becometh dumb,   *the nightingale*
       The rest complain of cares to come.

       The flowers do fade, and wanton fields,
10   To wayward winter reckoning yields,
       A honey tongue, a heart of gall,
       Is fancy's spring, but sorrow's fall.

       Thy gowns, thy shoes, thy beds of roses,
       Thy cap, thy kirtle, and thy poesies,
15   Soon break, soon wither, soon forgotten;
       In folly ripe, in reason rotten.

       Thy belt of straw and ivy buds,
       Thy coral clasps and amber studs,
       All these in me no means can move,
20   To come to thee, and be thy love.

1. Raleigh's *Reply* was published together with Marlowe's poem in Jaggard's collection.

But could youth last, and love still breed,
Had joys no date, nor age no need,
Then these delights my mind might move,
To live with thee, and be thy love.

The Tragical History of Dr. Faustus

Marlowe's play is the first dramatic rendition of the medieval legend of a man who sold his soul to the devil. Sixteenth-century readers associated him with a necromancer named Dr. Faustus, and Marlowe exploited this identification when he reworked the medieval plot for his play. Rejecting the usual learning available to ambitious men—philosophy, medicine, law, and theology—Marlowe's Faustus signs a contract with the devil, represented in this case by his servant, Mephostophilis; in exchange for his soul, Faustus gains superhuman powers for twenty-four years. He uses these powers to conjure the Pope in Rome into giving the Protestant Emperor Charles V authority over the church through a surrogate Pope, Bruno; but his powers are also deployed in the banal trickery of simple and even criminal characters. The play is enigmatic on points of doctrine. Mephostophilis describes hell not as a locale but rather as the state of mind of one who has rejected God—a description that Milton will later amplify—telling Faustus: "this is hell, nor am I out of it." And Faustus, having worshipped the devil, is nevertheless offered a chance to repent and find salvation even at the very end of his alloted life. But he rejects God's love in favor of a night with Helen of Troy, praising her in lines that are now famous: "Was this the face that launched a thousand ships, / And burnt the topless towers of Ilium?" The play concludes with a report of Faustus' mangled body, torn to bits by the demon to whom he had given his soul.

A short version of the play, in thirteen scenes, was published in 1604; known as the A text, it was probably used by touring companies. The longer B text, given here, was published in 1616, probably based on Marlowe's original manuscript but also incorporating revisions and additions by Marlowe or others, as (typically in this period) the play continued to evolve in performance.

The Tragical History of Dr. Faustus

Dramatis Personae

CHORUS	THE POPE
FAUSTUS	BRUNO
WAGNER, *Servant to Faustus*	RAYMOND, *King of Hungary*
GOOD ANGEL AND EVIL ANGEL	CHARLES, *the German Emperor*
VALDES ⎫ *Friends to Faustus*	MARTINO
CORNELIUS ⎭	FREDERICK
MEPHOSTOPHILIS	BENVOLIO
LUCIFER	SAXONY
BELZEBUB	DUKE OF VANHOLT
THE SEVEN DEADLY SINS	DUCHESS OF VANHOLT
CLOWN/ROBIN	SPIRITS IN THE SHAPES OF ALEXANDER
DICK	THE GREAT, DARIUS, PARAMOUR, AND
RAFE	HELEN
VINTNER	AN OLD MAN
CARTER	SCHOLARS, SOLDIERS, DEVILS, COURTIERS,
HOSTESS	CARDINALS, MONKS, CUPIDS

[*Enter Chorus.*]

CHORUS Not marching in the fields of Thrasimene,[1]
    Where Mars did mate the warlike Carthigens,
    Nor sporting in the dalliance of love
    In courts of kings where state is overturned,
5   Nor in the pomp of proud audacious deeds,
    Intends our muse to vaunt his heavenly verse.[2]
    Only this, gentles: we must now perform
    The form of Faustus' fortunes, good or bad.
    And now to patient judgments we appeal,
10   And speak for Faustus in his infancy.
    Now is he born, of parents base of stock,
    In Germany, within a town called Rhodes.
    At riper years to Wittenberg he went,
    Whereas his kinsmen chiefly brought him up.
15   So much he profits in divinity,
    The fruitful plot° of scholarism graced,   *field*
    That shortly he was graced with Doctor's name,
    Excelling all; and sweetly can dispute
    In th' heavenly matters of theology.
20   Till swol'n with cunning of a self-conceit,
    His waxen wings did mount above his reach,
    And melting, heavens conspired his overthrow.[3]
    For falling to a devilish exercise,
    And glutted now with learning's golden gifts,
25   He surfeits upon cursed necromancy.
    Nothing so sweet as magic is to him,
    Which he prefers before his chiefest bliss:
    And this the man that in his study sits.

Act 1

Scene One

[*Faustus in his study.*]

FAUSTUS Settle thy studies, Faustus, and begin
    To sound the depth of that thou wilt profess.
    Having commenced, be a divine in show,
    Yet level at the end of every art
5   And live and die in Aristotle's works.
    Sweet Analytics, 'tis thou hast ravished me.[4]
    Bene disserere est finis logices.
    Is "to dispute well logic's chiefest end"?

---

1. Trasimeno, a lake in Italy near Rome. The Carthaginian general Hannibal conquered Roman forces at Trasimeno in 217 B.C.; Marlowe's "Mars" is probably a reference to the Roman army, which "mated" or engaged the enemy opposition there.
2. These lines may refer to plays Marlowe had previously staged and whose subjects were war (*Tamburlaine*) and love (*Edward II, Dido, Queen of Carthage*).
3. Faustus is compared to the legendary figure of Icarus,

whose father, the master craftsman Daedalus, made him a pair of wings that were attached to his body with wax. Icarus flew too near the sun, the wax supporting his wings melted, and he fell to the sea. The legend is generally understood to signify the consequences of pride and presumption.
4. Aristotle (384–22 B.C.), the best known of the Greek philosophers, wrote on the natural and social sciences. His *Analytics* dealt with logic.

Affords this art no greater miracle?
10   Then read no more: thou hast attained that end.
A greater subject fitteth Faustus' wit.
Bid *on cai me on*° farewell. And Galen,[5] come.   *being and non-being*
Seeing, *ubi desinit philosophus, ibi incipit medicus*.
Be a physician, Faustus: heap up gold
15   And be eternized for some wondrous cure.
Summum bonum medicinae sanitas:
"The end of physic is our body's health."
Why, Faustus, hast thou not attained that end?
Is not thy common talk sound aphorisms?°   *wise sayings*
20   Are not thy bills hung up as monuments,
Whereby whole cities have escaped the plague,
And thousand desperate maladies been cured?
Yet art thou still but Faustus and a man.
Couldst thou make men to live eternally,
25   Or being dead, raise them to life again,
Then this profession were to be esteemed.
Physic, farewell. Where is Justinian?[6]
Si una eademque res legatur duobus,
Alter rem, alter valorem rei etc.,
30   A petty case of paltry legacies!
Exhaereditare filium non potest pater, nisi—
Such is the subject of the institute
And universal body of the law.
This study fits a mercenary drudge,
35   Who aims at nothing but external trash,
Too servile and illiberal for me.
When all is done Divinity is best.
Jerome's Bible![7] Faustus, view it well.
Stipendium peccati mors est. Ha! Stipendium etc.,
40   "The reward of sin is death."[8] That's hard.
Si pecasse negamus, fallimur, et nulla est in nobis veritas.
"If we say that we have no sin
We deceive ourselves, and there is no truth in us."[9]
Why then, belike, we must sin,
45   And so consequently die.
Ay, we must die, an everlasting death.
What doctrine call you this? *Che sera, sera.*
"What will be, shall be." Divinity, adieu!
These necromantic books are heavenly,
50   Lines, circles, scenes, letters and characters:

5. Greek physician (130–200) whose works on medicine were studied through the early modern period. Faustus welcomes his change of authorities with "where the philosopher ends, the physician begins."
6. Justinian, Emperor of Byzantium (483–565), codified all of Roman law; his *Institutes* provided the basis for civil law in England as well as on the continent. Faustus cites a principle of estate law: "if one and the same thing is

bequeathed to two people, one of them should have the thing itself, and the other the value of it"; and "the father may not disinherit the son."
7. Jerome (347–420), a theologian who translated the Greek Bible and some of the Hebrew Bible into Latin, also wrote on Christian doctrine.
8. Romans 6.23.
9. 1 John 1.8.

Ay, these are those that Faustus most desires.
Oh, what a world of profit and delight,
Of power, of honor, of omnipotence,
Is promised to the studious artisan!
55   All things that move between the quiet poles
Shall be at my command. Emperors and kings
Are but obeyed in their several provinces.
Nor can they raise the wind or rend the clouds.
But his dominion that exceeds in this
60   Stretcheth as far as doth the mind of man:
A sound magician is a demi-god.
Here, tire° my brains to get° a deity.   *use/engender*
   [*Enter Wagner.*]
Wagner, commend me to my dearest friends,
The German Valdes and Cornelius.
65   Request them earnestly to visit me.
WAGNER I will, sir.   [*Exit.*]
FAUSTUS Their conference will be a greater help to me
Than all my labors, plod I ne'er so fast.
   [*Enter the Good and Evil Angels.*]
GOOD ANGEL Oh Faustus, lay that damned book aside,
70   And gaze not on it lest it tempt thy soul
And heap God's heavy wrath upon thy head.
Read, read the scriptures: that is blasphemy.
EVIL ANGEL Go forward, Faustus, in that famous art
Wherein all nature's treasure is contained.
75   Be thou on earth as Jove[1] is in the sky,
Lord and commander of these elements.   [*Exeunt Angels.*]
FAUSTUS How am I glutted with conceit° of this!   *idea*
Shall I make spirits fetch me what I please,
Resolve me of all ambiguities,
80   Perform what desperate enterprise I will?
I'll have them fly to India for gold,
Ransack the ocean for orient pearl,
And search all corners of the new-found world
For pleasant fruits and princely delicates.
85   I'll have them read me strange philosophy,
And tell the secrets of all foreign kings.
I'll have them wall all Germany with brass,
And make swift Rhine circle fair Wittenberg.
I'll have them fill the public schools° with silk,   *college lecture halls*
90   Wherewith the students shall be bravely clad.
I'll levy soldiers with the coin they bring,
And chase the Prince of Parma from our land,
And reign sole king of all the provinces.
Yea, stranger engines for the brunt of war
95   Than was the fiery keel[2] at Antwerp's bridge
I'll make my servile spirits to invent.

---

1. Roman god of the heavens and king of the gods.   2. In 1585 a fireship destroyed the Duke of Parma's bridge across the river Scheldt in the city of Antwerp.

Come, German Valdes and Cornelius,
And make me blest with your sage conference.
[Enter Valdes and Cornelius.]
Valdes, sweet Valdes and Cornelius!
100   Know that your words have won me at the last
To practice magic and concealed arts.
Yet not your words only but mine own fantasy
That will receive no object° for my head,   *idea*
But ruminates on necromantic skill.
105   Philosophy is odious and obscure.
Both law and physic are for petty wits.
Divinity is basest of the three,
Unpleasant, harsh, contemptible and vile.
'Tis magic, magic that hath ravished me.
110   Then, gentle friends, aid me in this attempt,
And I, that have with subtle syllogisms
Gravelled the pastors of the German Church
And made the flowering pride of Wittenberg
Swarm to my problems as the infernal spirits
115   On sweet Musaeus³ when he came to hell,
Will be as cunning as Agrippa was,
Whose shadow made all Europe honor him.
VALDES   Faustus, these books, thy wit and our experience
Shall make all nations to canonize us,
120   As Indian moors obey their Spanish lords.
So shall the spirits of every element
Be always serviceable to us three.
Like lions shall they guard us when we please;
Like Almain rutters° with their horsemen's staves;   *German knights*
125   Or Lapland giants trotting by our sides.
Sometimes like women or unwedded maids,
Shadowing more beauty in their airy brows
Than has the white breasts of the queen of love.
From Venice shall they drag huge argosies,°   *merchant ships*
130   And from America the golden fleece⁴
That yearly stuffs old Philip's treasury
If learned Faustus will be resolute.
FAUSTUS   Valdes, as resolute am I in this
As thou to live, therefore object° it not.   *reject*
CORNELIUS   The miracles that magic will perform
Will make thee vow to study nothing else.
He that is grounded in Astrology,
Enriched with tongues,° well seen° in minerals,   *languages / educated*
Hath all the principles magic doth require.
140   Then doubt not, Faustus, but to be renowned,
And more frequented° for this mystery   *sought after*

3. Faustus wants to model himself on Musaeus, a legendary poet, said to have been a student of Orpheus, and Cornelius Agrippa of Nettesheim (1486–1535), a philosopher known for his works on scepticism and the occult.
4. The "golden fleece" refers to the treasure (the gold wool of a divine ram) sought and won by the legendary hero, Jason, and his companions, known as the Argonauts (from the name of their ship, the Argo). Faustus alludes to this treasure when he refers to the gold the King of Castile, Philip II, was taking from lands in the New World.

Than heretofore the Delphian oracle.[5]
The spirits tell me they can dry the sea,
And fetch the treasure of all foreign wracks,°   *wrecks*
145   Yea, all the wealth that our forefathers hid
Within the massy° entrails of the earth.   *massive*
Then tell me, Faustus, what shall we three want?
FAUSTUS   Nothing, Cornelius! Oh, this cheers my soul.
Come, show me some demonstrations magical,
150   That I may conjure in some bushy grove,
And have these joys in full possession.
VALDES   Then haste thee to some solitary grove,
And bear wise Bacon's and Albanus'[6] works,
The Hebrew Psalter and New Testament;
155   And whatsoever else is requisite
We will inform thee e're our conference cease.
CORNELIUS   Valdes, first let him know the words of art,
And then, all other ceremonies learned,
Faustus may try his cunning by himself.
VALDES   First I'll instruct thee in the rudiments,
And then wilt thou be perfecter than I.
FAUSTUS   Then come and dine with me, and after meat
We'll canvass every quiddity° thereof,   *question*
For ere I sleep, I'll try what I can do.
165   This night I'll conjure, though I die therefore.   [*Exeunt.*]

Scene Two

[*Enter two Scholars.*]
FIRST SCHOLAR   I wonder what's become of Faustus, that was wont to make our
        schools ring with *sic probo*.[7]
[*Enter Wagner.*]
SECOND SCHOLAR   That shall we presently know. Here comes his boy.
FIRST SCHOLAR   How now, sirrah, where's thy master?
WAGNER   God in heaven knows.
SECOND SCHOLAR   Why, dost not thou know then?
WAGNER   Yes, I know, but that follows not.
FIRST SCHOLAR   Go to, sirrah. Leave your jesting and tell us where he is.
WAGNER   That follows not by force of argument, which you, being licentiates,[8]
10   should stand upon. Therefore, acknowledge your error and be attentive.
SECOND SCHOLAR   Then you will not tell us?
WAGNER   You are deceived, for I will tell you. Yet if you were not dunces, you would
        never ask me such a question. For is he not *Corpus naturale*?[9] And is not that
        mobile? Then wherefore should you ask me such a question? But that I am

---

5. A shrine of Apollo, the god of the sun, music, and
medicine, in his temple at Delphi, where his priestess,
called the Pythia, spoke incoherent phrases that a priest
later interpreted as prophecies.
6. Roger Bacon (1214–1294) was an English Franciscan
monk and a lecturer at Oxford University who was interested in natural science, particularly alchemy. Albanus is

perhaps Pietro D'Abano (1250–1360), who was supposed
to be a sorcerer and was burned in effigy by the Inquisition after his death.
7. "Thus I prove."
8. Postgraduates.
9. A natural body.

15   by nature phlegmatic, slow to wrath and prone to lechery (to love, I would
say), it were not for you to come within forty foot of the place of execution,
although I do not doubt but to see you both hanged the next sessions. Thus,
having triumphed over you, I will set my countenance like a precision,[1] and
begin to speak thus: "Truly, my dear brethren, my master is within at dinner
20   with Valdes and Cornelius, as this wine, if it could speak, would inform your
worships. And so the Lord bless you, preserve you and keep you, my dear
brethren."   *[Exit.]*

FIRST SCHOLAR Oh Faustus, then I fear that which I have long suspected:
    That thou art fallen into that damned art
25   For which they two are infamous through the world.
SECOND SCHOLAR Were he a stranger, not allied to me,
    The danger of his soul would make me mourn.
    But come, let us go, and inform the Rector.
    It may be his grave counsel may reclaim him.
FIRST SCHOLAR I fear me nothing will reclaim him now.
SECOND SCHOLAR Yet let us see what we can do.   *[Exeunt.]*

Scene Three

[Thunder. Enter Lucifer and Four Devils. Faustus to them with this speech.]
FAUSTUS Now that the gloomy shadow of the night,
    Longing to view Orion's drizzling look,
    Leaps from th'Antarctic world unto the sky,
    And dims the welkin° with her pitchy breath,   *heaven*
5   Faustus, begin thine incantations
    And try if devils will obey thy hest,°   *command*
    Seeing thou hast prayed and sacrificed to them.
    Within this circle is Jehovah's name
    Forward and backward anagrammatized:
10   The abbreviated names of holy saints,
    Figures of every adjunct to the heavens,
    And characters of signs and evening stars,
    By which the spirits are enforced to rise.
    Then fear not, Faustus, to be resolute
15   And try the utmost magic can perform.[2]
    [Thunder.]
    Sint mihi dei acherontis propitii, valeat numen triplex Jehovae, ignei areii, aquatani
    spiritus salvete: orientis princeps Belzebub, inferni ardentis monarcha et demigor-
    gon, propitiamus vos, ut appareat, et surgat Mephostophilis (Dragon)[3] quod tu-
    meraris: per Jehovam, gehennam, et consecratam aquam quam nunc spargo;
20   *signumque crucis quod nunc facio; et per vota nostra ipse nunc surgat nobis*
    dicatus Mephostophilis.

---

1. Puritan.
2. Faustus styles himself an accomplished magician. He now repeats, in Latin, his command to Mephostophilis to appear in the guise of a friar: "May the gods of the underworld be kind to me; may the triple deity of Jehovah be gone; to the spirits of fire, air, and water, greetings. Prince of the east, Beelzebub, monarch of the fires below, and Demogorgon, we appeal to you so that Mephostophilis may appear and rise. Why do you delay? By Jehovah, hell and the hallowed water which I now sprinkle, and the sign of the cross, which I now make, and by our vows, let Mephostophilis himself now arise to serve us."
3. This appears to be a stage direction that was inserted into the playtext; it probably indicates that at this point the figure of a dragon should come on stage.

[*Enter a Devil.*]
  I charge thee to return and change thy shape.
  Thou art too ugly to attend on me.
  Go, and return an old Franciscan friar:
25 That holy shape becomes a devil best.   [*Exit Devil.*]
  I see there's virtue in my heavenly words.
  Who would not be proficient in this art?
  How pliant is this Mephostophilis!
  Full of obedience and humility,
30 Such is the force of magic and my spells.
  Now, Faustus, thou art conjuror laureate:[4]
  Thou canst command great Mephostophilis.
  Quin redis Mephostophilis fratris imagine.
 [*Enter Mephostophilis.*]
MEPHOSTOPHILIS Now, Faustus, what wouldst thou have me do?
FAUSTUS I charge thee wait upon me whilst I live,
  To do whatever Faustus shall command,
  Be it to make the moon drop from her sphere,
  Or the ocean to overwhelm the world.
MEPHOSTOPHILIS I am a servant to great Lucifer,
40 And may not follow thee without his leave.
  No more than he commands must we perform.
FAUSTUS Did not he charge thee to appear to me?
MEPHOSTOPHILIS No, I came now hither of mine own accord.
FAUSTUS Did not my conjuring speeches raise thee? Speak.
MEPHOSTOPHILIS That was the cause, but yet *per accidens;*°   *by accident*
  For when we hear one rack the name of God,
  Abjure the scriptures and his saviour Christ,
  We fly in hope to get his glorious soul.
  Nor will we come unless he use such means
50 Whereby he is in danger to be damned.
  Therefore the shortest cut for conjuring
  Is stoutly to abjure all godliness
  And pray devoutly to the price of hell.
FAUSTUS So Faustus hath already done, and holds this principle:
55 There is no chief but only Belzebub,
  To whom Faustus doth dedicate himself.
  This word "damnation" terrifies not me,
  For I confound hell in elysium.°   *heaven*
  My ghost be with the old philosophers.
60 But leaving these vain trifles of men's souls,
  Tell me, what is that Lucifer, thy lord?
MEPHOSTOPHILIS Arch-regent and commander of all spirits.
FAUSTUS Was not that Lucifer an angel once?

---

4. Faustus, stating he is a "conjurer laureate" or honored magician, asks again, in Latin: "Why do you not return, Mephostophilis, in the guise of a friar?"

MEPHOSTOPHILIS Yes, Faustus, and most dearly loved of God.

FAUSTUS How comes it then that he is prince of devils?

MEPHOSTOPHILIS Oh, by aspiring pride and insolence,
  For which God threw him from the face of heaven.

FAUSTUS And what are you that live with Lucifer?

MEPHOSTOPHILIS Unhappy spirits that fell with Lucifer,
70 Conspired against our God with Lucifer,
  And are for ever damned with Lucifer.

FAUSTUS Where are you damned?

MEPHOSTOPHILIS In hell.

FAUSTUS How comes it then that thou art out of hell?

MEPHOSTOPHILIS Why, this is hell, nor am I out of it.
  Think'st thou that I that saw the face of God
  And tasted the eternal joys of heaven,
  Am not tormented with ten thousand hells
  In being deprived of everlasting bliss?
80 Oh, Faustus, leave these frivolous demands,
  Which strike a terror to my fainting soul.

FAUSTUS What, is great Mephostophilis so passionate
  For being deprived of the joys of heaven?
  Learn thou of Faustus manly fortitude,
85 And scorn those joys thou never shalt possess.
  Go, bear these tidings to great Lucifer,
  Seeing Faustus hath incurred eternal death
  By desperate thoughts against Jove's deity.
  Say he surrenders up to him his soul,
90 So he will spare him four and twenty years,
  Letting him live in all voluptuousness,
  Having thee ever to attend on me,
  To give me whatsoever I shall ask,
  To tell me whatsoever I demand,
95 To slay mine enemies and to aid my friends
  And always be obedient to my will.
  Go, and return to mighty Lucifer,
  And meet me in my study at midnight,
  And then resolve me of thy master's mind.

MEPHOSTOPHILIS I will, Faustus.   [Exit.]

FAUSTUS Had I as many souls as there be stars,
  I'd give them all for Mephostophilis.
  By him I'll be great emperor of the world,
  And make a bridge through the air
105 To pass the ocean. With a band of men
  I'll join the hills that bind the Affrick shore,
  And make that country continent to Spain,
  And both contributory to my crown.
  The Emperor shall not live but by my leave,
110 Nor any potentate of Germany.
  Now that I have obtained what I desired,

I'll live in speculation of this art
Till Mephostophilis return again.   [*Exit.*]

Scene Four

[*Enter Wagner and the Clown.*]

WAGNER Come hither, sirrah boy.

CLOWN Boy? Oh, disgrace to my person! Zounds! "Boy" in your face! You have seen
many boys with beards, I am sure.

WAGNER Sirrah, hast thou no comings in?

CLOWN Yes, and goings out too, you may see, sir.

WAGNER Alas, poor slave. See how poverty jests in his nakedness. I know the villain's out of service and so hungry that I know he would give his soul to the
devil for a shoulder of mutton though it were blood-raw.

CLOWN Not so neither. I had need to have it well roasted, and good sauce to it, if I
10   pay so dear, I can tell you.

WAGNER Sirrah, wilt thou be my man and wait on me? And I will make thee go like
*Qui mihi discipulus.*5

CLOWN What, in verse?

WAGNER No, slave, in beaten silk and stavesacre.6

CLOWN Stavesacre? That's good to kill vermin. Then belike, if I serve you I shall be
lousy.

WAGNER Why, so thou shalt be whether thou dost it or no. For, sirrah, if thou dost
not presently bind thyself to me for seven years, I'll turn all the lice about
thee into familiars,7 and make them tear thee in pieces.

CLOWN Nay, sir, you may save yourself a labor, for they are as familiar with me as if
they paid for their meat and drink, I can tell you.

WAGNER Well, sirrah, leave your jesting and take these guilders.8

CLOWN Yes, marry, sir, and I thank you too.

WAGNER So, now thou art to be at an hour's warning, whensoever and wheresoever
25   the devil shall fetch thee.

CLOWN Here, take your guilders.

WAGNER Truly, I'll none of them.

CLOWN Truly but you shall.

WAGNER Bear witness I gave them him.

CLOWN Bear witness I give them you again.

WAGNER Not I. Thou art pressed. Prepare thyself, for I will presently raise up two
devils, to carry thee away: Banio, Belcher!

CLOWN Belcher? And Belcher come here, I'll belch him! I am not afraid of a devil.
[*Enter Two Devils and the Clown runs up and down crying.*]

WAGNER How now, sir, will you serve me now?

CLOWN Ay, good Wagner. Take away the devil then.

WAGNER Baliol and Belcher, spirits, away!   [*Exeunt Devils.*]

CLOWN What, are they gone? A vengeance on them! They have vile long nails.
There was a he-devil and a she-devil. I'll tell you how you shall know them:
all he-devils has horns, and all she-devils has clifts9 and cloven feet.

WAGNER Well, sirrah, follow me.

5. One who is my disciple.   8. Coins.
6. A poison.   9. Clefts.
7. Spirits.

CLOWN But, do you hear, if I should serve you, would you teach me to raise up
     Banio's and Belcheo's?
WAGNER I will teach thee to turn thyself to anything, to a dog, or a cat, or a mouse,
     or a rat, or anything.
CLOWN How? A Christian fellow to a dog or a cat, a mouse or a rat? No, no, sir, if
     you turn me into anything, let it be in the likeness of a little pretty frisking
     flea, that I may be here and there and everywhere. Oh, I'll tickle the pretty
     wenches' plackets![1] I'll be amongst them, i'faith.
WAGNER Well, sirrah, come.
CLOWN But do you hear, Wagner?
WAGNER How? Baliol and Belcher!
CLOWN Oh Lord, I pray, sir, let Banio and Belcher go sleep.
WAGNER Villain, call me Master Wagner, and see that you walk attentively and let
     your right eye be always diametrically fixed upon my left heel, that thou
55   mayest *Quasi vestigias nostras insistere.*[2]   [*Exit.*]
CLOWN God forgive me, he speaks Dutch fustian![3] Well, I'll follow him. I'll serve
     him, that's flat.   [*Exit.*]

                              Scene Five

          [*Enter Faustus in his study.*]
FAUSTUS Now, Faustus, must thou needs be damned?
          And canst thou not be saved?
          What boots it then to think on God or heaven?
          Away with such vain fancies and despair,
5   Despair in God and trust in Belzebub.°   the Devil
          Now go not backward. No, Faustus, be resolute.
          Why waverest thou? Oh, something soundeth in mine ears
          Abjure this magic, turn to God again.
          Ay, and Faustus will turn to God again.
10   To God? He loves thee not.
          The God thou servest is thine own appetite,
          Wherein is fixed the love of Belzebub.
          To him I'll build an altar and a church,
          And offer lukewarm blood of new-born babes.
          [*Enter the Good and Evil Angels.*]
GOOD ANGEL Sweet Faustus, leave that execrable art.
FAUSTUS Contrition, prayer, repentance, what of these?
GOOD ANGEL Oh, they are means to bring thee unto heaven.
EVIL ANGEL Rather illusions, fruits of lunacy,
          That make men foolish that do trust them most.
GOOD ANGEL Sweet Faustus, think of heaven and heavenly things.
EVIL ANGEL No, Faustus, think of honor and of wealth.   [*Exeunt Angels.*]
FAUSTUS Of wealth!
          Why, the signory of Emden[4] shall be mine!
          When Mephostophilis shall stand by me,

---

1. Petticoats.
2. Wagner mocks the Clown by telling him to walk "as if
to tread in our footsteps," knowing that the clown's magic will never be as powerful as his own.

3. Nonsense.
4. At this point in his career, Faustus aspires to the governorship of Emden, an important trading town in Germany, a pathetic exchange for his immortal soul.

25   What God can hurt thee, Faustus? Thou art safe.
            Cast no more doubts. Come, Mephostophilis,
            And bring glad tidings from great Lucifer.
            Is't not midnight? Come Mephostophilis!
            Veni, veni,° *Mephostophile!*   come, come
            [*Enter Mephostophilis.*]
30   Now tell me, what saith Lucifer, thy lord?
MEPHOSTOPHILIS That I shall wait on Faustus whilst he lives,
            So he will buy my service with his soul.
FAUSTUS Already Faustus hath hazarded that for thee.
MEPHOSTOPHILIS But now thou must bequeath it solemnly,
35   And write a deed of gift with thine own blood,
            For that security craves great Lucifer.
            If thou deny it, I will back to hell.
FAUSTUS Stay, Mephostophilis, and tell me
            What good will my soul do thy lord?
MEPHOSTOPHILIS Enlarge his kingdom.
FAUSTUS Is that the reason why he tempts us thus?
MEPHOSTOPHILIS *Solamen miseris, socios habuisse doloris.*[5]
FAUSTUS Why, have you any pain, that torture others?
MEPHOSTOPHILIS As great as have the human souls of men.
45   But tell me, Faustus, shall I have thy soul?
            And I will be thy slave and wait on thee,
            And give thee more than thou hast wit to ask.
FAUSTUS Ay, Mephostophilis, I'll give it thee.
MEPHOSTOPHILIS Then, Faustus, stab thy arm courageously,
50   And bind thy soul, that at some certain day
            Great Lucifer may claim it as his own,
            And then be thou as great as Lucifer.
FAUSTUS Lo, Mephostophilis, for love of thee
            I cut mine arm, and with my proper blood
55   Assure my soul to be great Lucifer's,
            Chief lord and regent of perpetual night.
            View here the blood that trickles from mine arm,
            And let it be propitious for my wish.
MEPHOSTOPHILIS But, Faustus, thou must write it in manner of a deed of gift.
FAUSTUS Ay, so I will. But, Mephostophilis,
            My blood congeals and I can write no more!
MEPHOSTOPHILIS I'll fetch thee fire to dissolve it straight.   [*Exit.*]
FAUSTUS What might the staying of my blood portend?
            Is it unwilling I should write this bill?
65   Why streams it not that I may write afresh?
            "Faustus gives to thee his soul": ah, there it stayed!
            Why shouldst thou not? Is not thy soul thine own?
            Then write again: "Faustus gives to thee his soul."
            [*Enter Mephostophilis with a chafer of coals.*]
MEPHOSTOPHILIS Here's fire. Come, Faustus, set it on.

5. Mephostophilis states that misery loves company in hell: "It is a comfort in wretchedness to have companions in woe."

FAUSTUS So, now my blood begins to clear again.
    Now will I make an end immediately.
MEPHOSTOPHILIS Oh what will not I do to obtain his soul!
FAUSTUS *Consummatum est:*[6] this bill is ended,
    And Faustus hath bequeathed his soul to Lucifer.
75   But what is this inscription on mine arm?
    Homo fuge!° Whither should I flee?   *Flee, O man*
    If unto heaven, he'll throw me down to hell.
    My senses are deceived: here's nothing writ!
    Oh, yes, I see it plain. Even here is writ
80   *Homo fuge.* Yet shall not Faustus fly.
MEPHOSTOPHILIS I'll fetch him somewhat to delight his mind.   *[Exit.]*
    [*Enter Devils, giving crowns and rich apparel to Faustus; they dance and then depart.
    Enter Mephostophilis.*]
FAUSTUS What means this show? Speak, Mephostophilis.
MEPHOSTOPHILIS Nothing, Faustus, but to delight thy mind,
    And let thee see what magic can perform.
FAUSTUS But may I raise such spirits when I please?
MEPHOSTOPHILIS Ay, Faustus, and do greater things than these.
FAUSTUS Then there's enough for a thousand souls.
    Here, Mephostophilis, receive this scroll,
    A deed of gift, of body and of soul:
90   But yet conditionally, that thou perform
    All covenants and articles between us both.
MEPHOSTOPHILIS Faustus, I swear by hell and Lucifer
    To effect all promises between us both.
FAUSTUS Then hear me read it, Mephostophilis.
95   On these conditions following:
    First, that Faustus may be a spirit in form and substance.
    Secondly, that Mephostophilis shall be his servant, and be by him commanded.
    Thirdly, that Mephostophilis shall do for him, and bring him whatsoever.
    Fourthly, that he shall be in his chamber or house invisible.
100   Lastly, that he shall appear to the said John Faustus at all times, in what
        shape and form soever he please.
    I, John Faustus of Wittenberg Doctor, by these presents, do give both body
        and soul to Lucifer, Prince of the East, and his minister Mephostophilis,
        and furthermore grant unto them that four and twenty years being
105   expired, and these articles above written being inviolate, full power to
        fetch or carry the said John Faustus, body and soul, flesh, blood or goods,
        into their habitation wheresoever.
    By me, John Faustus.
MEPHOSTOPHILIS Speak, Faustus, do you deliver this as your deed?
FAUSTUS Ay, take it, and the devil give thee good of it.
MEPHOSTOPHILIS So now, Faustus, ask me what thou wilt.
FAUSTUS First I will question with thee about hell.
    Tell me, where is the place that men call hell?
MEPHOSTOPHILIS Under the heavens.

6. Faustus speaks the last words of Jesus on the cross: "It is finished" (John 19.30), and then realizes he must try to avoid the consequences: "Flee, O man."

FAUSTUS Ay, so are all things else; but whereabouts?

MEPHOSTOPHILIS Within the bowels of these elements,
　　　　　Where we are tortured and remain for ever.
　　　　　Hell hath no limits, nor is circumscribed
　　　　　In one self place. But where we are is hell,
120　　　And where hell is there must we ever be.
　　　　　And to be short, when all the world dissolves
　　　　　And every creature shall be purified,
　　　　　All places shall be hell that is not heaven.

FAUSTUS Come, I think hell's a fable.

MEPHOSTOPHILIS Ay, think so still, till experience change thy mind.

FAUSTUS Why, dost thou think that Faustus shall be damned?

MEPHOSTOPHILIS Ay, of necessity, for here's the scroll
　　　　　In which thou hast given thy soul to Lucifer.

FAUSTUS Ay, and body too, but what of that?
130　　　Think'st thou that Faustus is so fond to imagine
　　　　　That after this life there is any pain?
　　　　　Tush, these are trifles and old wives' tales.

MEPHOSTOPHILIS But Faustus, I am an instance to prove the contrary,
　　　　　For I tell thee I am damned, and now in hell.

FAUSTUS How? Now in hell? Nay, and this be hell, I'll willingly be damned here.
　　　　　What! Sleeping, eating, walking and disputing? But leaving this, let me
　　　　　have a wife, the fairest maid in Germany, for I am wanton and lascivious,
　　　　　and can not live without a wife.

MEPHOSTOPHILIS How, a wife? I prithee, Faustus, talk not of a wife.

FAUSTUS Nay, sweet Mephostophilis, fetch me one, for I will have one.

MEPHOSTOPHILIS Well, thou wilt have one. Sit there till I come: I'll fetch thee a
　　　　　wife in the devil's name.

　　　　　[Enter a Devil dressed like a woman, with fireworks.]

FAUSTUS What sight is this?

MEPHOSTOPHILIS Tell, Faustus, how dost thou like thy wife?

FAUSTUS A plague on her for a hot whore.

MEPHOSTOPHILIS Tut, Faustus, marriage is but a ceremonial toy.
　　　　　If thou lovest me, think no more of it.
　　　　　I'll cull thee out the fairest courtesans
　　　　　And bring them every morning to thy bed.
150　　　She whom thine eye shall like, thy heart shall have,
　　　　　Be she as chaste as was Penelope,[7]
　　　　　As wise as Saba, or as beautiful
　　　　　As was bright Lucifer before his fall.
　　　　　Here, take this book, and peruse it well.
155　　　The iterating° of these lines brings gold,　　　　　　　　　*repetition*
　　　　　The framing of this circle on the ground
　　　　　Brings thunder, whirlwinds, storm and lightning.
　　　　　Pronounce this thrice devoutly to thyself
　　　　　And men in harness shall appear to thee,

7. Mephostophilis compares the ideal woman to Penelope, the wife of Odysseus, who waited 20 years for him to return from the Trojan wars, and to Saba, the wise Queen of Sheba, who taught King Solomon, known himself for his wisdom (1 Kings).

160   Ready to execute what thou commandest.

FAUSTUS Thanks, Mephostophilis. Yet fain would I have a book wherein I might
　　　behold all spells and incantations, that I might raise up spirits when I please.

MEPHOSTOPHILIS Here they are in this book.   [*There turn to them.*]

FAUSTUS Now would I have a book where I might see all characters and planets of
165　　the heavens, that I might know their motions and dispositions.

MEPHOSTOPHILIS Here they are too.   [*Turn to them.*]

FAUSTUS Nay, let me have one book more, and then I have done, wherein I might
　　　see all plants, herbs and trees that grow upon the earth.

MEPHOSTOPHILIS Here they be.

FAUSTUS Oh thou art deceived.

MEPHOSTOPHILIS Tut, I warrant thee.   [*Turn to them.*]

Act 2

Scene One

[*Enter Faustus in his study, and Mephostophilis.*]

FAUSTUS When I behold the heavens then I repent,
　　　And curse thee, wicked Mephostophilis,
　　　Because thou hast deprived me of those joys.

MEPHOSTOPHILIS 'Twas thine own seeking, Faustus, thank thyself.
5　　　But thinkst thou heaven is such a glorious thing?
　　　I tell thee, Faustus, it is not half so fair
　　　As thou or any man that breathes on earth.

FAUSTUS How prov'st thou that?

MEPHOSTOPHILIS 'Twas made for man; then he's more excellent.

FAUSTUS If heaven was made for man, 'twas made for me.
　　　I will renounce this magic and repent.

[*Enter the Good and Evil Angels.*]

GOOD ANGEL Faustus, repent. Yet God will pity thee.

EVIL ANGEL Thou art a spirit. God cannot pity thee.

FAUSTUS Who buzzeth in mine ears I am a spirit?
15　　　Be I a devil, yet God may pity me.
　　　Yea, God will pity me if I repent.

EVIL ANGEL Ay, but Faustus never shall repent.   [*Exeunt.*]

FAUSTUS My heart's so hardened I cannot repent.
　　　Scarce can I name salvation, faith or heaven,
20　　　But fearful echoes thunder in mine ears
　　　"Faustus, thou art damned." Then swords and knives,
　　　Poison, guns, halters and envenomed steel
　　　Are laid before me to dispatch myself.
　　　And long ere this I should have done the deed,
25　　　Had not sweet pleasure conquered deep despair.
　　　Have not I made blind Homer sing to me
　　　Of Alexander's love and Oenon's death?[1]
　　　And hath not he that built the walls of Thebes

---

1. Faustus claims he has made the poet Homer sing to him of the love of Alexander the Great (356–323 B.C.), who was married to Statira, daughter of the Emperor Darius of Persia; and of Oenone, a nymph of Mount Ida, who died from grief when her lover, Paris of Troy, deserted her for Helen, the wife of King Menalaus of Sparta.

With ravishing sound of his melodious harp
30   Made music with my Mephostophilis?[2]
Why should I die then, or basely despair?
I am resolved, Faustus shall not repent.
Come, Mephostophilis, let us dispute again,
And reason of divine astrology.
35   Speak, are there many spheres above the moon?
Are all celestial bodies but one globe,
As is the substance of this centric earth?[3]

MEPHOSTOPHILIS As are the elements, such are the heavens,
Even from the moon unto the empyrial orb,
40   Mutually folded in each other's spheres,
And jointly move upon one axle-tree,
Whose termine° is termed the world's wide pole.   *end point*
Nor are the names of Saturn, Mars or Jupiter
Feigned, but are erring stars.

FAUSTUS But have they all one motion, both *situ et tempore?*[4]

MEPHOSTOPHILIS All move from east to west in four and twenty hours upon the
poles of the world, but differ in their motions upon the poles of the zodiac.

FAUSTUS Tush, these slender trifles Wagner can decide. Hath Mephostophilis no
greater skill? Who knows not the double motion of the planets? That the
50   first is finished in a natural day? The second thus, as Saturn in thirty years,
Jupiter in twelve, Mars in four, the sun, Venus and Mercury in twenty-eight
days. Tush, these are freshmen's suppositions. But tell me, hath every sphere
a dominion or *intelligentia?*[5]

MEPHOSTOPHILIS Ay.

FAUSTUS How many heavens or spheres are there?

MEPHOSTOPHILIS Nine, the seven planets, the firmament, and the empyrial heaven.

FAUSTUS But is there not *coelum igneum et cristallinum?*

MEPHOSTOPHILIS No, Faustus, they be but fables.[6]

FAUSTUS Resolve me then in this one question. Why are not conjunctions, oppositions,
aspects, eclipses, all at one time, but in some years we have more, in some less?

MEPHOSTOPHILIS *Per inaequalem motum, respectu totius.*[7]

FAUSTUS Well, I am answered. Now tell me, who made the world?

MEPHOSTOPHILIS I will not.

FAUSTUS Sweet Mephostophilis, tell me.

MEPHOSTOPHILIS Move me not, Faustus.

FAUSTUS Villain, have not I bound thee to tell me anything?

MEPHOSTOPHILIS Ay, that is not against our kingdom, but this is.
Think on hell, Faustus, for thou art damned.

FAUSTUS Think, Faustus, upon God, that made the world.

MEPHOSTOPHILIS Remember this—   [*Exit.*]

FAUSTUS Ay, go, accursed spirit to ugly hell.

2. Faustus further claims that the legendary Amphion,
whose music built the walls of Thebes, also made music
with Mephostophilis, now Faustus's servant.
3. Faustus alludes to the Ptolemaic universe in which the
earth, at the center, is surrounded by concentric spheres,
beginning with the moon. Beyond the spheres of the stars
that were thought to move (the constellations) were the
spheres of the fixed stars.

4. In place and in time.
5. Guiding spirit.
6. Faustus asks whether there is a "fiery and crystalline
heaven" beyond the "empyrial heaven" Mephostophilis
has mentioned, and he is told it is a fiction.
7. Faustus asks why planetary and astral events do not occur
uniformly, and Mephostophilis answers that they do "with
respect to the whole" but each "by unequal motion."

'Tis thou hast damned distressed Faustus' soul.
Is't not too late?
[*Enter the Good and Evil Angels.*]
EVIL ANGEL Too late.
GOOD ANGEL Never too late, if Faustus will repent.
EVIL ANGEL If thou repent devils will tear thee in pieces.
GOOD ANGEL Repent, and they shall never raze° thy skin.   shave
[*Exeunt Angels.*]
FAUSTUS Ah, Christ my savior,
80   Seek to save distressed Faustus' soul.
[*Enter Lucifer, Belzebub and Mephostophilis.*]
LUCIFER Christ cannot save thy soul, for he is just.
        There's none but I have interest in the same.
FAUSTUS Oh what art thou that look'st so terribly?
LUCIFER I am Lucifer, and this is my companion prince in hell.
FAUSTUS Oh Faustus, they are come to fetch away thy soul.
BELZEBUB We are come to tell thee thou dost injure us.
LUCIFER Thou call'st on Christ contrary to thy promise.
BELZEBUB Thou shouldst not think on God.
LUCIFER Think on the devil.
BELZEBUB And his dam too.
FAUSTUS Nor will I henceforth. Pardon me in this,
        And Faustus vows never to look to heaven,
        Never to name God or to pray to him,
        To burn his scriptures, slay his ministers,
95   And make my spirits pull his churches down.
LUCIFER Do so, and we will highly gratify thee.
BELZEBUB Faustus, we are come from hell in person to show thee some pastime. Sit
        down and thou shalt behold the seven deadly sins appear to thee in their
        own proper shapes and likeness.
FAUSTUS That sight will be as pleasant to me as Paradise was to Adam the first day
        of his creation.
LUCIFER Talk not of Paradise or Creation, but mark this show. Talk of the devil
        and nothing else. Go, Mephostophilis, fetch them in.
[*Enter the Seven Deadly Sins.*]
BELZEBUB Now, Faustus, question them of their names and dispositions.
FAUSTUS That shall I soon. What art thou, the first?
PRIDE I am Pride. I disdain to have any parents. I am like to Ovid's flea.[8] I can creep
        into every corner of a wench. Sometimes like a periwig I sit upon her brow.
        Next, like a necklace I hang about her neck. Then, like a fan of feathers, I
        kiss her. And then turning myself to a wrought smock do what I list. But fie,
110   what a smell is here! I'll not speak a word for a king's ransome, unless the
        ground be perfumed and covered with cloth of Arras.[9]
FAUSTUS Thou art a proud knave indeed. What art thou, the second?
COVETOUSNESS I am Covetousness. Begotten of an old churl in a leather bag.
        And might I now obtain my wish, this house, you and all, should turn to
115   gold, that I might lock you safe into my chest. Oh, my sweet gold!

8. One of the poems of the Roman poet Ovid (43 B.C.–A.D.   9. Flemish cloth for tapestries.
18) describes the journey of a flea around a woman's body.

FAUSTUS And what art thou, the third?

ENVY I am Envy, begotten of a chimney-sweeper and an oyster-wife. I cannot read
     and therefore wish all books were burnt. I am lean with seeing others eat.
     Oh, that there would come a famine over all the world, that all might die,
120   and I live alone, then thou should'st see how fat I'd be. But must thou sit
     and I stand? Come down, with a vengeance!

FAUSTUS Out, envious wretch. But what art thou, the fourth?

WRATH I am Wrath. I had neither father nor mother. I leapt out of a lion's mouth
     when I was scarce an hour old, and ever since have run up and down the world
125   with this case of rapiers, wounding myself when I could get none to fight with-
     al. I was born in hell, and look to it, for some of you shall be my father.

FAUSTUS And what art thou, the fifth?

GLUTTONY I am Gluttony. My parents are all dead, and the devil a penny they
     have left me, but a small pension and that buys me thirty meals a day and
130   ten bevers:[1] a small trifle to suffice nature. I come of a royal pedigree; my
     father was a gammon of bacon and my mother was a hog's head of claret
     wine. My godfathers were these: Peter Pickle-herring and Martin Martle-
     mas-beef. But my godmother, oh, she was an ancient gentlewoman, and
     well-beloved in every good town and city. Her name was Mistress Margery
135   March-beer. Now, Faustus, thou hast heard all my progeny, wilt thou bid me
     to supper?

FAUSTUS No, I'll see thee hanged. Thou wilt eat up all my victuals.

GLUTTONY Then the devil choke thee.

FAUSTUS Choke thyself, Glutton. What art thou, the sixth?

SLOTH Hey ho, I am Sloth. I was begotten on a sunny bank where I have lain ever
     since, and you have done me great injury to bring me from thence. Let me
     be carried thither again by Gluttony and Lechery. I'll not speak another
     word for a king's ransom.

FAUSTUS And what are you, Mistress Minx, the seventh and last?

LECHERY Who, I sir? I am one that loves an inch of raw mutton better than an ell
     of fried stockfish,[2] and the first letter of my name begins with Lechery.

FAUSTUS Away to hell! Away, on, piper!   [Exeunt the Seven Deadly Sins.]

LUCIFER Now, Faustus, how dost thou like this?

FAUSTUS Oh, this feeds my soul.

LUCIFER Tut, Faustus, in hell is all manner of delight.

FAUSTUS Oh, might I see hell and return again safe, how happy were I then!

LUCIFER Faustus, thou shalt. At midnight I will send for thee. Meanwhile, peruse
     this book and view it throughly, and thou shalt turn thyself into what shape
     thou wilt.

FAUSTUS Thanks, mighty Lucifer. This will I keep as chary as my life.

LUCIFER Now, Faustus, farewell, and think on the devil.

FAUSTUS Farewell, great Lucifer. Come, Mephostophilis.

                                        [Exeunt omnes, several ways.]

                        Scene Two

[Enter the Clown.]

CLOWN What, Dick, look to the horses there till I come again. I have gotten one of
     Doctor Faustus' conjuring books, and now we'll have such knavery as't passes.

---

1. Snacks.

2. Lechery implies that she would prefer a short but energetic penis to a yard-long but dry one.

[*Enter Dick.*]

DICK What, Robin, you must come away and walk the horses.

ROBIN I walk the horses? I scorn't, faith. I have other matters in hand. Let the horses
5   walk themselves and they will. A *per se a, t.h.e. the: o per se o deny orgon,
gorgon*.[3] Keep further from me, O thou illiterate and unlearned hostler.

DICK 'Snails![4] What hast thou got there? A book? Why, thou canst not tell ne'er a
word on't.

ROBIN That thou shalt see presently. Keep out of the circle, I say, lest I send you
10   into the ostry[5] with a vengeance.

DICK That's like, faith. You had best leave your foolery, for, an my master come,
he'll conjure you, faith!

ROBIN My master conjure me? I'll tell thee what, an my master come here, I'll clap
as fair a pair of horns[6] on's head as e'er thou sawest in thy life.

DICK Thou need'st not do that, for my mistress hath done it.

ROBIN Ay, there be of us here, that have waded as deep into matters as other men, if
they were disposed to talk.

DICK A plague take you! I thought you did not sneak up and down after her for nothing. But I prithee tell me, in good sadness, Robin, is that a conjuring book?

ROBIN Do but speak what thou't have me to do, and I'll do't. If thou't dance naked,
put off thy clothes and I'll conjure thee about presently. Or if thou't go but
to the tavern with me, I'll give thee white wine, red wine, claret wine, sack,
muskadine, malmesey and whippincrust.[7] Hold, belly, hold; and we'll not
pay one penny for it.

DICK Oh brave! Prithee, let's to it presently, for I am as dry as a dog.

ROBIN Come, then, let's away.   [*Exeunt.*]

Act 3

Scene One

[*Enter the Chorus.*]

CHORUS Learned Faustus,
     To find the secrets of astronomy,
     Graven in the book of Jove's high firmament,
     Did mount him up to scale Olympus' top,
5   Where sitting in a chariot burning bright,
     Drawn by the strength of yoked dragons' necks,
     He views the clouds, the planets, and the stars,
     The tropic, zones, and quarters of the sky,
     From the bright circle of the horned moon,
10   Even to the height of *Primum Mobile*.[1]
     And whirling round with this circumference,
     Within the concave compass of the pole,
     From east to west his dragons swiftly glide,
     And in eight days did bring him home again.
15   Not long he stayed within his quiet house,
     To rest his bones after his weary toil,

---

3. Barely literate, Robin is trying to parse a Latin phrase, *atheo Demigorgon* ("godless Demigorgon").
4. Christ's nails.
5. Inn.
6. Sign of a cuckold.

7. Robin lists various kinds of wine; "whippencrust" is probably a corruption of "hippocras," a kind of sweet wine.
1. The outermost of the heavenly spheres. Faustus is pictured as viewing the heavens from Mount Olympus to the
circle of the moon and beyond, to the *primum mobile*.

But new exploits do hale him out again,
And mounted then upon a dragon's back,
That with his wings did part the subtle air,
20   He now is gone to prove cosmography,
That measures coasts and kingdoms of the earth;
And as I guess will first arrive at Rome,
To see the Pope and manner of his court,
And take some part of holy Peter's feast,
25   The which this day is highly solemnized.   [*Exit.*]

Scene Two

[*Enter Faustus and Mephostophilis.*]

FAUSTUS Having now, my good Mephostophilis,
Passed with delight the stately town of Trier,
Environed round with airy mountain tops,
With walls of flint, and deep entrenched lakes,
5   Not to be won by any conquering prince,
From Paris next coasting the realm of France
We saw the river Main fall into Rhine,
Whose banks are set with groves of fruitful vines;
Then up to Naples, rich Campania,
10   Whose buildings fair and gorgeous to the eye,
The streets straight forth and paved with finest brick,
Quarters the town in four equivolence.°   *parts*
There saw we learned Maro's golden tomb,[2]
The way he cut an English mile in length,
15   Thorough a rock of stone in one night's space.
From thence to Venice, Padua and the rest,
In midst of which a sumptuous temple stands,
That threats the stars with her aspiring top,
Whose frame is paved with sundry colored stones,
20   And roofed aloft with curious work in gold.
Thus hitherto hath Faustus spent his time.
But tell me now, what resting place is this?
Hast thou, as erst I did command,
Conducted me within the walls of Rome?
MEPHOSTOPHILIS I have, my Faustus, and for proof thereof,
This is the goodly palace of the Pope;
And cause we are no common guests,
I choose his privy chamber for our use.
FAUSTUS I hope his Holiness will bid us welcome.
MEPHOSTOPHILIS All's one, for we'll be bold with his venison.
But now, my Faustus, that thou may'st perceive
What Rome contains for to delight thine eyes,
Know that this city stands upon seven hills
That underprop the groundwork of the same.

---

2. Faustus' fiery chariot cut through rocks to go from Naples, where the Roman poet Publius Virgilius Maro, or Virgil, is buried, to Padua and Venice.

35   Just through the midst runs flowing Tiber's stream,
             With winding banks that cut it in two parts,
             Over the which four stately bridges lean,
             That make safe passage to each part of Rome.
             Upon the bridge called Ponto Angelo
40   Erected is a castle passing strong,
             Where thou shalt see such store of ordinance
             As that the double cannons forged of brass
             Do match the number of the days contained
             Within the compass of one complete year.
45   Beside the gates and high pyramides,
             That Julius Caesar brought from Africa.[3]

FAUSTUS Now by the kingdoms of infernal rule,
             Of Styx, or Acheron, and the fiery lake
             Of ever-burning Phlegethon,° I swear   *rivers in hell*
50   That I do long to see the monuments
             And situation of bright splendent Rome.
             Come, therefore, let's away.

MEPHOSTOPHILIS Now, stay, my Faustus. I know you'd see the Pope,
             And take some part of holy Peter's feast,
55   The which in state and high solemnity
             This day is held through Rome and Italy
             In honor of the Pope's triumphant victory.

FAUSTUS Sweet Mephostophilis, thou pleasest me.
             Whilst I am here on earth let me be cloyed
60   With all things that delight the heart of man.
             My four and twenty years of liberty
             I'll spend in pleasure and in dalliance,
             That Faustus' name, whilst this bright frame doth stand,
             May be admired through the furthest land.

MEPHOSTOPHILIS 'Tis well said, Faustus. Come then, stand by me,
             And thou shalt see them come immediately.

FAUSTUS Nay stay, my gentle Mephostophilis,
             And grant me my request, and then I go.
             Thou know'st within the compass of eight days
70   We viewed the face of heaven, of earth and hell.
             So high our dragons soared into the air,
             That looking down, the earth appeared to me
             No bigger than my hand in quantity.
             There did we view the kingdoms of the world,
75   And what might please mine eye, I there beheld.
             Then in this show let me an actor be,
             That this proud Pope may Faustus' cunning see.

MEPHOSTOPHILIS Let it be so, my Faustus, but first stay
             And view their triumphs° as they pass this way.   *procession*
80   And then devise what best contents thy mind

3. The Emperor Caligula brought an obelisk back from Heliopolis in Egypt, which stands before St. Peter's in Rome.

By cunning in thine art to cross the Pope,
Or dash the pride of this solemnity,
To make his monks and abbots stand like apes,
And point like antics° at his triple crown,   *clowns*
85   To beat the beads about the friars' pates,
Or clap huge horns upon the cardinals' heads,
Or any villainy thou canst devise,
And I'll perform it, Faustus. Hark, they come!
This day shall make thee be admired in Rome.

[*Enter the Cardinals and Bishops, some bearing crosiers, some the pillars, Monks and Friars, singing their procession. Then the Pope and Raymond, King of Hungary with Bruno[4] led in chains.*]

POPE   Cast down our footstool.
RAYMOND Saxon Bruno, stoop,
        Whilst on thy back his Holiness ascends
        Saint Peter's chair and state pontifical.
BRUNO   Proud Lucifer, that state belongs to me:
95   But thus I fall to Peter, not to thee.
POPE   To me and Peter shalt thou grovelling lie,
        And crouch before the papal dignity.
        Sounds trumpets then, for thus Saint Peter's heir
        From Bruno's back ascends Saint Peter's chair.

        [*A flourish while he ascends.*]
100   Thus, as the gods creep on with feet of wool
        Long ere with iron hands they punish men,
        So shall our sleeping vengeance now arise,
        And smite with death thy hated enterprise.
        Lord cardinals of France and Padua,
105   Go forthwith to our holy consistory,
        And read amongst the statutes decretal,
        What by the holy council held at Trent[5]
        The sacred synod hath decreed for them
        That doth assume the papal government,
110   Without election and a true consent.
        Away, and bring us word with speed!
FIRST CARDINAL We go, my lord.   [*Exeunt Cardinals.*]
POPE   Lord Raymond.
FAUSTUS Go, haste thee, gentle Mephostophilis,
115   Follow the cardinals to the consistory,
        And as they turn their superstitious books,
        Strike them with sloth and drowsy idleness,
        And make them sleep so sound that in their shapes
        Thyself and I may parly° with this Pope,   *speak*
120   This proud confronter of the Emperor,[6]
        And in despite of all his holiness

4. This character has no apparent historical counterpart or model.
5. The council of Trent, called to meet the challenges posed by the Protestant Reformation, was held between 1545 and 1563.
6. The Holy Roman Emperor, Charles V, Emperor from 1519.

Restore this Bruno to his liberty
And bear him to the states of Germany.

MEPHOSTOPHILIS Faustus, I go.

FAUSTUS Dispatch it soon,
The Pope shall curse that Faustus came to Rome.

[*Exeunt Faustus and Mephostophilis.*]

BRUNO Pope Adrian,[7] let me have some right of law:
I was elected by the Emperor.

POPE We will depose the Emperor for that deed,

130   And curse the people that submit to him.
Both he and thou shalt stand excommunicate,
And interdict from Church's privilege
And all society of holy men.
He grows too proud in his authority,

135   Lifting his lofty head above the clouds
And like a steeple overpeers the Church.
But we'll pull down his haughty insolence,
And, as Pope Alexander, our progenitor,
Stood on the neck of German Frederick,[8]

140   Adding this golden sentence to our praise,
That Peter's heirs should tread on emperors
And walk upon the dreadful adder's back,
Treading the lion and the dragon down,
And fearless spurn the killing basilisk,[9]

145   So will we quell that haughty schismatic,
And by authority apostolical
Depose him from his regal government.

BRUNO Pope Julius swore to princely Sigismond[1]
For him and the succeeding popes of Rome,

150   To hold the emperors their lawful lords.

POPE Pope Julius did abuse the Church's rites,
And therefore none of his decrees can stand.
Is not all power on earth bestowed on us?
And therefore though we would we cannot err.

155   Behold this silver belt, whereto is fixed
Seven golden seals fast sealed with seven seals,
In token of our seven-fold power from heaven,
To bind or loose, lock fast, condemn or judge,
Resign or seal, or what so pleaseth us.

160   Then he and thou, and all the world, shall stoop,
Or be assured of our dreadful curse,
To light as heavy as the pains of hell.

[*Enter Faustus and Mephostophilis, like the cardinals.*]

MEPHOSTOPHILIS Now tell me, Faustus, are we not fitted well?

---

7. Possibly Marlowe means Hadrian VI (1522–23), although he was Pope before the Council of Trent, after which the action of the play is supposed to have taken place.
8. Pope Alexander III (1159–81) forced Emperor Frederick Barbarossa to acknowledge his authority.

9. A mythical creature whose glance was lethal.
1. It is unclear to whom Marlowe refers; there was no Pope Julius during the reign of the Emperor Sigismund (1368–1436).

FAUSTUS Yes, Mephostophilis, and two such cardinals
165   Ne'er served a holy Pope as we shall do.
           But whilst they sleep within the consistory,
           Let us salute his reverend fatherhood.
RAYMOND Behold, my lord, the cardinals are returned.
POPE   Welcome, grave fathers, answer presently
170   What have our holy council there decreed
           Concerning Bruno and the Emperor,
           In quittance of their late conspiracy
           Against our state and papal dignity?
FAUSTUS Most sacred patron of the Church of Rome,
175   By full consent of all the synod
           Of priests and prelates, it is thus decreed:
           That Bruno and the German Emperor
           Be held as lollards[2] and bold schismatics
           And proud disturbers of the Church's peace.
180   And if that Bruno by his own assent,
           Without enforcement of the German peers,
           Did seek to wear the triple diadem
           And by your death to climb Saint Peter's chair,
           The statutes decretal have thus decreed:
185   He shall be straight condemned of heresy
           And on a pile of faggots burnt to death.
POPE   It is enough. Here, take him to your charge,
           And bear him straight to Ponto Angelo,
           And in the strongest tower enclose him fast.
190   Tomorrow, sitting in our consistory
           With all our college of grave cardinals,
           We will determine of his life or death.
           Here, take his triple crown along with you,
           And leave it in the Church's treasury.
195   Make haste again, my good lord cardinals,
           And take our blessing apostolical.
MEPHOSTOPHILIS So, so, was never devil thus blessed before.
FAUSTUS Away, sweet Mephostophilis, be gone:
           The cardinals will be plagued for this anon.
                                    [Exeunt Faustus and Mephostophilis.]
POPE   Go presently, and bring a banquet forth
           That we may solemnize Saint Peter's feast,
           And with Lord Raymond, King of Hungary,
           Drink to our late and happy victory.   [Exeunt.]

Scene Three

[A sennet[3] while the banquet is brought in, and then enter Faustus and Mephostophilis
in their own shapes.]

MEPHOSTOPHILIS Now, Faustus, come prepare thyself for mirth.
           The sleepy cardinals are hard at hand

2. Heretics; in England, followers of John Wycliffe   3. A trumpet call.
(1328?–1384).

To censure Bruno that is posted° hence,   *ridden*
And on a proud paced steed as swift as thought
5   Flies o'er the Alps to fruitful Germany,
There to salute the woeful Emperor.

FAUSTUS The Pope will curse them for their sloth today,
That slept both Bruno and his crown away.
But now, that Faustus may delight his mind,
10   And by their folly make some merriment,
Sweet Mephostophilis, so charm me here,
That I may walk invisible to all,
And do what e'er I please unseen of any.

MEPHOSTOPHILIS Faustus, thou shalt. Then kneel down presently:
15   Whilst on thy head I lay my hand,
And charm thee with this magic wand.
First wear this girdle, then appear
Invisible to all are here.
The planets seven, the gloomy air,
20   Hell and the Furies'⁴ forked hair,
Pluto's⁵ blue fire and Hecate's⁶ tree,
With magic spells so compass thee,
That no eye may thy body see.
So, Faustus, now for all their holiness,
25   Do what thou wilt, thou shalt not be discerned.

FAUSTUS Thanks, Mephostophilis. Now, friars, take heed
Lest Faustus make your shaven crowns to bleed.

MEPHOSTOPHILIS Faustus, no more. See where the cardinals come.
[*Enter the Pope and all the Lords. Enter the Cardinals with a book.*]

POPE   Welcome, lord cardinals. Come, sit down.
30   Lord Raymond, take your seat. Friars, attend
And see that all things be in readiness
As best beseems this solemn festival.

FIRST CARDINAL First, may it please your sacred Holiness,
To view the sentence of the reverend synod
35   Concerning Bruno and the Emperor?

POPE   What needs this question? Did I not tell you
Tomorrow we would sit i'the consistory
And there determine of his punishment?
You brought us word even now, it was decreed
40   That Bruno and the cursed Emperor
Were by the holy Council both condemned
For loathed lollards and base schismatics.
Then wherefore would you have me view that book?

FIRST CARDINAL Your Grace mistakes. You gave us no such charge.

RAYMOND Deny it not. We all are witnesses
That Bruno here was late delivered you,
With his rich triple crown to be reserved
And put into the Church's treasury.

4. Greek divinities instigating revenge.   6. Goddess representing death and the dark side of the
5. The Roman god of the underworld.   moon.

BOTH CARDINALS By holy Paul, we saw them not.
POPE   By Peter, you shall die
         Unless you bring them forth immediately.
         Hale° them to prison, lade their limbs with gyves!°   *take/chains*
         False prelates, for this hateful treachery,
         Cursed be your souls to hellish misery.
FAUSTUS So, they are safe. Now Faustus, to the feast.
         The Pope had never such a frolic guest.
POPE   Lord Archbishop of Rheims, sit down with us.
BISHOP I thank your Holiness.
FAUSTUS Fall to, and the devil choke you an you spare.
POPE   Who's that spoke? Friars, look about.
FRIARS Here's nobody, if it like your Holiness.
POPE   Lord Raymond, pray fall to. I am beholding
         To the Bishop of Milan for this so rare a present.
FAUSTUS I thank you, sir. [*Snatches it.*]
POPE   How now? Who snatched the meat from me?
         Villains, why speak you not?
         My good Lord Archbishop, here's a most dainty dish
         Was sent me from a cardinal in France.
FAUSTUS I'll have that too. [*Snatches it.*]
POPE   What lollards do attend our Holiness
         That we receive such great indignity? Fetch me some wine.
FAUSTUS Ay, pray do, for Faustus is a-dry.
POPE   Lord Raymond, I drink unto your grace.
FAUSTUS I pledge your grace. [*Snatches the glass.*]
POPE   My wine gone too? Ye lubbers,° look about   *louts*
         And find the man that doth this villainy,
         Or by our sanctitude you all shall die.
         I pray, my lords, have patience at this
         Troublesome banquet.
BISHOP Please it your Holiness, I think it be some ghost crept out of Purgatory, and
         now is come unto your Holiness for his pardon.
POPE   It may be so.
         Go, then, command our priests to sing a dirge
         To lay the fury of this same troublesome ghost.
         [*The Pope crosseth himself.*]
FAUSTUS How now? Must every bit be spiced with a cross?
         Nay then, take that.
         [*Faustus hits him a box of the ear.*]
POPE   Oh, I am slain! Help me, my lords.
         Oh come, and help to bear my body hence.
         Damned be this soul for ever for this deed!
                                                          [*Exeunt the Pope and his train.*]
MEPHOSTOPHILIS Now, Faustus, what will you do now?
         For I can tell you, you'll be cursed with bell, book and candle.
FAUSTUS Bell, book and candle, candle, book and bell,
         Forward and backward, to curse Faustus to hell.
         [*Enter the Friars with bell, book and candle, for the dirge.*]

FIRST FRIAR Come, brethren, let's about our business with good devotion.

95   [*sing*] Cursed be he that stole his Holiness' meat from the table. *Maledicat dominus.*[7]

Cursed be he that took his Holiness a blow on the face. *Maledicat dominus.*

Cursed be he that struck Friar Sandelo a blow on the pate. *Maledicat dominus.*

100   Cursed be he that disturbeth our holy dirge. *Maledicat dominus.*

Cursed be he that took away his Holiness' wine. *Maledicat dominus.*

Et omnes sancti.[8] Amen.

[*Faustus and Mephostophilis beat the Friars, fling fireworks among them and exeunt. Enter Chorus.*]

CHORUS When Faustus had with pleasure ta'en the view

Of rarest things and royal courts of kings,

105   He stayed his course and so returned home;

Where such as bear his absence but with grief,

I mean his friends and nearest companions,

Did gratulate his safety with kind words,

And in their conference of what befell,

110   Touching his journey through the world and air,

They put forth questions of astrology,

Which Faustus answered with such learned skill

As they admired and wondered at his wit.

Now is his fame spread forth in every land;

115   Amongst the rest, the Emperor is one,

Carolus the Fifth, at whose palace now

Faustus is feasted 'mongst his noblemen.

What there he did in trial of his art,

I leave untold: your eyes shall see performed.

Scene Four

[*Enter Robin the ostler*[9] *with a book in his hand.*]

ROBIN Oh this is admirable! Here I ha' stol'n one of Doctor Faustus' conjuring books, and, i'faith, I mean to search some circles for my own use. Now will I make all the maidens in our parish dance at my pleasure stark naked before me. And so by that means I shall see more than ere I felt or saw yet.

[*Enter Rafe calling Robin.*]

RAFE Robin, prithee come away! There's a gentleman tarries to have his horse, and he would have his things rubbed and made clean. He keeps such a chafing with my mistress about it, and she has sent me to look thee out. Prithee, come away!

ROBIN Keep out, keep out, or else you are blown up. You are dismembered, Rafe,
10   keep out, for I am about a roaring piece of work.

RAFE Come, what dost thou with that same book? Thou canst not read?

ROBIN Yes, my master and mistress shall find that I can read, he for his forehead, she for her private study. She's born to bear with me, or else my art fails.

RAFE Why, Robin, what book is that?

7. May God curse you.   9. Stableman.
8. And all the saints.

ROBIN   What book? Why, the most intolerable book for conjuring that ere was invented by any brimstone devil.

RAFE   Canst thou conjure with it?

ROBIN   I can do all these things easily with it. First, I can make thee drunk with ippocras at any tavern in Europe, for nothing. That's one of my conjuring works!

RAFE   Our master parson says that's nothing.

ROBIN   True, Rafe. And more, Rafe, if thou hast any mind to Nan Spit, our kitchen maid, then turn her and wind her to thy own use as often as thou wilt, and at midnight.

RAFE   Oh brave Robin! Shall I have Nan Spit, and to mine own use? On that con-
25   dition, I'll feed thy devil with horsebread as long as he lives, of free cost.

ROBIN   No more, sweet Rafe. Let's go and make clean our boots which lie foul upon our hands, and then to our conjuring, in the devil's name.

          [Exeunt. Re-enter Robin and Rafe with a silver goblet.]

ROBIN   Come, Rafe, did I not tell thee we were for ever made by this Doctor Faus-
          tus' book? Ecce signum,[1] here's a simple purchase for horse-keepers. Our
30   horses shall eat no hay as long as this lasts.

          [Enter the Vintner.]

RAFE   But, Robin, here comes the vintner.

ROBIN   Hush, I'll gull[2] him supernaturally. Drawer, I hope all is paid. God be with you. Come, Rafe.

VINTNER   Soft, sir, a word with you. I must yet have a goblet paid from you ere you go.

ROBIN   I, a goblet? Rafe, I a goblet? I scorn you, and you are but a etc. I, a goblet? Search me.

VINTNER   I mean so, sir, with your favor.

ROBIN   How say you now?

VINTNER   I must say somewhat to your fellow—you, sir.

RAFE   Me, sir? Me, sir? Search your fill. Now, sir, you may be ashamed to burden honest men with a matter of truth.

VINTNER   Well, t'one of you hath this goblet about you.

ROBIN   You lie, drawer. 'Tis afore me! Sirrah, you! I'll teach ye to impeach honest men. Stand by, I'll scour you for a goblet. Stand aside, you were best. I
45   charge you in the name of Belzebub. Look to the goblet, Rafe.

VINTNER   What mean you, sirrah?

ROBIN   I'll tell you what I mean. [He reads] Sanctobolorum Periphrasticon.[3] Nay, I'll tickle you, vintner—look to the goblet, Rafe. Polypragmos Belseborams fra-
          manto pacostiphos tostu Mephostophilis, Etc.

          [Enter Mephostophilis, who sets squibs[4] at their backs. They run about.]

VINTNER   O nomine Domine[5] what mean'st thou, Robin? Thou hast no goblet.

RAFE   Peccatum peccatorum[6] here's thy goblet, good vintner.

ROBIN   Misericordia pro nobis[7] what shall I do? Good devil, forgive me now and I'll never rob thy library more.

          [Enter to them Mephostophilis.]

MEPHOSTOPHILIS Vainish villains! Th'one like an ape, another like a bear, the
55   third an ass, for doing this enterprise.

---

1. "Behold, the sign"; i.e., of the truth.
2. Trick.
3. Gibberish.
4. Firecrackers.

5. In God's name.
6. Sin of sins.
7. Mercy on us.

Monarch of hell, under whose black survey
Great potentates do kneel with awful fear,
Upon whose altars thousand souls do lie,
How am I vexed with these villains' charms?
60   From Constantinople am I hither come,
Only for pleasure of these damned slaves.

ROBIN How, from Constantinople? You have had a great journey. Will you take six
pence in your purse to pay for your supper, and be gone?

MEPHOSTOPHILIS Well, villains, for your presumption I transform thee into an
65   ape and thee into a dog, and so be gone.   [*Exit.*]

ROBIN How, into an ape? That's brave! I'll have fine sport with the boys. I'll get
nuts and apples enow.

RAFE And I must be a dog!

ROBIN I'faith thy head will never be out of the potage pot.   [*Exeunt.*]

Act 4

Scene One

[*The Emperor's Court. Enter Martino and Frederick at several doors.*]

MARTINO What ho, officers, gentlemen!
Hie to the presence to attend the Emperor.
Good Frederick, see the rooms be voided straight.
His Majesty is coming to the hall;
5   Go back, and see the state in readiness.

FREDERICK But where is Bruno, our elected Pope,
That on a fury's back came post from Rome?
Will not his grace consort° the Emperor?   *greet*

MARTINO Oh yes, and with him comes the German conjuror,
10   The learned Faustus, fame of Wittenberg,
The wonder of the world for magic art.
And he intends to show great Carolus
The race of all his stout progenitors,
And bring in presence of his Majesty
15   The royal shapes and warlike semblances
Of Alexander and his beauteous paramour.[1]

FREDERICK Where is Benvolio?

MARTINO Fast asleep, I warrant you.
He took his rouse with stoups° of Rhenish wine   *large cups*
20   So kindly yesternight to Bruno's health,
That all this day the sluggard keeps his bed.

FREDERICK See, see, his window's ope. We'll call to him.

MARTINO What ho, Benvolio?

[*Enter Benvolio above at a window in his nightcap, buttoning.*]

BENVOLIO What a devil ail you two?

MARTINO Speak softly, sir, lest the devil hear you;
For Faustus at the court is late arrived,
And at his heels a thousand furies wait

---

1. Alexander the Great and his wife, Roxana.

           To accomplish whatsoever the Doctor please.

BENVOLIO What of this?

MARTINO Come, leave thy chamber first, and thou shalt see
           This conjuror perform such rare exploits
           Before the Pope and royal Emperor
           As never yet was seen in Germany.

BENVOLIO Has not the Pope enough of conjuring yet?
35   He was upon the devil's back late enough,
           And if he be so far in love with him,
           I would he would post with him to Rome again.

FREDERICK Speak, wilt thou come and see this sport?

BENVOLIO Not I.

MARTINO Wilt thou stand in thy window and see it, then?

BENVOLIO Ay, and I fall not asleep i' the meantime.

MARTINO The Emperor is at hand, who comes to see
           What wonders by black spells may compassed be.

BENVOLIO Well, go you, attend the Emperor. I am content for this once to thrust
45   my head out at a window, for they say if a man be drunk over night the dev-
           il cannot hurt him in the morning. If that be true, I have a charm in my
           head shall control him as well as the conjuror, I warrant you.

                                                 [Exeunt Martino and Frederick.]

Scene Two

[Sennet. Charles, the German Emperor, Bruno, Saxony, Faustus, Mephostophilis, Frederick, Martino, and Attendants. Benvolio still at the window.]

EMPEROR Wonder of men, renowned magician,
           Thrice-learned Faustus, welcome to our court.
           This deed of thine, in setting Bruno free
           From his and our professed enemy,
5   Shall add more excellence unto thine art,
           Than if by powerful necromantic spells
           Thou couldst command the world's obedience.
           For ever be beloved of Carolus;
           And if this Bruno thou hast late redeemed,
10   In peace possess the triple diadem
           And sit in Peter's chair, despite of chance,
           Thou shalt be famous through all Italy,
           And honored of the German Emperor.

FAUSTUS These gracious words, most royal Carolus,
15   Shall make poor Faustus to his utmost power
           Both love and serve the German Emperor,
           And lay his life at holy Bruno's feet.
           For proof whereof, if so your Grace be pleased,
           The Doctor stands prepared, by power of art,
20   To cast his magic charms that shall pierce through
           The ebon° gates of ever-burning hell,   *ebony*
           And hale the stubborn furies from their caves,
           To compass whatsoe'er your Grace commands.

BENVOLIO [*Aside*] Blood, he speaks terribly! But for all that, I do not greatly
25   believe him. He looks as like a conjuror as the Pope to a coster-monger.[2]
EMPEROR Then, Faustus, as thou late didst promise us,
     We would behold that famous conqueror,
     Great Alexander, and his paramour,
     In their true shapes and state majestical,
30   That we may wonder at their excellence.
FAUSTUS Your Majesty shall see them presently.
     Mephostophilis, away!
     And with a solemn noise of trumpets' sound,
     Present before this royal Emperor
35   Great Alexander and his beauteous paramour.
MEPHOSTOPHILIS Faustus, I will.
BENVOLIO Well, Master Doctor, an your devils come not away quickly, you shall
     have me asleep presently. Zounds, I could eat myself for anger, to think I
     have been such an ass all this while, to stand gaping after the devil's gover-
40   nor, and can see nothing.
FAUSTUS I'll make you feel something anon, if my art fail me not.
     My lord, I must forwarn your Majesty
     That when my spirits present the royal shapes
     Of Alexander and his paramour,
45   Your Grace demand no questions of the King,
     But in dumb silence let them come and go.
EMPEROR Be it as Faustus please, we are content.
BENVOLIO Ay, ay, and I am content too. And thou bring Alexander and his para-
     mour before the Emperor, I'll be Actaeon[3] and turn myself to a stag.
FAUSTUS And I'll play Diana, and send you the horns presently.
     [*Sennet. Enter at one the Emperor Alexander, at the other Darius. They meet. Darius
     is thrown down; Alexander kills him, takes off his crown, and, offering to go out, his
     Paramour meets him. He embraceth her and sets Darius' crown upon her head, and
     coming back, both salute the Emperor, who, leaving his state, offers to embrace them,
     which Faustus seeing, suddenly stays him. Then trumpets cease and music sounds.*]
     My gracious lord, you do forget yourself.
     These are but shadows, not substantial.
EMPEROR Oh pardon me, my thoughts are so ravished
     With sight of this renowned Emperor,
55   That in mine arms I would have compassed him.
     But, Faustus, since I may not speak to them,
     To satisfy my longing thoughts at full,
     Let me this tell thee: I have heard it said
     That this fair lady, whilst she lived on earth,
60   Had on her neck a little wart or mole.
     How may I prove that saying to be true?
FAUSTUS Your Majesty may boldly go and see.
EMPEROR Faustus, I see it plain,

---

2. Vegetable seller.
3. Mythical hunter, changed by the goddess Diana into a

stag because he had seen her naked as she bathed after a
hunt; he was then devoured by his own dogs.

And in this sight thou better pleasest me
65   Than if I gained another monarchy.

FAUSTUS Away, be gone.   *[Exit Show.]*
     See, see, my gracious lord, what strange beast is yon, that
          thrusts his head out at window?

EMPEROR Oh, wondrous sight! See, Duke of Saxony,
70   Two spreading horns most strangely fastened
     Upon the head of young Benvolio!⁴

SAXONY What, is he asleep? Or dead?

FAUSTUS He sleeps, my lord: but dreams not of his horns.

EMPEROR This sport is excellent. We'll call and wake him.
75   What ho, Benvolio!

BENVOLIO A plague upon you! Let me sleep awhile.

EMPEROR I blame thee not to sleep much, having such a head of thine own.

SAXONY Look up, Benvolio, 'tis the Emperor calls.

BENVOLIO The Emperor? Where? Oh, zounds, my head!

EMPEROR Nay, and thy horns hold, 'tis no matter for thy head, for that's armed
     sufficiently.

FAUSTUS Why, how now, Sir Knight? What, hanged by the horns? This most
     horrible! Fie, fie! Pull in your head for shame; let not all the world wonder
     at you.

BENVOLIO Zounds, Doctor, is this your villainy?

FAUSTUS Oh, say not so, sir. The Doctor has no skill,
     No art, no cunning, to present these lords
     Or bring before this royal Emperor
     The mighty monarch, warlike Alexander.
90   If Faustus do it, you are straight resolved
     In bold Actaeon's shape to turn a stag.
     And therefore, my lord, so please your majesty,
     I'll raise a kennel of hounds shall hunt him so
     As all his footmanship shall scarce prevail
95   To keep his carcass from their bloody fangs.
     Ho, Belimote, Argiron, Asterote!

BENVOLIO Hold, hold! Zounds, he'll raise up a kennel of devils, I think anon.
     Good my lord, entreat for me. 'Sblood, I am never never able to endure
     these torments.

EMPEROR Then, good Master Doctor,
     Let me entreat you to remove his horns:
     He has done penance now sufficiently.

FAUSTUS My gracious lord, not so much for injury done to me, as to delight your
     majesty with some mirth, hath Faustus justly requited this injurious knight;
105   which being all I desire, I am content to remove his horns. Mephostophilis,
     transform him. And hereafter, sir, look you speak well of scholars.

BENVOLIO *[Aside]* Speak well of ye? 'Sblood, and scholars be such cuckold-makers
     to clap horns of honest men's heads o' this order, I'll ne'er trust smooth faces
     and small ruffs more. But an I be not revenged for this, would I might be

---

4. To be "horned" was to be cuckolded. Benvolio, who has insulted scholars, is given horns by Faustus, who takes a scholar's revenge. The insult is introduced as a reflection on the myth of Diana and Actaeon.

110   turned to a gaping oyster and drink nothing but salt water.
EMPEROR Come, Faustus, while the Emperor lives,
        In recompense of this thy high desert,°   *merit*
        Thou shalt command the state of Germany,
        And live beloved of mighty Carolus.   [*Exeunt omnes.*]

                            Scene Three
    [*Enter Benvolio, Martino, Frederick and Soldiers.*]
MARTINO Nay, sweet Benvolio, let us sway thy thoughts
        From this attempt against the conjuror.
BENVOLIO Away, you love me not, to urge me thus.
        Shall I let slip° so great an injury,   *overlook*
5   When every servile groom jests at my wrongs,
        And in their rustic gambols proudly say
        Benvolio's head was graced with horns today?
        Oh, may these eyelids never close again
        Till with my sword I have that conjuror slain.
10   If you will aid me in this enterprise,
        Then draw your weapons and be resolute.
        If not, depart. Here will Benvolio die,
        But Faustus' death shall quit my infamy.
FREDERICK Nay, we will stay with thee, betide what may,
15   And kill that Doctor if he come this way.
BENVOLIO Then, gentle Frederick, hie° thee to the grove,   *take*
        And place our servants and our followers
        Close in an ambush there behind the trees.
        By this I know the conjuror is near:
20   I saw him kneel and kiss the Emperor's hand,
        And take his leave, laden with rich rewards.
        Then, soldiers, boldly fight. If Faustus die,
        Take you the wealth, leave us the victory.
FREDERICK Come, soldiers, follow me unto the grove.
25   Who kills him shall have gold and endless love.
                            [*Exit Frederick with the Soldiers.*]
BENVOLIO My head is lighter than it was by th'horns,
        But yet my heart more ponderous than my head,
        And pants until I see that conjuror dead.
MARTINO Where shall we place ourselves, Benvolio?
BENVOLIO Here will we stay to bide the first assault.
        Oh, were that damned hell-hound but in place,
        Thou soon shouldst see me quit my foul disgrace.
    [*Enter Frederick.*]
FREDERICK Close, close! The conjuror is at hand,
        And all alone comes walking in his gown.
35   Be ready then, and strike the peasant down.
BENVOLIO Mine be that honor, then. Now sword, strike home.
        For horns he gave, I'll have his head anon.
    [*Enter Faustus with a false head.*]
MARTINO See, see, he comes.

BENVOLIO No words. This blow ends all.

40   Hell take his soul; his body thus must fall.   [*Attacks Faustus.*]

FAUSTUS Oh!

FREDERICK Groan you, Master Doctor?

BENVOLIO Break may his heart with groans! Dear Frederick, see,
      Thus will I end his griefs immediately.   [*Cuts off his head.*]

MARTINO Strike with a willing hand: his head is off.

BENVOLIO The devil's dead! The Furies now may laugh.

FREDERICK Was this that stern aspect, that awful frown,
      Made the grim monarch of infernal spirits
      Tremble and quake at his commanding charms?

MARTINO Was this that damned head, whose heart conspired
      Benvolio's shame before the Emperor?

BENVOLIO Ay, that's the head, and here the body lies,
      Justly rewarded for his villainies.

FREDERICK Come, let's devise how we may add more shame

55   To the black scandal of his hated name.

BENVOLIO First, on his head, in quittance° of my wrongs,   *payment*
      I'll nail huge forked horns, and let them hang
      Within the window where he yoked° me first,   *overcame*
      That all the world may see my just revenge.

MARTINO What use shall we put his beard to?

BENVOLIO We'll sell it to a chimney-sweeper: it will wear

60   out ten birching° brooms, I warrant you.   *birch-twig*

FREDERICK What shall eyes do?

BENVOLIO We'll put out his eyes, and they shall serve for buttons to his lips, to

65   keep his tongue from catching cold.

MARTINO An excellent policy! And now, sirs, having divided him, what shall the
      body do?

      [*Faustus rises.*]

BENVOLIO Zounds, the devil's alive again!

FREDERICK Give him his head, for God's sake!

FAUSTUS Nay, keep it. Faustus will have heads and hands.
      I call your hearts to recompense this deed.
      Knew you not, traitors, I was limited
      For four and twenty years to breathe on earth?
      And had you cut my body with your swords,

75   Or hewed this flesh and bones as small as sand,
      Yet in a minute had my spirit returned,
      And I had breathed a man made free from harm.
      But wherefore do I dally° my revenge?   *delay*
      Asteroth, Belimoth, Mephostophilis!

      [*Enter Mephostophilis and other Devils.*]

80   Go, horse these traitors on your fiery backs,
      And mount aloft with them as high as heaven;
      Thence pitch them headlong to the lowest hell.
      Yet stay, the world shall see their misery,
      And hell shall after plague their treachery.

85   Go, Belimoth, and take this caitiff° hence,   *coward*
      And hurl him in some lake of mud and dirt.
      Take thou this other: drag him through the woods
      Amongst the pricking thorns and sharpest briars,
      Whilst with my gentle Mephostophilis,
90   This traitor flies unto some steepy rock,
      That rolling down may break the villain's bones,
      As he intended to dismember me.
      Fly hence, dispatch my charge immediately.
FREDERICK Pity us, gentle Faustus! Save our lives!
FAUSTUS Away!
FREDERICK He must needs go that the devil drives.
      [Exeunt Spirits with the Knights. Enter the Ambush Soldiers.]
FIRST SOLDIER Come, sirs, prepare yourselves in readiness.
      Make haste to help these noble gentlemen.
      I heard them parley with the conjuror.
SECOND SOLDIER See, where he comes. Dispatch and kill the slave.
FAUSTUS What's here? An ambush to betray my life!
      Then Faustus, try thy skill. Base peasants, stand!
      For lo, these trees remove at my command,
      And stand as bulwarks twixt yourselves and me,
105   To shield me from your hated treachery.
      Yet, to encounter this your weak attempt,
      Behold an army comes incontinent.°   *rapidly*
[Faustus strikes the door, and enter a devil playing on a drum; after him another bearing an ensign;[5] and divers with weapons; Mephostophilis with fireworks. They set upon the soldiers and drive them out.]

Scene Four

[Enter at several doors Benvolio, Frederick and Martino, their heads and faces bloody and besmeared with mud and dirt, all having horns on their heads.]
MARTINO What ho, Benvolio!
BENVOLIO Here! What, Frederick, ho!
FREDERICK Oh help me, gentle friend. Where is Martino?
MARTINO Dear Frederick, here,
5   Half smothered in a lake of mud and dirt,
      Through which the Furies dragged me by the heels.
FREDERICK Martino, see Benvolio's horns again!
MARTINO Oh misery! How now, Benvolio?
BENVOLIO Defend me, heaven! Shall I be haunted still?
MARTINO Nay, fear not, man; we have no power to kill.
BENVOLIO My friends transformed thus! Oh hellish spite!
      Your heads are all set with horns!
FREDERICK You hit it right:
      It is your own you mean. Feel on your head.
BENVOLIO Zounds, horns again!

5. Flag.

MARTINO Nay, chafe not, man. We all are sped.°   *done for*
BENVOLIO What devil attends this damned magician,
    That, spite of spite, our wrongs are doubled?
FREDERICK What may we do, that we may hide our shames?
BENVOLIO If we should follow him to work revenge,
    He'd join long asses' ears to these huge horns,
    And make us laughing stocks to all the world.
MARTINO What shall we then do, dear Benvolio?
BENVOLIO I have a castle joining near these woods,
25   And thither we'll repair and live obscure,
    Till time shall alter these our brutish shapes.
    Sith° black disgrace hath thus eclipsed our fame,   *since*
    We'll rather die with grief, than live with shame.   [*Exeunt omnes.*]

Scene Five

[*Enter Faustus and Mephostophilis.*]
FAUSTUS Now, Mephostophilis, the restless course
    That time doth run with calm and deadly foot,
    Shortening my days and thread of vital life,
    Calls for the payment of my latest years.
5   Therefore, sweet Mephostophilis, let us
    Make haste to Wittenberg.
MEPHOSTOPHILIS What, will you go on horseback, or on foot?
FAUSTUS Nay, till I am past this fair and pleasant green
    I'll walk on foot.
    [*Enter a Horse-Courser.*][6]
HORSE-COURSER I have been all this day seeking one master Fustian.[7] Mass, see
    where he is! God save you, Master Doctor.
FAUSTUS What, horse-courser! You are well met.
HORSE-COURSER Do you hear, sir? I have brought you forty dollars for your horse.
FAUSTUS I cannot sell him so. If thou likest him for fifty, take him.
HORSE-COURSER Alas, sir, I have no more. I pray you, speak for me.
MEPHOSTOPHILIS I pray you, let him have him. He is an honest fellow, and he
    has a great charge, neither wife nor child.
FAUSTUS Well, come, give me your money. My boy will deliver him to you. But I
    must tell you one thing before you have him: ride him not into the water at
20   any hand.
HORSE-COURSER Why, sir, will he not drink of all waters?
FAUSTUS Oh yes, he will drink of all waters; but ride him not into the water. Ride
    him over hedge or ditch or where thou wilt, but not into the water.
HORSE-COURSER Well, sir, now I am a made man for ever. I'll not leave my horse
25   for forty. If he had but the quality of hey ding ding, hey ding ding, I'd make
    a brave living on him. He has a buttock as slick as an eel. Well, God bye, sir.
    Your boy will deliver him me. But hark ye sir: if my horse be sick or ill at
    ease, if I bring his water to you, you'll tell me what is?
FAUSTUS Away, you villain! What, dost think I am a horse-doctor?
                                   [*Exit Horse-Courser.*]

6. Horse trader.   7. Bombast.

30   What art thou, Faustus, but a man condemned to die?
       Thy fatal time doth draw to final end:
       Despair doth drive distrust into my thoughts.
       Confound these passions with a quiet sleep.
       Tush, Christ did call the thief upon the cross;
35   Then rest thee, Faustus, quiet in conceit.
       [*Sleeps in his chair. Enter Horse-Courser all wet, crying.*]
HORSE-COURSER Alas, alas, Doctor Fustian quotha! Mass, Doctor Lopus[8] was
       never such a doctor. Has given me a purgation has purged me of forty dol-
       lars: I shall never see them more. But yet like an ass as I was, I would not be
       ruled by him, for he bade me I should ride him into no water. Now I, think-
40   ing my horse had had some rare quality that he would not have had me
       known of, I, like a venturous youth, rid him into the deep pond at the
       town's end. I was no sooner in the middle of the pond but my horse van-
       ished away, and I sat upon a bottle of hay, never so near drowning in my life.
       But I'll seek out my Doctor and have my forty dollars again, or I'll make it
45   the dearest horse. Oh, yonder is his snipper-snapper. Do you hear? You!
       Hey-pass, where's your master?
MEPHOSTOPHILIS Why, sir, what would you? You cannot speak with him.
HORSE-COURSER But I *will* speak with him.
MEPHOSTOPHILIS Why, he's fast asleep. Come some other time.
HORSE-COURSER I'll speak with him now, or I'll break his glass windows about his ears.
MEPHOSTOPHILIS I tell thee he has not slept this eight nights.
HORSE-COURSER And he have not slept this eight weeks I'll speak with him.
MEPHOSTOPHILIS See where he is fast asleep.
HORSE-COURSER Ay, this is he. God save ye, Master Doctor. Master Doctor!
55   Master Doctor Fustian! Forty dollars, forty dollars for a bottle of hay!
MEPHOSTOPHILIS Why, thou seest he hears thee not.
HORSE-COURSER So, ho, ho! So, ho, ho! [*Hollows in his ear.*]
       No, will you not wake? I'll make you wake e'er I go.
       [*He pulls him by the leg, and pulls it away.*]
       Alas, I am undone! What shall I do?
FAUSTUS Oh, my leg, my leg! Help, Mephostophilis. Call the officers. My leg, my leg!
MEPHOSTOPHILIS Come, villain, to the Constable.
HORSE-COURSER Oh lord, sir, let me go and I'll give you forty dollars more.
MEPHOSTOPHILIS Where be they?
HORSE-COURSER I have none about me. Come to my hostry and I'll give them you.
MEPHOSTOPHILIS Be gone, quickly!
       [*Horse-Courser runs away.*]
FAUSTUS What, is he gone? Farewell he. Faustus has his leg again, and the horse-
       courser, I take it, a bottle of hay for his labor. Well, this trick shall cost him
       forty dollars more.
       [*Enter Wagner.*]
FAUSTUS How now, Wagner, what news with thee?
WAGNER If it please you, the Duke of Vanholt[9] doth earnestly entreat your company,
       and hath sent some of his men to attend you with provision for your journey.

8. Dr. Lopez, Queen Elizabeth's physician, who was executed in 1594 for alleged complicity in an attempt to
murder the Queen. Marlowe died in 1593, so the reference is not his but one of a later editor.
9. The Duchy of Anholt in Germany.

FAUSTUS The Duke of Vanholt's an honorable gentleman, and one to whom I
must be no niggard[1] of my cunning. Come, away.   [*Exeunt.*]

Scene Six

[*Enter Clown, Dick, Horse-Courser and a Carter.*]

CARTER Come, my masters, I'll bring you to the best beer in Europe. What ho,
hostess. Where be these whores?

[*Enter Hostess.*]

HOSTESS How now, what lack you? What, my old guests, welcome!

CLOWN Sirrah Dick, dost thou know why I stand so mute?

DICK No, Robin, why is't?

CLOWN I am eighteen pence on the score.[2] But say nothing. See if she have forgotten me.

HOSTESS Who's this, that stands so solemnly by himself? What, my old guest?

CLOWN Oh, hostess, how do you? I hope my score stands still.

HOSTESS Ay, there's no doubt of that, for methinks you make no haste to wipe it out.

DICK Why, hostess, I say, fetch us some beer.

HOSTESS You shall presently. Look up into the hall there, ho!   [*Exit.*]

DICK Come, sirs, what shall we do now till mine hostess comes?

CARTER Marry, sir, I'll tell you the bravest tale how a conjuror served me. You
15   know Doctor Faustus?

HORSE-COURSER Ay, a plague take him. Here's some on's have cause to know
him. Did he conjure thee too?

CARTER I'll tell you how he served me. As I was going to Wittenberg t'other day,
with a load of hay, he met me and asked me what he should give me for as
20   much hay as he could eat. Now, sir, I, thinking that a little would serve his
turn, bade him take as much as he would for three-farthings. So he presently
gave me my money and fell to eating. And, as I am a cursen man, he never
left eating till he had eat up all my load of hay.

ALL Oh monstrous! Eat a whole load of hay?

CLOWN Yes, yes, that may be, for I have heard of one that has eat a load of logs.

HORSE-COURSER Now, sirs, you shall hear how villainously he served me. I went
to him yesterday to buy a horse of him, and he would by no means sell him
under forty dollars. So, sir, because I knew him to be such a horse as would
run over hedge and ditch and never tire, I gave him his money. So when I
30   had my horse, Doctor Fauster bade me ride him night and day and spare him
no time. But, quoth he, in any case ride him not into the water. Now, sir, I
thinking the horse had some quality that he would not have me know of,
what did I but ride him into a great river, and when I came just in the midst,
my horse vanished away, and I sat straddling upon a bottle of hay.

ALL Oh brave Doctor!

HORSE-COURSER But you shall hear how bravely I served him for it: I went me
home to his house, and there I found him asleep. I kept a-hallowing and
whooping in his ears, but all could not wake him. I, seeing that, took him by
the leg and never rested pulling, till I had pulled me his leg quite off, and
40   now 'tis at home in mine hostry.

---

1. Miser.   2. Eighteen pence in debt.

CLOWN And has the Doctor but one leg, then? That's excellent, for one of his devils turned me into the likeness of an ape's face.
CARTER Some more drink, hostess.
CLOWN Hark you, we'll into another room and drink a while, and then we'll go seek
45   out the Doctor.   [Exeunt omnes.]

Scene Seven

[Enter the Duke of Vanholt, his Duchess, Faustus and Mephostophilis.]

DUKE   Thanks, Master Doctor, for these pleasant sights. Nor know I how sufficiently to
recompense your great deserts in erecting that enchanted castle in the air, the
sight whereof so delighted me, as nothing in the world could please me more.
FAUSTUS I do think myself, my good lord, highly recompensed in that it pleaseth
5   your grace to think but well of that which Faustus hath performed. But, gracious lady, it may be that you have taken no pleasure in those sights. Therefore, I pray you tell me, what is the thing you most desire to have. Be it in
the world, it shall be yours. I have heard that great-bellied women do long
for things are rare and dainty.
LADY   True, Master Doctor, and since I find you so kind, I will make known unto
you what my heart desires to have; and were it now summer, as it is January, a dead time of the winter, I would request no better meat than a dish
of ripe grapes.
FAUSTUS This is but a small matter. Go, Mephostophilis, away.
                                                                  [Exit Mephostophilis.]
15   Madame, I will do more than this for your content.
[Enter Mephostophilis again with the grapes.]
Here, now taste ye these. They should be good, for they come from a far country, I can tell you.
DUKE   This makes me wonder more than all the rest, that at this time of the year,
when every tree is barren of his fruit, from whence you had these ripe grapes.
FAUSTUS Please it your grace, the year is divided into two circles over the whole
world, so that when it is winter with us, in the contrary circle it is likewise
summer with them, as in India, Saba and such countries that lie far East,
where they have fruit twice a year. From whence, by means of a swift spirit
that I have, I had these grapes brought as you see.
LADY   And trust me, they are the sweetest grapes that e'er I tasted.
[The Clowns bounce at the gate within.]
DUKE   What rude disturbers have we at the gate?
Go, pacify their fury. Set it ope,
And then demand of them what they would have.
[They knock again and call out to talk with Faustus.]
A SERVANT Why, how now, masters? What a coil[3] is there?
30   What is the reason you disturb the Duke?
DICK   We have no reason for it, therefore a fig for him.
SERVANT Why, saucy varlets, dare you be so bold?
HORSE-COURSER I hope, sir, we have wit enough to be more bold than welcome.
SERVANT It appears so. Pray be bold elsewhere,

3. Disturbance.

35   And trouble not the Duke.
DUKE   What would they have?
SERVANT They all cry out to speak with Doctor Faustus.
CARTER Ay, and we will speak with him.
DUKE   Will you, sir? Commit the rascals.
DICK   Commit with us! He were as good commit with his father as commit with us.
FAUSTUS I do beseech your grace let them come in.
          They are good subject for a merriment.
DUKE   Do as thou wilt, Faustus; I give thee leave.
FAUSTUS I thank your grace.
    [Enter the Clown, Dick, Carter and Horse-Courser.]
45   Why, how now, my good friends?
          Faith, you are too outrageous, but come near.
          I have procured your pardons. Welcome all.
CLOWN Nay, sir, we will be welcome for our money, and we will pay for what we
          take. What ho! Give's half-a-dozen of beer here, and be hanged.
FAUSTUS Nay, hark you. Can you tell me where you are?
CARTER Ay, marry can I. We are under heaven.
SERVANT Ay, but, sir sauce-box, know you in what place?
HORSE-COURSER Ay, ay, the house is good enough to drink in. Zounds, fill us
          some beer or we'll break all the barrels in the house and dash out all your
55   brains with your bottles.
FAUSTUS Be not so furious. Come, you shall have beer.
          My lord, beseech you give me leave awhile.
          I'll gage my credit, 'twill content your Grace.
DUKE   With all my heart, kind Doctor; please thyself.
60   Our servants and our court's at thy command.
FAUSTUS I humbly thank your Grace. Then fetch some beer.
HORSE-COURSER Ay, marry. There spake a doctor indeed, and faith, I'll drink a
          health to thy wooden leg for that word.
FAUSTUS My wooden leg? What dost thou mean by that?
CARTER Ha, ha, ha! Dost thou hear him, Dick? He has forgot his leg.
HORSE-COURSER Ay, ay, he does not stand much upon that.
FAUSTUS No, faith. Not much upon a wooden leg.
CARTER Good lord! That flesh and blood should be so frail with your worship. Do
          not you remember a horse-courser you sold a horse to?
FAUSTUS Yes, I remember I sold one a horse.
CARTER And do you remember you bid he should not ride into the water?
FAUSTUS Yes, I do very well remember that.
CARTER And do you remember nothing of your leg?
FAUSTUS No, in good sooth.
CARTER Then I pray remember your courtesy.[4]
FAUSTUS I thank you, sir.
CARTER 'Tis not so much worth. I pray you, tell me one thing.
FAUSTUS What's that?
CARTER Be both your legs bedfellows every night together?
FAUSTUS Wouldst thou make a colossus[5] of me, that thou askest me such questions?

4. Kindness   5. Huge statue.

CARTER No, truly, sir. I would make nothing of you, but I would fain know that.
  [*Enter Hostess with drink.*]
FAUSTUS Then I assure thee certainly they are.
CARTER I thank you, I am fully satisfied.
FAUSTUS But wherefore dost thou ask?
CARTER For nothing, sir: but methinks you should have a wooden bedfellow of
  one of 'em.
HORSE-COURSER Why, do you hear, sir? Did not I pull off one of your legs when
  you were asleep?
FAUSTUS But I have it again now I am awake. Look you here, sir.
ALL   Oh horrible! Had the Doctor three legs?
CARTER Do you remember, sir, how you cozened[6] me and eat up my load of—
  [*Faustus charms him dumb.*]
DICK   Do you remember how you made me wear an ape's—
HORSE-COURSER You whoreson conjuring scab, do you remember how you coz-
  ened me with a ho—
CLOWN Ha'you forgotten me? You think to carry it away with your hey-pass and re-
  pass. Do you remember the dog's fa—
  [*Faustus has charmed each dumb in turn; exeunt Clowns.*]
HOSTESS Who pays for the ale? Hear you, Master Doctor, now you have sent away
  my guests, I pray who shall pay me for my a—?   [*Exit Hostess.*]
LADY   My lord,
100   We are much beholding to this learned man.
DUKE   So are we, madam, which we will recompense
        With all the love and kindness that we may.
        His artful sport drives all sad thoughts away.   [*Exeunt.*]

Act 5

Scene One

[*Thunder and lightning. Enter Devils with covered dishes. Mephostophilis leads them
into Faustus' study. Then enter Wagner.*]

WAGNER I think my master means to die shortly.
        He hath made his will, and given me his wealth,
        His house, his goods, and store of golden plate,
        Besides two thousand ducats ready coined.
5   And yet methinks, if that death were near,
        He would not banquet and carouse and swill
        Amongst the students, as even now he doth,
        Who are at supper with such belly-cheer
        As Wagner ne'er beheld in all his life.
10   See where they come; belike the feast is ended.   [*Exit.*]
[*Enter Faustus, Mephostophilis and two or three Scholars.*]
FIRST SCHOLAR Master Doctor Faustus, since our conference about fair ladies,
        which was the beautifullest in all the world, we have determined with our-
        selves that Helen of Greece[1] was the admirablest lady that ever lived.
        Therefore Master Doctor, if you will do us so much favor, as to let us see that

---

6. Tricked.
1. The mythical queen of Menelaus, King of Sparta, who   was abducted by Paris, son of King Priam of Troy. The
                                                            action began the Trojan War.

15   peerless dame of Greece, whom all the world admires for majesty, we should
          think ourselves much beholding unto you.
FAUSTUS Gentlemen, for that I know your friendship is unfeigned,
          It is not Faustus' custom to deny
          The just request of those that wish him well.
20   You shall behold that peerless dame of Greece,
          No otherwise for pomp of majesty,
          Than when Sir Paris crossed the seas with her,
          And brought the spoils to rich Dardania.°   Troy
          Be silent then, for danger is in words.

        [Music sounds. Mephostophilis brings in Helen; she passeth over the stage.]

SECOND SCHOLAR Was this fair Helen, whose admired worth
          Made Greece with ten years wars afflict poor Troy?
THIRD SCHOLAR Too simple is my wit to tell her worth
          Whom all the world admires for majesty.
FIRST SCHOLAR Now we have seen the pride of nature's work,
30   We'll take our leaves, and for this blessed sight
          Happy and blest be Faustus evermore.

        [Enter an Old Man.]

FAUSTUS Gentlemen, farewell: the same wish I to you.

                                                              [Exeunt Scholars.]

OLD MAN Oh gentle Faustus, leave this damned art,
          This magic, that will charm thy soul to hell,
35   And quite bereave thee of salvation.
          Though thou hast now offended like a man,
          Do not persever in it like a devil.
          Yet, yet, thou hast an amiable° soul,   lovable
          If sin by custom grow not into nature:
40   Then, Faustus, will repentance come too late,
          Then thou art banished from the sight of heaven;
          No mortal can express the pains of hell.
          It may be this my exhortation
          Seems harsh and all unpleasant; let it not,
45   For, gentle son, I speak it not in wrath,
          Or envy of thee, but in tender love,
          And pity of thy future misery.
          And so have hope, that this my kind rebuke,
          Checking thy body, may amend thy soul.
FAUSTUS Where art thou, Faustus? Wretch, what hast thou done?
          Damned art thou, Faustus, damned: despair and die.
          Hell claims his right, and with a roaring voice
          Says "Faustus, come, thine hour is almost come"

        [Mephostophilis gives him a dagger.]

          And Faustus now will come to do thee right.
OLD MAN Oh stay, good Faustus, stay thy desperate steps.
          I see an angel hover o'er thy head,
          And with a vial full of precious grace,
          Offers to pour the same into thy soul.
          Then call for mercy and avoid despair.

FAUSTUS Ah my sweet friend, I feel thy words
    To comfort my distressed soul.
    Leave me awhile to ponder on my sins.

OLD MAN I leave thee, but with grief of heart,
    Fearing the ruin of thy hopeless soul.   [*Exit.*]

FAUSTUS Accursed Faustus, wretch, what hast thou done?
    I do repent, and yet I do despair.
    Hell strives with grace for conquest in my breast.
    What shall I do to shun the snares of death?

MEPHOSTOPHILIS Thou traitor, Faustus, I arrest thy soul
70   For disobedience to my sovereign lord.
    Revolt,[2] or I'll in piecemeal tear thy flesh.

FAUSTUS I do repent I e'er offended him.
    Sweet Mephostophilis, entreat thy lord
    To pardon my unjust presumption,
75   And with my blood again I will confirm
    The former vow I made to Lucifer.

MEPHOSTOPHILIS Do it then, Faustus, with unfeigned heart,
    Lest greater dangers do attend thy drift.

FAUSTUS Torment, sweet friend, that base and crooked age
80   That durst dissuade me from thy Lucifer,
    With greatest torment that our hell affords.

MEPHOSTOPHILIS His faith is great: I cannot touch his soul.
    But what I may afflict his body with
    I will attempt, which is but little worth.

FAUSTUS One thing, good servant, let me crave of thee,
    To glut the longing of my heart's desire,
    That I may have unto my paramour
    That heavenly Helen which I saw of late,
    Whose sweet embraces may extinguish clear
90   Those thoughts that do dissuade me from my vow,
    And keep my vow I made to Lucifer.

MEPHOSTOPHILIS This, or what else my Faustus shall desire,
    Shall be performed in twinkling of an eye.
    [*Enter Helen again, passing over between two Cupids.*]

FAUSTUS Was this the face that launched a thousand ships,
95   And burnt the topless towers of Ilium?
    Sweet Helen, make me immortal with a kiss.
    Her lips suck forth my soul: see where it flies.
    Come, Helen, come, give me my soul again.
    Here will I dwell, for heaven is in those lips,
100   And all is dross that is not Helena.
    [*Enter Old Man.*]
    I will be Paris,[3] and for love of thee
    Instead of Troy shall Wittenberg be sacked,
    And I will combat with weak Menelaus,

2. I.e., return to the terms of your bargain with the devil.
3. Faustus imagines he will be not only Paris, Helen's lover, but also the victor in combat with her husband, King Menelaus, as well as with the greatest of the Greek warriors, Achilles.

And wear thy colors on my plumed crest.
105   Yea, I will wound Achilles in the heel,
And then return to Helen for a kiss.
Oh, thou art fairer than the evening's air,
Clad in the beauty of a thousand stars.
Brighter art thou than flaming Jupiter,
110   When he appeared to hapless Semele:[4]
More lovely than the monarch of the sky,
In wanton Arethusa's[5] azure arms,
And none but thou shalt be my paramour.   [*Exeunt.*]

OLD MAN Accursed Faustus, miserable man,
115   That from thy soul exclud'st the grace of heaven,
And fliest the throne of his tribunal seat.
   [*Enter the Devils.*]
Satan begins to sift° me with his pride,   scrutinize
As in this furnace God shall try my faith.
My faith, vile hell, shall triumph over thee.
120   Ambitious fiends, see how the heavens smiles
At your repulse, and laughs your state to scorn.
Hence, hell, for hence I fly unto my God.   [*Exeunt.*]

Scene Two

[*Thunder. Enter Lucifer, Belzebub and Mephostophilis.*]

LUCIFER Thus from infernal Dis° do we ascend   hell
To view the subjects of our monarchy,
Those souls which sin seals the black sons of hell,
'Mong which as chief, Faustus, we come to thee,
5   Bringing with us lasting damnation
To wait upon thy soul. The time is come
Which makes it forfeit.

MEPHOSTOPHILIS   And this gloomy night,
Here in this room will wretched Faustus be.

BELZEBUB And here we'll stay,
10   To mark him how he doth demean himself.

MEPHOSTOPHILIS How should he, but in desperate lunacy?
Fond worldling, now his heart blood dries with grief.
His conscience kills it, and his laboring brain
Begets a world of idle fantasies
15   To overreach the devil. But all in vain:
His store of pleasures must be sauced with pain.
He and his servant Wagner are at hand.
Both come from drawing Faustus' latest will.
See where they come.

[*Enter Faustus and Wagner.*]

FAUSTUS Say, Wagner, thou hast perused my will:
How dost thou like it?

---

4. The mortal woman to whom Jupiter appeared as lightening.

5. A nymph beloved by the river-god Alpheus; no myth
describes her as Jupiter's lover.

WAGNER   Sir, so wondrous well
        As in all humble duty I do yield
        My life and lasting service for your love.
    [*Enter the Scholars.*]
FAUSTUS Gramercies, Wagner. Welcome, gentlemen.
FIRST SCHOLAR Now, worthy Faustus, methinks your looks are changed.
FAUSTUS Oh gentlemen!
SECOND SCHOLAR What ails Faustus?
FAUSTUS Ah, my sweet chamber-fellow, had I lived with thee
        Then had I lived still, but now must die eternally.
30   Look, sirs, comes he not? Comes he not?
FIRST SCHOLAR Oh, my dear Faustus, what imports this fear?
SECOND SCHOLAR Is all our pleasure turned to melancholy?
THIRD SCHOLAR He is not well with being oversolitary.
SECOND SCHOLAR If it be so, we'll have physicians, and Faustus shall be cured.
THIRD SCHOLAR 'Tis but a surfeit, sir; fear nothing.
FAUSTUS A surfeit of deadly sin, that hath damned both body and soul.
SECOND SCHOLAR Yet Faustus, look up to heaven, and remember mercy is infinite.
FAUSTUS But Faustus' offence can ne'er be pardoned, The serpent that tempted
        Eve may be saved, but not Faustus. Oh gentlemen, hear with patience and
40   tremble not at my speeches. Though my heart pant and quiver to remember
        that I have been a student here these thirty years, oh would I had never seen
        Wittenberg, never read book. And what wonders I have done all Germany
        can witness, yea all the world, for which Faustus hath lost both Germany
        and the world, yea heaven itself, heaven, the seat of God, the throne of the
45   blessed, the kingdom of joy, and must remain in hell for ever. Hell, oh hell
        for ever. Sweet friends, what shall become of Faustus, being in hell for ever?
SECOND SCHOLAR Yet Faustus, call on God.
FAUSTUS On God, whom Faustus hath abjured? On God, whom Faustus hath blas-
        phemed? Oh my God, I would weep, but the devil draws in my tears. Gush
50   forth blood instead of tears, yea, life and soul. Oh, he stays my tongue. I
        would lift up my hands, but see, they hold them, they hold them.
ALL   Who, Faustus?
FAUSTUS Why, Lucifer and Mephostophilis: Oh gentlemen, I gave them my soul
        for my cunning.
ALL   Oh, God forbid.
FAUSTUS God forbade it indeed, but Faustus hath done it. For vain pleasure of four
        and twenty years hath Faustus lost eternal joy and felicity. I writ them a bill
        with mine own blood, the date is expired: this is the time, and he will fetch me.
FIRST SCHOLAR Why did not Faustus tell us of this before, that divines might
60   have prayed for thee?
FAUSTUS Oft have I thought to have done so, but the devil threatened to tear me
        in pieces if I named God; to fetch me body and soul if I once gave ear to
        divinity, and now 'tis too late. Gentlemen, away, lest you perish with me.
SECOND SCHOLAR Oh what may we do to save Faustus?
FAUSTUS Talk not of me, but save yourselves and depart.
THIRD SCHOLAR God will strengthen me. I will stay with Faustus.
FIRST SCHOLAR Tempt not God, sweet friend, but let us into the next room and
        pray for him.

FAUSTUS Ay, pray for me, pray for me. And what noise soever you hear, come not
70   unto me, for nothing can rescue me.
SECOND SCHOLAR Pray thou, and we will pray, that God may have mercy upon thee.
FAUSTUS Gentlemen, farewell. If I live till morning, I'll visit you. If not, Faustus is
        gone to hell.
ALL   Faustus, farewell.   [*Exeunt Scholars.*]
MEPHOSTOPHILIS Ay, Faustus, now thou hast no hope of heaven,
        Therefore despair, think only upon hell,
        For that must be thy mansion, there to dwell.
FAUSTUS Oh, thou bewitching fiend, 'twas thy temptation
        Hath robbed me of eternal happiness.
MEPHOSTOPHILIS I do confess it, Faustus, and rejoice.
        'Twas I that, when thou were't i' the way to heaven,
        Dammed up thy passage; when thou took'st the book
        To view the scriptures, then I turned the leaves
        And led thine eye.
85   What, weep'st thou? 'Tis too late, despair. Farewell.
        Fools that will laugh on earth, must weep in hell.   [*Exit.*]
        [*Enter the Good and the Evil Angel at several doors.*]
GOOD ANGEL Oh Faustus, if thou hadst given ear to me,
        Innumerable joys had followed thee.
        But thou didst love the world.
EVIL ANGEL   Gave ear to me,
90   And now must taste hell's pains perpetually.
GOOD ANGEL Oh, what will all thy riches, pleasures, pomps,
        Avail thee now?
EVIL ANGEL   Nothing but vex thee more,
        To want in hell, that had on earth such store.
        [*Music while the throne descends.*]
GOOD ANGEL Oh, thou hast lost celestial happiness,
95   Pleasures unspeakable, bliss without end.
        Hadst thou affected sweet divinity,
        Hell, or the devil, had had no power on thee.
        Hadst thou kept on that way, Faustus, behold
        In what resplendent glory thou hadst sat
100   In yonder throne, like those bright shining saints,
        And triumphed over hell. That thou hast lost,
        And now, poor soul, must thy good angel leave thee:
        The jaws of hell are open to receive thee.   [*Exit.*]
        [*Hell is discovered.*]
EVIL ANGEL Now, Faustus, let thine eyes with horror stare
105   Into that vast perpetual torture-house.
        There are the furies tossing damned souls
        On burning forks. Their bodies broil in lead.
        There are live quarters broiling on the coals
        That ne'er can die. This ever-burning chair
110   Is for o'er-tortured souls to rest them in.
        These, that are fed with sops of flaming fire,
        Were gluttons, and loved only delicates,

And laughed to see the poor starve at their gates.
But yet all these are nothing. Thou shalt see
115   Ten thousand tortures that more horrid be.
FAUSTUS Oh, I have seen enough to torture me.
EVIL ANGEL Nay, thou must feel them, taste the smart of all:
        He that loves pleasure must for pleasure fall.
        And so I leave thee, Faustus, till anon.
120   Then wilt thou tumble in confusion.   [*Exit.*]
      [*The clock strikes eleven.*]
FAUSTUS Ah Faustus,
        Now hast thou but one bare hour to live,
        And then thou must be damned perpetually.
        Stand still, you ever-moving spheres of heaven,
125   That time may cease and midnight never come.
        Fair nature's eye, rise, rise again, and make
        Perpetual day. Or let this hour be but
        A year, a month, a week, a natural day,
        That Faustus may repent and save his soul.
130   *O lente, lente, currite noctis equi.*[6]
        The stars move still, time runs, the clock will strike.
        The devil will come, and Faustus must be damned.
        Oh, I'll leap up to my God: who pulls me down?
        See, see, where Christ's blood streams in the firmament.
135   One drop would save my soul, half a drop. Ah, my Christ!
        Ah, rend not my heart for naming of my Christ!
        Yet will I call on him. Oh, spare me, Lucifer!
        Where is it now? 'Tis gone:
        And see where God stretcheth out his arm,
140   And bends his ireful brows.
        Mountains and hills, come, come, and fall on me,
        And hide me from the heavy wrath of God.
        No, no. Then will I headlong run into the earth.
        Earth, gape! Oh no, it will not harbor me.
145   You stars that reigned at my nativity,
        Whose influence hath allotted death and hell,
        Now draw up Faustus like a foggy mist
        Into the entrails of yon laboring cloud,
        That when you vomit forth into the air
150   My limbs may issue from your smoky mouths,
        So that my soul may but ascend to heaven.
      [*The watch strikes.*]
        Ah! half the hour is past,
        'Twill all be past anon.°   *soon*
        Oh God, if thou wilt not have mercy on my soul,
155   Yet, for Christ's sake whose blood hath ransomed me,
        Impose some end to my incessant pain.
        Let Faustus live in hell a thousand years,

6. Faustus quotes from Ovid's *Amores* 1.13.40: "O slowly, slowly run, horses of the night."

A hundred thousand, and at last be saved.
Oh, no end is limited to damned souls.
160   Why wert thou not a creature wanting soul?
Or why is this immortal that thou hast?
Ah, Pythagoras' *metempsychosis*,[7] were that true
This soul should fly from me, and I be changed
Unto some brutish beast.
165   All beasts are happy, for when they die
Their souls are soon dissolved in elements,
But mine must live still to be plagued in hell.
Cursed be the parents that engendered me!
No, Faustus, curse thyself, curse Lucifer,
170   That hath deprived thee of the joys of heaven.
     [*The clock strikes twelve.*]
        Oh, it strikes, it strikes! Now body turn to air,
        Or Lucifer will bear thee quick to hell.
     [*Thunder and lightning.*]
        Oh soul, be changed into little water drops
        And fall into the ocean, ne'er be found.
     [*Thunder. Enter the Devils.*]
175   My God, my God, look not so fierce on me.
Adders and serpents, let me breathe awhile.
Ugly hell, gape not, come not, Lucifer!
I'll burn my books. Ah, Mephostophilis!   [*Exeunt with him.*]

Scene Three

[*Enter the Scholars.*]
FIRST SCHOLAR Come, gentlemen, let us go visit Faustus,
        For such a dreadful night was never seen
        Since first the world's creation did begin.
        Such fearful shrieks and cries were never heard.
5   Pray heaven the Doctor have escaped the danger.
SECOND SCHOLAR Oh help us, heaven! See, here are Faustus' limbs,
        All torn asunder by the hand of death.
THIRD SCHOLAR The devils whom Faustus served have torn him thus:
        For twixt the hours of twelve and one, methought
10   I heard him shriek and call aloud for help,
        At which self time the house seemed all on fire
        With dreadful horror of these damned fiends.
SECOND SCHOLAR Well, gentlemen, though Faustus' end be such.
        As every Christian heart laments to think on,
15   Yet, for he was a scholar once admired
        For wondrous knowledge in our German schools,
        We'll give his mangled limbs due burial,
        And all the students clothed in mourning black
        Shall wait upon his heavy funeral.   [*Exeunt.*]

---

7. The transmigration of souls. The Greek philosopher Pythagoras speculated that souls were reborn in other bodies in an endless progression.

Epilogue

[*Enter the Chorus.*]

CHORUS Cut is the branch that might have grown full straight,
    And burned is Apollo's laurel bough,
    That sometime grew within this learned man.
    Faustus is gone. Regard his hellish fall,
5   Whose fiendful fortune may exhort the wise
    Only to wonder at unlawful things,
    Whose deepness doth entice such forward wits,
    To practice more than heavenly power permits.

Terminat hora diem, Terminat Author opus.[8]
Finis.

William Shakespeare
1564–1616

English colonists venturing to the New World carried with them an English Bible; if they owned a single secular book, it was probably the works of Shakespeare. A humanist scripture of sorts, his works have never hardened into doctrine; rather, they have lent themselves to a myriad range of interpretations, each shaped by particular interests, tastes, and expectations. Ben Jonson's line— "He was not of an age, but for all time!"—describes the appeal Shakespeare has had for speakers of English and the many other languages into which his works have been translated.

Shakespeare was born in the provincial town of Stratford-on-Avon, a three-day journey from London by horse or carriage. His father, John Shakespeare, was a glover and local justice of the peace; his mother, Mary Arden, came from a family that owned considerable land in the county. He probably went to a local grammar school where he learned Latin and read histories of the ancient world. Jonson's disparaging comment, that Shakespeare knew "small Latin and less Greek," must not be taken too seriously. Shakespeare (unlike Jonson) was not classically inclined, but his mature works reveal a mind that was extraordinarily well informed and acutely aware of rhetorical techniques and logical argument. At eighteen, Shakespeare married Anne Hathaway, who was twenty-six; in the next three years they had a daughter, Susanna, and then twins, Hamnet and Judith. Six years later, perhaps after periods of teaching school in Stratford, he went to London, eventually (in 1594) to join one of the great theatrical companies of the day, the Chamberlain's Men. It was with this company that he began his career as actor, manager, and playwright. In 1599 the troupe began to put on plays at the Globe, an outdoor theater in Southwark, not far from the other principal theaters of the day—the Rose, the Bear Garden, and the Swan— and across the river from the city of London itself. Because these theaters were outside city limits, in a district known as "the liberties," they were free from the control of authorities responsible for civic order; in effect, the theater provided a place in which all kinds of ideas and ways of life, whether conventional or not, could be represented, examined, and criticized. When James I acceded to the throne in 1603, Shakespeare's company became the King's Men and played also at court and at Blackfriars, an indoor theater in London. Some critics think that the change in venue necessitated a degree of allusiveness and innuendo that was not evident in earlier productions.

8. The hour ends the day, the author ends the work.

During the years Shakespeare was writing for the theater, the populations of Europe were periodically devastated by the plague, and city authorities were obliged to close places of public gathering, including theaters. Shakespeare provided plays for seasons in which the theaters in London were open, composing them at lightning speed and helping to stage productions on very short notice. The plays that we now accept as Shakespeare's fall roughly into several general categories: first, the histories, largely based on the chronicles of the Tudor historian Raphael Holinshed, and the Roman plays, inspired by Plutarch's *Lives of the Ancient Romans*, written in Greek and translated by Sir Thomas North; second, the comedies, often set in the romantic world of the English countryside or an Italian town; third, the tragedies, some of which explore the dark legends of the past; and fourth, a group in the mixed genre of tragicomedy but also called, after critics in the nineteenth century, the romances. A fifth somewhat anomalous group—*All's Well That Ends Well, Measure for Measure,* and *Troilus and Cressida*—falls between comedy and satire; these plays are usually termed "problem comedies."

The early phase of Shakespeare's career, the decade beginning in the late 1580s, saw the first cycle of his English histories. In four plays (known as the first tetralogy) this cycle depicted events in the reigns of Henry VI and Richard III and concluded by dramatizing the accession of the first Tudor monarch, Henry VII. Fascinated by the fate of peoples governed by feeble or oppressive rulers, Shakespeare expressed his loathing of tyranny by showing how the misgovernment of a weak king can lead to despotic rule. The cycle ends with the death of the tyrant, Richard III, and the accession of the Duke of Richmond, later Henry VII (Elizabeth's grandfather)—an action that celebrates the founder of the Tudor dynasty and the providence that had selected this family to bring peace to England. A later play, *King John,* concerns an earlier monarch whose claim to the throne is suspect; here divine right, having validated the succession of the Tudor monarchy in the first tetralogy, is made doubtful by a monarch's own viciousness. The play implies a question that Shakespeare continues to ask of history for the rest of his career: in what sense may divine right to be understood as a principle of monarchic rule? History, as Shakespeare will go on to represent it, no longer clearly demonstrates the triumph of justice, but rather shows the interrelatedness of good and evil motives that end in morally ambiguous action. The first of the Roman plays, *The Tragedy of Titus Andronicus,* which tells of the Roman general's revenge for the rape of his daughter Lavinia, and the early comedies, *The Taming of the Shrew, The Comedy of Errors, Two Gentlemen of Verona,* and *Love's Labor's Lost,* which depicts the effects of mistaken identity and misunderstood speech, illustrate other themes that Shakespeare will continue to represent: the terrible consequences of the search for revenge and the unfortunate, as well as salutary, self-deceptions of love.

The second phase, culminating in productions around 1600, is marked by more and subtler comedy: *A Midsummer Night's Dream, The Merchant of Venice, The Merry Wives of Windsor, Much Ado About Nothing, As You Like It,* and *Twelfth Night.* These plays insert into plots that focus primarily on the courtship of young couples a dramatic commentary on darker kinds of human desire: a longing for possessions; a wish to control others, particularly children; and a self-love so intense that it leads to fantasy and delusion. A romantic tragedy of this period, *Romeo and Juliet,* shows how the gross unreason sustaining a family feud and a mysteriously malevolent fate combine to destroy the future of lovers. A second cycle of four English histories, beginning with the deposition of Richard II and ending in the triumphs of Henry V and the birth of Henry VI, reveals how Shakespeare complicates the genre. An ostensible motive for the second tetralogy was the celebration of an English monarchy that had been preserved through the ages by God's will. Yet the actions of even the least controversial of its kings are questionable: Henry V's conquest of France is driven by greed as much as by his claim to the French throne, which is represented as dubious even in the playtext. A second Roman play, *The Tragedy of Julius Caesar,* takes up the question of tyranny in relation to the liberty inherent in a republic; the play seems most tragic when its action suggests that the Roman people do not recognize the sacrifices that are necessary to preserve such freedom and even regard freedom itself as negligible. As a whole, these plays demonstrate the characteristics of Shakespeare's mature style. Certain recurring images unify the plays thematically and, more important, link them to contemporary habits of speech as well as to the intellectual discourse of the period. Visual images—the I and the eye of the lover—often clarify the language of love, and figures denoting the well-being of different kinds of "corporation," including the human body, the family, and the body politic, signal the comprehensive order that was supposed to govern relations among all the elements of creation.

Incorporating many of the themes in the "problem comedies," the tragedies of the same period preoccupied Shakespeare for the seven years following the accession of James I: *Hamlet*, *Othello*, *King Lear*, *Macbeth*, *Antony and Cleopatra*, and *Coriolanus*, together with *Timon of Athens*, a play that was apparently written in collaboration with Thomas Middleton. *All's Well That Ends Well* and *Measure for Measure* illustrate societies that contain rather than reject sordid or unregenerate characters, both noble and common, and thus provide opportunities for comic endings to situations that might otherwise have ended in tragedy. And making much of the need for order but exemplifying the deep disorder of the military societies of Greece and Troy, the characters in *Troilus and Cressida* reveal the extent to which Shakespeare could imagine language as ironic and the human spirit as utterly possessed by a cynical need to turn every occasion to its own advantage. These plays serve to introduce tragedies of unprecedented scope.

Featuring heroes who overreach the limits of their place in life and so fail to fulfill their obligations to themselves and their dependents, Shakespeare's later tragedies embrace a wider range of human experience than can be explained by traditional conceptions of sin and fate. Profoundly complex in their treatment of motivation and the operations of the will, the tragedies entertain the idea of a beneficent deity who both permits terrible suffering and infuses, to use Hamlet's words, a "special providence in the fall of a sparrow." They reveal the blinding egotism that causes fatal misperceptions of character, motive, and action; their heroes are at once terribly in error and also strangely sympathetic. The human capacity for evil is perhaps most fully realized in the characters of women: the bestial daughters of King Lear, Goneril and Regan; the diabolical Lady Macbeth; the shamelessly duplicitous Cleopatra. Yet even they are not entirely unsympathetic; in many ways their behavior responds to the challenges that other, essentially more authoritative characters represent. The romances—*Pericles, Cymbeline, The Winter's Tale*, and *The Tempest*—round out the final phase of Shakespeare's dramatic career, representing (like the comedies) the restoration of family harmony and (like the histories) the return of good government. The deeply troubling divisions within families and states that characterize the tragedies are the basis for the restorative unions in the romances. Their depiction of passages of time and space that allow providential recoveries of health and prosperity to both individual characters and whole bodies politic are largely owing to the intervention of women. Unlike the women of the tragedies, the daughters and wives of the romances are generative in the broadest sense. They heal their fathers and husbands by restoring to their futures the possibility of descendents and therefore of dynastic continuity. Their agency is, in turn, sustained by forces identified as divine and outside history. *Henry VIII*, a history, and *Two Noble Kinsmen*, a romance, both probably composed jointly with John Fletcher, conclude Shakespeare's career as a dramatist.

Shakespeare also wrote narrative and lyric poems of great power, notably *Venus and Adonis, The Rape of Lucrece*, and a cycle of 154 sonnets. In a bold departure from tradition the sonnets celebrate the poet's steadfast love for a young man (never identified), his competitive rivalry with another poet (sometimes identified as Christopher Marlowe), and his troubled relationship with a woman who has dark features. The cycle encourages an interpretation that accounts for its romantic elements, but it also thwarts any obvious construction of events. It is thought that most of the sonnets were composed in the mid-1590s, although they were not published until 1609, apparently without Shakespeare's oversight. Their order therefore cannot be assigned to Shakespeare, and for this reason alone their function as narrative must remain problematic. Still, the reader can trace their representation of successive relations between persons and themes: the young man, although himself derelict in the duties of friendship, will remain beloved by the poet and made immortal by his verse, while the dark lady, who is unscrupulous and afflicted with venereal disease, receives only expressions of desire and lust, shadowed by the poet's disdain and self-loathing.

In a sense, Shakespeare has always been up to date. True, his language is not what is heard today, and his characters are shaped by forces within his culture, not ours. Yet we continue to see his plays on stage and in film, sometimes as recreations of the productions that historians of theater think he knew and saw but more often as reconceived with the addition of modern costumes, settings, and music as well as some strategic cutting of the dramatic text. Earlier periods produced their own kinds of Shakespeare. The Restoration stage, with scenery that allowed audiences to imagine they were looking through a window to life itself, put on plays that were embellished and trimmed to satisfy the taste of the time. Some producers omitted characters who were considered superfluous (the porter in *Macbeth*); others added characters who were judged essential for balance (Miranda's sister, Dorinda, in *The Tempest*). *King Lear* acquired a happy ending when Edgar married Cordelia. No one production of any period has defined a play entirely; every director has had his or her vision of what Shakespeare meant an audience to see. These reinterpretations testify to the perennial vitality of a playwright who was indeed, as Jonson said, "for all time."

THE SONNETS

The entire sequence numbers 154 sonnets. The first fourteen encourage a young man to marry and have children and may have been commissioned by his family. Neither the young man nor his family has been identified, although some readers have thought Henry Wriosthesley, Earl of Southampton, a possible subject. Sonnet 20 initiates a long sequence of sonnets addressed to a young man as the poet's lover; whether he is the man who featured in the earlier sonnets on procreation is unclear, but it has generally been assumed so. Beginning with Sonnet 78, the poet complains that a rival poet is stealing his subject—the young man's virtue and grace—to the detriment of his own poetry. Who Shakespeare's rival is (or whether he is in fact a single person) is not known, although some readers have considered Christopher Marlowe a possibility. A final set of twenty-eight sonnets introduces a new character to the sequence, a figure often referred to as "the dark lady," who is the lover of both the poet and the young man. The threesome make up a dramatic unity that is fraught with tension and anguish.

SONNETS
1

From fairest creatures we desire increase,
That thereby beauty's rose might never die,
But as the riper° should by time decease,   *the older person*
His tender heir might bear his memory;
5   But thou, contracted° to thine own bright eyes,   *engaged, shrunk*
Feed'st thy light's flame with self-substantial fuel,
Making a famine where abundance lies,
Thyself thy foe, to thy sweet self too cruel.
Thou that art now the world's fresh ornament
10   And only herald to the gaudy spring,
Within thine own bud buriest thy content,

And, tender churl, mak'st waste in niggarding.°   *hoarding*
    Pity the world, or else this glutton be:
    To eat the world's due, by the grave and thee.[1]

18

Shall I compare thee to a summer's day?
Thou art more lovely and more temperate.
Rough winds do shake the darling buds of May,
And summer's lease hath all too short a date.°   *duration*
5   Sometimes too hot the eye of heaven shines,
And often is his gold complexion dimmed;
And every fair from fair sometimes declines,
By chance or nature's changing course untrimmed.°   *stripped bare*
But thy eternal summer shall not fade
10   Nor lose possession of that fair thou ow'st;°   *own*
Nor shall Death brag thou wanderest in his shade,
When in eternal lines° to time thou grow'st.   *of verse*
    So long as men can breathe or eyes can see,
    So long lives this, and this gives life to thee.

20

A woman's face with Nature's own hand painted
Hast thou, the master-mistress of my passion;[2]
A woman's gentle heart, but not acquainted
With shifting change, as is false women's fashion;
5   An eye more bright than theirs, less false in rolling,°   *straying*
Gilding the object whereupon it gazeth;
A man in hue, all hues in his controlling,[3]
Which steals men's eyes and women's souls amazeth.
And for a woman wert thou first created,
10   Till Nature, as she wrought thee, fell a-doting,°   *in love*
And by addition me of thee defeated,[4]
By adding one thing to my purpose nothing.
    But since she pricked thee out for women's pleasure,
    Mine be thy love and thy love's use their treasure.

29

When, in disgrace with fortune and men's eyes,
I all alone beweep my outcast state,
And trouble deaf heaven with my bootless° cries,   *unavailing*
And look upon myself and curse my fate,
5   Wishing me like to one more rich in hope,
Featured like him, like him with friends possessed,
Desiring this man's art and that man's scope,°   *powers*

1. Have pity on the world and do not consume your own substance, refusing to engender the child you owe now to the world and finally to the grave.
2. Feminine in appearance, the young man is both a master and a mistress of the poet's passion. This is the first of a series of sonnets in which Shakespeare addresses the young man in clearly erotic language.
3. A man in appearance, he determines the nature of what he sees, what is apparent to him.
4. The last four lines of the sonnet are full of double meanings: the thing loving nature adds to the young man is a penis; this points or "pricks" him out for women's pleasure or "use" (with the added suggestion that his body is capital, which through usury generates interest); but the poet reserves for himself the young man's love, which is beyond commerce and has no price.

With what I most enjoy contented least;
Yet in these thoughts myself almost despising,
10 Haply° I think on thee, and then my state,   *perhaps*
Like to the lark at break of day arising
From sullen earth, sings hymns at heaven's gate;
   For thy sweet love remembered such wealth brings
   That then I scorn to change° my state with kings.   *exchange*

55

Not marble nor the gilded monuments
Of princes shall outlive this powerful rhyme,
But you shall shine more bright in these contents
Than unswept stone besmeared with sluttish° time.   *dirty*
5 When wasteful war shall statues overturn,
And broils° root out the work of masonry,   *uprisings*
Nor° Mars his sword nor war's quick fire shall burn   *neither*
The living record of your memory.
'Gainst death and all-oblivious° enmity   *casting into oblivion*
10 Shall you pace forth; your praise shall still find room
Even in the eyes of all posterity
That wear this world out to the ending doom.°   *judgment day*
   So, till the judgment that yourself° arise,   *when you yourself*
   You live in this, and dwell in lovers' eyes.

60

Like as the waves make towards the pebbled shore,
So do our minutes hasten to their end;
Each changing place with that which goes before,
In sequent° toil all forwards do contend.°   *successive/strive*
5 Nativity, once in the main° of light,   *sea*
Crawls to maturity, wherewith being crowned,
Crookèd eclipses 'gainst his glory fight,
And Time that gave doth now his gift confound.°   *destroy*
Time doth transfix° the flourish set on youth   *puncture*
10 And delves° the parallels in beauty's brow,   *digs*
Feeds on the rarities of nature's truth,
And nothing stands but for his scythe to mow.
   And yet to times in hope my verse shall stand,
   Praising thy worth despite his cruel hand.

73

That time of year thou mayst in me behold
When yellow leaves, or none, or few, do hang
Upon those boughs which shake against the cold,
Bare ruined choirs[5] where late the sweet birds sang.
5 In me thou seest the twilight of such day
As after sunset fadeth in the west,
Which by and by black night doth take away,
Death's second self, that seals up all in rest.

---

5. The choir is the section of a church reserved for the singers in the choir. "Choir" puns on "quire," the gathering of pages in a book, and thus recalls the "leaves" in line 2.

In me thou seest the glowing of such fire
10   That on the ashes of his youth doth lie
As the deathbed whereon it must expire,
Consumed with that which it was nourished by.
  This thou perceiv'st, which makes thy love more strong,
  To love that well which thou must leave ere long.

87

Farewell! Thou art too dear for my possessing,
And like enough thou know'st thy estimate.°   *value*
The charter of thy worth gives thee releasing;[6]
My bonds in thee are all determinate.°   *ended*
5   For how do I hold thee but by thy granting,
And for that riches where is my deserving?
The cause of this fair gift in me is wanting,
And so my patent[7] back again is swerving.
Thyself thou gav'st, thy own worth then not knowing,
10   Or me, to whom thou gav'st it, else mistaking;
So thy great gift, upon misprision° growing,   *error*
Comes home again, on better judgment making.
  Thus have I had thee as a dream doth flatter,
  In sleep a king, but waking no such matter.

106

When in the chronicle of wasted° time   *past*
I see descriptions of the fairest wights,°   *people*
And beauty making beautiful old rhyme
In praise of ladies dead and lovely knights,
5   Then, in the blazon° of sweet beauty's best,   *catalogue*
Of hand, of foot, of lip, of eye, of brow,
I see their antique pen would have expressed
Even such a beauty as you master° now.   *possess*
So all their praises are but prophecies
10   Of this our time, all you prefiguring;
And, for° they looked but with divining eyes,   *because*
They had not skill enough your worth to sing.
  For we, which now behold these present days,
  Have eyes to wonder, but lack tongues to praise.[8]

116

Let me not to the marriage of true minds
Admit impediments. Love is not love
Which alters when it alteration finds,°   *in the beloved*
Or bends with the remover to remove.
5   O, no, it is an ever-fixèd mark°   *landmark*
That looks on tempests and is never shaken;
It is the star to every wandering bark,
Whose worth's unknown, although his height be taken.[9]

---

6. You are worth so much that you can pay off all obligations you owe me; in other words, I have no right to you.
7. Deed granting a monopoly.
8. The poets of antiquity could not describe your perfection

because they could only guess at it; we recognize your perfection but lack but the skill to describe it.
9. The star by which ships navigate by measuring its altitude
from the horizon (known values) is itself beyond valuation.

Love's not Time's fool, though rosy lips and cheeks
10   Within his bending sickle's compass° come;   *range*
Love alters not with his brief hours and weeks,
But bears it out even to the edge of doom.°   *judgment day*
    If this be error and upon me proved,
    I never writ, nor no man ever loved.

126

O thou, my lovely boy, who in thy power
Dost hold Time's fickle glass,° his sickle hour;   *hourglass*
Who hast by waning grown, and therein show'st
Thy lovers withering as thy sweet self grow'st;
5   If Nature, sovereign mistress over wrack,°   *destruction*
As thou goest onwards, still will pluck thee back,
She keeps thee to this purpose, that her skill
May Time disgrace and wretched minutes kill.[1]
Yet fear her, O thou minion° of her pleasure!   *slave*
10   She may detain, but not still keep, her treasure.
Her audit, though delayed, answered must be,
And her quietus° is to render thee.[2]   *settlement*

130[3]

My mistress' eyes are nothing like the sun;
Coral is far more red than her lips' red;
If snow be white, why then her breasts are dun;°   *brown*
If hairs be wires, black wires grow on her head.
5   I have seen roses damasked,° red and white,   *mingled*
But no such roses see I in her cheeks;
And in some perfumes is there more delight
Than in the breath that from my mistress reeks.
I love to hear her speak, yet well I know
10   That music hath a far more pleasing sound.
I grant I never saw a goddess go;
My mistress, when she walks, treads on the ground.
    And yet, by heaven, I think my love as rare
    As any she belied with false compare.[4]

138

When my love swears that she is made of truth
I do believe her, though I know she lies,
That she might think me some untutored youth,
Unlearnèd in the world's false subtleties.
5   Thus vainly thinking that she thinks me young,
Although she knows my days are past the best,

---

1. His lover's power can hold back time and prevent his sickle from mowing down his green youth; paradoxically, while others grow old, he grows young. Nature permits this expressly to defy Time.
2. Yet Nature owes you to Time and will pay her debt by handing you over at last. The sonnet ends short of the 14 lines the form demands, as if to emphasize the idea of brevity.

3. Sonnet 127 was the first to have a woman, not a man, as its principal subject; she is described as a woman of dark complexion.
4. The couplet suggests ironic or hyperbolic compliment: my mistress is exceptional in that she has set new standards for true beauty by a comparison that defies its standards.

Simply I credit her false-speaking tongue;
On both sides thus is simple truth suppressed.
But wherefore says she not she is unjust?
10   And wherefore say not I that I am old?
O, love's best habit is in seeming° trust,   *apparent*
And age in love loves not to have years told.
    Therefore I lie with her, and she with me,[5]
    And in our faults by lies we flattered be.

Othello

Othello (1604) is a tragedy both of its time and ahead of its time. Basing *Othello* on a novella from Giraldi Cinthio's *Hecatommithi* (1565), Shakespeare takes an Italian Renaissance tale of greed, lust, and brutality and turns it into a timeless tragedy of ingenious evil spiraling toward destruction, and love haunted by demonic jealousy. A brief plot synopsis of the novella will make the point. Lusting after Desdemona and resenting Cassio for being given the position of lieutenant by Othello, Iago sets about convincing Othello that his wife has been unfaithful with Cassio. When Desdemona meets with Othello's suspicious jealousy, she concludes that she should never have married a Moor. Iago and Othello together plot to kill her. Bludgeoning her to death with sandbags, they pull down the plaster from the ceiling to make it look like an accident. The remorseful Othello betrays Iago, who then fingers Othello. Desdemona's family catches up with Othello and gets their revenge.

Although Shakespeare gives Iago the twin motives of sexual jealousy (he suspects his wife Emilia of having slept with Othello) and resentment, the intelligence and cunning of Iago make him resemble a politically calculating reader of Machiavelli's *Prince* rather than a brutal thug. To match this villain, Shakespeare creates a noble hero—not only a great general and war hero but a man enthralled by his wife, reluctant to believe her guilty, and manipulated into blaming her by the false evidence of the handkerchief. Faced with the protean shape-shifting ability of Iago to make not only himself but also the people around him appear to be what they are not, Othello is less a coconspirator than a victim. He is also a victim of his own status as outsider, an element that the tragedy plays up from the very first scene, where Iago shouts in the streets to Brabantio, Desdemona's father, "the black ram is tupping your white ewe." Othello loves Desdemona with a passionate intensity that is only equalled by the terrifying jealousy by which he undoes them both, "when I love thee not, / Chaos is come again." Shakespeare's Desdemona is also far more complex than her counterpart in the Italian novella. Portrayed from the outset of the play as a woman unafraid of incurring her father's wrath for marrying the man she loves, she loves Othello to the end—preferring to die rather than to live without his love.

Shakespeare makes his audience question preconceptions about sex, race, and identity in ways that are still urgent today. The play represents the sexual relation between Othello and Desdemona as one that is both passionate and yet somehow, at least from the point of view of Iago and Brabantio, obscene. The only time we see the couple in the bedroom together is in the final scene, where they both meet their deaths at Othello's hand. He likens himself to the "base Indian" ("Judean" in the Folio) who "sacrificed all his tribe for a pearl of great price." Othello sees himself as a cultural other, like the Turk he has been fighting throughout the play. There is no getting around the play's obsession with Othello's blackness; the language and imagery repeatedly impress upon us the issue of the hero's race.

Finally, identity itself is a central theme of *Othello*. The play abounds in incongruities of identity. Othello the Moor of Venice is a bit like Nanook of Las Vegas. And Venice, a city known for its decadent courtesans, is here the home of a woman of complete faithfulness. From the first act, where Iago declares "I am not what I am," to his declaration of love for Othello at the

---

5. We deceive each other; we have sex with each other.

moment where the audience knows he is enacting the greatest hatred, Shakespeare allows his audience to see the deceptively manipulative role-playing involved in the struggle for power. But rather than achieving power, Iago destroys not only Othello and Desdemona but also Emilia and himself. Whether Iago's evil is unfathomable or not, there is certainly something about it that is beyond the control of his own amazing powers of strategy and improvisation. It is an evil strong enough to overtake and inhabit even a man as noble as Othello.

Othello, the Moor of Venice

The Names of the Actors

OTHELLO, *the Moor*
BRABANTIO, *a senator, father to Desdemona*
CASSIO, *an honorable lieutenant to Othello*
IAGO, *Othello's ancient, a villain*
RODERIGO, *a gulled gentleman*
DUKE OF VENICE
SENATORS *of Venice*
MONTANO, *Governor of Cyprus*
GENTLEMEN *of Cyprus*
LODOVICO AND GRATIANO, *kinsmen*
  to Brabantio, two noble Venetians

SAILORS
CLOWN
DESDEMONA, *daughter to Brabantio*
  and wife to Othello
EMILIA, *wife to Iago*
BIANCA, *a courtesan and mistress to Cassio*
A MESSENGER
A HERALD
A MUSICIAN
SERVANTS, ATTENDANTS, OFFICERS,
  SENATORS, MUSICIANS, GENTLEMEN

Scene: *Venice; a seaport in Cyprus*

Act 1[1]

Scene 1

[*Location: Venice. A street. Enter Roderigo and Iago.*]

RODERIGO Tush, never tell me! I take it much unkindly
      That thou, Iago, who hast had my purse
      As if the strings were thine, shouldst know of this.[2]
IAGO 'Sblood,[3] but you'll not hear me.
5   If ever I did dream of such a matter,
      Abhor me.
RODERIGO Thou toldst me thou didst hold him in thy hate.
IAGO Despise me
      If I do not. Three great ones of the city,
10   In personal suit to make me his lieutenant,
      Off-capped to him;° and by the faith of man,   *Othello*
      I know my price, I am worth no worse a place.
      But he, as loving his own pride and purposes,
      Evades them with a bombast circumstance[4]
15   Horribly stuffed with epithets of war,
      And, in conclusion,
      Nonsuits° my mediators. For, "Certes,"° says he,   *rejects/certainly*
      "I have already chose my officer."
      And what was he?

---

1. Our text is taken, and the notes are adapted, from David Bevington, ed., *The Complete Works of Shakespeare.*
2. I.e., Desdemona's elopement.
3. By His (Christ's) blood.
4. Wordy evasion. *Bombast* is cotton padding.

20   Forsooth, a great arithmetician,[5]
      One Michael Cassio, a Florentine,
      A fellow almost damned in a fair wife,[6]
      That never set a squadron in the field
      Nor the division of a battle knows
25   More than a spinster[7]—unless the bookish theoric,°   *theory*
      Wherein the togaed consuls° can propose°   *senators/discuss*
      As masterly as he. Mere prattle without practice
      Is all his soldiership. But he, sir, had th'election;
      And I, of whom his° eyes had seen the proof   *Othello's*
30   At Rhodes, at Cyprus, and on other grounds
      Christened° and heathen, must be beeled and calmed[8]   *Christian*
      By debitor and creditor.[9] This countercaster,[1]
      He, in good time,° must his lieutenant be,   *opportunely*
      And I—God bless the mark![2]—his Moorship's ancient.°   *ensign*
RODERIGO By heaven, I rather would have been his hangman.
IAGO Why, there's no remedy. 'Tis the curse of service;
      Preferment° goes by letter and affection,[3]   *promotion*
      And not by old gradation,[4] where each second
      Stood heir to th' first. Now, sir, be judge yourself
40   Whether I in any just term° am affined°   *respect/bound*
      To love the Moor.
RODERIGO   I would not follow him then.
IAGO O sir, content you.[5]
      I follow him to serve my turn upon him.
      We cannot all be masters, nor all masters
45   Cannot be truly° followed. You shall mark   *faithfully*
      Many a duteous and knee-crooking knave
      That, doting on his own obsequious bondage,
      Wears out his time, much like his master's ass,
      For naught but provender, and when he's old, cashiered.°   *dismissed*
50   Whip me[6] such honest knaves. Others there are
      Who, trimmed in forms and visages of duty,[7]
      Keep yet their hearts attending on themselves,
      And, throwing but shows of service on their lords,
      Do well thrive by them, and when they have lined their coats,[8]
55   Do themselves homage.[9] These fellows have some soul,
      And such a one do I profess myself. For, sir,
      It is as sure as you are Roderigo,
      Were I the Moor I would not be Iago.[1]

5. A man whose military knowledge is merely theoretical, based on books of tactics.
6. Cassio does not seem to be married, but his counterpart in Shakespeare's source does have a woman in his house.
7. A housewife, one whose regular occupation is spinning.
8. Left to leeward without wind, becalmed (a sailing metaphor).
9. A name for a system of bookkeeping, here used as a contemptuous nickname for Cassio.
1. Bookkeeper, one who tallies with *counters*, or "metal disks." Said contemptuously.
2. Perhaps originally a formula to ward off evil; here an expression of impatience.
3. Personal influence and favoritism.
4. Step-by-step seniority, the traditional way.
5. Don't you worry about that.
6. Whip, as far as I'm concerned.
7. Dressed up in the mere form and show of dutifulness.
8. Stuffed their purses.
9. Attend to self-interest solely.
1. If I were able to assume command, I certainly would not choose to remain a subordinate, or, I would keep a suspicious eye on a flattering subordinate.

In following him, I follow but myself—
60 Heaven is my judge, not I for love and duty,
But seeming so for my peculiar° end.   *particular*
For when my outward action doth demonstrate
The native° act and figure° of my heart   *innate/intent*
In compliment extern,² 'tis not long after
65 But I will wear my heart upon my sleeve
For daws³ to peck at. I am not what I am.⁴

RODERIGO What a full° fortune does the thick-lips⁵ owe°   *swelling/own*
     If he can carry 't thus!°   *carry this off*

IAGO   Call up her father.
Rouse him, make after him, poison his delight,
70 Proclaim him in the streets; incense her kinsmen,
And, though he in a fertile climate dwell,
Plague him with flies.⁶ Though that his joy be joy,⁷
Yet throw such changes of vexation° on 't   *vexing changes*
As it may lose some color.⁸

RODERIGO Here is her father's house. I'll call aloud.

IAGO Do, with like timorous° accent and dire yell   *frightening*
     As when, by night and negligence, the fire
     Is spied in populous cities.

RODERIGO What ho, Brabantio! Signor Brabantio, ho!

IAGO Awake! What ho, Brabantio! Thieves, thieves, thieves!
     Look to your house, your daughter, and your bags!
     Thieves, thieves!

[*Brabantio enters above at a window.*]⁹

BRABANTIO What is the reason of this terrible summons?
     What is the matter° there?   *your business*

RODERIGO Signor, is all your family within?

IAGO Are your doors locked?

BRABANTIO   Why, wherefore ask you this?

IAGO Zounds,¹ sir, you're robbed. For shame, put on your gown!
     Your heart is burst; you have lost half your soul.
     Even now, now, very now, an old black ram
90 Is tupping your white ewe.² Arise, arise!
     Awake the snorting° citizens with the bell,   *snoring*
     Or else the devil³ will make a grandsire of you.
     Arise, I say!

BRABANTIO   What, have you lost your wits?

RODERIGO Most reverend signor, do you know my voice?

BRABANTIO Not I. What are you?

RODERIGO My name is Roderigo.

BRABANTIO   The worser welcome.

---

2. Outward show (conforming in this case to the inner workings and intention of the heart).
3. Small crowlike birds, proverbially stupid and avaricious.
4. I am not one who wears his heart on his sleeve.
5. Elizabethans often applied the term "Moor" to Negroes.
6. Though he seems prosperous and happy now, vex him with misery.

7. Although he seems fortunate and happy.
8. That may cause it to lose some of its fresh gloss.
9. This stage direction, from the Quarto, probably calls for an appearance on the gallery above and rearstage.
1. By His (Christ's) wounds.
2. Covering, copulating with (said of sheep).
3. The devil was conventionally pictured as black.

I have charged thee not to haunt about my doors.
In honest plainness thou hast heard me say
My daughter is not for thee; and now, in madness,
100 Being full of supper and distempering° drafts,   *intoxicating*
Upon malicious bravery[4] dost thou come
To start° my quiet.   *disrupt*
RODERIGO Sir, sir, sir—
BRABANTIO   But thou must needs be sure
My spirits and my place[5] have in° their power   *have it in*
105 To make this bitter to thee.
RODERIGO   Patience, good sir.
BRABANTIO What tell'st thou me of robbing? This is Venice;
My house is not a grange.°   *country house*
RODERIGO   Most grave Brabantio,
In simple° and pure soul I come to you.   *sincere*
IAGO Zounds, sir, you are one of those that will not serve God if the devil bid you.
110 Because we come to do you service and you think we are ruffians, you'll have
your daughter covered with a Barbary[6] horse; you'll have your nephews[7] neigh
to you; you'll have coursers for cousins and jennets for germans.[8]
BRABANTIO What profane wretch art thou?
IAGO I am one, sir, that comes to tell you your daughter and the Moor are now mak-
115 ing the beast with two backs.
BRABANTIO Thou art a villain.
IAGO   You are—a senator.[9]
BRABANTIO This thou shalt answer.[1] I know thee, Roderigo.
RODERIGO Sir, I will answer anything. But I beseech you,
If 't be your pleasure and most wise° consent—   *well-informed*
120 As partly I find it is—that your fair daughter,
At this odd-even[2] and dull watch o' the night,
Transported with° no worse nor better guard   *by*
But with a knave of common hire,[3] a gondolier,
To the gross clasps of a lascivious Moor—
125 If this be known to you and your allowance°   *permission*
We then have done you bold and saucy° wrongs.   *insolent*
But if you know not this, my manners tell me
We have your wrong rebuke. Do not believe
That, from° the sense of all civility,°   *contrary to/decency*
130 I thus would play and trifle with your reverence.[4]
Your daughter, if you have not given her leave,
I say again, hath made a gross revolt,
Tying her duty, beauty, wit,° and fortunes   *intelligence*
In an extravagant° and wheeling° stranger[5]   *expatriate/vagabond*
135 Of here and everywhere. Straight° satisfy yourself.   *straightway*

---

4. With hostile intent to defy me.
5. My temperament and my authority of office.
6. From northern Africa (and hence associated with Othello).
7. I.e., grandsons.
8. You'll have stallions for kinsmen and ponies for relatives.

9. Said with mock politeness, as though the word itself were an insult.
1. Be held accountable for.
2. Between one day and the next, i.e., about midnight.
3. Than by a low fellow, a servant.
4. The respect due to you.
5. Foreigner.

If she be in her chamber or your house,
Let loose on me the justice of the state
For thus deluding you.
BRABANTIO Strike on the tinder,[6] ho!
140   Give me a taper! Call up all my people!
This accident° is not unlike my dream.   event
Belief of it oppresses me already.
Light, I say, light!   [Exit above.]
IAGO   Farewell, for I must leave you.
It seems not meet° nor wholesome to my place°   fitting / position
145   To be producted[7]—as, if I stay, I shall—
Against the Moor. For I do know the state,
However this may gall° him with some check,°   oppress / rebuke
Cannot with safety cast° him, for he's embarked° dismiss / engaged
With such loud reason[8] to the Cyprus wars,
150   Which even now stands in act,° that, for their souls,[9]   are going on
Another of his fathom[1] they have none
To lead their business; in which regard,[2]
Though I do hate him as I do hell pains,
Yet for necessity of present life°   livelihood
155   I must show out a flag and sign of love,
Which is indeed but sign. That you shall surely find him,
Lead to the Sagittary[3] the raisèd search,[4]
And there will I be with him. So farewell.   [Exit]
[Enter below, Brabantio in his nightgown[5] with servants and torches.]
BRABANTIO It is too true an evil. Gone she is;
160   And what's to come of my despisèd time[6]
Is naught but bitterness. Now, Roderigo,
Where didst thou see her?—O unhappy girl!—
With the Moor, sayst thou?—Who would be a father!—
How didst thou know 'twas she?—O, she deceives me
165   Past thought!—What said she to you?—Get more tapers.
Raise all my kindred.—Are they married, think you?
RODERIGO Truly, I think they are.
BRABANTIO O heaven! How got she out? O treason of the blood!
Fathers, from hence trust not your daughters' minds
170   By what you see them act. Is there not charms°   spells
By which the property° of youth and maidhood   nature
May be abused?° Have you not read, Roderigo,   deceived
Of some such thing?
RODERIGO   Yes, sir, I have indeed.
BRABANTIO Call up my brother.—O, would you had had her!—
175   Some one way, some another.—Do you know
Where we may apprehend her and the Moor?

6. Charred linen ignited by a spark from flint and steel, used to light torches or *tapers*.
7. Produced (as a witness).
8. Unanimous shout of confirmation (in the Senate).
9. To save themselves.
1. I.e., ability, depth of experience.
2. Out of regard for which.

3. An inn or house where Othello and Desdemona are staying, named for its sign of Sagittarius, or Centaur.
4. Search party roused out of sleep.
5. Dressing gown. (This costuming is specified in the Quarto text.)
6. I.e., remainder of life.

RODERIGO I think I can discover° him, if you please   *reveal*
    To get good guard and go along with me.
BRABANTIO Pray you, lead on. At every house I'll call;
180   I may command° at most.—Get weapons, ho!   *demand aid*
    And raise some special officers of night.—
    On, good Roderigo. I will deserve° your pains.   *reward*
                      [*Exeunt.*]

Scene 2

[*Location: Venice. Another street. Before Othello's lodgings. Enter Othello, Iago, attendants with torches.*]

IAGO Though in the trade of war I have slain men,
    Yet do I hold it very stuff[7] o' the conscience
    To do no contrived° murder. I lack iniquity   *premeditated*
    Sometimes to do me service. Nine or ten times
5   I had thought t' have yerked° him° here under the ribs.   *stabbed / Roderigo*
OTHELLO 'Tis better as it is.
IAGO   Nay, but he prated,
    And spoke such scurvy and provoking terms
    Against your honor
    That, with the little godliness I have,
10   I did full hard forbear him.[8] But, I pray you, sir,
    Are you fast married? Be assured of this,
    That the magnifico[9] is much beloved,
    And hath in his effect° a voice potential°   *command / powerful*
    As double as the Duke's. He will divorce you,
15   Or put upon you what restraint or grievance
    The law, with all his might to enforce it on,
    Will give him cable.°   *scope*
OTHELLO   Let him do his spite.
    My services which I have done the seigniory°   *government*
    Shall out-tongue his complaints. 'Tis yet to know°—   *not yet known*
20   Which, when I know that boasting is an honor,
    I shall promulgate—I fetch my life and being
    From men of royal siege,° and my demerits°   *rank / deserts*
    May speak unbonneted[1] to as proud a fortune
    As this that I have reached. For know, Iago,
25   But that I love the gentle Desdemona,
    I would not my unhousèd° free condition   *unconfined*
    Put into circumscription and confine°   *confinement*
    For the sea's worth.[2] But look, what lights come yond?
    [*Enter Cassio and certain officers[3] with torches.*]
IAGO Those are the raisèd father and his friends.
30   You were best go in.
OTHELLO   Not I. I must be found.

---

7. Essence, basic material (continuing the metaphor of *trade* from line 1).
8. I restrained myself with great difficulty from assaulting him.
9. Venetian grandee, i.e., Brabantio.

1. Without removing the hat, i.e., on equal terms (or "with hat off," "in all due modesty").
2. All the riches at the bottom of the sea.
3. The Quarto text calls for "Cassio with lights, officers with torches."

My parts, my title, and my perfect soul[4]
Shall manifest me rightly. Is it they?

IAGO By Janus,[5] I think no.

OTHELLO The servants of the Duke? And my lieutenant?

35   The goodness of the night upon you, friends!
What is the news?

CASSIO   The Duke does greet you, General,
And he requires your haste-post-haste appearance
Even on the instant.

OTHELLO   What is the matter,° think you?   *business*

CASSIO Something from Cyprus, as I may divine.°   *guess*

40   It is a business of some heat.° The galleys   *urgency*
Have sent a dozen sequent° messengers   *successive*
This very night at one another's heels,
And many of the consuls,° raised and met,   *senators*
Are at the Duke's already. You have been hotly called for;

45   When, being not at your lodging to be found,
The Senate hath sent about[6] three several° quests   *separate*
To search you out.

OTHELLO   'Tis well I am found by you.
I will but spend a word here in the house
And go with you.   [*Exit.*]

CASSIO   Ancient, what makes° he here?   *does*

IAGO Faith, he tonight hath boarded[7] a land carrack.°   *merchant ship*
If it prove lawful prize,° he's made forever.   *booty*

CASSIO I do not understand.

IAGO   He's married.

CASSIO   To who?
[*Enter Othello.*]

IAGO Marry,[8] to—Come, Captain, will you go?

OTHELLO Have with you.[9]

CASSIO Here comes another troop to seek for you.
[*Enter Brabantio, Roderigo, with officers and torches.*][1]

IAGO It is Brabantio. General, be advised.[2]
He comes to bad intent.

OTHELLO   Holla! Stand there!

RODERIGO Signor, it is the Moor.

BRABANTIO   Down with him, thief!
[*They draw on both sides.*]

IAGO You, Roderigo! Come, sir, I am for you.

OTHELLO Keep up° your bright swords, for the dew will rust them.   *sheathe*
Good signor, you shall more command with years
Than with your weapons.

---

4. My natural gifts, my position or reputation, and my
unflawed conscience.
5. Roman two-faced god of beginnings.
6. All over the city.
7. Gone aboard and seized as an act of piracy (with sexual
suggestion).

8. An oath, originally "by the Virgin Mary"; here used
with wordplay on *married*.
9. Let's go.
1. The Quarto text calls for "others with lights and
weapons."
2. Be on your guard.

BRABANTIO O thou foul thief, where hast thou stowed my daughter?
　　　　Damned as thou art, thou hast enchanted her!
65　　For I'll refer me to all things of sense,[3]
　　　　If she in chains of magic were not bound
　　　　Whether a maid so tender, fair, and happy,
　　　　So opposite to marriage that she shunned
　　　　The wealthy curlèd darlings of our nation,
70　　Would ever have, t' incur a general mock,
　　　　Run from her guardage[4] to the sooty bosom
　　　　Of such a thing as thou—to fear, not to delight.
　　　　Judge me the world if 'tis not gross in sense°　　　*obvious*
　　　　That thou hast practiced on her with foul charms,
75　　Abused her delicate youth with drugs or minerals°　　　*poisons*
　　　　That weakens motion.[5] I'll have 't disputed on;[6]
　　　　'Tis probable and palpable to thinking.
　　　　I therefore apprehend and do attach° thee　　　*arrest*
　　　　For an abuser of the world, a practicer
80　　Of arts inhibited° and out of warrant.°—　　　*black magic/illegal*
　　　　Lay hold upon him! If he do resist,
　　　　Subdue him at his peril.
OTHELLO　　　　　　　　　Hold your hands,
　　　　Both you of my inclining° and the rest.　　　*following*
　　　　Were it my cue to fight, I should have known it
85　　Without a prompter.—Whither will you that I go
　　　　To answer this your charge?
BRABANTIO To prison, till fit time
　　　　Of law and course of direct session[7]
　　　　Call thee to answer.
OTHELLO　　　　　　　　What if I do obey?
90　　How may the Duke be therewith satisfied,
　　　　Whose messengers are here about my side
　　　　Upon some present business of the state
　　　　To bring me to him?
OFFICER　　　　　　　　'Tis true, most worthy signor.
　　　　The Duke's in council, and your noble self,
95　　I am sure, is sent for.
BRABANTIO　　　　　　　How? The Duke in council?
　　　　In this time of the night? Bring him away.°　　　*right along*
　　　　Mine's not an idle° cause. The Duke himself,　　　*trifling*
　　　　Or any of my brothers of the state,
　　　　Cannot but feel this wrong as 'twere their own;
100　　For if such actions may have passage free,[8]
　　　　Bondslaves and pagans shall our statesmen be.
　　　　[*Exeunt.*]

---

3. Submit my case to creatures possessing common sense.
4. My guardianship of her.
5. Impair the vital faculties.

6. Argued in court by professional counsel, debated by experts.
7. Regular or specially convened legal proceedings.
8. Are allowed to go unchecked.

Scene 3

[*Location: Venice. A council chamber. Enter Duke and Senators and sit at a table, with lights, and Officers. The Duke and Senators are reading dispatches.*][9]

DUKE There is no composition° in these news   *consistency*
    That gives them credit.

FIRST SENATOR Indeed, they are disproportioned.°   *inconsistent*
    My letters say a hundred and seven galleys.

DUKE And mine, a hundred forty.

SECOND SENATOR   And mine, two hundred.
    But though they jump° not on a just° account—   *agree/exact*
    As in these cases, where the aim° reports   *conjecture*
    'Tis oft with difference—yet do they all confirm
    A Turkish fleet, and bearing up to Cyprus.

DUKE Nay, it is possible enough to judgment.
    I do not so secure me in the error
    But the main article I do approve[1]
    In fearful sense.

SAILOR [*within*]   What ho, what ho, what ho!
    [*Enter Sailor.*]

OFFICER A messenger from the galleys.

DUKE Now, what's the business?

SAILOR The Turkish preparation[2] makes for Rhodes.
    So was I bid report here to the state
    By Signor Angelo.

DUKE How say you by° this change?   *about*

FIRST SENATOR   This cannot be
20   By no assay° of reason. 'Tis a pageant°   *test/mere show*
    To keep us in false gaze.[3] When we consider
    Th' importancy of Cyprus to the Turk,
    And let ourselves again but understand
    That, as it more concerns the Turk than Rhodes,
25   So may he with more facile question bear it,[4]
    For that° it stands not in such warlike brace,°   *since/state*
    But altogether lacks th' abilities°   *means of defense*
    That Rhodes is dressed in°—if we make thought of this,   *equipped with*
    We must not think the Turk is so unskillful°   *careless*
30   To leave that latest° which concerns him first,   *last*
    Neglecting an attempt of ease and gain
    To wake° and wage° a danger profitless.   *stir up/risk*

DUKE Nay, in all confidence, he's not for Rhodes.

OFFICER Here is more news.
    [*Enter a Messenger.*]

MESSENGER The Ottomites, reverend and gracious,
    Steering with due course toward the isle of Rhodes,

---

9. The Quarto text calls for the Duke and senators to "sit at a table with lights and attendants."
1. I do not take such (false) comfort in the discrepancies that I fail to perceive the main point, i.e., that the Turkish fleet is threatening.

2. Fleet prepared for battle.
3. Looking the wrong way.
4. So also he (the Turk) can more easily capture it (Cyprus).

Have there injointed them[5] with an after° fleet.   *following*
FIRST SENATOR Ay, so I thought. How many, as you guess?
MESSENGER Of thirty sail; and now they do restem
40   Their backward course,[6] bearing with frank° appearance   *undisguised*
        Their purposes toward Cyprus. Signor Montano,
        Your trusty and most valiant servitor,°   *officer*
        With his free duty[7] recommends[8] you thus,
        And prays you to believe him.
DUKE 'Tis certain then for Cyprus.
        Marcus Luccicos, is not he in town?
FIRST SENATOR He's now in Florence.
DUKE Write from us to him, post-post-haste. Dispatch.
FIRST SENATOR Here comes Brabantio and the valiant Moor.
        [*Enter Brabantio, Othello, Cassio, Iago, Roderigo, and officers.*]
DUKE Valiant Othello, we must straight° employ you   *straightway*
        Against the general enemy[9] Ottoman.
        [*To Brabantio.*] I did not see you; welcome, gentle° signor.   *noble*
        We lacked your counsel and your help tonight.
BRABANTIO So did I yours. Good Your Grace, pardon me;
55   Neither my place° nor aught I heard of business   *official position*
        Hath raised me from my bed, nor doth the general care
        Take hold on me, for my particular° grief   *personal*
        Is of so floodgate[1] and o'erbearing nature
        That it engluts° and swallows other sorrows   *engulfs*
60   And it is still itself.[2]
DUKE   Why, what's the matter?
BRABANTIO My daughter! O, my daughter!
DUKE AND SENATORS   Dead?
BRABANTIO   Ay, to me.
        She is abused,° stol'n from me, and corrupted   *deceived*
        By spells and medicines bought of mountebanks;
        For nature so preposterously to err,
65   Being not deficient,° blind, or lame of sense,   *defective*
        Sans° witchcraft could not.   *without*
DUKE Whoe'er he be that in this foul proceeding
        Hath thus beguiled your daughter of herself,
        And you of her, the bloody book of law
        You shall yourself read in the bitter letter
70   After your own sense[3]—yea, though our proper° son   *my own*
        Stood in your action.[4]
BRABANTIO   Humbly I thank Your Grace.
        Here is the man, this Moor, whom now it seems
        Your special mandate for the state affairs
        Hath hither brought.
ALL   We are very sorry for 't.

5. Joined themselves.
6. Retrace their original course.
7. Freely given and loyal service.
8. Commends himself and reports to.
9. Universal enemy to all Christendom.

1. Overwhelming (as when floodgates are opened).
2. Remains undiminished.
3. According to your own interpretation.
4. Were under your accusation.

DUKE [*to Othello*]
75   What, in your own part, can you say to this?
BRABANTIO Nothing, but this is so.
OTHELLO Most potent, grave, and reverend signors,
    My very noble and approved° good masters: *esteemed*
    That I have ta'en away this old man's daughter,
80   It is most true; true, I have married her.
    The very head and front[5] of my offending
    Hath this extent, no more. Rude° am I in my speech,   *unpolished*
    And little blessed with the soft phrase of peace;
    For since these arms of mine had seven years' pith,[6]
85   Till now some nine moons wasted,[7] they have used
    Their dearest° action in the tented field;   *most valuable*
    And little of this great world can I speak
    More than pertains to feats of broils and battle,
    And therefore little shall I grace my cause
90   In speaking for myself. Yet, by your gracious patience,
    I will a round° unvarnished tale deliver   *plain*
    Of my whole course of love—what drugs, what charms,
    What conjuration, and what mighty magic,
    For such proceeding I am charged withal,°   *with*
95   I won his daughter.
BRABANTIO   A maiden never bold;
    Of spirit so still and quiet that her motion
    Blushed at herself;[8] and she, in spite of nature,
    Of years,[9] of country, credit,° everything,   *reputation*
    To fall in love with what she feared to look on!
100   It is a judgment maimed and most imperfect
    That will confess° perfection so could err   *concede (that)*
    Against all rules of nature, and must be driven
    To find out practices° of cunning hell   *plots*
    Why this should be. I therefore vouch° again   *assert*
105   That with some mixtures powerful o'er the blood,°   *passions*
    Or with some dram conjured to this effect,[1]
    He wrought upon her.
DUKE To vouch this is no proof,
    Without more wider° and more overt test°   *fuller / testimony*
    Than these thin habits[2] and poor likelihoods°   *weak inferences*
110   Of modern seeming[3] do prefer° against him.   *bring forth*
FIRST SENATOR But Othello, speak.
    Did you by indirect and forcèd courses[4]
    Subdue and poison this young maid's affections?
    Or came it by request and such fair question°   *conversation*
115   As soul to soul affordeth?
OTHELLO   I do beseech you,

---

5. Height and breadth, entire extent.
6. Since I was seven.
7. Until some nine months ago (since when Othello has evidently not been on active duty, but in Venice).
8. She blushed easily at herself. (*Motion* can suggest the impulse of the soul or of the emotions, or physical movement.)
9. I.e., difference in age.
1. Dose made by magical spells to have this effect.
2. Garments, i.e., appearances.
3. Commonplace assumption.
4. Means used against her will.

Send for the lady to the Sagittary
And let her speak of me before her father.
If you do find me foul in her report,
The trust, the office I do hold of you
120 Not only take away, but let your sentence
Even fall upon my life.
DUKE   Fetch Desdemona hither.
OTHELLO Ancient, conduct them. You best know the place.

[Exeunt Iago and attendants.]

And, till she come, as truly as to heaven
I do confess the vices of my blood,°   *passions*
125 So justly° to your grave ears I'll present   *accurately*
How I did thrive in this fair lady's love,
And she in mine.
DUKE Say it, Othello.
OTHELLO Her father loved me, oft invited me,
130 Still° questioned me the story of my life   *continually*
From year to year—the battles, sieges, fortunes
That I have passed.
I ran it through, even from my boyish days
To th' very moment that he bade me tell it,
135 Wherein I spoke of most disastrous chances,
Of moving accidents° by flood and field,   *stirring happenings*
Of hairbreadth scapes i' th' imminent deadly breach,⁵
Of being taken by the insolent foe
And sold to slavery, of my redemption thence,
140 And portance° in my travels' history,   *conduct*
Wherein of antres° vast and deserts idle,°   *caverns/barren*
Rough quarries,° rocks, and hills whose heads touch heaven,   *rock formations*
It was my hint° to speak—such was my process—   *opportunity*
And of the Cannibals that each other eat,
145 The Anthropophagi,⁶ and men whose heads
Do grow beneath their shoulders. These things to hear
Would Desdemona seriously incline;
But still the house affairs would draw her thence,
Which ever as she could with haste dispatch
150 She'd come again, and with a greedy ear
Devour up my discourse. Which I, observing,
Took once a pliant° hour, and found good means   *well-suiting*
To draw from her a prayer of earnest heart
That I would all my pilgrimage dilate,°   *relate in detail*
155 Whereof by parcels° she had something heard,   *piecemeal*
But not intentively.° I did consent,   *continuously*
And often did beguile her of her tears,
When I did speak of some distressful stroke
That my youth suffered. My story being done,
160 She gave me for my pains a world of sighs.
She swore, in faith, 'twas strange, 'twas passing° strange,   *exceedingly*

5. Death-threatening gaps made in a fortification.   6. Man-eaters (a term from Pliny's *Natural History*).

'Twas pitiful, 'twas wondrous pitiful.
She wished she had not heard it, yet she wished
That heaven had made her° such a man. She thanked me,   *created her to be*
165 And bade me, if I had a friend that loved her,
I should but teach him how to tell my story,
And that would woo her. Upon this hint° I spake.   *opportunity*
She loved me for the dangers I had passed,
And I loved her that she did pity them.
170 This only is the witchcraft I have used.
Here comes the lady. Let her witness it.
[*Enter Desdemona, Iago, and attendants.*]
DUKE I think this tale would win my daughter too.
Good Brabantio,
175 Take up this mangled matter at the best.[7]
Men do their broken weapons rather use
Than their bare hands.
BRABANTIO   I pray you, hear her speak.
If she confess that she was half the wooer,
Destruction on my head if my bad blame
180 Light on the man!—Come hither, gentle mistress.
Do you perceive in all this noble company
Where most you owe obedience?
DESDEMONA   My noble Father,
I do perceive here a divided duty.
To you I am bound for life and education;°   *upbringing*
185 My life and education both do learn° me   *teach*
How to respect you. You are the lord of duty;[8]
I am hitherto your daughter. But here's my husband,
And so much duty as my mother showed
To you, preferring you before her father,
190 So much I challenge° that I may profess   *claim*
Due to the Moor my lord.
BRABANTIO God be with you! I have done.
Please it Your Grace, on to the state affairs.
I had rather to adopt a child than get° it.   *beget*
195 Come hither, Moor. [*He joins the hands of Othello and Desdemona.*]
I here do give thee that with all my heart[9]
Which, but thou hast already, with all my heart°   *gladly*
I would keep from thee.—For your sake,° jewel,   *on your account*
I am glad at soul I have no other child,
200 For thy escape° would teach me tyranny,   *elopement*
To hang clogs[1] on them.—I have done, my lord.
DUKE Let me speak like yourself,[2] and lay a sentence[3]
Which, as a grice° or step, may help these lovers   *step*
Into your favor.
205 When remedies° are past, the griefs are ended   *hopes of remedy*

7. Make the best of a bad bargain.
8. To whom duty is due.
9. Wherein my whole affection has been engaged.
1. Blocks of wood fastened to the legs of criminals or con-

victs to inhibit escape.
2. As you would, in your proper temper.
3. Apply a maxim.

By seeing the worst, which late on hopes depended.[4]
To mourn a mischief° that is past and gone   *misfortune*
Is the next° way to draw new mischief on.   *nearest*
What° cannot be preserved when fortune takes,   *whatever*
210   Patience her injury a mockery makes.[5]
The robbed that smiles steals something from the thief;
He robs himself that spends a bootless grief.[6]

BRABANTIO So let the Turk of Cyprus us beguile,
We lose it not, so long as we can smile.
215   He bears the sentence well that nothing bears
But the free comfort which from thence he hears,
But he bears both the sentence and the sorrow
That, to pay grief, must of poor patience borrow.[7]
These sentences, to sugar or to gall,
220   Being strong on both sides, are equivocal.[8]
But words are words. I never yet did hear
That the bruisèd heart was piercèd through the ear.[9]
I humbly beseech you, proceed to th' affairs of state.

DUKE The Turk with a most mighty preparation makes for Cyprus. Othello, the
225   fortitude[1] of the place is best known to you; and though we have there a substitute[2] of most allowed[3] sufficiency, yet opinion, a sovereign mistress of
effects, throws a more safer voice on you.[4] You must therefore be content to
slubber[5] the gloss of your new fortunes with this more stubborn[6] and boisterous expedition.

OTHELLO The tyrant custom, most grave senators,
Hath made the flinty and steel couch of war
My thrice-driven° bed of down. I do agnize[7]   *thrice sifted*
A natural and prompt alacrity
I find in hardness,° and do undertake   *hardship*
235   These present wars against the Ottomites.
Most humbly therefore bending to your state,[8]
I crave fit disposition for my wife,
Due reference of place and exhibition,[9]
With such accommodation° and besort°   *provision/attendance*
240   As levels° with her breeding.°   *suits/upbringing*

DUKE Why, at her father's.

BRABANTIO   I will not have it so.

OTHELLO Nor I.

DESDEMONA   Nor I. I would not there reside,
To put my father in impatient thoughts

4. Which griefs were sustained until recently by hopeful
anticipation.
5. Patience laughs at the injury inflicted by fortune (and
thus eases the pain).
6. Indulges in unavailing grief.
7. A person well bears out your maxim who can enjoy
its platitudinous comfort, free of all genuine sorrow, but
anyone whose grief bankrupts his poor patience is left
with your saying and his sorrow, too. (*Bears the sentence*
also plays on the meaning, "receives judicial sentence.")
8. These fine maxims are equivocal, either sweet or bitter
in their application.

9. I.e., surgically lanced and cured by mere words of advice.
1. Strength.
2. Deputy.
3. Acknowledged.
4. General opinion, an important determiner of affairs,
chooses you as the best man.
5. Soil, sully.
6. Harsh, rough.
7. Know in myself, acknowledge.
8. Bowing to your authority.
9. Provision of appropriate place to live and allowance of
money.

By being in his eye. Most gracious Duke,
245   To my unfolding° lend your prosperous° ear,   *proposal/propitious*
And let me find a charter° in your voice,   *authorization*
T' assist my simpleness.
DUKE   What would you, Desdemona?
DESDEMONA   That I did love the Moor to live with him,
250   My downright violence and storm of fortunes[1]
May trumpet to the world. My heart's subdued
Even to the very quality of my lord.[2]
I saw Othello's visage in his mind,
And to his honors and his valiant parts°   *qualities*
255   Did I my soul and fortunes consecrate.
So that, dear lords, if I be left behind
A moth[3] of peace, and he go to the war,
The rites[4] for why I love him are bereft me,
And I a heavy interim shall support
260   By his dear[5] absence. Let me go with him.
OTHELLO   Let her have your voice.°   *consent*
Vouch with me, heaven, I therefor beg it not
To please the palate of my appetite,
Nor to comply with heat°—the young affects°   *sexual passion/desires*
265   In me defunct—and proper° satisfaction,   *personal*
But to be free° and bounteous to her mind.   *generous*
And heaven defend° your good souls that you think°   *forbid/should think*
I will your serious and great business scant
When she is with me. No, when light-winged toys
270   Of feathered Cupid seel[6] with wanton dullness
My speculative and officed instruments,[7]
That my disports corrupt and taint my business,[8]
Let huswives make a skillet of my helm,
And all indign° and base adversities   *unworthy, shameful*
275   Make head° against my estimation!°   *rise up/reputation*
DUKE   Be it as you shall privately determine,
Either for her stay or going. Th' affair cries haste,
And speed must answer it.
A SENATOR   You must away tonight.
DESDEMONA   Tonight, my lord?
DUKE   This night.
OTHELLO   With all my heart.
DUKE   At nine i' the morning here we'll meet again.
Othello, leave some officer behind,
And he shall our commission bring to you,
With such things else of quality and respect[9]

---

1. My plain and total breach of social custom, taking my future by storm and disrupting my whole life.
2. My heart is brought wholly into accord with Othello's virtues; I love him for his virtues.
3. I.e., one who consumes merely.
4. Rites of love (with a suggestion, too, of "rights," sharing).

5. Heartfelt. Also, costly.
6. I.e., make blind (as in falconry, by sewing up the eyes of the hawk during training).
7. Eyes and other faculties used in the performance of duty.
8. So that my sexual pastimes impair my work.
9. Of importance and relevance.

As doth import° you.   *concern*
OTHELLO   So please Your Grace, my ancient;
285   A man he is of honesty and trust.
      To his conveyance I assign my wife,
      With what else needful Your Good Grace shall think
      To be sent after me.
DUKE   Let it be so.
      Good night to everyone. [*To Brabantio.*] And, noble signor,
290   If virtue no delighted° beauty lack,   *delightful*
      Your son-in-law is far more fair than black.
FIRST SENATOR Adieu, brave Moor. Use Desdemona well.
BRABANTIO Look to her, Moor, if thou hast eyes to see.
      She has deceived her father, and may thee.
                    [*Exeunt Duke, Brabantio, Cassio, Senators, and officers.*]
OTHELLO My life upon her faith! Honest Iago,
      My Desdemona must I leave to thee.
      I prithee, let thy wife attend on her,
      And bring them after in the best advantage.[1]
      Come, Desdemona. I have but an hour
300   Of love, of worldly matters and direction,°   *instructions*
      To spend with thee. We must obey the time.[2]
                                                          [*Exit with Desdemona.*]
RODERIGO Iago—
IAGO What sayst thou, noble heart?
RODERIGO What will I do, think'st thou?
IAGO Why, go to bed and sleep.
RODERIGO I will incontinently° drown myself.   *immediately*
IAGO If thou dost, I shall never love thee after. Why, thou silly gentleman?
RODERIGO It is silliness to live when to live is torment; and then have we a pre-
      scription[3] to die when death is our physician.
IAGO O villainous![4] I have looked upon the world for four times seven years, and,
      since I could distinguish betwixt a benefit and an injury, I never found man
      that knew how to love himself. Ere I would say I would drown myself for the
      love of a guinea hen,[5] I would change my humanity with a baboon.
RODERIGO What should I do? I confess it is my shame to be so fond,[6] but it is not in
315   my virtue[7] to amend it.
IAGO Virtue? A fig![8] 'Tis in ourselves that we are thus or thus. Our bodies are our
      gardens, to the which our wills are gardeners; so that if we will plant nettles or
      sow lettuce, set hyssop[9] and weed up thyme, supply it with one gender[1] of herbs
      or distract it with[2] many, either to have it sterile with idleness[3] or manured
320   with industry—why, the power and corrigible authority[4] of this lies in our wills.

---

1. At the most favorable opportunity.
2. The urgency of the present crisis.
3. Right based on long-established custom. Also, doctor's
prescription
4. I.e., what perfect nonsense.
5. A slang term for a prostitute.
6. Infatuated.
7. Strength, nature.

8. To give a fig is to thrust the thumb between the first
and second fingers in a vulgar and insulting gesture.
9. An herb of the mint family.
1. Kind.
2. Divide it among.
3. Want of cultivation.
4. Power to correct.

If the beam[5] of our lives had not one scale of reason to poise[6] another of sensuality, the blood[7] and baseness of our natures would conduct us to most preposterous conclusions. But we have reason to cool our raging motions,[8] our carnal stings, our unbitted[9] lusts, whereof I take this that you call love to be a sect or
325   scion.[1]

RODERIGO It cannot be.

IAGO It is merely a lust of the blood and a permission of the will. Come, be a man. Drown thyself? Drown cats and blind puppies. I have professed me thy friend, and I confess me knit to thy deserving with cables of perdurable[2] toughness. I
330   could never better stead[3] thee than now. Put money in thy purse. Follow thou the wars; defeat thy favor[4] with an usurped[5] beard. I say, put money in thy purse. It cannot be long that Desdemona should continue her love to the Moor—put money in thy purse—nor he his to her. It was a violent commencement in her, and thou shalt see an answerable sequestration[6]—put but money
335   in thy purse. These Moors are changeable in their wills[7]—fill thy purse with money. The food that to him now is as luscious as locusts[8] shall be to him shortly as bitter as coloquintida.[9] She must change for youth; when she is sated with his body, she will find the error of her choice. She must have change, she must. Therefore put money in thy purse. If thou wilt needs damn thyself, do it a
340   more delicate way than drowning. Make[1] all the money thou canst. If sanctimony[2] and a frail vow betwixt an erring[3] barbarian and a supersubtle Venetian be not too hard for my wits and all the tribe of hell, thou shalt enjoy her. Therefore make money. A pox of drowning thyself! It is clean out of the way.[4] Seek thou rather to be hanged in compassing[5] thy joy than to be drowned and
345   go without her.

RODERIGO Wilt thou be fast[6] to my hopes if I depend on the issue?[7]

IAGO Thou art sure of me. Go, make money. I have told thee often, and I retell thee again and again, I hate the Moor. My cause is hearted;[8] thine hath no less reason. Let us be conjunctive[9] in our revenge against him. If thou canst cuckold
350   him, thou dost thyself a pleasure, me a sport. There are many events in the womb of time which will be delivered. Traverse,[1] go, provide thy money. We will have more of this tomorrow. Adieu.

RODERIGO Where shall we meet i' the morning?

IAGO At my lodging.

RODERIGO I'll be with thee betimes.° [He starts to leave.]   early

IAGO Go to, farewell.—Do you hear, Roderigo?

RODERIGO What say you?

---

5. Balance.
6. Counterbalance.
7. Natural passions.
8. Appetites.
9. Unbridled, uncontrolled.
1. Cutting or offshoot.
2. Very durable.
3. Assist.
4. Disguise your face.
5. The suggestion is that Roderigo is not man enough to have a beard of his own.
6. A corresponding separation or estrangement.
7. Carnal appetites.

8. Fruit of the carob tree (see Matthew 3:4), or perhaps honeysuckle.
9. Colocynth or bitter apple, a purgative.
1. Raise, collect.
2. Sacred ceremony.
3. Wandering, vagabond, unsteady.
4. Entirely unsuitable as a course of action.
5. Encompassing, embracing.
6. True.
7. Successful outcome.
8. Fixed in the heart, heartfelt.
9. United.
1. A military marching term.

IAGO No more of drowning, do you hear?
RODERIGO I am changed.
IAGO Go to, farewell. Put money enough in your purse.
RODERIGO I'll sell all my land.   [*Exit.*]
IAGO Thus do I ever make my fool my purse;
 For I mine own gained knowledge should profane
 If I would time expend with such a snipe[2]
365 But for my sport and profit. I hate the Moor;
 And it is thought abroad° that twixt my sheets   *rumored*
 He's done my office.[3] I know not if 't be true;
 But I, for mere suspicion in that kind,
 Will do as if for surety.[4] He holds me well;[5]
370 The better shall my purpose work on him.
 Cassio's a proper° man. Let me see now: *handsome*
 To get his place and to plume[6] up my will
 In double knavery—How, how?—Let's see:
 After some time, to abuse° Othello's ear   *deceive*
375 That he° is too familiar with his wife.   *Cassio*
 He hath a person and a smooth dispose°   *disposition*
 To be suspected, framed to make women false.
 The Moor is of a free° and open° nature, *frank / unsuspicious*
 That thinks men honest that but seem to be so,
380 And will as tenderly° be led by the nose   *readily*
 As asses are.
 I have 't. It is engendered. Hell and night
 Must bring this monstrous birth to the world's light.

                [*Exit.*]

Act 2

Scene 1

[*A seaport in Cyprus. An open place near the quay. Enter Montano and two Gentlemen.*]
MONTANO What from the cape can you discern at sea?
FIRST GENTLEMAN Nothing at all. It is a high-wrought flood.° *agitated sea*
 I cannot, twixt the heaven and the main,°   *ocean*
 Descry a sail.
MONTANO Methinks the wind hath spoke aloud at land;
 A fuller blast ne'er shook our battlements.
 If it hath ruffianed° so upon the sea,   *raged*
 What ribs of oak, when mountains° melt on them, *of water*
 Can hold the mortise?[7] What shall we hear of this?
SECOND GENTLEMAN A segregation° of the Turkish fleet. *dispersal*
 For do but stand upon the foaming shore,
 The chidden[8] billow seems to pelt the clouds;
 The wind-shaked surge, with high and monstrous mane,[9]

---

2. Woodcock, i.e., fool.
3. My sexual function as husband.
4. Act as if on certain knowledge.
5. Regards me favorably.
6. Put a feather in the cap of, i.e., glorify, gratify.

7. Hold their joints together.
8. I.e., rebuked, repelled (by the shore), and thus shot into the air.
9. The surf is like the mane of a wild beast.

Seems to cast water on the burning Bear[1]
15   And quench the guards of th' ever-fixèd pole.
I never did like molestation° view   *such a disturbance*
On the enchafèd° flood.   *angry*
MONTANO If that° the Turkish fleet   *if*
Be not ensheltered and embayed,° they are drowned;   *in a harbor*
20   It is impossible to bear it out.°   *survive*
Enter a [Third] Gentleman.
THIRD GENTLEMAN News, lads! Our wars are done.
The desperate tempest hath so banged the Turks
That their designment° halts.° A noble ship of Venice   *enterprise/is lame*
Hath seen a grievous wreck° and sufferance°   *shipwreck/damage*
25   On most part of their fleet.
MONTANO How? Is this true?
THIRD GENTLEMAN   The ship is here put in,
A Veronesa;[2] Michael Cassio,
Lieutenant to the warlike Moor Othello,
Is come on shore; the Moor himself at sea,
30   And is in full commission here for Cyprus.
MONTANO I am glad on 't. 'Tis a worthy governor.
THIRD GENTLEMAN But this same Cassio, though he speak of comfort
Touching the Turkish loss, yet he looks sadly°   *gravely*
And prays the Moor be safe, for they were parted
35   With foul and violent tempest.
MONTANO   Pray heaven he be,
For I have served him, and the man commands
Like a full° soldier. Let's to the seaside, ho!   *perfect*
As well to see the vessel that's come in
As to throw out our eyes for brave Othello,
40   Even till we make the main and th' aerial blue[3]
An indistinct regard.[4]
THIRD GENTLEMAN   Come, let's do so,
For every minute is expectancy°   *gives expectation*
Of more arrivance.°   *arrival*
[Enter Cassio.]
CASSIO Thanks, you the valiant of this warlike isle,
45   That so approve° the Moor! O, let the heavens   *honor*
Give him defense against the elements,
For I have lost him on a dangerous sea.
MONTANO Is he well shipped?
CASSIO His bark is stoutly timbered, and his pilot
50   Of very expert and approved allowance;°   *tested reputation*
Therefore my hopes, not surfeited to death,[5]
Stand in bold cure.[6]
          [A cry within:] "A sail, a sail, a sail!"

---

1. The constellation Ursa Minor or the Little Bear, which includes the polestar (and hence regarded as the *guards of th' ever-fixed pole* in the next line; sometimes the term *guards* is applied to the two "pointers" of the Big Bear or Dipper, which may be intended here.)
2. Fitted out in Verona for Venetian service, or possibly *Verennessa* (the Folio spelling), i.e., *verrinessa*, a cutter

(from *verrinare*, "to cut through").
3. The sea and the sky.
4. Indistinguishable in our view.
5. Overextended, worn thin through repeated application or delayed fulfillment.
6. In strong hopes of fulfillment.

CASSIO What noise?

A GENTLEMAN The town is empty. On the brow o' the sea[7]

55   Stand ranks of people, and they cry "A sail!"

CASSIO My hopes do shape him for[8] the governor.

[A shot within.]

SECOND GENTLEMAN They do discharge their shot of courtesy;[9]
       Our friends at least.

CASSIO   I pray you, sir, go forth,
       And give us truth who 'tis that is arrived.

SECOND GENTLEMAN I shall. [Exit.]

MONTANO But, good Lieutenant, is your general wived?

CASSIO Most fortunately. He hath achieved a maid
       That paragons° description and wild fame,°   surpasses / rumor
       One that excels the quirks° of blazoning[1] pens,   witty conceits
65   And in th' essential vesture of creation
       Does tire the enginer.[2]
       [Enter Second Gentleman.][3]
                            How now? Who has put in?°   to harbor

SECOND GENTLEMAN 'Tis one Iago, ancient to the General.

CASSIO He's had most favorable and happy speed.
       Tempests themselves, high seas, and howling winds,
70   The guttered° rocks and congregated sands—   jagged
       Traitors ensteeped° to clog the guiltless keel—   lying under water
       As° having sense of beauty, do omit°   as if / suspend
       Their mortal° natures, letting go safely by   deadly
       The divine Desdemona.

MONTANO   What is she?

CASSIO She that I spake of, our great captain's captain,
       Left in the conduct of the bold Iago,
       Whose footing° here anticipates our thoughts   landing
       A se'nnight's° speed. Great Jove, Othello guard,   week's
       And swell his sail with thine own powerful breath,
80   That he may bless this bay with his tall° ship,   splendid
       Make love's quick pants in Desdemona's arms,
       Give renewed fire to our extincted spirits,
       And bring all Cyprus comfort!
       [Enter Desdemona, Iago, Roderigo, and Emilia.]
                            O, behold,
       The riches of the ship is come on shore!
85   You men of Cyprus, let her have your knees.
       [The gentlemen make curtsy to Desdemona.]
       Hail to thee, lady! And the grace of heaven
       Before, behind thee, and on every hand
       Enwheel thee round!

DESDEMONA   I thank you, valiant Cassio.
       What tidings can you tell me of my lord?

7. Cliff-edge.
8. I hope it is.
9. Fire a salute in token of respect and courtesy.
1. Setting forth as though in heraldic language.
2. In her real, God-given, beauty, (she) defeats any

attempt to praise her. The enginer [engineer] is the poet,
one who devises.
3. So identified in the Quarto text here and in lines 57,
60, 67 and 95; the Folio calls him a gentleman.

CASSIO He is not yet arrived, nor know I aught
　　　But that he's well and will be shortly here.
DESDEMONA O, but I fear—How lost your company?
CASSIO The great contention of the sea and skies
　　　Parted our fellowship.
　　　[*Within: "A sail, a sail!" A shot.*]
　　　　　　　　　　　　　　But hark. A sail!
SECOND GENTLEMAN They give their greeting to the citadel.
　　　This likewise is a friend.
CASSIO 　　　　　　　　　　See for the news.
　　　[*Exit Second Gentleman.*]
　　　Good Ancient, you are welcome. [*Kissing Emilia.*]
　　　Welcome, mistress.
　　　Let it not gall your patience, good Iago,
100　That I extend° my manners; 'tis my breeding⁴　　　　　*give scope to*
　　　That gives me this bold show of courtesy.
IAGO Sir, would she give you so much of her lips
　　　As of her tongue she oft bestows on me,
　　　You would have enough.
DESDEMONA Alas, she has no speech!⁵
IAGO 　　　　　　　　　　　　In faith, too much.
　　　I find it still,° when I have list° to sleep.　　　　　*always / desire*
　　　Marry, before your ladyship, I grant,
　　　She puts her tongue a little in her heart
　　　And chides with thinking.⁶
EMILIA 　　　　　　　　　You have little cause to say so.
IAGO Come on, come on. You are pictures out of doors,⁷
　　　Bells⁸ in your parlors, wildcats in your kitchens,⁹
　　　Saints° in your injuries, devils being offended,　　　　*martyrs*
　　　Players° in your huswifery,° and huswives¹ in your beds.　*idlers / housekeeping*
DESDEMONA O, fie upon thee, slanderer!
IAGO Nay, it is true, or else I am a Turk.²
　　　You rise to play, and go to bed to work.
EMILIA You shall not write my praise.
IAGO 　　　　　　　　　　　　No, let me not.
DESDEMONA What wouldst write of me, if thou shouldst praise me?
IAGO O gentle lady, do not put me to 't,
120　For I am nothing if not critical.°　　　　　　　　　*censorious*
DESDEMONA Come on, essay.°—There's one gone to the harbor?　*try*
IAGO Ay, madam.
DESDEMONA I am not merry, but I do beguile
　　　The thing I am³ by seeming otherwise.
125　Come, how wouldst thou praise me?

4. Training in the niceties of etiquette.
5. She's not a chatterbox, as you allege.
6. In her thoughts only.
7. Silent and well-behaved in public.
8. Jangling, noisy, and brazen.

9. In domestic affairs. (Ladies would not do the cooking.)
1. Hussies (i.e., women are "busy" in bed, or unduly thrifty in dispensing sexual favors).
2. An infidel, not to be believed.
3. My anxious self.

IAGO I am about it, but indeed my invention
    Comes from my pate as birdlime[4] does from frieze—°   *coarse cloth*
    It plucks out brains and all. But my Muse labors,[5]
    And thus she is delivered:
130   If she be fair and wise, fairness and wit,
    The one's for use, the other useth it.[6]
DESDEMONA Well praised! How if she be black[7] and witty?
IAGO If she be black, and thereto have a wit,
    She'll find a white[8] that shall her blackness fit.[9]
DESDEMONA Worse and worse.
EMILIA How if fair and foolish?
IAGO She never yet was foolish that was fair,
    For even her folly[1] helped her to an heir.°   *to bear a child*
DESDEMONA These are old fond[2] paradoxes to make fools laugh i' th' alehouse.
140   What miserable praise hast thou for her that's foul[3] and foolish?
IAGO There's none so foul and foolish thereunto,°   *in addition*
    But does foul° pranks which fair and wise ones do.   *sluttish*
DESDEMONA O heavy ignorance! Thou praisest the worst best. But what praise
    couldst thou bestow on a deserving woman indeed, one that, in the authority
145   of her merit, did justly put on the vouch[4] of very malice itself?
IAGO She that was ever fair, and never proud,
    Had tongue at will, and yet was never loud,
    Never lacked gold and yet went never gay,°   *extravagantly clothed*
    Fled from her wish, and yet said, "Now I may,"[5]
150   She that being angered, her revenge being nigh,
    Bade her wrong stay[6] and her displeasure fly,
    She that in wisdom never was so frail
    To change the cod's head for the salmon's tail,[7]
    She that could think and ne'er disclose her mind,
155   See suitors following and not look behind,
    She was a wight, if ever such wight were—
DESDEMONA To do what?
IAGO To suckle fools and chronicle small beer.[8]
DESDEMONA O most lame and impotent conclusion! Do not learn of him, Emilia,
160   though he be thy husband. How say you, Cassio? Is he not a most profane and
    liberal[9] counselor?
CASSIO He speaks home,[1] madam. You may relish[2] him more in[3] the soldier than in
    the scholar.
    [Cassio and Desdemona stand together, conversing intimately.]

---

4. Sticky substance used to catch small birds.
5. Exerts herself. Also, prepares to deliver a child (with a following pun on "*delivered*" in line 130).
6. Her cleverness will make use of her beauty.
7. Dark-complexioned, brunette.
8. A fair person (with wordplay on "wight," a person).
9. With sexual suggestion of mating.
1. With added meaning of "lechery, wantonness."
2. Foolish.
3. Ugly.

4. Compel the approval.
5. Avoided temptation where the choice was hers.
6. Resolved to put up with her injury patiently.
7. To exchange a lackluster husband for a sexy lover(?) (*Cod's head* is slang for "penis.")
8. To nurse babies and keep petty household accounts.
9. Ribald and licentious.
1. Right to the target (a term from fencing).
2. Appreciate.
3. In the character of.

IAGO [*aside*] He takes her by the palm, Ay, well said,[4] whisper. With as little a web
165   as this will I ensnare as great a fly as Cassio. Aye, smile upon her, do; I will
gyve[5] thee in thine own courtship.[6] You say true;[7] 'tis so, indeed. If such tricks
as these strip you out of your lieutenantry, it had been better you had not kissed
your three fingers so oft, which now again you are most apt to play the sir[8] in.
Very good; well kissed! An excellent courtesy! 'Tis so, indeed. Yet again your
170   fingers to your lips? Would they were clyster pipes[9] for your sake! [*Trumpet
within.*] The Moor! I know his trumpet.

CASSIO 'Tis truly so.

DESDEMONA   Let's meet him and receive him.

CASSIO Lo, where he comes!

    [*Enter Othello and attendants.*]

OTHELLO O my fair warrior!

DESDEMONA   My dear Othello!

OTHELLO It gives me wonder great as my content
    To see you here before me. O my soul's joy,
    If after every tempest come such calms,
    May the winds blow till they have weakened death,
    And let the laboring bark climb hills of seas
180   Olympus-high, and duck again as low
    As hell's from heaven! If it were now to die,
    'Twere now to be most happy, for I fear
    My soul hath her content so absolute
    That not another comfort like to this
185   Succeeds in unknown fate.[1]

DESDEMONA   The heavens forbid
    But that our loves and comforts should increase
    Even as our days do grow!

OTHELLO Amen to that, sweet powers!
    I cannot speak enough of this content.
190   It stops me here; it is too much of joy.
    And this, and this, the greatest discords be
    [*They kiss.*][2]
    That e'er our hearts shall make!

IAGO [*aside*] O, you are well tuned now!
    But I'll set down[3] the pegs that make this music,
195   As honest as I am.[4]

OTHELLO Come, let us to the castle.
    News, friends! Our wars are done, the Turks are drowned.
    How does my old acquaintance of this isle?—
    Honey, you shall be well desired° in Cyprus;   *welcomed*
200   I have found great love amongst them. O my sweet,
    I prattle out of fashion,° and I dote   *incoherently*

---

4. Well done.
5. Fetter, shackle.
6. Courtesy, show of courtly manners.
7. That's right, go ahead.
8. The fine gentleman.

9. Tubes used for enemas and douches.
1. Can follow in the unknown future.
2. The direction is from the Quarto.
3. Loosen (and hence untune the instrument).
4. For all my supposed honesty.

In mine own comforts.—I prithee, good Iago,
Go to the bay and disembark my coffers.°   *chests*
Bring thou the master° to the citadel;   *ship's captain*
205 He is a good one, and his worthiness
Does challenge° much respect.—Come, Desdemona.—   *deserve*
Once more, well met at Cyprus!

    [*Exeunt Othello and Desdemona and all but Iago and Roderigo.*]

IAGO [*to an attendant*] Do thou meet me presently at the harbor. [*To Roderigo.*]
Come hither. If thou be'st valiant—as, they say, base men[5] being in love have
210 then a nobility in their natures more than is native to them—list[6] me. The
Lieutenant tonight watches on the court of guard.[7] First, I must tell thee this:
Desdemona is directly in love with him.

RODERIGO With him? Why, 'tis not possible.

IAGO Lay thy finger thus,[8] and let thy soul be instructed. Mark me with what vio-
215 lence she first loved the Moor, but[9] for bragging and telling her fantastical lies.
To love him still for prating? Let not thy discreet heart think it. Her eye must
be fed; and what delight shall she have to look on the devil? When the blood is
made dull with the act of sport,[1] there should be, again to inflame it and to give
satiety a fresh appetite, loveliness in favor,[2] sympathy[3] in years, manners, and
220 beauties—all which the Moor is defective in. Now, for want of these required
conveniences,[4] her delicate tenderness will find itself abused,[5] begin to heave
the gorge,[6] disrelish and abhor the Moor. Very nature[7] will instruct her in it
and compel her to some second choice. Now, sir, this granted—as it is a most
pregnant[8] and unforced position—who stands so eminent in the degree[9] of this
225 fortune as Cassio does? A knave very voluble,[1] no further conscionable[2] than
in putting on the mere form of civil and humane[3] seeming for the better compassing of his salt[4] and most hidden loose affection.[5] Why, none, why, none. A
slipper[6] and subtle knave, a finder out of occasions, that has an eye can stamp[7]
and counterfeit advantages,[8] though true advantage never present itself; a dev-
230 ilish knave. Besides, the knave is handsome, young, and hath all those requisites in him that folly[9] and green[1] minds look after. A pestilent complete
knave, and the woman hath found him[2] already.

RODERIGO I cannot believe that in her. She's full of most blessed condition.[3]

IAGO Blessed fig's end! The wine she drinks is made of grapes. If she had been
235 blessed, she would never have loved the Moor. Blessed pudding![4] Didst thou
not see her paddle with the palm of his hand? Didst not mark that?

---

5. Even lowly born men.
6. Listen to.
7. Guardhouse. (Cassio is in charge of the watch.)
8. I.e., on your lips
9. Only.
1. Sex.
2. Appearance.
3. Correspondence, similarity.
4. Things conducive to sexual compatibility.
5. Cheated, revolted.
6. Experience nausea.
7. Her very instincts.
8. Evident, cogent.
9. As next in line for.

1. Facile, glib.
2. Conscientious, conscience-bound.
3. Polite, courteous.
4. Licentious.
5. Passion.
6. Slippery.
7. An eye that can coin, create.
8. Favorable opportunities.
9. Wantonness.
1. Immature.
2. Sized him up, perceived his intent.
3. Disposition.
4. Sausage.

RODERIGO Yes, that I did; but that was but courtesy.

IAGO Lechery, by this hand. An index[5] and obscure prologue to the history of lust and foul thoughts. They met so near with their lips that their breaths embraced
240   together. Villainous thoughts, Roderigo! When these mutualities[6] so marshal the way, hard at hand[7] comes the master and main exercise, th' incorporate[8] conclusion. Pish! But, sir, be you ruled by me. I have brought you from Venice. Watch you[9] tonight; for the command, I'll lay 't upon you.[1] Cassio knows you not. I'll not be far from you. Do you find some occasion to anger Cassio, either
245   by speaking too loud, or tainting[2] his discipline, or from what other course you please, which the time shall more favorably minister.[3]

RODERIGO Well.

IAGO Sir, he's rash and very sudden in choler,[4] and haply[5] may strike at you. Provoke him that he may, for even out of that will I cause these of Cyprus to
250   mutiny,[6] whose qualification[7] shall come into no true taste[8] again but by the displanting of Cassio. So shall you have a shorter journey to your desires by the means I shall then have to prefer[9] them, and the impediment most profitably removed, without the which there were no expectation of our prosperity.

RODERIGO I will do this, if you can bring it to any opportunity.

IAGO I warrant[1] thee. Meet me by and by[2] at the citadel. I must fetch his necessaries ashore. Farewell.

RODERIGO Adieu.   [*Exit.*]

IAGO That Cassio loves her, I do well believe 't;
    That she loves him, 'tis apt° and of great credit.°   *probable/credibility*
260   The Moor, howbeit that I endure him not,
    Is of a constant, loving, noble nature,
    And I dare think he'll prove to Desdemona
    A most dear husband. Now, I do love her too,
    Not out of absolute lust—though peradventure
265   I stand accountant° for as great a sin—   *accountable*
    But partly led to diet° my revenge   *feed*
    For that I do suspect the lusty Moor
    Hath leaped into my seat, the thought whereof
    Doth, like a poisonous mineral, gnaw my innards;
270   And nothing can or shall content my soul
    Till I am evened with him, wife for wife,
    Or failing so, yet that I put the Moor
    At least into a jealousy so strong
    That judgment cannot cure. Which thing to do,
275   If this poor trash of Venice, whom I trace[3]
    For[4] his quick hunting, stand[5] the putting on,

---

5. Table of contents.
6. Exchanges, intimacies.
7. Closely following.
8. Carnal.
9. Stand watch.
1. I'll arrange for you to be appointed, given orders.
2. Disparaging.
3. Provide.
4. Wrath.
5. Perhaps.
6. Riot.

7. Appeasement.
8. Acceptable state.
9. Advance.
1. Assure.
2. Immediately.
3. Train, or follow (?), or perhaps *trash*, a hunting term, meaning to put weights on a hunting dog to slow him down.
4. To make more eager.
5. Respond properly when I incite him to quarrel.

I'll have our Michael Cassio on the hip,[6]
Abuse° him to the Moor in the rank garb°—   *slander/coarse manner*
For I fear Cassio with my nightcap[7] too—
280   Make the Moor thank me, love me, and reward me
For making him egregiously an ass
And practicing upon° his peace and quiet   *plotting against*
Even to madness. 'Tis here, but yet confused.
Knavery's plain face is never seen till used.   [*Exit.*]

Scene 2

[*Location: Cyprus. A street. Enter Othello's Herald with a proclamation.*]

HERALD It is Othello's pleasure, our noble and valiant general, that, upon certain
tidings now arrived, importing the mere perdition[8] of the Turkish fleet, every
man put himself into triumph:[9] some to dance, some to make bonfires, each
man to what sport and revels his addiction[1] leads him. For, besides these beneficial news, it is the celebration of his nuptial. So much was his pleasure should
be proclaimed. All offices[2] are open, and there is full liberty of feasting from
this present hour of five till the bell have told eleven. Heaven bless the isle of
Cyprus and our noble general Othello!

[*Exit.*]

Scene 3

[*Location: Cyprus. The citadel. Enter Othello, Desdemona, Cassio, and attendants.*]

OTHELLO Good Michael, look you to the guard tonight.
Let's teach ourselves that honorable stop°   *restraint*
Not to outsport° discretion.   *celebrate beyond*
CASSIO Iago hath direction what to do,
5   But notwithstanding, with my personal eye
Will I look to 't.
OTHELLO   Iago is most honest.
Michael, good night. Tomorrow with your earliest[3]
Let me have speech with you. [*To Desdemona.*] Come, my dear love,
The purchase made, the fruits are to ensue;
10   That profit's yet to come 'tween me and you.[4]—
Good night.
[*Exit Othello, with Desdemona and attendants.*]
[*Enter Iago.*]
CASSIO Welcome, Iago. We must to the watch.
IAGO Not this hour,[5] Lieutenant; 'tis not yet ten o' the clock. Our general cast[6] us
thus early for the love of his Desdemona; who[7] let us not therefore blame. He
15   hath not yet made wanton the night with her, and she is sport for Jove.
CASSIO She's a most exquisite lady.
IAGO And, I'll warrant her, full of game.

---

6. At my mercy, where I can throw him (a wrestling
term).
7. As a rival in my bed, as one who gives me cuckold's
horns.
8. Complete destruction.
9. Public celebration.
1. Inclination.

2. Rooms where food and drink are kept.
3. At your earliest convenience.
4. Though married, we haven't yet consummated our
love.
5. Not for an hour yet.
6. Dismissed.
7. Othello.

CASSIO Indeed, she's a most fresh and delicate creature.

IAGO What an eye she has! Methinks it sounds a parley[8] to provocation.

CASSIO An inviting eye, and yet methinks right modest.

IAGO And when she speaks, is it not an alarum[9] to love?

CASSIO She is indeed perfection.

IAGO Well, happiness to their sheets! Come, Lieutenant, I have a stoup[1] of wine, and here without[2] are a brace[3] of Cyprus gallants that would fain have a mea-
25   sure[4] to the health of black Othello.

CASSIO Not tonight, good Iago. I have very poor and unhappy brains for drinking. I could well wish courtesy would invent some other custom of entertainment.

IAGO O, they are our friends. But one cup! I'll drink for you.[5]

CASSIO I have drunk but one cup tonight, and that was craftily qualified[6] too, and
30   behold what innovation[7] it makes here.[8] I am unfortunate in the infirmity and dare not task my weakness with any more.

IAGO What, man? 'Tis a night of revels. The gallants desire it.

CASSIO Where are they?

IAGO Here at the door. I pray you, call them in.

CASSIO I'll do't, but it dislikes me.[9]   [Exit.]

IAGO If I can fasten but one cup upon him,
        With that which he hath drunk tonight already,
        He'll be as full of quarrel and offense[1]
        As my young mistress' dog. Now, my sick fool Roderigo,
40   Whom love hath turned almost the wrong side out,
        To Desdemona hath tonight caroused°   drunk off
        Potations pottle-deep;[2] and he's to watch.°   stand watch
        Three lads of Cyprus—noble swelling° spirits,   proud
        That hold their honors in a wary distance,[3]
45   The very elements° of this warlike isle—   typical sort
        Have I tonight flustered with flowing cups,
        And they watch° too. Now, 'mongst this flock of drunkards   are on guard
        Am I to put our Cassio in some action
        That may offend the isle.—But here they come.
        [Enter Cassio, Montano, and gentlemen; servants following with wine.]
50   If consequence do but approve my dream,[4]
        My boat sails freely both with wind and stream.°   current

CASSIO 'Fore God, they have given me a rouse° already.   large drink

MONTANA Good faith, a little one; not past a pint, as I am a soldier.

IAGO Some wine, ho!

55   [He sings.] "And let me the cannikin° clink, clink,   cup
        And let me the cannikin clink.

8. Calls for a conference, issues an invitation.
9. Signal calling men to arms (continuing the military metaphor of *parley,* line 21).
1. Measure of liquor, two quarts.
2. Outside.
3. Pair.
4. Gladly drink a toast.
5. In your place. (Iago will do the steady drinking to keep the gallants company while Cassio has only one cup.)

6. Diluted.
7. Disturbance, insurrection.
8. I.e., in my head.
9. I'm reluctant.
1. Readiness to take offense.
2. To the bottom of the tankard.
3. Are extremely sensitive of their honor.
4. If subsequent events will only substantiate my scheme.

A soldier's a man,
O, man's life's but a span;[5]
Why, then, let a soldier drink."

60   Some wine, boys!

CASSIO 'Fore God, an excellent song.

IAGO I learned it in England, where indeed they are most potent in potting.[6] Your Dane, your German, and your swag-bellied Hollander—drink, ho!—are nothing to your English.

CASSIO Is your Englishman so exquisite in his drinking?

IAGO Why, he drinks you,[7] with facility, your Dane dead drunk; he sweats not[8] to overthrow your Almain;[9] he gives your Hollander a vomit ere the next pottle can be filled.

CASSIO To the health of our general!

MONTANO I am for it, Lieutenant, and I'll do you justice.[1]

IAGO O sweet England! [He sings.]

"King Stephen was and-a worthy peer,
His breeches cost him but a crown;
He held them sixpence all too dear,
75   With that he called the tailor lown.°   lout

He was a wight of high renown,
And thou art but of low degree.
'Tis pride[2] that pulls the country down;
Then take thy auld° cloak about thee."   old

80   Some wine, ho!

CASSIO 'Fore God, this is a more exquisite song than the other.

IAGO Will you hear 't again?

CASSIO No, for I hold him to be unworthy of his place that does those things. Well, God's above all; and there be souls must be saved, and there be souls must not be saved.

IAGO It's true, good Lieutenant.

CASSIO For mine own part—no offense to the General, nor any man of quality[3]—I hope to be saved.

IAGO And so do I too, Lieutenant.

CASSIO Ay, but, by your leave, not before me; the lieutenant is to be saved before
90   the ancient. Let's have no more of this; let's to our affairs.—God forgive us our sins!—Gentlemen, let's look to our business. Do not think gentlemen, I am drunk. This is my ancient; this is my right hand, and this is my left. I am not drunk now. I can stand well enough, and speak well enough.

GENTLEMEN Excellent well.

CASSIO Why, very well then; you must not think then that I am drunk.   [Exit.]

MONTANO To th' platform, masters. Come, let's set the watch.[4]

---

5. Brief span of time. (Cf. Psalm 39.5 as rendered in the Book of Common Prayer: "Thou hast made my days as it were a span long.")
6. Drinking.
7. Drinks.
8. Need not exert himself.

9. German.
1. I'll drink as much as you.
2. Extravagance in dress.
3. Rank.
4. Mount the guard.

[*Exeunt Gentlemen.*]

IAGO You see this fellow that is gone before.
　　　He's a soldier fit to stand by Caesar
　　　And give direction; and do but see his vice.
100　'Tis to his virtue a just equinox,[5]
　　　The one as long as th' other. 'Tis pity of him.
　　　I fear the trust Othello puts him in,
　　　On some odd time of his infirmity,
　　　Will shake this island.
MONTANO　　　　　　　　But is he often thus?
IAGO 'Tis evermore the prologue to his sleep.
　　　He'll watch the horologe a double set,[6]
　　　If drink rock not his cradle.
MONTANO　　　　　　　　　It were well
　　　The General were put in mind of it.
　　　Perhaps he sees it not, or his good nature
110　Prizes the virtue that appears in Cassio
　　　And looks not on his evils. Is not this true?
　　　[*Enter Roderigo.*]
IAGO [*aside to him*] How now, Roderigo?
　　　I pray you, after the Lieutenant; go.　　　　　　　[*Exit Roderigo.*]
MONTANO And 'tis great pity that the noble Moor
115　Should hazard such a place as his own second
　　　With[7] one of an engraffed° infirmity.　　　　　　*inveterate*
　　　It were an honest action to say so
　　　To the Moor.
IAGO　　　　　　Not I, for this fair island.
　　　I do love Cassio well and would do much
120　To cure him of this evil. [*Cry within:* "Help! Help!"]
　　　　　　　　　But, hark! What noise?
　　　[*Enter Cassio, pursuing Roderigo.*][8]
CASSIO Zounds, you rogue! You rascal!
MONTANO What's the matter, Lieutenant?
CASSIO A knave teach me my duty? I'll beat the knave into a twiggen[9] bottle.
RODERIGO Beat me?
CASSIO Dost thou prate, rogue? [*He strikes Roderigo.*]
MONTANO Nay, good Lieutenant. [*Restraining him.*] I pray you, sir, hold your hand.
CASSIO Let me go, sir, or I'll knock you o'er the mazard.[1]
MONTANO Come, come, you're drunk.
CASSIO Drunk? [*They fight.*]
IAGO [*aside to Roderigo*]
130　Away, I say. Go out and cry a mutiny.[2]

　　　　　　　　　　　　　　　　　　　　[*Exit Roderigo.*]

　　　Nay, good Lieutenant—God's will, gentlemen—

---

5. Exact counterpart. (*Equinox* is an equal length of days and nights.)
6. Stay awake twice around the clock or *horologe*.
7. Risk giving such an important position as his second in command to.
8. The Quarto text reads, "driving in."

9. Wicker-covered. (Cassio vows to assail Roderigo until his skin resembles wickerwork or until he has driven Roderigo through the holes in a wickerwork.)
1. Head (literally, a drinking vessel).
2. Riot.

Help, ho!—Lieutenant—sir—Montano—sir—
Help, masters!°—Here's a goodly watch indeed!   *sirs*
[*A bell rings.*]³
Who's that which rings the bell?—Diablo,° ho!   *the devil*
135   The town will rise.° God's will, Lieutenant, hold!   *grow riotous*
You'll be ashamed forever.
[*Enter Othello and attendants with weapons*].

OTHELLO What is the matter here?

MONTANO   Zounds, I bleed still.
I am hurt to th' death. He dies! [*He thrusts at Cassio.*]

OTHELLO   Hold, for your lives!

IAGO Hold, ho! Lieutenant—sir—Montano—gentlemen—
140   Have you forgot all sense of place and duty?
Hold! The General speaks to you. Hold, for shame!

OTHELLO Why, how now, ho! From whence ariseth this?
Are we turned Turks, and to ourselves do that
Which heaven hath forbid the Ottomites?⁴
145   For Christian shame, put by this barbarous brawl!
He that stirs next to carve for⁵ his own rage
Holds his soul light;⁶ he dies upon his motion.⁷
Silence that dreadful bell. It frights the isle
From her propriety.° What is the matter, masters?   *proper state*
150   Honest Iago, that looks dead with grieving,
Speak. Who began this? On thy love, I charge thee.

IAGO I do not know. Friends all but now, even now,
In quarter⁸ and in terms° like bride and groom   *on good terms*
Devesting them° for bed; and then, but now—   *undressing*
155   As if some planet had unwitted men—
Swords out, and tilting one at others' breasts
In opposition bloody. I cannot speak°   *explain*
Any beginning to this peevish odds;°   *quarrel*
And would in action glorious I had lost
160   Those legs that brought me to a part of it!

OTHELLO How comes it, Michael, you are thus forgot?⁹

CASSIO I pray you, pardon me. I cannot speak.

OTHELLO Worthy Montano, you were wont° be civil;   *accustomed to be*
The gravity and stillness° of your youth   *sobriety*
165   The world hath noted, and your name is great
In mouths of wisest censure.° What's the matter   *judgment*
That you unlace¹ your reputation thus
And spend your rich opinion° for the name   *reputation*
Of a night-brawler? Give me answer to it.

MONTANO Worthy Othello, I am hurt to danger.
Your officer, Iago, can inform you—
While I spare speech, which something° now offends° me—   *somewhat/pains*

---

3. This direction is from the Quarto, as are *Exit Roderigo* at line 130, *They fight* at line 129, and *with weapons* at line 136.
4. Inflict on ourselves the harm that heaven has prevented the Turks from doing (by destroying their fleet).
5. Indulge, satisfy with his sword.

6. Places little value on his life.
7. If he moves.
8. In friendly conduct, within bounds.
9. Have forgotten yourself thus.
1. Undo, lay open (as one might loose the strings of a purse containing reputation).

Of all that I do know; nor know I aught
By me that's said or done amiss this night,
175   Unless self-charity be sometimes a vice,
And to defend ourselves it be a sin
When violence assails us.

OTHELLO   Now, by heaven,
My blood[2] begins my safer guides[3] to rule,
And passion, having my best judgment collied,°   *darkened*
180   Essays° to lead the way. Zounds, if I stir,   *undertakes*
Or do but lift this arm, the best of you
Shall sink in my rebuke. Give me to know
How this foul rout° began, who set it on;   *riot*
And he that is approved in° this offense,   *found guilty of*
185   Though he had twinned with me, both at a birth,
Shall lose me. What? In a town of[4] war
Yet wild, the people's hearts brim full of fear,
To manage° private and domestic quarrel?   *undertake*
In night, and on the court and guard of safety?[5]
190   'Tis monstrous. Iago, who began 't?

MONTANO [*to Iago*] If partially affined,[6] or leagued in office,[7]
Thou dost deliver more or less than truth,
Thou art no soldier.

IAGO   Touch me not so near.
I had rather have this tongue cut from my mouth
195   Than it should do offense to Michael Cassio;
Yet, I persuade myself, to speak the truth
Shall nothing wrong him. Thus it is, General.
Montano and myself being in speech,
There comes a fellow crying out for help,
200   And Cassio following him with determined sword
To execute[8] upon him. Sir, this gentleman [*indicating Montano.*]
Steps in to Cassio and entreats his pause.°   *him to stop*
Myself the crying fellow did pursue,
Lest by his clamor—as it so fell out—
205   The town might fall in fright. He, swift of foot,
Outran my purpose, and I returned, the rather°   *sooner*
For that I heard the clink and fall of swords
And Cassio high in oath, which till tonight
I ne'er might say before. When I came back—
210   For this was brief—I found them close together
At blow and thrust, even as again they were
When you yourself did part them.
More of this matter cannot I report.
But men are men; the best sometimes forget.°   *forget themselves*
215   Though Cassio did some little wrong to him,
As men in rage strike those that wish them best,[9]
Yet surely Cassio, I believe, received
From him that fled some strange indignity,

2. Passion (of anger).
3. I.e., reason.
4. Town garrisoned for.
5. At the main guardhouse or headquarters and on watch.

6. Made partial by some personal relationship.
7. In league as fellow officers.
8. Give effect to (his anger).
9. Even those who are well disposed.

Which patience could not pass.°   *overlook*

OTHELLO   I know, Iago,
220 Thy honesty and love doth mince this matter,
Making it light to Cassio. Cassio, I love thee,
But nevermore be officer of mine.

[Enter Desdemona, attended.]

Look if my gentle love be not raised up.
I'll make thee an example.

DESDEMONA What is the matter, dear?

OTHELLO   All's well now, sweeting;
Come away to bed. *[To Montano.]* Sir, for your hurts,
Myself will be your surgeon.[1]—Lead him off.

[Montano is led off.]

Iago, look with care about the town
And silence those whom this vile brawl distracted.
230 Come, Desdemona. 'Tis the soldiers' life
To have their balmy slumbers waked with strife.

[Exit with all but Iago and Cassio.]

IAGO What, are you hurt, Lieutenant?

CASSIO Ay, past all surgery.

IAGO Marry, God forbid!

CASSIO Reputation, reputation, reputation! O, I have lost my reputation! I have
lost the immortal part of myself, and what remains is bestial. My reputation,
Iago, my reputation!

IAGO As I am an honest man, I thought you had received some bodily wound; there
is more sense in that than in reputation. Reputation is an idle and most false
240 imposition,[2] oft got without merit and lost without deserving. You have lost no
reputation at all, unless you repute yourself such a loser. What, man, there are
more ways to recover[3] the General again. You are but now cast in his mood[4]—
a punishment more in policy[5] than in malice, even so as one would beat his
offenseless dog to affright an imperious lion.[6] Sue[7] to him again and he's yours.

CASSIO I will rather sue to be despised than to deceive so good a commander with
so slight,[8] so drunken, and so indiscreet an officer. Drunk? And speak parrot?[9]
And squabble? Swagger? Swear? And discourse fustian with one's own shadow?
O thou invisible spirit of wine, if thou hast no name to be known by, let us call
thee devil!

IAGO What was he that you followed with your sword? What had he done to you?

CASSIO I know not.

IAGO Is 't possible?

CASSIO I remember a mass of things, but nothing distinctly; a quarrel, but nothing
wherefore.[1] O God, that men should put an enemy in their mouths to steal
255 away their brains! That we should, with joy, pleasance, revel, and applause[2]
transform ourselves into beasts!

IAGO Why, but you are now well enough. How came you thus recovered?

1. Make sure you receive medical attention.
2. Thing artificially imposed and of no real value.
3. Regain favor with.
4. Dismissed in a moment of anger.
5. Done for expediency's sake and as a public gesture.
6. Would make an example of a minor offender to deter
more important and dangerous offenders.

7. Petition.
8. Worthless.
9. Talk nonsense, rant. (*Discourse fustian*, in the next
line, has much the same meaning.)
1. Why.
2. Desire for applause.

CASSIO It hath pleased the devil drunkenness to give place to the devil wrath. One unperfectness shows me another, to make me frankly despise myself.

IAGO Come, you are too severe a moraler.[3] As the time, the place, and the condition of this country stands, I could heartily wish this had not befallen; but since it is as it is, mend it for your own good.

CASSIO I will ask him for my place again; he shall tell me I am a drunkard. Had I as many mouths as Hydra,[4] such an answer would stop them all. To be now a sen-
265   sible man, by and by a fool, and presently a beast! O, strange! Every inordinate cup is unblessed, and the ingredient is a devil.

IAGO Come, come, good wine is a good familiar creature, if it be well used. Exclaim no more against it. And, good Lieutenant, I think you think I love you.

CASSIO I have well approved[5] it, sir. I drunk!

IAGO You or any man living may be drunk at a time,[6] man. I'll tell you what you shall do. Our general's wife is now the general—I may say so in this respect, for that[7] he hath devoted and given up himself to the contemplation, mark, and denotement[8] of her parts[9] and graces. Confess yourself freely to her; importune her help to put you in your place again. She is of so free,[1] so kind, so apt, so
275   blessed a disposition, she holds it a vice in her goodness not to do more than she is requested. This broken joint between you and her husband entreat her to splinter;[2] and, my fortunes against any lay[3] worth naming, this crack of your love shall grow stronger than it was before.

CASSIO You advise me well.

IAGO I protest,[4] in the sincerity of love and honest kindness.

CASSIO I think it freely;[5] and betimes in the morning I will beseech the virtuous Desdemona to undertake for me. I am desperate of my fortunes if they check[6] me here.

IAGO You are in the right. Good night, Lieutenant. I must to the watch.

CASSIO Good night, honest Iago.   [*Exit Cassio.*]

IAGO And what's he then that says I play the villain,
    When this advice is free[7] I give, and honest,
    Probal° to thinking, and indeed the course   reasonable
    To win the Moor again? For 'tis most easy
    Th' inclining° Desdemona to subdue°   willing/persuade
290   In any honest suit; she's framed as fruitful[8]
    As the free elements.[9] And then for her
    To win the Moor—were 't to renounce his baptism,
    All seals and symbols of redeemèd sin—
    His soul is so enfettered to her love
295   That she may make, unmake, do what she list,
    Even as her appetite[1] shall play the god
    With his weak function.[2] How am I then a villain,

---

3. Moralizer.
4. The Lernaean Hydra, a monster with many heads and the ability to grow two heads when one was cut off, slain by Hercules as the second of his twelve labors.
5. Proved.
6. At one time or another.
7. In view of this fact, that.
8. Both words mean "observation."
9. Qualities.
1. Generous.
2. Bind with splints.

3. Stake, wager.
4. Insist, declare.
5. Unreservedly.
6. Repulse.
7. Free from guile. Also, freely given.
8. Created as generous.
9. I.e., earth, air, fire, and water, unrestrained and spontaneous.
1. Her desire, or, perhaps, his desire for her.
2. Exercise of faculties (weakened by his fondness for her).

To counsel Cassio to this parallel[3] course
Directly to his good? Divinity of hell![4]
300　When devils will the blackest sins put on,°　　　　　　　　　　　*instigate*
They do suggest° at first with heavenly shows,　　　　　　　　　*tempt*
As I do now. For whiles this honest fool
Plies Desdemona to repair his fortune,
And she for him pleads strongly to the Moor,
305　I'll pour this pestilence into his ear,
That she repeals him[5] for her body's lust;
And by how much she strives to do him good,
She shall undo her credit with the Moor.
So will I turn her virtue into pitch,[6]
310　And out of her own goodness make the net
That shall enmesh them all.
　　　　　　　　　　[*Enter Roderigo.*]
　　　　　　　　　How now, Roderigo?
RODERIGO I do follow here in the chase, not like a hound that hunts, but one that
fills up the cry.[7] My money is almost spent; I have been tonight exceedingly
well cudgeled; and I think the issue will be I shall have so much[8] experience for
315　my pains, and so, with no money at all and a little more wit, return again to
Venice.
IAGO How poor are they that have not patience!
What wound did ever heal but by degrees?
Thou know'st we work by wit, and not by witchcraft,
320　And wit depends on dilatory time.
Does 't not go well? Cassio hath beaten thee,
And thou, by that small hurt, hast cashiered° Cassio.　　　　　　*dismissed*
Though other things grow fair against the sun,
Yet fruits that blossom first will first be ripe.[9]
325　Content thyself awhile. By the Mass, 'tis morning!
Pleasure and action make the hours seem short.
Retire thee; go where thou art billeted.
Away, I say! Thou shalt know more hereafter.
Nay, get thee gone.　　　　　　　　　　　　　[*Exit Roderigo.*]
330　Two things are to be done.
My wife must move° for Cassio to her mistress;　　　　　　　　*plead*
I'll set her on;
Myself the while to draw the Moor apart
And bring him jump° when he may Cassio find　　　　　　　　*precisely*
335　Soliciting his wife. Ay, that's the way.
Dull not device° by coldness° and delay.　　　　　[*Exit.*]　　*plot/lack of zeal*

Act 3

Scene 1

[*Location: Before the chamber of Othello and Desdemona. Enter Cassio and Musicians.*]

3. Corresponding to these facts and to his best interests.
4. Inverted theology of hell (which seduces the soul to its
damnation).
5. Attempts to get him restored.
6. Foul blackness. Also a snaring substance.

7. Merely takes part as one of the pack.
8. Just so much and no more.
9. Plans that are well prepared and set expeditiously in
motion will soonest ripen into success.

CASSIO Masters, play here—I will content your pains[1]—
 Something that's brief, and bid "Good morrow, General." [*They play.*]
 [*Enter Clown.*]
CLOWN Why, masters, have your instruments been in Naples, that they speak i' the
 nose[2] thus?
A MUSICIAN How, sir, how?
CLOWN Are these, I pray you, wind instruments?
A MUSICIAN Ay, marry, are they, sir.
CLOWN O, thereby hangs a tail.
A MUSICIAN Whereby hangs a tale, sir?
CLOWN Marry, sir, by many a wind instrument[3] that I know. But, masters, here's
 money for you. [*He gives money.*] And the General so likes your music that he
 desires you, for love's sake,[4] to make no more noise with it.
A MUSICIAN Well, sir, we will not.
CLOWN If you have any music that may not[5] be heard, to 't again; but, as they say,
15 to hear music the General does not greatly care.
A MUSICIAN We have none such, sir.
CLOWN Then put up your pipes in your bag, for I'll away.[6] Go, vanish into air, away!
                  [*Exeunt Musicians.*]
CASSIO Dost thou hear, mine honest friend?
CLOWN No, I hear not your honest friend; I hear you.
CASSIO Prithee, keep up[7] thy quillets.[8] There's a poor piece of gold for thee. [*He
 gives money.*] If the gentlewoman that attends the General's wife be stirring,
 tell her there's one Cassio entreats her a little favor of speech.[9] Wilt thou do
 this?
CLOWN She is stirring, sir. If she will stir[1] hither, I shall seem[2] to notify unto her.
CASSIO Do, good my friend.   [*Exit Clown.*]
 [*Enter Iago.*]
        In happy time,[3] Iago.
IAGO You have not been abed, then?
CASSIO Why, no. The day had broke
 Before we parted. I have made bold, Iago,
 To send in to your wife. My suit to her
30 Is that she will to virtuous Desdemona
 Procure me some access.
IAGO I'll send her to you presently;
 And I'll devise a means to draw the Moor
 Out of the way, that your converse and business
35 May be more free.
CASSIO I humbly thank you for 't.   [*Exit Iago.*]
      I never knew

1. Reward your efforts.
2. Sound nasal. Also sound like one whose nose has been attacked by syphilis. (Naples was popularly supposed to have a high incidence of venereal disease.)
3. With a joke on flatulence. The *tail* that hangs nearby the *wind instrument* suggests the penis.
4. Out of friendship and affection. Also, for the sake of lovemaking in Othello's marriage.
5. Cannot.
6. (Possibly a misprint, or a snatch of song?)
7. Do not bring out.
8. Quibbles, puns.
9. The favor of a brief talk.
1. Bestir herself (with a play on *stirring*, "rousing herself from rest").
2. Deem it good, think fit.
3. I.e., well met.

A Florentine⁴ more kind and honest.
[*Enter Emilia.*]

EMILIA Good morrow, good Lieutenant. I am sorry
For your displeasure;° but all will sure be well.   *fall from favor*
40   The General and his wife are talking of it,
And she speaks for you stoutly.° The Moor replies   *spiritedly*
That he you hurt is of great fame° in Cyprus   *importance*
And great affinity,° and that in wholesome wisdom   *family connection*
He might not but refuse you; but he protests° he loves you   *insists*
45   And needs no other suitor but his likings
To take the safest occasion by the front⁵
To bring you in again.

CASSIO   Yet I beseech you,
If you think fit, or that it may be done,
Give me advantage of some brief discourse
50   With Desdemon alone.

EMILIA   Pray you, come in.
I will bestow you where you shall have time
To speak your bosom° freely.   *thoughts*

CASSIO I am much bound to you.   [*Exeunt.*]

Scene 2

[*Location: The citadel. Enter Othello, Iago, and Gentlemen.*]

OTHELLO [*giving letters*] These letters give, Iago, to the pilot,
And by him do my duties° to the Senate.   *give my respects*
That done, I will be walking on the works;°   *fortifications*
Repair° there to me.   *return*

IAGO   Well, my good lord, I'll do 't.

OTHELLO This fortification, gentlemen, shall we see 't?

GENTLEMEN We'll wait upon° your lordship.   [*Exeunt.*]   *attend*

Scene 3

[*Location: The garden of the citadel. Enter Desdemona, Cassio, and Emilia.*]

DESDEMONA Be thou assured, good Cassio, I will do
All my abilities in thy behalf.

EMILIA Good madam, do. I warrant it grieves my husband
As if the cause were his.

DESDEMONA O, that's an honest fellow. Do not doubt, Cassio,
But I will have my lord and you again
As friendly as you were.

CASSIO   Bounteous madam,
Whatever shall become of Michael Cassio,
He's never anything but your true servant.

DESDEMONA I know 't. I thank you. You do love my lord;
You have known him long, and be you well assured
He shall in strangeness° stand no farther off   *aloofness*

---

4. I.e., even a fellow Florentine. (Iago is a Venetian; Cassio is a Florentine.)   5. Opportunity by the forelock.

Than in a politic[6] distance.

CASSIO   Ay, but, lady,
That policy may either last so long,
15   Or feed upon such nice and waterish diet,[7]
Or breed itself so out of circumstance,[8]
That, I being absent and my place supplied,[9]
My general will forget my love and service.

DESDEMONA Do not doubt° that. Before Emilia here   *fear*
20   I give thee warrant° of thy place. Assure thee,   *guarantee*
If I do vow a friendship I'll perform it
To the last article. My lord shall never rest.
I'll watch him tame[1] and talk him out of patience;[2]
His bed shall seem a school, his board° a shrift;°   *table/confessional*
25   I'll intermingle everything he does
With Cassio's suit. Therefore be merry, Cassio,
For thy solicitor° shall rather die   *advocate*
Than give thy cause away.°   *up*

Enter Othello and Iago at a distance].

EMILIA Madam, here comes my lord.

CASSIO Madam, I'll take my leave.

DESDEMONA Why, stay, and hear me speak.

CASSIO Madam, not now. I am very ill at ease,
Unfit for mine own purposes.

DESDEMONA Well, do your discretion.[3]   *[Exit Cassio.]*

IAGO Ha? I like not that.

OTHELLO   What dost thou say?

IAGO Nothing, my lord; or if—I know not what.

OTHELLO Was not that Cassio parted from my wife?

IAGO Cassio, my lord? No, sure, I cannot think it,
That he would steal away so guiltylike,
40   Seeing you coming.

OTHELLO   I do believe 'twas he.

DESDEMONA How now, my lord?
I have been talking with a suitor here,
A man that languishes in your displeasure.

OTHELLO Who is 't you mean?

DESDEMONA Why, your lieutenant, Cassio. Good my lord,
If I have any grace or power to move you,
His present reconciliation take;[4]
For if he be not one that truly loves you,
That errs in ignorance and not in cunning,°   *wittingly*
50   I have no judgment in an honest face.
I prithee, call him back.

OTHELLO   Went he hence now?

DESDEMONA Yes, faith, so humbled

---

6. Required by wise policy.
7. Or sustain itself at length upon such trivial and meager
technicalities.
8. Continually renew itself so out of chance events, or
yield so few chances for my being pardoned.
9. Filled by another person.

1. Tame him by keeping him from sleeping (a term from
falconry).
2. Past his endurance.
3. Act according to your own discretion.
4. Let him be reconciled to you right away.

That he hath left part of his grief with me
To suffer with him. Good love, call him back.

OTHELLO Not now, sweet Desdemon. Some other time.

DESDEMONA But shall 't be shortly?

OTHELLO   The sooner, sweet, for you.

DESDEMONA Shall 't be tonight at supper?

OTHELLO   No, not tonight.

DESDEMONA Tomorrow dinner,° then?   *noontime*

OTHELLO   I shall not dine at home.
     I meet the captains at the citadel.

DESDEMONA Why, then, tomorrow night, or Tuesday morn,
     On Tuesday noon, or night, on Wednesday morn.
     I prithee, name the time, but let it not
     Exceed three days. In faith, he's penitent;
     And yet his trespass, in our common reason°—   *judgments*
65   Save that, they say, the wars must make example
     Out of her best[5]—is not almost° a fault   *scarcely*
     T' incur a private check.[6] When shall he come?
     Tell me, Othello. I wonder in my soul
     What you would ask me that I should deny,
70   Or stand so mammering on.° What? Michael Cassio,   *wavering about*
     That came a-wooing with you, and so many a time,
     When I have spoke of you dispraisingly,
     Hath ta'en your part—to have so much to do
     To bring him in!° By 'r Lady, I could do much—   *restore him to favor*

OTHELLO Prithee, no more. Let him come when he will;
     I will deny thee nothing.

DESDEMONA   Why, this is not a boon.
     'Tis as I should entreat you wear your gloves,
     Or feed on nourishing dishes, or keep you warm,
     Or sue to you to do a peculiar° profit   *personal*
80   To your own person. Nay, when I have a suit
     Wherein I mean to touch° your love indeed,   *test*
     It shall be full of poise[7] and difficult weight,
     And fearful to be granted.

OTHELLO   I will deny thee nothing.
     Whereon,° I do beseech thee, grant me this,   *in return*
85   To leave me but a little to myself.

DESDEMONA Shall I deny you? No. Farewell, my lord.

OTHELLO Farewell, my Desdemona. I'll come to thee straight.°   *straightway*

DESDEMONA Emilia, come.—Be as your fancies° teach you;   *inclinations*
     Whate'er you be, I am obedient.   *[Exit with Emilia.]*

OTHELLO Excellent wretch![8] Perdition catch my soul
     But I do love thee! And when I love thee not,
     Chaos is come again.[9]

---

5. Were it not that, as the saying goes, military discipline requires making an example of the very best men. (*Her* refers to *wars* as a singular concept.)
6. Even a private reprimand.
7. Weight, heaviness; or equipoise, delicate balance involving hard choice.

8. A term of affectionate endearment.
9. I.e., My love for you will last forever, until the end of time when chaos will return. (But with an unconscious, ironic suggestion that, if anything should induce Othello to cease loving Desdemona, the result would be chaos.)

IAGO My noble lord—

OTHELLO   What dost thou say, Iago?

IAGO Did Michael Cassio, when you wooed my lady,
95   Know of your love?

OTHELLO He did, from first to last. Why dost thou ask?

IAGO But for a satisfaction of my thought;
      No further harm.

OTHELLO   Why of thy thought, Iago?

IAGO I did not think he had been acquainted with her.

OTHELLO O, yes, and went between us very oft.

IAGO Indeed?

OTHELLO Indeed? Ay, indeed. Discern'st thou aught in that?
110   Is he not honest?

IAGO   Honest, my lord?

OTHELLO   Honest. Ay, honest.

IAGO My lord, for aught I know.

OTHELLO What dost thou think?

IAGO   Think, my lord?

OTHELLO "Think, my lord?" By heaven, thou echo'st me,
      As if there were some monster in thy thought
      Too hideous to be shown. Thou dost mean something.
      I heard thee say even now, thou lik'st not that,
110   When Cassio left my wife. What didst not like?
      And when I told thee he was of my counsel°   *in my confidence*
      In my whole course of wooing, thou criedst "Indeed?"
      And didst contract and purse° thy brow together   *knit*
      As if thou then hadst shut up in thy brain
115   Some horrible conceit.° If thou dost love me,   *fancy*
      Show me thy thought.

IAGO My lord, you know I love you.

OTHELLO   I think thou dost;
      And, for° I know thou'rt full of love and honesty,   *because*
      And weigh'st thy words before thou giv'st them breath,
120   Therefore these stops° of thine fright me the more;   *pauses*
      For such things in a false disloyal knave
      Are tricks of custom,° but in a man that's just   *customary*
      They're close dilations,[1] working from the heart
      That passion cannot rule.[2]

IAGO   For° Michael Cassio,   *as for*
125   I dare be sworn I think that he is honest.

OTHELLO I think so too.

IAGO   Men should be what they seem;
      Or those that be not, would they might seem none![3]

OTHELLO Certain, men should be what they seem.

IAGO Why, then, I think Cassio's an honest man.

OTHELLO Nay, yet there's more in this.
      I prithee, speak to me as to thy thinkings,

1. Secret or involuntary expressions or delays.
2. I.e., that are too passionately strong to be restrained
(referring to the workings), or that cannot rule its own

passions (referring to the heart).
3. I.e., not to be men, or not seem to be honest.

As thou dost ruminate, and give thy worst of thoughts
The worst of words.

IAGO   Good my lord, pardon me.
Though I am bound to every act of duty,
135 I am not bound to that° all slaves are free to.[4]   *that which*
Utter my thoughts? Why, say they are vile and false,
As where's that palace whereinto foul things
Sometimes intrude not? Who has that breast so pure
But some uncleanly apprehensions
140 Keep leets and law days,[5] and in sessions sit
With° meditations lawful?°   *along with/innocent*

OTHELLO Thou dost conspire against thy friend,[6] Iago,
If thou but think'st him wronged and mak'st his ear
A stranger to thy thoughts.

IAGO   I do beseech you,
145 Though I perchance am vicious° in my guess—   *wrong*
As I confess it is my nature's plague
To spy into abuses, and oft my jealousy°   *suspicious nature*
Shapes faults that are not—that your wisdom then,°   *on that account*
From one[7] that so imperfectly conceits,°   *conjectures*
150 Would take no notice, nor build yourself a trouble
Out of his scattering° and unsure observance.   *random*
It were not for your quiet nor your good,
Nor for my manhood, honesty, and wisdom,
To let you know my thoughts.

OTHELLO   What dost thou mean?

IAGO Good name in man and woman, dear my lord,
Is the immediate° jewel of their souls.   *essential*
Who steals my purse steals trash; 'tis something, nothing;
'Twas mine, 'tis his, and has been slave to thousands;
But he that filches from me my good name
160 Robs me of that which not enriches him
And makes me poor indeed.

OTHELLO By heaven, I'll know thy thoughts.

IAGO You cannot, if° my heart were in your hand,   *even if*
175 Nor shall not, whilst 'tis in my custody.

OTHELLO Ha?

IAGO   O, beware, my lord, of jealousy.
It is the green-eyed monster which doth mock
The meat it feeds on.[8] That cuckold lives in bliss
Who, certain of his fate, loves not his wronger;[9]
But O, what damnèd minutes tells° he o'er   *counts*
170 Who dotes, yet doubts, suspects, yet fondly loves!

OTHELLO O misery!

IAGO Poor and content is rich, and rich enough,[1]

---

4. Free with respect to.
5. I.e., hold court, set up their authority in one's heart.
Leets are a kind of manor court; *law days* are the days
courts sit in session, or those sessions.
6. I.e., Othello.
7. I.e., myself, Iago.
8. Mocks and torments the heart of its victim, the man

who suffers jealously.
9. I.e., his faithless wife. (The unsuspecting cuckold is
spared the misery of loving his wife only to discover she is
cheating on him.)
1. To be content with what little one has is the greatest
wealth of all (proverbial).

But riches fineless° is as poor as winter   *boundless*
To him that ever fears he shall be poor.

175   Good God, the souls of all my tribe defend
From jealousy!

OTHELLO   Why, why is this?
Think'st thou I'd make a life of jealousy,
To follow still the changes of the moon
With fresh suspicions?² No! To be once in doubt

180   Is once° to be resolved.³ Exchange me for a goat   *once and for all*
When I shall turn the business of my soul
To such exsufflicate and blown⁴ surmises
Matching thy inference.° 'Tis not to make me jealous   *allegation*
To say my wife is fair, feeds well, loves company,

185   Is free of speech, sings, plays, and dances well;
Where virtue is, these are more virtuous.
Nor from mine own weak merits will I draw
The smallest fear or doubt of her revolt,⁵
For she had eyes, and chose me. No, Iago,

190   I'll see before I doubt; when I doubt, prove;
And on the proof, there is no more but this—
Away at once with love or jealousy.

IAGO I am glad of this, for now I shall have reason
To show the love and duty that I bear you

195   With franker spirit. Therefore, as I am bound,
Receive it from me. I speak not yet of proof.
Look to your wife; observe her well with Cassio.
Wear your eyes thus, not° jealous nor secure.°   *neither / certain*
I would not have your free and noble nature,

200   Out of self-bounty,⁶ be abused.° Look to 't.   *deceived*
I know our country disposition well;
In Venice they do let God see the pranks
They dare not show their husbands; their best conscience
Is not to leave 't undone, but keep 't unknown.

OTHELLO Dost thou say so?

IAGO She did deceive her father, marrying you;
And when she seemed to shake and fear your looks,
She loved them most.

OTHELLO   And so she did.

IAGO   Why, go to,⁷ then!
She that, so young, could give out such a seeming,°   *false appearance*

210   To seel⁸ her father's eyes up close as oak,⁹
He thought 'twas witchcraft! But I am much to blame.
I humbly do beseech you of your pardon
For too much loving you.

OTHELLO   I am bound¹ to thee forever.

---

2. To be constantly imagining new causes for suspicion, changing incessantly like the moon.
3. Free of doubt, having settled the matter.
4. Inflated and blown up, rumored about, or, spat out and flyblown, hence loathsome, disgusting.
5. Fear of her unfaithfulness.

6. Inherent or natural goodness and generosity.
7. An expression of impatience.
8. Blind (a term from falconry).
9. A close-grained wood.
1. Indebted (but perhaps with the ironic sense of "tied").

IAGO I see this hath a little dashed your spirits.
OTHELLO Not a jot, not a jot.
IAGO   I' faith, I fear it has.
    I hope you will consider what is spoke
    Comes from my love. But I do see you're moved.
    I am to pray you not to strain my speech
    To grosser issues° nor to larger reach°   *significances/scope*
220 Than to suspicion.
OTHELLO I will not.
IAGO   Should you do so, my lord,
    My speech should fall into such vile success°   *effect*
    Which my thoughts aimed not. Cassio's my worthy friend.
    My lord, I see you're moved.
OTHELLO   No, not much moved.
225 I do not think but Desdemona's honest.°   *chaste*
IAGO Long live she so! And long live you to think so!
OTHELLO And yet, how nature erring from itself—
IAGO Ay, there's the point! As—to be bold with you—
    Not to affect° many proposèd matches   *prefer*
230 Of her own clime, complexion, and degree,²
    Whereto we see in all things nature tends—
    Foh! One may smell in such a will° most rank,   *sensuality*
    Foul disproportion,° thoughts unnatural.   *abnormality*
    But pardon me. I do not in position°   *argument*
235 Distinctly speak of her, though I may fear
    Her will, recoiling° to her better³ judgment,   *reverting*
    May fall to match you with her country forms⁴
    And happily repent.⁵
OTHELLO   Farewell, farewell!
    If more thou dost perceive, let me know more.
240 Set on thy wife to observe. Leave me, Iago.
IAGO [*going*] My lord, I take my leave.
OTHELLO Why did I marry? This honest creature doubtless
    Sees and knows more, much more, than he unfolds.
IAGO [*returning*] My Lord, I would I might entreat your honor
245 To scan° this thing no farther. Leave it to time.   *scrutinize*
    Although 'tis fit that Cassio have his place—
    For, sure, he fills it up with great ability—
    Yet, if you please to hold him off awhile,
    You shall by that perceive him and his means.⁶
250 Note if your lady strain his entertainment⁷
    With any strong or vehement importunity;
    Much will be seen in that. In the meantime,
    Let me be thought too busy° in my fears—   *interfering*
    As worthy cause I have to fear I am—
255 And hold her free,⁸ I do beseech your honor.

2. Country, color, and social position.
3. I.e., more natural and reconsidered.
4. Undertake to compare you with Venetian norms of handsomeness.

5. Perhaps repent her marriage.
6. The method he uses (to regain his post).
7. Urge his reinstatement.
8. Regard her as innocent.

OTHELLO Fear not my government.°   *conduct*
IAGO I once more take my leave.   [*Exit.*]
OTHELLO This fellow's of exceeding honesty,
And knows all qualities,° with a learnèd spirit,   *natures*
260 Of human dealings. If I do prove her haggard,[9]
Though that her jesses[1] were my dear heartstrings,
I'd whistle her off and let her down the wind[2]
To prey at fortune.[3] Haply, for[4] I am black
And have not those soft parts of conversation[5]
265 That chamberers° have, or for I am declined   *gallants*
Into the vale of years—yet that's not much—
She's gone. I am abused,° and my relief   *deceived*
Must be to loathe her. O curse of marriage,
That we can call these delicate creatures ours
270 And not their appetites! I had rather be a toad
And live upon the vapor of a dungeon
Than keep a corner in the thing I love
For others' uses. Yet, 'tis the plague of great ones;
Prerogatived[6] are they less than the base.[7]
275 'Tis destiny unshunnable, like death.
Even then this forkèd[8] plague is fated to us
When we do quicken.[9] Look where she comes.

[*Enter Desdemona and Emilia.*]

If she be false, O, then heaven mocks itself!
I'll not believe 't.
DESDEMONA   How now, my dear Othello?
280 Your dinner, and the generous° islanders   *noble*
By you invited, do attend° your presence.   *await*
OTHELLO I am to blame.
DESDEMONA   Why do you speak so faintly?
Are you not well?
OTHELLO I have a pain upon my forehead here.
DESDEMONA Faith, that's with watching.° 'Twill away again.   *too little sleep*
[*She offers her handkerchief.*]
Let me but bind it hard, within this hour
It will be well.
OTHELLO   Your napkin° is too little.   *handkerchief*
Let it alone.° Come, I'll go in with you.   *never mind*
[*He puts the handkerchief from him, and it drops.*]
DESDEMONA I am very sorry that you are not well.

[*Exit with Othello.*]

EMILIA [*picking up the handkerchief*]
290 I am glad I have found this napkin.

---

9. Wild (like a wild female hawk).
1. Straps fastened around the legs of a trained hawk.
2. I'd let her go forever. (To release a hawk downwind
was to invite it not to return.)
3. Fend for herself in the wild.
4. Perhaps because.
5. Pleasing graces of social behavior.
6. Privileged (to have honest wives).

7. Ordinary citizens. (Socially prominent men are especially prone to the unavoidable destiny of being cuckolded and to the public shame that goes with it.)
8. An allusion to the horns of the cuckold.
9. Receive life. *Quicken* may also mean to swarm with maggots as the body festers, in which case these lines suggest that *even then*, in death, we are cuckolded by *forkèd* worms.

This was her first remembrance from the Moor.
My wayward° husband hath a hundred times   *capricious*
Wooed me to steal it, but she so loves the token—
For he conjured her she should ever keep it—
295   That she reserves it evermore about her
To kiss and talk to. I'll have the work ta'en out,[1]
And give 't Iago. What he will do with it
Heaven knows, not I;
I nothing but to please his fantasy.°   *whim*
[*Enter Iago.*]

IAGO How now? What do you here alone?

EMILIA Do not you chide. I have a thing for you.

IAGO You have a thing for me? It is a common thing[2]—

EMILIA Ha?

IAGO To have a foolish wife.

EMILIA O, is that all? What will you give me now
For that same handkerchief?

IAGO What handkerchief?

EMILIA What handkerchief?
Why, that the Moor first gave to Desdemona;
310   That which so often you did bid me steal.

IAGO Hast stolen it from her?

EMILIA No, faith. She let it drop by negligence,
And to th' advantage[3] I, being here, took 't up.
Look, here 'tis.

IAGO   A good wench! Give it me.

EMILIA What will you do with 't, that you have been so earnest
To have me filch it?

IAGO [*snatching it*]   Why, what is that to you?

EMILIA If it be not for some purpose of import,
Give 't me again. Poor lady, she'll run mad
When she shall lack° it.   *miss*

IAGO   Be not acknown on 't.[4]
320   I have use for it. Go, leave me.   [*Exit Emilia.*]
I will in Cassio's lodging lose[5] this napkin
And let him find it. Trifles light as air
Are to the jealous confirmations strong
As proofs of Holy Writ. This may do something.
325   The Moor already changes with my poison.
Dangerous conceits° are in their natures poisons,   *ideas*
Which at the first are scarce found to distaste,°   *be distasteful*
But with a little act° upon the blood   *action*
Burn like the mines of sulfur.
[*Enter Othello.*]
                          I did say so.
330   Look where he comes! Not poppy nor mandragora[6]

---

1. Design of the embroidery copied.
2. With bawdy suggestion; *common* suggests coarseness and availability to all comers, and *thing* is a slang term for the genitals.
3. Taking the opportunity.

4. Do not confess knowledge of it.
5. The Folio spelling, *loose,* is a normal spelling for "lose," but it may also contain the idea of "let go," "release."
6. An opiate made of the mandrake root.

Nor all the drowsy syrups of the world
Shall ever medicine thee to that sweet sleep
Which thou owedst° yesterday.   *you did own*

OTHELLO   Ha, ha, false to me?

IAGO Why, how now, General? No more of that.

OTHELLO Avaunt! Begone! Thou hast set me on the rack.
　　I swear 'tis better to be much abused
　　Than but to know 't a little.

IAGO   How now, my lord?

OTHELLO What sense had I of her stolen hours of lust?
　　I saw 't not, thought it not, it harmed not me.
340　I slept the next night well, fed well, was free° and merry;   *carefree*
　　I found not Cassio's kisses on her lips.
　　He that is robbed, not wanting° what is stolen,   *missing*
　　Let him not know 't and he's not robbed at all.

IAGO I am sorry to hear this.

OTHELLO I had been happy if the general camp,
　　Pioners[7] and all, had tasted her sweet body,
　　So° I had nothing known. O, now, forever   *provided*
　　Farewell the tranquil mind! Farewell content!
　　Farewell the plumèd troops and the big° wars   *stately*
350　That makes ambition virtue! O, farewell!
　　Farewell the neighing steed and the shrill trump,
　　The spirit-stirring drum, th' ear-piercing fife,
　　The royal banner, and all quality,°   *character*
　　Pride,° pomp, and circumstance° of glorious war!   *display/pageantry*
　　And O, you mortal engines,[8] whose rude throats
　　Th' immortal Jove's dread clamors° counterfeit,   *thunder*
　　Farewell! Othello's occupation's gone.

IAGO Is 't possible, my lord?

OTHELLO Villain, be sure thou prove my love a whore!
360　Be sure of it. Give me the ocular proof,
　　Or, by the worth of mine eternal soul,
　　Thou hadst been better have been born a dog
　　Than answer my waked wrath!

IAGO   Is 't come to this?

OTHELLO Make me to see 't, or at the least so prove it
365　That the probation° bear no hinge nor loop   *proof*
　　To hang a doubt on, or woe upon thy life!

IAGO My noble lord—

OTHELLO If thou dost slander her and torture me,
　　Never pray more; abandon all remorse;°   *pity*
370　On horror's head horrors accumulate;
　　Do deeds to make heaven weep, all earth amazed;
　　For nothing canst thou to damnation add
　　Greater than that.

IAGO   O grace! O heaven forgive me!
　　Are you a man? Have you a soul or sense?

---

7. Diggers of mines, the lowest grade of soldiers.　　　8. Cannon. (*Mortal* means "deadly.")

375 God b' wi' you; take mine office. O wretched fool,[9]
That lov'st to make thine honesty a vice!°   *failing*
O monstrous world! Take note, take note, O world,
To be direct and honest is not safe.
I thank you for this profit,° and from hence°   *instruction/henceforth*
380 I'll love no friend, sith° love breeds such offense.[1]   *since*

OTHELLO Nay, stay. Thou shouldst be honest.[2]

IAGO I should be wise, for honesty's a fool
And loses that° it works for.   *what*

OTHELLO   By the world,
I think my wife be honest and think she is not;
385 I think that thou art just and think thou art not.
I'll have some proof. My name, that was as fresh
As Dian's[3] visage, is now begrimed and black
As mine own face. If there be cords, or knives,
Poison, or fire, or suffocating streams,
390 I'll not endure it. Would I were satisfied!

IAGO I see, sir, you are eaten up with passion.
I do repent me that I put it to you.
You would be satisfied?

OTHELLO   Would? Nay, and I will.

IAGO And may; but how? How satisfied, my lord?
395 Would you, the supervisor,° grossly gape on?   *onlooker*
Behold her topped?

OTHELLO   Death and damnation! O!

IAGO It were a tedious difficulty, I think,
To bring them to that prospect. Damn them then,[4]
If ever mortal eyes do see them bolster[5]
400 More° than their own.° What then? How then?   *other/own eyes*
What shall I say? Where's satisfaction?
It is impossible you should see this,
Were they as prime° as goats, as hot as monkeys,   *wanton*
As salt° as wolves in pride,° and fools as gross   *lustful/heat*
405 As ignorance made drunk. But yet I say,
If imputation[6] and strong circumstances
Which lead directly to the door of truth
Will give you satisfaction, you might have 't.

OTHELLO Give me a living reason she's disloyal.

IAGO I do not like the office.
But sith° I am entered in this cause so far,   *since*
Pricked° to 't by foolish honesty and love,   *spurred*
I will go on. I lay with Cassio lately,
And being troubled with a raging tooth
415 I could not sleep. There are a kind of men
So loose of soul that in their sleeps will mutter

---

9. Iago addresses himself as a fool for having carried honesty too far.
1. Harm to the one who offers help and friendship.
2. It appears that you are. (But Iago replies in the sense of "ought to be.")

3. Diana, goddess of the moon and of chastity.
4. They would have to be really incorrigible.
5. Go to bed together, share a bolster.
6. Strong circumstantial evidence.

Their affairs. One of this kind is Cassio.
In sleep I heard him say, "Sweet Desdemona,
Let us be wary, let us hide our loves!"
420   And then, sir, would he grip and wring my hand,
Cry "O sweet creature!", then kiss me hard,
As if he plucked up kisses by the roots
That grew upon my lips; then laid his leg
Over my thigh, and sighed, and kissed, and then
425   Cried, "Cursèd fate that gave thee to the Moor!"

OTHELLO O monstrous! Monstrous!

IAGO   Nay, this was but his dream.

OTHELLO But this denoted a foregone conclusion.[7]
'Tis a shrewd doubt,[8] though it be but a dream.

IAGO And this may help to thicken other proofs
That do demonstrate thinly.

OTHELLO   I'll tear her all to pieces.

IAGO Nay, but be wise. Yet we see nothing done;
She may be honest yet. Tell me but this:
Have you not sometimes seen a handkerchief
Spotted° with strawberries in your wife's hand?   *embroidered*

OTHELLO I gave her such a one. 'Twas my first gift.

IAGO I know not that; but such a handkerchief—
I am sure it was your wife's—did I today
See Cassio wipe his beard with.

OTHELLO   If it be that—

IAGO If it be that, or any that was hers,
440   It speaks against her with the other proofs.

OTHELLO O, that the slave° had forty thousand lives!   *Cassio*
One is too poor, too weak for my revenge.
Now do I see 'tis true. Look here, Iago,
All my fond[9] love thus do I blow to heaven.
445   'Tis gone.
Arise, black vengeance, from the hollow hell!
Yield up, O love, thy crown and hearted° throne   *fixed in the heart*
To tyrannous hate! Swell, bosom, with thy freight,°   *burden*
For 'tis of aspics'° tongues!   *venomous serpents'*

IAGO   Yet be content.°   *calm*

OTHELLO O, blood, blood, blood!

IAGO Patience, I say. Your mind perhaps may change.

OTHELLO Never, Iago. Like to the Pontic Sea,[1]
Whose icy current and compulsive course
Ne'er feels retiring ebb, but keeps due on
455   To the Propontic[2] and the Hellespont,[3]
Even so my bloody thoughts with violent pace
Shall ne'er look back, ne'er ebb to humble love,

7. Concluded experience or action.
8. Suspicious circumstance.
9. Foolish (but also suggesting "affectionate").
1. Black Sea.

2. Sea of Marmora, between the Black Sea and the Aegean.
3. Dardanelles, straits where the Sea of Marmora joins with the Aegean.

Till that a capable° and wide revenge   *ample*
Swallow them up. Now, by yond marble[4] heaven,
460 [*Kneeling*.] In the due reverence of a sacred vow
I here engage my words.

IAGO   Do not rise yet.
[*He kneels*.][5] Witness, you ever-burning lights above,
You elements that clip° us round about,   *encompass*
Witness that here Iago doth give up
465 The execution° of his wit,° hands, heart,   *exercise / mind*
To wronged Othello's service. Let him command,
And to obey shall be in me remorse,[6]
What bloody business ever.° [*They rise*.]   *soever*

OTHELLO   I greet thy love,
Not with vain thanks, but with acceptance bounteous,
470 And will upon the instant put thee to 't.[7]
Within these three days let me hear thee say
That Cassio's not alive.

IAGO   My friend is dead;
'Tis done at your request. But let her live.

OTHELLO Damn her, lewd minx!° O, damn her, damn her!   *wanton*
475 Come, go with me apart. I will withdraw
To furnish me with some swift means of death
For the fair devil. Now art thou my lieutenant.

IAGO I am your own forever.   [*Exeunt*.]

Scene 4

[*Location: Before the citadel. Enter Desdemona, Emilia, and Clown*.]

DESDEMONA Do you know, sirrah,[8] where Lieutenant Cassio lies?

CLOWN I dare not say he lies[9] anywhere.

DESDEMONA Why, man?

CLOWN He's a soldier, and for me to say a soldier lies, 'tis stabbing.

DESDEMONA Go to. Where lodges he?

CLOWN To tell you where he lodges is to tell you where I lie.

DESDEMONA Can anything be made of this?

CLOWN I know not where he lodges, and for me to devise a lodging and say he lies here, or he lies there, were to lie in mine own throat.[1]

DESDEMONA Can you inquire him out, and be edified by report?

CLOWN I will catechize the world for him; that is, make questions, and by them answer.

DESDEMONA Seek him, bid him come hither. Tell him I have moved[2] my lord on his behalf and hope all will be well.

CLOWN To do this is within the compass of man's wit, and therefore I will attempt the doing it.   [*Exit Clown*.]

DESDEMONA Where should I lose that handkerchief, Emilia?

---

4. I.e., gleaming like marble and unrelenting.
5. In the Quarto text, Iago kneels here after Othello has knelt at line 460.
6. Pity (for Othello's wrongs).
7. To the proof.

8. A form of address to an inferior.
9. Lodges. (But the Clown makes the obvious pun.)
1. Lie egregiously and deliberately. Also, use the windpipe to speak a lie.
2. Petitioned.

EMILIA I know not, madam.

DESDEMONA Believe me, I had rather have lost my purse

20   Full of crusadoes;° and but my noble Moor   *gold coins*
    Is true of mind and made of no such baseness
    As jealous creatures are, it were enough
    To put him to ill thinking.

EMILIA   Is he not jealous?

DESDEMONA Who, he? I think the sun where he was born

25   Drew all such humors[3] from him.

EMILIA   Look where he comes.

    [*Enter Othello.*]

DESDEMONA I will not leave him now till Cassio
    Be called to him.—How is 't with you, my lord?

OTHELLO Well, my good lady. [*Aside.*] O, hardness to dissemble!—
    How do you, Desdemona?

DESDEMONA   Well, my good lord.

OTHELLO Give me your hand. [*She gives her hand.*] This hand is moist, my lady.

DESDEMONA It yet hath felt no age nor known no sorrow.

OTHELLO This argues fruitfulness and liberal heart.[4]
    Hot, hot, and moist. This hand of yours requires
    A sequester° from liberty, fasting and prayer,   *separation*
35   Much castigation,° exercise° devout;   *discipline/prayer*
    For here's a young and sweating devil here
    That commonly rebels. 'Tis a good hand,
    A frank[5] one.

DESDEMONA   You may indeed say so,
    For 'twas that hand that gave away my heart.

OTHELLO A liberal hand. The hearts of old gave hands,[6]
    But our new heraldry is hands, not hearts.[7]

DESDEMONA I cannot speak of this. Come now, your promise.

OTHELLO What promise, chuck?[8]

DESDEMONA I have sent to bid Cassio come speak with you.

OTHELLO I have a salt and sorry rheum[9] offends me;
    Lend me thy handkerchief.

DESDEMONA   Here, my lord. [*She offers a handkerchief.*]

OTHELLO That which I gave you.

DESDEMONA   I have it not about me.

OTHELLO Not?

DESDEMONA No, faith, my lord.

OTHELLO   That's a fault. That handkerchief

50   Did an Egyptian to my mother give.
    She was a charmer,° and could almost read   *sorceress*
    The thoughts of people. She told her, while she kept it
    'Twould make her amiable° and subdue my father   *desirable*

---

3. Refers to the four bodily fluids thought to determine temperament.
4. Gives evidence of amorousness, fecundity, and sexual freedom.
5. Generous, open (with sexual suggestion).
6. In former times, people would give their hearts when

they gave their hands to something.
7. In our decadent times, the joining of hands is no longer a badge to signify the giving of hearts.
8. A term of endearment.
9. Distressful head cold or watering of the eyes.

Entirely to her love, but if she lost it
55 Or made a gift of it, my father's eye
Should hold her loathèd and his spirits should hunt
After new fancies.° She, dying, gave it me,   *loves*
And bid me, when my fate would have me wived,
To give it her.[1] I did so; and take heed on 't;
60 Make it a darling like your precious eye.
To lose 't or give 't away were such perdition°   *loss*
As nothing else could match.

DESDEMONA   Is 't possible?

OTHELLO 'Tis true. There's magic in the web° of it.   *weaving*
A sibyl, that had numbered in the world
65 The sun to course two hundred compasses,[2]
In her prophetic fury[3] sewed the work;°   *embroidered pattern*
The worms were hallowed that did breed the silk,
And it was dyed in mummy[4] which the skillful
Conserved of[5] maidens' hearts.

DESDEMONA   I' faith! Is 't true?

OTHELLO Most veritable. Therefore look to 't well.

DESDEMONA Then would to God that I had never seen 't!

OTHELLO Ha? Wherefore?

DESDEMONA Why do you speak so startingly and rash?[6]

OTHELLO Is 't lost? Is 't gone? Speak, is 't out o' the way?°   *misplaced*

DESDEMONA Heaven bless us!

OTHELLO Say you?

DESDEMONA It is not lost; but what an if° it were?   *if*

OTHELLO How?

DESDEMONA I say it is not lost.

OTHELLO   Fetch 't, let me see 't.

DESDEMONA Why, so I can, sir, but I will not now.
This is a trick to put me from my suit.
Pray you, let Cassio be received again.

OTHELLO Fetch me the handkerchief! My mind misgives.

DESDEMONA Come, come,
85 You'll never meet a more sufficient° man.   *able*

OTHELLO The handkerchief!

DESDEMONA   I pray, talk° me of Cassio.   *talk to*

OTHELLO The handkerchief!

DESDEMONA   A man that all his time[7]
Hath founded his good fortunes on your love,
Shared dangers with you—

OTHELLO The handkerchief!

DESDEMONA I' faith, you are to blame.

OTHELLO Zounds!   [*Exit Othello.*]

EMILIA Is not this man jealous?

DESDEMONA I ne'er saw this before.

---

1. I.e., to my wife.
2. Annual circlings. (The *sibyl*, or prophetess, was 200 years old.)
3. Frenzy of prophetic inspiration.
4. Medicinal or magical preparation drained from mum-

mified bodies.
5. Prepared or preserved out of.
6. Disjointedly and impetuously, excitedly.
7. Throughout his career.

95   Sure, there's some wonder in this handkerchief.
       I am most unhappy in the loss of it.
EMILIA 'Tis not a year or two shows us a man.[8]
       They are all but° stomachs, and we all but food;   *nothing but*
       They eat us hungerly,° and when they are full   *hungrily*
100   They belch us.
                       [*Enter Iago and Cassio.*]
                       Look you, Cassio and my husband.
IAGO [*to Cassio*]
       There is no other way; 'tis she must do 't.
       And, lo, the happiness![9] Go and importune her.
DESDEMONA How now, good Cassio? What's the news with you?
CASSIO Madam, my former suit. I do beseech you
105   That by your virtuous° means I may again   *efficacious*
       Exist and be a member of his love
       Whom I, with all the office° of my heart,   *loyal service*
       Entirely honor. I would not be delayed.
       If my offense be of such mortal° kind   *fatal*
110   That nor° my service past, nor present sorrows,   *neither*
       Nor purposed merit in futurity
       Can ransom me into his love again,
       But to know so must be my benefit;[1]
       So shall I clothe me in a forced content,
115   And shut myself up in[2] some other course,
       To fortune's alms.[3]
DESDEMONA   Alas, thrice-gentle Cassio,
       My advocation° is not now in tune.   *advocacy*
       My lord is not my lord; nor should I know him,
       Were he in favor° as in humor° altered.   *appearance*/*mood*
120   So help me every spirit sanctified
       As I have spoken for you all my best
       And stood within the blank[4] of his displeasure
       For my free speech! You must awhile be patient.
       What I can do I will, and more I will
125   Than for myself I dare. Let that suffice you.
IAGO Is my lord angry?
EMILIA   He went hence but now,
       And certainly in strange unquietness.
IAGO Can he be angry? I have seen the cannon
130   When it hath blown his ranks into the air,
       And like the devil from his very arm
       Puffed his own brother—and is he angry?
       Something of moment[5] then. I will go meet him.
       There's matter in 't indeed, if he be angry.
DESDEMONA I prithee, do so. [*Exit Iago.*]

---

8. You can't really know a man even in a year or two of
experience (?), or, real men come along seldom (?).
9. In happy time, fortunately met.
1. Merely to know that my case is hopeless will have to
content me (and will be better than uncertainty).

2. Confine myself to.
3. Throwing myself on the mercy of fortune.
4. Within pointblank range. (The *blank* is the center of
the target.)
5. Of immediate importance, momentous.

Something, sure, of state,°   *state affairs*
Either from Venice, or some unhatched practice[6]
Made demonstrable here in Cyprus to him,
Hath puddled° his clear spirit; and in such cases   *muddied*
Men's natures wrangle with inferior things,
140   Though great ones are their object. 'Tis even so;
For let our finger ache, and it indues°   *induces*
Our other, healthful members even to a sense
Of pain. Nay, we must think men are not gods,
Nor of them look for such observancy°   *attentiveness*
145   As fits the bridal.[7] Beshrew me[8] much, Emilia,
I was, unhandsome° warrior as I am,   *unskillful*
Arraigning his unkindness with[9] my soul;
But now I find I had suborned the witness,[1]
And he's indicted falsely.

EMILIA   Pray heaven it be
150   State matters, as you think, and no conception
Nor no jealous toy° concerning you.   *fancy*

DESDEMONA Alas the day! I never gave him cause.

EMILIA But jealous souls will not be answered so;
They are not ever jealous for the cause,
155   But jealous for° they're jealous. It is a monster   *do because*
Begot upon itself,[2] born on itself.

DESDEMONA Heaven keep that monster from Othello's mind!

EMILIA Lady, amen.

DESDEMONA I will go seek him. Cassio, walk hereabout.
160   If I do find him fit, I'll move your suit
And seek to effect it to my uttermost.

CASSIO I humbly thank your ladyship.

                            [Exit Desdemona with Emilia.]

    [Enter Bianca.]

BIANCA Save° you, friend Cassio!   *God save*

CASSIO   What make° you from home?   *do*
How is 't with you, my most fair Bianca?
165   I' faith, sweet love, I was coming to your house.

BIANCA And I was going to your lodging, Cassio.
What, keep a week away? Seven days and nights?
Eightscore-eight[3] hours? And lovers' absent hours
More tedious than the dial[4] eightscore times?
170   O weary reckoning!

CASSIO   Pardon me, Bianca.
I have this while with leaden thoughts been pressed;
But I shall, in a more continuate° time,   *uninterrupted*
Strike off this score[5] of absence. Sweet Bianca,

---

6. As yet unexecuted or undiscovered plot.
7. Wedding (when a bridegroom is newly attentive to his bride).
8. A mild oath.
9. Before the bar of.
1. Induced the witness to give false testimony.

2. Generated solely from itself.
3. One hundred sixty-eight, the number of hours in a week.
4. A complete revolution of the clock.
5. Settle this account.

[*Giving her Desdemona's handkerchief.*]
    Take me this work out.[6]
BIANCA   O Cassio, whence came this?
175   This is some token from a newer friend.°   *mistress*
    To the felt absence now I feel a cause.
    Is 't come to this? Well, well.
CASSIO   Go to, woman!
    Throw your vile guesses in the devil's teeth,
    From whence you have them. You are jealous now
180   That this is from some mistress, some remembrance.
    No, by my faith, Bianca.
BIANCA   Why, whose is it?
CASSIO I know not, neither. I found it in my chamber.
    I like the work well. Ere it be demanded°—   *inquired for*
    As like° enough it will—I would have it copied.   *likely*
185   Take it and do 't, and leave me for this time.
BIANCA Leave you? Wherefore?
CASSIO I do attend here on the General,
    And think it no addition,[7] nor my wish,
    To have him see me womaned.
BIANCA Why, I pray you?
CASSIO Not that I love you not.
BIANCA But that you do not love me.
    I pray you, bring° me on the way a little,   *accompany*
    And say if I shall see you soon at night.
CASSIO 'Tis but a little way that I can bring you,
    For I attend here; but I'll see you soon.
BIANCA 'Tis very good. I must be circumstanced.[8]

                                        [*Exeunt omnes.*]

                        A c t   4

                        Scene 1

    [*Location: Before the citadel. Enter Othello and Iago.*]
IAGO Will you think so?
OTHELLO   Think so, Iago?
IAGO   What,
    To kiss in private?
OTHELLO   An unauthorized kiss!
IAGO Or to be naked with her friend in bed
    An hour or more, not meaning any harm?
OTHELLO Naked in bed, Iago, and not mean harm?
    It is hypocrisy against the devil.
    They that mean virtuously and yet do so,
    The devil their virtue tempts, and they tempt heaven.
IAGO If they do nothing, 'tis a venial° slip.   *pardonable*
10   But if I give my wife a handkerchief—
OTHELLO What then?

6. Copy this embroidery for me.   8. Be governed by circumstance, yield to your conditions.
7. I.e., addition to my reputation.

IAGO Why then, 'tis hers, my lord, and being hers,
    She may, I think, bestow 't on any man.
OTHELLO She is protectress of her honor too.
15   May she give that?
IAGO Her honor is an essence that's not seen;
    They have it[9] very oft that have it not.
    But, for the handkerchief—
OTHELLO By heaven, I would most gladly have forgot it.
20   Thou saidst—O, it comes o'er my memory
    As doth the raven o'er the infectious house,[1]
    Boding to all—he had my handkerchief.
IAGO Ay, what of that?
OTHELLO   That's not so good now.
IAGO   What
    If I had said I had seen him do you wrong?
25   Or heard him say—as knaves be such abroad,°   *around about*
    Who having, by their own importunate suit,
    Or voluntary dotage[2] of some mistress,
    Convincèd or supplied[3] them, cannot choose
    But they must blab—
OTHELLO   Hath he said anything?
IAGO He hath, my lord; but, be you well assured,
    No more than he'll unswear.
OTHELLO   What hath he said?
IAGO Faith, that he did—I know not what he did.
OTHELLO What? What?
IAGO Lie—
OTHELLO With her?
IAGO   With her, on her; what you will.
OTHELLO Lie with her? Lie on her? We say "lie on her" when they belie[4] her. Lie with her? Zounds, that's fulsome.[5]—Handkerchief—confessions—handkerchief!—To confess and be hanged for his labor—first to be hanged and then to confess.[6]—I tremble at it. Nature would not invest herself in such shadowing
40   passion without some instruction.[7] It is not words[8] that shakes me thus. Pish! Noses, ears, and lips.—Is 't possible?—Confess—handkerchief!—O devil!
    [*Falls in a trance.*]
IAGO Work on, My medicine, work! Thus credulous fools are caught,
    And many worthy and chaste dames even thus,
    All guiltless, meet reproach.—What, ho! My lord!
45   My lord! I say! Othello!
    [*Enter Cassio.*]
               How now, Cassio?
CASSIO What's the matter?

---

9. They enjoy a reputation for it.
1. Allusion to the belief that the raven hovered over a house of sickness or infection, such as one visited by the plague.
2. Willing infatuation.
3. Seduced or sexually gratified.
4. Slander.
5. Foul.

6. Othello reverses the proverbial *confess and be hanged;* Cassio is to be given no time to confess before he dies.
7. I.e., without some foundation in fact, nature would not have dressed herself in such an overwhelming passion that comes over me now and fills my mind with images, or in such a lifelike fantasy as Cassio had in his dream of lying with Desdemona.
8. Mere words.

IAGO My lord is fall'n into an epilepsy.
  This is his second fit. He had one yesterday.
CASSIO Rub him about the temples.
IAGO   No, forbear.
  The lethargy° must have his° quiet course.   *coma/its*
50 If not, he foams at mouth, and by and by
  Breaks out to savage madness. Look, he stirs.
  Do you withdraw yourself a little while.
  He will recover straight. When he is gone,
  I would on great occasion speak with you.

                    [Exit Cassio.]

55 How is it, General? Have you not hurt your head?
OTHELLO Dost thou mock me?[1]
IAGO   I mock you not, by heaven.
  Would you would bear your fortune like a man!
OTHELLO A hornèd man's a monster and a beast.
IAGO There's many a beast then in a populous city,
60 And many a civil° monster.   *city-dwelling*
OTHELLO Did he confess it?
IAGO Good sir, be a man.
  Think every bearded fellow that's but yoked[2]
  May draw with you.[3] There's millions now alive
65 That nightly lie in those unproper° beds   *shared*
  Which they dare swear peculiar.° Your case is better.[4] *their own*
  O, 'tis the spite of hell, the fiend's arch-mock,
  To lip° a wanton in a secure couch   *kiss*
  And to suppose her chaste! No, let me know,
70 And knowing what I am,[5] I know what she shall be.[6]
OTHELLO O, thou art wise. 'Tis certain.
IAGO   Stand you awhile apart;
  Confine yourself but in a patient list.[7]
  Whilst you were here o'erwhelmèd with your grief—
  A passion most unsuiting such a man—
75 Cassio came hither. I shifted him away,[8]
  And laid good 'scuse upon your ecstasy,°   *trance*
  Bade him anon return and here speak with me,
  The which he promised. Do but encave° yourself *conceal*
  And mark the fleers,° the gibes, and notable° scorns *sneers/obvious*
80 That dwell in every region of his face;
  For I will make him tell the tale anew,
  Where, how, how oft, how long ago, and when
  He hath and is again to cope° your wife.   *have sex with*
  I say, but mark his gesture. Marry, patience!
85 Or I shall say you're all-in-all in spleen,[9]
  And nothing of a man.

---

1. Othello takes Iago's question about hurting his head to
be a mocking reference to the cuckold's horns.
2. Married. Also, put into the yoke of infamy and cuckoldry.
3. Pull as you do, like oxen who are yoked, i.e., share your
fate as cuckold.
4. I.e., because you know the truth.

5. I.e., a cuckold.
6. Will happen to her.
7. Within the bounds of patience.
8. Used a dodge to get rid of him.
9. Utterly governed by passionate impulses.

OTHELLO   Dost thou hear, Iago?
I will be found most cunning in my patience;
But—dost thou hear?—most bloody.

IAGO   That's not amiss;
But yet keep time[1] in all. Will you withdraw?
[Othello stands apart.]

90   Now will I question Cassio of Bianca,
A huswife° that by selling her desires   *hussy*
Buys herself bread and clothes. It is a creature
That dotes on Cassio—as 'tis the strumpet's plague
To beguile many and be beguiled by one.

95   He, when he hears of her, cannot restrain°   *refrain*
From the excess of laughter. Here he comes.
[Enter Cassio.]
As he shall smile, Othello shall go mad;
And his unbookish° jealousy must conster°   *uninstructed/construe*
Poor Cassio's smiles, gestures, and light behaviors

100   Quite in the wrong.—How do you now, Lieutenant?

CASSIO The worser that you give me the addition°   *title*
Whose want[2] even kills me.

IAGO Ply Desdemona well and you are sure on 't.
[Speaking lower.] Now, if this suit lay in Bianca's power,

105   How quickly should you speed!

CASSIO *[laughing]*   Alas, poor caitiff!°   *wretch*

OTHELLO *[aside]* Look how he laughs already!

IAGO I never knew a woman love man so.

CASSIO Alas, poor rogue! I think, i' faith, she loves me.

OTHELLO Now he denies it faintly, and laughs it out.

IAGO Do you hear, Cassio?

OTHELLO   Now he importunes him
To tell it o'er. Go to![3] Well said,° well said.   *well done*

IAGO She gives it out that you shall marry her.
Do you intend it?

CASSIO Ha, ha, ha!

OTHELLO Do you triumph, Roman?[4] Do you triumph?

CASSIO I marry her? What? A customer?[5] Prithee, bear some charity to my wit;[6] do
not think it so unwholesome. Ha, ha, ha!

OTHELLO So, so, so, so! They laugh that win.[7]

IAGO Faith, the cry goes that you shall marry her.

CASSIO Prithee, say true.

IAGO I am a very villain else.[8]

OTHELLO Have you scored me?[9] Well.

CASSIO This is the monkey's own giving out. She is persuaded I will marry her out
of her own love and flattery,[1] not out of my promise.

---

1. Keep yourself steady (as in music).
2. The lack of which.
3. An expression of remonstrance.
4. The Romans were noted for their *triumphs* or triumphal
processions.
5. Prostitute.

6. Be more charitable to my judgment.
7. I.e., they that laugh last laugh best.
8. Call me a complete rogue if I'm not telling the truth.
9. Scored off me, beaten me, made up my reckoning,
branded me.
1. Self-flattery, self-deception.

OTHELLO Iago beckons° me. Now he begins the story.   *signals*

CASSIO She was here even now; she haunts me in every place. I was the other day talking on the seabank[2] with certain Venetians, and thither comes the bauble,[3] and, by this hand,[4] she falls me thus about my neck—
[*He embraces Iago.*]

OTHELLO Crying, "O dear Cassio!" as it were; his gesture imports it.

CASSIO So hangs and lolls and weeps upon me, so shakes and pulls me. Ha, ha, ha!

OTHELLO Now he tells how she plucked him to my chamber. O, I see that nose of yours, but not that dog I shall throw it to.[5]

CASSIO Well, I must leave her company.

IAGO Before me,[6] look where she comes.
[*Enter Bianca with Othello's handkerchief.*]

CASSIO 'Tis such another fitchew![7] Marry, a perfumed one.—What do you mean by this haunting of me?

BIANCA Let the devil and his dam[8] haunt you! What did you mean by that same handkerchief you gave me even now? I was a fine fool to take it. I must take out the work? A likely piece of work,[9] that you should find it in your chamber and

140   know not who left it there! This is some minx's token, and I must take out the work? There; give it your hobbyhorse.[1] [*She gives him the handkerchief.*] Wheresoever you had it, I'll take out no work on 't.

CASSIO How now, my sweet Bianca? How now? How now?

OTHELLO By heaven, that should be[2] my handkerchief!

BIANCA If you'll come to supper tonight, you may; if you will not, come when you are next prepared for.[3]

                                                                    [*Exit.*]

IAGO After her, after her.

CASSIO Faith, I must. She'll rail in the streets else.

IAGO Will you sup there?

CASSIO Faith, I intend so.

IAGO Well, I may chance to see you, for I would very fain speak with you.

CASSIO Prithee, come. Will you?

IAGO Go to. Say no more.   [*Exit Cassio.*]

OTHELLO [*advancing*] How shall I murder him, Iago?

IAGO Did you perceive how he laughed at his vice?

OTHELLO O, Iago!

IAGO And did you see the handkerchief?

OTHELLO Was that mine?

IAGO Yours, by this hand. And to see how he prizes the foolish woman your wife!

160   She gave it him, and he hath given it his whore.

OTHELLO I would have him nine years a-killing. A fine woman! A fair woman! A sweet woman!

---

2. Seashore.
3. Plaything.
4. I make my vow.
5. Othello imagines himself cutting off Cassio's nose and throwing it to a dog.
6. On my soul.
7. What a polecat she is! Just like all the others. (Polecats

were often compared with prostitutes because of their rank smell and presumed lechery.)
8. Mother.
9. A fine story.
1. Harlot.
2. Must be.
3. When I'm ready for you (i.e., never).

IAGO Nay, you must forget that.

OTHELLO Ay, let her rot and perish, and be damned tonight, for she shall not live.
165   No, my heart is turned to stone; I strike it, and it hurts my hand. O, the world
hath not a sweeter creature! She might lie by an emperor's side and command
him tasks.

IAGO Nay, that's not your way.[4]

OTHELLO Hang her! I do but say what she is. So delicate with her needle! An
170   admirable musician! O, she will sing the savageness out of a bear. Of so high
and plenteous wit and invention![5]

IAGO She's the worse for all this.

OTHELLO O, a thousand, a thousand times! And then, of so gentle a condition![6]

IAGO Ay, too gentle.[7]

OTHELLO Nay, that's certain. But yet the pity of it, Iago! O, Iago, the pity of it, Iago!

IAGO If you are so fond[8] over her iniquity, give her patent[9] to offend, for if it touch
not you it comes near nobody.

OTHELLO I will chop her into messes.[1] Cuckold me?

IAGO O, 'tis foul in her.

OTHELLO With mine officer?

IAGO That's fouler.

OTHELLO Get me some poison, Iago, this night. I'll not expostulate with her, lest
her body and beauty unprovide[2] my mind again. This night, Iago.

IAGO Do it not with poison. Strangle her in her bed, even the bed she hath contami-
185   nated.

OTHELLO Good, good! The justice of it pleases. Very good.

IAGO And for Cassio, let me be his undertaker.[3] You shall hear more by midnight.

OTHELLO Excellent good. [A trumpet within.] What trumpet is that same?

IAGO I warrant, something from Venice.
      [Enter Lodovico, Desdemona, and attendants.]
190   'Tis Lodovico. This comes from the Duke.
      See, your wife's with him.

LODOVICO God save you, worthy General!

OTHELLO   With all my heart, sir.[4]

LODOVICO [giving him a letter] The Duke and the senators of Venice greet you.

OTHELLO I kiss the instrument of their pleasures.
      [He opens the letter, and reads.]

DESDEMONA And what's the news, good cousin Lodovico?

IAGO I am very glad to see you, signor.
      Welcome to Cyprus.

LODOVICO I thank you. How does Lieutenant Cassio?

IAGO Lives, sir.

DESDEMONA Cousin, there's fall'n between him and my lord
      An unkind[5] breach; but you shall make all well.

---

4. I.e., the way you should think of her.
5. Imagination.
6. Wellborn and well-bred.
7. Generous, yielding (to other men).
8. Foolish.
9. License.

1. Portions of meat, i.e., bits.
2. Weaken, render unfit.
3. Undertake to dispatch him.
4. I thank you most heartily.
5. Unnatural, contrary to their natures; hurtful.

OTHELLO Are you sure of that?

DESDEMONA My lord?

OTHELLO [*reads*] "This fail you not to do, as you will—"

LODOVICO He did not call; he's busy in the paper.
    Is there division twixt my lord and Cassio?

DESDEMONA A most unhappy one. I would do much
    T' atone° them, for the love I bear to Cassio.   reconcile

OTHELLO Fire and brimstone!

DESDEMONA   My lord?

OTHELLO   Are you wise?

DESDEMONA What, is he angry?

LODOVICO   Maybe the letter moved him;
    For, as I think, they do command him home,
    Deputing Cassio in his government.°   office

DESDEMONA By my troth, I am glad on 't.°   of it

OTHELLO   Indeed?

DESDEMONA   My lord?

OTHELLO I am glad to see you mad.[6]

DESDEMONA   Why, sweet Othello—

OTHELLO [*striking her*] Devil!

DESDEMONA I have not deserved this.

LODOVICO My lord, this would not be believed in Venice,
    Though I should swear I saw 't. 'Tis very much.°   outrageous
    Make her amends; she weeps.

OTHELLO   O devil, devil!
    If that the earth could teem° with woman's tears,   breed
    Each drop she falls° would prove a crocodile.[7]   lets fall
    Out of my sight!

DESDEMONA   I will not stay to offend you. [*Going.*]

LODOVICO Truly, an obedient lady.
    I do beseech your lordship, call her back.

OTHELLO Mistress!

DESDEMONA [*returning*] My lord?

OTHELLO What would you with her, sir?

LODOVICO   Who, I, my lord?

OTHELLO Ay, you did wish that I would make her turn.[8]
    Sir, she can turn, and turn, and yet go on
230 And turn again; and she can weep, sir, weep;
    And she's obedient,[9] as you say, obedient,
    Very obedient.—Proceed you in your tears.—
    Concerning this, sir—O well-painted passion!—°   grief
    I am commanded home.—Get you away;
235 I'll send for you anon.—Sir, I obey the mandate
    And will return to Venice.—Hence, avaunt!

                                        [*Exit Desdemona.*]

    Cassio shall have my place. And, sir, tonight

---

6. I.e., I am glad to see that you are insane enough to
rejoice in Cassio's promotion. (Othello bitterly plays on
Desdemona's *I am glad.*)
7. Crocodiles were supposed to weep hypocritical tears for
their victims.
8. Othello implies that Desdemona is pliant and will do a
turn for any man.
9. With much the same sexual connotation as *turn*.

I do entreat that we may sup together.
You are welcome, sir, to Cyprus.—Goats and monkeys![1]
LODOVICO Is this the noble Moor whom our full Senate
    Call all in all sufficient? Is this the nature
    Whom passion could not shake? Whose solid virtue
    The shot of accident nor dart of chance
    Could neither graze nor pierce?
IAGO   He is much changed.
LODOVICO Are his wits safe? Is he not light of brain?
IAGO He's that he is. I may not breathe my censure
    What he might be. If what he might he is not,
    I would to heaven he were![2]
LODOVICO   What, strike his wife?
IAGO Faith, that was not so well; yet would I knew
250   That stroke would prove the worst!
LODOVICO   Is it his use?°   *custom*
    Or did the letters work upon his blood°   *passions*
    And new-create his fault?
IAGO   Alas, alas!
    It is not honesty in me to speak
    What I have seen and known. You shall observe him,
255   And his own courses will denote[3] him so
    That I may save my speech. Do but go after,
    And mark how he continues.
LODOVICO I am sorry that I am deceived in him.   *[Exeunt.]*

Scene 2

[Location: The Citadel. Enter Othello and Emilia.]
OTHELLO You have seen nothing then?
EMILIA Nor ever heard, nor ever did suspect.
OTHELLO Yes, you have seen Cassio and she together.
EMILIA But then I saw no harm, and then I heard
5   Each syllable that breath made up between them.
OTHELLO What, did they never whisper?
EMILIA Never, my lord.
OTHELLO Nor send you out o' the way?
EMILIA Never.
OTHELLO To fetch her fan, her gloves, her mask, nor nothing?
EMILIA Never, my lord.
OTHELLO That's strange.
EMILIA I durst, my lord, to wager she is honest,
    Lay down my soul at stake.° If you think other,   *as the wager*
15   Remove your thought; it doth abuse your bosom.°   *deceive you*
    If any wretch have put this in your head,
    Let heaven requite it with the serpent's curse![4]

---

1. The most lustful animals.
2. I dare not venture an opinion as to whether he's of unsound mind, as you suggest, but, if he isn't, then it might be better to wish he were in fact insane, since only that could excuse his wild behavior.

3. Actions will reveal.
4. The curse pronounced by God on the serpent for deceiving Eve, just as some man has done to Othello and Desdemona. (See Genesis 3.14.)

For if she be not honest, chaste, and true,
There's no man happy; the purest of their wives

20   Is foul as slander.

OTHELLO   Bid her come hither. Go.

[Exit Emilia.]

She says enough; yet she's a simple bawd
That cannot say as much.⁵ This° is a subtle whore,   *Desdemona*
A closet lock and key of villainous secrets.
And yet she'll kneel and pray; I have seen her do 't.
[Enter Desdemona and Emilia.]

DESDEMONA My lord, what is your will?

OTHELLO Pray you, chuck, come hither.

DESDEMONA What is your pleasure?

OTHELLO   Let me see your eyes.
Look in my face.

DESDEMONA   What horrible fancy's this?

OTHELLO *[to Emilia]* Some of your function,⁶ mistress.

30   Leave procreants° alone and shut the door;   *mating couples*
Cough or cry "hem" if anybody come.
Your mystery,° your mystery! Nay, dispatch.   *trade*

[Exit Emilia.]

DESDEMONA *[kneeling]* Upon my knees, what doth your speech import?
I understand a fury in your words,

35   But not the words.

OTHELLO Why, what art thou?

DESDEMONA   Your wife, my lord, your true
And loyal wife.

OTHELLO   Come, swear it, damn thyself,
Lest, being like one of heaven,⁷ the devils themselves
Should fear to seize thee. Therefore be double damned:

40   Swear thou art honest.

DESDEMONA   Heaven doth truly know it.

OTHELLO Heaven truly knows that thou art false as hell.

DESDEMONA To whom, my lord? With whom? How am I false?

OTHELLO *[weeping]* Ah, Desdemon! Away, away, away!

DESDEMONA Alas the heavy day! Why do you weep?

45   Am I the motive° of these tears, my lord?   *cause*
If haply you my father do suspect
An instrument of this your calling back,
Lay not your blame on me. If you have lost him,
I have lost him too.

OTHELLO   Had it pleased heaven

50   To try me with affliction, had they⁸ rained
All kinds of sores and shames on my bare head,
Steeped me in poverty to the very lips,
Given to captivity me and my utmost hopes,
I should have found in some place of my soul

5. Any procuress or go-between who couldn't make up as
plausible a story as Emilia's would have to be pretty stupid.
6. I.e., practice your chosen profession, that of bawd (by
guarding the door).
7. Looking like an angel.
8. I.e., heavenly powers.

55 A drop of patience. But, alas, to make me
A fixèd figure for the time of scorn[9]
To point his° slow and moving finger[1] at!   *its*
Yet could I bear that too, well, very well.
But there where I have garnered° up my heart,   *stored*
60 Where either I must live or bear no life,
The fountain° from the which my current runs   *spring*
Or else dries up—to be discarded thence!
Or keep it as a cistern° for foul toads   *cesspool*
To knot° and gender° in! Turn thy complexion there,[2]   *couple / engender*
65 Patience, thou young and rose-lipped cherubin—
Ay, there look grim as hell![3]

DESDEMONA I hope my noble lord esteems me honest.°   *chaste*

OTHELLO O, ay, as summer flies are in the shambles,°   *slaughterhouse*
That quicken° even with blowing.[4] O thou weed,   *come to life*
70 Who art so lovely fair and smell'st so sweet
That the sense aches at thee, would thou hadst ne'er been born!

DESDEMONA Alas, what ignorant sin[5] have I committed?

OTHELLO Was this fair paper, this most goodly book,
Made to write "whore" upon? What committed?
75 Committed? O thou public commoner!°   *prostitute*
I should make very forges of my cheeks,
That would to cinders burn up modesty,
Did I but speak thy deeds. What committed?
Heaven stops the nose at it and the moon winks;[6]
80 The bawdy[7] wind, that kisses all it meets,
Is hushed within the hollow mine[8] of earth
And will not hear 't. What committed?
Impudent strumpet!

DESDEMONA   By heaven, you do me wrong.

OTHELLO Are not you a strumpet?

DESDEMONA No, as I am a Christian.
If to preserve this vessel° for my lord   *body*
From any other foul unlawful touch
Be not to be a strumpet, I am none.

OTHELLO What, not a whore?

DESDEMONA No, as I shall be saved.

OTHELLO Is 't possible?

DESDEMONA O, heaven forgive us!

OTHELLO   I cry you mercy,° then.   *beg you pardon*
I took you for that cunning whore of Venice
That married with Othello. [*Calling out.*] You, mistress,
95 That have the office opposite to Saint Peter
And keep the gate of hell!
[*Enter Emilia.*]

---

9. Scornful world.
1. I.e., hour hand of the clock, moving so slowly it seems hardly to move at all. (Othello envisages himself as being eternally pointed at by the scornful world as the numbers on a clock are pointed at by the hour hand.)
2. Change your color, grow pale, at such a sight.
3. Even Patience, that rose-lipped cherub, will look grim and pale at this spectacle.
4. I.e., with the puffing up of something rotten in which maggots are breeding.
5. Sin in ignorance.
6. Closes her eyes. (The moon symbolizes chastity.)
7. Kissing one and all.
8. Cave (where the winds were thought to dwell).

                                  You, you, ay, you!
          We have done our course.[9] There's money for your pains.   [*He gives money.*]
          I pray you, turn the key and keep our counsel.   [*Exit.*]
EMILIA Alas, what does this gentleman conceive?°   *suppose*
100   How do you, madam? How do you, my good lady?
DESDEMONA Faith, half asleep.[1]
EMILIA Good madam, what's the matter with my lord?
DESDEMONA With who?
EMILIA Why, with my lord, madam.
DESDEMONA Who is thy lord?
EMILIA   He that is yours, sweet lady.
DESDEMONA I have none. Do not talk to me, Emilia.
          I cannot weep, nor answers have I none
          But what should go by water.[2] Prithee, tonight
          Lay on my bed my wedding sheets, remember;
110   And call thy husband hither.
EMILIA Here's a change indeed! [*Exit.*]
DESDEMONA 'Tis meet° I should be used so, very meet.   *fitting*
          How have I been behaved, that he might stick°   *attach*
          The small'st opinion° on my least misuse?°   *censure/misconduct*
[*Enter Iago and Emilia.*]
IAGO What is your pleasure, madam? How is 't with you?
DESDEMONA I cannot tell. Those that do teach young babes
          Do it with gentle means and easy tasks.
          He might have chid me so, for, in good faith,
          I am a child to chiding.
IAGO What is the matter, lady?
EMILIA Alas, Iago, my lord hath so bewhored her,
          Thrown such despite and heavy terms upon her,
          That true hearts cannot bear it.
DESDEMONA Am I that name, Iago?
IAGO What name, fair lady?
DESDEMONA Such as she said my lord did say I was.
EMILIA He called her whore. A beggar in his drink
          Could not have laid such terms upon his callet.°   *whore*
IAGO Why did he so?
DESDEMONA [*weeping*]
130   I do not know. I am sure I am none such.
IAGO Do not weep, do not weep. Alas the day!
EMILIA Hath she forsook so many noble matches,
          Her father and her country and her friends,
          To be called whore? Would it not make one weep?
DESDEMONA It is my wretched fortune.
IAGO   Beshrew° him for 't!   *curse*
          How comes this trick° upon him?   *delusion*
DESDEMONA   Nay, heaven doth know.
EMILIA I will be hanged if some eternal° villain,   *inveterate*

---

9. Business (with an indecent suggestion of "trick," turn   1. I.e., dazed.
at sex).   2. Be expressed by tears.

Some busy and insinuating° rogue,   *wheedling*
Some cogging,° cozening° slave, to get some office,   *cheating/defrauding*
140   Have not devised this slander. I will be hanged else.
IAGO   Fie, there is no such man. It is impossible.
DESDEMONA   If any such there be, heaven pardon him!
EMILIA   A halter° pardon him! And hell gnaw his bones!   *hangman's noose*
      Why should he call her whore? Who keeps her company?
145   What place? What time? What form?° What likelihood?   *appearance*
      The Moor's abused by some most villainous knave,
      Some base notorious knave, some scurvy fellow.
      O heaven, that such companions thou'dst unfold,[3]
      And put in every honest hand a whip
150   To lash the rascals naked through the world
      Even from the east to th' west!
IAGO   Speak within door.[4]
EMILIA   O, fie upon them! Some such squire° he was   *fellow*
      That turned your wit the seamy side without°   *wrong side out*
      And made you to suspect me with the Moor.
IAGO   You are a fool. Go to.[5]
DESDEMONA   Alas, Iago,
      What shall I do to win my lord again?
      Good friend, go to him; for, by this light of heaven,
      I know not how I lost him. Here I kneel. [*She kneels.*]
      If e'er my will did trespass 'gainst his love,
160   Either in discourse of thought or actual deed,
      Or that° mine eyes, mine ears, or any sense   *if*
      Delighted them° in any other form;   *took delight*
      Or that I do not yet,° and ever did,   *still*
      And ever will—though he do shake me off
165   To beggarly divorcement—love him dearly,
      Comfort forswear[6] me! Unkindness may do much,
      And his unkindness may defeat° my life,   *destroy*
      But never taint my love. I cannot say "whore."
      It does abhor[7] me now I speak the word;
170   To do the act that might the addition° earn   *title*
      Not the world's mass of vanity° could make me.   *showy splendor*
      [*She rises.*]
IAGO   I pray you, be content. 'Tis but his humor.°   *mood*
      The business of the state does him offense,
      And he does chide with you.
DESDEMONA   If 'twere no other—
IAGO   It is but so, I warrant. [*Trumpets within.*]
      Hark, how these instruments summon you to supper!
      The messengers of Venice stays the meat.°   *wait to dine*
      Go in, and weep not. All things shall be well.
                                          [*Exeunt Desdemona and Emilia.*]
      [*Enter Roderigo.*]

---

3. If only you would expose such fellows.   6. May heavenly comfort forsake.
4. I.e., not so loud.   7. Fill me with abhorrence. Also, make me whorelike.
5. I.e., that's enough.

How now, Roderigo?

RODERIGO I do not find that thou deal'st justly with me.

IAGO What in the contrary?

RODERIGO Every day thou daff'st me[8] with some device,[9] Iago, and rather, as it seems to me now, keep'st from me all conveniency[1] than suppliest me with the least advantage[2] of hope. I will indeed no longer endure it, nor am I yet per-
185   suaded to put up[3] in peace what already I have foolishly suffered.

IAGO Will you hear me, Roderigo?

RODERIGO Faith, I have heard too much, for your words and performances are no kin together.

IAGO You charge me most unjustly.

RODERIGO With naught but truth. I have wasted myself out of my means. The jewels you have had from me to deliver[4] Desdemona would half have corrupted a votarist.[5] You have told me she hath received them and returned me expectations and comforts of sudden respect[6] and acquaintance, but I find none.

IAGO Well, go to, very well.

RODERIGO "Very well"! "Go to"! I cannot go to,[7] man, nor 'tis not very well. By this hand, I think it is scurvy, and begin to find myself fopped[8] in it.

IAGO Very well.

RODERIGO I tell you 'tis not very well.[9] I will make myself known to Desdemona. If she will return me my jewels, I will give over my suit and repent my unlawful
200   solicitation; if not, assure yourself I will seek satisfaction[1] of you.

IAGO You have said now?[2]

RODERIGO Ay, and said nothing but what I protest intendment[3] of doing.

IAGO Why, now I see there's mettle in thee, and even from this instant do build on thee a better opinion than ever before. Give me thy hand, Roderigo. Thou hast
205   taken against me a most just exception; but yet I protest I have dealt most directly in thy affair.

RODERIGO It hath not appeared.

IAGO I grant indeed it hath not appeared, and your suspicion is not without wit and judgment. But, Roderigo, if thou hast that in thee indeed which I have greater
210   reason to believe now than ever—I mean purpose, courage, and valor—this night show it. If thou the next night following enjoy not Desdemona, take me from this world with treachery and devise engines[4] for my life.

RODERIGO Well, what is it? Is it within reason and compass?

IAGO Sir, there is especial commission come from Venice to depute Cassio in
215   Othello's place.

RODERIGO Is that true? Why, then Othello and Desdemona return again to Venice.

IAGO O, no; he goes into Mauritania and takes away with him the fair Desdemona, unless his abode be lingered here by some accident; wherein none can be so determinate[5] as the removing of Cassio.

8. You put me off.
9. Excuse, trick.
1. Advantage, opportunity.
2. Increase.
3. Submit to, tolerate.
4. Deliver to.
5. Nun.
6. Immediate consideration.
7. Roderigo changes Iago's go to, an expression urging patience, to I cannot go to, "I have no opportunity for suc-

cess in wooing."
8. Fooled, duped.
9. Roderigo changes Iago's very well, "all right, then," to not very well, "not at all good."
1. Repayment. (The term normally means settling of accounts in a duel.)
2. Have you finished?
3. Intention.
4. Plots against.
5. Conclusive.

RODERIGO How do you mean, removing of him?

IAGO Why, by making him uncapable of Othello's place—knocking out his brains.

RODERIGO And that you would have me to do?

IAGO Ay, if you dare do yourself a profit and a right. He sups tonight with a harlotry,[6] and thither will I go to him. He knows not yet of his honorable fortune.

225 If you will watch his going thence, which I will fashion to fall out[7] between twelve and one, you may take him at your pleasure. I will be near to second your attempt, and he shall fall between us. Come, stand not amazed at it, but go along with me. I will show you such a necessity in his death that you shall think yourself bound to put it on him. It is now high[8] suppertime, and the

230 night grows to waste.[9] About it.

RODERIGO I will hear further reason for this.

IAGO And you shall be satisfied.   [*Exeunt.*]

Scene 3

[*Location: The Citadel. Enter Othello, Lodovico, Desdemona, Emilia, and attendants.*]

LODOVICO I do beseech you, sir, trouble yourself no further.

OTHELLO O, pardon me; 'twill do me good to walk.

LODOVICO Madam, good night. I humbly thank your ladyship.

DESDEMONA Your honor is most welcome.

OTHELLO   Will you walk, sir?

5   O, Desdemona!

DESDEMONA My lord?

OTHELLO Get you to bed on th' instant. I will be returned forthwith. Dismiss your attendant there. Look 't be done.

DESDEMONA I will, my lord.

[*Exit Othello, with Lodovico and attendants.*]

EMILIA How goes it now? He looks gentler than he did.

DESDEMONA He says he will return incontinent,°   *immediately*
         And hath commanded me to go to bed,
         And bid me to dismiss you.

EMILIA   Dismiss me?

DESDEMONA It was his bidding. Therefore, good Emilia,

15   Give me my nightly wearing, and adieu.
         We must not now displease him.

EMILIA I would you had never seen him!

DESDEMONA So would not I. My love doth so approve him
         That even his stubbornness,° his checks,° his frowns—   *roughness/rebukes*

20   Prithee, unpin me—have grace and favor in them.
         [*Emilia prepares Desdemona for bed.*]

EMILIA I have laid those sheets you bade me on the bed.

DESDEMONA All's one.[1] Good faith, how foolish are our minds!
         If I do die before thee, prithee shroud me
         In one of these same sheets.

EMILIA   Come, come, you talk.°   *prattle*

6. Slut.
7. Occur.
8. Fully.

9. Wastes away.
1. All right. It doesn't really matter.

DESDEMONA My mother had a maid called Barbary.
  She was in love, and he she loved proved mad°   *wild*
  And did forsake her. She had a song of "Willow."
  An old thing 'twas, but it expressed her fortune,
  And she died singing it. That song tonight
30 Will not go from my mind; I have much to do
  But to go hang² my head all at one side
  And sing it like poor Barbary. Prithee, dispatch.
EMILIA Shall I go fetch your nightgown?°   *dressing gown*
DESDEMONA   No, unpin me here.
35 This Lodovico is a proper° man.   *handsome*
EMILIA A very handsome man.
DESDEMONA He speaks well.
EMILIA I know a lady in Venice would have walked barefoot to Palestine for a touch
  of his nether lip.
DESDEMONA [*singing*] "The poor soul sat sighing by a sycamore tree,
40 Sing all a green willow;³
  Her hand on her bosom, her head on her knee,
   Sing willow, willow, willow.
  The fresh streams ran by her and murmured her moans;
   Sing willow, willow, willow;
45 Her salt tears fell from her, and softened the stones—"
  Lay by these.
  [*Singing.*] "Sing willow, willow, willow—"
  Prithee, hie thee.° He'll come anon.°   *hurry/right away*
  [*Singing.*] "Sing all a green willow must be my garland.
50 Let nobody blame him; his scorn I approve—"
  Nay, that's not next.—Hark! Who is 't that knocks?
EMILIA It's the wind.
DESDEMONA [*singing*] "I called my love false love; but what said he then?
  Sing willow, willow, willow;
55 If I court more women, you'll couch with more men."
  So, get thee gone. Good night. Mine eyes do itch;
  Doth that bode weeping?
EMILIA   'Tis neither here nor there.
DESDEMONA I have heard it said so. O, these men, these men!
60 Dost thou in conscience think—tell me, Emilia—
  That there be women do abuse° their husbands   *deceive*
  In such gross kind?
EMILIA   There be some such, no question.
DESDEMONA Wouldst thou do such a deed for all the world?
EMILIA Why, would not you?
DESDEMONA   No, by this heavenly light!
EMILIA Nor I neither by this heavenly light;
65 I might do 't as well i' the dark.
DESDEMONA Wouldst thou do such a deed for all the world?
EMILIA The world's a huge thing. It is a great price

---

2. I can scarcely keep myself from hanging.   3. A conventional emblem of disappointed love.

For a small vice.

DESDEMONA Good troth, I think thou wouldst not.

EMILIA By my troth, I think I should, and undo 't when I had done. Marry, I would not do such a thing for a joint ring,[4] nor for measures of lawn,[5] nor for gowns, petticoats, nor caps, nor any petty exhibition.[6] But for all the whole world! Uds[7] pity, who would not make her husband a cuckold to make him a monarch? I should venture purgatory for 't.

DESDEMONA Beshrew me if I would do such a wrong
For the whole world.

EMILIA Why, the wrong is but a wrong i' the world, and having the world for your labor, 'tis a wrong in your own world, and you might quickly make it right.

DESDEMONA I do not think there is any such woman.

EMILIA Yes, a dozen, and as many
To th' vantage[8] as would store° the world they played[9] for.   populate
But I do think it is their husbands' faults
If wives do fall. Say that they slack their duties°   marital duties
And pour our treasures into foreign laps,[1]
85   Or else break out in peevish jealousies,
Throwing restraint upon us?[2] Or say they strike us,
Or scant our former having in despite?[3]
Why, we have galls,[4] and though we have some grace,
Yet have we some revenge. Let husbands know
90   Their wives have sense° like them. They see, and smell,   physical sense
And have their palates both for sweet and sour,
As husbands have. What is it that they do
When they change us for others? Is it sport?°   sexual pastime
I think it is. And doth affection° breed it?   passion
95   I think it doth. Is 't frailty that thus errs?
It is so, too. And have not we affections,
Desires for sport, and frailty, as men have?
Then let them use us well; else let them know,
The ills we do, their ills instruct us so.

DESDEMONA Good night, good night. God me such uses° send   practice
Not to pick bad from bad, but by bad mend![5]

[Exeunt.]

Act 5

Scene 1

[Location: A street in Cyprus. Enter Iago and Roderigo.]

IAGO Here stand behind this bulk.[6] Straight will he come.
Wear thy good rapier bare,° and put it home.   unsheathed
Quick, quick! Fear nothing. I'll be at thy elbow.

4. A ring made in separate halves.
5. Fine linen.
6. Gift.
7. God's.
8. In addition, to boot.
9. Gambled. Also, sported sexually.
1. I.e., are unfaithful, give what is rightfully ours (semen) to other women.

2. I.e., jealously restricting our freedom to see other men.
3. Reduce our allowance to spite us.
4. Are capable of resenting injury and insult.
5. Not to learn bad conduct from others' badness (as Emilia has suggested women learn from men), but to mend my ways by perceiving what badness is, making spiritual benefit out of evil and adversity.
6. Framework projecting from the front of a shop.

It makes us or it mars us. Think on that,
5   And fix most firm thy resolution.
RODERIGO Be near at hand. I may miscarry in 't.
IAGO Here, at thy hand. Be bold, and take thy stand.
        [Iago stands aside. Roderigo conceals himself.]
RODERIGO I have no great devotion to the deed;
        And yet he hath given me satisfying reasons.
10   'Tis but a man gone. Forth, my sword! He dies.
        [He draws.]
IAGO I have rubbed this young quat° almost to the sense,°   *pimple/raw*
        And he grows angry. Now, whether he kill Cassio
        Or Cassio him, or each do kill the other,
        Every way makes my gain. Live Roderigo,[7]
15   He calls me to a restitution large
        Of gold and jewels that I bobbed° from him   *swindled*
        As gifts to Desdemona.
        It must not be. If Cassio do remain,
        He hath a daily beauty in his life
20   That makes me ugly; and besides, the Moor
        May unfold° me to him; there stand I in much peril.   *expose*
        No, he must die. Be 't so. I hear him coming.
        [Enter Cassio.]
RODERIGO *[coming forth]* I know his gait, 'tis he.—Villain, thou diest!
        [He attacks Cassio.]
CASSIO That thrust had been mine enemy indeed,
25   But that my coat[8] is better than thou know'st.
        I will make proof° of thine.   *a test*
        [He draws, and wounds Roderigo.]
RODERIGO   O, I am slain! *[He falls.]*
        [Iago, from behind, wounds Cassio in the leg, and exit.]
CASSIO I am maimed forever. Help, ho! Murder! Murder!
        [Enter Othello.]
OTHELLO The voice of Cassio! Iago keeps his word.
RODERIGO O, villain that I am!
OTHELLO   It is even so.
CASSIO O, help, ho! Light! A surgeon!
OTHELLO 'Tis he. O brave Iago, honest and just,
        That hast such noble sense of thy friend's wrong!
        Thou teachest me. Minion,[9] your dear lies dead,
        And your unblest fate hies.° Strumpet, I come.   *hastens on*
35   Forth of° my heart those charms, thine eyes, are blotted;   *from out*
        Thy bed, lust-stained, shall with lust's blood be spotted.   *[Exit Othello.]*
        [Enter Lodovico and Gratiano.]
CASSIO What ho! No watch? No passage?° Murder! Murder!   *passers-by*
GRATIANO 'Tis some mischance. The voice is very direful.
CASSIO O, help!
LODOVICO Hark!

---

7. If Roderigo lives.
8. Possibly a garment of mail under the outer clothing, or simply a tougher coat than Roderigo expected.
9. Hussy (i.e., Desdemona).

RODERIGO O wretched villain!

LODOVICO Two or three groan. 'Tis heavy° night;   *thick, dark*
    These may be counterfeits. Let's think 't unsafe
    To come in° to the cry without more help.   *approach*
    [They remain near the entrance.]

RODERIGO Nobody come? Then shall I bleed to death.
    [Enter Iago in his shirtsleeves, with a light.]

LODOVICO Hark!

GRATIANO Here's one comes in his shirt, with light and weapons.

IAGO Who's there? Whose noise is this that cries on° murder?   *cries out*

LODOVICO We do not know.

IAGO   Did not you hear a cry?

CASSIO Here, here! For heaven's sake, help me!

IAGO   What's the matter?
    [He moves toward Cassio.]

GRATIANO *[to Lodovico]* This is Othello's ancient, as I take it.

LODOVICO *[to Gratiano]* The same indeed, a very valiant fellow.

IAGO *[to Cassio]* What° are you here that cry so grievously?   *who*

CASSIO Iago? O, I am spoiled,° undone by villains!   *ruined*
55   Give me some help.

IAGO O me, Lieutenant! What villains have done this?

CASSIO I think that one of them is hereabout,
    And cannot make° away.   *get*

IAGO   O treacherous villains!
    [To Lodovico and Gratiano.] What are you there? Come in, and
60   give some help. *[They advance.]*

RODERIGO O, help me there!

CASSIO That's one of them.

IAGO   O murderous slave! O villain!
    [He stabs Roderigo.]

RODERIGO O damned Iago! O inhuman dog!

IAGO Kill men i' the dark?—Where be these bloody thieves?—
    How silent is this town!—Ho! Murder, murder!—
    [To Lodovico and Gratiano.]
65   What may you be? Are you of good or evil?

LODOVICO As you shall prove us, praise° us.   *appraise*

IAGO Signor Lodovico?

LODOVICO He, sir.

IAGO I cry you mercy.[1] Here's Cassio hurt by villains.

GRATIANO Cassio?

IAGO How is 't, brother?

CASSIO My leg is cut in two.

IAGO Marry, heaven forbid!
    Light, gentlemen! I'll bind it with my shirt.
    [He hands them the light and tends to Cassio's wound.]
    [Enter Bianca.]

BIANCA What is the matter, ho? Who is 't that cried?

---

1. I beg your pardon.

IAGO Who is 't that cried?

BIANCA   O my dear Cassio!
My sweet Cassio! O Cassio, Cassio, Cassio!

IAGO O notable strumpet! Cassio, may you suspect
Who they should be that have thus mangled you?

CASSIO No.

GRATIANO I am sorry to find you thus. I have been to seek you.

IAGO Lend me a garter. [*He applies a tourniquet.*] So.—O, for a chair,°   litter
To bear him easily hence!

BIANCA Alas, he faints! O Cassio, Cassio, Cassio!

IAGO Gentlemen all, I do suspect this trash
To be a party in this injury.—
Patience awhile, good Cassio.—Come, come;
Lend me a light. [*He shines the light on Roderigo.*]
Know we this face or no?

90   Alas, my friend and my dear countryman
Roderigo! No.—Yes, sure.—O heaven! Roderigo!

GRATIANO What, of Venice?

IAGO Even he, sir. Did you know him?

GRATIANO Know him? Ay.

IAGO Signor Gratiano? I cry your gentle° pardon.   noble
These bloody accidents° must excuse my manners   sudden events
That so neglected you.

GRATIANO   I am glad to see you.

IAGO How do you, Cassio? O, a chair, a chair!

GRATIANO Roderigo!

IAGO He, he, 'tis he. [*A litter is brought in.*] O, that's well said;² the chair.
Some good man bear him carefully from hence;
I'll fetch the General's surgeon. [*To Bianca.*] For you, mistress,
Save you your labor.³ He that lies slain here, Cassio,
Was my dear friend. What malice° was between you?   enmity

CASSIO None in the world, nor do I know the man.

IAGO [*to Bianca*] What, look you pale?—O, bear him out o' th' air.⁴
[*Cassio and Roderigo are borne off.*]
Stay you,⁵ good gentlemen.—Look you pale, mistress?—
Do you perceive the gastness° of her eye?—   terror
Nay, if you stare,⁶ shall hear more anon.—

110   Behold her well; I pray you, look upon her.
Do you see, gentlemen? Nay, guiltiness
Will speak, though tongues were out of use.
[*Enter Emilia.*]

EMILIA 'Las, what's the matter? What's the matter, husband?

IAGO Cassio hath here been set on in the dark

115   By Roderigo and fellows that are scaped.
He's almost slain, and Roderigo dead.

EMILIA Alas, good gentleman! Alas, good Cassio!

IAGO This is the fruits of whoring. Prithee, Emilia,

---

2. Well done.
3. Never you mind tending Cassio.
4. Fresh air was thought to be dangerous for a wound.

5. Lodovico and Gratiano are evidently about to leave.
6. Iago pretends to interpret Bianca's wild looks as an involuntary confession of guilt.

Go know° of Cassio where he supped tonight.   *learn*
120   [*To Bianca.*] What, do you shake at that?
BIANCA He supped at my house, but I therefore shake not.
IAGO O, did he so? I charge you go with me.
EMILIA O, fie upon thee, strumpet!
BIANCA I am no strumpet, but of life as honest°   *chaste*
125   As you that thus abuse me.
EMILIA As I? Faugh! Fie upon thee!
IAGO Kind gentlemen, let's go see poor Cassio dressed.[7]—
      Come, mistress, you must tell 's another tale.
      Emilia, run you to the citadel
130   And tell my lord and lady what hath happed.—
      Will you go on afore? [*Aside.*] This is the night
      That either makes me or fordoes° me quite.   [*Exeunt.*]   *ruins*

Scene 2

[*Location: A bedchamber in the citadel.*
Enter Othello with a light, and Desdemona in her bed.][8]
OTHELLO It is the cause,[9] it is the cause, my soul.
      Let me not name it to you, you chaste stars!
      It is the cause. Yet I'll not shed her blood,
      Nor scar that whiter skin of hers than snow,
5   And smooth as monumental alabaster.[1]
      Yet she must die, else she'll betray more men.
      Put out the light, and then put out the light.[2]
      If I quench thee, thou flaming minister,[3]
      I can again thy former light restore,
10   Should I repent me;° but once put out thy light,   *change my mind*
      Thou cunning'st pattern[4] of excelling nature,
      I know not where is that Promethean heat[5]
      That can thy light relume.° When I have plucked thy rose,   *rekindle*
      I cannot give it vital growth again;
15   It needs must wither. I'll smell thee on the tree.
      [*He kisses her.*]
      O balmy breath, that dost almost persuade
      Justice to break her sword! One more, one more.
      Be thus when thou art dead, and I will kill thee,
      And love thee after. One more, and that's the last.
      [*He kisses her.*]
20   So sweet was ne'er so fatal. I must weep,
      But they are cruel° tears. This sorrow's heavenly;   *unrelenting*
      It strikes where it doth love.[6] She wakes.
DESDEMONA Who's there? Othello?
OTHELLO Ay, Desdemona.

7. Cassio's wounds dressed.
8. Either the curtains are drawn back to reveal the bed in a recessed area backstage or the bed is "thrust out" onstage as the scene begins.
9. Cause of justice, the offense itself, which Othello must correct as an agent of justice.
1. Used in making tombs and funeral monuments.

2. The torch or lamp . . . Desdemona's life.
3. Torch or lamp that serves me.
4. You skillfully wrought perfect example.
5. Divine fire (alluding to the theft of fire from heaven by Prometheus).
6. Compare Hebrews 12.6: "For whom the Lord loveth he chasteneth."

DESDEMONA Will you come to bed, my lord?

OTHELLO Have you prayed tonight, Desdemon?

DESDEMONA Ay, my lord.

OTHELLO If you bethink yourself of any crime°   *sin*

    Unreconciled as yet to heaven and grace,

30   Solicit° for it straight.°   *pray/immediately*

DESDEMONA Alack, my lord, what may you mean by that?

OTHELLO Well, do it, and be brief. I will walk by.

    I would not kill thy unprepgrèd spirit.

    No, heaven forfend!° I would not kill thy soul.   *forbid*

DESDEMONA Talk you of killing?

OTHELLO   Ay, I do.

DESDEMONA   Then heaven

    Have mercy on me!

OTHELLO   Amen, with all my heart!

DESDEMONA If you say so, I hope you will not kill me.

OTHELLO Humh!

DESDEMONA And yet I fear you; for you're fatal then

40   When your eyes roll so. Why I should fear I know not,

    Since guiltiness I know not; but yet I feel I fear.

OTHELLO Think on thy sins.

DESDEMONA   They are loves I bear to you.[7]

OTHELLO Ay, and for that thou diest.

DESDEMONA That death's unnatural that kills for loving.

45   Alas, why gnaw you so your nether lip?

    Some bloody passion shakes your very frame.

    These are portents; but yet I hope, I hope,

    They do not point on[8] me.

OTHELLO Peace, and be still!

DESDEMONA I will so. What's the matter?

OTHELLO That handkerchief which I so loved and gave thee

    Thou gav'st to Cassio.

DESDEMONA   No, by my life and soul!

    Send for the man and ask him.

OTHELLO Sweet soul, take heed, take heed of perjury.

55   Thou art on thy deathbed.

DESDEMONA Ay, but not yet to die.

OTHELLO   Yes, presently.°   *immediately*

    Therefore confess thee freely of thy sin;

    For to deny each article with oath

    Cannot remove nor choke the strong conception[9]

60   That I do groan withal.[1] Thou art to die.

DESDEMONA Then Lord have mercy on me!

OTHELLO   I say, amen.

DESDEMONA And have you mercy too! I never did

    Offend° you in my life; never loved Cassio   *wrong*

    But with such general warranty° of heaven   *sanction*

---

7. If I sinned, it was in loving you more than my father or more than God.

8. Point at, predict what is to happen to.

9. Belief in your guilt. Also, plan in my mind.

1. Groan at in sorrow. Also, as in giving birth.

65   As I might love. I never gave him token.

OTHELLO By heaven, I saw my handkerchief in 's hand.
        O perjured woman! Thou dost stone° heart,   *harden*
        And makes me call what I intend to do
        A murder, which I thought a sacrifice.
        I saw the handkerchief.

DESDEMONA   He found it, then.
        I never gave it him. Send for him hither;
        Let him confess a truth.

OTHELLO   He hath confessed.

DESDEMONA What, my lord?

OTHELLO That he hath used thee.

DESDEMONA   How? Unlawfully?

OTHELLO   Ay.

DESDEMONA He will not say so.

OTHELLO   No, his mouth is stopped;
        Honest Iago hath ta'en order° for 't.   *taken measures*

DESDEMONA O, my fear interprets. What, is he dead?

OTHELLO Had all his hairs been lives, my great revenge
        Had stomach for them all.

DESDEMONA Alas, he is betrayed and I undone!   [*She weeps.*]

OTHELLO Out, strumpet! Weep'st thou for him to my face?

DESDEMONA O, banish me, my lord, but kill me not!

OTHELLO Down, strumpet!

DESDEMONA Kill me tomorrow; let me live tonight!

OTHELLO Nay, if you strive—

DESDEMONA But half an hour!

OTHELLO   Being done,[2] there is no pause.

DESDEMONA But while I say one prayer!

OTHELLO   It is too late. [*Smothers her.*]

EMILIA [*at the door*] My lord, my lord! What, ho! My lord, my lord!

OTHELLO What noise is this? Not dead? Not yet quite dead?

90   I that am cruel am yet merciful;
        I would not have thee linger in thy pain. [*He dispatches her.*]
        So, so.

EMILIA [*within*] What, ho! My lord, my lord!

OTHELLO   Who's there?

EMILIA [*within*] O, good my lord, I would speak a word with you!

OTHELLO Yes, 'tis Emilia.—By and by.—She's dead.
        'Tis like° she comes to speak of Cassio's death.—   *likely that*
        The noise was here.[3] Ha! No more moving?
        Still as the grave. Shall she come in? Were 't good?—
        I think she stirs again. No. What's best to do?

100   If she come in, she'll sure speak to my wife.
        My wife! My wife! What wife? I have no wife.
        O, insupportable! O heavy hour!
        Methinks it should be now a huge eclipse
        Of sun and moon, and that th' affrighted globe

---

2. Since justice has begun its relentless course.

3. The Folio's *high* is possible, suggesting that the commotion of the attack on Cassio was loud.

Should yawn[4] at alteration.[5]

EMILIA [*within*]   I do beseech you
That I may speak with you, O, good my lord!

OTHELLO I had forgot thee. O, come in, Emilia.—
Soft,° by and by. Let me the curtains draw.—   *wait a minute*
[*He closes the bed-curtains and opens the door.*]
Where art thou?
[*Enter Emilia.*]
                                   What's the matter with thee now?

EMILIA O, my good lord, yonder's foul murders done!

OTHELLO What, now?

EMILIA But now, my lord.

OTHELLO It is the very error° of the moon;   *aberration, irregularity*
She comes more nearer earth than she was wont,
115   And makes men mad.

EMILIA Cassio, my lord, hath killed a young Venetian
Called Roderigo.

OTHELLO   Roderigo killed?
And Cassio killed?

EMILIA   No, Cassio is not killed.

OTHELLO Not Cassio killed? Then murder's out of tune,
120   And sweet revenge grows harsh.

DESDEMONA O, falsely, falsely murdered!

EMILIA O Lord, what cry is that?

OTHELLO That? What?

EMILIA Out[6] and alas, that was my lady's voice.
[*She opens the bed-curtains.*]
125   Help, help, ho, help! O lady, speak again!
Sweet Desdemona! O sweet mistress, speak!

DESDEMONA A guiltless death I die.

EMILIA O, who hath done this deed?

DESDEMONA Nobody; I myself. Farewell.
130   Commend me to my kind lord. O, farewell! [*She dies.*]

OTHELLO Why, how should she be murdered?

EMILIA   Alas, who knows?

OTHELLO You heard her say herself it was not I.

EMILIA She said so. I must needs report the truth.

OTHELLO She's like a liar gone to burning hell!
135   'Twas I that killed her.

EMILIA   O, the more angel she,
And you the blacker devil!

OTHELLO She turned to folly,[7] and she was a whore.

EMILIA Thou dost belie° her, and thou art a devil.   *slander*

OTHELLO She was false as water.

4. Gape in amazement, i.e., move in an earthquake. (According to Pliny, earthquakes often happen during eclipses.)
5. At these cataclysmic events in nature, well suited to express the horror of Desdemona's death.
6. A cry of dismay, intensifying *alas*.
7. I.e., wantonness, fleshly sin.

EMILIA   Thou art rash as fire to say
140   That she was false. O, she was heavenly true!
OTHELLO Cassio did top her. Ask thy husband else.[8]
        O, I were damned beneath all depth in hell
        But that I did proceed upon just grounds
        To this extremity. Thy husband knew it all.
EMILIA My husband?
OTHELLO   Thy husband.
EMILIA   That she was false to wedlock?
OTHELLO Ay, with Cassio. Nay, had she been true,
        If heaven would make me such another world
        Of one entire and perfect chrysolite,°   *precious topaz*
        I'd not have sold her for it.
EMILIA My husband?
OTHELLO Ay, 'twas he that told me on her first.
        An honest man he is, and hates the slime
        That sticks on filthy deeds.
EMILIA My husband?
OTHELLO What needs this iterance,° woman? I say thy husband.   *repetition*
EMILIA O mistress, villainy hath made mocks° with love!   *made sport*
        My husband say she was false?
OTHELLO   He, woman;
        I say thy husband. Dost understand the word?
        My friend, thy husband, honest, honest Iago.
EMILIA If he say so, may his pernicious soul
        Rot half a grain a day! He lies to th' heart.
        She was too fond of her most filthy bargain.
OTHELLO Ha? [*He draws.*]
EMILIA Do thy worst!
        This deed of thine is no more worthy heaven
        Than thou wast worthy her.
OTHELLO   Peace, you were best.[9]
EMILIA Thou hast not half that power to do me harm
        As I have to be hurt.° O gull!° O dolt!   *to endure hurt / dupe*
        As ignorant as dirt! Thou hast done a deed—
170   I care not for thy sword; I'll make thee known,
        Though I lost twenty lives.—Help! Help, ho, help!
        The Moor hath killed my mistress! Murder, murder!
        [*Enter Montano, Gratiano, and Iago.*]
MONTANO What is the matter? How now, General?
EMILIA O, are you come, Iago? You have done well,
175   That men must lay their murders on your neck.
GRATIANO What is the matter?
EMILIA [*to Iago*]
        Disprove this villain, if thou be'st a man.
        He says thou toldst him that his wife was false.
        I know thou didst not; thou'rt not such a villain.
180   Speak, for my heart is full.

---

8. I.e., if you don't believe me.   9. It would be best for you.

IAGO I told him what I thought, and told no more
    Than what he found himself was apt° and true.   *plausible*
EMILIA But did you ever tell him she was false?
IAGO I did.
EMILIA You told a lie, an odious, damnèd lie!
    Upon my soul, a lie, a wicked lie.
    She false with Cassio? Did you say with Cassio?
IAGO With Cassio, mistress. Go to, charm[1] your tongue.
EMILIA I will not charm my tongue; I am bound to speak.
190   My mistress here lies murdered in her bed—
ALL O heavens forfend!
EMILIA And your reports have set the murder on.
OTHELLO Nay, stare not, masters. It is true indeed.
GRATIANO 'Tis a strange truth.
MONTANO O monstrous act!
EMILIA   Villainy, villainy, villainy!
    I think upon 't—I think I smell 't! O villainy!
    I thought so then[2]—I'll kill myself for grief—
    O villainy, villainy!
IAGO What, are you mad? I charge you, get you home.
EMILIA Good gentlemen, let me have leave to speak.
    'Tis proper I obey him, but not now.
    Perchance, Iago, I will ne'er go home.
OTHELLO O! O! O! [*Othello falls on the bed.*][3]
EMILIA Nay, lay thee down and roar,
205   For thou hast killed the sweetest innocent
    That e'er did lift up eye.[4]
OTHELLO [*rising*]   O, she was foul!
    I scarce did know you, uncle. There lies your niece,
    Whose breath indeed these hands have newly stopped.
    I know this act shows° horrible and grim.   *looks*
GRATIANO Poor Desdemon! I am glad thy father's dead.
    Thy match was mortal to him, and pure grief
    Shore his old thread[5] in twain. Did he live now,
    This sight would make him do a desperate turn,°   *deed*
    Yea, curse his better angel from his side,
215   And fall to reprobance.[6]
OTHELLO 'Tis pitiful. But yet Iago knows
    That she with Cassio hath the act of shame
    A thousand times committed. Cassio confessed it;
    And she did gratify° his amorous works   *reward*
220   With that recognizance° and pledge of love   *token*
    Which I first gave her. I saw it in his hand;
    It was a handkerchief, an antique token
    My father gave my mother.
EMILIA O God! O heavenly God!
IAGO Zounds, hold your peace.

---

1. Keep silent (as though by a magic spell).
2. Perhaps in 3.3 and 4.2.
3. This direction is from the Quarto.
4. Lift her eyes to heaven.

5. Sheared the thread of his old age (as Atropos, one of the three Fates, was thought to do).
6. Damnation, i.e., suicide.

EMILIA   'Twill out, 'twill out! I peace?
   No, I will speak as liberal as the north.[7]
   Let heaven and men and devils, let them all,
   All, all, cry shame against me, yet I'll speak.
IAGO Be wise, and get you home.
EMILIA   I will not.
   [*Iago threatens Emilia.*]
GRATIANO   Fie,
230   Your sword upon a woman?
EMILIA O thou dull Moor! That handkerchief thou speak'st of
   I found by fortune and did give my husband;
   For often, with a solemn earnestness,
   More than indeed belonged° to such a trifle,   *was appropriate*
235   He begged of me to steal 't.
IAGO   Villainous whore!
EMILIA She give it Cassio? No, alas! I found it,
   And I did give 't my husband.
IAGO   Filth, thou liest!
EMILIA By heaven, I do not, I do not, gentlemen.
   O murderous coxcomb![8] What should such a fool
240   Do with so good a wife?
OTHELLO   Are there no stones[9] in heaven
   But what serves for the thunder?—Precious° villain!   *utter*
   [*He runs at Iago; Montano disarms Othello. Iago, from behind, stabs Emilia.*][1]
GRATIANO The woman falls! Sure he hath killed his wife.
EMILIA Ay, ay. O, lay me by my mistress' side.

                                   [*Exit Iago.*]

GRATIANO He's gone, but his wife's killed.
MONTANO 'Tis a notorious villain. Take you this weapon,
   Which I have here recovered from the Moor.
   Come, guard the door without. Let him not pass,
   But kill him rather. I'll after that same villain,
   For 'tis a damnèd slave.
   [*Exit with all but Othello and Emilia, who has been laid by Desdemona's side.*]
OTHELLO   I am not valiant neither,
250   But every puny whipster[2] gets my sword.
   But why should honor[3] outlive honesty?°   *integrity*
   Let it go all.
EMILIA   What did thy song bode, lady?
   Hark, canst thou hear me? I will play the swan,
   And die in music. [*She sings.*] "Willow, willow, willow."
255   Moor, she was chaste. She loved thee, cruel Moor.
   So come my soul to bliss as I speak true.
   So speaking as I think, alas, I die. [*She dies.*]
OTHELLO I have another weapon in this chamber;

---

7. Freely as the north wind (blows).
8. Fool (addressed to Othello).
9. Bolts, such as those used for thunderbolts.
1. The Quarto text reads, "The Moor runs at Iago. Iago kills his wife." The Quarto also specifies the exit of Iago below.

2. Contemptible fellow (one who is always ready to whip out his sword).
3. The bravery for which one enjoys a soldier's reputation.

It was a sword of Spain, the ice-brook's temper[4]—
260　O, here it is. [*He finds a sword.*] Uncle, I must come forth.
GRATIANO [*within*] If thou attempt it, it will cost thee dear.
　　　Thou hast no weapon, and perforce must suffer.
OTHELLO Look in upon me then and speak with me,
　　　Or, naked° as I am, I will assault thee.　　　　　　　　　　　　*unarmed*
　　　[*Enter Gratiano.*]
GRATIANO What is the matter?
OTHELLO　　　　　　　　　　Behold, I have a weapon;
　　　A better never did itself sustain
　　　Upon a soldier's thigh. I have seen the day
　　　That, with this little arm and this good sword,
　　　I have made my way through more impediments
270　Than twenty times your stop.[5] But O, vain boast!
　　　Who can control his fate? 'Tis not so now.
　　　Be not afraid, though you do see me weaponed;
　　　Here is my journey's end, here is my butt[6]
　　　And very seamark[7] of my utmost sail.
　　　[*Gratiano steps back.*]
275　Do you go back dismayed? 'Tis a lost° fear;　　　　　　　　　　*wasted*
　　　Man but a rush[8] against Othello's breast
　　　And he retires. Where should Othello go?
　　　[*He turns to Desdemona.*]
　　　Now, how dost thou look now? O ill-starred wench!
　　　Pale as thy smock! When we shall meet at compt,°　　　　　*Judgment Day*
280　This look of thine will hurl my soul from heaven,
　　　And fiends will snatch at it. Cold, cold, my girl?
　　　Even like thy chastity. O cursèd, cursèd slave![9]
　　　Whip me, ye devils,
　　　From the possession of this heavenly sight!
285　Blow me about in winds! Roast me in sulfur!
　　　Wash me in steep-down gulfs of liquid fire!
　　　O Desdemon! Dead, Desdemon! Dead! O! O!
　　　[*Enter Lodovico, Cassio (carried in a litter),*[1] *Montano, and Iago (prisoner), with officers.*]
LODOVICO Where is this rash and most unfortunate man?
OTHELLO That's he that was Othello. Here I am.
LODOVICO Where is that viper? Bring the villain forth.
　　　[*Iago is led forward.*]
OTHELLO I look down towards his feet;[2] but that's a fable.
　　　If that thou be'st a devil, I cannot kill thee.
　　　[*He wounds Iago.*]
LODOVICO Wrench his sword from him.　　[*Othello is disarmed.*]
IAGO　　　　　　　　　　　　　I bleed, sir, but not killed.
OTHELLO I am not sorry neither. I'd have thee live,
295　For in my sense[3] 'tis happiness to die.

---

4. Tempered in ice-cold water.
5. Power (to stop).
6. Goal, limit (an archery term).
7. Beacon (marking his destination or limit).
8. Wield no more than a reed.

9. Othello himself.
1. The Quarto specifies that Cassio is "in a chair."
2. I.e., to see if they are cloven, as the devil's are fabled to be.
3. To one who feels as I do.

LODOVICO O thou Othello, that was once so good,
 Fall'n in the practice[4] of a cursèd slave,°   *villain*
 What shall be said to thee?
OTHELLO   Why, anything.
 An honorable murderer, if you will,
300 For naught I did in hate, but all in honor.
LODOVICO This wretch hath part confessed his villainy.
 Did you and he consent° in Cassio's death?   *agree*
OTHELLO Ay.
CASSIO Dear General, I never gave you cause.
OTHELLO I do believe it, and I ask your pardon.
 Will you, I pray, demand that demi-devil
 Why he hath thus ensnared my soul and body?
IAGO Demand me nothing. What you know, you know.
 From this time forth I never will speak word.
LODOVICO What, not to pray?
GRATIANO Torments° will ope your lips.   *torture*
OTHELLO Well, thou dost best.
LODOVICO Sir, you shall understand what hath befall'n,
 Which, as I think, you know not. Here is a letter
315 Found in the pocket of the slain Roderigo;
 And here another. [*He produces letters.*] The one of them imports
 The death of Cassio, to be undertook
 By Roderigo.
OTHELLO O villain!
CASSIO   Most heathenish and most gross!°   *monstrous*
LODOVICO [*showing another paper*] Now here's another discontented paper
 Found in his pocket too. And this, it seems,
 Roderigo meant t' have sent this damnèd villain;
 But that belike° Iago in the interim   *most likely*
 Came in and satisfied him.[5]
OTHELLO O thou pernicious caitiff!—
 How came you, Cassio, by that handkerchief
 That was my wife's?
CASSIO   I found it in my chamber;
 And he himself confessed but even now
 That there he dropped it for a special purpose
330 Which wrought to his desire.[6]
OTHELLO   O fool, fool, fool!
CASSIO There is besides in Roderigo's letter
 How he upbraids Iago, that he made him
 Brave° me upon the watch, whereon it came[7]   *defy*
 That I was cast;° and even but now he spake,   *dismissed*
335 After long seeming dead, Iago hurt him,
 Iago set him on.
LODOVICO [*to Othello*] You must forsake this room and go with us.
 Your power and your command is taken off,°   *taken away*
 And Cassio rules in Cyprus. For this slave,

---

4. Through the plotting, into the snare.
5. Interposed and gave him satisfactory explanation.
6. Worked out as he wished, fitted in with his plan.
7. Whereof it came about.

340   If there be any cunning cruelty
     That can torment him much and hold him long,[8]
     It shall be his. You shall close prisoner rest°   *remain*
     Till that the nature of your fault be known
     To the Venetian state.—Come, bring away.
OTHELLO Soft you;° a word or two before you go.   *one moment*
     I have done the state some service, and they know't.
     No more of that. I pray you, in your letters,
     When you shall these unlucky° deeds relate,   *unfortunate*
     Speak of me as I am; nothing extenuate,
350   Nor set down aught in malice. Then must you speak
     Of one that loved not wisely but too well;
     Of one not easily jealous but, being wrought,[9]
     Perplexed° in the extreme; of one whose hand,   *distraught*
     Like the base Indian,[1] threw a pearl away
355   Richer than all his tribe; of one whose subdued[2] eyes,
     Albeit unusèd to the melting mood,
     Drops tears as fast as the Arabian trees
     Their medicinable gum.° Set you down this;   *myrrh*
     And say besides that in Aleppo once,
360   Where a malignant and a turbaned Turk
     Beat a Venetian and traduced the state,
     I took by th' throat the circumcisèd dog
     And smote him, thus. [*He stabs himself.*][3]
LODOVICO O bloody period!°   *end, conclusion*
GRATIANO   All that is spoke is marred.
OTHELLO I kissed thee ere I killed thee. No way but this,
     Killing myself, to die upon a kiss.
     [*He kisses Desdemona and dies.*]
CASSIO This did I fear, but thought he had no weapon;
     For he was great of heart.
LODOVICO [*to Iago*]   O Spartan dog,[4]
     More fell° than anguish, hunger, or the sea!   *cruel*
370   Look on the tragic loading of this bed.
     This is thy work. The object poisons sight;
     Let it be hid.[5] Gratiano, keep° the house,   *remain in*
     [*The bed curtains are drawn*]
     And seize upon the fortunes of the Moor,
     For they succeed on you.[6] [*To Cassio.*] To you, Lord Governor,
375   Remains the censure° of this hellish villain,   *sentencing*
     The time, the place, the torture. O, enforce it!
     Myself will straight aboard, and to the state
     This heavy act with heavy heart relate.   [*Exeunt.*]

8. Keep him alive a long time (during his torture).
9. Worked upon, worked into a frenzy.
1. This reading from the Quarto pictures an ignorant savage who cannot recognize the value of a precious jewel. The Folio reading, *Iudean* or *Judean*, i.e., infidel or disbeliever, may refer to Herod, who slew Mariam in a fit of jealousy, or to Judas Iscariot, the betrayer of Christ.

2. I.e., overcome by grief.
3. This direction is in the Quarto text.
4. Spartan dogs were noted for their savagery and silence.
5. I.e., draw the bed curtains. (No stage direction specifies that the dead are to be carried offstage at the end of the play.)
6. Take legal possession of Othello's property, which passes as though by inheritance to you.

OTHELLO IN CONTEXT
Ethnography in the Literature of Travel and Colonization

What would Shakespeare's audience have thought of the description of Othello as "the Moor"? Both the play itself and the literature on Africa that was available in English in the early modern period show that "Moor" was a synonym for "Negro." Two kinds of accounts of the Moors and North Africans were available to Shakespeare's audience: a kind of mythical travel literature inherited from such classical authors as Herodotus, Pliny, and Diodorus Siculus and more recent eyewitness accounts by seamen and traders who had traveled to Africa. While there were still many completely fantastical notions about non-European peoples such as Moors, Africans, and Turks, Leo Africanus's *History of Africa* enlightened sixteenth- and seventeenth-century European and English audiences about the peoples and customs of Africa.

This kind of writing, describing the physical features and social customs of a people, is called ethnography. The word comes from two Greek roots: *ethnos* ("nation") and *graphia* ("writing"). Rather than stressing the history of a people through time, ethnography reads as a timeless description of a people in space. Not surprisingly, ethnography was deployed mainly to describe cultural others, from the Scythians (the wild Northern Europeans of Book Four of Herodotus' *Histories*) to the Ethiopes of Philemon Holland's *Description of Africa*. Even within the British Isles, Spenser and other authors portrayed the Irish as barbarians because their language, customs, and religion were different from those of the English, who settled as colonists in Ireland.

Ethnography was also used to describe the people of the Caribbean. Columbus's description of the Caribes, or Canibes, gave rise to the word "cannibal." At the same time that Europeans traveled to and colonized the Americas, they also embarked on trade and took slaves in Africa. With the explorations of Portuguese navigators of the African coast came the exploitation of Africans as slaves in the plantations of the Caribbean. The British brought the first African slaves to Virginia in 1619. Leo Africanus himself was taken as a slave by Italian pirates. He was a learned man and was able to win his freedom through conversion. His accounts and those of eyewitnesses began to change the view of Africa as a place of such fantastical creatures as "men whose heads / Do grow beneath their shoulders" (*Othello* 1.3.145–46) to a place of prosperous kings and traders.

Peter Martyr

The Italian humanist Peter Martyr (Pietro Martire d'Anghiera, 1457?–1526) came to the court of Isabella and Ferdinand of Spain some time after 1480. Martyr became part of an intellectual movement that celebrated the consolidation of the monarchy's power over Spain and their conquests in the Americas. Although Martyr deplored the interventions of the French into Italy, he celebrated Spanish exploration and colonization around the world in *De Orbe Novo Decades* (1530). The style of this book has something in common with the tradition of travel writing and ethnography going back to Book 4 of Herodotus's *Histories* as well as Italian humanist letter writing as a method of disseminating information. Martyr himself never traveled beyond Europe, basing his accounts upon the reports of eyewitnesses.

Like Martyr, his English translator Richard Eden (1521?–1576) had a humanist education. Studying at Cambridge with Sir Thomas Smith prepared Eden for a life in government, in which he used his scholarship. He served as private secretary to Sir William Cecil in 1552 and gained a position in the English treasury of the Prince of Spain in 1554.

Eden added two eyewitness accounts of English voyages to Africa to his English translation of Martyr's work, *Decades of the New World* (1555). Although two papal bulls had given a monopoly over the West African coast to the Portuguese, two English seamen defied the ban: Thomas Windham voyaged to Guinea in 1553 and John Lok to Mina

Inigo Jones. *A Negro Nymph,* from the costume designs for Ben Jonson's *Masque of Blackness,* 1605. A designer of sets and costumes, Inigo Jones collaborated with Ben Jonson on many of his masques. In his notes on *The Masque of Blackness,* Jonson mentions Leo Africanus as a source. The ladies of the court painted their faces black to play the Negro Nymphs—among them Lady Mary Wroth, who would deploy metaphors of darkness and night to great effect in her poetry. Jones was also patronized by Lady Wroth's lover, William Herbert, the Earl of Pembroke, who financed the artist's journey to Italy where he studied Roman ruins and Palladio's buildings and writing on architecture. Jones became the first great English architect, designing such buildings as the earliest part of the Greenwich Hospital (1635) and the Church of Saint Paul, Covent Garden, with its square (1631–1638). In 1619 James I commissioned Jones to design the Banqueting House at Whitehall, the first English building to embody Palladian features such as rows of columns and symmetrical classical proportions. (See the engraving of the execution of Charles I before Jones's Banqueting House, page 728.)

(Elmina) in 1554–1555. The account of Windham's voyage is the source for the first excerpt here, a description of the court of Benin, a kingdom in what is now Nigeria. Eden introduces these two accounts with his own "brief description of Africa" and interjects his comments throughout the eyewitness reports, as in the next excerpted passage taken from "Second Voyage." Eden mixes his informants' observations with fanciful fables about the mythical Christian king of Ethiopia, Preseter John, derived from medieval legend, and outlandish and bizarre ethnographic fictions, from Pliny's *Historia Naturalis.* Eden's accounts of Africa were later republished in Richard Haklyut's monumental *Principal Navigations* (1589).

from *Decades of the New World*

[THE COURT OF BENIN]

When they came they were brought with a great company to the presence of the king [of Benin], who being a black Moor[1] (although not so black as the rest) sat in a great huge hall, long and wide, the walls made of earth without windows, the roof of thin boards, open in sundry places, like unto louvers to let in the air.

And here to speak of the great reverence they give to their king being such that if we would give as much to our Savior Jesus Christ, we should remove from our heads many plagues which we daily deserve for our contempt and impiety.
* * *

And now to speak somewhat of the communication that was between the king and our men, you shall first understand that he himself could speak the Portugal tongue, which he had learned of a child. Therefore after that he had commanded our men to stand up and demanded of them the cause of their coming into that country, they answered by Pinteado[2] that they were merchants traveling into those parts for the commodities of his country for exchange of wares which they had brought from their countries, being such as should be no less commodious for him and his people.

[THE PEOPLE OF AFRICA]

Now therefore I will speak somewhat of the people and their manners and manner of living, with also another brief description of Africa. It is to understand that the people which now inhabit the regions of the coast of Guinea, and the mid parts of Africa, as Libya the inner, and Nubia,[3] with diverse other great and large regions about the same, were in old time called Ethiopes and Nigrite, which we now call Moors, Moorens, or Negros, a people of beastly living, without a god, law, religion, or commonwealth, and so scorched and vexed with the heat of the sun, that in many places they curse it when it riseth.[4] * * *

But to speak somewhat more of Ethiopia. Although there are many nations of people so named, yet is Ethiopia chiefly divided into two parts, whereof the one is called Ethiopia under Egypt, a great and rich region. To this pertaineth the Island of Meroe, embraced round about with the streams of the river Nilus.[5] In this island women reigned in old time. Josephus writeth, that it was sometime

1. Inhabitants of northwestern Africa (Morocco and Algeria), who were Islamic. From the Middle Ages to the 17th century, Europeans thought of the Moors primarily as blacks, and so the word became a synonym for Negro; hence the term "Blackamoor."
2. Captain Antonianes Pinteado was a Portuguese mariner and guide whom Windham used as translator. Once a member of the King of Portugal's household, Pinteado was "forced by poverty" into England. Eden portrays Pinteado as "a man worthy to serve any prince most vilely used." Both Windham and the crew derisively called him "a Jew," and after Windham's death, Pinteado was made a prisoner and died on board ship.
3. Nubia is in northeastern Africa. At its height the kingdom stretched from the first cataract of the Nile in Egypt to Khartoum in Sudan. During the time of the Roman Emperor Diocletian, the Negro tribe the Nobatae settled in Nubia. The Nubian kingdom was converted to Christianity in the 6th century. After the Moslems moved into Nubia in 1366, Nubia was divided into smaller states.
4. Many Greek and Roman as well as early modern authors believed that Africans had black skin because of the intense heat of the sun. Sir Thomas Browne was one of the first to show this "common opinion" was an "error" in *Pseudodoxia Epidemica* (1646); see 6.10: "Of the Blackness of Negroes."
5. When the Nubians were expelled from Egypt in the 7th century B.C., they moved their capital to Meroe, which the Ethiopians conquered in A.D. 350. The site of ancient pyramids, Meroe, is on the Nile in Northern Sudan.

called Saba, and that the queen of Saba came from thence to Jerusalem to hear the wisdom of Solomon.[6] From hence toward the East reigneth the said Christian Emperor Prester John,[7] whom some call Papa Johannes, and others say that he is called Pean Juan (that is) great John, whose empire reacheth far beyond Nilus and is extended to the coasts of the Red Sea and Indian Sea. The middle of the region is almost in the 66 degrees of longitude, and 12 degrees of latitude. About this region inhabit the people called Clodii, Risophagi, Babilonii, Axiunite, Mosili, and Molibe. After these is the region called Trogloditica, whose inhabitants dwell in caves and dens, for these are their houses, and the flesh of serpents their meat, as writeth Pliny and Diodorus Siculus.[8] They have no speech, but rather a grinning and chattering. There are also people without heads, called Blemines, having their eyes and mouth in their breast. Likewise Strucophagi, and naked Ganphasantes; Satyrs also, which have nothing of men but only shape. Moreover Oripei, great hunters. Mennones also, and the region of Smyrnophara, which bringeth forth myrrh. After these is the region of Azania, in the which many elephants are found. A great part of the other regions of Africa that are beyond the equinoctial line, are now ascribed to the kingdom of Melinde,[9] whose inhabitants are accustomed to traffic with the nations of Arabie, and their kind is joined in friendship with the king of Portugal, and payeth tribute to Prester John.

The other Ethiope, called Ethiopia Interior (that is) the inner Ethiope, is not yet known for the greatness thereof, but only by the seacoasts. Yet is it described in this manner. First from the equinoctial toward the south is a great region of Ethiopians, which bringeth forth white elephants, tigers, and the beasts called Rhinocerontes. Also a region that bringeth forth plenty of cinnamon, lying between the branches of Nilus. Also the kingdom of Habech or Habassia,[1] a region of Christian men, lying both on this side and beyond Nilus. Here are also the Ethiopians, called Ichthiophagi (that is) such as live only by fish, and were sometimes subdued by the wars of great Alexander. Furthermore the Ethiopians calleth Rhapsii, and Anthropophagi, that are accustomed to man's flesh, inhabit the regions near unto the mountains called Montes Lunae (that is) the Mountains of the Moon.[2] Gazatia is under the Tropic of Capricorn.[3] After this followeth the front of Africa, the Cape of Buena Speranza, or Caput Bonae Spei (that is) the Cape of Good Hope,[4] by the which they pass that sail from Spain to Calicut. But by what names the capes and gulfs are called, for as much as the same are in every globe and card, it were here superfluous to rehearse them.

6. For the visit of the Queen of Sheba (Saba) to Solomon, see 1 Kings 10. See also *Antiquities of the Jews* by the Jewish historian Flavius Josephus (37–c. 95).
7. The medieval legend of Prester John placed this Christian king in either Asia or Africa. Marco Polo said that Prester John ruled over the Tartars, and some European writers thought of him as King of a Christian kingdom in either Ethiopia or India.
8. For Pliny, see *The History of the World* below. Diodorus Siculus (d. 21 B.C.) was a Sicilian author of a world history, including Ethiopia and North Africa, which is today considered unreliable.
9. Said to be in Arabia, 90 miles from Persia (Introduc-

tion to Martyr's *Decades*).
1. Possibly Abyssinia, another name for Ethiopia. In the 4th century the king of Northern Ethiopia was converted to Coptic Christianity, but later, in 451, the Alexandrian patriarch refused to recognize the Ethopian Christians as part of the Church. They believe that Christ has one nature in which his humanity is subsumed under his divinity.
2. This fantastical passage comes from Pliny.
3. The Southern Tropic.
4. The southern tip of Africa, around which the Portuguese sailed to India.

Pliny the Elder
from *The History of the World*[1]

All Ethiopia in general was in old time called Aetheria, afterwards Atlantia, and finally of Vulcan's son Aethops, it took the name Ethiopia. No wonder it is, that about the coasts thereof there be found both men and beasts of strange and monstrous shapes, considering the agility of the sun's fiery heat, so strong and powerful in those countries, which is able to frame bodies artificially of sundry proportions, and to imprint and grave[2] in them diverse forms. Certes, reported it is, that far within the country eastward there are a kind of people without any nose at all on their face, having their visage all plain and flat. Others again without any upper lip, and some tongueless. Moreover, there is a kind of them that want a mouth, framed apart from their nostrils, and at one and the same hole, and no more, taketh in breath, receiveth drink by drawing it in with an oaten straw; yea, and after the same manner feed themselves with the grains of oats, growing of their own accord without man's labor and tillage, for their only food. And others there be, who instead of speech and words, make signs, as well with nodding their heads, as moving their other members. There are also among them, that before the time of Ptolomaeus Lathyrus king of Egypt,[3] knew no use at all of fire.

Furthermore, writers there be, who have reported, that in the country near unto the mires and marshes from whence Nilus issueth, there inhabit those little dwarves called Pygmies * * * But then he [Dalion, the historian] telleth fabulous and incredible tales of those countries. Namely, that westward there are people called Nigroi, whose king hath but one eye, and that in the midst of his forehead. Also he talketh of the Agriophagi, who live most of panthers and lions flesh. Likewise of the Pomphagi, who eat all things whatsoever. Moreover, of the Anthopophagi, that feed on man's flesh. Furthermore, of the Cynamolgi,[4] who have heads like dogs. Over and besides, the Artabatites who wander and go up and down in the forests like four-footed savage beasts. Beyond whom, as he saith, be the Hesperioi and Perorsi, who, as we said before, were planted in the confines of Mauritania. In certain parts also of Ethiopia the people live off locusts only, which they powder with salt and hang up in smoke to harden, for their yearly provision, and these live not above 40 years at the most.

Leo Africanus

Born in Moorish Granada in the late 1480s and educated in Fez, to which his Moslem family fled in 1497, Al Hassan ibn Mohammed Al-Wezaz, Al-Fasi (Leo Africanus, 1488?–1552) was the first to write accurately about the interior of Africa. Captured by Italian pirates in the Mediterranean, he was at first enslaved and then presented to Pope Leo X, who freed him once he had converted to Christianity. In Rome, Leo Africanus learned Latin and taught Arabic. He wrote his history of Africa in 1526, but it was published in Venice only in 1550, when, according to one contemporary, Leo was living in Tunis, where he returned to his Moslem faith.

1. Pliny the Elder (Caius Plinius Secundus, A.D. 23–79) was a Roman naturalist from Cisalpine Gaul. His sole remaining work, the *Historia Naturalis*, is an encyclopedia of natural science, divided into 37 books, dealing with everything from the nature of the universe to geography, anthropology, and a history of the arts. Like the Greek historian Herodotus, Pliny knew more about Egypt than he did about the rest of Africa and had to rely on stories and legends for his accounts. The European view of Africa and Africans as wild, exotic, and unnatural derives from such accounts as the following from Book 6 of *The History of the World* (1601), the English translation of Pliny by Philemon Holland. This passage was Shakespeare's source for Othello's description of the "Anthropophagi" (man-eaters) in Othello 1.3.144–46.
2. Engrave.
3. Ptolomeus Lathyrus (d. 81 B.C.), King of Ancient Egypt of the Macedonian dynasty.
4. Dog-milkers.

Encouraged by Richard Haklyut, who called Leo's work "the very best," John Pory first translated it into English as *A Geographical History of Africa* in 1600. Leo's history, which first appeared in Italian, was already known in England through Latin and French editions. Sir Thomas Smith owned a French translation, and Ben Jonson mentions Leo's work as a source for his *Masque of Blackness*. According to Lois Whitney and Eldred Jones, strong circumstantial evidence suggests that Shakespeare knew Leo's *Geographical History* and that it provided the background material for references to Africa in *Othello* and *Antony and Cleopatra*.

Pory prefaced his translation with Leo's biography, excerpted here, which makes for fascinating reading. There are some parallels between Leo's life and Othello's. A North African Moor, Leo had visited many parts of Africa but lived much of his life in Italy. Leo was not only a scholar and traveler but also a soldier; as Pory relates, Leo "did . . . personally serve king Mahumet of Fez in his wars." Like Leo who often recited poems and stories, Othello told his "travel's history." Both Leo and many of the African kingdoms that he describes emerge from his work as civilized, learned, and prosperous in contrast to the stereotyped ethnographies, which had portrayed Africans as barbarous, ignorant, and poor. While Leo's account of Africa was well known to Shakespeare's generation and even the generation that followed, subsequent scholarship chose either to misrepresent it, as in Peter Heylyn's highly selective choice of uncomplimentary passages, or to ignore it, as in Samuel Coleridge's false assertion that "at that time . . . negroes were not known except as slaves."

from *The History and Description of Africa*

from JOHN PORY'S PREFACE

Give me leave (gentle readers) if not to present unto your knowledge, because some perhaps may as well be informed as myself; yet, to call to your remembrance, some few particulars, concerning this geographical history and John Leo the author thereof.

Who albeit by birth a Moor, and by religion for many years a Mahumetan; yet if you consider his parentage, wit, education, learning, employments, travels, and his conversion to Christianity, you shall find him not altogether unfit to undertake such an enterprise, not unworthy to be regarded.

First therefore his parentage seemeth not to have been ignoble, seeing (as in his second book himself testifieth) an uncle of his was so honorable a person and so excellent an orator and poet, that he was sent as a principal ambassador, from the king of Fez to the king of Tombuto.[1]

And whether this our author were born at Granada in Spain (as it is most likely) or in some part of Africa,[2] certain it is, that in natural sharpness and vivacity of wit, he most lively resembled those great and classical authors, Pomponius Mela, Justinus Historicus, Columella, Seneca, Quintilian, Orosius, Prudentius, Martial, Juvenal, Avicen, etc., reputed all for Spanish writers, as likewise Terentius Afer, Tertullian, Saint Augustine, Victor, Optatus, etc. known to be writers of Africa.[3] But amongst great variety which are to be found in the process of this notable discourse, I will here

---

1. Timbuktu, near the Niger, with the Sahara to the north. Settled in 1087, Timbuktu was a center for trade and Moslem culture.
2. Pory's hesitation is due to a passage in the Latin translation (Antwerp 1556) that can be translated as "Africa, unto which country I stand indebted for my birth." But in the original Italian edition, this passage simply states that Africa

was his "nurse," where he spent the early part of his life.
3. Pomponius Mela . . . Juvenal: Roman historians and rhetoricians; Avicen: the Arabic translator of Aristotle; Terentius Afer: a Roman writer of comedies, born in Carthage; Tertullian, Saint Augustine: the Church Fathers of late antiquity; Victorinus: a Neoplatonist convert to Christianity.

lay before your view our only pattern of his surpassing wit. In his second book therefore, if you peruse the description of Mount Teneves, you shall there find the learned and sweet Arabian verses of John Leo, not being then fully sixteen years of age, so highly esteemed by the prince of the same mountain that in recompense thereof, after bountiful entertainment, he dismissed him with gifts of great value.

Neither wanted he the best education that all Barbary could afford. For being even from his tender years trained up at the University of Fez, in grammar, poetry, rhetoric, philosophy, history, Cabala, astronomy, and other ingenuous sciences,[4] and having so great acquaintance and conversation in the king's court, how could he choose but prove in his kind a most accomplished and absolute man? So as I may justly say (if the comparison be tolerable) that as Moses was learned in all the wisdom of the Egyptians, so likewise was Leo, in that of the Arabians and Moors.

And that he was not meanly, but extraordinarily learned; let me keep silence, that the admirable fruits of his rare learning and this geographical history among the rest may bear record. Besides which, he wrote an Arabian grammar, highly commended by a great linguist of Italy who had the sight and examination thereof, as likewise a book of the lives of the Arabian philosophers and a discourse of the religion of Mahumet, with diverse excellent poems and other monuments of his industry, which are not come to light.

Now as concerning his employments, were they not such as might well beseem a man of good worth? For (to omit how many courts and camps of princes he had frequented) did not he, as himself in his third book witnesseth, personally serve king Mahumet of Fez in his wars against Arzilla?[5] And was he not at another time, as appeareth out of his second book, in service and honorable place under the same king of Fez, and sent ambassador by him to the king of Morocco? Yea, how often in regard of his singular knowledge and judgment in the laws of those countries, was he appointed and sometimes constrained at diverse strange cities and towns through which he traveled, to become a judge and arbiter in matters of greatest moment?

Moreover as touching his exceeding great travels, had he not at the first been a Moor and a Mahumetan in religion, and most skillful in the languages and customs of the Arabians and Africans, and for the most part traveled in caravans or under the authority, safe conduct, and commendation of great princes? I marvel much how ever he should have escaped so many thousands of imminent dangers. And (all the former notwithstanding) I marvel much more, how ever he escaped them. For how many desolate cold mountains and huge, dry, and barren deserts passed he? How often was he in hazard to have been captived or to have had his throat cut by the prowling Arabians and wild Moors? And how hardly many times escaped he the lion's greedy mouth and the devouring jaws of the crocodile? But if you will needs have a brief journal of his travels, you may see in the end of his eighth book, what he writeth for himself. Wherefore (saith he) if it shall please God to vouchsafe me longer life, I purpose to describe all the regions of Asia which I have traveled—to wit, Arabia Deserta, Arabia Petrea, Arabia Felix,[6] the Asian part of Egypt, Armenia, and some part of Tartaria—all which countries I saw and passed through in the time of my youth. Likewise I will describe my last voyages from Constantinople to Egypt and from

4. The University of Fez dated from the 13th-century Merinid dynasty. The Cabala, or Kabbala, was a system of occult wisdom and mystical interpretation of the Scriptures.

5. Leo served the Sultan Mohammed VI, who reigned in Fez (1508–1527), both in war and in diplomacy.
6. The ancients divided Arabia into three parts based on its principle place Petra, the desert, and the fertile area.

thence unto Italy, etc. Besides all which places he had also been at Tauris in Persia; and of his own country and other African regions adjoining and remote, he was so diligent a traveler that there was no kingdom, province, signory, or city, or scarcely any town, village, mountain, valley, river, or forest, etc. which he left unvisited. And so much the more credit and commendation deserveth this worthy history of his, in that it is (except the antiquities and certain other incidents) nothing else but a large itinerarium or journal of his African voyages, neither describeth he almost any one particular place, where himself had not sometime been an eyewitness.

But, not to forget his conversion to Christianity, amidst all these his busy and dangerous travels, it pleased the divine providence, for the discovery and manifestation of God's wonderful works and of his dreadful and just judgments performed in Africa (which before the time of John Leo, were either utterly concealed or unperfectly and fabulously reported both by ancient and late writers) to deliver this author of ours, and this present geographical history into the hands of certain Italian pirates about the isle of Gerbi, situated in the Gulf of Capes, between the cities of Tunis and Tripolis in Barbary. Being thus taken, the pirates presented him and his book unto Pope Leo the Tenth, who, esteeming of him as of a most rich and invaluable prize, greatly rejoiced at his arrival and gave him most kind entertainment and liberal maintenance, til such time as he had won him to be baptized in the name of Christ, and to be called John Leo, after the Pope's own name. And so during his abode in Italy, learning the Italian tongue, he translated this book thereinto, being before written in Arabic. Thus much of John Leo.

[ON THE CUSTOMS OF THE AFRICAN PEOPLE IN LIBYA]

Those five kinds of people before rehearsed, to wit, the people of Zenega, of Gansiga, of Terga, of Leuta, and of Bardeoa, are called of the Latins Numidae;[7] and they live all after one manner, that is to say, without all law and civility. Their garment is a narrow and base piece of cloth, wherewith scarce half their body is covered. Some of them wrap their heads in a kind of black cloth, as it were with a scarf, such as the Turks use, which is commonly called a turbant.[8] Such as well be discerned from the common sort, for gentlemen wear a jacket made of blue cotton with wide sleeves. And cotton cloth is brought unto them by certain merchants from the land of negros. They have no beasts fit to ride upon except their camels, unto whom nature, between the bunch standing upon the hinder part of their backs and their necks, hath allotted a place, which may fitly serve to ride upon, instead of a saddle. Their manner of riding is most ridiculous. For sometimes they lay their legs across upon the camel's neck, and sometimes again (having no knowledge nor regard of stirrups) they rest their feet upon a rope, which is cast over his shoulders. Instead of spurs they use a truncheon of a cubit's length, having at the one end thereof a goad, wherewith they prick only the shoulders of their camels. Those camels which they use to ride upon have a hole bored through the gristles of their nose, in the which a ring of leather is fastened, whereby as with a bit, they are more easily curbed and mastered, after which manner I have seen buffles[9] used in Italy. For beds, they lie upon mats made of sedge and bul-

---

7. Numidia, an ancient kingdom in North Africa, north of the Sahara, was at one time a province of the Roman Empire. Leo here gives a description of the Tuareg, a pastoral people on the western and central Sahara, now located in Algeria, Mali, and Niger. The alphabet of the Tuareg is related to ancient Phoenician script.
8. Tuareg men traditionally wore dark blue robes and turbans.
9. Buffaloes.

rushes. Their tents are covered for the most part with coarse chamlet[1] or with a harsh kind of wool which commonly groweth upon the boughs of their date trees. As for their manner of living, it would seem to any man incredible what hunger and scarcity this nation will endure. Bread they have none at all, neither use they any seething or roasting; their food is camel's milk only, and they desire no other dainties. For their breakfast they drink off a great cup of camel's milk; for supper they have certain dried flesh steeped in butter and milk, whereof each man, taking his share, eateth it out of his fist. And that this their meat may not stay long undigested in their stomachs, they sup off the foresaid broth wherein their flesh was steeped; for which purpose they use the palms of their hands as a most fit instrument framed by nature to the same end. After that, each one drinks his cup of milk, & so their supper hath an end. These Numidians, while they have any store of milk, regard water nothing at all, which for the most part happeneth in the spring of the year, all which time you shall find some among them that will neither wash their hands nor their faces. Which seemeth not altogether to be unlikely; for (as we said before) while their milk lasteth, they frequent not those places where water is common; yea, and their camels, so long as they may feed upon grass, will drink no water at all. They spend their whole days in hunting and thieving; for all their endeavor and exercise is to drive away the camels of their enemies; neither will they remain above three days in one place, by reason that they have not pasture any longer for the sustenance of their camels. And albeit (as is aforesaid) they have no civility at all, nor any laws prescribed unto them, yet have they a certain governor or prince placed over them, unto whom they render obedience and due honor, as unto their king. They are not only ignorant of all good learning and liberal sciences, but are likewise altogether careless and destitute of virtue, insomuch that you shall find scarce one amongst them all which is a man of judgment or counsel. And if any injured party will go to the law with his adversary, he must ride continually five or six days before he can come to the speech of any judge. This nation hath all learning and good disciplines in such contempt that they will not once vouchsafe to go out of their deserts for the study and attaining thereof; neither, if any learned man shall chance to come among them, can they love his company and conversation, in regard of their most rude and detestable behavior. Howbeit, if they can find any judge, which can frame himself to live and continue among them, to him they give [a] most large yearly allowance. Some allow their judge a thousand ducats yearly, some more, and some less, according as themselves think good. They that will seem to be accounted of the better sort, cover their heads (as I said before) with a piece of black cloth, part whereof, like a vizard or mask, reacheth down over their faces, covering all their countenance except their eyes; and this is their daily kind of attire. And so often as they put meat into their mouths they remove the said mask, which being done, they forthwith cover their mouths again, alleging this fond reason: for (say they) as it is unseemly for a man, after he hath received meat into his stomach, to vomit it out of his mouth again and to cast it upon the earth; even so it is an undecent part to eat meat with a man's mouth uncovered.

The women of this nation be gross, corpulent, and of a swart[2] complexion. They are fattest upon their breast and paps, but slender about the girdle-stead.[3] Very civil they are, after their manner, both in speech and gestures. Sometimes they will accept

---

1. Chamlet, a fabric made from a mixture of silk and camel's hair.

2. Dark.

3. Waist.

of a kiss; but whoso tempteth them farther, putteth his own life in hazard. For by reason of jealousy you may see them daily one to be the death and destruction of another, and that in such savage and brutish manner that in this case they will show no compassion at all. And they seem to be more wise in this behalf than diverse of our people, for they will by no means match themselves unto a harlot.

The liberality of this people hath at all times been exceeding great. And when any travelers may pass through their dry and desert territories, they will never repair unto their tents, neither will they themselves travel upon the common highway. And if any caravan or multitude of merchants will pass those deserts, they are bound to pay certain custom unto the prince of the said people, namely, for every camel's load a piece of cloth worth a ducat. Upon a time I remember that traveling in the company of certain merchants over the desert called by them Araoan, it was our chance there to meet with the prince of Zanaga; who, after he had received his due custom, invited the said company of merchants, for their recreation, to go and abide with him in his tents four or five days. Howbeit, because his tents were too far out of our way, and for that we should have wandered farther than we thought good, esteeming it more convenient for us to hold on our direct course, we refused his gentle offer, and for his courtesy gave him great thanks. But not being satisfied therewith, he commanded that our camels should proceed on forward, but the merchants he carried along with him and gave them very sumptuous entertainment at his place of abode. Where we were no sooner arrived but this good prince caused camels of all kinds and ostriches, which he had hunted and taken by the way, to be killed for his household provision. Howbeit we requested him not to make such daily slaughters of his camels, affirming moreover that we never used to eat the flesh of a gelt[4] camel, but when all other victuals failed us. Whereunto he answered that he should deal uncivilly, if he welcomed so worthy and so seldom seen guests with the killing of small cattle only. Wherefore he wished us to fall to such provision as was set before us. Here might you have seen great plenty of roasted and sudden flesh. Their roasted ostriches were brought to the table in wicker platters, being seasoned with sundry kinds of herbs and spices. Their bread made of mill and panick[5] was of a most savory and pleasant taste; and always at the end of dinner or supper we had plenty of dates and great store of milk served in. Yea, this bountiful and noble prince, that he might sufficiently show how welcome we were unto him, would together with his nobility always bear us company; howbeit we ever dined and supped apart by ourselves. Moreover he caused certain religious and most learned men to come unto our banquet, who, all the time we remained with the said prince, used not to eat any bread at all, but fed only upon flesh and milk. Whereat we being somewhat amazed, the good prince gently told us that they all were born in such places whereas no kind of grain would grow, howbeit that himself, for the entertainment of strangers, had great plenty of corn laid up in store. Wherefore he bade us to be of good cheer, saying that he would eat only of such things as his own native soil afforded, affirming moreover, that bread was yet in use among them at their feast of passover, and at other feasts also, whereupon they used to offer sacrifice. And thus we remained with him for the space of two days, all which time, what wonderful and magnificent cheer we had made us, would seem incredible to report. But the third day, being desirous to take our leave, the prince accompanied us to that place where we overtook our camels and company sent before. And this I dare most deeply take mine oath on, that we spent the said prince

---

4. Gelded, castrated.   5. Varieties of millet, or grain.

ten times more than our custom which he received came to.[6] We thought it not amiss here to set down this history to declare in some sort the courtesy and liberality of the said nation. Neither could the prince aforesaid understand our language nor we his, but all our speech to and fro was made by an interpreter. And this which we have here recorded as touching this nation is likewise to be understood of the other four nations above mentioned, which are dispersed over the residue of the Numidian deserts.

Edmund Spenser

In addition to writing some of the greatest English poetry, Edmund Spenser wrote a colonialist tract promoting England's subjugation of Ireland. Spenser first came to Ireland as secretary to Lord Grey de Wilton, Lord Deputy of Ireland, in 1580. Through government service, Spenser acquired his land and house in Kilcoman, property confiscated from Sir John of Desmond, an "Old English" aristocrat who had rebelled against English rule. The Old English had been Anglo-Normans who settled in Ireland in the twelfth century. In *A View of the Present State of Ireland*, Spenser writes about the customs of the Irish, among whom he finds the Old English to be the most troublesome because they have gone native and become "more Irish than O'Hanlon's breech." Drawing heavily on the ethnographic stereotypes of the medieval *Topography of Ireland* by Gerald of Wales, Spenser wrote his text as a dialogue between Irenius, ("Peaceful") a veteran of English service in Ireland, and Eudoxus ("Of good opinion"), a younger man who questions why English policy in Ireland has not worked. In the 1590s, when Spenser was writing this text, another Irish rebellion had broken out under the command of Hugh O'Neill. Spenser and his family were driven out of Kilcoman. Creating a view of the Irish as a separate race, Spenser compares Irish customs with those of Africans and Moors. The description of the Irish as barbarous prepares for the conclusion of the text in which he recommends a military solution to the colonization of Ireland. Though not published until 1633, *A View of the Present State of Ireland* was entered in the Stationer's Register in 1598 and circulated widely in manuscript.

from *A View of the Present State of Ireland*

Eudoxus. Believe me, this observation of yours, Irenius,[1] is very good and delightful; far beyond the blind conceit of some, who (I remember) have upon the same word *Farragh*, made a very blunt conjecture, as namely Master Stanyhurst,[2] who though he be the same countryman born, that should search more nearly into the secret of these things, yet hath strayed from the truth all the heavens wide (as they say), for he thereupon groundeth a very gross imagination, that the Irish should descend from the Egyptians which came into that island, first under the leading of one Scota the daughter of Pharaoh, whereupon they use (saith he) in all their battles to call upon the name of Pharaoh, crying Ferragh, Ferragh.[3] Surely he shoots wide on the bow hand and very far from the mark. For I would first know of him what ancient ground of authority he hath for such a senseless fable, and if he have any of the rude Irish

6. Leo is saying that the prince gave them much more than they paid in tribute.
1. Irenius, who has greater experience of Ireland then Eudoxus, has just asserted that the Irish battle cry "Ferragh" is from the Scottish word "Fergus," which means that the Irish are Scots. The 17th-century Irish language historian Geoffrey Keating points out in his *History of Ireland* that the Irish etymology of "Ferragh" is "faire ó" or "ó faire" ("take care").

2. Richard Stanyhurst (1547–1618), a Dubliner and Catholic, wrote *Description of Ireland* in Holinshed's *Chronicles*, as well as *De rebus in Hibernia gestis*, in which he dismisses the Egyptian origin of the Irish war cry.
3. The notion that the Irish were descended from the Egyptian Scota dates back to the 8th–century life of St. Abban and is repeated in the medieval Irish *Book of Invasions (Leabhar gabhála)*.

books, as it may be he hath, yet (me seems) that a man of his learning should not so lightly have been carried away with old wives' tales, from approvance of his own reason; for whether it be a smack of any learned judgment to say that Scota is like an Egyptian word, let the learned judge. But his Scota rather comes of the Greek *scotos*, that is, darkness, which hath not let him see the light of the truth.

Irenius. You know not, Eudoxus, how well Master Stanyhurst could see in the dark; perhaps he hath owls' or cats' eyes. But well I wot he seeth not well the very light in matters of more weight. ✳ ✳ ✳ There be other sorts of cries also used among the Irish, which savor greatly of the Scythian barbarism,[4] as their lamentations at their burials, with despairful outcries, and immoderate wailings, the which Master Stanyhurst might also have used for an argument to prove them Egyptians. For so in scripture it is mentioned, that the Egyptians lamented for the death of Joseph.[5] Others think this custom to come from the Spaniards, for that they do immeasurably likewise bewail their dead. But the same is not proper Spanish, but altogether heathenish, brought in thither first either by the Scythians, or the Moors that were Africans and long possessed that country. For it is the manner of all pagans and infidels to be intemperate in their wailings of their dead, for that they had no faith nor hope of salvation. And this ill custom also is specially noted by Diodorus Siculus,[6] to have been in the Scythians, and is yet amongst the Northern Scots at this day, as you may read in their chronicles.

Eudoxus. This is sure an ill custom also, but yet doth not so much concern civil reformation, as abuse in religion.[7]

✳ ✳ ✳

Eudoxus. It seemeth strange to me that the English should take more delight to speak that language than their own, whereas they should (me thinks) rather take scorn to acquaint their tongues thereto. For it hath ever been the use of the conqueror to despise the language of the conquered and to force him by all means to learn his. So did the Romans always use, insomuch that there is almost no nation in the world but is sprinkled with their language. It were good therefore (me seems) to search out the original cause of this evil; for, the same being discovered, a redress thereof will the more easily be provided. For I think it very strange that the English being so many, and the Irish so few, as they then were left, the fewer should draw the more unto their use.

Irenius. I suppose that the chief cause of bringing in the Irish language amongst them was especially their fostering[8] and marrying with the Irish, the which are two most dangerous infections; for first the child that sucketh the milk of the nurse must of necessity learn his first speech of her, the which being the first inured to his tongue, is ever after most pleasing unto him insomuch as though he afterwards be taught English, yet the smack of the first will always abide with him, and not only of speech but also of the manners and conditions. For besides that young children be like apes, which will affect and imitate what they see done before them, especially by their nurses whom they love so well, they moreover draw into themselves together with their suck even the nature and disposition of their nurses; for the mind fol-

---

4. Spenser claims both Irish and Scots are descended from the Scythians, described by Herodotus as a nomadic, barbarous people to the northwest of Greece.
5. Jacob, not Joseph (see Genesis 50.3).
6. Diodorus Siculus (d. 21 B.C.), a Sicilian author of a world history in Greek.
7. Irenius continues to discuss the Scythian, i.e., bar-

barous, character of Irish customs including going into battle naked, wearing glibs (masses of hair), and the women's riding facing right in the "old Spanish and as some say African" fashion, drinking blood and speaking the Irish language.
8. Gaelic custom of having children raised by clients, friends, or relatives to cement alliances.

loweth much the temperature of the body, and also the words are the image of the mind, so as they proceeding from the mind, the mind must needs be affected with the words. So that the speech being Irish, the heart must needs be Irish; for out of the abundance of the heart the tongue speaketh. The next is the marrying with the Irish, which how dangerous a thing it is in all commonwealths, appeareth to every simplest sense. And though some great ones have perhaps used such matches with their vassals and have of them nevertheless raised worthy issue, as Telamon did with Tocmissa, Alexander the Great with Roxanne, and Julius Caesar with Cleopatra,[9] yet the example is so perilous, as it is not to be adventured; for instead of those few good, I could count unto them infinite many evil. And indeed how can such matching but bring forth an evil race, seeing that commonly the child taketh most of his nature of the mother, besides speech, manners, and inclination, which are (for the most part) agreeable to the conditions of their mothers; for by them they are first framed and fashioned, so as what they receive once from them, they will hardly ever after forgo. Therefore are these evil customs of fostering and marrying with the Irish most carefully to be restrained; for of them two, the third evil, that is the custom of language (which I spake of), chiefly proceedeth.

Sir John Smith
from *The General History of Virginia, New England and the Summer Isles*[1]

Being thus satisfied with Europe and Asia, understanding of the wars in Barbary, he went from Gibraltar to Guta and Tanger, thence to Safee,[2] where growing into acquaintance with a French man-of-war,[3] the captain and some twelve more went to Morocco, to see the ancient monuments of that large renowned city. It was once the principal city in Barbary, situated in a goodly plain country, 14 miles from the great Mount Atlas and sixty miles from the Atlantic Sea, but now little remaining but the king's palace, which is like a city of itself, and the Christian church, on whose flat square steeple is a great brooch of iron, whereon is placed the three golden balls of Africa. The first is near three ells[4] in circumference, the next above it somewhat less, the uppermost the least over them, as it were, an half ball, and over all a pretty gilded pyramid. Against those golden balls hath been shot many a shot, their weight is recorded 700 weight of pure gold, hollow within, yet no shot did ever hit them, nor could ever any conspirator attain that honor as to get them down. They report the prince of Morocco betrothed himself to the king's daughter of Ethiopia, he dying before their marriage, she caused those three golden balls to be set up for his monument, and vowed virginity all her life. The Alfantica is also a place of note because it

9. All examples of interracial or cross-cultural marriages: the Phrygian Tecmessa with Greek Ajax, the Bactrian Roxana with the Macedonian Alexander, the Egyptian Cleopatra with the Roman Caesar.

1. Sir John Smith (1580–1631) spent his youth as a merchant's apprentice and then, at his father's death, set off to travel. He fought against the Turks in eastern Europe and was enslaved for a time in Turkey. On returning to England, he invested in the Virginia Company in 1606 and was appointed a member of the government council for the Jamestown settlement. He is probably best known for the much romanticized story of his being rescued from captivity by Pocahontas, the Indian princess and daughter of King Powhatan. After years of sea voyaging, warfare, and exploration, Smith returned to England. Among his many works of travel writing are *A Map of Virginia* (1612), *A Description of New England* (1616), and *The Generall Historie of Virginia New-England and the Summer Isles* (1624), from which the following passage describing the Barbary Coast (Tunisia and Morocco) is taken. Note Smith's mention of "that most excellent statesman, John de Leo,"—further evidence of how well known Leo Africanus' history of Africa was in early modern England.

2. From Gibraltar at the southern tip of Spain to Tangier in Morocco.

3. A large sailing ship equipped for warfare.

4. Twelve feet.

is environed with a great wall, wherein lie the goods of all the merchants securely guarded. The Juderea is also (as it were) a city of itself, where dwell the Jews. The rest for the most part is defaced, but by the many pinnacles and towers, with balls on their tops, hath much appearance of much sumptuousness and curiosity. There have been many famous universities, which are now but stables for fowls and beasts, and the houses in most parts lie tumbled one above another; the walls of earth are with the great fresh floods washed to the ground, nor is there any village in it, but tents for strangers, Larbes and Moors. Strange tales they will tell of a great garden, wherein were all sorts of birds, fishes, beasts, fruits and fountains, which for beauty, art and pleasure, exceeded any place known in the world, though now nothing but dunghills, pigeon houses, shrubs and bushes. There are yet many excellent fountains adorned with marble, and many arches, pillars, towers, ports and temples, but most only relics of lamentable ruins and sad desolation.

When Mully Hamet[5] reigned in Barbary he had three sons, Mully Sheck, Mully Sidan, and Mully Befferes—he, a most good and noble king that governed well with peace and plenty, til his empress, more cruel than any beast in Africa, poisoned him, her own daughter, Mully Sheck his eldest son born of a Portugal Lady, and his daughter, to bring Mully Sidan to the crown now reigning, which was the cause of all those brawls and wars that followed betwixt those brothers, their children, and a saint that start up, but he played the Devil.[6]

King Mully Hamet was not black, as many suppose, but Molata, or tawny, as are the most of his subjects, in every way noble, kind and friendly, very rich and pompous in state and majesty, though he sitteth not upon a throne nor chair of estate, but cross-legged upon a rich carpet, as doth the Turk, whose religion of Mahomet, with an incredible miserable curiosity they observe. His ordinary guard is at least 5,000 but in progress he goeth not with less than 20,000 horsemen, himself as rich in all his equipage as any prince in Christendom, and yet a contributor to the Turk. In all his kingdom were so few good artificers that he entertained from England, goldsmiths, plumbers, carvers and polishers of stone, and watchmakers, so much he delighted in the reformation of workmanship he allowed each of them ten shillings a day standing fee, linen, woolen, silks, and what they would for diet and apparel, and custom-free to transport or import what they would; for there were scare any of those qualities in his kingdoms, but those of which there are diverse of them living at this present in London. Amongst the rest, one Mr. Henry Archer, a watch-maker, walking in Morocco from the Alfantica to the Juderea, the way being very foul, met a great priest, or a Sante (as they call all great clergymen) who would have thrust him into the dirt for the way. But Archer, not knowing what he was, gave him a box on the ear; presently he was apprehended and condemned to have his tongue cut out and his hand cut off; but no sooner it was known at the king's court but 300 of his guard came and broke open the prison and delivered him, although the fact was next degree to treason. * * *

Fez also is a most large and plentiful country, the chief city is called Fez, divided into two parts, old Fez, containing about 80 thousand households, the other 4,000 pleasantly situated upon a river in the heart of Barbary, part upon hills, part upon plains, full of people and all sorts of merchandise. The great temple is called Carucer, in breadth seventeen arches, in length 120 born up with 2,500 white marble pillars.

---

5. Sultan of Morocco.
6. A reference to the "battle of the three kings" (1578) in Alcazarquivir, in which the Moroccan sultan (whose army was victorious), his Portuguese-supported rival, and Sebastian of Portugal (a religiously fervent prince who led an army of mercenaries to disaster) all perished.

Under the chief arch, where the tribunal is kept, hangeth a most huge lamp, compassed with 110 lesser; under the other also hang great lamps, and about some are burning fifteen hundred lights. They say they were all made of the bells the Arabians brought from Spain. It hath three gates of notable height, priests and officers so many that the circuit of the church, the yard, and other houses is little less than a mile and an half in compass. There are in this city 200 schools, 200 inns, 400 water mills, 600 water conduits, 700 temples and oratories, but fifty of them most stately and richly furnished. Their Alcazer[7] or Burse is walled about; it hath twelve gates and fifteen walks covered with tents to keep the sun from the merchants and them that come there. The king's palace, both for strength and beauty is excellent, and the citizens have many great privileges. Those two countries of Fez and Morocco are the best part of Barbary, abounding with people, cattle, and all good necessaries for man's use. For the rest, as the Larbes, or Mountainers, the kingdoms of Cocow, Algier, Tripoly, Tunis, and Egypt, there are so many large histories of them in diverse languages, especially that writ by that most excellent statesman, John de Leo [Africanus], who afterward turned Christian. The unknown countries of Ginny and Binne[8] this six and twenty years have been frequented with a few English ships only to trade, especially the river of Senega, by Captain Brimstead, Captain Brockit, Mr. Crump, and diverse others. Also the great river of Gambra, by Captain Jobson, who is returned in thither again in the year 1626 with Mr. William Grent and thirteen or fourteen others, to stay in the country, to discover some way to those rich mines of Gago or Tumbatu,[9] from whence is supposed the Moors of Barbary have their gold, and the certainty of those supposed descriptions and relations of those interior parts, which daily the more they are sought into, the more they are corrected. For surely, those interior parts of Africa are little known to either English, French, or Dutch, though they use much the coast; therefore we will make a little bold with the observations of the Portugals.

Seventeenth-Century Lyrics

Ben Jonson
1572–1637

Ben Jonson's life was full of changes and contradictions. His earliest biographer, William Drummond, called him "passionately kind and angry, careless either to gain or keep, vindictive, but, if he be well answered, at himself." His father was Protestant, but Jonson turned Catholic, only to recant that conversion later; nevertheless, in his last years he called himself a "beadsman." The stepson of a bricklayer, he became Poet Laureate. He wrote poems of praise to win the patronage of king and court but also skewered their follies in satire. Though often assuming the role of moralist in his poetry and plays, Jonson admitted that as a younger man he was "given to venery" and pleaded guilty to the charge of murder. He was attached to admiring younger poets, "the tribe of Ben," yet he also enjoyed feuds, such as those with fellow dramatists Marston and Dekker. While espousing Horatian spareness and an acute sense of meter in both criticism and poetry, Jonson also had a keen ear for the colloquial language of London.

---

7. A palace formed around a courtyard, here compared to a "Burse," or trading place.
8. Guinea and Benin, on the west coast of Africa.

9. Timbuktu, near the Niger with the Sahara to the north, a center of trade and Moslem culture.

Indeed, London was one of the few constants in Jonson's turbulent career. Born in Harts-Born Lane near Charing Cross, he was buried in Poets' Corner at Westminster Abbey. Jonson portrayed the city as the world of those who lived by their wits. He dramatized literary infighting in *Every Man Out of His Humour* (1599), greedy schemes in *Volpone* (1606), intellectual confidence scams in *The Alchemist* (1610), and antitheatrical Puritan preaching in *Bartholomew Fair* (1614). The London audience at the Hope Theatre was reported to have exclaimed at a performance of *Bartholomew Fair:* "O rare Ben Jonson!"

Jonson viewed writing as his profession; he became the first poet in England to earn a living by his art. His achievement was recognized by James I, who made Jonson the first Poet Laureate of England and granted him a pension for life. Before becoming laureate, Jonson depended on a whole string of patrons. With the new Stuart king in power, Jonson was able to use his claim of Scots descent to advantage. He was supported by Esme Stuart Seigneur D'Aubigny (a cousin of King James), to whom he dedicated his first tragedy, *Sejanus* (1603). His patrons included Sir Walter Raleigh and Lady Mary Wroth, to whom he dedicated *The Alchemist.* Jonson's most important break came when he received a commission for a court masque. In 1605 he wrote *The Masque of Blackness* starring the Queen herself. To gain some idea of the extravagance of these masques, consider that in 1617, while 12,000 pounds were spent on the entire administration of Ireland, 4,000 pounds were spent on a single masque, *Pleasure Reconciled to Virtue.* The masques were lavish ventures that required costumes, music, and magnificent scenery, which was designed by Inigo Jones, who introduced the Italian invention of perspective.

If the pursuit of patronage was crucial to Jonson's advancement, his satire of politics and power repeatedly put his career and even his life at risk. In 1603 Jonson was called before the Privy Council for *Sejanus;* the charges included "popery and treason." Jonson's *Epicoene, or the Silent Woman*—which climaxes in the revelation that the silent woman is really a boy—was suppressed because it lampooned a love affair of the King's first cousin, Lady Arbella Stuart. One observer complained of the 1613 *Irish Masque at Court* that it was "no time . . . to exasperate that nation by making ridiculous." Jonson was imprisoned twice for the offense that his plays gave to the powerful—once for the now lost *The Isle of Dogs* (1597) and another time for *Eastward Ho!* (1605), in which he made fun of King James's Scots accent.

Jonson took reckless risks, whose consequences he barely managed to escape. While imprisoned for the murder of Gabriel Spencer in 1598, Jonson became a Catholic. Following his conversion, Jonson pleaded guilty to manslaughter (later calling it the result of a duel) but went free by claiming benefit of clergy. This medieval custom originally allowed clerics to be judged by the bishop's court but, by Jonson's time, permitted anyone who could translate the Latin Bible to go free. Jonson left prison with his belongings confiscated, his thumb branded for the felony, and his reputation marked by his profession of an outlaw religion. Like any other Catholic in Elizabethan England, Jonson could be fined or have his property confiscated for not attending Anglican services. Indeed, he and his wife were interrogated for their nonattendance in 1605; Jonson was also charged with being "a poet, and by fame a seducer of youth to the Popish religion." Threatened again with loss of property and another prison term, Jonson complied with the Court's order that he take instruction in Protestantism.

Jonson had high regard for some of his contemporaries, as they did for him. Among these was John Donne, who wrote commendatory verses for *Volpone* and to whom Jonson wrote "Who shall doubt, Donne, whe'er I a poet be / When I dare send my epigrams to thee?" As an older man, Jonson held court at the Devil Tavern among his fellow poets as self-proclaimed *arbiter bibendi* (master of drinking), whose main object was "Not drinking much, but talking wittily." This vein of wit was carried on by Sir John Suckling's *A Session of Poets* and Herrick's *Prayer for Ben Jonson.* His servant Brome wrote an elegy for him, as did the many men of letters who contributed to *Jonsonius Virbius* ("Jonson Reborn"), the year after his death.

Ben Jonson's poetry is alternately urbane and sensuous, austere and moral—qualities which might at first seem opposed but which are often melded together in his verse, as in the concluding lines to *Song to Celia:*

'Tis no sin love's fruit to steal,
But the sweet theft to reveal:
To be taken, to be seen,
Those have crimes accounted been.

Both the erotic and the satiric impulses in Jonson's verse have classical roots. For example, the two-line poem *Fool or Knave* has the directness and wit of poems from the Greek Anthology: "Thy praise or dispraise is to me alike; / One doth not stroke me, nor the other strike." Or again, *On Something that Walks Somewhere* has the acerbic wit of the Latin poet Martial, upon whose poetry many of Jonson's own epigrams are modeled. Not only are his topics and timbres Latinate, but Jonson's meters are an attempt to reproduce the quantitative verse of Latin poetry, while all the while sounding perfectly natural. This fusion of perfect control and an offhanded spontaneity is echoed in the nonchalance of the tone of his personae, evoking the sprezzatura of Castiglione's *Courtier*. At times, Jonson's poetry achieves a paired-down simplicity, with the sound of conversational speech, something that has made him a favorite with contemporary English poets.

There is often a dramatic quality to Jonson's poetry; indeed, he conceived of his poetic universe as a kind of theater of mankind. In the preface to his *Epigrams*, Jonson writes mockingly of the audience for his verse, which would better suit the Roman Stoic sage Cato: "for why should they remit anything of their riot, their pride, their self-love, and other inherent graces, to consider truth or virtue? but with the trade of the world lend their long ears against men they love not, and hold their dear mountebank or jester in far better condition than all the study or studies of humanity. For such, I would rather know them by their vizards still, than they should publish their faces at their peril in my theatre, where Cato, if he lived, might enter without scandal."

On Something, That Walks Somewhere[1]

At court I met it, in clothes brave° enough,   *showy*
   To be a courtier; and looks grave enough,
To seem a statesman: as I near it came,
   It made me a great face, I asked the name.
"A lord," it cried, "buried in flesh, and blood,
   And such from whom let no man hope least good,
For I will do none; and as little ill,
   For I will dare none." Good lord, walk dead still.

On My First Daughter[1]

Here lies to each her parents' ruth,°   *grief*
Mary, the daughter of their youth;
Yet, all heaven's gifts, being heaven's due,
It makes the father, less, to rue.
5   At six months' end, she parted hence
With safety of her innocence;
Whose soul heaven's Queen (whose name she bears),
In comfort of her mother's tears,
Hath placed amongst her virgin-train;
10 Where, while that severed doth remain,
This grave partakes the fleshly birth;[2]
Which cover lightly, gentle earth.

1. This and the following four poems were all first printed in the collected *Works* of 1616 under the heading "Epigrams." An epigram is a short witty poem of invective or satire. Jonson's "Epigrams" include epitaphs, poems of praise, and a verse letter.
1. Probably written in the late 1590s.
2. While the soul is in heaven, the grave holds the body.

To John Donne

Donne, the delight of Phoebus,[1] and each Muse,
  Who, to thy one, all other brains refuse;[2]
Whose every work, of thy most early wit
  Came forth example, and remains so, yet;
Longer a-knowing than most wits do live;
  And which no affection praise enough can give!
To it,[3] thy language, letters, arts, best life,
  Which might with half mankind maintain a strife.
All which I meant to praise, and, yet, I would,
  But leave, because I cannot as I should.

On My First Son[1]

Farewell, thou child of my right hand,[2] and joy;
  My sin was too much hope of thee, loved boy.
Seven years thou wert lent to me, and I thee pay,
  Exacted by thy fate, on the just day.
O, could I lose all father, now![3] For why
  Will man lament the state he should envy?
To have so soon 'scaped world's and flesh's rage,
  And, if no other misery, yet age?
Rest in soft peace, and, asked, say, "Here doth lie
  Ben Jonson his best piece of poetry."
For whose sake, henceforth, all his vows be such,
  As what he loves may never like too much.[4]

Inviting a Friend to Supper[1]

Tonight, grave sir, both my poor house and I
  Do equally desire your company:
Not that we think us worthy such a guest,
  But that your worth will dignify our feast
5 With those that come; whose grace may make that seem
  Something, which else could hope for no esteem.
It is the fair acceptance, Sir, creates
  The entertainment perfect, not the cates.°   food
Yet shall you have, to rectify your palate,
10 An olive, capers, or some better salad
Ushering the mutton; with a short-legged hen
  If we can get her, full of eggs, and then
Lemons, and wine for sauce: to these, a coney°   rabbit
  Is not to be despaired of, for our money;
15 And though fowl now be scarce, yet there are clerks,°   scholars
  The sky not falling, think we may have larks.

---

1. God of poetry.
2. The Muses give the inspiration to your brain that they
deny to others.
3. In addition to your wit.
1. Benjamin, who died of the plague on his birthday in 1603.
2. In Hebrew, Benjamin means "son of the right hand;
dexterous, fortunate."

3. Let go of fatherly feeling.
4. "If you wish . . . to beware of sorrows that gnaw the
heart, to no man make yourself too much a comrade"
(Martial 12.34, lines 8–11).
1. Based on three poems of invitation by the Roman poet
Martial, 11.52, 5.78, and 10.48.

I'll tell you of more, and lie, so you will come:
    Of partridge, pheasant, woodcock, of which some
May yet be there; and godwit, if we can;
20   Knat, rail, and ruff,° too. Howsoe'er, my man   *gamebirds*
Shall read a piece of Virgil, Tacitus,
    Livy, or of some better book to us,
Of which we'll speak our minds, amidst our meat;
    And I'll profess no verses to repeat;
25 To this, if aught appear, which I not know of,
    That will the pastry, not my paper, show of.[2]
Digestive cheese and fruit there sure will be;
    But that, which most doth take my muse and me,
Is a pure cup of rich Canary wine,
30   Which is the Mermaid's,[3] now, but shall be mine:
Of which had Horace, or Anacreon tasted,
    Their lives, as do their lines, till now had lasted.[4]
Tobacco, nectar, or the Thespian spring
    Are all but Luther's beer to this I sing.[5]
35 Of this we will sup free, but moderately,
    And we will have no Poley, or Parrot by;[6]
Nor shall our cups make any guilty men,
    But, at our parting, we will be, as when
We innocently met. No simple word
40   That shall be uttered at our mirthful board
Shall make us sad next morning, or affright
    The liberty, that we'll enjoy tonight.

To Penshurst[1]

Thou art not, Penshurst, built to envious show,
    Of touch,° or marble; nor canst boast a row   *black marble*
Of polished pillars, or a roof of gold;
    Thou hast no lantern,° whereof tales are told,   *turret*
5   Or stair, or courts; but stand'st an ancient pile,[2]
    And these grudged at, art reverenced the while.
Thou joy'st in better marks, of soil, of air,
    Of wood, of water; therein thou art fair.
Thou hast thy walks for health, as well as sport:
10   Thy mount to which the dryads° do resort,   *wood nymphs*
Where Pan, and Bacchus their high feasts have made,[3]
    Beneath the broad beech and the chestnut shade;
That taller tree, which of a nut was set,
    At his great birth, where all the Muses met.
15   There, in the writhèd bark, are cut the names

---

2. Add to this that if there is any paper, it will only be that used to keep the pastry from sticking to the pan.
3. A famous tavern in Cheapside, London.
4. Horace praised wine in Latin verse, as did Anacreon in Greek.
5. The Thespian spring, inspiration of poetry, and all these things are but Luther's beer in comparison with Canary.
6. Government spies; talkative birds.
1. First published in the 1616 *Works* in "The Forest," a title

inspired by the Latin *silva* (timber), suggesting raw materials to be worked, used by classical authors for an improvised collection of poems. Penshurst was the Sidney family's house in Kent since 1552, the "great lord" (line 91) of which was Robert Sidney, Baron Sidney of Penshurst and Viscount of Lille, younger brother of Sir Philip Sidney.
2. The castle was built in 1340.
3. Pan was the god of forest, field, and pasture; Bacchus was the god of wine.

Of many a sylvan,° taken with his flames;   *wood sprite*
And thence, the ruddy satyrs oft provoke
    The lighter fauns, to reach thy Lady's oak.[4]
Thy copse,° too, named of Gamage, thou hast there,   *a small wood*
20   That never fails to serve thee seasoned deer
When thou wouldst feast, or exercise thy friends.
    The lower land, that to the river bends,
Thy sheep, thy bullocks, kine° and calves do feed;   *cows*
    The middle grounds thy mares and horses breed.
25 Each bank doth yield thee conies,° and the tops   *rabbits*
    Fertile of wood, Ashour and Sydney's copse,
To crown thy open table, doth provide
    The purpled pheasant with the speckled side;
The painted partridge lies in every field,
30   And, for thy mess, is willing to be killed.
And if the high-swoll'n Medway[5] fail thy dish,
    Thou hast thy ponds, that pay thee tribute fish:
Fat, agèd carps, that run into thy net.
    And pikes, now weary their own kind to eat,
35 As loath, the second draught, or cast to stay,
    Officiously, at first, themselves betray;
Bright eels, that emulate them, and leap on land,
    Before the fisher, or into his hand.
Then hath thy orchard fruit, thy garden flowers,
40   Fresh as the air, and new as are the hours.
The early cherry, with the later plum,
    Fig, grape, and quince, each in his time doth come;
The blushing apricot and woolly peach
    Hang on thy walls, that every child may reach.
45 And though thy walls be of the country stone,
    They're reared with no man's ruin, no man's groan;
There's none, that dwell about them, wish them down;
    But all come in, the farmer, and the clown,°   *peasant*
And no one empty-handed, to salute
50   Thy lord, and lady, though they have no suit.
Some bring a capon, some a rural cake,
    Some nuts, some apples; some that think they make
The better cheeses, bring'em; or else send
    By their ripe daughters, whom they would commend
55 This way to husbands; and whose baskets bear
    An emblem of themselves in plum, or pear.
But what can this (more than express their love)
    Add to thy free provisions, far above
The need of such? whose liberal board doth flow
60   With all that hospitality doth know!
Where comes no guest, but is allowed to eat
    Without his fear, and of thy lord's own meat;
Where the same beer, and bread, and self-same wine
    That is his lordship's shall be also mine,

---

4. In Greek mythology the satyr with a man's body and a
goat's legs was devoted to lechery. Robert Sidney's wife Bar-

bara Gamage was said to have given birth under this oak.
5. The local river.

65 And I not fain to sit (as some this day
　　At great men's tables) and yet dine away.
Here no man tells my cups; nor, standing by,
　　A waiter, doth my gluttony envy,
But gives me what I call, and lets me eat;
70 　　He knows below he shall find plenty of meat,
Thy tables hoard not up for the next day.
　　Nor, when I take my lodging, need I pray
For fire, or lights, or livery:° all is there,　　　　　　*provisions, food*
　　As if thou then wert mine, or I reigned here;
75 There's nothing I can wish, for which I stay.
　　That found King James, when, hunting late this way
With his brave son, the Prince, they saw thy fires
　　Shine bright on every hearth as the desires
Of thy Penates[6] had been set on flame
80 　　To entertain them; or the country came,
With all their zeal, to warm their welcome here.
　　What (great, I will not say, but) sudden cheer
Didst thou, then, make 'em! and what praise was heaped
　　On thy good lady, then, who therein reaped
85 The just reward of her high housewifery;
　　To have her linen, plate, and all things nigh,
When she was far, and not a room, but dressed
　　As if it had expected such a guest!
These, Penshurst, are thy praise, and yet not all.
90 　　Thy lady's noble, fruitful, chaste withall.
His children thy great lord may call his own,
　　A fortune, in this age, but rarely known.
They are, and have been, taught religion; thence
　　Their gentler spirits have sucked innocence.
95 Each morn and even, they are taught to pray,
　　With the whole household, and may every day
Read in their virtuous parents' noble parts
　　The mysteries of manners, arms, and arts.
Now, Penshurst, they that will proportion° thee　　　　*compare*
100 　　With other edifices, when they see
Those proud, ambitious heaps, and nothing else,
　　May say, their lords have built, but thy lord dwells.

Song to Celia

　　Drink to me only with thine eyes,
　　　　And I will pledge with mine;
　　Or leave a kiss but in the cup,
　　　　And I'll not look for wine.
5 　　The thirst that from the soul doth rise
　　　　Doth ask a drink divine;
　　But might I of Jove's nectar sup,
　　　　I would not change for thine.
　　I sent thee late a rosy wreath,
10 　　　　Not so much honoring thee

6. Household gods.

As giving it a hope that there
　　It could not withered be.
But thou thereon didst only breathe,
　　And sent'st it back on me;
15　Since when it grows, and smells, I swear,
　　Not of itself, but thee.

To the Memory of My Beloved, the Author, Mr. William Shakespeare, and What He Hath Left Us[1]

To draw no envy, Shakespeare, on thy name,
　　Am I thus ample[2] to thy book, and fame,
While I confess thy writings to be such,
　　As neither man, nor muse, can praise too much.
5　'Tis true, and all men's suffrage. But these ways
　　Were not the paths I meant unto thy praise;
For silliest ignorance on these may light,
　　Which, when it sounds at best, but echoes right;
Or blind affection, which doth ne'er advance
10　The truth, but gropes, and urgeth all by chance;
Or crafty malice, might pretend this praise,
　　And think to ruin, where it seemed to raise.
These are as some infamous bawd or whore
　　Should praise a matron. What could hurt her more?
15　But thou art proof against them, and indeed
　　Above the ill fortune of them, or the need.
I, therefore will begin. Soul of the age!
　　The applause! delight! the wonder of our stage!
My Shakespeare, rise; I will not lodge thee by
20　Chaucer, or Spenser, or bid Beaumont lie
A little further, to make thee a room;[3]
　　Thou art a monument without a tomb,
And art alive still while thy book doth live,
　　And we have wits to read, and praise to give.
25　That I not mix thee so, my brain excuses,
　　I mean with great, but disproportioned, Muses;
For, if I thought my judgment were of years,
　　I should commit thee surely with thy peers,
And tell how far thou didst our Lyly outshine,
30　Or sporting Kid, or Marlowe's mighty line.[4]
And though thou hadst small Latin, and less Greek,
　　From thence to honor thee, I would not seek
For names, but call forth thundering Aeschylus,
　　Euripides, and Sophocles to us,
35　Pacuvius, Accius, him of Cordova dead,
　　To life again, to hear thy buskin[5] tread

1. Prefixed to the first folio of Shakespeare's plays (1623).
2. From Latin *amplus*: copious; an *amplus orator* was one who spoke richly and with dignity.
3. Chaucer, Spenser, and Francis Beaumont were buried in Westminster Abbey; Shakespeare was buried in Stratford.
4. Lyly was an author of English prose comedies; Kyd and Marlowe were authors of English verse tragedies.
5. Boot worn by tragic actors. Jonson compares Shakespeare to tragedians of Ancient Greece (Aeschylus, Sophocles, Euripides) and Rome (Pacuvius, Accius, and "him of Cordova," Seneca).

And shake a stage; or, when thy socks[6] were on,
   Leave thee alone for the comparison
Of all that insolent Greece or haughty Rome
40   Sent forth, or since did from their ashes come.
Triumph, my Britain; thou hast one to show
   To whom all scenes of Europe homage owe.
He was not of an age, but for all time!
   And all the muses still were in their prime
45   When like Apollo he came forth to warm
   Our ears, or like a Mercury to charm![7]
Nature herself was proud of his designs,
   And joyed to wear the dressing of his lines,
Which were so richly spun, and woven so fit
50   As, since, she will vouchsafe no other wit.
The merry Greek, tart Aristophanes,
   Neat Terence, witty Plautus,[8] now not please,
But antiquated, and deserted lie,
   As they were not of Nature's family.
55   Yet must I not give Nature all; thy Art,
   My gentle Shakespeare, must enjoy a part.
For though the poet's matter, Nature be,
   His art doth give the fashion. And, that he,
Who casts to write a living line must sweat
60   (Such as thine are) and strike the second heat
Upon the Muses' anvil: turn the same,
   And himself with it, that he thinks to frame;[9]
Or for the laurel, he may gain a scorn;
   For a good poet's made as well as born.
65   And such wert thou! Look how the father's face
   Lives in his issue; even so, the race
Of Shakespeare's mind, and manners brightly shines
   In his well-turnèd, and true-filèd lines:
In each of which, he seems to shake a lance,[1]
70   As brandished at the eyes of ignorance.
Sweet Swan of Avon, what a sight it were
   To see thee in our waters yet appear,
And make those flights upon the banks of Thames,
   That so did take Eliza, and our James![2]
75   But stay, I see thee in the hemisphere
   Advanced, and made a constellation there!
Shine forth, thou star of poets, and with rage
   Or influence chide or cheer the drooping stage,[3]
Which, since thy flight from hence, hath mourned like night,
80   And despairs day, but for thy volume's light.

---

6. Symbols of comedy.
7. Apollo and Mercury were the gods of poetry and eloquence.
8. Aristophanes was an ancient Greek comic playwright;
Terence and Plautus were authors of Roman comedy.
9. See Horace, Ars Poetica 441: "return the ill-tuned verses to the anvil."

1. Pun on "Shake-speare."
2. Queen Elizabeth and King James.
3. Like an ancient hero, Shakespeare is given a place
among the stars; as the "rage" and "influence" of the
planets affect life on earth, Shakespeare affects the world
of the stage.

John Donne
1572–1631

John Donne wrote some of the most passionate love poems and most moving religious verse in the English language. Even his contemporaries wondered how one mind could express itself in such different modes. Eliciting a portrait of the artist as a split personality, Donne's letters mention the melancholic lover "Jack Donne," succeeded by the Anglican priest "Doctor Donne." Izaak Walton's *Life of Donne* (1640) portrays an earnest aspiring clergyman who wrote love poetry to his wife. Yet Donne actually wrote most of his poetry—both the love lyrics and the *Holy Sonnets*—before he entered the ministry at forty-three. An ambitious, talented, and handsome young man, Donne struggled to attain secular patronage; later he resigned himself to life in the church and, after his wife's death, came to terms with his own mortality.

Donne was born into a Catholic family. His mother was the great-niece of Sir Thomas More; she went into exile in Antwerp for a time to seek religious toleration. One of Donne's uncles was imprisoned in the Tower of London because he was a Jesuit priest. Donne wrote of his family that none "hath endured and suffered more in their persons and fortunes, for obeying the Teachers of Roman Doctrine, then it hath done." Donne and his brother Henry entered Hart Hall, Oxford, when they were just eleven and ten, young enough to be spared the required oath recognizing the Queen as head of the church. The Donne brothers later studied law at Lincoln's Inn, where Henry was arrested for harboring a priest in 1593. The priest was drawn and quartered; Henry died in Newgate prison of the plague.

Though shadowed by his brother's death, Donne's student years in London had their pleasures. Donne was distracted from studying law by "the worst voluptuousness . . . an Hydroptique immoderate desire of humane learning and languages." The young Donne was described by his friend Sir Richard Baker as "a great visitor of ladies, a great frequenter of Playes, a great writer of conceited Verses." Among these were Donne's erotic *Elegies*, including *To His Mistress Going to Bed* and *Love's Progress,* both of which were refused a license for publication in the 1633 edition of his collected verse.

Shortly after gaining a position as secretary to Sir Thomas Egerton, Lord Keeper of the Great Seal, in 1597, Donne met and fell in love with Ann More. His noble employer's niece, she was so far above Donne's station that they married secretly. When Ann's father heard the news, he asked Egerton to have Donne fired and saw to it that he was incarcerated. At this time, Donne is said to have written to Ann: *"John Donne, Ann Donne, un-done."* As a result of Donne's petition, the Court of Audience for Canterbury declared the marriage lawful; nevertheless, Ann was disinherited.

John and Ann made a love match, but their life was not easy. She bore twelve children in fifteen years, not counting miscarriages. Donne lamented the "poorness of [his] fortune and the greatness of [his] charge." After thirteen years of marriage, however, he could also still say: "we had not one another at so cheap a rate, as that we should ever be weary of one another." A few of the love poems in *Songs and Sonnets* express a mixture of bliss and hardship linked with their marriage.

Relations with friends and patrons also influenced Donne's poetry. He is said to have addressed several poems to Magdalen Herbert, mother of the poet George. Living in Mitcham near London, Donne cemented his friendship with Ben Jonson, who wrote two epigrams in praise of Donne in thanks for his Latin verses on *Volpone* (1607). Donne was also introduced to Lucy, Countess of Bedford, who asked Jonson to get her a copy of Donne's *Satires.* Donne not only addressed several verse letters to her but also enjoyed her poems. An even more generous patron was Sir Robert Drury, for the death of whose young daughter Elizabeth the poet composed *A Funeral Elegie,* the inspiration for his two *Anniversaries* (1612) on the nature of the cosmos and death.

Donne's writing from 1607 to 1611 dealt with theological and moral controversies. His *Pseudo-Martyr* (1610) argued that Catholics should take the Oath of Allegiance to the King and that resistance to him should not be glorified as a form of martyrdom. This work won him James I's advice to enter the ministry, but, still skeptical, Donne held off. He protested against sectarianism: "You know I never fettered nor imprisoned the word Religion . . . immuring it in a Rome, or a Wittenberg, or a Geneva." Donne also examined the morality of suicide in *Biathanatos* (written 1607, published 1646). His *Holy Sonnets* (some of which may have been written as early as 1608–1610) reveal an obsession with his own death and fear of damnation: "I dare not move my dim eyes any way, / Despair behind, and death before doth cast / Such terror."

Donne was plagued by professional bad luck until he became an Anglican priest. With the exception of Sir Robert Drury, Donne never found a dependable patron. His applications for secretaryships in Ireland and Virginia were unsuccessful. In search of the Earl of Somerset's patronage, Donne wrote an epithalamion for his marriage to Frances Howard and even volunteered to justify her earlier controversial divorce. Fortunately for Donne, his attempts to win a position through Somerset failed, since a year later the Earl fell from power. Giving up his long quest for secular preferment, Donne took holy orders in 1615. Once an Anglican priest, he was made a royal chaplain and received an honorary Doctorate of Divinity from Cambridge. Two years later, he became reader in divinity at his old law school Lincoln's Inn.

Prosperity was followed by tragic loss. Ann Donne died giving birth in 1617. The death of his wife turned Donne more completely toward God. His later prose viewed death from a different perspective from his earlier personal torment. Suffering from a recurring fever, he wrote *Devotions upon Emergent Occasions* (1624). In the midst of a major epidemic, at the height of his fever, distraught and sleepless, he realizes our common mortality: "never send to know for whom the bell tolls; it tolls for thee." He became a prolific and stirring preacher of sermons. Some of these, such as that urging the Company of the Virginia Plantation to spread the gospel (1622), were printed in his lifetime. One written just before his death shows confidence in God's forgiveness: "I cannot plead innocency of life, especially of my youth: But I am to be judged by a merciful God."

If Donne's life can be split into the secular and religious, his poetic sensibility cannot. His verse fuses flesh and spirit through metaphysical conceits that create fascinating connections between apparently unrelated topics. In Donne's erotic lyrics, sex excites spiritual ecstasy along with hot lust and seductive wit. Similarly, Donne's religious poems express his relation with God not as an intellectual construct but as an emotional need, articulated in intimate and even erotic language. Later ages did not always appreciate either Donne's sensuality or his intellectual extravagance; remarkably, none of his poems were included in the most important nineteenth-century anthology of poetry, Palgraves's *Golden Treasury*. Donne's fame was revived early in the twentieth century, when modernist poets, especially T. S. Eliot, took inspiration from Donne's complex mixture of immediacy and artifice, passion and subtle thought.

The Good Morrow[1]

I wonder by my troth, what thou, and I
Did, till we loved? Were we not weaned till then?
But sucked on country pleasures, childishly?
Or snorted we in the seven sleepers' den?[2]
5   'Twas so; but this, all pleasures fancies be.

1. Donne's love poems, written over a period of 20 years, cannot be dated with any certainty. They were first printed in 1633, scattered throughout the entire collection of poems. Then in the 1635 edition the love poems were printed as a group under the title *Songs and Sonnets*. There is no certainty that the titles were chosen by Donne.

2. Legendary cave where seven Ephesian youths were put to sleep by God to escape the persecution of Christians by the Emperor Decius (249).

If ever any beauty I did see,
Which I desired, and got, 'twas but a dream of thee.

And now good morrow to our waking souls,
Which watch not one another out of fear;
10   For love, all love of other sights controls,
And makes one little room, an everywhere.
Let sea-discoverers to new worlds have gone,
Let maps to others, worlds on worlds have shown,
Let us possess one world, each hath one, and is one.

15   My face in thine eye, thine in mine appears,
And true plain hearts do in the faces rest,
Where can we find two better hemispheres
Without sharp north, without declining west?
What ever dies, was not mixed equally;[3]
20   If our two loves be one, or, thou and I
Love so alike, that none do slacken, none can die.

Song

Go, and catch a falling star,
    Get with child a mandrake root,[1]
Tell me, where all past years are,
    Or who cleft the Devil's foot,
5   Teach me to hear mermaids singing,
Or to keep off envy's stinging,
        And find
        What wind
Serves to advance an honest mind.

10   If thou be borne to strange sights,
    Things invisible to see,
Ride ten thousand days and nights,[2]
    Till age snow white hairs on thee,
Thou, when thou return'st, will tell me
15   All strange wonders that befell thee,
        And swear
        No where
Lives a woman true, and fair.

If thou findest one, let me know,
20   Such a pilgrimage were sweet;
Yet do not, I would not go,
    Though at next door we might meet,
Though she were true, when you met her,
And last, till you write your letter,
25   Yet she
        Will be
False, ere I come, to two, or three.

3. According to ancient medicine, death was caused by
an imbalance of elements in the body.
1. A fork-rooted plant, resembling the human body in

its form.
2. See *Faerie Queene* 3.7.56–61, where Spenser's Squire of
Dames searches the country for a chaste woman.

The Undertaking

I have done one braver thing
    Than all the Worthies did,[1]
And yet a braver thence doth spring,
    Which is, to keep that hid.

5   It were but madness now to impart
    The skill of specular stone,[2]
When he which can have learned the art
    To cut it, can find none.

So, if I now should utter this,
10   Others (because no more
Such stuff to work upon, there is,)
    Would love but as before.

But he who loveliness within
    Hath found, all outward loathes,
15   For he who color loves, and skin,
    Loves but their oldest clothes.

If, as I have, you also do
    Virtue attired in woman see,
And dare love that, and say so too,
20   And forget the He and She;

And if this love, though placèd so,
    From profane men you hide,
Which will no faith on this bestow,
    Or, if they do, deride:

25   Then you have done a braver thing
    Than all the Worthies did;
And a braver thence will spring,
    Which is, to keep that hid.

The Sun Rising[1]

    Busy old fool, unruly Sun,
    Why dost thou thus
Through windows, and through curtains call on us?
Must to thy motions lovers' seasons run?
5   Saucy pedantic wretch, go chide
    Late schoolboys, and sour prentices,°   *apprentices*
Go tell court-huntsmen, that the king will ride,
Call country ants to harvest offices;
Love, all alike, no season knows, nor clime,
10   Nor hours, days, months, which are the rags of time.

      Thy beams, so reverend, and strong
      Why shouldst thou think?

---

1. The nine great military heroes of ancient and medieval legend and history.
2. Transparent stone of ancient times, but now lost, that required great skill to cut in strips.

1. In the tradition of the alba, a love song addressing the dawn, as in Ovid's *Amores* 1.13 and Petrarch's *Canzoniere* 188.

I could eclipse and cloud them with a wink,
But that I would not lose her sight so long:

15   If her eyes have not blinded thine,
     Look, and tomorrow late, tell me,
    Whether both th'Indias of spice and mine[2]
    Be where thou left'st them, or lie here with me.
    Ask for those kings whom thou saw'st yesterday,
20   And thou shalt hear, all here in one bed lay.

     She is all states, and all princes, I,
      Nothing else is.
    Princes do but play us; compared to this,
    All honor's mimic; all wealth alchemy.°   *fake science*
25   Thou sun art half as happy as we,
      In that the world's contracted thus;
    Thine age asks ease, and since thy duties be
    To warm the world, that's done in warming us.
    Shine here to us, and thou art everywhere;
30   This bed thy center is, these walls, thy sphere.

The Canonization[1]

For God's sake hold your tongue, and let me love,
  Or° chide my palsy, or my gout,   *either*
My five gray hairs, or ruined fortune flout,
    With wealth your state, your mind with arts improve,
5   Take you a course, get you a place,
      Observe his Honor, or his Grace,
Or the King's real, or his stampèd face[2]
    Contemplate, what you will, approve,
    So you will let me love.

10 Alas, alas, who's injured by my love?
    What merchant's ships have my sighs drowned?
Who says my tears have overflowed his ground?
    When did my colds a forward spring remove?
     When did the heats which my veins fill
15   Add one more to the plaguy bill?[3]
Soldiers find wars, and lawyers find out still
    Litigious men, which quarrels move
    Though she and I do love.

Call us what you will, we are made such by love;
20   Call her one, me another fly,
We are tapers° too, and at our own cost die,[4]   *candles*
    And we in us find the eagle and the dove.
     The phoenix riddle hath more wit[5]
     By us; we two being one, are it.

---

2. The East Indies was the source of spice; the West Indies was the source of gold.
1. The making of saints.
2. The King's actual face or his image stamped on coins.
3. Daily list of those who have died issued during out-breaks of the plague.
4. To die is to experience orgasm.
5. The mythical bird that was burned and reborn out of its own ashes, a symbol of perfection.

25   So to one neutral thing both sexes fit,
          We die and rise the same, and prove
          Mysterious by this love.

      We can die by it, if not live by love,
          And if unfit for tombs and hearse
30   Our legend be, it will be fit for verse;
          And if no piece of chronicle we prove,
              We'll build in sonnets pretty rooms;[6]
              As well a well wrought urn becomes
      The greatest ashes, as half-acre tombs,
35   And by these hymns, all shall approve
          Us canonized for love:

      And thus invoke us: You whom reverend love
          Made one another's hermitage;°   *refuge, retreat*
      You, to whom love was peace, that now is rage;
40   Who did the whole world's soul contract, and drove
              Into the glasses° of your eyes[7]   *lenses*
              (So made such mirrors, and such spies,
      That they did all to you epitomize)
          Countries, towns, courts: beg from above
45   A pattern of your love!

The Flea[1]

      Mark but this flea, and mark in this,
      How little that which thou deniest me is;
      It sucked me first,[2] and now sucks thee,
      And in this flea, our two bloods mingled be;
5   Thou know'st that this cannot be said
      A sin, nor shame, nor loss of maidenhead,
          Yet this enjoys before it woo,
          And pampered swells with one blood made of two,
          And this, alas, is more than we would do.

10   Oh stay, three lives in one flea spare,
      Where we almost, nay more than married are.
      This flea is you and I, and this
      Our marriage bed, and marriage temple is;
      Though parents grudge, and you, we are met,
15   And cloistered in these living walls of jet.°   *black*
          Though use make you apt to kill me,
          Let not to that, self murder added be,
          And sacrilege, three sins in killing three.

      Cruel and sudden, hast thou since
20   Purpled thy nail, in blood of innocence?
      Wherein could this flea guilty be,

6. A play on *stanza*, Italian for "room."
7. The lovers gazing into each other's eyes saw there a compact version or microcosm of the larger world or macrocosm.

1. Based on a poem attributed to Ovid, the poem plays on the belief that intercourse involved the mixing of bloods.
2. "Me it sucked first" in the 1635 edition.

Except in that drop which it sucked from thee?
Yet thou triumph'st, and say'st that thou
Find'st not thy self, nor me the weaker now;
25   'Tis true, then learn how false, fears be;
     Just so much honor, when thou yield'st to me,
     Will waste, as this flea's death took life from thee.

The Bait[1]

Come live with me, and be my love,
And we will some new pleasures prove
Of golden sands, and crystal brooks,
With silken lines, and silver hooks.

5   There will the river whispering run
Warmed by thy eyes, more than the sun.
And there the enamored fish will stay,
Begging themselves they may betray.

When thou wilt swim in that live bath,
10   Each fish, which every channel hath,
Will amorously to thee swim,
Gladder to catch thee, then thou him.

If thou, to be so seen, be'st loath,
By sun, or moon, thou darkenest both,
15   And if myself have leave to see,
I need not their light, having thee.

Let others freeze with angling reeds,
And cut their legs, with shells and weeds,
Or treacherously poor fish beset,
20   With strangling snare, or windowy net:

Let coarse bold hands, from slimy nest
The bedded fish in banks out-wrest,
Or curious traitors, sleave-silk flies[2]
Bewitch poor fishes' wandering eyes.

25   For thee, thou need'st no such deceit,
For thou thyself are thine own bait;
That fish, that is not catched thereby,
Alas, is wiser far than I.

A Valediction: Forbidding Mourning[1]

As virtuous men pass mildly away,
   And whisper to their souls, to go,
Whilst some of their sad friends do say,
   The breath goes now, and some say, no:

1. Parodies Marlowe's *The Passionate Shepherd to His Love* and Raleigh's *The Nymph's Reply*; see pages 499–501.
2. Artificial flies made from silk threads.

1. In his *Life of Dr. John Donne* (1640), Walton describes the occasion as Donne's farewell to his wife before his journey to France in 1611.

5   So let us melt, and make no noise,
        No tear-floods, nor sigh-tempests move,
    'Twere profanation° of our joys   *desecration*
        To tell the laity[2] of our love.

    Moving of th'earth brings harms and fears,
10   Men reckon what it did and meant,
    But trepidation of the spheres,[3]
        Though greater far, is innocent.

    Dull sublunary[4] lovers' love
        (Whose soul is sense) cannot admit
15   Absence, because it doth remove
        Those things which elemented° it.   *composed*

    But we by a love, so much refined,
        That our selves know not what it is,
    Inter-assurèd of the mind,
20   Care less, eyes, lips, and hands to miss.

    Our two souls therefore, which are one,
        Though I must go, endure not yet
    A breach, but an expansion,
        Like gold to airy thinness beat.[5]

25   If they be two, they are two so
        As stiff twin compasses[6] are two,
    Thy soul the fixed foot, makes no show
        To move, but doth, if th' other do.

    And though it in the center sit,
30   Yet when the other far doth roam,
    It leans, and hearkens after it,
        And grows erect, as that comes home.

    Such wilt thou be to me, who must
        Like th' other foot, obliquely run;
35   Thy firmness makes my circle just,°   *complete*
        And makes me end, where I begun.

The Ecstasy[1]

    Where, like a pillow on a bed,
        A pregnant bank swelled up, to rest
    The violet's reclining head,[2]
        Sat we two, one another's best.

5   Our hands were firmly cemented
        With a fast balm, which thence did spring,

---

2. The uninitiated.
3. Though the movement of the spheres is greater than an earthquake, we feel its effects less.
4. Under the sphere of the moon, hence sensual.
5. Gold was beaten to produce gold leaf. "Airy" suggests their love will become so fine that it will be spiritual.

6. A common emblem of constancy amidst change.
1. From *ekstasis* (Greek) meaning passion and the withdrawal of the soul from the body. A beautiful and secluded pastoral spot was a frequent setting for love poetry.
2. The violet was an emblem of faithfulness.

Our eye-beams twisted, and did thread
    Our eyes, upon one double string;[3]

So to intergraft our hands, as yet
10   Was all the means to make us one,
And pictures in our eyes to get
    Was all our propagation.[4]

As 'twixt two equal armies, Fate
    Suspends uncertain victory,
15   Our souls (which to advance their state
    Were gone out) hung 'twixt her and me.

And whilst our souls negotiate there,
    We like sepulchral statues lay;
All day, the same our postures were,
20   And we said nothing, all the day.

If any, so by love refined,
    That he soul's language understood,
And by good love were grown all mind,
    Within convenient distance stood,

25   He (though he knew not which soul spake
    Because both meant, both spake the same)
Might thence a new concoction[5] take,
    And part far purer than he came.

This ecstasy doth unperplex,
30   We said, and tell us what we love,
We see by this, it was not sex,
    We see, we saw not what did move:

But as all several souls contain
    Mixture of things, they know not what,
35   Love, these mixed souls, doth mix again,
    And makes both one, each this and that.

A single violet transplant,
    The strength, the color, and the size,
(All which before was poor and scant)
40   Redoubles still, and multiplies.

When love with one another so
    Interinanimates two souls,
That abler soul, which thence doth flow,
    Defects of loneliness controls.

45   We then, who are this new soul, know,
    Of what we are composed and made,
For, th' atomies° of which we grow,   *components, parts*
    Are souls, whom no change can invade.

---

3. The lovers are totally enthralled by gazing into each
other's eyes.
4. The act of reflecting each other's image was called
"making babies."
5. Refining of metals by heat.

But O alas, so long, so far
50   Our bodies why do we forbear?
They are ours, though they are not we, we are
        The intelligences, they the sphere.[6]

We owe them thanks, because they thus,
        Did us to us at first convey,
55   Yielded their forces, sense, to us,
        Nor are dross° to us, but allay.°   *refuse/a mixture*

On man heaven's influence works not so,
        But that it first imprints the air,[7]
So soul into the soul may flow,
60   Though it to body first repair.

As our blood labors to beget
        Spirits, as like souls as it can,
Because such fingers need to knit
        That subtle knot, which makes us man:[8]

65   So much pure lovers' souls descend
        T'affections,° and to faculties,°[9]   *feelings/powers*
Which sense may reach and apprehend,
        Else a great prince in prison lies.

To our bodies turn we then, that so
70   Weak men on love revealed may look;
Love's mysteries in souls do grow,
        But yet the body is his book.

And if some lover, such as we,
        Have heard this dialogue of one,
75   Let him still mark us, he shall see
        Small change, when we are to bodies gone.

from Holy Sonnets[1]
Divine Meditations

1

As due by many titles° I resign   *legal rights*
Myself to thee, Oh God, first I was made
By thee, and for thee, and when I was decayed
Thy blood bought that, the which before was thine,
5   I am thy son, made with thyself to shine,
Thy servant, whose pains thou has still repaid,
Thy sheep, thine image, and, till I betrayed

---

6. In Aristotelian cosmology, each planet moved in a sphere (the form of its motion around the earth) and was guided by an inner spiritual force, or intelligence.
7. An angel has to put on clothes of air to be seen by men; in hermetic medicine the air mediates the influence of the stars. Just as spirits need a material medium, so souls need the union of bodies.
8. In scholastic philosophy a human being is composed of

body and soul, and vapors called spirits produced by the blood link the body with the soul.
9. As the blood mediates between body and soul, so the lovers' feelings mediate between flesh and spirit.
1. The sonnets are printed in the sequence of the 1633 edition, which, according to Helen Gardner, represents Donne's order.

Myself, a temple of thy Spirit divine;
Why doth the devil then usurp in me?
10 Why doth he steal, nay ravish that's thy right?
Except thou rise and for thine own work fight,
Oh I shall soon despair, when I do see
That thou lov'st mankind well, yet wilt not choose me,
And Satan hates me, yet is loth to lose me.

5

If poisonous minerals, and if that tree,
Whose fruit threw death on else immortal us,
If lecherous goats, if serpents envious
Cannot be damned; alas, why should I be?
5   Why should intent or reason, born in me,
Make sins, else equal, in me more heinous?
And mercy being easy, and glorious
To God, in his stern wrath, why threatens he?
But who am I, that dare dispute with thee?
10 O God, Oh! of thine only worthy blood,
And my tears, make a heavenly Lethean[2] flood,
And drown in it my sins' black memory.
That thou remember them, some claim as debt,
I think it mercy, if thou wilt forget.

6

Death be not proud, though some have called thee
Mighty and dreadful, for thou are not so.
For, those, whom thou think'st thou dost overthrow,
Die not, poor death, nor yet canst thou kill me;
5   From rest and sleep, which but thy pictures be,
Much pleasure, then from thee, much more must flow,
And soonest our best men with thee do go,
Rest of their bones, and soul's delivery.
Thou art slave to fate, chance, kings, and desperate men,
10 And dost with poison, war, and sickness dwell,
And poppy,° or charms can make us sleep as well,   *a narcotic*
And better than thy stroke; why swell'st° thou then?   *grow in pride*
One short sleep past, we wake eternally,
And death shall be no more, Death thou shalt die.[3]

9

What if this present were the world's last night?
Mark in my heart, O soul, where thou dost dwell,
The picture of Christ crucified, and tell
Whether that countenance can thee affright,
5   Tears in his eyes quench the amazing light,
Blood fills his frowns, which from his pierced head fell,
And can that tongue adjudge thee unto hell,
Which prayed forgiveness for his foes' fierce spite?
No, no; but as in my idolatry[4]

2. Of Lethe, the river of forgetfulness in the underworld
of ancient mythology.
3. "The last enemy that shall be destroyed is death" (1

Corinthians 15.26).
4. Erotic devotion to women.

10 I said to all my profane mistresses,
 Beauty, of pity, foulness only is
 A sign of rigor:[5] so I say to thee,
 To wicked spirits are horrid shapes assigned,
 This beauteous form assures a piteous mind.

10

 Batter my heart, three-personed God;[6] for, you
 As yet but knock, breathe, shine, and seek to mend;
 That I may rise, and stand, o'erthrow me, and bend
 Your force, to break, blow, burn and make me new.
5 I, like an usurped town, to another due,
 Labor to admit you, but oh, to no end,
 Reason your viceroy° in me, me should defend,   *ruler*
 But is captived, and proves weak or untrue,
 Yet dearly I love you, and would be loved fain,°   *willingly*
10 But am betrothed unto your enemy,
 Divorce me, untie, or break that knot again,
 Take me to you, imprison me, for I
 Except you enthrall me, never shall be free,
 Nor ever chaste, except you ravish me.

⟶ ✦❈✦ ⟵

Lady Mary Wroth
1586–1640

Lady Mary Wroth was born the same year that her uncle Sir Philip Sidney died in battle. Like her uncle, she wrote brilliant sonnets and an entertaining and complex prose romance, but whereas his death and writing became the stuff of myth, she died in obscurity. Appreciated by the finest poets of her time, her writing was neglected for the next 300 years; she has only recently been rediscovered as one of the most compelling women writers of her age. Her *Pamphilia to Amphilanthus*, the first Petrarchan sonnet sequence in English by a woman, was first printed in 1621 but was not reprinted until 1977. Wroth's work has finally become available outside rare book libraries, thanks to Josephine Robert's editions of Wroth's complete poems (1983) and her prose romance *The Countess of Montgomeries Urania* (1995), along with Michael Brennan's edition of her pastoral tragicomedy *Love's Victory* (1988). Recent criticism has stressed the formal complexity and variety of her poetry and prose, their creation of female subjectivity, and their relationship to her life and social context, shedding new light on one of the most emotionally powerful and stylistically innovative authors of the Jacobean period.

  Mary Wroth was born into the cultivated and distinguished Sidney family. Mary and her mother, two brothers, and seven sisters lived at the family estate Penshurst in Kent. She sometimes visited her father in the Low Countries, where he commanded the English troops fighting for the Protestant cause against the Spanish. Ben Jonson sang the praises of Lady Mary's family and their way of life in *To Penshurst* (see page 657), a place where the

---

5. Beautiful women show compassion; only ugly ones refuse their lovers. 6. The Trinity: God the Father, Son, and Holy Spirit.

children not only enjoyed natural beauty—"broad beech" and "chest-nut shade"—but also learned the "mysteries of manners, arms and arts." Mary also spent a great deal of time in London with her aunt for whom she was named, Mary (Sidney) Herbert, Countess of Pembroke, hostess to and patron of a circle of poets that included George Chapman and Ben Jonson.

Mary found a mentor in her aunt, who herself wrote poems as well as translations of the Psalms and of Petrarch. Mary Herbert's translation of Petrarch's *Trionfo della Morte* ("Triumph of Death") portrays the poet's beloved Laura not as a passive object but as a lively and eloquent speaker. Mary Wroth's own sonnets similarly portray the woman as the suffering and desiring subject of love rather than the mute object that was common in earlier English Petrarchan poetry. Mary Wroth took the title of her *Urania* from a character in Philip Sidney's *The Countess of Pembrokes Arcadia,* whose publication had been overseen by his sister, Mary Sidney Herbert. Mary Wroth even created the character of the Queen of Naples as a fictional version of her aunt and perhaps saw *Urania* as a continuation of *Arcadia.*

When Mary married Sir Robert Wroth, Lord of Durance and Laughton House and juror for the Gunpowder Plot, she continued her close family ties with her aunt and father (yet another poet), but she also moved into the larger world of the Jacobean court. She served as Queen Anne's companion, and she became at once an observer and a center of attention in the aristocratic circle at court. In 1605, shortly after the first recorded performance of *Othello* at Whitehall, Lady Mary Wroth played in Ben Jonson's *Masque of Blackness,* in which she was presented to the court with Lady Frances Walsingham as the embodiment of gravity and dignity. Later, Wroth would deploy metaphors of darkness and night to great effect in her lyric poems.

It was in this court context that she attracted the attention of Ben Jonson, who not only wrote a poem complimenting her husband but also dedicated a sonnet and two epigrams to her. Jonson paid tribute to her as a subject and inspiration for poetry and as a powerfully moving poet in her own right. He claimed that since writing out her sonnets, he had "become / A better lover and much better poet." Dedicating his great play *The Alchemist* to her, he portrayed her as inheriting her uncle's mantle as poet: "To that Lady Most Deserving her Name and Blood, Lady Mary Wroth,"—a pun on her name, as Wroth was pronounced "worth." While she, too, punned on her married name in her poetry, Mary clung to her identity as a Sidney, using the Sidney device in her letters.

Her marriage was not particularly happy and pales in comparison with her literary friendship and love affair with her cousin William Herbert, by whom she had two illegitimate children, after she was widowed in 1614. During the years of her early widowhood she wrote the first part of her prose romance *Urania,* which was printed with *Pamphilia to Amphilanthus* in 1621. The *Urania* not only presents a fictional account of her relationship with her cousin and her parents' own happy marriage but also was read at the time as a criticism of the mores of the court. King James's courtiers, taking offense at the satire of their private lives, attacked her, prompting her to ask for the book to be removed from publication a few months after it first appeared. The early modern prejudice against women writing surfaces in Lord Denny's punning condescension to Wroth: "leave idle books alone / For wiser and worthier women have writ none."

Fortunately for us, she didn't take his advice and continued to write the second book of the *Urania,* which survives in manuscript. Indeed, no record of a warrant to recall the book survives. Her final years remain a mystery; she lived in retirement after her cousin's death. She left behind a body of poetry challenging the status quo of the court, proclaiming the suffering she had endured for love, and singing the beauty of spiritual love in a woman's voice. Imitating not only her uncle Philip's *Arcadia* but also the *Heptameron* of the French writer Marguerite de

Navarre, Mary Wroth made the prose romance a complex combination of novelistic fantasy, roman à clef, and social satire. The greatest English woman writer of her age, Mary Wroth fashioned a new voice and new perspectives within literary tradition that convey the fullness and complexity of her life as woman, lover, and writer.

from Pamphilia to Amphilanthus[1]

1

When night's black mantle could most darkness prove,
   And sleep death's image did my senses hire
   From knowledge of myself, then thoughts did move
   Swifter than those most swiftness need require:
5 In sleep, a chariot drawn by winged desire
   I saw, where sat bright Venus, Queen of love,
   And at her feet her son,[2] still adding fire
   To burning hearts which she did hold above,
But one heart flaming more than all the rest
10   The goddess held, and put it to my breast.
   "Dear son, now shut?"[3] said she, "thus must we win."
He her obeyed, and martyred my poor heart,
   I, waking, hoped as dreams it would depart;[4]
   Yet since, O me, a lover I have been.

16

Am I thus conquered? Have I lost the powers
   That to withstand, which joys to ruin me?
   Must I be still while it my strength devours
   And captive leads me prisoner, bound, unfree?
5 Love first shall leave men's fant'sies to them free,[5]
   Desire shall quench love's flames, spring hate sweet showers,
   Love shall loose all his darts, have sight, and see
   His shame, and wishings hinder happy hours.[6]
Why should we not Love's purblind° charms resist?   *totally blind*
10   Must we be servile, doing what he list?°   *wants*
   No, seek some host to harbor thee: I fly
Thy babish° tricks, and freedom do profess;   *childish*
   But O my hurt, makes my lost heart confess
   I love, and must. So farewell liberty.

39

Take heed mine eyes, how you your looks do cast,
   Lest they betray my heart's most secret thought;

1. The title means "From the All-loving One to the Dual Lover." First published in 1621, the sonnet sequence is here printed according to the numbering in Josephine Robert's 1983 edition.
2. Cupid. Compare the image of the chariot here with that in Petrarch's *Triumph of Love*.
3. Enclose that flaming heart within Pamphilia.

4. Pamphilia's experience of love is represented as a dream vision, a symbolic narrative in which the dreamer discovers hidden truth.
5. Before I surrender to Love, Love will allow men to realize their fantasies freely.
6. Cupid blindfolded was a popular figure in Renaissance iconography.

Be true unto yourselves for nothing's bought
More dear than doubt which brings a lover's fast.
5 Catch you all watching eyes, ere they be past,
    Or take yours fixed where your best love hath sought
    The pride of your desires; let them be taught
    Their faults for shame, they could no truer last;
Then look, and look with joy for conquest won,
10   Of those that searched your hurt in double kind;
    So you kept safe, let them themselves look blind;
    Watch, gaze, and mark 'til they to madness run,
While you, mine eyes, enjoy full sight of love
Contented that such happinesses move.

40

False hope which feeds but to destroy, and spill°   kill
    What it first breeds; unnatural to the birth
    Of thine own womb; conceiving but to kill,[7]
    And plenty gives to make the greater dearth,
5 So tyrants do who falsely ruling earth
    Outwardly grace them, and with profits fill,
    Advance those who appointed are to death
    To make their greater fall to please their will.
Thus shadow they their wicked vile intent,
10 Coloring evil with a show of good
    While in fair shows their malice so is spent;
    Hope kills the heart, and tyrants shed the blood.
For hope deluding brings us to the pride[8]
Of our desires the farther down to slide.

74. Song

Love a child is ever crying,
    Please him, and he straight is flying;
    Give him, he the more is craving,
    Never satisfied with having.

5 His desires have no measure,
    Endless folly is his treasure;
    What he promiseth he breaketh;
    Trust not one word that he speaketh.

He vows nothing but false matter,
10   And to cozen° you he'll flatter.   trick
    Let him gain the hand[9] he'll leave you,
    And still glory to deceive you.

He will triumph in your wailing,
    And yet cause be of your failing.

---

7. The image is of a miscarriage or infanticide.   9. Let him take control.
8. Arrogance, but also elation and pleasure.

15   These his virtues are, and slighter
        Are his gifts, his favors lighter.

        Feathers are as firm in staying,
            Wolves no fiercer in their preying;
            As a child then leave him crying,
20   Nor seek him so given to flying.

from *A Crown of Sonnets Dedicated to Love*[1]
77

        In this strange labyrinth how shall I turn?
            Ways° are on all sides while the way I miss: *paths*
            If to the right hand, there, in love I burn;
            Let me go forward, therein danger is;
5   If to the left, suspicion hinders bliss,
            Let me turn back, shame cries I ought return,
            Nor faint° though crosses with my fortunes kiss;[2]   *lose heart*
            Stand still is harder, although sure to mourn.[3]
        Thus let me take the right, or left-hand way,
10   Go forward, or stand still, or back retire;
            I must these doubts endure without allay°   *relief*
            Or help, but travail[4] find for my best hire.
        Yet that which most my troubled sense doth move
        Is to leave all, and take the thread of love.[5]

103

        My muse now happy, lay thyself to rest,
            Sleep in the quiet of a faithful love,
            Write you no more, but let these fant'sies move
            Some other hearts, wake not to new unrest;
5   But if you study, be those thoughts addressed
            To truth, which shall eternal goodness prove,
            Enjoying of true joy, the most, and best,
            The endless gain which never will remove.
        Leave the discourse to Venus, and her son
10   To young beginners, and their brains inspire
            With stories of great love, and from that fire
            Get heat to write the fortunes they have won,
        And thus leave off; what's past shows you can love,
        Now let your constancy your honor prove.

                                            Pamphilia.[6]

---

1. The crown (Italian *corona*) is a form in which the last
line of each poem is repeated as the first line of the next.
The last poem of the sequence ends with the first line of
the first poem.
2. Though troubles embrace my luck, or fate.
3. It is more difficult to do nothing, although this is sure
to make me mourn.
4. Hard work, with word play on "Travel," which occurs
in the 1621 text.

5. An allusion to the myth of Ariadne, beloved of Theseus, to whom she gave a thread to unwind behind him
on his path through the labyrinth so that, after slaying
the Minotaur, he could retrace his steps on his way out.
6. According to the 1621 *Urania*, when Pamphilia
accepts the keys to the Throne of Love, the virtue *Constancy* disappears and is transformed into Pamphilia's
breast.

Robert Herrick
1591–1674

The urbane and at times pagan poet Robert Herrick might seem an unlikely candidate for rural vicar, but such were his connections that he was promoted from deacon to priest in a day. He spent most of his life as vicar of the Devonshire parish of Dean, where he wrote poetry about country customs and church liturgy. A hundred and fifty years after his death, a writer in the *Quarterly Review* was able to find people in the village who could recite from memory Herrick's *Farewell to Dean Bourn:* "I never look to see / Dean, or thy warty incivility," lines that "they said he uttered as he crossed the brook, upon being ejected from the vicarage by Cromwell." Referring to Herrick's return to the vicarage after the Restoration, these locals "added with an air of innocent triumph, 'He did see it again.'" The villagers also recalled stories of how the bachelor vicar threw his sermon at the congregation one day for their inattention and how he taught his pet pig to drink from a tankard. Many of his best poems celebrate the landscape and the life of the country in the idealized tradition of pastoral poetry.

The son of a goldsmith in Cheapside, Herrick was apprenticed to the trade at age fourteen. After taking his B.A. from Cambridge in 1617, he returned to London, where he spent his poetic apprenticeship until he was appointed chaplain to the Duke of Buckingham in his failed expedition to aid the French Protestants of Rhé in 1627. Only a year later, Herrick moved to the vicarage at Dean, but many of his poems recount his London days, recalling the feasts frequented by Ben Jonson, whose verse "out-did the meat, out-did the frolic wine." The influence of Jonson's classical concision, wit, and urbanity can be felt in such poems as *Delight in Disorder*. While in London, Herrick also became friends with William Lawes, the court composer who wrote the music for Milton's masque *Comus*. When Lawes set Herrick's *To the Virgins to Make Much of Time* to music, this poem became one of the most popular drinking songs of the seventeenth century—often sung as a "catch," which meant that its words could be played with to produce ribald double meanings. His poems circulated in manuscript until his volume of verse was printed in 1648, with his secular poetry entitled *Hesperides* and his religious poetry entitled *Noble Numbers*. He first achieved a wide readership in the early nineteenth century with the romantic revival of interest in rural life and poetry.

The Argument of His Book[1]

> I sing of brooks, of blossoms, birds, and bowers,
> Of April, May, of June, and July flowers.
> I sing of Maypoles, hock carts, wassails, wakes,[2]
> Of bridegrooms, brides, and of their bridal cakes.
> 5   I write of youth, of love, and have access
> By these, to sing of cleanly wantonness.°   *carefree abandon*
> I sing of dews, of rains, and piece by piece,
> Of balm, of oil, of spice, and ambergris.[3]
> I sing of times trans-shifting;[4] and I write

---

1. All of Herrick's poems were published in 1648. The "Argument" introduces the book's themes.
2. Hock carts: harvest wagons; wassails: drinking toasts; wakes: celebrations in honor of the dedication of a parish church.
3. Secretion from the intestines of sperm whales, used to make perfume.
4. Times changing and passing; the cycle of the seasons.

10   How roses first came red, and lilies white.
       I write of groves, of twilights, and I sing
       The court of Mab,[5] and of the fairy king.
       I write of hell; I sing (and ever shall)
       Of Heaven, and hope to have it after all.

Delight in Disorder

       A sweet disorder in the dress
       Kindles in clothes a wantonness:
       A lawn° about the shoulders thrown   *scarf*
       Into a fine distraction;
5   An erring° lace, which here and there   *wandering*
       Enthralls the crimson stomacher:[1]
       A cuff neglectful, and thereby
       Ribbons to flow confusedly:
       A winning wave, deserving note,
10   In the tempestuous petticoat;
       A carelesse shoestring, in whose tie
       I see a wild civility:
       Do more bewitch me, than when art
       Is too precise[2] in every part.

To the Virgins, to Make Much of Time

       Gather ye rosebuds while ye may,
           Old time is still a-flying;[1]
       And this same flower that smiles today,
           Tomorrow will be dying.[2]

5   The glorious lamp of heaven, the sun,
           The higher he's a-getting;
       The sooner will his race be run,[3]
           And nearer he's to setting.

       That age is best, which is the first,
10   When youth and blood are warmer;
       But being spent, the worse, and worst
           Times still succeed the former.

       Then be not coy, but use your time,
           And while ye may, go marry;
15   For having lost but once your prime,
           You may for ever tarry.

Upon Julia's Clothes

       When as in silks my Julia goes,
           Then, then, me thinks, how sweetly flows

---

5. Queen of the fairies.
1. Ornamental covering for the chest worn under the lacing of the bodice.
2. "Precise" was often used to describe the strictness of
the Puritans.

1. The Latin tag *tempus fugit* ("time flies").
2. "Dying" was also a euphemism for orgasm.
3. In Greek mythology the sun was seen as the chariot of
Phoebus Apollo drawn across the sky each day as in a
race.

That liquefaction of her clothes.
Next, when I cast mine eyes and see
That brave° vibration each way free;   *splendid*
O how that glittering taketh me!

⁌ ⚎ ⌁

George Herbert
1593–1633

George Herbert spent the last three years of his life as a country parson. In an age in which such a church living was often a mere sinecure, Herbert had a genuine vocation, which he chose over other paths open to him through his talent and the connections of his distinguished Welsh family. His education and vocation were most influenced by his mother Magdalene Herbert, a woman with a great appreciation for poetry and strong devotion to the Church of England. When she died in 1627, John Donne gave the funeral sermon, extolling not only her grace, wit, and charm but especially her extraordinary charity to those who suffered from the plague of 1625, among whom was Donne himself. Herbert's mother had been widowed when he was just three years old. She brought up ten children, first in Oxford and then in London, where she saw to it that they were well read in the Bible and the classics.

Herbert studied at Cambridge University, where he became Reader in Rhetoric in 1616; in 1620 he was elected Public Orator, a post that he held for eight years. He wrote poetry and delivered public addresses in Latin and worked on the Latin version of Francis Bacon's *The Advancement of Learning*. Herbert also stood for Parliament and served there in 1624, when the Virginia Company, in which many of his friends and family were stockholders, was beset by financial difficulties and ultimately dissolved by James I.

Though his book *The Temple*, which included all his English poems, was not published until just after his death in 1633, Herbert was already writing verse as an undergraduate in 1610, when he dedicated two sonnets to his mother that advocated religious rather than secular love as the subject for poetry. His first published poems were written in Latin, commemorating the death of Prince Henry (1612). Herbert also wrote three different collections of Latin poems during his Cambridge years: *Musae Responsoriae*, polemical poems that defended the rites of the Church of England from Puritan criticism; *Passio discerpta*, religious verse that focused on Christ's passion and death in a style reminiscent of Crashaw; and *Lucas*, a collection of brief epigrams, such as this one on pride: "Each man is earth, and the field's child. Tell me, / Will you be a sterile mountain or a fertile valley?" The sardonic and mocking tone of these epigrams may surprise a reader of his English poems, but the wit and the rhetorical finish of his Latin poetry recur in his later verse.

Herbert's poetry is some of the most complex and innovative of all English verse. In a very pared-down style, enlivened by gentle irony, Herbert produces complexity of meaning through allegory and emblem, directly or more often indirectly alluding to biblical images, events, and insights, which take on their own moral and poetic meaning in the life of the speaker and the reader. Each of his poems is a kind of spiritual event, enacting in its form, both visual and aural, the very theological experiences and beliefs—or conflict of beliefs—expressed. Herbert allows us to make the spiritual journey with him through suffering and redemption, through doubt and hope. The meaning of one of his poems unravels like a discovery, each line and stanza raising alternative possibilities and altering the meaning of the one before. His spirituality is not a matter of easy acceptance but one of struggle, portrayed with wit, logic, and passion that recall the best of Donne's verse. The humility, subtle hesitancy, and whimsical irony are Herbert's alone, as when he addresses a love poem, *The Pearl*, to God:

I know the ways of pleasure, the sweet strains,
The lullings and the relishes of it . . .
My stuff is flesh, not brass; my senses live,
And grumble oft, that they have more in me
Then he that curbs them, being but one to five:
    Yet I love thee.

The Altar[1]

A broken ALTAR, Lord, thy servant rears,
Made of a heart, and cemented with tears:
    Whole parts are as thy hand did frame;
    No workman's tool has touched the same.[2]
5   A   HEART   alone
          Is   such   a   stone,
          As   nothing   but
          Thy power doth cut.
          Wherefore each part
10   Of my hard heart
          Meets in this frame,
          To praise thy Name.
    That, if I chance to hold my peace,
    These stones to praise thee may not cease.[3]
15   Oh let thy blessed SACRIFICE be mine,
    and sanctify this ALTAR to be thine.

Easter Wings[1]

Lord, who createdst man in wealth and store,[2]
Though foolishly he lost the same,
Decaying more and more,
Till he became
Most poor:
With thee
Oh let me rise
As larks, harmoniously,
And sing this day thy victories:
Then shall the fall[3] further the flight in me.

My tender age in sorrow did begin
And still with sickness and shame
Thou didst so punish sin,
That I became
Most thin.
With thee
Let me combine,
And feel this day thy victory:
For, if I imp[4] my wing on thine,
Affliction shall advance the flight in me.

1. All of Herbert's poems were published in *The Temple* (1633).
2. See Exodus 20.5, where God tells Moses: "And if thou wilt make me an altar of stone, thou shalt not build it of hewn stone: for if thou lift up thy tool upon it thou has polluted it."
3. See Luke 19.40: "I tell you that, if these should hold their peace, the stones would immediately cry out."

1. As in the first editions of Herbert, this poem is printed sideways to represent the shape of wings.
2. Plenty.
3. The human frailty of sin, as well as the speaker's own descent into sin and suffering, which Christ redeems through his rising from the dead on Easter.
4. In falconry, to insert feathers in a bird's wing.

Jordan (1)[1]

Who says that fictions only and false hair
Become a verse? Is there in truth no beauty?
Is all good structure in a winding stair?
May no lines pass, except they do their duty
5   Not to a true, but painted chair?

Is it no verse, except enchanted groves
And sudden arbors shadow coarse-spun lines?
Must purling° streams refresh a lover's loves?   *rippling*
Must all be veiled, while he that reads, divines,[2]
10   Catching the sense at two removes?

Shepherds are honest people; let them sing:
Riddle who list,[3] for me, and pull for prime:[4]
I envy no man's nightingale or spring;
Nor let them punish me with loss of rhyme,
15   Who plainly say, *My God, My King.*

The Collar

I struck the board,° and cried, "No more.   *table*
      I will abroad!
What? Shall I ever sigh and pine?
My lines and life are free; free as the road,
5   Loose as the wind, as large as store.°   *abundance*
      Shall I be still in suit?[1]
Have I no harvest but a thorn
To let me blood, and not restore
What I have lost with cordial[2] fruit?
10   Sure there was wine
      Before my sighs did dry it; there was corn
      Before my tears did drown it.
      Is the year only lost to me?
      Have I no bays[3] to crown it?
15 No flowers, no garlands gay? all blasted?
                          All wasted?
Not so, my heart; but there is fruit,
                          And thou hast hands.
      Recover all thy sigh-blown age
20 On double pleasures: leave thy cold dispute
Of what is fit and not forsake thy cage,
                          Thy rope of sands,
Which petty thoughts have made, and made to thee
      Good cable, to enforce and draw,
25   And be thy law,
While thou didst wink[4] and wouldst not see.

---

1. To cross the River Jordan symbolizes entering the Promised Land. This is one of two Herbert poems with this title.
2. To interpret what is obscure through magical insight or intuitive conjecture.
3. Whoever wants to may interpret.

4. Draw a lucky card, or hit upon a lucky guess.
1. Engaged in a lawsuit.
2. Invigorating to the heart.
3. The poet's laurel wreath.
4. Shut your eyes to.

Away! take heed:
I will abroad.
Call in thy death's head[5] there: tie up thy fears.
30   He that forbears
To suit and serve his need,
Deserves his load."
But as I raved and grew more fierce and wild
At every word,
35   Me thoughts I heard one calling, *Child!*
And I replied, *My Lord.*

Love (3)

Love bade me welcome: yet my soul drew back,
Guilty of dust and sin.
But quick-eyed Love, observing me grow slack°   slow, weak
From my first entrance in,
5   Drew nearer to me, sweetly questioning,
If I lacked anything.

"A guest," I answered, "worthy to be here":
Love said, "You shall be he."
"I the unkind, ungrateful? Ah my dear,
10   I cannot look on thee."
Love took my hand, and smiling did reply,
"Who made the eyes but I?"

"Truth Lord, but I marred them; let my shame
Go where it doth deserve."
15   "And know you not," says Love, "who bore the blame?"
"My dear, then I will serve."
"You must sit down," says Love, "and taste my meat."
So I did sit and eat.[1]

Richard Lovelace

1618–1657

In *To His Noble Friend*, Andrew Marvell portrays Richard Lovelace as an amorous and chivalrous courtier from a world destroyed by "Our Civil Wars." Marvell depicts the consternation that arose

When the beauteous ladies came to know
That their dear Lovelace was endangered so:
Lovelace that thawed the most congealèd breast
He who loved best and them defended best.

The dashing and handsome Lovelace was the last exemplar of courtly *sprezzatura* in the history of English poetry, recalling the eroticism and finesse of Wyatt and the chivalry of Sidney and

---

5. The skull as an emblem of human mortality.

1. The speaker takes Communion, which symbolizes union with God.

Raleigh. The voluptuousness and elegance that characterized his poetry no less than the Carolinian court was destroyed by the Puritan Revolution.

Lovelace's brief life was indeed endangered more than once—all because of his allegiance to the Royalist cause. After only two years at Cambridge University, he left school to fight in the army of King Charles I, serving as senior ensign in the First Scottish expedition of 1639 and captain in the second of 1640. Both expeditions were disasters for the King's forces. Lovelace was imprisoned twice, first in 1642 for presenting an anti-Parliamentary petition from his home county Kent and again in 1648, when Marvell's patron Lord Fairfax brought the Roundhead (Puritan) army right to the doors of Lovelace's country estate. During his first stint in prison, Lovelace wrote one of his most memorable poems, *To Althea, from Prison.* Released on bail, he lived a precarious life, aiding the King's cause by selling his property and giving money to supply arms. In 1649, when he was released from prison the second time, Lovelace was reduced to selling all of his property, even his family portraits.

Lovelace is a representative of the cultural milieu of the court of Charles I, which included many poets and painters of great distinction. The regime was graced by such poets as Sir John Suckling, Thomas Carew, Abraham Cowley, and Edmund Waller, sometimes referred to as the Cavalier poets, among whom Lovelace is considered the greatest. Lovelace admired not only the works of his fellow poets but also the paintings of Rubens, Van Dyck, and Lely, which adorned the court. Lovelace was great friends with, and wrote poems praising, Lely, who designed plates for Lovelace's two books of poems, published in 1649 and 1659. Lovelace enjoyed painting and music as a gentleman amateur, the characteristic persona of a Cavalier poet. His poems express a tone of extravagant passion tempered with courtly poise achieved through lush images conveying a sensuous *joie de vivre* and a perspective of brave insouciance mixed with self-deprecating irony. His deft rhythms create songlike poems with a spontaneous grace and ease, stylistic ideals of the Cavaliers.

We know nothing about Lovelace after 1649. His brother Philip had been colonel in the King's army but survived the Interregnum to become governor of New York in 1688. Of his brother William's death on the field of battle in the Civil War, Richard had written these Stoic lines to Philip:

> Iron decrees of Destiny
> Are ne'er wiped out with a wet eye.
> But this way you may gain the field,
> Oppose but sorrow, and 'twill yield;
> One gallant thorough made resolve
> Doth starry influence dissolve.

To Lucasta, Going to the Wars

Tell me not, sweet, I am unkind,
   That from the nunnery
Of thy chaste breast and quiet mind
   To war and arms I fly.

5   True, a new mistress now I chase,
   The first foe in the field;
And with a stronger faith embrace
   A sword, a horse, a shield.

Yet this inconstancy is such
10   As you too shall adore;
I could not love thee, dear, so much,
   Loved I not honor more.

1649

Love Made in the First Age: To Chloris[1]

In the nativity of time,
Chloris, it was not thought a crime
   In direct Hebrew for to woo.[2]
Now we make love, as all on fire,
5   Ring retrograde[3] our loud desire,
   And court in English backward too.

Thrice happy was that golden age,
When compliment was construed rage,[4]
   And fine words in the center hid;
10   When cursed *No* stained no maid's bliss,
And all discourse was summed in *Yes*,
   And nought forbade, but to forbid.

Love then unstinted, love did sip,
And cherries plucked fresh from the lip,
15   On cheeks and roses free he fed;
Lasses like autumn plums did drop,
And lads, indifferently did crop
   A flower, and a maidenhead.

Then unconfinèd each did tipple
20   Wine from the bunch, milk from the nipple;
   Paps tractable as udders were;
Then equally the wholesome jellies
Were squeezed from olive-trees, and bellies,
   Nor suits of trespass did they fear.

25   A fragrant bank of strawberries,
Diapered° with violet's eyes,   *decorated*
   Was table, tablecloth, and fare;
No palace to the clouds did swell
Each humble princess then did dwell
30   In the piazza[5] of her hair.

Both broken faith, and the cause of it,
All-damning gold was damned to the pit;
   Their troth sealed with a clasp and kiss,
Lasted until that extreme day,
35   In which they smiled their souls away,
   And, in each other breathed new bliss.

Because no fault, there was no tear;
No groan did grate the granting ear;
   No false foul breath their delicate smell:
40   No serpent kiss poisoned the taste,
Each touch was naturally chaste,
   And their mere sense a miracle.

1. "The First Age" refers to the golden age of Greek and
Roman mythology, a time of idyllic plenty in which there
was no need for laws or work.
2. Hebrew, which reads from right to left, was believed to
have been the original language.

3. In backward or reverse direction; an imitation of notes
in contrary motion.
4. When compliments were interpreted as passionate proposals.
5. A colonnade surrounding a square.

Naked as their own innocence,
And unembroidered[6] from offense
45   They went, above poor riches, gay;
On softer than the cygnet's° down,   *young swan's*
In beds they tumbled of their own;
    For each within the other lay.

Thus did they live: thus did they love,
50   Repeating only joys above;
    And angels were, but with clothes on,
Which they would put off cheerfully,
To bathe them in the galaxy,[7]
    Then gird them with the heavenly zone.[8]

55   Now, Chloris, miserably crave
The offered bliss you would not have;
    Which evermore I must deny,
Whilst ravished with these noble dreams
And crownèd with mine own soft beams,
60   Enjoying of myself I lie.

1659

━━◆◆━━

Andrew Marvell
1621–1678

Praised by his nephew for "joining the most peculiar graces of wit and learning" and berated by his antagonist Samuel Parker for speaking the language of "boat-swains and cabin boys," Andrew Marvell left little evidence for his biographers. Most of what remains of his verse has been bequeathed to posterity by virtue of a shady banking scheme on his part and an implausible claim by his housekeeper to be "Mrs. Marvell." Though she couldn't remember the date of his death, Mary Palmer tried to prove that she was the poet's wife to get at money that her master had squirrelled away in an account for some bankrupt acquaintances. To further her claim, she saw to it that Marvell's *Miscellaneous Poems* were published in 1681. In his own name, Marvell published only a few occasional poems and a satire attacking religious intolerance and political authoritarianism.

If it is thanks to Mrs. Palmer's rummaging through the poet's papers that such exquisite poems as *To His Coy Mistress* and *The Definition of Love* saw the light of day, it is largely thanks to T. S. Eliot that modern critical attention was turned to Marvell's poetry. The Augustans and Romantics neglected him, and it was not until Eliot that such features of Marvell's verse as Latinate gravity, metaphysical wit, and muscular syntax came to be fully appreciated. For ingenious ambiguity and sheer seductive sensuousness, Marvell is one of the greatest poets of all time.

As tantalizing as the verse is, it leaves little solid evidence of what was a very private life. Marvell grew up in a house surrounded by gardens in the Yorkshire town of Hull on the Humber, where his father was the Anglican rector. There is a story that Marvell once left university for London to flirt with Catholicism, but his father made sure he returned to Cambridge and

6. Not ornamented with the trappings of authority.   8. The zodiac of stars.
7. The Milky Way.

Protestantism. After his father's death, Marvell traveled in Holland, France, Italy, and Spain (1642–1647). He later tutored Mary Fairfax, daughter of Lord Fairfax of Nun-Appleton House (1650–1652), and taught William Dutton, Cromwell's ward (1653–1656). Initially recommended by Milton to serve as Assistant Latin Secretary in 1653, Marvell was first appointed Latin Secretary to the Council of State in 1657. He was elected Member of Parliament for Hull in 1659, a position he held until 1678. When Charles I returned to power, Marvell interceded on Milton's behalf and made sure his old friend and fellow poet was released from prison. Later in life, Marvell wrote satires criticizing the corruption of the Restoration regime, all but one published anonymously.

Marvell chose to keep his cards close to his chest in the ideologically volatile atmosphere of the Civil War and Restoration. A contemporary biographer remarked that Marvell "was wont to say that, he would not play the good-fellow in any man's company in whose hands he would not trust his life." He did not fight in the Civil War, since he was in Europe at the time, and as he later ambiguously maintained, "the Cause was too good to have been fought for." His strategy in dealing with change involved publicly siding with the faction in power while maintaining politically incorrect friendships and finding himself "inclinable to favor the weaker party"—whether it was a Royalist who had given his life for the King, such as Lord Hastings, or a Republican who went to prison for his convictions, such as Milton. Marvell wrote poems praising both royalists and revolutionaries. He was nothing if not tolerant.

He was also something of a chameleon, an assumer of numerous poetic personae and disguises. In *Tom May's Death*, Marvell satirized the Royalist turned Republican, here portrayed arriving in heaven drunk. Marvell equivocally praised Cromwell in *An Horatian Ode*, ironically maintaining that it was the Irish whom Cromwell had so brutally massacred who could "best affirm his praises." When he became tutor to Cromwell's ward William Dutton, Marvell wrote poems praising Cromwell in such slavishly glowing terms that the poet was made Latin Secretary to the Council of State.

The last word should go to Marvell, whose choice to translate the following chorus from Seneca's *Thyestes* shows his outlook on the vicissitudes of power:

> Climb at court for me that will
> Giddy favor's slippery hill;
> All I seek is to lie still,
> Settled in some secret nest.
> In calm leisure let me rest,
> And far off the public stage
> Pass away my silent age.
> Thus, when without noise, unknown,
> I have lived out all my span,
> I shall die without a groan,
> An old honest countryman,
> Who exposed to others' eyes,
> Into his own heart ne'er pries.
> Death to him's a strange surprise.

To His Coy Mistress[1]

Had we but world enough, and time,
This coyness, Lady, were no crime.
We would sit down, and think which way

1. A poem on the theme of *carpe diem* ("seize the day") that includes a blazon, or description of the lady from head to toe, and a logical argument: "If . . . But . . . Therefore."

To walk, and pass our long love's day.
5   Thou by the Indian Ganges' side
Shouldst rubies find: I by the tide
Of Humber would complain.[2] I would
Love you ten years before the flood:
And you should if you please refuse
10   Till the conversion of the Jews.[3]
My vegetable love should grow
Vaster then empires, and more slow.[4]
An hundred years should go to praise
Thine eyes, and on thy forehead gaze.
15   Two hundred to adore each breast:
But thirty thousand to the rest.
An age at least to every part,
And the last age should show your heart.
For Lady you deserve this State;
20   Nor would I love at lower rate.
    But at my back I always hear
Times wingèd chariot hurrying near:
And yonder all before us lie
Deserts of vast eternity.
25   Thy beauty shall no more be found;
Nor, in thy marble vault, shall sound
My echoing song: then worms shall try
That long preserved virginity:
And your quaint honor turn to dust;[5]
30   And into ashes all my lust.
The grave's a fine and private place,
But none, I think, do there embrace.
    Now, therefore, while the youthful hue
Sits on thy skin like morning dew,[6]
35   And while thy willing soul transpires
At every pore with instant fires,
Now let us sport us while we may;
And now, like amorous birds of prey,
Rather at once our time devour,
40   Than languish in his slow-chapped° power.   *slowly biting*
Let us roll all our strength, and all
Our sweetness, up into one ball:
And tear our pleasures with rough strife,
Thorough the iron gates of life.[7]
45   Thus, though we cannot make our sun
Stand still, yet we will make him run.[8]

2. Marvell grew up in Hull on the Humber River.
3. The end of time: the Flood occurred in the distant past, and Christians prophesied that Jews would convert to Christianity at the end of the world.
4. The "vegetable" was characterized only by growth, in contrast to the sensitive, which felt, and the rational, which could reason.
5. "Quaint honor," proud chastity. Note the pun on

queynte (Middle English), woman's genitals.
6. In the 1681 Folio, "dew" reads "glue," and in two manuscripts the rhymes in lines 33 and 34 are "glue" and "dew."
7. One manuscript reads "grates" for "gates."
8. Joshua made the sun stand still in the war against Gibeon (see Joshua 10.12).

The Definition of Love

My Love is of a birth as rare
As 'tis for object strange and high:
It was begotten by Despair
Upon Impossibility.

5   Magnanimous Despair alone
Could show me so divine a thing,
Where feeble Hope could ne'er have flown
But vainly flapped its tinsel wing.

And yet I quickly might arrive
10   Where my extended soul is fixed,
But Fate does iron wedges drive,
And always crowds itself betwixt.

For Fate with jealous eye does see
Two perfect loves, nor lets them close:°   *unite*
15   Their union would her ruin be,
And her tyrannic power depose.

And therefore her decrees of steel
Us as the distant poles have placed,
(Though Love's whole world on us doth wheel)
20   Not by themselves to be embraced.

Unless the giddy heaven fall,
And earth some new convulsion tear;
And, us to join, the world should all
Be cramped into a planisphere.[1]

25   As lines (so loves) oblique[2] may well
Themselves in every angle greet:
But ours so truly parallel,
Though infinite, can never meet.

Therefore the love which us doth bind,
30   But Fate so enviously debars,
Is the conjunction of the mind,
And opposition of the stars.[3]

The Garden

How vainly men themselves amaze
To win the palm, the oak, or bays,[1]
And their uncessant labors see

6. In the 1681 Folio, "dew" reads "glue," and in two manuscripts the rhymes in lines 33 and 34 are "glue" and "dew."
7. One manuscript reads "grates" for "gates."
8. Joshua made the sun stand still in the war against Gibeon (see Joshua 10.12).
1. A two-dimensional map of the globe.
2. Slanting at an angle other than a right angle, and also

veering away from right morals.
3. Conjunction: coming together in the same sign of the zodiac; union. Stars in opposition are diametrically opposed to one another.
1. Vainly: arrogantly, in vain. Amaze: bewilder, go mad. The palm, the oak, or bays: prizes symbolic of military, political, and poetic excellence.

Crowned from some single herb or tree,
5   Whose short and narrow-vergèd shade
Does prudently their toils upbraid,
While all flowers and all trees do close°   *unite*
To weave the garlands of repose.

Fair quiet, have I found thee here,
10   And innocence thy sister dear!
Mistaken long, I sought you then
In busy companies of men.
Your sacred plants, if here below,
Only among the plants will grow.
15   Society is all but rude,
To this delicious solitude.[2]

No white nor red[3] was ever seen
So am'rous as this lovely green.
Fond lovers, cruel as their flame,
20   Cut in these trees their mistress' name.
Little, alas, they know, or heed,
How far these beauties hers exceed!
Fair trees! whereso'er your barks I wound,
No name shall but your own be found.

25   When we have run our passion's heat,
Love hither makes his best retreat.
The gods, that mortal beauty chase,
Still in a tree did end their race.
Apollo hunted Daphne so,
30   Only that she might laurel grow,
And Pan did after Syrinx speed,
Not as a nymph, but for a reed.[4]

What wondrous life in this I lead!
Ripe apples drop about my head;
35   The luscious clusters of the vine
Upon my mouth do crush their wine;
The nectarine, and curious peach,
Into my hands themselves do reach;
Stumbling on melons, as I pass,
40   Insnared with flowers, I fall on grass.

Meanwhile the mind, from pleasure less,
Withdraws into its happiness:
The mind, that ocean where each kind
Does straight its own resemblance find,[5]

---

2. Compare to Katherine Philips's *A Country-life*: "Then welcome dearest solitude, / My great felicity; / Though some are pleased to call thee rude."
3. Colors used to describe the beloved's beauty.
4. As god of poetry, Apollo seeks the laurel (the bays), while Pan seeks the syrinx (pipe) of pastoral poetry. Apollo chased Daphne, who prayed to be saved from him

and was transformed into a laurel tree, just as Syrinx escaped Pan's lust when she was turned into a reed.
5. It was popularly believed that animals and plants on land had counterparts in the sea. This line describes the mind as innately possessing ideas, a concept of Platonic philosophy.

45   Yet it creates, transcending these,
      Far other worlds, and other seas,
      Annihilating all that's made
      To a green thought in a green shade.

      Here at the fountain's sliding foot,
50   Or at some fruit-tree's mossy root,
      Casting the body's vest aside,
      My soul into the boughs does glide:
      There like a bird it sits and sings,
      Then whets and combs its silver wings;
55   And, till prepared for longer flight,
      Waves in its plumes the various light.

      Such was that happy garden-state,
      While man there walked without a mate:
      After a place so pure and sweet,
60   What other help could yet be meet!
      But 'twas beyond a mortal's share
      To wander solitary there:
      Two paradises 'twere in one
      To live in paradise alone.

65   How well the skillful gardener drew
      Of flowers and herbs this dial new;[6]
      Where from above the milder sun
      Does through a fragrant zodiac run;
      And, as it works, th' industrious bee
70   Computes its time as well as we.[7]
      How could such sweet and wholesome hours
      Be reckoned but with herbs and flowers!

An Horatian Ode Upon Cromwell's Return from Ireland[1]

      The forward youth that would appear
      Must now forsake his muses dear,
            Nor in the shadows sing
            His numbers[2] languishing.
5   'Tis time to leave the books in dust,
      And oil th' unusèd armor's rust:
            Removing from the wall
            The corslet[3] of the hall.
      So restless Cromwell could not cease
10   In the inglorious arts of peace,
            But through adventurous war
            Urgèd his active star.

6. The garden is arranged as a floral sundial.
7. Computes its time: a pun on thyme.
1. Cromwell returned from his military campaign in Ireland in May 1650. After General Fairfax resigned as commander of the parliamentary army because he refused to invade Scotland, Cromwell assumed his position and attacked the Scots. This poem was printed in the 1681 edition but then was canceled from printed copies until 1776. The influence of Horace's Odes (especially I. 35, 37; IV. 4, 5, 14, 15) surfaces in the poised dignity of the verse and its subtly ambiguous attitude toward power.
2. Conformity to a rhythmical pattern in verse or music.
3. Defensive armor covering the upper body.

And, like the three-forked lightning, first
Breaking the clouds where it was nursed,
15   Did thorough his own side
          His fiery way divide:[4]
For 'tis all one to courage high
The emulous or enemy;
          And with such to enclose
20   Is more than to oppose.
Then burning through the air he went,
And palaces and temples rent:
          And Caesar's head at last
          Did through his laurels blast.[5]
25   'Tis madness to resist or blame
The force of angry heaven's flame:
          And, if we would speak true,
          Much to the man is due,
Who, from his private gardens, where
30   He lived reservèd and austere,
          As if his highest plot
          To plant the bergamot,[6]
Could by industrious valor climb
To ruin the great work of Time,
35   And cast the kingdom old
          Into another mold;
Though justice against fate complain,
And plead the ancient rights in vain:
          But those do hold or break,
40   As men are strong or weak.
Nature, that hateth emptiness,
Allows of penetration less:[7]
          And therefore must make room
          Where greater spirits come.
45   What field of all the Civil Wars,
Where his were not the deepest scars?
          And Hampton[8] shows what part
          He had of wiser art,
Where, twining subtle fears with hope,
50   He wove a net of such a scope,
          That Charles himself might chase
          To Carisbrooke's narrow case:
That thence the royal actor borne,
The tragic scaffold might adorn;
55   While round the armèd bands
          Did clap their bloody hands.

---

4. Cromwell's overtaking his rivals in Parliament is described as an elemental force similar to the "three-forked lightning" of Zeus.
5. Although lightning was thought not to strike the laurel (symbolizing the royal crown), Cromwell had struck down Charles I (Caesar).
6. A pear known as the "prince's pear."

7. Nature abhors not only a vacuum but even more so the penetration of one body's space by another body.
8. Hampton Court where Charles I was held captive before his execution in 1649. He had fled to Carrisbrooke Castle on the Isle of Wight, where he was betrayed to the Governor in 1647.

He nothing common did or mean
Upon that memorable scene:
    But with his keener eye
60   The axe's[9] edge did try;
Nor called the gods with vulgar spite
To vindicate his helpless right,
    But bowed his comely head,
    Down, as upon a bed.
65 This was that memorable hour
Which first assured the forcèd power.
    So when they did design
    The Capitol's first line,
A bleeding head where they begun,
70 Did fright the architects to run;
    And yet in that the State
    Foresaw it's happy fate.[1]
And now the Irish are ashamed
To see themselves in one year tamed:[2]
75   So much one man can do,
    That does both act and know.
They can affirm his praises best,
And have, though overcome, confessed
    How good he is, how just,
80   And fit for highest trust.[3]
Nor yet grown stiffer with command,
But still in the Republic's hand:
    How fit he is to sway
    That can so well obey.[4]
85 He to the commons' feet presents
A kingdom, for his first year's rents:
    And, what he may, forbears
    His fame to make it theirs:
And has his sword and spoils ungirt,
90 To lay them at the public's skirt.
    So when the falcon high
    Falls heavy from the sky,
She, having killed, no more does search,
But on the next green bough to perch;
95   Where, when he first does lure,
    The falconer has her sure.
What may not then our isle presume
While victory his crest does plume!
    What may not others fear
100   If thus he crown each year!

---

9. Marvell plays on the Latin "*acies*," the sharp edge of a sword, a keen glance, and the vanguard of battle.
1. In digging the foundations of the temple of Jupiter Capitolinum, the excavators found a human's head (*caput*), which was interpreted as prophesying that Rome should be the capitol of the Empire (see Livy, *Annals* I.55.6).

2. From August 1649 to his return to England in May 1650, Cromwell went on a savage military campaign that included the slaughter of Irish civilians.
3. An example of one of the many equivocal statements in this poem; of course, the Irish did not affirm Cromwell's greatness.
4. A saying attributed to the Athenian Solon the lawgiver.

A Caesar he ere long to Gaul,
To Italy an Hannibal,[5]
   And to all states not free
   Shall climactéric° be.   *period of change*
105   The Pict no shelter now shall find
Within his particolored mind;
   But from this valor sad°   *severe*
   Shrink underneath the plaid;[6]
Happy if in the tufted brake
110   The English hunter him mistake;
   Nor lay his hounds in near
   The Caledonian° deer.   *Scottish*
But thou the wars' and fortune's son
March indefatigably on;
115   And for the last effect
   Still keep thy sword erect:
Besides the force it has to fright
The spirits of the shady night,[7]
   The same arts that did gain
120   A power must it maintain.

Katherine Philips
1631–1664

Idolized as the "Matchless Orinda" in her own day, Katherine Philips is now taking her place in the history of English verse after two centuries of neglect. During her lifetime, her work circulated in manuscript among a close network of friends. The first edition of her poems appeared posthumously in 1664. The second edition of 1667 was evidently a commercial success, since it was reprinted in 1669, 1678, and 1710. The next complete edition of her poems did not appear until 1994.

John Keats esteemed Philips's *To Mrs. Mary Awbrey at Parting* as an example of "real feminine Modesty"; today, by contrast, critics praise her poems to women friends as reminiscent of the ancient Greek Sappho's erotic lyrics. By imitating Donne's love lyrics in her poems to women, Philips poetically conceives of these friendships as no less world-changing, no less ennobling and enthralling, than Donne's romantic liaisons. Some of the best poets of her own day were able to appreciate her as a fellow poet rather than as Keats's romanticized ideal woman. Marvell paid tribute to her by subtly alluding to lines of her poetry in one of his greatest poems, *The Garden*. And Henry Vaughan insisted that "No laurel grows, but for [her] brow."

Katherine Philips's work was particularly important for other women writers. Philips's lyric poetry influenced such other early modern women poets as Aphra Behn and Anne Killigrew. Yet it is impossible to pigeonhole Philips as stereotypically feminine. She wrote on public and political themes as well as personal subjects, endowing traditional genres such as the parting poem, the elegy, and the epitaph, with a particular directness and clarity all her own.

---

5. Neither Caesar nor Hannibal gave freedom to peoples whose countries they invaded and conquered.
6. Marvell uses "Picts" the ancient name for the Scots, creating a play on *picti* (Latin: painted) and particolored.

7. There was an ancient tradition of dead spirits being frightened by raised swords (Homer, *Odyssey* 11; Virgil, *Aeneid* 6). The dead spirits referred to here include the dead in the wars in Ireland and England, including the king.

Katherine Philips was born in London to a well-to-do Presbyterian family. Her father was a prosperous merchant, and her mother was the daughter of a Fellow of the Royal College of Physicians. Philips's father was wealthy enough to invest two hundred pounds for a thousand acres in Ulster, a scheme that was begun in 1642 by the Puritan Parliament but, ironically, not realized until the Restoration, when we find Katherine in Ireland pursuing lawsuits to obtain this land. As a girl, Katherine attended Mrs. Salmon's Presbyterian School, where she learned to love poetry and began to write verses. In 1646 her widowed mother married Sir Richard Philips, and the family moved to his castle in Wales. Philips herself married Sir Richard's kinsman James Philips, and they lived together for twelve years in the small Welsh town of Cardigan when not in London, where her husband served as Member of Parliament during the Interregnum.

However Presbyterian and Cromwellian were the associations of her family and marriage, she emerged after the Restoration as a complete Anglican. Not only did she write poetry against the regicide, such as *Upon the Double Murder of King Charles*, but she became a favorite author at court. She was encouraged to write poetry by her friend "Poliarchus," Sir Charles Cotterell, Master of Ceremonies in the Court of Charles II, who showed her poems to the royal family. An Anglo-Irish nobleman, the Earl of Orrery, encouraged her to complete a translation of Corneille's *Pompey* and actually produced and had the play printed in Dublin in 1663.

Katherine Philips developed friendships that became the theme of what most critics regard as her best poems. Perhaps the most intense of these friendships was that with Mrs. Anne Owen, the Lucasia of Philips's most passionate poems, several of which echo love poems by Donne. Her friend Sir Edward Dering, whom she called "the Noble Silvander," lamented Katherine Philips's death in recounting the extraordinary accomplishment of both her poetry and her life, which had attempted

> the most generous design . . . to unite all those of her acquaintance which she found worthy or desired to make so (among which later number she was pleased to give me a place) into one society, and by the bands of friendship to make an alliance more firm than what nature, our country or equal education can produce.

Friendship in Emblem,
or the Seal,[1]

TO MY DEAREST LUCASIA[2]

The hearts thus intermixèd speak
A love that no bold shock can break;
For joined and growing, both in one,
Neither can be disturbed alone.

5   That means a mutual knowledge too;
For what is't either heart can do,
Which by its panting sentinel°   guard
It does not to the other tell?

That friendship hearts so much refines,
10   It nothing but itself designs:

---

1. A symbolic picture, which appeared with a motto and a poem in such books as Geoffrey Whitney's *Choice of Emblems*. The central emblematic image of this poem is "the compasses" (line 21); another emblem is "those flames" (line 14).

2. Anne Owen, to whom many of Philips's poems are dedicated, was a neighbor of hers in Wales and a close friend from 1651 until Philips's death.

The hearts are free from lower ends,
For each point to the other tends.

They flame, 'tis true, and several ways,
But still those flames do so much raise,
15   That while to either they incline
They yet are noble and divine.

From smoke or hurt those flames are free,
From grossness or mortality:
The hearts (like Moses bush presumed)[3]
20   Warmed and enlightened, not consumed.

The compasses that stand above
Express this great immortal Love;[4]
For friends, like them, can prove this true,
They are, and yet they are not, two.

25   And in their posture is expressed
Friendship's exalted interest:
Each follows where the other leans,
And what each does, the other means.

And as when one foot does stand fast,
30   And t'other circles seeks to cast,
The steady part does regulate
And make the wanderer's motion straight:

So friends are only two in this,
T'reclaim each other when they miss:
35   For whose'er will grossly fall,
Can never be a friend at all.

And as that useful instrument
For even lines was ever meant;
So friendship from good angels[5] springs,
40   To teach the world heroic things.

As these are found out in design
To rule and measure every line;
So friendship governs actions best,
Prescribing law to all the rest.

45   And as in nature nothing's set
So just as lines and numbers met;
So compasses for these being made,
Do friendship's harmony persuade.

And like to them, so friends may own
50   Extension, not division:
Their points, like bodies, separate;
But head, like souls, knows no such fate.

---

3. See Exodus 3.2–5 for the burning bush from which God called Moses.
4. Compare the image of the compasses here to the "twin compasses" in Donne's A Valediction: Forbidding Mourn-ing, page 668.
5. Guardian spirits, with puns on angels, and angeli (Latin), messengers.

And as each part so well is knit,
That their embraces ever fit:
55   So friends are such by destiny,
And no third can the place supply.

There needs no motto to the seal:
But that we may the mine⁶ reveal
To the dull eye, it was thought fit
60   That friendship only should be writ.

But as there is degrees of bliss,
So there's no friendship meant by this,
But such as will transmit to fame
Lucasia's and Orinda's name.

Upon the Double Murder of King Charles
in Answer to a Libelous Rhyme Made by V. P.¹

I think not on the state, nor am concerned
Which way soever that great helm is turned,
But as that son whose father's danger nigh
Did force his native dumbness, and untie
5   The fettered organs: so here is a cause
That will excuse the breach of nature's laws.²
Silence were now a sin: nay passion now
Wise men themselves for merit would allow.
What noble eye could see, (and careless pass)
10   The dying lion kicked by every ass?
Hath Charles so broke God's laws, he must not have
A quiet crown, nor yet a quiet grave?
Tombs have been sanctuaries; thieves lie here
Secure from all their penalty and fear.
15   Great Charles his double misery was this,
Unfaithful friends, ignoble enemies;
Had any heathen been this prince's foe,
He would have wept to see him injured so.
His title was his crime, they'd reason good
20   To quarrel at the right they had withstood.
He broke God's laws, and therefore he must die,
And what shall then become of thee and I?
Slander must follow treason; but yet stay,
Take not our reason with our king away.
25   Though you have seized upon all our defense,
Yet do not sequester° our common sense.   excommunicate, confiscate

---

6. A mass of gold, a store of plenty, as well as a pun on the possessive pronoun meaning "my own" and perhaps also on "mind."

1. Vavasor Powell, a Fifth Monarchist who believed that Christ's second coming was imminent, and an ardent Republican, whose verses on the murder of the king are lost. According to Philips's poem, Powell argued that Charles I had usurped God's power.

2. Breaking the prohibition against women speaking on public affairs. See Margaret Tyler, Perspectives: Tracts on Women and Gender, page 706, for a defense of woman's ability to write about war, traditionally considered only appropriate to male authors.

But I admire not at this new supply:
No bounds will hold those who at scepters fly.
Christ will be King, but I ne'er understood,
His subjects built his kingdom up with blood,
(Except their own) or that he would dispense
With his commands, though for his own defense.
Oh! to what height of horror are they come,
Who dare pull down a crown, tear up a tomb![3]

30

To the Truly Noble, and Obliging Mrs. Anne Owen
(on My First Approaches)[1]

Madam,
As in a triumph conquerors admit
Their meanest captives to attend on it,[2]
Who, though unworthy, have the power confessed,
And justified the yielding of the rest:
So when the busy world (in hope t'excuse
Their own surprise) your conquests do peruse,
And find my name, they will be apt to say
Your charms were blinded, or else thrown away.
There is no honor got in gaining me,
Who am a prize not worth your victory.
But this will clear you, that 'tis general
The worst applaud what is admired by all.
But I have plots in't: for the way to be
Secure of fame to all posterity,
Is to obtain the honor I pursue,
To tell the world I was subdued by you.
And since in you all wonders common are,
Your votaries° may in your virtues share,   *devoted admirers*
While you by noble magic worth impart:
She that can conquer, can reclaim a heart.
Of this creation I shall not despair,
Since for your own sake it concerns your care:
For 'tis more honor that the world should know
You made a noble soul, than found it so.

5

10

15

20

To My Excellent Lucasia, on Our Friendship
17th. July 1651[1]

I did not live until this time
    Crowned my felicity,
When I could say without a crime,
    I am not thine, but thee.

3. Possibly a reference to the unearthing of the regicides'
bodies.
1. Mrs. Anne Owen of Orielton, Wales, was Philips's
close friend and the Lucasia of her poems; she was married to John Owen and was the heiress to the ancient seat
of Presaddfed in Anglesey.
2. Here, "triumph" means military victory and the triumphal procession that announced it.
1. Philips met her friend Anne Owen (called Lucasia) in
1651.

5 This carcass breathed, and walked, and slept,
  So that the world believed
There was a soul the motions kept;
  But they were all deceived.
For as a watch by art is wound
10 To motion, such was mine:
But never had Orinda found
  A soul till she found thine;
Which now inspires, cures and supplies,
  And guides my darkened breast:
15 For thou art all that I can prize,
  My joy, my life, my rest.
Nor bridegroom's nor crowned conqueror's mirth
  To mine compared can be:
They have but pieces of this earth,
20 I've all the world in thee.
Then let our flame still light and shine,
  (And no bold fear control)
As innocent as our design,
  Immortal as our soul.

The World

 We falsely think it due unto our friends,
That we should grieve for their too early ends:
He that surveys the world with serious eyes,
And strips her from her gross and weak disguise,[1]
5 Shall find 'tis injury to mourn their fate;
He only dies untimely who dies late.
For if 'twere told to children in the womb,
To what a stage of mischief they must come;
Could they foresee with how much toil and sweat
10 Men court that gilded nothing, being great;
What pains they take not to be what they seem,
Rating their bliss by others' false esteem,
And sacrificing their content, to be
Guilty of grave and serious vanity;
15 How each condition hath its proper thorns,
And what one man admires, another scorns;
How frequently their happiness they miss,
And so far from agreeing what it is,
That the same person we can hardly find,
20 Who is an hour together in a mind;
Sure they would beg a period of their breath,
And what we call their birth would count their death.
Mankind is mad; for none can live alone,
Because their joys stand by comparison:
25 And yet they quarrel at society,
And strive to kill they know not whom, nor why.

---

1. The Platonic notion that the body is a covering for the soul.

We all live by mistake, delight in dreams,
Lost to ourselves, and dwelling in extremes;
Rejecting what we have, though ne'er so good,
30 And prizing what we never understood.
Compared to our boisterous inconstancy
Tempests are calm, and discords harmony.
Hence we reverse the world, and yet do find
The God that made can hardly please our mind.
35 We live by chance, and slip into events;
Have all of beasts except their innocence.
The soul, which no man's power can reach, a thing
That makes each woman man, each man a king,
Doth so much loose, and from its height so fall,
40 That some contend to have no soul at all.
'Tis either not observed, or at the best
By passion fought withall, by sin depressed.
Freedom of will (God's image) is forgot;
And if we know it, we improve it not.
45 Our thoughts, though nothing can be more our own,
Are still unguided, very seldom known.
Time 'scapes our hands as water in a sieve,
We come to die ere we begin to live.
Truth, the most suitable and noble prize,
50 Food of our spirits, yet neglected lies.
Errors and shadows are our choice, and we
Owe our perdition to our own decree.
If we search truth, we make it more obscure;
And when it shines, we can't the light endure.
55 For most men who plod on, and eat, and drink,
Have nothing less their business than to think;
And those few that enquire, how small a share
Of truth they find! how dark their notions are!
That serious evenness that calms the breast,
60 And in a tempest can bestow a rest,
We either not attempt, or else decline,
By every trifle snatched from our design.
(Others he must in his deceits involve,
Who is not true unto his own resolve.)
65 We govern not ourselves, but loose the reins,
Courting our bondage to a thousand chains;
And with as many slaveries content,
As there are tyrants ready to torment,
We live upon a rack, extended still
70 To one extreme, or both, but always ill.
For since our fortune is not understood,
We suffer less from bad than from the good.
The sting is better dressed and longer lasts,
As surfeits are more dangerous than fasts.
75 And to complete the misery to us,
We see extremes are still contiguous.
And as we run so fast from what we hate,

Like squibs on ropes,[2] to know no middle state;
So (outward storms strengthened by us) we find
80   Our fortune as disordered as our mind.
But that's excused by this, it doth its part;
A treacherous world befits a treacherous heart.
All ill's our own; the outward storms we loathe
Receive from us their birth, or sting, or both;
85   And that our vanity be past a doubt,
'Tis one new vanity to find it out.
Happy are they to whom God gives a grave,
And from themselves as from his wrath doth save.
'Tis good not to be born; but if we must,
90   The next good is, soon to return to dust:
When th'uncaged[3] soul, fled to eternity,
Shall rest, and live, and sing, and love, and see.
Here we but crawl and grope, and play and cry;[4]
Are first our own, then other's enemy:
95   But there shall be defaced both stain and score,
For time, and death, and sin shall be no more.[5]

PERSPECTIVES

Tracts on Women and Gender

What is the nature of woman? Is she meant to be subordinate to man or an equal partner? What virtues is she capable of? Does she have intellectual ability, and if so, is it appropriate for her to write? How should she behave toward her husband? What are his responsibilities to her? What is the difference between a good woman and a bad one? What is the difference between manly behavior and womanly behavior? These are some of the questions that early modern English tracts on women and gender ask. Although we would not ask all of these questions in precisely the same way today, they are still of burning interest. The debate over these questions in early modern tracts on women sheds light on the representation of sex and gender in the poetry and drama of the period. By *sex* is meant the representation of biological difference; by *gender* is meant the representation of sex difference as it is socially constructed.

In the Middle Ages there were both attacks on women and defenses of them by both women and men, but intellectual and social changes modified the debate in the early modern period. One of the prominent medieval genres that continued to be imitated in the early modern period was the praise of exemplary women, such as Boccaccio's *De Claris Mulieribus* ("concerning famous women"), Chaucer's *Legend of Good Women*, and Christine de Pisan's *Le Livre de la Cité des Dames* (translated into English in 1521 as *The Book of the City of Ladies*). Renaissance humanism brought a new intellectual rigor to the genre. The German humanist Heinrich Cornelius Agrippa (1486–1535) stands out in the early Tudor controversy of the 1540s. Agrippa's *De Nobilitate et Praecellentia Foemenei Sexus* (translated in 1542 as *A Treatise of the Nobilitie and Excellencye of Woman Kynde*) not only lists Biblical and classical heroines but also examines how the place of women in society is determined by culture rather than nature: "And thus by these lawes, the women being subdued as it were by force of arms, are constrained to give place to men, and to obey their subduers, not by natural, nor divine necessity

---

2. A display of fireworks on a line.
3. Free from the body.

4. See 1 Corinthians 13.11–12.
5. See Revelation 21.4.

Title page from *The English Gentlewoman*, by Richard Brathwaite. 1631.

or reason, but by custom, education, fortune, and a certain tyrannical occasion." However, even a humanist author such as Erasmus, who had enlightened views on other social issues, had very strict views about the absolute subordination of wife to husband. Indeed, this subordination seems to have increased in intensity in the early modern period as the nuclear family headed by the father superseded the extended family, in which power was more dispersed throughout the network of kinship.

Among the learned, the new classical humanist education was still largely reserved for young men. Such changes moved the historian Joan Kelly Gadol to ask, "Did women have a Renaissance?" At the same time, some early modern women were educated enough to represent themselves in the debate on the nature of women, and they brought new perspectives to it. Margaret Tyler was one of the first English women to speak in defense of women as writers. Rachel Speght, the first polemical or argumentative woman writer in English, wrote her defense of women in response to a controversy set in motion by the publication of Joseph Swetnam's *An Arraignment of Lewd, Idle, Froward, and Unconstant Women* (1615). Swetnam was a misogynist (woman hater), but his tract had the virtue of eliciting defenses of women. Among these responses were *A Muzzle for Melastomus*, written from the theological perspective of Rachel Speght, and *Ester Hath Hanged Haman*, written from the more secular outlook of "Esther Sowernam" (a pen-name adopted to counter the "sweet" in the name Swetnam). Two other tracts of the 1620s, *Hic Mulier* ("the mannish woman") and *Haec Vir* ("the womanish man") humorously raised the problem of the blurring of genders and carried on a debate about the style of dress and behavior that men and women should adopt.

Whether these tracts take the form of an oration, a speech by one person, or a dialogue between two people (as in *Haec Vir*), they are all in lively conversation with each other, either directly or indirectly. They are also in a lively conversation with other texts in this period. Questions about marriage and a wife's relations with people other than her husband as well as a woman's speech and silence are dealt with directly in *Othello*. Representing only a fraction of the early modern literature on women and gender, these tracts attest to heightened interest in questions of gender, such as those posed by the speakers in Lady Mary Wroth's and Katherine Philips's poems.

◆━━ ◄✦► ━━◆

Desiderius Erasmus
1469?–1536

Erasmus was the author not only of the humorous *Encomium Morae* (*The Praise of Folly*), dedicated to his friend Thomas More, but also of numerous works on Christian morals. Although *The Praise of Folly* was translated into English only in 1551, Erasmus's *Coniugium* (c. 1523), a text on marriage, appeared in English as *A Mery Dialogue, Declaringe the Propertyes of Shrewde Shrewes, and Honest Wyves* as early as 1542. This text advocated wifely submissiveness but also domesticity for both men and women—concepts that influenced the English bourgeois notion of marriage. Richard Tavernour also translated Erasmus's writing on marriage as *A Ryght Frutefull Epystle Devised in Laude and Praise of Matrimony* (1534). The following passage from this text demonstrates a view of marriage as the closest possible bond between human beings—and, more than that, as a sacrament calling for the wife's sole loyalty to her husband and lasting even beyond death.

from In Laude and Praise of Matrimony

* * * if the most part of things (yea which be also bitter) are of a good man to be desired for none other purpose, but because they be honest, matrimony doubtless is chiefly to be desired whereof a man may doubt whether it hath more honesty than pleasure. For what thing is sweeter than with her to live, with whom ye may be most straightly coupled, not only in the benevolence of the mind, but also in the conjunction of the body? If a great delectation of mind be taken of the benevolence of our other kinsmen, since it is an especial sweetness to have one with whom ye may communicate the secret affections of your mind, with whom ye may speak even as it were with your own self, whom ye may safely trust, which supposeth your chances to be his, what felicity (think ye) have the conjunction of man and wife, than which no thing in the universal world may be found either greater or firmer. For with our other friends we be conjoined only with the benevolence of minds, with our wife we be coupled with most high love, with permixtion[1] of bodies, with the confederate band of the sacrament, and finally with the fellowship of all chances. Furthermore, in other friendships, how great simulation is there, how great falsity? Yea, they whom we

---

1. A thorough mixture or mingling.

judge our best friends, like as the swallows flee away when summer is gone, so they forsake us when fortune turneth her wheel. And sometime the fresher friend casts out the old. We hear of few whose fidelity endure till their lives' end. The wife's love is with no falsity corrupted, with no simulation obscured, with no chance of things minished,[2] finally with death only (nay not with death neither) withdrawn. She, the love of her parents, she, the love of her sisters, she, the love of her brethren, despiseth for the love of you, her only respect is to you, of you she hangeth,[3] with you she coveteth to die. * * *

* * * Do ye judge any pleasure to be compared with this so great a conjunction? If ye tarry at home there is at hand which shall drive away the tediousness of solitary being. If from home ye have one that shall kiss you when ye depart, long for you when ye be absent, receive you joyously when ye return. A sweet companion of youth, a kind solace of age. By nature yea any fellowship is delectable to man, as whom nature hath created to benevolence and friendship. This fellowship then how shall it not be most sweet, in which everything is common to them both? And contrarily, if we see the savage beasts also abhor[4] solitary living and delighted in fellowship, in my mind he is not once to be supposed a man, which abhoreth from[5] this fellowship most honest and pleasant of all. For what is more hateful than the man which (as though he were born only to himself) liveth for himself, seeketh for himself, spareth for himself, doth cost to himself, loveth no person, is loved of no person? Shall not such a monster be adjudged worthy to be cast out of all men's company into the mid sea with Timon the Athenian,[6] which because he fled all men's company, was called Misanthropus that is to say hate man. * * *

But I know well enough what among these, ye murmur against me. A blessed thing is wedlock, if all prove according to the desire, But what if a wayward wife chanceth?[7] What if an unchaste? What if unnatural children? There will run in your mind the examples of those whom wedlock have brought to utter destruction. Heap up as much as ye can, but yet these be the vices of men and not of wedlock. Believe me, an evil wife is not wont to chance, but to evil husbands. Put this unto it, that it lieth in you to choose out a good one. But what if after the marriage she be marred?[8] Of an evil husband (I will well) a good wife may be marred, but of a good, the evil is wont to be reformed and mended. We blame wives falsely. No man (if ye give any credence to men) had ever a shrew to his wife, but through his own default.[9]

——— ⪥◆⪤ ———

Barnabe Riche
1542–1617

A veteran of wars in the Low Countries and Ireland and author of twenty-six books, Barnabe Riche led a life as fraught with contention as his writing. Best known as the author of *His Farewell to Military Profession* (1581), which contains the source for Shakespeare's *Twelfth Night*, Riche was both a keen observer of contemporary social life and a spy. Alongside his attacks on shameless city women in *My Lady's Looking Glass* (1616) and *A New Description of Ireland* (1610), he also portrays Dublin ladies as critics of his work in *A*

2. Diminished, lessened in power.
3. In the sense of clinging, holding fast, adhering.
4. Hate.
5. Shrink with horror from.
6. The story of how Timon shunned society after his

friends abandoned him when he lost his wealth is told by Plutarch (the source for Shakespeare's *Timon of Athens*).
7. Comes about by chance.
8. Injured.
9. Fault.

True and Kind Excuse (1612)—an interesting episode documenting women's literacy in this period. His writing has the zealous spirit of reforming Protestantism and looks forward to the impassioned prose of radical dissenters in the Civil War. *My Lady's Looking Glass* was published by Thomas Adams, London, in 1616, and dedicated to Lady Saint Jones, wife of the Lord Deputy of Ireland. This text bears comparison with Riche's *Excellency of Good Women* (London, 1613), as well as numerous other Jacobean tracts on the conduct of women.

from My Lady's Looking Glass

But my promise was to give rules how to distinguish between a good woman and a bad, and promise is debt, but I must be well advised how I take the matter in hand; for we were better to charge a woman with a thousand defects in her soul, than with that one abuse of her body; and we must have two witnesses, besides our own eyes, to testify, or we shall not be believed: but I myself have thought of a couple that I hope will carry credit.

The first is the prophet Isaiah, that in his days challenged the daughters of Zion for their stretched-out necks, their wandering eyes, at their mincing and wanton demeanor as they passed through the streets: these signs and shows have ever been thought to be the special marks whereby to know a harlot.[1] But Solomon in a more particular manner better furnishes us with more assured notes, and to the end that we might the better distinguish the good woman from the bad, he delivereth their several qualities, and wherein they are opposite: and speaking of a good woman he saith, *She seeketh out wool and flax, and laboreth cheerfully with her hands: she overseeth the ways of her household, and eateth not the bread of idleness.*[2]

Solomon thinketh that a good woman should be a home *housewife*, he pointeth her out her housework. *She overseeth the ways of her household*, she must look to her children, her servants and family; but *the paths of a harlot* (he saith) *are movable, for now she is in the house, now in the streets, now she lies in wait in every corner*, she is still gadding from place to place, from person to person, from company to company; from custom to custom, she is evermore wandering: her feet are wandering, her eyes are wandering, her wits are wandering, *Her ways are like the ways of a serpent:* hard to be found out.[3]

A good woman (again) *opens her mouth with wisdom, the law of grace is in her tongue:* but *a harlot is full of words, she is loud and babbling*, saith Solomon.

She is bold, she is impudent, she is shameless, she cannot blush: and she that hath lost all these virtues hath lost her evidence of honesty: for the ornaments of a good woman are temperance in her mind, silence in her tongue, and bashfulness in her countenance.

It is not she that can lift up her heels highest in the dancing of a galliard,[4] she that is lavish of her lips or loose of her tongue.

Now if Solomon's testimony be good, the woman that is impudent, immodest, shameless, insolent, audacious, a night-walker, a company-keeper, a gadder from place to place, a reveller, a ramper, a roister, a rioter: she that has these properties, has the certain signs and marks of a harlot, as Solomon has avowed. Now what credit his words will carry in the Commissaries' court, I leave to those that be advocates, and proctors in women's causes.[5]

---

1. See Isaiah 3.16.
2. See Proverbs 31.13, 27.
3. See Proverbs 7.10–12.
4. A lively dance in triple time.

5. Commissaries' court: the court of a bishop's representative, which had jurisdiction over divorce and probate; advocates: pleaders, legal counselors; proctors: attorneys.

I have hitherto presented to your view the true resemblance of a harlot, as well what she is, as how she might be discerned: I would now give you the like notice of that notable *Strumpet, the whore of Babylon,*[6] that has made so many Kings and Emperors drunk with the cup of abominations, by whom the nations of the earth have so defiled themselves by their spiritual fornication, called in the Scripture by the name of *idolatry* (but now within the last five hundred years, amongst Christians) shadowed under the title of Popery. This harlot has her agents, Popes, Cardinals, Bishops, Abbots, Monks, Friars, Jesuits, Priests, with a number of other like, and all of them factors in her bands,[7] the professed enemies of the Gospel of Jesus Christ, that do superstitiously adore the crucifix, and are indeed enemies of the cross of Christ, and do tread his holy blood under their scornful feet: that build up devotion with ignorance, and do ring out their hot alarms in the ears of the unlearned, teaching that the light can be no light, that the Scriptures can be no Scriptures, nor the truth can be no truth, but by their allowance, and if they will say that high noon is midnight, we must believe them, and make no more ado but get us to bed.

❈

Margaret Tyler
flourished 1578

Margaret Tyler is best known today for the preface to her translation of Diego Ortunez de Calahorra's Spanish prose romance *The Mirrour of Princely Deedes and Knighthood,* Book I (1578), in which she argues that women have the ability to write on any subject. She was a waiting woman in the Catholic household of the Duke of Norfolk in the 1560s, where she may have read her translation aloud to the Duchess and her circle. In the preface to her translation, Tyler refers both to the "friends" who wanted her to return to her "old reading" and defends herself against potential critics who might object to her translating "matter more manlike than becometh my sex." She argues that she is more interested in virtue than in war and that, in any case, war affects women as much as it does men. The sixteenth-century humanist Vives had viewed romances as unsuitable for women readers, while male authors of romances often dedicated their work to women. Arguing for women's right to an education, Tyler reasons that if men can dedicate their texts to women, then women can read them, and that if women can read texts on such subjects as war and government, then they can write them.

from Preface to The First Part of the Mirror of Princely Deeds

Thou hast here, gentle Reader, the history of Trebatio, an Emperor in Greece: whether a true history of him indeed, or a feigned fable, I wot[1] not, neither did I greatly seek after it in the translation, but by me it is done into English for thy profit and delight. The chief matter therein contained, is of exploits of wars, and the parties therein named are especially renowned for their magnanimity and courage. * * * Such delivery as I have made I hope thou wilt friendly accept, the rather for that it is a woman's work, though in a story profane, and a matter more manlike than becometh my sex. But as for any manliness of the matter, thou knowest that it is not necessary for every trumpeter or drumstare[2] in the war to be a good fighter. They take wages only to incite others, though themselves have privy maims,[3] and are thereby recure-

---

6. An image from Revelation 17, taken by Protestants to symbolize the Roman Catholic Church.
7. Agents in her leagues, or covenants.

1. Know.
2. Drummer.
3. Secret weaknesses.

less.[4] So, gentle reader, if my travail in Englishing this author may bring thee to a liking of the virtues herein commended, and by example thereof in thy princes' and countries' quarrel to hazard thy person, and purchase good name, as for hope of well deserving myself that way, I neither bend my self thereto, nor yet fear the speech of people if I be found backward. I trust every man holds not the plough, which would that the ground were tilled, and it is no sin to talk of Robin Hood, though you never shot in his bow. Or be it that the attempt were bold to intermeddle in arms, as the ancient Amazons[5] did, and in this story Claridiana doth, and in other stories not a few, yet to report of arms is not so odious, but that it may be borne withall, not only in you men which yourselves are fighters, but in us women, to whom the benefit in equal part appertains of your victories, either the matter is so commendable that it carries no discredit from the homeliness of the speaker, or that it is so generally known, that it fits every man to speak thereof. * * * But my defense is by example of the best, amongst which, many have dedicated their labors, some stories, some of war, some physic, some law, some as concerning government, some divine matters, unto diverse ladies and gentlewomen. And if men may and do bestow such of their travails upon gentlewomen, then may we women read such of their works as they dedicate to us, and if we may read them, why not further wade in them to the search of truth. * * * But to return to whatever the truth is, whether that women may not at all discourse in learning, for men late in their claim to being sole possessioners of knowledge, or whether they may in some manner, that is by limitation or appointment in some kind of learning, my persuasion hath been thus, that it is all one for a woman to pen a story, as for a man to address his story to a woman. But amongst all my ill-willers, some I hope are not so straight that they would enforce me necessarily either not to write or to write of divinity. Whereas neither durst I trust mine own judgment sufficiently, if matter of controversy were handled, nor yet could I find any book in any tongue, which would not breed offense to some. But I perceive some may be rather angry to see their Spanish delight turned to all English pastime: they could well allow the story in Spanish, but they may not afford it so cheap, or they would have it proper to themselves. What natures such men be of, I list[6] not greatly to dispute, but my meaning hath been to make others partners of my liking, as I doubt not gentle reader, but if it shall please thee after serious matters to sport thyself with this Spaniard, that thou shalt find in him the just reward of malice and cowardice, with the good speed of honesty and courage, being able to furnish thee with sufficient store of foreign examples to both purposes. And as in such matters which have been rather devised to beguile time, than to breed matter of sad learning, he hath ever borne away any price which could season such delights with some profitable reading: so shalt thou have this stranger an honest man when need serveth, and at other times either a good companion to drive out a weary night, or a merry jest at thy board. And this much concerning this present story, that it is neither unseemly for a woman to deal in, neither greatly requiring a less staid age than mine is. But of these two points, gentle reader, I thought to give thee warning, lest perhaps understanding my name and years, there mightest be a wrong suspect[7] of my boldness and rashness, from which I would gladly free myself by this plain excuse, and if I may deserve thy good favor by like labor, when the choice is my own, I will have a special regard of thy liking. So I wish thee well.

Thine to use, M.T.[8]

4. Irrecoverable.
5. A tribe of female warriors described by Herodotus and other ancient Greek authors as living in Scythia.
6. Wish.
7. Suspicion.
8. Margaret Tyler.

Joseph Swetnam
flourished 1615

Little is known about Joseph Swetnam other than that he stirred up an enormous controversy over the question of women when he wrote *An Arraignment of Lewd, Idle, Froward, and Unconstant Women* (1615). The work was published anonymously with an introductory letter signed by "Thomas Tel-troth." Trotting out all the negative stereotypes of women he could jumble together, Swetnam constructed his mock treatise as a piece of raucous comedy, aimed at the lowest common denominator. Reading Swetnam's work as a serious diatribe against women, Rachel Speght and the pseudonymous Esther Sowernam and Constantia Munda produced critiques of misogyny. Speght unmasked Swetnam's authorship and identified him as a fencing master in Bristol. An anonymous comedy, *Swetnam the Woman-hater, Arraigned by Women* (1620), possibly by Thomas Heywood, dramatized the debate as a court trial with Swetnam prosecuting his case against women and the Amazon Atlanta (a soldier disguised as a woman) defending them. Swetnam is finally turned over to a court of women, who find him guilty and muzzle him (an obvious reference to Speght's *Muzzle for Melastomus*).

from The Arraignment of Lewd, Idle, Froward, and Inconstant Women

from *Chapter 2. The Second Chapter showeth the manner of such women as live upon evil report: it also showeth that the beauty of women has been the bane of many a man, for it hath overcome valiant and strong men, eloquent and subtle men. And in a word it hath overcome all men, as by examples following shall appear.*

First, that of Solomon unto whom God gave singular wit and wisdom, yet he loved so many women that he quite forgot his God which always did guide his steps, so long as he lived godly and ruled justly, but after he had glutted himself with women, then he could say, vanity of vanity all is but vanity. He also in many places of his book of Proverbs exclaims most bitterly against lewd women calling them all that naught is, and also displayeth their properties, and yet I cannot let men go blameless although women go shameless; but I will touch them both, for if there were not receivers then there would not be so many stealers: if there were not some knaves there would not be so many whores, for they both hold together to bolster each other's villainy, for always birds of a feather will flock together hand in hand to bolster each other's villainy.

Men, I say, may live without women, but women cannot live without men. For Venus, whose beauty was excellent fair, yet when she needeth man's help she took Vulcan, a clubfooted smith. And therefore if a woman's face glister,[1] and her gesture pierce the marble wall, or if her tongue be as smooth as oil or as soft as silk, and her words so sweet as honey, or if she were a very ape for wit, or a bag of gold for wealth, or if her personage have stolen away all that nature can afford, and if she be decked up in gorgeous apparel, then a thousand to one but she will love to walk where she may get acquaintance, and acquaintance bringeth familiarity, and familiarity setteth all follies abroad,[2] and twenty to one that if a woman love gadding but that she will pawn her honor to please her fantasy.

Man must be at all the cost and yet live by the loss. A man must take all the pains and women will spend all the gains. A man must watch and ward, fight and

---

1. Glitter, shine.   2. Flowing abroad.

defend, till the ground, labor in the vineyard, and look what he getteth in seven years; a woman will spread it abroad with a fork in one year, and yet little enough to serve her turn but a great deal too little to get her good will. Nay, if thou give her ever so much and yet if thy person please not her humor, then will I not give a half-penny for her honesty at the year's end.

For then her breast will be the harborer of an envious heart, and her heart the storehouse of poisoned hatred; her head will devise villainy, and her hands are ready to practice that which their heart desireth. Then who can but say that women are sprung from the devil, whose heads, hands and hearts, minds and souls are evil, for women are called the hook of all evil, because men are taken by them as a fish is taken in with the hook.

For women have a thousand ways to entice thee, and ten thousand ways to deceive thee, and all such fools as are suitors unto them; some they keep in hand with promises, and some they feed with flattery, and some they delay with dalliances, and some they please with kisses. They lay out the folds of their hair to entangle men into their love; betwixt their breasts is the vale of destruction, and in their beds there is hell, sorrow and repentance. Eagles do not eat men till they are dead, but women devour them alive, for a woman will pick thy pocket and empty thy purse, laugh in thy face and cut thy throat. They are ungrateful, perjured, full of fraud, flouting and deceit, unconstant, waspish,[3] toyish,[4] light, sullen, proud, discourteous and cruel, and yet they were by God created, and by nature formed, and therefore by policy and wisdom to be avoided, for good things abused are to be refused. Or else for a month's pleasure, she may make thee go stark naked. She will give thee roast meat, but she will beat thee with the spit. If thou hast crowns in thy purse, she will be thy heart's gold until she leave thee not a whit of white money. They are like summer birds, for they will abide no storm, but flock about thee in the pride of thy glory, and fly from thee in the storms of affliction; for they aim more at thy wealth than at thy person, and esteem more thy money than any man's virtuous qualities; for they esteem of a man without money as a horse does a fair stable without meat. They are like eagles which will always fly where the carrion is.

They will play the horse-leech to suck away thy wealth, but in the winter of thy misery, she will fly away from thee. Not unlike the swallow, which in the summer harboreth herself under the eaves of a house, and against winter flieth away, leaving nothing but dirt behind her.

Solomon saith, he that will suffer himself to be led away or to take delight in such women's company is like a fool which rejoiceth when he is led to the stocks. *Proverbs* 7.

Hosea, by marrying a lewd woman of light behavior was brought unto idolatry, *Hosea* 1. Saint Paul accounteth fornicators so odious, that we ought not to eat meat with them. He also showeth that fornicators shall not inherit the kingdom of Heaven, *1 Corinthians* the 9th and 11th verse.

And in the same chapter Saint Paul excommunicateth fornicators, but upon amendment he receiveth them again. Whoredom punished with death, *Deuteronomy* 22.21 and *Genesis* 38.24. Phineas a priest thrust two adulterers, both the man and the woman, through the belly with a spear, *Numbers* 25.

God detests the money or goods gotten by whoredom, *Deuteronomy* 23.17, 18. Whores called by diverse names, and the properties of whores, *Proverbs* 7.6 and 21. A

---

3. Spiteful   4. Frivolous, wanton.

whore envieth an honest woman, *Esdras* 16 and 24. Whoremongers God will judge, *Hebrews* 13 and 42. They shall have their portions with the wicked in the lake that burns with fire and brimstone, *Revelation* 21.8.

Only for the sin of whoredom God was sorry at heart, and repented that he ever made man, *Genesis* 6.67.

Saint Paul saith, to avoid fornication every man may take a wife, 1 *Corinthians* 6.9.

Therefore he which hath a wife of his own and yet goeth to another woman is like a rich thief which will steal when he has no need.

There are three ways to know a whore: by her wanton looks, by her speech, and by her gait. *Ecclesiasticus* 26.[5] and in the same chapter he saith, that we must not give our strength unto harlots, for whores are the evil of all evils, and the vanity of all vanities, they weaken the strength of a man and deprive the body of his beauty, it furroweth his brows and maketh the eyes dim, and a whorish woman causeth the fever and the gout; and at a word, they are a great shortening to a man's life.

For although they seem to be as dainty as sweet meat, yet in trial not so wholesome as sour sauce. They have wit, but it is all in craft; if they love it is vehement, but if they hate it is deadly.

Plato saith, that women are either angels or devils, and that they either love dearly or hate bitterly, for a woman hath no mean in her love, nor mercy in her hate, no pity in revenge, nor patience in her anger; therefore it is said, that there is nothing in the world which both pleases and displeases a man more than a woman, for a woman most delighteth a man and yet most deceiveth him, for as there is nothing more sweet to a man than a woman when she smiles, even so there is nothing more odious than the angry countenance of a woman.

Solomon in his 20th chapter of *Ecclesiastes*[6] saith, that an angry woman will foam at the mouth like a boar. If all this be true as most true it is, why shouldest thou spend one hour in the praise of women as some fools do, for some will brag of the beauty of such a maid, another will vaunt of the bravery of such a woman, that she goeth beyond all the women in the parish. Again, some study their fine wits how they may cunningly swooth[7] women, and with logic how to reason with them, and with eloquence to persuade them. They are always tempering their wits as fiddlers do their strings, who wrest them so high, that many times they stretch them beyond time, tune and reason.

Again, there are many that weary themselves with dallying, playing, and sporting with women, and yet they are never satisfied with the unsatiable desire of them; if with a song thou wouldest be brought asleep, or with a dance be led to delight, then a fair woman is fit for thy diet. If thy head be in her lap she will make thee believe that thou are hard by[8] God's seat, when indeed thou are just at hell gate.

Rachel Speght
1597?–?

The daughter of the rector of two London churches and the wife of a minister, Rachel Speght was only about nineteen years old when she wrote *A Muzzle for Melastomus, the Cynical Baiter*

---

5. Apocryphal book of the Old Testament.
6. A faulty citation: in Ecclesiasticus 25, an angry woman is compared to a bear.

7. Sway, woo.
8. Close to.

of, and Foul-Mouthed Barker Against Evah's Sex, or an Apologetical Answer to the Irreligious and Illiterate Pamphlet made by Io. Swu. and by him Intituled The Arraignment of Women. Speght interpreted Swetnam's *Arraignment* as a serious attack on women in order to show the faulty logic underpinning misogyny. Her title indicates the dual thrust of her analysis: the *irreligious* Swetnam has misinterpreted Scripture, and the *illiterate* pamphlet is logically confused and rhetorically flawed. She argues for a view of marriage as a mutual partnership and the relation between the sexes as one of greater equality. Modern critics have debated the implications of Speght's work: Barbara Lewalski has called Rachel Speght "the first self-proclaimed and positively identified female polemicist in England" while Ann Rosalind Jones has questioned whether Speght's work can be considered as feminist in the twentieth-century sense. All critics of early modern gender studies agree, however, that Speght was a learned and committed author. She alone of the participants in the Jacobean controversy about women affixed her own name to the title page. And she reiterated her authorship with the publication of her poetic dream-vision *Mortalities Memorandum* (1621), in which she defends women's education.

from A Muzzle for Melastomus

Of Woman's Excellency, with the causes of her creation, and of the sympathy which ought to be in man and wife each toward other

The work of creation being finished, this approbation thereof was given by God himself, that "All was very good."[1] If all, then woman, who—except man—is the most excellent creature under the canopy of heaven. But if it be objected by any:

First, that woman, though created good, yet by giving ear to Satan's temptations brought death and misery upon all her posterity.

Secondly, that "Adam was not deceived, but that the woman was deceived and was in the transgression."[2]

Thirdly, that St. Paul says "It were good for a man not to touch a woman."[3]

Fourthly and lastly, that of Solomon, who seems to speak against all of our sex: "I have found one man of a thousand, but a woman among them all I have not found,"[4] whereof in its due place.

To the first of these objections, I answer: that Satan first assailed the woman because where the hedge is lowest, most easy it is to get over, and she being the weaker vessel[5] was with more facility to be seduced—like as a crystal glass sooner receives a crack than a strong stone pot. Yet we shall find the offense of Adam and Eve almost to parallel; for as an ambitious desire to be made like God was the motive which caused her to eat, so likewise was it his, as may plainly appear by that *ironia:* "Behold, man is become as one of us"[6]—not that he was so indeed, but hereby his desire to attain a greater perfection than God had given him was reproved. Woman sinned, it is true, by her infidelity in not believing the word of God but giving credit to Satan's fair promises that "she should not die";[7] but so did the man, too. And if Adam had not approved of that deed which Eve had done, and been willing to tread the steps where she had gone, he—being her head—would have reproved her and have made the commandment a bit to restrain him from breaking his Maker's injunction. For if a man burn his hand in the fire, the bellows that blew the fire is

1. Genesis 1.31. References to the Bible are indicated in the margins of Speght's text.
2. 1 Timothy 2.14.
3. 1 Corinthians 7.1.
4. Ecclesiastes 7.28.
5. "The weaker vessel," a phrase taken from 1 Peter 3.7, is frequently used in early modern English sermons to describe woman.
6. Genesis 3.22. "Ironia," or irony, is a figure of speech in which the meaning is the opposite of that of the words used and the tone of which is often mocking.
7. Genesis 3.4.

not to be blamed, but himself rather for not being careful to avoid the danger. Yet if the bellows had not blown, the fire had not burned; no more is woman simply to be condemned for man's transgression. For by the free will which before his fall he enjoyed, he might have avoided and been free from being burned or singed with that fire which was kindled by Satan and blown by Eve. It therefore served not his turn a whit afterwards to say: "The woman which thou gavest me gave me of the tree, and I did eat."[8] For a penalty was inflicted upon him as well as on the woman, the punishment of her transgression being particular to her own sex and to none but the female kind, but for the sin of man the whole earth was cursed.[9] And he being better able than the woman to have resisted temptation, because the stronger vessel, was first called to account, to show that to whom much is given, of them much is required; and that he who was the sovereign of all creatures visible should have yielded greatest obedience to God.

True it is (as is already confessed) that woman first sinned, yet find we no mention of spiritual nakedness till man had sinned. Then it is said "Their eyes were opened,"[1] the eyes of their mind and conscience; and then perceived they themselves naked, that is, not only bereft of that integrity which they originally had, but felt the rebellion and disobedience of their members in the disordered motions of their now corrupt nature, which made them for shame to cover their nakednesse. Then (and not afore) it is said that they saw it, as if sin were imperfect and unable to bring a deprivation of a blessing received, or death on all mankind, till man (in whom lay the active power of generation) had transgressed. The offense, therefore, of Adam and Eve is by St. Austin[2] thus distinguished: "the man sinned against God and himself, the woman against God, herself and her husband"; yet in her giving of the fruit to eat had she no malicious intent towards him, but did therein show a desire to make her husband partaker of that happiness, which she thought by their eating they should both have enjoyed. This her giving Adam of that sauce, wherewith Satan had served her, whose sourness, afore he had eaten, she did not perceive, was that which made her sin to exceed his. Wherefore, that she might not of him who ought to honor her be abhorred,[3] the first promise that was made in Paradise, God makes to woman, that by her seed should the serpent's head be broken.[4] Whereupon Adam calls her *Hevah*, Life, that as the woman had been an occasion of his sin so should woman bring forth the Savior from sin, which was in the fullness of time accomplished.[5] By which was manifested that he is a Savior of believing women no less than of men, that so the blame of sin may not be imputed to his creature, which is good, but to the will by which Eve sinned; and yet by Christ's assuming the shape of man was it declared that his mercy was equivalent to both sexes. So that by Hevah's blessed seed, as St. Paul affirms, it is brought to pass that "male and female are all one in Christ Jesus."[6]

To the second objection I answer: that the Apostle does not hereby exempt man from sin, but only giveth to understand that the woman was the primary transgressor, and not the man; but that man was not at all deceived was far from his meaning. For he afterwards expressly saith that "in Adam all die, so in Christ shall all be made alive."[7]

---

8. Genesis 3.12.
9. Genesis 3.17.
1. Genesis 3.7.
2. Saint Augustine; this commonplace echoes parts of his sermon on Adam and Eve.

3. 1 Peter 3.7.
4. Genesis 3.15.
5. Galatians 4.4.
6. Galatians 3.28.
7. 1 Corinthians 15.22.

For the third objection, "It is good for a man not to touch a woman": the Apostle makes it not a positive prohibition but speaks it only because of the Corinth[ian]s' present necessity,[8] who were then persecuted by the enemies of the church. For which cause, and no other, he saith: "Art thou loosed from a wife? Seek not a wife"— meaning whilst the time of these perturbations should continue in their heat; "but if thou are bound, seek not to be loosed; if thou marriest, thou sinnest not," only increase thy care: "for the married careth for the things of this world. And I wish that you were without care that ye might cleave fast to the Lord without separation: for the time remaineth, that they which have wives be as though they had none, for the persecutors shall deprive you of them either by imprisonment, banishment or death." So that manifest it is, that the Apostle does not hereby forbid marriage, but only adviseth the Corinth[ian]s to forbear a while, till God in mercy should curb the fury of their adversaries. For (as Eusebius[9] writeth) Paul was afterward married himself, the which is very probable, being that interrogatively he saith: "Have we not power to lead about a wife being a sister, as well as the rest of the Apostles, and as the brethren of the Lord, and Cephas?"[1]

The fourth and last objection is that of Solomon: "I have found one man among a thousand, but a woman among them all have I not found.[2] For answer of which, if we look into the story of his life, we shall find therein a commentary upon this enigmatical[3] sentence included. For it is there said that Solomon had seven hundred wives and three hundred concubines, which number connected make one thousand. These women turning away his heart from being perfect with the Lord his God,[4] sufficient cause had he to say, that among the said thousand women found he not one upright. He saith not, that among a thousand women never any man found one worthy of commendation, but speaks in the first person singularly "I have not found," meaning in his own experience. For this assertion is to be held a part of the confession of his former follies, and no otherwise, his repentance being the intended drift of *Ecclesiastes*.

Thus having (by God's assistance) removed those stones whereat some have stumbled, others broken their shins, I will proceed toward the period of my intended task, which is to decipher the excellency of women. Of whose creation I will, for order's sake, observe: first, the efficient cause,[5] which was God; secondly, the material cause, or whereof she was made; thirdly, the formal cause, or fashion and proportion of her feature; fourthly and lastly, the final cause, the end or purpose for which she was made. To begin with the first.

The efficient cause of woman's creation was Jehovah the Eternal, the truth of which is manifest in Moses his narration of the six days' works, where he says, "God created them male and female."[6] And David, exhorting all "the earth to sing to the Lord" (meaning, by a metonymy,[7] "earth": all creatures that live on the earth, of whatever sex or nation) gives this reason: "For the Lord has made us."[8] That work then cannot choose but be good, yea very good, which is wrought by so excellent a workman as the Lord; for he, being a glorious Creator, must effect a worthy creature.

8. 1 Corinthians 7.
9. Eusebius (A.D. 260–340) was Bishop of Caesarea and a church historian. See *Ecclesiastical History* 3.30.
1. 1 Corinthians 9.5.
2. Ecclesiastes 7.30.
3. Mysterious.
4. 1 Kings 11.3.

5. The agent who makes something; see Aristotle's *Physics* 2.3.
6. Genesis 1.28 [27].
7. A figure of speech that substitutes one term for another to which it is closely related.
8. Psalms 100.3.

Bitter water cannot proceed from a pleasant sweet fountain, nor bad work from that workman which is perfectly good—and, in propriety, none but he.[9]

Secondly, the material cause, or matter whereof woman was made, was of a refined mold, if I may so speak. For man was created of the dust of the earth,[1] but woman was made of a part of man after that he was a living soul. Yet she was not produced from Adam's foot, to be his too low inferior; nor from his head to be his superior; but from his side, near his heart, to be his equal: that where he is lord, she may be lady. And therefore saith God concerning man and woman jointly: "Let them rule over the fish of the sea, and over the fowls of the heaven, and over every beast that moves upon the earth."[2] By which words he makes their authority equal, and all creatures to be in subjection to them both. This, being rightly considered, doth teach men to make such account of their wives as Adam did of Eve: "This is bone of my bone, and flesh of my flesh."[3] As also, that they neither do or wish any more hurt unto them, than unto their own bodies. For men ought to love their wives as themselves, because he that loves his wife loves himself;[4] and never did man hate his own flesh (which the woman is) unless a monster in nature.

Thirdly, the formal cause, fashion and proportion, of woman was excellent. For she was neither like the beasts of the earth, fowls of the air, fishes of the sea, or any other inferior creature; but man was the only object which she did resemble. For as God gave man a lofty countenance that he might look up toward Heaven, so did he likewise give unto woman. And as the temperature of man's body is excellent, so is woman's. For whereas other creatures, by reason of their gross humors, have excrements for their habit—as fowls their feathers, beasts their hair, fishes their scales—man and woman only have their skin clear and smooth.[5] And (that more is) in the image of God were they both created; yea and to be brief, all the parts of their bodies, both external and internal, were correspondent and meet each for other.

Fourthly and lastly, the final cause or end for which woman was made was to glorify God, and to be a collateral companion for man to glory God, in using her body and all the parts, powers and faculties thereof as instruments for his honor. As with her voice to sound forth his praises, like Miriam, and the rest of her company;[6] with her tongue not to utter words of strife, but to give good counsel unto her husband, the which he must not despise. For Abraham was bidden to give ear to Sarah his wife.[7] Pilate was willed by his wife not to have any hand in the condemning of Christ;[8] and a sin it was in him that he listened not to her; Leah and Rachel counseled Jacob to do according to the word of the Lord;[9] and the Shunamite put her husband in mind of harboring the prophet Elisha.[1] Her hands should be open, according to her ability, in contributing towards God's service and distressed servants, like to that poor widow who cast two mites into the treasury;[2] and as Mary Magdalene, Susanna and Joanna, the wife of Herod's steward, with many others which of their substance ministered unto Christ.[3] Her heart should be a receptacle for God's word, like Mary that treasured the sayings of Christ in her heart.[4] Her feet should be swift

9. Psalms 100.5; Matthew 19.7.
1. Genesis 2.7.
2. Genesis 1.26.
3. Genesis 2.23.
4. Ephesians 5.28.
5. Genesis 1.26
6. Exodus 15.20.

7. Genesis 21.12.
8. Matthew 27.19.
9. Genesis 31.16.
1. 2 Kings 4.9.
2. Mark 12.43.
3. Luke 8.
4. Luke 1.45.

in going to seek the Lord in his sanctuary, as Mary Magdalene made haste to seek Christ at his sepulcher.[5] Finally, no power external or internal ought woman to keep idle, but to employ it in some service of God, to the glory of her creator and comfort of her own soul.

The other end for which woman was made was to be a companion and helper for man; and if she must be a *helper*, and but a *helper*, then are those husbands to be blamed, which lay the whole burden of domestical affairs and maintenance on the shoulders of their wives. For, as yoke-fellows they are to sustain part of each other's cares, griefs and calamities. But as if two oxen be put into one yoke, the one being bigger than the other, the greater bears most weight; so the husband, being the stronger vessel, is to bear a greater burden than his wife. And therefore the Lord said to Adam: "In the sweat of your face shall you eat your bread, till you return to the dust."[6] And St. Paul says that "he that provideth not for his household is worse than an infidel."[7] Nature hath taught senseless creatures to help one another: as the male pigeon, when his hen is weary with sitting on her eggs and comes off from them, supplies her place, that in her absence they may receive no harm, until such time as she is fully refreshed. Of small birds, the cock always helps his hen to build her nest; and while she sits upon her eggs he flies abroad to get meat for her, who cannot then provide any for herself. The crowing cockerel helps his hen to defend her chickens from peril, and will endanger himself to save her and them from harm. Seeing then, that these unreasonable creatures by the instinct of nature bear such affection to each other, that without any grudge they willingly according to their kind help one another, I may reason, *a minore ad maius*,[8] that much more should man and woman, which are reasonable creatures, be helpers to each other in all things lawful, they having the law of God to guide them, his word to be a lantern to their feet and a light unto their paths, by which they are excited to a far more mutual participation of each other's burden than other creatures. So that neither the wife may say to her husband nor the husband to his wife: "I have no need of thee,"[9] no more than the members of the body may say to each other, between whom there is such a sympathy that if one member suffer, all suffer with it. Therefore though God bade Abraham forsake his country and kindred, yet he bade him not forsake his wife who, being "Flesh of his flesh, and bone of his bone," was to be copartner with him of whatsoever did betide him, whether joy or sorrow. Wherefore Solomon says "woe to him that is alone";[1] for when thoughts of discomfort, troubles of this world and fear of dangers do possess him, he wants a companion to lift him up from the pit of perplexity into which he is fallen.[2] For a good wife, saith Plautus, is the wealth of the mind and the welfare of the heart; and therefore a meet associate for her husband. And "woman," saith Paul, "is the glory of the man."[3]

Marriage is a merri-age, and this world's paradise, where there is mutual love. Our blessed Savior vouchsafed to honor a marriage with the first miracle that he wrought,[4] unto which miracle matrimonial estate may not unfitly be resembled. For as Christ turned water into wine, a far more excellent liquor (which, as the Psalmist saith, "Makes glad the hearts of man";[5] so the single man is changed by marriage from a bachelor to a husband, a far more excellent title: from a solitary life to a joyful

5. John 20.1.
6. Genesis 3.19.
7. 1 Timothy 5.8.
8. From the lesser to the greater.
9. 1 Corinthians 12.21.

1. Ecclesiastes 4.10.
2. Ecclesiastes 4.10.
3. 1 Corinthians 11.7.
4. John 2.
5. Psalms 104.15.

union and conjunction with such a creature as God had made meet for man, for whom none was fit till she was made. The enjoying of this great blessing made Pericles more unwilling to part from his wife than to die for his country; and Antonius Pius to pour forth that pathetic exclamation against death for depriving him of his dearly beloved wife: "O cruel hard-hearted death in bereaving me of her whom I esteemed more than my own life!"[6] "A virtuous woman," saith Solomon, "is the crown of her husband";[7] by which metaphor he shows both the excellency of such a wife and what account her husband is to make of her. For a king does not trample his crown under his feet, but highly esteems it, gently handles it and carefully lays it up as the evidence of his kingdom; and therefore when David destroyed Rabbah[8] he took off the crown from their king's head. So husbands should not account their wives as their vassals but as those that are "heirs together of the grace of life,"[9] and with all lenity and mild persuasions set their feet in the right way if they happen to tread awry, bearing with their infirmities, as Elkanah did with his wife's barrenness.[1]

The kingdom of God is compared to the marriage of a king's son;[2] John calleth the conjunction of Christ and his chosen a marriage;[3] and not few but many times does our blessed Savior in the Canticles[4] set forth his unspeakable love towards his church under the title of a husband rejoicing with his wife, and often vouchsafeth to call her his sister a spouse—by which is showed that with God "is no respect of persons," nations, or sexes.[5] For whosoever, whether it be man or woman, that doth "believe in the lord Jesus, such shall be saved."[6] And if God's love, even from the beginning, had not been as great toward woman as to man, then he would not have preserved from the deluge of the old world as many women as men. Nor would Christ after his resurrection have appeared to a woman first of all other, had it not been to declare thereby, that the benefits of his death and resurrection are as available, by belief, for women as for men; for he indifferently died for the one sex as well as the other.

※◆※

"Esther Sowernam"

The pen name Esther Sowernam comes from the Old Testament heroine Esther, who defended her people against Haman, and the antithesis of Joseph Swetnam's last name (sweet/sour). The full title of her text also parodies Swetnam's: *Ester Hath Hanged Haman; or An Answer to a Lewd Pamphlet, Entitled The Arraignment of Women. With the Arraignment of Lewd, Idle, Froward and Unconstant Men, and Husbands* (1617). On the whole the author of this pamphlet presents herself in a more secular light than Rachel Speght does. Sowernam's criticisms of misogyny are more psychological and social than moral and logical. Trained in classics as well as Scripture and a keen observer, Esther Sowernam finds that Swetnam has incorrectly stated that the Bible is the source of the statement that women are a necessary evil and finds that the true source is in Euripides' *Medea*. The occasion for Sowernam's writing is a dinner party at which Swetnam's book and Speght's response were discussed. Sowernam finds fault with both—Swetnam because he "damns all women" and Speght because she "undertaking to defend women doth

6. Antonius Pius (A.D. 86–161) Roman emperor, founded a charity for orphaned girls in honor of his wife. Plutarch writes about how Pericles (495–429 B.C.), ruler of Athens, greatly loved Aspasia.
7. Proverbs 7.4.
8. 1 Chronicles 20.2. Joab destroyed Rabbah, while David took the king's crown.

9. 1 Peter 3.7.
1. 1 Samuel 1.17.
2. Matthew 22.
3. Revelation 19.7.
4. The Song of Songs.
5. Romans 2.11.
6. John 3.18.

rather charge and condemn them." Sowernam cites the double standard by which men are excused for what women are judged harshly for in order to assert women's superiority. She argues that women are judged more severely because they are thought to be more virtuous in the first place. The second half of her pamphlet may have helped to inspire the comedy that spoofed the entire controversy, *Swetnam the Woman-Hater Arraigned By Women* (1620).

from **Ester Hath Hanged Haman**
from *Chapter 7. The answer to all objections which are material made against women*

As for that crookedness and frowardness[1] with which you charge women, look from whence they have it. For of themselves and their own disposition it doth not proceed, which is proved directly by your own testimony. For in your 46th page, line 15[16], you say: "A young woman of tender years is flexible, obedient, and subject to do anything, according to the will and pleasure of her husband." How cometh it then that this gentle and mild disposition is afterwards altered? Yourself doth give the true reason, for you give a great charge not to marry a widow. But why? Because, say you in the same page, "A widow is framed to the conditions[2] of another man." Why then, if a woman have froward conditions, they be none of her own, she was framed to them. Is not our adversary ashamed of himself to rail against women for those faults which do all come from men? Doth not he most grievously charge men to learn[3] their wives bad and corrupt behavior? For he saith plainly: "Thou must unlearn a widow, and make her forget and forego her former corrupt and disordered behavior." Thou must unlearn her; *ergo*, what fault she hath learned: her corruptness comes not from her own disposition but from her husband's destruction.

Is it not a wonder that your pamphlets are so dispersed? Are they not wise men to cast away time and money upon a book which cutteth their own throats? 'Tis pity but that men should reward you for your writing (if it be but as the Roman Sertorius[4] did the idle poet: he gave him a reward, but not for his writing—but because he should never write more). As for women, they laugh that men have no more able a champion. This author cometh to bait women or, as he foolishly saith, the "Bear-baiting of Women," and he bringeth but a mongrel cur who doth his kind[5] to brawl and bark, but cannot bite. The mild and flexible disposition of a woman is in philosophy proved in the composition of her body, for it is a maxim: *Mores animi sequntur temperaturam corporis* (the disposition of the mind is answerable to the temper of the body). A woman in the temperature of her body is tender, soft and beautiful, so doth her disposition in mind correspond accordingly: she is mild, yielding and virtuous. What disposition accidentally happeneth unto her is by the contagion of a froward husband, as Joseph Swetnam affirmeth.

And experience proveth. It is a shame for a man to complain of a froward woman—in many respects all concerning himself. It is a shame he hath no more government over the weaker vessel.[6] It is a shame he hath hardened her tender sides and gentle heart with his boisterous and Northern blasts. It is a shame for a man to publish and proclaim household secrets—which is a common practice amongst men, especially drunkards, lechers, and prodigal spendthrifts. These when they come home drunk, or are called in question for their riotous misdemeanors, they presently show themselves the right chil-

1. Perversity, unreasonableness.
2. Circumstances, character traits.
3. Teach.
4. Quintus Sertorius, Roman general, appointed governor

of Farther Spain in 83 B.C.
5. Nature.
6. From 1 Peter 3.7.

dren of Adam. They will excuse themselves by their wives and say that their unquietness and frowardness at home is the cause that they run abroad: an excuse more fitter for a beast than a man. If thou wert a man thou wouldst take away the cause which urgeth a woman to grief and discontent, and not by thy frowardness increase her distemperature.[7] Forbear thy drinking, thy luxurious riot, thy gaming and spending, and thou shalt have thy wife give thee as little cause at home as thou givest her great cause of disquiet abroad. Men which are men, if they chance to be matched with froward wives—either of their own making or others' marring[8]—they would make a benefit of the discommodity:[9] either try his skill to make her mild or exercise his patience to endure her cursedness; for all crosses are inflicted either for punishment of sins or for exercise of virtues. But humorous[1] men will sooner mar a thousand women than out of a hundred make one good.

And this shall appear in the imputation which our adversary chargeth upon our sex: to be lascivious, wanton and lustful. He saith: "Women tempt, allure and provoke men." How rare a thing is it for women to prostitute and offer themselves? How common a practice is it for men to seek and solicit women to lewdness? What charge do they spare? What travail do they bestow? What vows, oaths and protestations do they spend to make them dishonest? They hire panders, they write letters, they seal them with damnations and execrations to assure them of love when the end proves but lust. They know the flexible disposition of women, and the sooner to overreach them some will pretend they are so plunged in love that, except they obtain their desire, they will seem to drown, hang, stab, poison, or banish themselves from friends and country. What motives are these to tender dispositions? Some will pretend marriage, another offer continual maintenance; but when they have obtained their purpose, what shall a woman find?—just that which is her everlasting shame and grief: she hath made herself the unhappy subject to a lustful body and the shameful stall[2] of a lascivious tongue. Men may with foul shame charge woman with this sin which she had never committed, if she had not trusted; nor had ever trusted, if she had not been deceived with vows, oaths and protestations. To bring a woman to offend in one sin, how many damnable sins do they commit? I appeal to their own consciences. The lewd disposition of sundry men doth appear in this: if a woman or maid will yield to lewdness, what shall they want?[3]—but if they would live in honesty, what help shall they have? How much will they make of the lewd? How base an account of the honest? How many pounds will they spend in bawdy houses? But when will they bestow a penny upon an honest maid or woman, except it be to corrupt them?

Our adversary bringeth many examples of men which have been overthrown by women. It is answered before: the fault is their own. But I would have him, or anyone living, to show any woman that offended in this sin of lust, but that she was first solicited by a man.

Helen was the cause of Troy's burning: first, Paris did solicit her; next, how many knaves and fools of the male kind had Troy, which to maintain whoredom would bring their city to confusion?

When you bring in examples of lewd women and of men which have been stained by women, you show yourself both frantic and a profane irreligious fool to mention Judith,[4] for cutting off Holofernes' head, in that rank.

7. Disorder in mind and body.
8. Spoiling.
9. Inconvenience, disadvantageousness.
1. Moody.
2. Target.

3. Lack, need.
4. A wealthy, attractive widow who saved her people from Holofernes, an Assyrian general, by attracting and then killing him. (See The Book of Judith, part of the Catholic Bible, but viewed as apocryphal by Jews and Protestants.)

You challenge women for untamed and unbridled tongues; there was never woman was ever noted for so shameless, so brutish, so beastly a scold as you prove yourself in this base and odious pamphlet. Your blaspheme God, you rail at his creation, you abuse and slander his creatures; and what immodest or impudent scurrility is it which you do not express in this lewd and lying pamphlet?

Hitherto I have so answered all your objections against women that, as I have not defended the wickedness of any, so I have set down the true state of the question. As Eve did not offend without temptation of a serpent, so women do seldom offend but it is by provocation of men. Let not your impudency, nor your consorts' dishonesty, charge our sex hereafter with those sins of which you yourselves were the first procurers. I have, in my discourse, touched you, and all yours, to the quick. I have taxed you with bitter speeches; you will, perhaps, say I am a railing scold. In this objection, Joseph Swetnam, I will teach you both wit and honesty. The difference between a railing scold and an honest accuser is this: the first rageth upon passionate fury without bringing cause or proof, the other bringeth direct proof for what she allegeth. You charge women with clamorous words, and bring no proof; I charge you with blasphemy, with impudency, scurrility, foolery and the like. I show just and direct proof for what I say. It is not my desire to speak so much; it is your dessert to provoke me upon just cause so far. It is not railing to call a crow black, or a wolf a ravenor,[5] or a drunkard a beast; the report of the truth is never to be blamed: the deserver of such a report deserves the shame.

Now, for this time, to draw to an end. Let me ask according to the question of Cassian, *cui bono?*[6]—what have you gotten by publishing your pamphlet? Good I know you can get none. You have, perhaps, pleased the humors of some giddy, idle, conceited persons. But you have dyed yourself in the colors of shame, lying, slandering, blasphemy, ignorance, and the like.

The shortness of time and the weight of business call me away, and urge me to leave off thus abruptly; but assure yourself, where I leave now I will by God's grace supply the next term, to your small content. You have exceeded in your fury against widows, whose defense you shall hear of at the time aforesaid. In the mean space, recollect your wits; write out of deliberation, not out of fury; write out of advice, not out of idleness: forbear to charge women with faults which come from the contagion of masculine serpents.

— ⊨✧⊠ —

Hic Mulier
and
Haec Vir

Hic Mulier and *Haec Vir* were published anonymously within a week of each other in February 1620. *Hic Mulier*, the first of the two pamphlets to appear, begins with the complaint that "since the days of Adam women were never so masculine." The title introduces this theme by a gender switch of its own: *Hic Mulier*, Latin for "This Woman," uses the masculine form *hic* instead of the feminine *haec*. The title page contains illustrations of two such mannish women—one wearing a man's hat, which she admires in a mirror, and another sitting in a barber's chair to get her hair cut. Structured as a "brief declamation," or oration, the text argues

---

5. An animal who seizes in order to devour.

6. "To whose benefit," a phrase attributed by Cicero to Lucius Cassius.

that such activities as hair bobbing and wearing men's clothes are immoral and unnatural for women. Furthermore, such gender crossing is also a threat to the entire political order: "most pernicious to the commonwealth for she hath power by example to do it a world of injury."

As its subtitle boasts, *Haec Vir* was "an answer to the late book intituled *Hic Mulier*" and was represented as "a brief dialogue between Haec Vir the Womanish Man, and Hic Mulier the Man-Woman." The effeminate man and the hermaphroditic woman first misrecognize each other's gender. Once that is cleared up, the foppish man launches into a diatribe against the woman, who defends herself by arguing that "custom is an idiot." The first half of the dialogue reads like a proclamation of the equality of the sexes, with the bare-breasted, dagger-swinging Hic Mulier exclaiming, "We are as free-born as men, have as free election, and as free spirits, we are compounded of like parts and may with like liberty make benefit of our creations." Despite this bold challenge, the text as a whole makes a rather conservative case for the need for gender distinctions, the overturning of which was seen as an assault on hierarchy. The dialogue ends with both participants agreeing to exchange clothes and Latin pronouns so that men will again be manly and women subservient to them.

These pamphlets display the early modern fascination with, and loathing of, transvestism. Not only did the fashionable young male favorites of King James I's court resemble the womanish man of *Haec Vir*, but there were more than a few documented cases of women wearing breeches on the streets. One of these women, the notorious Mary Frith, was immortalized in Thomas Dekker and Thomas Middleton's comedy, *The Roaring Girl*. A few women were actually brought before ecclesiastical courts for "shamefully" putting on "man's apparel."

While conforming to the comic pattern of disrupting and then reestablishing the status quo, these pamphlets show that questions about custom, nature, and sex and gender roles were being asked in the early seventeenth century.

from Hic Mulier; or, The Man-Woman

So I present these masculine women in their deformities as they are, that I may call them back to the modest comeliness in which they were.

The modest comeliness in which they were? Why, did ever these mermaids, or rather mere-monsters,[1] that wear the Car-man's block,[2] the Dutchman's feather *upse-van-muffe*, the poor man's pate pouled by a Treene dish, the French doublet trussed with points, to Mary Aubries' light nether skirts, the fool's baldric, and the devil's poniard. Did they ever know comeliness or modesty? Fie, no, they never walked in those paths, for these at the best are sure but rags of gentry, torn from better pieces for their foul stains, or else the adulterate branches of rich stocks,[3] that taking too much sap from the root, are cut away, and employed in base uses; or, if not so, they are the stinking vapors drawn from dunghills, which nourished in the higher regions of the air, become meteors and false fires blazing and flashing therein, and amazing men's minds with their strange proportions, till the substance of their pride being spent, they drop down again to the place from whence they came, and there rot and consume unpitied, and unremembered.

And questionless it is true, that such were the first beginners of these last deformities, for from any purer blood would have issued a purer birth; there would have been some spark of virtue: some excuse for imitation; but this deformity has no agreement with goodness, nor any difference against the weakest reason: it is all base, all barbarous.

---

1. Pure monsters.
2. A merchant's hat. Descriptions of ridiculous fashions follow: the *upse-van-muffe* is an elaborate feathered hat; the pate pouled by a Treene dish is hair cut short to the

shape of a wooden dish; the French doublet is a man's close-fitting upper body garment tied with laces; baldric: fancy belt; poniard: dagger.
3. Trunks or stems.

Base, in the respect it offends men in the example, and God in the most unnatural use: barbarous, in that it is exorbitant from nature, and an antithesis to kind,[4] going astray (with ill-favored affectation) both in attire, in speech, in manners, and (it is to be feared) in the whole courses and stories of their actions. What can be more true and curious consent of the most fairest colors and the wealthy gardens which fill the world with living plants? Do but you receive virtuous inmates (as what palaces are more rich to receive heavenly messengers?) and you shall draw men's souls to you with that severe, devout, and holy adoration, that you shall never want praise, never love, never reverence.

But now methinks I hear the witty-offending great ones reply in excuse of their deformities: What, is there no difference amongst women? no distinction of places, no respect of honors, nor no regard of blood, or alliance? Must but a bare pair of shears pass between noble and ignoble, between the generous spirit and the base mechanic; shall we be all co-heirs of one honor, one estate, and one habit? O men, you are then too tyrannous, and not only injure nature, but also break the laws and customs of the wisest princes. Are not bishops known by their miters, princes by their crowns, judges by their robes, and knights by their spurs? But poor women have nothing (how great soever they be) to divide themselves from the enticing shows or moving images which do furnish most shops in the city. What is it that either the laws have allowed to the greatest ladies, custom found convenient, or their bloods or places challenged, which hath not been engrossed into the city with as great greediness, and pretense of true title; as if the surcease[5] from the imitation were the utter breach of their charter everlastingly.

For this cause, these apes of the city have enticed foreign nations to the cells, and there committing gross adultery with their gewgaws,[6] have brought out such unnatural conceptions, that the whole world is not able to make a *Democritus* big enough to laugh at their foolish ambitions.[7] Nay, the very art of painting (which to the last age shall ever be held in detestation) they have so cunningly stolen and hidden amongst their husbands' hoards of treasure, that the decayed stock of prostitution (having little other revenues) are hourly in bringing their action of *detinue*[8] against them. Hence (being thus troubled with these *Popeniars*,[9] and loath still to march in one rank with fools and *zanies*[1]) have proceeded these disguised deformities, not to offend the eyes of goodness, but to tire with ridiculous contempt the never to be satisfied appetites of these gross and unmannerly intruders. Nay, look if this very last edition of disguise, this which is so full of faults, corruptions, and false quotations, this bait which the devil had laid to catch the souls of wanton women, be not as frequent in the demi-palaces of burghers and citizens as it is either at masque, triumph, tilt-yard, or playhouse. Call but to account the tailors that are contained within the circumference of the walls of the city, and let but their heels and their hard reckonings be justly summed together, and it will be found they have raised more new foundations of this new disguise, and metamorphosed more modest old garments, to this new manner of short base and French doublet (only for the use of freemen's wives[2] and their children) in one month, than has been worn in court, suburbs, or country, since the unfortunate beginning of the first devilish invention.

---

4. The opposite of what is natural to the gender.
5. Cessation, stop.
6. Showy decorations.
7. Seneca recounts how Democritus laughed rather than cried at human life (*De tranquilitate animi* 15.2).

8. Legal action to recover personal property.
9. Popinjays, vain and empty people.
1. Parasites, those who play the fool for amusement.
2. Women married to men possessing the freedom of a city, borough, or corporation.

Let therefore the powerful Statute of Apparel[3] but lift his battle-axe, and crush the offenders in pieces, so as every one may be known by the true badge of their blood, or fortune; and then these *Chimeras* of deformity will be sent back to hell, and there burn to cinders in the flames of their own malice.

Thus, methinks, I hear the best offenders argue, nor can I blame a high blood to swell when it is coupled and counter-checked with baseness and corruption; yet this shows an anger passing near akin to envy, and alludes much to the saying of an excellent poet:

> Women never
> Love beauty in their sex, but envy ever.

They have Caesar's ambition, and desire to be one and one alone, but yet to offend themselves, to grieve others, is a revenge dissonant to reason, and as *Euripides* says, a woman of that malicious nature is a fierce beast, and most pernicious to the commonwealth, for she has power by example to do it a world of injury. But far be such cruelty from the softness of their gentle dispositions: O let them remember what the poet saith:

> Women be
> Fram'd with the same parts of the mind as men
> Nay Nature triumph'd in their beauty's birth,
> And women made the glory of the earth,
> The life of beauty, in whose simple breast,
> (As in her fair lodging) Virtue rests:
> Whose towering thoughts attended with remorse,
> Do make their fairness be of greater force.

But when they thrust virtue out of doors, and give a shameless liberty to every loose passion, that either their weak thoughts engender, or the discourse of wicked tongues can charm into their yielding bosoms (much too apt to be opened with any pick-lock of flattering and deceitful insinuation) then they turn maskers, mummers, nay monsters in their disguises, and so they may catch the bridle in their teeth, and run away with their rulers, they care not into what dangers they plunge either their fortunes or reputations, the disgrace of the whole sex, or the blot and obloquy of their private families, according to the saying of the poets

> Such is the cruelty of women-kind,
> When they have shaken off the shamefac'd band
> With which wise nature did them strongly bind,
> T'obey the bests of man's well-ruling hand
> That then all rule and reason they withstand
> To purchase a licentious liberty;
> But virtuous women wisely understand,
> That they were born to mild humility,
> Unless the heavens them lift to lawful sovereignty.[4]

To you therefore that are fathers, husbands, of sustainers of these new hermaphrodites, belongs the cure of this impostume;[5] it is you that give fuel to the flames of their wild indiscretion. You add the oil which makes their stinking lamps defile the

---

3. Laws governing dress that were intended to differentiate the aristocracy from the common people had been ennacted from the Middle Ages through to the early modern period.

4. Description of the tyranny of the Amazonian ruler Radigund in Spenser's *Faerie Queene* 5.5.25.
5. Abcess.

whole house with filthy smoke, and your purses purchase these deformities at rates both dear and unreasonable. Do you but hold close your liberal hands, or take a strict account of the employment of the treasure you give to their necessary maintenance, and these excesses will either cease, or else die smothered in prison in the tailors' trunks for want of redemption.

from Haec Vir; or, The Womanish Man

Hic-Mulier: Well, then to the purpose: first, you say, I am base in being a slave to novelty. What flattery can there be in freedom of election? Or what baseness to crown my delights with those pleasures which are most suitable to mine affections? Bondage or slavery is a restraint from those actions, which the mind (of its own accord) doth most willingly desire: to perform the intents and purposes of another's disposition, and that not but by mansuetude[1] or sweetness of entreaty; but by the force of authority and strength of compulsion. Now for me to follow change, according to the limitation of my own will and pleasure, there cannot be a greater freedom. Nor do I in my delight of change otherwise than as the whole world doth, or as becometh a daughter of the world to do. For what is the world, but a very shop or warehouse of change? Sometimes winter, sometimes summer; day and night: they hold sometimes riches, sometimes poverty, sometimes health, sometimes sickness: now pleasure; presently anguish; now honor; then contempt: and to conclude, there is nothing but change, which doth surround and mix with all our fortunes. And will you have poor woman such a fixed star, that she shall not so much as move or twinkle in her own sphere? That would be true slavery indeed, and a baseness beyond the chains of the worst servitude. Nature to everything she hath created hath given a singular delight in change, as to herbs, plants, and trees a time to wither and shed their leaves, a time to bud and bring forth their leaves, and a time for their fruits and flowers; to worms and creeping things a time to hide themselves in the pores and hollows of the earth, and a time to come abroad and suck the dew; to beasts liberty to choose their food, liberty to delight in their food, and liberty to feed and grow fat with their food. The birds have the air to fly in, the waters to bathe in, and the earth to feed on. But to man, both these and all things else, to alter, frame, and fashion, according to his will and delight shall rule him. Again, who will rob the eye of the variety of objects, the ear of the delight of sounds, the nose of smells, the tongue of taste, and the hand of feeling? And shall only woman, excellent woman, so much better in that she is something purer, be only deprived of this benefit? Shall she be the bondslave of time, the handmaid of opinion, or the strict observer of every frosty or cold benumbed imagination? It would be a cruelty beyond the rack or strapado.[2]

But you will say it is not change, but novelty, from which you deter us: a thing that doth avert the good, and erect the evil; prefer the faithless, and confound desert; that with the change of opinions breeds the change of states, and with continual alterations thrusts headlong forward both ruin and subversion. Alas (soft Sir) what can you christen by that new imagined title, when the words of a wise man are: *that what was done, is but done again: all things do change, and under the cope of heaven there is no new thing.*[3] So that whatsoever we do or imitate, it is neither slavish, base, nor a breeder of novelty.

1. Gentless, meekness.
2. Rack: a frame with a roller at either end on which a person would be tortured; strapado: a form of torture in which the victim's hands would be tied behind his or her back and the victim would then be suspended by a pulley with a sharp jolt.
3. Ecclesiastes 1.9.

Next, you condemn me of unnaturalness, in forsaking my creation, and con-temning[4] custom. How do I forsake my creation, that do all the right and offices due to my creation? I was created free, born free, and live free: what lets me then so to spin out my time, that I may die free?

To alter creation were to walk on my hands with my heels upward, to feed myself with my feet, or to forsake the sweet sound of sweet words, for the hissing noise of the serpent: but I walk with a face erected, with a body clothed, with a mind busied, and with a heart full of reasonable and devout cogitations; only offensive in attire, inas-much as it is a stranger to the curiosity of the present times, and an enemy to custom. Are we then bound to be the flatterers of time, or the dependents on custom? O mis-erable servitude chained only to baseness and folly! For then custom, nothing is more absurd, nothing more foolish. * * *

Cato Iunior held it for a custom, never to eat meat but sitting on the ground. The Venetians kiss one another ever at the first meeting; and even in this day it is a general received custom amongst our English, that when we meet or overtake any man in our travel or journeying, to examine him whither he rides, how far, to what purpose, and where he lodgeth? Nay, and with that unmannerly boldness of inquisi-tion, that it is a certain ground of a most insufficient quarrel, not to receive a full sat-isfaction of those demands which go far astray from good manners, or comely civility; and will you have us to marry ourselves to these mimic and most fantastic customs? It is a fashion or custom with us to mourn in black, yet the Argian[5] and Roman ladies ever mourned in white; and (if we will tie the action upon the signification of colors) I see not but we may mourn in green, blue, red or any simple color used in heraldry. For us to salute strangers with a kiss is counted but civility, but with foreign nations immodesty; for you to cut the hair of your upper lips, familiar here in England, every-where else almost thought unmanly. To ride on side-saddles at first was counted here abominable pride, and et cetera. I might instance in a thousand things that only cus-tom and not reason hath approved. To conclude, Custom is an idiot, and whoever dependeth wholly upon him, without the discourse of reason, will take from him his pied[6] coat, and become a slave indeed to contempt and censure.

But you say we are barbarous and shameless and cast off all softness, to run wild through a wilderness of opinions. In this you express more cruelty than in all the rest, because I do not stand with my hands on my belly like a baby[7] at Bartholomew Fair,[8] that move not my whole body when I should but only stir my head like Jack of the clock house[9] which has no joints, that is not dumb when wantons court me, as if ass-like I were ready for all burdens, or because I weep not when injury gripes me, like a worried deer in the fangs of many curs. Am I therefore barbarous or shameless? He is much injurious that so baptized us; we are as free-born as men, have as free election, and as free spirits, we are compounded of like parts, and may with like liberty make benefit of our creations; my countenance shall smile on the worthy, and frown on the ignoble, I will hear the wise, and be deaf to idiots, give counsel to my friend, but be dumb to flatterers, I have hands that shall be liberal to reward desert, feet that shall move swiftly to do good offices, and thoughts that shall ever accompany free-

---

4. Disdaining, despising.
5. Of Argos.
6. Spotted, motley.
7. Doll.

8. A popular carnival fair held every year from 1133 to 1865 at West Smithfield on August 24, the feast day of Saint Bartholomew.
9. Figure that strikes the bell of a clock.

dom and severity. If this be barbarous, let me leave the city and live with creatures of like simplicity.

* * *

Hic-Mulier: Therefore to take your proportion in a few lines, (my dear Feminine-Masculine) tell me what Charter, prescription or right of claim you have to those things you make our absolute inheritance? Why do you curl, frizzle and powder your hair, bestowing more hours and time in dividing lock from lock, and hair from hair, in giving every thread his posture, and every curl his true fence and circumference than ever Caesar did in marshalling his army, either at Pharsalia, in Spain, or Britain? Why do you rob us of our ruffs, our earrings, carkanets,[1] and mamillions,[2] of our fans and feathers, our busks and French bodies, nay, of our masks, hoods, shadows, and shapynas,[3] not so much as the very art of painting, but you have so greedily engrossed it, that were it not for that little fantastical sharp pointed dagger that hangs at your chins, and the cross hilt which guards your upper lip, hardly would there be any difference between the fair mistress and the foolish servant. But is this theft the uttermost of our spoil? Fie, you have gone a world further, and even ravished from us our speech, our actions, sports, and recreations. Goodness leave me, if I have not heard a man court his mistress with the same words that Venus did Adonis, or as near as the book could instruct him;[4] where are the tilts and tourneys, and lofty galliards[5] that were danced in the days of old, when men capered in the air like wanton kids on the tops of mountains, and turned above ground as if they had been compact of fire or a purer element?[6] Tut, all's forsaken, all's vanished, those motions showed more strength than art, and more courage than courtship; it was much too robustious, and rather spent the body than prepared it, especially where any defect before reigned; hence you took from us poor women our traverses and tourneys, our modest stateliness and curious slidings, and left us nothing but the new French garb of puppet hopping and setting. Lastly, poor shuttlecock[7] that was only a female invention, how have you taken it out of our hands, and made yourselves such lords and rulers over it, that though it be a very emblem of us, and our lighter despised fortunes, yet it dare now hardly come near us; nay, you keep it so imprisoned within your bed-chambers and dining rooms, amongst your pages and panders, that a poor innocent maid to give but a kick with her battledore,[8] were more than halfway to the ruin of her reputation. For this you have demolished the noble schools of horsemanship (of which many were in this city) hung up your arms to rust, glued up those swords in their scabbards that would shake all Christendom with the brandish, and entertained into your mind such softness, dullness, and effeminate niceness that it would even make *Heraclitus*[9] himself laugh against his nature to see how pulingly[1] you languish in this weak entertained sin of womanish softness. To see one of your gender either show himself (in the midst of his pride or riches) at a playhouse or public assembly; how (before he dare enter) with the Jacob's-staff of his own eyes and his

---

1. A jeweled or gold necklace.
2. Rounded protuberances (from French *mamelon*, nipple).
3. Disguises.
4. Venus, goddess of love, fell in love with the beautiful youth Adonis.
5. A brisk dance in triple time.
6. Men were thought to be dominated by dry humors and

women by humid ones.
7. A small piece of cork with feathers sticking out of it, batted back and forth in the game of battledoor and shuttlecock.
8. A small racket, used to hit a shuttlecock.
9. Heraclitus was said to weep whenever he went forth in public (See Seneca, *De tranquilitate animi* 15.2).
1. In a whining tone.

pages, he takes a full survey of himself, from the highest sprig in his feather, to the lowest spangle that shines in his shoestring: how he prunes and picks himself like a hawk set a-weathering, calls every several garment to auricular[2] confession, making them utter both their mortal great stains, and their venial and less blemishes, though the mote must be much less than an atom. Then to see him pluck and tug everything into the form of the newest received fashion; and by *Durer's* rules[3] make his leg answerable to his neck; his thigh proportionable with his middle, his foot with his hand, and a world of such idle disdained foppery. To see him thus patched up with symmetry, make himself complete, and even as a circle, and lastly, cast himself among the eyes of the people (as an object of wonder) with more niceness than a virgin goes to the sheets of her first lover would make patience herself mad with anger, and cry with the poet:

> O hominum mores, O gens, O tempora dura,
> Quantus in urbe dolor; quantus in orbe dolus![4]

Now since according to your own inference, even by the laws of nature, by the rules of religion, and the customs of all civil nations, it is necessary there be a distinct and special difference between man and woman, both in their habit and behaviors, what could we poor weak women do less (being far too weak by force to fetch back those spoils you have unjustly taken from us) than to gather up those garments you have proudly cast away, and therewith to clothe both our bodies and our minds; since no other means was left us to continue our names, and to support a difference? For to have held the way in which our forefathers first set us, or to have still embraced the civil modesty, or gentle sweetness of our soft inclinations; why, you had so far encroached upon us, and so over-bribed the world, to be deaf to any grant of restitution, that as at our creation, our whole sex was contained in man our first parent, so we should have had no other being, but in you, and your most effeminate quality. Hence we have preserved (though to our own shames) those manly things which you have forsaken, which would you again accept, and restore to us the blushes we laid by, when first we put on your masculine garments; doubt not but chaste thoughts and bashfulness will again dwell in us, and our palaces being newly gilt, trimmed, and re-edified, draw to us all the Graces, all the Muses,[5] which that you may more willingly do, and (as we of yours) grow into detestation of that deformity you have purloined, to the utter loss of your honors and reputations. Mark how the brave Italian poet,[6] even in the infancy of your abuses, most lively describes you:

> About his neck a Carknet[7] rich he ware
> Of precious Stones, all set in gold well tried;
> His arms that erst all warlike weapons bare,

---

2. Told privately, to the ear.
3. Albrecht Dürer (1471–1528), German painter and engraver, wrote a work on human proportions that was published after his death.
4. O customs of men, O people, O hard times / what great sadness in the city; what great fraud in the world.
5. The graces were the three sisters, Aglaia, Thalia, and Euphrosyne, viewed as bestowers of charm and beauty;

the muses were the nine daughters of Zeus and Memory who inspire poetry and the arts.
6. Ludovico Ariosto (1474–1532), whose description of Ruggiero's decadence when he is seduced by the sorceress Alcina in *Orlando Furioso* 7 is quoted here in the translation (1590) by Sir John Harington, Queen Elizabeth's godson.
7. Necklace.

In golden bracelets wantonly were tied:
Into his ears two rings conveyed are
Of golden wire, at which on either side,
Two Indian pearls, in making like two pears,
Of passing price were pendant at his ears.

His locks bedewed with water of sweet savor,
Stood curled round in order on his head;
He had such wanton womanish behavior,
At though in valor he had ne'er been bred:
So chang'd in speech, in manners and in favor,
So from himself beyond all reason led,
By these enchantments of this amorous dame;
He was himself in nothing, but in name.

Thus you see your injury to us is of an old and inveterate continuance, having taken such strong root in your bosoms, that it can hardly be pulled up, without some offense to the soil: ours young and tender, scarce freed from the swaddling clothes, and therefore may with as much ease be lost, as it was with little difficulty found. Cast then from you our ornaments, and put on your own armors. Be men in shape, men in show, men in words, men in actions, men in counsel, men in example: then will we love and serve you; then will we hear and obey you; then will we like rich jewels hang at your ears to take our instructions, like true friends follow you through all dangers, and like careful leeches[8] pour oil into your wounds. Then shall you find delight in our words; pleasure in our faces; faith in our hearts; chastity in our thoughts, and sweetness both in our inward and outward inclinations. Comeliness shall be then our study; fear our armor, and modesty our practice: then shall we be all your most excellent thoughts can desire, and have nothing in us less than impudence and deformity.

Haec-Vir. Enough: you have both raised my eyelids, cleared my sight, and made my heart entertain both shame and delight at an instant; shame in my follies past; delight in our noble and worthy conversion. Away then from me these light vanities, the only ensigns[9] of a weak and soft nature: and come you grave and solid pieces, which arm a man with fortitude and resolution: you are too rough and stubborn for a woman's wearing, we will here change our attires, as we have changed our minds, and with our attires, our names. I will no more be *Haec-Vir*, but *Hic Vir*, nor you *Hic-Mulier*, but *Haec Mulier*. From henceforth deformity shall pack to Hell; and if at any time he hide himself upon the earth, yet it shall be with contempt and disgrace. He shall have no friend but Poverty; no favorer but Folly, nor no reward but Shame. Henceforth we will live nobly like ourselves, ever sober, ever discreet, ever worthy; true men, and true women. We will be henceforth like well-coupled doves, full of industry, full of love: I mean, not of sensual and carnal love, but heavenly and divine love, which proceeds from God, whose inexpressible nature none is able to deliver in words, since is like his dwelling, high and beyond the reach of human apprehension.

[END OF PERSPECTIVES: TRACTS ON WOMEN AND GENDER]

8. Physicians.   9. Banners, signs.

The Execution of Charles I. Seventeenth-century German print.

<hr />

PERSPECTIVES

The Civil War, or the Wars of Three Kingdoms

The English Civil War arose out of citizens' revolutionary demands for their rights and those of their legislature, and out of England's attempt to dominate Ireland and Scotland. The armed conflicts that arose from the demand for political self-determination in every part of the British Isles would have consequences for centuries to come. During the period from 1639 to 1651, war raged not only in England but also in Ireland, Scotland, and Wales; hence, historians now prefer to call this period of conflict the Wars of Three Kingdoms. The origins of the conflict in England were between Parliament and a King who had an absolutist style of governing. Charles I reigned without Parliament from 1629 to 1640, a period referred to as the "Eleven Years' Tyranny." He also imposed unpopular heavy taxes in the form of ship money levies to build up the fleet. Even more controversial was his imposition of Anglican worship and episcopal authority on Puritans and Presbyterians, who felt that such ritual was tantamount to Roman Catholicism. The King placed two Anglican bishops on the court of Star Chamber, who used the arbitrary power of this body to enforce unpopular religious practices.

When the King decided to impose an Anglican liturgy on the Scottish Kirk in 1639, riots broke out in Edinburgh, and Scottish Lowlanders united in a National Covenant against English interference. In 1639 and 1640, Scottish military uprisings necessitated Charles I's recalling Parliament to ask for financial aid. The Parliament was already angered by the eleven-year shutdown by the King, his imposition of taxes without its consent, and his support for Archbishop Laud, whom Parliament viewed as too dictatorial and too high church, shutting out both Puritans (who elected their ministers and disdained Catholic sacraments) and Presbyterians (who favored central church government but not Anglo-Catholic authority or ritual). When Parliament refused after three weeks to grant the King's request for money, the King decided to dissolve the "Short Parliament." In the wake of the dissolution of Parliament, soldiers went on rampages against churches, smashing stained glass windows and altar rails that smacked to them of Roman Catholicism. In some places, soldiers mutinied against their aristocratic commanders.

When the Scots defeated the King's army in the fall of 1640, he had to recall Parliament to petition for more funds. Led by John Pym, the "Long Parliament" seized the opportunity to criticize the King. It passed a Bill of Attainder, condemning to death as a traitor the general of the King's army, Viscount Strafford, who had been accused of instigating the war against Scotland and of suggesting that an Irish Catholic army could be used against England. No proof of guilt was necessary, only assent from the House of Lords and the King. Despite the King's reluctance, the combined opposition of the House of Commons and armed mobs in London in the spring of 1641 pressured him into signing Strafford's death warrant.

That fall two rebellions broke out in Ireland—one organized by Catholic Irish gentry, another arising more spontaneously among the native Gaelic Irish in Ulster against Scots and English settlers who had dispossessed them of their land. Pym blamed the unrest on the King and his Catholic court. Although there was terrible violence, especially in the popular uprisings, the English press wildly exaggerated the extent of the bloodshed, claiming a figure for Protestant deaths in the North of Ireland that was greater than the number of Protestants then living in the whole country. Pym, the leader of the House of Commons, moved that Parliament should offer no help in repressing Irish rebellion unless Charles agreed to dismiss his guilty counselors. The next day, Oliver Cromwell moved that the Parliament empower the Puritan Earl of Essex to head the English militia. Attacks on the King became stronger: his irresponsibility and violation of the security and rights of the people mandated Parliament's wresting power from him. On May 12, Archbishop Laud was executed. Although the King made some concessions, by January 1642 he decided to impeach Pym, four other members of Commons, and one from the House of Lords for treason. However, the accused were safely hidden in the City, and the King left London, not to return until he was put on trial and beheaded six years later. Just on the eve of the outbreak of the war, the "Gentlewomen and Tradesmen's Wives of London" presented their petition to Parliament, complaining against Archbishop Laud's Anglicanism and the threat of violence from Ireland. The first part of the English Civil War (1642–1646), arising from the disputes between Parliament and the King, culminated in the victory of Parliament's New Model Army, headed by Sir Thomas Fairfax.

With the King defeated by the combined forces of the New Model Army and the Scots Covenanters in 1646, new conflicts arose between the army and the Parliament. Closely tied to the army, the Levellers, led by John Lilburne, agitated for a fundamental revision of the constitution: a single representative body, universal suffrage for men, and the abolition of monarchy and noble privilege. Colonel Ludlow, a leader of the republicans, opposed any negotiations with the King and petitioned Parliament to reform the constitution and to put the King on trial. When the House of Commons refused to listen to the army and continued to negotiate with the King, Colonels Ludlow, Ireton, and Pride purged Parliament, placing forty-five members under arrest and prohibiting another 186 from entering the House. This Rump Parliament set up a high court to try the King. On 27 January 1649, Charles I was condemned to death as a tyrant and traitor who had shed the blood of his people. John Bradshaw, President of the Court, proclaimed that the King was subject to the law and the law proceeded from Parliament. Arising out of these events came both the King's own memoir, *Eikon Basilike* ("the

Peter Paul Rubens. *Peace and War*. 1630. One of the greatest painters of the Flemish school, Rubens grew up in Antwerp, where he married and set up his studio. After the death of his wife in 1626, he entered the diplomatic service, traveling to Spain to negotiate a treaty between Philip IV and England in 1628. Idolized and knighted in London, Rubens painted *Peace and War* for Charles I to commemorate the English-Spanish peace treaty of 1629–30. Charles later walked to his death through the Banqueting Hall under a ceiling Rubens painted. *Peace and War* optimistically represents both the court of Charles I at its zenith and the hope for European peace that would be dashed ten years later. The painting is charged with movement. A satyr grasps the fruits of peace, while to the right, Minerva, goddess of wisdom, drives out Mars, god of war, and the fury Allecto. At the center, Peace extends her full breast to the baby Plutus, god of riches.

Royal Image"), ghostwritten and published after his execution by John Gauden, and Milton's militantly republican response *Eikonoklastes* ("Image-Breaker").

In the last stage of the civil war, the dead king's son, Charles II, attempted to regain power through Irish and Scottish aid. In Ireland the Marquis of Ormonde led a coalition of royalists that secured the support of Irish troops for the King in exchange for the free exercise of Catholicism. Before Charles II could land in Dublin, the English sent troops there to put down the uprising. Cromwell slaughtered many at the siege of Drogheda; his campaign throughout Munster killed many civilians. In the aftermath of Cromwell's conquest, what remained of an Irish intelligentsia was either exiled or killed off, and large numbers of native inhabitants were either thrown off their land onto poorer farming land in western Ireland or sent into indentured servitude in the Caribbean. Following policies begun by Elizabeth and James, Cromwell granted Irish land to English settlers. The late events of the war in Ireland are represented here by one of Cromwell's letters from his campaign in Ireland, and by *John O'Dwyer of the Glenn*, a translation of one of the many Irish-language laments for the devastation of the Cromwellian conquest.

In Scotland, Charles II found allies among Presbyterian Covenanters, infuriated with the English Parliament for executing a Scottish monarch, and in the Marquis of Montrose, who recruited the Highland clans. When the Covenanters met with Charles II for the Treaty of Breda in Holland, they imposed on him a promise to reestablish Presbyterianism as the religion of both England and Scotland, to reinstate the Scottish Parliament, and to repudiate his pledges to Ormonde and Montrose. When Charles landed in Scotland, he learned that Montrose, most loyal of all royalists, had been hanged and quartered as a traitor. The political intrigue of Argyle against Montrose can be seen in the Earl of Clarendon's account of Montrose's death. The Covenanters, fighting for Scotland rather than for the King, were defeated by Cromwell at Dunbar. The Scots' losses were so huge that Scottish royalism was revived for one last battle between the King's Cavaliers and Cromwell's Roundheads. Facing Cromwell's army at Worcester in 1651, the forces of Scots and English royalists were vastly outnumbered and easily defeated. Charles II escaped to France, where he remained until the Restoration. Two years later, Cromwell became Lord Protector of the Commonwealth.

John Gauden
1605–1662

John Gauden wrote the most influential account of the royalist cause, *Eikon Basilike* ("Royal Portrait"), advance copies of which were sold on the day of Charles I's execution in 1649. Although Gauden at first sided with Parliament and the Presbyterians, he did not agree to the abolition of the bishops. In 1647 supporters of Charles I, then confined at Hampton Court by Parliament, sought Gauden's help to revise the King's meditations for publication. When the manuscript was complete, Gauden showed it to the King, who hesitated about having it published under his name. Meanwhile, the King was preoccupied first by his attempts to escape and then by his confinement, trial, and execution. When Royston first printed the book in January 1649, he believed that King Charles was the author. Just months later, William Duggard published another edition based on a manuscript that had been revised by the King; Gauden's authorship remained publically unknown until 1690.

Throughout the interregnum, Gauden managed to keep his deanery at Brockton by conforming to Presbyterianism. With the Restoration in 1660, he was made Bishop of Exeter. In letters to Sir Edward Hyde, Gauden admitted his authorship and complained that his reward had not been sufficient. He was then promoted to the bishopric of Worcester, just a year before his death.

Eikon Basilike was written to influence public opinion and to guide the Prince of Wales, who waited in exile to regain his father's throne. A collection of meditations written in a lofty style, *Eikon Basilike* justified the King's views and evoked sympathy for his plight. The emblematic frontispiece shows the King in a saintly light—kneeling in prayer. Admirers of the work called it "most charitable, most heavenly" and "most pious, most ravishing." By the end of 1649, thirty-five editions had been printed in England. The most important of these, that of March 1649, added the King's prayers, the Prince of Wales's letter to his father, and an epitaph on the King's death. An English-language edition was published in Ireland in 1649, and twenty foreign language editions were published on the Continent for the English community in exile as well as their European supporters.

The text aroused both support and criticism. Parliament had the printer Duggard arrested but released him when he produced a license to publish the book. Parliament prohibited the further sale of the book in May 1649, but by the end of 1649, five clandestine editions and two responses had appeared. *The Princely Pellican* explained how Charles had come to write the book, and *Eikon Alethine* attacked it as a fraud. Milton wrote his own rebuttal in *Eikonoklastes*, a savagely satirical prosecution of the King. *Eikonoklastes* merely went through two editions, showing that it could not compete in popularity with *Eikon Basilike*.

from **Eikon Basilike**
from Chapter 4. Upon the Insolency of the Tumults

I never thought anything, except our sins, more ominously presaging all these mischiefs which have followed, than those tumults in London and Westminster soon after the convening of this Parliament which were not like a storm at sea, (which yet wants not its terror,) but like an earthquake, shaking the very foundation of all; than which nothing in the world hath more of horror.

As it is one of the most convincing arguments that there is a God, while His power sets bounds to the raging of the sea, so it is no less that He restrains the madness of the people. Nor does anything portend more God's displeasure against a nation than when He suffers the confluence and clamors of the vulgar to pass all boundaries of laws and reverence to authority.

Which those tumults did to so high degrees of insolence, that they spared not to invade the honor and freedom of the two Houses, menacing, reproaching, shaking, yea, and assaulting some members of both Houses as they fancied or disliked them; nor did they forbear most rude and unseemly deportments, both in contemptuous words and actions, to myself and my court.

Nor was this a short fit or two of shaking, as an ague, but a quotidian fever, always increasing to higher inflammations, impatient of any mitigation, restraint, or remission.

First, they must be a guard against those fears which some men scared themselves and others withal; when, indeed, nothing was more to be feared, and less to be used by wise men, than those tumultuary confluxes of mean and rude people who are taught first to petition, then to protect, then to dictate, at last to command and overawe the Parliament.

All obstructions of Parliament, that is, all freedom of differing in votes, and debating matters with reason and candor, must be taken away with these tumults. By these must the Houses be purged, and all rotten members (as they pleased to count them) cast out; by these the obstinacy of men, resolved to discharge their consciences, must be subdued; by these all factious, seditious, and schismatical proposals against government, ecclesiastical or civil, must be backed and abetted till they prevailed.

Generally, whoever had most mind to bring forth confusion and ruin upon Church and State used the midwifery of those tumults, whose riot and impatience was such as they would not stay the ripening and season of counsels, or fair production of acts, in the order, gravity, and deliberateness befitting a Parliament, but ripped up with barbarous cruelty, and forcibly cut out abortive notes, such as their inviters and encouragers most fancied.

Yea, so enormous and detestable were their outrages, that no sober man could be without infinite shame and sorrow to see them so tolerated and connived at by some, countenanced, encouraged, and applauded by others.

What good man had not rather want anything he most desired for the public good, than obtain it by such unlawful and irreligious means? But men's passions and God's directions seldom agree; violent designs and motions must have suitable engines; such as too much attend their own ends, seldom confine themselves to God's means. Force must crowd in what reason will not lead.

Who were the chief demagogues and patrons of tumults, to send for them, to flatter and embolden them, to direct and tune their clamorous importunities, some men yet living are too conscious to pretend ignorance. God in His due time will let these see that those were no fit means to be used for attaining His ends.

But as it is no strange thing for the sea to rage when strong winds blow upon it, so neither for multitudes to become insolent when they have men of some reputation for parts and piety to set them on.

That which made their rudeness most formidable was, that many complaints being made, and messages sent by myself and some of both Houses yet no order for redress could be obtained with any vigor and efficacy proportionable to the malignity of that now far-spread disease and predominant mischief.

Such was some men's stupidity, that they feared no inconvenience; others' petulancy, that they joyed to see their betters shamefully outraged and abused, while they knew their only security consisted in vulgar flattery, so insensible were they of mine or the two Houses common safety and honors.

Nor could ever any order be obtained impartially to examine, censure, and punish the known boutefeus[1] and impudent incendiaries, who boasted of the influence they had, and used to convoke those tumults as their advantages served.

Yea some, who should have been wiser statesmen, owned them as friends, commending their courage, zeal, and industry, which to sober men could seem no better than that of the devil, who goes about seeking whom he may deceive and devour.

I confess, when I found such a deafness, that no declaration from the bishops, who were first foully insolenced and assaulted, nor yet from other lords and gentlemen of honor, nor yet from myself, could take place for the due repression of these tumults, and securing not only our freedom in Parliament, but our very persons in the streets; I thought myself not bound by my presence to provoke them to higher boldness and contempts; I hoped by my withdrawing[2] to give time both for the ebbing of their tumultuous fury, and others regaining some degrees of modesty and sober sense.

Some may interpret it as an effect of pusillanimity[3] in any man, for popular terrors, to desert his public station; but I think it is hardiness beyond true valor for a wise man to set himself against the breaking in of a sea, which to resist at present threatens imminent danger, but to withdraw gives it space to spend its fury, and gains a fitter time to repair the breach. Certainly a gallant man had rather fight to great disadvantages for number and place in the field in an orderly way, than scuffle with an undisciplined rabble.

Some suspected and affirmed that I meditated a war, when I went from Whitehall only to redeem my person and conscience from violence: God knows I did not then think of a war. Nor will any prudent man conceive that I would, by so many former and some after acts, have so much weakened myself if I had purposed to engage in a war, which to decline by all means I denied myself in so many particulars. It is evident I had then no army to fly unto for protection and vindication.

Who can blame me, or any other, for withdrawing ourselves from the daily baitings of the tumults, not knowing whether their fury and discontent might not fly so high as to worry and tear those in pieces whom as yet they but played with in their paws? God, who is my sole judge, is my witness in heaven that I never had any thoughts of my going from my house at Whitehall if I could have had but any reasonable fair quarter. I was resolved to bear much, and did so; but I did not think myself bound to prostitute the majesty of my place and person, the safety of my wife and

1. Firebrands.
2. Charles decided to flee from London on the night of 10 January 1642, in response to rioting that erupted as a result of his failed attempts to arrest the five opposition leaders in the House of Commons. Charles returned to Whitehall only as a prisoner just before his execution.
3. Cowardice.

children, to those who are prone to insult most when they have objects and opportunity most capable of their rudeness and petulancy.

But this business of the tumults, whereof some have given already an account to God, others yet living know themselves desperately guilty, time and the guilt of many has so smothered up and buried, that I think it best to leave it as it is; only I believe the just avenger of all disorders will in time make those men and that city see their sin in the glass of their punishment. It is more than an even lay, that they may one day see themselves punished by that way they offended.

Had this Parliament, as it was in its first election and constitution, sat full and free, the members of both Houses, being left to their freedom of voting, as in all reason, honor, and religion they should have been, I doubt not but things would have been so carried as would have given no less good content to all good men than they wished or expected.

For I was resolved to hear reason in all things, and to consent to it as far as I could comprehend it; but as swine are to gardens and orderly plantations, so are tumults to Parliaments, and plebeian concourses to public counsels, turning all into disorders and sordid confusions.

I am prone sometimes to think that had I called this Parliament to any other place in England, as I might opportunely enough have done, the sad consequences in all likelihood, with God's blessing, might have been prevented. A Parliament would have been welcome in any place; no place afforded such confluence of various and vicious humors as that where it was unhappily convened. But we must leave all to God, who orders our disorders, and magnifies His wisdom most when our follies and miseries are most discovered.

John Milton
1608–1674

With the popularity of the royalist tract *Eikon Basilike* after the execution of Charles I, the new Puritan government needed to find someone to defend its cause against the growing support for the King. The Puritans found their man in the newly appointed Secretary for Foreign Tongues to the Council of State, John Milton. In *Eikonoklastes* ("Image Breaker"), Milton focused his attack on the arguments of *Eikon Basilike* more than on its authorship. He doubted whether the King wrote his own defense, but he chose to concentrate on a chapter-by-chapter refutation of the book's account of history—in terms of both events and the perspective on them. Milton also revealed that one the prayers attributed to the King was really Pamela's prayer from Sir Philip Sidney's prose romance *Arcadia*. For the Puritan Milton this was a shocking piece of paganism and plagiarism by one who presented himself as pious. Milton's language in *Eikonoklastes* is iconoclastic—mocking and sarcastic, marked by invective and sharply stinging *ad hominem* argument. One royalist called *Eikonoklastes* a "blackguardly book" in which Milton "blows his viper's breath upon those immortal devotions." Some royalists even viewed Milton's blindness as God's punishment for his having attacked the King. Shortly after the Restoration of Charles II in 1660 the House of Commons ordered the burning of *Eikonoklastes* and had Milton arrested. He was imprisoned for several months before being released through the aid of his friend Andrew Marvell. *Eikonklastes* was first published in October 1649; the second and final edition in Milton's lifetime appeared in 1650.

For more about Milton, see his principal listing, page 759.

from **Eikonoklastes**

from *Chapter 1. Upon the King's Calling This Last Parliament*

"The odium and offenses which some men's rigor, or remissness in church and state had contracted upon his government, he resolved to have expiated with better laws and regulations." And yet the worst of misdemeanors committed by the worst of all his favorites, in the height of their dominion, whether acts of rigor or remissness, he hath from time to time continued, owned, and taken upon himself by public declarations, as often as the clergy, or any other of his instruments felt themselves overburdened with the people's hatred. And who knows not the superstitious rigor of his Sunday's chapel, and the licentious remissness of his Sunday's theater;[1] accompanied with that reverend statute for dominical jigs and maypoles,[2] published in his own name, and derived from the example of his father James? Which testifies all that rigor in superstition, all that remissness in religion to have issued out originally from his own house, and from his own authority.

Much rather then may those general miscarriages in State, his proper sphere, be imputed to no other person chiefly than to himself. And which of all those oppressive acts, or impositions did he ever disclaim or disavow, till the fatal awe of this Parliament hung ominously over him. Yet here he smoothly seeks to wipe off all the envy of his evil government upon his substitutes, and under-officers: and promises, though much too late, what wonders he purposed to have done in the reforming of religion—a work wherein all his undertakings heretofore declare him to have had little or no judgment. Neither could his breeding, or his course of life acquaint him with a thing so spiritual. Which may well assure us what kind of reformation we could expect from him; either some politic form of an imposed religion, or else perpetual vexation, and persecution to all those that complied not with such a form.

The like amendment he promises in State; not a step further "than his reason and conscience told him was fit to be desired"; wishing "he had kept within those bounds, and not suffered his own judgment to have been overborne in some things," of which things one was the Earl of Strafford's execution.[3] And what signifies all this, but that still his resolution was the same, to set up an arbitrary government of his own; and that all Britain was to be tied and chained to the conscience, judgment, and reason of one man; as if those gifts had been only his peculiar and prerogative, entailed upon him with his fortune to be a king? When as doubtless no man so obstinate, or so much a tyrant, but professes to be guided by that which he calls his reason, and his judgment, though never so corrupted; and pretends also his conscience. In the meanwhile, for any Parliament or the whole nation to have either reason, judgment, or conscience, by this rule was altogether in vain, if it thwarted the king's will; which was easy for him to call by any other more plausible name. He himself hath

---

1. While observers such as the Spanish ambassador noted Charles's sincere piety, Milton considered traditional ritual "superstitious" ironically linking it to irreligious theater life. Like the Puritans, Milton abhorred Sunday theater performances, and in *Of Reformation* he attacked the bishops for promoting "gaming, jigging, wassailing, and mixed dancing" on Sundays.
2. The *Book of Sports* (1633) forbade bearbaiting and bullbaiting on Sundays, but also rebuked the Puritans for condemning other forms of recreation such as dancing and archery.

3. Thomas Wentworth, Earl of Strafford, was executed in May 1641. Charles had recalled Strafford from the Lord Deputyship in Ireland to help with the war against the Scots Covenanters. Parliament accused Wentworth of planning to use the Irish army to suppress the King's opponents in Scotland and England. Even though Strafford was successfully defended against the charges, Charles signed his death warrant, fearing retaliation against himself and the Queen for their part in a plot to rescue Strafford.

many times acknowledged to have no right over us but by law; and by the same law to govern us: but law in a free nation hath been ever public reason, the enacted reason of a Parliament; which he denying to enact, denies to govern us by that which ought to be our law; interposing his own private reason, which to us is no law. And thus we find these fair and specious promises, made upon the experience of many hard sufferings, and his most mortified retirements, being thoroughly sifted, to contain nothing in them much different from his former practices, so cross, and so averse to all his Parliaments, and both the nations of this island. What fruits they could in likelihood have produced in his restorement, is obvious to any prudent foresight.

And this is the substance of his first section, till we come to the devout of it, modeled into the form of a private psalter. Which they who so much admire, either for the matter or the manner, may as well admire the archbishop's late breviary,[4] and many other as good *Manuals*, and *Handmaids of Devotion*, the lip-work of every prelatical liturgist, clapped together, and quilted out of Scripture phrase, with as much ease, and as little need of Christian diligence, or judgment, as belongs to the compiling of any ordinary and salable piece of English divinity, that the shops value. But he who from such a kind of psalmistry, or any other verbal devotion, without the pledge and earnest of suitable deeds, can be persuaded of a zeal, and true righteousness in the person, hath much yet to learn; and knows not that the deepest policy of a tyrant hath been ever to counterfeit religious. And Aristotle in his *Politics*, hath mentioned that special craft among twelve other tyrannical sophisms.[5] Neither want we examples. Andronicus Comnenus the Byzantine Emperor, though a most cruel tyrant, is reported by Nicetas[6] to have been a constant reader of Saint Paul's Epistles; and by continual study had so incorporated the phrase and style of that transcendent apostle into all his familiar letters, that the imitation seemed to vie with the original. Yet this availed not to deceive the people of that empire; who notwithstanding his saint's vizard, tore him to pieces for his tyranny.

From stories of this nature both ancient and modern which abound, the poets also, and some English, have been in this point so mindful of decorum, as to put never more pious words in the mouth of any person, than of a tyrant. I shall not instance an abstruse author, wherein the King might be less conversant, but one whom we well know was the closet companion of these his solitudes, William Shakespeare, who introduces the person of Richard the Third, speaking in as high a strain of piety, and mortification, as is uttered in any passage of this book, and sometimes to the same sense and purpose with some words in this place, "I intended," saith he, "not only to oblige my friends but mine enemies." The like saith Richard, Act 2. Scene 1,

> I do not know that Englishman alive
> With whom my soul is any jot at odds,
> More than the infant that is born tonight;
> I thank my God for my humility.

Other stuff of this sort may be read throughout the whole tragedy, wherein the poet used not much license in departing from the truth of history, which delivers him a deep dissembler, not of his affections only, but of religion.

---

4. Milton's name for Archbishop Laud's *Prayer Book*, which the Puritans hated because of its similarity to Roman Catholic ritual.
5. See Aristotle, *Politics* 5.9.15, for the notion that care in religious ritual is a device of tyrants.
6. A 12th-century historian who recorded the cruelty of Comnenus's reign (1183–1185).

from *Chapter 4. Upon the Insolency of the Tumults*

And that the King was so emphatical and elaborate on this theme against tumults, and expressed with such a vehemence his hatred of them, will redound less perhaps, than he was aware, to the commendation of his government. For besides that in good governments they happen seldomest, and rise not without cause, if they prove extreme and pernicious, they were never counted so to monarchy, but to monarchical tyranny; and extremes one with another are at most antipathy. If then the King so extremely stood in fear of tumults, the inference will endanger him to be the other extreme. Thus far the occasion of this discourse against tumults; now to the discourse itself, voluble enough, and full of sentence,[1] but that, for the most part, either specious rather than solid, or to his cause nothing pertinent.

"He never thought any thing more to presage the mischiefs that ensued, than those tumults." Then was his foresight but short, and much mistaken. Those tumults were but the mild effects of an evil and injurious reign; not signs of mischiefs to come, but seeking relief for mischiefs past; those signs were to be read more apparent in his rage and purposed revenge of those free expostulations, and clamors of the people against his lawless government. "Not any thing," saith he, "portends more God's displeasure against a nation than when he suffers the clamors of the vulgar to pass all bounds of law & reverence to authority." It portends rather his displeasure against a tyrannous King, whose proud throne he intends to overturn by that contemptible vulgar; the sad cries and oppressions of whom his royalty regarded not. As for that supplicating people they did no hurt either to law or authority, but stood for it rather in the Parliament against whom they feared would violate it.

That "they invaded the honor and freedom of the two Houses," is his own officious accusation, not seconded by the Parliament, who had they seen cause, were themselves best able to complain. And if they "shook & menaced" any, they were such as had more relation to the Court, than to the Commonwealth; enemies, not patrons of the people. But if their petitioning unarmed were an invasion of both Houses, what was his entrance into the House of Commons, besetting it with armed men, in what condition then was the honor, and freedom of that House?

"They forbore not rude deportments, contemptuous words and actions to himself and his Court."

It was more wonder, having heard what treacherous hostility he had designed against the city, and his whole kingdom, that they forbore to handle him as people in their rage have handled tyrants heretofore for less offenses.

"They were not a short ague, but a fierce quotidian fever:" He indeed may best say it, who most felt it; for the shaking was within him; and it shook him by his own description "worse than a storm, worse then an earthquake, Belshazzar's Palsy."[2] Had not worse fears, terrors, and envies made within him that commotion, how could a multitude of his subjects, armed with no other weapon then petitions, have shaken all his joints with such a terrible ague. Yet that the Parliament should entertain the least fear of bad intentions from him or his party, he endures not; but would persuade

---

1. Significance, meaning.
2. In *Of Reformation,* Milton compares the feasting of Anglican bishops to that of Belshazzar in his palace in Babylon on the eve of the fall of the city to the Medes

and Persians. When King Belshazzar saw the mysterious writing on the wall that foretold his doom, "the joints of his loins were loosed, and his knees smote one against another" (Daniel 5.6).

us that "men scare themselves and others without cause;" for he thought fear would be to them a kind of armor, and his design was, if it were possible, to disarm all, especially of a wise fear and suspicion; for that he knew would find weapons.

He goes on therefore with vehemence to repeat the mischiefs done by these tumults. "They first petitioned, then protected, dictate next, and lastly overawe the Parliament. They removed obstructions, they purged the Houses, cast out rotten members." If there were a man of iron, such as Talus, by our poet Spenser, is feigned to be the page of Justice, who with his iron flail could do all this, and expeditiously, without those deceitful forms and circumstances of law, worse than ceremonies in religion; I say God send it down, whether by one Talus, or by a thousand.[3]

"But they subdued the men of conscience in Parliament, backed and abetted all seditious and schismatical proposals against government ecclesiastical and civil."

Now we may perceive the root of his hatred whence it springs. It was not the King's grace or princely goodness, but this iron flail the people, that drove the bishops out of their baronies, out of their cathedrals, out of the Lord's house, out of their copes and surplices, and all those papistical innovations,[4] threw down the High Commission and Star Chamber, gave us a triennial Parliament, and what we most desired;[5] in revenge whereof he now so bitterly inveighs against them; these are those seditious and scismatical proposals, then by him condescended to, as acts of grace, now of another name; which declares him, touching matters of Church and State, to have been no other man in the deepest of his solitude, than he was before at the highest of his sovereignty.

But this was not the worst of these tumults, they played the hasty "midwives," and "would not stay the ripening, but went straight to ripping up, and forcibly cut out abortive votes."

They would not stay perhaps the Spanish demurring, and putting off such wholesome acts and counsels, as the politic cabin at Whitehall had no mind to. But all this is complained here as done to the Parliament, and yet we heard not the Parliament at that time complain of any violence from the people, but from him. Wherefore intrudes he to plead the cause of Parliament against the people, while the Parliament was pleading their own cause against him; and against him were forced to seek refuge of the people? 'Tis plain then that those confluxes and resorts interrupted not the Parliament, nor by them were thought tumultuous, but by him only and his court faction.

"But what good Man had not rather want any thing he most desired for the public good, then attain it by such unlawful and irreligious means;" as much as to say, had not rather sit still and let his country be tyrannized, then that the people, finding no other remedy, should stand up like men and demand their rights and liberties. This is the artificialest piece of fineness to persuade men into slavery that the wit of court could have invented. But hear how much better the moral of this lesson would befit the teacher. What good man had not rather want a boundless and arbitrary power, and those fine flowers of the crown, called prerogatives, then for them to use force and perpetual vexation to his faithful subjects, nay to wade for them through blood and civil war? So that

---

3. Talus is the iron flail who ruthlessly cuts down all who oppose Artegal, the Knight of Justice, in Spenser's *Faerie Queene* 5, much of which is about the subjugation of Ireland by England.

4. Milton refers to the London petition calling for the abolition of the bishops' power, introduced into Parliament in December 1640, that resulted in their exclusion from the House of Lords.

5. The High Commission, the highest ecclesiastical court, investigated such matters as heresy, recusancy, and any writing against the Book of Common Prayer; Parliament abolished it on July 5, 1641. The Star Chamber was also abolished because it was viewed as a special tool of government favoring the special right of the sovereign above all other persons and the common law. A triennial Parliament is a parliament convened every three years.

this and the whole bundle of those following sentences may be applied better to the convincement of his own violent courses, then of those pretended tumults.

"Who were the chief demagogues to send for those tumults, some alive are not ignorant." Setting aside the affrightment of this goblin word; for the King by his leave cannot coin English as he could money, to be current (and tis believed this wording was above his known style and orthography, and accuses the whole composure to be conscious of some other author)[6] yet if the people "were sent for, emboldened and directed" by those "demagogues," who, saving his Greek, were good patriots, and by his own confession "Men of some repute for parts and piety," it helps well to assure us there was both urgent cause, and the less danger of their coming.

"Complaints were made, yet no redress could be obtained." The Parliament also complained of what danger they sat in from another party, and demanded of him a guard, but it was not granted. What marvel then if it cheered them to see some store of their friends, and in the Roman not the pettifogging sense, their clients so near about them; a defense due by nature both from whom it was offered, and to whom; as due as to their parents; though the Court stormed, and fretted to see such honor given to them, who were then best fathers of the Commonwealth. And both the Parliament and people complained, and demanded justice for those assaults, if not murders done at his own doors, by that crew of rufflers, but he, instead of doing justice on them, justified and abetted them in what they did, as in his public "Answer to a Petition from the City" may be read. Neither is it slightly to be passed over, that in the very place where blood was first drawn in this cause, as the beginning of all that followed, there was his own blood shed by the executioner. According to that sentence of divine justice, "In the place where dogs licked the blood of Naboth, shall dogs lick thy blood, even thine."

From hence he takes occasion to excuse that improvident and fatal error of his absenting from the Parliament. "When he found that no declaration of the bishops could take place against those tumults." Was that worth his considering, that foolish and self-undoing declaration of twelve cypher bishops, who were immediately appeached of treason for that audacious declaring?[7] The bishops peradventure were now and then pulled by the rochets,[8] and deserved another kind of pulling; but what amounted this to "the fear of his own person in the streets"? Did he not the very next day after his irruption into the House of Commons, than which nothing had more exasperated the people, go in his coach unguarded into the city? did he receive the least affront, much less violence in any of the streets, but rather humble demeanors, and supplications? Hence may be gathered, that however in his own guiltiness he might have justly feared, yet that he knew the people so full of awe and reverence to his person, as to dare commit himself single among the thickest of them, at a time when he had most provoked them. Besides in Scotland they had handled the Bishops in a more robustious manner; Edinburgh had been full of tumults,[9] two armies from thence had entered England against him;[1] yet after all this, he was not fearful, but very forward to take so long a journey to Edinburgh;[2] which argues first, as did also his rendition afterward to the Scotch Army,[3] that to England he continued still, as he was indeed, a stranger, and full of diffidence; to the Scots

6. Milton believed that Charles I could not have written *Eikon Basilike* because such passages as this one showed a word choice and style different from Charles's.
7. The Bishops' Exclusion Bill was Parliament's reaction to the assertion by 12 bishops that any legislation passed by the House of Lords when the bishops were absent was void.
8. Vestments.
9. When Charles attempted to force the Book of Common Prayer on the Scottish churches, the people rioted.
1. The first Scottish war ended with the Treaty of Berwick in June 1639, the second with the Treaty of Ripon in October 1640.
2. Charles went to Edinburgh in 1641, hoping to pit the Covenanters against their opponents.
3. Charles surrendered himself to the Scottish army commanders in May 1646.

only a native King,[4] in his confidence, though not in his dealing towards them. It shows us next beyond doubting, that all this his fear of tumults was but a mere color and occasion taken of his resolved absence from the Parliament, for some other end not difficult to be guessed. And those instances wherein valor is not to be questioned for not "scuffling with the sea, or an undisciplined rabble," are but subservient to carry on the solemn jest of his fearing tumults: if they discover not withall, the true reason why he departed; only to turn his slashing at the court gate, to slaughtering "in the field"; his disorderly bickering, to an orderly invading: which was nothing else but a more orderly disorder.

"Some suspected and affirmed, that he meditated a War when he went first from Whitehall." And they were not the worst heads that did so, nor did "any of his former acts weaken him" to that, as he alleges for himself, or if they had, they clear him only for the time of passing them, not for what ever thoughts might come after into his mind. Former actions of improvidence or fear, not with him unusual, cannot absolve him of all after meditations.

He goes on protesting his "no intention to have left Whitehall," had these horrid tumults given him but "fair quarter," as if he himself, his wife and children had been in peril. But to this enough hath been answered.

"Had this Parliament as it was in its first election," namely, with the Lord and Baron Bishops, "sat full and free," he doubts not but all had gone well. What warrant this of his to us? Whose not doubting was all good men's greatest doubt.

"He was resolved to hear reason, and to consent so far as he could comprehend." A hopeful resolution; what if his reason were found by oft experience to comprehend nothing beyond his own advantages, was this a reason fit to be intrusted with the common good of three nations?

"But," saith he, "as swine are to gardens, so are tumults to Parliaments." This the Parliament, had they found it so, could best have told us. In the meanwhile, who knows not that one great hog may do as much mischief in a garden, as many little swine.[5]

"He was sometimes prone to think that had he called this last Parliament to any other place in England, the sad consequences might have been prevented." But change of air changes not the mind. Was not his first Parliament at Oxford dissolved after two subsidies given him, and no justice received? Was not his last in the same place, where they sat with as much freedom, as much quiet from tumults, as they could desire, a Parliament both in his account, and their own, consisting of all his friends, that fled after him, and suffered for him, and yet by him nicknamed, and cashiered for a "mongrel Parliament that vexed his Queen with their base and mutinous motions," as his cabinet letter tells us?[6] Whereby the world may see plainly, that no shifting of place, no sifting of members to his own mind, no number, no paucity, no freedom from tumults, could ever bring his arbitrary wilfulness, and tyrannical designs to brook the least shape or similitude, the least counterfeit of a Parliament.

Finally instead of praying for his people as a good King should do, he prays to be delivered from them, as "from wild beasts, inundations, and raging seas, that had overborne all loyalty, modesty, laws, justice, and religion." God save the people from such intercessors.

4. Charles was born in Scotland, and he made special appeals to the Scots to be their king in both 1641 and 1646.
5. Milton may echo the identification of the hog with Henry VIII for his failure to carry out a thorough and consistent reformation in Anthony Gilby's *An Admonition to England and Scotland to Call Them to Repentance* (Geneva, 1558).

6. Charles called an opposition Parliament that met in Oxford in January 22, 1644, and that he ordered closed after disagreement with them. This Parliament first attempted a peaceful settlement with the Westminster Parliament and then declared it guilty of treason. The King called it his "mongrel Parliament."

＊━━ ☳◈☶ ━━＊

The Petition of Gentlewomen and Tradesmen's Wives

A month after the King tried to have the five chief members of Parliament arrested, two petitions were presented to the Commons by "Gentlewomen and Tradesmen's Wives" of London. In the first of these, dated 1 February 1642, the women complained about the lack of trade, which caused great want and blamed the "opposition of some bishops or lords" for the neglect of the women's earlier petitions. In the second petition, reprinted here, the women complain about threats to the security of the state posed by the bishops and Catholic lords in the House of Lords, the still not yet executed Archbishop Laud, and the Catholic Mass. From the London women's vantage point, the 1641 rebellion of the Catholics in Ireland demonstrated the risk to Puritans of attacks from Catholics (indistinguishable from Anglicans) within England. The violence unleashed by the more spontaneous and popular revolts in Ireland had been luridly portrayed and grossly exaggerated in the English press. Nevertheless, the Catholic revolt did bring much bloodshed, which increased with the Protestant retaliation. Interestingly, some of the Irish uprisings were led by women, a fact that would not have made any difference to the London women, even if they had known it.

The chief terms of the petition, like the chief terms of the Wars of the Three Kingdoms, were religious. Archbishop Laud is attacked here, but the King is not. Even the women's justification of their right to approach Parliament with a petition is articulated in religious terms. They argue that women are the same as men in Christ's eyes and that women have suffered as much religious persecution as men. If these women argue that women are equal to men, it is mainly insofar as they are believers in the Puritan practice of religion. Delegated by his fellow members to make a reply, Pym publicly reassured the women that their petition had been read and that they would receive "satisfaction . . . to [their] just and lawful desires." The next day, the House of Lords passed a bill excluding the Bishops, and so Parliament met at least one of the women petitioners' demands.

A True Copy of the Petition of the Gentlewomen and Tradesmen's Wives, In and About the City of London[1]

Delivered to the Honorable, the Knights, Citizens, and Burgesses of the House of Commons in Parliament, the 4th of February, 1642

Together with their several reasons why their sex ought thus to petition, as well as the men; and the manner how both their petition and reasons was delivered.

Likewise the answer which the Honorable Assembly sent to them by Mr. Pym,[2] as they stood at the house door.

To the Honorable Knights, Citizens and Burgesses,[3] of the House of Commons assembled in Parliament. The most humble Petition of the Gentlewomen, Tradesmen's Wives, and many others of the female sex, all inhabitants of the city of London, and the suburbs thereto.

With lowest submission showing,

1. Printed in the *Parliamentary History* ii.1074.
2. John Pym (1583?–1643) was a strong Puritan opponent of episcopacy and a leader of the House of Commons, one of the five members whom Charles I unsuc-

cessfully attempted to have arrested in 1642.
3. Members of Parliament representing boroughs or corporate towns.

That we also with all thankful humility acknowledging the unwearied pains, care and great charge, besides hazard of health and life, which you the noble worthies of this honorable and renowned assembly have undergone, for the safety both of church and commonwealth, for a long time already past; for which not only we your humble petitioners, and all well affected in this kingdom, but also all other good Christians are bound now and at all times acknowledge; yet notwithstanding that many worthy deeds have been done by you, great danger and fear do still attend us, and will, as long as Popish Lords and superstitious bishops are suffered to have their voice in the House of Peers, and that accursed and abominable idol of the Mass suffered in the kingdom, and that archenemy[4] of our prosperity and reformation lieth in the Tower, yet not receiving his deserved punishment.

All these under correction, gives us great cause to suspect that God is angry with us, and to be the chief causes why your pious endeavors for a further reformation proceedeth not with that success as you desire, and is most earnestly prayed for of all that wish well to true religion, and the flourishing estate both of king and kingdom; the insolencies of the papists and their abettors, raiseth a just fear and suspicion of sowing sedition, and breaking out into bloody persecution in this kingdom, as they have done in Ireland, the thoughts of which sad and barbarous events maketh our tender hearts to melt within us, forcing us humbly to petition to this honorable assembly, to make safe provision for yourselves and us, before it be too late.

And whereas we, whose hearts have joined cheerfully with all those petitions which have been exhibited unto you in the behalf of the purity of religion, and the liberty of our husbands' persons and estates, recounting ourselves to have an interest in the common privileges with them, do with the same confidence assure ourselves to find the same gracious acceptance with you, for easing of those grievances, which in regard of our frail condition, do more nearly concern us, and do deeply terrify our souls: our domestical dangers with which this kingdom is so much distressed, especially growing on us from those treacherous and wicked attempts already are such as we find ourselves to have as deep a share as any other.

We cannot but tremble at the very thoughts of the horrid and hideous facts which modesty forbids us now to name, occasioned by the bloody wars in Germany,[5] his Majesty's late Northern Army, how often did it affright our hearts, whilst their violence began to break out so furiously upon the persons of those whose husbands or parents were not able to rescue: we wish we had no cause to speak of those insolencies, and savage usage and unheard-of rapes, exercised upon our sex in Ireland, and have we not just cause to fear they will prove the forerunners of our ruin, except Almighty God by the wisdom and care of this Parliament be pleased to succor us, our husbands and children, which are as dear and tender unto us as the lives and blood of our hearts, to see them murdered and mangled and cut in pieces before our eyes, to see our children dashed against the stones, and the mothers' milk mingled with the infants' blood, running down the streets, to see our houses on flaming fire over our heads: oh how dreadful would this be?[6] We thought it misery enough (though nothing to that we have just cause to fear) but few years since for some of our sex, by

---

4. Archbishop Laud (1573–1645), who enforced forms of worship that were Anglican High Church, or similar to Roman Catholicism, and promoted church government by Anglican bishops. His policies and support for Charles I won Laud impeachment in 1642; in 1643 he was condemned to death by the Commons.
5. The Thirty Years War (1618–1648) was a European-wide war fought mainly in Germany between Protestant opponents to Hapsburg rule and Catholic supporters of the Holy Roman Empire.
6. While there was violence on both sides, woodcuts of the Irish rebellions in the English press sensationalized the violence of Catholics against Protestant settlers by depicting the murder of infants and attacks upon women.

unjust divisions from their bosom comforts, to be rendered in a manner widows, and the children fatherless, husbands were imprisoned from the society of their wives, even against the laws of God and nature, and little infants suffered in their fathers' banishments: thousands of our dearest friends have been compelled to fly from Episcopal persecutions into desert places amongst wild beasts, there finding more favor than in their native soil, and in the midst of all their sorrows such hath the pity of the Prelates[7] been, that our cries could never enter into their ears or hearts, not yet through multitudes of obstructions could never have access or come nigh to those royal mercies of our most gracious sovereign, which we confidently hope would have relieved us: but after all these pressures ended, we humbly signify that our present fears are, that unless the bloodthirsty faction of the Papists and Prelates be hindered in their designs, ourselves here in England as well as they in Ireland, shall be exposed to the misery which is more intolerable than that which is already past, as namely to the rage not of men alone, but of devils incarnate (as we may so say), besides the thralldom of our souls and consciences in matters concerning God, which of all things are most dear unto us.

Now the remembrance of all these fearful accidents aforementioned do strongly move us from the example of the woman of Tekoa (II Samuel 14.2–20)[8] to fall submissively at the feet of his Majesty, our dread sovereign, and cry Help, oh King, help oh ye the noble Worthies now sitting in Parliament: And we humbly beseech you, that you will be a means to his Majesty and the House of Peers, that they will be pleased to take our heartbreaking grievances into timely consideration, and to add strength and encouragement to your noble endeavors, and further that you would move his Majesty with our humble requests, that he would be graciously pleased according to the example of the good King Asa,[9] to purge both the court and kingdom of that great idolatrous service of the Mass, which is tolerated in the Queen's court, this sin (as we conceive) is able to draw down a greater curse upon the whole kingdom than all your noble and pious endeavors can prevent, which was the cause that the good and pious King Asa would not suffer idolatry in his own mother, whose example if it shall please his Majesty's gracious goodness to follow, in putting down Popery and idolatry both in great and small, in court and in the kingdom throughout, to subdue the Papists and their abettors, and by taking away the power of the Prelates, whose government by long and woeful experience we have found to be against the liberty of our conscience and the freedom of the Gospel, and the sincere profession and practice thereof, then shall our fears be removed, and we may expect that God will pour down his blessings in abundance both upon his Majesty, and upon this Honorable Assembly, and upon the whole land.

For which your new petitioners shall pray affectionately.

The reasons follow.

It may be thought strange and unbeseeming our sex to show ourselves by way of petition to this Honorable Assembly: but the matter being rightly considered, of the right and interest we have in the common and public cause of the church, it will, as we conceive (under correction) be found a duty commanded and required.

7. Churchmen, bishops.
8. The wise woman of Tekoa went before King David and urged him to act mercifully toward his son Absalom. King David had been failing to act decisively against rape and

murder within his own household.
9. Charles I is asked to banish Catholics and the Mass just as King Asa banished sodomites and idolatry in 1 Kings 15.8–12.

First, because Christ hath purchased us at as dear a rate as he hath done men, and therefore requireth the like obedience for the same mercy as of men.

Secondly, because in the free enjoying of Christ in his own laws, and a flourishing estate of the church and commonwealth, consisteth the happiness of women as well as men.

Thirdly, because women are sharers in the common calamities that accompany both church and commonwealth, when oppression is exercised over the church or kingdom wherein they live; and an unlimited power have been given to Prelates to exercise authority over the consciences of women, as well as men, witness Newgate, Smithfield,[1] and other places of persecution, wherein women as well as men have felt the smart of their fury.

Neither are we left without example in scripture, for when the state of the church, in the time of King Ahasuerus, was by the bloody enemies thereof sought to be utterly destroyed, we find that Esther the Queen and her maids fasted and prayed, and that Esther petitioned to the King in the behalf of the church:[2] and though she enterprised this duty with the hazard of her own life, being contrary to the law to appear before the King before she were sent for, yet her love to the church carried her through all difficulties, to the performance of that duty.

On which grounds we are emboldened to present our humble petition unto this Honorable Assembly, not weighing the reproaches which may and are by many cast upon us, who (not well weighing the premises) scoff and deride our good intent. We do it not out of any self-conceit, or pride of heart, as seeking to equal ourselves with men, either in authority or wisdom: But according to our places to discharge that duty we owe to God, and the cause of the church, as far as lieth in us, following herein the example of the men which have gone in this duty before us.

A relation of the manner how it was delivered, with their answer, sent by Mr. Pym.

This petition, with their reasons, was delivered the 4th of Feb. 1641/2, by Mrs. Anne Stagg, a gentlewoman and brewer's wife, and many others with her of like rank and quality, which when they had delivered it, after some time spent in reading of it, the Honorable Assembly sent them an answer by Mr. Pym, which was performed in this manner.

Mr. Pym came to the Commons door, and called for the women, and spake unto them in these words: Good women, your petition and the reasons have been read in the house; and is very thankfully accepted of, and is come in a seasonable time: You shall (God willing) receive from us all the satisfaction which we can possibly give to your just and lawful desires. We entreat you to repair to your houses, and turn your petition which you have delivered here into prayers at home for us; for we have been, are and shall be (to our utmost power) ready to relieve you, your husbands, and children, and to perform the trust committed unto us towards God, our King and country, as becometh faithful Christians and loyal subjects.

---

1. Persecutions at Smithfield and Newgate.
2. The Jewish Esther became the Queen of Ahasuerus and saved the Jews from Haman, who planned to massacre the Jews; see the Book of Esther and also *Ester Hath Hanged Haman* in Perspectives: Tracts on Women and Gender, page 717.

John Lilburne
1614?–1657

John Lilburne was one of the most tireless political reformers of the Civil War in England. His pamphlets against the Anglican Church in 1638 got him arrested and brought before the Star Chamber (the secret royal tribunal that judged and punished without a jury). Lilburne seized the opportunity to question the court's procedures by refusing to incriminate himself. With Cromwell's help in the House of Commons, Lilburne was released from prison and became a lieutenant in the Parliamentary army (1642–45), from which he resigned in objection to Presbyterianism as the state religion. Examined several times by the House of Commons for his criticisms of its policies and members, Lilburne became the chief exponent of the Levellers, derisively called such because of their egalitarianism. The Levellers wanted fundamental changes in the government, including universal suffrage, freedom of speech and religion, freedom from exorbitant taxation, care of the poor and aged, and trial by jury. Though a convinced antimonarchist, Lilburne even protested against the condemnation of Charles I without a proper trial.

The House of Commons rejected Leveller reforms in January 1648. This defeat, combined with Lilburne's fear that the Levellers would be brought to trial for their dissent, provoked his speech to Commons in February. This speech was published as *England's New Chains Discovered*. The first part (a selection from which is reprinted here) reviews the Levellers' concerns, and the second part criticizes the members of Parliament, who condemned Lilburne's speech as seditious. Lilburne went on to publish tracts criticizing Cromwell, monopolies, and enclosures but was ordered into exile by Parliament in 1652 only for attacking his uncle's business enemy, Sir Arthur Hesilrige, as a man "fit to be spewed out of all human society." In 1653, Lilburne returned to England in defiance of Cromwell and was arrested on arrival. His plight aroused popular petitions in his favor, and he was finally acquitted. Nevertheless, the government would not let him go free. Having converted to Quakerism, he died in confinement just a year before the death of Cromwell.

from England's New Chains Discovered

or, The serious apprehensions of a part of the People, in behalf of the Commonwealth; (being Presenters, Promoters, and Approvers of the Large Petition of September 11. 1648.)

Presented to the Supreme Authority of England, the Representers of the people in Parliament assembled.

By Lieut. Col. John Lilburn, and divers other Citizens of London, and Borough of Southwark; February 26. 1648. Whereunto his speech delivered at the Bar is annexed.

Since you have done the nation so much right, and yourselves so much honor as to declare that the people (under God) are the original of all just powers; and given us thereby fair grounds to hope, that you really intend their freedom and prosperity; yet the way thereunto being frequently mistaken, and through haste or error of judgment, those who mean the best, are many times misled so far to the prejudice of those that trust them, as to leave them in a condition nearest to bondage, when they have thought they had brought them into a way of freedom. And since woeful experience hath manifested this to be a truth, there seemeth no small reason that you should seriously lay to heart what at present we have to offer, for discovery and prevention of so great a danger.

And because we have been the first movers in and concerning an Agreement of the People,[1] as the most proper and just means for the settling the long and tedious distractions of this nation, occasioned by nothing more, than the uncertainty of our government; and since there hath been an Agreement prepared and presented by some officers of the army to this honorable House,[2] as what they thought requisite to be agreed unto by the people (you approving thereof) we shall in the first place deliver our apprehensions thereupon.

That an Agreement between those that trust, and those who are trusted, hath appeared a thing acceptable to this honorable House, his Excellency, and the officers of the army, is as much to our rejoicing, as we conceive it just in itself, and profitable for the Commonwealth,[3] and cannot doubt but that you will protect those of the people, who have no ways forfeited their birthright, in their proper liberty of taking this, or any other, as God and their own considerations[4] shall direct them.

Which we the rather mention, for that many particulars in the Agreement before you, are upon serious examination thereof, dissatisfactory to most of those who are very earnestly desirous of an Agreement, and many very material things seem to be wanting therein, which may be supplied in another: As

1. They are now much troubled there should be any intervals between the ending of this Representative, and the beginning of the next as being desirous that this present Parliament that hath lately done so great things in so short a time, tending to their liberties, should sit; until with certainty and safety they can see them delivered into the hands of another Representative, rather than to leave them (though never so small a time) under the dominion of a Council of State; a Constitution of a new and unexperienced nature, and which they fear, as the case now stands, may design to perpetuate their power, and to keep off Parliaments for ever.

2. They now conceive no less danger, in that it is provided that Parliaments for the future are to continue but 6 months, and a Council of State 18. In which time, if they should prove corrupt, having command of all forces by sea and land, they will have great opportunities to make themselves absolute and unaccountable: And because this is a danger, than which there cannot well be a greater; they generally incline to Annual Parliaments, bounded and limited as reason shall devise, not dissolvable, but to be continued or adjourned as shall seem good in their discretion, during that year, but no longer; and then to dissolve of course, and give way to those who shall be chosen immediately to succeed them, and in the intervals of their adjournments, to entrust an ordinary Committee of their own members, as in other cases limited and bounded with express instructions, and accountable to the next session, which will avoid all those dangers feared from a Council of State, as at present this is constituted.

3. They are not satisfied with the clause, wherein it is said, that the power of the Representatives shall extend to the erecting and abolishing of Courts of Justice; since the alteration of the usual way of trials by twelve sworn men of the neighborhood, may be included therein: a constitution so equal and just in itself, as that they conceive it ought to remain unalterable. Neither is it clear what is meant by these

1. The Levellers published their proposals for "An Agreement of the People" in *Foundations of Freedom* (15 December 1648). The beginning of this speech complains about how the government has betrayed the principles set forth in the Leveller "Agreement."
2. *An Agreement Prepared for the People of England* was submitted to Parliament on January 20, 1649.
3. Commonwealth, meaning both public good and body politic, and specifically the republican government established in England between the execution of Charles I in 1649 and the Restoration in 1660.
4. Attentive thoughts.

words, (viz.) That the Representatives have the highest final judgment. They conceiving that their authority in these cases, is only to make laws, rules, and directions for other courts and persons assigned by law for the execution thereof; unto which every member of the Commonwealth, as well those of the Representative, as others, should be alike subject; it being likewise unreasonable in itself, and an occasion of much partiality, injustice, and vexation to the people, that the law-makers should be law-executors.[5]

4. Although it doth provide that in the laws hereafter to be made, no person by virtue of any tenure, grant, charter, patent, degree, or birth, shall be privileged from subjection thereunto, or from being bound thereby, as well as others. Yet doth it not null and make void those present protections by law, or otherwise; nor leave all persons, as well Lords as others, alike liable in person and estate, as in reason and conscience they ought to be.[6]

5. They are very much unsatisfied with what is expressed as a reserve from the Representative, in matters of religion, as being very obscure, and full of perplexity, that ought to be most plain and clear; there having occurred no greater trouble to the nation about any thing than by the intermeddling of Parliaments in matters of religion.[7]

6. They seem to conceive it absolutely necessary, that there be in their agreement, a reserve from ever having any kingly government, and a bar against restoring the House of Lords, both which are wanting in the agreement which is before you.

7. They seem to be resolved to take away all known and burdensome grievances, as tithes,[8] that great oppression of the country's industry and hindrance of tillage: excise, and customs, those secret thieves, and robbers, drainers of the poor and middle sort of people, and the greatest obstructers of trade, surmounting all the prejudices of ship money, patents, and projects,[9] before this Parliament: also to take away all monopolizing companies of merchants, the hinderers and decayers of clothing and cloth-working, dying, and the like useful professions; by which thousands of poor people might be set at work, that are now ready to starve, were merchandising restored to its due and proper freedom: they conceive likewise that the three grievances before mentioned, (viz.) monopolizing companies, excise, and customs, do exceedingly prejudice shipping and navigation, and consequently discourage seamen, and mariners, and which have had no small influence upon the late unhappy revolts which have so much endangered the nation, and so much advantaged your enemies. They also incline to direct a more equal and less burdensome way for levying monies for the future, those other forementioned being so chargeable in the receipt, as that the very stipends and allowance to the officers attending thereupon would defray a very great part of the charge of the army; whereas now they engender and support a corrupt interest. They also have in mind to take away all imprisonment of disabled men, for debt; and to provide some effectual course to enforce all that are able to a

---

5. Lilburne is calling for a clear distinction between the power of the House of Commons to legislate and the power of the Courts to interpret the law.

6. The Commonwealth did not thoroughly abolish the privileges of the landed classes and so did not provide a government in which all classes would be treated equally under the law.

7. Lilburne criticizes the Commons for not completely separating Church and State, which he sees as a major danger, since the King's imposition of the rituals of the Anglican Church was one of the reasons the English Civil War was fought.

8. The tenth part of the annual produce of agriculture, due as payment for the Church.

9. "Ship money" was an ancient tax levied in time of war on maritime cities, which was revived by Charles I and applied to inland counties as well; patents were the sole right or license to sell or deal in a commodity; and projects were plans or schemes, here especially those by the government to get money.

speedy payment, and not suffer them to be sheltered in prisons, where they live in plenty, whilst their creditors are undone. They have also in mind to provide work, and comfortable maintenance for all sorts of poor, aged, and impotent people, and to establish some more speedy, less troublesome and chargeable way for deciding of controversies in law, whole families having been ruined by seeking right in the ways yet in being. All which, though of greatest and most immediate concernment to the people, are yet omitted in their Agreement before you.

These and the like are their intentions in what they purpose for an Agreement of the people, as being resolved (so far as they are able) to lay an impossibility upon all whom they shall hereafter trust, of ever wronging the Commonwealth in any considerable measure, without certainty of ruining themselves, and as conceiving it to be an improper tedious, and unprofitable thing for the people, to be ever running after their Representatives with petitions for redress of such grievances as may at once be removed by themselves, or to depend for these things so essential to their happiness and freedom, upon the uncertain judgments of several Representatives, the one being apt to renew what the other hath taken away.

Oliver Cromwell
1599–1658

Cromwell's brutal conquest of Ireland (1649–1650) was the culmination of a long military, political, and religiously zealous career and the turning point in his rise to the position of Lord Protector. He had risen steadily in the Parliamentary Army, serving in the early days of the Civil War as captain of a troop of horses and finally becoming the chief of the New Model Army. Not only did he have a genius for military strategy but he was one of those who "never stirred from their troops . . . but fought to the last minute." He and his men were both called "Ironsides" in tribute to their indomitability. As a member of Parliament, he argued vigorously for the Puritan cause, and when Parliament was purged of Presbyterians in 1649, Cromwell's power and that of his fellow Congregationalists or Independents increased. At the trial of Charles I in January 1649, Cromwell adamantly demanded execution. Afterward, when the new Commonwealth was set up, one of Parliament's first charges was to send Cromwell to subdue Ireland, where Irish Royalists and Rebels, once pitted against each other, had formed a coalition and were gaining ground.

Cromwell's treatment of the Irish tested the limits of the principles of the Puritan Revolution and left a legacy of devastation. Although Cromwell was a strong member of the English Parliament, he helped to bring about the abolition of both Irish and Scottish Parliaments with his military defeats of both kingdoms. In September 1644, Cromwell urged the Presbyterian Parliament to guarantee liberty of conscience to the Independents among his troops, but when the Catholics of New Ross, Ireland, called for similar toleration in October 1649, Cromwell refused them: "if by liberty of conscience, you mean a liberty to exercise the Mass, I judge it best to use plain dealing, and to let you know, where the Parliament of England have power, that will not be allowed of." Indeed during Cromwell's rule in England, only Jews and non-Anglican Protestants were tolerated. Furthermore, Cromwell escalated the policy (begun under Elizabeth and James) of giving lands confiscated from native Irish inhabitants to English colonists. The massacre of Drogheda—including civilians as well as troops—made the Irish remember Cromwell as cruel. In the following letter of September 17, 1649, Cromwell presents his troops' massacre of the people of Drogheda as "the righteous judgment of God." The same religious conviction that had made him and his New Model Army such valiant defenders of English liberty was used to justify Irish slaughter.

Cromwell also used his letters to keep Parliament informed of his progress, to ask for further supplies, and to promote his political power. He was to go on to defeat the Scots in 1650. Ultimately, his power grew to such an extent that in 1657 he became Lord Protector, assuming the pomp and trappings of royalty. When his son Richard succeeded him at his death in September 1658, it seemed as if Oliver Cromwell's rule had led to a new monarchy. His son proved a weak successor, and the Commonwealth was restored in May 1659, only to collapse with the Restoration of 1660. If Cromwell's participation in parliamentary politics and the New Model Army contributed to the cause of republican liberty, his conquest of Ireland marked one of the bleakest chapters in the English colonization of Ireland.

from Letters from Ireland

Relating the Several Great Success It Hath Pleased God to Give Unto the Parliament's Forces There, in the Taking of Drogheda, Trym, Dundalk, Carlingford, and the Nury . . . .

For the Honorable *William Lenthal* Esq;
Speaker of the Parliament of *England*

Sir,
Your army[1] being safely arrived at Dublin, and the enemy endeavoring to draw all his forces together about Trym and Tecroghan[2] (as my intelligence gave me); from whence endeavors were used by the Marquis of Ormonde, to draw Owen Roe O'Neal with his forces to his assistance, but with what success I cannot yet learn.[3] I resolved after some refreshment taken for our weather beaten men and horses, and accommodations for a march, to take the field; and accordingly upon Friday the thirtieth of August last, rendezvoused with eight regiments of foot, and six of horse, and some troops of dragoons, three miles on the north side of Dublin; the design was, to endeavor the regaining of Drogheda,[4] or tempting the enemy, upon his hazard of the loss of that place, to fight. Your army came before the town upon Monday following, where having pitched, as speedy course as could be was taken to frame our batteries,[5] which took up the more time, because divers of the battering guns were on shipboard. Upon Monday the ninth of this instant, the batteries began to play; whereupon I sent Sir Arthur Ashton the then Governor a summons, to deliver the town to the use of the Parliament of England; to the which I received no satisfactory answer, but proceeded that day to beat down the steeple of the church on the south side of the town, and to beat down a tower not far from the same place, which you will discern by the card[6] enclosed. Our guns not being able to do much that day, it was resolved to endeavor to do our utmost the next day to make breaches[7] assaultable, and by the help of God to storm them. The places pitched upon, were that part of the town wall next a church, called St. Marie's, which was the rather chosen, because we did hope that if we did enter and possess that church, we should be the better able to keep it against their horse and foot, until we could make way for the entrance of our horse,

1. The letter is addressed to Parliament from the commander of the parliamentary army, hence "your army."
2. A town and townland in County Meath, northwest of Dublin.
3. James Butler, Earl of Ormonde, represented Charles I in Ireland throughout the 1640s. At first opposed to the Catholic Confederation led by Owen Roe O'Neill (c. 1590–1649), Ormonde joined forces with O'Neill against

the incursion of Cromwell's army.
4. Drogheda (Droichead átha, "Bridge of the ford"), a city in County Louth, was under royalist command when Cromwell arrived there on 2 September 1649.
5. Platforms on which artillery was mounted.
6. Chart, map.
7. Gaps in fortifications.

which we did not conceive that any part of the town would afford the like advantage for that purpose with this. The batteries planted were two, one was for that part of the wall against the east end of the said church, the other against the wall on the south side; being somewhat long in battering, the enemy made six retrenchments, three of them from the said church to Duleek Gate, and three from the east end of the church to the town wall, and so backward. The guns after some two or three hundred shot, beat down the corner tower, and opened two reasonable good breaches in the east and south wall. Upon Tuesday the tenth of this instant, about five of the clock in the evening, we began the storm, and after some hot dispute, we entered about seven or eight hundred men, the enemy disputing it very stiffly with us; and indeed through the advantages of the place, and the courage God was pleased to give the defenders, our men were forced to retreat quite out of the breach, not without some considerable loss; Colonel Cassel being there shot in the head, whereof he presently died, and divers soldiers and officers doing their duty, killed and wounded. There was a tenalia[8] to flanker the south wall of the town, between Duleek Gate, and the corner tower before mentioned, which our men entered, wherein they found some forty or fifty of the enemy, which they put to the sword, and this they held; but it being without[9] the wall, and the sallyport[1] through the wall into that tenalia being choked up with some of the enemy which were killed in it, it proved of no use for our entrance into the town that way.

Although our men that stormed the breaches were forced to recoil, as before is expressed, yet being encouraged to recover their loss, they made a second attempt, wherein God was pleased to animate them, that they got ground of the enemy, and by the goodness of God, forced him to quit his entrenchments; and after a very hot dispute, the enemy having both horse and foot, and we only foot within the wall, the enemy gave ground, and our men became masters; but of their retrenchments and the church, which indeed although they made our entrance the more difficult, yet they proved of excellent use to us, so that the enemy could not annoy us with their horse, but thereby we had advantage to make good the ground, that so we might let in our own horse, which accordingly was done, though with much difficulty; the enemy retreated divers of them into the Mill-Mount, a place very strong and of difficult access, being exceeding high, having a good graft[2] and strongly pallisadoed;[3] the Governor Sir Arthur Ashton and divers considerable officers being there, our men getting up to them, were ordered by me to put them all to the sword; and indeed being in the heat of action, I forbade them to spare any that were in arms in the town, and I think that night they put to the sword about two thousand men, divers of the officers and soldiers being fled over the bridge into the other part of the town, where about one hundred of them possessed St. Peter's church steeple, some the west gate, and others, a round strong tower next the gate, called St. Sunday's. These being summoned to yield to mercy, refused; whereupon I ordered the steeple of St. Peter's church to be fired, where one of them was heard to say in the midst of the flames, "God damn me, God confound me, I burn, I burn." The next day the other two towers were summoned,[4] in one of which was about six or seven score, but they refused to yield themselves; and we knowing that hunger must compel them, set only good guards to secure them from running away, until their stomachs were come down.

---

8. A low fortification to protect the wall from the side.
9. Outside.
1. An opening for troops to pass through.

2. Ditch, moat.
3. Defended with a strong fence of pointed stakes.
4. Called to surrender.

From one of the said towers, notwithstanding their condition, they killed and wounded some of our men; when they submitted, their officers were knocked on the head, and every tenth man of the soldiers killed, and the rest shipped for the Barbados;[5] the soldiers in the other tower were all spared, as to their lives only, and shipped likewise for the Barbados. I am persuaded that this is a righteous judgment of God upon these barbarous wretches, who have imbrued their hands in so much innocent blood, and that it will tend to prevent the effusion of blood for the future, which are the satisfactory grounds to such actions, which otherwise cannot but work remorse and regret.

The officers and soldiers of this garrison were the flower of all their army; and their great expectation was that our attempting this place would put fair to ruin us; they being confident of the resolution of their men, and the advantage of the place; if we had divided our force into two quarters, to have besieged the north town and the south town, we could not have had such a correspondency between the two parts of our army, but that they might have chosen to have brought their army, and have fought with which part they pleased, and at the same time have made a sally with two thousand men upon us, and have left their walls manned, they having in the town the numbers specified in this inclosed, by some say near four thousand. Since this great mercy vouchsafed to us, I sent a party of horse and dragoons to Dundalk, which the enemy quitted, and we are possessed of; as also another castle they deserted between Trym and Drogheda, upon the Boynes.[6] I sent a party of horse and dragoons to a house within five miles of Trym, there being then in Trym some Scots companies which the Lord of Ards[7] brought to assist the Lord of Ormonde; but upon the news of Drogheda they ran away, leaving their great guns behind them, which we also have possessed. And now give me leave to say how it comes to pass that this work is wrought. It was set upon some of our hearts, that a great thing should be done, not by power, or might, but by the Spirit of God; and is it not so clear? That which caused your men to storm so courageously, it was the Spirit of God, who gave your men courage, and took it away again, and gave the enemy courage, and took it away again, and gave your men courage again, and therewith this happy success; and therefore it is good that God alone have all the glory.

It is remarkable, that these people at the first set up the Mass in some places of the town that had been monasteries; but afterwards grew so insolent, that the last Lord's day before the Storm,[8] the Protestants were thrust out of the great church, called St. Peter's, and they had public Mass there; and in this very place near one thousand of them were put to the sword, flying thither for safety: I believe all their friars were knocked on the head promiscuously, but two, the one of which was Father Peter Taaff (Brother to the Lord Taaff)[9] whom the Soldiers took the next day, and made an end of; the other was taken in the round tower, under the repute of lieutenant, and when he understood the officers in that tower had no quarter, he confessed he was a friar, but that did not save him. A great deal of loss in this business, fell upon Col. Hewson, Col. Cassel, and Colonel Ewers' regiments; Colonel Ewers having two field-officers in his regiment shot, Colonel Cassel and a captain of his

---

5. In the Cromwellian period in Ireland, not only men captured in battle but also women and children were sent into indentured servitude to English colonies in the Caribbean.
6. The Boyne River.
7. Hugh Montgomery (c. 1623–1663), 3rd Viscount of Ards.
8. I.e., Cromwell's attack on the town.
9. Theobald, 2nd Viscount Taaff (d. 1677). An uncle of Lord Taaff, Lucas was forced to surrender New Ross to Cromwell in October 1649.

regiment slain, Colonel Hewson's captain-lieutenant slain; I do not think we lost one hundred men upon the place, though many be wounded. I most humbly pray, the Parliament will be pleased this army may be maintained, and that a consideration may be had of them, and of the carrying on of the affairs here, as may give a speedy issue to this work, to which there seems to be a marvelous fair opportunity offered by God. And although it may seem very chargeable to the State of England to maintain so great a force, yet surely to stretch a little for the present, in following God's Providence, in hope the charge will not be long, I trust it will not be thought by any (that have no irreconcilable or malicious principles) unfit for me to move for a constant supply, which in humane probability, as to outward means, is most likely to hasten and perfect this work; and indeed, if God please to finish it here, as he hath done in England, the war is like to pay itself. We keep the field much, our tents sheltering us from the wet and cold, but yet the country sickness overtakes many, and therefore we desire recruits, and some fresh regiments of foot may be sent us; for it is easily conceived by what the garrisons already drink up, what our field army will come to, if God shall give more garrisons into our hands. Craving pardon for this great trouble, I rest,

Your most humble Servant,

Dublin, Sept. 17. 1649   O. CROMWELL

━━━━ ═◆═ ━━━━

John O'Dwyer of the Glenn
c. 1651

John O'Dwyer of the Glenn (*Seán O'Duibhir an Ghleanna*) is one of the most beautiful popular Irish-language songs commemorating the war against the Cromwellian conquest of Ireland and its aftermath. According to James Hardiman, who collected this song in his *Irish Minstrelsy, or Bardic Remains of Ireland* (1831), John O'Dwyer was "a distinguished officer who commanded in the Counties of Waterford and Tipperary in 1651." The poem is listed under the heading "Jacobite Relics," which places it in a long tradition of support for the Stuart kings, which began with the celebration of the accession of James I in elite bardic poetry and continued into the eighteenth century with support for Bonnie Prince Charlie in popular ballads.

The imagery of the natural world in *John O'Dwyer of the Glenn* symbolizes the state of Ireland. The lyric begins with a pastoral idyll, as the speaker describes awakening in the morning to the sound of birds singing. The intrusion of a fox signals the advent of war, and a sad old woman who stands by the side of the road reckoning her geese evokes Ireland weeping for those she has lost. Some of the geese (*geidh*), here referred to as "that prowler's spoil," died in battle; others, like the "wild geese" (*geidh fiádháin*) who left Ireland after the defeat of the Gaelic chiefs in 1603, fled to the Continent. John O'Dwyer and his men were said by Hardiman to have embarked for Spain.

The translation here is that of Thomas Furlong as printed in Hardiman's *Irish Minstrelsy.* The song originated in County Tipperary in the mid-seventeenth century, and there are more verses in Irish. It is still sung in both English and Irish. The best edition of the Irish text is that edited by Padraig de Brún and Breandán O Buachalla in *Nua-Dhuanaire* (1971), which also contains poems by such mid-seventeenth-century Irish poets as Piaras Feiritéar and Dáibhí O Bruadair.

John O'Dwyer of the Glenn

Blithe the bright dawn found me,
Rest with strength had crown'd me,

Sweet the birds sung round me,
    Sport was all their toil.
5   The horn its clang was keeping,
Forth the fox was creeping,
Round each dame stood weeping,
    O'er that prowler's spoil.
Hark, the foe is calling,
10   Fast the woods are falling,
Scenes and sights appalling
    Mark the wasted soil.[1]

War and confiscation
Curse the fallen nation;
15   Gloom and desolation
    Shade the lost land o'er.
Chill the winds are blowing,
Death aloft is going;
Peace or hope seems growing
20   For our race no more.
Hark the foe is calling,
Fast the woods are falling,
Scenes and sights appalling
    Throng our blood-stained shore.

25   Where's my goat to cheer me,[2]
Now it plays not near me;
Friends no more can hear me;
    Strangers round me stand.
Nobles once high-hearted,
30   From their homes have parted,
Scatter'd, scar'd and started
    By a base-born band.
Hark the foe is calling,
Fast the woods are falling;
35   Scenes and sights appalling
    Thicken round the land.

Oh! that death had found me
And in darkness bound me,
Ere each object round me
40   Grew so sweet, so dear.
Spots that once were cheering,
Girls beloved endearing,
Friends from whom I'm steering,
    Take this parting tear.
45   Hark, the foe is calling,
Fast the woods are falling;
Scenes and sights appalling
    Plague and haunt me here.

---

1. The falling woods are the old Irish families who have been thrown off their land, and the "wasted soil" is the country after war.

2. The goat stands for both Charles II in exile and the defeated Irish lords.

✦ ≖✦≖ ✦

The Story of Alexander Agnew

Alexander Agnew is seen by contemporary Scots writers such as Booker Prize–winning novelist James Kelman as something of a hero. An unrepentant freethinker, Agnew was the first man in Scots history publicly to deny the existence of God. Offending the Presbyterian laws of Scotland, Agnew was found guilty of blasphemy and hanged. The following journalistic account of his trial gives the sense of a man being driven to greater and greater levels of vitriolic sarcasm by the nitpicking detail of his Presbyterian examiners. Since the story begins with his refusing to go to church, saying, "Hang God, God was hanged long since," the ninth count against him—that he refused to say grace—seems oddly anticlimactic.

The story was printed in *Mercurius Politicus,* a pamphlet founded by Marchamont Needham in June 1650. In 1649, Parliament had had Needham arrested for the royalist *Mercurius Pragmaticus,* a pamphlet he had been editing since 1647, and ordered John Milton to examine Needham on his political views. Less than a year after his brush with the law, Needham reemerged as the editor of *Mercurius Politicus, the Common-Wealth of England Stated . . . With a Discourse of Excellencie of a Free-State, above a Kingly-Government.* Needham's editorial style has been described as slangy. For example, in Needham's first sentence in *Mercurius Politicus* 15, he refers to the Scots Prebyterians as "our gown'd Granado's." Needham clearly had it in for the Scots, whose independence he and his pamphlet's republican English audience saw as one of the greatest obstacles to the Commonwealth.

The Story of Alexander Agnew; or Jock of Broad Scotland[1]

Alexander Agnew, commonly called Jock of broad Scotland, being accused; forasmuch as by the Divine Law of Almighty God, and Acts of Parliament of this nation, the committers of the horrid crime of blasphemy are punished by death; nevertheless, in plain contempt of the said Laws and Acts of Parliament, the said Alexander Agnew uttered heinous and grievous blasphemies against the Omnipotent and Almighty God; and second and third persons of the Trinity, as the same is set down in diverse articles in manner following; to wit,

First, the said Alexander being desired to go to church answered, "Hang God, God was hanged long since." What had he to do with God? He had nothing to do with God. Secondly, he answered, he was nothing in God's common,[2] God gave him nothing, and he was no more obliged to God than to the Devil, and God was very greedy. Thirdly, when he was desired to seek anything in God's name, he said he would never seek anything for God's sake, and that it was neither God nor the Devil that gave the fruits of the ground, the wives of the country gave him his meat. Fourthly, being asked, wherein he believed, answered, he believed in white meal, water, and salt. Fifthly, being asked how many persons were in the Godhead, answered there was only one person in the Godhead who made all, but for Christ he was not God, because he was made, and came into the world after it was made, and died as other men, being nothing but a mere man.

Sixthly, he declared that he knew not whether God or the Devil had the greater power, but he thought the Devil had the greatest, "And when I die," said he, "let God and the Devil strive for my soul, and let him that is strongest take it." Seventhly, he denied there was a holy Ghost, or knew there was a Spirit, and denied he was a sinner or needed mercy. Eighthly, he denied he was a sinner and that he scorned to

---

1. From *Mercurius Politicus,* 3 July 1656.   2. Community.

seek God's mercy. Ninthly, he ordinarily mocked all exercise of God's worship, and invocation on his name, in derision saying, "Pray you to your God and I will pray to mine when I think time." And when he was desired by some to give thanks for his meat, he said, "Take a sackful of prayers to the mill and shell them, and grind them and take your breakfast of them." To others he said, "I will give you a twopence, and pray until a bowl of meal and one stone[3] of butter fall down from heaven through the house rigging to you." To others he said when bread and cheese was given him, and was laid on the ground by him, he said, "If I leave this, I will long cry to God before he give it me again." To others he said, "Take a bannock[4] and break it in two, and lay down the one half thereof, and ye will long pray to God before he put the other half to it again."

Tenthly, being posed whether or not he knew God or Christ, he answered, he had never had any profession, nor never would; he never had any religion, nor never would: also that there was no God nor Christ, and that he never received anything from God but from nature, which he said ever reigned, and ever would, and that to speak of God and their persons was an idle thing, and that he would never name such names, for he had shaken his cap of these things long since, and he denied that a man has a soul, or that there is a heaven or a hell, or that the Scriptures are the word of God. Concerning Christ he said, that he heard of such a man, but for the second person of the Trinity, he had been the second person of the Trinity, if the ministers had not put him in prison, and that he was no more obliged to God nor the Devil. And these aforesaid blasphemies are not rarely or seldom uttered by him, but frequently and ordinarily in several places where he resorted, to the entangling, deluding, and seducing of the common people: through the committing of which blasphemies he hath contravened the tenor of the said Laws and Acts of Parliament and incurred the pain of death mentioned therein, which ought to be inflicted upon him with all rigor, in manner specified in the indictment.

Which indictment being put to the knowledge of an assize,[5] the said Alexander Agnew called Jock of broad Scotland, was by the said assize, all in one voice, by the mouth of William Carlile, late baily[6] of Dumfrize their chancellor[7] found guilty of the crime of blasphemy mentioned in his indictment. For which the commissioners ordained him upon Wednesday, 21 May 1656, betwixt 2 and 4 hours in the afternoon to be taken to the ordinary place of execution for the burgh of Dumfrize, and there to be hanged on a gibbet while he be dead, and all his movable goods to be escheat.[8]

Edward Hyde, Earl of Clarendon
1609–1674

Bound up in the politics of his day, Edward Hyde was also often at odds with the powerful. From a long line of lawyers, he was neither noble nor wealthy by birth but rose to power through the law. Hyde played the observer in his roles as scholar, legislator, and diplomat. At law school at the Middle Temple in 1627 he complained that the whole country was a "sea of wine, and women, and quarrels, and gaming." A member of a humanist circle surrounding Sir Lucius Cary, Secretary

---

3. Fourteen pounds.
4. In Scotland and the North of England, a large round loaf of bread.
5. In Scotland, a trial by jury.

6. In Scotland, the chief magistrate of a county who functions as a sheriff.
7. In Scotland, the foreman of a jury.
8. Forfeited to the state.

of State under Charles I, Clarendon found them too naive about the realities of power. Entering Parliament in 1640, Hyde initially supported Parliament's curbs on royal absolutism, such as the impeachment of the King's man in Ireland, the Earl of Strafford. Later, however, fearing that parliamentary radicalism was a threat to the English constitution, Clarendon sided with the King. Serving Charles I closely throughout the 1640s by urging compromise with Parliament rather than war, Clarendon was no more comfortable among the King's followers than among the Parliamentarians. After the execution of Charles I, Clarendon was hired by Charles II in exile only when all other policies had been tried and failed. After the Restoration he held the position of Lord Chancellor until he was removed from power by Charles II's rakish courtiers, who resented his political ethos of moderation and tradition. Exiled in disgrace, he wrote the final version of *The History of the Rebellion and Civil Wars in England*, published a quarter century after his death (1702–1704).

Ironic detachment in tension with partisanship characterizes the history as it does his life. Strangely enough, neither his autobiography nor his history contains an account of how he abandoned the Parliamentarians for Charles I. Yet his scathing criticism of those who crossed the royalists—Presbyterians, Scots, Irish, Independents—reveals a private audience of like-minded royalists among family and friends. At times, Clarendon's irony escalates to sarcasm, as in his comments on the Scottish nobleman Argyle in the following account of the death of the great Scots military hero Montrose. Montrose's support of Charles I had thwarted Argyle's rise to power in Scotland. When Montrose returned to Scotland in 1649 as Charles II's Lieutenant General, Argyle succeeded in having him arrested on charges of heresy. A vacillating Charles II did not intervene, and Montrose was executed with theatrical brutality. As Martine Brownley has commented, there are "no unalloyed heroes or villains" in Clarendon's history, and so Montrose is portrayed in understated terms, and the narrative does not shrink from revealing Charles II's betrayal of his old ally. Clarendon's style eschews high rhetoric and opts for a middle style in a syntax uniting periods in a loose linear fashion. The poised detachment and sober gravity of his style produce the kind of authority that caused the German historian Ranke to say of Clarendon's *History of the Rebellion:* "the view of the event in England itself and in the educated world generally . . . has been determined by the book."

from True Historical Narrative of the Rebellion
[THE DEATH OF MONTROSE]

Permission was then given to him[1] to speak; and without the least trouble in his countenance, or disorder, upon all the indignities he had suffered, he told them, since the King had owned them so far as to treat with them, he had appeared before them with reverence, and bareheaded, which otherwise he would not have done: that he had done nothing of which he was ashamed, or had cause to repent; that the first Covenant he had taken,[2] and complied with it, and with them who took it, as long as the ends for which it was ordained were observed; but when he discovered, which was now evident to all the world, that private and particular men designed to satisfy their own ambition and interest, instead of considering the public benefit, and that under the pretence of reforming some errors in religion they resolved to abridge and take away the King's just power and lawful authority, he had withdrawn himself from that engagement: that for the League and Covenant,[3] he had never taken it, and therefore could not break it; and it was now too apparent to the whole Christian world what monstrous mischiefs it had produced: that when, under color of it, an army from Scotland had invaded England in assistance of the rebellion that was then against their lawful King, he had, by his

1. Montrose.
2. Montrose had sworn to the National Covenant of 1638, a pact drawn up by the Scots Presbyterians to drive out Anglicanism and the innovations of Archbishop Laud, particularly the English Book of Common Prayer.

3. The Solemn League and Covenant (1643) was an Anglo-Scottish alliance to establish a state Presbyterian Church in Scotland and Ireland and to pledge military aid against the King, both funding for the Scots Presbyterian forces in Ulster and the entrance of these forces into England.

majesty's command, received a commission from him to raise forces in Scotland, that he might thereby divert them from the other odious prosecution: that he had executed that commission with the obedience and duty that he owed to the King, and in all the circumstances of it had proceeded like a gentleman, and had never suffered any blood to be shed but in the heat of the battle; and that he saw many persons there whose lives he had saved: when the King commanded him, he laid down his arms, and withdrew out of the kingdom, which they could not have compelled him to have done. He said he was now again entered into the kingdom by his majesty's command and with his authority; and what success soever it might have pleased God to have given him, he would always have obeyed any command he should have received from him. He advised them to consider well of the consequence before they proceeded against him, and that all his actions might be examined and judged by the laws of the land, or those of nations.

As soon as he had ended his discourse he was ordered to withdraw, and after a short space was again brought in, and told by the Chancellor that he was on the morrow, being the one and twentieth of May 1650, to be carried to Edinborough cross, and there to be hanged upon a gallows thirty foot high, for the space of three hours, and then to be taken down, and his head to be cut off upon a scaffold, and hanged on Edinborough tollbooth, and his legs and arms to be hanged up in other public towns of the kingdom, and his body to be buried at the place where he was to be executed, except the Kirk should take off his excommunication, and then his body might be buried in the common place of burial. He desired that he might say somewhat to them, but was not suffered, and so was carried back to the prison.

That he might not enjoy any ease or quiet during the short remainder of his life, their ministers came presently to insult over him with all the reproaches imaginable, pronounced his damnation, and assured him that the judgment he was the next day to undergo was but an easy prologue to that which he was to undergo afterward. And after many such barbarities, they offered to intercede for him to the Kirk upon his repentance, and to pray with him; but he too well understood the form of their common prayers in those cases to be only the most virulent and insolent imprecations against the persons of those they prayed against ("Lord, vouchsafe yet to touch the obdurate heart of this proud incorrigible sinner, this wicked, perjured, traitorous, and profane person, who refuses to hearken to the voice of thy Kirk," and the like charitable expressions), and therefore he desired them to spare their pains, and to leave him to his own devotions. He told them that they were a miserable, deluded, and deluding people; and would shortly bring that poor nation under the most insupportable servitude ever people had submitted to. He told them he was prouder to have his head set upon the place it was appointed to be, than he could have been to have had his picture hung in the King's bedchamber: that he was so far from being troubled that his four limbs were to be hanged in four cities of the kingdom, that he heartily wished that he had flesh enough to be sent to every city in Christendom, as a testimony of the cause for which he suffered.

The next day they executed every part and circumstance of that barbarous sentence with all the inhumanity imaginable; and he bore it with all the courage and magnanimity, and the greatest piety, that a good Christian could manifest. He magnified the virtue, courage, and religion of the last King, exceedingly commended the justice and goodness and understanding of the present King, and prayed that they might not betray him as they had done his father. When he had ended all he meant to say, and was expecting to expire, they had yet one scene more to act of their tyranny. The hangman brought the book that had been published of his truly heroic actions whilst he had commanded in that kingdom, which book was tied in a small cord that was put about his neck. The marquis smiled at this new instance of their malice, and thanked them for it; and said he was pleased that it should be there, and was prouder of wearing it than ever he had been of the Garter;[4] and so renewing some devout ejaculations, he patiently endured the last act of the executioner.

Soon after, the officers who had been taken with him, Sir William Hurry, Sir Francis Hay, and many others of as good families as any in the kingdom, were executed, to the number of thirty or forty, in several quarters of the kingdom; many of them being suffered to be beheaded. There was one whom they thought fit to save, one Colonel Whitford; who, when he was brought to die, said, he knew the reason why he was put to death, which was only because he had killed Dorislaus at the Hague, who was one of those who had murdered the last King. One of the magistrates, who were present to see the execution, caused it to be suspended, till he presently informed the council what the man had said; and they thought fit to avoid the reproach, and so preserved the gentleman, who was not before known to have had a hand in that action.

Thus died the gallant Marquis of Montrose, after he had given as great a testimony of loyalty and courage as a subject can do, and performed as wonderful actions in several battles, upon as great inequality of numbers and as great disadvantages in respect of arms and other preparations for war, as hath been performed in this age. He was a gentleman of a very ancient extraction, many of whose ancestors had exercised the highest charges under the King in that kingdom, and had been allied to the Crown itself. He was of very good parts, which were improved by a good education: he had always a great emulation, or rather a great contempt, of the Marquis of Argyle (as he was too apt to contemn those he did not love), who wanted nothing but honesty and courage to be a very extraordinary man, having all other good talents in a great degree. He was in his nature fearless of danger, and never declined any enterprise for the difficulty of going through with it, but exceedingly affected those which seemed desperate to other men and did believe somewhat to be in him[self] which other men were not acquainted with, which made him live more easily towards those who were, or were willing to be, inferior to him, and towards whom he exercised wonderful civility and generosity, than with his superiors or equals. He was naturally jealous, and suspected those who did not concur with him in the way not to mean so well as he. He was not without vanity, but his virtues were much superior, and he well deserved to have his memory preserved and celebrated amongst the most illustrious persons of the age in which he lived.

The King received an account and information of all these particulars before he embarked from Holland, without any other apology for the affront and indignity to himself than that they assured him that the proceeding against the late Marquis of Montrose had been for his service. They who were most displeased with Argyle and his faction were not sorry for this inhuman and monstrous prosecution; which at the same time must render him the more odious, and had rid them of an enemy that they thought would have been more dangerous to them; and they persuaded the King, who was enough afflicted with the news and all the circumstances of it, that he might sooner take revenge upon that people by a temporary complying with them and going to them, than by staying away and absenting himself, which would invest them in an absolute dominion in that kingdom, and give them power to corrupt or destroy all those who yet remained faithful to him, and were ready to spend their lives in his service: and so he pursued his former resolution and embarked for Scotland.

[END OF PERSPECTIVES: THE CIVIL WAR, OR THE WARS OF THREE KINGDOMS]

---

4. The Order of the Garter is the oldest and most important order of knighthood in England, instituted by Edward III (c. 1346).

John Milton

1608–1674

While writing *Paradise Lost*, Milton would rise early to begin composing poetry; when his secretary arrived late, the old blind man would complain, "I want to be milked." Prodigious in his memory and ingenuity, austere in his frugality and discipline, Milton devoted his life to learning, politics, and art. He put his eloquence at the service of the Puritan Revolution, which brought on the beheading of a king and the institution of a republican commonwealth. Milton entered controversies on divorce and freedom of the press. He showed courage in defending the Puritan republic when he could have lost his life for doing so. Radical, scholar, sage—Milton is above all the great epic poet of England.

Milton's life was marked by a passionate devotion to his religious, political, and artistic ideals, a devotion that ran in his family. Milton's father was said to have been disinherited for his Protestantism by his own father, who was Roman Catholic. When the Civil War broke out, Milton sided with Cromwell while his brother fought for the King. The oldest of three children in a prosperous middle-class family, young John read Virgil, Ovid, and Livy; he especially loved "our sage and serious Spenser," whom he called "a better teacher than Aquinas." Milton later wrote that from the age of twelve he "hardly ever gave up reading for bed till midnight." After his first year at Christ's College, Cambridge, the poet was expelled. While in exile, Milton excoriated academia: "How wretchedly suited that place is to the worshippers of Phoebus! It is disgusting to be constantly subjected to the threats of a rough tutor and to other indignities my spirit cannot endure." Returning to Cambridge, he took his B.A. in 1629 and his M.A. in 1632. On vacations during these years he wrote two of his most musical lyrics, the erotic *L'Allegro* and the Platonic *Il Penseroso*. After leaving university, Milton lived with his parents in Berkshire, where he wrote *Lycidas*, a haunting elegy for the early death of his Cambridge friend Edward King, and *Comus*, a masque for the prominent noble Egerton family at Ludlow Castle.

After his mother's death in 1638, Milton traveled to Europe. He stayed longest in Italy, where his poems were greatly admired by the Florentine literati, who welcomed him into their academies. He later reflected that it was in Italy that he first sensed his vocation as an epic poet, hoping to "perhaps leave something so written, as they should not willingly let it die." Visiting Rome, Naples, and Venice, Milton collected Monteverdi's music, which he would later sing and play. He also met the famed astronomer Galileo, the censorship of whose works Milton would later protest. Concerned about political turmoil in England, he returned home at the outbreak of the Civil War.

From 1640 to 1660, Milton devoted himself to "the cause of real and substantial liberty," by which he meant religious, domestic, and civil liberties. Defending religious liberty, he decried Anglican hierarchy and ritualism—"the new vomited paganism of sensual idolatry"—in a series of tracts, including *Of Reformation* (1641) and *The Reason of Church Government* (1642).

That same year, Milton married seventeen-year-old Mary Powell, who came from a royalist Oxfordshire family. After only a month, she left Milton alone to his "philosophical" life for a more sociable one at home. Troubled by the unhappiness of his marriage, Milton wrote four treatises on divorce, for which he was publicly condemned. He argued that incompatibility should be grounds for divorce, that both husband and wife should be allowed to remarry, and that to maintain otherwise was contrary to reason and scripture. According to his nephew, whom Milton tutored during this time, he was interested in marrying another woman but by 1645 was reunited with Mary. They had a daughter soon afterward. They were joined for several years by Mary's family, who had lost their estate in the Civil War.

Along with "the true conception of marriage," Milton's concept of domestic liberty included "the sound education of children, and freedom of thought and speech." In *Of Education* (1644), opposing strictly vocational instruction, Milton called for the study of languages, rhetoric, poetry, philosophy, and science, the goal of which was "to perform justly, skillfully and magnanimously all of the offices both private and public of peace and war." In *Areopagitica* (1644), Milton fought against censorship before publication but counseled control of printed texts posing political or religious danger. In the 1640s, Milton steered a course midway between the religious conformity demanded by the once dissenting Presbyterians and the complete separation of church and state advocated by such radicals as Roger Williams, who ultimately went to America in search of greater toleration.

After Oliver Cromwell defeated the Royalists and the King was tried and executed by order of the "Rump" parliament purged of dissenters, Milton wrote *The Tenure of Kings and Magistrates* (1649) to argue that subjects could justly overthrow a tyrant. This tract won him the job of Latin Secretary to the Council of State, handling all correspondence to foreign governments. After the beheading of Charles I in 1649, *Eikon Basilike*, "the Royal Image" appeared, pieced together from the King's papers by his chaplain John Gauden. To counteract sympathy for the King's cause that this work might elicit, Milton wrote a chapter-by-chapter refutation of it entitled *Eikonoklastes, or Image-Breaker* (1649). Milton also defended Cromwell's government in three Latin works that were in some measure self-defenses: *First* and *Second Defense of the English People* (1651, 1654) and *Defense of Himself* (1656).

His eyes weakened by the strain of so much writing, Milton went blind. His wife Mary died, leaving three daughters and one son. The boy died soon after, in May 1652. That same month, Milton wrote a sonnet exhorting the Lord General Cromwell to "Help us to save free conscience from the paw of hireling wolves," a reference to ministers who wanted to exclude dissenters from a unified established church. Sounding the cry for liberty again in *Avenge, O Lord these Slaughtered Saints* (1655), Milton lamented the massacre of Italian Protestants. One of Milton's most beautiful and best-known sonnets, *Me thought I saw my late espoused saint*, is said to be about his second wife, Katherine Woodcock, who, after just two years of marriage, died following the birth of her child in 1558.

Cromwell died the same year, and his son Richard's succession to power began a period of political confusion. Milton continued to write political tracts, now even more radical in arguing for universal education and freedom from allegiance to *any* established church and against the abuse of church positions for money. In *De Doctrina Christiana* (written 1655–1660, published 1823), Milton set forth his individualistic theology; he was convinced that no one should be required to attend church and that everyone should interpret scripture in his own way. Committed to the cause of the republic even after the Restoration of Charles II, Milton published *The Ready and Easy Way to Establish a Free Commonwealth* in 1660. Shortly after its appearance, Milton went into hiding. The House of Commons ordered the burning of *Eikonoklastes* and had Milton arrested. He was held in prison for several months. For a time threatened with heavy fines and even death by hanging, Milton was finally released through the aid of his friend Andrew Marvell.

In the aftermath of the Restoration, Milton lived in obscurity and desolation. On the anniversary of Charles I's execution, Cromwell's body was dug up and hanged. More than a few of Milton's friends were either executed or forced into exile. The republic to which he had devoted his life's work had been defeated. Amid this experience of defeat, he worked on *Paradise Lost*, with its themes of fall, damnation, war in heaven, and future redemption for an erring humanity.

While writing his epic, he was much helped by the companionship and housekeeping of his young and amiable third wife Elizabeth Minshull, whom he married in 1663. Young pupils, secretaries, and his daughters read to him in many languages (some of which they didn't understand). The Miltons lived frugally on the money that he had saved from his salary as Latin Secretary (1649–1659). Milton had begun writing *Paradise Lost* by 1658–1659, but he only completed the first edition for publication in 1667. First conceiving of this work as a drama, he had written a soliloquy for the rebellious Lucifer in 1642, which later appeared near the opening of the epic's fourth book. Milton explained that he had put off writing *Paradise Lost* because it was "a work to be raised . . . by devout prayer to that eternal Spirit who can enrich with all utterance and knowledge."

In the last ten years of his life, Milton also wrote *Paradise Regained* (1671), a short epic about the temptation of Christ, based on the model of the Book of Job. Published in the same year was *Samson Agonistes*, a verse tragedy about the Biblical hero, who, betrayed by his lover Delilah, brought down destruction on himself as well as his enemies. In 1673 he published an expanded edition of his *Poems* (1645), to which he added his translations of the Psalms. Finally, in 1674, all twelve books of *Paradise Lost* as we know it were published. That same year, Milton died in a fit of gout and was buried in Saint Giles Cripplegate alongside his father.

Milton combined the traditional erudition of a Renaissance poet with the committed politics of a Puritan radical, both of which contributed to his crowning achievement, *Paradise Lost*. Milton draws on the Bible, Homer, Virgil, and Dante to create his own original sound and story. The vivid sensual imagery of *L'Allegro*, echoing Shakespeare and Spenser, suggests the pastoral idyll of Adam and Eve in Paradise. The intellectual rebelliousness of his prose works inflects the epic's dramatic embodiment of such problems as the origin of evil, sin, and death. Like *Samson Agonistes*, *Paradise Lost* reaches humanity's psychological depths: arrogance, despair, revenge, self-destruction, desire, and self-knowledge. Most of all, *Paradise Lost* dramatizes human wayfaring in the face of the Fall, not unlike Milton's own heroic perseverance in writing his epic after the loss of the world he had helped to create.

L'Allegro[1]

Hence loathèd Melancholy
   Of Cerberus,[2] and blackest midnight born,
In Stygian cave forlorn.
   'Mongst horrid shapes, and shreiks, and sights unholy,
5   Find out some uncouth° cell,   *unknown*
   Where brooding darkness spreads his jealous wings,
And the night-raven[3] sings;
   There under ebon shades, and low-brow'd rocks,
As ragged as thy Locks,
10   In dark Cimmerian[4] desert ever dwell.
But come thou goddess fair and free,
   In Heaven yclept° Euphrosyne,   *called*
And by men, heart-easing Mirth,
   Whom lovely Venus at a birth
15   With two sister Graces more
To ivy-crownèd Bacchus bore;[5]
   Or whether (as some sager sing)
The frolic wind that breathes the spring,
Zephyr with Aurora playing,
20   As he met her once a-Maying,[6]

---

1. The happy person. This and the companion poem *Il Penseroso* (the pensive one) were composed around 1631; they were first published in 1645.
2. For the underworld cave of the three-headed dog Cerberus, see Virgil, *Aeneid* 6.418. Milton makes Cerberus and Night the parents of Melancholy, which is the subject of *Il Penseroso*.
3. Ominous bird.

4. The Cimmerians lived at the extreme limit of the known world (see *Odyssey* 11.13–22).
5. The Graces: Euphrosyne (Mirth), Aglaia (Brightness), and Thalia (Bloom). Servius's commentary to the *Aeneid* makes Venus and Bacchus their parents.
6. Milton invented this parentage of the Graces by Aurora, the dawn, and Zephyr, the west wind.

There on beds of violets blue,
And fresh-blown roses washed in dew,
Filled her with thee a daughter fair,
So buxom,° blithe, and debonair.   *yielding*
25 Haste thee nymph, and bring with thee
Jest and youthful Jollity,
Quips and cranks,° and wanton wiles,   *jests*
Nods, and becks, and wreathèd smiles,
Such as hang on Hebe's[7] cheek,
30 And love to live in dimple sleek;
Sport that wrinkled Care derides,
And Laughter holding both his sides.
Come, and trip it as you go
On the light fantastic toe,
35 And in thy right hand lead with thee,
The mountain nymph, sweet Liberty;
And if I give thee honor due,
Mirth, admit me of thy crew
To live with her, and live with thee,
40 In unreprovèd pleasures free;
To hear the lark begin his flight,
And singing startle the dull night,
From his watch-tower in the skies,
Till the dappled dawn doth rise;
45 Then to come in spite of sorrow,
And at my window bid good morrow,
Through the sweetbriar, or the vine,
Or the twisted eglantine.°   *honey-suckle*
While the cock with lively din,
50 Scatters the rear of darkness thin,
And to the stack, or the barn door,
Stoutly struts his dames before,
Oft listening how the hounds and horn
Cheerly rouse the slumbring morn,
55 From the side of some hoar° hill,   *grey with mist*
Through the high wood echoing shrill.
Sometime walking not unseen
By hedge-row elms, on hillocks green,
Right against the eastern gate,
60 Where the great sun begins his state,°   *progress*
Robed in flames, and amber light,
The clouds in thousand liveries dight,°   *dressed*
While the plowman near at hand,
Whistles ore the furrowed land,
65 And the milkmaid singeth blithe,
And the mower whets his scythe,
And every shepherd tells his tale
Under the hawthorn in the dale.
Straight mine eye hath caught new pleasures

---

7. Goddess of youth and daughter of Zeus and Hera.

70	Whilst the landscape round it measures,	
	Russet lawns, and fallows° gray,	*plowed lands*
	Where the nibling flocks do stray,	
	Mountains on whose barren breast	
	The laboring clouds do often rest;	
75	Meadows trim with daisies pied,°	*variegated*
	Shallow brooks, and rivers wide.	
	Towers and battlements it sees	
	Bosomed high in tufted trees,	
	Where perhaps some beauty lies,	
80	The cynosure[8] of neighboring eyes.	
	Hard by, a cottage chimney smokes	
	From betwixt two agèd oaks,	
	Where Corydon and Thyrsis met,	
	Are at their savory dinner set	
85	Of herbs, and other country messes,	
	Which the neat-handed Phyllis dresses;	
	And then in haste her bower she leaves,	
	With Thestylis[9] to bind the sheaves;	
	Or if the earlier season lead	
90	To the tanned haycock° in the mead,	*heaps of hay*
	Sometimes with secure delight	
	The upland hamlets will invite,	
	When the merry bells ring round,	
	And the jocond rebecks° sound	*fiddles*
95	To many a youth, and many a maid,	
	Dancing in the checkered shade;	
	And young and old come forth to play	
	On a sunshine holiday,	
	Till the livelong daylight fail,	
100	Then to the spicy nut-brown ale,	
	With stories told of many a feat,	
	How fairy Mab[1] the junkets° eat,	*cream cheeses*
	She was pinched, and pulled she said,	
	And by the friar's lantern led	
105	Tells how the drudging goblin sweat,	
	To earn his cream-bowl duly set,	
	When in one night, ere glimpse of morn,	
	His shadowy flail hath threshed the corn	
	That ten day-laborers could not end;	
110	Then lies him down the lubber fiend.[2]	
	And stretched out all the chimney's length,	
	Basks at the fire his hairy strength;	
	And crop-full out of doors he flings,	
	Ere the first cock his matin rings.	
115	Thus done the tales, to bed they creep,	
	By whispering winds soon lulled asleep.	

8. The North Star, here meaning, the center of attention.
9. The shepherds' names are common in Renaissance pastoral.
1. Queen of the fairies, and the topic of Mercutio's

famous speech (*Romeo and Juliet* 1.4.54–95).
2. Slaving demon, like Robin Goodfellow called "lob of spirits" in *Midsummer Night's Dream* 2.1.16.

Towered cities please us then,
And the busy hum of men,
Where throngs of knights and barons bold,
120   In weeds° of peace high triumphs° hold,   *clothes/tournaments*
With store of ladies, whose bright eyes
Rain influence,[3] and judge the prize,
Of wit, or arms, while both contend
To win her grace, whom all commend.
125   There let Hymen[4] oft appear
In saffron robe, with taper clear,
And pomp, and feast, and revelry,
With mask, and antique pageantry;
Such sights as youthful poets dream
130   On summer eves by haunted stream.
Then to the well-trod stage anon,
If Jonson's learned sock[5] be on,
Or sweetest Shakespeare fancy's child,
Warble his native wood-notes wild,
135   And ever against eating cares
Lap me in soft Lydian airs,[6]
Married to immortal verse
Such as the meeting soul may pierce
In notes, with many a winding bout
140   Of linkèd sweetness long drawn out,
With wanton heed and giddy cunning,
The melting voice through mazes running,
Untwisting all the chains that tie
The hidden soul of harmony.
145   That Orpheus' self may heave his head
From golden slumber on a bed
Of heaped Elysian flowers, and hear
Such strains as would have won the ear
Of Pluto, to have quite set free
150   His half regained Eurydice.[7]
These delights, if thou canst give,
Mirth with thee, I mean to live.[8]

Il Penseroso[1]

Hence vain deluding joys,
    The brood of Folly without father bred,
How little you bestead,°   *help*
    Or fill the fixèd mind with all your toys;
5   Dwell in some idle brain,

3. In astrology, the process by which an ethereal fluid emanating from the stars ruled human fate.
4. Roman wedding god.
5. Low-heeled slipper of the comic actor in ancient Greece and Rome.
6. Plato considered the Lydian mode to be morally corrupting and loose; others found it a source of relaxed enjoyment.

7. When Orpheus attempted to rescue his wife Eurydice from Hades, he lost her by violating the command that he not look back to see if she were behind him.
8. The concluding lines recall the final couplet of Marlowe's lyric *The Passionate Shepherd to His Love:* "If these delights thy mind may move, / Then live with me, and be my love."
1. The pensive one.

And fancies fond with gaudy shapes possess,
As thick and numberless
    As the gay motes that people the sunbeams,
Or likest hovering dreams,
10   The fickle pensioners° of Morpheus'[2] train.   *guards*
But hail thou Goddess, sage and holy,
Hail divinest Melancholy,
Whose saintly visage is too bright
To hit° the sense of human sight,   *fit*
15   And therefore to our weaker view,
O'er laid with black staid Wisdom's hue;[3]
Black, but such as in esteem,
Prince Memnon's sister[4] might beseem,
Or that starred Ethiope Queen[5] that strove
20   To set her beauties praise above
The sea nymphs, and their powers offended.
Yet thou art higher far descended,
Thee bright-haired Vesta[6] long of yore,
To solitary Saturn bore;
25   His daughter she (in Saturn's reign
Such mixture was not held a stain)[7]
Oft in glimmering bowers, and glades
He met her, and in secret shades
Of woody Ida's inmost grove,
30   While yet there was no fear of Jove.
Come pensive nun, devout and pure,
Sober, steadfast, and demure,
All in a robe of darkest grain,
Flowing with majestic train,
35   And sable° stole of cypress lawn,°   *dark / fine linen*
Over thy decent shoulders drawn.
Come, but keep thy wonted state,
With even step, and musing gait,
And looks commercing with the skies,
40   Thy rapt soul sitting in thine eyes:
There held in holy passion still,
Forget thyself to marble,[8] till
With a sad leaden downward cast,
Thou fix them on the earth as fast.
45   And join with thee calm Peace, and Quiet,
Spare Fast, that oft with gods doth diet,
And hears the Muses in a ring,
Ay round about Jove's altar sing.
And add to these retired leisure;

2. God of dreams and son of Sleep.
3. Melancholy was governed by the black bile in the body
and manifested itself in a black face.
4. The Ethiopian Prince Memnon (*Odyssey* 11.521) had
a sister named Himera (Greek, "light of day").
5. Cassiopea was turned into a constellation because she
boasted that she was more beautiful than the Nereids.

6. Milton makes Vesta a mother; by tradition, she was a
virgin, daughter of Saturn, and goddess of the hearth.
7. The Golden Age was a time of plenty and sexual freedom.
8. Turning to stone through grief comes from the story of
Niobe.

50   That in trim gardens takes his pleasure;
      But first, and chiefest, with thee bring
      Him that yon soars on golden wing,
      Guiding the fiery-wheelèd throne,[9]
      The cherub Contemplation;[1]
55   And the mute Silence hist° along,   *a call*
      'Less Philomel[2] will deign a song,
      In her sweetest, saddest plight,
      Smoothing the rugged brow of night,
      While Cynthia[3] checks her dragon yoke,
60   Gently o'er th'accustomed oak;
      Sweet bird that shunn'st the noise of folly,
      Most musical, most melancholy!
      Thee chantress oft the woods among,
      I woo to hear thy evensong;
65   And missing thee, I walk unseen
      On the dry smooth-shaven green,
      To behold the wandring moon,
      Riding near her highest noon,
      Like one that had been led astray
70   Through the heaven's wide pathless way;
      And oft, as if her head she bowed,
      Stooping through a fleecy cloud.
      Oft on a plat° of rising ground,   *plot*
      I hear the far-off curfew sound,
75   Over some wide-watered shore,
      Swinging slow with sullen roar;
      Or if the air will not permit,
      Some still removèd place will fit,
      Where glowing embers through the room
80   Teach light to counterfeit a gloom,
      Far from all resort of mirth,
      Save the cricket on the hearth,
      Or the bellman's drowsy charm,[4]
      To bless the doors from nightly harm;
85   Or let my lamp at midnight hour,
      Be seen in some high lonely tower,
      Where I may oft out-watch the Bear,[5]
      With thrice great Hermes,[6] or unsphere[7]
      The spirit of Plato to unfold
90   What worlds, or what vast regions hold
      The immortal mind that hath forsook
      Her mansion in this fleshly nook;
      And of those demons that are found

9. See Ezekiel 1.4–6.
1. The angel Cherubim contemplate God.
2. The nightingale (Greek).
3. The moon goddess, another name for Hecate; for her dragons, see Ovid, *Metamorphoses* 7.218–19.
4. The night-watchman, or bellman, cries out the hours in a chant, or charm (from *carmen*, Latin for song).

5. The constellation of the Great Bear, which never sets, symbolizes perfection.
6. Hermes Trismegistus was believed to be the author of the Hermetica, texts of esoteric neoplatonism and magic.
7. To remove from the eternal sphere and make reappear on earth.

In fire, air, flood, or under ground,
95 Whose power hath a true consent
With planet, or with element.
Sometime let gorgeous Tragedy
In scepter'd pall° come sweeping by,   *robe*
Presenting Thebes, or Pelops line,
100 Or the tale of Troy divine.[8]
Or what (though rare) of later age
Ennobled hath the buskined stage.[9]
But, O sad virgin, that thy power
Might raise Musaeus[1] from his bower,
105 Or bid the soul of Orpheus[2] sing
Such notes as warbled to the string,
Drew iron tears down Pluto's cheek,
And made Hell grant what Love did seek.
Or call up him[3] that left half told
110 The story of Cambuscan bold,
Of Camball, and of Algarsife,
And who had Canace to wife,
That owned the virtuous° ring and glass,   *magical*
And of the wondrous horse of brass,
115 On which the Tartar king did ride;
And if aught else, great bards beside,[4]
In sage and solemn tunes have sung,
Of tourneys and of trophies hung;
Of forests, and enchantments drear,
120 Where more is meant then meets the ear.
Thus, Night, oft see me in thy pale career,
Till civil-suited Morn appear,
Not tricked and frounced[5] as she was wont,
With the Attic boy[6] to hunt,
125 But kerchiefed in a comely cloud,
While rocking winds are piping loud,
Or ushered with a shower still,°   *quiet*
When the gust hath blown his fill,
Ending on the rustling leaves,
130 With minute drops from off the eaves.
And when the sun begins to fling
His flaring beams, me, Goddess, bring
To archèd walks of twilight groves,
And shadows brown that Sylvan[7] loves
135 Of pine, or monumental oak,
Where the rude ax with heavèd stroke.

---

8. Thebes was the birthplace of Oedipus, tragic hero of Sophocles' *Oedipus Rex*. Pelops's descendants Agamemnon and Orestes are the subject of Aeschylus' tragedy *Oresteia*. Troy was the city destroyed by the Trojan War, the tragic consequences of which are the subject of Euripides' *The Trojan Women*.
9. The high boots of tragic actors. Compare *L'Allegro* line 132.
1. Prophet and poet, who studied with the mythic bard

Orpheus.
2. See *L'Allegro* 145–50.
3. Chaucer; the "story" is the unfinished *Squire's Tale*.
4. Lines 116–20 refer to Spenser's allegorical *Faerie Queene*.
5. Richly attired and wearing ringlets.
6. Cephalus, beloved of Aurora, who met him while he was hunting. (See Ovid, *Metamorphoses* 7.700–13.)
7. Roman god of the forest.

Was never heard the nymphs to daunt,
Or fright them from their hallowed haunt.
There in close covert by some brook,
140 Where no prophaner eye may look,
Hide me from day's garish eye,
While the bee with honeyed thigh,
That at her flowery work doth sing,
And the waters murmuring
145 With such consort° as they keep,   *musical harmony*
Entice the dewy-feathered sleep;
And let some strange mysterious dream
Wave at his wings in airy stream
Of lively portraiture displayed,
150 Softly on my eye-lids laid.
And as I wake, sweet music breathe
Above, about, or underneath,
Sent by some spirit to mortals good,
Or th'unseen genius° of the wood.   *presiding local god*
155 But let my due feet never fail
To walk the studious cloisters° pale,   *enclosure*
And love the high embowèd° roof,   *arched*
With antic pillars massy proof,°   *impenetrability*
And storied[8] windows richly dight,°   *decorated*
160 Casting a dim religious light.
There let the pealing organ blow
To the full voiced choir below,
In service high, and anthems clear,
As may with sweetness, through mine ear,
165 Dissolve me into ecstasies,
And bring all heaven before mine eyes.
And may at last my weary age
Find out the peaceful hermitage,
The hairy gown and mossy cell,
170 Where I may sit and rightly spell°   *find out about*
Of every star that heaven doth shew,
And every herb that sips the dew,
Till old experience do attain
To something like prophetic strain.
175 These pleasures Melancholy give,
And I with thee will choose to live.[9]

Lycidas

In this Monody[1] the Author bewails a learned Friend,[2] unfortunately drowned in his passage from Chester on the Irish Seas, 1637. And by occasion foretells the ruin of our corrupted Clergy then in their height.

8. With stories from the Bible.
9. See *L'Allegro* 151–52.
1. A mournful song sung by one voice. *Lycidas* is a pastoral elegy, a lament for the dead through language evoking nature and the rural life of shepherds. The first *Idyll* of Theocritus and Virgil's fifth *Eclogue* are classical prece-

dents for *Lycidas*. Shelley's *Adonais* and Arnold's *Thyrsis* are later examples of this form.
2. Edward King, who attended Cambridge when Milton did, and drowned 10 August 1637. He had planned to enter the clergy and had written some Latin poems.

Yet once more, O ye laurels, and once more
Ye myrtles brown, with ivy[3] never sear,°   withered
I come to pluck your berries harsh and crude,°   unripe
And with forced fingers rude,
5   Shatter your leaves before the mellowing year.
Bitter constraint, and sad occasion dear,
Compels me to disturb your season due:
For Lycidas is dead, dead ere his prime,[4]
Young Lycidas, and hath not left his peer:
10 Who would not sing for Lycidas? he knew
Himself to sing, and build the lofty rhyme.
He must not float upon his watery bier
Unwept, and welter° to the parching wind,   writhe
Without the meed° of some melodious tear.°   recompense/elegy
15   Begin then, sisters of the sacred well,[5]
That from beneath the seat of Jove doth spring,
Begin, and somewhat loudly sweep the string.
Hence with denial vain, and coy excuse,
So may some gentle Muse
20 With lucky words favor my destined urn,
And as he passes turn,
And bid fair peace be to my sable° shroud.   black
For we were nursed upon the self-same hill,
Fed the same flock; by fountain, shade, and rill.
25   Together both, ere the high lawns appeared
Under the opening eyelids of the morn,
We drove a field, and both together heard
What time the grayfly[6] winds her sultry horn,
Battening° our flocks with the fresh dews of night,   fattening
30 Oft till the star that rose, at evening, bright,
Toward heaven's descent had sloped his westering wheel.
Meanwhile the rural ditties were not mute,
Tempered to th' oaten flute,
Rough satyrs danced, and fauns with cloven heel,
35 From the glad sound would not be absent long,
And old Damaetas[7] lov'd to hear our song.
      But O the heavy change, now thou art gone,
Now thou art gone, and never must return!
Thee shepherd, thee the woods, and desert caves,
40 With wild thyme and the gadding° vine o'ergrown,   wandering
And all their echoes mourn.
The willows, and the hazle copses green,
Shall now no more be seen,
Fanning their joyous leaves to thy soft lays.
45 As killing as the canker° to the rose,   cankerworm
Or taint-worm[8] to the weanling herds that graze,

---

3. Laurels . . . myrtles . . . ivy: the leaves used to crown respectively poets, lovers, and scholars.
4. King ("Lycidas") was 25 when he died.
5. Sisters: the nine muses; well: Aganippe, on Mount Helicon, where there was an altar to Jove.

6. Name used to designate various kinds of insect.
7. "Damaetas" is etymologically derived from the Greek verb meaning "to tame"; thus a tutor is meant.
8. An intestinal worm that can kill newly weaned calves.

Or frost to flowers, that their gay wardrop wear,
When first the white thorn blows;
Such, Lycidas, thy loss to shepherd's ear.
50   Where were ye nymphs when the remorseless deep
Closed o'er the head of your loved Lycidas?
For neither were ye playing on the steep
Where your old Bards, the famous Druids,° lie,   *pagan Celtic priests*
Nor on the shaggy top of Mona[9] high,
55   Nor yet where Deva spreads her wizard stream:
Ay me, I fondly dream!
Had ye been there—for what could that have done?
What could the Muse[1] herself that Orpheus bore,
The Muse her self for her inchanting son
60   Whom universal nature did lament,
When by the rout that made the hideous roar
His gory visage down the stream was sent,
Down the swift Hebrus to the Lesbian shore.[2]
     Alas! What boots° it with incessant care   *avails*
65   To tend the homely slighted shepherd's trade,
And strictly meditate the thankless Muse,
Were it not better done as others use,
To sport with Amaryllis in the shade,
Or with the tangles of Neaera's hair?[3]
70   Fame is the spur that the clear spirit doth raise
(That last infirmity of noble mind)
To scorn delights, and live laborious days;
But the fair guerdon° when we hope to find,   *reward*
And think to burst out into sudden blaze,
75   Comes the blind Fury[4] with th'abhorred shears,
And slits the thin spun life. "But not the praise,"
Phoebus replied, and touched my trembling ears;[5]
"Fame is no plant that grows on mortal soil,
Nor in the glistering foil[6]
80   Set off to the world, nor in broad rumor lies,
But lives and spreds aloft by those pure eyes,
And perfet witness of all-judging Jove;
As he pronounces lastly on each deed,
Of so much fame in heaven expect thy meed."
85   O Fountain Arethuse, and thou honored flood,
Smooth-sliding Mincius, crowned with vocal reeds,
That strain I heard was of a higher mood.[7]
But now my oat proceeds,

9. The island of Anglesey; Deva: the river Dee, viewed as magical and prophetic by the inhabitants.
1. Calliope, Orpheus' mother.
2. Ovid, *Metamorphoses,* 11.1–55, relates how Orpheus was torn to pieces by the Thracian women and how his severed head floated down the Hebrus and was carried across to the island of Lesbos.
3. Amaryllis symbolizes erotic poetry (Virgil, *Eclogues* 2.14–5; Neaera: see *Eclogues* 3.3).
4. Atropos, one of the Fates, who cut the thread of life

spun by her sisters.
5. Echoing Virgil, *Eclogues* 6.3–4: "the Cynthian plucked my ear and warned me."
6. A reflecting leaf of gold or silver placed under a precious stone.
7. The "higher mood" is the lofty tone of Phoebus' speech. The invocation to the river Arethuse (in Sicily) and the Mincius (Virgil's native river) marks a return to pastoral.

And listens to the herald of the sea
90 That came in Neptune's plea.[8]
He asked the waves, and asked the felon° winds,   *savage*
"What hard mishap hath doomed this gentle swain?"
And questioned every gust of rugged wings
That blows from off each beakèd promontory;
95 They knew not of his story,
And sage Hippotades[9] their answer brings,
That not a blast was from his dungeon strayed,
The air was calm, and on the level brine,
Sleek Panope[1] with all her sisters played.
100 It was that fatal and perfidious bark,
Built in th' eclipse,° and rigged with curses dark,   *period of evil omen*
That sunk so low that sacred head of thine.
      Next Camus,[2] reverend sire, went footing slow,
His mantle hairy, and his bonnet sedge,[3]
105 Inwrought with figures dim, and on the edge
Like to that sanguine flower inscribed with woe.[4]
"Ah! who hath reft (quoth he) my dearest pledge?"°   *child*
Last came, and last did go,
The Pilot of the Galilean lake,[5]
110 Two massy keys he bore of metals twain,
(The golden opes, the iron shuts amain°)   *vehemently*
He shook his mitered[6] locks, and stern bespake,
"How well could I have spared for thee, young swain,
Enow° of such as for their bellies' sake,   *enough*
115 Creep and intrude, and climb into the fold?[7]
Of other care they little reckoning make,
Than how to scramble at the shearer's feast,
And shove away the worthy bidden guest.
Blind mouths![8] that scarce themselves know how to hold
120 A sheep-hook, or have learned aught else the least
That to the faithfull herdman's art belongs!
What recks it them?[9] What need they? They are sped;°   *satisfied*
And when they list,° their lean and flashy° songs   *please/insipid*
Grate on their scrannel° pipes of wretched straw,   *feeble*
125 The hungry sheep look up, and are not fed,
But swoln with wind, and the rank mist they draw,
Rot inwardly, and foul contagion spread.
Besides what the grim woolf[1] with privy° paw   *secret, hidden*
Daily devours apace, and nothing said,
130 But that two-handed engine at the door,

8. The herald Triton came to defend Neptune from blame for King's death.
9. God of winds, son of Hippotes.
1. One of the 50 Nereids (sea nymphs), mentioned by Virgil, *Aeneid* 5.240.
2. The River Cam, representing Cambridge University.
3. "Hairy" refers to the fur of the academic gown; "sedge" is a rushlike plant growing near water.
4. The hyacinth; see Ovid, *Metamorphoses* 10.214–6: "the flower bore the marks AI AI, letters of lamentation."

5. St. Peter bearing the keys of heaven given to him by Christ (Matthew 16.19).
6. Wearing a bishop's headdress.
7. See John 10.1: "He that entereth not by the door into the sheepfold, but climbeth up some other way, the same is a thief and a robber."
8. Milton's charge against the greed of the clergy.
9. What business is it of theirs?
1. The Roman Catholic Church.

Stands ready to smite once, and smite no more."[2]
   Return Alpheus,[3] the dread voice is past,
That shrunk thy streams; return Sicilian muse,
And call the vales, and bid them hither cast
135   Their bells, and flowerets of a thousand hues.
Ye valleys low where the mild whispers use,°   *often go*
Of shades and wanton winds, and gushing brooks,
On whose fresh lap the swart star[4] sparely looks,
Throw hither all your quaint enameled eyes,
140   That on the green turf suck the honeyed showers,
And purple all the ground with vernal flowers.
Bring the rathe° primrose that forsaken dies.   *early*
The tufted crow-toe,° and pale jessamine,°   *hyacinth/jasmine*
The white pink, and the pansie freaked° with jet,   *adorned*
145   The glowing violet.
The musk-rose, and the well attired woodbine,
With cowslips wan° that hang the pensive head,   *pale*
And every flower that sad embroidery wears:
Bid amaranthus[5] all his beauty shed,
150   And daffadillies fill their cups with tears,
To strew the laureate hearse where Lycid lies.
For so to interpose a little ease,
Let our frail thoughts dally with false surmise.[6]
Ay me! whilst thee the shores, and sounding seas
155   Wash far away, where'er thy bones are hurled,
Whether beyond the stormy Hebrides[7]
Where thou perhaps under the whelming tide
Visit'st the bottom of the monstrous world;
Or whether thou to our moist° vows denied,   *tearful*
160   Sleep'st by the fable of Bellerus[8] old,
Where the great vision of the guarded mount
Looks toward Namancos and Bayona's hold;[9]
Look homeward angel° now, and melt with ruth.°   *Michael/pity*
And, O ye dolphins, waft the haples youth.[1]
165   Weep no more, woeful shepherds weep no more,
For Lycidas your sorrow is not dead,
Sunk though he be beneath the wat'ry floor,
So sinks the day-star° in the ocean bed,   *the sun*
And yet anon repairs his drooping head,
170   And tricks° his beams, and with new spangled ore,°   *arrays/gold*
Flames in the forehead of the morning sky:
So Lycidas sunk low, but mounted high,
Through the dear might of him[2] that walked the waves

---

2. Indicates that the corrupted clergy will be punished;
see 1 Samuel 26.8.
3. The Arcadian hunter, who pursued Arethusa, the
nymph he loved, under the sea to Sicily.
4. The Dog-star, Sirius. Its rising brings on the dog-days
of heat.
5. The eternal flower (see *Paradise Lost*, 3.353–7).
6. The surmise is false since King's body drowned and will
have no hearse.
7. Islands off the northwest coast of Scotland.

8. A giant of Bellerium, the Latin name for Land's End.
9. Namancos: an ancient name for a district in northwestern Spain; Bayona: a fortress town about 50 miles
south of Cape Finisterre. The two names represent the
threat of Spanish Catholicism, against which St. Michael
guards England.
1. The dolphin is a symbol of Christ; waft: convey by
water.
2. Christ, who walks on the sea in Matthew 14.25–6.

175 Where other groves, and other streams along,
    With nectar pure his oozy lock's he laves,[3]
    And hears the unexpressive nuptial[4] song,
    In the blest kingdoms meek of joy and love.
    There entertain him all the saints above,
180 In solemn troops, and sweet societies
    That sing, and singing in their glory move,
    And wipe the tears for ever from his eyes.[5]
    Now Lycidas the shepherds weep no more;
    Henceforth thou art the genius° of the shore,   *local deity*
    In thy large recompense, and shalt be good
185 To all that wander in that perilous flood.
        Thus sang the uncouth° swain to th' oaks and rills, *unknown*
    While the still morn went out with sandals gray,
    He touched the tender stops of various quills,[6]
    With eager thought warbling his Doric° lay: *pastoral*
190 And now the sun had stretched out all the hills,[7]
    And now was dropped into the western bay;
    At last he rose, and twitch'd his mantle blue:[8]
    Tomorrow to fresh woods, and pastures new.

                                                            1638

How Soon Hath Time

    How soon hath time the subtle thief of youth,
        Stol'n on his wing my three and twentieth year![1]
    My hasting days fly on with full career,°   *speed*
    But my late spring no bud or blossom shew'th.
5   Perhaps my semblance° might deceive the truth,   *appearance*
        That I to manhood am arrived so near,
    And inward ripeness doth much less appear,
    That some more timely-happy spirits[2] endu'th.°   *gives, endows*
    Yet be it less or more, or soon or slow,
10   It shall be still° in strictest measure even,°   *always/level with*
    To that same lot, however mean or high,
    Toward which Time leads me, and the will of Heaven;
        All is, if I have grace to use it so,
        As ever in my great task Master's° eye.   *God's*

On the New Forcers of Conscience Under the Long Parliament[1]

    Because you have thrown off your prelate Lord,[2]
        And with stiff vows renounced his liturgy[3]

---

3. The brooks in Eden run with nectar, *Paradise Lost* 4.240; oozy: slimy from contact with the sea.
4. Relating to the marriage of the Lamb, or Christ, to the Church (Revelation 19.7).
5. See Revelation 7.17: "God shall wipe away all tears from their eyes"; see also Revelation 21.4.
6. Stops are the finger-holes in the pipes; quills are the hollow reeds of the shepherd's pipe.
7. The setting sun had shone over the hills and lengthened their shadows.

8. Blue is the traditional symbol of hope.
1. Written when Milton was 23, this sonnet was published in 1645.
2. Those individuals of Milton's age who have already achieved success.
1. Written c. 1646, but printed in 1673.
2. Refers to the abolishment of episcopacy in England in September 1646.
3. The House of Commons forbade the use of the *Book of Common Prayer* in August 1645.

To seize the widowed whore Plurality[4]
From them whose sin ye envied, not abhored,

5   Dare ye for this adjure° the civil sword   *entreat*
To force our consciences that Christ set free,[5]
And ride us with a classic hierarchy[6]
Taught ye by meer A. S. and Rutherford?[7]
Men whose life, learning, faith and pure intent

10   Would have been held in high esteem with Paul
Must now be named and printed heretics
By shallow Edwards[8] and Scotch what d'ye call:
But we do hope to find out all your tricks,
Your plots and packing worse then those of Trent[9]

15   That so the Parliament
May with their wholsome and preventive shears
Clip your phylacteries,[1] though balk° your ears,[2]   *stop short of*
And succor our just fears
When they shall read this clearly in your charge

20   *New presbyter* is but *old priest* writ large.[3]

When I Consider How My Light Is Spent[1]

When I consider how my light is spent,
Ere half my days, in this dark world and wide,
And that one talent which is death to hide,[2]
Lodged with me useless, though my soul more bent

5   To serve therewith my Maker, and present
My true account, lest he returning chide,
Doth God exact day-labor, light denied,
I fondly° ask; but Patience to prevent   *foolishly*
That murmur, soon replies, "God doth not need

10   Either man's work or his own gifts,[3] who best
Bear his mild yoke,[4] they serve him best, his state
Is kingly. Thousands at his bidding speed
And post o'er land and ocean without rest:
They also serve who only stand and wait."

---

4. The practice of holding more than one living identified with episcopacy but subsequently supported by the Presbyterian system.
5. Milton complains of the Westminster Assembly's attempt to impose Presbyterianism by force.
6. Parliament resolved that the English congregations were to be grouped in Presbyteries or "Classes," which could impose rules after the Scottish pattern.
7. A. S.: Dr. Adam Stewart, Scottish Presbyterian controversialist; Rutherford: Samuel Rutherford, author of pamphlets in defense of Presbyterianism.
8. Thomas Edwards, author of *Antapologia*, advocating strict Presbyterianism, and *Gangraena* (1646), which included a denunciation of Milton's views on divorce.
9. Comparing the overwhelming Presbyterian predominance in the Assembly to the anti-protestant Roman Catholic Council of Trent (1545–1563).
1. Small leather boxes containing scriptural texts worn by Jews as a mark of obedience. Christ in Matthew 23.5 uses

the phrase "make broad their phylacteries" in the sense "vaunt their own righteousness."
2. William Prynne, who had attacked one of the Bishops in print, actually did have both of his ears cut off. Milton's manuscript of this poem contains the line: "Crop ye as close as marginal P—'s ears."
3. "Priest" is etymologically a contracted form of Latin "presbyter" (an elder). The Presbyterians now appeared as dictatorial as the bishops had been.
1. Probably written around 1652, as Milton's blindness became complete.
2. In the parable of the talents, Jesus tells of a servant who is given a talent (a large sum of money) to keep for his master. He buries the money; his master condemns him for not having invested it wisely. Matthew 25.14–30.
3. See Job 22.2.
4. See Matthew 11.30: "My yoke is easy."

Methought I Saw My Late Espoused Saint[1]

Methought I saw my late espousèd saint°   *soul in heaven*
  Brought to me like Alcestis[2] from the grave,
  Whom Jove's great son to her glad husband gave,
  Rescued from death by force though pale and faint.
5 Mine as whom washed from spot of child-bed taint,
  Purification in the old Law[3] did save,
  And such, as yet once more I trust to have
  Full sight of her in Heaven without restraint,
  Came vested all in white, pure as her mind:
10 Her face was veiled, yet to my fancied sight,
  Love, sweetness, goodness, in her person shined
So clear, as in no face with more delight,
  But O, as to embrace me she enclined,
  I waked, she fled, and day brought back my night.[4]

Areopagitica

The title *Areopagitica* refers to the Areopagus, the ancient Athenian Council of State. Milton wrote *Areopagitica* to criticize the Parliamentary Ordinance of June 14, 1643 "to prevent and suppress the licence of printing." Although *Areopagitica* was unlicensed, Milton made the bold move of affixing his name to the title page, which made no mention of the printer. Also on the title page are these lines from Euripides' *Suppliant Women* (436–441):

  There is true Liberty when free born men
  Having to advise the public may speak free,
  Which he who can and will, deserv'd high praise,
  Who neither can nor will, may hold his peace;
  What can be juster in a state than this?

from Areopagitica[1]

A Speech of Mr. John Milton
for the Liberty of Unlicensed Printing,
to the Parliament of England

* * * Good and evil we know in the field of this world grow up together almost inseparably; and the knowledge of good is so involved and interwoven with the knowledge of evil, and in so many cunning resemblances hardly to be discerned, that those confused seeds which were imposed on Psyche as an incessant labor to cull out and sort asunder, were not more intermixed.[2] It was from out the rind of one apple tasted, that

1. The date of composition is placed at 1658; the poem appears as the last sonnet in the 1673 edition.
2. In Euripides' *Alcestis* she gives her life for her husband Admetus, but Hercules ("Jove's great son") wrestles with death and brings her back from the grave.
3. According to Leviticus 12.4–8, after bearing a female child, a woman shall be unclean "two weeks, as in her separation: and she shall continue in the blood of her purifying threescore and six days" (i.e., during this period "she shall touch no hallowed thing, nor come into the sanctuary"). Some critics construe this line as evidence that the sonnet is about the death of Milton's second wife Katherine Woodcock, who died three months after child-

birth in 1658.
4. In Virgil, Aeneas sees the ghost of his wife Creusa amid the ruins of Troy; when he tries to embrace her, "she withdrew into thin air . . . most like a winged dream" (*Aeneid* 2.791–794).
1. The Areopagus was the seat of the Council of State, organized as a judicial tribunal by Solon in the sixth century B.C. The Athenian orator Isocrates argues for its renewal in his *Areopagiticus*.
2. Furious over her son Cupid's love for Psyche, Venus ordered Psyche to sort out a huge mass of seeds, but the ants, sympathizing with her plight, sorted them for her. See Apuleius, *Golden Ass* 4–6.

the knowledge of good and evil, as two twins cleaving together, leaped forth into the world. And perhaps this is that doom which Adam fell into of knowing good and evil, that is to say, of knowing good by evil.[3]

As therefore the state of man now is, what wisdom can there be to choose, what continence to forbear without the knowledge of evil? He that can apprehend and consider vice with all her baits and seeming pleasures, and yet abstain, and yet distinguish, and yet prefer that which is truly better, he is the true wayfaring[4] Christian. I cannot praise a fugitive and cloistered virtue, unexercised and unbreathed, that never sallies out and sees her adversary, but slinks out of the race where that immortal garland is to be run for, not without dust and heat. Assuredly we bring not innocence into the world, we bring impurity much rather: that which purifies us is trial, and trial is by what is contrary. That virtue therefore which is but a youngling in the contemplation of evil, and knows not the utmost that vice promises to her followers, and rejects it, is but a blank virtue, not a pure; her whiteness is but an excremental[5] whiteness; which was the reason why our sage and serious poet Spenser, whom I dare be known to think a better teacher than Scotus or Aquinas, describing true temperance under the person of Guyon, brings him in with his palmer through the cave of Mammon and the bower of earthly bliss, that he might see and know, and yet abstain.[6]

Since therefore, the knowledge and survey of vice is in this world so necessary to the constituting of human virtue, and the scanning of error to the confirmation of truth, how can we more safely and with less danger scout into the regions of sin and falsity than by reading all manner of tractates and hearing all manner of reason? And this is the benefit which may be had of books promiscuously read.

But of the harm that may result hence, three kinds are usually reckoned. First is feared the infection that may spread; but then all human learning and controversy in religious points must remove out of the world, yea the Bible itself; for that ofttimes relates blasphemy not nicely,[7] it describes the carnal sense of wicked men not unelegantly, it brings in holiest men passionately murmuring against providence through all the arguments of Epicurus;[8] in other great disputes it answers dubiously and darkly to the common reader; and ask a Talmudist what ails the modesty of his marginal Keri, that Moses and all the prophets cannot persuade him to pronounce the textual Chetiv.[9] For these causes we all know the Bible itself put by the papist into the first rank of prohibited books. The ancientest fathers must be next removed, as Clement of Alexandria, and that Eusebian book of Evangelic preparation transmitting our ears through a hoard of heathenish obscenities to receive the Gospel. Who finds not that Irenaeus, Epiphanius, Jerome,[1] and others discover more heresies than they well confute, and that oft for heresy which is the truer opinion?[2]

---

3. See *Paradise Lost* 4.222: "Knowledge of Good bought dear by knowing ill."
4. The original reads "warfaring," but in several copies this is corrected by hand to "wayfaring."
5. Superficial.
6. Duns Scotus and Thomas Aquinas here represent types of the scholastic theologian. For the cave of Mammon, see *The Faerie Queene* 2.7 (the Palmer is not with Guyon in Mammon's Cave); the "Bower of Bliss," 2.12.
7. Delicately.
8. The Greek philosopher who propounded a morality based on pleasure.
9. Talmudist: a student of the Talmud, the Jewish commentaries on the Bible; Keri: marginal emendations of rabbinical scholars on the Chetiv, the text of the Bible.
1. Early apologists of Christianity: St. Clement of Alexandria (2nd century) and Eusebius, who describes pagan depravity to promote faith in Christianity, as do St. Irenaeus (2nd century), Epiphanius (4th century), and St. Jerome (early 5th century).
2. Milton goes on to argue that the effect of books depends upon the teacher, who, if really good, needs no books. Milton stresses the role of the reader: A wise person can find something instructive in even the worst books.

* * *

Impunity and remissness, for certain, are the bane of a commonwealth; but here the great art lies, to discern in what the law is to bid restraint and punishment, and in what things persuasion only is to work. If every action which is good or evil in man at ripe years, were to be under pittance and prescription and compulsion, what were virtue but a name, what praise could be then due to well-doing, what gramercy[3] to be sober, just, or continent?

Many there be that complain of divine providence for suffering Adam to transgress. Foolish tongues! when God gave him reason, he gave him freedom to choose, for reason is but choosing; he had been else a mere artificial Adam, such an Adam as he is in the motions.[4] We ourselves esteem not of that obedience, or love, or gift, which is of force. God therefore left him free, set before him a provoking object, ever almost in his eyes; herein consisted his merit, herein the right of his reward, the praise of his abstinence. Wherefore did he create passions within us, pleasures round about us, but that these rightly tempered are the very ingredients of virtue? They are not skilful considerers of human things who imagine to remove sin by removing the matter of sin. For, besides that it is a huge heap increasing under the very act of diminishing, though some part of it may for a time be withdrawn from some persons, it cannot from all, in such a universal thing as books are; and when this is done, yet the sin remains entire. Though ye take from a covetous man all his treasure, he has yet one jewel left—ye cannot bereave him of his covetousness. Banish all objects of lust, shut up all youth into the severest discipline that can be exercised in any hermitage, ye cannot make them chaste that came not thither so: such great care and wisdom is required to the right managing of this point.

Suppose we could expel sin by this means; look how much we thus expel of sin, so much we expel of virtue: for the matter of them both is the same; remove that, and ye remove them both alike. This justifies the high providence of God, who, though he command us temperance, justice, continence, yet pours out before us, even to a profuseness, all desirable things, and gives us minds that can wander beyond all limit and satiety. Why should we then affect a rigor contrary to the manner of God and of nature, by abridging or scanting those means which books freely permitted are, both to the trial of virtue and the exercise of truth?[5]

* * *

And lest some should persuade ye, Lords and Commons, that these arguments of learned men's discouragement at this your Order are mere flourishes, and not real, I could recount what I have seen and heard in other countries where this kind of inquisition tyrannizes; when I have sat among their learned men, for that honor I had, and been counted happy to be born in such a place of philosophic freedom as they supposed England was, while themselves did nothing but bemoan the servile condition into which learning amongst them was brought; that this was it which had damped the glory of Italian wits; that nothing had been there written now these many years but flattery and fustian. There it was that I found and visited the famous Galileo, grown old, a prisoner to the Inquisition[6] for thinking in astronomy otherwise

3. Thanks.
4. Puppet shows. For this statement about Adam, see *Paradise Lost* 3.103–28, page 822.
5. Milton argues that no intelligent person will be willing to take on the job of censorship and that an unintelligent person would be prone to commit serious errors. In addition to giving power to stupid people, censorship would

actually encourage people to read banned books and to adhere to the perverse opinions expressed in such books.
6. In 1633 the great Italian astronomer Galileo was tried by the Inquisition at Rome and forced to abjure his earlier assertion that his findings confirmed the Copernican heliocentric theory of the universe. He was under house arrest in Florence when Milton visited there in 1638–39.

than the Franciscan and Dominican licensers thought. And though I knew that England then was groaning loudest under the prelatical yoke, nevertheless I took it as a pledge of future happiness that other nations were so persuaded of her liberty.

Yet was it beyond my hope that those worthies were then breathing in her air, who should be her leaders to such a deliverance as shall never be forgotten by any revolution of time that this world hath to finish. When that was once begun, it was as little in my fear, that what words of complaint I heard among learned men of other parts uttered against the Inquisition, the same I should hear by as learned men at home uttered in time of Parliament against an order of licensing; and that so generally, that when I had disclosed myself a companion of their discontent, I might say, if without envy, that he whom an honest quaestorship had endeared to the Sicilians, was not more by them importuned against Verres,[7] than the favorable opinion which I had among many who honor ye, and are known and respected by ye, loaded me with entreaties and persuasions that I would not despair to lay together that which just reason should bring into my mind toward the removal of an undeserved thraldom upon learning.

That this is not, therefore, the disburdening of a particular fancy, but the common grievance of all those who had prepared their minds and studies above the vulgar pitch to advance truth in others, and from others to entertain it, thus much may satisfy. And in their name I shall for neither friend nor foe conceal what the general murmur is; that if it come to inquisitioning again and licensing, and that we are so timorous of ourselves and so suspicious of all men as to fear each book and the shaking of every leaf, before we know what the contents are; if some who but of late were little better than silenced from preaching, shall come now to silence us from reading, except what they please, it cannot be guessed what is intended by some but a second tyranny over learning; and will soon put it out of controversy that bishops and presbyters are the same to us both name and thing.

* * *

But I am certain that a state governed by the rules of justice and fortitude, or a church built and founded upon the rock of faith and true knowledge, cannot be so pusillanimous.[8] While things are yet not constituted in religion, that freedom of writing should be restrained by a discipline imitated from the prelates, and learnt by them from the Inquisition, to shut us up all again into the breast of a licenser, must needs give cause of doubt and discouragement to all learned and religious men. Who cannot but discern the fineness of this politic drift, and who are the contrivers: that while bishops were to be baited down, then all presses might be open; it was the people's birthright and privilege in time of parliament, it was the breaking forth of light.

But now, the bishops abrogated and voided out of the church, as if our reformation sought no more but to make room for others into their seats under another name, the episcopal arts begin to bud again; the cruse[9] of truth must run no more oil; liberty of printing must be enthralled again under a prelatical commission of twenty, the privilege of the people nullified; and, which is worse, the freedom of learning must groan again, and to her old fetters: all this the parliament yet sitting. Although their own late arguments and defenses against the prelates might remember them that this obstructing violence meets for the most part with an event utterly opposite to the end which it drives at; instead of suppressing sects and

---

7. Cicero exposed the corruption of Verres' government in 75 B.C.

8. Mean-spirited, cowardly.

9. Small vessel; see 1 Kings 17.12–16.

schisms, it raises them and invests them with a reputation: "The punishing of wits enhances their authority," saith the Viscount St. Albans,[1] "and a forbidden writing is thought to be a certain spark of truth that flies up in the faces of them who seek to tread it out."

This Order, therefore, may prove a nursing mother to sects, but I shall easily show how it will be a stepdame to Truth; and first by disenabling us to the maintenance of what is known already.

Well knows he who uses to consider, that our faith and knowledge thrives by exercise, as well as our limbs and complexion. Truth is compared in scripture to a streaming fountain;[2] if her waters flow not in a perpetual progression, they sicken into a muddy pool of conformity and tradition. A man may be a heretic in the truth; and if he believe things only because his pastor says so, or the Assembly so determines, without knowing other reason, though his belief be true, yet the very truth he holds becomes his heresy. There is not any burden that some would gladlier post off to another than the charge and care of their religion. There be, who knows not that there be, of protestants and professors who live and die in as arrant an implicit faith, as any lay papist of Loreto.[3]

A wealthy man addicted to his pleasure and to his profits, finds religion to be a traffic so entangled, and of so many piddling accounts, that of all mysteries[4] he cannot skill to keep a stock going upon that trade. What should he do? Fain he would have the name to be religious, fain he would bear up with his neighbors in that. What does he, therefore, but resolves to give over toiling, and to find himself out some factor to whose care and credit he may commit the whole managing of his religious affairs; some Divine of note and estimation that must be. To him he adheres, resigns the whole warehouse of his religion with all the locks and keys into his custody; and indeed makes the very person of that man his religion; esteems his associating with him a sufficient evidence and commendatory of his own piety. So that a man may say his religion is now no more within himself, but is become a dividual movable,[5] and goes and comes near him, according as that good man frequents the house. He entertains him, gives him gifts, feasts him, lodges him. His religion comes home at night, prays, is liberally supped, and sumptuously laid to sleep, rises, is saluted, and after the malmsey, or some well spiced brewage, and better breakfasted than he[6] whose morning appetite would have gladly fed on green figs between Bethany and Jerusalem, his religion walks abroad at eight, and leaves his kind entertainer in the shop trading all day without his religion.

Another sort there be, who, when they hear that all things shall be ordered, all things regulated and settled, nothing written but what passes through the customhouse of certain publicans[7] that have the tonnaging and the poundaging of all freespoken truth, will straight give themselves up into your hands, make 'em and cut 'em out what religion ye please. There be delights, there be recreations and jolly pastimes that will fetch the day about from sun to sun, and rock the tedious year as in a delightful dream. What need they torture their heads with that which others have taken so strictly and so unalterably into their own purveying? These are the fruits which a dull ease and cessation of our knowledge will bring forth among the people.

---

1. Sir Francis Bacon, An *Advertisement Touching the Controversies of the Church of England.*
2. See Psalms 85.11.
3. Professors: those who profess religion; Loreto: a Catholic shrine supposed to have been transported to Italy from the Holy Land.
4. Trades, crafts.
5. A separate piece of property.
6. For this description of Christ, see Mark 11.12–14.
7. Tax collectors.

How goodly, and how to be wished, were such an obedient unanimity as this, what a fine conformity would it starch us all into! Doubtless a staunch and solid piece of framework, as any January could freeze together.[8]

* * *

Truth indeed came once into the world with her divine Master, and was a perfect shape most glorious to look on. But when he ascended, and his apostles after him were laid asleep, then straight arose a wicked race of deceivers, who, as that story goes of the Egyptian Typhon with his conspirators, how they dealt with the good Osiris, took the virgin Truth, hewed her lovely form into a thousand pieces, and scattered them to the four winds.[9] From that time ever since, the sad friends of Truth, such as durst appear, imitating the careful search that Isis made for the mangled body of Osiris, went up and down gathering up limb by limb still as they could find them. We have not yet found them all, Lords and Commons, nor ever shall do, till her Master's second coming. He shall bring together every joint and member, and shall mold them into an immortal feature of loveliness and perfection. Suffer not these licensing prohibitions to stand at every place of opportunity, forbidding and disturbing them that continue seeking, that continue to do our obsequies to the torn body of our martyred saint.

We boast our light; but if we look not wisely on the sun itself, it smites us into darkness. Who can discern those planets that are oft combust, and those stars of brightest magnitude that rise and set with the sun, until the opposite motion of their orbs bring them to such a place in the firmament, where they may be seen evening or morning. The light which we have gained, was given us, not to be ever staring on, but by it to discover onward things more remote from our knowledge. It is not the unfrocking of a priest, the unmitering of a bishop, and the removing him from off the Presbyterian shoulders that will make us a happy nation; no, if other things as great in the church, and in the rule of life both economical and political, be not looked into and reformed, we have looked so long upon the blaze that Zwinglius[1] and Calvin hath beaconed up to us, that we are stark blind.

There be who perpetually complain of schisms and sects, and make it such a calamity that any man dissents from their maxims. It is their own pride and ignorance which causes the disturbing, who neither will hear with meekness, nor can convince, yet all must be suppressed which is not found in their syntagma.[2] They are the troublers, they are the dividers of unity, who neglect and permit not others to unite those dissevered pieces which are yet wanting to the body of Truth. To be still searching what we know not by what we know, still closing up truth to truth as we find it (for all her body is homogeneal[3] and proportional), this is the golden rule in theology as well as in arithmetic, and makes up the best harmony in a church; not the forced and outward union of cold and neutral and inwardly divided minds.

Lords and Commons of England, consider what nation it is whereof ye are, and whereof ye are the governors; a nation not slow and dull, but of a quick, ingenious, and piercing spirit, acute to invent, subtle and sinewy to discourse, not beneath the reach of any point the highest that human capacity can soar to. Therefore the studies of learning in her deepest sciences have been so ancient and so eminent among us that writers of good antiquity and ablest judgment have been persuaded that even the

---

8. Milton goes on to argue that censorship will make the clergy lazy and will hinder the Reformation's goal of seeking truth.
9. Typhon tore apart and scattered Osiris's body, and his wife Isis and son Horus collected it. The interpretation here is based on Plutarch's allegory in *Isis and Osiris*.
1. Ulrich Zwingli (1484–1531), the Protestant reformer of Zurich.
2. Systematic doctrinal treatise.
3. Homogeneous.

school of Pythagoras and the Persian wisdom took beginning from the old philosophy of this island.[4] And that wise and civil Roman, Julius Agricola, who governed once here for Caesar, preferred the natural wits of Britain before the labored studies of the French.[5] Nor is it for nothing that the grave and frugal Transylvanian[6] sends out yearly from as far as the mountainous borders of Russia and beyond the Hercynian wilderness,[7] not their youth, but their staid men to learn our language and our theologic arts.

Yet that which is above all this, the favor and the love of Heaven, we have great argument to think in a peculiar manner propitious and propending towards us. Why else was this nation chosen before any other, that out of her as out of Sion should be proclaimed and sounded forth the first tidings and trumpet of reformation to all Europe? And had it not been the obstinate perverseness of our prelates against the divine and admirable spirit of Wycliffe[8] to suppress him as a schismatic and innovator, perhaps neither the Bohemian Huss and Jerome,[9] no, nor the name of Luther, or of Calvin, had been ever known; the glory of reforming all our neighbors had been completely ours. But now, as our obdurate clergy have with violence demeaned the matter, we are become hitherto the latest and the backwardest scholars of whom God offered to have made us the teachers.

Now once again by all concurrence of signs, and by the general instinct of holy and devout men, as they daily and solemnly express their thoughts, God is decreeing to begin some new and great period in his Church, even to the reforming of reformation itself. What does he then but reveal himself to his servants, and, as his manner is, first to his Englishmen? I say as his manner is, first to us, though we mark not the method of his counsels and are unworthy. Behold now this vast city, a city of refuge, the mansion house of liberty, encompassed and surrounded with his protection. The shop of war hath not there more anvils and hammers waking, to fashion out the plates and instruments of armed justice in defense of beleaguered Truth, than there be pens and heads there, sitting by their studious lamps, musing, searching, revolving new notions and ideas wherewith to present, as with their homage and their fealty, the approaching reformation; others as fast reading, trying all things, assenting to the force of reason and convincement.

What could a man require more from a nation so pliant and so prone to seek after knowledge? What wants there to such a towardly[1] and pregnant soul but wise and faithful laborers to make a knowing people, a nation of prophets, of sages, and of worthies? We reckon more than five months yet to harvest; there need not be five weeks, had we but eyes to lift up; the fields are white already. Where there is much desire to learn, there of necessity will be much arguing, much writing, many opinions; for opinion in good men is but knowledge in the making. Under these fantastic terrors of sect and schism, we wrong the earnest and zealous thirst after knowledge and understanding which God hath stirred up in this city.

What some lament of, we rather should rejoice at, should rather praise this pious forwardness among men, to reassume the ill-deputed care of their religion into their own hands again. A little generous prudence, a little forbearance of one another, and

4. For the connection between the Druids and Zoroastrian and Pythagorean philosophy, see Pliny, *Natural History* 30.2.
5. See Tacitus, *Agricola* 21.
6. Seventeenth-century Transylvania was Protestant and independent.

7. South central Germany.
8. English Protestants viewed John Wycliff (1320?–84) as the initiator of the Reformation in England.
9. Jerome of Prague (c. 1365–1416), a disciple of Wycliff, and John Huss of Bohemia (1373–1415).
1. Promising.

some grain of charity might win all these diligences to join and unite into one general and brotherly search after truth; could we but forego this prelatical tradition of crowding free consciences and Christian liberties into canons and precepts of men. I doubt not, if some great and worthy stranger should come among us, wise to discern the mold and temper of a people, and how to govern it, observing the high hopes and aims, the diligent alacrity of our extended thoughts and reasonings in the pursuance of truth and freedom, but that he would cry out as Pyrrhus did, admiring the Roman docility and courage, "If such were my Epirots, I would not despair the greatest design that could be attempted to make a church or kingdom happy."[2]

Yet these are the men cried out against for schismatics and sectaries;[3] as if, while the temple of the Lord was building, some cutting, some squaring the marble, others hewing the cedars, there should be a sort of irrational men who could not consider there must be many schisms and many dissections made in the quarry and in the timber, ere the house of God can be built. And when every stone is laid artfully together, it cannot be united into a continuity, it can but be contiguous in this world; neither can every piece of the building be of one form; nay rather the perfection consists in this, that out of many moderate varieties and brotherly dissimilitudes that are not vastly disproportional, arises the goodly and the graceful symmetry that commends the whole pile and structure.

Let us, therefore, be more considerate builders, more wise in spiritual architecture, when great reformation is expected. For now the time seems come, wherein Moses, the great prophet, may sit in heaven rejoicing to see that memorable and glorious wish of his fulfilled, when not only our seventy elders, but all the Lord's people, are become prophets.

* * *

Methinks I see in my mind a noble and puissant nation rousing herself like a strong man after sleep, and shaking her invincible locks. Methinks I see her as an eagle muing[4] her mighty youth, and kindling her undazzled eyes at the full midday beam; purging and unscaling her long-abused sight at the fountain itself of heavenly radiance; while the whole noise of timorous and flocking birds, with those also that love the twilight, flutter about, amazed at what she means, and in their envious gabble would prognosticate a year of sects and schisms.

What should ye do then, should ye suppress all this flowery crop of knowledge and new light sprung up and yet springing daily in this city? Should ye set an oligarchy of twenty engrossers[5] over it, to bring a famine upon our minds again, when we shall know nothing but what is measured to us by their bushel? Believe it, Lords and Commons, they who counsel ye to such a suppressing, do as good as bid ye suppress yourselves; and I will soon show how.

* * *

And now the time in special is, by privilege, to write and speak what may help to the further discussing of matters in agitation. The temple of Janus with his two controversal faces might now not unsignificantly be set open.[6] And though all the winds of doctrine were let loose to play upon the earth, so Truth be in the field, we do injuriously by licensing and prohibiting to misdoubt her strength. Let her and Falsehood grapple; who ever knew Truth put to the worse, in a free and open encounter. Her confuting is

---

2. King Pyrrhus of Epirus defeated the Romans at Hereclea in 280 B.C.
3. Dividers of the church.
4. Renewing.

5. Monopolists.
6. The Roman god Janus's head had two faces looking in opposite directions. During times of war the gates of Janus were open.

the best and surest suppressing. He who hears what praying there is for light and clearer knowledge to be sent down among us, would think of other matters to be constituted beyond the discipline of Geneva, framed and fabriced already to our hands.[7]

Yet when the new light which we beg for shines in upon us, there be who envy and oppose, if it come not first in at their casements. What a collusion[8] is this, whenas we are exhorted by the wise man to use diligence, to seek for wisdom as for hidden treasures[9] early and late, that another order shall enjoin us to know nothing but by statute. When a man hath been laboring the hardest labor in the deep mines of knowledge, hath furnished out his findings in all their equipage, drawn forth his reasons as it were a battle ranged, scattered and defeated all objections in his way, calls out his adversary into the plain, offers him the advantage of wind and sun, if he please, only that he may try the matter by dint of argument; for his opponents then to skulk, to lay ambushments, to keep a narrow bridge of licensing where the challenger should pass, though it be valor enough in soldiership, is but weakness and cowardice in the wars of Truth.

For who knows not that Truth is strong, next to the Almighty. She needs no policies, nor stratagems, nor licensings to make her victorious—those are the shifts and the defenses that error uses against her power. Give her but room, and do not bind her when she sleeps, for then she speaks not true, as the old Proteus did, who spake oracles only when he was caught and bound,[1] but then rather she turns herself into all shapes except her own, and perhaps tunes her voice according to the time, as Micaiah did before Ahab,[2] until she be adjured into her own likeness.

Yet is it not impossible that she may have more shapes than one. What else is all that rank of things indifferent, wherein Truth may be on this side, or on the other, without being unlike herself? What but a vain shadow else is the abolition of those ordinances, that handwriting nailed to the cross;[3] what great purchase is this Christian liberty which Paul so often boasts of? His doctrine is, that he who eats, or eats not, regards a day, or regards it not, may do either to the Lord.[4] How many other things might be tolerated in peace and left to conscience, had we but charity, and were it not the chief stronghold of our hypocrisy to be ever judging one another. I fear yet this iron yoke of outward conformity hath left a slavish print upon our necks; the ghost of a linen decency[5] yet haunts us. We stumble and are impatient at the least dividing of one visible congregation from another, though it be not in fundamentals; and through our forwardness to suppress, and our backwardness to recover any enthralled piece of truth out of the gripe of custom, we care not to keep truth separated from truth, which is the fiercest rent and disunion of all. We do not see that while we still affect by all means a rigid external formality, we may as soon fall again into a gross conforming stupidity, a stark and dead congealment of "wood, and hay, and stubble"[6] forced and frozen together, which is more to the sudden degenerating of a church than many subdichotomies[7] of petty schisms.

Not that I can think well of every light separation, or that all in a church is to be expected "gold and silver and precious stones."[8] It is not possible for man to sever the wheat from the tares, the good fish from the other fry; that must be the angels' ministry

---

7. Discipline of Geneva: Calvinism; fabriced: fabricated.
8. Secret agreement for purposes of trickery; ambiguity in words or reasoning.
9. The wise man is Solomon; see Proverbs 8.11 and Matthew 13.44.
1. The story of Proteus is in *Odyssey* 384–93.
2. 1 Kings 22.

3. Colossians 2.14.
4. Romans 14.1–13.
5. A reference to the controversy over ecclesiastical vestments.
6. See 1 Corinthians 3.12.
7. Inconsequential divisions.
8. 1 Corinthians 3.12.

at the end of mortal things.[9] Yet if all cannot be of one mind,—as who looks they should be?—this doubtless is more wholesome, more prudent, and more Christian, that many be tolerated, rather than all compelled. I mean not tolerated popery and open superstition, which, as it extirpates all religions and civil supremacies, so itself should be extirpate, provided first that all charitable and compassionate means be used to win and regain the weak and the misled; that also which is impious or evil absolutely, either against faith or manners, no law can possibly permit, that intends not to unlaw itself; but those neighboring differences, or rather indifferences, are what I speak of, whether in some point of doctrine or of discipline, which though they may be many, yet need not interrupt "the unity of spirit," if we could but find among us the "bond of peace."[1]

In the meanwhile, if any one would write and bring his helpful hand to the slow-moving reformation which we labor under, if truth have spoken to him before others, or but seemed at least to speak, who hath so bejesuited us that we should trouble that man with asking license to do so worthy a deed? And not consider this, that if it come to prohibiting, there is not aught more likely to be prohibited than truth itself; whose first appearance to our eyes bleared and dimmed with prejudice and custom, is more unsightly and unplausible than many errors, even as the person is of many a great man slight and contemptible to see to. And what do they tell us vainly of new opinions, when this very opinion of theirs, that none must be heard but whom they like, is the worst and newest opinion of all others; and is the chief cause why sects and schisms do so much abound, and true knowledge is kept at distance from us; besides yet a greater danger which is in it. For when God shakes a kingdom with strong and healthful commotions to a general reforming, it is not untrue that many sectaries and false teachers are then busiest in seducing; but yet more true it is that God then raises to his own work men of rare abilities and more than common industry, not only to look back and revise what hath been taught heretofore, but to gain further and go on some new enlightened steps in the discovery of truth.

PARADISE LOST

Paradise Lost is about devastating loss attended by redemption. The reader's knowledge of the Fall creates a sense of tragic inevitability. And Satan, no less than Adam and Eve, appears in all the psychological complexity and verbal grandeur of a tragic hero. Indeed, there is even a manuscript in which Milton outlined the story as a tragedy. In that version, "Lucifer's contriving Adam's ruin" is Act 3. Following epic tradition, Milton places this part of the action at the forefront of his poem, beginning in medias res.

So powerful is Milton's opening portrayal of Satan that the Romantic poets thought Satan was the hero of the poem. Focusing on the first two books, the romantic reading sees him as a dynamic rebel. From a Renaissance point of view, Satan is more like an Elizabethan hero-villain, with his many soliloquies and his tortured psychology of brilliance twisted toward evil. Only in Book 9, however, does Milton say, "I now must change these notes to tragic," thereby signaling that he is about to narrate the fall of Adam and Eve. From this point on the poem follows Adam and Eve's tragic movement from sin to despair to the recognition of sin and the need for repentance. Adam and Eve's learning through suffering and the prophecy of the Son's redemption of sin make this a story of gain as well as loss, on the order of Aeschylean tragedy.

Like all epics, Paradise Lost is encyclopedic, combining many different genres. To read this poem is to have an education in everything from literary history to astronomy. Milton draws on a vast wealth of reading, with the Bible as his main source—not only Genesis, but

---

9. Matthew 13.24.   1. Ephesians 4.3.

also Exodus, the Prophets, Revelation, Saint Paul, and especially the Psalms, which he had translated. Milton also makes great use of biblical commentary from rabbinical, patristic, and contemporary sources. Early on, Milton had envisaged a poem about the Arthurian legend, and his choice of the nonmartial, seemingly unheroic biblical story of Adam and Eve marks a bold departure from epic tradition. While Spenser's *Faerie Queene* is Milton's most important vernacular model, among epic poets his closest affinity is with Virgil and Dante, both of whom had written of the underworld; Dante especially devoted himself to humanity's free choice of sin. Like Dante, Milton creates his poem as a microcosm of the natural universe. His ideal vision of the world before the Fall is one where day and night are equal and the sun is always in the same sign of the zodiac, an image that embodies in poetic astronomy the world of simplicity and perfection that humans have lost through sin. Milton does not choose between the earth-centered Ptolemaic and the heliocentric Copernican systems but presents both as alternative explanations for the order of the universe.

Although we know nothing about the order in which the parts of the poem were composed, we do know that Milton typically composed at night or in the early morning. Sometimes he lay awake unable to write a line; at others he was seized "with a certain impetus and *oestro*" [frenzy]. He would dictate forty lines from memory and then reduce them to half that number. According to his nephew, the poem was written from 1658 to 1663.

The one extant manuscript of the poem, which contains the first book, reveals that Milton revised for punctuation and spelling. There were two editions in Milton's lifetime, both printed by Samuel Simmons. The first edition, *Paradise Lost: A poem in ten books*, was printed in six different issues in 1667, 1668, and 1669. From the fourth issue of the poem on, such paratexts as "The Printer to Reader," "The Argument" (which stood altogether), and Milton's note on the verse appear. With the second octave edition of 1674, Milton divided Books 7 and 10 into two books each to create twelve books in all. Prefaced by dedicatory Latin verses, one of which was by his old friend Andrew Marvell, this 1674 edition, which appeared in the year of Milton's death, is the basis for the present text.

FROM **PARADISE LOST**[1]
Book 1
The Argument

This first Book proposes, first in brief, the whole Subject, Man's disobedience, and the loss thereupon of Paradise wherein he was plac't: Then touches the prime cause of his fall, the Serpent, or rather Satan in the Serpent; who revolting from God, and drawing to his side many Legions of Angels, was by the command of God driven out of Heaven with all his Crew into the great Deep. Which action past over, the Poem hastes into the midst of things,[2] presenting Satan with his Angels now fallen into Hell, describ'd here, not in the Centre (for Heaven and Earth may be suppos'd as yet not made, certainly not yet accurst) but in a place of utter darkness, fitliest call'd Chaos: Here Satan with his Angels lying on the burning Lake, thunder-struck and astonisht, after a certain space recovers, as from confusion, calls up him who next in Order and Dignity lay by him; they confer of thir miserable fall. Satan awakens all his Legions, who lay till then in the same manner confounded; They rise, thir Numbers, array of Battle, thir chief Leaders nam'd, according to the Idols known afterwards in Canaan and the Countries adjoining. To these Satan directs his Speech, comforts them with hope yet of regaining Heaven, but tells them lastly of a new World and new kind of Creature to be created, according to an ancient Prophecy or report

---

1. Our text is taken, and the notes are adapted, from John Carey and Alastair Fowler, eds., *The Poems of John Milton*.

2. Following Horace's rule that the epic should plunge "*in medias res*."

in Heaven; for that Angels were long before this visible Creation, was the opinion of many ancient Fathers. To find out the truth of this Prophecy, and what to determine thereon he refers to a full Council. What his Associates thence attempt. Pandemonium the Palace of Satan rises, suddenly built out of the Deep: The infernal Peers there sit in Council.

    Of Man's First Disobedience, and the Fruit
    Of that Forbidden Tree, whose mortal[3] taste
    Brought Death into the World, and all our woe,[4]
    With loss of *Eden*, till one greater Man[5]
5   Restore us, and regain the blissful Seat,
    Sing Heav'nly Muse,[6] that on the secret top
    Of *Oreb*, or of *Sinai*, didst inspire
    That Shepherd, who first taught the chosen Seed,[7]
    In the Beginning how the Heav'ns and Earth
10   Rose out of *Chaos*: Or if *Sion* Hill[8]
    Delight thee more, and *Siloa's* Brook[9] that flow'd
    Fast° by the Oracle of God; I thence   *close*
    Invoke thy aid to my advent'rous Song,
    That with no middle flight intends to soar
15   Above th' *Aonian* Mount,[1] while it pursues
    Things unattempted yet in Prose or Rhyme.[2]
    And chiefly Thou O Spirit, that dost prefer
    Before all Temples th' upright heart and pure,[3]
    Instruct me, for Thou know'st; Thou from the first
20   Wast present, and with mighty wings outspread
    Dove-like satst brooding on the vast Abyss
    And mad'st it pregnant:[4] What in me is dark
    Illumine, what is low raise and support;
    That to the highth of this great Argument°   *theme*
25   I may assert Eternal Providence,
    And justify[5] the ways of God to men.
      Say first, for Heav'n hides nothing from thy view
    Nor the deep Tract of Hell, say first what cause
    Mov'd our Grand[6] Parents in that happy State,

3. "Death-bringing" (Latin *mortalis*) but also "to mortals."
4. This definition of the first sin follows Calvin's Catechism.
5. Christ, in Pauline theology the second Adam (see Romans 5.19). The people and events referred to in these lines have a typological connection, i.e., the Christian interpretation of the Old Testament as a prefiguration of the New.
6. Rhetorically, lines 1–49 are the *invocatio*, consisting of an address to the Muse, and the *principium* that states the whole scope of the poem's action. The "Heavenly Muse," later addressed as the muse of astronomy Urania (7.1), is here identified with the Holy Spirit of the Bible, which inspires Moses.
7. The "Shepherd" is Moses, who was granted the vision of the burning bush on Mount Oreb (Exodus 3) and received the Law, either on Mount Oreb (Deuteronomy 4.10) or on its lower part, Mount Sinai (Exodus 19.20). Moses, the first Jewish writer, taught "the chosen seed," the children of Israel, about the beginning of the world in

Genesis.
8. The sanctuary, a place of ceremonial song but also (Isaiah 2.3) of oracular pronouncements.
9. A spring immediately west of Mount Zion and beside Calvary, often used as a symbol of the operation of the Holy Ghost.
1. Helicon, sacred to the Muses.
2. Ironically translating Ariosto's boast in the invocation to *Orlando Furioso*.
3. The Spirit is the voice of God, which inspired the Hebrew prophets.
4. Identifying the Spirit present at the creation (Genesis 1.2) with the Spirit in the form of a dove that descended on Jesus at the beginning of his ministry (John 1.32). Vast: large; deserted (Latin *vastus*).
5. Does not mean merely "demonstrate logically" but has its biblical meaning and implies spiritual rather than rational understanding.
6. Implies not only greatness, but also inclusiveness of generality or parentage.

30   Favor'd of Heav'n so highly, to fall off
     From thir Creator, and transgress his Will
     For° one restraint, Lords of the World besides?°   *because of/otherwise*
     Who first seduc'd them to that foul revolt?
     Th' infernal Serpent;[7] hee it was, whose guile
35   Stirr'd up with Envy and Revenge, deceiv'd
     The Mother of Mankind; what time his Pride
     Had cast him out from Heav'n, with all his Host
     Of Rebel Angels, by whose aid aspiring
     To set himself in Glory above his Peers,
40   He trusted to have equall'd the most High,[8]
     If he oppos'd; and with ambitious aim
     Against the Throne and Monarchy of God
     Rais'd impious War in Heav'n and Battle proud
     With vain attempt. Him the Almighty Power
45   Hurl'd headlong flaming from th' Ethereal Sky[9]
     With hideous ruin and combustion down
     To bottomless perdition, there to dwell
     In Adamantine Chains[1] and penal Fire,
     Who durst defy th' Omnipotent to Arms.
50   Nine times the Space that measures Day and Night[2]
     To mortal men, hee with his horrid crew
     Lay vanquisht, rolling in the fiery Gulf
     Confounded though immortal: But his doom
     Reserv'd him to more wrath; for now the thought
55   Both of lost happiness and lasting pain
     Torments him; round he throws his baleful° eyes   *evil, suffering*
     That witness'd huge affliction and dismay
     Mixt with obdúrate° pride and steadfast hate: *unyielding*
     At once as far as Angels' ken° he views   *power of vision*
60   The dismal° Situation waste and wild,   *dreadful, sinister*
     A Dungeon horrible, on all sides round
     As one great Furnace flam'd, yet from those flames
     No light, but rather darkness visible
     Serv'd only to discover sights of woe,[3]
65   Regions of sorrow, doleful shades, where peace
     And rest can never dwell, hope never comes
     That comes to all;[4] but torture without end
     Still urges,° and a fiery Deluge, fed   *presses*
     With ever-burning Sulphur unconsum'd:

7. "That old serpent, called the Devil, and Satan" (Revelation 12.9) both because Satan entered the body of a serpent to tempt Eve and because his nature is guileful and dangerous to humans.
8. Satan's crime was not his aspiring "above his peers" but aspiring "To set himself in [divine] Glory." Numerous verbal echoes relate lines 40–48 to the biblical accounts of the fall and binding of Lucifer, in 2 Peter 2.4, Revelation 20.1–2, and Isaiah 14.12–15: "Thou hast said . . . I will exalt my throne above the stars of God . . . I will be like the most High. Yet thou shalt be brought down to hell."

9. Mingling an allusion to Luke 10.18, "I beheld Satan as lightning fall from heaven," with one to Homer, *Iliad* 1.591, Hephaistos "hurled from the ethereal threshold."
1. 2 Peter 2.4; "God spared not the angels that sinned, but . . . delivered them into chains of darkness."
2. The devils fall for the same number of days that the Titans fall from heaven when overthrown by the Olympian gods (see Hesiod, *Theogony* 664–735).
3. See the account of the land of the dead in Job 10.22: "the light is as darkness."
4. The phrase echoes Dante's *Inferno*: "All hope abandon, ye who enter here."

70	Such place Eternal Justice had prepar'd	
	For those rebellious, here thir Prison ordained	
	In utter° darkness, and thir portion set	*complete, outer*
	As far remov'd from God and light of Heav'n	
	As from the Center thrice to th' utmost Pole.[5]	
75	O how unlike the place from whence they fell!	
	There the companions of his fall, o'erwhelm'd	
	With Floods and Whirlwinds of tempestuous fire,	
	He soon discerns, and welt'ring by his side	
	One next himself in power, and next in crime,	
80	Long after known in *Palestine*, and nam'd	
	Beëlzebub.[6] To whom th' Arch-Enemy,	
	And thence in Heav'n call'd Satan,[7] with bold words	
	Breaking the horrid silence thus began.[8]	
	If thou beest hee; But O how fall'n! how chang'd	
85	From him, who in the happy Realms of Light	
	Cloth'd with transcendent brightness didst outshine	
	Myriads though bright:[9] If he whom mutual league,	
	United thoughts and counsels, equal hope,	
	And hazard in the Glorious Enterprise,	
90	Join'd with me once, now misery hath join'd	
	In equal ruin: into what Pit thou seest	
	From what highth fall'n, so much the stronger prov'd	
	He with his Thunder: and till then who knew	
	The force of those dire Arms? yet not for those,	
95	Nor what the Potent Victor in his rage	
	Can else inflict, do I repent or change,	
	Though chang'd in outward luster; that fixt mind	
	And high disdain, from sense of injur'd merit,	
	That with the mightiest rais'd me to contend,	
100	And to the fierce contention brought along	
	Innumerable force of Spirits arm'd	
	That durst dislike his reign, and mee preferring,	
	His utmost power with adverse power oppos'd	
	In dubious Battle on the Plains of Heav'n,	
105	And shook his throne.[1] What though the field be lost?	
	All is not lost; the unconquerable Will,	
	And study° of revenge, immortal hate,	*pursuit*
	And courage never to submit or yield:	
	And what is else not to be overcome?	
110	That Glory[2] never shall his wrath or might	

5. Milton refers to the Ptolemaic universe in which the earth is at the center of ten concentric spheres. Milton draws attention to the numerical proportion, heaven-earth:earth-hell—i.e., earth divides the interval between heaven and hell in the proportion that Neoplatonists believed should be maintained between reason and concupiscence.
6. Hebrew, "Lord of the flies"; Matthew 12.24, "the prince of the devils."
7. Hebrew, "enemy." After his rebellion, Satan's "former name" (Lucifer) was no longer used (5.658).

8. Rhetorically, the opening of the action proper. The 41-line speech beginning here, the first speech in the book, exactly balances the last, which also is spoken by Satan and also consists of 41 lines (1.622–662).
9. The break in grammatical concord (between "him" and "didst") reflects Satan's doubt whether Beelzebub is present and so whether second-person forms are appropriate.
1. The Son's chariot, not Satan's armies, shakes heaven to its foundations, as we learn in Book 6. Throughout the present passage, Satan sees himself as the hero of a pagan epic.
2. Either "the glory of overcoming me" or "my glory of will."

Extort from me. To bow and sue for grace
With suppliant knee, and deify his power
Who from the terror of this Arm so late
Doubted° his Empire, that were low indeed,   *feared for*
115   That were an ignominy and shame beneath
This downfall; since by Fate the strength of Gods
And this Empyreal substance cannot fail,[3]
Since through experience of this great event
In Arms not worse, in foresight much advanc't,
120   We may with more successful hope resolve
To wage by force or guile eternal War
Irreconcilable to our grand Foe,
Who now triúmphs, and in th' excess of joy
Sole reigning holds the Tyranny of Heav'n.[4]
125   So spake th' Apostate Angel, though in pain,
Vaunting aloud, but rackt with deep despair:
And him thus answer'd soon his bold Compeer.°   *comrade*
     O Prince, O Chief of many Throned Powers,
That led th' imbattl'd Seraphim[5] to War
130   Under thy conduct, and in dreadful deeds
Fearless, endanger'd Heav'n's perpetual King;
And put to proof his high Supremacy,
Whether upheld by strength, or Chance, or Fate;[6]
Too well I see and rue the dire event,
135   That with sad overthrow and foul defeat
Hath lost us Heav'n, and all this mighty Host
In horrible destruction laid thus low,
As far as Gods and Heav'nly Essences
Can perish: for the mind and spirit remains
140   Invincible, and vigor soon returns,
Though all our Glory extinct, and happy state
Here swallow'd up in endless misery.
But what if he our Conqueror (whom I now
Of force° believe Almighty, since no less   *necessarily*
145   Than such could have o'erpow'rd such force as ours)
Have left us this our spirit and strength entire
Strongly to suffer and support our pains,
That we may so suffice° his vengeful ire,   *satisfy*
Or do him mightier service as his thralls
150   By right of War, whate'er his business be
Here in the heart of Hell to work in Fire,
Or do his Errands in the gloomy Deep;
What can it then avail though yet we feel
Strength undiminisht, or eternal being

3. Implying not only that as angels they are immortal, but
also that the continuance of their strength is assured by
fate.
4. An obvious instance of the devil's bias.
5. The traditional nine orders of angels are seraphim,
cherubim, thrones, dominions, virtues, powers, principalities, archangels, and angels, but Milton does not use
these terms systematically.
6. The main powers recognized in the devils' ideology.
God's power rests on a quality that does not occur to
Beelzebub: goodness.

155 To undergo eternal punishment?[7]
Whereto with speedy words th' Arch-fiend repli'd.
    Fall'n Cherub, to be weak is miserable
Doing or Suffering: but of this be sure,
To do aught good never will be our task,

160 But ever to do ill our sole delight,
As being the contrary to his high will
Whom we resist.[8] If then his Providence
Out of our evil seek to bring forth good,
Our labor must be to pervert that end,

165 And out of good still to find means of evil;
Which oft-times may succeed, so as perhaps
Shall grieve him, if I fail not, and disturb
His inmost counsels from thir destin'd aim.
But see the angry Victor hath recall'd

170 His Ministers of vengeance and pursuit
Back to the Gates of Heav'n: the Sulphurous Hail
Shot after us in storm, o'erblown hath laid°   subdued
The fiery Surge, that from the Precipice
Of Heav'n receiv'd us falling, and the Thunder,

175 Wing'd with red Lightning and impetuous rage,
Perhaps hath spent his shafts, and ceases now
To bellow through the vast and boundless Deep.
Let us not slip° th' occasion, whether scorn,   lose
Or satiate fury yield it from our Foe.

180 Seest thou yon dreary Plain, forlorn and wild,
The seat of desolation, void of light,
Save what the glimmering of these livid flames
Casts pale and dreadful? Thither let us tend
From off the tossing of these fiery waves,

185 There rest, if any rest can harbor there,
And reassembling our afflicted° Powers,   downcast
Consult how we may henceforth most offend°   harm
Our Enemy, our own loss how repair,
How overcome this dire Calamity,

190 What reinforcement we may gain from Hope,
If not what resolution from despair.
    Thus Satan talking to his nearest Mate
With Head up-lift above the wave, and Eyes
That sparkling blaz'd, his other Parts besides

195 Prone on the Flood, extended long and large
Lay floating many a rood,° in bulk as huge   six to eight yards
As whom the Fables name of monstrous size,
Titanian, or *Earth-born,* that warr'd on *Jove,*
Briareos or *Typhon,*[9] whom the Den

---

7. Existing eternally, merely so that our punishment may also be eternal.
8. This fundamental disobedience and disorientation make Satan's heroic virtue into the corresponding excess of vice. Lines 163–165 look forward to 12.470–78 and Adam's wonder at the astonishing reversal whereby God will turn the Fall into an occasion for good.

9. The serpent-legged *Briareos* was a Titan, the serpent-headed *Typhon* (Typhoeus) a Giant. Each was a son of Earth; each fought against Jupiter; and each was eventually confined beneath Aetna (see lines 232–37). Typhon was so powerful that when he first made war on the Olympians, they had to resort to metamorphoses to escape (Ovid, *Metamorphoses* 5.325–31 and 346–58).

200   By ancient *Tarsus*[1] held, or that Sea-beast
       Leviathan,[2] which God of all his works
       Created hugest that swim th' Ocean stream:
       Him haply slumb'ring on the *Norway* foam
       The Pilot of some small night-founder'd° Skiff,   *sunk in night*
205   Deeming some Island, oft, as Seamen tell,
       With fixed Anchor in his scaly rind
       Moors by his side under the Lee, while Night
       Invests° the Sea, and wished Morn delays: *wraps*
       So stretcht out huge in length the Arch-fiend lay
210   Chain'd on the burning Lake, nor ever thence
       Had ris'n or heav'd his head, but that the will
       And high permission of all-ruling Heaven
       Left him at large to his own dark designs,
       That with reiterated crimes he might
215   Heap on himself damnation, while he sought
       Evil to others, and enrag'd might see
       How all his malice serv'd but to bring forth
       Infinite goodness, grace and mercy shown
       On Man by him seduc't, but on himself
220   Treble confusion, wrath and vengeance pour'd.
       Forthwith upright he rears from off the Pool
       His mighty Stature; on each hand the flames
       Driv'n backward slope thir pointing spires, and roll'd
       In billows, leave i' th' midst a horrid° Vale.   *bristling*
225   Then with expanded wings he steers his flight
       Aloft, incumbent[3] on the dusky Air
       That felt unusual weight, till on dry Land
       He lights, if it were Land that ever burn'd
       With solid, as the Lake with liquid fire
230   And such appear'd in hue;[4] as when the force
       Of subterranean wind transports a Hill
       Torn from *Pelorus*,[5] or the shatter'd side
       Of thund'ring *AEtna*, whose combustible
       And fuell'd entrails thence conceiving Fire,
235   Sublim'd[6] with Mineral fury,[7] aid the Winds,
       And leave a singed bottom all involv'd°   *wreathed*
       With stench and smoke: Such resting found the sole
       Of unblest feet. Him follow'd his next Mate,
       Both glorying to have scap't the *Stygian*[8] flood
240   As Gods, and by thir own recover'd strength,
       Not by the sufferance of supernal Power.
          Is this the Region, this the Soil, the Clime,
       Said then the lost Arch-Angel, this the seat
       That we must change° for Heav'n, this mournful gloom   *exchange*

---

1. The biblical Tarsus was the capital of Cilicia, and both Pindar and Aeschylus describe Typhon's habitat as a Cilician cave or "den."

2. The monster of Job 41, identified in Isaiah's prophecy of judgement as "the crooked serpent" (Isaiah 27.1) but also sometimes thought of as a whale.

3. Pressing with his weight.

4. In the 17th century, "hue" referred to surface appearance and texture as well as color.

5. Pelorus and Aetna are volcanic mountains in Sicily.

6. Converted directly from solid to vapor by volcanic heat in such a way as to resolidify on cooling.

7. Disorder of minerals, or subterranean disorder.

8. Of the River Styx—i.e., hellish.

245 For that celestial light? Be it so, since he
Who now is Sovran can dispose and bid
What shall be right: fardest° from him is best   *farthest*
Whom reason hath equall'd, force hath made supreme
Above his equals. Farewell happy Fields
250 Where Joy for ever dwells: Hail horrors, hail
Infernal world, and thou profoundest Hell
Receive thy new Possessor: One who brings
A mind not to be chang'd by Place or Time.
The mind is its own place, and in itself
255 Can make a Heav'n of Hell, a Hell of Heav'n.⁹
What matter where, if I be still the same,
And what I should be, all but less than hee
Whom Thunder hath made greater? Here at least
We shall be free; th' Almighty hath not built
260 Here for his envy, will not drive us hence:
Here we may reign secure, and in my choice
To reign is worth ambition¹ though in Hell:
Better to reign in Hell, than serve in Heav'n.
But wherefore let we then our faithful friends,
265 Th' associates and copartners of our loss
Lie thus astonisht on th' oblivious Pool,²
And call them not to share with us their part
In this unhappy Mansion: or once more
With rallied Arms to try what may be yet
270 Regain'd in Heav'n, or what more lost in Hell?
　So *Satan* spake, and him *Beëlzebub*
Thus answer'd. Leader of those Armies bright,
Which but th' Omnipotent none could have foiled,
If once they hear that voice, thir liveliest pledge
275 Of hope in fears and dangers, heard so oft
In worst extremes, and on the perilous edge°   *front line*
Of battle when it rag'd, in all assaults
Thir surest signal, they will soon resume
New courage and revive, though now they lie
280 Groveling and prostrate on yon Lake of Fire,
As we erewhile, astounded and amaz'd;
No wonder, fall'n such a pernicious highth.
　He scarce had ceas't when the superior Fiend
Was moving toward the shore; his ponderous shield
285 Ethereal temper,³ massy, large and round,
Behind him cast; the broad circumference
Hung on his shoulders like the Moon, whose Orb
Through Optic Glass the *Tuscan* Artist⁴ views
At Ev'ning from the top of *Fesole*,

---

9. The view that heaven and hell are states of mind was held by Amaury de Bene, a medieval heretic often cited in 17th-century accounts of atheism.
1. Worth striving for (Latin *ambitio*). Satan refers not merely to a mental state but also to an active effort that is the price of power.
2. The pool attended by forgetfulness.

3. Tempered in celestial fire.
4. Galileo, who looked through a telescope ("optic glass"), had been placed under house arrest by the Inquisition near Florence, which is in the "Valdarno" or the Valley of the Arno, overlooked by the hills of "Fesole" or Fiesole.

290   Or in *Valdarno*, to descry new Lands,
         Rivers or Mountains in her spotty Globe.
         His Spear, to equal which the tallest Pine
         Hewn on *Norwegian* hills, to be the Mast
         Of some great Ammiral,° were but a wand,   *flagship*
295   He walkt with to support uneasy steps
         Over the burning Marl,° not like those steps   *ground*
         On Heaven's Azure, and the torrid Clime
         Smote on him sore besides, vaulted with Fire;
         Nathless° he so endur'd, till on the Beach   *nevertheless*
300   Of that inflamed Sea, he stood and call'd
         His Legions, Angel Forms, who lay intrans't
         Thick as Autumnal Leaves that strow the Brooks
         In *Vallombrosa*, where th' *Etrurian* shades
         High overarch't imbow'r;⁵ or scatter'd sedge
305   Afloat, when with fierce Winds *Orion* arm'd
         Hath vext the Red-Sea Coast,⁶ whose waves o'erthrew
         Busiris and his *Memphian* Chivalry,
         While with perfidious hatred they pursu'd
         The Sojourners of *Goshen*, who beheld
310   From the safe shore thir floating Carcasses
         And broken Chariot Wheels;⁷ so thick bestrown
         Abject and lost lay these, covering the Flood,
         Under amazement of thir hideous change.
         He call'd so loud, that all the hollow Deep
315   Of Hell resounded. Princes, Potentates,
         Warriors, the Flow'r of Heav'n, once yours, now lost,
         If such astonishment as this can seize
         Eternal spirits; or have ye chos'n this place
         After the toil of Battle to repose
320   Your wearied virtue,° for the ease you find   *strength*
         To slumber here, as in the Vales of Heav'n?
         Or in this abject posture have ye sworn
         To adore the Conqueror? who now beholds
         Cherub and Seraph rolling in the Flood
325   With scatter'd Arms and Ensigns,° till anon   *battle flags*
         His swift pursuers from Heav'n Gates discern
         Th' advantage, and descending tread us down
         Thus drooping, or with linked Thunderbolts
         Transfix us to the bottom of this Gulf.
330   Awake, arise, or be for ever fall'n.
               They heard, and were abasht, and up they sprung
         Upon the wing; as when men wont to watch

---

5. See Isaiah 34.4: "and all their host shall fall down, as the leaf falleth off from the vine, and as a falling fig from the fig tree." Fallen leaves were an enduring simile for the numberless dead; see Homer, *Iliad* 6.146; Virgil, *Aeneid* 6.309; Dante, *Inferno* 3.112. Milton adds an actual locality, Vallombrosa, again near Florence.
6. Commentators on Job 9.9 and Amos 5.8 interpreted the creation of Orion as a symbol of God's power to raise tempests and floods to execute his judgments. Thus Mil-

ton's transition to the Egyptians overwhelmed by God's judgment in lines 306–11 is a natural one. The Hebrew name for the Red Sea was "Sea of Sedge."
7. Contrary to his promise, the Pharaoh with his Memphian (i.e., Egyptian) charioteers pursued the Israelites—who had been in captivity in Goshen—across the Red Sea. The Israelites passed over safely; but the Egyptians' chariot wheels were broken (Exodus 14.25), and the rising sea engulfed them and cast their corpses on the shore.

On duty, sleeping found by whom they dread,
Rouse and bestir themselves ere well awake.
335 Nor did they not perceive the evil plight
In which they were, or the fierce pains not feel;
Yet to thir General's Voice they soon obey'd
Innumerable. As when the potent Rod
Of *Amram's* Son[8] in *Egypt's* evil day
340 Wav'd round the Coast, up call'd a pitchy cloud
Of *Locusts*, warping° on the Eastern Wind,   *floating*
That o'er the Realm of impious *Pharaoh* hung
Like Night, and darken'd all the Land of *Nile*:
So numberless were those bad Angels seen
345 Hovering on wing under the Cope° of Hell   *canopy*
'Twixt upper, nether, and surrounding Fires;
Till, as a signal giv'n, th' uplifted Spear
Of thir great Sultan waving to direct
Thir course, in even balance down they light
350 On the firm brimstone, and fill all the Plain;
A multitude, like which the populous North
Pour'd never from her frozen loins, to pass
Rhene or the *Danaw*, when her barbarous Sons
Came like a Deluge on the South, and spread
355 Beneath *Gibraltar* to the *Lybian* sands.[9]
Forthwith from every Squadron and each Band
The Heads and Leaders thither haste where stood
Thir great Commander; Godlike shapes and forms
Excelling human, Princely Dignities,
360 And Powers that erst in Heaven sat on Thrones;
Though of thir Names in heav'nly Records now
Be no memorial, blotted out and ras'd
By thir Rebellion, from the Books of Life.[1]
Nor had they yet among the Sons of *Eve*
365 Got them new Names, till wand'ring o'er the Earth,
Through God's high sufferance for the trial of man,
By falsities and lies the greatest part
Of Mankind they corrupted to forsake
God thir Creator, and th' invisible
370 Glory of him that made them, to transform
Oft to the Image of a Brute, adorn'd
With gay Religions° full of Pomp and Gold,   *ceremonies*
And Devils to adore for Deities:[2]
Then were they known to men by various Names,
375 And various Idols through the Heathen World.
Say, Muse, thir Names then known, who first, who last,
Rous'd from the slumber on that fiery Couch,
At thir great Emperor's call, as next in worth

8. Moses, who used his rod to bring down on the Egyptians a plague of locusts (Exodus 10.12–15).
9. The barbarian invasions of Rome began with crossings of the Rhine ("Rhene") and Danube ("Danaw") Rivers and spread to North Africa.

1. See Revelation 3.5 ("He that overcometh . . . I will not blot out his name out of the book of life") and Exodus 32.32–3.
2. The catalogue of gods here is an epic convention.

Came singly where he stood on the bare strand,
380   While the promiscuous crowd stood yet aloof?
The chief were those who from the Pit of Hell
Roaming to seek thir prey on earth, durst fix
Thir Seats long after next the Seat of God,
385   Thir Altars by his Altar, Gods ador'd
Among the Nations round, and durst abide
Jehovah thund'ring out of *Sion*, thron'd
Between the Cherubim; yea, often plac'd
Within his Sanctuary itself thir Shrines,
390   Abominations; and with cursed things
His holy Rites, and solemn Feasts profan'd,
And with thir darkness durst affront his light.
First *Moloch*,[3] horrid King besmear'd with blood
Of human sacrifice, and parents' tears,
Though for the noise of Drums and Timbrels° loud   *tambourines*
395   Thir children's cries unheard, that pass'd through fire
To his grim Idol. Him the *Ammonite*
Worshipt in *Rabba* and her wat'ry Plain,
In *Argob* and in *Basan*, to the stream
Of utmost *Arnon*.[4] Nor content with such
400   Audacious neighborhood, the wisest heart
Of *Solomon*[5] he led by fraud to build
His Temple right against the Temple of God
On that opprobrious Hill,[6] and made his Grove
The pleasant Valley of *Hinnom*, *Tophet* thence
405   And black *Gehenna* call'd, the Type of Hell.[7]
Next *Chemos*,[8] th' obscene dread of *Moab*'s Sons,
From *Aroar* to *Nebo*, and the wild
Of Southmost *Abarim*; in *Hesebon*
And *Horonaim*, *Seon*'s Realm, beyond
410   The flow'ry Dale of *Sibma* clad with Vines,
And *Eleale* to th' Asphaltic Pool.[9]
Peor[1] his other Name, when he entic'd
Israel in *Sittim* on thir march from *Nile*

---

3. Satan gathers twelve disciples: Moloch, Chemos, Baal-im, Ashtaroth, Astoreth, Thammuz, Dagon, Rimmon, Osiris, Isis, Horus, and Belial. The literal meaning of *Moloch* is "king."
4. Though ostensibly magnifying Moloch's empire, these lines look forward to his eventual defeat; for Rabba, the Ammonite royal city, is best known for its capture by David after his repentance (2 Samuel 12), while the Israelite conquest of the regions of Argob and Basan, as far as the boundary river Arnon, is recalled by Moses as particularly crushing (Deuteronomy 3.1–13).
5. Solomon's wives drew him into idolatry (1 Kings 11.5–7); but the "high places that were before Jerusalem . . . on the right hand of the mount of corruption which Solomon . . . had builded for Ashtoreth the abomination of the Zidonians, and for Chemosh the abomination of the Moabites, and Milcom the abomination of the children of Ammon" were later destroyed by Josiah (2 Kings 23.13–14).
6. The Mount of Olives, because of Solomon's idolatry

called "mount of corruption." Throughout the poem, Solomon functions as a type both of Adam and of Christ.
7. To abolish sacrifice to Moloch, Josiah "defiled Topheth, which is in the valley of the children of Hinnom" (2 Kings 23.10). Gehenna, for "Valley of Hinnom," is used in Matthew 10.28 as a name for hell.
8. "The abomination of Moab," associated with the neighboring god Moloch in 1 Kings 11.7.
9. Most of these places are named in Numbers 32 as the formerly Moabite inheritance assigned by Moses to the tribes of Reuben and Gad. Numbers 21.25–30 rejoices at the Israelite capture of Hesebon (Heshbon), a Moabite city which had been taken by the Amorite King Seon, or Sihon. Heshbon, Horonaim, "the vine of Sibmah," and Elealeh all figure in Isaiah's sad prophecy of the destruction of Moab (Isaiah 15.5, 16.8f). The Asphaltic Pool is the Dead Sea.
1. For the story of Peor, see Numbers 25.1–3 and Hosea 9.10.

	To do him wanton rites, which cost them woe.[2]
415	Yet thence his lustful Orgies he enlarg'd
	Even to that Hill of scandal, by the Grove
	Of *Moloch* homicide, lust hard by hate;
	Till good *Josiah*[3] drove them thence to Hell.
	With these came they, who from the bord'ring flood
420	Of old *Euphrates*[4] to the Brook that parts
	Egypt from *Syrian* ground, had general Names
	Of *Baalim* and *Ashtaroth*,[5] those male,
	These Feminine. For Spirits when they please
	Can either Sex assume, or both; so soft
425	And uncompounded is thir Essence pure,
	Not ti'd or manacl'd with joint or limb,
	Nor founded on the brittle strength of bones,
	Like cumbrous flesh; but in what shape they choose
	Dilated° or condens't, bright or obscure,
430	Can execute thir aery purposes,
	And works of love or enmity fulfil.
	For those the Race of *Israel* oft forsook
	Thir living strength,[6] and unfrequented left
	His righteous Altar, bowing lowly down
435	To bestial Gods; for which thir heads as low
	Bow'd down in Battle, sunk before the Spear
	Of despicable foes. With these in troop
	Came *Astoreth*, whom the *Phoenicians* call'd
	Astarte, Queen of Heav'n, with crescent Horns;[7]
440	To whose bright Image nightly by the Moon
	Sidonian Virgins paid thir Vows and Songs,
	In *Sion* also not unsung, where stood
	Her Temple on th' offensive Mountain, built
	By that uxorious King, whose heart though large,
445	Beguil'd by fair Idolatresses, fell
	To Idols foul. *Thammuz*[8] came next behind,
	Whose annual wound in *Lebanon* allur'd
	The *Syrian* Damsels to lament his fate
	In amorous ditties all a Summer's day,
450	While smooth *Adonis* from his native Rock
	Ran purple to the Sea, suppos'd with blood
	Of *Thammuz* yearly wounded: the Love-tale
	Infected *Sion's* daughters with like heat,

expanded (gloss for "Dilated°" at line 429)

2. A plague that killed 24,000 (Numbers 25.9).
3. Always a favorite with the Reformers because of his destruction of idolatrous images.
4. An area stretching from the northeast limit of Syria to the southwest limit of Canaan, the river Besor.
5. Baal is the general name for most idols; the Phoenician and Canaanite sun gods were collectively called Baalim (plural form). Astartes (Ishtars) were manifestations of the moon goddess.
6. See 1 Samuel 15.29: "Strength of Israel," a formulaic periphrasis for Jehovah.
7. The image of Astoreth or Astarte, the Sidonian (Phoenician) moon goddess and Venus, was the statue of a woman with the head of a bull above her head with horns resembling the crescent moon. "Queen of heaven": from Jeremiah 44.17–19.
8. The lover of Astarte. His identification with Adonis was based on St. Jerome's commentary on the passage in Ezekiel 8.14, drawn on by Milton in lines 454–456. The Syrian festival of Tammuz was celebrated after the summer solstice; the slaying of the young god by a boar was mourned as a symbol of the southward withdrawal of the sun and the death of vegetation. Each year when the River Adonis became discolored with red mud, it was regarded as a renewed sign of the god's wound.

Whose wanton passions in the sacred Porch
455   *Ezekiel* saw, when by the Vision led
His eye survey'd the dark Idolatries
Of alienated *Judah*. Next came one
Who mourn'd in earnest, when the Captive Ark
Maim'd his brute Image, head and hands lopt off
460   In his own Temple, on the grunsel° edge,   *threshold*
Where he fell flat, and sham'd his Worshippers:
Dagon his Name, Sea Monster, upward Man
And downward Fish:[9] yet had his Temple high
Rear'd in *Azotus*, dreaded through the Coast
465   Of *Palestine*, in *Gath* and *Ascalon*,
And *Accaron* and *Gaza's* frontier bounds.[1]
Him follow'd *Rimmon*, whose delightful Seat
Was fair *Damascus*, on the fertile Banks
Of *Abbana* and *Pharphar*, lucid streams.[2]
470   He also against the house of God was bold:
A Leper once he lost and gain'd a King,
Ahaz his sottish Conqueror, whom he drew
God's Altar to disparage and displace
For one of *Syrian* mode, whereon to burn
475   His odious off'rings, and adore the Gods
Whom he had vanquisht.[3] After these appear'd
A crew who under Names of old Renown,
Osiris, Isis, Orus and thir Train
With monstrous shapes and sorceries abus'd°   *deceived*
480   Fanatic *Egypt* and her Priests, to seek
Thir wand'ring Gods disguis'd in brutish forms
Rather than human.[4] Nor did *Israel* scape
Th' infection when thir borrow'd Gold compos'd
The Calf in *Oreb:*[5] and the Rebel King[6]
485   Doubl'd that sin in *Bethel* and in *Dan*,
Lik'ning his Maker to the Grazed Ox,[7]
Jehovah, who in one Night when he pass'd
From *Egypt* marching, equall'd with one stroke
Both her first born and all her bleating Gods.[8]

9. When the Philistines put the ark of the Lord, which they had captured, into the temple of Dagon, "on the morrow morning, behold, Dagon was fallen upon his face to the ground . . . and the head of Dagon and both the palms of his hands were cut off upon the threshold" (1 Samuel 5.4).

1. Divine vengeance on these Philistine cities is prophesied in Zephaniah 2.4.

2. When Elisha told Naaman that his leprosy would be cured if he washed in the Jordan, the Syrian was at first angry (2 Kings 5.12: "Are not Abana and Pharpar, rivers of Damascus, better than all the waters of Israel?") but then humbled himself and was cured.

3. After engineering the overthrow of Damascus by the Assyrians, the sottish (foolish) King Ahaz became interested in the cult of Rimmon and had an altar of the Syrian type put in the temple of the Lord (2 Kings 16.9–17).

4. Milton alludes to the myth of the Olympian gods fleeing from the Giant Typhoeus into Egypt and hiding in bestial forms (Ovid, *Metamorphoses* 5.319–31) afterward worshipped by the Egyptians.

5. Perhaps the most familiar of all Israelite apostasies was their worship of "a calf in Horeb" (Psalms 106.19) made by Aaron while Moses was away receiving the tables of the Law (Exodus 32).

6. Jeroboam, who led the revolt of the ten tribes of Israel against Rehoboam, Solomon's successor; he "doubled" Aaron's sin, since he made "two calves of gold," placing one in Bethel and the other in Dan (1 Kings 12.28–9).

7. "Thus they changed their glory into the similitude of an ox that eateth grass" (Psalms 106.20).

8. At the passover, Jehovah smote all the Egyptian firstborn, "both man and beast" (Exodus 12.12); presumably, this stroke would extend to their sacred animals.

490   *Belial* came last,[9] than whom a Spirit more lewd
Fell not from Heaven, or more gross to love
Vice for itself: To him no Temple stood
Or Altar smok'd; yet who more oft than hee
In Temples and at Altars, when the Priest
495   Turns Atheist, as did *Ely's* Sons, who fill'd
With lust and violence the house of God.[1]
In Courts and Palaces he also Reigns
And in luxurious Cities, where the noise
Of riot ascends above thir loftiest Tow'rs,
500   And injury and outrage: And when Night
Darkens the Streets, then wander forth the Sons
Of *Belial*, flown° with insolence and wine.[2]   *swollen*
Witness the Streets of *Sodom*, and that night
In *Gibeah*, when the hospitable door
505   Expos'd a Matron to avoid worse rape.[3]
These were the prime in order and in might;
The rest were long to tell, though far renown'd,
Th' *Ionian* Gods,[4] of *Javan's* Issue held
Gods, yet confest later than Heav'n and Earth
510   Thir boasted Parents; *Titan* Heav'n's first born
With his enormous° brood, and birthright seiz'd   *monstrous*
By younger *Saturn*, he from mightier *Jove*
His own and *Rhea's* Son like measure found;
So *Jove* usurping reign'd: these first in *Crete*
515   And *Ida* known,[5] thence on the Snowy top
Of cold *Olympus* rul'd the middle Air
Thir highest Heav'n; or on the *Delphian* Cliff,[6]
Or in *Dodona*, and through all the bounds
Of *Doric* Land;° or who with *Saturn* old   *Greece*
520   Fled over *Adria* to th' *Hesperian* Fields,
And o'er the *Celtic* roam'd the utmost Isles.[7]
All these and more came flocking; but with looks
Downcast and damp,° yet such wherein appear'd   *depressed*
Obscure some glimpse of joy, to have found thir chief
525   Not in despair, to have found themselves not lost
In loss itself; which on his count'nance cast
Like doubtful hue: but he his wonted pride
Soon recollecting,° with high words, that bore   *recovering*
Semblance of worth, not substance, gently rais'd
530   Thir fainting courage, and dispell'd thir fears.

9. Belial comes last, both because he had no local cult and because in the poem he is "timorous and slothful" (2.117). Properly, "Belial" is an abstract noun meaning "iniquity."

1. The impiety and fornication of Ely's sons are described in 1 Samuel 2.12–24.

2. The Puritans referred to their enemies as the Sons of Belial.

3. See Genesis 19 and Judges 19.

4. The Ionian Greeks were held by some to be the issue of

Javan the son of Japhet the son of Noah, on the basis of the Septuagint version of Genesis 10.

5. Jove was born and secretly reared on Mount Ida, in Crete.

6. Delphi was famed as the site of the Pythian oracle of Apollo, but cults of Ge, Poseidon, and Artemis were also celebrated there.

7. After Saturn's downfall he fled across the Adriatic Sea (Adria) to Italy (Hesperian Fields), France (the Celtic), and the British Isles (Utmost Isles).

Then straight commands that at the warlike sound
Of Trumpets loud and Clarions° be uprear'd   *shrill trumpets*
His mighty Standard; that proud honor claim'd
Azazel as his right, a Cherub tall:[8]

535   Who forthwith from the glittering Staff unfurl'd
Th' Imperial Ensign, which full high advanc't
Shone like a Meteor streaming to the Wind
With Gems and Golden lustre rich imblaz'd,[9]
Seraphic arms and Trophies: all the while

540   Sonorous metal blowing Martial sounds:
At which the universal Host upsent
A shout that tore Hell's Concave,° and beyond   *vault*
Frighted the Reign of *Chaos* and old Night.[1]
All in a moment through the gloom were seen

545   Ten thousand Banners rise into the Air
With Orient° Colors waving: with them rose   *brilliant*
A Forest huge of Spears: and thronging Helms
Appear'd, and serried° Shields in thick array   *locked together*
Of depth immeasurable: Anon they move

550   In perfect *Phalanx*[2] to the *Dorian*° mood   *solemn*
Of Flutes and soft Recorders; such as rais'd
To highth of noblest temper Heroes old
Arming to Battle, and instead of rage
Deliberate valor breath'd, firm and unmov'd

555   With dread of death to flight or foul retreat,
Nor wanting power to mitigate and swage°   *assuage*
With solemn touches, troubl'd thoughts, and chase
Anguish and doubt and fear and sorrow and pain
From mortal or immortal minds. Thus they

560   Breathing united force with fixed thought
Mov'd on in silence to soft Pipes that charm'd
Thir painful steps o'er the burnt soil; and now
Advanc't in view they stand, a horrid° Front   *bristling*
Of dreadful length and dazzling Arms, in guise

565   Of Warriors old with order'd Spear and Shield,
Awaiting what command thir mighty Chief
Had to impose: He through the armed Files
Darts his experienc't eye, and soon traverse°   *across*
The whole Battalion views, thir order due,

570   Thir visages and stature as of Gods;
Thir number last he sums. And now his heart
Distends with pride, and hard'ning in his strength
Glories: For never since created man,[3]
Met such imbodied° force, as nam'd with these   *united*

575   Could merit more than that small infantry

8. Azazel was one of the chief fallen angels who are the object of God's wrath in the apocryphal apocalypse The Book of Enoch. For the healing of the earth he is bound and cast into the same wilderness where the scapegoat was led (Enoch 10.4–8).

9. Adorned with heraldic devices.
1. Chaos and Night, rulers of the region of unformed matter between Heaven and Hell.
2. A square battle formation.
3. Since humanity was created.

Warr'd on by Cranes:[4] though all the Giant brood
Of *Phlegra* with th' Heroic Race were join'd
That fought at *Thebes* and *Ilium*, on each side
Mixt with auxiliar Gods;[5] and what resounds
580   In Fable or *Romance* of *Uther's* Son°   *King Arthur*
Begirt with *British* and *Armoric*[6] Knights;
And all who since, Baptiz'd or Infidel
Jousted in *Aspramont* or *Montalban*,
Damasco, or *Marocco*, or *Trebisond*,
585   Or whom *Biserta* sent from *Afric* shore
When *Charlemain* with all his Peerage fell
By *Fontarabbia*.[7] Thus far these beyond
Compare of mortal prowess, yet observ'd°   *obeyed*
Thir dread commander: he above the rest
590   In shape and gesture proudly eminent
Stood like a Tow'r; his form had yet not lost
All her Original brightness, nor appear'd
Less than Arch-Angel ruin'd, and th' excess
Of Glory obscur'd: As when the Sun new ris'n
595   Looks through the Horizontal misty Air
Shorn of his Beams, or from behind the Moon
In dim Eclipse disastrous twilight sheds
On half the Nations, and with fear of change
Perplexes Monarchs.[8] Dark'n'd so, yet shone
600   Above them all th' Arch-Angel: but his face
Deep scars of Thunder had intrencht, and care
Sat on his faded cheek, but under Brows
Of dauntless courage, and considerate° Pride   *deliberate*
Waiting revenge: cruel his eye, but cast
605   Signs of remorse and passion to behold
The fellows of his crime, the followers rather
(Far other once beheld in bliss) condemn'd
For ever now to have thir lot in pain,
Millions of Spirits for his fault amerc't°   *deprived*
610   Of Heav'n, and from Eternal Splendors flung
For his revolt, yet faithful how they stood,
Thir Glory wither'd. As when Heaven's Fire
Hath scath'd the Forest Oaks, or Mountain Pines,
With singed top thir stately growth though bare
615   Stands on the blasted Heath. He now prepar'd

4. When compared with the Devil's, any army would seem no bigger than pygmies ("that small infantry"), who were portrayed by Pliny as tiny men who fought with canes.
5. To amplify the heroic stature of the angels, Milton mentions a series of armies that had been thought worthy of epic treatment only to dismiss them. The Giants, who fought with the Olympians at Phlegra, join with the heroes of Thebes and Troy (Ilium).
6. From Brittany.
7. Aspramont was a castle near Nice, and Montalban was the castle of Rinaldo; these castles figure in Ariosto's *Orlando Furioso* and the romances concerned with chivalric wars between Christians and Saracens. Milton would know late versions of the Charlemagne legend. Charlemagne's whole rearguard, led by Roland, one of the 12 peers or paladins, was massacred at Roncesvalles, about 40 miles from Fontarabbia (Fuenterrabia).
8. The comparison is ironically double-edged, for the ominous solar eclipse presages not only disaster for creation but also the doom of the godlike ruler for whom the sun was a traditional symbol.

To speak; whereat thir doubl'd Ranks they bend
From wing to wing, and half enclose him round
With all his Peers: attention held them mute.
Thrice he assay'd, and thrice in spite of scorn,
620 Tears such as Angels weep, burst forth: at last
Words interwove with sighs found out thir way.
     O Myriads of immortal Spirits, O Powers
Matchless, but with th' Almighty, and that strife
Was not inglorious, though th' event° was dire,   *result*
625 As this place testifies, and this dire change
Hateful to utter: but what power of mind
Foreseeing or presaging, from the Depth
Of knowledge past or present, could have fear'd
How such united force of Gods, how such
630 As stood like these, could ever know repulse?
For who can yet believe, though after loss,
That all these puissant° Legions, whose exíle   *powerful*
Hath emptied Heav'n, shall fail to re-ascend
Self-rais'd, and repossess thir native seat?
635 For mee be witness all the Host of Heav'n,
If counsels different, or danger shunn'd
By me, have lost our hopes. But he who reigns
Monarch in Heav'n, till then as one secure
Sat on his Throne, upheld by old repute,
640 Consent or custom, and his Regal State
Put forth at full, but still his strength conceal'd,
Which tempted our attempt, and wrought our fall.
Henceforth his might we know, and know our own
So as not either to provoke, or dread
645 New War, provok't; our better part remains
To work in close° design, by fraud or guile   *secret*
What force effected not: that he no less
At length from us may find, who overcomes
By force, hath overcome but half his foe.
650 Space may produce new Worlds; whereof so rife°   *common*
There went a fame° in Heav'n that he ere long   *rumor*
Intended to create, and therein plant
A generation, whom his choice regard
Should favor equal to the Sons of Heaven:
655 Thither, if but to pry, shall be perhaps
Our first eruption, thither or elsewhere:
For this Infernal Pit shall never hold
Celestial Spirits in Bondage, nor th' Abyss
Long under darkness cover. But these thoughts
660 Full Counsel must mature: Peace is despair'd,
For who can think Submission? War then, War
Open or understood, must be resolv'd.
     He spake: and to confirm his words, out-flew
Millions of flaming swords, drawn from the thighs
665 Of mighty Cherubim; the sudden blaze
Far round illumin'd hell: highly they rag'd

Against the Highest, and fierce with grasped Arms
Clash'd on thir sounding shields the din of war,
Hurling defiance toward the Vault of Heav'n.
670   There stood a Hill not far whose grisly top
Belch'd fire and rolling smoke; the rest entire
Shone with a glossy scurf, undoubted sign
That in his womb was hid metallic Ore,
The work of Sulphur.⁹ Thither wing'd with speed
675 A numerous Brígad° hasten'd. As when bands   *brigade*
Of Píoners° with Spade and Pickax arm'd   *engineers*
Forerun the Royal Camp, to trench a Field,
Or cast a Rampart. *Mammon*¹ led them on,
Mammon, the least erected° Spirit that fell   *elevated*
680 From Heav'n, for ev'n in Heav'n his looks and thoughts
Were always downward bent, admiring more
The riches of Heav'n's pavement, trodd'n Gold,
Than aught divine or holy else enjoy'd
In vision beatific: by him first
685 Men also, and by his suggestion taught,
Ransack'd the Center, and with impious hands
Rifl'd the bowels of thir mother Earth
For Treasures better hid. Soon had his crew
Op'n'd into the Hill a spacious wound
690 And digg'd out ribs of Gold. Let none admire°   *wonder*
That riches grow in Hell; that soil may best
Deserve the precious bane. And here let those
Who boast in mortal things, and wond'ring tell
Of *Babel*, and the works of *Memphian* Kings,²
695 Learn how thir greatest Monuments of Fame,
And Strength and Art are easily outdone
By Spirits reprobate, and in an hour
What in an age they with incessant toil
And hands innumerable scarce perform.
700 Nigh on the Plain in many cells prepar'd,
That underneath had veins of liquid fire
Sluic'd° from the Lake, a second multitude   *led by channels*
With wondrous Art founded the massy Ore,
Severing each kind, and scumm'd the Bullion dross:
705 A third as soon had form'd within the ground
A various mould, and from the boiling cells
By strange conveyance fill'd each hollow nook:
As in an Organ from one blast of wind
To many a row of Pipes the sound-board breathes.
710 Anon out of the earth a Fabric huge

---

9. The traditional physiognomy of the fiend is in Milton's hell displaced onto the landscape. It is a dead or corrupt body imaged as scurf (i.e., scales, crust), belching, ransacked womb, bowels, entrails, and ribs.

1. In Matthew 6.24 and Luke 16.13, "Mammon" is an abstract noun meaning wealth, but later it was used as the name of "the prince of this world" (John 12.31). Medieval and Renaissance tradition often associated Mammon with Plutus, the Greek god of riches.

2. The Tower of Babel was built by the ambitious Nimrod. The works of Memphian kings, the Pyramids, were regarded as memorials of vanity.

Rose like an Exhalation,[3] with the sound
Of Dulcet Symphonies and voices sweet,
Built like a Temple, where *Pilasters*° round   *columns*
Were set, and Doric pillars overlaid

715   With Golden Architrave; nor did there want
Cornice or Frieze, with bossy° Sculptures grav'n;   *embossed*
The Roof was fretted° Gold. Not *Babylon*,[4]   *patterned*
Nor great *Alcairo* such magnificence
Equall'd in all thir glories,[5] to inshrine

720   *Belus*[6] or *Serapis*[7] thir Gods, or seat
Thir Kings, when *Egypt* with *Assyria* strove
In wealth and luxury. Th' ascending pile
Stood fixt her stately highth, and straight the doors
Op'ning thir brazen folds discover wide

725   Within, her ample spaces, o'er the smooth
And level pavement: from the arched roof
Pendant by subtle Magic many a row
Of Starry Lamps and blazing Cressets[8] fed
With *Naphtha* and *Asphaltus*[9] yielded light

730   As from a sky. The hasty multitude
Admiring enter'd, and the work some praise
And some the Architect: his hand was known
In Heav'n by many a Tow'red structure high,
Where Scepter'd Angels held thir residence,

735   And sat as Princes, whom the supreme King
Exalted to such power, and gave to rule,
Each in his Hierarchy, the Orders bright.
Nor was his name unheard or unador'd
In ancient *Greece*; and in *Ausonian* land

740   Men call'd him *Mulciber*;[1] and how he fell
From Heav'n, they fabl'd, thrown by angry *Jove*
Sheer o'er the Crystal Battlements: from Morn
To Noon he fell, from Noon to dewy Eve,
A Summer's day; and with the setting Sun

745   Dropt from the Zenith like a falling Star,
On *Lemnos* th' *Aegean* Isle:[2] thus they relate,
Erring; for he with this rebellious rout

3. Pandaemonium rises to music, since in the Renaissance it was believed that musical proportions governed the forms of architecture.

4. An ironic allusion to Ovid's description of the Palace of the Sun built by Mulciber (*Metamorphoses* 2. 1–4). Pandaemonium has a classical design, complete in every respect, like that of the ancient (but still surviving) gilt-roofed Pantheon, the most admired building of Milton's time. Doric is the oldest and simplest order of Greek architecture.

5. In traditional biblical exegesis, Babylon, a place of proud iniquity, was often a figure of Antichrist or of hell. Memphis (modern Cairo) was the most splendid city of heathen Egypt.

6. Bel, the Babylonian Baal; see lines 421–423n and Jeremiah 51.44: "I will punish Bel in Babylon."

7. An Egyptian deity.

8. Basketlike lamps.

9. *Naphtha* is an oily constituent of asphalt (asphaltus).

1. The Greek god Hephaistos, in Latin *Mulciber* or Vulcan, presided over all arts, such as metal-working, that required the use of fire. He built all the palaces of the gods. "Ausonian land" is the old Greek name for Italy. Milton emulates Homer's description of the daylong fall of Hephaistos (*Iliad* 1.591–95) and then deflates it in the casual but commanding dismissal of 2.746–48.

2. In Homer (*Iliad* 2.87–90) the Achaians going to a council are compared to bees, as are the Carthaginians; in Virgil (*Aeneid* 1.430–436). Milton also glances at Virgil's mock-epic account of the ideal social organization of the hive (*Georgics* 4.149–227).

Fell long before; nor aught avail'd him now
To have built in Heav'n high Tow'rs; nor did he scape
750   By all his Engines, but was headlong sent
With his industrious crew to build in hell.
Meanwhile the winged Heralds by command
Of Sovran power, with awful Ceremony
And Trumpets' sound throughout the Host proclaim
755   A solemn Council forthwith to be held
At *Pandaemonium*, the high Capitol
Of Satan and his Peers: thir summons call'd
From every Band and squared Regiment
By place or choice the worthiest; they anon
760   With hunderds and with thousands trooping came
Attended: all access was throng'd, the Gates
And Porches wide, but chief the spacious Hall
(Though like a cover'd field, where Champions bold
Wont ride in arm'd, and at the Soldan's° chair   *Sultan's*
765   Defi'd the best of *Paynim*° chivalry   *pagan*
To mortal combat or career with Lance)
Thick swarm'd, both on the ground and in the air,
Brusht with the hiss of rustling wings. As Bees
In spring time, when the Sun with *Taurus*[3] rides,
770   Pour forth thir populous youth about the Hive
In clusters; they among fresh dews and flowers
Fly to and fro, or on the smoothed Plank,
The suburb of thir Straw-built Citadel,
New rubb'd with Balm, expatiate° and confer   *debate*
775   Thir State affairs. So thick the aery crowd
Swarm'd and were strait'n'd; till the Signal giv'n,
Behold a wonder! they but now who seem'd
In bigness to surpass Earth's Giant Sons
Now less than smallest Dwarfs, in narrow room
780   Throng numberless, like that Pigmean Race
Beyond the *Indian* Mount, or Faery Elves,
Whose midnight Revels, by a Forest side
Or Fountain some belated Peasant sees,
Or dreams he sees, while over-head the Moon
785   Sits Arbitress, and nearer to the Earth
Wheels her pale course;[4] they on thir mirth and dance
Intent, with jocund Music charm his ear;
At once with joy and fear his heart rebounds.
Thus incorporeal Spirits to smallest forms
790   Reduc'd thir shapes immense, and were at large,
Though without number still amidst the Hall
Of that infernal Court. But far within
And in thir own dimensions like themselves

---

3. In Milton's time the sun entered the second sign of the zodiac in mid-April, according to the Julian calendar.
4. Echoing *A Midsummer Night's Dream* 2.1.28f and 141.

"The moon / Sits arbitress" because the moon-goddess was queen of faery.

secret

795 The great Seraphic Lords and Cherubim
In close° recess and secret conclave[5] sat   *secret*
A thousand Demi-Gods on golden seats,
Frequent° and full. After short silence then   *crowded*
And summons read, the great consult began.
The End of the First Book.

from **Book 2**

The Argument

The Consultation begun, Satan debates whether another Battle be to be hazarded for the recovery of Heaven: some advise it, others dissuade: A third proposal is preferr'd, mention'd before by Satan, to search the truth of that Prophecy or Tradition in Heaven concerning another world, and another kind of creature equal or not much inferior to themselves, about this time to be created: Thir doubt who shall be sent on this difficult search: Satan thir chief undertakes alone the voyage, is honor'd and applauded. The Council thus ended, the rest betake them several ways and to several employments, as thir inclinations lead them, to entertain the time till Satan return. He passes on his Journey to Hell Gates, finds them shut, and who sat there to guard them, by whom at length they are op'n'd, and discover[1] to him the great Gulf between Hell and Heaven; with what difficulty he passes through, directed by Chaos, the Power of that place, to the sight of this new World which he sought.

    High on a Throne of Royal State,[2] which far
Outshone the wealth of *Ormus* and of *Ind*,[3]
Or where the gorgeous East with richest hand
Show'rs on her Kings *Barbaric* Pearl and Gold,
5 Satan exalted sat, by merit rais'd
To that bad eminence; and from despair
Thus high uplifted beyond hope, aspires
Beyond thus high, insatiate to pursue
Vain War with Heav'n, and by success° untaught   *result*
10 His proud imaginations thus display'd.
    Powers and Dominions,[4] Deities of Heav'n,
For since no deep within her gulf can hold
Immortal vigor, though opprest and fall'n,
I give not Heav'n for lost. From this descent
15 Celestial Virtues rising, will appear
More glorious and more dread than from no fall
And trust themselves to fear no second fate:
Mee though just right and the fixt Laws of Heav'n
Did first create your Leader, next, free choice,
20 With what besides, in Counsel or in Fight,
Hath been achiev'd of merit, yet this loss

---

5. "Conclave" could refer to any assembly in secret session but already had the specifically ecclesiastical meaning on which Milton's satire here depends.
1. Disclose.
2. Compare Spenser's description of the bright throne of the Phaethonlike Lucifera, embodiment of pride in *The*

Faerie Queene Book 1, Canto 4.
3. India. Ormus, an island town in the Persian Gulf, was famous as a jewel market.
4. Two angelic orders mentioned by St. Paul in Colossians 1.16.

Thus far at least recover'd, hath much more
Establisht in a safe unenvied Throne
Yielded with full consent. The happier state
25 In Heav'n, which follows dignity, might draw
Envy from each inferior; but who here
Will envy whom the highest place exposes
Foremost to stand against the Thunderer's aim[5]
Your bulwark, and condemns to greatest share
30 Of endless pain? where there is then no good
For which to strive, no strife can grow up there
From Faction; for none sure will claim in Hell
Precedence, none, whose portion is so small
Of present pain, that with ambitious mind
35 Will covet more. With this advantage then
To union, and firm Faith, and firm accord,
More than can be in Heav'n, we now return
To claim our just inheritance of old,
Surer to prosper than prosperity
40 Could have assur'd us; and by what best way,
Whether of open War or covert guile,
We now debate; who can advise, may speak.
      He ceas'd, and next him *Moloch*, Scepter'd King
Stood up, the strongest and the fiercest Spirit
45 That fought in Heav'n; now fiercer by despair:
His trust was with th' Eternal to be deem'd
Equal in strength, and rather than be less
Car'd not to be at all; with that care lost
Went all his fear: of God, or Hell, or worse
50 He reck'd° not, and these words thereafter spake.   *cared*
      My sentence° is for open War: Of Wiles,   *opinion*
More unexpert,° I boast not: them let those   *inexperienced*
Contrive who need, or when they need, not now.
For while they sit contriving, shall the rest,
55 Millions that stand in Arms, and longing wait
The Signal to ascend, sit ling'ring here
Heav'n's fugitives, and for thir dwelling place
Accept this dark opprobrious Den of shame,
The Prison of his Tyranny who Reigns
60 By our delay? no, let us rather choose
Arm'd with Hell flames and fury[6] all at once
O'er Heav'n's high Tow'rs to force resistless way,
Turning our Tortures into horrid Arms
Against the Torturer; when to meet the noise
65 Of his Almighty Engine[7] he shall hear
Infernal Thunder, and for Lightning see
Black fire and horror shot with equal rage
Among his Angels; and his Throne itself

5. By identifying him with thunder, the attribute of Jupiter, Satan reduces God to a mere Olympian tyrant.
6. The violent yoking of concrete and abstract words is one of the most characteristic figures of Milton's style.
7. Machine of war, probably here referring to the Messiah's chariot or perhaps to his thunder.

Mixt with *Tartarean* Sulphur, and strange fire,[8]
70 His own invented Torments. But perhaps
The way seems difficult and steep to scale
With upright wing against a higher foe.
Let such bethink them, if the sleepy drench[9]
Of that forgetful Lake benumb not still,
75 That in our proper motion we ascend
Up to our native seat: descent and fall
To us is adverse. Who but felt of late
When the fierce Foe hung on our brok'n Rear
Insulting,° and pursu'd us through the Deep,   assaulting, exulting
80 With what compulsion and laborious flight
We sunk thus low? Th' ascent is easy then;
Th' event° is fear'd; should we again provoke   outcome
Our stronger, some worse way his wrath may find
To our destruction: if there be in Hell
85 Fear to be worse destroy'd: what can be worse
Than to dwell here, driv'n out from bliss, condemn'd
In this abhorred deep to utter woe;
Where pain of unextinguishable fire
Must exercise° us without hope of end   afflict
90 The Vassals[1] of his anger, when the Scourge
Inexorably, and the torturing hour
Calls us to Penance? More destroy'd than thus
We should be quite abolisht and expire.
What fear we then? what doubt we to incense
95 His utmost ire? which to the highth enrag'd,
Will either quite consume us, and reduce
To nothing this essential,° happier far   essence
Than miserable to have eternal being:
Or if our substance be indeed Divine,
100 And cannot cease to be, we are at worst
On this side nothing;[2] and by proof we feel
Our power sufficient to disturb his Heav'n,
And with perpetual inroads to Alarm,
Though inaccessible, his fatal Throne:
105 Which if not Victory is yet Revenge.
    He ended frowning, and his look denounc'd
Desperate revenge, and Battle dangerous
To less than Gods. On th' other side up rose
Belial, in act more graceful and humane;
110 A fairer person lost not Heav'n; he seem'd
For dignity compos'd and high exploit:
But all was false and hollow; though his Tongue
Dropt Manna, and could make the worse appear

---

8. In the classical underworld, Tartarus was the place of
the guilty. For "strange fire" see Leviticus 10.1–2: "Nadab
and Abihu, the sons of Aaron . . . offered strange fire
before the Lord, which he commanded them not. And
there went out fire from the Lord, and devoured them."
9. A draught of medicine for an animal.

1. Servants, slaves. Also an allusion to Romans 9.22:
"What if God, willing to show his wrath, and to make his
power known, endured with much longsuffering the vessels of wrath fitted to destruction . . . ?"
2. Already we are in the worst condition possible, short of
being nothing, being annihilated.

The better reason,[3] to perplex and dash
115 Maturest Counsels: for his thoughts were low;
To vice industrious, but to Nobler deeds
Timorous and slothful: yet he pleas'd the ear,
And with persuasive accent thus began.
　　　I should be much for open War, O Peers,
120 As not behind in hate; if what was urg'd
Main reason to persuade immediate War,
Did not dissuade me most, and seem to cast
Ominous conjecture on the whole success:
When he who most excels in fact° of Arms,　　　　　　*feat*
125 In what he counsels and in what excels
Mistrustful, grounds his courage on despair
And utter dissolution, as the scope
Of all his aim, after some dire revenge.
First, what Revenge? the Tow'rs of Heav'n are fill'd
130 With Armed watch, that render all access
Impregnable; oft on the bordering Deep
Encamp thir Legions, or with obscure[4] wing
Scout far and wide into the Realm of night,
Scorning surprise. Or could we break our way
135 By force, and at our heels all Hell should rise
With blackest Insurrection, to confound
Heav'n's purest Light, yet our great Enemy
All incorruptible would on his Throne
Sit unpolluted, and th' Ethereal mould
140 Incapable of stain would soon expel
Her mischief, and purge off the baser fire
Victorious.[5] Thus repuls'd, our final hope
Is flat° despair: we must exasperate　　　　　　　　*absolute*
Th' Almighty Victor to spend all his rage,
145 And that must end us, that must be our cure,
To be no more; sad cure; for who would lose,
Though full of pain, this intellectual being,
Those thoughts that wander through Eternity,
To perish rather, swallow'd up and lost
150 In the wide womb of uncreated night,
Devoid of sense and motion? and who knows,
Let this be good,[6] whether our angry Foe
Can give it, or will ever? how he can
Is doubtful; that he never will is sure.
155 Will he, so wise, let loose at once his ire,
Belike° through impotence, or unaware,　　　　　　*no doubt*
To give his Enemies thir wish, and end
Them in his anger, whom his anger saves
To punish endless? wherefore cease we then?

3. This was the claim of the Greek Sophists, who taught their students how to use rhetoric to win an argument.
4. "Obscure" is stressed on the first syllable here.
5. Criticizing Moloch's proposal to mix God's throne with sulphur (lines 68–9) and shoot "black fire" among

his angels. This "baser fire" Belial contrasts with the "ethereal" (derived from ether, the fifth and purest element) fire of the throne.
6. Suppose it is good to be destroyed.

160   Say they who counsel War, we are decreed,
       Reserv'd and destin'd to Eternal woe;
       Whatever doing, what can we suffer more,
       What can we suffer worse? is this then worst,
       Thus sitting, thus consulting, thus in Arms?
165   What when we fled amain,° pursu'd and strook°   *headlong/struck*
       With Heav'n's afflicting Thunder, and besought
       The Deep to shelter us? this Hell then seem'd
       A refuge from those wounds: or when we lay
       Chain'd on the burning Lake? that sure was worse.
170   What if the breath that kindl'd those grim fires
       Awak'd should blow them into sevenfold rage
       And plunge us in the flames? or from above
       Should intermitted vengeance arm again
       His red right hand to plague us? what if all
175   Her° stores were op'n'd, and this Firmament   *Hell's*
       Of Hell should spout her Cataracts of Fire,
       Impendent° horrors, threat'ning hideous fall   *threatening*
       One day upon our heads; while we perhaps
       Designing or exhorting glorious war,
180   Caught in a fiery Tempest shall be hurl'd
       Each on his rock transfixt, the sport and prey
       Of racking whirlwinds, or for ever sunk
       Under yon boiling Ocean, wrapt in Chains;
       There to converse with everlasting groans,
185   Unrespited, unpitied, unrepriev'd,
       Ages of hopeless end; this would be worse.
       War therefore, open or conceal'd, alike
       My voice dissuades; for what can force or guile
       With him, or who deceive his mind, whose eye
190   Views all things at one view? he from Heav'n's highth
       All these our motions° vain, sees and derides;   *schemes*
       Not more Almighty to resist our might
       Than wise to frustrate all our plots and wiles.
       Shall we then live thus vile, the race of Heav'n
195   Thus trampl'd, thus expell'd to suffer here
       Chains and these Torments? better these than worse
       By my advice; since fate inevitable
       Subdues us, and Omnipotent Decree,
       The Victor's will. To suffer, as to do,
200   Our strength is equal, nor the Law unjust
       That so ordains: this was at first resolv'd,
       If we were wise, against so great a foe
       Contending, and so doubtful what might fall.
       I laugh, when those who at the Spear are bold
205   And vent'rous, if that fail them, shrink and fear
       What yet they know must follow, to endure
       Exile, or ignominy, or bonds, or pain,
       The sentence of thir Conqueror: This is now
       Our doom; which if we can sustain and bear,
210   Our Supreme Foe in time may much remit

His anger, and perhaps thus far remov'd
Not mind us not offending, satisfi'd
With what is punisht; whence these raging fires
Will slack'n, if his breath stir not thir flames.
215   Our purer essence then will overcome
Thir noxious vapor, or enur'd° not feel,   *accustomed*
Or chang'd at length, and to the place conform'd
In temper[7] and in nature, will receive
Familiar the fierce heat, and void of pain;
220   This horror will grow mild, this darkness light,[8]
Besides what hope the never-ending flight
Of future days may bring, what chance, what change
Worth waiting, since our present lot appears
For happy though but ill, for ill not worst,[9]
225   If we procure not to ourselves more woe.
        Thus *Belial* with words cloth'd in reason's garb
Counsell'd ignoble ease, and peaceful sloth,
Not peace: and after him thus *Mammon* spake.
        Either to disinthrone the King of Heav'n
230   We war, if war be best, or to regain
Our own right lost: him to unthrone we then
May hope, when everlasting Fate shall yield
To fickle Chance, and *Chaos* judge the strife:
The former vain to hope argues as vain
235   The latter: for what place can be for us
Within Heav'n's bound, unless Heav'n's Lord supreme
We overpower? Suppose he should relent
And publish Grace to all, on promise made
Of new Subjection; with what eyes could we
240   Stand in his presence humble, and receive
Strict Laws impos'd, to celebrate his Throne
With warbl'd Hymns, and to his Godhead sing
Forc't Halleluiahs;[1] while he Lordly sits
Our envied Sovran, and his Altar breathes
245   Ambrosial[2] Odors and Ambrosial Flowers,
Our servile offerings. This must be our task
In Heav'n, this our delight; how wearisome
Eternity so spent in worship paid
To whom we hate. Let us not then pursue
250   By force impossible, by leave obtain'd
Unácceptable, though in Heav'n, our state
Of splendid vassalage, but rather seek
Our own good from ourselves, and from our own
Live to ourselves, though in this vast recess,
255   Free, and to none accountable, preferring

7. Temperament, the mixture or adjustment of humors. Thus the phrase means "adjusted psychologically and physically to the new environment."
8. Easy to bear, and illumination.
9. Though as far as happiness is concerned, the devils are but ill off, as far as evil is concerned, they could be worse.

1. The word "hallelujah" (Hebrew, "praise Jehovah") occurred in so many psalms that it came to mean a song of praise to God.
2. Fragrant and perfumed, immortal. Ambrosia was the fabled food or drink of the gods.

Hard liberty before the easy yoke
Of servile Pomp.[3] Our greatness will appear
Then most conspicuous, when great things of small,
Useful of hurtful, prosperous of adverse
260 We can create, and in what place soe'er
Thrive under evil, and work ease out of pain
Through labor and endurance. This deep world
Of darkness do we dread? How oft amidst
Thick clouds and dark doth Heav'n's all-ruling Sire
265 Choose to reside, his Glory unobscur'd,
And with the Majesty of darkness round
Covers his Throne; from whence deep thunders roar
Must'ring thir rage, and Heav'n resembles Hell?
As he our darkness, cannot we his Light
270 Imitate when we please? This Desert soil
Wants not her hidden lustre, Gems and Gold;
Nor want we skill or art, from whence to raise
Magnificence; and what can Heav'n show more?
Our torments also may in length of time
275 Become our Elements, these piercing Fires
As soft as now severe, our temper chang'd
Into their temper;[4] which must needs remove
The sensible of pain.[5] All things invite
To peaceful Counsels, and the settl'd State
280 Of order, how in safety best we may
Compose° our present evils, with regard   *order*
Of what we are and where, dismissing quite
All thoughts of War; ye have what I advise.
　　　He scarce had finisht, when such murmur fill'd
285 Th' Assembly, as when hollow Rocks retain
The sound of blust'ring winds, which all night long
Had rous'd the Sea, now with hoarse cadence lull
Sea-faring men o'erwatcht, whose Bark by chance
Or Pinnace anchors in a craggy Bay
290 After the Tempest: Such applause was heard
As *Mammon* ended, and his Sentence° pleas'd,   *opinion*
Advising peace: for such another Field
They dreaded worse than Hell: so much the fear
Of Thunder and the Sword of *Michaël*[6]
295 Wrought still within them; and no less desire
To found this nether Empire, which might rise
By policy,[7] and long process of time,
In emulation opposite to Heav'n.

3. In *Samson Agonistes* 271, Samson condemns those who are fonder of "bondage with ease than strenuous liberty." The antithesis is from the Roman historian, Sallust, who assigns it to an opponent of the dictator Sulla. See also Jesus' words in Matthew 11.28–30: "Come unto me. . . . For my yoke is easy."
4. Milton alludes to an idea of St. Augustine's, that the devils are bound to tormenting fires as if to bodies (*City of God*, 21.10).
5. The part of pain apprehended through the senses.
6. In the war in Heaven, Michael's two-handed sword felled "squadrons at once" and wounded even Satan. "Michael" here has three syllables.
7. Statesmanship, often in a bad sense, implying Machiavellian strategems. "Process" is stressed on the second syllable.

300	Which when *Beëlzebub*[8] perceiv'd, than whom,
	Satan except, none higher sat, with grave
	Aspect he rose, and in his rising seem'd
	A Pillar of State; deep on his Front° engraven *forehead*
	Deliberation sat and public care;
	And Princely counsel in his face yet shone,
305	Majestic though in ruin: sage he stood
	With *Atlantean*[9] shoulders fit to bear
	The weight of mightiest Monarchies; his look
	Drew audience and attention still as Night
	Or Summer's Noon-tide air, while thus he spake.
310	Thrones and Imperial Powers, off-spring of Heav'n,
	Ethereal Virtues; or these Titles now
	Must we renounce, and changing style be call'd
	Princes of Hell? for so the popular vote
	Inclines, here to continue, and build up here
315	A growing Empire; doubtless; while we dream,
	And know not that the King of Heav'n hath doom'd
	This place our dungeon, not our safe retreat
	Beyond his Potent arm, to live exempt
	From Heav'n's high jurisdiction, in new League
320	Banded against his Throne, but to remain
	In strictest bondage, though thus far remov'd,
	Under th' inevitable curb, reserv'd
	His captive multitude: For he, be sure,
	In highth or depth, still first and last will Reign
325	Sole King, and of his Kingdom lose no part
	By our revolt, but over Hell extend
	His Empire, and with Iron Sceptre rule
	Us here, as with his Golden those in Heav'n.
	What° sit we then projecting peace and war? *why*
330	War hath determin'd[1] us, and foil'd with loss
	Irreparable; terms of peace yet none
	Voutsaf't[2] or sought; for what peace will be giv'n
	To us enslav'd, but custody severe,
	And stripes, and arbitrary punishment
335	Inflicted? and what peace can we return,
	But to our power[3] hostility and hate,
	Untam'd reluctance,° and revenge though slow, *resistance*
	Yet ever plotting how the Conqueror least
	May reap his conquest, and may least rejoice
340	In doing what we most in suffering feel?[4]
	Nor will occasion want, nor shall we need
	With dangerous expedition to invade

8. Satan's closest associate.
9. Worthy of Atlas, who was forced by Jupiter to carry the heavens on his shoulders as a punishment for his part in the rebellion of the Titans.
1. Finished, but the context also activates a subsidiary meaning, "war has given us a settled aim."

2. "Vouchsafed": granted; Milton's spelling, "Voutsaf't," indicates the 17th-century pronunciation he preferred.
3. To the limit of our power.
4. How God may get the least happiness from our pain. Beelzebub portrays God as similar in his motives to the devils.

Heav'n, whose high walls fear no assault or Siege,
Or ambush from the Deep. What if we find
345   Some easier enterprise? There is a place
(If ancient and prophetic fame in Heav'n
Err not) another World, the happy seat
Of some new Race call'd *Man*, about this time
To be created like to us, though less
350   In power and excellence, but favor'd more
Of him who rules above;[5] so was his will
Pronounc'd among the Gods, and by an Oath,
That shook Heav'n's whole circumference, confirm'd.[6]
Thither let us bend all our thoughts, to learn
355   What creatures there inhabit, of what mould,
Or substance, how endu'd,° and what thir Power,   *gifted*
And where thir weakness, how attempted° best,   *attacked*
By force or subtlety: Though Heav'n be shut,
And Heav'n's high Arbitrator sit secure
360   In his own strength, this place may lie expos'd
The utmost border of his Kingdom, left
To their defense who hold it: here perhaps
Some advantageous act may be achiev'd
By sudden onset, either with Hell fire
365   To waste his whole Creation, or possess
All as our own, and drive as we were driven,
The puny° habitants, or if not drive,   *weak*
Seduce them to our Party, that thir God
May prove thir foe, and with repenting hand
370   Abolish his own works. This would surpass
Common revenge, and interrupt his joy
In our Confusion, and our Joy upraise
In his disturbance; when his darling Sons
Hurl'd headlong to partake with us,[7] shall curse
375   Thir frail Original,° and faded bliss,   *author*
Faded so soon. Advise if this be worth
Attempting, or to sit in darkness here
Hatching vain Empires. Thus *Beëlzebub*
Pleaded his devilish Counsel, first devis'd
380   By *Satan*, and in part propos'd: for whence,
But from the Author of all ill could Spring
So deep a malice, to confound the race
Of mankind in one root,[8] and Earth with Hell
To mingle and involve, done all to spite
385   The great Creator? But thir spite still serves
His glory to augment. The bold design
Pleas'd highly those infernal States,[9] and joy

5. The creation of humanity was the subject of a public oath by God, but the time of the creation was the subject of a rumor only ("it is not for you to know the times or season," Acts 1.7).
6. See Isaiah 13.12–3: "I will make a man more precious than fine gold. . . . Therefore I will shake the Heavens."
7. Share in our condition; also, take sides with us.
8. Adam, the root of the genealogical tree of man.
9. Estates of the realm, people of rank and authority.

Sparkl'd in all thir eyes; with full assent
They vote: whereat his speech he thus renews.

390   Well have ye judg'd, well ended long debate,
Synod[1] of Gods, and like to what ye are,
Great things resolv'd, which from the lowest deep
Will once more lift us up, in spite of Fate,
Nearer our ancient Seat; perhaps in view

395   Of those bright confines, whence with neighboring Arms
And opportune excursion we may chance
Re-enter Heav'n; or else in some mild Zone
Dwell not unvisited of Heav'n's fair Light
Secure, and at the bright'ning Orient beam

400   Purge off this gloom; the soft delicious Air,
To heal the scar of these corrosive Fires
Shall breathe her balm. But first whom shall we send
In search of this new world, whom shall we find
Sufficient? who shall tempt° with wand'ring feet   venture upon

405   The dark unbottom'd infinite Abyss
And through the palpable obscure[2] find out
His uncouth° way, or spread his aery flight   unknown
Upborne with indefatigable wings
Over the vast abrupt,[3] ere he arrive

410   The happy Isle; what strength, what art can then
Suffice, or what evasion bear him safe
Through the strict Senteries° and Stations thick   sentries
Of Angels watching round? Here he had need
All circumspection, and wee now no less

415   Choice in our suffrage;[4] for on whom we send,
The weight of all and our last hope relies.
      This said, he sat; and expectation held
His look suspense, awaiting who appear'd
To second, or oppose, or undertake

420   The perilous attempt; but all sat mute,
Pondering the danger with deep thoughts; and each
In other's count'nance read his own dismay
Astonisht: none among the choice and prime
Of those Heav'n-warring Champions could be found

425   So hardy as to proffer° or accept   offer
Alone the dreadful voyage; till at last
Satan, whom now transcendent glory rais'd
Above his fellows, with Monarchal pride
Conscious of highest worth, unmov'd thus spake.

430   O Progeny of Heav'n, Empyreal Thrones,
With reason hath deep silence and demur°   delay
Seiz'd us, though undismay'd: long is the way
And hard, that out of Hell leads up to light;

---

1. A meeting of councillors.
2. See Exodus 10.21: "The Lord said unto Moses, Stretch out thine hand toward heaven, that there may be darkness over the land of Egypt, even darkness which may be felt."

3. The adjective (precipitous, broken off) is here used as a noun and refers to the abyss between hell and heaven.
4. Care in our vote (to elect him).

	Our prison strong, this huge convex° of Fire,	*vault*
435	Outrageous to devour, immures us round	
	Ninefold, and gates of burning Adamant	
	Barr'd over us prohibit all egress.	
	These past, if any pass, the void profound	
	Of unessential° Night receives him next	*empty*
440	Wide gaping, and with utter loss of being	
	Threatens him, plung'd in that abortive gulf.	
	If thence he scape into whatever world,	
	Or unknown Region, what remains him less	
	Than⁵ unknown dangers and as hard escape.	
445	But I should ill become this Throne, O Peers,	
	And this Imperial Sov'ranty, adorn'd	
	With splendor, arm'd with power, if aught propos'd	
	And judg'd of public moment, in the shape	
	Of difficulty or danger could deter	
450	Mee from attempting. Wherefore do I assume	
	These Royalties, and not refuse to Reign,	
	Refusing⁶ to accept as great a share	
	Of hazard as of honor, due alike	
	To him who Reigns, and so much to him due	
455	Of hazard more, as he above the rest	
	High honor'd sits? Go therefore mighty Powers.	
	Terror of Heav'n, though fall'n; intend° at home,	*consider*
	While here shall be our home, what best may ease	
	The present misery, and render Hell	
460	More tolerable; if there be cure or charm	
	To respite° or deceive, or slack the pain	*rest*
	Of this ill Mansion: intermit no watch	
	Against a wakeful Foe, while I abroad	
	Through all the Coasts of dark destruction seek	
465	Deliverance for us all: this enterprise	
	None shall partake with me. Thus saying rose	
	The Monarch, and prevented all reply,	
	Prudent, lest from his resolution rais'd°	*encouraged*
	Others among the chief might offer now	
470	(Certain to be refus'd) what erst they fear'd;	
	And so refus'd might in opinion stand	
	His Rivals, winning cheap the high repute	
	Which he through hazard huge must earn. But they	
	Dreaded not more th' adventure than his voice	
475	Forbidding; and at once with him they rose;	
	Thir rising all at once was as the sound	
	Of Thunder heard remote. Towards him they bend	
	With awful° reverence prone; and as a God	*respectful*
	Extol him equal to the highest in Heav'n:	
480	Nor fail'd they to express how much they prais'd,	
	That for the general safety he despis'd	
	His own: for neither do the Spirits damn'd	

---

5. What awaits him except.   6. If I refuse.

Lose all thir virtue; lest bad men should boast[7]
Thir specious° deeds on earth, which glory excites,   *pretending*
485   Or close° ambition varnisht o'er with zeal.   *secret*
Thus they thir doubtful consultations dark
Ended rejoicing in their matchless Chief:
As when from mountain tops the dusky clouds
Ascending, while the North wind sleeps, o'erspread
490   Heav'n's cheerful face, the low'ring Element
Scowls o'er the dark'n'd lantskip° Snow, or show'r;   *landscape*
If chance the radiant Sun with farewell sweet
Extend his ev'ning beam, the fields revive,
The birds thir notes renew, and bleating herds
495   Attest thir joy, that hill and valley rings.
O shame to men! Devil with Devil damn'd
Firm concord holds, men only disagree
Of Creatures rational, though under hope
Of heavenly Grace; and God proclaiming peace,
500   Yet live in hatred, enmity, and strife
Among themselves, and levy cruel wars,
Wasting the Earth, each other to destroy:
As if (which might induce us to accord)
Man had not hellish foes anow° besides,   *enough*
505   That day and night for his destruction wait.
    The *Stygian* Council thus dissolv'd; and forth
In order came the grand infernal Peers:
Midst came thir mighty Paramount,° and seem'd   *ruler*
Alone th' Antagonist of Heav'n, nor less
510   Than Hell's dread Emperor with pomp Supreme,[8]
And God-like imitated State; him round
A Globe° of fiery Seraphim inclos'd   *band*
With bright imblazonry,° and horrent° Arms.   *heraldry/bristling*
Then of thir Session ended they bid cry
515   With Trumpet's regal sound the great result:
Toward the four winds four speedy Cherubim
Put to thir mouths the sounding Alchymy[9]
By Herald's voice explain'd: the hollow Abyss
Heard far and wide, and all the host of Hell
520   With deaf'ning shout, return'd them loud acclaim.
Thence more at ease thir minds and somewhat rais'd°   *encouraged*
By false presumptuous hope, the ranged powers[1]
Disband, and wand'ring, each his several way
Pursues, as inclination or sad choice
525   Leads him perplext, where he may likeliest find
Truce to his restless thoughts, and entertain
The irksome hours, till this great Chief return.
Part on the Plain, or in the Air sublime°   *uplifted*
Upon the wing, or in swift Race contend,

---

7. So that men ought not to boast.
8. Lines 510–520 may portray the English mob's easy gullibility and their passion (which Milton detested) for the
regalia of monarchy.

9. Trumpets made of the alloy brass, associated with
alchemy.
1. Armies drawn up in ranks.

530	As at th' *Olympian* Games or *Pythian* fields;[2]
	Part curb thir fiery Steeds, or shun the Goal
	With rapid wheels, or fronted Brígads form.
	As when to warn proud Cities war appears
	Wag'd in the troubl'd Sky, and Armies rush
535	To Battle in the Clouds, before each Van
	Prick forth the Aery Knights, and couch thir spears
	Till thickest Legions close; with feats of Arms
	From either end of Heav'n the welkin° burns.
	Others with vast *Typhoean*[3] rage more fell
540	Rend up both Rocks and Hills, and ride the Air
	In whirlwind; Hell scarce holds the wild uproar.
	As when *Alcides* from *Oechalia* Crown'd
	With conquest, felt th' envenom'd robe, and tore
	Through pain up by the roots *Thessalian* Pines,
545	And *Lichas* from the top of *Oeta* threw
	Into th' *Euboic* Sea.[4] Others more mild,
	Retreated in a silent valley, sing
	With notes Angelical to many a Harp
	Thir own Heroic deeds and hapless fall
550	By doom of Battle; and complain that Fate
	Free Virtue should enthrall to Force or Chance.
	Thir Song was partial,° but the harmony
	(What could it less when Spirits immortal sing?)
	Suspended° Hell, and took with ravishment
555	The thronging audience. In discourse more sweet
	(For Eloquence the Soul, Song charms the Sense,)
	Others apart sat on a Hill retir'd,
	In thoughts more elevate, and reason'd high
	Of Providence, Foreknowledge, Will, and Fate,
560	Fixt Fate, Free will, Foreknowledge absolute,
	And found no end, in wand'ring mazes lost.
	Of good and evil much they argu'd then,
	Of happiness and final misery,
	Passion and Apathy, and glory and shame,
565	Vain wisdom all, and false Philosophie:[5]
	Yet with a pleasing sorcery could charm
	Pain for a while or anguish, and excite
	Fallacious hope, or arm th' obdured° breast
	With stubborn patience as with triple steel.
570	Another part in Squadrons and gross° Bands,
	On bold adventure to discover wide
	That dismal World, if any Clime perhaps

sky (line 538)

prejudiced (line 552)

enthralled (line 554)

hardened (line 568)

dense (line 570)

2. Epic models for lines 528–569 include the sports of the Myrmidons during Achilles' absence from the war (Homer, *Iliad* 2.774ff.), the Greek funeral games of *Iliad* 23 and the Trojan of *Aeneid* 5, and the amusements of the blessed dead in Virgil's Elysium (*Aeneid* 6.642–59). To "shun the goal" (line 531) is to drive a chariot as close as possible around a post without touching it.
3. Like that of Typhon, the hundred-headed Titan. A pun, for "typhon" was also an English word meaning "whirlwind."

4. "Alcides" (Hercules) returning as victor from "Oechalia" (Ovid, *Metamorphoses* 9.136) put on a ritual robe that had inadvertently been soaked by his wife in corrosive poison. Mad with pain, he blamed his friend Lichas, who had brought the robe, and hurled him far into the "Euboic" (Euboean) Sea.
5. Directed against Stoicism, the most formidable ethical challenge to Christianity; "apathy," or complete freedom from passion, was a Stoic ideal.

Might yield them easier habitation, bend
Four ways thir flying March, along the Banks
575   Of four infernal Rivers that disgorge
Into the burning Lake thir baleful° streams;[6]   *evil*
Abhorred *Styx* the flood of deadly hate,
Sad *Acheron* of sorrow, black and deep;
Cocytus, nam'd of lamentation loud
580   Heard on the rueful stream; fierce *Phlegeton*
Whose waves of torrent fire inflame with rage.
Far off from these a slow and silent stream,
Lethe the River of Oblivion rolls
Her wat'ry Labyrinth, whereof who drinks,
585   Forthwith his former state and being forgets,
Forgets both joy and grief, pleasure and pain.
Beyond this flood a frozen Continent
Lies dark and wild, beat with perpetual storms
Of Whirlwind and dire Hail, which on firm land
590   Thaws not, but gathers heap, and ruin seems
Of ancient pile; all else deep snow and ice,
A gulf profound as that *Serbonian* Bog[7]
Betwixt *Damiata* and Mount *Casius* old,
Where Armies whole have sunk: the parching° Air   *withering*
595   Burns frore,° and cold performs th' effect of Fire.   *frozen*
Thither by harpy-footed Furies hal'd,[8]
At certain revolutions all the damn'd
Are brought: and feel by turns the bitter change
Of fierce extremes, extremes by change more fierce,
600   From Beds of raging Fire to starve° in Ice   *stifle*
Thir soft Ethereal warmth, and there to pine
Immovable, infixt, and frozen round,
Periods of time, thence hurried back to fire.
They ferry over this *Lethean* Sound
605   Both to and fro, thir sorrow to augment,
And wish and struggle, as they pass, to reach
The tempting stream, with one small drop to lose
In sweet forgetfulness all pain and woe,
All in one moment, and so near the brink;
610   But Fate withstands, and to oppose th' attempt
Medusa[9] with *Gorgonian* terror guards
The Ford, and of itself the water flies
All taste of living wight, as once it fled
The lip of *Tantalus.*[1] Thus roving on
615   In confus'd march forlorn, th' advent'rous Bands

---

6. This description of the four rivers of hell takes its broad outline from Virgil's (*Aeneid* 6), Dante's *Inferno* 14, and Spenser's *Faerie Queene* 2.7.56ff. Milton adds the detail of confluence in the "burning lake." The epithet or description attached to each river translates its Greek name (e.g., "Styx" means hateful).
7. Serbonis, a lake bordered by quicksands on the Egyptian coast.

8. Milton combines the hook-clawed Harpies of Dante and Virgil with the ancient Greek Furies, daughters of Acheron and Night and agencies of divine vengeance.
9. One of the Gorgons, mythical sisters with snakes for hair, whose look turned the beholder into stone.
1. In Homer's hell, Tantalus is tormented by thirst, standing in a pool that recedes whenever he tries to drink (*Odyssey* 11.582–92).

With shudd'ring horror pale, and eyes aghast
View'd first thir lamentable lot, and found
No rest: through many a dark and dreary Vale
They pass'd, and many a Region dolorous,
620   O'er many a Frozen, many a Fiery Alp,
Rocks, Caves, Lakes, Fens, Bogs, Dens, and shades of death,
A Universe of death, which God by curse
Created evil, for evil only good,
Where all life dies, death lives, and Nature breeds,
625   Perverse, all monstrous, all prodigious things,
Abominable, inutterable, and worse
Than Fables yet have feign'd, or fear conceiv'd,
Gorgons and *Hydras*, and *Chimeras* dire.[2]

* * *

from Book 3
The Argument

God *sitting on his Throne sees Satan flying towards this world, then newly created; shows him to the Son who sat at his right hand; foretells the success of Satan in perverting mankind; clears his own Justice and Wisdom from all imputation, having created Man free and able enough to have withstood his Tempter; yet declares his purpose of grace towards him, in regard he fell not of his own malice, as did Satan, but by him seduc't. The Son of God renders praises to his Father for the manifestation of his gracious purpose towards Man; but God again declares, that Grace cannot be extended towards Man without the satisfaction of divine Justice; Man hath offended the majesty of God by aspiring to Godhead, and therefore with all his Progeny devoted to death must die, unless some one can be found sufficient to answer for his offense, and undergo his Punishment. The Son of God freely offers himself a Ransom for Man: the Father accepts him, ordains his incarnation, pronounces his exaltation above all Names in Heaven and Earth; commands all the Angels to adore him; they obey, and hymning to thir Harps in full Choir, celebrate the Father and the Son. Meanwhile Satan alights upon the bare convex of this World's outermost Orb; where wand'ring he first finds a place since call'd The Limbo of Vanity; what persons and things fly up thither; thence comes to the Gate of Heaven, describ'd ascending by stairs, and the waters above the Firmament that flow about it: His passage thence to the Orb of the Sun; he finds there Uriel the Regent of that Orb, but first changes himself into the shape of a meaner Angel; and pretending a zealous desire to behold the new Creation and Man whom God had plac't there, inquires of him the place of his habitation, and is directed; alights first on Mount Niphates.*

Hail holy Light, offspring of Heav'n first-born,
Or of th' Eternal Coeternal beam
May I express thee unblam'd?[1] since God is Light,

---

2. The Hydra was many-headed, and the Chimeras breathed flame.

1. The light of the invocation has been interpreted as the Son of God, as physical light, and as the principal image of God and the divine emanation itself, according to the Platonic system. Milton proposes three images or forms of address, "offspring," "beam," and "stream," each of which associates the divine Light or Wisdom with a different aspect of deity. The blame could attach only to using the second name, "co-eternal beam"; it is this name that is justified by the implicit appeal to scriptural authority.

And never but in unapproached Light
5   Dwelt from Eternity, dwelt then in thee,
Bright effluence° of bright essence increate.[2]   *radiance*
Or hear'st thou rather[3] pure Ethereal stream,
Whose Fountain who shall tell? before the Sun,
Before the Heavens thou wert, and at the voice
10   Of God, as with a Mantle didst invest°   *cover*
The rising world of waters dark and deep,
Won from the void° and formless infinite.[4]   *chaos*
Thee I revisit now with bolder wing,
Escap't the *Stygian* Pool, though long detain'd
15   In that obscure sojourn, while in my flight
Through utter and through middle darkness borne[5]
With other notes than to th' *Orphean* Lyre
I sung of *Chaos* and *Eternal Night*,
Taught by the heav'nly Muse° to venture down   *Urania*
20   The dark descent, and up to reascend,
Though hard and rare:[6] thee I revisit safe,
And feel thy sovran vital Lamp; but thou
Revisit'st not these eyes, that roll in vain
To find thy piercing ray, and find no dawn;
25   So thick a drop serene[7] hath quencht thir Orbs,
Or dim suffusion° veil'd. Yet not the more   *cataract*
Cease I to wander where the Muses haunt
Clear Spring, or shady Grove, or Sunny Hill,
Smit with the love of sacred Song;[8] but chief
30   Thee *Sion*[9] and the flow'ry Brooks beneath
That wash thy hallow'd feet, and warbling flow,
Nightly I visit: nor sometimes forget
Those other two equall'd with me in Fate,
So were I equall'd with them in renown,
35   Blind *Thamyris* and blind *Maeonides*,
And *Tiresias* and *Phineus* Prophets old.[1]
Then feed on thoughts, that voluntary move
Harmonious numbers;° as the wakeful Bird[2]   *rhythmic measure*
Sings darkling,° and in shadiest Covert hid   *in the dark*

2. "God is Light," from 1 John 1.5. God "only hath immortality, dwelling in the light which no man can approach unto" (1 Timothy 6.16). "Essence increate," the uncreated divine essence. In the physics and metaphysics of Milton's time, light was regarded as an "accident" (quality), not a body or substance.
3. Do you prefer to be called.
4. See Genesis 1.1–5.
5. The "Stygian pool" and the "utter" (outer) darkness are hell; the "middle darkness" is chaos.
6. Alluding to the "fable of Orpheus, whom they faigne to have recovered his Euridice from Hell with his Musick, that is, Truth and Equity from darkenesse of Barbarisme and Ignorance with his profound and excellent Doctrines; but, that in the way to the upper-earth, she was lost againe" (Henry Reynolds, *Mythomystes*). "Other notes," because Milton, unlike Orpheus, claims not to have lost his Eurydice.

7. Literally translating *gutta serena*, the medical term for the form of blindness from which Milton suffered.
8. An allusion to Virgil's prayer that "smitten with a great love" of the Muses, he may be shown by them the secrets of nature (*Georgics* 2.475–489).
9. The mountain of scriptural inspiration.
1. Thamyris was a Thracian poet who fell in love with the Muses and challenged them to a contest in which the loser was to give the winner whatever he wanted. The Muses, having won, took Thamyris's eyes and his lyre. Maeonides was Homer's surname; the contrast between his outward blindness and inner vision was a commonplace. In *De Idea Platonica*, Milton writes of Tiresias that his "very blindness gave him boundless light." The Thracian king Phineus lost his sight because he had become too good a prophet.
2. The nightingale. The soul of Thamyris passed into a nightingale.

40   Tunes her nocturnal Note. Thus with the Year
      Seasons return, but not to me returns
      Day, or the sweet approach of Ev'n or Morn,
      Or sight of vernal bloom, or Summer's Rose,
      Or flocks, or herds, or human face divine;
45   But cloud instead, and ever-during dark
      Surrounds me, from the cheerful ways of men
      Cut off, and for the Book of knowledge[3] fair
      Presented with a Universal blanc°   *blank*
      Of Nature's works to me expung'd and ras'd,°   *erased*
50   And wisdom at one entrance quite shut out.
      So much the rather thou Celestial Light
      Shine inward, and the mind through all her powers
      Irradiate, there plant eyes, all mist from thence
      Purge and disperse, that I may see and tell
55   Of things invisible to mortal sight.
          Now had th' Almighty Father from above,
      From the pure Empyrean where he sits
      High Thron'd above all highth, bent down his eye,
      His own works and their works at once to view:
60   About him all the Sanctities of Heaven
      Stood thick as Stars, and from his sight receiv'd
      Beatitude past utterance; on his right
      The radiant image of his Glory sat,
      His only Son; On Earth he first beheld
65   Our two first Parents, yet the only two
      Of mankind, in the happy Garden plac't,
      Reaping immortal fruits of joy and love,
      Uninterrupted joy, unrivall'd love
      In blissful solitude; he then survey'd
70   Hell and the Gulf between, and *Satan* there
      Coasting the wall of Heav'n on this side Night
      In the dun° Air sublime,° and ready now   *dusky/aloft*
      To stoop with wearied wings, and willing feet
      On the bare outside of this World, that seem'd
75   Firm land imbosom'd without Firmament,[4]
      Uncertain which, in Ocean or in Air.
      Him God beholding from his prospect high,
      Wherein past, present, future he beholds,
      Thus to his only Son foreseeing spake.
80   Only begotten Son, seest thou what rage
      Transports our adversary, whom no bounds
      Prescrib'd, no bars of Hell, nor all the chains
      Heapt on him there, nor yet the main Abyss
      Wide interrupt° can hold; so bent he seems   *divided*
85   On desperate revenge, that shall redound
      Upon his own rebellious head. And now
      Through all restraint broke loose he wings his way

---

3. The Book of Nature.   4. The firmament or atmosphere, being inside the shell of
                                      the universe that Satan stands on, is invisible to him.

Not far off Heav'n, in the Precincts of light,
Directly towards the new created World,
90   And Man there plac't, with purpose to assay°   *test*
If him by force he can destroy, or worse,
By some false guile pervert; and shall pervert;
For Man will heark'n to his glozing° lies,   *flattering*
And easily transgress the sole Command,⁵
95   Sole pledge of his obedience: So will fall
Hee and his faithless Progeny: whose fault?
Whose but his own? ingrate, he had of mee
All he could have; I made him just and right,
Sufficient to have stood, though free to fall.
100   Such I created all th' Ethereal Powers
And Spirits, both them who stood and them who fail'd;
Freely they stood who stood, and fell who fell.
Not free, what proof could they have giv'n sincere
Of true allegiance, constant Faith or Love,
105   Where only what they needs must do, appear'd,
Not what they would? what praise could they receive?
What pleasure I from such obedience paid,
When Will and Reason (Reason also is choice)
Useless and vain, of freedom both despoil'd,
110   Made passive both, had serv'd necessity,
Not mee. They therefore as to right belong'd,
So were created, nor can justly accuse
Thir maker, or thir making, or thir Fate;
As if Predestination over-rul'd
115   Thir will, dispos'd by absolute Decree
Or high foreknowledge; they themselves decreed
Thir own revolt, not I: if I foreknew,
Foreknowledge had no influence on their fault,
Which had no less prov'd certain unforeknown.
120   So without least impulse or shadow of Fate,
Or aught by me immutably foreseen,
They trespass, Authors to themselves in all
Both what they judge and what they choose; for so
I form'd them free, and free they must remain,
125   Till they enthrall themselves: I else must change
Thir nature, and revoke the high Decree
Unchangeable, Eternal, which ordain'd
Thir freedom: they themselves ordain'd thir fall.
The first sort⁶ by thir own suggestion° fell,   *temptation*
130   Self-tempted, self-deprav'd: Man falls deceiv'd
By th' other first: Man therefore shall find grace,
The other none: in Mercy and Justice both,
Through Heav'n and Earth, so shall my glory excel,
But Mercy first and last shall brightest shine.
135   Thus while God spake, ambrosial fragrance fill'd

---

5. I.e., not to taste the fruit of the forbidden tree.   6. Satan and the rebel angels.

All Heav'n, and in the blessed Spirits elect[7]
Sense of new joy ineffable diffus'd:
Beyond compare the Son of God was seen
Most glorious, in him all his Father shone
140 Substantially express'd, and in his face
Divine compassion visibly appear'd,
Love without end, and without measure Grace,
Which uttering thus he to his Father spake.
     O Father, gracious was that word which clos'd
145 Thy sovran° sentence, that Man should find grace;   *sovereign*
For which both Heav'n and Earth shall high extol
Thy praises, with th' innumerable sound
Of Hymns and sacred Songs, wherewith thy Throne
Encompass'd shall resound thee ever blest.
150 For should Man finally be lost, should Man
Thy creature late so lov'd, thy youngest Son
Fall circumvented thus by fraud, though join'd
With his own folly? that be from thee far,
That far be from thee, Father, who art Judge
155 Of all things made, and judgest only right.
Or shall the Adversary[8] thus obtain
His end, and frustrate thine, shall he fulfil
His malice, and thy goodness bring to naught,
Or proud return though to his heavier doom,
160 Yet with revenge accomplish't and to Hell
Draw after him the whole Race of mankind,
By him corrupted? or wilt thou thyself
Abolish thy Creation, and unmake,
For him, what for thy glory thou hast made?
165 So should thy goodness and thy greatness both
Be question'd and blasphem'd without defense.
     To whom the great Creator thus repli'd.
O Son, in whom my Soul hath chief delight,[9]
Son of my bosom, Son who art alone
170 My word, my wisdom, and effectual might,
All hast thou spok'n as my thoughts are, all
As my Eternal purpose hath decreed:
Man shall not quite be lost, but sav'd who will,
Yet not of will in him, but grace in me
175 Freely voutsaf't;° once more I will renew   *vouchsafed*
His lapsed° powers, though forfeit and enthrall'd   *decayed*
By sin to foul exorbitant desires;
Upheld by me, yet once more he shall stand
On even ground against his mortal foe,
180 By me upheld, that he may know how frail
His fall'n condition is, and to me owe
All his deliv'rance, and to none but me.

---

7. The "elect angels" of 1 Timothy 5.21, explained in Milton's *De doctrina* 1.9 as angels "who have not revolted."
8. The literal meaning of "Satan."

9. Echoing Mark 1.11, the words out of the heavens at Jesus' baptism: "Thou art my beloved Son, in whom I am well pleased."

Some I have chosen of peculiar grace
Elect above the rest; so is my will:[1]
185 The rest shall hear me call, and oft be warn'd
Thir sinful state, and to appease betimes
Th' incensed Deity while offer'd grace
Invites; for I will clear thir senses dark,
What may suffice, and soft'n stony hearts
190 To pray, repent, and bring obedience due.
To Prayer, repentance, and obedience due,
Though but endeavor'd with sincere intent,
Mine ear shall not be slow, mine eye not shut.
And I will place within them as a guide
195 My Umpire *Conscience*, whom if they will hear,
Light after light well us'd they shall attain,
And to the end persisting, safe arrive.
This my long sufferance and my day of grace
They who neglect and scorn, shall never taste;
200 But hard be hard'n'd, blind be blinded more,
That they may stumble on, and deeper fall;
And none but such from mercy I exclude.
But yet all is not done; Man disobeying,
Disloyal breaks his fealty, and sins
205 Against the high Supremacy of Heav'n,
Affecting° God-head, and so losing all,   *seeking*
To expiate his Treason hath naught left,
But to destruction sacred and devote,°   *dedicated*
He with his whole posterity must die,
210 Die hee or Justice must; unless for him
Some other able, and as willing, pay
The rigid satisfaction, death for death.[2]
Say Heav'nly Powers, where shall we find such love,
Which of ye will be mortal[3] to redeem
215 Man's mortal crime, and just th' unjust to save,
Dwells in all Heaven charity° so dear?   *compassionate love*
    He ask'd, but all the Heav'nly Choir stood mute,
And silence was in Heav'n: on man's behalf
Patron or Intercessor none appear'd,
220 Much less that durst upon his own head draw
The deadly forfeiture, and ransom set.[4]
And now without redemption all mankind
Must have been lost, adjudg'd to Death and Hell
By doom° severe, had not the Son of God,   *judgment*

---

1. In *De doctrina* 1.4, Milton sets out an Arminian position, explicitly opposed to the Calvinist, on such doctrines as predestination, election, and reprobation, and he could be regarded as doing something similar here (lines 173–202); e.g., his God seems to make salvation depend on humans' will to avail themselves of grace, or on "prayer, repentance, and obedience" (line 191), whereas Calvinists regarded humans as incapable of contributing in any way to their own salvation. By the term "elect," Milton usually means no more than "whoever believes and continues in the faith."

2. Note that human death is here regarded by God not as a punishment, but as a "satisfaction" for the treason. See *De doctrina* 1.16: "The satisfaction of Christ is the complete reparation made by him . . . by the fulfilment of the Law, and payment of the required price for all mankind."

3. Is willing to be subject to death.

4. Put down the ransom price (by giving his own life).

225 In whom the fulness dwells of love divine,
     His dearest mediation thus renew'd.
        Father, thy word is past,[5] man shall find grace;
     And shall grace not find means, that finds her way,
     The speediest of thy winged messengers,
230 To visit all thy creatures, and to all
     Comes unprevented,° unimplor'd, unsought?   *unanticipated*
     Happy for man, so coming; he her aid
     Can never seek, once dead in sins and lost;
     Atonement for himself or offering meet,
235 Indebted and undone, hath none to bring:
     Behold mee then, mee for him, life for life
     I offer, on mee let thine anger fall;
     Account mee man; I for his sake will leave
     Thy bosom, and this glory next to thee
240 Freely put off, and for him lastly die
     Well pleas'd, on me let Death wreck all his rage;
     Under his gloomy power I shall not long
     Lie vanquisht; thou hast giv'n me to possess
     Life in myself for ever, by thee I live,[6]
245 Though now to Death I yield, and am his due
     All that of me can die, yet that debt paid,
     Thou wilt not leave me in the loathsome grave
     His prey, nor suffer my unspotted Soul
     For ever with corruption there to dwell;
250 But I shall rise Victorious, and subdue
     My vanquisher, spoil'd of his vaunted spoil;
     Death his death's wound shall then receive, and stoop
     Inglorious, of his mortal sting disarm'd.[7]
     I through the ample Air in Triumph high
255 Shall lead Hell Captive maugre° Hell, and show   *despite*
     The powers of darkness bound. Thou at the sight
     Pleas'd, out of Heaven shalt look down and smile,
     While by thee rais'd I ruin all my Foes,
     Death last, and with his Carcass glut the Grave:[8]
260 Then with the multitude of my redeem'd
     Shall enter Heav'n long absent, and return,
     Father, to see thy face, wherein no cloud
     Of anger shall remain, but peace assur'd,
     And reconcilement; wrath shall be no more
265 Thenceforth, but in thy presence Joy entire.
        His words here ended, but his meek aspéct
     Silent yet spake, and breath'd immortal love
     To mortal men, above which only shone
     Filial obedience: as a sacrifice
270 Glad to be offer'd, he attends° the will   *awaits*

---

5. Your word of honor is pledged.
6. See John 5.26: "As the Father hath life in himself: so hath he given to the Son to have life in himself."
7. See 1 Corinthians 15.55–6: "O death, where is thy sting? O grave, where is thy victory? The sting of death is sin; and the strength of sin is the law."
8. Alludes to 1 Corinthians 15.26: "The last enemy that shall be destroyed is death."

Of his great Father. Admiration seiz'd
All Heav'n, what this might mean, and whither tend
Wond'ring; but soon th' Almighty thus repli'd:
   O thou in Heav'n and Earth the only peace
275   Found out for mankind under wrath, O thou
My sole complacence! well thou know'st how dear
To me are all my works, nor Man the least
Though last created, that for him I spare
Thee from my bosom and right hand, to save,
280   By losing thee a while, the whole Race lost.
Thou therefore whom thou only canst redeem,
Thir Nature also to thy Nature join;
And be thyself Man among men on Earth,
Made flesh, when time shall be, of Virgin seed,
285   By wondrous birth: Be thou in *Adam's* room°   *place*
The Head of all mankind, though *Adam's* Son.
As in him perish all men, so in thee
As from a second root shall be restor'd,
As many as are restor'd, without thee none.[9]
290   His crime makes guilty all his Sons, thy merit
Imputed shall absolve them who renounce
Thir own both righteous and unrighteous deeds,[1]
And live in thee transplanted, and from thee
Receive new life. So Man, as is most just,
295   Shall satisfy for Man, be judg'd and die,
And dying rise, and rising with him raise
His Brethren, ransom'd with his own dear life.
So Heav'nly love shall outdo Hellish hate,
Giving to death, and dying to redeem,
300   So dearly to redeem what Hellish hate
So easily destroy'd, and still destroys
In those who, when they may, accept not grace.
Nor shalt thou by descending to assume
Man's Nature, lessen or degrade thine own.
305   Because thou hast, though Thron'd in highest bliss
Equal to God, and equally enjoying
God-like fruition, quitted[2] all to save
A world from utter loss, and hast been found
By Merit more than Birthright Son of God,
310   Found worthiest to be so by being Good,
Far more than Great or High; because in thee
Love hath abounded more than Glory abounds,
Therefore thy Humiliation shall exalt
With thee thy Manhood also to this Throne;
315   Here shalt thou sit incarnate, here shalt Reign

9. See 1 Corinthians 15.22: "As in Adam all die, even so in Christ shall all be made alive."
1. See *De doctrina* 1.22: "As therefore our sins are imputed to Christ, so the merits or righteousness of Christ are imputed to us through faith." If one simply renounced dependence on "righteous" deeds, one would be justified by faith alone; but for the "living faith"—faith issuing in works—that Milton believes necessary, one has to renounce (in a different sense) "unrighteous" deeds.
2. A pun, since "quitted" meant "redeemed, remitted" as well as "left."

Both God and Man, Son both of God and Man,
Anointed[3] universal King; all Power
I give thee, reign for ever, and assume
Thy Merits; under thee as Head Supreme
320 Thrones, Princedoms, Powers, Dominions I reduce:
All knees to thee shall bow, of them that bide
In Heaven, or Earth, or under Earth in Hell;
When thou attended gloriously from Heav'n
Shalt in the Sky appear, and from thee send
325 The summoning Arch-Angels to proclaim
Thy dread Tribunal: forthwith from all Winds
The living, and forthwith the cited° dead   *summoned*
Of all past Ages to the general Doom°   *judgment*
Shall hast'n, such a peal shall rouse thir sleep.
330 Then all thy Saints° assembl'd, thou shalt judge   *elect*
Bad men and Angels, they arraign'd shall sink
Beneath thy Sentence; Hell, her numbers full,
Thenceforth shall be for ever shut. Meanwhile
The World shall burn, and from her ashes spring
335 New Heav'n and Earth, wherein the just shall dwell
And after all thir tribulations long
See golden days, fruitful of golden deeds,
With Joy and Love triumphing, and fair Truth.[4]
Then thou thy regal Sceptre shalt lay by,
340 For regal Sceptre then no more shall need,
God shall be All in All. But all ye Gods,°   *angels*
Adore him, who to compass all this dies,
Adore the Son, and honor him as mee.
     No sooner had th' Almighty ceas't, but all
345 The multitude of Angels with a shout
Loud as from numbers without number, sweet
As from blest voices, uttering joy, Heav'n rung
With Jubilee, and loud Hosannas fill'd
Th' eternal Regions: lowly reverent
350 Towards either Throne they bow, and to the ground
With solemn adoration down they cast
Thir Crowns inwove with Amarant and Gold,
Immortal Amarant,[5] a Flow'r which once
In Paradise, fast by the Tree of Life
355 Began to bloom, but soon for man's offense
To Heav'n remov'd where first it grew, there grows,
And flow'rs aloft shading the Fount of Life,
And where the river of Bliss through midst of Heav'n
Rolls o'er *Elysian* Flow'rs her Amber stream;[6]
360 With these that never fade the Spirits elect
Bind thir resplendent locks inwreath'd with beams,

---

3. The "Anointed" in Hebrew is the Messiah.
4. The burning of Earth is based on 2 Peter 3.12ff.
5. "Amaranth" in Greek means "unwithering"; a purple flower that was a "symbol of immortality"; the amarantine crown was an ancient pagan symbol of untroubled tranquillity and health.
6. Allusion to Virgil, *Aeneid* 6.656–59, the description of spirits chanting in chorus beside the Eridanus, in the Elysian fields; "amber" was a standard of purity or clarity.

Now in loose Garlands thick thrown off, the bright
Pavement that like a Sea of Jasper shone
Impurpl'd with Celestial Roses smil'd.
365   Then Crown'd again thir gold'n Harps they took,
Harps ever tun'd, that glittering by thir side
Like Quivers hung, and with Preamble sweet
Of charming symphony they introduce
Thir sacred Song, and waken raptures high;
370   No voice exempt,° no voice but well could join   *debarred*
Melodious part, such concord is in Heav'n.
    Thee Father first they sung Omnipotent,
Immutable, Immortal, Infinite,[7]
Eternal King; thee Author of all being,
375   Fountain of Light, thyself invisible
Amidst the glorious brightness where thou sit'st
Thron'd inaccessible, but° when thou shad'st   *except*
The full blaze of thy beams, and through a cloud
Drawn round about thee like a radiant Shrine,
380   Dark with excessive bright thy skirts appear,
Yet dazzle Heav'n, that brightest Seraphim
Approach not, but with both wings veil thir eyes.
Thee next they sang of all Creation first,
Begotten Son, Divine Similitude,
385   In whose conspicuous count'nance, without cloud
Made visible, th' Almighty Father shines,
Whom else no Creature can behold;[8] on thee
Impresst th' effulgence of his Glory abides,
Transfus'd on thee his ample Spirit rests.
390   Hee Heav'n of Heavens and all the Powers therein
By thee created, and by thee threw down
Th' aspiring Dominations:° thou that day   *rebel angels*
Thy Father's dreadful Thunder didst not spare,
Nor stop thy flaming Chariot wheels, that shook
395   Heav'n's everlasting Frame, while o'er the necks
Thou drov'st of warring Angels disarray'd.
Back from pursuit thy Powers with loud acclaim
Thee only extoll'd, Son of thy Father's might,
To execute fierce vengeance on his foes:
400   Not so on Man; him through their malice fall'n,
Father of Mercy and Grace, thou didst not doom°   *judge*
So strictly, but much more to pity incline:
No sooner did thy dear and only Son
Perceive thee purpos'd not to doom frail Man
405   So strictly, but much more to pity inclin'd,[9]
Hee to appease thy wrath, and end the strife
Of Mercy and Justice in thy face discern'd,

---

7. Line 373 is transplanted in its entirety from Sylvester's
translation of Du Bartas's poem on creation.
8. See John 1.18 and 14.9.
9. Most editors say that "but" or "than" has to be supplied

before "He" (line 406). However, if "much more to pity
inclined" refers to the Son, the "but" immediately preceding is available for the main clause.

Regardless of the Bliss wherein hee sat
Second to thee, offer'd himself to die
410 For man's offense. O unexampl'd love,
Love nowhere to be found less than Divine!
Hail Son of God, Savior of Men, thy Name
Shall be the copious matter of my Song
Henceforth, and never shall my Harp thy praise
415 Forget, nor from thy Father's praise disjoin.
  Thus they in Heav'n, above the starry Sphere,
Thir happy hours in joy and hymning spent.
Meanwhile upon the firm opacous Globe
Of this round World, whose first convex divides
420 The luminous inferior Orbs, enclos'd
From *Chaos* and th' inroad of Darkness old,[1]
Satan alighted walks: a Globe far off
It seem'd, now seems a boundless Continent
Dark, waste, and wild, under the frown of Night
425 Starless expos'd, and ever-threat'ning storms
Of *Chaos* blust'ring round, inclement sky;
Save on that side which from the wall of Heav'n,
Though distant far, some small reflection gains
Of glimmering air less vext° with tempest loud: *tossed about*
430 Here walk'd the Fiend at large in spacious field.
As when a Vultur on *Imaus* bred,
Whose snowy ridge the roving *Tartar* bounds,
Dislodging from a Region scarce of prey
To gorge the flesh of Lambs or yeanling Kids
435 On Hills where Flocks are fed, flies toward the Springs
Of *Ganges* or *Hydaspes*, *Indian* streams;
But in his way lights on the barren Plains
Of *Sericana*, where *Chineses* drive
With Sails and Wind thir cany Waggons light:
440 So on this windy Sea of Land, the Fiend
Walk'd up and down alone bent on his prey,[2]
Alone, for other Creature in this place
Living or lifeless to be found was none,
None yet, but store hereafter from the earth
445 Up hither like Aereal vapors flew
Of all things transitory and vain, when Sin
With vanity had fill'd the works of men:[3]
Both all things vain, and all who in vain things
Built thir fond hopes of Glory or lasting fame,

1. The "starry Sphere," is either the sphere of the fixed stars or, more loosely, the stars and planets together. The stars are enclosed within the *primum mobile* or "first convex" (sphere). Both heaven and chaos lie outside that opaque ("opacous") shell.
2. The simile compares the vulture's journey to Satan's. One journey is from Imaus, (a mountain range said to run through Afghanistan), to the rivers of India; the other is from the "frozen continent" (2.587) of Tartarus, which did not keep Satan from roving, to Eden with its rivers. The "barren plains of Sericana" correspond to the *primum mobile* because both are stopping places and in both the elements are confused. (The Chinese use sails, the means of propulsion for ships, on their land vehicles; and the *primum mobile* is a "sea of land.")
3. In *Orlando Furioso* 34.73ff., a passage from which Milton quotes in *Of Reformation*, Ariosto tells how Astolfo searches for his lost wits in a Limbo of Vanity on the moon.

450   Or happiness in this or th' other life;
        All who have thir reward on Earth, the fruits
        Of painful Superstition and blind Zeal,
        Naught seeking but the praise of men, here find
        Fit retribution, empty as thir deeds;
455   All th' unaccomplisht works of Nature's hand,
        Abortive, monstrous, or unkindly mixt,
        Dissolv'd on Earth, fleet hither, and in vain,
        Till final dissolution, wander here,
        Not in the neighboring Moon, as some have dream'd;
460   Those argent Fields more likely habitants,
        Translated Saints,[4] or middle Spirits hold
        Betwixt th' Angelical and Human kind:
        Hither of ill-join'd Sons and Daughters born
        First from the ancient World those Giants came
465   With many a vain exploit, though then renown'd:[5]
        The builders next of *Babel* on the Plain
        Of *Sennaar,* and still with vain design
        New *Babels,* had they wherewithal, would build:[6]
        Others came single; he who to be deem'd
470   A God, leap'd fondly into *AEtna* flames,
        Empedocles, and hee who to enjoy
        Plato's Elysium, leap'd into the Sea,
        Cleombrotus,[7] and many more too long,
        Embryos, and Idiots, Eremites and Friars
475   White, Black and Grey, with all thir trumpery.[8]
        Here Pilgrims roam, that stray'd so far to seek
        In *Golgotha*[9] him dead, who lives in Heav'n;
        And they who to be sure of Paradise
        Dying put on the weeds of *Dominic,*
480   Or in *Franciscan* think to pass disguis'd;[1]
        They pass the Planets seven, and pass the fixt,
        And that Crystalline Sphere whose balance weighs
        The Trepidation talkt, and that first mov'd;[2]
        And now Saint *Peter* at Heav'n's Wicket seems
485   To wait them with his Keys, and now at foot
        Of Heav'n's ascent they lift thir Feet, when lo

---

4. Probably such as Enoch (Genesis 5.24) and Elijah (2 Kings 2).
5. The first group of fools are the Giants, "mighty men . . . of renown," born of the misunion of "sons of God" with "daughters of men" (Genesis 6.4).
6. At 12.45–47 the builders of Babel are said to have formed their "vain design" out of a desire for fame. "New Babels" suggests the New Babylon of anti-Papist propaganda.
7. Empedocles and Cleombrotus were not associated by classical writers but occur together in Lactantius' chapter on "Pythagoreans and Stoics who, Believing in the Immortality of the Soul, Foolishly Persuade a Voluntary Death" (*Divinae Institutiones* 3.18). Cleombrotus drowned himself after an unwise reading of Plato's *Phaedo;* Empedocles' motive was to conceal his own mortality.

8. Milton here satirizes a Catholic tradition that consigned cretins and unbaptized infants to a much debated *limbo infantum.* The friars were specified by robe color; "white" meant Carmelite, "black" Dominican, and "grey" Franciscan. The contemptuous juxtaposition of all three colors ridicules the importance assigned to external trappings. "Eremites" were Order of Friars Hermits.
9. The hill where Christ was crucified and buried.
1. Compare *Inferno* 27.67–84, in which Dante tells how Guido da Montefeltro hoped to get into heaven by virtue of Franciscan robes but found to his cost that absolution without repentance is vain.
2. In order of proximity to earth, the spheres passed are the seven planetary spheres; the eighth sphere, containing the "fixed" stars; the ninth, "crystalline sphere"; and the tenth sphere, the "first moved" or *primum mobile.*

A violent cross wind from either Coast
Blows them transverse ten thousand Leagues awry
Into the devious Air; then might ye see
490   Cowls, Hoods and Habits with thir weares tost
And flutter'd into Rags, then Reliques, Beads,
Indulgences, Dispenses,[3] Pardons, Bulls,
The sport of Winds: all these upwhirl'd aloft
Fly o'er the backside of the World far off
495   Into a *Limbo*° large and broad, since call'd   *empty region*
The Paradise of Fools, to few unknown
Long after, now unpeopl'd and untrod;
All this dark Globe the Fiend found as he pass'd,
And long he wander'd, till at last a gleam
500   Of dawning light turn'd thither-ward in haste
His travell'd steps; far distant he descries
Ascending by degrees magnific
Up to the wall of Heaven a Structure high,
At top whereof, but far more rich appear'd
505   The work as of a Kingly Palace Gate
With Frontispiece[4] of Diamond and Gold
Imbellisht; thick with sparkling orient° Gems   *brilliant*
The Portal shone, inimitable on Earth
By Model, or by shading Pencil drawn.
510   The Stairs were such as whereon *Jacob* saw
Angels ascending and descending, bands
Of Guardians bright, when he from *Esau* fled
To *Padan-Aram* in the field of *Luz*,
Dreaming by night under the open Sky,
515   And waking cri'd, *This is the Gate of Heav'n.*[5]
Each Stair mysteriously° was meant,[6] nor stood   *symbolically*
There always, but drawn up to Heav'n sometimes
Viewless, and underneath a bright Sea flow'd
Of Jasper, or of liquid Pearl, whereon
520   Who after came from Earth, sailing arriv'd,
Wafted by Angels, or flew o'er the Lake
Rapt in a Chariot drawn by fiery Steeds.
The Stairs were then let down, whether to dare
The Fiend by easy ascent, or aggravate
525   His sad exclusion from the doors of Bliss.
Direct against which op'n'd from beneath,
Just o'er the blissful seat of Paradise,
A passage down to th' Earth, a passage wide,
Wider by far than that of after-times
530   Over Mount *Sion*, and, though that were large,

---

3. A "dispense" or dispensation was an exemption from a solemn obligation by licence of an ecclesiastical dignitary, especially the Pope.
4. A decorated entrance or a pediment over the gate.
5. The unregenerate Jacob was terrified by the vision of a ladder reaching to heaven just after he had cheated Esau out of his father's blessing (Genesis 27–8). The experi-

ence awed him into belief and a vow to the Lord.
6. Jacob's ladder had been identified with Homer's golden chain linking the universe to Jupiter. Each "stair," or step, could be interpreted as a spiritual stage extending "from the supreme God even to the bottomest dregs of the universe."

Over the *Promis'd Land* to God so dear,
By which, to visit oft those happy Tribes,
On high behests his Angels to and fro
Pass'd frequent, and his eye with choice° regard   careful
535   From *Paneas* the fount of *Jordan's* flood
To *Beërsaba*,[7] where the *Holy Land*
Borders on *Egypt* and th' *Arabian* shore;
So wide the op'ning seem'd, where bounds were set
To darkness, such as bound the Ocean wave.
540   *Satan* from hence now on the lower stair
That scal'd by steps of Gold to Heaven Gate
Looks down with wonder at the sudden view
Of all this World at once. As when a Scout
Through dark and desert ways with peril gone
545   All night; at last by break of cheerful dawn
Obtains° the brow of some high-climbing Hill,   reaches
Which to his eye discovers unaware
The goodly prospect of some foreign land
First seen, or some renown'd Metropolis
550   With glistering Spires and Pinnacles adorn'd,
Which now the Rising Sun gilds with his beams.
Such wonder seiz'd, though after Heaven seen,
The Spirit malign, but much more envy seiz'd
At sight of all this World beheld so fair.[8] * * *

from Book 4
The Argument

Satan *now in prospect of* Eden, *and nigh the place where he must now attempt the bold
enterprise which he undertook alone against God and Man, falls into many doubts with himself, and many passions, fear, envy, and despair; but at length confirms himself in evil, journeys on to Paradise, whose outward prospect and situation is described, overleaps the
bounds, sits in the shape of a Cormorant on the Tree of Life, as highest in the Garden to
look about him. The Garden describ'd; Satan's first sight of Adam and Eve; his wonder at
thir excellent form and happy state, but with resolution to work thir fall; overhears thir discourse, thence gathers that the Tree of Knowledge was forbidden them to eat of, under
penalty of death; and thereon intends to found his Temptation, by seducing them to transgress: then leaves them a while, to know further of thir state by some other means. Meanwhile Uriel descending on a Sun-beam warns Gabriel, who had in charge the Gate of Paradise, that some evil spirit had escap'd the Deep, and past at Noon by his Sphere in the shape
of a good Angel down to Paradise, discovered after by his furious gestures in the Mount.
Gabriel promises to find him ere morning. Night coming on, Adam and Eve discourse of
going to thir rest: thir Bower describ'd; thir Evening worship. Gabriel drawing forth his
Bands of Night-watch to walk the round of Paradise, appoints two strong Angels to Adam's
Bower, lest the evil spirit should be there doing some harm to Adam or Eve sleeping; there*

7. "Paneas," is a later Greek name for Dan—not the city
of Dan but the spring of the same name, "the easternmost
fountain of Jordan." Beersaba was the southern limit of
Canaan, as Dan was the northern.
8. Seeing the archangel Uriel, Satan now disguises himself

as a cherub and asks the way to Eden. Uriel directs him,
not realizing who he is—"For neither Man nor Angel can
discern / Hypocrisy, the only evil that walks / Invisible,
except to God alone" (lines 682–5).

they find him at the ear of Eve, tempting her in a dream, and bring him, though unwilling, to Gabriel; by whom question'd, he scornfully answers, prepares resistance, but hinder'd by a Sign from Heaven, flies out of Paradise.

      O for that warning voice, which he who saw
      Th' *Apocalypse,* heard cry in Heav'n aloud,
      Then when the Dragon, put to second rout,
      Came furious down to be reveng'd on men,
5   *Woe to the inhabitants on Earth!*[1] that now,
      While time was, our first Parents had been warn'd
      The coming of thir secret foe, and scap'd
      Haply so scap'd his mortal snare; for now
      Satan, now first inflam'd with rage, came down,
10   The Tempter ere th' Accuser of man-kind,
      To wreck° on innocent frail man his loss   *avenge*
      Of that first Battle, and his flight to Hell:
      Yet not rejoicing in his speed, though bold,
      Far off and fearless, nor with cause to boast,
15   Begins his dire attempt, which nigh the birth
      Now rolling, boils in his tumultuous breast,
      And like a devilish Engine back recoils
      Upon himself; horror and doubt distract
      His troubl'd thoughts, and from the bottom stir
20   The Hell within him, for within him Hell
      He brings, and round about him, nor from Hell
      One step no more than from himself can fly
      By change of place: Now conscience wakes despair
      That slumber'd, wakes the bitter memory
25   Of what he was, what is, and what must be
      Worse; of worse deeds worse sufferings must ensue.
      Sometimes towards *Eden* which now in his view
      Lay pleasant,[2] his griev'd look he fixes sad,
      Sometimes towards Heav'n and the full-blazing Sun,
30   Which now sat high in his Meridian Tow'r:
      Then much revolving, thus in sighs began.
        O thou that with surpassing Glory crown'd,
      Look'st from thy sole Dominion like the God
      Of this new World; at whose sight all the Stars
35   Hide thir diminisht heads; to thee I call,
      But with no friendly voice, and add thy name
      O Sun, to tell thee how I hate thy beams
      That bring to my remembrance from what state
      I fell, how glorious once above thy Sphere;
40   Till Pride and worse Ambition threw me down
      Warring in Heav'n against Heav'n's matchless King:[3]
      Ah wherefore! he deserv'd no such return

---

1. The *Apocalypse* of St. John relates a vision of a second battle in heaven between Michael and "the Dragon," Satan.
2. The etymological meaning of "Eden" is "pleasure,

delight."
3. According to Edward Phillips, lines 32–41 were shown to him and some others "before the Poem was begun," when Milton intended to write a tragedy on the Fall.

From me, whom he created what I was
In that bright eminence, and with his good
45   Upbraided none;[4] nor was his service hard.
What could be less than to afford him praise,
The easiest recompense, and pay him thanks,
How due! yet all his good prov'd ill in me,
And wrought but malice; lifted up so high
50   I sdein'd° subjection, and thought one step higher   *disdained*
Would set me highest, and in a moment quit°   *pay off*
The debt immense of endless gratitude,
So burdensome, still paying, still to owe;
Forgetful what from him I still receiv'd,
55   And understood not that a grateful mind
By owing owes not, but still pays, at once
Indebted and discharg'd; what burden then?[5]
O had his powerful Destiny ordain'd
Me some inferior Angel, I had stood
60   Then happy; no unbounded hope had rais'd
Ambition. Yet why not? some other Power
As great might have aspir'd, and me though mean
Drawn to his part; but other Powers as great
Fell not, but stand unshak'n, from within
65   Or from without, to all temptations arm'd.
Hadst thou the same free Will and Power to stand?
Thou hadst: whom hast thou then or what to accuse,
But Heav'n's free Love dealt equally to all?
Be then his Love accurst, since love or hate,
70   To me alike, it deals eternal woe.
Nay curs'd be thou; since against his thy will
Chose freely what it now so justly rues.
Me miserable! which way shall I fly
Infinite wrath, and infinite despair?
75   Which way I fly is Hell; myself am Hell;
And in the lowest deep a lower deep
Still threat'ning to devour me opens wide,
To which the Hell I suffer seems a Heav'n.
O then at last relent: is there no place
80   Left for Repentance, none for Pardon left?
None left but by submission; and that word
Disdain forbids me, and my dread of shame
Among the Spirits beneath, whom I seduc'd
With other promises and other vaunts
85   Than to submit, boasting I could subdue
Th' Omnipotent. Ay me, they little know
How dearly I abide that boast so vain,
Under what torments inwardly I groan:
While they adore me on the Throne of Hell,
90   With Diadem and Sceptre high advanc'd
The lower still I fall, only Supreme

4. Demanded no return for his benefits; see James 1.5.   5. Simply by owning an obligation gratefully, one ceases
                                                           to owe it.

In misery; such joy Ambition finds.
But say I could repent and could obtain
By Act of Grace[6] my former state; how soon
95   Would highth recall high thoughts, how soon unsay
What feign'd submission swore: ease would recant
Vows made in pain, as violent and void.
For never can true reconcilement grow
Where wounds of deadly hate have pierc'd so deep:
100   Which would but lead me to a worse relapse,
And heavier fall: so should I purchase dear
Short intermission bought with double smart.
This knows my punisher; therefore as far
From granting hee, as I from begging peace:
105   All hope excluded thus, behold instead
Of us out-cast, exil'd, his new delight,
Mankind created, and for him this World.
So farewell Hope, and with Hope farewell Fear,
Farewell Remorse: all Good to me is lost;
110   Evil be thou my Good; by thee at least
Divided Empire with Heav'n's King I hold
By thee, and more than half perhaps will reign;
As Man ere long, and this new World shall know.
    Thus while he spake, each passion dimm'd his face,
115   Thrice chang'd with pale, ire, envy and despair,
Which marr'd his borrow'd visage, and betray'd
Him counterfeit, if any eye beheld.
For heav'nly minds from such distempers foul
Are ever clear. Whereof hee soon aware,
120   Each perturbation smooth'd with outward calm,
Artificer° of fraud; and was the first   *inventor*
That practis'd falsehood under saintly show,
Deep malice to conceal, couch't° with revenge: *hidden*
Yet not anough had practis'd to deceive
125   *Uriel* once warn'd; whose eye pursu'd him down
The way he went, and on th' *Assyrian* mount°   *Niphates*
Saw him disfigur'd, more than could befall
Spirit of happy sort: his gestures fierce
He mark'd and mad demeanor, then alone,
130   As he suppos'd, all unobserv'd, unseen.
So on he fares, and to the border comes
Of *Eden*, where delicious Paradise,
Now nearer, Crowns with her enclosure green,
As with a rural mound the champaign° head   *unenclosed, level*
135   Of a steep wilderness, whose hairy sides
With thicket overgrown, grotesque and wild,
Access deni'd; and over head up grew
Insuperable highth of loftiest shade,
Cedar, and Pine, and Fir, and branching Palm,
140   A Silvan Scene, and as the ranks ascend
Shade above shade, a woody Theatre

6. By concession of favor, not of right; often used for a formal pardon by Parliament.

Of stateliest view. Yet higher than thir tops
The verdurous wall of Paradise up sprung:
Which to our general Sire° gave prospect large   *Adam*
145   Into his nether Empire neighboring round.
And higher than that Wall a circling row
Of goodliest Trees loaden with fairest Fruit,
Blossoms and Fruits at once of golden hue
Appear'd, with gay enamell'd° colors mixt: *lustrous*
150   On which the Sun more glad impress'd his beams
Than in fair Evening Cloud, or humid Bow,°   *rainbow*
When God hath show'r'd the earth; so lovely seem'd
That Lantskip:° And of pure now purer air   *landscape*
Meets his approach, and to the heart inspires
155   Vernal delight and joy, able to drive
All sadness but despair: now gentle gales
Fanning thir odoriferous wings dispense
Native perfúmes, and whisper whence they stole
Those balmy spoils. As when to them who sail
160   Beyond the *Cape* of *Hope*, and now are past
Mozambic,[7] off at Sea North-East winds blow
Sabean[8] Odors from the spicy shore
Of *Araby* the blest, with such delay
Well pleas'd they slack thir course, and many a League
165   Cheer'd with the grateful smell old Ocean smiles.
So entertain'd those odorous sweets the Fiend
Who came thir bane, though with them better pleas'd
Than *Asmodeus* with the fishy fume,
That drove him, though enamor'd, from the Spouse
170   Of *Tobit's* Son, and with a vengeance sent
From *Media* post to *Egypt*, there fast bound.[9]
     Now to th' ascent of that steep savage° Hill   *wild*
Satan had journey'd on, pensive and slow;
But further way found none, so thick entwin'd,
175   As one continu'd brake, the undergrowth
Of shrubs and tangling bushes had perplext
All path of Man or Beast that pass'd that way:
One Gate there only was, and that look'd East
On th' other side: which when th' arch-felon saw
180   Due entrance he disdain'd, and in contempt,
At one slight bound high overleap'd all bound
Of Hill or highest Wall, and sheer within
Lights on his feet. As when a prowling Wolf,
Whom hunger drives to seek new haunt for prey,
185   Watching where Shepherds pen thir Flocks at eve
In hurdl'd Cotes° amid the field secure,   *shelters*

7. Mozambique, a Portuguese colony on the east coast of Africa; the trade route lay between Mozambique and Madagascar.
8. Of Saba or Sheba (now Yemen). Milton draws on the description of "Araby the blest"—"Arabia felix"—in Diodorus Siculus 3.46.
9. The apocryphal book Tobit relates the story of Tobit's son Tobias, who was sent into Media on an errand and there married Sara. Sara had previously been given to seven men, but all were killed by the jealous spirit Asmodeus before their marriages could be consummated. By the advice of Raphael, however, Tobias succeeded by creating a fishy smoke to drive away the devil Asmodeus.

Leaps o'er the fence with ease into the Fold:
Or as a Thief bent to unhoard the cash
Of some rich Burgher, whose substantial doors,
190   Cross-barr'd and bolted fast, fear no assault,
In at the window climbs, or o'er the tiles:
So clomb° this first grand Thief into God's Fold: *climbed*
So since into his Church lewd Hirelings[1] climb.
Thence up he flew, and on the Tree of Life,
195   The middle Tree and highest there that grew,
Sat like a Cormorant;[2] yet not true Life
Thereby regain'd, but sat devising Death
To them who liv'd; nor on the virtue thought
Of that life-giving Plant, but only us'd
200   For prospect,° what well us'd had been the pledge   *lookout*
Of immortality. So little knows
Any, but God alone, to value right
The good before him, but perverts best things
To worst abuse, or to thir meanest use.
205   Beneath him with new wonder now he views
To all delight of human sense expos'd
In narrow room Nature's whole wealth, yea more,
A Heaven on Earth: for blissful Paradise
Of God the Garden was, by him in the East
210   Of *Eden* planted; *Eden* stretch'd her Line
From *Auran* Eastward to the Royal Tow'rs
Of Great *Seleucia*, built by *Grecian* Kings,
Or where the Sons of *Eden* long before
Dwelt in *Telassar*:[3] in this pleasant soil
215   His far more pleasant Garden God ordain'd;
Out of the fertile ground he caus'd to grow
All Trees of noblest kind for sight, smell, taste;
And all amid them stood the Tree of Life,
High eminent, blooming Ambrosial Fruit
220   Of vegetable Gold; and next to Life
Our Death the Tree of Knowledge grew fast by,
Knowledge of Good bought dear by knowing ill.[4]
Southward through *Eden* went a River large,
Nor chang'd his course, but through the shaggy hill
225   Pass'd underneath ingulft, for God had thrown
That Mountain as his Garden mould high rais'd
Upon the rapid current, which through veins
Of porous Earth with kindly° thirst up-drawn,   *natural*
Rose a fresh Fountain, and with many a rill
230   Water'd the Garden;[5] thence united fell
Down the steep glade, and met the nether Flood,
Which from his darksome passage now appears,
And now divided into four main Streams,

1. Wicked men motivated only by material gain.
2. A voracious sea bird, often used to describe greedy clergy.
3. Auran was an eastern boundary of the land of Israel. Great Seleucia was built by Alexander's general Seleucus Nicator as a seat of government for his Syrian empire. The mention of Telassar prophesies war in Eden; see 2 Kings 14.11ff., where Telassar is an instance of lands destroyed utterly.
4. See Genesis 2.9.
5. See Genesis 2.10.

	Runs diverse, wand'ring many a famous Realm	
235	And Country whereof here needs no account,	
	But rather to tell how, if Art could tell,	
	How from that Sapphire Fount the crisped° Brooks,	*wavy*
	Rolling on Orient Pearl and sands of Gold,	
	With mazy error° under pendant shades	*wandering*
240	Ran Nectar, visiting each plant, and fed	
	Flow'rs worthy of Paradise which not nice° Art	*careful*
	In Beds and curious Knots, but Nature boon°	*bounteous*
	Pour'd forth profuse on Hill and Dale and Plain,	
	Both where the morning Sun first warmly smote	
245	The open field, and where the unpierc't shade	
	Imbrown'd° the noontide Bow'rs: Thus was this place,	*darkened*
	A happy rural seat of various view:	
	Groves whose rich Trees wept odorous Gums and Balm,	
	Others whose fruit burnisht with Golden Rind	
250	Hung amiable,° *Hesperian* Fables true,[6]	*lovely*
	If true, here only, and of delicious taste:	
	Betwixt them Lawns, or level Downs, and Flocks	
	Grazing the tender herb, were interpos'd,	
	Or palmy hillock, or the flow'ry lap	
255	Of some irriguous° Valley spread her store,	*well-watered*
	Flow'rs of all hue, and without Thorn the Rose:[7]	
	Another side, umbrageous° Grots and Caves	*shady*
	Of cool recess, o'er which the mantling Vine	
	Lays forth her purple Grape, and gently creeps	
260	Luxuriant; meanwhile murmuring waters fall	
	Down the slope hills, disperst, or in a Lake,	
	That to the fringed Bank with Myrtle crown'd,	
	Her crystal mirror holds, unite thir streams.	
	The Birds thir choir apply;° airs, vernal airs,[8]	*practice*
265	Breathing the smell of field and grove, attune	
	The trembling leaves, while Universal *Pan*[9]	
	Knit with the *Graces* and the *Hours* in dance	
	Led on th' Eternal Spring.[1] Not that fair field	
	Of *Enna*, where *Proserpin* gath'ring flow'rs	
270	Herself a fairer Flow'r by gloomy *Dis*	
	Was gather'd, which cost *Ceres* all that pain	
	To seek her through the world;[2] nor that sweet Grove	
	Of *Daphne* by *Orontes*, and th' inspir'd	
	Castalian Spring[3] might with this Paradise	
275	Of *Eden* strive; nor that *Nyseian* Isle	
	Girt with the River *Triton*, where old *Cham*,	
	Whom Gentiles *Ammon* call and *Lybian Jove*,	

6. Golden fruit like the legendary apples of the western islands, the Hesperides.

7. The thornless rose was used to symbolize the sinless state of humanity before the Fall; or the state of grace.

8. Breezes and melodies.

9. Pan (Greek for "all") was a symbol of universal nature.

1. Neoplatonists thought the triadic pattern of their dance expressed the movement underlying all natural generation.

2. The rape of Proserpina by Dis, the king of hell, was located in *Enna* by Ovid (*Fasti* 4.420ff.). The search for her made the world barren, and even when she was found, she was restored to Ceres—and fruitfulness to the world—only for half the year.

3. The grove called "Daphne" beside the River Orontes, near Antioch, had an Apolline oracle and a stream named after the famous Castalian spring of Parnassus.

Hid *Amalthea* and her Florid° Son,   *ruddy-complexioned*
Young *Bacchus*, from his Stepdame *Rhea's* eye;[4]
280 Nor where *Abassin* Kings thir issue Guard,
Mount *Amara*, though this by some suppos'd
True Paradise under the *Ethiop* Line
By *Nilus* head, enclos'd with shining Rock,
A whole day's journey high,[5] but wide remote
285 From this *Assyrian* Garden, where the Fiend
Saw undelighted all delight, all kind
Of living Creatures new to sight and strange:
Two of far nobler shape erect and tall,
Godlike erect, with native Honor clad
290 In naked Majesty seem'd Lords of all,
And worthy seem'd, for in thir looks Divine
The image of thir glorious Maker shone,[6]
Truth, Wisdom, Sanctitude severe and pure,
Severe, but in true filial freedom plac't;
295 Whence true autority in men; though both
Not equal, as thir sex not equal seem'd;
For contemplation hee and valor form'd,
For softness shee and sweet attractive Grace,
Hee for God only, shee for God in him:[7]
300 His fair large Front° and Eye sublime° declar'd   *forehead/uplifted*
Absolute rule; and Hyacinthine Locks
Round from his parted forelock manly hung
Clust'ring, but not beneath his shoulders broad:
Shee as a veil down to the slender waist
305 Her unadorned golden tresses wore
Dishevell'd, but in wanton ringlets wav'd
As the Vine curls her tendrils, which impli'd
Subjection, but requir'd with gentle sway,
And by her yielded, by him best receiv'd,
310 Yielded with coy° submission, modest pride,   *modest*
And sweet reluctant amorous delay.
Nor those mysterious parts were then conceal'd,
Then was not guilty shame: dishonest shame
Of Nature's works, honor dishonorable,
315 Sin-bred, how have ye troubl'd all mankind
With shows instead, mere shows of seeming pure,
And banisht from man's life his happiest life,
Simplicity and spotless innocence.
So pass'd they naked on, nor shunn'd the sight
320 Of God or Angel, for they thought no ill:
So hand in hand they pass'd, the loveliest pair
That ever since in love's imbraces met,

---

4. Ammon, King of Libya, had an illicit affair with a maiden Amaltheia, who gave birth to a marvelous son Dionysus (Bacchus). To protect mother and child from the jealousy of his wife Rhea, Ammon hid them on Nysa, an island near modern Tunis. The identifications of Ammon with the Libyan Jupiter and with Noah's son Ham were widely accepted.

5. Milton takes his description of Mount Amara from Peter Heylyn's *Cosmographie* 4.64.
6. See Genesis 1.27: "God created man in his own image."
7. See 1 Corinthians 11.3: "The head of every man is Christ; and the head of the woman is the man; and the head of Christ is God."

Adam the goodliest man of men since born
His Sons, the fairest of her Daughters *Eve*.

325 Under a tuft of shade that on a green
Stood whispering soft, by a fresh Fountain side
They sat them down, and after no more toil
Of thir sweet Gard'ning labor than suffic'd
To recommend cool *Zephyr*,[8] and made ease

330 More easy, wholesome thirst and appetite
More grateful, to thir Supper Fruits they fell,
Nectarine Fruits which the compliant boughs
Yielded them, side-long as they sat recline°   *lying down*
On the soft downy Bank damaskt with flow'rs:

335 The savory pulp they chew, and in the rind
Still as they thirsted scoop the brimming stream;
Nor gentle purpose,° nor endearing smiles   *conversation*
Wanted,° nor youthful dalliance as beseems   *lacked*
Fair couple, linkt in happy nuptial League,

340 Alone as they. About them frisking play'd
All Beasts of th' Earth, since wild, and of all chase
In Wood or Wilderness, Forest or Den;
Sporting the Lion ramp'd,° and in his paw   *reared up*
Dandl'd the Kid; Bears, Tigers, Ounces,° Pards°   *lynxes/leopards*

345 Gamboll'd before them, th' unwieldy Elephant
To make them mirth us'd all his might, and wreath'd
His Lithe Proboscis; close the Serpent sly
Insinuating,[9] wove with Gordian twine[1]
His braided train, and of his fatal guile

350 Gave proof unheeded; others on the grass
Coucht, and now fill'd with pasture gazing sat,
Or Bedward ruminating;[2] for the Sun
Declin'd was hasting now with prone career
To th' Ocean Isles,[3] and in th' ascending Scale

355 Of Heav'n the Stars that usher Evening rose:
When *Satan* still in gaze, as first he stood,
Scarce thus at length fail'd speech recover'd sad.
    O Hell! what do mine eyes with grief behold,
Into our room of bliss thus high advanc't

360 Creatures of other mould, earth-born perhaps,
Not Spirits, yet to heav'nly Spirits bright
Little inferior; whom my thoughts pursue
With wonder, and could love, so lively shines
In them Divine resemblance, and such grace

365 The hand that form'd them on thir shape hath pour'd.
Ah gentle pair, yee little think how nigh
Your change approaches, when all these delights
Will vanish and deliver ye to woe,
More woe, the more your taste is now of joy;

370 Happy, but for so happy ill secur'd

---

8. The west wind.
9. Penetrating by sinuous ways.
1. Coil, convolution, as difficult to undo as the Gordian

knot, which it took the hero Alexander to cut.
2. Chewing the cud before going to rest.
3. The Azores.

Long to continue, and this high seat your Heav'n
Ill fenc't for Heav'n to keep out such a foe
As now is enter'd; yet no purpos'd foe
To you whom I could pity thus forlorn
375 Though I unpitied: League with you I seek,
And mutual amity so strait,° so close,   *intimate*
That I with you must dwell, or you with me
Henceforth; my dwelling haply may not please
Like this fair Paradise, your sense, yet such
380 Accept your Maker's work; he gave it me,
Which I as freely give; Hell shall unfold,[4]
To entertain you two, her widest Gates,
And send forth all her Kings; there will be room,
Not like these narrow limits, to receive
385 Your numerous offspring; if no better place,
Thank him who puts me loath to this revenge
On you who wrong me not for him who wrong'd.
And should I at your harmless innocence
Melt, as I do, yet public reason[5] just,
390 Honor and Empire with revenge enlarg'd,
By conquering this new World, compels me now
To do what else though damn'd I should abhor.
      So spake the Fiend, and with necessity,
The Tyrant's plea, excus'd his devilish deeds.
395 Then from his lofty stand on that high Tree
Down he alights among the sportful Herd
Of those fourfooted kinds, himself now one,
Now other, as thir shape serv'd best his end
Nearer to view his prey, and unespi'd
400 To mark what of thir state he more might learn
By word or action markt: about them round
A Lion now he stalks with fiery glare,
Then as a Tiger, who by chance hath spi'd
In some Purlieu° two gentle Fawns at play,   *edge of a forest*
405 Straight couches close, then rising changes oft
His couchant watch, as one who chose his ground
Whence rushing he might surest seize them both
Gript in each paw: when *Adam* first of men
To first of women *Eve* thus moving speech,
410 Turn'd him° all ear to hear new utterance flow.   *Satan*
      Sole partner and sole part of all these joys,[6]
Dearer thyself than all; needs must the Power
That made us, and for us this ample World
Be infinitely good, and of his good
415 As liberal and free as infinite,
That rais'd us from the dust and plac't us here
In all this happiness, who at his hand
Have nothing merited, nor can perform

4. A blasphemous echo of Matthew 10.8 ("freely ye have received, freely give").
5. Reason of state, a perversion of the Ciceronian princi-
ple (*Laws* 3.3.8) that the good of the people is the supreme law.
6. The first "sole" means "only"; the second, "unrivalled."

Aught whereof hee hath need, hee who requires
420   From us no other service than to keep
This one, this easy charge, of all the Trees
In Paradise that bear delicious fruit
So various, not to taste that only Tree
Of Knowledge, planted by the Tree of Life,[7]
425   So near grows Death to Life, whate'er Death is,
Some dreadful thing no doubt; for well thou know'st
God hath pronounc't it death to taste that Tree,
The only sign of our obedience left
Among so many signs of power and rule
430   Conferr'd upon us, and Dominion giv'n
Over all other Creatures that possess
Earth, Air, and Sea.[8] Then let us not think hard
One easy prohibition, who enjoy
Free leave so large to all things else, and choice
435   Unlimited of manifold delights:
But let us ever praise him, and extol
His bounty, following our delightful task
To prune these growing Plants, and tend these Flow'rs,
Which were it toilsome, yet with thee were sweet.
440   To whom thus Eve repli'd. O thou for whom
And from whom I was form'd flesh of thy flesh,[9]
And without whom am to no end, my Guide
And Head, what thou hast said is just and right.[1]
For wee to him indeed all praises owe,
445   And daily thanks, I chiefly who enjoy
So far the happier Lot, enjoying thee
Preëminent by so much odds,° while thou   advantage
Like consort to thyself canst nowhere find.
That day I oft remember, when from sleep
450   I first awak't, and found myself repos'd
Under a shade on flow'rs, much wond'ring where
And what I was, whence thither brought, and how.
Not distant far from thence a murmuring sound
Of waters issu'd from a Cave and spread
455   Into a liquid Plain, then stood unmov'd
Pure as th' expanse of Heav'n; I thither went
With unexperienc't thought, and laid me down
On the green bank, to look into the clear
Smooth Lake, that to me seem'd another Sky.
460   As I bent down to look, just opposite,
A Shape within the wat'ry gleam appear'd
Bending to look on me, I started back,
It started back, but pleas'd I soon return'd,
Pleas'd it return'd as soon with answering looks

7. See Genesis 2.16ff.
8. See Genesis 1.28: "God said unto them . . . have
dominion over the fish of the sea, and over the fowl of
the air, and over every living thing that moveth upon the
earth."
9. See 1 Corinthians 11.9: "Neither was the man created

for the woman; but the woman for the man." See Genesis
2.23.
1. See 1 Corinthians 11.3: "The head of every man is
Christ; and the head of the woman is the man; and the
head of Christ is God."

465 Of sympathy and love; there I had fixt
Mine eyes till now, and pin'd with vain desire,[2]
Had not a voice thus warn'd me, What thou seest,
What there thou seest fair Creature is thyself,
With thee it came and goes: but follow me,
470 And I will bring thee where no shadow stays°   *awaits*
Thy coming, and thy soft imbraces, hee
Whose image thou art, him thou shalt enjoy
Inseparably thine, to him shalt bear
Multitudes like thyself, and thence be call'd
475 Mother of human Race: what could I do,
But follow straight, invisibly thus led?
Till I espi'd thee, fair indeed and tall,
Under a Platan, yet methought less fair,
Less winning soft, less amiably mild,
480 Than that smooth wat'ry image; back I turn'd,
Thou following cri'd'st aloud, Return fair *Eve*,
Whom fli'st thou? whom thou fli'st, of him thou art,
His flesh, his bone; to give thee being I lent
Out of my side to thee, nearest my heart
485 Substantial Life, to have thee by my side
Henceforth an individual° solace dear;   *inseparable*
Part of my Soul I seek thee, and thee claim
My other half: with that thy gentle hand
Seiz'd mine, I yielded, and from that time see
490 How beauty is excell'd by manly grace
And wisdom, which alone is truly fair.
    So spake our general Mother, and with eyes
Of conjugal attraction unreprov'd,°   *innocent*
And meek surrender, half imbracing lean'd
495 On our first Father, half her swelling Breast
Naked met his under the flowing Gold
Of her loose tresses hid: hee in delight
Both of her Beauty and submissive Charms
Smil'd with superior Love, as *Jupiter*
500 On *Juno* smiles, when he impregns° the Clouds   *impregnates*
That shed *May* Flowers; and press'd her Matron lip
With kisses pure: aside the Devil turn'd
For envy, yet with jealous leer malign
Ey'd them askance, and to himself thus plain'd.°   *complained*
505   Sight hateful, sight tormenting! thus these two
Imparadis't in one another's arms
The happier *Eden*, shall enjoy thir fill
Of bliss on bliss, while I to Hell am thrust,
Where neither joy nor love, but fierce desire,
510 Among our other torments not the least,
Still unfulfill'd with pain of longing pines;°   *troubles*
Yet let me not forget what I have gain'd
From thir own mouths; all is not theirs it seems:

2. Alluding to Ovid's story of the proud youth Narcissus, who was punished for his scornfulness by being made to fall in love with his own reflection in a pool.

One fatal Tree there stands of Knowledge call'd,
515   Forbidden them to taste: Knowledge forbidd'n?
Suspicious, reasonless. Why should thir Lord
Envy them that? can it be sin to know,
Can it be death? and do they only stand
By Ignorance, is that thir happy state,
520   The proof of thir obedience and thir faith?
O fair foundation laid whereon to build
Thir ruin! Hence I will excite thir minds
With more desire to know, and to reject
Envious commands, invented with design
525   To keep them low whom Knowledge might exalt
Equal with Gods; aspiring to be such,
They taste and die: what likelier can ensue?
But first with narrow search I must walk round
This Garden, and no corner leave unspi'd;
530   A chance but chance³ may lead where I may met
Some wand'ring Spirit of Heav'n, by Fountain side,
Or in thick shade retir'd, from him to draw
What further would be learnt. Live while ye may,
Yet happy pair; enjoy, till I return,
535   Short pleasures, for long woes are to succeed.
      So saying, his proud step he scornful turn'd,
But with sly circumspection, and began
Through wood, through waste, o'er hill, o'er dale his roam.
Meanwhile in utmost Longitude,⁴ where Heav'n
540   With Earth and Ocean meets, the setting Sun
Slowly descended, and with right aspect
Against the eastern Gate of Paradise
Levell'd his ev'ning Rays: it was a Rock
Of Alablaster,° pil'd up to the Clouds,   *alabaster*
545   Conspicuous far, winding with one ascent
Accessible from Earth, one entrance high;
The rest was craggy cliff, that overhung
Still as it rose, impossible to climb.⁵
Betwixt these rocky Pillars *Gabriel*⁶ sat
550   Chief of th' Angelic Guards, awaiting night;
About him exercis'd Heroic Games
Th' unarmed Youth of Heav'n, but nigh at hand
Celestial Armory, Shields, Helms, and Spears
Hung high with Diamond flaming, and with Gold.
555   Thither came *Uriel*, gliding through the Even
On a Sun-beam, swift as a shooting Star
In *Autumn* thwarts° the night, when vapors fir'd   *crosses*
Impress the Air, and shows the Mariner
From what point of his Compass to beware
560   Impetuous winds:⁷ he thus began in haste.
      Gabriel, to thee thy course by Lot hath giv'n

---

3. An accident and an opportunity.
4. The farthest west.
5. A possible source is the paradise of Mount Amara in Heylyn's *Cosmographie*.

6. "Strength of God," one of the four archangels ruling the corners of the world.
7. Shooting stars were thought to be a sign of storm because in falling they were thrust down by winds.

Charge and strict watch that to this happy place
No evil thing approach or enter in;
This day at highth of Noon came to my Sphere
565 A Spirit, zealous, as he seem'd, to know
More of th' Almighty's works, and chiefly Man
God's latest Image: I describ'd° his way   *observed*
Bent all on speed, and markt his Aery Gait;
But in the Mount that lies from *Eden* North,
570 Where he first lighted, soon discern'd his looks
Alien from Heav'n, with passions foul obscur'd:
Mine eye pursu'd him still, but under shade
Lost sight of him; one of the banisht crew
I fear, hath ventur'd from the Deep, to raise
575 New troubles; him thy care must be to find.
          To whom the winged Warrior thus return'd:
Uriel,[8] no wonder if thy perfect sight,
Amid the Sun's bright circle where thou sitst,
See far and wide: in at this Gate none pass
580 The vigilance here plac't, but such as come
Well known from Heav'n; and since Meridian hour
No Creature thence: if Spirit of other sort,
So minded, have o'erleapt these earthy bounds
On purpose, hard thou know'st it to exclude
585 Spiritual substance with corporeal bar.
But if within the circuit of these walks
In whatsoever shape he lurk, of whom
Thou tell'st, by morrow dawning I shall know.
          So promis'd hee, and *Uriel* to his charge
590 Return'd on that bright beam, whose point now rais'd
Bore him slope downward to the Sun now fall'n
Beneath th' *Azores*; whither the prime Orb,
Incredible how swift, had thither roll'd
Diurnal,° or this less volúbil[9] Earth   *in one day*
595 By shorter flight to th' East, had left him there
Arraying with reflected Purple and Gold
The Clouds that on his Western Throne attend:[1]
Now came still Ev'ning on, and Twilight gray
Had in her sober Livery all things clad;
600 Silence accompanied, for Beast and Bird,
They to thir grassy Couch, these to thir Nests
Were slunk, all but the wakeful Nightingale;
She all night long her amorous descant sung;
Silence was pleas'd: now glow'd the Firmament
605 With living Sapphires: *Hesperus*[2] that led
The starry Host, rode brightest, till the Moon
Rising in clouded Majesty, at length
Apparent Queen unveil'd her peerless light,
And o'er the dark her Silver Mantle threw.

8. "Light of God."
9. Capable of ready rotation on its axis.
1. The appearance of sunset can be regarded as caused
either by orbital motion of the sun about the earth or by
the earth's rotation (a lesser movement).
2. The evening star.

610   When *Adam* thus to *Eve*: Fair Consort, th' hour
             Of night, and all things now retir'd to rest
             Mind us of like repose, since God hath set
             Labor and rest, as day and night to men
             Successive, and the timely dew of sleep
615   Now falling with soft slumbrous weight inclines
             Our eye-lids; other Creatures all day long
             Rove idle unimploy'd, and less need rest;
             Man hath his daily work of body or mind
             Appointed, which declares his Dignity,
620   And the regard of Heav'n on all his ways;
             While other Animals unactive range,
             And of thir doings God takes no account.
             Tomorrow ere fresh Morning streak the East
             With first approach of light, we must be ris'n,
625   And at our pleasant labor, to reform
             Yon flow'ry Arbors, yonder Alleys green,
             Our walk at noon, with branches overgrown,
             That mock our scant manuring,° and require   *cultivating*
             More hands than ours to lop thir wanton growth:
630   Those Blossoms also, and those dropping Gums,
             That lie bestrown unsightly and unsmooth,
             Ask riddance, if we mean to tread with ease;
             Meanwhile, as Nature wills, Night bids us rest.
                 To whom thus *Eve* with perfect beauty adorn'd.
635   My Author° and Disposer, what thou bidd'st   *origin, creator*
             Unargu'd I obey; so God ordains,
             God is thy Law, thou mine: to know no more
             Is woman's happiest knowledge and her praise.
             With thee conversing I forget all time,
640   All seasons and thir change, all please alike.[3]
             Sweet is the breath of morn, her rising sweet,
             With charm° of earliest Birds; pleasant the Sun   *song*
             When first on this delightful Land he spreads
             His orient Beams, on herb, tree, fruit, and flow'r,
645   Glist'ring with dew; fragrant the fertile earth
             After soft showers; and sweet the coming on
             Of grateful Ev'ning mild, then silent Night
             With this her solemn Bird and this fair Moon,
             And these the Gems of Heav'n, her starry train:
650   But neither breath of Morn when she ascends
             With charm of earliest Birds, nor rising Sun
             On this delightful land, nor herb, fruit, flow'r,
             Glist'ring with dew, nor fragrance after showers,
             Nor grateful Ev'ning mild, nor silent Night
655   With this her solemn Bird, nor walk by Moon,
             Or glittering Star-light without thee is sweet.
             But wherefore all night long shine these, for whom
             This glorious sight, when sleep hath shut all eyes?

3. Time of day; not "seasons of the year," since it is still eternal spring.

        To whom our general Ancestor repli'd.

660   Daughter of God and Man, accomplisht *Eve*,
        Those have thir course to finish, round the Earth,
        By morrow Ev'ning, and from Land to Land
        In order, though to Nations yet unborn,
        Minist'ring light prepar'd, they set and rise;

665   Lest total darkness should by Night regain
        Her old possession, and extinguish life
        In Nature and all things, which these soft fires
        Not only enlighten, but with kindly heat
        Of various influence foment and warm,

670   Temper or nourish, or in part shed down
        Thir stellar virtue on all kinds that grow
        On Earth, made hereby apter to receive
        Perfection from the Sun's more potent Ray.[4]
        These then, though unbeheld in deep of night,

675   Shine not in vain, nor think, though men were none,
        That Heav'n would want spectators, God want praise;
        Millions of spiritual Creatures walk the Earth
        Unseen, both when we wake, and when we sleep:
        All these with ceaseless praise his works behold

680   Both day and night: how often from the steep
        Of echoing Hill or Thicket have we heard
        Celestial voices to the midnight air,
        Sole, or responsive each to other's note
        Singing thir great Creator: oft in bands

685   While they keep watch, or nightly rounding walk,
        With Heav'nly touch of instrumental sounds
        In full harmonic number join'd, thir songs
        Divide the night, and lift our thoughts to Heaven.

        Thus talking hand in hand alone they pass'd

690   On to thir blissful Bower; it was a place
        Chos'n by the sovran Planter, when he fram'd
        All things to man's delightful use; the roof
        Of thickest covert was inwoven shade
        Laurel and Myrtle, and what higher grew

695   Of firm and fragrant leaf; on either side
        Acanthus, and each odorous bushy shrub
        Fenc'd up the verdant wall; each beauteous flow'r,
        Iris all hues, Roses, and Jessamin°   *jasmine*
        Rear'd high thir flourisht heads between, and wrought

700   Mosaic; underfoot the Violet,
        Crocus, and Hyacinth with rich inlay
        Broider'd the ground, more color'd than with stone
        Of costliest Emblem:[5] other Creature here

---

4. In Neoplatonic astrology, Sol was said to accomplish the generation of new life by acting through each of the other planets in turn; their function was only to modulate his influence or to select from his complete spectrum of virtues. After the Fall, the influence of the stars becomes less "kindly" (benign; natural).

5. Any ornament of inlaid work; the other sense of "emblem" (pictorial symbol) also operates here, to draw attention to the emblematic properties of the flowers (the humility of the violet, prudence of the hyacinth, amiability of the jasmine, etc.). The bower as a whole is an emblem of true married love.

Beast, Bird, Insect, or Worm durst enter none;
705   Such was thir awe of Man. In shadier Bower
More sacred and sequester'd, though but feign'd,
Pan or *Silvanus* never slept, nor Nymph,
Nor *Faunus* haunted.[6] Here in close recess
With Flowers, Garlands, and sweet-smelling Herbs
710   Espoused *Eve* deckt first her Nuptial Bed,
And heav'nly Choirs the Hymenaean° sung,   *wedding hymn*
What day the genial° Angel to our Sire   *nuptial, generative*
Brought her in naked beauty more adorn'd,
More lovely than *Pandora,* whom the Gods
715   Endow'd with all thir gifts, and O too like
In sad event, when to the unwiser Son
Of *Japhet* brought by *Hermes,* she ensnar'd
Mankind with her fair looks, to be aveng'd
On him who had stole *Jove's* authentic fire.[7]
720   Thus at thir shady Lodge arriv'd, both stood,
Both turn'd, and under op'n Sky ador'd
The God that made both Sky, Air, Earth and Heav'n
Which they beheld, the Moon's resplendent Globe
And starry Pole:° Thou also mad'st the Night,   *sky*
725   Maker Omnipotent, and thou the Day,
Which we in our appointed work imploy'd
Have finisht happy in our mutual help
And mutual love, the Crown of all our bliss
Ordain'd by thee, and this delicious place
730   For us too large, where thy abundance wants
Partakers, and uncropt falls to the ground.
But thou hast promis'd from us two a Race
To fill the Earth, who shall with us extol
Thy goodness infinite, both when we wake,
735   And when we seek, as now, thy gift of sleep.
This said unanimous, and other Rites
Observing none, but adoration pure
Which God likes best, into thir inmost bower
Handed they went; and eas'd the putting off
740   These troublesome disguises which wee wear,
Straight side by side were laid, nor turn'd I ween
Adam from his fair Spouse, nor *Eve* the Rites
Mysterious of connubial Love refus'd:
Whatever Hypocrites austerely talk

---

6. Pan, Silvanus, and Faunus were confused, for all were represented as half man, half goat. Pan was a symbol of fecundity; Silvanus, god of woods, symbolized gardens and limits; Faunus, the Roman Pan, a wood god, and the father of satyrs, was an emblem of concupiscence.
7. Milton has followed Charles Estienne's version of the myth: "Pandora . . . is feigned by Hesiod the first woman—made by Vulcan at Jupiter's command—. . . she was called Pandora, either because she was 'endowed with all [the gods'] gifts,' or because she was endowed with gifts by all." She was "sent with a closed casket to Epimetheus, since Jupiter wanted revenge on the human race for the boldness of Prometheus, who had stolen fire from heaven and taken it . . . down to earth; and that Epimetheus received her and opened the casket, which contained every kind of evil, so that it filled the world with diseases and calamaties." Prometheus and Epimetheus were sons of Iapetus, the Titan son of Coelus and Terra. Milton identifies Iapetus with Iaphet (Noah's son).

745   Of purity and place and innocence,
         Defaming as impure what God declares
         Pure, and commands to some, leaves free to all.
         Our Maker bids increase,[8] who bids abstain
         But our Destroyer, foe to God and Man?
750   Hail wedded Love, mysterious Law, true source
         Of human offspring, sole propriety
         In Paradise of all things common else.
         By thee adulterous lust was driv'n from men
         Among the bestial herds to range, by thee
755   Founded in Reason, Loyal, Just, and Pure,
         Relations dear, and all the Charities°   *affections*
         Of Father, Son, and Brother first were known.
         Far be it, that I should write thee sin or blame,
         Or think thee unbefitting holiest place,
760   Perpetual Fountain of Domestic sweets,
         Whose bed is undefil'd and chaste pronounc't,[9]
         Present, or past, as Saints and Patriarchs us'd.
         Here Love his golden shafts imploys,[1] here lights
         His constant Lamp, and waves his purple wings,
765   Reigns here and revels; not in the bought smile
         Of Harlots, loveless, joyless, unindear'd,
         Casual fruition, nor in Court Amours,
         Mixt Dance, or wanton Mask, or Midnight Ball,
         Or Serenate, which the starv'd Lover sings
770   To his proud fair, best quitted with disdain.
         These lull'd by Nightingales imbracing slept,
         And on thir naked limbs the flow'ry roof
         Show'r'd Roses, which the Morn repair'd.° Sleep on,   *made up for*
         Blest pair; and O yet happiest if ye seek
775   No happier state, and know to know no more.[2]
            Now had night measur'd with her shadowy Cone
         Half way up Hill this vast Sublunar Vault,[3]
         And from thir Ivory Port the Cherubim
         Forth issuing at th' accustom'd hour stood arm'd
780   To thir night watches in warlike Parade,
         When *Gabriel* to his next in power thus spake.
            Uzziel,[4] half these draw off, and coast the South
         With strictest watch; these other wheel the North;
         Our circuit meets full West. As flame they part
785   Half wheeling to the Shield, half to the Spear.[5]

8. See Genesis 1.28.
9. See Hebrews 13.4: "Marriage is honourable in all, and the bed undefiled."
1. Cupid's "golden shafts" were sharp and gleaming and kindled love, while those of lead were blunt and put love to flight (Ovid, *Metamorphoses* 1.468–471).
2. Either "know that it is best not to seek new knowledge (by eating the forbidden fruit)" or "know how to limit your experience to the state of innocence."
3. The earth's shadow is a cone that appears to circle around it in diametrical opposition to the sun. When the axis of the cone reaches the meridian, it is midnight; but here it is only "Half way up," so the time is nine o'clock.
4. "Uzziel" (Strength of God) occurs in the Bible as an ordinary human name (e.g., Exodus 6.18), and so does "Zephon" (Searcher of Secrets: Numbers 26.15). "Ithuriel" (Discovery of God) is not from the Bible.
5. "Shield" for "left" and "spear" for "right" were ancient military terms.

From these, two strong and subtle Spirits he call'd
That near him stood, and gave them thus in charge.
   Ithuriel and *Zephon*, with wing'd speed
Search through this Garden, leave unsearcht no nook,
790   But chiefly where those two fair Creatures Lodge,
Now laid perhaps asleep secure° of harm.   *careless*
This Ev'ning from the Sun's decline arriv'd
Who tells of some infernal Spirit seen
Hitherward bent (who could have thought?) escap'd
795   The bars of Hell, on errand bad no doubt:
Such where ye find, seize fast, and hither bring.
   So saying, on he led his radiant Files,
Dazzling the Moon; these to the Bower direct
In search of whom they sought: him there they found
800   Squat like a Toad, close at the ear of *Eve*;
Assaying by his Devilish art to reach
The Organs of her Fancy, and with them forge
Illusions as he list, Phantasms° and Dreams,   *illusions*
Or if, inspiring venom, he might taint
805   Th' animal spirits[6] that from pure blood arise
Like gentle breaths from Rivers pure, thence raise
At least distemper'd,° discontented thoughts,   *vexed*
Vain hopes, vain aims, inordinate desires
Blown up with high conceits ingend'ring pride.
810   Him thus intent *Ithuriel* with his Spear
Touch'd lightly; for no falsehood can endure
Touch of Celestial temper, but returns
Of force to its own likeness: up he starts
Discover'd and surpris'd. As when a spark
815   Lights on a heap of nitrous[7] Powder, laid
Fit for the Tun[8] some Magazin to store
Against° a rumor'd War, the Smutty grain   *preparing for*
With sudden blaze diffus'd, inflames the Air:
So started up in his own shape the Fiend.
820   Back stepp'd those two fair Angels half amaz'd
So sudden to behold the grisly King;
Yet thus, unmov'd with fear, accost him soon.
   Which of those rebel Spirits adjudg'd to Hell
Com'st thou, escap'd thy prison, and transform'd,
825   Why satst thou like an enemy in wait
Here watching at the head of these that sleep?
   Know ye not then said *Satan*, fill'd with scorn,
Know ye not mee?[9] * * *

---

6. Spirits in this sense were fine vapors, regarded by some as a medium between body and soul, by others as a separate soul. Animal spirits (Latin *anima*, soul) ascended to the brain and issued through the nerves to impart motion to the body. Local movement of the animal spirits could also produce imaginative apparitions, by which angels were thought to affect the human mind.
7. Mixed with niter (potassium nitrate or saltpeter, an ingredient in gunpowder) to form an explosive.
8. In proper condition for casking, ready for use.
9. Ithuriel and Zephon take Satan to Gabriel, who orders him to return to Hell. Satan rises up to fight the assembled angels—"His Stature reacht the Sky, and on his Crest / Sat horror Plum'd"—but then God displays scales in heaven, showing victory tilting to Gabriel, and Satan flees.

from **Book 5**
The Argument

Morning approacht, Eve relates to Adam *her troublesome dream; he likes it not, yet comforts her: They come forth to thir day labors: Thir Morning Hymn at the Door of thir Bower. God to render Man inexcusable sends Raphael to admonish him of his obedience, of his free estate, of his enemy near at hand; who he is, and why his enemy, and whatever else may avail* Adam *to know.* Raphael *comes down to Paradise, his appearance describ'd, his coming discern'd by* Adam *afar off sitting at the door of his Bower; he goes out to meet him, brings him to his lodge, entertains him with the choicest fruits of Paradise got together by* Eve; *thir discourse at Table:* Raphael *performs his message, minds* Adam *of his state and of his enemy; relates at* Adam's *request who that enemy is, and how he came to be so, beginning from his first revolt in Heaven, and the occasion thereof; how he drew his Legions after him to the parts of the North, and there incited them to rebel with him, persuading all but only* Abdiel *a Seraph, who in Argument dissuades and opposes him, then forsakes him.*

from **Book 6**
The Argument

Raphael *continues to relate how* Michael *and* Gabriel *were sent forth to Battle against* Satan *and his Angels. The first fight describ'd:* Satan *and his Powers retire under Night: He calls a Council, invents devilish Engines, which in the second day's Fight put* Michael *and his Angels to some disorder; but they at length pulling up Mountains overwhelm'd both the force and Machines of* Satan: *Yet the Tumult not so ending, God on the third day sends Messiah his Son for whom he had reserv'd the glory of the Victory: Hee in the Power of his Father coming to the place, and causing all his Legions to stand still on either side, with his Chariot and Thunder driving into the midst of his Enemies, pursues them unable to resist towards the wall of Heaven; which opening they leap down with horror and confusion in the place of punishment prepar'd for them in the Deep: Messiah returns with triumph to his Father.*

from **Book 7**
The Argument

Raphael *at the request of* Adam *relates how and wherefore this world was first created; that God, after the expelling of* Satan *and his Angels out of Heaven, declar'd his pleasure to create another World and other Creatures to dwell therein; sends his Son with Glory and attendance of Angels to perform the work of Creation in six days: the Angels celebrate with Hymns the performance thereof, and his reascension into Heaven.*

from **Book 8**
The Argument

Adam *inquires concerning celestial Motions, is doubtfully answer'd, and exhorted to search rather things more worthy of knowledge:* Adam *assents, and still desirous to detain* Raphael, *relates to him what he remember'd since his own Creation, his placing in Paradise, his talk with God concerning solitude and fit society, his first meeting and Nuptials with* Eve, *his discourse with the Angel thereupon; who after admonitions repeated departs.*

Book 9

The Argument

Satan *having compast the Earth, with meditated guile returns as a mist by Night into Paradise, enters into the Serpent sleeping. Adam and Eve in the Morning go forth to thir labors, which Eve proposes to divide in several places, each laboring apart: Adam consents not, alleging the danger, lest that Enemy, of whom they were forewarn'd, should attempt her found alone: Eve loath to be thought not circumspect or firm enough, urges her going apart, the rather desirous to make trial of her strength; Adam at last yields: The Serpent finds her alone; his subtle approach, first gazing, then speaking, with much flattery extolling Eve above all other Creatures. Eve wond'ring to hear the Serpent speak, asks how he attain'd to human speech and such understanding not till now; the Serpent answers, that by tasting of a certain Tree in the Garden he attain'd both to Speech and Reason, till then void of both: Eve requires him to bring her to that Tree, and finds it to be the Tree of Knowledge forbidden: The Serpent now grown bolder, with many wiles and arguments induces her at length to eat; she pleas'd with the taste deliberates awhile whether to impart thereof to Adam or not, at last brings him of the Fruit, relates what persuaded her to eat thereof: Adam at first amaz'd, but perceiving her lost, resolves through vehemence[1] of love to perish with her; and extenuating[2] the trespass, eats also of the Fruit: The effects thereof in them both; they seek to cover thir nakedness; then fall to variance and accusation of one another.*

     No more of talk where God or Angel Guest
With Man, as with his Friend, familiar us'd
To sit indulgent, and with him partake
Rural repast, permitting him the while

5   Venial° discourse unblam'd: I now must change   *permissible*
Those Notes to Tragic; foul distrust, and breach
Disloyal on the part of Man, revolt,
And disobedience: On the part of Heav'n
Now alienated, distance and distaste,

10   Anger and just rebuke, and judgment giv'n,
That brought into this World a world of woe,
Sin and her shadow Death, and Misery
Death's Harbinger: Sad task, yet argument
Not less but more Heroic than the wrath

15   Of stern *Achilles* on his Foe pursu'd
Thrice Fugitive about *Troy* Wall; or rage
Of *Turnus* for *Lavinia* disespous'd,
Or *Neptune's* ire or *Juno's*, that so long
Perplex'd the *Greek* and *Cytherea's* Son;[3]

20   If answerable° style I can obtain   *equal, accountable*
Of my Celestial Patroness,[4] who deigns
Her nightly visitation unimplor'd,

---

1. The root meaning of Latin "vehementia" is mindlessness.
2. Carrying further, drawing out.
3. Achilles is "stern" in his "wrath" because he refused any covenant with Hector, and Turnus dies fighting Aeneas for the hand of Lavinia, whereas Messiah, more heroically, is not implacable in his anger. He issued his sole commandment "sternly" (8.333); but when it is disobeyed, he works for reconciliation. Similarly, God's

anger is distinguished from "Neptune's ire" and "Juno's" (which merely "perplexed" Odysseus and Aeneas) in that it is expressed in justice rather than in victimization.
4. The heavenly Muse, Urania. Both ancient and modern epics had always had war, or at least fighting, as a principal ingredient. (So has *Paradise Lost*, in the first half of the poem; but in the second half this subject is transcended.) Milton now glances unfavorably at the typical matter of the romantic epic.

And dictates to me slumb'ring, or inspires
Easy my unpremeditated Verse:
25   Since first this Subject for Heroic Song
Pleas'd me long choosing, and beginning late;
Not sedulous by Nature to indite
Wars, hitherto the only Argument
Heroic deem'd, chief maistry to dissect
30   With long and tedious havoc fabl'd Knights
In Battles feign'd; the better fortitude
Of Patience and Heroic Martyrdom
Unsung; or to describe Races and Games,
Or tilting Furniture, emblazon'd Shields,
35   Impreses[5] quaint, Caparisons[6] and Steeds;
Bases and tinsel Trappings, gorgeous Knights
At Joust and Tournament; then marshall'd Feast
Serv'd up in Hall with Sewers,° and Seneschals;°   *waiters/stewards*
The skill of Artifice or Office mean,
40   Not that which justly gives Heroic name
To Person or to Poem.[7] Mee of these
Nor skill'd nor studious, higher Argument
Remains, sufficient of itself to raise
That name,[8] unless an age too late, or cold
45   Climate, or Years damp my intended wing
Deprest; and much they may, if all be mine,
    Not Hers who brings it nightly to my Ear.
The Sun was sunk, and after him the Star
Of *Hesperus*,° whose Office is to bring   *the planet Venus*
50   Twilight upon the Earth, short Arbiter
Twixt Day and Night, and now from end to end
Night's Hemisphere had veil'd the Horizon round:
When *Satan* who late fled before the threats
Of *Gabriel* out of *Eden*,[9] now improv'd°   *intensified*
55   In meditated fraud and malice, bent
On Man's destruction, maugre what might hap
Of heavier on himself,[1] fearless return'd.
By Night he fled, and at Midnight return'd
From compassing the Earth, cautious of day,
60   Since *Uriel* Regent of the Sun descri'd
His entrance, and forewarn'd the Cherubim
That kept thir watch; thence full of anguish driv'n,
The space of seven continu'd Nights he rode
With darkness, thrice the Equinoctial Line
65   He circl'd, four times cross'd the Car of Night
From Pole to Pole, traversing each Colure;[2]
On th'eighth return'd, and on the Coast averse
From entrance or Cherubic Watch, by stealth

5. Heraldic devices, often with accompanying mottos.
6. Ornamented coverings spread over the saddle of a horse.
7. Artifice implies mechanic or applied art. It is beneath the dignity of epic to teach etiquette and social ceremony and heraldry.
8. The name of epic.
9. I.e., at the end of Book 4, a week earlier.

1. Despite the danger of heavier punishment.
2. By keeping to earth's shadow, Satan contrives to experience a whole week of darkness. The two colures were great circles, intersecting at right angels at the poles and dividing the equinoctial circle (the equator) into four equal parts.

70 Found unsuspected way. There was a place,
 Now not, though Sin, not Time, first wrought the change,
 Where *Tigris* at the foot of Paradise
 Into a Gulf shot under ground, till part
 Rose up a Fountain by the Tree of Life;
75 In with the River sunk, and with it rose
 Satan involv'd in rising Mist, then sought
 Where to lie hid; Sea he had searcht and Land
 From *Eden* over *Pontus,* and the Pool
 Maeotis, up beyond the River *Ob;*[3]
80 Downward as far Antarctic; and in length
 West from *Orontes* to the Ocean barr'd
 At *Darien,* thence to the Land where flows
 Ganges and *Indus:*[4] thus the Orb he roam'd
 With narrow search; and with inspection deep
85 Consider'd every Creature, which of all
 Most opportune might serve his Wiles, and found
 The Serpent subtlest Beast of all the Field.[5]
 Him after long debate, irresolute°   *undecided*
 Of thoughts revolv'd, his final sentence° chose *judgment*
 Fit Vessel, fittest Imp° of fraud, in whom   *offshoot*
90 To enter, and his dark suggestions hide
 From sharpest sight: for in the wily Snake,
 Whatever sleights none would suspicious mark,
 As from his wit and native subtlety
 Proceeding, which in other Beasts observ'd
95 Doubt° might beget of Diabolic pow'r   *suspicion*
 Active within beyond the sense of brute.
 Thus he resolv'd, but first from inward grief
 His bursting passion into plaints thus pour'd:
  O Earth, how like to Heav'n, if not preferr'd
100 More justly, Seat worthier of Gods, as built
 With second thoughts, reforming what was old!
 For what God after better worse would build?
 Terrestrial Heav'n, danc't round by other Heav'ns
 That shine, yet bear thir bright officious Lamps,
105 Light above Light, for thee alone, as seems,
 In thee concentring all thir precious beams
 Of sacred influence:[6] As God in Heav'n
 Is Centre, yet extends to all, so thou
 Centring receiv'st from all those Orbs; in thee,
110 Not in themselves, all thir known virtue appears
 Productive in Herb, Plant, and nobler birth
 Of Creatures animate with gradual life
 Of Growth, Sense, Reason, all summ'd up in Man.[7]

3. In his north-south circles, Satan passed Pontus (the Black Sea), the "pool / Maeotis" (the Sea of Azov), and the Siberian River Ob, which flows north into the Gulf of Ob and from there into the Arctic Ocean.
4. In his westward circling of the equinoctial line, he crossed the Syrian River Orontes, then the Pacific ("peaceful") "Ocean barred" by the Isthmus of Darien (Panama) and India.
5. See Genesis 3.1.
6. The case for an earth-centered universe, put at 8.86–114 by Raphael, is now put by Satan.
7. "Growth, sense, reason" are the activities of the vegetable, animal, and rational souls, respectively, in humans.

With what delight could I have walkt thee round,
115   If I could joy in aught, sweet interchange
Of Hill and Valley, Rivers, Woods and Plains,
Now Land, now Sea, and Shores with Forest crown'd,
Rocks, Dens, and Caves; but I in none of these
Find place or refuge; and the more I see
120   Pleasures about me, so much more I feel
Torment within me, as from the hateful siege°   *conflict*
Of contraries; all good to me becomes
Bane,° and in Heav'n much worse would be my state.   *poison*
But neither here seek I, no nor in Heav'n
125   To dwell, unless by maistring Heav'n's Supreme;
Nor hope to be myself less miserable
By what I seek, but others to make such
As I, though thereby worse to me redound:
For only in destroying I find ease
130   To my relentless thoughts; and him destroy'd,
Or won to what may work his utter loss,
For whom all this was made, all this will soon
Follow, as to him linkt in weal or woe,
In woe then: that destruction wide may range:[8]
135   To mee shall be the glory sole among
Th'infernal Powers, in one day to have marr'd
What he *Almight* styl'd, six Nights and Days
Continu'd making, and who knows how long
Before had been contriving, though perhaps
140   Not longer than since I in one Night freed
From servitude inglorious well nigh half
Th' Angelic Name, and thinner left the throng
Of his adorers: hee to be aveng'd,
And to repair his numbers thus impair'd,
145   Whether such virtue° spent of old now fail'd   *power*
More Angels to Create, if they at least
Are his Created, or to spite us more,
Determin'd to advance into our room
A Creature form'd of Earth, and him endow,
150   Exalted from so base original,
With Heav'nly spoils, our spoils; What he decreed
He effected; Man he made, and for him built
Magnificent this World, and Earth his seat,
Him Lord pronounc'd, and, O indignity!
155   Subjected to his service Angel wings,
And flaming Ministers to watch and tend
Thir earthy Charge: Of these the vigilance
I dread, and to elude, thus wrapt in mist
Of midnight vapor glide obscure, and pry
160   In every Bush and Brake, where hap may find
The Serpent sleeping, in whose mazy folds
To hide me, and the dark intent I bring.
O foul descent! that I who erst contended

---

8. The created cosmos will follow humans to destruction.

With Gods to sit the highest, am now constrain'd
165 Into a Beast, and mixt with bestial slime,
This essence to incarnate and imbrute,
That to the highth of Deity aspir'd;
But what will not Ambition and Revenge
Descend to? who aspires must down as low
170 As high he soar'd, obnoxious° first or last   *exposed*
To basest things. Revenge, at first though sweet,
Bitter ere long back on itself recoils;
Let it, I reck not, so it light well aim'd,
Since higher I fall short, on him who next
175 Provokes my envy, this new Favorite
Of Heav'n, this Man of Clay, Son of despite,
Whom us the more to spite his Maker rais'd
From dust: spite then with spite is best repaid.
   So saying, through each Thicket Dank or Dry,
180 Like a black mist low creeping, he held on
His midnight search, where soonest he might find
The Serpent: him fast sleeping soon he found
In Labyrinth of many a round self-roll'd,
His head the midst, well stor'd with subtle wiles:
185 Not yet in horrid Shade or dismal Den,
Nor nocent° yet, but on the grassy Herb   *harmful, guilty*
Fearless unfear'd he slept: in at his Mouth
The Devil enter'd, and his brutal sense,
In heart or head, possessing soon inspir'd
190 With act intelligential; but his sleep
Disturb'd not, waiting close° th' approach of Morn.   *concealed*
Now whenas sacred Light began to dawn
In *Eden* on the humid Flow'rs, that breath'd
Thir morning incense, when all things that breathe,
195 From th' Earth's great Altar send up silent praise
To the Creator, and his Nostrils fill
With grateful Smell, forth came the human pair
And join'd thir vocal Worship to the Choir
Of Creatures wanting voice; that done, partake
200 The season, prime for sweetest Scents and Airs:
Then cómmune how that day they best may ply
Thir growing work: for much thir work outgrew
The hands' dispatch of two Gard'ning so wide.
And *Eve* first to her Husband thus began.
205   *Adam*, well may we labor still to dress
This Garden, still to tend Plant, Herb and Flow'r,
Our pleasant task enjoin'd, but till more hands
Aid us, the work under our labor grows,
Luxurious by restraint; what we by day
210 Lop overgrown, or prune, or prop, or bind,
One night or two with wanton growth derides
Tending to wild. Thou therefore now advise
Or hear what to my mind first thoughts present,
Let us divide our labors, thou where choice
215 Leads thee, or where most needs, whether to wind

The Woodbine round this Arbor, or direct
The clasping Ivy where to climb, while I
In yonder Spring of Roses intermixt
With Myrtle, find what to redress till Noon:
220 For while so near each other thus all day
Our task we choose, what wonder if so near
Looks intervene and smiles, or object new
Casual discourse draw on, which intermits
Our day's work brought to little, though begun
225 Early, and th' hour of Supper comes unearn'd.
    To whom mild answer *Adam* thus return'd.
Sole *Eve*, Associate sole, to me beyond
Compare above all living Creatures dear,
Well hast thou motion'd,° well thy thoughts imploy'd   *proposed*
230 How we might best fulfil the work which here
God hath assign'd us, nor of me shalt pass
Unprais'd: for nothing lovelier can be found
In Woman, than to study household good,
And good works in her Husband to promote.
235 Yet not so strictly hath our Lord impos'd
Labor, as to debar us when we need
Refreshment, whether food, or talk between,
Food of the mind, or this sweet intercourse
Of looks and smiles, for smiles from Reason flow,
240 To brute deni'd, and are of Love the food,
Love not the lowest end of human life.
For not to irksome toil, but to delight
He made us, and delight to Reason join'd.
These paths and Bowers doubt not but our joint hands
245 Will keep from Wilderness with ease, as wide
As we need walk, till younger hands ere long
Assist us: But if much converse perhaps
Thee satiate, to short absence I could yield.
For solitude sometimes is best society,
250 And short retirement urges sweet return.
But other doubt possesses me, lest harm
Befall thee sever'd from me; for thou know'st
What hath been warn'd us, what malicious Foe
Envying our happiness, and of his own
255 Despairing, seeks to work us woe and shame
By sly assault; and somewhere nigh at hand
Watches, no doubt, with greedy hope to find
His wish and best advantage, us asunder,
Hopeless to circumvent us join'd, where each
260 To other speedy aid might lend at need;
Whether his first design be to withdraw
Our fealty from God, or to disturb
Conjugal Love, than which perhaps no bliss
Enjoy'd by us excites his envy more;
265 Or this, or worse,⁹ leave not the faithful side

9. Whether this or worse (be his first design).

That gave thee being, still shades thee and protects.
The Wife, where danger or dishonor lurks,
Safest and seemliest by her Husband stays,
Who guards her, or with her the worst endures.
270   To whom the Virgin° Majesty of *Eve*,   *chaste, innocent*
As one who loves, and some unkindness meets,
With sweet austere composure thus repli'd.
    Offspring of Heav'n and Earth, and all Earth's Lord,
That such an Enemy we have, who seeks
275 Our ruin, both by thee inform'd I learn,
And from the parting Angel over-heard
As in a shady nook I stood behind,
Just then return'd at shut of Ev'ning Flow'rs.
But that thou shouldst my firmness therefore doubt
280 To God or thee, because we have a foe
May tempt it, I expected not to hear.
His violence thou fear'st not, being such,
As wee, not capable of death or pain,
Can either not receive, or can repel.
285 His fraud is then thy fear, which plain infers
Thy equal fear that my firm Faith and Love
Can by his fraud be shak'n or seduc't;
Thoughts, which how found they harbor in thy breast,
Adam, misthought of her to thee so dear?
290   To whom with healing words *Adam* repli'd.
Daughter of God and Man, immortal *Eve*,
For such thou art, from sin and blame entire:°   *free*
Not diffident° of thee do I dissuade   *mistrustful*
Thy absence from my sight, but to avoid
295 Th' attempt itself, intended by our Foe.
For hee who tempts, though in vain, at least asperses°   *falsely charges*
The tempted with dishonor foul, suppos'd
Not incorruptible of Faith, not proof
Against temptation: thou thyself with scorn
300 And anger wouldst resent the offer'd wrong,
Though ineffectual found: misdeem not then,
If such affront I labor to avert
From thee alone, which on us both at once
The Enemy, though bold, will hardly dare,
305 Or daring, first on mee th' assault shall light.
Nor thou his malice and false guile contemn;
Subtle he needs must be, who could seduce
Angels, nor think superfluous others' aid.
I from the influence of thy looks receive
310 Access° in every Virtue, in thy sight   *increase*
More wise, more watchful, stronger, if need were
Of outward strength; while shame, thou looking on,
Shame to be overcome or over-reacht
Would utmost vigor raise, and rais'd unite.
315 Why shouldst not thou like sense within thee feel
When I am present, and thy trial choose
With me, best witness of thy Virtue tri'd.

So spake domestic *Adam* in his care
And Matrimonial Love; but *Eve,* who thought
320   Less° attribúted to her Faith sincere,   *too little*
Thus her reply with accent sweet renew'd.
     If this be our condition, thus to dwell
In narrow circuit strait'n'd by a Foe,
Subtle or violent, we not endu'd
325   Single with like defense, wherever met,
How are we happy, still in fear of harm?
But harm precedes not sin: only our Foe
Tempting affronts us with his foul esteem
Of our integrity: his foul esteem
330   Sticks no dishonor on our Front,° but turns   *forehead*
Foul on himself; then wherefore shunn'd or fear'd
By us? who rather double honor gain
From his surmise prov'd false, find peace within,
Favor from Heav'n, our witness from th' event.
335   And what is Faith, Love, Virtue unassay'd
Alone, without exterior help sustain'd?
Let us not then suspect our happy State
Left so imperfet by the Maker wise,
As not secure to single or combin'd.
340   Frail is our happiness, if this be so,
And *Eden* were no Eden[1] thus expos'd.
     To whom thus Adam fervently repli'd.
O Woman, best are all things as the will
Of God ordain'd them, his creating hand
345   Nothing imperfet or deficient left
Of all that he Created, much less Man,
Or aught that might his happy State secure,
Secure from outward force; within himself
The danger lies, yet lies within his power:
350   Against his will he can receive no harm.
But God left free the Will, for what obeys
Reason, is free, and Reason he made right,
But bid her well beware, and still erect,[2]
Lest by some fair appearing good surpris'd
355   She dictate false, and misinform the Will
To do what God expressly hath forbid.
Not then mistrust, but tender love enjoins,
That I should mind thee oft, and mind thou me.
Firm we subsist, yet possible to swerve,
360   Since Reason not impossibly may meet
Some specious object by the Foe suborn'd,
And fall into deception unaware,
Not keeping strictest watch, as she was warn'd.
Seek not temptation then, which to avoid
365   Were better, and most likely if from mee
Thou sever not: Trial will come unsought.
Wouldst thou approve° thy constancy, approve   *demonstrate*

---

1. I.e., no pleasure, the literal Hebrew meaning of "Eden."   2. Always attentive, but also with a glance at upright.

First thy obedience; th' other who can know,
Not seeing thee attempted, who attest?

370   But if thou think, trial unsought may find
Us both securer° than thus warn'd thou seem'st,   *more careless*
Go; for thy stay, not free, absents thee more;
Go in thy native innocence, rely
On what thou hast of virtue, summon all,

375   For God towards thee hath done his part, do thine.
       So spake the Patriarch of Mankind, but *Eve*
Persisted, yet submiss, though last, repli'd.
       With thy permission then, and thus forewarn'd
Chiefly by what thy own last reasoning words

380   Touch'd only, that our trial, when least sought,
May find us both perhaps far less prepar'd,
The willinger I go, nor much expect
A Foe so proud will first the weaker seek;
So bent, the more shall shame him his repulse.

385   Thus saying, from her Husband's hand her hand
Soft she withdrew, and like a Wood-Nymph light,
Oread or *Dryad*, or of *Delia's* Train,[3]
Betook her to the Groves, but *Delia's* self
In gait surpass'd and Goddess-like deport,

390   Though not as shee with Bow and Quiver arm'd,
But with such Gard'ning Tools as Art yet rude,
Guiltless° of fire had form'd, or Angels brought.[4]   *innocent, ignorant*
To Pales, or Pomona, thus adorn'd,
Likest she seem'd, Pomona when she fled

395   *Vertumnus*, or to *Ceres* in her Prime,
Yet Virgin of *Proserpina* from *Jove*.[5]
Her long and ardent look his Eye pursu'd
Delighted, but desiring more her stay.
Oft he to her his charge of quick return

400   Repeated, shee to him as oft engag'd
To be return'd by Noon amid the Bow'r,
And all things in best order to invite
Noontide repast, or Afternoon's repose.
O much deceiv'd, much failing, hapless *Eve*,

405   Of thy presum'd return! event perverse!
Thou never from that hour in Paradise
Found'st either sweet repast, or sound repose;
Such ambush hid among sweet Flow'rs and Shades
Waited with hellish rancor imminent

410   To intercept thy way, or send thee back
Despoil'd of Innocence, of Faith, of Bliss.
For now, and since first break of dawn the Fiend,
Mere° Serpent in appearance, forth was come,   *plain*
And on his Quest, where likeliest he might find

3. Oreads, were mountain nymphs, such as attended on Diana; dryads were wood nymphs. Neither class of nymphs were immortal.
4. Only as a result of the Fall did it become necessary for humans to have some means of warming themselves. There may also be an allusion to the fire stolen from heaven by Prometheus.
5. Pales was the Roman goddess of pastures; Pomona was the nymph or goddess of fruit trees, seduced by the disguised Vertumnus; Ceres was the goddess of corn and agriculture who bore Proserpina to Jove.

415	The only two of Mankind, but in them	
	The whole included Race, his purpos'd prey.	
	In Bow'r and Field he sought, where any tuft	
	Of Grove or Garden-Plot more pleasant lay,	
	Thir tendance° or Plantation for delight,	*object of care*
420	By Fountain or by shady Rivulet,	
	He sought them both, but wish'd his hap° might find	*chance*
	Eve separate, he wish'd, but not with hope	
	Of what so seldom chanc'd, when to his wish,	
	Beyond his hope, *Eve* separate he spies,	
425	Veil'd in a Cloud of Fragrance, where she stood,	
	Half spi'd, so thick the Roses bushing round	
	About her glow'd, oft stooping to support	
	Each Flow'r of slender stalk, whose head though gay	
	Carnation, Purple, Azure, or speckt with Gold,	
430	Hung drooping unsustain'd, them she upstays	
	Gently with Myrtle band, mindless the while,	
	Herself, though fairest unsupported Flow'r,	
	From her best prop so far, and storm so nigh.⁶	
	Nearer he drew, and many a walk travers'd	
435	Of stateliest Covert, Cedar, Pine, or Palm,	
	Then voluble and bold, now hid, now seen	
	Among thick-wov'n Arborets and Flow'rs	
	Imborder'd on each Bank, the hand° of *Eve*:	*handiwork*
	Spot more delicious than those Gardens feign'd	
440	Or of reviv'd *Adonis*, or renown'd	
	Alcinoüs, host of old *Laertes'* Son,	
	Or that, not Mystic, where the Sapient King	
	Held dalliance with his fair *Egyptian* Spouse.⁷	
	Much hee the Place admir'd, the Person more.	
445	As one who long in populous City pent,	
	Where Houses thick and Sewers annoy the Air,	
	Forth issuing on a Summer's Morn to breathe	
	Among the pleasant Villages and Farms	
	Adjoin'd, from each thing met conceives delight,	
450	The smell of Grain, or tedded° Grass, or Kine,°	*mown/cows*
	Or Dairy, each rural sight, each rural sound;	
	If chance with Nymphlike step fair Virgin pass,	
	What pleasing seem'd, for her now pleases more,	
	She most, and in her look sums all Delight.	
455	Such Pleasure took the Serpent to behold	
	This Flow'ry Plat,° the sweet recess of *Eve*	*piece of ground*
	Thus early, thus alone; her Heav'nly form	
	Angelic, but more soft, and Feminine,	
	Her graceful Innocence, her every Air	
460	Of gesture or least action overaw'd	
	His Malice, and with rapine sweet bereav'd	

6. See 4.270, page 838, where Proserpina (and by implication Eve) was "Herself a fairer Flow'r" when she was carried off by the king of hell.

7. "The sapient king" was Solomon (*Song of Solomon* 6.2). Milton alludes to Spenser's addition to the myth of Ado-

nis, that Venus keeps Adonis hidden in a secret garden (*The Faerie Queene* 3.6). "Laertes' son" was Odysseus; much-traveled as he was, he marveled when he saw the Garden of Alcinoüs (Homer, *Odyssey* 7).

His fierceness of the fierce intent it brought:
That space the Evil one abstracted stood
From his own evil, and for the time remain'd

465   Stupidly good, of enmity disarm'd,
Of guile, of hate, of envy, of revenge;
But the hot Hell that always in him burns,
Though in mid Heav'n, soon ended his delight,
And tortures him now more, the more he sees

470   Of pleasure not for him ordain'd: then soon
Fierce hate he recollects, and all his thoughts
Of mischief, gratulating,° thus excites.   *rejoicing*
    Thoughts, whither have ye led me, with what sweet
Compulsion thus transported to forget

475   What hither brought us, hate, not love, nor hope
Of Paradise for Hell, hope here to taste
Of pleasure, but all pleasure to destroy,
Save what is in destroying, other joy
To me is lost. Then let me not let pass

480   Occasion which now smiles, behold alone
The Woman, opportune° to all attempts,   *exposed*
Her Husband, for I view far round, not nigh,
Whose higher intellectual more I shun,
And strength, of courage haughty, and of limb

485   Heroic built, though of terrestrial mould,°   *formed of earth*
Foe not informidable, exempt from wound,
I not; so much hath Hell debas'd, and pain
Infeebl'd me, to what I was in Heav'n.
Shee fair, divinely fair, fit Love for Gods,

490   Not terrible, though terror be in Love
And beauty, not approacht by stronger hate,
Hate stronger, under show of Love well feign'd,
The way which to her ruin now I tend.
    So spake the Enemy of Mankind, enclos'd

495   In Serpent, Inmate bad, and toward *Eve*
Address'd his way, not with indented wave,
Prone on the ground, as since, but on his rear,
Circular base of rising folds, that tow'r'd
Fold above fold a surging Maze, his Head

500   Crested aloft, and Carbuncle his Eyes;[8]
With burnisht Neck of verdant Gold, erect
Amidst his circling Spires,° that on the grass   *coils*
Floated redundant:° pleasing was his shape,   *abundant to excess*
And lovely, never since of Serpent kind

505   Lovelier, not those that in *Illyria* chang'd
Hermione and *Cadmus,* or the God
In *Epidaurus;*[9] nor to which transform'd
Ammonian Jove, or *Capitoline* was seen,
Hee with *Olympias,* this with her who bore

8. "Carbuncle" or reddish eyes denoted rage.
9. Cadmus was turned into a serpent first; only after he had embraced his wife Hermione (Harmonia) in his new form did she too change (Ovid, *Metamorphoses* 4.572–603).

Aesculapius, the god of healing, once changed into a serpent to help the Romans in that form (Ovid, *Metamorphoses* 15.626–744).

510 *Scipio* the highth of Rome.[1] With tract oblique
    At first, as one who sought access, but fear'd
    To interrupt, side-long he works his way.
    As when a Ship by skilful Steersman wrought
    Nigh River's mouth or Foreland, where the Wind
515 Veers oft, as oft so steers, and shifts her Sail;
    So varied hee, and of his tortuous Train
    Curl'd many a wanton wreath in sight of *Eve*,
    To lure her Eye; shee busied heard the sound
    Of rustling Leaves, but minded not, as us'd
520 To such disport before her through the Field,
    From every Beast, more duteous at her call,
    Than at *Circean* call the Herd disguis'd.[2]
    Hee bolder now, uncall'd before her stood;
    But as in gaze admiring: Oft he bow'd
525 His turret Crest, and sleek enamell'd Neck,
    Fawning, and lick'd the ground whereon she trod.
    His gentle dumb expression turn'd at length
    The Eye of *Eve* to mark his play; he glad
    Of her attention gain'd, with Serpent Tongue
530 Organic, or impulse of vocal Air,
    His fraudulent temptation thus began.
        Wonder not, sovran Mistress, if perhaps
    Thou canst, who are sole Wonder, much less arm
    Thy looks, the Heav'n of mildness, with disdain,
535 Displeas'd that I approach thee thus, and gaze
    Insatiate, I thus single, nor have fear'd
    Thy awful brow, more awful thus retir'd.
    Fairest resemblance of thy Maker fair,
    Thee all things living gaze on, all things thine
540 By gift, and thy Celestial Beauty adore
    With ravishment beheld, there best beheld
    Where universally admir'd: but here
    In this enclosure wild, these Beasts among,
    Beholders rude, and shallow to discern
545 Half what in thee is fair, one man except,
    Who sees thee? (and what is one?) who shouldst be seen
    A Goddess among Gods, ador'd and serv'd
    By Angels numberless, thy daily Train.
        So gloz'd° the Tempter, and his Proem° tun'd;   *flattered/prelude*
550 Into the Heart of *Eve* his words made way,
    Though at the voice much marvelling; at length
    Not unamaz'd she thus in answer spake.
        What may this mean? Language of Man pronounc't
    By Tongue of Brute, and human sense exprest?[3]
555 The first at least of these I thought deni'd
    To Beasts, whom God on thir Creation-Day

---

1. Jupiter Ammon, the "Lybian Jove," as a serpent mated with Olympias to father Alexander the Great, just as the Roman Jupiter, Capitolinus, took the form of a snake to father the great general Scipio.
2. Homer's Circe changed men into beasts who surprised Odysseus's company by fawning on them like dogs (*Odyssey*

10.212–219).
3. Milton is unusually favorable to Eve in making her ask the serpent how it came by its voice. The Eve of Scriptural exegesis, by contrast, is carried away by the words and makes no inquiry into their source.

Created mute to all articulate sound;
The latter I demur,° for in thir looks   *hesitate about*
Much reason, and in thir actions oft appears.
560   Thee, Serpent, subtlest beast of all the field
I knew, but not with human voice endu'd;
Redouble then this miracle, and say,
How cam'st thou speakable of mute,⁴ and how
To me so friendly grown above the rest
565   Of brutal kind, that daily are in sight?
Say, for such wonder claims attention due.
     To whom the guileful Tempter thus repli'd.
Empress of this fair World, resplendent *Eve*,
Easy to mee it is to tell thee all
570   What thou command'st and right thou should'st be obey'd:
I was at first as other Beasts that graze
The trodden Herb, of abject° thoughts and low,   *mean-spirited*
As was my food, nor aught but food discern'd
Or Sex, and apprehended nothing high:
575   Till on a day roving the field, I chanc'd
A goodly Tree far distant to behold
Loaden with fruit of fairest colors mixt,
Ruddy and Gold: I nearer drew to gaze;
When from the boughs a savory odor blown,
580   Grateful to appetite, more pleas'd my sense
Than smell of sweetest Fennel, or the Teats
Of Ewe or Goat dropping with Milk at Ev'n,
Unsuckt of Lamb or Kid, that tend thir play.
To satisfy the sharp desire I had
585   Of tasting those fair Apples, I resolv'd
Not to defer; hunger and thirst at once,
Powerful persuaders, quick'n'd at the scent
Of that alluring fruit, urg'd me so keen.
About the mossy Trunk I wound me soon,
590   For high from ground the branches would require
Thy utmost reach or *Adam's:* Round the Tree
All other Beasts that saw, with like desire
Longing and envying stood, but could not reach.
Amid the Tree now got, where plenty hung
595   Tempting so nigh, to pluck and eat my fill
I spar'd not, for such pleasure till that hour
At Feed or Fountain never had I found.
Sated at length, ere long I might perceive
Strange alteration in me, to degree
600   Of Reason in my inward Powers, and Speech
Wanted not long, though to this shape retain'd.
Thenceforth to Speculations high or deep
I turn'd my thoughts, and with capacious mind
Consider'd all things visible in Heav'n,
605   Or Earth, or Middle, all things fair and good;
But all that fair and good in thy Divine

---

4. How did you become capable of speech from being dumb?

Semblance, and in thy Beauty's heav'nly Ray
United I beheld; no Fair° to thine   *beauty*
Equivalent or second, which compell'd
610   Mee thus, though importune perhaps, to come
And gaze, and worship thee of right declar'd
Sovran of Creatures, universal Dame.
    So talk'd the spirited[5] sly Snake; and *Eve*,
Yet more amaz'd unwary thus repli'd.
615   Serpent, thy overpraising leaves in doubt
The virtue° of that Fruit, in thee first prov'd: *power*
But say, where grows the Tree, from hence how far?
For many are the Trees of God that grow
In Paradise, and various, yet unknown
620   To us, in such abundance lies our choice,
As leaves a greater store of Fruit untoucht,
Still hanging incorruptible, till men
Grow up to thir provision, and more hands
Help to disburden Nature of her Birth.
625   To whom the wily Adder, blithe and glad.
Empress, the way is ready, and not long,
Beyond a row of Myrtles, on a Flat,
Fast by a Fountain, one small Thicket past
Of blowing° Myrrh and Balm; if thou accept   *blooming*
630   My conduct,° I can bring thee thither soon.   *guidance*
    Lead then, said Eve. Hee leading swiftly roll'd
In tangles, and made intricate seem straight,
To mischief swift. Hope elevates, and joy
    Bright'ns his Crest, as when a wand'ring Fire,
635   Compact° of unctuous vapor, which the Night   *made up*
Condenses, and the cold invirons round,
Kindl'd through agitation to a Flame,
Which oft, they say, some evil Spirit attends,
Hovering and blazing with delusive Light,
640   Misleads th' amaz'd Night-wanderer from his way
To Bogs and Mires, and oft through Pond or Pool,
There swallow'd up and lost, from succor far.
So glister'd the dire Snake, and into fraud
Led *Eve* our credulous Mother, to the Tree
645   Of prohibition, root of all our woe;
Which when she saw, thus to her guide she spake.
    Serpent, we might have spar'd our coming hither,
Fruitless to mee, though Fruit be here to excess,
The credit of whose virtue rest with thee,
650   Wondrous indeed, if cause of such effects.
But of this Tree we may not taste nor touch;
God so commanded, and left that Command
Sole Daughter of his voice;[6] the rest, we live
Law to ourselves, our Reason is our Law.
655   To whom the Tempter guilefully repli'd.
Indeed? hath God then said that of the Fruit

---

5. Endowed with an animating spirit, stirred up; also   6. A Hebraism for "voice sent from heaven."
energetic, enterprising, possessed by a spirit.

Of all these Garden Trees ye shall not eat,
Yet Lords declar'd of all in Earth or Air?[7]
   To whom thus *Eve* yet sinless. Of the Fruit
660 Of each Tree in the Garden we may eat,
But of the Fruit of this fair Tree amidst
The Garden, God hath said, Ye shall not eat
Thereof, nor shall ye touch it, lest ye die.
   She scarce had said, though brief, when now more bold
665 The Tempter, but with show of Zeal and Love
To Man, and indignation at his wrong,
New part puts on, and as to passion mov'd,
Fluctuates disturb'd, yet comely, and in act
Rais'd, as of some great matter to begin.
670 As when of old some Orator renown'd
In *Athens* or free *Rome*, where Eloquence
Flourish'd, since mute, to some great cause addrest,
Stood in himself collected, while each part,
Motion, each act won audience ere the tongue,
675 Sometimes in highth began, as no delay
Of Preface brooking through his Zeal of Right.[8]
So standing, moving, or to highth upgrown
The Tempter all impassion'd thus began.
   O Sacred, Wise, and Wisdom-giving Plant,
680 Mother of Science,° Now I feel thy Power   *knowledge*
Within me clear, not only to discern
Things in thir Causes, but to trace the ways
Of highest Agents, deem'd however wise.
Queen of this Universe, do not believe
685 Those rigid threats of Death; ye shall not Die:
How should ye? by the Fruit? it gives you Life
To° Knowledge: By the Threat'ner? look on mee,   *in addition to*
Mee who have touch'd and tasted, yet both live,
And life more perfet have attain'd than Fate
690 Meant mee, by vent'ring higher than my Lot.
Shall that be shut to Man, which to the Beast
Is open? or will God incense his ire
For such a petty Trespass, and not praise
Rather your dauntless virtue, whom the pain
695 Of Death denounc't, whatever thing Death be,
Deterr'd not from achieving what might lead
To happier life, knowledge of Good and Evil;
Of good, how just? of evil, if what is evil
Be real, why not known, since easier shunn'd?[9]
700 God therefore cannot hurt ye, and be just;
Not just, not God; not fear'd then, nor obey'd:
Your fear itself of Death removes the fear.
Why then was this forbid? Why but to awe,

7. Lines 655–58 closely follow Genesis. 3.1.
8. This simile blends oratorical, theatrical, and theological meanings. Thus "part" means "part of the body," "dramatic role," and "moral act"; "motion" means "gesture," "mime" (or "puppet-show"), and "instigation, persuasive force, inclination"; "act" means "action," "performance of

a play," and "the accomplished deed itself."
9. If the knowledge is good, how is it just to prohibit it? Here occurs the most egregious logical fallacy in speech. (For evil to be "shunned," it is not at all necessary that it should be "known" in the sense of being experienced.)

Why but to keep ye low and ignorant,
705   His worshippers; he knows that in the day
Ye Eat thereof, your Eyes that seem so clear,
Yet are but dim, shall perfetly be then
Op'n'd and clear'd, and ye shall be as Gods,
Knowing both Good and Evil as they know.[1]
710   That ye should be as Gods, since I as Man,
Internal Man,[2] is but proportion meet,
I of brute human, thee of human Gods.
So ye shall die perhaps, by putting off
Human, to put on Gods, death to be wisht,
715   Though threat'n'd, which no worse than this can bring.[3]
And what are Gods that Man may not become
As they, participating° God-like food?   *sharing*
The Gods are first, and that advantage use
On our belief, that all from them proceeds;
720   I question it, for this fair Earth I see,
Warm'd by the Sun, producing every kind,
Them nothing: If they° all things, who enclos'd   *if they produce*
Knowledge of Good and Evil in this Tree,
That who so eats thereof, forthwith attains
725   Wisdom without their leave? and wherein lies
Th' offense, that Man should thus attain to know?
What can your knowledge hurt him, or this Tree
Impart against his will if all be his?
Or is it envy, and can envy dwell
730   In heav'nly breasts?[4] these, these and many more
Causes import° your need of this fair Fruit.   *suggest*
Goddess humane, reach then, and freely taste.
      He ended, and his words replete with guile
Into her heart too easy entrance won:
735   Fixt on the Fruit she gaz'd, which to behold
Might tempt alone, and in her ears the sound
Yet rung of his persuasive words, impregn'd°   *impregnated*
With Reason, to her seeming, and with Truth;
Meanwhile the hour of Noon drew on, and wak'd
740   An eager appetite, rais'd by the smell
So savory of that Fruit, which with desire,
Inclinable now grown to touch or taste,
Solicited her longing eye;[5] yet first
Pausing a while, thus to herself she mus'd.
745   Great are thy Virtues, doubtless, best of Fruits,
Though kept from Man, and worthy to be admir'd,
Whose taste, too long forborne, at first assay
Gave elocution to the mute, and taught
The Tongue not made for Speech to speak thy praise:[6]

---

1. See Genesis 3.5.
2. The serpent's pretence is that his "inward powers" are human.
3. Satan offers a travesty of Christian mortification and death to sin; see *Colossians* 3.1–15: "ye have put off the old man with his deeds; And have put on the new man, which is renewed in knowledge after the image of him

that created him."
4. See Virgil, *Aeneid* 1.11; Satan is inviting Eve to participate in a pagan epic, complete with machinery of jealous gods.
5. For lines 735–43, see Genesis 3.6.
6. Eve has trusted Satan's account of the fruit and consequently argues from false premises, such as its magical power.

750 Thy praise hee also who forbids thy use,
    Conceals not from us, naming thee the Tree
    Of Knowledge, knowledge both of good and evil;
    Forbids us then to taste, but his forbidding
    Commends thee more, while it infers the good
755 By thee communicated, and our want:
    For good unknown, sure is not had, or had
    And yet unknown, is as not had at all.
    In plain° then, what forbids he but to know,   *plainly*
    Forbids us good, forbids us to be wise?
760 Such prohibitions bind not. But if Death
    Bind us with after-bands, what profits then
    Our inward freedom? In the day we eat
    Of this fair Fruit, our doom is, we shall die.
    How dies the Serpent? hee hath eat'n and lives,
765 And knows, and speaks, and reasons, and discerns,
    Irrational till then. For us alone
    Was death invented? or to us deni'd
    This intellectual food, for beasts reserv'd?
    For Beasts it seems: yet that one Beast which first
770 Hath tasted, envies not, but brings with joy
    The good befall'n him, Author unsuspect,[7]
    Friendly to man, far from deceit or guile.
    What fear I then, rather what know to fear[8]
    Under this ignorance of Good and Evil,
775 Of God or Death, of Law or Penalty?
    Here grows the Cure of all, this Fruit Divine,
    Fair to the Eye, inviting to the Taste,
    Of virtue° to make wise: what hinders then   *power*
    To reach, and feed at once both Body and Mind?
780   So saying, her rash hand in evil hour
    Forth reaching to the Fruit, she pluck'd, she eat:°   *ate*
    Earth felt the wound, and Nature from her seat
    Sighing through all her Works gave signs of woe,
    That all was lost. Back to the Thicket slunk
785 The guilty Serpent, and well might, for *Eve*,
    Intent now wholly on her taste, naught else
    Regarded, such delight till then, as seem'd,
    In Fruit she never tasted, whether true
    Or fancied so, through expectation high
790 Of knowledge, nor was God-head from her thought.[9]
    Greedily she ingorg'd without restraint,
    And knew not eating Death:[1] Satiate at length,
    And hight'n'd as with Wine, jocund and boon,°   *jolly*
    Thus to herself she pleasingly began.
795   O Sovran, virtuous, precious of all Trees
    In Paradise, of operation blest
    To Sapience,[2] hitherto obscur'd, infam'd,°   *defamed*

7. Eve means "informant not subject to suspicion."
8. What fear I, then—or rather (since I'm not allowed to
know anything) what do I know that is to be feared?
9. She expected to achieve godhead.
1. She knew not that she was eating death; "she was
unaware, while she ate death" or even "she 'knew'; not
eating (immediate) death."
2. "Sapience" is derived from Latin *sapientia* (discernment, taste) and ultimately from *sapere* (to taste).

And thy fair Fruit let hang, as to no end
Created; but henceforth my early care,
800 Not without Song, each Morning, and due praise
Shall tend thee, and the fertile burden ease
Of thy full branches offer'd free to all;
Till dieted by thee I grow mature
In knowledge, as the Gods who all things know;
805 Though others³ envy what they cannot give;
For had the gift been theirs, it had not here
Thus grown. Experience, next to thee I owe,
Best guide; not following thee, I had remain'd
In ignorance, thou op'n'st Wisdom's way,
810 And giv'st access, though secret she retire.
And I perhaps am secret; Heav'n is high,
High and remote to see from thence distinct
Each thing on Earth; and other care perhaps
May have diverted from continual watch
815 Our great Forbidder, safe with all his Spies
About him. But to *Adam* in what sort
Shall I appear? shall I to him make known
As yet my change, and give him to partake
Full happiness with mee, or rather not.
820 But keep the odds of Knowledge in my power
Without Copartner? so to add what wants
In Female Sex, the more to draw his Love,
And render me more equal, and perhaps,
A thing not undesirable, sometime
825 Superior: for inferior who is free?
This may be well: but what if God have seen,
And Death ensue? then I shall be no more,
And *Adam* wedded to another *Eve*,
Shall live with her enjoying, I extinct;
830 A death to think. Confirm'd then I resolve,
Adam shall share with me in bliss or woe:
So dear I love him, that with him all deaths
I could endure, without him live no life.
    So saying, from the Tree her step she turn'd,
835 But first low Reverence done, as to the power
That dwelt within, whose presence had infus'd
Into the plant sciential⁴ sap, deriv'd
From Nectar, drink of Gods. *Adam* the while
Waiting desirous her return, had wove
840 Of choicest Flow'rs a Garland to adorn
Her Tresses, and her rural labors crown,
As Reapers oft are wont thir Harvest Queen.
Great joy he promis'd to his thoughts, and new
Solace in her return, so long delay'd;
845 Yet oft his heart, divine° of something ill,   *prophet*
Misgave him; hee the falt'ring measure⁵ felt;
And forth to meet her went, the way she took

3. I.e., God. Eve's language is now full of lapses in logic   4. Endowed with knowledge.
and evasions in theology.   5. The rhythm of his own heart.

That Morn when first they parted; by the Tree
Of Knowledge he must pass; there he her met,
850   Scarce from the Tree returning; in her hand
A bough of fairest fruit that downy smil'd,
New gather'd, and ambrosial smell diffus'd.
To him she hasted, in her face excuse
Came Prologue, and Apology to prompt,[6]
855   Which with bland words at will she thus addrest.
  Hast thou not wonder'd, *Adam*, at my stay?
Thee I have misst, and thought it long, depriv'd
Thy presence, agony of love till now
Not felt, nor shall be twice, for never more
860   Mean I to try, what rash untri'd I sought,
The pain of absence from thy sight. But strange
Hath been the cause, and wonderful to hear:
This Tree is not as we are told, a Tree
Of danger tasted,° nor to evil unknown   *if tasted*
865   Op'ning the way, but of Divine effect
To open Eyes, and make them Gods who taste;
And hath been tasted such: the Serpent wise,
Or not restrain'd as wee, or not obeying,
Hath eat'n of the fruit, and is become,
870   Not dead, as we are threat'n'd, but thenceforth
Endu'd with human voice and human sense,
Reasoning to admiration, and with mee
Persuasively hath so prevail'd, that I
Have also tasted, and have also found
875   Th' effects to correspond, opener mine Eyes,
Dim erst, dilated Spirits, ampler Heart,
And growing up to Godhead; which for thee
Chiefly I sought, without thee can despise.
For bliss, as thou hast part, to me is bliss,
880   Tedious, unshar'd with thee, and odious soon.
Thou therefore also taste, that equal Lot
May join us, equal Joy, as equal Love;
Lest thou not tasting, different degree[7]
Disjoin us, and I then too late renounce
885   Deity for thee, when Fate will not permit.
  Thus *Eve* with Count'nance blithe her story told;
But in her Cheek distemper[8] flushing glow'd.
On th' other side, *Adam*, soon as he heard
The fatal Trespass done by *Eve*, amaz'd,
890   Astonied° stood and Blank, while horror chill   *stunned*
Ran through his veins, and all his joints relax'd;
From his slack hand the Garland wreath'd for *Eve*,
Down dropp'd, and all the faded Roses shed:
Speechless he stood and pale, till thus at length
895   First to himself he inward silence broke.

---

6. The expression on Eve's face is visible in advance as she approaches and so is like the prologue-speaker of a play. But it also remains on her face as she speaks, to help out her words, and so is like the prompter of the play. The actor prompted is apology, i.e., justification or defense personified.
7. Differing position in the scale of creatures.
8. A disordered condition due to disturbance of the temperament of the bodily humors.

O fairest of Creation, last and best
Of all God's Works, Creature in whom excell'd
Whatever can to sight or thought be form'd,
Holy, divine, good, amiable, or sweet!
900 How art thou lost, how on a sudden lost,
Defac't, deflow'r'd, and now to death devote?°   given over
Rather how hast thou yielded to transgress
The strict forbiddance, how to violate
The sacred Fruit forbidd'n! some cursed fraud
905 Of Enemy hath beguil'd thee, yet unknown,
And mee with thee hath ruin'd, for with thee
Certain my resolution is to Die;
How can I live without thee, how forgo
Thy sweet Converse and Love so dearly join'd,
910 To live again in these wild Woods forlorn?
Should God create another *Eve*, and I
Another Rib afford, yet loss of thee
Would never from my heart; no no, I feel
The Link of Nature draw me: Flesh of Flesh,
915 Bone of my Bone thou art, and from thy State
Mine never shall be parted, bliss or woe.
So having said, as one from sad dismay
Recomforted, and after thoughts disturb'd
Submitting to what seem'd remediless,
920 Thus in calm mood his Words to *Eve* he turn'd.
Bold deed thou hast presum'd, advent'rous *Eve*,
And peril great provok't, who thus hath dar'd
Had it been only coveting to Eye
That sacred Fruit, sacred° to abstinence,   devoted
925 Much more to taste it under ban to touch.
But past who can recall, or done undo?
Not God Omnipotent, nor Fate; yet so
Perhaps thou shalt not Die, perhaps the Fact°   crime, deed
Is not so heinous now, foretasted Fruit,
930 Profan'd first by the Serpent, by him first
Made common and unhallow'd ere our taste;
Nor yet on him found deadly, he yet lives,
Lives, as thou said'st, and gains to live as Man
Higher degree of Life, inducement strong
935 To us, as likely tasting to attain
Proportional ascent, which cannot be
But to be Gods, or Angels Demi-gods.
Nor can I think that God, Creator wise,
Though threat'ning, will in earnest so destroy
940 Us his prime Creatures, dignifi'd so high,
Set over all his Works, which in our Fall,
For us created, needs with us must fail,
Dependent made; so God shall uncreate,
Be frustrate, do, undo, and labor lose,
945 Not well conceiv'd of God, who though his Power
Creation could repeat, yet would be loath
Us to abolish, lest the Adversary

Triumph and say; Fickle their State whom God
Most Favors, who can please him long? Mee first
950   He ruin'd, now Mankind; whom will he next?
Matter of scorn, not to be given the Foe.
However I with thee have fixt my Lot,
Certain to undergo like doom;[9] if Death
Consort with thee, Death is to mee as Life;
955   So forcible within my heart I feel
The Bond of Nature draw me to my own,
My own in thee, for what thou art is mine;
Our State cannot be sever'd, we are one,
One Flesh; to lose thee were to lose myself.
960   So *Adam*, and thus *Eve* to him repli'd.
O glorious trial of exceeding Love,
Illustrious evidence, example high!
Ingaging me to emulate, but short
    Of thy perfection, how shall I attain,
965   *Adam*, from whose dear side I boast me sprung,
And gladly of our Union hear thee speak,
One Heart, one Soul in both; whereof good proof
This day affords, declaring thee resolv'd,
Rather than Death or aught than Death more dread
970   Shall separate us, linkt in Love so dear,
To undergo with mee one Guilt, one Crime,
If any be, of tasting this fair Fruit,
Whose virtue, for of good still good proceeds,
Direct, or by occasion[1] hath presented
975   This happy trial of thy Love, which else
So eminently never had been known.
Were it I thought Death menac't would ensue
This my attempt, I would sustain alone
The worst, and not persuade thee, rather die
980   Deserted, than oblige° thee with a fact   *make liable*
Pernicious to thy Peace, chiefly assur'd
Remarkably so late of thy so true,
So faithful Love unequall'd; but I feel
Far otherwise th' event,° nor Death, but Life   *result*
985   Augmented, op'n'd Eyes, new Hopes, new Joys,
Taste so Divine, that what of sweet before
Hath toucht my sense, flat seems to this, and harsh.
On my experience, *Adam*, freely taste,
And fear of Death deliver to the Winds.
990   So saying, she embrac'd him, and for joy
Tenderly wept, much won that he his Love
Had so ennobl'd, as of choice to incur
Divine displeasure for her sake, or Death.
In recompense (for such compliance bad
995   Such recompense best merits) from the bough
She gave him of that fair enticing Fruit
With liberal hand: he scrupl'd not to eat

9. Three separate meanings are possible: judgment, irrevocable destiny, and death.   1. I.e., directly or indirectly.

Against his better knowledge, not deceiv'd,
But fondly overcome with Female charm.[2]

1000 Earth trembl'd from her entrails, as again
In pangs, and Nature gave a second groan,
Sky low'r'd, and muttering Thunder, some sad drops
Wept at completing of the mortal Sin
Original;[3] while *Adam* took no thought,

1005 Eating his fill, nor *Eve* to iterate
Her former trespass fear'd, the more to soothe
Him with her lov'd society, that now
As with new Wine intoxicated both
They swim in mirth, and fancy that they feel

1010 Divinity within them breeding wings
Wherewith to scorn the Earth: but that false Fruit
Far other operation first display'd,
Carnal desire inflaming, hee on *Eve*
Began to cast lascivious Eyes, she him

1015 As wantonly repaid; in Lust they burn:
Till *Adam* thus 'gan *Eve* to dalliance move.
      Eve, now I see thou are exact of taste,
And elegant, of Sapience[4] no small part,
Since to each meaning savor[5] we apply,

1020 And Palate call judicious; I the praise
Yield thee, so well this day thou hast purvey'd.°   provided
Much pleasure we have lost, while we abstain'd
From this delightful Fruit, nor known till now
True relish, tasting; if such pleasure be

1025 In things to us forbidden, it might be wish'd,
For this one Tree had been forbidden ten.
But come, so well refresh't, now let us play,
As meet is, after such delicious Fare;
For never did thy Beauty since the day

1030 I saw thee first and wedded thee, adorn'd
With all perfections, so inflame my sense
With ardor to enjoy thee, fairer now
Than ever, bounty of this virtuous Tree.[6]
      So said he, and forbore not glance or toy°   caress

1035 Of amorous intent, well understood
Of° *Eve*, whose Eye darted contagious Fire.   by
Her hand he seiz'd, and to a shady bank,
Thick overhead with verdant roof imbowr'd
He led her nothing loath; Flow'rs were the Couch,

1040 Pansies, and Violets, and Asphodel,
And Hyacinth, Earth's freshest softest lap.
There they thir fill of Love and Love's disport
Took largely, of thir mutual guilt the Seal,

---

2. See 1 Timothy 2.14: "And Adam was not deceived, but the woman being deceived was in the transgression."
3. The only occurrence in *Paradise Lost* of the term "Original Sin." In his *De doctrina* (1.11) where Milton defines Original Sin as "the sin which is common to all men, that which our first parents, and in them all their posterity committed, when, casting off their obedience

to God, they tasted the fruit of the forbidden tree."
4. Wisdom, from Latin *sapere*, to taste.
5. Tastiness, understanding.
6. See Homer, *Iliad*. 14, where Hera, bent on deceiving Zeus, comes to him wearing Aphrodite's belt and seems more charming to him than ever before.

The solace of thir sin, till dewy sleep
1045   Oppress'd them, wearied with thir amorous play.
Soon as the force of that fallacious Fruit,
That with exhilarating vapor bland°   *pleasing*
About thir spirits had play'd, and inmost powers
Made err, was now exhal'd, and grosser sleep
1050   Bred of unkindly fumes,[7] with conscious dreams
Encumber'd, now had left them, up they rose
As from unrest, and each the other viewing,
Soon found thir Eyes how op'n'd, and thir minds
How dark'n'd;[8] innocence, that as a veil
1055   Had shadow'd them from knowing ill, was gone,
Just confidence, and native righteousness,
And honor from about them, naked left
To guilty shame: hee cover'd, but his Robe
Uncover'd more. So rose the *Danite* strong
1060   *Herculean Samson* from the Harlot-lap
Of *Philistean Dalilah*, and wak'd
Shorn of his strength, They destitute and bare
Of all thir virtue:[9] silent, and in face
Confounded long they sat, as struck'n mute,
1065   Till *Adam*, though not less than *Eve* abasht,
At length gave utterance to these words constrain'd.
        O *Eve*, in evil hour thou didst give ear
To that false Worm, of whomsoever taught
To counterfeit Man's voice, true in our Fall,
1070   False in our promis'd Rising; since our Eyes
Op'n'd we find indeed, and find we know
Both Good and Evil, Good lost, and Evil got,
Bad Fruit of Knowledge, if this be to know,
Which leaves us naked thus, of Honor void,
1075   Of Innocence, of Faith, of Purity,
Our wonted Ornaments now soil'd and stain'd,
And in our Faces evident the signs
Of foul concupiscence; whence evil store;
Even shame, the last of evils; of the first
1080   Be sure then. How shall I behold the face
Henceforth of God or Angel, erst with joy
And rapture so oft beheld? those heav'nly shapes
Will dazzle now this earthly, with thir blaze
Insufferably bright. O might I here
1085   In solitude live savage, in some glade
Obscur'd, where highest Woods impenetrable
To Star or Sun-light, spread thir umbrage broad,
And brown as Evening: Cover me ye Pines,
Ye Cedars, with innumerable boughs
1090   Hide me, where I may never see them more.
But let us now, as in bad plight, devise
What best may for the present serve to hide

7. Unnatural vapors or exhalations rising from the stomach to the brain.
8. See Genesis 3.7: "The eyes of them both were opened, and they knew that they were naked."
9. See Judges 16 for the story of Samson's betrayal by Delilah.

The Parts of each from other, that seem most
To shame obnoxious,° and unseemliest seen,   *exposed*
1095   Some Tree whose broad smooth Leaves together sew'd,
And girded on our loins, may cover round
Those middle parts, that this new comer, Shame,
There sit not, and reproach us as unclean.[1]
    So counsell'd hee, and both together went
1100   Into the thickest Wood, there soon they chose
The Figtree,[2] not that kind for Fruit renown'd,
But such as at this day to *Indians* known
In *Malabar* or *Decan* spreads her Arms
Branching so broad and long, that in the ground
1105   The bended Twigs take root, and Daughters grow
About the Mother Tree, a Pillar'd shade
High overarch't, and echoing Walks between;
There oft the *Indian* Herdsman shunning heat
Shelters in cool, and tends his pasturing Herds
1110   At Loopholes cut through thickest shade: Those Leaves
They gather'd, broad as Amazonian Targe,°   *shield*
And with what skill they had, together sew'd,
To gird thir waist, vain Covering if to hide
Thir guilt and dreaded shame; O how unlike
1115   To that first naked Glory. Such of late
Columbus found th' *American* so girt
With feather'd Cincture,° naked else and wild   *belt*
Among the Trees on Isles and woody Shores.
Thus fenc't, and as they thought, thir shame in part
1120   Cover'd, but not at rest or ease of Mind,
They sat them down to weep, nor only Tears
Rain'd at thir Eyes, but high Winds worse within
Began to rise, high Passions, Anger, Hate,
Mistrust, Suspicion, Discord, and shook sore
1125   Thir inward State of Mind, calm Region once
And full of Peace, now toss't and turbulent:
For Understanding rul'd not, and the Will
Heard not her lore, both in subjection now
To sensual Appetite, who from beneath
1130   Usurping over sovran Reason claim'd
Superior sway: From thus distemper'd breast,
Adam, estrang'd in look and alter'd style,
Speech intermitted thus to *Eve* renew'd.
    Would thou hadst heark'n'd to my words, and stay'd
1135   With me, as I besought thee, when that strange
Desire of wand'ring this unhappy Morn,
I know not whence possess'd thee; we had then
Remain'd still happy, not as now, despoil'd
Of all our good, sham'd, naked, miserable.
1140   Let none henceforth seek needless cause to approve°   *give proof of*
The Faith they owe;[3] when earnestly they seek
Such proof, conclude, they then begin to fail.

---

1. See Genesis 3.7.
2. Milton's description of the banyan or Indian fig comes
from Gerard's *Herball* (1597).
3. Be under obligation to render or possess.

To whom soon mov'd with touch of blame thus *Eve*.
What words have past thy Lips,[4] *Adam* severe,
1145   Imput'st thou that to my default, or will
Of wand'ring, as thou call'st it, which who knows
But might as ill have happ'n'd thou being by,
Or to thyself perhaps: hadst thou been there,
Or here th' attempt, thou couldst not have discern'd
1150   Fraud in the Serpent, speaking as he spake;
No ground of enmity between us known,
Why hee should mean me ill, or seek to harm.
Was I to have never parted from thy side?
As good have grown there still a lifeless Rib.
1155   Being as I am, why didst not thou the Head[5]
Command me absolutely not to go,
Going into such danger as thou said'st?
Too facile° then thou didst not much gainsay,   *permissive*
Nay, didst permit, approve, and fair dismiss.
1160   Hadst thou been firm and fixt in thy dissent,
Neither had I transgress'd, nor thou with mee.
    To whom then first incenst Adam repli'd.
Is this the Love, is this the recompense
Of mine to thee, ingrateful *Eve*, express't
1165   Immutable° when thou wert lost, not I,   *unchangeable*
Who might have liv'd and joy'd immortal bliss,
Yet willingly chose rather Death with thee:
And am I now upbraided, as the cause
Of thy transgressing? not enough severe,
1170   It seems, in thy restraint: what could I more?
I warn'd thee, I admonish'd thee, foretold
The danger, and the lurking Enemy
That lay in wait; beyond this had been force,
And force upon free Will hath here no place.
1175   But confidence then bore thee on, secure
Either to meet no danger, or to find
Matter of glorious trial; and perhaps
I also err'd in overmuch admiring
What seem'd in thee so perfet, that I thought
1180   No evil durst attempt thee, but I rue
That error now, which is become my crime,
And thou th' accuser. Thus it shall befall
Him who to worth in Woman overtrusting
Lets her Will rule; restraint she will not brook,
1185   And left to herself, if evil thence ensue,
Shee first his weak indulgence will accuse.
    Thus they in mutual accusation spent
The fruitless hours, but neither self-condemning,
And of thir vain contést appear'd no end.
        The End of the Ninth Book.

---

4. Echoes Odysseus's disapproval of a speech of Agamemnon's (*Iliad* 14.83).
5. Alludes to 1 Corinthians 11.3: "The head of every man

is Christ; and the head of the woman is the man; and the
head of Christ is God."

from **Book 10**
The Argument

Man's *transgression known, the Guardian Angels forsake Paradise, and return up to Heaven to approve thir vigilance, and are approv'd, God declaring that the entrance of Satan could not be by them prevented. He sends his Son to judge the Transgressors, who descends and gives Sentence accordingly; then in pity clothes them both, and reascends. Sin and Death sitting till then at the Gates of Hell, by wondrous sympathy feeling the success of Satan in this new World, and the sin by Man there committed, resolve to sit no longer confin'd in Hell, but to follow Satan thir Sire up to the place of Man: To make the way easier from Hell to this World to and fro, they pave a broad Highway or Bridge over Chaos, according to the Track that Satan first made; then preparing for Earth, they meet him proud of his success returning to Hell; thir mutual gratulation. Satan arrives at Pandemonium, in full assembly relates with boasting his success against Man; instead of applause is entertained with a general hiss by all his audience, transform'd with himself also suddenly into Serpents, according to his doom giv'n in Paradise; then deluded with a show of the forbidden Tree springing up before them, they greedily reaching to take of the Fruit, chew dust and bitter ashes. The proceedings of Sin and Death; God foretells the final Victory of his Son over them, and the renewing of all things; but for the present commands his Angels to make several alterations in the Heavens and Elements. Adam more and more perceiving his fall'n condition heavily bewails, rejects the condolement of Eve; she persists and at length appeases him: then to evade the Curse likely to fall on thir Offspring, proposes to Adam violent ways, which he approves not, but conceiving better hope, puts her in mind of the late Promise made them, that her Seed should be reveng'd on the Serpent, and exhorts her with him to seek Peace of the offended Deity, by repentance and supplication.*

      Meanwhile the heinous and despiteful act
      Of *Satan* done in Paradise, and how
      Hee in the Serpent had perverted *Eve*,
      Her Husband shee, to taste the fatal fruit,
5   Was known in Heav'n;[1] for what can scape the Eye
      Of *God* All-seeing, or deceive his Heart
      Omniscient, who in all things wise and just,
      Hinder'd not *Satan* to attempt the mind
      Of Man, with strength entire, and free will arm'd,
10   Complete to have discover'd and repulst
      Whatever wiles of Foe or seeming Friend.
      For still they knew, and ought to have still remember'd
      The high Injunction not to taste that Fruit,
      Whoever tempted; which they not obeying,
15   Incurr'd, what could they less, the penalty,
      And manifold[2] in sin, deserv'd to fall.
      Up into Heav'n from Paradise in haste
      Th' Angelic Guards ascended, mute and sad

---

1. Rhetorically, lines 1–16 function both as *principium*, stating the subject of the book, and as *initium*, introducing the first scene. They also sum up the theological content of Book 3, which will receive specific application in the present book, in the exchanges between the Father and the Son (lines 34–84) and between the Son and

Adam (lines 124ff.). Note the structural symmetry whereby the divine decrees of the third book are balanced by those of the third last.

2. Multiplied; alluding to Psalms 38.19: "they that hate me wrongfully are multiplied."

For Man, for of his state by this they knew,
20 Much wond'ring how the subtle Fiend had stol'n
Entrance unseen. Soon as th' unwelcome news
From Earth arriv'd at Heaven Gate, displeas'd
All were who heard, dim sadness did not spare
That time Celestial visages, yet mixt
25 With pity, violated not thir bliss.
About the new-arriv'd, in multitudes
Th' ethereal People ran, to hear and know
How all befell: they towards the Throne Supreme
Accountable made haste to make appear
30 With righteous plea, thir utmost vigilance,
And easily approv'd; when the most High
Eternal Father from his secret Cloud,
Amidst in Thunder utter'd thus his voice.
    Assembl'd Angels, and ye Powers return'd
35 From unsuccessful charge, be not dismay'd,
Nor troubl'd at these tidings from the Earth,
Which your sincerest care could not prevent,
Foretold so lately what would come to pass,
When first this Tempter cross'd the Gulf from Hell.
40 I told ye then he should prevail and speed°   succeed
On his bad Errand, Man should be seduc't
And flatter'd out of all, believing lies
Against his Maker; no Decree of mine
Concurring to necessitate his Fall,
45 Or touch with lightest moment of impulse
His free Will, to her own inclining left
In even scale.³ But fall'n he is, and now
What rests, but that the mortal Sentence pass
On his transgression. Death denounc't that day,
50 Which he presumes already vain and void,
Because not yet inflicted, as he fear'd,
By some immediate stroke; but soon shall find
Forbearance no acquittance ere day end.
Justice shall not return as bounty scorn'd.
55 But whom send I to judge them? whom but thee
Vicegerent Son, to thee I have transferr'd
All Judgment, whether in Heav'n, or Earth, or Hell.
Easy it may be seen that I intend
Mercy colleague with Justice, sending thee
60 Man's Friend, his Mediator, his design'd
Both Ransom and Redeemer voluntary,
And destin'd Man himself to judge Man fall'n.⁴
    So spake the Father, and unfolding bright
Toward the right hand his Glory, on the Son

3. "Moment" is a term applied to the smallest increment that could affect the equilibrium of a balance. If man had been protected from the tempter, then there would have been real interference with the free action of the scales of justice.

4. The double syntax—line 62 can be read as either "himself a man, destined to judge man" (primary) or "destined to judge man himself, man fallen"—mimes the close identification of Christ with humanity.

65 Blaz'd forth unclouded Deity; he full
    Resplendent all his Father manifest
    Express'd, and thus divinely answer'd mild.
        Father Eternal, thine is to decree,
    Mine both in Heav'n and Earth to do thy will
70 Supreme, that thou in mee thy Son belov'd
    May'st ever rest well pleas'd.[5] I go to judge
    On Earth these thy transgressors, but thou know'st,
    Whoever judg'd, the worst on mee must light,
    When time shall be, for so I undertook
75 Before thee; and not repenting, this obtain
    Of right, that I may mitigate thir doom
    On me deriv'd, yet I shall temper so
    Justice with Mercy, as may illustrate most
    Them fully satisfied, and thee appease.
80 Attendance none shall need, nor Train, where none
    Are to behold the Judgment, but the judg'd,
    Those two; the third[6] best absent is condemn'd,
    Convict° by flight, and Rebel to all Law: *convicted*
    Conviction to the Serpent none belongs.[7]
85   Thus saying, from his radiant Seat he rose
    Of high collateral° glory: him Thrones and Powers,   *side by side*
    Princedoms, and Dominations ministrant
    Accompanied to Heaven Gate, from whence
    Eden and all the Coast in prospect lay.
90 Down he descended straight; the speed of Gods
    Time counts not, though with swiftest minutes wing'd.
    Now was the Sun in Western cadence° low[8]   *falling*
    From Noon, and gentle Airs due at thir hour
    To fan the Earth now wak'd, and usher in
95 The Ev'ning cool, when he from wrath more cool
    Came the mild Judge and Intercessor both
    To sentence Man: the voice of God they heard
    Now walking in the Garden, by soft winds
    Brought to thir Ears, while day declin'd, they heard,
100 And from his presence hid themselves among
    The thickest Trees, both Man and Wife, till God
    Approaching, thus to Adam call'd aloud.
        Where art thou *Adam*, wont with joy to meet
    My coming seen far off? I miss thee here,
105 Not pleas'd, thus entertain'd with solitude,
    Where obvious duty erewhile appear'd unsought:
    Or come I less conspicuous, or what change
    Absents thee, or what chance detains? Come forth.
    He came, and with him *Eve*, more loath, though first
110 To offend, discount'nanc't both, and discompos'd;
    Love was not in thir looks, either to God

5. Echoing Matthew 3.17.
6. Satan.
7. "Conviction" has both the legal sense (proof of guilt)
and the theological (the condition of being convinced of sin).
8. Lines 92–123 follow Genesis 3.8–11.

Or to each other, but apparent guilt,
And shame, and perturbation, and despair,
Anger, and obstinacy, and hate, and guile.
115   Whence *Adam* falt'ring long, thus answer'd brief.
     I heard thee in the Garden, and of thy voice
Afraid, being naked, hid myself. To whom
The gracious Judge without revile repli'd.
     My voice thou oft hast heard, and hast not fear'd,
120 But still rejoic't, how is it now become
So dreadful to thee? that thou art naked, who
Hath told thee? hast thou eaten of the Tree
Whereof I gave thee charge thou shouldst not eat?
     To whom thus *Adam* sore beset repli'd.
125 O Heav'n! in evil strait this day I stand
Before my Judge, either to undergo
Myself the total Crime, or to accuse
My other self, the partner of my life;
Whose failing, while her Faith to me remains,
130 I should conceal, and not expose to blame
By my complaint; but strict necessity
Subdues me, and calamitous constraint,
Lest on my head both sin and punishment,
However insupportable, be all
135 Devolv'd;[9] though should I hold my peace, yet thou
Wouldst easily detect what I conceal.
This Woman whom thou mad'st to be my help,
And gav'st me as thy perfet gift, so good,
So fit, so acceptable, so Divine,
140 That from her hand I could suspect no ill,
And what she did, whatever in itself,
Her doing seem'd to justify the deed;
Shee gave me of the Tree, and I did eat.[1]
     To whom the sovran Presence thus repli'd.
145 Was shee thy God, that her thou didst obey
Before his voice, or was shee made thy guide,
Superior, or but equal, that to her
Thou didst resign thy Manhood, and the Place
Wherein God set thee above her made of thee,
150 And for thee, whose perfection far excell'd
Hers in all real° dignity:[2] Adorn'd   *regal*
She was indeed, and lovely to attract
Thy Love, not thy Subjection, and her Gifts
Were such as under Government well seem'd,
155 Unseemly to bear rule, which was thy part°   *role*
And person,° hadst thou known thyself aright.   *character*
     So having said, he thus to Eve in few:
Say Woman, what is this which thou hast done?

9. Caused to fall upon.
1. See Genesis 3.12.
2. See 1 Corinthians 11.8ff.: "For the man is not of the woman; but the woman of the man. Neither was the man created for the woman; but the woman for the man."

To whom sad *Eve* with shame nigh overwhelm'd,
160   Confessing soon, yet not before her Judge
Bold or loquacious, thus abasht repli'd.
        The Serpent me beguil'd and I did eat.[3]
        Which when the Lord God heard, without delay
To Judgment he proceeded on th' accus'd
165   Serpent though brute, unable to transfer
The Guilt on him who made him instrument
Of mischief, and polluted from the end
Of his Creation; justly then accurst,
As vitiated in Nature: more to know
170   Concern'd not Man (since he no further knew)
Nor alter'd his offense; yet God at last
To Satan first in sin his doom appli'd,
Though in mysterious° terms, judg'd as then best: *mystical*
And on the Serpent thus his curse let fall.
175   Because thou hast done this, thou art accurst
Above all Cattle, each Beast of the Field;
Upon thy Belly groveling thou shalt go,
And dust shalt eat all the days of thy Life.
Between Thee and the Woman I will put
180   Enmity, and between thine and her Seed;
Her Seed shall bruise thy head, thou bruise his heel.[4]
        So spake this Oracle, then verifi'd
When *Jesus* son of *Mary* second *Eve*,
Saw Satan fall like Lightning down from Heav'n,[5]
185   Prince of the Air; then rising from his Grave
Spoil'd Principalities and Powers, triumpht
In open show, and with ascension bright
Captivity led captive through the Air,[6]
The Realm itself of Satan long usurpt,
190   Whom he shall tread at last under our feet;[7]
Ev'n hee who now foretold his fatal bruise,
And to the Woman thus his Sentence turn'd.
        Thy sorrow I will greatly multiply
By thy Conception; Children thou shalt bring
195   In sorrow forth, and to thy Husband's will
Thine shall submit, hee over thee shall rule.
        On *Adam* last thus judgment he pronounc'd.
Because thou hast heark'n'd to the voice of thy Wife,
And eaten of the Tree concerning which
200   I charg'd thee, saying: Thou shalt not eat thereof,
Curs'd is the ground for thy sake, thou in sorrow
Shalt eat thereof all the days of thy Life;[8]
Thorns also and Thistles it shall bring thee forth
Unbid, and thou shalt eat th' Herb of the Field,

3. Repeating Genesis 3.13.
4. See Genesis 3.14ff.
5. "I beheld Satan as lightning fall from heaven" (Luke 10.18).
6. Psalms 68.18: "Thou hast ascended on high, thou hast

led captivity captive": applied to Christ in Ephesians 4.8.
7. See Romans 16.20: "And the God of peace shall bruise Satan under your feet shortly."
8. See Genesis 3.17.

205   In the sweat of thy Face shalt thou eat Bread,
     Till thou return unto the ground, for thou
     Out of the ground wast taken, know thy Birth,
     For dust thou art, and shalt to dust return.[9]
       So judg'd he Man, both Judge and Savior sent,
210   And th' instant stroke of Death denounc't that day
     Remov'd far off;[1] then pitying how they stood
     Before him naked to the air, that now
     Must suffer change, disdain'd not to begin
     Thenceforth the form of servant to assume,[2]
215   As when he wash'd his servants' feet, so now
     As Father of his Family he clad
     Thir nakedness with Skins of Beasts, or slain,
     Or as the Snake with youthful Coat repaid;
     And thought not much to clothe his Enemies:
220   Nor hee thir outward only with the Skins
     Of Beasts, but inward nakedness, much more
     Opprobrious, with his Robe of righteousness,
     Arraying cover'd from his Father's sight.
     To him with swift ascent he up return'd,
225   Into his blissful bosom reassum'd
     In glory as of old, to him appeas'd
     All, though all-knowing, what had past with Man
     Recounted, mixing intercession sweet.[3]

             * * *

            Th' other way *Satan* went down
415   The Causey° to Hell Gate; on either side   *causeway*
     Disparted *Chaos* over-built exclaim'd,
     And with rebounding surge the bars assail'd,
     That scorn'd his indignation: through the Gate,
     Wide open and unguarded, *Satan* pass'd,
420   And all about found desolate; for those
     Appointed to sit there,[4] had left thir charge,
     Flown to the upper World; the rest were all
     Far to th'inland retir'd, about the walls
     Of *Pandaemonium*, City and proud seat
425   Of *Lucifer*, so by allusion call'd,
     Of that bright Star to *Satan* paragon'd.°   *compared*
     There kept thir Watch the Legions, while the Grand
     In Council sat, solicitous° what chance   *anxious*
     Might intercept thir Emperor sent, so hee
430   Departing gave command, and they observ'd.
     As when the Tartar from his *Russian* Foe
     By *Astracan*[5] over the Snowy Plains
     Retires, or *Bactrian* Sophi[6] from the horns

---

9. See Genesis 3.18–9.
1. Christ removes the fear that physical death will follow the eating of the fruit on the same day.
2. See Phillipians. 2.7: "made himself of no reputation, and took upon him the form of a servant, and was made in the likeness of men."
3. Sin and Death now pave a highway across Chaos from

Hell to earth. Satan meets them and sends them on to dwell on earth; he heads home to Hell.
4. Sin and Death.
5. Astracan, or Astrakhan, was a Tartar kingdom and capital city near the outh of the Volga.
6. Persian king.

Of *Turkish* Crescent,[7] leaves all waste beyond
435   The Realm of *Aladule*,[8] in his retreat
To *Tauris* or *Casbeen*:[9] So these the late
Heav'n-banisht Host, left desert utmost Hell
Many a dark League, reduc't in careful Watch
Round thir Metropolis, and now expecting
440   Each hour their great adventurer from the search
Of Foreign Worlds: he through the midst unmark't,
In show Plebeian Angel militant
Of lowest order, pass't; and from the door
Of that *Plutonian*[1] Hall, invisible
445   Ascended his high Throne, which under state°   canopy
Of richest texture spread, at th' upper end
Was plac't in regal lustre. Down a while
He sat, and round about him saw unseen:
At last as from a Cloud his fulgent head
450   And shape Star-bright appear'd, or brighter, clad
With what permissive glory since his fall
Was left him, or false glitter: All amaz'd
At that so sudden blaze the Stygian throng
Bent thir aspect, and whom they wish'd beheld,
455   Thir mighty Chief return'd: loud was th' acclaim:
Forth rush'd in haste the great consulting Peers,
Rais'd from thir dark *Divan*,[2] and with like joy
Congratulant approach'd him, who with hand
Silence, and with these words attention won.
460   Thrones, Dominations, Princedoms, Virtues, Powers,
For in possession such, not only of right,
I call ye and declare ye now, return'd
Successful beyond hope, to lead ye forth
Triumphant out of this infernal Pit
465   Abominable, accurst, the house of woe,
And Dungeon of our Tyrant: Now possess,
As Lords, a spacious World, to our native Heaven
Little inferior, by my adventure hard
With peril great achiev'd. Long were to tell
470   What I have done, what suffer'd, with what pain
Voyag'd th' unreal, vast, unbounded deep
Of horrible confusion, over which
By Sin and Death a broad way now is pav'd
To expedite your glorious march; but I
475   Toil'd out my úncouth° passage, forc't to ride   strange
Th' untractable Abyss, plung'd in the womb
Of unoriginal° *Night* and *Chaos* wild,   uncreated
That jealous of thir secrets fiercely oppos'd
My journey strange, with clamorous uproar

480   Protesting Fate supreme; thence how I found
       The new created World, which fame in Heav'n
       Long had foretold, a Fabric wonderful
       Of absolute perfection, therein Man
       Plac't in a Paradise, by our exile
485   Made happy: Him by fraud I have seduc'd
       From his Creator, and the more to increase
       Your wonder, with an Apple; he thereat
       Offended, worth your laughter, hath giv'n up
       Both his beloved Man and all his World,
490   To Sin and Death a prey, and so to us,
       Without our hazard, labor, or alarm,
       To range in, and to dwell, and over Man
       To rule, as over all he should have rul'd.
       True is, mee also he hath judg'd, or rather
495   Mee not, but the brute Serpent in whose shape
       Man I deceiv'd: that which to mee belongs,
       Is enmity, which he will put between
       Mee and Mankind; I am to bruise his heel;
       His Seed, when is not set, shall bruise my head:
500   A World who would not purchase with a bruise,
       Or much more grievous pain? Ye have th' account
       Of my performance: What remains, ye Gods,
       But up and enter now into full bliss.
          So having said, a while he stood, expecting
505   Thir universal shout and high applause
       To fill his ear, when contrary he hears
       On all sides, from innumerable tongues
       A dismal universal hiss, the sound
       Of public scorn; he wonder'd, but not long
510   Had leisure, wond'ring at himself now more;
       His Visage drawn he felt to sharp and spare,
       His Arms clung to his Ribs, his Legs entwining
       Each other, till supplanted° down he fell   tripped
       A monstrous Serpent on his Belly prone,[3]
515   Reluctant,° but in vain: a greater power   resisting
       Now rul'd him, punisht in the shape he sinn'd,
       According to his doom: he would have spoke,
       But hiss for hiss return'd with forked tongue
       To forked tongue, for now were all transform'd
520   Alike, to Serpents all as accessories
       To his bold Riot: dreadful was the din
       Of hissing through the Hall, thick swarming now
       With complicated° monsters, head and tail,   compound
       Scorpion and Asp, and *Amphisbaena* dire,
525   *Cerastes* horn'd, *Hydrus,* and *Ellops* drear,
       And *Dipsas*[4] (not so thick swarm'd once the Soil

3. See the metamorphosis of Cadmus in Ovid, *Metamorphoses* 4.572–603, and the mutual interchange of serpentine forms in Dante's canto of the thieves, *Inferno* 25. 4. The amphisbaena is a serpent with a head at either end. The cerastes has four horns on its head. The hydrus is a water snake. The ellops, though sometimes identified as the swordfish, is mentioned as a serpent in Pliny, *Natural History* 32.5. The dipsas causes raging thirst by its bite.

Bedropt with blood of *Gorgon*, or the Isle
Ophiusa) but still greatest hee the midst,[5]
Now Dragon grown, larger than whom the Sun
530   Ingender'd in the *Pythian* Vale on slime,
Huge *Python*, and his Power no less he seem'd
Above the rest still to retain;[6] they all
Him follow'd issuing forth to th' open Field,
Where all yet left of that revolted Rout
535   Heav'n-fall'n, in station stood or just array,
Sublime° with expectation when to see   *uplifted*
In Triumph issuing forth thir glorious Chief;
They saw, but other sight instead, a crowd
Of ugly Serpents; horror on them fell,
540   And horrid sympathy; for what they saw,
They felt themselves now changing; down thir arms,
Down fell both Spear and Shield, down they as fast,
And the dire hiss renew'd, and the dire form
Catcht by Contagion, like in punishment,
545   As in thir crime. Thus was th' applause they meant,
Turn'd to exploding hiss, triumph to shame
Cast on themselves from thir own mouths. There stood
A Grove hard by, sprung up with this thir change,
His will who reigns above, to aggravate
550   Thir penance, laden with fair Fruit, like that
Which grew in Paradise, the bait of *Eve*
Us'd by the Tempter: on that prospect strange
Thir earnest eyes they fix'd, imagining
For one forbidden Tree a multitude
555   Now ris'n, to work them furder° woe or shame;   *further*
Yet parcht with scalding thirst and hunger fierce,
Though to delùde them sent, could not abstain,
But on they roll'd in heaps, and up the Trees
Climbing, sat thicker than the snaky locks
560   That curl'd *Megaera*:[7] greedily they pluck'd
The Fruitage fair to sight, like that which grew
Near that bituminous Lake where *Sodom* flam'd;[8]
This more delusive, not the touch, but taste
Deceiv'd; they fondly thinking to allay
565   Thir appetite with gust,° instead of Fruit   *taste*
Chew'd bitter Ashes, which th' offended taste
With spattering noise rejected: oft they assay'd,
Hunger and thirst constraining, drugg'd° as oft,   *nauseated*
With hatefullest disrelish writh'd thir jaws
570   With soot and cinders fill'd; so oft they fell
Into the same illusion, not as Man

---

5. When Perseus was bringing back the severed head of Medusa, drops of blood fell to earth and became serpents. "Ophiusa" means literally "full of serpents"; a name anciently given to several islands, including Rhodes and one of the Balearic group.
6. For the birth of Python from the slime remaining after the flood, see Ovid, *Metamorphoses* 1.438–440. Python was slain by Apollo. Satan's dragon shape is that of the "old dragon" of Christian apocalypse; see Revelation 12.9: "the great dragon was cast out, that old serpent, called the Devil, and Satan."
7. One of the Furies, often described as snaky-haired.
8. The allusion is to Josephus, *Wars* 4.8.4, where it is said that traces still remain of the divine fire that burnt Sodom, such as tasty-looking fruits that turned to ashes when plucked.

Whom they triumph'd, once lapst. Thus were they plagu'd
And worn with Famine long, and ceaseless hiss,
Till thir lost shape, permitted, they resum'd,
575   Yearly enjoin'd, some say, to undergo
This annual humbling certain number'd days,
To dash thir pride, and joy for Man seduc't.
However some tradition they dispers'd
Among the Heathen of thir purchase got,
580   And Fabl'd how the Serpent, whom they call'd
Ophion with Eurynome, the wide-
Encroaching Eve perhaps, had first the rule
Of high Olympus, thence by Saturn driv'n
And Ops, ere yet Dictaean Jove was born.[9]
585   Meanwhile in Paradise the hellish pair
Too soon arriv'd, Sin there in power before,
Once actual, now in body, and to dwell
Habitual habitant; behind her Death
Close following pace for pace, not mounted yet
590   On his pale Horse:[1] to whom Sin thus began.
        Second of Satan sprung, all conquering Death,
What think'st thou of our Empire now, though earn'd
With travail difficult, not better far
Than still at Hell's dark threshold to have sat watch,
595   Unnam'd, undreaded, and thyself half starv'd?
        Whom thus the Sin-born Monster answer'd soon.
To mee, who with eternal Famine pine,
Alike is Hell, or Paradise, or Heaven,
There best, where most with ravin I may meet;
600   Which here, though plenteous, all too little seems
To stuff this Maw, this vast unhide-bound Corpse.
        To whom th' incestuous Mother thus repli'd.
Thou therefore on these Herbs, and Fruits, and Flow'rs
Feed first, on each Beast next, and Fish, and Fowl,
605   No homely morsels, and whatever thing
The Scythe of Time mows down, devour unspar'd,
Till I in Man residing through the Race,
His thoughts, his looks, words, actions all infect,
And season him thy last and sweetest prey.
610   This said, they both betook them several ways,
Both to destroy, or unimmortal make
All kinds, and for destruction to mature
Sooner or later; which th' Almighty seeing
From his transcendent Seat the Saints among,
615   To those bright Orders utter'd thus his voice.
        See with what heat these Dogs of Hell advance
To waste and havoc° yonder World, which I   devastate
So fair and good created, and had still
Kept in that state, had not the folly of Man

9. Ophion and Eurynome ruled Olympus until the one yielded to Cronos (Saturn) and the other to Rhea (Ops). Their two successors then ruled the Titans, while Zeus lived in the Dictaean cave. See Apollonius Rhodius, *Arg-*

onautica 1.503–9.
1. See Revelation 6.8: "I looked, and behold a pale horse: and his name that sat on him was Death, and Hell followed with him."

620 Let in these wasteful Furies, who impute
Folly to mee, so doth the Prince of Hell
And his Adherents, that with so much ease
I suffer them to enter and possess
A place so heav'nly, and conniving seem
625 To gratify my scornful Enemies,
That laugh, as if transported with some fit
Of Passion, I to them had quitted° all,   *yielded*
At random yielded up to their misrule;
And know not that I call'd and drew them thither
630 My Hell-hounds, to lick up the draff° and filth   *refuse*
Which man's polluting Sin with taint hath shed
On what was pure, till cramm'd and gorg'd, nigh burst
With suckt and glutted offal, at one sling
Of thy victorious Arm, well-pleasing Son,
635 Both *Sin*, and *Death*, and yawning *Grave* at last
Through *Chaos* hurl'd, obstruct the mouth of Hell
For ever, and seal up his ravenous Jaws.
Then Heav'n and Earth renew'd shall be made pure
To sanctity that shall receive no stain:
640 Till then the Curse pronounc't on both precedes.[2]

* * *

Thus began
Outrage from lifeless things; but Discord first
Daughter of Sin, among th' irrational,
Death introduc'd through fierce antipathy:
710 Beast now with Beast gan war, and Fowl with Fowl,
And Fish with Fish; to graze the Herb all leaving,
Devour'd each other; nor stood much in awe
Of Man, but fled him, or with count'nance grim
Glar'd on him passing: these were from without
715 The growing miseries, which *Adam* saw
Already in part, though hid in gloomiest shade,
To sorrow abandon'd, but worse felt within,
And in a troubl'd Sea of passion tost,
Thus to disburd'n sought with sad complaint.
720 O miserable of happy! is this the end
Of this new glorious World, and mee so late
The Glory of that Glory, who now become
Accurst of blessed, hide me from the face
Of God, whom to behold was then my highth
725 Of happiness: yet well, if here would end
The misery, I deserv'd it, and would
My own deservings; but this will not serve;
All that I eat or drink, or shall beget,
Is propagated curse.[3] O voice once heard
730 Delightfully, *Increase and multiply*,[4]

---

2. See Genesis 3.17: "Cursed is the ground for thy sake."
God next commands the angels to make the earth turn
on its axis and so cause the change of seasons, and to disrupt the order of the planets, making their effect on the
world negative as well as positive.
3. Handed down from one generation to another. Food

prolongs life and thus extends the curse, while begetting
children hands it on. Note also that eating and sex are
jointly the concerns of the concupiscible faculty, which
was often regarded as the special field of operation of concupiscence or the "body of sin."
4. See Genesis 1.28.

Now death to hear! for what can I increase
Or multiply, but curses on my head?
Who of all Ages to succeed, but feeling
The evil on him brought by me, will curse
735   My Head; Ill fare our Ancestor impure,
For this we may thank *Adam*; but his thanks
Shall be the execration; so besides
Mine own that bide upon me, all from mee
Shall with a fierce reflux on mee redound,°   *overflow, come back*
740   On mee as on thir natural centre light
Heavy, though in thir place. O fleeting joys
Of Paradise, dear bought with lasting woes!
Did I request thee, Maker, from my Clay
To mould me Man, did I solicit thee
745   From darkness to promote me, or here place
In this delicious Garden? as my Will
Concurr'd not to my being, it were but right
And equal° to reduce me to my dust,   *just*
Desirous to resign, and render back
750   All I receiv'd, unable to perform
Thy terms too hard, by which I was to hold
The good I sought not. To the loss of that,
Sufficient penalty, why hast thou added
The sense of endless woes? inexplicable
755   Thy Justice seems; yet to say truth, too late
I thus contest; then should have been refus'd
Those terms whatever, when they were propos'd:
Thou didst accept them; wilt thou enjoy the good,
Then cavil the conditions? and though God
760   Made thee without thy leave, what if thy Son
Prove disobedient, and reprov'd, retort,
Wherefore didst thou beget me? I sought it not:
Wouldst thou admit for his contempt of thee
That proud excuse? yet him not thy election,°   *choice*
765   But Natural necessity begot.
God made thee of choice his own, and of his own
To serve him, thy reward was of his grace,
Thy punishment then justly is at his Will.
Be it so, for I submit, his doom° is fair,   *judgment*
770   That dust I am, and shall to dust return:[5]
O welcome hour whenever! why delays
His hand to execute what his Decree
Fix'd on this day? why do I overlive,
Why am I mockt with death, and length'n'd out
775   To deathless pain? How gladly would I meet
Mortality my sentence, and be Earth
Insensible, how glad would lay me down
As in my Mother's lap![6] There I should rest
And sleep secure; his dreadful voice no more

---

5. Alluding to Genesis 3.19.   6. Adam's lament echoes Job 3.

780 Would Thunder in my ears, no fear of worse
To mee and to my offspring would torment me
With cruel expectation. Yet one doubt
Pursues me still, lest all I cannot die,
Lest that pure breath of Life, the Spirit of Man
785 Which God inspir'd, cannot together perish
With this corporeal Clod; then in the Grave,
Or in some other dismal place, who knows
But I shall die a living Death? O thought
Horrid, if true! yet why? it was but breath
790 Of Life that sinn'd; what dies but what had life
And sin? the Body properly hath neither.
All of me then shall die:[7] let this appease
The doubt, since human reach no further knows.
For though the Lord of all be infinite,
795 Is his wrath also? be it, Man is not so,
But mortal doom'd. How can he exercise
Wrath without end on Man whom Death must end?
Can he make deathless Death? that were to make
Strange contradiction, which to God himself
800 Impossible is held, as Argument
Of weakness, not of Power. Will he draw out,
For anger's sake, finite to infinite
In punisht Man, to satisfy his rigor
Satisfi'd never; that were to extend
805 His Sentence beyond dust and Nature's Law,
By which all Causes else according still
To the reception of thir matter act,
Not to th' extent of thir own Sphere.[8] But say
That Death be not one stroke, as I suppos'd,
810 Bereaving sense, but endless misery
From this day onward, which I feel begun
Both in me, and without me, and so last
To perpetuity; Ay me, that fear
Comes thund'ring back with dreadful revolution
815 On my defenseless head; both Death and I
Am found Eternal, and incorporate° both,   *united, embodied*
Nor I on my part single, in mee all
Posterity stands curst:[9] Fair Patrimony
That I must leave ye, Sons; O were I able
820 To waste it all myself, and leave ye none!
So disinherited how would ye bless
Me now your Curse! Ah, why should all mankind
For one man's fault thus guiltless be condemn'd,

---

7. Adam's question is like Milton's in *De doctrina* 1.13: "What could be more absurd than that the mind, which is the part principally offending, should escape the threatened death; and that the body alone, to which immortality was equally allotted, before death came into the world by sin, should pay the penalty of sin by undergoing death, though not implicated in the transgression?" Milton's belief in the joint extinction and joint resurrection of man's body and mind was not an eccentric heresy but good biblical theology.
8. Adam tries to comfort himself with an argument drawn from medieval philosophy. Here Adam means that God would be going beyond a natural law, that any agent acts according to the powers of what receives its action, not according to its own powers.
9. Not only are Death and I double, two in one, but so also am I, since I am both myself and my descendants.

If guiltless? But from me what can proceed,
825   But all corrupt, both Mind and Will deprav'd,
Not to do only, but to will the same
With me? how can they then acquitted stand
In sight of God? Him after all Disputes
Forc't I absolve: all my evasions vain
830   And reasonings, though through Mazes, lead me still
But to my own conviction:[1] first and last
On mee, mee only, as the source and spring
Of all corruption, all the blame lights due;
So might the wrath. Fond wish! couldst thou support
835   That burden heavier than the Earth to bear,
Than all the World much heavier, though divided
With that bad Woman? Thus what thou desir'st,
And what thou fear'st, alike destroys all hope
Of refuge, and concludes thee miserable
840   Beyond all past example and future,
To *Satan* only like both crime and doom.
O Conscience, into what Abyss of fears
And horrors hast thou driv'n me; out of which
I find no way, from deep to deeper plung'd!
845   Thus *Adam* to himself lamented loud
Through the still Night, not now, as ere man fell,
Wholesome and cool and mild, but with black Air
Accompanied, with damps and dreadful gloom,
Which to his evil Conscience represented
850   All things with double terror: On the ground
Outstretcht he lay, on the cold ground, and oft
Curs'd his Creation, Death as oft accus'd
Of tardy execution, since denounc't
The day of his offense. Why comes not Death,
855   Said he, with one thrice àcceptable stroke
To end me? Shall Truth fail to keep her word,
Justice Divine not hast'n to be just?
But Death comes not at call, Justice Divine
Mends not her slowest pace for prayers or cries.
860   O Woods, O Fountains, Hillocks, Dales and Bow'rs,
With other echo late I taught your Shades
To answer, and resound far other Song.
Whom thus afflicted when sad Eve beheld,
Desolate where she sat, approaching nigh,
865   Soft words to his fierce passion she assay'd:
But her with stern regard he thus repell'd.
          Out of my sight, thou Serpent, that name best
Befits thee with him leagu'd, thyself as false
And hateful; nothing wants, but that thy shape,
870   Like his, and color Serpentine may show

---

1. Adam at last reaches full conviction of his sin; but being unable yet to pass to contrition, the next stage of repentance, he falls instead into despair. The present pas- sage should be compared with Satan's similar fall into conscience-stricken despair at 4.86–113.

Thy inward fraud, to warn all Creatures from thee
Henceforth; lest that too heav'nly form, pretended[2]
To hellish falsehood, snare them. But for thee
I had persisted happy, had not thy pride
875 And wand'ring vanity, when least was safe,
Rejected my forewarning, and disdain'd
Not to be trusted, longing to be seen
Though by the Devil himself, him overweening
To over-reach, but with the Serpent meeting
880 Fool'd and beguil'd, by him thou, I by thee,
To trust thee from my side, imagin'd wise,
Constant, mature, proof against all assaults,
And understood not all was but a show
Rather than solid virtue, all but a Rib
885 Crooked by nature, bent, as now appears,
More to the part siníster[3] from me drawn,
Well if thrown out, as supernumerary
To my just number found. O why did God,
Creator wise, that peopl'd highest Heav'n
890 With Spirits Masculine, create at last
This novelty on Earth, this fair defect
Of Nature, and not fill the World at once
With Men as Angels without Feminine,
Or find some other way to generate
895 Mankind?[4] this mischief had not then befall'n,
And more that shall befall, innumerable
Disturbances on Earth through Female snares,
And strait conjunction with this Sex: for either
He never shall find out fit Mate, but such
900 As some misfortune brings him, or mistake,
Or whom he wishes most shall seldom gain
Through her perverseness, but shall see her gain'd
By a far worse, or if she love, withheld
By Parents, or his happiest choice too late
905 Shall meet, already linkt and Wedlock-bound
To a fell° Adversary, his hate or shame: *bitter*
Which infinite calamity shall cause
To Human life, and household peace confound.
     He added not, and from her turn'd, but *Eve*
910 Not so repulst, with Tears that ceas'd not flowing,
And tresses all disorder'd, at his feet
Fell humble, and imbracing them, besought
His peace, and thus proceeded in her plaint.
     Forsake me not thus, *Adam*, witness Heav'n
915 What love sincere, and reverence in my heart
I bear thee, and unweeting° have offended,   *unintentionally*

---

2. Stretched in front as a covering serving as a mask.
3. Left; also corrupt, evil, base. The notion that woman is formed from a bent rib, and therefore crooked, had appeared in tracts like Swetnam's *The Arraignment of*

Lewd, Idle, Froward, and Inconstant Women (page 708).
4. Another ancient piece of antifeminism; see Euripides, *Hippolytus* 616ff. Aristotle had said in the *De generatione* that the female is a defective male.

Unhappily deceiv'd; thy suppliant
I beg, and clasp thy knees; bereave me not,
Whereon I live, thy gentle looks, thy aid,
920 Thy counsel in this uttermost distress,
My only strength and stay: forlorn of thee,
Whither shall I betake me, where subsist?
While yet we live, scarce one short hour perhaps,
Between us two let there be peace, both joining,
925 As join'd in injuries, one enmity
Against a Foe by doom express assign'd us,
That cruel Serpent: On me exercise not
Thy hatred for this misery befall'n,
On me already lost, mee than thyself
930 More miserable; both have sinn'd, but thou
Against God only, I against God and thee,
And to the place of judgment will return,
There with my cries importune Heaven, that all
The sentence from thy head remov'd may light
935 On me, sole cause to thee of all this woe,
Mee mee only just object of his ire.
    She ended weeping, and her lowly plight,
Immovable till peace obtain'd from fault
Acknowledg'd and deplor'd,[5] in *Adam* wrought
940 Commiseration; soon his heart relented
Towards her, his life so late and sole delight,
Now at his feet submissive in distress,
Creature so fair his reconcilement seeking,
His counsel whom she had displeas'd, his aid;
945 As one disarm'd, his anger all he lost,
And thus with peaceful words uprais'd her soon.
    Unwary, and too desirous, as before,
So now of what thou know'st not, who desir'st
The punishment all on thyself; alas,
950 Bear thine own first, ill able to sustain
His full wrath whose thou feel'st as yet least part,
And my displeasure bear'st so ill. If Prayers
Could alter high Decrees, I to that place
Would speed before thee, and be louder heard,
955 That on my head all might be visited,
Thy frailty and infirmer Sex forgiv'n,
To me committed and by me expos'd.
But rise, let us no more contend, nor blame
Each other, blam'd enough elsewhere,[6] but strive
960 In offices of Love, how we may light'n
Each other's burden in our share of woe;
Since this day's Death denounc't, if aught I see,
Will prove no sudden, but a slow-pac't evil,
A long day's dying to augment our pain,

5. Eve cannot be moved from Adam's feet until he forgives her.

6. Either "heaven" or the "place of judgment" of line 932.

965 And to our Seed (O hapless Seed!) deriv'd.
         To whom thus *Eve*, recovering heart, repli'd.
     Adam, by sad experiment I know
     How little weight my words with thee can find,
     Found so erroneous, thence by just event°   *consequence*
970 Found so unfortunate; nevertheless,
     Restor'd by thee, vile as I am, to place
     Of new acceptance, hopeful to regain
     Thy Love, the sole contentment of my heart
     Living or dying, from thee I will not hide
975 What thoughts in my unquiet breast are ris'n,
     Tending to some relief of our extremes,
     Or end, though sharp and sad, yet tolerable,
     As in our evils, and of easier choice.
     If care of our descent° perplex° us most,   *descendants / torment*
980 Which must be born to certain woe, devour'd
     By Death at last, and miserable it is
     To be to other cause of misery,
     Our own begott'n, and of our Loins to bring
     Into this cursed World a woeful Race,
985 That after wretched Life must be at last
     Food for so foul a Monster, in thy power
     It lies, yet ere Conception to prevent
     The Race unblest, to being yet unbegot.
     Childless thou art, Childless remain: So Death
990 Shall be deceiv'd his glut, and with us two
     Be forc'd to satisfy his Rav'nous Maw.
     But if thou judge it hard and difficult,
     Conversing, looking, loving, to abstain
     From Love's due Rites, Nuptial embraces sweet,
995 And with desire to languish without hope,[7]
     Before the present object° languishing   *Eve*
     With like desire, which would be misery
     And torment less than none of what we dread,
     Then both ourselves and Seed at once to free
1000 From what we fear for both, let us make short,
     Let us seek Death, or he not found, supply
     With our own hands his Office on ourselves;
     Why stand we longer shivering under fears,
     That show no end but Death, and have the power,
1005 Of many ways to die the shortest choosing,
     Destruction with destruction to destroy.
         She ended here, or vehement despair
     Broke off the rest; so much of Death her thoughts
     Had entertain'd, as dy'd her Cheeks with pale.
1010 But *Adam* with such counsel nothing sway'd,
     To better hopes his more attentive mind
     Laboring had rais'd, and thus to *Eve* replied.
         Eve, thy contempt of life and pleasure seems

---

7. See Dante, *Inferno* 4.42, "without hope we live in desire."

To argue in thee something more sublime
1015 And excellent than what thy mind contemns;
But self-destruction therefore sought, refutes
That excellence thought in thee, and implies,
Not thy contempt, but anguish and regret
For loss of life and pleasure overlov'd.
1020 Or if thou covet death, as utmost end
Of misery, so thinking to evade
The penalty pronounc't, doubt not but God
Hath wiselier arm'd his vengeful ire than so
To be forestall'd; much more I fear lest Death
1025 So snatcht will not exempt us from the pain
We are by doom to pay; rather such acts
Of contumacy° will provoke the Highest   *contempt*
To make death in us live: Then let us seek
Some safer resolution, which methinks
1030 I have in view, calling to mind with heed
Part of our Sentence, that thy Seed shall bruise
The Serpent's head; piteous amends, unless
Be meant, whom I conjecture, our grand Foe
Satan, who in the Serpent hath contriv'd
1035 Against us this deceit: to crush his head
Would be revenge indeed; which will be lost
By death brought on ourselves, or childless days
Resolv'd, as thou proposest; so our Foe
Shall 'scape his punishment ordain'd, and wee
1040 Instead shall double ours upon our heads.
No more be mention'd then of violence
Against ourselves, and wilful barrenness,
That cuts us off from hope, and savors only
Rancor and pride, impatience and despite,
1045 Reluctance° against God and his just yoke   *resistance*
Laid on our Necks. Remember with what mild
And gracious temper he both heard and judg'd
Without wrath or reviling; wee expected
Immediate dissolution, which we thought
1050 Was meant by Death that day, when lo, to thee
Pains only in Child-bearing were foretold,
And bringing forth, soon recompens't with joy,
Fruit of thy Womb: On mee the Curse aslope
Glanc'd on the ground, with labor I must earn
1055 My bread;[8] what harm? Idleness had been worse;
My labor will sustain me; and lest Cold
Or Heat should injure us, his timely care
Hath unbesought provided, and his hands
Cloth'd us unworthy, pitying while he judg'd;
1060 How much more, if we pray him, will his ear
Be open, and his heart to pity incline,[9]

8. Referring to Christ's words at lines 201–5.

9. Biblical diction; see Psalms 24.4, 119.36, 112; and 1 Peter 3.12.

And teach us further by what means to shun
Th' inclement Seasons, Rain, Ice, Hail and Snow,
Which now the Sky with various Face begins
1065   To show us in this Mountain, while the Winds
Blow moist and keen, shattering the graceful locks
Of these fair spreading Trees; which bids us seek
Some better shroud,° some better warmth to cherish   *shelter*
Our Limbs benumb'd, ere this diurnal Star[1]
1070   Leave cold the Night, how we his gather'd beams
Reflected, may with matter sere foment,[2]
Or by collision of two bodies grind
The Air attrite° to Fire, as late the Clouds   *ground down*
Justling° or pusht with Winds rude in thir shock   *jostling*
1075   Tine° the slant Lightning, whose thwart flame driv'n down   *ignite*
Kindles the gummy bark of Fir or Pine,
And sends a comfortable heat from far,
Which might supply° the Sun: such Fire to use,   *take the place of*
And what may else be remedy or cure
1080   To evils which our own misdeeds have wrought,
Hee will instruct us praying, and of Grace
Beseeching him, so as we need not fear
To pass commodiously this life, sustain'd
By him with many comforts, till we end
1085   In dust, our final rest and native home.
What better can we do, than to the place
Repairing where he judg'd us, prostrate fall
Before him reverent, and there confess
Humbly our faults, and pardon beg, with tears
1090   Watering the ground, and with our sighs the Air
Frequenting,° sent from hearts contrite, in sign   *filling*
Of sorrow unfeign'd, and humiliation meek.[3]
Undoubtedly he will relent and turn
From his displeasure; in whose look serene,
1095   When angry most he seem'd and most severe,
What else but favor, grace, and mercy shone?
    So spake our Father penitent, nor Eve
Felt less remorse: they forthwith to the place
Repairing where he judg'd them prostrate fell
1100   Before him reverent, and both confess'd
Humbly thir faults, and pardon begg'd, with tears
Watering the ground, and with thir sighs the Air
Frequenting, sent from hearts contrite, in sign
Of sorrow unfeign'd, and humiliation meek.[4]
    The End of the Tenth Book.

---

1. The sun.
2. Cherish; but alluding also to Latin *fomes* (tinder). Adam envisages making fire: focusing the sun's rays onto dry combustibles ("matter sere") with a parabolic mirror.
3. Having passed on from conviction of sin Adam, now "contrite" (line 1103), is ready for confession, the third stage of repentance. An allusion to the Penitential Psalm: "The sacrifices of God are a broken spirit: a broken and a contrite heart, O God, thou wilt not despise" (Psalms 51.17).
4. Repeating lines 1086–92, modulated into narrative discourse (only the last two verses remain identical).

from **Book 11**
The Argument

The Son of God present to his Father the Prayers of our first Parents now repenting, and intercedes for them: God accepts them, but declares that they must no longer abide in Paradise; sends Michael with a Band of Cherubim to dispossess them; but first to reveal to Adam future things; Michael's coming down. Adam shows to Eve certain ominous signs; he discerns Michael's approach, goes out to meet him: the Angel denounces thir departure. Eve's Lamentation. Adam pleads, but submits: The Angel leads him up to a high Hill, sets before him in vision what shall happ'n till the Flood.

Book 12
The Argument

The Angel Michael continues from the Flood to relate what shall succeed; then, in the mention of Abraham, comes by degrees to explain, who that Seed of the Woman shall be, which was promised Adam and Eve in the Fall; his Incarnation, Death, Resurrection, and Ascension; the state of the Church till his second Coming. Adam greatly satisfied and recomforted by these Relations and Promises descends the Hill with Michael; wakens Eve, who all this while had slept, but with gentle dreams compos'd to quietness of mind and submission. Michael in either hand leads them out of Paradise, the fiery Sword waving behind them, and the Cherubim taking thir Stations to guard the Place.

	As one who in his journey bates° at Noon,	*pauses*
	Though bent on speed, so here the Arch-Angel paus'd	
	Betwixt the world destroy'd and world restor'd,	
	If *Adam* aught perhaps might interpose;	
5	Then with transition sweet new Speech resumes.	
	Thus thou hast seen one World begin and end;	
	And Man as from a second stock proceed.[1]	
	Much thou hast yet to see, but I perceive	
	Thy mortal sight to fail; objects divine	
10	Must needs impair and weary human sense:	
	Henceforth what is to come I will relate,	
	Thou therefore give due audience, and attend.	
	This second source of Men, while yet but few,	
	And while the dread of judgment past remains	
15	Fresh in thir minds, fearing the Deity,	
	With some regard to what is just and right	
	Shall lead thir lives, and multiply apace,	
	Laboring° the soil, and reaping plenteous crop,	*tilling*
	Corn, wine and oil; and from the herd or flock,	
20	Oft sacrificing Bullock, Lamb, or Kid,	

---

1. "Stock," an ambiguity, refers not only to the literal replacement of one source of the human line of descent (Adam) by another (Noah), but also to the grafting of mankind onto the stem of Christ, according to the Pauline allegory of regeneration (Romans 11). The covenant with Noah was a type of the New Covenant.

With large Wine-offerings pour'd, and sacred Feast,
Shall spend thir days in joy unblam'd, and dwell
Long time in peace by Families and Tribes
Under paternal rule; till one shall rise[2]

25   Of proud ambitious heart, who not content
With fair equality, fraternal state,
Will arrogate Dominion undeserv'd
Over his brethren, and quite dispossess
Concord and law of Nature from the Earth;[3]

30   Hunting (and Men not Beasts shall be his game)
With War and hostile snare such as refuse
Subjection to his Empire tyrannous:[4]
A mighty Hunter thence he shall be styl'd
Before the Lord, as in despite of Heav'n,

35   Or from Heav'n claiming second Sovranty;[5]
And from Rebellion shall derive his name,
Though of Rebellion others he accuse.
Hee with a crew, whom like Ambition joins
With him or under him to tyrannize,

40   Marching from *Eden* towards the West, shall find
The Plain, wherein a black bituminous gurge°   *whirlpool*
Boils out from under ground, the mouth of Hell;
Of Brick, and of that stuff they cast to build
A City and Tow'r, whose top may reach to Heav'n;[6]

45   And get themselves a name, lest far disperst
In foreign Lands thir memory be lost,
Regardless whether good or evil fame.[7]
But God who oft descends to visit men
Unseen, and through thir habitations walks

50   To mark thir doings, them beholding soon,
Comes down to see thir City, ere the Tower
Obstruct Heav'n Tow'rs, and in derision sets
Upon thir Tongues a various Spirit to rase
Quite out thir Native Language, and instead

55   To sow a jangling noise of words unknown:
Forthwith a hideous gabble rises loud
Among the Builders; each to other calls
Not understood, till hoarse, and all in rage,
As mockt they storm;[8] great laughter was in Heav'n

---

2. Nimrod is not connected with the builders of the Tower in Genesis 10.8. The connection is made, however, in Josephus, *Antiquities* 1.4.2ff., where we also learn that Nimrod "changed the government into tyranny."
3. In *The Tenure of Kings and Magistrates*, Milton denies the natural right of kings and insists that their power is committed to them in trust by the people.
4. See *Eikonoklastes*: "The Bishops could have told him, that 'Nimrod,' the first that hunted after Faction is reputed, by ancient Tradition, the first that founded monarchy; whence it appeares that to hunt after Faction is more

properly the Kings Game."
5. "Before the Lord," Genesis 10.9; Milton takes it in a constitutional sense; see *The Tenure:* "To say Kings are accountable to none but God, is the overturning of all Law."
6. The materials of the Tower—brick with bitumen as mortar—are specified in Genesis 11.3.
7. See Genesis 11.4.
8. In the 17th century it was generally believed that the separation of language into distinct individual languages had its beginning at the confusion of tongues at Babel.

60   And looking down, to see the hubbub strange
        And hear the din; thus was the building left
        Ridiculous, and the work Confusion nam'd.[9]
            Whereto thus *Adam* fatherly displeas'd.
        O execrable Son so to aspire
65   Above his Brethren, to himself assuming
        Authority usurpt, from God not giv'n:
        He gave us only over Beast, Fish, Fowl
        Dominion absolute; that right we hold
        By his donation; but Man over men
70   He made not Lord; such title to himself
        Reserving, human left from human free.
        But this Usurper his encroachment proud
        Stays not on Man; to God his Tower intends
        Siege and defiance: Wretched man! what food
75   Will he convey up thither to sustain
        Himself and his rash Army, where thin Air
        Above the Clouds will pine his entrails gross,
        And famish him of breath, if not of Bread?
            To whom thus *Michael*. Justly thou abhorr'st
80   That Son, who on the quiet state of men
        Such trouble brought, affecting to subdue
        Rational Liberty;[1] yet know withal,
        Since thy original lapse, true Liberty
        Is lost, which always with right Reason dwells
85   Twinn'd, and from her hath no dividual° being: *separate*
        Reason in man obscur'd, or not obey'd,
        Immediately inordinate desires
        And upstart Passions catch the Government
        From Reason, and to servitude reduce
90   Man till then free. Therefore since hee permits
        Within himself unworthy Powers to reign
        Over free Reason, God in Judgment just
        Subjects him from without to violent Lords;
        Who oft as undeservedly enthral
95   His outward freedom: Tyranny must be,
        Though to the Tyrant thereby no excuse.
        Yet sometimes Nations will decline so low
        From virtue, which is reason, that no wrong,
        But Justice, and some fatal curse annext
100   Deprives them of thir outward liberty,
        Thir inward lost:[2] * * *

9. See Genesis 11.9, "Therefore is the name of it called Babel"; marginal gloss: "that is, Confusion."
1. Lines 80–101 recall the regicide tracts and follow St. Augustine's *City of God* 19.15, where we read that the derivation of servitude, whose mother is sin, is the "first cause of man's subjection to man: which notwithstanding comes not to pass but by the direction of the high- est, in whom is no injustice." For the connection between psychological and political enslavement, see 9.1127–31.
2. Michael goes on to describe the history of Israel, from Abraham to King David, then tells of the birth of the Messiah, who will crush Satan and defeat Sin and Death.

So spake th' Arch-Angel *Michaël*, then paus'd,
As at the World's great period;[3] and our Sire
Replete with joy and wonder thus repli'd.
    O goodness infinite, goodness immense![4]
470   That all this good of evil shall produce,
And evil turn to good; more wonderful
Than that which by creation first brought forth
Light out of darkness! full of doubt I stand,
Whether I should repent me now of sin
475   By mee done and occasion'd, or rejoice
Much more, that much more good thereof shall spring,
To God more glory, more good will to Men
From God, and over wrath grace shall abound.[5]
But say, if our deliverer up to Heav'n
480   Must reascend, what will betide the few
His faithful, left among th' unfaithful herd,
The enemies of truth; who then shall guide
His people, who defend? will they not deal
Worse with his followers than with him they dealt?
485   Be sure they will, said th' Angel; but from Heav'n
Hee to his own a Comforter will send,[6]
The promise of the Father, who shall dwell
His Spirit within them, and the Law of Faith
Working through love, upon thir hearts shall write,[7]
490   To guide them in all truth, and also arm
With spiritual Armor, able to resist
Satan's assaults, and quench his fiery darts,[8]
What Man can do against them, not afraid,
Though to the death, against such cruelties
495   With inward consolations recompens't,
And oft supported so as shall amaze
Thir proudest persecutors: for the Spirit
Pour'd first on his Apostles, whom he sends
To evangelize the Nations, then on all
500   Baptiz'd, shall them with wondrous gifts endue°   *endow*
To speak all Tongues, and do all Miracles,
As did thir Lord before them. Thus they win
Great numbers of each Nation to receive
With joy the tidings brought from Heav'n: at length
505   Thir Ministry perform'd, and race well run,
Thir doctrine and thir story written left,
They die; but in thir room, as they forewarn,

3. This is Michael's second pause; the first was at 12.2. The three divisions of Adam's instruction are meant to correspond to "three drops" of the well of life placed in his eyes (11.416). Here the pause is compared with the world's period the dawning of the present age, from the first to the second coming of Christ.
4. The Final Cause or end of the Fall: a greater "glory" for God and an opportunity for him to show his surpassing love through the sacrifice of Christ.
5. See Romans 5.20 ("where sin abounded, grace did much more abound") and 2 Corinthians 4.15.
6. The Holy Spirit. See John 14.18 and 15.26.
7. See Galations 5.6: "faith which worketh by love."
8. Alluding to the allegory in Ephesians 6.16: "Above all, taking the shield of faith, wherewith ye shall be able to quench all the fiery darts of the wicked."

Wolves shall succeed for teachers, grievous Wolves,[9]
Who all the sacred mysteries of Heav'n
510 To thir own vile advantages shall turn
Of lucre and ambition, and the truth
With superstitions and traditions taint,
Left only in those written Records pure,
Though not but by the Spirit understood.[1]
515 Then shall they seek to avail themselves of names,
Places and titles, and with these to join
Secular power, though feigning still to act
By spiritual, to themselves appropriating
The Spirit of God, promis'd alike and giv'n
520 To all Believers;[2] and from that pretense,
Spiritual Laws by carnal° power shall force   *worldly*
On every conscience; Laws which none shall find
Left them inroll'd, or what the Spirit within
Shall on the heart engrave.[3] What will they then
525 But force the Spirit of Grace itself, and bind
His consort Liberty; what, but unbuild
His living Temples, built by Faith to stand,[4]
Thir own Faith not another's: for on Earth
Who against Faith and Conscience can be heard
530 Infallible?[5] yet many will presume:
Whence heavy persecution shall arise
On all who in the worship persevere
Of Spirit and Truth; the rest, far greater part,
Will deem in outward Rites and specious forms
535 Religion satisfi'd; Truth shall retire
Bestuck with sland'rous darts, and works of Faith
Rarely be found: so shall the World go on,
To good malignant, to bad men benign,
Under her own weight groaning, till the day
540 Appear of respiration[6] to the just,
And vengeance to the wicked, at return
Of him so lately promis'd to thy aid,
The Woman's seed, obscurely then foretold,
Now amplier known thy Saviour and thy Lord,
545 Last in the Clouds from Heav'n to be reveal'd
In glory of the Father, to dissolve

---

9. "For I know this, that after my departing shall grievous wolves enter in among you, not sparing the flock" (Acts 20.29). See the simile comparing Satan to a wolf in the fold, at 4.183–87; see also *Lycidas* 113ff, page 771.
1. It was an important article of Protestant belief that in doctrinal matters the ultimate arbiter is individual conscience rather than mere authority.
2. The corruption of the Church through its pursuit of "secular power" is a subject Milton had dealt with in *Of Reformation.* In *De doctrina* 1.30 he condemns the enforcement of obedience to human opinions or authority.

3. The wolves will enforce laws written neither in Scripture nor in the individual conscience.
4. See 1 Corinthians 3.17: "The temple of God is holy, which temple ye are."
5. Even though the doctrine of papal infallibility was not formally adapted until 1870, there can be no doubt that Rome is Milton's main target here. In *A Treatise of Civil Power* he writes that the "Pope assumes infallibility over conscience and scripture."
6. Opportunity for breathing again; rest.

Satan with his perverted World, then raise
From the conflagrant° mass, purg'd and refin'd,   *burning*
New Heav'ns, new Earth, Ages of endless date
550 Founded in righteousness and peace and love,
To bring forth fruits Joy and eternal Bliss.
       He ended; and thus Adam last repli'd.
How soon hath thy prediction, Seer blest,
Measur'd this transient World, the Race of time,
555 Till time stand fixt: beyond is all abyss,
Eternity, whose end no eye can reach.
Greatly instructed I shall hence depart,
Greatly in peace of thought, and have my fill
Of knowledge, what this Vessel can contain;
560 Beyond which was my folly to aspire.
Henceforth I learn, that to obey is best,
And love with fear the only God, to walk
As in his presence, ever to observe
His providence, and on him sole depend,
565 Merciful over all his works, with good
Still overcoming evil, and by small
Accomplishing great things, by things deem'd weak
Subverting worldly strong, and worldly wise
By simply meek; that suffering for Truth's sake
570 Is fortitude to highest victory,
And to the faithful Death the Gate of Life;
Taught this by his example whom I now
Acknowledge my Redeemer ever blest.
       To whom thus also th' Angel last repli'd:
575 This having learnt, thou hast attain'd the sum
Of wisdom; hope no higher, though all the Stars
Thou knew'st by name, and all th' ethereal Powers,
All secrets of the deep, all Nature's works,
Or works of God in Heav'n, Air, Earth, or Sea,
580 And all the riches of this World enjoy'dst,
And all the rule, one Empire; only add
Deeds to thy knowledge answerable, add Faith,
Add Virtue, Patience, Temperance, add Love,
By name to come call'd Charity, the soul
585 Of all the rest:[7] then wilt thou not be loath
To leave this Paradise, but shalt possess
A paradise within thee, happier far.
Let us descend now therefore from this top
Of Speculation;[8] for the hour precise
590 Exacts our parting hence; and see the Guards,

---

7. Compare 2 Peter 1.5–7: "Add to your faith virtue;
and to virtue knowledge; and to knowledge temperance;
and to temperance patience; and to patience godliness;
and to godliness brotherly kindness; and to brotherly

kindness charity."
8. Vantage point but also height of theological speculation.

By mee encampt on yonder Hill, expect
Thir motion,[9] at whose Front a flaming Sword,
In signal of remove, waves fiercely round;
We may no longer stay: go, waken *Eve*;
595   Her also I with gentle Dreams have calm'd
Portending good, and all her spirits compos'd
To meek submission: thou at season fit
Let her with thee partake what thou hast heard,
Chiefly what may concern her Faith to know,
600   The great deliverance by her Seed to come
(For by the Woman's Seed)[1] on all Mankind,
That ye may live, which will be many days,[2]
Both in one Faith unanimous though sad,
With cause for evils past, yet much more cheer'd
605   With meditation on the happy end.
　　　He ended, and they both descend the Hill;
Descended, *Adam* to the Bow'r where *Eve*
Lay sleeping ran before, but found her wak't;
And thus with words not sad she him receiv'd.
610   Whence thou return'st, and whither went'st, I know;
For God is also in sleep, and Dreams advise,
Which he hath sent propitious, some great good
Presaging, since with sorrow and heart's distress
Wearied I fell asleep: but now lead on;
615   In mee is no delay; with thee to go,
Is to stay here; without thee here to stay,
Is to go hence unwilling; thou to mee
Art all things under Heav'n, all places thou,
Who for my wilful crime art banisht hence.[3]
620   This further consolation yet secure
I carry hence; though all by mee is lost,
Such favor I unworthy am voutsaf't,
By mee the Promis'd Seed shall all restore.
　　　So spake our Mother *Eve*, and *Adam* heard
625   Well pleas'd, but answer'd not; for now too nigh
Th' Arch-Angel stood, and from the other Hill
To thir fixt Station, all in bright array
The Cherubim descended; on the ground
Gliding meteorous,° as Ev'ning Mist   *meteoric*
630   Ris'n from a River o'er the marish° glides,   *marsh*
And gathers ground fast at the Laborer's heel
Homeward returning. High in Front advanc't,
The brandisht Sword of God before them blaz'd
Fierce as a Comet; which with torrid heat,
635   And vapor as the *Libyan* Air adust,°   *scorched*

---

9. Await deployment, marching orders.
1. Alluding to the birth of Jesus.
2. Adam lived to be 930 years of age (Genesis 5.5).
3. Eve has assimilated Michael's exhortation at 11.292:

"where [Adam] abides, think there thy native soil." There
is also a resonance with Eve's song at 4.635–56 (every
time of day is pleasing with Adam, none is pleasing without him).

Began to parch that temperate Clime; whereat
In either hand the hast'ning Angel caught
Our ling'ring Parents, and to th' Eastern Gate
Led them direct, and down the Cliff as fast
640　　To the subjected° Plain; then disappear'd.　　　　　　　　*underlying*
They looking back, all th' Eastern side beheld
Of Paradise, so late thir happy seat,
Wav'd over by that flaming Brand,[4] the Gate
With dreadful Faces throng'd and fiery Arms:
645　　Some natural tears they dropp'd, but wip'd them soon;
The World was all before them, where to choose
Thir place of rest, and Providence thir guide:[5]
They hand in hand with wand'ring steps and slow,
Through *Eden* took thir solitary way.

　　　　　　　　The End

---

4. See Genesis. 3.24: "a flaming sword which turned every way."

5. Note that "Providence" can be the object of "choose": decisions of faith lie ahead.

Thomas Bowles. *The Bubblers' Medley, or a Sketch of the Times.* 1720

The Restoration and
the Eighteenth Century

◄━━❈◆❈━━►

On 25 May 1660, Charles II set foot on the shore of Dover and brought his eleven-year exile to an end. The arrival was recorded by the great diarist Samuel Pepys, and his words preserve for us a form of the event:

> I went, and Mr. Mansell, and one of the King's footmen, with a dog that the King loved (which beshat the boat, which made us laugh, and methink that a king and all that belong to him are but just as others are), in a boat by ourselves, and so got on shore when the King did, who was received . . . with all imaginable love and respect at his entrance upon the land of Dover. Infinite the crowd of people and the horsemen, citizens, and noblemen of all sorts. The Mayor of the town came and gave him his white staff, the badge of his place, which the King did give him again. The Mayor also presented him from the town a very rich Bible, which he took and said it was the thing that he loved above all things in the world. . . . The shouting and joy expressed by all is past imagination.

Pepys captures and creates a brilliant mix of materials and experiences: his words compound jubilation and skepticism, images of authority and obeisance, tropes of spirituality and irony, and they remind us of the elements and passions by which all men live. Every gesture and exchange in this scene forecast the world to come, but what most signals the future is the paradox of remembering and forgetting that the diarist performs even as he records this scene. And all who witnessed the king's descent at Dover committed similar acts of memory and oblivion. Many of those (Pepys included) who were drunk with pleasure at the return of Charles Stuart had endorsed the destruction of his father eleven years before. The entire Restoration and the events that would follow over the ensuing years would prove a complex unfolding of memory and forgetfulness.

The jubilant crowds at Dover thought to make flux stop here: forever to banish the turbulence of civil war and political innovation, to restore all the old familiar forms, utterly to erase what had come between the death of the father and the restoration of the son. Charles II would soon institute an Act of Oblivion to those ends, forgiving proponents of rebellion by officially forgetting their misdeeds. But civil war and revolution would not be erased, nor could monarchy, the Anglican Church, aristocratic privilege, political patronage, and the old social hierarchies be revived as though nothing had intervened. Much of the old was brought back with the return of the Stuart monarchy, but the consequence of layering the present over a willfully suppressed past was an instability of feelings and forms that ensured the ever-changing triumph of different memories and different oblivions during the ensuing decades. No one celebrating the return of ancient ways in 1660 could have foreseen the ruptures and innovations that lay ahead in the next half of the century when crises of conspiracy and the birth of party politics would produce further shifts in monarchy, through a sequence of three ruling houses from three different countries. But even in 1660 the innocent acclaim on the shores of Dover was accompanied by hidden guilts and ironies, by vindictive desires, even for some by millenarian hopes. And while such stresses and tensions were unacknowledged in May 1660, they soon enough surfaced; and they unsettled not only the pleasures of this king's rule but the politics of an entire age.

MONARCHS, MINISTERS, EMPIRE

The coronation of Charles II in May 1661 marked the beginning of both the first and the eleventh year of his rule. The king's laws were named as if he had taken possession of the crown at the moment of his father's execution in 1649. And fictions, legal and not so legal, were to prove a hallmark of Stuart rule. The king openly proclaimed his love of parliaments, his devotion to the immemorial constitution of balance and moderation, his Protestant fervor, and his pious hopes for a national church. Yet he often postponed his parliaments; he claimed a tender conscience for Protestant dissenters, but he maneuvered for the toleration of Roman Catholics; he conducted an aggressive, nationalist program against European powers, but he signed a secret and deeply compromising treaty with Louis XIV; he took communion in the Anglican Church, but on his deathbed he sealed his own conversion to Catholicism; he was tenderly affectionate to his barren queen, yet he publicly flaunted his whoring tastes; he repeatedly exiled his unpopular brother James, Duke of York, while promoting and indulging his own bastard sons, yet he staunchly resisted any effort to displace his brother from the line of succession. The dominance of masquerade surely derived from Charles's temper, but fiction and falsehood were also the structural principles and aesthetic features of an entire world.

In December 1678, a series of events started to unfold that proved the very emblem of the masking, the fears, and the psychology of Charles II's rule. It began with legal depositions: one Titus Oates, a baker's son and self-anointed savior of a Protestant people, claimed to have knowledge of a secret plot to kill the king, crown his Catholic brother, and begin the wholesale conversion of English souls—and, just as frightening, English properties—to Rome. Oates offered to a public hungry for scandal and change a Popish plot and a familiar mix of images and idioms: priests and idols, the Roman Antichrist, conspiracy, murder, and mayhem. His depositions and fabrications played brilliantly on memories of the past and on fears of a future under a Catholic king. Nor did it help that the Duke of York's private secretary, Edward Coleman, was caught with treasonous correspondence in his chamber. The plot seemed compounded of sufficient truths to challenge the stability of the Crown. From the midst of the plot, and under the hand of the Earl of Shaftesbury, a political party emerged that took advantage of Popish facts and fears by proposing the Bill of Exclusion in Parliament that would bar the Duke of York and any future Catholic monarchs from the English throne. In the event, the bill failed, Charles died of natural causes, and the duke succeeded his brother in February 1685.

During James's brief reign, no plots, conspiracies, or political parties proved so costly to his rule as did the new king himself. He succeeded his brother in a mood of surprising public affirmation. At his accession, James returned the embrace of Anglican England by promising to honor the national church and that most beloved of Protestant properties, a tender conscience. There would be no forcing of religious uniformity in this reign. But soon enough James began to move against Anglican interests: he staffed his army with Catholic officers, he imposed Catholic officials on Oxford University, and he insisted that his Declarations of Toleration be read aloud from the pulpits of Anglican churches. Such a program challenged interest, property, and propriety, and it spelled the quick demise of Catholic rule.

As Duke of York, James had been famed for martial valor. But now, when confronted in November 1688 by the army of his Dutch son-in-law, William of Orange, he fled under cover of night to France. What had in part provoked James's flight were memories of the past—of civil war and of the execution of his father, Charles I. What had provoked the invasion by William of Orange was not merely the specter of Louis XIV hovering behind James's rule or the open presence of Jesuits at James's court. It was the birth of James Francis Edward Stuart, son of James II and Mary of Modena. Protestants would suffer not only the inconvenience of one Catholic monarch but the possibility of an endless Catholic succession. The prospect was too much to bear. Secret negotiations were begun between powerful English artistocrats—Whigs and Tories alike—and William, the governor (stadholder) of Holland, resulting in what many called the Glorious Revolution. But the deceits and pretenses—the gaps and silences—of this palace coup did not strike all contemporaries as glorious. The stadholder who chased a Catholic king from England was not only an invading hero (though some did call him William the Conqueror), he was also the son-in-law of James II. Those who clung to the binding ties of loyalty and gratitude accused William and Mary of deep impiety, indeed, of parricide.

But the astonishing invitation to William of Orange produced no bloodshed. What it did produce was a Protestant monarchy under the rule of King William III and Queen Mary. Members of Parliament, meeting to invent the laws that would sanctify this revolutionary change, decided that it would be best to say they had discovered the throne of England mysteriously vacant and that this William was no conqueror but a rightful claimant on a vacant throne. Of course, not everyone was pleased by such a revolution—sacred oaths had been broken, binding ties were cast aside, vows were juggled as mere words. Those who would not accept a convenient revolution were called Jacobites—that is, supporters of King James (*Jacobus* in Latin); they remained a force that would trouble British political life by threatening a Stuart restoration in the fervent but failed Jacobite rebellions of 1715 and 1745.

Most of William's subjects, though, were content with the evasions of this Glorious Revolution. Many were not content, though, with the program of European war in which the English were now plunged by their new king, intent on thwarting the ambitions of Louis XIV, his lifelong nemesis. The ruinous expense of war demanded taxes and fiscal innovation; it produced a stream of grumbling satire, complaint against Dutch favorites, and more than one conspiracy and attempted assassination. No such disaffection or turbulence disturbed the reign (1701–1714) of William's successor, Queen Anne. Her years were the twilight of Stuart monarchy, a time of political nostalgia and commercial confidence whose mood the young Alexander Pope captured in the lines of *Windsor-Forest* (1713), where softened memories and strategic elisions of the years of Stuart rule are mingled with images of triumph—of imperial expansion and a swelling commerce of domestic and foreign trade.

But luxury was not England's only import. At the death of Queen Anne an entire court and new ruling house were shipped to England from the German state of Hanover. George I was the grandson of James I; beyond lineage, George's communion in a Protestant Church was the virtue that most recommended his succession. He spoke no English, knew nothing of his new subjects, and could not be bothered to learn. Nor was he much implicated in the management of a state whose rule would successively become less the prerogative of kings than the business of ministers and the function of parties, interest, and corruption. This displacement of monarch by minister was cemented during the period caustically nicknamed "Robin's Reign": two decades (1721–1742), transversing the reigns of George I and George II, when politics were dominated by Robert Walpole, who bought loyalties, managed kings, and ran the state with such ruthless efficency as to earn him the new label "prime minister" (the phrase was meant as an insult, aimed at the perceived excess of his power in a government where ministers were only supposed to advise their colleagues and their king). The South Sea Bubble, a state-endorsed investment scheme which ruined many, was the making of Robert Walpole. As the only cabinet minister untainted by the scandal (he had initially argued against the scheme, then lost money in it), he was put in charge of the subsequent governmental housecleaning. Once empowered, he cheerfully shed his scruples, devising a political machine fueled by patronage that made his cronies rich, his opposition apoplectic. By the firmness of his rule and the prudence of his policies, Walpole consolidated a long period of Whig supremacy that supplanted the party contest of the preceding decades, when Whigs and Tories had see-sawed more swiftly in and out of power.

The parties had begun to crystallize during the Exclusion crisis of the early 1680s, when Whigs fought to bar the king's Catholic brother from the throne, and Tories upheld the established continuity of the Stuart line. Like "prime minister," the two party names began as insult, "Tory" denoting an Irish-Catholic bandit, "Whigs" identifying a group of Scotch rebels during the civil wars. Late in the eighteenth century, Samuel Johnson summed up their polarities: "The prejudice of the Tory is for establishment; the prejudice of the Whig is for innovation." "Establishment" meant preserving monarchic prerogatives, upholding the Anglican church, lamenting the advent of the Hanoverians, and—for some Tories, not all—actively yearning for the restoration of the Stuart line, and abetting the attempts to achieve this in the Jacobite rebellions of 1715 and 1745. Whig "innovation" entailed enthusiastic support for both the Glorious Revolution and the House of Hanover, for policies of religious tolerance, and for all measures that advanced the interests of the newly prosperous and powerful merchant class. In the late seventeenth century, party politics had begun for the first time to supplant long-running religious conflicts as the main articulation of interest and power. For all its noise and rage, the new structure produced a paradoxical calm, not by the suppression of difference but by its recognition. The division into parties amounted to a sanctioned fragmentation of the whole. Even during the reign of Anne, when party conflict was at its most feverish, what the machinery of the party seemed to ensure was the containment of partisan interest within the dynamic, even organic, coherence of the state.

During Walpole's "reign," portions of the two parties coalesced in an uneasy alliance. The arrogance, obstinacy, and efficacy of Walpole's methods galvanized an opposition consisting of both Tories and alienated Whigs; their endeavors acquired luster from the contributions of a remarkable array of writers (the Tories Jonathan Swift, Alexander Pope, John Gay, and Henry Fielding, and the Whig James Thomson) who opposed the prime minister on grounds of personality, principle, and of course self-interest. Walpole, recognizing that the best writers worked for the opposition, strove to suppress them by all the strategies of censorship he could devise. But by his greatness as a character and his force as an opponent, Walpole loomed for a long while as both literature's nemesis and its muse.

In fact, Walpole enforced the policies endorsed by only a fraction of his party—those moderate Whigs deeply interested in cultivating the country's wealth by commerce, deeply resistant to waging war. "My *politics*," he once wrote emphatically, "*are to keep free from all engagements, as long as we possibly can*"; by "engagements," he meant military commitments abroad. By the late 1730s, he discovered that he could keep free from them no longer. Britons feared that powers on the Continent—Spain, Austria, and above all France—were encroaching on their rights, and the popular clamor to wage European war prevailed. "When trade is at stake," the oppositionist William Pitt warned the British, "it is your last retrenchment; you must defend it or perish." Under the pressure of such sentiments Walpole eventually resigned, having led the state through two decades of comparative peace, growing national prosperity, and a new stability in government, but leaving behind him an army and a navy debilitated by disuse. Nonetheless, with trade at stake and the navy rebuilt, Britain embarked on a series of wars that ran almost unbroken for the rest of the century. Pitt presided brilliantly over many of them, wars waged directly or indirectly against France for trading privileges and territories abroad. By 1763, Britain had secured possession of Bengal in India, many islands and coastal territories in the Caribbean, and virtually all of North America (including Canada) east of the Mississippi, as well as half of all the international trade transpiring on the planet. So great was the impetus towards empire that even Britain's humiliating defeat in the American War of Independence (1775–1783) could not really halt the momentum; territories in India were still expanding, and settlement of Australia lay in the offing.

By now, the throne was occupied by the first Hanoverian monarch born in Britain—George III. His long reign (1760–1820) teemed with troubles: the popular scorn for his chosen ministers; the loss of the American war; the aftershocks of the French Revolution; the defiance of his heirs; the torments of his own slow-encroaching madness. But almost from beginning to end he ruled over the richest nation and the widest empire in the world. In 1740, a new song could be heard with a catchy refrain: "Rule, Britannia, rule the waves / Britons never will be slaves." The words were the work of the Scots-born poet James Thomson, now a proud adherent of "Britannia" by virtue of the Act of Union (1707) which had fused Scotland with England and Wales into a new nation, newly named: Great Britain. Over the ensuing years the song took hold because of the seductively prophetic ways in which it forecast Britain's greatness, and partly because of the proud but peculiar resonances of the refrain's last line. There, Thomson contrasts British liberties with the slave-like constraints supposedly suffered by subjects of absolute monarchy elsewhere. Less directly, "slaves" also points to those peoples upon whose subjugation British privilege and British prosperity were increasingly to depend. Throughout the century, Britons profited spectacularly from the capture, transport, sale, and labor of African slaves in current and former colonies; "no nation," William Pitt the Younger proclaimed in 1792, had "plunged so deeply into this guilt as Great Britain."

There were also whole populations whose condition often evoked the analogy of slavery in the minds of the few who paid reformist attention to their plight: the oppressed indigenous peoples of the colonies, and women and the poor at home. Conversation about such issues became louder and more purposeful near the end of the eighteenth century, as particular champions began to turn social questions into moral causes: John Wilkes on the widening of liberties and voting rights; Mary Wollstonecraft on the rights of women; William Blake (and later, William Cobbett) on the economic inequities of the whole social structure. The problems themselves did not even begin to find redress until the following century, but the emergence of such advocacies, quickened by the audacities of the French Revolution, marked a turning point toward the Romanticism that seized poetic and political imaginations in the 1790s. For most Britons of the eighteenth century, however, the new prosperity produced no special promptings of conscience. As their Restoration forebears had actively encouraged oblivion in an effort to anesthetize themselves to their past, men and women now sustained a moral and social oblivion that eased their use of others, and their pleasure in new wealth. Out of such adroitly managed oscillations, Britons fabricated a new sense of themselves as a nation and an empire.

This new construct was in large measure the work of a prominent breed of economic architects: the capital-wielding middle classes. For centuries, wealth had derived primarily from land: tenant farmers performed the labor; the landed gentry collected the often enormous profits. The new wealth was amassed, even created, by people situated between these two extremes, constituting what was often referred to as "the middling rank," "the middling station," or "the middling orders." What set the middling orders apart was the comparatively new way in which they made their money: not by landed inheritance, not by tenancy or wagework, but by the adroit deployment of money itself. Having acquired a sum by inheritance, wage, or loan, they used it as capital, investing it, along with their own efforts, in potentially lucrative enterprises: in shops, in factories, and in the enormous new financial structures (banks, stocks) that underwrote the nation's economic expansiveness. They hired helpers, reinvested profits, and when their schemes succeeded, they made their money grow. With wealth, of course, grew clout. The interests of the "City"—that is, of the eastern half of London where bustling merchants made their deals—increasingly shaped the affairs of state, the appetites for empire. Empire also shaped the progress of the arts: members of the middle class became the chief consumers and energetic producers of the period's most conspicuous new forms of literature: newspapers and novels. But nowhere were the new powers of the burgeoning bourgeoisie more striking than in the theater, that cultural site they often visited and ultimately revised.

MONEY, MANNERS, AND THEATRICS

No event more exactly and more economically signals the return of an aristocratic court to the center of English culture than the reopening of the London theaters in 1662. The intimacy, indeed the complicity, of court with theater throughout the early modern period was such that when in the 1640s Parliament took aim at monarchy, aristocracy, and privilege, it not only struck off the heads of the Earl of Strafford and Archbishop Laud, it also banished play acting and shut tight the doors of the London stage. But Puritans could not banish the theater from the English imagination, and no sooner were the playhouses closed than publishers issued new editions of old plays, and the theater made a secret return in domestic spaces and before private audiences. Print and memory would be the preservative of an entire culture. In 1660, monarchy and theater were restored in tandem. But this artistic restoration, like the political one that made it possible, irresistibly mingled the old with the new. Pepys captured all the excitement and splendor of this restoration; as usual he proves adroit at reckoning innovation:

> [T]he stage is now . . . a thousand times better and more glorious than heretofore. Now, wax-candles, and many of them; then, not above three pounds of tallow. Now, all things civil, no rudeness anywhere; then, as in a bear garden. Then, two or three fiddlers; now, nine or ten of the best. Then, nothing but rushes upon the ground and everything mean; and now all otherwise. Then the Queen seldom and the King never would come; now not the King only for state but all civil people do think they may come as well as any.

One reason that "all civil people" thought so was a matter of simple geography. Whereas the theaters of Shakespeare's day had been located in seedy districts on the outskirts of the city, this new and sumptuous theatrical world was ensconced in new neighborhoods strategically located for maximum social confluence, on the border between Westminster—home of the court—and the City of London, dwelling place of a "mighty band of citizens and prentices" whose sudden convergence with royalty seemed a dramatic innovation. They had all gathered to witness the most astonishing new spectacle of all: women on stage in a public theater.

Before the Restoration, aristocratic women had tantalized the court in private and privileged masquing; now the pleasures of display and consumption were democratized in several ways. For women, theatricality was no longer a pastime reserved for the very few but a plausible—though precarious—profession. For audiences at the new theaters, actresses represented the possibility of erotic spectacle for the price of a ticket—a chance to gaze on women who everyone knew were managing the pleasures, and often the policies, of kings and courtiers. Inevitably new strategies of theatricality suffused this audience, where women might model seductive conduct on the teasing combinations of concealment and display enacted before them. Pepys eavesdropped on the libertine Sir Charles Sedley in urgent banter with two women: "And one of the women would and did sit with her mask on, all the play. He would fain know who she was, but she would not tell; yet did give him many pleasant hints of her knowledge of him, by that means setting his brains at work to find out who she was, and did give him leave to use all means but pulling off her mask." Display and disguise not only animated the stage, they quickened social exchange in the intimate spaces of stalls and boxes. The traffic between revelation and concealment defined this theater. It drove the plots of plays and galvanzied audiences, modeling and scripting their fashions, their language, their lives.

In such a world the theater provided a national mask, a fantasy of empire and heroism, and yet at the same time sustained a critique of masquerade, a brutal exposure of deceptions rampant in the culture. On the one hand, the heroic drama displayed, indeed reveled in, outsized acts of conquest in exotic lands, valor, and virtue: on stage, princes slaughtered infidels by the thousands; virgins sustained honor through impossible ordeals of abduction and assault. Yet in 1667, at the same moment such dramas were thriving in the king's and the duke's playhouses, the royal fleet was being burned and sunk by a Dutch navy that breached all defenses, invading the very precincts and privacy of London's docks and shipyards. And while the fleet burned, the king busied himself with other depradations, sustaining a series of intrigues, some with the very actresses who wore such incomparable honor and virtue on the stage. (The mix of myth and mischief was popular in pictures too—for example, in the portrait of Barbara Villiers, Countess of Castlemaine, perhaps the most notorious of all the king's mistresses, gotten up in the guise of Minerva, Roman goddess of wisdom.) The heroic drama celebrated military conquest and colonial glory, and displayed them at a moment in national history that produced nothing so much as shame and humiliation: defeat at the hands of Dutch ships and Dutch commerce.

At the same time, but in a far different dramatic mode, the stage sustained a brilliant critique of a whole culture of incongruity, masquerade, and self-delusion. Restoration comedy took as its subject appetite and opportunism, social hypocrisy and sexual power play. The London audience watched scenes of seduction and connivance set in the very vicinities they had traversed to reach the playhouse: St. James's Park, Covent Garden. Such aristocratic libertines as Sir Charles Sedley and Lord Rochester, intent on their own intrigues, might admire themselves in a theatrical mirror, where the rake-hero conducted endless parry-and-thrust with his equals,

Sir Peter Lely (1616–1680). *Barbara Villiers, Countess of Castlemaine*. Ca. 1665. Theatricality disseminated: Charles II's favorite painter portrays Charles II's favorite mistress, in costume as Minerva, Roman goddess of wisdom, against a stormy background. Castlemaine's countenance was reproduced in less costly ways as well, in engravings from Lely's portraits that made the visage of the king's mistress possessible by ordinary mortals. The diarist Samuel Pepys records a visit to Lely's sumptuous studio, where he "saw the so-much-by-me-desired picture of my Lady Castlemaine, which is a most blessed picture and that I must have a copy of."

brutalized his inferiors, and laid hands and claim on any moveable object of desire: fruits and foodstuffs, silks and sonnets, housemaids and women of high estate. But the rakes in the playhouse might see themselves mocked as well. The best comic writers—Wycherley, Etherege, Behn, Congreve—showed the libertines equalled and often bested in cunning by the women they pursued, baffled where they would be most powerful, enslaved where they would be most free. In brilliant volleys of dialogue, these lovers mixed passion and poison in volatile measures, chasing one another through a maze of plots, counterplots, and subplots so convoluted as to suggest a world of calculation run mad. Over the thirty years of its triumphs, Restoration comedy, in an astounding fugue of excesses and depravities, laid bare the turbulence and toxins of this culture.

That the heroic drama, with all its exaggerations and flatteries, found a market, is hardly surprising; what is more puzzling is the commercial triumph of Restoration comedy, a theatrical mode that entertained by punishing and humiliating its audience—though it is hardly surprising that this theater should itself have fallen victim in the 1690s to prudery and what would come to be called "taste." In the wake of the Protestant revolution of 1688 that typed Stuart rule as the very emblem of self-indulgence, agents of moral improvement and social propriety made their assault on Restoration comedy the stalking horse for a broad program of Christian reform. Restoration comedy, which had erupted as a repudiation of Puritan prohibitions, now seemed to prompt a new wave of moral rectitude.

Under such pressures, the playhouse redirected its mirror, away from the aristocracy towards the upper strata of the "middling sort": London merchants, colonial profiteers. During the Restoration, the newly prosperous mercantile classes who converged with courtiers at the theater had watched themselves either derided or ignored on stage, their social pretensions and ineptitudes put down in the comedies, their commercial concerns absent from the heroic drama. In the early eighteenth century, they saw themselves glorified instead, in "domestic tragedy," which displayed the tribulations of commercial households, and in sentimental comedy, which sought by a mix of tears and modest laughter to inculcate family values and to portray the merchant class as the nation's moral core. Richard Steele's *The Conscious Lovers* (1722) sounded the fanfare for a newly theatric social self-conception. "We merchants," a businessman informs an aristocrat, "are a species of gentry that have grown into the world this last century, and are as honorable and almost as useful as you landed folk, that have always thought yourself so much above us."

Nor was the stage the only venue to promulgate this new cultural self-awareness. By its very title *The Spectator* (1711–1713), one of the most widely read periodicals of the century, assured its largely middle-class audience that they moved under the constant, thoughtful scrutiny of a virtual playgoer, the paper's fictive author, "Mr. Spectator," who made all London a kind of theater, in which he (and his eagerly imitative readers) might perpetually enjoy the privileges of making observations and forming judgments. The very energies that had been drained away from the stage now found a new home in the theatricalized world of commerce, fashion, manners, taste.

The cast members in this new theater were numerous, varied, and eager for direction, mostly because, as a "new species of gentry," they aspired to roles for which they had formerly been deemed unfit. Terms like "esquire" and "gentleman" had operated in previous centuries as proof of literal "entitlement." They were secured by registration with the College of Heralds, and they calibrated not merely monetary wealth but lineage, landholdings, education, and social standing. In the eighteenth century, men and women with sufficient money and nerve assumed these titles for themselves, confident enough that they might learn to play the part. "In our days," noted a 1730 dictionary, "all are accounted gentlemen that have money." But since "the money" was now so variously attainable—by shopkeeping, by manufacture, by international trade—the "middle station" was itself subdivided into many striations, and since the very point of capital was accumulation and improvement, ascent by emulation became a master plot in the new social theater. "Everyone," observed one commentator, "is flying from his inferiors in pursuit of his superiors, who fly from him with equal alacrity."

Amid the flux, fashion and commodity—what one wore, what one owned— mattered enormously. Wigs, fans, scarves, silks, petticoats, and jewels; china, silver, family portraits—these were the costumes, these the props of the new commercial theater, by which members of the middle orders pleased themselves and imitated the gentry. The commercial classes who had begun by catering to the aristocracy gradually became, in their waxing prosperity, their own best customers, selling garb and goods to one another. Shrewd marketers saw that novelty itself possessed an intrinsic and urgent appeal for people constantly in social flight, tirelessly engaged in remaking themselves. Advertising came into its own, filling the pages and underwriting the costs of the daily, weekly, and monthly periodicals. The listing of consumables became a prevalent mode of print, in everything from auction catalogues (the still-dominant houses of Christie's and Sotheby's got their start near the middle of the century) to poems and novels, where long lists of products and possessions became a means of recording the culture's appetites and at times of satirizing them. In the hands of Swift and Pope, the catalogue itself became a form of art. The taste in literary miscellany reflected a more general taste for omnivorous consumption: variety indexed abundance, and proved power. Tea from China, coffee from the Caribbean, tobacco from Virginia—all were relatively new, comparatively inexpensive, and enormously popular. In daily rituals of drink and smoke, the middling orders imbibed and inhaled a pleasing sense of their global reach, their comfortable centrality on a planet newly commercialized.

Commodities formed part of a larger discourse, involving speech and gesture as well as prop and costume. A cluster of precepts, gathered under the umbrella-term "politeness," supplied the stage directions, even at times the script, for the new social theater in which everyone was actor, and everyone was audience. Eager to shine in their recently acquired roles, the merchant classes pursued the polish implicit in the word "polite." They hired "dancing masters" to teach them graceful motions and proper manners; "bear leaders" (tutors) to guide their sons on the Grand Tour of France and Italy in the footsteps of the nobility; elocution coaches to help them purge inappropriate accents; teachers of painting and music to supply their daughters with marriageable competence. For the newly prosperous, politeness was the epitome of distinction: it went beyond gesture and accomplishment to suggest a state of mind, a refinement of perception, a mix of knowledge, responsiveness, and judgment often summarized as "taste." "The man of polite imagination," said the *Spectator*, "is let into a great many pleasures that the vulgar are not capable of receiving." Eager to gain access, middle-class readers avidly sought instruction.

Politeness (which Samuel Johnson once defined as "fictitious benevolence") required considerable self-control; the passions (rage, greed, lust) were to be contained and channeled into the appearance of abundant and abiding goodwill. The middle classes embraced such constraints partly to allay widespread suspicion of their commercial aggressions, their social ambitions. Their preoccupation with politeness has helped to foster a recurrent misimpression of the period: that, setting aside the occasional rake or wench, it was all manners and morals, dignity and decorum, fuss and formality, reason and enlightenment. Not so. Even among the merchant classes, politeness afforded only provisional concealment for roiling energies; amid the impoverished and the gentry, it held less purchase still. In no succeeding epoch until our own was language so openly and energetically obscene, drunkenness so rampant, sexual conduct so various and unapologetic. Even among the "officially" polite, the very failure of containment could produce a special thrill. In one of the century's most often-used phrases, a speaker announces that "I cannot forebear"—that is, cannot restrain myself—from saying or doing what the verb itself suggests were better left unsaid or undone. The formula declares helpless and pleasurable surrender to an unmastered impulse, and the condition was apparently endemic. James Boswell records the memorable self-summary of an elderly lawyer: "I have tried . . . in my time to be a philosopher, but—I don't know how—cheerfulness was always breaking in." Such "breakings-in" (and breakings-out) of feeling were common, even cherished. The scholar Donald Greene has argued well that the eighteenth century was less an "age of reason" (as has often been said) than an age of exuberance. Certainly much of what the middle classes read and wrote is a literature of outburst: of hilarity, of lament, of rage, of exaltation. The copious diaries that the century brought forth deal in all such exclamations; they are the prose of people who have chosen to write rather than repress the thoughts and actions that strict politeness might proscribe. Even the *Spectator*, that manual of polished taste, presents itself as the daily outpouring of a writer who, after maintaining an eccentric lifelong silence, has found that he can no longer keep his "discoveries"—moral, social, experiential—to himself.

Such self-publicizing was more complex for women than for men. When women represented their own lives—in manuscript (letters, journals) and increasingly in print—they sometimes chafed at the paradoxical mix of tantalizing possibilities and painful limitations that their privilege produced. Post-Restoration prosperity and politeness supplied women with many new venues for self-display and sociability, in playhouses and pleasure gardens, ballrooms, spas, and shops. Society exalted and paraded women as superior consumers: wearing the furs, fragrances, and fabrics of distant climes, they furnished evidence of empire, proud proof of their fathers' and husbands' economic attainments. They consumed print, too; near the start of the eighteenth century, male editors invented the women's periodical, and found the new genre immensely profitable. Increasingly, women not only purchased print but produced it, deploying their words and wit as a kind of cultural capital, which when properly expended might reap both cash and fame. During the eighteenth century, for the first time, books by women—of poems, of precepts, and above all of fiction— became not exotic but comparatively commonplace.

Still, books by women remained controversial, as did all manifestations of female autonomy and innovation. The very excitement aroused by women's new conspicuousness in the culture provoked counter-efforts at containment. Preachers and moralists argued endlessly that female virtue resided in domesticity. Marriage itself offered an age-old instrument of social control, newly retooled to meet the needs of ambitious merchants, for whom daughters were the very currency of social mobility. If parents could arrange the right marriage, the whole family's status promptly rose. The dowry that the bride brought with her was an investment in future possibilities: in the rank and connections that the union secured, in the inheritance that would descend to its heirs, in the annual income ("jointure") that the wife herself would receive following the death of the husband. Financially, a widow (or for that matter, a well-born woman who never married) was often far more independent than a wife, whose wedding led to a kind of sanctioned erasure. She possessed little or no control over marital property (including the wealth she had brought to the union); "in marriage," wrote the codifier of English law William Blackstone, "husband and wife are one person, and that person is the husband." The sums that the husband undertook to hand over to his wife were dubbed "pin money" (a suggestive trivialization): funds for managing the household, that sphere wherein, as the moral literature insisted, a woman might best deploy her innate talents and find her sanctioned satisfactions. These consisted first and foremost in producing children and in shaping their manners and morals. In a time of improvisatory birth control, precarious obstetrics, and high infant mortality, the bearing of children was a relentless, dangerous, and emotionally exhausting process. The upbringing of children provided more pleasure, and possessed a new cachet: the conduct literature endorsed busy, attentive child-rearing as the highest calling possible for women whose prosperity freed them from the need to work for wages. (Guidebooks for parents and pleasure books for children both had their origins in the eighteenth century.) Apart from the duties of motherhood and household management—the supervision of servants, meals, shopping, and social occasions—the woman of means was encouraged to pursue those pleasures for which her often deliberately constricted education had prepared her: music, embroidery, letter writing, and talk at the tea table—the domestic counterpart of the clubs and coffeehouses, where women were not permitted to appear.

In the late seventeenth century, the possibilities for women had seemed at moments more various and more audacious. In the plays of Aphra Behn, female characters pursued their pleasures with an almost piratical energy and ingenuity; in *A Serious Proposal to the Ladies* (1694), the feminist Mary Astell imagined academies where women could withdraw to pursue the pleasures of learning and escape the drudgeries of marriage. In the eighteenth century, though, despite women's increasing authorial presence, these early audacities tended to go underground. Protests by women against their secondary status are most overt in manuscript—in the acerbic poems and letters that Mary Wortley Montagu circulated among her friends, in the journal entries wherein the brewer's wife Hester Thrale vented her frustrations. In print, women's desire for autonomy became a tension in the text, rather than its explicit point or outcome. Novelists explored women's psyches with subtlety; their plots, however, nearly always culminated in marriage, and more rarely in catastrophe, as though those were the only alternatives. Even the Bluestocking Circle, an eminent late-century group of intellectual women, preached tenets of essential sexual difference and subordination; they argued (for example) in favor of improving girls' educations, but as a way of preparing them for better and happier work within the home rather than for adventures abroad. During the eighteenth century, the middle classes did much to spell out the gendered divison of labor—father as the family's champion in the marketplace, mother as cheerfully efficient angel in the house—that remained a cultural commonplace, among families who could afford it, for the next two hundred years.

Among the poor, such divisions were not tenable; most manual labor paid so little that everyone in the family had to work if all were to survive. Wives not only managed their frugal households; they also worked for wages, in fields, in shops, or in cottage manufacture of fabrics, gloves, basketry. Children often began wage work at age four or five, treading laundry, scaring crows, sweeping chimneys; boys began the more promising role of apprenticeships around the age of ten. For many of the poor, domestic service offered employment comparatively secure and endlessly demanding. Darker prospects included prostitution, and crime; shoplifting was punishable by death. In the case of the helplessly indigent, local government was responsible for providing relief; but the Poor Law provided large loopholes by which the parish could drive out any unwanted supplicant—an unwed mother, for example—who could not meet the intricate and restrictive criteria for legal residence. The poor had no vote, no voice in government; as the century progressed, their predicament attracted increasing attention and advocacy. Philanthropists instituted charity schools designed, in the words of their proponent Hannah More, "to train up the lower classes in habits of industry and piety." Two convictions informed even the most ambitious philanthropy: that poverty was part of a divine plan and that it was the fault of the indolent poor themselves; they thus found themselves caught between the rock of providence and the hard place of reproach. Yet charity schools did increase literacy, and with it perhaps the sense of possibilities. Other late-century developments, too, were mixed. Improvements in sanitation, medicine, and hygiene contributed to a surge in population, which in turn produced among the rural poor a labor surplus: too many people, too little work. At the same time, wealthy landholders increased the practice of "enclosure," acquiring and sequestering acreage formerly used by the poor for common pasturage and family farming. As a result, many rural families left the land on which they had worked for centuries, and traveled to alien terrain: the textile mills that capitalists had newly built, and the industrial cities developing rapidly around them.

As the poor became poorer, the very rich—landowning lords and gentry—became very much richer, both by the means they now shared with the middle class (capital investment in banks and stocks), and through their own long-held resources. Land increased in value, partly because there were now so many merchant families passionately eager to buy into the landscape and the life of their aristocratic betters, among whom the spectacle of emulation provoked amusement and revulsion. The landed gentry preserved their distance by many means: social practices (they often flaunted their adulteries, for example, as contrast to middle-class proprieties); artistic allegiance (with the advent of the bourgeois drama, aristocratic audiences defected from the theater to the opera house, where elaborate productions and myth-based plots sustained the aristocratic values of the heroic drama); and by the sheer ostentation of their leisure and the magnitude of their consumption. But the pivotal difference remained political: by the award of offices, by the control of elections, landowners maintained their stranglehold on local and national power, despite all the waxing wealth of trade.

At the same time, their very absorption in pleasure and power demanded a continual traffic with their inferiors. Merchants and shopkeepers catered to them; professionals managed their transactions; household servants contrived their comforts; aspiring artists sought to cultivate their taste and profit by their patronage. Transactions among the aristocracy and the middle classes took other forms as well. A lord low on money often found it lucrative to marry the daughter of a thriving merchant. And middle-class modes of life could exert a subtler magnetism, too—particularly for George III, who prized mercantile decorum over aristocratic swagger. In the portrait of his queen and her two eldest sons on the next page, the artist Johann Zoffany (himself an expensive German import) celebrates not their royal state but their domestic felicity: the heroic trappings (helmet, spear, turban) so conspicuous in Lely's portrait of the scandalous Lady Castlemaine (see page 912) are here reduced to the props of child's play in the domestic theater of family relations.

King George had commissioned Johann Zoffany in pursuit of precisely this effect. By his eager emulation of the middling orders, George III broke with monarchic traditions, but he inaugurated a new one that would be sustained and expanded in various ways by Queen Victoria in the nineteenth century and her successors in the twentieth. During George's reign, too, the middle classes began to pursue more practical convergence with the aristocracy: a wider distribution of voting rights, a firmer political power base. For the first time, the phrase "middle classes" itself came into use, as a way of registering this cohort's recognition of its own coherence and interests, its unique, often combative relations with the classes above and below; the plural ("classes") registered the abiding diversity—of income, of lifestyle—within the cohesion. In the years since the Restoration, the middle classes had moved themselves energetically, in the theater of social and economic relations, from a place in the audience towards center stage, exerting enormous power over the working lives of the poor, posing challenges to the elite. Increasingly, their money, manners, appetites, and taste came to be perceived as the essence of national life, as the part that might stand for the whole. "Trade," Henry Fielding remarked in 1751, "has indeed given a new face to the nation."

Johann Zoffany. *Queen Charlotte with her Two Eldest Sons.* 1764. Theatricality domesticated: a century after Lely painted the king's mistress in the garb of the goddess of wisdom, such mythological trappings are reduced to dress-up for George III's two young sons at play. Amid sumptuous furnishings, Zofanny's conversation piece emphasizes not the grandeur of the royal family but its intimacy and affection; a new era of majesty as "good example" has commenced.

It gave the nation new momentum, too, literal as well as figurative. The engineering marvels of the eighteenth century—the harnessing of steam power, the innovations in factory design, the acceleration of production—were instruments of capital. So were improvements in the rate of transport. Over the course of the century, the government collaborated with private investors to construct a proliferating network of smooth turnpikes and inland waterways: canal boats delivered coal and other cargo with new celerity; stagecoaches sped between cities on precise schedules with crowded timetables. Timekeeping itself became a source of national wealth and pride. During the 1660s, British clockmakers established themselves as the best in Europe. A century later, the clockmaker John Harrison invented the "marine chronometer," a large watch so sturdy and so precise that it could keep time to the minute throughout a voyage around the world, amid all vicissitudes of wind and weather. Harrison's invention made it possible accurately to calculate a ship's longitude, thus solving a problem that had bedeviled navigation for centuries (and sometimes sunk whole fleets). The innovation further paved the way for trade and empire-building, and did much to establish

Greenwich, a town just east of London, as the reference point for world time-keeping. Trade was giving a new face—a new distribution of power and priority—not only to the nation but also to the globe, placing Britain (so Britons liked to think) at its center.

FAITH AND KNOWLEDGE, THOUGHT AND FEELING

Clockwork functioned another way too: as a new, theologically unsettling metaphor for the relations between God and his creation. In his *Principia Mathematica* (1687), Isaac Newton set forth the mathematical principles—the laws of motion, the workings of gravity—by which, it turned out, the universe could be seen to operate more consistently and efficiently than even the finest clockwork. What need had this flawless mechanism for any further adjustments by its divine clockmaker? Some of Newton's admirers—though never the pious scientist himself—found in his discoveries the cue for a nearly omnivorous skepticism. The boldest deists and "freethinkers" dismissed Christianity as irrational fiction, to be supplanted by the stripped-down doctrine of "natural religion." In the intricate design of nature they found the proof of a creator whose existence and infinite wisdom, they argued, are all we know on earth and all we need to know. The fashion for such thought—at least in its purest form—proved fleeting. To most minds, the "argument from design" simply furnished further proof of God's benevolence. Amid such comfortable conviction, the blasphemies of a virtuoso skeptic like David Hume appeared an aberration, even an entertainment, rather than a trend. "There is a great cry about infidelity," Samuel Johnson remarked in 1775, "but there are, in reality, very few infidels." From deep belief and ingrained habit, Christianity retained its hold over the entire culture; though a few pietists voiced alarm, science tended to enhance faith, not destroy it.

Still, the relation of religion to public life had changed. In the mid-seventeenth century, politics was inevitably suffused with spirituality. Charles I had gone to the scaffold as an Anglican martyr; he had ruled according to the dictum "No bishop, no king." For many English men and women the war of Parliament against the king was a holy war; Puritans had typed Charles I as that "man of blood," Cromwell's army had gone to battle singing David's psalms. By the eighteenth century, ardors had cooled; no one went to war for creed alone. But that is not to say that these were lives bereft of the spiritual; deep religious feeling remained, even as violence of expression abated. The Restoration had reinstated Anglicanism as the national faith; its adherents were admitted to the full privileges of education and office. Over the ensuing century, the Church of England pursued a strategic but controversial mix of old exclusions and new accommodations. For dissenters (offspring of the Puritans), new laws proffered certain permissions (to teach, to congregate for public worship) in exchange for certain oaths. Catholics, by contrast, were kept beyond the pale; they received no such concessions until late in the eighteenth century, when even a limited act provoked angry Protestant riots. Early in the century, the Anglican faithful were divided between the "high flyers," who perennially claimed that the church was in danger of dilution, and the Latitudinarians, who argued that all kinds of dissent might finally be accommodated within the structure of the church. Latitudinarians prevailed, but as the Church of England broadened, it began to lose the force of its exclusiveness; attendance at services shrank markedly as the century advanced, but alternative forms of communal worship flourished. In the eighteenth century, evangelical religions came to occupy the crucial space of fervent spirituality that the church of Donne and Herbert had once claimed as its own. By mid-century, in the new movement called Methodism, John Wesley expressed a vehement response against the skeptical rationalism of the freethinkers and the monied complacency of the established church. Wesley preached the truth of scriptural revelation. He urged his followers to purge their sins methodically—by a constant self-monitoring, partly modeled on earlier Puritan practices—and enthusiastically, by attending revival meetings, hearing electrifying sermons. Wesley delivered some 40,000 sermons over the course of a phenomenally energetic life, and his no less relentless brother Charles composed some 6,000 hymns to quicken evangelical spirits. Methodism found its most ardent following among the poor, who discovered in the doctrine a sympathy for their condition and a recognition of their worth, epitomized in one of Charles Wesley's verses: "Our Savior by the rich unknown / Is worshipped by the poor alone." Their worship was loud and fervent; intensity of feeling attested authenticity of faith.

The middle class and gentry located their own fervor in the more polished idioms of sentiment and sensibility. The terms named a code of conduct and of feeling current in the mid-eighteenth century, when men and women increasingly came to pride themselves on an emotional responsiveness highly cultivated and conspicuously displayed: tears of pity at the spectacle of suffering, admiration for the achievements of art or the magnificence of nature. For many in the middle class, the cult of sentiment held out the appealing prospect of a democratization of manners; the elaborate protocols of the aristocracy might remain elusive, but pure *feeling* was surely more accessible, to anyone with the leisure and the training. For many women the cult afforded the added attraction of honoring that very susceptibility to feeling and that renunciation of reason that had long and pejoratively been gendered female. The sufferings of the poor, of children, of animals, became a testing ground for empathy; majestic mountains became favorite proving grounds for heightened response. The fashion for benevolence helped focus attention on the plight of the poor and the oppressed, prompting new charities and social movements. For many of the conventionally religious, sentimentality became an adjunct article of faith. They found their scriptures in treatises that posited proper feeling as a chief measure of human worth—Adam Smith's *Theory of Moral Sentiments* (1759); in sentimental dramas that modeled the cultivation (and the performance) of elaborate emotion; in novels that paid minute attention to the protagonist's every emotional nuance—Samuel Richardson's *Pamela* (1740–1741) and *Clarissa* (1747–1749); Laurence Sterne's *Life and Opinions of Tristram Shandy* (1759–1767) and *A Sentimental Journey* (1768); Henry Mackenzie's *The Man of Feeling* (1771); in travel books that transported readers geographically and emotionally by charged descriptions of mighty vistas. For both deists and pietists earlier in the century, nature had testified the existence of a God; for connoisseurs of the sublime near century's end, nature itself was beginning to serve as surrogate for the divine.

In the articulation of eighteenth-century faith and science, thought and feeling, the most conspicuous and continuous voice was that of the first person. The "I" was omnipresent, observing world and self alike: in the experiment-reports of the scientists and the thought-experiments of the philosophers; in the Methodists' self-monitoring, the sentimentalist's self-approbation, the sublimity-seekers' recorded raptures; in the copious autobiographical writings—diaries, letters, memoirs—of characters in novels and people in the real world. Always and everywhere, it seems, someone was setting down the nuances of his or her experience. The self-reckoning promulgated in the past by dissenters was now a broad cultural preoccupation. Its dominion may help to explain why the literature of this era famed for the dominance and delight of its conversation returns us, again and again, to a sense of fundamental solitude.

WRITERS, READERS, CONVERSATIONS

The century and a half from the English Civil Wars to the brink of the French Revolution brought startling change to the structures of politics, social relations, scientific knowledge, and the economy; and no change was more intimate to all these revolutions than the transformations in the relations between writers and readers. From our present perspective, perhaps no scene seems more familiar, even eternal, than that of reader with book in hand. We imagine Virgil's readers and Dante's, Austen's and Wilde's, Pound's and Pynchon's similarly situated, alone with a book, communing silently with an oracular author. But these configurations have changed radically from age to age—sometimes driven by shifts in technology, at other times by social changes. In the eighteenth century, the sea change in relations between writers and readers derived from new social transactions and a new marketplace of letters. And this change did much to shape the modern reckoning of the mix of the solitary and the social, the commerical and the therapeutic within the act of reading. In its refiguring of the social contract between writers and readers, the eighteenth century was nearly as eruptive as our own time with its marketplace of e-mail and Internet, where everyone can potentially operate as both consumer and purveyor—and no one knows for sure the shape of literary things to come.

In 1661, the Earl of Argyle wrote to his son with advice on books, their acquisition, and their proper use:

> Think no cost too much in purchasing rare books; next to that of acquiring good friends I look upon this purchase; but buy them not to lay by or to grace your library, with the name of such a manuscript, or by such a singular piece, but read, revolve him, and lay him up in your memory where he will be far the better ornament. Read seriously whatever is before you, and reduce and digest it to practice and observation, otherwise it will be Sisyphus's labor to be always revolving sheets and books at every new occurence which will require the oracle of your reading. Trust not to your memory, but put all remarkable, notable things you shall meet with in your books *sub slava custodia* [under the sound care] of pen and ink, but so alter the property by your own scholia and annotations on it, that your memory may speedily recur to the place it was committed to.

The earl's account displays all the elements of the traditional reading program of Renaissance humanism: book or manuscript as surrogate friend; as "ornament" of the gentleman's mind and library; as "oracle" of enduring truths; as "property" to be possessed, marked, transcribed, and committed to memory. In the decades that followed all these constructions remained in play, yet every one of the earl's crucial terms broadened in application to include print genres and transactions that Argyle would not have imagined: the periodical review, the monthly miscellany; epistolary fiction; the three-volume novel; as well as the coffeehouses and penny-lending libraries that broadly circulated these new forms of print. With these new genres and modes of distribution, the text's status as friend, ornament, oracle, and property changed markedly.

Nothing had demonstrated (some even thought created) the material force and oracular authority of print so much as the English Civil Wars. Sermons and prophecies bearing the names of "oracles" and "revelations" forecast the demise of the Beast, the triumph of Parliament, indeed the imminence of the thousand-year rule of Christ on earth. Nor had the Restoration of the Stuart monarchy wholly denatured print as prophecy—royalists and radicals continued to publish apocalyptic claims. And yet, over the ensuing decades the repeated threat of contest and rebellion began to exhaust both the authority of print as prophecy and the appetite of readers for a textual diet of frenzy and apocalypse. Not that party warfare in print forms declined, but rather that partisanship yoked political contest to forms of confrontation that cooled apocalyptic tempers and supplanted military combat with paper controversy. The uneven course of government censorship, the issuing and lapsing of the licensing laws that governed press freedom, meant that paper wars with their full armory of ephemera—pamphlets, broadsides, pasquinades—raged at moments of crisis and parliamentary inattention when printers might cash in on the market for opposition and confrontation.

But not all the action of print contest was situated in the gutter of journalism. Satire, that most venerable mode of attack and advocacy, flourished in England as it had in Augustan Rome. Horace and Juvenal were indeed the models for Dryden, Pope, and Swift, who not only translated the forms of Roman satire into native idioms but were themselves possessed by all the Roman delight in outrage and invective, in civic engagement and political contest. But the genius of satire is never solely political. Satirists always score their most important points by wit, by cool savagery, by the thrust and parry of language, by the most brilliant and damaging metaphors and rhymes. Their peers, their rivals, even their enemies ruefully conceded that Dryden, Pope, and Swift had brought the verse couplet and the prose sentence to an unprecedented suppleness and precision. Satire in the years of civil war and Stuart agitations had begun in politics; pamphlet wars, swelled by periodicals, continued to rage through the Georgian age. But the classic verse satire had moved to a more exalted ground where the aesthetic often overwhelmed the political, and satire itself became an object of admiration, even of theorizing, and of the most vivid and polite conversation.

"Conversation" had once meant the entire conduct of life itself; now, "conversation" had narrowed to signify social exchange; yet social exchange in its turn had expanded to govern the conduct of life itself. Many of the most striking literary developments in the period—its poetic modes and tastes, the popularity and prominence of letter and journal writing, the advent of the newspaper and the novel—can perhaps best be understood as new ways devised by writers for performing conversation on the page—conversation with readers, with other writers, and within the texts themselves. The cultural critic Mikhail Bakhtin has pinpointed as one key feature of the novel its "heteroglossia": its capacity to speak, almost concurrently, many different languages, in the various voices and viewpoints of its characters and narrators, the range of its concerns (across social ranks and geographical spaces), even the variabilities of its style (each with its own cultural connotations) from page to page, paragraph to paragraph. But in this respect as in so many, the novel, usually reckoned the greatest literary invention of the period, is the product of a time when virtually all modes of writing were involved with diversity and dialogue.

One of the most popular ways of buying and reading poetry, for example, was in the form of "miscellanies"—anthologies of work by many hands ancient and modern in many modes, brought together in intriguing juxtapositions. Such juxtapositions could also take place within a single poem. For poets, a crucial procedure was the "imitation"—a poem in English that closely echoes the tone, structure, and sequence of a classical model, while applying the predecessor's form and thought to contemporary topics. Where the Roman poet Juvenal, for example, begins his tenth Satire by declaring that wise men are hard to find even if you search every country from Spain to India (roughly the extent of the known Roman world), Samuel Johnson begins his imitation of Juvenal's poem (*The Vanity of Human Wishes*) this way:

> Let Observation, with extensive view,
> Survey mankind from China to Peru . . .

The known world, Johnson tacitly reminds his knowing reader, is much larger than it was when Juvenal wrote (and hence the rarity of discerning mortals will be all the more striking). The opening couplet prepares us for the poem's close, where it will turn out that moral possibilities are larger too: there, Johnson will supplant Juvenal's characteristically Roman resignation to "Fortune" with an expressly Christian reliance on the cardinal virtues (faith, hope, charity) as a means of protection from the delusions of desire. The writer of a poetic imitation always conducts at least a double dialogue: between poet and predecessor, and between the present writer and the ideal reader who knows enough of the "original" to savor the poetic exchange, the cultural cross talk, in all its echoes, divergences, and diversions.

Johnson here practices a more general kind of imitation as well, by casting his poem in heroic couplets: iambic pentameter lines paired in a sequence of successive rhymes. The rhymed pairs are often "closed," so that the moment of the rhyme coincides with and clinches the completion of a sentence and a thought. The verse form was called "heroic" because of its frequent use in the heroic drama and other high-aspiring poetry of the Restoration; the rhymed, closed pentameter was also thought to imitate, as closely as English allowed, the grandeur and the sonority of the lines in which ancient poets composed their epics. Throughout the century following Restoration, the heroic couplet prevailed as the most commonly used poetic structure, adaptable to all genres and occasions, deployed by every sort of poet from hacks to John Dryden and Alexander Pope, the supreme masters of the mode. It was in this form that Dryden translated Virgil's *Aeneid* (1697), and Pope translated Homer's *Iliad* (1715–1720) and *Odyssey* (1725–1726); it was in this form that they wrote original poems of high seriousness and savage satire; and it was in this form that they aspired (like many of their contemporaries) to write new epics of their own. Neither ever did; both complained intermittently that they lived in an unheroic age. But the mesh of mighty ancient models with trivial modern subjects produced a new mode of satire, the mock-heroic, and disclosed astonishing suppleness in the heroic couplet itself.

In the hands of Dryden, Pope, and many others, the mock mode—high style, low subject matter—performed brilliant accommodations and solved large problems. It allowed poets to turn what they perceived as the crassness of modern culture to satiric advantage. If the triviality of modern life prevented them from recapturing epic grandeur whole, they could at least strive to match the epic's inclusiveness, its capacity to encompass all the things and actions of the world: the accessories of a young woman's dressing table (Pope's *Rape of the Lock*); the clutter in a gutter after rain (Swift's *Description of a City Shower*); the glut of print itself and the folly of those who produce so much bad writing (Pope's *Dunciad*). After Pope's death, though, this vein of mockery seemed exhausted. The heroic couplet persisted in poetry to the end of the century; but other verse forms became prominent too, partly in the service of an even wider inclusiveness, of paying new kinds of attention to modes of life and literature that lay outside the heroic and the mock: the predicament of the poor, the pleasures of domesticity, the discoveries of science, the tones and textures of medieval English balladry, the modalities of melancholy, the improvisatory motions of human thought and feeling. Blank verse—iambic pentameter without rhyme— offered one manifestation of the impulse to open-endedness. James Thomson's *The Seasons* (1730) and William Cowper's *The Task* (1785), huge works in blank verse, are epic in their own kind: they mingle genres, and move from topic to topic, with the improvisatory energy of a barely stoppable train of thought. They perform the world's miscellany, the mind's conversation with itself and others, in a new poetic language—one that Wordsworth had absorbed by century's end, when he cast his *Prelude* in a capacious blank verse, and praised in the preface to *Lyrical Ballads* that kind of poetry which deploys "the real language" of "a man speaking to men."

In the new prose forms of the eighteenth century—both nonfiction and fiction—the dominion of miscellany, the centrality of conversation, is if anything more palpable than in poetry. The first daily newspaper and the first magazines both appeared early in the century, providing a regularly recurrent compendium of disparate items, intended to appeal to a variety of tastes and interests. These periodicals formed part of a larger and highly visible print mix: coffeehouses attracted a burgeoning clientele of urbanites by laying out copies of the current gazettes, mercuries, newsletters, playbooks and satiric verses. Customers took pleasure in the literary montage, the ever-shifting anthology on the tabletops (of which the pictorial medley on page 904 conveys a vivid visual idea). Coffeehouse customers gathered to consume new drink and new print in a commerce of pleasure, intellect, and gossip. Some read silently, others aloud to listeners who eagerly seized on texts and topics. Habits of social reading that would have been familiar to Chaucer and his audience (even to Virgil performing his epic at the court of Augustus Caesar) contributed to sociable debate on the persons and personalities of public life, foreign potentates, military campaigns, theatrical rivalries, monsters, and prodigies. In the eighteenth century, the papers and the consequent conversations broadened to encompass questions of personal conduct, relations between the sexes, manner and fashion. Writers of papers still claimed oracular authority: "Isaac Bickerstaff" of the *Tatler* dubbed himself the Censor of Great Britain, Mr. Spectator claimed to watch everyone who read his paper, and the *Athenian Gazette* dispensed advice as though with the authority of a supremely learned society. But writers made such claims at least partly with tongue in cheek; they knew that their oracular "truths" would trickle down into the commerce of conversation.

The press not only stimulated but also simulated conversation. Newspapers had always depended on "correspondents"—not (as now) professional reporters, but local letter writers who sent in the news of their parish and county in exchange for free copies of the paper. To read a newspaper was to read in part the work of fellow readers. Other periodicals—the scientific monthly as well as the journal of advice and the review of arts—adopted the practice of printing letters as a reliable source of copy and as an act and model of sociability. Printed correspondence ran longer, more ambitiously, and more lucratively. For the first time, the collected letters of the eminent became an attractive commercial genre (Pope was a pioneer), and travel books in the form of copious letters home sold by the thousands.

The printed letter would prove crucial too to the development of the newest form of all, the "novel." Aphra Behn had pioneered epistolary fiction in the Restoration, and Samuel Richardson recast the mode on an epic scale in *Pamela* and *Clarissa*, among the most important and talked-about fictions of the eighteenth century. In discussing the fate of his characters, Richardson's readers joined a conversation already in progress; Richardson's characters, in their lively exchange of letters, performed and modeled what their creator called "the converse of the pen."

Yet letters were only one among the many kinds of conversation that novelists contrived to carry on. "The rise of the novel"—the emergence over the course of the eighteenth century of so curious, capacious, and durable a genre—has long excited interest and controversy among scholars, who explain the phenomenon in various ways: by the emergence of a large middle-class readership with the money to obtain, the leisure to read, and the eagerness to absorb long narratives that mirrored their circumstances, their aspirations, and their appetites; by a tension between the aristocratic virtues central to older forms of fiction, and the constructs of human merit prized by a proud commercial culture; by the passion for journalistic and experiential fact (in newspapers, criminal autobiographies, scientific experiments, etc.), shading over imperceptibly into new practices of fiction.

All of these explanations are true, and each is revelatory when applied to particular clusters of novels. Still, definition and explanation remain elusive, as they clearly were for the genre's early readers and practitioners. The very word "novel"—identifying the genre by no other marks than newness itself—performs a kind of surrender in the face of a form whose central claim to novelty was its barely definable breadth. Mimicry, motion, and metamorphosis are the genre's stock in trade. Novels absorbed all the modes of literature around them: letters, diaries, memoirs, news items, government documents, drawings, verses, even sheet music all crop up within the pages of the early novels, one representational mode supplanting another with often striking speed. Novelists moved with equal alacrity through space: through England (Henry Fielding's *Tom Jones*), Britain more broadly (Tobias Smollett's *Humphry Clinker*), Europe (Smollett's *Roderick Random*), the entire globe as it is ordinarily mapped (Behn's *Oroonoko*, Defoe's *Robinson Crusoe*) or as it could be extraordinarily imagined (Swift's *Gulliver's Travels*). Traversing geographies, the genre crossed cultures too, mostly by means of mimicry, and parroted a range of accents, for purposes either of mockery—the malapropisms of a semiliterate housemaid, the fulminations of a Scots soldier, the outrage of an Irish cuckold—or of pathos: the lamentations of the African slave Oroonoko, the delirium of the violated Clarissa. Many novels, too, made a point of spanning the social spectrum, often compassing destitution and prosperity, labor and luxury within the career of a single ambitious character. Social mobility was perhaps the one plot element that novel readers savored most.

But the novel's supplest means of self-conveyance, its subtlest modes of conversation, were grounded in its attention to the workings of the mind. In his *Essay Concerning Human Understanding* (1690), the philosopher John Locke had explained the mind as a capacious, absorptive instrument engaged in constant motion, linking mixed memories, impressions, and ideas in a ceaseless chain of "associations." In the eighteenth century, novelists took Locke's cue; their works both mimicked the mind's capacity, heterogeneity, and associativeness, and explored them too, tracking over many pages the subtlest modulations in the characters' thoughts and feelings. Richardson famously boasted that his epistolary mode, featuring "familiar letters written as it were to the moment" by characters in their times of crisis, enabled him to track the course of their "hopes and fears" with unprecedented precision—and he trusted that the value of such a process would surely excuse the "bulk" of the huge novels themselves. In the nine volumes of Laurence Sterne's *Life and Opinions of Tristram Shandy*, the title narrator is so committed to following his digressive trains of thought wherever they may lead, that the pronouncement of his opinions leaves him preposterously little time to narrate his life. Moving widely over space, freely through society, minutely through time, and deeply into mind, the novelists devised new strategies for achieving that epic inclusiveness that writers sought, in various ways, throughout the century.

The new tactics of miscellany, the new conversations conducted by means of pen and printing press, poetry and prose, refigured the practices of reading that the Earl of Argyle had wished to transmit to his son. In the aristocratic world of Renaissance letters, the book as friend had intimated a sphere of male pedagogy and sociability. The grammar school classroom, the college lecture hall, the estate library, the world of the tutor and his high-born protégé, all these figured reading principally as the privilege and the pleasure of a limited few, mostly males in positions of some leisure, comfort, and power. The links between reading and power were sustained through patterns of production and consumption in which authors received benefits from aristocratic patrons, and manuscripts passed from hand to hand. Donne refused to imagine his verse circulating in any other fashion. After the Restoration, Dryden, Behn, and Pope all pursued the compensations of print, but they nonetheless remained eager to participate in patronage and coterie circulation. Even when printed, their satires purveyed the pleasurable sense of shared knowledge that had constituted the *frisson* of coterie reading. Printers and poets understood that concealing a public name behind initials and dashes provided safety from censors and litigants while at the same time garnering a market share among readers who pleased themselves by decoding "dangerous matter."

By the middle of the eighteenth century, the patronage model of literary production and the coterie mode of distribution had been complicated (some thought ruined) by the commerce of print. For print had become the principal mode of literary distribution. Samuel Johnson, a bookseller's son, thought of literature as print and rarely circulated a manuscript as a gesture of literary sociability. ("None but a blockhead," he famously intoned, "ever wrote except for money.") As a consequence of the dominance of print and its broad distribution, the audiences for texts proliferated into new mixtures. Readers from many strata could afford a penny paper; apprentices and merchants' daughters might read the same novel. Assumptions of commonality that had underwritten the intimate sociability of Renaissance reading had been exploded by civil conflict in the mid-seventeenth century, by the profusion of print and the proliferation of genres that drove and were driven by the appetite of contest and conversation. During the eighteenth century, the print marketplace generated audiences on a scale vaster than ever before, circulating widely across the boundaries of class and gender. Print may have cancelled some of the intimacies of the coterie, but it generated new convergences, even new consciousness—a public sphere in which aesthetics, politics, conduct, and taste were all objects of perpetual, often pleasurable debate. To an unprecedented extent, print furnished its readers with the substance for sustained conversation and continual contact.

It also kept them apart. Nothing was more evident to eighteenth-century men and women than the burgeoning of their domestic economy, the vastness of their colonial empire, and the growth in wealth and population which both entailed. The proliferation of consumables was evident in the village market, the Royal Exchange, and the bookstalls of country towns and capitol. The sheer bulk and variety of these consumables were strikingly evident in the length and scope of that capacious new genre, the novel. But even in the midst of abundance and sociability, eighteenth-century consumers were instructed in their paradoxical solitude. Defoe inscribes the condition of the novel as isolation—Robinson Crusoe, a man alone on an island, opines that human life "is, or ought to be, one universal act of solitude." And in nov-el after novel the very transactions of commerce produce isolation, as ambition and acquisition drive each character into the solitary, often melancholy corner of his or her own self-interest. The novel itself as a reading experience produced comparable sensations. Readers might now empathize with an entire world of fictional charac-ters; but in order to savor such imaginative pleasures, they spent long hours in the privacy of their own quarters, in silent acts of reading.

A sense of solitude underwrote all this century's celebrated gregariousness. This held true even for sociable transactions that might take place between a reader and a text. In the Renaissance, it had long been a practice to annotate texts with com-ments echoing and endorsing the author's oracular wisdom. Under the pressure of civil war, the dialogue between author and reader often became more heated as the manuscript marginalia expressed anger and outrage at the partisan zeal of the printed text. But one form of textual reverence persisted. Throughout the seventeenth cen-tury readers took pleasure in writing marginalia that epitomized the text, making its wisdom portable. They filled blank books with pithy sentences, "commonplaces" drawn from their favorite works and organized in ways that would allow them to recirculate these sayings in their own writing and conversation.

By the eighteenth century, print had managed to appropriate all these modes of study and sociability. Through print, the manuscript collation of wit and wisdom turned into popular commodities—the printed commonplace book, the miscellany, the anthology. Even annotation itself migrated from manuscript markings into print, as Swift and Pope (among others) found ways of exploding scholarly pretension and of rendering the breath of gossip and scandal in the elaborate apparatus of the print-ed page. By century's end, all of manuscript's august authority and its most cherished genres—letters and memoirs—had been commandeered by print. In the mid-1730s, Pope alarmed and outraged his contemporaries by publishing his letters as if they deserved to partake of eternity with Cicero's. By the early nineteenth century, even that most secretive mode of self-communion, the private journal, had made its way into the marketplace. In 1825, Pepys's *Diary* appeared in two large printed folios, lay-ing bare the elaborate machinery of public life, the secrets and scandals of the Restoration court, and the diarist's own experiences, transgressions, and sequestered musings, which he had written in shorthand code and shown to no one. The commu-nal and commodified medium of print had found yet another way to market signal acts of solitude.

CODA

Mrs. Abington as "Miss Prue" (1771), by the pre-eminent portraitist Sir Joshua Reynolds, shows a solitary figure engaged in intricate conversation with the viewer. Some of the intricacy inheres in the life history of the sitter, whose career many of the painting's first viewers would have known well. The daughter of a cobbler, Frances Abington had worked in childhood as a flower seller, in her early teens as a prostitute, and (beginning around age fifteen) as an actress, quickly establishing herself as "by far the most eminent performer in comedy of her day" (these words, and others to follow, are the testimony of contemporaries). When an unknown, she had married her music teacher; as fame increased, she carried on several well-publicized affairs with members of parliament and the aristocracy. By her sexual frankness, she scandalized—and of course fascinated—the multitudes. By her grace

Joshua Reynolds, *Mrs. Abington as "Miss Prue."* 1771. Restoration theatricality transposed and transformed.

and taste, she became "a favorite of the public" and "the high priestess of fashion"; her costumes on stage instantly set new trends among her audience. Reynolds, who greatly admired her, here captures the complexity of her character and reputation. Her dress is supremely stylish, her pose deliberately provocative. For a woman to lean casually over the back of a chair this way violated all propriety; in earlier portraits, only men had struck such a pose. The thumb at her lips suggests vulgarity verging on the lascivious. The portrait's title purports to explain such seeming aberrations: the actress here appears in her celebrated role as Miss Prue, the "silly, awkward country girl" in William Congreve's Restoration comedy *Love for Love* (1695), who comes to London with the intention, frankly lustful and loudly declared, of getting herself a husband. In Reynolds's painting, of course, Mrs. Abington plays a role more layered: a hybrid of Miss Prue, of the matchlessly fashionable figure into which the actress had transformed herself, and of the whole range of experiences, the prodigious lifelong motion from poverty to polish, which formed part of her self-creation and her fame. Impersonating Miss Prue some seventy-five years after the comedy's first production, Mrs. Abington here infuses Restoration wantonness with Georgian elegance, transgression with high taste, theatricality with self-assertive authenticity. Like the century she inhabits, she is miscellany incarnate.

Stuart Sherman and
Steven N. Zwicker

Samuel Pepys
1633–1703

Twice in his life, Samuel Pepys embarked on long projects that allowed him to use the methods of the bureaucrat with an inventiveness that amounted to genius. The longer project, which occupied him from his mid-twenties through his mid-fifties, was a fundamental restructuring of the Royal Navy. The shorter project began just a few months earlier. Starting on January 1, 1660, and continuing for the next nine years, Pepys devised the diary form as we know it today: a detailed, private, day-by-day account of daily doings.

Halfway through the diary, Pepys delights to describe himself as "a very rising man," and he wrote the diary in part to track his ascent. The rise began slowly. Born in London to a tailor and a butcher's sister, Pepys studied at Puritan schools; he then attended Magdalene College, Cambridge, as a scholarship student. His B.A. left him well educated but short on cash. A year later he married the fifteen-year-old Elizabeth St. Michel, a French Protestant whose poverty surpassed his own. By his mid-twenties (when the diary commences), neither his accomplishments nor his prospects were particularly striking: he was working as factotum for two powerful men, one of them his high-born cousin Edward Mountagu, First Earl of Sandwich, an important naval officer once devoted to Cromwell but recently turned Royalist.

The diary begins at a calendrical turning point (the first day of a new week, a new year, and a new decade) and on a kind of double bet: that the coming time would bring changes worth writing up, both in the life of the diarist and in the history of the state. The two surmises quickly proved true. As a schoolboy taught by Puritans, Pepys had attended and applauded the execution of Charles I, but the Restoration of Charles II was the making of him, and he recalibrated his loyalties readily enough. His cousin secured for him the Clerkship of the Acts in the Navy Office, a secretarial post that Pepys transformed into something more. By mastering the numberless details of shipbuilding and supplying—from the quality of timber to the composition of tar and hemp—he contrived to control costs and produce results to an extent unmatched by any predecessor.

He managed all these matters so carefully that he soon became the ruler of the Royal Navy, in effect if not in name. When the Test Act of 1673 forced Charles's Catholic brother James to resign as Lord High Admiral, Pepys took his place (in the newly created post of Admiralty Secretary) and ran the operation. He immediately launched a systematic reform of the institution, which he had come to see as dangerously slipshod. By devising (in the words of one biographer) "a rule for all things, great or small," and by enforcing the new disciplines through a method of tireless surveillance and correspondence with ports extending from the Thames to Tangier, Pepys made the navy immeasurably more efficient than ever before. His efforts were interrupted by the political tribulations of his patron James: Pepys spent two brief terms in prison on trumped-up charges of Catholic sympathies, and in 1688 the Glorious Revolution drove him from office into a prosperous retirement. At the height of his power, though, as his biographer Richard Ollard observes, Pepys was the "master builder" of the permanent, professional navy that made possible the expansion of trade and the conquest of colonies over the ensuing century. Energetic in his king's service and in his own (the taking of bribes was one of the perquisites of office that Pepys mastered most adroitly), the tailor's son functioned formidably as an early architect of empire.

Pepys's schooling and profession had immersed him in the two practices most central to earlier English diaries, Puritanism and financial bookkeeping. But where account books and religious diaries emphasize certain kinds of moment—exchanges of money and goods, instances of moral redemption and relapse—Pepys tries for something more comprehensive. He implicitly commits himself to tracking the whole day's experience: the motions of the body as it makes its way through the city in boats, in coaches, and on foot, and the motions of the mind as it shuttles between business and pleasure. He sustained his narrative over a virtually unbroken series of daily entries before stopping out of fear that his work on the diary had helped to damage his eyesight to the brink of blindness. "None of Pepys's contemporaries," writes his editor Robert Latham, "attempted a diary in the all-inclusive Pepysian sense and on the Pepysian scale." To the efficiency of the bookkeeper and the discipline of the Puritan, Pepys added the ardor of the virtuoso, eager (as he observes at one point) "to see any strange thing" and capable of finding wonder in ordinary things: music, plays, books, food, clothes, conversation. The phrase "with great pleasure" recurs in the diary as a kind of leitmotiv, and superlatives play leapfrog through the pages: many, many experiences qualify in turn as the "best" thing that the diarist ever ate, read, thought, saw, heard. To achieve the diary's seeming immediacy, Pepys put his entries through as many as five stages of revision, sometimes days or even months after the events recorded. Even at the final stage, in the bound, elegantly format-ted volumes of the diary manuscript, he often crammed new detail or comment into margins and between the lines. Comparable pressures operated in connection with the diary's complex privacy. Pepys took pains to secure secrecy for his text. He hid it from view in drawers or in cabinets. He wrote most of it in a secretarial shorthand, and where he most wanted secrecy, as in the accounts of his many flirtations and infidelities, he obscured things further by an impro-vised language made up of Spanish, French, Latin, and other tongues. (Elizabeth Pepys figures throughout the diary as a kind of muse and countermuse, the narrative's most recurrent and obsessive subject, and the person most urgently to be prevented from reading it.) At the same time, the manuscript makes notable gestures toward self-display. Pepys frequently shifts to a readily readable longhand, especially for names, places, titles of books, plays, and persons; at times even his secret sexual language opens out into longhand.

This ambivalent secrecy persisted past the diarist's death. Pepys bequeathed the manu-script to Magdalene College without calling any special attention to it. It was included among his many collections: of naval books and papers, of broadsheet ballads, and of instruc-tion manuals on shorthand methods—including the one Pepys used to write the diary. The manuscript kept its secrets long. In the early nineteenth century, the diary was discovered and painstakingly decoded (by a transcriber who, missing the connection between the manu-script and the shorthand manuals on adjacent shelves, treated the text as a million-word cryptogram); it was finally published, in a severely shortened and expurgated version, in 1825. Readers and reviewers soon called for more, recognizing that Pepys possessed (in the words of one reviewer) "the most indiscriminating, insatiable, and miscellaneous curiosity, that ever . . . supplied the pen, of a daily chronicler." Expanded (but still bowdlerized) edi-tions appeared throughout the century, and only in the 1970s did the semisecret manuscript make its way wholly into print.

from The Diary
[First Entries][1]

$16\frac{59}{60}$.

Blessed be God, at the end of the last year I was in very good health, without any sense of my old pain[2] but upon taking of cold.

---

1. England still adhered to the Old Style calendar, in which the new year officially began on March 25. Pepys wrote this "prelude" in early January 1659 according to the English reckoning, but 1660 (New Style) in the rest of Europe.

2. Pepys had suffered from stones in the bladder from babyhood until 1658, when he underwent a risky but suc-cessful operation.

I lived in Axe Yard,[3] having my wife and servant Jane, and no more in family than us three.

My wife, after the absence of her terms[4] for seven weeks, gave me hopes of her being with child, but on the last day of the year she hath them again. The condition of the state was thus. *Viz.* the Rump, after being disturbed by my Lord Lambert, was lately returned to sit again.[5] The officers of the army all forced to yield. Lawson lies still in the river and Monck is with his army in Scotland.[6] Only my Lord Lambert is not yet come in to the Parliament; nor is it expected that he will, without being forced to it.

The new Common Council of the City doth speak very high; and hath sent to Monck their sword-bearer, to acquaint him with their desires for a free and full Parliament, which is at present the desires and the hopes and expectation of all—22 of the old secluded members having been at the House door the last week to demand entrance; but it was denied them, and it is believed that they nor the people will not be satisfied till the House be filled.[7]

My own private condition very handsome; and esteemed rich, but indeed very poor, besides my goods of my house and my office, which at present is somewhat uncertain. Mr Downing master of my office.[8]

1 January 1659/60. Lord's Day. This morning (we lying lately in the garret) I rose, put on my suit with great skirts,[9] having not lately worn any other clothes but them.

Went to Mr. Gunning's church at Exeter House, where he made a very good sermon upon these words: that in the fullness of time God sent his Son, made of a woman, etc., showing that by "made under the law" is meant his circumcision, which is solemnized this day.[1]

Dined at home in the garret, where my wife dressed the remains of a turkey, and in the doing of it she burned her hand.

I stayed at home all the afternoon, looking over my accounts.

Then went with my wife to my father's; and in going, observed the great posts which the City hath set up[2] at the Conduit in Fleet Street.

Supped at my father's, where in came Mrs. Theophila Turner and Madam Morris[3] and supped with us. After that, my wife and I went home with them, and so to our own home.

---

3. In Westminster.
4. Menstrual periods.
5. John Lambert, a skilled general under Oliver Cromwell, now opposed the convening of the Rump Parliament, which had governed England since the fall of Cromwell's son Richard in 1659.
6. At this point, the political intentions and allegiance of General George Monck were the object of much speculation; he led his army back from Scotland into England on January 1 and became one of the principal engineers of the Restoration. Vice-Admiral John Lawson supported the Rump.
7. A Parliament that would include the "old secluded members"—the representatives expelled in 1648—was under-

stood to be a first step toward restoration of the monarchy.
8. Pepys was at this point a clerk in the office of the Exchequer.
9. I.e., with a long coat.
1. Peter Gunning had held illegal Anglican services during the Commonwealth. His sermon text is Galatians 4.4: "But, when the fullness of the time was come, God sent forth his Son, made of a woman, made under the law."
2. As defensive barriers during its opposition to the Rump Parliament.
3. A relative and a friend, respectively. "Mistress" ("Mrs.") was applied to unmarried as well as to married women; Theophila was eight years old.

[The Coronation of Charles II][4]

[23 April 1661] I lay with Mr. Shiply,[5] and about 4 in the morning I rose.

Coronation Day.

And got to the Abbey,[6] where I followed Sir J. Denham the surveyor with some company that he was leading in. And with much ado, by the favor of Mr Cooper his man, did get up into a great scaffold across the north end of the Abbey—where with a great deal of patience I sat from past 4 till 11 before the King came in. And a pleasure it was to see the Abbey raised in the middle, all covered with red and a throne (that is a chair) and footstool on the top of it. And all the officers of all kinds, so much as the very fiddlers, in red vests.

At last comes in the Dean and prebends of Westminster with the Bishops (many of them in cloth-of-gold copes); and after them the nobility all in their Parliament robes, which was a most magnificent sight. Then the Duke[7] and the King with a scepter (carried by my Lord of Sandwich) and sword and mond before him, and the crown too.

The King in his robes, bare-headed, which was very fine. And after all had placed themselves, there was a sermon and the service. And then in the choir at the high altar he passed all the ceremonies of the coronation—which, to my very great grief, I and most in the Abbey could not see. The crown being put upon his head, a great shout begun. And he came forth to the throne and there passed more ceremonies: as, taking the oath and having things read to him by the Bishop, and his lords (who put on their caps as soon as the King put on his crown) and bishops came and kneeled before him.

And three times the King-at-Arms went to the three open places on the scaffold and proclaimed that if any one could show any reason why Charles Stuart should not be King of England, that now he should come and speak.

And a general pardon also was read by the Lord Chancellor;[8] and medals flung up and down by my Lord Cornwallis—of silver; but I could not come by any.

But so great a noise, that I could make but little of the music; and indeed, it was lost to everybody. But I had so great a list[9] to piss, that I went out a little while before the King had done all his ceremonies and went round the Abbey to Westminster Hall, all the way within rails, and 10,000 people, with the ground covered with blue cloth—and scaffolds all the way. Into the hall I got—where it was very fine with hangings and scaffolds, one upon another, full of brave[1] ladies. And my wife in one little one on the right hand.

Here I stayed walking up and down; and at last, upon one of the side-stalls, I stood and saw the King come in with all the persons (but the soldiers) that were yesterday in the cavalcade;[2] and a most pleasant sight it was to see them in their several robes. And the King came in with his crown on and his scepter in his hand—under a canopy borne up by six silver staves, carried by Barons of the Cinqueports—and little bells at every end.

---

4. Charles II had returned to England in May 1660; he scheduled his coronation for St. George's Day, honoring England's patron saint.

5. Edward Shipley was steward to Pepys's cousin Edward Mountagu.

6. Westminster Abbey, site of English coronations.

7. Charles's brother James, Duke of York, later James II.

8. Charles II's Act of Oblivion forgave the crimes of all those on the parliamentary side, with the principal exception of those who had participated in the trial, sentencing, and execution of his father.

9. Desire.

1. Splendid.

2. The previous day's procession.

And after a long time he got up to the farther end, and all set themselves down at their several tables—and that was also a rare sight. And the King's first course carried up by the Knights of the Bath. And many fine ceremonies there was of the heralds leading up people before him and bowing; and my Lord of Albemarle's[3] going to the kitchen and eat[4] a bit of the first dish that was to go to the King's table.

But above all was these three Lords, Northumberland and Suffolk and the Duke of Ormond, coming before the courses on horseback and staying so all dinner-time; and at last, to bring up Dymock the King's champion, all in armor on horseback, with his spear and target carried before him. And a herald proclaim that if any dare deny Charles Stuart to be lawful King of England, here was a champion that would fight with him; and with those words the champion flings down his gauntlet; and all this he doth three times in his going up toward the King's table. At last, when he is come, the King drinks to him and then sends him the cup, which is of gold; and he drinks it off and then rides back again with the cup in his hand.

I went from table to table to see the bishops and all others at their dinner, and was infinite pleased with it. And at the lords' table I met with Will Howe and he spoke to my Lord for me and he did give him four rabbits and a pullet; and so I got it, and Mr. Creed and I got Mr. Mitchell to give us some bread and so we at a stall eat it, as everybody else did what they could get.[5]

I took a great deal of pleasure to go up and down and look upon the ladies—and to hear the music of all sorts; but above all, the 24 violins.

About 6 at night they had dined; and I went up to my wife and there met with a pretty lady (Mrs. Franklin, a doctor's wife, a friend of Mr. Bowyer's) and kissed them both—and by and by took them down to Mr. Bowyer's. And strange it is, to think that these two days have held up fair till now that all is done and the King gone out of the Hall; and then it fell a-raining and thundering and lightening as I have not seen it do some years—which people did take great notice of God's blessing of the work of these two days—which is a foolery, to take too much notice of such things.

I observed little disorder in all this; but only the King's footmen had got hold of the canopy and would keep it from the Barons of the Cinqueports; which they endeavored to force from them again but could not do it till my Lord Duke of Albemarle caused it to be put into Sir R. Pye's hand till tomorrow to be decided.

At Mr. Bowyer's, a great deal of company; some I knew, others I did not. Here we stayed upon the leads[6] and below till it was late, expecting to see the fireworks; but they were not performed tonight. Only, the City had a light like a glory round about it, with bonfires.

At last I went to King Street; and there sent Crockford to my father's and my house to tell them I could not come home tonight, because of the dirt and a coach could not be had.

And so after drinking a pot of ale alone at Mrs. Harper's, I returned to Mr. Bowyer's; and after a little stay more, I took my wife and Mrs. Franklin (who I proferred the civility of lying with my wife at Mrs. Hunt's tonight) to Axe Yard. In which, at the further end, there was three great bonfires and a great many great gallants, men and women; and they laid hold of us and would have us drink the King's

---

3. In 1660 Charles II had made George Monck Duke of Albemarle as a reward for his role in the Restoration.
4. Ate (pronounced "ett"), to test for poison.
5. Will Howe and John Creed served as clerks to Sand-

wich, whom the diarist invariably refers to as "my Lord." Miles Mitchell was a local bookseller.
6. Rooftop.

health upon our knee, kneeling upon a fagot; which we all did, they drinking to us one after another—which we thought a strange frolic. But these gallants continued thus a great while, and I wondered to see how the ladies did tipple.

At last I sent my wife and her bedfellow to bed, and Mr. Hunt and I went in with Mr. Thornbury (who did give the company all their wines, he being yeoman of the wine-cellar to the King) to his house; and there, with his wife and two of his sisters and some gallant sparks that were there, we drank the King's health and nothing else, till one of the gentlemen fell down stark drunk and there lay spewing. And I went to my Lord's pretty well. But no sooner a-bed with Mr. Shiply but my head begun to turn and I to vomit, and if ever I was foxed[7] it was now—which I cannot say yet, because I fell asleep and sleep till morning—only, when I waked I found myself wet with my spewing. Thus did the day end, with joy everywhere; and blessed be God, I have not heard of any mischance to anybody through it all, but only to Sergeant Glynne, whose horse fell upon him yesterday and is like to kill him; which people do please themselves with, to see how just God is to punish that rogue at such a time as this—he being now one of the King's sergeants and rode in the cavalcade with Maynard, to whom people wished the same fortune.[8]

There was also this night, in King Street, a woman had her eye put out by a boy's flinging of a firebrand into the coach.

Now after all this, I can say that besides the pleasure of the sight of these glorious things, I may now shut my eyes against any other objects, or for the future trouble myself to see things of state and show, as being sure never to see the like again in this world.

[24 April 1661] Waked in the morning with my head in a sad taking through the last night's drink, which I am very sorry for. So rise and went out with Mr. Creed to drink our morning draught, which he did give me in chocolate to settle my stomach. And after that to my wife, who lay with Mrs. Franklin at the next door to Mrs. Hunt's.

And they were ready, and so I took them up in a coach and carried the lady to Paul's[9] and there set her down; and so my wife and I home—and I to the office.

That being done, my wife and I went to dinner to Sir W. Batten;[1] and all our talk about the happy conclusion of these last solemnities.

After dinner home and advised with my wife about ordering things in my house; and then she went away to my father's to lie, and I stayed with my workmen, who do please me very well with their work.

At night set myself to write down these three days' diary; and while I am about it, I hear the noise of the chambers and other things of the fireworks, which are now playing upon the Thames before the King. And I wish myself with them, being sorry not to see them.

So to bed.

[THE FIRE OF LONDON]

[2 September 1666] Lord's Day. Some of our maids sitting up late last night to get things ready against our feast today, Jane called us up, about 3 in the morning, to tell us of a great fire they saw in the City. So I rose, and slipped on my nightgown, and went to her window, and thought it to be on the back side of Mark Lane at the fur-

---

7. Drunk.
8. Sir John Glynne and Sir John Maynard were lawyers who had served under Cromwell.

9. St. Paul's Cathedral.
1. Surveyor of the Navy.

thest; but being unused to such fires as followed, I thought it far enough off, and so went to bed again and to sleep. About 7 rose again to dress myself, and there looked out at the window and saw the fire not so much as it was, and further off. So to my closet[2] to set things to rights after yesterday's cleaning. By and by Jane comes and tells me that she hears that above 300 houses have been burned down tonight by the fire we saw, and that it was now burning down all Fish Street by London Bridge. So I made myself ready presently, and walked to the Tower and there got up upon one of the high places, Sir J. Robinson's little son going up with me; and there I did see the houses at that end of the bridge all on fire, and an infinite great fire on this and the other side the end of the bridge—which, among other people, did trouble me for poor little Mitchell and our Sarah on the bridge.[3] So down, with my heart full of trouble, to the Lieutenant of the Tower, who tells me that it begun this morning in the King's baker's house in Pudding Lane, and that it hath burned down St. Magnus's Church and most part of Fish Street already. So I down to the water-side and there got a boat and through bridge,[4] and there saw a lamentable fire. Poor Mitchell's house, as far as the Old Swan, already burned that way and the fire running further, that in a very little time it got as far as the Steelyard while I was there. Everybody endeavoring to remove their goods, and flinging into the river or bringing them into lighters[5] that lay off. Poor people staying in their houses as long as till the very fire touched them, and then running into boats or clambering from one pair of stair by the water-side to another. And among other things, the poor pigeons I perceive were loath to leave their houses, but hovered about the windows and balconies till they were some of them burned, their wings, and fell down.

Having stayed, and in an hour's time seen the fire rage every way, and nobody to my sight endeavoring to quench it, but to remove their goods and leave all to the fire; and having seen it get as far as the Steelyard, and the wind mighty high and driving it into the City, and everything, after so long a drought, proving combustible, even the very stones of churches, and among other things, the poor steeple by which pretty Mrs. Horsley lives, and whereof my old school-fellow Elborough is parson, taken fire in the very top and there burned till it fall down—I to Whitehall with a gentleman with me who desired to go off from the Tower to see the fire in my boat—to Whitehall, and there up to the King's closet in the chapel, where people came about me and I did give them an account dismayed them all; and word was carried in to the King, so I was called for and did tell the King and Duke of York what I saw, and that unless his Majesty did command houses to be pulled down, nothing could stop the fire. They seemed much troubled, and the King commanded me to go to my Lord Mayor from him and command him to spare no houses but to pull down before the fire every way. The Duke of York bid me tell him that if he would have any more soldiers, he shall; and so did my Lord Arlington afterward, as a great secret. Here meeting with Captain Cocke, I in his coach, which he lent me, and Creed with me, to Paul's; and there walked along Watling Street as well as I could, every creature coming away loaden with goods to save—and here and there sick people carried away in beds. Extraordinary good goods carried in carts and on backs. At last met my Lord Mayor in Canning Street, like a man spent, with a hankercher about his neck. To the King's message, he cried like a fainting woman, "Lord, what can I do? I am spent! People will not obey me. I have been pulling down houses. But the fire overtakes us

---

2. Private room, study.
3. London Bridge was lined with shops and houses, including the liquor shop of Pepys's friend Michael

Mitchell and the residence of his former servant Sarah.
4. Under the bridge.
5. Barges.

faster than we can do it." That he needed no more soldiers; and that for himself, he must go and refresh himself, having been up all night. So he left me, and I him, and walked home—seeing people all almost distracted and no manner of means used to quench the fire. The houses too, so very thick thereabouts, and full of matter for burning, as pitch and tar, in Thames Street—and warehouses of oil and wines and brandy and other things. Here I saw Mr. Isaac Houblon, that handsome man—prettily dressed and dirty at his door at Dowgate, receiving some of his brothers' things whose houses were on fire; and as he says, have been removed twice already, and he doubts (as it soon proved) that they must be in a little time removed from his house also—which was a sad consideration. And to see the churches all filling with goods, by people who themselves should have been quietly there at this time.

By this time it was about 12 a-clock, and so home and there find my guests, which was Mr. Wood and his wife, Barbary Shelden, and also Mr. Moone—she mighty fine, and her husband, for aught I see, a likely man. But Mr. Moone's design and mine, which was to look over my closet and please him with the sight thereof, which he hath long desired, was wholly disappointed, for we were in great trouble and disturbance at this fire, not knowing what to think of it. However, we had an extraordinary good dinner, and as merry as at this time we could be.

While at dinner, Mrs. Batelier came to inquire after Mr. Woolfe and Stanes (who it seems are related to them), whose houses in Fish Street are all burned, and they in a sad condition. She would not stay in the fright.

As soon as dined, I and Moone away and walked through the City, the streets full of nothing but people and horses and carts loaden with goods, ready to run over one another, and removing goods from one burned house to another—they now removing out of Canning Street (which received goods in the morning) into Lombard Street and further; and among others, I now saw my little goldsmith Stokes receiving some friend's goods, whose house itself was burned the day after. We parted at Paul's, he home and I to Paul's Wharf, where I had appointed a boat to attend me; and took in Mr. Carkesse and his brother, whom I met in the street, and carried them below and above bridge, to and again, to see the fire, which was now got further, both below and above, and no likelihood of stopping it. Met with the King and Duke of York in their barge, and with them to Queenhithe and there called Sir Richard Browne to them. Their order was only to pull down houses apace, and so below bridge at the water-side; but little was or could be done, the fire coming upon them so fast. Good hopes there was of stopping it at the Three Cranes above, and at Buttolph's Wharf below bridge, if care be used; but the wind carries it into the City, so as we know not by the water-side what it doth there. River full of lighters and boats taking in goods, and good goods swimming in the water; and only, I observed that hardly one lighter or boat in three that had the goods of a house in, but there was a pair of virginals[6] in it. Having seen as much as I could now, I away to Whitehall by appointment, and there walked to St. James's Park, and there met my wife and Creed and Wood and his wife and walked to my boat, and there upon the water again, and to the fire up and down, it still increasing and the wind great. So near the fire as we could for smoke; and all over the Thames, with one's face in the wind you were almost burned with a shower of firedrops—this is very true—so as houses were burned by these drops and flakes of fire, three or four, nay five or six houses, one from another. When we could endure no more upon the water, we to a little alehouse on

6. A small harpsichord.

the Bankside over against the Three Cranes, and there stayed till it was dark almost and saw the fire grow; and as it grow darker, appeared more and more, and in corners and upon steeples and between churches and houses, as far as we could see up the hill of the City, in a most horrid malicious bloody flame, not like the fine flame of an ordinary fire. Barbary and her husband away before us. We stayed till, it being dark-ish, we saw the fire as only one entire arch of fire from this to the other side the bridge, and in a bow up the hill, for an arch of above a mile long. It made me weep to see it. The churches, houses, and all on fire and flaming at once, and a horrid noise the flames made, and the cracking of houses at their ruin. So home with a sad heart, and there find everybody discoursing and lamenting the fire; and poor Tom Hayter[7] came with some few of his goods saved out of his house, which is burned upon Fish Street Hill. I invited him to lie at my house, and did receive his goods: but was deceived in his lying there, the noise coming every moment of the growth of the fire, so as we were forced to begin to pack up our own goods and prepare for their removal. And did by moonshine (it being brave,[8] dry, and moonshine and warm weather) car-ry much of my goods into the garden, and Mr. Hayter and I did remove my money and iron-chests into my cellar—as thinking that the safest place. And got my bags of gold into my office ready to carry away, and my chief papers of accounts also there, and my tallies into a box by themselves. So great was our fear, as Sir W. Batten had carts come out of the country to fetch away his goods this night. We did put Mr. Hayter, poor man, to bed a little; but he got but very little rest, so much noise being in my house, taking down of goods.

[3 September 1666] About 4 a-clock in the morning, my Lady Batten sent me a cart to carry away all my money and plate and best things to Sir W. Rider's at Bethnell Green; which I did, riding myself in my nightgown in the cart; and Lord, to see how the streets and the highways are crowded with people, running and riding and getting of carts at any rate to fetch away things. I find Sir W. Rider tired with being called up[9] all night and receiving things from several friends. His house full of goods—and much of Sir W. Batten and Sir W. Penn's.[1] I am eased at my heart to have my trea-sure so well secured. Then home with much ado to find a way. Nor any sleep all this night to me nor my poor wife. But then, and all this day, she and I and all my people laboring to get away the rest of our things, and did get Mr. Tooker to get me a lighter to take them in, and we did carry them (myself some) over Tower Hill, which was by this time full of people's goods, bringing their goods thither. And down to the lighter, which lay at the next quay above the Tower Dock. And here was my neighbor's wife, Mrs. Buckworth, with her pretty child and some few of her things, which I did will-ingly give way to be saved with mine. But there was no passing with anything through the postern,[2] the crowd was so great.

The Duke of York came this day by the office and spoke to us, and did ride with his guard up and down the City to keep all quiet (he being now general, and having the care of all).

This day, Mercer being not at home, but against her mistress's order gone to her mother's, and my wife going thither to speak with W. Hewer, met her there and was angry; and her mother saying that she was not a prentice girl, to ask leave every time

7. One of Pepys's clerks in the Navy Office.
8. Pleasant.
9. Called on, woken.

1. William Penn, Pepys's colleague on the Navy Board (and father of the founder of Pennsylvania).
2. Back or side gate.

she goes abroad, my wife with good reason was angry, and when she came home, bid her be gone again. And so she went away, which troubled me; but yet less than it would, because of the condition we are in fear of coming into in a little time, of being less able to keep one in her quality. At night, lay down a little upon a quilt of W. Hewer in the office (all my own things being packed up or gone); and after me, my poor wife did the like—we having fed upon the remains of yesterday's dinner, having no fire nor dishes, nor any opportunity of dressing anything.

[4 September 1666] Up by break of day to get away the remainder of my things, which I did by a lighter at the Iron Gate; and my hands so few, that it was the afternoon before we could get them all away.

Sir W. Penn and I to Tower Street, and there met the fire burning three or four doors beyond Mr. Howell's; whose goods, poor man (his trays and dishes, shovels, etc., were flung all along Tower Street in the kennels, and people working therewith from one end to the other), the fire coming on in that narrow street, on both sides, with infinite fury. Sir W. Batten, not knowing how to remove his wine, did dig a pit in the garden and laid it in there; and I took the opportunity of laying all the papers of my office that I could not otherwise dispose of. And in the evening Sir W. Penn and I did dig another and put our wine in it, and I my parmesan cheese as well as my wine and some other things.

The Duke of York was at the office this day at Sir W. Penn's, but I happened not to be within. This afternoon, sitting melancholy with Sir W. Penn in our garden and thinking of the certain burning of this office without extraordinary means, I did propose for the sending up of all our workmen from Woolwich and Deptford yards (none whereof yet appeared), and to write to Sir W. Coventry to have the Duke of York's permission to pull down houses rather then lose this office, which would much hinder the King's business. So Sir W. Penn he went down this night, in order to the sending them up tomorrow morning; and I wrote to Sir W. Coventry about the business, but received no answer.

This night Mrs. Turner (who, poor woman, was removing her goods all this day—good goods, into the garden, and knew not how to dispose of them)—and her husband supped with my wife and I at night in the office, upon a shoulder of mutton from the cook's, without any napkin or anything, in a sad manner but were merry. Only, now and then walking into the garden and saw how horridly the sky looks, all on a fire in the night, was enough to put us out of our wits; and indeed it was extremely dreadful—for it looks just as if it was at us, and the whole heaven on fire. I after supper walked in the dark down to Tower Street, and there saw it all on fire at the Trinity House on that side and the Dolphin Tavern on this side, which was very near us—and the fire with extraordinary vehemence. Now begins the practice of blowing up of houses in Tower Street, those next the Tower, which at first did frighten people more than anything; but it stopped the fire where it was done—it bringing down the houses to the ground in the same places they stood, and then it was easy to quench what little fire was in it, though it kindled nothing almost. W. Hewer this day went to see how his mother did, and comes late home, but telling us how he hath been forced to remove her to Islington, her house in Pye Corner being burned. So that it is got so far that way and all the Old Bailey, and was running down to Fleet Street. And Paul's is burned, and all Cheapside. I wrote to my father this night; but the post-house being burned, the letter could not go.

John Evelyn: from *Kalendarium*[1]

[2 September 1666] This fatal night about ten, began that deplorable fire, near Fish Street in London. 2: I had public prayers at home: after dinner the fire continuing, with my wife and son took coach and went to the Bankside in Southwark,[2] where we beheld that dismal spectacle, the whole City in dreadful flames near the water-side, and had now consumed all the houses from the bridge all Thames Street and upwards towards Cheapside, down to the Three Cranes, and so returned exceedingly astonished, what would become of the rest. 3: The fire having continued all this night (if I may call that night, which was as light as day for 10 miles round about after a dreadful manner) when conspiring with a fierce eastern wind, in a very dry season, I went on foot to the same place, when I saw the whole south part of the City burning from Cheapside to the Thames, and all along Cornhill (for it likewise kindled back against the wind, as well as forward) Tower Street, Fenchurch Street, Gracious Street and so along to Baynard Castle, and was now taking hold of St. Paul's Church, to which the scaffolds contributed exceedingly. The conflagration was so universal, and the people so astonished, that from the beginning (I know not by what desponding or fate), they hardly stirred to quench it, so as there was nothing heard or seen but crying out and lamentation, and running about like distracted creatures, without at all attempting to save even their goods; such a strange consternation there was upon them, so as it burned both in breadth and length, the churches, public halls, Exchange, hospitals, monuments, and ornaments, leaping after a prodigious manner from house to house and street to street, at great distance one from the other, for the heat (with a long set of fair and warm weather) had even ignited the air, and prepared the materials to conceive the fire, which devoured after an incredible manner, houses, furniture, and everything. Here we saw the Thames covered with goods floating, all the barges and boats laden with what some had time and courage to save, as on the other, the carts etc. carrying out to the fields, which for many miles were strewed with moveables of all sorts, and tents erecting to shelter both people and what goods they could get away: O the miserable and calamitous spectacle, such as haply the whole world had not seen the like since the foundation of it, nor to be outdone, till the universal conflagration of it. All the sky were of a fiery aspect, like the top of a burning oven, and the light seen above 40 miles round about for many nights. God grant mine eyes may never behold the like, who now saw above ten thousand houses all in one flame, the noise and crackling and thunder of the impetuous flames, the shrieking of women and children, the hurry of people, the fall of towers, houses and churches was like an hideous storm, and the air all about so hot and inflamed that at the last one was not able to approach it, so as they were forced to stand still, and let the flames consume

---

1. John Evelyn (1620–1706), versatile author (on air pollution, architecture, gardening, forestry, and other subjects), wrote up his life on a plan very different from that of his friend Pepys. His *Kalendarium*, commenced when he was 40 years old, narrates selected dates (and omits many), starting with his birth and ending shortly before his death; the thousand-page manuscript encompasses (in legible longhand) his extensive travels in Europe during the Civil Wars and his busy social, court, and civic life after the Restoration. Evelyn's vantage on the Fire of London (as on much else) contrasts with Pepys's. A land-owning gentleman, Evelyn dwelt at a remove from the City on a country estate across the river. A devout Anglican, he saw the catastrophe as an apocalypse steeped in biblical precedent and prophecy. A tireless projector of plans and improvements, he reckoned the City's losses and began to imagine its renewal. Nine days after the fire's outbreak, Evelyn presented the king and queen "with a survey of the ruins and a plot for a new city. . . . [They seemed] extremely pleased with what I had so early thought on"—though in the event, no unified plan for rebuilding was followed.

2. The southern bank of the Thames, across the river from the fire.

on which they did for near two whole miles in length and one in breadth. The clouds also of smoke were dismal, and reached upon computation near 50 miles in length. Thus I left it this afternoon burning, a resemblance of Sodom, or the last day.[3] It called to mind that of 4 *Heb: non enim hic habemus stabilem Civitatem:*[4] the ruins resembling the picture of *Troy: London* was,[5] but is no more. Thus I returned.

[4 September 1666] The burning still rages; I went now on horseback, and it was now gotten as far as the Inner Temple; all Fleet Street, Old Bailey, Ludgate Hill, Warwick Lane, Newgate, Paul's Chain, Watling Street now flaming and most of it reduced to ashes, the stones of Paul's flew like granados,[6] the lead melting down the streets in a stream, and the very pavements of them glowing with fiery redness, so as nor horse nor man was able to tread on them, and the demolitions had stopped all the passages, so as no help could be applied; the eastern wind still more impetuously driving the flames forwards. Nothing but the almighty power of God was able to stop them, for vain was the help of man. On the fourth it crossed towards Whitehall, but O the confusion was then at that court. It pleased his Majesty to command me among the rest to look after the quenching of Fetter Lane end, to preserve (if possible) that part of Holborn, whilst the rest of the gentlemen took their several posts, some at one part, some at another, for now they began to bestir themselves, and not till now, who till now had stood as men interdict, with their hands a cross,[7] and began to consider that nothing was like to put a stop, but the blowing up of so many houses, as might make a wider gap, than any had yet been made by the ordinary method of pulling them down with engines.[8] This some stout seamen proposed early enough to have saved the whole City; but some tenacious and avaricious men, aldermen etc., would not permit, because their houses must have been of the first. It was therefore now commanded to be practiced, and my concern being particularly for the Hospital of St. Bartholomew's near Smithfield, where I had many wounded and sick men, made me the more diligent to promote it;[9] nor was my care for the Savoy less. So as it pleased Almighty God by abating of the wind, and the industry of people, now when all was lost, infusing a new spirit into them (and such as had if exerted in time undoubtedly preserved the whole) that the fury of it began sensibly to abate, about noon, so as it came no farther than the Temple westward, nor than the entrance of Smithfield north; but continued all this day and night so impetuous toward Cripplegate, and the Tower, as made us even all despair. It also brake out again in the Temple: but the courage of the multitude persisting, and innumerable houses blown up with gunpowder, such gaps and desolations were soon made, as also by the former three days' consumption, as the back fire did not so vehemently urge upon the rest, as formerly. There was yet no standing near the burning and glowing ruins near a furlong's space. The coal and wood wharves and magazines of oil, rosin, chandler, etc.[1] did infinite mischief; so as the invective I but a little before dedicated to his Majesty and published, giving warning what might probably be the issue of suffering those shops to be

3. In Genesis, the Lord destroys the sinful city of Sodom by raining "fire and brimstone . . . out of heaven" (19.24). "The last day" is the Day of Judgment, when the city of Babylon (emblem of the corrupt world) "shall be utterly burned with fire" (Revelation 18.8).
4. For here we have no lasting city (Hebrews 13.14; the sentence continues: "but we seek one to come").
5. Echoing the *Aeneid*'s account of the fall of Troy: on the night the Greeks burn the city, a Trojan priest declares

fuit Ilium ("Troy was"; 2.325).
6. Grenades.
7. Immobilized, with their arms crossed (a conventional posture of passivity).
8. Machines.
9. Evelyn served on the Navy Board as a commissioner, charged with the care of sick and wounded seamen.
1. Different sorts of fuel, stored and sold in shops along the Thames.

in the City, was looked on as prophetic.[2] But there I left this smoking and sultry heap, which mounted up in dismal clouds night and day, the poor inhabitants dispersed all about St. George's, Moorfields, as far as Highgate, and several miles in circle, some under tents, others under miserable huts and hovels, without a rag, or any necessary utensils, bed or board, who from delicateness, riches and easy accommodations in stately and well-furnished houses, were now reduced to extremest misery and poverty. In this calamitous condition I returned with a sad heart to my house, blessing and adoring the distinguishing mercy of God, to me and mine, who in the midst of all this ruin, was like Lot, in my little Zoar, safe and sound.[3]

[Elizabeth Pepys and Deborah Willett]

[25 October 1668] *Lord's Day*. Up, and discoursing with my wife about our house and many new things we are doing of; and so to church I, and there find Jack Fen come, and his wife, a pretty black woman; I never saw her before, nor took notice of her now. So home and to dinner; and after dinner, all the afternoon got my wife and boy to read to me. And at night W. Batelier comes and sups with us; and after supper, to have my head combed by Deb, which occasioned the greatest sorrow to me that ever I knew in this world; for my wife, coming up suddenly, did find me embracing the girl con my hand sub su coats; and indeed, I was with my main in her cunny.[4] I was at a wonderful loss upon it, and the girl also; and I endeavored to put it off, but my wife was struck mute and grew angry, and as her voice came to her, grew quite out of order; and I do say little, but to bed; and my wife said little also, but could not sleep all night; but about 2 in the morning waked me and cried, and fell to tell me as a great secret that she was a Roman Catholic and had received the Holy Sacrament; which troubled me but I took no notice of it, but she went on from one thing to another, till at last it appeared plainly her trouble was at what she saw; but yet I did not know how much she saw and therefore said nothing to her. But after her much crying and reproaching me with inconstancy and preferring a sorry girl before her, I did give her no provocations but did promise all fair usage to her, and love, and foreswore any hurt that I did with her—till at last she seemed to be at ease again; and so toward morning, a little sleep; [26][5] and so I, with some little repose and rest, rose, and up and by water to Whitehall, but with my mind mightily troubled for the poor girl, whom I fear I have undone by this, my wife telling me that she would turn her out of door. However, I was obliged to attend the Duke of York, thinking to have had a meeting of Tangier today, but had not; but he did take me and Mr. Wren into his closet, and there did press me to prepare what I had to say upon the answers of my fellow-officers to his great letter; which I promised to do against his coming to town again the next week; and so to other discourse, finding plainly that he is in trouble and apprehensions of the reformers, and would be found to do what he can towards reforming himself.[6] And so thence to my Lord Sandwich; where after long stay, he

---

2. In 1661 Evelyn had warned of these dangers in a pamphlet entitled *Fumifugium: or the Inconveniency of the Air and Smoke of London Dissipated. Together with Some Remedies Humbly Proposed by J. E., Esq; to His Sacred Majesty, and to the Parliament Now Assembled.*

3. Lot, a prosperous inhabitant of Sodom, is warned by angels of the city's impending destruction. He escapes to Zoar, a small city nearby (Genesis 19.20–22).

4. I.e., with his hand under her petticoats and his hand in her vagina. Here as often, Pepys reports his illicit sexual activities in a "secret" language compounded of Latin, French, Spanish, and English.

5. Pepys wedges the new date into the margin, beside the run-on narrative.

6. The duke was Lord High Admiral of the navy; on his behalf Pepys had composed a letter to the Navy Board proposing reforms in response to parliamentary investigations of the disastrous Second Dutch War.

being in talk with others privately, I to him; and there he taking physic and keeping his chamber, I had an hour's talk with him about the ill posture of things at this time, while the King gives countenance to Sir Charles Sedley and Lord Buckhurst,[7] telling him their late story of running up and down the streets a little while since all night, and their being beaten and clapped up all night by the constable, who is since chid and imprisoned for his pains.

He tells me that he thinks his matters do stand well with the King—and hopes to have dispatch to his mind; but I doubt it, and do see that he doth fear it too. He told me my Lady Carteret's trouble about my writing of that letter[8] of the Duke of York's lately to the office; which I did not own, but declared to be of no injury to G. Carteret, and that I would write a letter to him to satisfy him therein. But this I am in pain how to do without doing myself wrong, and the end I had, of preparing a justification to myself hereafter, when the faults of the Navy come to be found out. However, I will do it in the best manner I can.

Thence by coach home and to dinner, finding my wife mightily discontented and the girl sad, and no words from my wife to her. So after dinner, they out with me about two or three things; and so home again, I all the evening busy and my wife full of trouble in her looks; and anon to bed—where about midnight, she wakes me and there falls foul on me again, affirming that she saw me hug and kiss the girl; the latter I denied, and truly; the other I confessed and no more. And upon her pressing me, did offer to give her under my hand that I would never see Mrs. Pearse[9] more, nor Knepp, but did promise her particular demonstrations of my true love to her, owning some indiscretion in what I did, but that there was no harm in it. She at last on these promises was quiet, and very kind we were, and so to sleep; [27] and in the morning up, but with my mind troubled for the poor girl, with whom I could not get opportunity to speak; but to the office, my mind mighty full of sorrow for her, where all the morning, and to dinner with my people and to the office all the afternoon; and so at night home and there busy to get some things ready against tomorrow's meeting of Tangier; and that being done and my clerks gone, my wife did towards bedtime begin to be in a mighty rage from some new matter that she had got in her head, and did most part of the night in bed rant at me in most high terms, of threats of publishing my shame; and when I offered to rise, would have rose too, and caused a candle to be lit, to burn by her all night in the chimney while she ranted; while I, that knew myself to have given some grounds for it, did make it my business to appease her all I could possibly, and by good words and fair promises did make her very quiet; and so rested all night and rose with perfect good peace, being heartily afflicted for this folly of mine that did occasion it; but was forced to be silent about the girl, which I have no mind to part with, but much less that the poor girl should be undone by my folly. [28] So up, with mighty kindness from my wife and a thorough peace; and being up, did by a note advise the girl what I had done and owned, which note I was in pain for till she told me that she had burned it. This evening, Mr. Spong came and sat late with me, and first told me of the instrument called parrallogram, which I must have one of, showing me his practice thereon by a map of England.[1]

---

7. Notorious libertines (Buckhurst was Nell Gwyn's current lover).
8. The "great letter" on naval reform.
9. Elizabeth Pearse, wife of a naval surgeon.
1. The parallelogram was a device for making copies of diagrams and maps on the same or on a different scale.

So by coach with Mr. Gibson[2] to Chancery Lane, and there made oath before a master of chancery to my Tangier account of fees; and so to Whitehall, where by and by a committee met; my Lord Sandwich there, but his report was not received, it being late; but only a little business done, about the supplying the place with victuals; but I did get, to my great content, my account allowed of fees, with great applause by my Lord Ashley and Sir W. Penn. Thence home, calling at one or two places, and there about our workmen, who are at work upon my wife's closet and other parts of my house, that we are all in dirt. So after dinner, with Mr. Gibson all the afternoon in my closet; and at night to supper and to bed, my wife and I at good peace, but yet with some little grudgings of trouble in her, and more in me, about the poor girl.

[14 November 1668] Up, and had a mighty mind to have seen or given a note to Deb or to have given her a little money; to which purpose I wrapped up 40s in a paper, thinking to give her; but my wife rose presently, and would not let me be out of her sight; and went down before me into the kitchen, and came up and told me that she was in the kitchen, and therefore would have me go round the other way; which she repeating, and I vexed at it, answered her a little angrily; upon which she instantly flew out into a rage, calling me dog and rogue, and that I had a rotten heart; all which, knowing that I deserved it, I bore with; and word being brought presently up that she was gone away by coach with her things, my wife was friends; and so all quiet, and I to the office with my heart sad, and find that I cannot forget the girl, and vexed I know not where to look for her—and more troubled to see how my wife is by this means likely for ever to have her hand over me, that I shall for ever be a slave to her; that is to say, only in matters of pleasure, but in other things she will make her business, I know, to please me and to keep me right to her—which I will labor to be indeed, for she deserves it of me, though it will be I fear a little time before I shall be able to wear Deb out of my mind. At the office all the morning, and merry at noon at dinner; and after dinner to the office, where all the afternoon and doing much business late; my mind being free of all troubles, I thank God, but only for my thoughts of this girl, which hang after her. And so at night home to supper, and there did sleep with great content with my wife. I must here remember that I have lain with my moher[3] as a husband more times since this falling-out then in I believe twelve months before—and with more pleasure to her than I think in all the time of our marriage before.

[20 November 1668] This morning up, with mighty kind words between my poor wife and I; and so to Whitehall by water, W. Hewer with me, who is to go with me everywhere until my wife be in condition to go out along with me herself; for she doth plainly declare that she dares not trust me out alone, and therefore made it a piece of our league that I should alway take somebody with me, or her herself; which I am mighty willing to, being, by the grace of God resolved never to do her wrong more.[4]

   We landed at the Temple, and there I did bid him call at my cousin Roger Pepys's lodgings, and I stayed in the street for him; and so took water again at the

2. A favorite assistant of Pepys's.
3. Spanish *mujer*: wife. For the first time, Pepys applies his secret language to Elizabeth.
4. Two nights earlier, Pepys had traced Deborah Willett to her new lodgings, and caressed her in his coach. The next day, Elizabeth told him that she knew about the assignation, and he signed a pledge "never to see or speak with Deb while I live."

Strand stairs and so to Whitehall, in my way I telling him plainly and truly my resolutions, if I can get over this evil, never to give new occasion for it. He is, I think, so
honest and true a servant to us both, and one that loves us, that I was not much troubled at his being privy to all this, but rejoiced in my heart that I had him to assist in
the making us friends; which he did do truly and heartily, and with good success—for
I did get him to go to Deb to tell her that I had told my wife all of my being with her
the other night, that so, if my wife should send, she might not make the business
worse by denying it. While I was at Whitehall with the Duke of York doing our ordinary business with him, here being also the first time the new treasurers, W. Hewer
did go to her and come back again; and so I took him into St. James's Park, and there
he did tell me he had been with her and found what I said about my manner of being
with her true, and had given her advice as I desired. I did there enter into more talk
about my wife and myself, and he did give me great assurance of several particular
cases to which my wife had from time to time made him privy of her loyalty and truth
to me after many and great temptations, and I believe them truly. I did also discourse
the unfitness of my leaving of my employment now in many respects, to go into the
country as my wife desires—but that I would labor to fit myself for it; which he thoroughly understands, and doth agree with me in it; and so, hoping to get over this
trouble, we about our business to Westminster Hall to meet Roger Pepys; which I did,
and did there discourse of the business of lending him 500*l* to answer some occasions
of his, which I believe to be safe enough; and so took leave of him and away by coach
home, calling on my coach-maker by the way, where I like my little coach mightily.
But when I came home, hoping for a further degree of peace and quiet, I find my wife
upon her bed in a horrible rage afresh, calling me all the bitter names; and rising, did
fall to revile me in the bitterest manner in the world, and could not refrain to strike
me and pull my hair; which I resolved to bear with, and had good reason to bear it.
So I by silence and weeping did prevail with her a little to be quiet, and she would
not eat her dinner without me; but yet by and by into a raging fit she fell again worse
than before, that she would slit the girl's nose; and at last W. Hewer came in and
came up, who did allay her fury, I flinging myself in a sad desperate condition upon
the bed in the blue room, and there lay while they spoke together; and at last it came
to this, that if I would call Deb "whore" under my hand,[5] and write to her that I hated her and would never see her more, she would believe me and trust in me—which I
did agree to; only, as to the name of "whore" I would have excused, and therefore
wrote to her sparing that word; which my wife thereupon tore it, and would not be
satisfied till, W. Hewer winking upon me, I did write so, with the name of a whore, as
that I did fear she might too probably have been prevailed upon to have been[6] a
whore by her carriage to me, and therefore, as such, I did resolve never to see her
more. This pleased my wife, and she gives it W. Hewer to carry to her, with a sharp
message from her. So from that minute my wife begun to be kind to me, and we to
kiss and be friends, and so continued all the evening and fell to talk of other matters
with great comfort, and after supper to bed.

 This evening comes Mr. Billup to me to read over Mr. Wren's alterations of
my draft of a letter for the Duke of York to sign, to the board; which I like mighty
well, they being not considerable, only in mollifying some hard terms which I
had thought fit to put in. From this to other discourse; I do find that the Duke of
York and his servant Mr. Wren do look upon this service of mine as a very sea-

sonable service to the Duke of York, as that which he will have to show to his enemies in his own justification of his care of the King's business. And I am sure I am heartily glad of it—both for the King's sake and the Duke of York's, and my own also—for if I continue, my work, by this means, will be the less, and my share in the blame[7] also.

He being gone, I to my wife again and so spent the evening with very great joy, and the night also, with good sleep and rest, my wife only troubled in her rest, but less than usual—for which the God of Heaven be praised. I did this night promise to my wife never to go to bed without calling upon God upon my knees by prayer; and I begun this night, and hope I shall never forget to do the like all my life—for I do find that it is much the best for my soul and body to live pleasing to God and my poor wife—and will ease me of much care, as well as much expense.

[31 May 1669] Up very betimes, and so continued all the morning, with W. Hewer, upon examining and stating my accounts, in order to the fitting myself to go abroad beyond sea,[8] which the ill condition of my eyes, and my neglect for a year or two, hath kept me behindhand in, and so as to render it very difficult now, and troublesome to my mind to do it; but I this day made a satisfactory entrance therein.[9] Dined at home, and in the afternoon by water to Whitehall, calling by the way at Mitchell's,[1] where I have not been many a day till just the other day; and now I met her mother there and knew her husband to be out of town. And here yo did besar ella, but have not opportunity para hazer mas[2] with her as I would have offered if yo had had it. And thence had another meeting with the Duke of York at Whitehall with the Duke of York on yesterday's work, and made a good advance; and so being called by my wife, we to the park, Mary Batelier, a Dutch gentleman, a friend of hers, being with us. Thence to the World's End, a drinking-house by the park, and there merry; and so home late.

And thus ends all that I doubt I shall ever be able to do with my own eyes in the keeping of my journal, I being not able to do it any longer, having done now so long as to undo my eyes almost every time that I take a pen in my hand; and therefore, whatever comes of it, I must forbear; and therefore resolve from this time forward to have it kept by my people in longhand, and must therefore be contented to set down no more than is fit for them and all the world to know; or if there be anything (which cannot be much, now my amours to Deb are past, and my eyes hindering me in almost all other pleasures), I must endeavor to keep a margin in my book open, to add here and there a note in shorthand with my own hand.[3] And so I betake myself to that course which is almost as much as to see myself go into my grave—for which, and all the discomforts that will accompany my being blind, the good God prepare me.

May. 31. 1669.   S. P.

---

7. For Navy Board misconduct.
8. Pepys and his wife planned a tour of Holland, Flanders, and France. Near journey's end, Elizabeth Pepys caught a fever; she died in London on 10 November 1669.
9. Pepys suffered from a painful combination of farsightedness and astigmatism which doctors did not know how to diagnose or to treat; he feared (mistakenly) that he was going blind.
1. Michael Mitchell sold liquor in a shop on London Bridge; his wife Betty is the "her" of the ensuing clauses.
2. I did kiss her but had no chance to do more.
3. Pepys never produced the continuation of his journal that he envisions here.

PERSPECTIVES

Reading Papers

Shakespeare never read a newspaper. In the early seventeenth century, the news was purveyed irregularly and improvisatorily. A breaking story or a sensational event might prompt a spate of ballads, broadsides, and bulletins, which would then abate until the next big thing hove into view. The news periodical, nascent on the Continent during Shakespeare's lifetime, arrived in England in 1620 in the form of English-language news sheets dispatched from Amsterdam. London publishers quickly took up the enterprise, to their considerable profit. Shakespeare's caustic contemporary Ben Jonson lived to witness their innovation; he promptly forecast an imminent glut of cheap and worthless information—fearing, with reason, that the new medium would supplant the theater as the public's favored oracle.

Even Jonson, though, could not have foreseen the quantities of print that would pour from presses decades later during the Civil Wars, when the instability of authority allowed innumerable newsbooks to appear, supporting every party in the conflict. During the Interregnum and Restoration, government tried through strict licensing laws to limit the flow and narrow the range of newsprint, but whenever those laws lapsed, innovations abounded: the first daily reports on proceedings in the House of Commons (1680), the first English newspaper outside London (1701), the first daily newspaper (1702), the first weekly journals (1713), melding the news with a miscellany of other departments. At the centennial of Shakespeare's death, London was producing some sixteen newspapers; a century later Britain possessed more than 350, in addition to legions of other periodicals purveying opinion and advice. The newspaper, the periodical essay, and the magazine had become confirmed habits in the lives of almost everyone who could read, and even of many who could not, since the papers were often read aloud, their contents discussed and debated, in public gathering places and household circles.

The periodical was a creature of the seventeenth century and a staple of the eighteenth. It punctuated the calendar with a new print pulse, and imparted to its readership a new sense of moving together in synchrony, in a rhythm that paradoxically combined the solitary and the social, the private and the public. The "mass ceremony" of reading the newspaper is generally performed (as the historian Benedict Anderson has observed) in "privacy, in the lair of the skull. Yet each communicant is well aware that the ceremony he performs is being replicated simultaneously by thousands (or millions) of others, of whose existence he is confident, yet of whose identity he has not the slightest notion." The periodical press, then, gave its readers a new way of seeing the world, and of seeing themselves in the world, as private beings and public entities; it prompted them (in Anderson's phrase) to imagine themselves as a community.

Monarchs and politicians tried hard to control the press, to dictate its views and to contain its criticisms, but in Britain the phenomenon proved too large for such arrant limitation. The news sheets and the essays helped create a new arena of political thought and action, separate from the older power centers of Court and Parliament, a public sphere of newly engaged readers who increasingly valued and deployed their own capacity to form collective opinions, and who increasingly expected their opinions to affect events. The freedom and copiousness of the press became a national boast, and abetted Britons in a conviction they were already cultivating: that they were participants in an ongoing narrative of commerce and taste, politeness, politics, and empire, protagonists in a story with numberless installments and no foreseeable end, unfolding at the center of the world.

Each newspaper in this section is introduced at its first appearance.

Periodical Personae

In print journalism it was primarily the news that sold the paper; in the periodical essay it was the voice: the idiosyncratic mix of assertion and deference, comedy and charisma, with which author addressed audience. Political writers had long known the advantages of using a mask or *persona*—a pen name, a fictitious character—as a means of both concealing their identity and expanding the appeal of their controversial arguments. In the early 1700s, the inventors of the periodical essay extended the tactic of the fictitious self into new territory. While collaborating on *The Tatler* and *The Spectator*, Richard Steele and Joseph Addison devised strategies for making the unreal author a real arbitrator in the culture, a teacher of taste and conduct, manners and morality, someone whom readers found it pleasurable to learn from, to identify with, even to "believe in," despite (and because of) his comically exaggerated quirks, his patent nonexistence. Working behind their carefully crafted masks, Addison and Steele sold so many papers and impressed so many readers that their mark became indelible. For the rest of the century, the periodical essayist's first task was to devise a persona unusual enough to define the paper, and engaging enough to sustain it.

The Tatler (1709–1711)

At age thirty-five, after a checkered career as soldier, poet, playwright, popular moralist, and Whig propagandist, Captain Richard Steele (1672–1729) was appointed editor of the *London Gazette*, the government's long-running newspaper. Evidently even this task did not sufficiently absorb his energies. Two years later, while still supervising the *Gazette*, he launched *The Tatler*, a periodical of his own that outstripped all its predecessors in commercial success and enduring appeal. It appeared three times a week, ran for two years and 271 numbers, spawned many imitators, and continued to sell (in a four-volume collected edition) for the rest of the century. The *Tatler*'s appeal derived in large measure from its putative author, Isaac Bickerstaff, Esquire, whose name Steele had borrowed from one of Swift's satires, but whose character he elaborated into that of a genial, perceptive, and comically self-congratulatory old man. The paper's commodious structure mirrored the gregariousness of its "author." Bickerstaff datelined his dispatches from the coffeehouses around London where papers were distributed, read, and discussed; he included letters (fictitious and authentic) from readers all over the country. The *Tatler*'s audience thus found itself absorbed into the paper several ways: they were its constant topic, they sometimes supplied its text, they constituted both its origin and its endpoint, and they gave it their unprecedented devotion. Steele soon made further discoveries of form under the influence of his school friend Joseph Addison (1672–1729), whom he had brought in (so one contemporary put it) as his "great and constant assistant." Addison and Steele found that Bickerstaff's private musings, dispatched "From my Own Apartment," were the most pleasing items of all, and so they often devoted whole papers to reprinting what their character was pleased to call his "lucubrations" (meditations by candlelight, late at night). John Gay summed up the strategy's success. Coffeehouse owners, Gay reported, "began to be sensible that the Esquire's lucubrations alone had brought them more customers than all their other newspapers put together." Bickerstaff's other "departments" diminished or disappeared, and "the Esquire's lucubrations," now running the full length of the paper, created the format and the fashion for the periodical essay, a unified piece on a single topic as opposed to the fragmentary "miscellany" from which Steele had started. By the time he stopped *The Tatler* (probably because of political pressures following the Whigs' fall from power), he and Addison had devised means and achieved ends with which they would experiment anew in the *Spectator*: ways of creating community shot through with solitude, of mixing sociability and meditation, morality and mirth.

Richard Steele: *from* Tatler No. 1
Tuesday, 12 April 1709

[Introducing Mr. Bickerstaff]

Quicquid agunt homines nostri farrago libelli.[1]

Though the other papers which are published for the use of the good people of England have certainly very wholesome effects, and are laudable in their particular kinds, they do not seem to come up to the main design of such narrations, which, I humbly presume, should be principally intended for the use of politic persons, who are so public-spirited as to neglect their own affairs to look into transactions of state. Now these gentlemen, for the most part, being persons of strong zeal and weak intellects,[2] it is both a charitable and necessary work to offer something whereby such worthy and well-affected members of the commonwealth may be instructed, after their reading, *what to think:* which shall be the end and purpose of this my paper, wherein I shall from time to time report and consider all matters of what kind soever that shall occur to me, and publish such my advices and reflections every Tuesday, Thursday, and Saturday in the week, for the convenience of the post.[3] I resolve also to have something which may be of entertainment to the fair sex, in honor of whom I have invented the title of this paper. I therefore earnestly desire all persons, without distinction, to take it in for the present *gratis*,[4] and hereafter at the price of one penny, forbidding all hawkers to take more for it at their peril. And I desire all persons to consider, that I am at a very great charge for proper materials for this work, as well as that before I resolved upon it, I had settled a correspondence in all parts of the known and knowing world. And forasmuch as this globe is not trodden upon by mere drudges of business only, but that men of spirit and genius are justly to be esteemed as considerable agents in it, we shall not upon a dearth of news present you with musty foreign edicts, or dull proclamations, but shall divide our relations of the passages which occur in action or discourse throughout this town, as well as elsewhere, under such dates of places as may prepare you for the matter you are to expect, in the following manner.

All accounts of gallantry,[5] pleasure, and entertainment shall be under the article of White's Chocolate House; poetry, under that of Will's Coffeehouse; learning, under the title of Grecian; foreign and domestic news you will have from St. James's Coffeehouse; and what else I have to offer on any other subject, shall be dated from my own apartment.[6]

I once more desire my reader to consider, that as I cannot keep an ingenious man to go daily to Will's, under two-pence each day merely for his charges; to White's, under sixpence; nor to the Grecian, without allowing him some Plain Spanish,[7] to be as able as others at the learned table; and that a good observer cannot speak with even Kidney[8] at St. James's without clean linen. I say, these considerations will, I

---

1. "Whatever people do [will furnish] the variety of our little book"; or (in the freer and more apt 18th-century translation by Thomas Percy) "Whate'er men do, or say, or think, or dream, / Our motley paper seizes for its theme" (Juvenal, *Satires* 1.85–86).
2. Bickerstaff mocks that category of men known as the "coffeehouse politicians," who spent long hours together discussing news.
3. These were the days on which the postal system carried mail from London to the provinces.
4. Steele distributed his first four numbers free, as a way of attracting readers.
5. Flirtation and self-display.
6. Steele exploits associations between topic and venue long familiar to his readers. Each of the coffeehouses he names catered to a clientele "specializing" in the pursuits he names. A journalist himself, Steele parodies the newspaper format that headed each item by the name of its (usually foreign) city of origin.
7. A kind of snuff, used as a stimulant to induce sneezing.
8. A waiter.

hope, make all persons willing to comply with my humble request (when my *gratis* stock is exhausted) of a penny apiece; especially since they are sure of some proper amusement, and that it is impossible for me to want means to entertain 'em, having, besides the force of my own parts, the power of divination, and that I can, by casting a figure, tell you all that will happen before it comes to pass.[9]

But this last faculty I shall use very sparingly, and speak but of few things 'till they are passed, for fear of divulging matters which may offend our superiors.[1] * * *

From my own apartment

I am sorry I am obliged to trouble the public with so much discourse, upon a matter which I at the very first mentioned as a trifle, *viz.* the death of Mr. Partridge, under whose name there is an almanac come out for the year 1709.[2] In one page of which, it is asserted by the said John Partridge, that he is still living, and not only so, but that he was also living some time before, and even at the instant when I writ of his death. I have in another place, and in a paper by itself, sufficiently convinced this man that he is dead, and if he has any shame, I don't doubt but that by this time he owns it to all his acquaintance: for though the legs and arms, and whole body, of that man may still appear and perform their animal functions; yet since, as I have elsewhere observed, his art is gone, the man is gone. I am, as I said, concerned that this little matter should make so much noise; but since I am engaged, I take myself obliged in honor to go on in my lucubrations, and by the help of these arts of which I am master, as well as my skill in astrological speculations, I shall, as I see occasion, proceed to confute other dead men, who pretend to be in being, that they are actually deceased. I therefore give all men fair warning to mend their manners, for I shall from time to time print bills of mortality; and I beg the pardon of all such who shall be named therein, if they who are good for nothing shall find themselves in the number of the deceased.

The Spectator (1711–1713)

In the weeks of the *Spectator*'s first appearance, readers marveled at both its contents and its pace. "We had at first . . . no manner of notion," the wit John Gay reported from London, "how a diurnal paper could be continued in the spirit and style of our present *Spectators*; but to our no small surprise we find them still rising upon us, and can only wonder from whence so prodigious a run of wit and learning can proceed." It proceeded (as Gay guessed) from the minds and pens of the same two writers who had shut down the *Tatler* just a few months before. For their second periodical collaboration, Addison and Steele considerably upped the ante. Not only did they undertake to publish a new number every day (something no essayist had hitherto attempted), they also devised a new persona, intricately linked with their triumphant earlier creation Isaac Bickerstaff. Where the *Tatler* had begun in gregariousness and modulated towards solitude (at "my own apartment"), the new paper started from an even farther remove, in the eccentric silence of Mr. Spectator, who declares at the outset that he has not spoken "three sentences together" since birth. Mr. Spectator carries his "own apartment"—his state of psychological apartness—with him, not at his residence but in his head; "the working of my own mind," he announces early on, "is the chief entertainment of my life."

---

9. To "cast a figure" is to work out a horoscope, an ability that the *Tatler*'s first readers would readily associate with the character "Isaac Bickerstaff." Jonathan Swift had originally created the character (in a series of pamphlets in 1708), as a way of satirizing the fashion for astrological almanacs, which purported to foretell the important events of the coming year. In Swift's first pamphlet, the fictitious astrologer Isaac Bickerstaff forecast the imminent death of the real (and very successful) astrologer John Partridge; in the second pamphlet, Bickerstaff declared blithely that his prophecy had come to pass. Partridge's subsequent, frantic protestations added relish to the joke.

1. Bickerstaff proceeds to supply first dispatches from White's, Will's, and St. James's coffeehouses.

2. In the 1709 issue of his annual almanac *Merlinus Liberatus*, Partridge had insisted that he was "still alive."

In his focused interiority, Mr. Spectator played out the principles of psychology that John Locke had propounded, but his extreme self-possession turned out to possess enormous rhetorical impact and commercial cachet as well. More than any other periodical persona, Mr. Spectator managed to embody and to allegorize the operations of the paper he inhabited. Like the paper he was everywhere, at once silent and articulate, fictitious in substance but impressive in effect, observant and absorbent of the culture, able to move into his readers' minds by the mysterious osmosis of reading itself, and to remain there, a disembodied monitor with a rapidly growing portfolio of daily essays. An anonymous pamphleteer reproached Mr. Spectator for the presumptuous "tyranny" of his surveillance, but the paper's tactics of reform remained in power for most of the century. It was read (and imitated) on the Continent, in the American colonies, and in remoter outposts like Sumatra, from whence a British trader wrote home to his daughter in London, admonishing her "to study the *Spectators*, especially those which relate to religion and domestic life. Next to the Bible you cannot read any writings so much to your purpose for the improvement of your mind and the conduct of your actions." The *Spectator*, Gay noted soon after the paper's debut, "is in everyone's hands, and a constant topic for our morning conversation at tea tables and coffeehouses." More than sixty years later, the Scots rhetorician Hugh Blair could only echo and elaborate on Gay's phrasing, in accordance with the paper's now long-established place in the British canon: "The *Spectator* . . . is a book which is in the hands of everyone, and which cannot be praised too highly. The good sense, and good writing, the useful morality, and the admirable vein of humor which abound in it, render it one of those standard books which have done the greatest honor to the English nation."

Joseph Addison: *from* Spectator No. 1
Thursday, 1 March 1711

[INTRODUCING MR. SPECTATOR]

Non fumum ex fulgore, sed ex fumo dare lucem
Cogitat, ut speciosa debinc miracula promat.[1]

I have observed, that a reader seldom peruses a book with pleasure 'till he knows whether the writer of it be a black or a fair man,[2] of a mild or choleric disposition, married or a bachelor, with other particulars of the like nature, that conduce very much to the right understanding of an author. To gratify this curiosity, which is so natural to a reader, I design this paper, and my next, as prefatory discourses to my following writings, and shall give some account in them of the several persons that are engaged in this work. As the chief trouble of compiling, digesting, and correcting will fall to my share, I must do myself the justice to open the work with my own history.

I was born to a small hereditary estate, which, according to the tradition of the village where it lies, was bounded by the same hedges and ditches in William the Conqueror's time[3] that it is at present, and has been delivered down from father to son whole and entire, without the loss or acquisition of a single field or meadow, during the space of six hundred years. There runs a story in the family, that when my mother was gone with child of me about three months, she dreamt that she was brought to bed of[4] a judge. Whether this might proceed from a lawsuit which was then depending in the family, or my father's being a justice of the peace, I cannot determine; for I am not so vain as to think it presaged any dignity that I should arrive

---

1. "He intends to produce not smoke from fire, but light from smoke, so that he may then put forth striking and amazing things" (Horace, *Ars Poetica* 143–144).
2. Of dark or light complexion.

3. The late 11th century, when William ruled as king of England.
4. Had given birth to. The silence of judges was proverbial.

at in my future life, though that was the interpretation which the neighborhood put upon it. The gravity of my behavior at my very first appearance in the world, and all the time that I sucked, seemed to favor my mother's dream: for, as she has often told me, I threw away my rattle before I was two months old, and would not make use of my coral[5] 'till they had taken away the bells from it.

As for the rest of my infancy, there being nothing in it remarkable, I shall pass it over in silence. I find that, during my nonage,[6] I had the reputation of a very sullen youth, but was always a favorite of my schoolmaster, who used to say, *that my parts were solid and would wear well*. I had not been long at the university before I distinguished myself by a most profound silence: for during the space of eight years, excepting in the public exercises of the college, I scarce uttered the quantity of an hundred words; and indeed do not remember that I ever spoke three sentences together in my whole life. Whilst I was in this learned body I applied myself with so much diligence to my studies that there are very few celebrated books, either in the learned or the modern tongues, which I am not acquainted with.

Upon the death of my father I was resolved to travel into foreign countries, and therefore left the university, with the character[7] of an odd unaccountable fellow that had a great deal of learning, if I would but show it. An insatiable thirst after knowledge carried me into all the countries of Europe, in which there was anything new or strange to be seen; nay, to such a degree was my curiosity raised, that having read the controversies of some great men concerning the antiquities of Egypt, I made a voyage to Grand Cairo, on purpose to take the measure of a pyramid; and as soon as I had set myself right in that particular, returned to my native country with great satisfaction.

I have passed my latter years in this city, where I am frequently seen in most public places, though there are not above half a dozen of my select friends that know me; of whom my next paper shall give a more particular account. There is no place of general resort, wherein I do not often make my appearance.[8] Sometimes I am seen thrusting my head into a round of politicians at Will's, and listening with great attention to the narratives that are made in those little circular audiences. Sometimes I smoke a pipe at Child's; and whilst I seem attentive to nothing but the *Post-Man*,[9] overhear the conversation of every table in the room. I appear on Sunday nights at St. James's Coffeehouse, and sometimes join the little committee of politics in the inner-room, as one who comes there to hear and improve. My face is likewise very well known at the Grecian, the Cocoa Tree, and in the theaters both of Drury Lane, and the Haymarket. I have been taken for a merchant upon the Exchange[1] for above these ten years, and sometimes pass for a Jew in the assembly of stock-jobbers at Jonathan's.[2] In short, wherever I see a cluster of people I always mix with them, though I never open my lips but in my own club.

Thus I live in the world, rather as a spectator of mankind than as one of the species; by which means I have made myself a speculative statesman, soldier,

---

5. Another sound maker for infants.
6. Childhood.
7. Reputation.
8. With a conspicuous openness to all parties and pursuits, Mr. Spectator distributes his visitations among some of London's favorite meeting places, including ones popular with Whigs (St. James's), Tories (the Cocoa Tree), authors (Child's), lawyers (the Grecian), and the news-obsessives he calls "politicians" (Will's).

9. A thrice-weekly newspaper, favored by Whigs.
1. The Royal Exchange was a large building containing many shops and serving as a meeting place for merchants. (For Addison's paean to the place, see *Spectator* No. 69, page 956).
2. Jonathan's coffeehouse, near the Royal Exchange, was a principal meeting place of merchants and stockbrokers ("stock-jobbers").

merchant, and artisan, without ever meddling with any practical part in life. I am very well versed in the theory of an husband or a father, and can discern the errors in the economy, business, and diversion of others, better than those who are engaged in them; as standers-by discover blots,[3] which are apt to escape those who are in the game. I never espoused any party with violence, and am resolved to observe an exact neutrality between the Whigs and Tories,[4] unless I shall be forced to declare myself by the hostilities of either side. In short, I have acted in all the parts of my life as a looker-on, which is the character I intend to preserve in this paper.

I have given the reader just so much of my history and character as to let him see I am not altogether unqualified for the business I have undertaken. As for other particulars in my life and adventures, I shall insert them in following papers as I shall see occasion. In the mean time, when I consider how much I have seen, read, and heard, I begin to blame my own taciturnity; and since I have neither time nor inclination to communicate the fullness of my heart in speech, I am resolved to do it in writing; and to print my self out, if possible, before I die. I have been often told by my friends that it is pity so many useful discoveries which I have made should be in the possession of a silent man. For this reason therefore, I shall publish a sheet-full of thoughts every morning, for the benefit of my contemporaries; and if I can any way contribute to the diversion or improvement of the country in which I live, I shall leave it, when I am summoned out of it, with the secret satisfaction of thinking that I have not lived in vain. * * *

The Female Spectator (April 1744–May 1746)

The Female Spectator was the first periodical written by a woman for women. Its author, Eliza Haywood (c. 1693–1756), had been an actress, a playwright, and the writer of some sixty romances, novels, and other narratives, many of them scandalous and some of them wildly successful. In the mid-1740s, after a long eclipse prompted in part by Alexander Pope's derision of her in the *Dunciad,* Haywood emerged in a new guise: no longer a purveyor of exotic thrills, she set up instead as a teacher of morality. *The Female Spectator* differed from its namesake in calendar (monthly rather than daily) and format: a pamphlet and not a sheet, each number presented an essay focused on a single topic with several illustrative fictional stories interspersed. The biggest difference, though, was in the new paper's point of view. Mr. Spectator had observed, described, and instructed "the fair sex" from without, as supremely self-confident male mentor. Haywood offered instead a running report from the interior of women's lives. Her vantage point proved popular. *The Female Spectator* continued to sell, in a four-volume collected edition, for more than two decades after its periodical run had ceased.

from Female Spectator Vol. 1, No. 1
[THE AUTHOR'S INTENT]

It is very much by the choice we make of subjects for our entertainment that the refined taste distinguishes itself from the vulgar and more gross. Reading is universally allowed to be one of the most improving as well as agreeable amusements; but then to render it so, one should, among the number of books which are perpetually issuing from the press, endeavor to single out such as promise to be most conducive to those ends. In order to be as little deceived as possible, I, for my own part, love to get as

---

3. In backgammon, a blot is a piece whose position puts it at risk of being taken.
4. Addison and Steele maintained "neutrality" more strictly in the *Spectator* than they had in the *Tatler,* which had incurred much controversy by its Whig partisanship.

well acquainted as I can with an author, before I run the risk of losing my time in perusing his work; and as I doubt not but most people are of this way of thinking, I shall, in imitation of my learned brother of ever precious memory,[1] give some account of what I am, and those concerned with me in this undertaking; and likewise of the chief intent of the lucubrations[2] hereafter communicated, that the reader, on casting his eye over the four or five first pages, may judge how far the book may or may not be qualified to entertain him, and either accept or throw it aside as he thinks proper. And here I promise that in the pictures I shall give of myself and associates, I will draw no flattering lines, assume no perfection that we are not in reality possessed of, nor attempt to shadow over any defect with an artificial gloss.

As a proof of my sincerity, I shall in the first place assure him that for my own part I never was a beauty, and am now very far from being young (a confession he will find few of my sex ready to make). I shall also acknowledge that I have run through as many scenes of vanity and folly as the greatest coquette of them all. Dress, equipage,[3] and flattery were the idols of my heart. I should have thought that day lost which did not present me with some new opportunity of showing myself. My life, for some years, was a continued round of what I then called pleasure, and my whole time engrossed by a hurry of promiscuous diversions. But whatever inconveniences such a manner of conduct has brought upon myself, I have this consolation, to think that the public may reap some benefit from it. The company I kept was not, indeed, always so well chosen as it ought to have been, for the sake of my own interest or reputation; but then it was general, and by consequence furnished me not only with the knowledge of many occurrences, which otherwise I had been ignorant of, but also enabled me, when the too great vivacity of my nature became tempered with reflection, to see into the secret springs which gave rise to the actions I had either heard or been witness of—to judge of the various passions of the human mind, and distinguish those imperceptible degrees by which they become masters of the heart, and attain the dominion over reason. A thousand odd adventures, which at the time they happened made slight impression on me, and seemed to dwell no longer on my mind than the wonder they occasioned, now rise fresh to my remembrance, with this advantage, that the mystery I then, for want of attention, imagined they contained, is entirely vanished, and I find it easy to account for the cause by the consequence.

With this experience, added to a genius[4] tolerably extensive, and an education more liberal than is ordinarily allowed to persons of my sex, I flattered myself that it might be in my power to be in some measure both useful and entertaining to the public; and this thought was so soothing to those remains of vanity not yet wholly extinguished in me, that I resolved to pursue it, and immediately began to consider by what method I should be most likely to succeed. To confine myself to any one subject, I knew could please but one kind of taste, and my ambition was to be as universally read as possible. From my observations of human nature, I found that curiosity had more or less a share in every breast; and my business, therefore, was to hit this reigning humor in such a manner as that the gratification it should receive from being made acquainted with other people's affairs should at the same time teach every one to regulate their own.

1. Addison and Steele's Mr. Spectator.
2. Writings by candlelight; Haywood pointedly picks up Isaac Bickerstaff's catchword for his essays in the *Tatler*.

3. Fancy carriages, servants, and furniture.
4. Talent, ability.

Having agreed within myself on this important point, I commenced author, by setting down many things which, being pleasing to myself, I imagined would be so to others; but on examining them the next day, I found an infinite deficiency both in matter and style, and that there was an absolute necessity for me to call in to my assistance such of my acquaintance as were qulaified for that purpose. The first that occurred to me, I shall distinguish by the name of Mira, a lady descended from a family to which wit seems hereditary, married to a gentleman every way worthy of so excellent a wife, and with whom she lives in so perfect a harmony, that having nothing to ruffle the composure of her soul, or disturb those sparkling ideas she received from nature and education, left me no room to doubt if what she favored me with would be acceptable to the public. The next is a widow of quality, who not having buried her vivacity in the tomb of her lord, continues to make one in all the modish diversions of the times, so far, I mean, as she finds them consistent with innocence and honor; and as she is far from having the least austerity in her behavior, nor is rigid to the failings she is wholly free from herself, those of her acquaintance who had been less circumspect scruple not to make her the confidante of secrets they conceal from all the world beside. The third is the daughter of a wealthy merchant, charming as an angel, but endued with so many accomplishments that to those who know her truly, her beauty is the least distinguished part of her. This fine young creature I shall call Euphrosyne, since she has all the cheerfulness and sweetness ascribed to that goddess.[5]

These three approved my design, assured me of all the help they could afford, and soon gave a proof of it in bringing their several essays; but as the reader, provided the entertainment be agreeable, will not be interested from which quarter it comes, whatever productions I shall be favored with from these ladies, or any others I may hereafter correspond with, will be exhibited under the general title of *The Female Spectator*, and how many contributors soever there may happen to be to the work, they are to be considered only as several members of one body, of which I am the mouth. * * *

━━◆═◆═◆━━

Getting, Spending, Speculating

The periodical essay was one commodity among many, in an economy whose energies were evident almost everywhere: in shops stocked with new (often exotic) goods; at outposts in remote countries where trade was gradually being transmuted into empire; at London banks, where the apparatus of transaction (loans, bills, draughts) was rapidly being refined; in nearby coffeehouses, where the agents and accumulators of wealth paused during busy days to absorb substances imported from abroad (coffee, tobacco, chocolate) as well as that home-crafted item of consumption, the periodical essay itself. The essayists often construed their audience as though it consisted *primarily* of merchants, shopkeepers, and customers—of people profoundly concerned with the course of commerce, whatever their gender or occupation. Defoe, Addison, and Steele all wrote to celebrate trade (its new profusions and possibilities), but also to regularize it, to render it respectable, to reconcile it with notions of human excellence originating in an earlier culture centered on aristocracy. The *Review*, the *Tatler*, and the *Spectator* all undertook (as the historian J. G. A. Pocock has elegantly argued) to redefine the idea of "virtue," to shift its focus of application from the classically defined obligations of the hereditary landowner to the prudent calculation of the urban merchant, alert to realities and

5. Euphrosyne is one of the three Graces, sister goddesses in Greek mythology who possess (and bestow) the gift of beauty.

The *Gentleman's Magazine* :

St JOHN's GATE.

Lond.Gazette
Lond.Journ
Fog's Journ.
Applebee's ::
Read's : : : :
Craftsman ::
H. Spectator
Lit Courier of
Grubstreet
Lyp.Poeta
Daily.Post
Q. Advertiser
St James's Eb.
Whitehall Eb
Lond. Eb Eg
Weekly Misc
General Eve.
Old Whig
D. Gazetteer
Lon. P. Post
Com. Sense

York News
Dublin 5 : :
Edinburgh 2
Bristol : : : : :
Norwich 2
Exeter 2 : :
Worcester
Northampton
Gloucester : :
Stamford : :
Nottingham
Burp Journ.
Chester ditto
Derby ditto
Ipswich do.
Reading do.
Leeds Merc
Newcastle C.
Canterbury
Durham
Kendal
Boston : : ¶
Barbados :
Jamaica &c

For JANUARY, 1738.

CONTAINING,

(More in Quantity, and greater Variety, than any Book of the Kind and Price).

I. ORIGINAL ESSAYS, Moral : The Character of a *Good Man*, by a late illustrious Lady. Of the Magistrate's Right to punish ye Death. Prescience consistent with Liberty. Whether Heaven and Hell be Local.
II. —— PHILOLOGICAL : Essay on Tragedy, with *Horace's* four Rules for ye Drama. Answers to Biblical Questions.
III. —— MATHEMATICKS : A new Astronomical Equation, discover'd by Mr *Facio*. A Method to find the Longitude and Latitude at Sea.
IV. —— THE Lady's Adventure, and Love Letters from a Protestant Gent. to a Catholic Lady.
V. ESSAYS from the Weekly Papers. *The Literary Courier of Grub-street*. Characters of News-Papers. Advice to Ladies on their Return to *London*. *Zenger's* Tryal for printing a Libel. Rules

of Physiognomy in chusing Husbands. The Widow describ'd. The Character of a Prince Royal, &c.
VI. POETRY. A Poem, inscrib'd to the *Dublin* Society, by Mr *Arbuckle*. Ode on the Death of P. *George* of *Denmark*, by the celebrated Mr *Alsop*. Prologue to *Venice preserv'd*, by a Person of Quality. The Blind Boy, with the Musick correct. Songs, Epigrams, Ænigmas, &c.
VII. HISTORICAL. The King's Speech; Addresses of the Lords and Commons. The Secrets of Free-Masonry.
VIII. LISTS of Births, Mariages, and Deaths, &c.
IX. FOREIGN AFFAIRS. Match of Don *Carlos* with the Princess Royal of *Poland*, &c. Caution to Mariners.
X. Price of Stocks. Bill of Mortality.
XI. Register of Books.
XII. TABLE of Contents.

By *SYLVANUS URBAN*, Gent.

LONDON: Printed by E. CAVE at St JOHN's GATE, and Sold by the Booksellers of Town and Country ; of whom may be had any former Month.

Where the *Review, Tatler,* and *Spectator* defined themselves *against* their print contemporaries, other periodicals took a different tack. With so much information, instruction, and entertainment flowing from so many sources, a desire developed for a digest that might organize it all. No one catered more adroitly to this new market than did Edward Cave, founder and editor of *Gentleman's Magazine*, a monthly pamphlet whose title coined a pivotal new term for print. "Magazine" meant a military storehouse of provisions and artillery; the *Gentleman's Magazine* promised an intellectual storehouse similarly well stocked. Cave promised "more in quantity, and greater variety, than any book of the kind and price." He delivered on the promise by publishing extracts and abstracts from many periodicals, but he soon cultivated a stable of his own writers (including the young Samuel Johnson) who furnished his readers with an ever-widening range of fresh materials: biographies, poetry, parliamentary debates. The *Magazine*'s logo presents it as a compendium of other papers, but Cave had in fact produced a true original, "one of the most successful and lucrative pamphlets" (wrote Johnson, whose observation still holds true) "which literary history has upon record." The title page depicts the 200 year-old gatehouse where the *Gentleman's Magazine* was composed, printed, and sold (the building's fortress-like appearance may entail a visual pun, conjuring up the military meaning of "magazine"). The building is flanked by the names of papers that the *Magazine* has incorporated, one way or another, into its own pages (London papers on the left, provincial and foreign ones on the right). The fictitious name "Sylvanus Urban" conjures up both countryside (*sylvanus*, "wooded") and city; as the bottom lines make clear, Cave aimed his appeal at audiences in both domains.

probabilities in an economy awash with speculation and controlled by credit, where "what one owned was promises": promises by entrepreneurs in search of capital; by stock-jobbers selling hopes of future prosperity; by the government whose operations depended on intricately structured loans from its own citizens. One central concern of the periodicals was how to commute promise into actual prosperity, rather than mere air.

In the selections in this section, Addison rejoices in the commercial and cultural confluence at the Royal Exchange (London's shopping center). In a more sentimental vein, Steele tracks the consequences of foreign trade in the lives and feelings of two lovers. Defoe, by contrast, is harder-headed, more closely analytic. Unlike the authors of the *Spectator,* he had spent years in business, making and losing fortunes. Surveying the shops of London, Defoe declares (as in virtually every *Review*) his passion for trade, but he asks what prospects the *present* patterns of consumption actually hold forth.

Joseph Addison: Spectator No. 69
Saturday, 19 May 1711

[ROYAL EXCHANGE[1]]

> *Hic segetes, illic veniunt felicius uvae:*
> *Arborei foetus alibi, atque injussa virescunt*
> *Gramina. Nonne vides, croceos ut Tmolus odores,*
> *India mittit ebur, molles sua thura Sabaei?*
> *At Chalybes nudi ferrum, virosaque Pontus*
> *Castorea, Eliadum palmas Epirus equarum?*
> *Continuo has leges aeternaque foedera certis*
> *Imposuit Natura locis . . .* [2]

There is no place in the town which I so much love to frequent as the Royal Exchange. It gives me a secret satisfaction, and in some measure gratifies my vanity, as I am an Englishman, to see so rich an assembly of countrymen and foreigners consulting together upon the private business of mankind, and making this metropolis a kind of emporium for the whole earth. I must confess I look upon high-change[3] to be a great council, in which all considerable nations have their representatives. Factors[4] in the trading world are what ambassadors are in the politic world; they negotiate affairs, conclude treaties, and maintain a good correspondence between those wealthy societies of men that are divided from one another by seas and oceans, or live on the different extremities of a continent. I have often been pleased to hear disputes adjusted between an inhabitant of Japan and an alderman of London, or to see a subject of the Great Mogul[5] entering into a league with one of the Czar of Mus-

1. The Exchange, a quadrangle of arcades and shops surrounding a huge courtyard, had functioned as a crucial site of London commerce since its creation in 1570. Destroyed in the Great Fire, it was rebuilt from a new design in 1669. The illustration on the next page depicts both the original building by Thomas Gresham (upper right corner) and the later structure with its more intricate, Baroque ornamentation. Statues of English kings occupy the second-floor arches. At the center of the courtyard, the statue of Charles II in the garb of a Roman emperor enacts that favored comparison (echoed by Addison in his essay's epigraph from Virgil) between contemporary Britain and the ancient Roman Empire.

2. "Corn grows more plentifully here, grapes there. In other places grow trees laden with fruit, and grasses unbidden. Do you not see how Tmolus sends us its saffron perfumes; India her ivory; the soft Sabaens their frankincense; but the naked Chalybes send us iron, the Pontus pungent beaver-oil, and Epirus prize-winning Olympic horses? These perpetual laws and eternal covenants Nature has imposed on certain places" (Virgil, *Georgics* 1.54–61).

3. In addition to housing shops, the Exchange was a central meeting place for international merchants, who frequently closed deals in the courtyard. "High change" was that period when trading was at its peak.

4. Commercial agents.

5. The Indian emperor.

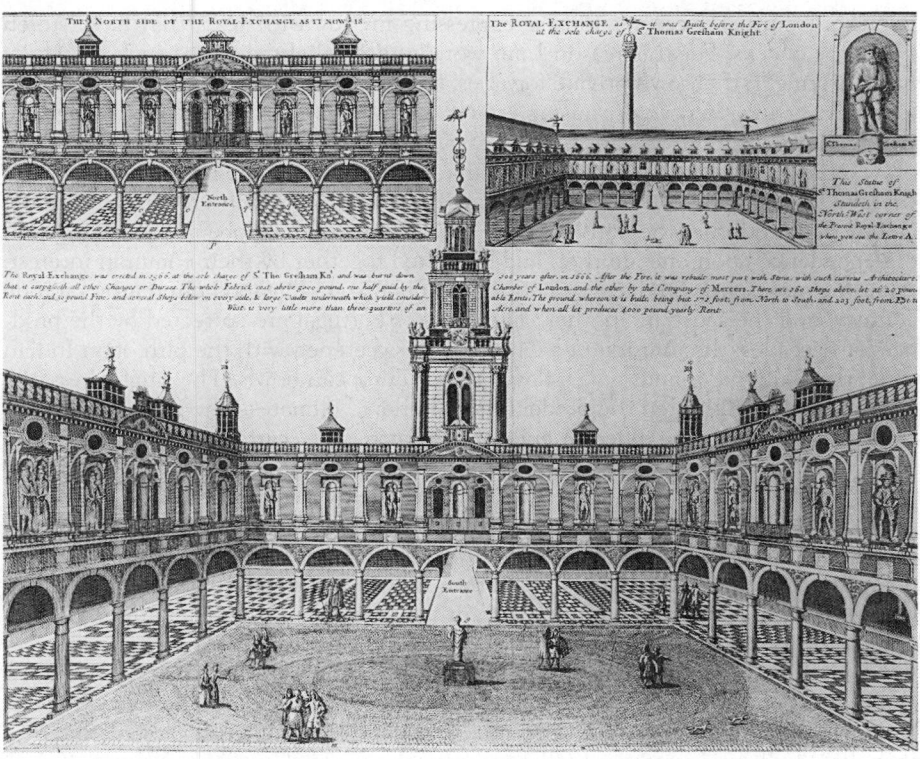

Sutton Nicholls. *The Royal Exchange*. 1712

covy.[6] I am infinitely delighted in mixing with these several ministers of commerce, as they are distinguished by their different walks and different languages. Sometimes I am jostled among a body of Armenians: sometimes I am lost in a crowd of Jews, and sometimes make one in a group of Dutchmen. I am a Dane, Swede, or Frenchman at different times, or rather fancy myself like the old philosopher,[7] who upon being asked what countryman he was, replied that he was a citizen of the world.

Though I very frequently visit this busy multitude of people, I am known to nobody there but my friend, Sir Andrew,[8] who often smiles upon me as he sees me bustling in the crowd, but at the same time connives at my presence without taking any further notice of me. There is indeed a merchant of Egypt, who just knows me by sight, having formerly remitted me some money to Grand Cairo;[9] but as I am not versed in the modern Coptic, our conferences go no further than a bow and a grimace.[1]

This grand scene of business gives me an infinite variety of solid and substantial entertainments. As I am a great lover of mankind, my heart naturally overflows with pleasure at the sight of a prosperous and happy multitude, insomuch that at many

6. A territory in west-central Russia (Moscow was its capital).
7. Diogenes the Cynic, credited for developing the concept of "cosmopolitanism"(citizenship in the universe), in which all beings are parts of a single whole.
8. Sir Andrew Freeport, a member of Mr. Spectator's

club: Whig merchant and ardent advocate (as his name implies) of free trade.
9. Where Mr. Spectator spent some time as a young man (see *Spectator* No. 1, page 951).
1. The word denoted an expression of politeness.

public solemnities I cannot forbear expressing my joy with tears that have stolen down my cheeks. For this reason I am wonderfully delighted to see such a body of men thriving in their own private fortunes, and at the same time promoting the public stock; or in other words, raising estates for their own families, by bringing into their country whatever is wanting, and carrying out of it whatever is superfluous.

Nature seems to have taken a particular care to disseminate her blessings among the different regions of the world, with an eye to this mutual intercourse and traffic among mankind, that the natives of the several parts of the globe might have a kind of dependence upon one another, and be united together by their common interest. Almost every degree produces something peculiar to it. The food often grows in one country, and the sauce in another. The fruits of Portugal are corrected by the products of Barbados; the infusion of a China plant sweetened with the pith of an Indian cane; the Philippic islands give a flavor to our European bowls. The single dress of a woman of quality is often the product of an hundred climates. The muff and the fan come together from the different ends of the Earth. The scarf is sent from the torrid zone, and the tippet from beneath the pole. The brocade petticoat rises out of the mines of Peru, and the diamond necklace out of the bowels of Indostan.

If we consider our own country in its natural prospect, without any of the benefits and advantages of commerce, what a barren uncomfortable spot of earth falls to our share! Natural historians tell us that no fruit grows originally among us, besides hips and haws, acorns and pig-nuts, with other delicacies of the like nature; that our climate of itself, and without the assistances of art, can make no further advances towards a plum than to a sloe,[2] and carries an apple to no greater a perfection than a crab;[3] that our melons, our peaches, our figs, our apricots, and cherries, are strangers among us, imported in different ages, and naturalized in our English gardens; and that they would all degenerate and fall away into the trash of our own country, if they were wholly neglected by the planter, and left to the mercy of our sun and soil. Nor has traffic more enriched our vegetable world, than it has improved the whole face of nature among us. Our ships are laden with the harvest of every climate; our tables are stored with spices, and oils, and wines; our rooms are filled with pyramids of China, and adorned with the workmanship of Japan; our morning's draught[4] comes to us from the remotest corners of the earth; we repair our bodies by the drugs of America, and repose ourselves under Indian canopies. My friend Sir Andrew calls the vineyards of France our gardens; the Spice Islands[5] our hotbeds; the Persians our silk weavers, and the Chinese our potters. Nature indeed furnishes us with the bare necessaries of life, but traffic gives us a great variety of what is useful, and at the same time supplies us with everything that is convenient and ornamental. Nor is it the least part of this our happiness, that whilst we enjoy the remotest products of the north and south, we are free from those extremities of weather which give them birth; that our eyes are refreshed with the green fields of Britain, at the same time that our palates are feasted with fruits that rise between the tropics.

For these reasons there are not more useful members in a commonwealth than merchants. They knit mankind together in a mutual intercourse of good offices, distribute the gifts of nature, find work for the poor, add wealth to the rich, and magnificence to the great. Our English merchant converts the tin of his own country into gold, and exchanges his wool for rubies. The Mahometans are clothed in our British manufacture, and the inhabitants of the frozen zone warmed with the fleeces of our sheep.

---

2. The berry of the blackthorn.   4. Drink.
3. Crabapple.   5. A cluster of islands in modern Indonesia.

When I have been upon the 'Change, I have often fancied one of our old kings[6] standing in person, where he is represented in effigy, and looking down upon the wealthy concourse of people with which that place is every day filled. In this case, how would he be surprised to hear all the languages of Europe spoken in this little spot of his former dominions, and to see so many private men, who in his time would have been the vassals of some powerful baron, negotiating like princes for greater sums of money than were formerly to be met with in the Royal Treasury! Trade, without enlarging the British territories, has given us a kind of additional empire: it has multiplied the number of the rich, made our landed estates infinitely more valuable than they were formerly, and added to them an accession of other estates as valuable as the lands themselves.

Richard Steele: Spectator No. 11
Tuesday, 13 March 1711

[INKLE AND YARICO[1]]

Dat veniam corvis, vexat censura columbas.[2]

Arietta is visited by all persons of both sexes who have any pretense to wit and gallantry. She is in that time of life which is neither affected with the follies of youth or infirmities of age; and her conversation is so mixed with gaiety and prudence that she is agreeable both to the young and the old. Her behavior is very frank, without being in the least blameable; and as she is out of the tract of any amorous or ambitious pursuits of her own, her visitants entertain her with accounts of themselves very freely, whether they concern their passions or their interests. I made her a visit this afternoon, having been formerly introduced to the honor of her acquaintance by my friend Will. Honeycomb,[3] who has prevailed upon her to admit me sometimes into her assembly, as a civil, inoffensive man. I found her accompanied with one person only, a commonplace talker who, upon my entrance, rose, and after a very slight civility sat down again; then turning to Arietta, pursued his discourse, which I found was upon the old topic of constancy in love. He went on with great facility in repeating what he talks every day of his life; and with the ornaments of insignificant laughs and gestures, enforced his arguments by quotations out of plays and songs, which allude to the perjuries of the fair, and the general levity[4] of women. Methought he strove to shine more than ordinarily in his talkative way, that he might insult my silence, and distinguish himself before a woman of Arietta's taste and understanding. She had often an inclination to interrupt him, but could find no opportunity, 'till the larum[5] ceased of itself; which it did not 'till he had repeated and murdered the celebrated story of the Ephesian matron.[6]

Arietta seemed to regard this piece of raillery as an outrage done to her sex, as indeed I have always observed that women, whether out of a nicer[7] regard to their

---

6. As depicted in the statues on the second story (see illustration on page 957).

1. Steele here elaborates on a 60-year-old traveler's tale, in such a way as to combine two of the *Spectator*'s central concerns: the transactions of love and power between men and women, and the impact of commerce on human conduct.

2. "Their verdict goes easy on the raven, but is severe on the dove" (Juvenal, *Satires* 2.63). The speaker, a woman, is complaining of how leniently men assess themselves, and how harshly they criticize women.

3. An aged member of Mr. Spectator's club, proud of his long-ago days as a Restoration rake, and still deeply interested in matters of the heart.

4. Lightness, fickleness.

5. The long-ringing alarm bell (of his talk).

6. The Roman story (told in Petronius's *Satyricon*, part 2) of a widow who, while mourning at the tomb of her newly deceased husband, succumbs to the attractions of a soldier standing nearby, and makes love with him on her husband's tomb.

7. More precise.

honor, or what other reason I cannot tell, are more sensibly touched with those general aspersions which are cast upon their sex, than men are by what is said of theirs.

When she had a little recovered herself from the serious anger she was in, she replied in the following manner.

"Sir, when I consider, how perfectly new all you have said on this subject is, and that the story you have given us is not quite two thousand years old, I cannot but think it a piece of presumption to dispute with you: but your quotations put me in mind of the fable of the lion and the man.[8] The man, walking with that noble animal, showed him, in the ostentation of human superiority, a sign of a man killing a lion. Upon which the lion said very justly, 'We lions are none of us painters, else we could show a hundred men killed by lions, for one lion killed by a man.' You men are writers, and can represent us women as unbecoming as you please in your works, while we are unable to return the injury. You have twice or thrice observed in your discourse that hypocrisy is the very foundation of our education; and that an ability to dissemble our affections is a professed part of our breeding. These, and such other reflections, are sprinkled up and down the writings of all ages, by authors who leave behind them memorials of their resentment against the scorn of particular women, in invectives against the whole sex. Such a writer, I doubt not, was the celebrated Petronius, who invented the pleasant aggravations of the frailty of the Ephesian lady; but when we consider this question between the sexes, which has been either a point of dispute or raillery ever since there were men and women, let us take facts from plain people, and from such as have not either ambition or capacity to embellish their narrations with any beauties of imagination. I was the other day amusing myself with Ligon's *Account of Barbados*; and, in answer to your well-wrought tale, I will give you (as it dwells upon my memory) out of that honest traveler, in his fifty-fifth page, the History of Inkle and Yarico.[9]

"Mr. Thomas Inkle[1] of London, aged 20 years, embarked in the Downs[2] on the good ship called the Achilles, bound for the West Indies, on the 16th of June 1647, in order to improve his fortune by trade and merchandise. Our adventurer was the third son of an eminent citizen, who had taken particular care to instill into his mind an early love of gain, by making him a perfect master of numbers, and consequently giving him a quick view of loss and advantage, and preventing the natural impulses of his passions, by prepossession towards his interests. With a mind thus turned, young Inkle had a person every way agreeable, a ruddy vigor in his countenance, strength in his limbs, with ringlets of fair hair loosely flowing on his shoulders. It happened, in the course of the voyage, that the Achilles, in some distress, put into a creek on the main of America, in search of provisions. The youth, who is the hero of my story, among others, went ashore on this occasion. From their first landing they were observed by a party of Indians, who hid themselves in the woods for that purpose. The English unadvisedly marched a great distance from the shore into the country, and were intercepted by the natives, who slew the greatest number of them. Our adventurer escaped among others, by flying

8. In Aesop's *Fables* (No. 219).
9. Richard Ligon's *True and Exact History of the Island of Barbados* (1657) includes a paragraph on a slave named Yarico and her misadventures in love, which Steele elaborates into the tale that follows.

1. Steele invents the name for this character; it means (perhaps prophetically) "linen tape," a common commodity.
2. A harbor on the southeastern coast of England.

into a forest. Upon his coming into a remote and pathless part of the wood, he threw himself, tired and breathless, on a little hillock, when an Indian maid rushed from a thicket behind him. After the first surprise, they appeared mutually agreeable to each other. If the European was highly charmed with the limbs, features, and wild graces of the naked American, the American was no less taken with the dress, complexion, and shape of an European, covered from head to foot. The Indian grew immediately enamored of him, and consequently solicitous for his preservation. She therefore conveyed him to a cave, where she gave him a delicious repast of fruits, and led him to a stream to slake his thirst. In the midst of these good offices, she would sometimes play with his hair, and delight in the opposition of its color to that of her fingers; then open his bosom, then laugh at him for covering it. She was, it seems, a person of distinction, for she every day came to him in a different dress, of the most beautiful shells, bugles, and bredes.[3] She likewise brought him a great many spoils, which her other lovers had presented to her; so that his cave was richly adorned with all the spotted skins of beasts, and most particolored feathers of fowls, which that world afforded. To make his confinement more tolerable, she would carry him in the dusk of the evening, or by the favor of moonlight, to unfrequented groves and solitudes, and show him where to lie down in safety, and sleep amidst the falls of waters, and melody of nightingales. Her part was to watch and hold him in her arms, for fear of her countrymen, and wake him on occasions to consult his safety. In this manner did the lovers pass away their time, till they had learned a language of their own, in which the voyager communicated to his mistress, how happy he should be to have her in his country, where she should be clothed in such silks as his waistcoat was made of, and be carried in houses drawn by horses, without being exposed to wind or weather. All this he promised her the enjoyment of, without such fears and alarms as they were there tormented with. In this tender correspondence these lovers lived for several months, when Yarico, instructed by her lover, discovered a vessel on the coast, to which she made signals, and in the night, with the utmost joy and satisfaction accompanied him to a ship's crew of his countrymen, bound for Barbados. When a vessel from the main arrives in that island, it seems the planters come down to the shore, where there is an immediate market of the Indians and other slaves, as with us of horses and oxen.

"To be short, Mr. Thomas Inkle, now coming into English territories, began seriously to reflect upon his loss of time, and to weigh with himself how many days' interest of his money he had lost during his stay with Yarico. This thought made the young man very pensive, and careful what account he should be able to give his friends of his voyage. Upon which considerations, the prudent and frugal young man sold Yarico to a Barbadian merchant; notwithstanding that the poor girl, to incline him to commiserate her condition, told him that she was with child by him; but he only made use of that information, to rise in his demands upon the purchaser."

I was so touched with this story, (which I think should be always a counterpart to the Ephesian matron) that I left the room with tears in my eyes; which a woman of Arietta's good sense did, I am sure, take for greater applause, than any compliments I could make her.

---

3. Tube-shaped glass beads and braiding.

A *Review of the State of the British Nation* (1704–1713)

Of the periodical commentators on the news, none was more formidable than Daniel Defoe, who single-handedly wrote his *Review* twice and sometimes thrice a week for nine years. The paper changed its name, its format, and its ostensible focus several times during its long run, but its general purposes remained the same throughout. Defoe wrote to celebrate trade, and to propose strategies for its improvement; to teach a rigorous piety and morality to a readership he saw as lax; and to advance by adroit advocacy the favorite programs of the paper's secret sponsor, Secretary of State Robert Harley (1661–1724). One of these was the Treaty of Union, whereby Scotland would merge under a single government with England and Wales to form the new national entity of Great Britain. Advocates of the measure construed it as a fair exchange, providing expanded trade for Scotland, enhanced security for England. In support of the cause, Defoe not only wrote copiously (pamphlets and essays as well as *Reviews*), he also persuaded Harley to send him to Scotland (where the prospect of Union was far from popular) to serve as chief strategist and propagandist. There, he argued energetically and successfully for passage of the treaty, while keeping his affiliation with Harley a close secret. When the Treaty of Union was ratified, the *Review* indulged in a moment of exultation, in the characteristic voice its creator had devised during his sustained periodic enterprise: that of a writer enmeshed in actual and volatile circumstance, deeply engaged with the politics, conduct, and commerce of the real world, sometimes embattled, often exasperated, occasionally exhausted, but ultimately indefatigable.

Daniel Defoe: *from* A Review of the State of the British Nation, Vol. 1, No. 43
Thursday, 8 January 1713

[WEAK FOUNDATIONS]

The subject of trade which I am now entered upon has this one excellency in it, for the benefit of the author, that really it can never be exhausted. * * * I remember some time ago I gave you a hint about the mighty alteration in the face of trade in this city; I cannot but touch it again on this occasion, because it relates to what I am upon. Let any man who remembers the glorious state of our trade about thirty or forty years past view but the streets of this opulent city and even the Exchange of London—nay, even our courts of law. It must of necessity put him in mind of Ezra 3.12, where the ancient men who had seen the old temple wept when they saw the weak foundations of the new.

However, to go on as I began and examine our new increase of commerce which we so must boast of: let me note a little to you with what mighty advantages the chasms, gaps, and breaches of our trade are filled up of late, and let us see it, I say, in the streets. Here, in the room of a trifling banker, or goldsmith, we are supplied with a most eminent brandy shop (Cheapside). There in the room of ditto you have a flaming shop[1] for white tea pots and luted earthen mugs (Cornhill), the most excellent offspring of that most valuable manufacture of earthenware. It is impossible that coffee, tea, and chocolate can be so advanced in their consumption without an eminent increase of those trades that attend them; whence we see the most noble shops in the city taken up with the valuable utensils of the tea table. The china warehouses are little marts within themselves (and by the way, are newly become markets of clandestine trade, of which I shall say more very quickly), and the eminent corner

---

1. A shop with a kiln for making earthenware.

houses in the chief streets of London are chosen out by the town tinkers to furnish us with tea kettles and chocolate pots—vide Catherine Street and Bedford Buildings. Two thousand pound is reckoned a small stock in copper pots and lacquered kettles, and the very fitting up one of these brazen people's shops with fine sashes,[2] etc., to set forth his ware, costs above 500£ sterling, which is more by half than the best draper or mercer's shop in London requires.

This certainly shows the increase of our trade. Brass locks for our chambers and parlors, brass knockers for our doors, and the like add to the luster of those shops, of which hereafter. And the same sash works, only finer and larger, are now used to range[3] your brass and copper, that the goldsmiths had always to set out their less valuable silver and gold plate. From hence, be pleased to look upon the druggists of the town who are the merchants of these things. Bucklers-Bury and Little Lombard Street were the places which a few years ago held the whole number, a very few excepted, of that difficult nice employment, whose number is now spread over the whole town and with the most capital stocks, whose whole employ is the furnishing us by wholesale and retail with these most valuable of all drugs, coffee, tea, and chocolate—the general furniture of a druggist's shop being now three bales of coffee, twelve boxes of chocolate, six large canisters of tea, and an hundred and fifty empty gilded boxes. In like manner the rest of the town—how gloriously it is supplied! How do pastry cooks and periwig makers, brandy shops and toy shops, succeed linen drapers, mercers, upholsterers, and the like. A hundred pounds to rent for a house to sell jellies and apple pies; two hundred pounds to fit up a brandy shop, and afterwards not a hundred pound stock to put into it. These I can show many instances of.

Look, gentlemen, upon the particular parts of your town, formerly eminent for the best of tradesmen! View the famous churchyard of St. Paul's where so many aldermen and lord mayors have been raised by the trade of broadcloth and mere woolen manufactures,[4] and on whose trades so many families of poor always depended, that Sir William Turner used to say his shop alone employed 50,000 poor people! What succeeds him? A most noble, and to be sure, a much more valuable vintner's warehouse, *Anglice*,[5] a tavern, more vulgarly a bawdyhouse. And the next draper's shop, a coffee house; what takes up the whole row there? and supplies the place of eighteen or nineteen topping drapers? Who can but observe it! Cane chair makers, gilders of leather, looking-glass shops, and peddlers or toy shops—manifold improvements of trade! and an eminent instance of the growth of our manufactures! * * *

Advertisements from the *Spectator*[1]

At the Lace Chamber on Ludgate Hill, kept by Mary Parsons, is a great quantity of Flanders lace, lately come over, to be sold off at great pennyworths[2] by wholesale or retail. She bought them there herself. [No. 200; Friday, 19 October 1711]

This day is published *The Court and City Vagaries*, being some late (and real) intrigues of several gentlemen and ladies. Written by one of the fair sex, price 6d. Sold by J. Baker in Paternoster Row. [No. 255; Saturday, 22 December 1711]

---

2. Windows made up of two sliding frames (common now, new and fancy at this time).
3. Display.
4. The trade in textiles had provided the foundation for many family fortunes and (hence) political careers.
5. In English.

1. Periodicals did not merely comment on commerce, they participated in it, earning much of their revenue from the advertisements that they printed at the conclusion of their main editorial matter.
2. At a terrific bargain.

The famous Italian water, for dying red and grey hairs of the head and eyebrows into a lasting brown or black; at 1, 2, or 4s. the bottle, with printed directions for the use of it. To be had at Mrs. Hannam's toyshop, at the sign of the Three Angels near the Half-Moon Tavern in Cheapside. [Vol. 8, No. 634; Friday, 17 December 1714]

The ladies that called at Mr. Charles Lillie's at the corner of Beauford Buildings,[3] in a hackney coach on Wednesday night, the 6th of this instant, about 10 o'clock, are desired to let him know where to direct to them, he being now able to give a particular account of what they enquired after. [No. 305; Tuesday, 19 February 1712]

Women and Men, Manners and Marriage

When Isaac Bickerstaff, in his first *Tatler*, undertook to teach his readers "what to think," politics was apparently what he most expected them to think about. Soon, though, he found a second focus: that cluster of questions today grouped under the rubric "gender." Bickerstaff, his imitators, and his successors strove constantly to instruct men and women as to who they were, what they should become, how they differed from each other, how they ought to interact, and how they might most happily merge in love and marriage. The *Tatler*, the *Review*, and the *Spectator* all urged men to supplant aggression with morality and grace; women to cultivate sound sense over mere caprice; and both sexes to ground their marriages in reciprocity, love, and reason, rather than financial gain or impulsive passion.

The essayists' instruction, though, was far from even-handed. "I will not meddle with the *Spectator*," Jonathan Swift wrote scornfully to Stella in 1711. "Let him *fair-sex* it to the world's end." Addison and Steele had used that phrase obsessively to describe, address, and instruct their female readers; it had by now become a kind of shorthand for a variable blend of courtesy and condescension endemic to the periodicals, almost all of which were written by men and directed at an audience in which males possessed a barely questioned sway. Nonetheless, women had for more than a decade occupied an important (albeit elusive) place in the periodical scheme of things, as purchasers, as readers, as participants. In the early 1690s, when John Dunton launched the first "question and answer" periodical, he quickly discovered that queries submitted by women were abundant, popular, and profitable. In the wake of his *Athenian Mercury*, almost all important periodicals devised strategies for incorporating "the fair sex" into their texts and even into their titles: Mr. Spectator sketched lines of identification between his silent, self-contained conduct, and the proper demeanor of the women whom he proposed to instruct; the *Tatler* proposed to "honor" (but also mocked) its female audience by its choice of title; many periodicals bore titles pitched even more explicitly at women: the *Female Tatler*, the *Ladies' Almanac*, the *Ladies' Magazine*, etc.

Such "inclusion" entailed obvious control. If the periodicals took up women's questions, they almost invariably supplied men's answers (even the *Ladies'* titles were mostly run by men). Eliza Haywood's *Female Spectator*, written not only for women but by a woman, offered something different. Far more fascinated with women's predicaments than with men's opinions, it helped foster a tradition of women's writing that grew richer and more various (encompassing novels and tracts as well as periodicals) as the century progressed.

---

3. Charles Lillie, a close associate of Addison's and Steele's, owned a perfume shop in the Strand. He had been one of the publishers and distributors of the *Tatler*, and sold the *Spectator* at his shop, where he also accepted advertisements for inclusion in the paper.

Richard Steele: *from* Tatler No. 104
Thursday, 8 December 1709

[JENNY DISTAFF NEWLY MARRIED[1]]

—*Garrit aniles*
Ex re Fabellas.—[2]

From My Own Apartment, December 7

My brother[3] Tranquillus being gone out of town for some days, my sister Jenny sent me word she would come and dine with me, and therefore desired me to have no other company. I took care accordingly, and was not a little pleased to see her enter the room with a decent and matronlike behavior, which I thought very much became her. I saw she had a great deal to say to me, and easily discovered in her eyes, and the air of her countenance, that she had abundance of satisfaction in her heart, which she longed to communicate. However, I was resolved to let her break into her discourse her own way, and reduced her to a thousand little devices and intimations to bring me to the mention of her husband. But finding I was resolved not to name him, she began of her own accord; my husband (said she) gives his humble service to you: to which I only answered, I hope he is well; and without waiting for a reply, fell into other subjects. She at last was out of all patience, and said (with a smile and manner that I thought had more beauty and spirit than I had ever observed before in her) I did not think, Brother, you had been so ill-natured. You have seen ever since I came in, that I had a mind to talk of my husband, and you won't be so kind as to give me an occasion. I did not know (said I) but it might be a disagreeable subject to you. You do not take me for so old-fashioned a fellow as to think of entertaining a young lady with the discourse of her husband. I know, nothing is more acceptable than to speak of one who is to be so; but to speak of one who is so! Indeed, Jenny, I am a better bred man than you think me. She showed a little dislike at my raillery; and by her bridling up, I perceived she expected to be treated hereafter not as Jenny Distaff, but Mrs. Tranquillus. I was very well pleased with this change in her humor; and upon talking with her on several subjects, I could not but fancy that I saw a great deal of her husband's way and manner in her remarks, her phrases, the tone of her voice, and the very air of her countenance. This gave me an unspeakable satisfaction, not only because I had found her an husband, from whom she could learn many things that were laudable, but also because I looked upon her imitation of him as an infallible sign that she entirely loved him. This is an observation that I never knew fail, though I do not remember that any other has made it. The natural shyness of her sex hindered her from telling me the greatness of her own passion; but I easily collected it, from the representation she gave me of his. I have everything, says she, in Tranquillus that I can wish for; and enjoy in him (what indeed you have told me were to be met with in a good husband) the fondness of a lover, the tenderness of a parent, and the intimacy of a friend. It transported me to see her eyes swimming in tears of affection when she spoke. And is there not, Dear Sister, said I, more pleasure in the

---

1. Jenny Distaff is Isaac Bickerstaff's half-sister. In some earlier *Tatlers* (Nos. 10 and 33), she appeared as an essayist in her own right, composing pieces for the paper whenever her brother was out of town. In more recent numbers (75, 79), Bickerstaff had told the story of arranging her marriage to "Tranquillus" ("the calm one"),

which he described as "a domestic affair of great importance, . . . no less than the disposal of my sister Jenny for life."
2. "He tells an old wives' tale very pertinently" (Horace, *Satires* 2.6.77–78).
3. Brother-in-law.

possession of such a man, than in all the little impertinencies[4] of balls, assemblies, and equipage, which it cost me so much pains to make you condemn? She answered, smiling, Tranquillus has made me a sincere convert in a few weeks, though I am afraid you could not have done it in your whole life. To tell you truly, I have only one fear hanging upon me, which is apt to give me trouble in the midst of all my satisfactions: I am afraid, you must know, that I shall not always make the same amiable appearance in his eye that I do at present. You know, Brother Bickerstaff, that you have the reputation of a conjurer; and if you have any one secret in your art to make your sister always beautiful, I should be happier than if I were mistress of all the worlds you have shown me in a starry night. Jenny (said I) without having recourse to magic, I shall give you one plain rule, that will not fail of making you always amiable to a man who has so great a passion for you, and is of so equal and reasonable a temper as Tranquillus. Endeavor to please, and you must please; be always in the same disposition as you are when you ask for this secret, and, you may take my word, you will never want it. An inviolable fidelity, good humor, and complacency of temper, outlive all the charms of a fine face, and make the decays of it invisible.

We discoursed very long upon this head, which was equally agreeable to us both; for I must confess, (as I tenderly love her) I take as much pleasure in giving her instructions for her welfare, as she herself does in receiving them. * * *

Joseph Addison: Spectator No. 128
Friday, 27 July 1711

[Variety of Temper[1]]

. . . Concordia discors.[2]

Women in their nature are much more gay and joyous than men; whether it be that their blood is more refined, their fibers more delicate, and their animal spirits more light and volatile; or whether, as some have imagined, there may not be a kind of sex in the very soul,[3] I shall not pretend to determine. As vivacity is the gift of women, gravity is that of men. They should each of them therefore keep a watch upon the particular bias which nature has fixed in their minds, that it may not draw too much, and lead them out of the paths of reason. This will certainly happen, if the one in every word and action affects the character of being rigid and severe, and the other of being brisk and airy. Men should beware of being captivated by a kind of savage philosophy, women by a thoughtless gallantry. Where these precautions are not observed, the man often degenerates into a cynic, the woman into a coquette; the man grows sullen and morose, the woman impertinent and fantastical.[4]

By what I have said we may conclude, men and women were made as counterparts to one another, that the pains and anxieties of the husband might be relieved by the sprightliness and good humor of the wife. When these are rightly tempered, care and cheerfulness go hand in hand; and the family, like a ship that is duly trimmed, wants neither sail nor ballast.

4. Irrelevancies, distractions.
1. Lady Mary Wortley Montagu praised this essay in a letter written to her husband shortly after it appeared: "One of the *Spectators* is very just, that says a man ought always to be on his guard against spleen and too severe a philosophy; a woman against levity and coquetry."

2. "Discordant concord" (i.e., harmony arising from difference; Lucan, *Pharsalia* 1.98).
3. In *Tatler* No. 172, Steele had asserted that "there is a sort of sex in souls" (i.e., an essential difference between men and women).
4. Irrelevant in her talk, preposterous in her thought.

Natural historians observe (for whilst I am in the country I must fetch my allusions from thence[5]) that only the male birds have voices; that their songs begin a little before feeding-time, and end a little after; that whilst the hen is covering her eggs, the male generally takes his stand upon a neighboring bough within her hearing; and by that means amuses and diverts her with his songs during the whole time of her sitting.

This contract among birds lasts no longer than till a brood of young ones arises from it; so that in the feathered kind, the cares and fatigues of the married state, if I may so call it, lie principally upon the female. On the contrary, as in our species the man and woman are joined together for life, and the main burden rests upon the former, nature has given all the little arts of soothing and blandishment to the female, that she may cheer and animate her companion in a constant and assiduous application to the making a provision for his family, and the educating of their common children. This however is not to be taken so strictly, as if the same duties were not often reciprocal, and incumbent on both parties; but only to set forth what seems to have been the general intention of Nature, in the different inclinations and endowments which are bestowed on the different sexes.

But whatever was the reason that man and woman were made with this variety of temper, if we observe the conduct of the fair sex, we find that they choose rather to associate themselves with a person who resembles them in that light and volatile humor which is natural to them, than to such as are qualified to moderate and counterbalance it. It has been an old complaint, that the coxcomb carries it[6] with them before the man of sense. When we see a fellow loud and talkative, full of insipid life and laughter, we may venture to pronounce him a female favorite. Noise and flutter are such accomplishments as they cannot withstand. To be short, the passion of an ordinary woman for a man, is nothing else but self-love diverted upon another object: she would have the lover a woman in every thing but the sex. I do not know a finer piece of satire on this part of womankind than those lines of Mr. Dryden,

> Our thoughtless sex is caught by outward form
> And empty noise, and loves itself in man.[7]

This is a source of infinite calamities to the sex, as it frequently joins them to men who in their own thoughts are as fine creatures as themselves; or if they chance to be good-humored, serve only to dissipate their fortunes, inflame their follies, and aggravate their indiscretions.

The same female levity is no less fatal to them after marriage than before. It represents to their imaginations the faithful prudent husband as an honest tractable and domestic animal, and turns their thoughts upon the fine gay gentleman that laughs, sings, and dresses so much more agreeably.

As this irregular vivacity of temper leads astray the hearts of ordinary women in the choice of their lovers and the treatment of their husbands, it operates with the same pernicious influence towards their children, who are taught to accomplish themselves in all those sublime perfections that appear captivating in the eye of their mother. She admires in her son what she loved in her gallant; and by that means contributes all she can to perpetuate herself in a worthless progeny.

The younger Faustina[8] was a lively instance of this sort of women. Notwithstanding she was married to Marcus Aurelius, one of the greatest, wisest, and best of

---

5. Mr. Spectator is visiting the country estate of his friend and club fellow, Sir Roger de Coverley.
6. Succeeds.
7. From John Dryden's tragedy *Oedipus* (1.1).

8. Annia Galeria Faustina (d. A.D. 175), wife of Marcus Aurelius (A.D. 121–180), cherished by her husband but dispraised by ancient writers as an unfaithful wife.

the Roman emperors, she thought a common gladiator much the prettier gentleman; and had taken such care to accomplish[9] her son Commodus according to her own notions of a fine man, that when he ascended the throne of his father, he became the most foolish and abandoned tyrant that was ever placed at the head of the Roman Empire, signalizing himself in nothing but the fighting of prizes, and knocking out men's brains. As he had no taste of true glory, we see him in several medals and statues which are still extant of him, equipped like an Hercules with a club and a lion's skin.

I have been led into this speculation by the characters I have heard of a country gentleman and his lady, who do not live many miles from Sir Roger. The wife is an old coquette, that is always hankering after the diversions of the town; the husband is a morose rustic, that frowns and frets at the name of it; the wife is overrun with affectation, the husband sunk into brutality. The lady cannot bear the noise of the larks and nightingales, hates your tedious summer days, and is sick at the sight of shady woods and purling streams; the husband wonders how any one can be pleased with the fooleries of plays and operas, and rails from morning to night at essenced[1] fops and tawdry courtiers. The children are educated in these different notions of their parents. The sons follow the father about his grounds, while the daughters read volumes of love letters and romances to their mother. By this means it comes to pass, that the girls look upon their father as a clown, and the boys think their mother no better than she should be.

How different are the lives of Aristus and Aspatia? The innocent vivacity of the one is tempered and composed by the cheerful gravity of the other. The wife grows wise by the discourses of the husband, and the husband good-humored by the conversations of the wife. Aristus would not be so amiable were it not for his Aspatia, nor Aspatia so much to be esteemed were it not for her Aristus. Their virtues are blended in their children, and diffuse through the whole family a perpetual spirit of benevolence, complacency, and satisfaction.

Eliza Haywood: *from* The Female Spectator, Vol. 1, No. 1
April 1744

[SEOMANTHE'S ELOPEMENT[1]]

Seomanthe, to her misfortune, was brought up under the tuition of her aunt Negratia,[2] a woman extremely sour by nature, but rendered yet more so by age and infirmity. Past all the joys of life herself, she looked with a malicious eye on every one who partook of them, censured the most innocent diversions in the severest manner, and the least complaisance between persons of different sexes was, with her, scandalous to the last degree. Her character was so well known that none but prudes, whose deformity was an antidote to desire (worn-out, superannuated rakes, who had outlived all sense of pleasure) and canting zealots,[3] whose bread depended on their hypocrisy, frequented her house. To this sort of company was the young, beautiful, and naturally gay Seomanthe condemned. She heard nothing but railing against that

---

9. Educate.
1. Perfumed.
1. Haywood tells this story to illustrate her point that it is sometimes wrong to blame young women for marrying unwisely; parents and other authorities "are sometimes,

by an over-caution, guilty of forcing them into things, which otherwise would be far distant from their thoughts."
2. The name means "unpleasing."
3. People pretending to fanatic piety.

way of life she knew was enjoyed by others of equal rank and fortune with herself, and which she had too much good sense to look upon as criminal. She thought people might be perfectly innocent, yet indulge themselves in sometimes going to a play or opera; nor could be brought to believe the court such a bugbear[4] as she was told it was: a laced coat and a toupee wig had double charms for her, as they were every day so much preached against; and she never saw a coach pass, wherein were gentlemen and ladies, but she wished to be among them, or a well-dressed beau, with whom she did not languish to be acquainted.

At length her desires were fulfilled. Close as she was kept, the report that Negratia had a young lady in her house, who was mistress of a large fortune on the day of marriage, reached the ears of one of those harpies who purchase to themselves a wretched sustenance, by decoying the unwary into everlasting ruin. This creature, who had been employed by one so far a gentleman as to be bred to no business, and whose whole estate was laid out on his back,[5] in hopes of appearing charming in the eyes of some moneyed woman, too truly guessed she had found in Seomanthe what she sought. She came to the house under the pretense of offering some lace, holland,[6] and fine tea, extraordinary cheap. Negratia being what is called a good housewife, and a great lover of bargains, readily admitted her; and while she was examining some of the goods at a small distance off, the artful woman put a letter into Seomanthe's hand, telling her it came from the finest gentleman in the world, who she was sure would die, if she did not favor him with an answer. The young lady took it, blushed, and put it in her bosom, but had not time to make any reply to the woman, Negratia that instant coming towards them. As nobody understood her business better, she managed it so that she was ordered to come again the next day, when she said she should have greater variety to show their ladyships. While she was packing up her bundles, she winked on Seomanthe, and at the same time gave her the most beseeching look; the meaning of which, young and unexperienced as she was, the destined victim but too well comprehended, and was, perhaps, no less impatient for the success of an adventure, the beginning of which afforded her infinite satisfaction.

She ran immediately to her chamber, shut herself in, and broke open her billet,[7] which she found stuffed with flames, darts, wounds, love, and death; the highest encomiums on her beauty, and the most vehement imprecations of not outliving his hope of obtaining her favor—expressions which would have excited only the laughter of a woman who knew the world, but drew tears into the eyes of the innocent Seomanthe. She imagined he had seen her either at church or looking out of the window, for she was permitted to show herself in no other place; and doubted not but all he had wrote to her of his love and despair, was no less true than what she had heard delivered from the pulpit. She looked upon herself as too much obliged by the passion he had for her, not to write an answer full of complaisance, and very dexterously gave it to the woman, on her coming the next day.

On the ensuing Sunday she saw a strange gentleman in the next pew to her; by the glances he stole at her every time he could do it without being taken notice of, she fancied him the person who had declared himself her lover, and was convinced her conjecture had not deceived her, when being kneeled down at her devotions, he

4. Danger (with the illusory connotation of "boogey-man").
5. Spent on clothing.

6. Imported fabric.
7. Letter.

found means, while everyone had their fans before their faces, to drop a letter on the bench she leaned upon. She was not so much taken up with the business she was employed about, as not to see it immediately, and throwing her handkerchief over it, clapped it into her pocket. The looks that passed between them afterwards, during the time of divine service, confirmed her in the opinion that he was no less charmed with her than he said he was; and him, that the sight of him had not destroyed the impression his letter by the old woman had made on her.

Both thought they had reason to be highly satisfied with this interview; but poor Seomanthe was up to the head and ears in love. The person of the man was agreeable enough, and, compared to those Negratia had suffered her to converse with, angelic. The prepossession she had for him, at least, rendered him so in her eyes, and she thought every moment an age till she got home to read this second billet, the contents of which were of the same nature with the former, only a postscript added, entreating she would contrive some means to let him entertain her with his passion, by word of mouth. He mentioned the woman who sold the things, and by whose means he at first made a discovery of it,[8] and gave the directions where she lived; begged a meeting there, if possible; at least an answer, whether he might be so happy or not; which, he told her, he would wait for himself early the next morning under her window, if she would be so good as to throw it out.

She sighed at reading it; thought her fate very hard that it was not in her power to comply with the first part of his request, but hesitated not in the least if she ought to grant the other. She snatched the first opportunity she could lay hold on to prepare a letter, in which she let him know how impossible it was for her to come out; but expressed such a regret at not being able to do so, as showed it would be no difficult matter to prevail on her to run the greatest lengths.

By the help of his adviser, he carried on a correspondence with her, which ended in her consenting to quit Negratia forever, and put herself under his protection. In fine, she packed up all her clothes and jewels, threw the former from the window to the woman, who stood ready to receive them on an appointed night; and having put the other into her pocket, exchanged one scene of hypocrisy for another, and flew from a life irksome for the present, to enter into one of lasting misery.

Early in the morning they were married, and it is possible passed some days in the usual transports of a bridal state. But when their place of abode was discovered by the friends and kindred of Seomanthe, who, distracted at her elopement, had searched the whole town, in how wretched a manner was she found! The villain had drawn her whole fortune out of the bank, robbed her of all her jewels and the best of her apparel, had shipped everything off, and was himself embarked she knew not to what place. The people of the house where they lodged, perceiving him, whom they expected to have been their paymaster, gone, seized on the few trifles he had left behind, as satisfaction for the rent, and were going to turn the unfortunate Seomanthe out of doors.

Not the sight of her distress, nor the lamentations she made, which were pitiful enough to have softened the most rugged hearts, had any effect on that of Negratia, who thought no punishment too severe for a person who had deceived her caution. But some others were of a more compassionate disposition. They took her home with them, and comforted her as well as they were able. She still lives with them a dependent on their courtesy, which she is obliged to purchase

---

8. I.e., had revealed his passion.

the continuance of, by rendering herself subservient to all their humors.[9] No news is yet arrived what course her wicked husband took; but it is supposed he is retired either to France or Holland, being almost as much in debt here, as all he wronged Seomanthe of would discharge; so that there is little probability of his ever returning, or if he did, that it would be at all to the satisfaction of his unhappy wife.

I was going on to recite some other instances of the mischiefs, which, for the most part, are the consequence of laying young people under too great a restraint, when Mira[1] came in, and seeing what I was about, took the pen out of my hand, and told me I had already said enough; if I proceeded to expatiate any farther on that head, I should be in danger of being understood to countenance an extreme on the other side,[2] which was much more frequently fatal to our sex.

I yielded to her superior judgment, and needed but few arguments to be convinced, that if unbridled youth were indulged in all the liberties it would take, we should scarce see anything but unhappy objects before maturity arrived.

Eliza Haywood: *from The Female Spectator,* Vol. 2, No. 10
February 1745

[WOMEN'S EDUCATION]

We[1] were beginning to lament the misfortunes our sex frequently fall into through the want of those improvements we are doubtless capable of, when a letter, left for us at our publisher's, was brought in which happened to be on that subject, and cannot anywhere be more properly inserted than in this place.

To the Female Spectator

Ladies,

Permit me to thank you for the kind and generous task you have undertaken in endeavoring to improve the minds and manners of our unthinking sex. It is the noblest act of charity you could exercise in an age like ours, where the sense of good and evil is almost extinguished, and people desire to appear more vicious than they really are, that so they may be less unfashionable. This humor, which is too prevalent in the female sex, is the true occasion of the many evils and dangers to which they are daily exposed. No wonder the men of sense disregard us! and the dissolute triumph over that virtue they ought to protect!

Yet I think it would be cruel to charge the ladies with all the errors they commit; it is most commonly the fault of a wrong education, which makes them frequently do amiss, while they think they act not only innocently but uprightly. It is therefore only the men—and the men of understanding, too—who, in effect, merit the blame of this, and are answerable for all the misconduct we are guilty of. Why do they call us silly women, and not endeavor to make us otherwise? God and Nature has endued them with means, and custom has established them in the power of rendering our minds such as they ought to be. How highly ungenerous is it then to give us a wrong turn, and then despise us for it!

---

9. Whims, moods.
1. One of the Female Spectator's collaborators.

2. I.e., in favor of leniency.
1. The Female Spectator and her collaborators.

The Mahometans indeed enslave their women, but then they teach them to believe their inferiority will extend to eternity. But our case is even worse than this; for while we live in a free country, and are assured from our excellent Christian principles that we are capable of those refined pleasures which last to immortality, our minds, our better parts, are wholly left uncultivated, and, like a rich soil neglected, bring forth nothing but noxious weeds.

There are, undoubtedly, no sexes in souls; and we are as able to receive and practice the impressions, not only of virtue and religion, but also of those sciences which the men engross to themselves, as they can be. Surely our bodies were not formed by the great Creator out of the finest mold, that our souls might be neglected like the coarsest of the clay?

O! would too imperious and too tenacious man be so just to the world as to be more careful of the education of those females to whom they are parents or guardians! Would they convince them in their infancy, that dress and show are not the essentials of a fine lady, and that true beauty is seated in the mind; how soon should we see our sex retrieve the many virtues which false taste has buried in oblivion! Strange infatuation! to refuse us what would so much contribute to their own felicity! Would not themselves reap the benefit of our amendment? Should we not be more obedient daughters, more faithful wives, more tender mothers, more sincere friends, and more valuable in every other station of life?

But, I find, I have let my pen run a much greater length than I at first intended. If I have said anything worthy your notice, or what you think the truth of the case, I hope you will mention this subject in some of your future essays; or if you find I have any way erred in my judgment, to set me right will be the greatest favor you can confer on,

Ladies,
Your constant reader,
And humble servant,
CLEORA

Hampton Court,
January 12, 1744–45

After thanking this lady for the favor of her obliging letter, we think it our duty to congratulate her on being one of those happy few who have been blessed with that sort of education which she so pathetically laments the want of in the greatest part of our sex.

Those men are certainly guilty of a great deal of injustice who think that all the learning becoming in a woman is confined to the management of her family; that is, to give orders concerning the table, take care of her children in their infancy, and observe that her servants do not neglect their business. All this, no doubt, is very necessary; but would it not be better if she performs those duties more through principle than custom? And will she be less punctual in her observance of them after she becomes a wife, for being perfectly convinced, before she is so, of the reasonableness of them, and why they are expected from her?

Many women have not been inspired with the least notion of even those requisites in a wife, and when they become so, continue the same loitering, lolloping, idle creatures they were before; and then the men are ready enough to condemn those who had the care of their education. * * *

[END OF PERSPECTIVES: READING PAPERS]

John Dryden

1631–1700

In his last years, Dryden often felt the need to defend his morals, his religion, his politics, even his writing. For nearly a quarter of a century, he had held high literary office and mingled with the great; he had curried royal favor and aristocratic patronage, bolstering officialdom, aiming to injure the Crown's enemies and to caress its friends. He wrote about politics and religion, about trade and empire; he wrote for the theater and for public occasions; he composed songs, fables, odes, and panegyrics, brilliant satire and savage polemic; he translated from many languages and formulated an idiomatic, familiar, and fluent prose style. Dryden virtually invented the idea of a commercial literary career; and through all the turns of a difficult public life, he fashioned from his own unlikely personality—from his privacy, self-doubts, and hesitations—a public figure of literary distinction. But he attained this celebrity at the cost of gossip and scandal, and in the last decade of his life (after the Glorious Revolution and his deposition from the Poet Laureateship) he faced suspicion and scorn.

The poet's beginnings give no hint of literary greatness or the likelihood of fame. He was born in 1631 in a country town and to comfortable circumstance; he was educated at Westminster School and graduated from Trinity College, Cambridge. He held minor public office in the 1650s but had written almost nothing before he was twenty-seven. Dryden then began his long career as public poet. He mourned the Lord Protector in 1659 (*Heroic Stanzas*) and then, in what looks like a convenient turn of allegiance, he celebrated the return of monarchy in 1660, writing poems to Charles II, to the Lord Chancellor, and to the Duchess of York; he praised the Royal Society (*To Doctor Charleton*) and defended the Royal Navy and its aristocratic high command (*Annus Mirabilis*, 1667).

The first years seem a series of calculated moves; and the combination of talent, application, and opportunity was crowned when Dryden was named Poet Laureate in 1667. But in addition to fashioning a career in the 1660s, Dryden also forged a new drama—an epic theater whose themes and language echoed the idioms of heroic verse—and a body of literary criticism that itself would have made his lasting reputation. Indeed, the great text of the first decade was the *Essay of Dramatic Poesy* (1668), Dryden's formulation of a pointedly English poetics and theater. Along with Sir Philip Sidney's *Defence of Poesy*, and Samuel Johnson's *Lives of the Poets*, Dryden's *Essay* is central to the long-standing canon of English literary criticism. Some of Dryden's early plays have been forgotten, but he worked steadily at a craft that would enable him to turn Milton's *Paradise Lost* into theater (*The State of Innocence*, 1677), create a superb adaptation of Shakespeare's *Antony and Cleopatra* in *All for Love* (1678), the finest of Restoration tragedies in *Don Sebastian* (1690), and the texts of one of England's first operas, *King Arthur* (1691), and last masques, *The Pilgrim* (1700).

By the late 1670s Dryden was famed as publicist for the Crown, and his theatrical work had come to dominate the stage; but he had hardly begun the career as satirist by which he is now best known. Its opening move was *Mac Flecknoe* (1676), and in the next few years Dryden fashioned masterpieces of literary mockery and political invective, poems that virtually created literary genres and dominated satire for decades to come. *Mac Flecknoe* allowed Dryden to ridicule and crush his rivals, all the while conjuring the suave tones and elegant manners of literary supremacy. In the abuse of rivals, only Pope surpasses Dryden as a master of scorn. But *Mac Flecknoe* was only the first act in a theater of invective. In the fall of 1681 Dryden wrote *Absalom and Achitophel*, a biblical allegory occasioned by the crisis of succession. The king had failed to beget a legitimate heir, and the king's Catholic brother waited ominously in the wings. It was Dryden's job to defend the Crown, to extenuate royal indulgence, and, especially, to defuse anxieties. With *Absalom and Achitophel*, Dryden wove together the Bible and contemporary politics with such deftness that mere diversionary tactics were spun into an incomparable allegory of envy, ambition, and misdeed. The satire was read, marked, circulated, and treasured as a masterpiece and a menace.

The masterpiece secured Dryden's fame; the menace exacted a cost. The poet had attacked powerful men: aristocrats, politicans, and their partisan hacks who intrigued against the Crown. They failed in the early 1680s to foment rebellion, but by 1688 they were able to effect a revolution that deposed Catholic monarchy and the Poet Laureate himself. Dryden was reputed a brilliant and damaging advocate of Stuart rule; he had collaborated with court publicity and polemic; he had even converted to Roman Catholicism after James ascended the throne. Indeed, Dryden wrote his longest and most elaborate original poem—*The Hind and the Panther* (1687)—in defense of that king's rule and religion, and of his own conversion to Roman Catholicism. Once James II had been chased into exile, the poet felt he had nowhere to turn. In 1688 Dryden was fifty-seven, an old man by contemporary standards. He was forced from office, his pension was cancelled, and he was driven back to the venues of commercial writing: the theater, translation, publication by subscription, even editing and anthologizing. He often expressed a keen sense of loss and abandonment in the 1690s, yet the decade would prove to be a remarkable phase of his career. Between his loss of the laureateship in 1689 and his death in 1700, Dryden wrote a series of superb translations that included selections from the satires of Juvenal and Persius, Ovid's *Metamorphoses* and *Amores*, Boccaccio's and Chaucer's tales. In these same years he wrote odes and epitaphs, and collaborated with his publisher Jacob Tonson in the new fashion for literary anthologies. Most remarkably, he produced *The Works of Virgil*, which set the standard for the translation of Latin poetry. He had come to his project late, and more than once he wrote of his inadequacy for this daunting task: "What Virgil wrote in the vigor of his age, in plenty and at ease, I have undertaken to translate in my declining years, struggling with wants, oppressed with sickness, curbed in my genius, liable to be misconstrued in all I write; and my judges . . . already prejudiced against me, by the lying character which has been given them of my morals." But Dryden's *Virgil* was a resounding, rehabilitating commercial and artistic success.

Nor were the twelve thousand lines of translated Virgil the close of this career. What followed was *Fables Ancient and Modern*, an anthology of original verse and new translations that included Ovid, Boccaccio, and Chaucer as well as a trial for what Dryden hoped would be his English Homer. He saw commercial opportunity in this new collection; but he must also have understood it as a crowning achievement in this life of theatricality and ventriloquism. He had begun by seeking a voice in the idioms and gestures of other poets; he now belonged wholly to himself as he casually turned their verse into his own. It is something of a paradox that a life of literary self-assertion, of aggressive, even calculating, careerism, should have closed with Dryden rummaging among other poets' verse, pausing over favorite lines, translating Ovid's Latin and Boccaccio's Italian into what was unmistakably his own voice. And the paradox of self-assertion ending in translation helps us to identify what is so particularly and so brilliantly Dryden's art. In the early modern world, writing meant belonging to others—to the authority of antiquity, to the opinions and fickle pleasure of patrons, to favor, to obligation, to taste, even to the emerging appetites of a reading public. Many of Dryden's contemporaries—Donne, Milton, Rochester—appeal to us by their seeming defiance of such self-denying ordinances. We read Dryden today not just for the skill with which he picked his way through political dangers or negotiated social minefields, not even for the savage cartooning of enemies or baroque praise of friends, but for the achievement of belonging to others as he became more exactly and more generously himself.

Absalom and Achitophel

Dryden wrote *Absalom and Achitophel* as a piece of propaganda; he was, after all, Poet Laureate. He may even have written it at the personal request of Charles II, and he surely intended to please the king, to entertain his friends, to embarrass their enemies. He performed these offices amidst tangled circumstances and under extraordinary partisan and civic pressures.

Charles had sired many children by many mistresses, but no heir by his wife. These habits and accidents of royal procreation had created a succession crisis: in the absence of a legitimate heir, the crown would pass to Charles's brother James, an openly professed Roman Catholic. This prospect excited every fear of absolute rule—of Popery, slavery, subjugation to France and to Rome. The crisis, in turn, helped crystallize an opposition of Protestants, rebels, republicans, and opportunists who mustered support for an audacious proposal: exclude the duke from succession and appoint as substitute the dim but charming, Protestant but (alas) bastard offspring of the king, James, Duke of Monmouth.

To bolster its program, the opposition made ingenious use of a conspiracy theory, widely entertained though largely false. In 1678 the mysterious murder of an eminent judge, a cloud of perjured witnesses, and a blizzard of broadsides, rumors, and innuendos persuaded many that the Queen, the Duke of York, and a band of Jesuits had conspired in a "Popish Plot" to kill the king and inaugurate Catholic rule. At the height of the mania, thirty-five Catholics were executed for their supposed complicity in this "plot." After the bloodletting, and in the face of much evidence to suggest that the plot itself was fiction, the rage subsided. The Whig opposition, now emerging from thuggery and faction into England's first organized political party, tested its powers by parliamentary maneuver. In 1680 its leader, the Earl of Shaftesbury, tried twice to pass a bill excluding Charles's brother James from the succession. In 1681 Shaftesbury publicly urged Charles to legitimate Monmouth. The king had had enough: he dismissed Parliament in March, and on July 2 had Shaftesbury imprisoned on charges of high treason. Four months later, a packed jury produced the verdict *ignoramus* ("we don't know").

Dryden's poem, appearing the week before the trial, told these busy stories in terms both daring and familiar. He cast the crisis as biblical drama: Charles became King David, Monmouth was David's wayward son Absalom, Shaftesbury the wily counselor Achitophel. Of course, factions of all sorts had long deployed parallels between England and Israel for instruction, for prophecy and exhortation, for mockery and even scandal. But no one had set all the possibilities of irony and celebration simultaneously in motion. Against the king's enemies Dryden turned their own rhetoric of scriptural sanctimony; in support of the king's friends he wrote hymns of praise; but on behalf of that complex client the king himself, Dryden discovered a way of portraying monarchy in a spirit at once appreciative, ironic, and delicately abrasive. In the poem's mischievous opening lines we hear these possibilities fully orchestrated. Charles's sexual energies, mapped as Davidic fecundity, are simultaneously grand and titillating, munificent and comic. Such mixtures of tone suffuse all the actions and arguments of Dryden's poem—its images of authority, its satiric portraits, its theories of governance, its monologues and declamations—all its traffic with the dangerous world of politics, plots, and promiscuity.

Absalom and Achitophel: A Poem.

—Si propiùs stes
Te capiet magis—[1]

To the Reader

    'Tis not my intention to make an apology for my poem: some will think it needs no excuse, and others will receive none. The design, I am sure, is honest, but he who

---

1. "If you stand closer, it will capture you more readily" (Horace, *Ars Poetica*, 361–362); Horace is here developing his argument that a poem works like a picture (*ut pictura poesis*).

draws his pen for one party must expect to make enemies of the other. For wit and fool are consequents of Whig and Tory, and every man is a knave or an ass to the contrary side. There's a treasury of merits in the fanatic church, as well as in the Papist, and a pennyworth to be had of saintship, honesty, and poetry, for the lewd, the factious, and the blockheads.[2] But the longest chapter in Deuteronomy has not curses enough for an anti-Bromingham.[3] My comfort is, their manifest prejudice to my cause will render their judgment of less authority against me. Yet if a poem have a genius, it will force its own reception in the world. For there's a sweetness in good verse, which tickles even while it hurts, and no man can be heartily angry with him who pleases him against his will. The commendation of adversaries is the greatest triumph of a writer, because it never comes unless extorted. But I can be satisfied on more easy terms: if I happen to please the more moderate sort, I shall be sure of an honest party and, in all probability, of the best judges, for the least concerned are commonly the least corrupt. And, I confess, I have laid in for those, by rebating[4] the satire (where justice would allow it) from carrying too sharp an edge. They who can criticize so weakly as to imagine I have done my worst may be convinced, at their own cost, that I can write severely with more ease than I can gently. I have but laughed at some men's follies, when I could have declaimed against their vices; and other men's virtues I have commended as freely as I have taxed[5] their crimes. And now, if you are a malicious reader, I expect you should return upon me that I affect to be thought more impartial than I am. But if men are not to be judged by their professions,[6] God forgive you commonwealthsmen[7] for professing so plausibly for the government. You cannot be so unconscionable as to charge me for not subscribing of my name, for that would reflect too grossly upon your own party, who never dare, though they have the advantage of a jury to secure them.[8] If you like not my poem, the fault may, possibly, be in my writing (though 'tis hard for an author to judge against himself); but, more probably, 'tis in your morals, which cannot bear the truth of it. The violent on both sides will condemn the character of Absalom as either too favorably or too hardly drawn. But they are not the violent whom I desire to please. The fault, on the right hand, is to extenuate, palliate, and indulge; and, to confess freely, I have endeavored to commit it. Besides the respect which I owe his birth, I have a greater for his heroic virtues; and David himself could not be more tender of the young man's life than I would be of his reputation. But since the most excellent natures are always the most easy,[9] and, as being such, are the soonest perverted by ill counsels, especially when baited with fame and glory, 'tis no more a wonder that he withstood not the temptations of Achitophel than it was for Adam not to have resisted the two devils, the serpent and the woman. The conclusion of the story I purposely forbore to prosecute, because I could not obtain from myself to show Absalom unfortunate.[1] The frame of it was cut out but for a picture to the waist; and if the draught be so far true, 'tis as much as I designed.

Absalom and Achitophel. A Poem.

2. Roman Catholic doctrine posited the existence in heaven of a fund of surplus "merits," accumulated through the goodness of Christ and the saints, on which ordinary mortals might draw for absolution. Dryden suggests that the dissenting Protestant sects ("the fanatic church"), like the Catholic ("Papist") church, confer forgiveness (even "saintship") too freely, and too cheaply.
3. Tory (Royalist). Deuteromony 28 includes a long list of curses against those who "shall not enter into the congregation of the Lord" because they have disobeyed his law.
4. Abating, softening.
5. Denounced.
6. What they say (profess).

7. Here and throughout the poem, Dryden conflates the supporters of Monmouth with the supporters of Cromwell, as enemies of the monarchy.
8. Dryden published his politically volatile poem anonymously. He accuses Whig writers of similar caution, and hence of greater cowardice, because the London juries that adjudicated cases of seditious libel were handpicked by Whig sheriffs for their bias in the party's favor.
9. Easily persuaded.
1. I.e., Dryden decided to leave off the end of the biblical story (in which Absalom is killed), because he could not bring himself to show Absalom's misfortune.

Were I the inventor, who am only the historian, I should certainly conclude the piece with the reconcilement of Absalom to David. And who knows but this may come to pass? Things were not brought to an extremity where I left the story. There seems yet to be room left for a composure;[2] hereafter, there may only be for pity. I have not so much as an uncharitable wish against Achitophel, but am content to be accused of a good-natured error and to hope with Origen[3] that the Devil himself may, at last, be saved. For which reason, in this poem he is neither brought to set his house in order nor to dispose of his person afterwards as he in wisdom shall think fit.[4] God is infinitely merciful, and his vicegerent[5] is only not so because he is not infinite.

The true end of satire is the amendment of vices by correction. And he who writes honestly is no more an enemy to the offender than the physician to the patient, when he prescribes harsh remedies to an inveterate disease; for those are only in order to prevent the surgeon's work of an *ense rescindendum*,[6] which I wish not to my very enemies. To conclude all, if the body politic have any analogy to the natural, in my weak judgment, an Act of Oblivion were as necessary in a hot, distempered state as an opiate would be in a raging fever.

Absalom and Achitophel: A Poem

In pious times, ere priestcraft did begin,
Before polygamy was made a sin;[7]
When man on many multiplied his kind,
Ere one to one was cursedly confined;
5   When Nature prompted, and no law denied
Promiscuous use of concubine and bride;
Then Israel's monarch, after Heaven's own heart,
His vigorous warmth did variously impart
To wives and slaves; and, wide as his command,
10   Scattered his Maker's image through the land.
Michal,[8] of royal blood, the crown did wear,
A soil ungrateful to the tiller's care:
Not so the rest, for several mothers bore
To godlike David several sons before.
15   But since like slaves his bed they did ascend,
No true succession could their seed attend.[9]
Of all this numerous progeny was none
So beautiful, so brave as Absolon:
Whether, inspired by some diviner lust,
20   His father got° him with a greater gust,°   *begot/pleasure*
Or that his conscious destiny made way
By manly beauty to imperial sway.

---

2. Reconciliation.
3. An early Christian theologian.
4. Dryden insinuatingly echoes the biblical account of Achitophel's disappointment and suicide (2 Samuel 23).
5. The king.
6. "Something to be cut out" in order to prevent infection of the whole organism. Dryden next suggests that an "Act of Oblivion" forgiving the rebels, like the one Charles II enacted at his Restoration, might constitute a gentler remedy.

7. "Priestcraft" is "religious fraud" (Johnson's *Dictionary*); Dryden mimics the anti-Catholicism of the Whigs, while insinuating that monogamy is an unnatural restriction imposed by power-hungry priests.
8. Daughter of David's predecessor King Saul; here she represents Charles's childless wife, Catherine of Braganza.
9. Their offspring could not succeed to the throne because of their illegitimacy.

Early in foreign fields he won renown,
With kings and states allied to Israel's crown:
25   In peace the thoughts of war he could remove,
And seemed as he were only born for love.
Whate'er he did was done with so much ease,
In him alone 'twas natural to please.
His motions all accompanied with grace;
30   And paradise was opened in his face.
With secret joy indulgent David viewed
His youthful image in his son renewed:
To all his wishes nothing he denied,
And made the charming Annabel[1] his bride.
35   What faults he had (for who from faults is free?)
His father could not, or he would not see.
Some warm excesses, which the law forbore,
Were construed youth that purged by boiling o'er:
And Amnon's murder,[2] by a specious name,
40   Was called a just revenge for injured fame.
Thus praised and loved the noble youth remained,
While David, undisturbed, in Sion[3] reigned.
But life can never be sincerely blest:
Heaven punishes the bad, and proves° the best.   tests
45   The Jews,[4] a headstrong, moody, murmuring race,
As ever tried th' extent and stretch of grace;
God's pampered people whom, debauched with ease,
No king could govern, nor no God could please
(Gods they had tried of every shape and size
50   That god-smiths could produce, or priests devise);
These Adam-wits, too fortunately free,
Began to dream they wanted° liberty;   lacked, desired
And when no rule, no precedent was found
Of men by laws less circumscribed and bound,
55   They led their wild desires to woods and caves,
And thought that all but savages were slaves.
They who when Saul was dead, without a blow,
Made foolish Ishbosheth[5] the crown forgo;
Who banished David did from Hebron bring,[6]
60   And with a general shout proclaimed him King:
Those very Jews, who, at their very best,
Their humor more than loyalty expressed,
Now wondered why so long they had obeyed
An idol monarch which their hands had made;
65   Thought they might ruin him they could create,
Or melt him to that golden calf, a state.
But these were random bolts; no formed design,

1. Anne, Countess of Buccleuch.
2. In 2 Samuel 8, Amnon rapes Absalom's half sister, and Absalom orders his murder; the correspondence with events in Monmouth's life is uncertain.
3. Jerusalem (hence, London).
4. The English.
5. Ishbosheth briefly succeeded his father Saul; correspondingly, Richard Cromwell was Protector for a few months after the death of his father, Oliver.
6. David ruled in Hebron seven years before becoming king of Israel. Charles had been crowned in Scotland in 1651.

Nor interest made the factious crowd to join:
The sober part of Israel, free from stain,
70 Well knew the value of a peaceful reign:
And, looking backward with a wise afright,
Saw seams of wounds, dishonest to the sight;
In contemplation of whose ugly scars
They cursed the memory of Civil Wars.
75 The moderate sort of men, thus qualified,
Inclined the balance to the better side:
And David's mildness managed it so well,
The bad found no occasion to rebel.
But when to sin our biased nature leans,
80 The careful Devil is still° at hand with means;   *always*
And providently pimps for ill desires:
The Good Old Cause[7] revived, a Plot requires.
Plots, true or false, are necessary things,
To raise up commonwealths and ruin kings.
85   Th' inhabitants of old Jerusalem
Were Jebusites:[8] the town so called from them;
And theirs the native right—
But when the chosen people grew more strong,
The rightful cause at length became the wrong:
90 And every loss the men of Jebus bore,
They still were thought God's enemies the more.
Thus, worn and weakened, well or ill content,
Submit they must to David's government:
Impoverished, and deprived of all command,
95 Their taxes doubled as they lost their land,
And, what was harder yet to flesh and blood,
Their gods disgraced, and burnt like common wood.[9]
This set the heathen priesthood in a flame;
For priests of all religions are the same:
100 Of whatsoe'er descent their godhead be,
Stock, stone, or other homely pedigree,
In his defense his servants are as bold
As if he had been born of beaten gold.
The Jewish rabbins,[1] though their enemies,
105 In this conclude them honest men and wise:
For 'twas their duty, all the learned think,
T' espouse his cause by whom they eat and drink.
From hence began that Plot,[2] the nation's curse,
Bad in itself, but represented worse:
110 Raised in extremes, and in extremes decried;
With oaths affirmed, with dying vows denied:
Not weighed or winnowed by the multitude,
But swallowed in the mass, unchewed and crude.
Some truth there was, but dashed and brewed with lies,

---

7. Popular name for the Cromwellian opposition to the
monarchy.
8. Jebusites inhabited Jerusalem before the Israelites;
here, they represent the Catholics.

9. Dryden alludes to a variety of anti-Catholic penal laws.
1. Anglican clergy.
2. The Popish Plot.

115 To please the fools, and puzzle all the wise.
   Succeeding times did equal folly call
   Believing nothing, or believing all.
   Th' Egyptian rites the Jebusites embraced,
   Where gods were recommended by their taste.[3]
120 Such savory deities must needs be good,
   As served at once for worship and for food.
   By force they could not introduce these gods,
   For ten to one[4] in former days was odds.
   So fraud was used (the sacrificer's trade):
125 Fools are more hard to conquer than persuade.
   Their busy teachers mingled with the Jews,
   And raked, for converts, even the court and stews:°   *brothels*
   Which Hebrew priests the more unkindly took,
   Because the fleece[5] accompanies the flock.
130 Some thought they God's anointed[6] meant to slay
   By guns, invented since full many a day:[7]
   Our author swears it not; but who can know
   How far the Devil and Jebusites may go?
   This Plot, which failed for want of common sense,
135 Had yet a deep and dangerous consequence:
   For, as when raging fevers boil the blood,
   The standing lake soon floats into a flood,
   And every hostile humor,[8] which before
   Slept quiet in its channels, bubbles o'er;
140 So several factions from this first ferment
   Work up to foam, and threat the government.
   Some by their friends, more by themselves thought wise,
   Opposed the power to which they could not rise.
   Some had in courts been great, and thrown from thence,
145 Like fiends were hardened in impenitence.
   Some, by their monarch's fatal mercy, grown,
   From pardoned rebels, kinsmen to the throne,
   Were raised in power and public office high:
   Strong bands, if bands ungrateful men could tie.
150 Of these the false Achitophel[9] was first:
   A name to all succeeding ages cursed:
   For close° designs and crooked counsels fit;   *secret*
   Sagacious, bold, and turbulent of wit:
   Restless, unfixed in principles and place;
155 In power unpleased, impatient of disgrace:
   A fiery soul, which working out its way, ⎫
   Fretted the pygmy body to decay: ⎬
   And o'er-informed the tenement of clay.[1] ⎭
   A daring pilot in extremity;

---

3. Here, and in the lines following, Dryden mocks the Catholic belief in transubstantiation.
4. Protestants to Catholics.
5. Tithe, paid by the "flock" (the parishioners).
6. The king.
7. Long since; Dryden playfully acknowledges this anachronism.

8. Bodily fluid, thought to determine temperament.
9. David's counselor, who encourages Absalom to rebel against his father; here representing Anthony Ashley Cooper, first Earl of Shaftesbury, counselor to both Cromwell and Charles II.
1. The body; Dryden contrasts Shaftesbury's large ambition with his small and sickly body.

160 Pleased with the danger, when the waves went high
He sought the storms; but for a calm unfit,
Would steer too nigh the sands, to boast his wit.
Great wits are sure to madness near allied;
And thin partitions do their bounds divide:
165 Else why should he, with wealth and honor blessed,
Refuse his age² the needful hours of rest?
Punish a body which he could not please;
Bankrupt of life, yet prodigal of ease?
And all to leave what with his toil he won,
170 To that unfeathered, two-legged thing, a son:
Got while his soul did huddled notions try;
And born a shapeless lump, like anarchy.
In friendship false, implacable in hate:
Resolved to ruin or to rule the state.
175 To compass this the triple bond³ he broke, ⎱
The pillars of the public safety shook, ⎰
And fitted Israel for a foreign yoke.
Then, seized with fear, yet still affecting° fame,   *desiring*
Usurped a patriot's all-atoning name.⁴
180 So easy still it proves in factious times,
With public zeal to cancel private crimes:
How safe is treason, and how sacred ill,
Where none can sin against the people's will:
Where crowds can wink,⁵ and no offense be known,
185 Since in another's guilt they find their own.
Yet fame deserved no enemy can grudge;
The statesman we abhor, but praise the judge.
In Israel's courts ne'er sat an Abbethdin⁶
With more discerning eyes, or hands more clean:
190 Unbribed, unsought, the wretched to redress,
Swift of dispatch, and easy of access.
Oh, had he been content to serve the crown,
With virtues only proper to the gown;
Or had the rankness of the soil been freed
195 From cockle,° that oppressed the noble seed: *weeds*
David for him his tuneful harp had strung,
And heaven had wanted one immortal song.⁷
But wild ambition loves to slide, not stand,
And fortune's ice prefers to virtue's land:
200 Achitophel, grown weary to possess°   *of possessing*
A lawful fame and lazy happiness,
Disdained the golden fruit to gather free,
And lent the crowd his arm to shake the tree.
Now, manifest° of crimes contrived long since,   *clearly guilty*
205 He stood at bold defiance with his prince:
Held up the buckler° of the people's cause   *shield*

2. Shaftesbury was 60 in 1681.
3. England's 1668 alliance with Sweden and Holland (against France).
4. Name that excuses anything.

5. Turn a blind eye.
6. Chief justice of the Jewish supreme court.
7. David would have composed one psalm fewer because he would be employed in writing praise of Achitophel.

Against the crown; and skulked behind the laws.
The wished occasion of the Plot he takes,
Some circumstances finds, but more he makes;
210   By buzzing emissaries fills the ears
Of list'ning crowds with jealousies and fears
Of arbitrary counsels brought to light,
And proves the King himself a Jebusite:
Weak arguments! which yet he knew full well
215   Were strong with people easy to rebel.
For, governed by the moon, the giddy Jews
Tread the same track when she the prime renews;[8]
And once in twenty years, their scribes record,
By natural instinct they change their lord.
220   Achitophel still wants a chief, and none
Was found so fit as warlike Absolon:
Not that he wished his greatness to create
(For politicians neither love nor hate),
But for he knew his title not allowed,
225   Would keep him still depending on the crowd,
That kingly power, thus ebbing out, might be
Drawn to the dregs of a democracy.[9]
Him he attempts with studied arts to please,
And sheds his venom in such words as these.
230   "Auspicious Prince! at whose nativity
Some royal planet ruled the southern sky;
Thy longing country's darling and desire;
Their cloudy pillar, and their guardian fire:
Their second Moses, whose extended wand
235   Divides the seas and shows the promised land:[1]
Whose dawning day, in every distant age,
Has exercised the sacred prophet's rage:
The people's prayer, the glad diviners' theme,
The young men's vision, and the old men's dream!
240   Thee, savior, thee, the nation's vows confess,
And, never satisfied with seeing, bless:
Swift, unbespoken pomps° thy steps proclaim,   *unsought honors*
And stammering babes are taught to lisp thy name.
How long wilt thou the general joy detain,
245   Starve and defraud the people of thy reign?
Content ingloriously to pass thy days
Like one of virtue's fools that feeds on praise;
Till thy fresh glories, which now shine so bright,
Grow stale and tarnish with our daily sight.
250   Believe me, royal youth, thy fruit must be
Or° gathered ripe, or rot upon the tree.   *either*
Heav'n has to all allotted, soon or late,
Some lucky revolution of their fate:

---

8. A lunar cycle lasts about 20 years; Dryden alludes to the constitutional crises of 1640, 1660, and 1680.
9. Like "commonwealth" and "state," a pejorative term used to suggest a government of mob rule.

1. On the way to Canaan, God's "promised land," Moses led the Israelites across the Red Sea and through the desert; they followed a pillar of cloud by day and a pillar of fire by night.

Whose motions, if we watch and guide with skill
255 (For human good depends on human will),
Our Fortune rolls as from a smooth descent,
And from the first impression takes the bent:
But, if unseized, she glides away like wind,
And leaves repenting folly far behind.[2]
260 Now, now she meets you with a glorious prize,
And spreads her locks before her as she flies.
Had thus old David, from whose loins you spring,
Not dared, when Fortune called him, to be King,
At Gath[3] an exile he might still remain,
265 And heaven's anointing oil had been in vain.
Let his successful youth your hopes engage,
But shun the example of declining age:
Behold him setting in his western skies,
The shadows length'ning as the vapors rise.
270 He is not now as when on Jordan's sand
The joyful people thronged to see him land,
Cov'ring the beach, and black'ning all the strand:[4]
But, like the Prince of Angels[5] from his height,
Comes tumbling downward with diminished light;
275 Betrayed by one poor plot to public scorn
(Our only blessing since his curst return),
Those heaps of people which one sheaf did bind,
Blown off and scattered by a puff of wind.
What strength can he to your designs oppose,
280 Naked of friends, and round beset with foes?
If Pharaoh's doubtful succor he should use,[6]
A foreign aid would more incense the Jews:
Proud Egypt would dissembled friendship bring,
Foment the war, but not support the King:
285 Nor would the royal party e'er unite
With Pharaoh's arms t' assist the Jebusite;
Or if they should, their interest soon would break,
And with such odious aid make David weak.
All sorts of men by my successful arts,
290 Abhorring kings, estrange their altered hearts
From David's rule; and 'tis the general cry,
'Religion, Commonwealth, and Liberty.'[7]
If you, as champion of the public good,
Add to their arms a chief of royal blood,
295 What may not Israel hope, and what applause
Might such a general gain by such a cause?
Not barren praise alone, that gaudy flower,
Fair only to the sight, but solid power:
And nobler is a limited command,

---

2. Fortune, represented as a woman with streaming hair, needs to be grasped at the first opportunity.
3. Brussels, where Charles spent the last phase of his exile.
4. Dryden refers to Charles's triumphant landing at Dover in May of 1660.

5. Lucifer (light-bearer) rebelled against God and was cast out from heaven.
6. I.e., if Charles should turn for assistance to Louis XIV, Catholic king of France.
7. A slogan of the Good Old Cause.

300 Giv'n by the love of all your native land,
Than a successive° title, long and dark,   *inherited*
Drawn from the moldy rolls of Noah's ark."
       What cannot praise effect in mighty minds,
When flattery soothes, and when ambition blinds!
305 Desire of power, on earth a vicious weed,
Yet, sprung from high, is of celestial seed:
In God 'tis glory, and when men aspire,
'Tis but a spark too much of heavenly fire.
Th' ambitious youth, too covetous of fame,
310 Too full of angel's metal[8] in his frame,
Unwarily was led from virtue's ways,
Made drunk with honor, and debauched with praise.
Half loath, and half consenting to the ill
(For royal blood within him struggled still),
315 He thus replied: "And what pretense have I
To take up arms for public liberty?
My father governs with unquestioned right;
The faith's defender, and mankind's delight:
Good, gracious, just, observant of the laws;
320 And heav'n by wonders has espoused his cause.
Whom has he wronged in all his peaceful reign?
Who sues for justice to his throne in vain?
What millions has he pardoned[9] of his foes,
Whom just revenge did to his wrath expose!
325 Mild, easy, humble, studious of our good,
Inclined to mercy, and averse from blood.
If mildness ill with stubborn Israel suit,
His crime is God's beloved attribute.
What could he gain, his people to betray,
330 Or change his right for arbitrary sway?
Let haughty Pharaoh curse, with such a reign,
His fruitful Nile, and yoke a servile train.
If David's rule Jerusalem displease,
The dog star[1] heats their brains to this disease.
335 Why then should I, encouraging the bad,
Turn rebel and run popularly mad?
Were he a tyrant who, by lawless might,
Oppressed the Jews and raised the Jebusite,
Well might I mourn; but nature's holy bands
340 Would curb my spirits and restrain my hands:
The people might assert their liberty,
But what was right in them were crime in me.
His favor leaves me nothing to require,
Prevents my wishes, and outruns desire.
345 What more can I expect while David lives?
All but his kingly diadem he gives;

---

8. Dryden puns on "angel" (a coin as well as a supernatural being) and on "metal/mettle" ("spriteliness, courage"—Johnson's *Dictionary*).

9. By the Act of Oblivion of 1660.
1. Sirius, which presides over the madness-inducing "dog days" of summer.

And that—" But there he paused; then sighing said,
"Is justly destined for a worthier head.
For when my father from his toils shall rest,
350   And late augment the number of the blest,
His lawful issue shall the throne ascend,
Or the collateral line[2] where that shall end.
His brother, though oppressed with vulgar spite,[3]
Yet dauntless and secure of native right,
355   Of every royal virtue stands possessed;
Still dear to all the bravest and the best.
His courage foes, his friends his truth proclaim;
His loyalty the King, the world his fame.
His mercy ev'n th' offending crowd will find,
360   For sure he comes of a forgiving kind.°   *family*
Why should I then repine at Heaven's decree,
Which gives me no pretense to royalty?
Yet O that Fate, propitiously inclined,
Had raised my birth, or had debased my mind;
365   To my large soul not all her treasure lent,
And then betrayed it to a mean descent.
I find, I find my mounting spirits bold,
And David's part disdains my mother's mold.
Why am I scanted by a niggard[4] birth?
370   My soul disclaims the kindred of her earth:
And, made for empire, whispers me within,
'Desire of greatness is a godlike sin.'"
       Him staggering so when Hell's dire agent found,[5]
While fainting Virtue scarce maintained her ground,
375   He pours fresh forces in, and thus replies:
       "Th' eternal God, supremely good and wise,
Imparts not these prodigious gifts in vain;
What wonders are reserved to bless your reign?
Against your will, your arguments have shown
380   Such virtue's only given to guide a throne.
Not that your father's mildness I condemn;
But manly force becomes the diadem.
'Tis true, he grants the people all they crave,
And more perhaps than subjects ought to have:
385   For lavish grants suppose° a monarch tame,   *suggest*
And more his goodness than his wit proclaim.
But when should people strive their bonds to break,
If not when kings are negligent or weak?
Let him give on till he can give no more,
390   The thrifty Sanhedrin[6] shall keep him poor:
And every shekel° which he can receive,   *coin*
Shall cost a limb of his prerogative.[7]

2. That which passed through Charles's brother, James.
3. The hostility of the common people.
4. Stingy; i.e., Monmouth's illegitimacy prevents him from acquiring all he desires.
5. The Miltonic inversion of syntax helps to link Achi-

tophel's speech to the temptation of Eve by Satan in Book 9 of *Paradise Lost*.
6. The Jewish council; here the English Parliament.
7. Royal privileges (which Parliament sought to limit).

To ply him with new plots shall be my care,
Or plunge him deep in some expensive war;
395   Which when his treasure can no more supply,
He must with the remains of kingship buy.
His faithful friends our jealousies and fears
Call Jebusites, and Pharaoh's pensioners:
Whom, when our fury from his aid has torn,
400   He shall be naked left to public scorn.
The next successor,[8] whom I fear and hate,
My arts have made obnoxious to the state;
Turned all his virtues to his overthrow,
And gained our elders[9] to pronounce a foe.
405   His right, for sums of necessary gold,
Shall first be pawned, and afterwards be sold:
Till time shall ever-wanting David draw,
To pass your doubtful title into law:
If not, the people have a right supreme
410   To make their kings, for kings are made for them.
All empire is no more than power in trust,
Which, when resumed, can be no longer just.
Succession, for the general good designed,
In its own wrong a nation cannot bind:
415   If altering that the people can relieve,
Better one suffer than a nation grieve.
The Jews well know their power: ere Saul they chose,
God was their King, and God they durst depose.[1]
Urge now your piety, your filial name,
420   A father's right, and fear of future fame;
The public good, that universal call
To which even Heav'n submitted, answers all.
Nor let his love enchant your generous mind;
'Tis Nature's trick to propagate her kind.
425   Our fond begetters, who would never die,
Love but themselves in their posterity.
Or let his kindness by th' effects be tried,
Or let him lay his vain pretense aside.
God said he loved your father; could he bring
430   A better proof than to anoint him King?
It surely showed he loved the shepherd well,
Who gave so fair a flock as Israel.
Would David have you thought his darling son?
What means he then to alienate° the crown?   *give away*
435   The name of godly he may blush to bear:
'Tis after God's own heart to cheat his heir.
He to his brother gives supreme command;
To you a legacy of barren land,[2]

---

8. James, Duke of York.
9. Shaftesbury's supporters, who included members of both the gentry and the aristocracy.
1. The prophet Samuel warned the Israelites that in choosing a king they would displace their true king, God (1 Samuel 8).
2. In 1678 Charles had promoted James and in the following year banished Monmouth.

Perhaps th' old harp on which he thrums his lays,[3]
440 Or some dull Hebrew ballad in your praise.
Then the next heir, a prince severe and wise,
Already looks on you with jealous eyes;
Sees through the thin disguises of your arts,
And marks your progress in the people's hearts.
445 Though now his mighty soul its grief contains,
He meditates revenge who least complains;
And like a lion, slumbering in the way,
Or sleep dissembling, while he waits his prey,
His fearless foes within his distance draws,
450 Constrains his roaring, and contracts his paws;
Till at the last, his time for fury found,
He shoots with sudden vengeance from the ground:
The prostrate vulgar passes o'er and spares,
But with a lordly rage his hunters tears.
455 Your case no tame expedients will afford;
Resolve on death, or conquest by the sword,
Which for no less a stake than life you draw;
And self-defense is nature's eldest law.
Leave the warm people no considering time,
460 For then rebellion may be thought a crime.
Prevail° yourself of what occasion gives,   *avail*
But try your title while your father lives:
And that your arms may have a fair pretense,
Proclaim you take them in the King's defense,
465 Whose sacred life each minute would expose
To plots from seeming friends and secret foes.
And who can sound the depth of David's soul?
Perhaps his fear his kindness may control.
He fears his brother, though he loves his son,
470 For plighted vows too late to be undone.
If so, by force he wishes to be gained,
Like women's lechery, to seem constrained:
Doubt not, but when he most affects the frown,
Commit a pleasing rape upon the crown.
475 Secure his person to secure your cause;
They who possess the prince, possess the laws."
    He said, and this advice above the rest,
With Absalom's mild nature suited best;
Unblamed of° life (ambition set aside),   *blameless in*
480 Not stained with cruelty, nor puffed with pride;
How happy had he been, if destiny
Had higher placed his birth, or not so high!
His kingly virtues might have claimed a throne,
And blessed all other countries but his own:
485 But charming greatness, since so few refuse,
'Tis juster to lament him than accuse.
Strong were his hopes a rival to remove,

---

3. David was said to have composed the Psalms.

With blandishments to gain the public love;
To head the faction while their zeal was hot,
490 And popularly prosecute the Plot.
To farther this, Achitophel unites
The malcontents of all the Israelites;
Whose differing parties he could wisely join,
For several ends, to serve the same design:
495 The best, and of the princes some were such,
Who thought the power of monarchy too much:
Mistaken men, and patriots in their hearts;
Not wicked, but seduced by impious arts.
By these the springs of property were bent,
500 And wound so high they cracked the government.
The next for interest sought t' embroil the state,
To sell their duty at a dearer rate;
And make their Jewish markets of the throne,
Pretending public good, to serve their own.
505 Others thought kings an useless heavy load,
Who cost too much, and did too little good.
These were for laying honest David by,
On principles of pure good husbandry.°   economy
With them joined all th' haranguers of the throng,
510 That thought to get preferment by the tongue.
Who follow next a double danger bring,
Not only hating David, but the King;
The Solymaean rout,[4] well versed of old
In godly faction, and in treason bold;
515 Cowering and quaking at a conqueror's sword,
But lofty° to a lawful prince restored;   arrogant
Saw with disdain an ethnic[5] plot begun,
And scorned by Jebusites to be outdone.
Hot Levites[6] headed these; who, pulled before
520 From th' ark, which in the judges' days they bore,[7]
Resumed their cant, and with a zealous cry
Pursued their old beloved theocracy:[8]
Where Sanhedrin and priest enslaved the nation,
And justified their spoils by inspiration;[9]
525 For who so fit for reign as Aaron's race,[1]
If once dominion they could found in grace?
These led the pack; though not of surest scent,
Yet deepest-mouthed against the government.
A numerous host of dreaming saints succeed;
530 Of the true old enthusiastic[2] breed:
'Gainst form and order they their power employ,

4. Solymas was another name for Jerusalem, hence, "the London mob."
5. Here, Catholic.
6. Dissenting clergymen.
7. The 1662 Act of Uniformity deprived Presbyterian clergy of their livings which they had acquired during the commonwealth (the judges' days, when they bore the ark).

8. I.e., sought to restore the commonwealth.
9. Members of dissenting sects sometimes claimed to be inspired directly by God.
1. Priests (who, in Jewish law, had to be descendants of Moses's brother Aaron).
2. A pejorative term, applied to those who claimed special inspiration.

Nothing to build and all things to destroy.
But far more numerous was the herd of such
Who think too little, and who talk too much.
535 These out of mere instinct, they knew not why,
Adored their fathers' God and property:
And, by the same blind benefit of fate,
The Devil and the Jebusite did hate:
Born to be saved, even in their own despite,°   *despite themselves*
540 Because they could not help believing right.
Such were the tools, but a whole Hydra³ more
Remains, of sprouting heads too long to score.
Some of their chiefs were princes of the land:
In the first rank of these did Zimri⁴ stand:
545 A man so various, that he seemed to be
Not one, but all mankind's epitome.
Stiff in opinions, always in the wrong;
Was everything by starts, and nothing long:
But, in the course of one revolving moon,
550 Was chemist, fiddler, statesman, and buffoon:
Then all for women, painting, rhyming, drinking,
Besides ten thousand freaks° that died in thinking.   *whims*
Blest madman, who could every hour employ,
With something new to wish, or to enjoy!
555 Railing° and praising were his usual themes;   *criticizing*
And both (to show his judgment) in extremes:
So over-violent, or over-civil,
That every man, with him, was god or devil.
In squand'ring wealth was his peculiar art:
560 Nothing went unrewarded but desert.°   *true worth*
Beggared by fools, whom still he found° too late: *found out*
He had his jest, and they had his estate.
He laughed himself from court, then sought relief
By forming parties, but could ne'er be chief:
565 For, spite of him, the weight of business fell
On Absalom and wise Achitophel:
Thus, wicked but in will, of means bereft,
He left not faction, but of that was left.
     Titles and names 'twere tedious to rehearse
570 Of lords below the dignity of verse.
Wits, warriors, commonwealthsmen, were the best:
Kind husbands and mere nobles all the rest.
And therefore, in the name of dullness, be
The well-hung Balaam⁵ and cold Caleb free.

---

3. Many-headed monster, who would sprout new heads every time one was cut off.
4. An Old Testament conspirator and regicide (1 Kings 16. 9–20); here, George Villiers, Second Duke of Buckingham, a prominent Whig. He had satirized the playwright Dryden in *The Rehearsal* (1671).
5. Balaam was a prophet who first resisted and then accepted God's will (Numbers 22–24); here, he probably represents Theophilus Hastings, Earl of Huntingdon, who initially supported Shaftesbury but was subsequently forgiven by Charles. *Well-hung*: Eloquent, or sexually impressive ("Lord Huntingdon," wrote one of the poem's early readers in a marginal inscription, "is said to have a swinging p——"). Caleb (a spy in Numbers 13) has been identified as either Lord Grey, whose wife was reputedly Monmouth's mistress, or Arthur Capel, an efficient administrator and ally of Shaftesbury.

575   And canting Nadab[6] let oblivion damn,
       Who made new porridge for the paschal lamb.[7]
       Let friendship's holy band some names assure:
       Some their own worth, and some let scorn secure.
       Nor shall the rascal rabble here have place,
580   Whom kings no titles gave, and God no grace:
       Not bull-faced Jonas,[8] who could statutes draw
       To mean rebellion, and make treason law.
       But he, though bad, is followed by a worse,
       The wretch who heaven's anointed dared to curse:
585   Shimei,[9] whose youth did early promise bring
       Of zeal to God, and hatred to his King;
       Did wisely from expensive sins refrain,
       And never broke the Sabbath, but for gain:
       Nor ever was he known an oath to vent,
590   Or curse, unless against the government.
       Thus heaping wealth by the most ready way
       Among the Jews, which was to cheat and pray;
       The city, to reward his pious hate
       Against his master, chose him magistrate:
595   His hand a vare° of justice did uphold;   *staff*
       His neck was loaded with a chain of gold.
       During his office, treason was no crime;
       The sons of Belial[1] had a glorious time:
       For Shimei, though not prodigal of pelf,[2]
600   Yet loved his wicked neighbor as himself:
       When two or three were gathered to declaim[3] ⎤
       Against the monarch of Jerusalem,   ⎬
       Shimei was always in the midst of them: ⎦
       And, if they cursed the King when he was by,
605   Would rather curse than break good company.
       If any durst his factious friends accuse,
       He packed a jury of dissenting Jews,
       Whose fellow-feeling in the godly cause
       Would free the suff'ring saint from human laws.
610   For laws are only made to punish those
       Who serve the King, and to protect his foes.
       If any leisure time he had from power
       (Because 'tis sin to misemploy an hour),
       His business was, by writing, to persuade
615   That kings were useless, and a clog to trade:

---

6. The priest Nadab tries to institute improper rites of worship, and is slain by God (Leviticus 10); probably William, Lord Howard of Escrick, a dissenting preacher.
7. Howard was said to have celebrated communion (the commemoration of Christ's sacrifice as "paschal lamb") not with bread and wine but with ale and roasted apples—a concoction known as "lamb's wool." Dissenters such as Howard referred disparagingly to the Anglican Book of Common Prayer as "porridge."
8. Sir William Jones, attorney general and fierce prosecu-

tor of alleged Popish plotters.
9. Shimei cursed David as he fled Absalom's rebellion. Here, he is Slingsby Bethel, one of London's sheriffs.
1. Rebellious, debauched men.
2. Free with money.
3. The description of Shimei echoes two of Christ's pronouncements: "Thou shalt love thy neighbor as thyself" (Matthew 22.39); "When two or three are gathered together in my name, there am I in the midst of them" (Matthew 18.20).

And that his noble style he might refine,
No Rechabite[4] more shunned the fumes of wine.
Chaste were his cellars, and his shrieval board[5]
The grossness of a city feast abhorred:
620 His cooks, with long disuse, their trade forgot;
Cool was his kitchen, though his brains were hot.
Such frugal virtue malice may accuse,
But sure 'twas necessary to the Jews:
For towns once burnt[6] such magistrates require
625 As dare not tempt God's providence by fire.
With spiritual food he fed his servants well,
But free from flesh that made the Jews rebel:
And Moses's laws he held in more account,
For forty days of fasting in the mount.[7]
630 To speak the rest, who better are forgot,
Would tire a well-breathed witness of the Plot:
Yet, Corah,[8] thou shalt from oblivion pass;
Erect thyself, thou monumental brass,°   *shamelessness*
High as the serpent of thy metal made,[9]
635 While nations stand secure beneath thy shade.
What though his birth were base, yet comets rise
From earthy vapors ere they shine in skies.
Prodigious actions may as well be done
By weaver's issue,[1] as by prince's son.
640 This arch-attestor for the public good
By that one deed ennobles all his blood.
Who ever asked the witnesses' high race,
Whose oath with martyrdom did Stephen[2] grace?
Ours was a Levite, and as times went then,
645 His tribe were God Almighty's gentlemen.
Sunk were his eyes, his voice was harsh and loud,
Sure signs he neither choleric° was, nor proud: *hot-tempered*
His long chin proved his wit; his saintlike grace
A church vermilion, and a Moses's face;[3]
650 His memory, miraculously great,
Could plots, exceeding man's belief, repeat;
Which therefore cannot be accounted lies,
For human wit could never such devise.
Some future truths are mingled in his book;
655 But where the witness failed, the prophet spoke:
Some things like visionary flights appear;

4. Rechabites drank no wine.
5. Sheriff's hospitality.
6. A reference to the Fire of London (1666).
7. Shimei attempts to justify his frugality by citing the precedent of Moses, who fasted on Mount Sinai before receiving the Ten Commandments.
8. A rebellious Levite; here, Titus Oates, the ambitious informer who did more than anyone to arouse suspicions of a "Popish Plot."

9. Moses set up a brass serpent that saved the Jews from dying of snakebite (Numbers 21).
1. Oates's father was a weaver.
2. The first Christian martyr, sworn against and stoned by false witness (Acts 6–7).
3. After Moses received the tables of the law on Mount Sinai, his face shone with divine illumination; Oates's face, by contrast, is flushed with debauchery.

The spirit caught him up, the Lord knows where,
And gave him his rabbinical degree
Unknown to foreign university.[4]
660   His judgment yet his memory did excel;
Which pieced his wondrous evidence so well,
And suited to the temper of the times,
Then groaning under Jebusitic crimes.
Let Israel's foes suspect his heav'nly call,
665   And rashly judge his writ apocryphal;[5]
Our laws for such affronts have forfeits made:
He takes his life, who takes away his trade.
Were I myself in witness Corah's place,
The wretch who did me such a dire disgrace
670   Should whet my memory, though once forgot,
To make him an appendix of my plot.
His zeal to heav'n made him his prince despise,
And load his person with indignities:
But zeal peculiar privilege affords,
675   Indulging latitude to deeds and words;
And Corah might for Agag's murder[6] call,
In terms as coarse as Samuel used to Saul.
What others in his evidence did join
(The best that could be had for love or coin)
680   In Corah's own predicament will fall:
For *witness* is a common name to all.
        Surrounded thus with friends of every sort,
Deluded Absalom forsakes the court:
Impatient of high hopes, urged with renown,
685   And fired with near possession of a crown:
Th' admiring crowd are dazzled with surprise,
And on his goodly person feed their eyes:
His joy concealed, he sets himself to show,
On each side bowing popularly low:
690   His looks, his gestures, and his words he frames,
And with familiar ease repeats their names.
Thus, formed by nature, furnished out with arts,
He glides unfelt into their secret hearts:
Then with a kind compassionating look,
695   And sighs bespeaking pity ere he spoke,
Few words he said, but easy those and fit:
More slow than Hybla° drops, and far more sweet.   honey
        "I mourn, my countrymen, your lost estate,
Though far unable to prevent your fate:
700   Behold a banished man, for your dear cause
Exposed a prey to arbitrary laws!
Yet O! that I alone could be undone,
Cut off from empire, and no more a son!

---

4. Oates pretended to hold a doctorate of divinity from the University of Salamanca.
5. Not part of the canon of biblical texts.

6. Oates denounced Lord Stafford, who was then executed, as Samuel denounced Agag, who was murdered by Saul (1 Samuel 15).

Now all your liberties a spoil are made,⎤
705   Egypt and Tyrus° intercept your trade, ⎬   *France and Holland*
And Jebusites your sacred rites invade. ⎦
My father, whom with reverence yet I name,
Charmed into ease, is careless of his fame:
And bribed with petty sums of foreign gold,
710   Is grown in Bathsheba's[7] embraces old:
Exalts his enemies, his friends destroys,
And all his pow'r against himself employs.
He gives, and let him give, my right away:
But why should he his own, and yours betray?
715   He only, he can make the nation bleed,
And he alone from my revenge is freed.
Take then my tears" (with that he wiped his eyes)
"'Tis all the aid my present power supplies:
No court informer can these arms accuse,
720   These arms may sons against their fathers use,
And 'tis my wish, the next successor's reign
May make no other Israelite complain."
    Youth, beauty, graceful action seldom fail:
But common interest always will prevail:
725   And pity never ceases to be shown
To him, who makes the people's wrongs his own.
The crowd (that still believe their kings oppress)
With lifted hands their young Messiah bless:
Who now begins his progress to ordain,[8]
730   With chariots, horsemen, and a numerous train:
From east to west his glories he displays:
And, like the sun, the promised land surveys.
Fame runs before him, as the morning star,
And shouts of joy salute him from afar:
735   Each house receives him as a guardian god,
And consecrates the place of his abode:
But hospitable treats did most commend
Wise Issachar,[9] his wealthy western friend.
This moving court, that caught the people's eyes,
740   And seemed but pomp, did other ends disguise:
Achitophel had formed it, with intent
To sound the depths, and fathom, where it went,
The people's hearts; distinguish friends from foes,
And try their strength before they came to blows:
745   Yet all was colored with a smooth pretense
Of specious love, and duty to their prince.
Religion, and redress of grievances,
Two names that always cheat and always please,
Are often urged, and good King David's life
750   Endangered by a brother and a wife.[1]

---

7. Louise de Kéroualle, Duchess of Portsmouth, Charles's French, Catholic mistress.
8. Monmouth traveled through the west of England in 1680, rallying popular support.

9. Thomas Thynne, a wealthy Whig.
1. Both James and Catherine were Catholic and were thought by some to be implicated in Popish plotting.

Thus, in a pageant show, a plot is made,
And peace itself is war in masquerade.
O foolish Israel! never warned by ill,
Still the same bait, and circumvented still!
755 Did ever men forsake their present ease,
In midst of health imagine a disease;
Take pains contingent mischiefs to foresee,
Make heirs for monarchs, and for God decree?
What shall we think! can people give away,
760 Both for themselves and sons, their native sway?
Then they are left defenseless to the sword
Of each unbounded, arbitrary lord:
And laws are vain, by which we right enjoy,
If kings unquestioned can those laws destroy.
765 Yet, if the crowd be judge of fit and just,
And kings are only officers in trust,
Then this resuming cov'nant was declared
When kings were made, or is forever barred:
If those who gave the scepter could not tie
770 By their own deed their own posterity,
How then could Adam bind his future race?
How could his forfeit on mankind take place?
Or how could heavenly justice damn us all,
Who ne'er consented to our father's fall?
775 Then kings are slaves to those whom they command,
And tenants to their people's pleasure stand.
Add, that the pow'r for property[2] allowed
Is mischievously seated in the crowd:
For who can be secure of private right,
780 If sovereign sway may be dissolved by might?
Nor is the people's judgment always true:
The most may err as grossly as the few,
And faultless kings run down by common cry
For vice, oppression, and for tyranny.
785 What standard is there in a fickle rout,
Which, flowing to the mark,° runs faster out?   high-water mark
Nor only crowds, but Sanhedrins may be
Infected with this public lunacy,
And share the madness of rebellious times,
790 To murder monarchs for imagined crimes.
If they may give and take whene'er they please,
Not kings alone (the Godhead's images),
But government itself at length must fall
To nature's state, where all have right to all.
795 Yet, grant our lords the people kings can make,
What prudent men a settled throne would shake?
For whatsoe'er their sufferings were before,
That change they covet makes them suffer more.
All other errors but disturb a state,

2. Political influence derived from ownership of land.

800 But innovation is the blow of fate.
     If ancient fabrics nod, and threat to fall,
     To patch the flaws, and buttress up the wall,
     Thus far 'tis duty; but here fix the mark:
     For all beyond it is to touch our ark.[3]
805 To change foundations, cast the frame anew,
     Is work for rebels who base ends pursue,
     At once divine and human laws control,
     And mend the parts by ruin of the whole.
     The tampering world is subject to this curse,
810 To physic their disease into a worse.
         Now what relief can righteous David bring?
     How fatal 'tis to be too good a king!
     Friends he has few, so high the madness grows;
     Who dare be such, must be the people's foes:
815 Yet some there were, ev'n in the worst of days;
     Some let me name, and naming is to praise.
         In this short file Barzillai[4] first appears;
     Barzillai crowned with honor and with years:
     Long since, the rising rebels he withstood
820 In regions waste, beyond the Jordan's flood:[5]
     Unfortunately brave to buoy the state,
     But sinking underneath his master's fate:
     In exile with his godlike prince he mourned;
     For him he suffered, and with him returned.
825 The court he practised, not the courtier's art:
     Large was his wealth, but larger was his heart:
     Which well the noblest objects knew to choose,
     The fighting warrior, and recording Muse.[6]
     His bed could once a fruitful issue boast:
830 Now more than half a father's name is lost:
     His eldest hope,[7] with every grace adorned,
     By me (so Heaven will have it) always mourned,
     And always honored, snatched in manhood's prime
     By unequal Fates, and Providence's crime:
835 Yet not before the goal of honor won,   ⎫
     All parts fulfilled of subject and of son;   ⎬
     Swift was the race, but short the time to run. ⎭
     Oh narrow circle, but of pow'r divine,
     Scanted in space, but perfect in thy line!
840 By sea, by land, thy matchless worth was known;
     Arms thy delight, and war was all thy own:
     Thy force, infused, the fainting Tyrians[8] propped:
     And haughty Pharaoh found his fortune stopped.
     O ancient honor, O unconquered hand,
845 Whom foes unpunished never could withstand!

---

3. To touch the ark was to commit sacrilege.
4. James Butler, Duke of Ormonde, loyal to Charles I and II.
5. I.e., in Ireland.
6. I.e., he gave money to support the Stuart cause and was

also a patron to authors.
7. Ormonde's eldest son, who died in 1680.
8. The Dutch, whom Ormonde's son had aided against the French.

But Israel was unworthy of thy name;
Short is the date of all immoderate fame.
It looks as Heaven our ruin had designed,
And durst not trust thy fortune and thy mind.
850   Now, free from earth, thy disencumbered soul
Mounts up, and leaves behind the clouds and starry pole:
From thence thy kindred legions mayst thou bring,
To aid the guardian angel of thy King.
Here stop, my Muse, here cease thy painful flight;
855   No pinions° can pursue immortal height: *wings*
Tell good Barzillai thou canst sing no more,
And tell thy soul she should have fled before;
Or fled she with his life, and left this verse
To hang on her departed patron's hearse?
860   Now take thy steepy flight from heaven, and see
If thou canst find on earth another *he;*
Another *he* would be too hard to find,
See then whom thou canst see not far behind:
Zadock[9] the priest, whom, shunning power and place,
865   His lowly mind advanced to David's grace:
With him the Sagan[1] of Jerusalem,
Of hospitable soul and noble stem;
Him of the western dome,[2] whose weighty sense
Flows in fit words and heavenly eloquence.
870   The prophets' sons[3] by such example led,
To learning and to loyalty were bred:
For colleges on bounteous kings depend,
And never rebel was to arts a friend.
To these succeed the pillars of the laws,
875   Who best could plead and best can judge a cause.
Next them a train of loyal peers ascend:
Sharp-judging Adriel,[4] the Muses' friend,
Himself a Muse—in Sanhedrin's debate
True to his prince, but not a slave of state:
880   Whom David's love with honors did adorn,
That from his disobedient son were torn.[5]
Jotham[6] of piercing wit and pregnant thought,
Indued° by nature, and by learning taught   *endowed*
To move assemblies, who but only tried
885   The worse awhile, then chose the better side;
Nor chose alone, but turned the balance too;
So much the weight of one brave man can do.
Hushai,[7] the friend of David in distress,
In public storms of manly steadfastness;

9. William Sancroft, Archbishop of Canterbury.
1. Henry Compton, Bishop of London.
2. John Dolben, Dean of Westminster ("the western dome").
3. Students of the Westminster School.
4. John Sheffield, Earl of Mulgrave, poet and a patron of Dryden.
5. In 1679 Mulgrave received two offices that had previ-

ously belonged to Monmouth.
6. George Savile, Marquis of Halifax, formerly a critic but now a supporter of Charles's policies, was instrumental in defeating the exclusion bill.
7. Laurence Hyde, Earl of Rochester, negotiated several European treaties and became the first Lord of the Treasury.

890   By foreign treaties he informed his youth,
      And joined experience to his native truth.
      His frugal care supplied the wanting throne,
      Frugal for that, but bounteous of his own:
      'Tis easy conduct when exchequers[8] flow,
895   But hard the task to manage well the low:
      For sovereign power is too depressed or high,
      When kings are forced to sell, or crowds to buy.
      Indulge one labor more, my weary Muse,
      For Amiel,[9] who can Amiel's praise refuse?
900   Of ancient race by birth, but nobler yet
      In his own worth, and without title great:
      The Sanhedrin long time as chief he ruled,
      Their reason guided and their passion cooled;
      So dexterous was he in the crown's defense,
905   So formed to speak a loyal nation's sense,
      That, as their band was Israel's tribes in small,
      So fit was he to represent them all.
      Now rasher charioteers the seat ascend,
      Whose loose careers his steady skill commend:
910   They like th' unequal ruler of the day,[1]
      Misguide the seasons and mistake the way;
      While he, withdrawn, at their mad labor smiles,
      And safe enjoys the sabbath of his toils.
        These were the chief, a small but faithful band ⎫
915   Of worthies, in the breach who dared to stand, ⎬
      And tempt th' united fury of the land. ⎭
      With grief they viewed such powerful engines bent,
      To batter down the lawful government:
      A numerous faction with pretended frights,
920   In Sanhedrins to plume° the regal rights: *pluck away*
      The true successor from the court removed:[2]
      The Plot by hireling witnesses improved.
      These ills they saw, and as their duty bound,
      They showed the King the danger of the wound:
925   That no concessions from the throne would please,
      But lenitives fomented[3] the disease:
      That Absalom, ambitious of the crown,
      Was made the lure to draw the people down:
      That false Achitophel's pernicious hate
930   Had turned the Plot to ruin Church and State:
      The council violent, the rabble worse:
      That Shimei taught Jerusalem to curse.
        With all these loads of injuries oppressed,
      And long revolving, in his careful breast,

8. Treasurers/treasuries.
9. Edward Seymour, speaker of the Commons (1673–1678) and treasurer of the Navy (1673–1681); opponent of exclusion.
1. Phaëthon, who drove (with disastrous results) the chariot of the sun that belonged to his father, Apollo.

2. In 1679, at the height of the furor over the Popish Plot, Charles II had ordered his brother to withdraw to the Continent, where James remained for six months.
3. I.e., soothing measures/medicines only encouraged the disease.

935 Th' event of things, at last, his patience tired,
Thus from his royal throne by Heav'n inspired,
The godlike David spoke: with awful fear
His train their Maker in their master hear.
    "Thus long have I, by native mercy swayed,
940 My wrongs dissembled, my revenge delayed:
So willing to forgive th' offending age,
So much the father did the king assuage.
But now so far my clemency they slight,
Th' offenders question my forgiving right.
945 That one was made for many, they contend:
But 'tis to rule, for that's a monarch's end.
They call my tenderness of blood my fear:
Though manly tempers can the longest bear.
Yet, since they will divert my native course,
950 'Tis time to show I am not good by force.
Those heaped affronts that haughty subjects bring,
Are burdens for a camel, not a king:
Kings are the public pillars of the state,
Born to sustain and prop the nation's weight:
955 If my young Samson⁴ will pretend a call
To shake the column, let him share the fall:
But O that yet he would repent and live!
How easy 'tis for parents to forgive!
With how few tears a pardon might be won
960 From Nature, pleading for a darling son!
Poor pitied youth, by my paternal care
Raised up to all the height his frame could bear:
Had God ordained his fate for empire born,
He would have given his soul another turn:
965 Gulled with a patriot's name, whose modern sense
Is one that would by law supplant his prince:
The people's brave,° the politicians' tool;   bully
Never was patriot yet, but was a fool.
Whence comes it that religion and the laws
970 Should more be Absalom's than David's cause?
His old instructor,⁵ ere he lost his place,
Was never thought indued with so much grace.
Good heavens, how faction can a patriot paint!
My rebel ever proves my people's saint:
975 Would they impose an heir upon the throne?
Let Sanhedrins be taught to give their own.
A king's at least a part of government,
And mine as requisite as their consent:
Without my leave a future king to choose,
980 Infers a right the present to depose:
True, they petition me t' approve their choice,

---

4. Monmouth, who threatens, Samson-like, to bring   5. Achitophel/Shaftesbury.
down the nation.

But Esau's hands suit ill with Jacob's voice.[6]
My pious subjects for my safety pray,
Which to secure they take my power away.
985   From plots and treasons Heaven preserve my years,
But save me most from my petitioners.
Unsatiate as the barren womb or grave;
God cannot grant so much as they can crave.
What then is left but with a jealous eye
990   To guard the small remains of royalty?
The law shall still direct my peaceful sway,
And the same law teach rebels to obey:
Votes shall no more established pow'r control,
Such votes as make a part exceed the whole:
995   No groundless clamors shall my friends remove,
Nor crowds have power to punish ere they prove:
For gods, and godlike kings, their care express,
Still to defend their servants in distress.
O that my power to saving were confined: ⎫
1000   Why am I forced, like Heaven, against my mind, ⎬
To make examples of another kind? ⎭
Must I at length the sword of justice draw?
O cursed effects of necessary law!
How ill my fear they by my mercy scan;[7]
1005   Beware the fury of a patient man.
Law they require, let law then show her face;
They could not be content to look on Grace,
Her hinder parts, but with a daring eye
To tempt the terror of her front, and die.
1010   By their own arts, 'tis righteously decreed,
Those dire artificers of death shall bleed.
Against themselves their witnesses will swear,
Till viper-like their mother Plot they tear:
And suck for nutriment that bloody gore
1015   Which was their principle of life before.
Their Belial with their Belzebub[8] will fight;
Thus on my foes, my foes shall do me right:
Nor doubt th' event: for factious crowds engage,
In their first onset, all their brutal rage;
1020   Then let 'em take an unresisted course,
Retire and traverse, and delude their force:
But when they stand all breathless, urge the fight,
And rise upon 'em with redoubled might:
For lawful pow'r is still superior found,
1025   When long driven back, at length it stands the ground."
       He said. Th' Almighty, nodding, gave consent;

6. In Genesis 27, Esau is a hunter and a "hairy man"; his younger brother Jacob steals his birthright by impersonating him before their blind father Isaac, covering his own smooth hands with rough goatskin. David/Charles here accuses his opposition of Esau-like violence and Jacob-like deception.

7. How wrong ("ill") they are to see ("scan") fear in my mercy.

8. Both devils.

And peals of thunder shook the firmament.
Henceforth a series of new time began,
The mighty years in long procession ran:
1030   Once more the godlike David was restored,
And willing nations knew their lawful lord.

1681   1681

COMPANION READING

*Charles II: His Majesty's Declaration to all His Loving Subjects,
Touching the Causes and Reasons that Moved Him
to Dissolve the Two Last Parliaments*[1]

It was with exceeding great trouble that We were brought to the dissolving of the two last Parliaments, without more benefit to Our people by the calling of them. But having done Our part in giving so many opportunities of providing for their good, it cannot be justly imputed to Us that the success hath not answered Our expectation.

We cannot at this time but take notice of the particular causes of Our dissatisfaction, which at the beginning of the last Parliament we did recommend to their care to avoid, and expected We should have no new cause to remember them.

We opened the last Parliament, which was held at Westminster, with as gracious expressions of Our readiness to satisfy the desires of Our good subjects and to secure them against all their just fears, as the weighty consideration, either of preserving the established religion, and the liberty and property of Our subjects at home, or of supporting Our neighbors and allies abroad, could fill Our heart with, or possibly require from Us.

And We do solemnly declare that We did intend, as far as would have consisted with the very being of the government, to have complied with anything that could have been proposed to Us to accomplish those ends.

We asked of them the supporting the alliances We had made for the preservation of the general peace in Christendom;[2] We recommended to them the further examination of the Plot;[3] We desired their advice and assistance concerning the preservation of Tangier;[4] We offered to concur in any remedies that could be proposed for the security of the Protestant religion, that might consist with preserving the succession of the Crown in its due and legal course of descent; to all which We met with most

---

1. In the wake of the "Popish Plot," the Whigs tried repeatedly to pass an exclusion bill barring the Catholic Duke of York from succeeding to the throne. In response, the increasingly exasperated Charles dissolved the Parliament twice in quick succession: On 18 January 1681, he dismissed the Commons at Westminster and called for a new Parliament at Oxford; on 28 March he abruptly dissolved this second Parliament after only seven days of bitterly contentious sessions. By his peremptory actions, the king had laid himself open to charges of arbitrary and despotic rule. In *His Majesty's Declaration*, Charles tried to lay these charges to rest. Recent votes in the House of Commons, he argued, had so encroached upon the king's prerogatives and the country's laws as to endanger the stability of the Restoration and revive the possibility of

civil war; throughout the pamphlet, Charles plays adroitly on his audience's memories of midcentury strife. Read aloud from pulpits throughout the land, this unusually direct statement by the monarch to his subjects made a considerable impression—though not so conclusive an impact as Dryden was willing to imagine in the closing lines of *Absalom and Achitophel*, where the king of Israel's arguments occasionally echo Charles's *Declaration*.
2. Charles had begun to cultivate—and to boast about—a defensive alliance with Spain against France.
3. At the first of the two Parliaments, Charles had consented to the execution of the one of the accused Popish "conspirators."
4. This seaport on the Straits of Gibraltar, claimed by the English, was now under attack by the Moors.

unsuitable returns from the House of Commons: addresses, in the nature of remonstrances, rather than of answers; arbitrary orders for taking Our subjects into custody, for matters that had no relation to privileges of Parliament; strange illegal votes, declaring diverse eminent persons to be enemies to the King and Kingdom, without any order or process of law, any hearing of their defense, or any proof so much as offered against them.[5] * * *

[The Parliamentary] Votes, instead of giving Us assistance to support our allies, or enable Us to preserve Tangier, tended rather to disable Us from contributing towards either, by Our own revenue or credit; not only exposing Us to all dangers that might happen either at home, or abroad, but endeavoring to deprive Us of the possibility of supporting the government itself, and to reduce Us to a more helpless condition than the meanest of Our subjects. * * *

These were some of the unwarrantable proceedings of the House of Commons, which were the occasion of Our parting with that Parliament.

Which We had no sooner dissolved, but We caused another to be forthwith assembled at Oxford; at the opening of which, We thought it necessary to give them warning of the errors of the former, in hopes to have prevented the like miscarriages; and We required of them to make the laws of the land their rule, as We did, and do, resolve they shall be Ours. We further added, that what We had formerly and so often declared concerning the succession, We could not depart from. But, to remove all reasonable fears that might arise from the possibility of a Popish successor's coming to the Crown, if means could be found that in such a case the administration of the government might remain in Protestant hands, We were ready to hearken to any expedient by which the religion established might be preserved, and the Monarchy not destroyed.

But contrary to Our offers and expectation, We saw that no expedient would be entertained but that of a total Exclusion, which, We had so often declared, was a point that, in Our own royal judgment, so nearly concerned Us both in honor, justice, and conscience, that We could never consent to it. In short, We cannot, after the sad experience We have had of the late Civil Wars, that murdered Our father of blessed memory and ruined the Monarchy, consent to a law that shall establish another most unnatural war, or at least make it necessary to maintain a standing force for the preserving the government and the peace of the Kingdom.

And We have reason to believe, by what passed in the last Parliament at Westminster, that if We could have been brought to give Our consent to a Bill of Exclusion, the intent was not to rest there, but to pass further, and to attempt some other great and important changes even in present. * * *

But, notwithstanding all this, let not the restless malice of ill men who are laboring to poison Our people, some out of fondness of their old beloved Commonwealth principles, and some out of anger at their being disappointed in the particular designs they had for the accomplishment of their own ambition and greatness, persuade any of Our good subjects that We intend to lay aside the use of Parliaments. For We do still declare that no irregularities in Parliaments shall ever make Us out of love with Parliaments, which We look upon as the best method for healing the distempers of the Kingdom, and the only means to preserve the Monarchy in that due credit and respect which it ought to have both at home and abroad.

5. At the first of the two Parliaments, the Whigs had demanded the expulsion of several "eminent persons" who had worked successfully to defeat an exclusion bill.

And for this cause We are resolved, by the blessing of God, to have frequent Parliaments, and, both in and out of Parliament, to use Our utmost endeavors to extirpate Popery, and to redress all the grievances of Our good subjects, and in all things to govern according to the laws of the Kingdom.

And We hope that a little time will so far open the eyes of all Our good subjects, that Our next meeting in Parliament shall perfect all that settlement and peace which shall be found wanting either in Church or State.

To which, as We shall contribute Our utmost endeavors, so We assure Ourself that We shall be assisted therein by the loyalty and good affections of all those who consider the rise and progress of the late troubles and confusions, and desire to preserve their country from a relapse.

And who cannot but remember that Religion, Liberty, and Property were all lost and gone when the Monarchy was shaken off, and could never be revived till that was restored.

Given at Our Court at Whitehall, the eighth day of April 1681.

Mac Flecknoe

In *Mac Flecknoe*, Dryden put on display a literary culture dangerously debased. The poem's title ("Son of Flecknoe") announces a royal succession in the kingdom of bad writing. A literary "father," the priest and minor poet Richard Flecknoe (c.1605–c.1677), anoints as his true heir Thomas Shadwell (1640–1692), a playwright whom Dryden loathed as a tiresome controversialist and an ardent (worse, successful) rival for public favor and aristocratic patronage. Dryden wages his attack in an idiom at once elevated and scandalous, in language whose allegiance alternates (even within a single line) between epic poetry and the privy. Like much libelous and bawdy verse, Dryden's demolitionary masterpiece circulated in manuscript for several years; it was eventually printed in a pirated edition (1682) by a publisher seeking to capitalize on the recent success of *Absalom and Achitophel*. Like that poem, *Mac Flecknoe* plays upon the question of monarchic succession, but stages it in such a way as to implicate bad politics in bad taste. Dryden maps a City of London where foul writing chokes the streets, and dim-witted citizens get—and applaud—the poet-monarchs they deserve.

Mac Flecknoe

> All human things are subject to decay,
> And, when Fate summons, monarchs must obey.
> This Flecknoe found, who, like Augustus, young
> Was called to empire,[1] and had governed long:
> 5 In prose and verse was owned, without dispute,
> Through all the realms of Nonsense, absolute.
> This aged prince, now flourishing in peace,
> And blest with issue of a large increase,
> Worn out with business, did at length debate
> 10 To settle the succession of the state:
> And, pondering which of all his sons was fit
> To reign, and wage immortal war with wit,
> Cried, " 'Tis resolved; for Nature pleads that he

---

1. Augustus became the first Roman emperor at the age of 32.

15 Should only rule, who most resembles me:
Sh—— alone my perfect image bears,
Mature in dullness from his tender years.
Sh—— alone, of all my sons, is he
Who stands confirmed in full stupidity.
The rest to some faint meaning make pretense,
20 But Sh—— never deviates into sense.
Some beams of wit on other souls may fall,
Strike through and make a lucid interval,
But Sh——'s genuine night admits no ray,
His rising fogs prevail upon the day.
25 Besides, his goodly fabric° fills the eye,   *large body*
And seems designed for thoughtless majesty:
Thoughtless as monarch oaks that shade the plain,
And, spread in solemn state, supinely reign.
Heywood and Shirley were but types of thee,[2]
30 Thou last great prophet of tautology:
Even I, a dunce of more renown than they,
Was sent before but to prepare thy way;
And coarsely clad in Norwich drugget[3] came
To teach the nations in thy greater name.[4]
35 My warbling lute, the lute I whilom° strung   *once*
When to King John of Portugal I sung,[5]
Was but the prelude to that glorious day
When thou on silver Thames didst cut thy way,
With well-timed oars before the royal barge,
40 Swelled with the pride of thy celestial charge;
And big with hymn, commander of an host,
The like was ne'er in Epsom blankets tossed.[6]
Methinks I see the new Arion[7] sail,
The lute still trembling underneath thy nail.
45 At thy well-sharpened thumb from shore to shore
The treble squeaks for fear, the basses roar:
Echoes from Pissing Alley[8] "Sh——" call,
And "Sh——" they resound from A—— Hall.[9]
About thy boat the little fishes throng,
50 As at the morning toast° that floats along.   *sewage*
Sometimes as prince of thy harmonious band
Thou wield'st thy papers in thy threshing hand.
St. André's feet[1] ne'er kept more equal time,
Not ev'n the feet of thy own *Psyche's* rhyme,
55 Though they in number as in sense excel;

2. Thomas Heywood and James Shirley, popular and prolific playwrights from the first half of the 17th century.
As "types," they foreshadow or prepare for Shadwell, just
as Old Testament figures such as Moses or Isaac were
interpreted in Christian theology as forerunners of Jesus.
3. Woolen cloth; Shadwell came from Norwich.
4. Here, Flecknoe is John the Baptist ("coarsely clad" in
camel's hair) to Shadwell's Jesus.
5. Flecknoe claimed that, during his travels in Europe,
he had been summoned to perform before the king of
Portugal.

6. A glance at two of Shadwell's plays: *Epsom Wells* and
The Virtuoso, in which Sir Samuel Hearty is tossed in a
blanket; tossing in blankets was also a means of inducing
childbirth.
7. Greek musician-poet rescued from drowning by music-
loving dolphins.
8. West of Temple Bar, it led from the Strand down to
the Thames.
9. Unidentified.
1. St. André, a French dancer who choreographed the
opera *Psyche* (1675), for which Shadwell wrote the libretto.

So just, so like tautology they fell,
That, pale with envy, Singleton foreswore
The lute and sword which he in triumph bore, ⎫
And vowed he ne'er would act Villerius[2] more. ⎭
60   Here stopped the good old sire, and wept for joy
In silent raptures of the hopeful boy.
All arguments, but most his plays, persuade,
That for anointed dullness he was made.
    Close to the walls which fair Augusta bind[3]
65   (The fair Augusta much to fears inclined[4]),
An ancient fabric,[5] raised t' inform the sight,
There stood of yore, and Barbican it hight:[6]
A watchtower once, but now, so Fate ordains,
Of all the pile an empty name remains.
70   From its old ruins brothel-houses rise,
Scenes of lewd loves and of polluted joys;
Where their vast courts the mother-strumpets keep
And, undisturbed by watch,° in silence sleep.[7]   *police*
Near these a nursery[8] erects its head,
75   Where queens[9] are formed and future heroes bred;
Where unfledged actors learn to laugh and cry,
Where infant punks° their tender voices try,   *prostitutes*
And little Maximins[1] the gods defy.
Great Fletcher never treads in buskins here,
80   Nor greater Jonson dares in socks appear.[2]
But gentle Simkin[3] just reception finds
Amidst this monument of vanished minds:
Pure clinches° the suburbian Muse[4] affords,   *puns*
And Panton[5] waging harmless war with words.
85   Here Flecknoe, as a place to fame well known,
Ambitiously designed his Sh——'s throne.
For ancient Dekker[6] prophesied long since, ⎫
That in this pile should reign a mighty prince, ⎬
Born for a scourge of wit, and flail of sense: ⎭
90   To whom true dullness should some *Psyches* owe,
But Worlds of *Misers* from his pen should flow;
Humorists and *Hypocrites*[7] it should produce,
Whole Raymond families, and tribes of Bruce.

2. John Singleton, one of the king's musicians; Villerius, a character in William Davenant's opera, *The Siege of Rhodes*.
3. The old wall of the City of London (Augusta).
4. Fears aroused by the Popish Plot.
5. Structure.
6. Was named; the Barbican, a medieval gatehouse, gave its name to a disreputable district of gaming and prostitution; adjoining it was Grub Street, the center of hack journalism.
7. Parodying Abraham Cowley, *Davideis* (1656), "Where their vast court the mother-waters keep, / And undisturbed by moons in silence sleep."
8. A training theater for the two main playhouses.
9. Dryden puns on queen (stage-monarch)/quean (prostitute). During the Restoration, actresses were often thought to moonlight as sexual companions.

1. Maximin is the fulminating protagonist of Dryden's *Tyrannic Love*.
2. John Fletcher and Ben Jonson, major playwrights of the previous generations. The buskin is the symbol of tragedy (Fletcher's forte) and the sock of comedy (Jonson's). Shadwell promoted himself as Jonson's successor in the tradition of "humors" comedy.
3. A clownish character in a series of popular farces.
4. I.e., the muse presiding over the disreputable area outside the City walls.
5. Another farce character.
6. Thomas Dekker (1570?–1632), prolific dramatist whose plays focused on London life.
7. Shadwell was the author of *The Miser* (1672), *The Humorists* (1671), and *The Hypocrite* (1669). Raymond and Bruce appear in *The Humorists* and *The Virtuoso*, respectively.

Now Empress Fame had published the renown
95   Of Sh——'s coronation through the town.
Roused by report of Fame, the nations meet,
From near Bunhill, and distant Watling Street.[8]
No Persian carpets spread th' imperial way,
But scattered limbs of mangled poets lay:
100   From dusty shops neglected authors come,
Martyrs of pies, and relics of the bum.[9]
Much Heywood, Shirley, Ogilby[1] there lay,
But loads of Sh—— almost choked the way.
Bilked stationers for yeomen stood prepared,
105   And H——[2] was captain of the guard.
The hoary prince in majesty appeared,
High on a throne of his own labors reared.
At his right hand our young Ascanius[3] sate,
Rome's other hope, and pillar of the state.
110   His brows thick fogs, instead of glories, grace,
And lambent° dullness played around his face.   *glowing*
As Hannibal did to the altars come,
Sworn by his sire a mortal foe to Rome,[4]
So Sh—— swore, nor should his vow be vain,
115   That he till death true dullness would maintain;
And in his father's right, and realm's defense,
Ne'er to have peace with wit, nor truce with sense.
The king himself the sacred unction[5] made,
As king by office, and as priest by trade:
120   In his sinister° hand, instead of ball,   *left*
He placed a mighty mug of potent ale;
Love's Kingdom[6] to his right he did convey,
At once his scepter and his rule of sway,[7]
Whose righteous lore the prince had practiced young,
125   And from whose loins[8] recorded Psyche sprung.
His temples last with poppies[9] were o'erspread,
That nodding seemed to consecrate his head:
Just at that point of time, if Fame not lie,
On his left hand twelve reverend owls[1] did fly.
130   So Romulus,[2] 'tis sung, by Tiber's brook,
Presage of sway from twice six vultures took.
Th' admiring throng loud acclamations make,
And omens of his future empire take.

---

8. Fame draws her crowd both from cemeteries (like Bunhill Fields) and from mercantile districts (like Watling Street); thus, these devotees of Shadwell include both the dead and the living.
9. Unsold books might be recycled as pie wrappers or as toilet paper; the bones of martyrs were often venerated as relics.
1. John Ogilby, printer, cartographer, and translator (like Dryden) of Virgil.
2. Henry Herringman, a prominent bookseller-publisher; he had published both Shadwell and Dryden.
3. The son of Aeneas, marked for greatness by a heaven-sent flame about his head.

4. According to Livy, Hannibal's father made the young boy swear himself Rome's enemy.
5. The oil with which the king was anointed during the coronation ceremony.
6. A play by Flecknoe.
7. Dryden parodies the rituals and props of the coronation ceremony.
8. Prounounced "lines" (a fact that permits Dryden a significant pun).
9. Symbolizing sleep.
1. Symbols of ignorance and darkness (because nocturnal).
2. Co-founder of Rome (through which the Tiber runs).

The sire then shook the honors[3] of his head,
135   And from his brows damps of oblivion shed
Full on the filial dullness: long he stood,   ⎫
Repelling from his breast the raging God;   ⎬
At length burst out in this prophetic mood: ⎭
      "Heavens bless my son, from Ireland let him reign
140   To far Barbados on the western main;[4]
Of his dominion may no end be known,
And greater than his father's be his throne.
Beyond *Love's Kingdom* let him stretch his pen!"
He paused, and all the people cried, "Amen."
145   "Then thus," continued he, "my son, advance
Still in new impudence, new ignorance.
Success let others teach, learn thou from me
Pangs without birth, and fruitless industry.
Let *Virtuosos* in five years be writ,
150   Yet not one thought accuse thy toil of wit.
Let gentle George[5] in triumph tread the stage,
Make Dorimant betray, and Loveit rage;
Let Cully, Cockwood, Fopling charm the pit,
And in their folly show the writer's wit.
155   Yet still thy fools shall stand in thy defense,
And justify° their author's want of sense.   prove
Let 'em be all by thy own model made
Of dullness, and desire no foreign aid:
That they to future ages may be known,
160   Not copies drawn, but issue[6] of thy own.
Nay let thy men of wit too be the same,
All full of thee, and differing but in name;
But let no alien S—dl—y[7] interpose
To lard with wit thy hungry *Epsom* prose.
165   And when false flowers of rhetoric thou would'st cull,
Trust nature, do not labor to be dull;
But write thy best, and top; and in each line,
Sir Formal's[8] oratory will be thine.
Sir Formal, though unsought, attends thy quill,
170   And does thy northern dedications[9] fill.
Nor let false friends seduce thy mind to fame,
By arrogating Jonson's hostile name.
Let father Flecknoe fire thy mind with praise,
And uncle Ogilby thy envy raise.
175   Thou art my blood, where Jonson has no part;
What share have we in nature or in art?
Where did his wit on learning fix a brand,

---

3. Ornaments, and by extension, hair—a Virgilian expression.
4. His kingdom will be the Atlantic Ocean.
5. Sir George Etherege, comic playwright; characters from his plays follow.
6. A pun: both progeny and printing.
7. Sir Charles Sedley, courtier, poet, and intimate of Dry-

den's circle; he wrote a prologue for *Epsom Wells*.
8. Sir Formal Trifle, a character in Shadwell's *The Virtuoso*, described by Shadwell as "the Orator, a florid coxcomb."
9. Both Flecknoe and Shadwell dedicated several of their works to the Duke and Duchess of Newcastle, (a town in the north of England).

And rail at arts he did not understand?
Where made he love in Prince Nicander's[1] vein,
180   Or swept the dust in *Psyche*'s humble strain?
Where sold he bargains,[2] "whip-stitch, kiss my arse,"
Promised a play and dwindled to a farce?
When did his Muse from Fletcher scenes purloin,
As thou whole Eth'rege dost transfuse to thine?
185   But so transfused as oil on waters flow,
His always floats above, thine sinks below.
This is thy province, this thy wondrous way,
New humors to invent for each new play:[3]
This is that boasted bias of thy mind,
190   By which one way, to dullness, 'tis inclined;
Which makes thy writings lean on one side still,
And in all changes that way bends thy will.
Nor let thy mountain belly make pretense
Of likeness; thine's a tympany[4] of sense.
195   A tun of man in thy large bulk is writ,
But sure thou'rt but a kilderkin[5] of wit.
Like mine thy gentle numbers feebly creep;
Thy tragic Muse gives smiles, thy comic sleep.
With whate'er gall thou sett'st thyself to write,
200   Thy inoffensive satires never bite.
In thy felonious heart, though venom lies,
It does but touch thy Irish[6] pen, and dies.
Thy genius calls thee not to purchase fame
In keen iambics,[7] but mild anagram:
205   Leave writing plays, and choose for thy command
Some peaceful province in acrostic land.
There thou may'st wings display and altars[8] raise,
And torture one poor word ten thousand ways.
Or if thou would'st thy diff'rent talents suit,
210   Set thy own songs, and sing them to thy lute."
He said, but his last words were scarcely heard, ⎫
For Bruce and Longvil had a trap prepared,[9] ⎬
And down they sent the yet declaiming bard. ⎭
Sinking he left his drugget robe behind,
215   Borne upwards by a subterranean wind.
The mantle fell to the young prophet's part,[1]
With double portion of his father's art.

c. 1676   1682

---

1. A character in *Psyche*.
2. "To sell bargains" is to respond to an innocent question with a coarse phrase, as in this line. Dryden sharpens the insult by quoting the slangy nonsense phrase "whip-stitch" from Shadwell's own play, *The Virtuoso*.
3. I.e., by these contemptible means, you purport to outdo Ben Jonson.
4. A swelling of the abdomen, caused by air or gas.
5. A tun was a large cask of wine; a kilderkin a quarter of a tun.
6. Neither Flecknoe nor Shadwell was actually Irish; Ireland was regarded in England as an abode of savages.

7. Sharp satire (written in iambic meter by classical satirists).
8. Dryden here mocks the practice of writing emblematic verse, poems in the shape of their subjects (e.g., George Herbert's *Easter Wings* and *The Altar*). He lumps this practice together with other forms of empty ingenuity.
9. In Shadwell's *The Virtuoso*, Bruce and Longvil open a trap door beneath the long-winded Sir Formal Trifle.
1. A burlesque of 2 Kings 2.8–14, in which the prophet Elijah is borne up to heaven, while his mantle falls to his successor, Elisha.

Aphra Behn

164?–1689

Aphra Behn's career was unprecedented, her output prodigious, her fame extensive, and her voice distinctive. Her origins, though, remain elusive. We know nothing certain about her birth, family, education, or marriage. She may have been born at the start or at the end of the 1640s, to parents of low or "gentle" station, named Johnson, Amies, or Cooper. Her Catholicism and her firm command of French suggest the possibility of a prosperous upbringing in a convent at home or abroad; the running argument against marriage for money that she sustains through much of her work suggests that her own marriage, to the otherwise unidentifiable "Mr. Behn," may have been obligatory and unhappy. In any case it was brief—and just possibly fictitious, since a widow could pursue a profession more freely than a spinster.

Behn's first appearances in the historical record suggest a propensity for self-invention. In 1663–1664, during a short stay with her family in the South American sugar colony of Surinam, a government agent there reported that she was conducting a flirtation with William Scott, an antimonarchist on the run from the Restoration. The agent referred to Scott as "Celadon" and Aphra as "Astraea," names the lovers may well have chosen for themselves from a popular French romance; Behn kept hers, as *nom de plume*, for the whole of her writing life. Within two years, her loyalties had shifted and her self-invention had grown more intricate. In 1666 Behn herself became the king's spy, sent from London to Antwerp to persuade her old flame Scott to turn informer against his fellow Republicans and to apprise King Charles of rebellious plots. She did useful but costly work, garnering good information that her handlers ignored and spending much money that they were slow to reimburse. Returning to England later that year, and threatened with imprisonment for debt, she wrote her supervisor, "I have cried myself dead and could find in my heart to break through all and get to the King and never rise till he were pleased to pay this, but I am sick and weak and unfit for it or a prison . . . Sir, if I have not the money tonight you must send me something to keep [sustain] me in prison, for I will not starve." The king paid up, and Behn forestalled any further threat of starvation by writing plays for money—the first woman in England to earn a living by her pen. She had been "forced to write for bread," she later declared, and she was "not ashamed to own it."

Throughout her career Behn transmuted such "shamelessness" into a positive point of pride and a source of literary substance. Many of her plays, poems, and fictions focus on the difficulty with which intelligent, enterprising women pursue their desires against the current of social convention. In the prologues, prefaces, postscripts, and letters by which she provided a running commentary on her work, Behn sometimes aligned herself with the large fraternity of male authors who "like good tradesmen" sell whatever is "in fashion," but she often stood apart to muse acerbically on her unique position as a *female* purveyor of literary product. Once, surveying the panoply of contemporary male playwrights, she declared that "except for our most unimitable Laureate [Dryden], I dare say I know of none that write at such a formidable rate, but that a woman may well hope to reach their greatest heights." "Formidable rate" suggests both speed and skill; Behn made good on both boasts, producing twenty plays in twenty years, along with much poetry (including fervent pro-Stuart propaganda), copious translations, one of the earliest epistolary novels in English, and a cluster of innovative shorter fiction. In her range and her dexterity, she approached the stature of the "unimitable Laureate" himself, who knew her and praised her repeatedly. With her greatest successes—the comedy *The Rover* (1677), the novella *Oroonoko* (1688)—she secured both an audience and a reputation that continued without pause well into the following century.

Other pieces worked less well. Changes in literary fashion often obliged Behn to try new modes; she switched to fiction, for example, in the 1680s, when plays became less lucrative.

Out of her vicissitudes—professional and personal, amorous, financial, literary—she fashioned a formidable celebrity, becoming the object of endless speculation in talk and in ink. "I value fame," she once wrote, and she cultivated it by what seemed an unprecedented frankness. ("All women together," wrote Virginia Woolf, "ought to let flowers fall upon the grave of Aphra Behn . . . for it was she who earned them the right to speak their minds.") In an age of libertines, when men like Rochester paraded their varied couplings in verse couplets, Behn undertook to proclaim and to analyze women's sexual desire, as manifested in her characters and in herself. Her disclosures, though, were intricately orchestrated. Living and writing at the center of a glamorous literary circle, Behn may have fostered, as the critic Janet Todd suggests, the "fantasy of a golden age of sexual and social openness," but she performed it for her readers rather than falling for it herself. Throughout her work Behn adroitly conceals the "self" that she purports to show and sell. She sometimes likens herself to those other female denizens of the theater, the mask-wearing prostitutes who roamed the audience in search of customers. The critic Catherine Gallagher has argued that Behn's literary persona—defiant, vulnerable, hypnotic—functions like the prostitute's vizard, promising the woman's "availability" as commodity while at the same time implying "the impenetrability of the controlling mind" behind the mask.

In Gallagher's reckoning, as in Woolf's, Behn's total career is more important than any particular work it produced. This is fitting tribute to a writer who, in an era of spectacular self-performers (Charles II, Dryden, Rochester), brought off, by virtue of her gender and her art, one of the most intricate performances of all. That performance now looks set for a long second run. After a hiatus in the nineteenth century, when both the writer and the work were dismissed as indecent, Behn's fame has undergone extraordinary revival. She dominates cultural-studies discourse as both a topic and a set of texts. The texts in particular are worth attending to: many are as astonishing as the career that engendered them.

The Disappointment[1]

One day the amorous Lysander,
By an impatient passion swayed,
Surprised fair Cloris, that loved maid,
Who could defend herself no longer.
5   All things did with his love conspire;
The gilded planet of the day,
In his gay chariot drawn by fire,
Was now descending to the sea,
And left no light to guide the world,
10   But what from Cloris' brighter eyes was hurled.

In a lone thicket made for love,
Silent as yielding maid's consent,
She with a charming languishment
Permits his force, yet gently strove;
15   Her hands his bosom softly meet,
But not to put him back designed,
Rather to draw 'em[2] on inclined;
Whilst he lay trembling at her feet,

1. Behn based this poem partly on a French source, *Sur une impuissance* (1661), itself derived in part from Ovid's poem on impotence in *Amores*, which also provided the model for Rochester's *Imperfect Enjoyment* (see page 1012). Behn's poem and Rochester's first appeared in the same volume, *Poems on Several Occasions* (1680); she later included hers, with alterations, in her own collection, *Poems on Several Occasions* (1684).
2. Behn's earlier version reads "him."

Resistance 'tis in vain to show;
20   She wants° the power to say, "Ah! What d'ye do?"   *lacks*

Her bright eyes sweet, and yet severe,
Where love and shame confusedly strive,
Fresh vigor to Lysander give;
And breathing faintly in his ear,
25   She cried, "Cease, cease your vain desire,
Or I'll call out—what would you do?
My dearer honor even to you
I cannot, must not give—retire,
Or take this life, whose chiefest part
30   I gave you with the conquest of my heart."

But he as much unused to fear,
As he was capable of love,
The blessed minutes to improve,
Kisses her mouth, her neck, her hair;
35   Each touch her new desire alarms,
His burning trembling hand he pressed
Upon her swelling snowy breast,
While she lay panting in his arms.
All her unguarded beauties lie
40   The spoils and trophies of the enemy.

And now without respect or fear,
He seeks the object of his vows,
(His love no modesty allows)
By swift degrees advancing—where
45   His daring hand that altar seized,
Where gods of love do sacrifice:
That awful° throne, that paradise   *awe-inspiring*
Where rage is calmed, and anger pleased;
That fountain where delight still flows,
50   And gives the universal world repose.

Her balmy lips encountering his,
Their bodies, as their souls, are joined;
Where both in transports unconfined
Extend themselves upon the moss.
55   Cloris half dead and breathless lay;
Her soft eyes cast a humid light,
Such as divides the day and night;
Or falling stars, whose fires decay:
And now no signs of life she shows,
60   But what in short-breathed sighs returns and goes.

He saw how at her length she lay;
He saw her rising bosom bare;
Her loose thin robes, through which appear
A shape designed for love and play;
65   Abandoned by her pride and shame,
She does her softest joys dispense,
Offering her virgin innocence
A victim to love's sacred flame;

While the o'er-ravished shepherd lies
70   Unable to perform the sacrifice.

Ready to taste a thousand joys,
The too transported hapless swain[3]
Found the vast pleasure turned to pain;
Pleasure which too much love destroys.
75   The willing garments by he laid,
And Heaven all opened to his view,
Mad to possess, himself he threw
On the defenseless lovely maid.
But oh what envying god conspires
80   To snatch his power, yet leave him the desire!

Nature's support[4] (without whose aid
She can no human being give)
Itself now wants the art to live.
Faintness its slackened nerves invade.
85   In vain the enraged youth essayed
To call its fleeting vigor back,
No motion 'twill from motion take.
Excess of love his love betrayed.
In vain he toils, in vain commands;
90   The insensible[5] fell weeping in his hand.

In this so amorous cruel strife,
Where love and fate were too severe,
The poor Lysander in despair
Renounced his reason with his life.
95   Now all the brisk and active fire
That should the nobler part inflame,
Served to increase his rage and shame,
And left no spark for new desire.
Not all her naked charms could move
100 Or calm that rage that had debauched° his love.   *corrupted*

Cloris returning from the trance
Which love and soft desire had bred,
Her timorous hand she gently laid
(Or° guided by design or chance)   *either*
105 Upon that fabulous Priapus,[6]
That potent god, as poets feign;
But never did young shepherdess,
Gathering of fern upon the plain,
More nimbly draw her fingers back,
110 Finding beneath the verdant leaves a snake,

Than Cloris her fair hand withdrew,
Finding that god of her desires
Disarmed of all his awful fires,
And cold as flowers bathed in the morning dew.

---

3. In English pastoral poetry, this is the conventional
term for the shepherd/lover.
4. I.e., the erect penis.

5. The unfeeling object.
6. Greek god of male fertility, often depicted as possessing
a permanent erection.

115   Who can the nymph's confusion guess?
    The blood forsook the hinder place,
    And strewed with blushes all her face,
    Which both disdain and shame expressed.
    And from Lysander's arms she fled,
120 Leaving him fainting on the gloomy bed.

    Like lightning through the grove she hies,
    Or Daphne from the Delphic god,[7]
    No print upon the grassy road
    She leaves, to instruct pursuing eyes.
125   The wind that wantoned in her hair,
    And with her ruffled garments played,
    Discovered in the flying maid
    All that the gods e'er made, if fair.
    So Venus, when her love was slain,
130 With fear and haste flew o'er the fatal plain.[8]

    The nymph's resentments none but I
    Can well imagine or condole.
    But none can guess Lysander's soul,
    But those who swayed his destiny.
135   His silent griefs swell up to storms,
    And not one god his fury spares;
    He cursed his birth, his fate, his stars;
    But more the shepherdess's charms,
    Whose soft bewitching influence
140 Had damned him to the hell of impotence.

                 1680

COMPANION READING

John Wilmot, Earl of Rochester: The Imperfect Enjoyment[1]

    Naked she lay, clasped in my longing arms,
    I filled with love, and she all over charms;
    Both equally inspired with eager fire,
    Melting through kindness, flaming in desire.
5   With arms, legs, lips close clinging to embrace,

7. Apollo, who pursued the nymph Daphne until she was turned into a laurel tree in order to escape his advances.
8. When her beloved Adonis was wounded by a boar, the goddess of love rushed to help him, but in vain.
1. John Wilmot, Earl of Rochester (1647–1680), was a lyric poet and satirist known for his many notorious escapades. Always living at odds with ordinary time, mostly ahead of it, he became Earl at age ten, when his father died, received his M.A. at Oxford at 14; conducted a Grand Tour of Europe during the next three years; tried to abduct his future wife Elizabeth Malet when he was 18, and was briefly imprisoned for the attempt; married her at 20; and died, after long libertinage and precipitate piety, at 33. Rochester's wit and beauty, the stupendous energies of his mind (erudite, inventive), of his language (adroit, obscene), of his body (alcoholic, bisexual), and his convictions (hedonistic, atheistic) fascinated the Restoration court. Before his death, Rochester asked his mother to burn his papers, and she did. Fewer than 100 poems survive. Rochester had never troubled to publish any of them himself; a pirated collection appeared a few months after his death. Yet these pieces, and the conflicting accounts of the life that produced them, have been enough to make him last. Soon after his death, Aphra Behn claimed in verse to have received a visit from his "lovely phantom." "The great, the god-like Rochester" comes before her in order both to praise and to correct her poetry. Since then he has haunted many—pietists, poets, and others—as object of veneration, or reproach, or both together.

She clips me to her breast, and sucks me to her face.
Her nimble tongue, Love's lesser lightning, played
Within my mouth, and to my thoughts conveyed
Swift orders that I should prepare to throw
10   The all-dissolving thunderbolt below.
My fluttering soul, sprung with the pointed kiss,
Hangs hovering o'er her balmy brinks of bliss.
But whilst her busy hand would guide that part
Which should convey my soul up to her heart,
15   In liquid raptures I dissolve all o'er,
Melt into sperm, and spend at every pore.
A touch from any part of her had done 't:
Her hand, her foot, her very look's a cunt.
    Smiling, she chides in a kind murmuring noise,
20   And from her body wipes the clammy joys,
When, with a thousand kisses wandering o'er
My panting bosom, "Is there then no more?"
She cries. "All this to love and rapture's due;
Must we not pay a debt to pleasure too?"
25   But I, the most forlorn, lost man alive,
To show my wished obedience vainly strive:
I sigh, alas! and kiss, but cannot swive.°   *screw*
Eager desires confound my first intent,
Succeeding shame does more success prevent,
30   And rage at last confirms me impotent.
Ev'n her fair hand, which might bid heat return
To frozen age, and make cold hermits burn,
Applied to my dead cinder, warms no more
Than fire to ashes could past flames restore.
35   Trembling, confused, despairing, limber, dry,
A wishing, weak, unmoving lump I lie.
This dart of love, whose piercing point, oft tried,
With virgin blood ten thousand maids have dyed,
Which nature still directed with such art
40   That it through every cunt reached every heart—
Stiffly resolved, 'twould carelessly invade
Woman or man, nor ought° its fury stayed:°   *anything/stopped*
Where'er it pierced, a cunt it found or made—
Now languid lies in this unhappy hour,
45   Shrunk up and sapless like a withered flower.
    Thou treacherous, base deserter of my flame,
False to my passion, fatal to my fame,
Through what mistaken magic dost thou prove
So true to lewdness, so untrue to love?
50   What oyster-cinder-beggar-common whore
Didst thou e'er fail in all thy life before?
When vice, disease, and scandal lead the way,
With what officious haste doest thou obey!
Like a rude, roaring hector° in the streets   *bully*
55   Who scuffles, cuffs, and justles all he meets,
But if his king or country claim his aid,

The rakehell villain shrinks and hides his head;
Ev'n so thy brutal valor is displayed,
Breaks every stew,° does each small whore invade,   *brothel*
60   But when great Love the onset does command,
Base recreant to thy prince, thou dar'st not stand.
Worst part of me, and henceforth hated most,
Through all the town a common fucking post,
On whom each whore relieves her tingling cunt
65   As hogs on gates do rub themselves and grunt,
Mayst thou to ravenous chancres° be a prey,   *syphilis sores*
Or in consuming weepings waste away;
May strangury and stone² thy days attend;
May'st thou never piss, who didst refuse to spend
70   When all my joys did on false thee depend.
          And may ten thousand abler pricks agree
          To do the wronged Corinna right for thee.

                                                                     1680

To Lysander at the Music-Meeting

It was too much, ye gods, to see and hear,
Receiving wounds both from the eye and ear.
One charm might have secured a victory;
Both, raised the pleasure even to ecstasy.
5   So ravished lovers in each other's arms,
Faint with excess of joy, excess of charms.
Had I but gazed and fed my greedy eyes,
Perhaps you'd pleased no farther than surprise.
That heav'nly form might admiration move,
10   But, not without the music, charmed° with love: *have charmed*
At least so quick the conquest had not been;
You stormed without, and harmony within.
Nor could I listen to the sound alone,
But I alas must look—and was undone:
15   I saw the softness that composed your face,
While your attention heightened every grace:
Your mouth all full of sweetness and content,
And your fine killing eyes of languishment:
Your bosom now and then a sigh would move,
20   (For music has the same effects with love).
Your body easy and all tempting lay,
Inspiring wishes which the eyes betray,
In all that have the fate to glance that way.
A careless and a lovely negligence,
25   Did a new charm to every limb dispense.
So look young angels, listening to the sound,
When the tuned spheres glad¹ all the heav'ns around:

---

2. Painful diseases of the bladder and urinary tract that block the flow of urine.
1. Gladden. In the Ptolemaic view of the universe that Behn invokes here, the heavens were composed of concentric crystalline spheres, whose motion produced a sublime music. Angels could hear it, humans could not.

So raptured lie amidst the wondering crowd,
So charmingly extended on a cloud.
30   When from so many ways love's arrows storm,
Who can the heedless heart defend from harm?
Beauty and music must the soul disarm;
Since harmony, like fire to wax, does fit
The softened heart impressions to admit:
35   As the brisk sounds of war the courage move,
Music prepares and warms the soul to love.
But when the kindling sparks such fuel meet,
No wonder if the flame inspired be great.

1684

To the Fair Clarinda, Who Made Love to Me,
Imagined More than Woman

Fair lovely maid, or if that title be
Too weak, too feminine for nobler thee,
Permit a name that more approaches truth,
And let me call thee, lovely charming youth.
5   This last will justify my soft complaint,
While that may serve to lessen my constraint;
And without blushes I the youth pursue,
When so much beauteous woman is in view.
Against thy charms we struggle but in vain,
10   With thy deluding form thou giv'st us pain,
While the bright nymph betrays us to the swain.[1]
In pity to our sex sure thou wert sent,
That we might love, and yet be innocent:
For sure no crime with thee we can commit;
15   Or if we should—thy form excuses it.
For who that gathers fairest flowers believes
A snake lies hid beneath the fragrant leaves.

Thou beauteous wonder of a different kind,
Soft Cloris with the dear Alexis[2] joined;
20   Whene'er the manly part of thee would plead
Thou tempts us with the image of the maid,
While we the noblest passions do extend
The love to Hermes, Aphrodite the friend.[3]

1688

APHRA BEHN IN CONTEXT
Coterie Writing

To Lysander, To the Fair Clarinda, A Letter to Mr. Creech: Some of Behn's poetry, like much other verse in the seventeenth century, proffered its readers the voyeuristic sense that they were

---

1. The conventional pastoral term for a male lover or a country lad.
2. "Cloris" is female, "Alexis" male.

3. Named after the offspring of these two gods, a hermaphrodite combines the characteristics of both sexes.

being let in on the poet's correspondence. Sometimes this was so. In literary families and in friendships, verse often served as a medium of communication. A poem might make its way first from the writer to a designated recipient, then to a larger circle of acquaintances, and finally (with or without the author's consent) to the printing press. The practice of circulating manuscripts has come to be called "coterie writing," and its antecedents were ancient. Theocritus, the Greek poet credited with inventing pastoral verse, cast many of his poems as expressions of love and friendship (sung rather than written) among shepherds and nymphs living in a Golden Age. The Greek names of these ardent Arcadians—all those swooning "Lysanders" and "Clarindas"— came down to the English poets through the *Eclogues* of Virgil, Theocritus's immeasurably influential Roman imitator. Another Roman, Horace, had pioneered the durable paradigm of the verse epistle, a wittily self-conscious poetic performance addressed to a real-life, explicitly identified contemporary. In the seventeenth century, the resurgence of coterie writing began with the work of Katherine Philips, who celebrated her friendships with women in poems published to great acclaim shortly after her early death. (Behn admired Philips enormously, but reworked the tradition by addressing many of her poems to men—lovers and literary colleagues—in a boldly specific, often sexual language that contrasted sharply with Philips's celebrated chastity.) Both men and women produced poems of friendship in great numbers, but for women writers the practice appears to have held a particular attraction. In addressing other women, they could enact a solidarity, cultivate a self-discovery, define and develop a resistance otherwise muted in a male-dominated world; they often depict themselves as building from female friendship what the critic Janet Todd calls "the last buttress against the irrationality always implied in the female condition." The equivocal "privacy" of the coterie poem made it a particularly supple medium, capable of combining fact and fiction, disguise and revelation, intimacy and declamation. The three practitioners sampled here worked many variations in this pliable, powerful mode of writing.

Mary, Lady Chudleigh[1]
To the Ladies

Wife and servant are the same,
But only differ in the name:
For when that fatal knot is tied,
Which nothing, nothing can divide:
5　When she the word *obey* has said,
And man by law supreme has made,
Then all that's kind is laid aside,
And nothing left but state° and pride:　　　　　　　　　*dignity*
Fierce as an Eastern Prince he grows,
10　And all his innate rigor shows:
Then but to look, to laugh, or speak,
Will the nuptial contract break.
Like mutes she signs alone must make,
And never any freedom take:
15　But still be governed by a nod,

1. Born Mary Lee, and wed at age 17 into a family as aristocratic as her own, Lady Chudleigh (1656–1710) lived and wrote in the west coast county of Devon. After years of dispatching manuscript verses among a widening circle of writing friends (including the laureate John Dryden and the pioneering feminist Mary Astell), Chudleigh made her first foray into print with *The Ladies Defense* (1701), a satiric retort to a parson who had exhorted all women (in her mocking paraphrase) to "give up their rea-

son, and their wills resign" to the dictates of their husbands. In her *Defense*, and in the two collections of shorter poems that followed (1703, 1710), Chudleigh sought to expand her coterie into a larger collective readership consisting of "all ingenious ladies": women willing, in defiance of male presumption and social convention, "to read and think, and think and read again," and thereby to "make it our whole business to be wise."

And fear her husband as her God:
Him still must serve, him still obey,
And nothing act, and nothing say,
But what her haughty lord thinks fit,
20 Who with the power, has all the wit.°   *intelligence*
Then shun, oh! shun that wretched state,
And all the fawning flatterers hate:
Value your selves, and men despise,
You must be proud, if you'll be wise.

                                                                  1703

To Almystrea[1]

                        1

Permit Marissa[2] in an artless lay
To speak her wonder, and her thanks repay:
Her creeping Muse can ne'er like yours ascend;
She has not strength for such a towering flight.
5   Your wit, her humble fancy does transcend;
She can but gaze at your exalted height:
Yet she believed it better to expose
        Her failures, than ungrateful prove;
            And rather chose
10   To show a want of sense, than want of love:
But taught by you, she may at length improve,
And imitate those virtues she admires.
Your bright example leaves a tract divine,
She sees a beamy brightness in each line,
15   And with ambitious warmth aspires,
Attracted by the glory of your name,
To follow you in all the lofty roads of fame.

                        2

Merit like yours can no resistance find,
But like a deluge overwhelms the mind;
20   Gives full possession of each part,
Subdues the soul, and captivates the heart.
Let those whom wealth, or interest[3] unite,
        Whom avarice, or kindred sway,[4]
        Who in the dregs of life delight,
25   And every dictate of their sense° obey,   *appetites*
Learn here to love at a sublimer rate,
To wish for nothing but exchange of thoughts,
            For intellectual joys,
            And pleasures more refined
30   Than earth can give, or fancy can create.
Let our vain sex be fond of glittering toys,
Of pompous titles, and affected noise,
Let envious men by barb'rous custom led

---

1. The name is an anagram for Mary Astell, feminist
author of *Some Reflections upon Marriage* (1700).
2. Chudleigh's pen name.

3. Self-interest, desire for power and material prosperity.
4. I.e., who are motivated by greed or desire for family
status.

Descant° on faults,   *expound*
35   And in detraction° find   *criticisms*
Delights unknown to a brave generous mind,
While we resolve a nobler path to tread,
    And from tyrannic custom free,
View the dark mansions of the mighty dead,
40   And all their close recesses see;
    Then from those awful shades retire,
        And take a tour above,
And there, the shining scenes admire,
    The opera of eternal love;
45 View the machines,[5] on the bright actors gaze,
Then in a holy transport, blest amaze,
To the great Author our devotion raise,
And let our wonder terminate in praise.

1703

Anne Finch, Countess of Winchilsea[1]
The Introduction

Did I my lines intend for public view,
How many censures would their faults pursue!
Some would, because such words they do affect,
Cry they're insipid, empty, uncorrect.
5   And many have attained, dull and untaught
The name of wit, only by finding fault.
True judges might condemn their want of wit,
And all might say they're by a woman writ.
Alas! A woman that attempts the pen,
10 Such an intruder on the rights of men,
Such a presumptuous creature is esteemed,
The fault can by no virtue be redeemed.
They tell us we mistake our sex and way;
Good breeding, fashion, dancing, dressing, play
15 Are the accomplishments we should desire;
To write, or read, or think, or to inquire
Would cloud our beauty, and exhaust our time,
And interrupt the conquests of our prime;
Whilst the dull manage of a servile house
20 Is held by some our utmost art, and use.
    Sure 'twas not ever thus, nor are we told
Fables,° of women that excelled of old;   *false stories*

---

5. The stage mechanisms used to move scenery and produce striking effects (including the appearances of gods and angels).

1. In the early 1680s, while serving as Maid of Honor to Mary of Modena (wife of the future James II), Anne Kingsmill (1661–1720) met and married Colonel Heneage Finch, and savored the splendors of the Stuart court. When that world vanished in the Revolution of 1688, she and her husband withdrew to his country estate, where she suffered recurrent depression, cultivated friendships, wrote poetry, and saw her work published in several miscellanies. In 1713, despite her wariness of the censures heaped on women writers, she published anonymously a collection of her own, *Miscellany Poems on Several Occasions*. (*The Introduction*, in which she most memorably confronts the censurers, remained like much of her verse unpublished until the 20th century.) The book brought her some fame in her own time and much more a century later, when William Wordsworth proclaimed his admiration for her work. Her poetry moves adroitly among polarities: city and country, satire and affection, solitude and friendship.

To whom, by the diffusive° hand of heaven   *scattering*
Some share of wit and poetry was given.
25   On that glad day, on which the Ark returned,[2]
The holy pledge for which the land had mourned,
The joyful tribes attend it on the way,
The Levites do the sacred charge convey,
Whilst various instruments before it play;
30   Here, holy virgins in the concert join,
The louder notes to soften, and refine,
And with alternate verse,[3] complete the hymn divine.
Lo! The young poet,[4] after God's own heart,
By Him inspired, and taught the Muse's art,
35   Returned from conquest, a bright chorus meets,
That sing his slain ten thousand in the streets.
In such loud numbers° they his acts declare,   *verses*
Proclaim the wonders of his early war,
That Saul upon the vast applause does frown,
40   And feels its mighty thunder shake the crown.[5]
What can the threatened judgment now prolong?[6]
Half of the kingdom is already gone:
The fairest half, whose influence guides the rest,
Have David's empire o'er their hearts confessed.
45   A woman[7] here leads fainting Israel on,
She fights, she wins, she triumphs with a song,
Devout, majestic, for the subject fit,
And far above her arms, exalts her wit,
Then to the peaceful, shady palm withdraws,
50   And rules the rescued nation with her laws.
How are we fal'n, fal'n by mistaken rules?
And education's, more than nature's fools,
Debarred from all improvements of the mind,
And to be dull, expected and designed°;   *intended*
55   And if someone would soar above the rest,
With warmer fancy[8] and ambition pressed,
So strong the opposing faction still appears,
The hopes to thrive can ne'er outweigh the fears.
Be cautioned then my Muse, and still retired;
60   Nor be despised, aiming to be admired;
Conscious of wants, still with contracted wing,
To some few friends and to thy sorrows sing;
For groves of laurel[9] thou wert never meant;
Be dark enough thy shades, and be thou there content.

                                                           1903

2. The Ark of the Covenant was a chest containing the stone tablets of the Ten Commandments. Recovered by King David, it was carried into Jerusalem by members of the Levite tribe (1 Chronicles 15).
3. Responsive singing: the male and the female choruses sing by turns, answering line with line.
4. David, who in his youth was skilled both as a fighter, conquering the Philistines, and as a harper, credited with composing the Psalms.
5. Saul, first king of Israel, had made David his general but tried to kill him after hearing the women of Israel singing, "Saul has slain his thousands, and David his ten thousands" (1 Samuel 18.7).
6. Postpone; the prophet Samuel had foretold an untimely end to Saul's reign.
7. Deborah, judge and prophet who led the Israelites to victory over the Canaanites (Judges 4–5).
8. Livelier imagination.
9. Tree whose leaves were used to crown celebrated poets.

Friendship Between Ephelia and Ardelia[1]

Eph.   What friendship is, Ardelia, show.
Ard.   'Tis to love, as I love you.
Eph.   This account, so short (though kind)
    Suits not my inquiring mind.
5   Therefore farther now repeat:
    What is friendship when complete?
Ard.   'Tis to share all joy and grief;
    'Tis to lend all due relief
    From the tongue, the heart, the hand;
10   'Tis to mortgage house and land;
    For a friend be sold a slave;
    'Tis to die upon a grave,
    If a friend therein do lie.
Eph.   This indeed, though carried high,
15   This, though more than e'er was done
    Underneath the rolling sun,
    This has all been said before.
    Can Ardelia say no more?
Ard.   Words indeed no more can show:
20   But 'tis to love, as I love you.

1713

A Ballad to Mrs. Catherine Fleming in London
from Malshanger Farm in Hampshire

From me, who whilom° sung the town,   *formerly*
    This second ballad comes;
To let you know we are got down
    From hurry, smoke, and drums:
5 And every visitor that rolls
In restless coach from Mall to Paul's,[1]
    With a fa-la-la-la-la-la.

And now were I to paint the seat[2]
    (As well-bred poets use°)   *do*
10 I should embellish our retreat,
    By favor of the Muse:
Though to no villa we pretend,
But a plain farm at the best end,
    With a fa-la etc.

15 Where innocence and quiet reigns,
    And no distrust is known;
His nightly safety none maintains,
    By ways they do in town,
Who rising loosen bolt and bar;
20 We draw the latch and out we are,
    With a fa-la etc.

---

1. "Ardelia" is Finch's pastoral pen name.
1. From Pall Mall, a fashionable promenade in London,
to St. Paul's Cathedral.
2. The "country seat": the farm.

For jarring sounds in London streets,
    Which still are passing by;
Where "Cowcumbers"[3] with "Sand ho" meets,
25   And for loud mastery vie:
The driver whistling to his team
Here wakes us from some rural dream,
    With a fa-la etc.

From rising hills through distant views,
30   We see the sun decline;
Whilst everywhere the eye pursues
    The grazing flocks and kine:
Which home at night the farmer brings,
And not the post's but sheep's bell rings,
35   With a fa-la etc.

We silver trouts and crayfish eat,
    Just taken from the stream;
And never think our meal complete,
    Without fresh curds and cream:
40 And as we pass by the barn floor,
We choose our supper from the door,
    With a fa-la etc.

Beneath our feet the partridge springs,
    As to the woods we go;
45 Where birds scarce stretch their painted wings,
    So little fear they show:
But when our outspread hoops° they spy,   *hoop skirts*
They look when we like them should fly,
    With a fa-la etc.

50   Through verdant circles as we stray,
    To which no end we know;
As we o'erhanging boughs survey,
    And tufted grass below:
Delight into the fancy falls,
55 And happy days and verse recalls,
    With a fa-la etc.

Oh! Why did I these shades forsake,
    And shelter of the grove;
The flowering shrub, the rustling brake,°   *thicket*
60   The solitude I love:
Where emperors have fixed their lot,
And greatly chose to be forgot,
    With a fa-la etc.

Then how can I from hence depart,
65   Unless my pleasing friend
Should now her sweet harmonious art
    Unto these shades extend:
And, like old Orpheus' powerful song,[4]

3. Cucumbers; these are the cries of street peddlers.   4. The mythological poet's music charmed trees and stones into motion.

70 Draw me and all my woods along,
    With a fa-la etc.

So charmed like Birnam's they would rise,
And march in goodly row,[5]
But since it might the town surprise
    To see me travel so,
75 I must from soothing joys like these,
Too soon return in open chaise°   carriage
    With a fa-la etc.

Meanwhile accept what I have writ,
    To show this rural scene;
80 Nor look for sharp satiric wit
    From off the balmy plain:
The country breeds no thorny bays,
    But mirth and love and honest praise,
    With a fa-la etc.

c. 1719   1929

Mary Leapor[1]
The Headache. To Aurelia

Aurelia, when your zeal makes known
Each woman's failing but your own,
How charming Silvia's teeth decay,
And Celia's hair is turning grey;
5 Yet Celia gay has sparkling eyes,
But (to your comfort) is not wise:
Methinks you take a world of pains
To tell us Celia has no brains.

    Now you wise folk, who make such a pother°   fuss
10 About the wit of one another,
With pleasure would your brains resign,
Did all your noddles° ache like mine.   heads

    Not cuckolds half my anguish know,
When budding horns[2] begin to grow;
15 Nor battered skull of wrestling Dick,
Who late was drubbed at singlestick;[3]

5. In Shakespeare's *Macbeth*, the forest of Birnam "comes" to Dunsinane (fulfilling the witches' prophecy) when soldiers carry boughs as camouflage.
1. The daughter of a gardener, Mary Leapor (1722–1746) worked as a kitchen maid, read voraciously, wrote plentifully, and sustained the tradition of the social poem (complete with pastoral pseudonyms) into a new era and a new register. Her manuscripts, circulating among neighbors, brought her the attention, friendship, and support of Bridget Freemantle, who undertook to arrange their publication. Leapor died of measles at age 24 before she could see her work in print. Her *Poems upon Several Occasions* appeared in 1748; its success prompted an addi-

tional volume three years later. Though the books were marketed as (in the words of one contemporary) the work of "a most extraordinary, uncultivated genius," the poems themselves prove otherwise. They display influences absorbed from Greek and Roman classics, Restoration drama, and Augustan literature—particularly Swift and Pope. Leapor transports these elements across boundary lines of class and gender to produce a new, arresting voice speaking from an old position: that of the woman who must labor in order to live.
2. Folklore held that the husband of an unfaithful wife would sprout horns from his forehead.
3. Beaten in a fencing match using short, heavy sticks.

Nor wretches that in fevers fry,
Not Sappho[4] when her cap's awry,
E'er felt such torturing pangs as I;
20 Not forehead of Sir Jeffrey Strife,
When smiling Cynthio kissed his wife.

  Not lovesick Marcia's languid eyes,
Who for her simpering Corin dies,
So sleepy look or dimly shine,
25 As these dejected eyes of mine:
Not Claudia's brow such wrinkles made
At sight of Cynthia's new brocade.

  Just so, Aurelia, you complain
Of vapors, rheums, and gouty pain;
30 Yet I am patient, so should you,
For cramps and headaches are our due:
We suffer justly for our crimes,
For scandal you, and I for rhymes;
Yet we (as hardened wretches do)
35 Still the enchanting vice pursue;
Our reformation ne'er begin
But fondly hug the darling sin.

  Yet there's a might difference too
Between the fate of me and you;
40 Though you with tottering age shall bow,
And wrinkles scar your lovely brow,
Your busy tongue may still proclaim
The faults of every sinful dame:
You still may prattle nor give o'er,
45 When wretched I must sin no more.
The sprightly Nine° must leave me then,   *Muses*
This trembling hand resign its pen:
No matron ever sweetly sung,
Apollo° only courts the young.   *god of poetry*
50 Then who would not (Aurelia, pray)
Enjoy his favors while they may?
Nor cramps nor headaches shall prevail:
I'll still write on, and you shall rail.

1748

An Essay on Woman

  Woman, a pleasing but a short-lived flower,
Too soft for business and too weak for power:
A wife in bondage, or neglected maid;
Despised, if ugly; if she's fair, betrayed.
5 'Tis wealth alone inspires every grace,
And calls the raptures to her plenteous face.

4. Apparently a mutual friend; the ensuing names, too, refer to either real or imaginary people, otherwise unidentified.

What numbers for those charming features pine,
If blooming acres round her temples twine![1]
Her lip the strawberry, and her eyes more bright
10   Than sparkling Venus in a frosty night;
Pale lilies fade and, when the fair appears,
Snow turns a negro[2] and dissolves in tears,
And, where the charmer treads her magic toe,
On English ground Arabian odors grow;
15   Till mighty Hymen° lifts his sceptred rod,   *god of marriage*
And sinks her glories with a fatal nod,
Dissolves her triumphs, sweeps her charms away,
And turns the goddess to her native clay.

　　But, Artemisia,[3] let your servant sing
20   What small advantage wealth and beauties bring.
Who would be wise, that knew Pamphilia's[4] fate?
Or who be fair, and joined to Sylvia's mate?
Sylvia, whose cheeks are fresh as early day,
As evening mild, and sweet as spicy May:
25   And yet that face her partial husband tires,
And those bright eyes, that all the world admires.
Pamphilia's wit who does not strive to shun,
Like death's infection or a dog-day's sun?
The damsels view her with malignant eyes,
30   The men are vexed to find a nymph so wise:
And wisdom only serves to make her know
The keen sensation of superior woe.
The secret whisper and the listening ear,
The scornful eyebrow and the hated sneer,
35   The giddy censures of her babbling kind,
With thousand ills that grate a gentle mind,
By her are tasted in the first degree,
Though overlooked by Simplicus and me.
Does thirst of gold a virgin's heart inspire,
40   Instilled by Nature or a careful sire?
Then let her quit extravagance and play,
The brisk companion and expensive tea,
To feast with Cordia in her filthy sty
On stewed potatoes or on mouldy pie;
45   Whose eager eyes stare ghastly at the poor,
And fright the beggars from her hated door;
In greasy clouts° she wraps her smokey chin,   *rags*
And holds that pride's a never-pardoned sin.

　　If this be wealth, no matter where it falls;
50   But save, ye Muses, save your Mira's[5] walls:

1. I.e., if her dowry includes valuable land.
2. I.e., seems black by comparison.
3. The name of an ancient ruler celebrated as a patron of literature; Leapor applies it to her friend and sponsor Bridget Freemantle.
4. The lines about "Pamphilia" suggest that she may serve here as Leapor's alter ego; the other pastoral names (Sylvia, Simplicus, etc.) conjure up acquaintances real or imaginary.
5. Leapor's pen name (derived from "Mary").

Still give me pleasing indolence and ease,
A fire to warm me and a friend to please.

Since, whether sunk in avarice or pride,
A wanton virgin or a starving bride,
55 Or° wondering crowds attend her charming tongue,   *whether*
Or, deemed an idiot, ever speaks the wrong;
Though Nature armed us for the growing ill
With fraudful cunning and a headstrong will;
Yet, with ten thousand follies to her charge,
60 Unhappy woman's but a slave at large.

                                                            1751

The Epistle of Deborah Dough

Dearly beloved Cousin, these
Are sent to thank you for your cheese;
The price of oats is greatly fell:
I hope your children all are well
5 (Likewise the calf you take delight in),
As I am at this present writing.
But I've no news to send you now;
Only I've lost my brindled° cow,   *spotted*
And that has greatly sunk my dairy.
10 But I forgot our neighbor Mary;
Our neighbor Mary—who, they say,
Sits scribble-scribble all the day,
And making—what—I can't remember;
But sure 'tis something like December;
15 A frosty morning—let me see—
O! Now I have it to a T:
She throws away her precious time
In scrawling nothing else but rhyme;[1]
Of which, they say, she's mighty proud,
20 And lifts her nose above the crowd;
Though my young daughter Cicely
Is taller by a foot than she,
And better learned (as people say);
Can knit a stocking in a day;
25 Can make a pudding, plump and rare;
And boil her bacon to an hair;
Will coddle° apples nice and green,   *cook*
And fry her pancakes—like a queen.

But there's a man, that keeps a dairy,
30 Will clip the wings of neighbor Mary:
Things wonderful they talk of him,
But I've a notion 'tis a whim.

---

1. A pun on "rime" (frost), which is why her work is "like December."

Howe'er, 'tis certain he can make
Your rhymes as thick as plums in cake;
35   Nay more, they say that from the pot
He'll take his porridge, scalding hot,
And drink 'em down;—and yet they tell ye
Those porridge shall not burn his belly;
A cheesecake o'er his head he'll throw,
40   And when 'tis on the stones below,
It shan't be found so much as quaking,
Provided 'tis of his wife's making.
From this some people would infer
That this good man's a conjuror:
45   But I believe it is a lie;
I never thought him so, not I,
Though Win'fred Hobble who, you know,
Is plagued with corns on every toe,
Sticks on his verse with fastening spittle,
50   And says it helps her feet a little.
Old Frances too his paper tears,
And tucks it close behind her ears;
And (as she told me t'other day)
It charmed her toothache quite away.

55   Now as thou'rt better learned than me,
Dear Cos', I leave it all to thee
To judge about this puzzling man,
And ponder wisely—for you can.

        Now Cousin, I must let you know
60   That, while my name is Deborah Dough,
I shall be always glad to see ye,
And what I have, I'll freely gi' ye.

        'Tis one o'clock, as I'm a sinner;
The boys are all come home to dinner,
65   And I must bid you now farewell.
I pray remember me to Nell;
And for your friend I'd have you know
Your loving Cousin,
                DEBORAH DOUGH

1751

Oroonoko

"I am very ill and have been dying this twelve month," Behn wrote an acquaintance late in 1687; she suffered from degenerative arthritis, and had some eighteen months' dying still to do. Now, near the end of her writing career, she set down a narrative of events that had pre-dated its beginnings, a story that she claimed to recall from the months she spent in 1663–1664 as a young woman in Surinam, an English colony on the northeastern coast of South America. A friend records that during the intervening decades Behn had often told the story of an African prince enslaved on the plantation where she dwelt; prompted by his love for a slave from his own country, he mounted a rebellion against his English masters. In *Oroonoko*, Behn displayed Surinam as a world where the appetites of trade and empire had brought several cultures—indigenous "Indians," colonizing Europeans, abducted Africans— into violent and precarious fusion.

Writing the narrative, Behn undertook volatile fusions of her own. On the title page, the single name "Oroonoko" sits above two subtitles in which both hero and text are implicitly split in two. The hero is both "royal" and a "slave"; the text's "true history" is so suffused with fictional conventions that for a long while historians suspected that Behn had never been to Surinam and had made the whole thing up (the truth of many of the story's details has been neither established nor refuted). Oroonoko and his beloved Imoinda play out the love-and-loss plot of a heroic romance—a genre favored by Restoration aristocracy—within the far more realistic context of a world driven by bourgeois imperatives and political aspirations. Behn's boldest fusion involves not only cultures, identities, and modes but also times. Oroonoko, "the chief actor in this history," comes to embody the history of Stuart sovereignty, playing the roles of all three kings to whom Behn had devoted her own obsessive loyalties: Charles I, whose 1649 execution haunts the narrative, particularly in its last few pages; Charles II, whose 1660 Restoration Behn pointedly invokes at the celebratory moment of the African prince's arrival at Surinam; and James II, the beleaguered Catholic king whose three-year reign was hurtling toward its close at the very moment of *Oroonoko*'s publication, and whose predicament as the embattled champion of an oppressed minority finds many echoes in the royal slave's rebellion and his fate.

Mapping all these convergences—of culture with culture, of monarch with slave, of man with woman—Behn places herself as narrator problematically near their center. The story is driven by her empathy for the slave couple, for whom she acts as mentor, friend, and advocate. Yet her empathy is complicated, perhaps even compromised. She shows less pity for less "royal" slaves, she acknowledges the possibility of her own complicity (however inadvertent) in her hero's pain, and she is oddly absent at the height of his suffering. She also participates in the profitable systems that enmesh him. Even before she tells his story, she presents herself as a kind of trader, who has brought back from Surinam butterflies for the Royal Society and exotic feathers for the dress of the "Indian Queen" in the popular heroic tragedy of that name. As Laura Brown points out, Behn's "treatment of slavery . . . is neither coherent nor fully critical." The narrative is by turns empathetic with the oppressed and complicit with the powerful; the crossing vectors of Behn's allegiance produce no conclusive sum.

In *Oroonoko*, cultural compounds prove unstable. Again and again in the story, human bodies are torn apart, and these sunderings foretell other dissolutions. Behn repeatedly reminds her readers that shortly after the events she narrates, the entire colony at Surinam disappeared: the English traded it away to the Dutch (they got New York in return). As colonist she laments this loss; as Tory, she anticipates another: the loss of James II in the parliamentary overthrow that would soon supplant the English Catholic with the Dutch Protestant William of Orange. Stuart rule, which had "ended" once with regicide, would end again (like the world of her youth in Surinam) with revolution.

Behn died shortly after publishing her narrative; she was buried in Westminster Abbey, where William would be crowned just five days later. After Behn's death, *Oroonoko* did more than any of her other works to sustain her fame. As a prose narrative and in an oft-revived dramatic adaptation, it became one of the touchstone texts for the antislavery movement that grew in England and America over the next century and a half. Only with the appearance of *Uncle Tom's Cabin* in the 1850s did the advocates of abolition find a more contemporary narrative that could take its place. Behn's intricately fictionalized "true history" had survived its initial moment and helped shape history thereafter.

Oroonoko
or
The Royal Slave
A True History

I do not pretend, in giving you the history of this royal slave, to entertain my reader with the adventures of a feigned hero, whose life and fortunes fancy may manage at the poet's pleasure; nor in relating the truth, design to adorn it with any accidents, but such as arrived in earnest to him. And it shall come simply into the world, recommended by its own proper merits, and natural intrigues; there being enough of reality to support it, and to render it diverting, without the addition of invention.

I was myself an eyewitness to a great part of what you will find here set down; and what I could not be witness of, I received from the mouth of the chief actor in this history, the hero himself, who gave us the whole transactions of his youth; and though I shall omit, for brevity's sake, a thousand little accidents of his life, which, however pleasant to us, where history was scarce, and adventures very rare, yet might prove tedious and heavy to my reader, in a world where he finds diversions for every minute, new and strange. But we who were perfectly charmed with the character of this great man were curious to gather every circumstance of his life.

The scene of the last part of his adventures lies in a colony in America called Surinam, in the West Indies.

But before I give you the story of this gallant slave, 'tis fit I tell you the manner of bringing them to these new colonies; for those they make use of there, are not natives of the place; for those we live with in perfect amity, without daring to command them; but on the contrary, caress them with all the brotherly and friendly affection in the world, trading with them for their fish, venison, buffaloes, skins, and little rarities; as marmosets, a sort of monkey as big as a rat or weasel, but of a marvelous and delicate shape, and has face and hands like an human creature; and cousheries,[1] a little beast in the form and fashion of a lion, as big as a kitten; but so exactly made in all parts like that noble beast, that it is it in miniature. Then for little parakeets, great parrots, macaws, and a thousand other birds and beasts of wonderful and surprising forms, shapes, and colors. For skins of prodigious snakes, of which there are some threescore yards in length; as is the skin of one that may be seen at His Majesty's Antiquaries,[2] where are also some rare flies,[3] of amazing forms and colors, presented to them by myself, some as big as my fist, some less; and all of various excellencies, such as art cannot imitate. Then we trade for feathers, which they order into all shapes, make themselves little short habits of them, and glorious wreaths for their heads, necks, arms, and legs, whose tinctures are inconceivable. I had a set of these presented to me, and I gave them to the King's Theater, and it was the dress of the *Indian Queen*,[4] infinitely admired by persons of quality, and were inimitable. Besides these, a thousand little knacks and rarities in nature, and some of art; as their baskets, weapons, aprons, etc. We dealt with them with beads of all colors, knives, axes, pins, and needles, which they used only as tools to drill holes with in their ears, noses, and lips, where they hang a great many little things; as long beads, bits of tin,

1. Other writers mention this animal, but its identity remains uncertain.
2. Probably the "Repository" (museum) of the Royal Society.
3. Butterflies.
4. A heroic drama (1664) by Robert Howard and John Dryden, celebrated for its sumptuous costumes and design.

brass, or silver, beat thin, and any shining trinket. The beads they weave into aprons about a quarter of an ell[5] long, and of the same breadth, working them very prettily in flowers of several colors of beads; which apron they wear just before them, as Adam and Eve did the fig leaves; the men wearing a long strip of linen, which they deal with us for. They thread these beads also on long cotton threads, and make girdles to tie their aprons to, which come twenty times or more about the waist and then cross, like a shoulder-belt, both ways, and round their necks, arms, and legs. This adornment, with their long black hair, and the face painted in little specks or flowers here and there, makes them a wonderful figure to behold. Some of the beauties which indeed are finely shaped, as almost all are, and who have pretty features, are very charming and novel; for they have all that is called beauty except the color, which is a reddish yellow; or after a new oiling, which they often use to themselves, they are of the color of a new brick, but smooth, soft, and sleek. They are extreme modest and bashful, very shy, and nice[6] of being touched. And though they are all thus naked, if one lives forever among them, there is not to be seen an indecent action or glance; and being continually used to see one another so unadorned, so like our first parents before the Fall, it seems as if they had no wishes; there being nothing to heighten curiosity, but all you can see, you see at once, and every moment see; and where there is no novelty, there can be no curiosity. Not but I have seen a handsome young Indian, dying for love of a very beautiful young Indian maid; but all his courtship was, to fold his arms, pursue her with his eyes, and sighs were all his language; while she, as if no such lover were present, or rather, as if she desired none such, carefully guarded her eyes from beholding him; and never approached him, but she looked down with all the blushing modesty I have seen in the most severe and cautious of our world. And these people represented to me an absolute idea of the first state of innocence, before man knew how to sin; and 'tis most evident and plain, that simple Nature is the most harmless, inoffensive, and virtuous mistress. 'Tis she alone, if she were permitted, that better instructs the world than all the inventions of man; religion would here but destroy that tranquillity they possess by ignorance, and laws would but teach them to know offense, of which now they have no notion. They once made mourning and fasting for the death of the English governor, who had given his hand to come on such a day to them, and neither came, nor sent; believing, when once a man's word was past, nothing but death could or should prevent his keeping it. And when they saw he was not dead, they asked him, what name they had for a man who promised a thing he did not do? The governor told them, such a man was a liar, which was a word of infamy to a gentleman. Then one of them replied, "Governor, you are a liar, and guilty of that infamy." They have a native justice which knows no fraud, and they understand no vice, or cunning, but when they are taught by the white men. They have plurality of wives which, when they grow old, they serve those that succeed them, who are young; but with a servitude easy and respected; and unless they take slaves in war, they have no other attendants.

Those on that continent where I was had no king; but the oldest war captain was obeyed with great resignation.

A war captain is a man who has led them on to battle with conduct[7] and success, of whom I shall have occasion to speak more hereafter, and of some other of their customs and manners, as they fall in my way.

5. Forty-five inches.
6. Shy.

7. Skillful management.

With these people, as I said, we live in perfect tranquillity and good understanding, as it behooves us to do; they knowing all the places where to seek the best food of the country, and the means of getting it; and for very small and invaluable trifles, supply us with what 'tis impossible for us to get; for they do not only in the wood, and over the savannahs, in hunting, supply the parts of hounds, by swiftly scouring through those almost impassable places, and by the mere activity of their feet, run down the nimblest deer, and other eatable beasts; but in the water, one would think they were gods of the rivers, or fellow citizens of the deep, so rare an art they have in swimming, diving, and almost living in water, by which they command the less swift inhabitants of the floods. And then for shooting, what they cannot take, or reach with their hands, they do with arrows, and have so admirable an aim, that they will split almost a hair; and at any distance that an arrow can reach, they will shoot down oranges and other fruit, and only touch the stalk with the darts' points, that they may not hurt the fruit. So that they being, on all occasions, very useful to us, we find it absolutely necessary to caress them as friends, and not to treat them as slaves; nor dare we do other, their numbers so far surpassing ours in that continent.

Those then whom we make use of to work in our plantations of sugar are Negroes, black slaves altogether, which are transported thither in this manner.

Those who want slaves make a bargain with a master, or captain of a ship, and contract to pay him so much apiece, a matter of twenty pound a head for as many as he agrees for, and to pay for them when they shall be delivered on such a plantation. So that when there arrives a ship laden with slaves, they who have so contracted go aboard, and receive their number by lot; and perhaps in one lot that may be for ten, there may happen to be three or four men; the rest, women and children; or be there more or less of either sex, you are obliged to be contented with your lot.

Coramantien,[8] a country of blacks so called, was one of those places in which they found the most advantageous trading for these slaves, and thither most of our great traders in that merchandise trafficked; for that nation is very warlike and brave, and having a continual campaign, being always in hostility with one neighboring prince or other, they had the fortune to take a great many captives; for all they took in battle were sold as slaves, at least, those common men who could not ransom themselves. Of these slaves so taken, the general only has all the profit; and of these generals, our captains and masters of ships buy all their freights.

The King of Coramantien was himself a man of a hundred and odd years old, and had no son, though he had many beautiful black wives; for most certainly, there are beauties that can charm of that color. In his younger years he had had many gallant men to his sons, thirteen of which died in battle, conquering when they fell; and he had only left him for his successor one grandchild, son to one of these dead victors; who, as soon as he could bear a bow in his hand, and a quiver at his back, was sent into the field, to be trained up by one of the oldest generals to war; where, from his natural inclination to arms, and the occasions given him, with the good conduct of the old general, he became, at the age of seventeen, one of the most expert captains, and bravest soldiers, that ever saw the field of Mars; so that he was adored as the wonder of all that world, and the darling of the soldiers. Besides, he was adorned with a native beauty so transcending all those of his gloomy race, that he struck an awe and reverence, even in those that knew not his quality; as he did in me, who beheld him with surprise and wonder, when afterwards he arrived in our world.

8. Koromantyn, a fort and trading post on the western coast of Africa (in modern Ghana).

He had scarce arrived at his seventeenth year when, fighting by his side, the general was killed with an arrow in his eye, which the Prince Oroonoko (for so was this gallant Moor[9] called) very narrowly avoided; nor had he, if the general, who saw the arrow shot, and perceiving it aimed at the Prince, had not bowed his head between, on purpose to receive it in his own body rather than it should touch that of the Prince, and so saved him.

'Twas then, afflicted as Oroonoko was, that he was proclaimed general in the old man's place; and then it was, at the finishing of that war, which had continued for two years, that the Prince came to court, where he had hardly been a month together, from the time of his fifth year to that of seventeen; and 'twas amazing to imagine where it was he learned so much humanity or, to give his accomplishments a juster name, where 'twas he got that real greatness of soul, those refined notions of true honor, that absolute generosity, and that softness that was capable of the highest passions of love and gallantry, whose objects were almost continually fighting men, or those mangled or dead; who heard no sounds but those of war and groans. Some part of it we may attribute to the care of a Frenchman of wit and learning, who finding it turn to very good account to be a sort of royal tutor to this young black, and perceiving him very ready, apt, and quick of apprehension, took a great pleasure to teach him morals, language, and science, and was for it extremely beloved and valued by him. Another reason was, he loved, when he came from war, to see all the English gentlemen that traded thither, and did not only learn their language but that of the Spaniards also, with whom he traded afterwards for slaves.

I have often seen and conversed with this great man, and been a witness to many of his mighty actions, and do assure my reader, the most illustrious courts could not have produced a braver man, both for greatness of courage and mind, a judgment more solid, a wit more quick, and a conversation more sweet and diverting. He knew almost as much as if he had read much: he had heard of, and admired the Romans; he had heard of the late Civil Wars in England, and the deplorable death of our great monarch,[1] and would discourse of it with all the sense, and abhorrence of the injustice imaginable. He had an extreme good and graceful mien, and all the civility of a well-bred great man. He had nothing of barbarity in his nature, but in all points addressed himself as if his education had been in some European court.

This great and just character of Oroonoko gave me an extreme curiosity to see him, especially when I knew he spoke French and English, and that I could talk with him. But though I had heard so much of him, I was as greatly surprised when I saw him as if I had heard nothing of him, so beyond all report I found him. He came into the room, and addressed himself to me, and some other women, with the best grace in the world. He was pretty tall, but of a shape the most exact that can be fancied; the most famous statuary[2] could not form the figure of a man more admirably turned from head to foot. His face was not of that brown, rusty black which most of that nation are, but a perfect ebony, or polished jet. His eyes were the most awful that could be seen, and very piercing, the white of them being like snow, as were his teeth. His nose was rising and Roman, instead of African and flat; his mouth, the finest shaped that could be seen, far from those great turned lips which are so natural to the rest of the Negroes. The whole proportion and air of his face was so noble and

9. The word originally meant "Moroccan," but was often used more generally for any person of African descent. Oroonoko's name may echo the river Orinoco in Venezuela, or the African god Oro.

1. Charles I, whose beheading in 1649 by sentence of the House of Commons marked the culmination of the wars between Royalists and Parliament.
2. Sculptor.

exactly formed that, bating[3] his color, there could be nothing in nature more beautiful, agreeable, and handsome. There was no one grace wanting that bears the standard of true beauty. His hair came down to his shoulders by the aids of art, which was, by pulling it out with a quill and keeping it combed, of which he took particular care. Nor did the perfections of his mind come short of those of his person, for his discourse was admirable upon almost any subject; and whoever had heard him speak, would have been convinced of their errors, that all fine wit is confined to the white men, especially to those of Christendom; and would have confessed that Oroonoko was as capable even of reigning well, and of governing as wisely, had as great a soul, as politic maxims,[4] and was as sensible of power as any prince civilized in the most refined schools of humanity and learning, or the most illustrious courts.

This prince, such as I have described him, whose soul and body were so admirably adorned, was (while yet he was in the court of his grandfather) as I said, as capable of love as 'twas possible for a brave and gallant man to be; and in saying that, I have named the highest degree of love; for sure, great souls are most capable of that passion.

I have already said the old general was killed by the shot of an arrow, by the side of this prince, in battle; and that Oroonoko was made general. This old dead hero had one only daughter left of his race; a beauty that, to describe her truly, one need say only, she was female to the noble male; the beautiful black Venus to our young Mars; as charming in her person as he, and of delicate virtues. I have seen an hundred white men sighing after her, and making a thousand vows at her feet, all vain and unsuccessful; and she was, indeed, too great for any but a prince of her own nation to adore.

Oroonoko coming from the wars (which were now ended) after he had made his court to his grandfather, he thought in honor he ought to make a visit to Imoinda, the daughter of his foster-father, the dead general; and to make some excuses to her, because his preservation was the occasion of her father's death; and to present her with those slaves that had been taken in this last battle, as the trophies of her father's victories. When he came, attended by all the young soldiers of any merit, he was infinitely surprised at the beauty of this fair Queen of Night, whose face and person was so exceeding all he had ever beheld; that lovely modesty with which she received him, that softness in her look and sighs, upon the melancholy occasion of this honor that was done by so great a man as Oroonoko, and a prince of whom she had heard such admirable things; the awfulness[5] wherewith she received him, and the sweetness of her words and behavior while he stayed, gained a perfect conquest over his fierce heart, and made him feel the victor could be subdued. So that having made his first compliments, and presented her a hundred and fifty slaves in fetters, he told her with his eyes that he was not insensible of her charms; while Imoinda, who wished for nothing more than so glorious a conquest, was pleased to believe she understood that silent language of new-born love; and from that moment, put on all her additions to beauty.

The Prince returned to court with quite another humor[6] than before; and though he did not speak much of the fair Imoinda, he had the pleasure to hear all his followers speak of nothing but the charms of that maid; insomuch that, even in the presence of the old king, they were extolling her, and heightening, if possible, the beauties they had found in her; so that nothing else was talked of, no other sound was heard in every corner where there were whisperers, but "Imoinda! Imoinda!"

---

3. Excepting.   5. Respect.
4. Shrewd principles or sayings.   6. Frame of mind.

'Twill be imagined Oroonoko stayed not long before he made his second visit; nor, considering his quality, not much longer before he told her he adored her. I have often heard him say that he admired by what strange inspiration he came to talk things so soft and so passionate, who never knew love, nor was used to the conversation of women; but (to use his own words) he said, most happily, some new, and till then unknown power instructed his heart and tongue in the language of love, and at the same time, in favor of him, inspired Imoinda with a sense of his passion. She was touched with what he said, and returned it all in such answers as went to his very heart, with a pleasure unknown before. Nor did he use those obligations ill that love had done him; but turned all his happy moments to the best advantage; and as he knew no vice, his flame aimed at nothing but honor, if such a distinction may be made in love; and especially in that country, where men take to themselves as many as they can maintain, and where the only crime and sin with woman is to turn her off, to abandon her to want, shame, and misery. Such ill morals are only practiced in Christian countries, where they prefer the bare name of religion; and, without virtue or morality, think that's sufficient. But Oroonoko was none of those professors; but as he had right notions of honor, so he made her such propositions as were not only and barely such; but, contrary to the custom of his country, he made her vows she should be the only woman he would possess while he lived; that no age or wrinkles should incline him to change, for her soul would be always fine, and always young; and he should have an eternal idea in his mind of the charms she now bore, and should look into his heart for that idea, when he could find it no longer in her face.

After a thousand assurances of his lasting flame, and her eternal empire over him, she condescended to receive him for her husband; or rather, received him, as the greatest honor the gods could do her.

There is a certain ceremony in these cases to be observed, which I forgot to ask him how performed; but 'twas concluded on both sides that, in obedience to him, the grandfather was to be first made acquainted with the design; for they pay a most absolute resignation to the monarch, especially when he is a parent also.

On the other side, the old king, who had many wives, and many concubines, wanted not court flatterers to insinuate in his heart a thousand tender thoughts for this young beauty; and who represented her to his fancy as the most charming he had ever possessed in all the long race of his numerous years. At this character his old heart, like an extinguished brand, most apt to take fire, felt new sparks of love and began to kindle; and now grown to his second childhood, longed with impatience to behold this gay thing, with whom, alas, he could but innocently play. But how he should be confirmed she was this wonder, before he used his power to call her to court (where maidens never came, unless for the King's private use) he was next to consider; and while he was so doing, he had intelligence brought him, that Imoinda was most certainly mistress to the Prince Oroonoko. This gave him some chagrin; however, it gave him also an opportunity, one day, when the Prince was a-hunting, to wait on a man of quality, as his slave and attendant, who should go and make a present to Imoinda, as from the Prince; he should then, unknown, see this fair maid, and have an opportunity to hear what message she would return the Prince for his present; and from thence gather the state of her heart, and degree of her inclination. This was put in execution, and the old monarch saw, and burned; he found her all he had heard, and would not delay his happiness, but found he should have some obstacle to overcome her heart; for she expressed her sense of the present the Prince had sent her, in terms so sweet, so soft and pretty, with an air of love and joy that could not be dissembled, insomuch that 'twas past doubt whether she loved Oroonoko entirely. This gave the old king some affliction, but he salved it with this, that the obedience the people pay their king was not at all inferior to what they paid their gods, and what love would not oblige Imoinda to do, duty would compel her to.

He was therefore no sooner got to his apartment, but he sent the royal veil to Imoinda, that is, the ceremony of invitation; he sends the lady, he has a mind to honor with his bed, a veil, with which she is covered and secured for the King's use; and 'tis death to disobey; besides, held a most impious disobedience.

'Tis not to be imagined the surprise and grief that seized this lovely maid at this news and sight. However, as delays in these cases are dangerous, and pleading worse than treason, trembling and almost fainting, she was obliged to suffer herself to be covered and led away.

They brought her thus to court; and the King, who had caused a very rich bath to be prepared, was led into it, where he sat under a canopy in state, to receive this longed for virgin; whom he having commanded should be brought to him, they (after disrobing her) led her to the bath and, making fast the doors, left her to descend. The King, without more courtship, bade her throw off her mantle and come to his arms. But Imoinda, all in tears, threw herself on the marble on the brink of the bath, and besought him to hear her. She told him, as she was a maid, how proud of the divine glory she should have been of having it in her power to oblige her king; but as by the laws he could not, and from his royal goodness would not take from any man his wedded wife, so she believed she should be the occasion of making him commit a great sin, if she did not reveal her state and condition, and tell him she was another's, and could not be so happy to be his.

The King, enraged at this delay, hastily demanded the name of the bold man that had married a woman of her degree without his consent. Imoinda, seeing his eyes fierce and his hands tremble, whether with age or anger I know not, but she fancied the last, almost repented she had said so much, for now she feared the storm would fall on the prince; she therefore said a thousand things to appease the raging of his flame, and to prepare him to hear who it was with calmness; but before she spoke, he imagined who she meant, but would not seem to do so, but commanded her to lay aside her mantle and suffer herself to receive his caresses; or by his gods, he swore, that happy man whom she was going to name should die, though it were even Oroonoko himself. "Therefore," said he, "deny this marriage, and swear thyself a maid." "That," replied Imoinda, "by all our powers I do, for I am not yet known to my husband." "'Tis enough," said the king, "'tis enough to satisfy both my conscience and my heart." And rising from his seat, he went and led her into the bath, it being in vain for her to resist.

In this time the Prince, who was returned from hunting, went to visit his Imoinda, but found her gone; and not only so, but heard she had received the royal veil. This raised him to a storm, and in his madness they had much ado to save him from laying violent hands on himself. Force first prevailed, and then reason. They urged all to him that might oppose his rage; but nothing weighed so greatly with him as the King's old age, incapable of injuring him with Imoinda. He would give way to that hope, because it pleased him most, and flattered best his heart. Yet this served not altogether to make him cease his different passions, which sometimes raged within him, and sometimes softened into showers. 'Twas not enough to appease him, to tell him his grandfather was old, and could not that way injure him, while he retained that awful[7] duty which the young men are used there to pay to their grave relations. He could not be convinced he had no cause to sigh and mourn for the loss of a mistress he could not with all his strength and courage retrieve. And he would often cry, "O my friends! Were she in walled cities, or confined from me in fortifications of the greatest strength; did enchantments or monsters detain her from me, I would venture through any hazard to free her. But here, in the arms of a feeble old man, my youth, my violent love, my trade in arms, and all my vast desire of glory avail me nothing. Imoinda is as irrecoverably lost to me as if she were snatched by the cold arms of death. Oh! she is never to be retrieved. If I would wait tedious years, till fate should bow the old king to his grave, even that would not leave me Imoinda free; but still that custom that makes it so vile a crime for a son to marry his father's wives or mistress would hinder my happiness; unless I would either ignobly set an ill precedent to my successors, or abandon my country and fly with her to some unknown world, who never heard our story."

But it was objected to him that his case was not the same; for Imoinda being his lawful wife, by solemn contract, 'twas he was the injured man, and might, if he so pleased, take Imoinda back, the breach of the law being on his grandfather's side; and that if he could circumvent him, and redeem her from the otan, which is the palace of the King's women, a sort of seraglio, it was both just and lawful for him so to do.

This reasoning had some force upon him, and he should have been entirely comforted, but for the thought that she was possessed by his grandfather. However, he loved so well that he was resolved to believe what most favored his hope, and to endeavor to learn from Imoinda's own mouth what only she could satisfy him in: whether she was robbed of that blessing, which was only due to his faith and love. But as it was very hard to get a sight of the women, for no men ever entered into the otan but when the King went to entertain himself with some one of his wives or mistresses, and 'twas death at any other time for any other to go in, so he knew not how to contrive to get a sight of her.

While Oroonoko felt all the agonies of love, and suffered under a torment the most painful in the world, the old king was not exempted from his share of affliction. He was troubled for having been forced by an irresistible passion to rob his son of a treasure he knew could not but be extremely dear to him, since she was the most beautiful that ever had been seen; and had besides all the sweetness and innocence of youth and modesty, with a charm of wit surpassing all. He found that however she was forced to expose her lovely person to his withered arms, she could only sigh and weep there, and think of Oroonoko; and oftentimes could not forbear speaking of him, though her life were, by custom, forfeited by owning her passion. But she spoke not of a lover only, but of a prince dear to him to whom she spoke; and of the praises of a man, who, till now, filled the old man's soul with joy at every recital of his bravery, or even his name. And 'twas this dotage on our young hero that gave Imoinda a thousand privileges to speak of him without offending, and this condescension in the old king that made her take the satisfaction of speaking of him so very often.

Besides, he many times inquired how the Prince bore himself; and those of whom he asked, being entirely slaves to the merits and virtues of the Prince, still answered what they thought conduced best to his service; which was, to make the old

7. Reverential.

king fancy that the Prince had no more interest in Imoinda, and had resigned her willingly to the pleasure of the King; that he diverted himself with his mathematicians, his fortifications, his officers, and his hunting.

This pleased the old lover, who failed not to report these things again to Imoinda, that she might, by the example of her young lover, withdraw her heart and rest better contented in his arms. But however she was forced to receive this unwelcome news, in all appearance, with unconcern and content, her heart was bursting within, and she was only happy when she could get alone, to vent her griefs and moans with sighs and tears.

What reports of the Prince's conduct were made to the King, he thought good to justify as far as possibly he could by his actions; and when he appeared in the presence of the King, he showed a face not at all betraying his heart; so that in a little time the old man, being entirely convinced that he was no longer a lover of Imoinda, he carried him with him, in his train to the otan, often to banquet with his mistress. But as soon as he entered one day into the apartment of Imoinda with the King, at the first glance from her eyes, notwithstanding all his determined resolution, he was ready to sink in the place where he stood; and had certainly done so, but for the support of Aboan, a young man who was next to him; which, with his change of countenance, had betrayed him, had the King chanced to look that way. And I have observed, 'tis a very great error in those who laugh when one says a Negro can change color; for I have seen them as frequently blush, and look pale, and that as visibly as ever I saw in the most beautiful white. And 'tis certain that both these changes were evident, this day, in both these lovers. And Imoinda, who saw with some joy the change in the Prince's face, and found it in her own, strove to divert the King from beholding either, by a forced caress, with which she met him, which was a new wound in the heart of the poor dying Prince. But as soon as the King was busied in looking on some fine thing of Imoinda's making, she had time to tell the Prince with her angry but love-darting eyes, that she resented his coldness, and bemoaned her own miserable captivity. Nor were his eyes silent, but answered hers again, as much as eyes could do, instructed by the most tender and most passionate heart that ever loved. And they spoke so well, and so effectually, as Imoinda no longer doubted but she was the only delight, and the darling of that soul she found pleading in them its right of love, which none was more willing to resign than she. And 'twas this powerful language alone that in an instant conveyed all the thoughts of their souls to each other, that they both found there wanted but opportunity to make them both entirely happy. But when he saw another door opened by Onahal, a former old wife of the King's who now had charge of Imoinda, and saw the prospect of a bed of state made ready with sweets and flowers for the dalliance of the King, who immediately led the trembling victim from his sight into that prepared repose, what rage, what wild frenzies seized his heart! Which forcing to keep within bounds, and to suffer without noise, it became the more insupportable and rent his soul with ten thousand pains. He was forced to retire to vent his groans, where he fell down on a carpet, and lay struggling a long time, and only breathing now and then, "O Imoinda!" When Onahal had finished her necessary affair within, shutting the door, she came forth to wait till the king called; and hearing some one sighing in the other room, she passed on, and found the Prince in that deplorable condition which she thought needed her aid. She gave him cordials but all in vain, till finding the nature of his disease by his sighs, and naming Imoinda. She told him he had not so much cause as he imagined to afflict himself; for if he knew the King so well as she did, he would not lose a moment in jealousy, and that she was confident that Imoinda bore, at this minute, part in his affliction. Aboan was of the same opinion; and both together persuaded him to reassume his courage; and all sitting down on the carpet, the Prince said so many obliging things to Onahal, that he half persuaded her to be of his party. And she promised him she would thus far comply with his just desires, that she would let Imoinda know how faithful he was, what he suffered, and what he said.

This discourse lasted till the King called, which gave Oroonoko a certain satisfaction; and with the hope Onahal had made him conceive, he assumed a look as gay as 'twas possible a man in his circumstances could do; and presently after, he was called in with the rest who waited without. The King commanded music to be brought, and several of his young wives and mistresses came all together by his command, to dance before him, where Imoinda performed her part with an air and grace so passing all the rest as her beauty was above them, and received the present ordained as a prize. The Prince was every moment more charmed with the new beauties and graces he beheld in this fair one; and while he gazed and she danced, Onahal was retired to a window with Aboan.

This Onahal, as I said, was one of the past mistresses of the old king; and 'twas these (now past their beauty) that were made guardians, or governants to the new and the young ones; and whose business it was, to teach them all those wanton arts of love with which they prevailed and charmed heretofore in their turn; and who now treated the triumphing happy ones with all the severity, as to liberty and freedom, that was possible, in revenge of those honors they rob them of; envying them those satisfactions, those gallantries and presents, that were once made to themselves, while youth and beauty lasted, and which they now saw pass regardless by, and paid only to the bloomings. And certainly, nothing is more afflicting to a decayed beauty than to behold in itself declining charms that were once adored, and to find those caresses paid to new beauties to which once she laid a claim; to hear them whisper as she passes by, "That once was a delicate woman." These abandoned ladies therefore endeavor to revenge all the despites and decays of time on these flourishing happy ones. And 'twas this severity that gave Oroonoko a thousand fears he should never prevail with Onahal to see Imoinda. But, as I said, she was now retired to a window with Aboan.

This young man was not only one of the best quality, but a man extremely well made and beautiful; and coming often to attend the King to the otan, he had subdued the heart of the antiquated Onahal, which had not forgot how pleasant it was to be in love. And though she had some decays in her face, she had none in her sense and wit; she was there agreeable still, even to Aboan's youth, so that he took pleasure in entertaining her with discourses of love. He knew also, that to make his court to these she-favorites was the way to be great; these being the persons that do all affairs and business at court. He had also observed that she had given him glances more tender and inviting than she had done to others of his quality. And now, when he saw that her favor could so absolutely oblige the Prince, he failed not to sigh in her ear, and to look with eyes all soft upon her, and give her hope that she had made some impressions on his heart. He found her pleased at this, and making a thousand advances to him; but the ceremony ending, and the King departing, broke up the company for that day, and his conversation.

Aboan failed not that night to tell the Prince of his success, and how advantageous the service of Onahal might be to his amour with Imoinda. The Prince was overjoyed with this good news, and besought him, if it were possible, to caress her, so as to engage her entirely; which he could not fail to do, if he complied with her desires. "For then," said the Prince, "her life lying at your mercy, she must grant you the request you make in my behalf." Aboan understood him, and assured him he would make love so effectually, that he would defy the most expert mistress of the art to find out whether he dissembled it or had it really. And 'twas with impatience they waited the next opportunity of going to the otan.

The wars came on, the time of taking the field approached, and 'twas impossible for the Prince to delay his going at the head of his army to encounter the enemy; so that every day seemed a tedious year, till he saw his Imoinda, for he believed he could not live if he were forced away without being so happy. 'Twas with impatience therefore that he expected the next visit the King would make; and, according to his wish, it was not long.

The parley of the eyes of these two lovers had not passed so secretly, but an old jealous lover could spy it; or rather, he wanted not flatterers who told him they observed it. So that the prince was hastened to the camp, and this was the last visit he found he should make to the otan; he therefore urged Aboan to make the best of this last effort, and to explain himself so to Onahal, that she, deferring her enjoyment of her young lover no longer, might make way for the Prince to speak to Imoinda.

The whole affair being agreed on between the Prince and Aboan, they attended the King, as the custom was, to the otan; where, while the whole company was taken up in beholding the dancing and antic[8] postures the women royal made to divert the King, Onahal singled out Aboan, whom she found most pliable to her wish. When she had him where she believed she could not be heard, she sighed to him, and softly cried, "Ah, Aboan! When will you be sensible of my passion? I confess it with my mouth, because I would not give my eyes the lie; and you have but too much already perceived they have confessed my flame. Nor would I have you believe that because I am the abandoned mistress of a king I esteem myself altogether divested of charms. No, Aboan; I have still a rest of beauty enough engaging, and have learned to please too well, not to be desirable. I can have lovers still, but will have none but Aboan." "Madam," replied the half-feigning youth, "you have already, by my eyes, found you can still conquer; and I believe 'tis in pity of me, you condescend to this kind confession. But, Madam, words are used to be so small a part of our country courtship, that 'tis rare one can get so happy an opportunity as to tell one's heart; and those few minutes we have are forced to be snatched for more certain proofs of love than speaking and sighing; and such I languish for."

He spoke this with such a tone that she hoped it true, and could not forbear believing it; and being wholly transported with joy, for having subdued the finest of all the King's subjects to her desires, she took from her ears two large pearls and commanded him to wear them in his. He would have refused them, crying, "Madam, these are not the proofs of your love that I expect; 'tis opportunity, 'tis a lone hour only, that can make me happy." But forcing the pearls into his hand, she whispered softly to him, "Oh! Do not fear a woman's invention when love sets her a-thinking." And pressing his hand she cried, "This night you shall be happy. Come to the gate of the orange groves, behind the otan, and I will be ready, about midnight, to receive you." 'Twas thus agreed, and she left him, that no notice might be taken of their speaking together.

8. Fantastic or grotesque.

The ladies were still dancing, and the King, laid on a carpet, with a great deal of pleasure was beholding them, especially Imoinda, who that day appeared more lovely than ever, being enlivened with the good tidings Onahal had brought her of the constant passion the Prince had for her. The Prince was laid on another carpet at the other end of the room, with his eyes fixed on the object of his soul; and as she turned or moved so did they; and she alone gave his eyes and soul their motions. Nor did Imoinda employ her eyes to any other use than in beholding with infinite pleasure the joy she produced in those of the Prince. But while she was more regarding him than the steps she took, she chanced to fall, and so near him as that leaping with extreme force from the carpet, he caught her in his arms as she fell; and 'twas visible to the whole presence, the joy wherewith he received her. He clasped her close to his bosom, and quite forgot that reverence that was due to the mistress of a king, and that punishment that is the reward of a boldness of this nature; and had not the presence of mind of Imoinda (fonder of his safety than her own) befriended him in making her spring from his arms and fall into her dance again, he had at that instant met his death; for the old king, jealous to the last degree, rose up in rage, broke all the diversion, and led Imoinda to her apartment, and sent out word to the Prince to go immediately to the camp; and that if he were found another night in court, he should suffer the death ordained for disobedient offenders.

You may imagine how welcome this news was to Oroonoko, whose unseasonable transport and caress of Imoinda was blamed by all men that loved him; and now he perceived his fault, yet cried that for such another moment, he would be content to die.

All the otan was in disorder about this accident; and Onahal was particularly concerned, because on the Prince's stay depended her happiness, for she could no longer expect that of Aboan. So that e'er they departed, they contrived it so that the Prince and he should come both that night to the grove of the otan, which was all of oranges and citrons, and that there they should wait her orders.

They parted thus, with grief enough, till night, leaving the King in possession of the lovely maid. But nothing could appease the jealousy of the old lover. He would not be imposed on, but would have it that Imoinda made a false step on purpose to fall into Oroonoko's bosom, and that all things looked like a design on both sides, and 'twas in vain she protested her innocence. He was old and obstinate, and left her more than half assured that his fear was true.

The King going to his apartment, sent to know where the Prince was, and if he intended to obey his command. The messenger returned and told him he found the Prince pensive, and altogether unpreparing for the campaign; that he lay negligently on the ground, and answered very little. This confirmed the jealousy of the King, and he commanded that they should very narrowly and privately watch his motions; and that he should not stir from his apartment, but one spy or other should be employed to watch him. So that the hour approaching, wherein he was to go to the citron grove, and taking only Aboan along with him, he leaves his apartment, and was watched to the very gate of the otan, where he was seen to enter, and where they left him, to carry back the tidings to the King.

Oroonoko and Aboan were no sooner entered but Onahal led the Prince to the apartment of Imoinda, who, not knowing anything of her happiness, was laid in bed. But Onahal only left him in her chamber to make the best of his opportunity, and took her dear Aboan to her own, where he showed the height of complaisance[9] for his prince, when, to give him an opportunity, he suffered himself to be caressed in bed by Onahal.

The Prince softly wakened Imoinda, who was not a little surprised with joy to find him there, and yet she trembled with a thousand fears. I believe he omitted saying nothing to this young maid that might persuade her to suffer him to seize his own and take the rights of love; and I believe she was not long resisting those arms where she so longed to be; and having opportunity, night and silence, youth, love and desire, he soon prevailed, and ravished in a moment what his old grandfather had been endeavoring for so many months.

'Tis not to be imagined the satisfaction of these two young lovers; nor the vows she made him, that she remained a spotless maid till that night; and that what she did with his grandfather had robbed him of no part of her virgin honor, the gods in mercy and justice having reserved that for her plighted lord, to whom of right it belonged. And 'tis impossible to express the transports he suffered while he listened to a discourse so charming from her loved lips, and clasped that body in his arms for whom he had so long languished; and nothing now afflicted him but his sudden departure from her; for he told her the necessity and his commands; but should depart satisfied in this, that since the old king had hitherto not been able to deprive him of those enjoyments which only belonged to him, he believed for the future he would be less able to injure him. So that abating the scandal of the veil, which was no otherwise so than that she was wife to another, he believed her safe even in the arms of the king, and innocent; yet would he have ventured at the conquest of the world, and have given it all, to have had her avoided that honor of receiving the royal veil. 'Twas thus, between a thousand caresses, that both bemoaned the hard fate of youth and beauty, so liable to that cruel promotion; 'twas a glory that could well have been spared here, though desired and aimed at by all the young females of that kingdom.

But while they were thus fondly employed, forgetting how time ran on and that the dawn must conduct him far away from his only happiness, they heard a great noise in the otan, and unusual voices of men; at which the Prince, starting from the arms of the frighted Imoinda, ran to a little battle-ax he used to wear by his side; and having not so much leisure as to put on his habit, he opposed himself against some who were already opening the door; which they did with so much violence that Oroonoko was not able to defend it, but was forced to cry out with a commanding voice, "Whoever ye are that have the boldness to attempt to approach this apartment thus rudely, know that I, the Prince Oroonoko, will revenge it with the certain death of him that first enters. Therefore stand back, and know this place is sacred to love and me this night; tomorrow 'tis the King's."

This he spoke with a voice so resolved and assured that they soon retired from the door, but cried, "'Tis by the King's command we are come; and being satisfied by thy voice, O Prince, as much as if we had entered, we can report to the King the truth of all his fears, and leave thee to provide for thy own safety, as thou art advised by thy friends."

At these words they departed, and left the Prince to take a short and sad leave of his Imoinda; who trusting in the strength of her charms, believed she should appease the fury of a jealous king by saying she was surprised, and that it was by force of arms

9. Desire to please.

he got into her apartment. All her concern now was for his life, and therefore she hastened him to the camp, and with much ado prevailed on him to go. Nor was it she alone that prevailed; Aboan and Onahal both pleaded, and both assured him of a lie that should be well enough contrived to secure Imoinda. So that at last, with a heart sad as death, dying eyes, and sighing soul, Oroonoko departed, and took his way to the camp.

It was not long after the King in person came to the otan, where beholding Imoinda with rage in his eyes, he upbraided her wickedness and perfidy, and threatening her royal lover, she fell on her face at his feet, bedewing the floor with her tears and imploring his pardon for a fault which she had not with her will committed, as Onahal, who was also prostrate with her, could testify that, unknown to her, he had broke into her apartment, and ravished her. She spoke this much against her conscience; but to save her own life, 'twas absolutely necessary she should feign this falsity. She knew it could not injure the Prince, he being fled to an army that would stand by him against any injuries that should assault him. However, this last thought of Imoinda's being ravished changed the measures of his revenge, and whereas before he designed to be himself her executioner, he now resolved she should not die. But as it is the greatest crime in nature amongst them to touch a woman after having been possessed by a son, a father, or a brother, so now he looked on Imoinda as a polluted thing, wholly unfit for his embrace; nor would he resign her to his grandson, because she had received the royal veil. He therefore removes her from the otan, with Onahal, whom he put into safe hands, with order they should be both sold off as slaves to another country, either Christian or heathen; 'twas no matter where.

This cruel sentence, worse than death, they implored might be reversed; but their prayers were vain, and it was put in execution accordingly, and that with so much secrecy that none, either without or within the otan, knew anything of their absence or their destiny.

The old king, nevertheless, executed this with a great deal of reluctance; but he believed he had made a very great conquest over himself when he had once resolved, and had performed what he resolved. He believed now that his love had been unjust, and that he could not expect the gods, or Captain of the Clouds (as they call the unknown power) should suffer a better consequence from so ill a cause. He now begins to hold Oroonoko excused and to say he had reason for what he did; and now everybody could assure the King, how passionately Imoinda was beloved by the Prince; even those confessed it now who said the contrary before his flame was abated. So that the King being old and not able to defend himself in war, and having no sons of all his race remaining alive but only this to maintain him on the throne; and looking on this as a man disobliged, first by the rape of his mistress, or rather, wife, and now by depriving him wholly of her, he feared, might make him desperate, and do some cruel thing, either to himself, or his old grandfather the offender; he began to repent him extremely of the contempt he had, in his rage, put on Imoinda. Besides, he considered he ought in honor to have killed her for this offense, if it had been one. He ought to have had so much value and consideration for a maid of her quality, as to have nobly put her to death, and not to have sold her like a common slave, the greatest revenge, and the most disgraceful of any, and to which they a thousand times prefer death, and implore it as Imoinda did, but could not obtain that honor. Seeing therefore it was certain that Oroonoko would highly resent this affront, he thought good to make some excuse for his rashness to him, and to that end he sent a messenger to the camp with orders to treat with him about the matter, to gain his pardon, and to endeavor to mitigate his grief; but that by no means he should tell him she was sold, but secretly put to death; for he knew he should never obtain his pardon for the other.

When the messenger came, he found the Prince upon the point of engaging with the enemy, but as soon as he heard of the arrival of the messenger he commanded him to his tent, where he embraced him and received him with joy; which was soon abated, by the downcast looks of the messenger, who was instantly demanded the cause by Oroonoko, who, impatient of delay, asked a thousand questions in a breath, and all concerning Imoinda. But there needed little return, for he could almost answer himself of all he demanded from his sighs and eyes. At last, the messenger casting himself at the Prince's feet and kissing them with all the submission of a man that had something to implore which he dreaded to utter, he besought him to hear with calmness what he had to deliver to him, and to call up all his noble and heroic courage to encounter with his words, and defend himself against the ungrateful things he must relate. Oroonoko replied, with a deep sigh and a languishing voice, "I am armed against their worst efforts—for I know they will tell me, Imoinda is no more—and after that, you may spare the rest." Then, commanding him to rise, he laid himself on a carpet under a rich pavilion, and remained a good while silent, and was hardly heard to sigh. When he was come a little to himself, the messenger asked him leave to deliver that part of his embassy which the Prince had not yet divined, and the Prince cried, "I permit thee." Then he told him the affliction the old king was in for the rashness he had committed in his cruelty to Imoinda, and how he deigned to ask pardon for his offense, and to implore the Prince would not suffer that loss to touch his heart too sensibly which now all the gods could not restore him, but might recompense him in glory which he begged he would pursue; and that death, that common revenger of all injuries, would soon even the account between him and a feeble old man.

Oroonoko bade him return his duty to his lord and master, and to assure him there was no account of revenge to be adjusted between them; if there were, 'twas he was the aggressor, and that death would be just, and, maugre[1] his age, would see him righted; and he was contented to leave his share of glory to youths more fortunate, and worthy of that favor from the gods. That henceforth he would never lift a weapon, or draw a bow, but abandon the small remains of his life to sighs and tears, and the continual thoughts of what his lord and grandfather had thought good to send out of the world, with all that youth, that innocence, and beauty.

After having spoken this, whatever his greatest officers and men of the best rank could do, they could not raise him from the carpet, or persuade him to action and resolutions of life, but commanding all to retire, he shut himself into his pavilion all that day, while the enemy was ready to engage; and wondering at the delay, the whole body of the chief of the army then addressed themselves to him, and to whom they had much ado to get admittance. They fell on their faces at the foot of his carpet, where they lay, and besought him with earnest prayers and tears to lead them forth to battle, and not let the enemy take advantages of them; and implored him to have regard to his glory, and to the world that depended on his courage and conduct. But he made no other reply to all their

---

1. In spite of; i.e., despite Oroonoko's youth, death will avenge the king by taking Oroonoko first.

supplications but this, that he had now no more business for glory; and for the world, it was a trifle not worth his care. "Go," continued he, sighing, "and divide it amongst you; and reap with joy what you so vainly prize, and leave me to my more welcome destiny."

They then demanded what they should do, and whom he would constitute in his room, that the confusion of ambitious youth and power might not ruin their order, and make them a prey to the enemy. He replied, he would not give himself the trouble; but wished them to choose the bravest man amongst them, let his quality or birth be what it would. "For, O my friends!" said he, "it is not titles make men brave, or good; or birth that bestows courage and generosity, or makes the owner happy. Believe this, when you behold Oroonoko, the most wretched, and abandoned by fortune of all the creation of the gods." So turning himself about, he would make no more reply to all they could urge or implore.

The army beholding their officers return unsuccessful, with sad faces and ominous looks that presaged no good luck, suffered a thousand fears to take possession of their hearts, and the enemy to come even upon them, before they would provide for their safety by any defense; and though they were assured by some, who had a mind to animate them, that they should be immediately headed by the Prince, and that in the meantime Aboan had orders to command as general, yet they were so dismayed for want of that great example of bravery that they could make but a very feeble resistance, and at last downright fled before the enemy, who pursued them to the very tents, killing them. Nor could all Aboan's courage, which that day gained him immortal glory, shame them into a manly defense of themselves. The guards that were left behind about the Prince's tent, seeing the soldiers flee before the enemy and scatter themselves all over the plain in great disorder, made such outcries as roused the prince from his amorous slumber, in which he had remained buried for two days without permitting any sustenance to approach him. But in spite of all his resolutions, he had not the constancy of grief to that degree as to make him insensible of the danger of his army; and in that instant he leapt from his couch and cried, "Come, if we must die, let us meet death the noblest way; and 'twill be more like Oroonoko to encounter him at an army's head, opposing the torrent of a conquering foe, than lazily, on a couch, to wait his lingering pleasure, and die every moment by a thousand wrecking thoughts; or be tamely taken by an enemy and led a whining, love-sick slave, to adorn the triumphs of Jamoan, that young victor, who already is entered beyond the limits I had prescribed him."

While he was speaking, he suffered his people to dress him for the field; and sallying out of his pavilion, with more life and vigor in his countenance than ever he showed, he appeared like some divine power descended to save his country from destruction; and his people had purposely put him on all things that might make him shine with most splendor, to strike a reverend awe into the beholders. He flew into the thickest of those that were pursuing his men, and being animated with despair, he fought as if he came on purpose to die, and did such things as will not be believed that human strength could perform, and such as soon inspired all the rest with new courage and new order. And now it was that they began to fight indeed, and so, as if they would not be outdone even by their adored hero, who turning the tide of the victory, changing absolutely the fate of the day, gained an entire conquest; and Oroonoko having the good fortune to single out Jamoan, he took him prisoner with his own hand, having wounded him almost to death.

This Jamoan afterwards became very dear to him, being a man very gallant and of excellent graces and fine parts, so that he never put him amongst the rank of captives, as they used to do, without distinction, for the common sale or market, but kept him in his own court, where he retained nothing of the prisoner but the name, and returned no more into his own country, so great an affection he took for Oroonoko; and by a thousand tales and adventures of love and gallantry, flattered his disease of melancholy and languishment, which I have often heard him say had certainly killed him, but for the conversation of this prince and Aboan, [and] the French governor he had from his childhood, of whom I have spoken before, and who was a man of admirable wit, great ingenuity and learning, all which he had infused into his young pupil. This Frenchman was banished out of his own country for some heretical notions he held; and though he was a man of very little religion, he had admirable morals, and a brave soul.

After the total defeat of Jamoan's army, which all fled, or were left dead upon the place, they spent some time in the camp, Oroonoko choosing rather to remain a while there in his tents, than enter into a palace, or live in a court where he had so lately suffered so great a loss. The officers therefore, who saw and knew his cause of discontent, invented all sorts of diversions and sports to entertain their prince: so that what with those amusements abroad and others at home, that is, within their tents, with the persuasions, arguments, and care of his friends and servants that he more peculiarly prized, he wore off in time a great part of that chagrin and torture of despair which the first effects of Imoinda's death had given him; insomuch as having received a thousand kind embassies from the King, and invitations to return to court, he obeyed, though with no little reluctance; and when he did so, there was a visible change in him, and for a long time he was much more melancholy than before. But time lessens all extremes, and reduces them to mediums and unconcern; but no motives or beauties, though all endeavored it, could engage him in any sort of amour, though he had all the invitations to it, both from his own youth and others' ambitions and designs.

Oroonoko was no sooner returned from this last conquest, and received at court with all the joy and magnificence that could be expressed to a young victor, who was not only returned triumphant but beloved like a deity, when there arrived in the port an English ship.

This person had often before been in these countries, and was very well known to Oroonoko, with whom he had trafficked for slaves, and had used to do the same with his predecessors.

This commander was a man of a finer sort of address and conversation, better bred and more engaging than most of that sort of men are; so that he seemed rather never to have been bred out of a court than almost all his life at sea. This captain therefore was always better received at court than most of the traders to those countries were; and especially by Oroonoko, who was more civilized, according to the European mode, than any other had been, and took more delight in the white nations, and, above all, men of parts and wit. To this captain he sold abundance of his slaves, and for the favor and esteem he had for him made him many presents, and obliged him to stay at court as long as possibly he could. Which the captain seemed to take as a very great honor done him, entertaining the Prince every day with globes and maps, and mathematical discourses and instruments; eating, drinking, hunting, and living with him with so much familiarity that it was not to be doubted but he had gained very greatly upon the heart of this gallant young man. And the captain, in return of all these mighty favors, besought the Prince to honor his vessel with his presence, some day or other, to dinner, before he should set sail; which he condescended to accept, and appointed his day. The captain, on his part, failed not to have all things in a readiness, in the most magnificent order he could possibly. And the day being come, the captain, in his boat richly adorned with carpets and velvet cushions, rowed to the shore to receive the Prince; with another longboat, where was placed all his music and trumpets, with which Oroonoko was extremely delighted, who met him on the shore, attended by his French governor, Jamoan, Aboan, and about an hundred of the noblest of the youths of the court. And after they had first carried the Prince on board, the boats fetched the rest off; where they found a very splendid treat, with all sorts of fine wines, and were as well entertained as 'twas possible in such a place to be.

The Prince having drunk hard of punch, and several sorts of wine, as did all the rest (for great care was taken they should want nothing of that part of the entertainment) was very merry, and in great admiration of the ship, for he had never been in one before; so that he was curious of beholding every place where he decently might descend. The rest, no less curious, who were not quite overcome with drinking, rambled at their pleasure fore and aft, as their fancies guided them: so that the captain, who had well laid his design before, gave the word and seized on all his guests; they clapping great irons suddenly on the Prince when he was leaped down in the hold to view that part of the vessel, and locking him fast down, secured him. The same treachery was used to all the rest; and all in one instant, in several places of the ship, were lashed fast in irons and betrayed to slavery. That great design over, they set all hands to work to hoist sail; and with as treacherous and fair a wind they made from the shore with this innocent and glorious prize, who thought of nothing less than such an entertainment.

Some have commended this act, as brave in the captain; but I will spare my sense of it, and leave it to my reader to judge as he pleases.

It may be easily guessed in what manner the Prince resented this indignity, who may be best resembled to a lion taken in a toil; so he raged, so he struggled for liberty, but all in vain; and they had so wisely managed his fetters that he could not use a hand in his defense, to quit himself of a life that would by no means endure slavery; nor could he move from the place where he was tied to any solid part of the ship against which he might have beat his head, and have finished his disgrace that way; so that being deprived of all other means, he resolved to perish for want of food. And pleased at last with that thought, and toiled and tired by rage and indignation, he laid himself down, and sullenly resolved upon dying, and refused all things that were brought him.

This did not a little vex the captain, and the more so because he found almost all of them of the same humor; so that the loss of so many brave slaves, so tall and goodly to behold, would have been very considerable. He therefore ordered one to go from him (for he would not be seen himself) to Oroonoko, and to assure him he was afflicted for having rashly done so inhospitable a deed, and which could not be now remedied, since they were far from shore; but since he resented it in so high a nature, he assured him he would revoke his resolution, and set both him and his friends ashore on the next land they should touch at; and of this the messenger gave him his oath, provided he would resolve to live. And Oroonoko, whose honor was such as he never had violated a word in his life himself, much less a solemn asseveration, believed in an instant what this man said, but replied he expected for a confirmation of this to have his shameful fetters dismissed. This demand was carried to the captain, who returned him answer that the offense had been so great which he had put upon the Prince, that he durst not trust him with liberty while he remained in the ship, for fear lest by a valor natural to him, and a revenge that would animate that valor, he might commit some outrage fatal to himself and the King his master, to whom his vessel did belong. To this Oroonoko replied, he would engage his honor to behave himself in all friendly order and manner, and obey the command of the captain, as he was lord of the King's vessel, and general of those men under his command.

This was delivered to the still doubting captain, who could not resolve to trust a heathen he said, upon his parole,[2] a man that had no sense or notion of the God that he worshipped. Oroonoko then replied he was very sorry to hear that the captain pretended to the knowledge and worship of any gods who had taught him no better principles, than not to credit as he would be credited; but they told him the difference of their faith occasioned that distrust: for the captain had protested to him upon the word of a Christian, and sworn in the name of a great God, which if he should violate, he would expect eternal torment in the world to come. "Is that all the obligation he has to be just to his oath?" replied Oroonoko. "Let him know I swear by my honor, which to violate, would not only render me contemptible and despised by all brave and honest men, and so give myself perpetual pain, but it would be eternally offending and diseasing all mankind, harming, betraying, circumventing, and outraging all men; but punishments hereafter are suffered by oneself; and the world takes no cognizances whether this god have revenged them, or not, 'tis done so secretly, and deferred so long; while the man of no honor suffers every moment the scorn and contempt of the honester world, and dies every day ignominiously in his fame, which is more valuable than life. I speak not this to move belief, but to show you how you mistake, when you imagine that he who will violate his honor will keep his word with his gods." So turning from him with a disdainful smile, he refused to answer him when he urged him to know what answer he should carry back to his captain; so that he departed without saying any more.

The captain pondering and consulting what to do, it was concluded that nothing but Oroonoko's liberty would encourage any of the rest to eat, except the Frenchman, whom the captain could not pretend to keep prisoner, but only told him he was secured because he might act something in favor of the Prince, but that he should be freed as soon as they came to land. So that they concluded it wholly necessary to free the Prince from his irons that he might show himself to the rest, that they might have an eye upon him, and that they could not fear a single man.

This being resolved, to make the obligation the greater, the captain himself went to Oroonoko; where, after many compliments, and assurances of what he had already promised, he receiving from the Prince his parole, and his hand, for his good behavior, dismissed his irons, and brought him to his own cabin; where, after having treated and reposed him a while, for he had neither eaten nor slept in four days before, he besought him to visit those obstinate people in chains, who refused all manner of sustenance; and entreated him to oblige them to eat, and assure them of their liberty the first opportunity.

Oroonoko, who was too generous not to give credit to his words, showed himself to his people, who were transported with excess of joy at the sight of their darling prince, falling at his feet, and kissing and embracing them, believing, as some divine

2. Word of honor.

oracle, all he assured them. But he besought them to bear their chains with that bravery that became those whom he had seen act so nobly in arms; and that they could not give him greater proofs of their love and friendship, since 'twas all the security the captain (his friend) could have against the revenge, he said, they might possibly justly take, for the injuries sustained by him. And they all, with one accord, assured him they could not suffer enough when it was for his repose and safety.

After this they no longer refused to eat, but took what was brought them and were pleased with their captivity, since by it they hoped to redeem the Prince, who, all the rest of the voyage, was treated with all the respect due to his birth, though nothing could divert his melancholy; and he would often sigh for Imoinda, and think this a punishment due to his misfortune, in having left that noble maid behind him that fatal night in the otan, when he fled to the camp.

Possessed with a thousand thoughts of past joys with this fair young person, and a thousand griefs for her eternal loss, he endured a tedious voyage, and at last arrived at the mouth of the river of Surinam, a colony belonging to the King of England, and where they were to deliver some part of their slaves. There the merchants and gentlemen of the country going on board to demand those lots of slaves they had already agreed on, and amongst those the overseers of those plantations where I then chanced to be, the captain, who had given the word, ordered his men to bring up those noble slaves in fetters, whom I have spoken of; and having put them, some in one, and some in other lots, with women and children (which they call pickaninnies), they sold them off as slaves to several merchants and gentlemen; not putting any two in one lot, because they would separate them far from each other; not daring to trust them together, lest rage and courage should put them upon contriving some great action, to the ruin of the colony.

Oroonoko was first seized on and sold to our overseer, who had the first lot, with seventeen more of all sorts and sizes, but not one of quality with him. When he saw this, he found what they meant; for, as I said, he understood English pretty well; and being wholly unarmed and defenseless, so as it was in vain to make any resistance, he only beheld the captain with a look all fierce and disdainful; upbraiding him with eyes that forced blushes on his guilty cheeks, he only cried in passing over the side of the ship, "Farewell, Sir! 'Tis worth my suffering to gain so true a knowledge both of you and of your gods by whom you swear." And desiring those that held him to forbear their pains, and telling them he would make no resistance, he cried, "Come, my fellow slaves, let us descend, and see if we can meet with more honor and honesty in the next world we shall touch upon." So he nimbly leapt into the boat, and showing no more concern, suffered himself to be rowed up the river with his seventeen companions.

The gentleman that bought him was a young Cornish gentleman, whose name was Trefry, a man of great wit and fine learning, and was carried into those parts by the Lord——, Governor, to manage all his affairs.[3] He reflecting on the last words of Oroonoko to the captain, and beholding the richness of his vest,[4] no sooner came into the boat, but he fixed his eyes on him; and finding something so extraordinary in his face, his shape and mien, a greatness of look, and haughtiness in his air, and finding he spoke English, had a great mind to be inquiring into his quality and fortune;

3. John Treffry (?–1674) supervised the plantation at Parham for Francis, Lord Willoughby (1613?–1686), a nobleman long involved with colonization, who received from Charles II both the governorship and a grant of land in Surinam; his appointment of Behn's father to the post of lieutenant-governor appears to account for her sojourn in the colony (though her father died en route).
4. Robe.

which, though Oroonoko endeavored to hide by only confessing he was above the rank of common slaves, Trefry soon found he was yet something greater than he confessed; and from that moment began to conceive so vast an esteem for him, that he ever after loved him as his dearest brother, and showed him all the civilities due to so great a man.

Trefry was a very good mathematician and a linguist, could speak French and Spanish, and in the three days they remained in the boat (for so long were they going from the ship to the plantation) he entertained Oroonoko so agreeably with his art and discourse, that he was no less pleased with Trefry, than he was with the Prince; and he thought himself, at least, fortunate in this, that since he was a slave, as long as he would suffer himself to remain so, he had a man of so excellent wit and parts for a master. So that before they had finished their voyage up the river, he made no scruple of declaring to Trefry all his fortunes and most part of what I have here related, and put himself wholly into the hands of his new friend, whom he found resenting all the injuries were done him, and was charmed with all the greatnesses of his actions, which were recited with that modesty and delicate sense, as wholly vanquished him, and subdued him to his interest. And he promised him on his word and honor, he would find the means to reconduct him to his own country again; assuring him, he had a perfect abhorrence of so dishonorable an action; and that he would sooner have died, than have been the author of such a perfidy. He found the Prince was very much concerned to know what became of his friends, and how they took their slavery; and Trefry promised to take care about the inquiring after their condition, and that he should have an account of them.

Though, as Oroonoko afterwards said, he had little reason to credit the words of a backearary,[5] yet he knew not why, but he saw a kind of sincerity and awful truth in the face of Trefry; he saw an honesty in his eyes, and he found him wise and witty enough to understand honor; for it was one of his maxims, "A man of wit could not be a knave or villain."

In their passage up the river they put in at several houses for refreshment, and ever when they landed numbers of people would flock to behold this man; not but their eyes were daily entertained with the sight of slaves, but the fame of Oroonoko was gone before him, and all people were in admiration of his beauty. Besides, he had a rich habit on, in which he was taken, so different from the rest, and which the captain could not strip him of because he was forced to surprise his person in the minute he sold him. When he found his habit made him liable, as he thought, to be gazed at the more, he begged Trefry to give him something more befitting a slave; which he did, and took off his robes. Nevertheless, he shone through all and his osenbrigs (a sort of brown holland suit he had on)[6] could not conceal the graces of his looks and mien; and he had no less admirers than when he had his dazzling habit on. The royal youth appeared in spite of the slave, and people could not help treating him after a different manner without designing it; as soon as they approached him they venerated and esteemed him; his eyes insensibly commanded respect, and his behavior insinuated it into every soul. So that there was nothing talked of but this young and gallant slave, even by those who yet knew not that he was a prince.

---

5. An African-derived term for "white master."

6. Osnaburg and holland were thick cotton or linen fabrics.

I ought to tell you, that the Christians never buy any slaves but they give them some name of their own, their native ones being likely very barbarous, and hard to pronounce; so that Mr. Trefry gave Oroonoko that of Caesar, which name will live in that country as long as that (scarce more) glorious one of the great Roman, for 'tis most evident, he wanted no part of the personal courage of that Caesar, and acted things as memorable, had they been done in some part of the world replenished with people and historians that might have given him his due. But his misfortune was to fall in an obscure world, that afforded only a female pen to celebrate his fame, though I doubt not but it had lived from others' endeavors, if the Dutch, who immediately after his time took that country,[7] had not killed, banished, and dispersed all those that were capable of giving the world this great man's life, much better than I have done. And Mr. Trefry, who designed it, died before he began it, and bemoaned himself for not having undertook it in time.

For the future therefore, I must call Oroonoko Caesar, since by that name only he was known in our western world, and by that name he was received on shore at Parham House, where he was destined a slave. But if the King himself (God bless him) had come ashore, there could not have been greater expectations by all the whole plantation, and those neighboring ones, than was on ours at that time; and he was received more like a governor than a slave. Notwithstanding, as the custom was, they assigned him his portion of land, his house, and his business, up in the plantation. But as it was more for form than any design to put him to his task, he endured no more of the slave but the name, and remained some days in the house, receiving all visits that were made him, without stirring towards that part of the plantation where the Negroes were.

At last, he would needs go view his land, his house, and the business assigned him. But he no sooner came to the houses of the slaves, which are like a little town by itself, the Negroes all having left work, but they all came forth to behold him, and found he was that prince who had, at several times, sold most of them to these parts; and, from a veneration they pay to great men, especially if they know them, and from the surprise and awe they had at the sight of him, they all cast themselves at his feet, crying out, in their language, "Live, O King! Long live, O King!" And kissing his feet, paid him even divine homage.

Several English gentlemen were with him; and what Mr. Trefry had told them was here confirmed, of which he himself before had no other witness than Caesar himself. But he was infinitely glad to find his grandeur confirmed by the adoration of all the slaves.

Caesar, troubled with their over-joy, and over-ceremony, besought them to rise, and to receive him as their fellow slave, assuring them, he was no better. At which they set up with one accord a most terrible and hideous mourning and condoling, which he and the English had much ado to appease. But at last they prevailed with them, and they prepared all their barbarous music, and everyone killed and dressed something of his own stock (for every family has their land apart, on which, at their leisure times, they breed all eatable things) and clubbing it together, made a most magnificent supper, inviting their grandee captain, their prince, to honor it with his presence, which he did, and several English with him, where they all waited on him,

7. In 1667 Surinam twice changed hands. The Dutch briefly captured the colony and the English won it back, but immediately ceded it to the Dutch (in exchange for New York) at the Treaty of Breda.

some playing, others dancing before him all the time, according to the manners of their several nations, and with unwearied industry endeavoring to please and delight him.

While they sat at meat Mr. Trefry told Caesar that most of these young slaves were undone in love, with a fine she-slave, whom they had had about six months on their land. The Prince, who never heard the name of love without a sigh, nor any mention of it without the curiosity of examining further into that tale which of all discourses was most agreeable to him, asked, how they came to be so unhappy, as to be all undone for one fair slave? Trefry, who was naturally amorous, and loved to talk of love as well as anybody, proceeded to tell him, they had the most charming black that ever was beheld on their plantation, about fifteen or sixteen years old, as he guessed; that, for his part, he had done nothing but sigh for her ever since she came; and that all the white beauties he had seen never charmed him so absolutely as this fine creature had done; and that no man of any nation ever beheld her, that did not fall in love with her; and that she had all the slaves perpetually at her feet; and the whole country resounded with the fame of Clemene, "for so," said he, "we have christened her. But she denies us all with such a noble disdain, that 'tis a miracle to see that she, who can give such eternal desires, should herself be all ice, and all unconcern. She is adorned with the most graceful modesty that ever beautified youth; the softest sigher—that, if she were capable of love, one would swear she languished for some absent happy man; and so retired, as if she feared a rape even from the God of Day,[8] or that the breezes would steal kisses from her delicate mouth. Her task of work some sighing lover every day makes it his petition to perform for her, which she accepts blushing, and with reluctance, for fear he will ask her a look for a recompense, which he dares not presume to hope, so great an awe she strikes into the hearts of her admirers." "I do not wonder," replied the Prince, "that Clemene should refuse slaves, being as you say so beautiful, but wonder how she escapes those who can entertain her as you can do. Or why, being your slave, you do not oblige her to yield." "I confess," said Trefry, "when I have, against her will, entertained her with love so long as to be transported with my passion even above decency, I have been ready to make use of those advantages of strength and force nature has given me. But oh! she disarms me, with that modesty and weeping so tender and so moving, that I retire, and thank my stars she overcame me." The company laughed at his civility to a slave, and Caesar only applauded the nobleness of his passion and nature, since that slave might be noble, or, what was better, have true notions of honor and virtue in her. Thus passed they this night, after having received from the slaves all imaginable respect and obedience.

The next day Trefry asked Caesar to walk, when the heat was allayed, and designedly carried him by the cottage of the fair slave, and told him, she whom he spoke of last night lived there retired. "But," says he, "I would not wish you to approach, for I am sure you will be in love as soon as you behold her." Caesar assured him he was proof against all the charms of that sex, and that if he imagined his heart could be so perfidious to love again after Imoinda, he believed he should tear it from his bosom. They had no sooner spoke, but a little shock dog,[9] that Clemene had presented her, which she took great delight in, ran out, and she, not knowing anybody

---

8. The sun.   9. A thick-haired dog.

was there, ran to get it in again, and bolted out on those who were just speaking of her. When seeing them she would have run in again, but Trefry caught her by the hand and cried, "Clemene, however you fly a lover, you ought to pay some respect to this stranger" (pointing to Caesar). But she, as if she had resolved never to raise her eyes to the face of a man again, bent them the more to the earth when he spoke, and gave the Prince the leisure to look the more at her. There needed no long gazing or consideration to examine who this fair creature was. He soon saw Imoinda all over her; in a minute he saw her face, her shape, her air, her modesty, and all that called forth his soul with joy at his eyes, and left his body destitute of almost life. It stood without motion, and, for a minute, knew not that it had a being. And I believe he had never come to himself, so oppressed he was with overjoy, if he had not met with this allay,[1] that he perceived Imoinda fall dead in the hands of Trefry. This awakened him, and he ran to her aid, and caught her in his arms, where, by degrees, she came to herself; and 'tis needless to tell with what transports, what ecstasies of joy, they both a while beheld each other, without speaking, then snatched each other to their arms, then gaze again, as if they still doubted whether they possessed the blessing they grasped. But when they recovered their speech, 'tis not to be imagined what tender things they expressed to each other, wondering what strange fate had brought them again together. They soon informed each other of their fortunes, and equally bewailed their fate; but at the same time, they mutually protested that even fetters and slavery were soft and easy, and would be supported with joy and pleasure, while they could be so happy to possess each other, and to be able to make good their vows. Caesar swore he disdained the empire of the world while he could behold his Imoinda, and she despised grandeur and pomp, those vanities of her sex, when she could gaze on Oroonoko. He adored the very cottage where she resided, and said, that little inch of the world would give him more happiness than all the universe could do, and she vowed, it was a palace, while adorned with the presence of Oroonoko.

Trefry was infinitely pleased with this novel,[2] and found this Clemene was the fair mistress of whom Caesar had before spoke; and was not a little satisfied, that Heaven was so kind to the Prince as to sweeten his misfortunes by so lucky an accident, and leaving the lovers to themselves, was impatient to come down to Parham House (which was on the same plantation) to give me an account of what had happened. I was as impatient to make these lovers a visit, having already made a friendship with Caesar, and from his own mouth learned what I have related, which was confirmed by his Frenchman, who was set on shore to seek his fortunes, and of whom they could not make a slave because a Christian, and he came daily to Parham Hill to see and pay his respects to his pupil prince. So that concerning and interesting myself in all that related to Caesar, whom I had assured of liberty as soon as the governor arrived, I hasted presently to the place where the lovers were, and was infinitely glad to find this beautiful young slave (who had already gained all our esteems, for her modesty and her extraordinary prettiness) to be the same I had heard Caesar speak so much of. One may imagine then, we paid her a treble respect; and though from her being carved in fine flowers and birds all over her body, we took her to be of quality before, yet, when we knew Clemene was Imoinda, we could not enough admire her.

---

1. Reduction; release.   2. New development.

I had forgot to tell you, that those who are nobly born of that country are so delicately cut and raced[3] all over the fore part of the trunk of their bodies, that it looks as if it were japanned;[4] the works being raised like high point[5] round the edges of the flowers. Some are only carved with a little flower or bird at the sides of the temples, as was Caesar; and those who are so carved over the body resemble our ancient Picts,[6] that are figured in the chronicles, but these carvings are more delicate.

From that happy day Caesar took Clemene for his wife, to the general joy of all people, and there was as much magnificence as the country would afford at the celebration of this wedding. And in a very short time after she conceived with child; which made Caesar even adore her, knowing he was the last of his great race. This new accident made him more impatient of liberty, and he was every day treating with Trefry for his and Clemene's liberty; and offered either gold, or a vast quantity of slaves, which should be paid before they let him go, provided he could have any security that he should go when his ransom was paid. They fed him from day to day with promises, and delayed him, till the Lord Governor should come, so that he began to suspect them of falsehood, and that they would delay him till the time of his wife's delivery, and make a slave of that too, for all the breed is theirs to whom the parents belong. This thought made him very uneasy, and his sullenness gave them some jealousies[7] of him, so that I was obliged, by some persons who feared a mutiny (which is very fatal sometimes in those colonies that abound so with slaves that they exceed the whites in vast numbers), to discourse with Caesar, and to give him all the satisfaction I possibly could. They knew he and Clemene were scarce an hour in a day from my lodgings, that they ate with me, and that I obliged them in all things I was capable of: I entertained him with the lives of the Romans, and great men, which charmed him to my company, and her, with teaching her all the pretty works that I was mistress of, and telling her stories of nuns, and endeavoring to bring her to the knowledge of the true God. But of all discourses Caesar liked that the worst, and would never be reconciled to our notions of the Trinity, of which he ever made a jest; it was a riddle, he said, would turn his brain to conceive, and one could not make him understand what faith was. However, these conversations failed not altogether so well to divert him, that he liked the company of us women much above the men, for he could not drink, and he is but an ill companion in that country that cannot. So that obliging him to love us very well, we had all the liberty of speech with him, especially myself, whom he called his Great Mistress; and indeed my word would go a great way with him. For these reasons, I had opportunity to take notice to him, that he was not well pleased of late, as he used to be, was more retired and thoughtful, and told him, I took it ill he should suspect we would break our words with him, and not permit both him and Clemene to return to his own kingdom, which was not so long away, but when he was once on his voyage he would quickly arrive there. He made me some answers that showed a doubt in him, which made me ask him, what advantage it would be to doubt? It would but give us a fear of him, and possibly compel us to treat him so as I should be very loath to behold: that is, it might occasion his confinement. Perhaps this was not so luckily spoke of me, for I perceived he resented that word, which I strove to soften again in vain. However, he assured me, that whatsoever resolutions he should take, he would act nothing upon the white people. And

3. Carved.
4. Varnished with a glossy black lacquer.
5. Intricate lace.
6. Ancient inhabitants of northern Britain, possibly so

named by the Romans because of the "pictures" (tattoos and other ornaments) they bore on their skin.
7. Suspicions.

as for myself, and those upon that plantation where he was, he would sooner forfeit his eternal liberty, and life itself, than lift his hand against his greatest enemy on that place. He besought me to suffer no fears upon his account, for he could do nothing that honor should not dictate, but he accused himself for having suffered slavery so long; yet he charged that weakness on love alone, who was capable of making him neglect even glory itself, and for which now he reproaches himself every moment of the day. Much more to this effect he spoke, with an air impatient enough to make me know he would not be long in bondage, and though he suffered only the name of a slave, and had nothing of the toil and labor of one, yet that was sufficient to render him uneasy, and he had been too long idle, who used to be always in action, and in arms. He had a spirit all rough and fierce, and that could not be tamed to lazy rest, and though all endeavors were used to exercise himself in such actions and sports as this world afforded, as running, wrestling, pitching the bar,[8] hunting and fishing, chasing and killing tigers of a monstrous size, which this continent affords in abundance; and wonderful snakes, such as Alexander[9] is reported to have encountered at the river of Amazons, and which Caesar took great delight to overcome; yet these were not actions great enough for his large soul, which was still panting after more renowned action.

Before I parted that day with him, I got, with much ado, a promise from him to rest yet a little longer with patience, and wait the coming of the Lord Governor, who was every day expected on our shore. He assured me he would, and this promise he desired me to know was given perfectly in complaisance to me, in whom he had an entire confidence.

After this, I neither thought it convenient to trust him much out of our view, nor did the country who feared him; but with one accord it was advised to treat him fairly, and oblige him to remain within such a compass, and that he should be permitted as seldom as could be to go up to the plantations of the Negroes; or if he did, to be accompanied by some that should be rather in appearance attendants than spies. This care was for some time taken, and Caesar looked upon it as a mark of extraordinary respect, and was glad his discontent had obliged them to be more observant to him. He received new assurance from the overseer, which was confirmed to him by the opinion of all the gentlemen of the country, who made their court to him. During this time that we had his company more frequently than hitherto we had had, it may not be unpleasant to relate to you the diversions we entertained him with, or rather he us.

My stay was to be short in that country, because my father died at sea, and never arrived to possess the honor was designed him (which was lieutenant-general of six and thirty islands, besides the continent[1] of Surinam), nor the advantages he hoped to reap by them, so that though we were obliged to continue on our voyage, we did not intend to stay upon the place. Though, in a word, I must say thus much of it, that certainly had his late Majesty,[2] of sacred memory, but seen and known what a vast and charming world he had been master of in that continent, he would never have parted so easily with it to the Dutch. 'Tis a continent whose vast extent was never yet known, and may contain more noble earth than all the universe besides; for they say it reaches from east to west, one way as far as China, and another to Peru. It

8. Hurling a heavy rod for purposes of exercise or sport.
9. Legends surrounding Alexander the Great included his encounter with the mythical woman warriors called

Amazons, and with the formidable snakes inhabiting their territories.
1. Mainland.
2. Charles II.

affords all things both for beauty and use; 'tis there eternal spring, always the very months of April, May, and June. The shades are perpetual, the trees, bearing at once all degrees of leaves and fruit from blooming buds to ripe autumn, groves of oranges, lemons, citrons, figs, nutmegs, and noble aromatics, continually bearing their fragrancies. The trees appearing all like nosegays adorned with flowers of different kind; some are all white, some purple, some scarlet, some blue, some yellow; bearing, at the same time, ripe fruit and blooming young, or producing every day new. The very wood of all these trees have an intrinsic value above common timber, for they are, when cut, of different colors, glorious to behold, and bear a price considerable, to inlay withal. Besides this, they yield rich balm and gums, so that we make our candles of such an aromatic substance as does not only give a sufficient light but, as they burn, they cast their perfumes all about. Cedar is the common firing, and all the houses are built with it. The very meat we eat, when set on the table, if it be native, I mean of the country, perfumes the whole room, especially a little beast called an armadillo, a thing which I can liken to nothing so well as a rhinoceros. 'Tis all in white armor so jointed that it moves as well in it as if it had nothing on. This beast is about the bigness of a pig of six weeks old. But it were endless to give an account of all the diverse wonderful and strange things that country affords, and which we took a very great delight to go in search of, though those adventures are oftentimes fatal and at least dangerous. But while we had Caesar in our company on these designs we feared no harm, nor suffered any.

As soon as I came into the country, the best house in it was presented me, called St. John's Hill. It stood on a vast rock of white marble, at the foot of which the river ran a vast depth down, and not to be descended on that side. The little waves still dashing and washing the foot of this rock made the softest murmurs and purlings in the world, and the opposite bank was adorned with such vast quantities of different flowers eternally blowing,[3] and every day and hour new, fenced behind them with lofty trees of a thousand rare forms and colors, that the prospect was the most ravishing that sands can create. On the edge of this white rock, towards the river, was a walk or grove of orange and lemon trees, about half the length of the Mall[4] here, whose flowery and fruity branches meet at the top, and hindered the sun, whose rays are very fierce there, from entering a beam into the grove, and the cool air that came from the river made it not only fit to entertain people in at all the hottest hours of the day, but refreshed the sweet blossoms, and made it always sweet and charming, and sure the whole globe of the world cannot show so delightful a place as this grove was. Not all the gardens of boasted Italy can produce a shade to out-vie this, which Nature had joined with Art to render so exceeding fine. And 'tis a marvel to see how such vast trees, as big as English oaks, could take footing on so solid a rock, and in so little earth, as covered that rock, but all things by nature there are rare, delightful, and wonderful. But to our sports.

Sometimes we would go surprising,[5] and in search of young tigers in their dens, watching when the old ones went forth to forage for prey, and oftentimes we have been in great danger, and have fled apace for our lives, when surprised by the dams. But once, above all other times, we went on this design, and Caesar was with us, who had no sooner stolen a young tiger from her nest, but going off, we encountered the

---

3. Blossoming.
4. A walk extending alongside London's St. James's Park.

5. I.e., surprise-attacking.

dam, bearing a buttock of a cow, which he[6] had torn off with his mighty paw, and going with it towards his den. We had only four women, Caesar, and an English gentleman, brother to Harry Martin, the great Oliverian.[7] We found there was no escaping this enraged and ravenous beast. However, we women fled as fast as we could from it, but our heels had not saved our lives if Caesar had not laid down his cub, when he found the tiger quit her prey to make the more speed towards him, and taking Mr. Martin's sword desired him to stand aside, or follow the ladies. He obeyed him, and Caesar met this monstrous beast of might, size, and vast limbs, who came with open jaws upon him, and fixing his awful stern eyes full upon those of the beast, and putting himself into a very steady and good aiming posture of defense, ran his sword quite through his breast down to his very heart, home to the hilt of the sword. The dying beast stretched forth her paw, and going to grasp his thigh, surprised with death in that very moment, did him no other harm than fixing her long nails in his flesh very deep, feebly wounded him, but could not grasp the flesh to tear off any. When he had done this, he hollowed to us to return, which, after some assurance of his victory, we did, and found him lugging out the sword from the bosom of the tiger, who was laid in her blood on the ground. He took up the cub, and with an unconcern, that had nothing of the joy or gladness of a victory, he came and laid the whelp at my feet. We all extremely wondered at his daring, and at the bigness of the beast, which was about the height of an heifer, but of mighty, great, and strong limbs.

Another time, being in the woods, he killed a tiger, which had long infested that part, and borne away abundance of sheep and oxen and other things, that were for the support of those to whom they belonged. Abundance of people assailed this beast, some affirming they had shot her with several bullets quite through the body, at several times, and some swearing they shot her through the very heart, and they believed she was a devil rather than a mortal thing. Caesar had often said he had a mind to encounter this monster, and spoke with several gentlemen who had attempted her, one crying, I shot her with so many poisoned arrows, another with his gun in this part of her, and another in that. So that he remarking all these places where she was shot, fancied still he should overcome her, by giving her another sort of a wound than any had yet done, and one day said (at the table), "What trophies and garlands, ladies, will you make me, if I bring you home the heart of this ravenous beast that eats up all your lambs and pigs?" We all promised he should be rewarded at all our hands. So taking a bow, which he chose out of a great many, he went up in the wood, with two gentlemen, where he imagined this devourer to be. They had not passed very far in it, but they heard her voice, growling and grumbling, as if she were pleased with something she was doing. When they came in view, they found her muzzling in the belly of a new ravished sheep which she had torn open, and seeing herself approached, she took fast hold of her prey with her forepaws, and set a very fierce raging look on Caesar, without offering to approach him, for fear, at the same time, of losing what she had in possession. So that Caesar remained a good while, only taking aim, and getting an opportunity to shoot her where he designed. 'Twas some time before he could accomplish it, and to wound her and not kill her would but have enraged her more, and endangered him. He had a quiver of arrows at his side, so that if one failed he could be supplied. At last, retiring a little, he gave her opportunity to

---

6. The "dam" is the cub's mother, but Behn has surprisingly shifted the gender of the pronoun from "she" to "he"; she will do so again in reference to another tiger in

the next paragraph.
7. Supporter of Oliver Cromwell.

eat, for he found she was ravenous, and fell to as soon as she saw him retire, being more eager of her prey than of doing new mischiefs. When he going softly to one side of her, and hiding his person behind certain herbage that grew high and thick, he took so good aim that, as he intended, he shot her just into the eye, and the arrow was sent with so good a will, and so sure a hand, that it stuck in her brain, and made her caper and become mad for a moment or two, but being seconded by another arrow, he fell dead upon the prey. Caesar cut him open with a knife, to see where those wounds were that had been reported to him, and why he did not die of them. But I shall now relate a thing that possibly will find no credit among men, because 'tis a notion commonly received with us that nothing can receive a wound in the heart and live; but when the heart of this courageous animal was taken out, there were seven bullets of lead in it, and the wounds seamed up with great scars, and she lived with the bullets a great while, for it was long since they were shot. This heart the conqueror brought up to us, and 'twas a very great curiosity, which all the country came to see; and which gave Caesar occasion of many fine discourses, of accidents in war and strange escapes.

At other times he would go a-fishing, and discoursing on that diversion, he found we had in that country a very strange fish, called a numb eel[8] (an eel of which I have eaten), that while it is alive, it has a quality so cold that those who are angling, though with a line of never so great a length, with a rod at the end of it, it shall, in the same minute the bait is touched by this eel, seize him or her that holds the rod with benumbedness, that shall deprive them of sense for a while. And some have fallen into the water, and others dropped as dead on the banks of the rivers where they stood, as soon as this fish touches the bait. Caesar used to laugh at this, and believed it impossible a man could lose his force at the touch of a fish; and could not understand that philosophy, that a cold quality should be of that nature. However, he had a great curiosity to try whether it would have the same effect on him it had on others, and often tried, but in vain. At last, the sought-for fish came to the bait as he stood angling on the bank; and instead of throwing away the rod, or giving it a sudden twitch out of the water, whereby he might have caught both the eel and have dismissed the rod before it could have too much power over him for experiment sake, he grasped it but the harder, and fainting fell into the river. And being still possessed of the rod, the tide carried him senseless as he was a great way, till an Indian boat took him up, and perceived, when they touched him, a numbness seize them, and by that knew the rod was in his hand, which with a paddle (that is, a short oar) they struck away, and snatched it into the boat, eel and all. If Caesar were almost dead with the effect of this fish, he was more so with that of the water, where he had remained the space of going a league, and they found they had much ado to bring him back to life. But at last they did, and brought him home, where he was in a few hours well recovered and refreshed, and not a little ashamed to find he should be overcome by an eel, and that all the people who heard his defiance would laugh at him. But we cheered him up and he, being convinced, we had the eel at supper, which was a quarter of an ell about, and most delicate meat, and was of the more value, since it cost so dear as almost the life of so gallant a man.

About this time we were in many mortal fears about some disputes the English had with the Indians, so that we could scarce trust ourselves, without great numbers, to go to any Indian towns or place where they abode, for fear they should fall upon us,

---

8. An electric eel.

as they did immediately after my coming away, and that it was in the possession of the Dutch, who used them not so civilly as the English, so that they cut in pieces all they could take, getting into houses, and hanging up the mother, and all her children about her, and cut a footman, I left behind me, all in joints, and nailed him to trees.

This feud began while I was there, so that I lost half the satisfaction I proposed, in not seeing and visiting the Indian towns. But one day, bemoaning of our misfortunes upon this account, Caesar told us we need not fear, for if we had a mind to go he would undertake to be our guard. Some would, but most would not venture. About eighteen of us resolved, and took barge, and after eight days arrived near an Indian town. But approaching it, the hearts of some of our company failed, and they would not venture on shore, so we polled who would, and who would not. For my part, I said, if Caesar would, I would go. He resolved, so did my brother and my woman, a maid of good courage. Now none of us speaking the language of the people, and imagining we should have a half diversion in gazing only and not knowing what they said, we took a fisherman that lived at the mouth of the river, who had been a long inhabitant there, and obliged him to go with us. But because he was known to the Indians, as trading among them, and being, by long living there, become a perfect Indian in color, we, who resolved to surprise them, by making them see something they never had seen (that is, white people) resolved only myself, my brother, and woman should go. So Caesar, the fisherman, and the rest, hiding behind some thick reeds and flowers, that grew on the banks, let us pass on towards the town, which was on the bank of the river all along. A little distant from the houses, or huts, we saw some dancing, others busied in fetching and carrying of water from the river. They had no sooner spied us but they set up a loud cry, that frighted us at first. We thought it had been for those that should kill us, but it seems it was of wonder and amazement. They were all naked, and we were dressed, so as is most commode for the hot countries, very glittering and rich, so that we appeared extremely fine. My own hair was cut short, and I had a taffeta cap, with black feathers, on my head. My brother was in a stuff[9] suit, with silver loops and buttons, and abundance of green ribbon. This was all infinitely surprising to them, and because we saw them stand still, till we approached them, we took heart and advanced, came up to them, and offered them our hands, which they took, and looked on us round about, calling still for more company; who came swarming out, all wondering, and crying out *tepeeme*, taking their hair up in their hands, and spreading it wide to those they called out to, as if they would say (as indeed it signified) "numberless wonders," or not to be recounted, no more than to number the hair of their heads. By degrees they grew more bold, and from gazing upon us round, they touched us, laying their hands upon all the features of our faces, feeling our breasts and arms, taking up one petticoat, then wondering to see another, admiring our shoes and stockings, but more our garters, which we gave them, and they tied about their legs, being laced with silver lace at the ends, for they much esteem any shining things. In fine, we suffered them to survey us as they pleased, and we thought they would never have done admiring us. When Caesar and the rest saw we were received with such wonder, they came up to us, and finding the Indian trader whom they knew (for 'tis by these fishermen, called Indian traders, we hold a commerce with them; for they love not to go far from home, and we never go to them), when they saw him therefore they set up a new joy, and cried, in their language, "Oh! here's our *tiguamy*, and we shall now know whether those things can

9. Woolen.

speak." So advancing to him, some of them gave him their hands, and cried, "*Amora tiguamy,*" which is as much as, "How do you," or "Welcome friend," and all, with one din, began to gabble to him, and asked, If we had sense, and wit? If we could talk of affairs of life, and war, as they could do? If we could hunt, swim, and do a thousand things they use? He answered them, we could. Then they invited us into their houses, and dressed venison and buffalo for us; and, going out, gathered a leaf of a tree, called a sarumbo leaf, of six yards long, and spread it on the ground for a tablecloth, and cutting another in pieces instead of plates, setting us on little bow Indian stools, which they cut out of one entire piece of wood, and paint in a sort of japan work. They serve everyone their mess on these pieces of leaves, and it was very good, but too high seasoned with pepper. When we had eaten, my brother and I took out our flutes and played to them, which gave them new wonder, and I soon perceived, by an admiration that is natural to these people, and by the extreme ignorance and simplicity of them, it were not difficult to establish any unknown or extravagant religion among them, and to impose any notions or fictions upon them. For seeing a kinsman of mine set some paper afire with a burning-glass, a trick they had never before seen, they were like to have adored him for a god, and begged he would give them the characters or figures of his name, that they might oppose it against winds and storms, which he did, and they held it up in those seasons, and fancied it had a charm to conquer them, and kept it like a holy relic. They are very superstitious, and called him the great *peeie,* that is, prophet. They showed us their Indian *peeie,* a youth of about sixteen years old, as handsome as Nature could make a man. They consecrate a beautiful youth from his infancy, and all arts are used to complete him in the finest manner, both in beauty and shape. He is bred to all the little arts and cunning they are capable of, to all the legerdemain tricks and sleight of hand whereby he imposes upon the rabble, and is both a doctor in physic and divinity. And by these tricks makes the sick believe he sometimes eases their pains, by drawing from the afflicted part little serpents, or odd flies, or worms, or any strange thing; and though they have besides undoubted good remedies for almost all their diseases, they cure the patient more by fancy than by medicines, and make themselves feared, loved, and reverenced. This young *peeie* had a very young wife, who seeing my brother kiss her, came running and kissed me; after this, they kissed one another, and made it a very great jest, it being so novel, and new admiration and laughing went round the multitude, that they never will forget that ceremony, never before used or known. Caesar had a mind to see and talk with their war captains, and we were conducted to one of their houses, where we beheld several of the great captains, who had been at council. But so frightful a vision it was to see them no fancy can create; no such dreams can represent so dreadful a spectacle. For my part I took them for hobgoblins, or fiends, rather than men. But however their shapes appeared, their souls were very humane and noble, but some wanted their noses, some their lips, some both noses and lips, some their ears, and others cut through each cheek, with long slashes, through which their teeth appeared; they had several other formidable wounds and scars, or rather dismemberings. They had *comitias,* or little aprons before them, and girdles of cotton, with their knives naked, stuck in it, a bow at their backs, and a quiver of arrows on their thighs, and most had feathers on their heads of diverse colors. They cried "*Amora tiguamy*" to us at our entrance, and were pleased we said as much to them. They feted us, and gave us drink of the best sort, and wondered, as much as the others had done before, to see us. Caesar was marveling as much at their faces, wondering how they should all be so wounded in war; he was impatient to know how they all came by those frightful marks of rage or malice, rather than wounds got in noble battle. They told us, by our interpreter, that when any war was waging, two men chosen out by some old captain, whose fighting was past, and who could only teach the theory of war, these two men were to stand in competition for the generalship, or Great War Captain, and being brought before the old judges, now past labor, they are asked, what they dare do to show they are worthy to lead an army? When he who is first asked, making no reply, cuts off his nose, and throws it contemptibly[1] on the ground, and the other does something to himself that he thinks surpasses him, and perhaps deprives himself of lips and an eye. So they slash on till one gives out, and many have died in this debate. And 'tis by a passive valor they show and prove their activity, a sort of courage too brutal to be applauded by our black hero; nevertheless he expressed his esteem of them.

In this voyage Caesar begot so good an understanding between the Indians and the English, that there were no more fears or heartburnings during our stay, but we had a perfect, open, and free trade with them. Many things remarkable, and worthy reciting, we met with in this short voyage, because Caesar made it his business to search out and provide for our entertainment, especially to please his dearly adored Imoinda, who was a sharer in all our adventures; we being resolved to make her chains as easy as we could, and to compliment the Prince in that manner that most obliged him.

As we were coming up again, we met with some Indians of strange aspects, that is, of a larger size, and other sort of features, than those of our country. Our Indian slaves, that rowed us, asked them some questions, but they could not understand us, but showed us a long cotton string with several knots on it, and told us, they had been coming from the mountains so many moons as there were knots. They were habited in skins of a strange beast, and brought along with them bags of gold dust, which, as well as they could give us to understand, came streaming in little small channels down the high mountains, when the rains fell, and offered to be the convoy to anybody, or persons, that would go to the mountains. We carried these men up to Parham, where they were kept till the Lord Governor came. And because all the country was mad to be going on this golden adventure, the governor, by his letters, commanded (for they sent some of the gold to him) that a guard should be set at the mouth of the river of Amazons (a river so called, almost as broad as the river of Thames), and prohibited all people from going up that river, it conducting to those mountains of gold. But we going off for England before the project was further prosecuted, and the Governor being drowned in a hurricane, either the design died, or the Dutch have the advantage of it. And 'tis to be bemoaned what His Majesty lost by losing that part of America.

Though this digression is a little from my story, however since it contains some proofs of the curiosity and daring of this great man, I was content to omit nothing of his character.

It was thus, for some time we diverted him. But now Imoinda began to show she was with child, and did nothing but sigh and weep for the captivity of her lord, herself, and the infant yet unborn, and believed, if it were so hard to gain the liberty of two, 'twould be more difficult to get that for three. Her griefs were so many darts in the great heart of Caesar, and taking his opportunity one Sunday, when all the whites were overtaken in drink, as there were abundance of several trades, and slaves

1. Contemptuously.

for four years,[2] that inhabited among the Negro houses, and Sunday was their day of debauch (otherwise they were a sort of spies upon Caesar), he went pretending out of goodness to them, to feast amongst them, and sent all his music, and ordered a great treat for the whole gang, about three hundred Negroes. And about a hundred and fifty were able to bear arms, such as they had, which were sufficient to do execution with spirits accordingly. For the English had none but rusty swords, that no strength could draw from a scabbard, except the people of particular quality, who took care to oil them and keep them in good order. The guns also, unless here and there one, or those newly carried from England, would do no good or harm, for 'tis the nature of that country to rust and eat up iron, or any metals but gold and silver. And they are very inexpert at the bow, which the Negroes and Indians are perfect masters of.

Caesar, having singled out these men from the women and children, made a harangue to them of the miseries and ignominies of slavery; counting up all their toils and sufferings, under such loads, burdens, and drudgeries as were fitter for beasts than men, senseless brutes than human souls. He told them it was not for days, months, or years, but for eternity; there was no end to be of their misfortunes. They suffered not like men who might find a glory and fortitude in oppression, but like dogs that loved the whip and bell,[3] and fawned the more they were beaten. That they had lost the divine quality of men, and were become insensible asses, fit only to bear. Nay worse, an ass, or dog, or horse having done his duty, could lie down in retreat, and rise to work again, and while he did his duty endured no stripes; but men, villainous, senseless men such as they, toiled on all the tedious week till black Friday, and then, whether they worked or not, whether they were faulty or meriting, they promiscuously, the innocent with the guilty, suffered the infamous whip, the sordid stripes, from their fellow slaves till their blood trickled from all parts of their body, blood whose every drop ought to be revenged with a life of some of those tyrants that impose it. "And why," said he, "my dear friends and fellow sufferers, should we be slaves to an unknown people? Have they vanquished us nobly in fight? Have they won us in honorable battle? And are we, by the chance of war, become their slaves? This would not anger a noble heart, this would not animate a soldier's soul. No, but we are bought and sold like apes, or monkeys, to be the sport of women, fools, and cowards, and the support of rogues, runagades, that have abandoned their own countries, for raping, murders, thefts, and villainies. Do you not hear every day how they upbraid each other with infamy of life below the wildest salvages, and shall we render obedience to such a degenerate race, who have no one human virtue left to distinguish them from the vilest creatures? Will you, I say, suffer the lash from such hands?" They all replied, with one accord, "No, no, no; Caesar has spoke like a great captain, like a great king."

After this he would have proceeded, but was interrupted by a tall Negro of some more quality than the rest. His name was Tuscan, who bowing at the feet of Caesar, cried, "My lord, we have listened with joy and attention to what you have said, and, were we only men, would follow so great a leader through the world. But oh! consider, we are husbands and parents too, and have things more dear to us than life: our wives and children unfit for travel, in these impassable woods, mountains, and bogs. We have not only difficult lands to overcome, but rivers to wade, and monsters to encounter, ravenous beasts of prey—" To this, Caesar replied, that honor was the

2. I.e., whites who, as punishment for crime or debt, had been forced into service for fixed periods of time.

3. Because rigorous training has taught them to cherish their punishment.

first principle in nature that was to be obeyed; but as no man would pretend to that, without all the acts of virtue, compassion, charity, love, justice, and reason, he found it not inconsistent with that, to take an equal care of their wives and children, as they would of themselves, and that he did not design, when he led them to freedom and glorious liberty, that they should leave that better part of themselves to perish by the hand of the tyrant's whip. But if there were a woman among them so degenerate from love and virtue to choose slavery before the pursuit of her husband, and with the hazard of her life to share with him in his fortunes, that such an one ought to be abandoned, and left as a prey to the common enemy.

To which they all agreed—and bowed. After this, he spoke of the impassable woods and rivers, and convinced them, the more danger, the more glory. He told them that he had heard of one Hannibal, a great captain, had cut his way through mountains of solid rocks,[4] and should a few shrubs oppose them, which they could fire before them? No, 'twas a trifling excuse to men resolved to die, or overcome. As for bogs, they are with a little labor filled and hardened, and the rivers could be no obstacle, since they swam by nature, at least by custom, from their first hour of their birth. That when the children were weary they must carry them by turns, and the woods and their own industry would afford them food. To this they all assented with joy.

Tuscan then demanded, what he would do? He said, they would travel towards the sea; plant a new colony, and defend it by their valor; and when they could find a ship, either driven by stress of weather, or guided by Providence that way, they would seize it, and make it a prize, till it had transported them to their own countries. At least, they should be made free in his kingdom, and be esteemed as his fellow sufferers, and men that had the courage and the bravery to attempt, at least, for liberty. And if they died in the attempt it would be more brave than to live in perpetual slavery.

They bowed and kissed his feet at this resolution, and with one accord vowed to follow him to death. And that night was appointed to begin their march; they made it known to their wives, and directed them to tie their hamaca[5] about their shoulder, and under their arm like a scarf; and to lead their children that could go, and carry those that could not. The wives who pay an entire obedience to their husbands obeyed, and stayed for them where they were appointed. The men stayed but to furnish themselves with what defensive arms they could get, and all met at the rendezvous, where Caesar made a new encouraging speech to them, and led them out.

But, as they could not march far that night, on Monday early, when the overseers went to call them all together to go to work, they were extremely surprised to find not one upon the place, but all fled with what baggage they had. You may imagine this news was not only suddenly spread all over the plantation, but soon reached the neighboring ones, and we had by noon about six hundred men, they call the militia of the county, that came to assist us in the pursuit of the fugitives. But never did one see so comical an army march forth to war. The men of any fashion would not concern themselves, though it were almost the common cause, for such revoltings are very ill examples, and have very fatal consequences oftentimes in many colonies. But they had a respect for Caesar, and all hands were against the Parhamites, as they called those of Parham Plantation, because they did not, in the first place, love the Lord Governor, and secondly, they would have it that Caesar was ill used, and baffled with.[6] And 'tis not impossible but some of the best in the country was of his counsel in this flight, and depriving us of all the slaves, so that they of the better sort would not meddle in the matter. The deputy governor,[7] of whom I have had no great occasion to speak, and who was the most fawning fair-tongued fellow in the world, and one that pretended the most friendship to Caesar, was now the only violent man against him, and though he had nothing, and so need fear nothing, yet talked and looked bigger than any man. He was a fellow whose character is not fit to be mentioned with the worst of the slaves. This fellow would lead his army forth to meet Caesar, or rather to pursue him. Most of their arms were of those sort of cruel whips they call cat-with-nine-tails; some had rusty useless guns for show; others old baskethilts, whose blades had never seen the light in this age, and others had long staffs, and clubs. Mr. Trefry went along rather to be a mediator than a conqueror in such a battle, for he foresaw and knew, if by fighting they put the Negroes into despair, they were a sort of sullen fellows that would drown or kill themselves before they would yield, and he advised that fair means was best. But Byam was one that abounded in his own wit, and would take his own measures.

It was not hard to find these fugitives, for as they fled they were forced to fire and cut the woods before them, so that night or day they pursued them by the light they made, and by the path they had cleared. But as soon as Caesar found he was pursued, he put himself in a posture of defense, placing all the women and children in the rear, and himself, with Tuscan by his side, or next to him, all promising to die or conquer. Encouraged thus, they never stood to parley, but fell on pell-mell upon the English, and killed some, and wounded a good many, they having recourse to their whips, as the best of their weapons. And as they observed no order, they perplexed the enemy so sorely, with lashing them in the eyes. And the women and children, seeing their husbands so treated, being of fearful cowardly dispositions, and hearing the English cry out, "Yield and live, yield and be pardoned," they all ran in amongst their husbands and fathers, and hung about them, crying out, "Yield, yield, and leave Caesar to their revenge," that by degrees the slaves abandoned Caesar, and left him only Tuscan and his heroic Imoinda, who, grown big as she was, did nevertheless press near her lord, having a bow, and a quiver full of poisoned arrows, which she managed with such dexterity that she wounded several, and shot the governor into the shoulder, of which wound he had like to have died but that an Indian woman, his mistress, sucked the wound, and cleansed it from the venom. But however, he stirred not from the place till he had parleyed with Caesar, who he found was resolved to die fighting, and would not be taken; no more would Tuscan, or Imoinda. But he, more thirsting after revenge of another sort, than that of depriving him of life, now made use of all his art of talking and dissembling, and besought Caesar to yield himself upon terms which he himself should propose, and should be sacredly assented to and kept by him. He told him, it was not that he any longer feared him, or could believe the force of two men, and a young heroine, could overcome all them, with all the slaves now on their side also, but it was the vast esteem he had for his person, the desire he had to serve so gallant a man, and to hinder himself from the reproach hereafter of having been the occasion of the death of a prince, whose valor and magnanimity deserved the empire of the world. He protested to him, he looked upon this action as gallant and brave, however tending to the prejudice of his lord and master, who would by it have lost so considerable a number of slaves, that this flight of his should be looked on as a heat of youth, and rashness of a too forward courage, and an unconsidered impatience of liberty, and no more; and that he labored in vain to accomplish

---

7. William Byam, who during a decade as administrator in Surinam had acquired a reputation for arrogance and severity.

that which they would effectually perform, as soon as any ship arrived that would touch on his coast. "So that if you will be pleased," continued he, "to surrender yourself, all imaginable respect shall be paid you; and yourself, your wife, and child, if it be here born, shall depart free out of our land." But Caesar would hear of no composition, though Byam urged, if he pursued and went on in his design, he would inevitably perish, either by great snakes, wild beasts, or hunger, and he ought to have regard to his wife, whose condition required ease, and not the fatigues of tedious travel, where she could not be secured from being devoured. But Caesar told him, there was no faith in the white men, or the gods they adored, who instructed them in principles so false that honest men could not live amongst them; though no people professed so much, none performed so little; that he knew what he had to do, when he dealt with men of honor, but with them a man ought to be eternally on his guard, and never to eat and drink with Christians without his weapon of defense in his hand, and, for his own security, never to credit one word they spoke. As for the rashness and inconsiderateness of his action he would confess the governor is in the right, and that he was ashamed of what he had done, in endeavoring to make those free, who were by nature slaves, poor wretched rogues, fit to be used as Christians' tools; dogs, treacherous and cowardly, fit for such masters, and they wanted only but to be whipped into the knowledge of the Christian gods to be the vilest of all creeping things, to learn to worship such deities as had not power to make them just, brave, or honest. In fine, after a thousand things of this nature, not fit here to be recited, he told Byam, he had rather die than live upon the same earth with such dogs. But Trefry and Byam pleaded and protested together so much, that Trefry believing the governor to mean what he said, and speaking very cordially himself, generously put himself into Caesar's hands, and took him aside, and persuaded him, even with tears, to live, by surrendering himself, and to name his conditions. Caesar was overcome by his wit and reasons, and in consideration of Imoinda, and demanding what he desired, and that it should be ratified by their hands in writing, because he had perceived that was the common way of contract between man and man amongst the whites. All this was performed, and Tuscan's pardon was put in, and they surrender to the governor, who walked peaceably down into the plantation with them, after giving order to bury their dead. Caesar was very much toiled with the bustle of the day, for he had fought like a Fury, and what mischief was done he and Tuscan performed alone, and gave their enemies a fatal proof that they durst do anything, and feared no mortal force.

But they were no sooner arrived at the place where all the slaves receive their punishments of whipping, but they laid hands on Caesar and Tuscan, faint with heat and toil; and surprising them, bound them to two several stakes, and whipped them in a most deplorable and inhumane manner, rending the very flesh from their bones; especially Caesar, who was not perceived to make any moan, or to alter his face, only to roll his eyes on the faithless governor, and those he believed guilty, with fierceness and indignation. And, to complete his rage, he saw every one of those slaves, who, but a few days before, adored him as something more than mortal, now had a whip to give him some lashes, while he strove not to break his fetters, though if he had, it were impossible. But he pronounced a woe and revenge from his eyes, that darted fire, that 'twas at once both awful and terrible to behold.

When they thought they were sufficiently revenged on him, they untied him, almost fainting with loss of blood from a thousand wounds all over his body, from which they had rent his clothes, and led him bleeding and naked as he was, and loaded him all over with irons, and then rubbed his wounds, to complete their cruelty, with Indian pepper, which had like to have made him raving mad, and in this condition made him so fast to the ground that he could not stir, if his pains and wounds would have given him leave. They spared Imoinda, and did not let her see this barbarity committed towards her lord, but carried her down to Parham, and shut her up, which was not in kindness to her, but for fear she should die with the sight, or miscarry, and then they should lose a young slave, and perhaps the mother.

You must know, that when the news was brought on Monday morning, that Caesar had betaken himself to the woods, and carried with him all the Negroes, we were possessed with extreme fear, which no persuasions could dissipate, that he would secure himself till night, and then, that he would come down and cut all our throats. This apprehension made all the females of us fly down the river, to be secured, and while we were away, they acted this cruelty. For I suppose I had authority and interest enough there, had I suspected any such thing, to have prevented it, but we had not gone many leagues, but the news overtook us that Caesar was taken, and whipped like a common slave. We met on the river with Colonel Martin, a man of great gallantry, wit, and goodness, and, whom I have celebrated in a character of my new comedy,[8] by his own name, in memory of so brave a man. He was wise and eloquent, and, from the fineness of his parts, bore a great sway over the hearts of all the colony. He was a friend to Caesar, and resented this false dealing with him very much. We carried him back to Parham, thinking to have made an accommodation; when we came, the first news we heard was that the governor was dead of a wound Imoinda had given him, but it was not so well. But it seems he would have the pleasure of beholding the revenge he took on Caesar, and before the cruel ceremony was finished, he dropped down, and then they perceived the wound he had on his shoulder was by a venomed arrow, which, as I said, his Indian mistress healed, by sucking the wound.

We were no sooner arrived, but we went up to the plantation to see Caesar, whom we found in a very miserable and inexpressible condition, and I have a thousand times admired how he lived, in so much tormenting pain. We said all things to him that trouble, pity, and good nature could suggest, protesting our innocence of the fact, and our abhorrence of such cruelties; making a thousand professions of services to him, and begging as many pardons for the offenders, till we said so much, that he believed we had no hand in his ill treatment, but told us, he could never pardon Byam. As for Trefry, he confessed he saw his grief and sorrow for his suffering, which he could not hinder, but was like to have been beaten down by the very slaves, for speaking in his defense. But for Byam, who was their leader, their head—and should, by his justice, and honor, have been an example to them—for him, he wished to live, to take a dire revenge of him, and said, "It had been well for him if he had sacrificed me, instead of giving me the contemptible whip." He refused to talk much, but begging us to give him our hands, he took them, and protested never to lift up his, to do us any harm. He had a great respect for Colonel Martin, and always took his counsel, like that of a parent, and assured him, he would obey him in anything but his revenge on Byam. "Therefore," said he, "for his own safety, let him speedily dispatch me, for if I could dispatch myself, I would not, till that justice were done to my injured person, and the contempt of a soldier. No, I would not kill myself, even after a whipping, but will be content to live with that infamy, and be pointed at by every grinning slave, till I have completed my revenge; and then you shall see that

8. *The Younger Brother: or the Amorous Jilt*, produced posthumously in 1696.

Oroonoko scorns to live with the indignity that was put on Caesar." All we could do could get no more words from him, and we took care to have him put immediately into a healing bath, to rid him of his pepper, and ordered a chirurgeon[9] to anoint him with healing balm, which he suffered, and in some time he began to be able to walk and eat. We failed not to visit him every day, and, to that end, had him brought to an apartment at Parham.

The governor was no sooner recovered, and had heard of the menaces of Caesar, but he called his council, who (not to disgrace them, or burlesque the government there) consisted of such notorious villains as Newgate[1] never transported, and possibly originally were such, who understood neither the laws of God or man, and had no sort of principles to make them worthy the name of men, but at the very council table would contradict and fight with one another, and swear so bloodily that 'twas terrible to hear and see them. (Some of them were afterwards hanged, when the Dutch took possession of the place; others sent off in chains.) But calling these special rulers of the nation together, and requiring their counsel in this weighty affair, they all concluded that (damn them) it might be their own cases, and that Caesar ought to be made an example to all the Negroes, to fright them from daring to threaten their betters, their lords and masters, and, at this rate, no man was safe from his own slaves, and concluded, *nemine contradicente*,[2] that Caesar should be hanged.

Trefry then thought it time to use his authority, and told Byam his command did not extend to his lord's plantation, and that Parham was as much exempt from the law as Whitehall; and that they ought no more to touch the servants of the Lord—— (who there represented the King's person) than they could those about the King himself; and that Parham was a sanctuary, and though his lord were absent in person, his power was still in being there, which he had entrusted with him, as far as the dominions of his particular plantations reached, and all that belonged to it; the rest of the country, as Byam was lieutenant to his lord, he might exercise his tyranny upon. Trefry had others as powerful, or more, that interested themselves in Caesar's life, and absolutely said he should be defended. So turning the governor, and his wise council, out of doors (for they sat at Parham House) we set a guard upon our landing place, and would admit none but those we called friends to us and Caesar.

The governor having remained wounded at Parham till his recovery was completed, Caesar did not know but he was still there, and indeed, for the most part, his time was spent there, for he was one that loved to live at other people's expense, and if he were a day absent, he was ten present there, and used to play, and walk, and hunt, and fish, with Caesar. So that Caesar did not at all doubt, if he once recovered strength, but he should find an opportunity of being revenged on him. Though, after such a revenge, he could not hope to live, for if he escaped the fury of the English mobile,[3] who perhaps would have been glad of the occasion to have killed him, he was resolved not to survive his whipping, yet he had, some tender hours, a repenting softness, which he called his fits of coward, wherein he struggled with love for the victory of his heart, which took part with his charming Imoinda there, but, for the most part, his time was passed in melancholy thought, and black designs. He considered, if he should do this deed, and die either in the attempt, or after it, he left his lovely Imoinda a prey, or at best a slave, to the enraged multitude; his great heart could not endure that thought. "Perhaps," said he, "she may be first ravished by every

---

9. Surgeon.
1. London prison from which convicts were sent to work in the colonies.

2. No one disagreeing.
3. Mob.

brute, exposed first to their nasty lusts, and then a shameful death." No, he could not live a moment under that apprehension, too insupportable to be borne. These were his thoughts, and his silent arguments with his heart, as he told us afterwards, so that now resolving not only to kill Byam, but all those he thought had enraged him, pleasing his great heart with the fancied slaughter he should make over the whole face of the plantation. He first resolved on a deed that (however horrid it at first appeared to us all), when we had heard his reasons, we thought it brave and just. Being able to walk and, as he believed, fit for the execution of his great design, he begged Trefry to trust him into the air, believing a walk would do him good, which was granted him, and taking Imoinda with him, as he used to do in his more happy and calmer days, he led her up into a wood where, after (with a thousand sighs, and long gazing silently on her face, while tears gushed, in spite of him, from his eyes), he told her his design first of killing her, and then his enemies, and next himself, and the impossibility of escaping, and therefore he told her the necessity of dying. He found the heroic wife faster pleading for death than he was to propose it, when she found his fixed resolution, and on her knees besought him not to leave her a prey to his enemies. He (grieved to death) yet pleased at her noble resolution, took her up, and embracing her with all the passion and languishment of a dying lover, drew his knife to kill this treasure of his soul, this pleasure of his eyes. While tears trickled down his cheeks, hers were smiling with joy she should die by so noble a hand, and be sent in her own country (for that's their notion of the next world) by him she so tenderly loved, and so truly adored in this, for wives have a respect for their husbands equal to what any other people pay a deity, and when a man finds any occasion to quit his wife, if he love her, she dies by his hand, if not, he sells her, or suffers some other to kill her. It being thus, you may believe the deed was soon resolved on, and 'tis not to be doubted, but the parting, the eternal leave-taking of two such lovers, so greatly born, so sensible,[4] so beautiful, so young, and so fond, must be very moving, as the relation of it was to me afterwards.

All that love could say in such cases being ended, and all the intermitting irresolutions being adjusted, the lovely, young, and adored victim lays herself down before the sacrificer, while he, with a hand resolved, and a heart breaking within, gave the fatal stroke, first cutting her throat, and then severing her yet smiling face from that delicate body, pregnant as it was with fruits of tenderest love. As soon as he had done, he laid the body decently on leaves and flowers, of which he made a bed, and concealed it under the same coverlid of nature, only her face he left yet bare to look on. But when he found she was dead, and past all retrieve, never more to bless him with her eyes and soft language, his grief swelled up to rage; he tore, he raved, he roared, like some monster of the wood, calling on the loved name of Imoinda. A thousand times he turned the fatal knife that did the deed toward his own heart, with a resolution to go immediately after her, but dire revenge, which now was a thousand times more fierce in his soul than before, prevents him, and he would cry out, "No, since I have sacrificed Imoinda to my revenge, shall I lose that glory which I have purchased so dear, as at the price of the fairest, dearest, softest creature that ever Nature made? No, no!" Then, at her name, grief would get the ascendant of rage, and he would lie down by her side, and water her face with showers of tears, which never were wont to fall from those eyes. And however bent he was on his intended slaughter, he had not power to stir from the sight of this dear object, now more beloved and more adored than ever.

4. Sensitive.

He remained in this deploring condition for two days, and never rose from the ground where he had made his sad sacrifice. At last, rousing from her side, and accusing himself with living too long now Imoinda was dead, and that the deaths of those barbarous enemies were deferred too long, he resolved now to finish the great work; but offering to rise, he found his strength so decayed, that he reeled to and fro, like boughs assailed by contrary winds, so that he was forced to lie down again, and try to summon all his courage to his aid. He found his brains turn round, and his eyes were dizzy, and objects appeared not the same to him as they were wont to do; his breath was short, and all his limbs surprised with a faintness he had never felt before. He had not eaten in two days, which was one occasion of this feebleness, but excess of grief was the greatest; yet still he hoped he should recover vigor to act his design, and lay expecting it yet six days longer, still mourning over the dead idol of his heart, and striving every day to rise, but could not.

In all this time you may believe we were in no little affliction for Caesar and his wife. Some were of opinion he was escaped never to return; others thought some accident had happened to him. But however, we failed not to send out a hundred people several ways to search for him. A party of about forty went that way he took, among whom was Tuscan, who was perfectly reconciled to Byam. They had not gone very far into the wood, but they smelt an unusual smell, as of a dead body, for stinks must be very noisome that can be distinguished among such a quantity of natural sweets, as every inch of that land produces. So that they concluded they should find him dead, or somebody that was so. They passed on towards it, as loathsome as it was, and made such a rustling among the leaves that lie thick on the ground, by continual falling, that Caesar heard he was approached, and though he had, during the space of these eight days, endeavored to rise, but found he wanted strength, yet looking up, and seeing his pursuers, he rose, and reeled to a neighboring tree, against which he fixed his back. And being within a dozen yards of those that advanced and saw him, he called out to them, and bid them approach no nearer, if they would be safe; so that they stood still, and hardly believing their eyes, that would persuade them that it was Caesar that spoke to them, so much was he altered, they asked him what he had done with his wife, for they smelt a stink that almost struck them dead. He, pointing to the dead body, sighing, cried, "Behold her there." They put off the flowers that covered her with their sticks, and found she was killed, and cried out, "Oh monster! that hast murdered thy wife." Then asking him, why he did so cruel a deed, he replied, he had no leisure to answer impertinent questions. "You may go back," continued he, "and tell the faithless governor he may thank Fortune that I am breathing my last, and that my arm is too feeble to obey my heart in what it had designed him." But his tongue faltering, and trembling, he could scarce end what he was saying. The English taking advantage by his weakness, cried, "Let us take him alive by all means." He heard them; and, as if he had revived from a fainting, or a dream, he cried out, "No, gentlemen, you are deceived, you will find no more Caesars to be whipped, no more find a faith in me. Feeble as you think me, I have strength yet left to secure me from a second indignity." They swore all anew, and he only shook his head, and beheld them with scorn. Then they cried out, "Who will venture on this single man? Will nobody?" They stood all silent while Caesar replied, "Fatal will be the attempt to the first adventurer, let him assure himself," and, at that word, held up his knife in a menacing posture. "Look ye, ye faithless crew," said he, "'tis not life I seek, nor am I afraid of dying," and, at that word, cut a piece of flesh from his own throat, and threw it at them, "yet still I would live if I could, till I had perfected my revenge. But oh! it cannot be. I feel life gliding from my eyes and heart, and, if I make not haste, I shall yet fall a victim to the shameful whip." At that, he ripped up his own belly, and took his bowels and pulled them out, with what strength he could, while some, on their knees imploring, besought him to hold his hand. But when they saw him tottering, they cried out, "Will none venture on him?" A bold English cried, "Yes, if he were the Devil" (taking courage when he saw him almost dead) and swearing a horrid oath for his farewell to the world he rushed on. Caesar with his armed hand met him so fairly, as stuck him to the heart, and he fell dead at his feet. Tuscan seeing that, cried out, "I love thee, oh Caesar, and therefore will not let thee die, if possible." And, running to him, took him in his arms, but at the same time, warding a blow that Caesar made at his bosom, he received it quite through his arm, and Caesar having not the strength to pluck the knife forth, though he attempted it, Tuscan neither pulled it out himself, nor suffered it to be pulled out, but came down with it sticking in his arm, and the reason he gave for it was because the air should not get into the wound. They put their hands across, and carried Caesar between six of them, fainted as he was, and they thought dead, or just dying, and they brought him to Parham, and laid him on a couch, and had the chirurgeon immediately to him, who dressed his wounds, and sewed up his belly, and used means to bring him to life, which they effected. We ran all to see him; and, if before we thought him so beautiful a sight, he was now so altered that his face was like a death's head blacked over, nothing but teeth and eye-holes. For some days we suffered nobody to speak to him, but caused cordials to be poured down his throat, which sustained his life, and in six or seven days he recovered his senses. For you must know, that wounds are almost to a miracle cured in the Indies, unless wounds in the legs, which rarely ever cure.

When he was well enough to speak, we talked to him, and asked him some questions about his wife, and the reasons why he killed her. And he then told us what I have related of that resolution, and of his parting, and he besought us we would let him die, and was extremely afflicted to think it was possible he might live. He assured us, if we did not dispatch him, he would prove very fatal to a great many. We said all we could to make him live, and gave him new assurances, but he begged we would not think so poorly of him, or of his love to Imoinda, to imagine we could flatter him to life again; but the chirurgeon assured him he could not live, and therefore he need not fear. We were all (but Caesar) afflicted at this news; and the sight was gashly.[5] His discourse was sad; and the earthly smell about him so strong, that I was persuaded to leave the place for some time (being myself but sickly, and very apt to fall into fits of dangerous illness upon any extraordinary melancholy). The servants, and Trefry, and the chirurgeons, promised all to take what possible care they could of the life of Caesar, and I, taking boat, went with other company to Colonel Martin's, about three days' journey down the river; but I was no sooner gone, but the governor taking Trefry about some pretended earnest business a day's journey up the river, having communicated his design to one Banister, a wild Irishman, and one of the council, a fellow of absolute barbarity, and fit to execute any villainy, but was rich, he came up to Parham, and forcibly took Caesar, and had him carried to the same post where he was whipped, and causing him to be tied to it, and a great fire made before him, he told him he should die like a dog, as he was. Caesar replied, this was the first piece of bravery that ever Banister did, and he never spoke sense till he pronounced that word, and, if he would keep it, he would declare, in the other world, that he was the

5. Ghastly.

only man, of all the whites, that ever he heard speak truth. And turning to the men that bound him, he said, "My friends, am I to die, or to be whipped?" And they cried, "Whipped! no; you shall not escape so well." And then he replied, smiling, "A blessing on thee," and assured them, they need not tie him, for he would stand fixed, like a rock, and endure death so as should encourage them to die. "But if you whip me," said he, "be sure you tie me fast."

He had learned to take tobacco, and when he was assured he should die, he desired they would give him a pipe in his mouth, ready lighted, which they did, and the executioner came, and first cut off his members,[6] and threw them into the fire. After that, with an ill-favored knife, they cut his ears and his nose, and burned them; he still smoked on, as if nothing had touched him. Then they hacked off one of his arms, and still he bore up, and held his pipe. But at the cutting off the other arm, his head sunk, and his pipe dropped, and he gave up the ghost, without a groan, or a reproach. My mother and sister were by him all the while, but not suffered to save him, so rude and wild were the rabble, and so inhuman were the justices, who stood by to see the execution, who after paid dearly enough for their insolence. They cut Caesar in quarters, and sent them to several of the chief plantations. One quarter was sent to Colonel Martin, who refused it, and swore he had rather see the quarters of Banister and the governor himself than those of Caesar on his plantations, and that he could govern his Negroes without terrifying and grieving them with frightful spectacles of a mangled king.

Thus died this great man, worthy of a better fate, and a more sublime wit than mine to write his praise. Yet, I hope, the reputation of my pen is considerable enough to make his glorious name to survive to all ages, with that of the brave, the beautiful, and the constant Imoinda.

1688

—— ✠ ——

Jonathan Swift
1667–1745

Arguably the greatest prose satirist in the history of English literature, Jonathan Swift was born in Dublin, the only son of English parents, seven months after his father died. In his infancy he was kidnapped by his nurse and did not see his mother for three years. With the future dramatist William Congreve he attended the Kilkenny School (Ireland's best), and in 1682 he began six years of study at Trinity College, Dublin. He received his B.A. degree in 1686. From 1689, Swift served as secretary to Sir William Temple (1628–1699), a retired diplomat whose father had befriended Swift's family. Swift worked at Temple's estate at Moor Park in Surrey for most of the next ten years. It was at Moor Park that Swift first experienced the vertigo, nausea, and hearing impairment of Ménière's syndrome, a disturbance of the inner ear that would plague him for the rest of his life and sometimes wrongly led him (and others) to question his mental stability. While working for Temple, Swift also wrote his first poems, undistinguished compositions that do not presage the literary acclaim that was to come.

Not content with his station in life, Swift took an M.A. degree from Oxford University in 1692; three years later, he was ordained a priest in the (Anglican) Church of Ireland and appointed to the undesirable prebendary of Kilroot, where he found the local Presbyterians unsympathetic and the salary meager. Added to professional discontent was personal disappointment: Swift was rejected in his marriage proposal to Jane "Varina" Waring, the daughter of an Anglican clergyman. Swift returned to Moor Park in 1696, and, after Temple died in 1699, held a series of ecclesiastical posts in Ireland, none of which fulfilled his ambition for an important position in England. In 1702 he was made Doctor of Divinity by his alma mater, Trinity College, Dublin.

While at Moor Park, Swift began to tutor an eight-year-old girl, Esther "Stella" Johnson, daughter of Sir William's late steward. Though she was nearly fourteen years Swift's junior, "Stella" would in time become his beloved companion and his most trusted friend. When she was eighteen, Swift described her as "one of the most beautiful, graceful, and agreeable young women in London." In 1701, at Swift's request, Stella and Sir William's spinster cousin, Rebecca Dingley, moved to Dublin, where they remained for the rest of their lives. Swift and Stella met regularly, but never alone. Although there has been much debate about the nature of their relationship, it is clear that Swift and Stella loved, trusted, and valued each other, whether or not they were ever secretly married (the evidence suggests they were not). Swift's *Journal to Stella* (composed 1710 to 1713) and the series of poems he composed for her birthdays reveal a playful intimacy and affection not seen in his more public writings.

Moor Park not only led him to Stella but was also the cradle of Swift's first major literary work: *A Tale of a Tub* (composed 1697 to 1698, published 1704), a brilliant satire on "corruptions in religion and learning," published with *The Battle of the Books*, Swift's mock-epic salvo in the debate between the Ancients and the Moderns. Like most of his subsequent works, *A Tale of a Tub* did not appear under Swift's name, though its ironic treatment of the church subsequently damaged his prospects for ecclesiastical preferment when his authorship became widely known.

In the first decade of the new century Swift placed his hopes for preferment with the Whigs, then in power, and became associated with the Whig writers Joseph Addison and Richard Steele, founder of the *Tatler*, a London periodical in which two of Swift's important early poems, *A Description of the Morning* (1709) and *A Description of a City Shower* (1710), first appeared. Swift's career as a political polemicist began when he rose to the defense of three Whig lords facing impeachment with his allegorical *Discourse of the Contests and Dissentions between the Nobles and Commons in Athens and Rome* (1701). His *Bickerstaff Papers* (1708–1709), witty parodies of the cobbler-turned-astrologer John Partridge, occasioned much laughter regardless of party allegiances. More importantly, Swift began to write a series of pamphlets on church affairs, including his ironical *Argument against Abolishing Christianity* (1708) and *A Letter . . . Concerning the Sacramental Test* (1709), which damaged his relationship with the Whigs.

While in London as an emissary for the Irish clergy in 1708, Swift met Esther "Vanessa" Vanhomrigh (pronounced "Vanummry") and, as with "Stella," acted as her mentor. Although his feelings for this attractive young woman (twenty-one years younger than he) clearly became more than paternal, Swift was eventually put off by her declaration of "inexpressible passion" and wrote *Cadenus and Vanessa* (composed 1713, published 1726) to cool the relationship.

Vehemently disagreeing with the Whig policies supporting the Dissenters (Protestants who were not members of the established church), because he feared they would weaken the Anglican church, Swift shifted his allegiance to the Tories in 1710 and soon became their principal spokesman and propagandist, taking charge of their weekly periodical the *Examiner* (1710–1711) and producing a series of highly effective political pamphlets, such as *The Conduct of the Allies* (1712), which called for an end to the War of Spanish Succession (1701–1713). Swift's years in London from 1710 to 1714, when he was an important lobbyist for the Church of Ireland and an influential agent of the Tory government, were the most exciting of his life.

In 1713 Swift was installed as Dean of Saint Patrick's Cathedral, Dublin—a prestigious appointment, but far short of the English bishopric he felt he deserved. Returning quickly to London, Swift became a vital presence in the Scriblerus Club—with Alexander Pope, John Arbuthnot, John Gay, Thomas Parnell, and Robert Harley, Earl of Oxford—which met in 1714. The influence of this group, with its love of parody, literary hoaxes, and the ridicule of false learning, is evident in *Gulliver's Travels*. Upon the death of Queen Anne in 1714 and the resultant fall of the Tory Ministry, Swift's hopes for further advancement were dashed, and he took up permanent residence in Ireland, where he conscientiously carried out his duties as Dean.

When Swift successfully defended Irish interests by writing *The Drapier's Letters* (1724–1725)—attacking a government plan to impose a new coin, "Wood's halfpence," that would devalue Ireland's currency and seriously damage the economy—he became a national hero. Thereafter, the people lit bonfires on his birthday and hailed him as a champion of Irish liberty, though he never ceased to regard Ireland as the land of his exile. From Dublin, he corresponded with Pope, Gay, Arbuthnot, and Henry St. John, Lord Bolingbroke; he enjoyed a long visit with his friends in England in 1726. While there, he encouraged Gay's *The Beggar's Opera* and Pope's *The Dunciad*, and arranged for the publication of his own masterpiece, *Gulliver's Travels* (1726).

When the death of George I the following year briefly created hopes of unseating "Prime Minister" Robert Walpole, Swift paid his final visit to England, where he assisted Pope in editing their joint *Miscellanies* in three volumes (1727, 1728, 1732). The years that followed in Dublin saw the production of many of Swift's finest poems, including *The Lady's Dressing Room* (1732), *A Beautiful Young Nymph Going to Bed* (1734), and *Verses on the Death of Dr. Swift* (composed 1731–1732, published 1739), his most celebrated poem. Swift continued to champion the cause of Irish political and economic freedom; with his like-minded friend Thomas Sheridan, he conducted a weekly periodical, the *Intelligencer* (1728). In 1729, he published his most famous essay, *A Modest Proposal*. Some years later, he supervised the publication of the first four volumes of his *Works* (1735) by the Dublin publisher George Faulkner.

When Swift reached his early seventies, his infirmities made him incapable of carrying out his clerical duties at Saint Patrick's; at seventy-five, he was found "of unsound mind and memory," and guardians were appointed to manage his affairs. In addition to ongoing debilities from Ménière's syndrome, he suffered from arteriosclerosis, aphasia, memory loss, and other diseases of old age; he was not insane, however, as many of his contemporaries believed. A devoted clergyman, Swift practiced the Christian charity he preached, giving more than half of his income to the needy; the founding of Ireland's first mental hospital through a generous provision in his will was the most famous of Swift's many benefactions.

Voltaire hailed Swift as the "English Rabelais," while Henry Fielding lauded him as the "English Lucian." Although the more delicate sensibilities of the nineteenth century eschewed his writings for their coarseness and truculence, twentieth-century readers have prized Swift's work for its intelligence, wit, and inventiveness. A committed champion of social justice and an untiring enemy of pride, Swift was a brilliant satirist in part because he was a thoroughgoing humanist.

A Description of a City Shower

"They say 'tis the best thing I ever writ, and I think so too," boasted Swift of his *Description of a City Shower* in 1710. It was first published in the *Tatler*, No. 238, on 17 October 1710, soon after its composition. Swift's closely observed rendering of London street life playfully mocks the English imitators of Virgil, especially John Dryden and his celebrated translation, *The Works of Virgil* (1697). We see, for example, Swift's mock-heroic effects based on Virgil's *Aeneid* (29–19 B.C.), most notably in comparing the timorous "beau" trapped in his sedan chair to the fierce Greek warriors hiding inside the Trojan Horse, and in calling to mind the storm that led to Queen Dido's seduction and eventual ruin (Dryden's translation 4.231–238). More importantly, just as Swift invoked the mock-pastoral in *A Description of the Morning*, so too does he create a mock-georgic mode in his *City Shower*. The division of the poem into portents, preliminaries, and deluge closely parallels the tempest scene in Virgil's *Georgics* (36–29 B.C.; book 1, 431–458, 483–538 in Dryden), so that Swift uses structural and verbal elements from a classical poem extolling the virtues of agriculture and rural life to depict the teeming diversity of the contemporary urban scene.

A Description of a City Shower

Careful observers may foretell the hour
(By sure prognostics) when to dread a shower.
While rain depends,° the pensive cat gives o'er   *is impending*
Her frolics, and pursues her tail no more.
5   Returning home at night you find the sink[1]
Strike your offended sense with double stink.
If you be wise, then go not far to dine,
You spend in coach-hire more than save in wine.
A coming shower your shooting corns[2] presage,
10   Old aches[3] throb, your hollow tooth will rage:
Sauntering in coffee-house is Dulman seen;
He damns the climate, and complains of spleen.[4]

Meanwhile the South,° rising with dabbled° wings,   *south wind/muddy*
A sable cloud athwart the welkin° flings;   *sky*
15   That swilled more liquor than it could contain,
And like a drunkard gives it up again.
Brisk Susan whips her linen from the rope,[5]
While the first drizzling shower is borne aslope:°   *at a slant*
Such is that sprinkling which some careless quean°   *hussy*
20   Flirts° on you from her mop, but not so clean: *flicks*
You fly, invoke the gods; then turning, stop
To rail; she singing, still whirls on her mop.
Nor yet the dust had shunned th' unequal strife,
But aided by the wind, fought still for life;
25   And wafted with its foe by violent gust,
'Twas doubtful which was rain, and which was dust.[6]
Ah! Where must needy poet seek for aid,
When dust and rain at once his coat invade?
Sole coat, where dust cemented by the rain
30   Erects the nap, and leaves a cloudy stain.
Now in contiguous drops the flood comes down,
Threatening with deluge this devoted° town.   *doomed*
To shops in crowds the daggled° females fly,   *muddied*
Pretend to cheapen° goods, but nothing buy.   *bargain for*
35   The Templer spruce,[7] while every spout's abroach,[8]
Stays till 'tis fair, yet seems to call a coach.
The tucked-up seamstress walks with hasty strides,
While streams run down her oiled umbrella's sides.
Here various kinds by various fortunes led,
40   Commence acquaintance underneath a shed.°   *shelter*

1. Sewer. The poem is built upon Swift's experiences in London: on November 8, 1710, Swift wrote to his beloved Stella (Esther Johnson) that "I will give ten shillings a week for my lodging; for I am almost stunk out of this with the sink, and it helps me to verses in my Shower." The parsimonious Swift normally spent around half this amount for lodgings.
2. The shooting pain in your corns.
3. Pronounced "aitches."

4. Dulman (a descriptive name) complains of melancholy or depression, then attributed to the spleen.
5. The typically named maid brings in her washing from the line.
6. Swift here parallels a line from Samuel Garth's popular satirical poem, *The Dispensary* (1699): "Tis doubtful which is sea, and which is sky" (5.176).
7. Well-dressed lawyer.
8. Drainpipe pouring water.

Triumphant Tories, and desponding Whigs,[9]
Forget their feuds, and join to save their wigs.
Boxed° in a chair[1] the beau impatient sits,   *confined*
While spouts run clattering o'er the roof by fits;
45   And ever and anon with frightful din
The leather sounds; he trembles from within.
So when Troy chairmen bore the wooden steed,
Pregnant with Greeks, impatient to be freed;
(Those bully Greeks, who, as the moderns do,
50   Instead of paying chairmen, run them through[2])
Laocoon struck the outside with his spear,
And each imprisoned hero quaked for fear.[3]

Now from all parts the swelling kennels[4] flow,
And bear their trophies with them as they go:
55   Filths of all hues and odors, seem to tell
What streets they sailed from, by the sight and smell.
They, as each torrent drives with rapid force
From Smithfield, or St. Pulchre's shape their course;[5]
And in huge confluent join at Snow Hill ridge,
60   Fall from the conduit prone to Holborn Bridge.[6]
Sweepings from butchers' stalls, dung, guts, and blood,
Drowned puppies, stinking sprats,° all drenched in mud,   *small fish*
Dead cats and turnip tops come tumbling down the flood.[7]
1710   1710

Stella's Birthday

Between 1719 and 1727 Swift wrote seven birthday poems to "Stella," his dear Esther Johnson. The one reprinted here is his first. Swift's earliest use of the name "Stella" in verse was in the first of this series of celebratory verses, which play on the obligation of the Poet Laureate to write an official "birthday ode" for the monarch every year. Placing himself in the role of her laureate, Swift may have chosen the name "Stella" to highlight the difference between his own uncontrived expressions of affection and those of the courtly Sir Philip Sidney in *Astrophel and Stella* (1591). Like Shakespeare's Sonnet 130 ("My mistress' eyes are nothing like the sun"), Swift's first poem on Stella's birthday violates the traditions of the conventional love lyric by calling attention to his beloved's considerable weight and age, only to suggest that his admiration of her lies in her deeper virtues. In his last birthday poem, Swift attempts to escape from the prospect of Stella's impending death, first by humor and then by the power of reason; when these fail, he tenderly acknowledges how much she means to him. Swift was to sail for England

9. 1710, the year this poem was written, was the first year of the Tory ministry under Queen Anne.
1. A sedan chair, carried by two men; this one has a leather roof.
2. With their swords.
3. When the Trojans carried the Greek's wooden horse into Troy, thinking that the opposing army had given up their siege, the priest Laocoon was suspicious, and struck the horse. See *Aeneid* 2.50–53.
4. Gutters, which were also open sewers.
5. Respectively, the cattle market and the parish west of the Newgate prison.
6. Snow Hill ridge extended down to Holborn Bridge,

which spanned Fleet ditch, used as an open sewer; from 1343, local butchers had been given permission to dump entrails in the Fleet.
7. These last three lines were intended against the licentious manner of modern poets, in making three rhymes together, which they call *Triplets*; and the last of the three was two, or sometimes more syllables longer, called an *Alexandrian*. These *Triplets* and *Alexandrians* were brought in by Dryden, and other poets in the reign of Charles II. They were the mere effect of haste, idleness, and want of money, and have been wholly avoided by the best poets since these verses were written [Swift's note].

less than a month after he gave those verses to her—both knew that they might never see each other again. Though more formal than the *Journal to Stella*, Swift's birthday verses were written primarily for Stella's enjoyment and for the entertainment of their small circle of intimate friends. Despite the private nature of these poems, Swift nevertheless authorized their publication in the third and last volume of the Pope-Swift *Miscellanies*, which appeared in March 1728.

Stella's Birthday, 1719
WRITTEN IN THE YEAR 1718/9[1]

Stella this day is thirty-four,[2]
(We shan't dispute a year or more):
However, Stella, be not troubled,
Although thy size and years are doubled,
5   Since first I saw thee at sixteen,[3]
The brightest virgin on the green.[4]
So little is thy form° declined;   *figure*
Made up° so largely in thy mind.   *compensated*

Oh, would it please the gods to *split*
10   Thy beauty, size, and years, and wit,
No age could furnish out a pair
Of nymphs so graceful, wise, and fair:
With half the luster of your eyes,
With half your wit, your years, and size:
15   And then before it grew too late,
How should I beg of gentle fate,
(That either nymph might have her swain),
To split my worship too in twain.

1719   1728

The Lady's Dressing Room

The first of Swift's so-called scatological poems, which have attracted much critical attention and amateur psychoanalysis, these verses enjoyed considerable popularity in Swift's lifetime, though some contemporaries condemned them as "deficient in point of delicacy, even to the highest degree." One of Swift's friends recorded in her memoirs that *The Lady's Dressing Room* made her mother "instantly" lose her lunch. Sir Walter Scott found in this poem (and other pieces by Swift) "the marks of an incipient disorder of the mind, which induced the author to dwell on degrading and disgusting subjects." If Pope's *The Rape of the Lock* describes Belinda at the "altar" of her dressing table undergoing "the sacred rites of pride" as she and her maid apply all manner of cosmetics to make her a beautiful "goddess" and arm her for the battle of the sexes, then *The Lady's Dressing Room* reveals the coarse realities of Celia's embodiment—a humorous and disturbing corrective to the pretense and false appearances on which her glorifi-

1. Until the calendar was reformed in 1751, the new year legally began on the Feast of the Annunciation (sometimes called "Lady Day") on March 25th, though January 1st was also commonly recognized as the start of the new year. Therefore, to avoid confusion, it was a widely accepted practice to write dates between January 1 and March 24 according to both methods of reckoning: 1718/19. Since Swift's poem was composed in February or March, we would say it was written in 1719.

2. Stella (Esther Johnson) actually celebrated her thirty-eighth birthday on 13 March 1719.
3. Swift first met Stella when she was eight years old; he may have "seen" her only when she grew from child to woman.
4. The village green, or common land, here implies a pastoral simplicity that suggests the natural innocence of their relationship.

cation depends. Although Swift assails the social and literary conventions that celebrate women for their superficial qualities, there is also a misogynistic quality to the poem, which may be attributable to his anger and disappointment over his beloved Stella's death in January 1728. Nevertheless, Strephon is ridiculed for being so naively idealistic about his lover and so easily deceived by appearances; once his secret investigations free him from his illusions, Strephon's permanent revulsion and rejection of all women show his inability to follow a middle course by appreciating women in their complex reality.

The Lady's Dressing Room

Five hours (and who can do it less in?)
By haughty Celia spent in dressing;
The goddess from her chamber issues,
Arrayed in lace, brocade, and tissues:
5 Strephon,[1] who found the room was void,
And Betty[2] otherwise employed,
Stole in, and took a strict survey,
Of all the litter as it lay:
Whereof, to make the matter clear,
10 An *inventory* follows here.

    And first, a dirty smock appeared,
Beneath the arm-pits well besmeared;
Strephon, the rogue, displayed it wide,
And turned it round on every side.
15 In such a case few words are best,
And Strephon bids us guess the rest;
But swears how damnably the men lie,
In calling Celia sweet and cleanly.

    Now listen while he next produces
20 The various combs for various uses,
Filled up with dirt so closely fixed,
No brush could force a way betwixt;
A paste of composition rare,
Sweat, dandruff, powder, lead,[3] and hair,
25 A forehead cloth with oil upon't
To smooth the wrinkles on her front;
Here alum flour[4] to stop the steams,
Exhaled from sour, unsavory streams;
There night-gloves made of Tripsy's[5] hide,
30 Bequeathed by Tripsy when she died;
With puppy water,[6] beauty's help,
Distilled from Tripsy's darling whelp.
Here gallipots° and vials placed,   *ointment jars*
Some filled with washes, some with paste;

1. Strephon and Celia are names usually associated with pastoral poetry, and are therefore used mockingly here.
2. A typical maidservant's name.
3. White lead face paint, used to whiten the skin.
4. Powdered alum used like modern antiperspirant.
5. Celia's lapdog; no fashionable lady was without such a pet.
6. A recipe for this cosmetic, made from the innards of a pig or a fat puppy, was given in the "Fop's Dictionary" in *Mundus Muliebris* [Womanly Make-up]: *Or, the Ladies' Dressing Room Unlocked* (1690), which Swift also used for other terms.

35   Some with pomatum,° paints, and slops,   *hair ointment*
       And ointments good for scabby chops.°   *lips or cheeks*
       Hard° by a filthy basin stands,   *close*
       Fouled with the scouring of her hands;
       The basin takes whatever comes,
40   The scrapings of her teeth and gums,
       A nasty compound of all hues,
       For here she spits, and here she spews.

       But oh! it turned poor Strephon's bowels,
       When he beheld and smelt the towels;
45   Begummed, bemattered, and beslimed;
       With dirt, and sweat, and ear-wax grimed.
       No object Strephon's eye escapes,
       Here, petticoats in frowzy° heaps;   *unkempt*
       Nor be the handkerchiefs forgot,
50   All varnished o'er with snuff[7] and snot.
       The stockings why should I expose,
       Stained with the moisture of her toes;
       Or greasy coifs and pinners° reeking,   *night caps*
       Which Celia slept at least a week in?
55   A pair of tweezers next he found
       To pluck her brows in arches round,
       Or hairs that sink the forehead low,
       Or on her chin like bristles grow.

       The virtues we must not let pass
60   Of Celia's magnifying glass;
       When frighted Strephon cast his eye on't,
       It showed the visage of a giant:[8]
       A glass that can to sight disclose
       The smallest worm in Celia's nose,
65   And faithfully direct her nail
       To squeeze it out from head to tail;
       For catch it nicely by the head,
       It must come out alive or dead.

       Why, Strephon, will you tell the rest?
70   And must you needs describe the chest?
       That careless wench! no creature warn her
       To move it out from yonder corner,
       But leave it standing full in sight,
       For you to exercise your spite!
75   In vain the workman showed his wit
       With rings and hinges counterfeit
       To make it seem in this disguise
       A cabinet to vulgar eyes;

7. Powdered tobacco, sniffed by fashionable men and women alike.
8. Cf. *Gulliver's Travels*, Part 2, "A Voyage to Brobding-nag," ch. 1: "This made me reflect upon the fair skins of our *English* ladies, who appear so beautiful to us, only because they are of our own size, and their defects not to be seen but through magnifying glass, where we find by experiment that the smoothest and whitest skins look rough and coarse, and ill colored."

Which Strephon ventured to look in,
80   Resolved to go through *thick and thin;*
He lifts the lid: there need no more,
He smelt it all the time before.

As, from within Pandora's box,
When Epimethus oped the locks,
85   A sudden universal crew
Of human evils upward flew;⁹
He still was comforted to find
That hope at last remained behind.

So, Strephon, lifting up the lid
90   To view what in the chest was hid,
The vapors flew from out the vent,
But Strephon cautious never meant
The bottom of the pan to grope,
And foul his hands in search of hope.

95   O! ne'er may such a vile machine°   construction
Be once in Celia's chamber seen!
O! may she better learn to keep
"Those secrets of the hoary deep."¹

As mutton cutlets, prime of meat,
100   Which though with art you salt and beat
As laws of cookery require,
And roast them at the clearest fire;
If from adown the hopeful chops
The fat upon a cinder drops,
105   To stinking smoke it turns the flame
Poisoning the flesh from whence it came;
And up exhales a greasy stench
For which you curse the careless wench:
So things which must not be expressed,
110   When *plumped°* into the reeking chest,   dropped
Send up an excremental smell
To taint the parts from which they fell:
The petticoats and gown perfume,
And waft a stink round every room.

115   Thus finishing his grand survey,
The swain disgusted slunk away,
Repeating in his amorous fits,
"Oh! Celia, Celia, Celia shits!"

But Vengeance, goddess never sleeping,
120   Soon punished Strephon for his peeping.
His foul imagination links
Each dame he sees with all her stinks:

---

9. In Greek mythology, Epimethus, acting against advice, opened the box Jove had given his wife Pandora, and all the evils and vices of the world flew out, leaving only hope in the box.
1. Quoting Milton's *Paradise Lost* 2.891, in which Sin is unleashing the chaotic forces of her infernal realm.

And if unsavory odors fly,
Conceives a lady standing by:
125 All women his description fits,
And both ideas jump° like wits   *join together*
By vicious fancy coupled fast,
And still appearing in contrast.

I pity wretched Strephon, blind
130 To all the charms of womankind;
Should I the queen of love refuse,
Because she rose from stinking ooze?[2]
To him that looks behind the scene,
Statira's but some pocky quean.[3]

135 When Celia in her glory shows,
If Strephon would but stop his nose,
Who now so impiously blasphemes
Her ointments, daubs, and paints and creams;
Her washes, slops, and every clout,[4]
140 With which she makes so foul a rout;[5]
He soon would learn to think like me,
And bless his ravished eyes to see
Such order from confusion sprung,
Such gaudy *tulips* raised from *dung.*

c. 1730   1732

COMPANION READING

Lady Mary Wortley Montagu: The Reasons that Induced
Dr. S. to write a Poem called "The Lady's Dressing Room"[1]

The Doctor in a clean starched band,
His golden snuff box in his hand,
With care his diamond ring displays
And artful shows its various rays,
5   While grave he stalks down —— street
His dearest Betty —— to meet.[2]
Long had he waited for this hour,

2. Venus, Roman goddess of sexual love and physical beauty, rose from the sea.
3. One of the heroines of Nathaniel Lee's highly popular tragedy *The Rival Queens* (1677); Swift's common slattern (quean) has had either smallpox or venereal disease.
4. Washes were either treated water used for the complexion or stale urine used as a detergent; clouts were rags.
5. Both of her skin and, presumably, of the men.
1. Lady Mary Wortley Montagu (1689–1762), born Mary Pierrepont, acquired her title at age one, lost her mother at age three, and fervently pursued a plan of self-education at odds with the conventional domesticating agenda laid out for young women of her rank. In 1712 she married, against her father's wishes, Edward Wortley Montagu, a Whig Member of Parliament who was later appointed ambassador to Turkey. Accompanying him on this assignment, she was to become fascinated by the Turkish practice of inoculating against smallpox, which she successfully championed in England on her return. She also reported eloquently in missives home on the gaps and continuities between British and Turkish culture. Her *Turkish Embassy Letters,* which she compiled from her writings during this sojourn, remain the foundation of her fame. Her life as a writer also yielded essays, short fiction, and a comedy, but she worked more steadily at verse, collaborating with Alexander Pope on some poems and combating him in others, after their friendship had disintegrated into a round of bitter, witty recriminations. In her riposte to Jonathan Swift's poem, Montagu mimics his iambic tetrameter and other mannerisms.
2. In Swift's poem, Betty is the maid's name, Celia, the mistress's.

Nor gained admittance to the bower,
Had joked and punned, and swore and writ,
10   Tried all his gallantry and wit,[3]
Had told her oft what part he bore
In Oxford's schemes in days of yore,[4]
But bawdy,° politics, nor satire   *obscenity*
Could move this dull hard hearted creature.
15   Jenny her maid could taste° a rhyme   *enjoy*
And, grieved to see him lose his time,
Had kindly whispered in his ear,
"For twice two pound you enter here;
My lady vows without that sum
20   It is in vain you write or come."
        The destined offering now he brought,
And in a paradise of thought,
With a low bow approached the dame,
Who smiling heard him preach his flame.
25   His gold she takes (such proofs as these
Convince most unbelieving shes)
And in her trunk rose up to lock it
(Too wise to trust it in her pocket)
And then, returned with blushing grace,
30   Expects the doctor's warm embrace.
        But now this is the proper place
Where morals stare me in the face,
And for the sake of fine expression
I'm forced to make a small digression.
35   Alas for wretched humankind,
With learning mad, with wisdom blind!
The ox thinks he's for saddle fit
(As long ago friend Horace writ[5])
And men their talents still mistaking,
40   The stutterer fancies his is speaking.
With admiration oft we see
Hard features heightened by toupée,
The beau affects° the politician,   *pretends to be*
Wit is the citizen's ambition,
45   Poor Pope philosophy displays on
With so much rhyme and little reason,
And though he argues ne'er so long
That all is right, his head is wrong.[6]
        None strive to know their proper merit
50   But strain for wisdom, beauty, spirit,
And lose the praise that is their due
While they've th' impossible in view.
So have I seen the injudicious heir

---

3. Montagu echoes Swift's poem *Cadenus and Vanessa*, where the clumsy lover "Had sighed and languished, vowed, and writ, / For pastime, or to show his wit" (542–543).
4. Swift had collaborated closely in the political schemes of Robert Harley, first Earl of Oxford (1661–1724).
5. "The ox desires the saddle" (Horace, *Epistles* 1.14.43).
6. Montagu ridicules Pope's conclusion to *An Essay on Man*: "Whatever IS, is RIGHT." See page 1193.

To add one window the whole house impair.
55   Instinct the hound does better teach,
Who never undertook to preach;
The frighted hare from dogs does run
But not attempts to bear a gun.
Here many noble thoughts occur
60   But I prolixity abhor,
And will pursue th' instructive tale
To show the wise in some things fail.
  The reverend lover with surprise ⎫
Peeps in her bubbies, and her eyes, ⎬
65   And kisses both, and tries—and tries. ⎭
The evening in this hellish play,
Beside his guineas thrown away,
Provoked the priest to that degree
He swore, "The fault is not in me.
70   Your damned close stool° so near my nose,   *chamber pot*
Your dirty smock, and stinking toes
Would make a Hercules as tame
As any beau that you can name."
  The nymph grown furious roared, "By God
75   The blame lies all in sixty odd,"[7]
And scornful pointing to the door
Cried, "Fumbler, see my face no more."
"With all my heart I'll go away,
But nothing done, I'll nothing pay.
80   Give back the money." "How," cried she,
"Would you palm such a cheat on me!
For poor four pound to roar and bellow—
Why sure you want some new Prunella?"[8]
"I'll be revenged, you saucy quean"°   *whore*
85   (Replies the disappointed Dean)
"I'll so describe your dressing room
The very Irish shall not come."
She answered short, "I'm glad you'll write.
You'll furnish paper when I shite."[9]

1734

Verses on the Death of Dr. Swift

"I have been several months writing near five hundred lines on a pleasant subject," wrote Swift to his friend John Gay in December 1731, "only to tell what my friends and enemies will say on me after I am dead." Swift completed what was to become his most celebrated poem by adding explanatory notes in the early months of 1732. It seems that Swift intended the *Verses* to be published after his death but showed the poem in manuscript to various friends. When

7. I.e., Swift's impotence derives not from her odors but from his age (65 at the time the poem was written).
8. "Prunella" is both a fabric used in clergy vestments (Swift was a clergyman), and the name of the promiscu-

ous, low-born heroine in Richard Estcourt's comic interlude *Prunella* (1708).
9. Compare line 118 of Swift's poem, page 1077.

the reputation of his *Verses* spread, Swift used the opportunity to publish a different autobiographical poem, *The Life and Genuine Character of Dr. Swift* (1733), which would satisfy public demand and make the eventual appearance of the *Verses* all the more surprising. Six years later, believing they were doing their friend a service, Alexander Pope and William King (1685–1763) published a version of the poem in which they edited out some of Swift's most self-aggrandizing and controversial lines. Swift was "much dissatisfied" with this London edition and responded by supervising the speedy publication of an unexpurgated text of the work in Dublin, though even he had the prudence to leave blank spaces for some of the names in his poem. Among the most controversial elements in the *Verses* were its direct attack on Prime Minister Robert Walpole and his government; the unflattering depiction of the court and singling out of Lady Suffolk and Queen Caroline for ridicule; and Swift's praise of Bolingbroke and Pulteney, leading opposition politicians. Swift's jaunty tetrameter carries an admixture of self-fashioning for posterity and moral instruction, a spirited apologia for his life and writings, and an idealized account of the principles by which he strove to live. *Verses on the Death of Dr. Swift* reveals its subject as a champion of liberty and embattled self-promoter, a humanistic preacher and an unsparing satirist.

Verses on the Death of Dr. Swift, D.S.P.D.[1]

Occasioned by Reading a Maxim in Rochefoucauld

Dans l'adversité de nos meilleurs amis nous trouvons quelque chose, qui ne nous deplaist pas.[2]

"In the adversity of our best friends, we find something that doth not displease us."

As Rochefoucauld his maxims drew
From Nature, I believe 'em true:
They argue° no corrupted mind   suggest
In him; the fault is in mankind.

5   This maxim more than all the rest
Is thought too base for human breast;
"In all distresses of our friends
We first consult our private ends,
While Nature kindly bent to ease us,
10   Points out some circumstance to please us."

If this perhaps your patience move°   strains
Let reason and experience prove.

We all behold with envious eyes,
Our equal raised above our size;
15   Who would not at a crowded show,
Stand high himself, keep others low?
I love my friend as well as you,
But would not have him stop my view;
Then let me have the higher post;
20   I ask but for an inch at most.

1. Dean of St. Patrick's, Dublin.
2. François, duc de La Rochefoucauld, *Réflexions ou Sen-* *tences et Maximes Morales* ("Reflections or Moral Aphorisms and Maxims," 1665).

If in a battle you should find,
One, whom you love of all mankind,
Had some heroic action done,
A champion killed, or trophy won;
25   Rather than thus be overtopped,
Would you not wish his laurels[3] cropped?

Dear honest Ned is in the gout,[4]
Lies racked with pain, and you without:[5]
How patiently you hear him groan!
30   How glad the case is not your own!

What poet would not grieve to see,
His brethren write as well as he?
But rather than they should excel,
He'd wish his rivals all in Hell.

35   Her end when emulation misses,
She turns to envy, stings, and hisses:
The strongest friendship yields to pride,
Unless the odds be on our side.

Vain humankind! Fantastic race!
40   Thy various follies, who can trace?
Self-love, ambition, envy, pride,
Their empire in our hearts divide:
Give others riches, power, and station,
'Tis all on me a usurpation.
45   I have no title to aspire;
Yet, when you sink, I seem the higher.
In Pope,[6] I cannot read a line,
But with a sigh, I wish it mine:
When he can in one couplet fix
50   More sense than I can do in six:
It gives me such a jealous fit,
I cry, "Pox take him, and his wit."

Why must I be outdone by Gay,[7]
In my own humorous, biting way?

55   Arbuthnot[8] is no more my friend,
Who dares to irony pretend;
Which I was born to introduce,
Refined it first, and showed its use.

St. John, as well as Pulteney[9] knows,
60   That I had some repute for prose;

---

3. In ancient times, laurel wreaths were given to poets, athletes, and war heroes to signify their preeminence.
4. A disease characterized by an inflammation of small joints, especially in the feet and hands.
5. Outside his room.
6. Alexander Pope, poet, satirist, and friend of Swift.
7. John Gay, poet and playwright, author of *The Beggar's Opera* (1728), friend of Swift, Pope, and Arbuthnot.

8. John Arbuthnot (1667–1735), physician to Queen Anne and member of Scriblerus Club along with Swift, Pope, and Gay; he was the principal author of *Memoirs of . . . Martinus Scriblerus* (1741).
9. Henry St. John Bolingbroke (1678–1751) and William Pulteney; both politicians—one a Tory, the other a Whig—were united in their opposition to Robert Walpole. See Swift's notes to lines 194 and 196.

And till they drove me out of date,
Could maul a minister of state:
If they have mortified my pride,
And made me throw my pen aside;
65   If with such talents Heaven hath blest 'em,
Have I not reason to detest 'em?

To all my foes, dear fortune, send
Thy gifts, but never to my friend:
I tamely can endure the first,
70   But, this with envy makes me burst.

Thus much may serve by way of proem,°   *preface*
Proceed we therefore to our poem.

The time is not remote, when I
Must by the course of nature die:
75   When I foresee my special friends,
Will try to find their private ends:
Though it is hardly understood,[1]
Which way my death can do them good;
Yet, thus methinks, I hear 'em speak;
80   "See, how the Dean begins to break:°   *weaken*
Poor gentleman, he droops apace,°   *quickly*
You plainly find it in his face:
That old vertigo in his head
Will never leave him, till he's dead:
85   Besides, his memory decays,
He recollects not what he says;
He cannot call his friends to mind;
Forgets the place where last he dined:
Plies you with stories o'er and o'er,
90   He told them fifty times before.
How does he fancy we can sit
To hear his out-of-fashioned wit?
But he takes up with younger folks,
Who for his wine will bear his jokes:
95   Faith,° he must make his stories shorter,   *in truth*
Or change his comrades once a quarter:
In half the time, he talks them round;[2]
There must another set be found.

"For poetry, he's past his prime,
100   He takes an hour to find a rhyme:
His fire° is out, his wit decayed,   *creative fire*
His fancy sunk, his muse a jade.[3]
I'd have him throw away his pen;
But there's no talking to some men."

---

1. Hard to understand.
2. Runs through his stock of stories and has to begin again.
3. The poet's muse—his inspiration (always female)—is here a worn-out horse or a disreputable or shrewish woman.

105   And then their tenderness appears,
             By adding largely to my years:
             "He's older than he would be reckoned,
             And well remembers Charles the Second."[4]

             "He hardly° drinks a pint of wine;   *barely*
110   And that, I doubt,° is no good sign.   *suspect*
             His stomach° too begins to fail: *appetite*
             Last year we thought him strong and hale;
             But now, he's quite another thing;
             I wish he may hold out till spring."

115   Then hug themselves, and reason thus:
             "It is not yet so bad with us."

             In such a case they talk in tropes,°   *figuratively*
             And by their fears express their hopes:
             Some great misfortune to portend,°   *predict*
120   No enemy can match a friend;
             With all the kindness they profess,
             The merit of a lucky guess
             (When daily "Howd'y's"[5] come of course,°   *routinely*
             And servants answer: "Worse and worse")
25   Would please 'em better than to tell
             That, God be praised, the Dean is well.
             Then he who prophesied the best,
             Approves° his foresight to the rest: *confirms*
             "You know, I always feared the worst,
130   And often told you so at first":
             He'd rather choose that I should die
             Than his prediction prove a lie.
             No one foretells I shall recover;
             But, all agree to give me over.°   *give up hope*

135   Yet should some neighbor feel a pain
             Just in the parts where I complain;
             How many a message would he send?
             What hearty prayers that I should mend?
             Inquire what regimen[6] I kept;
140   What gave me ease, and how I slept?
             And more lament, when I was dead,
             Than all the snivellers round my bed.

             My good companions, never fear,
             For though you may mistake a year;
145   Though your prognostics run too fast,
             They must be verified at last.

             "Behold the fatal day arrive!
             How is the Dean? He's just alive.

4. King Charles II died in 1685, when Swift was 18.   6. Prescribed pattern of living, exercising, and eating.
5. How does [is] he?

Now the departing prayer is read:
150   He hardly breathes. The Dean is dead.
Before the passing bell[7] begun,
The news through half the town has run.
O, may we all for death prepare!
What has he left? And who's his heir?
155   I know no more than what the news is,
'Tis all bequeathed to public uses.[8]
To public use! A perfect whim!
What had the public done for him?
Mere envy, avarice, and pride!
160   He gave it all.—But first he died.
And had the Dean, in all the nation,
No worthy friend, no poor relation?
So ready to do strangers good,
Forgetting his own flesh and blood?"

165   Now Grub Street wits[9] are all employed;
With elegies, the town is cloyed:
Some paragraph in every paper,
To curse the Dean, or bless the Drapier.[1]

The doctors tender of their fame,
170   Wisely on me lay all the blame:
"We must confess his case was nice,°   *difficult*
But he would never take advice;
Had he been ruled, for aught appears,
He might have lived these twenty years:
175   For when we opened him we found
That all his vital parts were sound."

From Dublin soon to London spread,[2]
'Tis told at court, the Dean is dead.

Kind Lady Suffolk[3] in the spleen,[4]
180   Runs laughing up to tell the Queen.
The Queen, so gracious, mild, and good,
Cries, "Is he gone? 'Tis time he should.
He's dead you say, why let him rot;

7. Death bell, rung to obtain prayers for the passing soul.
8. In fact, when Swift died he left a number of small personal bequests in addition to his large gifts to public charities.
9. Hack writers, paid to produce (often libelous) materials for London journals.
1. The Author imagines, that the Scribblers of the prevailing Party, which he always opposed, will libel him after his Death; but that others will remember him with gratitude, who consider the service he had done to Ireland, under the name of M. B. Drapier [Swift's note, referring to *The Drapier's Letters* (1724–1725), a series of essays he wrote to defend Ireland from the the British government's plan to impose a new coin, "Wood's half-pence," that would have devastated Ireland's economy].
2. The Dean supposeth himself to die in Ireland [Swift's note]; he did.
3. Mrs. Howard, afterwards Countess of Suffolk, then of the Bedchamber to the Queen, professed much friendship for the Dean. The Queen, then Princess, sent a dozen times to the Dean (then in London) with her command to attend her; which at last he did, by advice of all his friends. She often sent for him afterwards, and always treated him very graciously. He taxed her with a present worth ten pounds, which she promised before he should return to Ireland, but on his taking leave, the medals were not ready" [Swift's note].
4. The 18th-century equivalent of "depression."

I'm glad the medals were forgot.[5]
185 I promised them, I own;° but when?   *admit*
I only was a princess then;
But now as consort of the King,
You know 'tis quite a different thing."

Now, Chartres[6] at Sir Robert's levee,[7]
190 Tells, with a sneer, the tidings heavy:
"Why, is he dead without his shoes?"[8]
(Cries Bob)[9] "I'm sorry for the news;
Oh, were the wretch but living still,
And in his place my good friend Will;[1]
195 Or had a miter° on his head,   *bishop's hat*
Provided Bolingbroke[2] were dead."

Now Curll his shop from rubbish drains:
Three genuine tomes of Swift's remains.[3]
And then to make them pass the glibber,°   *sell better*
200 Revised by Tibbalds, Moore, and Cibber.[4]
He'll treat me as he does my betters:
Publish my will, my life, my letters,[5]
Revive the libels born to die;
Which Pope must bear, as well as I.

205 Here shift the scene, to represent
How those I love, my death lament.
Poor Pope will grieve a month; and Gay
A week; and Arbuthnot a day.

5. The medals were to be sent to the Dean in four months, but she forgot them, or thought them too dear [expensive]. The Dean, being in Ireland, sent Mrs. Howard a piece of Indian plaid made in that kingdom [Ireland]: which the Queen seeing took from her, and wore it herself, and sent to the Dean for as much as would clothe herself and her children, desiring he would send charge of it. He did the former. It cost thirty-five pounds, but he said he would have nothing except the medals. He was the summer following in England, was treated as usual, and she being then Queen, the Dean was promised a settlement in England, but returned as he went, and, instead of favor or medals, hath been ever since under her Majesty's displeasure [Swift's note].
6. Chartres is a most infamous, vile scoundrel, grown from a foot-boy, or worse, to a prodigious fortune [Swift's note]. Francis Charteris was convicted of rape, and pardoned by the prime minister, Robert Walpole, in 1730.
7. A morning audience held in the bedchamber of a person of distinction before or after rising.
8. I.e., in his bed, rather than meeting a violent death or being hanged.
9. Sir Robert Walpole, Chief Minister of State, treated the Dean, in 1726, with great distinction, invited him to dinner at Chelsea, with the Dean's friends chosen on purpose; appointed an hour to talk with him of Ireland, to which kingdom and people the Dean found him no great friend. . . . The Dean would see him no more [Swift's note].
1. Mr. William Pulteney, from being Mr. Walpole's inti-

mate friend, detesting his Administration, opposed his measures, and joined with my Lord Bolingbroke, to represent his conduct in an excellent paper, called the *Craftsman*, which is still continued [Swift's note].
2. Henry St. John, Lord Viscount Bolingbroke, Secretary of State to Queen Anne of blessed memory. He is reckoned the most universal genius in Europe; Walpole dreading his abilities, treated him most injuriously, working with King George, who forgot his promise of restoring the said Lord, upon the restless importunity of Walpole [Swift's note].
3. Edmund Curll hath been the most infamous bookseller of any age or country: his character in part may be found in Mr. Pope's *Dunciad*. He published three volumes all charged on [i.e., attributed to] the Dean, who never writ three pages of them: he hath used many of the Dean's friends in almost as vile a manner [Swift's note].
4. Three stupid verse writers in London, the last to the shame of the Court, and the highest disgrace to wit and learning, was made Laureate [Swift's note]. Lewis Theobald (1688–1744), Shakespearean scholar and poet; James Moore Smythe (1702–1734), playwright whom Pope accused of plagiarism; Colley Cibber (1671–1757), actor and playwright. All three men are satirized in Pope's *Dunciad*.
5. Curll is notoriously infamous for publishing the lives, letters, and last Wills and Testaments of the nobility and ministers of State, as well as of all the rogues who are hanged at Tyburn [Swift's note].

St. John himself will scarce forbear
210   To bite his pen, and drop a tear.
The rest will give a shrug and cry
"I'm sorry; but we all must die."
Indifference clad in wisdom's guise
All fortitude of mind supplies:
215   For how can stony bowels melt,[6]
In those who never pity felt;
When *we* are lashed, *they* kiss the rod,[7]
Resigning to the will of God.

The fools, my juniors by a year,
220   Are tortured with suspense and fear—
Who wisely thought my age a screen,
When death approached, to stand between:
The screen removed, their hearts are trembling,
They mourn for me without dissembling.

225   My female friends, whose tender hearts
Have better learnt to act their parts,
Receive the news in doleful dumps,
"The Dean is dead (*and what is trumps?*),
Then Lord have mercy on his soul.
230   (*Ladies, I'll venture for the vole*.[8])
Six deans they say must bear the pall.
(*I wish I knew which king to call*.)"
"Madam, your husband will attend
The funeral of so good a friend."
235   "No madam, 'tis a shocking sight,
And he's engaged tomorrow night!
My Lady Club would take it ill,
If he should fail her at quadrille.
He loved the Dean. (*I lead a heart*.)
240   But dearest friends, they say, must part.
His time was come, he ran his race;
We hope he's in a better place."

Why do we grieve that friends should die?
No loss more easy to supply.
245   One year is past; a different scene;
No further mention of the Dean;
Who now, alas, no more is missed
Than if he never did exist.
Where's now this fav'rite of Apollo?[9]
250   Departed; and his works must follow:
Must undergo the common fate;
His kind of wit is out of date.

---

6. I.e., how can one feel compassion.
7. Accept chastisement submissively; kissing a monarch's scepter or a state official's staff was a ritual of submission to authority.

8. All the tricks in the highly popular four-handed card game, quadrille.
9. Patron of poets.

Some country squire to Lintot[1] goes,
Inquires for Swift in verse and prose:
255 Says Lintot, "I have heard the name:
He died a year ago." "The same."
He searcheth all his shop in vain;
"Sir, you may find them in Duck Lane:[2]
I sent them with a load of books
260 Last Monday to the pastry-cook's.[3]
To fancy they could live a year!
I find you're but a stranger here.
The Dean was famous in his time
And had a kind of knack at rhyme:
265 His way of writing now is past;
The town hath got a better taste:
I keep no antiquated stuff;
But, spick and span I have enough.
Pray, do but give me leave to show 'em;
270 Here's Colley Cibber's birthday poem.[4]
This ode you never yet have seen
By Stephen Duck,[5] upon the Queen.
Then, here's a letter finely penned,
Against the *Craftsman*[6] and his friend;
275 It clearly shows that all reflection
On ministers, is disaffection.
Next, here's Sir Robert's vindication,[7]
And Mr Henley's last oration:[8]
The hawkers° have not got 'em yet,   *street sellers*
280 Your Honor please to buy a set?

"Here's Woolston's tracts,[9] the twelfth edition;
'Tis read by every politician:
The country members,[1] when in town,
To all their boroughs send them down:
285 You never met a thing so smart;
The courtiers have them all by heart:

---

1. Bernard Lintot (1675–1736), London publisher of Pope, Gay, and Steele, among others.
2. A place in London where old [i.e., remaindered] books are sold [Swift's note].
3. Wastepaper from unsold books was used to line baking tins. Cf. Dryden's *MacFlecknoe* (1682), who notes similar uses for old texts: "Martyrs of pies and relics of the bum" (line 101).
4. The Poet Laureate was required to write an ode for the monarch's birthday each year. Cibber's appointment as Laureate in 1730 was based on politics, not literary merit.
5. Stephen Duck (1705–1756), known as "the thresher poet," was a laborer whose poetry won him Queen Caroline's favor; Swift made fun of him in *On Stephen Duck, the Thresher, and Favorite Poet, A Quibbling Epigram* (1730).
6. From 1726, the principal periodical written in opposition to Robert Walpole's government. Its title was meant to indicate that Walpole was "a man of craft" (i.e.,

scheming and deceptive).
7. Walpole hires a set of Party scribblers, who do nothing else but write in his defense [Swift's note].
8. John Henley (1692–1756), known as "Orator Henley" for the Oratory he founded where "at set times, he delivereth strange speeches compiled by himself and his associates. . . . He is an absolute dunce, but generally reputed crazy" [Swift's note].
9. Woolston was a clergyman, but for want of bread, hath in several treatises, in the most blasphemous manner, attempted to turn our Savior and his miracles into ridicule. He is much caressed by many great courtiers, and by all the infidels, and his books read generally by the Court ladies [Swift's note]. Swift appears to conflate the identities of two contemporary clergymen: Thomas Woolston (1670–1733), a notorious Deist, and William Woollaston (1660–1724).
1. Members of Parliament from rural boroughs.

Those maids of honor (who can read)
Are taught to use them for their creed.
The reverend author's good intention
290   Hath been rewarded with a pension:
He doth an honor to his gown,
By bravely running priestcraft down:
He shows, as sure as God's in Gloucester,[2]
That Jesus was a grand impostor:
295   That all his miracles were cheats,
Performed as jugglers do their feats;
The church had never such a writer:
A shame he hath not got a miter!"

    Suppose me dead; and then suppose
300   A club assembled at the Rose;[3]
Where from discourse of this and that,
I grow the subject of their chat:
And while they toss my name about,
With favor some, and some without;
305   One quite indifferent in the cause
My character impartial draws:

    "The Dean, if we believe report,
Was never ill received at court;
As for his works in verse and prose,
310   I own myself no judge of those:
Nor can I tell what critics thought 'em;
But this I know, all people bought 'em;
As with a moral view designed
To cure the vices of mankind:
315   His vein, ironically grave,
Exposed the fool, and lashed the knave:
To steal a hint was never known,
But what he writ was all his own.[4]

    "He never thought an honor done him,
320   Because a duke was proud to own him:
Would rather slip aside, and choose
To talk with wits in dirty shoes:
Despised the fools with stars and garters,[5]
So often seen caressing Chartres:
325   He never courted men in station,
Nor persons had in admiration;°   *was in awe of*
Of no man's greatness was afraid,
Because he sought for no man's aid.
Though trusted long in great affairs,

2. A proverb derived from the number of monasteries there once were in that county.
3. The Rose Tavern, near Drury Lane Theatre, and therefore popular with playgoers.
4. Swift is here having fun with the reader, since this line claiming Swift's originality is stolen from Sir John Denham's elegy *On Mr. Abraham Cowley*: "To him no author was unknown / Yet what he wrote was all his own."
5. Worn by Knights of the Garter.

330   He gave himself no haughty airs;
       Without regarding private ends,
       Spent all his credit for his friends,
       And only chose the wise and good;
       No flatt'rers; no allies in blood;°   *relatives*
335   But succored virtue in distress,
       And seldom failed of good success;
       As numbers in their hearts must own,
       Who, but for him, had been unknown.

       "With princes kept a due decorum,
340   But never stood in awe before 'em:
       And to her Majesty, God bless her,
       Would speak as free as to her dresser,[6]
       She thought it his peculiar whim,
       Nor took it ill as come from him.
345   He followed David's lesson just,
       "In princes never put thy trust."[7]
       And, would you make him truly sour,
       Provoke him with a slave in power:
       The Irish senate, if you named,
350   With what impatience he declaimed!
       Fair LIBERTY was all his cry;
       For her he stood prepared to die;
       For her he boldly stood alone;
       For her he oft exposed his own.
355   Two kingdoms, just as factions led,
       Had set a price upon his head;
       But not a traitor could be found,
       To sell him for six hundred pound.[8]

       "Had he but spared his tongue and pen,
360   He might have rose like other men:
       But power was never in his thought,
       And wealth he valued not a groat;
       Ingratitude he often found,
       And pitied those who meant the wound;
365   But kept the tenor° of his mind,   *prevailing course*
       To merit well of humankind;
       Nor made a sacrifice of those
       Who still° were true, to please his foes.   *always*
       He labored many a fruitless hour
370   To reconcile his friends in power;
       Saw mischief by a faction brewing,
       While they pursued each other's ruin.

6. Queen Caroline and Lady Suffolk, one of the Ladies of
Her Majesty's bedchamber.
7. Psalm 146.3.
8. Two rewards of £300 each were offered in 1713 and

1724 for the revelation of the author of *The Public Spirit of
the Whigs* and *The Drapier's Fourth Letter*, respectively,
"but in neither kingdoms was the Dean discovered"
[Swift's note].

But finding vain was all his care,
He left the Court in mere° despair.[9]   *total*

375   "And, oh! how short are human schemes!
        Here ended all our golden dreams.
        What St. John's skill in state affairs,
        What Ormonde's valor,[1] Oxford's cares,
        To save their sinking country lent,
380   Was all destroyed by one event.
        Too soon that precious life was ended,[2]
        On which alone our weal° depended.   *well-being*
        When up a dangerous faction starts,[3]
        With wrath and vengeance in their hearts:
385   By *solemn league and covenant bound,*[4]
        To ruin, slaughter, and confound;
        To turn religion to a fable,
        And make the government a Babel:
        Pervert the law, disgrace the gown,
390   Corrupt the senate, rob the crown;
        To sacrifice old England's glory,
        And make her infamous in story.
        When such a tempest shook the land,
        How could unguarded virtue stand?

395   "With horror, grief, despair the Dean
        Beheld the dire destructive scene:
        His friends in exile, or the Tower,[5]
        Himself within the frown of power;
        Pursued by base, envenomed pens,[6]
400   Far to the land of slaves and fens;°   *Ireland*
        A servile race in folly nursed,
        Who truckle° most, when treated worst.   *cringe obsequiously*

        "By innocence and resolution,
        He bore continual persecution;
405   While numbers to preferment[7] rose;
        Whose merits were, to be his foes.
        When, *ev'n his own familiar*° *friends*   *close*
        Intent upon their private ends,

9. Under Queen Anne's Tory ministry, Swift tried to resolve differences between the Chancellor, Simon Harcourt (1661–1727), Lord Bolingbroke, and the Earl of Oxford, but was unsuccessful, and left London shortly before the collapse of their government.

1. James Butler (1665–1745), second Earl of Ormonde, succeeded Marlborough as commander in chief of the allied forces in 1712.

2. In the height of the quarrel between the ministers, the Queen [Anne] died [Swift's note].

3. When Queen Anne died, the Whigs were restored to power, "which they exercised with the utmost rage and revenge" [Swift's note]. Swift initially feared for his own safety, and considered emigrating to the island of Guernsey.

4. Alluding to the establishment of Scottish Presbyterianism in 1643, which Swift (as an Anglican) regretted.

5. The Tower of London, where convicted (or suspected) traitors were held.

6. Upon the Queen's death, the Dean returned to live in Dublin . . . numberless libels were writ against him in England, as a Jacobite; he was insulted in the street, and at nights was forced to be attended by his servants armed [Swift's note].

7. Places at the Court or in the church hierarchy, especially bishoprics.

Like renegadoes now he feels,
Against him lifting up their heels.[8]

"The Dean did by his pen defeat
An infamous, destructive cheat,[9]
Taught fools their interest to know,
And gave them arms to ward the blow.°   *defend themselves*
Envy hath owned it was his doing
To save that helpless land from ruin,
While they who at the steerage[1] stood,
And reaped the profit, sought his blood.

"To save them from their evil fate,
In him was held a crime of state.
A wicked monster on the bench,[2]
Whose fury blood could never quench;
As vile and profligate a villain,
As modern Scroggs, or old Tresilian;[3]
Who long all justice had discarded,
Nor feared he God, nor man regarded;[4]
Vowed on the Dean his rage to vent,
And make him of his zeal repent;
But heaven his innocence defends,
The grateful people stand his friends;
Not strains of law, nor judges' frown,
Nor topics° brought to please the crown,   *charges*
Nor witness hired, nor jury picked,
Prevail to bring him in convict.

"In exile[5] with a steady heart,
He spent his life's declining part;
Where folly, pride, and faction sway,
Remote from St. John, Pope, and Gay.

"His friendship there to few confined,
Were always of the middling kind:[6]
No fools of rank, a mongrel breed,
Who fain would pass for lords indeed:
Where titles give no right or power,

410
415
420
425
430
435
440

8. From Psalm 41.9: "Yea, mine own familiar friend, in whom I trusted, which did eat of my bread, hath lifted up his heel against me."
9. One Wood, a Hardware-man from England, had a patent for coining copper halfpence in Ireland, to the sum of £108,000, which in the consequence, must leave the kingdom without gold or silver [Swift's note]. Swift responded with *The Drapier's Letters* (1724–1725).
1. The helm (of the ship of state).
2. One Whitshed was then Chief Justice: he had some years before prosecuted a printer for a pamphlet writ by the Dean, to persuade the people of Ireland to wear their own manufactures. . . . He sat as Judge afterwards on the trial of the printer of the Drapier's Fourth Letter; but the Jury, against all he could say or swear, threw out the Bill [Swift's note].

3. Scroggs was Chief Justice under King Charles the Second: his judgment always varied in State trials, according to directions from the [royal] Court. Tresilian was a wicked Judge, hanged above three hundred years ago [Swift's note].
4. Cf. Luke 18.2: "There was in a city a judge, which feared not God, neither regarded man."
5. In Ireland, which he had reason to call a place of exile; to which country nothing could have driven him, but the Queen's death, who had determined to fix him in England [Swift's note].
6. The Dean was not acquainted with one single Lord spiritual or temporal. He only conversed with private gentlemen of the clergy or laity, and but a small number of either [Swift's note]; not entirely true.

And peerage is a withered flower,[7]
445 He would have held it a disgrace,
If such a wretch had known his face.
On rural squires, that kingdom's bane,
He vented oft his wrath in vain:
Biennial squires,[8] to market brought,
450 Who sell their souls and votes for naught;
The nation stripped, go joyful back,
To rob the church, their tenants rack,[9]
Go snacks° with thieves and rapparees,[1]   *divide the spoils*
And keep the peace,[2] to pick up fees:
455 In every job[3] to have a share,
A jail or barrack[4] to repair;
And turn the tax for public roads
Commodious to their own abodes.[5]

    "Perhaps I may allow the Dean
460 Had too much satire in his vein;
And seemed determined not to starve it,
Because no age could more deserve it.
Yet, malice never was his aim;
He lashed the vice but spared the name.[6]
465 No individual could resent,
Where thousands equally were meant.
His satire points at no defect,
But what all mortals may correct;
For he abhorred that senseless tribe,
470 Who call it humor when they jibe;
He spared a hump or crooked nose,
Whose owners set not up for beaux.
True, genuine dullness moved his pity,
Unless it offered to be witty.
475 Those who their ignorance confessed,
He ne'er offended with a jest;
But laughed to hear an idiot quote,
A verse from Horace, learned by rote.

    "He knew an hundred pleasant stories,
480 With all the turns of Whigs and Tories:
Was cheerful to his dying day,
And friends would let him have his way.

---

7. The peers of Ireland lost a great part of their jurisdiction by one single Act [of 1720], and tamely submitted to this infamous mark of slavery without the least resentment, or remonstrance [Swift's note].
8. The Parliament (as they call it) in Ireland meet but once in two years; and after giving five times more than they can afford, return home to reimburse themselves by all country jobs and oppressions, of which some few only are here mentioned [Swift's note].
9. I.e., torture by extortionate rent; "rack-rent" was an excessive rent nearly equal to the full value of the land.
1. The highwaymen in Ireland are, since the late wars there, usually called rapparees, which was a name given

to those Irish soldiers who in small parties used, at that time, to plunder the Protestants [Swift's note].
2. Act as magistrates.
3. Implying a business racket.
4. The army in Ireland is lodged in barracks, the building and repairing whereof, and other charges, have cost a prodigious sum to that unhappy kingdom [Swift's note].
5. There were complaints that the new system of public turnpike roads, then being established in England and in Ireland, was manipulated by estate owners so that the roads ran directly to their own properties.
6. Swift is being ironic, since the poem explicitly identifies many targets of his satire.

> "He gave the little wealth he had
> To build a house for fools and mad:[7]
485   And showed by one satiric touch,
> No nation wanted it so much:
> That kingdom he hath left his debtor,
> I wish it soon may have a better."

1731–1732   1739

Gulliver's Travels

Travels into Several Remote Nations of the World. In Four Parts. By Lemuel Gulliver—better known as *Gulliver's Travels*—was first published in late October 1726 and enjoyed instant success. One contemporary observer noted that "several thousands sold in a week," and Swift's London friends wrote to him in Dublin to say that everyone was reading and talking about Gulliver. Readers continue to be fascinated by Swift's masterpiece: since 1945, more than 500 books and scholarly articles have been devoted to *Gulliver's Travels*. Variously classified as an early novel, an imaginary voyage, a moral and political allegory, and even a children's story, Lemuel Gulliver's four journeys, representing the four directions of the globe, comprise a survey of the human condition: a comic, ironic, and sometimes harrowing answer to the question, "What does it mean to be a human being?"

In the first voyage, the diminutive citizens of Lilliput represent human small-mindedness and petty ambitions. Filled with self-importance, the Lilliputians are cruel, treacherous, malicious, and destructive. The perspective is reversed in the second voyage to Brobdingnag, land of giants, where Gulliver has the stature of a Lilliputian. He is humbled by his own helplessness and, finding the huge bodies of the Brobdingnagians grotesque, he realizes how repulsive the Lilliputians must have found him. When Gulliver gives the wise king an account of the political affairs of England—which manifest hypocrisy, avarice, and hatred—the enlightened monarch concludes that most of the country's inhabitants must be "the most pernicious race of little odious vermin that Nature ever suffered to crawl upon the surface of the earth." In the third voyage (which was written last), Gulliver visits the flying island of Laputa and the metropolis of Lagado, on an adjacent continent, where he encounters the misuse of human reason. In Laputa, those who are supposedly "wise" lack all common sense and practical ability; at Lagado, the Academy of Projectors is staffed by professors who waste both money and intelligence on absurd endeavors. Swift aims his satire at so-called intellectuals—especially the "virtuosi," or amateur scientists of the Royal Society—who live in the world of their own speculations and so fail to use their gifts for the common good. Throughout *Gulliver's Travels* that which is admirable is held up to expose corruption in the reader's world, and that which is deplorable is identified with the institutions and practices associated with contemporary Europe, particularly Britain.

Gulliver's fourth voyage (printed in its entirety below) finds him on the island of the Houyhnhnms, horses endowed with reason, whose highly rational and well-ordered (though emotionally sterile) society is contrasted with the violence, selfishness, and brutality of the Yahoos, irrational beasts who bear a disconcerting resemblance to humans. In his foolish pride, Gulliver believes that he can escape the human condition and live as a stoical Houyhnhnm, even when he returns to his family in England. Of course, Gulliver is neither Houyhnhnm nor Yahoo, but a man. His time in Houyhnhnm-land does not teach him to be more rational or

---

7. In his will, Swift made a large bequest to build a mental institution (the first in Ireland), St. Patrick's Hospital, which was opened in 1757.

compassionate, but makes him more foolish, derelict in his duties as husband, father, and citizen. Instead of seeking to become a better man, Gulliver strives to become what he is not—with results that are both tragic and farcical. Although the poet Edward Young charged Swift with having "blasphemed a nature little lower than that of the angels" in satirizing the follies of humankind, *Gulliver's Travels* reveals the Dean of Saint Patrick's to be more a humanist than a misanthrope. With brilliantly modulated ironic self-awareness, Swift's painful comedy of exposure to the truth of human frailty demonstrates that there is no room for the distortions of human pride in a world where our practices are so evidently at variance with our principles. Swift advances no program of social reform, but provokes a new recognition—literally, a rethinking—of our own humanity.

from Gulliver's Travels
from Part 3. *A Voyage to Laputa*
CHAPTER 5

The author permitted to see the grand Academy of Logado. The Academy largely[1] described. The arts wherein the professors employ themselves.

This Academy is not an entire single building, but a continuation of several houses on both sides of a street, which growing waste,[2] was purchased and applied to that use.

I was received very kindly by the Warden, and went for many days to the Academy. Every room has in it one or more projectors,[3] and I believe I could not be[4] in fewer than five hundred rooms.

The first man I saw was of a meager aspect, with sooty hands and face, his hair and beard long, ragged and singed in several places. His clothes, shirt, and skin were all of the same color. He had been eight years upon a project for extracting sunbeams out of cucumbers,[5] which were to be put into vials hermetically sealed, and let out to warm the air in raw, inclement summers. He told me, he did not doubt in eight years more, that he should be able to supply the Governor's gardens with sunshine at a reasonable rate; but he complained that his stock was low, and entreated me to give him something as an encouragement to ingenuity,[6] especially since this had been a very dear season for cucumbers. I made him a small present, for my Lord[7] had furnished me with money on purpose, because he knew their practice of begging from all who go to see them.

I went into another chamber, but was ready to hasten back, being almost overcome with a horrible stink. My conductor pressed me forward, conjuring me in a whisper to give no offense, which would be highly resented, and therefore I durst not so much as stop my nose. The projector of this cell was the most ancient student of

---

1. In general. The academy is a satire of the Royal Society, founded in 1662 for the purpose of scientific experimentation. Though many of its members made major contributions to science, the Society had a reputation for bizarre speculation. Swift had visited the Society in 1710 and here parodies actual experiments recorded in its *Philosophical Transactions;* he is also parodying the description of "Solomon's House," an academy of science in Francis Bacon's *New Atlantis* (1626).

2. Falling into disuse.
3. Those people undertaking the project.
4. Could not have been.
5. Stephen Hales (1677–1761), English botanist and physiologist, had recently investigated sunlight's agency in plant respiration. This and other studies were published in his *Vegetable Staticks* (1726).
6. His investigative powers.
7. The warden of the Academy.

the Academy. His face and beard were of a pale yellow; his hands and clothes daubed over with filth. When I was presented to him, he gave me a very close embrace (a compliment I could well have excused). His employment from his first coming into the Academy was an operation to reduce human excrement to its original food, by separating the several parts, removing the tincture which it receives from the gall, making the odor exhale, and scumming off the saliva. He had a weekly allowance from the Society of a vessel filled with human ordure,[8] about the bigness of a Bristol barrel.[9]

I saw another at work to calcine[1] ice into gunpowder, who likewise showed me a treatise he had written concerning the malleability of fire,[2] which he intended to publish.

There was a most ingenious architect who had contrived a new method for building houses, by beginning at the roof and working downwards to the foundation, which he justified to me by the like practice of those two prudent insects, the bee and the spider.

There was a man born blind, who had several apprentices in his own condition: their employment was to mix colors for painters, which their master taught them to distinguish by feeling and smelling.[3] It was indeed my misfortune to find them at that time not very perfect in their lessons, and the professor himself happened to be generally mistaken: this artist is much encouraged and esteemed by the whole fraternity.

In another apartment I was highly pleased with a projector, who had found a device of ploughing the ground with hogs, to save the charges of ploughs, cattle, and labor. The method is this; in an acre of ground you bury, at six inches distance, and eight deep, a quantity of acorns, dates, chestnuts, and other mast[4] or vegetables whereof these animals are fondest: then you drive six hundred or more of them into the field, where in a few days they will root up the whole ground in search of their food, and make it fit for sowing, at the same time manuring it with their dung; it is true upon experiment they found the charge and trouble very great, and they had little or no crop. However, it is not doubted that this invention may be capable of great improvement.

I went into another room, where the walls and ceiling were all hung round with cobwebs, except a narrow passage for the artist[5] to go in and out. At my entrance he called aloud to me not to disturb his webs. He lamented the fatal mistake the world had been so long in of using silkworms, while we had such plenty of domestic insects, who infinitely excelled the former, because they understood how to weave as well as spin. And he proposed farther, that by employing spiders, the charge[6] of dyeing silks would be wholly saved, whereof I was fully convinced when he showed me a vast number of flies most beautifully colored, wherewith he fed his spiders, assuring us, that the webs would take a tincture from them; and as he had them of all hues, he hoped to

8. Excrement.
9. A medium-size barrel, holding about 37 gallons.
1. Desiccate.
2. Cf. Rabelais, *Gargantua and Pantagruel* (1532–1564), bk. 5, ch. 22: "Others were cutting fire with a knife, and drawing water up in a net."
3. Based on Robert Boyle's account in *Experiments and Observations Upon Colors* (1665), of a blind man who

could distinguish colors.
4. Nuts.
5. Modeled on both the Frenchman M. Bon, who believed silk could be made from cobwebs, and Dr. Wall, who suggested that the excreta of ants fed on plant sap could be used as dye; both suggestions were published in the *Transactions of the Royal Society*.
6. Expense.

fit everybody's fancy, as soon as he could find proper food for the flies, of certain gums, oils, and other glutinous matter to give a strength and consistence to the threads.

There was an astronomer who had undertaken to place a sundial upon the great weathercock on the Town House,[7] by adjusting the annual and diurnal motions of the earth and sun, so as to answer and coincide with all accidental turnings of the wind.

I was complaining of a small fit of the colic, upon which my conductor led me into a room, where a great physician resided, who was famous for curing that disease by contrary operations from the same instrument. He had a large pair of bellows with a long slender muzzle of ivory. This he conveyed eight inches up the anus, and drawing in the wind, he affirmed he could make the guts as lank as a dried bladder. But when the disease was more stubborn and violent, he let in the muzzle while the bellows was full of wind, which he discharged into the body of the patient, then withdrew the instrument to replenish it, clapping his thumb strongly against the orifice of the fundament; and this being repeated three or four times, the adventitious wind would rush out, bringing the noxious along with it (like water put into a pump) and the patient recover. I saw him try both experiments upon a dog, but could not discern any effect from the former. After the latter, the animal was ready to burst, and made so violent a discharge, as was very offensive to me and my companions. The dog died on the spot, and we left the doctor endeavoring to recover him by the same operation.[8]

I visited many other apartments, but shall not trouble my reader with all the curiosities I observed, being studious of brevity.

I had hitherto seen only one side of the Academy, the other being appropriated to the advancers of speculative learning, of whom I shall say something when I have mentioned one illustrious person more, who is called among them *the universal artist*.[9] He told us he had been thirty years employing his thoughts for the improvement of human life. He had two large rooms full of wonderful curiosities, and fifty men at work. Some were condensing air into a dry, tangible substance, by extracting the niter,[1] and letting the aqueous or fluid particles percolate; others softening marble for pillows and pincushions; others petrifying the hoofs of a living horse to preserve them from foundering. The artist himself was at that time busy upon two great designs: the first, to sow land with chaff, wherein he affirmed the true seminal virtue to be contained, as he demonstrated by several experiments which I was not skillful enough to comprehend. The other was, by a certain composition of gums, minerals, and vegetables outwardly applied, to prevent the growth of wool upon two young lambs; and he hoped in a reasonable time to propagate the breed of naked sheep all over the kingdom.

We crossed a walk to the other part of the Academy, where, as I have already said, the projectors in speculative learning resided.

The first professor I saw was in a very large room, with forty pupils about him. After salutation, observing me to look earnestly upon a frame, which took up the greatest part of both the length and breadth of the room, he said perhaps I might

7. Town Hall.
8. Robert Hooke (1635–1703) produced artificial respiration in a dog (1667) by blowing air into its windpipe with a pair of bellows.

9. Possibly Robert Boyle (1627–1691), whose many scientific experiments investigated the nature of air, marble, petrifaction, agriculture, and sheep breeding.
1. Air was believed to contain nitrous matter.

wonder to see him employed in a project for improving speculative knowledge by practical and mechanical operations. But the world would soon be sensible[2] of its usefulness, and he flattered himself that a more noble exalted thought never sprang in any other man's head. Everyone knew how laborious the usual method is of attaining to arts and sciences; whereas by his contrivance, the most ignorant person at a reasonable charge, and with a little bodily labor, may write books in philosophy, poetry, politics, law, mathematics, and theology, without the least assistance from genius or study. He then led me to the frame, about the sides whereof all his pupils stood in ranks. It was twenty foot square, placed in the middle of the room. The superficies[3] was composed of several bits of wood, about the bigness of a die,[4] but some larger than others. They were all linked together by slender wires. These bits of wood were covered on every square with papers pasted on them, and on these papers were written all the words of their language in their several moods, tenses, and declensions, but without any order. The professor then desired me to observe, for he was going to set his engine[5] at work. The pupils at his command took each of them hold of an iron handle, whereof there were forty fixed round the edges of the frame, and giving them a sudden turn, the whole disposition of the words was entirely changed. He then commanded six and thirty of the lads to read the several lines softly as they appeared upon the frame; and where they found three or four words together that might make part of a sentence, they dictated to the four remaining boys who were scribes. This work was repeated three or four times, and at every turn the engine was so contrived, that the words shifted into new places, as the square bits of wood moved upside down.

Six hours a day the young students were employed in this labor, and the professor showed me several volumes in large folio already collected, of broken sentences, which he intended to piece together, and out of those rich materials to give the world a complete body of all arts and sciences; which however might be still improved, and much expedited, if the public would raise a fund for making and employing five hundred such frames in Lagado, and oblige the managers to contribute in common their several[6] collections.

He assured me, that this invention had employed all his thoughts from his youth, that he had emptied the whole vocabulary into his frame, and made the strictest computation of the general proportion there is in books between the numbers of particles, nouns, and verbs, and other parts of speech.

I made my humblest acknowledgments to this illustrious person for his great communicativeness, and promised if ever I had the good fortune to return to my native country, that I would do him justice, as the sole inventor of this wonderful machine; the form and contrivance of which I desired leave to delineate upon paper as in the figure here annexed. I told him, although it were the custom of our learned in Europe to steal inventions from each other,[7] who had thereby at least this advantage, that it became a controversy which was the right owner, yet I would take such caution, that he should have the honor entire without a rival.

---

2. Aware.
3. Surface.
4. Singular of dice.
5. Machine.
6. Individual.

7. No international patent agreement existed at this time, and the theft of inventions was common as nations competed in developing technology for commercial manufacturing and navigation on the open seas.

We next went to the school of languages, where three professors sat in consultation upon improving that of their own country.[8]

The first project was to shorten discourse by cutting polysyllables into one, and leaving out verbs and participles, because in reality all things imaginable are but nouns.

The other project was a scheme for entirely abolishing all words whatsoever; and this was urged as a great advantage in point of health as well as brevity. For, it is plain, that every word we speak is in some degree a diminution of our lungs by corrosion, and consequently contributes to the shortening of our lives. An expedient was therefore offered, that since words are only names for *things*, it would be more convenient for all men to carry about them such *things* as were necessary to express the particular business they are to discourse on.[9] And this invention would certainly have taken place, to the great ease as well as health of the subject,[1] if the women in conjunction with the vulgar and illiterate had not threatened to raise a rebellion, unless they might be allowed the liberty to speak with their tongues, after the manner of their forefathers; such constant irreconcilable enemies to science are the common people. However, many of the most learned and wise adhere to the new scheme of expressing themselves by *things*, which hath only this inconvenience attending it, that if a man's business be very great, and of various kinds, he must be obliged in proportion to carry a greater bundle of *things* upon his back, unless he can afford one or two strong servants to attend him. I have often beheld two of those sages almost sinking under the weight of their packs, like peddlers among us; who when they met in the streets would lay down their loads, open their sacks, and hold conversation for an hour together; then put up their implements, help each other to resume their burdens, and take their leave.

But for short conversations a man may carry implements in his pockets and under his arms, enough to supply him, and in his house he cannot be at a loss; therefore the room where company meet who practice this art, is full of all *things* ready at hand, requisite to furnish matter for this kind of artificial converse.[2]

Another great advantage proposed by this invention, was that it would serve as a universal language to be understood in all civilized nations, whose goods and utensils are generally of the same kind, or nearly resembling, so that their uses might easily be comprehended. And thus, ambassadors would be qualified to treat with foreign princes or ministers of state, to whose tongues they were utter strangers.

I was at the mathematical school, where the master taught his pupils after a method scarce imaginable to us in Europe. The proposition and demonstration were fairly written on a thin wafer, with ink composed of a cephalic[3] tincture. This the student was to swallow upon a fasting stomach, and for three days following eat noth-

8. The first secretary to the Royal Society, Thomas Spratt, in his *History* (1667) of that institution, recommended that such an Academy be founded, as the new style of science writing should strive to describe "so many *things* in an equal number of words." Although Swift burlesques this notion, he himself had published *Proposals for Correcting, Improving and Ascertaining the English Tongue* (1712), in which he suggested that an Academy be established with the aim of preserving culture and "fixing our language for ever."
9. The growth of scientific knowledge about the nature of the material world had encouraged suggestions that language should be made less abstract. In satirizing the projector, Swift alludes to John Locke's theory of language in Book 3 of *An Essay Concerning Human Understanding* (1690), where Locke argues that words stand for things only indirectly.
1. Both the individual practitioner and the people of the nation as a whole.
2. A reference to the Royal Society's attempt to collect one specimen or example of every thing in the world.
3. Of or for the head.

ing but bread and water. As the wafer digested, the tincture mounted to his brain, bearing the proposition along with it. But the success has not hitherto been answerable, partly by some error in the *quantum* or composition, and partly by the perverseness of lads, to whom this bolus[4] is so nauseous that they generally steal aside, and discharge it upwards before it can operate; neither have they been yet persuaded to use so long an abstinence as the prescription requires.

CHAPTER 10

The Luggnaggians commended. A particular description of the Struldbruggs, with many conversations between the author and some eminent persons upon that subject.[1]

The Luggnaggians are a polite and generous people, and although they are not without some share of that pride which is peculiar to all Eastern countries, yet they show themselves courteous to strangers, especially such who are countenanced by the Court. I had many acquaintance among persons of the best fashion, and being always attended by my interpreter, the conversation we had was not disagreeable.

One day in much good company, I was asked by a person of quality, whether I had seen any of their Struldbruggs or Immortals. I said I had not, and desired he would explain to me what he meant by such an appellation applied to a mortal creature. He told me, that sometimes, though very rarely, a child happened to be born in a family with a red circular spot in the forehead, directly over the left eyebrow, which was an infallible mark that it should never die. The spot, as he described it, was about the compass of a silver threepence, but in the course of time grew larger, and changed its color; for at twelve years old it became green, so continued till five and twenty, then turned to a deep blue; at five and forty it grew coal black, and as large as an English shilling, but never admitted any farther alteration. He said these births were so rare, that he did not believe there could be above eleven hundred Struldbruggs of both sexes in the whole kingdom, of which he computed about fifty in the metropolis, and among the rest a young girl born about three years ago. That these productions were not peculiar to any family, but a mere effect of chance, and the children of the Struldbruggs themselves, were equally mortal with the rest of the people.

I freely own myself to have been struck with inexpressible delight upon hearing this account: and the person who gave it me happening to understand the Balnibarbian language, which I spoke very well, I could not forbear breaking out into expressions perhaps a little too extravagant. I cried out as in a rapture: Happy nation where every child hath at least a chance for being immortal! Happy people who enjoy so many living examples of ancient virtue, and have masters ready to instruct them in the wisdom of all former ages! But, happiest beyond all comparison are those excellent Struldbruggs, who being born exempt from that universal calamity of human nature, have their minds free and disengaged, without the weight and depression of spirits caused by the continual apprehension of death. I discovered my admiration[2] that I had not observed any of these illustrious persons at Court, the black spot on

---

4. Mass of chewed food.
1. In order to return to England, Gulliver sails west on the Pacific from Balnibarbi (the country of which Lagado

is the capital) to Japan, stopping en route at the island of "Luggnagg," where he makes the following observations.
2. Expressed my surprise.

the forehead being so remarkable a distinction, that I could not have easily overlooked it; and it was impossible that his Majesty, a most judicious prince, should not provide himself with a good number of such wise and able counselors. Yet perhaps the virtue of those reverend sages was too strict for the corrupt and libertine manners of a Court. And we often find by experience that young men are too opinionative and volatile to be guided by the sober dictates of their seniors. However, since the King was pleased to allow me access to his royal person, I was resolved upon the very first occasion to deliver my opinion to him on this matter freely, and at large, by the help of my interpreter; and whether he would please to take my advice or no, yet in one thing I was determined, that his Majesty having frequently offered me an establishment in this country, I would with great thankfulness accept the favor, and pass my life here in the conversation of those superior beings the Struldbruggs, if they would please to admit me.

The gentleman to whom I addressed my discourse, because (as I have already observed) he spoke the language of Balnibarbi, said to me with a sort of a smile, which usually ariseth from pity to the ignorant, that he was glad of any occasion to keep me among them, and desired my permission to explain to the company what I had spoke. He did so, and they talked together for some time in their own language, whereof I understood not a syllable, neither could I observe by their countenances what impression my discourse had made on them. After a short silence the same person told me, that his friends and mine (so he thought fit to express himself) were very much pleased with the judicious remarks I had made on the great happiness and advantages of immortal life, and they were desirous to know in a particular manner, what scheme of living I should have formed to myself, if it had fallen to my lot to have been born a Struldbrugg.

I answered, it was easy to be eloquent on so copious and delightful a subject, especially to me who have been often apt to amuse myself with visions of what I should do if I were a king, a general, or a great lord; and upon this very case I had frequently run over the whole system how I should employ myself, and pass the time if I were sure to live for ever.

That, if it had been my good fortune to come into the world a Struldbrugg, as soon as I could discover my own happiness by understanding the difference between life and death, I would first resolve by all arts and methods whatsoever to procure myself riches. In the pursuit of which by thrift and management, I might reasonably expect in about two hundred years, to be the wealthiest man in the kingdom. In the second place, I would from my earliest youth apply myself to the study of arts and sciences, by which I should arrive in time to excel all others in learning. Lastly I would carefully record every action and event of consequence that happened in the public,[3] impartially draw the characters of the several successions of princes, and great ministers of state, with my own observations on every point. I would exactly set down the several changes in customs, language, fashions of dress, diet and diversions. By all which acquirements, I should be a living treasury of knowledge and wisdom, and certainly become the oracle of the nation.

I would never marry after threescore, but live in an hospitable manner, yet still on the saving side. I would entertain myself in forming and directing the minds of hopeful young men, by convincing them from my own remembrance, experience,

---

3. The state (from Latin *res publica*, the "public thing," from which derives the word *republic*).

and observation, fortified by numerous examples, of the usefulness of virtue in public and private life. But, my choice and constant companions should be a set of my own immortal brotherhood, among whom I would elect a dozen from the most ancient down to my own contemporaries. Where any of these wanted[4] fortunes, I would provide them with convenient lodges round my own estate, and have some of them always at my table, only mingling a few of the most valuable among you mortals, whom length of time would harden me to lose with little or no reluctance, and treat your posterity after the same manner, just as a man diverts himself with the annual succession of pinks and tulips in his garden, without regretting the loss of those which withered the preceding year.

These Struldbruggs and I would mutually communicate our observations and memorials through the course of time, remark the several gradations by which corruption steals into the world, and oppose it in every step, by giving perpetual warning and instruction to mankind; which, added to the strong influence of our own example, would probably prevent that continual degeneracy of human nature so justly complained of in all ages.

Add to all this, the pleasure of seeing the various revolutions of states and empires, the changes in the lower and upper world,[5] ancient cities in ruins, and obscure villages become the seats of kings. Famous rivers lessening into shallow brooks, the ocean leaving one coast dry, and overwhelming another, the discovery of many countries yet unknown. Barbarity overrunning the politest nations, and the most barbarous becoming civilized. I should then see the discovery of the longitude, the perpetual motion, the universal medicine,[6] and many other great inventions brought to the utmost perfection.

What wonderful discoveries should we make in astronomy, by outliving and confirming our own predictions, by observing the progress and returns of comets, with the changes of motion in the sun, moon, and stars.

I enlarged upon many other topics, which the natural desire of endless life and sublunary[7] happiness could easily furnish me with. When I had ended, and the sum of my discourse had been interpreted as before, to the rest of the company, there was a good deal of talk among them in the language of the country, not without some laughter at my expense. At last the same gentleman who had been my interpreter said, he was desired by the rest to set me right in a few mistakes, which I had fallen into through the common imbecility of human nature, and upon that allowance was less answerable for them. That, this breed of Struldbruggs was peculiar to their country, for there were no such people either in Balnibarbi or Japan, where he had the honor to be ambassador from his Majesty, and found the natives in both those kingdoms very hard to believe[8] that the fact was possible, and it appeared from my astonishment when he first mentioned the matter to me, that I received it as a thing wholly new, and scarcely to be credited. That in the two kingdoms above-mentioned, where during his residence he had conversed very much, he observed long life to be the universal desire and wish of mankind. That whoever had one foot in the grave, was sure to hold back the other as strongly as he could. That the oldest had still hopes of living one day longer, and looked on death as the greatest evil, from which nature always prompted him to retreat; only in this island of Luggnagg, the appetite

4. Lacked.
5. On the earth and in the heavens.
6. As at Lagado, Gulliver enumerates scientific quests Swift scoffed at: for a method of determining the longi-

tude of a ship at sea, for a perpetual motion machine, for one drug sufficient to cure all ills.
7. Earthly.
8. To convince.

for living was not so eager, from the continual example of the Struldbruggs before their eyes.

That the system of living contrived by me was unreasonable and unjust, because it supposed a perpetuity of youth, health, and vigor, which no man could be so foolish to hope, however extravagant he may be in his wishes. That the question therefore was not whether a man would choose to be always in the prime of youth, attended with prosperity and health, but how he would pass a perpetual life under all the usual disadvantages which old age brings along with it. For although few men will avow their desires of being immortal upon such hard conditions, yet in the two kingdoms before-mentioned of Balnibarbi and Japan, he observed that every man desired to put off death for some time longer, let it approach ever so late, and he rarely heard of any man who died willingly, except he were incited by the extremity of grief or torture. And he appealed to me whether in those countries I had traveled, as well as my own, I had not observed the same general disposition.

After this preface he gave me a particular account of the Struldbruggs among them. He said they commonly acted like mortals, till about thirty years old, after which by degrees they grew melancholy and dejected, increasing in both till they came to fourscore. This he learned from their own confession; for otherwise there not being above two or three of that species born in an age, they were too few to form a general observation by. When they came to fourscore years, which is reckoned the extremity of living in this country, they had not only all the follies and infirmities of other old men, but many more which arose from the dreadful prospect of never dying. They were not only opinionative, peevish, covetous, morose, vain, talkative, but uncapable of friendship, and dead to all natural affection, which never descended below their grandchildren. Envy and impotent desires are their prevailing passions. But those objects against which their envy seems principally directed, are the vices of the younger sort, and the deaths of the old. By reflecting on the former, they find themselves cut off from all possibility of pleasure; and whenever they see a funeral, they lament and repine that others have gone to an harbor of rest, to which they themselves never can hope to arrive. They have no remembrance of anything but what they learned and observed in their youth and middle age, and even that is very imperfect. And for the truth or particulars of any fact, it is safer to depend on common traditions than upon their best recollections. The least miserable among them appear to be those who turn to dotage, and entirely lose their memories; these meet with more pity and assistance, because they want many bad qualities which abound in others.

If a Struldbrugg happen to marry one of his own kind, the marriage is dissolved of course by the courtesy of the kingdom, as soon as the younger of the two comes to be fourscore. For the law thinks it a reasonable indulgence, that those who are condemned without any fault of their own to a perpetual continuance in the world, should not have their misery doubled by the load of a wife.[9]

As soon as they have completed the term of eighty years, they are looked on as dead in law; their heirs immediately succeed to their estates, only a small pittance is reserved for their support, and the poor ones are maintained at the public charge. After that period they are held incapable of any employment of trust or profit, they cannot purchase lands or take leases, neither are they allowed to be witnesses in any cause, either civil or criminal, not even for the decision of meres[1] and bounds.

9. Swift himself never married.   1. Property lines (at issue in property disputes).

At ninety they lose their teeth and hair, they have at that age no distinction of taste, but eat and drink whatever they can get, without relish or appetite. The diseases they were subject to, still continue without increasing or diminishing. In talking they forget the common appellation of things, and the names of persons, even of those who are their nearest friends and relations. For the same reason they never can amuse themselves with reading, because their memory will not serve to carry them from the beginning of a sentence to the end; and by this defect they are deprived of the only entertainment whereof they might otherwise be capable.

The language of this country being always upon the flux, the Struldbruggs of one age do not understand those of another, neither are they able after two hundred years to hold any conversation (farther than by a few general words) with their neighbors the mortals, and thus they lie under the disadvantage of living like foreigners in their own country. This was the account given me of the Struldbruggs, as near as I can remember. I afterwards saw five or six of different ages, the youngest not above two hundred years old, who were brought to me at several times by some of my friends; but although they were told that I was a great traveler, and had seen all the world, they had not the least curiosity to ask me a question; only desired I would give them *slumskudask*, or a token of remembrance, which is a modest way of begging, to avoid the law that strictly forbids it, because they are provided for by the public, although indeed with a very scanty allowance.

They are despised and hated by all sorts of people; when one of them is born, it is reckoned ominous, and their birth is recorded very particularly; so that you may know their age by consulting the registry, which however hath not been kept above a thousand years past, or at least hath been destroyed by time or public disturbances. But the usual way of computing how old they are, is, by asking them what kings or great persons they can remember, and then consulting history, for infallibly the last prince in their mind did not begin his reign after they were fourscore years old.

They were the most mortifying sight I ever beheld, and the women more horrible than the men. Besides the usual deformities in extreme old age, they acquired an additional ghastliness in proportion to their number of years, which is not to be described, and among half a dozen I soon distinguished which was the eldest, although there were not above a century or two between them.

The reader will easily believe, that from what I had heard and seen, my keen appetite for perpetuity of life was much abated. I grew heartily ashamed of the pleasing visions I had formed, and thought no tyrant could invent a death into which I would not run with pleasure from such a life. The king heard of all that had passed between me and my friends upon this occasion, and rallied me very pleasantly, wishing I would send a couple of Struldbruggs to my own country, to arm our people against the fear of death; but this it seems is forbidden by the fundamental laws of the kingdom, or else I should have been well content with the trouble and expense of transporting them.

I could not but agree that the laws of this kingdom, relating to the Struldbruggs, were founded upon the strongest reasons, and such as any other country would be under the necessity of enacting in the like circumstances. Otherwise, as avarice is the necessary consequent of old age, those Immortals would in time become proprietors of the whole nation, and engross the civil power, which, for want of abilities to manage, must end in the ruin of the public.

from *Part 4. A Voyage to the Country of the Houyhnhnms*[1]

CHAPTER 1

The author sets out as Captain of a ship. His men conspire against him, confine him a long time to his cabin, set him on shore in an unknown land. He travels up into the country. The Yahoos,[2] a strange sort of animal, described. The author meets two Houyhnhnms.

I continued at home with my wife and children about five months in a very happy condition, if I could have learned the lesson of knowing when I was well. I left my poor wife big with child, and accepted an advantageous offer made me to be Captain of the *Adventure*,[3] a stout merchantman of 350 tons: for I understood navigation well, and being grown weary of a surgeon's employment at sea, which however I could exercise upon occasion, I took a skillful young man of that calling, one Robert Purefoy,[4] into my ship. We set sail from Portsmouth upon the seventh day of September, 1710; on the fourteenth, we met with Captain Pocock[5] of Bristol, at Teneriffe,[6] who was going to the bay of Campeche, to cut logwood. On the sixteenth, he was parted from us by a storm; I heard since my return, that his ship foundered, and none escaped, but one cabin boy. He was an honest man, and a good sailor, but a little too positive in his own opinions, which was the cause of his destruction, as it hath been of several others. For if he had followed my advice, he might at this time have been safe at home with his family as well as myself.

I had several men died in my ship of calentures,[7] so that I was forced to get recruits out of Barbados, and the Leeward Islands, where I touched by[8] the direction of the merchants who employed me, which I had soon too much cause to repent; for I found afterwards that most of them had been buccaneers. I had fifty hands on board, and my orders were, that I should trade with the Indians in the South Sea, and make what discoveries I could. These rogues whom I had picked up debauched my other men, and they all formed a conspiracy to seize the ship and secure me; which they did one morning, rushing into my cabin, and binding me hand and foot, threatening to throw me overboard, if I offered to stir. I told them, I was their prisoner, and would submit. This they made me swear to do, and then unbound me, only fastening one of my legs with a chain near my bed, and placed a sentry at my door with his piece charged,[9] who was commanded to shoot me dead, if I attempted my liberty. They sent me down victuals and drink, and took the government of the ship to themselves. Their design was to turn pirates, and plunder the Spaniards, which they could not do till they got more men. But first they resolved to sell the goods in the ship, and then go to Madagascar[1] for recruits, several among them having died since my confinement.

---

1. Pronounced "whinnims," to mimic the sound of a horse's whinny, though some scholars have offered more complex interpretations of this name. With characteristic irony, Swift probably chose horses to represent rational creatures because the philosopher John Locke (1632–1704) and Bishop Edward Stillingfleet (1635–1699) had argued extensively about how one might distinguish man as a rational animal from an evidently irrational animal, such as a horse.
2. The name may be derived from similarly titled African or Guianan tribes. The animals represent sinful, fallen humanity, and their juxtaposition with the Houyhnhnms is designed to question belief in the innate rationality of humankind and the superiority of humans over other creatures.
3. The name of two ships of the notorious pirate Captain

William Kidd (d. 1701). Kidd, originally commissioned to capture pirates, was also subject to a mutiny.
4. "Pure faith," associating Gulliver with the overzealous Puritans.
5. Probably modeled on the dogmatic Captain Dampier (1652–1715), who had spent three years logcutting around the Campeche Bay, on the Yucatan Peninsula, in the Gulf of Mexico. His violent disagreements with his lieutenant led to a court martial.
6. One of the Canary Islands, off the northwestern coast of Africa.
7. Tropical fevers.
8. Landed according to.
9. Gun loaded.
1. A popular meeting place for pirates.

They sailed many weeks, and traded with the Indians, but I knew not what course they took, being kept close prisoner in my cabin, and expecting nothing less than to be murdered, as they often threatened me.

Upon the ninth day of May, 1711, one James Welch came down to my cabin; and said he had orders from the Captain to set me ashore. I expostulated with him, but in vain; neither would he so much as tell me who their new captain was. They forced me into the longboat, letting me put on my best suit of clothes, which were good as new, and a small bundle of linen, but no arms except my hanger;[2] and they were so civil as not to search my pockets, into which I conveyed what money I had, with some other little necessaries. They rowed about a league; and then set me down on a strand.[3] I desired them to tell me what country it was. They all swore, they knew no more than myself, but said, that the Captain (as they called him) was resolved, after they had sold the lading,[4] to get rid of me in the first place where they discovered land. They pushed off immediately, advising me to make haste, for fear of being overtaken by the tide, and bade me farewell.

In this desolate condition I advanced forward, and soon got upon firm ground, where I sat down on a bank to rest myself, and consider what I had best to do. When I was a little refreshed, I went up into the country, resolving to deliver myself to the first savages I should meet, and purchase my life from them by some bracelets, glass rings, and other toys,[5] which sailors usually provide themselves with in those voyages, and whereof I had some about me: the land was divided by long rows of trees, not regularly planted, but naturally growing; there was great plenty of grass, and several fields of oats. I walked very circumspectly for fear of being surprised, or suddenly shot with an arrow from behind or on either side. I fell into a beaten road, where I saw many tracks of human feet, and some of cows, but most of horses. At last I beheld several animals in a field, and one or two of the same kind sitting in trees. Their shape was very singular, and deformed, which a little discomposed me, so that I lay down behind a thicket to observe them better. Some of them coming forward near the place where I lay, gave me an opportunity of distinctly marking[6] their form. Their heads and breasts were covered with a thick hair, some frizzled and others lank; they had beards like goats, and a long ridge of hair down their backs, and the foreparts of their legs and feet, but the rest of their bodies were bare, so that I might see their skins, which were of a brown buff color. They had no tails, nor any hair at all on their buttocks, except about the anus; which, I presume, Nature had placed there to defend them as they sat on the ground; for this posture they used, as well as lying down, and often stood on their hind feet. They climbed high trees, as nimbly as a squirrel, for they had strong extended claws before and behind, terminating in sharp points, and hooked. They would often spring, and bound, and leap with prodigious agility. The females were not so large as the males; they had long lank hair on their heads, and only a sort of down on the rest of their bodies, except about the anus, and pudenda.[7] Their dugs[8] hung between their forefeet, and often reached almost to the ground as they walked. The hair of both sexes was of several colors, brown, red, black, and yellow. Upon the whole, I never beheld in all my travels so disagreeable an animal, nor one against which I naturally conceived so strong an antipathy. So that thinking I had seen enough, full of contempt and aversion, I got up and pursued

2. A short sword, typically hung from the belt.
3. The shore; in this context, apparently a spit extending into the sea.
4. Cargo.

5. Trinkets.
6. Observing.
7. Genitals.
8. Breasts.

the beaten road, hoping it might direct me to the cabin of some Indian. I had not gone far when I met one of these creatures full in my way, and coming up directly to me. The ugly monster, when he saw me, distorted several ways every feature of his visage, and stared as at an object he had never seen before; then approaching nearer, lifted up his forepaw, whether out of curiosity or mischief, I could not tell. But I drew my hanger, and gave him a good blow with the flat side of it; for I durst not strike him with the edge, fearing the inhabitants might be provoked against me, if they should come to know, that I had killed or maimed any of their cattle. When the beast felt the smart, he drew back, and roared so loud, that a herd of at least forty came flocking about me from the next field, howling and making odious faces; but I ran to the body of a tree, and leaning my back against it, kept them off, by waving my hanger. Several of this cursed brood getting hold of the branches behind leaped up into the tree, from whence they began to discharge their excrements on my head: however, I escaped pretty well, by sticking close to the stem of the tree, but was almost stifled with the filth, which fell about me on every side.

In the midst of this distress, I observed them all to run away on a sudden as fast as they could, at which I ventured to leave the tree, and pursue the road, wondering what it was that could put them into this flight. But looking on my left hand, I saw a horse walking softly in the field, which my persecutors having sooner discovered, was the cause of their flight. The horse started a little when he came near me, but soon recovering himself, looked full in my face with manifest tokens of wonder: he viewed my hands and feet, walking round me several times. I would have pursued my journey, but he placed himself directly in the way, yet looking with a very mild aspect, never offering the least violence. We stood gazing at each other for some time; at last I took the boldness to reach my hand towards his neck, with a design to stroke it, using the common style and whistle of jockeys when they are going to handle a strange horse. But this animal, seeming to receive my civilities with disdain, shook his head, and bent his brows, softly raising up his left forefoot to remove my hand. Then he neighed three or four times, but in so different a cadence, that I almost began to think he was speaking to himself in some language of his own.

While he and I were thus employed, another horse came up; who applying[9] himself to the first in a very formal manner, they gently struck each other's right hoof before, neighing several times by turns, and varying the sound, which seemed to be almost articulate. They went some paces off, as if it were to confer together, walking side by side, backward and forward, like persons deliberating upon some affair of weight, but often turning their eyes towards me, as it were to watch that I might not escape. I was amazed to see such actions and behavior in brute beasts, and concluded with myself, that if the inhabitants of this country were endued with a proportionable degree of reason, they must needs be the wisest people upon earth. This thought gave me so much comfort, that I resolved to go forward until I could discover some house or village, or meet with any of the natives, leaving the two horses to discourse together as they pleased. But the first, who was a dapple-grey, observing me to steal off, neighed after me in so expressive a tone, that I fancied myself to understand what he meant; whereupon I turned back, and came near him, to expect[1] his farther commands. But concealing my fear as much as I could, for I began to be in some pain,[2] how this adventure might terminate; and the reader will easily believe I did not much like my present situation.

---

9. Addressing.
1. Await.

2. Began to be worried.

The two horses came up close to me, looking with great earnestness upon my face and hands. The grey steed rubbed my hat all round with his right forehoof, and discomposed it so much, that I was forced to adjust it better, by taking it off, and settling it again; whereat both he and his companion (who was a brown bay) appeared to be much surprised; the latter felt the lappet[3] of my coat, and finding it to hang loose about me, they both looked with new signs of wonder. He stroked my right hand, seeming to admire the softness, and color; but he squeezed it so hard between his hoof and his pastern,[4] that I was forced to roar; after which they both touched me with all possible tenderness. They were under great perplexity about my shoes and stockings, which they felt very often, neighing to each other, and using various gestures, not unlike those of a philosopher,[5] when he would attempt to solve some new and difficult phenomenon.

Upon the whole, the behavior of these animals was so orderly and rational, so acute and judicious, that I at last concluded, they must needs be magicians, who had thus metamorphosed themselves upon some design, and seeing a stranger in the way, were resolved to divert themselves with him; or perhaps were really amazed at the sight of a man so very different in habit, feature, and complexion from those who might probably live in so remote a climate.[6] Upon the strength of this reasoning, I ventured to address them in the following manner: Gentlemen, if you be conjurers, as I have good cause to believe, you can understand any language; therefore I make bold to let your Worships know, that I am a poor distressed Englishman, driven by his misfortunes upon your coast, and I entreat one of you, to let me ride upon his back, as if he were a real horse, to some house or village, where I can be relieved. In return of which favor, I will make you a present of this knife and bracelet (taking them out of my pocket). The two creatures stood silent while I spoke, seeming to listen with great attention; and when I had ended, they neighed frequently towards each other, as if they were engaged in serious conversation. I plainly observed that their language expressed the passions[7] very well, and the words might with little pains be resolved into an alphabet more easily than the Chinese.

I could frequently distinguish the word *Yahoo*, which was repeated by each of them several times; and although it were impossible for me to conjecture what it meant, yet while the two horses were busy in conversation, I endeavored to practice this word upon my tongue; and as soon as they were silent, I boldly pronounced *Yahoo* in a loud voice, imitating, at the same time, as near as I could, the neighing of a horse; at which they were both visibly surprised, and the grey repeated the same word twice, as if he meant to teach me the right accent, wherein I spoke after him as well as I could, and found myself perceivably to improve every time, although very far from any degree of perfection. Then the bay tried me with a second word, much harder to be pronounced; but reducing it to the English *orthography*,[8] may be spelled thus, *Houyhnhnm*. I did not succeed in this so well as the former, but after two or three farther trials, I had better fortune; and they both appeared amazed at my capacity.

After some farther discourse, which I then conjectured might relate to me, the two friends took their leaves, with the same compliment of striking each other's hoof; and the grey made me signs that I should walk before him; wherein I thought it prudent to comply, till I could find a better director. When I offered to slacken my pace,

---

3. Lapel.
4. Part of a horse's foot between the fetlock (a projection of the lower leg) and the hoof.
5. Scientist.

6. Region.
7. Emotions.
8. Spelling.

he would cry *Hhuun, Hhuun;* I guessed his meaning, and gave him to understand, as well as I could, that I was weary, and not able to walk faster; upon which, he would stand a while to let me rest.

CHAPTER 2

The author conducted by a Houyhnhnm to his house. The house described. The author's reception. The food of the Houyhnhnms. The author in distress for want of meat, is at last relieved. His manner of feeding in that country.

Having traveled about three miles, we came to a long kind of building, made of timber stuck in the ground, and wattled across;[9] the roof was low, and covered with straw. I now began to be a little comforted, and took out some toys, which travelers usually carry for presents to the savage Indians of America and other parts, in hopes the people of the house would be thereby encouraged to receive me kindly. The horse made me a sign to go in first; it was a large room with a smooth, clay floor, and a rack[1] and manger extending the whole length on one side. There were three nags,[2] and two mares, not eating, but some of them sitting down upon their hams,[3] which I very much wondered at; but wondered more to see the rest employed in domestic business. The last seemed but ordinary cattle; however, this confirmed my first opinion, that a people who could so far civilize brute animals, must needs excel in wisdom all the nations of the world. The grey came in just after, and thereby prevented any ill treatment, which the others might have given me. He neighed to them several times in a style of authority, and received answers.

Beyond this room there were three others, reaching the length of the house, to which you passed through three doors, opposite to each other, in the manner of a vista;[4] we went through the second room towards the third; here the grey walked in first, beckoning me to attend:[5] I waited in the second room, and got ready my presents, for the master and mistress of the house: they were two knives, three bracelets of false pearl, a small looking glass, and a bead necklace. The horse neighed three or four times, and I waited to hear some answers in a human voice, but I heard no other returns than in the same dialect, only one or two a little shriller than his. I began to think that this house must belong to some person of great note among them, because there appeared so much ceremony before I could gain admittance. But, that a man of quality should be served all by horses, was beyond my comprehension. I feared my brain was disturbed by my sufferings and misfortunes: I roused myself, and looked about me in the room where I was left alone; this was furnished as the first, only after a more elegant manner. I rubbed mine eyes often, but the same objects still occurred. I pinched my arms and sides, to awake myself, hoping I might be in a dream. I then absolutely concluded, that all these appearances could be nothing else but necromancy[6] and magic. But I had no time to pursue these reflections; for the grey horse came to the door, and made me a sign to follow him into the third room, where I saw a very comely mare, together with a colt and foal, sitting on their haunches, upon mats of straw, not unartfully made, and perfectly neat and clean.

---

9. Filled in with twigs and branches.
1. Hayrack for the feed.
2. Ponies.
3. Buttocks.

4. Long, narrow view (usually between rows of trees).
5. Wait.
6. Sorcery.

The mare, soon after my entrance, rose from her mat, and coming up close, after having nicely[7] observed my hands and face, gave me a most contemptuous look; then turning to the horse, I heard the word *Yahoo* often repeated betwixt them; the meaning of which word I could not then comprehend, although it were the first I had learned to pronounce; but I was soon better informed, to my everlasting mortification: for the horse beckoning to me with his head, and repeating the word *Hhuun, Hhuun,* as he did upon the road, which I understood was to attend him, led me out into a kind of court, where was another building at some distance from the house. Here we entered, and I saw three of those detestable creatures, which I first met after my landing, feeding upon roots, and the flesh of some animals, which I afterwards found to be that of asses and dogs, and now and then a cow dead by accident or disease.[8] They were all tied by the neck with strong withes,[9] fastened to a beam; they held their food between the claws of their forefeet, and tore it with their teeth.

The master horse ordered a sorrel nag, one of his servants, to untie the largest of these animals, and take him into the yard. The beast and I were brought close together, and our countenances diligently compared, both by master and servant, who thereupon repeated several times the word *Yahoo.* My horror and astonishment are not to be described, when I observed, in this abominable animal, a perfect human figure; the face of it indeed was flat and broad, the nose depressed, the lips large, and the mouth wide. But these differences are common to all savage nations, where the lineaments of the countenance are distorted by the natives suffering[1] their infants to lie groveling on the earth, or by carrying them on their backs, nuzzling with their face against the mother's shoulders. The forefeet of the Yahoo differed from my hands in nothing else but the length of the nails, the coarseness and brownness of the palms, and the hairiness on the backs. There was the same resemblance between our feet, with the same differences, which I knew very well, though the horses did not, because of my shoes and stockings; the same in every part of our bodies, except as to hairiness and color, which I have already described.

The great difficulty that seemed to stick with the two horses, was, to see the rest of my body so very different from that of a Yahoo, for which I was obliged to my clothes, whereof they had no conception: the sorrel nag offered me a root, which he held (after their manner, as we shall describe in its proper place) between his hoof and pastern; I took it in my hand, and having smelt it, returned it to him as civilly as I could. He brought out of the Yahoo's kennel a piece of ass's flesh, but it smelt so offensively that I turned from it with loathing; he then threw it to the Yahoo, by whom it was greedily devoured. He afterwards showed me a wisp of hay, and a fetlock full of oats; but I shook my head, to signify, that neither of these were food for me. And indeed, I now apprehended, that I must absolutely starve, if I did not get to some of my own species: for as to those filthy Yahoos, although there were few greater lovers of mankind, at that time, than myself; yet I confess I never saw any sensitive[2] being so detestable on all accounts; and the more I came near them, the more hateful they grew, while I stayed in that country. This the master horse observed by my behavior, and therefore sent the Yahoo back to his kennel. He then

---

7. Closely.
8. The Yahoos eat food listed in Leviticus (11.3, 27, 39–40) as unclean, suggesting that they exemplify the human condition distorted and debased by sin.

9. Leashes.
1. Allowing.
2. "Having sense or perception, but not reason" (Johnson's *Dictionary*).

put his forehoof to his mouth, at which I was much surprised, although he did it with ease, and with a motion that appeared perfectly natural, and made other signs to know what I would eat; but I could not return him such an answer as he was able to apprehend; and if he had understood me, I did not see how it was possible to contrive any way for finding myself nourishment. While we were thus engaged, I observed a cow passing by, whereupon I pointed to her, and expressed a desire to let me go and milk her. This had its effect; for he led me back into the house, and ordered a mare-servant to open a room, where a good store of milk lay in earthen and wooden vessels, after a very orderly and cleanly manner. She gave me a large bowl full, of which I drank very heartily, and found myself well refreshed.

About noon I saw coming towards the house a kind of vehicle drawn like a sledge by four Yahoos. There was in it an old steed, who seemed to be of quality; he alighted with his hind feet forward, having by accident got a hurt in his left forefoot. He came to dine with our horse, who received him with great civility. They dined in the best room, and had oats boiled in milk for the second course, which the old horse ate warm, but the rest cold. Their mangers were placed circular in the middle of the room, and divided into several partitions, round which they sat on their haunches upon bosses[3] of straw. In the middle was a large rack with angles answering to every partition of the manger. So that each horse and mare ate their own hay, and their own mash of oats and milk, with much decency and regularity. The behavior of the young colt and foal appeared very modest, and that of the master and mistress extremely cheerful and complaisant[4] to their guest. The grey ordered me to stand by him, and much discourse passed between him and his friend concerning me, as I found by the stranger's often looking on me, and the frequent repetition of the word Yahoo.

I happened to wear my gloves, which the master grey observing, seemed perplexed, discovering signs of wonder what I had done to my forefeet; he put his hoof three or four times to them, as if he would signify, that I should reduce them to their former shape, which I presently did, pulling off both my gloves, and putting them into my pocket. This occasioned farther talk, and I saw the company was pleased with my behavior, whereof I soon found the good effects. I was ordered to speak the few words I understood, and while they were at dinner, the master taught me the names for oats, milk, fire, water, and some others; which I could readily pronounce after him, having from my youth a great facility in learning languages.

When dinner was done, the master horse took me aside, and by signs and words made me understand the concern he was in, that I had nothing to eat. Oats in their tongue are called *hlunnh*. This word I pronounced two or three times; for although I had refused them at first, yet upon second thoughts, I considered that I could contrive to make of them a kind of bread, which might be sufficient with milk to keep me alive, till I could make my escape to some other country, and to creatures of my own species. The horse immediately ordered a white mare-servant of his family to bring me a good quantity of oats in a sort of wooden tray. These I heated before the fire as well as I could, and rubbed them till the husks came off, which I made a shift[5] to winnow from the grain; I ground and beat them between two stones, then took water, and made them into a paste or cake, which I toasted at the fire, and ate warm with milk. It was at first a very insipid diet, although common enough in many parts of Europe, but grew tolerable by time; and having been often reduced to hard fare in

3. Piles or seats.
4. Courteous.

5. Attempted.

my life, this was not the first experiment I had made how easily nature is satisfied.[6] And I cannot but observe, that I never had one hour's sickness, while I stayed in this island. 'Tis true, I sometimes made a shift to catch a rabbit, or bird, by springes[7] made of Yahoos' hairs, and I often gathered wholesome herbs, which I boiled, or ate as salads with my bread, and now and then, for a rarity, I made a little butter, and drank the whey. I was at first at a great loss for salt; but custom soon reconciled the want of it; and I am confident that the frequent use of salt among us is an effect of luxury, and was first introduced only as a provocative to drink; except where it is necessary for preserving of flesh in long voyages, or in places remote from great markets. For we observe no animal to be fond of it but man:[8] and as to myself, when I left this country, it was a great while before I could endure the taste of it in anything that I ate.

This is enough to say upon the subject of my diet, wherewith other travelers fill their books, as if the readers were personally concerned whether we fared[9] well or ill. However, it was necessary to mention this matter, lest the world should think it impossible that I could find sustenance for three years in such a country, and among such inhabitants.

When it grew towards evening, the master horse ordered a place for me to lodge in; it was but six yards from the house, and separated from the stable of the Yahoos. Here I got some straw, and covering myself with my own clothes, slept very sound. But I was in a short time better accommodated, as the reader shall know hereafter, when I come to treat more particularly about my way of living.

CHAPTER 3

The author studious to learn the language, the Houyhnhnm his master assists in teaching him. The language described. Several Houyhnhnms of quality come out of curiosity to see the author. He gives his master a short account of his voyage.

My principal endeavor was to learn the language, which my master (for so I shall henceforth call him) and his children, and every servant of his house were desirous to teach me. For they looked upon it as a prodigy that a brute animal should discover[1] such marks of a rational creature. I pointed to everything, and inquired the name of it, which I wrote down in my journal book when I was alone, and corrected my bad accent, by desiring those of the family to pronounce it often. In this employment, a sorrel nag, one of the under servants, was very ready to assist me.

In speaking, they pronounce through the nose and throat, and their language approaches nearest to the High Dutch or German, of any I know in Europe; but is much more graceful and significant.[2] The Emperor Charles V made almost the same observation, when he said, that if he were to speak to his horse, it should be in High Dutch.[3]

The curiosity and impatience of my master were so great, that he spent many hours of his leisure to instruct me. He was convinced (as he afterwards told me) that I must be a Yahoo, but my teachableness, civility, and cleanliness astonished him; which were qualities altogether so opposite to those animals. He was most perplexed

---

6. A commonplace idea in ancient satire; Swift may here be mocking it.
7. Snares.
8. This is, of course, untrue, but Gulliver's subsequent dislike of salt indicates his dislike of human society in general.

9. A pun on "fare," meaning both food and "to get along."
1. Display.
2. Expressive.
3. I.e., German; Charles V of Spain (1500–1551) was believed to have said that he would address his God in Spanish, his mistress in Italian, and his horse in German.

about my clothes, reasoning sometimes with himself, whether they were a part of my body; for I never pulled them off till the family were asleep, and got them on before they waked in the morning. My master was eager to learn from whence I came, how I acquired those appearances of reason, which I discovered in all my actions, and to know my story from my own mouth, which he hoped he should soon do by the great proficiency I made in learning and pronouncing their words and sentences. To help my memory, I formed all I learned into the English alphabet, and writ the words down with the translations. This last, after some time, I ventured to do in my master's presence. It cost me much trouble to explain to him what I was doing; for the inhabitants have not the least idea of books or literature.

In about ten weeks' time I was able to understand most of his questions, and in three months could give him some tolerable answers. He was extremely curious to know from what part of the country I came, and how I was taught to imitate a rational creature, because the Yahoos (whom he saw I exactly resembled in my head, hands, and face, that were only visible), with some appearance of cunning, and the strongest disposition to mischief, were observed to be the most unteachable of all brutes. I answered, that I came over the sea, from a far place, with many others of my own kind, in a great hollow vessel made of the bodies of trees. That my companions forced me to land on this coast, and then left me to shift for myself. It was with some difficulty, and by the help of many signs, that I brought him to understand me. He replied, that I must needs be mistaken, or that I *said the thing which was not.* (For they have no word in their language to express lying or falsehood.) He knew it was impossible[4] that there could be a country beyond the sea, or that a parcel of brutes could move a wooden vessel whither they pleased upon water. He was sure no Houyhnhnm alive could make such a vessel, or would trust Yahoos to manage it.

The word *Houyhnhnm,* in their tongue, signifies a *horse,* and in its etymology, the *Perfection of Nature.* I told my master, that I was at a loss for expression, but would improve as fast as I could; and hoped in a short time I should be able to tell him wonders: he was pleased to direct his own mare, his colt and foal, and the servants of the family to take all opportunities of instructing me, and every day for two or three hours, he was at the same pains himself: several horses and mares of quality in the neighborhood came often to our house upon the report spread of a wonderful Yahoo, that could speak like a Houyhnhnm, and seemed in his words and actions to discover some glimmerings of reason. These delighted to converse with me; they put many questions, and received such answers as I was able to return. By all which advantages, I made so great a progress, that in five months from my arrival, I understood whatever was spoke, and could express myself tolerably well.

The Houyhnhnms who came to visit my master, out of a design of seeing and talking with me, could hardly believe me to be a right[5] Yahoo, because my body had a different covering from others of my kind. They were astonished to observe me without the usual hair or skin, except on my head, face, and hands; but I discovered that secret to my master, upon an accident, which happened about a fortnight before.

I have already told the reader, that every night when the family were gone to bed, it was my custom to strip and cover myself with my clothes: it happened one morning early, that my master sent for me, by the sorrel nag, who was his valet; when

---

4. The Houyhnhnm thus shows himself to be so dependent on reason that he is dogmatic in his ignorance, unable (like rationalists in religion) to accept what he does not know by his own reasoning.
5. True.

he came, I was fast asleep, my clothes fallen off on one side, and my shirt above my waist. I awaked at the noise he made, and observed him to deliver his message in some disorder; after which he went to my master, and in a great fright gave him a very confused account of what he had seen: this I presently discovered; for going as soon as I was dressed, to pay my attendance upon his Honor, he asked me the meaning of what his servant had reported, that I was not the same thing when I slept as I appeared to be at other times; that his valet assured him, some part of me was white, some yellow, at least not so white, and some brown.

I had hitherto concealed the secret of my dress, in order to distinguish myself as much as possible, from that cursed race of Yahoos; but now I found it in vain to do so any longer. Besides, I considered that my clothes and shoes would soon wear out, which already were in a declining condition, and must be supplied by some contrivance from the hides of Yahoos or other brutes; whereby the whole secret would be known: I therefore told my master, that in the country from whence I came, those of my kind always covered their bodies with the hairs of certain animals prepared by art, as well for decency, as to avoid inclemencies of air both hot and cold; of which, as to my own person, I would give him immediate conviction, if he pleased to command me; only desiring his excuse, if I did not expose those parts that Nature taught us to conceal. He said my discourse was all very strange, but especially the last part; for he could not understand why Nature should teach us to conceal what Nature had given. That neither himself nor family were ashamed of any parts of their bodies; but however I might do as I pleased. Whereupon, I first unbuttoned my coat, and pulled it off. I did the same with my waistcoat;[6] I drew off my shoes, stockings, and breeches. I let my shirt down to my waist, and drew up the bottom, fastening it like a girdle about my middle to hide my nakedness.

My master observed the whole performance with great signs of curiosity and admiration. He took up all my clothes in his pastern, one piece after another, and examined them diligently; he then stroked my body very gently, and looked round me several times, after which he said, it was plain I must be a perfect Yahoo; but that I differed very much from the rest of my species, in the softness, and whiteness, and smoothness of my skin, my want of hair in several parts of my body, the shape and shortness of my claws behind and before, and my affectation of walking continually on my two hinder feet. He desired to see no more, and gave me leave to put on my clothes again, for I was shuddering with cold.

I expressed my uneasiness at his giving me so often the appellation of *Yahoo*, an odious animal, for which I had so utter an hatred and contempt; I begged he would forbear applying that word to me, and take the same order in his family, and among his friends whom he suffered to see me. I requested likewise, that the secret of my having a false covering to my body might be known to none but himself, at least as long as my present clothing should last; for, as to what the sorrel nag his valet had observed, his Honor might command him to conceal it.

All this my master very graciously consented to,[7] and thus the secret was kept till my clothes began to wear out, which I was forced to supply by several contrivances, that shall hereafter be mentioned. In the meantime, he desired I would go on with my utmost diligence to learn their language, because he was more astonished at my

---

6. Vest.

7. The Houyhnhnms may have no word for "lying," but they can hide the truth.

capacity for speech and reason, than at the figure of my body, whether it were covered or no; adding, that he waited with some impatience to hear the wonders which I promised to tell him.

From thenceforward he doubled the pains he had been at to instruct me; he brought me into all company, and made them treat me with civility, because, as he told them privately, this would put me into good humor, and make me more diverting.

Every day when I waited on him, beside the trouble he was at in teaching, he would ask me several questions concerning myself, which I answered as well as I could; and by those means he had already received some general ideas, though very imperfect. It would be tedious to relate the several steps, by which I advanced to a more regular conversation: but the first account I gave of myself in any order and length, was to this purpose:

That, I came from a very far country, as I already had attempted to tell him, with about fifty more of my own species; that we traveled upon the seas, in a great hollow vessel made of wood, and larger than his Honor's house. I described the ship to him in the best terms I could, and explained by the help of my handkerchief displayed, how it was driven forward by the wind. That upon a quarrel among us, I was set on shore on this coast, where I walked forward without knowing whither, till he delivered me from the persecution of those execrable Yahoos. He asked me, who made the ship, and how it was possible that the Houyhnhnms of my country would leave it to the management of brutes? My answer was, that I durst proceed no farther in my relation, unless he would give me his word and honor that he would not be offended, and then I would tell him the wonders I had so often promised. He agreed; and I went on by assuring him, that the ship was made by creatures like myself, who in all the countries I had traveled, as well as in my own, were the only governing, rational animals; and that upon my arrival hither, I was as much astonished to see the Houyhnhnms act like rational beings, as he or his friends could be in finding some marks of reason in a creature he was pleased to call a Yahoo, to which I owned my resemblance in every part, but could not account for their degenerate and brutal nature. I said farther, that if good fortune ever restored me to my native country, to relate my travels hither, as I resolved to do, everybody would believe that I *said the thing which was not;* that I invented the story out of my own head; and with all possible respect to himself, his family, and friends, and under his promise of not being offended, our countrymen would hardly think it probable, that a Houyhnhnm should be the presiding creature of a nation, and a Yahoo the brute.

CHAPTER 4

The Houyhnhnms' notion of truth and falsehood. The author's discourse disapproved by his master. The author gives a more particular account of himself, and the accidents of his voyage.

My master heard me with great appearances of uneasiness in his countenance, because *doubting* or *not believing,* are so little known in this country, that the inhabitants cannot tell how to behave themselves under such circumstances. And I remember in frequent discourses with my master concerning the nature of manhood,[8] in other parts of the world, having occasion to talk of *lying,* and *false representation,* it was with much difficulty that he comprehended what I meant, although he

8. Human nature.

had otherwise a most acute judgment. For he argued thus: that the use of speech was to make us understand one another, and to receive information of facts; now if any one *said the thing which was not*, these ends were defeated; because I cannot properly be said to understand him, and I am so far from receiving information, that he leaves me worse than in ignorance, for I am led to believe a thing *black* when it is *white*, and *short* when it is *long*. And these were all the notions he had concerning that faculty of *lying*, so perfectly well understood, and so universally practiced among human creatures.

To return from this digression; when I asserted that the Yahoos were the only governing animal in my country, which my master said was altogether past his conception, he desired to know, whether we had Houyhnhnms among us, and what was their employment: I told him, we had great numbers, that in summer they grazed in the fields, and in winter were kept in houses, with hay and oats, where Yahoo servants were employed to rub their skins smooth, comb their manes, pick their feet, serve them with food, and make their beds. I understand you well, said my master; it is now very plain, from all you have spoken, that whatever share of reason the Yahoos pretend to, the Houyhnhnms are your masters;[9] I heartily wish our Yahoos would be so tractable. I begged his Honor would please to excuse me from proceeding any farther, because I was very certain that the account he expected from me would be highly displeasing. But he insisted in commanding me to let him know the best and the worst: I told him, he should be obeyed. I owned, that the Houyhnhnms among us, whom we called *horses*, were the most generous and comely animal we had, that they excelled in strength and swiftness; and when they belonged to persons of quality, employed in traveling, racing, or drawing chariots, they were treated with much kindness and care, till they fell into diseases, or became foundered in the feet;[1] but then they were sold, and used to all kind of drudgery till they died; after which their skins were stripped and sold for what they were worth, and their bodies left to be devoured by dogs and birds of prey.[2] But the common race of horses had not so good fortune, being kept by farmers and carriers and other mean people, who put them to greater labor, and fed them worse. I described as well as I could, our way of riding, the shape and use of a bridle, a saddle, a spur, and a whip, of harness and wheels. I added, that we fastened plates of a certain hard substance called *iron* at the bottom of their feet, to preserve their hoofs from being broken by the stony ways on which we often traveled.

My master, after some expressions of great indignation, wondered how we dared to venture upon a Houyhnhnm's back, for he was sure that the weakest servant in his house would be able to shake off the strongest Yahoo, or by lying down, and rolling upon his back, squeeze the brute to death. I answered, that our horses were trained up from three or four years old to the several uses we intended them for; that if any of them proved intolerably vicious, they were employed for carriages; that they were severely beaten while they were young, for any mischievous tricks; that the males, designed for the common use of riding or draft, were generally *castrated* about two years after their birth, to take down their spirits, and make them more tame and gentle; that they were indeed sensible of rewards and punishments; but his Honor would please to consider, that they had not the least tincture of reason any more than the Yahoos in this country.

---

9. Possibly a satire on the English love of horses.
1. Until their feet give in from overwork.
2. Swift mockingly paraphrases the *Iliad* 1.4–6: "The souls of mighty Chiefs untimely slain; / Whose limbs unburied on the naked shore, / Devouring dogs and hungry vultures tore" (Pope's translation).

It put me to the pains of many circumlocutions to give my master a right idea of what I spoke; for their language doth not abound in variety of words, because their wants and passions are fewer than among us. But it is impossible to express his noble resentment at our savage treatment of the Houyhnhnm race, particularly after I had explained the manner and use of *castrating* horses among us, to hinder them from propagating their kind, and to render them more servile. He said, if it were possible there could be any country where Yahoos alone were endued with reason, they certainly must be the governing animal, because reason will in time always prevail against brutal strength. But, considering the frame of our bodies, and especially of mine, he thought no creature of equal bulk was so ill-contrived for employing that reason in the common offices of life; whereupon he desired to know whether those among whom I lived, resembled me or the Yahoos of his country. I assured him, that I was as well shaped as most of my age, but the younger and the females were much more soft and tender, and the skins of the latter generally as white as milk. He said, I differed indeed from other Yahoos, being much more cleanly, and not altogether so deformed, but in point of real advantage, he thought I differed for the worse. That my nails were of no use either to my fore or hinder feet; as to my forefeet, he could not properly call them by that name, for he never observed me to walk upon them; that they were too soft to bear the ground; that I generally went with them uncovered, neither was the covering I sometimes wore on them of the same shape, or so strong as that on my feet behind. That I could not walk with any security, for if either of my hinder feet slipped, I must inevitably fall. He then began to find fault with other parts of my body, the flatness of my face, the prominence of my nose, mine eyes placed directly in front, so that I could not look on either side without turning my head, that I was not able to feed myself, without lifting one of my forefeet to my mouth, and therefore Nature had placed those joints to answer that necessity. He knew not what could be the use of those several clefts and divisions in my feet behind; that these were too soft to bear the hardness and sharpness of stones without a covering made from the skin of some other brute; that my whole body wanted a fence against heat and cold, which I was forced to put on and off every day with tediousness and trouble. And lastly, that he observed every animal in this country naturally to abhor the Yahoos, whom the weaker avoided, and the stronger drove from them. So that supposing us to have the gift of reason, he could not see how it were possible to cure that natural antipathy which every creature discovered[3] against us; nor consequently, how we could tame and render them serviceable. However, he would (as he said) debate that matter no farther, because he was more desirous to know my own story, the country where I was born, and the several actions and events of my life before I came hither.

I assured him, how extremely desirous I was that he should be satisfied in every point; but I doubted much, whether it would be possible for me to explain myself on several subjects whereof his Honor could have no conception, because I saw nothing in his country to which I could resemble[4] them. That, however, I would do my best, and strive to express myself by similitudes, humbly desiring his assistance when I wanted proper words; which he was pleased to promise me.

I said, my birth was of honest parents, in an island called England, which was remote from this country, as many days' journey as the strongest of his Honor's servants could travel in the annual course of the sun. That I was bred a surgeon, whose

3. Displayed.   4. Compare.

trade it is to cure wounds and hurts in the body, got by accident or violence; that my country was governed by a female man, whom we called a *Queen*. That I left it to get riches,[5] whereby I might maintain myself and family when I should return. That in my last voyage, I was commander of the ship, and had about fifty Yahoos under me, many of which died at sea, and I was forced to supply[6] them by others picked out from several nations. That our ship was twice in danger of being sunk; the first time by a great storm, and the second, by striking against a rock. Here my master interposed, by asking me, how I could persuade strangers out of different countries to venture with me, after the losses I had sustained, and the hazards I had run. I said, they were fellows of desperate fortunes, forced to fly from the places of their birth, on account of their poverty or their crimes. Some were undone by lawsuits; others spent all they had in drinking, whoring, and gaming; others fled for treason; many for murder, theft, poisoning, robbery, perjury, forgery, coining false money, for committing rapes or sodomy, for flying from their colors,[7] or deserting to the enemy, and most of them had broken prison; none of these durst return to their native countries for fear of being hanged, or of starving in a jail; and therefore were under a necessity of seeking a livelihood in other places.

During this discourse, my master was pleased often to interrupt me. I had made use of many circumlocutions in describing to him the nature of the several crimes, for which most of our crew had been forced to fly their country. This labor took up several days' conversation before he was able to comprehend me. He was wholly at a loss to know what could be the use or necessity of practicing those vices. To clear up which I endeavored to give him some ideas of the desire of power and riches, of the terrible effects of lust, intemperance, malice, and envy. All this I was forced to define and describe by putting of cases, and making suppositions. After which, like one whose imagination was struck with something never seen or heard of before, he would lift up his eyes with amazement and indignation. Power, government, war, law, punishment, and a thousand other things had no terms, wherein that language could express them, which made the difficulty almost insuperable to give my master any conception of what I meant. But being of an excellent understanding, much improved by contemplation and converse, he at last arrived at a competent knowledge of what human nature in our parts of the world is capable to perform, and desired I would give him some particular account of that land, which we call Europe, but especially, of my own country.

from CHAPTER 5

The author at his master's commands informs him of the state of England. The causes of war among the princes of Europe. The author begins to explain the English Constitution.

The reader may please to observe, that the following extract of many conversations I had with my master, contains a summary of the most material points, which were discoursed at several times for above two years; his Honor often desiring fuller satisfaction[8] as I farther improved in the Houyhnhnm tongue. I laid before him, as well as I could, the whole state of Europe; I discoursed of trade and manufactures, of arts and sciences; and the answers I gave to all the questions he made, as they arose upon sev-

---

5. Gulliver originally stated that he undertook his second and third voyages out of a desire to travel: he now reads all human motivation in the worst possible light.

6. Replace.

7. Deserting their regiment in the army.

8. Better explanation.

eral subjects, were a fund of conversation not to be exhausted. But I shall here only set down the substance of what passed between us concerning my own country, reducing it into order as well as I can, without any regard to time or other circumstances, while I strictly adhere to truth. My only concern is, that I shall hardly be able to do justice to my master's arguments and expressions, which must needs suffer by my want of capacity, as well as by a translation into our barbarous English.[9]

In obedience therefore to his Honor's commands, I related to him the Revolution under the Prince of Orange,[1] the long war with France[2] entered into by the said Prince, and renewed by his successor the present Queen, wherein the greatest powers of Christendom were engaged, and which still continued: I computed, at his request, that about a million of Yahoos might have been killed in the whole progress of it, and perhaps a hundred or more cities taken, and five times as many ships burnt or sunk.

* * * And, being no stranger to the art of war, I gave him a description of cannons, culverins,[3] muskets, carabines,[4] pistols, bullets, powder, swords, bayonets, battles, sieges, retreats, attacks, undermines, countermines,[5] bombardments, seafights; ships sunk with a thousand men, twenty thousand killed on each side; dying groans, limbs flying in the air, smoke, noise, confusion, trampling to death under horses' feet; flight, pursuit, victory; fields strewed with carcasses left for food to dogs, and wolves, and birds of prey; plundering, stripping, ravishing, burning, and destroying. And to set forth the valor of my own dear countrymen, I assured him, that I had seen them blow up a hundred enemies at once in a siege, and as many in a ship, and beheld the dead bodies drop down in pieces from the clouds, to the great diversion of all the spectators.

I was going on to more particulars, when my master commanded me silence. He said, whoever understood the nature of Yahoos might easily believe it possible for so vile an animal to be capable of every action I had named, if their strength and cunning equaled their malice. But as my discourse had increased his abhorrence of the whole species, so he found it gave him a disturbance in his mind, to which he was wholly a stranger before. He thought his ears being used to such abominable words, might by degrees admit them with less detestation. That although he hated the Yahoos of this country, yet he no more blamed them for their odious qualities, than he did a *gnnayh* (a bird of prey) for its cruelty, or a sharp stone for cutting his hoof. But when a creature pretending to reason could be capable of such enormities, he dreaded lest[6] the corruption of that faculty might be worse than brutality itself. He seemed therefore confident, that instead of reason, we were only possessed of some quality fitted to increase our natural vices; as the reflection from a troubled stream returns the image of an ill-shapen body, not only *larger*, but more *distorted*.

He added, that he had heard too much upon the subject of war, both in this, and some former discourses. There was another point which a little perplexed him at present. I had said, that some of our crew left their country on account of being ruined by *law*; that I had already explained the meaning of the word; but he was at a loss how it should come to pass, that the *law* which was intended for *every* man's preservation,

9. Presumably "barbarous," because English both lacks appropriate words to express Houyhnhnm concepts and has concepts (e.g., of lust, malice, envy) for which the other language has no words.
1. The Glorious Revolution of 1688 by which William of Orange, and his wife, Mary Stuart, ascended to the English throne in 1689.
2. The War of the League of Augsburg (1689–1697) and the War of the Spanish Succession (1701–1713), which Swift (as a good Tory) opposed.
3. Large cannons.
4. Short firearms.
5. Digging under fortification walls, and counter-digging by those inside the fort to stop the besiegers.
6. Worried that.

should be any man's ruin. Therefore he desired to be farther satisfied what I meant by *law*, and the dispensers thereof, according to the present practice in my own country; because he thought Nature and reason were sufficient guides for a reasonable animal, as we pretended to be, in showing us what we ought to do, and what to avoid.

I assured his Honor, that law was a science wherein I had not much conversed,[7] further than by employing advocates in vain, upon some injustices that had been done me; however, I would give him all the satisfaction I was able.

I said there was a society of men among us, bred up from their youth in the art of proving by words multiplied for the purpose, that white is black, and black is white, according as they are paid.[8] To this society all the rest of the people are slaves. For example, if my neighbor hath a mind to my cow, he hires a lawyer to prove that he ought to have my cow from me. I must then hire another to defend my right, it being against all rules of law that any man should be allowed to speak for himself.[9] Now in this case, I who am the true owner lie under two great disadvantages. First, my lawyer, being practiced almost from his cradle in defending falsehood, is quite out of his element when he would be an advocate for justice, which as an office unnatural, he always attempts with great awkwardness, if not with ill will. The second disadvantage is, that my lawyer must proceed with great caution, or else he will be reprimanded by the judges, and abhorred by his brethren, as one who would lessen the practice[1] of the law. And therefore I have but two methods to preserve my cow. The first is to gain over my adversary's lawyer with a double fee, who will then betray his client by insinuating that he hath justice on his side. The second way is for my lawyer to make my cause appear as unjust as he can, by allowing the cow to belong to my adversary; and this if it be skillfully done will certainly bespeak[2] the favor of the Bench.

Now, your Honor is to know that these judges are persons appointed to decide all controversies of property, as well as for the trial of criminals, and picked out from the most dexterous lawyers who are grown old or lazy, and having been biased all their lives against truth and equity, lie under such a fatal necessity of favoring fraud, perjury, and oppression, that I have known several of them refuse a large bribe from the side where justice lay, rather than injure the *Faculty*[3] by doing anything unbecoming their nature or their office.

It is a maxim among these lawyers, that whatever hath been done before, may legally be done again; and therefore they take special care to record all the decisions formerly made against common justice and the general reason of mankind. These, under the name of *precedents*, they produce as authorities to justify the most iniquitous opinions; and the judges never fail of directing accordingly.

In pleading, they studiously avoid entering into the *merits* of the cause; but are loud, violent, and tedious in dwelling upon all *circumstances* which are not to the purpose. For instance, in the case already mentioned; they never desire to know what claim or title my adversary hath to my cow, but whether the said cow were red or

---

7. Had not had much instruction.
8. Swift's satirical treatment of lawyers probably stems from his dislike of Lord Chief Justice Whitehead, who tried to force juries to give verdicts against Swift and the printer of two of his political pamphlets.
9. One of Swift's many references to Thomas More's *Utopia* (1516) in this discussion of the ideals of human and Houyhnhnm society. *Utopia* suggests that it is "better for each man to plead for his own cause, and tell the judge the same story he'd otherwise tell his lawyer." Other important sources for *Gulliver* include Lucian's *True*

History (mid-second century A.D.); Cyrano de Bergerac's *Histoire comique des états et empires de la lune* (1656); William Temple's essay *Of Heroick Virtue* (in *Miscellanea*, pt. 2, 1692); William Dampier's *New Voyage Round the World* (1697); and Lionel Wafer's *A New Voyage and Description of the Isthmus of America* (1699), which includes descriptions of monkeys Swift may have used for the Yahoos.
1. Both profession, and morally questionable dealing.
2. Gain.
3. Legal profession.

black, her horns long or short, whether the field I graze her in be round or square, whether she were milked at home or abroad, what diseases she is subject to, and the like; after which they consult *precedents*, adjourn the cause from time to time, and in ten, twenty, or thirty years come to an issue.

It is likewise to be observed that this society hath a peculiar cant[4] and jargon of their own, that no other mortal can understand, and wherein all their laws are written, which they take special care to multiply; whereby they have wholly confounded the very essence of truth and falsehood, of right and wrong; so that it will take thirty years to decide whether the field, left me by my ancestors for six generations, belong to me or to a stranger three hundred miles off.

In the trial of persons accused for crimes against the state the method is much more short and commendable: the judge first sends to sound the disposition of those in power, after which he can easily hang or save the criminal, strictly preserving all the forms of law.

Here my master, interposing, said it was a pity, that creatures endowed with such prodigious abilities of mind as these lawyers, by the description I gave of them, must certainly be, were not rather encouraged to be instructors of others in wisdom and knowledge. In answer to which, I assured his Honor, that in all points out of their own trade they were usually the most ignorant and stupid generation among us, the most despicable in common conversation, avowed enemies to all knowledge and learning, and equally disposed to pervert the general reason of mankind in every other subject of discourse, as in that of their own profession.

from CHAPTER 8

The author relateth several particulars of the Yahoos. The great virtues of the Houyhnhnms. The education and exercise of their youth. Their general Assembly.

* * * Having already lived three years in this country, the reader I suppose will expect that I should, like other travelers, give him some account of the manners and customs of its inhabitants, which it was indeed my principal study to learn.

As these noble Houyhnhnms are endowed by Nature with a general disposition to all virtues, and have no conceptions or ideas of what is evil in a rational creature, so their grand maxim is, to cultivate *Reason*, and to be wholly governed by it. Neither is *Reason* among them a point problematical as with us, where men can argue with plausibility on both sides of a question, but strikes you with immediate conviction, as it must needs do where it is not mingled, obscured, or discolored by passion and interest.[5] I remember it was with extreme difficulty that I could bring my master to understand the meaning of the word opinion, or how a point could be disputable, because *Reason* taught us to affirm or deny only where we are certain, and beyond our knowledge we cannot do either.[6] So that controversies, wranglings, disputes, and positiveness[7] in false or dubious propositions are evils unknown among the Houyhnhnms. In the like manner, when I used to explain to him our several systems of *natural philosophy*, he would laugh that a creature pretending to *Reason* should value itself upon the knowledge of other people's conjectures, and in things where that knowledge, if it were certain, could

---

4. Both insincere and specialist language.
5. Prejudice based on interest in personal benefit. Both Descartes (*Discourse on Method*) and Locke (*Essay Concerning Human Understanding*) wrote of the intuitive

nature of some knowledge.
6. Gulliver's master has clearly expressed "opinion" (i.e., prejudice) himself, however.
7. Assertiveness.

be of no use. Wherein he agreed entirely with the sentiments of Socrates, as Plato delivers them;[8] which I mention as the highest honor I can do that prince of philosophers. I have often since reflected what destruction such a doctrine would make in the libraries of Europe, and how many paths to fame would be then shut up in the learned world.

Friendship and benevolence are the two principal virtues among the Houyhnhnms, and these not confined to particular objects,[9] but universal to the whole race. For a stranger from the remotest part is equally treated with the nearest neighbor, and wherever he goes, looks upon himself as at home. They preserve *decency* and *civility* in the highest degrees, but are altogether ignorant of *ceremony*.[1] They have no fondness for their colts or foals, but the care they take in educating them proceedeth entirely from the dictates of *Reason*. And I observed my master to show the same affection to his neighbor's issue that he had for his own.[2] They will have it that *Nature* teaches them to love the whole species, and it is *Reason* only that maketh a distinction of persons, where there is a superior degree of virtue.

When the matron Houyhnhnms have produced one of each sex, they no longer accompany with[3] their consorts, except they lose one of their issue by some casualty, which very seldom happens: but in such a case they meet again. Or when the like accident befalls a person,[4] whose wife is past bearing, some other couple bestow him one of their own colts, and then go together a second time, till the mother be pregnant. This caution is necessary to prevent the country from being overburdened with numbers.[5] But the race of inferior Houyhnhnms bred up to be servants is not so strictly limited upon this article; these are allowed to produce three of each sex, to be domestics in the noble families.

In their marriages they are exactly careful to choose such colors as will not make any disagreeable mixture in the breed.[6] *Strength* is chiefly valued in the male, and *comeliness* in the female, not upon the account of *love*, but to preserve the race from degenerating; for where a female happens to excel in *strength*, a consort is chosen with regard to *comeliness*. Courtship, love, presents, jointures,[7] settlements, have no place in their thoughts, or terms whereby to express them in their language. The young couple meet and are joined, merely because it is the determination of their parents and friends: it is what they see done every day, and they look upon it as one of the necessary actions in a reasonable being. But the violation of marriage, or any other unchastity, was never heard of, and the married pair pass their lives with the same friendship, and mutual benevolence that they bear to others of the same species who come in their way; without jealousy, fondness, quarreling, or discontent.

In educating the youth of both sexes, their method is admirable, and highly deserveth our imitation. These are not suffered to taste a grain of *oats*, except upon certain days, till eighteen years old; nor *milk*, but very rarely; and in summer they graze two hours in the morning, and as many in the evening, which their parents likewise observe, but the servants are not allowed above half that time, and a great

8. I.e., that ethics (human nature) is worth studying, while the physical world is not, as we can never have certain knowledge of it: "Socrates: I am a friend of learning—the trees and the countryside won't teach me anything, but the people in the city do" *Phaedrus* (230d3–5).
9. To other, particular Houyhnhnms.
1. As are the Utopians.
2. As do men in Plato's *Republic* (461d).
3. Have sex with.

4. A male Houyhnhnm.
5. The Utopians are under no such restriction, knowing (as the Houyhnhnms do not) of other lands to which they can send their excess population.
6. In Plato's *Republic* (458d–461e), eugenic principles also control mating.
7. Marriage settlements for wives, should they survive their husbands.

part of their grass is brought home, which they eat at the most convenient hours, when they can be best spared from work.

Temperance, industry, exercise, and *cleanliness*, are the lessons equally enjoined to the young ones of both sexes, and my master thought it monstrous in us to give the females a different kind of education from the males, except in some articles of domestic management;[8] whereby as he truly observed, one half of our natives were good for nothing but bringing children into the world, and to trust the care of their children to such useless animals, he said, was yet a greater instance of brutality.

But the Houyhnhnms train up their youth to strength, speed, and hardiness, by exercising them in running races up and down steep hills, or over hard stony grounds, and when they are all in a sweat, they are ordered to leap over head and ears into a pond or a river. Four times a year the youth of certain districts meet to show their proficiency in running, and leaping, and other feats of strength or agility, where the victor is rewarded with a song made in his or her praise. On this festival the servants drive a herd of Yahoos into the field, laden with hay, and oats, and milk for a repast to the Houyhnhnms; after which, these brutes are immediately driven back again, for fear of being noisome to the assembly.

Every fourth year, at the *vernal equinox*, there is a Representative Council of the whole nation, which meets in a plain about twenty miles from our house, and continueth about five or six days. Here they inquire into the state and condition of the several districts, whether they abound or be deficient in hay or oats, or cows or Yahoos? And wherever there is any want (which is but seldom) it is immediately supplied by unanimous consent and contribution. Here likewise the regulation of children is settled: as for instance, if a Houyhnhnm hath two males, he changeth one of them with another who hath two females: and when a child hath been lost by any casualty, where the mother is past breeding, it is determined what family in the district shall breed another to supply the loss.

CHAPTER 9

A grand debate at the general Assembly of the Houyhnhnms, and how it was determined. The learning of the Houyhnhnms. Their buildings. Their manner of burials. The defectiveness of their language.

One of these grand Assemblies was held in my time, about three months before my departure, whither my master went as the Representative of our district. In this Council was resumed their old debate, and indeed, the only debate that ever happened in their country; whereof my master after his return gave me a very particular account.

The question to be debated, was, whether the Yahoos should be exterminated from the face of the earth. One of the *members* for the affirmative offered several arguments of great strength and weight, alleging, that as the Yahoos were the most filthy, noisome, and deformed animal which Nature ever produced, so they were the most restive and indocible,[9] mischievous, and malicious: they would privately suck the teats of the Houyhnhnms' cows, kill and devour their cats, trample down their oats and grass, if they were not continually watched, and commit a thousand other extravagancies. He took notice of a general tradition, that Yahoos had not been

8. In both Plato's *Republic* (451e6–7) and More's *Utopia*, the sexes receive the same education; Swift also began (but never completed) an essay entitled *Of the Education*

of Ladies (c. 1728).
9. Unteachable.

always in their country, but, that many ages ago, two of these brutes appeared together upon a mountain,[1] whether produced by the heat of the sun upon corrupted mud and slime, or from the ooze and froth of the sea, was never known.[2] That these Yahoos engendered, and their brood in a short time grew so numerous as to overrun and infest the whole nation. That the Houyhnhnms, to get rid of this evil, made a general hunting, and at last enclosed the whole herd; and destroying the elder, every Houyhnhnm kept two young ones in a kennel, and brought them to such a degree of tameness, as an animal so savage by nature can be capable of acquiring; using them for draft and carriage. That there seemed to be much truth in this tradition, and that those creatures could not be *ylnhniamshy* (or *aborigines* of the land) because of the violent hatred the Houyhnhnms, as well as all other animals, bore them; which although their evil disposition sufficiently deserved, could never have arrived at so high a degree, if they had been *aborigines*, or else they would have long since been rooted out. That the inhabitants taking a fancy to use the service of the Yahoos, had very imprudently neglected to cultivate the breed of *asses*, which were a comely animal, easily kept, more tame and orderly, without any offensive smell, strong enough for labor, although they yield to the other in agility of body; and if their braying be no agreeable sound, it is far preferable to the horrible howlings of the Yahoos.[3]

Several others declared their sentiments to the same purpose, when my master proposed an expedient to the assembly, whereof he had indeed borrowed the hint from me. He approved of the tradition, mentioned by the Honorable Member who spoke before, and affirmed, that the two Yahoos said to be first seen among them had been driven thither over the sea; that coming to land, and being forsaken by their companions, they retired to the mountains, and degenerating by degrees, became in process of time, much more savage than those of their own species in the country from whence these two originals came. The reason of his assertion was, that he had now in his possession a certain wonderful[4] Yahoo (meaning myself), which most of them had heard of, and many of them had seen. He then related to them, how he first found me: that my body was all covered with an artificial composure of the skins and hairs of other animals; that I spoke in a language of my own, and had thoroughly learned theirs; that I had related to him the accidents which brought me thither; that when he saw me without my covering, I was an exact Yahoo in every part, only of a whiter color, less hairy, and with shorter claws. He added, how I had endeavored to persuade him, that in my own and other countries the Yahoos acted as the governing, rational animal, and held the Houyhnhnms in servitude; that he observed in me all the qualities of a Yahoo, only a little more civilized by some tincture of reason, which however was in a degree as far inferior to the Houyhnhnm race, as the Yahoos of their country were to me;[5] that, among other things, I mentioned a custom we had of *castrating* Houyhnhnms when they were young, in order to render them tame; that the operation was easy and safe; that it was no shame to

---

1. Probably Milton's "steep savage Hill," the garden of Eden (*Paradise Lost*, 4.172).
2. Humans are supposed to be of divine origin, but the Yahoos represent such a degraded form of humanity that they (like, it was believed, insects on the Nile's banks) were formed from the action of the sun on mud.
3. The commonplace comparison of humans to asses was

one Swift had previously used in *A Tale of a Tub* (1704) and *The Battle of the Books* (1704).
4. Amazing, unusual.
5. Gulliver falls between the Houyhnhnms and the Yahoos in reason, as he did between the Lilliputians and the Brobdingnagians in size.

learn wisdom from brutes, as industry is taught by the ant, and building by the swallow. (For so I translate the word *lyhannh*, although it be a much larger fowl.) That this invention might be practiced upon the younger Yahoos here, which, besides rendering them tractable and fitter for use, would in an age put an end to the whole species without destroying life. That, in the meantime the Houyhnhnms should be exhorted to cultivate the breed of asses, which, as they are in all respects more valuable brutes, so they have this advantage, to be fit for service at five years old, which the others are not till twelve.

This was all my master thought fit to tell me at that time, of what passed in the grand Council. But he was pleased to conceal[6] one particular, which related personally to myself, whereof I soon felt the unhappy effect, as the reader will know in its proper place, and from whence I date all the succeeding misfortunes of my life. * * *

CHAPTER 10

The author's economy[7] and happy life among the Houyhnhnms. His great improvement in virtue, by conversing with them. Their conversations. The author hath notice given him by his master that he must depart from the country. He falls into a swoon for grief, but submits. He contrives and finishes a canoe, by the help of a fellow servant, and puts to sea at a venture.[8]

I had settled my little economy to my own heart's content. My master had ordered a room to be made for me after their manner, about six yards from the house, the sides and floors of which I plastered with clay, and covered with rush mats of my own contriving; I had beaten hemp, which there grows wild, and made of it a sort of ticking;[9] this I filled with the feathers of several birds I had taken with springes made of Yahoos' hairs, and were excellent food. I had worked[1] two chairs with my knife, the sorrel nag helping me in the grosser[2] and more laborious part. When my clothes were worn to rags, I made myself others with the skins of rabbits, and of a certain beautiful animal about the same size, called *nnuhnoh*, the skin of which is covered with a fine down. Of these I likewise made very tolerable stockings. I soled my shoes with wood which I cut from a tree, and fitted to the upper leather, and when this was worn out, I supplied it with the skins of Yahoos dried in the sun. I often got honey out of hollow trees, which I mingled with water,[3] or ate it with my bread. No man could more verify the truth of these two maxims, *That nature is very easily satisfied*; and, *That necessity is the mother of invention*. I enjoyed perfect health of body and tranquillity of mind; I did not feel the treachery or inconstancy of a friend, nor the injuries of a secret or open enemy. I had no occasion of bribing, flattering, or pimping, to procure the favor of any great man or of his minion. I wanted no fence[4] against fraud or oppression; here was neither physician to destroy my body, nor lawyer to ruin my fortune; no informer to watch my words and actions, or forge accusations against me for hire; here were no jibers, censurers, backbiters, pickpockets,

6. Another indication that the Houyhnhnms are not completely honest or candid.
7. Method of living.
8. Without further planning.
9. Sturdy material used for making mattress covering.

1. Made.
2. Heavier, larger.
3. Honey-sweetened water was a Utopian drink.
4. Defense.

highwaymen, housebreakers, attorneys, bawds, buffoons, gamesters, politicians, wits, splenetics, tedious talkers, controvertists, ravishers, murderers, robbers, virtuosos;[5] no leaders or followers of party and faction; no encouragers to vice, by seducement or examples; no dungeon, axes, gibbets, whipping posts, or pillories; no cheating shopkeepers or mechanics;[6] no pride, vanity, or affectation; no fops, bullies, drunkards, strolling whores, or poxes;[7] no ranting, lewd, expensive wives; no stupid, proud pendants; no importunate, overbearing, quarrelsome, noisy, roaring, empty, conceited, swearing companions; no scoundrels, raised from the dust upon the merit of their vices, or nobility thrown into it on account of their virtues; no lords, fiddlers, judges, or dancing masters.[8]

I had the favor of being admitted to[9] several Houyhnhnms, who came to visit or dine with my master; where his Honor graciously suffered me to wait in the room, and listen to their discourse. Both he and his company would often descend to ask me questions, and receive my answers. I had also sometimes the honor of attending my master in his visits to others. I never presumed to speak, except in answer to a question, and then I did it with inward regret, because it was a loss of so much time for improving myself; but I was infinitely delighted with the station of a humble auditor in such conversations, where nothing passed but what was useful, expressed in the fewest and most significant words; where (as I have already said) the greatest *decency* was observed, without the least degree of ceremony; where no person spoke without being pleased himself, and pleasing his companions; where there was no interruption, tediousness, heat,[1] or difference of sentiments. They have a notion, that when people are met together, a short silence doth much improve conversation: this I found to be true, for during those little intermissions of talk, new ideas would arise in their minds, which very much enlivened the discourse. Their subjects are generally on friendship and benevolence, or order and economy, sometimes upon the visible operations of Nature, or ancient traditions, upon the bounds and limits of virtue, upon the unerring rules of reason, or upon some determinations to be taken at the next great Assembly, and often upon the various excellencies of *poetry*. I may add without vanity, that my presence often gave them sufficient matter for discourse, because it afforded my master an occasion of letting his friends into the history of me and my country, upon which they were all pleased to descant in a manner not very advantageous to humankind; and for that reason I shall not repeat what they said: only I may be allowed to observe, that his Honor, to my great admiration, appeared to understand the nature of Yahoos much better than myself. He went through all our vices and follies, and discovered many which I had never mentioned to him, by only supposing what qualities a Yahoo of their country, with a small proportion of reason, might be capable of exerting; and concluded, with too much probability, how vile as well as miserable such a creature must be.

I freely confess, that all the little knowledge I have of any value, was acquired by the lectures I received from my master, and from hearing the discourses of him

---

5. One knowledgeable or interested in apparently trivial "scientific" pursuits.
6. Laborers.
7. Venereal diseases.
8. That necessary tutor for the socially aspiring, the danc-ing master (usually French), was a particular figure of fun; he usually accompanied himself on the fiddle.
9. Allowed to meet.
1. Heat of argument.

and his friends; to which I should be prouder to listen, than to dictate to the greatest and wisest assembly in Europe. I admired the strength, comeliness, and speed of the inhabitants; and such a constellation of virtues in such amiable persons produced in me the highest veneration. At first, indeed, I did not feel that natural awe which the Yahoos and all other animals bear towards them, but it grew upon me by degrees, much sooner than I imagined, and was mingled with a respectful love and gratitude, that they would condescend to distinguish me from the rest of my species.

When I thought of my family, my friends, my countrymen, or human race in general, I considered them as they really were, Yahoos in shape and disposition, perhaps a little more civilized, and qualified with the gift of speech, but making no other use of reason, than to improve and multiply those vices, whereof their brethren in this country had only the share that Nature allotted them. When I happened to behold the reflection of my own form in a lake or a fountain, I turned away my face in horror and detestation of myself,[2] and could better endure the sight of a common Yahoo, than of my own person. By conversing with the Houyhnhnms, and looking upon them with delight, I fell to imitate their gait and gesture, which is now grown into a habit, and my friends often tell me in a blunt way, that I *trot like a horse*; which, however, I take for a great compliment; neither shall I disown, that in speaking I am apt to fall into the voice and manner of the Houyhnhnms, and hear myself ridiculed on that account without the least mortification.

In the midst of all this happiness, when I looked upon myself to be fully settled for life, my master sent for me one morning a little earlier than his usual hour. I observed by his countenance that he was in some perplexity, and at a loss how to begin what he had to speak. After a short silence, he told me, he did not know how I would take what he was going to say; that in the last general Assembly, when the affair of the Yahoos was entered upon, the representatives had taken offense at his keeping a Yahoo (meaning myself) in his family more like a Houyhnhnm, than a brute animal. That he was known frequently to converse with me, as if he could receive some advantage or pleasure in my company; that such a practice was not agreeable to reason or Nature, or a thing ever heard of before among them. The Assembly did therefore *exhort* him, either to employ me like the rest of my species, or command me to swim back to the place from whence I came. That the first of these expedients was utterly rejected by all the Houyhnhnms who had ever seen me at his house or their own, for they alleged, that because I had some rudiments of reason, added to the natural pravity[3] of those animals, it was to be feared, I might be able to seduce them into the woody and mountainous parts of the country, and bring them in troops by night to destroy the Houyhnhnms' cattle, as being naturally of the ravenous[4] kind, and averse from labor.

My master added, that he was daily pressed by the Houyhnhnms of the neighborhood to have the Assembly's *exhortation* executed, which he could not put off much longer. He doubted[5] it would be impossible for me to swim to another country, and therefore wished I would contrive some sort of vehicle resembling those I had described to him, that might carry me on the sea, in which work I should have the

---

2. A mocking reversal both of a common pattern in pastoral love poetry and of the Greek myth of Narcissus.
3. Depravity.

4. Rapacious, predatory, or greedy.
5. Feared.

assistance of his own servants, as well as those of his neighbors. He concluded, that for his own part he could have been content to keep me in his service as long as I lived, because he found I had cured myself of some bad habits and dispositions, by endeavoring, as far as my inferior nature was capable, to imitate the Houyhnhnms.

I should here observe to the reader, that a decree of the general Assembly in this country is expressed by the word *hnhloayn*, which signifies an *exhortation*, as near as I can render it, for they have no conception how a rational creature can be *compelled*, but only advised, or *exhorted*, because no person can disobey reason, without giving up his claim to be a rational creature.

I was struck with the utmost grief and despair at my master's discourse, and being unable to support the agonies I was under, I fell into a swoon at his feet; when I came to myself, he told me, that he concluded I had been dead. (For these people are subject to no such imbecilities of nature.) I answered, in a faint voice, that death would have been too great an happiness; that although I could not blame the Assembly's *exhortation*, or the urgency[6] of his friends, yet in my weak and corrupt judgment, I thought it might consist[7] with reason to have been less rigorous. That I could not swim a league, and probably the nearest land to theirs might be distant above a hundred; that many materials, necessary for making a small vessel to carry me off, were wholly wanting in this country, which, however, I would attempt in obedience and gratitude to his Honor, although I concluded the thing to be impossible, and therefore looked on myself as already devoted to destruction. That the certain prospect of an unnatural death was the least of my evils: for, supposing I should escape with life by some strange adventure, how could I think with temper[8] of passing my days among Yahoos, and relapsing into my old corruptions, for want of examples to lead and keep me within the paths of virtue? That I knew too well upon what solid reasons all the determinations of the wise Houyhnhnms were founded, not to be shaken by arguments of mine, a miserable Yahoo; and therefore after presenting him with my humble thanks for the offer of his servants' assistance in making a vessel, and desiring a reasonable time for so difficult a work, I told him I would endeavor to preserve a wretched being; and, if ever I returned to England, was not without hopes of being useful to my own species, by celebrating the praises of the renowned Houyhnhnms, and proposing their virtues to the imitation of mankind.

My master in a few words made me a very gracious reply, allowed me the space of two *months* to finish my boat; and ordered the sorrel nag, my fellow servant (for so at this distance I may presume to call him) to follow my instructions, because I told my master, that his help would be sufficient, and I knew he had a tenderness for me.

In his company my first business was to go to that part of the coast, where my rebellious crew had ordered me to be set on shore. I got upon a height, and looking on every side into the sea, fancied I saw a small island, towards the northeast: I took out my pocket glass, and could then clearly distinguish it about five leagues off, as I computed; but it appeared to the sorrel nag to be only a blue cloud: for, as he had no conception of any country beside his own, so he could not be as expert in distinguishing remote objects at sea, as we who so much converse[9] in that element.

After I had discovered this island, I considered no farther; but resolved it should, if possible, be the first place of my banishment, leaving the consequence to Fortune.

---

6. Urging.
7. Be consistent.

8. Calmness.
9. Are familiar with.

I returned home, and consulting with the sorrel nag, we went into a copse at some distance, where I with my knife, and he with a sharp flint fastened very artificially, after their manner, to a wooden handle, cut down several oak wattles about the thickness of a walking staff, and some larger pieces. But I shall not trouble the reader with a particular description of my own mechanics; let it suffice to say, that in six weeks' time, with the help of the sorrel nag, who performed the parts that required most labor, I finished a sort of Indian canoe, but much larger, covering it with the skins of Yahoos well stitched together, with hempen threads of my own making. My sail was likewise composed of the skins of the same animal; but I made use of the youngest I could get, the older being too tough and thick, and I likewise provided myself with four paddles. I laid in a stock of boiled flesh, of rabbits and fowls, and took with me two vessels, one filled with milk, and the other with water.

I tried my canoe in a large pond near my master's house, and then corrected in it what was amiss; stopping all the chinks with Yahoos' tallow, till I found it staunch,[1] and able to bear me and my freight. And when it was as complete as I could possibly make it, I had it drawn on a carriage very gently by Yahoos, to the seaside, under the conduct of the sorrel nag, and another servant.

When all was ready, and the day came for my departure, I took leave of my master and lady, and the whole family, mine eyes flowing with tears, and my heart quite sunk with grief. But his Honor, out of curiosity, and perhaps (if I may speak it without vanity) partly out of kindness, was determined to see me in my canoe, and got several of his neighboring friends to accompany him. I was forced to wait above an hour for the tide, and then observing the wind very fortunately bearing towards the island, to which I intended to steer my course, I took a second leave of my master, but as I was going to prostrate myself to kiss his hoof, he did me the honor to raise it gently to my mouth. I am not ignorant how much I have been censured for mentioning this last particular. For my detractors are pleased to think it improbable, that so illustrious a person should descend to give so great a mark of distinction to a creature so inferior as I. Neither have I forgot, how apt some travelers are to boast of extraordinary favors they have received.[2] But if these censurers were better acquainted with the noble and courteous disposition of the Houyhnhnms, they would soon change their opinion.

I paid my respects to the rest of the Houyhnhnms in his Honor's company; then getting into my canoe, I pushed off from shore.

CHAPTER 11

The author's dangerous voyage. He arrives at New Holland, hoping to settle there. Is wounded with an arrow by one of the natives. Is seized and carried by force into a Portuguese ship. The great civilities of the captain. The author arrives at England.

I began this desperate voyage on February 15, 1715, at 9 o'clock in the morning. The wind was very favorable; however, I made use at first only of my paddles, but considering I should soon be weary, and that the wind might probably chop about,[3] I ventured to set up my little sail; and thus, with the help of the tide, I went at the rate of a league and a half an hour, as near as I could guess. My master and his friends continued[4] on

1. Watertight.
2. Swift heightens the absurdity of Gulliver's action, and draws attention to his later misanthropy.

3. Change direction.
4. Stayed.

the shore, till I was almost out of sight; and I often heard the sorrel nag (who always loved me) crying out, *Hnuy illa nyha maiah Yahoo*, Take care of thyself, gentle Yahoo.

My design was, if possible, to discover some small island uninhabited, yet sufficient by my labor to furnish me with the necessaries of life, which I would have thought a greater happiness than to be first minister in the politest court of Europe; so horrible was the idea I conceived of returning to live in the society and under the government of Yahoos. For in such a solitude as I desired, I could at least enjoy my own thoughts, and reflect with delight on the virtues of those inimitable Houyhnhnms, without any opportunity of degenerating into the vices and corruptions of my own species.

The reader may remember what I related when my crew conspired against me, and confined me to my cabin. How I continued there several weeks, without knowing what course we took, and when I was put ashore in the longboat, how the sailors told me with oaths, whether true or false, that they knew not in what part of the world we were. However, I did then believe us to be about ten degrees southward of the Cape of Good Hope, or about 45 degrees southern latitude, as I gathered from some general words I overheard among them, being I supposed to the southeast in their intended voyage to Madagascar. And although this were but little better than conjecture, yet I resolved to steer my course eastward, hoping to reach the southwest coast of New Holland, and perhaps some such island as I desired, lying westward of it. The wind was full west, and by six in the evening I computed I had gone eastward at least eighteen leagues, when I spied a very small island about half a league off, which I soon reached. It was nothing but a rock, with one creek, naturally arched by the force of tempests. Here I put in my canoe, and climbing a part of the rock, I could plainly discover[5] land to the east, extending from south to north. I lay all night in my canoe, and repeating my voyage early in the morning, I arrived in seven hours to the southwest point of New Holland.[6] This confirmed me in the opinion I have long entertained, that the maps and charts place this country at least three degrees more to the east than it really is;[7] which thought I communicated many years ago to my worthy friend Mr. Herman Moll, and gave him my reasons for it, although he hath rather chosen to follow other authors.[8]

I saw no inhabitants in the place where I landed, and being unarmed, I was afraid of venturing far into the country. I found some shellfish on the shore, and ate them raw, not daring to kindle a fire, for fear of being discovered by the natives. I continued three days feeding on oysters and limpets,[9] to save my own provisions, and I fortunately found a brook of excellent water, which gave me great relief.

On the fourth day, venturing out early a little too far, I saw twenty or thirty natives upon a height, not above five hundred yards from me. They were stark naked, men, women, and children, round a fire, as I could discover by the smoke. One of them spied me, and gave notice to the rest; five of them advanced towards me, leaving the women and children at the fire. I made what haste I could to the shore, and getting into my canoe, shoved off: the savages observing me retreat, ran after me; and before I could get far enough into the sea, discharged an arrow, which wounded me deeply on the inside of my left knee (I shall carry the mark to my grave). I appre-

5. Discern.
6. New Holland was the name the explorer Abel Tasman originally gave to the western coast of Australia. Gulliver seems to place the land of the Houyhnhnms west of southwestern Australia, in which case the distance he covers to reach New Holland is improbable (1,500 to 2,000 nautical miles in 16 hours). It is possible, however, that Gulliver is meant to have landed on Tasmania, thus putting the Houyhnhnms a short distance west of this island.
7. Dampier claimed that he had found New Holland further west than indicated in Tasman's charts.
8. This geographer's *New and Correct Map of the Whole World* (1719) was probably the basis for Swift's geography in *Gulliver's Travels*.
9. Small mollusks that attach themselves to rocks.

hended the arrow might be poisoned, and paddling out of the reach of their darts (being a calm day) I made a shift to suck the wound, and dress it as well as I could.

I was at a loss what to do, for I durst not return to the same landing place, but stood[1] to the north, and was forced to paddle; for the wind though very gentle was against me, blowing northwest. As I was looking about for a secure landing place, I saw a sail to the north-north-east, which appearing every minute more visible, I was in some doubt, whether I should wait for them or no; but at last my detestation of the Yahoo race prevailed, and turning my canoe, I sailed and paddled together to the south, and got into the same creek from whence I set out in the morning, choosing rather to trust myself among these *barbarians*, than live with European Yahoos. I drew up my canoe as close as I could to the shore, and hid myself behind a stone by the little brook, which, as I have already said, was excellent water.

The ship came within a half a league of this creek, and sent out her longboat with vessels to take in fresh water (for the place it seems was very well known) but I did not observe it till the boat was almost on shore, and it was too late to seek another hiding place. The seamen at their landing observed my canoe, and rummaging it all over, easily conjectured that the owner could not be far off. Four of them well armed searched every cranny and lurking hole, till at last they found me flat on my face behind the stone. They gazed a while in admiration[2] at my strange uncouth dress, my coat made of skins, my wooden-soled shoes, and my furred stockings; from whence, however, they concluded I was not a native of the place, who all go naked. One of the seamen in Portuguese bid me rise, and asked who I was. I understood that language very well, and getting upon my feet, said, I was a poor Yahoo, banished from the Houyhnhnms, and desired they would please to let me depart. They admired to hear me answer them in their own tongue, and saw by my complexion I must be a European; but were at a loss to know what I meant by Yahoos and Houyhnhnms, and at the same time fell a laughing at my strange tone in speaking, which resembled the neighing of a horse. I trembled all the while betwixt fear and hatred: I again desired leave to depart, and was gently moving to my canoe; but they laid hold on me, desiring to know, what country I was of? whence I came? with many other questions. I told them, I was born in England, from whence I came about five years ago, and then their country and ours were at peace. I therefore hoped they would not treat me as an enemy, since I meant them no harm, but was a poor Yahoo, seeking some desolate place where to pass the remainder of his unfortunate life.

When they began to talk, I thought I never heard or saw anything so unnatural; for it appeared to me as monstrous as if a dog or a cow should speak in England, or a Yahoo in Houyhnhnmland. The honest Portuguese were equally amazed at my strange dress, and the odd manner of delivering my words, which however they understood very well. They spoke to me with great humanity, and said they were sure their captain would carry me *gratis* to Lisbon, from whence I might return to my own country; that two of the seamen would go back to the ship, to inform the captain of what they had seen, and receive his orders; in the meantime, unless I would give my solemn oath not to fly,[3] they would secure me by force. I thought it best to comply with their proposal. They were very curious to know my story, but I gave them very little satisfaction; and they all conjectured, that my misfortunes had impaired my reason. In two hours the boat, which went loaden with vessels of water,

1. Steered.
2. Wonder, amazement.

3. Attempt to escape.

returned with the captain's commands to fetch me on board. I fell on my knees to preserve my liberty; but all was in vain, and the men having tied me with cords, heaved me into the boat, from whence I was taken into the ship, and from thence into the captain's cabin.

His name was Pedro de Mendez; he was a very courteous and generous person; he entreated me to give some account of myself, and desired to know what I would eat or drink; said, I should be used as well as himself, and spoke so many obliging things, that I wondered to find such civilities from a Yahoo. However, I remained silent and sullen; I was ready to faint at the very smell of him and his men. At last I desired something to eat out of my own canoe; but he ordered me a chicken and some excellent wine, and then directed that I should be put to bed in a very clean cabin. I would not undress myself, but lay on the bed clothes, and in half an hour stole out, when I thought the crew was at dinner, and getting to the side of the ship was going to leap into the sea, and swim for my life, rather than continue among Yahoos. But one of the seamen prevented me, and having informed the captain, I was chained to my cabin.

After dinner Don Pedro came to me, and desired to know my reason for so desperate an attempt: assured me he only meant to do me all the service he was able, and spoke so very movingly, that at last I descended[4] to treat him like an animal which had some little portion of reason. I gave him a very short relation of my voyage, of the conspiracy against me by my own men, of the country where they set me on shore, and of my three years' residence there. All which he looked upon as if it were a dream or a vision; whereat I took great offense; for I had quite forgot the faculty of lying, so peculiar to Yahoos in all countries where they preside, and consequently the disposition of suspecting truth in others of their own species. I asked him, whether it were the custom of his country to *say the thing that was not?* I assured him I had almost forgot what he meant by falsehood, and if I had lived a thousand years in Houyhnhnmland, I should never have heard a lie from the meanest servant; that I was altogether indifferent whether he believed me or no; but however, in return for his favors, I would give so much allowance to the corruption of his nature, as to answer any objection he would please to make, and then he might easily discover the truth.

The captain, a wise man, after many endeavors to catch me tripping in some part of my story, at last began to have a better opinion of my veracity.[5] But he added, that since I professed so inviolable an attachment to truth, I must give him my word of honor to bear him company in this voyage without attempting anything against my life, or else he would continue[6] me a prisoner till we arrived at Lisbon. I gave him the promise he required; but at the same time protested that I would suffer the greatest hardships rather than return to live among Yahoos.

Our voyage passed without any considerable accident.[7] In gratitude to the captain I sometimes sat with him at his earnest request, and strove to conceal my antipathy against human kind, although it often broke out, which he suffered to pass without observation. But the greatest part of the day, I confined myself to my cabin, to avoid seeing any of the crew. The captain had often entreated me to strip myself of

---

4. Condescended.
5. In the first edition, the sentence continues: "and the rather, because he confessed, he met with a Dutch Skipper, who pretended to have landed with five others of his crew upon a certain island or continent south of New Holland, where they went for fresh water, and observed a horse driving before him several animals exactly resembling those I had described under the name of Yahoos, with some other particulars, which the captain said he had forgot, because he then concluded them all to be lies." In 1735 Swift's Dublin publisher, George Faulkener, omitted these lines, probably because they contradicted Gulliver's later statement that no other European had visited this land.
6. Keep.
7. Incident.

my savage dress, and offered to lend me the best suit of clothes he had. This I would not be prevailed on to accept, abhorring to cover myself with anything that had been on the back of a Yahoo. I only desired he would lend me two clean shirts, which having been washed since he wore them, I believed would not so much defile me. These I changed every second day, and washed them myself.

We arrived at Lisbon, Nov. 5, 1715. At our landing the captain forced me to cover myself with his cloak, to prevent the rabble from crowding about me. I was conveyed to his own house, and at my earnest request, he led me up to the highest room backwards.[8] I conjured[9] him to conceal from all persons what I had told him of the Houyhnhnms, because the least hint of such a story would not only draw numbers of people to see me, but probably put me in danger of being imprisoned, or burnt by the Inquisition.[1] The captain persuaded me to accept a suit of clothes newly made, but I would not suffer the tailor to take my measure; however, Don Pedro being almost of my size, they fitted me well enough. He accoutered[2] me with other necessaries all new, which I aired for twenty-four hours before I would use them.

The captain had no wife, nor above three servants, none of which were suffered to attend at meals, and his whole deportment was so obliging, added to very good *human* understanding, that I really began to tolerate his company. He gained so far upon me, that I ventured to look out of the back window. By degrees I was brought into another room, from whence I peeped into the street, but drew my head back in a fright. In a week's time he seduced me down to the door. I found my terror gradually lessened, but my hatred and contempt seemed to increase. I was at last bold enough to walk the street in his company, but kept my nose well stopped with rue,[3] or sometimes with tobacco.

In ten days Don Pedro, to whom I had given some account of my domestic affairs, put it upon me as a point of honor and conscience, that I ought to return to my native country, and live at home with my wife and children. He told me, there was an English ship in the port just ready to sail, and he would furnish me with all things necessary. It would be tedious to repeat his arguments, and my contradictions. He said, it was altogether impossible to find such a solitary island as I had desired to live in; but I might command in my own house, and pass my time in a manner as recluse as I pleased.

I complied at last, finding I could not do better. I left Lisbon the 24th day of November, in an English merchantman, but who was the master I never inquired. Don Pedro accompanied me to the ship, and lent me twenty pounds. He took kind leave of me, and embraced me at parting, which I bore as well as I could. During this last voyage I had no commerce[4] with the master or any of his men, but pretending I was sick kept close in my cabin. On the fifth of December, 1715, we cast anchor in the Downs[5] about nine in the morning, and at three in the afternoon I got safe to my house at Redriff.

My wife and family received me with great surprise and joy, because they concluded me certainly dead; but I must freely confess the sight of them filled me only with hatred, disgust, and contempt, and the more by reflecting on the near alliance I

---

8. At the back of the house.
9. Appealed earnestly to.
1. Either because the Houyhnhnm hierarchy contradicted Genesis, in which man has dominion over the earth, or because Gulliver had been associating with diabolical powers, who could make humans appear to be horses (as

Gulliver himself had first believed).
2. Attired.
3. Strong-smelling shrub, used for medicinal purposes.
4. Interaction.
5. The sea off the North Downs in East Kent.

had to them. For, although since my unfortunate exile from the Houyhnhnm country, I had compelled myself to tolerate the sight of Yahoos, and to converse with Don Pedro de Mendez, yet my memory and imaginations were perpetually filled with the virtues and ideas of those exalted Houyhnhnms. And when I began to consider, that by copulating with one of the Yahoo species, I had become a parent of more, it struck me with the utmost shame, confusion, and horror.

As soon as I entered the house, my wife took me in her arms, and kissed me, at which, having not been used to the touch of that odious animal for so many years, I fell in a swoon for almost an hour. At the time I am writing it is five years since my last return to England: during the first year I could not endure my wife or children in my presence, the very smell of them was intolerable, much less could I suffer them to eat in the same room. To this hour they dare not presume to touch my bread, or drink out of the same cup, neither was I ever able to let one of them take me by the hand.[6] The first money I laid out was to buy two young stone-horses,[7] which I keep in a good stable, and next to them the groom is my greatest favorite; for I feel my spirits revived by the smell he contracts in the stable. My horses understand me tolerably well; I converse with them at least four hours every day. They are strangers to bridle or saddle, they live in great amity with me, and friendship to each other.

CHAPTER 12

The author's veracity. His design in publishing this work. His censure of those travelers who swerve from the truth. The author clears himself from any sinister ends in writing. An objection answered. The method of planting Colonies. His native country commended. The right of the Crown to those countries described by the author is justified. The difficulty of conquering them. The author takes his last leave of the reader, proposeth his manner of living for the future, gives good advice, and concludeth.

Thus, gentle reader,[8] I have given thee a faithful history of my travels for sixteen years, and above seven months, wherein I have not been so studious of ornament as of truth. I could perhaps like others have astonished thee with strange improbable tales; but I rather chose to relate plain matter of fact in the simplest manner and style, because my principal design was to inform, and not to amuse thee.

It is easy for us who travel into remote countries, which are seldom visited by Englishmen or other Europeans, to form descriptions of wonderful animals both at sea and land. Whereas a traveler's chief aim should be to make men wiser and better, and to improve their minds by the bad as well as good example of what they deliver concerning foreign places.[9]

I could heartily wish a law were enacted, that every traveler, before he were permitted to publish his voyages, should be obliged to make oath before the Lord High Chancellor that all he intended to print was absolutely true to the best of his knowledge; for then the world would no longer be deceived as it usually is, while some writers, to make their works pass the better upon the public, impose the grossest falsities on the unwary reader. I have perused several books of travels with great delight in my younger days; but having since gone over most parts of the globe, and been able to

---

6. Gulliver's unwillingness to share his bread or cup with his wife or children emphasizes his unchristian behavior.
7. Stallions.
8. Highly ironic, since the "gentle" readers must be Yahoos.
9. More's *Utopia* also argues that accounts of distant travels should provide useful lessons rather than fabulous tales.

contradict many fabulous accounts from my own observation, it hath given me a great disgust against this part of reading, and some indignation to see the credulity of mankind so impudently abused. Therefore since my acquaintance were pleased to think my poor endeavors might not be unacceptable to my country, I imposed on myself as a maxim, never to be swerved from, that I would *strictly adhere to truth*; neither indeed can I be ever under the least temptation to vary from it, while I retain in my mind the lectures and example of my noble master, and the other illustrious Houyhnhnms, of whom I had so long the honor to be an humble hearer.

>   —*Nec si miserum Fortuna Sinonem*
>   *Finxit, vanum etiam mendacemque improba finget.*[1]

I know very well how little reputation is to be got by writings which require neither genius nor learning, nor indeed any other talent, except a good memory or an exact journal. I know likewise, that writers of travels, like dictionary-makers, are sunk into oblivion by the weight and bulk of those who come last, and therefore lie uppermost.[2] And it is highly probable, that such travelers who shall hereafter visit the countries described in this work of mine, may, by detecting my errors (if there be any), and adding many new discoveries of their own, jostle me out of vogue, and stand in my place, making the world forget that ever I was an author. This indeed would be too great a mortification if I wrote for fame; but, as my sole intention was the PUBLIC GOOD,[3] I cannot be altogether disappointed. For who can read of the virtues I have mentioned in the glorious Houyhnhnms, without being ashamed of his own vices, when he considers himself as the reasoning, governing animal of his country? I shall say nothing of those remote nations where Yahoos preside, amongst which the least corrupted are the Brobdingnagians, whose wise maxims in morality and government it would be our happiness to observe. But I forbear descanting further, and rather leave the judicious reader to his own remarks and applications.

I am not a little pleased that this work of mine can possibly meet with no[4] censurers: for what objections can be made against a writer who relates only plain facts that happened in such distant countries, where we have not the least interest with respect either to trade or negotiations? I have carefully avoided every fault with which common writers of travels are often too justly charged. Besides, I meddle not the least with any *party*, but write without passion, prejudice, or ill-will against any man or number of men whatsoever. I write for the noblest end, to inform and instruct mankind, over whom I may, without breach of modesty, pretend to some superiority from the advantages I received by conversing so long among the most accomplished Houyhnhnms. I write without any view towards profit or praise. I never suffer a word to pass that may look like reflection,[5] or possibly give the least offense even to those who are most ready to take it. So that I hope I may with justice pronounce myself an author perfectly blameless, against whom the tribe of answerers, considerers, observers, reflecters, detecters, remarkers, will never be able to find matter for exercising their talents.[6]

---

1. "Nor, if cruel Fortune has made Sinon miserable, shall he also make him false and deceitful" (Virgil, *Aeneid* 2. 79–80). Swift cleverly employs the words that the Greek Sinon, the most famous liar in antiquity, used in the fraudulent tale he told to fool the Trojans into accepting *his* (wooden) horse.
2. The most current dictionary is the one most frequently used.
3. The English buccaneer and navigator William Dampi-

er professes a similar aim in the dedication to his *New Voyage Round the World* (1697).
4. Cannot possibly encounter any.
5. Criticism.
6. At this time it was common for historical and fictional accounts to be "applied" to contemporary situations or persons; by having Gulliver deny at such length that he is doing this, Swift draws attention to the possibility of making such connections.

I confess, it was whispered to me, that I was bound in duty as a subject of England, to have given in a memorial to a Secretary of State, at my first coming over; because, whatever lands are discovered by a subject belong to the Crown. But I doubt whether our conquests in the countries I treat of, would be as easy as those of Ferdinando Cortez over the naked Americans.[7] The Lilliputians, I think, are hardly worth the charge of a fleet and army to reduce them, and I question whether it might be prudent or safe to attempt the Brobdingnagians. Or whether an English army would be much at their ease with the Flying Island over their heads.[8] The Houyhnhnms, indeed, appear not to be so well prepared for war, a science to which they are perfect strangers, and especially against missive weapons.[9] However, supposing myself to be a minister of State, I could never give my advice for invading them. Their prudence, unanimity, unacquaintedness with fear, and their love of their country would amply supply all defects in the military art. Imagine twenty thousand of them breaking into the midst of an European army, confounding the ranks, overturning the carriages, battering the warriors' faces into mummy,[1] by terrible yerks[2] from their hinder hoofs. For they would well deserve the character given to Augustus; *Recalcitrat undique tutus*.[3] But instead of proposals for conquering that magnanimous nation, I rather wish they were in a capacity or disposition to send a sufficient number of their inhabitants for civilizing Europe, by teaching us the first principles of honor, justice, truth, temperance, public spirit, fortitude, chastity, friendship, benevolence, and fidelity. The *names* of all which virtues are still retained among us in most languages, and are to be met with in modern as well as ancient authors; which I am able to assert from my own small reading.

But I had another reason which made me less forward[4] to enlarge his Majesty's dominions by my discoveries. To say the truth, I had conceived a few scruples with relation to the distributive justice[5] of princes upon those occasions. For instance, a crew of pirates[6] are driven by a storm they know not whither, at length a boy discovers land from the topmast, they go on shore to rob and plunder; they see a harmless people, are entertained with kindness, they give the country a new name, they take formal possession of it for the king, they set up a rotten plank or a stone for a memorial, they murder two or three dozen of the natives, bring away a couple more by force for a sample, return home, and get their pardon. Here commences a new dominion acquired with a title by *divine right*. Ships are sent with the first opportunity, the natives driven out or destroyed, their princes tortured to discover their gold;[7] a free license given to all acts of inhumanity and lust, the earth reeking with the blood of its inhabitants; and this execrable crew of butchers employed in so pious an expedition, is a *modern colony* sent to convert and civilize an idolatrous and barbarous people.

---

7. In the 1520s, Cortés and 400 soldiers rapidly conquered the Aztec empire in Mexico.
8. These sentences refer to Gulliver's other travels: in Lilliput he encountered a miniature people; in Brobdingnag he met with giants; and in Laputa he encountered the Flying Island (able to force inhabitants below to submit either through starving them by blocking out the sun or by crushing them).
9. Anything thrown or shot through the air.
1. Pulp.
2. Kicks.
3. "He kicks back, well protected on every side" (Horace, *Satires* 2.i.20). While Gulliver refers admiringly to the horse's ability to defend itself, Swift recalls the context

for Horace's decision to use satire (rather than praise) when writing about Augustus: according to Horace, Augustus would kick out like a horse if he sensed servile flattery, so flattery was pointless. Gulliver's lavish praise of the Houyhnhnms backfires on him, not because the Houyhnhnms disliked it, but because his uncritical identification with them leaves him unable to cope with human society.
4. Eager.
5. Fairness with regard to the rights of the native people.
6. Referring to the first Spanish colonizers of America.
7. Montezuma was tortured by Cortés, and the Incan emperor Atahuallpa by Pizarro (1533).

But this description, I confess, doth by no means affect the British nation, who may be an example to the whole world for their wisdom, care, and justice in planting colonies;[8] their liberal endowments for the advancement of religion and learning; their choice of devout and able pastors to propagate Christianity; their caution in stocking their provinces with people of sober lives and conversations from this the mother kingdom;[9] their strict regard to the distribution of justice, in supplying the civil administration through all their colonies with officers of the greatest abilities, utter strangers to corruption; and to crown all, by sending the most vigilant and virtuous governors, who have no other views than the happiness of the people over whom they preside, and the honor of the King their master.

But, as those countries which I have described do not appear to have any desire of being conquered, and enslaved, murdered, or driven out by colonies, nor abound either in gold, silver, sugar, or tobacco; I did humbly conceive they were by no means proper objects of our zeal, our valor, or our interest. However, if those whom it more concerns, think fit to be of another opinion, I am ready to depose, when I shall be lawfully called, that no European did ever visit those countries before me. I mean, if the inhabitants ought to be believed.[1]

But as to the formality of taking possession in my Sovereign's name, it never came once into my thoughts; and if it had, yet as my affairs then stood, I should perhaps in point of prudence and self-preservation, have put it off to a better opportunity.

Having thus answered the *only* objection that can ever be raised against me as a traveler, I here take a final leave of my courteous readers, and return to enjoy my own speculations in my little garden at Redriff, to apply those excellent lessons of virtue which I learned among the Houyhnhnms, to instruct the Yahoos of my own family as far as I shall find them docible[2] animals, to behold my figure often in a glass, and thus if possible habituate myself by time to tolerate the sight of a human creature, to lament the brutality of Houyhnhnms in my own country, but always treat their persons with respect, for the sake of my noble master, his family, his friends, and the whole Houyhnhnm race, whom these of ours[3] have the honor to resemble in all their lineaments, however their intellectuals[4] came to degenerate.

I began last week to permit my wife to sit at dinner with me, at the farthest end of a long table, and to answer (but with the utmost brevity) the few questions I ask her. Yet the smell of a Yahoo continuing very offensive, I always keep my nose well stopped with rue, lavender, or tobacco leaves. And although it be hard for a man late in life to remove old habits, I am not altogether out of hopes in some time to suffer a neighbor Yahoo in my company, without the apprehensions I am yet under of his teeth or his claws.

My reconcilement to the Yahoo-kind in general might not be so difficult if they would be content with those vices and follies only, which Nature hath entitled them to. I am not in the least provoked at the sight of a lawyer, a pickpocket, a colonel, a fool, a lord, a gamester, a politician, a whoremonger, a physician, an evidence,[5] a suborner,[6] an attorney, a traitor, or the like: this is all according to the due course of things; but when I behold a lump of deformity and diseases both in body and mind,

8. Intended ironically.
9. Felons were commonly given a sentence of mandatory "transportation" to Britain's colonies.
1. The first edition continued: "unless a dispute may arise about the two Yahoos, said to have been seen many Ages ago on a mountain in Houyhnhnm-land, from whence the opinion is, that the race of those brutes hath descended; and these, for anything I know, may have been English, which indeed I was apt to suspect from the linea-

ments of their posterity's countenances, although very much defaced. But how far that will go to make out a title, I leave to the learned in colony law." Faulkener omitted this passage in the 1735 edition.
2. Teachable.
3. I.e., horses.
4. Intellects.
5. A (false) witness.
6. One who bribes another to commit a misdeed.

smitten with *pride*, it immediately breaks all the measures of my patience; neither shall I be ever able to comprehend how such an animal and such a vice could tally together. The wise and virtuous Houyhnhnms, who abound in all excellencies that can adorn a rational creature, have no name for this vice in their language, which hath no terms to express anything that is evil, except those whereby they describe the detestable qualities of their Yahoos, among which they were not able to distinguish this of pride, for want of thoroughly understanding human nature, as it showeth itself in other countries, where that animal presides. But I, who had more experience, could plainly observe some rudiments of it among the wild Yahoos.

But the Houyhnhnms, who live under the government of Reason, are no more proud of the good qualities they possess, than I should be for not wanting a leg or an arm, which no man in his wits would boast of, although he must be miserable without them. I dwell the longer upon this subject from the desire I have to make the society of an English Yahoo by any means not insupportable, and therefore I here entreat those who have any tincture of this absurd vice, that they will not presume to appear in my sight.[7]

FINIS

c. 1721–1725   1726

A Modest Proposal

In a letter written to Alexander Pope in August 1729, Swift described the condition of Ireland: "There have been three terrible years' dearth of corn [i.e., wheat], and every place strewn with beggars, but dearths are common in better climates, and our evils lie much deeper. Imagine a nation the two-thirds of whose revenues are spent out of it, and who are not permitted [by Britain] to trade with the other third, and where the pride of the women will not suffer them to wear their own manufactures even where they excel what come from abroad." Two months later, Swift published what is today his most famous political essay: *A Modest Proposal*. Swift had previously written a dozen or more tracts to help free Ireland from its desperate social, economic, and political plight. In *A Modest Proposal*, however, Swift wielded two favorite weapons from his armory of satirical techniques—irony and parody—with devastating effect. In creating a persona who combines a mixture of calculating rationality and misplaced compassion but does not comprehend the enormity of his plan, Swift aims his satire not only at the political arithmeticians (forerunners of today's social engineers and economic planners) and the exploitative and predatory absentee landlords living in England but at the Irish people as well. Believing Ireland to be its own worst enemy, Swift delineates a program of commercial cannibalism that institutionalizes the country's own self-destructive tendencies. Preserving a nation through the consumption of its children is self-defeating, however demographically logical, because it undermines the understanding of humanity upon which civil society depends. Swift thus highlights the futility of financial improvement unaccompanied by social and moral reform.

A Modest Proposal

FOR PREVENTING THE CHILDREN OF POOR PEOPLE IN IRELAND FROM BEING A BURDEN TO THEIR PARENTS OR COUNTRY, AND FOR MAKING THEM BENEFICIAL TO THE PUBLIC

It is a melancholy object to those who walk through this great town,[1] or travel in the country, when they see the streets, the roads, and cabin doors crowded with beggars of the female sex, followed by three, four, or six children, *all in rags,* and importuning every passenger[2] for an alms. These mothers, instead of being able to work for their

---

7. Gulliver thus falls into pride, the very vice he rejects.   2. Passerby.
1. Dublin.

honest livelihood, are forced to employ all their time in strolling,[3] to beg sustenance for their helpless infants, who, as they grow up, either turn thieves for want of work, or leave their dear native country to fight for the Pretender in Spain,[4] or sell themselves to the Barbados.[5]

I think it is agreed by all parties that this prodigious number of children, in the arms, or on the backs, or at the heels of their mothers, and frequently of their fathers, is in the present deplorable state of the kingdom a very great additional grievance; and therefore whoever could find out a fair, cheap, and easy method of making these children sound, useful members of the commonwealth would deserve so well of the public, as to have his statue set up for a preserver of the nation.

But my intention is very far from being confined to provide only for the children of professed beggars; it is of a much greater extent, and shall take in the whole number of infants at a certain age who are born of parents in effect as little able to support them as those who demand our charity in the streets.

As to my own part, having turned my thoughts for many years upon this important subject, and maturely weighed the several schemes of other projectors,[6] I have always found them grossly mistaken in their computation. It is true a child just dropped from its dam may be supported by her milk for a solar year with little other nourishment, at most not above the value of two shillings, which the mother may certainly get, or the value in scraps, by her lawful occupation of begging, and it is exactly at one year old that I propose to provide for them, in such a manner as instead of being a charge upon their parents or the parish, or wanting food and raiment for the rest of their lives, they shall, on the contrary, contribute to the feeding and partly to the clothing of many thousands.

There is likewise another great advantage in my scheme, that it will prevent those voluntary abortions, and that horrid practice of women murdering their bastard children, alas, too frequent among us, sacrificing the poor innocent babes, I doubt[7] more to avoid the expense than the shame, which would move tears and pity in the most savage and inhuman breast.

The number of souls in this kingdom being usually reckoned one million and a half, of these I calculate there may be about two hundred thousand couple whose wives are breeders, from which number I subtract thirty thousand couple who are able to maintain their own children, although I apprehend there cannot be so many under the present distresses of the kingdom; but this being granted, there will remain an hundred and seventy thousand breeders. I again subtract fifty thousand for those women who miscarry, or whose children die by accident or disease within the year.[8] There only remain a hundred and twenty thousand children of poor parents annually born: the question therefore is how this number shall be reared and provided for, which, as I have already said, under the present situation of affairs, is utterly impossible by all the methods hitherto proposed: for we can neither employ them in handicraft, or agriculture; we neither build houses (I mean in the country) nor cultivate land;[9] they can very seldom pick up a livelihood by stealing till they arrive at six

---

3. Wandering aimlessly.
4. Catholic Ireland was loyal to the Pretender, James Francis Edward Stuart (1688–1766), son of James II, who was deposed from the English throne in 1688 because of his Catholicism. Religious ties also made the Irish ideal recruits for France and Spain in their wars against England.
5. The impoverished Irish emigrated to the West Indies in large numbers, buying their passage by selling their

labor in advance to the sugar plantations.
6. Devisers of new "projects," usually of doubtful value.
7. Believe.
8. It is telling that Swift here projects an infant mortality rate of approximately 30 percent in a child's first year.
9. The vast estates of English absentee landlords, and British retention of Irish land for grazing sheep, rather than agriculture, contributed to Ireland's poverty.

years old, except where they are of towardly parts,[1] although, I confess they learn the rudiments much earlier, during which time they can however be properly looked upon only as *probationers*, as I have been informed by a principal gentleman in the County of Cavan, who protested to me, that he never knew above one or two instances under the age of six, even in a part of the kingdom so renowned for the quickest proficiency in that art.

I am assured by our merchants that a boy or a girl, before twelve years old, is no salable commodity, and even when they come to this age, they will not yield above three pounds, or three pounds and half-a-crown at most on the Exchange,[2] which cannot turn to account[3] either to the parents or kingdom, the charge of nutriment and rags having been at least four times that value.

I shall now therefore humbly propose my own thoughts, which I hope will not be liable to the least objection.

I have been assured by a very knowing American[4] of my acquaintance in London, that a young healthy child well nursed is at a year old a most delicious, nourishing, and wholesome food, whether stewed, roasted, baked, or boiled, and I make no doubt that it will equally serve in a fricassee or ragout.[5]

I do therefore humbly offer it to public consideration, that of the hundred and twenty thousand children already computed, twenty thousand may be reserved for breed, whereof only one fourth part to be males, which is more than we allow to sheep, black cattle, or swine, and my reason is that these children are seldom the fruits of marriage, a circumstance not much regarded by our savages, therefore one male will be sufficient to serve four females. That the remaining hundred thousand may at a year old be offered in sale to the persons of quality and fortune through the kingdom, always advising the mother to let them suck plentifully in the last month, so as to render them plump, and fat for a good table. A child will make two dishes at an entertainment for friends, and when the family dines alone, the fore or hind quarter will make a reasonable dish, and seasoned with a little pepper or salt will be very good boiled on the fourth day, especially in winter.

I have reckoned upon a medium, that a child just born will weigh 12 pounds, and in a solar year if tolerably nursed increaseth to 28 pounds.

I grant this food will be somewhat dear,[6] and therefore very proper for landlords, who, as they have already devoured most of the parents, seem to have the best title to the children.

Infants' flesh will be in season throughout the year, but more plentiful in March, and a little before and after, for we are told by a grave author,[7] an eminent French physician, that fish being a prolific diet,[8] there are more children born in Roman Catholic countries about nine months after Lent than at any other season; therefore reckoning a year after Lent, the markets will be more glutted than usual, because the number of Popish infants is at least three to one in this kingdom, and therefore it will have one other collateral advantage by lessening the number of Papists among us.

I have already computed the charge of nursing a beggar's child (in which list I reckon all cottagers,[9] laborers, and four-fifths of the farmers) to be about two shillings *per annum*, rags included, and I believe no gentleman would repine to give ten

1. Precocious.
2. At the market.
3. Be of value.
4. Some of the British believed that the harsh living conditions in America made the colonists adopt "savage" practices.
5. A fricassee is meat stewed in gravy, a ragout is a highly

seasoned French stew; such foreign dishes were becoming increasingly popular with fashionable Britons.
6. Both expensive and, of course, beloved.
7. The satirist François Rabelais, in *Gargantua and Pantagruel* (1532–1564), book 5, ch. 29.
8. One increasing fertility.
9. Tenant farmers.

shillings for the carcass of a good fat child, which, as I have said, will make four dishes of excellent nutritive meat, when he hath only some particular friend or his own family to dine with him. Thus the Squire will learn to be a good landlord and grow popular among his tenants, the mother will have eight shillings net profit, and be fit for work till she produces another child.

Those who are more thrifty (as I must confess the times require) may flay the carcass, the skin of which, artificially[1] dressed, will make admirable gloves for ladies and summer boots for fine gentlemen.

As to our City of Dublin, shambles[2] may be appointed for this purpose in the most convenient parts of it, and butchers we may be assured will not be wanting, although I rather recommend buying the children alive and dressing them hot from the knife,[3] as we do roasting pigs.

A very worthy person, a true lover of his country, and whose virtues I highly esteem, was lately pleased, in discoursing on this matter, to offer a refinement upon my scheme. He said that many gentlemen of this kingdom, having of late destroyed their deer, he conceived that the want of venison might be well supplied by the bodies of young lads and maidens, not exceeding fourteen years of age nor under twelve, so great a number of both sexes in every country being now ready to starve for want of work and service;[4] and these to be disposed of by their parents if alive, or otherwise by their nearest relations. But with due deference to so excellent a friend and so deserving a patriot, I cannot be altogether in his sentiments; for as to the males, my American acquaintance assured me from frequent experience that their flesh was generally tough and lean, like that of our schoolboys, by continual exercise, and their taste disagreeable, and to fatten them would not answer the charge. Then as to the females, it would, I think with humble submission, be a loss to the public, because they soon would become breeders themselves; and besides, it is not improbable that some scrupulous people might be apt to censure such a practice (although indeed very unjustly) as a little bordering upon cruelty which, I confess, hath always been with me the strongest objection against any project, however so well intended.

But in order to justify my friend, he confessed that this expedient was put into his head by the famous Psalmanazar,[5] a native of the island Formosa, who came from thence to London above twenty years ago, and in conversation told my friend that in his country when any young person happened to be put to death, the executioner sold the carcass to persons of quality as a prime dainty, and that, in his time, the body of a plump girl of fifteen, who was crucified for an attempt to poison the emperor, was sold to his Imperial Majesty's Prime Minister of State[6] and other great Mandarins of the Court, in joints from the gibbet,[7] at four hundred crowns. Neither indeed can I deny that if the same use were made of several plump young girls in this town, who, without one single groat[8] to their fortunes, cannot stir abroad without a chair,[9] and appear at the playhouse and assemblies[1] in foreign fineries which they never will pay for, the kingdom would not be the worse.

Some persons of a desponding spirit are in great concern about that vast number of poor people who are aged, diseased, or maimed, and I have been desired to employ my thoughts what course may be taken to ease the nation of so grievous an encumbrance.

---

1. Skillfully.
2. Places where meat is slaughtered and sold.
3. Skinning and gutting them immediately after killing.
4. Positions as servants.
5. George Psalmanazar, a Frenchman who pretended to be from Formosa (now Taiwan), wrote a book about its customs, the *Historical and Geographical Description of For-* *mosa* (1704), which was quickly exposed as fraudulent.
6. A reference to Robert Walpole.
7. Gallows.
8. Silver coin (issued 1351–1662) equal to four pennies.
9. A sedan chair, carried by two men.
1. Social gatherings.

But I am not in the least pain upon that matter, because it is very well known that they are every day dying, and rotting, by cold, and famine, and filth, and vermin, as fast as can be reasonably expected. And as to the younger laborers they are now in almost as hopeful a condition. They cannot get work, and consequently pine away for want of nourishment, to a degree that if at any time they are accidentally hired to common labor, they have not strength to perform it; and thus the country and themselves are in a fair way of being soon delivered from the evils to come.

I have too long digressed, and therefore shall return to my subject. I think the advantages by the proposal which I have made are obvious and many, as well as of the highest importance.

For first, as I have already observed, it would greatly lessen the number of Papists, with whom we are yearly overrun, being the principal breeders of the nation as well as our most dangerous enemies, and who stay at home on purpose with a design to deliver the kingdom to the Pretender, hoping to take their advantage by the absence of so many good Protestants, who have chosen rather to leave their country than stay at home, and pay tithes against their conscience, to an Episcopal curate.[2]

Secondly, the poorer tenants will have something valuable of their own, which by law may be made liable to distress,[3] and help to pay their landlords rent, their corn and cattle being already seized, and *money a thing unknown.*

Thirdly, whereas the maintenance of a hundred thousand children from two years old and upwards cannot be computed at less than ten shillings a piece *per annum*, the nation's stock will be thereby increased fifty thousand pounds *per annum*, besides the profit of a new dish introduced to the tables of all gentlemen of fortune in the kingdom who have any refinement in taste, and the money will circulate among ourselves, the goods being entirely of our own growth and manufacture.

Fourthly, the constant breeders, besides the gain of eight shillings sterling *per annum* by the sale of their children, will be rid of the charge of maintaining them after the first year.

Fifthly, this food would likewise bring great custom to taverns, where the vintners will certainly be so prudent as to procure the best receipts[4] for dressing it to perfection, and consequently have their houses frequented by all the fine gentlemen, who justly value themselves upon their knowledge in good eating; and a skillful cook who understands how to oblige his guests will contrive to make it as expensive as they please.

Sixthly, this would be a great inducement to marriage, which all wise nations have either encouraged by rewards or enforced by laws and penalties. It would increase the care and tenderness of mothers toward their children, when they were sure of a settlement for life to the poor babes, provided in some sort by the public to their annual profit instead of expense. We should see an honest emulation[5] among the married women, which of them could bring the fattest child to the market; men would become as fond of their wives, during the time of their pregnancy, as they are now of their mares in foal, their cows in calf, or sows when they are ready to farrow,[6] nor offer to beat or kick them (as it is too frequent a practice) for fear of a miscarriage.

---

2. The tithes, or ecclesiastical taxes, that supported the Church were avoided by the many "good" Protestants who absented themselves from Ireland on the grounds—spurious, Swift implies—of "conscience."

3. Seizure for debt.
4. Recipes.
5. Competition.
6. Give birth.

Many other advantages might be enumerated: for instance, the addition of some thousand carcasses in our exportation of barreled beef;[7] the propagation of swine's flesh, and improvement in the art of making good bacon, so much wanted among us by the great destruction of pigs, too frequent at our tables, which are no way comparable in taste or magnificence to a well-grown, fat yearling child, which roasted whole will make a considerable figure at a Lord Mayor's feast or any other public entertainment. But this and many others I omit, being studious of brevity.

Supposing that one thousand families in this city would be constant customers for infants' flesh, besides others who might have it at merry-meetings, particularly weddings and christenings, I compute that Dublin would take off annually about twenty thousand carcasses, and the rest of the kingdom (where probably they will be sold somewhat cheaper) the remaining eighty thousand.

I can think of no one objection that will possibly be raised against this proposal, unless it should be urged that the number of people will be thereby much lessened in the kingdom. This I freely own, and was indeed one principal design in offering it to the world. I desire the reader will observe that I calculate my remedy *for this one individual Kingdom of Ireland, and for no other that ever was, is, or, I think, ever can be upon earth.* Therefore let no man talk to me of other expedients:[8] *Of taxing our absentees at five shillings a pound; of using neither clothes nor household furniture, except what is of our own growth and manufacture; of utterly rejecting the materials and instruments that promote foreign luxury; of curing the expensiveness of pride, vanity, idleness, and gaming in our women; of introducing a vein of parsimony, prudence, and temperance; of learning to love our country, wherein we differ even from* LAPLANDERS, *and the inhabitants of* TOPINAMBOO;[9] *of quitting our animosities and factions, nor act any longer like the Jews, who were murdering one another at the very moment their city was taken;[1] of being a little cautious not to sell our country and consciences for nothing; of teaching landlords to have at least one degree of mercy toward their tenants. Lastly, of putting a spirit of honesty, industry, and skill into our shopkeepers, who, if a resolution could now be taken to buy our native goods, would immediately unite to cheat and exact upon us in the price, the measure, and the goodness, nor could ever yet be brought to make one fair proposal of just dealing, though often and earnestly invited to it.*

Therefore I repeat, let no man talk to me of these and the like expedients till he hath at least some glimpse of hope that there will ever be some hearty and sincere attempt to put them in practice.

But as to myself, having been wearied out for many years with offering vain, idle, visionary thoughts, and at length utterly despairing of success, I fortunately fell upon this proposal, which as it is wholly new, so it hath something solid and real, of no expense and little trouble, full in our own power, and whereby we can incur no danger in *disobliging* ENGLAND. For this kind of commodity will not bear exportation, the flesh being of too tender a consistence, to admit a long continuance in salt, *although perhaps I could name a country*[2] *which would be glad to eat up our whole nation without it.*

7. Pickled beef.
8. The kind of proposals Swift himself had made in earnest for remedying the poverty of Ireland; his *Proposal for the Universal Use of Irish Manufacture in Cloaths and Furniture . . . Utterly Rejecting and Renouncing Everything Wearable that Comes from England* (1720) is a typical example.
9. The inhabitants of the most hostile environments—the frozen north or the Brazilian jungle—love their countries more than the Irish.
1. According to one historian, when Jerusalem was besieged and captured by the Emperor Titus in A.D. 70, factional fighting inside the city contributed to its destruction.
2. England.

After all I am not so violently bent upon my own opinion as to reject any offer proposed by wise men, which shall be found equally innocent, cheap, easy, and effectual. But before something of that kind shall be advanced in contradiction to my scheme and offering a better, I desire the author or authors will be pleased maturely to consider two points. First, as things now stand, how they will be able to find food and raiment for an hundred thousand useless mouths and backs. And secondly, there being a round million of creatures in human figure throughout this kingdom whose whole subsistence put into a common stock would leave them in debt two millions of pounds sterling; adding those who are beggars by profession to the bulk of farmers, cottagers, and laborers with their wives and children, who are beggars in effect; I desire those politicians who dislike my overture, and may perhaps be so bold to attempt an answer, that they will first ask the parents of these mortals whether they would not at this day think it a great happiness to have been sold for food at a year old, in the manner I prescribe, and thereby have avoided such a perpetual scene of misfortunes as they have since gone through, by the oppression of landlords, the impossibility of paying rent without money or trade, the want of common sustenance, with neither house nor clothes to cover them from the inclemencies of the weather, and the most inevitable prospect of entailing[3] the like or greater miseries upon their breed forever.

I profess in the sincerity of my heart that I have not the least personal interest in endeavoring to promote this necessary work, having no other motive than the *public good of my country, by advancing our trade, providing for infants, relieving the poor, and giving some pleasure to the rich.* I have no children by which I can propose to get a single penny; the youngest being nine years old, and my wife past child-bearing.
1729   1729

COMPANION READING

William Petty: *from* Political Arithmetic[1]

from *Chapter 4. How to enable the people of England and Ireland to spend 5 millions worth of commodities more than now; and how to raise the present value of the lands and goods of Ireland from 2 to 3.*

This is to be done: 1. By bringing one million of the present 1,300 thousand of the people out of Ireland into England, though at the expense of a million of money. 2. That the remaining three hundred thousand left behind be all herdsmen and dairy women, servants to the owners of the lands and stock transplanted into England, all aged between 16 and 60 years, and to quit all other trades, but that of cattle, and to import nothing but salt and tobacco. Neglecting all housing, but what is fittest for these 300 thousand people, and this trade, though to the loss of 2 millions-worth of houses. Now

---

3. Bequeathing.
1. William Petty (1623–1687) represents the type of Englishman Swift had in mind in his implicit criticism of English rapaciousness in Ireland in *A Modest Proposal.* Petty, the son of a London clothier and weaver, was an extraordinary scholar and anatomist, and a charter member of the Royal Society. Appointed physician-general to the parliamentary army in Ireland in 1652, he obtained considerable property holdings in Ireland through his additional task of surveying lands forfeited by Roman Catholics. His new-found fortune enabled him to devote

his attention to his economic writings and to the Royal Society in London, though he was less than solicitous of his tenants in Ireland. Swift's friendship with Petty's children, Lord Shelburne and Lady Kerry, did not prevent him parodying Petty's *Political Arithmetic* (1691) in *A Modest Proposal.* Petty's suggestion that Ireland be turned into one huge farm to supply England by removing all the Irish was only one of many "political arithmetic" projects published during the Restoration and 18th century, reflecting English interest in "scientific" programs for social "improvement."

if a million of people be worth 70 pounds per head one with another, the whole are worth 70 millions; then the said people, reckoned as money at 5 percent interest, will yield 3 millions and a half per annum. 3. And if Ireland send into England 1 million and a half worth of effects (receiving nothing back), then England will be enriched from Ireland, and otherwise, 5 millions per annum more than now, which, at 20 year's purchase, is worth one hundred millions of pounds sterling, as was propounded. * * *

Postscript

If in this jealous age this essay should be taxed of an evil design to waste and dispeople Ireland, we say that the author of it intends not to be *Felo de se*,[4] and propound something quite contrary, by saying it is naturally possible in about 25 years to double the inhabitants of Great Britain and Ireland and make the people full as many as the territory of those kingdoms can with tolerable labor afford a competent livelihood unto, which I prove thus, (viz.)

1. The sixth part of the people are teeming women[5] of between 18 and 44 years old.
2. It is found by observation that but 1/3 part or between 30 and 40 of the teeming women are married.
3. That a teeming woman, at a medium, bear a child every two years and a half.
4. That in mankind at London, there are 14 males for 13 females, and because males are prolific[6] 40 years, and females but 25, there are in effect 560 males for 325 females.
5. That out of the mass of mankind there dies one out of 30 per annum.
6. That at Paris, where the christenings and the births are the same in number, the christenings are above 18,000 per annum, and consequently the births at London, which far exceed the christenings there, cannot be less than 19,000 where the burials are above 23,000.

As for Example

Of 600 people, the sixth part (viz. 100) are teeming women, which (if they were all married) might bear 40 children per annum (viz.) 20 more than do die out of 600, at the rate of one out of 30; and consequently in 16 years the increase will be 320, making the whole 920. And by the same reason, in the next 9 years, the said 920 will be 280 more, in all 1,200, viz. double of the original number of 600.

Upon these principles, if there be about 19,000 births per annum at London, the number of the married teeming women must be above 38,000; and of the whole stock of the teeming women must be above 114,000, and of the whole people six times as many viz. 684,000; which agrees well enough with 69,6000, which they have been elsewhere computed to be.

To conclude it is naturally possible, that all teeming women may be married, since there are in effect 560 males to 325 females; and since Great Britain and Ireland can with moderate labor, food, and other necessaries to near double the present people or to about 20 millions of heads, as shall when occasion requires it, be demonstrated. * * *   1691

---

4. Self-murder; literally, "felon of (one)self."   6. Capable of procreation.
5. Women capable of breeding.

Alexander Pope
1688–1744

"The life of a wit is a warfare upon earth; and the present spirit of the learned world is such, that to serve it . . . one must have the constancy of a martyr, and a resolution to suffer for its sake." Though still in his twenties when he wrote these words, Alexander Pope knew from painful experience their bitter truth. As a Roman Catholic, he could not vote, inherit or purchase land, attend a "public" school or a university, live within ten miles of London, hold public office, or openly practice his religion. He was obliged to pay double taxes. Such civil disenfranchisement barred him from receiving the literary patronage most talented writers depended upon for their livelihood. No wonder Pope wrote of "certain laws, by suff'rers thought unjust," by which he was "denied all posts of profit or of trust" (*Imitations of Horace, Epistle* 2. 2. 60–61). Despite whatever patriotism or loyalty to their country they may have felt, Catholics were widely regarded as alien and seditious. Pope's resentment of this attitude is evident in the *Epistle to Bathurst* (1733) when he calls the London Monument, which bears an inscription blaming the Great Fire of 1666 on a Papist conspiracy to destroy the capital, "a tall bully" who "lies."

Religion was not Pope's greatest impediment to success, however. When he was twelve, he contracted tuberculosis of the spine (Pott's disease), a condition that stunted his growth and left him humpbacked and deformed. At four feet six inches, he could not sit at an ordinary table with other adults unless his seat was raised. His constitution was so weakened that he frequently suffered from migraine headaches, asthma, nausea, and fevers. For much of his life, he could not hold his body upright without the help of stays, and he was unable to bathe, dress or undress, rise or go to bed by himself. Pope summarized his condition most succinctly in *An Epistle to Dr. Arbuthnot* (1735), when he wrote of "this long disease, my life."

Pope was born in London in 1688, the only child of his parents' marriage. Pope's *Epistle to Dr. Arbuthnot* includes a tribute to his father's equanimity and goodness; his mother is praised as "a noble wife." At the age of nine, Pope was sent to a school for Catholic boys but was expelled in his first year for writing a satire on his schoolmaster—a sign of things to come. When he was twelve, his family moved from the environs of London to Binfield, in the royal forest of Windsor; the effect of Windsor's "green retreats" on Pope's youthful imagination is apparent in the *Pastorals* (1709) and in *Windsor-Forest* (1713). At Binfield, he began to teach himself Greek and Latin with great determination, though the rigors of his studies made his sickness worse. Refusing to yield to his infirmity, he began, at fifteen, to journey into London to learn French and Italian. Pope spoke of these adolescent years as his "great reading period" when he "went through all the best critics, almost all the English, French, and Latin poets of any name . . . [and] Homer and some other of the Greek poets in the original." During this time Pope met his great friend John Caryll, at whose request he would write *The Rape of the Lock,* and Martha Blount, who was to become his lifelong intimate companion and to whom he addressed *Of the Characters of Women: An Epistle to a Lady* (1735).

Pope claimed that "as yet a child . . . I lisp'd in numbers [i.e., meter]." Certainly he was a precocious poet and his early efforts were encouraged by many, including the playwrights William Wycherley and William Congreve, to whom Pope dedicated his *Iliad* (1715–1720). If Pope had encouraging friends, he soon had detracting enemies as well. His first publication, the *Pastorals* (1709), occasioned a rivalry between Pope's Tory supporters and the Whig partisans of Ambrose Philips, whose *Pastorals* appeared in the same volume. Pope's next important poem, *An Essay on Criticism* (1711), brought a barrage of vituperative abuse from the critic John Dennis, who called Pope "a hunch-backed toad" and argued that his deformity was merely the outward sign of mental and moral ugliness. Undaunted, Pope continued to publish: the

Messiah (1712), *The Rape of the Lock* (1712, substantially enlarged in 1714), *Windsor-Forest* (1713), and *The Temple of Fame* (1715). With the publication of his *Works* (1717), Pope had proved himself master of a dazzling repertoire of poetic modes: pastoral and georgic, didactic, eclogue, mock-epic, allegorical dream-vision, heroic, and elegiac. No other living poet could display such dazzling versatility and comprehensive control.

There was still another area, however, in which Pope was proving the breathtaking range of his poetic gifts. Between 1713 and 1726, Pope devoted much of his creative energy to translating Homer's epics, the *Iliad* and the *Odyssey*, into heroic couplets. "Pope's Homer" not only won for him financial independence so that he could "live and thrive, / Indebted to no Prince or Peer alive" (*Imitations of Horace, Epistle* 2. 2), it also confirmed his reputation as the presiding poetic genius of his time. While he was working on the *Odyssey*, Pope produced a six-volume edition of Shakespeare's works (1725), which, though it contained some valuable insights, was very much an amateur effort. When Lewis Theobald, the leading Shakespeare scholar of the time, rather pedantically highlighted Pope's many editorial shortcomings in *Shakespeare Restored, or, a Specimen of the Many Errors Committed . . . by Mr. Pope* (1726), Pope's revenge was not far off: two years later, he published *The Dunciad*, a savagely satirical assault on Pope's critics and the bankrupt cultural values they embodied.

In the seventeen years between Dennis's attack and the publication of *The Dunciad*, Pope's appearance, talent, and character had been assailed in print more than fifty times. His enemies accused him of being obscene, seditious, duplicitous, venal, vain, blasphemous, libelous, ignorant, and a bad poet. Theobald's rebuke was the last straw, perhaps because it was the most justified. Pope's style of comic social criticism owed much to his membership in the Scriblerus Club with John Gay, Jonathan Swift, Dr. John Arbuthnot, Thomas Parnell, and Robert Harley, Earl of Oxford. The Scriblerians originally planned to produce a series entitled *The Works of the Unlearned*; although the group regularly met only for a short while in 1714, its members remained in contact. In addition to *The Dunciad*, the fruit of their exchanges may be seen in Swift's *Gulliver's Travels* (1726), Gay's *The Beggar's Opera* (1728), Pope's *Peri Bathous: Or, the Art of Sinking in Poetry* (1728), and Arbuthnot's and Pope's *Memoirs of the Extraordinary Life, Works, and Discoveries of Martinus Scriblerus* (1741).

An Essay on Man (1733–1734) showcased Pope's talent for philosophical poetry. This work and four *Moral Essays* (1731–1735) were originally intended to form part of a long poetic sequence on the nature of humankind that Pope had hoped would be his greatest work, though the project was abandoned. Between 1733 and 1738, Pope published more than a dozen *Imitations of Horace*. In these loose adaptations of Horace's epistles and satires, Pope invested his modern social criticism with the classical authority of a revered Roman poet. The *Moral Essays*, or "Epistles to Several Persons" as Pope called them, also show Pope assuming the mantle of Horace by using the familiar epistle as a vehicle for social commentary. Pope's Horatian poems are his most mature, elegant, and self-assured works.

In 1737, he published an authorized version of his letters, which he doctored to improve his reputation. His last years were a time of retirement at his villa at Twickenham, famous for its grotto of "Friendship and Liberty" and for the five-acre landscape garden Pope had designed. In *The New Dunciad* (1742), Pope shifted his attack from hack writers and low culture to all forms of hypocrisy and pretense. It was his final triumph. He worked with William Warburton on a new edition of his *Works* (1751), even as his many illnesses became still more overwhelming. Though he was a self-confessed "fool to Fame" (*Arbuthnot*), he told those gathered around his deathbed: "There is nothing that is meritorious but virtue and friendship." He was, as his enemies claimed, bellicose, self-indulgent, and self-aggrandizing. He was morally and physically courageous and had a great gift for friendship. Although it is no longer fashionable to call the first half of the eighteenth century the "Age of Pope," many of his contemporaries saw him as the predominant literary genius of his time. Today, most literary historians agree that the greatest English poet between John Milton and William Wordsworth was Alexander Pope.

An Essay on Criticism

Pope was only twenty-one years old when he wrote *An Essay on Criticism*, which was published anonymously in 1711. This aesthetic manifesto in heroic couplets is written in the tradition of Horace's *Ars Poetica* (c. 19 B.C.), Boileau's *Art poétique* (1674), and other verse essays delineating poetic principles and practices. Pope's chief contributions to the genre are his ringing epigrams and the playful ease with which he satirizes contemporary critics who lack genuine poetic understanding. The *Essay on Criticism* is divided into three parts: the first examines the rules of taste, their relationship to Nature, and the authority of classical authors. The second section (lines 201–559) considers the impediments preventing the attainment of the classical ideals outlined in part one. In the third part, Pope proposes an aesthetic and moral reformation to restore wit, sense, and taste to their former glory. While acknowledging the importance of precepts, Pope asserts the primacy of poetic genius and the power of imagination.

from An Essay on Criticism

'Tis hard to say, if greater want of skill
Appear in writing or in judging ill;
But, of the two, less dangerous is th' offense,
To tire our patience, than mislead our sense:°   *judgment*
5   Some few in that, but numbers err in this,
Ten censure wrong for one who writes amiss;
A fool might once himself alone expose,
Now one in verse makes many more in prose.[1]
'Tis with our judgments as our watches, none
10 Go just alike, yet each believes his own.
In poets as true genius is but rare,
True taste as seldom is the critic's share;
Both must alike from Heav'n derive their light,
These born to judge, as well as those to write.
15 Let such teach others who themselves excel,
And censure freely who have written well.
Authors are partial to their wit,[2] 'tis true,
But are not critics to their judgment too?
Yet if we look more closely, we shall find
20 Most have the seeds of judgment in their mind;
Nature affords at least a glimm'ring light;
The lines, though touched but faintly, are drawn right.
But as the slightest sketch, if justly traced, ⎤
Is by ill coloring but the more disgraced, ⎬
25 So by false learning is good sense defaced; ⎦
Some are bewildered in the maze of Schools,[3]
And some made coxcombs[4] Nature meant but fools.
In search of wit these lose their common sense,
And then turn critics in their own defense.
30 Each burns alike, who can, or cannot write,
Or° with a rival's or an eunuch's spite.[5]   *either*

---

1. I.e., many bad critics respond to one bad poet.
2. Both their writings and their (fancied) ability to write well.
3. Schools of criticism.

4. Conceited show-offs.
5. I.e., they either seek to compete or, knowing themselves sterile, criticize out of envy.

All fools have still° an itching to deride,[6]   *continually*
And fain° would be upon the laughing side: *gladly*
If Maevius scribble in Apollo's spite,[7]
35   There are, who judge still worse than he can write.
Some have at first for wits,° then poets past,   *intellectuals*
Turned critics next, and proved plain fools at last;
Some neither can for wits nor critics pass,
As heavy mules are neither horse nor ass.
40   Those half-learned witlings, num'rous in our isle,
As half-formed insects on the banks of Nile;
Unfinished things, one knows not what to call,
Their generation's so equivocal:[8]
To tell° 'em, would a hundred tongues require,   *count*
45   Or one vain wit's, that might a hundred tire.
But you who seek to give and merit° fame,   *deserve*
And justly bear a critic's noble name,
Be sure yourself and your own reach° to know,   *ability*
How far your genius, taste, and learning go;
50   Launch not beyond your depth, but be discrete,
And mark° that point where sense and dullness meet.   *note*
Nature to all things fixed the limits fit,
And wisely curbed proud man's pretending° wit: *aspiring*
As on the land while here the ocean gains,
55   In other parts it leaves wide sandy plains;
Thus in the soul while memory prevails,
The solid power of understanding fails;
Where beams of warm imagination play,
The memory's soft figures melt away.
60   One science only will one genius fit;[9]
So vast is Art, so narrow human wit;°   *understanding*
Not only bounded to peculiar° arts,   *particular*
But oft in those, confined to single parts.
Like kings we lose the conquests gained before,
65   By vain ambition still to make them more:
Each might his several province well command,
Would all but stoop to what they understand.
First follow NATURE, and your judgment frame
By her just standard, which is still° the same: *always*
70   Unerring Nature, still divinely bright,
One clear, unchanged, and universal light,
Life, force, and beauty, must to all impart,
At once the source, and end, and test of art.
Art from that fund each just supply provides,
75   Works without show,[1] and without pomp presides:
In some fair body thus th' informing soul[2]

6. The fool's perpetual itching suggests disease.
7. Maevius, a third-rate Roman poet, is set against Apollo, patron of good poetry.
8. Like the generation of insects on the banks of the Nile,
thought to occur spontaneously, through the action of
sun on mud.

9. The artist can hope only to succeed in one subject area
or object of study.
1. The suggestion that art should mask its presence came
from Horace.
2. The force that animates.

With spirits feeds, with vigor fills the whole,
Each motion guides, and every nerve sustains;
Itself unseen, but in th' effects, remains.
80   Some, to whom Heav'n in wit has been profuse,
Want° as much more, to turn it to its use;   *need*
For wit and judgment often are at strife,
Though meant each other's aid, like man and wife.
'Tis more to guide than spur the Muse's steed;[3]
85   Restrain his fury, than provoke his speed;
The winged courser,° like a gen'rous horse,   *swift horse*
Shows most true mettle° when you check his course.   *spirit*
     Those RULES of old discovered, not devised,
Are Nature still, but Nature *methodized;*
90   Nature, like Liberty, is but restrained
By the same laws which first herself ordained.
     Hear how learn'd Greece her useful rules indites,°   *composes*
When to repress, and when indulge our flights:
High on Parnassus'[4] top her sons she showed,
95   And pointed out° those arduous paths they trod,   *appointed*
Held from afar, aloft, th' immortal prize,
And urged the rest by equal steps to rise;
Just precepts thus from great examples giv'n,
She drew from them what they derived from Heav'n.
100 The gen'rous critic fanned the poet's fire,
And taught the world, with reason to admire.
Then criticism the Muse's handmaid proved,
To dress her charms,[5] and make her more beloved;
But following wits from that intention strayed;
105 Who could not win the mistress, wooed the maid;
Against the poets their own arms they turned,
Sure to hate most the men from whom they learned.
So modern 'pothecaries,° taught the art   *druggists*
By doctors' bills° to play the doctor's part,   *prescriptions*
110 Bold in the practice of mistaken° rules,   *misunderstood*
Prescribe, apply, and call their masters fools.
Some on the leaves of ancient authors prey,[6]
Nor time nor moths e'er spoiled so much as they:
Some dryly plain, without invention's° aid,   *imagination's*
115 Write dull receipts° how poems may be made: *recipes*
These leave the sense, their learning to display,
And those explain the meaning quite away.
     You then whose judgment the right course would steer,
Know well each ANCIENT'S proper character,[7]
120 His fable,° subject, scope° in every page,   *plot/intention*
Religion, country, genius of his age:
Without all these at once before your eyes,

---

3. Pegasus, the winged horse.
4. Mount Parnassus in Greece was sacred to the Muses.
5. Both dress and address, i.e., both interpret and adjust.
6. Textual commentators, depicted as literal bookworms

in continuation of the earlier insect metaphor.
7. An interest in the historical method in criticism was
on the rise.

Cavil° you may, but never criticize.   *quibble*
Be Homer's works your study, and delight,
125 Read them by day, and meditate by night,
Thence form your judgment, thence your maxims bring,
And trace the Muses upward to their spring;
Still with itself compared, his text peruse;
And let your comment be the Mantuan Muse.[8]
130   When first young Maro° in his boundless mind   *Virgil*
A work t' outlast immortal Rome designed,
Perhaps he seemed° above the critic's law,   *thought himself*
And but from Nature's fountains scorned to draw:
But when t' examine every part he came,
135 Nature and Homer were, he found, the same:
Convinced, amazed, he checks the bold design,⎤
And rules as strict his labored work confine, ⎬
As if the Stagyrite[9] o'erlooked each line. ⎦
Learn hence for ancient rules a just esteem;
140 To copy Nature is to copy them.

* * *

Of all the causes which conspire to blind
Man's erring judgment, and misguide the mind,
What the weak head with strongest bias[1] rules,
Is pride, the never-failing vice of fools.
205 Whatever Nature has in worth denied,
She gives in large recruits° of needful° pride;   *supplies/needed*
For as in bodies, thus in souls, we find
What wants° in blood and spirits, swelled with wind;   *is lacking*
Pride, where wit fails, steps in to our defense,
210 And fills up all the mighty void of sense!
If once right reason drives that cloud away,
Truth breaks upon us with resistless day;
Trust not yourself; but your defects to know,
Make use of every friend—and every foe.
215   A little learning is a dang'rous thing;
Drink deep, or taste not the Pierian spring:[2]
There shallow draughts[3] intoxicate the brain,
And drinking largely sobers us again.
Fired at first sight with what the Muse imparts,
220 In fearless youth we tempt° the heights of Arts,   *attempt*
While from the bounded° level of our mind,   *limited*
Short views we take, nor see the lengths behind,
But more advanced, behold with strange surprise
New, distant scenes of endless science[4] rise!
225 So pleased at first, the towering Alps we try,
Mount o'er the vales, and seem to tread the sky;

---

8. Virgil (born near Mantua) and his *Aeneid*, which took Homer's epics as models and was the best commentary on them.
9. Aristotle, whose *Poetics* provided the basis for later rules on poetry and epic writing.

1. Not only prejudice but a kind of bowling ball. (In bowls, the bias ball is one weighted to roll obliquely.)
2. Hippocrene, the stream associated with the Muses.
3. I.e., drinking small amounts.
4. Knowledge, subjects requiring study.

Th' eternal snows appear already past,
And the first clouds and mountains seem the last:
But those attained, we tremble to survey
230 The growing labors of the lengthened way,
Th' increasing prospect tires our wandering eyes,
Hills peep o'er hills, and Alps on Alps arise!

* * *

285   Thus critics, of less judgment than caprice,
Curious,° not knowing, not exact, but nice,°   *picky/fussy*
Form short ideas; and offend in arts
(As most in manners) by a love to parts.[5]
Some to conceit[6] alone their taste confine,
290 And glitt'ring thoughts struck out at every line;
Pleased with a work where nothing's just or fit;
One glaring chaos and wild heap of wit:
Poets like painters, thus, unskilled to trace
The naked Nature and the living grace,
295 With gold and jewels cover every part,
And hide with ornaments their want° of art.   *lack*
True wit is Nature to advantage dressed,
What oft was thought, but ne'er so well expressed,
Something, whose truth convinced at sight we find,
300 That gives us back the image of our mind:
As shades° more sweetly recommend the light,   *shadows*
So modest plainness sets off sprightly wit:
For works may have more wit than does 'em good,
As bodies perish through excess of blood.[7]
305   Others for language all their care express,
And value books, as women men, for dress:
Their praise is still—The style is excellent:
The sense, they humbly take upon content.°   *trust*
Words are like leaves; and where they most abound,
310 Much fruit of sense beneath is rarely found.
False eloquence, like the prismatic glass,
Its gaudy colors spreads on every place;
The face of Nature we no more survey,°   *observe*
All glares alike, without distinction gay:
315 But true expression, like th' unchanging sun, ⎫
Clears, and improves whate'er it shines upon, ⎬
It gilds all objects, but it alters none.   ⎭
Expression is the dress of thought,[8] and still
Appears more decent° as more suitable;   *correct*
320 A vile conceit° in pompous words expressed,   *idea*
Is like a clown° in regal purple dressed;   *peasant*
For different styles with different subjects sort,°   *belong*
As several garbs with Country, Town, and Court.[9]

---

5. Individual talents.
6. Extravagant use of metaphor.
7. Apoplexy, it was thought, was caused by such an excess.

8. It was generally held that a person's appearance reflected his or her inner self.
9. As various styles of dress suit country, mercantile, and courtly life.

Some by old words to fame have made pretense;[1]
325   Ancients in phrase, mere Moderns in their sense!
Such labored nothings, in so strange a style,
Amaze the unlearn'd, and make the learned smile.
Unlucky, as Fungoso in the play,[2]
These sparks[3] with awkward vanity display }
330   What the fine gentleman wore yesterday!
And but so mimic ancient wits at best,
As apes our grandsires in their doublets[4] dressed.
In words, as fashions, the same rule will hold;
Alike fantastic, if too new, or old;
335   Be not the first by whom the new are tried,
Nor yet the last to lay the old aside.
      But most by numbers[5] judge a poet's song,
And smooth or rough, with them, is right or wrong;
In the bright Muse though thousand charms conspire,°   *work together*
340   Her voice is all these tuneful fools admire,
Who haunt Parnassus but to please their ear, }
Not mend their minds; as some to church repair, }
Not for the doctrine, but the music there.
These equal syllables alone require,
345   Though oft the ear the open vowels tire,[6]
While expletives their feeble aid do join,
And ten low words oft creep in one dull line,
While they ring round the same unvaried chimes,
With sure returns of still expected rhymes.
350   Where-e'er you find the cooling western breeze,
In the next line, it whispers through the trees;
If crystal streams with pleasing murmurs creep,
The reader's threatened (not in vain) with sleep.
Then, at the last, and only couplet fraught
355   With some unmeaning thing they call a thought,
A needless Alexandrine[7] ends the song,
That like a wounded snake, drags its slow length along.
Leave such to tune their own dull rhymes, and know
What's roundly smooth, or languishingly slow;
360   And praise the easy vigor of a line,
Where Denham's strength, and Waller's sweetness join.[8]
True ease in writing comes from art, not chance,
As those move easiest who have learned to dance.
'Tis not enough no harshness gives offense,
365   The sound must seem an echo to the sense.[9]

1. Made a claim. Deliberately archaic language was used by Spenser and by a number of his 18th-century imitators.
2. In Ben Jonson's *Every Man Out of His Humor* (1599), this student lagged behind the fashions.
3. Hot-blooded young men, aspiring to fame and romantic conquest.
4. Close-fitting garment for the upper body.
5. Meter of verse, patterns of sound.
6. This line, like the couplets that follow, illustrates the fault it criticizes.
7. The 12 syllables and six stresses of an Alexandrine are illustrated in the next line.
8. Pope follows Dryden in his stylistic characterization of John Denham (1615–1669) and Edmund Waller (1606–1687), two poets greatly respected by writers of the early 18th century, especially for their work in heroic couplets.
9. The following nine lines exemplify the rule laid down here.

Soft is the strain when Zephyr° gently blows,   *the west wind*
And the smooth stream in smoother numbers flows;
But when loud surges lash the sounding shore,
The hoarse, rough verse should like the torrent roar.
370   When Ajax[1] strives, some rock's vast weight to throw,
The line too labors, and the words move slow;
Not so, when swift Camilla[2] scours the plain,
Flies o'er th' unbending corn, and skims along the main.°   *sea*
Hear how Timotheus'[3] varied lays surprise,
375   And bid alternate passions fall and rise!
While, at each change, the son of Lybian Jove[4]
Now burns with glory, and then melts with love;
Now his fierce eyes with sparkling fury glow;
Now sighs steal out, and tears begin to flow:
380   Persians and Greeks like turns of nature[5] found,
And the world's victor stood subdued by sound!
The pow'rs of music all our hearts allow;°   *admit to*
And what Timotheus was, is Dryden now.

* * *

c. 1709   1711

Windsor-Forest

"Mr. Pope has published a fine poem called Windsor Forest," wrote Jonathan Swift to his beloved Stella; "read it," he urged her in a letter sent just two days after the poem went on sale. Pope wrote *Windsor-Forest* in two distinct stages: the first part (lines 1–290) was composed in 1704–1705, but the remaining lines celebrating the imminent Peace of Utrecht (1713) that formally ended the long War of Spanish Succession were penned in late 1712 and early 1713. The Peace—a great triumph for the ruling Tory party and the last Stuart monarch, Queen Anne—recognized Great Britain as the world's leading naval power and greatly augmented its colonial and commercial empire at the expense of Spain and France. It would be wrong, however, to imagine that *Windsor- Forest* is half pastoral idyll and half Tory political propaganda; it is, rather, a thoroughgoing synthesis of the topographical, the moral, and the political. Pope's sources for *Windsor-Forest* include Virgil's *Eclogues* and *Georgics*, Ovid's *Metamorphoses*, the Bible, Spenser's *Faerie Queene*, Milton's *Paradise Lost*, Edmund Waller's *On St. James's Park* (1661), and Thomas Otway's *Windsor Castle* (1685). It is, however, Pope's comment on "the distinguishing excellence" of John Denham's *Cooper's Hill* (1642) that best explains Pope's own imaginative procedure in *Windsor-Forest*: "the descriptions of places, and images raised by the poet, are still [i.e., continually] tending to some hint, or leading into some reflection, upon moral life or political institution" (*Iliad* 16.466n). Windsor was the ideal setting for a political poem in which landscape evoked England's proud heritage: from William the Conqueror, who first established a royal residence at Windsor, to "great ANNA" (line 327), who made Windsor Castle her chief residence and frequently rode and hunted in the forest, this was a place suffused with English history. From this enclave of natural beauty and political tradition—the home of monarchs and the haven of Muses—Pope's myth-making genius created a triumphant vision of peace and prosperity, the dawning of a Golden Age.

1. The fabulously strong Greek hero in Homer's *Iliad*.
2. An Amazon warrior in Virgil's *Aeneid*.
3. Musician to Alexander the Great, as portrayed in Dry-

den's *Alexander's Feast* (1697).
4. Alexander the Great.
5. Similar changes of emotion.

Windsor-Forest
To the Right Honorable George Lord Lansdowne[1]

Non injussa cano: te nostrae, Vare, myricae
Te nemus omne canet; nec Phoebo gratior ulla est
Quam sibi quae Vari praescripsit pagina nomen. [2]

Thy forests, Windsor! and thy green retreats,
At once the monarch's and the Muse's seats,[3]
Invite my lays.° Be present, sylvan maids![4]   *prompt my poetry*
Unlock your springs, and open all your shades.
5   Granville commands: Your aid O Muses bring!
What Muse for Granville can refuse to sing?
   The groves of Eden, vanished now so long,
Live in description, and look green in song:[5]
These, were my breast inspired with equal flame,
10 Like them in beauty, should be like in fame.
Here hills and vales, the woodland and the plain,
Here earth and water seem to strive again,
Not chaos-like together crushed and bruised,
But as the world, harmoniously confused:
15 Where order in variety we see,
And where, though all things differ, all agree.
Here waving groves a checkered scene display,
And part admit and part exclude the day;
As some coy nymph her lover's warm address
20 Nor° quite indulges, nor can quite repress.   *neither*
There, interspersed in lawns° and opening glades,   *clearings*
Thin trees arise that shun each other's shades.
Here in full light the russet plains extend;
There wrapped in clouds the blueish hills ascend:
25 Ev'n the wild heath displays her purple dyes,[6]
And 'midst the desert° fruitful fields arise,   *uncultivated land*
That crowned with tufted trees[7] and springing corn,
Like verdant isles the sable waste adorn.
Let India boast her plants, nor envy we
30 The weeping amber or the balmy tree,
While by our oaks the precious loads are born,[8]
And realms commanded which those trees adorn.

---

1. George Granville (1667–1735), Baron Lansdowne, was himself a poet and playwright. A Tory politician close to Queen Anne, he became Secretary of War in 1710 and so was partly responsible both for British victory and for the peace that followed. Lord Lansdowne greatly admired Pope's poetry and encouraged him to publish a poem on the Peace.
2. Adapted from Virgil's sixth *Eclogue*, lines 9–12, in which the poet dedicates his pastoral poem to his friend Varus (like Lansdowne a prominent military figure): "I do not sing without purpose: our tamarisks, Varus, every grove will sing of you; nor is any page more pleasing to Apollo than one that begins with the name of Varus."
3. Windsor Forest, seat (country home) of Britain's mon-

archs since Norman times (and even fabled to be the site of the legendary King Arthur's court), in Pope's view was also home to the Muses because the 17th-century poets Sir John Denham and Abraham Cowley had lived nearby.
4. Dryads and naiads, spirits of the trees and water.
5. The Garden of Eden in Genesis was made "green in song" in Milton's (relatively) recent *Paradise Lost*.
6. Heather's purple blooms cover open moorland in late summer.
7. A cluster of trees; Pope borrowed the phrase from Milton's *L'Allegro* (1632).
8. British ships made of oak allowed Britain both to conquer distant countries and to carry goods from them.

Not proud Olympus[9] yields a nobler sight,
Though gods assembled grace his tow'ring height,
35   Than what more humble mountains offer here,
Where, in their blessings, all those gods appear.
See Pan with flocks, and fruits Pomona crowned,
Here blushing Flora[1] paints th' enameled ground,[2]
Here Ceres' gifts° in waving prospect stand,   *grain crops*
40   And nodding tempt the joyful reaper's hand,
Rich Industry sits smiling on the plains,
And Peace and Plenty tell, a STUART reigns.[3]
    Not thus the land appeared in ages past,[4]
A dreary desert and a gloomy waste,
45   To savage beasts and savage laws a prey,[5]
And kings more furious and severe than they:
Who claimed the skies, dispeopled° air and floods,   *depopulated*
The lonely lords of empty wilds and woods.
Cities laid waste, they stormed the dens and caves,
50   (For wiser brutes were backward° to be slaves.)   *unwilling*
What could be free, when lawless beasts obeyed,
And ev'n the elements[6] a tyrant swayed?
In vain kind seasons swelled the teeming grain,
Soft show'rs distilled, and suns grew warm in vain;
55   The swain with tears his frustrate labor yields,
And famished dies amidst his ripened fields.[7]
What wonder then, a beast or subject slain
Were equal crimes in a despotic reign;
Both doomed alike for sportive tyrants bled,
60   But while the subject starved, the beast was fed.
Proud Nimrod[8] first the bloody chase began,
A mighty hunter, and his prey was man.
Our haughty Norman boasts that barb'rous name,
And makes his trembling slaves the royal game.
65   The fields are ravished from th' industrious swains,
From men their cities, and from gods their fanes:[9]
The leveled towns with weeds lie covered o'er,
The hollow winds through naked temples roar;
Round broken columns clasping ivy twined;
70   O'er heaps of ruin stalked the stately hind;°   *female deer*
The fox obscene° to gaping tombs retires,   *loathsome*

And savage howlings till the sacred quires.[1]
Awed by his nobles, by his commons° cursed,   *commoners*
The oppressor ruled tyrannic where he durst,
75 Stretched o'er the poor, and church, his iron rod,
And served alike his vassals and his God.
Whom ev'n the Saxon spared, and bloody Dane,
The wanton victims of his sport remain.
But see the man who spacious regions gave
80 A waste for beasts, himself denied a grave![2]
Stretched on the lawn his second hope[3] survey,
At once the chaser and at once the prey.
Lo Rufus, tugging at the deadly dart,
Bleeds in the forest, like a wounded hart.[4]
85 Succeeding monarchs heard the subjects' cries,
Nor saw displeased the peaceful cottage rise.
Then gath'ring flocks on unknown° mountains fed,   *unfamiliar*
O'er sandy wilds were yellow harvests spread,
The forests wondered at th' unusual grain,
90 And secret transport touched the conscious swain.[5]
Fair Liberty, Britannia's goddess, rears
Her cheerful head, and leads the golden years.
   Ye vig'rous swains! while youth ferments your blood,[6]
And purer spirits swell the sprightly flood,
95 Now range the hills, the gameful woods beset,
Wind° the shrill horn, or spread the waving net.   *blow*
When milder Autumn Summer's heat succeeds,
And in the new-shorn field the partridge feeds,
Before his lord the ready spaniel bounds,
100 Panting with hope, he tries the furrowed grounds,
But when the tainted[7] gales the game betray,
Couched close[8] he lies, and meditates the prey;
Secure they trust th' unfaithful field, beset,
Till hov'ring o'er 'em sweeps the swelling net.
105 Thus (if small things we may with great compare)
When Albion° sends her eager sons to war,   *England*
Some thoughtless town, with ease and plenty blessed,
Near, and more near, the closing lines invest;°   *surround*
Sudden they seize th' amazed, defenseless prize,
110 And high in air Britannia's standard flies.
   See! from the brake° the whirring pheasant springs,   *bushes*
And mounts exulting on triumphant wings;
Short is his joy! he feels the fiery wound,

1. Choir stalls; Pope deliberately uses archaic spelling. His description of "quires," "broken columns," and "temples" also suggests grander buildings than the parish churches of this time, calling to mind the destruction of the abbeys during the Reformation.
2. Apparently, at William I's funeral, a knight had tried to stop the King from being buried in land he claimed to own. Pope suggests that this incident and the several royal deaths related to hunting in the forest (depicted in the following four lines) were divine vengeance.

3. Richard, second son of William the Conqueror [Pope's note].
4. William Rufus was accidentally killed by a friend's arrow while out hunting; a hart is a male deer.
5. Joy moves the peasant, well aware of what he has gained; this is a fairly new use of this sense of "conscious."
6. The blood is quickened by the animal spirits supposed to move in it.
7. With the animal's scent.
8. Crouching close to the ground.

Flutters in blood, and panting beats the ground.
115   Ah! what avail his glossy, varying dyes,
His purple crest, and scarlet-circled eyes,
The vivid green his shining plumes unfold;
His painted wings, and breast that flames with gold?
    Nor yet, when moist Arcturus[9] clouds the sky,
120   The woods and fields their pleasing toils deny.
To plains with well-breathed beagles we repair,
And trace the mazes of the circling hare.
(Beasts, urged by us, their fellow beasts pursue,
And learn of Man each other to undo.)
125   With slaught'ring guns th' unwearied fowler roves,
When frosts have whitened all the naked groves;
Where doves in flocks the leafless trees o'ershade,
And lonely woodcocks haunt the watry glade.
He lifts the tube, and levels with his eye;
130   Straight° a short thunder breaks the frozen sky.   *immediately*
Oft, as in airy rings they skim the heath,
The clam'rous lapwings feel the leaden death:
Oft as the mounting larks their notes prepare,
They fall, and leave their little lives in air.
135   In genial Spring, beneath the quiv'ring shade
Where cooling vapors breathe along the mead,
The patient fisher takes his silent stand
Intent, his angle trembling in his hand;
With looks unmoved, he hopes the scaly breed,
140   And eyes the dancing cork and bending reed.
Our plenteous streams a various race supply;
The bright-eyed perch with fins of Tyrian° dye,   *purple*
The silver eel, in shining volumes° rolled,   *coils*
The yellow carp, in scales bedropped with gold,
145   Swift trouts, diversified with crimson stains,
And pikes, the tyrants of the watry plains.
    Now Cancer glows with Phoebus' fiery car;[1]
The youth rush eager to the sylvan war;
Swarm o'er the lawns, the forest walks surround,
150   Rouse°the fleet hart, and cheer the opening° hound.   *flush out/baying*
Th' impatient courser° pants in ev'ry vein,   *fast horse*
And pawing, seems to beat the distant plain,
Hills, vales, and floods appear already crossed,
And ere he starts, a thousand steps are lost.
155   See! the bold youth strain up the threatening steep,
Rush through the thickets, down the valleys sweep,
Hang o'er their coursers' heads with eager speed,
And earth rolls back beneath the flying steed.
Let old Arcadia boast her ample plain,
160   Th' immortal Huntress, and her virgin train;
Nor envy, Windsor! since thy shades have seen

---

9. One of the stars in the Great Bear constellation; in antiquity, its rise with the sun in September was associated with bad weather.

1. The sun (Phoebus's chariot) enters the constellation of Cancer, the crab, on June 22.

As bright a goddess, and as chaste a Queen;
Whose care, like hers, protects the sylvan reign,[2]
The earth's fair light, and empress of the main.[3]
165 Here too, 'tis sung, of old Diana strayed,
And Cynthus' top[4] forsook for Windsor shade;
Here was she seen o'er airy wastes to rove,
Seek the clear spring, or haunt the pathless grove;
Here armed with silver bows, in early dawn,
170 Her buskined° virgins traced the dewy lawn.   *boot-wearing*
Above the rest a rural nymph was famed,
Thy offspring, Thames! the fair Lodona named
(Lodona's fate, in long oblivion cast,
The Muse shall sing, and what she sings shall last),
175 Scarce could the goddess from her nymph be known,
But by the crescent° and the golden zone,°   *moon/belt*
She scorned the praise of beauty, and the care;
A belt her waist, a fillet° binds her hair,   *headband*
A painted quiver on her shoulder sounds,
180 And with her dart the flying deer she wounds.
It chanced, as eager of the chase the maid
Beyond the forest's verdant limits strayed,
Pan saw and loved, and burning with desire
Pursued her flight; her flight increased his fire.
185 Not half so swift the trembling doves can fly,
When the fierce eagle cleaves the liquid° sky;   *transparent*
Not half so swiftly the fierce eagle moves,
When through the clouds he drives the trembling doves;
As from the god she flew with furious pace,
190 Or as the god, more furious, urged the chase.
Now fainting, sinking, pale, the nymph appears;
Now close behind his sounding steps she hears;
And now his shadow reached her as she run,
(His shadow lengthened by the setting sun)
195 And now his shorter breath with sultry air
Pants on her neck, and fans her parting hair.
In vain on Father Thames she calls for aid,
Nor could Diana help her injured maid.
Faint, breathless, thus she prayed, nor prayed in vain:
200 "Ah Cynthia! ah—though banished from thy train,
Let me, O let me, to the shades repair,
My native shades—there weep, and murmur there."
She said, and melting as in tears she lay,
In a soft, silver stream dissolved away.
205 The silver stream her virgin coldness keeps,
Forever murmurs, and forever weeps;
Still bears the name the hapless virgin bore,[5]

---

2. Queen Anne is compared both to the "immortal Huntress" Diana, goddess of chastity, and to Anne's illustrious forebear, the "virgin queen" Elizabeth I.
3. Like Diana, the moon goddess, who governed the tides, Britannia ruled the seas.

4. The mountain on which Diana was said to have been born.
5. I.e., Loddon, a river that runs through Windsor Forest and into the Thames.

And bathes the forest where she ranged before.
In her chaste current oft the goddess laves,°   *bathes*
210   And with celestial tears augments the waves.
Oft in her glass the musing shepherd spies
The headlong mountains and the downward skies,
The watry landscape of the pendant[6] woods,
And absent° trees that tremble in the floods;   *illusory*
215   In the clear azure gleam the flocks are seen,
And floating forests paint the waves with green.
Through the fair scene roll slow the lingering streams,
Then foaming pour along, and rush into the Thames.
     Thou too, great father° of the British floods!   *the Thames*
220   With joyful pride survey'st our lofty woods,
Where tow'ring oaks their growing honors rear,
And future navies on thy shores appear.
Not Neptune's self from all his streams receives
A wealthier tribute, than to thine he gives.
225   No seas so rich, so gay no banks appear,
No lake so gentle, and no spring so clear.
Nor Po so swells the fabling poets' lays,[7]
While led along the skies his current strays,
As thine, which visits Windsor's famed abodes,
230   To grace the mansion of our earthly gods.
Nor all his stars above a luster show,
Like the bright beauties on thy banks below;
Where Jove, subdued by mortal passion still,
Might change Olympus for a nobler hill.
235   Happy the man whom this bright court approves,
His sov'reign favors, and his country loves;
Happy next him who to these shades retires,
Whom Nature charms, and whom the Muse inspires,
Whom humbler joys of home-felt quiet please,
240   Successive study, exercise and ease.
He gathers health from herbs the forest yields,
And of their fragrant physic° spoils° the fields: *medicines/despoils*
With chemic art[8] exalts° the min'ral pow'rs,   *distills*
And draws° the aromatic souls of flow'rs.   *extracts*
245   Now marks the course of rolling orbs on high;
O'er figured worlds[9] now travels with his eye.
Of ancient writ unlocks the learned store,
Consults the dead, and lives past ages o'er.
Or wand'ring thoughtful in the silent wood,
250   Attends the duties of the wise and good,
T' observe a mean,[1] be to himself a friend,
To follow Nature, and regard his end.
Or looks on Heav'n with more than mortal eyes,
Bids his free soul expatiate in the skies,

6. Hanging; the woods both hang over the stream and, in
the stream's reflection, appear to stand upside down.
7. Both Virgil and Ovid compared the Po, a river in Italy,
to the winding constellation Eridanus, named for a river
in Greek mythology.

8. The skills of the chemist.
9. The earth or possibly the zodiac portrayed on a globe.
1. To maintain a steady, balanced course through life;
according to Aristotle, wisdom lay in following the "gold-
en mean," or middle way.

255   Amid her kindred stars familiar roam,
    Survey the region, and confess her home!
    Such was the life great Scipio[2] once admired,
    Thus Atticus,[3] and Trumbull[4] thus retired.
      Ye sacred Nine![5] that all my soul possess,
260   Whose Raptures fire me, and whose visions bless,
    Bear me, oh bear me to sequestered scenes,
    The bow'ry mazes and surrounding greens;
    To Thames's banks which fragrant breezes fill,
    Or where ye Muses sport on Cooper's Hill.
265   (On Cooper's Hill eternal wreaths shall grow,[6]
    While lasts the mountain, or while Thames shall flow)
    I seem through consecrated walks to rove,
    I hear soft music die along the grove;
    Led by the sound I roam from shade to shade,
270   By god-like poets venerable made:
    Here his first lays majestic Denham sung;[7]
    There the last numbers flowed from Cowley's tongue.[8]
    O early lost![9] what tears the river shed
    When the sad pomp along his banks was led?
275   His drooping swans on ev'ry note expire,
    And on his willows[1] hung each Muse's lyre.
      Since Fate relentless stopped their heav'nly voice,
    No more the forests ring, or groves rejoice;
    Who now shall charm the shades where Cowley strung
280   His living harp, and lofty Denham sung?
    But hark! the groves rejoice, the forest rings!
    Are these revived? Or is it Granville sings?
      'Tis yours, my Lord, to bless our soft retreats,
    And call the Muses to their ancient seats,
285   To paint anew the flow'ry sylvan scenes,
    To crown the forests with immortal greens,
    Make Windsor hills in lofty numbers rise,
    And lift her turrets nearer to the skies;
    To sing those honors you deserve to wear,
290   And add new luster to her silver star.[2]
      Here noble Surrey[3] felt the sacred rage,
    Surrey, the Granville of a former age:
    Matchless his pen, victorious was his lance;

2. Scipio Africanus, the Roman general who defeated Hannibal and the Carthaginians in 202 B.C. but declined political office, choosing eventually to retire to the country.

3. Titus Pomponius (109–32 B.C.), despite his friendship and correspondence with Cicero, refused to become involved in politics; he was called Atticus because he spent much time studying in Athens, which lies in the region of Attica.

4. Sir William Trumbull (1639–1716), Pope's elderly friend.

5. The Nine Muses, daughters of Mnemosyne (goddess of memory) and Zeus, each of whom presided over a different art or science.

6. Because commemorated in Sir John Denham's poem *Cooper's Hill* (1642).

7. Denham, described as "majestic" because of the (then unusual) style of the couplets in *Cooper's Hill*, lived near Windsor before the Civil War.

8. Mr. [Abraham] Cowley died at Chertsey, on the borders of the Forest, and was from thence conveyed to Westminster [Pope's note], where he was buried in state.

9. Cowley died at age 49.

1. Emblems of sorrow.

2. The star worn by members inducted into the highly prestigious Order of the Garter, founded by Edward III in Windsor Castle's Chapel of St. George.

3. Henry Howard, Earl of Surrey, one of the first refiners of the English poetry; famous in the time of Henry VIIIth for his sonnets, the scene of many of which is laid at Windsor [Pope's note].

Bold in the lists, and graceful in the dance:
295　In the same shades the Cupids tuned his lyre,
To the same notes of love, and soft desire:
Fair Geraldine,[4] bright object of his vow,
Then filled the groves, as heav'nly Myra[5] now.
　　Oh wouldst thou sing what heroes Windsor bore,
300　What kings first breathed upon her winding shore,[6]
Or raise old warriors whose adored remains
In weeping vaults[7] her hallowed earth contains!
With Edward's[8] acts adorn the shining page,
Stretch his long triumphs down through ev'ry age,
305　Draw monarchs chained, and Cressi's glorious field,[9]
The lilies[1] blazing on the regal shield.
Then, from her roofs when Verrio's colors fall,
And leave inanimate the naked wall;[2]
Still in thy song should vanquished France appear,
310　And bleed forever under Britain's spear.
　　Let softer strains ill-fated Henry[3] mourn,
And palms eternal flourish round his urn.
Here o'er the martyr-king the marble weeps,
And fast beside him, once-feared Edward[4] sleeps;
315　Whom not th' extended Albion could contain,
From old Belerium[5] to the northern main,
The grave unites; where ev'n the great find rest,
And blended lie th' oppressor and th' oppressed!
　　Make sacred Charles's tomb forever known,[6]
320　(Obscure the place, and uninscribed the stone)
Oh fact° accursed! What tears has Albion shed,　　　　　　　deed
Heav'ns! what new wounds, and how her old have bled?
She saw her sons with purple deaths[7] expire,
Her sacred domes° involved in rolling fire,　　　　　stately buildings
325　A dreadful series of intestine wars,[8]
Inglorious triumphs, and dishonest° scars.　　　　　　shameful
At length great ANNA° said—"Let discord cease!"　　　Queen Anne
She said, the world obeyed, and all was peace!

---

4. Lady Elizabeth Fitzgerald (1528?–1589) to whom Surrey was thought to have directed his love poems.
5. The poetic name Granville used for his female addressee.
6. Suggesting the etymological meaning of "Windsor."
7. Because of the seepage of water through the walls; similar natural phenomena explain the conceits in lines 307 and 313.
8. Edward III. born here [Pope's note].
9. The village in northern France where Edward III defeated the French; English triumph over the French (and other nations) was the theme of many of these paintings.
1. Emblem of France, but added to the English crest of arms.
2. In ceiling paintings at Windsor Castle, the artist Antonio Verrio (1639–1707) had depicted the surrender of France in 1356 to Edward the Black Prince, son of Edward III; the paintings were now starting to disintegrate.
3. Henry VI, murdered in 1471, was looked upon by some

in northern Britain (where he lived for some time as a fugitive) as a saint; the "palms" in line 32 are emblems of martyrdom.
4. Edward IV, responsible for Henry VI's murder, was buried in St. George's Chapel, Windsor, where Henry was later re-interred.
5. Land's End in Cornwall, the south-westernmost point in England.
6. Charles I, executed by the Puritans in 1649 and consequently considered by many a Christian and political martyr, was buried in St. George's Chapel without any service; his tomb remained unidentified until 1813.
7. Death from the Great Plague in 1665; this event, like the Great Fire of London (1666) and the 1688 Revolution alluded to in the following lines, was viewed by many as a result of God's wrath, possibly (as Pope here implies) visited on the nation as a result of Charles I's murder.
8. The civil wars during the reigns of Charles I, Cromwell (in Ireland), James II, and William III (in Ireland).

In that blessed moment, from his oozy bed
330   Old Father Thames advanced his rev'rend head.
His tresses dropped with dews, and o'er the stream
His shining horns[9] diffused a golden gleam:
Graved on his urn appeared the moon, that guides
His swelling waters, and alternate tides;
335   The figured streams in waves of silver rolled,
And on their banks Augusta° rose in gold.[1]   *London*
Around his throne the sea-born brothers[2] stood,
Who swell with tributary urns his flood.
First the famed authors of his ancient name,
340   The winding Isis and the fruitful Thame:[3]
The Kennet swift, for silver eels renowned;
The Loddon slow, with verdant alders crowned:
Cole, whose dark streams his flow'ry islands lave;
And chalky Wey, that rolls a milky wave:
345   The blue, transparent Vandalis° appears;   *the Wandle*
The gulphy Lee his sedgy tresses rears:
And sullen Mole, that hides his diving flood;
And silent Darent, stained with Danish blood.[4]
High in the midst, upon his urn reclined,
350   (His sea-green mantle waving with the wind)
The god appeared; he turned his azure eyes
Where Windsor domes and pompous turrets rise,
Then bowed and spoke; the winds forget to roar,
And the hushed waves glide softly to the shore.
355   Hail sacred peace![5] hail long-expected days,
That Thames's glory to the stars shall raise!
Though Tiber's streams immortal Rome behold,
Though foaming Hermus[6] swells with tides of gold,
From Heav'n itself though sev'nfold Nilus[7] flows,
360   And harvests on a hundred realms bestows;
These now no more shall be the Muse's themes,
Lost in my fame, as in the sea their streams.
Let Volga's banks[8] with iron squadrons° shine,   *cavalry*
And groves of lances glitter on the Rhine,
365   Let barb'rous Ganges[9] arm a servile train;
Be mine the blessings of a peaceful reign.
No more my sons shall dye with British blood
Red Iber's[1] sands, or Ister's[2] foaming flood;
Safe on my shore each unmolested swain

9. River gods often had bulls' horns, representing their strength, noisiness, and importance for agriculture.
1. A reference to Dryden's description of London's rebuilding after the Great Fire (in brick and white Portland stone) in *Annus Mirabilis* (1667), to which work the rest of this poem is indebted.
2. According to myth, all rivers were children of the sea gods Oceanus and Thethys.
3. The Thames was seen as the son of the Thame and the Isis rivers.
4. The Danes were defeated at Otford, on the Darent, in 1016.
5. The war of the Spanish Succession had begun in 1701;

peace treaties were signed at London in 1711, and at Utrecht in 1713.
6. An Italian river distinguished by Virgil.
7. Because of its delta, Ovid called the Nile *septemfluus.*
8. An allusion to the defeat of Charles XII of Sweden by the Russians in 1709 (though the battle did not take place near the Volga).
9. Alluding to the Mogul Emperor Aurangzeb's recent wars in India.
1. The Ebro in Spain, where the Allies had gained victory in 1710.
2. The Danube, where Marlborough achieved his famous victory at Blenheim in 1704.

370   Shall tend the flocks, or reap the bearded grain;
      The shady empire shall retain no trace
      Of war or blood, but in the sylvan chase,
      The trumpets sleep, while cheerful horns are blown,
      And arms employed on birds and beasts alone.
375   Behold! th' ascending villas[3] on my side
      Project long shadows o'er the crystal tide.
      Behold! Augusta's glitt'ring spires increase,
      And temples rise,[4] the beauteous works of peace.
      I see, I see where two fair cities[5] bend
380   Their ample bow,° a new Whitehall[6] ascend!   *riverbend*
      There mighty nations shall inquire their doom,[7]
      The world's great oracle in times to come;
      There kings shall sue, and suppliant states be seen
      Once more to bend before a British QUEEN.
385   Thy trees, fair Windsor! now shall leave their woods,
      And half thy forests rush into my floods,
      Bear Britain's thunder, and her cross[8] display,
      To the bright regions of the rising day;
      Tempt° icy seas, where scarce the waters roll,   *attempt*
390   Where clearer flames glow round the frozen pole;
      Or under southern skies exalt° their sails,   *raise*
      Led by new stars, and born by spicy gales!
      For me the balm[9] shall bleed, and amber flow,
      The coral redden, and the ruby glow,
395   The pearly shell its lucid globe infold,
      And Phoebus warm the ripening ore to gold.[1]
      The time shall come, when free as seas or wind
      Unbounded Thames[2] shall flow for all mankind,
      Whole nations enter with each swelling tide,
400   And seas but join the regions they divide;
      Earth's distant ends our glory shall behold,
      And the new world launch forth to seek the old.
      Then ships of uncouth form shall stem the tide,
      And feathered people crowd my wealthy side,[3]
405   And naked youths and painted chiefs admire
      Our speech, our color, and our strange attire!
      Oh stretch thy reign, fair Peace! from shore to shore,
      Till conquest cease, and slav'ry be no more:
      Till the freed[4] Indians in their native groves
410   Reap their own fruits and woo their sable loves,

3. Many new private country homes were being built along the Thames up from London at this time.
4. The fifty new churches [Pope's note], built on the queen's orders to meet the requirements of a growing London.
5. London and Westminster, separated by the Thames, were still distinct cities at this time.
6. There were plans afoot to rebuild the palace of Whitehall, which had largely burnt down in the fires of 1691 and 1697.
7. Fate or destiny. In lines 381–422 Pope makes extensive use of Isaiah chapter 60, which forecasts Zion's future glory.
8. St. George's cross which, with the cross of St. Andrew, made the new Union flag of Great Britain; Pope may also allude to recent British missionary work overseas.
9. Tree sap, often having soothing or healing properties.
1. Phoebus Apollo, god of the sun and patron of poets, was commonly believed to ripen metal into gold with his rays.
2. A wish that London may be made a FREE PORT [Pope's note]; many merchants proposed that customs duties be abolished to make Britain more open to international trade.
3. Four Iroquois Indian chiefs visited England in 1710, causing a sensation.
4. From Spanish oppression.

Peru once more a race of kings behold,
And other Mexicos be roofed with gold.
Exiled by thee from earth to deepest hell,
In brazen bonds shall barb'rous Discord dwell:
415   Gigantic Pride, pale Terror, gloomy Care,
And mad Ambition, shall attend her there.
There purple Vengeance bathed in gore retires,
Her weapons blunted, and extinct her fires:
There hateful Envy her own snakes shall feel,
420   And Persecution mourn her broken wheel:[5]
There Faction roar, Rebellion bite her chain,
And gasping Furies thirst for blood in vain.
    Here cease thy flight, nor with unhallowed lays
Touch the fair fame of Albion's golden days.
425   The thoughts of gods let Granville's verse recite,
And bring the scenes of opening fate to light.
My humble Muse, in unambitious strains,
Paints the green forests and the flow'ry plains,
Where Peace descending bids her olives spring,
430   And scatters blessings from her dove-like wing.
Ev'n I more sweetly pass my careless days,
Pleased in the silent shade with empty praise;
Enough for me, that to the list'ning swains
First in these fields I sung the sylvan strains.

1704–13   1713

The Rape of the Lock

"New things are made familiar, and familiar things are made new," wrote Samuel Johnson about the most accomplished poem of Pope's younger years. "The whole detail of a female day is brought before us invested with so much art of decoration that, though nothing is disguised, everything is striking."

Only a poet with formidable imaginative powers could have made a great mock-heroic poem out of such unpromising materials. When Robert, Lord Petre, cut a love-lock from the head of Arabella Fermor without her permission, the two young people, both in their early twenties, quarreled bitterly. Their families, leading members of the Roman Catholic gentry once on the friendliest terms, became seriously estranged. Pope's friend John Caryll, who saw himself as a mediator among the group, asked him "to write a poem to make a jest of it, and laugh them together."

Pope's first effort was a poem in two cantos, *The Rape of the Locke*, printed in 1712 with some of his other pieces and the work of other poets. Two years later, Pope separately published *The Rape of the Lock*, enlarged to five cantos by the addition of the "machinery" of the sylphs and gnomes, and by the game of Ombre. The poem reached its final form in 1717 when Pope added the moralizing declamation of Clarissa (5.7–35), a parody of the speech of Sarpedon to Glaucus in the *Iliad*. The mock-epic tenor of the five-canto poem was clearly influenced by Pope's translation of the *Iliad*, his main project while most of *The Rape of the Lock* was being composed. Other influences were Homer's *Odyssey*, Virgil's *Aeneid*, Milton's *Paradise Lost*, and Boileau's *Le Lutrin* (1674, 1683), a mock-heroic satire on clerical infighting over the placement of a lectern. Yoking together the mundanely trivial and the mythically heroic as he follows the course of Belinda's day, Pope produced a vivid, yet affectionate, mockery of the fashions and sexual mores common in his own social circle.

5. An instrument of torture.

The arming of the champion for war became the application of Belinda's (i.e., Arabella's) make-up for the battle of the sexes; the larger-than-life gods of classical mythology became miniature cartoon-like sylphs; Aeneas' voyage up the Tiber became Belinda's progress up the Thames; the depiction of Achilles' shield became the description of Belinda's petticoat; the test of single combat became the game of cards; the hero's journey to the underworld became the gnome's adventure in the Cave of Spleen; and the rape of Helen that started the Trojan War became the "rape" (stealing) of Belinda's hair that began an unpleasant social squabble. All the trappings of classical epic are here: the divine messenger appearing to the hero in a dream, the sacrifice to the gods, the inspirational speech to the troops before battle, the epic feast, the violent melee, and the final triumphant apotheosis. Throughout the poem, the enormous distance between the trivial *matter* and the heroic *manner* produces brilliantly comic results.

The Rape of the Lock

An Heroi-Comical Poem in Five Cantos

Nolueram, Belinda, *tuos violare capillos,*
Sed juvat hoc precibus me tribuisse tuis.

Martial[1]

To Mrs. Arabella Fermor
    Madam,
    It will be in vain to deny that I have some regard for this piece, since I dedicate it to you. Yet you may bear me witness, it was intended only to divert a few young ladies, who have good sense and good humor enough, to laugh not only at their sex's little unguarded follies, but at their own.[2] But as it was communicated with the air of a secret, it soon found its way into the world. An imperfect copy having been offered to a bookseller, you had the good nature for my sake to consent to the publication of one more correct; this I was forced to before I had executed half my design, for the *machinery* was entirely wanting to complete it.
    The *machinery,* Madam, is a term invented by the critics, to signify that part which the deities, angels, or demons, are made to act in a poem; for the ancient poets are in one respect like many modern ladies: let an action be never so trivial in itself, they always make it appear of the utmost importance. These machines I determined to raise on a very new and odd foundation, the Rosicrucian[3] doctrine of spirits.
    I know how disagreeable it is to make use of hard words before a lady; but 'tis so much the concern of a poet to have his works understood, and particularly by your sex, that you must give me leave to explain two or three difficult terms.
    The Rosicrucians are a people I must bring you acquainted with. The best account I know of them is in a French book called *Le Comte de Gabalis,*[4] which both in its title and size is so like a novel, that many of the fair sex have read it for one by mistake. According to these gentlemen, the four elements are inhabited by spirits, which they call Sylphs, Gnomes, Nymphs, and Salamanders.[5] The Gnomes, or Demons of Earth, delight in mischief; but the Sylphs, whose habitation is in the air, are the best-conditioned[6] creatures imaginable. For they say, any mortals may enjoy the most intimate familiarities with these gentle spirits, upon a condition very easy to all true adepts, an inviolate preservation of chastity.

---

1. "I did not wish, [Belinda,] to violate your locks, but I rejoice to have yielded this to your wishes" (Martial, *Epigrams* 12.84). Pope has substituted "Belinda" for Martial's "Polytimus."
2. I.e., at their own individual follies as well.
3. A secret society of the 17th and 18th centuries, devoted to the study of ancient religious, philosophical, and mystical doctrines.

4. Written in 1670 by the Abbé de Monfaucon de Villars, its approach to Rosicrucian philosophy was lighthearted. It was printed in duodecimo, a small "pocketbook" size common to many inexpensive novels.
5. Elemental spirits living in fire.
6. Best natured, having the best character.

As to the following cantos, all the passages of them are as fabulous,[7] as the vision at the beginning, or the transformation at the end (except the loss of your hair, which I always mention with reverence). The human persons are as fictitious as the airy ones; and the character of Belinda, as it is now managed, resembles you in nothing but in beauty.

If this poem had as many graces as there are in your person, or in your mind, yet I could never hope it should pass through the world half so uncensured as you have done. But let its fortune be what it will, mine is happy enough, to have given me this occasion of assuring you that I am, with the truest esteem,

Madam,

Your most obedient

humble servant.

A. Pope

CANTO 1

What dire offense from am'rous causes springs,
What mighty contests rise from trivial things,
I sing[8]—This verse to Caryll, Muse! is due;
This, ev'n Belinda may vouchsafe to view:
5   Slight is the subject, but not so the praise,
If she inspire, and he approve my lays.°   *verses*
       Say what strange motive, Goddess!° could compel   *his Muse*
A well-bred lord t' assault a gentle belle?
Oh say what stranger cause, yet unexplored,
10   Could make a gentle belle reject a lord?
In tasks so bold, can little men engage,
And in soft bosoms dwells such mighty rage?
       Sol through white curtains shot a tim'rous ray,
And op'd those eyes that must eclipse the day;
15   Now lapdogs[9] give themselves the rousing shake,
And sleepless lovers, just at twelve, awake:
Thrice rung the bell, the slipper knocked the ground,[1]
And the pressed watch returned a silver sound.[2]
Belinda still her downy pillow pressed,
20   Her guardian Sylph prolonged the balmy rest.
'Twas he had summoned to her silent bed
The morning dream that hovered o'er her head.
A youth more glitt'ring than a birthnight beau,[3]
(That ev'n in slumber caused her cheek to glow)
25   Seemed to her ear his winning lips to lay,
And thus in whispers said, or seemed to say:[4]
       "Fairest of mortals, thou distinguished care
Of thousand bright inhabitants of air!
If e'er one vision touched thy infant thought,
30   Of all the nurse and all the priest have taught,[5]

7. Fictional.
8. Pope begins with the ancient epic formula of "proposition" of the work as a whole, and "invocation" of the gods' assistance, continuing with the traditional epic questions.
9. Small dogs imported from Asia were highly fashionable ladies' pets at this time.
1. Belinda rings the bell and then finally bangs her slipper on the floor to call her maid.
2. The popular "pressed watch" chimed the hour and

quarter hours when its stem was pressed, saving its owner from striking a match to see the time.
3. On a royal birthday, courtiers' clothes were particularly extravagant.
4. His whispering recalls the serpent's temptation of Eve in Milton.
5. The nurse and priest were seen as two standard sources of superstition.

Of airy elves by moonlight shadows seen,
The silver token, and the circled green,[6]
Or virgins visited by angel pow'rs,[7]
With golden crowns and wreaths of heav'nly flow'rs,
35   Hear and believe! thy own importance know,
Nor bound thy narrow views to things below.
Some secret truths from learned pride concealed,
To maids alone and children are revealed:
What though no credit doubting wits may give?[8]
40   The fair and innocent shall still believe.
Know then, unnumbered spirits round thee fly,
The light militia of the lower sky;
These, though unseen, are ever on the wing,
Hang o'er the box, and hover round the ring.[9]
45   Think what an equipage[1] thou hast in air,
And view with scorn two pages and a chair.[2]
As now your own, our beings were of old,
And once enclosed in woman's beauteous mold;
Thence, by a soft transition, we repair
50   From earthly vehicles[3] to these of air.
Think not, when woman's transient breath is fled,
That all her vanities at once are dead:
Succeeding vanities she still regards,
And though she plays no more, o'erlooks the cards.
55   Her joy in gilded chariots, when alive,
And love of Ombre,[4] after death survive.
For when the fair in all their pride expire,
To their first elements[5] their souls retire:
The sprites of fiery termagants° in flame   *scolding women*
60   Mount up, and take a salamander's name.
Soft yielding minds to water glide away,
And sip with Nymphs, their elemental tea.
The graver prude sinks downward to a Gnome,
In search of mischief still on earth to roam.
65   The light coquettes in Sylphs aloft repair,
And sport and flutter in the fields of air.
    "Know farther yet; whoever fair and chaste
Rejects mankind, is by some Sylph embraced:
For spirits, freed from mortal laws, with ease
70   Assume what sexes and what shapes they please.[6]
What guards the purity of melting maids,[7]
In courtly balls, and midnight masquerades,

---

6. Withered circles in the grass and silver coins were supposed to be signs of fairies' presence.
7. Belinda is reminded of the many virgin saints, and particularly the Annunciation to the Virgin Mary.
8. Religious skepticism was on the increase.
9. The theater box and the equally fashionable drive round Hyde Park.
1. Carriage, horses, and attendants.
2. A sedan chair, carried by two chairmen.
3. Both the carriage, and the physical body.
4. Ombre (pronounced Omber) was an elaborate card game, introduced into England in the 17th century and

highly fashionable in the early 18th century. Given the general tenor of the poem, Pope may also be punning on the origin of the word "Ombre," from the Spanish *hombre*, meaning "man."
5. The four elements of fire, water, earth, and air were thought to make up all things; so an individual's character was determined by whichever element dominated his or her soul.
6. Cf. *Paradise Lost,* "For spirits when they please / Can either sex assume, or both" (1.423–424).
7. I.e., the chastity of weakening virgins.

Safe from the treach'rous friend, the daring spark,[8]
The glance by day, the whisper in the dark;
75 When kind occasion prompts their warm desires,
When music softens, and when dancing fires?
'Tis but their Sylph, the wise celestials know,
Though *Honor* is the word with men below.
        "Some nymphs there are, too conscious of their face,
80 For life predestined to the Gnomes' embrace.
These swell their prospects and exalt their pride,
When offers are disdained, and love denied.
Then gay ideas crowd the vacant brain;
While peers° and dukes, and all their sweeping train,   *aristocrats*
85 And garters, stars, and coronets[9] appear,
And in soft sounds, "your Grace"[1] salutes their ear.
'Tis these that early taint the female soul,
Instruct the eyes of young coquettes to roll,
Teach infant cheeks a bidden° blush to know,   *deliberate*
90 And little hearts to flutter at a beau.
        "Oft when the world imagine women stray,
The Sylphs through mystic mazes guide their way,
Through all the giddy circle they pursue,
And old impertinence° expel by new.   *frivolity*
95 What tender maid but must a victim fall
To one man's treat, but for another's ball?
When Florio speaks, what virgin could withstand,
If gentle Damon did not squeeze her hand?
With varying vanities, from ev'ry part,
100 They shift the moving toy shop[2] of their heart;
Where wigs with wigs, with sword knots sword knots strive,[3]
Beaus banish beaus, and coaches coaches drive.[4]
This erring mortals levity may call,
Oh blind to truth! the Sylphs contrive it all.
105   "Of these am I, who thy protection claim,
A watchful sprite, and Ariel is my name.
Late, as I ranged the crystal wilds of air,
In the clear mirror of thy ruling star
I saw, alas! some dread event impend,
110 Ere to the main° this morning sun descend.   *sea*
But Heav'n reveals not what, or how, or where:
Warned by thy Sylph, oh pious maid beware!
This to disclose is all thy guardian can.
Beware of all, but most beware of man!"
115   He said; when Shock,[5] who thought she slept too long,
Leapt up, and waked his mistress with his tongue.
'Twas then Belinda! if report say true,
Thy eyes first opened on a *billet-doux*;°   *love letter*

---

8. A bold, brash, and showy young man.
9. Emblems of noble rank.
1. Form of address for a duke or a duchess.
2. Where toys and trinkets are sold; "moving" here means easily changed, unstable.
3. Most men wore wigs in public; formally dressed men

tied ribbons to the hilt of their swords.
4. In word order and versification, these two lines mimic both Homer's and Ovid's description of heroic combat.
5. The shock or shough, a long-haired Icelandic poodle, fashionable as a lapdog.

Wounds, charms, and ardors, were no sooner read,
120   But all the vision vanished from thy head.
        And now, unveiled, the toilet° stands displayed,   *dressing table*
        Each silver vase in mystic order laid.
        First, robed in white, the nymph intent adores
        With head uncovered, the cosmetic pow'rs.
125   A heav'nly image[6] in the glass appears,
        To that she bends, to that her eyes she rears;°   *raises*
        Th' inferior priestess,[7] at her altar's side,
        Trembling, begins the sacred rites of pride.
        Unnumbered treasures ope at once, and here
130   The various off'rings of the world appear;
        From each she nicely culls with curious° toil,   *careful*
        And decks the goddess with the glitt'ring spoil.
        This casket India's glowing gems unlocks,
        And all Arabia° breathes from yonder box.   *eastern perfume*
135   The tortoise here and elephant unite,
        Transformed to combs, the speckled and the white.[8]
        Here files of pins extend their shining rows,
        Puffs, powders, patches, Bibles,[9] *billet-doux*.
        Now awful° beauty puts on all its arms;   *awe-inspiring*
140   The fair each moment rises in her charms,
        Repairs her smiles, awakens ev'ry grace,
        And calls forth all the wonders of her face;
        Sees by degrees a purer blush[1] arise,
        And keener lightnings[2] quicken in her eyes.
145   The busy Sylphs surround their darling care;
        These set the head, and those divide the hair,
        Some fold the sleeve, whilst others plait the gown;
        And Betty's praised for labors not her own.

Canto 2

Not with more glories, in th' ethereal plain,°   *sky*
        The sun first rises o'er the purpled main,
        Than issuing forth, the rival of his beams
        Launched on the bosom of the silver Thames.[1]
5   Fair nymphs, and well-dressed youths around her shone,
        But ev'ry eye was fixed on her alone.
        On her white breast a sparkling cross she wore,
        Which Jews might kiss, and infidels adore.[2]
        Her lively looks a sprightly mind disclose,
10   Quick as her eyes, and as unfixed as those:
        Favors to none, to all she smiles extends,
        Oft she rejects, but never once offends.

6. I.e., Belinda herself.
7. Belinda's maid, Betty.
8. Tortoise-shell and ivory.
9. Patches were small beauty spots of black silk, pasted onto the face to make the skin appear whiter. It was fashionable to own Bibles in very small format.
1. The even, artificial blush of rouge.
2. Caused by drops of belladonna (deadly nightshade),

which dilates the pupils.
1. Belinda takes a boat from London to Hampton Court, avoiding the dirt and squalor of the streets; her voyage compares with Aeneas's up the Tiber (*Aeneid* 7), or, alternatively, Cleopatra's up the Nile (*Antony and Cleopatra* 2.2).
2. Kissing the cross was the sign of religious conversion.

Bright as the sun, her eyes the gazers strike,
And, like the sun, they shine on all alike.
15 Yet graceful ease, and sweetness void of pride,
Might hide her faults, if belles had faults to hide:
If to her share some female errors fall,
Look on her face, and you'll forget 'em all.
     This nymph, to the destruction of mankind,
20 Nourished two locks which graceful hung behind
In equal curls, and well conspired to deck
With shining ringlets the smooth iv'ry neck.
Love in these labyrinths his slaves detains,
And mighty hearts are held in slender chains.
25 With hairy springes° we the birds betray,   *noose traps*
Slight lines° of hair surprise the finny prey,   *fishing lines*
Fair tresses man's imperial race ensnare,
And beauty draws us with a single hair.
     Th' adventurous Baron[3] the bright locks admired,
30 He saw, he wished, and to the prize aspired:
Resolved to win, he meditates the way,
By force to ravish, or by fraud betray;
For when success a lover's toil attends,
Few ask, if fraud or force attained his ends.
35   For this, ere Phoebus rose, he had implored
Propitious Heav'n, and ev'ry pow'r adored,°   *worshipped*
But chiefly *Love*—to *Love* an altar built,
Of twelve vast French romances, neatly gilt.
There lay three garters, half a pair of gloves;
40 And all the trophies of his former loves.
With tender *billet-doux* he lights the pyre,
And breathes three am'rous sighs to raise the fire.
Then prostrate falls, and begs with ardent eyes
Soon to obtain, and long possess the prize:
45 The pow'rs gave ear, and granted half his pray'r,
The rest the winds dispersed in empty air.[4]
     But now secure the painted vessel glides,
The sunbeams trembling on the floating tides,
While melting music steals upon the sky,
50 And softened sounds along the waters die.
Smooth flow the waves, the zephyrs° gently play,   *breezes*
Belinda smiled, and all the world was gay.
All but the Sylph—with careful° thoughts oppressed,   *worried*
Th' impending woe sat heavy on his breast.
55 He summons strait his denizens[5] of air;
The lucid squadrons round the sails repair:
Soft o'er the shrouds° aerial whispers breathe,   *ropes*
That seemed but zephyrs to the train beneath.
Some to the sun their insect wings unfold,
60 Waft on the breeze, or sink in clouds of gold.

---

3. Robert, Lord Petre (1690–1713), responsible for the
original incident.
4. Cf. *The Aeneid* 2.794–795, which Dryden translated:

"Apollo heard, and granting half his pray'r, / Shuffled in
winds the rest, and toss'd in empty air."
5. Naturalized foreigner.

Transparent forms, too fine for mortal sight,
Their fluid bodies half dissolved in light,
Loose to the wind their airy garments flew,
Thin glitt'ring textures of the filmy dew;
65   Dipped in the richest tincture of the skies,
Where light disports in ever-mingling dyes,
While ev'ry beam new transient colors flings,
Colors that change whene'er they wave their wings.
Amid the circle, on the gilded mast,
70   Superior by the head, was Ariel placed;[6]
His purple pinions opening to the sun,
He raised his azure wand, and thus begun:
    "Ye Sylphs and Sylphids,° to your chief give ear,   *female Sylphs*
Fays, Fairies, Genii, Elves, and Demons hear!
75   Ye know the spheres and various tasks assigned,
By laws eternal to th' aerial kind.
Some in the fields of purest ether[7] play,
And bask and whiten in the blaze of day.
Some guide the course of wandering orbs° on high,   *comets*
80   Or roll the planets through the boundless sky.
Some less refined, beneath the moon's pale light
Pursue the stars that shoot athwart the night,
Or suck the mists in grosser° air below,   *heavier*
Or dip their pinions in the painted bow,°   *rainbow*
85   Or brew fierce tempests on the wintry main,
Or o'er the glebe° distill the kindly rain.   *farmland*
Others on earth o'er human race preside,
Watch all their ways, and all their actions guide:
Of these the chief the care of nations own,
90   And guard with arms divine the British throne.
    "Our humbler province is to tend the fair,
Not a less pleasing, though less glorious care.
To save the powder from too rude° a gale,   *rough*
Nor let th' imprisoned essences° exhale,   *perfumes*
95   To draw fresh colors from the vernal flow'rs,
To steal from rainbows ere they drop in show'rs
A brighter wash;[8] to curl their waving hairs,
Assist their blushes, and inspire their airs;
Nay oft, in dreams, invention we bestow,
100   To change a flounce, or add a furbelow.°   *fringe*
    "This day, black omens threat the brightest fair
That e'er deserved a watchful spirit's care;
Some dire disaster, or° by force or sleight,°   *either/trick*
But what, or where, the fates have wrapped in night.
105   Whether the nymph shall break Diana's law,°   *virginity*
Or some frail China jar receive a flaw,
Or stain her honor, or her new brocade,
Forget her pray'rs, or miss a masquerade,
Or lose her heart, or necklace, at a ball;

---

6. Heroes of epics were typically taller than their men.   8. A cosmetic rinse.
7. Air beyond the moon.

110 Or whether Heav'n has doomed that Shock must fall.
Haste then ye spirits! to your charge° repair;   *duty*
The flutt'ring fan be Zephyretta's care;
The drops° to thee, Brillante, we consign;   *earrings*
And, Momentilla, let the watch be thine;
115 Do thou, Crispissa,[9] tend her fav'rite lock;
Ariel himself shall be the guard of Shock.
  "To fifty chosen Sylphs, of special note,
We trust th' important charge, the petticoat:
Oft have we known that sev'nfold fence[1] to fail,
120 Though stiff with hoops, and armed with ribs of whale.
Form a strong line about the silver bound,
And guard the wide circumference around.
  "Whatever spirit, careless of his charge,
His post neglects, or leaves the fair at large,
125 Shall feel sharp vengeance soon o'ertake his sins,
Be stopped in vials, or transfixed with pins;
Or plunged in lakes of bitter washes lie,
Or wedged whole ages in a bodkin's[2] eye:
Gums and pomatums° shall his flight restrain,   *ointments*
130 While clogged he beats his silken wings in vain;
Or alum styptics[3] with contracting power
Shrink his thin essence like a rivelled° flower.   *shriveled*
Or as Ixion[4] fixed, the wretch shall feel
The giddy motion of the whirling mill,[5]
135 In fumes of burning chocolate shall glow,
And tremble at the sea that froths below!"
  He spoke; the spirits from the sails descend;
Some, orb in orb, around the nymph extend,
Some thrid° the mazy ringlets of her hair,   *slid through*
140 Some hang upon the pendants of her ear;
With beating hearts the dire event they wait,
Anxious, and trembling for the birth of fate.

CANTO 3

Close by those meads forever crowned with flow'rs,
Where Thames with pride surveys his rising tow'rs,
There stands a structure of majestic frame,
Which from the neighb'ring Hampton takes its name.[1]
5 Here Britain's statesmen oft the fall foredoom
Of foreign tyrants, and of nymphs at home;
Here thou, great Anna! whom three realms obey,[2]
Dost sometimes counsel take—and sometimes tea.

---

9. The Latin *crispere* means "to curl."
1. Serving Belinda like the epic warrior's shield, her petticoat has seven layers bound together with a silver band (cf. *Iliad* 18 or *Aeneid* 8).
2. Blunt, thick needle; the Sylph, like the camel in Matthew 19.24, has difficulty getting through. Pope later plays on the various meanings of "bodkin," which also include a hair ornament and a dagger.
3. Astringents that stopped bleeding.
4. Having tried the chastity of Hera, Ixion was punished by being tied to a revolving wheel of fire.
5. For beating chocolate, a new and highly fashionable drink.
1. Hampton Court, about 15 miles upriver from London, was built in the 16th century by Cardinal Wolsey, and by Queen Anne's day was associated with wits as well as with statesmen.
2. The English Crown still maintained its ancient claim to rule France as well as Great Britain and Ireland.

       Hither the heroes and the nymphs resort,
10   To taste awhile the pleasures of a court;
       In various talk th' instructive hours they passed,
       Who gave the ball, or paid the visit last:
       One speaks the glory of the British Queen,
       And one describes a charming Indian screen;
15   A third interprets motions, looks, and eyes;
       At ev'ry word a reputation dies.
       Snuff, or the fan, supply each pause of chat,
       With singing, laughing, ogling, and all that.
          Meanwhile declining from the noon of day,
20   The sun obliquely shoots his burning ray;
       The hungry judges soon the sentence sign,
       And wretches hang that jurymen may dine;
       The merchant from th' Exchange° returns in peace,   *market*
       And the long labors of the toilette cease—
25   Belinda now, whom thirst of fame invites,
       Burns to encounter two advent'rous knights,
       At Ombre[3] singly to decide their doom;
       And swells her breast with conquests yet to come.
       Straight the three bands prepare in arms to join,
30   Each band the number of the Sacred Nine.[4]
       Soon as she spreads her hand, th' aerial guard
       Descend, and sit on each important card:
       First Ariel perched upon a Matador,[5]
       Then each, according to the rank they bore;
35   For Sylphs, yet mindful of their ancient race,
       Are, as when women, wondrous fond of place.°   *rank*
          Behold, four kings in majesty revered,
       With hoary whiskers[6] and a forky beard;
       And four fair queens whose hands sustain° a flow'r,   *hold*
40   Th' expressive emblem of their softer pow'r;
       Four knaves in garbs succinct,° a trusty band,   *girded up*
       Caps on their heads, and halberds in their hand;
       And particolored troops, a shining train,
       Draw forth to combat on the velvet plain.[7]
45   The skillful nymph reviews her force with care;
       "Let spades be trumps!" she said, and trumps they were.[8]
          Now move to war her sable Matadors,
       In show like leaders of the swarthy moors.
       Spadillio first, unconquerable lord!
50   Led off two captive trumps, and swept the board.
       As many more Manillio forced to yield,
       And marched a victor from the verdant field.

---

3. A card game played with 40 cards, similar to modern bridge: three players hold nine cards each and bid for tricks, with the highest bidder becoming the "ombre" (man) and choosing trumps.
4. Pope links the nine Muses to the nine cards each player holds.
5. The Matadores are the three cards of highest value; Belinda holds all three: when trumps are black, they are the Spadillio (ace of spades), Manillio (deuce of spades),

and Basto (ace of clubs).
6. Gray mustache. The royal figures on the cards now conduct a mock-epic review of their forces, and the whole game is described as an epic battle, with the characters appearing as on the cards.
7. The green velvet card table.
8. Cf. Genesis 1.3, "Then God said, 'Let there be light'; and there was light."

Him Basto followed, but his fate more hard
Gained but one trump and one plebeian card.
55 With his broad saber next, a chief in years,
The hoary majesty of spades appears;
Puts forth one manly leg, to sight revealed;
The rest his many-colored robe concealed.
The rebel knave who dares his prince engage,
60 Proves the just victim of his royal rage.
Ev'n mighty Pam[9] that kings and queens o'erthrew,
And mowed down armies in the fights of Lu,
Sad chance of war! now, destitute of aid,
Falls undistinguished by the victor spade!
65   Thus far both armies to Belinda yield;
Now to the Baron fate inclines the field.
His warlike amazon her host invades,
Th' imperial consort of the crown of spades.
The club's black tyrant first her victim died,
70 Spite of his haughty mien and barb'rous pride:
What boots the regal circle on his head,
His giant limbs in state unwieldy spread?
That long behind he trails his pompous robe,
And of all monarchs only grasps the globe?
75   The Baron now his diamonds pours apace;
Th' embroidered king who shows but half his face,
And his refulgent queen, with pow'rs combined,
Of broken troops an easy conquest find.
Clubs, diamonds, hearts, in wild disorder seen,
80 With throngs promiscuous strew the level green.
Thus when dispersed a routed army runs,
Of Asia's troops and Afric's sable sons,
With like confusion different nations fly,
Of various habit and of various dye,
85 The pierced battalions disunited fall,
In heaps on heaps; one fate o'erwhelms them all.
The knave of diamonds tries his wily arts,
And wins (oh shameful chance!) the queen of hearts.
At this, the blood the virgin's cheek forsook,
90 A livid paleness spreads o'er all her look;
She sees, and trembles at th' approaching ill,
Just in the jaws of ruin, and codille.[1]
And now (as oft in some distempered state)
On one nice trick[2] depends the gen'ral fate.
95 An ace of hearts steps forth: the king[3] unseen
Lurked in her hand, and mourned his captive queen.
He springs to vengeance with an eager pace,
And falls like thunder on the prostrate ace.
The nymph exulting fills with shouts the sky,
100 The walls, the woods, and long canals reply.

9. The knave or jack of clubs, which took precedence
over all trumps in the game of Lu, or Loo.
1. Literally "elbow": the defeat suffered by the ombre if
another player wins more tricks.

2. Trick applies in both its technical and general senses as
Belinda makes this careful maneuver.
3. The King of Hearts.

Oh thoughtless mortals! ever blind to fate,
Too soon dejected, and too soon elate!
Sudden these honors shall be snatched away,
And cursed forever this victorious day.
105   For lo! the board with cups and spoons is crowned,
The berries crackle, and the Mill turns round.[4]
On shining altars of Japan[5] they raise
The silver lamp; the fiery spirits blaze.
From silver spouts the grateful° liquors glide,   *pleasing*
110   While China's earth receives the smoking tide.
At once they gratify their scent and taste,
And frequent cups prolong the rich repast.
Straight° hover round the fair her airy band;   *immediately*
Some, as she sipped, the fuming liquor fanned,
115   Some o'er her lap their careful plumes displayed,
Trembling, and conscious of the rich brocade.
Coffee (which makes the politician wise,
And see through all things with his half-shut eyes)
Sent up in vapors[6] to the Baron's brain
120   New stratagems, the radiant lock to gain.
Ah cease rash youth! desist ere 'tis too late,
Fear the just gods, and think of Scylla's fate![7]
Changed to a bird, and sent to flit in air,
She dearly pays for Nisus' injured hair!
     But when to mischief mortals bend their will,
125   How soon they find fit instruments of ill!
Just then, Clarissa drew with tempting grace
A two-edged weapon from her shining case;
So ladies in romance assist their knight,
130   Present the spear, and arm him for the fight.
He takes the gift with rev'rence, and extends
The little engine° on his fingers' ends,   *instrument*
This just behind Belinda's neck he spread,
As o'er the fragrant steams she bends her head:
135   Swift to the lock a thousand sprites repair,
A thousand wings, by turns, blow back the hair,
And thrice they twitched the diamond in her ear,
Thrice she looked back, and thrice the foe drew near.
Just in that instant, anxious Ariel sought
140   The close recesses of the virgin's thought;
As on the nosegay in her breast reclined,
He watched th' ideas rising in her mind,
Sudden he viewed, in spite of all her art,
An earthly lover° lurking at her heart.   *Lord Petre*
145   Amazed, confused, he found his pow'r expired,
Resigned to fate, and with a sigh retired.
     The peer now spreads the glitt'ring forfex° wide,   *scissors*
T' enclose the lock; now joins it, to divide.

---

4. Grinding coffee beans.
5. Lacquered tables ("Japan" was a type of varnish originating in that country).
6. Both steam and vain imaginations.

7. Scylla plucked purple hair from the head of her father,
King Nisus, to offer to her lover, Minos, so destroying her
father's power. Minos rejected her impiety, and Scylla
was transformed into a bird.

Ev'n then, before the fatal engine closed,
150 A wretched Sylph too fondly interposed;
Fate urged the shears, and cut the Sylph in twain
(But airy substance soon unites again)[8]
The meeting points the sacred hair dissever
From the fair head, forever and forever!
155   Then flashed the living lightning from her eyes,
And screams of horror rend th' affrighted skies.
Not louder shrieks to pitying Heav'n are cast,
When husbands or when lapdogs breathe their last,
Or when rich china vessels, fall'n from high,
160 In glitt'ring dust and painted fragments lie!
    Let wreaths of triumph now my temples twine,
(The victor cried) the glorious prize is mine!
While fish in streams, or birds delight in air,
Or in a coach and six[9] the British fair,
165 As long as *Atalantis*[1] shall be read,
Or the small pillow grace a lady's bed,[2]
While visits shall be paid on solemn days,
When numerous wax lights[3] in bright order blaze,
While nymphs take treats, or assignations give,
170 So long my honor, name, and praise shall live!
    What time would spare, from steel receives its date,°   end
And monuments, like men, submit to fate!
Steel could the labor of the gods destroy,
And strike to dust th' imperial tow'rs of Troy;[4]
175 Steel could the works of mortal pride confound,
And hew triumphal arches to the ground.
What wonder then, fair nymph! thy hairs should feel
The conqu'ring force of unresisted steel?

CANTO 4

But anxious cares the pensive nymph oppressed,
And secret passions labored in her breast.
Not youthful kings in battle seized alive,
Not scornful virgins who their charms survive,
5 Not ardent lovers robbed of all their bliss,
Not ancient ladies when refused a kiss,
Not tyrants fierce that unrepenting die,
Not Cynthia when her manteau's° pinned awry,   gown's
E'er felt such rage, resentment, and despair,
10 As thou, sad virgin! for thy ravished hair.
    For, that sad moment, when the Sylphs withdrew,
And Ariel weeping from Belinda flew,
Umbriel, a dusky melancholy sprite

---

8. *Milton* lib. 6 [Pope's note], citing *Paradise Lost* 6.329–331, "The girding sword with discontinuous wound / Passed through him, but the ethereal substance closed / Not long divisible . . . ."
9. A carriage drawn by six horses; a symbol of wealth and prestige.
1. The scandalous *Atalantis: Secret Memoirs and Manners of Several Persons of Quality* (1709), by Mary Delarivière

Manley.
2. Said to be a place where ladies hid romance novels and other contraband.
3. Candles made of wax, rather than the cheaper tallow. Evening social visits were an essential part of the fashionable woman's routine.
4. Even Troy, fabled to have been built by Apollo and Poseidon, was destroyed by arms.

As ever sullied the fair face of light,
15   Down to the central earth, his proper scene,
Repaired to search the gloomy Cave of Spleen.[1]
Swift on his sooty pinions flits the Gnome,
And in a vapor[2] reached the dismal dome.
No cheerful breeze this sullen region knows,
20   The dreaded east[3] is all the wind that blows.
Here, in a grotto, sheltered close from air,
And screened in shades° from day's detested glare,   *shadows*
She sighs forever on her pensive bed,
Pain at her side, and Megrim° at her head.   *migraine*
25   Two handmaids wait the throne: alike in place,
But diff'ring far in figure and in face.
Here stood Ill-Nature like an ancient maid,
Her wrinkled form in black and white arrayed;
With store of pray'rs, for mornings, nights, and noons,
30   Her hand is filled; her bosom with lampoons.
There Affectation with a sickly mien
Shows in her cheek the roses of eighteen,
Practiced to lisp, and hang the head aside,
Faints into airs, and languishes with pride;
35   On the rich quilt sinks with becoming woe,
Wrapped in a gown, for sickness, and for show.
The fair ones feel such maladies as these,
When each new nightdress gives a new disease.
40   A constant vapor o'er the palace flies;
Strange phantoms rising as the mists arise;
Dreadful, as hermit's dreams in haunted shades,
Or bright as visions of expiring maids.[4]
Now glaring fiends, and snakes on rolling spires,°   *coils*
Pale specters, gaping tombs, and purple fires:
45   Now lakes of liquid gold, Elysian scenes,[5]
And crystal domes, and angels in machines.
Unnumbered throngs on ev'ry side are seen
Of bodies changed to various forms by Spleen.[6]
Here living teapots stand, one arm held out,
50   One bent; the handle this, and that the spout:
A pipkin[7] there like Homer's tripod walks;
Here sighs a jar, and there a goose pie[8] talks;
Men prove with child, as pow'rful fancy works,
And maids turned bottles, call aloud for corks.
55   Safe passed the Gnome through this fantastic band,
A branch of healing spleenwort[9] in his hand.

---

1. Named after the bodily organ, "spleen" was the current name for the fashionable affliction of melancholy or ill-humor. Umbriel's descent into the womb-like Cave of Spleen suggests the epic commonplace of the journey to the underworld.
2. "The spleen" was also called "the vapors."
3. The east wind was supposed to induce fits of spleen.
4. Religious visions of hell and heaven.
5. Elysium was the classical paradise, but this also recalls contemporary theater, which made much of scenic spec-

tacle and the use of machinery.
6. Hallucinations similar to those described in the following lines were common to those afflicted with spleen.
7. Small pot or pan. Hephaistos's "walking" tripods are described in the *Iliad* 18.439ff.
8. Alludes to a real fact, a Lady of distinction imagin'd herself in this condition [Pope's note].
9. Pope changes the golden bough that protected Aeneas on his trip through the underworld into a herb that was supposed to be good for the spleen.

Then thus addressed the pow'r—"Hail, wayward Queen!
Who rule the sex to fifty from fifteen,
Parent of vapors and of female wit,
60 Who give th' hysteric or poetic fit,
On various tempers act by various ways,
Make some take physic,° others scribble plays;[1]   *medicine*
Who cause the proud their visits to delay,
And send the godly in a pet° to pray.   *ill-humor*
65 A nymph there is that all thy pow'r disdains,
And thousands more in equal mirth maintains.
But oh! if e'er thy Gnome could spoil a grace,
Or raise a pimple on a beauteous face,
Like citron-waters° matrons' cheeks inflame,   *flavored brandy*
70 Or change complexions at a losing game;
If e'er with airy horns[2] I planted heads,
Or rumpled petticoats, or tumbled beds,
Or caused suspicion when no soul was rude,
Or discomposed the headdress of a prude,
75 Or e'er to costive° lapdog gave disease,   *constipated*
Which not the tears of brightest eyes could ease:
Hear me, and touch Belinda with chagrin;
That single act gives half the world the spleen."
     The goddess with a discontented air
80 Seems to reject him, though she grants his pray'r.
A wondrous bag with both her hands she binds,
Like that where once Ulysses held the winds;[3]
There she collects the force of female lungs,
Sighs, sobs, and passions, and the war of tongues.
85 A vial next she fills with fainting fears,
Soft sorrows, melting griefs, and flowing tears.
The Gnome rejoicing bears her gifts away,
Spreads his black wings, and slowly mounts to day.
     Sunk in Thalestris'[4] arms the nymph he found,
90 Her eyes dejected and her hair unbound.
Full o'er their heads the swelling bag he rent,
And all the furies issued at the vent.
Belinda burns with more than mortal ire,
And fierce Thalestris fans the rising fire.
95 "O wretched maid!" she spread her hands, and cried,
(While Hampton's echoes "Wretched maid!" replied)
"Was it for this you took such constant care
The bodkin, comb, and essence to prepare;
For this your locks in paper durance° bound,   *curling papers*
100 For this with tort'ring irons wreathed around?
For this with fillets[5] strained your tender head,
And bravely bore the double loads of lead?°   *wire supports*
Gods! shall the ravisher display your hair,

---

1. Melancholy was associated with artistic creativity.
2. A sign that a husband had been cuckolded.
3. Given to him by the wind god Aeolus (*Odyssey* 10.19ff.).

4. A queen of the Amazons; here Mrs. Morley, Arabella's second cousin.
5. Headbands, with reference to priestesses in the *Aeneid*.

While the fops envy, and the ladies stare!
105 Honor forbid! at whose unrivaled shrine
Ease, pleasure, virtue, all, our sex resign.
Methinks already I your tears survey,
Already hear the horrid things they say,
Already see you a degraded toast,[6]
110 And all your honor in a whisper lost!
How shall I, then, your helpless fame defend?
'Twill then be infamy to seem your friend!
And shall this prize, th' inestimable prize,
Exposed through crystal to the gazing eyes,
115 And heightened by the diamond's circling rays,
On that rapacious hand forever blaze?[7]
Sooner shall grass in Hyde Park Circus grow,[8]
And wits take lodgings in the sound of Bow;[9]
Sooner let earth, air, sea, to Chaos fall,
120 Men, monkeys, lapdogs, parrots, perish all!"
    She said; then raging to Sir Plume[1] repairs,
And bids her beau demand the precious hairs:
(Sir Plume, of amber snuffbox justly vain,
And the nice conduct of a clouded cane[2])
125 With earnest eyes, and round unthinking face,
He first the snuffbox opened, then the case,
And thus broke out—"My Lord, why, what the devil?
Z—ds![3] damn the lock! 'fore Gad, you must be civil!
Plague on't! 'tis past a jest—nay prithee, Pox!
130 Give her the hair"—he spoke, and rapped his box.
    "It grieves me much" (replied the Peer again)
"Who speaks so well should ever speak in vain.
But by this lock, this sacred lock I swear
(Which never more shall join its parted hair,
135 Which never more its honors shall renew,
Clipped from the lovely head where late it grew)
That while my nostrils draw the vital air,
This hand which won it shall forever wear."
He spoke, and speaking, in proud triumph spread
140 The long-contended honors[4] of her head.
    But Umbriel, hateful Gnome! forbears not so;
He breaks the vial whence the sorrows flow.
Then see! the nymph in beauteous grief appears,
Her eyes half-languishing, half-drowned in tears;
145 On her heaved bosom hung her drooping head,
Which, with a sigh, she raised; and thus she said:
    "Forever cursed be this detested day,[5]

6. A woman whose toast is often drunk, and who by implication is all too well known to her (male) toasters: (cf. Canto 5.10, and Fielding's *Tom Jones*, where Sophia is not pleased by reports that she has been Tom's toast, bk. 13, ch. 11).
7. I.e., mounted in a ring.
8. The fashion for driving coaches around Hyde Park prevented grass from growing there.

9. A commercial area around St. Mary-le-Bow, and not at all fashionable.
1. Sir George Browne, cousin of Arabella's mother.
2. Skilled use of a cane with a head of dark polished stone.
3. Zounds, a corruption of "God's wounds," a mild oath.
4. Her beautiful hair.
5. Echoing Achilles' lament for his slain friend Patroclus (*Iliad* 18.107ff.).

Which snatched my best, my fav'rite curl away!
Happy! ah ten times happy, had I been,
150   If Hampton Court these eyes had never seen!
Yet am not I the first mistaken maid,
By love of courts to num'rous ills betrayed.
Oh had I rather unadmired remained
In some lone isle, or distant northern land;
155   Where the gilt chariot never marks the way,
Where none learn Ombre, none e'er taste bohea!°   tea
There kept my charms concealed from mortal eye,
Like roses that in deserts bloom and die.
What moved my mind with youthful lords to roam?
160   O had I stayed, and said my pray'rs at home!
'Twas this, the morning omens seemed to tell;
Thrice from my trembling hand the patch box fell;
The tott'ring china shook without a wind,
Nay, Poll° sat mute, and Shock was most unkind!   her parrot
165   A Sylph too warned me of the threats of fate,
In mystic visions, now believed too late!
See the poor remnants of these slighted hairs!
My hands shall rend what ev'n thy rapine spares:
These, in two sable ringlets taught to break,°   divide
170   Once gave new beauties to the snowy neck.
The sister lock now sits uncouth, alone,
And in its fellow's fate foresees its own;
Uncurled it hangs, the fatal shears demands;
And tempts once more thy sacrilegious hands.
175   Oh hadst thou, cruel! been content to seize
Hairs less in sight, or any hairs but these!"

Canto 5

She said: the pitying audience melt in tears,
But Fate and Jove had stopped the Baron's ears.
In vain Thalestris with reproach assails,
For who can move when fair Belinda fails?
5   Not half so fixed the Trojan[1] could remain,
While Anna begged and Dido raged in vain.
Then grave Clarissa[2] graceful waved her fan;
Silence ensued, and thus the nymph began.
      "Say, why are beauties praised and honored most,
10   The wise man's passion, and the vain man's toast?
Why decked with all that land and sea afford,
Why angels called, and angel-like adored?
Why round our coaches crowd the white-gloved beaus,
Why bows the side box from its inmost rows?[3]
15   How vain are all these glories, all our pains,

---

1. Aeneas, fixed on his decision to leave Carthage and abandon Dido despite her pleas and those of her sister Anna (*Aeneid* 4.269–449).
2. A new character introduced . . . to open more clearly the moral of the poem, in a parody of the speech of Sarpedon to Glaucus in Homer [Pope's note in the 1717 edition]. Sarpedon's speech (*Iliad* 12) is a famous reflection on glory.
3. At the theater, gentlemen sat in the side boxes, ladies in the front boxes facing the stage.

Unless good sense preserve what beauty gains:
That men may say when we the front box grace,
Behold the first in virtue as in face!
Oh! if to dance all night, and dress all day,

20   Charmed the smallpox,[4] or chased old age away;
Who would not scorn what housewife's cares produce,
Or who would learn one earthly thing of use?
To patch, nay ogle, might become a saint,
Nor could it sure be such a sin to paint.

25   But since, alas! frail beauty must decay,
Curled or uncurled, since locks will turn to gray,
Since painted or not painted, all shall fade,
And she who scorns a man, must die a maid;
What then remains, but well our pow'r to use,

30   And keep good humor still whate'er we lose?
And trust me, dear! good humor can prevail,
When airs, and flights, and screams, and scolding fail.
Beauties in vain their pretty eyes may roll;
Charms strike the sight, but merit wins the soul."

35   So spoke the dame, but no applause ensued;
Belinda frowned, Thalestris called her prude.
"To arms, to arms!" the fierce virago[5] cries,
And swift as lightning to the combat flies.
All side in parties, and begin th' attack;

40   Fans clap, silks rustle, and tough whalebones crack;
Heroes' and heroines' shouts confus'dly rise,
And bass and treble voices strike the skies.
No common weapons in their hands are found,
Like gods they fight, nor dread a mortal wound.

45   So when bold Homer makes the gods engage,
And heav'nly breasts with human passions rage;
'Gainst Pallas,° Mars; Latona,[6] Hermes arms;   *Athena*
And all Olympus rings with loud alarms.
Jove's thunder roars, Heav'n trembles all around;

50   Blue Neptune storms, the bellowing deeps resound;
Earth shakes her nodding tow'rs, the ground gives way;
And the pale ghosts start at the flash of day!
       Triumphant Umbriel on a sconce's[7] height
Clapped his glad wings, and sat to view the fight:

55   Propped on their bodkin spears, the sprites survey
The growing combat, or assist the fray.
       While through the press enraged Thalestris flies,
And scatters deaths around from both her eyes,
A beau and witling° perished in the throng,   *little wit*

60   One died in metaphor, and one in song.
"O cruel Nymph! a living death I bear,"
Cried Dapperwit, and sunk beside his chair.
A mournful glance Sir Fopling upwards cast,

4. A common disease, which frequently left permanent facial scars.
5. Woman who behaves like a man.

6. Mother of Diana and Apollo.
7. Candlestick attached to the wall.

"Those eyes are made so killing"[8]—was his last:
65　Thus on Meander's flow'ry margin lies
　　Th' expiring swan, and as he sings he dies.[9]
　　　　When bold Sir Plume had drawn Clarissa down,
　　Chloe stepped in, and killed him with a frown;
　　She smiled to see the doughty hero slain,
70　But at her smile the beau revived again.
　　　　Now Jove suspends his golden scales in air,[1]
　　Weighs the men's wits against the lady's hair;
　　The doubtful beam long nods from side to side;
　　At length the wits mount up, the hairs subside.
75　　　　See fierce Belinda on the Baron flies,
　　With more than usual lightning in her eyes;
　　Nor feared the chief th' unequal fight to try,
　　Who sought no more than on his foe to die.[2]
　　But this bold lord, with manly strength indued,
80　She with one finger and a thumb subdued:
　　Just where the breath of life his nostrils drew,
　　A charge of snuff the wily virgin threw;
　　The Gnomes direct, to ev'ry atom just,
　　The pungent grains of titillating dust.
85　　　　Sudden, with starting tears each eye o'erflows,
　　And the high dome re-echoes to his nose.[3]
　　　　"Now meet thy fate," incensed Belinda cried,
　　And drew a deadly bodkin from her side.
　　(The same, his ancient personage to deck,
90　Her great–great–grandsire wore about his neck
　　In three seal rings; which after, melted down,
　　Formed a vast buckle for his widow's gown:
　　Her infant grandame's° whistle next it grew,　　　　　*grandmother's*
　　The bells she jingled, and the whistle blew;
95　Then in a bodkin[4] graced her mother's hairs,
　　Which long she wore, and now Belinda wears.)
　　　　"Boast not my fall" (he cried) "insulting foe!
　　Thou by some other shalt be laid as low.
　　Nor think, to die dejects my lofty mind;
100　All that I dread is leaving you behind!
　　Rather than so, ah let me still survive,
　　And burn in Cupid's flames—but burn alive."
　　　　"Restore the lock!" she cries; and all around
　　"Restore the lock!" the vaulted roofs rebound.
105　Not fierce Othello in so loud a strain
　　Roared for the handkerchief that caused his pain.
　　But see how oft ambitious aims are crossed,
　　And chiefs contend 'till all the prize is lost!
　　The lock, obtained with guilt, and kept with pain,

---

8. A line from Giovanni Bononcini's opera, *Camilla* (1696), which at this time was popular in London.
9. Meander: a river in Asia Minor. Swans were popularly believed to sing only on their death. This simile refers to Ovid's *Heroides*, 7, a lament from Dido to Aeneas.

1. To determine victory in battle; a convention found in both Homer and Virgil.
2. A standard metaphor for sexual climax.
3. Cf. his boast, 4.133–138.
4. A decorative pin, shaped like a dagger.

110   In ev'ry place is sought, but sought in vain:
       With such a prize no mortal must be blest,
       So Heav'n decrees! with Heav'n who can contest?
           Some thought it mounted to the lunar sphere,[5]
       Since all things lost on earth are treasured there.
115   There heroes' wits are kept in ponderous vases,
       And beaus' in snuffboxes and tweezer cases.
       There broken vows and deathbed alms are found,
       And lovers' hearts with ends of riband bound;
       The courtier's promises, and sick man's pray'rs,
120   The smiles of harlots, and the tears of heirs,
       Cages for gnats, and chains to yoke a flea;
       Dried butterflies, and tomes of casuistry.[6]
           But trust the Muse—she saw it upward rise,
       Though marked by none but quick poetic eyes:
125   (So Rome's great founder to the heav'ns withdrew,
       To Proculus alone confessed in view.[7])
       A sudden star, it shot through liquid air,
       And drew behind a radiant trail of hair.
       Not Berenice's locks first rose so bright,[8]
130   The heav'ns bespangling with disheveled light.
       The Sylphs behold it kindling as it flies,
       And pleased pursue its progress through the skies.
           This the beau monde shall from the Mall[9] survey,
       And hail with music its propitious ray.
135   This, the blest lover shall for Venus° take,   *the planet*
       And send up vows from Rosamonda's Lake.[1]
       This Partridge[2] soon shall view in cloudless skies,
       When next he looks through Galileo's eyes;[3]
       And hence th' egregious wizard shall foredoom
140   The fate of Louis, and the fall of Rome.
           Then cease, bright nymph! to mourn thy ravished hair
       Which adds new glory to the shining sphere!
       Not all the tresses that fair head can boast
       Shall draw such envy as the lock you lost.
145   For, after all the murders of your eye,
       When, after millions slain, yourself shall die;
       When those fair suns[4] shall set, as set they must,
       And all those tresses shall be laid in dust;
       This lock, the Muse shall consecrate to fame,
150   And mid'st the stars inscribe Belinda's name!

1711–1717   1712; 1714; 1717

---

5. Cf. Ariosto's *Orlando Furioso* (1516–1532), in which Orlando's lost wits are sought on the moon. See also *Paradise Lost* 3.444ff.
6. Subtle reasoning (often used of arguments justifying immoral conduct).
7. When Romulus was killed mysteriously, Proculus soothed popular grief by asserting that he had been taken up to heaven.
8. The Egyptian queen Berenice made an offering of her hair after her husband returned victorious from the wars;

when it disappeared from the temple, the court astronomer claimed it had been made into a new constellation.
9. A fashionable walk in St. James's Park.
1. Where lovers met in St. James's Park.
2. John Partridge was a ridiculous star-gazer, who in his almanacs every year, never failed to predict the downfall of the Pope and the King of France, then at war with the English [Pope's note].
3. I.e., a telescope.
4. I.e., her eyes

from An Essay on Man
In Four Epistles to Henry St. John, Lord Bolingbroke[1]
Epistle 1

TO THE READER

As the epistolary way of writing hath prevailed much of late, we have ventured to publish this piece composed some time since, and whose author chose this manner, notwithstanding his subject was high and of dignity, because of its being mixed with argument which of its nature approacheth to prose. This,[2] which we first give the reader, treats of the Nature and State of MAN, with respect to the UNIVERSAL SYSTEM;[3] the rest will treat of him with respect to his OWN SYSTEM, as an individual, and as a member of society, under one or other of which heads all ethics are included.

As he imitates no man, so he would be thought to vie with no man in these Epistles, particularly with the noted author of two lately published;[4] but this he may most surely say: that the matter of them is such as is of importance to all in general, and of offense to none in particular.

THE DESIGN

Having proposed to write some pieces on human life and manners, such as (to use my lord Bacon's expression) "come home to men's business and bosoms,"[5] I thought it more satisfactory to begin with considering Man in the abstract, his Nature and his State, since, to prove any moral duty, to enforce any moral precept, or to examine the perfection or imperfection of any creature whatsoever, it is necessary first to know what condition and relation it is placed in, and what is the proper end and purpose of its being.

The science[6] of human nature is, like all other sciences, reduced to a few clear points: there are not many *certain truths* in this world. It is therefore in the anatomy of the mind as in that of the body: more good will accrue to mankind by attending to the large, open, and perceptible parts, than by studying too much such finer nerves and vessels, the conformations and uses of which will forever escape our observation. The disputes are all upon these last, and, I will venture to say, they have less sharpened the wits than the hearts of men against each other, and have diminished the practice more than advanced the theory of morality. If I could flatter myself that this Essay has any merit, it is in steering betwixt the extremes of doctrines seemingly opposite, in passing over terms utterly unintelligible, and in forming a temperate yet not inconsistent, and a short yet not imperfect system of ethics.

1. "I believe," wrote Pope to his friend John Caryll, "that there is not in the whole course of the Scripture any precept so often and so strongly inculcated, as the trust and eternal dependence we ought to repose in that Supreme Being who is our constant preserver and benefactor." This is the theme of Pope's didactic and exhortatory *Essay on Man*, whose four epistles were published anonymously over eleven months in 1733–1734. For Pope, "to reason right is to submit" (line 164), not least because humankind occupies a middle ground—between angels and beasts—in a divinely ordered universe. Pope had intended the *Essay on Man* and the four *Moral Essays* (1731–1735) to be the first and last parts of a great poetic sequence on the nature of humankind, though he never completed the project. The *Essay* is addressed to Henry St. John, first Viscount Bolingbroke (1678–1751), a leading Tory statesman and political writer whom Pope described as "my guide, philosopher, and friend."
2. I.e., the first Epistle.
3. I.e., within the cosmic order, ordained by God.
4. I.e., Pope himself, whose *Epistle to Bathurst* (1733) and the first *Imitation of Horace* (1733) had recently been published. The *Essay on Man* was published anonymously; Pope uses his little address to the reader both to advertise his own work and to confuse his enemies about the identity of the poem's author.
5. From Bacon's Dedicatory Epistle in the collected edition of the *Essays* (1625).
6. Knowledge.

This I might have done in prose, but I chose verse, and even rhyme, for two reasons. The one will appear obvious: that principles, maxims, or precepts so written, both strike the reader more strongly at first, and are more easily retained by him afterwards. The other may seem odd, but is true: I found I could express them more shortly this way than in prose itself; and nothing is more certain, than that much of the force as well as grace of arguments or instructions depends on their conciseness. I was unable to treat this part of my subject more in detail without becoming dry and tedious, or more poetically, without sacrificing perspicuity to ornament, without wandering from the precision, or breaking the chain of reasoning. If any man can unite all these without diminution of any of them, I freely confess he will compass a thing above my capacity.

What is now published, is only to be considered as a general map of MAN, marking out no more than the greater parts, their extent, their limits, and their connection, but leaving the particular to be more fully delineated in the charts which are to follow. Consequently, these Epistles in their progress (if I have health and leisure to make any progress) will be less dry, and more susceptible of poetical ornament. I am here only opening the fountains, and clearing the passage. To deduce the rivers, to follow them in their course, and to observe their effects, may be a task more agreeable.

ARGUMENT

Of the Nature and State of Man, with respect to the UNIVERSE.

Of Man in the abstract.—I. That we can judge only with regard to our own system, being ignorant of the relations of systems and things, verses 17, etc. II. That Man is not to be deemed imperfect, but a being suited to his place and rank in the creation, agreeable to the general order of things, and conformable to ends and relations to him unknown, ver. 35, etc. III. That it is partly upon his ignorance of future events, and partly upon the hope of a future state, that all his happiness in the pres-ent depends, ver. 77, etc. IV. The pride of aiming at more knowledge, and pretending to more perfection, the cause of man's error and misery. The impiety of putting himself in the place of God, and judging of the fitness or unfitness, perfection or imperfection, justice or injustice of his dispensations, Ver. 113, etc. V. The absurdity of conceiting himself the final cause of the creation, or expecting that perfection in the *moral* world, which is not in the *natural*, Ver. 131, etc. VI. The unreasonableness of his complaints against Providence, while on the one hand he demands the perfections of the angels, and on the other the bodily qualifications of the brutes; though, to possess any of the sensitive faculties in a higher degree, would render him miserable, Ver. 173, etc. VII. That throughout the whole visible world, an universal order and gradation in the sensual and mental faculties is observed, which causes a subordination of creature to creature, and of all creatures to Man. The gradations of sense, instinct, thought, reflection, reason; that reason alone countervails all the other faculties, Ver. 207. VIII. How much farther this order and subordination of living creatures may extend, above and below us; were any part of which broken, not that part only, but the whole connected creation must be destroyed. Ver. 233. IX. The extravagance, madness, and pride of such a desire, Ver. 259. X. The consequence of all the absolute submission due to providence, both as to our present and future state, Ver. 281, etc. to the end.

> Awake, my ST. JOHN! leave all meaner° things   *base*
> To low ambition, and the pride of kings.
> Let us (since life can little more supply

5   Than just to look about us and to die)
       Expatiate free⁷ o'er all this scene of man;
       A mighty maze! but not without a plan;
       A wild, where weeds and flow'rs promiscuous° shoot,   *randomly mixed*
       Or garden, tempting with forbidden fruit.
       Together let us beat⁸ this ample field,
10   Try what the open, what the covert yield;
       The latent tracts, the giddy heights explore
       Of all who blindly creep, or sightless soar;⁹
       Eye nature's walks,° shoot folly as it flies,   *behaviors*
       And catch the manners living as they rise;
15   Laugh where we must, be candid° where we can;   *generous*
       But vindicate the ways of God to Man.¹

          1. Say first, of God above, or Man below,
       What can we reason, but from what we know?
       Of Man what see we, but his station here,
20   From which to reason, or to which refer?
       Through worlds unnumbered though the God be known,
       'Tis ours to trace him only in our own.
       He, who through vast immensity can pierce,
       See worlds on worlds compose one universe,
25   Observe how system into system runs,
       What other planets circle other suns,
       What varied being peoples° ev'ry star,   *inhabits*
       May tell why Heav'n has made us as we are.
       But of this frame the bearings, and the ties,
30   The strong connections, nice dependencies,
       Gradations just,² has thy° pervading soul   *the reader's*
       Looked through? or can a part contain the whole?
          Is the great chain,³ that draws all to agree,
       And drawn supports, upheld by God, or thee?

35   2. Presumptuous Man! the reason wouldst thou find,
       Why formed so weak, so little, and so blind!
       First, if thou canst, the harder reason guess,
       Why formed no weaker, blinder, and no less!
       Ask of thy mother earth, why oaks are made
40   Taller or stronger than the weeds they shade?
       Or ask of yonder argent fields above,
       Why Jove's satellites⁴ are less than Jove?
          Of systems possible, if 'tis confest
       That wisdom infinite must form the best,
45   Where all must full or not coherent be,⁵

---

7. Wander or speak unrestrainedly.
8. "Beat," "open," "covert" are all hunting terms: Pope imagines them to be searching out game by walking back and forth across open and wooded land.
9. There is a middle way appropriate to man between ignorance and presumption.
1. Cf. *Paradise Lost*, 1.24–26: "That to the highth of this great argument / I may assert eternal providence, / And justify the ways of God to men." Pope's mention of the

"garden, tempting with forbidden fruit" (line 8) also calls to mind the opening lines of Milton's epic.
2. "Connections," "dependencies," and "gradations" were key terms of the new sciences.
3. The Great Chain of Being linked all levels of creation, at the same time maintaining a fixed hierarchy.
4. Jupiter's moons. "Satellites" here has four syllables.
5. The Great Chain of Being could not be broken at any point.

And all that rises, rise in due degree;
Then, in the scale of reas'ning life, 'tis plain
There must be, somewhere, such a rank as Man;
And all the question (wrangle e'er so long)
50   Is only this, if God has placed him wrong?
        Respecting Man, whatever wrong we call,
May, must be right, as relative to all.
In human works, though labored on with pain,
A thousand movements scarce one purpose gain;
55   In God's, one single can its end produce;
Yet serves to second too some other use.
So Man, who here seems principal alone,
Perhaps acts second to some sphere unknown,
Touches some wheel, or verges to some goal;
60   'Tis but a part we see, and not a whole.
        When the proud steed shall know why Man restrains
His fiery course, or drives him o'er the plains;
When the dull ox, why now he breaks the clod,
Is now a victim, and now Egypt's god:[6]
65   Then shall Man's pride and dullness comprehend
His actions', passions', being's, use and end;
Why doing, suff'ring, checked, impelled; and why
This hour a slave, the next a deity.
        Then say not Man's imperfect, Heav'n in fault;
70   Say rather, Man's as perfect as he ought;
His knowledge measured to his state and place,
His time a moment, and a point his space.
If to be perfect in a certain sphere,°   *area of influence*
What matter, soon or late, or here or there?
75   The blest today is as completely so,
As who began a thousand years ago.

        3. Heav'n from all creatures hides the book of fate,
All but the page prescribed, their present state;
From brutes what men, from men what spirits° know: *angels*
80   Or who could suffer being here below?
The lamb thy riot° dooms to bleed today,   *extravagance*
Had he thy reason, would he skip and play?
Pleased to the last, he crops the flow'ry food,
And licks the hand just raised to shed his blood.
85   Oh blindness to the future! kindly giv'n,
That each may fill the circle marked by Heav'n;
Who sees with equal eye, as God of all,
A hero perish, or a sparrow fall,
Atoms or systems° into ruin hurled,   *solar systems*
90   And now a bubble burst, and now a world.
        Hope humbly then; with trembling pinions soar;
Wait the great teacher death, and God adore!
What future bliss, he gives not thee to know,

6. Apis, sacred bull of Memphis.

But gives that hope to be thy blessing now.
95   Hope springs eternal in the human breast:
Man never *is*, but always to *be* blest:
The soul, uneasy and confined from home,[7]
Rests and expatiates in a life to come.
      Lo! the poor Indian, whose untutored mind
100   Sees God in clouds, or hears him in the wind;
His soul proud science never taught to stray
Far as the solar walk, or milky way;
Yet simple nature to his hope has giv'n,
Behind the cloud-topped hill, an humbler Heav'n;
105   Some safer world in depth of woods embraced,
Some happier island in the watry waste,
Where slaves once more their native land behold,
No fiends torment, no Christians thirst for gold![8]
To be, contents his natural desire,
110   He asks no angel's wing, no seraph's fire;[9]
But thinks, admitted to that equal sky,
His faithful dog shall bear him company.

      4. Go, wiser thou! and in thy scale of sense
Weigh thy opinion against providence;
115   Call imperfection what thou fancy'st such,
Say, here he gives too little, there too much;
Destroy all creatures for thy sport or gust,°   *appetite*
Yet cry, If Man's unhappy, God's unjust;
If Man alone engross not Heav'n's high care,
120   Alone made perfect here, immortal there:
Snatch from his hand the balance and the rod,
Rejudge his justice, be the God of God!
      In pride, in reas'ning pride, our error lies;
All quit their sphere, and rush into the skies.
125   Pride still is aiming at the blest abodes,
Men would be angels, angels would be gods.
Aspiring to be gods, if angels fell,
Aspiring to be angels, men rebel;
And who but wishes to invert the laws
130   Of ORDER, sins against th' Eternal Cause.

      5. Ask for what end th' heav'nly bodies shine,
Earth for whose use? Pride answers, "'Tis for mine:
For me kind Nature wakes her genial° pow'r,   *generating*
Suckles each herb, and spreads out ev'ry flow'r;
135   Annual for me, the grape, the rose renew
The juice nectareous, and the balmy dew;
For me, the mine a thousand treasures brings;
For me, health gushes from a thousand springs;
Seas roll to waft me, suns to light me rise;

7. Away from its heavenly origin.
8. The Christian is meant to "thirst for God" (Psalm   42.2).
9. Seraphs were traditionally thought of as fiery.

140   My foot-stool earth, my canopy the skies."
          But errs not Nature from this gracious end,
        From burning suns when livid deaths descend,
        When earthquakes swallow, or when tempests sweep
        Towns to one grave, whole nations to the deep?
145   "No" ('tis replied) "the first Almighty cause[1]
        Acts not by partial, but by gen'ral laws;
        Th' exceptions few; some change since all began,
        And what created perfect?"—Why then Man?
        If the great end be human happiness,
150   Then Nature deviates; and can Man do less?
        As much that end a constant course requires
        Of show'rs and sunshine, as of Man's desires;
        As much eternal springs and cloudless skies,
        As men for ever temp'rate, calm, and wise.
155   If plagues or earthquakes break not Heav'n's design,
        Why then a Borgia, or a Catiline?[2]
        Who knows but he, whose hand the light'ning forms,
        Who heaves old ocean, and who wings the storms,
        Pours fierce ambition in a Caesar's mind,
160   Or turns young Ammon[3] loose to scourge mankind?
        From pride, from pride, our very reas'ning springs;
        Account for moral as for nat'ral things:
        Why charge we Heav'n in those, in these acquit?
        In both, to reason right is to submit.
165   Better for us, perhaps, it might appear,
        Were there all harmony, all virtue here;
        That never air or ocean felt the wind;
        That never passion discomposed the mind:
        But all subsists by elemental strife;
170   And passions are the elements of life.
        The gen'ral ORDER, since the whole began,
        Is kept in Nature, and is kept in Man.

          6. What would this Man? Now upward will he soar,
        And little less than angel, would be more;
175   Now looking downwards, just as grieved appears
        To want the strength of bulls, the fur of bears.
        Made for his use all creatures if he call,
        Say what their use, had he the pow'rs of all?
        Nature to these, without profusion kind,
180   The proper organs, proper pow'rs assigned;
        Each seeming want compensated of course,[4]
        Here with degrees of swiftness, there of force;
        All in exact proportion to the state;
        Nothing to add, and nothing to abate.

1. God the Creator.
2. Cesare Borgia (1476–1507), an Italian duke from a notoriously ruthless family. Lucius Sergius Catiline (d. 62 B.C.) plotted unsuccessfully against the Roman state.

3. Alexander the Great, King of Macedonia (336–323 B.C.) and conqueror of Asia Minor, Syria, Egypt, Babylonia, and Persia.
4. As is fitting, in the normal course of events.

185 Each beast, each insect, happy in its own;
Is Heav'n unkind to Man, and Man alone?
Shall he alone, whom rational we call,
Be pleased with nothing, if not blessed with all?
      The bliss of Man (could pride that blessing find)
190 Is not to act or think beyond mankind;
No pow'rs of body or of soul to share,
But what his nature and his state can bear.
Why has not Man a microscopic eye?
For this plain reason, Man is not a fly.
195 Say what the use, were finer optics giv'n,
T' inspect a mite, not comprehend the Heav'n?[5]
Or touch, if tremblingly alive all o'er,
To smart and agonize at ev'ry pore?
Or quick effluvia[6] darting through the brain,
200 Die of a rose in aromatic pain?
If Nature thundered in his op'ning ears,
And stunned him with the music of the spheres,
How would he wish that Heav'n had left him still
The whisp'ring zephyr,° and the purling rill?   *breeze*
205 Who finds not providence all good and wise,
Alike in what it gives, and what denies?

      7. Far as creation's ample range extends,
The scale of sensual, mental pow'rs ascends:
Mark how it mounts, to Man's imperial race,
210 From the green myriads in the peopled grass:
What modes of sight betwixt each wide extreme,
The mole's dim curtain, and the lynx's beam:
Of smell, the headlong lioness[7] between,
And hound sagacious on the tainted[8] green:
215 Of hearing, from the life that fills the flood,
To that which warbles through the vernal wood:
The spider's touch, how exquisitely fine!
Feels at each thread, and lives along the line:
In the nice bee, what sense so subtly true
220 From pois'nous herbs extracts the healing dew:[9]
How instinct varies in the grov'ling swine,
Compared, half-reas'ning elephant, with thine:
'Twixt that, and reason, what a nice barrier;[1]
Forever sep'rate, yet forever near!
225 Remembrance and reflection how allied;
What thin partitions sense from thought divide:
And middle natures, how they long to join,
Yet never pass th' insuperable line!

---

5. It was commonly believed that man alone of all the animals was able to look up to Heaven.
6. Epicurus (c.370–270 B.C.) and others believed that sensations reached the brain from the pores via streams of invisible particles.
7. Lions were, according to Pope, believed to hunt "by the ear, and not by the nostril."
8. Sagacious: of acute perception; tainted: i.e., with the smell of the hunted animal.
9. Honey had been thought to fall on flowers as dew and was used for medicinal purposes.
1. Fine distinction. "Barrier" is pronounced "bar-REAR."

Without this just gradation, could they be
230   Subjected these to those, or all to thee?
The pow'rs of all subdued by thee alone,
Is not thy reason all these pow'rs in one?

    8. See, through this air, this ocean, and this earth,
All matter quick,° and bursting into birth.   *living*
235   Above, how high progressive life may go!
Around, how wide! how deep extend below!
Vast chain of being, which from God began,
Natures ethereal, human, angel, Man,
Beast, bird, fish, insect! what no eye can see,
240   No glass° can reach! from infinite to thee,   *magnifying glass*
From thee to nothing!—On superior pow'rs
Were we to press, inferior might on ours:
Or in the full creation leave a void,
Where, one step broken, the great scale's destroyed:
245   From nature's chain whatever link you strike,
Tenth or ten thousandth, breaks the chain alike.
    And if each system in gradation roll,
Alike essential to th' amazing whole;
The least confusion but in one, not all
250   That system only, but the whole must fall.
Let earth unbalanced from her orbit fly,[2]
Planets and suns run lawless through the sky,
Let ruling angels from their spheres be hurled,[3]
Being on being wrecked, and world on world,
255   Heav'n's whole foundations to their center nod,
And Nature tremble to the throne of God:
All this dread ORDER break—for whom? for thee?
Vile worm!—oh madness, pride, impiety!

    9. What if the foot, ordained the dust to tread,
260   Or hand to toil, aspired to be the head?
What if the head, the eye, or ear repined
To serve mere engines to the ruling mind?
Just as absurd for any part to claim
To be another, in this gen'ral frame:
265   Just as absurd, to mourn the tasks or pains
The great directing MIND of ALL ordains.
    All are but parts of one stupendous whole,
Whose body, Nature is, and God the soul;
That, changed through all, and yet in all the same,
270   Great in the earth, as in th' ethereal frame,
Warms in the sun, refreshes in the breeze,
Glows in the stars, and blossoms in the trees,
Lives through all life, extends through all extent,
Spreads undivided, operates unspent,

2. Cf. *Paradise Lost* 7.242, where "Earth, self-balanced, on her center hung."

3. According to Thomas Aquinas (c.1225–1274), a sign of the end of the world.

275　Breathes in our soul, informs° our mortal part,　　　　　　　*permeates*
　　　As full, as perfect, in a hair as heart;
　　　As full, as perfect, in vile Man that mourns,
　　　As the rapt seraph that adores and burns;
　　　To him no high, no low, no great, no small;
280　He fills, he bounds, connects, and equals all.

　　　10. Cease then, nor ORDER imperfection name:[4]
　　　Our proper bliss depends on what we blame.
　　　Know thy own point: This kind, this due degree
　　　Of blindness, weakness, Heav'n bestows on thee.
285　Submit—In this, or any other sphere,
　　　Secure to be as blest as thou canst bear:
　　　Safe in the hand of one disposing Pow'r,
　　　Or° in the natal, or the mortal hour.　　　　　　　　　　*either*
　　　All nature is but art, unknown to thee;
290　All chance, direction, which thou canst not see;
　　　All discord, harmony, not understood;[5]
　　　All partial evil, universal good:[6]
　　　And, spite of pride, in erring reason's spite,
　　　One truth is clear, "Whatever Is, is RIGHT."

1733

An Epistle from Mr. Pope, to Dr. Arbuthnot

The *Epistle to Dr. Arbuthnot*, perhaps the most relaxed and engaging of all Pope's verse letters, is addressed to John Arbuthnot (1667–1735), who was physician to Queen Anne, a close friend of Pope and Swift, a valued member of the Scriblerus Club, and principal author of the *Memoirs of the Extraordinary Life, Works, and Discoveries of Martinus Scriblerus*, published with Pope's *Works* in 1741. Samuel Johnson described Arbuthnot as "the most universal genius," for he was a fine satirist, a skillful physician, an amateur mathematician, and a capable poet. Pope's epistle is an apology both for himself and for the satirist's art, written against those who had attacked his "person, morals, and family." He asserts the social role of the poet, includes moving autobiographical passages, and powerfully assails his enemies. This Horatian epistle, to the friend whose satires had delighted Pope and whose care had helped preserve and prolong Pope's own frail health, was published just seven weeks before the doctor died.

An Epistle from Mr. Pope, to Dr. Arbuthnot

Neque sermonibus vulgi dederis te, nec in Praemiis humanis spem posueris rerum tuarum: suis te oportet illecebris ipsa virtus trahat ad verum decus. Quid de te alii loquantur, ipsi videant, sed loquentur tamen.[1]

Tully

4. I.e., do not call order imperfection.
5. Here, as earlier in the poem, Pope invokes the Horatian principle of *concordia discors* (Horace, *Epistles* 1.12.19), a harmony of opposites.
6. In a letter to John Caryll in 1718, Pope wrote that "true piety would make us know, that all misfortunes may

as well be blessings."
1. You will not give yourself up to the flattery of the vulgar, nor hope for success in your affairs from mortal hands; virtue herself will lead to true honor; see that you follow her guidance. What others see fit to say of you let them say (Cicero, *De Re Publica* 6.23).

Advertisement

This paper is a sort of Bill of Complaint, begun many years since, and drawn up by snatches, as the several occasions offered. I had no thoughts of publishing it, till it pleased some persons of rank and fortune [the authors of *Verses to the Imitator of Horace*, and of an *Epistle to a Doctor of Divinity from a Nobleman at Hampton Court*][2] to attack in a very extraordinary manner, not only my writings (of which being public the public judge) but my person, morals, and family, whereof to those who know me not, a truer information may be requisite. Being divided between the necessity to say something of myself, and my own laziness to undertake so awkward a task, I thought it the shortest way to put the last hand to this Epistle. If it have anything pleasing, it will be that by which I am most desirous to please, the *truth* and the *sentiment*; and if anything offensive, it will be only to those I am least sorry to offend, the *vicious* or the *ungenerous*.

Many will know their own pictures in it, there being not a circumstance but what is true; but I have, for the most part spared their *names*, and they may escape being laughed at, if they please.

I would have some of them know, it was owing to the request of the learned and candid friend to whom it is inscribed, that I make not as free use of theirs as they have done of mine. However, I shall have this advantage, and honor, on my side, that whereas by their proceeding, any abuse may be directed at any man, no injury can possibly be done by mine, since a nameless character can never be found out, but by its *truth* and *likeness*.[3]

> Shut, shut the door, good John![4] fatigued I said,
> Tie up the knocker, say I'm sick, I'm dead,
> The Dog-star[5] rages! nay 'tis past a doubt,
> All Bedlam, or Parnassus,[6] is let out:
> 5   Fire in each eye, and papers in each hand,
> They rave, recite, and madden[7] round the land.
>   What walls can guard me, or what shades can hide?
> They pierce my thickets, through my grot[8] they glide,
> By land, by water,[9] they renew the charge,
> 10   They stop the chariot, and they board the barge.
> No place is sacred, not the church is free,
> Ev'n Sunday shines no Sabbath-day to me:
> Then from the Mint[1] walks forth the man of rhyme,
> Happy! to catch me, just at dinner time.
> 15   Is here a parson, much bemused in beer,[2]
> A maudlin poetess, a rhyming peer,

2. Lady Mary Wortley Montagu (1689–1762) and John Hervey (1696–1743), Baron Hervey of Ickworth.
3. I.e., its similarity to the original.
4. Pope's servant, John Serle.
5. Sirius, which appears in the heat of summer; Pope was finishing the poem in August 1734. The late summer was also the time for reciting poetry in classical Rome.
6. Bedlam (Bethlehem Hospital) was a London "lunatic" asylum; Parnassus was the mountain of the Muses.

7. A word Pope invented.
8. Pope's artificial grotto or cavern, his retreat, at Twickenham.
9. Pope's house at Twickenham was on the river Thames, and could be reached by boat from London.
1. Debtors were safe from the law in Southwark, London; on Sunday there were no arrests anywhere.
2. Laurence Eusden (1688–1730), Poet Laureate and parson given to drink.

A clerk, foredoomed his father's soul to cross,
Who pens a stanza when he should engross?°   *copy documents*
Is there, who locked from ink and paper, scrawls
20 With desp'rate charcoal round his darkened walls?
All fly to Twit'nam,° and in humble strain   *Twickenham*
Apply to me, to keep them mad or vain.
Arthur,[3] whose giddy son neglects the laws,
Imputes to me and my damned works the cause:
25 Poor Cornus° sees his frantic wife elope,   *cuckold*
And curses wit, and poetry, and Pope.[4]
     Friend to my life, (which did not you prolong,
The world had wanted many an idle Song)
What drop or nostrum° can this plague remove?   *medicines*
30 Or which must end me, a fool's wrath or love?
A dire dilemma! either way I'm sped,°   *hurried toward death*
If foes, they write, if friends, they read me dead.
Seized and tied down to judge, how wretched I!
Who can't be silent, and who will not lie;
35 To laugh were want of goodness and of grace,
And to be grave exceeds all pow'r of face.
I sit with sad civility, I read
With honest anguish, and an aching head;
And drop at last, but in unwilling ears,
40 This saving counsel, "Keep your piece nine years."[5]
     Nine years! cries he, who high in Drury Lane[6]
Lulled by soft zephyrs° through the broken pane,   *breezes*
Rhymes ere he wakes, and prints before term ends,[7]
Obliged by hunger and request of friends:[8]
45 "The piece you think is incorrect: why take it,
I'm all submission, what you'd have it, make it."
     Three things another's modest wishes bound,°   *encompass*
My friendship, and a prologue,[9] and ten pound.
     Pitholeon[1] sends to me: "You know his Grace,
50 I want a patron; ask him for a place."°   *paid position*
Pitholeon libeled me—"but here's a letter
Informs you, sir, 'twas when he knew no better.
Dare you refuse him? Curl[2] invites to dine,
He'll write a Journal, or he'll turn divine."[3]
55   Bless me! a packet.—"'Tis a stranger sues,

---

3. Arthur Moore; his son James Moore-Smythe had plagiarized from Pope's works.
4. Both the Pope and the author: as a nation, the British
were preoccupied with the threat of Roman Catholicism
without (from France and Spain) and within (from
Catholics like Pope).
5. Horace's advice to a poet eager to publish (*Ars Poetica*,
lines 386–389).
6. A bad neighborhood where writers lived in garrets.
7. Law court terms were the preferred publishing seasons.
8. It is the second reason, rather than the first, that the

aspiring poet gives in his prefaces.
9. To a play of his: a good way to show the public who
your friends were.
1. The name taken from a foolish Poet at Rhodes [Pope's
note].
2. Edmund Curll (1675–1747), a publisher notorious for
commissioning hacks to write libelous journals, full of
"news and scandal."
3. Pope may have meant Leonard Welsted (1688–1747),
who was planning a religious work.

A virgin tragedy, an orphan Muse."
If I dislike it, "Furies, death and rage!"
If I approve, "Commend it to the stage."
There (thank my stars) my whole commission ends,

60   The play'rs and I are, luckily, no friends.
Fired that the house° reject him, "'Sdeath I'll print it   *theater*
And shame the fools—your int'rest, sir, with Lintot."[4]
Lintot, dull rogue! will think your price too much.
"Not Sir, if you revise it, and retouch."

65   All my demurs but double his attacks,
At last he whispers "Do, and we go snacks."[5]
Glad of a quarrel, straight° I clap the door,   *immediately*
Sir, let me see your works and you no more.
       'Tis sung, when Midas' ears began to spring,[6]

70   Midas, a sacred person and a King),
His very Minister who spied them first,
(Some say his Queen) was forced to speak, or burst.
And is not mine, my friend, a sorer case,
When every coxcomb° perks° them in my face?   *fool/shoves*

75   "Good friend forbear! you deal in dang'rous things,
I'd never name Queens, Ministers, or Kings;
Keep close to ears,° and those let asses prick,[7]   *whisper it*
Tis nothing"—Nothing? if they bite and kick?
Out with it, Dunciad! let the secret pass,

80   That secret to each fool, that he's an ass:
The truth once told (and wherefore should we lie?),
The Queen of Midas slept, and so may I.
       You think this cruel? take it for a rule,
No creature smarts so little as a fool.

85   Let peals of laughter, Codrus![8] round thee break,
Thou unconcerned canst hear the mighty crack.[9]
Pit, box and gall'ry in convulsions hurled,
Thou stand'st unshook amidst a bursting world.
Who shames a scribbler? break one cobweb through,

90   He spins the slight, self-pleasing thread anew;
Destroy his fib, or sophistry; in vain,
The creature's at his dirty work again;
Throned in the center of his thin designs;
Proud of a vast extent of flimsy lines.

95   Whom have I hurt? has poet yet, or peer,
Lost the arched eyebrow, or Parnassian sneer?

---

4. Bernard Lintot (1675–1736), who published for Pope.
5. Share the profits.
6. King Midas grew ass's ears when he preferred Pan to Apollo in their music contest. One of those closest to him whispered the story to the earth, and it was in turn told by the reeds. Pope was also referring to that contemporary artistic dunce King George II, his wife Queen Caroline, and first minister Robert Walpole.

7. Presumably, their ears, as well as the poet.
8. A poet, perhaps fictional, ridiculed by Virgil and Juvenal.
9. "Mighty crack" was a phrase used by Addison to describe the collapse of the world; Pope showed how inadequate he thought it both in *Peri Bathous* and here, where it signals the failure of a play.

And has not Colley[1] still his Lord, and whore?
His butchers Henley, his Freemasons Moore?[2]
Does not one table Bavius[3] still admit?
100 Still to one bishop Philips[4] seem a wit?
Still Sappho[5]—"Hold! for God's sake—you'll offend:
No names—be calm—learn prudence of a friend:
I too could write, and I am twice as tall,
But foes like these!"—One flatt'rer's worse than all;
105 Of all mad creatures, if the learn'd are right,
It is the slaver kills, and not the bite.
A fool quite angry is quite innocent;
Alas! 'tis ten times worse when they *repent.*

One dedicates, in high heroic prose,
110 And ridicules beyond a hundred foes;
One from all Grub Street[6] will my fame defend,
And, more abusive, calls himself my friend.
This prints my letters,[7] that expects a bribe,
And others roar aloud, "Subscribe, subscribe."
115 There are, who to my person pay their court,
I cough like Horace, and though lean, am short,
Ammon's great son[8] one shoulder had too high,
Such Ovid's nose, and "Sir! you have an eye—"
Go on, obliging creatures, make me see
120 All that disgraced my betters, met in me:
Say for my comfort, languishing in bed,
"Just so immortal Maro° held his head:"   *Virgil*
And when I die, be sure you let me know
Great Homer died three thousand years ago.

125 Why did I write? what sin to me unknown
Dipped me in ink, my parents', or my own?
As yet a child, nor yet a fool to fame,
I lisped in numbers,° for the numbers came.   *verse, meter*
I left no calling for this idle trade,
130 No duty broke, no father disobeyed.
The Muse but served to ease some friend, not wife,
To help me through this long disease, my life,
To second, Arbuthnot! thy art and care,
And teach the being you preserved to bear.

---

1. Colley Cibber (1671–1757), actor, playwright, Poet Laureate; he replaced Lewis Theobald as the "hero" of *The Dunciad,* from where the "Parnassian sneer" comes.
2. John "Orator" Henley (1692–1756), a popular and unusual preacher, had set up an "oratory" in Newport Market, one of London's principal meat markets, causing enemies to claim that his audiences consisted only of ignorant butchers. James Moore-Smythe was a Freemason.
3. A bad poet who had attacked Virgil and Horace.

4. Ambrose Philips (c. 1675–1749), poet and secretary to the Bishop of Armagh.
5. Lady Mary Wortley Montagu, whom Pope had attacked previously under the name of this Greek lyric poet; from Arbuthnot's interjection, Pope seems to be implying that she was under Walpole's protection.
6. Home of literary hacks.
7. Forged or stolen (as Curll had in 1726).
8. Alexander the Great.

135   But why then publish? Granville[9] the polite,
   And knowing Walsh, would tell me I could write;
   Well-natured Garth inflamed with early praise,
   And Congreve loved, and Swift endured my lays;
   The courtly Talbot, Somers, Sheffield read,
140 Ev'n mitered Rochester would nod the head,
   And St. John's self (great Dryden's friends before)
   With open arms received one poet more.
   Happy my studies, when by these approved!
   Happier their author, when by these beloved!
145 From these the world will judge of men and books,
   Not from the Burnets, Oldmixons, and Cookes.[1]
    Soft were my numbers, who could take offense
   While pure description held the place of sense?
   Like gentle Fanny's[2] was my flow'ry theme,
150 A painted mistress, or a purling stream.
   Yet then did Gildon[3] draw his venal quill;
   I wished the man a dinner, and sat still:
   Yet then did Dennis rave in furious fret;[4]
   I never answered, I was not in debt:
155 If want provoked, or madness made them print,
   I waged no war with Bedlam or the Mint.
    Did some more sober critic come abroad?
   If wrong, I smiled; if right, I kissed the rod.[5]
   Pains, reading, study, are their just pretense,
160 And all they want is spirit, taste, and sense.
   Commas and points they set exactly right,
   And 'twere a sin to rob them of their mite.
   Yet ne'er one sprig of laurel graced these ribalds,[6]
   From slashing Bentley down to piddling Tibalds.[7]
165 Each wight who reads not, and but scans and spells,
   Each word-catcher that lives on syllables,
   Ev'n such small critics some regard may claim,
   Preserved in Milton's or in Shakespeare's name.
   Pretty! in amber to observe the forms
170 Of hairs, or straws, or dirt, or grubs, or worms;
   The things, we know, are neither rich nor rare,

9. Pope associates himself (and Dryden) with a number of important figures, friends, and patrons: George Granville, Baron Lansdowne (1666–1735); William Walsh (1663–1708); Sir Samuel Garth (1661–1719); William Congreve; Jonathan Swift; Charles Talbot, Duke of Shrewsbury (1660–1718); John Lord Somers (1651–1721); Francis Atterbury, Bishop of Rochester (1662–1732); Henry St. John, Viscount Bolingbroke (1678–1751).

1. Thomas Burnet, John Oldmixon, and Thomas Cooke: "authors of secret and scandalous history" [Pope's note]; Pope is comparing the greatness of his friends with the small-mindedness of those who attacked him.

2. Lord Hervey, court Vice Chamberlain, whom Pope thought effeminate, and later satirizes as Sporus (lines 305ff.).

3. Charles Gildon (1665–1724) had attacked *The Rape of the Lock*. Pope insinuates that Gildon writes to keep poverty at bay.

4. John Dennis (1657–1734), had attacked Pope; both, Gildon and Dennis, Pope thought, had acted at the instigation of Addison.

5. Accepted their criticism; kissing a monarch's scepter or an official's staff was a ritual of submission to authority.

6. Laurel: the poet's crown; ribalds: foolish jesters.

7. Richard Bentley (1662–1742), a classical scholar of great learning and bad temper, earned ridicule for his "corrected" edition of *Paradise Lost* (1732), while Lewis Theobald (1688–1744), sometime "hero" of *The Dunciad*, criticized Pope's edition of Shakespeare in his *Shakespeare Restored* (1726).

But wonder how the devil they got there?
   Were others angry? I excused them too;
Well might they rage; I gave them but their due.
175   A man's true merit 'tis not hard to find,
But each man's secret standard in his mind,
That casting-weight[8] pride adds to emptiness,
This, who can gratify? for who can *guess?*
The Bard[9] whom pilf'red pastorals renown,
180   Who turns a Persian tale for half a crown,[1]
Just writes to make his barrenness appear,
And strains from hard-bound brains eight lines a year:
He, who still wanting though he lives on theft,
Steals much, spends little, yet has nothing left:
185   And he, who now to sense, now nonsense leaning,
Means not, but blunders round about a meaning:
And he, whose fustian's° so sublimely bad,   *bombastic style*
It is not poetry, but prose run mad:
All these, my modest satire bad translate,
190   And owned, that nine such poets made a Tate.[2]
How did they fume, and stamp, and roar, and chafe?
And swear, not Addison himself was safe.
   Peace to all such! but were there one[3] whose fires
True genius kindles, and fair fame inspires,
195   Blest with each talent and each art to please,
And born to write, converse, and live with ease:
Should such a man, too fond to rule° alone,   *of ruling*
Bear, like the Turk, no brother near the throne,[4]
View him with scornful, yet with jealous eyes,
200   And hate for arts that caused himself to rise;
Damn with faint praise,[5] assent with civil leer,
And without sneering, teach the rest to sneer;
Willing to wound, and yet afraid to strike,
Just hint a fault, and hesitate dislike;
205   Alike reserved to blame, or to commend,
A tim'rous foe, and a suspicious friend,
Dreading ev'n fools, by flatterers besieged,
And so obliging that he ne'er obliged;
Like Cato, give his little Senate laws,[6]
210   And sit attentive to his own applause;
While wits and templars° ev'ry sentence raise,   *young lawyers*
And wonder with a foolish face of praise.
Who but must laugh, if such a man there be?

---

8. The weight that tips the balance.
9. Ambrose Philips wrote pastoral poems in imitation of Spenser and translated a book of *Persian Tales*. The fact that, in 1709, his pastorals were published in the same volume as Pope's occasioned a rivalry between the two poets.
1. A standard prostitute's charge.
2. Nahum Tate (1652–1715), playwright and poet.
3. Joseph Addison, here portrayed as Atticus, friend of Cicero. Pope respected Addison's abilities as a writer but

did not like him or his politics.
4. Turkish rulers killed close relatives who might be potential rivals.
5. Cf. William Wycherley's prologue to *The Plain Dealer* (1677): "And, with faint praises, one another damn."
6. Pope's prologue to Addison's play *Cato* (1713) included a version of this line. Now Pope turns the tables, and the noble Roman senator becomes the petty Addison, the senate, his coffeehouse clique.

Who would not weep, if Atticus were he!
215   What though my name stood rubric on the walls?
Or plastered posts, with claps in capitals?[7]
Or smoking forth, a hundred hawkers[8] load,
On wings of winds came flying all abroad?
I sought no homage from the race that write;
220   I kept, like Asian monarchs, from their sight:
Poems I heeded (now berhymed so long)
No more than thou, great George! a birthday song.[9]
I ne'er with wits or witlings passed my days,
To spread about the itch of verse and praise;
225   Nor like a puppy daggled° through the town,   *wandered*
To fetch and carry singsong up and down;
Nor at rehearsals sweat, and mouthed, and cried,
With handkerchief and orange[1] at my side:
But sick of fops, and poetry, and prate,
230   To Bufo left the whole Castalian State.[2]
       Proud, as Apollo on his forked hill,
Sat full-blown Bufo, puffed by ev'ry quill;
Fed with soft dedication all day long,
Horace and he went hand in hand in song.[3]
235   His library (where busts of poets dead
And a true Pindar stood without a head)[4]
Received of wits an undistinguished race,
Who first his judgment asked, and then a place:
Much they extolled his pictures, much his seat,°   *estate*
240   And flattered ev'ry day, and some days eat:
Till grown more frugal in his riper days,
He paid some bards with port, and some with praise,
To some a dry rehearsal was assigned,
And others (harder still) he paid in kind.[5]
245   Dryden alone (what wonder?) came not nigh,
Dryden alone escaped this judging eye:
But still the great have kindness in reserve,
He helped to bury whom he helped to starve.[6]
       May some choice patron bless each gray goose quill!
250   May ev'ry Bavius have his Bufo still!
So, when a statesman wants a day's defense,
Or envy holds a whole week's war with sense,
Or simple pride for flatt'ry makes demands;

7. Red lettering, or rubric, was often used by Lintot, Pope's publisher; "claps" were placards, pasted up around the city by booksellers.
8. Hawking by street criers was another way to publicize new works.
9. The Poet Laureate's official ode to the king.
1. Sold in the theaters for eating or throwing.
2. Poetry is the "Castalian State," named for the spring sacred to the Muses on Parnassus (the "forked hill"); it is left to "Bufo," a patron whose name derives from the Latin for toad and who was probably George Bubb Dod-

ington (1691–1762).
3. Dodington, a patron of literature, had been given the place of Maecenas, patron of Virgil and Horace, in a recent translation from Horace's *Odes*.
4. In *Peri Bathous* (1728), Pope ridiculed those antiquaries who exhibited headless statues, claiming they were busts of great poets.
5. I.e., he read or gave them his own poetry.
6. Mr. Dryden, after having liv'd in exigencies, had a magnificent funeral bestow'd upon him by the contributions of several persons of quality [Pope's note].

May dunce by dunce be whistled off my hands!
255   Blest be the Great! for those they take away,
And those they left me—For they left me Gay,[7]
Left me to see neglected genius bloom,
Neglected die! and tell it on his tomb;
Of all thy blameless life the sole return
260   My verse, and Queensb'ry[8] weeping o'er thy urn!
Oh let me live my own! and die so too!
("To live and die is all I have to do"):[9]
Maintain a poet's dignity and ease,
And see what friends, and read what books I please.
265   Above a patron, though I condescend
Sometimes to call a minister my friend:
I was not born for courts or great affairs,
I pay my debts, believe, and say my pray'rs,
Can sleep without a poem in my head,
270   Nor know, if Dennis be alive or dead.
        Why am I asked, what next shall see the light?
Heav'ns! was I born for nothing but to write?
Has life no joys for me? or (to be grave)
Have I no friend to serve, no soul to save?
275   "I found him close with Swift"—"Indeed? no doubt"
(Cries prating Balbus[1]) "something will come out."
'Tis all in vain, deny it as I will.
"No, such a genius never can lie still,"
And then for mine obligingly mistakes
280   The first Lampoon Sir Will. or Bubo[2] makes.
Poor guiltless I! and can I choose but smile,
When ev'ry coxcomb knows me by my *style*?
        Cursed be the verse, how well soe'er it flow,
That tends to make one worthy man my foe,
285   Give virtue scandal, innocence a fear,
Or from the soft-eyed virgin steal a tear!
But he, who hurts a harmless neighbor's peace,
Insults fall'n worth, or beauty in distress,
Who loves a lie, lame slander helps about,
290   Who writes a libel, or who copies out:
That fop whose pride affects a patron's name,
Yet absent, wounds an author's honest fame;
Who can your merit selfishly approve,
And show the sense of it, without the love;
295   Who has the vanity to call you friend,
Yet wants the honor injured to defend;[3]
Who tells whate'er you think, whate'er you say,
And, if he lie not, must at least betray:

---

7. John Gay, poet, playwright, and friend of Pope; it was apparently his failure to win patronage that prompted him to write *The Beggar's Opera* (1728).
8. The Duke and Duchess of Queensberry were Gay's patrons.

9. Slightly adapted from *Of Prudence* (1668) by Sir John Denham.
1. A Roman lawyer.
2. Sir William Yonge (d. 1755) and Dodington.
3. I.e., lacks the honor when you are injured to defend you.

Who to the Dean and silver bell can swear,
300   And sees at Cannons what was never there:[4]
Who reads but with a lust to misapply,
Make satire a lampoon, and fiction, lie.
A lash like mine no honest man shall dread,
But all such babbling blockheads in his stead.
305   Let Sporus[5] tremble—"What? that thing of silk,
Sporus, that mere white curd of ass's milk?
Satire or sense alas! can Sporus feel?
Who breaks a butterfly upon a wheel?"[6]
Yet let me flap this bug with gilded wings,
310   This painted child of dirt that stinks and stings;
Whose buzz the witty and the fair annoys,
Yet wit ne'er tastes, and beauty ne'er enjoys,
So well-bred spaniels civilly delight
In mumbling of the game they dare not bite.
315   Eternal smiles his emptiness betray,
As shallow streams run dimpling all the way.
Whether in florid impotence he speaks,
And, as the prompter breathes, the puppet squeaks;
Or at the ear of Eve,[7] familiar toad,
320   Half froth, half venom, spits himself abroad,
In puns, or politics, or tales, or lies,
Or spite, or smut, or rhymes, or blasphemies.
His wit all seesaw between that and this,
Now high, now low, now master up, now miss,
325   And he himself one vile antithesis.
Amphibious Thing! that acting either part,
The trifling head, or the corrupted heart!
Fop at the toilet,[8] flatt'rer at the board,°   *dining table*
Now trips a Lady, and now struts a Lord.
330   Eve's tempter thus the Rabbins° have expressed,   *Jewish scholars*
A cherub's face, a reptile all the rest;
Beauty that shocks you, parts that none will trust,
Wit that can creep, and pride that licks the dust.
    Not fortune's worshipper, nor fashion's fool,
335   Not lucre's madman, nor ambition's tool,
Not proud, nor servile, be one poet's praise
That, if he pleased, he pleased by manly ways;
That flatt'ry, ev'n to kings, he held a shame,
And thought a lie in verse or prose the same:
340   That not in fancy's maze he wandered long,
But stooped° to truth, and moralized his song: *pounced upon*
That not for fame, but virtue's better end,
He stood° the furious foe, the timid friend,   *withstood*

4. I.e., who misapplies satirical references in Pope's *Epistle to Burlington*. Pope was upset by the willful misreading of "Timon's villa" in the poem as Cannons, estate of the Duke of Chandos.
5. A boy, Nero's favorite sexual partner; here, Lord Hervey, confidante of Queen Caroline.

6. The rack, an instrument of torture.
7. In the fourth book of Milton [*Paradise Lost* 4.800] the devil is represented in this posture [Pope's note]. "Eve" is Queen Caroline, with whom Hervey is both familiar and a familiar (a witch's pet).
8. Dressing table.

The damning critic, half-approving wit,
345   The coxcomb hit, or fearing to be hit;
Laughed at the loss of friends he never had,
The dull, the proud, the wicked, and the mad;
The distant threats of vengeance on his head,
The blow unfelt, the tear he never shed;[9]
350   The tale revived, the lie so oft o'erthrown;
Th' imputed trash, and dullness not his own;
The morals blackened when the writings 'scape;
The libeled person, and the pictured shape;[1]
Abuse on all he loved, or loved him, spread,
355   A friend in exile, or a father, dead;
The whisper that to greatness still too near,
Perhaps, yet vibrates on his Sovereign's ear—
Welcome for thee, fair virtue! all the past:
For thee, fair virtue! welcome ev'n the last!
360   "But why insult the poor, affront the great?"
A knave's a knave, to me, in ev'ry state,
Alike my scorn, if he succeed or fail,
Sporus at court, or Japhet[2] in a jail,
A hireling scribbler, or a hireling peer,
365   Knight of the post[3] corrupt, or of the shire,
If on a pillory, or near a throne,
He gain his prince's ear, or lose his own.
    Yet soft by nature, more a dupe than wit,
Sappho[4] can tell you how this man was bit°   *deceived*
370   This dreaded sat'rist Dennis will confess
Foe to his pride, but friend to his distress:[5]
So humble, he has knocked at Tibbald's door,
Has drunk with Cibber, nay has rhymed for Moore.[6]
Full ten years slandered, did he once reply?
375   Three thousand suns went down on Welsted's lie:
To please a mistress, one aspersed his life;
He lashed him not, but let her be his wife:
Let Budgell[7] charge low Grubstreet on his quill,
And write whate'er he pleased, except his will;
380   Let the two Curlls[8] of town and court, abuse
His father, mother, body, soul, and Muse.
Yet why? that father held it for a rule
It was a sin to call our neighbor fool,
That harmless mother thought no wife a whore,—

9. *A Pop upon Pope* (1728) tried to humiliate Pope by pretending he had been whipped.
1. Pope was frequently vilified in print by his enemies. His deformity and Roman Catholicism were often mocked—he was even caricatured as a hunchbacked ape wearing the papal crown.
2. Japhet Crook, a forger.
3. A person who supported himself by giving false evidence.
4. Lady Mary Wortley Montagu hurt Pope, who had been very close to her, by switching loyalties to Hervey.

5. In Dennis's old age, Pope had publicly supported his work.
6. Or rather, Moore-Smythe plagiarized from him.
7. Eustace Budgell (1686–1737); the *Grub Street Journal* accused him of forging the will of Dr. Matthew Tindal to make himself inheritor.
8. Pope uses Edmund Curll's name as a derogatory epithet for Hervey. Curll, an unscrupulous publisher, is attacked in *The Dunciad* and in Swift's *Verses on the Death of Dr. Swift.*

385   Hear this! and spare his family, James Moore!
        Unspotted names! and memorable long,
        If there be force in virtue, or in song.
            Of gentle blood (part shed in honor's cause,
        While yet in Britain honor had applause)
390   Each parent sprung—"What Fortune, pray?"—Their own,
        And better got than Bestia's[9] from the throne.
        Born to no pride, inheriting no strife,
        Nor marrying discord in a noble wife,
        Stranger to civil and religious rage,
395   The good man walked innoxious through his Age.
        No courts he saw, no suits would ever try,
        Nor dared an oath, nor hazarded a lie:[1]
        Unlearn'd, he knew no schoolman's subtle art,
        No language, but the language of the heart.
400   By nature honest, by experience wise,
        Healthy by temp'rance and by exercise:
        His life, though long, to sickness past unknown,
        His death was instant, and without a groan.
        Oh grant me thus to live, and thus to die!
405   Who sprung from kings shall know less joy than I.
            O Friend!° may each domestic bliss be thine!   Arbuthnot
        Be no unpleasing melancholy mine:
        Me, let the tender office long engage
        To rock the cradle of reposing age,
410   With lenient arts extend a mother's breath,[2]
        Make languor smile, and smooth the bed of death,
        Explore the thought, explain the asking eye,
        And keep a while one parent from the sky!
        On cares like these if length of days attend,
415   May Heav'n, to bless those days, preserve my friend,
        Preserve him social, cheerful, and serene,
        And just as rich as when he served a Queen![3]
        Whether that blessing be denied, or giv'n,
        Thus far was right, the rest belongs to Heav'n.

1731–1734   1735

━━◄═╳═►━━

William Hogarth
1697–1764

"I had naturally a good eye," William Hogarth remembered near his life's end. "Shows of all sorts gave me uncommon pleasure when an infant." The "shows" (spectacles) that filled his eye in the turbulent London neighborhood of Smithfield where he grew up suffused his art for

9. A Roman consul who accepted bribes for peace, suggesting the Duke of Marlborough's rewards from Queen Anne.
1. Pope's father refused to take oaths against the Pope, which would have helped him avoid anti-Catholic

measures.
2. Pope's mother died two years before the poem was published, but he retained these lines, written in 1731.
3. Arbuthnot had been physician to Queen Anne.

life: the antics of actors and the raucousness of audiences at Bartholomew Fair; the chicanery and pathos of prostitutes and thieves; the casual injustice of constables and magistrates. Above all, he watched his father fail. Richard Hogarth, a classical scholar, spent four years as a prisoner for debt, when his coffeehouse (catering to learned men and specializing in Latin conversation) failed to cover its own expenses. The debtor's family was effectually imprisoned too, and Hogarth, in his early teens during the ordeal, never forgot. "The emphasis throughout his work" (notes his biographer Ronald Paulson) "is on prisons, real and metaphorical. Even when he is not dealing with people who are in a prison . . . he portrays rooms that are more like prison cells than boudoirs or parlors."

At age seventeen, Hogarth was apprenticed to a silver engraver, ornamenting platters, rings, tableware, and the like. Finding the work dull, he switched to copper engraving, the technique by which book illustrators and printmakers created and reproduced their pictures. Late in his twenties he commenced his career as painter. His first great successes combined both craft and art. Hogarth produced the series of six pictures that make up *A Harlot's Progress* first as a set of paintings in oil, then as a sequence of copper engravings aimed at wider distribution. If *A Harlot's Progress* launched his popularity, *A Rake's Progress* (engraved in 1735 from canvases painted the year before) clinched his reputation as Britain's most masterly, mocking delineator of contemporary vice and folly. Though he continued for a while to nurture conventional ambitions as a painter of portraits and historical subjects catering to aristocratic tastes, Hogarth came gradually to recognize the originality, force, and commercial viability of his satrical engravings. As he later expressed it (in his own idiosyncratic syntax), he had discovered a style pitched between "the sublime and the grotesque," and had devised "a more new way of proceeding, viz. painting and engraving modern moral subjects, a field unbroke up in any country or any age. . . . Provided I could strike the passions, and by small sums from many, by means of prints which I could engrave from my pictures myself, I could secure my property to myself." Hogarth managed to "strike the passions" both ways: by depicting them vividly in the countenance of his characters, and by igniting them in his audience. He also managed, better than any predecessor, to "secure his property to himself." He petitioned Parliament to pass the Engraver's Copyright Act (often called "Hogarth's Act"), which protected printmakers from the then rampant piratical reproduction of their work, and which thereby (in Hogarth's proud words) "made prints a considerable article and trade in this country, there being more business of that kind done in this town than in Paris or anywhere else." The engravings of *A Rake's Progress* were first published, pointedly, the day after Hogarth's Act became the law of the land.

Early in his career, Hogarth had been praised as a "Shakespeare in painting," and admirers noted repeatedly the literary force of his graphic art; only he, wrote one, could "teach pictures to speak and to think." Hogarth had appropriated the very idea of an instructive moral "progress" from John Bunyan's phenomenally popular religious narrative *Pilgrim's Progress*, but he made the journey at once darker and more satiric. Bunyan's Mr. Christian progresses through Vanity Fair and other dangers toward the Celestial City; Hogarth's protagonists remain mired within the Vanity Fair of contemporary London; their "progress" takes them downward to degradation and death. His art also helped shape a newer form of narrative, the novel. Like the novel, Hogarth's sequences abound in suggestive subplots, telling asides, and startling revelations, played out in the tiniest details carefully placed. Novelists as different from one another as Samuel Richardson, Henry Fielding, and Laurence Sterne valued him as a friend, sought him as a collaborator, and embraced him as a past master in their own moral and narrative mode. "I almost dare affirm," wrote Fielding, "that those two works of his, which he calls *The Rake's* and *The Harlot's Progress*, are calculated more to serve the cause of virtue, and for the preservation of mankind, than all the folios of morality which have ever been written."

A Rake's Progress

Plate 1: Tom Rakewell's father (depicted in the portrait above the mantle) has recently died. The old man was miserly: he wore a coat and fur hat indoors so as not to incur the costs of a fire; he saved broken junk (in the open chest); he nearly starved his housecat (lower left). The young man is profligate: he has torn open doors and cabinets in search of sequestered wealth; he is being measured for new and ostentatious clothes; he is trying to pay off the raging mother of Sarah Young, the weeping woman (at right) whom he has made pregnant.

Plate 2: Nearly unrecognizable in his new elegance, Rakewell (the tallest figure in the picture) surrounds himself with instructors and tradespeople eager to sell their services. In the foreground
(from left to right) are a composer, a fencing master, a dance teacher (with fiddle), a hired killer
(in black; the note in Tom's hand, from "William Stab," vouches for the assassin as "a man of hon-
or"); a huntsman (with horn); and a jockey, whose trophy cup bears the suggestive name of the
winning horse: "Silly Tom." The two moping Englishmen at the back may be miffed to find themselves supplanted by the fashionable foreigners in front of them. The painting above the mantle
depicts the Judgment of Paris, that indolent princeling whose unrestrained desires precipitated the
catastrophe of the Trojan War.

Plate 3: Rakewell (sprawled at left) has bought himself an orgy. All the Roman portraits in the upper right corner have been defaced, except that of the emperor Nero, who looks out over the havoc like some patron saint of vandalism (his reputed incendarism is re-enacted by the woman standing at the back near the shattered mirror, holding a candle flame to the map of the world). One prostitute caresses Tom while conveying away his watch; in the foreground opposite, a woman disrobes in preparation for an obscene dance that will likely involve the reflective platter and large candle held by the cross-eyed lackey in the doorway. Admonitions to the orgiasts lie at hand, in the form of the chicken's carcass (lower right corner), stripped and forked; and in the person of the ballad singer, tattered, pregnant, and ignored, whose song bears the telling title "Black Joke."

Plate 4: Carried in his sedan chair to a night of gaming at White's Chocolate House and gambling club (rear left), Tom is stopped by a bailiff who serves him with a notice of arrest for debt. He receives aid not from the revellers in the distance but from Sarah Young, the abandoned woman whose mother he tried to buy off in Plate 1. Reversing that gesture, she seeks to secure his release by offering the money she has earned by making ribbons and caps (sample wares hang at her side). On a ladder a lamplighter, distracted by the goings-on, carelessly (and emblematically) spills his flammable fluid onto Rakewell's head.

Plate 5: Intent on wealth, not the love Sarah offers, Rakewell weds an old woman in a dim, disin-
tegrating church where light and faith are in scant supply. On the left, the "Poor's Box," receptacle
of charity, has long been shut (a cobweb covers its lid); on the right wall, the table of commandments is cracked. The one-eyed bride appears to wink at the grim parson; Rakewell proffers her
the ring while eying her maid. On the floor, a canine couple parodies the human ceremony; in
the back, a woman with churchkeys flailing tries to prevent the intrusion of Sarah Young, holding
the child Rakewell has sired; Sarah's mother does vigorous but unavailing battle.

Plate 6: During a night of gambling, Rakewell has evidently lost the fortune he acquired by his calculating marriage. Wigless, frantic, he falls to one knee and curses his lot; his rage is replicated (as were his nuptials) by a dog on the floor to his right. The croupier at rear center, carrying the candles, echoes the "world-burning" woman in Plate 3. This time, though, the building is actually on fire. The lantern-bearing watchman at left has come to give warning. Most of the gamblers are too immersed in their own operations to notice either Rakewell's anguish or their own danger.

Plate 7: In the wake of his losses, Rakewell has at last been imprisoned for debt, unable to pay the "garnish" (or customary bribe) that the jailer behind him expects, or even the cost of a beer. The note on the table—"I have read your play and find it will not do"—rejects his last poor, literary attempt at solvency. His wife rails, Sarah faints, his daughter tugs at Sarah's skirts, and his cellmates embody futilities even more preposterous than his own playwriting. The impoverished man at left has devised "a new scheme for paying the debts of the nation." The man seated at the stove is an alchemist, vainly trying to transmute base metals into gold; before his imprisonment, he also built himself a pair of wings (upper left), but they, like Rakewell's upward aspirations, have produced only debt and confinement, not flight and freedom.

Plate 8: Rakewell has been moved from debtor's prison to Bethlehem Royal Hospital (better known as Bedlam), London's asylum for the insane. Grinning outright for the first time in the series, Tom claws at his head while guards restrain him. Sarah Young, weeping, has come to give him comfort. The other two women are here to amuse themselves (at the cost of two pence per visit, Bedlam had become one of London's most popular entertainments). Some inmates display lunatic religious zeal; others have gone mad in pursuit of science. The man drawing the world on the wall seeks a solution to the longitude, the navigational problem that had obsessed Britons for many decades. Behind the open door of the central cell, a naked madman sits and thinks he's king. In a later revision (1763), Hogarth superimposed upon the longitudinist's globe an emblem of Britannia, as though empire and madhouse were now one.

Mind and God

Nature, and Nature's Laws lay hid in Night.
God said, *Let Newton be!* and All was *Light*.

So wrote Alexander Pope, capturing in a couplet the awe with which many of his contemporaries regarded the accomplishments of Isaac Newton. The lines, intended for Newton's tomb, compass his whole career. Pope's last word evokes one of the scientist's early breakthroughs: the discovery that sunlight, for all its seeming "whiteness," teemed with colors, whose operations could be mathematically described. Later, in his masterwork *Naturalis Philosophiae Principia Mathematica* (The Mathematical Principles of Natural Philosophy, 1687), Newton had expounded "Nature's Laws" on a scale and with a precision heretofore unmatched, pinpointing, in compact mathematical formulas, the laws governing gravity and motion, both on earth and throughout the heavens. In Pope's replaying of Genesis, Newton himself becomes a principle, not merely the interpreter of Creation but virtually synonomous with it: God's luminous word, from which revelation follows. For numberless admirers, the name of Newton figured forth not only the intricate simplicities of "Nature's Laws," but also the astonishing, hitherto unsuspected capacity of the human mind to shed light upon the works of God.

The human mind itself promptly became the object of new investigation, Newtonian in its ambitions and its methods. Two years after the *Principia* appeared, John Locke published his *Essay Concerning Human Understanding* (1689), a work comparably influential, in which he sought answers to key questions of epistemology: what do we know? and by what means do we come to know it? Locke, like Newton, brought luster to the scientific approach championed by the Royal Society (of which both men were members): empiricism, the conviction that truth could be attained solely through experiment and experience. The intimate interplay of those two crucial elements is nicely registered in Albert Einstein's account of the way that Newton did his work: "The conceptions which he used to reduce the material of experience to order seemed to flow spontaneously from experience itself, from the beautiful experiments which he ranged in order like playthings and describes with an affectionate wealth of detail." Locke imported empiricism from the physical sciences into the realms of philosophy and psychology. Striving to found a science of mind, to make sense of the running encounter between the material world and human perception, Locke and his successors found in experience both a method for investigating epistemological problems and the core of their solution: for these thinkers, experience is how we know, it is what we know, and it is how we can learn more about the processes of our knowing. The human mind is intrinsically (though not methodically) empiricist in its ways of gathering its "wealth of detail" about the world.

Under the mind's new scrutinies, God's place and primacy fell open to new questions. Empiricism itself was seen to cut two ways. On the one hand, as Newton and the vast majority of his followers delightedly proclaimed, experimental observation was revealing a universal architecture so exquisite as to prove both the existence and the matchless artistry of God the architect; this route from reason to religious faith became known as the "argument from design." On the other hand, discovery was beginning to conjure up alternative possibilities unsettling to faith: of a God not wholly supreme but subject to nature's inexorable laws; or of laws so efficiently self-sustaining that they needed no God to enforce them. In some of its modes, empiricism itself could be seen to imperil faith, since direct experience or demonstration of the divine proved elusive in a science that limited itself to the observation of material, mechanical causes and effects. For Newton, Locke, and countless other inquirers, empiricism promised to explain the ways of God; but they had begun a process which, in other hands, might threaten to explain God away.

The clash between science and theology gathered force in the mid-nineteenth century, when discoveries in geology (the age of the Earth) and biology (evolution) rendered Scripture strongly suspect. But contention between faith and science was manifest much earlier. At the start of the nineteenth century, William Blake briefly sketched the lines of struggle in his private notebook. "Newton's particles of light," he wrote

> Are sands upon the Red sea shore,
> Where Israel's tents do shine so bright.

Against the arrogance of inquiry, Blake insists upon humility and awe; biblical revelation trumps all the small advancements of human knowledge. Pope had gestured in this direction some seven decades earlier. He suggested, in his *Essay on Man*, that for "superior beings" (angels, God), the sight of Newton unfolding "all Nature's law" might provide the same kind of amazement and amusement that we mortals derive from the antics of a performing ape—a creature who knows more than we might expect, but far less than we ourselves. So great (Pope argues) is the difference between human and divine capacities. Throughout the eighteenth century, in works suffused by the concepts of Newton and of Locke, the relations between mind and God were brilliantly explicated and newly contested, as poets and philosophers undertook, from varying vantages and factions, to sing God's praise, to parse his ways, to work toward him by reason or (in rare instances) to reason him out of existence altogether.

⤖❖⤖

Isaac Newton
1642–1727

Albert Einstein summed up Newton's abilities as follows: "In one person, he combined the experimenter, the theorist, the mechanic, and, not least, the artist in exposition." Einstein praises magnificently, and omits much. Newton also combined in his one person a supreme mathematician, an obsessive alchemist, a forceful administrator, and (perhaps most importantly, in his own view) an ardent theologian, eager to discover and expound the place of God in his creation. His voluminous, unorthodox writings on the subject remained unpublished in his lifetime. By denying the full divinity of Christ, Newton accorded God *more* authority than did conventional Anglicanism. His views, if known, would have toppled him from the public eminences he enjoyed: as Lucasian Professor of Mathematics at Cambridge, as Master of the Mint in London, as President of the Royal Society. Still, Newton's first admirers found in his scientific work exhilarating support for a more mainstream theology: the strongest foundation yet for the argument from design. It was the business of natural philosophy, Newton repeatedly insisted, "to deduce causes from effects, until we come to the First Cause, which is certainly not mechanical." Newton's own scientific revelations gave rise to a passionate interest in "natural religion"—a faith in God's existence and benevolence, grounded in the orderliness and beauty of the natural world. One of that faith's adherents was the ambitious young classicist and clergyman Richard Bentley (1662–1742), who, having been been commissioned to deliver a series of lectures defending Christianity against atheism, found in Newton's recently published *Principia* abundant new evidence for his own arguments about the divine "origin and frame of the universe." While preparing his lectures for the press, Bentley sent Newton a set of questions, in order to make sure that he was correctly understanding and deploying the *Principia*. Newton's four replies (the first is excerpted here) map the convergence that interests him most, between the discoveries of science and the majesty of God.

from **Letter to Richard Bentley**

10 December 1692

Sir,

When I wrote my treatise about our system, I had an eye upon such principles as might work with considering men for the belief of a Deity, and nothing can rejoice me more than to find it useful for that purpose. But if I have done the public any service this way, 'tis due to nothing but industry and a patient thought.

As to your first query, it seems to me, that if the matter of our sun and planets and all the matter in the universe was evenly scattered throughout all the heavens, and every particle had an innate gravity towards all the rest,[1] and the whole space throughout which this matter was scattered was but finite, the matter on the outside of this space would by its gravity tend towards all the matter on the inside, and by consequence fall down to the middle of the whole space, and there compose one great spherical mass. But if the matter was evenly diffused through an infinite space, it would never convene into one mass, but some of it convene into one mass and some into another so as to make an infinite number of great masses scattered at great distances from one to another throughout all that infinite space. And thus might the sun and fixed stars be formed, supposing the matter were of a lucid[2] nature. But how the matter should divide itself into two sorts, and that part of it which is fit to compose a shining body should fall down into one mass and make a sun, and the rest which is fit to compose an opaque body should coalesce not into one great body like the shining matter but into many little ones; or, if the sun was at first an opaque body like the planets, or the planets lucid bodies like the sun, how he alone should be changed into a shining body whilst all they continue opaque, or all they be changed into opaque ones whilst he remains unchanged, I do not think explicable by mere natural causes but am forced to ascribe it to the counsel[3] and contrivance of a voluntary agent. The same power, whether natural or supernatural, which placed the sun in the center of the orbs[4] of the six primary planets, placed Saturn in the center of the orbs of his five secondary planets,[5] and Jupiter in the center of the orbs of his four secondary ones, and the Earth in the center of the moon's orb; and therefore, had this cause been a blind one without contrivance and design, the sun would have been a body of the same kind with Saturn, Jupiter and the Earth; that is without light and heat. Why there is one body in our system qualified to give light and heat to all the rest I know no reason but because the author of the system thought it convenient, and why there is but one body of this kind I know no reason but because one was sufficient to warm and enlighten all the rest. For the Cartesian hypothesis[6] of suns losing their light and then turning into comets and comets into planets can have no place in my system and is plainly erroneous, because it's certain that comets as often as they appear to us descend into the system of our planets lower than the orb of Jupiter and sometimes lower than the orbs of Venus and Mercury, and yet never stay here but always return from the sun with the same degrees of motion by which they approached him.

---

1. Newton did not endorse this premise. "You sometimes speak," he wrote Bentley in his second letter, "of gravity as essential and inherent to matter: pray do not ascribe that notion to me, for the cause of gravity is what I do not pretend to know."
2. Light-producing.
3. Deliberate design.

4. Orbits.
5. I.e., Saturn's moons; Newton states the numbers of planets and their moons then known.
6. A theory put forth by the French mathematician and philosopher René Descartes (1596–1650) in his highly influential treatises on physics, which Newton's *Principia* had challenged.

To your second query I answer that the motions which the planets now have could not spring from any natural cause alone but were impressed by an intelligent agent. For since comets descend into the region of our planets and here move all manner of ways, going sometimes the same way with the planets, sometimes the contrary way, and sometimes in cross ways in planes inclined to the plane of the ecliptic at all kinds of angles, it's plain that there is no natural cause which could determine all the planets both primary and secondary to move the same way and in the same plane without any considerable variation.[7] This must have been the effect of counsel. Nor is there any natural cause which could give the planets those just degrees of velocity in proportion to their distances from the sun and other central bodies about which they move and to the quantity of matter contained in those bodies, which were requisite to make them move in concentric orbs about those bodies. Had the planets been as swift as comets in proportion to their distances from the sun (as they would have been, had their motions been caused by their gravity, whereby the matter at the first formation of the planets might fall from the remotest regions towards the sun), they would not move in concentric orbs but in such eccentric ones as the comets move in. Were all the planets as swift as Mercury or as slow as Saturn or his satellites, or were their several velocities otherwise much greater or less than they are (as they might have been had they arose from any other cause than their gravity), or had their distances from the centers about which they move been greater or less than they are with the same velocities; or had the quantity of matter in the sun or in Saturn, Jupiter, and the Earth and by consequence their gravitating power been greater or less than it is, the primary planets could not have revolved about the sun nor the secondary ones about Saturn, Jupiter and the Earth in concentric circles as they do, but would have moved in hyperbolas or parabolas or in ellipses very eccentric. To make this system therefore, with all its motions, required a cause which understood and compared together the quantities of matter in the several bodies of the sun and planets and the gravitating powers resulting from thence, the several distances of the primary planets from the sun and secondary ones from Saturn, Jupiter, and the Earth, and the velocities with which these planets could revolve at those distances about those quantities of matter in the central bodies. And to compare and adjust all these things together in so great a variety of bodies argues that cause to be not blind and fortuitous, but very well skilled in mechanics and geometry.

To your third query I answer that it may be represented that the sun may, by heating those planets most which are nearest to him, cause them to be better concocted[8] and more condensed by concoction. But when I consider that our Earth is much more heated in its bowels below the upper crust by subterraneous fermentations of mineral bodies than by the sun, I see not why the interior parts of Jupiter and Saturn might not be as much heated, concocted, and coagulated by those fermentations as our Earth is, and therefore this various density should have some other cause than the various distances of the planets from the sun; and I am confirmed in this

---

7. Newton oversimplifies: the planes of the planets actually incline to each other by as much as five degrees. Newton's biographer Richard Westfall, "reveal above all a determination to find God in nature," even to impose God upon nature. All the phenomena that Newton here attributes to the intervention of divine "counsel" and "skill" were explained scientifically over the course of the next centu-

ry by physicists applying and extending Newton's own system, so that (as the most brilliant of the extenders, Pierre Simon Laplace, is said to have remarked to Napoleon) the hypothesis of divine intervention was no longer necessary.

8. Purified by heat (and hence made denser by the absence of the extraneous matter that the heat has annihilated).

opinion by considering that the planets of Jupiter and Saturn, as they are rarer[9] than the rest, so they are vastly greater and contain a far greater quantity of matter and have many satellites about them, which qualifications surely arose not from their being placed at so great a distance from the sun, but were rather the cause why the Creator placed them at that great distance. For by their gravitating powers they disturb one another's motions very sensibly, as I find by some late observations of Mr. Flamsteed,[1] and had they been placed much nearer to the sun and to one another they would by the same powers have caused a considerable disturbance in the whole system. * * *

Lastly, I see nothing extraordinary in the inclination of the Earth's axis for proving a Deity unless you will urge it as a contrivance for winter and summer and for making the Earth habitable towards the poles, and that the diurnal rotations of the sun and planets, as they could hardly arise from any cause purely mechanical, so by being determined all the same way with the annual and menstrual[2] motions they seem to make up that harmony in the system which (as I explained above) was the effect of choice rather than of chance.

There is yet another argument for a Deity which I take to be a very strong one, but till the principles on which 'tis grounded be better received I think it more advisable to let it sleep. I am

Your most humble servant to command
IS. NEWTON

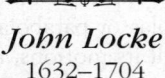

John Locke
1632–1704

In the preface to his *Essay Concerning Human Understanding*, Locke depicts "the incomparable Mr. Newton" as one of the "master builders" of the new science, and himself as a mere "under-laborer," busy "clearing the ground a little, and removing some of the rubbish that lies in the way to knowledge." The eighteenth century, though, tended to venerate the two thinkers equally, Newton as master explicator of the cosmos, Locke as master inquirer into the mind. Starting from the claim that "simple ideas," acquired early, constituted the building blocks of thought, Locke constructed a system of the mind of comparable in intricacy with Newton's universe, but of greater idiosyncrasy (since the content of consciousness differed from person to person, and indeed determined individual identity). Part of Locke's appeal lay in the comparative accessibility of his empiricism. His experiments, unlike Newton's, required neither telescope nor prism, calculus nor genius: readers could perform them (as Locke repeatedly suggested) in the laboratories of their minds, using their own perceptions and memories as raw material. More than any other text, Locke's *Essay* spurred that fascination with the first person which suffuses so much eighteenth-century writing: autobiographies, essays, diaries, travel journals, philosophic treatises, novels. Locke described the workings of the mind so persuasively that in effect he changed them too, prompting an analytic self-consciousness that had not obtained in the same kind and to the same degree before his book appeared.

9. Less dense.
1. John Flamsteed (1646–1719), astronomer and director of the Royal Greenwich Observatory, had recently supplied Newton with these data; the two men later quarrelled bitterly over Flamsteed's reluctance to make available the immense, precise, and urgently needed records of his celestial observations.
2. Monthly.

from An Essay Concerning Human Understanding

[ON IDEAS¹]

Every man being conscious to himself that he thinks, and that which his mind is employed about whilst thinking being the *ideas* that are there, 'tis past doubt, that men have in their minds several *ideas*, such as are those expressed by the words *whiteness, hardness, sweetness, thinking, motion, man, elephant, army, drunkenness,* and others. It is in the first place then to be inquired, how he comes by them? I know it is a received doctrine, that men have native *ideas* and original characters² stamped upon their minds, in their very first being. This opinion I have at large examined already, and I suppose what I have said in the foregoing book³ will be much more easily admitted, when I have shown whence the understanding may get all the *ideas* it has, and by what ways and degrees they may come into the mind; for which I shall appeal to everyone's own observation and experience.

Let us then suppose the mind to be, as we say, white paper, void of all characters, without any *ideas.* How comes it to be furnished? Whence comes it by that vast store, which the busy and boundless fancy of man has painted on it, with an almost endless variety? Whence has it all the materials of reason and knowledge? To this I answer, in one word, from *experience.* In that, all our knowledge is founded, and from that it ultimately derives itself. Our observation employed either about *external, sensible objects, or about the internal operations of our minds, perceived and reflected on by ourselves, is that which supplies our understandings with all the materials of thinking.* These two are the fountains of knowledge, from whence all the *ideas* we have, or can naturally have, do spring.

First, *our senses,* conversant about particular sensible objects, do *convey into the mind,* several distinct *perceptions* of things, according to those various ways, wherein those objects do affect them; and thus we come by those *ideas* we have of *yellow, white, heat, cold, soft, hard, bitter, sweet,* and all those which we call sensible qualities, which when I say the senses convey into the mind, I mean, they from external objects convey into the mind what produces there those *perceptions.* This great source of most of the *ideas* we have, depending wholly upon our senses and derived by them to the understanding, I call SENSATION.

Secondly, the other fountain from which experience furnisheth the understanding with *ideas* is the *perception of the operations of our own minds* within us, as it is employed about the *ideas* it has got; which operations, when the soul comes to reflect on, and consider, do furnish the understanding with another set of *ideas,* which could not be had from things without; and such are *perception, thinking, doubting, believing, reasoning, knowing, willing,* and all the different actings of our own minds; which we being conscious of, and observing in ourselves, do from these receive into our understandings, as distinct *ideas,* as we do from bodies affecting our senses. This source of *ideas* every man has wholly in himself. And though it be not sense, as having nothing to do with external objects, yet it is very like it, and might properly enough be called internal sense. But as I call the other *sensation,* so I call this REFLECTION, the *ideas* it affords being such only, as the mind gets by reflecting on its own operations within itself. By REFLECTION then, in the following part of this discourse, I would be understood to mean, that notice which the mind takes of its own operations, and the manner of them, by reason whereof there come to be *ideas* of these operations in the

---

1. All selections are from Book 2, "Of Ideas"; chapter and section numbers follow each section, in brackets. Most of Locke's italics have been retained.

2. Inscriptions.
3. In which Locke denied the existence of "innate principles," received by the soul "in its very first being" (1.2.1).

understanding. These two, I say, *viz.* external, material things, as the objects of SEN-SATION, and the operations of our own minds within, as the objects of REFLECTION, are, to me, the only originals,[4] from whence all our *ideas* take their beginnings. The term *operations* here I use in a large sense, as comprehending not barely the actions of the mind about its *ideas*, but some sort of passions arising sometimes from them, such as is the satisfaction or uneasiness arising from any thought.

The understanding seems to me not to have the least glimmering of any *ideas*, which it doth not receive from one of these two. *External objects furnish the mind with the ideas of sensible qualities*, which are all those different perceptions they produce in us; and the *mind furnishes the understanding with ideas of its own operations*.

These, when we have taken a full survey of them, and their several modes, combinations, and relations, we shall find to contain all our whole stock of *ideas*; and that we have nothing in our minds which did not come in one of these two ways. Let anyone examine his own thoughts, and thoroughly search into his understanding, and then let him tell me, whether all the original *ideas* he has there are any other than of the objects of his *senses*, or of the operations of his mind, considered as objects of his *reflection*; and how great a mass of knowledge soever he imagines to be lodged there, he will, upon taking a strict view, see that he has *not any* idea *in his mind, but what one of these two have imprinted*; though, perhaps, with infinite variety compounded and enlarged by the understanding, as we shall see hereafter.

He that attentively considers the state of a *child*, at his first coming into the world, will have little reason to think him stored with plenty of *ideas*, that are to be the matter of his future knowledge. 'Tis by degrees he comes to be furnished with them. And though the *ideas* of obvious and familiar qualities imprint themselves before the memory begins to keep a register of time and order, yet 'tis often so late, before some unusual qualities come in the way, that there are few men that cannot recollect the beginning of their acquaintance with them; and if it were worthwhile, no doubt a child might be so ordered as to have but a very few, even of the ordinary *ideas*, till he were grown up to a man. But all that are born into the world being surrounded with bodies that perpetually and diversely affect them, variety of *ideas*, whether care be taken about it or no, are imprinted on the minds of children. *Light* and *colors* are busy at hand everywhere, when the eye is but open; *sounds* and some *tangible qualities* fail not to solicit their proper senses, and force an entrance to the mind; but yet, I think, it will be granted easily, that if a child were kept in a place where he never saw any other but black and white till he were a man, he would have no more *ideas* of scarlet or green, than he that from his childhood never tasted an oyster, or a pineapple, has of those particular relishes.

Men then come to be furnished with fewer or more simple *ideas* from without, according as the *objects* they converse with[5] afford greater or less variety; and from the operation of their minds within, according as they more or less *reflect* on them. For, though he that contemplates the operations of his mind cannot but have plain and clear *ideas* of them; yet unless he turn his thoughts that way, and considers them *attentively*, he will no more have clear and distinct *ideas* of all the *operations of his mind*, and all that may be observed therein, than he will have all the particular *ideas* of any landscape, or of the parts and motions of a clock, who will not turn his eyes to it, and with attention heed all the parts of it. The picture or clock may be so placed that they may come in his way every day; but yet he will have but a confused *idea* of all the parts they are made up of, till he *applies himself with attention*, to consider them each in particular. [1.1–7]

4. Origins.   5. Encounter.

* * *

But to return to the matter in hand, the *ideas* we have of substances, and the ways we come by them; I say *our specific* ideas *of substances are nothing else but a collection of a certain number of simple* ideas, *considered as united in one thing.* These *ideas* of substances, though they are commonly called simple apprehensions, and the names of them simple terms, yet in effect, are complex and compounded. Thus the *idea* which an *English*man signifies by the name *swan* is white color, long neck, red beak, black legs, and whole feet, and all these of a certain size, with a power of swimming in the water, and making a certain kind of noise, and, perhaps, to a man who has long observed those kind of birds, some other properties, which all terminate in sensible simple *ideas*, all united in one common subject.

Besides the complex *ideas* we have of material sensible substances, of which I have last spoken, by the simple *ideas* we have taken from those operations of our own minds, which we experiment[6] daily in ourselves, as thinking, understanding, willing, knowing, and power of beginning motion, etc. co-existing in some substance, we are able to frame *the complex* idea *of an immaterial spirit*. And thus by putting together the *ideas* of thinking, perceiving, liberty, and power of moving themselves and other things, we have as clear a perception and notion of immaterial substances, as we have of material. For putting together the *ideas* of thinking and willing, or the power of moving or quieting corporeal motion, joined to substance, of which we have no distinct *idea*, we have the *idea* of an immaterial spirit; and by putting together the *ideas* of coherent solid parts, and a power of being moved, joined with substance, of which likewise we have no positive *idea*, we have the *idea* of matter. The one is as clear and distinct an *idea*, as the other: the *idea* of thinking, and moving a body, being as clear and distinct *ideas*, as the *ideas* of extension, solidity, and being moved. [23.14–15]

* * *

If we examine the *idea* we have of the incomprehensible Supreme Being, we shall find that we come by it the same way; and that the complex *ideas* we have both of God, and separate spirits, are made up of the simple *ideas* we receive from *reflection;* *v.g.* having, from what we experiment in ourselves, got the *ideas* of existence and duration; of knowledge and power; of pleasure and happiness; and of several other qualities and powers, which it is better to have than to be without; when we would frame an *idea* the most suitable we can to the Supreme Being, we enlarge every one of these with our *idea* of infinity; and so putting them together, make our complex *idea of God*. For that the mind has such a power of enlarging some of its *ideas*, received from sensation and reflection, has been already showed. [23.33]

[ON IDENTITY]

Personal identity consists, not in the identity of substance, but, as I have said, in the identity of *consciousness*, wherein, if Socrates and the present Mayor of Queenborough agree, they are the same person. If the same Socrates waking and sleeping do not partake of the same *consciousness*, Socrates waking and sleeping is not the same person. And to punish Socrates waking, for what sleeping Socrates thought, and waking Socrates was never conscious of, would be no more of right, than to punish one twin for what his brother-twin did, whereof he knew nothing, because their outsides were so like that they could not be distinguished; for such twins have been seen.

But yet possibly it will still be objected, suppose I wholly lose the memory of some parts of my life, beyond a possibility of retrieving them, so that perhaps I shall

6. Experience.

never be conscious of them again; yet am I not the same person that did those actions, had those thoughts, that I was once conscious of, though I have now forgot them? To which I answer, that we must here take notice what the word *I* is applied to, which in this case is the man only. And the same man being presumed to be the same person, *I* is easily here supposed to stand also for the same person. But if it be possible for the same man to have distinct incommunicable consciousness at different times, it is past doubt the same man would at different times make different persons; which, we see, is the sense of mankind in the solemnest declaration of their opinions, human laws not punishing the *mad man* for the *sober man's* actions, nor the *sober man* for what the *mad man* did, thereby making them two persons; which is somewhat explained by our way of speaking in *English*, when we say such an one *is not himself*, or is *besides himself*; in which phrases it is insinuated, as if those who now, or, at least, first used them, thought that *self* was changed, the *self* same person was no longer in that man.

But yet 'tis hard to conceive that Socrates the same individual man should be two persons. To help us a little in this, we must consider what is meant by *Socrates*, or the same individual *man.*

First, it must be either the same individual, immaterial, thinking substance: in short, the same numerical soul, and nothing else.

Secondly, or the same animal,[7] without any regard to an immaterial soul.

Thirdly, or the same immaterial spirit united to the same animal.

Now take which of these suppositions you please, it is impossible to make personal identity to consist in anything but consciousness, or reach any farther than that does.

For by the first of them, it must be allowed possible that a man born of different women, and in distant times, may be the same man. A way of speaking, which whoever admits, must allow it possible for the same man to be two distinct persons, as any two that have lived in different ages without the knowledge of one another's thoughts.

By the second and third, Socrates in this life, and after it, cannot be the same man any way, but by the same consciousness; and so making *human identity* to consist in the same thing wherein we place *personal identity*, there will be no difficulty to allow the same man to be the same person. But then they who place *human identity* in consciousness only, and not in something else, must consider how they will make the infant Socrates the same man with Socrates after the resurrection. But whatsoever to some men makes a *man*, and consequently the same individual man, wherein perhaps few are agreed, personal identity can by us be placed in nothing but consciousness (which is that alone which makes what we call *self*) without involving us in great absurdities.

But is not a man drunk and sober the same person? Why else is he punished for the fact[8] he commits when drunk, though he be never afterwards conscious of it? Just as much the same person, as a man that walks, and does other things in his sleep, is the same person, and is answerable for any mischief he shall do in it. Human laws punish both with a justice suitable to their way of knowledge: because in these cases, they cannot distinguish certainly what is real, what counterfeit; and so the ignorance in drunkeness or sleep is not admitted as a plea. For though punishment be annexed to personality, and personality to consciousness, and the drunkard perhaps be not conscious of what he did, yet human judicatures justly punish him; because the fact is proved against him, but what of consciousness cannot be proved for him. But in the

---

7. Physical, living body.   8. Deed.

great day,[9] wherein the secrets of all hearts shall be laid open, it may be reasonable to think, no one shall be made to answer for what he knows nothing of; but shall receive his doom, his conscience accusing or excusing him. [27.19–22]

1671–1689   1689

⟶ ⟐ ⟵

Isaac Watts
1674–1748

"As his mind was capacious, his curiosity excursive, and his industry continual," wrote Samuel Johnson in praise of the dissenting minister Isaac Watts, "his writings are very numerous." Watts produced books of poetry, logic, theology, philosophy, and science, but the writings that have mattered most are the hymns and psalm translations (about seven hundred in all) that he began composing in his early twenties. In his philosophical writings, Watts worked hard to absorb the innovations of Newton's physics and Locke's psychology; in his hymns, an older structure of piety prevails. One of empiricism's chief effects was to entangle truth with time, to make knowledge a consequence of *process* (a series of experiments, a sequence of ideas). In Watts's hymns, truth is eternal; the mind's chief tasks are to register God's greatness and to praise it aright. The singing of hymns, and of psalms awkwardly translated from the Hebrew, had been a practice of long standing in Protestant congregations. Watts brought to these forms a new clarity and grace, in verses he carefully crafted, week after week, for the immediate use and pleasure of his congregants. He sought (he once explained) to achieve an "ease of numbers [i.e., meter] and smoothness of sound, and . . . to make the sense plain and obvious." In print, the simplicity of his style gradually won a wider attention, extending far beyond local circles of dissent. As the religious historian and poet Donald Davie has pointed out, Watts's hymns and psalms probably touched more minds (and certainly resounded in more throats) over the course of the eighteenth century than any of the texts we now deem greater hits: *Gulliver's Travels*, Johnson's *Dictionary*, Thomson's *Seasons*. In his lifetime and for more than a century after, Watts was reckoned the English, Christian successor to that ancient king of Israel traditionally credited with creating the Psalms. "Were David to speak English," Watts's brother once remarked to him, "he would choose to make use of your style."

A Prospect of Heaven Makes Death Easy[1]

There is a land of pure delight
    Where saints immortal reign;
Infinite day excludes the night,
    And pleasures banish pain.

5   There everlasting spring abides,
        And never-withering flowers:
Death like a narrow sea divides
    This heav'nly land from ours.

Sweet fields beyond the swelling flood
10   Stand dressed in living green:
So to the Jews old Canaan stood,
    While Jordan rolled between.[2]

9. I.e., Judgment Day.
1. From *Hymns and Spiritual Songs* (1707).
2. In Joshua 3, the children of Israel, at the end of their 40-year journey in the desert, see the promised land of Canaan across the River Jordan.

But timorous mortals start° and shrink   *tremble*
    To cross this narrow sea,
15   And linger shivering on the brink,
    And fear to launch away.

O! could we make our doubts remove,°   *withdraw*
    Those gloomy doubts that rise,
And see the Canaan that we love,
20   With unbeclouded eyes:

Could we but climb where Moses stood,[3]
    And view the landskip° o'er,   *landscape*
Not Jordan's stream, nor death's cold flood
    Should fright us from the shore.

1707

The Hurry of the Spirits, in a Fever and Nervous Disorders[1]

My frame of nature is a ruffled sea,
And my disease the tempest. Nature feels
A strange commotion to her inmost center;
The throne of reason shakes. "Be still, my thoughts;
5 Peace and be still." In vain my reason gives
The peaceful word, my spirit strives in vain
To calm the tumult and command my thoughts.
This flesh, this circling blood, these brutal powers
Made to obey, turn rebels to the mind,
10 Nor hear its laws. The engine° rules the man.   *body*
Unhappy change! When nature's meaner springs,
Fired to impetuous ferments, break all order;
When little restless atoms rise and reign
Tyrants in sovereign uproar, and impose
15 Ideas on the mind; confused ideas
Of non-existents and impossibles,
Who can describe them? Fragments of old dreams,
Borrowed from midnight, torn from fairy fields
And fairy skies, and regions of the dead,
20 Abrupt, ill-sorted. O 'tis all confusion!
If I but close my eyes, strange images
In thousand forms and thousand colors rise,
Stars, rainbows, moons, green dragons, bears and ghosts,
An endless medley rush upon the stage
25 And dance and riot wild in reason's court
Above control. I'm in a raging storm,
Where seas and skies are blended, while my soul
Like some light worthless chip of floating cork
Is tossed from wave to wave: now overwhelmed

---

3. Having led the Israelites to the end of their desert journey, Moses on his last day of life climbed the mountain of Nebo, and surveyed the entire promised land (Deuteronomy 34.1–4).

1. Not a hymn but an autobiographical poem, the first in a sequence entitled *Thoughts and Meditations in a Long Sickness, 1712 and 1713*, published decades later in Watts' *Reliquiae Juveniles* (writings in youth).

30   With breaking floods, I drown, and seem to lose
       All being; now high-mounted on the ridge
       Of tall foaming surge, I'm all at once
       Caught up into the storm, and ride the wind,
       The whistling wind; unmanageable steed,
35   And feeble rider! Hurried many a league
       Over the rising hills of roaring brine,
       Through airy wilds unknown, with dreadful speed
       And infinite surprise, till some few minutes
       Have spent the blast, and then perhaps I drop
40   Near to the peaceful coast. Some friendly billow
       Lodges me on the beach, and I find rest.
       Short rest I find; for the next rolling wave
       Snatches me back again; then ebbing far
       Sets me adrift, and I am borne off to sea,
45   Helpless, amidst the bluster of the winds,
       Beyond the ken of shore.

       Ah, when will these tumultuous scenes be gone?
       When shall this weary spirit, tossed with tempests,
       Harassed and broken, reach the ports of rest,
50   And hold it firm? When shall this wayward flesh
       With all th' irregular springs of vital movement
       Ungovernable, return to sacred order,
       And pay their duties to the ruling mind?

1712   1734

Against Idleness and Mischief[1]

       How doth the little busy bee
          Improve each shining hour,
       And gather honey all the day
          From every opening flower!

5   How skillfully she builds her cell!
          How neat she spreads the wax!
       And labors hard to store it well
          With the sweet food she makes.

       In works of labor, or of skill,
10   I would be busy too;
       For Satan finds some mischief still°   *always*
          For idle hands to do.

       In books, or work, or healthful play,
          Let my first years be passed.
15   That I may give for every day
          Some good account at last.

1715

---

1. From *Divine Songs Attempted in Easy Language, for the Use of Children*. The poems in this durable little collection were memorized by numberless children in the 18th and 19th centuries, including Lewis Carroll's Alice. Wandering through Wonderland, she is commanded by its inhabitants (as she doubtless was in school) to recite these verses, and discovers to her dismay that the lines come out all wrong.

Man Frail, and God Eternal[1]

Our God, our help in ages past,
   Our hope for years to come,
Our shelter from the stormy blast,
   And our eternal home.

5   Under the shadow of thy throne
   Thy saints have dwelt secure.
Sufficient is thine arm alone,
   And our defense is sure.

Before the hills in order stood,
10   Or earth received her frame,
From everlasting thou art God,
   To endless years the same.

Thy word commands our flesh to dust,
   Return, ye sons of men.
15   All nations rose from earth at first,
   And turn to earth again.

A thousand ages in thy sight
   Are like an evening gone;
Short as the watch that ends the night,
20   Before the rising sun.

The busy tribes of flesh and blood
   With all their lives and cares
Are carried downwards by thy flood,
   And lost in following years.

25   Time, like an ever-rolling stream
   Bears all its sons away.
They fly forgotten, as a dream
   Dies at the opening day.

Like flowery fields the nations stand
30   Pleased with the morning light.
The flowers beneath the mower's hand
   Lie withering ere 'tis night.

Our God, our help in ages past,
   Our hope for years to come,
35   Be thou our guard while troubles last,
   And our eternal home.

1. An imitation of Psalm 90, lines 1–6; from *The Psalms of David Imitated in the Language of the New Testament, and Applied to the Christian State and Worship*. As the title indicates, Watts intended not merely to translate the Psalms, but to recast them. In his preface, he declares himself "the first who hath brought down the royal author [King David] into the common affairs of the Christian life, and let the psalmist of Israel into the Church of Christ, without anything of a Jew about him."

Joseph Addison
1672–1719

The ideas of Newton and Locke became widely known not through their own writings (which were voluminous and often dense, but through various popularizations: lectures, demonstrations, explanatory handbooks, the popular press. One of the chief disseminators was the *Spectator,* the phenomenally successful series of daily essays composed by Joseph Addison and Richard Steele (for more on the *Spectator,* see page 949). Addison in particular undertook to inculcate the ideas of Newton and Locke, sometimes directly by quotation and commentary, but more often indirectly, by absorption and a kind of tacit transmission. "The working of my own mind," Mr. Spectator announces early on, "is the general entertainment of my life," and he recommends this notably Lockean "entertainment" to his readers too; his own name honors Locke's reckoning of sight as the mind's chief instrument for the gathering of ideas. In the following extract, Addison pays comparably implicit homage to Newton, in an ode that quickly became one of the touchstones of eighteenth-century devotion. Though Addison places his poem in a tradition that combines Aristotle with the Psalms, Newton is powerfully present too, in the depiction of a heaven whose silent motions proclaim to human reason the perfection of God's design.

from Spectator No. 465
Saturday, 23 August 1712[1]

* * * The last method which I shall mention for the giving life to a man's faith is frequent retirement from the world, accompanied with religious meditation. When a man thinks of any thing in the darkness of the night, whatever deep impressions it may make in his mind, they are apt to vanish as soon as the day breaks about him. The light and noise of the day, which are perpetually soliciting his senses and calling off his attention, wear out of his mind the thoughts that imprinted themselves in it with so much strength during the silence and darkness of the night. A man finds the same difference as to himself in a crowd and in a solitude; the mind is stunned and dazzled amidst that variety of objects which press upon her in a great city: she cannot apply herself to the consideration of those things which are of the utmost concern to her. The cares or pleasures of the world strike in with every thought, and a multitude of vicious examples give a kind of justification to our folly. In our retirements everything disposes us to be serious. In courts and cities we are entertained with the works of men, in the country with those of God. One is the province of art, the other of nature. Faith and devotion naturally grow in the mind of every reasonable man, who sees the impressions of divine power and wisdom in every object on which he casts his eye. The Supreme Being has made the best arguments for his own existence, in the formation of the heavens and the earth, and these are arguments which a man of sense cannot forbear attending to, who is out of the noise and hurry of human affairs. Aristotle says,[2] that should a man live under ground, and there converse with works of art and mechanism, and should afterwards be brought up into the open day, and see the several glories of the heaven and earth, he would

---

1. Addison often set Saturdays aside for particularly serious topics, as a way of preparing his readers for the religious solemnities of Sunday (the only day on which the *Spectator* did not appear). He devotes the present paper to

"the proper means of strengthening and confirming" Christian faith.
2. Addison paraphrases lines quoted by Cicero from *De Philosophia,* a work of Aristotle's long lost.

immediately pronounce them the works of such a being as we define God to be. The Psalmist has very beautiful strokes of poetry to this purpose, in that exalted strain, "The heavens declare the glory of God: and the firmament showeth his handiwork. One day telleth another: and one night certifieth another. There is neither speech nor language: but their voices are heard among them. Their sound is gone out into all lands: and their words into the ends of the world."[3] As such a bold and sublime manner of thinking furnishes very noble matter for an ode, the reader may see it wrought into the following one.

1

    The spacious firmament on high,
    With all the blue ethereal sky,
    And spangled heav'ns, a shining frame,
    Their great original proclaim:
5   Th' unwearied sun, from day to day,
    Does his Creator's power display,
    And publishes to every land
    The works of an almighty hand.

2

    Soon as the evening shades prevail,
10 The moon takes up the wondrous tale,
    And nightly to the list'ning earth
    Repeats the story of her birth:
    Whilst all the stars that round her burn,
    And all the planets, in their turn,
15 Confirm the tidings as they roll,
    And spread the truth from pole to pole.

3

    What though, in solemn silence, all
    Move round the dark terrestrial ball?
    What though nor real voice nor sound
20 Amid their radiant orbs be found?
    In reason's ear they all rejoice,
    And utter forth a glorious voice,
    For ever singing, as they shine,
    "The hand that made us is divine."

George Berkeley
1685–1753

For Locke, "ideas" are formed in the mind out of its ongoing encounter with the very real world outside it, where swans swim and elephants plod. For George Berkeley—clergyman, poet, traveler, and philosopher—ideas are all there is. *Esse est percipi,* he argues throughout his philosophical writings: to be is to be perceived. "All those bodies which compose the mighty frame of the world, have not any subsistence without a mind"—a mind engaged in the act of perceiving them. What, then, accounts for the apparent independence and conti-

3. Psalm 19.1–4.

nuity of real objects (trees, to take one of Berkeley's recurrent examples), which seem to remain in place even when no mortal observes them? Berkeley's answer: one mind *is* perpetually engaged in perceiving them. The mind of God creates the ideas, sustains them, renders them consistent with themselves and independent of our intermittent human perceptions. In Berkeley's argument, this divine activity both constitutes proof of God's existence (since such an "infinite mind" is necessary to explain why the world appears to us as it does), and lies at the core of God's benevolence. Berkeley expounded his theory of "immaterialism" in his *Essay Towards a New Theory of Vision* (1709) and *Treatise Concerning the Principles of Human Knowledge* (1710), before recasting it in the more compact, accessible, and popular format of *Three Dialogues Between Hylas and Philonous*. Philonous ("Lover of mind") voices Berkeley's views, while Hylas ("Wooden") expresses the bemused incredulity with which Berkeley's readers continued to greet the philosopher's radical unmaking and reweaving of the fabric of everyday life. Scoffers tended to overlook the solution Berkeley was proffering to an abiding theological problem. Newton's cosmology had given rise (despite his own piety) to the unsettling image of the Clockmaker God, who having made the universe a perfectly efficient mechanism, could now let it run without further intervention. Newton addressed this problem in part by insisting that God had to intervene at intervals in order to adjust his system. Berkeley's God, by contrast, is no clockmaker at all; having authored the world in the beginning, he continues to make it anew at every moment by the creative act of his continual perception.

from Three Dialogues Between Hylas and Philonous

HYLAS But do you in earnest think, the real existence of sensible things consists in their being actually perceived? If so, how comes it that all mankind distinguish between them? Ask the first man you meet, and he shall tell you, *to be perceived* is one thing, and *to exist* is another.

PHILONOUS I am content, Hylas, to appeal to the common sense of the world for the truth of my notion. Ask the gardener why he thinks yonder cherry tree exists in the garden, and he shall tell you, because he sees and feels it; in a word, because he perceives it by his senses. Ask him why he thinks an orange tree not to be there, and he shall tell you, because he does not perceive it. What he perceives by sense, that he terms a real being, and saith it *is*, or *exists*; but that which is not perceivable, the same, he saith, hath no being.

HYLAS Yes, Philonous, I grant the existence of a sensible thing consists in being perceivable, but not in being actually perceived.

PHILONOUS And what is perceivable but an idea? And can an idea exist without being actually perceived? These are points long since agreed between us.

HYLAS But be your opinion never so true, yet surely you will not deny it is shocking, and contrary to the common sense of men. Ask the fellow whether yonder tree hath an existence out of his mind: what answer think you he would make?

PHILONOUS The same that I should myself, to wit, that it doth exist out of his mind. But then to a Christian it cannot surely be shocking to say, the real tree existing without his mind is truly known and comprehended by (that is, *exists in*) the infinite mind of God. Probably he may not at first glance be aware of the direct and immediate proof there is of this, inasmuch as the very being of a tree, or any other sensible thing, implies a mind wherein it is. But the point itself he cannot deny. The question between the materialists[1] and me is not whether things have a real

---

1. Those who assert the existence of matter, independent of perception.

existence out of the mind of this or that person, but whether they have an absolute existence, distinct from being perceived by God, and exterior to all minds. This indeed some heathens and philosophers have affirmed, but whoever entertains notions of the Deity suitable to the Holy Scriptures will be of another opinion.

HYLAS But according to your notions, what difference is there between real things, and chimeras formed by the imagination, or the visions of a dream, since they are all equally in the mind?

PHILONOUS The ideas formed by the imagination are faint and indistinct; they have besides an entire dependence on the will. But the ideas perceived by sense, that is, real things, are more vivid and clear, and being imprinted on the mind by a spirit distinct from us, have not a like dependence on our will. There is therefore no danger of confounding these with the foregoing: and there is as little of confounding them with the visions of a dream, which are dim, irregular, and confused. And though they should happen to be never so lively and natural, yet by their not being connected, and of a piece with the preceding and subsequent transactions of our lives, they might easily be distinguished from realities. In short, by whatever method you distinguish *things* from *chimeras* on your own scheme, the same, it is evident, will hold also upon mine. For it must be, I presume, by some perceived difference, and I am not for depriving you of any one thing that you perceive.

HYLAS But still, Philonous, you hold, there is nothing in the world but spirits and ideas. And this, you must needs acknowledge, sounds very oddly.

PHILONOUS I own the word *idea,* not being commonly used for *thing,* sounds something out of the way. My reason for using it was, because a necessary relation to the mind is understood to be implied by that term; and it is now commonly used by philosophers to denote the immediate objects of the understanding. But however oddly the proposition may sound in words, yet it includes nothing so very strange or shocking in its sense, which in effect amounts to no more than this, to wit, that there are only things perceiving, and things perceived; or that every unthinking being is necessarily, and from the very nature of its existence, perceived by some mind; if not by any finite created mind, yet certainly by the infinite mind of God, in whom "we live, and move, and have our being."[2] Is this as strange as to say, the sensible qualities are not on the objects, or that we cannot be sure of the existence of things, or know anything of their real natures, though we both see and feel them, and perceive them by all our senses?

HYLAS And in consequence of this, must we not think there are no such things as physical or corporeal causes but that a spirit is the immediate cause of all the phenomena in nature? Can there be anything more extravagant than this?

PHILONOUS Yes, it is infinitely more extravagant to say, a thing which is inert, operates on the mind, and which is unperceiving, is the cause of our perceptions. Besides, that which to you, I know not for what reason, seems so extravagant, is no more than the Holy Scriptures assert in a hundred places. In them God is represented as the sole and immediate author of all those effects which some heathens and philosophers are wont to ascribe to nature, matter, fate, or the like unthinking principle. This is so much the constant language of Scripture, that it were needless to confirm it by citations. * * *

2. Acts 17.28.

—— ⫻ ——

David Hume
1711–1776

As he lay dying at home in his native city of Edinburgh, David Hume entertained a visitor by conjuring up, with characteristic cheerfulness, a scenario in the afterlife. He imagined himself begging the fatal ferryman Charon for a little more time: "Have a little patience, good Charon, I have been endeavoring to open the eyes of the public. If I live a few years longer, I may have the satisfaction of seeing the downfall of some of the prevailing systems of superstition." The "prevailing system" which Hume had become most notorious for attacking was the Christian religion, whose favorite tenets—providence, miracles, the argument from design, the afterlife itself—he had called into question, with increasing audacity, over the course of his work. But he had also done much damage to newer systems of thought, notably Locke's. Locke had regarded personal identity as coherent and continuous, the consequence of lifelong experiences and ideas accumulated in the memory. Hume, in his early, massive *Treatise of Human Nature* (1739–1740), waived all this away as an arrant fiction—though perhaps a necessary one, since empiricism properly pursued reveals so radical an incoherence in mortal minds that empiricists themselves must intermittently abandon philosophy in order to go about their daily lives. Like many of his empiric predecessors Hume argued that knowledge of the real world "must be founded entirely on experience"; more than any predecessor he was willing to entertain (and to entertain with) the doubts and demolitions arising from that premise. In his own lifetime, his skepticism did not prove as contagious as he had hoped. The *Treatise*, he recalled wryly, "fell *deadborn from the press*, without reaching such distinction as even to excite a murmur among the zealots." Though his attempt to recast his chief arguments more succinctly in *An Enquiry Concerning Human Understanding* (1748) prompted a somewhat livelier response, he eventually made his fortune not as a philosopher but as author of the highly successful *History of England* (1754–1763). He faced the general indifference or hostility to his arguments as blithely as he later greeted death, continually refining his views and revising his prose. He knew himself out of sync with his times. When, in his fantasy, he forecasts to Charon the imminent downfall of superstition, the ferryman responds, "You loitering rogue, that will not happen these many hundred years. Do you fancy I will grant you a lease for so long a term? Get into the boat this instant, you lazy loitering rogue." More than two hundred years later, the artful mischief of Hume's work has secured him some such lease. His writings, lucid and elusive, forthright and sly, demand (and receive) continual reassessment; his skepticism has proven more powerful than his contemporaries suspected, and he figures as perhaps the wittiest and most self-possessed philosophical troublemaker since Socrates.

from A Treatise of Human Nature
[THE MIND AS THEATER[1]]

There are some philosophers,[2] who imagine we are every moment intimately conscious of what we call our *self*; that we feel its existence and its continuance in existence; and are certain, beyond the evidence of a demonstration, both of its perfect identity and simplicity. The strongest sensation, the most violent passion, say they, instead of distracting us from this view, only fix it the more intensely, and make us consider their influence on *self* either by their pain or pleasure. To attempt a farther

---

1. From Book 1, section 6, "Of Personal Identity."
2. Notably Joseph Butler, an Anglican bishop who argued in *The Analogy of Religion* (1736) that the existence of the self is a truth of which every person is continually (and correctly) certain.

proof of this were to weaken its evidence; since no proof can be derived from any fact, of which we are so intimately conscious; nor is there anything of which we can be certain, if we doubt of this.

Unluckily all these positive assertions are contrary to that very experience which is pleaded for them, nor have we any idea of *self*, after the manner it is here explained. For from what impression could this idea be derived? This question 'tis impossible to answer without a manifest contradiction and absurdity; and yet 'tis a question, which must necessarily be answered, if we would have the idea of self pass for clear and intelligible. It must be some one impression, that gives rise to every real idea. But self or person is not any one impression, but that to which our several impressions and ideas are supposed to have a reference. If any impression gives rise to the idea of self, that impression must continue invariably the same through the whole course of our lives, since self is supposed to exist after that manner. But there is no impression constant and invariable. Pain and pleasure, grief and joy, passions and sensations succeed each other, and never all exist at the same time. It cannot, therefore, be from any of these impressions, or from any other, that the idea of self is derived; and consequently there is no such idea.

But farther, what must become of all our particular perceptions upon this hypothesis? All these are different, and distinguishable, and separable from each other, and may be separately considered, and may exist separately, and have no need of anything to support their existence. After what manner, therefore, do they belong to self; and how are they connected with it? For my part, when I enter most intimately into what I call *myself*, I always stumble on some particular perception or other, of heat or cold, light or shade, love or hatred, pain or pleasure. I never can catch *myself* at any time without a perception, and never can observe anything but the perception. When my perceptions are removed for any time, as by sound sleep, so long am I insensible of *myself*, and may truly be said not to exist. And were all my perceptions removed by death, and could I neither think, nor feel, nor see, nor love, nor hate after the dissolution of my body, I should be entirely annihilated, nor do I conceive what is farther requisite to make me a perfect nonentity. If anyone upon serious and unprejudiced reflection, thinks he has a different notion of *himself*, I must confess I can reason no longer with him. All I can allow him is, that he may be in the right as well as I, and that we are essentially different in this particular. He may, perhaps, perceive something simple and continued, which he calls *himself*; though I am certain there is no such principle in me.

But setting aside some metaphysicians of this kind, I may venture to affirm of the rest of mankind, that they are nothing but a bundle or collection of different perceptions, which succeed each other with an inconceivable rapidity, and are in a perpetual flux and movement. Our eyes cannot turn in their sockets without varying our perceptions. Our thought is still more variable than our sight; and all our other senses and faculties contribute to this change; nor is there any single power of the soul which remains unalterably the same, perhaps for one moment. The mind is a kind of theater, where several perceptions successively make their appearance: pass, re-pass, glide away, and mingle in an infinite variety of postures and situations. There is properly no *simplicity* in it at one time, nor *identity* in different; whatever natural propension we may have to imagine that simplicity and identity. The comparison of the theater must not mislead us. They are the successive perceptions only, that constitute the mind; nor have we the most distant notion of the place where these scenes are represented, or of the materials, of which it is composed. * * *

[PHILOSOPHY AND COMMON LIFE³]

But what have I here said, that reflections very refined and metaphysical have little or no influence upon us? This opinion I can scarce forbear retracting, and condemning from my present feeling and experience. The *intense* view of these manifold contradictions and imperfections in human reason has so wrought upon me, and heated my brain, that I am ready to reject all belief and reasoning, and can look upon no opinion even as more probable or likely than another. Where am I, or what? From what causes do I derive my existence, and to what condition shall I return? Whose favor shall I court, and whose anger must I dread? What beings surround me? and on whom have I any influence, or who have any influence on me? I am confounded with all these questions, and begin to fancy myself in the most deplorable condition imaginable, environed with the deepest darkness, and utterly deprived of the use of every member and faculty.

Most fortunately it happens, that since reason is incapable of dispelling these clouds, nature herself suffices to that purpose, and cures me of this philosophical melancholy and delirium, either by relaxing this bent of mind, or by some avocation and lively impression of my senses, which obliterate all these chimeras. I dine, I play a game of backgammon, I converse, and am merry with my friends; and when after three or four hour's amusement, I would return to these speculations, they appear so cold, and strained, and ridiculous, that I cannot find in my heart to enter into them any farther.

Here then I find myself absolutely and necessarily determined to live, and talk, and act like other people in the common affairs of life. But notwithstanding that my natural propensity, and the course of my animal spirits and passions reduce me to this indolent belief in the general maxims of the world, I still feel such remains of my former disposition, that I am ready to throw all my books and papers into the fire, and resolve never more to renounce the pleasures of life for the sake of reasoning and philosophy. For these are my sentiments in that splenetic⁴ humor, which governs me at present. I may, nay I must yield to the current of nature, in submitting to my senses and understanding; and in this blind submission I show most perfectly my skeptical disposition and principles. But does it follow, that I must strive against the current of nature, which leads me to indolence and pleasure; that I must seclude myself, in some measure, from the commerce and society of men, which is so agreeable; and that I must torture my brain with subtleties and sophistries, at the very time that I cannot satisfy myself concerning the reasonableness of so painful an application, nor have any tolerable prospect of arriving by its means at truth and certainty? Under what obligation do I lie of making such an abuse of time? And to what end can it serve either for the service of mankind, or for my own private interest? No: if I must be a fool, as well as those who reason or believe anything *certainly* are, my follies shall at least be natural and agreeable. Where I strive against my inclination, I shall have a good reason for my resistance; and will no more be led a wandering into such dreary solitudes, and rough passages, as I have hitherto met with.

3. From Book 1, section 7: "Conclusion of This Book." The first book of the *Treatise* serves as a long prelude to the whole; in concluding it, Hume considers the "manifest contradictions" between the assumptions on which ordinary people lead their lives, and the volatile questions raised by "refined reasoning" (rigorous philosophic inquiry). Pinpointing these contradictions in himself, he contemplates the precariousness of his enterprise, and the intricacy of his motives for undertaking it.
4. Depressive, irritable.

There are the sentiments of my spleen[5] and indolence; and indeed I must confess, that philosophy has nothing to oppose to them, and expects a victory more from the returns of a serious good-humored disposition, than from the force of reason and conviction. In all the incidents of life we ought still to preserve our skepticism. If we believe, that fire warms, or water refreshes, 'tis only because it costs us too much pains to think otherwise. Nay if we are philosophers, it ought only to be upon skeptical principles, and from an inclination, which we feel to the employing ourselves after that manner. Where reason is lively, and mixes itself with some propensity, it ought to be assented to. Where it does not, it never can any title to operate upon us.

At the time, therefore, that I am tired with amusement and company, and have indulged a *reverie* in my chamber, or in a solitary walk by a riverside, I feel my mind all collected within itself, and am naturally *inclined* to carry my view into all those subjects, about which I have met with so many disputes in the course of my reading and conversation.[6] I cannot forbear having a curiosity to be acquainted with the principles of moral good and evil, the nature and foundation of government, and the cause of those several passions and inclinations, which actuate and govern me. I am uneasy to think I approve of one object, and disapprove of another; call one thing beautiful, and another deformed; decide concerning truth and falsehood, reason and folly, without knowing upon what principles I proceed. I am concerned for the condition of the learned world, which lies under such a deplorable ignorance in all these particulars. I feel an ambition to arise in me of contributing to the instruction of mankind, and of acquiring a name by my inventions and discoveries. These sentiments spring up naturally in my present disposition; and should I endeavor to banish them, by attaching myself to any other business or diversion, I *feel* I should be a loser in point of pleasure; and this is the origin of my philosophy.

1734–1737   1739–1740

from An Enquiry Concerning Human Understanding[1]
from *Section 10: Of Miracles*

A miracle is a violation of the laws of nature; and as a firm and unalterable experience has established these laws, the proof against a miracle, from the very nature of the fact, is as entire as any argument from experience can possibly be imagined. Why is it more than probable that all men must die; that lead cannot, of itself, remain suspended in the air; that fire consumes wood, and is extinguished by water; unless it be, that these events are found agreeable to the laws of nature, and there is required a violation of these laws, or in other words, a miracle to prevent them? Nothing is esteemed a miracle, if it ever happen in the common course of nature. It is no miracle that a man, seemingly in good health, should die on a sudden; because such a kind of death, though more unusual than any other, has yet been frequently observed to happen. But it is a miracle that a dead man should come to life; because that has never been observed in any age or country. There must, therefore, be a uniform experience against every miraculous event, otherwise the event would not merit that appella-

---

5. Despondency.
6. In the list that follows, Hume names many of the topics he will take up later in the *Treatise*.
1. Hume wrote this essay in the mid-1730s, intending to include it in his *Treatise*; conscious of its volatility, he withheld it for a dozen years, publishing it for the first

time in his *Philosophical Essays Concerning Human Understanding* (1748); ten years later a revised version of the work appeared, under the new title *An Enquiry....* The essay proved at least as explosive as he had anticipated, prompting a spate of refutations; for Samuel Johnson's view, see page 1285).

tion. And as a uniform experience amounts to a proof, there is here a direct and full *proof*, from the nature of the fact, against the existence of any miracle; nor can such a proof be destroyed, or the miracle rendered credible, but by an opposite proof, which is superior.

The plain consequence is (and it is a general maxim worthy of our attention), "That no testimony is sufficient to establish a miracle, unless the testimony be of such a kind, that its falsehood would be more miraculous than the fact which it endeavors to establish; and even in that case there is a mutual destruction of arguments, and the superior only gives us an assurance suitable to that degree of force which remains after deducting the inferior." When anyone tells me, that he saw a dead man restored to life, I immediately consider with myself, whether it be more probable, that this person should either deceive or be deceived, or that the fact, which he relates, should really have happened. I weigh the one miracle against the other; and according to the superiority which I discover, I pronounce my decision, and always reject the greater miracle. If the falsehood of his testimony would be more miraculous than the event which he relates, then, and not till then, can he pretend to command my belief or opinion.

In the foregoing reasoning we have supposed, that the testimony, upon which a miracle is founded, may possibly amount to an entire proof, and that the falsehood of that testimony would be a real prodigy. But it is easy to show that we have been a great deal too liberal in our concession, and that there never was a miraculous event established on so full an evidence.

For *first*, there is not to be found, in all history, any miracle attested by a sufficient number of men, of such unquestioned good sense, education, and learning, as to secure us against all delusion in themselves; of such undoubted integrity, as to place them beyond all suspicion of any design to deceive others; of such credit and reputation in the eyes of mankind, as to have a great deal to lose in case of their being detected in any falsehood; and at the same time, attesting facts performed in such a public manner and in so celebrated a part of the world, as to render the detection unavoidable. All which circumstances are requisite to give us a full assurance in the testimony of men.

Secondly. We may observe in human nature a principle which, if strictly examined, will be found to diminish extremely the assurance which we might, from human testimony, have, in any kind of prodigy. The maxim by which we commonly conduct ourselves in our reasonings is that the objects of which we have no experience resemble those of which we have; that what we have found to be most usual is always most probable; and that where there is an opposition of arguments, we ought to give the preference to such as are founded on the greatest number of past observations. But though, in proceeding by this rule, we readily reject any fact which is unusual and incredible in an ordinary degree; yet in advancing farther, the mind observes not always the same rule; but when anything is affirmed utterly absurd and miraculous, it rather the more readily admits of such a fact, upon account of that very circumstance which ought to destroy all its authority. The passion of *surprise* and *wonder*, arising from miracles, being an agreeable emotion, gives a sensible tendency towards the belief of those events from which it is derived. And this goes so far, that even those who cannot enjoy this pleasure immediately, nor can believe those miraculous events, of which they are informed, yet love to partake of the satisfaction at second-hand or by rebound, and place a pride and delight in exciting the admiration of others.

With what greediness are the miraculous accounts of travelers received, their descriptions of sea and land monsters, their relations of wonderful adventures, strange men, and uncouth manners? But if the spirit of religion join itself to the love of wonder, there is an end of common sense; and human testimony, in these circumstances, loses all pretensions to authority. A religionist may be an enthusiast,[2] and imagine he sees what has no reality. He may know his narrative to be false, and yet persevere in it, with the best intentions in the world, for the sake of promoting so holy a cause; or even where this delusion has not place, vanity, excited by so strong a temptation, operates on him more powerfully than on the rest of mankind in any other circumstances; and self-interest with equal force. His auditors may not have, and commonly have not, sufficient judgment to canvass his evidence. What judgment they have, they renounce by principle, in these sublime and mysterious subjects; or if they were ever so willing to employ it, passion and a heated imagination disturb the regularity of its operations. Their credulity increases his impudence; and his impudence overpowers their credulity. * * *

Thirdly. It forms a strong presumption against all supernatural and miraculous relations, that they are observed chiefly to abound among ignorant and barbarous nations; or if a civilized people has ever given admission to any of them, that people will be found to have received them from ignorant and barbarous ancestors, who transmitted them with that inviolable sanction and authority, which always attend received opinions. When we peruse the first histories of all nations, we are apt to imagine ourselves transported into some new world, where the whole frame of nature is disjointed, and every element performs its operations in a different manner from what it does at present. Battles, revolutions, pestilence, famine, and death are never the effect of those natural causes which we experience. Prodigies, omens, oracles, judgments, quite obscure the few natural events that are intermingled with them. But as the former grow thinner every page, in proportion as we advance nearer the enlightened ages, we soon learn that there is nothing mysterious or supernatural in the case, but that all proceeds from the usual propensity of mankind towards the marvelous, and that, though this inclination may at intervals receive a check from sense and learning, it can never be thoroughly extirpated from human nature. * * *

Upon the whole, then, it appears that no testimony for any kind of miracle has ever amounted to a probability, much less to a proof; and that, even supposing it amounted to a proof, it would be opposed by another proof; derived from the very nature of the fact, which it would endeavor to establish. It is experience only which gives authority to human testimony; and it is the same experience which assures us of the laws of nature. When, therefore, these two kinds of experience are contrary, we have nothing to do but subtract the one from the other, and embrace an opinion, either on one side or the other, with that assurance which arises from the remainder. But according to the principle here explained, this subtraction, with regard to all popular religions, amounts to an entire annihilation; and therefore we may establish it as a maxim, that no human testimony can have such force as to prove a miracle, and make it a just foundation for any such system of religion. * * *

What we have said of miracles may be applied, without any variation, to prophecies; and indeed, all prophecies are real miracles, and as such only can be admitted as proofs of any revelation. If it did not exceed the capacity of human nature to foretell future events, it would be absurd to employ any prophecy as an argument for a divine

---

2. Fanatic.

mission or authority from heaven. So that, upon the whole, we may conclude, that the *Christian religion* not only was at first attended with miracles, but even at this day cannot be believed by any reasonable person without one. Mere reason is insufficient to convince us of its veracity. And whoever is moved by *faith* to assent to it, is conscious of a continued miracle in his own person, which subverts all the principles of his understanding, and gives him a determination to believe what is most contrary to custom and experience.

c. 1736   1748

Christopher Smart
1722–1771

"Newton . . . is more of error than of the truth, but I am of the Word of God," wrote Christopher Smart in his astonishing poem *Jubilate Agno* ("Rejoice in the Lamb"). For Smart, as for a growing number of Christians in the century's second half, the Newtonian "error" consisted in a commitment to materialist science, to an empiricism which investigated the physical world and sought its seeming system, rather than submitting to faith in a God who worked by will and sometimes by miracle, free of any fixed laws of nature. Smart composed *Jubilate Agno* in his late thirties, while confined in a madhouse; after a brilliant career as a classical scholar at Cambridge, and an auspicious start in London as a literary adventurer (poet, editor, translator, essayist), he suffered a derangement whose chief symptom was his compulsion to pray spontaneously in public places (he was too much "of the Word of God" to be socially acceptable). Released from the asylum after five years, Smart recast much material from the *Jubilate Agno* in his *Song of David* (1763); following Watts's precedent, he published a translation of the Psalms (1767) and (while imprisoned for debt at the very end of his life) a book of *Hymns for the Amusement of Children* (1771). *Jubilate Agno* remained in manuscript and unknown for a century and a half after the poet's death. Smart called it "my Magnificat," *magnificat* being the title of the liturgical hymn first uttered by the Virgin Mary upon learning that she would conceive a son: "My Soul doth magnify the Lord" (Luke 1.46–55). Structured like a responsive prayer, Smart's poem moves rapidly across a wide range of reference, from the scriptural and mystical to the local and the homely ("God be gracious to Baumgarden"—a London bassoon player). But Smart returns repeatedly to a preoccupation touched on in the poem's title: to the animal world as emblem and embodiment of God's grace and greatness (in Smart's time natural history was among the branches of knowledge least touched by the new science, and most inflected by faith and folklore). In the excerpts below, Smart punningly pinpoints the animal essences of languages ancient and modern, then depicts the feline who kept him company during his years of confinement, singing Jeoffry's praises with such exuberance as to make *magnificat* seem a latent, sacred, and affectionate pun.

from Jubilate Agno
[ANIMALS IN LANGUAGE[1]]

625   For the power of some animal is predominant in every language.
           For the power and spirit of a CAT is in the Greek.

---

1. These selections come from Fragment B of Smart's manuscript. Some pages of Smart's manuscript contain long sequences of lines beginning "Let"; other pages contain lines beginning "For," with clear enough indications that the "Let" and "For" lines were meant to be dovetailed and read alternately, in the form of responsive prayer. For the two excerpts printed here, though, lines beginning "Let" have not been found—and may never have been written.

For the sound of a cat is in the most useful preposition κατ' ευχην.[2]

For the pleasantry of a cat at pranks is in the language ten thousand times over.[3]

For JACK UPON PRANCK is in the performance of περι together or separate.[4]

630   For Clapperclaw[5] is in the grappling of the words upon one another in all the modes of versification.

For the sleekness of a Cat is in his αγλαιηφι.[6]

For the Greek is thrown from heaven and falls upon its feet.[7]

For the Greek when distracted from the line is sooner restored to rank and rallied into some form than any other.

For the purring of a Cat is his τρυζει.[8]

635   For his cry is in ουαι,[9] which I am sorry for.

For the Mouse (Mus) prevails in the Latin.[1]

For Edi-mus, bibi-mus, vivi-mus—ore-mus.[2]

For the Mouse is a creature of great personal valor.

For—this is a true case—Cat takes female mouse from the company of male—male mouse will not depart, but stands threat'ning and daring.

640   For this is as much as to challenge, if you will let her go, I will engage you, as prodigious a creature as you are.

For the Mouse is of an hospitable disposition.

For bravery and hospitality were said and done by the Romans rather than others.

For two creatures the Bull and the Dog prevail in the English.

For all the words ending in -ble are in the creature. Invisi-ble, Incompre-hensi-ble, ineffa-ble, A-ble.

645   For the Greek and Latin are not dead languages, but taken up and accepted for the sake of him that spoke them.

For can is (canis[3]) is cause and effect a dog.

For the English is concise and strong. Dog and Bull again.

For Newton's notion of colors is αλογος,[4] unphilosophical.

[My Cat Jeoffry]

695   For I will consider my Cat Jeoffry.

For he is the servant of the Living God duly and daily serving him.

For at the first glance of the glory of God in the East he worships in his way.

For is this done by wreathing his body seven times round with elegant quickness.

For then he leaps up to catch the musk, which is the blessing of God upon his prayer.

700   For he rolls upon prank to work it in.

For having done duty and received blessing he begins to consider himself.

For this he performs in ten degrees.

---

2. Greek *kat' euchen:* "according to prayer."
3. The syllable *kat* appears in many word forms.
4. Greek *perikato* means "upside down" (as, probably, does "Jack Upon Pranck").
5. To claw, scratch.
6. *Aglaiefi:* "beauty."
7. Perhaps an allusion to the Greek poetic term *catalexis,* the shortening or omission of a "foot" from a line of verse; the prefix *cata-* means "down."

8. *Truzei:* "murmur."
9. *Ouai:* exclamation of lament ("ah!").
1. Partly because (as Smart illustrates in line 637), the syllable *mus* means "mouse" and is also the suffix for first person plural present-tense conjugations.
2. "We eat, we drink, we live—let us pray."
3. Latin: dog.
4. *Alogos:* literally, "without the Word."

For first he looks upon his fore-paws to see if they are clean.

For secondly he kicks up behind to clear away there.

705 For thirdly he works it upon stretch with the fore-paws extended.

For fourthly he sharpens his paws by wood.

For fifthly he washes himself.

For sixthly he rolls upon wash.

For seventhly he fleas himself, that he may not be interrupted upon the beat.

710 For eighthly he rubs himself against a post.

For ninthly he looks up for his instructions.

For tenthly he goes in quest of food.

For having considered God and himself he will consider his neighbor.

For if he meets another cat he will kiss her in kindness.

715 For when he takes his prey he plays with it to give it chance.

For one mouse in seven escapes by his dallying.

For when his day's work is done his business more properly begins.

For he keeps the Lord's watch in the night against the adversary.

For he counteracts the powers of darkness by his electrical skin and glaring eyes.

720 For he counteracts the Devil, who is death, by brisking about the life.

For in his morning orisons he loves the sun and the sun loves him.

For he is of the tribe of Tiger.

For the Cherub Cat is a term of the Angel Tiger.

For he has the subtlety and hissing of a serpent, which in goodness he suppresses.

725 For he will not do destruction, if he is well-fed, neither will he spit without provocation.

For he purrs in thankfulness, when God tells him he's a good Cat.

For he is an instrument for the children to learn benevolence upon.

For every house is incomplete without him and a blessing is lacking in the spirit.

For the Lord commanded Moses concerning the cats at the departure of the Children of Israel from Egypt.[5]

730 For every family had one cat at least in the bag.

For the English Cats are the best in Europe.

For he is the cleanest in the use of his fore-paws of any quadrupede.

For the dexterity of his defense is an instance of the love of God to him exceedingly.

For he is the quickest to his mark of any creature.

735 For he is tenacious of his point.

For he is a mixture of gravity and waggery.

For he knows that God is his Savior.

For there is nothing sweeter than his peace when at rest.

For there is nothing brisker than his life when in motion.

740 For he is of the Lord's poor and so indeed is he called by benevolence perpetually—Poor Jeoffry! poor Jeoffry! the rat has bit thy throat.

For I bless the name of the Lord Jesus that Jeoffry is better.

For the divine spirit comes about his body to sustain it in complete cat.

For his tongue is exceeding pure so that it has in purity what it wants in music.

5. "Take your flocks and your herds," says the Egyptian Pharaoh when demanding the Israelites' departure (Exodus 12.32); Smart adds the Lord and the cats.

For he is docile and can learn certain things.
745   For he can set up with gravity which is patience upon approbation.
For he can fetch and carry, which is patience in employment.
For he can jump over a stick which is patience upon proof positive.
For he can spraggle° upon waggle at the word of command.   *sprawl*
For he can jump from an eminence into his master's bosom.
750   For he can catch the cork and toss it again.
For he is hated by the hypocrite and miser.
For the former is afraid of detection.
For the latter refuses the charge.
For he camels his back to bear the first notion of business.
755   For he is good to think on, if a man would express himself neatly.
For he made a great figure in Egypt for his signal services.
For he killed the Ichneumon-rat° very pernicious by land.   *mongoose*
For his ears are so acute that they sting again.
For from this proceeds the passing quickness of his attention.
760   For by stroking of him I have found out electricity.
For I perceived God's light about him both wax and fire.
For the Electrical fire is the spiritual substance, which God sends from
    heaven to sustain the bodies both of man and beast.
For God has blessed him in the variety of his movements.
For, though he cannot fly, he is an excellent clamberer.
765   For his motions upon the face of the earth are more than any other
    quadrupede.
For he can tread to all the measures upon the music.
For he can swim for life.
For he can creep.

c. 1758–1763   1939

—◦—≒◦≓—◦—

William Cowper
1731–1800

Like Christopher Smart, William Cowper suffered madness, loved animals, wrote hymns, and invented capacious new structures for religious verse. But where Smart wrote to celebrate his sure salvation, Cowper wrote out of the certainty that he was damned—unworthy of redemption and predestined for hellfire. The conviction first took hold in 1763, when a paralyzing panic cut him off from impending attachments (to a new job he was about to secure, a beloved woman he was soon to marry) and prompted several attempts at suicide. The course of recovery took him first to an asylum, then through a conversion to Calvinism, then to the household of Mary Unwin, who loved and looked after him for the next four decades, and finally into partnership with Unwin's neighbor, the austere hymn-writer John Newton, with whom Cowper collaborated for years on a new collection of religious song, the *Olney Hymns* (it included, along with several of Cowper's still-sung texts, Newton's perdurable *Amazing Grace*). A second, sharper attack of madness, ten years after the first, deepened Cowper's conviction of his doom but also ushered in years of plentiful poetic composition. Seizing any small occasion (a fish dinner, the death of a pet bird) to produce a short, often comic piece of verse, Cowper wrote poems to hold terror at bay. As his output increased, his ambition did too. *The Task,* a massive mock-epic grounded in the comforts of Cowper's rural retirement (sofa, garden, seasons) but ranging satirically over the whole wide world, surprised even its author by its scope and popularity. Spurred by its success, Cowper undertook to translate Homer's epics, hoping to surpass Pope's attempts earlier in the century. In a passage near the midpoint of the poem (printed here), Newton appears briefly as the embodiment of Cowper's deepest hope, that the mind might merge with God through a science immersed in faith—"philosophy baptized." In his last, autobiographical poem, *The Cast-away*, Cowper draws a darker picture, of a mind sundered from its maker by distance and despair.

Light Shining out of Darkness[1]

God moves in a mysterious way,
　　His wonders to perform;
He plants his footsteps in the sea,
　　And rides upon the storm.

5　　Deep in unfathomable mines
　　Of never-failing skill,
He treasures up his bright designs,
　　And works his sov'reign will.

Ye fearful saints[2] fresh courage take,
10　　The clouds ye so much dread
Are big with mercy, and shall break
　　In blessings on your head.

Judge not the Lord by feeble sense,
　　But trust him for his grace;
15　Behind a frowning providence,
　　He hides a smiling face.

His purposes will ripen fast,
　　Unfolding every hour;
The bud may have a bitter taste,
20　　But sweet will be the flower.

Blind unbelief is sure to err,
　　And scan his work in vain;
God is his own interpreter,
　　And he will make it plain.

c. 1773　　　　　　　　　　　　　　　　　　　　　　　　　　　　　1774

from The Task
["PHILOSOPHY BAPTIZED"[1]]

God never meant that man should scale the heav'ns
By strides of human wisdom. In his works
Though wond'rous, he commands us in his word
To seek *him* rather, where his mercy shines.
225　The mind indeed enlightened from above
Views him in all. Ascribes to the grand cause
The grand effect. Acknowledges with joy

---

1. Written and first published during the period of Cowper's collaboration with John Newton; later included in their *Olney Hymns* (1779).

2. Cowper addresses those who (according to Calvinist theology) are predestined for salvation.
1. From Book 3, The Garden.

His manner, and with rapture tastes his style.
But never yet did philosophic° tube   *scientific*
230   That brings the planets home into the eye
Of observation, and discovers, else°   *otherwise*
Not visible, his family of worlds,
Discover him that rules them; such a veil
Hangs over mortal eyes, blind from the birth
235   And dark in things divine. Full often too
Our wayward intellect, the more we learn
Of nature, overlooks her author more,
From instrumental causes proud to draw
Conclusions retrograde and mad mistake.
240   But if his word once teach us, shoot a ray
Through all the heart's dark chambers, and reveal
Truths undiscerned but by that holy light,
Then all is plain. Philosophy baptized
In the pure fountain of eternal love
245   Has eyes indeed; and viewing all she sees
As meant to indicate a God to man,
Gives *him* his praise, and forfeits not her own.
Learning has borne such fruit in other days
On all her branches. Piety has found
250   Friends in the friends of science, and true prayer
Has flowed from lips wet with Castalian dews.[2]
Such was thy wisdom, Newton, childlike sage!
Sagacious reader of the works of God,
And in his word sagacious. * * *

1783–1785   1785

The Cast-away[1]

Obscurest night involved° the sky,   *encompassed*
    Th' Atlantic billows roared,
When such a destined° wretch as I   *doomed*
    Washed headlong from on board
5   Of friends, of hope, of all bereft,
His floating home for ever left.

No braver chief[2] could Albion° boast   *Britain*
    Than he with whom he went,
Nor ever ship left Albion's coast
10   With warmer wishes sent.
He loved them both, but both in vain,
Nor him beheld, nor her again.

2. I.e., from poets (who have drunk of the inspirational
Castalian spring on the mountain of the Muses).
1. Cowper based this poem on a mariner's account, in a
popular travel book, of having watched helplessly as a
shipmate was hurled overboard during a storm: "We were
the more grieved at his unhappy fate, as we . . . conceived
from the manner in which he swam that he might continue sensible, for a considerable time longer, of the hor-

ror attending his irretrievable situation." Cowper collates
the doomed man's situation with his own, which he conceived as also "irretrievable"; the poem, left in manuscript at his death, is his last surviving original poem in
English.
2. George Anson, commander of the naval squadron in
which the sailor was lost.

Not long beneath the whelming brine
　　Expert to swim, he lay,
15　Nor soon he felt his strength decline
　　Or courage die away;
But waged with Death a lasting strife
Supported by despair of life.

He shouted, nor his friends had failed
20　　To check the vessel's course,
But so the furious blast prevailed
　　That, pitiless perforce,
They left their outcast mate behind,
And scudded still before the wind.

25　Some succor yet they could afford,
　　And, such as storms allow,
The cask, the coop, the floated cord
　　Delayed not to bestow;
But he, they knew, nor ship nor shore,
30　Whate'er they gave, should visit more.

Nor, cruel as it seemed, could he
　　Their haste, himself, condemn,
Aware that flight, in such a sea,
　　Alone could rescue them;
35　Yet bitter felt it still to die
Deserted, and his friends so nigh.

He long survives who lives an hour
　　In ocean, self-upheld,
And so long he, with unspent power,
40　　His destiny repelled,
And ever, as the minutes flew,
Entreated help, or cried, Adieu!

At length, his transient respite past,
　　His comrades, who before
45　Had heard his voice in every blast,
　　Could catch the sound no more;
For then, by toil subdued, he drank
The stifling wave, and then he sank.

No poet wept him: but the page
50　　Of narrative[3] sincere
That tells his name, his worth,° his age,　　　　　　　　rank
　　Is wet with Anson's tear,
And tears by bards or heroes shed
Alike immortalize the dead.

55　I therefore purpose not or dream,
　　Descanting on his fate,
To give the melancholy theme
　　A more enduring date,

---

3. The log book of the ship from which he fell.

But misery still delights to trace
60   Its semblance in another's case.

No voice divine the storm allayed,
   No light propitious shone,
When, snatched from all effectual aid,
   We perished, each, alone;
65   But I beneath a rougher sea,
And whelmed in deeper gulphs than he.

1799
                                                    1804

[END OF PERSPECTIVES: MIND AND GOD]

Thomas Gray
1716–1771

Toward the end of his most famous poem, *Elegy Written in a Country Churchyard,* Thomas Gray commends the quietude with which the villagers have led their ordinary lives:

> Along the cool sequestered vale of life
> They kept the noiseless tenor of their way.

Tenor here means "course," and the line incorporates a notable revision: Gray had originally written "silent tenor," and then written the new adjective "noiseless" above the old, without crossing out "silent." In retrospect, this manuscript moment of alternate possibilities looks emblematic. Sickly, shy, and melancholic, Gray was often drawn toward silence but never settled there. Words—in ancient literature and in modern history, in talk and correspondence with his friends, in the varied idioms of his own compelling poems—exerted too strong a fascination. The fascination started early. At age nine, having weathered a bleak childhood in the troubled London household of his irascible father and doting mother, he entered the privileged precincts of Eton College, where his uncles worked and where he hit upon the satisfactions that would fill his life: passionate reading (in the classics first and foremost) and passionate friendships, with three schoolmates in particular: Richard West, Thomas Ashton, and Horace Walpole, son of the notorious prime minister Robert Walpole. Dubbing themselves the Quadruple Alliance, the four friends piqued themselves on a collective erudition, refinement, and wit that set them off from their contemporaries. The links among them mattered enormously in Gray's life of writing: West inspired his poems; Walpole sponsored their publication; and all Gray's friendships, at Eton and beyond, drew from Gray a steady flow of virtuosic letters. Gray's affections took form and motion partly from their containment. He was homosexual; yet there is no evidence that he ever physically consummated the great passions of his life—for Walpole, for West, and, in his last years, for the young Swiss scion Charles-Victor de Bonstatten.

After nine years at Eton, Gray was admitted to Cambridge. He found university life far less pleasing, with its drudgeries, pressures, and solitudes, but Cambridge ultimately afforded him a few new friendships and a permanent sanctuary. After a Grand Tour of Europe, undertaken in Walpole's company (the two men quarreled en route, after which they were estranged for five years), Gray returned to the university, ostensibly to learn law, but in fact to pursue his own private program of study. He read widely, copiously, and systematically in many subjects (botany, zoology, and music, as well as literature and history), making himself one of the most learned scholars alive, and eventually becoming (in 1768) Regius Professor of Modern History. He never delivered a lecture, and continued to spend much of his time alone reading, but thoroughgoing privacy had long ceased to be an option. In his late thirties, Gray had stumbled, reluctantly, into enormous poetic fame. He had written Latin verse when young; in 1742, the year his beloved West died of tuberculosis, he commenced English poetry in earnest. The *Elegy*'s completion took five years or more; its publication in 1751 (a "distress" the poet had hoped to avoid) brought upon Gray an instantaneous, massive, and baffling celebrity. As if in recoil, he veered onto an alternate poetic path, carefully crafting over the ensuing years a set of intricate Pindaric odes, including *The Bard* and *The Progress of Poesy*; the two poems were printed, on Walpole's own press, in 1754. They provoked both admiration, as a new embodiment of poetic sublimity, and derision, as gratuitously labored, showily obscure. In the years following their murky reception, Gray wrote only a few poems, and published none. He pursued other studies (including Norse literature); fell in love one final time; and died abruptly, mourned deeply by his friends and widely by a public whose thoughts and feelings about death itself he had done much to shape. In one early version of the *Elegy* the line about silence appears as an admonition addressed by the poet to himself: "Pursue the silent tenor of thy doom." In his letters (published posthumously) and in his poems, Gray worked for that doom a delicate but decisive reversal.

Elegy Written in a Country Churchyard

The curfew tolls the knell of parting day,
The lowing herd wind slowly o'er the lea,
The plowman homeward plods his weary way,
And leaves the world to darkness and to me.

5 Now fades the glimmering landscape on the sight,
And all the air a solemn stillness holds,
Save where the beetle wheels his droning flight,
And drowsy tinklings lull the distant folds;

Save that from yonder ivy-mantled tower
10 The moping owl does to the moon complain
Of such as, wand'ring near her secret bower,
Molest her ancient solitary reign.

Beneath those rugged elms, that yew-tree's shade,
Where heaves the turf in many a mouldering heap,
15 Each in his narrow cell for ever laid,
The rude forefathers of the hamlet sleep.

The breezy call of incense-breathing morn,
The swallow twitt'ring from the straw-built shed,
The cock's shrill clarion, or the echoing horn,
20 No more shall rouse them from their lowly bed.

For them no more the blazing hearth shall burn,
Or busy housewife ply her evening care:
No children run to lisp their sire's return,
Or climb his knees the envied kiss to share.

25 Oft did the harvest to their sickle yield,
Their furrow oft the stubborn glebe° has broke;   *clod of earth*

How jocund did they drive their team afield!
How bowed the woods beneath their sturdy stroke!

30 Let not Ambition mock their useful toil,
    Their homely joys, and destiny obscure;
    Nor Grandeur hear, with a disdainful smile,
    The short and simple annals of the poor.

    The boast of heraldry, the pomp of power,
    And all that beauty, all that wealth e'er gave,
35 Awaits alike th' inevitable hour.
    The paths of glory lead but to the grave.

    Nor you, ye Proud, impute to these the fault,
    If Mem'ry o'er their tomb no trophies raise,
    Where through the long-drawn isle and fretted vault
40 The pealing anthem swells the note of praise.

    Can storied urn or animated bust
    Back to its mansion call the fleeting breath?
    Can Honor's voice provoke the silent dust,
    Or Flatt'ry soothe the dull cold ear of Death?

45 Perhaps in this neglected spot is laid
    Some heart once pregnant with celestial fire;
    Hands, that the rod of empire might have swayed,
    Or waked to ecstasy the living lyre.

    But Knowledge to their eyes her ample page
50 Rich with the spoils of time did ne'er unroll;
    Chill Penury repressed their noble rage,
    And froze the genial current of the soul.

    Full many a gem of purest ray serene,
    The dark unfathomed caves of ocean bear:
55 Full many a flower is born to blush unseen,
    And waste its sweetness on the desert air.

    Some village-Hampden[1] that with dauntless breast
    The little tyrant of his fields withstood;
    Some mute inglorious Milton here may rest,
60 Some Cromwell guiltless of his country's blood.

    Th' applause of listening senates to command,
    The threats of pain and ruin to despise,
    To scatter plenty o'er a smiling land,
    And read their hist'ry in a nation's eyes,

65 Their lot forbade: nor circumscribed alone
    Their growing virtues, but their crimes confined;
    Forbade to wade through slaughter to a throne,
    And shut the gates of mercy on mankind,

---

1. John Hampden (1594–1643), Parliamentary statesman and general in the Civil Wars, famed for his firm defiance of Charles I.

The struggling pangs of conscious truth to hide,
70   To quench the blushes of ingenuous shame,
Or heap the shrine of Luxury and Pride
With incense kindled at the Muse's flame.[2]

Far from the madding crowd's ignoble strife,
Their sober wishes never learned to stray;
75   Along the cool sequestered vale of life
They kept the noiseless tenor of their way.

Yet ev'n these bones from insult to protect
Some frail memorial still erected nigh,
With uncouth rhymes and shapeless sculpture decked,
80   Implores the passing tribute of a sigh.

Their name, their years, spelt by th' unlettered muse,
The place of fame and elegy supply:
And many a holy text around she strews,
That teach the rustic moralist to die.

85   For who to dumb Forgetfulness a prey,
This pleasing anxious being e'er resigned,
Left the warm precincts of the cheerful day,
Nor cast one longing ling'ring look behind?

On some fond breast the parting soul relies,
90   Some pious drops the closing eye requires;
Ev'n from the tomb the voice of nature cries,
Ev'n in our ashes live their wonted fires.

For thee, who mindful of th' unhonored dead
Dost in these lines their artless tale relate;
95   If chance, by lonely Contemplation led,
Some kindred spirit shall inquire thy fate,

Haply some hoary-headed swain may say,
"Oft have we seen him at the peep of dawn
Brushing with hasty steps the dews away
100   To meet the sun upon the upland lawn.

"There at the foot of yonder nodding beech
That wreathes its old fantastic roots so high,
His listless length at noontide would he stretch,
And pore upon the brook that babbles by.

2. According to Gray's friend William Mason, the poem originally concluded at this juncture with the following four stanzas, preserved in a manuscript at Eton College:

The thoughtless world to majesty may bow
Exalt the brave, and idolize success,
But more to innocence their safety owe
Than power and genius e'er conspired to bless.

And thou, who mindful of the unhonored dead
Dost in these notes their artless tale relate
By night and lonely contemplation led
To linger in the gloomy walks of fate,

Hark how the sacred calm, that broods around
Bids ev'ry fierce tumultuous passion cease
In still small accents whisp'ring from the ground
A grateful earnest of eternal peace.

No more with reason and thyself at strife;
Give anxious cares and endless wishes room
But through the cool sequestered vale of life
Pursue the silent tenor of thy doom.

105   "Hard by yon wood, now smiling as in scorn,
        Mutt'ring his wayward fancies he would rove,
        Now drooping, woeful wan, like one forlorn,
        Or crazed with care, or crossed in hopeless love.

        "One morn I missed him on the 'customed hill,
110   Along the heath and near his favorite tree;
        Another came; nor yet beside the rill,
        Nor up the lawn, nor at the wood was he;

        "The next with dirges due in sad array
        Slow through the church-way path we saw him borne.
115   Approach and read (for thou can'st read) the lay,
        Graved on the stone beneath yon aged thorn."

The Epitaph

Here rests his head upon the lap of earth
A youth to fortune and to fame unknown.
Fair Science frowned not on his humble birth,
120 *And Melancholy marked him for her own.*

Large was his bounty, and his soul sincere,
Heaven did a recompense as largely send:
He gave to Mis'ry all he had, a tear,
He gained from Heav'n ('twas all he wished) a friend.

125 *No farther seek his merits to disclose,*
Or draw his frailties from their dread abode,
(There they alike in trembling hope repose)
The bosom of his Father and his God.

1746–1750   1751

Samuel Johnson
1709–1784

Samuel Johnson was born among books—his father sold them, not very successfully, at the family's combined home and shop in the market town of Lichfield. The son went on to create some of the most celebrated books of his age: an entire *Dictionary*, an edition of Shakespeare, a travel book, philosophical fictions, two eminent series of essays, a thick cluster of biographies. Despite his output, Johnson suffered from a chronic sense that he was underusing his talent, and throughout his *oeuvre* he wrote about "human unsuccess" (in W. H. Auden's phrase) with an empathy and acuity that few have matched before or since.

    Johnson's struggles began early. An infection in infancy, followed by an attack of scrofula at age two, left his face scarred and his sight and hearing permanently impaired; by the age of eight a nervous disorder, probably Tourette's syndrome, brought on the compulsive gesticulations and intermittent muttering that would afflict him throughout his life, making him appear bizarre or even repellent at first encounter—until (as many testified) the stunning moment when he would begin to speak. His impressiveness had begun early, too. In childhood, the speed with which he acquired knowledge and the force with which he retained it astonished classmates and teachers, and also his parents, whose desire to show off his attainments often made him miserable. Johnson found more congenial mentors in his cousin, the rakish but learned young clergyman Cornelius Ford, at whose home he spent about half a year at age sixteen, and in Gilbert Walmesley, a middle-aged Lichfield lawyer, who welcomed Johnson often to his ample table and to the intelligent, disputatious company there assembled. Under Ford's and Walmesley's influence, Johnson undertook an intense but improvisatory program of reading, mostly in his father's shop. He read with a ferocious concentration that locked the texts into lifelong memory. "In this irregular manner," he later recalled, "I had looked into a great many books, which were not commonly known at the university, where they seldom read any books but what are put into their hands by their tutors; so that when I came to Oxford, Dr. Adams, now master of Pembroke College, told me, I was the best qualified for the university that he had ever known come there."

Despite such qualifications, Johnson's time at Oxford ushered in not triumph but frustration, and an oppressive sense of failure. Though he continued to be admired for his reading, and began to be noted for his writing, Johnson left the university after only thirteen months, "miserably poor" and unable to pay the fees, unbearably depressed and incapable of envisioning a viable future. After a melancholy year at home, during which his father died in debt, Johnson tried his hand at a variety of jobs beneath his earlier expectations: as assistant at a grammar school (he applied for three such positions, secured one, and left it in disgust after six months), and as occasional contributor to *The Birmingham Journal*. At Birmingham, he befriended the merchant Harry Porter and his wife Elizabeth ("Tetty"); she saw past his awkwardness at their first encounter, remarking to her daughter, "This is the most sensible man that I ever saw in my life." In 1735, ten months after her husband's death, she and Johnson married, despite wariness in both families at their difference in age (she was twenty years his senior). The new husband and wife tried to start a country boarding school, but it attracted only a handful of students. Early in 1737, Johnson decided to try something new: the life of a freelance writer in London.

The generic term for such a life was "Grub Street": it identified both an actual London street where some writers lived and plied their trade, and also the painful state of mind in which almost all of them did so, eking out precarious incomes from whatever assignments they could drum up. From the first, Johnson fared a little better than most. He attached himself immediately to Edward Cave, founder of the flourishing *Gentleman's Magazine*, in which Johnson's writing appeared plentifully over the next decade: essays, poems, short biographies, reviews, and voluminous, ingeniously fictionalized reports of debates in Parliament (authentic transcriptions were prohibited by law). The work provided some security but no prosperity: Johnson and his wife lived in poverty for many years. The struggle fueled articulate rage: in his poem *London* (1738), Johnson inveighed against the corruption of Robert Walpole's Whig government and the cruelties of the city. Among his Grub Street colleagues he found a friend who, far more than himself, had made a sense of injury the basis of both life and art. The poet Richard Savage, generous, brilliant, and unstable, believed himself the abandoned offspring of a wealthy countess, and squandered much of his short life in the vain pursuit of recognition and redress. In *The Life of Richard Savage* (1744), published soon after his friend's early death, Johnson for the first time orchestrated many of the elements that would make his own work great: a commitment to biographical precision rather than routine panegyric; an analysis of expectation, self-delusion, and disappointment; a deep sympathy combined with nuanced judgment.

Savage was a memoir of Grub Street, but not yet for Johnson a valedictory. For two more years he continued his life of anonymous publication, narrow income, and declining spirits— "lost," as a friend lamented, "both to himself and the world." Then a new project found him. In 1746, the bookseller Robert Dodsley, struck by the erudition evident in Johnson's unsigned pieces, persuaded him to create a new dictionary of English, and assembled a consortium of publishers to finance (and profit from) the enormous undertaking. Johnson and his wife promptly moved from cramped and squalid quarters to a three-story house complete with a well-lit garret. There, with the help of six part-time assistants, Johnson made his lexicon, compiling word lists, tracking shifts and gradations of meaning, devising definitions, and illustrating them with quotations culled from the authors he most admired. The writer who (as Adam Smith later testified) "knew more books than any man alive" now decanted them discriminatingly into the two folio volumes of his *Dictionary* (1755), so as to make the work not only a standard reference for the language but also a compendium of its literature and its learning. The task took Johnson longer than he'd anticipated—seven years, not three—but during this span he had busied himself in other ways as well: publishing *The Vanity of Human Wishes* (1749), a long poem on the pain of disillusion; witnessing the long-postponed production of his tragedy *Irene* (which brought him welcome added income); and composing, twice a week for two years, the periodical essay called *The Rambler* (1750–1752), the most formidable and famous instance of the genre since Addison and Steele had set down the *Spectator* forty years before. Johnson had embarked on the *Dictionary* as a virtual unknown; he emerged from the project with lasting fame, and a double measure of celebratory sobriquets: he was widely known as "Dictionary Johnson," and was sometimes referred to simply (without surname) as "the Rambler."

As an epitome of his character the second label was perhaps more apt. A restlessness closely connected with loneliness had marked Johnson's mind since childhood. During the years of the *Dictionary*'s making, the loneliness had deepened. In 1752 Tetty died, and despite the strains in a marriage that had been differently difficult for both of them, Johnson mourned her obsessively for the rest of his days. He also contrived new sources of companionship, at home and in the wider world. He housed under his roof a group of eccentric, often difficult characters, including the ungainly man of medicine Robert Levet; the Jamaican servant Francis Barber; the blind Anna Williams, who waited up late every night to keep him company in his final cup of tea, often after he had spent long hours in more elevated society. He established what amounted to a second residence in the more polished household of the brewer Henry Thrale and his witty wife Hester, who welcomed and pampered not only Johnson but also the accomplished people who now rejoiced to rotate in his orbit: the actor David Garrick (who had been his pupil in the failed school and his companion on the road to London); the painter Joshua Reynolds; the politician and orator Edmund Burke; the writer Oliver Goldsmith; and Johnson's ardent young protégé and future biographer James Boswell. At the Thrales' country seat, and at the London clubs he formed to stave off solitude, Johnson sat surrounded by luminaries, savoring and often dominating the conversation. He talked (as Boswell noted) "for victory," and he generally secured it by a kind of surprise attack, a witty demolition of his companions' most familiar premises and casual assumptions. He won his listeners over by texture as well as text: by the spontaneous clarity and force of his utterance (as lexicographer he had defined every word he spoke); by the depth and energy of his voice.

Writing was by contrast largely solitary. Johnson's work pattern in the decade after the *Dictionary* recapitulated that of the one before: one ambitious, overarching project— this time an edition of all Shakespeare's plays (1665)—punctuated by shorter writings of lasting significance: a new periodical essay called *The Idler* (1758–1760); the philosophical tale *Rasselas, Prince of Abyssinia* (1759). In 1762 Johnson received a royal pension from George III in recognition of the *Dictionary*, assuring him an income of £300 a year for the remainder of his life. The pension brought Johnson a new security, along with the occasional accusation that his subsequent political pamphlets, generally favorable to the regime, amounted to paid propaganda. In fact, Johnson's politics throughout his life correlated fairly well with the views he implicitly espoused in the distinction he once drew for Boswell: "The prejudice of the Tory is for establishment; the prejudice of the Whig is for innovation." Born into a world where Whigs had long prevailed, Johnson early committed himself to Tory ways of thought: he cherished precedent, defended "subordination" (social hierarchy), and opposed Whiggish innovation with seriocomic fervor. What remained most notable about his politics was their compassion. "From first to last," John Wain remarks, Johnson "rooted his life among the poor and outcast"; in his work he argued the causes of prostitutes and slaves, of anyone sunk by the "want of necessaries" into "motionless despondence."

In the wake of his pension, Johnson's writing grew sparser, and markedly more social, compassing gestures to and for people he valued. He continued an ingrained habit of churning out prose for his friends to use under their own names: dictating law briefs for lawyers, composing sermons for preachers. He carried on an abundant and affectionate correspondence with Hester Thrale. With Boswell as companion, he traveled to the Scottish Highlands, and on his return published his account of that gregarious trip, A Journey to the Western Islands (1775). His final large work was social in a different sense. He accepted a commission to provide Prefaces Biographical and Critical for an anthology of English poets of the past hundred and fifty years. These included predecessors who had influenced him, contemporaries he had known, successors he regarded with admiration or alarm. To write their biographies, to analyze their works, was in a sense to live over his own literary life, and to reenter, at length and for the last time, the world of reading and of writing in which he'd now made his way for almost seven decades.

"Our social comforts drop away," Johnson lamented when his friend Levet died in 1782; his own last years were marred by loss. Successive deaths shrunk his contentious household; his friendship with Hester Thrale disintegrated under the pressure of her passion for a man of whom Johnson disapproved; a stroke temporarily deprived him of speech and ushered in his final difficult illness. At his death, an admirer remarked that Johnson had left "a chasm, which not only nothing can fill up, but which nothing has a tendency to fill up. Johnson is dead. Let us go to the next best:—there is nobody: no man can be said to put you in mind of Johnson." Biographers rushed in to fill the chasm, with the testimony of friends and of detractors, and with transcriptions of the hypnotic talk that many of them (notably Boswell and Thrale) had begun to record decades before. For most of the nineteenth century the fame of Johnson's talk far surpassed that of his writing. In recent decades scholars and readers have redressed the balance, finding in Johnson's prose and verse the richest repositories of his thought. Throughout a life of arduous struggle, prodigious accomplishment, and (in the end) near-matchless celebrity, Johnson wrote most eloquently and most feelingly—even in the Dictionary, even in literary criticism—of human vulnerabilities: to hope and disappointment, suffering and loss.

The Vanity of Human Wishes

In his Life of Pope, Johnson defines the imitation, a poetic form much in vogue during the late seventeenth and early eighteenth centuries, as a "mode . . . in which the ancients are familiarized by adapting their sentiments to modern topics. . . . It is a kind of middle composition between translation and original design, which pleases when the thoughts are unexpectedly applicable and the parallels lucky." The Vanity of Human Wishes is Johnson's most sustained and successful endeavor in the mode. In the second century A.D., the Roman poet Juvenal had written an enduring satire on human ambition and failure, drawing vivid instances from history and from contemporary life. Johnson does the same, replacing the Roman's ancient examples with modern ones, supplanting his Stoic "sentiments" with a Christian credo. Johnson produced his imitation quickly, composing the whole of it in his mind before writing any of it down. It was the first work to appear under his own name, after more than a decade of abundant but anonymous publications. Its title and text sound themes that would preoccupy him for the remainder of his writing life: the dangers of desire, the inevitability of disappointment, the necessity of faith. The Vanity of Human Wishes is Johnson's signature poem in more ways than one.

The Vanity of Human Wishes
The Tenth Satire of Juvenal Imitated

Let Observation, with extensive view,
Survey mankind, from China to Peru;
Remark each anxious toil, each eager strife,
And watch the busy scenes of crowded life;
5   Then say how hope and fear, desire and hate,
O'erspread with snares the clouded maze of fate,
Where wav'ring man, betrayed by vent'rous pride,
To tread the dreary paths without a guide,
As treach'rous phantoms in the mist delude,
10   Shuns fancied ills, or chases airy[1] good;
How rarely reason guides the stubborn choice,
Rules the bold hand, or prompts the suppliant voice;
How nations sink, by darling schemes oppressed,
When vengeance listens to the fool's request.
15   Fate wings with every wish th' afflictive dart,
Each gift of nature, and each grace of art,
With fatal heat impetuous courage glows,
With fatal sweetness elocution flows,
Impeachment stops the speaker's pow'rful breath,
20   And restless fire precipitates on death.
    But scarce observed, the knowing and the bold
Fall in the gen'ral massacre of gold;
Wide-wasting pest! that rages unconfined,
And crowds with crimes the records of mankind;
25   For gold his sword the hireling ruffian draws,
For gold the hireling judge distorts the laws;
Wealth heaped on wealth, nor truth nor safety buys,
The dangers gather as the treasures rise.
    Let hist'ry tell where rival kings command,
30   And dubious title shakes the madded land,
When statutes° glean the refuse of the sword,   *tax laws*
How much more safe the vassal than the lord;
Low skulks the hind° beneath the rage of pow'r,   *rural laborer*
And leaves the wealthy traitor in the Tow'r,[2]
35   Untouched his cottage, and his slumbers sound,
Though confiscation's vultures hover round.
    The needy traveler, secure and gay,
Walks the wild heath, and sings his toil away.
Does envy seize thee? crush th' upbraiding joy,
40   Increase his riches and his peace destroy;
Now fears in dire vicissitude invade,
The rustling brake° alarms, and quiv'ring shade,   *thicket*
Nor light nor darkness bring his pain relief,
One shows the plunder, and one hides the thief.
45   Yet still one gen'ral cry the skies assails,

---

1. "Wanting reality; having no steady foundation in truth or nature" (Johnson's *Dictionary*).   2. The Tower of London.

And gain and grandeur load the tainted gales;
Few know the toiling statesman's fear or care,
Th' insidious rival and the gaping heir.
    Once more, Democritus,[3] arise on earth,
50 With cheerful wisdom and instructive mirth,
See motley[4] life in modern trappings dressed,
And feed with varied fools th' eternal jest:
Thou who couldst laugh where want enchained caprice,
Toil crushed conceit, and man was of a piece;
55 Where wealth unloved without a mourner died,
And scarce a sycophant was fed by pride;
Where ne'er was known the form of mock debate,
Or seen a new-made mayor's unwieldy state;
Where change of fav'rites made no change of laws,
60 And senates heard before they judged a cause;
How wouldst thou shake at Britain's modish tribe,
Dart the quick taunt, and edge the piercing gibe?
Attentive truth and nature to descry,°   *discern*
And pierce each scene with philosophic eye.
65 To thee were solemn toys or empty show,
The robes of pleasure and the veils of woe:
All aid the farce, and all thy mirth maintain,
Whose joys are causeless, or whose griefs are vain.
    Such was the scorn that filled the sage's mind,
70 Renewed at ev'ry glance on humankind;
How just that scorn ere yet thy voice declare,
Search every state, and canvass every prayer.
    Unnumbered suppliants crowd Preferment's gate,
Athirst for wealth, and burning to be great;
75 Delusive Fortune hears th' incessant call,
They mount, they shine, evaporate, and fall.[5]
On every stage the foes of peace attend,
Hate dogs their flight, and insult mocks their end.
Love ends with hope, the sinking statesman's door
80 Pours in the morning worshiper no more;
For growing names the weekly scribbler lies,
To growing wealth the dedicator flies,
From ev'ry room descends the painted face,
That hung the bright Palladium[6] of the place,
85 And smoked in kitchens, or in auctions sold,
To better features yields the frame of gold;
For now no more we trace in ev'ry line
Heroic worth, benevolence divine:
The form distorted justifies the fall,
90 And detestation rids th' indignant wall.
    But will not Britain hear the last appeal,
Sign her foes' doom, or guard her fav'rites' zeal?

---

3. Ancient Greek philosopher who laughed at the follies
of humanity.
4. Multicolored clothes worn by jesters.

5. The image is that of Fortune's wheel.
6. A statue of Pallas Athene, guardian of Troy.

Through Freedom's sons no more remonstrance rings,
Degrading nobles and controlling kings;
95   Our supple tribes° repress their patriot throats,   *of voters*
And ask no questions but the price of votes;
With weekly libels and septennial ale,[7]
Their wish is full to riot and to rail.
In full-blown dignity, see Wolsey[8] stand,
100 Law in his voice, and fortune in his hand:
To him the church, the realm, their pow'rs consign,
Through him the rays of regal bounty shine,
Turned by his nod the stream of honor flows,
His smile alone security bestows:
105 Still to new heights his restless wishes tow'r,
Claim leads to claim, and pow'r advances pow'r;
Till conquest unresisted ceased to please,
And rights submitted, left him none to seize.
At length his sov'reign frowns—the train of state
110 Mark the keen glance, and watch the sign to hate.
Wheree'er he turns he meets a stranger's eye,
His suppliants scorn him, and his followers fly;
At once is lost the pride of awful state,
The golden canopy, the glitt'ring plate,
115 The regal palace, the luxurious board,
The liv'ried army, and the menial lord.
With age, with cares, with maladies oppressed,
He seeks the refuge of monastic rest.
Grief aids disease, remembered folly stings,
120 And his last sighs reproach the faith of kings.
Speak thou, whose thoughts at humble peace repine,
Shall Wolsey's wealth, with Wolsey's end be thine?
Or liv'st thou now, with safer pride content,
The wisest justice on the banks of Trent?[9]
125 For why did Wolsey near the steeps° of fate,   *precipices*
On weak foundations raise th' enormous weight?
Why but to sink beneath misfortune's blow,
With louder ruin to the gulfs below?
What gave great Villiers[1] to th' assassin's knife,
130 And fixed disease on Harley's[2] closing life?
What murdered Wentworth, and what exiled Hyde,[3]
By kings protected, and to kings allied?
What but their wish indulged in courts to shine,
And pow'r too great to keep, or to resign?

---

7. Drink offered to voters as bribes during campaigns for
Parliament, held every seven years.
8. Cardinal Wolsey (1475–1530), Henry VIII's Lord
Chancellor, who was dismissed and imprisoned for failing
to procure the King a divorce from Catherine of Aragon.
9. The river that divides northern from southern England; it is near Lichfield, Johnson's birthplace.
1. George Villiers (1592–1628), first Duke of Buckingham and a favorite of James I, was stabbed to death.

2. Robert Harley (1661–1724), first Earl of Oxford and
leading statesman during the reign of Queen Anne, was
impeached when George I succeeded to the throne in
1714.
3. Thomas Wentworth (1593–1641), first Earl of Strafford and adviser to Charles I, was executed at the beginning of the English Civil War. Edward Hyde (1609–
1674), first Earl of Clarendon, served Charles II but then
fell from favor.

135   When first the college rolls receive his name,
    The young enthusiast[4] quits his ease for fame;
    Through all his veins the fever of renown
    Burns from the strong contagion of the gown;[5]
    O'er Bodley's dome[6] his future labors spread,
140   And Bacon's mansion[7] trembles o'er his head.
    Are these thy views? proceed, illustrious youth,
    And virtue guard thee to the throne of Truth!
    Yet should thy soul indulge the gen'rous heat,
    Till captive Science° yields her last retreat;   *knowledge*
145   Should Reason guide thee with her brightest ray,
    And pour on misty Doubt resistless day;
    Should no false Kindness lure to loose delight,
    Nor Praise relax, nor Difficulty fright;
    Should tempting Novelty thy cell refrain,
150   And Sloth effuse her opiate fumes in vain;
    Should Beauty blunt on fops her fatal dart,
    Nor claim the triumph of a lettered heart;
    Should no disease thy torpid veins invade,
    Nor Melancholy's phantoms haunt thy shade;
155   Yet hope not life from grief or danger free,
    Nor think the doom of man reversed for thee:
    Deign on the passing world to turn thine eyes,
    And pause awhile from letters, to be wise;
    There mark what ills the scholar's life assail,
160   Toil, envy, want, the patron,[8] and the jail.
    See nations slowly wise, and meanly just,
    To buried merit raise the tardy bust.
    If dreams yet flatter, once again attend,
    Hear Lydiat's life, and Galileo's end.[9]
165   Nor deem, when learning her last prize bestows,
    The glitt'ring eminence exempt from foes;
    See when the vulgar 'scape, despised or awed,
    Rebellion's vengeful talons seize on Laud.[1]
    From meaner minds, though smaller fines content,
170   The plundered palace or sequestered rent;
    Marked out by dangerous parts° he meets the shock, *abilities*
    And fatal Learning leads him to the block:
    Around his tomb let Art and Genius weep,
    But hear his death, ye blockheads, hear and sleep.
175   The festal blazes, the triumphal show,
    The ravished standard, and the captive foe,
    The senate's thanks, the gazette's pompous tale,

---

4. "One of hot imagination" (Johnson's *Dictionary*).
5. Scholastic dress (but also a reference to the poisoned garment that killed Hercules).
6. The Bodleian Library, Oxford.
7. "There is a tradition, that the study of friar Bacon [Roger Bacon, a medieval philosopher] built an arch over the bridge, will fall, when a man greater than Bacon shall pass under it" [Johnson's note].

8. Johnson originally wrote "garret," but changed it to "patron" after enduring the neglect of Lord Chesterfield (see his letter to Chesterfield, page 1278).
9. Thomas Lydiat (1572–1646) was a distinguished but impoverished mathematician. The astronomer Galileo Galilei (1564–1642) was silenced by the Inquisition.
1. William Laud (1572–1645), Archbishop of Canterbury under Charles I, was beheaded by the Parliamentarians.

With force resistless o'er the brave prevail.
Such bribes the rapid Greek[2] o'er Asia whirled,
180 For such the steady Romans shook the world;
For such in distant lands the Britons shine,
And stain with blood the Danube or the Rhine;
This pow'r has praise, that virtue scarce can warm,
Till fame supplies the universal charm.
185 Yet Reason frowns on War's unequal game,
Where wasted nations raise a single name,
And mortgaged states their grandsires' wreaths[3] regret,
From age to age in everlasting debt;
Wreaths which at last the dear-bought right convey
190 To rust on medals, or on stones decay.
     On what foundation stands the warrior's pride,
How just his hopes let Swedish Charles[4] decide;
A frame of adamant, a soul of fire,
No dangers fright him, and no labors tire;
195 O'er love, o'er fear, extends his wide domain,
Unconquered lord of pleasure and of pain;
No joys to him pacific scepters yield,
War sounds the trump, he rushes to the field;
Behold surrounding kings their pow'r combine,
200 And one capitulate, and one resign;
Peace courts his hand, but spreads her charms in vain;
"Think nothing gained," he cries, "till nought remain,
On Moscow's walls till Gothic standards fly,
And all be mine beneath the polar sky."
205 The march begins in military state,
And nations on his eye suspended wait;
Stern Famine guards the solitary coast,
And Winter barricades the realms of Frost;
He comes, not want and cold his course delay—
210 Hide, blushing Glory, hide Pultowa's day:
The vanquished hero leaves his broken bands,
And shows his miseries in distant lands;
Condemned a needy supplicant to wait,
While ladies interpose, and slaves debate.
215 But did not Chance at length her error mend?
Did no subverted empire mark his end?
Did rival monarchs give the fatal wound?
Or hostile millions press him to the ground?
His fall was destined to a barren strand,
220 A petty fortress, and a dubious hand;[5]
He left the name, at which the world grew pale,
To point a moral, or adorn a tale.

---

2. Alexander the Great.
3. Garlands of victory.
4. Charles XII of Sweden, whose precarious military career ended at the Battle of Pultowa (1709). After his defeat by the Russians, Charles attempted to forge an alliance with the Turks.
5. Charles XII of Sweden was thought to have been killed by one of his own officers during a siege of little military consequence.

All times their scenes of pompous woes afford,
From Persia's tyrant[6] to Bavaria's lord.[7]
225   In gay hostility, and barb'rous pride,
With half mankind embattled at his side,
Great Xerxes comes to seize the certain prey,
And starves exhausted regions in his way;
Attendant Flattery counts his myriads o'er,
230   Till counted myriads soothe his pride no more;
Fresh praise is tried till madness fires his mind,
The waves he lashes, and enchains the wind;
New pow'rs are claimed, new pow'rs are still bestowed,
Till rude resistance lops the spreading god;
235   The daring Greeks deride the martial show,
And heap their valleys with the gaudy foe;
Th' insulted sea with humbler thoughts he gains,
A single skiff to speed his flight remains;
Th' encumbered oar scarce leaves the dreaded coast
240   Through purple billows and a floating host.
        The bold Bavarian, in a luckless hour,
Tries the dread summits of Cesarean power,
With unexpected legions bursts away,
And sees defenseless realms receive his sway;
245   Short sway! fair Austria spreads her mournful charms,
The queen, the beauty, sets the world in arms;
From hill to hill the beacon's rousing blaze
Spreads wide the hope of plunder and of praise;
The fierce Croatian, and the wild Hussar,
250   And all the sons of ravage crowd the war;
The baffled prince in honor's flattering bloom
Of hasty greatness finds the fatal doom,
His foes' derision, and his subjects' blame,
And steals to death from anguish and from shame.
255   Enlarge my life with multitude of days,
In health, in sickness, thus the suppliant prays;
Hides from himself his state, and shuns to know,
That life protracted is protracted woe.
Time hovers o'er, impatient to destroy,
260   And shuts up all the passages of joy:
In vain their gifts the bounteous seasons pour,
The fruit autumnal, and the vernal flow'r,
With listless eyes the dotard views the store,
He views, and wonders that they please no more;
265   Now pall the tasteless meats, and joyless wines,
And Luxury° with sighs her slave resigns.   *voluptuousness*
Approach, ye minstrels, try the soothing strain,

---

6. Xerxes (?519–465 B.C.) invaded Greece with a large army and navy. In order to transport his troops, he built a bridge of boats across the Hellespont. When a storm broke up this bridge, Xerxes ordered the wind and water to be punished. The Persian army was defeated at the Battle of Plataea, the navy at the Battle of Salamis.
7. Charles Albert (1697–1745), Elector of Bavaria, was defeated by Empress Maria Theresa, whose army included Austrian colonists from Croatia and Hungarian cavalry called "jussars."

Diffuse the tuneful lenitives[8] of pain:
No sounds alas would touch th' impervious ear,
270 Though dancing mountains witnessed Orpheus[9] near;
Nor lute nor lyre his feeble pow'rs attend,
Nor sweeter music of a virtuous friend,
But everlasting dictates crowd his tongue,
Perversely grave, or positively wrong.
275 The still returning tale, and ling'ring jest,
Perplex the fawning niece and pampered guest,
While growing hopes scarce awe the gathering sneer,
And scarce a legacy can bribe to hear;
The watchful guests still hint the last° offense,   *latest*
280 The daughter's petulance, the son's expense,
Improve his heady rage with treach'rous skill,
And mold his passions till they make his will.
    Unnumbered maladies his joints invade,
Lay siege to life and press the dire blockade;
285 But unextinguished Avarice still remains,
And dreaded losses aggravate his pains;
He turns, with anxious heart and crippled hands,
His bonds of debt, and mortgages of lands;
Or views his coffers with suspicious eyes,
290 Unlocks his gold, and counts it till he dies.
    But grant, the virtues of a temp'rate prime
Bless with an age exempt from scorn or crime;
An age that melts with unperceived decay,
And glides in modest innocence away;
295 Whose peaceful day Benevolence endears,
Whose night congratulating Conscience cheers;
The gen'ral favorite as the gen'ral friend:
Such age there is, and who shall wish its end?
    Yet ev'n on this her load Misfortune flings,
300 To press the weary minutes' flagging wings:
New sorrow rises as the day returns,
A sister sickens, or a daughter mourns.
Now kindred Merit fills the sable bier,
Now lacerated Friendship claims a tear.
305 Year chases year, decay pursues decay,
Still drops some joy from with'ring life away;
New forms arise, and different views engage,
Superfluous lags the vet'ran on the stage,
Till pitying Nature signs the last release,
310 And bids afflicted worth retire to peace.
    But few there are whom hours like these await,
Who set unclouded in the gulfs of fate.
From Lydia's monarch should the search descend,
By Solon cautioned to regard his end,[1]

---

8. "Anything medicinally applied to ease pain" (Johnson's *Dictionary*).
9. In Greek mythology, the musician Orpheus charmed wild beasts and moved mountains.

1. Solon, Greek philosopher and legislator, warned the wealthy King Croesus of Lydia that no one should count himself happy until reaching the end of life.

315   In life's last scene what prodigies surprise,
     Fears of the brave, and follies of the wise?
     From Marlborough's eyes the streams of dotage flow,[2]
     And Swift expires a driveler and a show.[3]
        The teeming mother, anxious for her race,
320   Begs for each birth the fortune of a face:
     Yet Vane could tell what ills from beauty spring;
     And Sedley cursed the form that pleased a king.[4]
     Ye nymphs of rosy lips and radiant eyes,
     Whom Pleasure keeps too busy to be wise,
325   Whom Joys with soft varieties invite,
     By day the frolic, and the dance by night,
     Who frown with vanity, who smile with art,
     And ask the latest fashion of the heart,
     What care, what rules your heedless charms shall save,
330   Each nymph your rival, and each youth your slave?
     Against your fame with fondness hate combines,
     The rival batters, and the lover mines.
     With distant voice neglected Virtue calls,
     Less heard and less, the faint remonstrance falls;
335   Tired with contempt, she quits the slipp'ry reign,
     And Pride and Prudence take her seat in vain.
     In crowd at once, where none the pass defend,
     The harmless Freedom, and the private Friend.
     The guardians yield, by force superior plied;
340   By Interest, Prudence; and by Flattery, Pride.
     Now beauty falls betrayed, despised, distressed,
     And hissing Infamy proclaims the rest.
        Where then shall Hope and Fear their objects find?
     Must dull Suspense corrupt the stagnant mind?
345   Must helpless man, in ignorance sedate,°   *calm*
     Roll darkling° down the torrent of his fate?   *in the dark*
     Must no dislike alarm, no wishes rise,
     No cries attempt the mercies of the skies?
     Inquirer, cease, petitions yet remain,
350   Which Heav'n may hear, nor deem religion vain.
     Still raise for good the supplicating voice,
     But leave to Heav'n the measure and the choice,
     Safe in his power, whose eyes discern afar
     The secret ambush of a specious prayer.
355   Implore his aid, in his decisions rest,
     Secure whate'er he gives, he gives the best.
     Yet when the sense of sacred presence fires,
     And strong devotion to the skies aspires,
     Pour forth thy fervors for a healthful mind,
360   Obedient passions, and a will resigned;
     For love, which scarce collective man can fill;

---

2. John Churchill (1650–1722), first Duke of Marlborough, hero of the War of the Spanish Succession, lived for six years after suffering two paralytic strokes.
3. Jonathan Swift, who declined into senility, was thought to have been exhibited by his servant for money.
4. Anne Vane (1705–1736) was the mistress of the Prince of Wales, Catherine Sedley (1657–1717) of James II.

For patience sov'reign o'er transmuted ill;
For faith, that panting for a happier seat,
Counts death kind Nature's signal of retreat:
365   These goods for man the laws of Heav'n ordain,
These goods he grants, who grants the power to gain;
With these celestial wisdom calms the mind,
And makes the happiness she does not find.

1748   1749

A Short Song of Congratulation[1]

Long expected one and twenty
    Ling'ring year at last is flown,
Pomp and pleasure, pride and plenty,
    Great Sir John, are all your own.

5   Loosened from the minor's tether,
    Free to mortgage or to sell,
Wild as wind, and light as feather
    Bid the slaves of thrift farewell.[2]

Call the Bettys, Kates, and Jennys
10   Ev'ry name that laughs at care,
Lavish of your grandsire's guineas,
    Show the spirit of an heir.

All that prey on vice and folly
    Joy to see their quarry fly,
15   Here the gamester light and jolly
    There the lender grave and sly.

Wealth, Sir John, was made to wander,
    Let it wander as it will;
See the jockey, see the pander,
20   Bid them come, and take their fill.

When the bonny blade carouses,
    Pockets full, and spirits high,
What are acres? What are houses?
    Only dirt, or wet or dry.

25   If the guardian or the mother
    Tell the woes of willful waste,
Scorn their counsel and their pother,
    You can hang or drown at last.

1780   1794

The Rambler

In the midst of working on his *Dictionary*, Johnson took on an ambitious additional task: he wrote *The Rambler*, a twice-weekly periodical essay which he sustained for two full years

1. Written for Sir John Lade (1759–1838), the nephew of Johnson's close friend Henry Thrale.

2. Sir John fulfilled Johnson's predictions: he made a scandalous marriage and then squandered his inheritance.

(1750–1752). The project brought him needed income and also a useful respite from the strains of lexicography. *The Rambler's* most famous antecedent was Addison and Steele's the *Spectator* (1711–1713), and though Johnson would later praise Addison's prose as a "model of the middle style . . . always equable and always easy," he chose for his own essays a mode more astringent: a large, often Latinate vocabulary, intricately balanced sentences, a steady alertness to the human propensity for self-delusion, a willingness to confront rather than ingratiate. Pressures of production could run high (Johnson later claimed that he sometimes wrote his essay with the printer's messenger standing at his side, waiting to take the text to the press), and speed of output may have helped shape the results. Many *Ramblers*, with their formidably wrought prose and surprising turns of thought, manage to seem imposing and improvisatory at the same time. Free to choose his topics, working under relentlessly recurrent deadlines, Johnson drew on four decades dense with reading and thought, during which (in the words of his biographer John Hawkins) he had "accumulated a fund of moral science that was more than sufficient for such an undertaking," and had become "in a very eminent degree qualified for the office of an instructor of mankind in their greatest and most important concerns." Readers proved eager for the instruction. More than any of his earlier writings, *The Rambler* established Johnson's style, his substance, and his fame.

Rambler No. 4

[ON FICTION]

Saturday, 31 March 1750

Simul et jucunda et idonea dicere vitae.

Horace, *Ars Poetica* 1.334

And join both profit and delight in one.

Creech

The works of fiction with which the present generation seems more particularly delighted are such as exhibit life in its true state, diversified only by accidents that daily happen in the world, and influenced by passions and qualities which are really to be found in conversing with mankind.

This kind of writing may be termed not improperly the comedy of romance, and is to be conducted nearly by the rules of comic poetry. Its province is to bring about natural events by easy means, and to keep up curiosity without the help of wonder: it is therefore precluded from the machines[1] and expedients of the heroic romance, and can neither employ giants to snatch away a lady from the nuptial rites, nor knights to bring her back from captivity; it can neither bewilder its personages in deserts, nor lodge them in imaginary castles.

I remember a remark made by Scaliger upon Pontanus,[2] that all his writings are filled with the same images; and that if you take from him his lillies and his roses, his satyrs and his dryads, he will have nothing left that can be called poetry. In like manner, almost all the fictions of the last age will vanish, if you deprive them of a hermit and a wood, a battle and a shipwreck.

Why this wild strain of imagination found reception so long, in polite and learned ages, it is not easy to conceive; but we cannot wonder that, while readers

---

1. "Supernatural agency in poems" (Johnson's *Dictionary*).
2. The Renaissance humanist Julius Caesar Scaliger

(1484–1558) criticized the poetry of Giovanni Pontano (1426–1503).

could be procured, the authors were willing to continue it: for when a man had by practice gained some fluency of language, he had no further care than to retire to his closet,[3] let loose his invention, and heat his mind with incredibilities; a book was thus produced without fear of criticism, without the toil of study, without knowledge of nature, or acquaintance with life.

The task of our present writers is very different; it requires, together with that learning which is to be gained from books, that experience which can never be attained by solitary diligence, but must arise from general converse, and accurate observation of the living world. Their performances have, as Horace expresses it, *plus oneris quantum veniae minus*, little indulgence, and therefore more difficulty.[4] They are engaged in portraits of which every one knows the original, and can detect any deviation from exactness of resemblance. Other writings are safe, except from the malice of learning, but these are in danger from every common reader; as the slipper ill executed was censured by a shoemaker who happened to stop in his way at the Venus of Apelles.[5]

But the fear of not being approved as just copiers of human manners, is not the most important concern that an author of this sort ought to have before him. These books are written chiefly to the young, the ignorant, and the idle, to whom they serve as lectures of conduct, and introductions into life. They are the entertainment of minds unfurnished with ideas, and therefore easily susceptible of impressions; not fixed by principles, and therefore easily following the current of fancy; not informed by experience, and consequently open to every false suggestion and partial account.

That the highest degree of reverence should be paid to youth, and that nothing indecent should be suffered to approach their eyes or ears, are precepts extorted by sense and virtue from an ancient writer, by no means eminent for chastity of thought.[6] The same kind, though not the same degree of caution, is required in every thing which is laid before them, to secure them from unjust prejudices, perverse opinions, and incongruous combinations of images.

In the romances formerly written, every transaction and sentiment was so remote from all that passes among men, that the reader was in very little danger of making any applications to himself; the virtues and crimes were equally beyond his sphere of activity; and he amused himself with heroes and with traitors, deliverers and persecutors, as with beings of another species, whose actions were regulated upon motives of their own, and who had neither faults nor excellencies in common with himself.

But when an adventurer is leveled with the rest of the world, and acts in such scenes of the universal drama, as may be the lot of any other man, young spectators fix their eyes upon him with closer attention, and hope by observing his behavior and success to regulate their own practices, when they shall be engaged in the like part.

For this reason these familiar histories may perhaps be made of greater use than the solemnities of professed morality, and convey the knowledge of vice and virtue with more efficacy than axioms and definitions. But if the power of example is so great, as to take possession of the memory by a kind of violence, and produce effects almost without the intervention of the will, care ought to be taken that, when the choice is unrestrained, the best examples only should be exhibited; and that which is likely to operate so strongly, should not be mischievous or uncertain in its effects.

3. Study.
4. Horace, *Epistles* 2.1.170.
5. In his *Natural History*, Pliny the Elder tells this story of the famous painter Apelles.
6. Johnson refers to the opening lines of Juvenal's fourteenth satire.

The chief advantage which these fictions have over real life is, that their authors are at liberty, though not to invent, yet to select objects, and to cull from the mass of mankind those individuals upon which the attention ought most to be employed; as a diamond, though it cannot be made, may be polished by art, and placed in such a situation as to display that lustre which before was buried among common stones.

It is justly considered as the greatest excellency of art, to imitate nature; but it is necessary to distinguish those parts of nature, which are most proper for imitation: greater care is still required in representing life, which is so often discolored by passion, or deformed by wickedness. If the world be promiscuously[7] described, I cannot see of what use it can be to read the account; or why it may not be as safe to turn the eye immediately upon mankind, as upon a mirror which shows all that presents itself without discrimination.

It is therefore not a sufficient vindication of a character, that it is drawn as it appears, for many characters ought never to be drawn; nor of a narrative, that the train of events is agreeable to observation and experience, for that observation which is called knowledge of the world will be found much more frequently to make men cunning than good. The purpose of these writings is surely not only to show mankind, but to provide that they may be seen hereafter with less hazard; to teach the means of avoiding the snares which are laid by Treachery for Innocence, without infusing any wish for that superiority with which the betrayer flatters his vanity; to give the power of counteracting fraud, without the temptation to practice it; to initiate youth by mock encounters in the art of necessary defense, and to increase prudence without impairing virtue.

Many writers, for the sake of following nature, so mingle good and bad qualities in their principal personages, that they are both equally conspicuous; and as we accompany them through their adventures with delight, and are led by degrees to interest ourselves in their favor, we lose the abhorrence of their faults, because they do not hinder our pleasure, or, perhaps, regard them with some kindness for being united with so much merit.

There have been men indeed splendidly wicked, whose endowments threw a brightness on their crimes, and whom scarce any villainy made perfectly detestable, because they never could be wholly divested of their excellencies; but such have been in all ages the great corrupters of the world, and their resemblance ought no more to be preserved, than the art of murdering without pain.

Some have advanced, without due attention to the consequences of this notion, that certain virtues have their correspondent faults, and therefore that to exhibit either apart is to deviate from probability. Thus men are observed by Swift to be "grateful in the same degree as they are resentful."[8] This principle, with others of the same kind, supposes man to act from a brute impulse, and pursue a certain degree of inclination, without any choice of the object; for otherwise, though it should be allowed that gratitude and resentment arise from the same constitution of the passions, it follows not that they will be equally indulged when reason is consulted; yet unless that consequence be admitted, this sagacious maxim becomes an empty sound, without any relation to practice or to life.

Nor is it evident, that even the first motions to these effects are always in the same proportion. For pride, which produces quickness of resentment, will obstruct gratitude, by unwillingness to admit that inferiority which obligation implies; and it is very unlikely that he who cannot think he receives a favor will acknowledge or repay it.

7. Indiscriminately.

8. In fact, it was Pope who made this observation, in the *Miscellanies* he coauthored with Swift.

It is of the utmost importance to mankind that positions of this tendency should be laid open and confuted; for while men consider good and evil as springing from the same root, they will spare the one for the sake of the other, and in judging, if not of others at least of themselves, will be apt to estimate their virtues by their vices. To this fatal error all those will contribute, who confound the colors of right and wrong, and instead of helping to settle their boundaries, mix them with so much art, that no common mind is able to disunite them.

In narratives where historical veracity has no place, I cannot discover why there should not be exhibited the most perfect idea of virtue; of virtue not angelical, nor above probability, for what we cannot credit we shall never imitate, but the highest and purest that humanity can reach, which, exercised in such trials as the various revolutions of things shall bring upon it, may, by conquering some calamities, and enduring others, teach us what we may hope, and what we can perform. Vice, for vice is necessary to be shown, should always disgust; nor should the graces of gaiety, or the dignity of courage, be so united with it, as to reconcile it to the mind. Wherever it appears, it should raise hatred by the malignity of its practices, and contempt by the meanness of its stratagems; for while it is supported by either parts[9] or spirit, it will be seldom heartily abhorred. The Roman tyrant was content to be hated, if he was but feared;[1] and there are thousands of the readers of romances willing to be thought wicked, if they may be allowed to be wits. It is therefore to be steadily inculcated, that virtue is the highest proof of understanding, and the only solid basis of greatness; and that vice is the natural consequence of narrow thoughts, that it begins in mistake, and ends in ignominy.

Rambler No. 60

[ON BIOGRAPHY]

Saturday, 13 October 1750

—Quid sit pulchrum, quid turpe, quid utile, quid non,
Plenius et melius Chrysippo et Crantore dicit.

Horace, *Epistles*, 1.2.3–4.

Whose works the beautiful and base contain;
Of vice and virtue more instructive rules,
Than all the sober sages of the schools.

Francis

All joy or sorrow for the happiness or calamities of others is produced by an act of the imagination, that realizes the event however fictitious, or approximates[1] it however remote, by placing us, for a time, in the condition of him whose fortune we contemplate; so that we feel, while the deception lasts, whatever motions would be excited by the same good or evil happening to ourselves.

Our passions are therefore more strongly moved, in proportion as we can more readily adopt the pains or pleasures proposed to our minds, by recognizing them as once our own, or considering them as naturally incident to our state of life. It is not easy for the most artful writer to give us an interest in happiness or misery, which we think ourselves never likely to feel, and with which we have never yet been made

9. Abilities.
1. The Roman historian Suetonius reports this of the
emperor Caligula.
1. Bring close.

acquainted. Histories of the downfall of kingdoms, and revolutions of empires, are read with great tranquility; the imperial tragedy pleases common auditors only by its pomp of ornament, and grandeur of ideas; and the man whose faculties have been engrossed by business, and whose heart never fluttered but at the rise or fall of stocks, wonders how the attention can be seized, or the affections agitated by a tale of love.

Those parallel circumstances, and kindred images, to which we readily conform our minds, are, above all other writings, to be found in narratives of the lives of particular persons; and therefore no species of writing seems more worthy of cultivation than biography, since none can be more delightful or more useful, none can more certainly enchain the heart by irresistible interest, or more widely diffuse instruction to every diversity of condition.

The general and rapid narratives of history, which involve a thousand fortunes in the business of a day, and complicate innumerable incidents in one great transaction, afford few lessons applicable to private life, which derives its comforts and its wretchedness from the right or wrong management of things which nothing but their frequency makes considerable, *parva, si non fiant quotidie,* says Pliny,[2] and which can have no place in those relations which never descend below the consultation of senates, the motions of armies, and the schemes of conspirators.

I have often thought that there has rarely passed a life of which a judicious and faithful narrative would not be useful. For, not only every man has, in the mighty mass of the world, great numbers in the same condition with himself, to whom his mistakes and miscarriages, escapes and expedients, would be of immediate and apparent use; but there is such an uniformity in the state of man, considered apart from adventitious and separable decorations and disguises, that there is scarce any possibility of good or ill, but is common to humankind. A great part of the time of those who are placed at the greatest distance by fortune, or by temper, must unavoidably pass in the same manner; and though, when the claims of nature are satisfied, caprice, and vanity, and accident, begin to produce discriminations and peculiarities, yet the eye is not very heedful, or quick, which cannot discover the same causes still terminating their influence in the same effects, though sometimes accelerated, sometimes retarded, or perplexed by multiplied combinations. We are all prompted by the same motives, all deceived by the same fallacies, all animated by hope, obstructed by danger, entangled by desire, and seduced by pleasure.

It is frequently objected to relations of particular lives, that they are not distinguished by any striking or wonderful vicissitudes. The scholar who passed his life among his books, the merchant who conducted only his own affairs, the priest, whose sphere of action was not extended beyond that of his duty, are considered as no proper objects of public regard, however they might have excelled in their several stations, whatever might have been their learning, integrity, and piety. But this notion arises from false measures of excellence and dignity, and must be eradicated by considering that, in the esteem of uncorrupted reason, what is of most use is of most value.

It is, indeed, not improper to take honest advantages of prejudice, and to gain attention by a celebrated name; but the business of the biographer is often to pass slightly over those performances and incidents, which produce vulgar greatness, to lead the thoughts into domestic privacies, and display the minute details of daily life, where exterior appendages are cast aside, and men excel each other only by prudence and by virtue. The account of Thuanus is, with great propriety, said by its author to have been written, that it might lay open to posterity the private and familiar character of that

---

2. "Matters which would be trivial were they not part of a daily routine" (Pliny the Younger, *Epistles* 3.1).

man, *cujus ingenium et candorem ex ipsius scriptis sunt olim semper miraturi*,[3] whose candor and genius will to the end of time be by his writings preserved in admiration.

There are many invisible circumstances which, whether we read as inquirers after natural or moral knowledge, whether we intend to enlarge our science,[4] or increase our virtue, are more important than public occurrences. Thus Sallust, the great master of nature, has not forgot, in his account of Catiline, to remark that "his walk was now quick, and again slow," as an indication of a mind revolving something with violent commotion.[5] Thus the story of Melancthon[6] affords a striking lecture on the value of time, by informing us, that when he made an appointment, he expected not only the hour, but the minute to be fixed, that the day might not run out in the idleness of suspense; and all the plans and enterprises of De Witt are now of less importance to the world, than that part of his personal character which represents him as "careful of his health, and negligent of his life."[7]

But biography has often been allotted to writers who seem very little acquainted with the nature of their task, or very negligent about the performance. They rarely afford any other account than might be collected from public papers, but imagine themselves writing a life when they exhibit a chronological series of actions or preferments; and so little regard the manners or behavior of their heroes, that more knowledge may be gained of a man's real character, by a short conversation with one of his servants, than from a formal and studied narrative, begun with his pedigree, and ended with his funeral.

If now and then they condescend to inform the world of particular facts, they are not always so happy as to select the most important. I know not well what advantage posterity can receive from the only circumstance by which Tickell has distinguished Addison from the rest of mankind, the irregularity of his pulse:[8] nor can I think myself overpaid for the time spent in reading the life of Malherb,[9] by being enabled to relate, after the learned biographer, that Malherb had two predominant opinions; one, that the looseness of a single woman might destroy all her boast of ancient descent; the other, that the French beggars made use very improperly and barbarously of the phrase "noble gentleman," because either word included the sense of both.

There are, indeed, some natural reasons why these narratives are often written by such as were not likely to give much instruction or delight, and why most accounts of particular persons are barren and useless. If a life be delayed till interest and envy are at an end, we may hope for impartiality, but must expect little intelligence; for the incidents which give excellence to biography are of a volatile and evanescent kind, such as soon escape the memory, and are rarely transmitted by tradition. We know how few can portray a living acquaintance, except by his most prominent and observable particularities, and the grosser features of his mind; and it may be easily imagined how much of this little knowledge may be lost in imparting it, and how soon a succession of copies will lose all resemblance of the original.

---

3. Johnson quotes from a commentary affixed by Nicolas Rigault to the *History of His Own Time* by the French historian Jacques-Auguste de Thou (1553–1617). The Latin is translated by the words that follow.
4. Knowledge.
5. Johnson quotes from an account by the Roman historian Sallust of Catiline's conspiracy against Rome.
6. Johnson quotes from a biography of the Protestant theologian Philip Melancthon (1497–1560) by Joachim

Camerarius.
7. Johnson quotes the essayist Sir William Temple's verdict on the Dutch statesman Jan de Witt (1625–1672).
8. Thomas Tickell prefixed a biography of Joseph Addison to his edition of Addison's *Works* (1721).
9. Johnson refers to the biography of the French poet Francois de Malherbe (1555–1628) by the Marquis de Racan.

If the biographer writes from personal knowledge, and makes haste to gratify the public curiosity, there is danger lest his interest, his fear, his gratitude, or his tenderness, overpower his fidelity, and tempt him to conceal, if not to invent. There are many who think it an act of piety to hide the faults or failings of their friends, even when they can no longer suffer by their detection; we therefore see whole ranks of characters adorned with uniform panegyric, and not to be known from one another, but by extrinsic and casual circumstances. "Let me remember," says Hale, "when I find myself inclined to pity a criminal, that there is likewise a pity due to the country."[1] If we owe regard to the memory of the dead, there is yet more respect to be paid to knowledge, to virtue, and to truth.

Idler No. 31[1]

[ON IDLENESS]

Saturday, 18 November 1758

Many moralists have remarked, that pride has of all human vices the widest dominion, appears in the greatest multiplicity of forms, and lies hid under the greatest variety of disguises; of disguises, which, like the moon's "veil of brightness," are both its "luster and its shade,"[2] and betray it to others, though they hide it from ourselves.

It is not my intention to degrade pride from this pre-eminence of mischief, yet I know not whether idleness may not maintain a very doubtful and obstinate competition.

There are some that profess idleness in its full dignity, who call themselves the Idle, as Busiris in the play "calls himself the Proud";[3] who boast that they do nothing, and thank their stars that they have nothing to do; who sleep every night till they can sleep no longer, and rise only that exercise may enable them to sleep again; who prolong the reign of darkness by double curtains, and never see the sun but to "tell him how they hate his beams";[4] whose whole labor is to vary the postures of indulgence, and whose day differs from their night but as a couch or chair differs from a bed.

These are the true and open votaries of idleness, for whom she weaves the garlands of poppies, and into whose cup she pours the waters of oblivion; who exist in a state of unruffled stupidity,[5] forgetting and forgotten; who have long ceased to live, and at whose death the survivors can only say, that they have ceased to breathe.

But idleness predominates in many lives where it is not suspected, for being a vice which terminates in itself, it may be enjoyed without injury to others, and is therefore not watched like fraud, which endangers property, or like pride, which naturally seeks its gratifications in another's inferiority. Idleness is a silent and peaceful

---

1. Johnson quotes from the biography of Sir Matthew Hale (1609–1676), eminent jurist and religious writer, by Gilbert Burnet.

1. *The Idler* (1758–1760) bears a more self-deprecating title than *The Rambler;* other circumstances, too, suggest that Johnson intended a less imposing performance in this series of periodical essay than in its predecessor. The new pieces appeared not twice but once a week, and not as an independent sheet but as a department within a weekly newspaper called *The Universal Chronicle* (which achieved little eminence apart from Johnson's contribution). The *Idlers* were shorter than the *Ramblers*, and

dealt more often in light topics and comic touches. Boswell opined that the second series had "less body and more spirit . . . more variety of real life, and greater facility of language." His judgment is hardly definitive; the comparison has been assayed, with varying results, many times since.

2. Both quotations come from Samuel Butler's poem *Hudibras* (1663–1678), 2.1.905 and 908.

3. *Busiris* (1719) by Edward Young.

4. Milton, *Paradise Lost* 4.37.

5. Stupor.

quality, that neither raises envy by ostentation, nor hatred by opposition; and therefore nobody is busy to censure or detect it.

As pride sometimes is hid under humility, idleness is often covered by turbulence and hurry. He that neglects his known duty and real employment, naturally endeavors to crowd his mind with something that may bar out the remembrance of his own folly, and does any thing but what he ought to do with eager diligence, that he may keep himself in his own favor.

Some are always in a state of preparation, occupied in previous measures, forming plans, accumulating materials, and providing for the main affair. These are certainly under the secret power of idleness. Nothing is to be expected from the workman whose tools are forever to be sought. I was once told by a great master, that no man ever excelled in painting, who was eminently curious[6] about pencils[7] and colors.

There are others to whom idleness dictates another expedient, by which life may be passed unprofitably away without the tediousness of many vacant hours. The art is, to fill the day with petty business, to have always something in hand which may raise curiosity, but not solicitude, and keep the mind in a state of action, but not of labor.

This art has for many years been practiced by my old friend Sober,[8] with wonderful success. Sober is a man of strong desires and quick imagination, so exactly balanced by the love of ease, that they can seldom stimulate him to any difficult undertaking; they have, however, so much power, that they will not suffer him to lie quite at rest, and though they do not make him sufficiently useful to others, they make him at least weary of himself.

Mr. Sober's chief pleasure is conversation; there is no end of his talk or his attention; to speak or to hear is equally pleasing; for he still fancies that he is teaching or learning something, and is free for the time from his own reproaches.

But there is one time at night when he must go home, that his friends may sleep; and another time in the morning, when all the world agrees to shut out interruption. These are the moments of which poor Sober trembles at the thought. But the misery of these tiresome intervals, he has many means of alleviating. He has persuaded himself that the manual arts are undeservedly overlooked; he has observed in many trades the effects of close thought, and just ratiocination. From speculation he proceeded to practice, and supplied himself with the tools of a carpenter, with which he mended his coal-box very successfully, and which he still continues to employ, as he finds occasion.

He has attempted at other times the crafts of the shoemaker, tinman, plumber, and potter; in all these arts he has failed, and resolves to qualify himself for them by better information. But his daily amusement is chemistry. He has a small furnace, which he employs in distillation, and which has long been the solace of his life. He draws oils and waters, and essences and spirits, which he knows to be of no use; sits and counts the drops as they come from his retort, and forgets that, while a drop is falling, a moment flies away.

Poor Sober! I have often teased him with reproof, and he has often promised reformation; for no man is so much open to conviction as the idler, but there is none on whom it operates so little. What will be the effect of this paper I know not; perhaps he will read it and laugh, and light the fire in his furnace; but my hope is that he will quit his trifles, and betake himself to rational and useful diligence.

6. "Difficult to please" (Johnson's *Dictionary*).
7. Brushes.

8. Johnson's friends believed that the portrait of Sober was autobiographical.

Idler No. 32
[ON SLEEP]

Saturday, 25 November 1758

Among the innumerable mortifications that waylay human arrogance on every side may well be reckoned our ignorance of the most common objects and effects, a defect of which we become more sensible by every attempt to supply it. Vulgar and inactive minds confound familiarity with knowledge, and conceive themselves informed of the whole nature of things when they are shown their form or told their use; but the speculatist, who is not content with superficial views, harasses himself with fruitless curiosity, and still as he inquires more perceives only that he knows less.

Sleep is a state in which a great part of every life is passed. No animal has been yet discovered, whose existence is not varied with intervals of insensibility; and some late philosophers have extended the empire of sleep over the vegetable world.

Yet of this change so frequent, so great, so general, and so necessary, no searcher has yet found either the efficient or final cause; or can tell by what power the mind and body are thus chained down in irresistible stupefaction; or what benefits the animal receives from this alternate suspension of its active powers.

Whatever may be the multiplicity or contrariety of opinions upon this subject, nature has taken sufficient care that theory shall have little influence on practice. The most diligent inquirer is not able long to keep his eyes open; the most eager disputant will begin about midnight to desert his argument, and once in four and twenty hours, the gay and the gloomy, the witty and the dull, the clamorous and the silent, the busy and the idle, are all overpowered by the gentle tyrant, and all lie down in the equality of sleep.

Philosophy has often attempted to repress insolence by asserting that all conditions are leveled by death; a position which, however it may deject the happy, will seldom afford much comfort to the wretched. It is far more pleasing to consider that sleep is equally a leveler with death; that the time is never at a great distance, when the balm of rest shall be effused alike upon every head, when the diversities of life shall stop their operation, and the high and the low shall lie down together.

It is somewhere recorded of Alexander, that in the pride of conquests, and intoxication of flattery, he declared that he only perceived himself to be a man by the necessity of sleep. Whether he considered sleep as necessary to his mind or body it was indeed a sufficient evidence of human infirmity; the body which required such frequency of renovation gave but faint promises of immortality; and the mind which, from time to time, sunk gladly into insensibility had made no very near approaches to the felicity of the supreme and self-sufficient nature.

I know not what can tend more to repress all the passions that disturb the peace of the world than the consideration that there is no height of happiness or honor from which man does not eagerly descend to a state of unconscious repose; that the best condition of life is such that we contentedly quit its good to be disentangled from its evils; that in a few hours splendor fades before the eye and praise itself deadens in the ear; the senses withdraw from their objects, and reason favors the retreat.

What then are the hopes and prospects of covetousness, ambition and rapacity? Let him that desires most have all his desires gratified, he never shall attain a state which he can, for a day and a night, contemplate with satisfaction, or from which, if he had the power of perpetual vigilance, he would not long for periodical separations.

All envy would be extinguished if it were universally known that there are none to be envied, and surely none can be much envied who are not pleased with themselves. There is reason to suspect that the distinctions of mankind have more show than value when it is found that all agree to be weary alike of pleasures and of cares, that the powerful and the weak, the celebrated and obscure, join in one common wish, and implore from nature's hand the nectar of oblivion.

Such is our desire of abstraction from ourselves that very few are satisfied with the quantity of stupefaction which the needs of the body force upon the mind. Alexander himself added intemperance to sleep, and solaced with the fumes of wine the sovereignty of the world. And almost every man has some art by which he steals his thoughts away from his present state.

It is not much of life that is spent in close attention to any important duty. Many hours of every day are suffered to fly away without any traces left upon the intellects. We suffer phantoms to rise up before us, and amuse ourselves with the dance of airy images, which after a time we dismiss forever, and know not how we have been busied.

Many have no happier moments than those that they pass in solitude, abandoned to their own imagination, which sometimes puts sceptres in their hands or mitres on their heads, shifts the scene of pleasure with endless variety, bids all the forms of beauty sparkle before them, and gluts them with every change of visionary luxury.

It is easy in these semi-slumbers to collect all the possibilities of happiness, to alter the course of the sun, to bring back the past, and anticipate the future, to unite all the beauties of all seasons, and all the blessings of all climates, to receive and bestow felicity, and forget that misery is the lot of man. All this is a voluntary dream, a temporary recession from the realities of life to airy fictions; an habitual subjection of reason to fancy.

Others are afraid to be alone, and amuse themselves by a perpetual succession of companions, but the difference is not great; in solitude we have our dreams to ourselves, and in company we agree to dream in concert. The end sought in both is forgetfulness of ourselves.

A Dictionary of the English Language

Johnson's *Dictionary* struck its first readers as a nearly superhuman accomplishment; it seems one still. "A dictionary of the English language," observed one early reviewer, had never before "been attempted with the least degree of success"; the closest antecedents to Johnson's project were the national dictionaries of France and Italy, and these had been composed by whole academies of scholars, working collectively over the course of decades. Here, by contrast, was the seven years' labor of a single author (aided only by six part-time amanuenses): 40,000 words defined with unprecedented exactitude, and illustrated with more than 114,000 passages drawn from English prose and poetry of the previous 250 years. Ninety years earlier, members of the newly founded Royal Society for Improving Natural Knowledge had dreamed of such a resource; Johnson produced it by empirical methods much like the ones they promulgated. He spent his first years on the project accumulating data, rereading the English writers he valued most, marking any passage that strikingly illuminated the workings of a particular word. He then worked from this heap of collected evidence to the fine-honed, sharply distinguished conclusions of his definitions. The results have been variously and accurately described as the first standard English dictionary; as one of the final fruits of Renaissance humanism; as a commonplace-book (or database) of important English writing from Sidney to Pope; as a massive map of its author's mind. The key to that map resides in the *Dictionary*'s Preface, where Johnson measures the grandeur of his aspirations against the limitations of his achievement. In this mix of personal memoir and linguistic meditation, lexicography becomes a local instance of the vanity of human wishes. Human language, massive, metamorphic, and intractable, overmatches the human desire to codify and contain it, to fix it once and for all.

from A Dictionary of the English Language
from *Preface*
[ON METHOD]

It is the fate of those who toil at the lower employments of life to be rather driven by the fear of evil than attracted by the prospect of good; to be exposed to censure, without hope of praise; to be disgraced by miscarriage or punished for neglect, where success would have been without applause and diligence without reward.

Among these unhappy mortals is the writer of dictionaries; whom mankind have considered not as the pupil but the slave of science, the pioneer[1] of literature, doomed only to remove rubbish and clear obstructions from the paths through which learning and genius press forward to conquest and glory, without bestowing a smile on the humble drudge that facilitates their progress. Every other author may aspire to praise; the lexicographer can only hope to escape reproach, and even this negative recompense has been yet granted to very few.

I have, notwithstanding this discouragement, attempted a dictionary of the English language which, while it was employed in the cultivation of every species of literature, has itself been hitherto neglected; suffered to spread, under the direction of chance, into wild exuberance; resigned to the tyranny of time and fashion; and exposed to the corruptions of ignorance, and caprices of innovation.

When I took the first survey of my undertaking, I found our speech copious without order, and energetic without rules: wherever I turned my view, there was perplexity to be disentangled and confusion to be regulated; choice was to be made out of boundless variety, without any established principle of selection; adulterations were to be detected without a settled test of purity; and modes of expression to be rejected or received without the suffrages[2] of any writers of classical reputation or acknowledged authority.

Having therefore no assistance but from general grammar, I applied myself to the perusal of our writers; and, noting whatever might be of use to ascertain or illustrate any word or phrase, accumulated in time the materials of a dictionary, which, by degrees, I reduced to method, establishing to myself in the progress of the work such rules as experience and analogy suggested to me; experience, which practice and observation were continually increasing; and analogy, which, though in some words obscure, was evident in others.

[ON DEFINITIONS AND EXAMPLES]

That part of my work on which I expect malignity most frequently to fasten is the explanation; in which I cannot hope to satisfy those who are perhaps not inclined to be pleased, since I have not always been able to satisfy myself. To interpret a language by itself is very difficult; many words cannot be explained by synonyms because the idea signified by them has not more than one appellation; nor by paraphrase,

---

1. "One whose business is to level the road, throw up works, or sink mines in military operations" (Johnson's *Dictionary*).   2. Votes, testimonies.

because simple ideas cannot be described. When the nature of things is unknown, or the notion unsettled and indefinite, and various in various minds, the words by which such notions are conveyed or such things denoted will be ambiguous and perplexed. And such is the fate of hapless lexicography that not only darkness, but light, impedes and distresses it; things may be not only too little, but too much known, to be happily illustrated. To explain requires the use of terms less abstruse than that which is to be explained, and such terms cannot always be found; for as nothing can be proved but by supposing something intuitively known and evident without proof, so nothing can be defined but by the use of words too plain to admit a definition.

Other words there are, of which the sense is too subtle and evanescent to be fixed in a paraphrase; such are all those which are by the grammarians termed expletives, and, in dead languages, are suffered to pass for empty sounds, of no other use than to fill a verse or to modulate a period,[1] but which are easily perceived in living tongues to have power and emphasis, though it be sometimes such as no other form of expression can convey. * * *

The solution of all difficulties and the supply of all defects must be sought in the examples subjoined to the various senses of each word, and ranged according to the time of their authors.

When first I collected these authorities, I was desirous that every quotation should be useful to some other end than the illustration of a word; I therefore extracted from philosophers principles of science; from historians remarkable facts; from chemists complete processes; from divines striking exhortations; and from poets beautiful descriptions. Such is design while it is yet at a distance from execution. When the time called upon me to range this accumulation of elegance and wisdom into an alphabetical series, I soon discovered that the bulk of my volumes would fright away the student, and was forced to depart from my scheme of including all that was pleasing or useful in English literature, and reduce my transcripts very often to clusters of words in which scarcely any meaning is retained; thus to the weariness of copying, I was condemned to add the vexation of expunging. Some passages I have yet spared which may relieve the labor of verbal searches, and intersperse with verdure and flowers the dusty deserts of barren philology.

The examples, thus mutilated, are no longer to be considered as conveying the sentiments or doctrine of their authors; the word for the sake of which they are inserted, with all its appendant clauses, has been carefully preserved; but it may sometimes happen, by hasty detruncation, that the general tendency of the sentence may be changed: the divine may desert his tenets, or the philosopher his system. * * *

[CONCLUSION]

A large work is difficult because it is large, even though all its parts might singly be performed with facility; where there are many things to be done, each must be allowed its share of time and labor in the proportion only which it bears to the whole; nor can it be expected that the stones which form the dome of a temple should be squared and polished like the diamond of a ring.

Of the event of this work, for which, having labored it with so much application, I cannot but have some degree of parental fondness, it is natural to form conjectures. Those who have been persuaded to think well of my design will require that it should fix our language and put a stop to those alterations which time and chance have hitherto been suffered to make in it without opposition. With this consequence I will

---

1. Clause or sentence.

confess that I flattered myself for a while; but now begin to fear that I have indulged expectation which neither reason nor experience can justify. When we see men grow old and die at a certain time one after another, from century to century, we laugh at the elixir that promises to prolong life to a thousand years; and with equal justice may the lexicographer be derided, who being able to produce no example of a nation that has preserved their words and phrases from mutability, shall imagine that his dictionary can embalm his language and secure it from corruption and decay, that it is in his power to change sublunary nature, and clear the world at once from folly, vanity, and affectation. * * *

The great pest of speech is frequency of translation. No book was ever turned from one language into another without imparting something of its native idiom; this is the most mischievous and comprehensive innovation; single words may enter by thousands and the fabric of the tongue continue the same, but new phraseology changes much at once; it alters not the single stones of the building but the order of the columns.[1] If an academy should be established for the cultivation of our style, which I, who can never wish to see dependence multiplied, hope the spirit of English liberty will hinder or destroy, let them, instead of compiling grammars and dictionaries, endeavor, with all their influence, to stop the license of translators, whose idleness and ignorance, if it be suffered to proceed, will reduce us to babble a dialect of France.

If the changes that we fear be thus irresistible, what remains but to acquiesce with silence, as in the other insurmountable distresses of humanity? It remains that we retard what we cannot repel, that we palliate what we cannot cure. Life may be lengthened by care, though death cannot be ultimately defeated: tongues, like governments, have a natural tendency to degeneration; we have long preserved our constitution, let us make some struggles for our language.

In hope of giving longevity to that which its own nature forbids to be immortal, I have devoted this book, the labor of years, to the honor of my country, that we may no longer yield the palm[2] of philology without a contest to the nations of the Continent. The chief glory of every people arises from its authors: whether I shall add anything by my own writings to the reputation of English literature must be left to time: much of my life has been lost under the pressures of disease; much has been trifled away; and much has always been spent in provision for the day that was passing over me; but I shall not think my employment useless or ignoble if by my assistance foreign nations and distant ages gain access to the propagators of knowledge, and understand the teachers of truth; if my labors afford light to the repositories of science, and add celebrity to Bacon, to Hooker, to Milton, and to Boyle.

When I am animated by this wish, I look with pleasure on my book, however defective, and deliver it to the world with the spirit of a man that has endeavored well. That it will immediately become popular I have not promised to myself: a few wild blunders and risible absurdities, from which no work of such multiplicity was ever free, may for a time furnish folly with laughter, and harden ignorance in contempt; but useful diligence will at last prevail, and there never can be wanting some who distinguish desert,[3] who will consider that no dictionary of a living tongue ever can be perfect, since while it is hastening to publication some words are budding and some falling away; that a whole life cannot be spent upon syntax and etymology, and that even a whole life would not be sufficient; that he whose design includes whatever language

---

1. In classical architecture, the five "orders" are Doric, Ionic, Corinthian, Tuscan, and Composite.

2. Crown (symbol of victory).

3. Merit.

can express, must often speak of what he does not understand; that a writer will sometimes be hurried by eagerness to the end, and sometimes faint with weariness under a task, which Scaliger compares to the labors of the anvil and the mine;[4] that what is obvious is not always known, and what is known is not always present; that sudden fits of inadvertency will surprise vigilance, slight avocations will seduce attention, and casual eclipses of the mind will darken learning; and that the writer shall often in vain trace his memory at the moment of need for that which yesterday he knew with intuitive readiness, and which will come uncalled into his thoughts tomorrow.

In this work, when it shall be found that much is omitted, let it not be forgotten that much likewise is performed; and though no book was ever spared out of tenderness to the author, and the world is little solicitous to know whence proceeded the faults of that which it condemns; yet it may gratify curiosity to inform it, that the *English Dictionary* was written with little assistance of the learned, and without any patronage of the great; not in the soft obscurities of retirement or under the shelter of academic bowers, but amidst inconvenience and distraction, in sickness and in sorrow. It may repress the triumph of malignant criticism to observe that if our language is not here fully displayed, I have only failed in an attempt which no human powers have hitherto completed. If the lexicons of ancient tongues, now immutably fixed and comprised in a few volumes, are yet, after the toil of successive ages, inadequate and delusive; if the aggregated knowledge, and cooperating diligence of the Italian academicians did not secure them from the censure of Beni;[5] if the embodied critics of France, when fifty years had been spent upon their work, were obliged to change its economy and give their second edition another form, I may surely be contented without the praise of perfection, which, if I could obtain, in this gloom of solitude, what would it avail me? I have protracted my work till most of those whom I wished to please have sunk into the grave, and success and miscarriage are empty sounds: I therefore dismiss it with frigid tranquility, having little to fear or hope from censure or from praise.

[SOME ENTRIES][1]

FUNK. n.s. A stink. A low word.

IMAGINÁTION. n.s. [*imaginatio*, Lat. *imagination*, Fr. from *imagine*.]

1. Fancy; the power of forming ideal pictures; the power of representing things absent to one's self or others.

> *Imagination* I understand to be the representation of an individual thought. Imagination is of three kinds: joined with belief of that which is to come; joined with memory of that which is past; and of things present, or as if they were present: for I comprehend in this imagination feigned and at pleasure, as if one should imagine such a man to be in the vestments of a pope, or to have wings.   —Bacon

> Our simple apprehension of corporal objects, if present, is sense; if absent, *imagination:* when we would perceive a material object, our fancies present us with its idea.   —Glanville

> O whither shall I run, or which way fly
> The sight of this so horrid spectacle,

---

4. Johnson refers to a poem, *Against the Compilers of the Lexicons,* by the great Renaissance scholar Joseph Justus Scaliger.
5. Paolo Beni criticized the Italian dictionary published in 1612 by the Accademia della Crusca.

1. All entries are from the fourth edition of Johnson's *Dictionary* (1773), the last which Johnson prepared. Each entry is presented complete, with etymology, definitions, illustrations.

> Which erst my eyes beheld, and yet behold!
> For dire *imagination* still pursues me. —Milton

> Where beams of warm *imagination* play,
> The memory's soft figures melt away. —Pope

2. Conception; image in the mind; idea.

> Sometimes despair darkens all her *imaginations;* sometimes the active passion of love
> cheers and clears her invention. —Sidney

> Princes have but their titles for their glories,
> An outward honor for an inward toil;
> And, for unfelt *imaginations*,
> They often feel a world of restless cares. —Shakespeare, *Richard III*

> Better I were distract,
> So should my thoughts be severed from my griefs;
> And woes, by wrong *imaginations*, lose
> The knowledge of themselves. —Shakespeare, *King Lear*

> His *imaginations* were often as just as they were bold and strong. —Dennis

3. Contrivance; scheme.

> Thou hast seen all their vengeance, and all their *imaginations* against me.
> —Bible (Lamentations 3.60)

4. An unsolid or fanciful opinion.

> We are apt to think that space, in itself, is actually boundless; to which *imagination*,
> the idea of space, of itself leads us. —Locke

JÚDGMENT. n.s. [*jugement*, Fr.]

1. The power of discerning the relations between one term or one proposition and
another.

> O *judgment!* thou art fled to brutish beasts,
> And men have lost their reason. —Shakespeare, *Julius Caesar*

> The faculty, which God has given man to supply the want of certain knowledge, is
> *judgment*, whereby the mind takes any proposition to be true or false, without per-
> ceiving a demonstrative evidence in the proofs. —Locke

> *Judgment* is that whereby we join ideas together by affirmation or negation; so, this
> tree is high. —Watts

2. Doom; the right or power of passing judgment.

> If my suspect be false, forgive me, God;
> For *judgment* only doth belong to thee. —Shakespeare, *Henry VI*

3. The act of exercising judicature; judicatory.

> They gave *judgment* upon him. —Bible (2 Kings)

> When thou, O Lord, shalt stand disclosed
> In majesty severe,
> And sit in *judgment* on my soul,
> O how shall I appear? —Addison's *Spectator*

4. Determination; decision.

> Where distinctions or identities are purely material, the *judgment* is made by the imagination, otherwise by the understanding. —Glanville's *Scepsis*

> We shall make a certain *judgment* what kind of dissolution that earth was capable of. —Burnet's *Theory*

> Reason ought to accompany the exercise of our senses, whenever we would form a just *judgment* of things proposed to our inquiry. —Watts

5. The quality of distinguishing propriety and impropriety; criticism.

> *Judgment*, a cool and slow faculty, attends not a man in the rapture of poetical composition. —Dennis

> 'Tis with our *judgments* as our watches, none
> Go just alike; yet each believes his own. —Pope

6. Opinion; notion.

> I see men's *judgments* are
> A parcel of their fortunes, and things outward
> Draw the inward quality after them,
> To suffer all alike. —Shakespeare, *Antony and Cleopatra*

> When she did think my master loved her well,
> She, in my *judgment*, was as fair as you. —Shakespeare

7. Sentence against a criminal.

> When he was brought again to th' bar, to hear
> His knell rung out, his *judgment*, he was stirred
> With agony. —Shakespeare, *Henry VIII*

> The chief priests informed me, desiring to have *judgment* against him. —Bible (Acts 25.15)

> On Adam last this *judgment* he pronounced. —Milton

8. Condemnation. This is a theological use.

> The *judgment* was by one to condemnation; but the free gift is of many offenses unto justification. —Bible (Romans 5.16)

> The precepts, promises, and threatenings of the Gospel will rise up in *judgment* against us, and the articles of our faith will be so many articles of accusation.
> —Tillotson

9. Punishment inflicted by Providence, with reference to some particular crime.

> This *judgment* of the heavens that makes us tremble,
> Touches us not with pity. —Shakespeare, *King Lear*

> We cannot be guilty of greater uncharitableness, than to interpret afflictions as punishments and *judgments*: it aggravates the evil to him who suffers, when he looks upon himself as the mark of divine vengeance. —Addison's *Spectator*

10. Distribution of justice.

> The Jews made insurrection against Paul, and brought him to the *judgment* seat.
> —Bible (Acts 18.12)

Your dishonor
Mangles true *judgment*, and bereaves the state
Of that integrity which should become it.   —Shakespeare's *Coriolanus*

In *judgments* between rich and poor, consider not what the poor man needs, but what is his own.   —Taylor

A bold and wise petitioner goes strait to the throne and *judgment* seat of the monarch.
                                                                    —Arbuthnot and Pope

11. Judiciary law; statute.

If ye hearken to these *judgments*, and keep and do them, the Lord thy God shall keep unto thee the covenant.   —Bible (Deuteronomy)

12. The last doom.

The dreadful *judgment* day
So dreadful will not be as was his sight.   —Shakespeare's *Henry VI*

LEXICÓGRAPHER. n.s. [λεξικον and γραφειν; *lexicographe*, Fr.] A writer of dictionaries; a harmless drudge, that busies himself in tracing the original, and detailing the signification of words.

Commentators and *lexicographers* acquainted with the Syriac language, have given these hints in their writings on scripture.   —Watt's *Improvement of the Mind*

VACÚITY. n.s. [*vacuitas*; from *vacuus*, Lat. *vacuité*, Fr.]

1. Emptiness; state of being unfilled.

Hunger is such a state of *vacuity*, as to require a fresh supply of aliment.
                                                                    —Arbuthnot

2. Space unfilled; space unoccupied.

In filling up *vacuities*, turning out shadows and ceremonies, by explicit prescription of substantial duties, which those shadows did obscurely represent.
                                                                    —Hammond's *Fund*

He, that seat soon failing, meets
A vast *vacuity*.   —Milton

Body and space are quite different things, and a *vacuity* is interspersed among the particles of matter.   —Bentley

God, who alone can answer all our longings, and fill every *vacuity* of our soul, should entirely possess our heart.   —Rogers

Redeeming still at night these *vacuities* of the day.   —Fell

3. Inanity; want of reality.

The soul is seen, like other things, in the mirror of its effects: but if they'll run behind the glass to catch at it, their expectations will meet with *vacuity* and emptiness.
                                                                    —Glanville

LETTERS
To Lord Chesterfield[1]

My Lord: 7 February 1755

I have been lately informed by the proprietor of *The World* that two papers in which my Dictionary is recommended to the public were written by your Lordship.[2] To be so distinguished is an honor which, being very little accustomed to favors from the great, I know not well how to receive, or in what terms to acknowledge.

When upon some slight encouragement I first visited your Lordship I was overpowered like the rest of mankind by the enchantment of your adress, and could not forbear to wish that I might boast myself *le vainqueur du vainqueur de la terre*,[3] that I might obtain that regard for which I saw the world contending; but I found my attendance so little encouraged, that neither pride nor modesty would suffer me to continue it. When I had once adressed your Lordship in public, I had exhausted all the art of pleasing which a retired and uncourtly scholar can possess. I had done all that I could, and no man is well pleased to have his all neglected, be it ever so little.

Seven years, my lord, have now passed since I waited in your outward rooms or was repulsed from your door, during which time I have been pushing on my work through difficulties of which it is useless to complain, and have brought it at last to the verge of publication without one act of assistance, one word of encouragement, or one smile of favor. Such treatment I did not expect, for I never had a patron before.

The shepherd in Virgil grew at last acquainted with Love, and found him a native of the rocks.[4] Is not a patron, my lord, one who looks with unconcern on a man struggling for life in the water and when he has reached ground encumbers him with help?[5] The notice which you have been pleased to take of my labors, had it been early, had been kind; but it has been delayed till I am indifferent and cannot enjoy it, till I am solitary and cannot impart it, till I am known and do not want it.

I hope it is no very cynical asperity not to confess obligation where no benefit has been received, or to be unwilling that the public should consider me as owing that to a patron, which providence has enabled me to do for myself.

Having carried on my work thus far with so little obligation to any favorer of learning I shall not be disappointed though I should conclude it, if less be possible, with less, for I have been long wakened from that dream of hope, in which I once boasted myself with so much exultation, my Lord, your Lordship's most humble, most obedient servant,

                                                                              S.J.

To Hester Thrale

Dear Madam: Bolt Court, Fleetstreet, June 19, 1783

I am sitting down in no cheerful solitude to write a narrative which would once have affected you with tenderness and sorrow, but which you will perhaps pass over now

---

1. Philip Dormer Stanhope (1694–1773), fourth Earl of Chesterfield, a politician and man of letters renowned for his elegant manners and his knowledge of the polite world. In 1747 Johnson had dedicated his *Plan of a Dictionary* to Chesterfield but had received neither financial nor moral support from him during the long years of labor on the *Dictionary*.
2. Chesterfield had contributed two essays to Robert Dodsley's periodical *The World*. In these essays he praised the forthcoming *Dictionary* in such a way as to imply that

he had been its enlightened sponsor.
3. "The conqueror of the world's conqueror" (the opening line of the epic *Alaric*, by Georges de Scudéry).
4. Johnson alludes to a pastoral poem by Virgil (*Eclogue* 8), in which Love is described as coming from a land of "flinty crags."
5. In his *Dictionary*, Johnson defines "patron" as "commonly a wretch who supports with insolence, and is paid with flattery."

with the careless glance of frigid indifference.[1] For this diminution of regard however, I know not whether I ought to blame you, who may have reasons which I cannot know, and I do not blame myself who have for a great part of human life done you what good I could, and have never done you evil.

I had been disordered in the usual way, and had been relieved by the usual methods, by opium and cathartics,[2] but had rather lessened my dose of opium.

On Monday the 16 I sat for my picture,[3] and walked a considerable way with little inconvenience. In the afternoon and evening I felt myself light and easy, and began to plan schemes of life. Thus I went to bed, and in a short time waked and sat up as has been long my custom when I felt a confusion and indistinctness in my head which lasted, I suppose about half a minute. I was alarmed and prayed God, that however he might afflict my body he would spare my understanding. This prayer, that I might try the integrity of my faculties, I made in Latin verse. The lines were not very good, but I knew them not to be very good, I made them easily, and concluded myself to be unimpaired in my faculties.

Soon after I perceived that I had suffered a paralytic stroke, and that my speech was taken from me. I had no pain, and so little dejection in this dreadful state that I wondered at my own apathy, and considered that perhaps death itself when it should come, would excite less horror than seems now to attend it.

In order to rouse the vocal organs I took two drams. Wine has been celebrated for the production of eloquence; I put myself into violent motion, and, I think, repeated it. But all was vain; I then went to bed, and, strange as it may seem, I think, slept. When I saw light, it was time to contrive what I should do. Though God stopped my speech he left me my hand, I enjoyed a mercy which was not granted to my Dear Friend Lawrence,[4] who now perhaps overlooks me as I am writing and rejoices that I have what he wanted.[5] My first note was necessarily to my servant, who came in talking, and could not immediately comprehend why he should read what I put into his hands.

I then wrote a card to Mr. Allen,[6] that I might have a discreet friend at hand to act as occasion should require. In penning this note I had some difficulty, my hand, I know not how nor why, made wrong letters. I then wrote to Dr. Taylor[7] to come to me, and bring Dr. Heberden, and I sent to Dr. Brocklesby, who is my neighbor. My physicians are very friendly and very disinterested; and give me great hopes, but you may imagine my situation. I have so far recovered my vocal powers, as to repeat the Lord's Prayer with no very imperfect articulation. My memory, I hope, yet remains as it was. But such an attack produces solicitude for the safety of every faculty.

How this will be received by you, I know not, I hope you will sympathize with me, but perhaps

> My Mistress gracious, mild, and good,
> Cries, Is he dumb? 'tis time he should.[8]

But can this be possible, I hope it cannot. I hope that what, when I could speak, I spoke of You, and to You, will be in a sober and serious hour remembered by You, and surely it cannot be remembered but with some degree of kindness. I have loved You with vir-

---

1. As she became more and more attached to Gabriel Piozzi, an Italian musician, Hester Thrale (correctly sensing how angry Johnson would be) began to disengage from their close friendship. Though he knew something had gone wrong, Johnson did not learn of the love affair until a year later, when Mrs. Thrale wrote to inform him of her marriage.
2. Purgatives.
3. Johnson's portrait was being painted.

4. Johnson's favorite physician, Dr. Thomas Lawrence, had died earlier that month after suffering a stroke.
5. Lacked.
6. Johnson's printer and neighbor, Edmund Allen.
7. The clergyman John Taylor, one of Johnson's oldest and closest friends.
8. Johnson adapts a couplet from Swift's *Verses on the Death of Dr. Swift:* "The Queen, so gracious, mild and good, / Cries, 'Is he gone? 'Tis time he should'" (lines 181–182).

tuous affection, I have honoured You with sincere esteem. Let not all our endearment be forgotten, but let me have in this great distress your pity and your prayers. You see I yet turn to You with my complaints as a settled and unalienable friend, do not, do not drive me from You, for I have not deserved either neglect or hatred.

To the girls,[9] who do not write often, for Susy has written only once, and Miss Thrale owes me a letter, I earnestly recommend as their guardian and friend, that they remember their Creator in the days of their youth.[1]

I suppose You may wish to know how my disease is treated by the physicians. They put a blister upon my back, and two from my ear to my throat, one on a side. The blister on the back has done little, and those on the throat have not risen. I bullied, and bounced, (it sticks to our last sand)[2] and compelled the apothecary to make his salve according to the Edinburgh dispensatory[3] that it might adhere better. I have two on now of my own prescription. They likewise give me salt of hartshorn, which I take with no great confidence, but am satisfied that what can be done, is done for me.

O God, give me comfort and confidence in Thee, forgive my sins, and if it be thy good pleasure, relieve my diseases for Jesus Christ's sake. Amen.

I am almost ashamed of this querulous letter, but now it is written, let it go. I am Madam, Your most humble servant,

SAM. JOHNSON

To Hester Thrale Piozzi

Madam: July 2, 1784

If I interpret your letter right, You are ignominiously married,[1] if it is yet undone, let us once talk together. If You have abandoned your children and your religion, God forgive your wickedness; if You have forfeited your fame, and your country, may your folly do no further mischief.[2]

If the last act is yet to do, I, who have loved you, esteemed you, reverenced you, and served you, I who long thought You the first of humankind, entreat that before your fate is irrevocable, I may once more see You. I was, I once was, Madam, most truly yours,

SAM. JOHNSON

I will come down if you permit it.

To Hester Thrale Piozzi

Dear Madam: London, July 8, 1784

What You have done, however I may lament it, I have no pretense to resent, as it has not been injurious to me. I therefore breathe out one sigh more of tenderness perhaps useless, but at least sincere.

I wish that God may grant You every blessing, that you may be happy in this world for its short continuance, and eternally happy in a better state. And whatever I

---

9. Hester Thrale's four surviving daughters: Hester Maria ("Miss Thrale"), Susanna ("Susy"), Sophia, and Cecilia.
1. "Remember now thy Creator in the days of thy youth, while the evil days come not" (Ecclesiastes 12.1).
2. "Time, that on all things lays his lenient hand, / Yet tames not this; it sticks to our last sand" (Pope, *Epistle to Cobham*, lines 224–225).

3. Medical manual.
1. Hester Thrale had written on June 30 to inform Johnson of her marriage to Gabriel Piozzi.
2. Johnson's objections to Gabriel Piozzi include the fact that he is a musician (and therefore socially inferior), a Catholic, and an Italian.

can contribute to your happiness, I am very ready to repay for that kindness which soothed twenty years of a life radically wretched.

Do not think slightly of the advice which I now presume to offer. Prevail upon Mr. Piozzi to settle in England. You may live here with more dignity than in Italy, and with more security. Your rank will be higher, and your fortune more under your own eye. I desire not to detail all my reasons; but every argument of prudence and interest is for England, and only some phantoms of imagination seduce you to Italy.

I am afraid, however, that my counsel is vain, yet I have eased my heart by giving it.

When Queen Mary took the resolution of sheltering herself in England, the Archbishop of St. Andrew's attempting to dissuade her,[1] attended on her journey and when they came to the irremeable[2] stream that separated the two kingdoms, walked by her side into the water, in the middle of which he seized her bridle, and with earnestness proportioned to her danger and his own affection, pressed her to return. The Queen went forward.—If the parallel reaches thus far; may it go no further. The tears stand in my eyes.

I am going into Derbyshire,[3] and hope to be followed by your good wishes, for I am with great affection, Your most humble servant,

SAM. JOHNSON

Any letters that come for me hither, will be sent me.

James Boswell
1740–1795

"I have discovered," James Boswell announced at age twenty-two in the journal he had just commenced, "that we may be in some degree whatever character we choose." The possibilities opened up by this discovery both exhilarated and troubled him. Neither the "choosing" nor the "being" turned out to be as simple as he expected, in part because some alternate choice always beckoned. In the pages of his journal, Boswell performed his excited choices and anxious reconsiderations. The oscillation did much to drive the intricate comedy and intermittent pathos, the energetic posing and fervent self-scrutiny of the diaries he kept all his adult life, and of the published books he crafted from them.

Boswell's parents had chosen their own characters early, and had stuck to them assiduously. His father was a Scots laird—heir to an ancient family and a landed estate—and a distinguished jurist, serving as justice on Scotland's highest courts. His mother was an impassioned Calvinist, who numbered among her many strictures an abhorrence of the theater; the actors' freedom of character-choice, which made the playhouse for her a place of sinful deception, would make it the site of a lifelong enchantment for her son. Boswell's parents had chosen firmly for their firstborn too. James was to become, like his father, an eminent lawyer and respectable landowner.

Boswell chafed at the narrowness of the scheme. Struggling (he later recalled) "against paternal affection, ambition, interest," he ran away to London for a short spell at age eighteen

---

1. Johnson draws on a semifictional account of Mary Queen of Scots' fateful decision to take refuge in England. According to this version, she crossed the river on horseback, attended by John Hamilton, Archbishop of

St. Andrews.
2. "Admitting no return" (Johnson's *Dictionary*).
3. The home of John Taylor.

and returned there at twenty-two, seeking a commission as a soldier with the king's personal bodyguard, a post that would have secured him lifelong residence in the city, flashy uniforms, and ample opportunities to display himself in them. While Boswell waited for this prospect to materialize (it never did), he found his real calling. He started to keep a copious journal, narrating each day in succession, dispatching the text in weekly packets to his friend John Johnston back home in Scotland. After Samuel Johnson befriended the young diarist, six months into his London stay, the friendship gave Boswell's journal a new purpose (to record the conversations of this dazzling talker) and his life a new direction. Returning to Scotland in 1766, Boswell took up the life his father had mapped for him, settling in Edinburgh, and becoming (as he haughtily informed his disreputable friend John Wilkes) "a Scottish lawyer, a Scottish laird, and a Scottish married man." In each of these roles, though, he repeatedly broke character. He went down to London almost every spring, ostensibly to cultivate his legal practice but really to renew his old absorptions: in theater, in sexual adventure, in the spellbinding company of Johnson and the group of artists, writers, and thinkers who surrounded him.

Boswell yearned to join their number not merely as admirer but as eminent author, and he soon did. Over the ensuing years, he produced much journalism and some verse, as well as three books in which he explored with increasing audacity the potential of his own diary as a public text—as a vehicle of entertainment, instruction, profit, and fame. He pursued for the journal form a print authority it had not previously possessed, devising ways for it to encroach upon, even to colonize, territory and tasks traditionally reserved to other genres: travel book, "character" sketch, biography. In his first attempt, *An Account of Corsica . . . and Memoirs of Pascal Paoli* (1769), he recast his original travel journal (rearranging the entries, dropping the dates) to produce a heroic portrait of his friend the liberator. In his second experiment, *A Journal of a Tour to the Hebrides with Samuel Johnson* (1785), which appeared the year after Johnson's death, the imperative to portraiture was even more pronounced. The public craved accounts of the lost titan, and this time Boswell met that demand a different way. He presented his journal *as* a journal, with scrupulously dated, plentifully narrated consecutive entries rich in the "minute details of daily life" that Johnson himself had stipulated as the criteria for good biography. The book struck readers as startlingly new. Some mocked it for its minutiae ("How are we all with rapture touched," exclaimed one versifier, "to see / Where, when, and at what hour, you swallowed tea!"), while many praised its veracity and abundance.

There was much more where that came from. In *The Life of Samuel Johnson, LL.D.* (1791), Boswell deployed the *Tour*'s techniques on a massive scale. Drawing on his diaries, and on years of arduous research among Johnson's many acquaintances, Boswell built a thousand-page biography that is largely a book of talk, of conversations diligently recorded and deftly dramatized, the culmination of the textual theater that Boswell had long practiced in manuscript. Johnson's capacious mind and imposing presence find embodiment in a text dense with accumulated time, told and retold over the span of almost three decades that stretches from Boswell's first Johnsonian journal entry to the biography's publication. Pleased with the book's commercial success, stung by charges that he had been either too partial to Johnson or too critical of him, Boswell worked at two further editions (in which his footnotes swelled with new information and rebuttals). He died at fifty-five, unmade by alcoholism, by venereal disease, and by the violent depressions that accompanied his ongoing uncertainty as to what he might "be" and had become.

His books sustained his fame, though ever since the *Life*'s first appearance, readers have debated the degree of its accuracy and the merits of its portraiture. Two centuries later, Boswell's biography has become a touchstone text for the problem of the "documentary"—the question of how art and "fact" should merge in representations of historical events. Over the past eighty years the debate has been deepened by the unexpected recovery of Boswell's original papers, including the diaries that he drew on and boasted of in his published books. The papers had long been given up for lost, but masses of them had actually been stashed and forgotten by various descendants in odd receptacles (cabinet, croquet box, grain loft) on estates scattered across Scotland and Ireland. The papers' recovery took more than twenty years; the process of their publication continues. Taken together, Boswell's papers and his published works make it possible to trace the intricate course by which the flux of his energetic, agitated life became fixed in text.

The Life of Samuel Johnson, LL.D.

[INTRODUCTION; BOSWELL'S METHOD]

To write the Life of him who excelled all mankind in writing the lives of others, and who, whether we consider his extraordinary endowments or his various works, has been equaled by few in any age, is an arduous, and may be reckoned in me a presumptuous task.

Had Dr. Johnson written his own life, in conformity with the opinion which he has given, that every man's life may be best written by himself;[1] had he employed in the preservation of his own history, that clearness of narration and elegance of language in which he has embalmed so many eminent persons, the world would probably have had the most perfect example of biography that was ever exhibited. But although he at different times, in a desultory manner, committed to writing many particulars of the progress of his mind and fortunes, he never had preserving diligence enough to form them into a regular composition. Of these memorials a few have been preserved; but the greater part was consigned by him to the flames, a few days before his death.

As I had the honor and happiness of enjoying his friendship for upwards of twenty years; as I had the scheme of writing his life constantly in view; as he was well apprised of this circumstance, and from time to time obligingly satisfied my inquiries, by communicating to me the incidents of his early years; as I acquired a facility in recollecting, and was very assiduous in recording, his conversation, of which the extraordinary vigor and vivacity constituted one of the first features of his character; and as I have spared no pains in obtaining materials concerning him, from every quarter where I could discover that they were to be found, and have been favored with the most liberal communications by his friends; I flatter myself that few biographers have entered upon such a work as this with more advantages; independent of literary abilities, in which I am not vain enough to compare myself with some great names who have gone before me in this kind of writing. * * *

Instead of melting down my materials into one mass, and constantly speaking in my own person, by which I might have appeared to have more merit in the execution of the work, I have resolved to adopt and enlarge upon the excellent plan of Mr. Mason, in his *Memoirs* of Gray.[2] Wherever narrative is necessary to explain, connect, and supply, I furnish it to the best of my abilities; but in the chronological series of Johnson's life, which I trace as distinctly as I can, year by year, I produce, wherever it is in my power, his own minutes,[3] letters, or conversation, being convinced that this mode is more lively, and will make my readers better acquainted with him, than even most of those were who actually knew him, but could know him only partially; whereas there is here an accumulation of intelligence from various points, by which his character is more fully understood and illustrated.

Indeed I cannot conceive a more perfect mode of writing any man's life than not only relating all the most important events of it in their order, but interweaving

1. In *Idler* No. 84.
2. William Mason constructed his *Memoirs* of Thomas Gray (1775) around a selection of the poet's letters.
3. Memoranda.

what he privately wrote, and said, and thought; by which mankind are enabled as it were to see him live, and to "live o'er each scene"[4] with him, as he actually advanced through the several stages of his life. Had his other friends been as diligent and ardent as I was, he might have been almost entirely preserved. As it is, I will venture to say that he will be seen in this work more completely than any man who has ever yet lived.

And he will be seen as he really was; for I profess to write, not his panegyric, which must be all praise, but his Life; which, great and good as he was, must not be supposed to be entirely perfect. To be as he was, is indeed subject of panegyric enough to any man in this state of being; but in every picture there should be shade as well as light, and when I delineate him without reserve, I do what he himself recommended, both by his precept[5] and his example. * * *

What I consider as the peculiar value of the following work is the quantity that it contains of Johnson's conversation; which is universally acknowledged to have been eminently instructive and entertaining; and of which the specimens that I have given upon a former occasion have been received with so much approbation that I have good grounds for supposing that the world will not be indifferent to more ample communications of a similar nature. * * *

I am fully aware of the objections which may be made to the minuteness on some occasions of my detail of Johnson's conversation, and how happily it is adapted for the petty exercise of ridicule, by men of superficial understanding and ludicrous fancy;[6] but I remain firm and confident in my opinion, that minute particulars are frequently characteristic,[7] and always amusing, when they relate to a distinguished man. I am therefore exceedingly unwilling that anything, however slight, which my illustrious friend thought it worth his while to express, with any degree of point,[8] should perish. * * *

Of one thing I am certain, that considering how highly the small portion which we have of the table talk and other anecdotes of our celebrated writers[9] is valued, and how earnestly it is regretted that we have not more, I am justified in preserving rather too many of Johnson's sayings than too few; especially as from the diversity of dispositions it cannot be known with certainty beforehand, whether what may seem trifling to some, and perhaps to the collector himself, may not be most agreeable to many; and the greater number that an author can please in any degree, the more pleasure does there arise to a benevolent mind.

To those who are weak enough to think this a degrading task, and the time and labor which have been devoted to it misemployed, I shall content myself with opposing the authority of the greatest man of any age, Julius Caesar, of whom Bacon observes, that "in his book of Apothegms which he collected, we see that he esteemed it more honor to make himself but a pair of tables, to take the wise and pithy words of others, than to have every word of his own to be made an apothegm or an oracle."

Having said thus much by way of introduction, I commit the following pages to the candor of the Public.

---

4. "To wake the soul by tender strokes of art, / To raise the genius, and to mend the heart, / To make mankind in conscious virtue bold, / Live o'er each scene, and be what they behold" (lines 1–4 of Pope's prologue to Addison's *Cato*).
5. Boswell proceeds to quote from *Rambler* No. 60 (see page 1264) in which Johnson articulates his biographical principles.
6. Boswell's Hebridean journal had already been parodied

in print for its "minuteness" and "detail."
7. Revealing of character.
8. "Remarkable turn of words or thought" (Johnson's *Dictionary*).
9. E.g., Joseph Spence's *Anecdotes, Observations and Characters of Books and Men, Collected from the Conversation of Mr. Pope*, which (though unpublished until 1820) Johnson drew on for his *Life* of Pope.

[CONVERSATIONS ABOUT HUME]

[21 July 1763] Next morning I found him alone, and have preserved the following fragments of his conversation. Of a gentleman[1] who was mentioned, he said, "I have not met with any man for a long time who has given me such general displeasure. He is totally unfixed in his principles, and wants to puzzle other people." I said his principles had been poisoned by a noted infidel writer,[2] but that he was, nevertheless, a benevolent good man. JOHNSON: "We can have no dependence upon that instinctive, that constitutional goodness which is not founded upon principle. I grant you that such a man may be a very amiable member of society. I can conceive him placed in such a situation that he is not much tempted to deviate from what is right; and as every man prefers virtue, when there is not some strong incitement to transgress its precepts, I can conceive him doing nothing wrong. But if such a man stood in need of money, I should not like to trust him; and I should certainly not trust him with young ladies, for *there* there is always temptation. Hume and other skeptical innovators are vain men, and will gratify themselves at any expense. Truth will not afford sufficient food to their vanity; so they have betaken themselves to error. Truth, Sir, is a cow which will yield such people no more milk, and so they are gone to milk the bull. If I could have allowed myself to gratify my vanity at the expense of truth, what fame might I have acquired. Everything which Hume has advanced against Christianity had passed through my mind long before he wrote. Always remember this, that after a system is well settled upon positive evidence, a few partial objections ought not to shake it. The human mind is so limited that it cannot take in all the parts of a subject, so that there may be objections raised against anything. There are objections against a *plenum*, and objections against a *vacuum*;[3] yet one of them must certainly be true."

I mentioned Hume's argument against the belief of miracles, that it is more probable that the witnesses to the truth of them are mistaken, or speak falsely, than that the miracles should be true. JOHNSON: "Why, Sir, the great difficulty of proving miracles should make us very cautious in believing them. But let us consider; although God has made Nature to operate by certain fixed laws, yet it is not unreasonable to think that he may suspend those laws, in order to establish a system highly advantageous to mankind. Now the Christian religion is a most beneficial system, as it gives us light and certainty where we were before in darkness and doubt. The miracles which prove it are attested by men who had no interest in deceiving us; but who, on the contrary, were told that they should suffer persecution, and did actually lay down their lives in confirmation of the truth of the facts which they asserted. Indeed, for some centuries the heathens did not pretend to deny the miracles; but said they were performed by the aid of evil spirits. This is a circumstance of great weight. Then, Sir, when we take the proofs derived from prophecies which have been so exactly fulfilled, we have most satisfactory evidence. Supposing a miracle possible, as to which, in my opinion, there can be no doubt, we have as strong evidence for the miracles in support of Christianity, as the nature of the thing admits."

At night Mr. Johnson and I supped in a private room at the Turk's Head coffeehouse, in the Strand. "I encourage this house (said he); for the mistress of it is a good civil woman, and has not much business."

1. Boswell's friend George Dempster.
2. The skeptical philosopher David Hume.
3. According to the scientific theory of the *plenum*, all space is full (*plenus*) of matter; the opposing theory postulated that there are parts of space that are empty (*vacuus*) of matter.

"Sir, I love the acquaintance of young people; because, in the first place, I don't like to think myself growing old. In the next place, young acquaintances must last longest, if they do last; and then, Sir, young men have more virtue than old men; they have more generous sentiments in every respect. I love the young dogs of this age: they have more wit and humor and knowledge of life than we had; but then the dogs are not so good scholars. Sir, in my early years I read very hard. It is a sad reflection, but a true one, that I knew almost as much at eighteen as I do now. My judgment, to be sure, was not so good; but I had all the facts. I remember very well, when I was at Oxford, an old gentleman said to me, 'Young man, ply your book diligently now, and acquire a stock of knowledge; for when years come upon you, you will find that poring upon books will be but an irksome task.'"

* * *

[26 October 1769] When we were alone, I introduced the subject of death, and endeavored to maintain that the fear of it might be got over. I told him that David Hume said to me, he was no more uneasy to think he should *not be* after this life, than that he *had not been* before he began to exist. JOHNSON: "Sir, if he really thinks so, his perceptions are disturbed; he is mad: if he does not think so, he lies. He may tell you, he holds his finger in the flame of a candle, without feeling pain; would you believe him? When he dies, he at least gives up all he has." BOSWELL: "Foote,[4] Sir, told me, that when he was very ill he was not afraid to die." JOHNSON: "It is not true, Sir. Hold a pistol to Foote's breast, or to Hume's breast, and threaten to kill them, and you'll see how they behave." BOSWELL: "But may we not fortify our minds for the approach of death?" Here I am sensible I was in the wrong, to bring before his view what he ever looked upon with horror; for although when in a celestial frame, in his *Vanity of Human Wishes*,[5] he has supposed death to be "kind Nature's signal for retreat," from this state of being to "a happier seat," his thoughts upon this awful change were in general full of dismal apprehensions. His mind resembled the vast amphitheater, the Colosseum at Rome. In the center stood his judgment, which, like a mighty gladiator, combated those apprehensions that, like the wild beasts of the Arena, were all around in cells, ready to be let out upon him. After a conflict, he drove them back into their dens; but not killing them, they were still assailing him. To my question, whether we might not fortify our minds for the approach of death, he answered, in a passion, "No, Sir, let it alone. It matters not how a man dies, but how he lives. The act of dying is not of importance, it lasts so short a time." He added (with an earnest look), "A man knows it must be so, and submits. It will do him no good to whine."

I attempted to continue the conversation. He was so provoked that he said, "Give us no more of this"; and was thrown into such a state of agitation, that he expressed himself in a way that alarmed and distressed me, showed an impatience that I should leave him, and when I was going away, called to me sternly, "Don't let us meet tomorrow."

I went home exceedingly uneasy. All the harsh observations which I had ever heard made upon his character crowded into my mind; and I seemed to myself like the man who had put his head into the lion's mouth a great many times with perfect safety, but at last had it bit off.

---

4. Samuel Foote (1721–1771), actor, playwright, and theatrical manager.

5. Johnson's imitation of Juvenal's tenth satire, lines 363–4 (see page 1260).

[DINNER WITH WILKES]

[May 1776] I am now to record a very curious incident in Dr. Johnson's life, which fell under my own observation; of which *pars magna fui*,[1] and which I am persuaded will, with the liberal-minded, be much to his credit.

My desire of being acquainted with celebrated men of every description had made me, much about the same time, obtain an introduction to Dr. Samuel Johnson and to John Wilkes, Esq.[2] Two men more different could perhaps not be selected out of all mankind. They had even attacked one another with some asperity in their writings; yet I lived in habits of friendship with both. I could fully relish the excellence of each; for I have ever delighted in that intellectual chemistry which can separate good qualities from evil in the same person.

Sir John Pringle,[3] "mine own friend and my Father's friend," between whom and Dr. Johnson I in vain wished to establish an acquaintance, as I respected and lived in intimacy with both of them, observed to me once, very ingeniously, "It is not in friendship as in mathematics, where two things, each equal to a third, are equal between themselves. You agree with Johnson as a middle quality, and you agree with me as a middle quality; but Johnson and I should not agree." Sir John was not sufficiently flexible, so I desisted, knowing, indeed, that the repulsion was equally strong on the part of Johnson, who, I know not from what cause, unless his being a Scotchman, had formed a very erroneous opinion of Sir John. But I conceived an irresistible wish, if possible, to bring Dr. Johnson and Mr. Wilkes together. How to manage it was a nice[4] and difficult matter.

My worthy booksellers[5] and friends, Messieurs Dilly in the Poultry, at whose hospitable and well-covered table I have seen a greater number of literary men than at any other, except that of Sir Joshua Reynolds, had invited me to meet Mr. Wilkes and some more gentlemen on Wednesday, May 15. "Pray," said I, "let us have Dr. Johnson."—"What, with Mr. Wilkes? not for the world," said Mr. Edward Dilly, "Dr. Johnson would never forgive me."—"Come," said I, "if you'll let me negotiate for you, I will be answerable that all shall go well." DILLY: "Nay, if you will take it upon you, I am sure I shall be very happy to see them both here."

Notwithstanding the high veneration which I entertained for Dr. Johnson, I was sensible that he was sometimes a little actuated by the spirit of contradiction, and by means of that I hoped I should gain my point. I was persuaded that if I had come upon him with a direct proposal, "Sir, will you dine in company with Jack Wilkes?" he would have flown into a passion, and would probably have answered, "Dine with Jack Wilkes, Sir! I'd as soon dine with Jack Ketch."[6] I therefore, while we were sitting quietly by ourselves at his house in an evening, took occasion to open my plan thus:—"Mr. Dilly, Sir, sends his respectful compliments to you, and would be happy if you would do him the honor to dine with him on Wednesday next along with me, as I must soon go to Scotland." JOHNSON: "Sir, I am obliged to Mr. Dilly. I will wait upon him:" BOSWELL: "Provided, Sir, I suppose, that the company which he is to have is agreeable to you." JOHNSON: "What do you mean, Sir? What do you take me

---

1. "I was no small part." (Virgil, *Aeneid* 2.5).
2. John Wilkes (1727–1797), libertine, satirist, and radical politician, had been expelled from Parliament for blasphemous and seditious libel. Johnson considered Wilkes an unprincipled philanderer and demagogue.
3. John Pringle (1707–1782), distinguished physician and

president of the Royal Society. Johnson disliked Pringle's freethinking religious views and his pro-American political convictions.
4. Delicate.
5. Publishers.
6. Famous 17th-century hangman.

for? Do you think I am so ignorant of the world, as to imagine that I am to prescribe to a gentleman what company he is to have at his table?" BOSWELL: "I beg your pardon, Sir, for wishing to prevent you from meeting people whom you might not like. Perhaps he may have some of what he calls his patriotic[7] friends with him." JOHNSON: "Well, Sir, and what then? What care I for his *patriotic friends?* Poh!" BOSWELL: "I should not be surprised to find Jack Wilkes there." JOHNSON: "And if Jack Wilkes *should* be there, what is that to *me*, Sir? My dear friend, let us have no more of this. I am sorry to be angry with you; but really it is treating me strangely to talk to me as if I could not meet any company whatever, occasionally." BOSWELL: "Pray forgive me, Sir. I meant well. But you shall meet whoever comes, for me." Thus I secured him, and told Dilly that he would find him very well pleased to be one of his guests on the day appointed.

Upon the much-expected Wednesday, I called on him about half an hour before dinner, as I often did when we were to dine out together, to see that he was ready in time, and to accompany him. I found him buffeting[8] his books, as upon a former occasion, covered with dust and making no preparation for going abroad. "How is this, Sir?" said I. "Don't you recollect that you are to dine at Mr. Dilly's?" JOHNSON: "Sir, I did not think of going to Dilly's: it went out of my head. I have ordered dinner at home with Mrs. Williams."[9] BOSWELL: "But, my dear Sir, you know you were engaged to Mr. Dilly, and I told him so. He will expect you, and will be much disappointed if you don't come." JOHNSON: "You must talk to Mrs. Williams about this."

Here was a sad dilemma. I feared that what I was so confident I had secured would yet be frustrated. He had accustomed himself to show Mrs. Williams such a degree of humane attention, as frequently imposed some restraint upon him; and I knew that if she should be obstinate, he would not stir. I hastened downstairs to the blind lady's room and told her I was in great uneasiness, for Dr. Johnson had engaged to me to dine this day at Mr. Dilly's, but that he had told me he had forgotten his engagement, and had ordered dinner at home. "Yes, Sir," said she, pretty peevishly, "Dr. Johnson is to dine at home." "Madam," said I "his respect for you is such that I know he will not leave you unless you absolutely desire it. But as you have so much of his company, I hope you will be good enough to forgo it for a day; as Mr. Dilly is a very worthy man, has frequently had agreeable parties at his house for Dr. Johnson, and will be vexed if the Doctor neglects him today. And then, Madam, be pleased to consider my situation; I carried the message, and I assured Mr. Dilly that Dr. Johnson was to come, and no doubt he has made a dinner, and invited a company, and boasted of the honor he expected to have. I shall be quite disgraced if the Doctor is not there." She gradually softened to my solicitations, which were certainly as earnest as most entreaties to ladies upon any occasion, and was graciously pleased to empower me to tell Dr. Johnson, "That all things considered, she thought he should certainly go." I flew back to him, still in dust, and careless of what should be the event,[1] "indifferent in his choice to go or stay";[2] but as soon as I had announced to him Mrs. Williams's consent, he roared, "Frank, a clean shirt," and was very soon dressed. When I had him fairly[3] seated in a hackney coach

---

7. Those in favor of diminishing the power of the monarch and supporting the rights of the American colonists. Johnson had recently written a political tract called *The Patriot* (1774) in which he attacked Wilkes and his supporters.
8. Vigorously cleaning.

9. An elderly blind woman who lived in Johnson's house as one of several dependents.
1. Not caring how the matter turned out.
2. Boswell adapts a line from Addison's *Cato:* "Indiff'rent in his choice to sleep or die" (5.1).
3. Securely.

with me, I exulted as much as a fortune hunter who has got an heiress into a post chaise with him to set out for Gretna Green.[4]

When we entered Mr. Dilly's drawing room, he found himself in the midst of a company he did not know. I kept myself snug and silent, watching how he would conduct himself. I observed him whispering to Mr. Dilly, "Who is that gentleman, Sir?"—"Mr. Arthur Lee."—JOHNSON: "Too, too, too" (under his breath), which was one of his habitual mutterings. Mr. Arthur Lee could not but be very obnoxious to Johnson, for he was not only a *patriot* but an *American*. He was afterwards minister from the United States at the court of Madrid. "And who is the gentleman in lace?"—"Mr. Wilkes, Sir." This information confounded him still more; he had some difficulty to restrain himself, and taking up a book, sat down upon a window seat and read, or at least kept his eye upon it intently for some time, till he composed himself. His feelings, I dare say, were awkward enough. But he no doubt recollected his having rated[5] me for supposing that he could be at all disconcerted by any company, and he, therefore, resolutely set himself to behave quite as an easy man of the world, who could adapt himself at once to the disposition and manners of those whom he might chance to meet.

The cheering sound of "Dinner is upon the table" dissolved his reverie, and we *all* sat down without any symptom of ill humor. There were present, besides Mr. Wilkes, and Mr. Arthur Lee, who was an old companion of mine when he studied physics at Edinburgh, Mr. (now Sir John) Miller, Dr. Lettsom, and Mr. Slater, the druggist. Mr. Wilkes placed himself next to Dr. Johnson and behaved to him with so much attention and politeness that he gained upon him insensibly.[6] No man eat[7] more heartily than Johnson, or loved better what was nice and delicate. Mr. Wilkes was very assiduous in helping him to some fine veal. "Pray give me leave, Sir—It is better here—A little of the brown—Some fat, Sir—A little of the stuffing—Some gravy—Let me have the pleasure of giving you some butter—Allow me to recommend a squeeze of this orange, or the lemon, perhaps, may have more zest."—"Sir, Sir, I am obliged to you, Sir," cried Johnson, bowing, and turning his head to him with a look for some time of "surly virtue,"[8] but, in a short while, of complacency.

Foote being mentioned, Johnson said, "He is not a good mimic." One of the company added, "A merry Andrew, a buffoon." JOHNSON: "But he has wit[9] too, and is not deficient in ideas, or in fertility and variety of imagery, and not empty of reading;[1] he has knowledge enough to fill up his part. One species of wit he has in an eminent degree, that of escape. You drive him into a corner with both hands; but he's gone, Sir, when you think you have got him—like an animal that jumps over your head. Then he has a great range for his wit; he never lets truth stand between him and a jest, and he is sometimes mighty coarse. Garrick is under many restraints from which Foote is free." WILKES: "Garrick's wit is more like Lord Chesterfield's." JOHNSON: "The first time I was in company with Foote was at Fitzherbert's.[2] Having no good opinion of the fellow, I was resolved not to be pleased; and it is very difficult to please a man against his will. I went on eating my dinner pretty sullenly, affecting not

---

4. A village just across the border in Scotland; it was the common destination of eloping couples who could thereby bypass the formalities and restrictions of the Anglican Church.
5. Chided.
6. Imperceptibly.

7. Ate (pronounced "ett").
8. Boswell quotes from Johnson's poem *London*.
9. Intelligence, cleverness.
1. Devoid of learning.
2. William Fitzherbert (1712–1772), landowner and politician.

to mind him. But the dog was so very comical, that I was obliged to lay down my knife and fork, throw myself back upon my chair, and fairly laugh it out. No, Sir, he was irresistible. He upon one occasion experienced, in an extraordinary degree, the efficacy of his powers of entertaining. Amongst the many and various modes which he tried of getting money, he became a partner with a small-beer brewer, and he was to have a share of the profits for procuring customers amongst his numerous acquaintance. Fitzherbert was one who took his small beer;[3] but it was so bad that the servants resolved not to drink it. They were at some loss how to notify[4] their resolution, being afraid of offending their master, who they knew liked Foote much as a companion. At last they fixed upon a little black boy, who was rather a favorite, to be their deputy and deliver their remonstrance; and having invested him with the whole authority of the kitchen, he was to inform Mr. Fitzherbert, in all their names, upon a certain day, that they would drink Foote's small beer no longer. On that day Foote happened to dine at Fitzherbert's, and this boy served at table; he was so delighted with Foote's stories, and merriment, and grimace,[5] that when he went downstairs, he told them, 'This is the finest man I have ever seen. I will not deliver your message. I will drink his small beer.'"

Somebody observed that Garrick could not have done this. WILKES: "Garrick would have made the small beer still smaller. He is now leaving the stage; but he will play Scrub[6] all his life." I knew that Johnson would let nobody attack Garrick but himself, as Garrick once said to me, and I had heard him praise his liberality; so to bring out his commendation of his celebrated pupil, I said, loudly, "I have heard Garrick is liberal." JOHNSON: "Yes, Sir, I know that Garrick has given away more money than any man in England that I am acquainted with, and that not from ostentatious views. Garrick was very poor when he began life; so when he came to have money, he probably was very unskillful in giving away, and saved when he should not. But Garrick began to be liberal as soon as he could; and I am of opinion, the reputation of avarice which he has had, has been very lucky for him and prevented his having many enemies. You despise a man for avarice, but do not hate him. Garrick might have been much better attacked for living with more splendor than is suitable to a player: if they had had the wit to have assaulted him in that quarter, they might have galled him more. But they have kept clamoring about his avarice, which has rescued him from much obloquy and envy."

Talking of the great difficulty of obtaining authentic information for biography, Johnson told us, "When I was a young fellow I wanted to write the *Life of Dryden*, and in order to get materials, I applied to the only two persons then alive who had seen him; these were old Swinney, and old Cibber.[7] Swinney's information was no more than this, "That at Will's coffeehouse Dryden had a particular chair for himself, which was set by the fire in winter, and was then called his winter-chair; and that it was carried out for him to the balcony in summer, and was then called his summer-chair." Cibber could tell no more but "that he remembered him a decent old man, arbiter of critical disputes at Will's." You are to consider that Cibber was then at a great distance from Dryden, had perhaps one leg only in the room, and

---

3. Weak beer.
4. Express.
5. Exaggerated facial expressions (Foote specialized in caricatures of his contemporaries).
6. A character in George Farquhar's comedy, *The Beaux'*

Stratagem.
7. Owen Mac Swiney and Colley Cibber, actors from the first half of the 18th century. Cibber was also a poet, playwright, and the author of a widely read autobiography (his *Apology*).

durst not draw in the other." BOSWELL: "Yet Cibber was a man of observation?" JOHNSON: "I think not." BOSWELL: "You will allow his *Apology* to be well done." JOHNSON: "Very well done, to be sure, Sir. That book is a striking proof of the justice of Pope's remark:

> Each might his several province well command,
> Would all but stoop to what they understand."[8]

BOSWELL: "And his plays are good." JOHNSON: "Yes; but that was his trade; *l'esprit du corps:* he had been all his life among players and play-writers. I wondered that he had so little to say in conversation, for he had kept the best company, and learnt all that can be got by the ear. He abused Pindar[9] to me, and then showed me an ode of his own, with an absurd couplet, making a linnet soar on an eagle's wing. I told him that when the ancients made a simile, they always made it like something real."

Mr. Wilkes remarked, that "among all the bold flights of Shakespeare's imagination, the boldest was making Birnam Wood march to Dunsinane,[1] creating a wood where there never was a shrub; a wood in Scotland! ha! ha! ha!" And he also observed that "the clannish slavery of the Highlands of Scotland was the single exception to Milton's remark[2] of 'The mountain nymph, sweet Liberty,' being worshipped in all hilly countries." "When I was at Inverary," said he, "on a visit to my old friend, Archibald, Duke of Argyle, his dependents congratulated me on being such a favorite of his Grace. I said, 'It is then, gentlemen, truly lucky for me; for if I had displeased the Duke, and he had wished it, there is not a Campbell among you but would have been ready to bring John Wilkes's head to him in a charger. It would have been only

Off with his head! So much for Aylesbury.[3]

I was then member[4] for Aylesbury." * * *

Mr. Arthur Lee mentioned some Scotch who had taken possession of a barren part of America, and wondered why they should choose it. JOHNSON: "Why, Sir, all barrenness is comparative. The *Scotch* would not know it to be barren." BOSWELL: "Come, come, he is flattering the English. You have now been in Scotland, Sir, and say if you did not see meat and drink enough there." JOHNSON: "Why yes, Sir; meat and drink enough to give the inhabitants sufficient strength to run away from home." All these quick and lively sallies were said sportively, quite in jest, and with a smile, which showed that he meant only wit. Upon this topic he and Mr. Wilkes could perfectly assimilate; here was a bond of union between them, and I was conscious that as both of them had visited Caledonia,[5] both were fully satisfied of the strange narrow ignorance of those who imagine that it is a land of famine. But they amused themselves with persevering in the old jokes. When I claimed a superiority for Scotland over England in one respect, that no man can be arrested there for a debt merely because another swears it against him; but there must first be the judgment of a court of law ascertaining its

---

8. Pope, *Essay on Criticism*, lines 66–67.
9. Spoke disparagingly of the ancient Greek poet Pindar, famous for his odes.
1. In Act 5 of *Macbeth*. In his *Journey to the Western Islands* (1775), Johnson had commented repeatedly on the treelessness of Scotland.

2. In his poem *L'Allegro* (36).
3. Wilkes adapts Colley Cibber's popular version of Shakespeare's *Richard III*, which contains the line, "Off with his head. So much for Buckingham."
4. Of Parliament.
5. Scotland (from the Roman name for North Britain).

justice; and that a seizure of the person, before judgment is obtained, can take place only if his creditor should swear that he is about to fly from the country, or, as it is technically expressed, is *in meditatione fugae*. WILKES: "That, I should think, may be safely sworn of all the Scotch nation." JOHNSON (to Mr. Wilkes): "You must know, Sir, I lately took my friend Boswell and showed him genuine civilized life in an English provincial town. I turned him loose at Lichfield, my native city, that he might see for once real civility: for you know he lives among savages in Scotland, and among rakes in London." WILKES: "Except when he is with grave, sober, decent people like you and me." JOHNSON (smiling): "And we ashamed of him."

They were quite frank and easy. Johnson told the story of his asking Mrs. Macaulay[6] to allow her footman to sit down with them, to prove the ridiculousness of the argument for the equality of mankind; and he said to me afterwards, with a nod of satisfaction, "You saw Mr. Wilkes acquiesced." Wilkes talked with all imaginable freedom of the ludicrous title given to the Attorney General, *Diabolus Regis*,[7] adding, "I have reason to know something about that officer; for I was prosecuted for a libel."[8] Johnson, who many people would have supposed must have been furiously angry at hearing this talked of so lightly, said not a word. He was now, *indeed*, "a good-humored fellow."

After dinner we had an accession[9] of Mrs. Knowles, the Quaker lady, well known for her various talents, and of Mr. Alderman Lee. Amidst some patriotic groans, somebody (I think the Alderman) said, "Poor old England is lost." JOHNSON: "Sir, it is not so much to be lamented that Old England is lost, as that the Scotch have found it."[1] WILKES: "Had Lord Bute governed Scotland only, I should not have taken the trouble to write his eulogy, and dedicate *Mortimer* to him."[2]

Mr. Wilkes held a candle to show a fine print of a beautiful female figure which hung in the room, and pointed out the elegant contour of the bosom with the finger of an arch connoisseur. He afterwards, in a conversation with me, waggishly insisted that all the time Johnson showed visible signs of a fervent admiration of the corresponding charms of the fair Quaker.

This record, though by no means so perfect as I could wish, will serve to give a notion of a very curious interview, which was not only pleasing at the time, but had the agreeable and benignant effect of reconciling any animosity, and sweetening any acidity, which in the various bustle of political contest, had been produced in the minds of two men, who though widely different, had so many things in common— classical learning, modern literature, wit, and humor, and ready repartee—that it would have been much to be regretted if they had been forever at a distance from each other.

Mr. Burke gave me much credit for this successful *negotiation* and pleasantly said that "there was nothing to equal it in the whole history of the *Corps Diplomatique*."

6. Catherine Macaulay, author of a controversial *History of England* (1763–1783). In order to test her egalitarian principles, Johnson had proposed that she invite her footman to join them at dinner. "I thus, Sir, showed her the absurdity of the levelling doctrine," he told Boswell. "She has never liked me since."

7. The King's Devil.

8. See n. 2, page 1287.

9. I.e., these additional guests arrived: Mary Morris Knowles (1733–1807), a highly accomplished needlewoman whose "sutile pictures" Johnson praised in a letter to Mrs. Thrale; and William Lee (1739–1795), merchant, diplomat, and the only American ever elected an alderman of London.

1. Soon after succeeding to the throne in 1760, George III made his former tutor, the Scottish Earl of Bute, Prime Minister of Britain. The appointment unleashed a flood of anti-Scottish propaganda.

2. As part of a sustained campaign against Bute's government, Wilkes had chosen to reprint a 1731 play called *The Fall of Mortimer* and had prefaced it with a mock-respectful dedication to the prime minister.

I attended Dr. Johnson home, and had the satisfaction to hear him tell Mrs. Williams how much he had been pleased with Mr. Wilkes's company, and what an agreeable day he had passed.

[CONVERSATIONS AT STREATHAM AND THE CLUB][1]

[30 March 1778] I mentioned that I had in my possession the Life of Sir Robert Sibbald, the celebrated Scottish antiquary, and founder of the Royal College of Physicians at Edinburgh, in the original manuscript in his own handwriting; and that it was I believed the most natural and candid account of himself that ever was given by any man. As an instance, he tells that the Duke of Perth, then Chancellor of Scotland, pressed him very much to come over to the Roman Catholic faith; that he resisted all his Grace's arguments for a considerable time, till one day he felt himself, as it were, instantaneously convinced, and with tears in his eyes ran into the Duke's arms, and embraced the ancient religion; that he continued very steady in it for some time, and accompanied his Grace to London one winter, and lived in his household; that there he found the rigid fasting prescribed by the church very severe upon him; that this disposed him to reconsider the controversy, and having then seen that he was in the wrong, he returned to Protestantism. I talked of some time or other publishing this curious life. MRS. THRALE: "I think you had as well let alone that publication. To discover[2] such weakness exposes a man when he is gone." JOHNSON: "Nay, it is an honest picture of human nature. How often are the primary motives of our greatest actions as small as Sibbald's, for his re-conversion." MRS. THRALE: "But may they not as well be forgotten?" JOHNSON: "No, Madam, a man loves to review his own mind. That is the use of a diary, or journal." LORD TRIMLESTOWN: "True, Sir. As the ladies love to see themselves in a glass, so a man likes to see himself in his journal." BOSWELL: "A very pretty allusion." JOHNSON: "Yes, indeed." BOSWELL: "And as a lady adjusts her dress before a mirror, a man adjusts his character by looking at his journal." I next year found the very same thought in Atterbury's *Funeral Sermon on Lady Cutts*, where, having mentioned her *Diary*, he says, "In this glass she every day dressed her mind." This is a proof of coincidence, and not of plagiarism; for I had never read that sermon before.

Next morning, while we were at breakfast, Johnson gave a very earnest recommendation of what he himself practiced with the utmost conscientiousness: I mean a strict attention to truth, even in the most minute particulars. "Accustom your children," said he, "constantly to this; if a thing happened at one window, and they, when relating it, say that it happened at another, do not let it pass, but instantly check them; you do not know where deviation from truth will end." BOSWELL: "It may come to the door: and when once an account is at all varied in one circumstance, it may by degrees be varied so as to be totally different from what really happened." Our lively hostess, whose fancy was impatient of the rein,[3] fidgeted at this, and ventured to say, "Nay, this is too much. If Mr. Johnson should forbid me to drink tea, I would comply, as I should feel the restraint only twice a day; but little variations in narrative must happen a thousand times a day, if one is not perpetually watching." JOHNSON: "Well, Madam, and you *ought* to be perpetually watching. It is more from carelessness about truth than from intentional lying, that there is so much falsehood in the world."

1. These were two of Johnson's favorite venues of conversation. Streatham was the country estate of Henry and Hester Thrale, where Johnson and his friends were often guests. The Club was a group of distinguished thinkers, writers, artists, and statesman that met weekly.
2. Reveal.
3. Whose imagination did not like to be restrained.

In his review of Dr. Warton's *Essay on the Writings and Genius of Pope*, Johnson has given the following salutary caution upon this subject:

"Nothing but experience could evince[4] the freqency of false information, or enable any man to conceive that so many groundless reports should be propagated, as every man of eminence may hear of himself. Some men relate what they think, as what they know; some men of confused memories and habitual inaccuracy ascribe to one man what belongs to another; and some talk on, without thought or care. A few men are sufficient to broach falsehoods, which are afterwards innocently diffused by successive relaters."

Had he lived to read what Sir John Hawkins and Mrs. Piozzi have related concerning himself[5] how much would he have found his observation illustrated. He was indeed so much impressed with the prevalence of falsehood, voluntary or unintentional, that I never knew any person who upon hearing an extraordinary circumstance told, discovered more of the *incredulus odi*.[6] He would say, with a significant look and decisive tone, "It is not so. Do not tell this again." He inculcated upon all his friends the importance of perpetual vigilance against the slightest degrees of falsehood; the effect of which, as Sir Joshua Reynolds observed to me, has been, that all who were of his *school* are distinguished for a love of truth and accuracy, which they would not have possessed in the same degree, if they had not been acquainted with Johnson.

Talking of ghosts, he said, "It is wonderful that five thousand years have now elapsed since the creation of the world, and still it is undecided whether or not there has ever been an instance of the spirit of any person appearing after death. All argument is against it; but all belief is for it."

He said, "John Wesley's[7] conversation is good, but he is never at leisure. He is always obliged to go at a certain hour. This is very disagreeable to a man who loves to fold his legs and have out his talk, as I do."

On Friday, April 3, I dined with him in London, in a company where were present several eminent men, whom I shall not name, but distinguish their parts in the conversation by different letters.[8]

F: "I have been looking at this famous antique marble dog of Mr. Jennings, valued at a thousand guineas, said to be Alcibiades's dog."[9] JOHNSON: "His tail then must be docked.[1] That was the mark of Alcibiades's dog." E: "A thousand guineas! The representation of no animal whatever is worth so much. At this rate a dead dog would indeed be better than a living lion." JOHNSON: "Sir, it is not the worth of the thing, but of the skill in forming it which is so highly estimated. Everything that enlarges the sphere of human powers, that shows man he can do what he thought he could not do, is valuable. The first man who balanced a straw upon his nose; Johnson,[2] who rode upon three horses at a time; in short, all such men deserved the applause of mankind, not on account of the use of what they

---

4. Prove, serve as evidence of.
5. Boswell refers to the two rival biographies, Sir John Hawkins's *Life of Samuel Johnson LL.D.* (1787) and Hester Thrale Piozzi's *Anecdotes of the Late Samuel Johnson LL.D.* (1786).
6. Hostile incredulity.
7. Co-founder (1703–1791) of the Methodist movement.
8. "F" stands for John Fitzpatrick, Earl of Upper Ossory, an Irish nobleman; "E" for Edmund Burke, statesman and political theorist; "R" for Richard Brinsley Sheridan, playwright; "C" or George Fordyce, a chemist; "P" for Sir Joshua Reynolds ("Painter").
9. A marble statue purchased in Rome by the collector Henry Jennings, it was called after an antique sculpture in the Uffizi, Florence.
1. Clipped.
2. An acrobatic rider (no relation).

did, but of the dexterity which they exhibited." BOSWELL: "Yet a misapplication of time and assiduity is not to be encouraged. Addison, in one of his *Spectators*, commends the judgment of a king, who, as a suitable reward to a man that by long perseverance had attained to the art of throwing a barleycorn through the eye of a needle, gave him a bushel of barley." JOHNSON: "He must have been a king of Scotland, where barley is scarce." F: "One of the most remarkable antique figures of an animal is the boar at Florence." JOHNSON: "The first boar that is well made in marble should be preserved as a wonder. When men arrive at a facility of making boars well, then the workmanship is not of such value, but they should however be preserved as examples, and as a greater security for the restoration of the art, should it be lost."

E: "We hear prodigious complaints at present of emigration. I am convinced that emigration makes a country more populous." J: "That sounds very much like a paradox." E: "Exportation of men, like exportation of all other commodities, makes more be produced." JOHNSON: "But there would be more people were there not emigration, provided there were food for more." E: "No; leave a few breeders, and you'll have more people than if there were no emigration." JOHNSON: "Nay, Sir, it is plain there will be more people, if there are more breeders. Thirty cows in good pasture will produce more calves than ten cows, provided they have good bulls." E: "There are bulls enough in Ireland."[3] JOHNSON (smiling): "So, Sir, I should think from your argument." * * *

E: "The Irish language is not primitive; it is Teutonic, a mixture of the northern tongues: it has much English in it." JOHNSON: "It may have been radically Teutonic; but English and High Dutch have no similarity to the eye, though radically the same. Once, when looking into Low Dutch, I found, in a whole page, only one word similar to English; *stroem*, like *stream*, and it signified *tide*." E: "I remember having seen a Dutch sonnet, in which I found this word, *roesnopies*. Nobody would at first think that this could be English; but, when we inquire, we find *roes*, rose, and *nopie*, knob; so we have *rosebuds*."

JOHNSON: "I have been reading Thicknesse's travels, which I think are entertaining." BOSWELL: "What, Sir, a good book?" JOHNSON: "Yes, Sir, to read once; I do not say you are to make a study of it and digest it; and I believe it to be a true book in his intention. All travelers generally mean to tell truth; though Thicknesse observes, upon Smollett's account[4] of his alarming a whole town in France by firing a blunderbuss, and frightening a French nobleman till he made him tie on his portmanteau, that he would be loath to say Smollett had told two lies in one page; but he had found the only town in France where these things could have happened. Travelers must often be mistaken. In everything, except where mensuration can be applied, they may honestly differ. There has been, of late, a strange turn in travelers to be displeased."

E: "From the experience which I have had—and I have had a great deal—I have learnt to think *better* of mankind." JOHNSON: "From my experience I have found them worse in commercial dealings, more disposed to cheat, than I had any notion of; but more disposed to do one another good than I had conceived." J: "Less just and more beneficent." JOHNSON: "And really it is wonderful, consider-

3. An "Irish bull" was a foolish blunder.
4. Philip Thicknesse, *A Year's Journey through France and*

Spain (1777); Tobias Smollett, *Travels in France and Italy* (1766).

ing how much attention is necessary for men to take care of themselves, and ward off immediate evils which press upon them, it is wonderful how much they do for others. As it is said of the greatest liar, that he tells more truth than falsehood; so it may be said of the worst man, that he does more good than evil." BOSWELL: "Perhaps from experience men may be found *happier* than we suppose." JOHNSON: "No, Sir; the more we inquire, we shall find men the less happy." P: "As to thinking better or worse of mankind from experience, some cunning people will not be satisfied unless they have put men to the test, as they think. There is a very good story told of Sir Godfrey Kneller, in his character of a justice of the peace. A gentleman brought his servant before him, upon an accusation of having stolen some money from him; but it having come out that he had laid it purposely in the servant's way, in order to try his honesty, Sir Godfrey sent the master to prison." JOHNSON: "To resist temptation once is not a sufficient proof of honesty. If a servant, indeed, were to resist the continued temptation of silver lying in a window, as some people let it lie, when he is sure his master does not know how much there is of it, he would give a strong proof of honesty. But this is a proof to which you have no right to put a man. You know, humanly speaking, there is a certain degree of temptation which will overcome any virtue. Now, in so far as you approach temptation to a man, you do him an injury; and, if he is overcome, you share his guilt." P: "And, when once overcome, it is easier for him to be got the better of again." BOSWELL: "Yes, you are his seducer; you have debauched him. I have known a man resolve to put friendship to the test by asking a friend to lend him money merely with that view, when he did not want it." JOHNSON: "That is very wrong, Sir. Your friend may be a narrow man, and yet have many good qualities: narrowness may be his only fault. Now you are trying his general character as a friend, by one particular singly, in which he happens to be defective, when, in truth, his character is composed of many particulars."

E: "I understand the hogshead[5] of claret, which this society was favored with by our friend the Dean, is nearly out; I think he should be written to, to send another of the same kind. Let the request be made with a happy ambiguity of expression, so that we may have the chance of his sending *it* also as a present." JOHNSON: "I am willing to offer my services as secretary on this occasion." P: "As many as are for Dr. Johnson being secretary hold up your hands.—Carried unanimously." BOSWELL: "He will be our Dictator." JOHNSON: "No, the company is to dictate to me. I am only to write for wine; and I am quite disinterested, as I drink none; I shall not be suspected of having forged the application. I am no more than humble *scribe*." E: "Then you shall *prescribe*." BOSWELL: "Very well. The first play of words today." J: "No, no; the *bulls* in Ireland." JOHNSON: "Were I your Dictator you should have no wine. It would be my business *cavere ne quid detrimenti Respublica caperet*,[6] and wine is dangerous. Rome was ruined by luxury" (smiling). E: "If you allow no wine as Dictator, you shall not have me for your master of horse."[7]

1791

5. A large barrel.
6. "To ensure that no harm befall the republic." Johnson quotes from the *Senatus Consultum Ultimum*, a declaration of public emergency by the Roman senate. This declaration suspended ordinary laws and appointed a dictator for the duration of the emergency.
7. Under the emergency decree, the master of the horse served as second in command to the dictator.

Hester Salusbury Thrale Piozzi
1740–1821

Hester Salusbury Thrale Piozzi: the litany of last names tells some of her story. She was born to the Salusburys, an aristocratic and in some branches wealthy Welsh family; both her parents could claim the bloodline, neither of them the wealth. So she was wed at age twenty-three to Henry Thrale, a successful English brewer twelve years her senior, for whom she neither felt nor feigned love. She accepted his proposal in order to secure for her family a large bequest that hinged on her being married. Nonetheless, she threw herself with a will into domestic life at Streatham, Henry's estate six miles outside London. She bore twelve children and mourned eight of them, dead in infancy or childhood. She worked hard helping her husband to advance his endless commercial and political aspirations. And she hosted frequent gatherings of eminent houseguests, with Samuel Johnson the most frequent and most eminent of them all. Johnson had met the Thrales in 1765 and valued them both, Henry for his affability, Hester for her wide curiosity, sharp conversation, and attentive care. For nearly two decades she made Streatham Johnson's second home, and a center of British intellectual life.

Hester Thrale had always read and written plentifully, and in her early twenties had published some short verse in newspapers. During her marriage to Thrale her writing remained mostly a matter of manuscript—occasional poems, innumerable letters, and two sustained autobiographical documents: *The Family Book,* in which she recorded the progress of her offspring, and *Thraliana,* a text more her own, in which she recorded talk, thought, experience, feeling, "and in fine, every thing that struck me at the time." Johnson had recommended the practice, and her husband had given her the handsomely bound blank books in which to pursue it. In those volumes she detailed (among many other things) her intricate connection and her frequent exasperation with both men.

At Henry's death in 1781, much changed. Helped by Johnson, Hester Thrale managed and then sold the brewery. Despite objections by Johnson, and by almost all her family and friends, she fell deeply in love for the only time in her life, with the Italian musician Gabriel Piozzi. Foreign, Roman Catholic, irascible, and not rich, Piozzi combined traits that alienated virtually everyone in Thrale's once cohesive world. Friends marveled at the sudden prevalence of passion in a woman who had once been, as one of them lamented, "the best mother, the best wife, the best friend, the most amiable member of society. . . . I am myself convinced that the poor woman is mad." So were many others, but in the summer of 1784, the "poor woman" married her beloved and departed with him for Italy, leaving in her wake a cacophony, in gossip and newsprint, of scandal and scorn.

In her new marriage and new country, Hester Piozzi launched her career as published author. She produced *Anecdotes of the Late Samuel Johnson* (1786), culled from *Thraliana;* a collection of Johnson's *Letters* (1788); *Observations and Reflections* (1789), reworked from her journal of a tour through Europe; and *British Synonymy* (1794), an anecdotal survey of the overlapping meanings of English words. Piozzi's books brought her equivocal fame at best, heavily mixed with retrospectives on her history as celebrated hostess and social renegade. She spent her last decades in England, Wales, and (after Piozzi's death) at Bath, where she once reported with amusement that a tourist had "brought his son here, that he might see the *first woman in England.* So I am now grown one of the curiosities of Bath, it seems, and *one of the Antiquities.*" Her writing, though, has too much edge to pass as harmless "curiosity." When her *Anecdotes of Johnson* first appeared, Horace Walpole voiced a common complaint: "Her panegyric is loud in praise of her hero; and almost every fact she relates disgraces him." Walpole exaggerates, but the push-pull that he points to is one aspect that makes her work still fascinating. Again and again she immerses herself energetically in the conventional roles assigned to women ("best mother," "best wife," "best friend"), then steps aside to examine them askance, to question, to debunk, even to renounce them. Vibrating between acquiescence and anger, sentimentality and acerbity, Hester Salusbury Thrale Piozzi struck a note of her own, making for herself an interesting life, and a various and idiosyncratic body of work.

from The Family Book

[ON HER DAUGHTER'S PROGRESS]

Hester Maria Thrale born on the 17th September 1764 at her father's house, Southwark.[1]

This is to serve as a memorandum of her corporeal and mental powers at the age of two years, to which she is arrived this 17 September 1766. She can walk and run alone up and down all smooth places though pretty steep, and though the backstring[2] is still kept on it is no longer of use. She is perfectly healthy, of a lax constitution, and is strong enough to carry a hound-puppy two months old quite across the lawn at Streatham; also to carry a bowl[3] such as are used on bowling greens up the mount to the tubs.[4] She is neither remarkably big nor tall, being just 34 inches high, but eminently pretty. She can speak most words and speak them plain enough too, but is no great talker. She repeats the Pater Noster,[5] the three Christian virtues[6] and the signs of the zodiac in Watt's verses;[7]; she likewise knows them on the globe perfectly well. She can tell all her letters great and small and spell little words as D,o,g, Dog, C,a,t, Cat etc. She knows her nine figures and the simplest combinations of 'em as 3, 4, 34; 6, 8, 68; but none beyond a hundred. She knows all the heathen deities by their attributes and counts 20 without missing one. Signed—H. L. Thrale.

Sponsors[8] to H. M. T.: Mrs. Salusbury, Mrs. Nesbitt, and Sir John Lade.

* * *

Hester Maria Thrale,   London 17 March 1767.

Six months have now elapsed since I wrote down an account of what she could do; the following is for a record of the amazing improvements made in this last half year; her person has however undergone no visible change. She cannot read at all, but knows the compass as perfectly as any mariner upon the seas; is mistress of the solar system, can trace the orbits, and tell the arbitrary marks of the planets as readily as Dr. Bradley.[9] The comets she knows at sight when represented upon paper, and all the chief constellations on the celestial globe. The signs of the zodiac she is thoroughly acquainted with, as also the difference between the ecliptic and equator. She has too by the help of the dissected maps acquired so nice a knowledge of geography as to be well able to describe not only the four quarters of the world, but almost, nay, I do think every nation on the terrestrial globe, and all the principal islands in all parts of the world. These—with the most remarkable seas, gulfs, straits, etc.—she has so full an acquaintance with, that she discovers them colored, or penciled, separate or together in any scale small or great, map or globe. She can repeat likewise the names of all the capital cities in Europe besides those of Persia and India—China I mean; also the 3 Christian virtues in English, the 4 cardinal ones in Latin[1], the 1st page of Lily's Grammar[2] to the bottom, the seven days of the week, the 12 months of

---

1. In this borough across the river from London, the Thrales owned a city home adjacent to their brewery.
2. A cord at the back of the pinafore, sometimes held like a leash to keep the infant from harm.
3. A bowling ball.
4. Watering troughs.
5. The Lord's Prayer.

6. Faith, hope, and charity (1 Corinthians 13.13).
7. Isaac Watts, poet and hymnist whose *Divine Songs for the Use of Children* (1715) includes a poem on the zodiac.
8. Godparents.
9. James Bradley (1693–1762), eminent astronomer.
1. Prudence, temperance, fortitude, and justice.
2. A Latin textbook.

the Year, the twos of the multiplication table, the four points of the compass, the four quarters of the world, the Pater Noster, the Nicene Creed and the Decalogue;[3] the responses of the church catechism to the end of the duty to our neighbor, and the names of the richest, wisest, and meekest man, etc. She has also in these last six months learned to distinguish colors, and to name them; as also to tell a little story with some grace and emphasis, as the story of the Fall of Man, of Perseus and Andromeda, of the Judgment of Paris, and two or three more. These are certainly uncommon performances of a baby 2 years and 6 months only; but they are most strictly true. She cannot however read at all. * * *

17 September 1767. A little blue-cover book will now best show the further acquisitions of Hester M. Thrale who has this day completed the second and begun the third[4] year of her life by repeating all the responses in that book by heart—this 17 September 1767 at Brighthelmstone.[5] She is yet a miserable poor speller, and can scarce read a word.

* * *

17 December 1768. Hester Maria Thrale is this day four years and a quarter old. I have made her up a little red book to which I must appeal for her progress in improvements. She went through it this day quite well. The astronomical part is the hardest. She can now read tolerably, but not at sight, and has a manner of reading that is perfectly agreeable, free from tone or accent. At 3 years and a half however she wrote some cards to her friends with a print taken from the picture which Zoffany[6] drew of her at 20 months old; but as I lay in[7] soon after, the writing was totally forgotten, and is now all to begin again. She has this day repeated her catechism quite through, her Latin grammar to the end of the 5 declensions, a fable in Phaedrus, an epigram in Martial,[8] the revolutions, diameters, and distance of the planets. She is come vastly forward in sense and expression and once more I appeal to her little red book. With regard to her person, it is accounted exquisitely pretty. Her hair is sandy, her eyes of a very dark blue, and their luster particularly fine; her complexion delicate, and her carriage[9] uncommonly genteel. Her temper is not so good; reserved to all, insolent where she is free, and sullen to those who teach or dress or do anything towards her. Never in a passion, but obstinate to that uncommon degree that no punishment except severe smart[1] can prevail on her to beg pardon if she has offended.

[ON THE DEATH OF HER SON]

[March 1776] On Thursday the 21st they all[1] rose well and lively, and Queeney went with me to fetch her sister from school for a week. She seemed sullen all the way there and back but not sick, so I huffed her and we got home in good time to dress for dinner, when we expected Sir Robert Cotton and the Davenants.[2] Harry however had seen a play of his friend Murphy's[3] advertised, and teased me so to let him see it that I could not resist his importunity, and treated one of our principle clerks to go

---

3. The Ten Commandments.

4. I.e., completed the third and begun the fourth.

5. Brighton, a popular seaside resort, where the Thrales kept a house for use each autumn.

6. Johann Zoffany (1733–1810), a portraitist much in demand by royal, aristocratic, and merchant families (see his portrait of Queen Charlotte and her children, page 918).

7. Gave birth (to her fourth child) and convalesced.

8. Phaedrus translated Aesop's *Fables* from Greek into Latin; Martial was a Roman poet celebrated for his short,

witty verses.

9. Bearing

1. I.e., a whipping (with a rod that was kept on the nursery mantle).

1. I.e., the three children now at home: Hester ("Queeney"), Henry (the only son, now nine years old), and Sophy (four); the sister at school was Susan (five).

2. Cousins of Hester Thrale.

3. Arthur Murphy (1727–1805), Irish actor, playwright, and friend of the family.

with him. He came home at 12 o'clock half mad with delight, and in such spirits, health, and happiness that nothing ever exceeded. Queeney however drooped all afternoon, complained of the headache, and Mr. Thrale was so cross at my giving Harry leave to go to the play, instead of showing him to Sir Robert, that I passed an uneasy time of it, and could not enjoy the praises given to Susan, I was so fretted about the two eldest. When Harry came home so happy, however, all was forgotten, and he went to rest in perfect tranquility. Queeney however felt hot, and I was not at all pleased with her, but on Friday morning the boy rose quite cheerful and did our little business with great alacrity. Count Manucci[4] came to breakfast by appointment. We were all to go show him the Tower[5] forsooth, so Queeney made light of her illness and pressed me to take her too. There was one of the ships bound for Boston now in the river with our beer aboard.[6] Harry ran to see the blaze in the morning and coming back to the counting-house, "I see," he says to our first clerk, "I see your porter[7] is good, Mr. Perkins, for it *burns* special well." Well by this time we set out for the Tower, Papa and Manucci and the children and I. Queeney was not half well, but Harry continued in high spirits both among the lions and the arms, repeating passages from the English history, examining the artillery and getting into every mortar[8] till he was as black as the ground. Count Manucci observed his pranks, and said he must be a soldier with him; but Harry would not fight for the Grand Duke of Tuscany because he was a Papist, and "Look here," said he, showing the instruments of torture to the Count, "what those Spanish Papists intended for *us*." From the place we drove to Moore's Carpet Manufactory, where the boy was still active, attentive, and lively. But as Queeney's looks betrayed the sickness she would fain have concealed, we drove homewards, taking in our way Brooke's Menagerie, where I just stopped to speak about my peafowl. Here Harry was happy again with a lion intended for a show who was remarkably tame, and a monkey so beautiful and gentle, that I was as much pleased with him as the children. Here we met a Mr. Hervey who took notice of the boy how *well* he looked. "Yes," said I, "if the dirt were scraped off him." It was now time to get home, and Harry after saying how hungry he was, instantly "pounced" as he called it on a piece of cold mutton and spent the afternoon among us all recounting the pleasures of the day. He went to bed that night as perfectly well as ever I saw man, woman, or child in my life. Queeney however took some rhubarb, and went on drooping and felt feverish. I looked at her two or three times in the night too, and found her hot and feverish, but her dear brother slept as cool and comfortable as possible, and on the morning of the next fatal day, Saturday 23rd of March 1776, he rose in perfect health, went to the baker for his roll and watched the drawing it out of the oven, carried it to *Bachelor's Hall*, as he called it where the young clerks live down the brewhouse yard; there he got butter, and cooked a merry breakfast among them. After this he returned with two penny cakes he had bought for the little girls, and distributed them between them in his pleasant manner for[9] minuets that he made them dance. I was all this while waiting on Queeney, who seemed far from well, and I was once very impatient at the noise the maids and children made in the nursery, by laughing excessively at his antic tricks. By this time I came down to my dressing room to tutor Sophy till the clock struck ten which is my regular breakfast hour. I had scarce made the tea when Moll came to tell me Queeney was better, and Harry

---

4. A Florentine nobleman whom the Thrales had first met in Paris.
5. Of London.
6. Carrying a cargo of beer from the Thrale brewery; while in the river, the ship had caught fire.
7. Dark beer.
8. Canon.
9. In exchange for.

making a figure of 5:10,[1] so we always called his manner of twisitng about when anything ailed him. When I got to the nursery, there was Harry crying as if he had been
whipped instead of ill, so I reproved him for making such a bustle about nothing, and
said, "See how differently your sister behaves," who though in earnest far from well,
had begged to make breakfast for Papa and Mr. Baretti,[2] while I was employed above.
The next thing I did was to send for Mr. Lawrence of York Buildings, to whom Nurse
was always partial.[3] My note expressed to him that both the eldest children were ill,
but Hetty *worst*. Presently, however, finding the boy inclined to vomit, I administered a large wine glass of emetic wine, which however did nothing *any way*, though
he drank small liquids with avidity. And now, seeing his sickness increase, and his
countenance begin to alter, I sent out Sam with orders not to come back without
some physician—Jebb, Bromfield, Pinkstan, or Lawrence of Essex Street, whichever
he could find. In the mean time I plunged Harry into water as hot as could easily be
borne, up to his middle, and had just taken him out of the tub and laid him in a warm
bed, when Jebb came, and gave him first hot wine, then usquebaugh,[4] then Daffy's
Elixir,[5] so fast that it alarmed me, though I had not notion of *Death* having seen him
so perfectly well at 9 o'clock. He then had poultices made with mustard put to his
feet, and strong broth and wine clysters[6] injected, but we could get no evacuation *any*
way, and the inclination to vomit still continuing, Jebb gave him five grains of
ipecacuanha[7] and then drove away to call Heberden's help.[8] The child all this while
spoke well and brisk, sat upright to talk with the doctors, and said he had no pain
now but his breath was short. This I attributed to the hot things he had taken, and
thought Jebb in my heart far more officious than wise. I was however all confusion,
distress, and perplexity, and Mr. Thrale bid me not cry so, for I should look like a hag
when I went to Court next day. He often saw Harry in the course of the morning,
and apprehended no danger at all. No more did Baretti, who said he should be
whipped for frighting his mother for nothing. Queeney had for some time been laid
down on her own bed, and got up fancying herself better. But soon a universal shriek
called us all together to Harry's bedside, where he struggled a moment—thrusting his
finger down his throat to excite vomiting—and then, turning to Nurse, said very distinctly, "Don't scream so—I *know* I must die."

   This however I did not hear. Lady Lade, who I believe had been here half the
morning watching the event, asked me kindly what she should do for me. I replied,
"Oh take me these two little girls away—they distract me." She accordingly then carried them off and set 'em safe at Kensington, where they are still. This most dreadful
of all our misfortunes, which they say happened about 3 o'clock or 4, on the 23rd day
of March 1776, had such an effect on poor Queeney that I expected her to follow
him. Jebb however did something for her, and advising speedy change of scene, I rose
in the morning of the 30th after a sleepless night, and in a sort of desperation drove
away with her to Bath, which little journey did her infinite service. Baretti kindly
offered to go with me, so he conducted the troop and diverted Queeney's melancholy
with all the tricks he could think on. She is now—though not recovered—yet I hope
out of danger (as the phrase is). I saw the little girls at Kensington yesterday as I came
home. This is the 9th of April 1776.

---

1. I.e., bent in half, with knees pulled in to the chest.
2. Giuseppe Baretti (1719–1789), Italian scholar and
author, a close friend of Henry Thrale.
3. Herbert Lawrence was a local physician; "Nurse" took
care of the Thrale children.
4. Whiskey.
5. A laxative.
6. Enemas.
7. A purgative.
8. William Heberden, one of the best physicians in London.

[ON HER MARRIAGE AND HOUSEHOLD]

25 September 1778. My eldest daughter Hester Maria was measured, and found of a pleasing and sufficient height. She was this last birthday, 17 September 1778, fourteen years old. She is very pretty still, but is of a pale complection. Her person, mind, and temper have never indeed suffered any considerable changes. Her face and figure are very lovely, her mind very highly cultivated, and her temper haughty and contemptuous. She is blue-eyed, fair-haired, has a good set of teeth, good shape, and the carriage of a girl of fashion. Books are her delight, and she chooses her own studies now for me, who do not interfere much—nor would she suffer[1] me. She is my Mistress completely, but has I think no great influence over her Papa. We kept her birthday merrily, gave old Nurse money, and she treated the servants with a dance. If my Master's mad management does not bereave us all of all our property,[2] she stands foremost now to inherit our possessions, and *mine* thank God are entailed.[3] Little as they are, and greatly as Mr. Thrale despises them, they may become our best friends, and he will take the swiftest methods to make them so, by feeding the brew house with its own flesh till it perishes with a sudden and dreadful ruin.

* * *

This is the last day of the year 1778. My children are all about me and my house is full of friends. Susan and I read two acts of Molière's *Bourgeois*[4] today. She understands it to a miracle, and translates with some idea even of giving an English turn to the idiom, or an English idiom to the phrase. Sophy reads English narrative to amuse herself perfectly well without any tone or drawl; they both work well, and write very prettily, spelling as exactly as myself. Sue can do sums in the three first rules of arithmetic; pounds, shillings, and pence quite readily, and pretends to tinkle the harpsichord, but I think she has for that affair neither ear nor fingers. Susan's geographical and grammatical knowledge amazes even me, but she never will dance I think. When Sophy gets a good master[5] she will be eminent in that art. Hester is well—and beautiful, Susan is a pretty girl as need be, Cecilia is much liked, and Harriett quite a cherubim. Sophy is much the plainest as to countenance but her form is most complete and her temper enchanting. Hester and Susan are touchy, moody, and capricious.

Mr. Thrale is once more happy in his mind, and at leisure to be so in love with S.S.[6] that it is comical. She is a charming young creature; everybody must love her. We have her, and F. Browne and Murphy and Seward and the Davenants and Johnson here, besides Tom Cotton and occasional comers in.

I think I am again pregnant, I think I am; then let us conclude the old year with humble thanks to almighty God for all his mercies through Jesus Christ our Lord, and most of all for the health of my dear children, and for the boon I hope I have obtained by my prayers and tears—that I shall never follow any more of my offspring to the grave—Amen Lord Jesus!

Amen!

if so—I will not fret about this rival this S.S. no I won't.[7]

1766–1778   1976

1. Allow.
2. "My Master" is Henry Thrale, who often spent more capital than his brewery could afford, in an obsessive attempt to surpass his competitors.
3. Secured by law to be inherited by her husband and children. She is mistaken here, and later reclaimed the property for herself and her second husband.
4. The comedy *Le Bourgeois Gentilhomme* (1671) by the French playwright Molière.
5. Teacher.
6. Sophia Streatfield (1754–1835); noted for her beauty and for her accomplished Greek scholarship, she had become a family friend, a godparent to Henrietta, and an obsession of Henry Thrale's.
7. The Family Book ends here.

from Thraliana

[FIRST ENTRIES]

It is many years since Doctor Samuel Johnson advised me to get a little book, and write in it all the little anecdotes which might come to my knowledge, all the observations I might make or hear; all the verses never likely to be published, and in fine every thing which struck me at the time. Mr. Thrale has now treated me with a repository, and provided it with the pompous title of Thraliana.[1] I must endeavor to fill it with nonsense new and old. 15 September 1776.

Bob Lloyd[2] used to say that a parent or other person devoted to the care and instruction of youth, led the life of a finger post, still fixed to one disagreeable spot himself, while his whole business was only to direct others in the way.

An old man's child, says Johnson, leads much the same sort of life as a child's dog, teased like that with fondness through folly, and exhibited like that to every company, through idle and empty vanity.

I have heard Johnson observe that as education is often compared to agriculture, so it resembles it chiefly in this: that though no one can tell whether the crop may answer the culture,[3] yet if nothing be sowed, we all see that no crop can be obtained.

* * *

[Brighton, July–August 1780] I have picked up Piozzi[4] here, the great Italian singer; he shall teach Hester. She will have some powers in the musical way I believe. Her voice though not strong is sweet and flexible, her taste correct, and her expression pleasing. The other two girls leave me tomorrow; they will do very well; Susan is three parts a Beauty, and quite a Scholar for ten Years old. * * *

I dread the general election more than ever. Mr. Thrale is now well enough to canvass in person, and 'twill kill him.[5] Had it happened when he *could not absolutely* have stirred, we would have done it for him, but now! Well! One should not however anticipate misfortunes, they will come time enough.

* * *

[8 August 1780] Piozzi is become a prodigious favorite with me. He is so intelligent a creature, so discerning, one can't help wishing for his good opinion. His singing surpasses everybody's for taste, tenderness, and true elegance. His hand on the fortepiano too is so soft, so sweet, so delicate, every tone goes to one's heart I think, and fills the mind with emotions one would not be without, though inconvenient enough sometimes. I made him sing yesterday, and though he says his voice is gone, I cannot somehow or other get it out of my ears—odd enough!

These were the Verses he sung to me.

> Amor—non sò che sia,
>   Ma sò che è un traditor;
> Cosa è la gelosia?
>   Non l'hò provato ancor.
>
> La donna mi vien detto
>   Fà molto sospirar;

1. He had given his wife six leather-bound volumes, each displaying the "pompous title" on its cover, on a red label stamped with gold lettering.
2. A poet.
3. I.e., will prove worth the care expended on it.
4. "He is amazingly like my father" [Thrale's note]. Born near Venice, Gabriel Piozzi (1740–1809) had now lived in England for about four years, giving concerts and teaching voice.
5. Henry Thrale was running for Parliament; he ended up finishing third in a field of three.

> Ed Io poveretto,
>   Men' voglio innamorar.

I instantly translated them for him, and made him sing them in English thus
all'Improviso.

> For Love—I can't abide it,
>   The treacherous rogue I know;
> Distrust!—I never tried it
>   Whether t'would sting or no.

> For Flavia many sighs are,
>   Sent up by sad despair.
> And yet poor simple I Sir
>   Am hasting to the snare.

[October–November 1780] Here is Sophy Streatfield again, handsomer than
ever, and flushed with new conquests: the Bishop of Chester feels her power I am
sure. She showed me a letter from him that was as tender, and had all the *tokens* upon
it as strong as ever I remember to have seen 'em. I repeated to her out of Pope's
Homer. "Very well Sophy," says I,

> "Range undisturbed among the hostile crew,
>   But touch not *Hinchliffe*, Hinchliffe is *my* due."[6]

"Miss Streatfield," says my Master, "could have quoted these lines *in the Greek*."
His saying so piqued me; and piqued me because it was true. I wish I understood
Greek! Mr. Thrale's preference of her to me never vexed me so much as my consciousness—or fear at least—that he had *reason* for his preference. She has ten
times my beauty, and five times my scholarship. Wit and knowledge has she
none.

How fond some people are of riding in a carriage! Those most I think who had
from beginning least chance of keeping one. Johnson dotes on a coach; so do many
people indeed. I never get into any vehicle, but for the sake of being conveyed to
some place, or some person. The motion is unpleasing to me in itself, and the strait-
ness[7] of the room makes it inconvenient. Conversation too is almost wholly precluded, the grinding of the wheels hinders one from hearing, and the necessity of raising
one's voice makes it less comfortable to talk. A book is better than a friend in a carriage—and a carriage is the only place where it is so.

* * *

[10 December 1780] We have got a sort of literary curiosity amongst us; the foul
copy of Pope's Homer,[8] with all his old intended verses, sketches, emendations etc.
Strange that a man should keep such things! Stranger still that a woman should write
such a book as this; put down every occurrence of her life, every emotion of her
heart, and call it a *Thraliana* forsooth—but then I mean to destroy it.

All wood and wire behind the scenes[9] sure enough! One sees that Pope labored
as hard—

---

6. "Rage uncontrolled through all the hostile crew / But
touch not Hector; Hector is my due"; Achilles's instructions to Patroclus in Pope's translation of Homer's *Iliad*
(16.113). John Hinchliffe was Bishop of Peterborough
and a friend of the family.

7. Narrowness
8. The manuscript draft of Pope's translation of the *Iliad*.
Johnson was consulting it for his biography of Pope.
9. I.e., backstage at a theater.

as if the Stagyrite o'erlooked each line[1]

indeed, and how very little effect those glorious verses at the end of the 8th book of the *Iliad* have upon one, when one sees 'em all in their cradles and clouts;[2] and "light" changed for "bright"—and then the whole altered again, and the line must end with "night"—and Oh Dear! thus—*torturing one poor word a thousand ways*.[3]

Johnson says 'tis pleasant to see the progress of such a mind. True; but 'tis a malicious pleasure, such as men feel when they watch a woman at her toilet[4] and

see by degrees a purer blush arise, *etc*.[5]

Wood and wire once more! Wood and wire!—

* * *

[January 1781] What an odd partiality I have for a rough character! and even for the hard parts of a soft one! Fanny Burney[6] has secured my heart. I now love her with a fond and firm affection, besides my esteem of her parts,[7] and my regard for her father. Her lofty spirit—dear Creature!—has quite subdued mine; and I adore her for the pride which once revolted me. There is no true affection, no friendship in the sneakers and fawners. 'Tis not for obsequious civility that I delight in Johnson or Hinchliffe, Sir Richard Jebb or Piozzi, who has as much spirit *in his way* as the best of them—great solidity of mind too I think, some sarcasm, and wonderful discernment in that rough Italian. I will do him all the service I can.

[10 January 1781] I will now write out the Characters of the people who are intended to have their portraits hung up in the Library here at Streatham.[8] * * *

My own and my eldest daughter's portraits in one picture come next, and are to be placed over the chimney.[9]

> In features so placid, so smooth, so serene,
> What trace of the wit or the Welsh-woman's seen?
> Of the temper sarcastic, the flattering tongue,
> The sentiment right—with th' occasion still wrong.
> What trace of the tender, the rough, the refined,
> The soul in which all contrarieties joined?
> Where though merriment loves over method to rule,
> Religion resides, and the virtues keep school;
> Till when tired we condemn her dogmatical air,
> Like a rocket she rises, and leaves us to stare.
> To such contradictions d'ye wish for a clue?
> Keep vanity still—that vile passion—in view.
> For 'tis thus the slow miner his fortune to make,
> Of arsenic thin scattered pursues the pale track;
> Secure where that poison pollutes the rich ground,
> That it points to the soil where some silver is found.

1. Pope's *Essay on Criticism* (line 138). The "Stagyrite" is Aristotle, the Greek philosopher Pope here invokes as the ultimate arbiter of literary judgment.
2. Diapers.
3. Dryden, *Mac Flecknoe* (line 208).
4. Dressing table.
5. From Pope's description of Belinda in *The Rape of the Lock* (1.143).
6. Daughter of the musicologist Charles Burney, and author of the novel *Evelina, or a Young Lady's Entrance into the World* (1778), which brought her to the attention and admiration of the Streatham circle.
7. Intellect.
8. The 13 paintings, by Sir Joshua Reynolds, had been commissioned by Henry Thrale. They depicted his wife, daughter, and distinguished friends, including Johnson, Burke, Baretti, and Reynolds himself. A "character" is a word portrait; Hester Thrale wrote one in verse for each person Reynolds depicted.
9. Her verse self-portrait follows.

The portrait of my eldest daughter deserves better lines than these which follow. She is a valuable girl.

> Of a virgin so tender the face or the fame,
> Alike would be injured by praise or by blame.
> To the world's fiery trial too early consigned,
> She soon shall experience it, cruel or kind.
>
> His concern thus the anxious enameller hides,
> And his well finished work to the furnace confides;
> But jocund resumes it secure from decay,
> If the colors stand firm on the dangerous day.

* * *

One Page more I see ends the 3d Volume of Thraliana! strange farrago as it is of sense, nonsense, public, private follies—but chiefly my own—and *I* the little Hero etc. Well! but who should be the Hero of an *Ana?* Let me vindicate my own vanity if it be with my last pen. This volume will be finished at Streatham and be left there—where I may never more return to dwell!

Mr. Thrale *may* die,[1] and not leave me sufficient to keep Streatham open as it has been kept, and I shall hate to live in it with more thought about expenses than I have done. I *may* indeed be left sole mistress of the brewhouse to manage for my girls, but that I hardly think will be the case; and if not so, why Farewell pretty Streatham, where I have spent many a merry hour, and many a sad one.

My poor little old Aunt at Bath is dying too, and I am dolt enough to be sincerely sorry, the more as her past kindnesses claim that personal attendance from me, which Mr. Thrale will not permit me to pay her—poor, little, old, insipid, useless creature! May God Almighty in his mercy, pity, receive and bless her, as a most inoffensive atom of humanity—for whom his only Son consented to be crucified, and among whose flock she has most innocently fed for sixty or seventy years.—

Here closes the third volume

Streatham
Monday 29 January 1781.

[The Death of Henry Thrale; Marriage to Gabriel Piozzi]

[Sunday 18 March 1781] Well! Now I have experienced the delights of a London winter spent in the bosom of flattery, gaiety, and Grosvenor Square. 'Tis a poor thing however, and leaves a void in the mind; but I have had my compting-house[2] duties to attend, my sick Master to watch, my little children to look after—and how much good have I done in any way? Not a scrap as I can see. The pecuniary affairs have gone on perversely: how should they choose when the sole proprietor is incapable of giving orders, yet not so far incapable as to be set aside! Distress, fraud, folly meet me at every turn, and I am not able to fight against them all, though endued with an iron constitution which shakes not by sleepless nights, or days severely fretted. Mr. Thrale talks now of going to Spa and Italy again. How shall we drag him thither? A man who cannot keep awake four hours at a stroke, who can scarce retain the Feces etc. Well! This will indeed be a trial of one's patience; and who must go with us on this

---

1. He had suffered a series of strokes.
2. Bookkeeping. During her husband's final illness,

Thrale was helping to manage the brewery.

expedition? Mr. Johnson! He will indeed be the only happy person of the party. He values nothing under heaven but his own mind, which is a spark *from* Heaven; and *that* will be invigorated by the addition of new ideas. If Mr. Thrale dies on the road, Johnson will console himself by learning *how it is* to travel with a corpse—and after all, such reasoning is the true philosophy—one's heart is a mere encumbrance. Would I could leave mine behind. The children shall go to their sisters at Kensington. Mrs. Cumyns[3] may take care of 'em all. God grant us a happy Meeting! Some *where* and some *time!*

Baretti should attend I think. There is no man who has so much of *every* language, and can manage so well with Johnson, and is so tidy on the road, so active too to obtain good accommodations. He is the man in the world I think whom I most abhor, and who hates, and professes to hate me the most. But what does that signify? He will be careful of Mr. Thrale and Hester whom he *does* love—and he won't strangle me I suppose. It will be very convenient to have him. Somebody we must have. Croza would court our Daughter, and Piozzi could not talk to Johnson, nor I suppose do one any good, but sing to one—and how should we sing *songs in a strange land?* Baretti must be the man, and I will beg it of him as a favor. Oh the triumph he will have! and the lies that he will tell!

If I die abroad I shall leave all my papers in charge with Fanny Burney. I have at length conquered all her scruples, and won her confidence and her heart. 'Tis the most valuable conquest I ever *did* make, and dearly, very dearly, do I love my little *Tayo,* so the people at Otaheite[4] call a *bosom friend.* She is now satisfied of my affection, and has no reserves, no ill opinion, no further notion I shall insult her sweetness. I now respect her caution, and esteem her above all living women. Mrs. Byron will half break her heart at my going. Mrs. Lambart is going herself.[5]

No danger of all these distresses it seems. Mr. Thrale died on the 4th of April 1781.[6]

* * *

[20 September 1782] Now! That little dear discerning creature Fanny Burney says I'm in love with Piozzi—very likely! He is so amiable, so honorable, so much above his situation by his abilities, that if

> Fate hadn't fast bound her
> With Styx nine times round her
> Sure Music and Love were victorious.[7]

But if he is ever so worthy, ever so lovely, he is *below me* forsooth. In what is he below me? In virtue—I would I were above him. In understanding—I would mine were from this instant under the guardianship of his. In birth—to be sure, he is below me in birth, and so is almost every man I know, or have a chance to know. But he is below me in fortune—is mine sufficient for us both? More than amply so. Does he deserve it by his conduct in which he has always united warm notions of honor with cool attention to economy, the spirit of a gentleman with the talents of a professor?

---

3. A childhood friend, who now ran a school which Sophia and Susan Thrale attended.
4. Tahiti, where Burney's brother James had traveled on one of Captain James Cook's expeditions.
5. Sophia Byron and Elizabeth Lambart were Thrale's close friends and frequent correspondents.

6. Thrale set down these two sentences at the center of a blank page.
7. Pope, *Ode for Music, on St. Cecelia's Day* (lines 90–92). The passage describes Eurydice, momentarily freed from her imprisonment in the underworld by the enchanting music of her lover Orpheus.

How shall any man deserve fortune if he does not? But I am the guardian of five daughters by Mr. Thrale, and must not disgrace their name and family. Was then the man my mother chose for me of higher extraction than him I have chosen for myself? No. But his fortune was higher. I wanted fortune then perhaps, do I want it now? Not at all. But I am not to think about myself. I married the first time to please my mother, I must marry the second time to please my daughter.[8] I have always sacrificed my own choice to that of others, so I must sacrifice it again. But why? Oh because I am a woman of superior understanding, and must not for the world degrade myself from my situation in life. But if I have superior understanding, let me at least make use of it for once, and rise to the rank of a human being conscious of its own power to discern good from ill. The person who has uniformly acted by the will of others, has hardly that dignity to boast. * * *

[4 November 1782] Sir Richard Musgrave[9] has sent me proposals of marriage from Ireland. His wife is dying at least if not dead, and he is in haste for a better. He will get *me* to be sure!! a likely matter! when my head is full of nothing but my children—my heart of my beloved Piozzi! * * *

[Brighthelmstone, Saturday, 16 November 1782] For him I have been contented to reverse the laws of Nature, and request of my child that concurrence which at my age (and a widow) I am not required either by divine or human institutions to ask even of a parent. The life I gave her she may now more than repay, only by agreeing to what she will with difficulty prevent, and which if she does prevent, will give her lasting remorse—for those who stab *me* shall hear me groan—whereas if she will—but how can she?—gracefully, or even compassionately consent, if she will go abroad with me upon the chance of his death or mine preventing our union, and live with me till she is of age—perhaps there is no heart so callous by avarice, no soul so poisoned by prejudice, no head so feathered by foppery, that will forbear to excuse her when she returns to the rich and the gay, for having saved the life of a mother through compliance extorted by anguish, contrary to the received opinions of the world.

[Brighthelmstone, 19 November 1782] What is above written, though intended only to unload my heart by writing it, I showed in a transport of passion to Queeney and to Burney. Sweet Fanny Burney cried herself half blind over it, said there was no resisting such pathetic eloquence, and that if she was the daughter instead of the friend, she should be even tempted to attend me to the altar. But that while she possessed her reason, nothing should seduce her to approve what reason itself would condemn: that children, religion, situation, country and character—besides the diminution of fortune by the certain loss of £800 a year were too much to sacrifice to any *one* man. If however I were resolved to make the sacrifice, *à la bonne heure!*[1] It was an astonishing proof of an attachment, very difficult for mortal man to repay.

I will talk no more of it.

* * *

[29 January 1783] Adieu to all that's dear, to all that's lovely. I am parted from my Life, my Soul! my Piozzi: *Sposo promesso! Amante adorato! Amico senza equale.*[2] If I can get health and strength to write my story here, 'tis all I wish for now! Oh Misery!

The cold dislike of my eldest daughter I thought might wear away by familiarity with his merit, and that we might live tolerably together or at least part friends, but no. Her aversion increased daily, and she communicated it to the others. They treat-

---

8. Queeney, who objected vehemently to the prospect of her mother's marriage to Piozzi.
9. Irish baronet and member of Parliament, whom Thrale had met at Bath in 1776.
1. Fine! Good for you! (French.)
2. Promised husband, adored lover, friend without equal.

ed *me* insolently, and *him* very strangely—running away whenever he came as if they saw a serpent, and plotting with their governess, a cunning Italian, how to invent lies to make me hate him, and twenty such narrow tricks. By these means the notion of my partiality took air—and whether Miss Thrale sent him word slyly, or not I cannot tell; but on the 25 January 1783 Mr. Crutchley[3] came hither to *conjure* me not to go to Italy: he had heard *such* things he said, and by *means* next to *miraculous*. The next day, Sunday 26, Fanny Burney came, said I must marry him instantly, or give him up; that my reputation would be lost else. I actually groaned with anguish, threw myself on the bed in an agony which my fair daughter beheld with frigid indifference. She had indeed never by one tender word endeavored to dissuade me from the match, but said coldly that if I *would* abandon my children, I *must;* that their father had not deserved such treatment from me; that I should be punished by Piozzi's neglect, for that she knew he hated me, and that I turned out my offspring to chance for his sake like puppies in a pond to swim or drown according as Providence pleased; that for her part she must look herself out a place like the other servants, for my face would she never see more. "Nor write to me?" said I. "I shall not Madam," replied she with a cold sneer, "easily find *out your address*, for you are going you know not whither I believe." Susan and Sophy said nothing at all, but they taught the two little ones to cry, "Where are you going Mama? Will you leave us, and die as our poor papa did?" There was no standing *that*, so I wrote my lover word that my mind was all distraction, and bid him come to me the next morning my birthday, 27 January. Mean time I took a vomit, and spent the Sunday night in torture not to be described. My falsehood to my Piozzi, my strong affection for him, the incapacity I felt in myself to resign the man I so adored, the hopes I had so cherished, inclined me strongly to set them all at defiance, and go with him to Church to sanctify the promises I had so often made him, while the idea of abandoning the children of my first husband, who left me so nobly provided for, and who depended on my attachment to his offspring, awakened the voice of conscience, and threw me on my knees to pray for *his* direction who was hereafter to judge my conduct.

His grace illuminated me, his power strengthened me; and I flew to my daughter's bed in the morning and told, told her my resolution to resign my own, my dear, my favorite purposes; and to prefer my children's interest to my love. She questioned my ability to make the sacrifice; said one word from him would undo all my[4] * * *

[27 June 1784] My daughters parted with me at last prettily enough *considering* (as the phrase is). We shall perhaps be still better friends apart than together. Promises of correspondence and kindness were very sweetly reciprocated, and the eldest wished for Piozzi's safe return obligingly.[5]

I fancy two days more will absolutely bring him to Bath—The present moments are critical and dreadful, and would shake stronger nerves than mine. Oh Lord strengthen me to do thy will I pray.

[28 June] I am not *yet sure* of seeing him again—not *sure* he lives, not *sure* he loves me, *yet*. Should any thing happen *now*!! Oh I will not trust myself with such a fancy—it will either kill me, or drive me distracted.

3. Jeremiah Crutchley, one of the executors of Henry Thrale's will.

4. The remainder of the entry is lost, because the next page is missing. Informed of Thrale's decision, Piozzi left for Italy. Negotiations between mother and daughter continued for another year, until Queeney finally capitu-

lated on the grounds that Thrale's agitation was endangering her health. The daughters were to remain in England, looked after by the trustees of their father's estate; the mother would reside with her new husband in Italy.

5. He was now returning from Italy to England.

[2 July] The happiest day of my whole life I think. Yes, *quite* the happiest.[6] My Piozzi came home yesterday and dined with me. But my spirits were too much agitated, my heart too much dilated, I was too painfully happy *then*. My sensations are more quiet today, and my felicity less tumultuous. I have spent the night as I ought in prayer and Thanksgiving. Could I have slept, I had not deserved such blessings. May the Almighty but preserve them to me! He lodges at our old house on the South Parade. His companion Mecci[7] is a faithless treacherous fellow—but no matter! 'Tis all over now.

[Bath, 25 July] I am returned from church the happy wife of my lovely, my faithful Piozzi, subject of my prayers, object of my wishes, my sighs, my reverence, my esteem.

His nerves have been horribly shaken, but he lives, he loves me, and will be mine *for ever*. He has sworn it in the face of God and the whole Christian Church: Catholics, Protestants, all are witnesses. May he who has preserved us thus long for each other give us a long life together—and so I hope and trust he will through the merits of Jesus Christ. Amen.

[3 September] Wellbeck Street, Cavendish Square, London] I have now been six weeks married, and enjoyed greater and longer felicity than I ever yet experienced. To crown all, my dear daughters Susanna and Sophia have spent the day with myself and my amiable husband. We part in peace, and love, and harmony, and tomorrow I set off for the finest country in the world, in company with the most excellent man in it.

Some natural tears they dropped, but wiped 'em soon. Milton.[8]

* * *

[THE DEATH OF JOHNSON]

[Milan, January 1785] The new year is begun. May God prosper it to my husband, my children, and myself. I went to church and prayed most fervently for their happiness.

My Piozzi is not well. He has no disorder though that shortens life, notwithstanding the uneasiness it occasions him. Strong fibers with weak nerves produce all his sufferings, and add to his natural irritability. The constant complaints too which he makes of his health take off from the envy his situation would otherwise provoke, but he is best on a journey. I shall like to go to Venice in the spring—if nothing prevents me, *which I should like still better*. Praying for children is wrong however, and I will do it no more. I used to weary Heaven with requests for pregnancy, and now!! all I begged for are in the grave almost, and those that are left, love not *me*.

I had letters the other day indeed of which I ought not to complain. Susan and Sophy's kindness *should* compensate for the frigidity of their elder sister, and Mr. Cator says all of them are well.

Oh poor Dr. Johnson!!![9]

[25 January 1785] I have recovered myself sufficiently to think what will be the consequence to me of Johnson's death, but must wait the event as all thoughts on the future in this world are vain.

---

6. For Johnson's admonitory letter on this same date, see page 1280.
7. Francesco Mecci, a teacher of Italian, whom Thrale apparently suspected of trying to prevent the marriage.

8. From the description of Adam and Eve as they prepare to depart from paradise (*Paradise Lost* 12.645).
9. He had died 13 December 1785.

Six people have already undertaken to write his life I hear, of which Sir John Hawkins, Mr. Boswell, Tom Davies, and Dr. Kippis are four. Piozzi says he would have me add to the number, and so I would; but that I think my anecdotes too few, and am afraid of saucy answers if I send to England for others. The saucy answers *I* should disregard, but my heart is made vulnerable by my late marriage, and I am certain that to spite me, they would insult my husband. Poor Johnson! I see they will leave *nothing untold* that I labored so long to keep secret; and I was so very delicate in trying to conceal his fancied insanity,[1] that I retained no proofs of it—or hardly any—nor ever mentioned it in these books, lest by dying first *they* might be printed and the secret (for such I thought it) discovered.

I used to tell him in jest that his biographers would be at a loss concerning some orange peel he used to keep in his pocket,[2] and many a joke we had about the Lives that would be published. "Rescue me out of all their hands, my dear, and do it *yourself*," said he. "Taylor, Adams, and Hector[3] will furnish you with juvenile anecdotes, and Baretti will give you all the rest that you have not already—for I think Baretti is a liar only when he speaks of himself." "Oh!" said I, "Baretti told me yesterday that you got by heart six pages of Machiavel's *History*[4] once, and repeated 'em thirty years afterwards word for word." "O why this indeed is a *gross* lie," says Johnson. "I never read the book at all." "Baretti too told me of *you*" (said I) "that you once kept sixteen cats in your chamber, and yet they scratched your legs to such a degree, you were forced to use mercurial plasters[5] for some time after." "Why this" (replied Johnson) "is an unprovoked lie indeed. I thought the fellow would not have broken through divine and human laws thus, to make Puss his heroine. But I see I was mistaken."

1776–1808   1951

---

1. Johnson had confided to her more than to others how deeply and how often he feared the loss of his faculties.
2. He used it as a laxative.
3. Johnson's childhood friends.

4. Niccolò Machiavelli's history of Florence, *Storie Fiorentine* (1520–1525).
5. Bandages soaked in mercury.

Thomas Phillips. *Lord Byron,* 1814.

The Romantics and Their Contemporaries

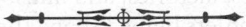

LITERATURE AND THE AGE: "NOUGHT WAS LASTING"

Reviewing Mary Shelley's *Frankenstein* in 1818, *The Edinburgh Magazine* remarked that "never was a wilder story imagined." Even so, the reviewer went on, "like most of the fictions of this age, it has an air of reality attached to it, by being connected with the favourite projects and passions of the times. The real events of the world have, in our day, too, been of so wondrous and gigantic a kind,—the shiftings of the scenes in our stupendous drama have been so rapid and various, that Shakespeare himself, in his wildest flights, has been completely distanced by the eccentricities of actual existence." The turbulent world and whirl of real events shaped the years of the "Romantic" period. It was marked on the one end by the revolutions in America and France, and on the other, by the reform of Parliament to extend the vote and reconfigure representation, by the emergence of the modern industrial state, and by the abolition of slavery in British colonies. In the early 1820s, Lord Byron protested:

> Talk not of seventy years as age; in seven
>   I have seen more changes, down from monarchs to
> The humblest individual under heaven,
>   Than might suffice a moderate century through.
> I knew that nought was lasting, but now even
>   Change grows too changeable without being new:
> Nought's permanent among the human race . . . (*Don Juan* 11.81)

As the nod toward monarchs indicates, the French Revolution of the 1790s cast a long shadow across British consciousness. Its events had announced a radical break in historical continuity—a sudden, cataclysmic overthrow of a monarchy surrounded by high culture, and the eruption of new social order that no one knew how to "read." New, challenging, and often contradictory energies reverberated across Britain and Europe. Enthusiasts heralded the fall of an oppressive aristocracy and the birth of democratic and egalitarian ideals, a new era, shaped by "the rights of man" rather than the entailments of wealth and privilege, while skeptics and reactionaries rued the end of chivalry, lamented the erosion of order, and foresaw the decline of civilization.

Yet whatever side one took, the upheaval bore a stark realization: politically, socially, economically, and philosophically, an irrevocable tide of new ideas had risen against seemingly entrenched structures. "It was now known," as historian E. J. Hobsbawm puts it, "that revolution in a single country could be a European phenomenon, that its doctrines could spread across the frontiers. . . . It was now known that social revolution was possible, that nations existed as something independent of states, peoples as something independent of their rulers, and even that the poor existed as something independent of the ruling classes." Other challenges appeared, framed in the rhetoric of the Revolution debate and animated by appeals to moral law and natural principle. There were arguments for and against the rights of women (not for the vote, but for better principles of education and improved social attitudes); debates over the abolition of Britain's slave trade and of slavery in its colonies (a moral blight but also a source of enormous and widespread commercial profit); movements for social and political remedies for the poor (versus the traditional spiritual consolations); and a newly emergent class consciousness among discontented workers in Britain's fields, mines, factories, and mills.

Polemical essays and pamphlets helped shape the controversies, and so did various forms of literary writing: sonnets and songs, ballads and poetic epistles, tales and plays, the sensationally turned narrative and the didactic novel. Even literature not forged in the social and political turbulence was caught by a sense of revolution. The first generation of writers (those who made their marks in the 1790s and the first decade of the new century) included William Blake, William Wordsworth, Samuel Taylor Coleridge, and Walter Scott, as well as several remarkable women: Anna Barbauld, Hannah More, Mary Wollstonecraft, Ann Radcliffe, Joanna Baillie, and Mary Robinson. The second generation (emerging before 1820) adds the younger voices and visions of Percy Shelley, Mary Shelley, John Keats, Lord Byron, John Clare. It also witnesses the emergence of international literary celebrity, first and foremost in the charismatic figure of Lord Byron, then extending in the 1820s to the adored Felicia Hemans and at last to venerable Wordsworth, who would become a beloved Poet Laureate in 1843. All these writers were invigorated by a sense of participating in the modern world, of defining its values, and of claiming a place for writers as its instructors, prophets, critics, and inspirers. In 1792 Wollstonecraft urged "a REVOLUTION in female manners," and at the end of the decade, Wordsworth's Preface to the second edition of *Lyrical Ballads* announced his break with "known habits of association" in the genre of poetry—a program, as his collaborator Coleridge later said, of "awakening the mind's attention from the lethargy of custom" (*Biographia Literaria*, 1817). The post-Revolutionary poet "strips the veil of familiarity from the world," declared Shelley in *A Defence of Poetry*, a document he concluded by designating poets the "unacknowledged legislators of the world." This enthusiasm inspired innovations in content and literary form. Lyric, epic, and autobiography became radically subjective, spiraling inward to psychological dramas of mind and memory, or projecting outward into prophecies and visions of new worlds formed by new values. Other hybrid forms, such as political ballads and polemical narrative, emerged to address pressing issues of the day, while novelists were producing new kinds of female heroines and new narrative structures to represent family and social life. Still other writers developed forms such as the personal essay, the travelogue, or the journal, to join the personal and the political, the social and the domestic, the world of feeling to the world of thought, and both to the world of action.

ROMANCE, ROMANTICISM, AND THE POWERS OF THE IMAGINATION

In this vibrant culture of new imaginative possibilities, "Imagination" itself became a subject of reflection, and often debate. Eighteenth-century philosophy and science had put a rigorous emphasis on objective, verifiable truth and the common basis of our experience in a world of concrete, measurable physical realities. Over the century, however, there emerged a competing interest in individual variations, subjective filterings, and the mind's independence of physical realities, or even creative transformation of them: not just a recorder or mirror, the mind was an active, synthetic, dynamic, even visionary power—of particular importance to poets. Poets tended to define "Imagination" against what it was not, even categorically the opposite of: thus, imagination vs. reality; imagination vs. reason; vs. science; vs. the understanding (especially its "fixities" and "certainties"); vs. mere "fancy"; even vs. religious truth. Blake declared its priority: "What is now proved was once, only imagin'd" (*The Marriage of Heaven and Hell*); it is imagination that can "see a World in a Grain of Sand / And a Heaven in a Wild Flower" (*Auguries of Innocence*). Deeming Wordsworth too wedded to observation and description, he scribbled in the margin of Wordsworth's 1815 *Poems*, "One Power alone makes a Poet.—Imagination The Divine Vision." Yet Wordsworth had moods in which he shared Blake's sense of imagination as most potent when severed from ordinary senses and experiences: "Imagination—here the Power so called / Through sad incompetence of human speech, / That awful Power rose from the mind's abyss / Like an unfathered vapour" (1850 *Prelude* Book 6), he writes at a pivotal moment in a work that is the story of imagination, celebrated in his conclusion as the ultimate synthesizing power: "Imagination . . . in truth, / Is but another name for absolute strength / And clearest insight, and amplitude of mind, / And reason in her most exalted mood" (1805 *Prelude* 13.167–70).

Coleridge defined "Primary Imagination" as "the living Power and prime Agent of all human Perception," analogous to but a lesser power than divine creation. Poetry is written by the "secondary Imagination," an "echo" of the Primary "coexisting with conscious will": it dissolves and diffuses the materials of perception "in order to recreate," and thus shows itself "in the balance or reconciliation of opposite or discordant qualities," among these, the general and the individual, the new and the familiar, emotion and order, judgment and enthusiasm, rationality and passion, the artificial and the natural (*Biographia Literaria* chs. 13, 14). Percy Shelley, who also liked binaries, contrasted "Imagination" to "Reason" in the first paragraph of his *Defence of Poetry*, and following Coleridge, coordinated their powers: "Reason is to imagination as the instrument to the agent, as the body to the spirit, as the shadow to the substance." Byron, when he wasn't dramatizing the torments of imagination, was inclined to look wryly: "Imagination droops her pinion, / And the sad truth which hovers o'er my desk / Turns what was once romantic to burlesque" (*Don Juan* 4.3); "And as for other love, the illusion's o'er; / And money, that most pure imagination, / Gleams only through the dawn of its creation" (12.2). Keats proposed the imagination as a link to the ideal world at the dawn of creation: "The Imagination may be compared to Adam's dream—he awoke and found it truth," he suggested, referring to the dream of Eve. But he was ultimately more interested in the way imagination operates on real perception: "probably every mental pursuit takes its reality and worth from the ardour of the pursuer—being in itself a nothing." And like his contemporaries, he was drawn by the involvement of imagination with disease, deviance, delusion, egotism, escapism.

As Keats's analogy of Adam's dream suggests, male imagination often projects an eroticized female or feminized object. How did women writers participate in the discussion? Though not always, they tended to a more skeptical view, accenting dangers, a corruption of rational capacity and moral judgment, an alliance with destructive (rather than creative) passion. This impulse was not just resistance to male schemes of gender; it was also fueled by a discourse of rational education and intellectual dissent that included both men and women. "The imagination should not be allowed to debauch the understanding before it has gained strength, or vanity will become the forerunner of vice," cautioned Wollstonecraft in *A Vindication of the Rights of Woman;* the best books are those "which exercise the understanding and regulate the imagination." When Jane Austen describes Emma's vain, egotistical illusions, she pointedly terms her an "imaginist . . . on fire with speculation and foresight!—especially with such a ground-work of anticipation as her mind had already made" (*Emma,* vol. 3, ch. 3).

In her widely read *Plays on the Passions* Joanna Baillie summons the word to name trouble and torment: "strange imaginations," "dark imaginations . . . frightful . . . / The haunt of damned spirits," "the worst imagination" of a "madden'd brain," "a wild imagination / Which has o'erreach'd . . . judgment." Mary Robinson recognized how, Hamlet-wise, "pall'd imagination, sick'ning, spurns / The sanity of reason!" (*The Sicilian Lover,* 15.23–24). When Mary Shelley recalls, "My imagination, unbidden, possessed and guided me, gifting the successive images that arose in my mind with a vividness far beyond the usual bounds of reverie," the gift was *Frankenstein.* Men often wrote about these dangers, but usually in a pattern of alternation with enthusiastic, idealizing, visionary projections.

Imagination was a heady romance—an inspiring force, a dangerous seduction. Not coincidentally, the issues often took shape in the language of romance. The rapid changes, new demands, and confusions of the age often pressed writers into imagining worlds elsewhere, an impulse summed in the prestige of the mode from which the "Romantic" era gets its name: the "Romance." In 1755 Samuel Johnson's great *Dictionary* defined it thus: "A military fable of the middle ages; a tale of wild adventures in war and love." Under this appeal, the subtitle "A Romance" graced a host of titles in the Romantic era. Radcliffe perfected the gothic romance novel; Scott elaborated the poetic romance and virtually defined the historical romance, while Byron made his name and fame in exotic quest romance: his first success, *Childe Harold's Pilgrimage* (1812), was subtitled "A Romaunt" (an old "romance" spelling), confirming the aura of the main title. In a variety of genres—ballad, narrative poem, novel—Romance turned to other places and times, or shaped timeless, ahistorical tales of quest and desire, love and adventure. A medieval idiom, which flourished into a "gothic" vogue, supplied vivid language for Radcliffe's novels, Coleridge's *Christabel* and *The Rime of the Ancyent Marinere* (in the patently antiqued version of 1798), Scott's *Lay of the Last Minstrel* (1805), Byron's *Childe Harold,* Keats's *La Belle Dame Sans Mercy* and *The Eve of St. Agnes* (1820), and Hemans's many poems of the age of the Crusades. Romance could inhabit the even more distant pasts of Anglo-Saxon legend or classical mythology. Percy Shelley and Keats turned to the landscapes and myths of ancient Greece as resources of imagination before the age of Christian "truth." As the settings of many of these works indicate, Romance is also fascinated with foreign worlds. *Childe Harold,* Coleridge's *Kubla Khan,* and Hemans's *Tales, and Historic Scenes* testify to the vogue of Eastern materials. Byron intrigued readers with a lexicon of "jelicks" and "baracans," "giaours" and "viziers" (*Don Juan*). "Queen of far-away!" Keats hailed "Romance" itself.

In its various forms and stories, Romances shared a feature that Victorians would take as exemplary of the literary (if not the polemical) imagination of the age: a turn, even an escape, from the tumultuous and confusing here-and-now of England. The appeal lay not only in exotic settings and remote ages themselves but also in the free-dom these licensed to explore superstitions and customs that had been dismissed by Enlightenment thinkers who championed faith in "Reason," progress, and universal truths. These historically distant worlds were often sites for prophecy of renewed worlds and alternative values. Defined against "neoclassical" values of proportion, rational order, balanced harmony, and a reverence for the traditions that conveyed these values, the adjective "romantic" had long stood for a recurrent impulse in the history of the arts: a passion for the wild, the unfamiliar, the irregular, the irrational, even anti-rational. Johnson's *Dictionary* offered a suggestive cluster for "romantick": "1) resembling the tales of romances; wild. 2) Improbable; false. 3) Fanciful; full of wild scenery." All these senses infuse one powerful model for the male Romantic poet: the enraptured, entranced "bard." Descended from the Old Testament prophet, Englished by Milton and elaborated in the eighteenth-century ode, the bard emerged in the Romantic era as an electrically visionary poet and prophet for the age. Poets as various and as different from one another as Blake, Wordsworth, Coleridge, Shelley, and Keats assume a bardic stance to credit their dreams, hopes, and visions, even as socially oriented reformists, such as Wollstonecraft advocating "the rights of woman" or Wilberforce arguing for the abolition of slavery, adopt bardic tones to project a better, more moral world.

There was another landscape in the Romantic age that overlapped with these exotic worlds: the psychic terrain of imagination. And here a second definition John-son supplies for "romance"—"A lie; a fiction"—casts its shadow. Romance is not only the genre of enchanted dreams and inspired visions, but also of superstitions and spells, delusions and nightmares. Coleridge said that the poetry he wrote for *Lyrical Ballads* was devoted to "persons and characters supernatural, or at least romantic"; hence the nightmare worlds and sensations of demonic possession in *The Rime of the Ancyent Marinere* and *Christabel*. Infused with sensations of supernatural power, or fed by opiated fantasies, the magical mystery tours of supernatural romance may hold the keys to paradise or the passage to hell, or both by turns—as they do in Thomas De Quincey's bizarrely romantic autobiography, *Confessions of an English Opium Eater*. The genre of romance fairly bristles with complexities. Acutely aware of the chaos of their historical moment, writers often make the attraction to another world a critical theme: "magic casements," said Keats, "opening on the foam / Of perilous seas, in faery lands forlorn" (*Ode to a Nightingale*). The dubiously magic casements, moreover, may turn into mirrors: Romances often reflect, and reflect on, the world seemingly escaped or effaced from consciousness. The most celebrated romancers were hardly uncritical practitioners of the genre. Byron casts *Childe Harold* as a quest romance, but its path turns repeatedly to modern life, in particular the Napoleonic wars that were ravaging Europe.

At the same time, the prestige of "romance" and "romanticism" posed problems for women writers. Keats suggests one of these when he portrays "Romance" itself as a dangerous seductress (a "Queen of far-away," a "Fair plumed Syren") and opposes her allure to the demands of epic and tragedy (by which male poets claimed their fame). The critique of "Romance" could be tinged with sexism—an irony, since many women writers were inclined to criticize the genre, too. Clara Reeve, Wollstonecraft, Barbauld, and Hannah More—whose opinions divided, often sharply, on a variety of political and social issues—found common ground on the dangers of "Romance." Especially in the popular form of the novel, they felt it encouraged too much

John Martin. *The Bard,* 1817. "Ruin seize thee, ruthless King!" According to the legend retold in Thomas Gray's 1757 ode *The Bard,* in the thirteenth century Edward I attempted to stamp out Welsh resistance to English power by ordering the court poets or bards put to death. John Martin's large canvas captures the sublime moment at which the last bard denounced the invading monarch before leaping into the river Conway below.

"sensibility"—the cultivation of emotional refinement over rational intellect—and fed an appetite for fantasy over sound judgment. Insofar as "Romances" deal in "the wild and extravagant," worried Reeve in *The Progress of Romance* (1785), they are "dangerous" for young readers: "they create and encourage the wildest excursions of imagination." "Novels . . . tend to make women the creatures of sensation," warned Wollstonecraft's *Rights of Woman* (1792); "their character is thus formed in the mould of folly." The genre enfeebled reason and stimulated illusions about "romantic love" that held perilous social consequences. By 1810, Barbauld was willing to argue that good novels could teach good values, but she was still cautious about the power of "romances . . . to impress false ideas on the mind." Urging women to cultivate the Enlightenment values of "Reason" and intellectual strength, these female critics also challenged romance stereotypes proffered as universal truth: the ideals of "feminine" silence, self-sacrifice, passivity, and unquestioning obedience; the ideology of female life contained in the domestic sphere.

There were still more ways that Romance exoticism intersected with the socially immediate world. Encounters with outcasts of all kinds—refugees, the poor, abandoned and fallen women, discharged soldiers, sailors, vagrants, peasants, north-country shepherds and smallholders, abject slaves—supplied the unusual and unexpected, and at the same time provoked social self-reflection. Foreign cultures might be close to home, as in the ballads enthusiastically collected by Scott in *Minstrelsy of the Scottish Border* (1802–1803) and his subsequent use of Highland materials in the series of novels begun with *Waverley*. Scots poet Robert Burns packaged himself as a primitive bard: the son of a tenant-farmer and tenant-farmer himself, a heavy-drinking, illegitimate-child-siring, native genius whose dialect verse and egalitarian sentiments seemed to make him the very voice of the people. William Wordsworth produced incidents from rural life in *Lyrical Ballads,* and his sister Dorothy Wordsworth captured the dialects in her journal. John Clare wrote of rural life in a rural idiom and himself embodied the figure of the peasant poet. Meanwhile, the "wild scenery" of Johnson's definition was caught in new travel books and records of "tours," while "tourists"—a word that emerged around 1800—began to delight in locales ignored by previous generations, or thought unpleasantly rough. Once-isolated Wales became so flooded by tourists that by 1833 a Welsh grammar carried an appendix of useful phrases: "I long to see the monastery"; "Is there a waterfall in this neighbourhood?"

This romance of novelty interplays with a powerful sense of a past that might be renewed. Writers created hybrid forms, building on models anywhere from the middle ages through the eighteenth century. Byron remained loyal to neoclassic poets such as Pope and Dryden, even as he gave their forms new vibrancy and reveled in contemporary political satire. Literary tradition was a cherished, if daunting, national heritage. Many admired Chaucer's tale-telling and descriptive detail; others worked variations on Spenser's allegorical epic, *The Faerie Queene.* Hazlitt honored Spenser as "the poet of our waking dreams," and the Spenserian stanza that conveyed these dreams shaped more than a few new "romances"—among them, Byron's *Childe Harold,* Hemans's *Forest Sanctuary,* Keats's *Eve of St. Agnes,* Shelley's *Revolt of Islam* and his homage to Keats, *Adonais.* Shakespeare and Milton were the great progenitors. Shakespeare was admired for the intensity of his imagery, his spectacular versatility, his unparalleled characterizations, as well as his mastery of "organic" (as opposed to "mechanical") aesthetic form, a concept elaborated in the criticism of Coleridge. He was an early inspiration for Coleridge's lectures and poetry; Wordsworth, Byron, and Hemans could hardly write without alluding to him; Keats named him his "Presider," and De Quincey wrote vivid essays about him. For this generation of writers, Milton's revolutionary politics provided an example of antimonarchal courage, and *Paradise Lost* was indisputably the most important poem in English literature. Milton's Eve focuses the feminist grievances of Wollstonecraft's *Rights of Woman,* while for poets, as Byron declares in *Don Juan,* "the word 'Miltonic' mean[s] 'sublime,'" stimulating epic ambitions in works as diverse as Blake's *Milton* and *Jerusalem,* Charlotte Smith's *Emigrants,* Wordsworth's *Prelude,* Percy Shelley's *Prometheus Unbound,* Keats's *Hyperion,* and Byron's *Don Juan.* Milton's Satan, an epitome of the "sublime," is echoed and doubled everywhere, and along with Milton's God and Adam, casts his shadow across the fable of masculine ambition and heroic alienation that Wollstonecraft's daughter Mary Shelley creates for *Frankenstein.*

At the same time (as the protagonist of *Frankenstein* demonstrates), Romantic creativity also defined itself—often defiantly—against tradition, experimenting with new forms and genres. Blake writes visionary epics; Wordsworth spends half a century on his poetic autobiography, "a thing unprecedented in Literary history," he said. Mary Shelley fuses several myths into a complex, interlocking structure of tales and tellers to form *Frankenstein.* Byron interplays stand-up patter with a tale of adventure to shape his burlesque *Don Juan,* "a poem totally of its own species . . . at once the stamp of originality and a defiance of imitation," Percy Shelley exclaimed to him. Individual experience, simultaneously the most exotic and most common region of all, led to excavations of the depths of the single self—which is to say, the unfolding of a self conceived as having depths and mysterious recesses. Reading Wordsworth's *Tintern Abbey*, Keats found "Genius" in its "dark Passages." In the Prospectus to *The Recluse* (1814), Wordsworth himself proclaimed

> Not Chaos, not
> The darkest pit of lowest Erebus,
> Nor aught of blinder vacancy—scooped out
> By help of dreams, can breed such fear and awe
> As fall upon us often when we look
> Into our Minds, into the Mind of Man,
> My haunt, and the main region of my Song.

Byron jibed that Keats's *Sleep and Poetry* was "an ominous title," but when Wordsworth named "the Mind" as his subject, Keats understood completely, and even women poets participated. This post-Enlightenment, bourgeois Protestant individualism moved beyond the rhetorical first-person of eighteenth-century poetry to produce the "I" as an individual authority, for whom the mind, in all its creative powers and passionate testimony of deeply registered sensations, became a compelling focus. The "I" could sponsor extravagant self-display (Robinson and Byron), prophetic self-elevation (Blake and Shelley), poignant song (Hemans), internal debate (Keats), or what Keats, thinking of Wordsworth, called the "egotistical sublime." Many of its forms defined a radical or alienated subjectivity. Wollstonecraft wrote as a nonconformist, Cowper and Hemans were famous for the melancholy autobiography that haunts their poetry, while poets such as Byron, Coleridge, and Shelley cultivated the "I" as antihero: the exile, the damned visionary, the alienated idealist, the outcast, whose affiliates were Cain, Satan, even the paradoxical figure of Napoleon—all joined by the passion of mind and the torments of imagination.

Whether cast as experiment and innovation or allied with liberty and revolution, these new expressive forms were sharpened by a sense of modernity, with their writers often viewing old forms and traditions as tyranny or, at the very least, as the strictures of custom and habit. Revoking the neoclassical argument of Dryden (in the seventeenth century) that the poet is responsible for "putting bounds to a wilde overflowing Fancy," Wordsworth asserted in the Preface to *Lyrical Ballads* (1800) that poetry should be a "spontaneous overflow of powerful feelings," and explained, in a later version, that in his poems "the feeling . . . gives importance to the action and situation, and not the action and situation to the feeling." Framing "incidents of common life," he made the agents of feeling such socially disenfranchised figures as children, bereft mothers, impoverished shepherds, beggars, veterans, and the rural destitute. In a lecture "On the Living Poets" (1818), William Hazlitt sneered at this "mixed rabble of . . . convicts, female vagrants, gipsies, . . . ideot boys and mad mothers . . . peasants, pedlars," but Wordsworth's revolution was to treat them all as vehicles of worthy imagination and passion. Hazlitt had no trouble linking this program to "the sentiments and opinions which produced the French revolution" as well as its "principles and events":

> The change in the belles-lettres was as complete, and . . . as startling, as the change in politics, with which it went hand in hand. . . . According to the prevailing notions, all was to be natural and new. Nothing that was established was to be tolerated. . . . Kings

and queens were dethroned from their rank and station in legitimate tragedy or epic poetry, as they were decapitated elsewhere; rhyme was looked upon as a relic of the feudal system, and regular metre was abolished along with regular government.

THE FRENCH REVOLUTION AND ITS REVERBERATIONS

In the 1780s, the American Revolution was a recent memory for the British, at once an inspiration to political progressives, an embarrassment for the prestige of the Empire, and a worry to a conservative ruling class concerned about the arrival of democratic ideas on British shores. When the next Revolution exploded in France only twelve miles across the Channel, rather than a hemisphere away, the press of radical, violent, and inevitable change seemed imminent. With the fall of the Bastille prison, a symbol of royal tyranny, on July 14, 1789, and the *Declaration of the Rights of Man* that soon followed, British consciousness was dominated by French events. Conservatives were alarmed, while liberals welcomed the early phase as a repetition of England's "Glorious Revolution" of 1688, an overdue end to feudal abuse and the inauguration of constitutional government. Radicals hoped for a more thorough-going renovation: "Bliss was it in that dawn to be alive, / But to be young was very heaven!" Wordsworth said in retrospect, in a passage from his poetic autobiography that he published in 1809, and again in 1815 under the title *French Revolution as it Appeared to Enthusiasts at its Commencement*. Everything was infused with "the attraction of a country in Romance!" He was not the only one in rapture. Southey recalled how "a visionary world seemed to open. . . . Old things seemed passing away, and nothing was dreamt of but the regeneration of the human race." Burns was certain that "man to man the world o'er / Shall be brithers for a' that." In their own idioms, Wollstonecraft, Blake, and Charles Lamb joined the chorus, and in subsequent generations, Byron and Percy Shelley continued to hope that what was started in France could be continued elsewhere with better consequences.

Better consequences, because millenarian dreams were soon undermined by harsh developments: the overthrow of the French monarchy in August 1792 and in the next month, the massacre of more than a thousand prisoners by a Paris mob. When extremist Jacobins prevailed over moderate Girondins, the French Revolution fragmented into the Reign of Terror. Louis XVI was guillotined in January 1793, Queen Marie Antoinette in October. In February 1793, France declared war on Britain and Britain reciprocated, throwing the political ideals of Wordsworth and his generation into sharp conflict with their love of country. Except for the brief interlude of the deceptive Peace of Amiens (1802–1803: "Peace in a week, war in a month," a British diplomat commented), Britain was at war with France until the final defeat of Napoleon at Waterloo in 1815. The shock of these events lasted for decades, and lent retroactive credit to the conservative polemic of Edmund Burke's *Reflections on the Revolution in France*, published in 1790, after the arrest and imprisonment of the royal family. In 1790 Burke seemed a sentimental hysteric to political opponents and was quickly subject to sarcastic challenge in Wollstonecraft's *Vindication of the Rights of Men* (1790) and Tom Paine's *Rights of Man* (1791). In 1793 radical philosopher William Godwin's *Political Justice*, though not directly about the Revolution, offered a vision of a society governed by individual reason, without the oppression of social institutions or private property. But the course of the Revolution confirmed Burke's alarm.

Under the systematic Terror of Robespierre (1793–1794), thousands of aristocrats, their employees, the clergy, and ostensible opponents of the Revolution were guillotined, the violence swallowing up Robespierre himself in 1794. British unease

Thomas Rowlandson, after a drawing by Lord George Murray. *The Contrast, 1792.*

increased when France offered to support all revolutions abroad, and then invaded the Netherlands and the German states in 1794, Italy in 1796, and republican Switzerland in 1798. Now "Oppressors in their turn," Wordsworth wrote, "Frenchmen had changed a war of self-defense / For one of conquest, losing sight of all / Which they had struggled for" (1805 *Prelude* 10: 791–794). In 1799 Napoleon, a general who consolidated his power in the Italian and Swiss campaigns, staged a coup d'etat and was named First Consul for life. The Revolution had evolved into a military dictatorship, its despotism confirmed when Napoleon crowned himself Emperor in 1804. A complex personality—a nightmare to entrenched monarchies; a charismatic military genius; a ruthless, egotistical imperialist—he generated nearly two decades of war that ravaged the Continent. Although war barely reached Britain, it was a constant threat, cost thousands of British lives and sent its economy into turmoil.

When Napoleon invaded the Iberian Peninsula in 1807, British support for the spontaneous resistance of the Portuguese and Spanish peoples enabled former radicals to return to the patriotic fold, to see their country as the champion of liberty against French imperialism. Napoleon's actions, claimed Coleridge, produced a "national unanimity unexampled in our history since the reign of Elizabeth . . . and made us all once more Englishmen." English self-definition was energized, the contest with France drawing on historical antagonisms that went back for centuries. Unlike the English, the French rejected their monarchy; if France could thus claim to be the first modern nation in the old world, Britain could feel superior to a country defined by the Terror and then Napoleon. National self-definition had strong literary manifestations. Hemans began her career with patriotic anthems celebrating Britain's support for the "noble" (and highly "romantic") Spanish resistance, and across these decades she published *Welsh Melodies, Greek Songs, Songs of Spain, National Lyrics*, and even the canonical American anthem, "The Landing of the Pilgrim Fathers" (our "Thanksgiving" hymn). Thomas Moore wrote *Irish Melodies* (1807–1834) and championed the grievances of Ireland. Byron wrote *Hebrew Melodies* (1815), got involved with Italian liberation movements, and in his last real-life romance, died in Greece where he had gone to aid the revolution against the Ottoman Empire.

Yet even as this literature tamed class differences into a general culture of songs for the salon, or made nationalism itself a vivid "romance," continuing disturbances pointed to those excluded from Coleridge's idealized whole of "us all . . . Englishmen." Its fears heightened by the threat of invasion, the government clamped down on any form of political expression that hinted at French ideas. Efforts to reform Parliament begun in the 1780s were stifled, as was the movement to abolish the slave trade, and even moderates were silenced by accusations of "Jacobinism" (sympathy with Revolutionary extremists). In 1791 authorities in Birmingham connived at three days of riots by a loyal "Church and King" mob against Dissenters who had held a dinner to commemorate the Fall of the Bastille. When his house and laboratory were sacked, the eminent chemist and nonconformist Joseph Priestley fled to London and then emigrated to America. In 1792 Paine fled to France; he was tried and convicted in absentia of sedition for writing *The Rights of Man*, and his publishers and booksellers were regularly prosecuted. In 1794, twelve London radicals were arrested, including a novelist and playwright, Thomas Holcroft, and Horne Tooke, a philologist whose publications seemed a dangerous attempt to democratize language. Charged with high treason, they were defended by Godwin and acquitted, but the trial was a harbinger of repression to come.

In 1794 the government suspended the long-established right of habeas corpus, which required the state to show cause for imprisonment and to conduct trials in a timely fashion; now anyone suspected of a crime could be jailed indefinitely. The Gagging Acts of 1795 targeted radical lecturers and societies, defining any criticism of the monarchy as treason and squelching political organization by limiting the size of meetings called to discuss reform. The Combination Act of 1799 forbade workmen, under penalty of conspiracy charges, to unionize or even to associate for purposes of collective bargaining. All these laws were enforced by government spies. Coleridge and Wordsworth, walking and conversing on the coastal hills of the Bristol Channel and plotting nothing more revolutionary than poems for *Lyrical Ballads*, looked suspicious enough to warrant tailing by a government informer. Coleridge was amused that their talk of the philosopher Spinoza was reported as references to "Spy Nozy," but actual radicals suffered severer consequences, for the government was also deploying *agents provocateurs* to incite them into capital offences. These infiltrators played a major role in plotting the Pentridge Rising of 1817 and the Cato Street Conspiracy of 1820, a scheme to murder cabinet ministers (a prime minister had been assassinated in 1812) and stage a coup d'état. "Cato Street" was "exposed" and its radical conspirators hanged or sent to prison in Australia, but the ultimate conspirator had been the government. Policy was still more severe outside England: in Edinburgh, delegates to the first British Convention of reformers were arrested for sedition and doomed to sentences in Australia; in Ireland, where Britain had more troops than on the Continent, a peasants' rebellion was crushed in a bloodbath (1798). Rather than international "fraternity," it was repression at home and wars abroad that defined the legacy of the French Revolution. When Napoleon was finally defeated in 1815 and the Bourbons were restored to the throne of France, the result was to reinforce reactionary measures and despotic monarchies all over Europe.

In the England of 1815, a further affliction was visited on the poor, among whom were many veterans, by Parliament's passage of the Corn Laws. Because importing grain had been impossible during the war years, prices for native grain soared; the Corn Laws now restricted imports in order to sustain the artificially high prices, a boon for landlords and a disaster for the poor, for whom bread was a chief article of diet. Bad harvests further raised costs. For the first time, in the estimate of the *Morning Chronicle*, protests and petitions erupted from "a majority of the adult male population of England," igniting food riots across the country. Under the unreformed electoral system, petitions to Parliament were the only recourse for those without representatives. In 1800 only males, and only five percent of them, were allowed to vote; only Anglicans, members of the state Church, could serve in the House of Lords. Workers did not have a vote, or even a representative in Parliament. The worker-populated cities of Leeds, Manchester, Birmingham, and Sheffield did not have a vote, whereas depopulated "rotten boroughs," consisting of one or two houses owned by a single landlord, enjoyed one or even two representatives in Parliament. As the Prince Regent returned from the opening of Parliament in January 1817, he found his carriage surrounded by a hostile crowd and stoned.

Workers were also being displaced by new machinery; they sometimes retaliated with attacks on the machines themselves, actions punishable by death (Byron's first speech in the House of Lords was against such a measure, the Frame-breaking Bill provoked by weavers' riots). Throughout the 1820s, farmworkers, angry at their degraded conditions, erupted into sporadic violence, culminating in a great uprising in 1830, in which barns burned across the countryside, and laborers again attacked machinery. The unemployed starved to death. Men scrambled for employment, while women and children, because they were deemed tractable and obedient, found it at pitiful wages. Prevailing attitudes and institutions were inadequate to ameliorate the misery and consequent disruptions. Since Elizabethan times, England had relied on a network of parishes and justices of the peace: local notables, serving in a largely volunteer capacity that enhanced their status, who kept records, assisted the needy, and administered everyday justice. Indigent newcomers to the cities could not easily be returned to their home parishes for support; they were needed as workers. And the parish system left out many: Irish Catholic immigrants, members of dissenting sects, and those lapsed from an Anglicanism that had failed to build churches for the new populations and at worst seemed remote from their concerns. When Lord John Manners declared that "the only means of Christianizing Manchester" was to revive the monasteries, he made clear the inadequacy of the current state Church to supply moral authority, social structure, and needed assistance.

No wonder that it was in Manchester that the modern vocabulary of class struggle emerged. The eighteenth-century ideal of stable social "orders" and "ranks" was challenged by a growing antagonism between successful capitalist entrepreneurs and their workers. In August 1819, nearly a hundred thousand mill-workers and their families gathered at nearby St. Peter's Field for a peaceful demonstration with banners and parades, capped by an address by the radical "Orator" Hunt calling for Parliamentary reform. Alarmed by the spectacle, the local ruling class sent their drunken, sabre-wielding militia to charge the rally and arrest Hunt. Hunt offered no resistance, but the militia struck out at the jeering though unarmed crowd and, backed by mounted Hussars, in ten minutes left an official toll of eleven dead, including one trampled child, and more than four hundred injured, many from sabre wounds. Unreported injuries and later deaths from injury undoubtedly added to the official toll. This pivotal event in nineteenth-century economic and political strife was immediately dubbed "Peterloo" by the left press—a sardonic echo of the celebrated British triumph over Napoleon at Waterloo, four years before. Parliament did not reform, but instead consolidated the repressive measures of previous decades into the notorious Six Acts at the end of 1819. These Acts outlawed demonstrations, empowered magistrates to enter private houses in search of arms, prohibited meetings of more than fifty unless all participants were residents of the parish in which the meeting was held, increased the prosecution of blasphemous or seditious libel (defined as language "tending to bring into hatred or contempt" the monarchy or government), and raised the newspaper tax, thus constricting the circulation of William Cobbett's radical *Political Register* by tripling its price.

THE MONARCHY

Outraged by the situation summed by "Peterloo," Percy Shelley mordantly surveyed *England in 1819*, the title of a sonnet whose language rendered it unpublishable, even in a radical newspaper such as his friend Leigh Hunt's *Examiner*. It began:

> An old, mad, blind, despised, and dying King,
> Princes, the dregs of their dull race, who flow
> Through public scorn,—mud from a muddy spring,—
> Rulers who neither see, nor feel, nor know . . .

The Lear-like king who inspired this contempt was George III, Washington's antagonist in the American Revolution. He had had an episode of mental instability in 1765 and another in 1788: he talked incessantly and rarely slept, and once his eldest son tried to throttle him. The episode at once epitomized their antagonism and reflected the political conflicts of the late Georgian era. The King lived a domestic life and his successive administrations were firmly Tory—that is, socially and politically "conservative," committed to the constitutional power of the monarchy and the Church, and opposed to concessions of greater religious and political liberties. The Prince lived extravagantly at taxpayers' expense, with a devout Roman Catholic mistress whom he secretly and unconstitutionally married. In 1787 he obtained an extra £10,000 from the King, a relief from Parliament of £100,000 to pay his debts, and an additional £60,000 to build his residence, Carlton House—a total equivalent to almost seven million dollars today. But because his comparative political flexibility held out the hope of some reforms, he was backed by the opposition party, the liberal Whigs. He expected the crown in 1788, but the King unexpectedly recovered, hanging on until November 1810, when he relapsed and became permanently mad. In January 1811 the Prince was appointed "Regent."

In this new position of power, he focused all the contradictions and tensions of the time. In 1812, the *Morning Post* addressed him in the loyalist hyperbole that earned it the nickname of the "Fawning Post": "You are the glory of the People . . . You breathe eloquence, you inspire the Graces—You are an Adonis in loveliness." Leigh and John Hunt replied in *The Examiner*, denouncing "this Adonis in Loveliness" as "a corpulent gentlemen of fifty . . . a man who had just closed half a century without one single claim on the gratitude of his country or the respect of posterity."

Thomas Lawrence. *Corona-
tion Portrait of the Prince
Regent (George IV), 1820.*

Their scathing rejoinder earned them two-year sentences for libel and fines of £500 each, but Leigh continued to edit *The Examiner* from his prison cell, which he transformed into a gentleman's parlor, where he was visited as a hero by Byron, Moore, Keats, and Lamb.

Meanwhile, the Prince Regent was transforming the face of London. He and his architects recreated Regent's Park in the north and St. James Park in the south, linking them by extending Regent Street, built Trafalgar Square, elevated Buckingham House into Buckingham Palace, and erected the Hyde Park arch. The "metropolitan improvements" bespoke impressive city planning, but also deliberately demarcated the boundaries between rich and poor. The Gothic/Chinese/Indian fantasy of his beloved retreat, the Brighton Pavilion, spoke even more loudly of his distance from the everyday life of his subjects. By 1815, when a mere £150 a year provided a comfortable living for many, he was £339,000 in debt, an extravagance that brought contempt on the monarchy. The pathos of George III attracted sympathy, whereas the son's conduct alienated the nation. On his accession to power, he abandoned his Whig friends, separated his estranged Queen Caroline from their daughter Charlotte, and was absent from Charlotte when she died in childbirth in 1817. In 1820, when George III died and he at last became King, he attempted to divorce Caroline by initiating a sordid investigation of her escapades abroad. The scandal rebounded on a man excoriated, in the Hunts' words, as "a libertine over head and heels in debt and disgrace, a despiser of domestic ties," and provided yet another handle for attacks upon him. The personal elegance that had made him "the first gentleman of Europe" had dissipated; already in 1813, Beau Brummell, an aristocratic "dandy" whose impeccable style and social assurance made him a paragon of the era, responded to a slight by the Regent by loudly inquiring of a fellow dandy, "who's your fat friend?" The Prince was too fat to mount his horse by 1816; by 1818 it was reported that "Prinny has let loose his belly which now reaches his knees." Of his official Coronation portrait, Moore acidly noted that it was "disgraceful both to the King & the painter—a lie upon canvas." It was inevitable that satiric sketches would compete for fame.

INDUSTRIAL ENGLAND AND "NEVER-RESTING LABOUR"

In the decades of this royal extravagance, the general population was rapidly expanding, accompanied by grim social misery. By 1750, the population of England and Wales was around five-and-a-half million; at the turn of the century, when the first census was taken, it was about eight million, with most of the increase in the last two decades. Scotland registered another million and a half, Ireland more than five million. Traditionally viewed as an index to a nation's wealth, population now loomed as a danger, inspiring the dire prophecy of Thomas Malthus's *On the Principle of Population As It Affects the Future Improvement of Society* (1798): "population, when unchecked, increases in a geometrical ratio. Subsistence increases only in an arithmetical ratio. A slight acquaintance with numbers will show the immensity of the first power in comparison of the second." The increase continued: by 1831 the population of Great Britain neared fourteen million.

The numbers do not tell the whole story. Ever since the end of the eighteenth century and then with postwar acceleration, the economic base of England had begun to shift from agriculture, controlled by wealthy aristocrats (the landlords), to manufacture, controlled by new-money industrialists. The war against France fueled a surge: "A race of merchants and manufacturers and bankers and loan jobbers and contractors" was born, remarked William Cobbett in 1802. Factories and mills invaded the countryside, pumped small towns into burgeoning cities, and cities into teeming metropolises. In 1800 only London—with about ten percent of the entire population of England and Wales—had more than a hundred thousand people. By 1837, when Victoria was crowned, there were five such cities, and London was growing by as much as twenty percent a decade. Even more staggering was the growth of the new industrial cities of the north. Manchester's population increased fivefold in fifty years, to 142,000 in 1831. Cobbett denounced these developments as "infernal," and many of his contemporaries, alarmed by the new concentrations of people and their demands for wages, food, and housing, feared a repetition at home of the mob violence of France.

This unprecedented concentration was the result of several converging factors. The 1790s had been racked by poor harvests, and harvests were bad again in 1815. Scarcities were aggravated by the Corn Laws and an increase of "Enclosure acts"—

the consolidation and privatization of the old common fields into larger and more efficient farms. The modernizing did improve agricultural yield and animal husbandry, thus offsetting in some measure Malthus's prediction of an inadequate food supply, but it also produced widespread dislocation and misery. The pattern of country landholding changed. Smallholders, whether independent but modest farmers or proprietors of estates up to a thousand acres, fell away, while the great estates prospered in size and number: "the big bull frog grasps all," Cobbett pungently remarked. Meanwhile, the farmers and herdsmen whom the enclosure acts rendered landless had to settle for meager subsistence wages in the country or migrate to the cities. The census of 1811 revealed for the first time that a majority of families were engaged in nonagricultural employment. The yeomen who had represented the mythic heart of sturdy English freedom became day laborers, while others sank into poverty. The reform of the farms eroded centuries-old social structures. Sending the Whig leader in Parliament a copy of *Lyrical Ballads* that he hoped might call attention to the plight of the rural poor, Wordsworth lamented that without a "little tract of land" as "a kind of permanent rallying point" in their hardships, "the bonds of domestic feeling ... have been weakened, and in innumerable instances entirely destroyed."

Uprooted families were pulled by hopes of employment to the new factory towns. Cotton made modern Manchester. By 1802 there were more than fifty spinning mills, and the once-provincial city had become one of the commercial capitals of Europe. Textiles produced in vast quantities by power looms eliminated skilled hand-weavers, and extinguished the traditional supplement to the income of the cottager. The city did not incorporate until 1838, and no regulations controlled manufacture, sanitation, or housing; the unchecked boom enriched the few master manufacturers and immiserated the workers. The factories required a workforce disciplined to the constant output of the machines they tended; families accustomed to the ebb and flow of agricultural rhythms found themselves plunged into a world of industrial clock-time. Twelve-to-fifteen-hour shifts, strict discipline, capricious firings, dangerous and unsanitary conditions, injuries, and ruined health were the rule of the day. Children were the preferred staff for the mills, and youngsters of five worked in the mines, their little bodies ideal for hauling coal in the narrow shafts. Workers were often further victimized by debts to their employers for housing and food. There was no philosophy of government restraint and regulation of these practices; all was "laissez-faire," the doctrine associated with Adam Smith's enormously influential *Wealth of Nations* (1777) that national wealth would flourish if businesses were left to operate with unfettered self-interest. By the 1780s there was a measurable gulf between rich and poor, ever more apparent in Manchester in the contrast between the homes of the wealthy in the suburbs and the slums by the polluted city river. "The town is abominably filthy," declared a visitor in 1808, "the Steam Engine is pestiferous, the Dyehouses noisome and offensive, and the water of the river as black as ink or the Stygian lake."

The twin agricultural and industrial revolutions recast both the town and the country and altered the relationship between them. To obtain the waterpower to drive them, early mills and factories were set by rivers, thereby converting peaceful valleys into sites of production. Gas lighting, first used in such buildings, made possible twenty-four-hour operation, and the resulting spectacle affected contemporaries as a weird and ominous splendor. In regions that were once the "assured domain of calm simplicity / And pensive quiet," wrote Wordsworth in *The Excursion* (1814):

> an unnatural light,
> Prepared for never-resting Labour's eyes,
> Breaks from a many-windowed Fabric huge;
> And at the appointed hour a Bell is heard—
> Of harsher import than the Curfew-knoll
> That spake the Norman Conqueror's stern behest,
> A local summons to unceasing toil!
> Disgorged are now the Ministers of day;
> And, as they issue from the illumined Pile,
> A fresh Band meets them, at the crowded door,—
> And in the Courts—and where the rumbling Stream,
> That turns the multitude of dizzy wheels,
> Glares, like a troubled Spirit, in its bed
> Among the rocks below. Men, Maidens, Youths,
> Mother and little Children, Boys and Girls,
> Enter, and each the wonted task resumes
> Within this Temple—where is offered up
> To Gain—the Master Idol of the Realm,
> Perpetual sacrifice.   (8. 169–187)

Industry invaded the most picturesque quarters of the British Isles. A center of tourism, Wales was also home to oppressive slate mines. Richard Pennant of North Wales epitomised the fortunes made in the trade in slaves and new-world commodities. Using the profits from his family's Jamaican sugar plantations, Pennant developed and mechanized the slate quarries on his estates. Elected to Parliament from Liverpool in 1783, he led the planters' defense of the slave trade while boosting the market for slate at home. Slate was an ideal roofing material, and the spread of education created a need for slate blackboards; at Port Penrhyn, the town Pennant established to ship slate, a hundred thousand writing slates were manufactured each year. In the eighteenth century, the quarries employed six hundred and the manufactory thirty more; by 1820 the workforce was a thousand, and it expanded rapidly over the next two decades. The concurrent discovery on the estate of minerals useful to the manufacture of Herculaneum pottery in Liverpool generated still more income. The profits underwrote Penryhn Castle, a lush Norman fantasy constructed (from 1821) by Pennant's heir.

The rhetoric of an 1832 history of Wales obscures the dislocations entailed by the progress it lauds: "About forty years ago, this part of the country bore a most wild, barren, and uncultivated appearance, but it is now covered with handsome villas, well built farm houses, neat cottages, rich meadows, well-cultivated fields, and flourishing plantations; bridges have been built, new roads made, bogs and swampy grounds drained and cultivated, neat fences raised, and barren rocks covered with woods." At Portmadoc, about twelve miles south of the sublime scenery of Mount Snowdon in Wales, William Madocks was performing one of the celebrated technological feats of the day, building a massive embankment (1808–1811), draining the tidal estuary behind it, enlarging the harbor, and founding a model village named after himself, Tremadoc—a project on which Percy Shelley enthusiastically collaborated, until he and his household fled from Wales in 1813 in the wake of a murderous attack. Popular biography ascribed the incident to Shelley's propensity to hallucination, but underlying it were genuine conflicts between idealist radicalism, paternalistic planning, local privilege, and labor unrest.

If Romantic poetry is famous for celebrating "Nature," this affection coincides with the peril to actual nature by modern industry. "Our feeling for nature," wrote Friedrich Schiller in the 1790s, "is like the feeling of an invalid for health." Industry scarred previously rural communities. Visiting Scotland in 1803 with her brother, Dorothy Wordsworth noted of one village: "a pretty place it once has been, but a manufactory is established there; and a townish bustle and ugly stone houses are fast taking the place of the brown-roofed thatched cottages." Of the famous Carron Ironworks, "seen at a distance," she noted, "the sky above them was red with a fiery light." Industry ringed even their beloved Lake District, and on its coast the shafts of the coal mines owned by the employer of Wordsworth's father, Sir James Lowther, ran ever deeper and longer, until they extended under the sea and even caused the collapse of houses in Whitehaven, the planned port city from which the coal was shipped.

The need to bring coal and iron into conjunction spurred improvements in transport. In 1759 the Duke of Bridgewater cut an eleven-mile canal between his colliery at Worsley and Manchester; two years later an extension linked Manchester to the sea. Soon canals transected the country; in 1790–1794 alone, eighty-one Acts for the construction of canals were passed. The cost of carriage was drastically cut, and the interior of England opened for commerce. By 1811 there were steamboats on the rivers; by 1812 locomotives were hauling coal. Large-scale road-building followed, including arteries between Shrewsbury and Holyhead (the port of departure for Ireland) and another between Carlisle and Glasgow in Scotland. During these years, a Scotsman, John Macadam, developed the road surface that bears his name. Across the country, distant regions were joined by a web of new roads and the Royal Mail coaches that ran along them on regular schedules. Decades later, remembering coach travel as it was in 1812, De Quincey recalled the new sensation of speed: "we saw it, we felt it as a thrilling; and this speed was not the product of blind insensate agencies, that had no sympathy to give, but was incarnated in the fiery eyeballs of an animal, in his dilated nostril, spasmodic muscles, and echoing hoofs" (*The English Mail-Coach, or the Glory of Motion* [1849]).

In this age of acceleration, the British Empire was expanding, too. Economically and politically, it had become the preeminent world power. The American colonies had been lost, but Canada and the West Indies remained, and Australia, New Zealand, and India marked a global reach. British forces subjugated natives, defeated rival French ambitions, and held the Turks and Russians in check, while the East India Company, originally a trading organization, gradually assumed administrative control of the subcontinent, even to the point of collecting taxes to protect British interests. The Company penetrated every aspect of British life: Warren Hastings, the first governor-general of India, was tried for cruelty and corruption, having amassed a fortune of over £400,000 in India. His trial, lasting from 1788 to 1795, was a *cause célèbre*, establishing the fame of the prosecutors even though he was acquitted. While his profits were exceptional, they marked a trend of great numbers of younger sons seeking fortunes in India. In a pattern common to north-country boys with the right connections, Wordsworth's family destined his younger brother John for service with the East India Company. "I will work for you," he said to William, "and you shall attempt to do something for the world." Although John lost his life in 1805 in the wreck of a tradeship, so widespread was the phenomenon of English fortunes based on Indian gain that "nabob," Hindi for "vicegerent" or "governor," entered the vernacular as a synonym for a wealthy man.

CONSUMERS AND COMMODITIES

Even more remarkable was the role of the East India Company as the prototype for later colonial rule. At a time when Oxford and Cambridge graduates were preparing for clerical orders, the Company college at Haileybury trained its students for their foreign service. Malthus taught there; both James Mill and son John Stuart Mill worked for the Company; Lamb was a clerk in the home office in London. And thousands more indirectly derived livelihoods or pleasures from the Company's activities. Napoleon sneered at Britain as "a nation of shopkeepers," taking this phrase from Smith's *Wealth of Nations:* "To found a great empire for the sole purpose of raising up a people of customers, may at first sight appear a project fit only for a nation of shopkeepers." But Smith's mercantile empire was a perspicuous forecast, confirmed in 1823 by Byron when he named England's pride as its "haughty shopkeepers, who sternly dealt / Their goods and edicts out from pole to pole, / And made the very billows pay them toll" (*Don Juan* 10:65).

Cotton and tea were major goods. So was opium, and behind the dreams of Coleridge's *Kubla Khan*, Keats's *Ode to a Nightingale* (whose poet compares his state of sensation to intoxication by "some dull opiate"), and De Quincey's *Confessions of an English Opium Eater* were grim realities. Laudanum, opium dissolved in alcohol, was widely prescribed for a variety of complaints; it was the chief ingredient in a host of sedatives for children, especially of the poor, whose families had to leave them at home while they worked. It was also a cheap intoxicant. When Marx said that "religion was the opium of the masses," he was not using a random metaphor. Opium virtually defined foreign profiteering. De Quincey's uncle was a colonel in Bengal, in the military service of the East India Company, which reaped enormous profits from producing opium and smuggling it into China against the prohibition of the Chinese government. A Member of Parliament remarked: "If the Chinese are to be poisoned by opium, I would rather they were poisoned for the benefit of our Indian subjects than for the benefit of any other Exchequer." But the profits accrued less to Indian subjects than to the ruling British, even as the Opium Wars served the larger purpose of opening China to Lancashire cotton, as India had been opened earlier: the Wars concluded with the annexation of Hong Kong, and the opening of five treaty ports to British commerce. Meanwhile, the persistence of slave labor in British colonial plantations (not abolished until 1833) continued to raise ethical questions about the traffic in their commodities. International affairs inescapably cast their shadow on national life: "By foreign wealth are British morals chang'd," charged Barbauld in 1791, "And Afric's sons, and India's, smile aveng'd."

As morals adjusted in relation to economic opportunities, the empire also fed a growing appetite for the exotic among those shut up in urban squalor, or merely in an increasingly routinized commercial life. For those who had the wherewithal, the era proffered a new world of objects, which had begun to proliferate in the late eighteenth century. An exemplary instance of the success of marketing joined to new technological advance is Josiah Wedgwood (1730–1795), whose cream-colored earthenware became known as "Queen's ware" because of Queen Charlotte's patronage in 1765, and, aided by that éclat, soon enjoyed a worldwide sale. In the 1770s he discovered how quickly high art could be transformed into status commodity, and began to produce imitation Greek vases, in vogue because of recent excavations at Herculaneum and Pompeii. The Wedgwood fortune enabled Josiah's sons to offer Coleridge an annuity of £150 so that he could devote himself to literature.

Alfred Bird, inventor of "Bird's Custard," pinned up in his Birmingham shop a telling motto mixing morality and the new imperatives of trade: "Early to bed. Early to rise / Stick to your work . . . And Advertise." From the late eighteenth century on, fashion magazines with colored plates advertised to provincial residents the latest styles of the capital. Even as she denounced the enslavement of women by "the perpetual fluctuation of fashion," Mary Hays conceded that "this constant variation of mode is serviceable to commerce, and promotes a brisk circulation of money" (*Letters and Essays*, 1793). This stimulus reached its acme with the arrival of *The Forget Me Not, a Christmas and New Year's Present for 1823*. More than sixty annuals emerged to capitalize on this pioneering venture, bearing such titles as *The Book of Beauty*. Partly because they targeted female readers, they were hospitable to female authors, including Shelley and Hemans. And becuase they paid so well, they also attracted male writers: Wordsworth, Coleridge, Southey, Lamb, and Scott published in them, even though literary contributions were subordinated to the engravings that were their most compelling feature. The elegantly produced annuals were best-sellers (*The Literary Souvenir* attained a circulation of fifteen thousand); copies were shipped across the empire months in advance.

Not only women and city-dwellers were seduced by the lure of shop windows, magazines, and circulating catalogues. Cobbett hurled jeremiads at the prosperous farmers who aspired to a gentility that set them apart from the workers they had once fed as part of the family:

> Everything about this farm-house was formerly the scene of *plain manners* and *plentiful living*. . . . But all appeared to be in a state of decay and nearly of disuse. There appeared to have been hardly any *family* in that house, where formerly there were, in all probability, from ten to fifteen men, boys, and maids: and, which was the worst of all, there was a *parlour*. Aye, and a *carpet* and a *bell-pull* too! . . . And, there were the decanters, the glasses, the "dinner-set" of crockery-ware, and all just in the true stock-jobber style. And I dare say it has been 'Squire Charington and the Miss Charingtons; and not plain Master Charington, and his son Hodge, and his daughter Betty Charington, all of whom this accursed system has, in all likelihood, transmuted into a species of mock gentlefolks, while it has ground the labourers down into real slaves. (*Rural Rides*, 20 October 1825)

This revolution in manners and family structure reduced "family" to its biological nucleus, replacing the economic unit that enfolded laborers, servants, and dependents. This was but one manifestation of the "acceleration" and "agitation" that, in De Quincey's words, characterized the period well before the French Revolution.

AUTHORSHIP, AUTHORITY, AND "ROMANTICISM"

In this fast-moving world, the fortunes of writers, too, began to rise and fall with new speed. Writing in *The Edinburgh Review* in 1829, the critic Francis Jeffrey meditated on "the perishable nature of modern literary fame":

> Since the beginning of our critical career, we have seen a vast deal of beautiful poetry pass into oblivion, in spite of our feeble efforts to recall or retain it in remembrance. The tuneful quartos of Southey are already little better than lumber:—And the rich melodies of Keats and Shelley,—and the fantastical emphasis of Wordsworth,—and the plebeian pathos of Crabbe, are melting fast from the fields of our vision. The novels of Scott have put out his poetry. Even the splendid strains of Moore are fading into distance and dimness, except where they have been married to immortal music; and the blazing star of Byron himself is receding from its place of pride. . . . The two who have the longest withstood this rapid withering of the laurel, and with the least marks of decay on their branches, are Rogers and Campbell; neither of them, it may be remarked, voluminous writers, and both distinguished rather for the fine taste and consummate elegance of their writ-

ings, than for the fiery passion, and disdainful vehemence, which seemed for a time to be so much more in favour with the public. . . . If taste and elegance, however, be titles to enduring fame, we might venture securely to promise that rich boon to the author before us.

The author before Jeffrey as he wrote was Felicia Hemans, a poet widely admired on both sides of the Atlantic but by the end of the century forgotten, except for a few anthology favorites. Meanwhile, with nearly three decades of reviewing experience, Jeffrey was unable to predict the durable fame of some of the writers who by the century's end would be deemed quintessential "romantics": Byron, Wordsworth, Keats, and Shelley. And he misguessed about Rogers and Campbell, though it is clear he would have attributed their demise to degraded public taste rather than intrinsic faults. What Jeffrey helps us see is that naming a literary canon is a matter of selection from a wide field, motivated by personal values. Other than Hemans, for instance, he thinks of English literary tradition as defined by men—even though Jane Austen and Mary Shelley proved to have as much durability as anyone in his census (Austen's novels and Shelley's *Frankenstein* have never been out of print). He also prefers literature of "fine taste" and "elegance" to the fiery passion and disdainful vehemence that other readers would admire in Byron and Shelley.

It was the conservative Jeffrey who first attempted to assess the "new poets," in the inaugural issue of the *Edinburgh* (1802). Here he castigates Southey as a member of a heretical "sect of poets, that has established itself in this country within these ten or twelve years, and is looked upon, we believe, as one of its chief champions and apostles." His polemical intent was to brand with all the excesses of the French Revolution a group he called "the Lakers" (from their residence in the Lake District): Southey, Wordsworth, and Coleridge. Well before Hazlitt, Jeffrey was blaming "the revolution in our literature" on "the agitations of the French revolution, and the discussion as well as the hopes and terrors to which it gave occasion." "A splenetic and idle discontent with the existing institutions of society, seems to be at the bottom of all their serious and peculiar sentiments"; "the ambition of Mr. Southey and some of his associates" is not "of that regulated and manageable sort which usually grows up in old established commonwealths," but "of a more undisciplined and revolutionary character which looks, we think with a jealous and contemptuous eye on the old aristocracy of the literary world."

By the Regency, the revolutionary "Lake School" was joined by the upstart "Cockney School," a term of insult fixed on Londoners Hazlitt, Hunt, and Keats, by the Scotsman John Gibson Lockhart, writing in *Blackwood's* in 1817, partly in response to Hunt's celebration of a vigorous school of "Young Poets" in essays he was writing for *The Examiner*. Hunt was a radical; Lockhart despised his politics. In 1821 ex-Laker and now Poet Laureate Southey identified still a third school. His youthful radicalism well behind him, he denounced the men "of diseased hearts and depraved imaginations" who formed "the Satanic School, . . . characterized by a Satanic spirit of pride and audacious impiety." Provoked by the allusion to himself and Percy Shelley, Byron responded with satiric attacks against both Southey personally and the establishment politics he had come to espouse. All these classifications were politically motivated—in most cases sneers at innovators and nonconformists or class-inflected put-downs. The designation of a "Romantic School" was not a product of the age itself, but was applied much later in the century—by literary historians with their own Victorian motivations and nostalgia.

With no sense of a monolithic movement that could be called "Romanticism," the polemical terms of the age itself mark a field animated by differences of location, class, gender, politics, and audience. The boundaries that appear rigid at one moment re-form when the perspective shifts: to Lockhart, Lakers (whom he respected) and

Cockneys were distinct; to Byron, a champion of Pope, Keats was both "a tadpole of the Lakes" and a Cockney brat who "abused Pope and Swift." And except for Hunt and Scott, most of these men bonded across class and political lines in their contempt of "Blue Stockings" (intellectual women) and female writers, even as these women were defining themselves for and against the stigmatized precedent of Wollstonecraft. Liberals, conservatives, and radicals; Byron and Shelley, self-exiled aristocrats in Italy; Wordsworth, Coleridge, and Southey praising domesticity in the Lakes; Keats, Hazlitt, and Hunt, an apprentice surgeon and working journalists, all precariously middle-class Londoners; women novelists, poets, and essayists, Blue Stockings and Wollstonecraftians, moralizers and rebels: the array is diverse and engaged in a contest for attention too keen to call debate or conversation.

The difficulty of specifying the term "Romantic" arises in part because it hovers between chronological and conceptual references. Its literature emerges in the social and literary ferment of the 1780s, a benchmark being the publication of Blake's *Songs of Innocence* in the climactic year of 1789. The period's close is usually seen in the 1830s—the decade in which George IV died, as did several writers who defined the age: Scott, Lamb, Coleridge, Hemans. By this time, too, Keats, Byron, and Percy Shelley, Austen, and most of the first generation were dead. In the same decade, Alfred Lord Tennyson's poetic career began, and Victoria was crowned Queen. Yet the temporal boundaries are fluid: "Romantic" Keats and "Victorian" Thomas Carlyle were born the same year, 1795, and Wordsworth's major poem, *The Prelude*, though he worked on it for a half century beginning in 1797 or so, was not published until the year of his death, 1850, the same year that Tennyson's quintessentially Victorian *In Memoriam* appeared. Much of Keats's poetry appeared for the first time after 1848, reviving interest in him among a new generation of readers.

Yet even with these ambiguous boundaries, the "Romantic" movement, from its first description in the nineteenth century until the mid-1980s, was characterized by men's writing. This was also a dominant spirit of the age, during which the powers of literary production—publishers, booksellers, reviews, and the press—were men's domains and not always open to female authors, and the culture as a whole was not receptive to female authority. Wollstonecraft's *Rights of Woman* (1792) was one of the first analyses to define "women" as an oppressed class that cut across national distinctions and historical differences—oppressed by lack of education, by lack of legal rights and access to gainful employment, as well as by a "prevailing opinion" about their character: that women were made to feel and be felt, rather than to think; their duty was to bear children and be domestic drudges, to obey their fathers and their husbands without complaint. Women writers faced more than a few challenges. One was the pervasive cultural attitude that a woman who presumed to authority, published her views, and even aspired to make a living as an author was grossly immodest, decidedly "unfeminine," and probably a truant from her domestic calling. Many women published anonymously, under male pseudonyms, with the proper title "Mrs." or, as in Austen's case, under an anonymous and socially modest signature, "by a Lady" (not one of Austen's novels bore her name). They also maintained propriety by hewing to subjects and genres deemed "feminine"—not political polemic, epic poetry, science or philosophy but children's books, conduct literature, travel writing (if it was clear they had proper escorts), household hints, cookbooks, novels of manners, and poems of sentiment and home, of patriotism and religious piety. Women who transgressed provoked harsh discipline. When Barbauld ventured an anti-imperialist poem, *Eighteen Hundred and Eleven*, the Tory *Quarterly Review* exercised reproof precisely in terms of the gender-genre transgression:

Mrs. Barbauld turned satirist! . . . We had hoped, indeed, that the empire might have been saved without the intervention of a lady-author. . . . Her former works have been of some utility; her "Lessons for Children," her "Hymns in Prose," her "Selections from the Spectator," . . . but we must take the liberty of warning her to desist from satire . . . writing any more pamphlets in verse. (June 1812)

Barbauld took this advice to heart, and published no more. About fifteen years earlier, Anglican arbiter Richard Polwhele viciously listed a whole set of contemporary female writers in his poem *The Unsex'd Females,* with virulent animosity to Wollstonecraft. They are "unsex'd" by their public stance, parading what "ne'er our fathers saw."

The Tory *British Critic,* on the occasion of praising Hemans's excellence "in painting the strength and the weaknesses of her own lovely sex" and the "womanly nature throughout all her thoughts and her aspirations," kept up the surveillance, taking the opportunity to despise anything that advertised the intellectual and critical authority of women. It opened its review of Hemans (1823) not with a discussion of the work at hand but with an assault on the world that was changing before its eyes, against which it invokes every counterauthority, from divine creation, to modern science, to Shakespeare, to the language of ridicule and disgust:

> We heartily abjure Blue Stockings. We make no compromise with any variation of the colour, from sky-blue to Prussian blue, blue stockings are an outrage upon the eternal fitness of things. It is a principle with us to regard an Academicienne of this Society, with the same charity that a cat regards a vagabond mouse. We are inexorable to special justifications. We would fain make a fire in Charing-Cross, of all the bas bleus in the kingdom, and albums, and commonplace books, as accessaries [sic] before or after the fact, should perish in the conflagration.
>
> Our forefathers never heard of such a thing as a Blue Stocking, except upon their sons' legs; the writers of Natural History make no mention of the name. . . . Shakspeare, who painted all sorts and degrees of persons and things, who compounded or created thousands, which, perhaps, never existed, except in his own prolific mind, even he, in the wildest excursion of his fancy never dreamed of such an extraordinary combination as a Blue Stocking! No!

The extraordinary combination, however, was there to stay, and even with all these constraints, women writers thrived. More, Barbauld, Mary Robinson, Charlotte Smith, and Maria Edgeworth stand out among those who earned both reputation and a living through poetry, novels, and tracts on education and politics, freely crossing the borders between public and private spheres, male and female realms.

POPULAR PROSE

When *The Edinburgh Review* was founded in 1802 as an organ of liberal political opinion, it raised the status of periodical writing. "To be an Edinburgh Reviewer," opined William Hazlitt, who freelanced in the journal, "is, I suspect, the highest rank in modern literary society." By the end of the decade, the rival Tory *Quarterly Review* arrived on the scene. The quarterlies favored an authoritative, anonymous voice, while new monthly magazines revived the lighter manner of the eighteenth-century "familiar essay." *Blackwood's* (founded 1817) printed raffish conversations set in a nearby tavern, and the *London* (founded 1820) hosted Lamb's essays and De Quincey's *Confessions of an English Opium Eater.* Whether the topic was imaginative literature, social observation, science, or political commentary, the personality of the essayist and the literary performance—by turns meditative, autobiographical, analytical, whimsical, terse and expansive—were what commanded attention. "All the great geniuses of the day are Periodical," declared John Wilson, writing in *Blackwood's* in 1829—a self-interested judgment, but true insofar as it acknowledges the new importance of the periodical essay. Meanwhile, beneath the realm of the respectable journals, though not out of their anxious sight, thrived William Cobbett, who published a weekly newspaper, the *Political Register* (founded 1802), its price low enough to evade the stamp tax (thus becoming known as "The Two-Penny Trash"). It reached a circulation of forty or fifty thousand and helped make him the most widely read writer of his era, and surely the most prolific, with an output estimated at more than twenty million words.

If later decades tended to represent "Romanticism" largely as an age of poetry, in the age itself, poetry, traditionally the genre of prestige, had to compete with prose, and not just the engaging new essay form, but also, and quite emphatically, the once-disreputable novel. The novel had begun to command new attention after the success of Godwin's political romance from the 1790s, *Caleb Williams*, and new respect after the critical and popular success of Scott's *Waverley* (1814). With dozens of works of narrative fiction over the next two decades, Scott perfected the genre of historical "romance"—"the interest of which turns upon marvelous and uncommon incidents," he said in a review of Austen. As the occasion indicates, the novel was also a genre in which women achieved considerable success—perhaps why, in addition to its status as a "low" form, Sir Walter kept his authorship of the *Waverley* novels anonymous. In *Waverley*, Scott spoofed the gothic devices that animated Ann Radcliffe's sensational "gothic" novels. But Radcliffe was remarkably popular; the genre that she perfected in the 1790s caught everyone's attention, including publishers'. She received the unheard of sum of £500 for *The Mysteries of Udolpho* (1794), topped by £600 for *The Italian* (1797), and achieved unprecedented fame for a novelist of any sex. Edgeworth's regional-historical novels, their career launched in 1800 with *Castle Rackrent* and extending over a quarter century, also caught the attention of Scott, who dubbed her "the great Maria" both out of admiration for a genre that shaped his own ventures and in recognition of her considerable financial success. Hannah More's only novel, *Coelebs in Search of a Wife* (1808), ran through twelve editions in its first year, and before her death in 1833 had sold thirty thousand copies in America alone. Shelley produced a durable masterpiece with *Frankenstein* (1818 and 1831), while Austen's novels caught public interest with their sharp social observation and stories of heroines coming of age in a world of finely calibrated social codes and financial pressures. With Scott, she would be deemed one of the major figures in the genre.

Throughout the years, social turmoil and technological change fostered a proliferation of writing. In the Preface to *Lyrical Ballads* (1800) Wordsworth deplored the "multitude of causes unknown to former times . . . now acting with a combined force to blunt the discriminating powers of the mind," and diagnosed the most virulent as "the great national events which are daily taking place, and the encreasing accumulation of men in cities, where the uniformity of their occupations produces a craving for extraordinary incident which the rapid communication of intelligence hourly gratifies." Newspapers, daily and Sunday, multiplied to meet this craving. In 1814 the London *Times* converted to a steam press, and doubled circulation. Newspaper sales reached thirty million, with yet more readers in the coffee-houses and subscription reading-rooms that took papers that taxes rendered too expensive for individual purchase. Parliamentary commissions and boards of review collected information and compiled statistics and summaries as never before on every aspect of the nation's economy and policies, and the press disseminated them. Cobbett ceaselessly lambasted the fundholders who profited from the debts incurred by the war, even as those who had fought suffered from the postwar depression; John Wade investigated sinecures, aristocratic incomes, pluralism in the Church, corruption in Parliament, and the expenditures of the civil list, and published his findings in the sensational *Black Book* (1820), available in sixpenny installments that sold ten thousand copies each.

THE PRESS, invented much about the same time with the *Reformation*, hath done more mischief to the discipline of our Church, than all the doctrine can make amends for. 'Twas an happy time, when all learning was in manuscript, and some little officer did keep the keys of the library! Now, since PRINTING came into the world, such is the mischief, that *a man cannot write a book but presently he is answered!* There have been ways found out to fine not the people, but even the *grounds and fields where they assembled*: but no art yet could prevent these SEDITIOUS MEETINGS OF LETTERS! Two or three brawny fellows in a corner, with mere ink and elbow-grease, do more harm than an *hundred systematic divines*. Their ugly printing *letters*, that look but like so many rotten teeth, how oft have they been pulled out by the public tooth-drawers! And yet these rascally operators of the press have got a trick to fasten them again in a few minutes, that they grow as firm a set, and as biting and talkative as ever! O PRINTING! how hast thou *"disturbed the peace!"* Lead, when moulded into ballets, is not so mortal as when founded into *letters!* There was a mistake sure in the story of Cadmus; and the *serpent's teeth* which he sowed, were nothing else but the *letters* which he invented.
Marvell's Rehearsal transprosed, 4to, 1672.

Being marked only with *four and twenty letters,—variously transposed* by the help of a PRINTING PRESS,—PAPER works miracles. The Devil dares no more come near a *Stationer's* heap, or a *Printer's Office*, than *Rats* dare put their noses into a Cheesemonger's Shop.
A Whip for the Devil, 1669. p. 92.

George Cruikshank. *The Press*, from the satirical pamphlet *The Political Showman—at Home!* by William Hone, 1821.

The explosion of readers at once liberated authors from patronage and exposed them to the turbulent and precarious world of the literary marketplace. In 1812 Jeffrey reckoned that among "the higher classes" there were twenty thousand readers, but at least "two hundred thousand who read for amusement and instruction, among the middling classes of society," defining "middling" as those "who do not aim at distinction or notoriety beyond the circle of their equals in fortune or station." Faced with an audience fissured along class lines, he thought that it was "easy to see" which group an author should please. But others looked to the growing number of literate poor who lacked traditional education, vast numbers whose allegiance was fought over by radicals like Cobbett and Paine and conservatives such as More, whose *Cheap Repository Tracts* (1795–1799) were circulated by the millions.

Such journalism diffused and intensified troubled perceptions of the functioning of society and one's place in it. "The beginning of Inquiry is Disease," intoned Carlyle; he inveighed against "the diseased self-conscious state of Literature" but this self-consciousness was its character. Uncertain of the audience(s) by whom they would be read, writers resorted to an ironic wavering that sought to forestall being pinned down to a position and dismissed, or devised various strategies to seduce assent: the development of the authorial "I" whom readers might come to trust as an authentic percipient, personae that insiders would be able to penetrate, and codings that would deepen a sense of solidarity among a constituency. Wordsworth had made his name with the highly personal, but culturally resonant, lyric outpouring of "Lines, Composed a few miles above Tintern Abbey, On Revisiting the Banks of they Wye during a Tour, July 13, 1798" (*Lyrical Ballads*, 1798); he celebrated his return from France in 1802 with a sonnet "Composed in the Valley, near Dover, On the Day of Landing," rejoicing in familiar sights of rivers and boys at play: "All, all are English." In a neighboring sonnet in the same collection, though, he complained, "The world is too much with us," running our lives with "getting and spending" and alienating our hearts from "Nature."

Wordsworth remained ambivalent about developing a voice and a literature that would gain popular reception, and continued to resent those, such as Scott, who were more successful in these terms. But the new world and the new literatures were finding remarkable sympathy in many quarters. Scott's first romance, *The Lay of the Last Minstrel* (1805), sold well over 2,000 copies within a year of publication, and nearly 10,000 more by 1807. His publisher offered him 1,000 guineas, sight unseen, for his next poetic romance, *Marmion* (1808). Scott said the sum "made men's hair stand on end," but the bargain was a good one on both sides: by 1811 it had sold 28,000 copies. These figures were topped by Byron, who, Scott good-naturedly conceded, drove him from the field of poetry, while his own *Waverley* novels proved still more popular. Over his lifetime, Scott made about £80,000 from his writing. That Byron's *Corsair* (1814) could sell 10,000 copies on the day of publication testifies to the mechanisms of production, publicity, and sales the book trade commanded. Byron was not embarrassed to seek £2600 for *Childe Harold IV* (1818). It must have galled Wordsworth that his publisher gave Thomas Moore 3,000 guineas for *Lalla Rookh*, more than had ever been offered for a single poem. Yet along with these stunning successes, other careers were more modestly compensated, and poets, at least, did not often enjoy the degree of prosperity that the novelists did.

The volatility of the market and of public taste points to salient qualities of the period: a heightened awareness of differences and boundaries, and of the energies generated along their unstable edges, and even more, a heightened awareness of time and history, public and cultural as well as personal. "Romanticism" denotes less a unified concept, or even a congeries of ideas, than an era and a literature of clashing systems, each plausibly claiming allegiance, in a world of rapid change.

Anna Laetitia Barbauld

1743–1825

Barbauld's long career exemplifies that of the professional woman of letters: a respected poet (and not only on conventionally feminine themes), a writer on radical causes throughout the 1790s, an early welcomer of Coleridge (who presented her with a prepublication copy of *Lyrical Ballads*), and a friend of Priestley, Hannah More, and Joanna Baillie. The daughter of John Aikin, master of Warrington Academy, a celebrated institution of English Dissenting culture where she lived between the ages of fifteen and thirty, Anna Laetitia Aikin is said to have learned to read English by the age of three, Italian and French not long afterwards, and Greek and Latin while still a child. Her first volume of *Poems* (1773) went through five editions in four years; in the same year, she published *Miscellaneous Pieces in Prose* with her brother John, later editor of the *Monthly Magazine*, an influential radical journal. In 1774 she married Rochemont Barbauld, a Dissenting clergyman, with whom she ran a school. Samuel Johnson derided the activity as the waste of a fine education, but it led to her often reprinted *Lessons for Children* (1778) and *Hymns in Prose for Children* (1781). After the increasing mental instability of her husband led to the closing of their school, she undertook ambitious editorial projects. In 1794 she produced an edition of Akenside, one of Collins in 1797, and in 1804 a six-volume edition of the *Correspondence of Samuel Richardson*, followed by a fifty-volume set of *The British Novelists* (1810), with biographical introductions and a sophisticated preface arguing for the instructive value of a genre derided as mere entertainment, as well as a popular anthology for young women, *The Female Speaker* (1811). Like Wollstonecraft, she believed that young women should be educated to become wives and mothers. Her lively domestic realism is shown in her poem *Washing-Day* (1797), which moves from mock-epic to personal recollection to its concluding instance of a recent scientific advance, the Montgolfier brothers' balloon ascent, effortlessly crossing the conventional boundaries of private and public, feminine and masculine, realms; *The First Fire* likewise surprisingly joins a celebration of the domestic hearth to a vista of geological process. Barbauld thus consistently opens up traditional themes and poetic forms in the service of a powerful social and poetic vision.

The Mouse's Petition to Dr. Priestley[1]

O hear a pensive prisoner's prayer,
    For liberty that sighs;
And never let thine heart be shut
    Against the wretch's cries!

5 For here forlorn and sad I sit,
    Within the wiry grate;
And tremble at the approaching morn,
    Which brings impending fate.

If e'er thy breast with freedom glowed,
10   And spurned a tyrant's chain,
Let not thy strong oppressive force
    A free-born mouse detain!

1. The full title in early editions is *The Mouse's Petition, Found in the trap where he had been confined all night*, accompanied by a motto from Virgil's *Aeneid* (6.853): "Parcere subjectis & debellare superbos" [To spare the conquered, and subdue the proud]. Joseph Priestley (1733–1804), political radical and eminent chemist who discovered oxygen, had been testing the properties of gases on captured household mice. Tradition has it that Barbauld's petition succeeded, and this mouse was released.

O do not stain with guiltless blood
    Thy hospitable hearth;
15   Nor triumph that thy wiles betrayed
    A prize so little worth.

The scattered gleanings of a feast
    My frugal meals supply;
But if thine unrelenting heart
20   That slender boon deny,—

The cheerful light, the vital air,
    Are blessings widely given;
Let nature's commoners enjoy
    The common gifts of heaven.

25   The well-taught philosophic mind
    To all compassion gives:
Casts round the world an equal eye,
    And feels for all that lives.

If mind,—as ancient sages taught,—
30   A never-dying flame,
Still shifts through matter's varying forms,
    In every form the same;

Beware, lest in the worm you crush
    A brother's soul you find;
35   And tremble lest thy luckless hand
    Dislodge a kindred mind.

Or, if this transient gleam of day
    Be *all* of life we share,
Let pity plead within thy breast
40   That little *all* to spare.

So may thy hospitable board
    With wealth and peace be crowned;
And every charm of heartfelt ease
    Beneath thy roof be found.

45   So when destruction lurks unseen,
    Which men, like mice, may share,
May some kind angel clear thy path,
    And break the hidden snare.

1771   1773

On a Lady's Writing

Her even lines her steady temper show,
Neat as her dress, and polished as her brow;
Strong as her judgment, easy as her air;
Correct though free, and regular though fair:
And the same graces o'er her pen preside,
That form her manners and her footsteps guide.

                                            1773

Inscription for an Ice-House[1]

Stranger, approach! within this iron door
Thrice locked and bolted, this rude arch beneath
That vaults with ponderous stone the cell; confined
By man, the great magician, who controuls
5   Fire, earth and air, and genii of the storm,
And bends the most remote and opposite things
To do him service and perform his will,—
A giant sits; stern Winter; here he piles,
While summer glows around, and southern gales
10 Dissolve the fainting world, his treasured snows°   *sherberts*
Within the rugged cave.—Stranger, approach!
He will not cramp thy limbs with sudden age,
Nor wither with his touch the coyest flower
That decks thy scented hair. Indignant here,
15 Like fettered Sampson[2] when his might was spent
In puny feats to glad the festive halls
Of Gaza's wealthy sons; or he who sat
Midst laughing girls submiss, and patient twirled
The slender spindle in his sinewy grasp;[3]
20 The rugged power, fair Pleasure's minister,
Exerts his art to deck the genial board;
Congeals the melting peach, the nectarine smooth,
Burnished and glowing from the sunny wall:
Darts sudden frost into the crimson veins
25 Of the moist berry; moulds the sugared hail:
Cools with his icy breath our flowing cups;
Or gives to the fresh dairy's nectared bowls
A quicker zest. Sullen he plies his task,
And on his shaking fingers counts the weeks
30 Of lingering Summer, mindful of his hour
To rush in whirlwinds forth, and rule the year.

c. 1793   1825

To a Little Invisible Being
Who Is Expected Soon to Become Visible

Germ of new life, whose powers expanding slow
For many a moon their full perfection wait,—
Haste, precious pledge of happy love, to go
Auspicious borne through life's mysterious gate.

5 What powers lie folded in thy curious frame,—
Senses from objects locked, and mind from thought!
How little canst thou guess thy lofty claim
To grasp at all the worlds the Almighty wrought!

1. The ice-house, where blocks of ice were kept cold in the warmer months, was the commonest form of refrigeration before the twentieth century.
2. Judges 16 relates the imprisonment of the blinded Samson in Gaza, forced to make "sport" for the Philistines; the story forms the subject of Milton's tragedy, *Samson Agonistes* (1671).
3. Hercules, who served a term as slave to Queen Omphale, during which time he performed women's tasks.

And see, the genial season's warmth to share,
10 Fresh younglings shoot, and opening roses glow!
Swarms of new life exulting fill the air,—
Haste, infant bud of being, haste to blow!°   *bloom*

For thee the nurse prepares her lulling songs,
The eager matrons count the lingering day;
15 But far the most thy anxious parent longs
On thy soft cheek a mother's kiss to lay.

She only asks to lay her burden down,
That her glad arms that burden may resume;
And nature's sharpest pangs her wishes crown,
20 That free thee living from thy living tomb.

She longs to fold to her maternal breast
Part of herself, yet to herself unknown;
To see and to salute the stranger guest,
Fed with her life through many a tedious moon.

25 Come, reap thy rich inheritance of love!
Bask in the fondness of a Mother's eye!
Nor wit nor eloquence her heart shall move
Like the first accents of thy feeble cry.

Haste, little captive, burst thy prison doors!
30 Launch on the living world, and spring to light!
Nature for thee displays her various stores,
Opens her thousand inlets of delight.

If charmed verse of muttered prayers had power,
With favouring spells to speed thee on thy way,
35 Anxious I'd bid my beads° each passing hour,   *tell my rosary*
Till thy wished smile thy mother's pangs o'erpay.
c. 1795   1825

To the Poor[1]

Child of distress, who meet'st the bitter scorn
Of fellow men to happier prospects born,
Doomed art and nature's various stores to see
Flow in full cups of joy,—and not for thee,
5 Who seest the rich, to heaven and fate resign'd,
Bear *thy* afflictions with a patient mind;
Whose bursting heart disdains unjust controll,
Who feel'st oppression's iron in thy soul,
Who drag'st the load of faint and feeble years,
10 Whose bread is anguish and whose water tears—
Bear, bear thy wrongs, fulfil thy destined hour,
Bend thy meek neck beneath the foot of power!

---

1. Barbauld wrote that this poem was "inspired by indignation on hearing sermons in which the poor are addressed in a manner which evidently shows the design of making religion an engine of government."

But when thou feel'st the great deliverer nigh,
And thy freed spirit mounting seeks the sky,
15 Let no vain fears thy parting hour molest,
No whispered terrors shake thy quiet breast,
Think not their threats can work thy future woe,
Nor deem the Lord above, like Lords below.
Safe in the bosom of that love repose
20 By whom the sun gives light, the ocean flows,
Prepare to meet a father undismayed,
Nor fear the God whom priests and kings have made.

1795   1825

Washing-Day

". . . And their voice,
Turning again towards childish treble, pipes
And whistles in its sound."[1]

The Muses are turned gossips; they have lost
The buskined° step, and clear, high-sounding phrase,   *tragic*
Language of gods. Come, then, domestic Muse,
In slipshod measure° loosely prattling on   *loose metres*
5 Of farm or orchard, pleasant curds and cream,
Or drowning flies, or shoe lost in the mire
By little whimpering boy, with rueful face;
Come, Muse, and sing the dreaded Washing-day.
Ye who beneath the yoke of wedlock bend,
10 With bowed soul, full well ye ken the day
Which week, smooth sliding after week, brings on
Too soon;—for to that day nor peace belongs,
Nor comfort; ere the first gray streak of dawn,
The red-armed washers come and chase repose.
15 Nor pleasant smile, nor quaint device of mirth,
E'er visited that day: the very cat,
From the wet kitchen's scared and reeking° hearth,   *smoking*
Visits the parlor,—an unwonted guest.
The silent breakfast-meal is soon despatched;
20 Uninterrupted, save by anxious looks
Cast at the lowering° sky, if sky should lower.   *threatening*
From that last evil, O preserve us, heavens!
For should the skies pour down, adieu to all
Remains of quiet: then expect to hear
25 Of sad disasters,—dirt and gravel stains
Hard to efface, and loaded lines at once
Snapped short,—and linen-horse° by dog thrown down, *drying rack for sheets*
And all the petty miseries of life.
Saints have been calm while stretched upon the rack,
30 And Guatimozin[2] smiled on burning coals;

---

1. Shakespeare, loosely quoted from *As You Like It* (2.7 161–63), Jaques's speech on the seven ages of man. 2. Cuauhtemoc, the last Aztec emperor of Mexico, tortured and executed by Cortés in 1525.

But never yet did housewife notable°   *efficient*
Greet with a smile a rainy washing-day.
But grant the welkin° fair, require not thou   *the heavens*
Who call'st thyself perchance the master there,
35   Or study swept, or nicely dusted coat,
Or usual 'tendance,—ask not, indiscreet,
Thy stockings mended, though the yawning rents
Gape wide as Erebus;[3] nor hope to find
Some snug recess impervious: shouldst thou try
40   The 'customed garden-walks, thine eyes shall rue
The budding fragrance of thy tender shrubs,
Myrtle or rose, all crushed beneath the weight
Of coarse checked apron,—with impatient hand
Twitched off when showers impend: or crossing lines
45   Shall mar thy musings, as the wet, cold sheet
Flaps in thy face abrupt. Woe to the friend
Whose evil stars have urged him forth to claim
On such a day the hospitable rites!
Looks, blank at best, and stinted courtesy,
50   Shall he receive. Vainly he feeds his hopes
With dinner of roast chicken, savory pie,
Or tart, or pudding:—pudding he nor tart
That day shall eat; nor, though the husband try,
Mending what can't be helped, to kindle mirth
55   From cheer deficient, shall his consort's brow
Clear up propitious: the unlucky guest
In silence dines, and early slinks away.
I well remember, when a child, the awe
This day struck into me; for then the maids,
60   I scarce knew why, looked cross, and drove me from them:
Nor soft caress could I obtain; nor hope
Usual indulgences; jelly or creams,
Relic of costly suppers, and set by
For me their petted one, or buttered toast,
65   When butter was forbid; or thrilling tale
Of ghost or witch or murder,—so I went
And sheltered me beside the parlor fire:
There my dear grandmother, eldest of forms,
Tended the little ones, and watched from harm,
70   Anxiously fond, though oft her spectacles
With elfin cunning hid, and oft the pins
Drawn from her ravelled stockings, might have soured
One less indulgent.—
At intervals my mother's voice was heard,
75   Urging despatch: briskly the work went on,
All hands employed to wash, to rinse, to wring,
To fold, and starch, and clap, and iron, and plait.
Then would I sit me down, and ponder much

3. In Greek mythology, the dark passage through which souls enter Hades.

Why washings were. Sometimes through hollow bowl
80   Of pipe amused we blew, and sent aloft
The floating bubbles; little dreaming then
To see, Montgolfier,[4] thy silken ball
Ride buoyant through the clouds,—so near approach
The sports of children and the toils of men.
85   Earth, air, and sky, and ocean hath its bubbles,
And verse is one of them,—this most of all.

          1797

The First Fire
October 1st, 1815

Ha, old acquaintance! many a month has past
Since last I viewed thy ruddy face; and I,
Shame on me! had mean time well nigh forgot
That such a friend existed. Welcome now!—
5   When summer suns ride high, and tepid airs
Dissolve in pleasing langour; then indeed
We think thee needless, and in wanton pride
Mock at thy grim attire and sooty jaws,
And breath sulphureous, generating spleen,—
10   As Frenchmen say; Frenchmen, who never knew
The sober comforts of a good coal fire.
—Let me imbibe thy warmth, and spread myself
Before thy shrine adoring:—magnet thou
Of strong attraction, daily gathering in
15   Friends, brethren, kinsmen, variously dispersed,
All the dear charities of social life,
To thy close circle. Here a man might stand,
And say, This is my world! Who would not bleed
Rather than see thy violated hearth
20   Prest by a hostile foot? The winds sing shrill;
Heap on the fuel! Not the costly board,
Nor sparkling glass, nor wit, nor music, cheer
Without thy aid. If thrifty thou dispense
Thy gladdening influence, in the chill saloon
25   The silent shrug declares th' unpleased guest.
—How grateful to belated traveller
Homeward returning, to behold the blaze
From cottage window, rendering visible
The cheerful scene within! There sits the sire,
30   Whose wicker chair, in sunniest nook enshrined,
His age's privilege,—a privilege for which
Age gladly yields up all precedence else
In gay and bustling scenes,—supports his limbs.
Cherished by thee, he feels the grateful warmth
35   Creep through his feeble frame and thaw the ice

---

4. In 1783, in France, the Montgolfier brothers launched the first hot-air balloon.

Of fourscore years, and thoughts of youth arise.
—Nor less the young ones press within, to see
Thy face delighted, and with husk of nuts,
Or crackling holly, or the gummy pine,
40   Feed thy immortal hunger: cheaply pleased
They gaze delighted, while the leaping flames
Dart like an adder's tongue upon their prey;
Or touch with lighted reed thy wreaths of smoke;
Or listen, while the matron sage remarks
45   Thy bright blue scorching flame and aspect clear,
Denoting frosty skies. Thus pass the hours,
While Winter spends without his idle rage.

—Companion of the solitary man,
From gayer scenes withheld! With thee he sits,
50   Converses, moralizes; musing asks
How many eras of uncounted time
Have rolled away since thy black unctuous° food   oily
Was green with vegetative life, and what
This planet then: or marks, in sprightlier mood,
55   Thy flickering smiles play round the illumined room,
And fancies gay discourse, life, motion, mirth,
And half forgets he is a lonely creature.

—Nor less the bashful poet loves to sit
Snug, at the midnight hour, with only thee
60   Of his lone musings conscious. Oft he writes,
And blots, and writes again; and oft, by fits,
Gazes intent with eyes of vacancy
On thy bright face; and still at intervals,
Dreading the critic's scorn, to thee commits,
65   Sole confidant and safe, his fancies crude.

—O wretched he, with bolts and massy bars
In narrow cell immured, whose green, damp walls,
That weep unwholesome dews, have never felt
Thy purifying influence! Sad he sits
70   Day after day till in his youthful limbs
Life stagnates, and the hue of hope is fled
From his wan cheek. And scarce less wretched he,—
When wintry winds blow loud and frosts bite keen,—
The dweller of the clay-built tenement,
75   Poverty-struck, who, heart[h]less, strives to raise
From sullen turf, or stick plucked from the hedge,
The short-lived blaze; while chill around him spreads
The dreary fen, and Ague, sallow-faced,
Stares through the broken pane;—assist him, ye
80   On whose warm roofs the sun of plenty shines,
And feel a glow beyond material fire!

1815   1825

The Rights of Man and
the Revolution Controversy

"The Revolution in France," wrote Percy Shelley, "overthrew the hierarchy, the aristocracy, and the monarchy, and the whole of that peculiarly insolent and oppressive system on which they were based." Celebrated international center of high culture and progressive philosophy, eighteenth-century France was also a country of profound social inequalities and oppression. Dissatisfaction had been growing against the corrupt and inefficient aristocracy, who relentlessly taxed the lower classes (the "Third Estate": peasants, serfs, yeomen, industrial workers and economically independent bourgeoisie) without granting them political power. Tensions mounted in the 1780s as the government went bankrupt and tried to hold on with more taxation and the imprisonment of dissidents, without trial, in the Bastille prison in Paris. Open rebellion broke out with the storming of the Bastille in 1789 and radiated into a series of cataclysmic events watched from across the English Channel, and witnessed by some English visitors to France, with a mixture of interest, sympathy, and horror.

Support for the Revolution was a coterie enthusiasm in England rather than widespread, but it was still of concern to the government and allied institutions. Following the American Revolution, and close to the centenary of Britain's "Glorious Revolution" of 1688, this latest upheaval underscored to European monarchies the insecurity of long-standing alliances of church, state, and aristocracy, and seemed to herald an inevitable movement of "the spirit of the age" toward liberalism and democracy. Political idealists took fire, enchanted by the bold reformation of French life, including not only a new government but also new street names, a new calendar (Year I beginning 21 September 1792) with new month names, new deities (the goddesses Reason, Liberty), and new national festivals to replace the old religious holidays. "Bliss was it in that dawn to be alive!" exclaimed William Wordsworth in a retrospect published in 1809 (cf. *Prelude* 10.689). But the dream proved short-lived as the French Republic descended into factionalism, extremist purges, internal violence, terrorism, and imperialist war-mongering: the monarchy was overthrown in August 1792, thousands of artistocrats and suspected sympathizers were massacred in September, Louis XVI was guillotined in January 1793, and Queen Marie Antoinette in October. Wordsworth and others fell into disenchantment and despair ("The scenes that I witnessed during the earlier years of the French Revolution when I was resident in France," he wrote in 1835, "come back on me with appalling violence"). Conservatives sounded the alarm and, citing the likelihood of a French invasion, the British government enacted a series of repressive measures in the 1790s—suspending civil rights, spying on and harassing political groups, outlawing and vigorously prosecuting some kinds of assembly and publication. France and Britain declared war, and the countries remained on hostile terms, often at war, through the 1790s and the rise of Napoleon, who was finally defeated by the British at Waterloo in 1815. The Revolution and its sequels had such a profound effect on British political life that in 1823 Samuel Taylor Coleridge could say, "We are not yet aware of the consequences of that event. We are too near it."

Helen Maria Williams
1762–1827

When Helen Maria Williams died in Paris in 1827, the *Gentleman's Magazine* in England remembered her as "pre-eminent among the violent female devotees of the Revolution." Of

Scots and Welsh descent, Williams made her appearance in London literary circles with the publication of *Edwin and Eltruda* (1782). Subsequent works fixed her reputation as a poet of liberal opinions, among them *Peru* (1784), a critique of imperialism, and *A Poem on the Bill lately passed for regulating the Slave Trade* (1788). A poem on the Bastille in her only novel, *Julia* (1790), signaled her enthusiasm for the Revolution. She visited Paris in 1790, returned in 1791, and settled there in 1792. A close friend of the moderate Girondins, she was imprisoned in 1793, but her support for the principles of the Revolution never wavered. The salon she ran until 1816 was a magnet for many expatriates, including Paine and Wollstonecraft; Wordsworth bore a letter of introduction to her from Charlotte Smith when he arrived in 1791. Her *Letters Written in France in the Summer of 1790* were followed by further volumes of *Letters from France* (1792–1796), and *A Tour in Switzerland* (1798), which recorded the impact of the Revolution on the Swiss republic. Her admiration for Napoleon dimmed only when he crowned himself Emperor in 1804. Her disillusion can be seen in two later works, published in 1815 and 1819, which carry her account of French life through to the restoration of Louis XVIII, but by then her public identification with radicalism was set. Such sentiments, when joined with her enduring affair with the Unitarian radical John Hurford Stone, tarnished her standing at home, provoking Horace Walpole to call her "a scribbling trollop." But Williams's devotion had produced an unparalleled eyewitness narrative of more than twenty-five turbulent years; perhaps no English subject knew so many of those who shaped the course of the Revolution.

from Letters Written in France, in the Summer of 1790,
to a Friend in England, Containing Various Anecdotes Relative to the French Revolution[1]

[ARRIVAL IN PARIS]

I arrived at Paris, by a very rapid journey, the day before the federation;[2] and when I am disposed to murmur at the evils of my destiny, I shall henceforth put this piece of good fortune into the opposite scale, and reflect how many disappointments it ought to counterbalance. Had the packet which conveyed me from Brighton to Dieppe failed a few hours later; had the wind been contrary; in short, had I not reached Paris at the moment I did reach it, I should have missed the most sublime spectacle which, perhaps, was ever represented on the theatre of this earth.

[A DEPICTION OF A FEDERATION]

I promised to send you a description of the federation: but it is not to be described! One must have been present, to form any judgment of a scene, the sublimity of which depended much less on its external magnificence than on the effect it produced on the minds of the spectators. "The people, sure, the people were the sight!" I may tell you of pavilions, of triumphal arches, of altars on which incense was burnt, of two hundred thousand men walking in procession; but how am I to give you an adequate idea of the behaviour of the spectators? How am I to paint the impetuous feelings of that immense, that exulting multitude? Half a million people assembled at a spectacle, which furnished every image that can elevate the mind of man; which connected the enthusiasm of moral sentiment with the solemn pomp of religious ceremonies; which addressed itself at once to the imagination, the understanding, and the heart!

The Champ de Mars[3] was formed into an immense amphitheatre, round which were erected forty rows of seats, raised one above another with earth, on which

---

1. The selections here are drawn from volume 1, letters 1, 2, 4, and 5.
2. The Festival of the Federation was held in Paris on 14 July 1790, to celebrate the anniversary of the fall of the

Bastille and the new constitution.
3. "The Field of Mars," the former military parade ground on the left bank of the Seine.

wooden forms were placed. Twenty days' labour, animated by the enthusiasm of the people, accomplished what seemed to require the toil of years. Already in the Champ de Mars the distinctions of rank were forgotten; and, inspired by the same spirit, the highest and lowest orders of citizens gloried in taking up the spade, and assisting the persons employed in a work on which the common welfare of the state depended. Ladies took the instruments of labour in their hands, and removed a little of the earth, that they might be able to boast that they also had assisted in the preparations at the Champ de Mars; and a number of old soldiers were seen voluntarily bestowing on their country the last remains of their strength. A young Abbé of my acquaintance told me, that the people beat a drum at the door of the convent where he lived, and obliged the Superior to let all the Monks come out and work in the Champ de Mars. The Superior with great reluctance acquiesced, "Quant à moi," said the young Abbé, "je ne demandois pas mieux" ["As for me, I desired nothing better"].[4]

At the upper end of the amphitheatre a pavilion was built for the reception of the King, the Queen, their attendants, and the National Assembly,[5] covered with striped tent-cloth of the national colours, and decorated with streamers of the same beloved tints, and fleur de lys. The white flag was displayed above the spot where the King was seated. In the middle of the Champ de Mars L'Autel de la Patrie[6] was placed, on which incense was burnt by priests dressed in long white robes, with sashes of national ribbon. Several inscriptions were written on the altar, but the words visible at the greatest distance were, La Nation, la Loi, et le Roi [The Nation, the Law, and the King].

At the lower end of the amphitheatre, opposite to the pavilion, three triumphal arches were erected, adorned with emblems and allegorical figures.

The procession marched to the Champ de Mars, through the central streets of Paris. At La Place de Louis Quinze, the escorts, who carried the colours, received under their banners, ranged in two lines, the National Assembly, who came from the Tuilleries. When the procession passed the street where Henry the Fourth was assassinated,[7] every man paused as if by general consent: the cries of joy were suspended, and succeeded by a solemn silence. This tribute of regret, paid from the sudden impulse of feeling at such a moment, was perhaps the most honourable testimony to the virtues of that amiable Prince which his memory has yet received.

In the streets, at the windows, and on the roofs of the houses, the people, transported with joy, shouted and wept as the procession passed. Old men were seen kneeling in the streets, blessing God that they had lived to witness that happy moment. The people ran to the doors of their houses loaded with refreshments, which they offered to the troops; and crouds of women surrounded the soldiers, and holding up their infants in their arms, and melting into tears, promised to make their children imbibe, from their earliest age, an inviolable attachment to the principles of the new constitution.

[A Visit to the Bastille Prison]

Before I suffered my friends at Paris to conduct me through the usual routine of convents, churches, and palaces, I requested to visit the Bastille; feeling a much stronger desire to contemplate the ruins of that building than the most perfect edifices in

4. The translations of French phrases in the letters are by Williams herself, who wanted her work to reach as broad an audience as possible.
5. The legislative assembly made up of the third estate, or commons, that by declaring itself the governing body of the nation had precipitated the revolution in 1789.
6. The Altar of the Fatherland.
7. The king of France known for his love of his people, assassinated in 1610.

Paris. When we got into the carriage, our French servant called to the coachman, with an air of triumph, "A la Bastille—mais nous n'y resterons pas" ["To the Bastille,—but we shall not remain there"]. We drove under that porch which so many wretches have entered never to repass, and alighting from the carriage descended with difficulty into the dungeons, which were too low to admit of our standing upright, and so dark that we were obliged at noon-day to visit them with the light of a candle. We saw the hooks of those chains by which the prisoners were fastened round the neck, to the walls of their cells; many of which being below the level of the water, are in a constant state of humidity; and a noxious vapour issued from them, which more than once extinguished the candle, and was so insufferable that it required a strong spirit of curiosity to tempt one to enter. Good God! and to these regions of horror were human creatures dragged at the caprice of despotic power. What a melancholy consideration, that

> ————Man! proud man,
> Drest in a little brief authority,
> Plays such fantastic tricks before high heaven,
> As make the angels weep.[8]————

There appears to be a greater number of these dungeons than one could have imagined the hard heart of tyranny itself would contrive; for, since the destruction of the building, many subterraneous cells have been discovered underneath a piece of ground which was inclosed within the walls of the Bastille, but which seemed a bank of solid earth before the horrid secrets of this prison-house were disclosed. Some skeletons were found in these recesses, with irons still fastened on their decaying bones.

After having visited the Bastille, we may indeed be surprized, that a nation so enlightened as the French, submitted so long to the oppressions of their government; but we must cease to wonder that their indignant spirits at length shook off the galling yoke.

Those who have contemplated the dungeons of the Bastille, without rejoicing in the French revolution, may, for aught I know, be very respectable persons, and very agreeable companions in the hours of prosperity; but, if my heart were sinking with anguish, I should not fly to those persons for consolation. Sterne[9] says, that a man is incapable of loving one woman as he ought, who has not a sort of an affection for the whole sex; and as little should I look for particular sympathy from those who have no feelings of general philanthropy. If the splendour of a despotic throne can only shine like the radiance of lightning, while all around is involved in gloom and horror, in the name of heaven let its baleful lustre be extinguished for ever. May no such strong contrast of light and shade again exist in the political system of France! but may the beams of liberty, like the beams of day, shed their benign influence on the cottage of the peasant, as well as on the palace of the monarch! May liberty, which for so many ages past has taken pleasure in softening the evils of the bleak and rugged climates of the north, in fertilizing a barren soil, in clearing the swamp, in lifting mounds against the inundations of the tempest, diffuse her blessings also on the genial land of France, and bid the husbandman rejoice under the shade of the olive and the vine!

8. Isabella's tirade against the tyranny of Angelo, the agent of the Duke, in Shakespeare's *Measure for Measure* 2.2.117–123.

9. Laurence Sterne, author of *Tristram Shandy* (1759–1767) and *A Sentimental Journey* (1768).

from **Letters from France**[1]

[THE EXECUTION OF THE KING]

Paris, Feb. 10, 1793

The faction of the anarchists desired that the French king should be put to death without the tedious forms of a trial. This opinion, however, was confined to the summit of the Mountain,[2] that elevated region, where aloof from all the ordinary feelings of our nature, no one is diverted from his purpose by the weakness of humanity, or the compunction of remorse; where urbanity is considered as an aristocratical infringement of les grands principes, and mercy as a crime de leze-nation [treason].

The trial of the king was decreed by the National Convention, and the eleventh of December was fixed upon for that purpose. Lewis the sixteenth had supported his long imprisonment with fortitude; and, when he heard that the day for his trial was fixed, he said with great calmness, "Eh bien! qu'on me guillotine si on veut; je suis preparé" ["Well! let them *guillotine* me if they will; I am prepared"].

A short time after the taking of the Bastille the king was observed reading the history of Charles the first.[3] "Why, sire," said an attendant, "do you read that history? it will make you melancholy." "Je me mets dans l'esprit," replied the king, "qu'un jour je finirai comme lui" ["I feel an impression on my mind, that one day I shall end like him"]. It appears that the French queen has also chosen a model for her behaviour, in the last scene of life, from the English annals; for since her imprisonment she has been employed in reading the history of Mary queen of Scots.[4] Marie Antoinette, however, is in no danger of sharing the same fate: if she were, her haughty indignant spirit, which preferred the chance of losing empire and life to the certainty of retaining any thing less than absolute dominion, would probably meet death with becoming dignity, feeling, that "to be weak is to be miserable, doing or suffering."[5]

* * * History will, indeed, condemn Lewis the sixteenth. The evidence of his guilt is clear; and the historian will fulfil his duty in passing sentence upon his memory; for the historian has not, like the judge, the prerogative to pardon. But Lewis the sixteenth will not stand alone at the bar of posterity. His judges also must appear at that tribunal; on them, also, the historian will pass sentence. He will behold the same men acting at once as accusers, party, and judge; he will behold the unfortunate monarch deprived, not only of his inviolability as a king, but of his rights as a citizen; and perhaps the irrevocable decree of posterity may reverse that of the National Convention.

The detail of the interrogation which the French king underwent at the bar of the National Convention is too well known to need repetition.—He was conducted back to the Temple about six in the evening: the night was dark; but the town was illuminated; and those objects which appeared only half formed, and were seen indistinctly, imagination finished and filled up, as best suited the gloomy impressions of the moment. By the way, since the second of September, when the whole town was

1. The selections here are from the second edition (1796), volume 4, letters 1 and 5.
2. Term for the radical Jacobin deputies, who sat on the high benches in the left of the National Convention.
3. The civil war between Charles I, king of Great Britain from 1625, and the Parliamentary forces under Oliver Cromwell, culminated in his execution on 30 January 1649.

4. Daughter of James V of Scotland, Mary became queen as an infant; in 1558 she married the Dauphin of France; a romantic figure, for the next three decades, she was the Roman Catholic threat to Elizabeth for the throne of Britain. Imprisoned from 1569 and tried for treason in 1586, she was beheaded in 1587.
5. Paraphrasing Milton's Satan, *Paradise Lost* 1.156–57.

lighted up for security, an illumination at Paris appears no gaudy pageant, which beams the symbol of public festivity; but is considered as the harbinger of danger—the signal of alarm—the tocsin of night. A considerable number of horse as well as foot-guards formed the escort of the king; and the trampling of the horses' feet—the hoarse sounds of the collected multitude—the beating of drums—the frequent report of fire-arms—all conspired to excite the most solemn emotions. The long page of human history rushed upon the mind—age after age arose to memory, in sad succession, like the line of Banquo;[6] and each seemed disfigured by crimes or darkened by calamity. The past was clouded with horror—a great experiment was about to be made for the future; but it was impossible to reflect, without trembling anxiety, that the stake was human happiness, and that the issue was doubtful, while all that could be calculated with certainty was, that millions must perish in the trial. It is asserted that the philosophers of France produced the revolution; I believe this to be an error. They, indeed, have disseminated the principles which form the basis of the new fabric of French government; but the ancient system was overthrown, not because it was unphilosophical, but because it could be upheld no longer. The revolution was the effect of imperious necessity; for, whatever permanent good may result from a change of government, the temporary evil is so certain, that every age is disposed to leave that work to a succeeding generation. The instinct of the people teaches them, that in framing a new government they can only hope, like Moses, to see the promised land, but not to enter it. They may plant the seeds of general prosperity, sown with toil and trouble, and bathed in blood; but the blooming vegetation and the golden fruit belong to another race of men.

The defence of Lewis the sixteenth * * * though it failed to prove his innocence, at least interested the humane part of the audience in behalf of his misfortunes: and such of that audience as reflected, that he who now stood an arraigned criminal at the bar of the Convention, had, four years ago, the destiny of twenty-five millions of people at the disposal of his will, felt that, whatever were his sins against the nation, he was already punished enough. * * * The attention of all Europe was fixed in anxious suspense on the issue of this important trial; and the situation of Lewis the sixteenth excited universal sympathy. But at Paris it cast a peculiar horror—a sort of local gloom over the whole city; it seemed as if the National Convention had chosen the very means most proper to re-kindle the dying flame of loyalty. We remembered that the king had betrayed his people, till, by the rigour of their resentment, they made us lose the sense of his guilt in the greatness of his calamities. They wished us to feel indignation at his offence, and they compelled us to weep for his misfortunes. They called on our abhorrence of the ungenerous use he had made of the power with which he was entrusted, and we saw how little magnanimous was the use which they made of theirs. Their decision seemed at once so cruel and so impolitic, that it is not surprising if, instead of appearing to foreign nations in the light of a painful sacrifice made to public security, it bore the aspect of public security sacrificed to inhumanity and vengeance. It were, however, an error to believe, either that Lewis the sixteenth fell the victim of that barbarous thirst for his blood displayed by the chiefs of the Mountain, or that he was devoted to death by the pusillanimity of those who were influenced by considerations of their own personal safety. No; while we admire the heroic courage of such as, in defiance of the popular outcry, pleased with pathetic eloquence the cause of mercy; while we love the humanity of Brissot, the philosophy of Condorcet, we must admit, that amongst those who voted for the death of Lewis

6. See Shakespeare, *Macbeth*, 4.1.112–24.

the sixteenth are found men equally incapable of being actuated by fear or by vengeance; men, who, considering the king's death as essential to security of the republic, pronounced the fatal sentence in the bitterness of their souls, and as the performance of a cruel duty which their country imperiously required.

The proposition of an appeal to the departments was rejected, because it was apprehended, that such an appeal might lead to civil war. * * * The French king received the intelligence of his approaching fate without dismay. He displayed far more firmness upon the scaffold than he had done upon the throne, and atoned for the weakness and inconsistency of his conduct in life, by the calmness and fortitude of his behaviour in death. The evening before his execution, his family, from whom he had been separated since the commencement of his trial, were conducted to the tower of the Temple, and allowed the sad indulgence of a last interview, unmolested by the presence of his guards. * * * Ah, surely, amidst the agonies of final separation from those to whom we are bound by the strongest ties of nature and affection! surely when we cling to those we love, in the unutterable pang of a last embrace—in such moments the monarch must forget his crown, and the regrets of disappointed ambition must be unfelt amidst the anguish which overwhelms the broken heart. * * *

The king had sufficient firmness to avoid seeing his family on the morning of his execution! He desired the queen might be told that he was unable to bear the sight of her and his children in those last moments! he took a ring off his finger, which contained some of his own hair, of the queen's, and of his two children, and desired it might be given to the queen. He called the municipal officers round him, and told them, it was his dying request, that Clery, his valet-de-chambre, might remain with his son. He then said to Santerre, "Marchons" ["Let us go"]; and after crossing, with a hurried pace, the inner court of the Temple, he got into the mayor's carriage, which was in waiting, and was attended by his confessor.

It is certain that many of those acts of illegal power, which brought the unhappy monarch to the scaffold, were dictated by the fanatical and discontented clergy which swarmed about his palace; by non-juring bishops and archbishops; men who, having lost their wealth and their influence by the revolution, prompted the king to run all risks in order to gratify their own resentment. * * *

The calmness which Lewis the sixteenth displayed on this great trial of human fortitude, is attributed not only to the support his mind received from religious faith, but also to the hope which it is said he cherished, even till his last moment, that the people, whom he meant to address from the scaffold, would demand that his life might be spared. And his confessor, from motives of compassion, had encouraged him in this hope. After ascending the scaffold with a firm step, twice the unhappy monarch attempted to speak, and twice Santerre prevented him from being heard, by ordering the drums to beat immediately. * * * Then it was that despair seized upon the mind of the unfortunate monarch—his countenance assumed a look of horror—twice with agony he repeated, "Je suis perdu! je suis perdu!" ["I am undone! I am undone!"] His confessor mean time called to him from the foot of the scaffold, "Louis, fils de St. Louis, montez au ciel" ["Son of St. Louis, ascend to heaven!"]; and in one moment he was delivered from the evils of mortality.

The executioner held up the bleeding head, and the guards cried "Vive la Republique!" ["Long live the Republic!"] Some dipt their handkerchiefs in the blood—but the greater number, chilled with horror at what had passed, desired the commandant would lead them instantly from the spot. The hair was sold in separate tresses at the foot of the scaffold.

["WHAT THEN IS THE CONCLUSION OF THE WHOLE MATTER?"]

Paris, March 1793

* * * The destruction of the monarchy in France on the 10th of August—the horrors of the massacre of the 2d of September,[7] and then the death of the king, finally alienated the minds of Englishmen from the French revolution; rendered popular a war, which otherwise no minister would have dared to undertake; disgusted all wise, and shocked all humane men; and left to us, and all who had espoused the cause, no hope but that Heaven, which knows how to bring good out of evil, would watch over an event so interesting to the welfare of mankind as the French revolution; nor suffer the folly and vice of the agents concerned in it, to spoil the greatest and noblest enterprise ever undertaken by a nation.

A variety of secondary causes operated, in conjunction with these primary ones, to alienate the minds of our countrymen from the French revolution. It is curious, and may be useful to trace a few of them.

Those who have long held the first rank in any society are always reluctant to yield up their place, or suffer others, who were below, to be raised above them. Accustomed to regard their own constitution as the perfection of civil polity, the English found a new source of disapprobation of the French institution: they forgot that their dearest privileges, trial by jury, the liberty of the press, and other advantages, had once been regarded by foreign nations as audacious novelties; and had scandalized the despots of Europe and their degraded subjects, as much as the new experiments of the French did at present. It was a common saying in France, under the old system, that "Le roi d'Angleterre / Regne dans l'enfer" ["The king of England reigns in hell"] and the freedom of speech, and of writing on public affairs, the dearest rights of Englishmen, were constantly represented as absurd and noxious privileges, that occasioned eternal commotion in the state, and *disturbed the peace of government*. In spite of these facts, when circumstances arose that hurt their national vanity, by exalting a rival people, many of our countrymen appear to have forgotten the ancient history of England—the nations seemed to have changed sides, and Englishmen talked of France as Frenchmen were wont to talk of England. But truth changes not with the fashions of the times. It was not to be forgotten, that the English had been the first *bold experimenters* in the science of government in modern Europe—the first who carried into practical execution the calumniated principle of EQUALITY—the first people who formally brought a monarch to the scaffold—the first asserters of the neglected *rights of man*. In the common law of England, and the commentaries of the older lawyers on it, I have found all the fundamental principles of the French declaration des droits de l'homme [of the rights of man].

But, said some, we made our revolution without bloodshed, and theirs has been a continued scene of confusion and murder. It is true, the revolution of 1688 was accomplished with little trouble; but it produced the wars of 1715 and 1745, in the last of which the metropolis very nearly fell into the hands of the enemy; a circumstance that would have placed a popish despot on the throne, and annihilated the liberties of England. And it is to be observed, that the revolution of 1688 was but one of many events that formed the English constitution. That system was the fruit of the labours of ages of struggle and confusion. The establishment of our liberties cost us

---

7. Between 2 and 6 September 1792, more than a thousand prisoners, aristocrats, priests, and purported sympathizers were seized from the Paris jails and summarily executed.

many wars—and amidst the civil dissensions caused by the contest of principles against ancient error, our history records a sad catalogue of crimes and cruelties committed on all sides. Whoever, Madam, will examine these annals, will soon be convinced, that we have not much ground to reproach our neighbours. In France, indeed, a greater number of events have been crowded into a shorter space of time; and the enormities in France have been committed at a period, when, by means of the facility of communication, all public events are more widely and rapidly circulated than in former ages; circumstances that alter the appearance, but not the reality, of the case. We now enjoy the blessings of freedom, and have forgotten the price it cost our ancestors to obtain it. But no people ever travelled to the temple of Liberty by a path strewed with roses; nor has established tyranny ever yielded to reason and justice, till after a severe struggle. I do not pretend to justify the French, but I do not see much right that we at least have to condemn them. We cannot even reproach them with the fate of Louis the sixteenth, without calling up to remembrance that of Charles the first. * * *

If the destruction of the monarchy was absolutely necessary, certainly the death of the king was not; and France might have struck surrounding nations with reverence at her sublime clemency, in place of shocking all Europe by a condemnation, the justice of which was at best doubtful, and which the generality of them at present consider as an atrocious crime. * * * However much indisposed our countrymen were to the French from preceding reasons, it is certain that the death of the king alone prepared their minds for war, and completed the triumph of the enemies of France in England. * * *

Whether France will finally be able to extricate herself from an intestine, as well as external war, which now assail her at once—whether she will be able to support her republic; or, fatigued with anarchy, repose herself in limited monarchy; or finally, overwhelmed by her foes, be forced to accept that constitution which they choose to give her, are points that surpass my powers to decide. Were I to conjecture, I would say, that she will succeed in maintaining her own freedom, but not in communicating it to her neighbours. But should she even be overpowered by her enemies, and should continental despots wish to load her with the most galling chains, I cannot forget, Madam, that Britain is concerned in this transaction! And this recollection cheers my mind; for a free and generous people cannot condemn twenty-five millions of men to be slaves! No: the severest sentence that England can suffer to be pronounced, even on her rival, would be, "Let France be delivered from the dominion of a ferocious mob—let her be delivered from anarchy, and restored to reason and lawful sway!" Thus terminate how it will, I trust the French revolution will promote the good of France, and this prospect consoles me amidst the present evils. * * *

When I said that the French revolution began in wisdom, I admitted that it came afterwards into the hands of fools. But *the foundation was laid in wisdom*. I must intreat you to mark that circumstance; for if even the superstructure should fall, the foundation would remain. The BASTILLE, though honoured by Mr. Burke with the title of the *king's castle* (a shocking satire on every humane and just prince), will never be rebuilt in France; and the declaration of the rights of man will remain eternal, as the truths it contains. In the early ages of the world, the revolutions of the states, and the incursions of barbarians, often overwhelmed knowledge, and occasioned *the loss of principles:* but since the invention of printing has diffused science over Europe, and accumulated the means of extending and preserving truth, PRINCIPLES can no more be lost. Like vigorous seeds committed to the bosom of the fertile earth, accidental circumstances may prevent their vegetation for a time, but they will remain alive, and ready to spring up at the first favourable moment.

What then is the conclusion of the whole matter? This, surely, that PRINCIPLES are never to be abandoned, however unsuccessful may be the attempt to carry them into *practice*. We in England, however, have had practical experience of the good effects of right principles: our maxims of liberty have proved their intrinsic worth, by counteracting even the natural defects of our country. They have made, as Addison happily expresses, "our bleak rocks and barren mountains smile"; and on the careful preservation of these maxims depends the continuance of the blessings they have procured us. But I must conclude:

> O Liberty! expand thy vital ray,
> O'er the dark globe diffuse celestial day;
> Glad distant regions by thy blissful voice,
> Till India's wilds and Afric's sands rejoice;
> Thy spirit breathe, wide as creation's space;
> Exalt, illume, inspire the human race;
> As heaven's own æther thro' expansion whirl'd,
> Attracts, sublimes, and animates the world.[8]

Thus wishes a worthy member of the British Senate, and such are your wishes and mine.

ADIEU

━━━━ ✠ ━━━━

Edmund Burke
1729–1797

A political writer and Irish member of Parliament for nearly thirty years, famous for electrifying oratory, Edmund Burke embodied the debates of his century. Although he was allied with the Whigs and not the Tories, and with them often advocated liberal and reform clauses, his politics were never of a piece. The son of a Protestant minister and a Catholic mother, he castigated Britain's handling of Ireland, urging the emancipation of Irish trade, the Irish Parliament, and Irish Catholics. He endorsed William Wilberforce's movement for the abolition of the slave trade, worked for the reform of the East India Company's abuses in India, and argued for better treatment of and greater autonomy for the American colonies. Yet he also supported Britain's right to tax the colonies and was a celebrated opponent of the French Revolution, denouncing it as an unparalleled disaster in modern history.

"Burke never shows his powers, except he is in a passion. The French Revolution was alone a subject fit for him," remarked Samuel Taylor Coleridge. Burke's best known work is *Reflections on the Revolution in France*, published in 1790, after the arrest and imprisonment of Louis XVI and Marie Antoinette but before the Terror and their execution. (Wordsworth, who as a young man saw the Revolution heralding a new golden age in human history, was horrified by the Terror and later praised the "Genius of Burke.") Selling quickly and widely (5,500 copies in seventeen days and 30,000 in the next few years), *Reflections* provoked strong

---

8. Attributed by Williams to John Courtenay (1738–1816), dissenter, abolitionist, supporter of the French Revolution. The prior reference is to Joseph Addison (1672–1719), poet, Whig statesman, and essayist.

James Gillray. *Smelling out a Rat,* 1790.

reactions, pro and con. It was championed throughout Europe for a principled conservatism that revered an idealized past and historical continuity, and on this basis defended the moral authority of a nation's institutions: the monarchy, the aristocracy, the church, and the constitution that guaranteed their power. A famous passage dramatized the arrest and imprisonment of the royal family, with a dignified queen as tragic heroine. Sympathizers with the Revolution immediately produced rebuttals, among the first, Mary Wollstonecraft's *Vindication of the Rights of Men*, and the most influential, Tom Paine's *Rights of Man*.

from Reflections on the Revolution in France
["THIS STRANGE CHAOS"]

All circumstances taken together, the French Revolution is the most astonishing that has hitherto happened in the world. The most wonderful things are brought about in many instances by means the most absurd and ridiculous; in the most ridiculous modes; and, apparently, by the most contemptible instruments. Everything seems out of nature in this strange chaos of levity and ferocity, and of all sorts of crimes jumbled together with all sorts of follies. In viewing this monstrous tragi-comic scene, the most opposite passions necessarily succeed, and sometimes mix with each other in the mind; alternate contempt and indignation; alternate laughter and tears; alternate scorn and horror.

It cannot however be denied, that to some this strange scene appeared in quite another point of view. Into them it inspired no other sentiments than those of exultation and rapture. They saw nothing in what has been done in France, but a firm and temperate exertion of freedom; so consistent, on the whole, with morals and with piety as to make it deserving not only of the secular applause of dashing Machiavelian politicians,[1] but to render it a fit theme for all the devout effusions of sacred eloquence.

[THE CONSTITUENT PARTS OF A STATE]

The constituent parts of a state are obliged to hold their public faith with each other, and with all those who derive any serious interest under their engagements, as much as the whole state is bound to keep its faith with separate communities. Otherwise competence and power would soon be confounded, and no law be left but the will of a prevailing force. On this principle the succession of the crown has always been what it now is, an hereditary succession by law: in the old line it was a succession by the common law; in the new by the statute law, operating on the principles of the common law, not changing the substance, but regulating the mode, and describing the persons. Both these descriptions of law are of the same force, and are derived from an equal authority, emanating from the common agreement and original compact of the state, *communi sponsione reipublicae*,[2] and as such are equally binding on king and people too, as long as the terms are observed, and they continue the same body politic.

[LEVELLERS CAN NEVER EQUALISE]

Your present confusion, like a palsy, has attacked the fountain of life itself. Every person in your country, in a situation to be actuated by a principle of honour, is disgraced and degraded, and can entertain no sensation of life, except in a mortified and humiliated indignation. But this generation will quickly pass away. The next generation of the nobility will resemble the artificers and clowns, and money-jobbers, usurers, and Jews, who will be always their fellows, sometimes their masters. Believe me, Sir, those who attempt to level,[3] never equalise. In all societies, consisting of various descriptions of citizens, some description must be uppermost. The levellers therefore only change and pervert the natural order of things.

[THE REAL RIGHTS OF MEN]

Far am I from denying in theory, full as far is my heart from withholding in practice, (if I were of power to give or to withhold,) the *real* rights of men.[4] In denying their false claims of right, I do not mean to injure those which are real, and are such as their pretended rights would totally destroy. If civil society be made for the advantage of man, all the advantages for which it is made become his right. It is an institution of beneficence; and law itself is only beneficence acting by a rule. Men have a right to live by that rule; they have a right to do justice, as between their fellows,

---

1. Niccolo Machiavelli (1469–1527), Florentine statesman, was famous for *The Prince*, a handbook on power; "Machiavelian" came to refer to a cynical politics of cunning, manipulation, and duplicity.
2. Burke summons the Latin phrase "common compact of the state" to give classical Roman republican authority to the principle of rule based on mutual agreement.
3. An allusion to the Levellers, the radical republicans of

the English Civil War period of the 1640s, who advocated principles that were to shape democratic movements in Burke's day: universal suffrage for men, a written constitution, proportional representation in a single governing body, and the abolition of the monarchy and class privileges.
4. An allusion to the French Revolutionary Assembly's Declaration of the Rights of Man.

whether their fellows are in public function or in ordinary occupation. They have a right to the fruits of their industry; and to the means of making their industry fruitful. They have a right to the acquisitions of their parents; to the nourishment and improvement of their offspring; to instruction in life, and to consolation in death. Whatever each man can separately do, without trespassing upon others, he has a right to do for himself; and he has a right to a fair portion of all which society, with all its combinations of skill and force, can do in his favour. In this partnership all men have equal rights; but not to equal things. He that has but five shillings in the partnership, has as good a right to it, as he that has five hundred pounds has to his larger proportion. But he has not a right to an equal dividend in the product of the joint stock; and as to the share of power, authority, and direction which each individual ought to have in the management of the state, that I must deny to be amongst the direct original rights of man in civil society.

[THE ARREST AND IMPRISONMENT OF THE KING AND QUEEN]

History will record, that on the morning of the 6th of October, 1789, the king and queen of France, after a day of confusion, alarm, dismay, and slaughter, lay down, under the pledged security of public faith, to indulge nature in a few hours of respite, and troubled, melancholy repose. From this sleep the queen was first startled by the voice of the sentinel at her door, who cried out to her to save herself by flight—that this was the last proof of fidelity he could give—that they were upon him, and he was dead. Instantly he was cut down. A band of cruel ruffians and assassins, reeking with his blood, rushed into the chamber of the queen, and pierced with a hundred strokes of bayonets and poniards the bed, from whence this persecuted woman had but just time to fly almost naked, and, through ways unknown to the murderers, had escaped to seek refuge at the feet of a king and husband, not secure of his own life for a moment.

This king, to say no more of him, and this queen, and their infant children, (who once would have been the pride and hope of a great and generous people,) were then forced to abandon the sanctuary of the most splendid palace in the world, which they left swimming in blood, polluted by massacre, and strewed with scattered limbs and mutilated carcases. Thence they were conducted into the capital of their kingdom. Two had been selected from the unprovoked, unresisted, promiscuous slaughter, which was made of the gentlemen of birth and family who composed the king's body guard. These two gentlemen, with all the parade of an execution of justice, were cruelly and publicly dragged to the block, and beheaded in the great court of the palace. Their heads were stuck upon spears, and led the procession; whilst the royal captives who followed in the train were slowly moved along, amidst the horrid yells, and shrilling screams, and frantic dances, and infamous contumelies, and all the unutterable abominations of the furies of hell, in the abused shape of the vilest of women. After they had been made to taste, drop by drop, more than the bitterness of death, in the slow torture of a journey of twelve miles, protracted to six hours, they were, under a guard, composed of those very soldiers who had thus conducted them through this famous triumph, lodged in one of the old palaces of Paris, now converted into a bastile for kings.

Is this a triumph to be consecrated at altars? to be commemorated with grateful thanksgiving? to be offered to the divine humanity with fervent prayer and enthusiastic ejaculation? * * *

Such treatment of any human creatures must be shocking to any but those who are made for accomplishing revolutions. But I cannot stop here. Influenced by the inborn feelings of my nature, and not being illuminated by a single ray of this new sprung modern light, I confess to you, Sir,[5] that the exalted rank of the persons suffering, and particularly the sex, the beauty, and the amiable qualities of the descendant of so many kings and emperors, with the tender age of royal infants, insensible only through infancy and innocence of the cruel outrages to which their parents were exposed, instead of being a subject of exultation, adds not a little to my sensibility on that most melancholy occasion.

I hear that the august person,[6] who was the principal object of our preacher's triumph, though he supported himself, felt much on that shameful occasion. As a man, it became him to feel for his wife and his children, and the faithful guards of his person, that were massacred in cold blood about him; as a prince, it became him to feel for the strange and frightful transformation of his civilized subjects, and to be more grieved for them than solicitous for himself. It derogates little from his fortitude, while it adds infinitely to the honour of his humanity. I am very sorry to say it, very sorry indeed, that such personages are in a situation in which it is not becoming in us to praise the virtues of the great.

I hear, and I rejoice to hear, that the great lady[7] the other object of the triumph, has borne that day, (one is interested that beings made for suffering should suffer well,) and that she bears all the succeeding days, that she bears the imprisonment of her husband, and her own captivity, and the exile of her friends, and the insulting adulation of addresses, and the whole weight of her accumulated wrongs, with a serene patience, in a manner suited to her rank and race, and becoming the offspring of a sovereign distinguished for her piety and her courage: that, like her, she has lofty sentiments; that she feels with the dignity of a Roman matron;[8] that in the last extremity she will save herself from the last disgrace; and that, if she must fall, she will fall by no ignoble hand.[9]

It is now sixteen or seventeen years since I saw the queen of France, then the dauphiness [princess], at Versailles;[1] and surely never lighted on this orb, which she hardly seemed to touch, a more delightful vision. I saw her just above the horizon, decorating and cheering the elevated sphere she just began to move in,—glittering like the morning-star, full of life, and splendour, and joy. Oh! what a revolution! and what a heart must I have to contemplate without emotion that elevation and that fall! Little did I dream when she added titles of veneration to those of enthusiastic, distant, respectful love, that she should ever be obliged to carry the sharp antidote against disgrace concealed in that bosom; little did I dream that I should have lived to see such disasters fallen upon her in a nation of gallant men, in a nation of men of honour, and of cavaliers. I thought ten thousand swords must have leaped from their

---

5. *Reflections* is framed as a letter to a "gentleman in Paris."
6. King Louis XVI. The preacher is Richard Price (1723–1791), to whose *Discourse on the Love of our Country* Burke is replying.
7. Queen Marie Antoinette.
8. The women of ancient Rome were famous for dignified self-possession in the face of adversity; Marie Antoinette was the daughter of the Empress of Austria, Maria Theresa.

9. The ancient Roman course of action in defeat was to take one's own life (cf. below: "the sharp antidote to disgrace concealed in that bosom"—a small knife or poison). Such hope was not realized for Marie Antoinette, who was beheaded in a noisy public event in 1793 (three years after the publication of *Reflections*).
1. The royal palace outside Paris from 1682 until the ejection of the royal family here described.

scabbards to avenge even a look that threatened her with insult. But the age of chivalry is gone. That of sophisters, economists, and calculators, has succeeded; and the glory of Europe is extinguished for ever. Never, never more shall we behold that generous loyalty to rank and sex, that proud submission, that dignified obedience, that subordination of the heart, which kept alive, even in servitude itself, the spirit of an exalted freedom. The unbought grace of life, the cheap defence of nations, the nurse of manly sentiment and heroic enterprise, is gone! It is gone, that sensibility of principle, that chastity of honour, which felt a stain like a wound, which inspired courage whilst it mitigated ferocity, which ennobled whatever it touched, and under which vice itself lost half its evil, by losing all its grossness.

This mixed system of opinion and sentiment had its origin in the ancient chivalry; and the principle, though varied in its appearance by the varying state of human affairs, subsisted and influenced through a long succession of generations, even to the time we live in. If it should ever be totally extinguished, the loss I fear will be great. It is this which has given its character to modern Europe. It is this which has distinguished it under all its forms of government, and distinguished it to its advantage, from the states of Asia, and possibly from those states which flourished in the most brilliant periods of the antique world. It was this, which, without confounding ranks, had produced a noble equality, and handed it down through all the gradations of social life. It was this opinion which mitigated kings into companions, and raised private men to be fellows with kings. Without force or opposition, it subdued the fierceness of pride and power; it obliged sovereigns to submit to the soft collar of social esteem, compelled stern authority to submit to elegance, and gave a dominating vanquisher of laws to be subdued by manners.

But now all is to be changed. All the pleasing illusions, which made power gentle and obedience liberal, which harmonized the different shades of life, and which, by a bland assimilation, incorporated into politics the sentiments which beautify and soften private society, are to be dissolved by this new conquering empire of light and reason.[2] All the decent drapery of life is to be rudely torn off. All the super-added ideas, furnished from the wardrobe of a moral imagination, which the heart owns, and the understanding ratifies, as necessary to cover the defects of our naked, shivering nature, and to raise it to dignity in our own estimation, are to be exploded as a ridiculous, absurd, and antiquated fashion.

On this scheme of things, a king is but a man, a queen is but a woman; a woman is but an animal, and an animal not of the highest order. All homage paid to the sex[3] in general as such, and without distinct views, is to be regarded as romance and folly. Regicide, and parricide, and sacrilege, are but fictions of superstition, corrupting jurisprudence by destroying its simplicity. The murder of a king, or a queen, or a bishop, or a father, are only common homicide; and if the people are by any chance, or in any way, gainers by it, a sort of homicide much the most pardonable, and into which we ought not to make too severe a scrutiny.

On the scheme of this barbarous philosophy, which is the offspring of cold hearts and muddy understandings, and which is as void of solid wisdom as it is destitute of all taste and elegance, laws are to be supported only by their own terrors,

2. A sarcastic reference to the Enlightenment ideology of Reason championed by political reformers and revolutionaries alike.

3. Women; a common usage.

and by the concern which each individual may find in them from his own private speculations, or can spare to them from his own private interests. In the groves of *their* academy,[4] at the end of every vista, you see nothing but the gallows. Nothing is left which engages the affections on the part of the commonwealth. On the principles of this mechanic philosophy, our institutions can never be embodied, if I may use the expression, in persons; so as to create in us love, veneration, admiration, or attachment. But that sort of reason which banishes the affections is incapable of filling their place. These public affections, combined with manners, are required sometimes as supplements, sometimes as correctives, always as aids to law. The precept given by a wise man, as well as a great critic, for the construction of poems, is equally true as to states:—*Non satis est pulchra esse poemata, dulcia sunto*.[5] There ought to be a system of manners in every nation, which a well-formed mind would be disposed to relish. To make us love our country, our country ought to be lovely.

But power, of some kind or other, will survive the shock in which manners and opinions perish; and it will find other and worse means for its support. The usurpation which, in order to subvert ancient institutions, has destroyed ancient principles, will hold power by arts similar to those by which it has acquired it. When the old feudal and chivalrous spirit of *fealty*,[6] which, by freeing kings from fear, freed both kings and subjects from the precautions of tyranny, shall be extinct in the minds of men, plots and assassinations will be anticipated by preventive murder and preventive confiscation, and that long roll of grim and bloody maxims, which form the political code of all power, not standing on its own honour, and the honour of those who are to obey it. Kings will be tyrants from policy, when subjects are rebels from principle.

When ancient opinions and rules of life are taken away, the loss cannot possibly be estimated. From that moment we have no compass to govern us; nor can we know distinctly to what port we steer. Europe, undoubtedly, taken in a mass, was in a flourishing condition the day on which your revolution was completed. How much of that prosperous state was owing to the spirit of our old manners and opinions is not easy to say; but as such causes cannot be indifferent in their operation, we must presume, that, on the whole, their operation was beneficial.

We are but too apt to consider things in the state in which we find them, without sufficiently adverting to the causes by which they have been produced, and possibly may be upheld. Nothing is more certain, than that our manners, our civilization, and all the good things which are connected with manners and with civilization, have, in this European world of ours, depended for ages upon two principles; and were indeed the result of both combined; I mean the spirit of a gentleman, and the spirit of religion. The nobility and the clergy, the one by profession, the other by patronage, kept learning in existence, even in the midst of arms and confusions, and whilst governments were rather in their causes, than formed. Learning paid back what it received to nobility and to priesthood; and paid it with usury,[7] by enlarging their ideas, and by furnishing their minds. Happy if they had all continued to know their indissoluble union, and their proper place! Happy if learning, not debauched by

---

4. In ancient Greece, philosophers and students met outside under the shade of the trees.
5. "It is not enough that poems be beautiful, they must be sweet [tender, touching]" (Horace, *Ars Poetica*).
6. Medieval ideal of a vassal's obligation of fidelity to his

lord; by extension, the faithful allegiance that secures social order both from fear of violent revolt and from preventive lordly tyranny.
7. Interest; a positive term.

ambition, had been satisfied to continue the instructor, and not aspired to be the master! Along with its natural protectors and guardians, learning will be cast into the mire, and trodden down under the hoofs of a swinish multitude.[8]

["This Great Drama"]

[W]hen kings are hurled from their thrones by the Supreme Director[9] of this great drama, and become the objects of insult to the base, and of pity to the good, we behold such disasters in the moral, as we should behold a miracle in the physical, order of things. We are alarmed into reflection; our minds (as it has long since been observed) are purified by terror and pity;[1] our weak, unthinking pride is humbled under the dispensations of a mysterious wisdom. Some tears might be drawn from me, if such a spectacle were exhibited on the stage. I should be truly ashamed of finding in myself that superficial, theatric sense of painted distress, whilst I could exult over it in real life. With such a perverted mind, I could never venture to show my face at a tragedy. People would think the tears that Garrick formerly, or that Siddons not long since, have extorted from me, were the tears of hypocrisy;[2] I should know them to be the tears of folly.

Indeed the theatre is a better school of moral sentiments than churches, where the feelings of humanity are thus outraged. Poets who have to deal with an audience not yet graduated in the school of the rights of men, and who must apply themselves to the moral constitution of the heart, would not dare to produce such a triumph as a matter of exultation. There, where men follow their natural impulses, they would not bear the odious maxims of a Machiavelian policy, whether applied to the attainment of monarchical or democratic tyranny. They would reject them on the modern, as they once did on the ancient stage, where they could not bear even the hypothetical proposition of such wickedness in the mouth of a personated tyrant, though suitable to the character he sustained. No theatric audience in Athens would bear what has been borne, in the midst of the real tragedy of this triumphal day; a principal actor weighing, as it were in scales hung in a shop of horrors,—so much actual crime against so much contingent advantage,—and after putting in and out weights, declaring that the balance was on the side of the advantages. They would not bear to see the crimes of new democracy posted as in a ledger against the crimes of old despotism, and the book-keepers of politics finding democracy still in debt, but by no means unable or unwilling to pay the balance. In the theatre, the first intuitive glance, without any elaborate process of reasoning, will show, that this method of political computation would justify every extent of crime. They would see, that on these principles, even where the very worst acts were not perpetrated, it was owing rather to the fortune of the conspirators, than to their parsimony in the expenditure of treachery and blood. They would soon see, that criminal means once tolerated are soon preferred. They present a shorter cut to the object than through the highway of the moral virtues. Justifying perfidy and murder for public benefit, public benefit would soon become the pretext, and perfidy and murder the end;

---

8. Among the several rebuttals provoked by *Reflections* was *The Reply of the Swinish Multitude to Mr. Burke*.
9. God.
1. In his extended metaphor of the "great drama," Burke refers to Aristotle's argument in *Poetics* for the salutary effect of drama in its controlled release of sensations of pity and fear.
2. David Garrick (1717–1779) and Sarah Siddons (1755–1831) were two of the leading actors of the age, both celebrated for their performances in Shakespeare's tragedies; "hypocrisy" is in the same metaphor system, derived from a Greek word for "stage-acting."

until rapacity, malice, revenge, and fear more dreadful than revenge, could satiate their insatiable appetites. Such must be the consequences of losing, in the splendour of these triumphs of the rights of men, all natural sense of wrong and right.

[THE CONTRACT OF SOCIETY]

To avoid therefore the evils of inconstancy and versatility, ten thousand times worse than those of obstinacy and the blindest prejudice, we have consecrated the state, that no man should approach to look into its defects or corruptions but with due caution; that he should never dream of beginning its reformation by its subversion; that he should approach to the faults of the state as to the wounds of a father, with pious awe and trembling solicitude. By this wise prejudice we are taught to look with horror on those children of their country, who are prompt rashly to hack that aged parent in pieces, and put him into the kettle of magicians, in hopes that by their poisonous weeds, and wild incantations, they may regenerate the paternal constitution, and renovate their father's life.[3]

Society is indeed a contract. Subordinate contracts for objects of mere occasional interest may be dissolved at pleasure—but the state ought not to be considered as nothing better than a partnership agreement in a trade of pepper and coffee, calico or tobacco, or some other such low concern, to be taken up for a little temporary interest, and to be dissolved by the fancy of the parties. It is to be looked on with other reverence; because it is not a partnership in things subservient only to the gross animal existence of a temporary and perishable nature. It is a partnership in all science; a partnership in all art; a partnership in every virtue, and in all perfection. As the ends of such a partnership cannot be obtained in many generations, it becomes a partnership not only between those who are living, but between those who are living, those who are dead, and those who are to be born. Each contract of each particular state is but a clause in the great primæval contract of eternal society, linking the lower with the higher natures, connecting the visible and invisible world, according to a fixed compact sanctioned by the inviolable oath which holds all physical and all moral natures, each in their appointed place. This law is not subject to the will of those, who by an obligation above them, and infinitely superior, are bound to submit their will to that law. The municipal corporations of that universal kingdom are not morally at liberty at their pleasure, and on their speculations of a contingent improvement, wholly to separate and tear asunder the bands of their subordinate community, and to dissolve it into an unsocial, uncivil, unconnected chaos of elementary principles. It is the first and supreme necessity only, a necessity that is not chosen, but chooses, a necessity paramount to deliberation, that admits no discussion, and demands no evidence, which alone can justify a resort to anarchy. This necessity is no exception to the rule; because this necessity itself is a part too of that moral and physical disposition of things, to which man must be obedient by consent or force: but if that which is only submission to necessity should be made the object of choice, the law is broken, nature is disobeyed, and the rebellious are outlawed, cast forth, and exiled, from this world of reason, and order, and peace, and virtue, and fruitful penitence, into the antagonist world of madness, discord, vice, confusion, and unavailing sorrow.

---

3. Manipulated by the sorceress Medea, the daughters of Pelias, King of Thessaly, took this course of action, not realizing that Medea was in league with Pelias's dispossessed half-nephew, Jason.

+→ ☰◈☰ →+

Mary Wollstonecraft
1759–1797

Wollstonecraft was living on her own in London on Bastille Day, 14 July 1789, writing for and serving on the staff of the *Analytical Review,* enjoying a lively circle of artists, writers, and intellectuals gathered around Joseph Johnson, its politically radical publisher. A *Vindication of the Rights of Men* (published by Johnson) appeared anonymously, in two printings in rapid succession in late 1790, leading a flood of responses to Burke's *Reflections on the Revolution in France,* which had appeared only weeks earlier. Her title refers to the Declaration of the Rights of Man voted by the French Constituent Assembly in August 1789. Caustic, trenchant, and frequently sarcastic, *Rights of Men* made her reputation when the second edition bore her name in 1791. Concerned chiefly to refute Burke's arguments for the hereditary succession of the crown, the inviolability of a national constitution, and the necessary alliance of church and state, Wollstonecraft also drew notice for her collateral arguments about the property of the poor, and for her bitter critiques of naval impressment, antipoaching laws, slavery, and Burke's attitudes about women and gender, which had already irritated her in his widely influential *Inquiry into the Origin of Our Ideas of the Sublime and Beautiful* (1757), where the feminine was equated with the qualities of "beautiful"—proportion, smoothness, delicacy, and smallness.

For more about Wollstonecraft, see her principal listing, page 1469.

from A Vindication of the Rights of Men
in a Letter to the Right Honourable Edmund Burke;
Occasioned by his Reflections on the Revolution in France

Mr. Burke's Reflections on the French Revolution first engaged my attention as the transient topic of the day. * * * My indignation was roused by the sophistical arguments, that every moment crossed me, in the questionable shape[1] of natural feelings and common sense. * * * I have confined my strictures, in a great measure, to the grand principles at which he has levelled many ingenious arguments in a very specious garb.

[SENSIBILITY]

Sensibility is the *manie* of the day,[2] and compassion the virtue which is to cover a multitude of vices, whilst justice is left to mourn in sullen silence, and balance truth in vain.

In life, an honest man with a confined understanding is frequently the slave of his habits and the dupe of his feelings, whilst the man with a clearer head and colder heart makes the passions of others bend to his interest; but truly sublime is the character that acts from principle. * * * All your pretty flights arise from your pampered sensibility; and that, vain of this fancied pre-eminence of organs, you foster every

---

1. A sardonic allusion to Hamlet's first address to his father's ghost: "Angels and ministers of grace defend us! / Be thou a spirit of health or goblin damned, / Bring with thee airs from heaven or blasts from hell, / Be thy intents wicked or charitable, / Thou com'st in such a questionable shape / That I will speak to thee" (*Hamlet* 1.4.39–44).

2. A reference to the "Cult of Sensibility," the elevation of feelings over rationality, particularly by poets and sentimental novelists of both sexes, but with a general sense that such culture is primarily the province of women and men of "feminine" character. *Manie,* a quasi-medical term, combines the senses of emotional hyperactivity and mania, a cultural craze.

emotion till the fumes, mounting to your brain, dispel the sober suggestions of reason. It is not in this view surprising, that when you should argue you become impassioned, and that reflection inflames your imagination, instead of enlightening your understanding.

Quitting now the flowers of rhetoric, let us, Sir, reason together.[3] * * *

The birthright of man, to give you, Sir, a short definition of this disputed right, is such a degree of liberty, civil and religious, as is compatible with the liberty of every other individual with whom he is united in a social compact, and the continued existence of that compact.[4]

Liberty, in this simple, unsophisticated sense, I acknowledge, is a fair idea that has never yet received a form in the various governments that have been established on our bounteous globe; the demon of property has ever been at hand to encroach on the sacred rights of men, and to fence round with awful pomp laws that war with justice. * * * If there is any thing like argument, or first principles, in your wild declamation, behold the result:—that we are to reverence the rust of antiquity, and term the unnatural customs, which ignorance and mistaken self-interest have consolidated, the sage fruit of experience: nay, that, if we do discover some errors, our *feelings* should lead us to excuse, with blind love, or unprincipled filial affection, the venerable vestiges of ancient days. These are gothic notions of beauty[5]—the ivy is beautiful, but, when it insidiously destroys the trunk from which it receives support, who would not grub it up? * * *

The civilization which has taken place in Europe has been very partial, and, like every custom that an arbitrary point of honour has established, refines the manners at the expence of morals, by making sentiments and opinions current in conversation that have no root in the heart, or weight in the cooler resolves of the mind.—And what has stopped its progress?—hereditary property—hereditary honours. The man has been changed into an artificial monster by the station in which he was born, and the consequent homage that benumbed his faculties like the torpedo's touch;[6]—or a being, with a capacity of reasoning, would not have failed to discover, as his faculties unfolded, that true happiness arose from the friendship and intimacy which can only be enjoyed by equals; and that charity is not a condescending distribution of alms, but an intercourse of good offices and mutual benefits, founded on respect for justice and humanity.

[AUTHORITY, SLAVERY, AND NATURAL RIGHTS]

Are we to seek for the rights of men in the ages when a few marks were the only penalty imposed for the life of a man, and death for death when the property of the rich was touched? when—I blush to discover the depravity of our nature—when a

---

3. A parody of Isaiah: "Come now, and let us reason together, saith the Lord: though your sins be as scarlet, they shall be as white as snow" (1.18). Rhetoric, the ornamental art of language, may displace or distort reason; cf. Wollstonecraft's remarks on her style in Introduction to *Rights of Woman*, page 1473.

4. An allusion to the notion of "social compact" in political philosophy. John Locke's *Two Treatises on Government* (1690) defines the "*original Compact*," whereby every man "with others incorporates into *one Society*": "by consenting with others to make one Body Politick under one Government, [he] puts himself under an obligation to every one of that Society, to submit to the determination of the *majority*, and to be concluded by it"

(2.97). Jean-Jacques Rousseau's *Social Contract* (1762) similarly argues that a free acceptance of this contract involves the surrender of the individual to the State, their reciprocal obligations, and their legal equality. Although Rousseau distrusted democracy and preferred monarchy, this work would be cited as the philosophical basis for the "democratic despotism" fostered by the French Revolution.

5. A reference to the "gothic" aesthetic of the 18th century, which admired the gloomy, wild, and untamed, and adored ivy-covered ruins (preferably of medieval gothic architecture); ivy is a parasite.

6. The numbing electric discharges of the torpedo, a ray fish; *torpedo* in Latin means *numbness*.

deer was killed![7] Are these the laws that it is natural to love, and sacrilegious to invade?—Were the rights of men understood when the law authorized or tolerated murder?—or is power and right the same in your creed? * * *

It is necessary emphatically to repeat, that there are rights which men inherit at their birth, as rational creatures, who were raised above the brute creation by their improvable faculties; and that, in receiving these, not from their forefathers but, from God, prescription can never undermine natural rights.

A father may dissipate his property without his child having any right to complain;—but should he attempt to sell him for a slave, or fetter him with laws contrary to reason; nature, in enabling him to discern good from evil, teaches him to break the ignoble chain, and not to believe that bread becomes flesh, and wine blood, because his parents swallowed the Eucharist[8] with this blind persuasion.

There is no end to this implicit submission to authority—some where it must stop, or we return to barbarism; and the capacity of improvement, which gives us a natural sceptre on earth, is a cheat, an ignis-fatuus,[9] that leads us from inviting meadows into bogs and dunghills. And if it be allowed that many of the precautions, with which any alteration was made, in our government, were prudent, it rather proves its weakness that substantiates an opinion of the soundness of the stamina, or the excellence of the constitution.

But on what principle Mr. Burke could defend American independence, I cannot conceive;[1] for the whole tenor of his plausible arguments settles slavery on an everlasting foundation. Allowing his servile reverence for antiquity, and prudent attention to self-interest, to have the force which he insists on, the slave trade ought never to be abolished;[2] and, because our ignorant forefathers, not understanding the native dignity of man, sanctioned a traffic that outrages every suggestion of reason and religion, we are to submit to the inhuman custom, and term an atrocious insult to humanity the love of our country, and a proper submission to the laws by which our property is secured.—Security of property! Behold, in a few words, the definition of English liberty. And to this selfish principle every nobler one is sacrificed.—The Briton takes place of the man, and the image of God is lost in the citizen! But it is not that enthusiastic flame which in Greece and Rome consumed every sordid passion: no, self is the focus; and the disparting rays rise not above our foggy atmosphere. But softly—it is only the property of the rich that is secure; the man who lives by the sweat of his brow has no asylum from oppression. * * * It is a farce to pretend that a man fights *for his country, his hearth, or his altars,* when he has neither liberty nor property.—His property is in his nervous arms—and they are compelled to pull a strange rope at the surly command of a tyrannic boy, who probably obtained his rank on account of his family connections, or the prostituted vote of his father, whose interest in a borough, or voice as a senator, was acceptable to the minister.[3] * * *

---

7. From 1389 to 1831, British law restricted the right to kill game to wealthy landlords and leaseholders; poaching, a theft of game often motivated by desperate hunger, was punishable by death.

8. Catholic theology stressed that the communion bread and wine are inwardly transformed into Christ's body and blood. Wollstonecraft was religious; her contempt issues from a general English disdain of Roman Catholicism as well as from her Enlightenment deism, which distrusted the institutional authority of an established Church.

9. Latin for false/foolish fire; the name for nighttime lights over marshlands supposedly caused by spontaneous combustion of gases released by the decay of organic material; by extension, a deceptive guiding light, an illusory ideal.

1. Burke's *Speech on Conciliation with America* (22 March 1775) defended the American Revolution on principles of traditional British liberties (e.g., taxation by consent and representation).

2. The institution of slavery in ancient Greece and Rome poses a contradiction to Burke's support in the 1780s of the parliamentary movement to abolish the slave trade.

3. A reference to impressment, the conscription of men into naval service; men of means could buy their way out or pay for a substitute; "nervous" means "well strung, vigorous."

Misery, to reach your heart, I perceive, must have its cap and bells;[4] your tears are reserved, very *naturally* considering your character, for the declamation of the theatre, or for the downfall of queens, whose rank alters the nature of folly, and throws a graceful veil over vices that degrade humanity; whilst the distress of many industrious mothers, whose *helpmates* have been torn from them, and the hungry cry of helpless babes, were vulgar sorrows that could not move your commiseration, though they might extort an alms. * * *

A brutal attachment to children has appeared most conspicuous in parents who have treated them like slaves, and demanded due homage for all the property they transferred to them, during their lives. It has led them to force their children to break the most sacred ties; to do violence to a natural impulse, and run into legal prostitution to increase wealth or shun poverty.[5] * * * It appears to be a natural suggestion of reason, that a man should be freed from implicit obedience to parents and private punishments, when he is of an age to be subject to the jurisdiction of the laws of his country; and that the barbarous cruelty of allowing parents to imprison their children, to prevent their contaminating their noble blood by following the dictates of nature when they chose to marry, or for any misdemeanor that does not come under the cognizance of public justice, is one of the most arbitrary violations of liberty.[6]

Who can recount all the unnatural crimes which the *laudable, interesting* desire of perpetuating a name has produced? The younger children have been sacrificed to the eldest son; sent into exile, or confined in convents, that they might not encroach on what was called, with shameful falsehood, the *family* estate.[7] Will Mr Burke call this parental affection reasonable or virtuous?—No; it is the spurious offspring of over-weening, mistaken pride—and not that first source of civilization, natural parental affection, that makes no difference between child and child, but what reason justifies by pointing out superior merit.

Another pernicious consequence which unavoidably arises from this artificial affection is, the insuperable bar which it puts in the way of early marriages. It would be difficult to determine whether the minds or bodies of our youth are most injured by this impediment. Our young men become selfish coxcombs. * * *

The same system has an equally pernicious effect on female morals.—Girls are sacrificed to family convenience, or else marry to settle themselves in a superior rank, and coquet, without restraint, with the fine gentleman whom I have already described.

[Romance and Chivalry]

Whether the glory of Europe is set, I shall not now enquire; but probably the spirit of romance and chivalry is in the wane; and reason will gain by its extinction.

From observing several cold romantic characters I have been led to confine the term romantic to one definition—false, or rather artificial, feelings. Works of genius

---

4. A court-jester's bell-tipped hat; hence, any device of foolish entertainment.
5. Marriage for financial reasons rather than mutual love, affection, and esteem—a frequent term in Wollstonecraft's *Rights of Woman*, used earlier by Daniel Defoe in *Conjugal Lewdness: or, Matrimonial Whoredom* (1727).
6. In her *Letters Written in France in the Summer of 1790*, Helen Maria Williams tells the story of one family that suffered such injustice (chs. 16–22); until 1791, it was

possible for a French citizen to imprison another without trial by using a "lettre de cachet" signed by the king. Wordsworth tells a story based on Williams of French parental tyranny against young lovers at the end of Book 9 of the 1805 *Prelude* (556–935).
7. A reference to primogeniture, a system to preserve the family estate by restricting inheritance to the first-born son, abolished in the French Revolution.

are read with a prepossession in their favour, and sentiments imitated, because they were fashionable and pretty, and not because they were forcibly felt.

In modern poetry the understanding and memory often fabricate the pretended effusions of the heart, and romance destroys all simplicity; which, in works of taste, is but a synonymous word for truth. This romantic spirit has extended to our prose, and scattered artificial flowers over the most barren heath; or a mixture of verse and prose producing the strangest incongruities. The turgid bombast of some of your periods[8] fully proves these assertions; for when the heart speaks we are seldom shocked by hyperbole, or dry raptures. * * * I am led very often to doubt your sincerity, and to suppose that you have said many things merely for the sake of saying them well. * * * The mock dignity and haughty stalk, only reminds me of the ass in the lion's skin.

A sentiment of this kind glanced across my mind when I read the following exclamation. "Whilst the royal captives, who followed in the train, were slowly moved along, amidst the horrid yells, and shrilling screams, and frantic dances, and infamous contumelies, and all the unutterable abominations of the furies of hell, in the abused shape of the vilest of women."[9] Probably you mean women who gained a livelihood by selling vegetables or fish, who never had any advantages of education; or their vices might have lost part of their abominable deformity, by losing part of their grossness.[1] The queen of France—the great and small vulgar, claim our pity; they have almost insuperable obstacles to surmount in their progress towards true dignity of character; still I have such a plain downright understanding that I do not like to make a distinction without a difference. But it is not very extraordinary that *you* should, for throughout your letter you frequently advert to a sentimental jargon, which has long been current in conversation, and even in books of morals, though it never received the *regal* stamp of reason. A kind of mysterious instinct is *supposed* to reside in the soul, that instantaneously discerns truth, without the tedious labour of ratiocination. This instinct, for I know not what other name to give it, has been termed *common sense*, and more frequently *sensibility*, and, by a kind of *indefeasible* right, it has been *supposed*, for rights of this kind are not easily proved, to reign paramount over the other faculties of the mind, and to be an authority from which there is no appeal. * * * It is to this instinct, without doubt, that you allude, when you talk of the "moral constitution of the heart."

In the name of the people of England, you say, " * * * In England we have not yet been completely emboweled of our natural entrails; we still feel within us, and we cherish and cultivate those inbred sentiments which are the faithful guardians, the active monitors of our duty, the true supporters of all liberal and manly morals."— What do you mean by inbred sentiments? From whence do they come? How were they bred? Are they the brood of folly, which swarms like the insects on the banks of the Nile, when mud and putrefaction have enriched the languid soil? Were these *inbred* sentiments faithful guardians of our duty when the church was an asylum for murderers, and men worshipped bread as a God? when slavery was authorized by law to fasten her fangs on human flesh, and the iron eat into the very soul? If these sentiments are not acquired, if our passive dispositions do not expand into virtuous affections and passions, why are not the Tartars in the first rude horde endued with sentiments white and *elegant* as the driven snow? Why is passion or heroism the child of reflection, the consequence of dwelling with intent contemplation on one object?

8. Sentences.   1. Echoing Burke's *Reflections*, page 1360.
9. See Burke's *Reflections*, page 1359.

The appetites are the only perfect inbred powers that I can discern; and they like instincts have a certain aim, they can be satisfied—but improveable reason has not yet discovered the perfection it may arrive at—God forbid!

[BURKE'S VIEW OF WOMEN]

Where is the dignity, the infallibility of sensibility, in the fair ladies, whom, if the voice of rumour is to be credited, the captive negroes curse in all the agony of bodily pain, for the unheard of tortures they invent? It is probable that some of them, after the sight of a flagellation, compose their ruffled spirits and exercise their tender feelings by the perusal of the last imported novel.—How true these tears are to nature, I leave you to determine. But these ladies may have read your Enquiry concerning the origin of our ideas of the Sublime and Beautiful, and, convinced by your arguments, may have laboured to be pretty, by counterfeiting weakness.[2]

You may have convinced them that *littleness* and *weakness* are the very essence of beauty; and that the Supreme Being, in giving women beauty in the most supereminent degree, seemed to command them, by the powerful voice of Nature, not to cultivate the moral virtues that might chance to excite respect, and interfere with the pleasing sensations they were created to inspire. Thus confining truth, fortitude, and humanity, within the rigid pale of manly morals, they might justly argue, that to be loved, woman's high end and great distinction! they should "learn to lisp, to totter in their walk, and nickname God's creatures."[3] Never, they might repeat after you, was any man, much less a woman, rendered amiable by the force of those exalted qualities, fortitude, justice, wisdom, and truth; and thus forewarned of the sacrifice they must make to those austere, unnatural virtues, they would be authorized to turn all their attention to their persons, systematically neglecting morals to secure beauty. * * * You have clearly proved that one half of the human species, at least, have not souls; and that Nature, by making women *little, smooth, delicate, fair* creatures, never designed that they should exercise their reason to acquire the virtues that produce opposite, if not contradictory, feelings. The affection they excite, to be uniform and perfect, should not be tinctured with the respect which moral virtues inspire, lest pain should be blended with pleasure, and admiration disturb the soft intimacy of love. This laxity of morals in the female world is certainly more captivating to a libertine[4] imagination than the cold arguments of reason, that give no sex to virtue. If beautiful weakness be interwoven in a woman's frame, if the chief business of her life be (as you insinuate) to inspire love, and Nature has made an eternal distinction between the qualities that dignify a rational being and this animal perfection, her duty and happiness in this life must clash with any preparation for a more exalted state. So that Plato and Milton were grossly mistaken in asserting that human love led to heavenly, and was only an exaltation of the same affection.[5]

2. In his influential treatise on aesthetics, *A Philosophical Enquiry into the Origin of Our Ideas of the Sublime and Beautiful* (1757), Burke genders these categories, with the sublime, characterized by sensations of pain, danger, and terror, as masculine; and the beautiful, characterized by qualities evoking heterosexual love—smallness, delicacy to the point of fragility, smoothness, proportion, softness—as feminine; see ch. 3.9 and 14. Wollstonecraft's sneer at "fair ladies" aims at both class status ("ladies" are aristocrats) and the "delicacy" that can abide the violent abuse of the slaves whose labor enables their luxury.

3. The traditional notion that reason is a male capacity allows women to excuse their immoral conduct on grounds of not knowing any better and to claim that their only responsibility is to make themselves attractive objects for men's love. The phrase in quotation is from Hamlet's misogynist diatribe at Ophelia, whom he suspects of treachery (3.1.145–50), also quoted by Burke in *Sublime and Beautiful* ch.3.9.

4. Unconstrained, sensual.

5. See Plato (5th–4th c. B.C.), *Symposium* (Diotima's lesson, 201d ff., esp. 210–11), and Raphael's lesson to Adam in Milton's *Paradise Lost:* "Love refines / The thoughts, and heart enlarges, . . . is the scale / By which to heav'nly Love thou may'st ascend" (8.589–592). Wollstonecraft elaborates the arguments of this section in *Rights of Woman* (1792).

[THE RICH AND THE POOR]

The rich and weak, a numerous train, will certainly applaud your system, and loudly celebrate your pious reverence for authority and establishments—they find it pleasanter to enjoy than to think; to justify oppression than correct abuses.—*The rights of men* are grating sounds that set their teeth on edge; the impertinent enquiry of philosophic meddling innovation. If the poor are in distress, they will make some *benevolent* exertions to assist them; they will confer obligations, but not do justice. Benevolence is a very amiable specious quality; yet the aversion which men feel to accept a right as a favour, should rather be extolled as a vestige of native dignity, than stigmatized as the odious offspring of ingratitude. The poor consider the rich as their lawful prey; but we ought not too severely to animadvert on[6] their ingratitude. When they receive an alms they are commonly grateful at the moment; but old habits quickly return, and cunning has ever been a substitute for force. * * *

Among all your plausible arguments, and witty illustrations, your contempt for the poor always appears conspicuous, and rouses my indignation. The following paragraph in particular struck me, as breathing the most tyrannic spirit, and displaying the most factitious feelings. "Good order is the foundation of all good things. To be enabled to acquire, the people, without being servile, must be tractable and obedient. The magistrate must have his reverence, the laws their authority. The body of the people must not find the principles of natural subordination by art rooted out of their minds. They *must* respect that property of which they *cannot* partake. *They must labour to obtain what by labour can be obtained; and when they find, as they commonly do, the success disproportioned to the endeavour, they must be taught their consolation in the final proportions of eternal justice.* Of this consolation, whoever deprives them, deadens their industry, and strikes at the root of all acquisition as of all conservation. He that does this, is the cruel oppressor, the merciless enemy, of the poor and wretched; at the same time that, by his wicked speculations, he exposes the fruits of successful industry, and the accumulations of fortune, (ah! there's the rub)[7] to the plunder of the negligent, the disappointed, and the unprosperous."

This is contemptible hard-hearted sophistry, in the specious form of humility, and submission to the will of Heaven.—It is, Sir, *possible* to render the poor happier in this world, without depriving them of the consolation which you gratuitously grant them in the next. They have a right to more comfort than they at present enjoy; and more comfort might be afforded them, without encroaching on the pleasures of the rich: not now waiting to enquire whether the rich have any right to exclusive pleasures. What do I say?—encroaching! No; if an intercourse were established between them, it would impart the only true pleasure that can be snatched in this land of shadows, this hard school of moral discipline.

I know, indeed, that there is often something disgusting in the distresses of poverty, at which the imagination revolts, and starts back to exercise itself in the more attractive Arcadia of fiction.[8] The rich man builds a house, art and taste give it the highest finish. His gardens are planted, and the trees grow to recreate the fancy of the planter, though the temperature of the climate may rather force him to avoid the dangerous damps they exhale, than seek the umbrageous retreat. Every thing on the estate is cherished but man;—yet, to contribute to the happiness of man, is the most sublime of all enjoyments. But if, instead of sweeping pleasure-grounds, obelisks, temples, and elegant cottages, as

6. Censure.
7. The flaw in the argument; the phrase is from *Hamlet* 3.1.65, referring to the way the attraction of suicide is thwarted by fear of the afterlife.
8. In ancient Greece, a region of pastoral simplicity, beauty, and harmony.

objects for the eye,[9] the heart was allowed to beat true to nature, decent farms would be scattered over the estate, and plenty smile around. Instead of the poor being subject to the griping hand of an avaricious steward, they would be watched over with fatherly solicitude, by the man whose duty and pleasure it was to guard their happiness, and shield from rapacity the beings who, by the sweat of their brow, exalted him above his fellows.

I could almost imagine I see a man thus gathering blessings as he mounted the hill of life; or consolation, in those days when the spirits lag, and the tired heart finds no pleasure in them. It is not by squandering alms that the poor can be relieved, or improved—it is the fostering sun of kindness, the wisdom that finds them employments calculated to give them habits of virtue, that meliorates their condition. * * *

Why cannot large estates be divided into small farms? these dwellings would indeed grace our land. Why are huge forests still allowed to stretch out with idle pomp and all the indolence of Eastern [Asian] grandeur? Why does the brown waste meet the traveller's view, when men want work? But commons cannot be enclosed without *acts of parliament* to increase the property of the rich![1] Why might not the industrious peasant be allowed to steal a farm from the heath? This sight I have seen;—the cow that supported the children grazed near the hut, and the cheerful poultry were fed by the chubby babes, who breathed a bracing air, far from the diseases and the vices of cities. Domination blasts all these prospects; virtue can only flourish amongst equals, and the man who submits to a fellow-creature, because it promotes his worldly interest, and he who relieves only because it is his duty to lay up a treasure in heaven,[2] are much on a par, for both are radically degraded by the habits of their life.

In this great city, that proudly rears its head, and boasts of its population and commerce, how much misery lurks in pestilential corners, whilst idle mendicants assail, on every side, the man who hates to encourage impostors, or repress, with angry frown, the plaints of the poor! How many mechanics, by a flux of trade or fashion, lose their employment; whom misfortunes, not to be warded off, lead to the idleness that vitiates their character and renders them afterwards averse to honest labour! Where is the eye that marks these evils, more gigantic than any of the infringements of property, which you piously deprecate? Are these remediless evils? And is the humane heart satisfied with turning the poor over to *another* world, to receive the blessings this could afford? * * *

What were the outrages of a day[3] to these continual miseries? Let those sorrows hide their diminished head before the tremendous mountain of woe that thus defaces our globe![4] Man preys on man; and you mourn * * * for the empty pageant of a name, when slavery flaps her wing, and the sick heart retires to die in lonely wilds, far from the abodes of men. Did the pangs you felt for insulted nobility, the anguish that rent your heart when the gorgeous robes were torn off the idol human weakness had set up [Queen Marie Antoinette], deserve to be compared with the long-drawn sigh of melancholy reflection, when misery and vice are thus seen to haunt our steps, and swim on the top of

9. A reference to the 18th-century vogue of landscaping on aristocratic estates, which frequently involved vast rearrangements of topography and the addition of picturesque enhancements such as pillars, classical temples, instant ruins, quaint cottages.

1. "Brown waste" is arable but untilled land; Wollstonecraft may also be alluding to Lancelot "Capability" Brown, a famous landscaper of aristocratic estates, who devised, among other "improvements," idle, though picturesque, stretches of forests and plains. In the 18th century, Parliament enacted a series of extreme "enclosure" acts, deeding to private ownership formerly public lands (the "commons" being the least arable of these), on

which the poor lived, grew crops, and pastured livestock.
2. See Jesus' instruction to "lay up for yourselves treasures in heaven, where neither moth nor rust doth corrupt, and where thieves do not break through nor steal" (Matthew 6.20). Wollstonecraft is referring to charity motivated by self-interest, the belief that such acts will count in one's favor in the judgment of Heaven.
3. The 6th of October (1789) [Wollstonecraft's note]; see Burke, *Reflections*, page 61.
4. In *Paradise Lost*, Satan notes how "all the Stars / Hide thir diminisht heads" at the sight of the noonday sun, "that with surpassing Glory crown'd, / Look'st from [its] sole dominion like the God / Of this new World" (4.32–35).

every cheering prospect? Why is our fancy to be appalled by terrific perspective of a hell beyond the grave?—Hell stalks abroad;—the lash resounds on the slave's naked sides; and the sick wretch, who can no longer earn the sour bread of unremitting labour, steals to a ditch to bid the world a long good night—or, neglected in some ostentatious hospital, breathes his last amidst the laugh of mercenary attendants.

Such misery demands more than tears—I pause to recollect myself; and smother the contempt I feel rising for your rhetorical flourishes and infantine sensibility.

Thomas Paine
1737–1809

"These are the times that try men's souls," declared Thomas Paine in a pamphlet that was read to George Washington's suffering and discouraged troops before the battle of Trenton. Paine was already famous for *Common Sense* (1776), urging the colonies to revolt from Britain; selling briskly, more than 100,000 copies in three months, it was a critical inspiration for the Declaration of Independence and the American Revolution. Born in England, and with only a grammar-school education, Paine wandered through various unsatisfactory jobs until he met Benjamin Franklin in London. At thirty-seven, with letters of introduction from Franklin, he sailed to America, where he launched his career as a writer with articles on women's rights and the abolition of slavery. After he returned to England in 1787, he shuttled back and forth to France, and when Edmund Burke's *Reflections on the Revolution in France* appeared in 1790, he quickly began his rebuttal, *The Rights of Man*, published early the next year. Burke wrote eloquent prose for the educated elite; Paine's simple, electric style was framed for the common reader, and his tract, priced cheaply, was an immediate and widespread success, selling 200,000 copies by 1793—but not without cost. Paine's incitement to revolution over reform and his attack on monarchies sent his bookseller to jail and led to his own indictment for treason. Fleeing to France in 1792 (just after the September Massacres), he was warmly received, elected to the National Assembly and given honorary citizenship. But he soon got into trouble for criticizing the execution of Louis XVI. Imprisoned by the Jacobins, he only narrowly escaped the guillotine himself through the intercession of James Monroe, then American ambassador to France. Convicted in absentia in England, he could not return without imprisonment, so he went back to America. There he completed *The Age of Reason* (1792–1795), a case for Deism begun during his imprisonment in France. Its strident denunciation of institutionalized Christianity and the Bible cost Paine sympathetic readers, however, and his reputation fell further in 1796 when he attacked Washington and federalism. He died in 1809, impoverished, angry, and ostracized. Denounced as an atheist, he was denied a consecrated burial, but in 1819, William Cobbett, a sympathetic English radical, exhumed his remains and took them to England.

from The Rights of Man
Being an answer to Mr. Burke's attack on the French Revolution
["MAN HAS NO PROPERTY IN MAN"]

There never did, there never will, and there never can, exist a Parliament, or any description of men, or any generation of men, in any country, possessed of the right or the power of binding and controuling posterity to the *"end of time."* * * * Every age and generation must be as free to act for itself *in all cases* as the ages and generations which preceded it. The vanity and presumption of governing beyond the grave is the most ridiculous and insolent of all tyrannies. Man has no property in man; neither has any generation a property in the generations which are to follow. The Parliament or the people of 1688,[1] or of any other period, had no more right to dispose of the people of the present day, or to bind or to controul them *in any shape whatever*, than the Parliament or the people of the present day have to dispose of, bind or controul those who are to live a hundred or a thousand years hence. Every generation is, and must be, competent to all the purposes which its occasions require. It is the living, and not the dead, that are to be accommodated. When man ceases to be, his power and his wants cease with him; and having no longer any participation in the concerns of this world, he has no longer any authority in directing who shall be its governors, or how its Government shall be organised, or how administered.

I am not contending for nor against any form of Government, nor for nor against any party, here or elsewhere. That which a whole Nation chooses to do, it has a right to do. Mr. Burke says, No. Where, then does the right exist? I am contending for the rights of the *living*, and against their being willed away, and controuled and contracted for, by the manuscript assumed authority of the dead; and Mr. Burke is contending for the authority of the dead over the rights and freedom of the living. There was a time when Kings disposed of their Crowns by will upon their death-beds, and consigned the people, like beasts of the field, to whatever successor they appointed. This is now so exploded as scarcely to be remembered, and so monstrous as hardly to be believed; but the Parliamentary clauses upon which Mr. Burke builds his political church are of the same nature.

The laws of every country must be analogous to some common principle. In England no parent or master, nor all the authority of Parliament, omnipotent as it has called itself, can bind or controul the personal freedom even of an individual beyond the age of twenty-one years. On what ground of right, then, could the Parliament of 1688, or any other Parliament, bind all posterity for ever?

Those who have quitted the world, and those who are not yet arrived at it, are as remote from each other as the utmost stretch of mortal imagination can conceive. What possible obligation, then, can exist between them; what rule or principle can be laid down that of two non-entities, the one out of existence and the other not in, and who never can meet in this world, the one should controul the other to the end of time? * * * It is the nature of man to die, and he will continue to die as long as he continues to be born. But Mr. Burke has set up a sort of political Adam, in whom all posterity are bound for ever; he must, therefore, prove that his Adam possessed such a power, or such a right. * * * It requires but a very small glance of thought to perceive that altho' laws made in one generation often continue in force through succeeding generations, yet that they continue to derive their force from the consent of the living. A law not repealed continues in force, not because it *cannot* be repealed, but because it *is not* repealed; and the non-repealing passes for consent.

[PRINCIPLES, NOT PERSONS]

Mr. Burke shows that he is ignorant of the springs and principles of the French Revolution. It was not against Louis XVI., but against the despotic principles of the government, that the Nation revolted. These principles had not their origin in him, but in the original establishment, many centuries back; and they were become too deeply rooted to be removed, and the Augean stable of parasites and plunderers too abom-

---

1. In the Glorious Revolution of 1688 (so named by the Whigs), Parliament deposed James II and installed William and Mary in the monarchy, along with a bill of rights that shifted the balance of power from the monarchy to Parliament.

inably filthy to be cleansed,[2] by anything short of a complete and universal Revolution. When it becomes necessary to do a thing, the whole heart and soul should go into the measure, or not attempt it. That crisis was then arrived, and there remained no choice but to act with determined vigour, or not to act at all. The King was known to be the friend of the Nation, and this circumstance was favourable to the enterprise.[3] Perhaps no man bred up in the style of an absolute King, ever possessed a heart so little disposed to the exercise of that species of power as the present King of France. But the principles of the Government itself still remained the same. The Monarch and the Monarchy were distinct and separate things; and it was against the established despotism of the latter, and not against the person or principles of the former, that the revolt commenced, and the Revolution has been carried.

Mr. Burke does not attend to the distinction between *men* and *principles;* and, therefore, he does not see that a revolt may take place against the despotism of the latter, while there lies no charge of despotism against the former.

The natural moderation of Louis XVI contributed nothing to alter the hereditary despotism of the Monarchy. All the tyrannies of former reigns, acted under that hereditary despotism, were still liable to be revived in the hands of a successor. It was not the respite of a reign that would satisfy France, enlightened as she then was become. A casual discontinuance of the *practice* of despotism, is not a discontinuance of its *principles;* the former depends on the virtue of the individual who is in immediate possession of the power; the latter, on the virtue and fortitude of the nation. In the case of Charles I and James II of England, the revolt was against the personal despotism of the men;[4] whereas in France, it was against the hereditary despotism of the established government. But men who can consign over the rights of posterity for ever on the authority of a mouldy parchment, like Mr. Burke, are not qualified to judge of this Revolution. It takes in a field too vast for their views to explore, and proceeds with a mightiness of reason they cannot keep pace with.

But there are many points of view in which this Revolution may be considered. When despotism has established itself for ages in a country, as in France, it is not in the person of the King only that it resides. It has the appearance of being so in show, and in nominal authority; but it is not so in practice and in fact. It has its standard everywhere. Every office and department has its despotism, founded upon custom and usage. Every place has its Bastille, and every Bastille its despot.[5] The original hereditary despotism resident in the person of the King, divides and subdivides itself into a thousand shapes and forms, till at last the whole of it is acted by deputation. This was the case in France; and against this species of despotism, proceeding on

2. One of Hercules' labors was to purge the notoriously filthy stables of King Augeas—hence, a place of entrenched corruption.
3. In the 1770s and 1780s, Louis XVI tried unsuccessfully to initiate some reforms, including moderate taxation of the nobility. After the fall of the Bastille in July 1789, he withdrew his troops, reinstated his reform-minded director of the treasury (ousted by reactionary factions), and outwardly accepted the Revolution.
4. Charles I, son of James I (successor of Elizabeth I), was unpopular for imposing exorbitant taxes, suspending Parliament, and harshly oppressing religious dissent; defeated in the 1640s Civil War with Parliament, he was beheaded for "high treason and other high crimes" in 1649. The monarchy was restored in 1660, and his

Roman Catholic son James II became king in 1685, but was soon forced from office for his attempt to restore absolute monarchy and Catholicism as the state religion. Seven powerful nobles, with the consent of Parliament, invited William III of Orange (grandson of Charles I) to invade England to protect its liberties and become joint monarch with Charles's Protestant daughter, Mary; William advanced bloodlessly to London with 15,000 troops, and Parliament proclaimed him and Mary monarchs in 1689.
5. The Bastille was France's infamous prison, holding many political prisoners, mostly without trial; it was the icon of the abuse of power that fomented the Revolution, which began with the storming of the Bastille and the liberation of its prisoners on 14 July 1789.

through an endless labyrinth of office till the source of it is scarcely perceptible, there is no mode of redress. It strengthens itself by assuming the appearance of duty, and tyrannises under the pretence of obeying.

When a man reflects on the condition which France was in from the nature of her Government, he will see other causes for revolt than those which immediately connect themselves with the person or character of Louis XVI. There were, if I may so express it, a thousand despotisms to be reformed in France, which had grown up under the hereditary despotism of the monarchy, and became so rooted as to be in great measure independent of it. Between the Monarchy, the Parliament, and the Church, there was a *rivalship* of despotism; besides the feudal despotism operating locally, and the ministerial despotism operating everywhere. But Mr. Burke, by considering the King as the only possible object of a revolt, speaks as if France was a village, in which everything that passed must be known to its commanding officer, and no oppression could be acted but what he could immediately controul. Mr. Burke might have been in the Bastille his whole life, as well under Louis XVI as Louis XIV,[6] and neither the one nor the other have known that such a man as Mr. Burke existed. The despotic principles of the Government were the same in both reigns, though the dispositions of the men were as remote as tyranny and benevolence.

What Mr. Burke considers as a reproach to the French Revolution (that of bringing it forward under a reign more mild than the preceding ones) is one of its highest honours. The Revolutions that have taken place in other European countries, have been excited by personal hatred. The rage was against the man, and he became the victim. But, in the instance of France we see a revolution generated in the rational contemplation of the rights of man, and distinguishing from the beginning between persons and principles.

But Mr. Burke appears to have no idea of principles when he is contemplating Governments. "Ten years ago," says he, "I could have felicitated France on her having a Government, without inquiring what the nature of that Government was, or how it was administered." Is this the language of a rational man? Is it the language of a heart feeling as it ought to feel for the rights and happiness of the human race? On this ground, Mr. Burke must compliment all the Governments in the world, while the victims who suffer under them, whether sold into slavery, or tortured out of existence, are wholly forgotten. It is power, and not principles, that Mr. Burke venerates.

* * *

As to the tragic paintings by which Mr. Burke has outraged his own imagination, and seeks to work upon that of his readers, they are very well calculated for theatrical representation, where facts are manufactured for the sake of show, and accommodated to produce, through the weakness of sympathy, a weeping effect. But Mr. Burke should recollect that he is writing history, and not *plays*, and that his readers will expect truth, and not the spouting rant of high-toned exclamation.

When we see a man dramatically lamenting in a publication intended to be believed that *"The age of chivalry is gone! that The glory of Europe is extinguished for ever! that the unbought grace of life* (if any one knows what it is), *the cheap defence of nations, the nurse of manly sentiment and heroic enterprise is gone!"* and all this

6. Louis XVI's ancestor (1638–1715), known as the Sun King, a notorious spendthrift, advocate of the divine right of kings, and patron of the arts.

because the Quixote age of chivalry nonsense is gone, what opinion can we form of his judgment, or what regard can we pay to his facts?[7] In the rhapsody of his imagination he has discovered a world of windmills, and his sorrows are that there are no Quixotes to attack them. But if the age of Aristocracy, like that of Chivalry, should fall (and they had originally some connection), Mr. Burke, the trumpeter of the order, may continue his parody to the end, and finish with exclaiming: "*Othello's occupation's gone!*"[8]

Notwithstanding Mr. Burke's horrid paintings, when the French Revolution is compared with the Revolutions of other countries, the astonishment will be that it is marked with so few sacrifices; but this astonishment will cease when we reflect that *principles*, and not *persons*, were the meditated objects of destruction. The mind of the nation was acted upon by a higher stimulus than what the consideration of persons could inspire, and sought a higher conquest than could be produced by the downfall of an enemy. Among the few who fell there do not appear to be any that were intentionally singled out. They all of them had their fate in the circumstances of the moment. * * * From his violence and his grief, his silence on some points and his excess on others, it is difficult not to believe that Mr. Burke is sorry, extremely sorry, that arbitrary power, the power of the Pope[9] and the Bastille, are pulled down.

Not one glance of compassion, not one commiserating reflection that I can find throughout his book, has he bestowed on those who lingered out the most wretched of lives, a life without hope in the most miserable of prisons. It is painful to behold a man employing his talents to corrupt himself. Nature has been kinder to Mr. Burke than he is to her. He is not affected by the reality of distress touching his heart, but by the showy resemblance of it striking his imagination. He pities the plumage, but forgets the dying bird.[1] Accustomed to kiss the aristocratical hand that hath purloined him from himself, he degenerates into a composition of art, and the genuine soul of nature forsakes him. His hero or his heroine must be a tragedy-victim expiring in show, and not the real prisoner of misery, sliding into death in the silence of a dungeon.

[THE DOCTRINE OF EQUAL RIGHTS]

If the mere name of antiquity is to govern in the affairs of life, the people who are to live an hundred or a thousand years hence, may as well take us for a precedent, as we make a precedent of those who lived an hundred or a thousand years ago. The fact is, that portions of antiquity, by proving everything, establish nothing. It is authority against authority all the way, till we come to the divine origin of the rights of man at the creation. Here our inquiries find a resting-place, and our reason finds a home. If a dispute about the rights of man had arisen at the distance of an hundred years from the creation, it is to this source of authority they must have referred, and it is to this same source of authority that we must now refer.

---

7. Paine is quoting Burke's *Reflections*, page 1361, and alluding to Cervantes' Don Quixote, a country gentleman who, overfed on chivalric romances, sets out in search of knightly adventure and winds up tilting at windmills in lieu of real opponents.
8. Othello utters this cry, when, falsely convinced of his wife's infidelity, he feels he has nothing more to live for (*Othello* 3.3.354).

9. Pre-Revolutionary France was Catholic (like Burke's Ireland), and so answerable to the Pope, at least in theory.
1. Perhaps the most famous sentence in this tract. Royalty frequently ornamented itself with elaborate plumage (feathers); Paine's point is that Burke is so wrapped up in the disgrace of the royal family that he neglects the misery of the state that sustains it, and which itself is dying from poverty and corruption.

Though I mean not to touch upon any sectarian principle of religion, yet it may be worth observing, that the genealogy of Christ is traced to Adam. Why then not trace the rights of man to the creation of man? I will answer the question. Because there have been upstart Governments, thrusting themselves between and presumptuously working to *un-make* man.

If any generation of men ever possessed the right of dictating the mode by which the world should be governed for ever, it was the first generation that existed; and if that generation did it not, no succeeding generation can show any authority for doing it, nor can set any up. The illuminating and divine principle of the equal rights of man (for it has its origin from the Maker of man) relates, not only to the living individuals, but to generations of men succeeding each other. Every generation is equal in rights to the generations which preceded it, by the same rule that every individual is born equal in rights with his contemporary.

Every history of the creation, and every traditionary account, whether from the lettered or unlettered world, however they may vary in their opinion or belief of certain particulars, all agree in establishing one point, *the unity of man;* by which I mean that men are all of *one degree*, and consequently that all men are born equal, and with equal natural rights, in the same manner as if posterity had been continued by *creation* instead of *generation*, the latter being only the mode by which the former is carried forward; and consequently every child born into the world must be considered as deriving its existence from God. The world is as new to him as it was to the first man that existed, and his natural right in it is of the same kind.

The Mosaic account of the creation,[2] whether taken as divine authority or merely historical, is fully up to this point, *the unity or equality of man.* The expressions admit of no controversy. "And God said, Let us make man in our own image. In the image of God created he him; male and female created he them." The distinction of sexes is pointed out, but no other distinction is even implied. If this be not divine authority, it is at least historical authority, and shows that the equality of man, so far from being a modern doctrine, is the oldest upon record. * * *

It is not among the least of the evils of the present existing Governments in all parts of Europe that man, considered as man, is thrown back to a vast distance from his Maker, and the artificial chasm filled up by a succession of barriers, or sort of turnpike gates, through which he has to pass. I will quote Mr. Burke's catalogue of barriers that he has set up between Man and his Maker. Putting himself in the character of a herald, he says: *We fear God—we look with* AWE *to kings—with affection to Parliaments—with duty to magistrates—with reverence to priests, and with respect to nobility.* Mr. Burke has forgotten to put in "*chivalry*." He has also forgotten to put in Peter.[3]

The duty of man is not a wilderness of turnpike gates, through which he is to pass by tickets from one to the other. It is plain and simple, and consists but of two points. His duty to God, which every man must feel; and with respect to his neighbour, to do as he would be done by. If those to whom power is delegated do well, they will be respected; if not, they will be despised; and with regard to those to whom no power is delegated, but who assume it, the rational world can know nothing of them.

---

2. Moses (adj. Mosaic) was traditionally thought to be the author of Genesis. Paine's ensuing quotation is patched from Genesis 1.26–27; in Genesis 2, which Milton follows

in *Paradise Lost*, God creates man first, and woman second.
3. In popular Christian lore, St. Peter keeps the gates to Heaven, deciding whom to admit.

[THE REPUBLICAN SYSTEM]

When we survey the wretched condition of Man, under the monarchical and hereditary systems of Government, dragged from his home by one power, or driven by
another, and impoverished by taxes more than by enemies, it becomes evident that
those systems are bad, and that a general Revolution in the principle and construction of Governments is necessary.

What is Government more than the management of the affairs of a Nation? It is
not, and from its nature cannot be, the property of any particular man or family, but
of the whole community, at whose expence it is supported; and though by force and
contrivance it has been usurped into an inheritance, the usurpation cannot alter the
right of things. Sovereignty, as a matter of right, appertains to the Nation only, and
not to any individual; and a Nation has at all times an inherent, indefeasible right to
abolish any form of Government it finds inconvenient, and to establish such as
accords with its interest, disposition, and happiness. The romantic and barbarous distinction of men into Kings and subjects, though it may suit the conditions of
courtiers, cannot that of citizens; and is exploded by the principle upon which Governments are now founded. Every citizen is a member of the sovereignty, and, as such,
can acknowledge no personal subjection: and his obedience can be only to the laws.

* * * In this view of Government, the Republican system, as established by America and France, operates to embrace the whole of a Nation. * * * What we formerly
called Revolutions, were little more than a change of persons, or an alteration of local
circumstances. They rose and fell like things of course, and had nothing in their existence or their fate that could influence beyond the spot that produced them. But what
we now see in the world, from the Revolutions of America and France, are a renovation
of the natural order of things, a system of principles as universal as truth and the existence of man, and combining moral with political happiness and national prosperity.

++ =◊= ++

William Godwin
1756–1836

Husband of Mary Wollstonecraft and father of Mary Wollstonecraft Shelley, William Godwin
has his own claim to fame as the author of *An Enquiry Concerning Political Justice*, an intellectually if not politically influential work published in the wake of the execution of Louis XVI of
France. The son of a dissenting minister, Godwin entered this profession in 1778, but under
the influence of Enlightenment philosophy, he was beset by religious doubts, and in 1782 he
left the calling for political writing. *Political Justice*, begun in 1791 and published in 1793, is
one of the most emphatic English statements of "anarchist" political philosophy: the disdain of
governmental institutions and their legal apparatus as the source of manifold evils and corruptions. In a kind of radical Protestantism, Godwin placed faith in the capacity of man to be
guided by private judgment, arguing that rational men, pursuing common good, would cease to
need government, law, and religion. He went so far as to abolish marriage and private property. This work appalled conservatives but for a time had a strong following, including William
Wordsworth, Samuel Taylor Coleridge, Lord Byron, and Percy Shelley. "No work in our time
gave such a blow to the philosophical mind of the country," wrote William Hazlitt in *The Spirit of the Age* (1825); "Tom Paine was considered for the time as Tom Fool to him; . . . Edmund
Burke a flashy sophist." For Wordsworth's account of his romance and disillusionment with
Godwinian philosophy, see *The Prelude* 10:805–865. *Political Justice* was revised and expanded

in 1796 and saw a third edition in 1798, in an atmosphere of increasing censorship of "seditious" writing. Excerpts here are from the first edition, the one that blazed on the scene of English debate in the wake of the Terror.

from An Enquiry Concerning Political Justice and Its Influence on General Virtue and Happiness

from *Of Justice*

If justice have any meaning, it is just that I should contribute every thing in my power to the benefit of the whole. * * * Justice is a rule of conduct originating in the connection of one percipient being with another. A comprehensive maxim which has been laid down upon the subject is, "that we should love our neighbour as ourselves."[1] But this maxim, though possessing considerable merit as a popular principle, is not modelled with the strictness of philosophical accuracy.

In a loose and general view I and my neighbour are both of us men; and of consequence entitled to equal attention. But in reality it is probable that one of us is a being of more worth and importance than the other. A man is of more worth than a beast; because, being possessed of higher faculties, he is capable of a more refined and genuine happiness. In the same manner the illustrious archbishop of Cambray was of more worth than his chambermaid, and there are few of us that would hesitate to pronounce, if his palace were in flames, and the life of only one of them could be preserved, which of the two ought to be preferred.[2]

But there is another ground of preference, beside the private consideration of one of them being farther removed from the state of a mere animal. We are not connected with one or two percipient beings, but with a society, a nation, and in some sense with the whole family of mankind. Of consequence that life ought to be preferred which will be most conducive to the general good. In saving the life of Fenelon, suppose at the moment when he was conceiving the project of his immortal Telemachus, I should be promoting the benefit of thousands, who have been cured by the perusal of it of some error, vice and consequent unhappiness. Nay, my benefit would extend farther than this, for every individual thus cured has become a better member of society, and has contributed in his turn to the happiness, the information and improvement of others.

Supposing I had been myself the chambermaid, I ought to have chosen to die, rather than that Fenelon should have died. The life of Fenelon was really preferable to that of the chambermaid. But understanding is the faculty that perceives the truth of this and similar propositions; and justice is the principle that regulates my conduct accordingly. It would have been just in the chambermaid to have preferred the archbishop to herself. To have done otherwise would have been a breach of justice.

Supposing the chambermaid had been my wife, my mother or my benefactor. This would not alter the truth of the proposition. The life of Fenelon would still be more valuable than that of the chambermaid; and justice, pure, unadulterated justice,

---

1. The second of the great Commandments, according to Jesus (Mark 12.31).
2. In a later edition, Godwin changed "chambermaid" to "valet" (a male personal attendant). Archbishop of Cambrai; François Fénelon lost favor in the court of Louis XIV upon the publication of *Télémaque* (1699), a didactic romance that indirectly criticized the king's policies by urging humane internationalism and stressing the king's obligations to the welfare of his subjects.

would still have preferred that which was most valuable. Justice would have taught me to save the life of Fenelon at the expence of the other. What magic is there in the pronoun "my," to overturn the decisions of everlasting truth? My wife or my mother may be a fool or a prostitute, malicious, lying or dishonest. If they be, of what consequence is it that they are mine?

"But my mother endured for me the pains of child bearing, and nourished me in the helplessness of infancy." When she first subjected herself to the necessity of these cares, she was probably influenced by no particular motives of benevolence to her future offspring. Every voluntary benefit however entitles the bestower to some kindness and retribution. But why so? Because a voluntary benefit is an evidence of benevolent intention, that is, of virtue. It is the disposition of the mind, not the external action, that entitles to respect. But the merit of this disposition is equal, whether the benefit was conferred upon me or upon another. I and another man cannot both be right in preferring our own individual benefactor, for no man can be at the same time both better and worse than his neighbour. My benefactor ought to be esteemed, not because he bestowed a benefit upon me, but because he bestowed it upon a human being. His desert will be in exact proportion to the degree, in which that human being was worthy of the distinction conferred. Thus every view of the subject brings us back to the consideration of my neighbour's moral worth and his importance to the general weal, as the only standard to determine the treatment to which he is entitled. Gratitude therefore, a principle which has so often been the theme of the moralist and the poet, is no part either of justice or virtue. * * *

Now the same justice, that binds me to any individual of my fellow men, binds me to the whole. If, while I confer a benefit upon one man, it appear, in striking an equitable balance, that I am injuring the whole, my action ceases to be right and becomes absolutely wrong. But how much am I bound to do for the general weal, that is, for the benefit of the individuals of whom the whole is composed? Every thing in my power. What to the neglect of the means of my own existence? No; for I am myself a part of the whole. Beside, it will rarely happen but that the project of doing for others every thing in my power, will demand for its execution the preservation of my own existence; or in other words, it will rarely happen but that I can do more good in twenty years than in one. If the extraordinary case should occur in which I can promote the general good by my death, more than by my life, justice requires that I should be content to die. * * * I hold my person as a trust in behalf of mankind. I am bound to employ my talents, my understanding, my strength and my time for the production of the greatest quantity of general good. Such are the declarations of justice, so great is the extent of my duty.

But justice is reciprocal. If it be just that I should confer a benefit, it is just that another man should receive it, and, if I withhold from him that to which he is entitled, he may justly complain. My neighbour is in want of ten pounds that I can spare. There is no law of political institution that has been made to reach this case, and to transfer this property from me to him. But in the eye of simple justice, unless it can be shewn that the money can be more beneficially employed, his claim is as complete, as if he had my bond in his possession, or had supplied me with goods to the amount. * * *

Society is nothing more than an aggregation of individuals. Its claims and its duties must be the aggregate of their claims and duties, the one no more precarious and arbitrary than the other. What has the society a right to require from me? The question is already answered: every thing that it is my duty to do. * * * What is it that the society is bound to do for its members? Every thing that can contribute to their welfare. But the nature of their welfare is defined by the nature of mind. That will most contribute to it, which enlarges the understanding, supplies incitements to virtue, fills us with a generous consciousness of our independence, and carefully removes whatever can impede our exertions.

Should it be affirmed, "that it is not in the power of any political system to secure to us these advantages," the conclusion I am drawing will still be incontrovertible. * * * There is one thing that political institutions can assuredly do, they can avoid positively counteracting the true interests of their subjects.

from *Of Revolutions*

No question can be more important than that which respects the best mode of effecting revolutions. Before we enter upon it however, it may be proper to remove a difficulty which has suggested itself to the minds of some men, how far we ought generally speaking to be the friends of revolution; or, in other words, whether it be justifiable in a man to be the enemy of the constitution of his country.

"We live," it will be said, "under the protection of this constitution; and protection, being a benefit conferred, obliges us to a reciprocation of support in return."

To this it may be answered, first, that this protection is a very equivocal thing; and, till it can be shown that the vices, from the effects of which it protects us, are not for the most part the produce of that constitution, we shall never sufficiently understand the quantity of benefit it includes. * * * Affection to my countrymen will be much better proved, by my exertions to procure them a substantial benefit, than by my supporting a system which I believe to be fraught with injurious consequences.

He who calls upon me to support the constitution must found his requisition upon one of two principles. It has a claim upon my support either because it is good, or because it is British. * * * He that desires a revolution for its own sake is to be regarded as a madman. He that desires it from a thorough conviction of its usefulness and necessity has a claim upon us for candour and respect. As to the demand upon me for support to the English constitution, because it is English, there is little plausibility in this argument. It is of the same nature as the demand upon me to be a Christian, because I am a Briton, or a Mahometan, because I am a native of Turkey. * * * If men reason and reflect, it must necessarily happen that either the Englishman or the Turk will find his government to be odious and his religion false. For what purpose employ his reason, if he must for ever conceal the conclusions to which it leads him? How would man have arrived at his present attainments, if he had always been contented with the state of society in which he happened to be born? In a word, either reason is the curse of our species, and human nature is to be regarded with horror; or it becomes us to employ our understanding and to act upon it, and to follow truth wherever it may lead us. It cannot lead us to mischief, since utility, as it regards percipient beings, is the only basis of moral and political truth.

* * * The true instruments for changing the opinions of men are argument and persuasion. The best security for an advantageous life is free and unrestricted discussion. In that field truth must always prove the successful champion. If then we would improve the social institutions of mankind, we must write, we must argue, we must converse. To this business there is no close; in this pursuit there should be no pause. Every method should be employed,—not so much positively to allure the attention of mankind, or persuasively to invite them to the adoption of our opinions—as to

remove every restraint upon thought, and to throw open the temple of science and the field of enquiry to all the world. * * * The phalanx of reason is invulnerable; it advances with deliberate and determined pace; and nothing is able to resist it. But when we lay down our arguments, and take up our swords, the case is altered. Amidst the barbarous pomp of war and the clamorous din of civil brawls, who can tell whether the event[1] shall be prosperous or miserable?

We must therefore carefully distinguish between informing the people and inflaming them. Indignation, resentment and fury are to be deprecated; and all we should ask is sober thought, clear discernment and intrepid discussion. Why were the revolutions of America and France a general concert of all orders and descriptions of men, without so much (if we bear in mind the multitudes concerned) as almost a dissentient voice; while the resistance against our Charles the first divided the nation into two equal parts?[2] Because the latter was the affair of the seventeenth century, and the former happened in the close of the eighteenth. Because in the case of America and France philosophy had already developed some of the great principles of political truth, and Sydney and Locke and Montesquieu and Rousseau had convinced a majority of reflecting and powerful minds of the evils of usurpation.[3] If these revolutions had happened still later, not one drop of the blood of one citizen would have been shed by the hands of another, nor would the event have been marked so much perhaps as with one solitary instance of violence and confiscation.

There are two principles therefore which the man who desires the regeneration of his species ought ever to bear in mind, to regard the improvement of every hour as essential in the discovery and dissemination of truth, and willingly to suffer the lapse of years before he urges the reducing his theory into actual execution. With all his caution it is possible that the impetuous multitude will run before the still and quiet progress of reason. * * * But, if his caution be firmly exerted, there is no doubt that he will supersede many abortive attempts, and considerably prolong the general tranquility.

from *Of the Enjoyment of Liberty*
["EVILS OF COHABITATION—AND MARRIAGE"]

Cohabitation is not only an evil as it checks the independent progress of mind; it is also inconsistent with the imperfections and propensities of man. It is absurd to expect that the inclinations and wishes of two human beings should coincide through any long period of time. To oblige them to act and to live together, is to subject them to some inevitable portion of thwarting, bickering, and unhappiness. This cannot be otherwise, so long as man has failed to reach the standard of absolute perfection. The supposition that I must have a companion for life, is the result of a complication of vices. It is the dictates of cowardice, and not of fortitude. It flows from the desire of being loved and esteemed for something that is not desert.

1. Outcome.
2. A reference to the parliamentary resistance, and then English Civil Wars of the 1640s, concluding in the execution of Charles I.
3. Algernon Sydney, English politician who took Parliament's side in the English Civil Wars. After the Restoration, he joined the opposition to Charles II; he was executed in 1683. In 1698, his influential liberal *Discourses Concerning Government* was published. John Locke's *Two Treatises on Civil Government* (1690), in part a justification of the Glorious Revolution of 1688, set forth the

qualified rights of revolution, of property, the rights to the products of one's labor, and a system of governmental checks and balances. Influenced by Locke, Charles Montesquieu wrote *The Spirit of the Laws* (1748), an analysis of three types of government—monarchy, republic, despotism—also advocating a separation and balance of powers. The political philosophy of Rousseau is best known from *The Social Contract* (1762), an argument for the voluntary submission of social subjects to a common good, determined by rational reflection.

But the evil of marriage as it is practised in European countries lies deeper than this. The habit is, for a thoughtless and romantic youth of each sex to come together, to see each other for a few times and under circumstances full of delusion, and then to vow to each other eternal attachment. What is the consequence of this? In almost every instance they find themselves deceived. They are reduced to make the best of an irretrievable mistake. They are presented with the strongest imaginable temptation to become the dupes of falsehood. They are led to conceive it their wisest policy to shut their eyes upon realities, happy if by any perversion of intellect they can persuade themselves that they were right in their first crude opinion of their companion. The institution of marriage is a system of fraud; and men who carefully mislead their judgments in the daily affair of their life, must always have a crippled judgment in every other concern. We ought to dismiss our mistake as soon as it is detected; but we are taught to cherish it. We ought to be incessant in our search after virtue and worth; but we are taught to check our enquiry, and shut our eyes upon the most attractive and admirable objects. Marriage is law, and the worst of all laws. Whatever our understandings may tell us of the person from whose connexion we should derive the greatest improvement, of the worth of one woman and the demerits of another, we are obliged to consider what is law, and not what is justice.

Add to this, that marriage is an affair of property, and the worst of all properties. So long as two human beings are forbidden by positive institution to follow the dictates of their own mind, prejudice is alive and vigorous. So long as I seek to engross one woman to myself, and to prohibit my neighbor from proving his superior desert and reaping the fruits of it, I am guilty of the most odious of all monopolies. Over this imaginary prize men watch with perpetual jealousy, and one man will find his desires and his capacity to circumvent as much excited, as the other is exited to traverse his projects and frustrate his hopes. As long as this state of society continues, philanthropy will be crossed and checked in a thousand ways, and the still augmenting stream of abuse will continue to flow.

The abolition of marriage will be attended with no evils. We are apt to represent it to ourselves as the harbinger of brutal lust and depravity. But it really happens in this as in other cases, that the positive laws which are made to restrain our vices, irritate and multiply them. Not to say, that the same sentiments of justice and happiness which in a state of equal property would destroy the relish for luxury, would decrease our inordinate appetites of every kind, and lead us universally to prefer the pleasures of intellect to the pleasures of sense.

The intercourse[1] of the sexes will in such a state fall under the same system as any other species of friendship. Exclusively of all groundless and obstinate attachments, it will be impossible for me to live in the world without finding one man of worth superior to that of any other whom I have an opportunity of observing. To this man I shall feel a kindness in exact proportion to my appreciation of his worth. The case will be precisely the same with respect to the female sex. I shall assiduously cultivate the intercourse of that woman whose accomplishments shall strike me in the most powerful manner. "But it may happen that other men will feel for her the same preference that I do." This will create no difficulty. We may all enjoy her conversation; and we shall all be wise enough to consider the sensual intercourse as a very trivial object. This, like every other affair in which two persons are concerned, must be regulated in each successive instance by the unforced consent of either party. It is a mark of the extreme depravity of our present habits, that we are inclined to suppose

---

1. Social interaction.

the sensual intercourse [of] any wife material to the advantages arising from the purest affection. Reasonable men now eat and drink, not from the love of pleasure, but because eating and drinking are essential to our healthful existence. Reasonable men then will propagate their species, not because a certain sensible pleasure is annexed to this action, but because it is right the species should be propagated; and the manner in which they exercise this function will be regulated by the dictates of reason and duty.

Such are some of the considerations that will probably regulate the commerce of the sexes. It cannot be definitively affirmed whether it will be known in such a state of society who is the father of each individual child. But is may be affirmed that such knowledge will be of no importance. It is aristocracy, self love and family pride that teach us to set a value upon it at present. I ought to prefer no human being to another, because that being is my father, my wife, or my son, but because, for reasons which equally appeal to all understandings, that being is entitled to preference. One among the measures which will successively be dictated by the spirit of democracy, and that probably at no great distance, is the abolition of surnames.

⊷ ⸎ ⊶

The Anti-Jacobin

In thirty-six numbers between November 1797 and July 1798 *The Anti-Jacobin,* or *Weekly Examiner,* under the editorship of William Gifford, defended Pitt's government by brilliantly lampooning any and all signs of radical opposition. Avowedly devoted to combating the spread of subversive ideas, George Ellis, John Hookham Frere, George Canning, and their fellows deployed a wit as pointed as it was exuberant against political figures and at writers such as Wordsworth and Charles Lamb suspected of dangerous sympathies. Robert Southey's *The Widow* (1796) offered an irresistible target: Frere and Canning derided its classical Sapphic meter as an "absurdity" in true English verse, even as they denounced Southey's "new topics of invective against the pride of property"—a characteristic juxtaposition of abstract republican philanthropy with Jacobin conduct, whether real or imagined. Their burlesque, *The Friend of Humanity and the Knife-Grinder,* appeared in *The Anti-Jacobin* on November 27, 1797. It was illustrated by the leading caricaturist of the day, James Gillray, with an instantly recognizable portrait of James Tierney, Member of Parliament and of the reformist society, The Friends of the People. The piece caused a sensation. As late as 1890, an editor could say of it: "perhaps no lines in the English language have been more effective, or oftener quoted." They endure as a vivid index of the charged climate in which the poems of the Romantics emerged.

from The Anti-Jacobin
[THE FRIEND OF HUMANITY AND THE KNIFE-GRINDER]

In the specimen of JACOBIN POETRY which we gave in our last number was developed a principle, perhaps one of the most universally recognised in the Jacobin creed; namely, "that the animadversion of *human law* upon *human actions* is for the most part nothing but *gross oppression;* and that, in all cases of the administration of *criminal justice,* the truly benevolent mind will consider only the *severity of the punishment,* without any reference to the *malignity of the crime.*" This principle has of late years been laboured with extraordinary industry, and brought forward in a variety of shapes, for the edification of the public. It has been inculcated in bulky quartos, and illustrated in popular novels. It remained only to fit it with a poetical dress, which had been attempted in the INSCRIPTION for CHEPSTOW CASTLE, and which (we flatter ourselves) was accomplished in that for MRS. BROWNRIGG'S CELL.[1]

Another principle, no less devoutly entertained, and no less sedulously disseminated, is the *natural and eternal warfare of the POOR and the RICH*. In those orders and gradations of society, which are the natural result of the original difference of talents and of industry among mankind, the Jacobin sees nothing but a graduated scale of violence and cruelty. He considers every rich man as an oppressor, and every person in a lower situation as the victim of avarice, and the slave of aristocratical insolence and contempt. These truths he declares loudly, not to excite compassion, or to soften the consciousness of superiority in the higher, but for the purpose of aggravating discontent in the inferior orders.

A human being, in the lowest state of penury and distress, is a treasure to the reasoner of this cast. He contemplates, he examines, he turns him in every possible light, with a view of extracting from the variety of his wretchedness new topics of invective against the pride of property. He, indeed (if he is a true Jacobin), refrains from *relieving* the object of his compassionate contemplation; as well knowing that every diminution from the general mass of human misery must proportionably diminish the force of his argument.

This principle is treated at large by many authors. It is versified in sonnets and elegies without end. We trace it particularly in a poem by the same author [Southey] from whom we borrowed our former illustration of the Jacobin doctrine of crimes and punishments. In this poem, the pathos of the matter is not a little relieved by the absurdity of the metre. ∗ ∗ ∗ The learned reader will perceive that the metre is SAPPHIC, and affords a fine opportunity for his *scanning* and *proving*, if he has not forgotten them.

The Widow

Sapphics

Cold was the night wind; drifting fast the snows fell;
Wide were the downs, and shelterless and naked;
When a poor wand'rer struggled on her journey,
    Weary and way-sore.

5   Drear were the downs, more dreary her reflections;
Cold was the night wind, colder was her bosom:
She had no home, the world was all before her,[2]
    She had no shelter.

Fast o'er the heath a chariot rattled by her:
10   "Pity me!" feebly cried the poor night wanderer.
"Pity me, strangers! lest with cold and hunger
    Here I should perish.

Once I had friends—but they have all forsook me!
Once I had parents—they are now in heaven!
15   I had a home once—I had once a husband—
    Pity me, strangers!

1. The first issue of the *Anti-Jacobin*, 20 November 1797, had parodied Robert Southey's sympathetic "Inscription for the Apartment in Chepstow Castle, where Henry Marten, the Regicide, was imprisoned thirty years" with an "Inscription for the Door of the Cell in Newgate, where Mrs. Brownrigg, the 'Prentice-cide,' was confined previous to her Execution." Henry Marten was a republican who signed the death warrant of Charles I; he was imprisoned at the Restoration in 1660.

2. See Milton, *Paradise Lost* 12.646–47, page 903.

I had a home once—I had once a husband—
I am a widow, poor and broken-hearted!"
Loud blew the wind, unheard was her complaining;
20   On drove the chariot.

Then on the snow she laid her down to rest her;
She heard a horseman: "Pity me!" she groaned out.
Loud was the wind, unheard was her complaining;
                  On went the horseman.

25   Worn out with anguish, toil, and cold and hunger,
Down sunk the wanderer; sleep had seized her senses:
There did the traveller find her in the morning—
                  God had released her.

—*Robert Southey [1796]*

We proceed to give our IMITATION, which is of the *Amoeboean* or *Collocutory* kind.[3]

Sapphics

The Friend of Humanity and the Knife-Grinder

Friend of Humanity:

"Needy Knife-grinder! whither are you going?
Rough is the road, your wheel is out of order—
Bleak blows the blast; your hat has got a hole in't,
                  So have your breeches!

5   Weary Knife-grinder! little think the proud ones,
Who in their coaches roll along the turnpike-
-road, what hard work 'tis crying all day 'Knives and
                  Scissars to grind O!'

Tell me, Knife-grinder, how you came to grind knives?
10   Did some rich man tyrannically use you?
Was it the squire? or parson of the parish?
                  Or the attorney?

Was it the squire, for killing of his game? or
Covetous parson, for his tithes° distraining?   *Church tax*
15   Or roguish lawyer, made you lose your little
                  All in a lawsuit?

(Have you not read the Rights of Man, by Tom Paine?)
Drops of compassion tremble on my eyelids,
Ready to fall, as soon as you have told your
20   Pitiful story."

Knife-Grinder:

"Story! God bless you! I have none to tell, sir,
Only last night a-drinking at the Chequers,
This poor old hat and breeches, as you see, were
                  Torn in a scuffle.

3. A poem composed in strophes with alternating speakers; a dialogue.

James Gillray. Illustration to *The Friend of Humanity and the Knife Grinder*, 1797.

25   Constables came up for to take me into
        Custody; they took me before the justice;
        Justice Oldmixon put me in the parish-
                        -Stocks for a vagrant.

        I should be glad to drink your Honour's health in
30   A pot of beer, if you will give me sixpence;
        But for my part, I never love to meddle
                        With politics, sir."

Friend of Humanity:

        "*I give* thee sixpence! I will see thee damned first—
        Wretch! whom no sense of wrongs can rouse to vengeance—
35   Sordid, unfeeling, reprobate, degraded,
        Spiritless outcast!"
        [*Kicks the Knife-grinder, overturns his wheel, and exit in a transport
            of Republican enthusiasm and universal philanthropy.*]

William Blake

1757–1827

It was from Blake's *Marriage of Heaven and Hell* that a sensationally transgressive rock band of the 1960s, the Doors, took their name:

> If the doors of perception were cleansed
> every thing would appear to man as it is: In-
> -finite.

But unlike the Doors, Blake needed no pharmaceutical assistance in cleansing his vision. His eccentricity and imaginative intensity, which seemed like madness to more than a few contemporaries, emerged from a childhood punctuated by such events as beholding God's face pressed against his window, seeing angels among the haystacks, and being visited by the Old Testament prophet Ezekiel. When his favorite brother died in 1787, Blake claimed that he saw his "released spirit ascend heavenwards, clapping its hand for joy." Soon after, he reports, this spirit visited him with a critical revelation of the method of "Illuminated Printing" that he would use in his major poetical works.

Rebellious, unconventional, fiercely idealistic, Blake became a celebrity in modern counterculture—Allen Ginsberg and many of the Beat poets of the 1950s and 1960s cited him as a major influence. But for a good part of the nineteenth century, he was known only to a coterie. He did not support himself as a poet but got by on patronage and commissions for engraving and painting. His projects included the Book of Job and other scenes from the Bible; Chaucer's Canterbury Pilgrims; characters in Spenser's *Faerie Queene*; Milton's *L'Allegro, Il Penseroso, Paradise Lost*, and *Paradise Regained*; Gray's *The Bard*; Young's *Night Thoughts*; and Blair's *The Grave*. His obscurity as a poet was due in part to the difficulty of his work after the mid-1790s but chiefly to the very limited issue of his books, a consequence of the painstaking and time-consuming process of "Illuminated Printing." He hoped to reach a wider audience with a private exhibition of his illustrations in 1809, but his adventurous originality, coupled with his cantankerous and combative personality, left him ignored, except by one of the radical journals, *The Examiner*, which called him a lunatic in a vicious review. At the time of his death, he was impoverished and almost entirely unknown except to a small group of younger painters. Only in 1863 did interest begin to grow, thanks to Alexander Gilchrist's biography, *The Life of William Blake: Pictor Ignotus*, its second volume a selection of poems edited by Dante Gabriel Rossetti. The revival was fanned by the enthusiasm of the Pre-Raphaelite circle and subsequent essays by Algernon Charles Swinburne, William Michael Rossetti (Dante Gabriel's brother), and William Butler Yeats.

Although Blake had no formal education, he was an avid reader, immersing himself in English poetry, the Bible, and works of mysticism and philosophy, as well as a study of Greek, Latin, and Hebrew. With precocious talent as a sketcher, he hoped to become a painter, but his father could not afford the tuition, and so apprenticed him at age fourteen as an engraver. During this seven-year term, Blake found time to write the poems gathered into his first publication, *Poetical Sketches* (1783), his only unilluminated volume. The later illuminated books, by contrast, were not products of the letter-press, but of a process of hand-etching designs onto copper plates, using these plates to ink-print pages that were then individually hand-colored and hand-bound into volumes. So labor-intensive a method was not adaptable to any production of quantity: there are, for instance, only twenty-seven known copies of *Songs of Innocence and of Experience* and only nine of *The Marriage of Heaven and Hell*. Yet Blake was committed to the product. By involving his verbal text with pictures and pictorial embellishments, he created books of extraordinary beauty and an innovative "composite art" of word and image.

In this art, the script is visually meaningful—flowing versus starkly blocked letters, for instance—and the pictorial elements play a significant role, sometimes illustrating, sometimes adding another perspective or an ironic comment on the verbal text, sometimes even presenting contradictory information. We hope to suggest the value of this composite art with several black-and-white plates, and our transcriptions follow their linear arrangements. We urge you to consult the illuminated editions as well, for a vitally important dimension abides in Blake's total designs.

Blake's popularity is based chiefly on his earlier and most accessible works from the 1790s. *Songs of Innocence and of Experience* (1789–1794) was much admired in his own day by Samuel Taylor Coleridge, Charles Lamb, and William Wordsworth (even though Blake deemed him too enamored of "Natural Piety"—faith in the natural world as spiritual and poetic resource: "I see in Wordsworth the Natural man rising up against the Spiritual Man Continually, & then he is No Poet but a heathen Philosopher at Enmity against all true Poetry or Inspiration"). *Songs* is notable not only for a concern with the different ways children and adults see and understand their world (a theme that would occupy Wordsworth, too) but also for its acid critiques of social evils, political injustice, and their agents, the triumvirate of "God & his Priest & King" (in the voice of a too-experienced chimney sweeper). Reflecting Blake's familiarity with the range of freethinking contemporary biblical commentary that became the "Higher Criticism," *The Marriage of Heaven and Hell* (1790) brings visionary energy and poetic extravagance to a trenchant argument for imaginative freedom over psychological inhibition, conventional morality, and institutionalized authority. It is also one of the first Romantic-era appropriations of Milton's *Paradise Lost*, the archetypal story of right and wrong, sin and punishment. Blake takes as an important effect a common reaction (including even Alexander Pope): that Satan and the scenes in Hell provide far more exciting and imaginatively powerful reading than the Angels and God's court in Heaven. "The reason Milton wrote in fetters when / he wrote of Angels & God, and at liberty when of / Devils & Hell," proposes Blake's "Voice of the Devil," is "because he was a true Poet and / of the Devils party without knowing it." Unfettering himself from Milton's moral machinery with this outrageously subversive commentary, Blake presents devils who are a lot more fun than his angels. Indeed, the *Proverbs of Hell* offer their wisdom with a kind of transgressive glee, sarcastic levity, and diabolical wit that anticipates the sly aphorisms of Oscar Wilde and the exuberance of American Beat poetry.

Visions of the Daughters of Albion (1793), a potent commentary on the tyranny of rape and sexual possession, reflects Blake's admiration for Mary Wollstonecraft, whose *Vindication of the Rights of Woman* had been published to controversial reception the year before. These works and others of this decade emerge from Blake's involvement with the London circle gathered around bookseller Joseph Johnson, including Wollstonecraft, William Godwin, Tom Paine, and Dr. Joseph Priestley—a radical political group of artists and religious dissenters joined by their sociopolitical criticism and a general support of the French Revolution. Like many of this group, Blake read the revolutions in America and France as heralds of a new millennium, and thus inspired, he produced a sequence of (sometimes abstruse) visionary works celebrating the overthrow of tyranny: *The French Revolution* (1791), *America: A Prophecy* (1793), *Europe: A Prophecy* (1794), and *The Book of Urizen* (1794). His later "prophetic" works—*Milton* (1804) and *Jerusalem* (1804–1820)—develop some of these themes with an increasingly esoteric vocabulary and elaborate personal mythology, and are notoriously difficult to read, although they contain passages of impressive energy and imagination.

An emblematic episode from 1803 suggests the real-life consequences of Blake's uncompromising visions. When a drunken dragoon trespassed onto his cottage garden and refused to leave, Blake vigorously ejected him. In consequence, he was arrested on a spiteful accusation of seditious threats against the crown; with England at war with France, this was a capital offense for which the penalty could have been death. Blake's trial ended in an acquittal loudly applauded by the spectators, but the ordeal exacerbated his memory of having been arrested in 1780 under the suspicion of being a spy for France while on a riverboat sketching excursion, and it crystallized his anger at state authority. Energizing all Blake's works is his commitment to imagination and the potency of visionary idealism, sharpened by resistance to psychological, ideological, institutional, and political tyrannies.

[Plate 1]

The voice of one crying in the
Wilderness[1]

[Plate 2]

All Religions Are One[2]

[Plate 3]

The Argument
As the true meth-
-od of knowledge
is experiment,
the true faculty
of knowing must
be the faculty which
experiences. This
faculty I treat of.

[Plate 4]

PRINCIPLE 1st
That the Poetic Genius is
the true Man, and that
the body or outward form
of Man is derived from the
Poetic Genius. Likewise
that the forms of all things
are derived from their
Genius, which by the
Ancients was calld an
Angel & Spirit & Demon.

[Plate 5]

PRINCIPLE 2d
As all men are alike in
outward form, So (and
with the same infinite
variety) all are alike in
the Poetic Genius

[Plate 6]

PRINCIPLE 3d
No man can think
write or speak from his
heart, but he must intend
truth. Thus all sects of
Philosophy are from the
Poetic Genius, adapted
to the weaknesses of
every individual.

---

1. The prophecy of Isaiah 40.3, which Matthew 3.3 takes to refer to John the Baptist; Blake places himself in this line of visionary authority.
2. Blake asserts that religious sects are only various forms of a central truth, divined by the poet's imagination. He did not subscribe his name to the potentially heretical *All Religions Are One* but presents its argument and principles as if from the voice of a biblical prophet speaking to the modern age.

[Plate 7]

PRINCIPLE 4ᵗʰ

As none by trave
ling over known
lands can find out
the unknown, So,
from already ac
quired knowledge,
Man could not ac
quire more; there
fore an universal
Poetic Genius exists.

[Plate 8]

PRINCIPLE 5ᵗʰ

The Religions of all Nat-
-ions are derived from each
Nations different reception
of the Poetic Genius which
is every where call'd the Spi
rit of Prophecy

[Plate 9]

PRINCIPLE 6ᵗʰ

The Jewish & Chris-
tian Testaments are
An original derivati-
-on from the Poetic Ge-
nius: this is necessary
from the confined natu
re of bodily sensation

[Plate 10]

PRINCIPLE 7ᵗʰ

As all men are alike
(tho' infinitely vari
ous) So all Religions:
& as all similars have
one source,
    The true Man is the
source, he being the
Poetic Genius

SONGS OF INNOCENCE AND OF EXPERIENCE

Blake's most popular work appeared in two phases. In 1789 he published *Songs of Innocence;* five years later he bound these poems with a set of new poems in a volume titled *Songs of Innocence and of Experience Shewing the two contrary States of the Human Soul.* "Innocence" and "Experience" are definitions of consciousness that rethink Milton's existential-mythic states of "Paradise" and the "Fall." Blake's categories are modes of perception that tend to coordinate with a chronological story that would become standard in Romanticism: childhood is a time and a state of protected "innocence," but it is a qualified innocence, not immune to the fallen world and its institutions. This world sometimes impinges on childhood itself, and in any event becomes known through "experience," a state of being marked by the loss of childhood vitality, by fear and inhibition, by social and political corruption, and by the manifold oppression of Church, State, and the ruling classes. The volume's "Contrary States" are sometimes signaled by patently repeated or contrasted titles: in *Innocence, Infant Joy*, in *Experience, Infant Sorrow*; in *Innocence, The Lamb*, in *Experience, The Fly* and *The Tyger*.

These contraries are not constructed as simple oppositions, however. Unlike Milton's narrative of the Fall from Paradise, Blake shows either state of soul possible at any moment. Some children, even infants, have already lost their innocence through a soiling contact with the world; some adults, particularly joyously visionary poets, seem able to retain a kind of innocent vitality even as they enter the world of experience. Moreover, the values of "Innocence" and "Experience" are themselves complex. At times, the innocent state of soul reflects a primary, untainted vitality of imagination; but at other times, Blake, like Mary Wollstonecraft, implicates innocence with dangerous ignorance and vulnerability to oppression. Thus, in their rhetorical structure, the poems may present an innocent speaker against dark ironies that a more experienced reader, alert to social and political evil, will grasp. But just as trickily, experience can also define an imagination self-darkened by its own "mind-forg'd manacles." Blake's point is not that children are pure and adults fallen, or that children are naive and adults perspicacious. The contrary possibilities coexist, with different plays and shades of emphasis in different poems. And these values are often further complicated by the ambiguous significance of the illustrations that accompany and often frame the poems' texts. Sometimes these illustrations sustain the speaker's tone and point of view (e.g., *The Lamb*), and sometimes (e.g., *The Little Black Boy*) they offer an ironic counter-commentary.

from SONGS OF INNOCENCE AND OF EXPERIENCE

SHEWING THE TWO CONTRARY STATES OF THE HUMAN SOUL

from *Songs of Innocence*

Introduction

    Piping down the valleys wild
    Piping songs of pleasant glee
    On a cloud I saw a child
    And he laughing said to me.

5   Pipe a song about a Lamb:
    So I piped with merry chear,
    Piper, pipe that song again—
    So I piped, he wept to hear.

    Drop thy pipe thy happy pipe
10   Sing thy songs of happy chear,
    So I sang the same again
    While he wept with joy to hear

    Piper sit thee down and write
    In a book that all may read—
15   So he vanish'd from my sight
    And I pluck'd a hollow reed

    And I made a rural pen,
    And I stain'd the water clear,
    And I wrote my happy songs,
20   Every child may joy to hear

The Ecchoing Green

The Sun does arise,
And make happy the skies.
The merry bells ring
To welcome the Spring.
5   The sky-lark and thrush,
The birds of the bush,
Sing louder around,
To the bells chearful sound
While our sports shall be seen
10 On the Ecchoing Green.

Old John with white hair
Does laugh away care,
Sitting under the oak,
Among the old folk,
15 They laugh at our play,
And soon they all say,
Such such were the joys
When we all girls & boys,
In our youth time were seen,
20 On the Ecchoing Green.

Till the little ones weary
No more can be merry
The sun does descend,
And our sports have an end:
25 Round the laps of their mothers
Many sisters and brothers,
Like birds in their nest,
Are ready for rest:
And sport no more seen,
30 On the darkening Green.

The Lamb

Little Lamb who made thee
Dost thou know who made thee
Gave thee life & bid thee feed,
By the stream & o'er the mead;
5   Gave thee clothing of delight,
Softest clothing wooly bright;
Gave thee such a tender voice,
Making all the vales rejoice:
Little Lamb who made thee
10 Dost thou know who made thee

Little Lamb, I'll tell thee.
Little Lamb, I'll tell thee;
He is called by thy name
For he calls himself a Lamb:
15 He is meek & he is mild,

William Blake. *The Lamb,* from *Songs of Innocence.*

He became a little child:
I a child & thou a lamb,
We are called by his name.
    Little Lamb God bless thee
20   Little Lamb God bless thee

The Little Black Boy

My mother bore me in the southern wild,
And I am black, but O! my soul is white
White as an angel is the English child:
But I am black as if bereav'd of light.

5   My mother taught me underneath a tree
And sitting down before the heat of day,
She took me on her lap and kissed me,
And, pointing to the east, began to say.

Look on the rising sun: there God does live
10 And gives his light and gives his heat away.
And flowers and trees and beasts and men recieve
Comfort in morning joy in the noon day.

William Blake. *The Little Black Boy*, from *Songs of Innocence*. In some copies, Blake tints the black boy's skin as light as the English boy's; in others, he colors them differently. While the heavenly scene (right) shows both boys sheltered by the tree and welcomed by Christ, it also puts the black boy outside the inner circle formed by the curve of Christ's body and the praying English boy. He is not part of this configuration of prayer, but rather a witness to it, stroking the hair of the English boy who has no regard for him.

And we are put on earth a little space
That we may learn to bear the beams of love.
15 And these black bodies and this sun-burnt face
Is but a cloud, and like a shady grove.

For when our souls have learn'd the heat to bear
The cloud will vanish we shall hear his voice
Saying: come out from the grove, my love & care,
20 And round my golden tent like lambs rejoice.

Thus did my mother say, and kissed me.
And thus I say to little English boy.
When I from black and he from white cloud free,
And round the tent of God like lambs we joy:

25 Ill shade him from the heat till he can bear,
To lean in joy upon our fathers knee
And then Ill stand and stroke his silver hair,
And be like him and he will then love me.

The Chimney Sweeper[1]

When my mother died I was very young
And my father sold me while yet my tongue
Could scarcely cry weep weep weep weep.[2]
So your chimneys I sweep & in soot I sleep.

5   Theres little Tom Dacre, who cried when his head
That curl'd like a lambs back, was shav'd, so I said:
Hush Tom never mind it, for when your head's bare
You know that the soot cannot spoil your white hair

And so he was quiet, & that very night,
10   As Tom was a sleeping he had such a sight,
That thousands of sweepers Dick, Joe, Ned & Jack
Were all of them lock'd up in coffins of black,

And by came an Angel who had a bright key,
And he open'd the coffins & set them all free.
15   Then down a green plain leaping laughing they run
And wash in a river and shine in the Sun.

Then naked & white, all their bags left behind,
They rise upon clouds, and sport in the wind
And the Angel told Tom if he'd be a good boy,
20   He'd have God for his father & never want joy

And so Tom awoke and we rose in the dark
And got with our bags & our brushes to work.
Tho' the morning was cold, Tom was happy & warm
So if all do their duty they need not fear harm.[3]

The Divine Image

To Mercy Pity Peace and Love,
All pray in their distress:
And to these virtues of delight
Return their thankfulness.

5   For Mercy Pity Peace and Love
Is God our father dear:
And Mercy Pity Peace and Love,
Is Man his child and care.

For Mercy has a human heart
10   Pity, a human face:

---

1. Chimney-sweeps were young children, mostly boys, whose impoverished parents sold them into the business, or who were orphans, outcasts, or illegitimate children with no other means of living. It was filthy, health-ruining labor, aggravated by overwork and inadequate clothing, food, and shelter. Among the hazards were burns, permanently blackened skin, deformed legs, black lung disease, and cancer of the scrotum. Protective legislation passed in 1788 was never enforced. Blake's outrage at this exploitation also sounds in "London." Admiring the poem, Charles Lamb sent it to James Montgomery (a topical poet and radical-press editor) for inclusion in *The Chimney-Sweeper's Friend, and Climbing Boy's Album* (1824), which he was assembling for the Society for Ameliorating the Condition of Infant Chimney-Sweepers.

2. With a relevant pun, the child's lisping street cry advertising his trade, "sweep! sweep!"

3. A typical conduct homily.

And Love, the human form divine,
And Peace, the human dress.

Then every man, of every clime
That prays in his distress,
15   Prays to the human form divine
Love Mercy Pity Peace.

And all must love the human form,
In heathen, turk or jew.
Where Mercy, Love & Pity dwell,
20   There God is dwelling too.

HOLY THURSDAY[1]

Twas on a Holy Thursday their innocent faces clean
The children walking two & two in red & blue & green[2]
Grey headed beadles[3] walkd before with wands as white as snow
Till into the high dome of Pauls they like Thames waters flow

5   O what a multitude they seemd these flowers of London town
Seated in companies they sit with radiance all their own
The hum of multitudes was there but multitudes of lambs
Thousands of little boys & girls raising their innocent hands

Now like a mighty wind they raise to heaven the voice of song
10   Or like harmonious thunderings the seats of heaven among
Beneath them sit the aged men wise guardians of the poor
Then cherish pity lest you drive an angel from your door[4]

COMPANION READING

Charles Lamb: from *The Praise of Chimney-Sweepers*[1]

I like to meet a sweep; understand me,—not a grown sweeper, (old chimney-sweepers are by no means attractive,) but one of those tender novices, blooming through their first nigritude, the maternal washings not quite effaced from the

1. One of the poems with a marked companion in *Experience* (see page 1402). Holy Thursday in the calendar of England's official state religion celebrated the Ascension; it was customary to conduct the children in London's charity schools, many of them orphans, to services at St. Paul's, the chief Anglican cathedral.
2. The colors denote different school uniforms.
3. Minor officials charged with ushering and preserving order at services.
4. A conduct homily, perhaps echoing Hebrews 13.1–2: "Let brotherly love continue. Be not forgetful to entertain strangers: for thereby some have entertained angels unawares."
1. Published in *London Magazine*, May 1822, under pseudonym "Elia." Charles Lamb (1775–1834) was born in London, the son of a legal clerk; his brother John and sister Mary, his literary collaborator and companion, were more than a decade older. At seven he entered Christ's Hospital, a charity school where he become a lifelong friend of Coleridge, to whose *Poems on Various Subjects* he con-

tributed in 1796–1797. Unlike Coleridge, Lamb, a stammerer, did not distinguish himself academically or go on to university. Shortly after leaving school he joined his brother briefly as a clerk at the South Sea House, moving in 1792 to the East India House, where he remained until his retirement in 1825. His early writings had little success, but Lamb persevered with a self-mocking resilience. In 1796, in a fit of the insanity that ran through the family, Mary fatally stabbed their mother and wounded their father. To prevent her from being committed to an asylum, Charles assumed responsibility for her care. Though her derangements periodically recurred, the weekly suppers that they hosted gathered a diverse group of London artists and intellectuals. Radicals such as Godwin, Hazlitt, and Leigh Hunt mixed with Wordsworth, Coleridge, and Southey, as Charles moved among them, smoking, drinking, and making outrageous puns. Such evenings concentrated the delights of city life that Lamb celebrated in his essays and letters. For more by Lamb, see the Companion Readings under William Wordsworth (page 1558).

cheek: such as come forth with the dawn, or somewhat earlier, with their little professional notes sounding like the *peep peep* of a young sparrow; or liker to the matin lark should I pronounce them, in their aërial ascents not seldom anticipating the sun-rise?

I have a kindly yearning toward these dim specks—poor blots—innocent blacknesses.

I reverence these young Africans of our own growth,—these almost clergy imps, who sport their cloth without assumption; and from their little pulpits, (the tops of chimneys,) in the nipping air of a December morning, preach a lesson of patience to mankind.

When a child, what a mysterious pleasure it was to witness their operation! to see a chit no bigger than one's-self, enter, one knew not by what process, into what seemed the *fauces Averni*,[2]—to pursue him in imagination, as he went sounding on through so many dark stifling caverns, horrid shades!—to shudder with the idea that "now, surely, he must be lost for ever!"—to revive at hearing his feeble shout of discovered day-light—and then (O fulness of delight!) running out of doors, to come just in time to see the sable phenomenon emerge in safety, the brandished weapon of his art victorious like some flag waved over a conquered citadel! I seem to remember having been told that a bad sweep was once left in a stack with his brush, to indicate which way the wind blew. It was an awful spectacle certainly; not much unlike the old stage direction in Macbeth, where the "Apparition of a child crowned, with a tree in his hand, rises."[3]

Reader, if thou meetest one of these small gentry in thy early rambles, it is good to give him a penny. It is better to give him twopence. If it be starving weather, and to the proper troubles of his hard occupation a pair of kibed[4] heels (no unusual accompaniment) be superadded, the demand on thy humanity will surely rise to a tester.[5] * * *

In one of the state-beds at Arundel Castle,[6] a few years since, under a ducal canopy, (that seat of the Howards is an object of curiosity to visitors, chiefly for its beds, in which the late duke was especially a connoisseur,) encircled with curtains of delicatest crimson, with starry coronets inwoven, folded between a pair of sheets whiter and softer than the lap where Venus lulled Ascanius,[7] was discovered by chance, after all methods of search had failed, at noon-day, fast asleep, a lost chimney-sweeper. The little creature, having somehow confounded his passage among the intricacies of those lordly chimneys, by some unknown aperture had alighted upon this magnificent chamber; and, tired with his tedious explorations, was unable to resist the delicious invitement to repose, which he there saw exhibited; so creeping between the sheets very quietly, laid his black head upon the pillow, and slept like a young Howard.

Such is the account given to the visitors at the Castle. But I cannot help seeming to perceive a confirmation of what I had just hinted at in this story. A high instinct was at work in the case, or I am mistaken. Is it probable that a poor child of that description, with whatever weariness he might be visited, would

---

2. The Jaws of Avernus (a phrase from Vergil's *Aeneid*, 6.201); Lake Avernus, near Naples, was thought to lead to the underworld.
3. Cf. *Macbeth* Act 4.1; the crowned child is a sign that a line other than childless Macbeth's will become Scotland's kings.

4. Ulcerated and inflamed from exposure to the cold.
5. Sixpence.
6. Home of the Howard family, Dukes of Norfolk.
7. Aeneas's young son (*Aeneid* bk. 1) who, protected by Venus, escaped with his father from burning Troy.

have ventured, under such a penalty as he would be taught to expect, to uncover the sheets of a Duke's bed, and deliberately to lay himself down between them, when the rug, or the carpet, presented an obvious couch still far above his pretensions? Is this probable, I would ask, if the great power of nature, which I contend for, had not been manifested within him, prompting to the adventure? Doubtless this young nobleman (for such my mind misgives me that he must be) was allured by some memory, not amounting to full consciousness, of his condition in infancy, when he was used to be lapped by his mother, or his nurse, in just such sheets as he there found, into which he was now but creeping back as into his proper *incunabula* [cradle clothes] and resting-place. By no other theory than by this sentiment of a pre-existent state (as I may call it), can I explain a deed so venturous, and indeed upon any other system, so indecorous, in this tender but unseasonable sleeper.

My pleasant friend Jem White[8] was so impressed with a belief of metamorphoses like this frequently taking place, that in some sort to reverse the wrongs of fortune in these poor changelings, he instituted an annual feast of chimney-sweepers, at which it was his pleasure to officiate as host and waiter. * * * O it was a pleasure to see the sable younkers lick in the unctuous meat, with *his* more unctuous sayings— how he would fit the tit-bits to the puny mouths, reserving the lengthier links for the seniors—how he would intercept a morsel even in the jaws of some young desperado, declaring it "must to the pan again to be browned, for it was not fit for a gentleman's eating"—how he would recommend this slice of white bread, or that piece of kissing-crust,[9] to a tender juvenile, advising them all to have a care of cracking their teeth, which were their best patrimony,—how genteelly he would deal about the small ale, as if it were wine, naming the brewer, and protesting, if it were not good, he should lose their custom; with a special recommendation to wipe the lip before drinking. Then we had our toasts—"The King,"—"the Cloth,"— which, whether they understood or not, was equally diverting and flattering;—and for a crowning sentiment, which never failed, "May the Brush supersede the Laurel!" All these, and fifty other fancies, which were rather felt than comprehended by his guests, would he utter, standing upon tables, and prefacing every sentiment with—"Gentlemen, give me leave to propose so and so," which was a prodigious comfort to those young orphans; every now and then stuffing into his mouth (for it did not do to be squeamish on these occasions) indiscriminate pieces of those reeking sausages, which pleased them mightily, and was the savouriest part, you may believe, of the entertainment.

> Golden lads and lasses must,
> As chimney-sweepers, come to dust.[1]

James White is extinct, and with him these suppers have long ceased. He carried away with him half the fun of the world when he died—of my world at least. His old clients look for him among the pens; and missing him, reproach the altered feast of St. Bartholomew, and the glory of Smithfield departed for ever.

---

8. James White, Lamb's schoolmate at Christ's Hospital, a London school for orphans and poor children, also attended by Coleridge and Leigh Hunt.
9. Overhanging crust that touches, or kisses, the crust of another loaf of bread during baking.

1. A couplet from a song in Shakespeare's *Cymbeline* (4.2.262–63); "dust" is both literal for the chimney-sweepers' soot and metaphorical for the return of the body after death to elemental earth.

William Blake. *The Fly*, from *Songs of Experience*.

from *Songs of Experience*
The Fly[1]

Little Fly
Thy summer's play,
My thoughtless hand   15
Has brush'd away.[3]

5   Am not I
A fly like thee?
Or art not thou
A man like me?

For I dance
10   And drink & sing:
Till some blind hand
Shall brush my wing.

If thought is life
And strength & breath:[2]
And the want
Of thought is death;

Then am I
A happy fly,
If I live,
20   Or if I die.

---

1. Blake's plate arranges two columns of verse, with stanzas 1–3 in the left, and stanzas 5 and 6 in the right, placed opposite 1 and 2, respectively; this arrangement allows a reading of the stanzas in an alternative order of left to right: 1-4-2-5-3.

2. Cf. Descartes' famous statement: "I think, therefore I am."
3. Cf. the blinded Gloucester's bitterly rueful comment in *King Lear*: "As flies to wanton boys, are we to th' gods, / They kill us for their sport" (4.1.36–37).

The CLOD & the PEBBLE

Love seeketh not Itself to please,
Nor for itself hath any care;
But for another gives its ease,
And builds a Heaven in Hells despair.[1]

5   So sung a little Clod of Clay
       Trodden with the cattles feet:
       But a Pebble of the brook,
       Warbled out these metres meet.

Love seeketh only Self to please
10 To bind another to Its delight:
Joys in anothers loss of ease,
And builds a Hell in Heavens despite.[2]

HOLY THURSDAY[1]

Is this a holy thing to see,
In a rich and fruitful land
Babes reducd to misery
Fed with cold and usurous hand?

5   Is that trembling cry a song?
Can it be a song of joy?
And so many children poor?
It is a land of poverty!

And their sun does never shine,
10 And their fields are bleak & bare,
And their ways are fill'd with thorns
It is eternal winter there.

For where-e'er the sun does shine,
And where-e'er the rain does fall:
15 Babe can never hunger there,
Nor poverty the mind appall.

The Tyger

Tyger Tyger, burning bright,
In the forests of the night;[1]
What immortal hand or eye,
Could frame thy fearful symmetry?

---

1. Cf. I Corinthians 13.4: "Charity suffereth long, and is kind; charity envieth not; charity vaunteth not itself, is not puffed up."
2. Cf. Satan's rebellious declaration in *Paradise Lost*: "The mind is its own place, and in itself / Can make a Heaven of Hell, a Hell of Heaven" (1. 254–55).
1. See *Holy Thursday* in *Songs of Innocence*, page 1398.
1. Not just a time of day but a metaphysical location, characterized by forest mazes—the terrain that conducts to Hell in Dante's *Inferno*. Cf. "midnight streets" in *London*, line 13.

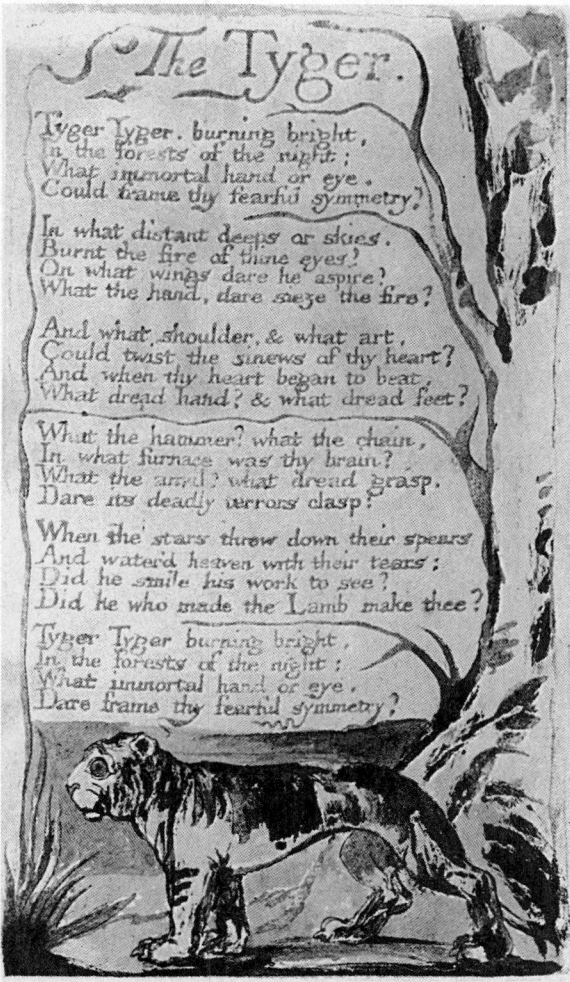

William Blake. *The Tyger,* from *Songs of Experience.* In some copies, Blake colors the tiger in lurid tones; in others, the tiger is colored in pastels.

5   In what distant deeps or skies,
       Burnt the fire of thine eyes?
       On what wings dare he aspire?[2]
       What the hand dare sieze the fire?

       And what shoulder & what art,
10   Could twist the sinews of thy heart?
       And when thy heart began to beat,
       What dread hand? & what dread feet?[3]

2. An allusion to Icarus, who, with his father Dedalus, fashioned wings of feathers and wax to escape from prison. Icarus became enchanted with flight and, ignoring his father's cautions, soared too close to the sun;

the wax melted and he fell to his death in the sea.
3. One engraving has, "What dread hand Formd thy dread feet?"

What the hammer? what the chain,
In what furnace was thy brain?
15   What the anvil? what dread grasp,
Dare its deadly terrors clasp!

When the stars threw down their spears
And water'd heaven with their tears:[4]
Did he smile his work to see?[5]
20   Did he who made the Lamb make thee?[6]

Tyger Tyger burning bright,
In the forests of the night:
What immortal hand or eye,
Dare frame thy fearful symmetry?

The Chimney Sweeper[1]

A little black thing among the snow:
Crying weep, weep, in notes of woe!
Where are thy father & mother? say?
They are both gone up to the church to pray.

5   Because I was happy upon the heath
And smil'd among the winters snow:
They clothed me in the clothes of death,
And taught me to sing the notes of woe.

And because I am happy & dance & sing,
10   They think they have done me no injury:
And are gone to praise God & his Priest & King
Who make up a heaven of our misery.[2]

The SICK ROSE

O Rose thou art sick.
The invisible worm,
That flies in the night
In the howling storm:

5   Has found out thy bed
Of crimson joy:
And his dark secret love
Does thy life destroy.

---

4. In the war in Heaven, *Paradise Lost* (bk. 6), Satan, rebelling against God's authority, is defeated by the Son and driven down to Hell. Blake's verb leaves it undecidable whether the stars "threw down their spears" in desperate surrender or in defiance.
5. In a notebook draft, Blake wrote "did he laugh his work to see."
6. An allusion to Jesus, "The Lamb of God" (John 1.29

and 1.36) and, indirectly, to the poem in *Songs of Innocence*, with Blake as the maker.
1. See *The Chimney Sweeper* in *Songs of Innocence*, page 1397.
2. In both senses: construct their happiness from the elements of our misery; create an illusion of heavenly will in our misery.

AH! SUN-FLOWER[1]

Ah Sun-flower! weary of time,
Who countest the steps of the Sun:
Seeking after that sweet golden clime
Where the travellers journey is done

5   Where the Youth pined away with desire,
And the pale Virgin shrouded in snow:
Arise from their graves and aspire
Where my Sun-flower wishes to go.

The GARDEN of LOVE

I went to the Garden of Love.
And saw what I never had seen:
A Chapel was built in the midst,
Where I used to play on the green.

5   And the gates of this Chapel were shut,
And Thou shalt not, writ over the door;[1]
So I turnd to the Garden of Love,
That so many sweet flowers bore.

And I saw it was filled with graves,
10 And tomb-stones where flowers should be:
And Priests in black gowns, were walking their rounds,
And binding with briars, my joys & desires.[2]

LONDON

I wander thro' each charter'd street,[1]
Near where the charter'd Thames does flow
And mark in every face I meet
Marks of weakness, marks of woe.

5   In every cry of every Man,
In every Infants cry of fear,
In every voice; in every ban,[2]
The mind-forg'd manacles I hear[3]

How the Chimney-sweepers cry
10 Every blackning Church appalls.[4]

---

1. In Ovid's *Metamorphosis* (4.192), a nymph spurned by Apollo, the sun god, so pined for him that she turned into a sunflower. Blake personifies the sunflower as a heliotrope—a plant that turns to follow the sun.
1. An ironic parody of the syntax of the Ten Commandments.
2. An allusion to the crown of thorns that was part of Jesus' torture.
1. A charter is a grant of liberty or privilege, as in Magna Carta (1215). A charter is exclusive: granted to some, it thereby forbids others. Whether rights were chartered or natural was contested in the 1790s.
2. Several meanings are involved: political prohibition, public condemnation, curse, announcement of marriage.

3. The forgers of these fetters are both the authorities of Church and state (Blake originally wrote "german forged," referring to the German descent of King George III) and the individual selves who internalize this oppression with fetters of fear or compliance. Between this "hear" and its rhyming repetition at the end of line 13, note the acrostic of the first letters of the third stanza.
4. The capital C makes it clear that this is the institutional Church of England. Blake's adjective involves the literal blackening of soot with the imagery of moral evil; "appalls" continues the indictment, by drawing into the sense of "dismay" (to which the Church is immune) the literal meaning, "make pale"—that is, clean the soot out of; this color-moral extends into the next stanza's "blasts" and "blights."

And the hapless Soldiers sigh
Runs in blood down Palace walls

But most thro' midnight streets I hear
How the youthful Harlots curse[5]
15   Blasts the new-born Infants tear
And blights with plagues the Marriage hearse[6]

The Human Abstract

Pity would be no more,
If we did not make somebody Poor:
And Mercy no more could be,
If all were as happy as we:

5   And mutual fear brings peace:
Till the selfish loves increase.
Then Cruelty knits a snare,
And spreads his baits with care.

He sits down with holy fears,
10   And waters the ground with tears:
Then Humility takes its root
Underneath his foot.

Soon spreads the dismal shade
Of Mystery over his head;
15   And the Catterpiller and Fly,
Feed on the Mystery.

And it bears the fruit of Deceit,
Ruddy and sweet to eat:
And the Raven his nest has made
20   In its thickest shade.

The Gods of the earth and sea,
Sought thro' Nature to find this Tree
But their search was all in vain:
There grows one in the Human Brain

A POISON TREE[1]

I was angry with my friend:
I told my wrath, my wrath did end.
I was angry with my foe:
I told it not, my wrath did grow.

5   And I waterd it in fears,
Night & morning with my tears:
And I sunned it with smiles.
And with soft deceitful wiles.

And it grew both day and night.
10   Till it bore an apple bright.

---

5. Many of the prostitutes in London were desperately poor girls barely out of childhood, abandoned or disowned by their families.

6. An allusion to prenatal blindness caused by sexually transmitted diseases.
1. Originally titled "Christian Forbearance."

William Blake. *A Poison Tree,* from *Songs of Experience.*

And my foe beheld it shine.
And he knew that it was mine.

And into my garden stole.
When the night had veild the pole.
15   In the morning glad I see.
My foe outstretchd beneath the tree.

A DIVINE IMAGE

Cruelty has a Human Heart
And Jealousy a Human Face
Terror, the Human Form Divine
And Secrecy, the Human Dress

5   The Human Dress, is forged in Iron
The Human Form, a fiery Forge.
The Human Face, a Furnace seal'd
The Human Heart, its hungry Gorge.

THE MARRIAGE OF HEAVEN AND HELL

The Marriage of Heaven and Hell is Blake's first, though hardly systematic, attempt to present a philosophical vision. His aim is to challenge, even outrage, conventional ideologies of good and evil and the moral rewards of Heaven and Hell. His immediate target is the teachings of Emanuel Swedenborg (1688–1772), a visionary theologian he initially admired but then found fault with: it is Swedenborg's *Memorable Relations*, solemn reports of encounters with angels and devils in his *Treatise Concerning Heaven and Hell* (1778), that are satirized in Blake's *Memorable Fancies*. Most of Blake's targets are still recognizable: scientific materialists like Locke who value reason and the information of the senses over imagination; pious moral philosophies that regard the body and soul as distinct, antithetical entities; conventional strictures, keyed to such philosophies, that shame the body and sexuality. Although Blake assails orthodox Christian pieties, his argument is not with religion per se: he is intensely spiritual, believing in visionary prophecy, presenting the prophets Isaiah and Ezekiel as inspirational allies and fellow poets, and admiring Jesus, not as the enforcer of the Ten Commandments but as a compassionate rebel whose "virtue" is precisely that he "acted from im-/-pulse and not from rules." Blake's poem wields the allied genres of satire, enlightenment treatise, and prophecy (of spiritual revolution, signaled by political revolution). The verse lines in the text below vary from standard editorial transcriptions by following the linear arrangement of Blake's plates. Square brackets to the left give the plate number in Blake's illuminated book.

[Plate 1]

THE
MARRIAGE
of
HEAVEN
and
HELL

[Plate 2]

The Argument.[1]

Rintrah[2] roars & shakes his fires in the burdend air;
Hungry clouds swag° on the deep   *sink; lie heavily*

Once meek, and in a perilous path,
The just man[3] kept his course along
5   The vale of death.
Roses are planted where thorns grow.
And on the barren heath
Sing the honey bees.

Then the perilous path was planted:
10   And a river, and a spring
On every cliff and tomb;
And on the bleached bones[4]
Red clay brought forth.[5]

1. An "Argument" is normally a prose summary of a verse passage to follow; Blake deploys the term both inversely and deceptively: he is using poetry to summarize the prose that follows and not really providing a simplified summary at all.
2. A Blake-name for a wrathful poet-prophet of the Old-Testament type and herald (like John the Baptist) of a new messianic era, this figure is Blake's persona for rebuking the present aridity of society and predicting restorative revolution.
3. An allegorical figure for the spiritual pilgrim and prophet, the original inhabitant of Paradise trying to keep faith after the Fall, helped by Christ (who plants the perilous paths) and thwarted by the villains of the Christian Church.
4. See Ezekiel 37, an account of the resurrection of life

from a valley of bones ("can these bones live?").
5. A literal translation of "Adam"; also a reference to the blood of revolutionary violence, and thus its role in redemption (Christ is sometimes called the second Adam). Isaiah 5 prophesies assault by devouring fire and a "roaring" army (30), and chapters 34–35, to which Blake refers on plate 3, prophesy "the day of the Lord's vengeance" on Edom—the destruction of the armies, the dominion of wild beasts, and a land reduced to deserts and thorns and then restored to fertility and the rebirth of faith: "the desert shall . . . blossom as the rose . . . in the wilderness shall waters break out . . . And an highway shall be there . . . called The way of holiness."

Till the villain left the paths of ease,
15   To walk in perilous paths, and drive
The just man into barren climes.

Now the sneaking serpent walks
In mild humility.
And the just man rages in the wilds[6]
20   Where lions roam.

Rintrah roars & shakes his fires in the
        burdend air;
Hungry clouds swag on the deep.

[Plate 3]   As a new heaven is begun, and it is now thir-
-ty-three years since its advent:[7] the Eternal Hell[8]
revives. And lo! Swedenborg is the Angel sitting
at the tomb: his writings are the linen clothes folded
up.[9] Now is the dominion of Edom,[1] & the return of
Adam into Paradise; see Isaiah XXXIV & XXXV Chap:[2]
        Without Contraries is no progression. Attraction
and Repulsion, Reason and Energy, Love and
Hate, are necessary to Human existence.
        From these contraries spring what the religious call
Good & Evil. Good is the passive that obeys Reason
Evil is the active springing from Energy.
        Good is Heaven. Evil is Hell.

[Plate 4]   The voice of the
                        Devil[3]
        All   Bibles   or   sacred   codes,   have   been
the causes of the following Errors.
        1. That Man has two real existing princi-
ples Viz: a Body & a Soul.
        2. That Energy, calld Evil, is alone from the
Body, & that Reason, calld Good, is alone from
the Soul.

---

6. Compare to epigraph for *All Religions Are One*. The voice from the wilderness is prophesied in Isaiah 40.3 and taken by Matthew (3.3) to refer to John the Baptist.

7. In 1757, 33 years before he began this poem in 1790, Blake was born and Swedenborg claimed to have witnessed the Last Judgment and the advent of "New Heaven." At age 33, Christ was crucified and resurrected—hence Blake's sly reference to himself in 1790 in the role of Christ-like prophet.

8. As various sects prophesy new heavens, Hell remains eternal. Blake is also referring to his anti-Swedenborgian writing as the countercreation of his own "Bible of Hell" (see plate 24).

9. See John 20.4–14 for the discovery of Christ's empty sepulchre, the empty burial linens folded and two angels sitting where the body was, and then the appearance of the resurrected body of Christ. Blake puts Swedenborg in the comically ironic situation of announcing his teachings as no longer useful, cast off.

1. See Genesis 27.40: "Edom" is another name for Esau, the honest brother duped out of his inheritance by the trickery of Jacob; their father Isaac assures Esau that "it shall come to pass when thou shalt have the dominion, that thou shalt break [Jacob's] yoke from off thy neck." Isaiah 63 presents the allegory of an Edomite (Esau's descendant) "red in apparel"—bloodspattered from a vengeful trampling down of the rebellious Israelites. "Edom," like "Adam," means "red earth," a literal pun that in the early 1790s would evoke the blood of political revolution that precedes (in Blake's myth) Adam's return to Paradise.

2. In addition to the chapters and verses named (see Argument), Blake is also, defiantly, recalling Isaiah 5.20, which records the warning "Woe unto them that call evil good and good evil."

3. Not necessarily Blake's own voice, but an antidote to conventionally "sacred codes"—"what the religious call Good & Evil." In such codes, Good is restraint, obedience, prohibition, and rationality, and "Evil" is its judgment on principles of pleasure, bodily desire, imagination, and rebellion. The diabolic voice argues that Good is only a synonym for sterility unto death and that Evil is energy, freedom, and life.

3. That God will torment Man in Eternity for following his Energies.

But the following Contraries to these are True

1. Man has no Body distinct from his Soul for that calld Body is a portion of Soul discernd by the five Senses, the chief inlets of Soul in this age.

2. Energy is the only life and is from the Body and Reason is the bound or outward circumference of Energy.

3. Energy is Eternal Delight

[Plate 5]   Those who restrain desire, do so because theirs is weak enough to be restrained; and the restrainer or reason usurps its place & governs the unwilling.

And being restraind it by degrees becomes passive till it is only the shadow of desire.

The history of this is written in Paradise Lost. & the Governor or Reason is call'd Messiah.[4]

And the original Archangel or possessor of the command of the heavenly host is call'd the Devil or Satan and his children are call'd Sin & Death[5]

But in the Book of Job Miltons Messiah is call'd Satan.[6]

For this history has been adopted by both parties

It indeed appear'd to Reason as if Desire was cast out, but the Devil's account is, that the Messi-

[Plate 6]   ah fell. & formed a heaven of what he stole from the Abyss

This is shewn in the Gospel, where he prays to the Father to send the comforter or Desire that Reason may have Ideas to build on,[7] the Jehovah of the Bible being no other than he   who dwells in flaming fire.

Know that after Christs death, he became Jehovah.

But in Milton; the Father is Destiny, the Son, a Ratio of the five senses.[8] & the Holy-ghost, Vacuum![9]

Note. The reason Milton wrote in fetters when he wrote of Angels & God, and at liberty when of

4. Blake is referring to the value of "Reason" in *Paradise Lost*, the highest mental capacity, through which man knows God, and thus the agency by which "lower" faculties such as passion and appetite are disciplined.

5. A reference to Satan's status as Archangel Lucifer before his fall from Heaven along with the rebel faction he commanded in the war against God (see *Paradise Lost* 6:824ff.). In Bk. 2.746–814, Milton provides a lurid account of the birth of Satan's children: first his daughter Sin, and then their incestuous son, Death.

6. In the Book of Job, God tests Job's faith by allowing Satan to torment him.

7. An ironic twist on Christ's assurance that after his earthly death he will send the Holy Ghost as comforter; see John 14.16–17.

8. Blake puns on the Latin meanings of "sum" and "Reason." He argues that philosophical and theological exaltations of reason demote the creative power of imagination.

9. Milton was skeptical of the Trinitarian completion of divinity by the Holy Ghost, but Blake here satirizes what he sees as imaginative emptiness.

Devils & Hell, is because he was a true Poet and of the Devils party[1] without knowing it

A Memorable Fancy

As I was walking among the fires of hell, de-lighted with the enjoyments of Genius; which to An-gels look like torment and insanity. I collected some of their Proverbs: thinking that as the sayings used in a nation, mark its character, so the Proverbs of Hell, shew the nature of Infernal wisdom better than any description of buildings or garments

When I came home, on the abyss of the five sen-ses, where a flat sided steep frowns over the pre-sent world. I saw a mighty Devil folded in black clouds hovering on the sides of the rock, with cor-

[Plate 7]   -roding fires[2] he wrote the following sentence now per-cieved by the minds of men, & read by them on earth.

How do you know but ev'ry Bird that cuts the airy way, Is an immense world of delight, clos'd by your senses five?[3]

Proverbs of Hell.[4]

In seed time learn, in harvest teach, in winter enjoy.
Drive your cart and your plow over the bones of the dead.
The road of excess leads to the palace of wisdom.
Prudence is a rich ugly old maid courted by Incapacity.
He who desires but acts not, breeds pestilence.
The cut worm forgives the plow.
Dip him in the river who loves water.
A fool sees not the same tree that a wise man sees.
He whose face gives no light, shall never become a star.
Eternity is in love with the productions of time.
The busy bee has no time for sorrow.
The hours of folly are measur'd by the clock, but of wis-dom: no clock can measure.
All wholsom food is caught without a net or a trap.
Bring out number weight & measure in a year of dearth

1. Both the Devil's point of view and the political faction he led against the authority of God. This "Note" is a famous example of what was later called "Romantic Satanism" and its reading *Paradise Lost* against Milton's avowed "Argument."
2. Casting himself and other poets as Devils, Blake refers to his process of book production, whereby he etched his designs on copper plates with an acid-resistant fluid, then washed the plate in acid so that the designs emerged in relief. Hand-colored, this relief plate was then used to print the pages. See plate 14 for a reference to the symbolic value of this method.

3. These lines allude to verses by Thomas Chatterton: "How dydd I know that eve'ry darte, / That cutte the Airie waie, / Myghte nott find passage toe my harte, / And close myne eyes for aie?" (*Bristowe Tragedie*). At age 17, Chatterton committed suicide in despair of success and thereby won celebrity in the Romantic era as a martyred genius (see, e.g., William Wordsworth's *Resolution and Independence*, 43–50).
4. Blake's diabolic version of the Old Testament's Book of Proverbs as well as his satire on the *Aphorisms* of Kaspar Lavater (1788), a Swiss moralist and friend of Henry Fuseli, an artist who was also Blake's friend.

No bird soars too high. if he soars with his own wings.
A dead body. revenges not injuries.
The most sublime act is to set another before you.
If the fool would persist in his folly he would become
Folly is the cloke of knavery.   [wise
Shame is Prides cloke.

[Plate 8]   Proverbs of Hell
Prisons are built with stones of Law, Brothels with
          bricks of Religion.
The pride of the peacock is the glory of God.
5   The lust of the goat is the bounty of God.
The wrath of the lion is the wisdom of God.
The nakedness of woman is the work of God.
Excess of sorrow laughs. Excess of joy weeps.
The roaring of lions, the howling of wolves the raging
10   of the stormy sea, and the destructive sword, are
          portions of eternity too great for the eye of man.
The fox condemns the trap. not himself.
Joys impregnate. Sorrows bring forth.
Let man wear the fell of the lion. woman the fleece of
15   the sheep.
The bird a nest, the spider a web, man friendship.
The selfish smiling fool. & the sullen frowning fool. shall
          be both thought wise, that they may be a rod.
What is now proved was once, only imagin'd.
20   The rat, the mouse, the fox, the rabbet; watch the roots,
          the lion, the tyger, the horse, the elephant, watch
          the fruits.
The cistern contains: the fountain overflows
One thought. fills immensity.
25   Always be ready to speak your mind, and a base man
          will avoid you.
Every thing possible to be believ'd is an image of truth.
The eagle never lost so much time. as when he submit-
          -ted to learn of the crow.

[Plate 9]   Proverbs of Hell
The fox provides for himself. but God provides for the lion.
Think in the morning. Act in the noon, Eat in the even-
          -ing, Sleep in the night.
5   He who has sufferd you to impose on him knows you.
As the plow follows words, so God rewards prayers.
The tygers of wrath are wiser than the horses of in-
Expect poison from the standing water.   [-struction
You never know what is enough unless you know what is
10   more than enough.
Listen to the fools reproach! it is a kingly title!
The eyes of fire, the nostrils of air, the mouth of water,
          the beard of earth.
The weak in courage is strong in cunning.

15 The apple tree never asks the beech how he shall grow,
     nor the lion, the horse, how he shall take his prey.
The thankful reciever bears a plentiful harvest.
If others had not been foolish. we should be so.
The soul of sweet delight. can never be defil'd,
20 When thou seest an Eagle, thou seest a portion of Ge
     -nius. lift up thy head!
As the catterpiller chooses the fairest leaves to lay
     her eggs on, so the priest lays his curse on
     the fairest joys.
25 To create a little flower is the labour of ages.
Damn, braces: Bless relaxes.
The best wine is the oldest. the best water the newest
Prayers plow not! Praises reap not!
Joys laugh not! Sorrows weep not!

[Plate 10]   Proverbs of Hell
The head Sublime, the heart Pathos, the genitals Beauty
     the hands & feet Proportion.
As the air to a bird or the sea to a fish, so is contempt
     to the contemptible.
The crow wish'd every thing was black, the owl, that eve-
     -ry thing was white.
Exuberance is Beauty.
If the lion was advised by the fox. he would be cunning.
10 Improvent makes strait roads, but the crooked roads
     without Improvement. are roads of Genius.
Sooner murder an Infant in its cradle than nurse unact
     -ed desires
Where man is not nature is barren.
15 Truth can never be told so as to be understood and
     not be believd.
                    Enough! or Too much

[Plate 11]   The ancient Poets animated all sensible objects
with Gods or Geniuses, calling them by the names and
adorning them with the properties of woods, rivers,
mountains, lakes, cities, nations, and whatever their
enlarged & numerous senses could percieve.
     And particularly they studied the genius of each
city & country. placing it under its mental deity.
     Till a system was formed, which some took ad-
vantage of & enslav'd the vulgar by attempting to
realize or abstract the mental deities from their
objects: thus began Priesthood.
     Choosing forms of worship from poetic tales.
     And at length they pronouncd that the Gods
had orderd such things.
     Thus   men   forgot   that   All   deities   reside
in the human breast.

[Plate 12]   A Memorable Fancy.

The Prophets Isaiah and Ezekiel dined with
me, and I asked them how they dared so roundly to
assert. that God spake to them; and whether they
did not think at the time, that they would be mis-
-understood, & so be the cause of imposition.

Isaiah answer'd. I saw no God, nor heard
any, in a finite organical perception; but my sen-
-ses discover'd the infinite in every thing, and as I
was then perswaded, & remain confirmd; that the
voice of honest indignation is the voice of God, I
cared not for consequences but wrote.

Then I asked: does a firm perswasion that a
thing is so, make it so?

He replied. All poets believe that it does. &
in ages of imagination this firm perswasion remo
ved mountains; but many are not capable of a
firm perswasion of any thing.

Then Ezekiel said. The philosophy of the east
taught the first principles of human perception
some nations held one principle for the origin &
some another; we of Israel taught that the Poetic
Genius (as you now call it) was the first principle
and all the others merely derivative, which was the
cause of our despising the Priests & Philosophers
of other countries. and prophecying that all Gods

[Plate 13]   would at last be proved to originate in ours & to be the
tributaries of the Poetic Genius, it was this. that our
great poet King David desired so fervently & invokes
so patheticly, saying by this he conquers enemies &
governs kingdoms; and we so loved our God. that we
cursed in his name all the deities of surrounding
nations, and asserted that they had rebelled; from
these opinions the vulgar came to think that all nati-
-ons would at last be subject to the jews.

This said he, like all firm perswasions, is come to
pass, for all nations believe the jews code and wor-
-ship the jews god, and what greater subjection can be

I heard this with some wonder. & must confess
my own conviction. After dinner I ask'd Isaiah to favour the world with his lost works, he said none of
equal value was lost. Ezekiel said the same of his.

I also asked Isaiah what made him go naked and
barefoot three years?[5] he answerd, the same that made
our friend Diogenes the Grecian.

---

5. See Isaiah 20.2; the Lord instructs Isaiah to walk "naked and barefoot."

I then asked Ezekiel. why he eat dung, & lay so
long on his right & left side?[6] he answerd, the desire
of raising other men into a perception of the infinite
this the North American tribes practise. & is he honest who resists his genius or conscience. only for
the sake of present ease or gratification?

[Plate 14]   The ancient tradition that the world will be con-
-sumed in fire at the end of six thousand years[7]
is true. as I have heard from Hell.

For the cherub with his flaming sword is
hereby commanded to leave his guard at tree of
life,[8] and when he does, the whole creation will
be consumed and appear infinite. and holy
whereas it now appears finite & corrupt.

This will come to pass by an improvement of
sensual enjoyment.

But first the notion that man has a body
distinct from his soul, is to be expunged; this
I shall do, by printing in the infernal method, by
corrosives, which in Hell are salutary and medicinal, melting apparent surfaces away, and
displaying the infinite which was hid.

If the doors of perception were cleansed
every thing would appear to man as it is: In-
-finite.

For man has closed himself up, till he sees
all things thro' narrow chinks of his cavern.[9]

[Plate 15]   A Memorable Fancy[1]
I was in a Printing house in Hell & saw the
method in which knowledge is transmitted from generation to generation.

6. See Ezekiel 4. Ezekiel is instructed to act out with his
body the siege of Jerusalem by lying on his left side for
390 days to represent the years of Israel's iniquity and for
40 days on his right side for the years of the iniquity of
the house of Judah; he is also ordered to eat barley cakes
mixed with dung. Diogenes, famous for searching in daylight with a lantern for one honest man, was a 4th-centu-
ry Greek Cynic philosopher who led a severely ascetic
life. Blake alludes to these extraordinary actions to reflect
the eccentricity often associated with visionary prophets.
7. This prophetic tradition is represented in the Book of
Revelation and based on the translation of the six days of
creation into six millennia (see 2 Peter 3.8); Blake relates
this symbolism to his own era of the American and
French revolutions.
8. See Genesis 3.24. After evicting Adam and Eve from
Eden, God "placed at the east of the garden of Eden cheru-
bims, and a flaming sword which turned every way, to keep
the way of the tree of life" (this is one of the last images in
Book 12 of *Paradise Lost*). Blake in turn imagines the
expulsion of this angelic policeman and the restoration of
Adam to the garden, free from sexual shame.
9. A reference to Plato's allegory of the Cave (*Republic* 7),

which compares the human mind to a cavern where men
sit with their backs to the aperture of daylight, appre-
hending only shadows cast by firelight on the wall. A
more immediate reference for Blake is Locke's description in his *Essay Concerning Human Understanding*
(1690–1700) of "external and internal sensation" as "the
only passages . . . of knowledge to the understanding . . .
the windows by which light is let into [the] dark room" of
the mind: "understanding is not much unlike a closet
wholly shut from light, with only some little openings
left, to let in external visible resemblances, or ideas of
things without" (2.11.17).
1. The caverns continue the imagery of plate 14. The
allegory is cryptic but seems to refer to Blake's creative
process: in the first cavern, a figure of diabolic energy is
clearing away the rubbish of wasted systems; the second
chamber is undergoing artistic restoration; the third is
being made into a place for liberated imagination; in the
fourth and fifth chambers, the metal plates for Blake's
book-making processes are being formed; in the sixth,
men take possession of these books, imaging the decline
from energy to system.

In the first chamber was a Dragon-Man, clear-
-ing away the rubbish from a caves mouth; within, a
number of Dragons were hollowing the cave.

In the second chamber was a Viper folding round
the rock & the cave, and others adorning it with gold
silver and precious stones.

In the third chamber was an Eagle, with wings
and feathers of air, he caused the inside of the cave
to be infinite, around were numbers of Eagle like
men, who built palaces in the immense cliffs.

In the fourth chamber were Lions of flaming fire
raging around & melting the metals into living fluids.

In the fifth chamber were Unnam'd forms, which
cast the metals into the expanse.

There they were reciev'd by Men who occupied
the sixth chamber, and took the forms of books &
were arranged in libraries.

[Plate 16]   The Giants who formed this world into its
sensual existence and now seem to live in it
in chains; are in truth. the causes of its life
& the sources of all activity, but the chains
are, the cunning of weak and tame minds which
have power to resist energy. according to the pro-
-verb, the weak in courage is strong in cunning.

Thus one portion of being, is the Prolific. the
other, the Devouring: to the devourer it seems as
if the producer was in his chains, but it is not so;
he only takes portions of existence and fancies
that the whole.

But the Prolific would cease to be Prolific
unless the Devourer as a sea reciev'd the excess
of his delights.

Some will say, Is not God alone the Prolific?
I answer. God only Acts & Is, in existing beings
or Men.

These two classes of men are always upon
earth. & they should be enemies: whoever tries

[Plate 17]   to reconcile them seeks to destroy existence.
Religion is an endeavour to reconcile the two.

Note. Jesus Christ did not wish to unite
but to separate them, as in the Parable of sheep and
goats! & he says I came not to send Peace but a
Sword.[2]

Messiah or Satan or Tempter was formerly
thought to be one of the Antediluvians[3] who are our
Energies.

---

2. The Prolific (diabolical creators) and the Devourers (sterile pious reasoners) accord with the parable of the sheep and goats (Matthew 25.32–33): Jesus, the Shepherd, separates the sheep on his right hand, admitting them to his kingdom, and the goats on his left, condemn-ing them to the punishment of everlasting fire—having cautioned, "think not that I am come to send peace on earth: I came not to send peace, but a sword" (10.34).
3. Inhabitants of the earth "before the flood" survived by Noah.

A Memorable Fancy[4]

An Angel came to me and said. O pitiable foolish young man! O horrible! O dreadful state! consider the hot burning dungeon thou art preparing for thyself to all eternity, to which thou art going in such career.

I said. perhaps you will be willing to shew me my eternal lot & we will contemplate together upon it and see whether your lot or mine is most desirable.

So he took me thro' a stable & thro' a church & down into the church vault at the end of which was a mill: thro' the mill we went, and came to a cave. down the winding cavern we groped our tedi--ous way till a void boundless as a nether sky ap--peard beneath us & we held by the roots of trees and hung over this immensity: but I said, if you please we will commit ourselves to this void, and see whether providence is here also, if you will not I will? but he answerd, do not presume O young-man but as we here remain behold thy lot which will soon appear when the darkness passes away
So I remaind with him sitting in the twisted

[Plate 18]

root of an oak; he was suspended in a fungus which hung with the head downward into the deep:

By degrees we beheld the infinite Abyss, fiery as the smoke of a burning city; beneath us at an immense distance was the sun, black but shining round it were fiery tracks on which revolv'd vast spiders, crawling after their prey; which flew or rather swum in the infinite deep, in the most ter--rific shapes of animals sprung from corruption. & the air was full of them, & seemd composed of them; these are Devils. and are called Powers of the air. I now asked my companion which was my eternal lot? he said, between the black & white spiders

But now, from between the black & white spiders a cloud and fire burst and rolled thro the deep blackning all beneath, so that the nether deep grew black as a sea & rolled with a terrible noise: be--neath us was nothing now to be seen but a black tempest, till looking east between the clouds & the waves, we saw a cataract of blood mixed with fire and not many stones throw from us appeard and sunk again the scaly fold of a monstrous serpent. at last to the east, distant about three degrees[5] ap--peard a fiery crest above the waves slowly it rear--ed like a ridge of golden rocks till we discoverd two globes of crimson fire, from which the sea

---

4. In this Memorable Fancy, a kind of dream allegory, Blake wages an elaborately comic argument with a pious Swedenborgian Angel, the voice of conventional moral-ity and religion. The geography of their fantastic tour images the decline of Christianity, beginning in the sta-ble of Christ's birth and the church founded in His name, and descending into the vault, the cave, the mill, and the abyss—into the rigidity of institutional religion.
5. The longitudinal position of Paris, heart of the French Revolution, relative to London.

fled away in clouds of smoke, and now we saw, it was the head of Leviathan.[6] his forehead was divided into streaks of green & purple like those on a tygers forehead: soon we saw his mouth & red gills hang just above the raging foam, tinging the black deep with beams of blood, advancing toward

[Plate 19]   us with all the fury of a spiritual exsitence.

My friend the Angel climb'd up from his station into the mill; I remain'd alone, & then this appearance was no more, but I found myself sitting on a pleasant bank beside a river by moon light hearing a harper who sung to the harp. & his theme was, The man who never alters his opinion is like standing water, & breeds reptiles of the mind.

But I arose, and sought for the mill & there I found my Angel, who surprised asked me, how I escaped?

I answerd. All that we saw was owing to your metaphysics: for when you ran away, I found myself on a bank by moonlight hearing a harper, But now we have seen my eternal lot, shall I shew you yours? he laughd at my proposal; but I by force suddenly caught him in my arms, & flew westerly thro' the night, till we were elevated above the earths shadow: then I flung myself with him directly into the body of the sun, here I clothed myself in white,[7] & taking in my hand Swedenborgs volumes sunk from the glorious clime, and passed all the planets till we came to saturn, here I staid to rest & then leap'd into the void, between saturn & the fixed stars.

Here said I! is your lot, in this space, if space it may be calld. Soon we saw the stable and the church, & I took him to the altar and open'd the Bible, and lo! it was a deep pit, into which I de--scended driving the Angel before me, soon we saw seven houses of brick,[8] one we enterd; in it were a

[Plate 20]   number of monkeys, baboons, & all of that species chaind by the middle, grinning and snatching at one another, but witheld by the shortness of their chains:[9] however I saw that they sometimes grew nu merous, and then the weak were caught by the strong and with a grinning aspect first coupled with & then devourd, by plucking off first one limb & then ano-

6. A beast described in the Bible (Job 41.1, Isaiah 27.1, Psalms 104.26), and alluded to by Thomas Hobbes (1588–1679) in his famous treatise on government, *Leviathan, or the Matter, Form, and Power of a Commonwealth, Ecclesiastical and Civil* (1651), written during the commonwealth and defending a secular monarchy; Hobbes argues that appetitive self-interest must be controlled only by the laws and institutions of government, whose authority is agreed upon by common contract. In Blake's view, this vision of the state is monstrous.
7. In Revelation 7.9, those who have been redeemed appear before the throne of Christ in white robes.
8. The seven churches to whom John addresses the Book of Revelation (1.4).
9. Blake's satire of theological dispute.

-ther till the body was left a helpless trunk. this after grinning & kissing it with seeming fondness they de--vourd too; and here & there I saw one savourily pic--king the flesh off of his own tail; as the stench ter--ribly annoyd us both we went into the mill, & I in my hand brought the skeleton of a body, which in the mill was Aristotles Analytics.[1]

So the Angel said: thy phantasy has imposed upon me & thou oughtest to be ashamed.

I answerd: we impose upon one another. & it is but lost time to converse with you whose works are only Analytics

Opposition is true Friendship[2]

[Plate 21]   I have always found that Angels have the vani--ty to speak of themselves as the only wise; this they do with a confident insolence sprouting from systema--tic reasoning:

Thus Swedenborg boasts that what he writes is new: tho' it is only the Contents or Index of already publish'd books

A man carried a monkey about for a shew, & be--cause he was a little wiser than the monkey, grew vain, and conciev'd himself as much wiser than se--ven men. It is so with Swedenborg: he shews the folly of churches & exposes hypocrites, till he im--agines that all are religious, & himself the single

[Plate 22]   one on earth that ever broke a net.

Now hear a plain fact: Swedenborg has not writ--ten one new truth: Now hear another: he has written all the old falshoods.

And now hear the reason. He conversed with Angels who are all religious. & conversed not with Devils who all hate religion for he was incapable thro' his conceited notions.

Thus Swedenborgs writings are a recapitulation of all superficial opinions, and an analysis of the more sublime. but no further.

Have now another plain fact: Any man of mechani--cal talents may from the writings of Paracelsus or Ja--cob Behmen,[3] produce ten thousand volumes of equal value with Swedenborg's, and from those of Dante or Shakespear, an infinite number.

But when he has done this, let him not say that he knows better than his master, for he only holds a can--dle in sunshine.

---

1. A "skeleton" both in the sense of an abstract summary and as a symbolic comment on the lifeless form of knowl-edge represented by Aristotle's treatise on logic as the highest kind of mental discipline. Compare the reference to "bleached bones" in the Argument.
2. This motto appears in only three of the nine known copies of the poem.
3. Paracelsus (1493–1541) was a Swiss physician, occultist, and alchemist; Behmen is Jakob Boehme (1575–1624), a German mystic, who believed that God was knowable from the unity of the natural world.

A Memorable Fancy

Once I saw a Devil in a flame of fire, who arose be
fore an Angel that sat on a cloud, and the Devil ut-
-terd these words.

The worship of God is. Honouring his gifts in other
men each according to his genius. and loving the

[Plate 23]

greatest men best, those who envy or calumniate
great men hate God, for there is no other God.

The Angel hearing this became almost blue
but mastering himself he grew yellow, & at last
white pink & smiling. and then replied,

Thou Idolater, is not God One? & is not he
visible in Jesus Christ? and has not Jesus Christ
given his sanction to the law of ten commandments
and are not all other men fools sinners & nothings?

The Devil answer'd; bray a fool in a morter with
wheat yet shall not his folly be beaten out of him[4]
if Jesus Christ is the greatest man, you ought to
love him in the greatest degree; now hear how he
has given his sanction to the law of ten command
-ments: did he not mock at the sabbath, and so
mock the sabbaths God? murder those who were
murderd because of him? turn away the law from
the woman taken in adultery? steal the labor of
others to support him? bear false witness when
he omitted making a defence before Pilate? covet
when he pray'd for his disciples, and when he bid
them shake off the dust of their feet against such
as refused to lodge them? I tell you, no virtue
can exist without breaking these ten commandments: Jesus was all virtue, and acted from im-

[Plate 24]

-pulse: not from rules.[5]

When he had so spoken, I beheld the Angel who
stretched out his arms embracing the flame of fire
& he was consumed and arose as Elijah.[6]

Note. This Angel, who is now become a Devil, is
my particular friend: we often read the Bible to-
-gether in its infernal or diabolical sense which
the world shall have if they behave well.

I have also: **The Bible of Hell**:[7] which the world
shall have whether they will or no.

One Law for the Lion & Ox is Oppression

1790–1793   1793–1825

---

4. See Proverbs 27.22: "Though thou shouldest bray
[crush] a fool in a mortar among wheat with a pestle, yet
will not his foolishness depart from him."
5. For Jesus' breaking of Jewish law, see John 8.2–11, and
Matthew 9.14–17, 12.1–8, and 27.11–14.

6. See 2 Kings 2.11: "there appeared a chariot of fire, and
horses of fire, and . . . Elijah went up by a whirlwind into
heaven."
7. Blake's own scripture—that is, his illuminated poems.

VISIONS OF THE DAUGHTERS OF ALBION

Although "Albion," a mythical name for England, gives this poem the aura of a fable, its immediate context is Wollstonecraft's *Rights of Woman* (1792). Blake presents a chorus comprised of the Daughters of Albion (oppressed Englishwomen) and three characters: Oothoon, "the soft soul of America," that is, freedom and new hope; Theotormon ("God-Tormented"), her lover; and Bromion, who rapes her. Theotormon, paralyzed by jealousy (sexual possessiveness), binds Bromion and Oothoon back-to-back in his cave, and sits at the entry weeping. The remainder of the poem consists of the monologues of the three characters in this unchanging situation. Bromion expresses a tyrant's ideology of violent oppression and terror; Theotormon laments the debilitating effects of religious strictures; Oothoon inveighs against egotism and envisions love free from sexual and economic oppression. Like Wollstonecraft, Blake means to shock the sons of Albion by linking sexual tyranny and oppression to slavery, including the ravages of colonialism and the exploitation of children. The poem concludes with the Daughters of Albion echoing Oothoon's woe, but its subtitle, "The Eye sees more than the Heart knows," invites a regard of Oothoon's long soliloquy not only as a potent detailing of the oppression her heart knows well but also as a visionary hymn to unfettered love infused with a passionate hope for transformation. Square brackets at the front of lines indicate the plate number in Blake's illuminated book.

VISIONS
of
the Daughters of
Albion

[Plate ii]   The Eye sees more than the Heart knows.

[Plate iii]   The Argument[1]
                   I loved Theotormon
                   And I was not ashamed
                   I trembled in my virgin fears
5   And I hid in Leutha's vale![2]

                   I plucked Leutha's flower,[3]
                   And I rose up from the vale;
                   But the terrible thunders tore
                   My virgin mantle in twain.

[Plate 1]   *Visions*

ENSLAV'D,[4] the Daughters of Albion weep: a trembling lamentation
Upon their mountains; in their valleys. sighs toward America.[5]

For the soft soul of America, Oothoon[6] wanderd in woe,
5   Along the vales of Leutha seeking flowers to comfort her;
And thus she spoke to the bright Marygold of Leutha's vale

        Art thou a flower! art thou a nymph! I see thee now a flower:
        Now a nymph! I dare not pluck thee from thy dewy bed!

        The Golden nymph replied; pluck thou my flower Oothoon the mild
10   Another flower shall spring, because the soul of sweet delight
        Can never pass away. she ceas'd & closd her golden shrine.

---

1. Oothoon's description of herself before being raped.
2. A world of sexual shyness and sexual desire.
3. Traditional image for sexual initiation.
4. Blake's inscription of this word with large letters advertises the affinity of sexual slavery and chattel slavery, a recurrent theme in Wollstonecraft's *Rights of Woman*

(1792) and Thompson and Wheeler's *Appeal* (1825).
5. A country that has already revolted against tyranny.
6. An evocation of Oi-thona, the name of the "virgin of the waves" in James Macpherson's *Ossian*, who is kidnapped and raped by a rejected suitor.

Then Oothoon pluck'd the flower saying, I pluck thee from thy bed,
Sweet flower, and put thee here to glow between my breasts
And thus I turn my face to where my whole soul seeks.

15   Over the waves she went in wing'd exulting swift delight;
And over Theotormons reign, took her impetuous course.

Bromion rent her with his thunders.[7] on his stormy bed
Lay the faint maid, and soon her woes appalld his thunders hoarse

Bromion spake. behold this harlot[8] here on Bromions bed
20   And let the jealous dolphins sport around the lovely maid:
Thy soft American plains are mine, and mine thy north & south:
Stampt with my signet are the swarthy children of the sun:[9]
They are obedient, they resist not, they obey the scourge:
Their daughters worship terrors and obey the violent:[1]

[Plate 2]   Now thou maist marry Bromions harlot, and protect the child
Of Bromions rage, that Oothoon shall put forth in nine moons
                                                      [time
Then storms rent Theotormons limbs; he rolled his waves around.
5   And folded his black jealous waters round the adulterate pair
Bound back to back in Bromions caves[2] Terror & meekness dwell
At entrance Theotormon sits wearing the threshold hard
With secret tears; beneath him sound like waves on a desart shore
The voice of slaves beneath the sun, and children bought with money,
10   That shiver in religious caves beneath the burning fires
Of lust, that belch incessant from the summits of the earth

Oothoon weeps not: she cannot weep! her tears are locked up;
But she can howl incessant, writhing her soft snowy limbs.
And calling Theotormons Eagles to prey upon her flesh.

15   I call with holy voice! kings of the sounding air,
Rend away this defiled bosom that I may reflect.
The image of Theotormon on my pure transparent breast.

The Eagles at her call descend & rend their bleeding prey;
Theotormon severely smiles. her soul reflects the smile;
20   As the clear spring mudded with feet of beasts grows pure & smiles

The Daughters of Albion hear her woes, & eccho back her sighs.

Why does my Theotormon sit weeping upon the threshold;
And Oothoon hovers by his side, perswading him in vain:
I cry arise O Theotormon for the village dog

7. The imagery conveys both his wrath and the physical violence of rape.
8. "Harlot" reflects the common prejudice that despises the rape victim as fallen, soiled, blamable. In *Rights of Woman*, Wollstonecraft observes that rape, or even seduction out of wedlock, was often a prelude to prostitution: "A woman who has lost her honour, imagines that she cannot fall lower, and as for recovering her former station, it is impossible; no exertion can wash this stain away. Losing thus every spur, and having no other means

of support, prostitution becomes her only refuge."
9. Referring to the branding of African slaves.
1. A tyrant's ideology: the victims of tyranny actually crave such treatment.
2. As in *The Marriage of Heaven and Hell*, these caves image the imprisoned mind—a prison evident in Theotormon's jealous regard of the rapist and his victim as "the adulterate pair" and his susceptibility to Bromion's taunting presentation of Oothoon to him for marriage, pregnant by Bromion.

25 Barks at the breaking day, the nightingale has done lamenting,
The lark does rustle in the ripe corn, and the Eagle returns
From nightly prey, and lifts his golden beak to the pure east;
Shaking the dust from his immortal pinions to awake
The sun that sleeps too long. Arise my Theotormon I am pure.
30 Because the night is gone that clos'd me in its deadly black.
They told me that the night & day were all that I could see;
They told me that I had five senses to inclose me up.
And they inclos'd my infinite brain into a narrow circle.
And sunk my heart into the Abyss, a red round globe hot burning
35 Instead of morn arises a bright shadow, like an eye
In the eastern cloud; instead of night a sickly charnel house;
That Theotormon hears me not! to him the night and morn
Are both alike: a night of sighs, a morning of fresh tears;

[Plate 3]   And none but Bromion can hear my lamentations.

With what sense is it that the chicken shuns the ravenous hawk
With what sense does the tame pigeon measure out the expanse?
With what sense does the bee form cells? have not the mouse & frog
5 Eyes and ears and sense of touch? yet are their habitations,
And, their pursuits, as different as their forms and as their joys:
Ask the wild ass why he refuses burdens: and the meek camel
Why he loves man: is it because of eye ear mouth or skin
Or breathing nostrils? No, for these the wolf and tyger have.
10 Ask the blind worm the secrets of the grave, and why her spires
Love to curl round the bones of death! and ask the rav'nous snake
Where she gets poison: & the wing'd eagle why he loves the sun
And then tell me the thoughts of man, that have been hid of old.

Silent I hover all the night, and all day could be silent.
15 If Theotormon once would turn his loved eyes upon me;
How can I be defild when I reflect thy image pure?
Sweetest the fruit that the worm feeds on. & the soul prey'd on by woe
The new wash'd lamb ting'd with the village smoke & the bright swan
By the red earth[3] of our immortal river: I bathe my wings.
20 And I am white and pure to hover round Theotormons breast.

Then Theotormon broke his silence. and he answered.

Tell me what is the night or day to one oerflowd with woe?
Tell me what is a thought? & of what substance is it made?
Tell me what is a joy? & in what gardens do joys grow?
25 And in what rivers swim the sorrows? and upon what mountains
[Plate 4]   Wave shadows of discontent? and in what houses dwell the wretched
Drunken with woe forgotten, and shut up from cold despair.

Tell me where dwell the thoughts forgotten till thou call them forth
Tell me where dwell the joys of old? & where the ancient loves?

3. An evocation of Adam, whose name means literally "red earth."

5   And when will they renew again & the night of oblivion past?
     That I might traverse times & spaces far remote and bring
     Comforts into a present sorrow and a night of pain
     Where goest thou O thought? to what remote land is thy flight?
     If thou returnest to the present moment of affliction
10   Wilt thou bring comforts on thy wings. and dews and honey and balm;
     Or poison From the desart wilds, from the eyes of the envier.

Then Bromion said: and shook the cavern with his lamentation

     Thou knowest that the ancient trees seen by thine eyes have fruit;
     But knowest thou that trees and fruits flourish upon the earth
15   To gratify senses unknown? trees beasts and birds unknown:
     Unknown, not unpercievd, spread in the infinite microscope,
     In places yet unvisited by the voyager, and in worlds
     Over another kind of seas, and in atmospheres unknown?
     Ah! are there other wars, beside the wars of sword and fire!
20   And are there other sorrows, beside the sorrows of poverty?
     And are there other joys, besides the joys of riches and ease?
     And is there not one law for both the lion and the ox?[4]
     And is there not eternal fire, and eternal chains?
     To bind the phantoms of existence from eternal life?

25   Then Oothoon waited silent all the day, and all the night,
[Plate 5]   But when the morn arose, her lamentation renewd.
     The Daughters of Albion hear her woes, & eccho back her sighs.

     O Urizen! Creator of men! mistaken Demon of heaven:[5]
     Thy joys are tears! thy labour vain, to form men to thine image.
5   How can one joy absorb another? are not different joys
     Holy, eternal, infinite! and each joy is a Love.

     Does not the great mouth laugh at a gift? & the narrow eyelids mock
     At the labour that is above payment, and wilt thou take the ape
     For thy councellor? or the dog for a schoolmaster to thy children?
10   Does he who contemns poverty, and he who turns with abhorrence
     From usury: feel the same passion or are they moved alike?
     How can the giver of gifts experience the delights of the merchant?
     How the industrous citizen the pains of the husbandman.
     How different far the fat fed hireling with hollow drum;
15   Who buys whole corn fields into wastes, and sings upon the heath:
     How different their eye and ear! how different the world to them!
     What are his nets & gins & traps, & how does he surround him
     With cold floods of abstraction, and with forests of solitude,
     To build him castles and high spires, where kings & priests may dwell.

---

4. See the last line of *The Marriage of Heaven and Hell.*
5. Oothoon wonders if the limitations of both Bromion and Theotormon are the work of Urizen, a creator of men in his own image: his name sounds like "your reason" (and so evokes the constraints of sterile rationality) as well as "horizon" (derived from the Greek word for outward limit, or boundary circle).

20   Till she who burns with youth and knows no fixed lot; is bound
      In spells of law to one she loaths: and must she drag the chain
      Of life, in weary lust! must chilling murderous thoughts, obscure
      The clear heaven of her eternal spring! to bear the wintry rage
      Of a harsh terror driv'n to madness, bound to hold a rod
25   Over her shrinking shoulders all the day; & all the night
      To turn the wheel of false desire: and longings that wake her womb
      To the abhorred birth of cherubs in the human form
      That live a pestilence & die a meteor & are no more.
      Till the child dwell with one he hates, and do the deed he loaths
30   And the impure scourge force his seed into its unripe birth
      E'er yet his eyelids can behold the arrows of the day.

      Does the whale worship at thy footsteps as the hungry dog?
      Or does he scent the mountain prey, because his nostrils wide
      Draw in the ocean? does his eye discern the flying cloud
35   As the ravens eye? or does he measure the expanse like the vulture?
      Does the still spider view the cliffs where eagles hide their young?
      Or does the fly rejoice, because the harvest is brought in?
      Does not the eagle scorn the earth & despise the treasures beneath?
      But the mole knoweth what is there, & the worm shall tell it thee.
40   Does not the worm erect a pillar in the mouldering church yard?
[Plate 6]   And a palace of eternity in the jaws of the hungry grave
      Over his porch these words are written. Take thy bliss O Man!
      And sweet shall be thy taste, & sweet thy infant joys renew!

      Infancy, fearless, lustful, happy! nestling for delight
5   In laps f pleasure; Innocence! honest, open, seeking
      The vigorous joys of morning light; open to virgin bliss.
      Who taught thee modesty, subtil modesty! child of night & sleep
      When thou awakest. wilt thou dissemble all thy secret joys
      Or wert thou not awake when all this mystery was disclos'd!
10   Then comst thou forth a modest virgin knowing to dissemble
      With nets found under thy night pillow, to catch virgin joy,
      And brand it with the name of whore: & sell it in the night,
      In silence, ev'n without a whisper, and in seeming sleep:
      Religious dreams and holy vespers, light thy smoky fires:
15   Once were thy fires lighted by the eyes of honest morn
      And does my Theotormon seek this hypocrite modesty!
      This knowing, artful, secret, fearful, cautious, trembling hypocrite.
      Then is Oothoon a whore indeed! and all the virgin joys
      Of life are harlots: and Theotormon is a sick mans dream
20   And Oothoon is the crafty slave of selfish holiness.

      But Oothoon is not so, a virgin fill'd with virgin fancies
      Open to joy and to delight where ever beauty appears
      If in the morning sun I find it: there my eyes are fix'd
[Plate 7]   In happy copulation; if in evening mild wearied with work,
      Sit on a bank and draw the pleasures of this free born joy.

The moment of desire! the moment of desire! The virgin
That pines for man; shall awaken her womb to enormous joys
5   In the secret shadows of her chamber; the youth shut up from
The lustful joy, shall forget to generate. & create an amorous image
In the shadows of his curtains and in the folds of his silent pillow.
Are not these the places of religion? the rewards of continence?
The self enjoyings of self denial? Why dost thou seek religion?
10   Is it because acts are not lovely, that thou seekest solitude,
Where the horrible darkness is impressed with reflections of desire.

Father of Jealousy,[6] be thou accursed from the earth!
Why hast thou taught my Theotormon this accursed thing?
Till beauty fades from off my shoulders, darken'd and cast out,
15   A solitary shadow wailing on the margin of non-entity.

I cry, Love! Love! Love! happy happy Love! free as the mountain wind!
Can that be Love, that drinks another as a sponge drinks water?
That clouds with jealousy his nights, with weepings all the day:
To spin a web of age around him, grey and hoary! dark!
20   Till his eyes sicken at the fruit that hangs before his sight.
Such is self-love that envies all! a creeping skeleton
With lamplike eyes watching around the frozen marriage bed.

But silken nets and traps of adamant will Oothoon spread,
And catch for thee girls of mild silver, or of furious gold:
25   I'll lie beside thee on a bank & view their wanton play
In lovely copulation bliss on bliss with Theotormon:
Red as the rosy morning, lustful as the first born beam,
Oothoon shall view his dear delight, nor e'er with jealous cloud
Come in the heaven of generous love; nor selfish blightings bring.

30
[Plate 8]   Does the sun walk in glorious raiment. on the secret floor
Where the cold miser spreads his gold? or does the bright cloud drop
On his stone threshold? does his eye behold the beam that brings
Expansion to the eye of pity? or will he bind himself
Beside the ox to thy hard furrow? does not that mild beam blot
5   The bat, the owl, the glowing tyger, and the king of night.
The sea fowl takes the wintry blast, for a cov'ring to her limbs:
And the wild snake, the pestilence to adorn him with gems & gold.
And trees & birds, & beasts, & men, behold their eternal joy.
Arise you little glancing wings. and sing your infant joy!
10   Arise and drink your bliss, for every thing that lives is holy![7]

Thus every morning wails Oothoon. but Theotormon sits
Upon the margind ocean conversing with shadows dire.

The Daughters of Albion hear her woes, & eccho back her sighs.

The End

1793

6. Urizen, who creates men with this passion; as in *Oth-ello*, "jealousy" refers specifically to sexual possessive-ness.

7. In some editions of *The Marriage of Heaven and Hell*, Blake appended "A Song of Liberty," of which this decla-ration is the concluding line.

Letters
To Dr. John Trusler[1]

23 August 1799

Rev'd Sir,

I really am sorry that you are fall'n out with the Spiritual World, Especially if I should have to answer for it. I feel very sorry that your Ideas & Mine on Moral Painting differ so much as to have made you angry with my method of Study. If I am wrong, I am wrong in good company. I had hoped your plan comprehended All Species of this Art, & Especially that you would not regret that Species which gives Existence to Every other, namely, Visions of Eternity. You say that I want somebody to Elucidate my Ideas. But you ought to know that What is Grand is necessarily obscure to Weak men. That which can be made Explicit to the Idiot is not worth my care. The wisest of the Ancients considered what is not too Explicit as the fittest for Instruction, because it rouses the faculties to act. I name Moses, Solomon, Esop, Homer, Plato.

But as you have favor'd me with your remarks on my Design, permit me in return to defend it against a mistaken one, which is, That I have supposed Malevolence without a Cause.[2] Is not Merit in one a Cause of Envy in another, & Serenity & Happiness & Beauty a Cause of Malevolence? But Want of Money & the Distress of A Thief can never be alleged as the Cause of his Thieving, for many honest people endure greater hardships with Fortitude. We must therefore seek the Cause elsewhere than in want of Money, for that is the Miser's passion, not the Thief's.

I have therefore proved your Reasonings Ill-proportion'd, which you can never prove my figures to be; they are those of Michael Angelo, Rafael & the Antique, & of the best living Models. I perceive that your Eye is perverted by Caricature Prints, which ought not to abound so much as they do. Fun I love, but too much Fun is of all things the most loathsome. Mirth is better than Fun, & Happiness is better than Mirth. I feel that a Man may be happy in This World. And I know that This World Is a World of IMAGINATION & Vision. I see Every thing I paint In This World, but Everybody does not see alike. To the Eyes of a Miser a Guinea is more beautiful than the Sun, & a bag worn with the use of Money has more beautiful proportions than a Vine filled with Grapes. The tree which moves some to tears of joy is in the Eyes of others only a Green thing that stands in the way. Some See Nature all Ridicule & Deformity, & by these I shall not regulate my proportions; & Some Scarce see Nature at all. But to the Eyes of the Man of Imagination, Nature is Imagination itself. As a man is, So he Sees. As the Eye is formed, such are its Powers. You certainly Mistake, when you say that the Visions of Fancy are not to be found in This World. To Me This World is all One continued Vision of Fancy or Imagination & I feel Flattered when I am told so. What is it sets Homer, Virgil & Milton in so high a rank of Art. Why is the Bible more Entertaining & Instructive than any other book? Is it not because they are addressed to the Imagination, which is Spiritual Sensation, & but mediately to the Understanding or Reason? Such is True Painting and such <was> alone valued by the Greeks & the best modern Artists. Consider what Lord Bacon

---

1. Rev. Dr. John Trusler (1735–1820), clergyman and minor man of letters, was interested in Blake as an illustrator for his books, but the two proved incompatible, Trusler deeming Blake's designs too much "in the other world, or the World of Spirits, which accords not with my Intentions, which, whilst living in This World, Wish to follow the Nature of it."

2. A reference to one of the illustrations Blake submitted to Trusler.

says: "Sense sends over to Imagination before Reason have judged, & Reason sends over to Imagination before the Decree can be acted." See Advancem[ent] of Learning Part 2, P. 47 of first Edition.[3]

But I am happy to find a Great Majority of Fellow Mortals who can Elucidate My Visions & Particularly they have been Elucidated by Children, who have taken a greater delight in contemplating my Pictures than I even hoped. Neither Youth nor Childhood is Folly or Incapacity. Some Children are Fools & so are some Old Men. But There is a vast Majority on the side of Imagination or Spiritual Sensation.

To Engrave after another Painter is infinitely more laborious than to Engrave ones own Inventions. And of the Size you require my price has been Thirty Guineas & I cannot afford to do it for less. I had Twelve for the Head I sent you as a Specimen, but after my own designs I could do at least Six times the quantity of labour in the same time which will account for the difference of price as also that Chalk Engraving is at least six times as laborious as Aqua tinta. I have no objection to Engraving after another Artist. Engraving is the profession I was apprenticed to, & should never had attempted to live by any thing else, If orders had not come in for my Designs & Paintings, which I have the pleasure to tell you are Increasing Every Day. Thus If I am a Painter it is not to be attributed to Seeking after. But I am contented whether I live by painting or Engraving.

I am Revd Sir, Your very obedient servant,

WILLIAM BLAKE

To Thomas Butts[1]

22 November 1802

Dear Sir,

* * * I will bore you more with some Verses which My Wife desires me to Copy out & send you with her kind love & Respect; they were Composed above a twelve-month ago, while walking from Felpham to Lavant to meet my Sister:

> With happiness stretch'd across the hills
> In a cloud that dewy sweetness distills,
> With a blue sky spread over with wings
> And a mild Sun that mounts & sings,
> 5   With trees & fields full of Fairy elves
> And little devils who fight for themselves,
> Rememb'ring the Verses that Hayley sung[2]
> When my heart knock'd against the root of my tongue,
> With Angels planted in Hawthorn bowers
> 10   And God himself in the passing hours,
> With Silver Angels across my way

---

3. Referring to Francis Bacon's *Advancement of Learning* (1605). Although Blake seems to agree with Bacon here, he despised Bacon's commitment to patronage, scientific reason, and the monarchy. In his later works, "Bacon & Newton & Locke" are an infernal trinity of materialism.

1. Thomas Butts (1757–1845), a government worker and real estate entrepreneur, was a lifelong friend and patron of Blake. Blake produced 80 biblical illustrations for him from 1800 to 1805, and twenty-one watercolors of the Book of Job from 1805 to 1810. Altogether, Butts purchased about two hundred pictures and ten illuminated

books, a collection so voluminous that it spilled out of his home and into his greenhouse.

2. William Hayley (1745–1820), minor poet and patron of art, was Blake's patron and neighbor in Felpham (on the English channel) from 1800 to 1803. He commissioned him to illustrate his *Life of Cowper* (another poet) and his *Essay on Sculpture*. He disapproved of Blake's visionary bent and urged him toward more conventional modes. As with Trusler, the relationship proved uncongenial, and the two had a falling out. When, however, Blake was arrested for treason (the cottage garden episode), Hayley contributed to his defense.

And Golden Demons that none can stay,
With my Father hovering upon the wind
And my Brother Robert just behind
15 And my Brother John the evil one
In a black cloud making his moan;[3]
Tho' dead, they appear upon my path,
Notwithstanding my terrible wrath;
They beg, they intreat, they drop their tears,
20 Fill'd full of hopes, fill'd full of fears;
With a thousand Angels upon the Wind
Pouring disconsolate from behind
To drive them off, & before my way
A frowning Thistle implores my stay.
25 What to others a trifle appears
Fills me full of smiles or tears;
For double the vision my Eyes do see,
And a double vision is always with me.[4]
With my inward Eye 'tis an old Man grey;
30 With my outward, a Thistle across my way.
"If thou goest back," the thistle said,
"Thou art to endless woe betray'd;
For here does Theotormon lower,°   brood
And here is Enitharmon's bower,
35 And Los the terrible thus hath sworn,[5]
Because thou backward dost return,
Poverty, Envy, old age & fear
Shall bring thy Wife upon a bier;
And Butts shall give what Fuseli gave,[6]
40 A dark black Rock & a gloomy Cave."

I struck the Thistle with my foot,
And broke him up from his delving root.
"Must the duties of life each other cross?
Must every joy be dung & dross?
45 Must my dear Butts feel cold neglect
Because I give Hayley his due respect?
Must Flaxman look upon me as wild,
And all my friends be with doubts beguil'd?[7]
Must my Wife live in my Sister's bane,[8]

3. The spirits of Blake's father (d. 1784); his favorite brother Robert (1767–1787); and brother John (b. 1760), who had enlisted in the army, was once apprenticed to a gingerbread maker, but fell into poverty and alcoholism, and died young.
4. "Single vision" (see 1.88) is mere sense perception or "Newton's sleep"—the sleep of imagination in the domain of mathematical reason; "double [or twofold] vision" is perception infused with individual imagination.
5. Theotormon is one of the four sons of Enitharmon and Los, both figures in Blake's later poetry. Enitharmon, the spirit of Beauty, is the twin and consort of Los, the spirit of poetry and imagination. In this letter, this Blakean trinity emerges to support his fidelity to poetic genius.
6. Henry Fuseli, a neoclassical painter and lifelong friend; he frequently employed Blake as an engraver of his own

paintings, and like almost everyone else, had a falling out with him over matters of artistic vision, in consequence of which he ceased to employ him by 1802—hence the snippiness here and the worry that Butts will turn out the same way, as someone who would push Blake into a gloomy Cave devoid of imagination.
7. John Flaxman (1755–1826), one of England's major sculptors, was a close friend and supporter of Blake in his early career, subsidizing the printing of his first, unillustrated, volume, Poetical Sketches, in 1783. Like Hayley, he urged Blake to devote himself to drawing and engraving and to forgo his grand visionary paintings and prophetic illuminated poems.
8. Blake's sister was living with him and his wife at Felpham while he worked for Hayley, and did not get along with his wife.

50   Or my Sister survive on my Love's pain?
      The curses of Los, the terrible shade,
      And his dismal terrors make me afraid."

      So I spoke & struck in my wrath
      The old man weltering upon my path.
55   Then Los appeared in all his power;
      In the Sun he appear'd, descending before
      My face in fierce flames; in my double Sight[9]
      'Twas outward a Sun, inward Los in his might.

      "My hands are labour'd day and night,
60   And Ease comes never in my sight.
      My Wife has no indulgence given
      Except what comes to her from Heaven.
      We eat little, we drink less;
      This Earth breeds not our happiness.
65   Another Sun feeds our life's streams,
      We are not warmed with thy beams;
      Thou measurest not the Time to me,
      Nor yet the Space that I do see;
      My Mind is not with thy light array'd.
70   Thy terrors shall not make me afraid."

      When I had my Defiance given,
      The Sun stood trembling in heaven;
      The Moon that glowed remote below,
      Became leprous & white as snow;
75   And every soul of men on the Earth
      Felt affliction & sorrow & sickness & dearth.
      Los flam'd in my path, & the Sun was hot
      With the bows of my Mind & the Arrows of Thought.
      My bowstring fierce with Ardour breathes;
80   My arrows glow in their golden sheaves;
      My brothers & father march before;
      The heavens drop with human gore.

      Now I a fourfold vision see,
      And a fourfold vision is given to me;
85   'Tis fourfold in my supreme delight
      And threefold in soft Beulah's night
      And twofold Always. May God us keep
      From Single vision & Newton's sleep![1]

9. See "double vision," n. 4 to line 28.

1. In Blake's hierarchy, fourfold vision is pure visionary inspiration, with no reliance on the physical senses and the material world; threefold vision is the deep source of poetic vision: the subconscious, the world of dreams, figuratively "Beulah's night." Beulah, which means "married," is an important spiritual location in Blake's later poetry. In the Bible, it is the name given to Zion in Isaiah 62.4 when it is restored to God's favor. In John Bunyan's dream allegory,

Pilgrim's Progress from This World to That Which Is to Come (1678–1684), the country of Beulah is the Earthly Paradise, which wayfaring Christians gain after a long journey of toils and challenges, and where they abide until they cross the River of Death into the Celestial City. For "twofold" and "Single," see note 4 to line 28. "Newton's sleep" is the dormancy of imagination in the scientific (empirical) mind, referring to Isaac Newton (1642–1727), discoverer of the law of gravity and formulator of the laws of modern physics.

I also enclose you some Ballads by Mr. Hayley,[2] with prints to them by Your H^mble Servt. I should have sent them before now but could not get any thing done for You to please myself; for I do assure you that I have truly studied the two little pictures I now send, & do not repent of the time I have spent upon them.

God bless you.

> Yours,
> W. B.

P.S. I have taken the liberty to trouble you with a letter to my Brother, which you will be so kind as to send or give him, & oblige yours, W. B.

The Abolition of Slavery and the Slave Trade

Slavery and the slave trade provoked sharp controversy in the age of Romanticism, and literary writing played a major role in shaping public opinion. From 1783 to 1793 more than 300,000 slaves were sold in the British colonies, at a value of over £15,000,000. A "triangular trade" flourished, whereby British merchants financed expeditions to the African Gold Coast to buy or kidnap human cargo, to be shipped (the "Middle Passage") under brutal conditions to markets in the West Indies and South America. About 13 percent of this cargo died, while the survivors suffered heat, cramped quarters, fettering, physical abuse, poor sanitation, and disease. In *Thoughts Upon the African Slave Trade* (1788), John Newton guessed that on the voyages he captained, one-fourth of the slave-cargo was lost, not counting those who died right after capture. With the profits, which usually exceeded a hundred percent of the initial investment, traders filled their ships with exotic colonial goods—tobacco, sugar, molasses, rum, spices, cotton—which they sold in Europe, also at tremendous profits. Moral opposition to this trade, spearheaded by the Quakers and Evangelical Christian sects, was invigorated by Lord Mansfield's ruling in 1772 declaring the absence of any legal basis for slavery in England. Over the 1770s, several abolitionist tracts appeared, and by the end of the decade, bills were being introduced in Parliament to regulate the trade. National attention was galvanized by the scandal of the slave ship *Zong* (1781) whose captain ordered 133 weak and diseased slaves ejected into shark-infested waters in order to collect on a policy that held the insurer liable for cargo jettisoned in order to salvage the remainder.

In the 1780s the Quakers continued to petition Parliament and distribute pamphlets, while other abolitionists wrote tracts challenging the scriptural as well as economic justifications for slavery, and reformed slave-traders published memoirs detailing the horrors of the trade. By the end of the decade, William Wilberforce was heading a Parliamentary investigation and the former slave Olaudah Equiano's *Interesting Narrative* quickly became a best-seller. But the advent of the French Revolution in 1789 increased fear of slave-revolts, and Wilberforce's first bill for abolition was defeated in 1791.

Yet the abolition movement persisted. In 1792 Edmund Burke's *Sketch of a Negro Code* gave a plan for orderly abolition and emancipation, and in 1793 Wilberforce's second bill for abolition at least won in the House of Commons. By the end of the decade, the British treasury

---

2. *Designs to a Series of Ballads written by William Hayley* (1802), for which Blake did 14 engravings.

was reeling under the cost of regulating the trade and defending the plantation owners. The abolition movement achieved its first major success in 1807, when Parliament ended British participation in the trade. Wilberforce's stirring *Letter on the Abolition of the Slave Trade* (1807) commemorated the moral importance of the event and helped sustain the movement for abolishing slavery itself (still legal in the colonies)—as did Thomas Clarkson's gripping *History of the Abolition of the African Slave-Trade by the British Parliament* (1808), which detailed the horrors of the trade both for the slaves and the seamen. By the 1820s, the movement was benefiting from the increasing involvement of women, who were horrified by the often violent and sexually abusive treatment of female slaves. In 1823 Clarkson and Wilberforce founded the influential *Anti-Slavery Monthly Reporter*, which relentlessly publicized all the horrors, and Parliament seriously addressed the issue, with Foreign Secretary George Canning arguing that "the spirit of the Christian religion is hostile to slavery." The year 1831 was a critical one, marked not only by a massive slave rebellion in Jamaica, with severe reprisals against slaves and sympathetic missionaries, but also by the publication of former slave Mary Prince's autobiography, with searing reports of atrocities, especially to female slaves. The Reform Parliament of 1832 proved hospitable to emancipation, and in 1833 it passed the Emancipation Bill, liberating 800,000 slaves in British colonies and compensating the owners with more than £20,000,000.

It was the planters and the merchants in Bristol and Liverpool, who were enjoying immense profits, who opposed abolition. Supported by their Standing Committee in Parliament, they justified slavery by arguing that Africans had already enslaved each other on their own continent; that they were mental and moral primitives, animals and heathens, to whom plantation life brought a work-ethic, civilized behavior, and the grace of Christian religion; and finally, that British abolition would not end the trade, only leave the profits to other nations. Their literary propaganda tended toward the genre of "romance," pastoral stories with happy endings in which slaves are grateful and planters benevolent. Their appeals to social stability were amplified by alarm at the French Revolution, and in 1791 a massive slave revolt in Santo Domingo made it possible to link abolitionism to Jacobinism and to embarrass at least the Evangelical abolitionists, who tended to be critical of the Revolution.

Abolitionists came from differing, often opposed political groups: Tory, Evangelical, Quaker, Unitarian, Dissenter, Nonconformist, radical. Some, such as Anna Barbauld, Mary Wollstonecraft, and Tom Paine, energized abolitionism with related commitments to social reform and the new philosophies of "the rights of man" and "the rights of woman." Wordsworth's excoriation of slavery in *The Prelude* powerfully sounds this note. But others, including the Parliamentarians Burke and Wilberforce and most Evangelical Christians, were politically conservative, often wealthy; wanting to avoid the revolutionary cast of "rights of man" arguments, the Evangelicals instead condemned slavery as a moral blight on a Christian nation and advocated Parliamentary reform. They refuted the planters' claims of kind treatment on slave-ships and plantations, and vividly purveyed what amounts to a pornography of atrocities, even as the moral stress was on common humanity and Christian values. With their own version of African primitivism, their fables evoked sympathy for the slaves' childlike simplicity and the pathos of their destroyed families, their physical tortures and suffering. In these narratives, redemption for the slaves appears not through rebellion, but through the salvational processes of Christian conversion, forbearance, and an appeal to enlightened authority.

Many well-known writers produced abolitionist literature, rallying support by using vivid individual stories to exemplify the broad social and ethical issues involved. The texts that follow show the range of literary resources, and the range of viewpoints, employed by writers who composed poems, essays, and stories as part of the protracted struggle over abolition.

⊷ ≖◊≖ ⊷

Olaudah Equiano
c. 1745–1797

In the Parliamentary inquiry into the condition of the slave trade in 1788–1789, evidence came almost exclusively from the traders. Olaudah Equiano's *Interesting Narrative* was crucial for presenting dramatic evidence from the slaves' harrowing experiences. Born to a high-ranking, prosperous, slave-owning family of the Ebo tribe, in the region of modern Nigeria, Equiano was kidnapped by freelance slavers at age ten, shipped first to Barbados, then North America. The disorienting effects of this brutal experience are reflected in the series of names he was given by successive owners: on the slave-ship he was "Michael," then named "Jacob" by a Virginia plantation owner, and then dubbed "Gustavus Vassa," after a sixteenth-century Swedish hero, when he was purchased by Lieutenant Michael Pascal of the British navy. Pascal took him to England in 1757, and then to Canada where he fought in the Seven Years' war in 1758; he was baptized in 1759, and worked for the British navy in the Mediterranean as a servant and gunner's mate. Pascal then sold him to an American Quaker merchant, Robert King, on whose trading ships he worked. With profits from private trade conducted by his own initiative and entrepreneurial skill, he earned enough from the system he abhorred to purchase his freedom, for £70, in 1766. Subsequent adventures took him on a Grand Tour of the Mediterranean, to the Caribbean, and even on an expedition to the Arctic in 1773 (seeking a polar route to India), where a shipmate was young Horatio Nelson (later, one of England's celebrated naval heroes). At various times, Equiano managed a plantation in Central America, earned a living as a hairdresser in London, and worked for the Sierra Leone project (a planned colony for freed slaves in Africa), until he protested against financial mismanagement and was dismissed.

Once settled in England, he renewed his commitment to Christianity and worked with the Evangelicals, campaigned tirelessly for abolition, and became an acquaintance of the founder of the radical working-class London Corresponding Society. In 1792 Equiano married an English woman with whom he had two daughters, and was well enough off at his death in 1797 to leave his one surviving daughter an inheritance of £950 on her twenty-first birthday in 1816. Equiano's *Interesting Narrative* witnesses the cruelty of the Middle Passage, the violence of slavery, and the uncertain status of even the free black; at the same time, it is a vivid picaresque adventure, a religious conversion narrative, and a document of surprising social mobility. A story of triumph as well as oppression, the *Narrative* has a complexity the more compelling for its seeming artlessness. It was an immediate sensation, selling 5,000 copies the first year, and going through thirty-six editions over the next half century. Published as far afield as Germany and Russia, it was influential in promoting abolition, a cause that Equiano continued to serve as a devoted public speaker until the end of his life.

From The Interesting Narrative of the Life of Olaudah Equiano
or Gustavus Vassa, the African
[THE SLAVE SHIP AND ITS CARGO]

The first object that saluted my eyes when I arrived on the coast was the sea, and a slave ship, which was then riding at anchor, and waiting for its cargo.[1] These filled me with astonishment, that was soon converted into terror, which I am yet at a loss to describe, and much more the then feelings of my mind when I was carried on board. I was immediately handled and tossed up to see if I was sound, by some of the

---

1. Captured by slavers along with his sister, Equiano was soon separated from her and sold to different masters over a period of several months before reaching the African coast for shipment to Barbados.

crew; and I was now persuaded that I had got into a world of bad spirits, and that they were going to kill me. Their complexions too, differing so much from ours, their long hair, and the language they spoke, which was very different from any I had ever heard, united to confirm me in this belief. Indeed such were the horrors of my views and fears at the moment, that if ten thousand worlds had been my own, I would have freely parted with them all to have exchanged my condition with the meanest slave in my own country. When I looked round the ship too, and saw a large furnace or copper boiling and a multitude of black people, of every description, chained together, every one of their countenances expressing dejection and sorrow, I no longer doubted of my fate; and, quite overpowered with horror and anguish, I fell motionless on the deck, and fainted. When I recovered a little, I found some black people about me, who I believed were some of those who brought me on board, and had been receiving their pay: they talked to me in order to cheer me, but all in vain. I asked them if we were not to be eaten by those white men with horrible looks, red faces, and long hair. They told me I was not: and one of the crew brought me a small portion of spirituous liquor in a wine glass; but, being afraid of him, I would not take it out of his hand. One of the blacks therefore took it from him and gave it to me, and I took a little down my palate, which, instead of reviving me, as they thought it would, threw me into the greatest consternation at the strange feeling it produced, having never tasted any such liquor before.

Soon after this the blacks who brought me on board went off, and left me abandoned to despair. I now saw myself deprived of all chance of returning to my native country, or even the least glimpse of gaining the shore, which I now considered as friendly; and I even wished for my former slavery, in preference to my present situation, which was filled with horrors of every kind, still heightened by my ignorance of what I was to undergo. I was not long suffered to indulge my grief. I was soon put down under the decks, and there I received such a salutation in my nostrils as I had never experienced in my life: so that, with the loathsomeness of the stench, and with my crying together, I became so sick and low that I was not able to eat, nor had I the least desire to taste any thing. I now wished for the last friend, death, to relieve me; but soon, to my grief, two of the white men offered me eatables; and, on my refusing to eat, one of them held me fast by the hands, and laid me across, I think, the windlass, and tied my feet, while the other flogged me severely. I had never experienced any thing of this kind before, and although, not being used to the water, I naturally feared that element the first time I saw it, yet nevertheless, could I have got over the nettings, I would have jumped over the side, but I could not; and besides the crew used to watch us very closely, who were not chained down to the decks, lest we should leap into the water. I have seen some of these poor African prisoners most severely cut for attempting to do so, and hourly whipped for not eating. This indeed was often the case with myself. In a little time after, amongst the poor chained men, I found some of my own nation, which in a small degree gave ease to my mind. I inquired of these what was to be done with us. They gave me to understand we were to be carried to these white people's country to work for them. I was then a little revived, and thought if it were no worse than working, my situation was not so desperate. But still I feared I should be put to death, the white people looked and acted, as I thought, in so savage a manner; for I had never seen among any people such instances of brutal cruelty: and this is not only shewn towards us blacks, but also to some of the whites themselves. One white man in particular I saw, when we were permitted to be on deck, flogged so unmercifully with a large rope near the foremast, that he died in consequence of it; and they tossed him over the side as they would have done a brute. This made me fear these people the more; and I expected nothing less than to be treated in the same manner. I could not help expressing my fearful apprehensions to some of my countrymen; I asked them if these people had no country, but lived in this hollow place, the ship. They told me they did not, but came from a distant one. "Then," said I, "how comes it, that in all our country we never heard of them?" They told me, because they lived so very far off. I then asked, where their women were: had they any like themselves. I was told they had. "And why," said I, "do we not see them?" They answered, because they were left behind. I asked how the vessel could go. They told me they could not tell; but that there was cloth put upon the masts by the help of the ropes I saw, and then the vessel went on; and the white men had some spell or magic they put in the water, when they liked, in order to stop the vessel. I was exceedingly amazed at this account, and really thought they were spirits. I therefore wished much to be from amongst them, for I expected they would sacrifice me; but my wishes were in vain, for we were so quartered that it was impossible for any of us to make our escape.

[EQUIANO, AGE 12, REACHES ENGLAND]

One morning, when I got upon deck, I perceived it covered over with the snow that fell overnight. As I had never seen any thing of the kind before, I thought it was salt; so I immediately ran down to the mate and desired him, as well as I could, to come and see how somebody in the night had thrown salt all over the deck. He, knowing what it was, desired me to bring some of it down to him; accordingly I took up a handful of it, which I found very cold indeed; and when I brought it to him he desired me to taste it. I did so, and was surprised above measure. I then asked him what it was; he told me it was snow; but I could not by any means understand him. He asked me if we had no such thing in our country; and I told him "No." I then asked him the use of it, and who made it; he told me a great man in the heavens, called God: but here again I was to all intents and purposes at a loss to understand him; and the more so, when a little after I saw the air filled with it, in a heavy shower, which fell down on the same day.

After this I went to church; and having never been at such a place before, I was again amazed at seeing and hearing the service. I asked all I could about it; and they gave me to understand it was "worshiping God, who made us and all things." I was still at a loss, and soon got into an endless field of inquiries, as well as I was able to speak and ask about things. However, my dear little friend Dick[2] used to be my best interpreter; for I could make free with him and he always instructed me with pleasure. And from what I could understand by him of this God, and in seeing that these white people did not sell one another as we did, I was much pleased: and in this I thought they were much happier than we Africans. I was astonished at the wisdom of the white people in all things which I beheld; but I was greatly amazed at their not sacrificing, not making any offerings, and at their eating with unwashen hands, and touching of the dead. I also could not help remarking the particular slenderness of their women, which I did not at first like, and I thought them not so modest and shamefaced as the African women.

I had often seen my master Dick employed in reading; and I had a great curiosity to talk to the books, as I thought they did; and so to learn how all things had a beginning. For that purpose I have often taken up a book and talked to it, and then put my ears to it, when alone, in hopes it would answer me; and I have been very much concerned when I found it remaining silent.

---

2. Richard Baker, an American boy four or five years older than Equiano.

[Employment in the West Indies]

I had the good fortune to please my master in every department in which he employed me; and there was scarcely any part of his business, or household affairs, in which I was not occasionally engaged. I often supplied the place of a clerk, in receiving and delivering cargoes to the ships, in tending stores, and delivering goods; and, besides this, I used to shave and dress my master, when convenient, and take care of his horse; and when it was necessary, which was very often, I worked likewise on board of his different vessels. By these means I became very useful to my master, and saved him, as he used to acknowledge, above a hundred pounds a year. Nor did he scruple to say I was of more advantage to him than any of his clerks; tho' their usual wages in the West-Indies are from sixty to a hundred pounds current a year.

I have sometimes heard it asserted that a negro cannot earn his master the first cost; but nothing can be further from the truth. I suppose nine tenths of the mechanics throughout the West-Indies are negro slaves; and I well know the coopers[3] among them earn two dollars a-day; the carpenters the same, and oftentimes more; also the masons, smiths, and fishermen, &c. and I have known many slaves whose masters would not take a thousand pounds current for them. But surely this assertion refutes itself: for, if it be true, why do the planters and merchants pay such a price for slaves? And, above all, why do those, who make this assertion, exclaim the most loudly against the abolition of the slave trade? So much are men blinded, and to such inconsistent arguments are they driven by mistaken interest! I grant, indeed, that slaves are sometimes, by half-feeding, half-clothing, over-working, and stripes,[4] reduced so low, that they are turned out as unfit for service, and left to perish in the woods, or to expire on a dunghill.

My master was several times offered by different gentlemen one hundred guineas[5] for me; but he always told them he would not sell me, to my great joy: and I used to double my diligence and care for fear of getting into the hands of these men, who did not allow a valuable slave the common support of life. Many of them used to find fault with my master for feeding his slaves so well as he did; although I often went hungry, and an Englishman might think my fare very indifferent: but he used to tell them he always would do it, because the slaves thereby looked better and did more work.

While I was thus employed by my master, I was often a witness to cruelties of every kind, which were exercised on my unhappy fellowslaves. I used frequently to have different cargoes of new negroes in my care for sale; and it was almost a constant practice with our clerks, and other whites, to commit violent depredations on the chastity of the female slaves; and to these atrocities I was, though with reluctance, obliged to submit at all times, being unable to help them. When we have had some of these slaves on board my master's vessels to carry them to other islands, or to America, I have known our mates commit these acts most shamefully, to the disgrace not of christians only, but of men. I have even known them gratify their brutal passion with females not ten years old; and these abominations some of them practised to such a scandalous excess, that one of our captains discharged the mate and others on that account. And yet in Montserrat[6] I have seen a negro-man staked to the ground, and cut most shockingly, and then his ears cut off, bit by bit, because he had been con-

---

3. Barrel-makers.
4. Lashings and the welts they leave.
5. The guinea coin, first struck in 1663 by a company of merchants chartered by the British crown to obtain slaves

from the Guinea coast of Africa (hence the name), was worth 21 shillings; made of gold, it often traded for more than its face value and connoted a certain prestige.
6. Island in the British West Indies.

nected with a white woman, who was a common prostitute! As if it were no crime in the whites to rob an innocent African girl of her virtue; but most heinous in a black man only to gratify a passion of nature, where the temptation was offered by one of a different colour, though the most abandoned woman of her species.

[THE PERILS OF BEING A FREEMAN]

I have since often seen in Jamaica and other islands, free men, whom I have known in America, thus villainously trepanned[7] and kept in bondage. I have heard of two similar practices even in Philadelphia: and were it not for the benevolence of the Quakers in that city, many of the sable race, who now breathe the air of liberty, would, I believe, be groaning under some planter's chains. These things opened my mind to a new scene of horror, to which I had been before a stranger. Hitherto I had thought only slavery dreadful; but the state of a free negro appeared to me now equally so at least, and in some respects even worse; for they live in constant alarm for their liberty, which is but nominal; and they are universally insulted and plundered without the possibility of redress; such being the equity of the West-Indian laws, that no free negro's evidence will be admitted in their courts of justice. * * *

I determined to make every exertion to obtain my freedom, and to return to Old England. For this purpose I thought a knowledge of Navigation might be of use to me; for, though I did not intend to run away unless I should be ill used, yet, in such a case, if I understood navigation, I might attempt my escape in our sloop, which was one of the swiftest sailing vessels in the West-Indies, and I could be at no loss for hands to join me. Had I made this attempt, I had intended to go in her to England; but this, as I said, was only to be in the event of my meeting with any ill usage. I therefore employed the mate of our vessel to teach me Navigation, for which I agreed to give him twenty-four dollars, and actually paid him part of the money down; though when the captain, some time after, came to know that the mate was to have such a sum for teaching me, he rebuked him, and said it was a shame for him to take any money from me. However, my progress in this useful art was much retarded by the constancy of our work.

Had I wished to run away I did not want opportunities, which frequently presented themselves; and particularly at one time, soon after this. When we were at the island of Guadaloupe there was a large fleet of merchantmen bound for Old France; and seamen then being very scarce, they gave from fifteen to twenty pounds a man for the run. Our mate and all the white sailors left our vessel on this account, and went aboard of the French ships. They would have had me also to go with them, for they regarded me, and swore to protect me, if I would go: and, as the fleet was to sail the next day, I really believe I could have got safe to Europe at that time. However, as my master was kind, I would not attempt to leave him; still remembering the old maxim, that *honesty is the best policy,* I suffered them to go without me. Indeed my captain was much afraid of my leaving him and the vessel at that time, as I had so fair an opportunity: but, I thank God, this fidelity of mine turned out much to my advantage hereafter, when I did not in the least think of it; and made me so much in favour with the captain, that he used now and then to teach me some parts of Navigation himself. But some of our passengers, and others, seeing this, found much fault with him for it, saying it was a very dangerous thing to let a negro know Navigation; and thus I was hindered again in my pursuits.

7. Betrayed.

[MANUMISSION]

When we had unladen the vessel, and I had sold my venture,[8] finding myself master of about forty-seven pounds, I consulted my true friend, the Captain, how I should proceed in offering my master the money for my freedom.[9] He told me to come on a certain morning, when he and my master would be at breakfast together. Accordingly, on that morning I went, and met the Captain there, as he had appointed. When I went in I made my obeisance to my master, and with my money in my hand, and many fears in my heart, I prayed him to be as good as his offer to me, when he was pleased to promise me my freedom as soon as I could purchase it. This speech seemed to confound him; he began to recoil; and my heart that instant sunk within me. "What," said he, "give you your freedom? Why, where did you get the money? Have you got forty pounds sterling?" "Yes, sir," I answered. "How did you get it?" replied he. I told him, "very honestly." The Captain then said he knew I got the money very honestly and with much industry, and that I was particularly careful. On which my master replied, I got money much faster than he did; and said he would not have made me the promise which he did, had he thought I should have got the money so soon. "Come, come," said my worthy Captain, clapping my master on the back, "Come, Robert, (which was his name) I think you must let him have his freedom. You have laid your money out very well; you have received good interest for it all this time, and here is now the principal at last. I know GUSTAVUS has earned you more than a hundred a year, and he will still save you money, as he will not leave you. Come, Robert, take the money." My master then said, he would not be worse than his promise; and, taking the money, told me to go to the Secretary at the Register Office, and get my manumission[1] drawn up.

These words of my master were like a voice from heaven to me: in an instant all my trepidation was turned into unutterable bliss, and I most reverently bowed myself with gratitude, unable to express my feelings, but by the overflowing of my eyes, and a heart replete with thanks to God; while my true and worthy friend, the Captain, congratulated us both with a peculiar degree of heartfelt pleasure. As soon as the first transports of my joy were over, and that I had expressed my thanks to these my worthy friends in the best manner I was able, I rose with a heart full of affection and reverence, and left the room, in order to obey my master's joyful mandate of going to the Register Office. As I was leaving the house I called to mind the words of the Psalmist, in the 126th Psalm, and like him, "I glorified God in my heart, in whom I trusted."[2] These words had been impressed on my mind from the very day I was forced from Deptford[3] to the present hour, and I now saw them, as I thought, fulfilled and verified.

My imagination was all rapture as I flew to the Register Office; and in this respect, like the apostle Peter (whose deliverance from prison was so sudden and extraordinary, that he thought he was in a vision)[4] I could scarcely believe I was awake. Heavens! who could do justice to my feelings at this moment? Not conquering heroes themselves, in the midst of a triumph—Not the tender mother who has just regained her long-lost infant, and presses it to her heart—Not the weary, hungry

8. The stock he was permitted to trade for himself.
9. In 1763 Equiano was sold to Robert King, a Quaker merchant, and thereafter served in the West Indies in one of his ships under Captain Thomas Farmer.
1. The formal liberation of a slave.
2. Psalm 126 celebrates release from captivity; the phrase

Equiano quotes does not appear there, though it echoes several other psalms (28, 33, 86, 125).
3. A borough southeast of London, where in 1762 Captain Michael Henry Pascal sold Equiano back into slavery, after several years' service.
4. Acts 12.9 [Equiano's note].

mariner, at the sight of the desired friendly port—Not the lover, when he once more embraces his beloved mistress, after she has been ravished from his arms!—All within my breast was tumult, wildness, and delirium! My feet scarcely touched the ground; for they were winged with joy, and, like Elijah, as he rose to Heaven, they "were with lightning sped as I went on."[5] Every one I met I told of my happiness, and blazed about the virtue of my amiable master and Captain. * * *

In short, the fair as well as black people immediately styled me by a new appellation,—to me the most desirable in the world,—which was "Freeman," and, at the dances I gave, my Georgia superfine blue clothes made no indifferent appearance, as I thought. Some of the sable females, who formerly stood aloof, now began to relax and appear less coy; but my heart was still fixed on London, where I hoped to be ere long. So that my worthy Captain, and his owner, my late master, finding that the bent of my mind was towards London, said to me, "We hope you won't leave us, but that you will still be with the vessels." Here gratitude bowed me down; and none but the generous mind can judge of my feelings, struggling between inclination and duty. However, notwithstanding my wish to be in London, I obediently answered my benefactors that I would go in the vessel, and not leave them; and from that day I was entered on board as an able-bodied seaman, at thirty-six shillings per month, besides what perquisites I could make.[6] My intention was to make a voyage or two, entirely to please these my honoured patrons; but I determined that the year following, if it pleased God, I would see Old England once more, and surprise my old master, Captain Pascal, who was hourly in my mind: for I still loved him, notwithstanding his usage to me, and I pleased myself with thinking of what he would say when he saw what the Lord had done for me in so short a time, instead of being, as he might perhaps suppose, under the cruel yoke of some planter.

✦ ✦ ✦

Mary Prince
c. 1788–after 1833

The History of Mary Prince, a West Indian Slave, Related by Herself is the earliest known slave narrative by a woman. Sponsored by the Anti-Slavery Society to galvanize support for abolition, especially from Britain's women, its saga of overwork, abuse, and sexual violence was chronicled in unprecedented depth and detail. Prince's *History* was a sensation, reaching a third edition the year it was published, 1831.

Prince was born a slave on a farm in Bermuda, a British colony whose major industries were shipbuilding and salting, and whose population was half slave. In her childhood, she was treated with relative kindness, but things changed dramatically when she was twelve. She was sold to sadistic, sexually abusive new owners. After several years of brutality, she was sold to an even more ghastly situation in the "cruel, horrible" salt ponds of Turks Island, about 200 miles northeast of Bermuda, where her labor left her legs covered with boils and eventually crippled her with rheumatism. Perpetually beaten, and sexually assaulted by an "indecent master," she requested to be sold to a merchant from Antigua, who was impressed by her reputation as a good worker. Overworked and exhausted, she began to rebel at her status there, and suffered imprisonment and repeated beatings and floggings. In 1827, with the help of abolitionist sympathizers, she escapted from these owners, when they took her to London. There Thomas

---

5. In 2 Kings (2.11), Elijah has a vision of a chariot of fire and is carried to Heaven in a whirlwind.

6. Equiano has the right to trade for himself and to receive tips.

Pringle, a Methodist and secretary of the Anti-Slavery Society, employed her as a domestic servant. He also edited her *History* as publicity for the movement; it sparked a national controversy when attacked in *Blackwood's Edinburgh Magazine* and *The Glasgow Courier* as fraudulent propaganda by a loose-moraled liar. Libel suits erupted, Prince's owner suing Pringle, and Pringle suing *Blackwood's*. *Blackwood's* declined to cross-examine her, letting her statement stand, but Pringle lost the other case because he couldn't produce witnesses from the West Indies to substantiate the allegations of *The History*. Even so, *The History* commanded wide readership, influencing the cause not only in its representation of general atrocities, but also in its image of Prince's individual resilience and determination. "All slaves want to be free," she declared in the final paragraph; "to be free is very sweet.... I can tell by myself what other slaves feel, and by what they have told me. The man that says slaves be quite happy in slavery—that they don't want to be free—that man is either ignorant or a lying person. I never heard a slave say so."

from The History of Mary Prince, a West Indian Slave
Related by Herself

It was night when I reached my new home. The house was large, and built at the bottom of a very high hill; but I could not see much of it that night. I saw too much of it afterwards. The stones and the timber were the best things in it; they were not so hard as the hearts of the owners.[1]

Before I entered the house, two slave women, hired from another owner, who were at work in the yard, spoke to me, and asked who I belonged to? I replied, "I am come to live here." "Poor child, poor child!" they both said; "you must keep a good heart, if you are to live here."—When I went in, I stood up crying in a corner. Mrs. I—— came and took off my hat, a little black silk hat Miss Pruden[2] made for me, and said in a rough voice, "You are not come here to stand up in corners and cry, you are come here to work." She then put a child into my arms, and, tired as I was, I was forced instantly to take up my old occupation of a nurse.—I could not bear to look at my mistress, her countenance was so stern. She was a stout tall woman with a very dark complexion, and her brows were always drawn together into a frown. I thought of the words of the two slave women when I saw Mrs. I——, and heard the harsh sound of her voice.

The person I took the most notice of that night was a French Black called Hetty, whom my master took in privateering[3] from another vessel, and made his slave. She was the most active woman I ever saw, and she was tasked to her utmost. A few minutes after my arrival she came in from milking the cows, and put the sweet-potatoes on for supper. She then fetched home the sheep, and penned them in the fold; drove home the cattle, and staked them about the pond side;[4] fed and rubbed down my master's horse, and gave the hog and the fed cow[5] their suppers; prepared the beds, and undressed the children, and laid them to sleep. I liked to look at her and watch all her doings, for hers was the only friendly face I had as yet seen, and I felt glad that she was there. She gave me my supper of potatoes and milk, and a blanket to sleep upon, which she spread for me in the passage before the door of Mrs. I——'s chamber.

1. These strong expressions, and all of a similar character in this little narrative, are given verbatim as uttered by Mary Prince [Thomas Pringle's note].
2. Prince's first owner, Mrs. Williams, had fallen on hard times and hired her out at age 12 to Mrs. Pruden; with Mrs. Williams's death, she was sold to "Captain I—."

3. Sanctioned raiding of enemy ships by armed private vessels.
4. The cattle on a small plantation in Bermuda are, it seems, often thus staked or tethered, both night and day, in situations where grass abounds. [Pringle's note].
5. A cow fed for slaughter. [Pringle's note].

I got a sad fright, that night. I was just going to sleep, when I heard a noise in my mistress's room; and she presently called out to inquire if some work was finished that she had ordered Hetty to do. "No, Ma'am, not yet," was Hetty's answer from below. On hearing this, my master started up from his bed, and just as he was, in his shirt, ran down stairs with a long cow-skin in his hand.[6] I heard immediately after, the cracking of the thong, and the house rang to the shrieks of poor Hetty, who kept crying out, "Oh, Massa! Massa! me dead. Massa! have mercy upon me—don't kill me outright."—This was a sad beginning for me. I sat up upon my blanket, trembling with terror, like a frightened hound, and thinking that my turn would come next. At length the house became still, and I forgot for a little while all my sorrows by falling fast asleep.

The next morning my mistress set about instructing me in my tasks. She taught me to do all sorts of household work; to wash and bake, pick cotton and wool, and wash floors, and cook. And she taught me (how can I ever forget it!) more things than these; she caused me to know the exact difference between the smart of the rope, the cart-whip, and the cow-skin, when applied to my naked body by her own cruel hand. And there was scarcely any punishment more dreadful than the blows I received on my face and head from her hard heavy fist. She was a fearful woman, and a savage mistress to her slaves.

There were two little slave boys in the house, on whom she vented her bad temper in a special manner. One of these children was a mulatto,[7] called Cyrus, who had been bought while an infant in his mother's arms; the other, Jack, was an African from the coast of Guinea, whom a sailor had given or sold to my master. Seldom a day passed without these boys receiving the most severe treatment, and often for no fault at all. Both my master and mistress seemed to think that they had a right to ill-use them at their pleasure; and very often accompanied their commands with blows, whether the children were behaving well or ill. I have seen their flesh ragged and raw with licks.—Lick—lick—they were never secure one moment from a blow, and their lives were passed in continual fear. My mistress was not contented with using the whip, but often pinched their cheeks and arms in the most cruel manner. My pity for these poor boys was soon transferred to myself; for I was licked, and flogged, and pinched by her pitiless fingers in the neck and arms, exactly as they were. To strip me naked—to hang me up by the wrists and lay my flesh open with the cow-skin, was an ordinary punishment for even a slight offence. My mistress often robbed me too of the hours that belong to sleep. She used to sit up very late, frequently even until morning; and I had then to stand at a bench and wash during the greater part of the night, or pick wool and cotton; and often I have dropped down overcome by sleep and fatigue, till roused from a state of stupor by the whip, and forced to start up to my tasks.

Poor Hetty, my fellow slave, was very kind to me, and I used to call her my Aunt; but she led a most miserable life, and her death was hastened (at least the slaves all believed and said so), by the dreadful chastisement she received from my master during her pregnancy. It happened as follows. One of the cows had dragged the rope away from the stake to which Hetty had fastened it, and got loose. My master flew into a terrible passion, and ordered the poor creature to be stripped quite naked, notwithstanding her pregnancy, and to be tied up to a tree in the yard. He then flogged her as hard as he could lick, both with the whip and cow-skin, till she was all

---

6. A thong of hard twisted hide, known by this name in the West Indies [Pringle's note].

7. A person of mixed African and Caucasion descent.

over streaming with blood. He rested, and then beat her again and again. Her shrieks were terrible. The consequence was that poor Hetty was brought to bed before her time, and was delivered after severe labour of a dead child. She appeared to recover after her confinement, so far that she was repeatedly flogged by both master and mistress afterwards; but her former strength never returned to her. Ere long her body and limbs swelled to a great size; and she lay on a mat in the kitchen, till the water burst out of her body and she died. All the slaves said that death was a good thing for poor Hetty; but I cried very much for her death. The manner of it filled me with horror. I could not bear to think about it; yet it was always present to my mind for many a day.

After Hetty died all her labours fell upon me, in addition to my own. I had now to milk eleven cows every morning before sunrise, sitting among the damp weeds; to take care of the cattle as well as the children; and to do the work of the house. There was no end to my toils—no end to my blows. I lay down at night and rose up in the morning in fear and sorrow; and often wished that like poor Hetty I could escape from this cruel bondage and be at rest in the grave. But the hand of God whom then I knew not, was stretched over me; and I was mercifully preserved for better things. It was then, however, my heavy lot to weep, weep, weep, and that for years; to pass from one misery to another, and from one cruel master to a worse. But I must go on with the thread of my story.

One day a heavy squall of wind and rain came on suddenly, and my mistress sent me round the corner of the house to empty a large earthen jar. The jar was already cracked with an old deep crack that divided it in the middle, and in turning it upside down to empty it, it parted in my hand. I could not help the accident, but I was dreadfully frightened, looking forward to a severe punishment. I ran crying to my mistress, "O mistress, the jar has come in two." "You have broken it, have you?" she replied; "come directly here to me." I came trembling; she stripped and flogged me long and severely with the cow-skin; as long as she had strength to use the lash, for she did not give over till she was quite tired.—When my master came home at night, she told him of my fault; and oh, frightful! how he fell a swearing. After abusing me with every ill name he could think of, (too, too bad to speak in England,) and giving me several heavy blows with his hand, he said, "I shall come home to-morrow morning at twelve, on purpose to give you a round hundred." He kept his word—Oh sad for me! I cannot easily forget it. He tied me up upon a ladder, and gave me a hundred lashes with his own hand, and master Benjy[8] stood by to count them for him. When he had licked me for some time he sat down to take breath; then after resting, he beat me again and again, until he was quite wearied, and so hot (for the weather was very sultry), that he sank back in his chair, almost like to faint. While my mistress went to bring him drink, there was a dreadful earthquake.[9] Part of the roof fell down, and every thing in the house went—clatter, clatter, clatter. Oh I thought the end of all things near at hand; and I was so sore with the flogging, that I scarcely cared whether I lived or died. The earth was groaning and shaking; every thing tumbling about; and my mistress and the slaves were shrieking and crying out, "The earthquake! the earthquake!" It was an awful day for us all. * * *

Some little time after this, one of the cows got loose from the stake, and eat one of the sweet-potatoe slips.[1] I was milking when my master found it out. He came to me, and without any more ado, stooped down, and taking off his heavy boot, he struck

---

8. Captain I—'s son, about Prince's age.   1. A cutting, rooted and planted.
9. An earthquake shook Bermuda on 19 February 1801.

me such a severe blow in the small of my back, that I shrieked with agony, and thought I was killed; and I feel a weakness in that part to this day. The cow was frightened at his violence, and kicked down the pail and spilt the milk all about. My master knew that this accident was his own fault, but he was so enraged that he seemed glad of an excuse to go on with his ill usage. I cannot remember how many licks he gave me then, but he beat me till I was unable to stand, and till he himself was weary.

After this I ran away and went to my mother, who was living with Mr. Richard Darrel.[2] My poor mother was both grieved and glad to see me; grieved because I had been so ill used, and glad because she had not seen me for a long, long while. She dared not receive me into the house, but she hid me up in a hole in the rocks near, and brought me food at night, after every body was asleep. My father, who lived at Crow-Lane, over the salt-water channel, at last heard of my being hid up in the cavern, and he came and took me back to my master. Oh I was loth, loth to go back; but as there was no remedy, I was obliged to submit.

When we got home, my poor father said to Cap. I——, "Sir, I am sorry that my child should be forced to run away from her owner; but the treatment she has received is enough to break her heart. The sight of her wounds has nearly broke mine.—I entreat you, for the love of God, to forgive her for running away, and that you will be a kind master to her in future." Capt. I—— said I was used as well as I deserved, and that I ought to be punished for running away. I then took courage and said that I could stand the floggings no longer; that I was weary of my life, and therefore I had run away to my mother; but mothers could only weep and mourn over their children, they could not save them from cruel masters—from the whip, the rope, and the cow-skin. He told me to hold my tongue and go about my work, or he would find a way to settle me. He did not, however, flog me that day.

—⊷ ⊱⟐⟐⟐⊰ ⊶—

Thomas Bellamy
1745–1800

Thomas Bellamy had various careers, as a hosier, a bookseller's clerk, magazine publisher, writer, and proprietor of a circulating library. In 1789 he wrote *The Benevolent Planters* in support of the anti-abolitionist West Indian lobby. Staged at the Theatre Royal, Haymarket, with some of the leading actors of the day, his playlet presents a world of kindly paternal masters whose slaves proclaim their happiness and gratitude.

The Benevolent Planters
A Dramatic Piece

Scene, Jamaica

Characters
Planters: GOODWIN, STEADY, HEARTFREE
Slaves: ORAN, SELIMA
Archers, &c. &c.

2. Captain Darrell had purchased Prince and her mother, and then gave Prince to his daughter-in-law, Mrs. Williams.

Prologue (By a Friend)[1]

AN AFRICAN SAILOR   To Afric's torrid clime, where every day
              The sun oppresses with his scorching ray,
              My birth I owe; and here for many a year,
              I tasted pleasure free from every care.
5   There 'twas my happy fortune long to prove
              The fond endearments of parental love.
              ' Twas there my Adela, my favourite maid,
              Return'd my passion, love with love repaid.
              Oft on the banks where golden rivers flow,
10   And aromatic woods enchanting grow,
              With my lov'd Adela I pass'd the day,
              While suns on suns roll'd unperceiv'd away.
              But ah! this happiness was not to last,
              Clouds now the brightness of my fate o'ercast;
15   For the white savage fierce upon me sprung,
              Wrath in his eye, and fury on his tongue,
              And dragg'd me to a loathsome vessel near,
              Dragg'd me from every thing I held most dear,
              And plung'd me in the horrors of despair.
20   Insensible to all that pass'd around,
              Till, in a foreign clime, myself I found,
              And sold to slavery!—There with constant toil,
              Condemn'd in burning suns to turn the soil.
              Oh! if I told you what I suffer'd there,
25   From cruel masters, and the lash severe,
              Eyes most unus'd to melt, would drop the tear.
              But fortune soon a kinder master gave,
              Who made me soon forget I was a slave,
              And brought me to this land, this generous land,°   *Jamaica*
30   Where, they inform me, that an hallow'd band,
              Impelled by soft humanity's kind laws,
              Take up with fervent zeal the Negroe's cause,
              And at this very moment, anxious try,
              To stop the widespread woes of slavery.
35   But of this hallow'd band a part appears,
              Exult my heart, and flow my grateful tears.
              Oh sons of mercy! whose extensive mind
              Takes in at once the whole of human kind,
              Who know the various nations of the earth,
40   To whatsoever clime they owe their birth,
              Or of whatever colour they appear,
              All children of one gracious Parent are.
              And thus united by paternal love,
              To all mankind, of all the friend you prove.
45   With fervent zeal pursue your godlike plan,
              And man deliver from the tyrant man!
              What tho' at first you miss the wish'd-for end,

1. Spoken by John Philip Kemble, a leading tragic actor, as "An African Sailor." In the play Kemble performed Olah, whose beloved, Selima, was performed by his wife.

Success at last your labours will attend.
Then shall your worth, extoll'd in grateful strains,
50   Resound through Gambia's and Angola's plains.[2]
Nations unborn your righteous zeal shall bless,
To them the source of peace and happiness.
Oh mighty Kannoah, thou most holy power,
Whom humbly we thy sable race adore!
55   Prosper the great design—thy children free
From the oppressor's hand, and give them liberty!

Scene 1

A Room in Goodwin's House; Enter Goodwin, meeting Steady and Heartfree.

GOODWIN Good morrow, neighbours, friend Steady,[3] is your jetty tribe ready for the diversions?

STEADY My tribe is prepared and ready to meet thine, and my heart exults on beholding so many happy countenances. But an added joy is come home to my bosom. This English friend, who, some time since, came to settle among us, in order that he might exhibit to his brother Planters, the happy effects of humanity, in the treatment of those who, in the course of human chance, are destined to the bonds of slavery, has honoured my dwelling with his presence, and gladdened my heart with his friendship.

HEARTFREE A cause like the present, makes brothers of us all, and may heaven increase the brothers of humanity—Friend Steady informs me, that we are to preside as directors of the different diversions.

GOODWIN It is our wish to prevent a repetition of disorders, that last year disturbed the general happiness. They were occasioned by the admission of one of those games, which, but too often, begin in sport, and end in passion. The offenders, however, were soon made sensible of the folly of attacking each other without provocation, and with no other view than to shew their superior skill, in an art, which white men have introduced among them.[4]

HEARTFREE If that art was only made use of as a defence against the attacks of an unprincipled and vulgar violence, no man could with propriety form a wish of checking its progress. But while it opens another field where the gambler fills his pocket at the expence of the credulous and unsuspecting, whose families too often mourn in poverty and distress the effects of their folly; every member of society will hold up his hand against it, if his heart feels as it ought. I am sorry likewise to add, that too many recent instances of its fatal effects among my own countrymen, have convinced me of the guilt and folly of venturing *a life* to display *a skill*.

GOODWIN We are happy to find our union strengthened by corresponding sentiments.

HEARTFREE The sports, I find, are to continue six days; repeat your design, respecting the successful archers.

STEADY The archers, friend, to the number of twelve, consist of selected slaves, whose honest industry and attachment have rendered them deserving of reward. They are to advance in pairs, and the youth who speeds the arrow surest, is to be proclaimed victor.

2. Gambia: northwest African country, with a strong British colonial presence. Angola: Portuguese colony on the southwest coast.
3. "Friend" evokes the Quaker term of address; Bellamy

may be trying to suggest that not all Quakers were adamant abolitionists.
4. Perhaps boxing or duelling.

HEARTFREE And what is his reward?

STEADY A portion of land for himself, and his posterity—freedom for his life, and the maiden of his heart.

HEARTFREE Generous men! humanity confers dignity upon authority. The grateful Africans have hearts as large as ours, and shame on the degrading lash, when it can be spared—Reasonable obedience is what we expect, and let those who look for more, feel and severely feel the sting of disappointment.

STEADY Will your poor fellow attend the festival?

HEARTFREE He will. I respect your feelings for the sorrows of the worthy Oran.

GOODWIN Oran, did you say? What know you of him; pardon my abruptness, but relate his story, it may prove a task of pleasure.

HEARTFREE By the fate of war,[5] Oran had been torn from his beloved Selima. The conquerors were on the point of setting fire to the consuming pile to which he was bound, while the partner of his heart, who was devoted[6] to the arms of the chief of the adverse party, was rending the air with her cries; at this instant a troop of Europeans broke in upon them, and bore away a considerable party to their ships; among the rest was the rescued Oran, who was happily brought to our mart, where I had the good fortune to become his master—he has since served me well and affectionately. But sorrow for his Selima is so deeply rooted in his feeling bosom, that I fear I shall soon lose an excellent domestic and as valuable a friend, whose only consolation springs from a sense of dying in the possession of Christian principles, from whence he acknowledges to have drawn comforts inexpressible.

GOODWIN And comfort he shall still draw from a worldly as well as a heavenly source. For know, I can produce the Selima he mourns. She has told me her story, which is indeed a tale of woe. Inward grief has preyed upon her mind, and like her faithful Oran, she is bending to her grave. But happiness, love, and liberty shall again restore them.

HEARTFREE When the mind has made itself up to misery—discoveries admitting of more than hope, ought ever to be made with caution. But you have a heart to feel for the distress of another, and conduct to guide you in giving relief to sorrow; leave me to my poor fellow, and do you prepare his disconsolate partner.

GOODWIN I'll see her immediately, and when we take our seats on the plain of sports, we will communicate to each other the result of our considerations.

STEADY Till then, my worthy associates, farewell. [*Exeunt*]

Scene II

Another Apartment in Goodwin's house. Enter Goodwin and Selima.

GOODWIN Come, my poor disconsolate, be composed, and prepare to meet your friends on those plains, where you never shall experience sorrow; but on the contrary, enjoy every happiness within the power of thy grateful master to bestow; you once told me, Selima, that my participation of your griefs abated their force; will you then indulge me with that pleasing tho' mournful Song you have made, on the loss of him, who, perhaps, may one day be restored?

SELIMA Good and generous Master! ever consoling me with hope, can I deny you who have given me mind, taught me your language, comforted me with the

---

5. Tribal warfare in Africa.   6. Destined.

knowledge of books, and made me every thing I am? Prepared too, my soul for joys, which you say are to succeed the patient bearing of human misery. Oh, Sir, with what inward satisfaction do I answer a request in every way grateful to my feelings!

SONG. SET TO MUSIC BY MR. REEVE[7]

How vain to me the hours of ease,
   When every daily toil is o'er;
In my sad heart no hope I find,
   For Oran is, alas! no more.

Not sunny Africa could please,
   Nor friends upon my native shore,
To me the dreary world's a cave,
   For Oran is, alas! no more.

In bowers of bliss beyond the moon,
   The white man says, his sorrow's o'er,
And comforts me with soothing hope,
   Tho' Oran is, alas, no more.

O come then, messenger of death,
   Convey me to yon starry shore,
Where I may meet with my true love,
   And never part with Oran more.

GOODWIN There's my kind Selima! and now attend to a discovery, on which depends your future happiness; not only liberty, but love awaits you.

SELIMA The first I want not—the last can never be! for where shall I find another Oran?

GOODWIN O my good girl, your song of sorrow shall be changed into that of gladness. For know—the hours of anguish are gone by, your Oran lives, and lives but to bless his faithful Selima.

SELIMA [after a pause] To that invisible Being who has sustained my suffering heart, I kneel, overwhelmed with an awful[8] sense of his protecting power. But how?

GOODWIN As we walk on, I will explain every thing. You soon will embrace your faithful Oran, and his beloved Selima shall mourn no more. [Exeunt.]

Scene III

An open Plain.

[On one side a range of men-slaves; on the other a range of women-slaves—at some distance, seated on decorated chairs, Heartfree, Goodwin, and Steady—twelve archers close the line on the men-side, meeting the audience with Oran at their head, distinguished from the rest by a rich dress—Oran, advancing to the front of the stage, stands in a dejected posture.]

HEARTFREE Now let the air echo to the sound of the enlivening instruments, and beat the ground to their tuneful melody; while myself and my two worthy friends,

7. William Reeve (1757–1815), actor and composer.   8. Awe-filled.

who since our last festival have reaped the benefit of your honest labours, in full goblets drink to your happiness.

[*Flourish of music, and a dance.*]

HEARTFREE Now let the archers advance in pairs, and again, in replenished cups, health and domestic peace to those who surest speed the arrow.

[*Flourish. Here the archers advance in pairs to the middle of the Stage, and discharge their arrows through the side wings—the victor is saluted by two female slaves, who present to him the maiden of his choice—then a flourish of music, and the parties fall back to the side. After the ceremony has been repeated five times to as many pair of archers, and Oran and Almaboe only remain to advance as the sixth pair, Oran appears absorbed in grief, which is observed with evident concern by Heartfree.*]

HEARTFREE Why Oran, with looks divided between earth and heaven, dost thou appear an alien among those who are encompassed with joy and gladness? Though your beloved Selima is torn from your widowed arms, yet it is a duty you owe yourself, as a man, an obligation due to me, as your friend, to take to your bosom one whom I have provided for you. A contest with Almaboe is needless; he has fixed on his partner, to whom, according to your request, he is now presented. [*A flourish of music—two female slaves advance with a third, who is presented to Almaboe—the parties embrace.*] It remains, therefore, for you to comply with the wishes of those who honour your virtues, and have respected your sorrows.

ORAN Kind and benevolent masters; I indeed came hither unwillingly, to draw the bow, with a heart already pierced with the arrow of hopeless anguish. You have done generously by my friend, to whom I meant to have relinquished the victor's right, had the chance been mine. For alas, Sirs! Selima was my first and only love; and when I lost her, joy fled from a bosom it will never again revisit. The short date of my existence is therefore devoted alone to that Power whom you have taught me to revere. Sacred to gratitude, and sacred to her whose beckoning spirit seems at this moment to call on me from yonder sky—

GOODWIN What say you, Oran, if I should produce a maiden whose virtues will bring you comfort, and whose affection you will find as strong as hers, whose loss you so feelingly deplore?

ORAN O Sirs! had you but known my Selima, you would not attempt to produce her equal! Poor lost excellence! Yes, thy spirit, released from all its sufferings, is now looking down upon its Oran! But let not imagination too far transport me: perhaps she yet lives, a prey to brutal lust. [*Turns to Almaboe.*] Brother of my choice, and friend of my adverse hour, long may your Coanzi be happy in the endearments of her faithful Almaboe. And O my friend! when thy poor Oran is no more, if [it] chance that Selima yet lives, if blessed Providence *should* lead her to these happy shores, if she should escape the cruel enemy, and be brought hither with honour unsullied;[9] tell her how much she owes to these generous men; comfort her afflicted spirit, and teach her to adore the God of truth and mercy.

9. Not sexually compromised either by rape or forced consent.

ALMABOE Oran must himself endeavour to live for that day, and not by encouraging despair, sink self-devoted to the grave.[1] The same Providence, my friend, which has turned the terrors of slavery into willing bondage, may yet restore thy Selima.

ORAN The words of Almaboe come charged with the force of truth, and erring Oran bends to offended Heaven! Yet erring Oran must still feel his loss, and erring Oran must for ever lament it.

GOODWIN It is true, Oran, our arguments to urge thee to be happy, have hitherto proved fruitless. But know, thou man of sorrow, we are possessed of the means which will restore thee to thyself and to thy friends. Hear, then, the important secret, and know, that thy Selima yet lives!

ORAN [after a pause] Yet lives! Selima yet lives! what my Selima! my own dear angel! O speak again, your words have visited my heart, and it is lost in rapture.

HEARTFREE Nay, Oran, but be calm.

ORAN I am calm—Heaven will permit me to support my joy, but do you relieve me from suspence.

GOODWIN Let the instruments breathe forth the most pleasing strains—Advance, my happy virgins, with your charge, and restore to Oran his long-lost Selima. You receive her pure as when you parted, with a mind released from the errors of darkness, and refined by its afflictions.

[Soft music—Selima comes down the stage, attended by six virgins in fancied dresses, who present her to Oran—the lovers embrace—flourish of music, and a shout.]

ORAN Lost in admiration, gratitude, and love, Oran has no words, but can only in silence own the hand of Heaven; while to his beating heart he clasps his restored treasure. And O my masters! for such, though free, suffer me still to call you; let my restored partner and myself bend to such exalted worth; while for ourselves, and for our surrounding brethren, we declare, that you have proved yourselves *The Benevolent Planters*, and that under subjection like yours,

SLAVERY IS BUT A NAME

SONG. TO THE TUNE OF *RULE BRITANNIA*.[2]

In honour of this happy day,
    Let Afric's sable sons rejoice;
To mercy we devote the lay,
    To heaven-born mercy raise the voice.
Long may she reign, and call each heart her own,
And nations guard her sacred throne.

Fair child of heaven, our rites approve,
    With smiles attend the votive song,
Inspire with universal love,
    For joy and peace to thee belong.
Long may'st thou reign, and call each heart thy own,
While nations guard thy sacred throne.

---

1. By suicide; "devoted" means "doomed."

2. A famous song, written by James Thomson in 1740, with music by Thomas Arne.

•┼ ⲉ◆Ǝ ┼•

William Cowper
1731–1800

The son of a rector and a mother who traced her descent to Henry III and John Donne, Cowper was beset through his life with manic, sometimes suicidal depressions, aggravated by his attraction to sects emphasizing man's original sin. He studied law but found poetry more congenial, and with the Evangelical minister and abolitionist John Newton published a volume of hymns in 1779, including Newton's great hymn *Amazing Grace*. He followed with a series of moral satires in the early 1780s, and his most famous poem, *The Task* (1785), whose second book opens with a strong critique of slavery. Feeling deeply the moral blight of slavery as an institution sustained only by greed, Cowper responded to Wilberforce's call for popular abolitionist literature with four ballads in 1788 that were widely reprinted. The poet of *The Morning Dream* envisions the goddess Britannia sailing west to a "slave-cultured island" to confront the cruel "Demon" of slave-ownership, who sickens and dies at her sight; the balladeer of *Pity for Poor Africans*, insisting that he is "shock'd at the purchase of slaves," justifies his participation by arguing that foreigners will not give up the trade: "He shar'd in the plunder, but he pitied the man." *Sweet Meat Has Sour Sauce: or, The Slave-Trader in the Dumps*, printed here, is the ditty of a trader lamenting the inevitable abolition of his business and trying to unload his gear. And *The Negro's Complaint*, the most popular of the group in part because of its stark wood-cut illustrations, doubly refutes the view of slaves as subhuman: its slave-speaker not only expresses his own profound humanity but also exposes the inhumanity of the "iron-hearted" masters, whom he calls "slaves of gold." Cowper grew so depressed with his involvement in the slavery issue that eventually he had to stop writing about it. His last poem, written shortly before his death, is the beautifully melancholy *The Castaway* (see page 1242).

Sweet Meat Has Sour Sauce
or, The Slave-Trader in the Dumps

<blockquote>

A trader I am to the African shore,
But since that my trading is like to be o'er,
I'll sing you a song that you ne'er heard before,
        Which nobody can deny, deny,
5   Which nobody can deny.

When I first heard the news it gave me a shock,
Much like what they call an electrical knock,
And now I am going to sell off my stock,
        Which nobody can deny.

10 'Tis a curious assortment of dainty regales,°   *choice pieces*
To tickle the Negroes with when the ship sails—
Fine chains for the neck, and a cat with nine tails,[1]
        Which nobody can deny.

Here's supple-jack plenty, and store of rat-tan,[2]
15 That will wind itself round the sides of a man,
As close as a hoop round a bucket or can,
        Which nobody can deny.

</blockquote>

---

1. Cat-o'-nine-tails: a whip made with nine knotted lashes.

2. Both supple-jack (a woody vine) and rattan (a climbing palm) were used to make whips, canes, and ropes.

Here's padlocks and bolts, and screws for the thumbs,
That squeeze them so lovingly till the blood comes;
20 They sweeten the temper like comfits or plums,
            Which nobody can deny.

When a Negro his head from his victuals withdraws,
And clenches his teeth and thrusts out his paws,
Here's a notable engine to open his jaws,[3]
25   Which nobody can deny.

Thus going to market, we kindly prepare
A pretty black cargo of African ware,
For what they must meet with when they get there,
            Which nobody can deny.

30 'Twould do your heart good to see 'em below
Lie flat on their backs all the way as we go,[4]
Like sprats on a gridiron, scores in a row,[5]
            Which nobody can deny.

But ah! if in vain I have studied an art
35 So gainful to me, all boasting apart,
I think it will break my compassionate heart,
            Which nobody can deny.

For oh! how it enters my soul like an awl!
This pity, which some people self-pity call,
40 Is sure the most heart-piercing pity of all,
            Which nobody can deny.

So this is my song, as I told you before;
Come, buy off my stock, for I must no more
Carry Caesars and Pompeys to Sugar-cane shore,[6]
45   Which nobody can deny, deny,
            Which nobody can deny.

Hannah More
1745–1833

Poet and essayist More published 114 Cheap Repository Tracts between 1795 and 1798. With simple language cast into stories, ballads, poems, dialogues, sermons, prayers, parables, and moral tales, she strove, with an Evangelical view, "to improve the habits, and raise the principles of the common people . . . not only to counteract vice and profligacy on the one hand, but error, discontent, and false religion on the other." Among her concerns were quelling political discontent and class antagonisms and shaping public opinion in favor of abolition. Priced at a halfpenny, and marketed not only in shops but also at fairs and on street corners, the Tracts sold quickly and

---

3. Force-feeding of a slave meaning to starve to death.
4. A reference to the tortuous tight-packing of slave-cargo; see illustration, page 1462.
5. Sprats are herrings (metaphorically, insignificant people); a gridiron is a griddle—an image of slaves cooking

in hot cargo-holds.
6. Caesar and Pompey were famous ancient Romans (many slaves were royalty in their African cultures); "Sugar-cane shore" is the West Indies.

widely, over two million in the first year alone. They were purchased in bulk by preachers for their congregations, landlords for their tenants and laborers, and missionaries for their work in Africa and India, and disseminated in hospitals, prisons, the armed forces, and the workhouses.

More had first treated the issue in *Slavery: A Poem* (1788), a 356-line polemical oration aimed at creating support for Wilberforce in Parliament. Eager to involve a popular audience, she devoted four of her Tracts to slavery. The most popular and most frequently reprinted were *The Sorrows of Yamba* (More's authorship is debated) and *The Black Prince,* perhaps coauthored by More and her mentor John Newton, whose own *Authentic Narrative* (1764) vividly recounted his conversion from slave-trading to Evangelical Christianity and abolition. The Tracts repeat such a conversion in the lives of the slaves. When the tortured slavewoman Yamba attempts suicide, she is prevented by a missionary who converts her to Christianity, teaching her patient endurance and ultimate salvation.

An additional work by More is included in A "Vindication" in Context: The Wollstonecraft Controversy and the Rights of Women, page 1497.

The Sorrows of Yamba
or, The Negro Woman's Lamentation

In St. Lucia's distant isle,[1]
   Still with Afric's love I burn;
Parted many a thousand mile,
   Never, never to return.

5   Come, kind death! and give me rest;
   Yamba has no friend but thee;
Thou canst ease my throbbing breast;
   Thou canst set the Prisoner free.

Down my cheeks the tears are dripping,
10   Broken is my heart with grief;
Mangled my poor flesh with whipping,
   Come, kind death, and bring relief.

Born on Afric's golden coast,[2]
   Once I was as blest as you;
15   Parents tender I could boast,
   Husband dear, and children too.

Whity man he came from far,
   Sailing o'er the briny flood;
Who with help of British Tar,°   *seaman*
20   Buys up human flesh and blood.

With the baby at my breast
   (Other too were sleeping by)
In my hut I sat at rest,
   With no thought of danger nigh.

25   From the brush at even-tide,
   Rush'd the fierce man-stealing crew;
Seiz'd the children by my side,
   Seiz'd the wretched Yamba too.

1. In the British West Indies.
2. An evocation of an idyllic world (golden age) and iron-
ically a naming of "Gold Coast," a British West African colony (now Ghana) trading chiefly in gold and slaves.

Then for love of filthy gold,
    Strait they bore me to the sea,
Cramm'd me down a slave-ship's hold,
    Where were hundreds stow'd like me.

Naked on the platform lying,
    Now we cross the tumbling wave;
Shrieking, sickening, fainting, dying;
    Deed of shame for Britons brave!

At the savage Captain's beck,
    Now, like brutes, they make us prance;
Smack the cat° about the deck,   *whip*
    And in scorn they make us dance.

Nauseous horse-beans they bring nigh,
    Sick and sad we cannot eat;
Cat must cure the sulks, they cry,
    Down their throats we'll force the meat.[3]

I, in groaning pass'd the night,
    And did roll my aching head;
At the break of morning light
    My poor child was cold and dead.

Happy, happy, there she lies;
    Thou shalt feel the lash no more;
Thus full many a Negro dies,
    Ere we reach the destin'd shore.

Thee, sweet infant, none shall sell;
    Thou hast gain'd a wat'ry grave;
Clean escap'd the tyrants fell,°   *fierce*
    While thy mother lives a slave.

Driven like cattle to a fair,
    See, they sell us, young and old;
Child from mother too they tear,
    All for love of filthy gold.

I was sold to Massa° hard,   *Master*
    Some have Massas kind and good:
And again my back was scarr'd,
    Bad and stinted was my food.

Poor and wounded, faint and sick,
    All expos'd to burning sky,
Massa bids me grass to pick,
    And I now am near to die.

What, and if to death he send me,
    Savage murder tho' it be,
British laws shall not befriend me,
    They protect not slaves like me.

3. Forced feeding; horse-beans are food for horses.

Mourning thus my wretched state
    (Ne'er may I forget the day)
75   Once in dusk of evening late,
    Far from home I dar'd to stray.

Dar'd, alas! with impious haste,
    Tow'rds the roaring sea to fly;
Death itself I longed to taste,
80   Long'd to cast me in and die.

There I met upon the Strand,
    English missionary good;
He had Bible book in hand;
    Which poor me no understand.

85   Led by pity from afar,
    He had left his native ground;
Thus, if some inflict a scar,
    Others fly to cure the wound.

Strait he pull'd me from the shore,
90   Bid me no self-murder do;
Talk'd of state when life is o'er,
    All from Bible good and true.

Then he led me to his cot,°   cottage
    Sooth'd and pity'd all my woe;
95   Told me 'twas the Christian's lot
    Much to suffer here below.

Told me then of God's dear Son
    (Strange and wondrous is the Story)
What sad wrong to him was done,
100   Tho' he was the Lord of Glory.

Told me too, like one who knew him
    (Can such love as this be true?)
How he died for them that slew him,
    Died for wretched Yamba too.

105   Freely he his mercy proffer'd
    And to Sinners he was sent;
E'en to Massa pardon's offered;
    O, if Massa would repent!

Wicked deed full many a time,
110   Sinful Yamba too hath done;
But she wails to God her crime,
    But she trusts his only Son.

O, ye slaves whom Massas beat,
    Ye are stain'd with guilt within;
115   As ye hope for Mercy sweet,
    So forgive your Massas' sin.

* * *

125   Now I'll bless my cruel capture
         (Hence I've known a Saviour's name)
      Till my grief is turn'd to rapture,
         And I half forget the blame.

      But tho' here a convert rare
130   Thanks her God for Grace divine;
      Let not man the glory share:
         Sinner still the guilt is thine.

      Here an injur'd Slave forgives,
         There a host for vengeance cry;
135   Here a single Yamba lives,
         There a thousand droop and die.

      Only now baptiz'd am I,
         By good Missionary man:
      Lord, my nature purify,
140   As no outward water can!
                  * * *
      But tho' death this hour may find me,
         Still with Afric's love I burn;
155   (There I've left a spouse behind me)
         Still to native land I turn.

      And when Yamba sinks in death,
         This my latest prayer shall be,
      While I yield my parting breath,
160   *O, that Afric might be free!*

      Cease, ye British sons of murder!
         Cease from forging Afric's chain:
      Mock your Saviour's name no further,
         Cease your savage lust of gain.

165   Ye that boast *"Ye rule the waves,"*
         Bid no Slave-ship soil the sea;
      Ye, that *"never will be slaves,"*
         Bid poor Afric's land be free.[4]

      Where ye gave to war its birth,
170   Where your traders fix'd their den,
      There go publish *"Peace on Earth,"*
         Go, proclaim *"good will to men."*[5]

      Where ye once have carried slaughter,
         Vice, and slavery, and sin;
175   Seiz'd on Husband, Wife, and Daughter,
         Let the Gospel enter in.

      Thus, where Yamba's native home,
         Humble hut of rushes stood;
      Oh, if there should chance to roam
180   Some dear Missionary good;

---

4. The quotations are from the British imperialist hymn, *Rule Britannia*. See also page 1449.

5. Quoting the angels' proclamation of the birth of Jesus in Luke (2.14).

Tho' in Afric's distant land,
  Still shalt see the man I love;
Join him to the Christian band,
  Guide his soul to the realms above.

185   There no fiend again shall sever
  Those whom God hath join'd and blest:
There they dwell with him for ever,
  There *the weary are at rest.*[6]

━━╼╪╾━━

Thomas Clarkson
1760–1846

"The grand mover of the main efforts for the abolition of the Slave Trade," in Dorothy Wordsworth's phrase, Thomas Clarkson was the hero of the movement. In 1785, while a student at Cambridge University, he wrote a prize-winning essay, *On the Slavery and Commerce of the Human Species*, its moral arguments supported with a litany of atrocities documented in the West Indies. When it was published in 1786, one slave owner protested, "I declare to God, I do not believe that a series of more abominable falsehoods ever blotted a page in the wide history of human depravity!" The next year, Clarkson joined with the English Quakers' Anti-Slavery Society, and at its behest began an arduous investigation of atrocities, centering his research in Bristol and Liverpool, whose merchants were financing and thriving on the trade. Often at great personal risk, Clarkson gathered detailed information, from the devastating effects on the seamen impressed into the brutal service, to the abuse of the slaves and the conditions aboard ship, to the conduct of the slave-markets. This labor supplied William Wilberforce with critical material for his Parliamentary campaign. In the 1790s, Clarkson traveled to France to urge the Revolutionary government to abolish its slave trade and colonial slavery, agitated in England for a boycott of West Indian sugar and tea, and continued to document the atrocities that the planters' lobby continued to deny and excoriate as falsehoods, working himself into physical collapse in 1794. His most famous work, the *History of . . . the Abolition of the African Slave-Trade* (1808), helped fuel the movement for the abolition of slavery itself, a cause in which Clarkson remained active.

from The History of the Rise, Progress, & Accomplishment of the Abolition of the African Slave-Trade by the British Parliament
["The Nature of the Evil"]

This may be seen by examining it in three points of view: First, As it has been proved to arise on the continent of Africa in the course of reducing the inhabitants of it to slavery; Secondly, In the course of conveying them from thence to the lands or colonies of other nations; And, Thirdly, In continuing them there as slaves.

To see it as it has been shown to arise in the first case, let us suppose ourselves on the Continent just mentioned. Well then: We are landed; we are already upon our travels; we have just passed through one forest; we are now come to a more open place, which indicates an approach to habitations. And what object is that, which first obtrudes itself upon our sight? Who is that wretched woman, whom we discover under that noble tree, wringing her hands, and beating her breast, as if in the agonies

---

6. Job, tormented by Satan on a mission from God as a test of his faith, longs for death, where "the wicked cease from troubling; and . . . the weary be at rest" (3.17).

of despair? Three days has she been there at intervals to look and to watch, and this is the fourth morning, and no tidings of her children yet. Beneath its spreading boughs they were accustomed to play: But alas! the savage man-stealer interrupted their playful mirth, and has taken them for ever from her sight.

But let us leave the cries of this unfortunate woman, and hasten into another district: And what do we first see here? Who is he that just now started across the narrow pathway, as if afraid of a human face? What is that sudden rustling among the leaves? Why are those persons flying from our approach, and hiding themselves in yon darkest thicket? Behold, as we get into the plain, a deserted village! The rice-field has been just trodden down around it. An aged man, venerable by his silver beard, lies wounded and dying near the threshold of his hut. War, suddenly instigated by avarice, has just visited the dwellings which we see. The old have been butchered, because unfit for slavery, and the young have been carried off, except such as have fallen in the conflict, or have escaped among the woods behind us. * * *

Let us examine the state of the unhappy Africans, reduced to slavery in this manner, while on board the vessels, which are to convey them across the ocean to other lands. And here I must observe at once, that, as far as this part of the evil is concerned, I am at a loss to describe it. Where shall I find words to express properly their sorrow, as arising from the reflection of being parted for ever from their friends, their relatives, and their country? Where shall I find language to paint in appropriate colours the horror of mind brought on by thoughts of their future unknown destination, of which they can augur nothing but misery from all that they have yet seen? How shall I make known their situation, while labouring under painful disease, or while struggling in the suffocating holds of their prisons, like animals inclosed in an exhausted receiver?[1] How shall I describe their feelings as exposed to all the personal indignities, which lawless appetite or brutal passion may suggest? How shall I exhibit their sufferings as determining to refuse sustenance and die, or as resolving to break their chains, and, disdaining to live as slaves, to punish their oppressors? How shall I give an idea of their agony, when under various punishments and tortures for their reputed crimes? Indeed every part of this subject defies my powers, and I must therefore satisfy myself and the reader with a general representation, or in the words of a celebrated member of Parliament [Wilberforce], that "Never was so much human suffering condensed in so small a space."

I come now to the evil, as it has been proved to arise in the third case; or to consider the situation of the unhappy victims of the trade, when their painful voyages are over, or after they have been landed upon their destined shores. And here we are to view them first under the degrading light of cattle.[2] We are to see them examined, handled, selected, separated, and sold. Alas! relatives are separated from relatives, as if, like cattle, they had no rational intellect, no power of feeling the nearness of relationship, nor sense of the duties belonging to the ties of life! We are next to see them labouring, and this for the benefit of those, to whom they are under no obligation, by any law either natural or divine, to obey. We are to see them, if refusing the commands of their purchasers, however weary, or feeble, or indisposed, subject to corporal punishments, and, if forcibly resisting them, to death. We are to see them in a state of general degradation and misery. The knowledge, which their oppressors have of their own crime in having violated the rights of nature, and of the disposition of

---

1. Emptied tank.
2. Clarkson's analogy to cattle evokes "chattel," a synonym for "slave" that shares an etymology with "cattle" and "capital."

the injured to seek all opportunities of revenge, produces a fear which dictates to them the necessity of a system of treatment by which they shall keep up a wide distinction between the two, and by which the noble feelings of the latter shall be kept down, and their spirits broken. We are to see them again subject to individual persecution, as anger, or malice, or any bad passion may suggest. Hence the whip; the chain; the iron-collar. Hence the various modes of private torture, of which so many accounts have been truly given. Nor can such horrible cruelties be discovered so as to be made punishable, while the testimony of any number of the oppressed is invalid against the oppressors, however they may be offences against the laws. And; lastly, we are to see their innocent offspring, against whose personal liberty the shadow of an argument cannot be advanced, inheriting all the miseries of their parents' lot.

* * * While the miseries endured by the unfortunate Africans excite our pity on the one hand, the vices, which are connected with them, provoke our indignation and abhorrence on the other. The Slave-trade, in this point of view, must strike us as an immense mass of evil on account of the criminality attached to it. * * * Is not that man made morally worse, who is induced to become a tyger to his species, or who, instigated by avarice, lies in wait in the thicket to get possession of his fellow-man? Is no injustice manifest in the land, where the prince, unfaithful to his duty, seizes his innocent subjects, and sells them for slaves? Are no moral evils produced among those communities, which make war upon other communities for the sake of plunder, and without any previous provocation or offence?

* * * The counterpart of the evil is to be seen in the conduct of those, who purchase the miserable natives in their own country, and convey them to distant lands. And here questions, similar to the former, may be asked. Do they experience no corruption of their nature, or become chargeable with no violation of right, who, when they go with their ships to this continent, know the enormities which their visits there will occasion, who buy their fellow-creature man, and this, knowing the way in which he comes into their hands, and who chain, and imprison, and scourge him? Do the moral feelings of those persons escape without injury, whose hearts are hardened? And can the hearts of those be otherwise than hardened, who are familiar with the tears and groans of innocent strangers forcibly torn away from every thing that is dear to them in life, who are accustomed to see them on board their vessels in a state of suffocation and in the agonies of despair, and who are themselves in the habits of the cruel use of arbitrary power?

The counterpart of the evil in its third branch is to be seen in the conduct of those, who, when these miserable people have been landed, purchase and carry them to their respective homes. And let us see whether a mass of wickedness is not generated also in the present case. Can those have nothing to answer for, who separate the faithful ties which nature and religion have created? Can their feelings be otherwise than corrupted, who consider their fellow-creatures as brutes, or treat those as cattle, who may become the temples of the Holy Spirit, and in whom the Divinity disdains not himself to dwell? Is there no injustice in forcing men to labour without wages? Is there no breach of duty, when we are commanded to clothe the naked, and feed the hungry, and visit the sick and in prison, in exposing them to want, in torturing them by cruel punishment, and in grinding them down by hard labour, so as to shorten their days? Is there no crime in adopting a system, which keeps down all the noble faculties of their souls, and which positively debases and corrupts their nature? Is there no crime in perpetuating these evils among their innocent offspring? And finally, besides all these crimes, is there not naturally in the familiar sight of the exercise, but more especially in the exercise itself, of uncontroulled power, that which vitiates the internal man? In seeing misery stalk daily over the land, do not all become insensibly hardened? By giving birth to that misery themselves, do they not become abandoned? In what state of society are the corrupt appetites so easily, so quickly, and so frequently indulged, and where else, by means of frequent indulgence, do these experience such a monstrous growth? Where else is the temper subject to such frequent irritation, or passion to such little controul? Yes; if the unhappy slave is in an unfortunate situation, so is the tyrant who holds him. * * *

* * * If we were to take the vast extent of space occupied by these crimes and sufferings from the heart of Africa to its shores, and that which they filled on the continent of America and the islands adjacent, and were to join the crimes and sufferings in one to those in the other by the crimes and sufferings which took place in the track of the vessels successively crossing the Atlantic, we should behold a vast belt as it were of physical and moral evil, reaching through land and ocean to the length of nearly half the circle of the globe.

[THE RECRUITMENT OF SEAMEN FOR THE SLAVE-SHIPS]

The young mariner if a stranger to the port [of Bristol] and unacquainted with the nature of the Slave-trade, was sure to be picked up. The novelty of the voyages, the superiority of the wages in this over any other trades, and the privileges of various kinds, were set before him. Gulled in this manner he was frequently enticed to the boat, which was waiting to carry him away. If these prospects did not attract him, he was plied with liquor till he became intoxicated, when a bargain was made over him between the landlord and the mate. After this his senses were kept in such a constant state of stupefaction by the liquor, that in time the former might do with him what he pleased. Seamen also were boarded in these houses, who, when the slave-ships were going out, but at no other time, were encouraged to spend more than they had money to pay for; and to these, when they had thus exceeded, but one alternative was given, namely, a slave-vessel, or a jail. These distressing scenes I found myself obliged frequently to witness, for I was no less than nineteen times occupied in making these hateful rounds. And I can say from my own experience, and all the information I could collect from Thompson and others, that no such practices were in use to obtain seamen for other trades.

The treatment of the seamen employed in the Slave-trade had so deeply interested me, and now the manner of procuring them, that I was determined to make myself acquainted with their whole history; for I found by report, that they were not only personally ill-treated, * * * but that they were robbed by artifice of those wages, which had been held up to them as so superior in this service. * * * On whatever branch of the system I turned my eyes, I found it equally barbarous. The trade was, in short, one mass of iniquity from the beginning to the end. * * *

In pursuing another object, which was that of going on board the slave-ships, and learning their construction and dimensions, I was greatly struck, and indeed affected, by the appearance of two little sloops, which were fitting out for Africa, the one of only twenty-five tons, which was said to be destined to carry seventy; and the other of only eleven, which was said to be destined to carry thirty slaves. I was told also that which was more affecting, namely, that these were not to act as tenders on the coast, by going up and down the rivers, and receiving three or four slaves at a time, and then carrying them to a large ship, which was to take them to the West

Indies, but that it was actually intended, that they should transport their own slaves themselves. * * * In the vessel of twenty-five tons, the length of the upper part of the hold, or roof, of the room, where the seventy slaves were to be stowed, was but little better than ten yards, or thirty-one feet. The greatest breadth of the bottom, or floor, was ten feet four inches, and the least five. Hence, a grown person must sit down all the voyage, and contract his limbs within the narrow limits of three square feet. In the vessel of eleven tons, the length of the room for the thirty slaves was twenty-two feet. The greatest breadth of the floor was eight, and the least four. The whole height from the keel to the beam was but five feet eight inches, three feet of which were occupied by ballast, cargo, and provisions, so that two feet eight inches remained only as the height between the decks. Hence, each slave would have only four square feet to sit in, and, when in this posture, his head, if he were a full-grown person, would touch the ceiling, or upper deck.

[CLARKSON'S NIGHTMARES]

At Bristol my feelings had been harassed by the cruel treatment of the seamen, which had come to my knowledge there: but now I was doomed to see this treatment over again in many other melancholy instances; and additionally to take in the various sufferings of the unhappy slaves. These accounts I could seldom get time to read till late in the evening, and sometimes not till midnight, when the letters containing them were to be answered. The effect of these accounts was in some instances to overwhelm me for a time in tears, and in others to produce a vivid indignation, which affected my whole frame. Recovering from these, I walked up and down the room. I felt fresh vigour, and made new determinations of perpetual warfare against this impious trade. I implored strength that I might proceed. I then sat down, and continued my work as long as my wearied eyes would permit me to see. Having been agitated in this manner, I went to bed: but my rest was frequently broken by the visions which floated before me. When I awoke, these renewed themselves to me, and they flitted about with me for the remainder of the day. Thus I was kept continually harassed: my mind was confined to one gloomy and heart-breaking subject for months. It had no respite, and my health began now materially to suffer.

[THE DEFENSE OF THE TRADE IN PARLIAMENT]

The public papers began to be filled with such statements as were thought most likely to influence the members of the house of commons, previously to the discussion of the question [bill for abolition].

The first impression attempted to be made upon them was with respect to the slaves themselves. It was contended, and attempted to be shown by the revival of the old argument of human sacrifices in Africa, that these were better off in the islands than in their own country. It was contended also, that they were people of very inferior capacities, and but little removed from the brute creation; whence an inference was drawn, that their treatment, against which so much clamour had arisen, was adapted to their intellect and feelings.

The next attempt was to degrade the abolitionists in the opinion of the house, by showing the wildness and absurdity of their schemes. It was again insisted upon that emancipation was the real object of the former; so that thousands of slaves would be let loose in the islands to rob or perish, and who could never be brought back again into habits of useful industry.

An attempt was then made to excite their pity in behalf of the planters. The abolition, it was said, would produce insurrections among the slaves. But insurrections would produce the massacre of their masters; and, if any of these should happily escape from butchery, they would be reserved only for ruin.

An appeal was then made to them on the ground of their own interest and of that of the people, whom they represented. It was stated that the ruin of the islands would be the ruin of themselves and of the country. Its revenue would be half annihilated. Its naval strength would decay. Merchants, manufacturers and others would come to beggary. But in this deplorable situation they would expect to be indemnified for their losses. Compensation indeed must follow. It could not be withheld. But what would be the amount of it? The country would have no less than from eighty to a hundred millions to pay the sufferers; and it would be driven to such distress in paying this sum as it had never before experienced.

The last attempt was to show them that a regulation of the trade was all that was now wanted. While this would remedy the evils complained of, it would prevent the mischief which would assuredly follow the abolition. The planters had already done their part. The assemblies of the different islands had most of them made wholesome laws upon the subject. The very bills passed for this purpose in Jamaica and Grenada had arrived in England, and might be seen by the public: the great grievances had been redressed: no slave could now be mutilated or wantonly killed by his owner; one man could not now maltreat, or bruise, or wound the slave of another; the aged could not now be turned off to perish by hunger. There were laws also relative to the better feeding and clothing of the slaves. It remained only that the trade to Africa should be put under as wise and humane regulations as the slavery in the islands had undergone.

[COUNTER-TESTIMONY FROM A SLAVE-SHIP INVESTIGATOR]

Having said thus much on the subject of procuring slaves in Africa, he would now go to that of the transportation of them. * * * This was the most wretched part of the whole subject. He was incapable of impressing the house with what he felt upon it. A description of their conveyance was impossible. So much misery condensed in so little room was more than the human imagination had ever before conceived. Think only of six hundred persons linked together, trying to get rid of each other, crammed in a close vessel with every object that was nauseous and disgusting, diseased, and struggling with all the varieties of wretchedness. It seemed impossible to add any thing more to human misery. Yet shocking as this description must be felt to be by every man, the transportation had been described by several witnesses from Liverpool to be a comfortable conveyance. Mr. Norris had painted the accommodations on board a slaveship in the most glowing colours. He had represented them in a manner which would have exceeded his attempts at praise of the most luxurious scenes. Their apartments, he said, were fitted up as advantageously for them as circumstances could possibly admit: they had several meals a day; some, of their own country provisions, with the best sauces of African cookery; and, by way of variety, another meal of pulse, according to the European taste. After breakfast they had water to wash themselves, while their apartments were perfumed with frankincense and lime-juice. Before dinner they were amused after the manner of their country: instruments of music were introduced: the song and the dance were promoted: games of chance were furnished them: the men played and sang, while the women

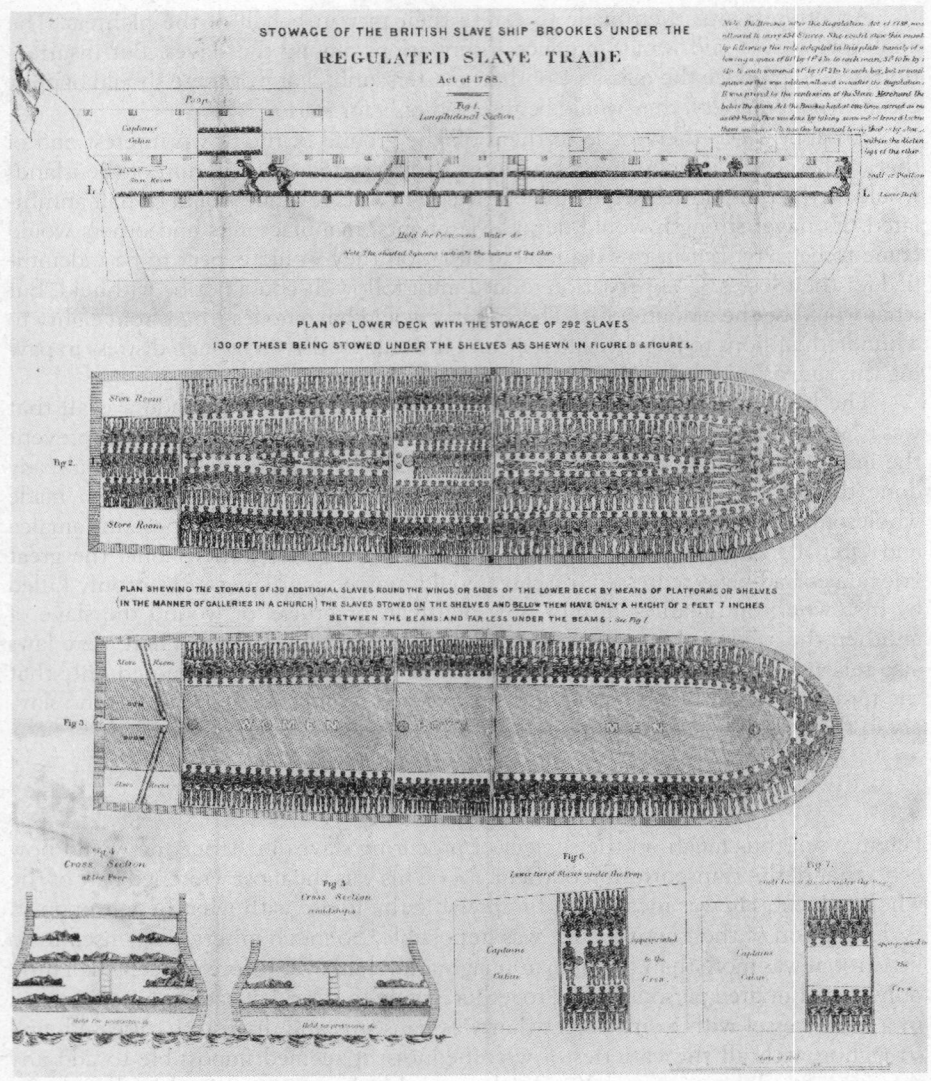

Packing methods on a slave ship. Illustration to *The History of the Rise, Progress, & Accomplishment of the Abolition of the African Slave-Trade by the British Parliament,* by Thomas Clarkson, 1808.

and girls made fanciful ornaments from beads, with which they were plentifully supplied. They were indulged in all their little fancies, and kept in sprightly humour. Another of them had said, when the sailors were flogged, it was out of the hearing of the Africans, lest it should depress their spirits. He by no means wished to say that such descriptions were wilful misrepresentations. If they were not, it proved that interest or prejudice was capable of spreading a film over the eyes thick enough to occasion total blindness.

Others, however, and these men of the greatest veracity, had given a different account. What would the house think, when by the concurring testimony of these the true history was laid open? The slaves who had been described as rejoicing in their captivity, were so wrung with misery at leaving their country, that it was the constant practice to set sail in the night, lest they should know the moment of their departure. With respect to their accommodation, the right ancle of one was fastened to the left ancle of another by an iron fetter; and if they were turbulent, by another on the wrists. Instead of the apartments described, they were placed in niches, and along the decks, in such a manner, that it was impossible for any one to pass among them, however careful he might be, without treading upon them. Sir George Yonge had testified, that in a slave-ship, on board of which he went, and which had not completed her cargo by two hundred and fifty, instead of the scent of frankincense being perceptible to the nostrils, the stench was intolerable. The allowance of water was so deficient, that the slaves were frequently found gasping for life, and almost suffocated. The pulse with which they had been said to be favoured, were absolutely English horse-beans. The legislature of Jamaica had stated the scantiness both of water and provisions, as a subject which called for the interference of parliament. As Mr. Norris had said, the song and the dance were promoted, he could not pass over these expressions without telling the house what they meant. It would have been much more fair if he himself had explained the word *promoted*. The truth was, that, for the sake of exercise, these miserable wretches, loaded with chains and oppressed with disease, were forced to dance by the terror of the lash, and sometimes by the actual use of it. "I," said one of the evidences, "was employed to dance the men, while another person danced the women." Such then was the meaning of the word *promoted*; and it might also be observed with respect to food, that instruments were sometimes carried out, in order to force them to eat; which was the same sort of proof, how much they enjoyed themselves in this instance also. With respect to their singing, it consisted of songs of lamentation for the loss of their country. While they sung they were in tears: so that one of the captains, more humane probably than the rest, threatened a woman with a flogging because the mournfulness of her song was too painful for his feelings. Perhaps he could not give a better proof of the sufferings of these injured people during their passage, than by stating the mortality which accompanied it. This was a species of evidence which was infallible on this occasion. Death was a witness which could not deceive them; and the proportion of deaths would not only confirm, but, if possible, even aggravate our suspicion of the misery of the transit. It would be found, upon an average of all the ships, upon which evidence had been given, that, exclusively of such as perished before they sailed from Africa, not less than twelve and a half per cent. died on their passage: besides these, the Jamaica report stated that four and a half per cent. died while in the harbours, or on shore before the day of sale, which was only about the space of twelve or fourteen days after their arrival there; and one third more died in the seasoning:[3] and this in a climate exactly similar to their own, and where, as some of the witnesses pretended, they were healthy and happy. Thus, out of every lot of one hundred, shipped from Africa, seventeen died in about nine weeks, and not more than fifty lived to become effective labourers in our islands.

["REFLECTIONS ON THIS GREAT EVENT"]

With respect to the end obtained by this contest, or the great measure of the abolition of the Slave-trade as it has now passed, I know not how to appreciate its impor-

3. Breaking-in.

tance. To our own country, indeed, it is invaluable. We have lived, in consequence of it, to see the day, when it has been recorded as a principle in our legislation, that commerce itself shall have its moral boundaries. We have lived to see the day, when we are likely to be delivered from the contagion of the most barbarous opinions.

* * * though nature shrinks from pain, and compassion is engendered in us when we see it become the portion of others, yet what is physical suffering compared with moral guilt? The misery of the oppressed is, in the first place, not contagious like the crime of the oppressor. Nor is the mischief, which it generates, either so frightful or so pernicious. The body, though under affliction, may retain its shape; and, if it even perish, what is the loss of it but of worthless dust? But when the moral springs of the mind are poisoned, we lose the most excellent part of the constitution of our nature, and the divine image is no longer perceptible in us. Nor are the two evils of similar duration. By a decree of Providence, for which we cannot be too thankful, we are made mortal. Hence the torments of the oppressor are but temporary; whereas the immortal part of us, when once corrupted, may carry its pollutions with it into another world.

But independently of the quantity of physical suffering and the innumerable avenues to vice in more than a quarter of the globe, which this great measure will cut off, there are yet blessings, which we have reason to consider as likely to flow from it. Among these we cannot overlook the great probability, that Africa, now freed from the vicious and barbarous effects of this traffic, may be in a better state to comprehend and receive the sublime truths of the Christian religion. Nor can we overlook the probability, that, a new system of treatment necessarily springing up in our islands, the same bright sun of consolation may visit her children there. But here a new hope rises to our view. Who knows but that emancipation, like a beautiful plant, may, in its due season, rise out of the ashes of the abolition of the Slave-trade, and that, when its own intrinsic value shall be known, the seed of it may be planted in other lands? And looking at the subject in this point of view, we cannot but be struck with the wonderful concurrence of events as previously necessary for this purpose, namely, that two nations, England and America, the mother and the child, should, in the same month of the same year, have abolished this impious traffic; nations, which at this moment have more than a million of subjects within their jurisdiction to partake of the blessing; and one of which, on account of her local situation and increasing power, is likely in time to give, if not law, at least a tone to the manners and customs of the great continent, on which she is situated.

Reader! Thou art now acquainted with the history of this contest! Rejoice in the manner of its termination! And, if thou feelest grateful for the event, retire within thy closet,[4] and pour out thy thanksgivings to the Almighty for this his unspeakable act of mercy to thy oppressed fellow-creatures.

———❈———

William Wordsworth
1770–1850

When they were all living in the Lake District of England, the Wordsworths and Coleridge became close friends with Thomas Clarkson and his wife, and were inspired by Clarkson's intense commitment to abolition. William Wordsworth's sonnet *To Thomas Clarkson*, pub-

---

4. Private sitting room. This is the closing paragraph of the *History*.

lished in 1807, honors his heroic persistence in behalf of the Abolition Bill. *To Toussaint L'Ouverture* honors François Dominique Toussaint (1743?–1803), a self-educated slave freed shortly before the 1791 revolt in San Domingo, who became a leader of the revolutionaries (dubbed "L'Ouverture" for his skill in "opening" gaps in enemy ranks, he adopted this as a surname). In 1801, he conquered San Domingo and became governor of the whole island. When, in 1802, he resisted Napoleon's attempt to re-establish French rule and slavery, he was arrested and dungeoned in the French Alps, where he died in April 1803, after ten months of cold and hunger. Wordsworth published his sonnet in *The Morning Post* in February 1803, and then in *Poems* of 1807 under "Sonnets Dedicated to Liberty." *Humanity*—written decades later, in 1829, before colonial emancipation, and published soon after, in 1835—demonstrates his unwavering moral revulsion at slavery and contempt for the economic justifications for it. But in a letter of 1833, he joined the now Tory Poet Laureate Southey in declining to contribute to a volume of antislavery poetry, expressing qualified sympathy for the planters, who, he suggests, have been too one-sidedly villainized.

For more about Wordsworth, see the principal listing on page 1520.

To Toussaint L'Ouverture

Toussaint, the most unhappy man of men!
Whether the whistling Rustic tend his plough
Within thy hearing, or thy head be now
Pillowed in some deep dungeon's earless den;—
5   O miserable Chieftain! where and when
Wilt thou find patience? Yet die not; do thou
Wear rather in thy bonds a cheerful brow:
Though fallen thyself, never to rise again,
Live, and take comfort. Thou hast left behind
10   Powers that will work for thee; air, earth, and skies;
There's not a breathing of the common wind
That will forget thee; thou hast great allies;
Thy friends are exultations, agonies,
And love, and man's unconquerable mind.

1802   1807

To Thomas Clarkson

*On the Final Passing of the Bill for the Abolition of the Slave Trade,
March, 1807*

Clarkson! it was an obstinate Hill to climb;
How toilsome—nay, how dire—it was, by Thee
Is known,—by none, perhaps, so feelingly:
But Thou, who, starting in thy fervent prime,
5   Didst first lead forth this pilgrimage sublime,
Hast heard the constant Voice its charge repeat,
Which, out of thy young heart's oracular seat,
First roused thee.—O true yoke-fellow of Time,
With unabating effort, see, the palm
10   Is won, and by all Nations shall be worn!
The bloody Writing is forever torn;
And Thou henceforth shalt have a good Man's calm,
A great Man's happiness; thy zeal shall find
Repose at length, firm Friend of human kind!

1807   1807

Letter to Mary Ann Rawson[1]

Dear Madam,

Your letter which I lose no time in replying to, has placed me under some embarrassment, as I happen to possess some Mss verses of my own upon the subject to which you solicit my attention. But I frankly own to you, that neither with respect to this subject nor to the kindred one, the Slavery of the children in the Factories,[2] which is adverted to in the same Poem, am I prepared to add to the excitement already existing in the public mind upon these, and so many other points of legislation and government. Poetry, if good for any thing, must appeal forcibly to the Imagination and the feelings; but what at this period we want above every thing, is patient examination and sober judgement. It can scarcely be necessary to add that my mind revolts as strongly as any one's can, from the law that permits one human being to sell another. It is in principle monstrous, but it is not the worst thing in human nature. Let precipitate advocates for its destruction bear this in mind. But I will not enter farther into the question than to say, that there are three parties—the Slave—the Slave owner—and the imperial Parliament, or rather the people of the British Islands, acting through that Organ. Surely the course at present pursued is hasty, intemperate, and likely to lead to gross injustice. Who in fact are most to blame? the people—who, by their legislation, have sanctioned not to say encouraged, slavery. But now we are turning round at once upon the planters, and heaping upon them indignation without measure, as if we wished that the Slaves should believe that their Masters alone were culpable—and they alone fit objects of complaint and resentment.

Excuse haste and believe me Dear Madam
respectfully yours,
Wm Wordsworth

+→ ⊰◆⊱ ←+

The Edinburgh Review

One of the most influential quarterly journals of the day, *The Edinburgh* Review was edited by its co-founder Francis Jeffrey (1773–1850) from its inception in 1802 until 1829. Although Jeffrey tended to conservative standards as a literary critic (famously attacking the Lake school for presenting peasants sympathetically), the *Edinburgh* was an important organ for liberal political opinion and was committed to supporting the Whigs in their parliamentary campaign for reform. Among its other co-founders, Henry Brougham (1778–1868) was a leader in the abolitionist movement, and Sydney Smith (1771–1845) excoriated the slave trade as an "enormous wickedness." Although England had abolished the trade in 1807, other countries, including France and the United States, remained involved, and slavery was still legal in Eng-

1. Wordsworth wrote this letter about May 1833 to Mary Ann Rawson, an original member of the Sheffield Female anti-Slavery Society, founded in 1825; in 1826 she began collecting pieces for an anthology of antislavery prose and poetry, *The Bow in the Cloud*, which she published in 1834, after colonial Emancipation, in a small edition of 500 copies.
2. A Parliamentary commission issued a shocking report

in 1832 about child labor in the factories that led to the "Act of 1833," which prevented those under 9 from such labor and limited those under 13 to 48 hours a week, with no more than 9 hours in any one day; it also required these children to receive at least two hours of schooling a day. It failed in its goal to secure a 10-hour day for teenagers.

land's colonies. Reports such as the one below (October 1821) kept public attention focused on the atrocities.

from Abstract of the Information laid on the Table of the House of Commons, on the Subject of the Slave Trade

The French ship Le Rodeur, of two hundred tons burden, sailed from the port of Havre for the river Calabar on the coast of Africa, where she arrived after a prosperous voyage, and anchored at Bonny on the fourteenth of March. Her crew, of twenty-two men, had enjoyed perfect health; and this continued during her stay of three weeks, while she received on board one hundred and sixty negroes, with whom she set sail for Guadaloupe[1] on the sixth of April. No traces of any epidemy had been perceived among the natives; the cargo (as it is called), no more than the crew, exhibited any symptoms of disease; and the first fortnight of the voyage to the West Indies promised a continuance of all the success which had seemed to attend the earlier stages of the expedition. The vessel had now approached the line,[2] when a frightful malady broke out. At first the symptoms were slight, little more than a redness of the eyes; and this being confined to the negroes, was ascribed to the want of air in the hold, and the narrow space between the decks, into which so large a number of those unhappy beings were crowded; something, too, was imagined to arise from the scarcity of water, which had thus early begun to be felt, and pressed chiefly upon the slaves; for they were allowed only eight ounces, which was soon reduced to half a wine glass per day. By the surgeon's advice, therefore, they were suffered, for the first time, to breathe the purer air upon the deck, where they were brought in succession; but many of these poor creatures being affected with that mighty desire of returning to their native country, which is so strong as to form a disease, termed *Nostalgia* by the physicians, no sooner found they were at liberty, than they threw themselves into the sea, locked in each other's arms, in the vain hope, known to prevail among them, of thus being swiftly transported again to their homes. With the view of counteracting this propensity, the Captain ordered several who were stopt in the attempt, to be shot or hanged in the sight of their companions; but this terrible example was unavailing to deter them; and it became necessary, once more, to confine them entirely to the hold.

The disease proved to be a virulent ophthalmia, and it now spread with irresistible rapidity among the Africans, all of whom were seized; but it soon attacked the crew; and its ravages were attended, perhaps its violence exasperated, by a dysentery, which the use of rain-water was found to have produced. A sailor who slept near the hatch communicating with the hold, was the first who caught it; next day a landsman was taken ill; and in three days more, the Captain and almost all the rest of the crew were infected. The resources of medicine were tried in vain; the sufferings of the people, and the number of the blind, were daily increasing; and they were in constant expectation that the negroes, taking advantage of their numbers, would rise and destroy them. From this danger they were only saved by the mutual hatred of the tribes to which these unfortunate beings belonged, and which was so fierce and inextinguishable, that, even under the load of chains and sickness, they were ready every instant, in their fury, to tear one another in pieces. * * *

The consternation now became general and horrid; but it did not preclude calculation; for, thirty-six of the negroes having become quite blind, were *thrown into the*

---

1. In the Caribbean.   2. Equator.

sea and drowned, in order to save the expense of supporting slaves rendered unsaleable, and to obtain grounds for a claim against the under-writers.[3] * * *

The reader may think that we have been going back to the times when the slave-trade flourished under the protection of the law in England and France; and that we have been citing from the writings of some political author, some advocate for the abolition. Not so. All these horrors darken the history of the year 1819; and the tale is almost all told incidentally by the scientific compilers of a Medical Journal. Yes—in 1819 * * * twelve years after England had forbidden the traffic—eight years after she had declared it a crime—and four years after France, first by law, and then by solemn treaty, had become a party to its positive, unqualified, immediate abolition.

Dreadful as are the scenes disclosed in the case of the Rodeur, there are even worse horrors in the Parliamentary Papers of which the abstract lies before us. In March 1820, the Tartar, commanded by Sir George Collier, boarded a French vessel, called La Jeune Estelle of Martinique, after a long chase. The captain admitted that he had been engaged in the slave-trade, but denied that he had any slaves on board, declaring that he had been plundered of his cargo. The English officers, however, observed that all the French seamen appeared agitated and alarmed; and this led to an examination of the hold. Nothing, however, was found; and they would have departed with the belief that the captain's story was a true one, had not a sailor happened to strike a cask, and hear, or fancy he heard, a faint voice issue from within. The cask was opened, and two negro girls were found crammed into it, and in the last stage of suffocation. Being brought upon the deck of the Tartar, they were recognised by a person who had before seen them in the possession of an American who had died on the coast. An investigation now took place; and it was ascertained that they formed part of a cargo of fourteen slaves, whom the French captain had carried off by an attack which he and his crew made on the American's property after his decease. This led to a new search of the slave-ship for the other twelve, whom he was thus proved to have obtained by the robbery; when a platform was discovered, on which the negroes must have been laid in a space twenty-three inches in height, and beneath it a negro was found, not, however, one of the twelve, jammed into the crevice between two water casks. Still there were no traces of those twelve slaves; and the French captain persisted in his story, that he had been plundered by a Spanish pirate. But suddenly a most horrible idea darted across the minds of the English officers and men; they recollected that, when the chase began, they had seen several casks floating past them, which, at the time, they could not account for; but now, after the examination of the one which remained on board the Jeune Estelle, little doubt could be entertained that those casks contained the wretched slaves, whom the infernal monster had thus thrown overboard, to prevent the detection that would have ensued, either upon their being found in his ship, or by their bodies floating exposed on the sea. * * *

May we not then appeal to the body of our most enlightened European neighbours, and call upon them to stimulate their rulers not only to follow the example set by England and America in classing the slave-trade among heinous crimes, but to join them in that measure which, if those three great maritime powers adopt it, must speedily become the law of all nations? That the French people at large are prepared for such a step, there can be little reason to doubt. All their ablest statesmen have the most sound views upon

---

3. The notorious precedent was the case of the slave ship Zong (1781), whose captain ordered 133 weak and diseased slaves ejected into shark-infested waters in order to collect on a policy that held the insurer liable for cargo jettisoned in order to salvage the remainder. The insurance trial (not about the captain's criminal liability but the underwriter's financial liability) was presided over by Mansfield, who ruled in favor of the captain.

this important question; and the remains of prejudice with respect to the means, when so generous an anxiety is entertained for the attainment of the object, must soon give way to the enlightened genius of the age; and certainly, what has passed in America, is calculated to assist in dispelling those prejudices beyond any thing we can conceive.

Our attention has, in this article, been confined to the portion of the Parliamentary Papers which treats of the French slave-trade, as out of all comparison the most important in every point of view. Much to lament and to amend is, however, contained in the correspondence with Spain, Portugal, and the Netherlands; and it is to be hoped that our Government, acting under the control of the almost unanimous opinion upon this subject entertained both by Parliament and the country, will be enabled, before long, to obtain some more satisfactory arrangements with those three powers. The late Revolutions, and the establishment of a popular constitution in Portugal and Spain, afford additional grounds for such expectations.

[END OF PERSPECTIVES: THE ABOLITION OF SLAVERY AND THE SLAVE TRADE]

Mary Wollstonecraft
1759–1797

It is hard to imagine how anyone advocating the education of young women, the virtues of sense over sensibility, chastity for men as well as women, school uniforms, and regular physical exercise, could be reviled as a radical revolutionary, an atheist, a slut, and a pathologically castrating threat to masculine authority. But Mary Wollstonecraft suffered all these abuses. The attacks were provoked, in part, by her principled, frequently caustic refutation in *A Vindication of the Rights of Men* of Edmund Burke's *Reflections on the Revolution in France*. She went further in her *Vindication of the Rights of Woman*, a trenchant critique of the ideologies of gender in such culturally revered works as Milton's *Paradise Lost* and the admired "conduct" literature of the day—advice to young women on how to be attractive to men and cultivate the Christian virtues of submission, obedience, and service. It was not only Wollstonecraft's publications that provoked censure; it was also her private life, taken to be the basis of her ideas. The litany included helping a sister run away from an abusive husband (an assault on the social institution and religious sacrament of marriage); her financial independence and career as a professional writer (very unfeminine); her enamored pursuit of Swiss artist Henry Fuseli in the early 1790s (most immodest) and the outright sinfulness of her tempestuous affair with American adventurer Gilbert Imlay a few years later; her out-of-wedlock daughter by Imlay; the two attempts at suicide provoked by Imlay's infidelities; her affair with William Godwin and a premarital pregnancy. When she died from complications in childbirth, her detractors intuited divine judgment.

A brilliant thinker and conversationalist, a prolific polemical writer, a commanding social presence, Wollstonecraft led a life of passionate commitments, and was one of the most impressive figures of the radical circle in England in the 1790s. Born in 1759, she spent a childhood suffering the consequences of her father's failures at various enterprises, as he squandered a large inheritance and sought refuge in drink; more than once she defended her mother from his drunken rages. To escape, she became a lady's companion in Bath but returned after two years to nurse her mother. After her mother's death, she left home for good, supporting herself with eye-straining work as a seamstress and then as a schoolmistress in North London with a friend and another sister. When the school failed, Wollstonecraft wrote to pay off her debts, publishing *Thoughts on the Education of Daughters* in 1786; she worked for a year as a governess in an Irish aristocratic family, during which time she wrote her first novel, *Mary, A Fiction*.

Determined to make a living as a writer, she returned to London where she met Joseph Johnson, a radical bookseller, who in 1788, published *Mary* and her book for children, *Original Stories from Real Life*, and in 1789, her anthology, *The Female Reader* (under a male pen name). He also hired her to work for and write articles for *The Analytic Review* and to produce translations of German and French moral philosophers. In London Wollstonecraft became part of Johnson's lively circle of artists, writers, liberal political thinkers, progressive philosophers, and religious Dissenters—among them, Anna Laetitia Barbauld, Thomas Paine, William Blake, Joel Barlow, Joseph Priestley, Fuseli, and her future husband, Godwin. Blake and Robert Southey were completely enamored of her, though Godwin was at first put off by her forwardness in conversation. In 1790 Johnson published *A Vindication of the Rights of Men*, written quickly to respond to Edmund Burke's *Reflections on the Revolution in France;* this was anonymous, and when Wollstonecraft signed her name to the second edition in 1791, her fame was established.

She began *Rights of Woman* the same year and early in 1792 spent time with Talleyrand, the French minister of education, on his visit to London; she dedicated *Rights of Woman* to him when its second edition was published later that year. Her reasonable, modest proposals for the improved education and social development of young women were etched with acid comparisons of the state of women to that of plantation and harem slaves, equally oppressed, tyrannized, and brutalized by morally illegitimate masters. Wollstonecraft called for a "revolution in female manners," arguing that no agenda for "the rights of man" could claim moral authority if it entailed the unchanged degradation of women. At the end of 1792, she left on her own for Paris, partly to wean herself from her crush on Fuseli and partly to witness Revolutionary France. Here she met Helen Maria Williams, and within a few months, Imlay, dashing veteran of the American Revolution. Paris in 1793 was a dangerous world, still reeling from the September massacres of 1792 and the arrest and trial of Louis XVI, who was beheaded in January 1793. Over the course of this year, the Reign of Terror beheaded thousands more, including Wollstonecraft's friend Madame Roland and Queen Marie Antoinette in October. Wollstonecraft left Paris to seek safety in the suburbs, but returned to register as Imlay's wife at the American embassy in order to gain protection as an American citizen, France being at war with England. Early in 1794, she and Imlay went to Le Havre, where their daughter Fanny was born. They all returned to Paris; then Imlay went to London, leaving wife and daughter behind.

Wollstonecraft's *Historical and Moral View of the Origin and Progress of the French Revolution* was published later that year. On returning to London, she was devastated to discover Imlay living with an actress. He prevented her attempted suicide, and to distance himself from her, sent her (with Fanny and a French nurse) on a business trip to Scandinavia during the summer of 1795. She returned in October to find him living with yet another actress and again attempted suicide, jumping off a bridge into the Thames. Imlay left for Paris with his new amour in November, and Wollstonecraft, ever resourceful, decided to publish her letters to him recording her experiences in Scandinavia. When *Letters Written during a Short Residence in Sweden, Norway, and Denmark* appeared the following year, Godwin exclaimed, "If ever there was a book calculated to make a man in love with its author, this appears to me to be the book." They renewed their friendship in January 1796 and by the summer, "friendship melting into love," they became lovers. When she became pregnant at the end of the year, they set aside principle and decided to marry. They were wed in March, but insisted on keeping separate residences. Mary Wollstonecraft Godwin—the future Mary Shelley—was born in August; in ten days, her mother, having suffered agonizing pain from poisoning by an incompletely expelled placenta, was dead, at age thirty-seven.

When Godwin published a *Memoir* of her and her unfinished novel, *The Wrongs of Woman, or Maria* in 1798, both works fed anti-Jacobin attacks on her ideas and moral character. His grief clouded his judgment about what he could recount without offending propriety, and the *Memoir* proved a scandal, embarrassing even those who had welcomed *Rights of*

Woman. An anonymous *Defence of the Character and Conduct of the Late Mary Wollstonecraft Godwin* (often credited to Mary Hays, her friend and fellow feminist), appeared in 1803, but the defense could hardly rest. Hays did not feel safe including her in her *Female Biography, or Memoirs of Illustrious and Celebrated Women of all Ages and Countries* (also 1803), even though she found space for the Lesbian Sappho and Marat's assassin Charlotte Corday. Decades later, in 1869, John Stuart Mill forgot to mention *Rights of Woman* in his *Subjection of Women*. Attacks on Wollstonecraft's character and conduct persisted well into the 1970s, not only stigmatizing the arguments of her writing but providing anti-feminists with fuel to impugn any advocacy of women's rights. Yet there always persisted a community of admiration for her courage and intelligence, including (for better or worse) Percy Shelley, and over ensuing decades, such women of intellect as George Eliot, Emma Goldman, and Virginia Woolf.

Selections from *A Vindication of the Rights of Men* are included in Perspectives: The Rights of Man and the Revolution Controversy, page 1365.

A VINDICATION OF THE RIGHTS OF WOMAN

With the French Revolutionary Assembly's Declaration of the Rights of Man granting participatory citizenship only to men, Wollstonecraft's "second *Vindication*" responds to a concern of many progressive women, namely, that the vibrant declarations of the "Rights of Man" were all too serious about the *fraternity* of "liberty, fraternity, equality." Bluntly comparing marriage to slavery and tyrannical oppression, Wollstonecraft boldly challenges the ideology that sustains and frequently idealizes this subjection: the view of women's subordination as a universal fact of nature, human history, rational philosophy, and divine ordination. She proceeds first to identify this view as a sociocultural text, a "prevailing opinion," and then to subject it to a sharp critical reading. This textual critique is embedded in the overt literary criticism that fills her pages, incisive and often sarcastic examinations of the attitudes about gender in long-standing misogynist myths (Pandora) and in the most influential works of her day: John Milton's *Paradise Lost* (and its informing biblical stories), Alexander Pope's second *Moral Essay*, "Of the Characters of Women" (1735), Samuel Richardson's *Clarissa* (1747–1748), Jean-Jacques Rousseau's influential education novel, *Émile* (1762) and *Julie, ou la Nouvelle Héloïse* (1791), Dr. John Gregory's *A Father's Legacy to His Daughters* (1774), Dr. James Fordyce's *Sermons to Young Women* (1765). Her literary criticism extends to an unforgiving focus on a set of interlocked key terms used to flatter women into subjection—"innocent," "delicate," "feminine," "beautiful"—embellished with praise for their "fair defects" of character (an oxymoron she despises) and reverence for them as "angels" or "girls," rather than rationally capable, intelligent, mature adults.

Wollstonecraft's argument for a gender-neutral capacity of "reason" simultaneously draws on eighteenth-century rationalist philosophy and democratizes the Miltonic value of "Reason" as the highest mental capacity. For Milton, this capacity is located in men only; Wollstonecraft argues that this hierarchical arrangement is not a divine but a social formation. She counters that if God is Reason, He surely would not have created women without this capacity, the source of both virtuous conduct and spiritual salvation—a religious argument Wollstonecraft uses not only to refute appeals to divine ordination, but also to invest her social polemic with what she hopes will be an unimpeachable moral foundation. Alongside this moral argument, her *Vindication* wields the discourse of tyranny and revolution that already had currency with her male colleagues, allowing her to point out the reactionary attitudes about women that may be tolerated, even supported, by progressive political thinkers.

from A Vindication of the Rights of Woman
Introduction

After considering the historic page, and viewing the living world with anxious solicitude, the most melancholy emotions of sorrowful indignation have depressed my spirits, and I have sighed when obliged to confess, that either nature has made a great difference between man and man, or that the civilization which has hitherto taken place in the world has been very partial. I have turned over various books written on the subject of education, and patiently observed the conduct of parents and the management of schools; but what has been the result?—a profound conviction that the neglected education of my fellow-creatures is the grand source of the misery I deplore; and that women, in particular, are rendered weak and wretched by a variety of concurring causes, originating from one hasty conclusion. The conduct and manners of women, in fact, evidently prove that their minds are not in a healthy state; for, like the flowers which are planted in too rich a soil, strength and usefulness are sacrificed to beauty; and the flaunting leaves, after having pleased a fastidious eye, fade, disregarded on the stalk, long before the season when they ought to have arrived at maturity.—One cause of this barren blooming I attribute to a false system of education, gathered from the books written on this subject by men who, considering females rather as women than human creatures, have been more anxious to make them alluring mistresses than affectionate wives and rational mothers; and the understanding of the sex has been so bubbled[1] by this specious homage, that the civilized women of the present century, with a few exceptions, are only anxious to inspire love, when they ought to cherish a nobler ambition, and by their abilities and virtues exact respect.

In a treatise, therefore, on female rights and manners, the works which have been particularly written for their improvement must not be overlooked; especially when it is asserted, in direct terms, that the minds of women are enfeebled by false refinement; that the books of instruction, written by men of genius, have had the same tendency as more frivolous productions; and that, in the true style of Mahometanism, they are treated as a kind of subordinate beings, and not as a part of the human species,[2] when improveable reason is allowed to be the dignified distinction which raises men above the brute creation, and puts a natural sceptre in a feeble hand.

Yet, because I am a woman, I would not lead my readers to suppose that I mean violently to agitate the contested question respecting the equality or inferiority of the sex; but as the subject lies in my way, and I cannot pass it over without subjecting the main tendency of my reasoning to misconstruction, I shall stop a moment to deliver, in a few words, my opinion.—In the government of the physical world it is observable that the female in point of strength is, in general, inferior to the male. This is the law of nature; and it does not appear to be suspended or abrogated in favour of woman. A degree of physical superiority cannot, therefore, be denied—and it is a noble prerogative! But not content with this natural pre-eminence, men endeavour to sink us still lower, merely to render us alluring objects for a moment; and women, intoxicated by the adoration which men, under the influence of their senses, pay them, do not seek to obtain a durable interest in their hearts, or to become the friends of the fellow creatures who find amusement in their society.

I am aware of an obvious inference:—from every quarter have I heard exclamations against masculine women; but where are they to be found? If by this appellation men mean to inveigh against their ardour in hunting, shooting, and gaming, I shall most cordially join in the cry; but if it be against the imitation of manly virtues, or, more properly speaking, the attainment of those talents and virtues, the exercise of

---

1. Gas-filled; deluded.
2. A Western misconception that the sacred texts of

Islam stated that women lack souls and therefore have no afterlife in Heaven.

which ennobles the human character, and which raise females in the scale of animal being, when they are comprehensively termed mankind;—all those who view them with a philosophic eye must, I should think, wish with me, that they may every day grow more and more masculine.

This discussion naturally divides the subject. I shall first consider women in the grand light of human creatures, who, in common with men, are placed on this earth to unfold their faculties; and afterwards I shall more particularly point out their peculiar designation.

I wish also to steer clear of an error which many respectable writers have fallen into; for the instruction which has hitherto been addressed to women, has rather been applicable to *ladies*, if the little indirect advice, that is scattered through Sandford and Merton, be excepted;[3] but, addressing my sex in a firmer tone, I pay particular attention to those in the middle class, because they appear to be in the most natural state.[4] Perhaps the seeds of false-refinement, immorality, and vanity, have ever been shed by the great. Weak, artificial beings, raised above the common wants and affections of their race, in a premature unnatural manner, undermine the very foundation of virtue, and spread corruption through the whole mass of society! As a class of mankind they have the strongest claim to pity; the education of the rich tends to render them vain and helpless, and the unfolding mind is not strengthened by the practice of those duties which dignify the human character.—They only live to amuse themselves, and by the same law which in nature invariably produces certain effects, they soon only afford barren amusement.

But as I purpose taking a separate view of the different ranks of society, and of the moral character of women, in each, this hint is, for the present, sufficient; and I have only alluded to the subject, because it appears to me to be the very essence of an introduction to give a cursory account of the contents of the work it introduces.

My own sex, I hope, will excuse me, if I treat them like rational creatures, instead of flattering their *fascinating* graces, and viewing them as if they were in a state of perpetual childhood, unable to stand alone. I earnestly wish to point out in what true dignity and human happiness consists—I wish to persuade women to endeavour to acquire strength, both of mind and body, and to convince them that the soft phrases, susceptibility of heart, delicacy of sentiment, and refinement of taste, are almost synonymous with epithets of weakness, and that those beings who are only the objects of pity and that kind of love, which has been termed its sister, will soon become objects of contempt.

Dismissing then those pretty feminine phrases, which the men condescendingly use to soften our slavish dependence, and despising that weak elegancy of mind, exquisite sensibility, and sweet docility of manners, supposed to be the sexual characteristics of the weaker vessel, I wish to shew that elegance is inferior to virtue, that the first object of laudable ambition is to obtain a character as a human being, regardless of the distinction of sex; and that secondary views should be brought to this simple touchstone.

This is a rough sketch of my plan; and should I express my conviction with the energetic emotions that I feel whenever I think of the subject, the dictates of experience and reflection will be felt by some of my readers. Animated by this important

3. The tutor in Thomas Day's popular children's story, *The History of Sandford and Merton* (1786–1789, influenced by Rousseau's *Émile*), tells several moral tales.

4. "Ladies" are upper-class; Wollstonecraft suggests that the middle class is the most "natural" state because it has not been corrupted by extremes of wealth or poverty.

object, I shall disdain to cull my phrases or polish my style;—I aim at being useful, and sincerity will render me unaffected; for, wishing rather to persuade by the force of my arguments, than dazzle by the elegance of my language, I shall not waste my time in rounding periods,[5] or in fabricating the turgid bombast of artificial feelings, which, coming from the head, never reach the heart.—I shall be employed about things, not words!—and, anxious to render my sex more respectable members of society, I shall try to avoid that flowery diction which has slided from essays into novels, and from novels into familiar letters and conversation.

These pretty superlatives, dropping glibly from the tongue, vitiate the taste, and create a kind of sickly delicacy that turns away from simple unadorned truth; and a deluge of false sentiments and over-stretched feelings, stifling the natural emotions of the heart, render the domestic pleasures insipid, that ought to sweeten the exercise of those severe duties, which educate a rational and immortal being for a nobler field of action.

The education of women has, of late, been more attended to than formerly; yet they are still reckoned a frivolous sex, and ridiculed or pitied by the writers who endeavour by satire or instruction to improve them. It is acknowledged that they spend many of the first years of their lives in acquiring a smattering of accomplishments; meanwhile strength of body and mind are sacrificed to libertine notions of beauty, to the desire of establishing themselves,—the only way women can rise in the world,—by marriage. And this desire making mere animals of them, when they marry they act as such children may be expected to act:—they dress; they paint, and nickname God's creatures.[6]—Surely these weak beings are only fit for a seraglio![7]— Can they be expected to govern a family with judgment, or take care of the poor babes whom they bring into the world?

If then it can be fairly deduced from the present conduct of the sex,[8] from the prevalent fondness for pleasure which takes place of ambition and those nobler passions that open and enlarge the soul; that the instruction which women have hitherto received has only tended, with the constitution of civil society, to render them insignificant objects of desire—mere propagators of fools!—if it can be proved that in aiming to accomplish them, without cultivating their understandings, they are taken out of their sphere of duties, and made ridiculous and useless when the short-lived bloom of beauty is over,[9] I presume that *rational* men will excuse me for endeavouring to persuade them to become more masculine and respectable.

Indeed the word masculine is only a bugbear: there is little reason to fear that women will acquire too much courage or fortitude; for their apparent inferiority with respect to bodily strength, must render them, in some degree, dependent on men in the various relations of life; but why should it be increased by prejudices that give a sex to virtue,[1] and confound simple truths with sensual reveries?

Women are, in fact, so much degraded by mistaken notions of female excellence, that I do not mean to add a paradox when I assert, that this artificial weakness produces a propensity to tyrannize, and gives birth to cunning, the natural opponent of strength, which leads them to play off those contemptible infantine airs that undermine esteem even whilst they excite desire. Let men become more chaste and mod-

---

5. Crafting elaborate sentences—the oratorical style for which Burke was famous.

6. A reference to Hamlet's misogynist diatribe at Ophelia, whom he suspects of treachery: "God hath given you one face, and you make yourselves another. You jig and amble, and you lisp; you nickname God's creatures and make your wantonness [seem] your ignorance" (*Hamlet*

3.1.145–48). Cf. *Rights of Men*, page 1370, n.3.

7. Harem.

8. The female sex, a common usage.

9. A lively writer . . . asks what business women turned of forty have to do in the world? [Wollstonecraft's note.]

1. The prevailing opinion that only men have the rational and hence moral capacity for virtuous behavior.

est, and if women do not grow wiser in the same ratio, it will b*
weaker understandings. It seems scarcely necessary to say, that I*ar that they have
in general. Many individuals have more sense than their male re*peak of the sex
ing preponderates where there is a constant struggle for an equi*and, as noth-
has naturally more gravity, some women govern their husbands *, without it
themselves, because intellect will always govern.   degrading

from *Chapter 1. The Rights and Involved Duties of Mankin*

In the present state of society it appears necessary to go back to fir*red
search of the most simple truths, and to dispute with some prevailing p*
inch of ground. To clear my way, I must be allowed to ask some plain q*in
the answers will probably appear as unequivocal as the axioms on which*
built; though, when entangled with various motives of action, they are f*
tradicted, either by the words or conduct of men.

In what does man's pre-eminence over the brute creation consist? Th*
as clear as that a half is less than the whole; in Reason.

What acquirement exalts one being above another? Virtue; we spontaneou*

For what purpose were the passions implanted? That man by struggli*
them might attain a degree of knowledge denied to the brutes; whispers Expe*

Consequently the perfection of our nature and capability of happiness, must *
mated by the degree of reason, virtue, and knowledge, that distinguish the indivi*
and direct the laws which bind society: and that from the exercise of reason, knowledge
and virtue naturally flow, is equally undeniable, if mankind be viewed collectively.

The rights and duties of man thus simplified, it seems almost impertinent to attempt to illustrate truths that appear so incontrovertible; yet such deeply rooted prejudices have clouded reason, and such spurious qualities have assumed the name of virtues, that it is necessary to pursue the course of reason as it has been perplexed and involved in error, by various adventitious circumstances, comparing the simple axiom with casual deviations.

Men, in general, seem to employ their reason to justify prejudices, which they have imbibed, they can scarcely trace how, rather than to root them out. The mind must be strong that resolutely forms its own principles; for a kind of intellectual cowardice prevails which makes many men shrink from the task, or only do it by halves. Yet the imperfect conclusions thus drawn, are frequently very plausible, because they are built on partial experience, on just, though narrow, views. * * *

The civilization of the bulk of the people of Europe is very partial; nay, it may be made a question, whether they have acquired any virtues in exchange for innocence, equivalent to the misery produced by the vices that have been plastered over unsightly ignorance, and the freedom which has been bartered for splendid slavery. The desire of dazzling by riches, the most certain pre-eminence that man can obtain, the pleasure of commanding flattering sycophants, and many other complicated low calculations of doting self-love, have all contributed to overwhelm the mass of mankind, and make liberty a convenient handle for mock patriotism. For whilst rank and titles are held of the utmost importance, before which Genius "must hide its diminished head,"[1] it is, with a few exceptions, very unfortunate for a nation when a

---

1. A sardonic reference to Satan's noting how "all the Stars / Hide thir diminisht heads" at the sight of the noonday sun "that with surpassing Glory crown'd, / Look'st from [its] sole dominion like the God / Of this new World" (*Paradise Lost* 4.32–35). Wollstonecraft also quotes this phrase in *Rights of Men*; see page 1372.

...hout rank or property, pushes himself forward to notice.—Alas!
...isery have thousands suffered to purchase a cardinal's hat for an
...e adventurer, who longed to be ranked with princes, or lord it over
...ng the triple crown![2] * * *

...an set the regal character in a more contemptible point of view, than
...imes that have elevated men to the supreme dignity.—Vile intrigues,
...mes, and every vice that degrades our nature, have been the steps to this
...d eminence; yet millions of men have supinely allowed the nerveless limbs
...rity of such rapacious prowlers to rest quietly on their ensanguined thrones.[3]
...t but a pestilential vapour can hover over society when its chief director is
...tructed in the invention of crimes, or the stupid routine of childish cere-
...s? Will men never be wise?—will they never cease to expect corn from tares,
...gs from thistles?[4]

It is impossible for any man, when the most favourable circumstances concur, to
quire sufficient knowledge and strength of mind to discharge the duties of a king,
ntrusted with uncontrouled power; how then must they be violated when his very
elevation is an insuperable bar to the attainment of either wisdom or virtue; when all
the feelings of a man are stifled by flattery, and reflection shut out by pleasure! Surely it is madness to make the fate of thousands depend on the caprice of a weak fellow
creature, whose very station sinks him *necessarily* below the meanest of his subjects!
But one power should not be thrown down to exalt another—for all power inebriates
weak man; and its abuse proves that the more equality there is established among
men, the more virtue and happiness will reign in society. But this and any similar
maxim deduced from simple reason, raises an outcry—the church or the state is in
danger, if faith in the wisdom of antiquity is not implicit; and they who, roused by
the sight of human calamity, dare to attack human authority, are reviled as despisers
of God, and enemies of man. These are bitter calumnies, yet they reached one of the
best of men,[5] whose ashes still preach peace, and whose memory demands a respectful
pause, when subjects are discussed that lay so near his heart.—

After attacking the sacred majesty of Kings, I shall scarcely excite surprise by
adding my firm persuasion that every profession, in which great subordination of
rank constitutes its power, is highly injurious to morality.

A standing army, for instance, is incompatible with freedom; because subordination and rigour are the very sinews of military discipline; and despotism is necessary
to give vigour to enterprizes that one will directs. A spirit inspired by romantic
notions of honour, a kind of morality founded on the fashion of the age, can only be
felt by a few officers, whilst the main body must be moved by command, like the
waves of the sea; for the strong wind of authority pushes the crowd of subalterns forward, they scarcely know or care why, with headlong fury.

---

2. Papal crown.

3. "Could there be a greater insult offered to the rights of
man than the beds of justice in France, when an infant
was made the organ of the detestable Dubois!" [Woll-
stonecraft's note.] Guillaume Dubois (1656–1723) was
foreign affairs advisor to Philippe II, Duc d'Orleans, the
appointed regent (acting ruler) of France during the
minority of Louis XV (1710–1774), who became king at
age five (Louis XVI, king in 1792, was his grandson and
successor).

4. See Jesus' Sermon on the Mount: "Beware of false
prophets. . . . Ye shall know them by their fruits. Do men
gather . . . figs of thistles? (Matthew 7.15–16); tares:
weeds. See also Shakespeare, *Hamlet* (2.2.310).

5. Dr. Price [Wollstonecraft's note]. "Calumnies" are
maliciously false charges. Wollstonecraft's friend
Richard Price, dissenting minister and radical political
writer, championed the American and French Revolutions. His lecture to the Revolution Society in 1789, *A
Discourse on the Love of our Country*, provoked sharp criticism in Burke's *Reflections on the Revolution in France*
and spirited defense in Wollstonecraft's *Vindication of the
Rights of Men*.

Besides, nothing can be so prejudicial to the morals of the inhabitants of country towns as the occasional residence of a set of idle superficial young men, whose only occupation is gallantry, and whose polished manners render vice more dangerous, by concealing its deformity under gay ornamental drapery. An air of fashion, which is but a badge of slavery, and proves that the soul has not a strong individual character, awes simple country people into an imitation of the vices, when they cannot catch the slippery graces, of politeness. Every corps is a chain of despots, who, submitting and tyrannizing without exercising their reason, become dead weights of vice and folly on the community. A man of rank or fortune, sure of rising by interest, has nothing to do but to pursue some extravagant freak; whilst the needy *gentleman*, who is to rise, as the phrase turns, by his merit, becomes a servile parasite or vile pander.

Sailors, the naval gentlemen, come under the same description, only their vices assume a different and a grosser cast. They are more positively indolent, when not discharging the ceremonials of their station; whilst the insignificant fluttering of soldiers may be termed active idleness. More confined to the society of men, the former acquire a fondness for humour and mischievous tricks; whilst the latter, mixing frequently with well-bred women, catch a sentimental cant.—But mind is equally out of the question, whether they indulge the horse-laugh, or polite simper.

May I be allowed to extend the comparison to a profession where more mind is certainly to be found; for the clergy have superior opportunities of improvement, though subordination almost equally cramps their faculties? The blind submission imposed at college to forms of belief serves as a novitiate to the curate, who must obsequiously respect the opinion of his rector or patron, if he mean to rise in his profession. Perhaps there cannot be a more forcible contrast than between the servile dependent gait of a poor curate and the courtly mien of a bishop. And the respect and contempt they inspire render the discharge of their separate functions equally useless.

It is of great importance to observe that the character of every man is, in some degree, formed by his profession. A man of sense may only have a cast of countenance that wears off as you trace his individuality, whilst the weak, common man has scarcely ever any character, but what belongs to the body; at least, all his opinions have been so steeped in the vat consecrated by authority, that the faint spirit which the grape of his own vine yields cannot be distinguished.

Society, therefore, as it becomes more enlightened, should be very careful not to establish bodies of men who must necessarily be made foolish or vicious by the very constitution of their profession.

from *Chapter 2. The Prevailing Opinion of a Sexual Character Discussed*

To account for, and excuse the tyranny of man, many ingenious arguments have been brought forward to prove, that the two sexes, in the acquirement of virtue, ought to aim at attaining a very different character: or, to speak explicitly, women are not allowed to have sufficient strength of mind to acquire what really deserves the name of virtue. Yet it should seem, allowing them to have souls, that there is but one way appointed by Providence to lead *mankind* to either virtue or happiness.

If then women are not a swarm of ephemeron[1] triflers, why should they be kept in ignorance under the specious name of innocence? Men complain, and with reason,

---

1. Flying insect that lives for only a day.

of the follies and caprices of our sex, when they do not keenly satirize our headstrong passions and groveling vices.—Behold, I should answer, the natural effect of ignorance! The mind will ever be unstable that has only prejudices to rest on, and the current will run with destructive fury when there are no barriers to break its force. Women are told from their infancy, and taught by the example of their mothers, that a little knowledge of human weakness, justly termed cunning, softness of temper, *outward* obedience, and a scrupulous attention to a puerile kind of propriety, will obtain for them the protection of man; and should they be beautiful, every thing else is needless, for, at least, twenty years of their lives.

Thus Milton describes our first frail mother; though when he tells us that women are formed for softness and sweet attractive grace,[2] I cannot comprehend his meaning, unless, in the true Mahometan strain, he meant to deprive us of souls, and insinuate that we were beings only designed by sweet attractive grace, and docile blind obedience, to gratify the senses of man when he can no longer soar on the wing of contemplation.

How grossly do they insult us who thus advise us only to render ourselves gentle, domestic brutes! For instance, the winning softness so warmly, and frequently, recommended, that governs by obeying. What childish expressions, and how insignificant is the being—can it be an immortal one? who will condescend to govern by such sinister methods! "Certainly," says Lord Bacon, "man is of kin to the beasts by his body; and if he be not of kin to God by his spirit, he is a base and ignoble creature!"[3] Men, indeed, appear to me to act in a very unphilosophical manner when they try to secure the good conduct of women by attempting to keep them always in a state of childhood. Rousseau was more consistent when he wished to stop the progress of reason in both sexes, for if men eat of the tree of knowledge, women will come in for a taste; but, from the imperfect cultivation which their understandings now receive, they only attain a knowledge of evil.[4]

Children, I grant, should be innocent; but when the epithet is applied to men, or women, it is but a civil term for weakness. For if it be allowed that women were destined by Providence to acquire human virtues, and by the exercise of their understandings, that stability of character which is the firmest ground to rest our future hopes upon, they must be permitted to turn to the fountain of light, and not forced to shape their course by the twinkling of a mere satellite. Milton, I grant, was of a very different opinion; for he only bends to the indefeasible right of beauty, though it would be difficult to render two passages which I now mean to contrast, consistent. But into similar inconsistencies are great men often led by their senses.

> To whom thus Eve with *perfect beauty* adorn'd.
> "My Author and Disposer, what thou bidst
> *Unargued* I obey; So God ordains;
> God is *thy law, thou mine:* to know no more
> Is Woman's *happiest* knowledge and her *praise.*"[5]

These are exactly the arguments that I have used to children; but I have added, your reason is now gaining strength, and, till it arrives at some degree of maturity, you must look up to me for advice—then you ought to *think*, and only rely on God.

---

2. See Satan's first view of Adam and Eve in *Paradise Lost:* "Not equal, as thir sex not equal seem'd; / For contemplation hee and valor form'd; / For softness shee and sweet attractive Grace, / He for God only, shee for God in him" (4.296–99). Fordyce quotes these lines in *Sermons to Young Women,* ch. 13.

3. Francis Bacon , *Essay* (1606) 16: "Of Atheism."

4. See Rousseau's *Émile* (1.1): "Only reason teaches us good from evil."

5. *Paradise Lost* 4.634–38; Wollstonecraft's emphases.

Yet in the following lines Milton seems to coincide with me; when he makes Adam thus expostulate with his Maker.

> Hast thou not made me here thy substitute,
> And these inferior far beneath me set?
> Among *unequals* what society
> Can sort, what harmony or true delight?
> Which must be mutual, in proportion due
> Giv'n and receiv'd; but in *disparity*
> The one intense, the other still remiss
> Cannot well suit with either, but soon prove
> Tedious alike: of *fellowship* I speak
> Such as I seek, fit to participate
> All rational delight[6]—

In treating, therefore, of the manners of women, let us, disregarding sensual arguments, trace what we should endeavour to make them in order to co-operate, if the expression be not too bold, with the supreme Being.

By individual education, I mean, for the sense of the word is not precisely defined, such an attention to a child as will slowly sharpen the senses, form the temper, regulate the passions as they begin to ferment, and set the understanding to work before the body arrives at maturity; so that the man may only have to proceed, not to begin, the important task of learning to think and reason. * * *

In fact, it is a farce to call any being virtuous whose virtues do not result from the exercise of its own reason. This was Rousseau's opinion respecting men: I extend it to women, and confidently assert that they have been drawn out of their sphere by false refinement, and not by an endeavour to acquire masculine qualities. Still the regal homage which they receive is so intoxicating, that till the manners of the times are changed, and formed on more reasonable principles, it may be impossible to convince them that the illegitimate power, which they obtain, by degrading themselves, is a curse, and that they must return to nature and equality, if they wish to secure the placid satisfaction that unsophisticated affections impart. But for this epoch we must wait—wait, perhaps, till kings and nobles, enlightened by reason, and, preferring the real dignity of man to childish state, throw off their gaudy hereditary trappings: and if then women do not resign the arbitrary power of beauty—they will prove that they have *less* mind than man.

I may be accused of arrogance; still I must declare what I firmly believe, that all the writers who have written on the subject of female education and manners from Rousseau to Dr. Gregory, have contributed to render women more artificial, weak characters, than they would otherwise have been; and, consequently, more useless members of society.[7] * * * My objection extends to the whole purport of those books, which tend, in my opinion, to degrade one half of the human species, and render women pleasing at the expense of every solid virtue.

Though, to reason on Rousseau's ground, if man did attain a degree of perfection of mind when his body arrived at maturity, it might be proper, in order to make a

---

6. *Paradise Lost* 8.381–91; Wollstonecraft's emphases.
7. In *Émile*, ch. 5, "Sophy or Woman," Rousseau advises that a "woman's education must . . . be planned in relation to man. To be pleasing in his sight, to win his respect and love, to train him in childhood, to tend him in manhood, to counsel and console, to make his life pleasant

and happy"; at any state of life, she "will always be in subjection to a man, or to man's judgment, and she will never be free to set her own opinion above his." Dr. John Gregory (1724–1773) wrote a popular English conduct book, *A Father's Legacy to His Daughters* (1774).

man and his wife *one*, that she should rely entirely on his understanding; and the graceful ivy, clasping the oak that supported it, would form a whole in which strength and beauty would be equally conspicuous. But, alas! husbands, as well as their help-mates, are often only overgrown children; nay, thanks to early debauchery, scarcely men in their outward form—and if the blind lead the blind, one need not come from heaven to tell us the consequence.[8] * * *

Probably the prevailing opinion, that woman was created for man, may have taken its rise from Moses's poetical story;[9] yet, as very few, it is presumed, who have bestowed any serious thought on the subject, ever supposed that Eve was, literally speaking, one of Adam's ribs, the deduction must be allowed to fall to the ground; or, only be so far admitted as it proves that man, from the remotest antiquity, found it convenient to exert his strength to subjugate his companion, and his invention to shew that she ought to have her neck bent under the yoke, because the whole creation was only created for his convenience or pleasure.

Let it not be concluded that I wish to invert the order of things; I have already granted, that, from the constitution of their bodies, men seem to be designed by Providence to attain a greater degree of virtue. I speak collectively of the whole sex; but I see not the shadow of a reason to conclude that their virtues should differ in respect to their nature. In fact, how can they, if virtue has only one eternal standard? I must therefore, if I reason consequentially, as strenuously maintain that they have the same simple direction, as that there is a God.

It follows then that cunning should not be opposed to wisdom, little cares to great exertions, or insipid softness, varnished over with the name of gentleness, to that fortitude which grand views alone can inspire.

I shall be told that woman would then lose many of her peculiar graces, and the opinion of a well known poet might be quoted to refute my unqualified assertion. For Pope has said, in the name of the whole male sex,

> Yet ne'er so sure our passion to create,
> As when she touch'd the brink of all we hate.

In what light this sally[1] places men and women, I shall leave to the judicious to determine; meanwhile I shall content myself with observing, that I cannot discover why, unless they are mortal, females should always be degraded by being made subservient to love or lust.

To speak disrespectfully of love is, I know, high treason against sentiment and fine feelings; but I wish to speak the simple language of truth, and rather to address the head than the heart. To endeavour to reason love out of the world, would be to out Quixote Cervantes, and equally offend against common sense;[2] but an endeavour to restrain this tumultuous passion, and to prove that it should not be allowed to dethrone superior powers, or to usurp the sceptre which the understanding should ever coolly wield, appears less wild.

Youth is the season for love in both sexes; but in those days of thoughtless enjoyment provision should be made for the more important years of life, when reflection

---

8. See Jesus' admonition, "if the blind lead the blind, both shall fall into the ditch" (Matthew 15.14). "Rousseau's ground" is given in *Émile*, ch. 5.
9. The first five books of the Old Testament are traditionally attributed to Moses; Genesis gives two versions of the creation of woman: in 1:27, God creates man and woman simultaneously; in 2:21–23, the one followed by Milton, God creates Eve out of Adam's rib.

1. The "sally" (an attack by besieged troops; an outburst of wit) is from Pope's *Epistle II, to a Lady*, "Of the Characters of Women" (1735), 51–52.
2. To outdo Cervantes' comic hero Don Quixote in ineffectual idealism, including the ideals of courtly love.

takes place of sensation. But Rousseau, and most of the male writers who have followed his steps, have warmly inculcated that the whole tendency of female education
ought to be directed to one point:—to render them pleasing.[3]

Let me reason with the supporters of this opinion who have any knowledge of
human nature, do they imagine that marriage can eradicate the habitude of life? The
woman who has only been taught to please will soon find that her charms are oblique
sunbeams, and that they cannot have much effect on her husband's heart when they
are seen every day, when the summer is passed and gone. Will she then have sufficient native energy to look into herself for comfort, and cultivate her dormant faculties? or, is it not more rational to expect that she will try to please other men; and, in
the emotions raised by the expectation of new conquests, endeavour to forget the
mortification her love or pride has received? When the husband ceases to be a
lover—and the time will inevitably come, her desire of pleasing will then grow languid, or become a spring of bitterness; and love, perhaps, the most evanescent of all
passions, gives place to jealousy or vanity.

I now speak of women who are restrained by principle or prejudice; such women,
though they would shrink from an intrigue with real abhorrence, yet, nevertheless,
wish to be convinced by the homage of gallantry that they are cruelly neglected by
their husbands; or, days and weeks are spent in dreaming of the happiness enjoyed by
congenial souls till their health is undermined and their spirits broken by discontent.
How then can the great art of pleasing be such a necessary study? it is only useful to a
mistress; the chaste wife, and serious mother, should only consider her power to
please as the polish of her virtues, and the affection of her husband as one of the
comforts that render her task less difficult and her life happier.—But, whether she be
loved or neglected, her first wish should be to make herself respectable, and not to
rely for all her happiness on a being subject to like infirmities with herself. * * *

Women ought to endeavour to purify their heart; but can they do so when their
uncultivated understandings make them entirely dependent on their senses for
employment and amusement, when no noble pursuit sets them above the little vanities of the day, or enables them to curb the wild emotions that agitate a reed over
which every passing breeze has power? To gain the affections of a virtuous man is
affectation necessary? Nature has given woman a weaker frame than man; but, to
ensure her husband's affections, must a wife, who by the exercise of her mind and
body whilst she was discharging the duties of a daughter, wife, and mother, has
allowed her constitution to retain its natural strength, and her nerves a healthy
tone, is she, I say, to condescend to use art and feign a sickly delicacy in order to
secure her husband's affection? Weakness may excite tenderness, and gratify the
arrogant pride of man; but the lordly caresses of a protector will not gratify a noble
mind that pants for, and deserves to be respected. Fondness is a poor substitute for
friendship!

In a seraglio, I grant, that all these arts are necessary; the epicure must have his
palate tickled, or he will sink into apathy; but have women so little ambition as to be
satisfied with such a condition? Can they supinely dream life away in the lap of pleasure, or the languor of weariness, rather than assert their claim to pursue reasonable
pleasures and render themselves conspicuous by practising the virtues which dignify
mankind? Surely she has not an immortal soul who can loiter life away merely
employed to adorn her person, that she may amuse the languid hours, and soften the

3. See *Émile*, ch. 5.

cares of a fellow-creature who is willing to be enlivened by her smiles and tricks, when the serious business of life is over.

Besides, the woman who strengthens her body and exercises her mind will, by managing her family and practising various virtues, become the friend, and not the humble dependent of her husband; and if she, by possessing such substantial qualities, merit his regard, she will not find it necessary to conceal her affection, nor to pretend to an unnatural coldness of constitution to excite her husband's passions. In fact, if we revert to history, we shall find that the women who have distinguished themselves have neither been the most beautiful nor the most gentle of their sex. * * *

I own it frequently happens that women who have fostered a romantic unnatural delicacy of feeling,[4] waste their lives in *imagining* how happy they should have been with a husband who could love them with a fervid increasing affection every day, and all day. But they might as well pine married as single—and would not be a jot more unhappy with a bad husband than longing for a good one. That a proper education; or, to speak with more precision, a well stored mind, would enable a woman to support a single life with dignity, I grant; but that she should avoid cultivating her taste, lest her husband should occasionally shock it, is quitting a substance for a shadow. To say the truth, I do not know of what use is an improved taste, if the individual be not rendered more independent of the casualties of life; if new sources of enjoyment, only dependent on the solitary operations of the mind, are not opened. People of taste, married or single, without distinction, will ever be disgusted by various things that touch not less observing minds. On this conclusion the argument must not be allowed to hinge; but in the whole sum of enjoyment is taste to be denominated a blessing? * * *

But to view the subject in another point of view. Do passive indolent women make the best wives? Confining our discussion to the present moment of existence, let us see how such weak creatures perform their part? Do the women who, by the attainment of a few superficial accomplishments, have strengthened the prevailing prejudice, merely contribute to the happiness of their husbands? Do they display their charms merely to amuse them? And have women, who have early imbibed notions of passive obedience, sufficient character to manage a family or educate children? So far from it, that, after surveying the history of woman, I cannot help, agreeing with the severest satirist, considering the sex as the weakest as well as the most oppressed half of the species. What does history disclose but marks of inferiority, and how few women have emancipated themselves from the galling yoke of sovereign man?—So few, that the exceptions remind me of an ingenious conjecture respecting Newton: that he was probably a being of a superior order, accidentally caged in a human body.[5] Following the same train of thinking, I have been led to imagine that the few extraordinary women who have rushed in eccentrical directions out of the orbit prescribed to their sex, were *male* spirits, confined by mistake in female frames. But if it be not philosophical to think of sex when the soul is mentioned, the inferiority must depend on the organs; or the heavenly fire, which is to ferment the clay, is not given in equal portions.[6] * * *

---

4. For example, the herd of novelists [Wollstonecraft's note, attacking the influence of popular sentimental fiction].

5. Isaac Newton (1642–1727), brilliant physicist and mathematician.

6. In the 18th century, the question whether the soul was marked by a sexual character, like the body, was widely debated. "Clay" is a familiar figure for the body.

from *Chapter 3. The Same Subject Continued*

If it be granted that woman was not created merely to gratify the appetite of man, or to be the upper servant, who provides his meals and takes care of his linen, it must follow, that the first care of those mothers or fathers, who really attend to the education of females, should be, if not to strengthen the body, at least, not to destroy the constitution by mistaken notions of beauty and female excellence; nor should girls ever be allowed to imbibe the pernicious notion that a defect can, by any chemical process of reasoning, become an excellence. In this respect, I am happy to find, that the author of one of the most instructive books, that our country has produced for children, coincides with me in opinion; I shall quote his pertinent remarks to give the force of his respectable authority to reason.[1]

But should it be proved that woman is naturally weaker than man, whence does it follow that it is natural for her to labour to become still weaker than nature intended her to be? Arguments of this cast are an insult to common sense, and savour of passion. The *divine right* of husbands, like the divine right of kings, may, it is to be hoped, in this enlightened age, be contested without danger, and, though conviction may not silence many boisterous disputants, yet, when any prevailing prejudice is attacked, the wise will consider, and leave the narrow-minded to rail with thoughtless vehemence at innovation.

The mother, who wishes to give true dignity of character to her daughter, must, regardless of the sneers of ignorance, proceed on a plan diametrically opposite to that which Rousseau has recommended with all the deluding charms of eloquence and philosophical sophistry: for his eloquence renders absurdities plausible, and his dogmatic conclusions puzzle, without convincing, those who have not ability to refute them.

Throughout the whole animal kingdom every young creature requires almost continual exercise, and the infancy of children, conformable to this intimation, should be passed in harmless gambols, that exercise the feet and hands, without requiring very minute direction from the head, or the constant attention of a nurse. In fact, the care necessary for self-preservation is the first natural exercise of the understanding, as little inventions to amuse the present moment unfold the imagination. But these wise designs of nature are counteracted by mistaken fondness or blind zeal. The child is not left a moment to its own direction, particularly a girl, and thus rendered dependent—dependence is called natural.

To preserve personal beauty, woman's glory! the limbs and faculties are cramped with worse than Chinese bands,[2] and the sedentary life which they are

1. "If women are in general feeble both in body and mind, it arises less from nature than from education. We encourage a vicious indolence and inactivity, which we falsely call delicacy; instead of hardening their minds by the severer principles of reason and philosophy, we breed them to useless arts, which terminate in vanity and sensuality. In most of the countries which I had visited, they are taught nothing of an higher nature than a few modulations of the voice, or useless postures of the body; their time is consumed in sloth or trifles, and trifles become the only pursuits capable of interesting them. We seem to forget, that it is upon the qualities of the female sex that our own domestic comforts and the education of our children must depend. And what are the comforts or the education which a race of beings, corrupted from their infancy, and unacquainted with all the duties of life, are fitted to bestow? To touch a musical instrument with useless skill, to exhibit their natural or affected graces to the eyes of indolent and debauched young men, to dissipate their husband's patrimony [his inheritance as well as his children's] in riotous and unnecessary [sic] expences, these are the only arts cultivated by women in most of the polished nations I had seen. And the consequences are uniformly such as may be expected to proceed from such polluted sources, private misery and public servitude . . . ." Mr. [Thomas] Day's *Sandford and Merton*, Vol III [Wollstonecraft's note].

2. The Chinese practice of binding girls' feet to keep them delicately small often left them crippled for life, reinforcing dependency.

condemned to live, whilst boys frolic in the open air, weakens the muscles and relaxes the nerves.—As for Rousseau's remarks, which have since been echoed by several writers, that they have naturally, that is from their birth, independent of education, a fondness for dolls, dressing, and talking[3]—they are so puerile as not to merit a serious refutation. That a girl, condemned to sit for hours together listening to the idle chat of weak nurses, or to attend at her mother's toilet,[4] will endeavour to join the conversation, is, indeed, very natural; and that she will imitate her mother or aunts, and amuse herself by adorning her lifeless doll, as they do in dressing her, poor innocent babe! is undoubtedly a most natural consequence. For men of the greatest abilities have seldom had sufficient strength to rise above the surrounding atmosphere; and, if the page of genius have always been blurred by the prejudices of the age, some allowance should be made for a sex, who, like kings, always see things through a false medium.

Pursuing these reflections, the fondness for dress, conspicuous in women, may be easily accounted for, without supposing it the result of a desire to please the sex on which they are dependent. The absurdity, in short, of supposing that a girl is naturally a coquette, and that a desire connected with the impulse of nature to propagate the species, should appear even before an improper education has, by heating the imagination, called it forth prematurely, is so unphilosophical, that such a sagacious observer as Rousseau would not have adopted it, if he had not been accustomed to make reason give way to his desire of singularity, and truth to a favorite paradox.[5] * * *

I have, probably, had an opportunity of observing more girls in their infancy than J. J. Rousseau[6]—I can recollect my own feelings, and I have looked steadily around me; yet, so far from coinciding with him in opinion respecting the first dawn of the female character, I will venture to affirm, that a girl, whose spirits have not been damped by inactivity, or innocence tainted by false shame, will always be a romp, and the doll will never excite attention unless confinement allows her no alternative. Girls and boys, in short, would play harmlessly together, if the distinction of sex was not inculcated long before nature makes any difference.—I will go further, and affirm, as an indisputable fact, that most of the women, in the circle of my observation, who have acted like rational creatures, or shewn any vigour of intellect, have accidentally been allowed to run wild—as some of the elegant formers of the fair sex would insinuate. * * *

I once knew a weak woman of fashion, who was more than commonly proud of her delicacy and sensibility. She thought a distinguishing taste and puny appetite the height of all human perfection, and acted accordingly.—I have seen this weak sophisticated being neglect all the duties of life, yet recline with self-complacency on a sofa, and boast of her want of appetite as a proof of delicacy that extended to, or, perhaps, arose from, her exquisite sensibility: for it is difficult to render intelligible such ridiculous jargon.—Yet, at the moment, I have seen her insult a worthy old gentlewoman, whom unexpected misfortunes had made dependent on her ostentatious bounty, and who, in better days, had claims on her gratitude. Is it possible that a human creature could have become such a weak and depraved being, if, like the Sybarites,[7] dissolved in luxury, every thing like virtue had not been worn away, or

---

3. See *Émile*, ch. 5.
4. Grooming and dressing.
5. See *Émile*, ch. 5.
6. Wollstonecraft was the eldest sister in a family with

three girls and had also worked as a governess.
7. The inhabitants of a 5th-century Greek colony in Italy famed for luxurious decadence.

never impressed by precept, a poor substitute, it is true, for cultivation of mind, though it serves as a fence against vice?

Such a woman is not a more irrational monster than some of the Roman emperors, who were depraved by lawless power. Yet, since kings have been more under the restraint of law, and the curb, however weak, of honour, the records of history are not filled with such unnatural instances of folly and cruelty, nor does the despotism that kills virtue and genius in the bud, hover over Europe with that destructive blast which desolates Turkey, and renders the men, as well as the soil, unfruitful.[8] * * *

It is time to effect a revolution in female manners—time to restore to them their lost dignity—and make them, as a part of the human species, labour by reforming themselves to reform the world. It is time to separate unchangeable morals from local manners.—If men be demi-gods—why let us serve them! And if the dignity of the female soul be as disputable as that of animals—if their reason does not afford sufficient light to direct their conduct whilst unerring instinct is denied—they are surely of all creatures the most miserable! and, bent beneath the iron hand of destiny, must submit to be a *fair defect* in creation. But to justify the ways of Providence respecting them, by pointing out some irrefragable reason for thus making such a large portion of mankind accountable and not accountable, would puzzle the subtilest casuist.[9] * * *

I must relieve myself by drawing a different picture.

Let fancy now present a woman with a tolerable understanding, for I do not wish to leave the line of mediocrity, whose constitution, strengthened by exercise, has allowed her body to acquire its full vigour; her mind, at the same time, gradually expanding itself to comprehend the moral duties of life, and in what human virtue and dignity consist.

Formed thus by the discharge of the relative duties of her station, she marries from affection, without losing sight of prudence, and looking beyond matrimonial felicity, she secures her husband's respect before it is necessary to exert mean arts to please him and feed a dying flame, which nature doomed to expire when the object became familiar, when friendship and forbearance take place of a more ardent affection.—This is the natural death of love, and domestic peace is not destroyed by struggles to prevent its extinction. I also suppose the husband to be virtuous; or she is still more in want of independent principles.

Fate, however, breaks this tie.—She is left a widow, perhaps, without a sufficient provision; but she is not desolate! The pang of nature is felt; but after time has softened sorrow into melancholy resignation, her heart turns to her children with redoubled fondness, and anxious to provide for them, affection gives a sacred heroic cast to her maternal duties. She thinks that not only the eye sees her virtuous efforts from whom all her comfort now must flow, and whose approbation is life; but her imagination, a little abstracted and exalted by grief, dwells on the fond hope that the eyes which her trembling hand closed, may still see how she subdues every wayward passion to fulfil the double duty of being the father as well as the mother of her children. Raised to heroism by misfortunes, she represses the first faint dawning of a natural inclination, before it ripens into love, and in the bloom of life forgets her sex—forgets the pleasure of an awakening passion, which might again have been inspired and returned. She no longer thinks of pleasing, and conscious dignity prevents her from priding herself on account of the praise which her conduct demands. Her children have her love, and her brightest hopes are beyond the grave, where her imagination often strays.

---

8. Both the hot, dusty winds from the deserts to the south and the infamously despotic Ottoman Empire.
9. For "fair defect," see *Paradise Lost* 8.891–92; Milton begins his epic invoking divine inspiration to "justify the ways of God to men" (1.26); a casuist is one who debates ethical questions with overtones of dishonesty.

I think I see her surrounded by her children, reaping the reward of her care. The intelligent eye meets hers, whilst health and innocence smile on their chubby cheeks, and as they grow up the cares of life are lessened by their grateful attention. She lives to see the virtues which she endeavoured to plant on principles, fixed into habits, to see her children attain a strength of character sufficient to enable them to endure adversity without forgetting their mother's example.

The task of life thus fulfilled, she calmly waits for the sleep of death, and rising from the grave, may say—Behold, thou gavest me a talent—and here are five talents.[1]

I wish to sum up what I have said in a few words, for I here throw down my gauntlet, and deny the existence of sexual virtues, not excepting modesty.[2] For man and woman, truth, if I understand the meaning of the word, must be the same; yet the fanciful female character, so prettily drawn by poets and novelists, demanding the sacrifice of truth and sincerity, virtue becomes a relative idea, having no other foundation than utility, and of that utility men pretend arbitrarily to judge, shaping it to their own convenience.

Women, I allow, may have different duties to fulfil; but they are *human* duties, and the principles that should regulate the discharge of them, I sturdily maintain, must be the same. * * *

from *Chapter 13. Some Instances of the Folly Which the Ignorance of Women Generates; with Concluding Reflections on the Moral Improvement That a Revolution in Female Manners Might Naturally Be Expected to Produce*
[CONCLUDING REFLECTIONS]

That women at present are by ignorance rendered foolish or vicious, is, I think, not to be disputed; and, that the most salutary effects tending to improve mankind might be expected from a REVOLUTION in female manners, appears, at least, with a face of probability, to rise out of the observation. For as marriage has been termed the parent of those endearing charities which draw man from the brutal herd, the corrupting intercourse that wealth, idleness, and folly, produce between the sexes, is more universally injurious to morality than all the other vices of mankind collectively considered. To adulterous lust the most sacred duties are sacrificed, because before marriage, men, by a promiscuous intimacy with women, learned to consider love as a selfish gratification—learned to separate it not only from esteem, but from the affection merely built on habit, which mixes a little humanity with it. Justice and friendship are also set at defiance, and that purity of taste is vitiated which would naturally lead a man to relish an artless display of affection rather than affected airs. But that noble simplicity of affection, which dares to appear unadorned, has few attractions for the libertine, though it be the charm, which by cementing the matrimonial tie, secures to the pledges of a warmer passion the necessary parental attention; for children will never

---

1. An extravagant rewriting of Jesus' parable of the talents (Matthew 25.15–28), on the duty to make good use of God's gifts. A master, having given one servant five talents (a talent is a silver coin worth about $1,000 today), another two, and another only one, is pleased to learn that first two have doubled their money; but he is so enraged at the timidity of the third servant, who has only buried his talent, that he takes the money away from him

and gives it to the first servant.
2. Wollstonecraft is using an image of male warfare: to throw down one's gauntlet, the glove of combat armor, is a challenge to combat. By "sexual virtues," she means sex-specific; "modesty" (usually regarded as a "feminine" characteristic) refers to the general moral discipline of self-restraint and respect for others desirable in both sexes.

be properly educated till friendship subsists between parents. Virtue flies from a house divided against itself—and a whole legion of devils take up their residence there.[1]

The affection of husbands and wives cannot be pure when they have so few sentiments in common, and when so little confidence is established at home, as must be the case when their pursuits are so different. That intimacy from which tenderness should flow, will not, cannot subsist between the vicious.

Contending, therefore, that the sexual distinction which men have so warmly insisted upon, is arbitrary, I have dwelt on an observation, that several sensible men, with whom I have conversed on the subject, allowed to be well founded; and it is simply this, that the little chastity to be found amongst men, and consequent disregard of modesty, tend to degrade both sexes; and further, that the modesty of women, characterized as such, will often be only the artful veil of wantonness instead of being the natural reflection of purity, till modesty be universally respected.[2]

From the tyranny of man, I firmly believe, the greater number of female follies proceed; and the cunning, which I allow makes at present a part of their character, I likewise have repeatedly endeavoured to prove, is produced by oppression.

Were not dissenters,[3] for instance, a class of people, with strict truth, characterized as cunning? And may I not lay some stress on this fact to prove, that when any power but reason curbs the free spirit of man, dissimulation is practised, and the various shifts of art are naturally called forth? Great attention to decorum, which was carried to a degree of scrupulosity, and all that puerile bustle about trifles and consequential solemnity, which Butler's caricature of a dissenter, brings before the imagination, shaped their persons as well as their minds in the mould of prim littleness.[4] I speak collectively, for I know how many ornaments to human nature have been enrolled amongst sectaries; yet, I assert, that the same narrow prejudice for their sect, which women have for their families, prevailed in the dissenting part of the community, however worthy in other respects; and also that the same timid prudence, or headstrong efforts, often disgraced the exertions of both. Oppression thus formed many of the features of their character perfectly to coincide with that of the oppressed half of mankind; or is it not notorious that dissenters were, like women, fond of deliberating together, and asking advice of each other, till by a complication of little contrivances, some little end was brought about? A similar attention to preserve their reputation was conspicuous in the dissenting and female world, and was produced by a similar cause.

Asserting the rights which women in common with men ought to contend for, I have not attempted to extenuate their faults; but to prove them to be the natural consequence of their education and station in society. If so, it is reasonable to suppose that they will change their character, and correct their vices and follies, when they are allowed to be free in a physical, moral, and civil sense.[5]

1. An allusion to Jesus' lesson that "if a house be divided against itself, that house cannot stand" (Mark 3.25).
2. By chastity and modesty, Wollstonecraft means sexual self-control and self-discipline; male chastity entails fidelity, not sexual self-denial, in marriage.
3. Those who dissented from the established Church of England to form independent religious sects; many of Wollstonecraft's friends were dissenters.
4. Samuel Butler's mock-heroic, satirical poem Hudibras (1663–1678) takes aim at Puritans (dissenters who

formed the commonwealth government after the execution of Charles I); Sir Hudibras, pedant and hypocrite, is a country justice who sets out to reform England of various popular entertainments.
5. I had further enlarged on the advantages which might reasonably be expected to result from an improvement in female manners, towards the general reformation of society; but it appeared to me that such reflections would more properly close the last volume. [Wollstonecraft's note; no further volumes were published].

Let woman share the rights and she will emulate the virtues of man; for she must grow more perfect when emancipated, or justify the authority that chains such a weak being to her duty.—If the latter, it will be expedient to open a fresh trade with Russia for whips; a present which a father should always make to his son-in-law on his wedding day, that a husband may keep his whole family in order by the same means; and without any violation of justice reign, wielding this sceptre, sole master of his house, because he is the only being in it who has reason:—the divine, indefeasible earthly sovereignty breathed into man by the Master of the universe. Allowing this position, women have not any inherent rights to claim; and, by the same rule, their duties vanish, for rights and duties are inseparable.

Be just then, O ye men of understanding! and mark not more severely what women do amiss, than the vicious tricks of the horse or the ass for whom ye provide provender—and allow her the privileges of ignorance, to whom ye deny the rights of reason, or ye will be worse than Egyptian task-masters, expecting virtue where nature has not given understanding!

A "VINDICATION" IN CONTEXT
The Wollstonecraft Controversy and the Rights of Women

Wollstonecraft's *Vindication of the Rights of Woman* challenged an age when women had no legal standing as daughters or wives, being under the coverture (legal identity) of their fathers and husbands. They could not own property, form contracts, or conduct business. "Obedience" was expected behavior, sanctioned by religion, law, and custom; a rebellious daughter (one, for instance, refusing her father's choice of her husband) could be disowned; divorce was granted only by husbands, who retained custody of all property (including dowry) as well as the children (a prime reason many women remained in abusive marriages). Female suffrage was so outrageous a notion that it could not be debated for another century or so. Far from having any power to change the law by vote, women did not even have legal status, or any representatives for their concerns in Parliament. It was not until 1870 that The Married Woman's Property Act was passed, allowing such women to keep their earnings, and not until 1882 that it was amended to allow them to keep the property, including personal property, that they brought to the marriage (dowry) or acquired during it; this act also gave a woman the right to enter legal contracts and to sue in courts, as well as a legally distinct identity from her husband.

England was not alone in the 1790s in resisting change: even in France the case for women's rights fared so poorly with the Revolutionary government that its champions were sent to the guillotine. French women did not secure the vote until 1944, nearly a century after American feminists presented the Declaration of Sentiments and Resolutions at Seneca Falls. The way was paved for these changes by the constant debate from the 1790s onward over systems of female education, women's rights, and social policy—a debate that even among women involved ideologically disparate, even opposed, commitments. When Maria Edgeworth proposed to Anna Barbauld that they coedit a periodical featuring "the literary ladies of the present day," Barbauld declined on the question of common cause: "There is no bond of union among literary women, any more than among literary men; different sentiments and different connections separate them much more than the joint interest of their sex would unite them. Mrs. Hannah More would not write along with you or me, and we should probably hesitate at joining Miss Hays, or if she were living, Mrs. Godwin" [Wollstonecraft]. Our selections from this tremendous body of literature show the wide range of concerns in this debate and the wide range of responses it involved, in particular to Wollstonecraft—a lightning rod in this charged atmosphere.

━━━━◆━━━━

Catherine Macaulay
1731–1791

The daughter of a wealthy landowner in Kent and an heiress of a London banker, Macaulay grew up in comfort, and was left well off at the death of her husband, an eminent London obstetrician, in 1776. Her major work is the controversial eight-volume *History of England from the Accession of James I to that of the Brunswick Line* (the current monarchy), published over twenty years (1763–1783). Its defense of Cromwell's regicidal government and its generally antimonarchal Whig sympathies endeared her to Wollstonecraft, poet Thomas Gray, and even Prime Minister William Pitt, even as it earned Edmund Burke's contempt of her as a "republican Virago." Not surprisingly, her political writings were more popular in France and America than in England. In 1785, she visited George and Martha Washington at Mount Vernon and later corresponded with them, as well as with John Adams and Benjamin Franklin. But as with Wollstonecraft, her politics produced enemies and vicious misogynist attacks on her private life, attacks gleefully sharpened by her marriage in 1779, at the age of fifty-seven, to a twenty-one-year-old William Graham.

    Letters on Education, published in 1790, deeply influenced Wollstonecraft, who called Macaulay "the woman of the greatest abilities, undoubtedly, that this country has ever produced." She did not live to see the publication of *Rights of Woman*, in which Wollstonecraft praises her "strong and clear" intellect and echoes many of her polemics: the attack on the gender ideologies proffered by Rousseau and Pope and on the cultural systems that educate women into "a state of slavery"; a disdain of "coquetry" (the female art of manipulating men through their passions); a scathing critique of the language of female compliments; and advocacy of coeducation and a gender-neutral standard of "rational" conduct.

from Letters on Education
from Letter 22. No Characteristic Difference in Sex

The great difference that is observable in the characters of the sexes, Hortensia,[1] as they display themselves in the scenes of social life, has given rise to much false speculation on the natural qualities of the female mind.—For though the doctrine of innate ideas, and innate affections, are in a great measure exploded by the learned, yet few persons reason so closely and so accurately on abstract subjects as, through a long chain of deductions, to bring forth a conclusion which in no respect militates with their premises.

    It is a long time before the crowd give up opinions they have been taught to look upon with respect. * * * It is from such causes that the notion of a sexual difference in the human character has, with very few exceptions, universally prevailed from the

---

1. The fictitious recipient of the letter.

earliest times, and the pride of one sex, and the ignorance and vanity of the other, have helped to support an opinion which a close observation of Nature, and a more accurate way of reasoning, would disprove.

It must be confessed, that the virtues of the males among the human species, though mixed and blended with a variety of vices and errors, have displayed a bolder and a more consistent picture of excellence than female nature has hitherto done. It is on these reasons that, when we compliment the appearance of a more than ordinary energy in the female mind, we call it masculine; and hence it is, that Pope has elegantly said *a perfect woman's but a softer man*.[2] And if we take in the consideration, that there can be but one rule of moral excellence for beings made of the same materials, organized after the same manner, and subjected to similar laws of Nature, we must either agree with Mr. Pope, or we must reverse the proposition, and say, that *a perfect man is a woman formed after a coarser mold*. The difference that actually does subsist between the sexes, is too flattering for men to be willingly imputed to accident; for what accident occasions, wisdom might correct; and it is better, says Pride, to give up the advantages we might derive from the perfection of our fellow associates, than to own that Nature has been just in the equal distribution of her favours. These are the sentiments of the men: but mark how readily they are yielded to by the women; not from humility I assure you, but merely to preserve with character those fond vanities on which they set their hearts. No; suffer them to idolize their persons, to throw away their life in the pursuit of trifles, and to indulge in the gratification of the meaner passions, and they will heartily join in the sentence of their degradation.

Among the most strenuous asserters of a sexual difference in character, Rousseau is the most conspicuous, both on account of that warmth of sentiment which distinguishes all his writings, and the eloquence of his compositions: but never did enthusiasm and the love of paradox, those enemies to philosophical disquisition, appear in more strong opposition to plain sense than in Rousseau's definition of this difference.[3] He sets out with a supposition, that Nature intended the subjection of the one sex to the other; that consequently there must be an inferiority of intellect in the subjected party; but as man is a very imperfect being, and apt to play the capricious tyrant, Nature, to bring things nearer to an equality, bestowed on the woman such attractive graces, and such an insinuating address, as to turn the balance on the other scale. Thus Nature, in a giddy mood, recedes from her purposes, and subjects prerogative to an influence which must produce confusion and disorder in the system of human affairs. Rousseau saw this objection; and in order to obviate it, he has made up a moral person of the union of the two sexes, which, for contradiction and absurdity, outdoes every metaphysical riddle that was ever formed in the schools. In short, it is not reason, it is not wit; it is pride and sensuality that speak in Rousseau, and, in this instance, has lowered the man of genius to the licentious pedant. * * * for so little did a wise and just Providence intend to make the condition of slavery an unalterable law of female nature, that in the same proportion as the male sex have consulted the interest of their own happiness, they have relaxed in their tyranny over women; and such is

---

2. A slight misquotation of *Epistle II*, "Of the Characters of Women": "Heaven, when it strives to polish all it can / Its last best work, but forms a softer man" (271–272).

3. Referring to Rousseau's arguments throughout *Émile*, especially ch. 5 ("Sophy").

their use in the system of mundane creation, and such their natural influence over the male mind, that were these advantages properly exerted, they might carry every point of any importance to their honour and happiness. However, till that period arrives in which women will act wisely, we will amuse ourselves in talking of their follies.

The situation and education of women, Hortensia, is precisely that which must necessarily tend to corrupt and debilitate both the powers of mind and body. From a false notion of beauty and delicacy, their system of nerves is depraved before they come out of their nursery; and this kind of depravity has more influence over the mind, and consequently over morals, than is commonly apprehended. But it would be well if such causes only acted towards the debasement of the sex; their moral education is, if possible, more absurd than their physical. The principles and nature of virtue, which is never properly explained to boys, is kept quite a mystery to girls. They are told indeed, that they must abstain from those vices which are contrary to their personal happiness, or they will be regarded as criminals, both by God and man; but all the higher parts of rectitude, every thing that ennobles our being, and that renders us both innoxious and useful, is either not taught, or is taught in such a manner as to leave no proper impression on the mind. This is so obvious a truth, that the defects of female education have ever been a fruitful topic of declamation for the moralist; but not one of this class of writers have laid down any judicious rules for amendment. Whilst we still retain the absurd notion of a sexual excellence, it will mitigate against the perfecting a plan of education for either sex. The judicious Addison animadverts on the absurdity of bringing a young lady up with no higher idea of the end of education than to make her agreeable to a husband, and confining the necessary excellence for this happy acquisition to the mere graces of person.[4]

Every parent and tutor may not express himself in the same manner as is marked out by Addison; yet certain it is, that the admiration of the other sex is held out to women as the highest honour they can attain; and whilst this is considered as their *summum bonum* [highest good] and the beauty of their persons the chief *desideratum* [thing wanted] of men, Vanity, and its companion Envy, must taint, in their characters, every native and every acquired excellence. Nor can you, Hortensia, deny, that these qualities, when united to ignorance, are fully equal to the engendering and riveting all those vices and foibles which are peculiar to the female sex; vices and foibles which have caused them to be considered, in ancient times, as beneath cultivation, and in modern days have subjected them to the censure and ridicule of writers of all descriptions, from the deep thinking philosopher to the man of ton[5] and gallantry, who, by the bye, sometimes distinguishes himself by qualities which are not greatly superior to those he despises in women. Nor can I better illustrate the truth of this observation than by the following picture, to be found in the polite and gallant Chesterfield. "Women," says his Lordship, "are only children of a larger growth. They have an entertaining tattle, sometimes wit; but for solid reasoning, and good sense, I never in my life knew one that had it, or who acted or reasoned in consequence of it for four and twenty hours together. A man of sense only trifles with them, plays with

---

4. Joseph Addison (1672–1719), essayist and poet. Macaulay wrongly attributes to Addison an unsigned essay on this subject in *The Spectator* by his collaborator, Richard Steele. Animadverts: criticizes.
5. Fashion.

them, humours and flatters them, as he does an engaging child; but he neither consults them, nor trusts them in serious matters." [6]

⊷ ⊷⊱⊰⊱ ⊶

Richard Polwhele
1760–1838

Reverend Polwhele was educated at Oxford, first training for the law. He wrote poetry, histories, journalism, theological tracts, and translations of Greek literature, and was a frequent contributor to some leading conservative journals of his day, including the *Anti-Jacobin*. Among his mother's friends were two outspoken writers about the situation of women, Hannah More and Catherine Macaulay, whom he met in 1777. He participated in an elaborate birthday celebration for Macaulay, writing an ode for her that he included in his first volume of poetry, published in 1777. *The Unsex'd Females* appeared in 1798, at the end of a decade of vigorous debate about women's rights inaugurated by Macaulay's *Letters on Education* (1790) and Wollstonecraft's *Rights of Woman* (1792).

By 1798, both Macaulay and Wollstonecraft were dead, and a reactionary political climate as well as the scandal of Wollstonecraft's life had dealt "rights of woman" a serious setback. The only voices to command popular sympathy were calls for female education in modest, virtuous intelligence, trained to the values of piety, obedience, and domestic duty, and devoted to the formation of Christian daughters, wives, and mothers. Fresh from reading Godwin's memoir of Wollstonecraft, Polwhele, with tones tipping from nasty to horrified, castigated its revelations in a review for the *European Magazine* and in *The Unsex'd Females*. With an explicit political agenda, the poem casts radicals such as Wollstonecraft as "unnatural," "licentious," anti-Christian revolutionaries, driven by the ideology of godless "Reason." Yet the animosities extend to a strange sorority. In addition to Wollstonecraft and her allies, Helen Maria Williams and Mary Hays, its indictment includes women of quite different views, having in common with the radicals only a public voice: poet and novelist Charlotte Smith, initially a sympathizer with the French Revolution, but famous by 1793 for *The Emigrants* (a long poem expressing her outrage at the massacre of French aristocrats and her sympathy for those forced to flee) and by the decade's end, an outspoken reactionary; Anna Barbauld, an abolitionist, but no revolutionary, no fan of Wollstonecraft, and very qualified on women's rights; Mary Robinson, advocate of abolition but not primarily a political writer; Anne Yearsley, advocate for the poor and an abolitionist but also a voice of anti-Revolution sympathies in *Reflections on the Death of Louis XVI* (1793) and *An Elegy on Marie Antoinette* (1795). So as not to seem flatly misogynist, Polwhele ends his poem celebrating conservative eighteenth-century bluestocking women, a "kindred train" who "influence" through "modest virtue," and allied with such conservatives as Horace Walpole, Joshua Reynolds, Samuel Johnson, and Edmund Burke: the "Queen of the Blues" Elizabeth Montagu (1720–1800), scholar and poet Elizabeth Carter (1717–1806), poet and educational theorist Hester Chapone (1727–1801), poet Anna Seward (1743–1809), woman of letters Hester Thrale Piozzi (1741–1821), novelists Frances Burney (1752–1840) and Anne Radcliffe (1764–1823). He ventriloquizes his praise through the voice of their disciple Hannah More, whose views on the "natural" differences of the sexes and their separate spheres he warmly endorses. Polwhele's numerous footnotes, which nearly overwhelm his poem, are not supplementary but an important part of his polemic. Some of these notes, especially ones on the question of women's rights and ones relevant to other writers in this volume, are included in the excerpt here.

---

6. *Letters to His Son* no. 294 (16 Nov. 1752), also cited in *Rights of Woman*, ch. 4. Philip Chesterfield (1694–1773), statesman, author, and wit, wrote letters of advice to his illegitimate son from age five until his own death; published in 1774, these became famous (or infamous) for their comments on sexual behavior and rituals.

from The Unsex'd Females

Thou, who with all the poet's genuine rage,
Thy "fine eye rolling" o'er "this aweful age,"[1]
Where polish'd life unfolds its various views,
Hast mark'd the magic influence of the muse;
5   Sever'd, with nice precision, from her beam
Of genial power, her false and feeble gleam;
Expos'd the Sciolist's[2] vain-glorious claim,
And boldly thwarted Innovation's aim,
Where witlings wildly think, or madly dare,[3]
10   With Honor, Virtue, Truth, announcing war;
Survey with me, what ne'er our fathers saw,
A female band despising NATURE's law,[4]
As "proud defiance"[5] flashes from their arms,
And vengeance smothers all their softer charms.
15   *I* shudder at the new unpictur'd scene,
Where unsex'd woman vaunts the imperious mien;
Where girls, affecting to dismiss the heart,
Invoke the Proteus of petrific art;[6]
With equal ease, in body or in mind,
20   To Gallic freaks or Gallic faith[7] resign'd,
The crane-like neck, as Fashion bids, lay bare,
Or frizzle, bold in front, their borrow'd hair;°   *wigs*
Scarce by a gossamery film carest,
Sport, in full view, the meretricious breast;[8]
25   Loose the chaste cincture,[9] where the graces shone,
And languish'd all the Loves, the ambrosial zone;

---

1. The addressee is another Tory conservative scourge, Thomas James Mathias, whose long satirical poem *The Pursuits of Literature* (1794–1797), also encased in footnotes, inspired Polwhele's. In his Preface to the 4th dialogue of this popular poem (16 editions), Mathias lamented that "our *unsexed* female writers now instruct, or confuse, us and themselves, in the labyrinth of politics, or turn us wild with Gallic frenzy"—French-inspired ideas and fashions. He begins representing himself "not unconscious of this awful age" (1.7), echoing Milton's representation of himself and other visionary poets as chastisers of their own age, "fall'n on evil days" (*Paradise Lost* 7.25). Theseus in *A Midsummer Night's Dream* describes "the poet's eye, in a fine frenzy rolling" (5.1.12).
2. Displayer of superficial learning.
3. "Greatly think, or nobly die." Pope [Polwhele's note, slightly misquoting l.10 of *Elegy to the Memory of an Unfortunate Lady*, about a woman who seems to have committed suicide in despair of love].
4. Nature is the grand basis of all laws human and divine: and the woman, who has no regard to nature, either in the decoration of her person, or the culture of her mind, will soon "walk after the flesh, in the lust of uncleanness, and despise government" [Polwhele's note, quoting 2 Peter 2:10; Rousseau and other defenders of sexual inequality routinely invoke "Natural" or "Nature's" law].
5. "A troop came next, who crowns and armour wore, / And proud defiance in their looks they bore." Pope. The Amazonian band—the female Quixotes of the new philosophy, are, here, too justly characterised [Polwhele's

note]. The quotation is from *The Temple of Fame* (1711, ll.342–343), the troop answering "the direful trump of Slander." The Amazons, legendary race of warrior women from Scythia, near the Black Sea, frequently assailed the Greeks; they were fabled to have burnt off the right breast (*a*, without; *mazos*, breast) to facilitate use of bow or javelin; the term is used, not always disparagingly, for any "masculine" woman, or, disparagingly, as a synonym for virago. Quixotes (from Cervantes' hero) are impractical idealists.
6. Proteus: god able to change shapes at will; petrific: able to turn to stone, as if a Medusa, an unfeeling woman.
7. French fashions and the new French (Godless) religion.
8. To "sport a face," is a cant phrase in one of our Universities, by which is meant an impudent obtrusion of a man's person in company. It is not inapplicable, perhaps, to the open bosom—a fashion which we have never invited or sanctioned. The fashions of France, which have been always imitated by the English, were, heretofore, unexceptionable in a moral point of view; since, however ridiculous or absurd, they were innocent. But they have now their source among prostitutes—among women of the most abandoned character. [Polwhele's note]. Meretricious: whorish. An 18th-century French aristocratic fashion was a fancy-gown neckline plunged below the bosom, displaying it bare.
9. A wide belt surrounding the waist and sometimes the bosom, as a girdle; it is "chaste" for concealing breasts and hips.

As lordly domes inspire dramatic rage,
Court prurient Fancy to the private stage;
With bliss botanic[1] as their bosoms heave,
30 Still pluck forbidden fruit, with mother Eve,
For puberty in sighing florets pant,
Or point the prostitution of a plant;
Dissect[2] its organ of unhallow'd lust,
And fondly gaze the titillating[3] dust;
35 With liberty's sublimer views expand,
And o'er the wreck of kingdoms[4] sternly stand;
And, frantic, midst the democratic storm,
Pursue, Philosophy! thy phantom-form.
    Far other is the female shape and mind,
40 By modest luxury heighten'd and refin'd;
Those limbs, that figure, tho' by Fashion grac'd,
By Beauty polish'd, and adorn'd by Taste;
That soul, whose harmony perennial flows,
In Music trembles, and in Color glows;
45 Which bids sweet Poesy reclaim the praise
With faery light to gild fastidious days,
From sullen clouds relieve domestic care,
And melt in smiles the withering frown of war.
Ah! once the female Muse, to NATURE true,
50 The unvalued store from FANCY, FEELING drew;
Won, from the grasp of woe, the roseate hours,
Cheer'd life's dim vale, and strew'd the grave with flowers.
    But lo! where, pale amidst the wild,[5] she draws

1. Botany has lately become a fashionable amusement with the ladies. But how the study of the sexual system of plants can accord with female modesty, I am not able to comprehend. I had first written: "More eager for illicit knowlege [sic] pant, / With lustful boys anatomize a plant; / The virtues of its dust prolific speak, / Or point its pistill with unblushing cheek." I have, several times, seen boys and girls botanizing together [Polwhele's note]. Such judgment of the immodesty of botanizing was probably fueled by Erasmus Darwin, whose popular poem, *The Botanic Garden*, especially Part II, *The Loves of the Plants* (1789; 1791), is explicit about sexual organs and activity.
2. Miss Wollstonecraft does not blush to say, in an introduction to a book designed for the use of young ladies, that, "in order to lay the axe at the root of corruption, it would be proper to familiarize the sexes to an unreserved discussion of those topics, which are generally avoided in conversation from a principle of false delicacy; and that it would be right to speak of the organs of generation as freely as we mention our eyes or our hands." To such language our botanizing girls are doubtless familiarized: and, they are in a fair way of becoming worthy disciples of Miss W. If they do not take heed to their ways, they will soon exchange the blush of modesty for the bronze of impudence [Polwhele's note, alluding to Luke 3.9]. He misrepresents Wollstonecraft's statement in "Introductory Address to Parents," *Elements of Morality, For the Use of Children* (1792): concerned with masturbation and other "impure" practices, she contends that "the most efficacious method to root out this dreadful evil, which poisons the source of human happiness, would be to speak to children of the organs of generation as freely as we speak of the other parts of the body, and explain to them the noble use which they were designed for, and how they may be injured." In *Rights of Woman* (ch. 7: "Modesty") she refutes as "absurd" the "gross idea" that botany is inconsistent with female modesty, and lists it among the subjects that boys and girls might study together (ch. 12: "On National Education").
3. "Each pungent grain of titillating dust." Pope; "The prolific dust"—of the botanist [Polwhele's note, alluding to the "Charge of *Snuff*"—"The pungent Grains of titillating Dust"—Belinda hurls at her adversary in *The Rape of the Lock* (5.84)].
4. The female advocates of Democracy in this country, though they have had no opportunity of imitating the French ladies, in their atrocious acts of cruelty; have yet assumed a stern serenity in the contemplation of those savage excesses. "To express their abhorrence of royalty, they (the French ladies) threw away the character of their sex, and bit the amputated limbs of their murdered countrymen.—I say this on the authority of a young gentleman who saw it.—I am sorry to add, that the relation, accompanied with looks of horror and disgust, only provoked a contemptuous smile from an illuminated British fair-one." See Robinson [Polwhele's note, quoting *Proofs of a Conspiracy*].
5. "A wild, where flowers and weeds promiscuous shoot; / A garden tempting with forbidden fruit." Pope [Polwhele's note, quoting *Essay on Man* (1733): *Epistle I*, 7–8].

Each precept cold from sceptic Reason's[6] vase;
55   Pours with rash arm the turbid stream along,
        And in the foaming torrent whelms the throng.[7]
            Alas! her pride sophistic° flings a gloom,   *specious*
        To chase, sweet Innocence! thy vernal bloom,
        Of each light joy to damp the genial glow,
60   And with new terrors clothe the groupe of woe,
        Quench the pure daystar° in oblivion deep,   *sun*
        And, Death! restore thy "long, unbroken sleep."[8]
            See Wollstonecraft, whom no decorum checks,
        Arise, the intrepid champion of her sex;
65   O'er humbled man assert the sovereign claim,
        And slight the timid blush[9] of virgin fame.
            "Go, go (she cries) ye tribes of melting maids,
        Go, screen your softness in sequester'd shades;
        With plaintive whispers woo the unconscious grove,
70   And feebly perish, as depis'd ye love.
        What tho' the fine Romances of Rousseau
        Bid the frame flutter, and the bosom glow;
        Tho' the rapt Bard, your empire fond to own,
        Fall prostrate and adore your living throne,
75   The living throne his hands presum'd to rear,
        Its seat a simper, and its base a tear;[1]
        Soon shall the sex disdain the illusive sway,
        And wield the sceptre in yon blaze of day;
        Ere long, each little artifice discard,
80   No more by weakness[2] winning fond regard;
        Nor eyes, that sparkle from their blushes, roll,
        Nor catch the languors of the sick'ning soul,
        Nor the quick flutter, nor the coy reserve,
        But nobly boast the firm gymnastic nerve;[3]
85   Nor more affect with Delicacy's fan
        To hide the emotion from congenial man;
        To the bold heights where glory beams, aspire,
        Blend mental energy with Passion's fire,
        Surpass their rivals in the powers of mind

6. A troubled stream only, can proceed from the vase of scepticism [Polwhele's note, alluding to the Revolutionaries' (Godless) ideology of "Reason"].

7. "Raging waves, foaming out their own shame"—St. Jude. Such were those infamous publications of Paine and others, which, like the torrents of December, threatened to sweep all before them—to overwhelm the multitude [Polwhele's note].

8. "We, the great, the valiant and the wise, / When once the seal of death hath clos'd our eyes, / Shut in the hollow tomb obscure and deep, / Slumber, to wake no more, one long unbroken sleep." Moschus [Polwhele's note; Moschus: 2nd-century B.C. Greek pastoral poet, whom he translated in a well-received publication of 1786].

9. That Miss Wollstonecraft was a sworn enemy to blushes, I need not remark. But many of my readers, perhaps, will be astonished to hear, that at several of our boarding-schools for young ladies, a blush incurs a penalty [Polwhele's note].

1. According to Rousseau, the empire of women is the empire of softness—of address: their commands, are caresses; their menaces, are tears. [Polwhele's note, referring to Rousseau's views on women in *La Nouvelle Heloise* (1760) and *Émile* (1762), both criticized by Wollstonecraft in *Rights of Woman*.]

2. "Like monarchs, we have been flattered into imbecillity, by those who wish to take advantage of our weakness," says Mary Hays (*Essays and Letters*, p. 92). But, whether flattered or not, women were always weak: and female weakness hath accomplished, what the force of arms could not effect [Polwhele's note, quoting her passionate endorsement of Wollstonecraft's *Rights of Woman*]. Hays's feminist *Appeal to the Men of Great Britain on Behalf of Women* appeared anonymously in 1798.

3. Miss Wollstonecraft seriously laments the neglect of all muscular exercises, at our female Boarding-schools [Polwhele's note].

90   And vindicate *the Rights of womankind.*"
           She spoke: and veteran BARBAULD[4] caught the strain,
       And deem'd her songs of Love, her Lyrics vain;
       And ROBINSON[5] to Gaul her Fancy gave,
       And trac'd the picture of a Deist's grave!
95   And charming SMITH[6] resign'd her power to please,
       Poetic feeling and poetic ease;
       And HELEN,[7] fir'd by Freedom, bade adieu
       To all the broken visions of Peru.
       And YEARSLEY,[8] who had warbled, Nature's child,
100   Midst twilight dews, her minstrel ditties wild,

4. Here . . . I have formed a groupe of female Writers; whose productions have been appreciated by the public as works of learning or genius—though not praised with that extravagance of panegyric, which was once a customary tribute to the literary compositions of women. In this country, a female author was formerly esteemed a Phenomenon in Literature: and she was sure of a favourable reception among the critics, in consideration of her sex. This species of gallantry, however, conveyed no compliment to her understanding. It implied such an inferiority of woman in the scale of intellect as was justly humiliating: and critical forbearance was mortifying to female vanity. At the present day, indeed, our literary women are so numerous, that their judges, wa[i]ving all complimentary civilities, decide upon their merits with the same rigid impartiality as it seems right to exercise towards the men. The tribunal of criticism is no longer charmed into complacence by the blushes of modest apprehension. It no longer imagines the pleading eye of feminine diffidence that speaks a consciousness of comparative imbecillity, or a fearfulness of having offended by intrusion. Experience hath drawn aside the flimsy veil of affected timidity, that only served to hide the smile of complacency; the glow of self-gratulation. Yet, alas! the crimsoning blush of modesty, will be always more attractive, than the sparkle of confident intelligence.—Mrs. Barbauld stands the most conspicuous figure in the groupe. She is a veteran in Literature . . . Her poetry . . . is certainly, chaste and elegant. . . . I was sorry to find Mrs. B. . . . classed with such females as a Wollstonecraft. . . . But though Mrs. B. has lately published several political tracts, which if not discreditable to her talents and virtues, can by no means add to her reputation, yet, I am sure, she must reprobate, with me, the alarming eccentricities of Miss Wollstonecraft [Polwhele's note].
5. In Mrs. Robinson's Poetry, there is a peculiar delicacy: but her Novels, as literary compositions, have no great claim to approbation—As containing the doctrines of Philosophism, they merit the severest censure. Would that, for the sake of herself and her beautiful daughter (whose personal charms are only equalled by the elegance of her mind) would, that, for the sake of the public morality, Mrs. Robinson were persuaded to dismiss the gloomy phantom of annihilation; to think seriously of a future retribution; and to communicate to the world, a recantation of errors that originated in levity, and have been nursed by pleasure! I have seen her, "glittering like the morning-star, full of life, and splendor and joy!" Such, and more glorious, may I meet her again, when the just "shall shine forth as the brightness of the firmament, and as the stars for ever and ever!" [Polwhele, quoting Burke's famous description of his first sight of princess Marie

Antoinette; see *Reflections*, pages 62–63.] "Philosophism" refers to the Enlightenment ideology of progress and human perfectibility through reason.
6. The Sonnets of Charlotte Smith, have a pensiveness peculiarly their own. It is not the monotonous plaintiveness of Shenstone, the gloomy melancholy of Gray, or the meek subdued spirit of Collins. It is a strain of wild, yet softened sorrow, that breathes a romantic air, without losing, for a moment, its mellowness. Her images, often original, are drawn from nature: the most familiar, have a new and charming aspect. Sweetly picturesque, she creates with the pencil of a Gilpin, and infuses her own soul into the landscape. There is so uncommon a variety in her expression, that I could read a thousand of such sonnets without lassitude. In general, a very few Sonnets fatigue attention, partly owing to the sameness of their construction. Petrarch, indeed, I can relish for a considerable time: but Spenser and Milton soon produce somnolence. . . . But why does she suffer her mind to be infected with the Gallic mania? [Polwhele's note]. For Smith's sonnets, see the Companion Readings to Wordsworth, page 1562. Other references are to the 18th-century poets William Shenstone, Thomas Gray, and William Collins, and to William Gilpin (1724–1804), author of illustrated picturesque tours of Britain.
7. Miss Helen Williams is, doubtless, a true poet. But is it not extraordinary, that such a genius, a female and so young, should have become a politician—that the fair Helen, whose notes of love have charmed the moonlight vallies, should stand forward, an intemperate advocate for Gallic licentiousness—that such a woman should import with her, a blast more pestilential than that of Avernus, though she has so often delighted us with melodies, soft as the sighs of the Zephyr, delicious as the airs of Paradise? [Polwhele's note]. See Williams's *Letters from France* (1792–1796), page 1347; her long political poem condemning imperial conquest, *Peru*, was published in 1784. Avernus is a lake in Italy thought to be the gate to the underworld; zephyr is the spring breeze.
8. Mrs. Yearsley's [sic] Poems, as the product of an untutored milk-woman, certainly entitled her to patronage: and patronage she received, from Miss H. More, liberal beyond example. Yet, such is the depravity of the human heart, that this milk-woman had no sooner her hut cheered by the warmth of benevolence, than she spurned her benefactor from her door. . . . My business, however, with Mrs. Y. is to recall her, if possible, from her Gallic wanderings—if an appeal to native ingenuousness be not too late; if the fatal example of the Arch-priestess of female Libertinism, have any influence on a mind once stored with the finest moral sentiment [Polwhele's note]. The "fatal example" is Wollstonecraft.

(Tho' soon a wanderer from her meads and milk,
She long'd to rustle, like her sex, in silk)
Now stole that modish grin, the sapient sneer,
And flippant HAYS[9] assum'd a cynic leer * * *

1798

— ✠ —

Hannah More
1745–1833

More came from a High Church–Tory family, and though she would turn Evangelical and become a vigorous abolitionist, her politics never swung left. In *Village Politics* (1792), she criticized the French Revolution and the "Rights of Man," hewing to the Evangelical line that the lot of the poor was to be improved by philanthropy and faith in ultimate salvation. "Rights of women! We shall be hearing of the Rights of Children next!" she scoffed on hearing of Wollstonecraft's *Rights of Woman*. Yet she shared many of its principles: the value of rationality, modesty, chastity, and "practical education" over trivial "accomplishments" like needlework, painting, dancing, and musical performance. Her life, moreover, was not conducted in the traditional "female sphere" of hearth and home. As a child, she learned Latin (a man's language) and mathematics from a father who wanted his daughters to be capable of self-sufficiency as teachers. She later learned French, Italian, and Spanish from her elder sisters. As a young woman, she came to London and entered a lively literary world, becoming friends with Samuel Johnson, actor David Garrick, and Horace Walpole, as well as the women of the Bluestocking Club, celebrated in her long poem *The Bas Bleu* (1786). She was a successful writer even before she gained an annuity of £200 in compensation for a reneged engagement; with this income she was able to live independently, never marrying, and devoting herself to philanthropy and writing, the latter with considerable financial success.

First published in 1799, *Strictures on Female Education* went through thirteen editions and was in demand for decades, selling 19,000 copies. Even more popular (eight editions in its first two months) was her didactic "conduct" novel of 1809, *Coelebs in Search of a Wife*—an easy target for Byron (see *Don Juan* 1.16, page 1688). Like Wollstonecraft, More was willing to condescend to this genre for propaganda. An ideal and idealist young man in quest of an ideal wife, Coelebs auditions several near and not so near Misses until he finds perfection in quiet, proper, prudent Lucilla, blessed with skills in household management and given to compassionate visits to the poor to read to them from the Bible. *Strictures* sets the didactic curriculum, arguing for rational education, Christian virtue, the "separate spheres" of male and female life, and the subordination of women to men.

Another work by More appears in Perspectives: The Abolition of Slavery and the Slave Trade, page 1452.

---

9. Mary Hays from her "Letters and Essays" . . . is evidently a Wollstonecraftian. "I cannot mention (says she) the admirable advocate for the rights of women, without pausing to pay a tribute of grateful respect, in the name of my sex, to the virtue and talents of a writer, who with equal courage and ability, hath endeavoured to rescue the female mind from those prejudices which have been the canker of genuine virtue. . . . The rights of woman and the name of Wollstonecraft, will go down to posterity with reverence." Mary Hays ridicules "the good lady who studied her Bible, and obliged her children to say their prayers, and go statedly to church." Her expressions respecting the European Governments are, in a high degree, inflammatory [Polwhele's note]. The attacks on Wollstonecraft continue in subsequent notes, recounting her infatuation with the married Fuseli, her affair with Imlay, her suicide attempts despite a young daughter, her premarital affair with Godwin, and her lack of church attendance or death-bed conversion. "I cannot but think, that the Hand of Providence is visible, in her life, her death and in [Godwin's] Memoirs. . . . As she was given up to her 'heart's lusts,' and let 'to follow her own imaginations,' that the fallacy of and the effects of an irreligious conduct, might be manifested to the world; and as she died a death that strongly marked the distinction of the sexes, by pointing out the destiny of women and the diseases to which they are liable."

from Strictures on the Modern System of Female Education;
with a View of the Principles and Conduct Prevalent among Women of Rank and Fortune

from *Introduction*

It is a singular injustice which is often exercised towards women, first to give them a very defective education, and then to expect from them the most undeviating purity of conduct;—to train them in such a manner as shall lay them open to the most dangerous faults, and then to censure them for not proving faultless. Is it not unreasonable and unjust, to express disappointment if our daughters should, in their subsequent lives, turn out precisely that very kind of character for which it would be evident to an unprejudiced by-stander that the whole scope and tenour of their instruction had been systematically preparing them?

Some reflections on the present erroneous system are here with great deference submitted to public consideration. The author is apprehensive that she shall be accused of betraying the interests of her sex by laying open their defects; but surely an earnest wish to turn their attention to objects calculated to promote their true dignity, is not the office of an enemy. So to expose the weakness of the land, as to suggest the necessity of internal improvement, and to point out the means of effectual defence, is not treachery, but patriotism. * * *

Let it not be suspected that the author arrogantly conceives *herself* to be exempt from that natural corruption of the heart which it is one chief object of this slight work to exhibit; that she superciliously erects herself into the impeccable censor of her sex and of the world; as if from the critic's chair she were coldly pointing out the faults and errors of another order of beings, in whose welfare she had not that lively interest which can only flow from the tender and intimate participation of fellow-feeling.

Bath, March 14, 1799

from *Chapter 8. On Female Study*

Will it not be ascribed to a captious singularity, if I venture to remark that real knowledge and real piety, though they may have gained in many instances, have suffered in others from that profusion of little, amusing, sentimental books with which the youthful library overflows? Abundance has its dangers as well as scarcity. In the first place, may not the multiplicity of these alluring little works increase the natural reluctance to those more dry and uninteresting studies, of which, after all, the rudiments of every part of learning *must* consist? And, secondly, is there not some danger (though there are many honourable exceptions) that some of those engaging narratives may serve to infuse into the youthful heart a sort of spurious goodness, a confidence of virtue, a parade of charity? And that the benevolent actions with the recital of which they abound, when they are not made to flow from any source but *feeling,* may tend to inspire a self-complacency, a self-gratulation, a "stand by, for I am holier than thou?" May not the success with which the good deeds of the little heroes are uniformly crowned; the invariable reward which is made the instant concomitant of well-doing, furnish the young reader with false views of the condition of life, and the nature of the divine dealings with men? May they not help to suggest a false standard of morals, to infuse a love of popularity and an anxiety for praise, in the place of that simple and unostentatious rule of doing whatever good we do, *because it is the will of*

God? The universal substitution of this principle would tend to purify the worldly morality of many a popular little story. And there are few dangers which good parents will more carefully guard against than that of giving their children a mere political piety; that sort of religion which just goes to make people more respectable, and to stand well with the world; a religion which is to save appearances without inculcating realities; a religion which affects to "preach peace and good will to men," but which forgets to give "glory to God in the highest."[1]

There is a certain precocity of mind which is much helped on by these superficial modes of instruction; for frivolous reading will produce its correspondent effect, in much less time than books of solid instruction; the imagination being liable to be worked upon, and the feelings to be set a going, much faster than the understanding can be opened and the judgment enlightened. A talent for conversation should be the result of instruction, not its precursor: it is a golden fruit when suffered to ripen gradually on the tree of knowledge; but if forced in the hot-bed of a circulating library,[2] it will turn out worthless and vapid in proportion as it was artificial and premature. Girls who have been accustomed to devour a multitude of frivolous books, will converse and write with a far greater appearance of skill, as to style and sentiment, at twelve or fourteen years old, than those of a more advanced age, who are under the discipline of severer studies; but the former having early attained to that low standard which had been held out to them, become stationary; while the latter, quietly progressive, are passing through just gradations to a higher strain of mind; and those who early begin with talking and writing like women, commonly end with thinking and acting like children.

I would not, however, prohibit such works of imagination as suit this early period. When moderately used, they serve to stretch the faculties and expand the mind; but I should prefer works of vigorous genius and pure unmixed fable to many of those tame and more affected moral stories, which are not grounded on Christian principle. I should suggest the use, on the one hand, of original and acknowledged fictions; and, on the other, of accurate and simple facts; so that truth and fable may ever be kept separate and distinct in the mind. * * *

This suggestion is, however, by no means intended to exclude works of taste and imagination, which must always make the ornamental part, and of course a very considerable part of female studies. It is only intimated, that they should not form them entirely and exclusively. For what is called dry tough reading, independent of the knowledge it conveys, is useful as a habit, and wholesome as an exercise. Serious study serves to harden the mind for more trying conflicts; it lifts the reader from sensation to intellect; it abstracts her from the world and its vanities; it fixes a wandering spirit and fortifies a weak one; it divorces her from matter; it corrects that spirit of trifling which she naturally contracts from the frivolous turn of female conversation and the petty nature of female employments. * * *

Far be it from me to desire to make scholastic ladies or female dialecticians; but there is little fear that the kind of books here recommended, if thoroughly studied, and not superficially skimmed, will make them pedants, or induce conceit; for by showing them the possible powers of the human mind, you will bring them to see the

---

1. An ingenious (and in many respects useful) French Treatise on Education has too much encouraged this political piety [More's note; her quotations are from Luke 2.14].

2. Lending libraries that flourished from the 1790s carried stores of popular fiction, much of it written by and for women.

littleness of their own: and surely to get acquainted with the mind, to regulate, to inform it; to show it its own ignorance and its own weakness, does not seem the way to puff it up. But let her who is disposed to be elated with her literary acquisitions check the rising vanity by calling to mind the just remark of Swift, "that after all her boasted acquirements, a woman will, generally speaking, be found to possess less of what is called learning than a common school-boy."[3]

Neither is there any fear that this sort of reading will convert ladies into authors. The direct contrary effect will be likely to be produced by the perusal of writers who throw the generality of readers at such an unapproachable distance as to check presumption, instead of exciting it. Who are those ever-multiplying authors, that with unparalleled fecundity are overstocking the world with their quick-succeeding progeny? They are NOVEL-WRITERS: the easiness of whose productions is at once the cause of their own fruitfulness, and of the almost infinitely numerous race of imitators to whom they give birth. Such is the frightful facility of this species of composition, that every raw girl, while she reads, is tempted to fancy that she can also write. And as Alexander, on perusing the Iliad, found by congenial sympathy the image of Achilles stamped on his own ardent soul, and felt himself the hero he was studying; and as Corregio, on first beholding a picture which exhibited the perfection of the graphic art, prophetically felt all his own future greatness, and cried out in rapture, "And I, too, am a painter!" so a thorough-paced novel-reading Miss, at the close of every tissue of hackneyed adventures, feels within herself the stirring impulse of corresponding genius, and triumphantly exclaims, "And I, too, am an author!" The glutted imagination soon overflows with the redundance of cheap sentiment and plentiful incident, and by a sort of arithmetical proportion, is enabled by the perusal of any three novels, to produce a fourth; till every fresh production, like the prolific progeny of Banquo, is followed by "Another, and another, and another!"[4] Is a lady, however destitute of talents, education, or knowledge of the world, whose studies have been completed by a circulating library, in any distress of mind? the writing a novel suggests itself as the best soother of her sorrows! Does she labour under any depression of circumstances? writing a novel occurs as the readiest receipt for mending them! and she solaces her imagination with the conviction that the subscription which has been extorted by her importunity, or given to her necessities, has been offered as a homage to her genius; and this confidence instantly levies a fresh contribution for a succeeding work. Capacity and cultivation are so little taken into the account, that writing a book seems to be now considered as the only sure resource which the idle and the illiterate have always in their power.

May the Author be indulged in a short digression, while she remarks, though rather out of its place, that the corruption occasioned by these books has spread so wide, and descended so low, as to have become one of the most universal, as well as most pernicious, sources of corruption among us. Not only among milliners, mantua-makers, and other trades where numbers work together, the labour of one girl is frequently sacrificed that she may be spared to read those mischievous books to the others; but she has been assured by clergymen who have witnessed the fact, that they are

---

3. From *Letter to a Young Lady* (1727) by Jonathan Swift: "Those who are commonly called Learned Women have lost all manner of Credit by their impertinent Talkativeness and Conceit of themselves; but there is an easy remedy for this, if you once consider, that after all the pains you may be at, you can never arrive in point of learning to the perfection of a School-boy."

4. References are to the famous anecdote of Alexander the Great's sympathy with the Greek hero Achilles in Homer's epic of the Trojan War; the Italian Renaissance painter; and to the vision of Banquo's royal heirs that frustrates Macbeth (4.1).

procured and greedily read in the wards of our hospitals! an awful hint, that those who teach the poor to read, should not only take care to furnish them with principles which will lead them to abhor corrupt books, but that they should also furnish them with such books as shall strengthen and confirm their principles.[5]

from *Chapter 14. The Practical Use of Female Knowledge, with a Sketch of the Female Character, and a Comparative View of the Sexes*

The chief end to be proposed, in cultivating the understandings of women is to qualify them for the practical purposes of life. Their knowledge is not often, like the learning of men, to be reproduced in some literary composition, and never in any learned profession; but it is to come out in conduct: it is to be exhibited in life and manners. A lady studies, not that she may qualify herself to become an orator or a pleader; not that she may learn to debate, but to act. She is to read the best books, not so much to enable her to talk to them, as to bring the improvement which they furnish to the rectification of her principles and the formation of her habits. The great uses of study to a woman are to enable her to regulate her own mind, and to be instrumental to the good of others. * * *

But there is one *human* consideration which would perhaps more effectually tend to damp in an aspiring woman the ardours of literary vanity—I speak not of real genius, though there the remark often applies—than any which she will derive from motives of humility, or propriety, or religion; which is, that in the judgment passed on her performances, she will have to encounter the mortifying circumstance of having her sex always taken into account, and her highest exertions will probably be received with the qualified approbation *that it is really extraordinary for a woman*. Men of learning, who are naturally disposed to estimate works in proportion as they appear to be the result of art, study, and institution, are inclined to consider even the happier performances of the other sex as the spontaneous productions of a fruitful but shallow soil, and to give them the same kind of praise which we bestow on certain salads, which often draw from us a sort of wondering commendation, not, indeed, as being worth much in themselves, but because, by the lightness of the earth, and a happy knack of the gardener, these indifferent cresses spring up in a night, and therefore we are ready to wonder they are no worse.

As to men of sense, however, they need be the less hostile to the improvement of the other sex, as they themselves will be sure to be gainers by it; the enlargement of the female understanding being the most likely means to put an end to those petty and absurd contentions for equality which female smatterers so anxiously maintain. I say smatterers, for between the first class of both sexes the question is much more rarely and always more temperately agitated. Cooperation, and not competition, is, indeed, the clear principle we wish to see reciprocally adopted by those higher minds in each sex which really approximate the nearest to each other. The more a woman's understanding is improved, the more obviously she will discern that there can be no happiness in any society where there is a perpetual struggle for power; and the more her judgment is rectified, the more accurate views will she take of the station she was born to fill, and the more readily will she accommodate herself to it. * * *

5. The above facts furnish no argument on the side of those who would keep the poor in ignorance. Those who cannot *read* can *hear*, and are likely to hear to worse purpose than those who have been better taught. And that ignorance furnishes no security for integrity either in morals or politics, the late revolts in more than one country, remarkable for the ignorance of the poor, fully illustrate. It is earnestly hoped that the above facts may tend to impress ladies with the importance of superintending the instruction of the poor, and of making it an indispensable part of their charity to give them moral and religious books [More's note].

There is this singular difference between a woman vain of her wit, and a woman vain of her beauty; * * * she who is vain of her genius, more liberal at least in her vanity, is jealous for the honour of her whole sex, and contends for the equality of their pretensions as a body, in which she feels that her own are involved as an individual. The beauty vindicates her own rights, the wit the rights of women; * * * and while the more selfish though more moderate beauty "would but be Queen for life," the public-spirited wit struggles to abrogate the Salique law of intellect, and to enthrone "a whole sex of Queens."[1]

At the revival of letters in the sixteenth and the following century, the controversy about this equality was agitated with more warmth than wisdom; and the process was instituted and carried on, on the part of the female complainant, with that sort of acrimony which always raises a suspicion of the justice of any cause; for violence commonly implies doubt, and invective indicates weakness rather than strength. * * * Among the innovations of this innovating period, the imposing term of *rights* has been produced to sanctify the claim of our female pretenders,[2] with a view not only to rekindle in the minds of women a presumptuous vanity, dishonourable to their sex, but produced with a view to excite in their hearts an impious discontent with the post which God has assigned them in this world.[3]

But *they* little understand the true interests of woman who would lift her from the important duties of her allotted station, to fill, with fantastic dignity, a loftier but less appropriate niche. Nor do they understand her true happiness, who seek to annihilate distinctions from which she derives advantages, and to attempt innovations which would depreciate her real value. Each sex has its proper excellences, which would be lost were they melted down into the common character by the fusion of the new philosophy. Why should we do away distinctions which increase the mutual benefits and enhance the satisfactions of life? Whence, but by carefully preserving the original marks of difference, stamped by the hand of the Creator, would be derived the superior advantage of mixed society? Is either sex so abounding in perfection, as to be independent on the other for improvement? Have men no need to have their rough angles filed off, and their harshnesses and asperities smoothed and polished by assimilating with beings of more softness and refinement? Are the ideas of women naturally so *very* judicious, are their principles so *invincibly* firm, are their views so *perfectly* correct, are their judgments so *completely* exact, that there is occasion for no additional weight, no superadded strength, no increased clearness, none of that enlargement of mind, none of that additional invigoration, which may be derived from the aids of the stronger sex? What identity could advantageously supersede such an enlivening opposition, such an interesting variety of character? * * *

Natural propensities best mark the designations of Providence as to their application. The fin was not more clearly bestowed on the fish that he should swim, nor the wing given to the bird that he should fly, than superior strength of body and a firmer texture of mind were given to man, that he might preside in the deep and daring scenes of action and of council; in the complicated arts of government, in the contention of arms, in the intricacies and depths of science, in the bustle of commerce, and in those professions which demand a higher reach and a

---

1. Pope's *Epistle II*, "of the Characters of Women," assumes that "ev'ry Lady would be Queen for life" and shudders at the thought of "a whole Sex of Queens! / Pow'r all their end" (218–220). Salique (Salic) law, deriving from old French law, excludes females from the line of succession to a throne.

2. False claimants, especially to a throne; More is also suggesting "fantasizers" and dissemblers.
3. This was written soon after the publication of a work intitled "The Rights of Woman" [More's note, referring to Wollstonecraft's *Vindication*].

wider range of powers. The true value of woman is not diminished by the imputation of inferiority in those talents which do not belong to her, of those qualities in which her claim to excellence does not consist. She has other requisites, better adapted to answer the end and purposes of her being, from "Him who does all things well;" who suits the agent to the action; who accommodates the instrument to the work.

Let not, then, aspiring, because ill-judging, woman view with pining envy the keen satirist, hunting vice through all the doublings and windings of the heart; the sagacious politician, leading senates, and directing the fate of empires; the acute lawyer, detecting the obliquities of fraud; and the skilful dramatist, exposing the pretensions of folly; but let her ambition be consoled by reflecting, that those who thus excel, to all that Nature bestows and books can teach, must add besides that consummate knowledge of the world to which a delicate woman has no fair avenues, and which, even if she could attain, she would never be supposed to have come honestly by.

In almost all that comes under the description of polite letters, in all that captivates by vivid imagery or warms by just and affecting sentiment, women are excellent. They possess in a high degree that delicacy and quickness of perception, and that nice discernment between the beautiful and defective which comes under the denomination of taste. Both in composition and in action they excel in details; but they do not so much generalise their ideas as men, nor do their minds seize a great subject with so large a grasp. They are acute observers, and accurate judges of life and manners, as far as their own sphere of observation extends, but they describe a smaller circle. A woman sees the world, as it were, from a little elevation in her own garden, whence she makes an exact survey of home scenes, but takes not in that wider range of distant prospects which he who stands on a loftier eminence commands.

◆—◆≡◆—◆

William Thompson and *Anna Wheeler*
1775–1833   1785–post-1848?

Karl Marx's *Manifesto of the Communist Party*, published in London in 1848, assured proletarians that they "have nothing to lose but their chains" and closed with the call, "Working Men of All Countries, Unite!" In these ringing phrases, English socialists heard a striking echo of the "Address to Women" that concluded William Thompson and Anna Wheeler's *Appeal*: "Women of England! women, in whatever country ye breathe—wherever ye breathe, degraded—awake! . . . O wretched slaves of such wretched masters! Awake, arise, shake off these fetters!" The work of two leading socialists of the 1820s, *Appeal* is the most important English feminist document between Wollstonecraft's *Rights of Woman* (1792) and John Stuart Mill's *Subjection of Women* (1869).

Born into Protestant Irish gentry, Thompson came of age during the tumultuous era of the French Revolution. At his father's death in 1814, he inherited the family's thousand-acre estate and prosperous businesses, including a fleet of trading vessels. He did not fall into step with Protestant capitalism, however, but agitated for Catholic Emancipation, denounced the division between laborers and "idle classes," and experimented with socialist alternatives, including organizing the 700 vagrants on the family estate into a highly successful experimental community. He then went to London, where he befriended leading social theorists John Stuart Mill, Jeremy Bentham, and Robert Owen. He published books on labor and wealth, including *An Inquiry into the Principles of the Distribution of Wealth Most Conducive to Human Happiness, Applied to the Newly Proposed System of Voluntary Equality of Wealth* (1824). Another London friend was Anna Wheeler, whose family, like his, was Irish gentry. A "reigning beauty" in her youth, she married a pampered Irish nobleman at age 15, bore six children (only two surviving infancy), and still found time to read widely, especially in philosophy and social theory. Increasingly disaffected from her idle, heavily drinking husband, she left him in 1812, eventually heading for London and France, where she met leading socialists and feminists. A dynamic figure in the movement for women's rights, she struck Benjamin Disraeli as "very clever, but awefully revolutionary."

Thompson and Wheeler were deeply concerned over the indifference of some of their socialist friends to women's rights. Some were even opposed—for instance, Bentham's disciple, James Mill, whose *Article on Government* for the 1824 *Encyclopedia Britannica* (a separate pamphlet in 1825) argued against political representation for women, contending that their interests were "involved" and "included" with their fathers or their husbands and had no separate claim. Thompson and Wheeler immediately began a refutation, publishing it in 1825. He was the author named on the title page of this *Appeal*, but his introduction credits Wheeler as co-author: he is the scribe of their "feelings, sentiments, and reasonings" and the work is their "joint property." Patently allied with Wollstonecraft's *Rights of Woman*, *Appeal* expands her social analysis into a critique of the underlying economic system. As the full title suggests, it also expands Wollstonecraft's discourse of female slavery. The blunt comparisons of English women to Turkish harem-slaves and the plantation slaves of the new world ally the polemic with the moral consensus fueling the expanding movement for the abolition of colonial slavery.

APPEAL of One Half the Human Race, WOMEN, Against the Pretensions of the Other Half, MEN, To Retain Them in Political, and Thence in CIVIL AND DOMESTIC SLAVERY

"'Tis all stern duty on the female side;
On man's, mere sensual gust and surly pride."[1]

from *Introductory Letter to Mrs. Wheeler*

The days of dedication and patronage are gone by. It is *not* with the view of obtaining the support of your name or your influence to the cause of truth and humanity that these lines are addressed to you. * * * I address you then simply to perform towards you a debt of justice. * * * Anxious that you should take up the cause of your proscribed sex, and state to the world in writing, in your own name, what you have so often and so well stated in conversation, and under feigned names in such of the periodical publications of the day as would tolerate such a theme, I long hesitated to arrange our common ideas, even upon a branch of the subject like the present. Anxious that the hand of a woman should have the honor of raising from the dust that neglected banner which a woman's hand nearly thirty years ago unfolded boldly, in face of the prejudices of thousands of years, and for which a woman's heart bled, and her life was all but the sacrifice—I hesitated to write. Were courage the quality wanting, you would have shown, what every day's experience proves, that women have more fortitude in endurance than men. Were comprehensiveness of mind, above the narrow views which too often marred Mary Wolstoncroft's [sic] pages and narrowed their usefulness, the quality wanting,—above the timidity and impotence of conclu-

---

1. A slight misquotation of Dryden's *Palamon and Arcite; or, The Knight's Tale, From Chaucer* (3.230–31) in *Fables Ancient and Modern; Translated into Verse* (1700); the virgin Emily begs the goddess Cynthia to accept her as a votress, pleading, "Like Death, thou know'st, I loath the Nuptial state, / And Man, the Tyrant of our Sex, I hate, / A lowly Servant, but a lofty Mate. / Where Love is Duty, on the Female side; / On theirs meer sensual Gust, and sought with surly Pride" (227–32); "Gust" is appetite. In *Rights of Woman*, ch. 6, Wollstonecraft quotes 230–31 correctly, using these lines to gloss the lack of "satisfaction" that any woman of delicate affections would confront "in a union with such a man."

sion accompanying the gentle eloquence of Mary Hays, addressed, about the same time that Mary Wolstonecroft wrote, in the shape of an "*Appeal*" to the then closed ears of unreasoning men;[2] yours was the eye which no prejudice obscured, open to the rays of truth from whatever quarter they might emanate. But leisure and resolution to undertake the drudgery of the task were wanting. A few only therefore of the following pages are the exclusive produce of your mind and pen, and written with your own hand. The remainder are our joint property, I being your interpreter and the scribe of your sentiments. * * *

You look forward, as I do, to a state of society very different from that which now exists, in which the effort of all is to out wit, supplant, and snatch from each other; where interest is systematically opposed to duty; where the so-called system of morals is little more than a mass of hypocrisy preached by knaves, unpractised by them, to keep their slaves, male as well as female, in blind uninquiring obedience; and where the whole motley fabric is kept together by fear and blood. You look forward to a better aspect of society, where the principle of benevolence shall supersede that of fear; where restless and anxious individual competition shall give place to mutual co-operation and joint possession; where individuals in large numbers, male and female, forming voluntary associations, shall become a mutual guarantee to each other for the supply of all useful wants, and form an unsalaried and uninsolvent insurance company against all insurable casualties; where perfect freedom of opinion and perfect equality will reign amongst the co-operators; and where the children of all will be equally educated and provided for by the whole, even these children longer the slaves of individual caprice.

In truth, under the present arrangements of society, the principle of individual competition remaining, as it is, the master-key and moving principle of the whole social organization, *individual* wealth the great object sought after by all, and the quantum of happiness of each individual (other things being equal) depending on the quantum of wealth, the means of happiness, possessed by each; it seems impossible—even were all unequal legal and unequal moral restraints removed, and were no secret current of force or influence exerted to baffle new regulations of equal justice—that women should attain to equal happiness with men. Two circumstances—permanent inferiority of strength, and occasional loss of time in gestation and rearing infants—must eternally render the average exertions of women in the race of the competition for wealth less successful than those of men. The pleasant compensation that men now affect to give for these two natural sources of inferior accumulation of wealth on the part of women (aggravated a thousand degrees by their exclusions from knowledge and almost all means of useful exertions, (the very lowest only excepted)), is the existing system of marriage; under which, for the mere faculty of eating, breathing and living, in whatever degree of comfort husbands may think fit, women are reduced to domestic slavery, without will of their own, or power of locomotion, otherwise than as permitted by their respective masters. * * *

With you I would equally elevate both sexes. Really enlightened women, disdaining equally the submissive tricks of the slave and the caprices of the despot,

2. Mary Hays, disciple and friend of Wollstonecraft, published her feminist polemic, *Appeal to the Men of Great Britain in Behalf of Women* anonymously in 1798, by which time Wollstonecraft was a scandal and the English political climate increasingly conservative as it confronted growing social unrest at home and the emergence of Napoleon abroad. Despite her numerous defenses of Wollstonecraft, Hays felt it unwise to include her in her *Female Biography, or Memoirs of Illustrious and Celebrated Women of all Ages and Countries* (1803).

breathing freely only in the air of the esteem of equals, and of mutual, *unbought, uncommanded,* affection, would find it difficult to meet with associates worthy of them in men as now formed, full of ignorance and vanity, priding themselves on a *sexual* superiority, entirely independent of any merit, any superior qualities, or pretensions to them, claiming respect from the strength of their arm and the lordly faculty of producing beards attached by nature to their chins! No: unworthy of, as incapable of appreciating, the delight of the society of such women, are the great majority of the existing race of men. The pleasures of mere animal appetite, the pleasures of commanding (the prettier and more helpless the slave, the greater these pleasures of the brute), are the only pleasures which the majority of men seek for from women, are the only pleasures which their education and the hypocritical system of morals with which they have been necessarily imbued, permit them to expect. * * *

Even under the present arrangements of society, founded as they all are on the basis of individual competition, nothing could be more easy than to put the *rights* of women, political and civil, on a perfect equality with those of men. It is only to abolish all prohibitory and exclusive laws,—statute or what are called "common,"—the remnants of the barbarous customs of our ignorant ancestors; particularly the horrible and odious inequality and indissolubility of that disgrace of civilization, the present marriage code. Women then might exert in a free career with men their faculties of mind and body, to whatever degree developed, in pursuit of happiness by means of exertion, as men do. But this would not raise women to an equality of happiness with men: their rights might be equal, but not their happiness, because unequal powers under free competition must produce unequal effects.

In truth, the system of the most enlightened of the school of those reformers called political economists, is still founded on exclusions. Its basis is too narrow for human happiness. A more comprehensive system, founded on equal benevolence, on the true development of the principle of Utility, is wanting.[3] Let the *competitive* political economists be satisfied with the praise of causing the removal of some of the rubbish of ignorant restrictions, under the name of laws, impeding the development of human exertion in the production of wealth. To build up a new fabric of social happiness, comprehending equally the interests of all existing human beings, has never been contemplated by them, and is altogether beyond the scope of their little theories; aiming at the utmost at increasing the number of what they style the happy middling orders, but leaving the great bulk of human beings to eternal ignorance and toil, requited by the mere means of prolonging from day to day an unhealthy and precarious existence. To a new science, the *social science,* or the science of promoting human happiness, that of political economy, or the mere science of producing wealth by individual competition, must give way.

from Part 2
[ON DAUGHTERS]

Business, professions, political concerns, local affairs, the whole field of sciences and arts, are open to the united and mutually sympathizing efforts of the males. To their mutual judgments and speculations, the disposal of the family income and capital are

---

3. The philosophy of utilitarianism, formulated by contemporaries Jeremy Bentham and James Mill, that there is no inherent right and wrong; the only issue is consequence, whether an action contributes to "the happiness of man."

intrusted. From all these commanding sources of intellectual and muscular activity, the daughters, like the little children, are excluded, previous care having been taken, by shutting them out from all means of intellectual culture, and from the view of and participation in the real incidents of active life, to render them as unfit for, as unambitious of, such high occupations. Confined, like other domestic animals, to the house and its little details, their "sober wishes" are never permitted "to stray" into the enlarged plains of general speculation and action. The dull routine of domestic incidents is the world to them. * * *

So much more completely is the interest of the sons involved than that of the daughters in the interest of fathers, that as soon as the daughters become adult, they, necessarily operated upon by the system under which they live, look out of their artificial cages of restraint and imbecility, to catch glances at the world with the hope of freedom from parental control, by leaving behind them the very name of their fathers, and vainly hoping for happiness without independence, in the gratification of one passion, love, round which their absurd training for blind male sensuality, has caused all their little anxieties to centre. The adult sons go in and out of the father's house when they choose: they are frequently treated with liberality as visitors or equals. But the adult daughters are, for the most part, under as much restraint as little children: they must ask leave to open the door or take a walk: not one of their actions that does not depend on the will of another: they are never permitted, like the sons, to regulate their conduct by their own notions of propriety and prudence and to restrain them where necessary, like rational beings, from a regard to their consequences: every thing is prescribed to them: their reason and foresight are not cultivated like those of the sons; and the despotism which creates their imbecility, adduces its own work as a justification of its unrelenting pressure and of its eternal duration. To marriage therefore, as the only means allowed them of emerging from paternal control; as the only means of gratifying one passion, to which all their thoughts have been exclusively directed, but which they are at the same time told it is highly improper they should wish to enjoy; as the only means of obtaining, through cunning and blandishment, that direction of their own voluntary actions, which all rational beings ought to possess, and which is the sure and only basis of intelligence and morals; to marriage, as the fancied haven of pleasure and freedom—the freedom of the slave to-be-sure, to be acquired not by right but by coaxing, by the influence of passions inapplicable to the cold despotism of the fathers—daughters look forward. No sooner adult, than their home and their name are daughters anxious to get rid of, because the retaining of them is made incompatible with the only views of happiness presented to them.

[On Wives]

By way of distinguishing and honoring this class of the proscribed half of the human race, man condescends to enter into what he calls a *contract* with certain women, for certain purposes, the most important of which is, the producing and rearing of children to maturity. Each man yokes a woman to his establishment, and calls it a *contract*. Audacious falsehood! A contract! where are any of the attributes of contracts, of equal and just contracts, to be found in this transaction? A contract implies the voluntary assent of both the contracting parties. Can even both the parties, man and woman, by agreement alter the terms, as to *indissolubility* and *inequality*, of this pretended contract? No. Can any individual man divest himself, were he even so inclined, of his power of despotic control? He cannot. Have women been consulted as to the terms of this pretended contract? A contract, all of whose enjoyments—wherever nature has not imposed a physical bar on the depravity of selfishness—are on one side, while all of its pains and privations are on the other! A contract, giving all power, arbitrary will and unbridled enjoyment to the one side; to the other, unqualified obedience, and enjoyments meted out or withheld at the caprice of the ruling and enjoying party. Such a contract, as the owners of *slaves* in the West Indies and every other slave-polluted soil, enter into with their slaves—the law of the stronger imposed on the weaker, *in contempt* of the interests and wishes of the weaker. * * *

As soon as adult daughters become wives, their civil rights disappear; they fall back again, and remain all their lives—should their owners and directors live so long—into the state of children or idiots, the passive property of their owners; protected by the law in some few respects only, like other slaves, from the excessive abuse of despotic power.

Woman is then compelled, in marriage, by the possession of superior strength on the part of men, by the want of knowledge, skill and wealth, by the positive, cruel, partial, and cowardly enactments of law, by the terrors of superstition, by the mockery of a pretended vow of obedience, and to crown all, and as the result of all, by the force of an unrelenting, unreasoning, unfeeling, public opinion, to be the literal unequivocal *slave* of the man who may be styled her husband. I say emphatically the slave; for a slave is a person whose actions and earnings, instead of being, under his own control, liable only to equal laws, to public opinion, and to his own calculations, under these, of his own interest, are under the arbitrary control of any other human being, by whatever name called. This is the essence of slavery, and what distinguishes it from freedom. A domestic, a civil, a political slave, in the plain unsophisticated sense of the word—in no metaphorical sense—is every married woman. No matter with what wealth she may be surrounded, with what dainties she may be fed, with what splendor of trappings adorned, with what voluptuousness her corporeal, mental, or moral sweets may be gathered; that high prerogative of human nature, the faculty of self-government, the basis of intellectual development, without which no moral conduct can exist, is to her wanting. * * * Till laws afford married women the same protection against the restraints and violence of the men to whom they are married, that they affect to afford them against all other individuals; till they afford them the same protection against the restraints and violence of their husbands, that their husbands enjoy against their caprices and violence, the social condition of the civilized wife will remain more completely slavish than that of the female slave of the West Indies.

[EXHORTATION TO MEN]

Be consistent, men! Ye stronger half of the race, be at length rational! Three or four thousand years have worn threadbare your vile cloak of hypocrisy. Even women, your poor, weak, contented slaves, at whose impotence of penetration, the result of your vile exclusions, you have been accustomed to laugh, begin to see through it and to shudder at the loathsomeness beneath. Cast aside this tattered cloak before it leaves you naked and exposed. Clothe yourselves with the new garments of sincerity. Be rational human beings, not mere male sexual creatures. Cast aside the ferocious brute of your nature: give up the pleasures of the brute, those of mere lust and command, for the pleasures of the rational being. So shall you enjoy the love of your *equals*, enlightened, benevolent, graceful, like yourselves, founded on an appreciation of your real merits: so shall you be happy. For the intercourse of the *bought* prostitute, or of the *commanded* household slave, you shall have full and equal participation in the compounded and associated pleasures of sense, intellect and benevolence. To the highest enjoyments of which your nature is susceptible, there is no shorter road than the simple road of equal justice.

[WHAT DO WOMEN WANT?]

The simple and modest request is, that they may be permitted equal enjoyments with men, *provided they can by the free and equal development and exercise of their faculties procure for themselves such enjoyments*. They ask the same means that men possess of acquiring every species of knowledge, of unfolding every one of their faculties of mind and body that can be made tributary to their happiness. They ask every facility of access to every art, occupation, profession, from the highest to the lowest, without one exception, to which their inclination and talents may direct and may fit them to occupy. They ask the removal of *all* restraints and exclusions not applicable to men of equal capacities. They ask for perfectly equal political, civil and domestic rights. They ask for equal obligations and equal punishments from the law with men in case of infraction of the same law by either party. They ask for an equal system of morals, founded on utility instead of caprice and unreasoning despotism, in which the same action attended with the same consequences, whether done by man or woman, should be attended with the same portion of approbation or disapprobation; in which every pleasure, accompanied or followed by no preponderant evil, should be equally permitted to women and to men; in which every pleasure accompanied or followed by preponderant evil should be equally censured in women and in men.

* * *

Women of England! women, in whatever country ye breathe—wherever ye breathe, degraded—awake! Awake to the contemplation of the happiness that awaits you when all your faculties of mind and body shall be fully cultivated and developed; when every path in which ye can exercise those improved faculties shall be laid open and rendered delightful to you, even as to them who now ignorantly enslave and degrade you. If degradation from long habitude have lost its sting, if the iron have penetrated so deeply into your frame that it has been gradually taken up into the system and mingles unperceived amidst the fluids of your life; if the prostration of reason and the eradication of feeling have kept pace within you, so that you are insensible alike to what you suffer and to what you might enjoy,—your case were all but hopeless. Nothing less, then, than the sight presented before your eyes, of the superior happiness enjoyed by other women, under arrangements of perfect equality with men, could arouse you. Such a sight, even under such circumstances, would excite your envy and kindle up all your extinct desires. But you are not so degraded. The unvaried despotism of so many thousand years, has not so entirely degraded you, has not been able to extinguish within you the feelings of nature, the love of happiness and of equal justice. The united exertions of law, superstition, and pretended morals of past ages of ignorance, have not entirely succeeded. * * *

Nor will your fellow-creatures, men, long resist the change. They are too deeply concerned to continue long to oppose what palpably tends to their happiness: they are too deeply concerned not to be compelled to re-consider the barbarous systems of law and morals under which they have been brought up. In justice, in pity to them, submit no longer; no longer *willingly* submit to their caprices. Though your bodies may be a little longer kept in servitude, degrade not yourselves by the repetition of superfluous vows of obedience: cease to kiss the rod: let your *minds* be henceforth free. The morn of loosening your physical chains will not be far distant.

O woman, from your auspicious hands may the new destiny of your species proceed! The collective voices of your sex raised against oppression will ultimately make men themselves your advocates and debtors. Reflect then seriously on your miserable and degraded position—your youth, your beauty, your feelings, your opinions, your actions, your time, your few years' fever of meritricious life—all made tributary to the appetites and passions of men. Whatever pleasures you enjoy, are permitted you for man's sake. Nothing is your own; protection of person and of property are alike withheld from you. Nothing is yours, but secret pangs, the bitter burning tears of regret, the stifled sobs of outraged nature thrown back upon your own hearts, where the vital principle itself stands checked, or is agitated with malignant passions, until body and mind become the frequent prey to overwhelming disease; now finding vent in sudden phrensy, now plunged in pining melancholy, or bursting the weak tenement of reason, seeking relief in self-destruction.

How many thousand of your sex *daily* perish thus unpitied and unknown; often victims of pressing want, always of privation and the arbitrary laws of heartless custom; condemned to cheerless solitude, or an idiot round of idle fashionable pursuits; your morning of life perhaps passed by, and with it the lingering darling hope of sympathy expired—puppets once of doting ignorant parents, whose tenderness for you outlived not your first youth; who, careless of your future fate, "launched you into life without an oar," indigent and ignorant, to eat the tear-steeped bread of dependence as wives, sisters, hired mistresses or unpitied prostitutes! This is the fate of the many, nay, of all your sex, subject only to those shades of difference arising from very peculiar circumstances or the accident of independent fortune; though even here the general want of knowledge, withheld from your sex, keeps even those individuals who are favored by fortune bowed to the relentless yoke which man's laws, his superstitions, and hypocritical morality, have prepared for you.

For once then instruct man in what is good, wash out the foul stain, equally disgraceful to both sexes—that your sex has unbounded influence in making men to do evil, but cannot induce them to do good.

How many Thaises are there, who, vain of the empire they hold over the passions of men, exercise at all risks this contemptible and pernicious influence—the only influence permitted them—in stimulating these masters of the world to destroy cities; and, regardless of the whispers of conscience and humanity, often shake men's tardy resolutions to repair the evils they have caused![1]—Shall none be found with sufficient knowledge and elevation of mind to persuade men to do good, to make the most certain step towards the regeneration of degraded humanity, by opening a free course for justice and benevolence, for intellectual and social enjoyments, by no colour, by no sex to be restrained? As your bondage has chained down man to the ignorance and vices of despotism, so will your liberation reward him with knowledge, with freedom and with happiness.[2]

[END OF PERSPECTIVES: THE WOLLSTONECRAFT CONTROVERSY
AND THE RIGHTS OF WOMEN]

1. Probably the 4th-century B.C. Athenian courtesan, patronized by Alexander the Great and then by the King of Egypt; she was said to have accompanied Alexander on his conquests. Another Thais was a 1st-century Alexandrian, famous for her beauty, wealth, and sexual indulgences, who repented and converted to Christianity and a life of piety.
2. The last paragraph of *Appeal*.

Joanna Baillie
1762–1851

In 1824, Blackwood's *Edinburgh Magazine* observed the influence of Baillie's plays on Lord Byron: "the dark shadows of his Lordship's imagination have received a deeper gloom from his early acquaintance with those wild and midnight forests, in which the passion of De Monfort [*De Monfort*, 1798] consummated its dreadful purpose, and the dim aisles in which it met its retribution." The influence is also reflected in his Lordship's nervous admiration. In 1813, Byron insisted that Baillie could not have "a more enthusiastic admirer than myself," and he was eager to meet her; in 1817, in the throes of rewriting his gothic closet drama *Manfred*, he mulled over Voltaire's reply to a question about "why no woman has ever written even a tolerable tragedy": "Ah (said the Patriarch) the composition of a tragedy requires *testicles*." "If this be true," Byron comments to his publisher, "Lord knows what Joanna Baillie does—I suppose she borrows them." Byron's regard for Baillie's potency was shared (without the regendering speculation) by many of her contemporaries, including William Wordsworth, who called her "the bold enchantress," Anna Laetitia Barbauld, Maria Edgeworth, Robert Southey, Samuel Taylor Coleridge, Felicia Hemans, who dedicated *Records of Woman* to her, and Sir Walter Scott, who deemed her the finest English dramatist since Shakespeare.

Born in 1762 in Scotland, Baillie traced her ancestry to the famously brave-hearted patriot William Wallace. She never married and lived her adult life with her unmarried sister. Her first literary efforts were poetry, published anonymously in 1790 as *Poems: Wherein it is Attempted to Describe Certain Views of Nature and Rustic Manners.* This was unsuccessful, and she turned to drama, with *Plays on the Passions,* as it is commonly known; the full title was *A Series of Plays in Which it is Attempted to Delineate the Stronger Passions of the Mind.* This appeared in three installments from 1798 to 1812. The first one was anonymous, and a curious public speculated about the identity of the author, believing it to be a man; Samuel Rogers, writing for *The Monthly Review,* insisted that the "Introductory Discourse" could have been written only by a man, and ascribed it to Baillie's brother. The program Baillie gave of "unveiling the human mind under the dominion of . . . strong and fixed passions" was echoed two years later by Wordsworth in his Preface to *Lyrical Ballads* (1800), which announces his similar devotion to tracing "the essential passions of the heart" in states of excitement. Although *De Monfort* attracted the leading actors of the day, including Sarah Siddons, John Philip Kemble, and Edmund Kean, the psychological emphases and philosophical introspectiveness of Baillie's plays were ill-suited to popular theater, and however much they impressed other poets, they were not successful on the stage. Baillie continued to write and publish plays over the next three decades, conceiving them as dramas for "the mental theatre of the reader," in Byron's words, taking a cue from Charles Lamb's essay on the unsuitability of Shakespeare's tragedies for stage representation (1811). In 1821, she published *Metrical Legends of Exalted Characters,* including "chronicles" of her ancestors Wallace and Lady Griselda Baillie, and she put out an expanded edition of her poems in 1840 under the title *Fugitive Verses.* Some of these pieces show her skill at the poetry in Scots dialect that Robert Burns popularized, while others follow the program of her dramas, voicing passion, sometimes in stormy moods, but often in quieter and more domestic scenes.

London

It is a goodly sight through the clear air,
From Hampstead's heathy height[1] to see at once

---

1. Hampstead heath, to the north, offers a view of London.

England's vast capital in fair expanse,
Towers, belfries,° lengthen'd streets, and structures fair.   *bell-towers*
5   St. Paul's high dome[2] amidst the vassal bands
Of neighb'ring spires, a regal chieftain stands,
And over fields of ridgy roofs appear,
With distance softly tinted, side by side,
In kindred grace, like twain of sisters dear,
10 The Towers of Westminster, her Abbey's pride;[3]
While, far beyond, the hills of Surrey shine[4]
Through thin soft haze, and show their wavy line.
View'd thus, a goodly sight! but when survey'd
Through denser air when moisten'd winds prevail,
15 In her grand panoply° of smoke array'd,   *armor*
While clouds aloft in heavy volumes sail,
She is sublime.—She seems a curtain'd gloom
Connecting heaven and earth,—a threat'ning sign of doom.
With more than natural height, rear'd in the sky
20 'Tis then St. Paul's arrests the wondering eye;
The lower parts in swathing mist conceal'd,
The higher through some half spent shower reveal'd,
So far from earth removed, that well, I trow,°   *believe*
Did not its form man's artful structure show,
25 It might some lofty alpine peak be deem'd,
The eagle's haunt, with cave and crevice seam'd.
Stretch'd wide on either hand, a rugged screen,
In lurid dimness, nearer streets are seen
Like shoreward billows of a troubled main,°   *open sea*
30 Arrested in their rage. Through drizzly rain,
Cataracts of tawny sheen pour from the skies,
Of furnace smoke black curling columns rise,
And many tinted vapours, slowly pass
O'er the wide draping of that pictured mass.

35   So shows by day this grand imperial town,
And, when o'er all the night's black stole is thrown,
The distant traveller doth with wonder mark
Her luminous canopy athwart the dark,
Cast up, from myriads of lamps that shine
40 Along her streets in many a starry line:—
He wondering looks from his yet distant road,
And thinks the northern streamers° are abroad.   *northern lights*
"What hollow sound is that?" approaching near,
The roar of many wheels breaks on his ear.
45 It is the flood of human life in motion!
It is the voice of a tempestuous ocean!

---

2. London's chief Anglican cathedral.
3. Westminster, a city within London, is the seat of government, the location of Westminster Palace (Parliament), Buckingham Palace (the royal family home), and Westminster Abbey, an imposing gothic church.
4. County southwest of London.

With sad but pleasing awe his soul is fill'd,
Scarce heaves his breast, and all within is still'd,
As many thoughts and feelings cross his mind,—
50 Thoughts, mingled, melancholy, undefined,
Of restless, reckless man, and years gone by,
And Time fast wending to Eternity.

1790, 1840

Thunder

Spirit of strength! to whom in wrath 'tis given,
To mar the earth and shake its vasty dome,
Behold the sombre robes whose gathering folds,
Thy secret majesty conceal. Their skirts
5 Spread on mid air move slow and silently,
O'er noon-day's beam thy sultry shroud is cast,
Advancing clouds from every point of heaven,
Like hosts° of gathering foes in pitchy volumes, *armies*
Grandly dilated, clothe the fields of air,
10 And brood° aloft o'er the empurpled earth. *hover*
Spirit of strength! it is thy awful hour;
The wind of every hill is laid to rest,
And far o'er sea and land deep silence reigns.

Wild creatures of the forest homeward hie,
15 And in their dens with fear unwonted° cower; *unaccustomed*
Pride in the lordly palace is put down,
While in his humble cot° the poor man sits *cottage*
With all his family round him hush'd and still,
In awful expectation. On his way
20 The traveller stands aghast and looks to heaven.
On the horizon's verge thy lightning gleams,
And the first utterance of thy deep voice
Is heard in reverence and holy fear.

From nearer clouds bright burst more vivid gleams,
25 As instantly in closing darkness lost;
Pale sheeted flashes cross the wide expanse
While over boggy moor or swampy plain,
A streaming cataract of flame appears,
To meet a nether fire from earth cast up,
30 Commingling terribly; appalling gloom
Succeeds, and lo! the rifted° centre pours *fissured*
A general blaze, and from the war of clouds,
Red, writhing falls the embodied bolt of heaven.
Then swells the rolling peal, full, deep'ning, grand,
35 And in its strength lifts the tremendous roar,
With mingled discord, rattling, hissing, growling;
Crashing like rocky fragments downward hurl'd,
Like the upbreaking of a ruined world,

In awful majesty the explosion bursts
40 Wide and astounding o'er the trembling land.
Mountain, and cliff, repeat the dread turmoil,
And all, to man's distinctive senses known,
Is lost in the immensity of sound.
Peal after peal succeeds with waning strength,
45 And hush'd and deep each solemn pause between.

Upon the lofty mountain's side
The kindled forest blazes wide;
Huge fragments of the rugged steep
Are tumbled to the lashing deep;
50 Firm rooted in his cloven rock,
Crashing falls the stubborn oak.
The lightning keen in wasteful ire
Darts fiercely on the pointed spire,
Rending in twain the iron-knit stone,
55 And stately towers to earth are thrown.
No human strength may brave the storm,
Nor shelter screen the shrinking form,
Nor castle wall its fury stay,
Nor massy gate impede its way:
60 It visits those of low estate,°   *the poor*
It shakes the dwellings of the great,
It looks athwart the vaulted tomb,
And glares upon the prison's gloom.
Then dungeons black in unknown light,
65 Flash hideous on the wretches' sight,
And strangely groans the downward cell,
Where silence deep is wont to dwell.

Now eyes, to heaven up-cast, adore,
Knees bend that never bent before,
70 The stoutest hearts begin to fail,
And many a manly face is pale;
Benumbing fear awhile up-binds,
The palsied action of their minds,
Till waked to dreadful sense they lift their eyes,
75 And round the stricken corse° shrill shrieks of horror rise.   *corpse*

Now rattling hailstones, bounding as they fall
To earth, spread motley winter o'er the plain;
Receding peals sound fainter on the ear,
And roll their distant grumbling far away:
80 The lightning doth in paler flashes gleam,
And through the rent cloud, silvered with his rays,
The sun on all this wild affray° looks down,   *tumult, quarrel*
As, high enthroned above all mortal ken,°   *understanding*
A higher Power beholds the strife of men.

1790, 1840

Robert Burns
1759–1796

A "striking example of native genius bursting through the obscurity of poverty and the obstructions of laborious life" exclaimed the *Edinburgh Magazine* when Burns's *Poems, Chiefly in the Scottish Dialect* appeared from provincial Kilmarnock in 1786. Yet the reality of the "heaven-taught plow-man" was more complex. A tenant farmer like his father, Burns planned to accept a position on a Jamaican plantation until the success of his poetry provided another means of escape from a hard existence. Though poor, Burns was well read; his poems, if "chiefly" in dialect, were never exclusively so: the accents and forms of folk culture play against a range of polite English genres. Fame brought Burns to Edinburgh, where he enlarged and reprinted his book. On the profits, Burns returned to farming and married Jean Armour, who had borne him children in 1786 and 1788.

The farm failed, as had its three predecessors, and Burns moved his family to Dumfries, where he obtained the post of exciseman, or tax-inspector. Government employment might seem anomalous for one who championed the American and French Revolutions, who believed in the goodness of man against the tenets of the Scots church, which he repeatedly satirized, and flamboyantly defied in his many erotic escapades, but Burns fulfilled his duties responsibly. An invitation in 1787 to contribute to *The Scots Musical Museum* intensified his sense of his Scots identity: for the next six years Burns became "absolutely crazed," as he put it, with collecting and editing traditional songs for the successive volumes, and wrote more than two hundred himself, new or adapted. When the fourth volume was finished in 1792, Burns agreed to participate in a *Select Collection of Scottish Airs,* a far more genteelly refining version of Scottish poetry. The more earthy energies of Burns's poetry appear in the posthumously published *Merry Muses of Caledonia* (1799–1800), a collection printed at least partly from Burns's papers following his early death from heart disease at the age of thirty-seven. The second version of *Comin' Thro' the Rye* and *The Fornicator* appeared in this work.

To a Mouse
On Turning Her Up in Her Nest with the Plough, November, 1785

	Wee, sleekit,° cowrin, tim'rous beastie,	*sleek*
	O, what a panic's in thy breastie!	
	Thou need na start awa sae° hasty	*so*
	Wi' bickering brattle!°	*scurry*
5	I wad be laith° to rin an' chase thee,	*loath*
	Wi' murdering pattle!°	*plough-scraper*
	I'm truly sorry man's dominion	
	Has broken Nature's social union,	
	An' justifies that ill opinion	
10	Which makes thee startle	
	At me, thy poor, earth-born companion	
	An' fellow mortal!	
	I doubt na, whyles,° but thou may thieve;	*sometimes*
	What then? poor beastie, thou maun° live!	*must*
15	A daimen icker in a thrave°	*odd ear in 24 sheaves*
	'S a sma' request;	

I'll get a blessin wi' the lave,°   rest
    An' never miss 't!

Thy wee-bit housie, too, in ruin!
20   Its silly wa's° the win's are strewin!   feeble walls
    An' naething, now, to big° a new ane,   build
        O' foggage° green!   coarse grass
    An' bleak December's win's ensuin,
        Baith snell° an' keen!   bitter

25   Thou saw the fields laid bare an' waste,
    An' weary winter comin fast,
    An' cozie here, beneath the blast,
        Thou thought to dwell,
    Till crash! the cruel coulter° past   plow-blade
30   Out thro' thy cell.

That wee bit heap o' leaves an' stibble,°   stubble
Has cost thee monie a weary nibble!
Now thou's turned out, for a' thy trouble,
    But° house or hald,°   without / goods
35   To thole° the winter's sleety dribble,   endure
        An' cranreuch° cauld!   hoarfrost

But Mousie, thou art no thy lane,°   not alone
In proving foresight may be vain:
The best-laid schemes o' mice an' men
40   Gang aft agley,°   go oft awry
An' lea'e us nought but grief an' pain,
    For promis'd joy!

Still thou art blest, compared wi' me!
The present only toucheth thee:
45   But och! I backward cast my e'e,
        On prospects drear!
    An' forward, tho' I canna see,
        I guess an' fear!

1785   1786

Comin' Thro' the Rye (1)[1]

CHORUS

O, Jenny's a' weet, poor body,
    Jenny's seldom dry:
    She draigl't° a' her petticoatie,   bedraggled
    Comin thro' the rye!

5   Comin thro' the rye, poor body,
        Comin thro' the rye,
    She draigl't a' her petticoatie,
        Comin thro' the rye!

1. A revision and expansion of an old song, also popular in various bawdy versions, as in the second version which follows, with obscenities tactfully hyphenated by the 1800 publisher.

Gin° a body meet a body   if
10   Comin thro' the rye,
Gin a body kiss a body,
Need a body cry?

Gin a body meet a body
Comin thro' the glen,
15   Gin a body kiss a body,
Need the warld ken?°   know

CHORUS

1796

Comin' Thro' the Rye (2)

CHORUS

O gin a body meet a body,
Comin throu the rye;
Gin a body f—k a body,
Need a body cry.

5   Comin' thro' the rye, my jo,°   sweetheart
An' comin' thro' the rye;
She fand a staun° o' staunin' graith,°   stand/tools
Comin' thro' the rye.

Gin a body meet a body,
10   Comin' thro' the glen;
Gin a body f—k a body,
Need the warld ken.

Gin a body meet a body,
Comin' thro' the grain;
15   Gin a body f—k a body,
C—t's a body's ain.°   own

Gin a body meet a body,
By a body's sel,
What na body f—s a body,
20   Wad a body tell.

Mony a body meets a body,
They dare na weel avow;
Mony a body f—s a body,
Ye wadna think it true.

1799–1800

A Red, Red Rose[1]

O, my luve is like a red, red rose,
That's newly sprung in June.
O, my luve is like the melodie,
That's sweetly play'd in tune.

---

1. This poem incorporates elements of several old ballads and folk songs, a common practice of amalgamation at which Burns had great success.

5   As fair art thou, my bonie lass,
           So deep in luve am I,
       And I will luve thee still, my dear,
           Till a' the seas gang° dry.   *go*

       Till a' the seas gang dry, my dear,
10   And the rocks melt wi' the sun!
       And I will luve thee still, my dear,
           While the sands o' life shall run.

       And fare thee weel, my only luve,
           And fare thee weel a while!
15   And I will come again, my luve,
           Tho' it were ten thousand mile!

1794   1796

Auld Lang Syne

       Should auld acquaintance be forgot,
           And never brought to mind?
       Should auld acquaintance be forgot,
           And auld lang syne!°   *long ago times*

                           CHORUS
5   For auld lang syne, my dear,
                  For auld lang syne,
              We'll tak a cup o' kindness yet
                  For auld lang syne!

       And surely ye'll be° your pint-stowp,°   *buy/pint-cup*
10   And surely I'll be mine,
       And we'll tak a cup o' kindness yet
           For auld lang syne!

                           CHORUS
       We twa hae run about the braes,°   *slopes*
           And pou'd° the gowans° fine,   *pulled/daisies*
15   But we've wander'd monie a weary fit°   *foot*
           Sin'° auld lang syne.   *since*

                           CHORUS
       We twa hae paidl'd in the burn[1]
           Frae morning sun till dine,°   *dinner (noon)*
       But seas between us braid° hae roar'd   *broad*
20   Sin' auld lang syne.

                           CHORUS
       And there's a hand, my trusty fiere,°   *friend*
           And gie's a hand o' thine,
       And we'll tak a right guid-willie waught°   *good-will swig*
           For auld lang syne!

                           CHORUS
25   For auld lang syne, my dear,
                  For auld lang syne,
              We'll tak a cup o' kindness yet
                  For auld lang syne!

1788   1796

---

1. Stream; waters used for brewing. "Burns" would especially appreciate the double sense.

The Fornicator. A New Song
Tune, Clout the Caldron

Ye jovial boys who love the joys
    The blissful joys of lovers;
Yet dare avow with dauntless brow,
    When the bony lass discovers:[1]
5   I pray draw near and lend an ear,
        And welcome in a Frater,°   *brother*
For I've lately been on quarantine,
    A proven Fornicator.

Before the Congregation wide
10   I pass'd the muster fairly,[2]
My handsome Betsey by my side,[3]
    We gat° our ditty° rarely;   *received / reproof*
But my downcast eye by chance did spy
    What made my lips to water,
15   Those limbs so clean where I, between
        Commenc'd a Fornicator.

With rueful face and signs of grace
        I pay'd the buttock-hire,[4]
The night was dark and thro the park
20   I could not but convoy her;
A parting kiss, what could I less,
        My vows began to scatter,
My Betsey fell—lal de dal lal lal,
    I am a Fornicator.

25   But for her sake this vow I make,
        And solemnly I swear it,
That while I own a single crown,
        She's welcome for to share it;
And my roguish boy his Mother's joy,
30   And the darling of his Pater,°   *father*
For him I boast my pains and cost,
    Although a Fornicator.

Ye wenching blades whose hireling jades[5]
    Have tipt you off blue-boram,[6]
35   I tell you plain, I do disdain
        To rank you in the Quorum;
But a bony lass upon the grass
        To teache her esse Mater,°   *to be a mother*
And no reward but for regard,
40   O that's a Fornicator.

Your warlike kings and heroes bold,
    Great Captains and Commanders;

---

1. Reveals her pregnancy.
2. In the Scottish Church those found guilty of fornication were required to sit, clothed in black, for three successive Sundays on a raised "stool of repentance."
3. Usually taken as Elizabeth Paton, with whom Burns

had an illegitimate child.
4. There was a six-pound fine for fornication.
5. Worn-out horses, a contemptuous term for women.
6. Infected you with syphilis. The term probably derives from the notorious Blue Boar Tavern in London.

Your mighty Cèsars fam'd of old,
    And Conquering Alexanders;
45   In fields they fought and laurels bought
    And bulwarks strong did batter,
But still they grac'd our noble list
    And ranked Fornicator!!!

1784–1785   1799

✦ ✦ ✦

William Wordsworth
1770–1850

Meeting Wordsworth in 1815, Byron told his wife that he had "but one feeling . . . reverence!" The exemplar of "plain living and high thinking," Wordsworth provided an image of poetry and "the Poet" as at once humble and exalted, domestic and severely moral. By the end of his life he had become a cultural institution, respected even by those who opposed his politics. Admirers made pilgrimages to his home at Rydal Mount in the Lake District. His beginnings were less auspicious. Born in the Lake District, Wordsworth was the son of the steward of Lord Lonsdale, the dominant landowner of the beautiful but isolated region. The death of Wordsworth's mother when he was eight years old broke a stable middle-class family life; William and his three brothers were sent to Hawkshead to school, and his sister Dorothy sent to live with various distant relatives. His father died five years later, at which point Lord Lonsdale resisted paying the monies owed to him; the children did not receive their inheritance until 1802, when a new Lord Lowther, who became Wordsworth's patron, succeeded to the title. "The props of my affection were removed, / And yet the building stood," Wordsworth exclaimed in a passage of the *Prelude* that readers have taken to refer obliquely to these early losses and separations; "taught to feel, perhaps too much, / The self-sufficing power of Solitude," Wordsworth developed a potent myth of himself as a "favoured being" shaped by the severe but mysteriously benevolent ministry of Nature.

In 1787 Wordsworth entered St. John's College, Cambridge, taking his degree in 1791 without distinction. As his autobiographical poem *The Prelude* testifies, his travels left deeper impressions than his studies: a summer walking tour in 1790 that brought him to France a year after the fall of the Bastille, then a trip through North Wales in 1791, and a year-long stay in France (1791–1792). There he became an active partisan in the heady early phase of the Revolution. "Bliss was it in that dawn to be alive, / But to be young was very Heaven!" as he wrote in *The Prelude*. The millenarian hopes of a new era were suffused with personal attachments: he had a love affair with Annette Vallon, who bore their daughter in December 1792. By then, lack of funds had forced him back to England, and the English declaration of war against France precluded his return until 1802. In him as in many of his generation, the war produced a crisis of loyalties, aggravated by the increasing violence of revolutionary France. "Sick, wearied out with contrarieties," Wordsworth recovered "a saving intercourse with [his] true self" only through the struggles that his poetry records.

A turning point came in 1795, when a small legacy of £900 from a friend enabled Wordsworth to devote himself to poetry. He reunited with Dorothy, and met Coleridge; in 1797 brother and sister moved to Alfoxden, to be near Coleridge at Nether Stowey. "[B]uoyant spirits / . . . were our daily portion when we first / Together wantoned in wild poesy," Wordsworth later wrote; comfortably housed, free to wander the countryside, Wordsworth and Coleridge collaborated on the poems that became *Lyrical Ballads*, published anonymously in

1798 to mixed reviews. The strangeness of *The Rime of the Ancyent Marinere* disconcerted some readers, and the audacious simplicity of Wordsworth's subjects and style offended more. But others felt the "power and pathos" of the poetry, even (in Hazlitt's words) "the sense of a new style and a new spirit." In 1800 Wordsworth published a second edition under his own name, adding a volume containing *Michael* and the "Lucy" poems and others written during the cold and lonely winter that he and Dorothy had passed in Germany in 1798–1799. A new Preface, defending his principles and repudiating the expectations of his readers, set the terms of his reception and continued to govern the charges against him by critics such as Francis Jeffrey for decades afterwards.

In late 1799 William and Dorothy returned to the Lakes and settled in the beautiful Grasmere valley, where they remained together for the rest of their lives: first at Dove Cottage, then, after 1813, at the more spacious Rydal Mount. In 1802 their household had expanded when Wordsworth married a childhood friend, and the tenor of their life was steady thereafter, though the years were marred by grave losses—his brother John drowned in 1805, when the ship he captained went down in a storm, two of his five children died in 1812, and a rift with Coleridge was not patched up until the 1820s. Harsh reviews of *Poems, in Two Volumes* (1807) and *The Excursion* (1814) paradoxically attested to Wordsworth's emerging centrality, and the publication of his revised and reordered *Poems* in 1815 asserted his claim to enter the canon of English poetry. Wordsworth continued to write and publish almost to the end of his long life. Though his increasingly conservative politics led some of the next generation to regard him as having betrayed his republican youth, and put him in opposition to the democratic and commercializing spirit of post-Reform Bill England, his reputation grew steadily, and in 1843 he was appointed Poet Laureate.

The Prelude, the poem that has most compelled modern readers, was published posthumously. Wordsworth had held back the work ("Title not yet fixed upon") that he had referred to variously as "the poem to Coleridge," "the poem on the growth of my own mind," and "the poem on my own poetical education," in part because he thought it "unprecedented" that an author should talk so much about himself, in part so as to bequeath its copyright as a legacy to his family. Reserving his most intimate and ambitious poem while revising it across four decades must have affected his often touchy attitude to his critics; by the time *The Prelude* appeared in 1850, the same year as Tennyson's *In Memoriam*, not even the "jacobinical" strain that Thomas Macaulay detected could much alter the image of him. For the Victorians, Wordsworth was the poet of nature, whose writings made the Lake District a tourist spot (much to his disgruntlement) and provided a moral philosophy of life, of childhood and "joy in widest commonalty spread," and above all, of memory and consolation. It was chiefly Wordsworth's "healing power" that led Matthew Arnold to declare in 1879 that Wordsworth stood third only to Milton and Shakespeare in English poetry since the Renaissance. Twentieth-century readers have been captivated by the visionary power of his language, those transient moments when "forms and substances . . . through the turnings intricate of verse, / Present themselves as objects recognized, / In flashes, and with a glory scarce their own." In Wordsworth's sustained effort in *The Prelude* to trace the growth of his mind while attending to experiences lying beyond and beneath the rational mind's grasp—"Points have we all of us within our souls / Where all stand single; this I feel, and make / Breathings for incommunicable powers"—some critics have discerned the beginnings of modern subjectivity. For Geoffrey Hartman, Wordsworth is "the most isolated figure among the great English poets." Other readers, though, have found in the tensions and ambivalences of Wordsworth's project a particularly rich embodiment of the strains of the pivotal decades in which he wrote, and he remains a crucial focus for understanding the vivid and contradictory currents of his age.

Other writing by Wordsworth appears in Perspectives: The Abolition of Slavery and the Slave Trade, page 1465.

LYRICAL BALLADS

In spring 1798 the young Wordsworth and Coleridge had been near neighbors in Somerset for almost a year. In the fall of 1797, they had decided to pay for a brief walking tour by collaborating on a poem to be sold to the *Monthly Magazine*. Uncompleted at the time, *The Rime of the Ancyent Marinere* became the opening poem of a more substantial enterprise: *Lyrical Ballads, with a few other poems*, the joint collection they published anonymously in October 1798. The exchange that nourished the project had been so close that Coleridge said that the two poets regarded the volume as "one work, in kind, though not in degree, as an ode is one work; and that our different poems are stanzas, good, relatively rather than absolutely," though of the twenty-three poems he wrote only four. A friend, the Bristol bookseller Joseph Cottle, agreed to pay the poets £30 for the copyright; before the book appeared they had departed for Germany, Coleridge to study philosophy at Göttingen and Wordsworth to learn German at Goslar, in hopes of later earning money as a translator. Priced at five shillings, the volume sold steadily and earned favorable reviews, but the simplicity of style, the focus on rural life and language, and the obscurity of the *Ancyent Marinere* provoked memorably sharp criticism. The volume had been prefixed by an Advertisement describing the majority of the poems as "experiments" to "ascertain how far the language of conversation in the middle and lower classes of society is adapted to the purposes of poetic pleasure." Attacking "the gaudiness and inane phraseology of many modern writers," and anticipating that "readers of superior judgment" would find that many of the poems would not "suit their taste," the Advertisement deliberately positioned the volume as an affront to "pre-established codes of decision," and thereby claimed for its authors the status of innovators.

Returned from Germany in 1800 and living in the Lake District, Wordsworth planned a second edition, which he sold to Longman, an established London publisher. He now dominated the project: the whole collection was published under his name alone, and Wordsworth replaced the Advertisement with an extended Preface vindicating his principles. A new second volume was made up entirely of his poems; the archaisms of the *Ancyent Marinere* were trimmed, and the poem, retitled *The Ancient Mariner: A Poet's Reverie*, was moved from the head of the first volume to the twenty-third position, accompanied by a condescending note ("The Poem of my Friend has indeed great defects"). The expanded collection sold quickly, and by 1802 a revised third edition appeared, with a significant addition to the Preface, "What is a poet?" The harsh critique by Francis Jeffrey in the newly founded *Edinburgh Review* (page 1555) may be seen as sealing the notoriety that Wordsworth had been courting; it surely helped propel the final edition of *Lyrical Ballads* in 1805, after which the contents were dispersed among the author's separate publications. Years later, in 1843, Wordsworth dictated notes on the circumstances of the poems' composition; these notes, recorded by Isabella Fenwick, are indicated as "[I.F.]."

FROM LYRICAL BALLADS (1798)
Simon Lee[1]
The Old Huntsman, with an incident in which he was concerned.

In the sweet shire of Cardigan,
Not far from pleasant Ivor-hall,
An old man dwells, a little man,
I've heard he once was tall.

---

1. "This old man had been huntsman to the squires of Alfoxden. . . . The old man's cottage stood upon the common, a little way from the entrance to Alfoxden Park. . . . I have, after an interval of 45 years, the image of the old man as fresh before my eyes as if I had seen him yesterday [I.F.]. Wordsworth has relocated the poem from Somersetshire, where he and his sister Dorothy lived from 1797–1798, to Cardiganshire, a former county of southwest Wales. A huntsman manages the hunt and has charge of the hounds. In the Preface of 1800, Wordsworth said he wrote the poem to provoke his readers' feelings "from ordinary moral sensations."

5 Of years he has upon his back,
 No doubt, a burthen weighty;
 He says he is three score and ten,°   *seventy years old*
 But others say he's eighty.

 A long blue livery-coat° has he,   *servant's uniform*
10 That's fair behind, and fair before;
 Yet, meet him where you will, you see
 At once that he is poor.
 Full five and twenty years he lived
 A running huntsman merry;
15 And, though he has but one eye left,
 His cheek is like a cherry.

 No man like him the horn could sound,
 And no man was so full of glee;
 To say the least, four counties round
20 Had heard of Simon Lee;
 His master's dead, and no one now
 Dwells in the hall of Ivor;
 Men, dogs, and horses, all are dead;
 He is the sole survivor.

25 His hunting feats have him bereft
 Of his right eye, as you may see:
 And then, what limbs those feats have left
 To poor old Simon Lee!
 He has no son, he has no child,
30 His wife, an aged woman,
 Lives with him, near the waterfall,
 Upon the village common.[2]

 And he is lean and he is sick,
 His little body's half awry
35 His ancles they are swoln and thick;
 His legs are thin and dry.
 When he was young he little knew
 Of husbandry or tillage;
 And now he's forced to work, though weak,
40 —The weakest in the village.

 He all the country could outrun,
 Could leave both man and horse behind;
 And often, ere the race was done,
 He reeled and was stone-blind.
45 And still there's something in the world
 At which his heart rejoices;
 For when the chiming hounds are out,
 He dearly loves their voices![3]

---

2. Common lands were progressively being enclosed as private property. Wordsworth successfully fought the enclosure of Grasmere's commons.

3. The expression when the hounds were out, "I dearly love their voices," was word for word from his own lips [I.F.].

Old Ruth works out of doors with him,
50 And does what Simon cannot do;
For she, not over stout° of limb,   *hardy*
Is stouter of the two.
And though you with your utmost skill
From labour could not wean them,
55 Alas! 'tis very little, all
Which they can do between them.

Beside their moss-grown hut of clay,
Not twenty paces from the door,
A scrap of land they have, but they
60 Are poorest of the poor.
This scrap of land he from the heath
Enclosed when he was stronger;
But what avails the land to them,
Which they can till no longer?

65 Few months of life has he in store,
As he to you will tell,
For still, the more he works, the more
His poor old ancles swell.
My gentle reader, I perceive
70 How patiently you've waited,
And I'm afraid that you expect
Some tale will be related.

O reader! had you in your mind
Such stores as silent thought can bring,
75 O gentle° reader! you would find   *kind, well-born*
A tale in every thing.
What more I have to say is short,
I hope you'll kindly take it;
It is no tale; but should you think,
80 Perhaps a tale you'll make it.

One summer-day I chanced to see
This old man doing all he could
About the root of an old tree,
A stump of rotten wood.
85 The mattock° totter'd in his hand;   *pick-ax*
So vain was his endeavour
That at the root of the old tree
He might have worked for ever.

"You're overtasked, good Simon Lee,
90 Give me your tool" to him I said;
And at the word right gladly he
Received my proffer'd aid.
I struck, and with a single blow
The tangled root I sever'd,
95 At which the poor old man so long
And vainly had endeavour'd.

The tears into his eyes were brought,
And thanks and praises seemed to run
So fast out of his heart, I thought
100   They never would have done.
—I've heard of hearts unkind, kind deeds
With coldness still returning.
Alas! the gratitude of men
Has oftner left me mourning.

1798   1798

We Are Seven[1]

A simple child, dear brother Jim,
That lightly draws its breath,
And feels its life in every limb,
What should it know of death?

5   I met a little cottage girl,
She was eight years old, she said;
Her hair was thick with many a curl
That cluster'd round her head.

She had a rustic, woodland air,
10   And she was wildly clad;
Her eyes were fair, and very fair,
—Her beauty made me glad.

"Sisters and brothers, little maid,
How many may you be?"
15   "How many? seven in all," she said,
And wondering looked at me.

"And where are they, I pray you tell?"
She answered, "Seven are we,
And two of us at Conway° dwell,   *Welsh seaport*
20   And two are gone to sea.

"Two of us in the church-yard lie,
My sister and my brother,
And in the church-yard cottage, I
Dwell near them with my mother."

25   "You say that two at Conway dwell,
And two are gone to sea,
Yet you are seven; I pray you tell
Sweet Maid, how this may be?"

Then did the little Maid reply,
30   "Seven boys and girls are we;

1. The little girl who is the heroine I met within the area of Goodrich Castle in the year 1793. . . . I composed it while walking in the grove at Alfoxden. My friends will not deem it too trifling to relate that while walking to and fro I composed the last stanza first having begun with the last line [I.F.]. Coleridge wrote the first stanza. Wordsworth's own mother died when he was turning eight, the age of the girl in the poem.

Two of us in the church-yard lie,
Beneath the church-yard tree."

"You run about, my little Maid,
Your limbs they are alive;
35   If two are in the church-yard laid,
Then ye are only five."

"Their graves are green, they may be seen,"
The little Maid replied,
"Twelve steps or more from my mother's door,
40   And they are side by side.

"My stockings there I often knit,
My 'kerchief there I hem;
And there upon the ground I sit—
I sit and sing to them.

45   "And often after sunset, Sir,
When it is light and fair,
I take my little porringer,°   porridge-bowl
And eat my supper there.

"The first that died was little Jane;
50   In bed she moaning lay,
Till God released her of her pain,
And then she went away.

"So in the church-yard was she laid;
And all the summer dry,
55   Together round her grave we played,
My brother John and I.

"And when the ground was white with snow,
And I could run and slide,
My brother John was forced to go,
60   And he lies by her side."

"How many are you then," said I,
"If they two are in Heaven?"
The little Maiden did reply,
"O Master! we are seven."

65   "But they are dead; those two are dead!
Their spirits are in heaven!"
'Twas throwing words away; for still
The little Maid would have her will,
And said, "Nay, we are seven!"

1798   1798

Lines Written in Early Spring

I heard a thousand blended notes,
While in a grove I sate reclined,
In that sweet mood when pleasant thoughts
Bring sad thoughts to the mind.

5   To her fair works did nature link
     The human soul that through me ran;
     And much it griev'd my heart to think
     What man has made of man.

     Through primrose-tufts, in that sweet bower,
10   The periwinkle trail'd its wreathes;
     And 'tis my faith that every flower
     Enjoys the air it breathes.

     The birds around me hopp'd and play'd:
     Their thoughts I cannot measure,°   *assess, put in meters*
15   But the least motion which they made,
     It seem'd a thrill of pleasure.

     The budding twigs spread out their fan,
     To catch the breezy air;
     And I must think, do all I can,
20   That there was pleasure there.

     If I these thoughts may not prevent,
     If such be of my creed the plan,
     Have I not reason to lament
     What man has made of man?

1798   1798

Expostulation and Reply[1]

     "Why William, on that old grey stone,
     Thus for the length of half a day,
     Why William, sit you thus alone,
     And dream your time away?

5   "Where are your books? that light bequeath'd
     To beings else forlorn and blind!
     Up! Up! and drink the spirit breath'd
     From dead men to their kind.

     You look round on your mother earth,
10   As if she for no purpose bore you;
     As if you were her first-born birth,
     And none had lived before you!"

     One morning thus, by Esthwaite lake,[2]
     When life was sweet I knew not why,
15   To me my good friend Matthew spake,
     And thus I made reply.

     "The eye it cannot chuse but see,
     We cannot bid the ear be still;

---

1. This and the following poem opened the second edition of *Lyrical Ballads*. They are companion pieces that Wordsworth claimed "arose out of a conversation with a friend who was somewhat unreasonably attached to modern books of Moral Philosophy" ("Advertisement," 1798)— probably William Hazlitt, who visited him in 1798 and argued about metaphysics. Wordsworth later noted the poem's popularity among Quakers, whose worship is typically informal and spontaneous.
2. At Hawkshead, where Wordsworth went to school.

20   Our bodies feel, where'er they be,
Against, or with our will.

"Nor less I deem that there are powers,
Which of themselves our minds impress,
That we can feed this mind of ours,
In a wise passiveness.

25   "Think you, mid all this mighty sum
Of things for ever speaking,
That nothing of itself will come,
But we must still be seeking?

"—Then ask not wherefore, here, alone,
30   Conversing as I may,
I sit upon this old grey stone,
And dream my time away."

1798   1798

The Tables Turned

An Evening Scene, on the Same Subject

Up! up! my friend, and clear your looks,
Why all this toil and trouble?[1]
Up! up! my friend, and quit your books,
Or surely you'll grow double.°   *doubled over*

5   The sun above the mountain's head,
A freshening lustre mellow,
Through all the long green fields has spread,
His first sweet evening yellow.

Books! 'tis a dull and endless strife,
10   Come, hear the woodland linnet,°   *finch*
How sweet his music; on my life
There's more of wisdom in it.

And hark! how blithe the throstle° sings!   *thrush*
And he is no mean preacher;
15   Come forth into the light of things,
Let Nature be your teacher.

She has a world of ready wealth,
Our minds and hearts to bless—
Spontaneous wisdom breathed by health,
20   Truth breathed by chearfulness.

One impulse from a vernal wood
May teach you more of man;
Of moral evil and of good,
Than all the sages can.

25   Sweet is the lore which nature brings;
Our meddling intellect

---

1. A joking reference to the witches' incantation in *Macbeth* (4.1.10).

Misshapes the beauteous forms of things;
—We murder to dissect.

Enough of science and of art;°   *liberal arts*
30   Close up these barren leaves;°   *pages*
Come forth, and bring with you a heart
That watches and receives.

1798   1798

Old Man Travelling
Animal Tranquility and Decay[1]

A SKETCH

The little hedge-row birds,
That peck along the road, regard him not.
He travels on, and in his face, his step,
His gait, is one expression; every limb,
5   His look and bending figure, all bespeak
A man who does not move with pain, but moves
With thought—He is insensibly subdued
To settled quiet: he is one by whom
All effort seems forgotten, one to whom
10   Long patience has such mild composure given,
That patience now doth seem a thing, of which
He hath no need. He is by nature led
To peace so perfect, that the young behold
With envy, what the old man hardly feels.[2]
15   —I asked him whither he was bound, and what
The object of his journey; he replied
"Sir! I am going many miles to take
A last leave of my son, a mariner,
Who from a sea-fight has been brought to Falmouth,[3]
20   And there is dying in an hospital."

1798   1798

Tintern Abbey

"No poem of mine was composed under circumstances more pleasant for me to remember than this. I began it upon leaving Tintern, after crossing the Wye, and concluded it just as I was entering Bristol in the evening, after a ramble of 4 or 5 days, with my sister. Not a line of it was altered, and not any part of it written down till I reached Bristol." So Wordsworth recalled in 1843, but he had been practicing the gestures of the poem for some time: a manuscript fragment of 1796–1797 underlies the seemingly spontaneous opening and one of its central formulations: "Yet once again do I behold the forms / Of these huge mountains, and yet once again, / Standing beneath these elms, I hear thy voice, / Beloved Derwent, that peculiar voice / Heard in the stillness of the evening air, / Half-heard and half-created." Wordsworth first visited the

1. In 1800 the main title was discarded. "Animal" involves two nearly antithetical senses: mere physical existences; spiritually "animated" life.
2. Lines 15–20 were dropped in 1815 and after. The sub-
title "A Sketch" was dropped in 1845.
3. On the south coast of Cornwall. The journey is more than 120 miles.

Wye valley in August 1793, on a solo walking tour; the return with his sister in July 1798 prompted this spacious meditation on time and memory, in which the ruined Abbey, a famous picturesque destination, does not appear. Instead, it is replaced by the inward "fluxes and refluxes of the mind" that shape the poem, which concludes the 1798 *Lyrical Ballads*. In 1800 Wordsworth added a note on the elevated manner: "I have not ventured to call this Poem an Ode; but it was written with a hope that in the transitions, and the impassioned music of the versification, would be found the principal requisites of that species of composition."

Lines Written a Few Miles above Tintern Abbey
On Revisiting the Banks of the Wye during a Tour, July 13, 1798

Five years have passed; five summers, with the length
Of five long winters! and again I hear
These waters, rolling from their mountain-springs
With a sweet inland murmur.[1]—Once again
5   Do I behold these steep and lofty cliffs,
Which on a wild secluded scene impress
Thoughts of more deep seclusion; and connect
The landscape with the quiet of the sky.
The day is come when I again repose
10   Here, under this dark sycamore, and view
These plots of cottage-ground, these orchard-tufts,
Which, at this season, with their unripe fruits,
Among the woods and copses lose themselves,
Nor, with their green and simple hue, disturb
15   The wild green landscape. Once again I see
These hedge-rows, hardly hedge-rows, little lines
Of sportive wood run wild; these pastoral farms
Green to the very door; and wreathes of smoke
Sent up, in silence, from among the trees,
20   With some uncertain notice, as might seem,
Of vagrant dwellers in the houseless woods,
Or of some hermit's cave, where by his fire
The hermit° sits alone.   *religious recluse*

Though absent long,
These forms of beauty have not been to me,
25   As is a landscape to a blind man's eye:
But oft, in lonely rooms, and mid the din
Of towns and cities, I have owed to them,
In hours of weariness, sensations sweet,
Felt in the blood, and felt along the heart,
30   And passing even into my purer mind
With tranquil restoration:—feelings too
Of unremembered pleasure; such, perhaps,
As may have had no trivial influence
On that best portion of a good man's life;
35   His little, nameless, unremembered acts
Of kindness and of love. Nor less, I trust,
To them I may have owed another gift,

---

1. The river is not affected by the tides a few miles above Tintern [Wordsworth's note, 1798].

Of aspect more sublime; that blessed mood,
In which the burthen° of the mystery,[2]   *burden*
40   In which the heavy and the weary weight
Of all this unintelligible world
Is lighten'd:—that serene and blessed mood,
In which the affections gently lead us on,
Until, the breath of this corporeal frame,
45   And even the motion of our human blood
Almost suspended, we are laid asleep
In body, and become a living soul:
While with an eye made quiet by the power
Of harmony, and the deep power of joy,
50   We see into the life of things.

                      If this
Be but a vain belief, yet, oh! how oft,
In darkness, and amid the many shapes
Of joyless day-light; when the fretful stir
Unprofitable, and the fever of the world,
55   Have hung upon the beatings of my heart,[3]
How oft, in spirit, have I turned to thee
O sylvan Wye! Thou wanderer through the wood
How often has my spirit turned to thee!

And now, with gleams of half-extinguish'd thought.
60   With many recognitions dim and faint,
And somewhat of a sad perplexity,
The picture of the mind revives again:
While here I stand, not only with the sense
Of present pleasure, but with pleasing thoughts
65   That in this moment there is life and food
For future years. And so I dare to hope
Though changed, no doubt, from what I was, when first
I came among these hills; when like a roe
I bounded o'er the mountains, by the sides
70   Of the deep rivers, and the lonely streams,
Wherever nature led; more like a man
Flying from something that he dreads, than one
Who sought the thing he loved. For nature then
(The coarser pleasures of my boyish days,
75   And their glad animal movements all gone by,)
To me was all in all.—I cannot paint
What then I was. The sounding cataract
Haunted me like a passion: the tall rock,
The mountain, and the deep and gloomy wood,
80   Their colours and their forms, were then to me
An appetite: a feeling and a love,
That had no need of a remoter charm,

---

2. Keats thought this phrase the core of Wordsworth's
"genius." See his letter of 3 May 1818 (page 1774).
3. Echoing Macbeth's sense of life's fitful fever (3.2.23)

and Hamlet's view of life as "weary, stale, flat, and
unprofitable" (1.2.133).

By thought supplied, or any interest
Unborrowed from the eye.—That time is past,
85   And all its aching joys are now no more,
And all its dizzy raptures. Not for this
Faint° I, nor mourn nor murmur: other gifts   *lose heart*
Have followed, for such loss, I would believe,
Abundant recompence. For I have learned
90   To look on nature, not as in the hour
Of thoughtless youth, but hearing oftentimes
The still, sad music of humanity,
Not harsh nor grating, though of ample power
To chasten and subdue. And I have felt
95   A presence that disturbs me with the joy
Of elevated thoughts; a sense sublime
Of something far more deeply interfused,
Whose dwelling is the light of setting suns,
And the round ocean, and the living air,
100   And the blue sky, and in the mind of man,
A motion and a spirit, that impels
All thinking things, all objects of all thought,
And rolls through all things. Therefore am I still
A lover of the meadows and the woods,
105   And mountains; and of all that we behold
From this green earth; of all the mighty world
Of eye and ear, both what they half-create,[4]
And what perceive; well pleased to recognize
In nature and the language of the sense,
110   The anchor of my purest thoughts, the nurse,
The guide, the guardian of my heart, and soul
Of all my moral being.

                    Nor, perchance,
If I were not thus taught, should I the more
Suffer my genial° spirits to decay: *creative*
115   For thou art with me, here, upon the banks
Of this fair river; thou, my dearest Friend,[5]
My dear, dear Friend, and in thy voice I catch°   *sense, arrest*
The language of my former heart, and read
My former pleasures in the shooting lights
120   Of thy wild eyes. Oh! yet a little while
May I behold in thee what I was once,
My dear, dear Sister! And this prayer I make,
Knowing that Nature never did betray
The heart that loved her; 'tis her privilege,
125   Through all the years of this our life, to lead
From joy to joy: for she can so inform
The mind that is within us, so impress

---

4. This line has a close resemblance to an admirable line of Young, the exact expression of which I cannot recollect [Wordsworth's note]. He is thinking of Edward Young's "half create the wondrous world they see" (*The*

Complaint or Night Thoughts [1744], 6.427).
5. His sister Dorothy. The language echoes Psalm 23: "Yea, though I walk through the valley of the shadow of death, I will fear no evil: for thou art with me."

With quietness and beauty, and so feed
With lofty thoughts, that neither evil tongues,[6]
130 Rash judgments, nor the sneers of selfish men,
Nor greetings where no kindness is, nor all
The dreary intercourse of daily life,
Shall e'er prevail against us, or disturb
Our chearful faith that all which we behold
135 Is full of blessings. Therefore let the moon
Shine on thee in thy solitary walk;
And let the misty mountain winds be free
To blow against thee: and in after years,
When these wild ecstasies shall be matured
140 Into a sober pleasure, when thy mind
Shall be a mansion for all lovely forms,
Thy memory be as a dwelling-place
For all sweet sounds and harmonies; Oh! then,
If solitude, or fear, or pain, or grief,
145 Should be thy portion,° with what healing thoughts   dowry, bequest
Of tender joy wilt thou remember me,
And these my exhortations! Nor, perchance,
If I should be, where I no more can hear
Thy voice, nor catch from thy wild eyes these gleams
150 Of past existence, wilt thou then forget
That on the banks of this delightful stream
We stood together; and that I, so long
A worshipper of Nature, hither came,
Unwearied in that service: rather say
155 With warmer love, oh! with far deeper zeal
Of holier love. Nor wilt thou then forget,
That after many wanderings, many years
Of absence, these steep woods and lofty cliffs,
And this green pastoral landscape, were to me
160 More dear, both for themselves, and for thy sake.
1798   1798

FROM **LYRICAL BALLADS (1800, 1802)**
from **Preface**[1]

The First Volume of these Poems has already been submitted to general perusal.[2] It was published, as an experiment which, I hoped, might be of some use to ascertain how far, by fitting to metrical arrangement a selection of the real language of men in a state of vivid sensation, that sort of pleasure and that quantity of pleasure may be imparted, which a Poet may rationally endeavor to impart. * * *

They who have been accustomed to the gaudiness and inane phraseology of many modern writers, if they persist in reading this book to its conclusion, will, no doubt, frequently have to struggle with feelings of strangeness and aukwardness: they

6. An echo of Milton's claim to "Sing with mortal voice, unchang'd / To hoarse or mute, though fall'n on evil days, / . . . and evil tongues" (*Paradise Lost* 7.24–26).
1. The Preface first appeared in the edition of 1800. The

text given here is the revised preface of 1802.
2. That is, *Lyrical Ballads*, 1798, which formed the first volume in the two-volume edition of 1800.

will look round for poetry, and will be induced to inquire by what species of courtesy these attempts can be permitted to assume that title. * * * I hope, therefore, the Reader will not censure me, if I attempt to state what I have proposed to myself to perform.

[THE PRINCIPAL OBJECT OF THE POEMS. HUMBLE AND RUSTIC LIFE]

The principal object, then, proposed in these poems was to chuse incidents and situations from common life, and to relate or describe them, throughout, as far as was possible, in a selection of language really used by men, and, at the same time, to throw over them a certain colouring of imagination, whereby ordinary things should be presented to the mind in an unusual way; and further, and above all, to make these incidents and situations interesting by tracing in them, truly though not ostentatiously, the primary laws of our nature: chiefly as far as regards the manner in which we associate ideas in a state of excitement. Low and rustic life was generally chosen, because in that condition the essential passions of the heart find a better soil in which they can attain their maturity, are less under restraint, and speak a plainer and more emphatic language; because in that condition of life our elementary feelings co-exist in a state of greater simplicity and consequently may be more accurately contemplated and more forcibly communicated; because the manners of rural life germinate from those elementary feelings; and from the necessary character of rural occupations, are more easily comprehended, and are more durable; and, lastly, because in that condition the passions of men are incorporated with the beautiful and permanent forms of nature. The language, too, of these men has been adopted (purified indeed from what appear to be its real defects, from all lasting and rational causes of dislike or disgust) because such men hourly communicate with the best objects from which the best part of language is originally derived; and because, from their rank in society and the sameness and narrow circle of their intercourse, being less under the influence of social vanity they convey their feelings and notions in simple and unelaborated expressions. Accordingly, such a language, arising out of repeated experience and regular feelings, is a more permanent, and a far more philosophical language, than that which is frequently substituted for it by Poets, who think that they are conferring honour upon themselves and their art, in proportion as they separate themselves from the sympathies of men, and indulge in arbitrary and capricious habits of expression, in order to furnish food for fickle tastes, and fickle appetites of their own creation.[3]

["THE SPONTANEOUS OVERFLOW OF POWERFUL FEELINGS"]

[A]ll good poetry is the spontaneous overflow of powerful feelings: but though this be true, Poems to which any value can be attached, were never produced on any variety of subjects but by a man who, being possessed of more than usual organic sensibility, had also thought long and deeply. For our continued influxes of feeling are modified and directed by our thoughts, which are indeed the representatives of all our past feelings; and, as by contemplating the relation of these general representatives to each other we discover what is really important to men, so, by the repetition and continuance of this act, our feelings will be connected with important subjects, till at length, if we be originally possessed of much sensibility,

---

3. It is worth while here to observe that the affecting parts of Chaucer are almost always expressed in language pure and universally intelligible even to this day [Wordsworth's note].

such habits of mind will be produced that, by obeying blindly and mechanically the impulses of those habits, we shall describe objects, and utter sentiments, of such a nature, and in such connection with each other, that the understanding of the reader must necessarily be in some degree enlightened, and his affections ameliorated.

I have said that each of these poems has a purpose. * * * I should mention one other circumstance which distinguishes these Poems from the popular Poetry of the day; it is this, that the feeling therein developed gives importance to the action and situation, and not the action and situation to the feeling. * * * I will not suffer a sense of false modesty to prevent me from asserting, that I point my Reader's attention to this mark of distinction, far less for the sake of these particular Poems than from the general importance of the subject. The subject is indeed important! For the human mind is capable of being excited without the application of gross and violent stimulants; and he must have a very faint perception of its beauty and dignity who does not know this, and who does not further know, that one being is elevated above another in proportion as he possesses this capability. It has therefore appeared to me, that to endeavor to produce or enlarge this capability is one of the best services in which, at any period, a Writer can be engaged; but this service, excellent at all times, is especially so at the present day. For a multitude of causes, unknown to former times, are now acting with a combined force to blunt the discriminating powers of the mind, and, unfitting it for all voluntary exertion to reduce it to a state of almost savage torpor. The most effective of these causes are the great national events which are daily taking place, and the encreasing accumulation of men in cities, where the uniformity of their occupations produces a craving for extraordinary incident, which the rapid communication of intelligence hourly gratifies.[4] To this tendency of life and manners the literature and theatrical exhibitions of the country have conformed themselves. The invaluable works of our elder writers, I had almost said the works of Shakespear and Milton, are driven into neglect by frantic novels, sickly and stupid German Tragedies, and deluges of idle and extravagant stories in verse.[5]—When I think upon this degrading thirst after outrageous stimulation, I am almost ashamed to have spoken of the feeble effort with which I have endeavoured to counteract it; and, reflecting upon the magnitude of the general evil, I should be oppressed with no dishonorable melancholy, had I not a deep impression of certain inherent and indestructible qualities of the human mind, and likewise of certain powers in the great and permanent objects that act upon it which are equally inherent and indestructible; and did I not further add to this impression a belief, that the time is approaching when the evil will be systematically opposed, by men of greater powers, and with far more distinguished success.

[THE LANGUAGE OF POETRY]

Having dwelt thus long on the subjects and aim of these Poems, I shall request the Reader's permission to apprize him of a few circumstances relating to their *style*, in order, among other reasons, that he may not censure me for not having performed what I never attempted. The reader will find that personifications of abstract ideas rarely occur in these volumes; and, I hope, are utterly rejected as an ordinary device

---

4. That is, the rapid increase in daily newspaper production at this time. The "events" include the war with France, the Irish rebellion, and the sedition trials at home.

5. For example, sentimental melodramas and the popular Gothic novels of Ann Radcliffe and "Monk" Lewis.

to elevate the style, and raise it above prose. I have proposed to myself to imitate, and, as far as is possible, to adopt the very language of men; and assuredly such personifications do not make any natural or regular part of that language. They are, indeed, a figure of speech occasionally prompted by passion, and I have made use of them as such; but have endeavoured utterly to reject them as a mechanical device of style, or as a family language which Writers in metre seem to lay claim to by prescription. I have wished to keep my Reader in the company of flesh and blood, persuaded that by so doing I shall interest him. Others who pursue a different track will interest him likewise; I do not interfere with their claim, I only wish to prefer a claim of my own. There will also be found in these volumes little of what is usually called poetic diction; as much pains has been taken to avoid it as others ordinarily take to produce it; this I have done for the reason already alleged, to bring my language near to the language of men, and further, because the pleasure which I have proposed to myself to impart is of a kind very different from that which is supposed by many persons to be the proper object of poetry. I do not know how without being culpably particular I can give my Reader a more exact notion of the style in which I wished these poems to be written, than by informing him that I have at all times endeavoured to look steadily at my subject; consequently, I hope that there is in these Poems little falsehood of description, and my ideas are expressed in language fitted to their respective importance. Something I must have gained by this practice, as it is friendly to one property of all good poetry, namely, good sense; but it has necessarily cut me off from a large portion of phrases and figures of speech which from father to son have long been regarded as the common inheritance of Poets. * * *

To illustrate the subject in a general manner, I will here adduce a short composition of Gray,[1] who was at the head of those who, by their reasonings, have attempted to widen the space of separation betwixt Prose and Metrical composition, and was more than any other man curiously elaborate in the structure of his own poetic diction.

> In vain to me the smiling mornings shine,
> And reddening Phœbus° lifts his golden fire: sun god
> The birds in vain their amorous descant° join,   song
> Or chearful fields resume their green attire:
> These ears alas! for other notes repine;°   languish
> *A different object do these eyes require;*
> *My lonely anguish melts no heart but mine;*
> *And in my breast the imperfect joys expire;*
> Yet Morning smiles the busy race to cheer,
> And new-born pleasure brings to happier men;
> The fields to all their wonted tribute bear;
> To warm their little loves the birds complain.
> *I fruitless mourn to him that cannot hear*
> *And weep the more because I weep in vain.*

It will easily be perceived, that the only part of this Sonnet which is of any value is the lines printed in Italics; it is equally obvious, that, except in the rhyme, and in

---

1. Thomas Gray (1716–1771) is best known for *Elegy Written in a Country Church-Yard* (page 1245). The poem Wordsworth quotes (adding italics) is *Sonnet On the Death of Richard West* (1775). Grey had said to West that "the language of the age is never the language of poetry."

the use of the single word "fruitless" for fruitlessly, which is so far a defect, the language of these lines does in no respect differ from that of prose.

By the foregoing quotation I have shewn that the language of Prose may yet be well adapted to Poetry; and I have previously asserted that a large portion of the language of every good poem can in no respect differ from that of good Prose. I will go further. I do not doubt that it may be safely affirmed, that there neither is, nor can be, any essential difference between the language of prose and metrical composition.[2]

[What Is a Poet?]

What is a Poet? To whom does he address himself? And what language is to be expected from him? He is a man speaking to men: a man, it is true, endued with more lively sensibility, more enthusiasm and tenderness, who has a greater knowledge of human nature, and a more comprehensive soul, than are supposed to be common among mankind; a man pleased with his own passions and volitions, and who rejoices more than other men in the spirit of life that is in him; delighting to contemplate similar volitions and passions as manifested in the goings-on of the Universe, and habitually impelled to create them where he does not find them. To these qualities he has added a disposition to be affected more than other men by absent things as if they were present; an ability of conjuring up in himself passions, which are indeed far from being the same as those produced by real events, yet (especially in those parts of the general sympathy which are pleasing and delightful) do more nearly resemble the passions produced by real events, than anything which, from the motions of their own minds merely, other men are accustomed to feel in themselves; whence, and from practice, he has acquired a greater readiness and power in expressing what he thinks and feels, and especially those thoughts and feelings which, by his own choice, or from the structure of his own mind, arise in him without immediate external excitement.

But, whatever portion of this faculty we may suppose even the greatest Poet to possess, there cannot be a doubt that the language which it will suggest to him, must in liveliness and truth, fall far short of that which is uttered by men in real life, under the actual pressure of those passions, certain shadows of which the Poet thus produces, or feels to be produced, in himself. However exalted a notion we would wish to cherish of the character of a Poet, it is obvious, that while he describes and imitates passions, his situation is altogether slavish and mechanical, compared with the freedom and power of real and substantial action and suffering. So that it will be the wish of the Poet to bring his feelings near to those of the persons whose feelings he describes, nay, for short spaces of time perhaps, to let himself slip into an entire delusion, and even confound and identify his own feelings with theirs; modifying only the language which is thus suggested to him, by a consideration that he describes for a particular purpose, that of giving pleasure. Here, then, he will apply the principle on which I have so much insisted, namely, that of selection; on this he will depend for removing what would otherwise be painful or disgusting in the passion; he will feel that there is no necessity to trick out or to elevate nature: and, the more industriously he applies this principle, the deeper will be his faith that no words which his fancy or imagination can suggest, will be to be compared with those which are the emanations of reality and truth.

---

2. Wordsworth's footnote says that he means "Poetry" as opposed to "Prose, and synonymous with metrical composition"; he concedes that "much confusion has been introduced into criticism by this contradistinction of Poetry and Prose, instead of the more philosophical one of Poetry and Matter of fact, or Science. The only strict antithesis to Prose is Metre; nor is this, in truth, a *strict* antithesis; because lines and passages of metre so naturally occur in writing prose, that it would be scarcely possible to avoid them, even were it desirable."

["EMOTION RECOLLECTED IN TRANQUILLITY"]

I have said that Poetry is the spontaneous overflow of powerful feelings; it takes its origin from emotion recollected in tranquillity: the emotion is contemplated till, by a species of reaction, the tranquillity gradually disappears, and an emotion, kindred to that which was before the subject of contemplation, is gradually produced, and does itself actually exist in the mind. In this mood successful composition generally begins.

There was a Boy[1]

There was a Boy; ye knew him well, ye Cliffs
And Islands of Winander![2] many a time,
At evening, when the earliest stars had just begun
To move along the edges of the hills,
5   Rising or setting, would he stand alone,
Beneath the trees, or by the glimmering lake,
And there, with fingers interwoven, both hands
Press'd closely palm to palm and to his mouth
Uplifted, he, as through an instrument,
10   Blew mimic hootings to the silent owls
That they might answer him. And they would shout
Across the wat'ry vale and shout again
Responsive to his call, with quivering peals,
And long halloos, and screams, and echoes loud
15   Redoubled and redoubled, a wild scene
Of mirth and jocund din! And, when it chanced
That pauses of deep silence mock'd his skill,
Then, sometimes, in that silence, while he hung
Listening, a gentle shock of mild surprize
20   Has carried far into his heart the voice
Of mountain-torrents; or the visible scene
Would enter unawares into his mind
With all its solemn imagery, its rocks,
Its woods, and that uncertain heaven receiv'd
25   Into the bosom of the steady lake.
    Fair are the woods, and beauteous is the spot,
The vale where he was born: the Church-yard hangs
Upon a slope above the village school;[3]
And there along that bank where I have pass'd
30   At evening, I believe, that near his grave
A full half-hour together I have stood,
Mute—for he died when he was ten years old.

1797–1798   1800

---

1. First drafted in Germany in 1798 in the first person, these lines were later assimilated to *The Prelude* Book 5 as an example of education by "Nature." In his collection of 1815, Wordsworth had this poem lead off the subsection "Poems of the Imagination," commenting in his Preface that it displayed "one of the earliest processes of Nature in the development of this faculty. Guided by one of my own primary consciousnesses, I have presented a commu-

tation and transfer of internal feelings, co-operating with external accidents, to plant, for immortality, images of sound and sight, in the celestial soil of the Imagination."
2. Windermere, in the Lake District.
3. Hawkshead Grammar School, which Wordsworth attended as a child in the Lake district village of Esthwaite.

Strange fits of passion have I known[1]

Strange fits of passion have I known,
And I will dare to tell,
But in the lover's ear alone,
What once to me befel.

5 When she I lov'd, was strong and gay
And like a rose in June,
I to her cottage bent my way,
Beneath the evening moon.

Upon the moon I fix'd my eye,
10 All over the wide lea;
My horse trudg'd on, and we drew nigh
Those paths so dear to me.

And now we reach'd the orchard plot,
And, as we climb'd the hill,
15 Towards the roof of Lucy's cot°   cottage
The moon descended still.

In one of those sweet dreams I slept,
Kind Nature's gentlest boon!
And, all the while, my eyes I kept
20 On the descending moon.

My horse mov'd on; hoof after hoof
He rais'd, and never stopp'd:
When down behind the cottage roof
At once the planet dropp'd.

25 What fond and wayward thoughts will slide
Into a Lover's head—
"O mercy!" to myself I cried,
"If Lucy should be dead!"[2]

1798–1799   1800

Song (She dwelt among th' untrodden ways)

She dwelt among th' untrodden ways
   Beside the springs of Dove,[1]
A Maid whom there were none to praise
   And very few to love:

5 A Violet by a mossy stone
   Half-hidden from the Eye![2]
—Fair, as a star when only one
   Is shining in the sky!

1. This and the three following lyrics, all written during a
lonely winter that William and Dorothy spent in Germany, compose four of five lyrics traditionally called the
"Lucy Poems." Lucy has not been conclusively identified.
The name "Lucy" comes from the Latin "lux" (light);
"Lucina" is an old name for the goddess of the moon.
2. A manuscript from 1799 shows a final stanza later

deleted: "I told her this: her laughter light / Is ringing in
my ears: / And when I think upon that night / My eyes
are dim with tears."
1. A river in England.
2. See Gray's Elegy in a Country Churchyard, page 1246:
"Full many a flower is born to blush unseen" (55).

She *liv'd* unknown, and few could know
10   When Lucy ceas'd to be;
But she is in her Grave, and Oh!
      The difference to me!

1798   1800

Three years she grew in sun and shower

Three years she grew in sun and shower,
Then Nature said, "A lovelier flower
On earth was never sown;
This Child I to myself will take
5   She shall be mine, and I will make
A Lady of my own.

"Myself will to my darling be
Both law and impulse, and with me
The Girl in rock and plain,
10   In earth and heaven, in glade and bower,
Shall feel an overseeing power
To kindle or restrain.

"She shall be sportive as the fawn
That wild with glee across the lawn
15   Or up the mountain springs,
And hers shall be the breathing balm,
And hers the silence and the calm
Of mute insensate things.

"The floating clouds their state shall lend
20   To her; for her the willow bend,
Nor shall she fail to see
Even in the motions of the storm
Grace that shall mould the Maiden's form
By silent sympathy.

25   "The stars of midnight shall be dear
To her, and she shall lean her ear
In many a secret place
Where rivulets dance their wayward round,
And beauty born of murmuring sound
30   Shall pass into her face.

"And vital feelings of delight
Shall rear her form to stately height,
Her virgin bosom swell,
Such thoughts to Lucy I will give
35   While she and I together live
Here in this happy dell."

Thus Nature spake—The work was done —
How soon my Lucy's race was run!
She died, and left to me
40   This heath, this calm and quiet scene,
The memory of what has been,
And never more will be.

1798–1799   1800

Song (A slumber did my spirit seal)[1]

A slumber did my spirit seal;
    I had no human fears:
She seem'd a thing that could not feel
    The touch of earthly years.

5   No motion has she now, no force
    She neither hears nor sees
Roll'd round in earth's diurnal° course,   *daily*
    With rocks, and stones, and trees.

1798–1799   1800

Lucy Gray[1]

Oft I had heard of Lucy Gray,
And when I cross'd the Wild,
I chanc'd to see at break of day
The solitary Child.

5   No Mate, no comrade Lucy knew;
She dwelt on a wild Moor,
The sweetest Thing that ever grew
Beside a human door!

You yet may spy the Fawn at play,
10   The Hare upon the Green;
But the sweet face of Lucy Gray
Will never more be seen.

"To-night will be a stormy night,
You to the Town must go,
15   And take a lantern, Child, to light
Your Mother thro' the snow."

"That, Father! will I gladly do;
'Tis scarcely afternoon—
The Minster°-clock has struck two,   *church*
20   And yonder is the Moon."[2]

At this the Father rais'd his hook
And snapp'd a faggot-band;°   *bundle of firewood*
He plied his work; and Lucy took
The lantern in her hand.

25   Not blither is the mountain roe,
With many a wanton° stroke   *frolicsome*
Her feet disperse the powd'ry snow
That rises up like smoke.

---

1. Coleridge wrote to a friend, "Some months ago Wordsworth transmitted to me a most sublime Epitaph. Whether it had any reality, I cannot say. Most probably, in some gloomier moment he had fancied the moment in which his Sister might die."

1. Founded on a circumstance told me by my Sister, of a little girl who, not far from Halifax in Yorkshire, was bewildered in a snow-storm. . . . Her footsteps were traced by her parents to the middle of the lock of a canal, and no other vestige of her, backward or forward, could be traced. The body, however, was found in the canal. The way in which the incident was treated & the spiritualizing of the character might furnish hints for contrasting the imaginative influences which I have endeavoured to throw over common life with Crabbe's matter of fact style of treating subjects of the same kind. [I.F., referring to poet George Crabbe.] In 1815, Wordsworth changed the title to *Lucy Gray, or Solitude.*

2. Wordsworth remarked that "the day-moon" is something "no town or village girl would ever notice" (1816).

The storm came on before its time,
30   She wander'd up and down,
And many a hill did Lucy climb
But never reach'd the Town.

The wretched Parents all that night
Went shouting far and wide;
35   But there was neither sound nor sight
To serve them for a guide.

At day-break on a hill they stood
That overlook'd the Moor;
And thence they saw the Bridge of Wood,
40   A furlong° from their door.   220 yards

And now they homeward turn'd, and cry'd
"In Heaven we all shall meet!"
When in the snow the Mother spied
The print of Lucy's feet.

45   Then downward from the steep hill's edge
They track'd the footmarks small;
And through the broken hawthorn-hedge,
And by the long stone-wall;

And then an open field they cross'd,
50   The marks were still the same;
They track'd them on, nor ever lost,
And to the Bridge they came.

They follow'd from the snowy bank
Those footmarks, one by one,
55   Into the middle of the plank,
And further there were none.

Yet some maintain that to this day
She is a living Child,
That you may see sweet Lucy Gray
60   Upon the lonesome Wild.

O'er rough and smooth she trips along,
And never looks behind;
And sings a solitary song
That whistles in the wind.

1798–1799   1800

Poor Susan[1]

At the corner of Wood-Street, when day-light appears,
There's a Thrush that sings loud, it has sung for three years:
Poor Susan has pass'd by the spot, and has heard
In the silence of morning the song of the bird.

---

1. The title was changed to *The Reverie of Poor Susan* in 1815. The poem is set in London's mercantile district.

5   'Tis a note of enchantment; what ails her? She sees
       A mountain ascending, a vision of trees;
       Bright volumes of vapour through Lothbury glide,
       And a river flows on through the vale of Cheapside.

       Green pastures she views in the midst of the dale,
10   Down which she so often has tripp'd with her pail,
       And a single small cottage, a nest like a dove's,
       The one only dwelling on earth that she loves.

       She looks, and her heart is in Heaven, but they fade,
       The mist and the river, the hill and the shade;
15   The stream will not flow, and the hill will not rise,
       And the colours have all pass'd away from her eyes.

       Poor Outcast! return—to receive thee once more
       The house of thy Father will open its door,
       And thou once again, in thy plain russet gown,
20   May'st hear the thrush sing from a tree of its own.[2]

1798   1800

Nutting[1]

       It seems a day
       (I speak of one from many singled out)
       One of those heavenly days that cannot die;
       When forth I walked from our cottage-door,[2]
5   And with a wallet o'er my shoulder slung,
       A nutting-crook in hand; and turn'd my steps
       Towards the distant wood, a Figure quaint,
       Trick'd out in proud disguise of Beggar's weeds°   clothing
       Put on for the occasion, by advice
10   And exhortation of my frugal Dame.
       Motley accoutrement! of power to smile
       At thorns, and brakes, and brambles, and, in truth,
       More ragged than need was. Among the woods,
       And o'er the pathless rocks, I forc'd my way
15   Until, at length, I came to one dear nook
       Unvisited, where not a broken bough
       Droop'd with its wither'd leaves, ungracious sign
       Of devastation, but the hazels rose
       Tall and erect, with milk-white clusters hung,
20   A virgin scene![3]—A little while I stood,
       Breathing with such suppression of the heart
       As joy delights in; and with wise restraint

2. Charles Lamb felt this last stanza "threw a kind of dubiety upon Susan's moral conduct"; it was dropped after 1800.
1. Intended as part of a poem on my own life, but struck out as not being wanted there. Like most of my schoolfellows I was an impassioned nutter. For this pleasure, the vale of Esthwaite, abounding in coppice-wood, furnished a very wide range. The verses arose out of the remembrance of feelings I had when a boy [I.F.].

2. The house at which I boarded during the time I was at School [Wordsworth's note]; supervised by Ann Tyson, the Dame of line 10.
3. The moral terrain of the bower entails two precedents: Spenser's "Bower of Blisse" in *The Faerie Queene*, a dangerously seductive pleasure garden, and the Garden of Eden in Milton's *Paradise Lost*, which Satan invades to ravage Eve.

Voluptuous, fearless of a rival, eyed

The banquet; or beneath the trees I sate

25 Among the flowers, and with the flowers I play'd;

A temper known to those, who, after long

And weary expectation, have been bless'd

With sudden happiness beyond all hope.—

—Perhaps it was a bower beneath whose leaves

30 The violets of five seasons re-appear

And fade, unseen by any human eye,

Where fairy water-breaks[4] do murmur on

For ever, and I saw the sparkling foam,

And with my cheek on one of those green stones

35 That, fleec'd with moss, beneath the shady trees,

Lay round me, scatter'd like a flock of sheep,

I heard the murmur and the murmuring sound,

In that sweet mood when pleasure loves to pay

Tribute to ease, and, of its joy secure

40 The heart luxuriates with indifferent things,   *tree stumps*

Wasting its kindliness on stocks° and stones,

And on the vacant air. Then up I rose,

And dragg'd to earth both branch and bough, with crash

And merciless ravage: and the shady nook

45 Of hazels, and the green and mossy bower

Deform'd and sullied, patiently gave up

Their quiet being: and unless I now

Confound my present feelings with the past,

Even then, when from[5] the bower I turn'd away,

50 Exulting, rich beyond the wealth of kings

I felt a sense of pain when I beheld

The silent trees, and saw the intruding sky.—

Then, dearest Maiden![6] move along these shades°   *shadows, spirits*

In gentleness of heart; with gentle hand

55 Touch,—for there is a Spirit in the woods.

1798–1799   1800

Michael

Sending a copy of the 1800 *Lyrical Ballads* to Charles James Fox, leader of the Whig opposition in Parliament, Wordsworth drew attention to *Michael*: "I have attempted to draw a picture of the domestic affections . . . amongst a class of men who are now almost confined to the North of England. They are small independent *proprietors* of land here called statesmen, men of respectable education who daily labour on their own little properties. The domestic affections will always be strong amongst men who live in a country not crowded with population, if these men are placed above poverty. But if they are proprietors of small estates, which have descended to them from their ancestors, the power which these affections will acquire . . . is inconceivable by those who have only had an opportunity of observing hired labourers, farmers, and the manufacturing Poor.

---

4. Wordsworth's coinage for "little rapids."
5. Later revised to "ere from," making the "sense of pain" precede rather than coincide with "exulting."
6. In a much longer manuscript draft, Wordsworth pre-

ceded this poem with the story of a "Lucy" who had been ravaging a bower—her ungentle, unmaidenly action pro-voking her companion to recount this episode from his past, seemingly to admonish her with his remorse.

Their little tract of land serves as a kind of permanent rallying point for their domestic feelings, as a tablet upon which they are written which makes them objects of memory in a thousand instances when they would otherwise be forgotten"; *Michael* shows "that men who do not wear fine cloaths can feel deeply." Later that year Wordsworth wrote to a friend, "I have attempted to give a picture of a man, of strong mind and lively sensibility, agitated by two of the most powerful affections of the human heart; the parental affection, and the love of property, *landed* property, including the feelings of inheritance, home, and personal and family independence." Wordsworth drew on two local tales, one of "the son of an old couple having become dissolute and run away from his parents" (who once owned Dove Cottage, Wordsworth's home at the time); and one of "an old shepherd having been seven years in building up a sheepfold in a solitary valley." The austere biblical aura of the "covenant" between Michael and his son evokes Old Testament prototypes, and Luke is the Gospel that contains the parable of the Prodigal Son (15.11–32). In focusing on contemporary conditions and refusing to provide any relief except in Michael's "comfort in the strength of love," Wordsworth significantly revises the genre of pastoral.

Michael

A Pastoral Poem

If from the public way you turn your steps
Up the tumultuous brook of Green-head Gill,[1]
You will suppose that with an upright path
Your feet must struggle; in such bold ascent
5   The pastoral Mountains front you, face to face.
But, courage! for around that boisterous Brook
The mountains have all open'd out themselves,
And made a hidden valley of their own.
No habitation can be seen; but such
10   As journey thither find themselves alone
With a few sheep, with rocks and stones, and kites°   *hawks*
That overhead are sailing in the sky.

It is in truth an utter solitude;
Nor should I have made mention of this Dell
15   But for one object which you might pass by,
Might see and notice not. Beside the brook
There is a straggling heap of unhewn stones!
And to that place a story appertains,
Which, though it be ungarnish'd with events,
20   Is not unfit, I deem, for the fire-side,
Or for the summer shade. It was the first,
The earliest of those tales that spake to me
Of Shepherds, dwellers in the valleys, men
Whom I already lov'd; not verily
25   For their own sakes, but for the fields and hills
Where was their occupation and abode.
And hence this Tale, while I was yet a boy
Careless of books, yet having felt the power
Of Nature, by the gentle agency
30   Of natural objects, led me on to feel
For passions that were not my own, and think

---

1. Green-head Gill (valley) and the poem's other settings are near Wordsworth's cottage at Grasmere.

At random and imperfectly indeed
On man; the heart of man, and human life.
Therefore, although it be a history
35   Homely and rude, I will relate the same
For the delight of a few natural hearts,
And with yet fonder feeling, for the sake
Of youthful Poets, who among these Hills
Will be my second self when I am gone.

40   Upon the Forest-side in Grasmere Vale
There dwelt a Shepherd, Michael was his name,
An old man, stout of heart, and strong of limb.
His bodily frame had been from youth to age
Of an unusual strength; his mind was keen
45   Intense and frugal, apt for all affairs,
And in his Shepherd's calling he was prompt
And watchful more than ordinary men.
Hence had he learn'd the meaning of all winds,
Of blasts of every tone, and often-times,
50   When others heeded not, He heard the South°   *south wind*
Make subterraneous music, like the noise
Of Bagpipers on distant Highland hills;
The Shepherd, at such warning, of his flock
Bethought him, and he to himself would say
55   The winds are now devising work for me!
And truly at all times the storm, that drives
The Traveller to a shelter, summon'd him
Up to the mountains: he had been alone
Amid the heart of many thousand mists
60   That came to him, and left him, on the heights.
So liv'd he till his eightieth year was pass'd.

And grossly that man errs, who should suppose
That the green Valleys, and the Streams and Rocks
Were things indifferent to the Shepherd's thoughts.
65   Fields, where with chearful spirits he had breath'd
The common air; the hills, which he so oft
Had climb'd, with vigorous steps; which had impress'd
So many incidents upon his mind
Of hardship, skill or courage, joy or fear;
70   Which, like a book, preserv'd the memory
Of the dumb animals, whom he had sav'd,
Had fed or shelter'd, linking to such acts,
So grateful in themselves, the certainty
Of honourable gains; these fields, these hills
75   Which were his living Being, even more
Than his own Blood—what could they less? had laid
Strong hold on his affections, were to him
A pleasurable feeling of blind love,
The pleasure which there is in life itself.

80   He had not passed his days in singleness.
He had a Wife, a comely Matron, old

Though younger than himself full twenty years.
She was a woman of a stirring life
Whose heart was in her house: two wheels she had
85 Of antique form; this large, for spinning wool,
That small for flax; and if one wheel had rest,
It was because the other was at work.
The Pair had but one Inmate° in their house,   *resident*
An only Child, who had been born to them
90 When Michael telling° o'er his years began   *counting*
To deem that he was old, in Shepherd's phrase,
With one foot in the grave. This only son,
With two brave sheep dogs tried° in many a storm,   *tested*
The one of an inestimable worth,
95 Made all their Household. I may truly say,
That they were as a proverb in the vale
For endless industry. When day was gone,
And from their occupations out of doors
The Son and Father were come home, even then
100 Their labour did not cease, unless when all
Turn'd to the cleanly supper-board, and there
Each with a mess of pottage° and skimm'd milk,   *stew*
Sate round the basket pil'd with oaten cakes,
And their plain home-made cheese. Yet when their meal
105 Was ended, LUKE (for so the Son was nam'd)
And his old Father, both betook themselves
To such convenient work as might employ
Their hands by the fire-side; perhaps to card°   *comb out*
Wool for the House-wife's spindle, or repair
110 Some injury done to sickle, flail, or scythe,
Or other implement of house or field.

Down from the ceiling, by the chimney's edge,
That in our ancient uncouth country style
Did with a huge projection overbrow
115 Large space beneath, as duly as the light
Of day grew dim, the House-wife hung a lamp;
An aged utensil, which had perform'd
Service beyond all others of its kind.
Early at evening did it burn and late,
120 Surviving Comrade of uncounted Hours
Which going by from year to year had found
And left the Couple neither gay perhaps
Nor chearful, yet with objects and with hopes
Living a life of eager industry.
125 And now, when LUKE was in his eighteenth year,
There by the light of this old lamp they sate,
Father and Son, while late into the night
The House-wife plied her own peculiar work,
Making the cottage thro' the silent hours
130 Murmur as with the sound of summer flies.
Not with a waste of words, but for the sake
Of pleasure, which I know that I shall give

To many living now, I of this Lamp
Speak thus minutely: for there are no few
135 Whose memories will bear witness to my tale.
This Light was famous in its neighbourhood,
And was a public Symbol of the life,
That thrifty Pair had liv'd. For, as it chanc'd,
Their Cottage on a plot of rising ground
140 Stood single, with large prospect North and South,
High into Easedale, up to Dunmal-Raise,
And Westward to the village near the Lake;
And from this constant light so regular
And so far seen, the House itself by all
145 Who dwelt within the limits of the vale,
Both old and young, was nam'd The Evening Star.

Thus living on through such a length of years,
The Shepherd, if he lov'd himself, must needs
Have lov'd his Help-mate; but to Michael's heart
150 This Son of his old age was yet more dear—
Effect which might perhaps have been produc'd
By that instinctive tenderness, the same
Blind Spirit, which is in the blood of all,
Or that a child, more than all other gifts,
155 Brings hope with it, and forward-looking thoughts,
And stirrings of inquietude, when they
By tendency of nature needs must fail.
From such, and other causes, to the thoughts
Of the old Man his only Son was now
160 The dearest object that he knew on earth.
Exceeding was the love he bare to him,
His Heart and his Heart's joy! For oftentimes
Old Michael, while he was a babe in arms,
Had done him female service, not alone
165 For dalliance and delight, as is the use
Of Fathers, but with patient mind enforc'd
To acts of tenderness; and he had rock'd
His cradle, as with a woman's gentle hand.

And in a later time, ere yet the Boy
170 Had put on Boy's attire, did Michael love,
Albeit of a stern unbending mind,
To have the young one in his sight, when he
Had work by his own door, or when he sate
With sheep before him on his Shepherd's stool,
175 Beneath that large old Oak, which near their door
Stood, and from its enormous breadth of shade
Chosen for the Shearer's covert from the sun,
Thence in our rustic dialect was call'd
The CLIPPING TREE,[2] a name which yet it bears.
180 There, while they two were sitting in the shade,

2. Clipping is the word used in the North of England for shearing [Wordsworth's note].

With others round them, earnest all and blithe,
Would Michael exercise his heart with looks
Of fond correction and reproof bestow'd
Upon the child, if he disturb'd the sheep
185　By catching at their legs, or with his shouts
Scar'd them, while they lay still beneath the shears.

And when by Heaven's good grace the Boy grew up
A healthy Lad, and carried in his cheek
Two steady roses that were five years old,
190　Then Michael from a winter coppice° cut　　　　　　　　*grove of small trees*
With his own hand a sapling, which he hoop'd
With iron, making it throughout in all
Due requisites a perfect Shepherd's Staff,
And gave it to the Boy; wherewith equipp'd
195　He as a Watchman oftentimes was plac'd
At gate or gap, to stem or turn the flock,
And to his office prematurely call'd
There stood the urchin, as you will divine,
Something between a hindrance and a help,
200　And for this cause not always, I believe,
Receiving from his Father hire of praise.
Though nought was left undone which staff or voice,
Or looks, or threatening gestures, could perform.
But soon as Luke, full ten years old, could stand
205　Against the mountain blasts, and to the heights,
Not fearing toil, nor length of weary ways,
He with his Father daily went, and they
Were as companions, why should I relate
That objects which the Shepherd loved before
210　Were dearer now? that from the Boy there came
Feelings and emanations, things which were
Light to the sun and music to the wind;
And that the Old Man's heart seemed born again.
Thus in his Father's sight the Boy grew up:
215　And now, when he had reached his eighteenth year,
He was his comfort and his daily hope.

While this good household thus were living on
From day to day, to Michael's ear there came
Distressful tidings. Long before the time
220　Of which I speak, the Shepherd had been bound
In surety° for his Brother's Son, a man　　　　　　　　*guaranteed a loan*
Of an industrious life, and ample means;
But unforeseen misfortunes suddenly
Had press'd upon him, and old Michael now
225　Was summon'd to discharge the forfeiture,°　　　　　　*collateral*
A grievous penalty, but little less
Than half his substance. This un-look'd for claim,
At the first hearing, for a moment took
More hope out of his life than he supposed
230　That any old man ever could have lost.

As soon as he had gather'd so much strength
That he could look his trouble in the face,
It seem'd that his sole refuge was to sell
A portion of his patrimonial fields.
235   Such was his first resolve; he thought again,
And his heart fail'd him. "Isabel," said he,
Two evenings after he had heard the news,
"I have been toiling more than seventy years,
And in the open sun-shine of God's love
240   Have we all liv'd; yet if these fields of ours
Should pass into a Stranger's hand, I think
That I could not lie quiet in my grave.
Our lot is a hard lot; the Sun itself
Has scarcely been more diligent than I,
245   And I have liv'd to be a fool at last
To my own family. An evil Man
That was, and made an evil choice, if he
Were false to us; and if he were not false,
There are ten thousand to whom loss like this
250   Had been no sorrow. I forgive him—but
'Twere better to be dumb than to talk thus.
When I began, my purpose was to speak
Of remedies and of a chearful hope.
Our Luke shall leave us, Isabel; the land
255   Shall not go from us, and it shall be free;°   *not mortgaged*
He° shall possess it, free as is the wind   *Luke*
That passes over it. We have, thou knowest,
Another Kinsman, he will be our friend
In this distress. He is a prosperous man,
260   Thriving in trade, and Luke to him shall go,
And with his Kinsman's help and his own thrift,
He quickly will repair this loss, and then
May come again to us. If here he stay,
What can be done? Where every one is poor
265   What can be gained?" At this the old Man paus'd,
And Isabel sate silent, for her mind
Was busy, looking back into past times.
There's Richard Bateman, thought she to herself,[3]
He was a parish-boy° at the church-door   *on welfare*
270   They made a gathering for him, shillings, pence,
And halfpennies, wherewith the Neighbours bought
A Basket, which they fill'd with Pedlar's wares,
And with this Basket on his arm, the Lad
Went up to London, found a Master° there,   *employer*
275   Who out of many chose the trusty Boy
To go and overlook his merchandise
Beyond the seas, where he grew wond'rous rich,
And left estates and monies to the poor,
And at his birth-place, built a Chapel, floor'd

---

3. The story alluded to here is well known in the country [Wordsworth's note, 1802].

280　With Marble, which he sent from foreign lands.
　　　These thoughts, and many others of like sort,
　　　Pass'd quickly thro' the mind of Isabel,
　　　And her face brighten'd. The old Man was glad,
　　　And thus resum'd. "Well! Isabel, this scheme
285　These two days, has been meat and drink to me.
　　　Far more than we have lost is left us yet.
　　　—We have enough—I wish indeed that I
　　　Were younger, but this hope is a good hope.
　　　—Make ready Luke's best garments, of the best
290　Buy for him more, and let us send him forth
　　　To-morrow, or the next day, or to-night:
　　　—If he could go, the Boy should go to-night."

　　　Here Michael ceas'd, and to the fields went forth
　　　With a light heart. The House-wife for five days
295　Was restless° morn and night, and all day long　　　*without rest*
　　　Wrought on with her best fingers to prepare
　　　Things needful for the journey of her Son.
　　　But Isabel was glad when Sunday came
　　　To stop her in her work; for, when she lay
300　By Michael's side, she through the last two nights
　　　Heard him, how he was troubled in his sleep:
　　　And when they rose at morning she could see
　　　That all his hopes were gone. That day at noon
　　　She said to Luke, while they two by themselves
305　Were sitting at the door, "Thou must not go,
　　　We have no other Child but thee to lose,
　　　None to remember—do not go away,
　　　For if thou leave thy Father he will die."[4]
　　　The Lad made answer with a jocund voice,
310　And Isabel, when she had told her fears,
　　　Recover'd heart. That evening her best fare
　　　Did she bring forth, and all together sate
　　　Like happy people round a Christmas fire.

　　　Next morning Isabel resum'd her work,
315　And all the ensuing week the house appear'd
　　　As chearful as a grove in Spring: at length
　　　The expected letter from their Kinsman came,
　　　With kind assurances that he would do
　　　His utmost for the welfare of the Boy,
320　To which requests were added, that forthwith
　　　He might be sent to him. Ten times or more
　　　The letter was read over; Isabel
　　　Went forth to shew it to the neighbours round:
　　　Nor was there at that time on English Land
325　A prouder heart than Luke's. When Isabel
　　　Had to her house return'd, the Old Man said,

4. Echoing the story of Joseph in Genesis 44.22: "The lad cannot leave his father: for if he should leave his father, his father would die."

"He shall depart to-morrow." To this word
The House-wife answered, talking much of things
Which, if at such short notice he should go,
330   Would surely be forgotten. But at length
She gave consent, and Michael was at ease.

Near the tumultuous brook of Green-head Gill,
In that deep Valley, Michael had design'd
To build a Sheep-fold;[5] and, before he heard
335   The tidings of his melancholy loss,
For this same purpose he had gathered up
A heap of stones, which close to the brook side
Lay thrown together, ready for the work.
With Luke that evening thitherward he walk'd;
340   And soon as they had reach'd the place he stopp'd,
And thus the Old Man spake to him. "My Son,
To-morrow thou wilt leave me; with full heart
I look upon thee, for thou art the same
That wert a promise to me ere thy birth,
345   And all thy life hast been my daily joy.
I will relate to thee some little part
Of our two histories; 'twill do thee good
When thou art from me, even if I should speak
On things thou canst not know of.—After thou
350   First cam'st into the world—as oft befalls
To new-born infants, thou didst sleep away
Two days, and blessings from thy Father's tongue
Then fell upon thee. Day by day pass'd on,
And still I lov'd thee with encreasing love.
355   Never to living ear came sweeter sounds
Than when I heard thee by our own fire-side
First uttering without words a natural tune,
While thou, a feeding babe, didst in thy joy
Sing at thy Mother's breast. Month followed month,
360   And in the open fields my life was pass'd
And on the mountains, else I think that thou
Hadst been brought up upon thy father's knees.
—But we were playmates, Luke; among these hills,
As well thou know'st, in us the old and young
365   Have play'd together, nor with me didst thou
Lack any pleasure which a boy can know."

Luke had a manly heart; but at these words
He sobb'd aloud. The Old Man grasp'd his hand,
And said, "Nay do not take it so—I see
370   That these are things of which I need not speak.
—Even to the utmost I have been to thee
A kind and a good Father: and herein
I but repay a gift which I myself

---

5. A sheepfold in these mountains is an unroofed building of stone walls, with different divisions. It is generally placed by the side of a brook [Wordsworth's note, 1802]. "The Sheepfold . . . remains, or rather ruins of it," Wordsworth remarked in 1843.

Receiv'd at others' hands, for, though now old
375   Beyond the common life of man, I still
Remember them who lov'd me in my youth.
Both of them sleep together: here they liv'd,
As all their Forefathers had done, and when
At length their time was come, they were not loth
380   To give their bodies to the family mold.
I wish'd that thou should'st live the life they liv'd.
But 'tis a long time to look back, my Son,
And see so little gain from sixty years.
These fields were burthen'd° when they came to me;   *mortgaged*
385   'Till I was forty years of age, not more
Than half of my inheritance was mine.
I toil'd and toil'd; God bless'd me in my work,
And 'till these three weeks past the land was free.
—It looks as if it never could endure
390   Another Master. Heaven forgive me, Luke,
If I judge ill for thee, but it seems good
That thou should'st go." At this the Old Man paus'd;
Then, pointing to the Stones near which they stood,
Thus, after a short silence, he resum'd:
395   "This was a work for us, and now, my Son,
It is a work for me. But, lay one Stone—
Here, lay it for me, Luke, with thine own hands.
I for the purpose brought thee to this place.
Nay, Boy, be of good hope:—we both may live
400   To see a better day. At eighty-four
I still am strong and stout;°—do thou thy part;   *hardy*
I will do mine[6]—I will begin again
With many tasks that were resign'd to thee;
Up to the heights, and in among the storms,
405   Will I without thee go again, and do
All works which I was wont to do alone,
Before I knew thy face.—Heaven bless thee, Boy!
Thy heart these two weeks has been beating fast
With many hopes—it should be so—yes—yes—
410   I knew that thou could'st never have a wish
To leave me, Luke, thou hast been bound to me
Only by links of love, when thou art gone
What will be left to us!—But, I forget
My purposes. Lay now the corner-stone,
415   As I requested, and hereafter, Luke,
When thou art gone away, should evil men
Be thy companions, let this sheep-fold be
Thy anchor and thy shield; amid all fear
And all temptation, let it be to thee
420   An emblem of the life thy Fathers liv'd,
Who, being innocent, did for that cause

---

6. "Nature . . . hath done her part; / Do thou but thine," Raphael instructs Adam about his responsibility for Eve (*Paradise Lost* 8.561–62); "God toward thee hath done his part, do thine," Adam cautions Eve, before she goes off alone in Eden, the prelude to her Fall (9.375).

Bestir them in good deeds. Now, fare thee well—
When thou return'st, thou in this place wilt see
A work which is not here, a covenant
425 'Twill be between us—but, whatever fate
Befall thee, I shall love thee to the last,
And bear thy memory with me to the grave."

The Shepherd ended here; and Luke stoop'd down,
And as his Father had requested, laid
430 The first stone of the Sheep-fold; at the sight
The Old Man's grief broke from him, to his heart
He press'd his Son, he kissed him and wept;
And to the House together they return'd.

Next morning, as had been resolv'd, the Boy
435 Began his journey, and when he had reach'd
The public Way, he put on a bold face;
And all the Neighbours, as he pass'd their doors
Came forth with wishes and with farewell pray'rs,
That follow'd him 'till he was out of sight.

440 A good report did from their Kinsman come,
Of Luke and his well-doing; and the Boy
Wrote loving letters, full of wond'rous news,
Which, as the House-wife phrased it, were throughout
The prettiest letters that were ever seen.
445 Both parents read them with rejoicing hearts.
So, many months pass'd on: and once again
The Shepherd went about his daily work
With confident and chearful thoughts; and now
Sometimes when he could find a leisure hour
450 He to that valley took his way, and there
Wrought at the Sheep-fold. Meantime Luke began
To slacken in his duty; and, at length
He in the dissolute city gave himself
To evil courses: ignominy and shame
455 Fell on him, so that he was driven at last
To seek a hiding-place beyond the seas.

There is a comfort in the strength of love;
'Twill make a thing endurable, which else
Would break the heart:—Old Michael found it so.
460 I have convers'd with more than one who well
Remember the Old Man, and what he was
Years after he had heard this heavy news.
His bodily frame had been from youth to age
Of an unusual strength. Among the rocks
465 He went, and still look'd up upon the sun,
And listen'd to the wind; and as before
Perform'd all kinds of labour for his Sheep,
And for the land, his small inheritance.
And to that hollow Dell from time to time
470 Did he repair, to build the Fold of which

His flock had need. 'Tis not forgotten yet
The pity which was then in every heart
For the Old Man—and 'tis believed by all
That many and many a day he thither went,
475   And never lifted up a single stone.

There, by the Sheep-fold, sometimes was he seen
Sitting alone, with that his faithful Dog,
Then old, beside him, lying at his feet.
The length of full seven years from time to time
480   He at the building of this Sheep-fold wrought,
And left the work unfinished when he died.

Three years, or little more, did Isabel,
Survive her Husband: at her death the estate
Was sold, and went into a Stranger's hand.
485   The Cottage which was nam'd The Evening Star
Is gone, the ploughshare has been through the ground
On which it stood;[7] great changes have been wrought
In all the neighbourhood, yet the Oak is left
That grew beside their Door; and the remains
490   Of the unfinished Sheep-fold may be seen
Beside the boisterous brook of Green-head Gill.

1800   1800

COMPANION READINGS

Francis Jeffrey: from *A Review of Robert Southey's* Thalaba[1]

Poetry has this much, at least, in common with religion, that its standards were fixed long ago, by certain inspired writers, whose authority it is no longer lawful to call in question; and that many profess to be entirely devoted to it, who have no *good works* to produce in support of their pretensions. * * * The author who is now before us, belongs to a *sect* of poets, that has established itself in this country within these ten or twelve years, and is looked upon, we believe, as one of its chief champions and apostles. The peculiar doctrines of this sect, it would not, perhaps, be very easy to explain; but, that they are *dissenters* from the established systems in poetry and criticism, is admitted, and proved indeed, by the whole tenor of their compositions. Though they lay claim, we believe, to a creed and a revelation of their own, there can be little doubt, that their doctrines are of *German* origin, and have been derived from some of the great modern reformers in that country. Some of their leading principles, indeed, are probably of an earlier date, and seem to have been borrowed from the great apostle of Geneva.[2] * * *

    The disciples of this school boast much of its originality, and seem to value themselves very highly, for having broken loose from the bondage of ancient authority,

---

7. The grazing fields have been enclosed for agriculture; also evoking the strife between the herdsman Abel and his farming brother Cain.

1. Francis Jeffrey (1773–1850) was editor and chief literary critic for *The Edinburgh Review*, one of the most influential liberal journals of the age. Jeffrey's literary tastes were more neoclassical than modern, and his attacks on Wordsworth's principles persisted for decades.

Wordsworth's fellow "Lake Poet" Robert Southey was committed to political reform in his youth. His *Thalaba, the Destroyer* (1801) is a verse romance set in the East, involving magic, vengeance, and vampires.

2. Referring chiefly to Goethe and to German poets of sensational verse narrative. The apostle of Geneva is Rousseau.

and re-asserted the independence of genius. Originality, however, we are persuaded, is rarer than mere alteration; and a man may change a good master for a bad one, without finding himself at all nearer to independence. * * * The productions of this school, we conceive, are so far from being entitled to the praise of originality, that they cannot be better characterised, than by an enumeration of the sources from which their materials have been derived. The greater part of them, we apprehend, will be found to be composed of the following elements: 1. The antisocial principles, and distempered sensibility of Rousseau—his discontent with the present constitution of society—his paradoxical morality, and his perpetual hankerings after some unattainable state of voluptuous virtue and perfection. 2. The simplicity and energy (*horresco referens* [I dread to say it]) of Kotzebue and Schiller. 3. The homeliness and harshness of some of Cowper's language and versification, interchanged occasionally with the *innocence* of Ambrose Philips, or the quaintness of Quarles and Dr Donne.[3] * * *

The authors, of whom we are now speaking [Southey, Wordsworth, and Coleridge], have, among them, unquestionably, a very considerable portion of poetical talent, and have, consequently, been enabled to seduce many into an admiration of the false taste (as it appears to us) in which most of their productions are composed. They constitute, at present, the most formidable conspiracy that has lately been formed against sound judgment in matters poetical; and are entitled to a larger share of our censorial notice, than could be spared for an individual delinquent. * * *

Their most distinguishing symbol, is undoubtedly an affection of great simplicity and familiarity of language. They disdain to make use of the common poetical phraseology, or to ennoble their diction by a selection of fine or dignified expressions. There would be too much *art* in this, for that great love of nature with which they are all of them inspired; and their sentiments, they are determined shall be indebted, for their effect, to nothing but their intrinsic tenderness or elevation. There is something very noble and conscientious, we will confess, in this plan of composition; but the misfortune is, that there are passages in all poems, that can neither be pathetic nor sublime; and that, on these occasions, a neglect of the embellishments of language is very apt to produce absolute meanness and insipidity. * * * It is in such passages, accordingly, that we are most frequently offended with low and inelegant expressions; and that the language, which was intended to be simple and natural, is found oftenest to degenerate into mere slovenliness and vulgarity. * * *

One of their own authors, indeed, has very ingeniously set forth, (in a kind of manifesto that preceded one of their most flagrant acts of hostility), that it was their capital object "to adapt to the uses of poetry, the ordinary language of conversation among the middling and lower orders of the people." What advantages are to be gained by the success of this project, we confess ourselves unable to conjecture. The language of the higher and more cultivated orders may fairly be presumed to be better than that of their inferiors: at any rate, it has all those associations in its favour, by means of which, a style can ever appear beautiful or exalted, and is adapted to the purposes of poetry, by having been long consecrated to its use. The language of the vulgar, on the other hand, has all the opposite associations to contend with; and must seem unfit for poetry, (if there were no other reason), merely because it has scarcely ever been employed in it. A great genius may indeed overcome these disad-

---

3. August von Kotzebue was famed for his sentimental plays. Ambrose Phillips (1675–1749) was admired and ridiculed for his sweet verses; Francie Quarles was best known for *Emblems* (1635), a book of devotional poems with quaint illustrations. John Donne (1572–1631) wrote boldly experimental poetry known for its passion, its rough meters, and extravagant wit.

vantages; but we can scarcely conceive that he should court them. We may excuse a certain homeliness of language in the productions of a ploughman or a milkwoman;[4] but we cannot bring ourselves to admire it in an author, who has had occasion to indite odes to his college bell, and inscribe hymns to the Penates.[5]

But the mischief of this new system is not confined to the depravation of language only; it extends to the sentiments and emotions, and leads to the debasement of all those feelings which poetry is designed to communicate. It is absurd to suppose, that an author should make use of the language of the vulgar, to express the sentiments of the refined. His professed object, in employing that language, is to bring his compositions nearer to the true standard of nature; and his intention to copy the sentiments of the lower orders, is implied in his resolution to make use of their style. Now, the different classes of society have each of them a distinct character, as well as a separate idiom; and the names of the various passions to which they are subject respectively, have a signification that varies essentially, according to the condition of the persons to whom they are applied. The love, or grief, or indignation of an enlightened and refined character, is not only expressed in a different language, but is in itself a different emotion from the love, or grief, or anger, of a clown,[6] a tradesman, or a market-wench. The things themselves are radically and obviously distinct; and the representation of them is calculated to convey a very different train of sympathies and sensations to the mind. The question, therefore, comes simply to be—which of them is the most proper object for poetical imitation? It is needless for us to answer a question, which the practice of all the world has long ago decided irrevocably. The poor and vulgar may interest us, in poetry, by their *situation*; but never, we apprehend, by any sentiments that are peculiar to their condition, and still less by any language that is characteristic of it. The truth is, that is impossible to copy their diction or their sentiments correctly, in a serious composition; and this, not merely because poverty makes men ridiculous, but because just taste and refined sentiment are rarely to be met with among the uncultivated part of mankind; and a language, fitted for their expression, can still more rarely form any part of their "ordinary conversation."

∗ ∗ ∗ It has been argued, indeed, (for men will argue in support of what they do not venture to practice), that as the middling and lower orders of society constitute by far the greater part of mankind, so, their feelings and expressions should interest more extensively, and may be taken, more fairly than any other, for the standards of what is natural and true. To this, it seems obvious to answer, that the arts that aim at exciting admiration and delight, do not take their models from what is ordinary, but from what is excellent; and that our interest in the representation of any event, does not depend upon our familiarity with the original, but on its intrinsic importance, and the celebrity of the parties it concerns. The sculptor employs his art in delineating the graces of Antinous or Apollo, and not in the representation of those ordinary forms that belong to the crowd of his admirers. When a chieftain perishes in battle, his followers mourn more for him, than for thousands of their equals that may have fallen around him. ∗ ∗ ∗

The qualities of style and imagery, however, form but a small part of the characteristics by which a literary faction is to be distinguished. The subject and object of their compositions, and the principles and opinions they are calculated to support, constitute a far more important criterion, and one to which it is usually altogether

4. Alluding to the popularity of Robert Burns, Scots farmer poet (see page 1515) and Anne Yearsley, "the poetical milkwoman."
5. A sarcastic reference to Southey's mock ode *The*

Chapel-Bell (1793) and his long *Hymn to the Penates* (1796); penates were Roman household deities.
6. A peasant.

easy to refer. Some poets are sufficiently described as the flatterers of greatness and power, and others as the champions of independence. One set of writers is known by its antipathy to decency and religion; another, by its methodistical cant and intolerance. Our new school of poetry has a moral character also; though it may not be possible, perhaps, to delineate it quite so concisely.

A splenetic and idle discontent with the existing institutions of society, seems to be at the bottom of all their serious and peculiar sentiments. Instead of contemplating the wonders and the pleasures which civilization has created for mankind, they are perpetually brooding over the disorders by which its progress has been attended. They are filled with horror and compassion at the sight of poor men spending their blood in the quarrels of princes, and brutifying their sublime capabilities in the drudgery of unremitting labour. For all sorts of vice and profligacy in the lower orders of society, they have the same virtuous horror, and the same tender compassion. While the existence of these offences overpowers them with grief and confusion, they never permit themselves to feel the smallest indignation or dislike towards the offenders. The present vicious constitution of society alone is responsible for all these enormities: the poor sinners are but the helpless victims or instruments of its disorders, and could not possibly have avoided the errors into which they have been betrayed. Though they can bear with crimes, therefore, they cannot reconcile themselves to punishments; and have an unconquerable antipathy to prisons, gibbets, and houses of correction, as engines of oppression, and instruments of atrocious injustice. While the plea of moral necessity is thus artfully brought forward to convert all the excesses of the poor into innocent misfortunes, no sort of indulgence is shown to the offences of the powerful and rich. Their oppressions, and seductions, and debaucheries, are the theme of many an angry verse; and the indignation and abhorrence of the reader is relentlessly conjured up against those perturbators of society, and scourges of mankind.

It is not easy to say, whether the fundamental absurdity of this doctrine, or the partiality of its application, be entitled to the severest reprehension.

1802

Charles Lamb: from *Letter to William Wordsworth*[1]

[Jan. 30, 1801]

Thanks for your Letter and Present. I had already borrowed your second volume.[2] What most please me are, the Song of Lucy. * * * *Simon's sickly daughter* in the Sexton made me cry.[3] * * * I will mention one more: the delicate and curious feeling in the wish for the Cumberland Beggar, that he may have about him the melody of Birds, altho' he hear them not. Here the mind knowingly passes a fiction upon herself, first substituting her own feelings for the Beggar's, and, in the same breath detecting the fallacy, will not part with the wish.— * * * I will just add that it appears to me a fault in the Beggar, that the instructions conveyed in it are too direct and like a lecture:[4] they don't slide into the mind of the reader, while he is imagining no such matter. An intelligent reader

---

1. For Lamb, see page 1398. At the time of these letters, Lamb was an old friend of Coleridge and a newer acquaintance of the Wordsworths; he had published a novel and some verses, but his major career as an essayist was still to come.
2. Wordsworth had sent the two-volume *Lyrical Ballads* (1800) to Lamb, who knew the poems in the first volume from the 1798 edition. The poems he discusses are newly published in volume 2.
3. Referring to *Song* (*She dwelt among th'untrodden ways*) and *To a Sexton*, where the charnel house worker is chastised for disturbing the bones of the dead, including Simon's daughter.
4. The poem includes a polemic by Wordsworth against forcing beggars into miserable workhouses (lines 177–178).

finds a sort of insult in being told, I will teach you how to think upon this subject. * * * There is implied an unwritten compact between Author and reader; I will tell you a story, and I suppose you will understand it. * * * —I am sorry that Coleridge has christened his Ancient Marinere "a poet's Reverie"—it is as bad as Bottom the Weaver's declaration that he is not a Lion but only the scenical representation of a Lion.[5] What new idea is gained by this Title, but one subversive of all credit, which the tale should force upon us, of its truth? For me, I was never so affected with any human Tale. After first reading it, I was totally possessed with it for many days.—I dislike all the miraculous part of it, but the feelings of the man under the operation of such scenery dragged me along like Tom Piper's magic whistle. I totally differ from your idea that the Marinere should have had a character and profession. This is a Beauty in Gulliver's Travels, where the mind is kept in a placid state of little wonderments; but the Ancient Marinere undergoes such Trials, as overwhelm and bury all individuality or memory of what he was, like the state of a man in a Bad dream, one terrible peculiarity of which is: that all consciousness of personality is gone. Your other observation is I think as well a little unfounded: the Marinere from being conversant in supernatural events *has* acquired a supernatural and strange cast of *phrase*, eye, appearance, &c. which frighten the wedding guest. You will excuse my remarks, because I am hurt and vexed that you should think it necessary, with a prose apology,[6] to open the eyes of dead men that cannot see. To sum up a general opinion of the second vol.—I do not feel any one poem in it so forcibly as the Ancient Marinere, the Mad Mother, and the Lines at Tintern Abbey in the first.—I could, too, have wished the Critical preface had appeared in a separate treatise. All its dogmas are true and just, and most of them new, *as* criticism. But they associate a *diminishing* idea with the Poems which follow, as having been written for *Experiment* on the public taste, more than having sprung (as they must have done) from living and daily circumstances.—I am prolix, because I am gratified in the opportunity of writing to you, and I don't well know when to leave off. I ought before this to have reply'd to your very kind invitation into Cumberland.[7] With you and your Sister I could gang any where. But I am afraid whether I shall ever be able to afford so desperate a Journey. Separate from the pleasure of your company, I don't much care if I never see a mountain in my life. I have passed all my days in London, until I have formed as many and intense local attachments, as any of you mountaineers can have done with dead nature. The Lighted shops of the Strand and Fleet Street, the innumerable trades, tradesmen and customers, coaches, waggons, playhouses, all the bustle and wickedness round about Covent Garden, the very women of the Town, the Watchmen, drunken scenes, rattles,—life awake, if you awake, at all hours of the night, the impossibility of being dull in Fleet Street, the crowds, the very dirt & mud, the Sun shining upon houses and pavements, the print shops, the old book stalls, parsons cheap'ning books, coffee houses, steams of soups from kitchens, the pantomimes, London itself a pantomime and a masquerade,—all these things work themselves into my mind and feed me, without a power of satiating me. The wonder of these sights impells me into night-walks about her crowded streets, and I often shed tears in the motley Strand from fulness of joy at so much Life.—All these emotions must be strange to you. So are your rural emotions to me. But consider, what must I have been doing all my life, not to have lent great portions of my heart with usury to such scenes?————

---

5. In 1800, the poem was subtitled "A Poet's Reverie." In Shakespeare's *Midsummer Night's Dream* (5.1), Snug the Joiner says this, on Bottom's fervent recommendation, fearing that the ladies in the audience will take him for a real lion (5.1.220 ff; cf. Bottom, 3.1.35–45).
6. The Preface of 1800.
7. In the Lake District.

Charles Lamb: from Letter to Thomas Manning[1]

[Feb. 15, 1801]

I had need be cautious henceforward what opinion I give of the "Lyrical Ballads." All the North of England are in a turmoil. Cumberland and Westmoreland have already declared a state of war.[2] I lately received from Wordsworth a copy of the second volume, accompanied by an acknowledgement of having received from me many months since a copy of a certain Tragedy,[3] with excuses for not having made any acknowledgement sooner, it being owing to an "almost insurmountable aversion from Letter-writing." This letter I answered in due form and time, and enumerated several of the passages which had most affected me, adding, unfortunately, that no single piece had moved me so forcibly as the "Ancient Mariner," "The Mad Mother," or the "Lines at Tintern Abbey." The Post did not sleep a moment. I received almost instantaneously a long letter of four sweating pages from my Reluctant Letter-Writer, the purport of which was, that he was sorry his 2d vol. had not given me more pleasure (Devil a hint did I give that it had *not pleased me*), and "was compelled to wish that my range of sensibility was more extended, being obliged to believe that I should receive large influxes of happiness and happy Thoughts" (I suppose from the L. B.)—With a deal of stuff about a certain Union of Tenderness and Imagination, which in the sense he used Imagination was not the characteristic of Shakspeare, but which Milton possessed in a degree far exceeding other Poets: which Union, as the highest species of Poetry, and chiefly deserving that name, "He was most proud to aspire to;" then illustrating the said Union by two quotations from his own 2d vol. (which I had been so unfortunate as to miss) [quotes *Michael* 349–53]. These lines [52–53] were thus undermarked, and then followed "This Passage, as combining in an extraordinary degree that Union of Imagination and Tenderness which I am speaking of, I consider as one of the Best I ever wrote!" * * * good Poetry: but after one has been reading Shakspeare twenty of the best years of one's life, to have a fellow start up, and prate about some unknown quality, which Shakspeare possessed in a degree inferior to Milton and *somebody else!!* This was not to be *all* my castigation. Coleridge, who had not written to me some months before, starts up from his bed of sickness to reprove me for my hardy presumption: four long pages, equally sweaty and more tedious, came from him; assuring me that, when the works of a man of true genius such as W. undoubtedly was, do not please me at first sight, I should suspect the fault to lie "in me and not in them," etc. etc. etc. etc. etc. What am I to do with such people? I certainly shall write them a very merry Letter. Writing to *you*, I may say that the 2d vol. has no such pieces. * * * It is full of original thinking and an observing mind, but it does not often make you laugh or cry.—It too artfully aims at simplicity of expression. And you sometimes doubt if Simplicity be not a cover for Poverty. The best Piece in it I will send you, being *short*. I have grievously offended my friends in the North by declaring my undue preference; but I need not fear you:— [quotes *Song (She dwelt among th'untrodden ways)*]. This is choice and genuine, and so are many, many more. But one does not like to have 'em rammed down one's throat. "Pray, take it—it's very good—let me help you—eat faster."

1. One of Lamb's closest friends, Manning (1772–1840), mathematician and traveler, was considered the first scholar of Chinese literature in Europe; he was the first and, for many years, only Englishman to enter the holy city of Lhasa, Tibet.
2. Coleridge was living in Cumberland county, the Wordsworths in Westmoreland.
3. By Lamb.

SONNETS, 1802–1807[1]
Prefatory Sonnet

Nuns fret not at their Convent's narrow room;[2]
And Hermits are contented with their Cells;
And Students with their pensive Citadels;
Maids at the Wheel, the Weaver at his Loom,
Sit blithe and happy; Bees that soar for bloom,   5
High as the highest Peak of Furness-fells,°   *mountains*
Will murmur by the hour in Foxglove bells:
In truth, the prison, into which we doom
Ourselves, no prison is: and hence for me,
In sundry moods, 'twas pastime to be bound   10
Within the Sonnet's scanty plot of ground:
Pleas'd if some Souls (for such there needs must be)
Who have felt the weight of too much liberty,
Should find brief solace there, as I have found.

The world is too much with us

The world is too much with us; late and soon,
Getting and spending, we lay waste our powers:
Little we see in nature that is ours;
We have given our hearts away, a sordid boon!
The Sea that bares her bosom to the moon;   5
The Winds that will be howling at all hours
And are up-gathered now like sleeping flowers;
For this, for everything, we are out of tune;
It moves us not. Great God! I'd rather be
A Pagan° suckled in a creed outworn;   *pre-Christian*   10
So might I, standing on this pleasant lea,
Have glimpses that would make me less forlorn;
Have sight of Proteus rising from the sea;
Or hear old Triton blow his wreathed horn.[1]

Composed upon Westminster Bridge, Sept. 3, 1802[1]

Earth has not anything to shew more fair:
Dull would he be of soul who could pass by

1. William Bowles and Charlotte Smith had revived sonnet writing at the end of the 18th century. Wordsworth's first publication was his sonnet *On seeing Miss Helen Maria Williams Weep at a Tale of Distress* (1787) and he was impressed by this revival as well as by Milton's political sonnets. He composed may of the sonnets in this section in 1802, when he briefly visited France during the Peace of Amiens to settle affairs with Annette Vallon, prior to his marriage. Other sonnets from this period are included in Perspectives: The Abolition of Slavery and the Slave Trade, page 1465.
2. In 1802 Wordsworth praised Milton's sonnets for their "energetic and varied flow of sound crowding into narrow room more of the combined effect of rhyme and blank verse than can be done by any other kind of verse that I know of." He particulary liked Milton's stanzaic and linear enjambments (see his own wit about this device in line 10 where *bound* is thus unbound). For another sonnet on sonnet writing, see Keats's *Incipet altera sonneta*, page 1764.

1. Proteus is the shape-changing herdsman of the sea; Triton, usually depicted blowing a conch shell, is a sea deity. Cf. the personified "Sea" in line 5.

1. Composed on the roof of a coach, on my way to France [Wordsworth's note, 1843]. For a description of the circumstances, see Dorothy Wordsworth's *Grasmere Journals*, July 1802, page 1628. Wordsworth misremembered the date as September (the time of his return, not his departure), and gave the year as 1803 (corrected to 1802 in the edition of 1838). His evasiveness about the date may have had to do with his anxiety about his reunion with—and final departure from—Annette Vallon and their daughter Caroline.

A sight so touching in its majesty:
This City now doth like a garment wear
5   The beauty of the morning; silent, bare,
Ships, towers, domes, theatres, and temples lie
Open unto the fields, and to the sky;
All bright and glittering in the smokeless air.
Never did sun more beautifully steep
10   In his first splendour, valley, rock, or hill;
Ne'er saw I, never felt, a calm so deep!
The river glideth at his own sweet will:
Dear God! the very houses seem asleep;
And all that mighty heart is lying still!

It is a beauteous Evening[1]

It is a beauteous Evening, calm and free;
The holy time is quiet as a Nun
Breathless with adoration; the broad sun
Is sinking down in its tranquillity;
5   The gentleness of heaven is on the Sea:[2]
Listen! the mighty Being is awake
And doth with his eternal motion make
A sound like thunder—everlastingly.
Dear Child! dear Girl! that walkest with me here,[3]
10   If thou appear'st untouch'd by solemn thought,
Thy nature is not therefore less divine:
Thou liest in Abraham's bosom[4] all the year;
And worshipp'st at the Temple's inner shrine,
God being with thee when we know it not.

COMPANION READINGS

Charlotte Smith: from *Elegiac Sonnets*[1]

To Melancholy. Written on the Banks of the Arun, October, 1785

When latest Autumn spreads her evening veil
And the grey mists from these dim waves arise,
I love to listen to the hollow sighs,
Thro' the half leafless wood that breathes the gale.
5   For at such hours the shadowy phantom pale,
Oft seems to fleet before the poet's eyes;

---

1. This was composed on the beach near Calais, in the autumn of 1802 [Wordsworth's note, 1843].
2. In 1836 Wordsworth changed "is on" to "broods o'er."
3. Wordsworth's daughter Caroline.
4. Christ's description of the resting place for heaven-bound souls (Luke 16.22).
1. Charlotte Smith was born in 1749; a disastrous marriage when she was sixteen culminated in her spendthrift husband's imprisonment for debt in 1783. Pregnant with her twelfth child, Smith was left to support herself and her family by her pen. The successful first edition of *Ele-*

giac Sonnets (1784) led to eight more, ever-expanding editions by 1800. Though the ten novels she produced in those years were far more lucrative, poetry was the more exalted genre, and she was admired for the sonnets, her substantial blank-verse poem *The Emigrants* (1793), and her final work, *Beachy-Head,* published in 1807, the year of her death. Coleridge acknowledged Bowles and Smith as "they who first made the Sonnet popular in English," and Wordsworth was reading her sonnets in 1802 as he worked on his own sonnet sequence.

Strange sounds are heard, and mournful melodies,
As of night wanderers, who their woes bewail!
Here, by his native stream, at such an hour,
10   Pity's own Otway,[2] I methinks could meet,
         And hear his deep sighs swell the sadden'd wind!
Oh Melancholy!—such thy magic power,
         That to the soul these dreams are often sweet,
         And soothe the pensive visionary mind!

1789

Far on the Sands

Far on the sands, the low, retiring tide,
         In distant murmurs hardly seems to flow,
And o'er the world of waters, blue and wide,
         The sighing summer-wind, forgets to blow.
5 As sinks the day star in the rosy West,
         The silent wave, with rich reflection glows;
Alas! can tranquil nature give *me* rest,
         Or scenes of beauty, soothe me to repose?
Can the soft lustre of the sleeping main,
10   Yon radiant heaven, or all creation's charms,
"Erase the written troubles of the brain,"[1]
         Which Memory tortures, and which Guilt alarms?
Or bid a bosom transient quiet prove,
That bleeds with vain remorse, and unextinguish'd love!

1800

To Tranquillity

In this tumultuous sphere, for thee unfit,
         How seldom art thou found—Tranquillity!
         Unless 'tis when with mild and downcast eye
By the low cradles, thou delight'st to sit,
5 Of sleeping infants—watching the soft breath,
         And bidding the sweet slumberers easy lie;
Or sometimes hanging o'er the bed of death,
         Where the poor languid sufferer—hopes to die.
Oh! beauteous sister of the halcyon peace![1]
10   I sure shall find thee in that heavenly scene
         Where care and anguish shall their power resign;
Where hope alike, and vain regret shall cease;
         And Memory—lost in happiness serene,
Repeat no more—that misery has been mine!

1789

2. Thomas Otway (1652–1685), author of the dramas *The Orphan* and *Venice Preserved*, was known for the pathos of his work.

1. Macbeth asks his wife's doctor, "Canst thou not minister to a mind diseased, / Pluck from the memory of a rooted sorrow, / Raze out the written troubles of the brain?" He replies, "Therein the patient / Must minister to himself" (5.3.39–46).

1. When her husband perished in a shipwreck, Halcyone threw herself into the sea; in pity the gods changed the pair into kingfishers and calmed the sea for a brief interval each year so they could mate. A halcyon peace is a blessed interval of calm amid adversity.

Written in the Church Yard at Middleton in Sussex

Press'd by the Moon, mute arbitress of tides,
    While the loud equinox its power combines,
    The sea no more its swelling surge confines,
But o'er the shrinking land sublimely rides.
5   The wild blast, rising from the Western cave,
    Drives the huge billows from their heaving bed;
    Tears from their grassy tombs the village dead,
And breaks the silent sabbath of the grave![1]
With shells and sea-weed mingled, on the shore
10   Lo! their bones whiten in the frequent wave;
    But vain to them the winds and waters rave;
They hear the warring elements no more:
While I am doom'd—by life's long storm opprest,
To gaze with envy, on their gloomy rest.

1789

On being cautioned against walking on an headland overlooking the sea, because it was frequented by a lunatic

Is there a solitary wretch who hies
    To the tall cliff, with starting pace or slow,
And, measuring, views with wild and hollow eyes
    Its distance from the waves that chide below;
5   Who, as the sea-born gale with frequent sighs
    Chills his cold bed upon the mountain turf,
With hoarse, half-utter'd lamentation, lies
    Murmuring responses to the dashing surf?
In moody sadness, on the giddy brink,
10   I see him more with envy than with fear;
He has no *nice felicities* that shrink[1]
    From giant horrors; wildly wandering here,
He seems (uncursed with reason) not to know
The depth or the duration of his woe.

1800

THE PRELUDE

Now regarded as Wordsworth's major work, *The Prelude* was unknown in his lifetime except to a small circle of family and friends. Though the poem was largely complete by 1805, Wordsworth continued to rework and polish the poem for the remaining forty-five years of his life, in an ongoing and intense self-inquiry into his childhood and youth. Published posthu-

---

1. Middleton is a village on the margin of the sea. . . . There were formerly several acres of ground between its small church and the sea, which now, by its continual encroachments, approaches within a few feet of this half-ruined and humble edifice. The wall, which once surrounded the church-yard, is entirely swept away, many of the graves broken up, and the remains of bodies interred washed into the sea; whence human bones are found among the sand and shingles on the shore [Smith's note, 1800].

1. "'Tis delicate felicity that shrinks / When rocking winds are loud." Walpole [Smith's note, 1800]; compare Milton's *Il Penseroso*: "while rocking winds are piping loud" (line 126); Smith's reference to Walpole is uncertain.

mously in 1850, *The Prelude* incorporates passages first written in the late 1790s. In a poignant passage of Book 4 (1805), Wordsworth compared his enterprise, "Incumbent o'er the surface of past time," to that of a man "who hangs down-bending from the side / Of a slow-moving Boat," incapable of distinguishing what resides below from what is reflected from above, and repeatedly "cross'd by gleam / Of his own image" (4.247–264). On first reading, *The Prelude* appears a paean to the recovery of the past; on closer acquaintance it is a great and self-conscious testimony to the construction of the past out of the urgent needs of the present. To compose the poem was also to compose the poet, to create Wordsworth as The Poet, a meditative and resolute figure who had struggled through years of family disruption and revolutionary turmoil to a position of authority.

The Prelude evolved in three principal versions. Isolated in Germany in the coldest winter of the century in 1798–1799, Wordsworth wrote several passages drawing on his childhood experiences in nature, sketches for *The Recluse*, a philosophic poem that Coleridge had urged him to write. By the time he and his sister Dorothy had settled in Grasmere, he had completed the text now known as *The Two-Part Prelude* of 1799, almost a thousand lines of blank verse narrating his life from schooldays through the age of seventeen.

In 1801 Wordsworth began to revise his poem, though it was not until 1804 that he set to work in earnest. An initial plan to write it in five books quickly gave way to a greater expansion into thirteen books, allowing Wordsworth to include an account of his experiences in France and the crisis that followed the failure of his hopes for the French Revolution. The full version finished in 1805 combines earlier and later material, not always in chronological order, suggesting that the sequence of Wordsworth's life is less important than the imperatives shaping its argument. Further revised over the years, the poem was finally published by Wordsworth's widow in 1850. This was the only known text until 1926, when Ernest de Selincourt published that of 1805, the version printed here.

Part confession, a crisis-autobiography descended from Saint Augustine's exemplary *Confessions*, *The Prelude* is also a consciously English document. Exceptionally personal, it is also a representative story of one seduced by youthful radicalism from his native heritage and returning from his errors to become a national poet. To that degree, *The Prelude* stands as a rejoinder to Rousseau's notorious *Confessions*, but its chief parallel is Milton's *Paradise Lost*, with which it regularly challenges comparison. *The Prelude* turns epic inward even as it claims the growth of the poet's mind as an exalted subject. But *The Prelude* is not everywhere epic and prophetic: it is also an epistle to Coleridge, intimate and domestic, a record of friendship. The result is a shifting interplay between high genre and familiar, between the adult poet looking back and trying to explain and the child from whose sense of the mysterious the poem derives its originating power. "So wide appears / The vacancy between me and those days," Wordsworth wrote of his childhood, "Which yet have such self-presence in my mind / That, sometimes, when I think of them, I seem / Two consciousnesses, conscious of myself / And of some other Being" (2.28–33). As he tries to close the gap in the act of writing, the ungraspable, elusive vacancies generate a structure that circles back in its large patterns, animated throughout by countermovements that uncannily create the effect of authenticity:

> As oftentimes a River, it might seem,
> Yielding in part to old remembrances,
> Part sway'd by fear to tread an onward road
> That leads direct to the devouring sea,
> Turns and will measure back his course, far back
> Towards the very regions which he cross'd
> In his first outset; so have we long time
> Made motions retrograde, in like pursuit
> Detain'd.   (9.1–9)

FROM THE PRELUDE, OR GROWTH OF A POET'S MIND

Book First. Introduction, Childhood, and School time

Oh there is blessing in this gentle breeze[1]
That blows from the green fields and from the clouds
And from the sky: it beats against my cheek
And seems half conscious of the joy it gives.
5   O welcome Messenger! O welcome Friend!
A Captive greets thee, coming from a house
Of bondage,[2] from yon City's walls set free,
A prison where he hath been long immured.
Now I am free, enfranchis'd and at large,
10   May fix my habitation where I will.
What dwelling shall receive me? In what Vale
Shall be my harbour? Underneath what grove
Shall I take up my home, and what sweet stream
Shall with its murmurs lull me to my rest?
15   The earth is all before me:[3] with a heart
Joyous, nor scar'd at its own liberty
I look about, and should the guide I chuse
Be nothing better than a wandering cloud
I cannot miss my way. I breathe again;
20   Trances of thought and mountings of the mind
Come fast upon me: it is shaken off,
As by miraculous gift 'tis shaken off,
That burthen of my own unnatural self,
The heavy weight of many a weary day
25   Not mine, and such as were not made for me.
Long months of peace (if such bold word accord
With any promises of human life)
Long months of ease and undisturb'd delight
Are mine in prospect: whither shall I turn
30   By road or pathway or through open field,
Or shall a twig or any floating thing
Upon the river, point me out my course?
       Enough that I am free; for months to come
May dedicate myself to chosen tasks;
35   May quit the tiresome sea, and dwell on shore,
If not a settler on the soil, at least
To drink wild water, and to pluck green herbs,
And gather fruits fresh from their native bough.
Nay more, if I may trust myself, this hour
40   Hath brought a gift that consecrates my joy;
For I, methought, while the sweet breath of Heaven
Was blowing on my body, felt within
A corresponding mild creative breeze,

1. Lines 1–54, which Wordsworth later called his "glad preamble" (7.4), were composed in late 1799 or 1800. Nature itself is his inspiring Muse or spirit ("spiritus" in Latin means both "spirit" and "breeze").
2. Cf. Exodus 13.14: "the Lord brought us out from Egypt,
from the house of bondage."
3. Compare the ending of *Paradise Lost*, when Adam and Eve leave Eden: "the world was all before them" (12.646ff, page 903).

A vital breeze which travell'd gently on
45 O'er things which it had made, and is become
A tempest, a redundant° energy   *abounding*
Vexing its own creation. 'Tis a power
That does not come unrecognis'd, a storm,
Which, breaking up a long continued frost
50 Brings with it vernal° promises, the hope   *springtime*
Of active days, of dignity and thought,
Of prowess in an honorable field,
Pure passions, virtue, knowledge, and delight,
The holy life of music and of verse.
55   Thus far, O Friend! did I, not used to make
A present joy the matter of my Song,[4]
Pour out, that day, my soul in measur'd strains,
Even in the very words which I have here
Recorded: to the open fields I told
60 A prophecy: poetic numbers° came   *verses*
Spontaneously, and cloth'd in priestly robe
My spirit, thus singled out, as it might seem,
For holy services: great hopes were mine;
My own voice chear'd me, and, far more, the mind's
65 Internal echo of the imperfect sound:
To both I listen'd, drawing from them both
A chearful confidence in things to come.
       Whereat, being not unwilling now to give
A respite to this passion, I paced on
70 Gently, with careless steps, and came erelong
To a green shady place where down I sate
Beneath a tree, slackening my thoughts by choice
And settling into gentler happiness.
'Twas Autumn, and a calm and placid day,
75 With warmth as much as needed from a sun
Two hours declin'd towards the west, a day
With silver clouds, and sunshine on the grass
And, in the shelter'd grove where I was couch'd,
A perfect stillness. On the ground I lay
80 Passing through many thoughts, yet mainly such
As to myself pertain'd. I made a choice
Of one sweet Vale° whither my steps should turn   *Grasmere*
And saw, methought, the very house and fields
Present before my eyes: nor did I fail
85 To add, meanwhile, assurance of some work
Of glory, there forthwith to be begun,[5]
Perhaps, too, there perform'd. Thus, long I lay
Chear'd by the genial pillow of the earth
Beneath my head, sooth'd by a sense of touch
90 From the warm ground, that balanced me, though lost
Entirely, seeing nought, nought hearing, save

<hr>

4. The poem is addressed to Coleridge; in the Preface to   "emotion recollected in tranquillity."
Lyrical Ballads, Wordsworth describes poetic creation as   5. *The Recluse* (never finished).

When here and there, about the grove of Oaks
Where was my bed, an acorn from the trees
Fell audibly, and with a startling sound.
95   Thus occupied in mind, I linger'd here
Contented, nor rose up until the sun
Had almost touch'd the horizon; bidding then
A farewell to the City° left behind,   *Goslar, Germany*
Even on the strong temptation of that hour
100   And with its chance equipment, I resolved
To journey towards the Vale which I had chosen.
It was a splendid evening: and my soul
Did once again make trial of her strength
Restored to her afresh; nor did she want
105   Eolian visitations; but the harp[6]
Was soon defrauded, and the banded host
Of harmony dispers'd in straggling sounds
And, lastly, utter silence. "Be it so,
It is an injury," said I, "to this day
110   To think of any thing but present joy."
So like a Peasant I pursued my road
Beneath the evening sun; nor had one wish
Again to bend the sabbath of that time
To a servile yoke. What need of many words?
115   A pleasant loitering journey, through two days
Continued, brought me to my hermitage.°   *secluded dwelling*
    I spare to speak, my Friend, of what ensued,
The admiration and the love, the life
In common things; the endless store of things
120   Rare, or at least so seeming, every day
Found all about me in one neighbourhood,
The self-congratulation,° the complete   *rejoicing*
Composure, and the happiness entire.
But speedily a longing in me rose
125   To brace myself to some determin'd aim,
Reading or thinking, either to lay up
New stores, or rescue from decay the old
By timely interference, I had hopes
Still higher, that with a frame of outward life,
130   I might endue,° might fix in a visible home   *endow*
Some portion of those phantoms of conceit°   *mental images*
That had been floating loose about so long,
And to such Beings temperately deal forth
The many feelings that oppress'd my heart.
135   But I have been discouraged: gleams of light
Flash often from the East, then disappear
And mock me with a sky that ripens not
Into a steady morning: if my mind,
Remembering the sweet promise of the past,
140   Would gladly grapple with some noble theme,

---

6. The Aeolian harp, named for Aeolus, mythic god of the winds, resounds at the wind's touch.

Vain is her wish; where'er she turns she finds
Impediments from day to day renew'd.
       And now it would content me to yield up
Those lofty hopes a while for present gifts
145 Of humbler industry. But, O dear Friend!
The Poet, gentle creature as he is,
Hath, like the Lover, his unruly times;
His fits when he is neither sick nor well,
Though no distress be near him but his own
150 Unmanageable thoughts. The mind itself,
The meditative mind, best pleased, perhaps,
While she, as duteous as the Mother Dove,
Sits brooding,[7] lives not always to that end
But hath less quiet instincts, goadings-on
155 That drive her, as in trouble, through the groves.
With me is now such passion, which I blame
No otherwise than as it lasts too long.
       When, as becomes a man who would prepare
For such a glorious work, I through myself
160 Make rigorous inquisition, the report
Is often chearing; for I neither seem
To lack, that first great gift! the vital soul,
Nor general truths which are themselves a sort
Of Elements and Agents, Under-Powers,
165 Subordinate helpers of the living mind.
Nor am I naked in external things,
Forms, images; nor numerous other aids
Of less regard, though won perhaps with toil,
And needful to build up a Poet's praise.
170 Time, place, and manners;° these I seek, and these   customs
I find in plenteous store; but nowhere such
As may be singled out with steady choice;
No little Band of yet remember'd names
Whom I, in perfect confidence, might hope
175 To summon back from lonesome banishment
And make them inmates in the hearts of men
Now living, or to live in times to come.
Sometimes, mistaking vainly, as I fear,
Proud spring-tide swellings for a regular sea
180 I settle on some British theme, some old
Romantic tale, by Milton left unsung:[8]
More often, resting at some gentle place
Within the groves of Chivalry, I pipe
Among the Shepherds, with reposing Knights
185 Sit by a Fountain-side, and hear their tales.
Sometimes, more sternly mov'd, I would relate
How vanquish'd Mithridates northward pass'd,

---

7. In *Paradise Lost*, the epic narrator asks for inspiration from the Holy Spirit who, at Creation, "Dove-like satst brooding on the vast Abyss / And mad'st it pregnant" (1.21–2).

8. Milton considered writing an epic about Arthurian knights before settling on his biblical theme; a "Romantic" tale is a story of knightly adventure.

And, hidden in the cloud of years, became
That Odin, Father of a Race by whom
190   Perish'd the Roman Empire:[9] how the Friends
And Followers of Sertorius, out of Spain
Flying, found shelter in the Fortunate Isles;[1]
And left their usages, their arts, and laws
To disappear by a slow gradual death;
195   To dwindle and to perish one by one
Starved in those narrow bounds: but not the Soul
Of Liberty, which fifteen hundred years
Surviv'd, and when the European° came   *Spanish conquerors*
With skill and power that could not be withstood,
200   Did like a pestilence maintain its hold,
And wasted down by glorious death that Race
Of natural Heroes: or I would record
How in tyrannic times some unknown Man,
Unheard of in the Chronicles of Kings,
205   Suffer'd in silence for the love of truth:
How that one Frenchman,[2] through continued force
Of meditation on the inhuman deeds
Of the first Conquerors of the Indian Isles,
Went single in his ministry across
210   The Ocean, not to comfort the Oppress'd,
But, like a thirsty wind, to roam about,
Withering the Oppressor: how Gustavus found
Help at his need in Dalecarlia's Mines;[3]
How Wallace fought for Scotland,[4] left the name
215   Of Wallace to be found like a wild flower,
All over his dear Country, left the deeds
Of Wallace, like a Family of Ghosts,
To people the steep rocks and river banks,
Her natural sanctuaries, with a local soul
220   Of independence and stern liberty.
Sometimes it suits me better to shape out
Some Tale from my own heart, more near akin
To my own passions and habitual thoughts,
Some variegated story, in the main
225   Lofty, with interchange of gentler things;
But deadening admonitions will succeed,
And the whole beauteous Fabric seems to lack
Foundation, and, withal, appears throughout
Shadowy and unsubstantial. Then, last wish,
230   My last and favorite aspiration! then

9. In his *Decline and Fall of the Roman Empire* (1776–1788), Edward Gibbon had proposed that the Norse god Odin had originally been a tribal chieftain who had attacked Rome, his story taking on elements from the historical figure of King Mithridates, a Near Eastern king defeated by the Romans in the 1st century B.C.
1. The Canary Islands. Sertorius was a Roman general and ally of Mithridates, slain in 72 B.C.

2. In the 1560s Dominique de Gourges avenged Spanish cruelties to his countrymen in Florida.
3. Gustavus I of Sweden (1496–1530) planned his country's liberation from Danish rule, while hiding in the Dalecarlia mines of Sweden.
4. William Wallace was a Scottish hero who fought for the liberty of his country; he was executed by the British in 1305.

I yearn towards some philosophic Song
Of Truth that cherishes° our daily life;   *holds dear*
With meditations passionate from deep
Recesses in man's heart, immortal verse
235 Thoughtfully fitted to the Orphean lyre;[5]
But from this awful° burthen I full soon   *solemn*
Take refuge, and beguile myself with trust
That mellower years will bring a riper mind
And clearer insight. Thus from day to day
240 I live, a mockery of the brotherhood
Of vice and virtue, with no skill to part
Vague longing that is bred by want of power
From paramount impulse not to be withstood,
A timorous capacity from prudence;
245 From circumspection infinite delay.
Humility and modest awe themselves
Betray me, serving often for a cloak
To a more subtle selfishness, that now
Doth lock my functions up in blank reserve,°   *inertia*
250 Now dupes me by an over anxious eye
That with a false activity beats off
Simplicity and self-presented truth.
—Ah! better far than this, to stray about
Voluptuously° through fields and rural walks,   *luxuriantly*
255 And ask no record of the hours, given up
To vacant musing, unreprov'd neglect
Of all things, and deliberate holiday:
Far better never to have heard the name
Of zeal and just ambition, than to live
260 Thus baffled by a mind that every hour
Turns recreant to her task, takes heart again
Then feels immediately some hollow thought
Hang like an interdict upon her hopes.
This is my lot; for either still I find
265 Some imperfection in the chosen theme;
Or see of absolute accomplishment
Much wanting, so much wanting in myself,
That I recoil and droop, and seek repose
In indolence from vain perplexity,
270 Unprofitably travelling towards the grave,
Like a false Steward who hath much receiv'd
And renders nothing back.[6]—Was it for this
That one, the fairest of all Rivers,[7] lov'd
To blend his murmurs with my Nurse's song
275 And from his alder shades and rocky falls,
And from his fords and shallows sent a voice

---

5. In Greek myth, Orpheus singing and playing on his lyre could enthrall the natural world as well as people. Coleridge later praised *The Prelude* as "an Orphic Tale indeed."
6. An allusion to the parable of the steward who fails to use his talents (literally a coin, metaphorically, God-given abilities), Matthew 25.14–30.
7. The Derwent, which flows behind Wordsworth's childhood residence in Cockermouth, Cumberland.

That flow'd along my dreams? For this didst Thou,
O Derwent! travelling over the green Plains
Near my sweet birth-place,[8] didst thou, beauteous Stream,
280   Make ceaseless music through the night and day
Which with its steady cadence tempering
Our human waywardness, composed my thoughts
To more than infant softness, giving me,
Among the fretful dwellings of mankind,
285   A knowledge, a dim earnest of the calm
Which Nature breathes among the hills and groves.
     When, having left his Mountains, to the Towers
Of Cockermouth that beauteous River came,
Behind my Father's House he pass'd, close by,
290   Along the margin of our Terrace Walk.
He was a Playmate whom we dearly lov'd.
Oh! many a time have I, a five years' Child,
A naked Boy, in one delightful Rill,
A little Mill-race sever'd from his stream,
295   Made one long bathing of a summer's day,
Bask'd in the sun, and plunged, and bask'd again,
Alternate all a summer's day, or cours'd
Over the sandy fields, leaping through groves
Of yellow grunsel,° or when crag and hill,   *ragweed*
300   The woods, and distant Skiddaw's[9] lofty height,
Were bronz'd with a deep radiance, stood alone
Beneath the sky, as if I had been born
On Indian Plains,° and from my Mother's hut   *in America*
Had run abroad in wantonness, to sport,
305   A naked Savage, in the thunder shower.
     Fair seed-time had my soul, and I grew up
Foster'd alike by beauty and by fear;
Much favor'd in my birth-place, and no less
In that beloved Vale[1] to which, erelong,
310   I was transplanted. Well I call to mind,
('Twas at an early age, ere I had seen
Nine summers) when upon the mountain slope
The frost, and breath of frosty wind had snapp'd
The last autumnal crocus, 'twas my joy
315   To wander half the night among the Cliffs
And the smooth Hollows, where the woodcocks ran
Along the open turf. In thought and wish,
That time, my shoulder all with springes° hung,   *bird-traps*
I was a fell destroyer. On the heights
320   Scudding away from snare to snare, I plied
My anxious visitation, hurrying on,
Still hurrying, hurrying onward: moon and stars
Were shining o'er my head; I was alone

---

8. Quoting Coleridge's *Frost at Midnight* (28).
9. At 3053 feet, the fourth-highest peak of the Lake District, nine miles east of Cockermouth.

1. Esthwaite, location of the village of Hawkshead, where Wordsworth went to school, 35 miles from Cockermouth.

And seem'd to be a trouble to the peace
325   That was among them. Sometimes it befel
In these night-wanderings, that a strong desire
O'erpower'd my better reason, and the bird
Which was the captive of another's toils°   *labors, snares*
Became my prey; and, when the deed was done,
330   I heard among the solitary hills
Low breathings coming after me, and sounds
Of undistinguishable motion, steps
Almost as silent as the turf they trod.
    Nor less in spring-time when on southern banks
335   The shining sun had from her knot of leaves
Decoy'd the primrose flower, and when the Vales
And woods were warm, was I a plunderer then
In the high places, on the lonesome peaks
Where'er, among the mountains and the winds,
340   The Mother Bird had built her lodge. Though mean
My object, and inglorious, yet the end
Was not ignoble. Oh! when I have hung
Above the raven's nest, by knots of grass,
And half-inch fissures in the slippery rock
345   But ill sustain'd, and almost, as it seem'd,
Suspended by the blast which blew amain,
Shouldering the naked crag; Oh! at that time,
While on the perilous ridge I hung alone,
With what strange utterance did the loud dry wind
350   Blow through my ears! the sky seem'd not a sky
Of earth, and with what motion mov'd the clouds!
    The mind of man is framed even like the breath
And harmony of music. There is a dark
Invisible workmanship that reconciles
355   Discordant elements, and makes them move
In one society. Ah me! that all
The terrors, all the early miseries,
Regrets, vexations, lassitudes, that all
The thoughts and feelings which have been infus'd
360   Into my mind should ever have made up
The calm existence that is mine when I
Am worthy of myself. Praise to the end!
Thanks likewise for the means! But I believe
That Nature, oftentimes, when she would frame
365   A favor'd Being, from his earliest dawn
Of infancy doth open out the clouds,
As at the touch of lightning, seeking him
With gentlest visitation: not the less,
Though haply° aiming at the self-same end,   *perhaps*
370   Does it delight her sometimes to employ
Severer interventions, ministry
More palpable, and so she dealt with me.
    One evening (surely I was led by her)
I went alone into a Shepherd's Boat,

375   A Skiff that to a Willow tree was tied
       Within a rocky Cave, its usual home.
       'Twas by the Shores of Patterdale, a Vale
       Wherein I was a Stranger, thither come,
       A School-boy Traveller, at the Holidays.
380   Forth rambled from the Village Inn alone
       No sooner had I sight of this small Skiff,
       Discover'd thus by unexpected chance,
       Than I unloos'd her tether and embark'd.
       The moon was up, the Lake was shining clear
385   Among the hoary mountains: from the Shore
       I push'd, and struck the oars and struck again
       In cadence, and my little Boat mov'd on
       Even like a Man who walks with stately step
       Though bent on speed. It was an act of stealth
390   And troubled pleasure: nor without the voice
       Of mountain echoes did my Boat move on,
       Leaving behind her still on either side
       Small circles glittering idly in the moon
       Until they melted all into one track
395   Of sparkling light. A rocky steep uprose
       Above the Cavern of the Willow tree
       And now, as suited one who proudly row'd
       With his best skill, I fix'd a steady view
       Upon the top of that same craggy ridge,
400   The bound of the horizon, for behind
       Was nothing but the stars and the grey sky.
       She was an elfin Pinnace;° lustily   *a small boat*
       I dipp'd my oars into the silent Lake,
       And, as I rose upon the stroke, my Boat
405   Went heaving through the water, like a Swan,
       When from behind that craggy Steep, till then
       The bound of the horizon, a huge Cliff,
       As if with voluntary power instinct,°   *endowed*
       Uprear'd its head: I struck, and struck again,
410   And, growing still in stature, the huge Cliff
       Rose up between me and the stars, and still,
       With measur'd motion, like a living thing,
       Strode after me. With trembling hands I turn'd,
       And through the silent water stole my way
415   Back to the Cavern of the Willow tree.
       There, in her mooring-place, I left my Bark
       And, through the meadows homeward went with grave
       And serious thoughts: and after I had seen
       That spectacle, for many days my brain
420   Work'd with a dim and undetermin'd sense
       Of unknown modes of being: in my thoughts
       There was a darkness, call it solitude,
       Or blank desertion, no familiar shapes
       Of hourly objects, images of trees,
425   Of sea, or sky, no colours of green fields;

But huge and mighty Forms that do not live
Like living men mov'd slowly through my mind
By day and were the trouble of my dreams.
    Wisdom and Spirit of the Universe!
430 Thou Soul that art the Eternity of Thought!
And giv'st to forms and images a breath
And everlasting motion! not in vain,
By day or starlight thus from my first dawn
Of Childhood didst Thou intertwine for me
435 The passions that build up our human Soul,
Not with the mean and vulgar° works of Man,   *lowly and ordinary*
But with high objects, with enduring things,
With life and nature, purifying thus
The elements of feeling and of thought,
440 And sanctifying by such discipline
Both pain and fear until we recognise
A grandeur in the beatings of the heart.
    Nor was this fellowship vouchsaf'd to me
With stinted kindness. In November days
445 When vapours, rolling down the valleys, made
A lonely scene more lonesome; among woods
At noon, and 'mid the calm of summer nights,
When by the margin of the trembling Lake
Beneath the gloomy hills I homeward went
450 In solitude, such intercourse was mine;
'Twas mine among the fields both day and night,
And by the waters all the summer long.
—And in the frosty season, when the sun
Was set, and, visible for many a mile,
455 The cottage windows through the twilight blaz'd,
I heeded not the summons:—happy time
It was indeed for all of us; to me
It was a time of rapture: clear and loud
The village clock toll'd six; I wheel'd about,
460 Proud and exulting, like an untired horse,
That cares not for its home.—All shod with steel
We hiss'd along the polish'd ice, in games
Confederate, imitative of the chace,
And woodland pleasures, the resounding horn,
465 The Pack, loud bellowing, and the hunted hare.
So through the darkness and the cold we flew,
And not a voice was idle: with the din,
Meanwhile, the precipices rang aloud,
The leafless trees, and every icy crag
470 Tinkled like iron, while the distant hills
Into the tumult sent an alien sound
Of melancholy, not unnoticed, while the stars,
Eastward, were sparkling clear, and in the west,
The orange sky of evening died away.
475   Not seldom from the uproar I retired
Into a silent bay, or sportively

Glanced sideway, leaving the tumultuous throng,
To cut across the image of a star
That gleam'd upon the ice: and oftentimes,
480 When we had given our bodies to the wind,
And all the shadowy banks, on either side,
Came sweeping through the darkness, spinning still
The rapid line of motion; then at once
Have I, reclining back upon my heels,
485 Stopp'd short, yet still the solitary Cliffs
Wheel'd by me, even as if the earth had roll'd
With visible motion her diurnal° round;   daily
Behind me did they stretch in solemn train
Feebler and feebler, and I stood and watch'd
490 Till all was tranquil as [   ]²
       Ye Presences of Nature, in the sky
Or on the earth! Ye Visions of the hills!
And Souls of lonely places! can I think
A vulgar hope was yours when Ye employ'd
495 Such ministry, when Ye through many a year
Haunting me thus among my boyish sports,
On caves and trees, upon the woods and hills,
Impress'd upon all forms the characters°   marks, signs
Of danger or desire, and thus did make
500 The surface of the universal earth
With triumph, and delight, and hope, and fear
Work like a sea.
                    Not uselessly employ'd,
I might pursue this theme through every change
Of exercise and play, to which the year
505 Did summon us in its delightful round.
—We were a noisy crew; the sun in heaven
Beheld not vales more beautiful than ours
Nor saw a race, in happiness and joy
More worthy of the fields where they were sown.
510 I would record with no reluctant voice
The woods of autumn and their hazel bowers
With milk-white clusters hung; the rod and line,
True symbol of the foolishness of hope,
Which with its strong enchantment led us on
515 By rocks and pools, shut out from every star
All the green summer, to forlorn cascades
Among the windings of the mountain-brooks.
—Unfading recollections! at this hour
The heart is almost mine with which I felt
520 From some hill-top, on sunny afternoons,
The Kite high up among the fleecy clouds
Pull at its rein, like an impatient Courser,°   race-horse
Or, from the meadows sent on gusty days
Beheld her breast the wind, then suddenly
525 Dash'd headlong; and rejected by the storm.

2. Wordsworth left the end of this line blank in 1805. In 1809, it was completed as "a dreamless sleep."

Ye lowly Cottages in which we dwelt,
A ministration of your own was yours,
A sanctity, a safeguard, and a love!
Can I forget you, being as ye were
530 So beautiful among the pleasant fields
In which ye stood? Or can I here forget
The plain and seemly countenance with which
Ye dealt out your plain comforts? Yet had ye
Delights and exultations of your own.
535 Eager and never weary we pursued
Our home amusements by the warm peat fire
At evening; when with pencil and with slate,
In square divisions parcell'd out, and all
With crosses and with cyphers scribbled o'er,°   *tic-tac-toe*
540 We schemed and puzzled, head opposed to head,
In strife too humble to be named in Verse;
Or round the naked Table, snow-white deal,°   *pine*
Cherry, or maple, sate in close array,
And to the combat, Lu or Whist,° led on   *card games*
545 A thick-ribb'd Army, not as in the world
Neglected and ungratefully thrown by
Even for the very service they had wrought,
But husbanded through many a long campaign.
Uncouth assemblage was it, where no few
550 Had changed their functions, some, plebean cards,
Which Fate beyond the promise of their birth
Had glorified, and call'd to represent
The persons of departed Potentates.
Oh! with what echoes on the Board they fell!
555 Ironic Diamonds; Clubs, Hearts, Diamonds, Spades,
A congregation piteously akin;
Cheap matter did they give to boyish wit,
Those sooty Knaves, precipitated down
With scoffs and taunts, like Vulcan out of Heaven,
560 The paramount Ace, a moon in her eclipse,
Queens, gleaming through their splendour's last decay,
And Monarchs, surly at the wrongs sustain'd
By royal visages. Meanwhile, abroad
The heavy rain was falling, or the frost
565 Raged bitterly, with keen and silent tooth,
And, interrupting the impassion'd game,
From Esthwaite's neighbouring Lake the splitting ice,
While it sank down towards the water, sent,
Among the meadows and the hills, its long
570 And dismal yellings, like the noise of wolves
When they are howling round the Bothnic Main.°   *Baltic sea*
Nor, sedulous³ as I have been to trace
How Nature by extrinsic passion first
Peopled my mind with beauteous forms or grand,
575 And made me love them, may I well forget

---

3. Diligent; revising Milton's claim that he is "Not sedulous by Nature" to treat epic themes (*Paradise Lost* 9.27).

How other pleasures have been mine, and joys
Of subtler origin; how I have felt
Not seldom, even in that tempestuous time,
Those hallow'd and pure motions of the sense
580 Which seem, in their simplicity, to own
An intellectual charm, that calm delight
Which, if I err not, surely must belong
To those first-born affinities that fit
Our new existence to existing things
585 And, in our dawn of being, constitute
The bond of union betwixt life and joy.
     Yes, I remember, when the changeful earth,
And twice five seasons on my mind had stamp'd
The faces of the moving year, even then,
590 A Child, I held unconscious intercourse
With the eternal Beauty, drinking in
A pure organic pleasure from the lines
Of curling mist, or from the level plain
Of waters colour'd by the steady clouds.
595   The Sands of Westmoreland, the Creeks and Bays
Of Cumbria's⁴ rocky limits, they can tell
How when the Sea threw off his evening shade
And to the Shepherd's hut beneath the crags
Did send sweet notice of the rising moon,
600 How I have stood to fancies such as these,
Engrafted in the tenderness of thought,
A stranger, linking with the spectacle
No conscious memory of a kindred sight,
And bringing with me no peculiar sense
605 Of quietness or peace, yet have I stood,
Even while mine eye has mov'd o'er three long leagues
Of shining water, gathering, as it seem'd,
Through every hair-breadth of that field of light,
New pleasure, like a bee among the flowers.
610   Thus, often in those fits of vulgar° joy   *ordinary*
Which through all seasons, on a child's pursuits
Are prompt attendants, 'mid that giddy bliss
Which, like a tempest, works along the blood
And is forgotten; even then I felt
615 Gleams like the flashing of a shield: the earth
And common face of Nature spake to me
Rememberable things: sometimes, 'tis true,
By chance collisions, and quaint accidents
Like those ill-sorted unions, work suppos'd
620 Of evil-minded fairies, yet not vain,
Nor profitless, if haply they impress'd
Collateral° objects and appearances,   *subordinate*
Albeit lifeless then, and doom'd to sleep
Until maturer seasons call'd them forth

4. Lake District counties.

625 To impregnate and to elevate the mind.
And if the vulgar joy by its own weight
Wearied itself out of the memory
The scenes which were a witness of that joy
Remained, in their substantial lineaments
630 Depicted on the brain, and to the eye
Were visible, a daily sight: and thus,
By the impressive discipline of fear,
By pleasure, and repeated happiness,
So frequently repeated, and by force
635 Of obscure feelings representative
Of joys that were forgotten, these same scenes,
So beauteous and majestic in themselves,
Though yet the day was distant, did at length
Become habitually dear; and all
640 Their hues and forms were by invisible links
Allied to the affections.
                      I began
My Story early, feeling as I fear,
The weakness of a human love, for days
Disown'd by memory, ere the birth of spring
645 Planting my snow-drops among winter snows.
Nor will it seem to thee, my Friend! so prompt
In sympathy, that I have lengthen'd out,
With fond and feeble tongue, a tedious tale.
Meanwhile, my hope has been that I might fetch
650 Invigorating thoughts from former years,
Might fix the wavering balance of my mind,
And haply meet reproaches, too, whose power
May spur me on, in manhood now mature,
To honorable toil. Yet should these hopes
655 Be vain, and thus should neither I be taught
To understand myself, nor thou to know
With better knowledge how the heart was fram'd
Of him thou lovest, need I dread from thee
Harsh judgments, if I am so loth to quit
660 Those recollected hours that have the charm
Of visionary things, and lovely forms,
And sweet sensations that throw back our life
And almost make our Infancy itself
A visible scene on which the sun is shining.
665   One end hereby, at least, hath been attain'd—
My mind hath been reviv'd, and if this mood
Desert me not, I will forthwith bring down,
Through later years, the story of my life.
The road lies plain before me; 'tis a theme
670 Single, and of determin'd bounds; and hence
I chuse it rather, at this time, than work
Of ampler or more varied argument.[5]

5. Wordsworth wrote this last paragraph in 1804, further explaining why he is not following Coleridge's advice to write a major philosophical epic.

from **Book Second. School time continued**
[Two Consciousnesses]

Thus far, O Friend! have we, though leaving much
Unvisited, endeavour'd to retrace
My life through its first years, and measur'd back
The way I travell'd when I first began
5   To love the woods and fields: the passion yet
Was in its birth, sustain'd, as might befal,
By nourishment that came unsought; for still,
From week to week, from month to month we liv'd
A round of tumult: duly were our games
10   Prolong'd in summer till the daylight fail'd;
No chair remain'd before the doors, the bench
And threshold steps were empty; fast asleep
The Labourer, and the Old Man who had sate,
A later lingerer, yet the revelry
15   Continued, and the loud uproar: at last,
When all the ground was dark, and the huge clouds
Were edged with twinkling stars, to bed we went
With weary joints, and with a beating mind.
Ah! is there one who ever has been young,
20   And needs a monitory voice to tame
The pride of virtue, and of intellect?
And is there one, the wisest and the best
Of all mankind, who does not sometimes wish
For things which cannot be, who would not give,
25   If so he might, to duty and to truth
The eagerness of infantine desire?
A tranquillizing spirit presses now
On my corporeal frame: so wide appears
The vacancy between me and those days,
30   Which yet have such self-presence in my mind
That, sometimes, when I think of them, I seem
Two consciousnesses, conscious of myself
And of some other Being.

[Blessed Infant Babe]

Bless'd the infant Babe,[1]
(For with my best conjectures I would trace
The progress of our being) blest the Babe,
240   Nurs'd in his Mother's arms, the Babe who sleeps
Upon his Mother's breast, who, when his soul
Claims manifest kindred with an earthly soul,
Doth gather passion from his Mother's eye!
Such feelings pass into his torpid life
245   Like an awakening breeze, and hence his mind

---

1. Wordsworth has been discussing how hard it is "to analyse a soul" when no clear beginning can be found for one's habits and desires, or even for any "obvious and particular thought." He then moves on to this general speculation in psychobiography.

Even [in the first trial of its powers,]²
Is prompt and watchful, eager to combine
In one appearance, all the elements
And parts of the same object, else detach'd
250 And loth to coalesce. Thus, day by day,
Subjected to the discipline of love,
His organs and recipient faculties
Are quicken'd, are more vigorous, his mind spreads,
Tenacious of the forms which it receives.
255 In one beloved presence, nay and more,
In that most apprehensive habitude°   *capacity to assimilate*
And those sensations which have been deriv'd
From this beloved Presence, there exists
A virtue which irradiates and exalts
260 All objects through all intercourse of sense.
No outcast he, bewilder'd and depress'd:
Along his infant veins are interfus'd
The gravitation and the filial bond
Of nature, that connect him with the world.
265 Emphatically such a Being lives,
An inmate of this *active* universe;
From nature largely he receives; nor so
Is satisfied, but largely gives again,
For feeling has to him imparted strength,
270 And powerful in all sentiments of grief,
Of exultation, fear, and joy, his mind,
Even as an agent of the one great mind,
Creates, creator and receiver both,
Working but in alliance with the works
275 Which it beholds.——Such, verily, is the first
Poetic spirit of our human life;
By uniform controul of after years
In most abated and suppress'd, in some,
Through every change of growth or of decay,
280 Pre-eminent till death.
                              From early days,
Beginning not long after that first time
In which, a Babe, by intercourse of touch,
I held mute dialogues with my Mother's heart,
I have endeavour'd to display the means
285 Whereby the infant sensibility,
Great birth-right of our Being, was in me
Augmented and sustain'd. Yet is a path
More difficult before me, and I fear
That in its broken windings we shall need
290 The chamois'° sinews, and the eagle's wing: *mountain antelope*
For now a trouble came into my mind
From unknown causes. I was left alone,
Seeking the visible world, nor knowing why.

2. This line was completed decades later.

The props of my affections were remov'd,
295   And yet the building stood, as if sustain'd
By its own spirit!³ All that I beheld
Was dear to me, and from this cause it came,
That now to Nature's finer influxes°   influences, impressions
My mind lay open, to that more exact
300   And intimate communion which our hearts
Maintain with the minuter properties
Of objects which already are belov'd,
And of those only.

from Book Sixth. Cambridge, and the Alps

[TRAVELLING IN THE ALPS. SIMPLON PASS]

Yet still in me, mingling with these delights°   of travel
Was something of stern mood, an under thirst
490   Of vigour, never utterly asleep.
Far different dejection once was mine,
A deep and genuine sadness then I felt:
The circumstances I will here relate
Even as they were. Upturning with a Band
495   Of Travellers, from the Valais we had clomb
Along the road that leads to Italy;
A length of hours, making of these our guides
Did we advance, and having reach'd an Inn
Among the mountains, we together ate
500   Our noon's repast, from which the Travellers rose,
Leaving us at the Board. Erelong we follow'd,
Descending by the beaten road that led
Right to a rivulet's edge, and there broke off.
The only track now visible was one
505   Upon the further side, right opposite,
And up a lofty Mountain. This we took
After a little scruple,° and short pause,   hesitation
And climb'd with eagerness, though not, at length,
Without surprize and some anxiety
510   On finding that we did not overtake
Our Comrades gone before. By fortunate chance,
While every moment now encreas'd our doubts,
A Peasant met us and from him we learn'd
That to the place which had perplex'd us first
515   We must descend, and there should find the road
Which in the stony channel of the Stream
Lay a few steps, and then along its Banks,
And, further, that thenceforward all our course
Was downwards, with the current of that Stream.
520   Hard of belief we questioned him again,
And all the answers which the Man return'd

---

3. Perhaps an oblique reference to the death of Wordsworth's mother when he was almost eight years old.

To our inquiries, in their sense and substance,
Translated by the feelings which we had,
Ended in this, that we had cross'd the Alps.
525   Imagination! lifting up itself
Before the eye and progress of my Song
Like an unfather'd vapour; here that Power,
In all the might of its endowments, came
Athwart me; I was lost as in a cloud,
530 Halted without a struggle to break through,
And now[1] recovering to my Soul I say
I recognize thy glory; in such strength
Of usurpation, in such visitings
Of awful° promise, when the light of sense   *awe-filled*
535 Goes out in flashes that have shewn to us
The invisible world, doth Greatness make abode,
There harbours whether we be young or old.
Our destiny, our nature, and our home
Is with infinitude, and only there;
540 With hope it is, hope that can never die,
Effort, and expectation, and desire,
And something evermore about to be.
The mind beneath such banners militant
Thinks not of spoils, trophies nor of aught
545 That may attest its prowess, blest in thoughts
That are their own perfection and reward,
Strong in itself, and in the access of joy
Which hides it like the overflowing Nile.
    The dull and heavy slackening which ensu'd
550 Upon those tidings by the Peasant given
Was soon dislodg'd; downwards we hurried fast,
And enter'd with the road which we had miss'd
Into a narrow chasm: the brook and road
Were fellow-travellers in this gloomy Pass,
555 And with them did we journey several hours
At a slow step. The immeasurable height
Of woods decaying, never to be decay'd,
The stationary blasts of waterfalls,
And every where along the hollow rent
560 Winds thwarting winds, bewilder'd and forlorn,
The torrents shooting from the clear blue sky,
The rocks that mutter'd close upon our ears,
Black drizzling crags that spake by the way-side
As if a voice were in them, the sick sight
565 And giddy prospect of the raving stream,
The unfetter'd clouds, and region of the heavens,
Tumult and peace, the darkness and the light
Were all like workings of one mind, the features
Of the same face, blossoms upon one tree,
570 Characters° of the great Apocalyps,   *signs, letters*

1. This apostrophe was written in 1804, fourteen years after the disappointment of the missed climax.

The types and symbols of Eternity,
Of first and last, and midst, and without end.[2]
    That night our lodging was an Alpine House,
An Inn or Hospital, as they are named,
575   Standing in that same valley by itself
And close upon the confluence of two streams,
A dreary Mansion, large beyond all need,
With high and spacious rooms, deafen'd and stunn'd
By noise of waters, making innocent Sleep
580   Lie melancholy among weary bones.
    Uprisen betimes, our journey we renew'd
Led by the Stream, ere noon-day magnified
Into a lordly River, broad and deep,
Dimpling along in silent majesty,
585   With mountains for its neighbours, and in view
Of distant mountains and their snowy tops,
And thus proceeding to Locarno's Lake,
Fit resting-place for such a Visitant.
——Locarno, spreading out in width like Heaven,
590   And Como, thou a treasure by the earth
Kept to itself, a darling bosom'd up
In Abyssinian[3] privacy, I spake
Of thee, thy chesnut woods, and garden plots
Of Indian corn tended by dark-eyed Maids,
595   Thy lofty steeps, and path-ways roof'd with vines
Winding from house to house, from town to town,
Sole link that binds them to each other, walks
League after league, and cloistral avenues
Where silence is, if music be not there:
600   While yet a Youth, undisciplined in Verse,
Through fond ambition of my heart, I told
Your praises; nor can I approach you now,
Ungreeted by a more melodious Song,
Where tones of learned Art and Nature mix'd
605   May frame enduring language. Like a breeze
Or sunbeam over your domain I pass'd
In motion without pause; but Ye have left
Your beauty with me, an impassion'd sight
Of colours and of forms, whose power is sweet
610   And gracious, almost might I dare to say,
As virtue is, or goodness, sweet as love
Or the remembrance of a noble deed,
Or gentlest visitations of pure thought
When God, the Giver of all joy, is thank'd
615   Religiously, in silent blessedness,
Sweet as this last itself, for such it is.

---

2. Milton's terms for God (*Paradise Lost* 5.165), echoing God's description of himself in the book of Revelation (the Apocalypse) as "Alpha and Omega, the beginning and the ending"—the first and last letters of the Greek alphabet. "Types" are people or events that foreshadow God's future works.
3. Abyssinia was a legendary location for Paradise.

Are memorable, but from him lock'd up,
Being written in a tongue he cannot read;
So that he questions the mute leaves with pain
And half upbraids their silence. But that night
55   When on my bed I lay I was most mov'd
And felt most deeply in what world I was;
My room was high and lonely, near the roof
Of a large Mansion or Hotel, a spot
That would have pleas'd me in more quiet times
60   Nor was it wholly without pleasure then.
With unextinguish'd taper I kept watch,
Reading at intervals; the fear gone by
Press'd on me almost like a fear to come;
I thought of those September Massacres,
65   Divided from me by a little month,[3]
And felt and touch'd them, a substantial dread;
The rest was conjured up from tragic fictions
And mournful Calendars° of true history,   records
Remembrances and dim admonishments.
70   "The horse is taught his manage° and the wind   paces
Of heaven wheels round and treads in his own steps,[4]
Year follows year, the tide returns again,
Day follows day, all things have second birth;
The earthquake is not satisfied at once."
75   And in such way I wrought upon myself
Until I seem'd to hear a voice that cried
To the whole City, "Sleep no more."[5] To this
Add comments of a calmer mind, from which
I could not gather full security,
80   But at the best it seemed a place of fear,
Unfit for the repose of night,
Defenceless as a wood where tigers roam.
          Betimes next morning to the Palace Walk
Of Orleans I repair'd and entering there
85   Was greeted, among divers° other notes,   various
By voices of the Hawkers in the crowd
Bawling, *Denunciation of the crimes*
Of Maximilian Robespierre: the speech
Which in their hands they carried was the same
90   Which had been recently pronounced the day
When Robespierre, well-knowing for what mark
Some words of indirect reproof had been
Intended, rose in hardihood and dared
The Man who had an ill surmise of him
95   To bring his charge in openness: whereat
When a dead pause ensued and no one stirr'd,
In silence of all present, from his seat

3. Between September 2 and 7, a newly powerful radical faction of the Republican government organized massacres in which 3,000 prisoners were executed.
4. The National Convention of France now met at a for-
mer riding school near the Tuileries.
5. The quotation recalls Macbeth's guilty fantasy after he has murdered his king: "Methought I heard a voice cry 'Sleep no more!'" (*Macbeth* 2.2.35).

<blockquote>

Louvet walked singly through the avenue
And took his station in the Tribune,° saying   *rostrum*
100   "I, Robespierre, accuse thee"! 'Tis well known
What was the issue of that charge, and how
Louvet was left alone without support
Of his irresolute Friends:[6] but these are things
Of which I speak only as they were storm
105   Or sunshine to my individual mind,
No further. Let me then relate that now
In some sort seeing with my proper° eyes   *own*
That Liberty, and Life and Death would soon
To the remotest corners of the Land
110   Lie in the arbitriment° of those who ruled   *government*
The capital City, what was struggled for,
And by what combatants victory must be won,
The indecision on their° part whose aim   *Girondin moderates*
Seem'd best, and the straight-forward path of those
115   Who in attack or in defense alike
Were strong through their impiety,° greatly I   *the Jacobin radicals*
Was agitated; yea I could almost
Have pray'd that throughout earth upon all souls
Worthy of liberty, upon every soul
120   Matured to live in plainness and in truth
The gift of tongues might fall,[7] and men arrive
From the four quarters of the winds to do
For France what without help she could not do,
A work of honour: think not that to this
125   I added work of safety; from such thought
And the least fear about the end of things
I was as far as Angels are from guilt.
       Yet did I grieve, nor only grieved, but thought
Of opposition and of remedies,
130   An insignificant Stranger, and obscure,
Mean° as I was, and little graced with powers   *humble*
Of eloquence even in my native speech,
And all unfit for tumult and intrigue,
Yet would I willingly have taken up
135   A service at this time for cause so great,
However dangerous. Inly I revolved
How much the destiny of man had still°   *always*
Hung upon single persons, that there was,
Transcendant to all local patrimony,
140   One Nature, as there is one Sun in heaven,
That objects, even as they are great, thereby
Do come within the reach of humblest eyes,
That Man was only weak through his mistrust
And want of hope, where evidence divine

</blockquote>

---

6. In the National Convention, on 29 October 1792, the moderate Girondist J. B. Louvet de Couvray accused Robespierre of dictatorial behavior and aspirations. The phrase "walked singly" in line 98 evokes the solitary resis-

tance of archangel Abdiel to Satan's revolt against God (*Paradise Lost* 5.877ff).
7. Apostles began to speak in tongues at Pentacost, miraculously understood by foreigners of many languages (Acts 2).

145   Proclaim'd to him that hope should be most sure,
That, with desires heroic and firm sense,
A Spirit thoroughly faithful to itself,
Unquenchable, unsleeping, undismay'd,[8]
Was as an instinct among men, a stream
150   That gather'd up each petty straggling rill
And vein of water, glad to be roll'd on
In safe obedience, that a mind whose rest
Was where it ought to be, in self-restraint,
In circumspection and simplicity,
155   Fell rarely in entire discomfiture
Below its aim, or met with from without
A treachery that defeated it, or foil'd.
    —On the other side I call'd to mind those truths
Which are the common-places of the Schools,
160   A theme° for Boys, too trite even to be felt,   *essay subject*
Yet with a revelation's liveliness
In all their comprehensive bearings known
And visible to Philosophers of old,
Men who, to business of the world untrain'd,
165   Liv'd in the Shade, and to Harmodius known
And his Compeer Aristogiton,[9] known
To Brutus, that tyrannic Power is weak,
Hath neither gratitude, nor faith, nor love,
Nor the support of good or evil men
170   To trust in, that the Godhead which is ours
Can never utterly be charm'd° or still'd,   *expelled*
That nothing hath a natural right to last
But equity and reason, that all else
Meets foes irreconcilable, and at best
175   Doth live but by variety of disease.
        Well might my wishes be intense, my thoughts
Strong and perturb'd, not doubting at that time,
Creed which ten shameful years have not annull'd,
But that the virtue of one paramount mind
180   Would have abash'd those impious crests, have quell'd
Outrage and bloody power, and in despite
Of what the People were through ignorance
And immaturity, and, in the teeth
Of desperate opposition from without,
185   Have clear'd a passage for just government,
And left a solid birth-right to the State,
Redeem'd according to example given
By ancient Lawgivers.
                In this frame of mind
Reluctantly to England I return'd,[1]
190   Compell'd by nothing less than absolute want

8. Again evoking Abdiel's faithful heroism (*Paradise Lost* 5.897–99).
9. Harmodius and Aristogiton were killed when they tried to overthrow the tyrant Hippias in 514 B.C. in Athens. Brutus was the idealistic assassin of Julius Caesar, who seemed ready in 44 B.C. to name himself emperor.
1. Wordsworth returned to England late in 1792.

Of funds for my support, else, well assured
That I both was and must be of small worth,
No better than an alien in the Land,
I doubtless should have made a common cause
195   With some who perish'd, haply° perish'd too,[2]   *perhaps*
A poor mistaken and bewilder'd offering,
Should to the breast of Nature have gone back
With all my resolutions, all my hopes,
A Poet only to myself, to Men
200   Useless, and even, beloved Friend, a soul
To thee unknown.[3]

[FURTHER EVENTS IN FRANCE]

In France, the Men who for their desperate ends
Had pluck'd up mercy by the roots were glad
Of this new enemy. Tyrants, strong before
310   In devilish pleas were ten times stronger now,[4]
And thus beset with Foes on every side
The goaded Land wax'd mad; the crimes of few
Spread into madness of the many, blasts
From hell came sanctified like airs from heaven;[5]
315   The sternness of the Just,[6] the faith of those
Who doubted not that Providence had times
Of anger and vengeance, theirs who throned
The human understanding paramount
And made of that their God,[7] the hopes of those
320   Who were content to barter short-lived pangs
For a paradise of ages, the blind rage
Of insolent tempers, the light vanity
Of intermeddlers, steady purposes
Of the suspicious, slips of the indiscreet,
325   And all the accidents of life were press'd
Into one service, busy with one work;
The Senate was heart-stricken, not a voice
Uplifted, none to oppose or mitigate:
Domestic carnage now fill'd all the year
330   With Feast-days; the Old Man from the chimney-nook,
The Maiden from the bosom of her Love,
The Mother from the Cradle of her Babe,
The Warrior from the Field, all perish'd,
Friends, enemies, of all parties, ages, ranks,
335   Head after head, and never heads enough

---

2. Wordsworth's revolutionary sympathies were with the moderate Girondins, almost all of whom were executed or committed suicide following Robespierre's rise to power.
3. Wordsworth met Coleridge in 1795.
4. After France declared war on England in February 1793, England joined the coalition against France led by Austria and Prussia. Except for a brief peace in 1802, England would be at war with France until 1815.

5. Echoing Hamlet's uncertainty about whether his murdered father's ghost brings "airs from heaven or blasts from hell" (*Hamlet* 1.4.41).
6. Referring obliquely to Robespierre's associate Louis St. Just, a leader of the Terror.
7. "La Raison" (Reason) was embodied as a symbolic goddess of the Republic, and churches were turned into Temples of Reason.

For those who bade them fall: they found their joy,
They made it, ever thirsty.—As a Child,
(If light desires of innocent little Ones
May with such heinous appetites be match'd)
340 Having a toy, a windmill, though the air
Do of itself blow fresh, and makes the vane
Spin in his eyesight, he is not content,
But with the play-thing at arm's length, he sets
His front against the blast, and runs amain°   *full force*
345 To make it whirl the faster.
                              In the depth
Of these enormities, even thinking minds
Forgot at seasons whence they had their being,
Forgot that such a sound was ever heard
As Liberty, upon earth; yet all beneath
350 Her innocent authority was wrought,
Nor could have been without her blessed name.
The illustrious Wife of Roland, in the hour
Of her composure, felt that agony
And gave it vent in her last words.[8] O Friend!
355 It was a lamentable time for man
Whether a hope had e'er been his or not,
A woful time for them whose hopes did still
Outlast the shock, most woful for those few—
They had the deepest feeling of the grief—
360 Who still were flatter'd,° and had trust in man.   *deluded*
Meanwhile, the Invaders fared as they deserv'd;
The Herculean Commonwealth had put forth her arms
And throttled with an infant Godhead's might
The snakes about her cradle:[9] that was well
365 And as it should be, yet no cure for those
Whose souls were sick with pain of what would be
Hereafter brought in charge against mankind;
Most melancholy at that time, O Friend!
Were my day thoughts, my dreams were miserable;
370 Through months, through years, long after the last beat
Of those atrocities (I speak bare truth,
As if to thee alone in private talk)
I scarcely had one night of quiet sleep,
Such ghastly visions had I of despair
375 And tyranny and implements of death,
And long orations which in dreams I pleaded
Before unjust Tribunals, with a voice
Labouring, a brain confounded, and a sense
Of treachery and desertion in the place
380 The holiest that I knew of, my own soul.

8. Madame Roland, an important supporter of the Girondins, was guillotined in November 1793. Her famous last words were: "O Liberté, que des crimes l'on commet en ton nom!" ("O Liberty, what crimes are committed in your name!").

9. As an infant in his cradle, Hercules strangled the two serpents sent by Hera to destroy him, just as the infant Republic had repelled foreign invasions.

[THE DEATH OF ROBESPIERRE AND RENEWED OPTIMISM] [1]

the scene appear'd
So gay and chearful, when a Traveller
Chancing to pass, I carelessly inquired
If any news were stirring: he replied
In the familiar language of the day
535   That "*Robespierre was dead.*" Nor was a doubt,
On further question, left within my mind
But that the tidings were substantial truth,
That he and his supporters all were fallen.
    Great was my glee of spirit, great my joy
540   In vengeance, and eternal justice, thus
Made manifest. "Come now ye golden times,"
Said I, forth-breathing on those open Sands
A Hymn of triumph, "as the morning comes
Out of the bosom of the night, come Ye:
545   Thus far our trust is verified; behold!
They who with clumsy desperation brought
A river of blood, and preach'd that nothing else
Could cleanse the Augean Stable,[2] by the might
Of their own helper have been swept away;
550   Their madness is declared and visible,
Elsewhere will safety now be sought,[3] and Earth
March firmly towards righteousness and peace."
Then schemes I framed more calmly, when and how
The madding Factions might be tranquillised,
555   And though through hardships manifold and long,
The mighty renovation would proceed:
Thus, interrupted by uneasy bursts
Of exultation, I pursued my way
Along that very Shore which I had skimm'd
560   In former times, when, spurring from the Vale
Of Nightshade and St Mary's mouldering Fane°   *shrine*
And the Stone Abbot, after circuit made
In wantonness of heart, a joyous Crew
Of School-boys, hastening to their distant home,
565   Along the margin of the moonlight Sea,
We beat with thundering hoofs the level Sand.
           * * *
    O pleasant exercise of hope and joy![4]
690   For great were the auxiliars° which then stood   *allies*
Upon our side, we who were strong in love;

1. Wordsworth is back in England, spending the summer on the coast near Peele Castle. On 28 July 1794, Robespierre and 21 of his associates were guillotined. Wordsworth is walking near the shore when he learns of Robespierre's death.
2. In one of his 12 labors, Hercules cleaned the filthy stable of King Augeus, by diverting two rivers through the stable.
3. Instead of with Robespierre's Committee of Public

Safety, which had instigated the Terror.
4. Wordsworth's renewed faith in the French Republic extended to hope for peaceful reforms in England. Here he recalls his first enthusiasm for the Revolution; he published this passage in Coleridge's journal *The Friend* in 1809 and again in his *Poems* of 1815, as "French Revolution as It Appeared to Enthusiasts at Its Commencement," classing it with "Poems of the Imagination."

Bliss was it in that dawn to be alive,
But to be young was very heaven: O times,
In which the meagre, stale, forbidding ways
695   Of custom, law and statute took at once
The attraction of a Country in Romance;
When Reason seem'd the most to assert her rights
When most intent on making of herself
A prime Enchanter to assist the work
700   Which then was going forwards in her name:
Not favor'd spots alone, but the whole earth
The beauty wore of promise, that which sets,
To take an image which was felt, no doubt,
Among the bowers of paradise itself,
705   The budding rose above the rose full blown.
What temper° at the prospect did not wake   *temperament*
To happiness unthought-of? The inert
Were rouz'd, and lively natures rapt° away.   *carried, enraptured*
They who had fed their childhood upon dreams,
710   The Play-fellows of Fancy, who had made
All powers of swiftness, subtlety, and strength
Their ministers, used to stir in lordly wise
Among the grandest objects of the sense
And deal with whatsoever they found there
715   As if they had within some lurking right
To wield it:—they too, who, of gentle mood,
Had watch'd all gentle motions, and to these
Had fitted their own thoughts, schemers more mild,
And in the region of their peaceful selves—
720   Did now find helpers to their heart's desire,
And stuff at hand, plastic° as they could wish,   *malleable*
Were call'd upon to exercise their skill,
Not in Utopia, subterraneous fields,
Or some secreted Island Heaven knows where;
725   But in the very world which is the world
Of all of us, the place on which in the end
We find our happiness, or not at all.

[BRITAIN DECLARES WAR ON FRANCE.
THE RISE OF NAPOLEON AND IMPERIALIST FRANCE]

In the main outline, such, it might be said
Was my condition, till with open war
Britain opposed the Liberties of France:[5]
760   This threw me first out of the pale° of love,   *boundary*
Sour'd, and corrupted upwards to the source
My sentiments, was° not, as hitherto,   *this was*
A swallowing up of lesser things in great;
But change of them into their opposites,
765   And thus a way was open'd for mistakes

5. France declared war on Holland and England on 1 February 1793. Ten days later, England reciprocated.

And false conclusions of the intellect
As gross in their degree and in their kind
Far, far more dangerous. What had been a pride
Was now a shame; my likings and my loves
770 Ran in new channels, leaving old ones dry,
And thus a blow which in maturer age
Would but have touch'd the judgement struck more deep
Into sensations near the heart: meantime,
As from the first, wild theories were afloat
775 Unto the subtleties of which at least
I had but lent a careless ear, assured
Of this, that time would soon set all things right,
Prove that the multitude had been oppress'd,
And would be so no more.
                                But when events
780 Brought less encouragement, and unto these
The immediate proof of principles no more
Could be entrusted, while the events themselves,
Worn out in greatness and in novelty,
Less occupied the mind and sentiments,
785 Could through my understanding's natural growth
No longer justify themselves through faith
Of inward consciousness, and hope that laid
Its hand upon its object; evidence
Safer, of universal application, such
790 As could not be impeach'd was sought elsewhere.
      And now, become Oppressors in their turn,
Frenchmen had changed a war of self-defense
For one of conquest, losing sight of all
Which they had struggled for; and mounted up
795 Openly in the view of earth and heaven
The scale of Liberty.[6] I read her doom,
Vex'd inly somewhat, it is true, and sore,
But not dismay'd, nor taking to the shame
Of a false Prophet; but, rouz'd up, I stuck
800 More firmly to old tenets, and to prove
Their temper,° strain'd them more, and thus in heat   *test their strength*
Of contest did opinions every day
Grow into consequence till round my mind
They clung, as if they were the life of it.
805 This was the time when all things tended fast
To depravation; the Philosophy
That promised to abstract the hopes of man
Out of his feelings, to be fix'd thenceforth
For ever in a purer element
810 Found ready welcome.[7] Tempting region that
For Zeal to enter and refresh herself

---

6. Initially fighting only in self-defense, by late 1794 France was clearly the aggressor in wars on several foreign fronts.

7. A reference to William Godwin's *Political Justice* (1793), which argued for the power of individual rational judgment to bring about reform.

Where passions had the privilege to work,
And never hear the sound of their own names:
But, speaking more in charity, the dream
815 Was flattering° to the young ingenuous mind,   *seductive*
Pleas'd with extremes, and not the least with that
Which makes the human Reason's naked self
The object of its fervour: what delight!
How glorious! in self-knowledge and self-rule
820 To look through all the frailties of the world
And, with a resolute mastery shaking off
The accidents of nature, time, and place
That make up the weak being of the past,
Build social freedom on its only basis,
825 The freedom of the individual mind,
Which, to the blind restraint of general laws
Superior, magisterially adopts
One guide, the light of circumstances, flash'd
Upon an independent intellect.
830   For, howsoe'er unsettled, never once
Had I thought ill of human kind, or been
Indifferent to its welfare; but, enflamed
With thirst of a secure intelligence
And sick of other passion, I pursued
835 A higher nature, wish'd that man should start
Out of the worm-like° state in which he is,   *caterpillar-like*
And spread abroad the wings of Liberty,
Lord of himself in indisturb'd delight—
A noble aspiration, yet° I feel   *even now*
840 The aspiration, but with other thoughts
And happier; for I was perplex'd and sought
To accomplish the transition by such means
As did not lie in nature, sacrificed
The exactness of a comprehensive mind
845 To scrupulous and microscopic views
That furnish'd out materials for a work
Of false imagination, placed beyond
The limits of experience and of truth.
     Enough, no doubt, the advocates themselves
850 Of ancient institutions had performed
To bring disgrace upon their° very names,   *the institutions'*
Disgrace of which custom and written law
And sundry moral sentiments, as props
And emanations of these institutes,
855 Too justly bore a part. A veil had been
Uplifted; why deceive ourselves? 'Twas so,
'Twas even so, and sorrow for the man,
Who either had not eyes wherewith to see,
Or seeing hath forgotten. Let this pass;
860 Suffice it that a shock had then been given
To old opinions; and the minds of all men
Had felt it; that my mind was both let loose,

Let loose and goaded. After what hath been
Already said of patriotic love,
865   And hinted at in other sentiments
We need not linger long upon this theme.
This only may be said, that from the first
Having two natures in me, joy the one
The other melancholy, and withal
870   A happy man, and therefore bold to look
On painful things, slow somewhat too and stern
In temperament, I took the knife in hand
And stopping not at parts less sensitive,
Endeavour'd with my best of skill to probe
875   The living body of society
Even to the heart: I push'd without remorse
My speculations forward; yea, set foot
On Nature's holiest places. Time may come
When some dramatic Story may afford
880   Shapes livelier to convey to thee, my Friend,
What then I learn'd, or think I learn'd of truth
And the errors into which I was betray'd
By present objects, and by reasonings false
From the beginning, inasmuch as drawn
885   Out of a heart which had been turn'd aside
From nature by external accidents,
And which was thus confounded more and more,
Misguiding and misguided. Thus I fared,
Dragging all passions, notions, shapes of faith
890   Like culprits to the bar,° suspiciously   courtroom
Calling the mind to establish in plain day
Her titles and her honours, now believing,
Now disbelieving, endlessly perplex'd
With impulse, motive, right and wrong, the ground
895   Of moral obligation, what the rule
And what the sanction, till, demanding proof
And seeking it in every thing, I lost
All feeling of conviction, and in fine°   in the end
Sick, wearied out with contrarieties,
900   Yielded up moral questions in despair,
And for my future studies, as the sole
Employment of the inquiring faculty,
Turn'd towards mathematics, and their clear
And solid evidence.—Ah! then it was
905   That Thou, most precious Friend! about this time
First known to me, didst lend a living help
To regulate my soul, and then it was,
That the beloved Woman,[8] in whose sight
Those days were pass'd, now speaking in a voice
910   Of sudden admonition like a brook

---

8. After a long separation, Dorothy Wordsworth and her brother were able to realize their dream of sharing a household
in September 1795; Coleridge lived nearby.

That does but cross a lonely road, and now
Seen, heard, and felt, and caught at every turn,
Companion never lost through many a league,
Maintain'd for me a saving intercourse°   communion
915   With my true self: for, though impair'd and changed,
Much, as it seem'd, I was no further changed
Than as a clouded, not a waning moon.
She in the midst of all preserv'd me still
A Poet, made me seek beneath that name
920   My office upon earth, and nowhere else,
And lastly, Nature's self, by human love
Assisted, through the weary labyrinth
Conducted me again to open day,
Revived the feelings of my earlier life,
925   Gave me that strength, and knowledge full of peace,
Enlarged, and never more to be disturb'd,
Which through the steps of our degeneracy,
All degradation of this age, hath still
Upheld me, and upholds me at this day°   1804
930   In the catastrophe (for so they dream,
And nothing less) when finally, to close
And rivet up the gains of France, a Pope
Is summon'd in, to crown an Emperor;
This last opprobrium° when we see the dog   disgrace
935   Returning to his vomit,[9] when the sun
That rose in splendour, was alive, and moved
In exultation among living clouds
Hath put his function and his glory off,
And, turn'd into a gewgaw, a machine,°   stage machine
940   Sets like an opera phantom. * * *

COMPANION READING

William Wordsworth: from The Prelude (1850)

[APOSTROPHE TO EDMUND BURKE][1]

Genius of Burke! forgive the pen seduced
By specious wonders, and too slow to tell
Of what the ingenuous, what bewildered men,
515   Beginning to mistrust their boastful guides,
And wise men, willing to grow wiser, caught,
Rapt auditors! from thy most eloquent tongue—
Now mute, for ever mute in the cold grave.
I see him,—old, but vigorous in age,—
520   Stand like an oak whose stag-horn branches start

---

9. In November 1804 Pope Pius VII attended Napoleon's coronation as Emperor; as Pius was about to crown him, Napoleon snatched the crown and put it on himself. Wordsworth alludes to 2 Peter 2.22: the persistently evil man is like a dog "turned to his own vomit again."

1. This passage, composed in 1832, appears in Book 7 of the 1850 Prelude, as Wordsworth pauses before Parliament and remembers Burke's parliamentary career and his anti-revolutionary Reflections on the Revolution in France (see page 1357).

Out of its leafy brow, the more to awe
The younger brethren of the grove. But some—
While he forewarns, denounces, launches forth,
Against all systems built on abstract rights,
525   Keen ridicule; the majesty proclaims
Of Institutes and Laws, hallowed by time;
Declares the vital power of social ties
Endeared by Custom; and with high disdain,
Exploding upstart Theory, insists
530   Upon the allegiance to which men are born—
Some—say at once a froward° multitude—   *willful*
Murmur (for truth is hated, where not loved)
As the winds fret within the Aeolian cave,
Gall'd by their monarch's chain.[2] The times were big
535   With ominous change, which, night by night, provoked
Keen struggles, and black clouds of passion raised;
But memorable moments intervened,
When Wisdom, like the Goddess° from Jove's brain,   *Athena*
Broke forth in armour of resplendent words,
540   Startling the Synod.° Could a youth, and one   *Parliament*
In ancient story versed, whose breast had heaved
Under the weight of classic eloquence,
Sit, see, and hear, unthankful, uninspired?

-----

from Book Eleventh. Imagination, How Impaired and Restored

[IMAGINATION RESTORED BY NATURE]

Long time hath Man's unhappiness and guilt
Detain'd us; with what dismal sights beset
For the outward view, and inwardly oppress'd
With sorrow, disappointment, vexing thoughts,
5   Confusion of the judgement, zeal decay'd
And lastly, utter loss of hope itself,
And things to hope for. Not with these began
Our Song; and not with these our Song must end:
Ye motions of delight that through the fields
10   Stir gently, breezes and soft airs that breathe
The breath of paradise, and find your way
To the recesses of the soul! Ye Brooks
Muttering along the stones, a busy noise
By day, a quiet one in silent night,
15   And you, Ye Groves, whose ministry it is
To interpose the covert of your shades,
Even as a sleep, betwixt the heart of man
And the uneasy world, 'twixt man himself,
Not seldom, and his own unquiet heart,
20   Oh! that I had a music and a voice,
Harmonious as your own, that I might tell

2. The wind god Aeolus kept the winds chained in a cave.

What ye have done for me. The morning shines,
Nor heedeth Man's perverseness; Spring returns,
I saw the Spring return when I was dead
25 To deeper hope, yet had I joy for her,
And welcomed her benevolence, rejoiced
In common with the Children of her Love,
Plants, insects, beast in field, and bird in bower.
So neither were complacency° nor peace   satisfaction
30 Nor tender yearnings wanting° for my good   lacking
Through those distracted times; in Nature still
Glorying, I found a counterpoise in her,
Which, when the spirit of evil was at height
Maintain'd for me a secret happiness;
35 Her I resorted to, and lov'd so much
I seem'd to love as much as heretofore;
And yet this passion, fervent as it was,
Had suffer'd change; how could there fail to be
Some change, if merely hence, that years of life
40 Were going on, and with them loss or gain
Inevitable, sure alternative.
    This History, my Friend, hath chiefly told
Of intellectual° power, from stage to stage   mental and spiritual
Advancing, hand in hand with love and joy,
45 And of imagination teaching truth
Until that natural graciousness of mind
Gave way to over-pressure of the times
And their disastrous issues. What avail'd,
When Spells forbade the Voyager to land,
50 The fragrance which did ever and anon
Give notice° of the Shore, from arbours breathed   reports
Of blessed sentiment and fearless love?
What did such sweet remembrances avail,
Perfidious then, as seem'd, what serv'd they then?
55 My business was upon the barren seas,
My errand was to sail to other coasts:
Shall I avow that I had hope to see,
I mean that future times would surely see
The man to come parted as by a gulph
60 From him who had been, that I could no more
Trust the elevation which had made me one
With the great Family that here and there
Is scatter'd through the abyss of ages past,
Sage, Patriot, Lover, Hero; for it seem'd
65 That their best virtues were not free from taint
Of something false and weak which could not stand
The open eye of Reason. Then I said,
Go to the Poets; they will speak to thee
More perfectly of purer creatures, yet
70 If Reason be nobility in man
Can aught be more ignoble than the man
Whom they describe, would fasten if they may

Upon our love by sympathies of truth.
   Thus strangely did I war against myself.

["SPOTS OF TIME." TWO MEMORIES FROM CHILDHOOD AND LATER REFLECTIONS][1]

In truth, this degradation, howsoe'er
Induced, effect in whatsoe'er degree
245   Of custom, that prepares such wantonness
As makes the greatest things give way to least,
Of any other cause which hath been named,
Or, lastly, aggravated by the times,
Which with their passionate sounds might often make
250   The milder minstrelsies of rural scenes
Inaudible, was transient; I had felt
Too forcibly, too early in my life
Visitings of imaginative power,
For this to last: I shook the habit off
255   Entirely and for ever, and again
In Nature's presence stood, as I stand now,
A sensitive and a creative Soul.
   There are in our existence spots of time,
Which with distinct preeminence retain
260   A renovating Virtue,° whence, depress'd   *power*
By false opinion and contentious thought,
Or aught of heavier or more deadly weight
In trivial occupations, and the round
Of ordinary intercourse, our minds
265   Are nourish'd, and invisibly repair'd,
A virtue by which pleasure is enhanced
That penetrates, enables us to mount
When high, more high, and lifts us up when fallen.
This efficacious spirit chiefly lurks
270   Among those passages of life in which
We have had deepest feeling that the mind
Is lord and master, and that outward sense
Is but the obedient servant of her will.
Such moments, worthy of all gratitude,
275   Are scatter'd every where, taking their date
From our first childhood; in our childhood even
Perhaps are most conspicuous. Life with me
As far as memory can look back, is full
Of this beneficent influence. At a time
280   When scarcely (I was then not six years old)
My hand could hold a bridle, with proud hopes
I mounted, and we rode towards the hills:
We were a pair of Horsemen; honest James[2]

1. This sequence, which concludes Book 11, was drafted
in 1799. Originally placed early in Book 1 of the *Two-
Part Prelude*, the discussion of "spots of time" explores the
way memories can have a restorative power on the imagination. By transferring these early memories to this late
point in his autobiography, Wordsworth empowers them
to enact what they describe—the revivification of poetic
powers through recollection.
2. Later identified as "an ancient servant of my father's
house."

Was with me, my encourager and guide.
285 We had not travell'd long ere some mischance
Disjoin'd me from my Comrade, and through fear
Dismounting, down the rough and stony Moor
I led my Horse, and, stumbling on, at length
Came to a bottom,° where in former times   *dell*
290 A Murderer had been hung in iron chains.
The Gibbet mast was moulder'd down, the bones
And iron case were gone; but on the turf
Hard by, soon after that fell deed was wrought
Some unknown hand had carved the Murderer's name.
295 The monumental writing was engraven
In times long past, and still, from year to year,
By superstition of the neighbourhood
The grass is clear'd away; and to this hour
The letters are all fresh and visible.
300 Faltering, and ignorant where I was, at length
I chanced to espy those characters inscribed
On the green sod: forthwith I left the spot
And, reascending the bare Common,° saw   *field*
A naked Pool that lay beneath the hills,
305 The Beacon on the summit, and more near
A Girl who bore a Pitcher on her head
And seem'd with difficult steps to force her way
Against the blowing wind. It was, in truth,
An ordinary sight; but I should need
310 Colours and words that are unknown to man
To paint the visionary dreariness
Which, while I look'd all round for my lost Guide,
Did at that time invest the naked Pool,
The Beacon on the lonely Eminence,
315 The Woman, and her garments vex'd and toss'd
By the strong wind. When in a blessed season
With those two dear Ones,[3] to my heart so dear,
When in the blessed time of early love,
Long afterwards, I roam'd about
320 In daily presence of this very scene;
Upon the naked pool and dreary crags,
And on the melancholy Beacon, fell
The spirit of pleasure, and youth's golden gleam;
And think ye not with radiance more divine
325 From these remembrances, and from the power
They left behind? So feeling comes in aid
Of feeling, and diversity of strength
Attends us, if but once we have been strong.
Oh! mystery of Man, from what a depth
330 Proceed thy honours! I am lost, but see
In simple childhood something of the base
On which thy greatness stands, but this I feel,

---

3. His sister and Mary Hutchinson, whom he would marry in 1802.

That from thyself it is that thou must give,
Else never canst receive. The days gone by

335   Come back upon me from the dawn almost
Of life: the hiding-places of my power
Seem open; I approach, and then they close;[4]
I see by glimpses now; when age comes on
May scarcely see at all, and I would give,

340   While yet we may, as far as words can give,
A substance and a life to what I feel:
I would enshrine the spirit of the past
For future restoration. Yet another
Of these to me affecting incidents
With which we will conclude.

345   One Christmas-time,
The day before the Holidays began,
Feverish, and tired, and restless, I went forth
Into the fields, impatient for the sight
Of those two Horses which should bear us home,

350   My Brothers and myself.[5] There was a Crag,
An Eminence, which from the meeting point
Of two high-ways ascending, overlook'd
At least a long half-mile of those two roads,
By each of which the expected Steeds might come,

355   The choice uncertain. Thither I repair'd,
Up to the highest summit: 'twas a day
Stormy, and rough and wild, and on the grass
I sate, half shelter'd by a naked wall:
Upon my right hand was a single sheep,

360   A whistling hawthorn on my left, and there
With those Companions at my side, I watch'd,
Straining my eyes intensely, as the mist
Gave intermitting prospect of the wood
And plain beneath. Ere I to School return'd

365   That dreary time, ere I had been ten days
A Dweller in my Father's House, he died
And I and my two Brothers, Orphans then,
Followed his Body to the Grave.[6] The event
With all the sorrow which it brought appear'd

370   A chastisement; and when I call'd to mind
That day so lately pass'd, when from the crag
I look'd in such anxiety of hope,
With trite reflections of morality,
Yet in the deepest passion, I bow'd low

375   To God, who thus corrected my desires;
And afterwards, the wind and sleety rain
And all the business of the elements,
The single sheep, and the one blasted tree,

---

4. In the 1850 text, this line became "I would approach them, but they close" (12.280).
5. December 1783; William and his two brothers were away from home at Hawkshead Grammar School.
6. Wordsworth's father died on 30 December 1783; his mother had died five years earlier.

380   And the bleak music of that old stone wall,
The noise of wood and water, and the mist
Which on the line of each of those two Roads
Advanced in such indisputable shapes,[7]
All these were spectacles and sounds to which
I often would repair, and thence would drink
385   As at a fountain: and I do not doubt
That in this later time, when storm and rain
Beat on my roof at midnight, or by day
When I am in the woods, unknown to me
The workings of my spirit thence are brought.
390   Thou wilt not languish here, O Friend! for whom
I travel in these dim uncertain ways;
Thou wilt assist me as a pilgrim gone
In quest of highest truth. Behold me then
Once more in Nature's presence, thus restored
395   Or otherwise, and strengthen'd once again
(With memory left of what had been escaped)
To habits of devoutest sympathy.

from Book Thirteenth. Conclusion

[CLIMBING MOUNT SNOWDON. MOONLIT VISTA. MEDITATION ON "MIND,"
"SELF," "IMAGINATION," "FEAR," AND "LOVE"]

In one of these excursions, travelling then
Through Wales, on foot, and with a youthful Friend,[1]
I left Bethkelet's huts at couching-time,°   *bedtime*
And westward took my way to see the sun
5   Rise from the top of Snowdon. Having reach'd
The Cottage at the Mountain's foot, we there
Rouz'd up the Shepherd, who by ancient right
Of office is the Stranger's usual Guide,
And after short refreshment sallied forth.
10   —It was a Summer's night, a close warm night,
Wan, dull and glaring,° with a dripping mist   *clammy*
Low-hung and thick that cover'd all the sky,
Half-threatening storm and rain: but on we went
Uncheck'd, being full of heart and having faith
15   In our tried Pilot. Little could we see,
Hemm'd round on every side with fog and damp,
And, after ordinary Traveller's chat
With our Conductor, silently we sunk
Each into commerce with his private thoughts:
20   Thus did we breast the ascent, and by myself
Was nothing either seen or heard the while
Which took me from my musings, save that once

7. An echo of Hamlet's cry to his father's ghost: "Thou
com'st in such a questionable shape / That I will speak to
thee" (*Hamlet* 1.4.43–44).
1. Robert Jones, the friend with whom Wordsworth had

toured Europe in 1790. During a walking tour of North
Wales in the summer of 1791, they climbed Mount
Snowdon, the highest peak in Wales, starting from the
village of Beddgelert, four miles away.

The Shepherd's Cur did to his own great joy
Unearth a hedge-hog in the mountain crags
25   Round which he made a barking turbulent.
This small adventure, (for even such it seem'd
In that wild place and at the dead of night)
Being over and forgotten, on we wound
In silence as before. With forehead bent
30   Earthward, as if in opposition set
Against an enemy, I panted up
With eager pace, and no less eager thoughts.
Thus might we wear perhaps an hour away,
Ascending at loose distance each from each,
35   And I, as chanced, the foremost of the Band,
When at my feet the ground appear'd to brighten,
And with a step or two seem'd brighter still,
Nor had I time to ask the cause of this,
For instantly a Light upon the turf
40   Fell like a flash: I look'd about, and lo!
The Moon stood naked in the Heavens, at height
Immense above my head, and on the shore
I found myself of a huge sea of mist,
Which meek and silent, rested at my feet:
45   A hundred hills their dusky backs upheaved
All over this still Ocean,[2] and beyond,
Far, far beyond, the vapours shot themselves,
In headlands, tongues, and promontory shapes
Into the Sea, the real Sea,° that seem'd   *the Irish Sea*
50   To dwindle and give up its majesty,
Usurp'd upon as far as sight could reach.
Meanwhile the Moon look'd down upon this shew
In single glory, and we stood, the mist
Touching our very feet: and from the shore
55   At distance not the third part of a mile
Was a blue chasm, a fracture in the vapour,
A deep and gloomy breathing-place thro' which
Mounted the roar of waters, torrents, streams
Innumerable, roaring with one voice.
60   The universal spectacle throughout
Was shaped for admiration and delight,
Grand in itself alone, but in that breach
Through which the homeless voice of waters rose,
That dark deep thorough-fare had Nature lodg'd
65   The Soul, the Imagination of the whole.
    A meditation rose in me that night
Upon the lonely Mountain when the scene
Had pass'd away, and it appear'd to me
The perfect image of a mighty Mind,
70   Of one that feeds upon infinity,

---

2. Echoing Milton's description of God's creation of land from the sea (*Paradise Lost* 7.285–877).

That is exalted by an underpresence,
The sense of God, or whatsoe'er is dim
Or vast in its own being; above all
One function of such mind had Nature there
75 Exhibited by putting forth, in midst
Of circumstance most awful° and sublime,   *awe-inspiring*
That domination which she oftentimes
Exerts upon the outward face of things,
So molds them and endues, abstracts, combines
80 Or by abrupt and unhabitual influence
Doth make one object so impress itself
Upon all others, and pervade them so
That even the grossest minds must see and hear
And cannot chuse but feel. The Power which these
85 Acknowledge when thus moved, which Nature thus
Thrusts forth upon the senses, is the express
Resemblance, in the fullness of its strength
Made visible, a genuine Counterpart
And Brother of the glorious faculty
90 Which higher minds bear with them as their own;
This is the very spirit in which they deal
With all the objects of the universe.
They from their native selves can send abroad
Like transformation, for themselves create
95 A like existence, and whene'er it is
Created for them catch it by an instinct;
Them the enduring and the transient both
Serve to exalt; they build up greatest things
From least suggestions; ever on the watch,
100 Willing to work and to be wrought upon,
They need not extraordinary calls
To rouze them, in a world of life they live
By sensible impressions not enthrall'd,
But quicken'd, rouz'd, and made thereby more fit
105 To hold communion with the invisible world.
Such minds are truly from the Deity;
For they are Powers; and hence the highest bliss
That can be known is theirs, the consciousness
Of whom they are habitually infused
110 Through every image, and through every thought,
And all impressions: hence religion, faith,
And endless occupation for the soul
Whether discursive or intuitive,
Hence sovereignty within and peace at will,
115 Emotion which best foresight need not fear,
Most worthy then of trust when most intense:
Hence chearfulness in every act of life,
Hence truth in moral judgements and delight
That fails not in the external universe.
120   Oh! who is he that hath his whole life long
Preserved, enlarged this freedom in himself!

For this alone is genuine Liberty.
Witness, ye Solitudes! where I received
My earliest visitations, careless then

125   Of what was given me, and which now I roam
A meditative, oft a suffering Man,
And yet, I trust, with undiminish'd powers,
Witness, whatever falls my better mind,
Revolving with the accidents of life,

130   May have sustain'd, that, howsoe'er misled,
I never, in the quest of right and wrong,
Did tamper with myself° from private aims;   *my conscience*
Nor was in any of my hopes the dupe
Of selfish passions; nor did wilfully

135   Yield ever to mean cares and low pursuits;
But rather did with jealousy° shrink back   *vigilance*
From every combination that might aid
The tendency, too potent in itself,
Of habit to enslave the mind, I mean

140   Oppress it by the laws of vulgar° sense,   *mere*
And substitute a universe of death,
The falsest of all worlds, in place of that
Which is divine and true. To fear and love,
To love, as first and chief, for there fear ends,

145   Be this ascribed; to early intercourse,
In presence of sublime and lovely Forms,
With the adverse principles of pain and joy,
Evil, as one° is rashly named by those   *i.e., pain*
Who know not what they say. From love, for here

150   Do we begin and end, all grandeur comes,
All truth and beauty, from pervading love,
That gone, we are as dust. Behold the fields
In balmy spring-time, full of rising flowers
And blissful Creatures: see that Pair, the Lamb

155   And the Lamb's Mother, and their tender ways
Shall touch thee to the heart: in some green bower
Rest, and be not alone, but have thou there
The One who is thy choice of all the world;
There linger, lull'd, and lost, and rapt away,

160   Be happy to thy fill: thou call'st this love,
And so it is; but there is higher love
Than this, a love that comes into the heart
With awe and a diffusive° sentiment;   *bountiful*
Thy love is human merely; this proceeds

165   More from the brooding Soul, and is divine.
        This love more intellectual° cannot be   *spiritual*
Without Imagination, which in truth
Is but another name for absolute strength
And clearest insight, amplitude of mind,

170   And reason in her most exalted mood.
This faculty hath been the moving soul
Of our long labour: we have traced the stream

From darkness, and the very place of birth
In its blind cavern, whence is faintly heard
175 The sound of waters, follow'd it to light
And open day, accompanied its course
Among the ways of Nature; afterwards
Lost sight of it, bewilder'd and engulph'd,
Then given it greeting, as it rose once more
180 With strength, reflecting in its solemn breast
The works of man and face of human life,
And lastly, from its progress have we drawn
The feeling of life endless, the one thought
By which we live, Infinity and God.
185 Imagination having been our theme,
So also hath that intellectual love,
For they are each in each, and cannot stand
Dividually.° —Here must thou be, O Man!   *separately*
Strength to thyself; no Helper hast thou here;
190 Here keepest thou thy individual state:
No other can divide with thee this work,
No secondary hand can intervene
To fashion this ability; 'tis thine,
The prime and vital principle is thine
195 In the recesses of thy nature, far
From any reach of outward fellowship,
Else 'tis not thine at all.—But joy to him,
O joy to him who here hath sown, hath laid
Here the foundations of his future years!
200 For all that friendship, all that love can do,
All that a darling countenance can look
Or dear voice utter to complete the man,
Perfect him, made imperfect in himself,
All shall be his: and he whose soul hath risen
205 Up to the height of feeling intellect
Shall want no humbler tenderness, his heart
Be tender as a nursing Mother's heart,
Of female softness shall his life be full,
Of little loves and delicate desires,
210 Mild interests and gentlest sympathies.

[CONCLUDING RETROSPECT AND PROPHECY]

Having now
Told what best merits mention, further pains
Our present labour seems not to require
370 And I have other tasks. Call back to mind
The mood in which this Poem was begun,
O Friend! the termination of my course
Is nearer now, much nearer; yet even then
In that distraction and intense desire
375 I said unto the life which I had lived,
Where art thou? Hear I not a voice from thee

Which 'tis reproach to hear?[3] Anon I rose
As if on wings, and saw beneath me stretch'd
Vast prospect of the world which I had been
380 And was; and hence this Song which like a lark
I have protracted, in the unwearied Heavens
Singing, and often with more plaintive voice
Attemper'd to the sorrows of the earth;
Yet centring all in love, and in the end
385 All gratulant° if rightly understood.   *expressing joy*
    Whether to me shall be allotted life,
And with life power to accomplish aught of worth
Sufficient to excuse me in men's sight
For having given this Record of myself
390 Is all uncertain: but, beloved Friend,
When, looking back, thou seest in clearer view
Than any sweetest sight of yesterday
That summer when on Quantock's grassy Hills[4]
Far ranging, and among the sylvan Coombs°   *small valleys*
395 Thou in delicious words with happy heart
Didst speak the Vision of that Ancient Man,
The bright-eyed Mariner, and rueful woes
Didst utter of the Lady Christabel
And I, associate in such labour, walk'd
400 Murmuring of him who, joyous hap! was found,
After the perils of his moonlight ride
Near the loud Waterfall; or her who sate
In misery near the miserable Thorn;[5]
When thou dost to that summer turn thy thoughts,
405 And hast before thee all which then we were,
To thee, in memory of that happiness
It will be known, by thee at least, my Friend,
Felt, that the history of a Poet's mind
Is labour not unworthy of regard.
410 To thee the work shall justify itself.
    The last, and later portions of this Gift
Which I for Thee design have been prepared
In times which have from those wherein we first
Together wanton'd in wild Poesy,
415 Differ'd thus far, that they have been, O Friend,
Times of much sorrow, of a private grief
Keen and enduring,[6] which the frame of mind
That in this meditative History
Hath been described, more deeply makes me feel;
420 Yet likewise hath enabled me to bear
More firmly; and a comfort now, a hope,
One of the dearest which this life can give,

3. Recalling Coleridge's urging that he should undertake a major philosophical epic, Book 1.625–72.
4. The Wordsworths lived near Coleridge in the Quantock Hills above Alfoxden, in Somerset, from 1797–1798.
5. Referring to the lyrical ballads Wordsworth wrote at that time, and to Coleridge's *Rime of the Ancyent Mariner* and *Christabel*.
6. Wordsworth's younger brother John drowned on a shipwreck on 5 February 1805.

Is mine; that Thou art near and wilt be soon
Restored to us in renovated health:[7]
425   When, after the first mingling of our tears,
'Mong other consolations we may find
Some pleasure from this Offering of my love.
      Oh! yet a few short years of useful life,
And all will be complete, thy race be run,
430   Thy monument of glory will be raised;
Then, though, too weak to tread the ways of truth,
This Age fall back to old idolatry,
Though men return to servitude as fast
As the tide ebbs, to ignominy and shame
435   By Nations° sink together, we shall still   nation by nation
Find solace in the knowledge which we have,
Bless'd with true happiness if we may be
United helpers forward of a day
Of firmer trust, joint-labourers in the work,
440   (Should Providence such grace to us vouchsafe)
Of their redemption, surely yet to come.
Prophets of Nature, we to them will speak
A lasting inspiration, sanctified
By reason and by truth: what we have loved
445   Others will love; and we may teach them how,
Instruct them how the mind of man becomes
A thousand times more beautiful than the earth
On which he dwells, above this Frame of things
(Which 'mid all revolutions in the hopes
450   And fears of men doth still remain unchanged)
In beauty exalted, as it is itself
Of substance and of fabric more divine.

I wandered lonely as a cloud[1]

I wandered lonely as a cloud
That floats on high o'er vales and hills,
When all at once I saw a crowd,
A host, of golden daffodils;
5   Beside the lake, beneath the trees,
Fluttering and dancing in the breeze.

Continuous as the stars that shine
And twinkle on the milky way,
They stretched in never-ending line
10   Along the margin of a bay:
Ten thousand saw I at a glance,
Tossing their heads in sprightly dance.

The waves beside them danced; but they
Outdid the sparkling waves in glee:—

7. Coleridge had gone to the Mediterranean island of
Malta for his health.

1. Compare Dorothy Wordsworth's *Grasmere Journal*, 15
April 1802, page 1627.

15   A Poet could not but be gay,
        In such a jocund company:
        I gazed—and gazed—but little thought
        What wealth the show to me had brought:

        For oft when on my couch I lie
20   In vacant or in pensive mood,
        They flash upon that inward eye
        Which is the bliss of solitude;[2]
        And then my heart with pleasure fills,
        And dances with the daffodils.

1804/1815   1807/1815

My heart leaps up

        My heart leaps up when I behold
          A Rainbow in the sky:
        So was it when my life began;
        So is it now I am a Man;
5   So be it when I shall grow old,
          Or let me die!
        The Child is Father of the Man;
        And I could wish my days to be
        Bound each to each by natural piety.

1802   1807

Ode: Intimations of Immortality[1]

In a letter from 1814, Wordsworth remarks, "The poem rests entirely on two recollections of childhood, one that of a splendour in the objects of sense which is passed away, and the other an indisposition to bend to the law of death as applying to our particular case. A Reader who has not a vivid recollection of these feelings having existed in his mind cannot understand that Poem." In 1843 he recalled, "Two years at least passed between the writing of the four first stanzas and the remaining part. To the attentive and competent reader the whole sufficiently explains itself; but there may be no harm in adverting here to particular feelings or *experiences* of my own mind on which the structure of the poem partly rests. Nothing was more difficult for me in childhood than to admit the notion of death as a state applicable to my own being. I have said elsewhere—

        A simple child,
    That lightly draws its breath,
    And feels its life in every limb,
    What should it know of death!— [*We Are Seven*, 1–4]

But it was not so much from feelings of animal vivacity that my difficulty came as from a sense of the indomitableness of the Spirit within me. I used to brood over the stories of Enoch and Elijah, and almost to persuade myself that, whatever might become of others, I should be translated, in something of the same way, to heaven.[2] With a feeling congenial to this, I was often unable to think of external things as having external existence, and I communed with all that I saw as something not apart from, but inherent in, my own immaterial nature. Many times while going to school have I grasped at a wall or tree to recall myself from this abyss of idealism

---

2. Lines 21–22 were composed by Wordsworth's wife. He thought them the "two best lines," though Coleridge called them "mental bombast."
1. A version published in 1807 was titled simply *Ode*, with an epigraph from Virgil's *Fourth* (*Messianic*) *Eclogue*: *Paulò majora canamus* (Let us sing of somewhat higher things). The long title and epigraph from *My heart leaps up* were added in 1815, and the Latin phrase was dropped.
2. Old Testament prophets: Enoch did not die, but was taken directly to heaven (Genesis 5.24) and Elijah was carried to heaven in a chariot of fire (2 Kings 2.11).

to the reality. At that time I was afraid of such processes. In later periods of life I have deplored, as we have all reason to do, a subjugation of an opposite character, and have rejoiced over the remembrances, as is expressed in the lines—

> Obstinate questionings
> Of sense and outward things,
> Fallings from us, vanishings; etc. [141–43]

To that dream-like vividness and splendour which invest objects of sight in childhood, every one, I believe, if he would look back, could bear testimony, and I need not dwell upon it here: but having in the poem regarded it as presumptive evidence of a prior state of existence, I think it right to protest against a conclusion, which has given pain to some good and pious persons, that I meant to inculcate such a belief. It is far too shadowy a notion to be recommended to faith, as more than an element in our instincts of immortality. But let us bear in mind that, though the idea is not advanced in revelation, there is nothing there to contradict it, and the fall of Man presents an analogy in its favour. Accordingly, a pre-existent state has entered into the popular creeds of many nations; and, among all persons acquainted with classic literature, is known as an ingredient in Platonic philosophy. Archimedes said that he could move the world if he had a point whereon to rest his machine. Who has not felt the same aspirations as regards the world of his own mind? Having to wield some of its elements when I was impelled to write this poem on the 'Immortality of the Soul,' I took hold of the notion of pre-existence as having sufficient foundation in humanity for authorising me to make for my purpose the best use of it I could as a Poet." [I. F.]

Ode
Intimations of Immortality from Recollections of Early Childhood

> The Child is Father of the Man;
> And I could wish my days to be
> Bound each to each by natural piety.

1

There was a time when meadow, grove, and stream,
The earth, and every common sight,
　　　　To me did seem
　　　　Apparelled in celestial light,
5　　The glory and the freshness of a dream.
It is not now as it hath been of yore;—
　　　　Turn wheresoe'er I may,
　　　　　By night or day,
The things which I have seen I now can see no more.

2

10　　　　The Rainbow comes and goes,
　　　　And lovely is the Rose,
　　　　The Moon doth with delight
Look round her when the heavens are bare,
　　　　Waters on a starry night
15　　　　Are beautiful and fair;
　　　　The sunshine is a glorious birth;
　　　　But yet I know, where'er I go,
That there hath past away a glory from the earth.

3

Now, while the birds thus sing a joyous song,
20　　　　And while the young lambs bound

small drum

As to the tabor's° sound,
To me alone there came a thought of grief:
A timely utterance gave that thought relief,
        And I again am strong:
25   The cataracts blow their trumpets from the steep;
No more shall grief of mine the season wrong;
I hear the Echoes through the mountains throng,
The Winds come to me from the fields of sleep,
        And all the earth is gay;
30   Land and sea
        Give themselves up to jollity,
        And with the heart of May
        Doth every Beast keep holiday;—
            Thou Child of Joy,
35   Shout round me, let me hear thy shouts, thou happy Shepherd-boy!

4

Ye blessèd Creatures, I have heard the call
        Ye to each other make; I see
The heavens laugh with you in your jubilee;
        My heart is at your festival,

flower wreath

40   My head hath its coronal,°
The fulness of your bliss, I feel—I feel it all.
        Oh evil day! if I were sullen
        While Earth herself is adorning,
            This sweet May-morning,
45   And the Children are culling
            On every side,
        In a thousand valleys far and wide,
        Fresh flowers; while the sun shines warm,
And the Babe leaps up on his Mother's arm:—
50   I hear, I hear, with joy I hear!
—But there's a Tree, of many, one,
A single Field which I have looked upon,
Both of them speak of something that is gone:
            The Pansy³ at my feet
55   Doth the same tale repeat:
Whither is fled the visionary gleam?
Where is it now, the glory and the dream?⁴

5

Our birth is but a sleep and a forgetting:

the sun

The Soul that rises with us, our life's Star,°
60   Hath had elsewhere its setting,
            And cometh from afar:
        Not in entire forgetfulness,
        And not in utter nakedness,
But trailing clouds of glory do we come⁵
65   From God, who is our home:
Heaven lies about us in our infancy!

---

3. From the French *pensée*, "thought," this flower is its
emblem.
4. A sounding of the "Ubi sunt" trope of elegiac literary
tradition. In 1802, Wordsworth stopped writing the ode

at this point and did not resume for two years.
5. Revising a famous line in Thomas Gray's *Elegy Written
in a Country Churchyard* (1751): "The paths of glory lead
but to the grave."

Shades of the prison-house begin to close
   Upon the growing Boy,
But He beholds the light, and whence it flows,
70   He sees it in his joy;
The Youth, who daily farther from the east
   Must travel, still is Nature's Priest,
   And by the vision splendid
   Is on his way attended;
75 At length the Man perceives it die away,
And fade into the light of common day.

6

Earth fills her lap with pleasures of her own;
Yearnings she hath in her own natural kind,
And, even with something of a Mother's mind,
80   And no unworthy aim,
   The homely° Nurse doth all she can   *simple*
To make her Foster-child, her Inmate° Man,   *resident*
   Forget the glories he hath known,
And that imperial palace whence he came.

7

85 Behold the Child among his new-born blisses,
A six years' Darling of a pigmy size!
See, where 'mid work of his own hand he lies,
Fretted by sallies of his mother's kisses,
With light upon him from his father's eyes!
90 See, at his feet, some little plan or chart,
Some fragment from his dream of human life,
Shaped by himself with newly-learned art;
   A wedding or a festival,
   A mourning or a funeral;
95   And this hath now his heart,
   And unto this he frames his song:
     Then will he fit his tongue
To dialogues of business, love, or strife;
   But it will not be long
100   Ere this be thrown aside,
   And with new joy and pride
The little Actor cons another part;
Filling from time to time his "humorous stage"[6]
With all the Persons, down to palsied Age,
105 That Life brings with her in her equipage;
   As if his whole vocation
   Were endless imitation.

8

Thou, whose exterior semblance doth belie
   Thy Soul's immensity;
110 Thou best Philosopher, who yet dost keep
Thy heritage, thou Eye among the blind,
That, deaf and silent, read'st the eternal deep,
Haunted for ever by the eternal mind,—

6. A phrase from the dedicatory sonnet for Samuel Daniel's *Musophilus* (1599), referring to the different character types of Renaissance drama, defined by their "humors" (natural temperaments).

            Mighty Prophet! Seer blest!
115   On whom those truths do rest,
        Which we are toiling all our lives to find,
        In darkness lost, the darkness of the grave;
        Thou, over whom thy Immortality
        Broods like the Day, a Master o'er a Slave,
120   A Presence which is not to be put by;
        Thou little Child, yet glorious in the might
        Of heaven-born freedom on thy being's height,
        Why with such earnest pains dost thou provoke
        The years to bring the inevitable yoke,
125   Thus blindly with thy blessedness at strife?
        Full soon thy Soul shall have her earthly freight,
        And custom lie upon thee with a weight,
        Heavy as frost, and deep almost as life!

                        9

            O joy! that in our embers
130   Is something that doth live,
            That Nature yet remembers
            What was so fugitive!
        The thought of our past years in me doth breed
        Perpetual benediction: not indeed
135   For that which is most worthy to be blest—
        Delight and liberty, the simple creed
        Of Childhood, whether busy or at rest,
        With new-fledged hope still fluttering in his breast:—
            Not for these I raise
140   The song of thanks and praise;
            But for those obstinate questionings
            Of sense and outward things,
            Fallings from us, vanishings;
            Blank misgivings of a Creature
145   Moving about in worlds not realised,°   *seeming unreal*
        High instincts before which our mortal nature
        Did tremble like a guilty Thing surprised:
            But for those first affections,
            Those shadowy recollections,
150   Which, be they what they may,
        Are yet the fountain light of all our day,
        Are yet a master light of all our seeing;
            Uphold us, cherish, and have power to make
        Our noisy years seem moments in the being
155   Of the eternal Silence: truths that wake,
            To perish never;
        Which neither listlessness, nor mad endeavour,
            Nor Man nor Boy,
        Nor all that is at enmity with joy,
160   Can utterly abolish or destroy!
            Hence in a season of calm weather
            Though inland far we be,
        Our Souls have sight of that immortal sea
            Which brought us hither,

165   Can in a moment travel thither,
       And see the Children sport upon the shore,
       And hear the mighty waters rolling evermore.

                    10

       Then sing, ye Birds, sing, sing a joyous song!
         And let the young Lambs bound
170   As to the tabor's sound!
       We in thought will join your throng,
         Ye that pipe and ye that play,
         Ye that through your hearts to-day
         Feel the gladness of the May!
175   What though the radiance which was once so bright
       Be now for ever taken from my sight,
         Though nothing can bring back the hour
       Of splendour in the grass, of glory in the flower;
         We will grieve not, rather find
180   Strength in what remains behind;
         In the primal sympathy
         Which having been must ever be;
         In the soothing thoughts that spring
         Out of human suffering;
185   In the faith that looks through death,
       In years that bring the philosophic mind.

                    11

       And O, ye Fountains, Meadows, Hills, and Groves,
       Forebode not any severing of our loves!
       Yet in my heart of hearts I feel your might;
190   I only have relinquished one delight
       To live beneath your more habitual sway.
       I love the Brooks which down their channels fret,
       Even more than when I tripped lightly as they;
       The innocent brightness of a new-born Day
195   Is lovely yet;
       The Clouds that gather round the setting sun
       Do take a sober colouring from an eye
       That hath kept watch o'er man's mortality;
       Another race hath been, and other palms° are won.   prizes
200   Thanks to the human heart by which we live,
       Thanks to its tenderness, its joys, and fears,
       To me the meanest° flower that blows can give   humblest
       Thoughts that do often lie too deep for tears.

1802–1804/1815   1807/1815

The Solitary Reaper[1]

Behold her, single in the field,
Yon solitary Highland Lass!
Reaping and singing by herself;

---

1. Suggested by Wordsworth's reading in manuscript of "a beautiful sentence" in Thomas Wilkinson's *Tours to the British Mountains* (1824): "Passed a female who was reaping alone: she sung in Erse [Scottish Gaelic] as she bended over her sickle; the sweetest human voice I ever heard: her strains were tenderly melancholy, and felt delicious, long after they were heard no more."

Stop here, or gently pass!
5 Alone she cuts, and binds the grain,
And sings a melancholy strain;
O listen! for the Vale profound
Is overflowing with the sound.

No Nightingale did ever chaunt
10 More welcome notes to weary bands
Of Travellers in some shady haunt,
Among Arabian Sands:
No sweeter voice was ever heard[2]
In spring-time from the Cuckoo-bird,
15 Breaking the silence of the seas
Among the farthest Hebrides.°   *Scottish islands*

Will no one tell me what she sings?—
Perhaps the plaintive numbers flow
For old, unhappy, far-off things,
20 And battles long ago:
Or is it some more humble lay,
Familiar matter of today?
Some natural sorrow, loss, or pain,
That has been, and may be again!

25 Whate'er the theme, the Maiden sang
As if her song could have no ending;
I saw her singing at her work,
And o'er the sickle bending;—
I listen'd till I had my fill.[3]
30 And, as I mounted up the hill,
The music in my heart I bore,
Long after it was heard no more.

1805   1807

Surprized by joy

Surprized by joy—impatient as the Wind
I turned to share the transport—Oh! with whom
But thee, long buried in the silent Tomb,
That spot which no vicissitude can find?[1]
5 Love, faithful love, recalled thee to my mind—
But how could I forget thee? Through what power,
Even for the least division of an hour,
Have I been so beguiled as to be blind
To my most grievous loss!—That thought's return
10 Was the worst pang that sorrow ever bore,
Save one, one only, when I stood forlorn,
Knowing my heart's best treasure was no more;
That neither present time, nor years unborn
Could to my sight that heavenly face restore.

1812–1815   1815

---

2. In 1836 this line became "A voice so thrilling ne'er
was heard."
3. In 1820 this became "I listened, motionless and still."

1. The Wordsworths' daughter Catherine, who died in
1812 at age 3.

Dorothy Wordsworth

1771–1855

Dorothy Wordsworth would probably be surprised at her presence in this anthology, for unlike just about everyone else in our pages, she did not think of herself primarily as a writer, and she did not aspire to publication. Her brother William Wordsworth did put a few of her poems in his volumes (including *Address to a Child* and *Floating Island*), specifying them as "By my Sister"—an apt credit, for this was Dorothy's own chief self-identification. When friends urged her to publish her remarkable account of her community's response to a local tragedy (*George and Sarah Green*, 1808), she protested that she had written it only at her brother's urging and only as a local record; "I should detest the idea of setting myself as an Author," she said. Similar encouragement for her journals of her tours of Scotland and Europe was similarly rebuffed, Dorothy insisting that she had written only for the amusement of family and friends. When she began her Grasmere journal, she told herself that she was writing to give William "pleasure."

Born in the Lake District of England in 1771, Dorothy Wordsworth lived happily there with her four brothers until 1778, when their mother died. Their father, who was often absent on business, felt unable to sustain the household and sent the boys away to school and Dorothy to live with a series of distant relatives, in situations ranging from happy to bleak. She saw her brothers rarely and especially missed William, with whom she was closest, less than two years his junior. As soon as they were reunited in 1787, they longed to have a home together, and in 1795, with the advantage of William's legacy from a college friend, they were able to realize this dream. They first lived in southwest England, in Dorset, as a quasi-family with a friend's young son as their ward. Moving to Alfoxden in 1797 to be near Samuel Taylor Coleridge, they became acquainted with Charles and Mary Lamb and Robert Southey. During their summer tour of the Wye valley in 1798, William wrote *Tintern Abbey* with its homage to Dorothy's companionship and her continuing inspiration to him. They spent the next winter miserably in Goslar, Germany (following Coleridge there on a scheme to learn the language); after they returned to England, they settled at the end of 1799 in Grasmere, in their beloved native Lake District, where they remained together for the rest of their lives.

Dorothy began her Grasmere journal in May 1800, just as William was beginning to court their childhood friend, Mary Hutchinson, and she left off at the beginning of 1803, a few months after Mary and William returned from their honeymoon. There was never any question about her remaining in the household: Mary married *them*. A beloved aunt to their children, Dorothy was really more a third parent. She not only shared the domestic labors but functioned for William as companion, encourager, sounding board, secretary, and (along with Mary) perpetual transcriber of his drafts into fair-copy. In 1829 she was stricken by the first in a series of devastating illnesses, with relapses and new afflictions occurring over the next six years, each event wracking her with pain and leaving her further debilitated. By 1835 it was clear that her temperament and mental acuity were also afflicted, a pre-senile dementia akin to Alzheimer's disease. Cared for with affection by her family, she lived a kind of invalid half-life, with lucid intervals, for the next twenty years, surviving her brother by five.

This demise is especially poignant, given the intelligence, sensitivity, and physical vitality with which she had impressed everyone. It was not until the end of the nineteenth century that her poems and journals were collected and published, and for a long time the journals were treated as subordinate documents, read chiefly for information about Coleridge, William, and the circumstances of the poems he wrote between 1798 and 1802. Placed alongside these poems, however, some of Dorothy's passages suggest that William may have been inspired as much by her language as by events and appearances in the external world; and recently,

Dorothy Wordsworth has come to light as a writer in her own right. Her Grasmere journal is a fascinating chronicle of early nineteenth-century life in the Lake District—full of brilliantly detailed descriptions of nature (admired by Virginia Woolf), accounts of domestic life and household labors, precise observations of the people, the social textures and economic distresses of rural England. In the cast of characters that cross her pages—children, neighbors, local laborers, tinkers and itinerants, beggars and vagrants, abandoned wives and mothers, a leech-gatherer, discharged and often injured soldiers, sailors, and veterans—Dorothy Wordsworth captures, as much as her brother hoped his poetry would, the "language really used by men" (and women). In addition to journals, records of tours, numerous letters, and ceaseless secretarial work and manuscript transcription for William, Dorothy wrote about thirty poems. Composed sporadically from 1805 to 1840, these often allude to or converse with her brother's poetry, sometimes marking different investments of imagination, giving alternative views of the world they share, or showing a different sensibility—one less solitary and more social in orientation, less visionary than domestic in idiom, and more self-effacing and self-discrediting in character, especially about the vocation and practice of writing poetry.

Address to a Child

During a boisterous Winter Evening in a high wind[1]

What way does the wind come? what way does he go?
He rides over the water and over the snow,
Through wood, and through vale; and o'er rocky height
Which the goat cannot climb takes his sounding flight.[2]
5 He tosses about in every bare tree,
As, if you look up you plainly may see
But how he will come, and whither he goes
There's never a Scholar in England knows.

He will suddenly stop in a cunning nook
10 And rings a sharp larum:°—but if you should look   call to arms
There's nothing to see but a cushion of snow,
Round as a pillow and whiter than milk
And softer than if it were cover'd with silk.

Sometimes he'll hide in the cave of a rock;
15 Then whistle as shrill as the buzzard cock;
—Yet seek him and what shall you find in his place
Nothing but silence and empty space
Save in a corner a heap of dry leaves
That he's left for a bed for beggars or thieves.

20 As soon as 'tis daylight tomorrow with me
You shall go to the orchard & then you will see
That he has been there, & made a great rout,°   debacle
And cracked the branches, & strew'd them about:
Heaven grant that he spare but that one upright twig

---

1. Written 1806 for nephew Johnny (see letter to Lady Beaumont, page 1630); in late 1805 she commented to Lady Beaumont: "what a fearful thing a windy night is now at our house! I am too often haunted with dreadful images of Shipwrecks and the Sea when I am in bed and hear a stormy wind"—evoking the loss of her beloved brother John in a shipwreck in 1805. Published unsigned in William's *Poems*, 1815; our text follows this version, with significant variants from the ms. ("An address to a Child in a high wind") indicated in footnotes.
2. In the manuscript, these lines read: "Through the valley, and over the hill / And roars as loud as a thundering Mill" (waterfall where a mill is located).

25 That look'd up at the sky so proud & so big
 All last summer, as well you know
 Studded with apples, a beautiful shew!

 Hark! over the roof he makes a pause
 And growls as if he would fix his claws
30 Right in the slates, and with a huge rattle
 Drive them down like men in a battle.
 —But let him range round; he does us no harm
 We build up the fire; we're snug and warm,
 Untouch'd by his breath see the candle shines bright,
35 And burns with a clear and steady light;
 Books have we to read,—hush! that half-stifled knell,
 Methinks 'tis the sound of the eight o'clock bell.[3]

 Come, now we'll to bed, and when we are there
 He may work his own will, & what shall we care.
40 He may knock at the door—we'll not let him in
 May drive at the windows—we'll laugh at his din
 Let him seek his own home wherever it be
 Here's a cozy warm house for Edward and me.[4]

1806   1815

Irregular Verses[1]

 Ah Julia! ask a Christmas rhyme
 Of *me* who in the golden time
 Of careless, hopeful, happy youth
 Ne'er strove to decorate the truth,
5 Contented to lay bare my heart
 To one dear Friend, who had her part
 In all the love and all the care
 And every joy that harboured there.
 —To her I told in simple prose
10 Each girlish vision, as it rose
 Before an active busy brain
 That needed neither spur nor rein,
 That still enjoyed the present hour
 Yet for the *future* raised a tower
15 Of bliss more exquisite and pure
 Bliss that (so deemed we) should endure
 Maxims of caution, prudent fears
 Vexed not the projects of those years
 Simplicity our steadfast theme,
20 No works of Art adorned our scheme.—
 A cottage in a verdant dell,

3. In the manuscript, lines 34–37 read: "Old Madam has brought us plenty of coals / And the Glazier has closed up all the holes / In every window that Johnny broke / And the walls are tighter than Molly's new cloak."
4. In the manuscript, the synonym *canny* is used instead of *cozy*; and Johnny's name was used (the pseudonym

protects his privacy).
1. Written in 1829 as Christmas-verses to her 20-year-old goddaughter, daughter of her childhood friend Jane Pollard, later Mrs. Marshall. Dorothy Wordsworth encouraged Julia Marshall's efforts to write poetry. "Irregular" means not metrically regular.

A foaming stream, a crystall Well,
A garden stored with fruit and flowers
And sunny seats and shady bowers,
25 A file of hives for humming bees
Under a row of stately trees
And, sheltering all this faery ground,
A belt of hills must wrap it round,
Not stern or mountainous, or bare,
30 Nor lacking herbs to scent the air;
Nor ancient trees, nor scattered rocks,
And pastured by the blameless flocks
That print their green tracks to invite
Our wanderings to the topmost height.

35   Such was the spot I fondly framed
When life was new, and hope untamed:[2]
There with my one dear Friend would dwell,
Nor wish for aught beyond the dell.
   Alas! the cottage fled in air,
40 The streamlet never flowed:
—Yet did those visions pass away[3]
So gently that they seemed to stay,
Though in our riper years we each pursued a different way.

   —We parted, sorrowful; by duty led;
45 My Friend, ere long a happy Wife
Was seen with dignity to tread
The paths of usefulness, in active life;
And such her course through later days;
The same her honour and her praise;
50 As thou canst witness, thou dear Maid,
One of the Darlings of her care;[4]
Thy *Mother* was that Friend who still repaid
Frank confidence with unshaken truth:
This was the glory of her youth,
55 A brighter gem than shines in prince's diadem.

   You ask why in that jocund time
Why did I not in jingling rhyme
Display those pleasant guileless dreams
That furnished still exhaustless themes?
60 —I *reverenced* the Poet's skill,
And *might have* nursed a mounting Will
To imitate the tender Lays°   songs
Of them who sang in Nature's praise;
But bashfulness, a struggling shame
65 A fear that elder heads might blame
—Or something worse—a lurking pride
Whispering my playmates would deride

2. Cf. W. Wordsworth's, *Elegiac Stanzas* (1806): "Such, in the fond illusion of my heart, / Such Picture would I at that time have made" (29–30).
3. Cf. W. Wordsworth's *Poor Susan* (page 1543): "The stream will not flow, and the hill will not rise, / And the colours have all passed away from her eyes!" (15–16).
4. Jane Marshall bore eleven children.

Stifled ambition, checked the aim
If e'er by chance "the numbers came"[5]
70   —Nay even the mild maternal smile,
That oft-times would repress, beguile
The over-confidence of youth,
Even that dear smile, to own the truth,
Was dreaded by a fond self-love;
75   "'Twill glance on me—and to reprove
Or," (sorest wrong in childhood's school)
"Will *point* the sting of ridicule."[6]

And now, dear Girl, I hear you ask
Is this your lightsome, chearful task?
80   You tell us tales of forty years,
Of hopes extinct, of childish fears,
Why cast among us thoughts of sadness
When we are seeking mirth and gladness?[7]
Nay, ill those words befit the Maid
85   Who pleaded for my Christmas rhyme
Mirthful she is; but placid—staid—
Her heart beats to no giddy chime
Though it with Chearfulness keep time
For Chearfulness, a willing guest,
90   Finds ever in her tranquil breast
A fostering home, a welcome rest.
And well she knows that, casting *thought* away,
We lose the best part of our day;
That joys of youth remembered when our youth is past
95   Are joys that to the end of life will last;[8]

And if this poor memorial strain,
Breathed from the depth of years gone by,
Should touch her Mother's heart with tender pain,
Or call a tear into her loving eye,
100   She will not check the tear or still the rising sigh.
—The happiest heart is given to sadness;
The saddest heart feels deepest gladness.

Thou dost not ask, thou dost not need
A verse from me; nor wilt thou heed
105   A greeting masked in laboured rhyme
From one whose heart has still kept time
With every pulse of thine

1829

---

5. From Pope's *Epistle To Dr. Arbuthnot* (1735): "Why did I write? what sin to me unknown / Dipt me in Ink, my Parents', or my own? / As yet a Child, nor yet a Fool to Fame, / I lisp'd in Numbers, for the Numbers came" (125–128). Also involved are W. Wordsworth's recollection of his promise as a poet at the beginning of *The Prelude*: "To the open fields I told / A prophesy; poetic numbers came / Spontaneously, and clothed in priestly robe / My spirit, thus singled out, as it might seem, / For holy services" (1.59–63), itself alluding to Milton's claim to "feed on thoughts, that voluntary move / Harmonious numbers" (*Paradise Lost* 3.36–37), blessed by a "Celestial Patroness"

who "inspires / Easy . . . unpremeditated Verse" (9.21–24).
6. An imaginary reproof; her mother died when she was seven, before the era of friendship with Jane recounted here.
7. Along with ll.101–102, compare to W. Wordsworth's *Resolution and Independence*: "We Poets in our youth begin in gladness; / But thereof come in the end despondency and madness" (48–49) and Shelley's similar sentiment in *To a Sky-Lark* (88–90), along with the same, probably allusive, rhyme (101–103).
8. A hope frequently voiced in W. Wordsworth's poetry, e.g., *Tintern Abbey*, 64–65: "in this moment there is life and food / For future years" (page 1531).

Thoughts on My Sick-bed[1]

And has the remnant of my life
Been pilfered of this sunny Spring?
And have its own prelusive sounds
Touched in my heart no echoing string?

5   Ah! say not so—the hidden life
Couchant° within this feeble frame   *lying down*
Hath been enriched by kindred gifts,
That, undesired, unsought-for, came

With joyful heart in youthful days
10   When fresh each season in its Round
I welcomed the earliest Celandine[2]
Glittering upon the mossy ground;

With busy eyes I pierced the lane
In quest of known and *unknown* things,
15   —The primrose a lamp on its fortress rock,
The silent butterfly spreading its wings,

The violet betrayed by its noiseless breath,
The daffodil dancing in the breeze,
The carolling thrush, on his naked perch,
20   Towering above the budding trees.[3]

Our cottage-hearth no longer our home,
Companions of Nature were we,
The Stirring, the Still, the Loquacious, the Mute—
To all we gave our sympathy.

25   Yet never in those careless days
When spring-time in rock, field, or bower
Was but a fountain of earthly hope
A promise of fruits & the *splendid* flower.[4]

No! then I never felt a bliss
30   That might with *that* compare
Which, piercing to my couch of rest,
Came on the vernal air.

When loving Friends an offering brought,
The first flowers of the year,
35   Culled from the precincts of our home,
From nooks to Memory dear.[5]

1. Written in spring 1832, by which time Dorothy was
being stricken with a series of debilitating illnesses.
2. A resilient flower, addressed by William in *The Small
Celandine* (1804; 1807) as an emblem of inevitable old
age.
3. A bouquet of loaded references to William's poems:
The Primrose of the Rock (c. 1831, about a flower on the
Grasmere-Rydal road); *To a Butterfly* ("Stay near me")
and *To a Butterfly* ("I've watched you") (both 1802;
1807); *Song* ("*She dwelt among th'untrodden ways*") (page
1539: "a violet by a mossy stone, half hidden from the

eye"); *I wandered lonely as a cloud* (page 1609: "golden daffodils . . . dancing in the breeze").
4. W. Wordsworth's "Intimations" *Ode* (page 1615):
"Though nothing can bring back the hour / Of splendour
in the grass, of glory in the flower; / We will grieve not,
rather find / Strength in what remains behind" (177–80).
5. "Intimations" *Ode:* "The fulness of your bliss, I feel—I
feel it all. / O evil day! if I were sullen / While Earth herself is adorning, / This sweet May-morning, / And the
Children are culling / On every side, / In a thousand valleys far and wide, / Fresh flowers" (41–48); page 1612.

With some sad thoughts the work was done,[6]
Unprompted and unbidden,
But joy it brought to my *hidden* life,
40   To consciousness no longer hidden.

I felt a Power unfelt before,
Controlling weakness, languor, pain;
It bore me to the Terrace walk
I trod the Hills again;—

45   No prisoner in this lonely room,
I *saw* the green Banks of the Wye,
Recalling thy prophetic words,
Bard, Brother, Friend from infancy![7]

No need of motion, or of strength,[8]
50   Or even the breathing air:
—I thought of Nature's loveliest scenes;
And with Memory I was there.

1832

When Shall I Tread Your Garden Path?[1]

When shall I tread your garden path?
Or climb your sheltering hill?
When shall I wander, free as air,
And track the foaming rill?

5   A prisoner on my pillowed couch
Five years in feebleness I've lain,
Oh! shall I e'er with vigorous step
Travel the hills again?
           To Mr Carter DW
           Novr 11—1835

Lines Written (Rather Say *Begun*) on the Morning of Sunday April 6th

The Third Approach of Spring-Time Since My Illness Began.
It Was a Morning of Surpassing Beauty.

The worship of this sabbath morn,
How sweetly it begins!
With the full choral hymn of birds
Mingles no sad lament for sins.

5   The air is clear, the sunshine bright.
The dew-drops glitter on the trees;
My eye beholds a perfect Rest,
I hardly hear a stirring breeze.

A robe of quiet overspreads
10   The living lake and verdant field;

---

6. W. Wordsworth's *Lines Written in Early Spring* (page 1526: "I sate reclined, / In that sweet mood when pleasant thoughts / Bring sad thoughts to the mind") and *Three Years She Grew* (page 1540: "Thus nature spake— The work was done— / How soon my Lucy's race was run! / She died").

7. See *Tintern Abbey* (pages 1530ff.), especially 111ff.
8. W. Wordsworth's *A slumber did my spirit seal* (page 1541: "No motion has she now, no force").
1. Addressed to John Carter, William's assistant in the stamp office and their handyman for more than 40 years.

The very earth seems sanctified,
Protected by a holy shield.

The steed, now vagrant on the hill,
Rejoices in this sacred day,
15 Forgetful of the plough—the goad—
And, though subdued, is happy as the gay.

A chastened call of bleating lambs
Drops steadily from that lofty Steep;
—I could believe this sabbath peace
20 Was felt even by the mother sheep.[1]

Conscious that they are safe from man
On this glad day of punctual rest,
By God himself—his work being done—
Pronounced the holiest and the best

25 'Tis but a fancy, a fond thought,
To which a waking dream gave birth,
Yet heavenly, in this brilliant Calm,
—Yea *heavenly* is the spirit of earth—

Nature attunes the pious heart
30 To gratitude and fervent love
By visible stillne[ss] the chearful voice
Of living things in budding trees & in the air above.

Fit prelude are these lingering hours
To man's appointed, holy task
35 Of prayer and social gratitude:
They prompt our hearts in faith to ask,

Ask humbly for the precious boon
Of pious hope and fixed content
And pardon, sought through trust in Him
40 Who died to save the Penitent.

And now the chapel bell invites
The Old, the Middle-aged, and Young
To meet beneath those sacred walls,
And give to pious thought a tongue

45 That simple bell of jingling tone
To careless ears unmusical,
Speaks to the Serious in a strain
That might their wisest hours recal.

Alas! my feet no more may join
50 The chearful sabbath train;
But if I inwardly lament
Soon may a will subdued all grief restrain.[2]

---

1. In another copy, Dorothy replaces all the subsequent
stanzas with this last one: "Thus have ye passed one gladsome hour / But [earnest?] youth exhausts its power / The
weary limbs, the panting breast / The throbbing head /
Plead piteously for rest."
2. In yet another copy, Dorothy writes *resigned* instead of
subdued.

No prisoner am I on this couch
My mind is free to roam,
55 And leisure, peace, and loving Friends
Are the best treasures of an earthly home.

Such gifts are mine: then why deplore
The body's gentle slow decay,
A warning mercifully sent
60 To fix my hopes upon a surer stay?

from The Grasmere Journals
[HOME ALONE]

May 14 1800 [*Wednesday*]. Wm and John set off into Yorkshire[1] after dinner at 1/2 past 2 o'clock—cold pork in their pockets. I left them at the turning of the Low-wood bay under the trees. My heart was so full that I could hardly speak to W when I gave him a farewell kiss. I sate a long time upon a stone at the margin of the lake, & after a flood of tears my heart was easier. The lake looked to me I knew not why dull and melancholy, the weltering on the shores seemed a heavy sound. I walked as long as I could amongst the stones of the shore. The wood rich in flowers. A beautiful yel-low, palish yellow flower, that looked thick round & double, and smelt very sweet— I supposed it was a ranunculus—Crowfoot, the grassy-leaved Rabbit-toothed white flower, strawberries, Geranium—scentless violet, anemones two kinds, orchises, primroses. The heckberry very beautiful. * * * Met a blind man, driving a very large beautiful Bull & a cow—he walked with two sticks. Came home by Clappersgate. The valley very green, many sweet views up to Rydale head when I could juggle away the fine houses, but they disturbed me even more than when I have been happier— one beautiful view of the Bridge, without Sir Michaels.[2] Sate down very often, tho' it was cold. I resolved to write a journal of the time till W & J return, and I set about keeping my resolve because I will not quarrel with myself, & because I shall give Wm Pleasure by it when he comes home again. At Rydale a woman of the village, stout & well dressed, begged a halfpenny—she had never she said done it before, but these hard times—Arrived at home with a bad head-ach, set some slips of privett. The evening cold had a fire—my face now flame-coloured. It is nine o'clock. I shall soon go to bed. A young woman begged at the door—she had come from Manchester on Sunday morn with two shillings & a slip of paper which she supposed a Bank note— it was a cheat. She had buried her husband & three children within a year & a half—all in one grave—burying very dear—paupers all put in one place—20 shillings paid for as much ground as will bury a man—a stone to be put over it or the right will be lost—11/6 each time the ground is opened.[3] Oh! that I had a letter from William!

Sunday [*18th.*] Went to church, slight showers, a cold air. The mountains from this window look much greener & I think the valley is more green than ever. The corn

1. William and younger brother John, who lived with them at Dove Cottage in 1800; the trip through York-shire was to visit childhood friend Mary Hutchinson, whom William would marry in October 1802.
2. Rydal Hall, the home of Sir Michael le Fleming; in 1813, the Wordsworth household would move to Rydal

Mount, the substantial residence next door, where they lived the rest of their lives.
3. Eleven shillings, 6 pence; dear: expensive. William and Dorothy lived modestly but comfortably on £130–140 a year.

begins to shew itself. The ashes are still bare. * * * A little girl from Coniston came to beg. She had lain out all night—her step-mother had turned her out of doors.

[THE GRASMERE MAILMAN]

Monday Morning 8th February 1802. It was very windy & rained very hard all the morning. William worked at his poem & I read a little in Lessing and the Grammar.[4] A chaise came past to fetch Ellis the Carrier who had hurt his head. After dinner (i.e. we set off at about 1/2 past 4) we went towards Rydale[5] for letters. It was a cold *"Cauld Clash"*—the Rain had been so cold that it hardly melted the snow. We stopped at Park's to get some straw in William's shoes. The young mother was sitting by a bright wood fire with her youngest child upon her lap & the other two sate on each side of the chimney. The light of the fire made them a beautiful sight, with their innocent countenances, their rosy cheeks & glossy curling hair. We sate & talked about poor Ellis, and our journey over the Hawes. It had been reported that we came over in the night. Willy told us of 3 men who were once lost in crossing that way in the night, they had carried a lantern with them—the lantern went out at the Tarn[6] & they all perished. Willy had seen their cloaks drying at the public house in Patterdale[7] the day before their funeral. We walked on very wet through the clashy cold roads in bad spirits at the idea of having to go as far as Rydale, but before we had come again to the shore of the Lake, we met our patient, bow-bent Friend with his little wooden box at his Back. "Where are you going?" said he. "To Rydale for letters.—I have two for you in my Box." We lifted up the lid & there they lay. Poor Fellow, he straddled & pushed on with all his might but we soon outstripped him far away when we had turned back with our letters. We were very thankful that we had not to go on, for we should have been sadly tired. In thinking of this I could not help comparing lots with him! He goes at that slow pace every morning, & after having wrought a hard days work returns at night, however weary he may be, takes it all quietly, & though perhaps he neither feels thankfulness, nor pleasure when he eats his supper, & has no luxury to look forward to but falling asleep in bed, yet I daresay he neither murmurs nor thinks it hard. He seems mechanized to labour.

[A VISION OF THE MOON]

[*18 March 1802*] * * * As we came along Ambleside vale in the twilight—it was a grave evening—there was something in the air that compelled me to serious thought—the hills were large, closed in by the sky. It was nearly dark * * * night was come on & the moon was overcast. But as I climbed Moss the moon came out from behind a Mountain Mass of Black clouds—O the unutterable darkness of the sky & the Earth below the Moon! & the glorious brightness of the moon itself! There was a vivid sparkling streak of light at this end of Rydale water but the rest was very dark & Loughrigg fell and Silver How were white & bright as if they were covered with hoar frost.[8] The moon retired again & appeared & disappeared several times before I reached home. Once there was no moonlight to be seen but upon the Island house &

---

4. William's poem is *The Pedlar*, abandoned as an independent piece and later incorporated into the first part of Book 1 of his long poem, *The Excursion* (1814). Lessing (1729–1781) is a German dramatist, art theorist, and critic; "the Grammar" is most likely a German grammar (Dorothy had learned German in Germany).
5. About a mile away.

6. Mountain lake.
7. An inn in the village several miles away, reached by treacherous pass over the high mountains.
8. The places mentioned are White Moss Common, Rydale water (a lake nearby Grasmere Lake and the Common), and two peaks to the south of these lakes, Loughrigg and Silver How.

the promontory of the Island where it stands, "That needs must be a holy place" &c—&c.[9] I had many many exquisite feelings and when I saw this lowly Building in the waters among the dark & lofty hills, with that bright soft light upon it—it made me more than half a poet. I was tired when I reached home. I could not sit down to reading & tried to write verses but alas! I gave up expecting William & went soon to bed. Fletcher's carts came home late.[1]

[A FIELD OF DAFFODILS]

Thursday 15th. [*April 1802*] * * * When we were in the woods beyond Gowbarrow[2] park we saw a few daffodils close to the water side, we fancied that the lake had float- ed the seeds ashore & that the little colony had so sprung up—But as we went along there were more & yet more & at last under the boughs of the trees, we saw that there was a long belt of them along the shore, about the breadth of a country turn- pike road.[3] I never saw daffodils so beautiful they grew among the mossy stones about & about them, some rested their heads upon these stones as on a pillow for weariness & the rest tossed & reeled & danced & seemed as if they verily laughed with the wind that blew upon them over the Lake, they looked so gay ever glancing ever changing. This wind blew directly over the lake to them. There was here & there a little knot & a few stragglers a few yards higher up but they were so few as not to dis- turb the simplicity & unity & life of that one busy highway. We rested again & again. The Bays were stormy, & we heard the waves at different distances and in the middle of the water like the Sea.

[A BEGGAR WOMAN FROM COCKERMOUTH[4]]

Tuesday 4th May [*1802*]. William had slept pretty well & though he went to bed ner- vous & jaded in the extreme he rose refreshed. I wrote the Leech Gatherer[5] for him which he had begun the night before & of which he wrote several stanzas in bed this Monday morning. It was very hot, we called at Mr Simpson's door as we passed but did not go in. We rested several times by the way, read & repeated the Leech Gath- erer. We were almost melted before we were at the top of the hill. * * * William & I ate a Luncheon, then went on towards the Waterfall. It is a glorious wild solitude under that lofty purple crag. It stood upright by itself. Its own self and its shadow below, one mass—all else was sunshine. We went on further. A Bird at the top of the crags was flying round & round & looked in thinness & transparency, shape & motion, like a moth. We climbed the hill but looked in vain for a shade except at the foot of the great waterfall, & there we did not like to stay on account of the loose stones above our heads. We came down & rested upon a moss covered Rock, rising out of the bed of the River. There we lay ate our dinner & stayed there till about 4 o clock or later. Wm & C[6] repeated & read verses. I drank a little Brandy & water & was in Heaven. The Stags horn is very beautiful & fresh springing upon the fells. Mountain ashes, green. * * * On the Rays we met a woman with 2 little girls one in

9. Perhaps recalling an early draft of Coleridge's *Kubla Khan*, line 14 (see page 1657), or William's feeling in *Home at Grasmere* that "dwellers in this holy place / Must need themselves be hallow'd" (lines 366–67).
1. William's ride, via the mail carrier.
2. Several miles away in another part of the Lake district, near Patterdale on Ullswater.
3. Dorothy erased the next words, "the end we did not see." Cf. W. Wordsworth's poem, *I wandered lonely as a*

cloud (page 1609): "They stretched in never-ending line."
4. The town where Dorothy and her brothers were born and spent their childhood before the break-up of the household.
5. The early, working title for *Resolution and Independence*.
6. Coleridge, whom they met up with on their excursion.

her arms the other about 4 years old walking by her side, a pretty little thing, but half starved. She had on a pair of slippers that had belonged to some gentlemans child, down at the heels it was not easy to keep them on but, poor thing! young as she was, she walked carefully with them. Alas too young for such cares & such travels. The Mother when we accosted her told us that her husband had left her & gone off with another woman & how she *"pursued"* them. Then her fury kindled & her eyes rolled about. She changed again to tears. She was a Cockermouth woman 30 years of age— a child at Cockermouth when I was. I was moved & gave her a shilling—I believe 6ᵈ more than I ought to have given.[7] We had the crescent moon with the "auld moon in her arms."[8] We rested often— always upon the Bridges. Reached home at about 10 o clock.

[THE CIRCUMSTANCES OF "COMPOSED UPON WESTMINISTER BRIDGE"[9]]

[*27 July 1802*] * * * After various troubles & disasters we left London on Saturday morning at 1/2 past 5 or 6. * * * we mounted the Dover Coach at Charing Cross. It was a beautiful morning. The City, St Pauls, with the River & a multitude of little Boats, made a most beautiful sight as we crossed Westminster Bridge. The houses were not overhung by their cloud of smoke & they were spread out endlessly, yet the sun shone so brightly with such a pure light that there was even something like the purity of one of nature's own grand Spectacles.

[THE CIRCUMSTANCES OF "IT IS A BEAUTEOUS EVENING"[1]]

[*1 August 1802*] * * * We walked by the sea-shore almost every Evening with Annette & Caroline or Wm & I alone.[2] * * * there was always light, & life, & joy upon the Sea.—One night, though, I shall never forget. The day had been very hot, & William & I walked alone together upon the pier—the sea was gloomy for there was a blackness over all the sky except when it was overspread with lightning which often revealed to us a distant vessel. Near us the waves roared & broke against the pier, & as they broke & as they travelled towards us, they were interfused with green-ish fiery light. The more distant sea always black & gloomy. It was also beautiful on the calm hot night to see the little Boats row out of harbour with wings of fire & the sail boats with the fiery track which they cut as they went along & which closed up after them with a hundred thousand sparkles balls shootings, & streams of glowworm light. Caroline was delighted.

[THE HOUSEHOLD IN WINTER, WITH WILLIAM'S NEW WIFE. GINGERBREAD]

[*25 December 1802*] * * * It is today Christmas-day Saturday 25th December 1802. I am 31 years of age.—It is a dull frosty day. * * *

Tuesday January 11th [*1803*] A very cold day. Wm promised me he would rise as soon as I had carried him his Breakfast but he lay in bed till between 12 & one. We

7. Six pence; Dorothy inserted "30 years of age—a child at Cockermouth when I was" to explain the generosity.
8. A line from *Sir Patrick Spence*, also quoted by Coleridge in his epigraph for *Dejection: An Ode.*
9. See page 1561; William and Dorothy are on their way to Calais, France, sailing from Dover, to settle affairs with Annette Vallon and her daughter by William, Caroline,

prior to William's marriage to Mary Hutchinson in October. The City is Westminster, a district of London where Parliament, Westminster Abbey, and Buckingham Palace are located; St. Paul's is the chief Anglican church. Westminster Bridge crosses the Thames river.
1. See William's sonnet, page 1562.
2. Without Annette, that is.

talked of walking, but the blackness of the Cold made us slow to put forward & we did not walk at all. Mary read the Prologue to Chaucer's tales to me, in the morning William was working at his poem to C.[3] Letter from Keswick & from Taylor on Wm's marriage. C poorly, in bad spirits. Canaries.[4] Before tea I sate 2 hours in the parlour— read part of The Knight's Tale with exquisite delight. Since Tea Mary has been down stairs copying out Italian poems for Stuart. Wm has been working beside me, & here ends this imperfect summary. I will take a nice Calais Book[5] & *will* for the future write regularly &, if I can legibly, so much for this my resolution on Tuesday night, January 11th 1803. Now I am going to take Tapioca for my supper, & Mary an Egg. William some cold mutton—his poor chest is tired.

Wednesday 12th. Very cold, & cold all the week.

Sunday the 16th. Intensely cold. Wm had a fancy for some ginger-bread I put on Molly's Cloak & my Spenser,[6] and we walked towards Matthew Newtons.[7] I went into the house. The blind Man & his Wife & Sister were sitting by the fire, all dressed very clean in their Sunday's Clothes, the sister reading. They took their little stock of gingerbread out of the cubboard & I bought 6 pennyworth. They were so grateful when I paid them for it that I could not find it in my heart to tell them we were going to make Gingerbread ourselves. I had asked them if they had no thick "No" answered Matthew "there was none on Friday but we'll *endeavour* to get some." The next Day the woman came just when we were baking & we bought 2 pennyworth.

LETTERS
To Jane Pollard[1]
[A SCHEME OF HAPPINESS]

16 Feb. 1793

* * * [William] is steady and sincere in his attachments, has both these Virtues in an eminent degree; and a sort of violence of Affection if I may so Term it which demonstrates itself every moment of the Day when the Objects of his affection are present with him, in a thousand almost imperceptible attentions to their wishes, in a sort of restless watchfulness which I know not how to describe, a Tenderness that never sleeps, and at the same Time such a Delicacy of Manners as I have observed in few Men. I hope you will one day be much better acquainted with him than you are at present, much as I have talked to you about him. I look forward with full confidence to the Happiness of receiving you in my little Parsonage,[2] I hope you will spend at least a year with me. I have laid the particular scheme of happiness for each Season. When I think of Winter I hasten to furnish our little Parlour, I close the Shutters, set out the Tea-table, brighten the Fire. When our Refreshment is ended I produce our Work, and William brings his book to our Table and contributes at once to our Instruction and amusement, and at Intervals we lay aside the Book and each hazard

---

3. *The Prelude*, known during William's lifetime as *Poem to Coleridge*, his addressee; *The Knight's Tale* is one of Chaucer's *Canterbury Tales*.

4. Canary Islands, where Coleridge was hoping to go for his health.

5. A blank notebook purchased in Calais; Dorothy did not continue her journal.

6. Heavy overcoat.

7. A gingerbread shop in Grasmere.

1. Jane Pollard (1771–1847), later Mrs. John Marshall, close childhood friend.

2. Dorothy imagines that she will keep house for William, who planned a career in the Church before receiving the bequest in 1795 that enabled him to attempt a career as a poet.

our observations upon what has been read without the fear of Ridicule or Censure. We talk over past days, we do not sigh for any Pleasures beyond our humble Habitation "The central point of all our joys."[3] Oh Jane! with such romantic dreams as these I amuse my fancy during many an hour which would otherwise pass heavily along, for kind as are my Uncle and Aunt,[4] much as I love my sweet little Cousins, I cannot help heaving many a Sigh at the Reflection that I have passed one and twenty years of my Life, and that the first six years only of this Time was spent in the Enjoyment of the same Pleasures that were enjoyed by my Brothers, and that I was then too young to be sensible of the Blessing. We have been endeared to each other by early misfortune. We in the same moment lost a father, a mother, a home, we have been equally deprived of our patrimony by the cruel Hand of lordly Tyranny.[5] These afflictions have all contributed to unite us closer by the Bonds of affection notwithstanding we have been compelled to spend our youth far asunder. "We drag at each remove a lengthening Chain"[6] this Idea often strikes me very forcibly. Neither absence nor Distance nor Time can ever break the Chain that links me to my Brothers. * * *

To Lady Beaumont

[HER POETRY, WILLIAM'S POETRY]

Grasmere. Saturday afternoon 4 o'clock. April 20th [1806]

* * * I am truly glad that my Brother's manuscript poems give you so much pleasure—I was sure that you would be deeply impressed by the Ode.[7] The last time I read it over, I said: "Lady Beaumont will like this." I long to know your opinion and Sir George's of Benjamin, the Waggoner;[8] I *think* you will be pleased with it, but cannot be so sure of this—And you would persuade *me* that I am capable of writing poems that might give pleasure to others besides my own particular friends!! indeed, indeed you do not know me thoroughly; you think far better of me than I deserve—I must tell you the history of those two little things which William in his fondness read to you.[9] I happened to be writing a letter one evening when he and my Sister were last at Park house, I laid down the pen and thinking of little Johnny (then in bed in the next room) I muttered a few lines of that address to him about the Wind, and having paper before me, wrote them down, and went on till I had finished. The other lines I wrote in the same way, and as William knows every thing that I do, I shewed them to him when he came home, and he was very much pleased; but this I attributed to his partiality; yet because they gave him pleasure and for the sake of the children I ventured to hope that I might do something more at some time or other. Do not think that I was ever bold enough to hope to compose verses for the pleasure of grown persons. Descriptions, Sentiments, or little stories for children was all I could be ambitious of doing, and I did try one story,[1] but failed so sadly that I was completely discouraged. Believe me, since I received your let-

3. Quoted from William's *Descriptive Sketches* (1793), l.571.
4. She had been living with her uncle William Cookson and his wife in Norfolk, in northeast England, since 1788.
5. Their mother died in 1778, their father in 1783; she had been separated from her brothers since 1778. Their inheritance was tied up in legal wrangling for several years, complicated by a debt owed by Lord Lowther, whose family did not settle it until 1803.
6. Oliver Goldsmith, *The Traveller, or A Prospect of Soci-*

ety (1755–1764): "Where'er I roam, whatever realms to see, / My heart untravelled fondly returns to thee; / Still to my brother turns with ceaseless pain, / And drags at each remove a lengthening chain" (7–10).
7. *Ode: Intimations of Immortality* (see page 1610), written 1802 and 1804, pub. as *Ode* in 1807.
8. Published 1819.
9 *An Address to a Child* (page 1618) and *To My Niece Dorothy, a Sleepless Baby.*
1. *Mary Jones and Her Pet Lamb.*

ter I have made several attempts (could I do less as you requested that I would *for your sake?*) and have been obliged to give it up in despair; and looking into my mind I find nothing there, even if I had the gift of language and numbers,[2] that I could have the vanity to suppose could be of any use beyond our own fireside, or to please, as in your case, a few partial friends; but I have no command of language, no power of expressing my ideas, and no one was ever more inapt at molding words into regular metre. I have often tried when I have been walking alone (muttering to myself as is my Brother's custom) to express my feelings in verse; feelings, and *ideas* such as they were, I have never wanted at those times; but prose and rhyme and blank verse were jumbled together and nothing ever came of it. As to those two little things which I did write, I was very unwilling to place them beside my Brother's poems, but he insisted upon it, and I was obliged to submit; and though you have been pleased with them I cannot but think that it was chiefly owing to the spirit which William gave them in the reading and to your kindness for me. I have said far more than enough on this subject * * *

Believe me affectionately yours, D. Wordsworth.

My Brother has a copy of my Journal of our Scotch Tour[3] which I have desired him to leave with you when it comes from the Bookbinders, but perhaps you may be too much engaged to find time to read it. My Sister begs her kind remembrances. Excuse blunders and scrawling and this torn paper. I have a very inconvenient desk to write upon * * *

To Mrs Thomas Clarkson[4]

[Household Labors]

Thursday Evening December 8 [1808]

* * * I will not attempt to detail the height and depth and number of our sorrows in connection with the smoky chimneys. They are in short so very bad that if they cannot be mended we must leave the house,[5] beautiful as everything will soon be out of doors, dear as is the vale where we have so long lived. The labour of the house is literally doubled. Dishes are washed, and no sooner set into the pantry than they are covered with smoke.—Chairs—carpets—the painted ledges of the rooms, all are ready for the reception of soot and smoke, requiring endless cleaning, and are never clean. This is not certainly the worst part of the business, but the smarting of the eyes etc. etc. you may guess at, and I speak of these other discomforts as more immediately connected with myself. In fact we have seldom an hour's leisure (either Mary or I) till after 7 o'clock (when the children go to bed), for all the time that we have for sitting still in the course of the day we are obliged to employ in scouring (and many of our evenings also). We are regularly thirteen in family, and on Saturdays and Sundays 15 (for when Saturday morning is not very stormy Hartley and Derwent[6] come). I include the servants in the number, but as you may judge, in the most convenient house there would be work enough for two maids and a little Girl. In ours there is far too much. We keep a cow—the stable is two short field lengths from the house, and the cook has both to fodder, and clean after the cow. We have also two pigs, bake all our bread at home and though we do not *wash all* our clothes, yet we wash a part

---

2. Metrical verse.
3. With William and Coleridge in late summer 1803.
4. Catherine Clarkson (1772–1856), wife of Thomas

Clarkson, the abolitionist.
5. New, more spacious family quarters in Grasmere.
6. Coleridge's sons, both at school nearby.

every week, and mangle or iron the whole. This is a tedious tale and I should not have troubled you with it but to let you see plainly that idleness has nothing to do with my putting off to write to you. * * * William and Mary (alas! all involved in smoke) in William's study, where she is writing for him (he dictating). He is engaged in a work which occupies all his thoughts. It will be a pamphlet of considerable length, entitled The Convention of Cintra brought to the Test of Principles and the People of England justified from the Charge of Prejudging, or something to that effect.[7] I believe it will first appear in the *Courier* in different sections. Mr De Quincey,[8] whom you would love dearly, as I am sure I do, is beside me, quietly turning over the leaves of a Greek book—and God be praised *we* are breathing a clear air, for the night is calm, and this room (the Dining-room) only smokes very much in a high wind. Mr De Q. will stay with us, we hope, at least till the Spring. We feel often as if he were one of the Family—he is loving, gentle, and happy—a very good scholar, and an acute Logician—so much for his mind and manners. His person is *unfortunately* diminutive, but there is a sweetness in his looks, especially about the eyes, which soon overcomes the oddness of your first feeling at the sight of so very little a Man. John[9] sleeps with him and is passionately fond of him. * * *

Believe me evermore your affectionate D. W.

To Mrs Thomas Clarkson

[A PROSPECT OF PUBLISHING]

Kendal,[1] Sunday 9 Dec. 1810

My dear Friend, * * * I cannot express what pain I feel in refusing to grant any request of yours, and above all one in which dear Mr Clarkson joins so earnestly, but indeed I cannot have that narrative[2] published. My reasons are entirely disconnected with myself, much as I should detest the idea of setting myself up as an Author. I should not object on that score as if it had been an invention of my own it might have been published without a name, and nobody would have thought of me. But on account of the Family of the Greens I cannot consent. Their story was only represented to the world in that narrative which was drawn up for the collecting of the subscription, so far as might tend to produce the end desired, but by publishing this narrative of mine I should bring the children forward to notice as Individuals, and we know not what injurious effect this might have upon them. Besides it appears to me that the events are too recent to be published in delicacy to others as well as to the children. I should be the more hurt at having to return such an answer to your request, if I could believe that the story would be of that service to the work which Mr Clarkson imagines. I cannot believe that it would do much for it. Thirty or forty years hence when the Characters of the children are formed and they can be no longer objects of curiosity,

7. William's pamphlet was one of many criticisms of the British agreement of August 1808, by which Napoleon's imperialist army, halted by Spanish resistance and British forces, was given safe passage home from Spain with their booty, in British ships. Many Britons sympathized with the "noble Spaniards."
8. Thomas De Quincey was helping William with the Cintra pamphlet.
9. Her nephew Johnny.
1. A town about 20 miles from Grasmere.
2. *A Narrative concerning George and Sarah Green of the*

Parish of Grasmere (1808). George and Sarah Green perished in a snowstorm, leaving behind six children. The *Narrative* was written to raise funds for the orphans beyond the minimal parish allotment; the hope was to place them with local families and secure them an education. The narrative circulated to several prominent people, including Scott, Southey, Baillie, DeQuincey, and several of the aristocracy. William did publish a poem on the death of George and Sarah, and De Quincey gave his version of the events some decades later in a magazine article and again in *Recollections of the Lakes*.

if it should be thought that any service would be done, it is my present wish that it should then be published whether I am alive or dead. * * *

yours affectionately D. W.

I am called to dinner.

To William Johnson[3]
[MOUNTAIN-CLIMBING WITH A WOMAN]

October 21st, 1818.

* * * we all dined together in the romantic Vale of Borrowdale, at the house of a female friend, an unmarried Lady, who, bewitched with the charms of the rocks, and streams, and mountains of that secluded spot, has there built herself a house, and though she is admirably fitted for society, and has as much enjoyment when surrounded by her friends as any one *can* have, her chearfulness has never flagged, though she has lived more than the year round alone in Borrowdale, at six miles distance from Keswick, with bad roads between.[4] You will guess that she has resources within herself; such indeed she has. She is a painter and labours hard in depicting the beauties of her favorite Vale; she is also found of music and of reading, and has a reflecting mind; besides (though before she lived in Borrowdale she was no great walker) she is become an active climber of the hills, and I must tell you of a feat that she and I performed on Wednesday the 7th of this month. * * * Miss Barker proposed that * * * she and I should go to Seathwaite beyond the Black lead mines at the head of Borrowdale, and thence up a mountain called at the top *Ash Course* * * * At the top of Ash Course Miss Barker had promised that I should see a magnificent prospect; but we had some miles to travel to the foot of the mountain, and accordingly went thither in a cart—Miss Barker, her maid, and myself. We departed before nine o'clock, the sun shone; the sky was clear and blue; and light and shade fell in masses upon the mountains; the fields below *glittered* with the dew, where the beams of the sun could reach them; and every little stream tumbling down the hills seemed to add to the chearfulness of the scene.

We left our cart at Seathwaite and proceeded, with a man to carry our provisions, and a kind neighbour of Miss Barker's, a statesman shepherd of the vale, as our companion and guide. We found ourselves at the top of Ash Course without a weary limb, having had the fresh air of autumn to help us up by its invigorating power, and the sweet warmth of the unclouded sun to tempt us to sit and rest by the way. From the top of Ash Course we beheld a prospect which would indeed have amply repaid us for a *toilsome* journey, if such it had been; and a sense of thankfulness for the continuance of that vigour of body, which enabled me to climb the high mountain, as in the days of my youth, inspiring me with fresh chearfulness, added a delight, a charm to the contemplation of the magnificent scenes before me, which I cannot describe.

* * * We had attained the object of our journey; but our ambition mounted higher. We saw the summit of Scaw Fell, as it seemed, very near to us; we were indeed, three parts up that mountain, and thither we determined to go. We found the distance greater than it had appeared to us, but our courage did not fail; however, when we came nearer we perceived that in order to attain that summit we must make a

great dip, and that the ascent afterwards would be exceedingly steep and difficult, so that we might have been benighted if we had attempted it; therefore, unwillingly, we gave it up, and resolved, instead, to ascend another point of the same mountain, called *the Pikes*, and which, I have since found, the measurers of the mountains estimate as higher than the larger summit which bears the name of Scaw Fell, and where the Stone Man is built which we, at the time, considered as the point of highest honour. The sun had never once been overshadowed by a cloud during the whole of our progress from the centre of Borrowdale; at the summit of the Pike there was not a breath of air to stir even the papers which we spread out containing our food. There we ate our dinner in summer warmth; and the stillness seemed to be not of this world. We paused, and kept silence to listen, and not a sound of any kind was to be heard. We were far above the reach of the cataracts of Scaw Fell; and not an insect was there to hum in the air. The Vales before described lay in view, and side by side with Eskdale, we now saw the sister Vale of Donnerdale terminated by the Duddon Sands. But the majesty of the mountains below and close to us, is not to be conceived. We now beheld the whole mass of Great Gavel from its base, the Den of Wasdale at our feet, the gulph immeasurable, Grasmere and the other mountains of Crummock, Ennerdale and *its* mountains, and the sea beyond.

While we were looking round after dinner our Guide said that we must not linger long, for we should have a storm. We looked in vain to espy the traces of it; for mountains, vales, and the sea were all touched with the clear light of the sun. "It is there," he said, pointing to the sea beyond Whitehaven, and, sure enough, we there perceived a light cloud, or mist, unnoticeable but by a shepherd, accustomed to watch all mountain bodings. We gazed around again and yet again, fearful to lose the remembrance of what lay before us in that lofty solitude; and then prepared to depart. Meanwhile the air changed to cold, and we saw the tiny vapour swelled into mighty masses of cloud which came boiling over the mountains. Great Gavel, Helvellyn, and Skiddaw were wrapped in storm; yet Langdale and the mountains in that quarter were all bright with sunshine. Soon the storm reached us; we sheltered under a crag, and almost as rapidly as it had come, it passed away, and left us free to observe the goings-on of storm and sunshine in other quarters—Langdale had now its share, and the Pikes were decorated by two splendid rainbows; Skiddaw also had its own rainbows, but we were glad to see them and the clouds disappear from that mountain. * * * we, indeed, were hardly at all wetted; and before we found ourselves again upon that part of the mountain called Ash Course every cloud had vanished from every summit.

Do not think we here gave up our spirit of enterprise. No! I had heard much of the grandeur of the view of Wasdale from Stye Head, the point from which Wasdale is first seen in coming by the road from Borrowdale; but though I had been in Wasdale I had never entered the dale by that road, and had often lamented that I had not seen what was so much talked of by travellers. Down to that Pass (for we were yet far above it) we bent our course by the side of Ruddle Gill, a very deep red chasm in the mountains which begins at a spring—that spring forms a stream, which must, at times, be a mighty torrent, as is evident from the channel which it has wrought out—thence by Sprinkling Tarn to Stye Head; and there we sate and looked down into Wasdale. We were now upon Great Gavel which rose high above us. Opposite was Scaw Fell and we heard the roaring of the stream from one of the ravines of that mountain, which, though the bending of Wasdale Head lay between us and Scaw Fell, we could look into, as it were, and the depth of the ravine appeared tremendous; it was black and the crags were awful.

We now proceeded homewards by Stye head Tarn along the road into Borrowdale. Before we reached Stonethwaite a few stars had appeared, and we travelled home in our cart by moonlight.

I ought to have described the last part of our ascent to Scaw Fell Pike. There, not a blade of grass was to be seen—hardly a cushion of moss, and that was parched and brown; and only growing rarely between the huge blocks and stones which cover the summit and lie in heaps all round to a great distance, like skeletons or bones of the earth not wanted at the creation, and there left to be covered with never-dying lichens, which the clouds and dews nourish; and adorn with colours of the most vivid and exquisite beauty, and endless in variety. No gems or flowers can surpass in colouring the beauty of some of these masses of stone which no human eye beholds except the shepherd led thither by chance or traveller by curiosity; and how seldom must this happen! The other eminence is that which is visited by the adventurous traveller, and the shepherd has no temptation to go thither in quest of his sheep; for on the Pike there is no food to tempt them. We certainly were singularly fortunate in the day; for when we were seated on the summit our Guide, turning his eyes thoughtfully round, said to us, "I do not know that in my whole life I was ever at any season of the year so high up on the mountains on so calm a day." Afterwards, you know, we had the storm which exhibited to us the grandeur of earth and heaven commingled, yet without terror; for we knew that the storm would pass away; for so our prophetic guide assured us. I forget to tell you that I espied a ship upon the glittering sea while we were looking over Eskdale. "Is it a ship?" replied the Guide. "A ship, yes, it can be nothing else, don't you see the shape of it?" Miss Barker interposed, "It is a ship, of that I am certain. I cannot be mistaken, I am so accustomed to the appearance of ships at sea." The Guide dropped the argument; but a moment was scarce gone when he quietly said, "Now look at your ship, it is now a horse." So indeed it was—a horse with a gallant neck and head. We laughed heartily, and, I hope when again inclined to positiveness, I may remember the ship and the horse upon the glittering sea; and the calm confidence, yet submissiveness, of our wise Man of the Mountains, who certainly had more knowledge of clouds than we, whatever might be our knowledge of ships. To add to our uncommon performance on that day Miss Barker and I each wrote a letter from the top of the Pike to our far distant friend in S. Wales, Miss Hutchinson. I believe that you are not much acquainted with the Scenery of this Country, except in the Neighbourhood of Grasmere, your duties when you were a resident here, having confined you so much to that one Vale; I hope, however, that my long story will not be very dull; and even I am not without a further hope, that it may awaken in you a desire to spend a long holiday among the mountains, and explore their recesses.

⊷ ⇌⬦⇌ ⊶

Samuel Taylor Coleridge
1772–1834

"Come back into memory, like as thou wert in the dayspring of thy fancies, with hope like a fiery column before thee—the dark pillar not yet turned—Samuel Taylor Coleridge—Logician, Metaphysician, Bard!—How have I seen the casual passer through the cloisters stand still, entranced with admiration . . . while the walls of the old Grey Friars re-echoed to the accents of the *inspired charity-boy!*" When Charles Lamb thus memorialized his former schoolfellow, Coleridge had more than a decade yet to live, but he had already made himself into the mythic Romantic figure of promise and failure whom Lamb salutes.

Born in 1772, the last child of the vicar of Ottery St. Mary's in Devon, Coleridge developed a reputation for precocity even before the death of his father led to his enrollment at Christ's Hospital, a London boarding school for the sons of distressed families, where Lamb met him. A brilliant career at Jesus College, Cambridge, ended in an unhappy attempt to enlist in the army under an assumed name, and he left without a degree in 1794. With Robert Southey, a fellow Oxford enthusiast for poetry and radical politics, he planned an ideal democratic community on the banks of the Susquehanna in Pennsylvania, to be named "Pantisocracy," or equal rule by all. The project collapsed over a dispute whether they would have servants, but not before Coleridge had cemented the social bonds by becoming engaged to Sara Fricker, the sister of Southey's fiancée; the marriage proved unhappy. Coleridge later minimized his youthful "squeaking baby-trumpet of sedition," but he founded a short-lived antigovernment periodical, *The Watchman* (1796); to earn a living, he was pointing in the unorthodox direction of the Unitarian ministry until he was relieved by a moderate annuity of £150 from the Wedgwoods, of the famous pottery firm. In 1796 he published *Poems on Various Subjects*, containing the poem later titled *The Eolian Harp*, and in 1797 he began the collaboration with Wordsworth that produced *Lyrical Ballads* (1798), headed by *The Rime of the Ancyent Marinere*, as the poem was called in its archaizing first version. Before the volume was published, Coleridge and the Wordsworths departed for Germany, where Coleridge studied philosophy at Göttingen. Charges of plagiarism have swirled ever since around the readings of Kant, Schiller, Schelling, and Fichte that animated his lifelong effort to combat what he regarded as the spiritless mechanical world of eighteenth-century British empiricism.

In 1800 Coleridge followed the Wordsworths to the Lake District, where his love for Sara Hutchinson, sister of Wordsworth's future wife, sharpened his estrangement from his own wife. He became addicted to laudanum (opium dissolved in alcohol), a standard medical remedy for the rheumatic pains he suffered, but the stomach disorders it produced increased his dependency. The physiology of addiction was not understood in his day, and what was a widespread social phenomenon Coleridge regarded as an individual moral flaw. His inability to break the habit produced a spiral of depression: guilt, a paralytic doubt of his strength of will, the fear that he was unworthy of love. By 1802, in *Dejection: An Ode*, he declared the failure of his "genial spirits" and "shaping spirit of Imagination," but he carried on an active public career. An important political commentator in the newspapers, he also undertook another periodical, *The Friend* (1809–1810), saw his play *Remorse* succeed at Drury Lane (1813), and gave a series of brilliant lectures on Shakespeare, Milton, poetry, drama, and philosophy (1808–1818). That these enterprises often fell short of the triumphant fullness he forecast for them fixed the myth of promise unfulfilled, even as his accomplishments won increasing influence. From 1816 on, he lived in a London suburb under the care of a young doctor, James Gillman, and he flourished in this stable environment. The fabled talk of the "Sage of Highgate," as Carlyle called him, "had a charm much more than literary, a charm almost religious and prophetic." If the "practical intellects of the world did not much heed him," Carlyle continued, "to the rising spirits of the young generation he had this dusky sublime character; and sat there as a kind of *Magus*." Coleridge became, in the judgment of John Stuart Mill, one of the two seminal minds of the nineteenth century, the idealist, Christian, philosopher of organic unity around whose work the opposition to Benthamite utilitarianism crystalized.

In the final decades of his life, Coleridge joined new work and the gathering of old into a substantial body of publication. *Christabel*, long known by reputation, appeared with Byron's enthusiastic sponsorship, in 1816, together with *Kubla Khan*; 1817 brought *Sibylline Leaves*, Coleridge's collected poems, including the marginal-gloss version of the lyrical ballad now titled *The Rime of the Ancient Mariner*, and *Biographia Literaria*, the account of his "literary life and opinions" that has provided the starting-point for much twentieth-century literary criticism. In a series of works, Coleridge advocated a network of conservative principles continuous with but far evolved from the Jacobin associations that had led him to urge anonymous publication of the *Lyrical Ballads* because "Wordsworth's name is nothing, and mine stinks": two *Lay Sermons* (1816–1817), articulating his views in the debate over reform, *The Friend*, expanded in 1818 into a three-volume collection of essays on "politics, morals, and religion," *Aids to Reflection* (1825), emphasizing Christianity as "personal revelation," and *On the Constitution of Church and State* (1830), which outlined conceptions of national culture (and the "clerisy" responsible for preserving it) that resonate throughout the Victorian period. *Table Talk* (1836) posthumously captured the echoes of his voice, but Coleridge has enjoyed a resurrection in our own day. As new scholarly editions bring more of Coleridge's writings to light, they deepen the fascination of a man who was the author of some of the most suggestive poems in the language and an erudite philosopher, a poet who in the *Biographia Literaria* transformed the role of the critic, a theorist of the unifying imagination whose works and life are marked by fragments and discontinuities, a believer in the unity of all whose own method has been aptly described as marginal glosses on the works of others, and an idealist engaged with the daily politics of a turbulent era.

The Eolian Harp[1]

Composed at Clevedon, Somersetshire.

My pensive Sara![2] thy soft cheek reclined
Thus on mine arm, most soothing sweet it is
To sit beside our cot,° our cot o'ergrown   cottage
With white-flowered jasmin, and the broad-leaved myrtle,
5   (Meet emblems they of Innocence and Love!)
And watch the clouds, that late were rich with light,
Slow saddening round, and mark the star of eve
Serenely brilliant (such should wisdom be)
Shine opposite! How exquisite the scents
10 Snatched from yon bean-field! and the world so hushed!
The stilly murmur of the distant sea
Tells us of silence.
                         And that simplest lute,
Placed length-ways in the clasping casement, hark!
How by the desultory breeze caressed,
15 Like some coy maid half yielding to her lover,
It pours such sweet upbraiding,° as must needs   reproach
Tempt to repeat the wrong! And now, its strings
Boldlier swept, the long sequacious° notes   rhythmic, flowing
Over delicious surges sink and rise,
20 Such a soft floating witchery of sound
As twilight Elfins make, when they at eve
Voyage on gentle gales from Fairy-Land,
Where Melodies round honey-dropping flowers,
Footless and wild, like birds of Paradise,[3]

---

1. Named after Aeolus, the Greek god of winds, the harp consisted of a guitarlike box, set in an open window where the breeze would cause its strings to sound. Originally titled *Effusium xxxv Composed August 20th, at Clevedon, Sumersetshire*.

2. Sara Fricker, Coleridge's new bride. This poem was written during Coleridge's honeymoon.
3. Birds of the New Guinea islands famed for their colorful plumage.

25   Nor pause, nor perch, hovering on untamed wing!
      O the one life within us and abroad,
      Which meets all motion and becomes its soul,
      A light in sound, a sound-like power in light
      Rhythm in all thought, and joyance everywhere—
30   Methinks, it should have been impossible
      Not to love all things in a world so filled;
      Where the breeze warbles, and the mute still air
      Is Music slumbering on her instrument.[4]

      And thus, my love! as on the midway slope
35   Of yonder hill I stretch my limbs at noon,
      Whilst through my half-closed eyelids I behold
      The sunbeams dance, like diamonds, on the main,
      And tranquil muse upon tranquillity;
      Full many a thought uncalled and undetained,
40   And many idle flitting phantasies,
      Traverse my indolent and passive brain,
      As wild and various as the random gales
      That swell and flutter on this subject lute!

      And what if all of animated nature
45   Be but organic harps diversely framed,
      That tremble into thought, as o'er them sweeps
      Plastic and vast, one intellectual breeze,
      At once the Soul of each, and God of All?

      But thy more serious eye a mild reproof
50   Darts, O beloved woman! nor such thoughts
      Dim and unhallowed dost thou not reject,
      And biddest me walk humbly with my God.
      Meek daughter in the family of Christ!
      Well hast thou said and holily dispraised
55   These shapings of the unregenerate mind;
      Bubbles that glitter as they rise and break
      On vain Philosophy's aye-babbling spring.
      For never guiltless may I speak of him,
      The Incomprehensible! save when with awe
60   I praise him, and with Faith that inly feels;
      Who with his saving mercies healed me,
      A sinful and most miserable man,
      Wildered and dark, and gave me to possess
      Peace, and this cot, and thee, heart-honored Maid!

1795–1817   1796, 1817

This Lime-Tree Bower My Prison

In the June of 1797, some long-expected Friends[1] paid a visit to the author's cottage; and on the morning of their arrival, he met with an accident, which disabled him

---

4. The eight lines beginning "O the one life" were added to the poem in 1817.

1. Among them was Charles Lamb, to whom the poem is addressed.

from walking during the whole time of their stay. One evening, when they had left him for a few hours, he composed the following lines in the garden-bower.

Well, they are gone, and here must I remain,
This lime-tree bower my prison! I have lost
Beauties and feelings, such as would have been
Most sweet to my remembrance even when age
5   Had dimmed mine eyes to blindness! They, meanwhile,
Friends, whom I never more may meet again,
On springy heath, along the hill-top edge,
Wander in gladness, and wind down, perchance,
To that still roaring dell,° of which I told;   *deep hollow*
10   The roaring dell, o'erwooded, narrow, deep,
And only speckled by the mid-day sun;
Where its slim trunk the ash from rock to rock
Flings arching like a bridge;—that branchless ash,
Unsunned and damp, whose few poor yellow leaves
15   Ne'er tremble in the gale, yet tremble still,
Fanned by the waterfall! and there my friends
Behold the dark green file of long lank weeds,
That all at once (a most fantastic sight!)
Still nod and drip beneath the dripping edge
20   Of the blue clay-stone.

                    Now, my friends emerge
Beneath the wide wide Heaven—and view again
The many-steepled tract magnificent
Of hilly fields and meadows, and the sea,
With some fair bark,° perhaps, whose sails light up   *small boat*
25   The slip of smooth clear blue betwixt two Isles
Of purple shadow! Yes! they wander on
In gladness all; but thou, methinks, most glad,
My gentle-hearted Charles! for thou hast pined
And hungered after Nature, many a year,
30   In the great City pent, winning thy way
With sad yet patient soul, through evil and pain
And strange calamity![2] Ah! slowly sink
Behind the western ridge, thou glorious sun!
Shine in the slant beams of the sinking orb,
35   Ye purple heath-flowers! richlier burn, ye clouds!
Live in the yellow light, ye distant groves!
And kindle, thou blue ocean! So my Friend
Struck with deep joy may stand, as I have stood,
Silent with swimming sense; yea, gazing round
40   On the wide landscape, gaze till all doth seem
Less gross than bodily; and of such hues
As veil the Almighty Spirit, when yet he makes
Spirits perceive his presence.

2. The fit of insanity in which Mary Lamb, Charles's sister, had killed their mother the year before.

A delight

Comes sudden on my heart, and I am glad
45   As I myself were there! Nor in this bower,
This little lime-tree bower, have I not marked
Much that has soothed me. Pale beneath the blaze
Hung the transparent foliage; and I watched
Some broad and sunny leaf, and loved to see
50   The shadow of the leaf and stem above
Dappling its sunshine! And that walnut-tree
Was richly tinged, and a deep radiance lay
Full on the ancient ivy, which usurps
Those fronting elms, and now, with blackest mass
55   Makes their dark branches gleam a lighter hue
Through the late twilight: and though now the bat
Wheels silent by, and not a swallow twitters,
Yet still the solitary humble bee
Sings in the bean-flower! Henceforth I shall know
60   That Nature ne'er deserts the wise and pure;
No plot so narrow, be but Nature there,
No waste so vacant, but may well employ
Each faculty of sense, and keep the heart
Awake to Love and Beauty! and sometimes
65   'Tis well to be bereft of promised good,
That we may lift the Soul, and contemplate
With lively joy the joys we can not share.
My gentle-hearted Charles! when the last rook
Beat its straight path along the dusky air
70   Homewards, I blest it! deeming, its black wing
(Now a dim speck, now vanishing in light)
Had crossed the mighty orb's dilated glory,
While thou stood'st gazing; or when all was still,
Flew creeking o'er thy head, and had a charm
75   For thee, my gentle-hearted Charles, to whom
No sound is dissonant which tells of Life.

1797   1800

The Rime of the Ancient Mariner[1]
In Seven Parts

Facile credo, plures esse Naturas invisibiles quam visibiles
in rerum universitate. Sed horum omnium familiam quis
nobis enarrabit, et gradus et cognationes et discrimina et
singulorum munera? Quid agunt? quae loca habitant?
Harum rerum notitiam semper ambivit ingenium hu-
manum, nunquam attigit. Juvat, interea, non diffiteor,
quandoque in animo, tanquam in Tabulâ, majoris et me-
lioris mundi imaginem contemplari: ne mens assuefacta

---

1. When he finally published *The Rime* under his own name in 1817, Coleridge added the extensive glosses printed in the left margins, as well as the Latin epigraph.

hodiernae vitae minutiis se contrahat nimis, et tota subsi-
dat in pusillas cogitationes. Sed veritati interea invigilan-
dum est, modusque servandus, ut certa ab incertis, diem a
nocte, distinguamus.[2]

T. Burnet. Archaeol. Phil. p. 68.

Part 1

An ancient Mariner
meeteth three gallants
bidden to a wedding
feast, and detaineth
one.

It is an ancient Mariner,
And he stoppeth one of three.
"By thy long gray beard and glittering eye,
Now wherefore stopp'st thou me?

"The Bridegroom's doors are opened wide,   5
And I am next of kin;
The guests are met, the feast is set:
May'st hear the merry din."

He holds him with his skinny hand,
"There was a ship," quoth he.   10
"Hold off! unhand me, graybeard loon!"
Eftsoons° his hand dropt he.   *immediately*

The wedding-guest is
spellbound by the eye
of the old sea-faring
man, and constrained
to hear his tale.

He holds him with his glittering eye—
The wedding-guest stood still,
And listens like a three years' child: 15
The Mariner hath his will.

The wedding-guest sat on a stone:
He can not choose but hear;
And thus spake on that ancient man,
The bright-eyed Mariner.   20

The ship was cheered, the harbor cleared,
Merrily did we drop
Below the kirk,° below the hill.   *church*
Below the light-house top.

The Mariner tells how
the ship sailed
southward with a good
wind and fair weather,
till it reached the line.

The sun came up upon the left,   25
Out of the sea came he!
And he shone bright, and on the right
Went down into the sea.

Higher and higher every day,
Till over the mast at noon—   30

2. From the English theologian Thomas Burnet's *Archae-
ologiae Philosophicae* (1692): "I can easily believe that
there are more invisible creatures in the universe than
visible ones. But who will tell us to what family each
belongs, their ranks and relationships, and what their distinguishing characteristics may be? What do they do?
Where do they live? The human mind has always circled
around these matters without finding satisfaction. But I
do not doubt that it is beneficial sometimes to contemplate in the mind, as in a picture, the image of a grander
and better world; for if the mind becomes used to the
trival things of everyday life, it may limit itself too much
and decline completely into worthless thinking. Meanwhile, however, we must be on the lookout for the truth,
keeping a sense of proportion so that we can distinguish
what is sure from what is uncertain, and day from night."

The Wedding-Guest here beat his breast,
For he heard the loud bassoon.

The wedding-guest
heareth the bridal
music; but the mariner
continueth his tale.

The bride hath paced into the hall,
Red as a rose is she;
Nodding their heads before her goes   35
The merry minstrelsy.

The Wedding-Guest he beat his breast,
Yet he can not choose but hear;
And thus spake on that ancient man,
The bright-eyed Mariner.   40

The ship drawn by a
storm toward the south
pole.

And now the storm-blast came, and he
Was tyrannous and strong:
He struck with his o'ertaking wings,
And chased us south along.

With sloping masts and dipping prow,   45
As who pursued with yell and blow
Still treads the shadow of his foe,
And forward bends his head,
The ship drove fast, loud roared the blast,
And southward aye we fled.   50

And now there came both mist and snow,
And it grew wondrous cold:
And ice, mast-high, came floating by,
As green as emerald.

The land of ice, and of
fearful sounds where
no living thing was to
be seen.

And through the drifts the snowy clifts   55
Did send a dismal sheen:
Nor shapes of men nor beast we ken°—   *saw*
The ice was all between.

The ice was here, the ice was there,
The ice was all around: 60
It cracked and growled, and roared and howled,
Like noises in a swound!°   *swoon*

Till a great seabird
called the Albatross,
came through the
snow fog, and was
received with great joy
and hospitality.

At length did cross an Albatross,
Through the fog it came;
As if it had been a Christian soul,   65
We hailed it in God's name.

It ate the food it ne'er had eat,
And round and round it flew.
The ice did split with a thunder-fit;
The helmsman steered us through!   70

And lo! the Albatross
proveth a bird of good
omen, and followeth
the ship as it returneth
northward through fog
and floating ice.

And a good south wind sprung up behind;
The Albatross did follow,
And every day, for food or play,
Came to the mariner's hollo!

In mist or cloud, on mast or shroud,°   *supporting rope*   75
It perched for vespers nine;
Whiles all the night, through fog-smoke white,
Glimmered the white moon-shine.

The ancient Mariner
inhospitably killeth
the pious bird of good
omen.

"God save thee, ancient Mariner!
From the fiends, that plague thee thus!—   80
Why look'st thou so?"—With my cross-bow
I shot the Albatross.

Part 2

The Sun now rose upon the right:
Out of the sea came he,
Still hid in mist, and on the left   85
Went down into the sea.

And the good south wind still blew behind,
But no sweet bird did follow,
Nor any day for food or play
Came to the mariners' hollo!   90

His shipmates cry out
against the ancient
Mariner, for killing the
bird of good luck.

And I had done a hellish thing,
And it would work 'em woe:
For all averred, I had killed the bird
That made the breeze to blow.
Ah wretch! said they, the bird to slay,   95
That made the breeze to blow!

But when the fog
cleared off, they justify
the same, and thus
make themselves
accomplices in the
crime.

Nor dim nor red, like God's own head,
The glorious Sun uprist:
Then all averred, I had killed the bird
That brought the fog and mist.   100
'Twas right, said they, such birds to slay,
That bring the fog and mist.

The fair breeze contin-
ues; the ship enters the
Pacific Ocean, and sails
northward, even until it
reaches the Line.

The fair breeze blew, the white foam flew
The furrow followed free;
We were the first that ever burst   105
Into that silent sea.

The ship hath been
suddenly becalmed.

Down dropt the breeze, the sails dropt down,
'Twas sad as sad could be;
And we did speak only to break
The silence of the sea!   110

All in a hot and copper sky,
The bloody Sun, at noon,
Right up above the mast did stand,
No bigger than the Moon.

Day after day, day after day,   115
We stuck, nor breath nor motion;

And the Albatross
begins to be avenged.

As idle as a painted ship
Upon a painted ocean.

Water, water, everywhere,
And all the boards did shrink;   120
Water, water, everywhere,
Nor any drop to drink.

A spirit had followed
them; one of the
invisible inhabitants of
this planet, neither
departed souls nor
angels; concerning
whom the learned Jew,
Josephus, and the
Platonic Constantino-
politan, Michael
Psellus, may be
consulted. They are
very numerous, and
there is no climate or
element without one
or more.

The very deep did rot: O Christ!
That ever this should be!
Yea, slimy things did crawl with legs   125
Upon the slimy sea.

About, about, in reel and rout
The death-fires° danced at night;   *phosphorescent plankton*
The water, like a witch's oils,
Burnt green, and blue and white.   130

And some in dreams assured were
Of the spirit that plagued us so;
Nine fathoms deep he had followed us
From the land of mist and snow.

And every tongue, through utter drought,   135
Was withered at the root;
We could not speak, no more than if
We had been choked with soot.

The ship-mates, in
their sore distress,
would fain throw the
whole guilt on the
ancient Mariner; in
sign whereof they hang
the dead sea-bird
round his neck.

Ah! well a-day! what evil looks
Had I from old and young!   140
Instead of the cross, the Albatross
About my neck was hung.

Part 3

There passed a weary time. Each throat
Was parched, and glazed each eye.
A weary time! a weary time!   145
How glazed each weary eye,
When looking westward, I beheld
A something in the sky.

The ancient Mariner
beholdeth a sign in the
element afar off.

At first it seemed a little speck,
And then it seemed a mist;   150
It moved and moved, and took at last
A certain shape, I wist.°   *knew*

A speck, a mist, a shape, I wist!
And still it neared and neared:
As if it dodged a water-sprite,   155
It plunged and tacked and veered.

At its nearer approach,
it seemeth him to be a
ship; and at a dear
ransom he freeth his
speech from the bonds
of thirst.

With throats unslaked, with black lips baked,
We could not laugh nor wail;
Through utter drought all dumb we stood!

I bit my arm, I sucked the blood,   160
And cried, A sail! A sail!

A flash of joy;

With throats unslaked, with black lips baked,
Agape they heard me call:
Gramercy!° they for joy did grin,   *many thanks*
And all at once their breath drew in,   165
As they were drinking all.

And horror follows.
For can it be a ship
that comes onward
without wind or tide?

See! see! (I cried) she tacks no more!
Hither to work us weal;°   *benefit*
Without a breeze, without a tide,
She steadies with upright keel!   170

The western wave was all a-flame.
The day was well nigh done!
Almost upon the western wave
Rested the broad bright Sun;
When that strange shape drove suddenly   175
Betwixt us and the Sun.

It seemeth him but the
skeleton of a ship.

And straight the sun was flecked with bars,
(Heaven's Mother send us grace!)
As if through a dungeon-grate he peered
With broad and burning face.   180

And its ribs are seen as
bars on the face of the
setting Sun.

Alas! (thought I, and my heart beat loud)
How fast she nears and nears!
Are those her sails that glance in the Sun,
Like restless gossameres?°   *cobwebs*

The spectre-woman
and her death-mate,
and no other on board
the skeleton-ship.

Are those her ribs through which the Sun   185
Did peer, as through a grate?
And is that Woman all her crew?
Is that a DEATH? and are there two?
Is DEATH that woman's mate?

Like vessel, like crew!

Her lips were red, her looks were free,   190
Her locks were yellow as gold:
Her skin was as white as leprosy,
The Night-Mair LIFE-IN-DEATH was she,
Who thicks man's blood with cold.

DEATH and LIFE-IN-
DEATH have diced for
the ship's crew, and she
(the latter) winneth
the ancient Mariner.

The naked hulk alongside came,   195
And the twain were casting dice;
"The game is done! I've, I've won!"
Quoth she, and whistles thrice.

No twilight within the
courts of the Sun.

The Sun's rim dips; the stars rush out:
At one stride comes the dark;   200
With far-heard whisper, o'er the sea,
Off shot the spectre-bark.

At the rising of the
Moon.

We listened and looked sideways up!
Fear at my heart, as at a cup,
My life-blood seemed to sip!   205

The stars were dim, and thick the night,
The steersman's face by his lamp gleamed white;
From the sails the dew did drip—
Till clomb above the eastern bar
The horned Moon, with one bright star   210
Within the nether tip.

One after another,

One after one, by the star-dogged Moon,
Too quick for groan or sigh,
Each turned his face with a ghastly pang,
And cursed me with his eye.   215

His ship-mates drop
down dead.

Four times fifty living men
(And I heard nor sigh nor groan),
With heavy thump, a lifeless lump,
They dropped down one by one.

But LIFE-IN-DEATH
begins her work on the
ancient Mariner.

The souls did from their bodies fly,—   220
They fled to bliss or woe!
And every soul, it passed me by,
Like the whizz of my cross-bow!

Part 4

The wedding-guest
feareth that a spirit is
talking to him.

"I fear thee, ancient Mariner!
I fear thy skinny hand!   225
And thou art long, and lank, and brown,
As is the ribbed sea-sand.

I fear thee and thy glittering eye,
And thy skinny hand, so brown."—

But the ancient
Mariner assureth him
of his bodily life, and
proceedeth to relate
his horrible penance.

Fear not, fear not, thou wedding-guest!   230
This body dropt not down.

Alone, alone, all, all alone,
Alone on a wide wide sea!
And never a saint took pity on
My soul in agony.   235

He despiseth the
creatures of the calm.

The many men, so beautiful!
And they all dead did lie:
And a thousand thousand slimy things
Lived on; and so did I.

And envieth that they
should live, and so
many lie dead.

I looked upon the rotting sea,   240
And drew my eyes away;
I looked upon the rotting deck,
And there the dead men lay.

I looked to heaven, and tried to pray;
But or ever a prayer had gusht,   245
A wicked whisper came, and made
My heart as dry as dust.

I closed my lids, and kept them close,
And the balls like pulses beat;
For the sky and the sea, and the sea and the sky 250

Lay like a load on my weary eye,
And the dead were at my feet.

The cold sweat melted from their limbs,
Nor rot nor reek did they:
The look with which they looked on me   255
Had never passed away.

An orphan's curse would drag to hell
A spirit from on high;
But oh! more horrible than that
Is the curse in a dead man's eye!   260
Seven days, seven nights, I saw that curse,
And yet I could not die.

The moving Moon went up the sky,
And nowhere did abide:
Softly she was going up,   265
And a star or two beside—

Her beams bemocked the sultry main°   *open sea*
Like April hoar-frost spread;
But where the ship's huge shadow lay,
The charmed water burnt alway   270
A still and awful red.

Beyond the shadow of the ship,
I watched the water-snakes:
They moved in tracks of shining white,
And when they reared, the elfish light   275
Fell off in hoary° flakes.   *frosty*

Within the shadow of the ship
I watched their rich attire:
Blue, glossy green, and velvet black,
They coiled and swam; and every track   280
Was a flash of golden fire.

O happy living things! no tongue
Their beauty might declare:
A spring of love gushed from my heart,
And I blessed them unaware: 285
Sure my kind saint took pity on me,
And I blessed them unaware.

The selfsame moment I could pray;
And from my neck so free
The Albatross fell off, and sank   290
Like lead into the sea.

Part 5

Oh sleep! it is a gentle thing,
Beloved from pole to pole!
To Mary Queen the praise be given!
She sent the gentle sleep from Heaven,   295
That slid into my soul.

The marginal glosses:

But the curse liveth for him in the eye of the dead men.

In his loneliness and fixedness he yearneth towards the journeying Moon, and the stars that still sojourn, yet still move onward; and everywhere the blue sky belongs to them, and is their appointed rest, and their native country and their own natural homes, which they enter unannounced, as lords that are certainly expected, and yet there is a silent joy at their arrival.

By the light of the Moon he beholdeth God's creatures of the great calm.

Their beauty and their happiness.

He blesseth them in his heart.

The spell begins to break.

By grace of the holy Mother, the ancient Mariner is refreshed with rain.

The silly° buckets on the deck,   *simple*
That had so long remained,
I dreamt that they were filled with dew;
And when I awoke, it rained.   300

My lips were wet, my throat was cold,
My garments all were dank;
Sure I had drunken in my dreams,
And still my body drank.

I moved, and could not feel my limbs: 305
I was so light—almost
I thought that I had died in sleep,
And was a blessed ghost.

He heareth sounds and   And soon I heard a roaring wind:
seeth strange sights   It did not come anear;   310
and commotions in the   But with its sound it shook the sails,
sky and the element.   That were so thin and sere.°   *withered*

The upper air burst into life!
And a hundred fire-flags sheen,°   *gleamed*
To and fro they were hurried about!   315
And to and fro, and in and out,
The wan stars danced between.

And the coming wind did roar more loud,
And the sails did sigh like sedge;°   *rush-like grass*
And the rain poured down from one black cloud;   320
The Moon was at its edge.

The thick black cloud was cleft, and still
The Moon was at its side:
Like waters shot from some high crag,
The lightning fell with never a jag,   325
A river steep and wide.

The bodies of the   The loud wind never reached the ship,
ship's crew are   Yet now the ship moved on!
inspired, and the ship   Beneath the lightning and the moon
moves on.   The dead men gave a groan.   330

They groaned, they stirred, they all uprose,
Nor spake, nor moved their eyes;
It had been strange, even in a dream,
To have seen those dead men rise.

The helmsman steered, the ship moved on;   335
Yet never a breeze up blew;
The mariners all 'gan work the ropes,
Where they were wont to do;
They raised their limbs like lifeless tools—
We were a ghastly crew.   340

The body of my brother's son
Stood by me, knee to knee:

The body and I pulled at one rope,
But he said naught to me.

But not by the souls of
the men, nor by
daemons of earth or
middle air, but by a
blessed troop of angelic
spirits, sent down by
the invocation of the
guardian saint.

"I fear thee, ancient Mariner!"   345
Be calm, thou Wedding-Guest!
'Twas not those souls that fled in pain,
Which to their corses came again,
But a troop of spirits blest:

For when it dawned—they dropped their arms,   350
And clustered round the mast;
Sweet sounds rose slowly through their mouths,
And from their bodies passed.

Around, around, flew each sweet sound
Then darted to the Sun;   355
Slowly the sounds came back again,
Now mixed, now one by one.

Sometimes a-dropping from the sky
I heard the sky-lark sing;
Sometimes all little birds that are,   360
How they seemed to fill the sea and air
With their sweet jargoning!°   *warbling*

And now 'twas like all instruments,
Now like a lonely flute;
And now it is an angel's song,   365
That makes the heavens be mute.
It ceased; yet still the sails made on

A pleasant noise till noon,
A noise like of a hidden brook
In the leafy mouth of June,   370
That to the sleeping woods all night
Singeth a quiet tune.

Till noon we quietly sailed on,
Yet never a breeze did breathe:
Slowly and smoothly went the ship,   375
Moved onward from beneath.

The lonesome spirit
from the South Pole
carries on the ship as
far as the line, in
obedience to the
angelic troop, but still
requireth vengeance.

Under the keel nine fathom deep,
From the land of mist and snow,
The spirit slid: and it was he
That made the ship to go.   380
The sails at noon left off their tune,
And the ship stood still also.

The Sun, right up above the mast,
Had fixed her to the ocean:
But in a minute she 'gan stir,   385
With a short uneasy motion—
Backwards and forwards half her length
With a short uneasy motion.

Then like a pawing horse let go,
She made a sudden bound:
It flung the blood into my head,
And I fell down in a swound.   390

How long in that same fit I lay,
I have not to declare;
But ere my living life returned,   395
I heard, and in my soul discerned
Two voices in the air.

The Polar Spirit's fellow daemons, the invisible inhabitants of the element, take part in his wrong; and two of them relate, one to the other, that penance long and heavy for the ancient Mariner hath been accorded to the Polar Spirit, who returneth southward.

"Is it he?" quoth one, "Is this the man?
By him who died on cross,
With his cruel bow he laid full low   400
The harmless Albatross.

"The spirit who bideth by himself
In the land of mist and snow,
He loved the bird that loved the man
Who shot him with his bow."   405

The other was a softer voice,
As soft as honeydew.
Quoth he, "The man hath penance done,
And penance more will do."

Part 6

First voice.

"But tell me, tell me! speak again,   410
Thy soft response renewing—
What makes that ship drive on so fast?
What is the ocean doing?"

Second voice.

"Still as a slave before his lord,
The ocean hath no blast;   415
His great bright eye most silently
Up to the Moon is cast—

If he may know which way to go:
For she guides him smooth or grim.
See, brother, see! how graciously   420
She looketh down on him."

First voice.

"But why drives on that ship so fast,
Without or wave or wind?"

Second voice.

"The air is cut away before,
And closes from behind.   425

The Mariner hath been cast into a trance; for the angelic power causeth the vessel to drive northward faster than human life could endure.

Fly, brother, fly! more high, more high!
Or we shall be belated:
For slow and slow that ship will go,
When the Mariner's trance is abated."

The supernatural
motion is retarded; the
Mariner awakes, and
his penance begins
anew.

I woke, and we were sailing on   430
As in a gentle weather:
'Twas night, calm night, the moon was high;
The dead men stood together.

All stood together on the deck,
For a charnel-dungeon fitter: 435
All fixed on me their stony eyes,
That in the Moon did glitter.

The pang, the curse, with which they died,
Had never passed away:
I could not draw my eyes from theirs,   440
Nor turn them up to pray.

The curse is finally
expiated.

And now this spell was snapped: once more
I viewed the ocean green,
And looked far forth, yet little saw
Of what had else been seen—   445

Like one, that on a lonesome road
Doth walk in fear and dread,
And having once turned round walks on,
And turns no more his head;
Because he knows, a frightful fiend   450
Doth close behind him tread.

But soon there breathed a wind on me,
Nor sound nor motion made:
Its path was not upon the sea,
In ripple or in shade.   455

It raised my hair, it fanned my cheek
Like a meadow-gale of spring—
It mingled strangely with my fears,
Yet it felt like a welcoming.

Swiftly, swiftly flew the ship,   460
Yet she sailed softly too:
Sweetly, sweetly blew the breeze—
On me alone it blew.

And the ancient
Mariner beholdeth his
native country.

Oh! dream of joy! is this indeed
The light-house top I see?   465
Is this the hill? is this the kirk?
Is this mine own countree?

We drifted o'er the harbor-bar,
And I with sobs did pray—
O let me be awake, my God!   470
Or let me sleep alway.

The harbor-bay was clear as glass,
So smoothly it was strewn!
And on the bay the moonlight lay,
And the shadow of the moon.   475

The rock shone bright, the kirk no less,
That stands above the rock:
The moonlight steeped in silentness
The steady weathercock.

And the bay was white with silent light,   480
Till rising from the same,
Full many shapes, that shadows were,
In crimson colors came.

*The angelic spirits
leave the dead bodies,*

A little distance from the prow
Those crimson shadows were: 485
I turned my eyes upon the deck—
Oh, Christ! what saw I there!

*And appear in their
own forms of light.*

Each corse lay flat, lifeless and flat,
And, by the holy rood!°   *cross*
A man all light, a seraph-man,°   *angel* 490
On every corse there stood.

This seraph-band, each waved his hand:
It was a heavenly sight!
They stood as signals to the land,
Each one a lovely light;   495

This seraph-band, each waved his hand,
No voice did they impart—
No voice; but oh! the silence sank
Like music on my heart.

But soon I heard the dash of oars,   500
I heard the Pilot's cheer;
My head was turned perforce away,
And I saw a boat appear.

The Pilot and the Pilot's boy,
I heard them coming fast: 505
Dear Lord in Heaven! it was a joy
The dead men could not blast.

I saw a third—I heard his voice:
It is the Hermit good!
He singeth loud his godly hymns   510
That he makes in the wood.
He'll shrieve° my soul, he'll wash away   *absolve*
The Albatross's blood.

Part 7

*The Hermit of the
wood,*

This Hermit good lives in that wood
Which slopes down to the sea.   515
How loudly his sweet voice he rears!
He loves to talk with mariners
That come from a far countree.

He kneels at morn, and noon, and eve
He hath a cushion plump: 520

It is the moss that wholly hides
The rotted old oak-stump.

The skiff-boat neared: I heard them talk,
"Why, this is strange, I trow!
Where are those lights so many and fair,   525
That signal made but now?"

Approacheth the ship
with wonder.

"Strange, by my faith!" the Hermit said—
"And they answered not our cheer!
The planks looked warped! and see those sails,
How thin they are and sere!   530
I never saw aught like to them,
Unless perchance it were

"Brown skeletons of leaves that lag
My forest-brook along;
When the ivy-tod° is heavy with snow,   *bush*   535
And the owlet whoops to the wolf below,
That eats the she-wolf's young."

"Dear Lord! it hath a fiendish look—
(The Pilot made reply)
I am a-feared"—"Push on, push on!"   540
Said the Hermit cheerily.

The boat came closer to the ship,
But I nor spake nor stirred;
The boat came close beneath the ship,
And straight a sound was heard.   545

The ship suddenly
sinketh.

Under the water it rumbled on,
Still louder and more dread:
It reached the ship, it split the bay;
The ship went down like lead.

The ancient Mariner is
saved in the Pilot's
boat.

Stunned by that loud and dreadful sound,   550
Which sky and ocean smote,
Like one that hath been seven days drowned
My body lay afloat;
But swift as dreams, myself I found
Within the Pilot's boat.   555

Upon the whirl, where sank the ship,
The boat spun round and round;
And all was still, save that the hill
Was telling of the sound.

I moved my lips—the Pilot shrieked   560
And fell down in a fit;
The holy Hermit raised his eyes,
And prayed where he did sit.

I took the oars: the Pilot's boy,
Who now doth crazy go,   565
Laughed loud and long, and all the while

His eyes went to and fro.
"Ha! ha!" quoth he, "full plain I see,
The Devil knows how to row."

And now, all in my own countree,   570
I stood on the firm land!
The Hermit stepped forth from the boat,
And scarcely he could stand.

The ancient Mariner earnestly entreateth the Hermit to shrieve him; and the penance of life falls on him.

"O shrieve me, shrieve me,[6] holy man!"
The Hermit crossed his brow.   575
"Say quick," quoth he, "I bid thee say—
What manner of man art thou?"

Forthwith this frame of mine was wrenched
With a woful agony,
Which forced me to begin my tale;   580
And then it left me free.

And ever and anon throughout his future life an agony constraineth him to travel from land to land.

Since then, at an uncertain hour,
That agony returns:
And till my ghastly tale is told,
This heart within me burns.   585

I pass, like night, from land to land;
I have strange power of speech;
That moment that his face I see,
I know the man that must hear me:
To him my tale I teach.   590

What loud uproar bursts from that door!
The wedding-guests are there:
But in the garden-bower the bride
And bride-maids singing are:
And hark the little vesper-bell,   595
Which biddeth me to prayer!

O Wedding-Guest! this soul hath been
Alone on a wide wide sea:
So lonely 'twas, that God himself
Scarce seemed there to be.   600

O sweeter than the marriage-feast,
'Tis sweeter far to me,
To walk together to the kirk
With a goodly company!—

To walk together to the kirk,   605
And all together pray,
While each to his great Father bends,
Old men, and babes, and loving friends,
And youths and maidens gay!

6. Hear confession and give absolution.

And to teach, by his
own example, love and
reverence to all things
that God made and
loveth.

Farewell, farewell! but this I tell   610
To thee, thou Wedding-Guest!
He prayeth well who loveth well
Both man and bird and beast.

He prayeth best, who loveth best
All things both great and small;   615
For the dear God who loveth us,
He made and loveth all.

The Mariner, whose eye is bright,
Whose beard with age is hoar,
Is gone: and now the Wedding-Guest   620
Turned from the bridegroom's door.

He went like one that hath been stunned,
And is of sense forlorn:
A sadder and a wiser man,
He rose the morrow morn.   625

1797/1817   1817

COMPANION READING

Samuel Taylor Coleridge: from *Table Talk*

May 31, 1830. Mrs. Barbauld once told me that she admired the Ancient Mariner
very much, but that there were two faults in it, it was improbable, and had no moral.
As for the probability, I owned that that might admit some question; but as to the
want of a moral, I told her that in my own judgment the poem had too much; and
that the only, or chief fault, if I might say so, was the obtrusion of the moral sentiment so openly on the reader as a principle or cause of action in a work of such pure
imagination. It ought to have had no more moral than the Arabian Nights' tale of
the merchant's sitting down to eat dates by the side of a well, and throwing the shells
aside, and lo! a genie starts up, and says he *must* kill the aforesaid merchant, *because*
one of the date shells had, it seems, put out the eye of the genie's son.

Kubla Khan[1]

Or, A Vision in a Dream. A Fragment.

The following fragment is here published at the request of a poet of great and
deserving celebrity,[2] and, as far as the author's own opinions are concerned, rather
as a psychological curiosity, than on the ground of any supposed *poetic* merits.

In the summer of the year 1797, the Author, then in ill health, had retired to
a lonely farm-house between Porlock and Linton, on the Exmoor confines of Somerset and Devonshire. In consequence of a slight indisposition, an anodyne[3] had
been prescribed, from the effect of which he fell asleep in his chair at the moment
that he was reading the following sentence, or words of the same substance, in
"Purchas's Pilgrimage":[4] "Here the Khan Kubla commanded a palace to be built,

---

1. Kubla Khan was the grandson of Genghis Khan and
Emperor of China in the 13th century.
2. Byron.
3. A painkiller, probably laudanum.

4. A collection of often fantastical accounts of foreign
lands compiled by Samuel Purchas (1613). As a boy,
Coleridge was an avid reader of such literature.

and a stately garden thereunto: and thus ten miles of fertile ground were inclosed with a wall." The author continued for about three hours in a profound sleep, at least of the external senses, during which time he has the most vivid confidence, that he could not have composed less than from two to three hundred lines; if that indeed can be called composition in which all the images rose up before him as things, with a parallel production of the correspondent expressions, without any sensation or consciousness of effort. On awaking he appeared to himself to have a distinct recollection of the whole, and taking his pen, ink, and paper, instantly and eagerly wrote down the lines that are here preserved. At this moment he was unfortunately called out by a person on business from Porlock, and detained by him above an hour, and on his return to his room, found, to his no small surprise and mortification, that though he still retained some vague and dim recollection of the general purport of the vision, yet, with the exception of some eight or ten scattered lines and images, all the rest had passed away like the images on the surface of a stream into which a stone had been cast, but, alas! without the after restoration of the latter:

> Then all the charm
> Is broken—all that phantom-world so fair
> Vanishes, and a thousand circlets spread,
> And each mis-shape[s] the other. Stay awhile,
> Poor youth! who scarcely dar'st lift up thine eyes—
> The stream will soon renew its smoothness, soon
> The visions will return! And lo! he stays,
> And soon the fragments dim of lovely forms
> Come trembling back, unite, and now once more
> The pool becomes a mirror.[5]

Yet from the still surviving recollections in his mind, the Author has frequently purposed to finish for himself what had been originally, as it were, given to him. Σαμερον αδιον ασω:[6] but the to-morrow is yet to come.

As a contrast to this vision, I have annexed a fragment of a very different character, describing with equal fidelity the dream of pain and disease.[7]

(1816)

Kubla Khan

In Xanadu did Kubla Khan
A stately pleasure-dome decree:
Where Alph, the sacred river, ran
Through caverns measureless to man
5 Down to a sunless sea.
So twice five miles of fertile ground
With walls and towers were girdled round:
And there were gardens bright with sinuous rills,
Where blossomed many an incense-bearing tree;
10 And here were forests ancient as the hills,
Enfolding sunny spots of greenery.

5. From Coleridge's *The Picture* (lines 91–100).
6. From Theocritus, *Idylls*, line 145: "I'll sing a sweeter song tomorrow."
7. *The Pains of Sleep*.

But oh! that deep romantic chasm which slanted
Down the green hill athwart a cedarn cover!
A savage place! as holy and enchanted
15 As e'er beneath a waning moon was haunted
By woman wailing for her demon-lover!
And from this chasm, with ceaseless turmoil seething,
As if this earth in fast thick pants were breathing,
A mighty fountain momently was forced:
20 Amid whose swift half-intermitted burst
Huge fragments vaulted like rebounding hail,
Or chaffy grain beneath the thresher's flail:
And mid these dancing rocks at once and ever
It flung up momently the sacred river.
25 Five miles meandering with a mazy motion
Through wood and dale the sacred river ran,
Then reached the caverns measureless to man,
And sank in tumult to a lifeless ocean:
And 'mid this tumult Kubla heard from far
30 Ancestral voices prophesying war!
        The shadow of the dome of pleasure
        Floated midway on the waves;
        Where was heard the mingled measure
        From the fountain and the caves.
35 It was a miracle of rare device,
A sunny pleasure-dome with caves of ice!

        A damsel with a dulcimer
        In a vision once I saw:
        It was an Abyssinian maid,
40   And on her dulcimer she played,
        Singing of Mount Abora.
        Could I revive within me
        Her symphony and song,
        To such a deep delight 'twould win me,
45 That with music loud and long,
I would build that dome in air,
That sunny dome! those caves of ice!
And all who heard should see them there,
And all should cry, Beware! Beware!
50 His flashing eyes, his floating hair!
Weave a circle round him thrice,
And close your eyes with holy dread,
For he on honey-dew hath fed,
And drunk the milk of Paradise.

1797–1798   1816

Frost at Midnight

The Frost performs its secret ministry,
Unhelped by any wind. The owlet's cry
Came loud—and hark, again! loud as before.

The inmates of my cottage, all at rest,
5   Have left me to that solitude, which suits
Abstruser musings: save that at my side
My cradled infant slumbers peacefully.
'Tis calm indeed! so calm, that it disturbs
And vexes meditation with its strange
10 And extreme silentness. Sea, hill, and wood
This populous village! Sea, and hill, and wood,
With all the numberless goings on of life,
Inaudible as dreams! the thin blue flame
Lies on my low burnt fire, and quivers not;
15 Only that film,[1] which fluttered on the grate,
Still flutters there, the sole unquiet thing.
Methinks, its motion in this hush of nature
Gives it dim sympathies with me who live,
Making it a companionable form,
20 Whose puny flaps and freaks the idling Spirit
By its own moods interprets, everywhere
Echo or mirror seeking of itself,
And makes a toy of Thought.

                                But O! how oft,
How oft, at school, with most believing mind,
25 Presageful, have I gazed upon the bars,
To watch that fluttering stranger! and as oft
With unclosed lids, already had I dreamt
Of my sweet birth-place, and the old church-tower,
Whose bells, the poor man's only music, rang
30 From morn to evening, all the hot fair-day,
So sweetly, that they stirred and haunted me
With a wild pleasure, falling on mine ear
Most like articulate sounds of things to come!
So gazed I, till the soothing things I dreamt
35 Lulled me to sleep, and sleep prolonged my dreams!
And so I brooded all the following morn,
Awed by the stern preceptor's° face, mine eye   *teacher's*
Fixed with mock study on my swimming book:
Save if the door half opened, and I snatched
40 A hasty glance, and still my heart leaped up,
For still I hoped to see the stranger's face,
Townsman, or aunt, or sister more beloved,
My playmate when we both were clothed alike![2]

    Dear Babe, that sleepest cradled by my side,
45 Whose gentle breathings, heard in this deep calm,
Fill up the interspersed vacancies
And momentary pauses of the thought!
My babe so beautiful! it thrills my heart

---

1. A piece of soot. "In all parts of the kingdom these films   some absent friend" (Coleridge's note).
are called *strangers* and supposed to portend the arrival of   2. Boys and girls wore the same clothes until age 5.

With tender gladness, thus to look at thee,
50   And think that thou shalt learn far other lore
And in far other scenes! For I was reared
In the great city, pent 'mid cloisters dim,
And saw naught lovely but the sky and stars.
But *thou*, my babe! shalt wander like a breeze
55   By lakes and sandy shores, beneath the crags
Of ancient mountain, and beneath the clouds,
Which image in their bulk both lakes and shores
And mountain crags: so shalt thou see and hear
The lovely shapes and sounds intelligible
60   Of that eternal language, which thy God
Utters, who from eternity doth teach
Himself in all, and all things in himself.
Great universal Teacher! he shall mould
Thy spirit, and by giving make it ask.

65   Therefore all seasons shall be sweet to thee,
Whether the summer clothe the general earth
With greenness, or the redbreast sit and sing
Betwixt the tufts of snow on the bare branch
Of mossy apple-tree, while the nigh thatch
70   Smokes in the sun-thaw; whether the eave-drops fall
Heard only in the trances of the blast,
Or if the secret ministry of frost
Shall hang them up in silent icicles,
Quietly shining to the quiet Moon.

February 1798   1798

Dejection: An Ode[1]

Late, late yestreen I saw the new Moon,
        With the old Moon in her arms;
And I fear, I fear, my Master dear!
        We shall have a deadly storm.

Ballad of Sir Patrick Spence[2]

1

Well! If the Bard was weather-wise, who made
        The grand old ballad of Sir Patrick Spence,
            This night, so tranquil now, will not go hence
    Unroused by winds, that ply a busier trade
5   Than those which mould yon cloud in lazy flakes,
        Or the dull sobbing draft, that moans and rakes
            Upon the strings of this Aeolian lute,[3]

1. *Dejection* evolved from a long verse-letter that Coleridge wrote to Sara Hutchinson in April 1802, after hearing the opening stanzas of Wordsworth's *Ode: Intimations of Immortality* (see page 1610). Cutting the verse letter by half, Coleridge published it on October 4, 1802, Wordsworth's wedding day and the seventh anniversary of his own unhappy marriage.

2. A traditional ballad printed in Thomas Percy's *Reliques of Ancient Poetry* (1765), which profoundly influenced both Coleridge and Wordsworth.

3. An instrument named after Aeolus, the Greek god of winds; see *The Eolian Harp*, page 1637.

Which better far were mute.
For lo! the New-moon winter-bright!
10   And overspread with phantom light,
(With swimming phantom light o'erspread
But rimmed and circled by a silver thread)
I see the old Moon in her lap, foretelling
The coming on of rain and squally blast.
15   And oh! that even now the gust were swelling,
And the slant night-shower driving loud and fast!
Those sounds which oft have raised me, whilst they awed,
And sent my soul abroad,
Might now, perhaps, their wonted impulse give,
20   Might startle this dull pain, and make it move and live!

2

A grief without a pang, void, dark, and drear,
A stifled, drowsy, unimpassioned grief,
Which finds no natural outlet, no relief,
In word, or sigh, or tear—
25   O Lady! in this wan and heartless mood,
To other thoughts by yonder throstle° woo'd,   *thrush*
All this long eve, so balmy and serene,
Have I been gazing on the western sky,
And its peculiar tint of yellow green:
30   And still I gaze—and with how blank an eye!
And those thin clouds above, in flakes and bars,
That give away their motion to the stars;
Those stars, that glide behind them or between,
Now sparkling, now bedimmed, but always seen:
35   Yon crescent Moon, as fixed as if it grew
In its own cloudless, starless lake of blue;
I see them all so excellently fair,
I see, not feel how beautiful they are!

3

My genial° spirits fail;   *creative*
40   And what can these avail
To lift the smothering weight from off my breast?
It were a vain endeavor,
Though I should gaze forever
On that green light that lingers in the west:
45   I may not hope from outward forms to win
The passion and the life, whose fountains are within.

4

O Lady! we receive but what we give,
And in our life alone does Nature live:
Ours is her wedding-garment, ours her shroud!
50   And would we aught behold, of higher worth,
Than that inanimate° cold world allowed   *soulless*
To the poor loveless ever-anxious crowd,
Ah! from the soul itself must issue forth,
A light, a glory, a fair luminous cloud
55   Enveloping the Earth—
And from the soul itself must there be sent

A sweet and potent voice, of its own birth,
Of all sweet sounds the life and element!

5

O pure of heart; thou need'st not ask of me

60 What this strong music in the soul may be!
What, and wherein it doth exist,
This light, this glory, this fair luminous mist,
This beautiful and beauty-making power.
      Joy, virtuous Lady! Joy that ne'er was given,

65 Save to the pure, and in their purest hour,
Life, and Life's effluence, cloud at once and shower
Joy, Lady! is the spirit and the power
Which wedding Nature to us gives in dower,
      A new Earth and new Heaven,

70 Undreamt of by the sensual and the proud—
Joy is the sweet voice, Joy the luminous cloud—
      We in ourselves rejoice!
And thence flows all that charms or ear or sight,
      All melodies the echoes of that voice,

75 All colors a suffusion from that light.

6

There was a time when, though my path was rough,
      This joy within me dallied with distress,
And all misfortunes were but as the stuff
      Whence Fancy made me dreams of happiness:

80 For hope grew round me, like the twining vine,
And fruits, and foliage, not my own, seemed mine.
But now afflictions bow me down to earth:
Nor care I that they rob me of my mirth,
      But oh! each visitation

85 Suspends what nature gave me at my birth,
      My shaping spirit of Imagination.
For not to think of what I needs must feel,
      But to be still and patient, all I can;
And haply by abstruse research to steal

90 From my own nature all the natural man—
      This was my sole resource, my only plan:
Till that which suits a part infects the whole,
And now is almost grown the habit of my soul.

7

Hence, viper thoughts, that coil around my mind,
95   Reality's dark dream!
I turn from you, and listen to the wind,
      Which long has raved unnoticed. What a scream
Of agony by torture lengthened out
That lute sent forth! Thou Wind, that ravest without,

100 Bare craig, or mountain-tairn,° or blasted tree,   *pond*
Or pine-grove whither woodman never clomb,
Or lonely house, long held the witches' home,
      Methinks were fitter instruments for thee,
Mad Lutanist! who in this month of showers,

105 Of dark-brown gardens, and of peeping flowers,

Mak'st Devils' yule,° with worse than wintry song,   *Christmas*
The blossoms, buds, and timorous leaves among.
   Thou Actor, perfect in all tragic sounds!
Thou mighty Poet, e'en to frenzy bold!
110   What tell'st thou now about?
      'Tis of the rushing of a host in rout,
   With groans of trampled men, with smarting wounds—
At once they groan with pain, and shudder with the cold!
But hush! there is a pause of deepest silence!
115   And all that noise, as of a rushing crowd,
With groans and tremulous shudderings—all is over—
   It tells another tale, with sounds less deep and loud!
      A tale of less affright,
      And tempered with delight,
120 As Otway's self had framed the tender lay,[4]
      'Tis of a little child,
      Upon a lonesome wild,
Not far from home, but she hath lost her way:
And now moans low in bitter grief and fear,
125 And now screams loud, and hopes to make her mother hear.

8

'Tis midnight, but small thoughts have I of sleep;
Full seldom may my friend such vigils keep!
Visit her, gentle Sleep! with wings of healing,
   And may this storm be but a mountain-birth,°   *short-lived*
130 May all the stars hang bright above her dwelling,
   Silent as though they watched the sleeping Earth!
      With light heart may she rise,
      Gay fancy, cheerful eyes,
Joy lift her spirit, joy attune her voice;
135 To her may all things live, from pole to pole,
Their life the eddying of her living soul!
   O simple spirit, guided from above,
Dear Lady! friend devoutest of my choice,
Thus mayest thou ever, evermore rejoice.

1802   1802

Work Without Hope
Lines Composed 21st February, 1825

All Nature seems at work. Slugs leave their lair—
The bees are stirring—birds are on the wing—
And Winter slumbering in the open air,
Wears on his smiling face a dream of Spring!
5 And I, the while, the sole unbusy thing,
Nor honey make, nor pair, nor build, nor sing.

Yet well I ken° the banks where amaranths° blow,   *know / fadeless flowers*
Have traced the fount whence streams of nectar flow.

---

4. Thomas Otway, author of *The Orphan* (1680) and other tragedies noted for their pathos. In earlier versions the reference is to "William," probably alluding to Wordsworth's *Lucy Gray* (see page 1541).

10   Bloom, O ye amaranths! bloom for whom ye may,
     For me ye bloom not! Glide, rich streams, away!
     With lips unbrightened, wreathless brow, I stroll:
     And would you learn the spells that drowse my soul?
     Work without Hope draws nectar in a sieve,
     And Hope without an object cannot live.

1825   1828

Constancy to an Ideal Object

     Since all that beat about in Nature's range,
     Or° veer or vanish; why shouldst thou remain   *either*
     The only constant in a world of change,
     O yearning Thought! that liv'st but in the brain?
5   Call to the Hours, that in the distance play,
     The faery people of the future day—
     Fond Thought! not one of all that shining swarm
     Will breathe on thee with life-enkindling breath,
     Till when, like strangers shelt'ring from a storm,
10   Hope and Despair meet in the porch of Death!
     Yet still thou haunt'st me; and though well I see,
     She is not thou, and only thou art she,
     Still, still as though some dear embodied Good,
     Some living Love before my eyes there stood
15   With answering look a ready ear to lend,
     I mourn to thee and say—"Ah! loveliest friend!
     That this the meed of all my toils might be,
     To have a home, an English home, and thee!"
     Vain repetition! Home and Thou are one.
20   The peacefull'st cot,° the moon shall shine upon,   *cottage*
     Lulled by the thrush, and wakened by the lark,
     Without thee were but a becalmed bark,°   *boat*
     Whose Helmsman on an ocean waste and wide
     Sits mute and pale his mouldering helm beside.

25   And art thou nothing? Such thou art, as when
     The woodman winding westward up the glen
     At wintry dawn, where o'er the sheep-track's maze
     The viewless° snow-mist weaves a glist'ning haze,   *invisible*
     Sees full before him, gliding without tread,
30   An image with a glory round its head;[1]
     The enamored rustic worships its fair hues,
     Nor knows he makes the shadow, he pursues!

                                                                     1828

Epitaph

     Stop, Christian Passer-by—Stop, child of God,
     And read with gentle breast. Beneath this sod
     A poet lies, or that which once seem'd he—

---

1. Coleridge refers to the phenomenon in which a walker in the mountains, the sun behind him, casts a magnified self-image onto the mists before him. See *Dejection: An Ode*, line 54.

O lift one thought in prayer for S. T. C.;
5   That he who many a year with toil of breath
Found death in life, may here find life in death!
Mercy for° praise—to be forgiven for° fame   *instead of*
He ask'd, and hoped, through Christ. Do thou the same!
1833   1834

from Biographia Literaria
or, Biographical Sketches of My Literary Life and Opinions[1]

from Chapter 13

[IMAGINATION AND FANCY]

Thus far had the work been transcribed for the press, when I received the following letter from a friend,[2] whose practical judgement I have had ample reason to estimate and revere, and whose taste and sensibility preclude all the excuses which my self-love might possibly have prompted me to set up in plea against the decision of advisers of equal good sense, but with less tact and feeling.

Dear C.

You ask my opinion concerning your Chapter on the Imagination, both as to the impressions it made on myself, and as to those which I think it will make on the PUBLIC, *i.e. that part of the public, who from the title of the work and from its forming a sort of introduction to a volume of poems, are likely to constitute the great majority of your readers.*

As to myself, and stating in the first place the effect on my understanding, your opinions and method of argument were not only so new to me, but so directly the reverse of all I had ever been accustomed to consider as truth, that even if I had comprehended your premises sufficiently to have admitted them, and had seen the necessity of your conclusions, I should still have been in that state of mind, which in your note, p. 75, 76, you have so ingeniously evolved, as the antithesis to that in which a man is, when he makes a bull.[3] In your own words, I should have felt as if I had been standing on my head.

The effect on my feelings, on the other hand, I cannot better represent, than by supposing myself to have known only our light airy modern chapels of ease, and then for the first time to have been placed, and left alone, in one of our largest Gothic cathedrals in a gusty moonlight night of autumn. "Now in glimmer, and now in gloom;"[4] often in palpable darkness not without a chilly sensation of terror; then suddenly emerging into broad yet visionary

1. In 1803 Coleridge contemplated writing "my metaphysical works *as my life*, & *in my life*—intermixed with all the other events of history of the mind and fortunes of S.T. Coleridge." Nothing came of this characteristically Romantic interfusion of personal experience and philosophical generalization until 1815, when Coleridge decided to prefix to a collected edition of his poems "a general preface . . . on the principles" of criticism. Wordsworth's *Poems* (1815), with an extensive essay supplementary to the *Lyrical Ballads* Preface of 1800–1802, further prompted Coleridge to clarify his theoretical divergences from his former collaborator. The resulting *Biographia Literaria*, grown from preface to an independent two-volume work, is an extraordinary text: a revisionary autobiography, in which Coleridge minimizes his youthful radicalism; a philosophical argument to establish the freedom of the will, yet so enmeshed in the material exigencies of book production that publication was delayed for two years; a meditation on original genius heavily indebted to recent German thought; and, in Chapter 13, a comic masquerade that has proved one of the seminal passages for subsequent literary studies. In his sustained, probing commentary on Wordsworth, unprecedented in discussions of modern literature, Coleridge confirmed Wordsworth's stature and, at the same time, by claiming to understand Wordsworth better than he did himself, institutionalized the role of the critic as the reader who completes the poet's task.

2. Coleridge wrote the letter himself.

3. That is, when he unwittingly contradicts himself, thereby leaving himself open to ridicule.

4. From his poem *Christabel*, line 169.

lights with coloured shadows, of fantastic shapes yet all decked with holy insignia and mystic symbols; and ever and anon coming out full upon pictures and stone-work images of great men, with whose names I was familiar, but which looked upon me with countenances and an expression, the most dissimilar to all I had been in the habit of connecting with those names. Those whom I had been taught to venerate as almost super-human in magnitude of intellect, I found perched in little fret-work niches, as grotesque dwarfs; while the grotesques, in my hitherto belief, stood guarding the high altar with all the characters of Apotheosis.[5] *In short, what I had supposed substances were thinned away into shadows, while every where shadows were deepened into substances:*

> If substance may be call'd what shadow seem'd,
> For each seem'd either!

Milton[6]

Yet after all, I could not but repeat the lines which you had quoted from a MS. poem of your own in the FRIEND,[7] *and applied to a work of Mr. Wordsworth's though with a few of the words altered:*

> ————An orphic tale indeed,
> A tale obscure of high and passionate thoughts
> To a strange music chaunted![8]

Be assured, however, that I look forward anxiously to your great book on the CON-STRUCTIVE PHILOSOPHY,[9] *which you have promised and announced: and that I will do my best to understand it. Only I will not promise to descend into the dark cave of Trophonius*[1] *with you, there to rub my own eyes, in order to make the sparks and figured flashes, which I am required to see.*

So much for myself. But as for the PUBLIC, *I do not hesitate a moment in advising and urging you to withdraw the Chapter from the present work, and to reserve it for your announced treatises on the Logos or communicative intellect in Man and Deity.*[2] *First, because imperfectly as I understand the present Chapter, I see clearly that you have done too much, and yet not enough. You have been obliged to omit so many links, from the necessity of compression, that what remains, looks (if I may recur to my former illustration) like the fragments of the winding steps of an old ruined tower. Secondly, a still stronger argument (at least one that I am sure will be more forcible with you) is, that your readers will have both right and reason to complain of you. This Chapter, which cannot, when it is printed, amount to so little as an hundred pages, will of necessity greatly increase the expense of the work; and every reader who, like myself, is neither prepared or perhaps calculated for the study of so abstruse a subject so abstrusely treated, will, as I have before hinted, be almost entitled to accuse you of a sort of imposition on him. For who, he might truly observe, could from your title-page, viz.* "𝔐𝔶 𝔏𝔦𝔱𝔢𝔯𝔞𝔯𝔶 𝔏𝔦𝔣𝔢 𝔞𝔫𝔡 𝔒𝔭𝔦𝔫𝔦𝔬𝔫𝔰," *published too as introductory to a volume of miscellaneous poems, have anticipated, or even conjectured, a long treatise on ideal Realism, which holds the same relation in abstruseness to Plotinus, as Plotinus does to*

---

5. Divinity.
6. *Paradise Lost*, 2.669–70, misquoted.
7. A journal produced by Coleridge in the years 1809–1810.
8. *To William Wordsworth*, lines 45–47 (variant), referring to the 1805 *Prelude*.
9. Perhaps the *Logic* or *Opus Maximum*, perhaps a more general reference to Coleridge's Kantian model of systematic philosophy.

1. Legendary architect of the temple of Apollo at Delphi. After his death an oracle was consecrated to him; visitors were dragged into a cave filled with strange sounds and glaring lights, where they received the oracle's messages.
2. The Word of God, associated with the incarnation of Jesus Christ. Coleridge announced a study of the Gospel of John as part of a work that never appeared, the *Logosophia*.

Plato.[3] *It will be well, if already you have not too much of metaphysical disquisition in your work, though as the larger part of the disquisition is historical, it will doubtless be both interesting and instructive to many to whose* unprepared *minds your speculations on the esemplastic power*[4] *would be utterly unintelligible. Be assured, if you do publish this Chapter in the present work, you will be reminded of Bishop Berkley's Siris,*[5] *announced as an Essay on Tar-water, which beginning with Tar ends with the Trinity, the omne scibile [everything knowable] forming the interspace. I say in the* present *work. In that greater work to which you have devoted so many years, and study so intense and various, it will be in its proper place. Your prospectus will have described and announced both its contents and their nature; and if any persons purchase it, who feel no interest in the subjects of which it treats, they will have themselves only to blame.*

I could add to these arguments one derived from pecuniary[6] *motives, and particularly from the probable effects on the sale of your present publication; but they would weigh little with you compared with the preceding. Besides, I have long observed, that arguments drawn from your own personal interests more often act on you as narcotics than as stimulants, and that in money concerns you have some small portion of pignature in your moral idiosyncracy, and like these amiable creatures, must occasionally be pulled backward from the boat in order to make you enter it. All success attend you, for if hard thinking and hard reading are merits, you have deserved it.*

Your affectionate, &c.

In consequence of this very judicious letter, which produced complete conviction on my mind, I shall content myself for the present with stating the main result of the Chapter, which I have reserved for that future publication, a detailed prospectus of which the reader will find at the close of the second volume.

The IMAGINATION then I consider either as primary, or secondary. The primary IMAGINATION I hold to be the living Power and prime Agent of all human Perception, and as a repetition in the finite mind of the eternal act of creation in the infinite I AM. The secondary I consider as an echo of the former, co-existing with the conscious will, yet still as identical with the primary in the *kind* of its agency, and differing only in *degree*, and in the *mode* of its operation. It dissolves, diffuses, dissipates, in order to re-create; or where this process is rendered impossible, yet still at all events it struggles to idealize and to unify. It is essentially *vital*, even as all objects (*as* objects) are essentially fixed and dead.

FANCY, on the contrary, has no other counters to play with, but fixities and definites. The Fancy is indeed no other than a mode of Memory emancipated from the order of time and space; and blended with, and modified by that empirical phenomenon of the will, which we express by the word CHOICE. But equally with the ordinary memory it must receive all its materials ready made from the law of association.

Whatever more than this, I shall think it fit to declare concerning the powers and privileges of the imagination in the present work, will be found in the critical

---

3. Coleridge saw himself as an "ideal realist," rejecting the Platonic distinction between the essence and appearance of things, for an idea of the world intuited whole by the indwelling human spirit, a position derived from Plato's inheritor Plotinus. The perceptions of that Spirit are thus both ideal and real at once.
4. A term of Coleridge's own invention; "esemplastic" means unifying or synthesizing.

5. George Berkeley (1685–1753), Irish bishop and philosopher. *Siris* (1744) begins with a chemical description of the medicinal advantages of tar and proceeds from there to reflections on theology. It impressed Coleridge as an example of philosophy tied to the empirical truths of the natural sciences.
6. Financial.

essay on the uses of the Supernatural in poetry and the principles that regulate its introduction: which the reader will find prefixed to the poem of 𝕿𝖍𝖊 𝕬𝖓𝖈𝖎𝖊𝖓𝖙 𝕸𝖆𝖗𝖎𝖓𝖊𝖗.

from *Chapter 14*

[OCCASION OF THE *LYRICAL BALLADS*—PREFACE TO THE SECOND EDITION—
THE ENSUING CONTROVERSY]

During the first year that Mr. Wordsworth and I were neighbours, our conversations turned frequently on the two cardinal points of poetry, the power of exciting the sympathy of the reader by a faithful adherence to the truth of nature, and the power of giving the interest of novelty by the modifying colours of imagination. The sudden charm, which accidents of light and shade, which moon-light or sun-set diffused over a known and familiar landscape, appeared to represent the practicability of combining both. These are the poetry of nature. The thought suggested itself (to which of us I do not recollect) that a series of poems might be composed of two sorts. In the one, the incidents and agents were to be, in part at least, supernatural; and the excellence aimed at was to consist in the interesting of the affections by the dramatic truth of such emotions, as would naturally accompany such situations, supposing them real. And real in *this* sense they have been to every human being who, from whatever source of delusion, has at any time believed himself under supernatural agency. For the second class, subjects were to be chosen from ordinary life; the characters and incidents were to be such, as will be found in every village and its vicinity, where there is a meditative and feeling mind to seek after them, or to notice them, when they present themselves.

In this idea originated the plan of the "Lyrical Ballads"; in which it was agreed, that my endeavours should be directed to persons and characters supernatural, or at least romantic; yet so as to transfer from our inward nature a human interest and a semblance of truth sufficient to procure for these shadows of imagination that willing suspension of disbelief for the moment, which constitutes poetic faith. Mr. Wordsworth, on the other hand, was to propose to himself as his object, to give the charm of novelty to things of every day, and to excite a feeling analogous to the supernatural, by awakening the mind's attention from the lethargy of custom, and directing it to the loveliness and the wonders of the world before us; an inexhaustible treasure, but for which in consequence of the film of familiarity and selfish solicitude we have eyes, yet see not, ears that hear not, and hearts that neither feel nor understand.

With this view I wrote the "Ancient Mariner," and was preparing among other poems, the "Dark Ladie," and the "Christabel," in which I should have more nearly realized my ideal, than I had done in my first attempt. But Mr. Wordsworth's industry had proved so much more successful, and the number of his poems so much greater, that my compositions, instead of forming a balance, appeared rather an interpolation of heterogeneous matter. Mr. Wordsworth added two or three poems written in his own character, in the impassioned, lofty, and sustained diction, which is characteristic of his genius. In this form the *Lyrical Ballads* were published; and were presented by him, as an *experiment*,[1] whether subjects, which from their nature rejected the usual ornaments and extra-colloquial style of poems in general, might not be so managed in the language of ordinary life as to produce the pleasurable interest, which it is the peculiar business of poetry to impart. To the second edition he added a preface of

---

1. "Experiments" is Wordsworth's term in the Advertisement to the 1798 *Lyrical Ballads*.

considerable length; in which notwithstanding some passages of apparently a contrary import, he was understood to contend for the extension of this style to poetry of all kinds, and to reject as vicious and indefensible all phrases and forms of style that were not included in what he (unfortunately, I think, adopting an equivocal expression) called the language of *real life*. From this preface, prefixed to poems in which it was impossible to deny the presence of original genius, however mistaken its direction might be deemed, arose the whole long continued controversy. For from the conjunction of perceived power with supposed heresy I explain the inveteracy[2] and in some instances, I grieve to say, the acrimonious passions, with which the controversy has been conducted by the assailants.

Had Mr. Wordsworth's poems been the silly, the childish things, which they were for a long time described as being; had they been really distinguished from the compositions of other poets merely by meanness of language and inanity of thought; had they indeed contained nothing more than what is found in the parodies and pretended imitations of them; they must have sunk at once, a dead weight, into the slough of oblivion, and have dragged the preface along with them. But year after year increased the number of Mr. Wordworth's admirers. They were found too not in the lower classes of the reading public, but chiefly among young men of strong sensibility and meditative minds; and their admiration (inflamed perhaps in some degree by opposition) was distinguished by its intensity, I might almost say, by its *religious* fervour. These facts, and the intellectual energy of the author, which was more or less consciously felt, where it was outwardly and even boisterously denied, meeting with sentiments of aversion to his opinions, and of alarm at their consequences, produced an eddy of criticism, which would of itself have borne up the poems by the violence, with which it whirled them round and round. With many parts of this preface in the sense attributed to them and which the words undoubtedly seem to authorise, I never concurred; but on the contrary objected to them as erroneous in principle, and as contradictory (in appearance at least) both to other parts of the same preface, and to the author's own practice in the greater number of the poems themselves. Mr. Wordsworth in his recent collection has, I find, degraded this prefatory disquisition to the end of his second volume, to be read or not at the reader's choice.[3] But he has not, as far as I can discover, announced any change in his poetic creed. [At] all events, considering it as the source of a controversy, in which I have been honored more, than I deserve, by the frequent conjunction of my name with his, I think it expedient to declare once for all, in what points I coincide with his opinions, and in what points I altogether differ. But in order to render myself intelligible I must previously, in as few words as possible, explain my ideas, first, of a POEM; and secondly, of POETRY itself, in *kind*, and in *essence*.

[PHILOSOPHIC DEFINITIONS OF A POEM AND POETRY]

A poem is that species of composition, which is opposed to works of science, by proposing for its *immediate* object pleasure, not truth; and from all other species (having *this* object in common with it) it is discriminated by proposing to itself such delight from the *whole*, as is compatible with a distinct gratification from each component *part*. * * *

But if this should be admitted as a satisfactory character of a poem, we have still to seek for a definition of poetry. The writings of PLATO, and Bishop TAYLOR, and the

---

2. Deep-seated prejudice.

3. *Poems* (1815), the edition in which Wordsworth represented his works.

Theoria Sacra of BURNET,[4] furnish undeniable proofs that poetry of the highest kind may exist without metre, and even without the contra-distinguishing objects of a poem. The first chapter of Isaiah (indeed a very large proportion of the whole book) is poetry in the most emphatic sense; yet it would be not less irrational than strange to assert, that pleasure, and not truth, was the immediate object of the prophet. In short, whatever *specific* import we attach to the word, poetry, there will be found involved in it, as a necessary consequence, that a poem of any length neither can be, or ought to be, all poetry. * * *

What is poetry? is so nearly the same question with, what is a poet? that the answer to the one is involved in the solution of the other. For it is a distinction resulting from the poetic genius itself, which sustains and modifies the images, thoughts, and emotions of the poet's own mind. The poet, described in ideal per-fection, brings the whole soul of man into activity, with the subordination of its faculties to each other, according to their relative worth and dignity. He diffuses a tone, and spirit of unity, that blends, and (as it were) *fuses*, each into each, by that synthetic and magical power, to which we have exclusively appropriated the name of imagination. This power, first put in action by the will and understanding, and retained under their irremissive, though gentle and unnoticed, controul (*laxis effer-tur habenis* [guided by loose reins]) reveals itself in the balance or reconciliation of opposite or discordant qualities: of sameness, with difference; of the general, with the concrete; the idea, with the image; the individual, with the representative; the sense of novelty and freshness, with old and familiar objects; a more than usual state of emotion, with more than usual order; judgement ever awake and steady self-possession, with enthusiasm and feeling profound or vehement; and while it blends and harmonizes the natural and the artificial, still subordinates art to nature; the manner to the matter; and our admiration of the poet to our sympathy with the poetry. * * *

Finally, GOOD SENSE is the BODY of poetic genius, FANCY its DRAPERY, MOTION its LIFE, and IMAGINATION the SOUL that is every where, and in each; and forms all into one graceful and intelligent whole.

from *Chapter 17*

[EXAMINATION OF THE TENETS PECULIAR TO MR. WORDSWORTH.
RUSTIC LIFE AND POETIC LANGUAGE]

As far then as Mr. Wordsworth in his preface contended, and most ably contended, for a reformation in our poetic diction, as far as he has evinced the truth of passion, and the *dramatic* propriety of those figures and metaphors in the original poets, which stript of their justifying reasons, and converted into mere artifices of connection or ornament, constitute the characteristic falsity in the poetic style of the moderns; and as far as he has, with equal acuteness and clearness, pointed out the process in which this change was effected, and the resemblances between that state into which the reader's mind is thrown by the pleasureable confusion of thought from an unaccus-tomed train of words and images; and that state which is induced by the natural language of empassioned feeling; he undertook a useful task, and deserves all praise, both for the attempt and for the execution. * * *

4. The Greek philosopher Plato, Jeremy Taylor, author of *Holy Living* and *Holy Dying* (1650–51), and the 17th-century theologian Thomas Burnet are singled out for the poetical quality of their prose writing.

My own differences from certain supposed parts of Mr. Wordsworth's theory ground themselves on the assumption, that his words had been rightly interpreted, as purporting that the proper diction for poetry in general consists altogether in a language taken, with due exceptions, from the mouths of men in real life, a language which actually constitutes the natural conversation of men under the influence of natural feelings. * * * The poet informs his reader, that he had generally chosen *low and rustic* life; but not *as* low and rustic, or in order to repeat that pleasure of doubtful moral effect, which persons of elevated rank and of superior refinement oftentimes derive from a happy *imitation* of the rude unpolished manners and discourse of their inferiors. * * * He chose low and rustic life, "because in that condition the essential passions of the heart find a better soil, in which they can attain their maturity, are less under restraint, and speak a plainer and more emphatic language; because in that condition of life our elementary feelings coexist in a state of greater simplicity, and consequently may be more accurately contemplated, and more forcibly communicated; because the manners of rural life germinate from those elementary feelings; and from the necessary character of rural occupations are more easily comprehended, and are more durable; and lastly, because in that condition the passions of men are incorporated with the beautiful and permanent forms of nature."

Now it is clear to me, that in the most interesting of the poems, in which the author is more or less dramatic, as the "Brothers," "Michael," "Ruth," the "Mad Mother," &c. the persons introduced are by no means taken *from low or rustic life* in the common acceptation of those words; and it is not less clear, that the sentiments and language, as far as they can be conceived to have been really transferred from the minds and conversation of such persons, are attributable to causes and circumstances not necessarily connected with "their occupations and abode." The thoughts, feelings, language, and manners of the shepherd-farmers in the vales of Cumberland and Westmoreland,[1] as far as they are actually adopted in those poems, may be accounted for from causes, which will and do produce the same results in *every* state of life, whether in town or country. As the two principal I rank that INDEPENDENCE, which raises a man above servitude, or daily toil for the profit of others, yet not above the necessity of industry and a frugal simplicity of domestic life; and the accompanying unambitious, but solid and religious EDUCATION, which has rendered few books familiar, but the bible, and the liturgy or hymn book. * * *

I am convinced, that for the human soul to prosper in rustic life, a certain vantage-ground is pre-requisite. It is not every man, that is likely to be improved by a country life or by country labours. Education, or original sensibility, or both, must pre-exist, if the changes, forms, and incidents of nature are to prove a sufficient stimulant. And where these are not sufficient, the mind contracts and hardens by want of stimulants; and the man becomes selfish, sensual, gross, and hard-hearted. * * *

I adopt with full faith the principle of Aristotle,[2] that poetry as poetry is essentially *ideal*, that it avoids and excludes all *accident*; that its apparent individualities of rank, character, or occupation must be *representative* of a class; and that the *persons* of poetry must be clothed with *generic* attributes, with the *common* attributes of the class; not with such as one gifted individual might *possibly* possess, but such as from his situation it is most probable before-hand, that he *would* possess. If my premises are

---

1. Counties in the northwest of England known together as the Lake District.

2. Author of the earliest known treatise on the theory of poetry (5th century B.C.), the *Poetics*.

right, and my deductions legitimate, it follows that there can be no *poetic* medium between the swains of Theocritus[3] and those of an imaginary golden age.

The characters of the vicar and the shepherd-mariner in the poem of the BROTH-ERS, those of the shepherd of Green-head Gill in the "MICHAEL," have all the verisimilitude and representative quality, that the purposes of poetry can require. They are persons of a known and abiding class, and their manners and sentiments the natural product of circumstances common to the class. * * *

On the other hand, in the poems which are pitched at a lower note, as the "Harry Gill," "Idiot Boy," &c. the *feelings* are those of human nature in general; though the poet has judiciously laid the *scene* in the country, in order to place *himself* in the vicinity of interesting images, without the necessity of ascribing a sentimental perception of their beauty to the persons of his drama. * * *

In the "Thorn," the poet himself acknowledges in a note the necessity of an introductory poem, in which he should have pourtrayed the character of the person from whom the words of the poem are supposed to proceed: a superstitious man moderately imaginative, of slow faculties and deep feelings, "a captain of a small trading vessel, for example, who being past the middle age of life, had retired upon an annuity, or small independent income, to some village or country town of which he was not a native, or in which he had not been accustomed to live. Such men having nothing to do become credulous and talkative from indolence." But in a poem, still more in a lyric poem (and the NURSE in Shakspeare's Romeo and Juliet alone prevents me from extending the remark even to dramatic *poetry,* if indeed the Nurse itself can be deemed altogether a case in point) it is not possible to imitate truly a dull and garrulous discourser, without repeating the effects of dulness and garrulity. * * *

Still more must I hesitate in my assent to the sentence which immediately follows the former citation[:] * * * "The language too of these men is adopted (purified indeed from what appears to be its real defects, from all lasting and rational causes of dislike or disgust) because such men hourly communicate with the best objects from which the best part of language is originally derived; and because, from their rank in society, and the sameness and narrow circle of their intercourse, being less under the action of social vanity, they convey their feelings and notions in simple and unelaborated expressions." To this I reply; that a rustic's language, purified from all provincialism and grossness, and so far re-constructed as to be made consistent with the rules of grammar (which are in essence no other than the laws of universal logic, applied to Psychological materials) will not differ from the language of any other man of common-sense, however learned or refined he may be, except as far as the notions, which the rustic has to convey, are fewer and more indiscriminate. This will become still clearer, if we add the consideration (equally important though less obvious) that the rustic, from the more imperfect development of his faculties, and from the lower state of their cultivation, aims almost solely to convey *insulated facts,* either those of his scanty experience or his traditional belief; while the educated man chiefly seeks to discover and express those *connections* of things, or those relative *bearings* of fact to fact, from which some more or less general law is deducible. For *facts* are valuable to a wise man, chiefly as they lead to the discovery of the in-dwelling *law,* which is the true *being* of things, the sole solution of their modes of existence, and in the knowledge of which consists our dignity and our power.

3. Greek poet, 3rd century B.C. His *Idylls* are the origin of the Western pastoral tradition.

As little can I agree with the assertion, that from the objects with which the rustic hourly communicates, the best part of language is formed. For first, if to communicate with an object implies such an acquaintance with it, as renders it capable of being discriminately reflected on; the distinct knowledge of an uneducated rustic would furnish a very scanty vocabulary. The few things, and modes of action, requisite for his bodily conveniences, would alone be individualized; while all the rest of nature would be expressed by a small number of confused, general terms. Secondly, I deny that the words and combinations of words derived from the objects, with which the rustic is familiar, whether with distinct or confused knowledge, can be justly said to form the best part of language. It is more than probable, that many classes of the brute creation possess discriminating sounds, by which they can convey to each other notices of such objects as concern their food, shelter, or safety. Yet we hesitate to call the aggregate of such sounds a language, otherwise than metaphorically. The best part of human language, properly so called, is derived from reflection on the acts of the mind itself. It is formed by a voluntary appropriation of fixed symbols to internal acts, to processes and results of imagination, the greater part of which have no place in the consciousness of uneducated man; though in civilized society, by imitation and passive remembrance of what they hear from their religious instructors and other superiors, the most uneducated share in the harvest which they neither sowed or reaped. * * *

The positions, which I controvert, are contained in the sentences—"*a selection of the* REAL *language of men;*"—"*the language of these men* (i.e. men in low and rustic life) *I propose to myself to imitate, and as far as possible, to adopt the very language of men.*" "*Between the language of prose and that of metrical composition, there neither is, nor can be any essential difference.*" It is against these exclusively, that my opposition is directed.

I object, in the very first instance, to an equivocation in the use of the word "real." Every man's language varies, according to the extent of his knowledge, the activity of his faculties, and the depth or quickness of his feelings. Every man's language has, first, its *individualities*; secondly, the common properties of the *class* to which he belongs; and thirdly, words and phrases of *universal* use. The language of Hooker, Bacon, Bishop Taylor, and Burke, differ from the common language of the learned class only by the superior number and novelty of the thoughts and relations which they had to convey. The language of Algernon Sidney[4] differs not at all from that, which every well educated gentleman would wish to write, and (with due allowances for the undeliberateness, and less connected train, of thinking natural and proper to conversation) such as he would wish to talk. Neither one or the other differ half as much from the general language of cultivated society, as the language of Mr. Wordsworth's homeliest composition differs from that of a common peasant. For "real" therefore, we must substitute *ordinary*, or *lingua communis* [common language]. And this, we have proved, is no more to be found in the phraseology of low and rustic life, than in that of any other class. Omit the peculiarities of each, and the result of course must be common to all. * * *

Neither is the case rendered at all more tenable by the addition of the words, "*in a state of excitement.*" For the nature of a man's words, when he is strongly affected by joy, grief, or anger, must necessarily depend on the number and quality of the general truths, conceptions and images, and of the words expressing them, with which his mind had been previously stored. For the property of passion is not to *create*; but to

---

4. Richard Hooker (1554–1600) wrote *The Laws of Ecclesiastical Polity*; he and Bishop Taylor were both known for their style as well as their ideas, as were the philosophers Francis Bacon (1561–1626) and Edmund Burke. The republican Algernon Sidney was executed for his supposed complicity in the so-called Rye House Plot to assassinate Charles II in 1683. Coleridge refers to his *Discourses on Government* (1698).

set in increased activity. At least, whatever new connections of thoughts or images, or (which is equally, if not more than equally, the appropriate effect of strong excitement) whatever generalizations of truth or experience, the heat of passion may produce; yet the terms of their conveyance must have pre-existed in his former conversations, and are only collected and crowded together by the unusual stimulation. It is indeed very possible to adopt in a poem the unmeaning repetitions, habitual phrases, and other blank counters, which an unfurnished or confused understanding interposes at short intervals, in order to keep hold of his subject which is still slipping from him, and to give him time for recollection; or in mere aid of vacancy, as in the scanty companies of a country stage the same player pops backwards and forwards, in order to prevent the appearance of empty spaces, in the procession of Macbeth, or Henry VIIIth. But what assistance to the poet, or ornament to the poem, these can supply, I am at a loss to conjecture. Nothing assuredly can differ either in origin or in mode more widely from the *apparent* tautologies[5] of intense and turbulent feeling, in which the passion is greater and of longer endurance, than to be exhausted or satisfied by a single representation of the image or incident exciting it. Such repetitions I admit to be a beauty of the highest kind; as illustrated by Mr. Wordsworth himself from the song of Deborah [Judges 5.27]. *"At her feet he bowed, he fell, he lay down; at her feet he bowed, he fell; where he bowed, there he fell down dead."*

1815   1817

━━━━━◆━━━━━

George Gordon, Lord Byron
1788–1824

"Mad—bad—and dangerous to know," pronounced Lady Caroline Lamb, before becoming his lover; a "splendid and imperishable excellence of sincerity and strength," declared Matthew Arnold: the fascination that made Byron the archetypal Romantic, in Europe even more than in Britain, grew from both judgments. He was born in London in 1788, the son of Captain John "Mad Jack" Byron and his second wife, Catherine Gordon, a Scots heiress. The Captain quickly ran through her fortune and departed; Byron and his mother withdrew to Aberdeen in 1789. He passed the next ten years in straitened circumstances, sensitive to the clubfoot with which he had been born, left with a mother who displaced resentment against her absconded husband onto him, and tended by a Calvinist nurse whom he later said had early awakened his sexuality. In 1798 his great-uncle the fifth Baron Byron, "the wicked Lord," died childless, and just after his tenth birthday Byron unexpectedly inherited his title. He asked his mother "whether she perceived any difference in him since he had been made a lord, as he perceived none himself," but the difference shaped the poet.

Byron and his mother returned to England and moved into Newstead Abbey, near Nottingham, the now debt-ridden estate presented to the Byrons by Henry VIII; to the lonely boy, the Gothic hall embodied his tempestuous family heritage. In 1801 Byron was sent to school at Harrow; in the same year he probably met his half-sister Augusta. He entered Trinity College, Cambridge, in 1805, living extravagantly and entangling himself with moneylenders, but also making enduring friendships.

Byron's first published volume, *Hours of Idleness*, appeared in 1807, when he was nineteen; the lofty pose he struck in announcing himself as "Lord Byron: A Minor" provoked a savage notice from the *Edinburgh Review*, to which he retaliated in 1809 with a satire in Popean

---

5. Pointless repetitions.

couplets, *English Bards and Scotch Reviewers*. "Written when I was very young and very angry," Byron later confessed to Coleridge, the poem "has been a thorn in my side ever since; more particularly as almost all the Persons animadverted upon became subsequently my acquaintances, and some of them my friends." He suppressed the fifth edition, but so memorable were its attacks on Coleridge, Southey, Wordsworth, Scott, and others that pirated editions continued to appear. Byron took his seat in the House of Lords that same year, and then departed on a grand tour shaped by the Napoleonic wars, which barred much of Europe. He sailed to Lisbon, crossed Spain, and proceeded to Greece and Albania, through country little known to Western Europeans. There he began *Childe Harold's Pilgrimage*. In March 1810 he sailed for Constantinople, visited the site of Troy and swam the Hellespont in imitation of the mythical Greek lover, Leander. In the East, Byron found a world in which the love of an older aristocrat for a beautiful boy was accepted, and he also developed a political identity as the Western hero who would liberate Greece from the Turks.

Byron returned to London in July 1811, but too late to see his mother before she died. In February 1812 he made his first speech in the House of Lords, denouncing the death penalty proposed for weavers who had smashed the machines they blamed for their loss of work. Byron's parliamentary activity was superseded the next month when the first two cantos of *Childe Harold's Pilgrimage* appeared and he "woke to find himself famous." The poem joined the immediacy of a travelogue to the disillusionment of a speaker who voiced the melancholy of a generation wearied by prolonged war. Despite Byron's claim that Harold was a fiction designed merely to connect a picaresque narrative, readers took him as the mouthpiece of an author speaking passionately of his own concerns. The magnetism of this personality offset the cynicism the poem displayed: the handsome, aristocratic poet, returned from exotic travels, himself became a figure of force. Byron followed this success with a series of "Eastern" tales that added to his aura: one of them, *The Corsair* (1814), written in ten days, sold ten thousand copies on the day of publication. *Hebrew Melodies* (1815) contains some of Byron's most famous lyrics (*She walks in beauty*) and accorded with the vogue for nationalist themes. Byron was both a sensational commercial success and a noble who gave away his copyrights because aristocrats do not write for money. Like all myths, "Byron" embodied contradictions more than he resolved them.

This literary celebrity was enhanced by Byron's lionizing in Whig society. Liaisons with Lady Caroline Lamb and the "autumnal" Lady Oxford magnified his notoriety, but it was his relationship with his half-sister Augusta, now married, that gave rise to most scandal; her daughter Medora, born in 1814 and given the name of the heroine of *The Corsair*, was widely thought to be Byron's, and probably was. Seeking to escape these agitating affairs, and also to repair his debts, Byron proposed to Annabella Milbanke. They married in January 1815; their daughter Augusta Ada was born at the end of the year, but a few weeks later Annabella left Byron to live with her parents, amid rumors of insanity, incest, and sodomy. Pirated editions of Byron's poems on the separation made marital discord into public scandal.

In April 1816 Byron quit England, bearing the pageant of his bleeding heart, in Matthew Arnold's famous phrase, across Europe. He settled in Geneva, near Percy Bysshe Shelley and Mary Godwin, who had eloped two years before. They had been joined by Mary's stepsister, Claire Clairmont, with whom Byron resumed an affair he had begun in England. Poetry was as much in the air as romance: Byron reported that Shelley "dosed him with Wordsworth physic even to nausea"; the influence and resistance the phrase shows are both evident in the third canto of *Childe Harold* (1816). He wrote *The Prisoner of Chillon* at this time and began the closet-drama *Manfred* (1817). At the end of the summer the Shelley party left for England, where Claire gave birth to Byron's illegitimate daughter Allegra; in October Byron departed for Venice, where he rented a palazzo on the Grand Canal.

Byron described his Venetian life in brilliant letters, some of which were meant for circulation in the circle of his publisher John Murray. To a ceaseless round of sexual activity, he joined substantial literary productivity. He studied Armenian, completed *Manfred,* and visited Rome, gathering materials for a fourth canto of *Childe Harold* (1818). The canto was his longest and most sublime, and its invocation of Freedom's torn banner streaming "*against* the wind" fixed his revolutionary reputation. Yet Byron began to feel trapped by the modes that had won him popularity; determining to "repel charges of monotony and mannerism," he wrote *Beppo*, a comic verse tale of a Venetian *ménage-à-trois* (1818). In its colloquial, digressive ease, Byron was testing the form of his greatest poem, *Don Juan*, at once fictional autobiography, picaresque narrative, literary burlesque, and exposure of social, sexual, and religious hypocrisies. The first two cantos were published in 1819 in an expensive edition meant to forestall charges of blasphemy and bearing neither the author's nor the publisher's name. The authorship was nonetheless known: *Blackwood's Magazine* criticized Byron for "a filthy and impious" attack on his wife, and the second canto, which turns to shipwreck and cannibalism, redoubled charges of nihilism. Shocking the proprieties of one audience, Byron moved toward another; the poem sold well in increasingly cheap editions.

In April 1819 Byron met his "last attachment," Countess Teresa Gamba Guiccioli, nineteen years old and married to a man nearly three times her age. Through her family, Byron was initiated into the Carbonari, a clandestine revolutionary organization devoted to achieving Italian independence from Austria. While continuing *Don Juan*, he wrote *Marino Faliero, Sardanapalus*, and *The Two Foscari* (all 1821), historical dramas exploring the relationship between the powerful individual and the postrevolutionary state. To the same year belongs *Cain*, a "mystery" drama refused copyright for its unorthodoxy and immediately pirated by radicals.

When Teresa's father and brother were exiled for their part in an abortive uprising, she followed them, and Byron reluctantly went with her to Pisa. There he reunited with Percy Shelley, with whom he planned a radical journal, *The Liberal*. The first number contained *The Vision of Judgment*, a devastating rebuttal to a eulogy of George III by Robert Southey, in the preface to which the poet laureate had alluded to Byron as the head of a "Satanic School."

Restive in the domesticity of life with Teresa, Byron agreed to act as agent of a London committee aiding the Greeks in their struggle for independence. In July 1823 he left for Cephalonia, an island in western Greece. Clear of debt and now attentive to his literary income, Byron devoted his fortune to the cause. Philhellenic idealism was soon confronted by motley reality, but Byron founded, paid, and trained a brigade of soldiers. A serious illness in February 1824, followed by the usual remedy of bleeding, weakened him; in April he contracted a fever, treated by further bleeding, from which he died on 19 April at the age of thirty-six. Deeply mourned, he became a Greek national hero, and throughout Europe his name became synonymous with Romanticism. In England, the stunned reaction of the young Tennyson spoke for many: on hearing the news, he sadly wrote on a rock "Byron is dead." As Arnold later recalled, in placing Byron with Wordsworth as the great English poets of the century, he had "subjugated" his readers, and his influence was immense and lasting.

She walks in beauty[1]

1

She walks in beauty, like the night
   Of cloudless climes and starry skies;
And all that's best of dark and bright
   Meet in her aspect and her eyes:
5 Thus mellow'd to that tender light
   Which heaven to gaudy day denies.

2

One shade the more, one ray the less,
   Had half impair'd the nameless grace
Which waves in every raven tress,

---

1. The first poem in *Hebrew Melodies*, a collection initiated by the Jewish composer Isaac Nathan, and published with his music. The subject is Anne Wilmot, the wife of Byron's cousin, whom he had seen at a party wearing "mourning, with dark spangles on her dress."

10   Or softly lightens o'er her face;
        Where thoughts serenely sweet express
        How pure, how dear their dwelling-place.

                        3

        And on that cheek, and o'er that brow,
        So soft, so calm, yet eloquent,
15   The smiles that win, the tints that glow,
        But tell of days in goodness spent,
        A mind at peace with all below,
        A heart whose love is innocent!

1814   1815

So, we'll go no more a–roving

                        1

        So, we'll go no more a–roving[1]
        So late into the night,
        Though the heart be still as loving,
        And the moon be still as bright.

                        2

5   For the sword outwears its sheath,
        And the soul wears out the breast,
        And the heart must pause to breathe,
        And love itself have rest.

                        3

        Though the night was made for loving,
10   And the day returns too soon,
        Yet we'll go no more a roving
        By the light of the moon.

1817   1830

FROM CHILDE HAROLD'S PILGRIMAGE
from Canto 3[1]
[THUNDERSTORM IN SWITZERLAND][2]

                        92

860   Thy sky is changed!—and such a change! Oh night,
        And storm, and darkness, ye are wondrous strong,

1. The poem first appeared in a letter Byron wrote from Venice to Thomas Moore: "The Carnival—that is, the latter part of it—and sitting up late o'nights, had knocked me up a little. But it is over—and it is now Lent . . . though I did not dissipate much upon the whole, yet I find 'the sword wearing out the scabbard,' though I have but just turned the corner of twenty-nine."

1. The first two cantos of *Childe Harold's Pilgrimage* appeared in 1812. As their subtitle "A Romaunt" indicated, Byron had adopted the form of romance for his unnervingly contemporary poem. The Spenserian stanzas and mock-archaisms—a "childe" is a youth of noble birth—played discordantly against the account of his travels in 1809–1811 through Spain (and his acerbic commentary on the Peninsular War; see Introduction, pages 1322–1323) and then on into parts of Greece unfrequented by Westerners. The overwhelming success of the poem

ensured that Byron would be identified with Childe Harold. Byron protested, but the connection is reinforced by the manuscripts themselves, which disclose that Childe Harold was once Childe Burun, an ancient form of his family name. Canto 3, published in 1816, is independent, though the continuity reflects the degree to which protagonist and poet had come to figure each other. Byron left England on 25 April 1816, and wrote the opening stanzas while crossing the Channel.

2. "The thunder-storms to which these lines refer occurred on the thirteenth of June, 1816, at midnight. I have seen among the Acroceraunian mountains of Chimari several more terrible, but none more beautiful" [Byron's note]. Byron had settled in the Villa Diodati on 10 June, near the Shelley party; a few days after these storms Mary Shelley began *Frankenstein* in Byron's new residence.

Yet lovely in your strength, as is the light
Of a dark eye in woman! Far along,
From peak to peak, the rattling crags among
865 Leaps the live thunder! Not from one lone cloud,
But every mountain now hath found a tongue,
And Jura answers, through her misty shroud,
Back to the joyous Alps, who call to her aloud![3]

93

And this is in the night:—Most glorious night!
870 Thou wert not sent for slumber! let me be
A sharer in thy fierce and far delight,—
A portion of the tempest and of thee!
How the lit lake shines, a phosphoric sea,
And the big rain comes dancing to the earth!
875 And now again 'tis black,—and now, the glee
Of the loud hills shakes with its mountain-mirth,
As if they did rejoice o'er a young earthquake's birth.

94

Now, where the swift Rhone cleaves his way between
Heights which appear as lovers who have parted
880 In hate, whose mining depths so intervene,
That they can meet no more, though broken-hearted!
Though in their souls, which thus each other thwarted,
Love was the very root of the fond rage
Which blighted their life's bloom, and then departed:
885 Itself expired, but leaving them an age
Of years all winters,—war within themselves to wage.[4]

95

Now, where the quick Rhone thus hath cleft his way,
The mightiest of the storms hath ta'en his stand:
For here, not one, but many, make their play,
890 And fling their thunder-bolts from hand to hand,
Flashing and cast around: of all the band,
The brightest through these parted hills hath fork'd
His lightnings, as if he did understand,
That in such gaps as desolation work'd,
895 There the hot shaft should blast whatever therein lurk'd.

96

Sky, mountains, river, winds, lake, lightnings! ye!
With night, and clouds, and thunder, and a soul
To make these felt and feeling, well may be
Things that have made me watchful; the far roll
900 Of your departing voices, is the knoll
Of what in me is sleepless,—if I rest.
But where of ye, oh tempests! is the goal?
Are ye like those within the human breast?
Or do ye find, at length, like eagles, some high nest?

---

3. The Jura mountains, to the north and west of Geneva, form the boundary between Switzerland and France; the Alps run to the east and south.
4. This description of the landscape in terms of lovers who have parted in hate obliquely recalls Byron's separation from his wife and illustrates his tendency to turn nature into sublime self-projection.

97

905 Could I embody and unbosom now
That which is most within me,—could I wreak
My thoughts upon expression, and thus throw
Soul, heart, mind, passions, feelings, strong or weak,
All that I would have sought, and all I seek,
910 Bear, know, feel, and yet breathe—into *one* word,
And that one word were Lightning, I would speak;
But as it is, I live and die unheard,
With a most voiceless thought, sheathing it as a sword.

from Canto 4[1]
[THE COLOSSEUM. THE DYING GLADIATOR]

139

And here the buzz of eager nations ran,
In murmur'd pity, or loud-roar'd applause,
1245 As man was slaughter'd by his fellow man.[2]
And wherefore slaughter'd? wherefore, but because
Such were the bloody Circus' genial laws,
And the imperial pleasure. Wherefore not?
What matters where we fall to fill the maws°   stomachs
1250 Of worms—on battle-plains or listed spot?
Both are but theatres where the chief actors rot.

140

I see before me the Gladiator lie:
He leans upon his hand—his manly brow
Consents to death, but conquers agony,
1255 And his droop'd head sinks gradually low—
And through his side the last drops, ebbing slow
From the red gash, fall heavy, one by one,
Like the first of a thunder-shower; and now
The arena swims around him—he is gone,
1260 Ere ceased the inhuman shout which hail'd the wretch who won.

141

He heard it, but he heeded not—his eyes
Were with his heart, and that was far away:
He reck'd not of the life he lost nor prize,
But where his rude hut by the Danube lay,
1265 *There* were his young barbarians all at play,
There was their Dacian mother[3]—he, their sire,
Butcher'd to make a Roman holiday—

---

1. Byron began Canto 4 in June 1817, and published it in April 1818. In the dedication he announced that the reader would find "less of the pilgrim" than in the preceding cantos: "I had become weary," he declared in ending the division between the narrator and Harold, "of drawing a line which every one seemed determined not to perceive." Canto 4 is spoken in his own person and carries the account of his travels into Italy.
2. Byron is viewing the partly ruined Colosseum, a vast amphitheater completed about A.D. 80; throughout the period of the Roman Empire, it was the site of gladiatorial combats in which prisoners of war or slaves fought to the death. Spectators could signal mercy to the defeated by waving handkerchiefs; turning thumbs down doomed the combatant.
3. The Dacians, a people north of the Danube River in what is now Romania, harried the Romans until their defeat by the Emperor Trajan (A.D. 101–107).

All this rush'd with his blood—Shall he expire
And unavenged?—Arise! ye Goths, and glut your ire![4]

142

1270   But here, where Murder breathed her bloody steam;
And here, where buzzing nations choked the ways,
And roar'd or murmur'd like a mountain stream
Dashing or winding as its torrent strays;
Here, where the Roman millions' blame or praise
1275   Was death or life, the playthings of a crowd,
My voice sounds much—and fall the stars' faint rays
On the arena void—seats crush'd—walls bow'd—
And galleries, where my steps seem echoes strangely loud.

143

A ruin—yet what ruin! from its mass
1280   Walls, palaces, half-cities, have been rear'd;
Yet oft the enormous skeleton ye pass,
And marvel where the spoil could have appear'd.
Hath it indeed been plunder'd, or but clear'd?
Alas! developed,° opens the decay,   *disclosed*
1285   When the colossal fabric's form is near'd:
It will not bear the brightness of the day,
Which streams too much on all years, man, have reft° away.   *ravaged*

144

But when the rising moon begins to climb
Its topmost arch, and gently pauses there;
1290   When the stars twinkle through the loops of time,
And the low night-breeze waves along the air
The garland forest, which the gray walls wear,
Like laurels on the bald first Caesar's head;[5]
When the light shines serene but doth not glare,
1295   Then in this magic circle raise the dead:
Heroes have trod this spot—'tis on their dust ye tread.

145

"While stands the Coliseum, Rome shall stand;
When falls the Coliseum, Rome shall fall;
And when Rome falls—the World."[6] From our own land
1300   Thus spake the pilgrims o'er this mighty wall
In Saxon times, which we are wont to call
Ancient;[7] and these three mortal things are still
On their foundations, and unalter'd all;

---

4. The Goths were Germanic tribes who overran the Roman Empire in the 5th century A.D. The vivid stanza was inspired by the statue of a dying Gaul in the Capitoline Museum, in Byron's day thought to represent a dying gladiator.
5. The Roman historian Suetonius records that Julius Caesar (102–44 B.C.) was particularly gratified by a decree of the Roman Senate that permitted him to wear a laurel wreath, the traditional symbol of victory, at all times, because it hid his baldness.
6. A note directs the reader to chapter 71 of *The Decline and Fall of the Roman Empire*, by Edward Gibbon

(1737–1794), a work Byron had known since adolescence: "Reduced to its naked majesty, the Flavian amphitheatre was contemplated with awe and admiration by the pilgrims of the North: and their rude enthusiasm broke forth in a sublime proverbial expression, which is recorded in the eighth century in the fragments of the venerable Bede."
7. The Anglo-Saxon kingdoms in Britain, established following the withdrawal of the Romans in the 4th century A.D., consolidated into one Saxon kingdom that existed until the Norman Conquest of 1066.

> Rome and her Ruin past Redemption's skill,
1305 The World, the same wide den—of thieves, or what ye will.

Don Juan

"Give me a poem," Byron's publisher John Murray wrote him in January 1817, "a good Venetian tale describing manners formerly from the story itself, and now from your own observations." The response was *Beppo*, which Byron based on an anecdote that he had heard from the husband of his mistress, turning it into a seemingly effortless comparison of Italian and British manners. Its success led Murray to ask in July 1818: "Have you not another lively tale like *Beppo*? Or will you not give me some prose in three volumes?—all the adventures that you have undergone, seen, heard of, or imagined, with your reflections on life and manners." In the same week Byron had begun *Don Juan*; his own inclination consorted with the publisher's sketch of a suitable "work to open [his] campaign" for fall sales.

For a work of which he remarked "I *have* no plan—I *had* no plan—but I had or have materials," Byron found an ideal model in the seriocomic Italian romances of the fifteenth and sixteenth centuries by Pulci, Berni, and Ariosto. Their episodic, digressive mode, flexible enough to incorporate a wide range of moods and stylistic levels, enabled Byron to stage aspects of himself that had not appeared in the titanism of his Eastern tales and the loftiness of *Childe Harold's Pilgrimage*. He sought to treat public issues with the conversational fluency of a skeptical intelligence engaged with the ordinary materiality of the world: brand names and ship's pumps, indigestion and thinning hair, literary rivalries and reviewers. Byron regarded the story as a "hinge" on which to mount his reflections, and as the poem proceeds its title character retreats before the ceaseless inventions of the narrator, who both is and is not Byron. "If people contradict themselves," he wrote, "can I / Help contradicting them, and everybody, / Even my veracious self?" Truth's streams, he continued, "cut through such canals of contradiction, / That she must often navigate o'er fiction" (15.88). Such teasing of the borders between fiction and fact intrigued readers, and enhanced the allure of the figure of "Byron" the words create. *Don Juan* is a seemingly inexhaustible improvisatory monologue—sixteen cantos were published between 1819 and 1823, with a fragmentary seventeenth left uncompleted at Byron's death. Through a range of voices, by allusion and quotation, and in the number of perspectives entertained or denounced by the narrator, the poem generates a sense of dialogue and exchange. As the critic Jerome McGann has argued, the poem superimposes three historical levels: Juan's own story is set in the late eighteenth century and was planned to end in the French Revolution; the narrator's reminiscences arise from Byron's years of fame in Regency London (1812–1816); lastly, the narrator's commentary engages the post-Napoleonic moment of the actual writing (1818–1823). As it proceeds, *Don Juan* depicts Greek pirates and Turkish harems, Russian armies and Spanish families, British highwaymen and British aristocrats, story and commentary together building a critical portrait of the Europe of Byron's era, torn by revolution and now subsiding into the conservative restoration the poet condemns. Though he might have begun the poem intending only "to giggle and make giggle," Byron's purposes deepened as he advanced against the opposition of his friends and publisher.

Byron intensifies the sense that he is speaking in *Don Juan*—forms of the first-person pronoun occur almost two thousand times—and he repeatedly reminds the reader of his capricious playing with form, but the poem is personal in a more specific way as well. Readers familiar with Byron's life—and his celebrity had assured that many were—could perceive in Juan's mother, Donna Inez, a caricature of Byron's estranged wife Annabella, Lady Byron. The account of Juan's youth with Inez also draws on Byron's childhood, "an only son left with an only mother" (1.37). Like Wordsworth's *Prelude*, *Don Juan* is autobiography—but in the form of oblique and theatricalized fiction. It is also picaresque adventure, satire, and mock-Homeric epic, whose hero belies the legacy of his name, seduced more often than seducing, kind-hearted rather than ruthless and conniving. Byron's genre-crossing revision of literary tradition made "something wholly new & relative to the age," as Shelley recognized.

Much of the poem's power arises from Byron's fluent handling of ottava rima, the eight-line stanza form rhyming *abababcc*. He credited *The Monks and the Giants* (1817) by his friend John Hookham Frere with having shown him its possibilities, but Frere's work shows little of Byron's deftness. Byron employed a fantastic wealth of rhymes ("Plato" with "potato," "intellectual" with "hen-peck'd you all"), often emphasizing the snap of the concluding couplet for comic surprise, but he could also downplay the rhymes and enjamb lines to yield a rhythm like blank verse. "The most readable poem of its length ever written," Virginia Woolf observed of *Don Juan*, because its "method is a discovery by itself . . . an elastic shape which will hold whatever you choose to put in it." "Like all free and easy things," she added, "only the skilled and mature really bring them off successfully. But Byron was full of ideas—a quality that gives his verse a toughness." The rare combination of ease and power to which both Shelley and Woolf point keeps *Don Juan* subversively fresh today.

from DON JUAN
Dedication[1]

1

Bob Southey! You're a poet, Poet-laureate,[2]
    And representative of all the race,
Although 'tis true that you turn'd out a Tory at
    Last,—yours has lately been a common case,—
5   And now, my Epic Renegade! what are ye at?
    With all the Lakers,[3] in and out of place?
A nest of tuneful persons, to my eye
Like "four and twenty Blackbirds in a pye;[4]

2

"Which pye being open'd they began to sing"
10   (This old song and new simile holds good),
"A dainty dish to set before the King,"
    Or Regent, who admires such kind of food;—
And Coleridge, too, has lately taken wing,
    But like a hawk encumber'd with his hood,—
15   Explaining metaphysics to the nation—
I wish he would explain his Explanation.[5]

3

You, Bob! are rather insolent, you know,
    At being disappointed in your wish
To supersede all warblers here below,

1. Byron sent the Dedication to his publisher in November 1818 with Canto 1 of *Don Juan*. When Cantos 1-2 were published together, anonymously, in 1819 Byron removed the Dedication because he did not want "to attack the dog [Southey] so fiercely without putting my name." It appeared for the first time in the 1832–1833 edition of Byron's works.
2. Robert Southey became Poet Laureate in 1813. He earned Byron's contempt for having abandoned his early republican principles and for his malicious gossip in 1816 about Byron, Shelley, Claire Clairmont, and Mary Shelley: "The Son of a Bitch . . . said that Shelley and I 'had formed a League of Incest and practiced our precepts

with &c'." The phrase "Epic Renegade" (line 5) glances both at Southey's political reversal and his series of epic poems such as *Thalaba* (1801) and *The Curse of Kehama* (1810).
3. The collective term applied by *The Edinburgh Review* to Coleridge, Southey, and Wordsworth, from their common residence in the Lake District.
4. Henry James Pye (1745–1813) was the Poet Laureate before Southey; his very first official ode had provoked the nursery-rhyme parody Byron repeats here.
5. Referring to Coleridge's *The Statesman's Manual* (1816) and *Biographia Literaria* (1817).

20   And be the only Blackbird in the dish;
    And then you overstrain yourself, or so,
    And tumble downward like the flying fish
Gasping on deck, because you soar too high, Bob,
    And fall, for lack of moisture quite a-dry, Bob![6]

4

25   And Wordsworth, in a rather long "Excursion"[7]
    (I think the quarto holds five hundred pages),
Has given a sample from the vasty version
    Of his new system to perplex the sages;
'Tis poetry—at least by his assertion,
30   And may appear so when the dog-star rages—
And he who understands it would be able
To add a story to the Tower of Babel.[8]

5

You—Gentlemen! by dint of long seclusion
    From better company, have kept your own
35   At Keswick,[9] and, through still continued fusion
    Of one another's minds, at last have grown
To deem as a most logical conclusion,
    That Poesy has wreaths for you alone:
There is a narrowness in such a notion,
40   Which makes me wish you'd change your lakes for ocean.

6

I would not imitate the petty thought,
    Nor coin my self-love to so base a vice,
For all the glory your conversion brought,
    Since gold alone should not have been its price.
45   You have your salary; was't for that you wrought?
    And Wordsworth has his place in the Excise.[1]
You're shabby fellows—true—but poets still,
And duly seated on the immortal hill.°   *Parnassus*

7

Your bays° may hide the baldness of your brows—   *laurel wreaths*
50   Perhaps some virtuous blushes;—let them go—
To you I envy neither fruit nor boughs—
    And for the fame you would engross below,
The field is universal, and allows
    Scope to all such as feel the inherent glow:
55   Scott, Rogers, Campbell, Moore, and Crabbe,[2] will try
'Gainst you the question with posterity.

6. A "dry bob" was slang for sex without ejaculation.
7. Wordsworth's nine-book poem *The Excursion* had appeared in 1814.
8. To punish human presumption, God destroys the Tower of Babel and institutes the multiplicity of languages (Genesis 11.1–9); note the pun on "story."
9. The town where Southey lived, to which Coleridge and his family moved in 1800; Wordsworth lived nearby in Grasmere.
1. In March 1813 Wordsworth obtained a sinecure as distributor of tax stamps for Westmoreland through the aid of his patron, the Earl of Lonsdale, to whom he dedicated

The Excursion.
2. In ranking the living poets in an 1813 journal, Byron declared Walter Scott the "Monarch of Parnassus," Samuel Rogers (1763–1855) next, Thomas Moore (1779–1852) and Thomas Campbell (1777–1844) third, "Southey-Wordsworth-Coleridge" below these. George Crabbe (1754–1832) he elsewhere praised for being "free" of the "wrong revolutionary poetical system" that he and his contemporaries exemplified: "and if I had to begin again—I would model myself accordingly— Crabbe's the man."

8

For me, who, wandering with pedestrian Muses,[3]
   Contend not with you on the winged steed,
I wish your fate may yield ye, when she chooses,
60   The fame you envy, and the skill you need;
And recollect a poet nothing loses
   In giving to his brethren their full meed°   *reward*
Of merit, and complaint of present days
Is not the certain path to future praise.

9

65 He that reserves his laurels for posterity
   (Who does not often claim the bright reversion)
Has generally no great crop to spare it, he
   Being only injured by his own assertion;
And although here and there some glorious rarity
70   Arise like Titan from the sea's immersion,
The major part of such appellants go
To—God knows where—for no one else can know.

10

If, fallen in evil days on evil tongues,
   Milton appeal'd to the Avenger, Time,[4]
75 If Time, the Avenger, execrates his wrongs,
   And makes the word "Miltonic" mean "*sublime,*"
He deign'd not to belie his soul in songs,
   Nor turn his very talent to a crime;
He did not loathe the Sire to laud the Son,
80 But closed the tyrant-hater he begun.[5]

11

Think'st thou, could he—the blind Old Man—arise
   Like Samuel from the grave, to freeze once more
The blood of monarchs with his prophecies,[6]
   Or be alive again—again all hoar
85 With time and trials, and those helpless eyes,
   And heartless daughters[7]—worn—and pale—and poor;
Would *he* adore a sultan? *he* obey
The intellectual eunuch Castlereagh?[8]

12

Cold-blooded, smooth-faced, placid miscreant!
90 Dabbling its sleek young hands in Erin's° gore,   *Ireland's*
And thus for wider carnage taught to pant,
   Transferr'd to gorge upon a sister shore,

3. The "musa pedestris" of the Latin poet Horace (65–8
B.C.) signals a humble, as opposed to exalted or epic, style
(*Satires* 2.6.17).
4. Recalling the invocation to Book 7 of *Paradise Lost:*
"On evil days though fall'n, and evil tongues" (26).
5. Milton, who had supported the Commonwealth party
that overthrew Charles I in 1649, remained loyal to principle and did not praise Charles II after the Restoration
in 1660.
6. King Saul, attacked by the Philistines, raises the ghost
of the prophet Samuel to ask advice, only to learn that he
has disobeyed the Lord and will be delivered to the ene-

my (1 Samuel 28).
7. "Milton's two elder daughters are said to have robbed
him of his books, besides cheating and plaguing him in
the economy of his house" [Byron's note].
8. The Irish nobleman Robert Stewart, Marquis of Londonderry and Viscount Castlereagh, as chief secretary for
Ireland (1799–1801) suppressed the Irish rebellion and
secured the Act of Union with England that ended the
Irish Parliament; he became Foreign Secretary of Britain
(1812–1822). He was instrumental in arranging the balance of power in post-Napoleonic Europe, for which he
was detested by Byron and the liberals.

The vulgarest tool that Tyranny could want,
    With just enough of talent, and no more,
To lengthen fetters by another fix'd,
And offer poison long already mix'd.⁹

13

An orator of such set trash of phrase
    Ineffably—legitimately vile,¹
That even its grossest flatterers dare not praise,
    Nor foes—all nations—condescend to smile,—
Not even a sprightly blunder's spark can blaze
    From that Ixion grindstone's ceaseless toil,²
That turns and turns to give the world a notion
Of endless torments and perpetual motion.

14

A bungler even in its disgusting trade,
    And botching, patching, leaving still behind
Something of which its masters are afraid,
    States to be curb'd, and thoughts to be confined,
Conspiracy or Congress to be made—³
    Cobbling at manacles for all mankind—
A tinkering slave-maker, who mends old chains,
With God and man's abhorrence for its gains.

15

If we may judge of matter by the mind,
    Emasculated to the marrow *It*
Hath but two objects, how to serve, and bind,
    Deeming the chain it wears even men may fit,
Eutropius⁴ of its many masters,—blind
    To worth as freedom, wisdom as to wit,
Fearless—because *no* feeling dwells in ice,
Its very courage stagnates to a vice.

16

Where shall I turn me not to *view* its bonds,
    For I will never *feel* them;—Italy!
Thy late reviving Roman soul desponds
    Beneath the lie this State-thing breathed o'er thee—
Thy clanking chain, and Erin's yet green wounds,
    Have voices—tongues to cry aloud for me.
Europe has slaves—allies—kings—armies still,
And Southey lives to sing them very ill.

---

9. His opponents regarded Castlereagh as the pawn of the Austrian foreign minister, Prince Metternich.

1. Castlereagh's poor speaking was notorious: "It is the first time indeed since the Normans," Byron wrote in the Preface to Cantos 6–8, "that England has been insulted by a *Minister* (at least) who could not speak English, and that Parliament permitted itself to be dictated to in the language of Mrs. Malaprop" [the character from R. B. Sheridan's *The Rivals* (1773) who has given her name to verbal slips].

2. In Greek mythology Ixion is punished in Hades by being chained to a perpetually rolling wheel.

3. In 1814 Austria, Russia, Prussia, and England formed the Quadruple Alliance; after the fall of Napoleon, Castlereagh and Metternich reestablished the "legitimate" governments of Europe at the Congress of Vienna (1815), restoring the Bourbons in France and acknowledging Ferdinand VII in Spain.

4. The career of Eutropius, a eunuch who became a magistrate and general in the Eastern Roman Empire (395–408), is narrated by Gibbon, *Decline and Fall* (ch. 32). Byron's denunciation of Castlereagh as a "eunuch" and an "It" may hint private knowledge. Castlereagh's suicide in 1822, officially attributed to overwork, was preceded by an attempt to blackmail him on the grounds of homosexuality: sodomy was a capital crime.

17

Meantime—Sir Laureate—I proceed to dedicate,
130   In honest simple verse, this song to you.
And, if in flattering strains I do not predicate,
    'Tis that I still retain my "buff and blue";[5]
My politics as yet are all to educate:
    Apostasy's so fashionable, too,
135   To keep *one* creed's a task grown quite Herculean;
Is it not so, my Tory, ultra-Julian?[6]

from Canto 1

1

I want a hero: an uncommon want,
    When every year and month sends forth a new one,
Till, after cloying the gazettes with cant,
    The age discovers he is not the true one;
5   Of such as these I should not care to vaunt,
    I'll therefore take our ancient friend Don Juan—
We all have seen him, in the pantomime,
Sent to the devil somewhat ere his time.[1]

2

Vernon, the butcher Cumberland, Wolfe, Hawke,
10   Prince Ferdinand, Granby, Burgoyne, Keppel, Howe,[2]
Evil and good, have had their tithe of talk,
    And fill'd their sign-posts then, like Wellesley now;[3]
Each in their turn like Banquo's monarchs stalk,
    Followers of fame, "nine farrow" of that sow:[4]
15   France, too, had Buonaparté and Dumourier
Recorded in the Moniteur and Courier.[5]

3

Barnave, Brissot, Condorcet, Mirabeau,
    Petion, Clootz, Danton, Marat, La Fayette,[6]
Were French, and famous people, as we know;
20   And there were others, scarce forgotten yet,
Joubert, Hoche, Marceau, Lannes, Desaix, Moreau,

5. Buff and blue were the colors adopted by the Whigs and by the *Edinburgh Review*.
6. Julian was raised as a Christian, but on becoming Roman emperor in 361 he revived the worship of the pagan gods. He was killed in battle in 363. See Gibbon, *Decline and Fall* (ch. 23).
1. Popular melodrama portrayed Don Juan as a seducer who ends in hell; Byron plays against his own reputation as notorious lover by presenting Juan as an innocent boy overwhelmed by women. His attention may have been drawn to the figure by Coleridge's discussion in *Biographia Literaria* (ch. 23). Note that the pronunciation of "Juan" is Anglicized into two syllables, as the rhymes with "true one" and "new one" indicate. "Inez" rhymes with "fine as" and "Jóse" with "nosey."
2. A roll call of recent military heroes. The Duke of Cumberland commanded the forces that defeated the Stuart army at Culloden in 1745; he earned the title "Butcher" for his subsequent suppression of Jacobitism in Scotland.
3. Arthur Wellesley, Duke of Wellington, born in Ire-

land, the most celebrated British general of his time. Granted a peerage for his victory over the French at Talavera (1808), he commanded the British forces at Waterloo.
4. In Shakespeare's *Macbeth* (4.1), the witches show Macbeth a vision of future Scots kings descended from the murdered Banquo, establishing the triumph of his line and the frustration of Macbeth's ambitions.
5. Charles Dumouriez was a French general and Girondist; suspected by the Jacobins in 1793, he fled to the Austrians whom he had defeated the year before. He settled in England in 1804, and advised the British in their war against Buonaparte. The *Moniteur* and *Courier* were French newspapers.
6. All figures of the French Revolution. Jean Baptiste, Baron von Cloots, a zealot, dropped his title and took the pseudonym Anacharsis; elected to the Convention in 1792, he voted for the King's death and was himself executed in 1794. Byron wrote that he meant Juan "to finish as *Anacharsis Clootz*—in the French Revolution."

With many of the military set,
Exceedingly remarkable at times,
But not at all adapted to my rhymes.

4

25   Nelson was once Britannia's god of war,
        And still should be so, but the tide is turn'd;
There's no more to be said of Trafalgar,
        'Tis with our hero quietly inurn'd;[7]
Because the army's grown more popular,
30   At which the naval people are concern'd;
Besides, the prince is all for the land-service,
Forgetting Duncan, Nelson, Howe, and Jervis.[8]

5

Brave men were living before Agamemnon[9]
        And since, exceeding valorous and sage,
35   A good deal like him too, though quite the same none;
        But then they shone not on the poet's page,
And so have been forgotten:—I condemn none,
        But can't find any in the present age
Fit for my poem (that is, for my new one);
40   So, as I said, I'll take my friend Don Juan.

6

Most epic poets plunge "in medias res"
        (Horace makes this the heroic turnpike road),[1]
And then your hero tells, whene'er you please,
        What went before—by way of episode,
45   While seated after dinner at his ease,
        Beside his mistress in some soft abode,
Palace, or garden, paradise, or cavern,
Which serves the happy couple for a tavern.

7

That is the usual method, but not mine—
50   —My way is to begin with the beginning;
The regularity of my design
        Forbids all wandering as the worst of sinning,
And therefore I shall open with a line
        (Although it cost me half an hour in spinning)
55   Narrating somewhat of Don Juan's father,
And also of his mother, if you'd rather.

8

In Seville was he born, a pleasant city,
        Famous for oranges and women—he
Who has not seen it will be much to pity,
60   So says the proverb—and I quite agree;
Of all the Spanish towns is none more pretty,

---

7. Horatio Nelson, admiral and viscount, died in the Battle of Trafalgar (1805) at which he defeated the French fleet.
8. Byron plays the four distinguished British admirals against the Regent's support of the army.
9. An adaptation of Horace (Odes 4.9.25–28): "Many

heroes lived before Agamemnon; but all are overwhelmed in unending night, unwept, unknown, because they lacked a sacred bard" (trans. by C. E. Bennett).
1. In his Ars Poetica Horace recommends that the epic poet begin dramatically, like Homer, by taking the audience directly "into the midst of things."

Cadiz perhaps—but that you soon may see:—
Don Juan's parents lived beside the river,
A noble stream, and call'd the Guadalquivir.

9

65   His father's name was Jóse—*Don*, of course,
        A true Hidalgo,° free from every stain   *nobleman*
Of Moor or Hebrew blood, he traced his source
        Through the most Gothic gentlemen of Spain;
A better cavalier ne'er mounted horse,
70   Or, being mounted, e'er got down again,
Than Jóse, who begot our hero, who
Begot—but that's to come————Well, to renew:

10

His mother was a learned lady, famed
        For every branch of every science known—
75   In every Christian language ever named,
        With virtues equall'd by her wit alone,
She made the cleverest people quite ashamed,
        And even the good with inward envy groan,
Finding themselves so very much exceeded
80   In their own way by all the things that she did.

11

Her memory was a mine: she knew by heart
        All Calderon and greater part of Lopé,[2]
So that if any actor miss'd his part
        She could have served him for the prompter's copy;
85   For her Feinagle's were an useless art,[3]
        And he himself obliged to shut up shop—he
Could never make a memory so fine as
That which adorn'd the brain of Donna Inez.

12

Her favourite science was the mathematical,
90   Her noblest virtue was her magnanimity,
Her wit (she sometimes tried at wit) was Attic° all,   *refined*
        Her serious sayings darken'd to sublimity;
In short, in all things she was fairly what I call
        A prodigy—her morning dress was dimity,°   *plain cotton*
95   Her evening silk, or, in the summer, muslin,
And other stuffs, with which I won't stay puzzling.

13

She knew the Latin—that is, "the Lord's prayer,"
        And Greek—the alphabet—I'm nearly sure;
She read some French romances here and there,
100   Although her mode of speaking was not pure;
For native Spanish she had no great care,
        At least her conversation was obscure;
Her thoughts were theorems, her words a problem,
As if she deem'd that mystery would ennoble 'em.

---

2. Pedro Calderón de la Barca (1600–1681) and Lopé de   3. Gregor von Feinagle (1765–1819) lectured on
Vega (1562–1635), Spanish dramatists.   mnemonics.

14

105 She liked the English and the Hebrew tongue,
       And said there was analogy between 'em;
     She proved it somehow out of sacred song,
       But I must leave the proofs to those who've seen 'em,
     But this I heard her say, and can't be wrong,
110   And all may think which way their judgments lean 'em,
     "'Tis strange—the Hebrew noun which means 'I am,'[4]
     The English always use to govern d—n."

15

     Some women use their tongues—she *look'd* a lecture,
       Each eye a sermon, and her brow a homily,
115 An all-in-all-sufficient self-director,
       Like the lamented late Sir Samuel Romilly,
     The Law's expounder, and the State's corrector,
       Whose suicide was almost an anomaly—[5]
     One sad example more, that "All is vanity,"—
120 (The jury brought their verdict in "Insanity.")

16

     In short, she was a walking calculation,
       Miss Edgeworth's novels stepping from their covers,
     Or Mrs. Trimmer's books on education,
       Or "Coelebs' Wife" set out in quest of lovers,[6]
125 Morality's prim personification,
       In which not Envy's self a flaw discovers;
     To others' share let "female errors fall,"[7]
     For she had not even one—the worst of all.

17

     Oh! she was perfect past all parallel—
130   Of any modern female saint's comparison;
     So far above the cunning powers of hell,
       Her guardian angel had given up his garrison;
     Even her minutest motions went as well
       As those of the best time-piece made by Harrison:[8]
135 In virtues nothing earthly could surpass her,
     Save thine "incomparable oil," Macassar![9]

18

     Perfect she was, but as perfection is
       Insipid in this naughty world of ours,
     Where our first parents never learn'd to kiss

---

4. "God," *Yahweh* in Hebrew, which God renders to Moses as "I AM THAT I AM" (Exodus 3.14).
5. Romilly (1757–1818), a liberal member of Parliament, accepted a retainer to represent Byron in the separation proceedings but then switched to Lady Byron. The stanza shows that even his suicide did not soften Byron's resentment; Murray refused to print it in the first edition.
6. Maria Edgeworth was a popular Irish novelist and educational writer; Sarah Trimmer (1741–1810) was a popular writer on education and of children's books. *Coelebs in Search of a Wife* (1809)—its title deliberately misquoted by Byron—was the only novel of Hannah More, for whom see page 1498.
7. Alexander Pope, *The Rape of the Lock* (1714), 2.17.
8. In 1762 the English clockmaker John Harrison claimed the government prize of £20,000 for a chronometer accurate enough to determine longitude.
9. Byron cites the advertisements of the firm A. Rowland and Son for this widely used hair-oil.

140   Till they were exiled from their earlier bowers,
  Where all was peace, and innocence, and bliss
   (I wonder how they got through the twelve hours)
  Don Jóse, like a lineal son of Eve,
  Went plucking various fruit without her leave.

        19
145   He was a mortal of the careless kind,
   With no great love for learning, or the learn'd,
  Who chose to go where'er he had a mind,
   And never dream'd his lady was concern'd;
  The world, as usual, wickedly inclined
150   To see a kingdom or a house o'erturn'd,
  Whisper'd he had a mistress, some said *two*,
  But for domestic quarrels *one* will do.

        20
  Now Donna Inez had, with all her merit,
   A great opinion of her own good qualities;
155 Neglect, indeed, requires a saint to bear it,
   And such, indeed, she was in her moralities;
  But then she had a devil of a spirit,
   And sometimes mix'd up fancies with realities,
  And let few opportunities escape
160 Of getting her liege lord into a scrape.

        21
  This was an easy matter with a man
   Oft in the wrong, and never on his guard;
  And even the wisest, do the best they can,
   Have moments, hours, and days, so unprepared,
165 That you might "brain them with their lady's fan";[1]
   And sometimes ladies hit exceeding hard,
  And fans turn into falchions° in fair hands,   *swords*
  And why and wherefore no one understands.

        22
  'Tis pity learned virgins ever wed
170   With persons of no sort of education,
  Or gentlemen, who, though well born and bred,
   Grow tired of scientific conversation:
  I don't choose to say much upon this head,
   I'm a plain man, and in a single station,
175 But—Oh! ye lords of ladies intellectual,
  Inform us truly, have they not hen-peck'd you all?

        23
  Don Jóse and his lady quarrell'd—*why*,
   Not any of the many could divine,
  Though several thousand people chose to try,
180   'Twas surely no concern of theirs nor mine;
  I loathe that low vice—curiosity;

---

1. Shakespeare, *1 Henry IV*, 2.3.23.

But if there's any thing in which I shine,
   'Tis in arranging all my friends' affairs,
Not having, of my own, domestic cares.

24

185 And so I interfered, and with the best
   Intentions, but their treatment was not kind;
I think the foolish people were possess'd,
   For neither of them could I ever find,
Although their porter afterwards confess'd—
190   But that's no matter, and the worst's behind,
For little Juan o'er me threw, down stairs,
A pail of housemaid's water unawares.

25

A little curly-headed, good-for-nothing,
   And mischief-making monkey from his birth;
195 His parents ne'er agreed except in doting
   Upon the most unquiet imp on earth;
Instead of quarrelling, had they been but both in
   Their senses, they'd have sent young master forth
To school, or had him soundly whipp'd at home,
200 To teach him manners for the time to come.

26

Don Jóse and the Donna Inez led
   For some time an unhappy sort of life,
Wishing each other, not divorced, but dead;
   They lived respectably as man and wife,
205 Their conduct was exceedingly well-bred,
   And gave no outward signs of inward strife,
Until at length the smother'd fire broke out,
And put the business past all kind of doubt.

27

For Inez call'd some druggists, and physicians,
210   And tried to prove her loving lord was *mad*,[2]
But as he had some lucid intermissions,
   She next decided he was only *bad*;
Yet when they ask'd her for her depositions,
   No sort of explanation could be had,
215 Save that her duty both to man and God
Required this conduct—which seem'd very odd.

28

She kept a journal, where his faults were noted,
   And open'd certain trunks of books and letters,
All which might, if occasion served, be quoted;
220   And then she had all Seville for abettors,
Besides her good old grandmother (who doted);
   The hearers of her case became repeaters,
Then advocates, inquisitors, and judges,
Some for amusement, others for old grudges.

---

2. As Byron believed Lady Byron had tried to do; stanzas 27 and 28 replay details of their separation.

29

225 And then this best and meekest woman bore
          With such serenity her husband's woes,
     Just as the Spartan ladies did of yore,
          Who saw their spouses kill'd, and nobly chose
     Never to say a word about them more—
230   Calmly she heard each calumny that rose,
     And saw *his* agonies with such sublimity,
     That all the world exclaim'd, "What magnanimity!"

30

     No doubt this patience, when the world is damning us,
          Is philosophic in our former friends;
235 'Tis also pleasant to be deem'd magnanimous,
          The more so in obtaining our own ends;
     And what the lawyers call a "*malus animus*"°   *ill will*
          Conduct like this by no means comprehends:
     Revenge in person's certainly no virtue,
240 But then 'tis not *my* fault, if *others* hurt you.

31

     And if our quarrels should rip up old stories,
          And help them with a lie or two additional,
     I'm not to blame, as you well know—no more is
          Any one else—they were become traditional;
245 Besides, their resurrection aids our glories
          By contrast, which is what we just were wishing all:
     And science profits by this resurrection—
     Dead scandals form good subjects for dissection.

32

     Their friends had tried at reconciliation,
250   Then their relations, who made matters worse.
     ('Twere hard to tell upon a like occasion
          To whom it may be best to have recourse—
     I can't say much for friend or yet relation):
          The lawyers did their utmost for divorce,
255 But scarce a fee was paid on either side
     Before, unluckily, Don Jóse died.

33

     He died: and most unluckily, because,
          According to all hints I could collect
     From counsel learned in those kinds of laws,
260   (Although their talk's obscure and circumspect)
     His death contrived to spoil a charming cause;
          A thousand pities also with respect
     To public feeling, which on this occasion
     Was manifested in a great sensation.

34

265 But ah! he died; and buried with him lay
          The public feeling and the lawyers' fees:
     His house was sold, his servants sent away,
          A Jew took one of his two mistresses,
     A priest the other—at least so they say:
270   I ask'd the doctors after his disease—

He died of the slow fever call'd the tertian,°   *malaria*
And left his widow to her own aversion.

35

Yet Jóse was an honourable man,
   That I must say, who knew him very well;
Therefore his frailties I'll no further scan,
   Indeed there were not many more to tell:
And if his passions now and then outran
   Discretion, and were not so peaceable
As Numa's (who was also named Pompilius),[3]
He had been ill brought up, and was born bilious.

36

Whate'er might be his worthlessness or worth,
   Poor fellow! he had many things to wound him.
Let's own—since it can do no good on earth—
   It was a trying moment that which found him
Standing alone beside his desolate hearth,
   Where all his household gods lay shiver'd round him
No choice was left his feelings or his pride,
Save death or Doctors' Commons[4]—so he died.

37

Dying intestate,° Juan was sole heir   *without a will*
   To a chancery suit, and messuages,° and lands,   *houses*
Which, with a long minority and care,
   Promised to turn out well in proper hands:
Inez became sole guardian, which was fair,
   And answer'd but to nature's just demands;
An only son left with an only mother
Is brought up much more wisely than another.

38

Sagest of women, even of widows, she
   Resolved that Juan should be quite a paragon,
And worthy of the noblest pedigree:
   (His sire was of Castile, his dam from Aragon.)
Then for accomplishments of chivalry,
   In case our lord the king should go to war again,
He learn'd the arts of riding, fencing, gunnery,
And how to scale a fortress—or a nunnery.

39

But that which Donna Inez most desired,
   And saw into herself each day before all
The learned tutors whom for him she hired,
   Was, that his breeding should be strictly moral:
Much into all his studies she enquired,
   And so they were submitted first to her, all,
Arts, sciences, no branch was made a mystery
To Juan's eyes, excepting natural history.

---

3. The second king of Rome, renowned for his piety.   4. The court that presided over divorces.

40

The languages, especially the dead,
   The sciences, and most of all the abstruse,
315 The arts, at least all such as could be said
   To be the most remote from common use,
In all these he was much and deeply read;
   But not a page of any thing that's loose,
Or hints continuation of the species,
320 Was ever suffer'd, lest he should grow vicious.

41

His classic studies made a little puzzle,
   Because of filthy loves of gods and goddesses,
Who in the earlier ages raised a bustle,
   But never put on pantaloons or bodices;
325 His reverend tutors had at times a tussle,
   And for their Aeneids, Iliads, and Odysseys,
Were forced to make an odd sort of apology,
For Donna Inez dreaded the Mythology.

42

Ovid's a rake, as half his verses show him,
330   Anacreon's morals are a still worse sample,
Catullus scarcely has a decent poem,
   I don't think Sappho's Ode a good example,
Although Longinus tells us there is no hymn
   Where the sublime soars forth on wings more ample;
335 But Virgil's songs are pure, except that horrid one
Beginning with "Formosum Pastor Corydon."[5]

43

Lucretius' irreligion is too strong
   For early stomachs, to prove wholesome food;
I can't help thinking Juvenal was wrong,
340   Although no doubt his real intent was good,
For speaking out so plainly in his song,
   So much indeed as to be downright rude;
And then what proper person can be partial
To all those nauseous epigrams of Martial?[6]

44

345 Juan was taught from out the best edition,
   Expurgated by learned men, who place,
Judiciously, from out the schoolboy's vision,
   The grosser parts; but fearful to deface

5. Byron rehearses the classical erotic poets: the Roman Ovid (43 B.C.–A.D. 18), author of the *Amores* and *The Art of Love*; Anacreon, 6th-century B.C.; the lyric poet Catullus (c. 84–54 B.C.); Sappho, the 7th-century B.C. Greek poet called "the Tenth Muse" by Plato, whose ode beginning "To me he seems like a god / as he sits facing you" (trans. by Willis Barnstone) was praised by Longinus in his essay *On the Sublime* (1st century B.C.). The final reference is to the second Eclogue of Virgil (70–19 B.C.), a homoerotic text beginning: "Corydon the shepherd burned for lovely Alexis, / His master's beloved."
6. *De Rerum Natura* ("On the Nature of Things"), by the 1st century B.C. Roman poet Lucretius, argues a materialistic view of the world; the 16 satires of Juvenal (c. A.D. 60–130) sternly denounce Roman society; the epigrams of Martial (A.D. 40–104) are witty but often blunt.

Too much their modest bard by this omission,
350   And pitying sore his mutilated case,
They only add them all in an appendix,
        Which saves, in fact, the trouble of an index;[7]

45

For there we have them all "at one fell swoop,"
        Instead of being scatter'd through the pages;
355   They stand forth marshall'd in a handsome troop,
        To meet the ingenuous youth of future ages,
Till some less rigid editor shall stoop
        To call them back into their separate cages,
Instead of standing staring altogether,
360   Like garden gods—and not so decent either.

46

The Missal too (it was the family Missal)
        Was ornamented in a sort of way
Which ancient mass-books often are, and this all
        Kinds of grotesques illumined; and how they,
365   Who saw those figures on the margin kiss all,
        Could turn their optics to the text and pray,
Is more than I know—but Don Juan's mother
Kept this herself, and gave her son another.

47

Sermons he read, and lectures he endured,
370   And homilies, and lives of all the saints;
To Jerome and to Chrysostom inured,[8]
        He did not take such studies for restraints;
But how faith is acquired, and then ensured,
        So well not one of the aforesaid paints
375   As Saint Augustine in his fine Confessions,
Which make the reader envy his transgressions.[9]

48

This, too, was a seal'd book to little Juan—
        I can't but say that his mamma was right,
If such an education was the true one.
380   She scarcely trusted him from out her sight;
Her maids were old, and if she took a new one,
        You might be sure she was a perfect fright,
She did this during even her husband's life—
I recommend as much to every wife.

49

385   Young Juan wax'd in goodliness and grace;
        At six a charming child, and at eleven

---

7. "Fact. There is, or was, such an edition, with all the obnoxious epigrams of Martial placed by themselves at the end" [Byron's note].
8. St. Jerome (340–420), translator of the Vulgate, and St. John Chrysostom (c. 345–407) were both known for

their asceticism.
9. In his *Confessions* (397–398) Augustine describes his life in Carthage, "a hissing cauldron of lust," before his conversion to Christianity.

With all the promise of as fine a face
     As e'er to man's maturer growth was given:
He studied steadily, and grew apace,
390   And seem'd, at least, in the right road to heaven,
For half his days were pass'd at church, the other
Between his tutors, confessor, and mother.

50

At six, I said, he was a charming child,
     At twelve he was a fine, but quiet boy;
395 Although in infancy a little wild,
     They tamed him down amongst them: to destroy
His natural spirit not in vain they toil'd.
     At least it seem'd so; and his mother's joy
Was to declare how sage, and still, and steady,
400 Her young philosopher was grown already.

51

I had my doubts, perhaps I have them still,
     But what I say is neither here nor there:
I knew his father well, and have some skill
     In character—but it would not be fair
405 From sire to son to augur good or ill:
     He and his wife were an ill-sorted pair—
But scandal's my aversion—I protest
Against all evil speaking, even in jest.

52

For my part I say nothing—nothing—but
410   This I will say—my reasons are my own—
That if I had an only son to put
     To school (as God be praised that I have none),
'Tis not with Donna Inez I would shut
     Him up to learn his catechism alone,
415 No—no—I'd send him out betimes to college,
For there it was I pick'd up my own knowledge.

53

For there one learns—'tis not for me to boast,
     Though I acquired—but I pass over that,
As well as all the Greek I since have lost:
420   I say that there's the place—but "Verbum sat,"[1]
I think I pick'd up too, as well as most,
     Knowledge of matters—but no matter what—
I never married—but, I think, I know
That sons should not be educated so.

54

425 Young Juan now was sixteen years of age,
     Tall, handsome, slender, but well knit: he seem'd
Active, though not so sprightly, as a page;
     And every body but his mother deem'd

1. Proverbial: "A word to the wise suffices."

Him almost man; but she flew in a rage
430   And bit her lips (for else she might have scream'd)
If any said so, for to be precocious
Was in her eyes a thing the most atrocious.

                    55
Amongst her numerous acquaintance, all
         Selected for discretion and devotion,
435   There was the Donna Julia, whom to call
         Pretty were but to give a feeble notion
Of many charms in her as natural
         As sweetness to the flower, or salt to ocean,
Her zone to Venus,[2] or his bow to Cupid,
440   (But this last simile is trite and stupid.)

                    56
The darkness of her Oriental eye
         Accorded with her Moorish origin;
(Her blood was not all Spanish, by the by;
         In Spain, you know, this is a sort of sin.)
445   When proud Granada fell, and, forced to fly,
         Boabdil[3] wept, of Donna Julia's kin
Some went to Africa, some stay'd in Spain,
Her great great grandmamma chose to remain.

                    57
She married (I forget the pedigree)
450   With an Hidalgo, who transmitted down
His blood less noble than such blood should be;
         At such alliances his sires would frown,
In that point so precise in each degree
         That they bred in and in, as might be shown,
455   Marrying their cousins—nay, their aunts, and nieces,
Which always spoils the breed, if it increases.

                    58
This heathenish cross restored the breed again,
         Ruin'd its blood, but much improved its flesh;
For from a root the ugliest in Old Spain
460   Sprung up a branch as beautiful as fresh;
The sons no more were short, the daughters plain:
         But there's a rumour which I fain would hush,
'Tis said that Donna Julia's grandmamma
Produced her Don more heirs at love than law.

                    59
465   However this might be, the race went on
         Improving still through every generation,
Until it centred in an only son,
         Who left an only daughter; my narration
May have suggested that this single one
470   Could be but Julia (whom on this occasion

---

2. The belt ("zone") of Venus made its wearer sexually
attractive.

3. Mohammed XI, the last Moorish king of Granada,
expelled by Ferdinand and Isabella in 1492.

I shall have much to speak about), and she
Was married, charming, chaste, and twenty-three.

60

Her eye (I'm very fond of handsome eyes)
    Was large and dark, suppressing half its fire
475   Until she spoke, then through its soft disguise
    Flash'd an expression more of pride than ire,
And love than either; and there would arise
    A something in them which was not desire,
But would have been, perhaps, but for the soul
480   Which struggled through and chasten'd down the whole.

61

Her glossy hair was cluster'd o'er a brow
    Bright with intelligence, and fair, and smooth;
Her eyebrow's shape was like th' aërial bow,
    Her cheek all purple with the beam of youth,
485   Mounting, at times, to a transparent glow,
    As if her veins ran lightning; she, in sooth,
Possess'd an air and grace by no means common:
Her stature tall—I hate a dumpy woman.

62

Wedded she was some years, and to a man
490   Of fifty, and such husbands are in plenty;
And yet, I think, instead of such a ONE
    'Twere better to have TWO of five-and-twenty,
Especially in countries near the sun:
    And now I think on't, "mi vien in mente,"°   *it comes to mind*
495   Ladies even of the most uneasy virtue
Prefer a spouse whose age is short of thirty.

63

'Tis a sad thing, I cannot choose but say,
    And all the fault of that indecent sun,
Who cannot leave alone our helpless clay,
500   But will keep baking, broiling, burning on,
    That howsoever people fast and pray,
    The flesh is frail, and so the soul undone:
What men call gallantry, and gods adultery,
Is much more common where the climate's sultry.

64

505   Happy the nations of the moral North!
    Where all is virtue, and the winter season
Sends sin, without a rag on, shivering forth
    ('Twas snow that brought St. Anthony to reason);[4]
Where juries cast up what a wife is worth,
510   By laying whate'er sum, in mulct,° they please on   *penalty*
The lover, who must pay a handsome price,
Because it is a marketable vice.

---

4. As Byron realized in correcting proofs, it was St. Francis of Assisi (1181?–1226) who cast himself into ditches full of snow to quell his desires.

from **Canto 11**[1]

[JUAN IN ENGLAND][2]

21

Through Groves, so call'd as being void of trees,
    (Like *lucus* from *no* light);[3] through prospects named
Mount Pleasant, as containing nought to please,
    Nor much to climb; through little boxes framed
165 Of bricks, to let the dust in at your ease,
    With "To be let,"° upon their doors proclaim'd;   *rented*
Through "Rows" most modestly call'd "Paradise,"
Which Eve might quit without much sacrifice;—

22

Through coaches, drays, choked turnpikes, and a whirl
170   Of wheels, and roar of voices, and confusion;
Here taverns wooing to a pint of "purl,"°   *gin and beer*
    There mails° fast flying off like a delusion;   *mail-coaches*
There barbers' blocks with periwigs in curl
    In windows; here the lamplighter's infusion
175 Slowly distill'd into the glimmering glass
    (For in those days we had not got to gas—);[4]

23

Through this, and much, and more, is the approach
    Of travellers to mighty Babylon:
Whether they come by horse, or chaise, or coach,
180   With slight exceptions, all the ways seem one.
I could say more, but do not choose to encroach
    Upon the Guide-book's privilege. The sun
Had set some time, and night was on the ridge
Of twilight, as the party cross'd the bridge.

24

185 That's rather fine, the gentle sound of Thamis°—   *River Thames*
    Who vindicates a moment, too, his stream—
Though hardly heard through multifarious "damme's."
    The lamps of Westminster's more regular gleam,
The breadth of pavement, and yon shrine[5] where fame is
190   A spectral resident—whose pallid beam
In shape of moonshine hovers o'er the pile—
Make this a sacred part of Albion's isle.

25

The Druids' groves are gone—so much the better:
    Stone-Henge[6] is not—but what the devil is it?—
195 But Bedlam still exists with its sage fetter,

---

1. Byron composed Canto 11 in October 1822. John Hunt published Cantos 9–11 together in August 1823, again anonymously.
2. Having distinguished himself at Ismail, Juan is sent to St. Petersburg, where he becomes the favorite of the Empress Catherine the Great, whose sexual appetite was notorious. Amply rewarded but exhausted, Juan is sent on a diplomatic mission to England to restore his declining health. Juan's journey across Europe enabled Byron lightly to revisit the materials of *Childe Harold's Pilgrimage*, and his arrival in England returns the poem, in a vivid act

of memory, to the Regency England in which Byron had shined. Here Juan is approaching London.
3. In a famous ancient false etymology, it was speculated that the Latin word for "grove," *lucus*, derived from the lack of light (*lux*) under the trees.
4. Gas came into use in London in 1812.
5. Westminster Abbey, filled with monuments to the famous.
6. Interest in the ancient Celtic Druids, to whom the oak was sacred, and Stonehenge, the Druid stone circle on Salisbury Plain, had grown in the 18th century.

That madmen may not bite you on a visit;
　　The Bench too seats or suits full many a debtor;
　　　The Mansion House too (though some people quiz it)
　　To me appears a stiff yet grand erection;
200　　But then the Abbey's worth the whole collection.[7]

26

The line of lights too up to Charing Cross,
　　Pall Mall,[8] and so forth, have a coruscation°　　　　　*sparkle*
Like gold as in comparison to dross,
　　Match'd with the Continent's illumination,
205　　Whose cities Night by no means deigns to gloss.
　　The French were not yet a lamp-lighting nation,
　　And when they grew so—on their new-found lantern,
　　Instead of wicks, they made a wicked man turn.[9]

27

A row of gentlemen along the streets
210　　Suspended, may illuminate mankind,
As also bonfires made of country seats;
　　But the old way is best for the purblind:
The other looks like phosphorus on sheets,
　　A sort of ignis fatuus° to the mind,　　　　　*will o' the wisp*
215　　Which, though 'tis certain to perplex and frighten,
　　Must burn more mildly ere it can enlighten.

28

But London's so well lit, that if Diogenes
　　Could recommence to hunt his *honest man*,[1]
And found him not amidst the various progenies
220　　Of this enormous city's spreading spawn,
'Twere not for want of lamps to aid his dodging his
　　Yet undiscover'd treasure. What *I* can,
I've done to find the same throughout life's journey,
But see the world is only one attorney.

* * *

65[2]

His morns he pass'd in business—which dissected,
　　Was like all business, a laborious nothing,
515　　That leads to lassitude, the most infected
　　And Centaur Nessus garb of mortal clothing,[3]
And on our sofas makes us lie dejected,
　　And talk in tender horrors of our loathing
All kinds of toil, save for our country's good—.
520　　Which grows no better, though 'tis time it should.

66

His afternoons he pass'd in visits, luncheons,
　　Lounging, and boxing; and the twilight hour

---

7. London sites: Bedlam, a corruption of Bethlehem Hospital for the insane; the Bench, the Court of Common Pleas; the Mansion House, the residence of the Lord Mayor.
8. Juan is proceeding to the fashionable West End.
9. A punning capsule history, from the rationalism of the Enlightenment to the hanging of offending persons from lampposts during the French Revolution.
1. The Greek philosopher Diogenes the Cynic (c.

423–323 B.C.) took a lantern in broad daylight to search for an honest man.
2. The intervening stanzas record Juan's enthusiastic reception by high society.
3. When her husband Hercules was unfaithful, Deianira sent him the tunic of the Centaur Nessus, whom he had killed, believing it to be a love charm. Instead Hercules died in agony.

In riding round those vegetable puncheons
    Call'd "Parks," where there is neither fruit nor flower
525   Enough to gratify a bee's slight munchings;
      But after all it is the only "bower,"
(In Moore's phrase) where the fashionable fair
Can form a slight acquaintance with fresh air.

67

Then dress, then dinner, then awakes the world!
530   Then glare the lamps, then whirl the wheels, then roar
Through street and square fast flashing chariots hurl'd
    Like harness'd meteors; then along the floor
Chalk mimics painting; then festoons are twirl'd;
    Then roll the brazen thunders of the door,
535   Which opens to the thousand happy few
An earthly Paradise of "Or Molu."[4]

* * *

74

585   Our hero, as a hero, young and handsome,
    Noble, rich, celebrated, and a stranger,
Like other slaves of course must pay his ransom
    Before he can escape from so much danger
As will environ a conspicuous man.[5] Some
590   Talk about poetry, and "rack and manger,"°   *rack and ruin*
And ugliness, disease, as toil and trouble;—
I wish they knew the life of a young noble.

75

They are young, but know not youth—it is anticipated;
    Handsome but wasted, rich without a sou;
595   Their vigour in a thousand arms is dissipated;
    Their cash comes *from*, their wealth goes to a Jew;
Both senates see their nightly votes participated
    Between the tyrant's and the tribunes' crew;[6]
And having voted, dined, drank, gamed, and whored,
600   The family vault receives another lord.

Stanzas[1]

When a man hath no freedom to fight for at home,
    Let him combat for that of his neighbours;
Let him think of the glories of Greece and of Rome,
    And get knock'd on the head for his labours.

5   To do good to mankind is the chivalrous plan,
    And is always as nobly requited;
Then battle for freedom wherever you can,
    And, if not shot or hang'd, you'll get knighted.

1820   1830

---

4. Gilded bronze, an ornamental material popular in the Regency.
5. Echoing Samuel Butler's satiric poem, *Hudibras* (1663–1678), "Ah me! what perils do environ / The man who meddles with cold iron" (pt. 1, ch. 3).
6. The tyrants are the Tories, in power; the tribunes, rep-

resentatives of the people, are the opposition Whigs and radicals.
1. Sent to Thomas Moore in a letter of 5 November 1820, the poem reflects—with his usual irony—Byron's involvement with the Carbonari, rebels against Austrian domination of Italy.

On This Day I Complete My Thirty-Sixth Year
Missolonghi, Jan. 22. 1824[1]

'Tis time this heart should be unmoved,
    Since others it hath ceased to move:
Yet, though I cannot be beloved,
    Still let me love!

5   My days are in the yellow leaf;[2]
    The flowers and fruits of love are gone;
The worm, the canker, and the grief
    Are mine alone!

The fire that on my bosom preys
10   Is lone as some volcanic isle;
No torch is kindled at its blaze—
    A funeral pile!

The hope, the fear, the jealous care,
    The exalted portion of the pain
15   And power of love, I cannot share,
    But wear the chain.

But 'tis not *thus*—and 'tis not *here*—
    Such thoughts should shake my soul, nor *now*,
Where glory decks the hero's bier,
20   Or binds his brow.

The sword, the banner, and the field,
    Glory and Greece, around me see!
The Spartan, borne upon his shield,[3]
    Was not more free.

25   Awake! (not Greece—she *is* awake!)
    Awake, my spirit! Think through *whom*
Thy life-blood tracks its parent lake,
    And then strike home!

Tread those reviving passions down,
30   Unworthy manhood!—unto thee
Indifferent should the smile or frown
    Of beauty be.

If thou regret'st thy youth, *why* live?
    The land of honourable death
35   Is here:—up to the field, and give
    Away thy breath!

Seek out—less often sought than found—
    A soldier's grave, for thee the best;
Then look around, and choose thy ground,
40   And take thy rest.

1824

---

1. Two weeks earlier, Byron had arrived in Missolonghi, a marshy town in western Greece, to support the Greeks in their war against Turkish rule. The poem is the final entry in his Missolonghi journal; he died from a fever and the ignorant medical practice of the day on April 19. The poem reflects Byron's feelings for his 15-year-old page, Loukas Chalandritsanos.

2. Echoing Shakespeare, *Macbeth*, 5.3.22.

3. Spartan warriors were exhorted not to drop their shields and flee battle but to return either with their shields or carried, dead, upon them.

Percy Bysshe Shelley
1792–1822

One of the most radically visionary of the Romantics, Percy Shelley has always had counter-cultural prestige. In the nineteenth century, Karl Marx and Friedrich Engels praised his "prophetic genius," and in the twentieth century, Paul Foot, head of England's Socialist Workers Party, edited an inexpensive volume of his political writing both to answer "the enthusiasm of the members of the SWP for Shelley's revolutionary writings" and to give socialists a means to disseminate their views not "with dogmatic propaganda but with the poetry which carries revolutionary ideas through the centuries." With William Blake he was a celebrity in the youth culture of the 1960s.

Shelley's esteem in these disparate countercultures emerges from a selective reading of his work and life, whose full range complicates and challenges partisan evaluation. Variously described as a selflessly devoted, often misunderstood idealist and as appallingly selfish, Shelley was always a risk-taker, and could be careless about the consequences. As an Oxford undergraduate, he collaborated with a friend on *The Necessity of Atheism*, a pamphlet that got them promptly expelled after they sent it to every university professor and administrative official, as well as every bishop in the United Kingdom. His first long poem, *Queen Mab*, included a vitriolic attack on "Priestcraft" and "Kingcraft" that earned him celebrity in the radical press and infamy in the conservative press; well into the nineteenth century, these atheist and revolutionary passages were expurgated. This censorship was part of the refashioning of Shelley in the Victorian period. In a well-orchestrated campaign by his grieving widow and devoted disciples of his poetry, he was made safe for parlors, refurbished from a dangerous thinker into an impossibly delicate visionary given to chanting at sky-larks, "Hail to thee, blithe Spirit!"

Shelley's life is marked by idealism, scandal, and passionate but shifting emotional commitments, especially to women. Grandson of a wealthy landowner and son of a member of Parliament, he was born into conservative aristocracy. Expected to continue in this world, he was sent to the best schools. But he began to rebel early. At Eton (1804–1810), he challenged the tyrannical system of "fagging," whereby upperclassmen had the privilege of abusing their juniors. He no sooner enrolled in Oxford, in 1810, than he got himself expelled for that pamphlet on atheism, an event that at once surprised him and enraged his father. He took off for London, where he met Harriet Westbrook and, believing her oppressed by her father, convinced her to elope with him in August 1811 (he was eighteen, she sixteen). The next year, he was in Ireland irritating its Protestant aristocracy by distributing pamphlets urging Catholic emancipation and improved conditions for its large population of the poor. Eager to meet William Godwin, author of *Political Justice*, he returned to London, and began *Queen Mab*, a Godwinian dream vision. In 1813 Harriet bore a daughter, and he published *Mab* at his own expense. At once celebrated (and pirated) by the radical press and denounced by the Tory press, this poem would be linked to Shelley for the rest of his life, its infamy persisting even into his obituaries.

In the heat of his Godwinian enthusiasms and mindful of Godwin's disdain of the institution of marriage, Shelley allowed himself to tire of Harriet and become enamored of Godwin and Wollstonecraft's beautiful, intelligent daughter Mary. In July 1814, he and Mary eloped to France, accompanied by her stepsister Claire Clairmont. After a six-week tour of Europe, marveling at the Alps and dismayed by the ravages of the Napoleonic wars, they returned to England and the scandal of their elopement. In December Harriet bore her second child by Percy but declined his invitation to join their menage as a platonic sister. When Shelley's grandfather died at the beginning of 1815, he gained a modest fortune of £1000 per year, one-fifth of which was paid directly to Harriet and a good portion of which he would always spend on philanthropy and loans to friends. Mary's first child, a daughter, was born prematurely in February, and died within a few weeks, an event that devastated her. During this year, they experiment-ed with an "open" relationship, in which Percy had a romance with Claire and she with his college friend T. J. Hogg (collaborator on the pamphlet on atheism). Still at odds with their fathers, Mary and Percy were further strained by debts and a constant shift of residences to avoid their creditors and the bailiffs. Percy wrote *Alastor*, a somewhat equivocally framed story of a young visionary poet alienated by life in the world who seeks visionary fulfillment, finding this ultimately in death. Their second child, William, was born early in 1816.

They left for Switzerland in May 1816 with Claire to meet Lord Byron, now Claire's lover. During this summer, Mary wrote *Frankenstein*, and Percy wrote *Hymn to Intellectual Beauty* and *Mont Blanc*, and toured the lakes with Byron. At the summer's end, the Shelley party returned to England and several catastrophes. Mary's half-sister Fanny Imlay committed suicide in October on discovering that Godwin was not her father, and in November, Harriet, pregnant by a new lover and in despair over rejection by him as well as her husband, drowned herself. Percy and Mary were now able to marry, but the scandal of his life and political writings cost him custody of his children by Harriet—an extraordinary ruling in an age when fathers automatically had cus-tody. He was shocked by this judgment, which deepened his self-mythology as an idealist perse-cuted by social and political injustice and despised by a world unable to appreciate his "beautiful idealisms of moral excellence" (as he would phrase it in the Preface to *Prometheus Unbound*).

Over the course of 1817, Shelley consoled himself with new political writing and his friendship with Leigh Hunt, minor poet and editor of the radical newspaper *The Examiner;* through Hunt he met John Keats. Mary was pregnant again, and Clara was born in September. In 1818 they moved to Europe. Eager to spend as much time as possible with Byron, now in Italy, Percy subjected his family to much arduous travel during an oppressively hot summer. Clara did not fare well and died in September. The year 1819 was a productive one for Shel-ley's writing. He finished *Prometheus Unbound*, an epic "closet-drama" begun the year before about the Titan's war with his oppressor; he wrote *The Cenci*, a Jacobean political tragedy of incestuous rape, parricide, and persecution; several other political poems, including *The Mask of Anarchy*, in reaction to the infamous "Peterloo Massacre" of a peaceful workers' rally; a long proto-Marxist political pamphlet, *A Philosophical View of Reform*; and a witty satire of Wordsworth (*Peter Bell the Third*), energized by dismay at the middle-aged poet's didacticism and swing to the political right. He also composed one of his most famous poems, *Ode to the West Wind*, an impassioned cry for spiritual transformation rendered in the astonishingly intri-cate, overflowing verse of terza-rima sonnet-stanzas. The death of William in June, at age three and a half, wrenched the Shelleys with a grief only partly allayed by the birth, five months lat-er, of a second son, Percy Florence—the only one of their children to survive.

Shelley continued to write poetry over the next two years, including *To a Sky-Lark*, and *Adonais*, an elegy for Keats, representing him as a martyr to vicious, politically motivated reviews. Increasingly identifying with this myth himself, and despairing of his bid for poetic fame, in 1821 he began his *Defence of Poetry* (published posthumously by Mary in 1840), in which he set forth his views on the relation of poets both to their immediate social and histor-ical circumstances and to the "Eternity" that authorized their visions and would vindicate their merits. He was also becoming infatuated with Jane Williams, who with her common-law husband Edward had joined their circle in Pisa, Italy. The Williamses and the Shelleys decided to live together on the Bay of Spezia in the summer of 1822. More and more alienated from Mary, who was understandably moody (pregnant for the fifth time in six years and still grieving for her first three children), Percy frequently left her behind to enjoy excursions with the Williamses or Jane alone. He was charmed by their company, jealous of their relationship, and in love with Jane, to whom he addressed a set of beautiful lyrics interwoven with his affection for her, his resentment of Edward, and his withdrawal from Mary. Mary suffered a nearly fatal miscarriage in June. In July, Percy and Edward sailed to Leghorn to greet Leigh Hunt, who was joining Shelley and Byron in Italy to establish *The Liberal*, a journal of opinion and the arts.

On the sail back, Percy and Edward were caught in a sudden storm, and both drowned. Byron wrote to his publisher, sponsor of the most influential Tory periodical of the day, *The Quarterly Review* (which had savaged Shelley): "You are all brutally mistaken about Shelley who was without exception—the *best* and least selfish man I ever knew.—I never knew one who was not a beast in comparison." Whether or not one shares this judgment of the man, Shelley's accomplishment as an artist has always compelled admiration. Wordsworth, who thought him too fantastic by half and who was famously sparing in praise of other poets, judged Shelley "one of the best *artists* of us all . . . in workmanship of style."

Mont Blanc
Lines Written in the Vale of Chamouni[1]

1

The everlasting universe of things
Flows through the mind, and rolls its rapid waves,
Now dark—now glittering—now reflecting gloom—
Now lending splendour, where from secret springs
5 The source of human thought its tribute brings
Of waters,—with a sound but half its own.
Such as a feeble brook will oft assume
In the wild woods, among the mountains lone,
Where waterfalls around it leap for ever,
10 Where woods and winds contend, and a vast river
Over its rocks ceaselessly bursts and raves.[2]

2

Thus thou, Ravine of Arve—dark, deep Ravine—
Thou many-coloured, many-voiced vale,
Over whose pines and crags and caverns sail
15 Fast cloud-shadows and sunbeams: awful° scene,   awesome
Where Power in likeness of the Arve comes down
From the ice gulfs that gird his secret throne,
Bursting through these dark mountains like the flame
Of lightning through the tempest;—thou dost lie,—
20 Thy giant brood of pines around thee clinging,
Children of elder° time, in whose devotion   older and earlier
The chainless winds still come and ever came
To drink their odours, and their mighty swinging
To hear, an old and solemn harmony;

1. At nearly 16,000 ft. in the French Alps, Mont Blanc is the highest peak in Europe, a must-see on everyone's Grand Tour as the epitome of "the sublime"—a vast scene at once exciting and defeating adequate perception and representation; its summit had been attained only a few times by 1816. In Mary's *History of a Six Weeks' Tour*, Percy said the poem "was composed under the immediate impression of the deep and powerful feelings excited by the objects which it attempts to describe; and, as an undisciplined overflowing of the soul, rests its claim to approbation on an attempt to imitate the untamable wildness and inaccessible solemnity from which those feelings sprang." The "imitation" involves a dizzying play of imagery and language: wildly dilated and piled-up syntaxes, dazzling verbal transformations and a welter of sublime negatives (e.g. *unknown, infinite, unearthly, unfathomable, viewless*).

Amid this drama, Shelley poses questions of the mind's ability to perceive and comprehend transcendent power, and ultimately its existence. He portrays the perceiving "mind" with metaphors drawn from the landscape before him, as he stands on a bridge over the River Arve, a deep ravine, and the valley below, the mountain and glacier above. Echoing with a difference Wordsworth's love for "all the mighty world / Of eye, and ear,—both what they half create, / And what perceive; well pleased to recognise / In nature and the language of the sense / The anchor of my purest thoughts" (*Tintern Abbey* 105–109, page 1532), Shelley's poetry alludes to and contests this philosophy of "Nature."

2. Coleridge's *Kubla Khan* (pub. 1816) 17–21, page 1655; the landscape of this poem also appears at 122.

25   Thine earthly rainbows stretched across the sweep
      Of the etherial waterfall, whose veil
      Robes some unsculptured image;[3] the strange sleep
      Which, when the voices of the desart fail,
      Wraps all in its own deep eternity;—
30   Thy caverns echoing to the Arve's commotion,
      A loud, lone sound no other sound can tame;
      Thou art pervaded with that ceaseless motion
      Thou art the path of that unresting sound—
      Dizzy Ravine! and when I gaze on thee,
35   I seem, as in a trance sublime and strange
      To muse on my own separate phantasy,°   *fantasy, delusion*
      My own, my human Mind, which passively
      Now renders and receives fast influencings,
      Holding an unremitting interchange
40   With the clear universe of things around;
      One legion of wild thoughts, whose wandering wings
      Now float above thy darkness, and now rest
      Where that° or thou° art no unbidden guest,   *thy darkness / ravine*
      In the still cave of the witch Poesy,
45   Seeking among the shadows that pass by,
      Ghosts of all things that are, some shade of thee,
      Some phantom, some faint image; till the breast
      From which they fled recalls them, thou art there![4]

                      3

      Some say that gleams of a remoter world
50   Visit the soul in sleep,[5]—that death is slumber,
      And that its shapes the busy thoughts outnumber
      Of those who wake and live.—I look on high;
      Has some unknown omnipotence unfurled
      The veil of life and death?[6] or do I lie
55   In dream, and does the mightier world of sleep
      Spread far around and inaccessibly
      Its circles? For the very spirit fails,
      Driven like a homeless cloud from steep to steep
      That vanishes among the viewless° gales!   *unseeing, invisible*
60   Far, far above, piercing the infinite sky,
      Mont Blanc appears, still, snowy, and serene—
      Its subject mountains their unearthly forms
      Pile around it, ice and rock; broad vales between
      Of frozen floods, unfathomable deeps,
65   Blue as the overhanging heaven, that spread
      And wind among the accumulated steeps;

3. Rocks behind the waterfall in shapes not sculpted by human artistry.

4. An allusion to Plato's allegory in *Republic* 7, which compares the mind to a cave in which our sense of reality consists of the shadows cast by firelight on its walls, ignorant of the light of "Reality" outside. Shelley's difficult syntax blurs the distinction of inner and outer, human mind and Ravine.

5. Inverting Wordsworth's philosophy of Platonic amnesia in stanza 5 of the "Intimations" *Ode* (see pages 1612–1613), Shelley entertains the idea that this spiritual reality is not forgotten but visits the soul in sleep.

6. The screen of phenomena separating physical from spiritual reality (lifted in sleep, in daydreams and visions).

A desart peopled by the storms alone,
Save° when the eagle brings some hunter's bone,   except
And the wolf tracts° her there—how hideously   tracks, traces
70   Its shapes are heaped around: rude, bare, and high,
Ghastly, and scarred, and riven!°—Is this the scene   split
Where the old Earthquake-daemon taught her young
Ruin?[7] Were these their toys? or did a sea
Of fire envelop once this silent snow?
75   None can reply—all seems eternal now.
The wilderness has a mysterious tongue
Which teaches awful doubt,°—or faith so mild,   awe-filled questioning
So solemn, so serene, that man may be,
But for such faith, with nature reconciled.[8]
80   Thou hast a voice, great Mountain, to repeal
Large codes of fraud and woe; not understood
By all, but which the wise and great and good
Interpret, or make felt, or deeply feel.

4

The fields, the lakes, the forests, and the streams,
85   Ocean, and all the living things that dwell
Within the daedal earth,[9] lightning and rain,
Earthquake and fiery flood, and hurricane,
The torpor of the year when feeble dreams
Visit the hidden buds, or dreamless sleep
90   Holds every future leaf and flower; the bound
With which from that detested trance they leap;
The works and ways of man, their death and birth,
And that of him, and all that his may be;
All things that move and breathe with toil and sound
95   Are born and die; revolve, subside, and swell.
Power dwells apart in its tranquillity,
Remote, serene, and inaccessible:
And *this*, the naked countenance of earth,
On which I gaze, even these primaeval mountains
100   Teach the adverting mind. The glaciers creep
Like snakes that watch their prey, from their far fountains,
Slow rolling on; there, many a precipice,
Frost and the sun in scorn of mortal power
Have piled: dome, pyramid, and pinnacle,
105   A city of death, distinct with many a tower
And wall impregnable of beaming ice.
Yet not a city, but a flood of ruin
Is there, that from the boundary of the sky

7. In Greek mythology daemons are (often playful) spirits, usually personifications of natural forces.
8. Shelley first wrote "In such wise faith with Nature reconciled," then revised to "But for such faith" and lower-
cased "nature." The sense is ambiguous: "But for" may
indicate "Only by means of" faith in Nature over the
"Large codes of fraud and woe" promulgated by institutional religions (81). Or it may mean "Except for": man

might be reconciled to the mysteries of nature's violent
power, did it not require a bland faith in a nature that is
unknowable and perhaps indifferent to human needs and
values.
9. The adjective derives from Daedalus, architect of the
famous labyrinth in Crete, and of wings for flight that he
crafted with feathers and wax; hence, a wonderfully
wrought, inspired creation.

Rolls its perpetual stream; vast pines are strewing
110   Its destined path, or in the mangled soil
Branchless and shattered stand: the rocks, drawn down
From yon remotest waste, have overthrown
The limits of the dead and living world,
Never to be reclaimed. The dwelling-place
115   Of insects, beasts, and birds, becomes its spoil;
Their food and their retreat for ever gone,
So much of life and joy is lost. The race
Of man flies far in dread; his work and dwelling
Vanish, like smoke before the tempest's stream,
120   And their place is not known.[1] Below, vast caves
Shine in the rushing torrents' restless gleam,
Which from those secret chasms in tumult welling
Meet in the vale; and one majestic River,
The breath and blood of distant lands, for ever
125   Rolls its loud waters to the ocean-waves,
Breathes its swift vapours to the circling air.

5

Mont Blanc yet gleams on high:—the power is there,
The still and solemn power, of many sights,
And many sounds, and much of life and death.
130   In the calm darkness of the moonless nights,
In the lone glare of day, the snows descend
Upon that Mountain; none beholds them there,
Nor when the flakes burn in the sinking sun,
Or the star-beams dart through them:—Winds contend
135   Silently there, and heap the snow, with breath
Rapid and strong, but silently! Its home
The voiceless lightning in these solitudes
Keeps innocently, and like vapour broods
Over the snow. The secret strength of things
140   Which governs thought, and to the infinite dome
Of heaven is as a law, inhabits thee!
And what were thou,° and earth, and stars, and sea,   *Mont Blanc*
If to the human mind's imaginings
Silence and solitude were vacancy?

23 July 1816   1817

Hymn to Intellectual Beauty[1]

1

The awful shadow of some unseen Power
Floats, though unseen, amongst us, visiting

---

1. Echoing Psalm 103: "As for man, his days are as grass . . . For the wind passeth over it, and it is gone; and the place thereof shall know it no more" (15–16).
1. Composed the same summer as *Mont Blanc* (1816), *Hymn* shares its metaphysics. "Intellectual" refers to the ideal Platonic spirit apprehended by the mind, over the faint and fleeting information of the senses; Shelley may have taken this term from Wollstonecraft's lament in *Rights of Woman* over the low cultural esteem of women's "intellectual beauty" (ch. 3). As in *Mont Blanc*, "unseen Power" is evoked by a rhetoric of negation, unanswered questions, and merely proximate similes.

    This various world with as inconstant wing
    As summer winds that creep from flower to flower.—
5   Like moonbeams that behind some piny mountain shower,°   *(verb)*
        It visits with inconstant glance
        Each human heart and countenance;
    Like hues and harmonies of evening,—
        Like clouds in starlight widely spread,—
10   Like memory of music fled,—
        Like aught that for its grace may be
    Dear, and yet dearer for its mystery.

2

    Spirit of BEAUTY, that dost consecrate
        With thine own hues all thou dost shine upon
15   Of human thought or form,—where art thou gone?
    Why dost thou pass away, and leave our state,
    This dim vast vale of tears, vacant and desolate?—
        Ask why the sunlight not for ever
        Weaves rainbows o'er yon mountain river;
20   Why aught should fail and fade that once is shown;
        Why fear and dream and death and birth
        Cast on the daylight of this earth
        Such gloom,—why man has such a scope
    For love and hate, despondency and hope?

3

25   No voice from some sublimer world hath ever
        To sage or poet these responses given—
        Therefore the names of God and ghost and Heaven,
    Remain the records of their° vain endeavour,   *sages and poets*
    Frail spells—whose uttered charm might not avail to sever
30   From all we hear and all we see,
        Doubt, chance, and mutability.[2]
    Thy light alone like mist o'er mountains driven,
        Or music by the night wind sent
        Through strings of some still instrument,[3]
35   Or moonlight on a midnight stream,
    Gives grace and truth to life's unquiet dream.

4

    Love, Hope, and Self-esteem, like clouds depart
        And come, for some uncertain moments lent.
        Man were° immortal, and omnipotent,   *would be*
40   Didst thou,° unknown and awful as thou art,   *if thou didst*
    Keep with thy glorious train firm state within his heart.
        Thou messenger of sympathies
        That wax and wane in lovers' eyes—
    Thou, that to human thought art nourishment,

---

2. Although some "responses" have been given to the questions in stanza 2, even the potent vocabulary of institutional religions has been unable to allay all doubts and fears.

3. An aeolian or "wind" harp; see Coleridge's *The Eolian Harp*, page 1637.

45   Like darkness to a dying flame![4]
            Depart not—as thy shadow came:
            Depart not, lest the grave should be,
       Like life and fear, a dark reality!

                            5
       While yet a boy, I sought for ghosts, and sped
50   Through many a listening chamber, cave and ruin,
            And starlight wood, with fearful steps pursuing
       Hopes of high talk with the departed dead.[5]
       I called on poisonous names with which our youth is fed.[6]
            I was not heard—I saw them not—
55   When musing deeply on the lot
       Of life at that sweet time when winds are wooing
            All vital things that wake to bring
            News of birds and blossoming,—
            Sudden, thy shadow fell on me;
60   I shrieked, and clasped my hands in exstasy!

                            6
       I vowed that I would dedicate my powers
            To thee and thine—have I not kept the vow?
            With beating heart and streaming eyes, even now
       I call the phantoms of a thousand hours
65   Each from his voiceless grave: they have in visioned bowers
            Of studious zeal or love's delight
            Outwatched with me the envious night—
       They know that never joy illumed my brow
            Unlinked with hope that thou wouldst free
70   This world from its dark slavery,
            That thou, O awful LOVELINESS,
       Wouldst give whate'er these words cannot express.

                            7
       The day becomes more solemn and serene
            When noon is past—there is a harmony
75   In autumn, and a lustre in its sky,
       Which through the summer is not heard or seen,
       As if it could not be, as if it had not been!
            Thus let thy power, which like the truth
            Of Nature on my passive youth
80   Descended, to my onward life supply
            Its calm—to one who worships thee,
            And every form containing thee,
            Whom, SPIRIT fair, thy spells did bind
       To fear° himself, and love all humankind.   *revere, fear for*

1816   1817

---

4. Darkness aesthetically nourishes a flame by offsetting
its glow, even as the flame ultimately dies into darkness;
thus Intellectual Beauty nourishes frail human intellect.
5. An alignment of his childhood with Wordsworth's
shadowy recollection in the "Intimations" *Ode* of a boy-

hood sense of a spiritual reality behind the veil of phenomena; see especially lines 141–147 (page 1614).
6. The vocabulary for divinity in institutional religions;
see line 27. Shelley is referring to boyhood experiments
in conjuration.

Ozymandias[1]

I met a traveller from an antique land
Who said: "Two vast and trunkless° legs of stone   *lacking a torso*
Stand in the desert. . . . Near them on the sand,
Half sunk, a shattered visage° lies, whose frown,   *face*
5   And wrinkled lip, and sneer of cold command,
Tell that its sculptor well those passions read
Which yet survive, stamped on these lifeless things,
The hand that mocked them, and the heart that fed.[2]
And on the pedestal, these words appear:
10   "My name is Ozymandias, King of Kings:
Look on my works, ye Mighty, and despair!"[3]
Nothing beside remains. Round the decay
Of that colossal[4] Wreck, boundless and bare,
The lone and level sands stretch far away."

1817   1818

The Mask of Anarchy

On 16 August 1819, nearly 100,000 millworkers and their families gathered at Saint Peter's Field outside Manchester for a peaceful demonstration, capped by an address by radical Henry "Orator" Hunt calling for parliamentary reform, especially greater representation for the working classes. Alarmed by the spectacle, the local ruling class sent their drunken, sabre-wielding militia to charge the rally and to arrest Hunt; they brutally wounded hundreds, a dozen fatally. It is unclear whether the Home Office (internal security) collaborated in advance with the Manchester elite to suppress the reform movement, or whether, along with the Prince Regent (later George IV), it merely offered congratulations after the fact. The opposition press, notably *The Examiner* (published by Shelley's friends Leigh and John Hunt, no relation to Orator), fueled public outrage with a relentless flow of reports, beginning with eyewitness accounts of what came to be dubbed the "Peterloo Massacre" in sardonic parody of the celebrated English victory at Waterloo, and continuing through Hunt's triumphant entry and subsequent trial in London (he was convicted and sent to prison for two years).

An expatriate in Italy at the time, Shelley was inspired by a self-described "torrent of indignation" to write *The Mask of Anarchy*, which he sent to Leigh Hunt on September 23, 1819, hoping for publication in *The Examiner*. Hunt was already immersed in a series of articles defending Shelley from defamations in the Tory press provoked by *The Revolt of Islam* (another political poem); he backed off from *The Mask* as too risky, notwithstanding its politics of nonviolent resistance. To print a popular ballad advocating the rights of the poor and envisioning the overthrow of a corrupt and tyrannical government would guarantee prosecution, fines, imprisonment, perhaps even exile to Australia; the Hunts had already been jailed and

---

1. Ozymandias (the Greek name for Ramses II) reigned from 1292–1225 B.C.; he is thought to be the pharaoh of Exodus whom Moses challenged. The story of the statue and its inscription is taken from the Greek historian Diodorus Siculus, 1st century B.C.
2. The sculptor read well those passions that survive his hand (that mocked them) and the tyrant's heart (that fed them); "mocked": "imitated," with a sense of caricature or derision. The passions survive both on the images of the stone fragments and in the hearts of modern tyrants; Shelley published this sonnet in 1818 in Leigh Hunt's

radical journal, *The Examiner*.
3. According to Diodorus, this is the actual boast; by Shelley's time, its language echoes ironically against the subsequent application of this title to Christ.
4. An adjective derived from "colossus," the term in antiquity for any large statue; there were several such of 50–60 feet in ancient Egypt. Shelley is also recalling the depiction of Julius Caesar by one of the conspirators in his assassination: "he doth bestride the narrow world / Like a Colossus" (*Julius Caesar* 1.2.135–136).

heavily fined for prior "libels," and here was Shelley likening "Murder" to the Tory Foreign Secretary Castlereagh (also reviled by Byron in the unpublishable Dedication of *Don Juan*, see pages 1683–1684), "Hypocrisy" to Sidmouth the Home Secretary, and "Fraud" to Lord Chancellor Eldon (who had deprived Shelley of his children by Harriet). Leigh Hunt waited to print the poem until 1832, ten years after Shelley's death and just after the passage of the Reform Bill, when Shelley's hotter rhetoric could be viewed with historical distance and its cooler advice admired as prophetic of the nonviolent persuasion by which reform had been won. By this time, too, the notoriety of "Peterloo" was undisputed as a breach of the right of peaceful assembly. Even so, Hunt felt it best to cancel the names Eldon and Sidmouth, as well as the subtitle. Shelley's main title ironically echoes Eldon's condemnation of the rally as "an overt act of treason" posing a "shocking choice between military government and anarchy"; he turns the word back on the government itself, to name its tyranny. "Mask" builds on *The Examiner*'s reference to the government's "Brazen Masks of power" (22 August) and also puns on the literary-theatrical genre of the "masque" (Shelley called the poem *Masque of Anarchy* in a letter to Hunt, who used this title in 1832). Thus he describes government officials as parading in a "ghastly masquerade" (27), a spectacle that travesties the court-masques of the early seventeenth century, performances for the court and the aristocracy that typically celebrated the structures of order and authority that defined their power.

The Mask of Anarchy
Written on the Occasion of the Massacre at Manchester

As I lay asleep in Italy
There came a voice from over the Sea
And with great power it forth led me
To walk in the visions of Poesy.

5   I met Murder on the way—
He had a mask like Castlereagh—
Very smooth he looked, yet grim;
Seven bloodhounds followed him.[1]

All were fat; and well they might
10   Be in admirable plight,
For one by one, and two by two,
He tossed them human hearts to chew
Which from his wide cloak he drew.

Next came Fraud, and he had on,
15   Like Eldon, an ermined gown;
His big tears, for he wept well,
Turned to mill-stones as they fell:[2]

And the little children, who
Round his feet played to and fro,
20   Thinking every tear a gem,
Had their brains knocked out by them.

---

1. Castlereagh, Tory Foreign Secretary and leader in the House of the Commons, was known for his violent suppression of political unrest in Ireland and his support of the reactionary Holy Alliance in Europe and of Austria's domination of Italy. In 1815 he secured England's support for the postponement of the abolition of the slave trade by seven European nations; the pro-war faction in Parliament was known as "bloodhounds" (cf. "hawks"). 2. Eldon was Lord Chancellor (an office identified by its ermine gown) and famous for his public shedding of tears.

Clothed with the Bible, as with light,
And the shadows of the night,
Like Sidmouth, next, Hypocrisy
25   On a crocodile rode by.[3]

And many more Destructions played
In this ghastly masquerade,
All disguised, even to the eyes,
Like Bishops, lawyers, peers, or spies.

30   Last came Anarchy: he rode
On a white horse splashed with blood;
He was pale even to the lips,
Like Death in the Apocalypse.[4]

And he wore a kingly crown,
35   And in his grasp a sceptre° shone;   *royal staff*
On his brow this mark I saw—
"I AM GOD, AND KING, AND LAW!"

With a pace stately and fast
Over English land he passed,
40   Trampling to a mire of blood
The adoring multitude.

And a mighty troop around
With their trampling shook the ground,
Waving each a bloody sword,
45   For the service of their Lord.

And with glorious triumph, they
Rode through England proud and gay
Drunk as with intoxication
Of the wine of desolation.

50   O'er fields and towns, from sea to sea,
Passed the Pageant swift and free,
Tearing up and trampling down,
Till they came to London town.

And each dweller, panic-stricken,
55   Felt his heart with terror sicken,
Hearing the tempestuous cry
Of the triumph of Anarchy.

For with pomp to meet him came,
Clothed in arms like blood and flame,
60   The hired Murderers who did sing
"Thou art God, and Law, and King!

3. Sidmouth was Home Secretary (officer of internal security). The crocodile, fabled to weep as it devours its prey, symbolizes hypocrisy; Sidmouth had used provocateurs to incite illegal action among discontented workers (who were then arrested, jailed, deported, or executed); he also spent millions to build churches to teach spiritual patience to the starving poor rather than improve their material conditions.

4. See St. John the Divine's vision of the fourth horseman of the Apocalypse: "behold a pale horse: and his name that sat on him was Death" (Revelation 6.8). Shelley is also evoking Benjamin West's famous painting, *Death on a Pale Horse* (which he may have seen in London in late 1817 or read about in the press), depicting a crowd trampled by crowned Death and his sword-wielding army.

We have waited, weak and lone,
For thy coming, Mighty One!
Our purses are empty, our swords are cold,
65   Give us glory, and blood, and gold."

Lawyers and priests, a motley° crowd,   *ragtag*
To the earth their pale brows bowed;
Like a bad prayer not over loud,
Whispering—"Thou art Law and God!"

70   Then all cried with one accord,
"Thou art King, and God, and Lord;
Anarchy, to Thee we bow,
Be thy name made holy now!"

And Anarchy the Skeleton
75   Bowed and grinned to every one,
As well as if his education
Had cost ten millions to the Nation.

For he knew the Palaces
Of our Kings were rightly his;
80   His the sceptre, crown, and globe,°   *royal emblems*
And the gold-inwoven robe.

So he sent his slaves before
To seize upon the Bank and Tower,[5]
And was proceeding with intent
85   To meet his pensioned Parliament,

When one fled past, a maniac maid,
And her name was Hope, she said,
But she looked more like Despair,
And she cried out in the air:

90   "My father Time is weak and grey
With waiting for a better day;
See how idiot-like he stands,
Fumbling with his palsied hands![6]

He has had child after child
95   And the dust of death is piled
Over every one but me—
Misery! oh Misery!"

Then she lay down in the street,
Right before the horses' feet,
100   Expecting, with a patient eye,
Murder, Fraud, and Anarchy—

When between her and her foes
A mist, a light, an image rose,
Small at first, and weak, and frail
105   Like the vapour of a vale:

5. The Bank of England is the national treasury; the Tower of London houses the crown jewels. Parliament had been bought off with bribes and other lucrative corruption.
6. A dig at George III.

Till as clouds grow on the blast,
Like tower-crowned giants striding fast,
And glare with lightnings as they fly,
And speak in thunder to the sky,

110   It grew—a Shape arrayed in mail°   *suit of armor*
Brighter than the Viper's scale,
And upborne on wings whose grain°   *pattern*
Was as the light of sunny rain.

On its helm, seen far away,
115   A planet, like the Morning's,° lay;   *Venus as morning star*
And those plumes its light rained through,
Like a shower of crimson dew.

With step as soft as wind it passed
O'er the heads of men—so fast
120   That they knew the presence there,
And looked,—but all was empty air.

As flowers beneath May's footstep waken
As stars from Night's loose hair are shaken
As waves arise when loud winds call
125   Thoughts sprung where'er that step did fall.

And the prostrate multitude
Looked—and ankle-deep in blood,
Hope, that maiden most serene,
Was walking with a quiet mien;°   *appearance*

130   And Anarchy, the ghastly birth,
Lay dead earth upon the earth
The Horse of Death tameless as wind
Fled, and with his hoofs did grind
To dust the murderers thronged behind.

135   A rushing light of clouds and splendour,
A sense awakening and yet tender,
Was heard and felt—and at its close
These words of joy and fear arose

As if their Own indignant Earth,
140   Which gave the sons of England birth,
Had felt their blood upon her brow,
And shuddering with a mother's throe

Had turned every drop of blood
By which her face had been bedewed
145   To an accent unwithstood,—
As if her heart had cried aloud:

"Men of England, heirs of Glory,
Heroes of unwritten story,
Nurslings of one mighty Mother,
150   Hopes of her and one another!

Rise, like Lions after slumber
In unvanquishable number!
Shake your chains to Earth, like dew
Which in sleep had fallen on you—
155   Ye are many, they are few.

What is Freedom? ye can tell
That which Slavery is, too well—
For its very name has grown
To an echo of your own.

160   'Tis to work and have such pay
As just keeps life from day to day
In your limbs, as in a cell
For the tyrants' use to dwell:

So that ye for them are made
165   Loom and plough and sword and spade;
With or without your own will, bent
To their defence and nourishment.

'Tis to see your children weak
With their mothers pine° and peak°   long / waste away
170   When the winter winds are bleak,—
They are dying whilst I speak.

'Tis to hunger for such diet
As the rich man in his riot
Casts to the fat dogs that lie
175   Surfeiting beneath his eye.

'Tis to let the Ghost of Gold[7]
Take from Toil a thousand fold
More than e'er its substance could
In the tyrannies of old.

180   Paper coin—that forgery
Of the title deeds which ye
Hold to something of the worth
Of the inheritance of Earth.

'Tis to be a slave in soul,
185   And to hold no strong control
Over your own wills, but be
All that others make of ye.

And, at length when ye complain
With a murmur weak and vain,
190   'Tis to see the Tyrant's crew
Ride over your wives and you—
Blood is on the grass like dew!

---

7. Debased paper money; though standard legal tender today, in Shelley's day its use as wages was controversial and devastating. Paper could be issued without adequate backing and thus subject to inflation. The doubly evil effect was to
depress the cost of labor to employers and the purchasing worth of the workers' wages.

Then it is to feel revenge,
Fiercely thirsting to exchange
195   Blood for blood—and wrong for wrong—
Do not thus when ye are strong!

Birds find rest in narrow nest,
When weary of their winged quest;
Beasts find fare in woody lair
200   When storm and snow are in the air;

Horses, oxen, have a home
When from daily toil they come;
Household dogs, when the wind roars,
Find a home within warm doors;[8]

205   Asses, swine, have litter spread,
And with fitting food are fed;
All things have a home but one—
Thou, O Englishman, hast none![9]

This is Slavery!—savage men,
210   Or wild beasts within a den,
Would endure not as ye do—
But such ills they never knew.

What art thou, Freedom? O! could slaves
Answer from their living graves
215   This demand, tyrants would flee
Like a dream's dim imagery;

Thou art not, as impostors say,
A shadow soon to pass away,
A superstition, and a name
220   Echoing from the cave of Fame.°   *Rumor*

For the labourer, thou art bread
And a comely table spread,
From his daily labour come
To a neat and happy home.

225   Thou art clothes, and fire, and food
For the trampled multitude—
No—in countries that are free
Such starvation cannot be
As in England now we see!

230   To the rich thou art a check;
When his foot is on the neck
Of his victim, thou dost make
That he treads upon a snake.[1]

8. This stanza is only in *The Masque of Anarchy* (1832).
9. Ironically echoing Jesus' cautions to a scribe who wants to join his ministry: "The foxes have holes, and the birds of the air have nests; but the Son of man hath no where to lay his head" (Matthew 8.20).

1. A famous image from the American Revolutionary flag, whose motto was "Don't Tread on Me!"

Thou art Justice—ne'er for gold
235   May thy righteous laws be sold
As laws are in England—thou
Shield'st alike the high and low.

Thou art Wisdom: Freemen never
Dream that God will damn for ever
240   All who think those things untrue
Of which Priests make such ado.

Thou art Peace—never by thee
Would blood and treasure wasted be
As tyrants wasted them, when all
245   Leagued to quench thy flame in Gaul.°   *Revolutionary France*

What if English toil and blood
Was poured forth, even as a flood?
It availed, Oh, Liberty!
To dim but not extinguish thee.

250   Thou art Love—the rich have kissed
Thy feet, and, like him following Christ,
Give their substance to the free
And through the rough world follow thee,[2]

Or turn their wealth to arms, and make
255   War for thy beloved sake
On wealth and war and fraud—whence they
Drew the power which is their prey.

Science, Poetry, and Thought,
Are thy lamps; they make the lot
260   Of the dwellers in a cot°   *cottage*
So serene, they curse it not.

Spirit, Patience, gentleness,
All that can adorn and bless
Art thou—let deeds, not words, express
265   Thine exceeding loveliness.

Let a great Assembly be
Of the fearless and the free
On some spot of English ground
Where the plains stretch wide around.

270   Let the blue sky overhead,
The green earth on which ye tread,
All that must eternal be,
Witness the solemnity.

From the corners uttermost
275   Of the bounds of English coast,
From every hut, village, and town

---

2. An allusion to Jesus' counsel to a rich young man, who rejects it: "If thou wilt be perfect go and sell that thou hast, and give to the poor, and thou shalt have treasure in heaven: and come and follow me" (Matthew 19.21).

Where those who live and suffer moan
For others' misery or their own;

From the workhouse[3] and the prison
280   Where, pale as corpses newly risen,
Women, children, young and old,
Groan for pain, and weep for cold—

From the haunts of daily life
Where is waged the daily strife
285   With common wants and common cares
Which sows the human heart with tares[4]

Lastly, from the palaces
Where the murmur of distress
Echoes, like the distant sound
290   Of a wind alive around

Those prison halls of wealth and fashion,
Where some few feel such compassion
For those who groan and toil and wail
As must make their brethren pale—

295   Ye who suffer woes untold
Or° to feel, or to behold   *either*
Your lost country bought and sold
With a price of blood and gold—

Let a vast assembly be,
300   And with great solemnity
Declare with measured words that ye
Are, as God has made ye, free!

Be your strong and simple words
Keen to wound as sharpened swords,
305   And wide as targes° let them be,   *shields*
With their shade to cover ye.

Let the tyrants pour around
With a quick and startling sound,
Like the loosening of a sea
310   Troops of armed emblazonry.

Let the charged artillery drive
Till the dead air seems alive
With the clash of clanging wheels,
And the tramp of horses' heels.

315   Let the fixed bayonet
Gleam with sharp desire to wet
Its bright point in English blood,
Looking keen as one for food.

3. In a system to replace begging and alms-giving, the poor
were forced into workhouses where they labored for meager
wages in miserable conditions, often with families separated.

4. See Jesus' parable of the tares (weeds) in the wheat
field, Matthew 13.24–30.

Let the horsemen's scimitars°   *curved Turkish swords*
320   Wheel and flash, like sphereless stars°   *lacking an orbit*
    Thirsting to eclipse their burning
    In a sea of death and mourning.

    Stand ye calm and resolute,
    Like a forest close and mute,
325   With folded arms, and looks which are
    Weapons of an unvanquished war,

    And let Panic, who outspeeds
    The career of armed steeds
    Pass, a disregarded shade
330   Through your phalanx° undismayed.   *arrayed troops*

    Let the Laws of your own land,
    Good or ill, between ye stand,
    Hand to hand, and foot to foot,
    Arbiters of the dispute,

335   The old laws of England—they
    Whose reverend heads with age are grey,
    Children of a wiser day;
    And whose solemn voice must be
    Thine own echo—Liberty!

340   On those who first should violate
    Such sacred heralds in their state
    Rest the blood that must ensue,
    And it will not rest on you.

    And, if then the tyrants dare,
345   Let them ride among you there,
    Slash and stab and maim and hew,—
    What they like, that let them do.

    With folded arms and steady eyes,
    And little fear and less surprise,
350   Look upon them as they slay
    Till their rage has died away.

    Then they will return with shame
    To the place from which they came,
    And the blood thus shed will speak
355   In hot blushes on their cheek.

    Every woman in the land
    Will point at them as they stand—
    They will hardly dare to greet
    Their acquaintance in the street.

360   And the bold, true warriors
    Who have hugged Danger in wars
    Will turn to those who would be free,
    Ashamed of such base company.

And that slaughter to the Nation
365   Shall steam up like inspiration,
Eloquent, oracular,
A volcano heard afar;

And these words shall then become
Like Oppression's thundered doom
370   Ringing through each heart and brain
Heard again—again—again!

Rise like lions after slumber,
In unvanquishable number!
Shake your chains to earth like dew
375   Which in sleep had fallen on you—
Ye are many—they are few."

1819   1832

Ode to the West Wind[1]

1

O wild West Wind, thou breath of Autumn's being,
Thou from whose unseen presence the leaves dead
Are driven like ghosts from an enchanter fleeing,

Yellow, and black, and pale, and hectic° red,   *feverish*
5   Pestilence-stricken multitudes![2] O Thou
Who chariotest to their dark wintry bed

The winged seeds, where they lie cold and low,
Each like a corpse within its grave, until
Thine azure sister of the Spring° shall blow   *spring wind*

10   Her clarion° o'er the dreaming earth, and fill   *shrill trumpet*
(Driving sweet buds like flocks to feed in air)
With living hues and odours plain and hill:

Wild Spirit, which art moving everywhere;
Destroyer and Preserver;[3] hear, O hear!

2

15   Thou on whose stream, mid the steep sky's commotion,
Loose clouds like earth's decaying leaves are shed,
Shook from the tangled boughs of heaven and ocean,[4]

Angels° of rain and lightning! there are spread   *messengers*
On the blue surface of thine airy surge,
20   Like the bright hair uplifted from the head

---

1. There is a long tradition, as old as the Bible, of wind as metaphor of life and inspiration—particularly the West Wind, as bearer of new weather, the harbinger of future seasons, events, and transformations, not only in the natural weather, but by symbolic extension, in emotional, spiritual, and political life. The Latin word for "wind," *spiritus*, also means "breath" (1) and soul or spirit (13.61–62), as well as being the root-word for "inspiration" (a taking-in of energy).

2. An allusion to a traditional epic simile (Milton, Dante, Virgil) comparing the dead to wind-driven fallen leaves.
3. Titles for major Hindu gods, Siva the Destroyer and Vishnu the Preserver.
4. Blending the imagery of leaves with that of ocean tumult, the "tangled boughs of Heaven and Ocean" suggest both waterspouts and huge clouds formed of heaven's winds and ocean vapors.

Of some fierce Maenad, even from the dim verge
Of the horizon to the zenith's height,
The locks of the approaching storm.[5] Thou dirge° *funeral chant*

Of the dying year, to which this closing night
Will be the dome of a vast sepulchre,
Vaulted with all thy congregated might

Of vapours, from whose solid atmosphere
Black rain, and fire, and hail, will burst: Oh hear!

3

Thou who didst waken from his summer dreams
The blue Mediterranean, where he lay,
Lulled by the coil of his crystalline streams,

Beside a pumice° isle in Baiae's bay, *volcanic*
And saw in sleep old palaces and towers
Quivering within the wave's intenser day,

All overgrown with azure moss, and flowers
So sweet, the sense faints picturing them![6] Thou
For whose path the Atlantic's level powers

Cleave themselves into chasms, while far below
The sea-blooms and the oozy woods which wear
The sapless foliage of the ocean, know

Thy voice, and suddenly grow grey with fear,
And tremble and despoil themselves:[7] O hear!

4

If I were a dead leaf thou mightest bear;
If I were a swift cloud to fly with thee;
A wave to pant beneath thy power, and share

The impulse of thy strength, only less free
Than thou, O uncontrollable! if even
I were as in my boyhood, and could be

The comrade of thy wanderings over heaven,
As then, when to outstrip thy skiey speed
Scarce seemed a vision,—I would ne'er have striven

As thus with thee in prayer in my sore need.
Oh lift me as a wave, a leaf, a cloud!
I fall upon the thorns of life![8] I bleed!

A heavy weight of hours has chained and bowed
One too like thee—tameless, and swift, and proud.

---

5. The Greek god of wine Bacchus was attended by Maenads, female votaries who danced in wild worship. Viewing a sculpture of them in Florence, Shelley commented: "The tremendous spirit of superstition aided by drunkenness . . . seems to have caught them in its whirlwinds, and to bear them over the earth as the rapid volutions of a tempest have the ever-changing trunk of a water-spout. . . . Their hair, loose and floating, seems caught in tempest of their own tumultuous motion." Associated in general with vegetation, Bacchus was fabled to die in the autumn and be reborn in the spring.
6. Ruins of imperial Roman villas in the Bay of Baiae, west of Naples.
7. In a note, Shelley says he is alluding to the seasonal change (despoiling) of seaweed, a process he imagines as instigated by the autumn wind.
8. A risky self-comparison to Jesus' torture by a crown of thorns; compare to *Adonais* 305–306.

5

Make me thy lyre,[9] even as the forest is:
What if my leaves are falling like its own?
The tumult of thy mighty harmonies

60   Will take from both a deep autumnal tone,
Sweet though in sadness. Be thou, Spirit fierce,
My spirit! Be thou me, impetuous one![1]

Drive my dead thoughts over the universe,
Like withered leaves, to quicken a new birth;
65   And, by the incantation of this verse,

Scatter, as from an unextinguished hearth
Ashes and sparks, my words among mankind!
Be through my lips to unawakened earth

The trumpet of a prophecy! O Wind,
70   If Winter comes, can Spring be far behind?

1819   1820

To a Sky-Lark

Hail to thee, blithe Spirit!
    Bird thou never wert—
That from Heaven or near it
    Pourest thy full heart
5   In profuse strains of unpremeditated art.[1]

Higher still and higher
    From the earth thou springest,
Like a cloud of fire;
    The blue deep thou wingest,
10   And singing still dost soar, and soaring ever singest.

In the golden lightning
    Of the sunken sun,
O'er which clouds are bright'ning,
    Thou dost float and run,
15   Like an unbodied joy whose race is just begun.

The pale purple even°   evening
    Melts around thy flight;
Like a star of Heaven,
    In the broad daylight
20   Thou art unseen, but yet I hear thy shrill delight—

Keen as are the arrows
    Of that silver sphere°   morning star
Whose intense lamp narrows
    In the white dawn clear
25   Until we hardly see—we feel, that it is there.

---

9. A wind-harp, an image used again in A *Defence* (page 1726), and in Coleridge's *The Eolian Harp* (see page 1637).
1. Shelley hazards the ungrammatical objective case ("me" instead of "I") not only to chime with "Be" but also to represent himself as an object.
1. The skylark sings only in flight; Shelley evokes Milton's thanks to his "Celestial patroness," who "inspires / Easy [his] unpremeditated Verse" (*Paradise Lost* 9.21–24).

All the earth and air
　　With thy voice is loud,
　As, when night is bare,
　　From one lonely cloud
30　The moon rains out her beams, and Heaven is overflowed.

　What thou art we know not;
　　What is most like thee?
　From rainbow clouds there flow not
　　Drops so bright to see
35　As from thy presence showers a rain of melody:—

　Like a Poet hidden
　　In the light of thought,
　Singing hymns unbidden,
　　Till the world is wrought
40　To sympathy with hopes and fears it heeded not:

　Like a high-born maiden
　　In a palace tower,
　Soothing her love-laden
　　Soul in secret hour
45　With music sweet as love which overflows her bower:

　Like a glow-worm golden
　　In a dell of dew,
　Scattering unbeholden
　　Its aerial hue
50　Among the flowers and grass which screen it from the view:

　Like a rose embowered
　　In its own green leaves,
　By warm winds deflowered,
　　Till the scent it gives
55　Makes faint with too much sweet these heavy-winged thieves:

　Sound of vernal° showers　　　　　　　　　　　*springtime*
　　On the twinkling grass,
　Rain-awakened flowers,
　　All that ever was,
60　Joyous and clear and fresh,—thy music doth surpass.

　Teach us, Sprite° or Bird,　　　　　　　　　　*spirit, fairy*
　　What sweet thoughts are thine:
　I have never heard
　　Praise of love or wine
65　That panted forth a flood of rapture so divine.

　Chorus Hymeneal°　　　　　　　　　　　*wedding song*
　　Or triumphal° chaunt,　　　　　　　　　　　*military*
　Matched with thine, would be all
　　But an empty vaunt—
70　A thing wherein we feel there is some hidden want.

　What objects are the fountains
　　Of thy happy strain?
　What fields, or waves, or mountains?

What shapes of sky or plain?
75   What love of thine own kind? what ignorance of pain?

With thy clear keen joyance
    Languor cannot be:
Shadow of annoyance
    Never came near thee:
80   Thou lovest—but ne'er knew love's sad satiety.°   (over)fullness

Waking or asleep,
    Thou of death must deem
Things more true and deep
    Than we mortals dream,
85   Or how could thy notes flow in such a crystal stream?

We look before and after,[2]
    And pine for what is not:
Our sincerest laughter
    With some pain is fraught;
90   Our sweetest songs are those that tell of saddest thought.

Yet if we could scorn
    Hate and pride and fear,
If we were things born
    Not to shed a tear,
95   I know not how thy joy we ever should come near.

Better than all measures
    Of delightful sound,
Better than all treasures
    That in books are found,
100   Thy skill to poet were, thou scorner of the ground!

Teach me half the gladness
    That thy brain must know,
Such harmonious madness
    From my lips would flow
105   The world should listen then—as I am listening now.[3]
1820   1820

A Defence of Poetry

Shelley was called to the *Defence* by an extravagant essay published in 1820 by his friend
Thomas Love Peacock. Peacock described a fall from the grandeur of former ages into a modern poetry marked by triviality, vulgarity, and a studious ignorance "of history, society, and
human nature": Wordsworth gives us "the phantastical parturition of the moods of his own
mind"; "Scott digs up the poachers and cattle-stealers of the ancient border. Lord Byron cruizes

2. Echoing Hamlet's comment on the human capability
of "looking before and after" (4.4.34), as well as alluding
to Wordsworth's use of this phrase in Preface to *Lyrical
Ballads* (1802 addition), just after declaring that "the
Poet, singing a song in which all human beings join with
him, rejoices in the presence of truth as our visible friend

and hourly companion."
3. Alluding to Wordsworth's rhyme in *Resolution and
Independence*: "We Poets in our youth begin in gladness; /
But thereof come in the end despondency and madness"
(48–49). See also the last lines of Coleridge's *Kubla Khan*,
page 1657.

for thieves and pirates," and Coleridge "superadds the dreams of crazy theologians and the mysticisms of German metaphysics." Replete with "obsolete customs, and exploded superstitions . . . the whining of exaggerated feeling, and the cant of factitious sentiment," such poetry, Peacock argued, lacks relevance to modern civilization, which is being shaped by the intellectual power of "mathematicians, astronomers, chemists, moralists, metaphysicians, historians, politicians, and political economists." Even as Shelley recognized the playful taunting of Peacock's essay, he also knew that such views had currency in contemporary Utilitarian philosophies. He began his *Defence* early the next year, but put it aside in the distraction of other projects and a tumultuous personal life. Left unfinished at his death, the fragment did not appear until Mary Shelley published it in 1840.

"Poets are the unacknowledged legislators of the world," Shelley famously concluded, releasing the poet from having to defend his vocation and anointing him as visionary legislator in his own right. Yet what makes *A Defence* so compelling is not any skillful, coherent legal argumentation toward this verdict, but its welter of impassioned, often conflicting arguments and its evocative, often contradictory images for poetic authority and value. On the one hand, a radical dualism invests all truth in "the eternal, the infinite, and the one"—a transcendent realm to which the poet's imagination has visionary access. This is a theme elaborated throughout Shelley's career. Shelley concedes the frustration of any artist who would convey his visions: "the mind in creation is as a fading coal. . . . when composition begins, inspiration is already on the decline, and the most glorious poetry that has ever been communicated to the world is probably a feeble shadow of the original conception." On the other hand, this inevitability has not thwarted poets, Shelley among them, from laboring to make beautiful poems in order to awaken readers' minds to higher values—a precondition for effective political action. In this other line of defense, poetry is not just weak communication of truths beyond the reach of words but is a force of revelation and vital creation in itself. It is not surprising to discover that many of the *Defence*'s sentences, including the celebration of the "electric life" of inspired words and of poets as "unacknowledged legislators," were ones Shelley first drafted for his political pamphlet (also unfinished) *A Philosophical Review of Reform*.

from A Defence of Poetry
or Remarks Suggested by an Essay Entitled "The Four Ages of Poetry"

According to one mode of regarding those two classes of mental action which are called reason and imagination, the former may be considered as mind contemplating the relations borne by one thought to another, however produced; and the latter as mind acting upon those thoughts so as to color them with its own light, and composing from them, as from elements, other thoughts, each containing within itself the principle of its own integrity. The one is the τὸ ποιεῖν,[1] or the principle of synthesis, and has for its object those forms which are common to universal nature and existence itself; the other is the τὸ λογίζειν,[2] or principle of analysis, and its action regards the relations of things simply as relations; considering thoughts not in their integral unity, but as the algebraical representations which conduct to certain general results. Reason is the enumeration of quantities already known; imagination is the perception of the value of those quantities, both separately and as a whole. Reason respects the differences, and imagination the similitudes of things. Reason is to imagination as the instrument to the agent, as the body to the spirit, as the shadow to the substance.

---

1. "Making something," the derivation of "poet." Sir Philip Sidney refers to the poet as "maker" in his late 16th-century *Defense of Poesie*.
2. The logic or reason.

Poetry, in a general sense, may be defined to be "the expression of the imagi-nation"; and poetry is connate with the origin of man. Man is an instrument over which a series of external and internal impressions are driven, like the alterna-tions of an ever-changing wind over an Aeolian lyre,[3] which move it by their motion to ever-changing melody. But there is a principle within the human being (and perhaps within all sentient beings) which acts otherwise than in lyre, and produces not melody alone, but harmony, by an internal adjustment of the sounds and motions thus excited to the impressions which excite them. It is as if the lyre could accommodate its chords to the motions of that which strikes them, in a determined proportion of sound—even as the musician can accommodate his voice to the sound of the lyre. A child at play by itself will express its delight by its voice and motions, and every inflection of tone and every gesture will bear exact relation to a corresponding antitype in the pleasurable impressions which awak-ened it. It will be the reflected image of that impression; and as the lyre trembles and sounds after the wind has died away, so the child seeks, by prolonging in its voice and motions the duration of the effect, to prolong also a consciousness of the cause. In relation to the objects which delight a child, these expressions are what poetry is to higher objects.

The savage (for the savage is to ages what the child is to years) expresses the emotions produced in him by surrounding objects in a similar manner; and language and gesture, together with plastic[4] or pictorial imitation, become the image of the combined effect of those objects and his apprehension of them. Man in society, with all his passions and his pleasures, next becomes the object of the passions and plea-sures of man; an additional class of emotions produces an augmented treasure of expression; and language, gesture, and the imitative arts become at once the repre-sentation and the medium, the pencil and the picture, the chisel and the statue, the chord and the harmony. The social sympathies, or those laws from which, as from its elements, society results, begin to develop themselves from the moment that two human beings coexist; the future is contained within the present as the plant within the seed; and equality, diversity, unity, contrast, mutual dependence, become the principles alone capable of affording the motives according to which the will of a social being is determined to action (inasmuch as he is social), and constitute plea-sure in sensation, virtue in sentiment, beauty in art, truth in reasoning, and love in the intercourse of kind. Hence men, even in the infancy of society, observe a certain order in their words and actions distinct from that of the objects and the impres-sions represented by them, all expression being subject to the laws of that from which it proceeds.

But let us dismiss those more general considerations which might involve an inquiry into the principles of society itself, and restrict our view to the manner in which the imagination is expressed upon its forms.

In the youth of the world, men dance and sing and imitate natural objects, observing[5] in these actions (as in all others) a certain rhythm or order. And, although all men observe a similar, they observe not the same order in the motions of the dance, in the melody of the song, in the combinations of language, in the series of their imitations of natural objects. For there is a certain order or rhythm belonging to each of these classes of mimetic representation, from which the hear-

3. Wind harp.
4. Shaping.

5. Seeing and following, obeying.

er and the spectator receive an intenser and purer pleasure than from any other. The sense of an approximation to this order has been called taste by modern writers. Every man in the infancy of art observes an order which approximates more or less closely to that from which this highest delight results. But the diversity is not sufficiently marked as that its gradations should be sensible, except in those instances where the predominance of this faculty of approximation to the beautiful (for so we may be permitted to name the relation between this highest pleasure and its cause) is very great. Those in whom it exists to excess are poets, in the most universal sense of the word; and the pleasure resulting from the manner in which they express the influence of society or nature upon their own minds, communicates itself to others, and gathers a sort of reduplication from the community. Their language is vitally metaphorical; that is, it marks the before unapprehended relations of things, and perpetuates their apprehension, until words which represent them, become through time signs for portions or classes of thought instead of pictures of integral thoughts; and then, if no new poets should arise to create afresh the associations which have been thus disorganized, language will be dead to all the nobler purposes of human intercourse.

These similitudes or relations are finely said by Lord Bacon to be "the same footsteps of nature impressed upon the various subjects of the world"—and he considers the faculty which perceives them as the storehouse of axioms common to all knowledge.[6] In the infancy of society every author is necessarily a poet, because language itself is poetry; and to be a poet is to apprehend the true and the beautiful, in a word, the good which exists in the relation subsisting, first between existence and perception, and secondly between perception and expression. Every original language near to its source is in itself the chaos of a cyclic poem:[7] the copiousness of lexicography and the distinctions of grammar are the works of a later age, and are merely the catalogue and the form of the creations of poetry.

But Poets, or those who imagine and express this indestructible order, are not only the authors of language and of music, of the dance and architecture and statuary and painting; they are the institutors of laws, and the founders of civil society, and the inventors of the arts of life, and the teachers who draw into a certain propinquity with the beautiful and the true that partial apprehension of the agencies of the invisible world which is called religion. Hence all original religions are allegorical, or susceptible of allegory, and like Janus have a double face of false and true. Poets, according to the circumstances of the age and nation in which they appeared, were called in the earlier epochs of the world, legislators or prophets. A poet essentially comprises and unites both these characters. For he not only beholds intensely the present as it is, and discovers those laws according to which present things ought to be ordered, but he beholds the future in the present, and his thoughts are the germs of the flower and the fruit of latest time. Not that I assert poets to be prophets in the gross sense of the word, or that they can foretell the form as surely as they foreknow the spirit of events; such is the pretence of superstition, which would make poetry an attribute of prophecy, rather than prophecy an attribute of poetry.[8]

6. In a note, Shelley cites Francis Bacon's *Of the Advancement of Learning* (1605) Book 3, ch. 1.

7. An extended set of poems, not necessarily by the same author, dealing with a common subject, event, or character. The term *cyclic poets* (which Shelley uses in *A Defence*) was first applied to a series of Greek epic poems supplementing Homer's *Iliad*; the most famous example of the genre in British literature is "the Arthurian Cycle," dealing with the court of King Arthur.

8. Sidney's *Defence* observes that the Roman word for poet, *vates*, means "prophet" or "oracle."

A Poet participates in the eternal, the infinite, and the one; as far as relates to his conceptions, time and place and number are not. The grammatical forms which express the moods of time, and the difference of persons and the distinction of place are convertible with respect to the highest poetry without injuring it as poetry and the choruses of Aeschylus, and the Book of Job, and Dante's Paradise would afford, more than any other writings, examples of this fact, if the limits of this essay did not forbid citation.[9] The creations of sculpture, painting, and music, are illustrations still more decisive.

Language, colour, form, and religious and civil habits of action are all the instruments and materials of poetry; they may be called poetry[1] by that figure of speech which considers the effect as a synonym of the cause. But poetry in a more restricted sense expresses those arrangements of language, and especially metrical language, which are created by that imperial faculty whose throne is curtained within the invisible nature of man. And this springs from the nature itself of language, which is a more direct representation of the actions and passions of our internal being, and is susceptible of more various and delicate combinations, than colour, form, or motion, and is more plastic and obedient to the control of that faculty of which it is the creation. For language is arbitrarily produced by the imagination, and has relation to thoughts alone; but all other materials, instruments and conditions of art have relations among each other which limit and interpose between conception and expression. The former is as a mirror which reflects, the latter as a cloud which enfeebles, the light of which both are mediums of communication. Hence the fame of sculptors, painters and musicians (although the intrinsic powers of the great masters of these arts may yield in no degree to that of those who have employed language as the hieroglyphic of their thoughts) has never equalled that of poets in the restricted sense of the term, as two performers of equal skill will produce unequal effects from a guitar and a harp. The fame of legislators and founders of religions (so long as their institutions last) alone seems to exceed that of poets in the restricted sense; but it can scarcely be a question whether, if we deduct the celebrity which their flattery of the gross opinions of the vulgar usually conciliates, together with that which belonged to them in their higher character of poets, any excess will remain. * * *

Poetry is ever accompanied with pleasure: all spirits on which it falls, open themselves to receive the wisdom which is mingled with its delight. * * * it acts in a divine and unapprehended manner, beyond and above consciousness; and it is reserved for future generations to contemplate and measure the mighty cause and effect in all the strength and splendour of their union. * * * no living poet ever arrived at the fulness of his fame; the jury which sits in judgement upon a poet, belonging as he does to all time, must be composed of his peers: it must be impanelled by Time from the selectest of the wise of many generations. A Poet is a nightingale, who sits in darkness and sings to cheer its own solitude with sweet sound; his auditors are as men entranced by the melody of an unseen musician, who feel that they are moved and softened, yet know not whence or why[2]. * * *

---

9. In addition to Job, referring to the Greek tragedian (525–456 B.C.), and *Paradiso*, the third and final part of Dante's epic *Divina Commedia* (completed 1321).
1. In the general sense of creative imagination and creative arts.
2. Compare *To a Sky-Lark*, especially 36–40 and 101–105 (pages 1723 and 1724).

The whole objection * * * of the immorality of poetry rests upon a misconception of the manner in which poetry acts to produce the moral improvement of man.[3] Ethical science[4] arranges the elements which poetry has created, and propounds schemes and proposes examples of civil and domestic life. Nor is it for want of admirable doctrines that men hate, and despise, and censure, and deceive, and subjugate one another. But poetry acts in another and diviner manner. It awakens and enlarges the mind itself by rendering it the receptacle of a thousand unapprehended combinations of thought. Poetry lifts the veil from the hidden beauty of the world, and makes familiar objects be as if they were not familiar; it re-produces all that it represents, and the impersonations clothed in its Elysian light[5] stand thenceforward in the minds of those who have once contemplated them as memorials of that gentle and exalted content[6] which extends itself over all thoughts and actions with which it co-exists. The great secret of morals is love, or a going out of our own[7] nature, and an identification of ourselves with the beautiful which exists in thought, action, or person, not our own. A man, to be greatly good, must imagine intensely and comprehensively; he must put himself in the place of another and of many others; the pains and pleasures of his species must become his own. The great instrument of moral good is the imagination; and poetry administers to the effect by acting upon the cause.

Poetry enlarges the circumference of the imagination by replenishing it with thoughts of ever new delight, which have the power of attracting and assimilating to their own nature all other thoughts, and which form new intervals and interstices whose void forever craves fresh food. Poetry strengthens the faculty which is the organ of the moral nature of man, in the same manner as exercise strengthens a limb. A poet therefore would do ill to embody his own conceptions of right and wrong (which are usually those of his place and time) in his poetical creations (which participate in neither). By this assumption of the inferior office of interpreting the effect, in which perhaps after all he might acquit himself but imperfectly, he would resign a glory in the participation of the cause. There was little danger that Homer, or any of the eternal poets, should have so far misunderstood themselves as to have abdicated this throne of their widest dominion. Those in whom the poetical faculty, though great, is less intense (as Euripides, Lucan, Tasso, Spenser) have frequently affected[8] a moral aim, and the effect of their poetry is diminished in exact proportion to the degree in which they compel us to advert to this purpose.[9] * * *

We have more moral, political and historical wisdom than we know how to reduce into practice; we have more scientific and economical knowledge than can be accommodated to the just distribution of the produce which it multiplies. The poetry in these systems of thought is concealed by the accumulation of facts and calculating processes. There is no want of knowledge respecting what is wisest and best in morals, government, and political economy, or at least what is wiser and better

3. In the previous paragraph, Shelley defended poetry from the charge of immorality (leveled famously by Plato in *The Republic*, renewed by the English Puritans of the 17th century and the Evangelicals of Shelley's own age) for depicting characters "remote from moral perfection" and thus offering no "edifying pattern for general imitation" by their readers. Throughout, *A Defence* also counters Plato's other charge, that all art is only representation, and thus a diminishment of Ideal Truth.
4. Moral philosophy.
5. In Greek myth, Elysium is the abode of the blessed after death.
6. Noun: both "content" and "contentment."

7. In the argument of Plato's *Symposium*, a key sentence reads, "Love, therefore, and every thing else that desires anything, desires that which is absent and beyond his reach, that which it has not, that which is not itself, that which it wants" (Shelley's translation); "wants" means both "desires" and "lacks."
8. Adopted.
9. Euripides: Greek tragedian, 5th century B.C.; Lucan: Roman epic poet, A.D. 1st century; Torquato Tasso: Italian epic poet, 16th century; Edmund Spenser: 16th-century English poet, best known for the romance epic, *The Faerie Queene*.

than what men now practise and endure. But we let "*I dare not* wait upon *I would*, like the poor cat i'the adage."[1] We want the creative faculty to imagine that which we know; we want the generous impulse to act that which we imagine; we want the poetry of life:[2] our calculations have outrun conception; we have eaten more than we can digest. The cultivation of those sciences which have enlarged the limits of the empire of man over the external world, has, for want of the poetical faculty, proportionally circumscribed those of the internal world; and man, having enslaved the elements, remains himself a slave. To what but a cultivation of the mechanical arts in a degree disproportioned to the presence of the creative faculty (which is the basis of all knowledge) is to be attributed the abuse of all invention for abridging and combining labour, to the exasperation of the inequality of mankind? From what other cause has it arisen that these inventions, which should have lightened, have added a weight to the curse imposed on Adam?[3] Poetry, and the principle of Self (of which money is the visible incarnation) are the God and Mammon of the world.[4]

The functions of the poetical faculty are twofold: by one it creates new materials of knowledge and power and pleasure; by the other it engenders in the mind a desire to reproduce and arrange them according to a certain rhythm and order which may be called the beautiful and the good. The cultivation of poetry is never more to be desired than in periods when, from an excess of the selfish and calculating principle, the accumulation of the materials of external life exceed the quantity of the power of assimilating them to the internal laws of human nature. The body has then become too unwieldy for that which animates it.

Poetry is indeed something divine. It is at once the centre and circumference of knowledge;[5] it is that which comprehends all science, and that to which all science must be referred. It is at the same time the root and blossom of all other systems of thought. It is that from which all spring, and that which adorns all; and that which, if blighted, denies the fruit and the seed, and withholds from the barren world the nourishment and the succession of the scions of the tree of life. It is the perfect and consummate surface and bloom of all things; it is as the odour and the colour of the rose to the texture of the elements which compose it, as the form and splendour of unfaded beauty to the secrets of anatomy and corruption. What were [would be] Virtue, Love, Patriotism, Friendship, etc., what were the scenery of this beautiful Universe which we inhabit; what were our consolations on this side of the grave, and what were our aspirations beyond it,—if Poetry did not ascend to bring light and fire from those eternal regions where the owl-winged faculty of calculation dare not ever soar? Poetry is not like reasoning, a power to be exerted according to the determination of the will. A man cannot say, "I will compose poetry." The greatest poet even cannot say it: for the mind in creation is as a fading coal which some invisible influence, like an inconstant wind, awakens to transitory brightness. This power arises

1. *Macbeth* 1.7.44–45.
2. In these declarations, "want" means "lack" and "need," shaded by a sense of "desire," "wish for."
3. The Lord says to Adam, in punishment for his sin, "cursed is the ground for thy sake; in sorrow shalt thou eat of it all the days of thy life; thorns also and thistles shall it bring forth. . . . In the sweat of thy face shalt thou eat bread, till thou return unto the ground; . . . dust thou art, and unto dust shalt thou return" (Genesis 3.17–19).
4. Mammon is the false idol of money and worldly goods, against whom Jesus cautions, "Ye cannot serve God and mammon" (Luke 16.13). Keats told Shelley the year before he wrote his *Defence,* "A modern work it is said must have a purpose, which may be the God—*an artist* must serve Mammon—he must have 'self concentration' selfishness perhaps. You I am sure will forgive me for sincerely remarking that you might curb your magnanimity and be more of an artist" (see page 1779).
5. Shelley is evoking the description of God, often attributed to St. Augustine (A.D. 4th–5th century), as the circle whose center is everywhere and circumference nowhere.

from within, like the colour of a flower which fades and changes as it is developed, and the conscious portions of our natures are unprophetic either of its approach or its departure. Could this influence be durable in its original purity and force, it is impossible to predict the greatness of the results; but when composition begins, inspiration is already on the decline, and the most glorious poetry that has ever been communicated to the world is probably a feeble shadow of the original conceptions of the poet. I appeal to the greatest poets of the present day whether it is not an error to assert that the finest passages of poetry are produced by labour and study. The toil and the delay recommended by critics can be justly interpreted to mean no more than a careful observation of the inspired moments, and an artificial connection of the spaces between their suggestions by the intertexture of conventional expressions—a necessity only imposed by a limitedness of the poetical faculty itself. For Milton conceived the Paradise Lost as a whole before he executed it in portions. We have his own authority also for the muse having "dictated" to him the "unpremeditated song."[6] And let this be an answer to those who would allege the fifty-six various readings of the first line of the Orlando Furioso.[7] Compositions so produced are to poetry what mosaic is to painting. The instinct and intuition of the poetical faculty is still more observable in the plastic and pictorial arts: a great statue or picture grows under the power of the artist as a child in the mother's womb, and the very mind which directs the hands in formation is incapable of accounting to itself for the origin, the gradations, or the media of the process.

Poetry is the record of the best and happiest moments of the happiest and best minds. We are aware of evanescent visitations of thought and feeling sometimes associated with place or person, sometimes regarding our own mind alone, and always arising unforeseen and departing unbidden, but elevating and delightful beyond all expression; so that even in the desire and the regret they leave, there cannot but be pleasure, participating as it does in the nature of its object. It is, as it were, the interpenetration of a diviner nature through our own, but its footsteps are like those of a wind over sea, which the morning calm erases, and whose traces remain only as on the wrinkled sand which paves it. These and corresponding conditions of being are experienced principally by those of the most delicate sensibility and the most enlarged imagination; and the state of mind produced by them is at war with every base desire. The enthusiasm of virtue, love, patriotism, and friendship is essentially linked with emotions; and whilst they last, self appears as what it is, an atom to a Universe. Poets are not only subject to these experiences as spirits of the most refined organization, but they can colour all that they combine with the evanescent hues of this etherial world; a word or a trait in the representation of a scene or a passion will touch the enchanted chord, and reanimate, in those who have ever experienced these emotions, the sleeping, the cold, the buried image of the past. Poetry thus makes immortal all that is best and most beautiful in the world; it arrests the vanishing apparitions which haunt the interlunations[8] of life, and veiling them or [either] in language or in form, sends them forth among mankind, bearing sweet news of kindred joy to those with whom their sisters abide—abide, because there is no portal of expression from the caverns of the spirit

---

6. In Paradise Lost, Milton says that his celestial muse "dictates to me slumb'ring, or inspires / Easy my unpremeditated verse" (9.23–24); compare To a Sky-

Lark, 5 (page 1722).
7. Epic poem by Italian poet Ariosto (1632).
8. The dark intervals between the old and new moons.

which they inhabit into the universe of things.[9] Poetry redeems from decay the visitations of the divinity in man.

Poetry turns all things to loveliness: it exalts the beauty of that which is most beautiful, and it adds beauty to that which is most deformed; it marries exultation and horror, grief and pleasure, eternity and change; it subdues to union under its light yoke all irreconcilable things.[1] It transmutes all that it touches, and every form moving within the radiance of its presence is changed by wondrous sympathy to an incarnation of the spirit which it breathes; its secret alchemy turns to potable gold the poisonous waters which flow from death through life; it strips the veil of familiarity from the world, and lays bare the naked and sleeping beauty which is the spirit of its forms.

All things exist as they are perceived: at least in relation to the percipient. "The mind is its own place, and of itself can make a heaven of hell, a hell of heaven."[2] But poetry defeats the curse which binds us to be subjected to the accident of surrounding impressions. And whether it spreads its own figured curtain or withdraws life's dark veil from before the scene of things, it equally creates for us a being within our being.[3] It makes us the inhabitant of a world to which the familiar world is a chaos. It reproduces the common universe of which we are portions and percipients, and it purges from our inward sight the film of familiarity which obscures from us the wonder of our being. It compels us to feel that which we perceive, and to imagine that which we know. It creates anew the universe after it has been annihilated in our minds by the recurrence of impressions blunted by reiteration. It justifies that bold and true word of Tasso: *Non merita nome di creatore, se non Iddio ed il Poeta.*[4]

A Poet, as he is the author to others of the highest wisdom, pleasure, virtue, and glory, so he ought personally to be the happiest, the best, the wisest, and the most illustrious of men. As to his glory, let time be challenged to declare whether the fame of any other institutor of human life be comparable to that of a poet. That he is the wisest, the happiest, and the best, inasmuch as he is a poet, is equally incontrovertible: the greatest poets have been men of the most spotless virtue, of the most consummate prudence, and (if we would look into the interior of their lives) the most fortunate of men. And the exceptions, as they regard those who possessed the poetic faculty in a high yet inferior degree, will be found on consideration to confirm rather than destroy the rule. Let us for a moment stoop to the arbitration of popular breath, and usurping and uniting in our own persons the incompatible characters of accuser, witness, judge and executioner, let us decide without trial, testimony, or form, that certain motives of those who are "there sitting where we dare not soar,"[5] are reprehensible. Let us assume that Homer was a drunkard, that Virgil was a flatterer, that Horace was a cow-

9. Poetry is valuable because it articulates not only what the poet apprehends—those "vanishing apparitions"—but also their "sisters" in the spiritual selves of ordinary mankind, who would lack connection to what is "best and most beautiful in the world" and "the universe of things," were it not for poetry. In his *Defense*, Sidney calls the inner potential for understanding the "foreconceit," and grants poets similar power.

1. Coleridge's description of imagination, *Biographia Literaria* (1817), the end of ch. 14 (see page 1669).

2. A small but significant misquotation of Satan's boast in Hell, *Paradise Lost* 1.254–55; Milton wrote "in itself" (not "of"), in order to set up, along with the second half of the chiasmus that Shelley goes on to deflect, the horri-

bly ironic return of this boast of mind over place when Satan beholds Eve and Eden in the morning (9.467–70).

3. For these possibilities, recall *Mont Blanc* 53–54 (page 1705).

4. *None merits the name of creator except God and the Poet;* from Serassi's *Life of Torquato Tasso* (1785). Sidney's *Apology* refers to God as the "Maker of [the] maker" (punning on the Greek root for "poet".

5. "Those" are the poets whose reprehensible motives Shelley is willing to concede for the sake of argument. His quotation adapts Satan's sneering reminder to his former peers of his former state in Heaven: "ye knew me once no mate / For you, there sitting where ye durst not soar" (*Paradise Lost* 4.428–29).

ard, that Tasso was a madman, that Lord Bacon was a peculator, that Raphael was a libertine, that Spenser was a Poet Laureate.[6] It is inconsistent with this division of our subject to cite living poets, but posterity has done ample justice to the great names now referred to. Their errors have been weighed and found to have been dust in the balance; if their sins "were as scarlet, they are now white as snow"; they have been washed in the blood of the mediator and redeemer, Time.[7] Observe in what a ludicrous chaos the imputations of real or fictitious crime have been confused in the contemporary calumnies against poetry and poets; consider how little is as it appears—or appears as it is; look to your own motives, and judge not, lest ye be judged.[8]

Poetry, as has been said, differs in this respect from logic: that it is not subject to the controul of the active power of the mind, and that its birth and recurrence has no necessary connection with the consciousness or will. It is presumptuous to determine that these are the necessary conditions of all mental causation, when mental effects are experienced insusceptible of being referred to them.[9] The frequent recurrence of the poetical power, it is obvious to suppose, may produce in the mind a habit of order and harmony correlative with its own nature and with its effects upon other minds. But in the intervals of inspiration (and they may be frequent without being durable) a poet becomes a man, and is abandoned to the sudden reflux of the influences under which others habitually live. But as he is more delicately organized than other men, and sensible to pain and pleasure (both his own and that of others), in a degree unknown to them,[1] he will avoid the one [pain] and pursue the other [pleasure] with an ardor proportioned to this difference. And he renders himself obnoxious to calumny, when he neglects to observe the circumstances under which these objects of universal pursuit and flight have disguised themselves in one another's garments.

But there is nothing necessarily evil in this error, and thus cruelty, envy, revenge, avarice, and the passions purely evil, have never formed any portion of the popular imputations on the lives of poets.

I have thought it most favourable to the cause of truth to set down these remarks according to the order in which they were suggested to my mind by a consideration of the subject itself, instead of following that of the treatise that excited me to make them public. Thus although devoid of the formality of a polemical reply, if the views which they contain be just, they will be found to involve a refutation of the doctrines

6. All charges that have been made against these poets. Homer: epic poet of ancient Greece; Horace: Roman lyric poet and satirist, 1st century B.C.; Virgil: Roman pastoral and epic poet, 1st century B.C., sometimes accused of being an apologist for Roman imperialism; Bacon: English Renaissance philosopher, essayist, statesman, and scientist, whose public career was ruined by his conviction for accepting bribes (a peculator is an embezzler); Raphael: 16th century Italian painter (a libertine is given to immoral sensual indulgence); for Tasso and Spenser, see n. 9, page 1729. The first Poet Laureate, a royally bestowed office and honor, was Dryden (1670–1689), but because the position is associated with royal patronage and often the defense or celebration of the monarchy, other court poets, including Spenser, have been retroactively accorded the title. Shelley uses the charge against Spenser to sneer at one particular "living poet," the current Laureate, Robert Southey (cf. Byron's Dedication to Don Juan, page 1681).

7. See Isaiah: "Come now, and let us reason together,

saith the Lord: though your sins be as scarlet, they shall be as white as snow" (1.18); and Revelation: those in white robes at the throne of God "came out of great tribulation, and have washed their robes, and made them white in the blood of the Lamb" (i.e., Christ; 7.14).

8. See Christ's admonition, "Judge not, that ye be not judged. For with what judgment ye judge, ye shall be judged" (Matthew 7.1–2); by "contemporary calumnies," slanders and lies intended to ruin reputations, Shelley is referring to attacks on himself and others in Tory journals, especially The Quarterly. In the Preface of his panegyric on the death of King George III (1820), Poet Laureate Southey described Shelley's circle in Italy, which included Byron, as a "League of Incest," and their poetry as the work of "the Satanic School."

9. The plural pronouns refer to "consciousness and will" in the previous sentence.

1. An echo of Wordsworth's Preface to Lyrical Ballads; see page 1537.

of "The Four Ages of Poetry" so far at least as regards the first division of the subject. I can readily conjecture what should have moved the gall of the learned and intelligent author of that paper; I confess myself like him unwilling to be stunned by the *Theseids* of the hoarse Codri of the day. Bavius and Maevius undoubtedly are, as they ever were, insufferable persons. But it belongs to a philosophical critic to distinguish rather than confound.[2]

The first part of these remarks has related to poetry in its elements and principles; and it has been shown, as well as the narrow limits assigned them would permit, that what is called poetry in a restricted sense has a common source with all other forms of order and of beauty according to which the materials of human life are susceptible of being arranged, and which is poetry in a universal sense.

The second part will have for its object an application of these principles to the present state of the cultivation of poetry, and a defense of the attempt to idealize the modern forms of manners and opinions, and compel them into a subordination to the imaginative and creative faculty.[3] For the literature of England, an energetic development of which has ever preceded or accompanied a great and free development of the national will, has arisen, as it were, from a new birth. In spite of the low-thoughted envy which would undervalue contemporary merit, our own will be a memorable age in intellectual achievements, and we live among such philosophers and poets as surpass beyond comparison any who have appeared since the last national struggle for civil and religious liberty.[4] The most unfailing herald, companion, and follower of the awakening of a great people to work a beneficial change in opinion or institution, is poetry. At such periods there is an accumulation of the power of communicating and receiving intense and impassioned conceptions respecting man and nature. The persons in whom this power resides may often (as far as regards many portions of their nature) have little apparent correspondence with that spirit of good of which they are the ministers. But even whilst they deny and abjure, they are yet compelled to serve the power which is seated on the throne of their own soul. It is impossible to read the compositions of the most celebrated writers of the present day without being startled with the electric life which burns within their words.[5] They measure the circumference and sound the depths of human nature with a comprehensive and all-penetrating spirit, and they are themselves perhaps the most sincerely astonished at its manifestations, for it is less their spirit than the spirit of the age. Poets are the hierophants[6] of an unapprehended inspiration, the mirrors of the gigantic shadows which futurity casts upon the present, the words which express what they understand not; the trumpets which sing to battle, and feel not what they inspire; the influence which is moved not, but moves.[7] Poets are the unacknowledged legislators of the world.

---

2. Theseids are epic poems about Theseus, hero of ancient Greek legend; one of the worst and longest, by Roman poet Codrus (*Codri*, the plural, names poems of this type), was savaged by Juvenal and other satirists. Two other inferior Roman poets, Bavius and Maevius, were satirized by Virgil and Horace; the names became bywords for bad poetry. In the 1790s William Gifford (who would go on to edit *The Anti-Jacobin* and *The Quarterly*) gave the titles *The Baviad* and *The Maeviad* to his devastating mock-heroic satires of the sentimental-aesthetic poetry of the day.

3. Never drafted.
4. The Civil Wars of the 1640s, concluding in the execution of Charles I, and the Glorious Revolution of the late 1680s, unseating James II. Among "philosophers and poets," Shelley has Byron and himself in mind.
5. Again, himself and Byron.
6. Ancient priests who interpret sacred mysteries; oracles of revelation.
7. Aristotle (Greek philosopher, 4th century B.C.) described God as the "Unmoved Mover" of the universe.

Felicia Hemans
1793–1835

A best-selling poet in England and America through most of the nineteenth century, Felicia Hemans (née Browne) was a prolific writer. In addition to numerous publications in magazines and gift-books, she produced nineteen volumes of poems and plays between 1808 and 1834. Lord Byron, with whom she shared the publisher John Murray, was sensitive to the competition. In letters to Murray, he tags her "your feminine *He-Man*" or "Mrs. Hewoman's," his punning turning her commercial prowess into a monstrous mockery of sexual identity. Byron preferred women in their place, not his. "I do not despise Mrs. Heman—but if [she] knit blue stockings instead of wearing them it would be better," he declared to Murray, referring to the "blue-stockings," a derisive term for learned women.

Born in Liverpool in 1793, the year of the Terror in France and the execution of its king and queen, Felicia Hemans was raised in the distant calms of North Wales. Under the devoted tutelage of her mother, she became a child prodigy, learning Latin, German, French, and Italian, devouring Shakespeare, and quickly developing a talent for writing; when she was fourteen, her parents underwrote the publication of her first volume. Learning of her talents and beauty, Percy Shelley ventured a correspondence, but (fortunately for young Felicia Browne) her mother intervened and nothing came of his overture. The romance that did blossom was with Captain Alfred Hemans, a veteran of the Peninsular Campaign in Spain in which her brothers also served. They married in 1812, the year of her nineteenth birthday and third volume, *The Domestic Affections*. By 1818, she had produced three more volumes to favorable reviews, as well as five sons. Just before the birth of the last, the Captain left for Italy for reasons unclear; the story was ill health. In any event, they never saw each other again, the breach mirroring her father's desertion of his wife and children in 1810, for a fresh start in Canada. The collapse of her own and her mother's marriages haunts the idealism of home for which "Mrs. Hemans" was becoming famous, shadowing it with repeated stories of men's unreliability or treachery and the necessity of maternal responsibility.

Determined to support herself and her sons with her writing, Hemans returned to her mother's home in Wales. With no wifely obligations or husband to "obey," and with sisters, mother, and brothers to help care for her boys and run the home, Hemans had considerable time to read, study, write, and publish. There was a related cultural advantage. As a daughter under "the maternal wing" and an "affectionate, tender, and vigilant mother" herself (as prefaces to her works later in the century put it), the professional writer was immunized against the stigma of "unfeminine" independence. The death of her mother in 1827 was a deep and devastating grief, aggravated by the disintegration of her home as sons grew up and brothers and sisters married or moved away. Her health suffered, and after a long decline, she died in Dublin in 1835, a few months before her forty-second birthday. William Wordsworth warmly honored her in the memorial verses of his *Extempore Effusion*, even as he indicated his discomfort with her ignorance of household skills and her affectation of being a "literary lady."

Among Hemans's most successful volumes, both critically and commercially, were *Tales, and Historic Scenes* (1819), *The Forest Sanctuary* (1825), *Records of Woman* (1828), which she dedicated to Joanna Baillie, and *Songs of the Affections* (1830). She was popular well into the Victorian age, especially among women. By the middle of our century, she was remembered only by a few favorite poems, including *The Homes of England*, *The Landing of the Pilgrim Fathers* ("The breaking waves dashed high, / On a stern and rockbound coast") and *Casabianca* ("The boy stood on the burning deck")—this last a parlor-recitation and school-assembly favorite, as well as the subject of multiple parodies. By the 1980s, she was virtually forgotten.

In the recent recovery of the "lost" women writers of the Romantic era, however, her work has received fresh attention, especially for its reflection of many of the key social, psychological, and emotional concerns for women in her day. These involve not only woman's culturally celebrated roles as a patient, devoted, and often long-suffering lover, wife, and mother, but also persistent tensions within these definitions. Some readers still read her poetry as celebrating traditional gender values: women's place at home and her value in upholding "domestic affections," religious faith, and patriotic sentiment. But to others this same poetry seems only tenuously conservative and far from replete—haunted by sensations of the futility and vulnerability of the very ideals it celebrates, invaded by sadness, melancholy, betrayal, suffering, and violence, and repeatedly staging women's heroism in scenes of defeat and death. Hemans's imagination was particularly tuned to conflicts besetting women who achieve fame in nontraditional roles, especially as artists, typically at great cost in personal happiness.

FROM TALES AND HISTORIC SCENES, IN VERSE
The Wife of Asdrubal

"This governor, who had braved death when it was at a distance, and protested that the sun should never see him survive Carthage,[1] this fierce Asdrubal, was so mean-spirited, as to come alone, and privately throw himself at the conqueror's feet. The general, pleased to see his proud rival humbled, granted his life, and kept him to grace his triumph. The Carthaginians in the citadel no sooner understood that their commander had abandoned the place, than they threw open the gates, and put the proconsul in possession of Byrsa. The Romans had now no enemy to contend with but the nine hundred deserters, who, being reduced to despair, retired into the temple of Esculapius, which was a second citadel within the first: there the proconsul attacked them; and these unhappy wretches, finding there was no way to escape, set fire to the temple. As the flames spread, they retreated from one part to another, till they got to the roof of the building: there Asdrubal's wife appeared in her best apparel, as if the day of her death had been a day of triumph; and after having uttered the most bitter imprecations against her husband, whom she saw standing below with Emilianus,[2]—'Base coward!' said she, 'the mean things thou hast done to save thy life shall not avail thee; thou shalt die this instant, at least in thy two children.' Having thus spoken, she drew out a dagger, stabbed them both, and while they were yet struggling for life, threw them from the top of the temple, and leaped down after them into the flames."

Ancient Universal History. [London, 1736–1744]

The sun sets brightly—but a ruddier glow
O'er Afric's heaven the flames of Carthage throw;
Her walls have sunk, and pyramids of fire
In lurid splendor from her domes aspire;
5   Sway'd by the wind, they wave—while glares the sky
As when the desert's red Simoom° is nigh;   *desert wind*
The sculptured altar, and the pillar'd hall,
Shine out in dreadful brightness ere they fall;
Far o'er the seas the light of ruin streams,
10   Rock, wave, and isle, are crimson'd by its beams;

1. Carthage was a powerful city-state on Africa's northern coast; its control of the western Mediterranean was challenged by the Roman empire, which finally destroyed it in the Third Punic War (149–46 B.C.).

2. Scipio Africanus Minor, the Roman general (son of Aemilius Paullus). The surviving Carthaginians were sold into slavery, and Asdrubal lived comfortably as a state prisoner in Italy.

While captive thousands, bound in Roman chains,
Gaze in mute horror on their burning fanes;°   *temples*
And shouts of triumph, echoing far around,
Swell from the victor's tents with ivy crown'd.[3]

15 But mark! from yon fair temple's loftiest height
What towering form bursts wildly on the sight,
All regal in magnificent attire,
And sternly beauteous in terrific ire?
She might be deem'd a Pythia[4] in the hour
20 Of dread communion and delirious power;
A being more than earthly, in whose eye
There dwells a strange and fierce ascendancy.
The flames are gathering round—intensely bright,
Full on her features glares their meteor-light,
25 But a wild courage sits triumphant there,
The stormy grandeur of a proud despair;
A daring spirit, in its woes elate,
Mightier than death, untameable by fate.
The dark profusion of her locks unbound,
30 Waves like a warrior's floating plumage round;
Flush'd is her cheek, inspired her haughty mien,
She seems th' avenging goddess of the scene.

Are those *her* infants, that with suppliant-cry
Cling round her, shrinking as the flame draws nigh,
35 Clasp with their feeble hands her gorgeous vest,
And fain would rush for shelter to her breast?
Is that a mother's glance, where stern disdain,
And passion awfully vindictive, reign?

Fix'd is her eye on Asdrubal, who stands,
40 Ignobly safe, amidst the conquering bands;
On him, who left her to that burning tomb,
Alone to share her children's martyrdom;
Who when his country perish'd, fled the strife,
And knelt to win the worthless boon of life.
45 "Live, traitor, live!" she cries, "since dear to thee,
E'en in thy fetters, can existence be!
Scorn'd and dishonour'd, live!—with blasted name,
The Roman's triumph° not to grace, but shame.   *victory parade*
O slave in spirit! bitter be thy chain
50 With tenfold anguish to avenge my pain!
Still may the manès° of thy children rise   *avenging spirits*
To chase calm slumber from thy wearied eyes;
Still may their voices on the haunted air
In fearful whispers tell thee to despair,
55 Till vain remorse thy wither'd heart consume,
Scourged by relentless shadows of the tomb!

---

3. It was a Roman custom to adorn the tents of victors
with ivy [Hemans's note].
4. Priestess and medium of Apollo at the oracle of Delphi,
whose entranced, frenzied communications required
interpretation by male priests.

E'en now my sons shall die—and thou, their sire,
In bondage safe, shalt yet in them expire.
Think'st thou I love them not?—'Twas thine to fly—
60   'Tis mine with these to suffer and to die.
Behold their fate!—the arms that cannot save
Have been their cradle, and shall be their grave."

Bright in her hand the lifted dagger gleams,
Swift from her children's hearts the life-blood streams;
65   With frantic laugh she clasps them to the breast
Whose woes and passions soon shall be at rest;
Lifts one appealing, frenzied glance on high,
Then deep midst rolling flames is lost to mortal eye.

1819

Evening Prayer, at a Girls' School[1]

"Now in thy youth, beseech of Him
    Who giveth, upbraiding not,
That his light in thy heart becomes not dim,
    And his love be unforgot;
And thy God, in the darkest of days, will be
Greenness, and beauty, and strength to thee."
                                        —*Bernard Barton*[2]

Hush! 'tis a holy hour—the quiet room
    Seems like a temple, while yon soft lamp sheds
A faint and starry radiance, through the gloom
    And the sweet stillness, down on fair young heads,
5   With all their clustering locks, untouched by care,
    And bowed, as flowers are bowed in night, in prayer.

Gaze on—'tis lovely! Childhood's lip and cheek,
    Mantling° beneath its earnest brow of thought—   *blushing*
Gaze—yet what seest thou in those fair, and meek,
10   And fragile things, as but for sunshine wrought?—
Thou seest what grief must nurture for the sky,
What Death must fashion for Eternity!

Oh! joyous creatures! that will sink to rest,
    Lightly, when those pure orisons° are done,   *prayers*
15   As birds with slumber's honey-dew opprest,
    Midst the dim folded leaves, at set of sun—
Lift up your hearts! though yet no sorrow lies
Dark in the summer-heaven of those clear eyes.

Though fresh within your breasts the untroubled springs
20   Of hope make melody where'er ye tread,
And o'er your sleep bright shadows, from the wings
    Of spirits visiting but youth, be spread—
Yet in those flute-like voices, mingling low,

---

1. First published in a gift-book annual, this poem was frequently anthologized in the 19th century.
2. From *The Ivy, Addressed to a Young Friend.* Barton, "the Quaker poet," first sponsored by Quakers, would later secure a pension after he dedicated *Household Verses* (1845) to Queen Victoria.

Is woman's tenderness—how soon her wo!

25 Her lot° is on you—silent tears to weep,   *fate*
      And patient smiles to wear through suffering's hour,
   And sumless riches, from affection's deep,
      To pour on broken reeds—a wasted shower!
   And to make idols, and to find them clay,
30 And to bewail that worship.[3]—Therefore pray!

   Her lot is on you—to be found untir'd,
      Watching the stars out by the bed of pain,
   With a pale cheek, and yet a brow inspir'd,
      And a true heart of hope, though hope be vain;
35 Meekly to bear with wrong, to cheer decay,
   And, oh! to love through all things—therefore pray!

   And take the thought of this calm vesper° time,   *evening prayer*
      With its low murmuring sounds and silvery light,
   On through the dark days fading from their prime,
40   As a sweet dew to keep your souls from blight!
   Earth will forsake—oh! happy to have given
   Th'unbroken heart's first fragrance unto Heaven.

1826   1829

from RECORDS OF WOMAN[1]

Indian Woman's Death-Song

An Indian woman, driven to despair by her husband's desertion of her for another wife, entered a canoe with her children, and rowed it down the Mississippi towards a cataract. Her voice was heard from the shore singing a mournful death-song, until overpowered by the sound of the waters in which she perished. The tale is related in Long's "Expedition to the source of St Peter's River."[2]

> Non, je ne puis vivre avec un coeur brisé. Il faut que je
> retrouve la joie, et que je m'unisse aux esprits libres de l'air.
>
> *Bride of Messina*, Translated by Madame de Staël[3]

Let not my child be a girl, for very sad is the life of a woman.

The Prairie[4]

Down a broad river of the western wilds,
Piercing thick forest glooms, a light canoe
Swept with the current: fearful was the speed

---

3. These metaphors were clichés in Hemans's day; "suffering's hour" is any affliction and particularly childbirth; "broken reeds" are children who die young; "idols" of "clay" are those (probably husbands) who prove unworthy of the worship they court.

1. Hemans's most popular volume was first published in 1828, with a dedication to Baillie; as in Wollstonecraft, "Woman" identifies a universal category. Along with the *Records of Woman*, there was a section of *Miscellaneous Poems* that included *The Graves of a Household* and *The Homes of England*.

2. William Hippolytus Keating, *Narrative of an Expedition to the Source of St. Peter's River* (1824) which includes notes from Stephen Long's narrative of his explorations in the American plains states in the 1820s.

3. In *De L'Allemagne* (1810); "No, I cannot live with a broken heart. I must regain joy and join the free spirits of the air."

4. From ch. 26 of *The Prairie* (1827), novel by American James Fenimore Cooper; spoken by the third wife of a Sioux Chief, who has proposed a fourth marriage to a "white" Mexican woman captured by his tribe, promising her status as favorite. The third wife never fully recovers from this betrayal and her sense of inferiority to the white woman.

        Of the frail bark, as by a tempest's wing
5   Borne leaf-like on to where the mist of spray
        Rose with the cataract's thunder.—Yet within,
        Proudly, and dauntlessly, and all alone,
        Save that a babe lay sleeping at her breast,
        A woman stood: upon her Indian brow
10   Sat a strange gladness, and her dark hair wav'd
        As if triumphantly. She press'd her child,
        In its bright slumber, to her beating heart,
        And lifted her sweet voice, that rose awhile
        Above the sound of waters, high and clear,
15   Wafting a wild proud strain, her song of death.

        Roll swiftly to the Spirit's land, thou mighty stream and free!
        Father of ancient waters,[5] roll! and bear our lives with thee!
        The weary bird that storms have toss'd, would seek the sunshine's calm,
        And the deer that hath the arrow's hurt, flies to the woods of balm.

20   Roll on!—my warrior's eye hath look'd upon another's face,
        And mine hath faded from his soul, as fades a moonbeam's trace;
        My shadow comes not o'er his path, my whisper to his dream,
        He flings away the broken reed—roll swifter yet, thou stream!

        The voice that spoke of other days is hush'd within *his* breast,
25   But *mine* its lonely music haunts, and will not let me rest;
        It sings a low and mournful song of gladness that is gone,
        I cannot live without that light—Father of waves! roll on!

        Will he not miss the bounding step that met him from the chase?°   hunt
        The heart of love that made his home an ever sunny place?
30   The hand that spread the hunter's board, and deck'd his couch of yore?—
        He will not!—roll, dark foaming stream, on to the better shore!

        Some blessed fount amidst the woods of that bright land must flow,
        Whose waters from my soul may lave the memory of this wo;
        Some gentle wind must whisper there, whose breath may waft away
35   The burden of the heavy night, the sadness of the day.

        And thou, my babe! tho' born, like me, for woman's weary lot,
        Smile!—to that wasting of the heart, my own! I leave thee not;
        Too bright a thing art *thou* to pine in aching love away,
        Thy mother bears thee far, young Fawn! from sorrow and decay.

40   She bears thee to the glorious bowers where none are heard to weep,
        And where th' unkind one hath no power again to trouble sleep;
        And where the soul shall find its youth, as wakening from a dream,—
        One moment, and that realm is ours—On, on, dark rolling stream!

Joan of Arc, in Rheims

Jeanne d'Arc avait eu la joie de voir à Chalons quelques amis de son enfance. Une
joie plus ineffable encore l'attendait à Rheims, au sein de son triomphe: Jacques
d'Arc, son père y se trouva, aussitot que de troupes de Charles VII y furent entreés; et

---

5. "Father of waters," the Indian name for the Mississippi [Hemans's note].

comme les deux frères de notre Héroine l'avaient accompagnés, elle se vit, pour un instant au milieu de sa famille, dans les bras d'un père vertueux. *Vie de Jeanne d'Arc*.[1]

> Thou hast a charmed cup, O Fame!
>   A draught that mantles° high,   *expands*
> And seems to lift this earth-born frame
>   Above mortality:
> Away! to me—a woman—bring
> Sweet waters from affection's spring.[2]

That was a joyous day in Rheims of old,
When peal on peal of mighty music roll'd
Forth from her throng'd cathedral; while around,
A multitude, whose billows made no sound,
5   Chain'd to a hush of wonder, tho' elate
With victory, listen'd at their temple's gate.
And what was done within?—within, the light
    Thro' the rich gloom of pictured windows flowing,
Tinged with soft awfulness a stately sight,
10   The chivalry of France, their proud heads bowing
In martial vassalage!—while midst that ring,
And shadow'd by ancestral tombs, a king
Receiv'd his birthright's crown. For this, the hymn
    Swell'd out like rushing waters, and the day
15   With the sweet censer's misty breath grew dim,
        As thro' long aisles it floated o'er th' array
Of arms and sweeping stoles. But who, alone
And unapproach'd, beside the altar-stone,
With the white banner, forth like sunshine streaming,
20   And the gold helm, thro' clouds of fragrance gleaming,
Silent and radiant stood?—the helm was rais'd,
And the fair face reveal'd, that upward gaz'd,
    Intensely worshipping:—a still, clear face,
Youthful, but brightly solemn!—Woman's cheek
25   And brow were there, in deep devotion meek,
        Yet glorified with inspiration's trace
On its pure paleness; while, enthron'd above,
The pictur'd virgin, with her smile of love,
Seem'd bending o'er her votaress.—That slight form!
30   Was that the leader thro' the battle storm?
Had the soft light in that adoring eye,

---

1. "Joan of Arc had the pleasure of seeing at Chalons some childhood friends. A still more exquisite pleasure awaited her at Rheims in the scene of her triumph: Jacques d'Arc, her father, arrived there just as the troops of Charles VII made their entry; and as the two brothers of our Heroine had accompanied him, she found herself for a moment, in the midst of her family, in the arms of a good father" [Jean Masson, *Life of Joan of Arc* (1712)]. French national heroine and later saint, Jeanne d'Arc (1412–1431), inspired by what she took to be holy voices, encouraged the Dauphin (prince and claimant to the throne) to throw off the English claim to France. She led

his troops against the siege of Orleans and conducted him to the cathedral at Rheims, where he was crowned Charles VII and she received acclaim. She continued to lead the war against the English, but suffered defeats and was taken prisoner in 1430; with Charles's cowardly acquiescence, she was turned over to the French ecclesiastical court, which tried her for witchcraft, blasphemy, and dressing in male armor; uneasy about punishing so popular a heroine, however, they handed her over to the English, who burned her at the stake in the marketplace at Rouen.

2. The first stanza of *Woman and Fame*, page 1745.

Guided the warrior where the swords flash'd high?
'Twas so, even so!—and thou, the shepherd's child,
Joanne,[3] the lowly dreamer of the wild!
35 Never before, and never since that hour,
Hath woman, mantled° with victorious power,   *flushed, covered*
Stood forth as *thou* beside the shrine didst stand,
Holy amidst the knighthood of the land;
And beautiful with joy and with renown,
40 Lift thy white banner o'er the olden crown,
Ransom'd for France by thee!

     The rites are done.
Now let the dome with trumpet-notes be shaken,
And bid the echoes of the tombs awaken,
 And come thou forth, that Heaven's rejoicing sun
45 May give thee welcome from thine own blue skies,
 Daughter of victory!—A triumphant strain,
A proud rich stream of warlike melodies,
 Gush'd thro' the portals of the antique fane,°   *temple*
And forth she came.—Then rose a nation's sound—
50 Oh! what a power to bid the quick heart bound,
The wind bears onward with the stormy cheer
Man gives to glory on her high career!
Is there indeed such power?—far deeper dwells
In one kind household voice, to reach the cells
55 Whence happiness flows forth!—The shouts that fill'd
The hollow heaven tempestuously, were still'd
One moment; and in that brief pause, the tone,
As of a breeze that o'er her home had blown,
Sank on the bright maid's heart.—"Joanne!"—Who spoke
60   Like those whose childhood with *her* childhood grew
Under one roof?—"Joanne!"—*that* murmur broke
 With sounds of weeping forth!—She turn'd—she knew
Beside her, mark'd from all the thousands there,
In the calm beauty of his silver hair,
65 The stately shepherd; and the youth, whose joy
From his dark eye flash'd proudly; and the boy,
The youngest-born, that ever lov'd her best:
"Father! and ye, my brothers!"—On the breast
Of that grey sire she sank—and swiftly back,
70 Ev'n in an instant, to their native track
Her free thoughts flowed.—She saw the pomp no more—
The plumes, the banners:—to her cabin-door,
And to the Fairy's fountain in the glade,[4]
Where her young sisters by her side had play'd,
75 And to her hamlet's chapel, where it rose
Hallowing the forest unto deep repose,
Her spirit turn'd.—The very wood-note, sung

3. Hemans's hybrid of the French "Jeanne" and the English "Joan."
4. A beautiful fountain near Domremi, believed to be
haunted by fairies, and a favourite resort of Jeanne d'Arc
in her childhood [Hemans's note].

In early spring-time by the bird, which dwelt
Where o'er her father's roof the beech-leaves hung,
80   Was in her heart; a music heard and felt,
Winning her back to nature.[5]—She unbound
     The helm of many battles from her head,
And, with her bright locks bow'd to sweep the ground,
     Lifting her voice up, wept for joy, and said,—
85   "Bless me, my father, bless me! and with thee,
To the still cabin and the beechen-tree,
Let me return!"[6]
               Oh! never did thine eye
Thro' the green haunts of happy infancy
Wander again, Joanne!—too much of fame
90   Had shed its radiance on thy peasant-name;
And bought alone by gifts beyond all price,[7]
The trusting heart's repose, the paradise
Of home with all its loves, doth fate allow
The crown of glory unto woman's brow.[8]

1826   1828

The Graves of a Household

They grew in beauty, side by side,
    They filled one home with glee;—
Their graves are sever'd far and wide,
    By mount, and stream, and sea.[1]

5   The same fond mother bent at night
    O'er each fair sleeping brow;
She had each folded flower in sight,—
    Where are those dreamers now?

One, midst the forest of the west,
10   By a dark stream is laid—
The Indian knows his place of rest,
    Far in the cedar shade.

The sea, the blue lone sea, hath one,
    He lies where pearls lie deep;
15 *He* was the lov'd of all, yet none
    O'er his low bed may weep.

One sleeps where southern vines are drest
    Above the noble slain:
He wrapt his colours round his breast
20   On a blood-red field of Spain.[2]

5. The world of nature and also her deepest female "nature" as daughterly maid, before her days of fame.
6. Compare to Jesus' parable of the prodigal son, Luke 15.11–32.
7. Salvation through Christ is a promise "great beyond price" (2 Peter).
8. "Thou never from that hour in Paradise / Found'st either sweet repast, or sound repose," Milton writes of Eve as she leaves Adam's side (*Paradise Lost* 9.406–407).
1. Hemans's younger brother died in Canada in 1821.
2. Hemans's brothers and husband had served in the war in Spain against Napoleon; her first long poem was *England and Spain, or Valour and Patriotism* (1808).

And one—o'er *her* the myrtle showers
   Its leaves, by soft winds fann'd;
She faded midst Italian flowers,—
   The last of that bright band.

25   And parted thus they rest, who play'd
   Beneath the same green tree;
Whose voices mingled as they pray'd
   Around one parent knee!

They that with smiles lit up the hall,
30   And cheer'd with song the hearth,—
Alas, for love! if *thou* wert all,
   And naught beyond, oh, earth!

1825   1828

Corinne at the Capitol[1]

"Les femmes doivent penser qu'il est dans cette carrière bien
peu de sorts qui puissent valoir la plus obscure vie d'une
femme aimée et d'une mère heureuse."

                        —*Madame de Staël*[2]

Daughter of th' Italian heaven!
Thou, to whom its fires are given,
Joyously thy car hath roll'd
Where the conqueror's pass'd of old;
5   And the festal sun that shone,
O'er three hundred triumphs gone,[3]
Makes thy day of glory bright,
With a shower of golden light.

Now thou tread'st th' ascending road,
10   Freedom's foot so proudly trode;
While, from tombs of heroes borne,
From the dust of empire shorn,
Flowers upon thy graceful head,

1. Hemans's title comes from Book II of Madame de Staël's *Corinne, ou l'Italie* (1807); quickly translated into English, this novel was immensely popular, especially with women, not only Hemans, but also Jane Austen and Mary Godwin (Shelley), Elizabeth Barrett (Browning), George Eliot, and Harriet Beecher (Stowe). It was read as the definitive story of female "genius"—as an inspirational and cautionary tale about creative achievement at the cost of domestic happiness. De Staël was famous for her intellect, her social charm, her essays, her forthright conversation (including blunt criticism of Napoleon), and her salons, which were attended by political and literary celebrities. Her heroine, Corinne, half English and half Italian, is a famous performing poet living in Italy, where she meets the English Lord Nelvil. With him, we see her for the first time, at the Roman Capitol, celebrated in all her glorious genius. De Staël elaborates her triumphant perfor-

mance, transcribing "Corinne's Improvisation at the Capitol," and concluding in a female apotheosis: "No longer a fearful woman, she was an inspired priestess, joyously devoting herself to the cult of genius." Corinne and Nelvil fall in love, but she declines his proposal of marriage, fearing a too-constrained life as an English wife. He returns to England and marries her half sister, a fully proper English maid. When Corinne learns of this, she dies of grief.
2. From *De L'influence des Passions* (1796): "Women should consider that in this career there are very few destinies equal in worth to the most obscure life of a beloved wife and a happy mother."
3. The trebly hundred triumphs.—Byron [Hemans's note, referring to *Childe Harold's Pilgrimage*, 4.731, a comment on the number of triumphs (victory parades), in ancient Rome.]

Chaplets° of all hues, are shed,   *head-wreaths*
15 In a soft and rosy rain,
Touch'd with many a gemlike stain.

Thou hast gain'd the summit now!
Music hails thee from below;—
Music, whose rich notes might stir
20 Ashes of the sepulchre;
Shaking with victorious notes
All the bright air as it floats.
Well may woman's heart beat high
Unto that proud harmony!

25 Now afar it rolls—it dies—
And thy voice is heard to rise
With a low and lovely tone
In its thrilling power alone;
And thy lyre's deep silvery string,
30 Touch'd as by a breeze's wing,
Murmurs tremblingly at first,
Ere the tide of rapture burst.

All the spirit of thy sky
Now hath lit thy large dark eye,
35 And thy cheek a flush hath caught
From the joy of kindled thought;
And the burning words of song
From thy lip flow fast and strong,
With a rushing stream's delight
40 In the freedom of its might.

Radiant daughter of the sun!
Now thy living wreath is won.
Crown'd of Rome!—Oh! art thou not
Happy in that glorious lot?—
45 Happier, happier far than thou,
With the laurel on thy brow,[4]
She that makes the humblest hearth
Lovely but to one on earth!

1830

Woman and Fame

Happy—happier far than thou,
With the laurel on thy brow;
She that makes the humblest hearth
Lovely but to one on earth.[1]

Thou hast a charmed cup, O Fame!
A draught° that mantles° high,   *drink/blushes*

---

4. The laurel wreath is a public honor for glorious accomplishment; laurel is the badge of Apollo, classical god of poetry (whence "Poet Laureate").

1. The final lines of Hemans's *Corinne at the Capitol.*

And seems to lift this earthly frame
    Above mortality.
5   Away! to me—a woman—bring
    Sweet waters from affection's spring.[2]

Thou hast green laurel-leaves that twine
    Into so proud a wreath;[3]
For that resplendent gift of thine,
10   Heroes have smiled in death.
Give *me* from some kind hand a flower,
The record of one happy hour!

Thou hast a voice, whose thrilling tone
    Can bid each life-pulse beat,
15   As when a trumpet's note hath blown,
    Calling the brave to meet:
But mine, let mine—a woman's breast,
By words of home-born love be bless'd.

A hollow sound is in thy song,
20   A mockery in thine eye,
To the sick heart that doth but long
    For aid, for sympathy;
For kindly looks to cheer it on,
For tender accents that are gone.

25   Fame, Fame! thou canst not be the stay
    Unto the drooping reed,
The cool fresh fountain, in the day
    Of the soul's feverish need;
Where must the lone one turn or flee?—
30   Not unto thee, oh! not to thee!
1827–1829   1829

John Clare
1793–1864

The horizon of John Clare's world was defined by the village of Helpston, Northamptonshire, in which he was born, the son of a barely literate farmhand and an illiterate mother. His formal education was sparse, though his poetry shows his knowledge of Milton and Thomson and he read Wordsworth, Coleridge, Keats, and Byron (two late long poems are entitled *Childe Harold* and *Don Juan*). By the "indefatigable savings of a penny and a halfpenny," the young Clare purchased fairy tales from hawkers, recalling that "I firmly believed every page I read and considerd I possessd in these the chief learning and literature of the country." His own writing was produced swiftly and with few revisions in time seized from agricultural labor, then hid "with all secresy possible" in "an old unused cubbard" or hole in the wall.

---

2. These lines provide the epigraph for *Joan of Arc, in Rheims*.

3. See n. 4 to *Corinne at the Capitol*.

Clare's condition placed him in the line of those "natural geniuses" eagerly sought by eighteenth-century primitivism: Stephen Duck "The Thresher Poet" (1705–1756), Robert Bloomfield (*The Farmer's Boy*, 1800), Ann Yearsley "The Milkmaid Poet" (1752–1806) and Robert Burns (1759–1796) had all been fit into the stereotype of the peasant poet. In 1817 Keats's publisher John Taylor saw Clare's proposal to publish a volume of poetry by subscription; in 1820 his firm brought out *Poems Descriptive of Rural Life and Scenery*, marketing it as the work of a young "Northamptonshire Peasant," a description that fixed Clare's regional and class identity. The book enjoyed both critical and popular success, going through four editions in a year. The vogue that brought Clare attention quickly came to constrain him: his Evangelical patron disapproved of his social criticism and "vulgar" manner, and Taylor sought to broaden his appeal by standardizing his language and cutting his poems. Clare's pungent dialect usages—which illustrate by contrast how thoroughly Wordsworth "purified" the "language really used by men" in *Lyrical Ballads*—and belief "that what ever is intellig[i]ble to others is grammer and what ever is commonsense is not far from correctness" offended the norms of polite literature. "Grammer in learning," Clare adamantly insisted to Taylor in a phrase that by linking style and politics makes clear the twin offenses he posed to the urban book-buying public, "is like Tyranny in government—confound the bitch Ill never be her slave." Taylor found himself in the awkward position of intermediary between an audience for poetry increasingly represented by genteel women and a prickly lower-class male writer: "*false delicasy* damn it I hate it beyond every thing those primpt up misses brought up in those seminaries of mysterious wickedness (Boarding Schools) what will please 'em? why we well know—but while their heart & soul loves to extravagance (what we dare not mention) false delicasy's seriousness muscles [muzzles] up the mouth & condemns it." If that explosion reminds one of the "rodomontade" with which Keats defended his sexually more explicit revisions to *The Eve of St. Agnes*, the distance between the literariness of Keats, whom Clare admired, and Clare's plainness is manifest in his objection that Keats "keeps up a constant alusion or illusion to the grecian mythology & there I cannot follow . . . the frequency of such classical accompaniment makes it wearisome to the reader where behind every rose bush he looks for a Venus & under every laurel a thrumming Appollo."

New editions of Clare's writings have freed his texts from the emendations of their first publication and have brought unpublished materials to view, winning him the audience he missed in his own time. As illustration, we print two versions of *Written in November*, the first from the manuscripts edited by Eric Robinson and David Powell, the source of our texts, the second as the poem appeared in *The Village Minstrel* (1821).

Written in November (1)

Autumn I love thy latter end to view
In cold novembers day so bleak & bare
When like lifes dwindled thread worn nearly thro
Wi lingering pottering° pace & head bleached bare　　*dawdling, uncertain*
5　Thou like an old man bids the world adieu
I love thee well & often when a child
Have roamd the bare brown heath a flower to find
& in the moss clad vale & wood bank wild
Have cropt the little bell flowers paley blue
10　That trembling peept the sheltering bush behind
When winnowing north winds cold & blealy° blew　　*coldly, bleakly*
How have I joyd wi dithering° hands to find　　*shivering*
Each fading flower & still how sweet the blast
Would bleak novembers hour Restore the joy thats past

Written in November (2)

Autumn, I love thy parting look to view
   In cold November's day, so bleak and bare,
When, thy life's dwindled thread worn nearly thro',
   With ling'ring pott'ring pace, and head bleach'd bare,
5   Thou, like an old man, bidd'st the world adieu.
   I love thee well: and often, when a child,
Have roam'd the bare brown heath a flower to find;
   And in the moss-clad vale, and wood-bank wild
Have cropt the little bell-flowers, pearly blue,
10   That trembling peep the shelt'ring bush behind.
When winnowing north-winds cold and bleaky blew,
   How have I joy'd, with dithering hands, to find
Each fading flower; and still how sweet the blast,
Would bleak November's hour restore the joy that's past.

c. 1812   1821

Clock a Clay°

lady-bug

In the cowslips peeps° I lye[1]   *primrose blossoms*
Hidden from the buzzing fly
While green grass beneath me lies
Pearled wi' dew like fishes eyes
5 Here I lye a Clock a clay
Waiting for the time o' day[2]

While grassy forests quake surprise
And the wild wind sobs and sighs
My gold home rocks as like to fall
10 On its pillars green and tall
When the pattering rain drives bye
Clock a Clay keeps warm and dry

Day by day and night by night
All the week I hide from sight
15 In the cowslips peeps I lye
In rain and dew still warm and dry
Day and night and night and day
Red black spotted clock a clay

My home it shakes in wind and showers
20 Pale green pillar top't wi' flowers
Bending at the wild winds breath
Till I touch the grass beneath
Here still I live lone clock a clay
Watching for the time of day

c. 1848   1873

---

1. Cf. Ariel's song in Shakespeare, *The Tempest*, 5.1.89: "In a cowslip's bell I lie."   2. Refers to the children's game of counting the taps needed to make the lady-bug fly away home.

"I Am"

I am—yet what I am, none cares or knows;
    My friends forsake me like a memory lost:—
I am the self-consumer of my woes;—
    They rise and vanish in oblivion's host,
5   Like shadows in love's frenzied stifled throes:—
And yet I am, and live—like vapours tost

Into the nothingness of scorn and noise,—
    Into the living sea of waking dreams,
Where there is neither sense of life or joys,
10   But the vast shipwreck of my lifes esteems;
Even the dearest, that I love the best
Are strange—nay, rather stranger than the rest.

I long for scenes, where man hath never trod
    A place where woman never smiled or wept
15 There to abide with my Creator, God;
And sleep as I in childhood, sweetly slept,
Untroubling, and untroubled where I lie,
The grass below—above the vaulted sky.

c. 1842   1848

John Keats
1795–1821

"A thing of beauty is a joy for ever"; "tender is the night"; "Beauty is truth; truth Beauty"—these phrases are so well known that we may forget that they once sprung from the imagination of John Keats. Keats's brief career ran only from 1814, when he wrote his first poem, to 1820, when he revised his sonnet *Bright Star* on board a ship to Italy. "Oh, for ten years, that I may overwhelm / Myself in poesy," he said in 1816. Not even getting this decade, his active life as a writer stopped around his twenty-fourth birthday. At age twenty-four, Chaucer had yet to write anything, and if Shakespeare had died at twenty-four, he would be known only (if at all) by a few early works. What if Keats had lived until 1881, like that Victorian sage Thomas Carlyle, also born in 1795?

The drama of Keats is not just the poignancy of genius cut off in youth but also his humble origins—a focus of ridicule during and after his lifetime by class-conscious reviewers and aristocratic poets. Son of a livery-stable keeper who had married the owner's daughter and inherited the suburban London business, Keats was sent to the progressive Enfield School. Here he was tutored and befriended by Charles Cowden Clark, the headmaster's son, who introduced him to literature, music, the theater. When Keats was nine years old, his father died in a riding accident and his mother remarried immediately; her commitment to her children was as erratic as it was doting, and her presence at home was inconstant. Keats was deeply attached to her and devastated when she disappeared for four years, leaving them all with his grandmother. When she returned sick and consumptive, he nursed her, and she died when he was fourteen; the welter of emotions she left in him is reflected in the series of adored, inconstant women around which so much of his poetry revolves. The children were remanded to the guardianship of a practical businessman whose chief concern was to apprentice the boys to some viable trade. Unimaginative himself and unsympathetic to any passion for learning and poetry, he apprenticed Keats to a London hospital surgeon in the grim days before anesthesia. Keats stayed with this training long enough to be licensed as an apothecary (more a general practitioner than a druggist), but he frequently took time off to read and to write poetry. When he came of age in 1817, he gave up medicine and set out to make a living as a poet.

Keats was already enjoying the society of Clarke and his circle of politically progressive thinkers, artists, poets, journalists, and publishers, many of whom became close friends—among them Leigh Hunt, also a poet as well as a radical journalist. Hunt launched Keats's career, publishing him in his weekly paper, *The Examiner,* and advertising him as one of the rising young poets. It was through Hunt that Keats met some of the chief nonestablishment writers of the day—William Wordsworth, William Hazlitt, Charles Lamb, Percy Shelley—and the controversial painter Benjamin Robert Haydon. His inaugural volume, published in 1817, included twenty sonnets, a favorite form for him, as well as Spenserian stanzas, odes, verse epistles, romance fragments, and meditative long poems on the subject of poetry itself. The writers that mattered most to him were Spenser (his first poem, written in 1814, was a deft "Imitation of Spenser" in Spenserian stanzas), Shakespeare, and ambivalently, Milton, and among his contemporaries, Wordsworth and Byron, though again with intelligent ambivalence. Keats warmly dedicated the 1817 *Poems* to Hunt and in a long concluding piece (*Sleep and Poetry*) voiced sharp criticism of what he saw as the arid formalism of eighteenth-century neoclassical poetry, which still had prestige with conservative or aristocratic writers, Byron among the latter. Byron never forgave Keats for this tirade, and it immediately provoked the Tory journalists, who were only too eager to jab at their political enemy Hunt through his protégé. Published in a year when civil rights were weakened and the radical publisher William Hone brought to trial, *Poems* was viciously ridiculed in reviews marked by social snobbery and political prejudice and Keats was indelibly tagged "the Cockney Poet"—one of Hunt's suburban radicals. He was stung, but determined to prove himself with his next effort, *Endymion,* initiated as part of a contest with Hunt and Shelley to see who could write a 4,000-line poem by the end of 1817. The only one to complete the challenge, Keats set off with a sense that it would be "a test" or "trial" of his talents. "A thing of beauty is a joy for ever" begins this tale of a shepherd-prince who dreams of a goddess, and on waking is profoundly alienated from ordinary life in the world. Book I narrates this episode; over the course of the next three books, Endymion dreams of her again, loses her, searches high (more dreams) and low (underground to the Bower of Venus and Adonis and several other labyrinthine terrains), and finally gives up, falling for a maid he finds abandoned in the woods. She turns out to be his goddess in disguise, and his dream comes true. This is the last time in Keats's poetry that dreams are so happily realized.

During 1818 Keats nursed his beloved brother Tom, dying of tuberculosis, the disease that had killed their mother and that would kill Keats himself three years later (already he was suffering from a chronically sore throat). Tom died at the end of 1818, and Keats sought relief in his poetry. In a burst of inspiration that lasted well into the fall of 1819 (when he revised *Hyperion*), he produced the work that established his fame: *The Eve of St. Agnes* (a part serious, part ironic romance), *La Belle Dame sans Merci* (a romance with a vengeance), *Lamia* (a wickedly satirical, bitter romance), all the Great Odes, and a clutch of brilliant sonnets, including *Bright Star*. Although (unlike most of his contemporaries) he wrote no prefaces, defenses, self-promoting polemics, or theoretical essays, his letters display a critical intelligence as brilliant as the poetic talent. A number of their off-the-cuff formulations—the "finer tone" of repetition, "negative capability," "the camelion Poet," "the egotistical sublime," truth "proved upon our pulses"—have become standard terms in literary criticism and theory, and from their first publication, after his death, his letters have been admired for their generosity and playfulness, their insight, their candor, and their critical penetration.

His health worsening over the course of 1819, Keats suffered a major lung hemorrhage early in 1820; with the accuracy of his medical training, he read his "death warrant" and was devastated. For despite the shaky reception of *Poems* and *Endymion*, he was optimistic about his forthcoming volume and full of enthusiasm for new writing (journalism or plays); he was also deeply in love with the girl next door, Fanny Brawne, whom he secretly betrothed and hoped to marry once he was financially capable. He sailed to Italy in September, seeking health in a warmer climate, but died at the end of the next February, four months after his twenty-fifth birthday—far from Fanny and his friends and in such despair of fame that he asked his tombstone to be inscribed "Here lies one whose name was writ in water." Yet he did live long enough to see some favorable reviews of his 1820 volume. Shelley's fable of Keats killed by hostile reviewers in *Adonais*, though often retold as truth, could not have been more out of tune with Keats's own resilience. "This is a mere matter of the moment," he assured his brother George, adding, "I think I shall be among the English Poets after my death."

On First Looking into Chapman's Homer[1]

Much have I travell'd in the realms of gold,
   And many goodly states and kingdoms seen;
   Round many western islands have I been
Which bards in fealty to Apollo° hold.   *God of poetry*
5 Oft of one wide expanse had I been told
   That deep-brow'd Homer ruled as his demesne;°   *realm*
   Yet did I never breathe its pure serene°   *clear sky*
Till I heard Chapman speak out loud and bold:
Then felt I like some watcher of the skies
10   When a new planet swims into his ken;[2]
Or like stout Cortez when with eagle eyes
   He star'd at the Pacific—and all his men
Look'd at each other with a wild surmise—
   Silent, upon a peak in Darien.[3]

1816   1816, 1817

COMPANION READINGS

Alexander Pope: Homer's Iliad[1]
from *Book 5*
[THE ARMOR OF DIOMEDES, A GREEK WARRIOR]

High on his helm celestial lightnings play,
His beamy shield emits a living ray;
Th' unwearied blaze incessant streams supplies,
Like the red star that fires th' autumnal skies,

1. Written the morning after Keats had stayed up all night with Clarke reading George Chapman's vibrant translation (c. 1611–1614) of Homer at a time when Pope's rendering in polished heroic couplets was the standard. Keats describes his reading as a Homeric voyage through the Greek isles where classical literature had its golden age. In *The Apology for Poetry* (1595), Sidney wrote that poets "deliver a golden" world from the "brazen" world of nature. Keats extends the language of traveling in "realms of gold" to Renaissance-era voyages

of discovery to the New World in quest of gold by adventurers such as the conquistador of Mexico, Cortez.
2. Uranus was discovered in 1781; ken: range of apprehension.
3. Mountain range in eastern Panama.
1. When Books 1–4 of Pope's *Iliad* were published in 1715 (book 5 in 1716), he was acclaimed the greatest poet of the age; the successful sale inaugurated the first poetic career in England able to sustain itself independent of political or aristocratic patronage.

5   When fresh he rears his radiant orb to sight,
       And bath'd in Ocean, shoots a keener light.
       Such glories Pallas[2] on the chief bestow'd,
       Such, from his arms, the fierce effulgence flow'd:
       Onward she drives him, furious to engage,
10   Where the fight burns, and where the thickest rage.

George Chapman: Homer's Iliad[1]
from *Book 5*

From his bright helme and shield did burne a most unwearied fire,
Like rich Autumnus' golden lampe, whose brightnesse men admire
Past all the other host of starres, when, with his cheaerfull face
Fresh washt in loftir ocean waves he doth the skies enchase.
5   To let whose glory lose no sight, still Pallas made him turne
Where tumult most expresst his powre, and where the fight did burne.

On Seeing the Elgin Marbles[1]

My spirit is too weak—mortality
     Weighs heavily on me like unwilling sleep,
     And each imagined pinnacle and steep
Of godlike hardship, tells me I must die
5   Like a sick eagle looking at the sky.
     Yet 'tis a gentle luxury to weep
     That I have not the cloudy winds to keep
Fresh for the opening of the morning's eye.
Such dim-conceived glories of the brain
10   Bring round the heart an undescribable feud;
So do these wonders a most dizzy pain
     That mingles Grecian grandeur with the rude
Wasting of old time—with a billowy main°   *sea*
     A sun—a shadow of a magnitude.

1817   1817, 1818

Sonnet: When I have fears

When I have fears that I may cease to be[1]
     Before my pen has glean'd my teeming brain,
     Before high piled books in charact'ry°   *written symbols*

---

2. Pallas Athene, an epithet of Athena, Greek Goddess of War (and later, wisdom).

1. Chapman uses the fourteener, an iambic seven-beat line, most common in ballad verse (as two lines of four and three beats). Although both Pope and Chapman turn Homer's unrhymed lines into couplets, Keats preferred Chapman's rougher, less balanced lines and direct language.

1. Keats viewed these sculptural fragments from the Athenian Parthenon with Haydon, a champion of Lord Elgin's purchase of them in 1806 from the Turks, then occupying Greece. Elgin (hard *g*) was motivated both by admiration for their powerful beauty and a desire to preserve them from erosion and the further peril of supply-

ing mortar and target practice for Turkish soldiers. Their aesthetic value was debated (some found them crude and even inauthentic), and their purchase by the British government in 1816 for deposit in the British Museum (they are still there) was (and still is) controversial. Keats's sonnet appeared in *The Examiner* in 1817 (the text used here) and in Haydon's *Annals of the Fine Arts* in 1818.

1. Keats's sonnet plays several allusive echoes: Shakespeare's "When I do count the clock that tells the time"; Wordsworth's "few could know / When Lucy ceased to be" (*She dwelt among th'untrodden ways;* see page 1539); Milton's sonnet, "When I consider how my light is spent / Ere half my days, in this dark world and wide . . ."

Hold like rich garners the full-ripened grain;
5   When I behold upon the night's starred face,
Huge cloudy symbols of a high romance,
And think that I may never live to trace
Their shadows with the magic hand of chance;
And when I feel, fair creature of an hour,
10   That I shall never look upon thee more,
Never have relish in the fairy power
Of unreflecting love—then on the shore
Of the wide world I stand alone and think,
Till love and fame to nothingness do sink.

January 1818

The Eve of St. Agnes

Keats began this poem in the early winter months of 1819, setting it on St. Agnes' Eve, when, according to legend, a young virgin who has performed certain rituals may dream of her future husband. Agnes is the patron saint of virgins, but her story is rather more violent. A thirteen-year-old Christian martyr in early fourth-century Rome, she was condemned to a night of rape in the brothels before her execution. This first stage of the sentence was prevented by a miraculous storm of thunder and lightning, a climate that Keats writes into the end of his poem. Working in the intricate form of Spenserian stanzas, repopularized by Byron's *Childe Harold's Pilgrimage* (1812–1818), Keats spins an ironic romance—at once indulging the traditional pleasures of the genre (love, imagination, gorgeous sensuality with a spiritual aura) and bringing a playful, sometimes satiric, sometimes darkly shaded perspective to its illusions. With *Romeo and Juliet* in mind, Keats at first portrayed the sexual desire of his hero and heroine, but his publishers, worried about indecency, forced him to revise. Though he complied with angry reluctance, the imagery of stars and flowers in stanza 36 shows his skill in retaining some of the original pulsation.

The Eve of St. Agnes

1

St. Agnes' Eve—Ah, bitter chill it was!
The owl, for all his feathers, was a-cold;
The hare limp'd trembling through the frozen grass,
And silent was the flock in woolly fold:
5   Numb were the Beadsman's fingers, while he told
His rosary,[1] and while his frosted breath,
Like pious incense from a censer old,
Seem'd taking flight for heaven, without a death,
Past the sweet Virgin's picture, while his prayer he saith.

2

10 His prayer he saith, this patient, holy man;
Then takes his lamp, and riseth from his knees,
And back returneth, meagre, barefoot, wan,
Along the chapel aisle by slow degrees:
The sculptur'd dead, on each side, seem to freeze,
15 Emprison'd in black, purgatorial rails:
Knights, ladies, praying in dumb orat'ries,°   *chapels*

---

1. A pensioner paid to say prayers, this beadsman is saying a rosary in the estate's cold chapel for the salvation of the aristocrats partying indoors.

He passeth by; and his weak spirit fails
To think how they may ache in icy hoods and mails.

3

20   Northward he turneth through a little door,
And scarce three steps, ere Music's golden tongue
Flatter'd to tears this aged man and poor;
But no—already had his deathbell rung;
The joys of all his life were said and sung:
His was harsh penance on St. Agnes' Eve:
25   Another way he went, and soon among
Rough ashes sat he for his soul's reprieve,
And all night kept awake, for sinners' sake to grieve.

4

That ancient Beadsman heard the prelude soft;
And so it chanc'd, for many a door was wide,
30   From hurry to and fro. Soon, up aloft,
The silver, snarling trumpets 'gan to chide:
The level chambers, ready with their pride,
Were glowing to receive a thousand guests:
The carved angels, ever eager-eyed,
35   Star'd, where upon their heads the cornice rests,
With hair blown back, and wings put cross-wise on their breasts.

5

At length burst in the argent° revelry,   *silvery*
With plume, tiara, and all rich array,
Numerous as shadows haunting fairily
40   The brain, new stuff'd, in youth with triumphs gay
Of old romance.[2] These let us wish away,
And turn, sole-thoughted, to one Lady there,
Whose heart had brooded, all that wintry day,
On love, and wing'd St. Agnes' saintly care,
45   As she had heard old dames full many times declare.

6

They told her how, upon St. Agnes' Eve,
Young virgins might have visions of delight,
And soft adorings from their loves receive
Upon the honey'd middle of the night,
50   If ceremonies due they did aright;
As, supperless to bed they must retire,
And couch supine their beauties, lily white;
Nor look behind, nor sideways, but require°   *beseech*
Of Heaven with upward eyes for all that they desire.[3]

7

55   Full of this whim was thoughtful Madeline:[4]
The music, yearning like a God in pain

2. The literary genre.
3. Keats's publishers forced him to cancel as too explicitly erotic a stanza that followed this one, recounting the fable of a maid's "future lord" appearing in her dreams, bringing "delicious food even to her lips": "Viands, and wine, and fruit, and sugared cream, / To touch her palate with the fine extreme / Of relish; the soft music heard;

and then / More pleasures followed in a dizzy stream, / Palpable almost; then to wake again / Warm in the virgin morn, no weeping Magdalen"—i.e., Mary Magdalen, the prostitute befriended by Jesus; in Keats's day hospitals for unwed mothers were called Magdalens.
4. A name derived from Magdalen.

She scarcely heard: her maiden eyes divine,
Fix'd on the floor, saw many a sweeping train°   *long skirt*
Pass by—she heeded not at all: in vain
60 Came many a tiptoe, amorous cavalier,
And back retir'd; not cool'd by high disdain,
But she saw not: her heart was otherwise:
She sigh'd for Agnes' dreams, the sweetest of the year.

8

She danc'd along with vague, regardless eyes,
65 Anxious her lips, her breathing quick and short:[5]
The hallow'd hour was near at hand: she sighs
Amid the timbrels,° and the throng'd resort   *tambourines*
Of whisperers in anger, or in sport;
'Mid looks of love, defiance, hate, and scorn,
70 Hoodwink'd° with faery fancy; all amort,°   *blinded/dead*
Save to St. Agnes and her lambs unshorn,
And all the bliss to be before to-morrow morn.[6]

9

So, purposing each moment to retire,
She linger'd still. Meantime, across the moors,
75 Had come young Porphyro,[7] with heart on fire
For Madeline. Beside the portal doors,
Buttress'd from moonlight,[8] stands he, and implores
All saints to give him sight of Madeline,
But for one moment in the tedious hours,
80 That he might gaze and worship all unseen:
Perchance speak, kneel, touch, kiss—in sooth such things have been.

10

He ventures in: let no buzz'd whisper tell:
All eyes be muffled, or a hundred swords
Will storm his heart,[9] Love's fev'rous citadel:
85 For him, those chambers held barbarian hordes,
Hyena foemen, and hot-blooded lords,
Whose very dogs would execrations howl
Against his lineage: not one breast affords
Him any mercy, in that mansion foul,
90 Save one old beldame,[1] weak in body and in soul.

11

Ah, happy chance! the aged creature came,
Shuffling along with ivory-headed wand,°   *staff*
To where he stood, hid from the torch's flame,
Behind a broad hall-pillar, far beyond

---

5. Originally: "Her anxious mouth full pulped with rosy thoughts."
6. It was a custom at St. Agnes' Day mass, during the singing of Agnus Dei (Lamb of God), to bless two white unshorn lambs, whose wool nuns then spun and wove.
7. From porphyra, "purple," a precious dye for garments of the nobility; "purple blood" signifies royalty and nobility; a porphyre is a purple-colored serpent. Moreover, Porphyry (3rd c. A.D.), famous antagonist of Christianity, instituted Neoplatonism throughout the Roman Empire a few decades before the martyrdom of St. Agnes.

8. Hidden in the shadow of a buttress (the external architecture that supports the castle walls).
9. Keats echoes Burke's famous account of the arrest of Marie Antoinette: "A band of cruel ruffians and assassins . . . rushed into the chamber of the queen, and pierced with an hundred strokes of bayonets and poniards the bed, from whence this persecuted woman had but just time to fly almost naked" (see *Reflections*, page 1359).
1. Grandmother or old nurse; Keats's Angela evokes Juliet's nurse Angelica in *Romeo and Juliet*, also go-between for the lovers.

95   The sound of merriment and chorus bland:°   soft
        He startled her; but soon she knew his face,
        And grasp'd his fingers in her palsied hand,
        Saying, "Mercy, Porphyro! hie thee from this place;
        They are all here to-night, the whole blood-thirsty race!

                                12
100   "Get hence! get hence! there's dwarfish Hildebrand;
        He had a fever late, and in the fit
        He cursed thee and thine, both house and land:
        Then there's that old Lord Maurice, not a whit
        More tame for his grey hairs—Alas me! flit!
105   Flit like a ghost away."—"Ah, Gossip° dear,   confidant
        We're safe enough; here in this arm-chair sit,
        And tell me how"—"Good Saints! not here, not here;
        Follow me, child, or else these stones will be thy bier."°   coffin-platform

                                13
        He follow'd through a lowly arched way,
110   Brushing the cobwebs with his lofty plume,
        And as she mutter'd "Well-a—well-a-day!"
        He found him in a little moonlight room,
        Pale, lattic'd, chill, and silent as a tomb.
        "Now tell me where is Madeline," said he,
115   "O tell me, Angela, by the holy loom
        Which none but secret sisterhood may see,
        When they St. Agnes' wool are weaving piously."

                                14
        "St. Agnes! Ah! it is St. Agnes' Eve—
        Yet men will murder upon holy days:
120   Thou must hold water in a witch's sieve,
        And be liege-lord of all the Elves and Fays,°   fairies
        To venture so: it fills me with amaze
        To see thee, Porphyro!—St. Agnes' Eve!
        God's help! my lady fair the conjuror plays
125   This very night: good angels her deceive!
        But let me laugh awhile, I've mickle° time to grieve."   much

                                15
        Feebly she laugheth in the languid moon,
        While Porphyro upon her face doth look,
        Like puzzled urchin on an aged crone
130   Who keepeth clos'd a wond'rous riddle-book,
        As spectacled she sits in chimney nook.
        But soon his eyes grew brilliant, when she told
        His lady's purpose; and he scarce could brook°   hold back
        Tears, at the thought of those enchantments cold,
135   And Madeline asleep in lap of legends old.

                                16
        Sudden a thought came like a full-blown rose,
        Flushing his brow, and in his pained heart
        Made purple riot: then doth he propose
        A stratagem, that makes the beldame start:
140   "A cruel man and impious thou art:

Sweet lady, let her pray, and sleep, and dream
Alone with her good angels, far apart
From wicked men like thee. Go, go!—I deem
Thou canst not surely be the same that thou didst seem."

17

145 "I will not harm her, by all saints I swear,"
Quoth Porphyro: "O may I ne'er find grace
When my weak voice shall whisper its last prayer,
If one of her soft ringlets I displace.
Or look with ruffian passion in her face:
150 Good Angela, believe me by these tears;
Or I will, even in a moment's space,
Awake, with horrid shout, my foemen's ears,
And beard° them, though they be more fang'd than wolves and bears." *defy*

18

"Ah! why wilt thou affright a feeble soul?
155 A poor, weak, palsy-stricken, churchyard thing,
Whose passing-bell° may ere the midnight toll; *death-knell*
Whose prayers for thee, each morn and evening,
Were never miss'd."—Thus plaining,° doth she bring *lamenting*
A gentler speech from burning Porphyro;
160 So woeful, and of such deep sorrowing,
That Angela gives promise she will do
Whatever he shall wish, betide her weal or woe.

19

Which was, to lead him, in close secrecy,
Even to Madeline's chamber, and there hide
165 Him in a closet,° of such privacy *private room*
That he might see her beauty unespied,
And win perhaps that night a peerless bride,
While legion'd fairies pac'd the coverlet,
And pale enchantment held her sleepy-eyed.
170 Never on such a night have lovers met,
Since Merlin paid his Demon all the monstrous debt.[2]

20

"It shall be as thou wishest," said the Dame:
"All cates° and dainties shall be stored there *delicacies*
Quickly on this feast-night: by the tambour frame[3]
175 Her own lute thou wilt see: no time to spare,
For I am slow and feeble, and scarce dare
On such a catering trust my dizzy head.
Wait here, my child, with patience; kneel in prayer
The while: Ah! thou must needs the lady wed,
180 Or may I never leave my grave among the dead."

21

So saying, she hobbled off with busy fear.
The lover's endless minutes slowly pass'd;

2. In Arthurian legend, the magician Merlin had his powers turned against him by the enchantress Vivien, who
treacherously repaid his love by imprisoning him in a
cave, where he died.
3. Frame for needlework embroidery, shaped like a tam-
bourine.

The dame return'd, and whisper'd in his ear
To follow her; with aged eyes aghast
185   From fright of dim espial.[4] Safe at last,
Through many a dusky gallery, they gain
The maiden's chamber, silken, hush'd, and chaste;
Where Porphyro took covert, pleas'd amain.°   *fully*
His poor guide hurried back with agues° in her brain.   *trembling*

22

190   Her falt'ring hand upon the balustrade,°   *bannister*
Old Angela was feeling for the stair,
When Madeline, St. Agnes' charmed maid,
Rose, like a mission'd spirit,[5] unaware:
With silver taper's° light, and pious care,   *candle's*
195   She turn'd, and down the aged gossip led
To a safe level matting. Now prepare,
Young Porphyro, for gazing on that bed;
She comes, she comes again, like ring-dove fray'd° and fled.   *frightened*

23

Out went the taper° as she hurried in;   *candle*
200   Its little smoke, in pallid moonshine, died:
She clos'd the door, she panted, all akin
To spirits of the air, and visions wide:
No utter'd syllable, or, woe betide!
But to her heart, her heart was voluble,°   *beating audibly*
205   Paining with eloquence her balmy side;
As though a tongueless nightingale should swell
Her throat in vain, and die, heart-stifled, in her dell.[6]

24

A casement° high and triple-arch'd there was,   *window*
All garlanded with carven imag'ries
210   Of fruits, and flowers, and bunches of knot-grass,
And diamonded with panes of quaint device,
Innumerable of stains and splendid dyes,
As are the tiger-moth's deep-damask'd wings;
And in the midst, 'mong thousand heraldries,°   *genealogical emblems*
215   And twilight saints, and dim emblazonings,
A shielded scutcheon blush'd with blood of queens and kings.[7]

25

Full on this casement shone the wintry moon,
And threw warm gules° on Madeline's fair breast, *red*
As down she knelt for heaven's grace and boon;°   *favor*
220   Rose-bloom fell on her hands, together prest,
And on her silver cross soft amethyst,
And on her hair a glory,° like a saint: *halo*

4. Being espied, even in dim light.
5. Commissioned, as if an angel-messenger.
6. In a story in Ovid's *Metamorphoses*, Tereus, after raping his wife's sister Philomela, cut out her tongue to prevent her reporting the crime; but she wove its imagery into a robe that her sister understood, and was so enraged that she butchered her and Tereus's son and fed him a dinner made from the flesh. With Tereus on the verge of violent revenge, all three were turned into birds, Philomela into a nightingale; her name means "lover of honey, sweetness, song."
7. Scutcheon: shield; although "blood" aptly evokes bloodshed, here it refers to Madeline's royal bloodline.

She seem'd a splendid angel, newly drest,
Save wings, for heaven:—Porphyro grew faint:
225 She knelt, so pure a thing, so free from mortal taint.

26

Anon his heart revives: her vespers done,
Of all its wreathed pearls her hair she frees;
Unclasps her warmed jewels one by one;
Loosens her fragrant bodice;[8] by degrees
230 Her rich attire creeps rustling to her knees:
Half-hidden, like a mermaid in sea-weed,
Pensive awhile she dreams awake, and sees,
In fancy, fair St. Agnes in her bed,
But dares not look behind, or all the charm is fled.[9]

27

235 Soon, trembling in her soft and chilly nest,
In sort of wakeful swoon, perplex'd she lay,
Until the poppied° warmth of sleep oppress'd   *fragrant, narcotic*
Her soothed limbs, and soul fatigued away;
Flown, like a thought, until the morrow-day;
240 Blissfully haven'd both from joy and pain;
Clasp'd like a missal where swart Paynims pray;[1]
Blinded alike from sunshine and from rain,
As though a rose should shut, and be a bud again.

28

Stol'n to this paradise,[2] and so entranced,
245 Porphyro gazed upon her empty dress,
And listen'd to her breathing, if it chanced
To wake into a slumberous tenderness;
Which when he heard, that minute did he bless,
And breath'd himself: then from the closet crept,
250 Noiseless as fear in a wide wilderness,
And over the hush'd carpet, silent, stept,
And 'tween the curtains peep'd, where, lo!—how fast she slept.

29

Then by the bed-side, where the faded moon
Made a dim, silver twilight, soft he set
255 A table, and, half anguish'd, threw thereon
A cloth of woven crimson, gold, and jet:—
O for some drowsy Morphean amulet![3]
The boisterous, midnight, festive clarion,
The kettle-drum, and far-heard clarionet,
260 Affray° his ears, though but in dying tone:—   *frighten*
The hall door shuts again, and all the noise is gone.

---

8. Keats tested some even more erotic phrasing: "bursting
boddice"; "her boddice and her bosom bare."
9. Evoking the myth of Orpheus and Eurydice, with
Madeline in the male role of the lover who wins the
opportunity to lead his dead beloved back to life from
Hades, on the condition that he not look back at her
until they reach the upper world. Orpheus violated this
injunction and lost Eurydice forever.

1. Clasped shut and held like a prayer-book concealed
from the sight of hostile, dark-skinned pagans (Muslims);
"clasped" also suggests "arrested," with "pray" punning as
"prey" (on), or persecute.
2. Alluding to Satan's entry into the Garden of Eden to
corrupt Eve.
3. Sleep-inducing charm; Morpheus is the divine agent
of sleep.

30

And still she slept an azure-lidded sleep,
In blanched linen, smooth, and lavender'd,
While he from forth the closet brought a heap
265   Of candied apple, quince, and plum, and gourd;°   *melon*
With jellies soother⁴ than the creamy curd,
And lucent syrops, tinct° with cinnamon;   *clear syrups, tinged*
Manna° and dates, in argosy° transferr'd   *rare food / merchant fleet*
From Fez; and spiced dainties, every one,
270   From silken Samarcand to cedar'd Lebanon.⁵

31

These delicates he heap'd with glowing hand
On golden dishes and in baskets bright
Of wreathed silver: sumptuous they stand
In the retired quiet of the night,
275   Filling the chilly room with perfume light.—
"And now, my love, my seraph° fair, awake!   *angel*
Thou art my heaven, and I thine eremite:°   *hermit*
Open thine eyes, for meek St. Agnes' sake,
Or I shall drowse beside thee, so my soul doth ache."

32

280   Thus whispering, his warm, unnerved° arm   *weak, unmanned*
Sank in her pillow. Shaded was her dream
By the dusk curtains:—'twas a midnight charm
Impossible to melt as iced stream:
The lustrous salvers° in the moonlight gleam: *trays*
285   Broad golden fringe upon the carpet lies:
It seem'd he never, never could redeem
From such a steadfast spell his lady's eyes;
So mus'd awhile, entoil'd in woofed° phantasies.   *woven*

33

Awakening up, he took her hollow lute,—
290   Tumultuous,—and, in chords that tenderest be,
He play'd an ancient ditty, long since mute,
In Provence call'd, "La belle dame sans mercy":⁶
Close to her ear touching the melody;—
Wherewith disturb'd, she utter'd a soft moan:
295   He ceased—she panted quick—and suddenly
Her blue affrayed° eyes wide open shone: *frayed, afraid*
Upon his knees he sank, pale as smooth-sculptured stone.

34

Her eyes were open, but she still beheld,
Now wide awake, the vision of her sleep:
300   There was a painful change, that nigh expell'd
The blisses of her dream so pure and deep
At which fair Madeline began to weep,

---

4. A Keats-coinage: smoother and more soothing.
5. All major places in the British trade in exotic goods, the luxuries of the feudal aristocracy: Fez in northern Morocco was a source of sugar; the ancient Persian city of Samarkand was famous for its silk markets, and Lebanon renowned for its fine cedar timber.

6. Provence is a region of southern France famed for troubadours; in the poem by Alain Chartier (1424; translated by Chaucer), a lady earns this title for her determined refusal of a suitor. In a few months, Keats would write his own ballad of a lady "sans mercy"/"sans merci": see n. 1 to *La Belle Dame sans Mercy* (page 1762).

And moan forth witless° words with many a sigh;   *uncomprehending*
While still her gaze on Porphyro would keep;
305 Who knelt, with joined hands and piteous eye,
Fearing to move or speak, she look'd so dreamingly.

35

"Ah, Porphyro!" said she, "but even now
Thy voice was at sweet tremble in mine ear,
Made tuneable with every sweetest vow;
310 And those sad eyes were spiritual and clear:
How chang'd thou art! how pallid, chill, and drear!
Give me that voice again, my Porphyro,
Those looks immortal, those complainings° dear!   *laments*
Oh leave me not in this eternal woe,
315 For if thou diest, my Love, I know not where to go."

36

Beyond a mortal man impassion'd far
At these voluptuous accents, he arose,
Ethereal, flush'd, and like a throbbing star
Seen mid the sapphire heaven's deep repose;
320 Into her dream he melted, as the rose
Blendeth its odour with the violet,—[7]
Solution° sweet: meantime the frost-wind blows   *fusion*
Like Love's alarum,° pattering the sharp sleet   *Cupid's warning*
Against the window-panes; St. Agnes' moon hath set.

37

325 'Tis dark: quick pattereth the flaw-blown° sleet: *storm-driven*
"This is no dream, my bride, my Madeline!"
'Tis dark: the iced gusts still rave and beat:
"No dream, alas! alas! and woe is mine!
Porphyro will leave me here to fade and pine.—
330 Cruel! what traitor could thee hither bring?
I curse not, for my heart is lost in thine,
Though thou forsakest a deceived thing;—
A dove forlorn and lost with sick unpruned° wing."   *bedraggled*

38

"My Madeline! sweet dreamer! lovely bride!
335 Say, may I be for aye° thy vassal blest?[8]   *ever*
Thy beauty's shield, heart-shaped and vermeil° dyed?   *vermillion*
Ah, silver shrine, here will I take my rest
After so many hours of toil and quest,
A famish'd pilgrim,—saved by miracle.
340 Though I have found, I will not rob thy nest
Saving of thy sweet self; if thou think'st well
To trust, fair Madeline, to no rude infidel.°   *unbeliever*

39

"Hark! 'tis an elfin-storm from faery land,
Of haggard° seeming, but a boon indeed: *wild, bewitched*

---

7. Keats's publishers refused his revision of 314–322, in
which Porphyro's "arms encroaching slow . . . zon'd her,
heart to heart" as he spoke into "her burning ear," and
then "with her wild dream . . . mingled as a rose / Marry-
eth its odour to a violet."
8. Keats would tell Fanny Brawne (25 July 1819): "the
very first week I knew you I wrote myself your vassal"
(page 1778). Vassal: devoted servant.

345   Arise—arise! the morning is at hand;—
    The bloated wassaillers will never heed:—
    Let us away, my love, with happy speed;
    There are no ears to hear, or eyes to see,—
    Drown'd all in Rhenish and the sleepy mead:°   *sweet wine*
350   Awake! arise! my love, and fearless be,
  For o'er the southern moors I have a home for thee."

40

    She hurried at his words, beset with fears,
    For there were sleeping dragons all around,
    At glaring watch, perhaps, with ready spears—
355   Down the wide stairs a darkling° way they found.— *dark, in the dark*
    In all the house was heard no human sound.
    A chain-droop'd lamp was flickering by each door;
    The arras,° rich with horseman, hawk, and hound,   *tapestry*
    Flutter'd in the besieging wind's uproar;
360 And the long carpets rose along the gusty floor.

41

    They glide, like phantoms, into the wide hall;
    Like phantoms to the iron porch they glide;
    Where lay the Porter,° in uneasy sprawl,   *gate-keeper*
    With a huge empty flagon by his side:
365   The wakeful bloodhound rose, and shook his hide,
    But his sagacious eye an inmate owns:[9]
    By one, and one, the bolts full easy slide:—
    The chains lie silent on the footworn stones;—
  The key turns, and the door upon its hinges groans.

42

370   And they are gone: ay, ages long ago
    These lovers fled away into the storm.
    That night the Baron dreamt of many a woe,
    And all his warrior-guests, with shade and form
    Of witch, and demon, and large coffin-worm,
375   Were long be-nightmar'd. Angela the old
    Died palsy-twitch'd, with meagre face deform;
    The Beadsman, after thousand aves told,[1]
  For aye unsought for slept among his ashes cold.

1819   1820

La Belle Dame sans Mercy[1]

  Ah, what can ail thee, wretched wight,°   *fellow*
    Alone and palely loitering;

---

9. Recognizes one of the usual dwellers (i.e., Madeline).
1. "Ave Maria" ("Hail Mary") prayers, part of the rosary ritual.
1. Published in Hunt's aesthetic (as opposed to political) journal, *The Indicator*; a version in a letter of April 1819, with slight differences in title, "La Belle Dame sans Merci," some words and stanza ordering, became, after it was first published in 1848, the preferred version, in part because it was shorn of association with Hunt. Our text is the version published in the Romantic era. The letter text, its French title taken from a medieval poem (see *Eve*

of *St. Agnes* 292, page 1760), gives the lady both more agency and more remorse. "La Belle Dame" means "the beautiful lady"; "Merci" suggests "Mercy" but carries a sense of gracious obligation. Both words derive from the medieval French *merces*, price paid or wages, suggesting the economy of exchange (the granting of sexual favor in exchange for gifts and service) that courted women are expected to honor. Keats situates the "Belle Dame" of his literary ballad in a long literary tradition of "femmes fatales," temptresses whose seduction proves fatal.

The sedge° is wither'd from the lake,   *marsh grass*
   And no birds sing.

5   Ah, what can ail thee wretched wight,
      So haggard and so woe-begone?
The squirrel's granary is full,
      And the harvest's done.

I see a lily on thy brow,
10   With anguish moist and fever dew;
And on thy cheeks a fading rose
      Fast withereth too.[2]

I met a Lady in the meads°[3]   *meadows*
      Full beautiful, a fairy's child;
15   Her hair was long, her foot was light,
      And her eyes were wild.

I set her on my pacing steed,[4]
      And nothing else saw all day long;
For sideways would she lean, and sing
20   A fairy's song.

I made a garland for her head,
      And bracelets too, and fragrant zone;°   *belt*
She look'd at me as° she did love,   *while, as if*
      And made sweet moan.

25   She found me roots of relish sweet,
      And honey wild, and manna dew;[5]
And sure in language strange she said,
      I love thee true.

She took me to her elfin grot,°   *grotto*
30   And there she gaz'd and sighèd deep,
And there I shut her wild sad eyes—
      So kiss'd to sleep.

And there she slumber'd on the moss,
      And there I dream'd, ah woe betide,
35   The latest° dream I ever dream'd   *last, most recent*
      On the cold hill side

I saw pale kings, and princes too,
      Pale warriors, death-pale were they all;
Who cry'd—"La belle Dame sans mercy
40   Hath thee in thrall!"°   *enslaved, enthralled*

I saw their starv'd lips in the gloom
      With horrid warning gapèd wide,
And I awoke, and found me here
      On the cold hill side.

2. Traditional emblems: the lily, death; the rose, love.
3. This stanza seems to begin the wretched wight's reply to his questioner, but the initial questioner may be continuing with his own story.
4. In the letter text, this stanza was transposed with the next.

5. In Exodus 16, God feeds the Israelites in the wilderness with a miraculous dew that hardens into food called manna; the context here may recall lines Keats marked in *Paradise Lost* describing fallen angel Belial's sophistry: "all was false and hollow, though his Tongue / Dropt Manna" (2.112–113).

45   And this is why I sojourn here
            Alone and palely loitering,
        Though the sedge is wither'd from the lake,
            And no birds sing.

1819   1820

Incipit Altera Sonneta[1]

I have been endeavouring to discover a better sonnet stanza than we have. The legitimate does not suit the language over-well from the pouncing rhymes—the other
kind appears too elegaiac[2]—and the couplet at the end of it has seldom a pleasing
effect—I do not pretend to have succeeded—it will explain itself—

        If by dull rhymes our English° must be chain'd,   *English language*
        And, like Andromeda,[3] the Sonnet sweet
        Fetter'd in spite of pained loveliness;
        Let us find out, if we must be constrain'd,
5   Sandals more interwoven & complete
        To fit the naked foot of Poesy;[4]
        Let us inspect the Lyre[5], & weigh the stress
        Of every chord & see what may be gain'd
        By ear industrious & attention meet;°   *appropriate*
10   Misers of sound & syllable, no less
        Than Midas of his coinage,[6] let us be
        Jealous of dead leaves in the bay wreath Crown;[7]
        So if we may not let the Muse be free,
        She will be bound with Garlands of her own.

1819   1836; 1848

THE ODES OF 1819

In Keats's career of ode-writing (from *Ode to Apollo*, 1814, to *Ode to Fanny*, 1820), there is a
remarkable group composed in a burst of inspiration between April and September 1819 that
is often regarded as his highest achievement. Except for *Ode on Indolence*, first published in
1848, all appeared, though not as a sequence, in Keats's 1820 volume. The order of composition is not known, beyond the fact that *Ode to Psyche* was written in April, the others probably
in May, and *To Autumn* the last, in September. They reflect personal, cultural, and political
contexts of 1819, having to do with everything from the Elgin Marbles controversy, to the
widespread use of opium as a painkiller, to social misery and political unrest, to Keats's grief

---

1. Latin: "Here begins another Sonnet"; Keats's heading
for this poem in a letter, to his brothers (30 April 1819),
in which this sonnet appears. Although every sonnet
implicitly comments on sonnet tradition, Keats's *Incipit*,
like Wordsworth's *Nuns fret not* (page 1561), is an
explicit reading of the tradition and his relation to it.
Keats had written more than 60 sonnets by this point
(not counting ones embedded in longer poems), but he
would write only a few more after. Several allusions to
Ovid's *Metamorphoses* reflect his concern with formal
transformation.
2. The Petrarchan ("legitimate") sonnet opens with
"pouncing rhymes": abbaabba; the "other" kind, the
Shakespearean sonnet, deploys three "elegiac" stanzas
(quatrains rhymed abab; cdcd; efef).

3. In Ovid's fable, beautiful Andromeda was fettered to a
rock to be ravaged by a sea serpent; she was rescued by
Perseus on his winged horse, Pegasus, an emblem of poetic inspiration.
4. Alluding to "poetic feet"—that is, meter.
5. The instrument of Apollo, god of poetry.
6. When Ovid's miserly king got his wish that everything
he touched would turn to gold, he found he was unable to
eat.
7. A head-wreath of bay laurel, first bestowed on military
victors, then on poets (hence, "poet laureate"); in *Metamorphoses*, when the nymph Daphne escapes Apollo's
amorous pursuit by turning into a laurel, he takes the laurel as his emblem.

over one brother's death and the other's emigration to America, to his nagging sensation that he was doomed to die young. Their language is enriched by literary allusion, as dense as it is casual, ranging through the Bible, Keats's earlier poetry and the hostile reviews of it, and favorite writers: Spenser, Shakespeare, Milton, Thomson, Collins, Chatterton, Coleridge, and Wordsworth. Even so, the odes also have an independent appeal that has made them, like Shakespeare's sonnets, general primers of the pleasure of reading poetry—of discovering how verbal nuance and reverberation, and complex interplays of imagery, shape a dynamic process of thought. Nineteenth-century readers admired the beautiful phrases and sensuous language—the tactile, auditory, visual qualities, even sensations of smell and taste. Readers in our century have added an enthusiasm for the intellectual complexity and mental drama, variously described as a poetry of "internal debate," a structure of "paradox" and "contradiction," a "rhetoric of irony" or a poetics of "indeterminacy."

Keats once suggested that "a question is the best beacon toward a little speculation," and that knowledge was less a matter of "resting places and seeming sure points of Reasoning" than of "question and answer—a little pro and con." The key questions in his odes—"Was it a vision, or a waking dream?"; "What leaf-fringed legend haunts about thy shape . . . ?"; "Where are the songs of spring?"—are met less with answers than with pro and con: a poet's mind as a "rosy sanctuary" and a place of mere "shadowy thought"; a bird-song that evokes "full-throated ease" and "easeful death"; a world of art in which human figures are both "for ever young" and a "cold pastoral"; an intensity of "Beauty" that is always a "Beauty that must die"; a sensuous "indolence" that cannot stay "sheltered from annoy" of busy thoughts; an autumn that is inextricably a season of ripe fruition and of death.

Ode to a Nightingale[1]

1

My heart aches, and a drowsy numbness pains
  My sense, as though of hemlock I had drunk,
Or emptied some dull opiate to the drains
  One minute past, and Lethe-wards had sunk:[2]
5 'Tis not through envy of thy happy lot,
  But being too happy in thine happiness,—
    That thou, light-winged Dryad° of the trees,   *wood-nymph*
        In some melodious plot
Of beechen green, and shadows numberless,
10   Singest of summer in full-throated ease.

2

O, for a draught of vintage!° that hath been   *wine*
  Cool'd a long age in the deep-delved earth,
Tasting of Flora and the country green,
  Dance, and Provençal song, and sunburnt mirth![3]
15 O for a beaker full of the warm South,

1. First published in *Annals of the Fine Arts*, 1819. Keats's stanza incorporates sonnet elements: a Shakespearean quatrain (abab) followed by a Petrarchan sestet (cdecde), also the form of the odes on "Melancholy" and "Indolence." The nightingale in literary tradition (including Milton, Charlotte Smith, Wordsworth, Coleridge) often evokes Ovid's story of Philomela, who had been raped by her brother-in-law Tereus, who cut out her tongue to ensure her silence. After she revealed the crime by weaving the story into a robe, the gods changed her into a nightingale. Keats was also inspired by an actual nightingale's song at the house where he was living.

2. In small doses hemlock is a sedative; in large doses, such as Socrates', it is fatal; an opiate is any sense-duller, particularly opium, widely used as a painkiller; Lethe is the mythic river of the underworld whose waters produce forgetfulness of previous life.

3. *Deep-delved* alludes to the magician Merlin's dwelling "in a deep delve, farre from the view of day, / That of no living wight he mote be found" (*Faerie Queene* 3.3.7). Flora: Roman goddess of flowers. Provençal: region in southern France famed for troubadours.

Full of the true, the blushful Hippocrene,[4]
     With beaded bubbles winking at the brim,
          And purple-stained mouth;
     That I might drink, and leave the world unseen,[5]
20   And with thee fade away into the forest dim:

                              3

     Fade far away, dissolve, and quite forget
     What thou among the leaves hast never known,
     The weariness, the fever, and the fret
     Here, where men sit and hear each other groan;
25   Where palsy shakes a few, sad, last gray hairs,
     Where youth grows pale, and spectre-thin, and dies;[6]
          Where but to think is to be full of sorrow
          And leaden-eyed despairs,
     Where Beauty cannot keep her lustrous eyes,
30   Or new Love pine at them beyond to-morrow.

                              4

     Away! away! for I will fly to thee,
     Not charioted by Bacchus and his pards,[7]
     But on the viewless wings of Poesy,
     Though the dull brain perplexes and retards:
35   Already with thee! tender is the night,
          And haply° the Queen-Moon is on her throne,   *happily, perhaps*
          Cluster'd around by all her starry Fays;°   *fairies*
               But here there is no light,
     Save what from heaven is with the breezes blown
40   Through verdurous glooms and winding mossy ways.

                              5

     I cannot see what flowers are at my feet,
          Nor what soft incense hangs upon the boughs,
     But, in embalmed darkness, guess each sweet
     Wherewith the seasonable month endows
45   The grass, the thicket, and the fruit-tree wild;
          White hawthorn, and the pastoral eglantine;
          Fast fading violets cover'd up in leaves;
               And mid-May's eldest child,
     The coming musk-rose, full of dewy wine,
50   The murmurous haunt of flies on summer eves.[8]

                              6

     Darkling° I listen; and, for many a time   *in the dark*
     I have been half in love with easeful Death,

---

4. Hippocrene: the fountain of the muses on Mount Helicon.
5. "Unseen" can modify both "I" and "world."
6. An echo of Wordsworth's memory in *Tintern Abbey* of himself in "darkness, and amid the many shapes / Of joyless day-light; when the fretful stir / Unprofitable, and the fever of the world, / Have hung upon the beatings of my heart" (52–55); see page 1531, and Keats's remarks on *Tintern Abbey* in the letter of 3 May 1818 (pages 1774–1776). Both poets recall Macbeth's envy of Duncan "in his grave; / After life's fitful fever he sleeps well"

(*Macbeth* 3.322–323). Also echoed is Wordsworth's image of an ideal life "from diminution safe and weakening age; / While man grows old, and dwindles, and decays" (*Excursion* 4.759–760).
7. Bacchus, god of wine and revelry, whose chariot is drawn by leopards.
8. This guessing of flowers echoes Oberon's description in *A Midsummer Night's Dream* of a verdant bank where one may find a snake-skin whose juices make a sleeper fall in love with whatever is first seen on waking (2.1.249–58).

Call'd him soft names in many a mused rhyme,
    To take into the air my quiet breath;
55 Now more than ever seems it rich to die,
    To cease upon the midnight with no pain,
      While thou art pouring forth thy soul abroad
        In such an ecstasy!
    Still wouldst thou sing, and I have ears in vain—
60   To thy high requiem° become a sod.   *funeral mass*

7

Thou wast not born for death, immortal Bird!
    No hungry generations tread thee down;
    The voice I hear this passing night was heard
    In ancient days by emperor and clown:°   *rustic, peasant*
65 Perhaps the self-same song that found a path
    Through the sad heart of Ruth, when, sick for home,
      She stood in tears amid the alien corn;[9]
        The same that oft-times hath
    Charm'd magic casements, opening on the foam
70   Of perilous seas, in faery lands forlorn.

8

Forlorn! the very word is like a bell
    To toll me back from thee to my sole self!
    Adieu! the fancy cannot cheat so well[1]
    As she is fam'd to do, deceiving elf.
75 Adieu! adieu! thy plaintive anthem fades
    Past the near meadows, over the still stream,
      Up the hill-side; and now 'tis buried deep
        In the next valley-glades:
    Was it a vision, or a waking dream?
    Fled is that music:—Do I wake or sleep?

Ode on a Grecian Urn[1]

1

Thou still unravish'd bride of quietness,
    Thou foster-child of silence and slow time,
Sylvan° historian, who canst thus express   *woodland*
    A flowery tale more sweetly than our rhyme:
5 What leaf-fring'd legend haunts about thy shape
    Of deities or mortals, or of both,

---

9. See Ruth 1–2: compelled by famine to leave her home, Ruth eked out a living as a gleaner in far-away fields.
1. The adieu echoes the opening line of Charlotte Smith's *On the Departure of the Nightingale* (1784), "Sweet poet of the woods!—a long adieu!" The closing question bears several echoes: *Psyche* 5–6; the opening of Spenser's Amoretti 77: "Was it a dreame, or did I see it playne?"; Hazlitt's remark that "Spenser was the poet of our waking dreams," his "music . . . lulling the senses into a deep oblivion of the jarring noises of the world from which we have no wish ever to be recalled" (*On Chaucer and Spenser*, 1818); a spellbound lover's confusion in *Midsummer Night's Dream*: "Are you sure / That we are awake? It seems to me / That yet we sleep, we dream" (4.1.194–96); Wordsworth's lament in the "Intimations" Ode, "Whither is fled the visionary gleam? / Where is it now, the glory and the dream?" (56–57), and his phrase "waking dream" in *Yarrow Visited* (pub. 1815).
1. First published in *Annals of the Fine Arts*. Keats is not describing any particular urn but three scenes on a representative one. The first is an image of revelry and sexual pursuit; the second (stanzas 2–3) is either a detail of this or another: a piper, and a lover in pursuit of a fair maid; in both, the story of Pan is implied. The third (stanza 4) is a sacrificial ritual, perhaps inspired by one of the Elgin Marble friezes.

In Tempe or the dales of Arcady?[2]
What men or gods are these? What maidens loth?
What mad pursuit? What struggle to escape?
10   What pipes and timbrels?° What wild ecstasy?   *tambourines*

      2

Heard melodies are sweet, but those unheard
Are sweeter; therefore, ye soft pipes, play on;
Not to the sensual° ear, but, more endear'd,   *physical*
Pipe to the spirit ditties of no tone:
15 Fair youth, beneath the trees, thou canst not leave
Thy song, nor ever can those trees be bare;
Bold Lover, never, never canst thou kiss,
Though winning near the goal—yet, do not grieve;
She cannot fade, though thou hast not thy bliss,
20 For ever wilt thou love, and she be fair!

      3

Ah, happy, happy° boughs! that cannot shed   *joyous, fortunate*
Your leaves, nor ever bid the Spring adieu;
And, happy melodist, unwearied,
For ever piping songs for ever new;
25 More happy love! more happy, happy love!
For ever warm and still to be enjoy'd,
For ever panting, and for ever young;
All breathing human passion far above,
That leaves a heart high-sorrowful and cloy'd,
30 A burning forehead, and a parching tongue.

      4

Who are these coming to the sacrifice?
To what green altar, O mysterious priest,[3]
Lead'st thou that heifer lowing at the skies,
And all her silken flanks with garlands drest?
35 What little town by river or sea shore,
Or mountain-built with peaceful citadel,°   *fortress*
Is emptied of this folk, this pious morn?
And, little town, thy streets for evermore
Will silent be; and not a soul to tell
40 Why thou art desolate, can e'er return.

      5

O Attic shape! Fair attitude!° with brede°   *pose / intricate design*
Of marble men and maidens overwrought,[4]
With forest branches and the trodden weed;
Thou, silent form, dost tease us out of thought
45 As doth eternity: Cold Pastoral!
When old age shall this generation waste,

---

2. A design of leaves frames a "legend" or caption on some vases; Tempe and Arcadia are districts of ancient Greece famed for beauty and serenity, where the gods often recreated.
3. That is, "unknown"; also denoting religious "mysteries" or rites.

4. The urn, made in Attica (where Athens is located), is "overwrought" (overlaid) with its design; Keats may be implying "over-elaborated," with a hint of psychological or emotional anguish in the frozen figures; thus "brede" puns on what cannot happen, "breed."

Thou shalt remain, in midst of other woe
Than ours, a friend to man, to whom thou say'st,
Beauty is truth, truth beauty,—that is all
50   Ye know on earth, and all ye need to know.[5]

Ode on Melancholy[1]

1

No, no, go not to Lethe,° neither twist   *river of forgetfulness*
    Wolf's-bane, tight-rooted, for its poisonous wine;
Nor suffer thy pale forehead to be kiss'd
    By nightshade, ruby grape of Proserpine;[2]
5   Make not your rosary of yew-berries,[3]
    Nor let the beetle, nor the death-moth be
        Your mournful Psyche,[4] nor the downy owl
A partner in your sorrow's mysteries;°   *secret rites*
    For shade to shade will come too drowsily,
10   And drown the wakeful anguish of the soul.

2

But when the melancholy fit shall fall
    Sudden from heaven like a weeping cloud,
That fosters the droop-headed flowers all,
    And hides the green hill in an April shroud;
15 Then glut thy sorrow on a morning rose,
    Or on the rainbow of the salt sand-wave,
    Or on the wealth of globed peonies;
Or if thy mistress some rich anger shows,
    Emprison her soft hand, and let her rave,
20   And feed deep, deep upon her peerless eyes.

3

She[5] dwells with Beauty—Beauty that must die;
    And Joy, whose hand is ever at his lips

5. In the 1820 volume, but in no other draft, quotation marks are placed around "Beauty is truth, truth beauty." Keats ponders the relation between "beauty" and "truth" throughout his career.

1. In May 1819, Keats paraphrased a couplet from Wordsworth's "Intimations" Ode: "Nothing can bring back the hour / Of splendour in the grass and glory in the flower" (cf. 177–178; page 1615), commenting, "I once thought this a Melancholist's dream." "Melancholy" is a traditional term for "the blues," or even "black" moods; Hamlet is famously "The Melancholy Dane." Robert Burton's treatise, *Anatomy of Melancholy* (1621), which Keats studied, offers an elaborate medical analysis of melancholy as well as an anthology of notable remarks. Taking a stock subject for poets in the 18th century (Charlotte Smith's sonnet *To Melancholy* among them; see page 1562), Keats prizes melancholy as a sensibility that accepts, even relishes, the evanescence of joy, pleasure, and beauty—their imminent flux into their opposites rendering such sensations all the more exquisite. He originally began the ode with a macabre, mock-heroic stanza about the quest for the goddess Melancholy: "Though you should build a bark

of dead men's bones, / And rear a phantom gibbet for a mast, / Stitch creeds together for a sail, with groans / To fill it out, bloodstained and aghast; / Although your rudder be a Dragon's tail, / Long sever'd, yet still hard with agony, / Your cordage large uprootings from the skull / Of bald Medusa: certes you would fail / To find the Melancholy, whether she / Dreameth in any isle of Lethe dull . . ."

2. Wolf's-bane and nightshade are poisons; Proserpine (or Persephone) was abducted to the underworld by its ruler, Hades, but an appeal by her mother Ceres (goddess of grain) allowed her an annual sojourn in the upper world from spring to fall—a fable of seasonal flux relevant to the aesthetic of Melancholy.

3. The yew-tree is an emblem of death; rosary: prayer beads.

4. In Greek, "Psyche" means both "soul" and "butterfly" (its emblem); the markings on the death's-head moth resemble a human skull; the beetle may be the scarab, a jewel-bug placed in tombs by the ancient Egyptians as a portent of resurrection.

5. A double reference, to the mistress and to the goddess Melancholy.

Bidding adieu; and aching Pleasure nigh,
    Turning to poison while the bee-mouth sips:
25   Ay, in the very temple of Delight
      Veil'd Melancholy has her sovran shrine,
        Though seen of none save him whose strenuous tongue
    Can burst Joy's grape against his palate fine;°   *sensitive, refined*
      His soul shall taste the sadness of her might,
30   And be among her cloudy trophies hung.

To Autumn[1]

1

Season of mists and mellow fruitfulness,
    Close bosom-friend of the maturing sun;
Conspiring with him how to load and bless
    With fruit the vines that round the thatch-eaves[2] run;
5   To bend with apples the moss'd cottage-trees,
      And fill all fruit with ripeness to the core;
        To swell the gourd, and plump the hazel shells
With a sweet kernel; to set budding more,
    And still more, later flowers for the bees,
10   Until they think warm days will never cease,
        For Summer has o'er-brimm'd their clammy cells.

2

Who hath not seen thee oft amid thy store?
    Sometimes whoever seeks abroad may find
Thee sitting careless on a granary floor,
15   Thy hair soft-lifted by the winnowing wind;
Or on a half-reap'd furrow sound asleep,
    Drowsed with the fume of poppies, while thy hook°   *scythe*
      Spares the next swath and all its twined flowers:
And sometimes like a gleaner thou dost keep
20   Steady thy laden head across a brook;
    Or by a cider-press, with patient look,
      Thou watchest the last oozings hours by hours.

3

Where are the songs of Spring? Ay, where are they?[3]
    Think not of them, thou hast thy music too,—
25   While barred clouds bloom the soft-dying day,

---

1. Composed 19–21 September 1819 in Winchester, a tranquil village in southern England, from which Keats wrote to a friend: "How beautiful the season is now— How fine the air. A temperate sharpness about it. . . . I never lik'd stubble fields so much as now—Aye better than the chilly green of the spring. Somehow a stubble plain looks warm—in the same way that some pictures look warm—this struck me so much in my sunday's walk that I composed upon it." The ode evokes two competing but related senses of autumn: the social context of harvest bounty; and the symbolic association with death—

the reaper as grim reaper, autumn as the presage of winter (see Shakespeare's sonnet, "That time of year thou may'st in me behold"). Among other poems echoed are Thomson's *Autumn* in *The Seasons* (1740) and the last stanza of Coleridge's *Frost at Midnight*.
2. The eaves of thatched cottage roofs.
3. A self-conscious sounding of the "Ubi sunt" trope ("where are they now?"), which traditionally prefaces a nostalgic lament for lost worlds, the implied answer being "gone"; cf. Wordsworth's version at the end of stanza 4 of *Ode: Intimations* (page 1612).

And touch the stubble-plains with rosy hue;
Then in a wailful choir the small gnats mourn
     Among the river sallows,[4] borne aloft
     Or sinking as the light wind lives or dies;
30   And full-grown lambs loud bleat from hilly bourn;°   boundary, region
     Hedge-crickets sing; and now with treble soft°   faint high pitch
     The red-breast whistles from a garden-croft;°   enclosure
     And gathering swallows twitter in the skies.

This living hand[1]

This living hand, now warm and capable
Of earnest grasping, would, if it were cold
and in the icy silence of the tomb,
So haunt thy days and chill thy dreaming nights
5   That thou would wish thine own hea[r]t[2] dry of blood
So in my veins red life might stream again,
and thou be conscience-calm'd—see here it is—
I hold it towards you—

c. 1819   1898

Bright Star[1]

Bright Star, would I were stedfast as thou art—
     Not in lone splendor hung aloft the night,
     And watching, with eternal lids apart,
     Like nature's patient, sleepless Eremite,°   hermit
5   The moving waters at their priestlike task
     Of pure ablution° round earth's human shores,   ritual washing
     Or gazing on the new soft-fallen masque[2]
     Of snow upon the mountains and the moors—
No—yet still stedfast, still unchangeable
10   Pillow'd upon my fair love's ripening breast,
To feel for ever its soft swell and fall.
     Awake for ever in a sweet unrest,
     Still, still to hear her tender-taken breath,
And so live ever—or else swoon to death—

1820   1838

---

4. Willows (an emblem of death).
1. A mysterious fragment, context unknown; "hand" is also a term for the character of one's "handwriting."
2. Keats inserted "heat" as superscript between "thine" and "own"; his characteristic dropping of "r" in handwriting makes it possible that he meant "heart," which best fits the context (although "heat" is relevant).
1. In summer 1818, Keats remarked that the scenery of the lake country "refine[s] one's sensual vision into a sort of north star which can never cease to be open lidded and stedfast over the wonders of the great Power"; sometime

before summer 1819, he drafted this sonnet, then wrote this revised version in early autumn 1820 into the volume of Shakespeare's poems he took to Italy; perhaps the last poetry he wrote, its title in 19th-century editions was "Keats's last sonnet." The opening recalls the heroic self-description of Julius Caesar: "I could be well moved . . . but I am constant as the Northern Star, / Of whose true-fixed and resting quality / There is no fellow in the firmament" (Julius Caesar 3.1.58–62).
2. Punning on "mask," the word used in the 1819 draft.

LETTERS[1]

To George and Thomas Keats[2]

["INTENSITY" AND "NEGATIVE CAPABILITY"]

December 1818

My dear Brothers

[21 Dec.] * * * I saw Kean return to the public in Richard III,[3] & finely he did it.
* * * Hone the publisher's trial, you must find very amusing; & as Englishmen very
encouraging—his <u>Not Guilty</u> is a thing, which not to have been, would have
dulled still more Liberty's Emblazoning—Lord Ellenborough has been paid in his
own coin—Wooler & Hone have done us an essential service[4]—I spent Friday
evening with Wells & went the next morning to see <u>Death on the Pale horse.</u>[5] It
is a wonderful picture, when West's age is considered; But there is nothing to be
intense upon; no women one feels mad to kiss; no face swelling into reality. the
excellence of every Art is its intensity, capable of making all disagreeables evaporate, from their being in close relationship with Beauty & Truth—Examine King
Lear[6] & you will find this examplified throughout; but in this picture we have
unpleasantness without any momentous depth of speculation excited, in which to
bury its repulsiveness. * * *

[?27 Dec.] * * * I had not a dispute but a disquisition with Dilke, on various subjects;[7] several things dovetailed in my mind, & at once it struck me, what quality
went to form a Man of Achievement especially in Literature & which Shakespeare posessed so enormously—I mean <u>Negative Capability</u>, that is when man is
capable of being in uncertainties, Mysteries, doubts, without any irritable reaching after fact & reason[8]—Coleridge, for instance, would let go by a fine isolated
verisimilitude caught from the Penetralium of mystery, from being incapable of
remaining content with half knowledge.[9] This pursued through Volumes would

---

1. In order to convey the character of Keats's letter-writing,
idiosyncrasies of spelling, punctuation, and capitalization are
for the most part preserved. Our insertions for clarity appear
in square brackets [ ]; words or letters canceled by Keats that
still seem interesting are inside angled brackets < >.
2. The brothers had lived together since 1816; George
(1797–1841) had taken Tom to Teignmouth, Devonshire for his health.
3. Edmund Kean (1787–1833), charismatic and scandal-
ridden actor who revolutionized the Shakespearean stage
with his passionate performances. Richard III was one of
his celebrated roles; Keats had just published an article
on him in The Champion.
4. Referring to two notorious prosecutions. William Hone
had just been found not guilty on three counts of blasphemous libel for his parodies of the liturgy, of which nearly
100,000 copies had sold. A conservative Lord Chief Justice Ellenborough, who had earlier sentenced John and
Leigh Hunt for libel, presided at two of his trials and was
humiliated by the loudly applauded verdict. Thomas
Wooler, politician, journalist, and editor of the radical
weekly The Black Dwarf, was acquitted on similar charges
the previous June. The trials were well attended and

extremely amusing because the "offenses" had to be read
into the record, thus gaining audience not only in the
courtroom but also in reports in the "legitimate" press.
5. Wells was a schoolmate of Tom; Death on a Pale Horse,
by American painter Benjamin West, is based on the
image in Revelation of the fourth horseman of the Apocalypse.
6. West's painting of the storm scene in the play, not the
play itself.
7. Disquisition: legalese for formal inquiry. Charles Dilke
(1789–1864), government worker and amateur scholar,
was a new friend.
8. "Negative Capability," Keats's most famous formulation, is a self-conscious oxymoron, wittily defined by its
refrain from positing certainties of "fact & reason"; compare Keats's antipathy to egotistical assertions of "certain
philosophy," "resting places and seeming sure points of
Reasoning" (letters to Reynolds, 3 Feb. and 3 May 1818).
9. In 1817, Coleridge published Biographia Literaria and a
volume of poems (Sibylline Leaves), in which The Rime of
the Ancient Mariner appears with an explanatory marginal
gloss. "Penetralium" is Keats's faux-Latin singular of
"penetralia," the inmost chamber of a temple.

perhaps take us no further than this, that with a great poet the sense of Beauty overcomes every other consideration, or rather obliterates all consideration.

Shelley's poem is out & there are words about its being objected too, as much as Queen Mab was. Poor Shelley I think he has his Quota of good qualities, in sooth la!![1] Write soon to your most sincere friend & affectionate Brother

John

To John Hamilton Reynolds[2]
[WORDSWORTH AND "THE WHIMS OF AN EGOTIST"]

3 February 1818

My dear Reynolds,

* * * It may be said that we ought to read our Contemporaries. that Wordsworth &c should have their due from us. but for the sake of a few fine imaginative or domestic passages, are we to be bullied into a certain Philosophy engendered in the whims of an Egotist—Every man has his speculations, but every man does not brood and peacock over[3] them till he makes a false coinage and deceives himself—Many a man can travel to the very bourne of Heaven,[4] and yet want confidence to put down his halfseeing. Sancho[5] will invent a Journey heavenward as well as any body. We hate poetry that has a palpable design upon us—and if we do not agree, seems to put its hand in its breeches pocket.[6] Poetry should be great & unobtrusive, a thing which enters into one's soul, and does not startle it or amaze it with itself but with its subject.—How beautiful are the retired flowers! how would they lose their beauty were they to throng into the highway crying out, "admire me I am a violet! dote upon me I am a primrose!["] * * * I will cut all this—I will have no more of Wordsworth or Hunt in particular. * * * I don't mean to deny Wordsworth's grandeur & Hunt's merit, but I mean to say we need not be teazed with grandeur & merit—when we can have them uncontaminated & unobtrusive. Let us have the old Poets, & robin Hood Your letter and its sonnets gave me more pleasure than will the 4th Book of Childe Harold & the whole of any body's life & opinions.[7] * * *

Y^r sincere friend and Coscribbler
John Keats.

1. Shelley was forced to withdraw *Laon and Cythna* (1817), an epic featuring the incestuous love of its sibling hero and heroine; the outcry was as heated as that against *Queen Mab* (1813), a visionary political epic attacking "Kingcraft, Priestcraft, and Statecraft." Keats's "sooth la!" ("the truth!") echoes the voice of Cleopatra as she tries, ineptly, to help Antony put on his armor after their night of debauchery (*Antony and Cleopatra* 4.4.8).
2. John Hamilton Reynolds (1794–1852), lawyer and poet, became one of Keats's closest friends; he introduced him to many others who would become friends, and to the publishers, Taylor and Hessey, who published *Endymion* and the 1820 volume.

3. To strut about ostentatiously; the OED credits Keats's usage here as the first instance of this verbal sense.
4. Alluding to Hamlet's description of the afterlife as the "undiscovered country, from whose bourn / No traveler returns" (*Hamlet* 3.1. 79–80); bourn: region.
5. Down-to-earth squire to the idealistic hero of Cervantes' *Don Quixote*.
6. Put away one's fist and refuse to fight.
7. Reynolds had just sent Keats some sonnets on Robin Hood; in response, Keats wrote *Robin Hood* and *Lines on the Mermaid Tavern*. The 4th canto of Byron's sensationally popular serial epic *Childe Harold's Pilgrimage* would be published in April.

To John Hamilton Reynolds

[WORDSWORTH, MILTON, AND "DARK PASSAGES"]

3 May 1818

My dear Reynolds.

What I complain of is that I have been in so an uneasy a state of Mind as not to be fit to write to an invalid. I cannot write to any length under a dis-guised feeling. I should have loaded you with an addition of gloom, which I am sure you do not want. I am now thank God in a humour to give you a good groats worth—for Tom, after a Night without a Wink of sleep, and overburdened with fever, has got up after a refreshing day sleep and is better than he has been for a long time. * * * Were I to study physic or rather Medicine again,—I feel it would not make the least difference in my Poetry; when the Mind is in its infancy a Bias is in reality a Bias, but when we have acquired more strength, a Bias becomes no Bias. Every department of knowledge we see excel-lent and calculated towards a great whole. I am so convinced of this, that I am glad at not having given away my medical Books, which I shall again look over to keep alive the little I know thitherwards. * * * An extensive knowledge is needful to thinking people—it takes away the heat and fever; and helps, by widening speculation, to ease the Burden of the Mystery:[8] a thing I begin to understand a little, and which weighed upon you in the most gloomy and true sentence in your Letter. The difference of high Sensations with and without knowledge appears to me this—in the latter case we are falling continually ten thousand fathoms deep and being blown up again without wings and with all [the] horror of a <bare> shouldered Creature—in the former case, our shoulders are fledge<d>, and we go thro' the same <air> and space without fear.[9] This is running one's rigs[1] on the score of abstracted benefit—when we come to human Life and the affections it is impossible how a parallel of breast and head can be drawn—(you will forgive me for thus privately heading <treading> out my depth and take it for treading as schoolboys head <tread> the water<s>)—it is impossible to know how far knowledge will console [us] for the death of a friend and the ill "that flesh is heir [to"][2] * * *

You seem by that to have been going through with a more painful and acute <test> zest the same labyrinth that I have—I have come to the same conclusion thus far. My Branchings out therefrom have been numerous: one of them is the consideration of Wordsworth's genius and as a help, in the manner of gold being the meridian Line of worldly wealth,—how he differs from Milton.[3]—And here I have nothing but surmises, from an uncertainty whether Miltons apparently less anxiety for Humanity proceeds from his seeing further or no than Wordsworth: And whether Wordsworth has in truth epic passion<s>, and martyrs himself to the human heart, the main region of his song[4]—In regard to his genius alone—we find

8. An allusion to Wordsworth's recollection in *Tintern Abbey* of that "blessed mood / In which the burthen of the mystery, / In which the heavy and the weary weight / Of all this unintelligible world, / Is lightened" (37–41).
9. Milton describes the angels in *Paradise Lost* as having "Shoulders fledge with wings" (3.627); even so, Satan is blown about in Chaos: "Flutt'ring his pennons vain plumb down he drops / Ten thousand fadom deep," then propelled "As many miles aloft" (2.933–38).
1. On a ship, running one's rigs means going at top speed; Keats's next image of treading water suggests a shipwreck

on this abstract value.
2. Alluding to Hamlet's longing for death as a way to "end / The heartache, and the thousand natural shocks / That flesh is heir to!" (*Hamlet* 3.1.61–63).
3. Keats treats Milton as the gold standard for assessing wealth, or the meridian line of longitude used by sailors to take their bearings.
4. In the "Prospectus" to *The Excursion*, Wordsworth aligned his epic with *Paradise Lost*, but declared "the Mind of Man" as the "haunt, and the main region of [his] song" (40–41).

what he says true as far as we have experienced and we can judge no further but by larger experience—for axioms in philosophy are not axioms until they are proved upon our pulses: We read fine—things but never feel them to [the] full until we have gone the same steps as the Author.—I know this is not plain; you will know exactly my meaning when I say, that now I shall relish Hamlet more than I ever have done—Or, better—You are sensible no man can set down Venery[5] as a bestial or joyless thing until he is sick of it and therefore all philosophizing on it would be mere wording. Until we are sick, we understand not;—in fine, as Byron says, "Knowledge is Sorrow"; and I go on to say that "Sorrow is Wisdom"—and further for aught we can know for certainty! "Wisdom is folly"[6]—So you see how I have run away from Wordsworth, and Milton. * * * I will return to Wordsworth— whether or no he has an extended vision or a circumscribed grandeur—whether he is an eagle in his nest, or on the wing—And to be more explicit and to show you how tall I stand by the giant, I will put down a simile of human life as far as I now perceive it; that is, to the point to which I say we both have arrived at—Well—I compare human life to a large Mansion of Many Apartments, two of which I can only describe, the doors of the rest being as yet shut upon me—The first we step into we call the infant or thoughtless Chamber, in which we remain as long as we do not think—We remain there a long while, and notwithstanding the doors of the second Chamber remain wide open, showing a bright appearance, we care not to hasten to it; but are at length imperceptibly impelled by the awakening of the thinking principle—within us—we no sooner get into the second Chamber, which I shall call the Chamber of Maiden-Thought, than we become intoxicated with the light and the atmosphere, we see nothing but pleasant wonders, and think of delay-ing there for ever in delight: However among the effects this breathing is father of is that tremendous one of sharpening one's vision into the <head> heart and nature of Man—of convincing ones nerves that the World is full of Misery and Heartbreak, Pain, Sickness and oppression—whereby This Chamber of Maiden Thought becomes gradually darken'd and at the same time on all sides of it many doors are set open—but all dark—all leading to dark passages—We see not the bal-lance of good and evil.[7] We are in a Mist—We are now in that state—We feel the "burden of the Mystery," To this point was Wordsworth come, as far as I can con-ceive when he wrote "Tintern Abbey" and it seems to me that his Genius is explo-rative of those dark Passages. Now if we live, and go on thinking, we too shall explore them. he is a Genius and superior [to] us, in so far as he can, more than we, make discoveries, and shed a light in them—Here I must think Wordsworth is deeper than Milton—though I think it has depended more upon the general and gregarious advance of intellect, than individual greatness of Mind—From the Par-adise Lost and the other Works of Milton, I hope it is not too presuming, even between ourselves to say, his Philosophy, human and divine, may be tolerably understood by one not much advanced in years, In his time englishmen were just

5. Venery: sexual debauchery; Keats may have indulged himself thus when he visited Bailey at Oxford.
6. A mismemory or deliberate reversing of the complaint of Byron's tormented scholar-magician Manfred: "Sorrow is knowledge: they who know the most / Must mourn the deepest o'er the fatal truth, / The tree of knowledge is not that of life" (*Manfred* 1.1.10). Where Manfred alludes to Adam and Eve's gain of knowledge in tandem with a

death sentence, Keats blends the phrase to echo the famous conclusion of Thomas Gray's *Ode on a Distant Prospect of Eton College* (1747): "where ignorance is bliss, / 'Tis folly to be wise."
7. In the "Prospectus" to *The Excursion* Wordsworth stat-ed his Miltonic "intent / To weigh the good and evil of our mortal state".

emancipated from a great superstition—and Men had got hold of certain points and resting places in reasoning which were too newly born to be doubted, and too much \<oppressed\> opposed by the Mass of Europe not to be thought etherial and authentically divine—who could gainsay his ideas on virtue, vice, and Chastity in Comus, just at the time of the dismissal of Cod-pieces and a hundred other disgraces?[8] who would not rest satisfied with his hintings at good and evil in the Paradise Lost, when just free from the inquisition and burrning in Smithfield?[9] The Reformation produced such immediate and great benefits, that Protestantism was considered under the immediate eye of heaven, and its own remaining Dogmas and superstitions, then, as it were, regenerated, constituted those resting places and seeming sure points of Reasoning—from that I have mentioned, Milton, whatever he may have thought in the sequel, appears to have been content with these by his writings[1]—He did not think into the human heart, as Wordsworth has done—Yet Milton as a Philosop[h]er, had sure as great powers as Wordsworth—What is then to be inferr'd? O many things—It proves there is really a grand march of intellect—, It proves that a mighty providence subdues the mightiest Minds to the service of the time being, whether it be in human Knowledge or Religion—Tom has spit a leetle blood this afternoon, and that is rather a damper—but I know—the truth is there is something real in the World Your third Chamber of Life shall be a lucky and a gentle one—stored with the wine of love— and the Bread of Friendship[2] * * *

Your affectionate friend
John Keats.

To Richard Woodhouse[3]

[THE "CAMELION POET" VS. THE "EGOTISTICAL SUBLIME"]

27 October 1818

My dear Woodhouse,

Your Letter gave me a great satisfaction; more on account of its friendliness, than any relish of that matter in it which is accounted so acceptable in the 'genus irritabile'[4] The best answer I can give you is in a clerklike manner to make some observations on two principle points, which seem to point like indices into the midst of the whole pro and con, about genius, and views and achievements and ambition and cœtera. 1st As to the poetical Character itself, (I mean that sort of which, if I am any thing, I am a

8. The "superstition" was the old theory, enforced by the Catholic Church, of the earth as the center of the universe. In Milton's lifetime, Protestant scientists such as Copernicus overturned this theory, even as society abandoned such archaic fashions in clothing as codpieces. *Comus* (1634) depicts the temptation of a lady's virtue by the enchanter Comus.

9. The medieval Church established the Inquisition to seek out heretics, who were often burned at the stake. Smithfield, northwest of London, was a notorious site of public executions in the 16th and 17th centuries, especially under the reign of Catholic Queen Mary.

1. The "sequel" is the later writings; the Reformation was

a series of religious revolutions in the 16th century that resulted, often with violent warfare, in a variety of Protestant sects, including the Anglican Church.

2. A consciously secular application of the emblems of the Christian Eucharist.

3. Legal and literary adviser to Keats's second publishers, Woodhouse was a great admirer of Keats and assiduously preserved or transcribed his letters, manuscripts, and proof-sheets, as well as collected anecdotes. This is one of Keats's most famous letters, written after he had weathered a summer of negative reviews in highly visible journals.

4. Horace's term for poets, "the irritable tribe" (*Epistles* 2.2.102).

Member; that sort distinguished from the wordsworthian or egotistical sublime;[5] which is a thing per se and stands alone[6] it is not itself—it has no self—it is every thing and nothing—It has no character—it enjoys light and shade; it lives in gusto, be it foul or fair, high or low, rich or poor, mean or elevated—It has as much delight in conceiving an Iago as an Imogen.[7] What shocks the virtuous philosop[h]er, delights the camelion[8] Poet. It does no harm from its relish of the dark side of things any more than from its taste for the bright one; because they both end in speculation. A Poet is the most unpoetical of any thing in existence; because he has no Identity— he is continually in for[ming?]—and filling some other Body—The Sun, the Moon, the Sea and Men and Women who are creatures of impulse are poetical and have about them an unchangeable attribute—the poet has none; no identity—he is certainly the most unpoetical of all God's Creatures. If then he has no self, and if I am a Poet, where is the Wonder that I should say I would <right> write no more? Might I not at that very instant [have] been cogitating on the Characters of saturn and Ops?[9] It is a wretched thing to confess; but is a very fact that not one word I ever utter can be taken for granted as an opinion growing out of my identical nature—how can it, when I have no nature? When I am in a room with People if I ever am free from speculating on creations of my own brain, then not myself goes home to myself: but the identity of every one in the room begins to press upon me that, I am in a very little time an[ni]hilated—not only among Men; it would be the same in a Nursery of children: I know not whether I make myself wholly understood: I hope enough so to let you see that no dependence is to be placed on what I said that day.

In the second place I will speak of my views, and of the life I purpose to myself— I am ambitious of doing the world some good: if I should be spared that may be the work of maturer years—in the interval I will assay to reach to as high a summit in Poetry as the nerve bestowed upon me will suffer. The faint conceptions I have of Poems to come brings the blood frequently into my forehead—All I hope is that I may not lose all interest in human affairs—that the solitary indifference I feel for applause even from the finest Spirits, will not blunt any acuteness of vision I may have. I do not think it will—I feel assured I should write from the mere yearning and fondness I have for the Beautiful even if my night's labours should be burnt every morning and no eye ever shine upon them. But even now I am perhaps not speaking from myself; but from some character in whose soul I now live. I am sure however that this next sentence is from myself. I feel your anxiety, good opinion and friendliness in the highest degree, and am

Your's most sincerely
John Keats

5. By "Character" Keats means not only the poet's personality but also the degree to which a poet's identity, biases, philosophy, etc. are visible in his work. In Keats's day, Shakespeare was admired, by Coleridge and others, for the invisibility of this "character"; in an influential lecture of 1818 (attended by Keats), Hazlitt called Shakespeare "the least of an egotist that it was possible to be. He was nothing in himself; but . . . all that others were." Milton and Wordsworth were typically summoned for contrast, as poets of egotism.

6. A foolish soldier in Shakespeare's *Troilus and Cressida* is described as "a very man per se" who "stands alone" (1.2.15–16).

7. William Hazlitt's *On Gusto* begins, "Gusto in art is power or passion defining any object." Iago is the scheming villain of *Othello*; Imogen is the virtuous heroine of *Cymbeline*.

8. Chameleon, a creature able to change color according to circumstance.

9. Keats had remarked to Woodhouse that he felt preempted by the great poets of the past. In Greek mythology, Saturn is the king of the Titan gods and Ops a harvest goddess; cast out of heaven by the revolt of their children, the fallen Titans focus the major part of the poem Keats was working on during these months, *Hyperion*.

To Fanny Brawne[1]
["You Take Possession of Me"]

25 July 1819 Sunday Night.

My sweet Girl,

I hope you did not blame me much for not obeying your request of a Letter on Saturday: we have had four in our small room playing at cards night and morning leaving me no undisturb'd opportunity to write. * * * Brown to my sorrow confirms the account you give of your ill health. You cannot conceive how I ache to be with you: how I would die for one hour—for what is in the world? I say you cannot conceive; it is impossible you should look with such eyes upon me as I have upon you: it cannot be. Forgive me if I wander a little this evening, for I have been all day employ'd in a very abstr[a]ct Poem[2] and I am in deep love with you—two things which must excuse me. I have, believe me, not been an age in letting you take possession of me; the very first week I knew you I wrote myself your vassal; but burnt the Letter as the very next time I saw you I thought you manifested some dislike to me. If you should ever feel for Man at the first sight what I did for you, I am lost. Yet I should not quarrel with you, but hate myself if such a thing were to happen—only I should burst if the thing were not as fine as a Man as you are as a Woman. Perhaps I am too vehement, then fancy me on my knees, especially when I mention a part of you Letter which hurt me; you say speaking of Mr Severn[3] "but you must be satisfied in knowing that I admired you much more than your friend." My dear love, I cannot believe there ever was or ever could be any thing to admire in me especially as far as sight goes—I cannot be admired, I am not a thing to be admired. You are, I love you; all I can bring you is a swooning admiration of your Beauty. I hold that place among Men which snubnos'd brunettes with meeting eyebrows do among women— they are trash to me—unless I should find one among them with a fire in her heart like the one that burns in mine. You absorb me in spite of myself—you alone: for I look not forward with any pleasure to what is call'd being settled in the world; I tremble at domestic cares—yet for you I would meet them, though if it would leave you the happier I would rather die than do so. I have two luxuries to brood over in my walks, your Loveliness and the hour of my death. O that I could have possession of them both in the same minute.[4] I hate the world: it batters too much the wings of my self-will, and would I could take a sweet poison from your lips to send me out of it. From no others would I take it. I am indeed astonish'd to find myself so careless of all cha[r]ms but yours—remembering as I do the time when even a bit of ribband was a matter of interest with me. What softer words can I find for you after this—

---

1. When Keats met Fanny Brawne (1800–1865) in the summer 1818, he was charmed and vexed by her almost at once. They fell in love within a few months and became engaged at the end of the year, but kept it secret pending Keats's financial ability to make a formal offer. His first letters to her were written from a working vacation with Brown on the Isle of Wight in the summer of 1819. As a tenant in Brown's apartment in Hampstead, Keats lived next door to the Brawnes from October 1819 to May 1820, and they cared for him in their own quarters later that summer. He saw Fanny Brawne for the last time on 13 September 1820, just before he left for Italy. Her identity became public in 1878 when his surviving letters to her were first published, a sensational event that damaged both their reputations.

2. The remodeling of *Hyperion* into *The Fall of Hyperion*.

3. Joseph Severn (1793–1879), an artist; he went with Keats to Rome, and Keats died in his arms.

4. Compare *Bright Star*, page 1771.

what it is I will not read. Nor will I say more here, but in a Postscript answer any thing else you may have mentioned in your Letter in so many words—for I am distracted with a thousand thoughts. I will imagine you Venus tonight and pray, pray, pray to your star like a Hethen.

Your's ever, fair Star,
John Keats.

To Percy Bysshe Shelley
["An Artist Must Serve Mammon"]

16 August 1820

My dear Shelley,

I am very much gratified that you, in a foreign country, and with a mind almost over occupied, should write to me in the strain of the Letter beside me. If I do not take advantage of your invitation it will be prevented by a circumstance I have very much at heart to prophesy.[5] There is no doubt that an english winter would put an end to me, and do so in a lingering hateful manner, therefore I must either voyage or journey to Italy as a soldier marches up to a battery. My nerves at present are the worst part of me, yet they feel soothed when I think that come what extreme may, I shall not be destined to remain in one spot long enough to take a hatred of any four particular bed-posts. I am glad you take any pleasure in my poor Poem;[6]—which I would willingly take the trouble to unwrite, if possible, did I care so much as I have done about Reputation. I received a copy of the Cenci, as from yourself from Hunt. There is only one part of it I am judge of; the Poetry, and dramatic effect, which by many spirits now a days is considered the mammon.[7] A modern work it is said must have a purpose, which may be the God—an artist must serve Mammon—he must have "self concentration" selfishness perhaps. You I am sure will forgive me for sincerely remarking that you might curb your magnanimity and be more of an artist, and "load every rift" of your subject with ore.[8] The thought of such discipline must fall like cold chains upon you, who perhaps never sat with your wings furl'd for six Months together. And is not this extraordina[r]y talk for the writer of Endymion? whose mind was like a pack of scattered cards—I am pick'd up and sorted to a pip.[9] My Imagination is a Monastry and I am its Monk—you must explain my [metaphysics] to yourself. I am in expectation of Prometheus[1] every day. Could I have my own wish for its interest effected you would have it still in manuscript—or be but now putting an end to the second act.

---

5. Learning of Keats's grave ill health from Hunt, Shelley offered him hospitality in the warmer climate of Italy; Keats accepted the invitation, first going to Rome, where he died.
6. Sympathetic to the sting of negative reviews, Shelley had written some encouraging remarks about *Endymion*.
7. The false idol of money and worldly goods, against whom Jesus cautions, "Ye cannot serve God and mammon" (Matthew 6.24). In the Preface of *The Cenci*

(1820), a tragedy of incestuous rape, tyranny, and parricide, Shelley proffered a moral judgment of its heroine Beatrice Cenci.
8. From the ceiling of the Palace of Mammon in Spenser's *Faerie Queene* hang stalactites "Embost with massy gold of glorious gift, / And with rich metall loaded every rift, / That heavy ruine they did seeme to threat" (2.7.28).
9. Arranged in order; pips are marks on playing cards.
1. Shelley's epic, *Prometheus Unbound*, just published.

I remember you advising me not to publish my first-blights, on Hampstead heath[2]—I am returning advice upon your hands. Most of the Poems in the volume I send you have been written above two years, and would never have been publish'd but from a hope of gain;[3] so you see I am inclined enough to take your advice now. I must exp[r]ess once more my deep sense of your kindness, adding my sincere thanks and respects for Mrs Shelley. In the hope of soon seeing you I remain

most sincerely yours,
John Keats—

To Charles Brown
[KEATS'S LAST LETTER][4]

Rome. 30 November 1820.

My dear Brown,

'Tis the most difficult thing in the world to me to write a letter. My stomach continues so bad, that I feel it worse on opening any book,—yet I am much better than I was in Quarantine.[5] Then I am afraid to encounter the proing and conning of any thing interesting to me in England. I have a habitual feeling of my real life having past, and that I am leading a posthumous existence. God knows how it would have been—but it appears to me—however, I will not speak of that subject. I must have been at Bedhampton nearly at the time you were writing to me from Chichester—how unfortunate—and to pass on the river too![6] There was my star predominant! I cannot answer any thing in your letter, which followed me from Naples to Rome, because I am afraid to look it over again. I am so weak (in mind) that I cannot bear the sight of any hand writing of a friend I love so much as I do you. Yet I ride the little horse,[7]—and, at my worst, even in Quarantine, summoned up more puns, in a sort of desperation, in one week than in any year of my life. There is one thought enough to kill me—I have been well, healthy, alert &c, walking with her[8]—and now—the knowledge of contrast, feeling for light and shade, all that information (primitive sense) necessary for a poem are great enemies to the recovery of the stomach. There, you rogue, I put you to the torture,—but you must bring your philosophy to bear—as I do mine, really—or how should I be able to live? Dr Clarke is very attentive to me; he says, there is very little the matter with my lungs, but my stomach, he says, is very bad. I am well disappointed in hearing good news from George,—for it runs in my head we shall all die young.[9] I have not written to x x x x x yet, which he must think

2. Many of the pieces in Keats's 1817 *Poems* took inspiration from the landscape of Hampstead Heath; Keats met Shelley through Hunt, who lived there.
3. The 1820 volume; Keats was eager for financial "gain" as a requisite for marriage to Fanny Brawne.
4. Charles Brown (1787–1842), a man of various literary and amorous pursuits, was a close friend, traveling companion, and housemate. He cared assiduously for Keats after his first major hemorrhage in February 1820, but left for his usual summer vacation in May. When Keats realized that he had to go to Italy for his health, his earnest wish was that

Brown would accompany him, but he could not be located.
5. The ship on which Keats sailed was held for quarantine outside Naples, in oppressive summer weather.
6. The towns are near Portsmouth harbor, from which Keats would sail.
7. Recommended by Keats's doctor in Rome as exercise.
8. Fanny Brawne; Brown deleted her name, as well as those of Keats's friends, when he included the letter in a biography of Keats.
9. Tom died at 19, George lived to his mid-40s, and the youngest, Fanny, lived into her 80s.

very neglectful; being anxious to send him a good account of my health, I have delayed it from week to week. If I recover, I will do all in my power to correct the mistakes made during sickness; and if I should not, all my faults will be forgiven. I shall write to x x x to-morrow, or next day. I will write to x x x x x in the middle of next week. Severn is very well, though he leads so dull a life with me. Remember me to all friends, and tell x x x x I should not have left London without taking leave of him, but from being so low in body and mind. Write to George as soon as you receive this, and tell him how I am, as far as you can guess;—and also a note to my sister— who walks about my imagination like a ghost—she is so like Tom. I can scarcely bid you good bye even in a letter. I always made an awkward bow.

God bless you!
John Keats.

Gustave Doré. *Ludgate Hill,* from *London: A Pilgrimage,* 1872.

The Victorian Age

◆━◆◆◆━◆

1832–1901

> Never since the beginning of Time was there, that we hear or read
> of, so intensely self-conscious a Society. Our whole relations to the
> Universe and to our fellow-man have become an Inquiry, a Doubt.
>
> —*Thomas Carlyle, 1831*

Nothing characterizes Victorian society so much as its quest for self-definition. The sixty-three years of Victoria's reign were marked by momentous and intimidating social changes, startling inventions, prodigious energies; the rapid succession of events produced wild prosperity and unthinkable poverty, humane reforms and flagrant exploitation, immense ambitions and devastating doubts. Between 1800 and 1850 the population doubled from nine to eighteen million, and Britain became the richest country on earth, the first urban, industrial society in history. For some, it was a period of great achievement, deep faith, indisputable progress. For others, it was "an age of destruction," religious collapse, vicious profiteering. To almost everyone it was apparent that, as Sir Henry Holland put it in 1858, "we are living in *an age of transition.*"

But what Matthew Arnold called the "multitudinousness" of British culture overwhelmed all efforts to give the era a collective identity or a clear sense of purpose. Dazzled and dazed by their steam-powered printing presses, their railways and telegraphs, journalism and junk mail, Victorians suffered from both future shock and the information explosion. For the first time a nation had become self-consciously modern: people were sure only of their differences from previous generations, certain only that traditional ways of life were fast being transformed into something perilously unstable and astonishingly new. As the novelist William Makepeace Thackeray noted, "We are of the time of chivalry. . . . We are of the age of steam."

VICTORIA AND THE VICTORIANS

In an unpredictable, tumultuous era, the stern, staid figure of Queen Victoria came to represent stability and continuity. The adjective "Victorian" was first used in 1851 to celebrate the nation's mounting pride in its institutions and commercial success. That year, the global predominance of British industry had emerged incontestably at the original "world's fair" in London, the "Great Exhibition of the Works of Industry of All Nations," which Prince Albert helped organize. Arrayed for the world to see in a vast "Crystal Palace" of iron and glass, the marvels of British manufacture achieved a regal stature of their own and cast their allure upon the monarchy in turn. In the congratulatory rhetoric that surrounded the event, the conservative, retiring queen emerged as the durable symbol of her dynamic, aggressively businesslike realm.

Sunlight Soap advertisement commemorating the 1897 Jubilee of Victoria's reign.

In succeeding decades, the official portraits of Queen Victoria, gradually aging, reflected her country's sense of its own maturation as a society and world power. Etched by conflict with her prime ministers, the birth of nine children, and the early death of her beloved Prince Albert, Victoria's once pretty face became deeply lined and heavily jowled. Represented as a fairytale teenaged queen at her coronation in 1837, she radiated a youthful enthusiasm that corresponded to the optimism of the earlier 1830s. It seemed a decade of new beginnings. Settling into the role of fertile matron-monarch, she offered a domestic image to match the booming productivity of the 1850s. Reclusive after Albert died in 1861, she eventually took on the austere role of the black-satined Empress of India, projecting a world-weary glumness that lent gravity to the imperial heyday of the 1870s. Finally, as the aged, venerated Widow of Windsor, she became a universal icon, prompting the nostalgic worldwide spectacles of the Golden and Diamond Jubilees in 1887 and 1897. When Victoria died in 1901, after the longest reign in English history, a newspaper wrote: "Few of us, perhaps, have realized till now how large a part she had in the life of everyone of us; how the thread of her life [bound] the warp of the nation's progress."

During the seven decades of her rule, Victoria's calm profile, stamped on currency and displayed in offices and outposts from London to Bombay, presided over the expansion of Britain into the world's greatest empire. Economically and politically, Britannia ruled not only the waves but more than a quarter of the globe's landmass. Among its domains were Canada, Australia, New Zealand, South Africa, the Indian subcontinent and Ceylon, Malaya, Hong Kong, Singapore, Burma, Jamaica, Trinidad,

British Guiana, Bermuda, the Bahamas, Rhodesia, Kenya, Uganda, and Nigeria. By the 1890s one out of every four people on earth was a "subject" of Queen Victoria.

Victoria stood not only for England and Empire, but also for Duty, Family, and, especially, Propriety. "We have come to regard the Crown as the head of our morality" wrote the historian Walter Bagehot. As a description of behavior, "Victorian" signifies social conduct governed by strict rules, formal manners, and rigidly defined gender roles. Relations between the sexes were hedged about with sexual prudery and an intense concern for maintaining the appearance of propriety in public, whatever the private facts. But although she was presented as the ultimate role model, Victoria herself could not escape the contradictions of her era. The most powerful woman on earth, she denounced "this mad, wicked folly of Women's Rights." Her quiet reserve restored the dignity of the monarchy after the rakish ways of George IV, but she allowed advertisers to trade shamelessly on her image and product endorsements. Her face was universally known, featured on everything from postage stamps to tea trays, yet after Albert's death she lived in seclusion, rarely seeing either her ministers or the public. An icon of motherhood, she detested pregnancy, childbirth, and babies. As an emblem of Britain's greatness, Queen Victoria gave her subjects the public identity and purpose that privately they—and she, in her diaries—recognized as an unfulfilled ideal.

The Victorians have left us a contradictory picture of themselves. On the one hand, they were phenomenally energetic, dedicated to the Gospel of Work and driven by a solemn sense of duty to the Public Good. Popular authors like Dickens and Trollope churned out three-volume novels, engaged in numerous philanthropic projects, devoured twelve-course dinners, took twenty-mile walks, and produced a voluminous correspondence. Explorers and missionaries such as Burton, Speke, Stanley, and Livingston took enormous risks to map uncharted territory or spread Christianity "in darkest Africa." Although an invalid, Florence Nightingale revamped the entire British military medical and supply system from her bedroom office. All this activity was sustained by belief in its implicit moral benefit. In matters of character Victorians prized respectability, earnestness, a sense of duty and public service; most would have regarded an industrious, pious conventionality as the best road not only to material recompense but to heavenly rewards as well.

Yet the fabled self-confidence of this overachieving society often rings hollow. Their literature conveys an uneasy sense that their obsession with work was in part a deliberate distraction, as if Victorians were discharging public responsibilities in order to ease nagging doubts about their religious faith, about changing gender roles, about the moral quandaries of class privilege and imperial rule. Much of the era's social conservatism, such as its resistance to women's rights and to class mobility, may be traced to the fear of change. They struggled to dominate the present moment in order to keep an uncertain future at bay. Few questioned that tremendous advances were taking place in science, public health, transportation, and the general standard of living, but each new idea or discovery seemed to have unexpected, distressing repercussions.

The critic J. A. Froude remarked in 1841 that "the very truths which have come forth have produced doubts . . . this dazzle has too often ended in darkness." Discoveries in geology, biology, and textual scholarship shattered belief in the literal truth of the Bible. The Industrial Revolution shifted power from the landed aristocracy toward an insecure, expanding middle class of businessmen and professionals, impoverishing millions of once-rural laborers along the way. Strident, riotous campaigns to extend voting rights to males of the middle and working classes produced fears of armed insurrection. Coupled with the agitations for and against trade unions, women's equality, socialism, and the separation of church and state, the fitful transformation of Britain's political and economic structure often teetered on the brink of open class warfare. In the national clamor for reform, every sector of the population fought for its privileges and feared for its rights. The following pages introduce the Victorian period by looking at several key issues: the era's energy and invention, its doubts about religion and industrialism, its far-reaching social reforms, its conflicted fascination with Empire, the commercialization and expansion of the reading public, and the period's vigorous self-scrutiny in the mirror of literature.

THE AGE OF ENERGY AND INVENTION

> The most salient characteristic of life in this latter portion of the 19th century is its SPEED.
>
> —*W. R. Greg*, Life at High Pressure, *1875*

The "newness" of Victorian society—its speed, progress, and triumphant ingenuity—was epitomized by the coming of the railway. Until the 1830s, the fastest ways to travel or transport goods were still the most ancient ones, by sail or horse. But on seeing the first train pass through the Rugby countryside in 1839, Thomas Arnold astutely remarked: "Feudality is gone forever." The earliest passenger railway line opened in 1830 between Liverpool and Manchester; by 1855, eight thousand miles of track had been laid. Speeds of fifty miles per hour were soon routine; the journey from London to Edinburgh that had taken two weeks in 1800 now took less than a day.

Carrying passengers, freight, newspapers, and mail, the railways helped create a national consciousness by linking once-remote parts of the country into a single economy and culture. Networks of information, distribution, and services moved news, goods, and people from one end of Britain to the other to the rhythm of the railway timetable. The accelerating pace of life that railways introduced became one of the defining features of the age.

Moreover, the railway irrevocably altered the face of the landscape. Its bridges, tunnels, cuttings, crossings, viaducts, and embankments permanently scarred a rural landscape whose fields, hedgerows, and highways were rooted deep in history. In the cities, engineers and entrepreneurs carved room for vast railyards and stations by demolishing populous districts. Discharging commodities and crowds, the railways transformed town centers everywhere, bolstering local economies and stimulating construction as they arrived, but depriving once-thriving coaching inns and former mail routes of traffic and trade. Underground trains restructured the experience of travel within the city as well: the world's first subway line opened in 1863 in London; a complete inner London system was operating by 1884. Finally, railway-sponsored mass tourism eroded the regional distinctiveness and insularity of individual places. The inventor of the organized excursion, Thomas Cook, saw his advertising slogan, "RAILWAYS FOR THE MILLIONS," turned into a simple statement of fact.

Optimistic social prophets envisioned all classes reaping the fruits of the Industrial Revolution. The widespread Victorian belief in Progress was sustained by many factors, including rising incomes, the greater availability of goods, the perception of surplus production, and the leading role of Britain in world affairs. Many people were

Robert Howlett. *Portrait of Isambard Kingdom Brunel and Launching Chains of the Great Eastern,* 1857. Howlett's interest in contemporary subjects, ranging from steamships and Crimean War heroes to telescopic views of the moon, exemplified the belief that as a new medium itself, photography was supremely suited to capture "progress" in all its manifestations. In his portrait of Brunel, the audacious engineer who designed the Great Western Railway and the world's largest steamship, *The Great Eastern,* Howlett evoked both industrial might and Victorian self-confidence; the man of genius dominates the chains that dwarf him.

awed by the sheer size of industrial achievement: the heaviest ships, the longest tunnels, the biggest warehouses, the most massive factory outputs ever known all contributed to a sublimity of scale that staggered the public's imagination.

Every decade brought impressive innovations that transformed the rhythms of everyday life. The first regular Atlantic steamship crossings began in 1838, flouting the age-old dependence on wind and tide, importing tea from China, cotton from India or Alabama, beef from Australia, and exporting to world markets finished goods ranging from Sheffield cutlery and Manchester textiles to Pear's Soap and the latest Dickens novel.

Equally momentous in its own way was Henry Fox Talbot's discovery between 1839 and 1841 of how to produce and print a photographic negative. The technology of his "sun-pictures" revolutionized the entire visual culture and changed the human relationship to the past. A moment in time could now be "fixed" forever. Thus, more than a century later, we have photographic records of many subsequent innovations: the construction of the London sewer system; the laying of the transatlantic cable in 1865, putting London and New York in almost instantaneous contact via telegraph; the popularity in the 1890s of bicycles, gramophones, electric trams, and the first regular motion picture shows; and in the year of Victoria's death, 1901, Marconi's first transatlantic wireless radio message.

Capturing the public mood, Disraeli wrote in 1862: "It is a privilege to live in this age of rapid and brilliant events. What an error to consider it a utilitarian age. It is one of infinite romance." For the growing middle class there was an Aladdin-like sense of wonderment at the astounding abundance of *things:* an incredible hodge-podge of inventions, gimmicks, and gadgets began to make up the familiar parapher-nalia of modern life, including chain stores, washing and sewing machines, postage stamps, canned foods, toothpaste, sidewalk newsstands, illustrated magazines and newspapers, typewriters, breakfast cereal, slide projectors, skin creams, diet pills, shampoo, ready-to-wear clothes, sneakers (called "plimsolls"), and even a cumber-some prototype computer, designed by Charles Babbage.

Victorian architecture, interior design, and clothing embodied the obsession with plenitude, presenting a bewildering variety of prefabricated, highly ornamented styles. A house might feature Gothic revival, neoclassical, Egyptian, Moorish, baronial, or Arts-and-Crafts motifs, every inch of its interior covered with wallpapers, etchings, draperies, carvings, lacework, and knickknacks. Though fashions varied, men and women were usually as well upholstered as their furniture, tightly buttoned from top to toe in sturdy fabrics, their clothes complexly layered on the outside (men's waistcoats, jackets, cravats, and watches) and inside (women's crinolines, petticoats, bustles, corsets, and drawers).

In a Protestant culture that linked industriousness with godliness, both capitalism and consumerism were fueled by prevailing religious attitudes. For Thomas Carlyle, work itself had a divine sanction: "Produce! Produce!" he wrote in *Sartor Resartus:* "Were it but the pitifullest infinitesimal fraction of a Product, produce it in God's name!" His compatriots obliged: by 1848 Britain's output of cotton cloth and iron was more than half of the world total, and the coal output two-thirds of world production. At the Great Exhibition of 1851, when Britain was dubbed "the workshop of the world," the display struck the Reverend Charles Kingsley as triumphant evidence of God's will: "If these forefathers of ours could rise from their graves this day they would be inclined to see in our hospitals, in our railroads, in the achievements of our physical science . . . proofs of the kingdom of God . . . vaster than any of which they had dreamed."

But for Karl Marx, laboring to write *Das Kapital* (1867) at a desk in the British Museum Reading Room, it was not enough to find God in the material world. He saw that through the hoopla of the marketplace, products had acquired a "mystical char-acter" and "theological niceties" of their own. Yet Marx did not regard commodities as proof of God's existence; instead, he argued that they functioned as deities in their own right. An ignored subversive stationed at the heart of the empire, Marx per-ceived how status-filled objects seemed to take on lives that defined human social relations, even as they degraded the workers that produced them. Looking around at the wonders of British industry, Marx decided that people had become, finally, less important than things. For him, it was the Age of Commodity Fetishism.

THE AGE OF DOUBT

It was the age of science, new knowledge, searching criticism, fol-lowed by multiplied doubts and shaken beliefs.

—John Morley

Despite their reverence for material accomplishment and the tenets of organized reli-gion, the Victorians were deeply conflicted in their beliefs and intentions. In retro-spect, the forces that shook the foundations of Victorian society might be summed up in two names, Marx and Darwin: though he was virtually unknown at the time, Marx's radical critique of unbridled free enterprise brought to the most acute level contemporary analyses of economic injustice and the class system. Darwin's staggering evolutionary theories implied that biblical accounts of creation could not be literally true. But well before either had published a word, British thought was in crisis: "The Old has passed away," wrote Carlyle in 1831, "but, alas, the New appears not in its stead." In his 1851 novel *Yeast*, Charles Kingsley described how deluged the Victorians felt by challenges to their faith and social order: "The various stereotyped systems . . . received by tradition [are] breaking up under them like ice in a thaw," he wrote; "a thousand facts and notions, which they know not how to classify, [are] pouring in on them like a flood."

The Crisis of Faith

In the midst of this tumult, the Victorians were troubled by Time. On the one hand, there was not enough of it: the accelerated pace of change kept people too busy to assimilate the torrent of new ideas and technologies. In the 1880s the essayist F. R. Harrison contended that Victorians were experiencing "a life lived so full . . . that we have no time to reflect where we have been and whither we intend to go." On the other hand, there was too much time: well before Darwin, scientists were showing that vast eons of geological and cosmic development had preceded human history, itself suddenly lengthening due to such discoveries as the Neanderthal skeletons found in 1856.

Their sense of worth diminished by both time clocks and time lines, Victorians felt they had little opportunity for reflection and often took scant comfort in it. Matthew Arnold complained of "this strange disease of modern life with its sick hurry, its divided aims." Yet this climate of anxious uncertainty provoked intense religious fervor, and debates about church doctrine and the proper forms of Christian worship occupied the national consciousness throughout the century. "This is the age of experiment," wrote the historian E. P. Hood in 1850, regarding the constant testing of belief, "but the cheerful fact is, that almost all men are yearning after a faith."

The most influential group were the "Evangelicals," a term which covers not only "dissenting" or "nonconformist" Protestant sects outside the Church of England (such as Methodists, Presbyterians, Congregationalists, and Baptists), but also the Evangelical party or "Low Church" faction within the Church of England. Anti-Catholic, Bible-oriented, concerned with humanitarian issues, and focused on the salvation of individual souls within a rigid framework of Christian conduct, Evangelicalism dominated the religious and often the social life of working- and middle-class Britons. Evangelicals practiced self-denial and frugality; they rejected most forms of entertainment as sinful or frivolous, and regarded any but the simplest church service as a "popish" throwback to Catholicism, which they abhorred on nationalistic as well as religious grounds. It was Evangelicalism that was largely responsible for the freeing of slaves in the British colonies in 1833, for the strictness of Victorian morality at home, and for British missionary zeal abroad.

At the other end of the spectrum were the Anglo-Catholics of the Tractarian or Oxford Movement, which flourished in the 1830s and 1840s. Through an appeal to early church history, they sought to revitalize the power and spiritual intensity of the Church of England, insisting on the authority of the Church hierarchy, and reaffirming the Church's traditional position as a grace-granting intermediary between

Christians and their God. The movement collapsed when its leader, John Henry Newman, converted to Roman Catholicism in 1845. But the antirational, romantic spirit of this small group left a substantial legacy in the renewed ritualism of "High Church" practices. Gothic revival architecture, the burning of altar candles and incense, the resplendent vestments of the clergy—all these were aspects of a religious apprehension of sensuous beauty and mysticism that had not been seen in England since before the Reformation. This "High Church" aestheticism came into direct and ongoing conflict with "Low Church" sobriety.

The crisis of religious doubt occasioned by biblical scholarship and scientific discoveries hit Christian belief hard. But it prompted an array of coping strategies and new ideas about the position of human beings in the universe that remain significant to this day. Most Victorian authors and intellectuals found a way to reassert religious ideas. Thus George Eliot, for instance, maintained that an Evangelical sense of duty and ethics was essential as a social "glue" to prevent the disintegration of society in the absence of religious authority. That it was still an era which *wanted* to believe is evident from the huge success of Tennyson's *In Memoriam* (1850), in which the poet's hard-won religious faith finally triumphs over science-induced despair. Extending evolutionary theory to spiritual advantage, Tennyson hoped man might transcend animality by encouraging his divine soul to "Move upward, working out the beast, / And let the ape and tiger die." Even Darwin's defender Thomas Huxley, who coined the word "agnostic," also celebrated Auguste Comte's positivism and "the Religion of Humanity." Huxley spoke for many who had renounced organized religion but not spiritual impulses when he said that Carlyle's *Sartor Resartus* "led me to know that a deep sense of religion was compatible with the entire absence of theology." Finally, some artists and writers used Christian icons as an avant-garde protest against the secular direction of modern life. "The more materialistic science becomes," said the artist Edward Burne-Jones, "the more angels shall I paint."

The Industrial Catastrophe

In principle, the Victorian crisis of faith should at least have pleased the Utilitarians. The creed of these atheistic, rationalist followers of Jeremy Bentham was strictly practical: measure all human endeavor by its ability to produce "the greatest happiness for the greatest number." Sharing a committed, "can do" philosophy of social reform, Utilitarianism and Evangelicalism were the two dominant ideologies shaping early and mid-Victorian life. But despite the significant changes they effected in government and education during the 1820s and 1830s, even the Utilitarians ran out of self-assurance and moral steam in the morass of mid-Victorian cultural ferment.

A few energetic idealists dreamed of leveling age-old inequalities. "Glory to Man in the highest!" wrote Swinburne in 1869, "for Man is the master of things." But here too a form of evolutionary theory was undercutting the conventional pieties of social discourse. "Love thy neighbor" had no more moral authority for the "Social Darwinist" than it had historical accuracy for the textual scholar. Summed up in the phrase "survival of the fittest"—coined by the philosopher Herbert Spencer in 1852, seven years before *The Origin of Species* appeared—Social Darwinism viewed as dangerous any attempt to regulate the supposedly immutable laws of society. Evolutionary forces decreed that only the fittest should survive in capitalist competition as well as in nature. Applied to nations and races as well as individuals, this theory supported the apparent destiny of England to prosper and rule the world.

Social Darwinism was a brutal offshoot of the influential economic theory of laissez-faire capitalism. Drawing on Adam Smith's *The Wealth of Nations* (1776), businessmen argued that the unfettered pursuit of self-interest, in the form of unrestricted competition in a free market, would be best for society. This was an idea that Utilitarians and many Evangelicals rejected in favor of legislative regulation, since their view of the imperfections of humanity indicated that one person's self-interest was likely to mean another's exploitation. The desperate need to protect the poor and disadvantaged, and the difficulty of doing so, was cause for much soul-searching, particularly among those who had made a religion of social reform.

Concern about the fairness and efficacy of the social structure was exacerbated by the unprecedented rate of urbanization. "Our age is preeminently the age of great cities" declared historian Robert Vaughan in 1843. At the beginning of the nineteenth century only one-fifth of the British population lived in cities; by the end of the century, more than three-quarters did. Such vast numbers of people crowding into the cities created hideous problems of housing, sanitation, and disease. For the poor, living and working conditions were appalling, particularly in the 1830s and 1840s when neither housing nor factories were regulated. Industrial workers labored six days a week, for as many as fourteen or sixteen hours a day, in stifling, deafening, dangerous workshops, then went home to unheated rooms they often shared with other families, six or seven people to a bed of rags. Drinking water often came from rivers filled with industrial pollution and human waste. Without job security, health-care, or pensions, the injured, the sick, and the aged fell by the wayside. In manufacturing cities the competition for survival was indeed intense: the life expectancy among working people in Manchester in 1841 was about twenty years.

Joseph Paxton. The Crystal Palace, site of the Great Exhibition of 1851, after its re-erection at Sydenham, c. 1855.

Foreign visitors in particular were struck with wonder and horror at the conjunction of so much misery and so much wealth. "From this filthy sewer pure gold flows," marveled the French historian Alexis de Tocqueville: "From this foul drain the greatest stream of human industry flows out to fertilize the whole world." Friedrich Engels spent a year in Manchester, producing the most detailed and shocking firsthand account of Victorian industrial life, *The Condition of the Working Class in England in 1844*. Karl Marx, who lived in England for thirty-four years, worked his observations into his famous theory of "surplus labor value." Under the current system, he said, wretched factory hands would never receive adequate payment for the wealth they created by transforming raw materials into precious commodities. Like many people at the time, both liberal and conservative, Marx expected that violent class warfare was imminent.

On average real wages went up and prices went down in Victoria's reign, with per capita income doubling between 1800 and 1860. But the boom-and-bust cycles of free trade made for unsteady wages, seesaw prices, sudden layoffs, and volatile labor relations, as Britain made a lurching transition to an industrial and commercial economy. There were serious depressions or slowdowns almost every decade, but the worst took place during "the Hungry Forties." Scarce food, widespread unemployment, and general despair provoked riots and fears of revolution. The statesman Charles Greville noted in his diary in 1842, "There is an immense and continually increasing population, no adequate demand for labor . . . no confidence, but a universal alarm, disquietude, and discontent." An American observer of the industrial scene named Henry Coleman remarked, "Every day that I live I thank Heaven that I am not a poor man with a family in England." When the economy recovered, many fled. Between the years 1850 and 1880, three million emigrants left Britain, two-thirds for the United States.

THE AGE OF REFORM

The whole meaning of Victorian England is lost if it is thought of as a country of stuffy complacency and black top-hatted moral priggery. Its frowsty crinolines and dingy hansom cabs, its gas-lit houses and over-ornate draperies, concealed a people engaged in a tremendously exciting adventure—the daring experiment of fitting industrial man into a democratic society.

—*Historian David Thompson, 1950*

Despite crushing problems and the threat of social breakdown, the Victorian period can justly be called an age of reform. Each of the issues that threatened to bring the country into open conflict or destroy the social fabric was in the course of the century addressed peacefully through legislation: voting rights were extended, working conditions improved, and women's rights began to gain ground, without the bloody revolutions or insurrections that struck France in 1838, 1848, and 1870, and Germany in 1848. As fears of revolution receded, the subtler worries of Mill and Arnold, based on their observation of American democracy, seemed more to the point. How could liberty of thought be preserved in a mass culture dedicated to majority rule? How could the best ideas elevate, rather than succumb to, the lowest common denominator?

Politics and Class

The key to the century's relatively peaceful progress was the passage of legislation for political and social reform. The start of the Victorian era is often dated 1832, five years before Victoria's coronation, because in that year the First Reform Bill was enacted. It gave representation to the new industrial towns, such as Manchester, Birmingham, and Leeds, all cities of over 100,000 inhabitants that had lacked a single seat in Parliament. It also enlarged the electorate by about 50 percent, granting the vote to some propertied portions of the middle class. Still, only one in six adult males could vote, and the aristocracy retained parliamentary control. Agitation for reform continued, especially in the Chartist movement of 1838–1848. Taking its name from the People's Charter of 1838, it was a loose alliance of artisans and factory workers that called for sweeping reforms, including universal male suffrage, the secret ballot, equal electoral districts, and annual elections. Chartism was the world's first independent working-class movement, its membership swelling into the millions during the depressions of the 1840s. The Chartists presented giant petitions, signed by one to five million people, to Parliament in 1839, 1842, and 1848. But each time they were rejected, and the movement collapsed after a government show of force effectively defused the demonstrations accompanying the petition of 1848.

The lot of workers was to improve piecemeal, not through the grand political reorganization envisioned by Chartism, as Parliament grudgingly passed acts regulating food, factories, and the right to unionize. An important breakthrough came with the repeal of the Corn Laws in 1846. The laws levied tariffs on the importation of foreign grain; they were sponsored by the landed aristocracy to protect the high price of their home-grown grains (called "corn" in Britain). Therefore, as the poet Thomas Hood wrote in 1842, "bread was dear and flesh and blood were cheap." The new urban business interests fought the protectionist tariffs in the name of "Free Trade." They preferred a stable, better-fed workforce to one that rioted or starved in times of scarcity, but they also wanted cheap bread to keep their workers' wages down. Later, the Public Health acts of 1848 and 1869 improved the availability of tea, sugar, and beer. In the 1870s the importation of wheat from the United States and refrigerated beef and fruit from Australia and New Zealand meant that the new custom of having large bacon-and-egg breakfasts could be observed even by the working classes.

Beginning in 1833, a crucial series of Factory Acts slowly curtailed the horrors of industrial labor. The 1833 Act provided for safety inspections of machinery, prohibited the employment of children under nine, and limited the work week to forty-eight hours for children under twelve. Though the law was poorly enforced, a trend had begun. The Ten Hours Act of 1847 limited the time women and children could work daily in textile factories, and ensuing acts gradually regulated safety and working conditions in other industries. Workers' political power increased when the Second Reform Bill (1867) doubled the electorate, including all male urban householders. During this period employers also felt increasing pressure from extra-legal trade union movements, including miners, textile workers, and women garment workers. An uncomprehending middle class (including Dickens and Gaskell) often regarded unionists as anarchists and murderers. But trade unions were finally legalized in 1871, and the first working-class Members of Parliament were unionist miners elected in 1874. By the 1890s there were 1.5 million trade union members, many of them part of the growing Socialist movement, and the foundations of the modern Labour Party had been laid.

Thus the high hopes of Chartism had in a sense succeeded, many of its supposedly dangerous demands eventually met. As Engels noted, these changes also benefited the middle class who resisted them, as people realized the value—social as well as economic—of reduced hostilities and improved cooperation between classes. Everyone also gained from related reforms that reflected weakening class barriers and increasing social mobility. In 1870 the Education Act initiated nationally funded public education in England and Wales. In the 1880s, middle-class investigators and social workers spearheaded the "discovery of poverty" in London's East End, one of a range of efforts that brought better housing, nutrition, and education to the poor. Finally, the nation as a whole benefited from what historian Asa Briggs has called "the one great political invention in Victorian England"—a civil service staffed through open examinations rather than patronage.

By the last decades of the century, Britain had become a more democratic and pluralistic society; it enjoyed greater freedom in matters of religion, political views, and intellectual life than any other country. Overall, the middle class were the chief generators and beneficiaries of social change. Outsiders before 1832, they became key players in the Victorian period. Though they never dominated politics, which remained largely an aristocratic preserve, they set the tone and agenda for the era's socioeconomic evolution.

"The Woman Question"

Still, one group found almost all doors closed against it. Throughout much of Victoria's reign, women had few opportunities for higher education or satisfying employment: from scullery maids to governesses, female workers of all ranks were severely exploited, and prior to the 1870s married women had no legal rights. What contemporaries called "the Woman Question" was hotly debated in every decade, but only at the end of the century were the first women allowed to vote in local elections. Full female suffrage came only after World War I. Despite articulate champions such as Harriet Martineau and John Stuart Mill, and the examples of successful women such as George Eliot, the Brontës, Florence Nightingale, and the Queen herself, proponents of women's rights made slow headway against prevailing norms. Victorians were quick to note that theirs was the first era in which women writers achieved literary prominence, producing works widely recognized to be equal in stature to those by men. But many regarded this "brain-work" as a serious aberration that unfitted women for motherhood. The medical establishment backed the conventional view that women were physically and intellectually inferior, a "weaker sex" that would buckle under the weight of strong passion, serious thought, or vigorous exercise. Only in their much-vaunted "femininity" did women have an edge, as nurturers of children and men's better instincts.

The ideal Victorian woman was supposed to be domestic and pure, selflessly motivated by the desire to serve others rather than fulfill her own needs. In particular, her duty was to soothe the savage beast her husband might become as he fought in the jungle of free trade. Her role prescribed by Coventry Patmore's wildly popular poem, *The Angel in the House* (1854–1862), the model woman would provide her family with an uplifting refuge from the moral squalor of the working world. Only a small portion of the nation's women could afford to remain at home, but the constant celebration of home and hearth by politicians, the press, and respected authors made conspicuous domesticity the expected role for well-born and well-married women. Many upper- and middle-class women spent their days paying social calls or acquiring "female accomplishments" such as needlework, sketching, or flower-arranging. Though this leisure played an important part in generating new literary markets targeted at women, it provoked devastating satires of time-wasting females by Elizabeth Barrett Browning, Charles Dickens, and Florence Nightingale, among others. By the 1860s, with the birth of the department store and modern advertising, leisured women were also for the first time wooed as consumers and portrayed as smart shoppers.

Though their contribution was minimized, women were in fact heavily involved in the labor force, making up one-third of all workers, and 90 percent of the nation's largest labor category, household servants. For so-called "redundant" women who could not find husbands or work, the situation was especially grim. Low wages and unemployment drove tens of thousands of girls and women into prostitution, which, due to the growth of the military and repressive Victorian sexual mores, became one more "boom industry" whose workers reaped few rewards.

If a woman's life was economically precarious outside marriage, her existence was legally terminated within that bond. A woman lost the few civil rights she had as she became "one body" with her husband. Married women had, at the start of the era, no legal right to custody of their own children or to own property. The Divorce and Matrimonial Causes Act of 1857 established a civil divorce court in London, and subsequent acts created protection against assault, desertion, and cruelty, but only a wealthy few could afford legal proceedings. The Married Women's Property Acts of 1870 and 1882, however, gave women the right to possess wages they earned after marriage, as well as any property they owned before it.

Gradually, with the aid of male allies, women created educational opportunities for themselves. The first women's college opened in London in 1848, and the first women's colleges opened at Cambridge in 1869 and at Oxford in 1879—though women were not allowed to take Oxbridge degrees. Elizabeth Blackwell, the first woman M.D., became an accredited physician both in Britain and the United States in 1859; by 1895 there were 264 women doctors. In the 1890s, the much-parodied image of the liberated "New Woman" began circulating in the press. By then many young women were braving a conservative backlash to take new positions in office work, the civil service, nursing, and teaching. They also enjoyed the social freedom that accompanied their expanding role in the economy. The novelist Walter Besant wrote admiringly in 1897 of the "personal independence that is the keynote of the situation. . . . The girls go off by themselves on their bicycles; they go about as they please. . . . For the first time in man's history it is regarded as a right and proper thing to trust a girl as a boy insists on being trusted."

The uphill battle that feminists faced is conveyed in the cautious motto of a national-market periodical for women. Published from 1890 to 1912, *Woman* magazine declared its mission: "Forward, but not too fast." Antisuffragists of both sexes found willing allies among those who regarded women as weak and unworldly, better equipped for housekeeping than speechmaking. As the nineteenth century waned, many women and most men would still have endorsed Dickens's parodic view of the public woman, Mrs Jellyby in *Bleak House:* she is so focused on missionary work in Africa that she cannot see the lamentable state of her family in the very next room.

THE AGE OF EMPIRE

I contend that we are the first race in the world, and the more of
the world we inhabit, the better it is for the human race.

—*Cecil Rhodes*

With the prime meridian conveniently located at Greenwich, just southeast of London, Victorians could measure all the world in relation to a British focal point, culturally as well as geographically. Abroad, as at home, it was an Englishman's duty to rule
whatever childlike or womanly peoples he came across, for their own good. For Queen
Victoria, the mission of empire was obvious: "to protect the poor natives and advance
civilization." The conviction of innate superiority was reinforced by the implacable
desire of British business to dominate world markets. The vast size of Britain's naval
and commercial fleets and its head start in industrial production helped the cause,
and Britain's military and commercial might was unsurpassed. Victorian advertising
reveals the global realities and hopes of the emerging merchant empires. Tetley's tea
ads depicted their plantations in Ceylon, as well as the ships, trains, and turbanned
laborers that secured "the largest sale in the world." Pear's Soap advertising campaigns
kept up with British expeditionary forces worldwide, finding potential customers in
temporary adversaries such as the "Fuzzy-Wuzzies" of the Sudanese wars, or the Boers
of South Africa. One advertiser even challenged convention by speaking of "Brightest Africa"—because of the continent's vast market potential.

Yet the empire was hard to assemble and expensive—monetarily and morally—
to maintain. Slavery was abolished in British dominions in 1833, but many fortunes
still depended on the cheap production of sugar at West Indian plantations, as well as
slave-produced cotton from the United States. Thus British implication in the slave
trade remained a volatile issue. All Britain took sides in the Governor Eyre scandal of
1865, when the acting governor of Jamaica imposed severe martial law to put down a
rebellion by plantation workers. Carlyle, Dickens, and Ruskin supported the executions and floggings, while John Stuart Mill sought to have Eyre tried for murder.

Closer to home, the perennial "Irish Question" resurfaced urgently during the
potato famine of 1845–1847. Through the British government's callousness and
ineptitude, a million and a half Irish died of starvation and disease and an equal number emigrated. In the wake of this disaster, the Irish engaged in rebellions, uprisings,
and massive political efforts to gain parliamentary "Home Rule" for Ireland. But concern about the unity of the Empire, the safety of Protestants in the north of Ireland,
and the supposed inability of the Irish to govern themselves led Parliament to defeat
all efforts at Irish autonomy during Victoria's reign.

The Asian empire captured the popular imagination for the first time through
the so-called "Indian Mutiny" of 1857–1859, a broad-based rebellion against the East
India Company, the commercial entity that ruled most of India. The gory details of
Indian atrocities, followed by equally bloody and more extensive British reprisals,
filled the press and inflamed the public. The crown now took possession, and henceforth British policy was much more guarded, attempting to respect local institutions
and practices. Later, as Rudyard Kipling recorded in his novel *Kim* (1901), India
became an important setting for the "Great Game" of espionage to prevent foreign
destabilization of British interests worldwide.

THE FORMULA OF BRITISH CONQUEST

PEARS SOAP IS THE BEST

REG^D COPYRIGHT

PEARS' SOAP IN THE SOUDAN.

"Even if our invasion of the Soudan has done nothing else it has at any rate left the Arab something to puzzle his fuzzy head over, for the legend
          PEARS' SOAP IS THE BEST,
inscribed in huge white characters on the rock which marks the farthest point of our advance towards Berber,
will tax all the wits of the Dervishes of the Desert to translate."—Phil-Robinson, War Correspondent
(in the Soudan) of the Daily Telegraph in London, 1884.

"The Formula of British Conquest." Pears' Soap advertisement from *Illustrated London News,* 27 August 1887. *Source:* Harvard College Library.

In the second half of the century, frequent and often bungled conflicts riveted public attention. The Crimean War of 1854–1856, in which Britain fought on the side of Turkey to prevent Russian expansion in the Middle East, cost 21,000 British lives but made little change in the European balance of power. "Some one had blunder'd," as Tennyson wrote in *The Charge of the Light Brigade.* The newspapers' exposure of the gross mismanagement of the war effort, however, led to improved supply systems, medical care, and weapons, and the rebuilding of the armed forces, all of which served Britain in ensuing colonial wars. A veteran of the Crimea, General George Gordon, rose to fame in 1860, capturing Peking and protecting far-flung Britons in the Second Opium War. But in 1884 he and several thousand others were massacred at Khartoum in the Sudan after a year's siege by religiously inspired rebels. Governmental dithering caused the British relief force to arrive two days too late. On another front, the Boer War of 1899–1902 stimulated war mania at home but tarnished Britain's image throughout the world. In pursuit of freer access to South African gold and diamond mines, the world's greatest military power bogged down in a guerilla war that ended only when British forces herded Afrikaner civilians into concentration camps, where 20,000 died.

Many viewed these conflicts as part of "the White Man's burden," as Kipling phrased it: the duty to spread British order and culture throughout the world. Yet imperialism had many opponents. In 1877 the Liberal leader William Gladstone argued that the Empire was a drain on the economy and population, serving only "to compromise British character in the judgment of the impartial world." Even Queen Victoria complained of the "overbearing and offensive behavior" of the Indian Civil Service for "trying to trample on the people and continually reminding them and making them feel that they are a conquered people." Like the growth of Victorian cities, the unplanned agglomeration of British colonies involved such a haphazard mixture of economic expansion, high-minded sentiment, crass exploitation, political expediency, and blatant racism that it apparently had no clear rationale. "We seem," said Cambridge historian J. R. Seeley in 1883, "to have conquered and peopled half the world in a fit of absence of mind."

Victorians did not only go to the ends of the earth; they saw the world's abundance come home to them. Britain and especially London became a magnet for all manner of people and things, a world within a world. There were many distinguished foreign sojourners at the center of empire. Among the artists, exiles, and expatriots who visited or stayed were the deposed French emperor Louis Napoleon, the painters Vincent Van Gogh and James McNeill Whistler, and the writers Arthur Rimbaud, Paul Verlaine, and Stephen Crane. Many of the era's great images and cultural moments came from outsiders: London was memorably painted by Claude Monet, anatomized by Henry James, serenaded by Frédéric Chopin and Franz Liszt, and entertained by Buffalo Bill. It received possibly its most searching critique from Karl Marx and Friedrich Engels, who drafted the *Communist Manifesto* there in 1847. Not only the country's prosperity and cultural prestige attracted people, but also its tolerance and democracy. Despite the wage slavery and imperialist ideology that he saw only too clearly, Engels was forced to admit: "England is unquestionably the freest—that is, the least unfree—country in the world, North America not excepted."

THE AGE OF READING

> Even idleness is eager now,—eager for amusement; prone to excursion-trains, art-museums, periodical literature, and exciting novels.
>
> —*George Eliot*

Publishing became a major industry in the Victorian period. Magazines, newspapers, novels, poetry, histories, travel narratives, sporting news, scandal sheets, and penny cyclopedias kept people entertained and informed as never before. A thriving commercial literary culture was built on rising literacy rates, with as many as 97 percent of both sexes able to read by 1900. The expansion of the reading public went hand-in-hand with new print technologies, including steam-powered presses, the introduction of cheaper wood-pulp (instead of rag-based) paper, and, eventually, mechanized typesetting. Illustrations were widely used, notably in serialized fiction, where they helped unpracticed readers to follow the story. After 1875 wood engravings gave way to photogravure, and in the 1880s halftone printing enabled photographs to replace hand-drawn works as the primary means of visual communication. Colored illustrations were hand-tinted at first, often by poor women and children working at home; later chromolithography made colored reproductions of artwork possible. British publishing gradually transformed itself into a modern industry with worldwide distribution and influence. Copies of *The Times* circulated in uncharted Africa; illustrations torn from magazines adorned bushmen's huts in the Great Karoo.

Readers' tastes varied according to class, income, and education. The well-educated but unintellectual upper class formed only a small portion of the Victorian reading public. As the historian Walter Bagehot noted at the time, "A great part of the 'best' English people keep their minds in a state of decorous dullness." At the other end of the social scale, working-class literacy rates were far below the general standard but increased as working hours diminished, housing improved, and public libraries spread. The appetite for cheap literature steadily grew, feeding on a diet of religious tracts, self-help manuals, reprints of classics, penny newspapers, and the expanding range of sensational entertainment: "penny dreadfuls and shilling shockers," serials, bawdy ballads, and police reports of lurid crimes.

It was the burgeoning middle class, however, that formed the largest audience for new prose and poetry, and produced the authors to meet an increasing demand for books that would edify, instruct, and entertain. This was the golden age of the English novel, but poetry and serious nonfiction also did a brisk trade, as did "improving" works on religion, science, philosophy, and economics. But new books, especially fiction, were still a luxury in the earlier Victorian period. Publishers inflated prices so that readers would rent novels and narrative poems—just as people rent videos today—from commercial circulating libraries, which provided a larger and steadier income than individual sales. The collaboration between publishers and libraries required authors to produce "three deckers," long novels packaged in three separate volumes that thereby tripled rental fees and allowed three readers to peruse a single novel at one time. An economical alternative was to buy the successive "numbers" of a book as they appeared in individual, illustrated monthly installments. This form of publication became common with the tremendous success of Dickens's first novel *Pickwick Papers*, which came out in parts in 1836 and 1837. By the 1860s most novels were serialized in weekly or monthly magazines, giving the reader a wealth of additional material for about the same price.

The serialization of novels had a significant impact on literary form. Most of the major novelists, including Dickens, Thackeray, Collins, Gaskell, Trollope, and Eliot, had to organize their work into enticing, coherent morsels that kept characters and story lines clear from month to month, and left readers eager to buy the next installment. Authors felt pressure to keep ahead of deadlines, often not knowing which turn a story might take. But they also enjoyed the opportunity to stay in the public eye, to weave in references to current events, or to make adjustments based on sales and reviews. For their part, readers experienced literature as an ongoing part of their lives. They had time to absorb and interpret their reading, and even to influence the outcome of literary events: throughout his career, Dickens was badgered by readers who wanted to see more of one character, less of another, or prevent the demise of a third.

The close relationship authors shared with their public had its drawbacks: writers had to censor their content to meet the prim standards of "circulating library morality." In keeping with the Evangelical temper of the times, middle-class Victorian recreation centered on the home, where one of the most sacred institutions was

A NOVEL FACT.

Old-fashioned Party (with old-fashioned prejudices). "AH! VERY CLEVER, I DARE SAY. BUT I SEE IT'S WRITTEN BY A LADY, AN'
I WANT A BOOK THAT MY *DAUGHTERS* MAY READ. GIVE ME SOMETHING ELSE!"

Cartoon from *Punch* magazine, 1867.

the family reading circle. Usually wives or daughters read aloud to the rest of the household. Any hint of impropriety, anything that might bring "a blush to the cheek of the Young Person"—as Dickens warily satirized the trend—was aggressively ferreted out by publishers and libraries. Even revered poets such as Tennyson and Barrett Browning found themselves edited by squeamish publishers.

A better testimony to the intelligence and perceptiveness of the Victorian reading public is the fact that so many of today's classics were bestsellers then, including the novels of the Brontës, Dickens, and George Eliot; the poetry of Tennyson, Elizabeth and Robert Browning, and Christina Rossetti; and the essays of Carlyle, Ruskin, and Arnold. These works were addressed to readers who had an impressive level of literary and general culture, kept up to snuff by the same magazines and reviews in which the best fiction, poetry, and prose appeared. Educated Victorians had an insatiable appetite for "serious" literature on religious issues, socioeconomic theory, scientific developments, and general information of all sorts. It was an era of outstanding, influential periodicals that combined entertaining writing with intellectual substance: politically oriented quarterlies such as the Whig *Edinburgh Review* and the Benthamite *Westminster Review;* more varied monthlies such as *Fraser's Magazine,* where Carlyle's *Sartor Resartus* first appeared, and *Cornhill,* which published works by Ruskin, Thackeray, Eliot, Trollope, and Hardy; the satirical weekly *Punch,* still published today; and Dickens's low-priced weeklies *Household Words* and *All the Year Round* for a more general readership. As a rule, the public had faith in the press, regarding it as a forum essential to the progress and management of democracy. At the same time, as political and cultural power broadened, the press took seriously its new role as creator, shaper, and transmitter of public opinion.

Celebrated authors were hailed as heroes, regarded as public property, and respected as sages; they inspired a passionate adulation. Robert Browning first approached Elizabeth Barrett by writing her a fan letter. The public sought instruction and guidance from authors, who were alternately flattered and dismayed by the responsibilities thrust upon them. The critic Walter Houghton points out that "every writer had his congregation of devoted or would-be devoted disciples who read his work in much the spirit they had once read the Bible." Robert Browning lived to see an international proliferation of Browning Societies, dedicated to expounding his supposed moral teachings. Hero worship was yet another Victorian invention.

THE AGE OF SELF-SCRUTINY

The energy of Victorian literature is its most striking trait, and self-exploration is its favorite theme. Victorians produced a staggeringly large body of literature, renowned for its variety and plenitude. Their writing is distinguished by its particularity, eccentricity, long-windedness, earnestness, ornateness, fantasy, humor, experimentation, and self-consciousness. As befits a scientific age, most authors exhibited a willingness to experiment with new forms of representation, coupled with a penchant for realism, a love of closely observed detail: Tennyson was famous for his myopic descriptions of flowers; Browning transcribed tics of speech like a clinical psychologist; Eliot compared her scenes to Dutch genre paintings; and Dickens indignantly defended the accuracy of his characterization and the plausibility of his plots. Sustained labor was as important as keen observation: "lyric" poems ran to hundreds of lines, novels spanned a thousand pages, essayists constructed lengthy paragraphs with three or four generous sentences. One single book, alternately discredited and revered, underpinned the whole literary enterprise. The King James Version of the Bible shaped the cadences, supplied the imagery, and proposed the structures through which Victorians apprehended the universe; knowledge of it immensely deepens one's appreciation of the time.

Like the photographic close-ups invented by Julia Margaret Cameron, much Victorian literature tries to get at what Matthew Arnold called "the buried life" of individuals struggling for identity in a commercial, technocratic society. In the 1830s Carlyle was already alluding to "these autobiographical times of ours." Autobiography rapidly assumed new importance as a literary form, driven by the apparent necessity of each person working out a personal approach to the universe and a position within the culture. As Matthew Arnold announced in 1853, "the dialogue of the mind with itself has commenced."

Often written under intense emotional pressure, nonfiction prose on social or aesthetic issues turned into an art form as personal as lyric poetry, expressing the writers' interior lives as well as their ideas. Yet the very variety of disguised or semiautobiographical forms (such as the dramatic monologue) suggests that introspection produced its own moral perplexities. In a culture that stressed action, production, civic duty, and family responsibility, such apparently self-indulgent self-scrutiny might well seem unworthy: "I sometimes hold it half a sin / To put in words the grief I feel" said Tennyson about the loss of his best friend. Thus the guilty confessional impulse was forced underground to reemerge almost everywhere: in first-person narratives, devotional poems, travelogues, novels of religious or emotional crisis, intimate essays, dramatic lyrics, fictionalized memoirs, and recollections of famous people and places.

The Major Genres

Victorian literature is remarkable in that there were three great literary genres: non-fiction prose emerged as the artistic equal of poetry and fiction. Topical and influential in their day, the criticism and essays of such writers as Carlyle, Mill, Newman, Ruskin, Darwin, Arnold, Nightingale, Pater, and Wilde achieved classic status by virtue of their distinctive styles and force of intellect. In richly varied rhythms they record the process of original minds seeking to understand the relation of individuals to nature and culture in the new industrial world. Though their works might be categorized as religion, politics, aesthetics, or science, all these authors wrote revealingly of their intellectual development, and all explored the literary resources of the language, from simile and metaphor to fable and fantasy. Oscar Wilde argued for the supreme creativity of the autobiographical critic-as-artist: "That is what the highest criticism really is, the record of one's own soul." His teacher Walter Pater remarked simply that prose is "the special and opportune art of the modern world."

Poets struggled to refute this sentiment. Poetry commanded more respect than prose as a literary genre, but despite the immense success of Tennyson, it gradually lost ground in popularity. Whether this occurred because of, or in spite of, poetry's deliberate cultivation of a mass audience is difficult to say. But whereas Romantic poets were greeted as visionaries, praised for opening dazzling new vistas onto the self and nature, Victorian poets were encouraged to keep their ideas down to earth, to offer practical advice about managing the vicissitudes of heart and soul in a workaday world. The Romantic emphasis on self-expression gave way to more qualified soul-searching with an eye toward moral content that the public could grasp and apply. Carlyle's famous admonition in *Sartor Resartus* set the tone for the period: "Close thy *Byron;* open thy *Goethe*." In other words, forget the self-indulgent quest for happiness or self-knowledge associated with Byronic heroes; strive instead to improve society and practice greater artistic control; know your work and do it.

Whether they felt guilty, inspired, infuriated, or amused over their audience's thirst for instruction, Victorian poets took advantage of it to expand the resources of poetry in English. Though there are obvious lines of influence from the Romantics—Keats to Tennyson, Shelley to Browning, Wordsworth to Arnold—the innovations are perhaps even more striking. Eclectic poets introduced their readers to a bewildering variety of rhythms, stanzas, topics, words, and ideas that had not been seen in poetry before. Contemporary social concerns vied with—and sometimes merged into—Greek mythology and Arthurian legend as subject matter. Swinburne and Hopkins engaged in verbal pyrotechnics that produced new meters amid an ecstasy of sound; Elizabeth Barrett Browning unleashed stormy feminist lyrics marked by a dazzling intellect; Arnold captured readers with his startling emotional honesty; Christina Rossetti whittled her lines down to a thought-teasing purity; Arthur Symons and William Ernest Henley adapted French *vers libre* to create modern "free verse."

Perhaps the most important development was the rise of the dramatic monologue. Almost every poet found occasion to speak through characters apparently quite foreign in time, place, or social situation. Tennyson's liquid vowel sounds and Browning's clotted consonant clusters are trademarks of very different styles, but both poets use their distinctive music to probe the psychology of the speakers in their dramatic poems. Adapting the sound of their lines to fit the rhythms of their speakers' thoughts, poets acquired a more conversational tone and expanded the psychological range of their craft. While Browning was preoccupied with extreme psychological states, many poets shared his desire to represent a person or event from multiple perspectives, through shifting voices and unreliable narrators. These relativistic approaches also encouraged poets to experiment with new angles of vision suggested by the initially disorienting array of developments in visual culture. Photography, panoramas, stereopticons, impressionist painting, illustrated newspapers, and the mass reproduction of art images all left their mark on poetic practice. The ultimate effect was to engender poems whose ability to please or even communicate depended on the active participation of the reader.

Though nonfiction prose and poetry flourished, the Victorian era is still considered the great age of British fiction. Novelists strove to embody the character and genius of the time. The novel's triumphant adaptation of practically any material into "realistic" narrative and detail fueled an obsession with storytelling that spilled over into anecdotal painting, program music, and fictive or autobiographical frames for essays and histories. The novels themselves generally explored the relation between individuals and their society through the mechanism of a central love plot, around which almost any subject could be investigated, including the quest for self-knowledge, religious crises, industrialism, education, women's roles, crime and punishment, or the definition of gentlemanliness.

Convoluted by later standards, Victorian novels received their most famous assessment from Henry James, who regarded them as "loose baggy monsters." The English novel, he said, is "a treasure house of detail, but an indifferent whole." Shrewd as the observation was, it overlooks the thematic density that unifies Dickens's sprawling three-deckers; the moral consciousness that registers every nuance of thought in George Eliot's rural panoramas; the intricate narrative structures and ardent self-questioning that propel the tormented romances of the Brontës. Their novels work within an established social frame, focusing on the characters' freedom to act within fairly narrow moral codes in an unpredictable universe; they deal with questions of social responsibility and personal choice, the impulses of passion and the dictates of conscience. Yet even as they portrayed familiar details of contemporary social life, novelists challenged the confines of "realist" fiction, experimenting with multiple perspectives, unreliable narrators, stories within stories, direct appeals to the reader, and strange extremes of behavior.

The Role of Art in Society

"The past for poets, the present for pigs." This polemical statement by the painter Samuel Palmer sums up much of the period's literary debate. Because Victorian times seemed so thoroughly to break from the past, "modern" became a common but often prejudicial word. Was there anything of lasting artistic value to be found in ordinary everyday life? Many writers felt there was not; they preferred to indulge instead in what Tennyson called the "passion of the past." Most poetry shunned the details of contemporary urban existence, and even the great novelists like Dickens, Eliot, and Thackeray situated much of their work in the pre-Victorian world of their parents. Some of this writing was escapist, but many authors saw in earlier times a more ethically and aesthetically coherent world that could serve as a model for Victorian social reform. The Pre-Raphaelite painters and their literary allies sought out medieval models, while Matthew Arnold returned to the Greco-Roman classics: "They, at any rate, knew what they wanted in art, and we do not."

But another group vigorously disagreed; they stressed the importance of creating an up-to-date art that would validate or at least grapple with the uniqueness of Victorian life. In *Aurora Leigh* Elizabeth Barrett Browning contended that "this live throbbing age" should take precedence over all other topics: "if there's room for poets in this world," she said, "Their sole work is to represent the age / Their age, not Charlemagne's." In 1850 the critic F. G. Stephens argued that poets should emphasize "the poetry of the things about us; our railways, factories, mines, roaring cities, steam vessels, and the endless novelties and wonders produced every day." As the century wore on, there was a broadening in social scope: the life of the working classes became a serious literary topic, and in the 1870s and 1880s "naturalist" writers probed the structures of everyday life at near-subsistence level. Thomas Hardy wrote searching studies of rural life; George Gissing, whose first wife was a prostitute, documented in harsh detail "the nether world" of backstreet London.

Whether they favored the past or present as a literary landscape, whether they criticized or lauded the times they lived in, most Victorian writers felt at home in their era. Though they had their own interests, they did not act as alienated outcasts but addressed social needs and responded to the public desire for instruction and reassurance. They recognized the force of John Stuart Mill's remark: "Whatever we may think or affect to think of the present age, we cannot get out of it; we must suffer with its sufferings, and enjoy with its enjoyments; we must share in its lot."

Amid all this energetic literary production, a substantial portion of readers demanded to know if literature had any value at all. Utilitarians regarded art as a waste of time and energy, while Evangelicals were suspicious of art's appeal to the senses and emotions rather than the soul and the conscience. "All poetry is misrepresentation," said the founder of Utilitarianism, Jeremy Bentham, who could not see how fanciful words might be of service to humanity. Such was the temper of the time that writers strove mightily to prove that audiences could derive moral and religious benefit from impractical things like circuses or watercolors. Even secular critics sought to legitimize art's role in society by contending that if religion failed, literature would take its place as a guiding light. "Literature is but a branch of Religion," said Carlyle; "in our time, it is the only branch that still shows any greenness." "More and more," said Arnold, "mankind will discover that we have to turn to poetry to interpret life for us, to console us, to sustain us."

The great expectations most Victorians had for their literature inevitably produced reactions against such moral earnestness. In the theater, a huge variety of comedies, melodramas, pantomimes, and music-hall skits amused all classes; 150,000 people a day went to theaters in London during the 1860s. Yet in comparison to other literary forms, little of lasting value remains. Though leading authors such as Browning, Tennyson, and Henry James tried their hand at writing for the stage, it was not until the 1890s, with the sophisticated wit of Oscar Wilde, the subtle social inquiry of Arthur Wing Pinero, and the provocative "problem plays" of Bernard Shaw, that British theater offered more than light entertainment for the masses. The way for serious drama had been prepared by the wonderfully clever musicals of W. S. Gilbert and Arthur Sullivan, which satirized such topics as Aestheticism (*Patience*,

1881), the House of Lords (*Iolanthe*, 1882), and the struggle for sexual equality (*Princess Ida*, 1884). Victorian social drama came into its own late in the era, when it began directly to explore its own relevance, dissecting social and theatrical conventions even as it questioned whether art could—or should—teach anything at all.

Doubts about the mission of art to improve society culminated in the Aesthetic Movement of the 1880s and 1890s, whose writers sought to show, in Oscar Wilde's words, that "there is no such thing as a moral or an immoral book. Books are well written or badly written. That is all." In an era of practicality, art declared its freedom by positing its sheer uselessness. Wilde argued that it is "through Art, and through Art only, that we can shield ourselves from the sordid perils of actual existence." Thus many authors at the end of the Victorian period renounced the values that characterize the age as a whole.

And yet the Aesthetes were still quintessentially Victorian in feeling that, as writers, they had to expose their inner being, whether uplifting or shocking, to the public gaze. In their thoughts and deeds, but especially in their words, writers were expected to harness their autobiographical impulses to society's need for guidance and amusement—or even outrage. "I never travel without my diary," one of Wilde's characters remarks: "One should always have something sensational to read in the train."

Every generalization about the Victorians comes with a ready-made contradiction: they were materialist but religious, self-confident but insecure, monstrous exploiters who devoted themselves to humane reforms; they were given to blanket pronouncements about the essential nature of sexes and races, the social order, and the Christian universe, but they relentlessly probed the foundations of their thought; they demanded a moral literature and thrilled to mindless page-turners. Yet in all these matters they were constantly concerned with rules, codes of duty and behavior, their places in a complex and often frustrating social order. Even the alienated rebels of the 1890s cared intensely (a favorite word) what people thought and how shocking their calculated transgressions might make them.

For a few decades after World War I, the Victorians' obsession with the tightly buttoned structures of everyday life seemed their only legacy, offering an easy target for Modernists who sought to declare their own free-thinking independence. "Queen Victoria was like a great paper-weight," wrote H. G. Wells, "that for half a century sat upon men's minds, and when she was removed their ideas began to blow about all over the place haphazardly." But the end of the Victorian period is now almost a century past, and the winds of change have blown many Victorian ideas back into favor. More and more readers delight to discover beneath the stiff manners and elaborate conventions of a bygone era an anxious, humorous, dynamic people very much like ourselves.

Thomas Carlyle

1795–1881

Thomas Carlyle was a difficult and cranky character whose imaginative, eccentric works of history and social criticism had an immense influence on his fellow Victorians. Mill, Tennyson, Browning, Dickens, Ruskin, and many others idolized him. George Eliot believed that even if all Carlyle's books were burnt, "it would be only like cutting down an oak after its acorns have sown a forest. For there is hardly a superior or active mind of this generation that has not been modified by Carlyle's writings; there has hardly been an English book written for the last ten or twelve years that would not have been different if Carlyle had not lived."

Carlyle was born in the small village of Ecclefechan in Scotland, the eldest son of a stonemason and his wife who gave their numerous children a strict Calvinist upbringing. From his devout and self-disciplined parents, Carlyle learned early the value of hard work, and he later preached the Gospel of Work to his generation. His parents recognized his exceptional abilities and sent him to the University of Edinburgh to study for the ministry.

Religious doubts, however, prevented him from seeking ordination; at nineteen he wrote, "I am growing daily and hourly more lukewarm about this preaching business." He tried schoolteaching instead, but hated it, and feared that his youth was "hurrying darkly and uselessly away." Tormented by ill health and his lack of a vocation, Carlyle gradually turned to a literary career. Inspired by German literature and philosophy, he began reviewing and translating.

In 1821 Carlyle met Jane Welsh. Middle-class, well-educated, and with literary aspirations of her own, Jane did not at first take Carlyle seriously as a suitor, but he was determined to marry her. Prophetically, he wrote to a friend that he expected their marriage to be "the most turbulent, incongruous thing on earth—a mixture of honey and wormwood" with "thunder and lightning and furious storms—all mingled together into the same season—and the sunshine always in the *smallest* quantity!" Despite this gloomy forecast, they married in 1826, embarking on one of the century's most famous, and most speculated about, marriages. Jane was sharp-tongued and high-strung, Thomas was perpetually irritable, depressed, and complaining, yet they stayed together for nearly forty years. Samuel Butler rather nastily remarked that "it was very good of God to let Carlyle and Mrs. Carlyle marry one another and so make only two people miserable instead of four, besides being very amusing."

In 1828 they left the social and intellectual pleasures of Edinburgh for six years of self-imposed exile in Craigenputtoch, a bleak, remote sheep farm. Here Carlyle wrote the essays that would begin to make his name, *Signs of the Times*, *On History*, and *Characteristics*, as well as his first book, *Sartor Resartus* (1833–1834), a symbolic autobiography that records Carlyle's struggle to find meaning in life after his loss of faith. In 1834 the Carlyles moved to London, to a house in Chelsea where they spent the rest of their lives. The bustling city was a great contrast to the lonely farm, providing more access to stimulating books and friendships, but Carlyle continued to struggle with poverty, poor health, and insomnia. He set to work on his chronicle of *The French Revolution* (1837), the most dramatic and apocalyptic event in recent European history. In impassioned and impressionistic prose, he traced the downfall of an aristocracy of corrupt impostors, who had to be swept away to allow for the rebirth of a healthy society. In their destruction he read a warning for England, whose leaders seemed to be abandoning the country to democracy and laissez-faire capitalism.

Julia Margaret Cameron. *Thomas Carlyle*, 1867. The greatest of Victorian portrait photographers, Cameron lived near Tennyson on the Isle of Wight, and by virtue of her irrepressible personality managed to get his many distinguished visitors to sit through grueling photo sessions in her drafty greenhouse. Tennyson once brought the American poet Longfellow to her, saying "You will have to do whatever she tells you. I will come back soon and see what is left of you." Cameron's portrait of Carlyle conveys not only his stern prophetic power but also her own sense of photography's ability to discover a transcendent energy in simple human features: "My mortal but yet divine! Art of photography."

After completing the first of three volumes, Carlyle suffered a catastrophic setback: he lent the manuscript to his friend John Stuart Mill, whose housemaid accidentally burned it in the fireplace. Carlyle was devastated, but he forced himself to begin again. Rewriting was torture: Carlyle called *The French Revolution* "a wild savage Book" that "has come out of my own soul; born in blackness, whirl-wind and sorrow."

Yet, to his own surprise, this was the book that finally brought him widespread public recognition and some relief from financial strain. He enjoyed the admiration, and savored his new role as Sage and Prophet—though he complained that nobody listened when he addressed his contemporaries on a variety of social issues. Invited to give a series of lectures, later published as *On Heroes and Hero-Worship* (1841), Carlyle offered historical examples of what he considered true leadership. Then, in *Past and Present* (1843), he contrasted the coherent social and religious fabric of life in the Middle Ages with the chaos of the modern world. Democracy, to Carlyle, meant the breakdown of political order, the "despair of finding any heroes to govern you." He urged the "Captains of Industry" to become modern heroes, as feudal lords had been in an idealized medieval past, and to reestablish a sense of human community in mechanized England.

Carlyle believed that strong leaders were the only hope for social reform. Turning to history once again for examples, he wrote about *Oliver Cromwell* (1845) and *Frederick the Great* (1858–1865). Six volumes long, *Frederick* was hailed as Carlyle's masterpiece, and Carlyle was elected Rector of Edinburgh University. While he was in Scotland delivering his inaugural speech in 1866, Jane Welsh Carlyle died. In his grief, Carlyle wrote a moving memoir of his wife, to which he added others, including portraits of his friend Edward Irving, and Wordsworth; these were published after his death as *Reminiscences* (1881).

Although Carlyle continued to have public honors heaped upon him in old age, a reaction against his authoritarianism had begun as early as 1850, when he published the *Latter-Day Pamphlets*, a jeremiad against democracy, and *Shooting Niagara, and After?* (1867), an attack on the Second Reform Bill. While he remained an important figure, admired and respected, he was frustrated at feeling, as the critic G. B. Tennyson has put it, "everywhere honored and nowhere heeded." Carlyle's lifelong insistence on divine purpose at work in the universe was deeply attractive to a society in the grip of social unrest and religious malaise—but few were willing to accept the tasks that Carlyle claimed God had set for them. Carlyle's reputation rests on his vigorous denunciation of a materialist society and his rousing calls for social reform. Like a biblical prophet, Carlyle exhorts his followers to mend their ways. In powerfully idiosyncratic language, he condemns laziness and greed, alienation and mechanization, and urges the necessity for spiritual rebirth.

from Past and Present[1]
Midas[2]
[The Condition of England]

The condition of England, on which many pamphlets are now in the course of publication, and many thoughts unpublished are going on in every reflective head, is justly regarded as one of the most ominous, and withal one of the strangest, ever seen in this world. England is full of wealth, of multifarious produce, supply for human want in every kind; yet England is dying of inanition. With unabated bounty the land of England blooms and grows; waving with yellow harvests; thick-studded with workshops, industrial implements, with fifteen millions of workers, understood to be the strongest, the cunningest and the willingest our Earth ever had; these men are here; the work they have done, the fruit they have realised is here, abundant, exuberant on every hand of us: and behold, some baleful fiat as of Enchantment has gone forth, saying, "Touch it not, ye workers, ye master-workers, ye master-idlers; none of you can touch it, no man of you shall be the better for it; this is enchanted fruit!" On the poor workers such fiat falls first, in its rudest shape; but on the rich master-workers too it falls; neither can the rich master-idlers, nor any richest or highest man escape, but all are like to be brought low with it, and made "poor" enough, in the money sense or a far fataler one.

Of these successful skilful workers some two millions, it is now counted, sit in Workhouses, Poor-law Prisons;[3] or have "out-door relief"[4] flung over the wall to them,—the workhouse Bastille being filled to bursting, and the strong Poor-law bro-

---

1. *Past and Present* (1843) was Carlyle's response to the crisis of poverty and class estrangement during the Hungry 'Forties. Unemployment among industrial workers, combined with appalling conditions for the relief of the poor, had led to violent rioting. Even the Chartist movement's more peaceful attempts to address social and economic injustices through political reform aroused fears of revolution. Carlyle called for strong leaders to take charge. He contrasted the selfish indifference of laissez-faire industrialists and privileged aristocrats to the responsible paternalism of feudal lords and medieval monks. Medieval inequality and lack of personal freedom, he argued, were preferable to the modern "liberty to starve."
2. From Book 1, ch. 1. Midas was a legendary king who was granted his wish that everything he touched might

turn to gold; belatedly he realized he could not eat, for food became gold in his mouth.
3. Under the Poor Law Amendment Act of 1834, workhouses were established to provide relief to the poor. To deter loafers, the workhouses were made as unpleasant as possible: the standard of living was deliberately rendered worse than that of the lowest paid worker, and the inmates were expected to perform prison labor, such as picking oakum or breaking stones. Men and women were housed separately so that families were broken up.
4. Under the system of "outdoor relief," which existed prior to the Poor Law Amendment Act of 1834, each parish provided for its own poor through minimum allowances.

ken asunder by a stronger. They sit there, these many months now; their hope of deliverance as yet small. In workhouses, pleasantly so-named, because work cannot be done in them. Twelve-hundred-thousand workers in England alone; their cunning right-hand lamed, lying idle in their sorrowful bosom; their hopes, outlooks, share of this fair world, shut-in by narrow walls. They sit there, pent up, as in a kind of horrid enchantment; glad to be imprisoned and enchanted, that they may not perish starved. The picturesque Tourist, in a sunny autumn day, through this bounteous realm of England, descries the Union Workhouse on his path. "Passing by the Work-house of St. Ives in Huntingdonshire, on a bright day last autumn," says the pic-turesque Tourist, "I saw sitting on wooden benches, in front of their Bastille and within their ring-wall and its railings, some half-hundred or more of these men. Tall robust figures, young mostly or of middle age; of honest countenance, many of them thoughtful and even intelligent-looking men. They sat there, near by one another; but in a kind of torpor, especially in a silence, which was very striking. In silence: for, alas, what word was to be said? An Earth all lying round, crying, Come and till me, come and reap me;—yet we here sit enchanted! In the eyes and brows of these men hung the gloomiest expression, not of anger, but of grief and shame and manifold inarticulate distress and weariness; they returned my glance with a glance that seemed to say, "Do not look at us. We sit enchanted here, we know not why. The Sun shines and the Earth calls; and, by the governing Powers and Impotences of this Eng-land, we are forbidden to obey. It is impossible, they tell us!" There was something that reminded me of Dante's Hell in the look of all this; and I rode swiftly away."

So many hundred thousands sit in workhouses: and other hundred thousands have not yet got even workhouses; and in thrifty Scotland itself, in Glasgow or Edin-burgh City, in their dark lanes, hidden from all but the eye of God, and of rare Benevolence the minister of God, there are scenes of woe and destitution and desola-tion, such as, one may hope, the Sun never saw before in the most barbarous regions where men dwelt. Competent witnesses, the brave and humane Dr. Alison,[5] who speaks what he knows, whose noble Healing Art in his charitable hands becomes once more a truly sacred one, report these things for us: these things are not of this year, or of last year, have no reference to our present state of commercial stagnation, but only to the common state. Not in sharp fever-fits, but in chronic gangrene of this kind is Scotland suffering. A Poor-law, any and every Poor-law, it may be observed, is but a temporary measure; an anodyne, not a remedy: Rich and Poor, when once the naked facts of their condition have come into collision, cannot long subsist together on a mere Poor-law. True enough:—and yet, human beings cannot be left to die! Scotland too, till something better come, must have a Poor-law, if Scotland is not to be a byword among the nations. O, what a waste is there; of noble and thrice-noble national virtues; peasant Stoicisms, Heroisms; valiant manful habits, soul of a Nation's worth,—which all the metal of Potosi[6] cannot purchase back; to which the metal of Potosi, and all you can buy with *it*, is dross and dust!

Why dwell on this aspect of the matter? It is too indisputable, not doubtful now to any one. Descend where you will into the lower class, in Town or Country, by what avenue you will, by Factory Inquiries, Agricultural Inquiries, by Revenue Returns, by Mining-Labourer Committees, by opening your own eyes and looking,

5. William Pulteney Alison, Scottish physician and author of *Observations on the Management of the Poor in Scotland* (1840).

6. Bolivian city noted for its silver, tin, lead, and copper mines.

the same sorrowful result discloses itself: you have to admit that the working body of this rich English Nation has sunk or is fast sinking into a state, to which, all sides of it considered, there was literally never any parallel. At Stockport Assizes,—and this too has no reference to the present state of trade, being of date prior to that,—a Mother and a Father are arraigned and found guilty of poisoning three of their children, to defraud a "burial-society" of some 3l.8s. due on the death of each child: they are arraigned, found guilty; and the official authorities, it is whispered, hint that perhaps the case is not solitary, that perhaps you had better not probe farther into that department of things. This is in the autumn of 1841; the crime itself is of the previous year or season. "Brutal savages, degraded Irish," mutters the idle reader of Newspapers; hardly lingering on this incident. Yet it is an incident worth lingering on; the depravity, savagery and degraded Irishism being never so well admitted. In the British land, a human Mother and Father, of white skin and professing the Christian religion, had done this thing; they, with their Irishism and necessity and savagery, had been driven to do it. Such instances are like the highest mountain apex emerged into view; under which lies a whole mountain region and land, not yet emerged. A human Mother and Father had said to themselves, What shall we do to escape starvation? We are deep sunk here, in our dark cellar; and help is far.—Yes, in the Ugolino Hunger-tower stern things happen; best-loved little Gaddo fallen dead on his Father's knees![7]—The Stockport Mother and Father think and hint: Our poor little starveling Tom, who cries all day for victuals, who will see only evil and not good in this world: if he were out of misery at once; he well dead, and the rest of us perhaps kept alive? It is thought, and hinted; at last it is done. And now Tom being killed, and all spent and eaten, Is it poor little starveling Jack that must go, or poor little starveling Will?—What a committee of ways and means!

In starved sieged cities, in the uttermost doomed ruin of old Jerusalem fallen under the wrath of God, it was prophesied and said, "The hands of the pitiful women have sodden their own children."[8] The stern Hebrew imagination could conceive no blacker gulf of wretchedness; that was the ultimatum of degraded god-punished man. And we here, in modern England, exuberant with supply of all kinds, besieged by nothing if it be not by invisible Enchantments, are we reaching that?——How come these things? Wherefore are they, wherefore should they be?

Nor are they of the St. Ives workhouses, of the Glasgow lanes, and Stockport cellars, the only unblessed among us. This successful industry of England, with its plethoric wealth, has as yet made nobody rich; it is an enchanted wealth, and belongs yet to nobody. We might ask, Which of us has it enriched? We can spend thousands where we once spent hundreds; but can purchase nothing good with them. In Poor and Rich, instead of noble thrift and plenty, there is idle luxury alternating with mean scarcity and inability. We have sumptuous garnitures for our Life, but have forgotten to *live* in the middle of them. It is an enchanted wealth; no man of us can yet touch it. The class of men who feel that they are truly better off by means of it, let them give us their name!

Many men eat finer cookery, drink dearer liquors,—with what advantage they can report, and their Doctors can: but in the heart of them, if we go out of the dyspeptic stomach, what increase of blessedness is there? Are they better, beautifuler,

---

7. Count Ugolino and his sons and grandsons were starved to death in a tower by his political opponents; in Canto 33 of the *Inferno* Dante implies that Ugolino, out

of starvation and desperation, cannibalized his children's corpses.
8. Cf. Lamentations 4.10.

stronger, braver? Are they even what they call "happier"? Do they look with satisfaction on more things and human faces in this God's-Earth; do more things and human faces look with satisfaction on them? Not so. Human faces gloom discordantly, disloyally on one another. Things, if it be not mere cotton and iron things, are growing disobedient to man. The Master Worker is enchanted, for the present, like his Workhouse Workman; clamours, in vain hitherto, for a very simple sort of "Liberty": the liberty "to buy where he finds it cheapest, to sell where he finds it dearest." With guineas jingling in every pocket, he was no whit richer; but now, the very guineas threatening to vanish, he feels that he is poor indeed. Poor Master Worker! And the Master Unworker, is not he in a still fataler situation? Pausing amid his game-preserves, with awful eye,—as he well may! Coercing fifty-pound tenants;[9] coercing, bribing, cajoling; "doing what he likes with his own." His mouth full of loud futilities, and arguments to prove the excellence of his Corn–law;[1] and in his heart the blackest misgiving, a desperate half-consciousness that his excellent Corn-law is indefensible, that his loud arguments for it are of a kind to strike men too literally *dumb*.

To whom, then, is this wealth of England wealth? Who is it that it blesses; makes happier, wiser, beautifuler, in any way better? Who has got hold of it, to make it fetch and carry for him, like a true servant, not like a false mock-servant; to do him any real service whatsoever? As yet no one. We have more riches than any Nation ever had before; we have less good of them than any Nation ever had before. Our successful industry is hitherto unsuccessful; a strange success, if we stop here! In the midst of plethoric plenty, the people perish; with gold walls, and full barns, no man feels himself safe or satisfied. Workers, Master Workers, Unworkers, all men, come to a pause; stand fixed, and cannot farther. Fatal paralysis spreading inwards, from the extremities, in St. Ives workhouses, in Stockport cellars, through all limbs, as if towards the heart itself. Have we actually got enchanted, then; accursed by some god?—

Midas longed for gold, and insulted the Olympians. He got gold, so that whatsoever he touched became gold,—and he, with his long ears, was little the better for it. Midas had misjudged the celestial music-tones; Midas had insulted Apollo and the gods: the gods gave him his wish, and a pair of long ears, which also were a good appendage to it. What a truth in these old Fables!

from *Gospel of Mammonism*[1]
[THE IRISH WIDOW]

One of Dr. Alison's Scotch facts struck us much. A poor Irish Widow, her husband having died in one of the Lanes of Edinburgh, went forth with her three children, bare of all resource, to solicit help from the Charitable Establishments of that City. At this Charitable Establishment and then at that she was refused; referred from one to the other, helped by none;—till she had exhausted them all; till her strength and heart failed her: she sank down in typhus-fever; died, and infected her Lane with fever, so that "seventeen other persons" died of fever there in consequence. The humane Physician asks thereupon, as with a heart too full for speaking, Would it not have been *economy* to help this poor Widow? She took typhus-fever, and killed seventeen of you!—Very curious. The forlorn Irish Widow applies to her fellow-crea-

---

9. The Reform Bill of 1832 enfranchised tenants who paid 50 pounds or more in annual rent.
1. The Corn Laws regulated the import of grain into England. Intended to protect domestic agriculture, they also limited food supplies and raised food prices.
1. From Book 3, ch. 2.

tures, as if saying, "Behold I am sinking, bare of help: ye must help me! I am your sister, bone of your bone; one God made us: ye must help me!" They answer, "No, impossible; thou art no sister of ours." But she proves her sisterhood; her typhus-fever kills *them*: they actually were her brothers, though denying it! Had human creature ever to go lower for a proof?

For, as indeed was very natural in such case, all government of the Poor by the Rich has long ago been given over to Supply-and-demand, Laissez-faire and such-like,[2] and universally declared to be "impossible." "You are no sister of ours; what shadow of proof is there? Here are our parchments, our padlocks, proving indisputably our money-safes to be *ours*, and you to have no business with them. Depart! It is impossible!"—Nay, what wouldst thou thyself have us do? cry indignant readers. Nothing, my friends,—till you have got a soul for yourselves again. Till then all things are "impossible." Till then I cannot even bid you buy, as the old Spartans would have done, two-pence worth of powder and lead, and compendiously shoot to death this poor Irish Widow: even that is "impossible" for you. Nothing is left but that she prove her sisterhood by dying, and infecting you with typhus. Seventeen of you lying dead will not deny such proof that she *was* flesh of your flesh; and perhaps some of the living may lay it to heart.

from *Labour*[1]
[KNOW THY WORK]

For there is a perennial nobleness, and even sacredness, in Work. Were he never so benighted, forgetful of his high calling, there is always hope in a man that actually and earnestly works: in Idleness alone is there perpetual despair. Work, never so Mammonish,[2] mean, *is* in communication with Nature; the real desire to get Work done will itself lead one more and more to truth, to Nature's appointments and regulations, which are truth.

The latest Gospel in this world is, Know thy work and do it. "Know thyself": long enough has that poor "self" of thine tormented thee; thou wilt never get to "know" it, I believe! Think it not thy business, this of knowing thyself; thou art an unknowable individual: know what thou canst work at; and work at it, like a Hercules![3] That will be thy better plan.

It has been written, "an endless significance lies in Work"; a man perfects himself by working. Foul jungles are cleared away, fair seedfields rise instead, and stately cities; and withal the man himself first ceases to be a jungle and foul unwholesome desert thereby. Consider how, even in the meanest sorts of Labour, the whole soul of a man is composed into a kind of real harmony, the instant he sets himself to work! Doubt, Desire, Sorrow, Remorse, Indignation, Despair itself, all these like helldogs lie beleaguering the soul of the poor dayworker, as of every man: but he bends himself with free valour against his task, and all these are stilled, all these shrink murmuring far off into their caves. The man is now a man. The blessed glow of Labour in him, is it not as purifying fire, wherein all poison is burnt up, and of sour smoke itself there is made bright blessed flame!

2. The free trade philosophy of British industrialists who believed in the market's ability to regulate itself, and in the right to do business unhampered by government regulation.

1. From Book 3, ch. 9.
2. Mammon is the personification of material wealth. "Ye cannot serve God and mammon" (Matthew 7.24).
3. Hercules had to perform twelve labors.

Destiny, on the whole, has no other way of cultivating us. A formless Chaos, once set it *revolving*, grows round and ever rounder; ranges itself, by mere force of gravity, into strata, spherical courses; is no longer a Chaos, but a round compacted World. What would become of the Earth, did she cease to revolve? In the poor old Earth, so long as she revolves, all inequalities, irregularities disperse themselves; all irregularities are incessantly becoming regular. Hast thou looked on the Potter's wheel,—one of the venerablest objects; old as the Prophet Ezechiel and far older? Rude lumps of clay, how they spin themselves up, by mere quick whirling, into beautiful circular dishes. And fancy the most assiduous Potter, but without his wheel; reduced to make dishes, or rather amorphous botches, by mere kneading and baking! Even such a Potter were Destiny, with a human soul that would rest and lie at ease, that would not work and spin! Of an idle unrevolving man the kindest Destiny, like the most assiduous Potter without wheel, can bake and knead nothing other than a botch; let her spend on him what expensive colouring, what gilding and enamelling she will, he is but a botch. Not a dish; no, a bulging, kneaded, crooked, shambling, squint-cornered, amorphous botch,—a mere enamelled vessel of dishonour! Let the idle think of this.

Blessed is he who has found his work; let him ask no other blessedness. He has a work, a life-purpose; he has found it, and will follow it! How, as a free-flowing channel, dug and torn by noble force through the sour mud-swamp of one's existence, like an ever-deepening river there, it runs and flows;—draining-off the sour festering water, gradually from the root of the remotest grass-blade; making, instead of pestilential swamp, a green fruitful meadow with its clear-flowing stream. How blessed for the meadow itself, let the stream and *its* value be great or small! Labour is Life: from the inmost heart of the Worker rises his god-given Force, the sacred celestial Life-essence breathed into him by Almighty God; from his inmost heart awakens him to all nobleness,—to all knowledge, "self-knowledge" and much else, so soon as Work fitly begins. Knowledge? The knowledge that will hold good in working, cleave thou to that; for Nature herself accredits that, says Yea to that. Properly thou hast no other knowledge but what thou hast got by working: the rest is yet all a hypothesis of knowledge; a thing to be argued of in schools, a thing floating in the clouds, in endless logic-vortices, till we try it and fix it. "Doubt, of whatever kind, can be ended by Action alone."

Captains of Industry[1]

If I believed that Mammonism with its adjuncts was to continue henceforth the one serious principle of our existence, I should reckon it idle to solicit remedial measures from any Government, the disease being insusceptible of remedy. Government can do much, but it can in nowise do all. Government, as the most conspicuous object in Society, is called upon to give signal of what shall be done; and, in many ways, to preside over, further, and command the doing of it. But the Government cannot do, by all its signaling and commanding, what the Society is radically indisposed to do. In the long-run every Government is the exact symbol of its People, with their wisdom and unwisdom; we have to say, Like People like Government.—The main substance of this immense Problem of Organising Labour, and first of all of Managing the Working Classes, will, it is very clear, have to be solved by those who stand practically in the middle of

---

1. From Book 4, ch. 4.

it; by those who themselves work and preside over work. Of all that can be enacted by any Parliament in regard to it, the germs must already lie potentially extant in those two Classes, who are to obey such enactment. A Human Chaos *in* which there is no light, you vainly attempt to irradiate by light shed *on* it: order never can arise there.

But it is my firm conviction that the "Hell of England" will *cease* to be that of "not making money"; that we shall get a nobler Hell and a nobler Heaven! I anticipate light *in* the Human Chaos, glimmering, shining more and more; under manifold true signals from without That light shall shine. Our deity no longer being Mammon,—O Heavens, each man will then say to himself: "Why such deadly haste to make money? I shall not go to Hell, even if I do not make money! There is another Hell, I am told!" Competition, at railway-speed, in all branches of commerce and work will then abate:—good felt-hats for the head, in every sense, instead of seven-feet lath-and-plaster hats on wheels, will then be discoverable! Bubble-periods,[2] with their panics and commercial crises, will again become infrequent; steady modest industry will take the place of gambling speculation. To be a noble Master, among noble Workers, will again be the first ambition with some few; to be a rich Master only the second. How the Inventive Genius of England, with the whirr of its bobbins and billy-rollers[3] shoved somewhat into the backgrounds of the brain, will contrive and devise, not cheaper produce exclusively, but fairer distribution of the produce at its present cheapness! By degrees, we shall again have a Society with something of Heroism in it, something of Heaven's Blessing on it; we shall again have, as my German friend[4] asserts, "instead of Mammon-Feudalism with unsold cotton-shirts and Preservation of the Game, noble just Industrialism and Government by the Wisest!"

It is with the hope of awakening here and there a British man to know himself for a man and divine soul, that a few words of parting admonition, to all persons to whom the Heavenly Powers have lent power of any kind in this land, may now be addressed. And first to those same Master-Workers, Leaders of Industry; who stand nearest and in fact powerfulest, though not most prominent, being as yet in too many senses a Virtuality rather than an Actuality.

The Leaders of Industry, if Industry is ever to be led, are virtually the Captains of the World! if there be no nobleness in them, there will never be an Aristocracy more. But let the Captains of Industry consider: once again, are they born of other clay than the old Captains of Slaughter; doomed forever to be no Chivalry, but a mere gold-plated *Doggery*,—what the French well name *Canaille*, "Doggery" with more or less gold carrion at its disposal? Captains of Industry are the true Fighters, henceforth recognisable as the only true ones: Fighters against Chaos, Necessity and the Devils and Jötuns;[5] and lead on Mankind in that great, and alone true, and universal warfare; the stars in their courses fighting for them, and all Heaven and all Earth saying audibly, Well done! Let the Captains of Industry retire into their own hearts, and ask solemnly, If there is nothing but vulturous hunger, for fine wines, valet reputation and gilt carriages, discoverable there? Of hearts made by the Almighty God I will not believe such a thing. Deep-hidden under wretchedest god-forgetting Cants, Epicurisms, Dead-Sea Apisms;[6] forgotten as under foulest fat Lethe

---

2. Ups and downs in the stock market.
3. Machines that prepare cotton or wool for spinning.
4. Teufelsdröckh, the central character in *Sartor Resartus*.
5. Giants in Norse mythology.

6. An Islamic myth held that a tribe living near the Dead Sea were turned into apes because they refused to heed the prophecies of Moses.

mud and weeds, there is yet, in all hearts born into this God's-World, a spark of the Godlike slumbering. Awake, O nightmare sleepers; awake, arise, or be forever fallen! This is not playhouse poetry; it is sober fact. Our England, our world cannot live as it is. It will connect itself with a God again, or go down with nameless throes and fire-consummation to the Devils. Thou who feelest aught of such a Godlike stirring in thee, any faintest intimation of it as through heavy-laden dreams, follow it, I conjure thee. Arise, save thyself, be one of those that save thy country.

Bucaniers, Chactaw Indians, whose supreme aim in fighting is that they may get the scalps, the money, that they may amass scalps and money: out of such came no Chivalry, and never will! Out of such came only gore and wreck, infernal rage and misery; desperation quenched in annihilation. Behold it, I bid thee, behold there, and consider! What is it that thou have a hundred thousand-pound bills laid-up in thy strong-room, a hundred scalps hung-up in thy wigwam? I value not them or thee. Thy scalps and thy thousand-pound bills are as yet nothing, if no nobleness from within irradiate them; if no Chivalry, in action, or in embryo ever struggling towards birth and action, be there.

Love of men cannot be bought by cash-payment; and without love men cannot endure to be together. You cannot lead a Fighting World without having it regiment-ed, chivalried: the thing, in a day, becomes impossible; all men in it, the highest at first, the very lowest at last, discern consciously, or by a noble instinct, this necessity. And can you any more continue to lead a Working World unregimented, anarchic? I answer, and the Heavens and Earth are now answering, No! The thing becomes not "in a day" impossible; but in some two generations it does. Yes, when fathers and mothers, in Stockport hunger-cellars, begin to eat their children, and Irish widows have to prove their relationship by dying of typhus-fever; and amid Governing "Corporations of the Best and Bravest," busy to preserve their game by "bushing," dark millions of God's human creatures start up in mad Chartisms, impracticable Sacred-Months, and Manchester Insurrections;[7]—and there is a virtual Industrial Aristocracy as yet only half-alive, spell-bound amid money-bags and ledgers; and an actual Idle Aristocracy seemingly near dead in somnolent delusions, in trespasses and double-barrels; "sliding," as on inclined-planes, which every new year they *soap* with new Hansard's-jargon[8] under God's sky, and so are "sliding," ever faster, towards a "scale" and balance-scale whereon is written *Thou art found Wanting:*—in such days, after a generation or two, I say, it does become, even to the low and simple, very palpably impossible! No Working World, any more than a Fighting World, can be led on without a noble Chivalry of Work, and laws and fixed rules which follow out of that,—far nobler than any Chivalry of Fighting was. As an anarchic multitude on mere Supply-and-demand, it is becoming inevitable that we dwindle in horrid suici-dal convulsion and self-abrasion, frightful to the imagination, into *Chactaw* Workers. With wigwams and scalps,—with palaces and thousand-pound bills; with savagery, depopulation, chaotic desolation! Good Heavens, will not one French Revolution and Reign of Terror suffice us, but must there be two? There will be two if needed; there will be twenty if needed; there will be precisely as many as are needed. The Laws of Nature will have themselves fulfilled. That is a thing certain to me.

Your gallant battle-hosts and work-hosts, as the others did, will need to be made loyally yours; they must and will be regulated, methodically secured in their just share

---

7. Manchester was the site of Chartist agitation in 1838–1839; in 1819, charging cavalry had killed a dozen people at an outdoor workers' meeting.

8. *Hansard* is the official record of Parliamentary debate.

of conquest under you;—joined with you in veritable brotherhood, sonhood, by quite other and deeper ties than those of temporary day's wages! How would mere red-coated regiments, to say nothing of chivalries, fight for you, if you could discharge them on the evening of the battle, on payment of the stipulated shillings,—and they discharge you on the morning of it! Chelsea Hospitals,[9] pensions, promotions, rigorous lasting covenant on the one side and on the other, are indispensable even for a hired fighter. The Feudal Baron, much more,—how could he subsist with mere temporary mercenaries round him, at sixpence a day; ready to go over to the other side, if sevenpence were offered? He could not have subsisted;—and his noble instinct saved him from the necessity of even trying! The Feudal Baron had a Man's Soul in him; to which anarchy, mutiny, and the other fruits of temporary mercenaries, were intolerable: he had never been a Baron otherwise, but had continued a Chactaw and Bucanier. He felt it precious, and at last it became habitual, and his fruitful enlarged existence included it as a necessity, to have men round him who in heart loved him; whose life he watched over with rigour yet with love; who were prepared to give their life for him, if need came. It was beautiful; it was human! Man lives not otherwise, nor can live contented, anywhere or anywhen. Isolation is the sum-total of wretchedness to man. To be cut off, to be left solitary: to have a world alien, not your world; all a hostile camp for you; not a home at all, of hearts and faces who are yours, whose you are! It is the frightfulest enchantment; too truly a work of the Evil One. To have neither superior, nor inferior, nor equal, united manlike to you. Without father, without child, without brother. Man knows no sadder destiny. "How is each of us," exclaims Jean Paul,[1] "so lonely in the wide bosom of the All!" Encased each as in his transparent "ice-palace"; our brother visible in his, making signals and gesticulations to us;—visible, but forever unattainable: on his bosom we shall never rest, nor he on ours. It was not a God that did this; no!

Awake, ye noble Workers, warriors in the one true war: all this must be remedied. It is you who are already half-alive, whom I will welcome into life; whom I will conjure, in God's name, to shake off your enchanted sleep, and live wholly! Cease to count scalps, gold-purses; not in these lies your or our salvation. Even these, if you count only these, will not long be left. Let bucaniering be put far from you; alter, speedily abrogate all laws of the bucaniers, if you would gain any victory that shall endure. Let God's justice, let pity, nobleness and manly valour, with more gold-purses or with fewer, testify themselves in this your brief Life-transit to all the Eternities, the Gods and Silences. It is to you I call; for ye are not dead, ye are already half-alive: there is in you a sleepless dauntless energy, the prime-matter of all nobleness in man. Honour to you in your kind. It is to you I call: ye know at least this, That the mandate of God to His creature man is: Work! The future Epic of the World rests not with those that are near dead, but with those that are alive, and those that are coming into life.

Look around you. Your world-hosts are all in mutiny, in confusion, destitution; on the eve of fiery wreck and madness! They will not march farther for you, on the sixpence a day and supply-and-demand principle: they will not; nor ought they, nor can they. Ye shall reduce them to order, begin reducing them. To order, to just subordination; noble loyalty in return for noble guidance. Their souls are driven nigh mad; let yours be sane and ever saner. Not as a bewildered bewildering mob; but as a firm regimented mass, with real captains over them, will these men march any more. All human interests, combined human endeavours, and social growths in this world,

---

9. A home and hospital for disabled soldiers.   1. Jean Paul Richter (1763–1825), German writer.

have, at a certain stage of their development, required organising: and Work, the grandest of human interests, does now require it.

God knows, the task will be hard: but no noble task was ever easy. This task will wear away your lives, and the lives of your sons and grandsons: but for what purpose, if not for tasks like this, were lives given to men? Ye shall cease to count your thousand-pound scalps, the noble of you shall cease! Nay the very scalps, as I say, will not long be left if you count only these. Ye shall cease wholly to be barbarous vulturous Chactaws, and become noble European Nineteenth-Century Men. Ye shall know that Mammon, in never such gigs[2] and flunky "respectabilities," is not the alone God; that of himself he is but a Devil, and even a Brute-god.

Difficult? Yes, it will be difficult. The short-fibre cotton; that too was difficult. The waste cotton-shrub, long useless, disobedient, as the thistle by the wayside,—have ye not conquered it: made it into beautiful bandana webs; white woven shirts for men; bright-tinted air-garments wherein flit goddesses? Ye have shivered mountains asunder, made the hard iron pliant to you as soft putty: the Forest-giants, Marsh-jötuns bear sheaves of golden-grain; Aegir the Sea-demon himself stretches his back for a sleek highway to you, and on Firehorses and Windhorses ye career. Ye are most strong. Thor red-bearded, with his blue sun-eyes, with his cheery heart and strong thunder-hammer, he and you have prevailed. Ye are most strong, ye Sons of the icy North, of the far East,—far marching from your rugged Eastern Wildernesses, hitherward from the gray Dawn of Time! Ye are Sons of the Jötun-land; the land of Difficulties Conquered. Difficult? You must try this thing. Once try it with the understanding that it will and shall have to be done. Try it as ye try the paltrier thing, making of money! I will bet on you once more, against all Jötuns, Tailor-gods, Double-barrelled Law-wards, and Denizens of Chaos whatsoever!
1843   1843

The Industrial Landscape

"The most fundamental transformation of human life in the history of the world"—this is how the historian Eric Hobsbawm describes the Industrial Revolution. In economic terms, the arrival of the "Machine Age" was a huge success: thanks to its technological preeminence, Britain's wealth and prosperity increased enormously. This increase, coupled with pride in the improvements themselves, created a sense of excitement, of living in stirring times, and bolstered the optimistic conviction that further progress was certain. But the rapidity with which industrialization took place was also profoundly disorienting. Overnight, it seemed, the world had been transformed.

The first wave of the Industrial Revolution took place in the cotton industry. During the eighteenth century, new inventions had changed the technique of spinning and speeded up production of thread. This in turn had created a demand for more weavers. But with the development of steam-powered looms in the 1820s, weaving began to be done in factories rather than at home, and handloom weavers became obsolete. Large numbers of people found themselves without a job. Rural workers flocked to the cities to find work, and the population burgeoned in northern cities such as Manchester, Liverpool, Leeds, Birmingham, Sheffield, and Glasgow.

Britain grew richer, but it was not the poor who benefited from this revolution. In the early decades of the century, before legislation was passed to address some of the worst evils of the factory system, workers—including children—toiled for up to sixteen hours a day, six days a week, under inhuman conditions: deafening noise, poor ventilation, dangerous machinery,

---

2. A two-wheeled, one-horse carriage.

John Leech. *Horseman pursued by a train engine named "Time."*

demanding overseers, and no insurance or benefits to protect them in the event of an accident or illness. Periodic economic depressions resulted in massive unemployment: being "in work" was bad enough, but being out of work could mean actual starvation.

The factory system disrupted not only traditional patterns of work but also family life. As more and more women and children were employed in factories, mills, and mines, there was an inevitable loss of paternal authority. Women had always worked, but never before had their labor been so visible. The "factory girl" became a focus for fears about promiscuity and the undermining of the family structure.

The overcrowded conditions in the cities created urban slums of unimaginable wretchedness. Whole families—sometimes several families—might live in a single room. Tens of thousands of people lived in damp cellars. Because of the lack of sanitation, raw sewage overflowed everywhere, and fresh water was often impossible to obtain. When typhoid and cholera broke out, epidemics spread rampantly among the inhabitants of these foul dens; contagion was impossible to avoid.

Industrial pollution was another byproduct of the machine age. Factories spewed smoke into the air, and cities dumped sewage directly into the rivers. The outlying areas of Birmingham came to be known as "The Black Country." In *Contrasts* (1836) A. W. N. Pugin vividly depicted the sheer ugliness of a landscape dominated by smokestacks. In *The Storm-Cloud of the Nineteenth Century* (1884) John Ruskin denounced the devastation wrought by industrialism: "Blanched Sun,—blighted grass,—blinded man."

The second phase of the Industrial Revolution was brought about by the railway boom of the 1840s. The spreading network of rails linked the cities, and allowed the iron and coal industries to flourish. The railroad transfigured the landscape in ways that were terribly disruptive but also immensely thrilling. More than any other technological innovation, it symbolized the dizzying speed with which Britain was changing.

Psychologically, it was hard to assimilate such a rapidly altering environment. Many people felt that the world of their childhood had been obliterated. In 1860 the novelist William Makepeace Thackeray voiced this sense of bewilderment:

It was only yesterday; but what a gulf between now and then! *Then* was the old world. Stage-coaches, more or less swift, riding-horses, pack-horses, highwaymen, knights in armour, Norman invaders, Roman legions, Druids, Ancient Britons painted blue, and so forth—all these belong to the old period. . . . But your railroad starts the new era. . . . We who lived before railways, and survive out of the ancient world, are like Father Noah and his family out of the Ark.

Writers throughout the nineteenth century shared Thackeray's wistful longing for a romanticized past. Pugin, Carlyle, Tennyson, Morris, and many others used their vision of an idealized medieval England, aesthetically pleasing and socially harmonious, as a device to castigate the evils of industrialization.

This harking back to the past was not mere nostalgia: it reflected the trauma of the experience of industrialization. The transformation from a rural agrarian economy to a machine-dominated system of factories, mines, and railroads meant a very real shift in ancient patterns of life. The clock rather than the natural rhythms of the seasons now dictated working-class existence, and the laissez-faire pursuit of profit changed the relations between masters and men. Despite the huge accumulation of national wealth, the gulf between rich and poor had never been wider. In 1844 Friedrich Engels observed that "class warfare is so open and shameless that it has to be seen to be believed." Hunger, misery, and hopelessness found expression in strikes and trade union activity. The Chartist movement, in which the workers hoped for some relief from their distress by presenting a list of demands to Parliament, fizzled. Far from gaining middle-class compassion, it aroused hostility, and even fears of a revolution in Britain.

Among the key literary responses to the "condition of England" question were Carlyle's *Past and Present* (1843), Elizabeth Gaskell's *Mary Barton* (1848) and *North and South* (1855), and Dickens's *Hard Times* (1854). Their writing helped to focus attention on the human costs of the Industrial Revolution. In an effort to prick the consciences of their readers, they dramatized the sufferings of factory workers, and tried to put a human face on the inflammatory figure of the Chartist; they warned of the dangers of selfish individualism, and urged sympathy, communication, and benevolent leadership as remedies for class alienation.

The Steam Loom Weaver

In traditional bawdy ballads, the lovers meet under a hedge or by a stream, and their agrarian pursuits—herding sheep, milking cows, grinding corn, weaving cotton by hand—provide the pastoral setting and imagery for a sexual encounter. But the Industrial Revolution sent tens of thousands of rural people to live and work in cities. This humorous working-class ballad takes its imagery from the new industrial occupations of the factories, where steam engines powered the weavers' looms in cotton mills. Broadside ballads like this one were printed on flimsy paper and sold in the street for a penny or less; in the early nineteenth century, they were the most common form of reading matter for the urban poor.

The Steam Loom Weaver

One morning in summer I did ramble,
In the pleasant month of June,
The birds did sing the lambkins play,
Two lovers walking in their bloom,
5   The lassie was a steam loom weaver,
The lad an engine driver keen,
All their discourse was about weaving.
And the getting up of steam.

She said my loom is out of fettle,
10   Can you right it yes or no,
You say you are an engine driver,

Which makes the steam so rapid flow;
My lambs and jacks[1] are out of order,
My laith in motion has not been,
15   So work away without delay,
And quickly muster up the steam.

I said fair maid you seem determined,
No longer for to idle be,
Your healds and laith[2] I'll put in motion,
20   Then work you can without delay,
She said young man a pair of pickers,[3]
A shuttle too I want you ween,
Without these three I cannot weave,
So useless would be the steam.

25   Dear lass these things I will provide,
But when to labour will you begin
As soon my lad as things are ready
My loom shop you can enter in.
A shuttle true and pickers too,
30   This young man did provide amain.
And soon her loom was put in tune
So well it was supplied with steam.

Her loom worked well the shuttle flew,
His nickers play'd the tune nick-nack,
35   Her laith did move with rapid motion,
Her temples, healds, long-lambs and jacks,
Her cloth beam rolled the cloth up tight,
The yarn beam emptied soon its seam,
The young man cried your loom works, light
40   And quickly then off shot the steam.

She said young man another web,
Upon the beam let's get don't strike,
But work away while yet it's day,
This steam loom weaving well I like.
45   He said good lass I cannot stay,
But if a fresh warp you will beam
If ready when I come this way,
I'd strive for to get up the steam.

c. 1830

━◆━

Fanny Kemble
1809–1893

The Liverpool and Manchester Railway, opened in 1830, was Britain's first passenger railway, built despite powerful opposition. During the debates in Parliament it had been argued that cows would cease to give milk, hens would be prevented from laying, and horses would become extinct

---

1. Jacks are levers that raise the harness supporting the warp threads; lambs are foot pedals that operate the jacks.
2. Healds are loops through which the warp threads pass;
the laith is the supporting stand of the loom.
3. Pickers are attachments to the picking stick which propels the shuttle through the warp threads.

if this monstrosity were allowed to deface the countryside. Fanny Kemble, a popular young actress, was the first woman to ride on the steam locomotive. She was accompanied by George Stephenson himself, the engineer who had designed the railroad. Her vivid description captures the startling newness of the experience, and the sense of traveling at astonishing speeds.

from Record of a Girlhood
[FIRST RIDE ON A STEAM ENGINE]

Liverpool, August 26th

My dear H———,

A common sheet of paper is enough for love, but a foolscap extra[1] can alone contain a railroad and my ecstasies. * * * We were introduced to the little engine which was to drag us along the rails. She (for they make these curious little fire-horses all mares) consisted of a boiler, a stove, a small platform, a bench, and behind the bench a barrel containing enough water to prevent her being thirsty for fifteen miles,—the whole machine not bigger than a common fire-engine. She goes upon two wheels, which are her feet, and are moved by bright steel legs called pistons; these are propelled by steam, and in proportion as more steam is applied to the upper extremities (the hip-joints, I suppose) of these pistons, the faster they move the wheels; and when it is desirable to diminish the speed, the steam, which unless suffered to escape would burst the boiler, evaporates through a safety-valve into the air. The reins, bit, and bridle of this wonderful beast—a small steel handle, which applies or withdraws the steam from its legs or pistons, so that a child might manage it. The coals, which are its oats, were under the bench, and there was a small glass tube affixed to the boiler, with water in it, which indicates by its fulness or emptiness when the creature wants water, which is immediately conveyed to it from its reservoirs. There is a chimney to the stove, but as they burn coke there is none of the dreadful black smoke which accompanies the progress of a steam-vessel. This snorting little animal, which I felt rather inclined to pat, was then harnessed to our carriage, and, Mr. Stephenson having taken me on the bench of the engine with him, we started at about ten miles an hour. * * * You can't imagine how strange it seemed to be journeying on thus, without any visible cause of progress other than the magical machine, with its flying white breath and rhythmical, unvarying pace, between these rocky walls, which are already clothed with moss and ferns and grasses; and when I reflected that these great masses of stone had been cut asunder to allow our passage thus far below the surface of the earth, I felt as if no fairy tale was ever half so wonderful as what I saw. * * * * * * He explained to me the whole construction of the steam-engine, and said he could soon make a famous engineer of me, which, considering the wonderful things he *has* achieved, I dare not say is impossible. * * * The engine having received its supply of water * * * set off at its utmost speed, thirty-five miles an hour, swifter than a bird flies (for they tried the experiment with a snipe). You cannot conceive what that sensation of cutting the air was; the motion is as smooth as possible, too. I could either have read or written. * * * When I closed my eyes this sensation of flying was quite delightful, and strange beyond description; yet, strange as it was, I had a perfect sense of security, and not the slightest fear * * * [as] this brave little she-dragon of ours flew on.

1830   1878

___

1. An extra-long sheet of writing paper.

┉ 〓◈〓 ┉

Thomas Babington Macaulay
1800–1859

Not everyone deplored the high human cost of rapid industrialization: the historian Thomas Babington Macaulay saw it as evidence of social progress. He was a firm believer in "the natural tendency of society to improvement," and he took great pride in the material achievements of his age. He expressed his views forcefully in reviewing Robert Southey, whose *Colloquies on the Progress and Prospects of Society* (1829) had criticized industrialism and urged a return to a romanticized rural past. In reply, Macaulay argued that in the nineteenth century "people live longer because they are better fed, better lodged, better clothed, and better attended in sickness, and that these improvements are owing to that increase of national wealth which the manufacturing system has produced."

from A Review of Southey's Colloquies
[THE NATURAL PROGRESS OF SOCIETY]

History is full of the signs of this natural progress of society. We see in almost every part of the annals of mankind how the industry of individuals, struggling up against wars, taxes, famines, conflagrations, mischievous prohibitions, and more mischievous protections, creates faster than governments can squander, and repairs whatever invaders can destroy. We see the wealth of nations increasing, and all the arts of life approaching nearer and nearer to perfection, in spite of the grossest corruption and the wildest profusion on the part of rulers.

The present moment is one of great distress. But how small will that distress appear when we think over the history of the last forty years; a war, compared with which all other wars sink into insignificance;[1] taxation, such as the most heavily taxed people of former times could not have conceived; a debt larger than all the public debts that ever existed in the world added together; the food of the people studiously rendered dear; the currency imprudently debased, and imprudently restored. Yet is the country poorer than in 1790? We firmly believe that, in spite of all the misgovernment of her rulers, she has been almost constantly becoming richer and richer. Now and then there has been a stoppage, now and then a short retrogression; but as to the general tendency there can be no doubt. A single breaker may recede; but the tide is evidently coming in.

If we were to prophesy that in the year 1930 a population of fifty millions, better fed, clad, and lodged than the English of our time, will cover these islands, that Sussex and Huntingdonshire will be wealthier than the wealthiest parts of the West Riding of Yorkshire now are, that cultivation, rich as that of a flower garden, will be carried up to the very tops of Ben Nevis and Helvelyn,[2] that machines constructed on principles yet undiscovered will be in every house, that there will be no highways but railroads, no traveling but by steam, that our debt, vast as it seems to us, will appear to our great-grandchildren a trifling encumbrance, which might easily be paid off in a year or two, many people would think us insane. We prophesy nothing; but this we say: If any person had told the Parliament which met in perplexity and terror after the crash in 1720 that in 1830 the wealth of England would surpass all their wildest

---

1. The Napoleonic Wars, which took place from 1792 until 1815.   2. Mountains in Scotland and the Lake District of England.

dreams, that the annual revenue would equal the principal of that debt which they considered as an intolerable burden, that for one man of ten thousand pounds then living there would be five men of fifty thousand pounds, that London would be twice as large and twice as populous, and that nevertheless the rate of mortality would have diminished to one-half of what it then was, that the post office would bring more into the exchequer than the excise and customs had brought in together under Charles the Second,[3] that stage coaches would run from London to York in twenty-four hours, that men would be in the habit of sailing without wind, and would be beginning to ride without horses, our ancestors would have given as much credit to the prediction as they gave to *Gulliver's Travels*. Yet the prediction would have been true; and they would have perceived that it was not altogether absurd, if they had considered that the country was then raising every year a sum which would have purchased the fee-simple[4] of the revenue of the Plantagenets, ten times what supported the Government of Elizabeth, three times what, in the time of Cromwell,[5] had been thought intolerably oppressive. To almost all men the state of things under which they have been used to live seems to be the necessary state of things. We have heard it said that five per cent is the natural interest of money, that twelve is the natural number of a jury, that forty shillings is the natural qualification of a county voter. Hence it is that, though in every age everybody knows that up to his own time progressive improvement has been taking place, nobody seems to reckon on any improvement during the next generation. We cannot absolutely prove that those are in error who tell us that society has reached a turning point, that we have seen our best days. But so said all who came before us, and with just as much apparent reason. "A million a year will beggar us," said the patriots of 1640. "Two millions a year will grind the country to powder," was the cry in 1660. "Six millions a year, and a debt of fifty millions!" exclaimed Swift, "the high allies have been the ruin of us." "A hundred and forty millions of debt!" said Junius;[6] "well may we say that we owe Lord Chatham more than we shall ever pay, if we owe him such a load as this." "Two hundred and forty millions of debt!" cried all the statesmen of 1783 in chorus; "what abilities, or what economy on the part of a minister, can save a country so burdened?" We know that if, since 1783, no fresh debt had been incurred, the increased resources of the country would have enabled us to defray that debt at which Pitt, Fox, and Burke[7] stood aghast, nay, to defray it over and over again, and that with much lighter taxation than what we have actually borne. On what principle is it that, when we see nothing but improvement behind us, we are to expect nothing but deterioration before us?

It is not by the intermeddling of Mr Southey's idol, the omniscient and omnipotent State, but by the prudence and energy of the people, that England has hitherto been carried forward in civilization; and it is to the same prudence and the same energy that we now look with comfort and good hope. Our rulers will best promote the improvement of the nation by strictly confining themselves to their own legitimate duties, by leaving capital to find its most lucrative course, commodities their fair price, industry and intelligence their natural reward, idleness and folly their nat-

---

3. Reigned 1660–1685.
4. Complete ownership of their estates. The Plantagenets ruled England from 1154 to 1399.
5. Elizabeth reigned from 1558 to 1603. Oliver Cromwell was Lord Protector from 1653 to 1658.

6. Pseudonym of a political commentator (active from 1769 to 1772) who supported William Pitt, Earl of Chatham. Pitt led the costly war against France.
7. William Pitt, Charles James Fox, and Edmund Burke were 18th-century statesmen.

ural punishment, by maintaining peace, by defending property, by diminishing the price of law, and by observing strict economy in every department of the State. Let the Government do this: the People will assuredly do the rest.

1830

⊷ ⚌⚉⚌ ⊶

Parliamentary Papers ("Blue Books")

Factories, mills, and mines all employed women and children as cheap labor. They often worked grueling hours under appalling conditions, for wages that barely enabled them to subsist. Their misery attracted the attention of various official fact-finding commissions, whose horrifying reports, known as the "Blue Books," revealed that five-year-old children slaved in pitch-dark mines for twelve hours a day, and that pregnant and half-naked women crawled through mineshafts hauling heavy loads of coal. Such investigations helped bring about the 1833 and 1842 Factory Acts that prohibited the employment of children under nine, and limited those under twelve to forty-eight hours of work per week. In the following passages young girls testify before Parliamentary commissions about the circumstances of their lives.

Testimony of Hannah Goode, a Child Textile Worker

I work at Mr. Wilson's mill. I attend the drawing-head.[1] I get 5s. 9d. It is four or five years since we worked double hours. We only worked an hour over then. We got a penny for that. We went in the morning at six o'clock by the mill clock. It is about half past five by our clock at home when we go in, and we are about a quarter too fast by Nottingham. We come out at seven by the mill. The clock is in the engine-house. It goes like other clocks. I think the youngest child is about seven. There are only two males in the mill. I dare say there are twenty under nine years. They go in when we do and come out when we do. The smallest children work at the cards,[2] and doffing the spinning bobbins.[3] I work in that room. We never stop to take our meals, except at dinner. It has gone on so this six years and more. It is called an hour for dinner from coming out to going in. We have a full hour. Some stop in, if they have a mind. The men stop half an hour at dinner-time to clean the wheels. The children stop to clean their own work; that may take them five or ten minutes or so. That is taken out of the dinner-time. William Crookes is overlooker in our room; he is cross-tempered sometimes. He does not beat me; he beats the little children if they do not do their work right. They want beating now and then. He has a strap; he never beats them with any thing else, except his hand. The children are in a middling way as to goodness. I have sometimes seen the little children drop asleep or so, but not lately. If they are catched asleep they get the strap. They are always very tired at night. I have weakened[4] them sometimes to prevent Crookes seeing them; not very often, because they don't often go to sleep. Sometimes they play about the street when they come out; sometimes they go home. The girls often go home and sew. I sit up often till nine or ten o'clock at

---

1. The drawing-frame, a machine which drew out, or lengthened, the wool after it had been carded.
2. Work at the carding machine, which consisted of rollers studded with wires to comb the wool and remove debris.

3. Removing the full bobbins or spindles of wool, and taking them to other machines to be made into thread.
4. Wakened.

home, picking the spinners waste. I get 2½d. a pound for that. I can pick about half a pound a night, working very hard. I have known the people complain of their children getting beat. There is no rule about not beating the children. When the engine stops, all stops except the reeling. The reelers are all grown up. I can read a little; I can't write. I used to go to school before I went to the mill; I have [not] since. I am sixteen. We have heard nothing in our mill about not working so long.

1833

Testimony of Ann and Elizabeth Eggley, Child Mineworkers

Ann Eggley, eighteen years old.———I'm sure I don't know how to spell my name. We go at four in the morning, and sometimes at half-past four. We begin to work as soon as we get down. We get out after four, sometimes at five, in the evening. We work the whole time except an hour for dinner, and sometimes we haven't time to eat. I hurry[1] by myself, and have done so for long. I know the corves are very heavy they are the biggest corves anywhere about. The work is far too hard for me; the sweat runs off me all over sometimes. I am very tired at night. Sometimes when we get home at night we have not power to wash us, and then we go to bed. Sometimes we fall asleep in the chair. Father said last night it was both a shame and a disgrace for girls to work as we do, but there was nought else for us to do. I have tried to get wind-ing[2] to do, but could not. I begun to hurry when I was seven and I have been hurrying ever since. I have been 11 years in the pit. The girls are always tired. I was poorly twice this winter; it was with headache. I hurry for Robert Wiggins; he is not akin to me. I riddle[3] for him. We all riddle for them except the littlest when there is two. We don't always get enough to eat and drink, but we get a good supper. I have known my father go at two in the morning to work when we worked at Twibell's, where there is a day-hole to the pit, and he didn't come out till four. I am quite sure that we work constantly 12 hours except on Saturdays. We wear trousers and our shifts[4] in the pit, and great big shoes clinkered and nailed. The girls never work naked to the waist in our pit. The men don't insult us in the pit. The conduct of the girls in the pit is good enough sometimes, and sometimes bad enough. I never went to a day-school. I went a little to a Sunday-school, but I soon gave it over. I thought it too bad to be con-fined both Sundays and week-days. I walk about and get the fresh air on Sundays. I have not learnt to read. I don't know my letters. I never learnt nought. I never go to church or chapel; there is no church or chapel at Gawber, there is none nearer than a mile. If I was married I would not go to the pits, but I know some married women that do. The men do not insult the girls with us, but I think they do in some. I have never heard that a good man came into the world who was God's Son to save sinners. I never heard of Christ at all. Nobody has ever told me about him, nor have my father and mother ever taught me to pray. I know no prayer: I never pray. I have been taught nothing about such things.

Elizabeth Eggley, sixteen years old.———I am sister to the last witness. I hurry in the same pit, and work for my father. I find my work very much too hard for me. I hurry alone. It tires me in my arms and back most. We go to work between four and five in the morning. If we are not there by half past five we are not allowed to

---

1. A hurrier pushed carriages loaded with ore through the mineshafts. These handtrucks, called corves, weighed as much as 800 pounds.

2. Helping to hoist the coal up the shaft to the surface.
3. Sift the coal through a sieve.
4. Loose-fitting undergarments.

go down at all. We come out at four, five, or six at night as it happens. We stop in generally 12 hours, and sometimes longer. We have to hurry only from the bank-face down to the horse-gate and back. I am sure it is very hard work and tires us very much; it is too hard for girls to do. We sometimes go to sleep before we get to bed. We haven't a very good house; we have but two rooms for all the family. I have never been to school except four times, and then I gave over because I could not get things to go in.[5] I cannot read: I do not know my letters. I don't know who Jesus Christ was. I never heard of Adam either. I never heard about them at all. I have often been obliged to stop in bed all Sunday to rest myself. I never go to church or chapel.

1842

━ ◄◆► ━

Charles Dickens
1812–1870

The most popular novelist of his century, Dickens combined dramatic plots and brilliantly comic characters to explore themes of all kinds, including the human costs of industrialism and materialism. Two of his portrayals of the new industrial landscape are given here. During the "railway mania" of the 1840s, nearly nine thousand miles of new track were laid across Britain. In 1842 the young Queen Victoria took her first railway journey, and was "quite charmed by it"—though she was also criticized for having risked her life. The railroads were a visible symbol of progress, but as Dickens dramatizes in his novel *Dombey and Son,* their construction brought about a vast demolition of neighborhoods and upheaval of the landscape. In the later novel *Hard Times,* Dickens portrays industrial Manchester as "Coketown" because of the coal residue that blackened the city. He emphasizes the dreary regimentation and the loss of personal identity produced by the mechanization of labor. The workers who tended the machines were called "hands," a term that aptly symbolized their dehumanization. But, as Dickens insists throughout *Hard Times,* oppressive working conditions were only part of the problem; the factory system also fostered alienation and hostility between classes, and the masters were apparently content for their workers to be deprived of education, religion, and even entertainment.

from Dombey and Son
[THE COMING OF THE RAILWAY]

The first shock of a great earthquake had, just at that period, rent the whole neighbourhood to its centre.[1] Traces of its course were visible on every side. Houses were knocked down; streets broken through and stopped; deep pits and trenches dug in the ground; enormous heaps of earth and clay thrown up; buildings that were undermined and shaking, propped by great beams of wood. Here, a chaos of carts, overthrown and jumbled together, lay topsy-turvy at the bottom of a steep unnatural hill; there, confused treasures of iron soaked and rusted in something that had accidentally become a pond. Everywhere were bridges that led nowhere; thoroughfares that were wholly impassable; Babel towers[2] of chimneys, wanting half their height; temporary wooden

---

5. I.e., proper clothing.
1. Dickens is describing the construction of the London-Birmingham railway, which demolished many buildings in Camden Town, an area in London he knew as a boy. The

line opened in 1838.
2. The tower of Babel was supposed to have been built high enough to reach heaven (Genesis 11).

houses and enclosures, in the most unlikely situations; carcases of ragged tenements, and fragments of unfinished walls and arches, and piles of scaffolding, and wilderness-es of bricks, and giant forms of cranes, and tripods straddling above nothing. There were a hundred thousand shapes and substances of incompleteness, wildly mingled out of their places, upside down, burrowing in the earth, aspiring in the air, moulder-ing in the water, and unintelligible as any dream. Hot springs and fiery eruptions, the usual attendants upon earthquakes, lent their contributions of confusion to the scene. Boiling water hissed and heaved within dilapidated walls; whence, also, the glare and roar of flames came issuing forth; and mounds of ashes blocked up rights of way, and wholly changed the law and custom of the neighbourhood.

In short, the yet unfinished and unopened Railroad was in progress; and, from the very core of all this dire disorder, trailed smoothly away, upon its mighty course of civilisation and improvement.

But as yet, the neighbourhood was shy to own the Railroad. One or two bold speculators had projected streets; and one had built a little, but had stopped among the mud and ashes to consider farther of it. A bran-new Tavern, redolent of fresh mortar and size, and fronting nothing at all, had taken for its sign The Railway Arms; but that might be rash enterprise—and then it hoped to sell drink to the workmen. So, the Excavators' House of Call had sprung up from a beer-shop; and the old-estab-lished Ham and Beef Shop had become the Railway Eating House, with a roast leg of pork daily, through interested motives of a similar immediate and popular descrip-tion. Lodging-house keepers were favourable in like manner; and for the like reasons were not to be trusted. The general belief was very slow. There were frowzy fields, and cow-houses, and dunghills, and dustheaps, and ditches, and gardens, and sum-mer-houses, and carpet-beating grounds, at the very door of the Railway. Little tumuli[3] of oyster shells in the oyster season, and of lobster shells in the lobster season, and of broken crockery and faded cabbage leaves in all seasons, encroached upon its high places. Posts, and rails, and old cautions to trespassers, and backs of mean hous-es, and patches of wretched vegetation, stared it out of countenance. Nothing was the better for it, or thought of being so. If the miserable waste ground lying near it could have laughed, it would have laughed it to scorn, like many of the miserable neighbours.

1846

from Hard Times
[COKETOWN]

Coketown, to which Messrs Bounderby and Gradgrind[1] now walked, was a triumph of fact; it had no greater taint of fancy in it than Mrs Gradgrind herself. Let us strike the key-note, Coketown, before pursuing our tune.

It was a town of red brick, or of brick that would have been red if the smoke and ashes had allowed it; but, as matters stood it was a town of unnatural red and black like the painted face of a savage. It was a town of machinery and tall chimneys, out of which interminable serpents of smoke trailed themselves for ever and ever, and

---

3. Artificial mounds. Oysters, a luxury today, were popular with poor people in Dickens's day; in *Pickwick Papers* Sam Weller says: "Poverty and oysters always seem to go together."

1. Bounderby is a mill owner; Gradgrind runs a school on Utilitarian principles.

never got uncoiled. It had a black canal in it, and a river that ran purple with ill-smelling dye, and vast piles of building full of windows where there was a rattling and a trembling all day long, and where the piston of the steam-engine worked monotonously up and down, like the head of an elephant in a state of melancholy madness. It contained several large streets all very like one another, and many small streets still more like one another, inhabited by people equally like one another, who all went in and out at the same hours, with the same sound upon the same pavements, to do the same work, and to whom every day was the same as yesterday and tomorrow, and every year the counterpart of the last and the next.

These attributes of Coketown were in the main inseparable from the work by which it was sustained; against them were to be set off, comforts of life which found their way all over the world, and elegancies of life which made, we will not ask how much of the fine lady, who could scarcely bear to hear the place mentioned. The rest of its features were voluntary, and they were these.

You saw nothing in Coketown but what was severely workful. If the members of a religious persuasion built a chapel there—as the members of eighteen religious persuasions had done—they made it a pious warehouse of red brick, with sometimes (but this only in highly ornamented examples) a bell in a bird-cage on the top of it. The solitary exception was the New Church; a stuccoed edifice with a square steeple over the door, terminating in four short pinnacles like florid wooden legs. All the public inscriptions in the town were painted alike, in severe characters of black and white. The jail might have been the infirmary, the infirmary might have been the jail, the town-hall might have been either, or both, or anything else, for anything that appeared to the contrary in the graces of their construction. Fact, fact, fact, everywhere in the material aspect of the town; fact, fact, fact, everywhere in the immaterial. The M'Choakumchild school was all fact, and the school of design was all fact, and the relations between master and man were all fact, and everything was fact between the lying-in hospital and the cemetery, and what you couldn't state in figures, or show to be purchaseable in the cheapest market and saleable in the dearest, was not, and never should be, world without end, Amen.[2]

A town so sacred to fact, and so triumphant in its assertion, of course got on well? Why no, not quite well. No? Dear me!

No. Coketown did not come out of its own furnaces, in all respects like gold that had stood the fire. First, the perplexing mystery of the place was, Who belonged to the eighteen denominations? Because, whoever did, the labouring people did not. It was very strange to walk through the streets on a Sunday morning, and note how few of *them* the barbarous jangling of bells that was driving the sick and nervous mad, called away from their own quarter, from their own close rooms, from the corners of their own streets, where they lounged listlessly, gazing at all the church and chapel going, as at a thing with which they had no manner of concern. Nor was it merely the stranger who noticed this, because there was a native organization in Coketown itself, whose members were to be heard of in the House of Commons every session, indignantly petitioning for acts of parliament that should make these people religious by main force. Then, came the Teetotal Society, who complained that these same people *would* get drunk, and showed in tabular statements that they did get drunk, and proved at tea parties that no inducement, human or Divine (except a medal),

2. The conclusion of the Anglican form of the Lord's Prayer.

would induce them to forego their custom of getting drunk. Then, came the chemist and druggist, with other tabular statements, showing that when they didn't get drunk, they took opium. Then, came the experienced chaplain of the jail, with more tabular statements, outdoing all the previous tabular statements, and showing that the same people *would* resort to low haunts, hidden from the public eye, where they heard low singing and saw low dancing, and mayhap joined in it; and where A. B., aged twenty-four next birthday, and committed for eighteen months' solitary, had himself said (not that he had ever shown himself particularly worthy of belief) his ruin began, as he was perfectly sure and confident that otherwise he would have been a tip-top moral specimen. Then, came Mr Gradgrind and Mr Bounderby, the two gentlemen at this present moment walking through Coketown, and both eminently practical, who could, on occasion, furnish more tabular statements derived from their own personal experience, and illustrated by cases they had known and seen, from which it clearly appeared—in short it was the only clear thing in the case—that these same people were a bad lot altogether, gentlemen; that do what you would for them they were never thankful for it, gentlemen; that they were restless, gentlemen; that they never knew what they wanted; that they lived upon the best, and bought fresh butter, and insisted on Mocha coffee, and rejected all but prime parts of meat, and yet were eternally dissatisfied and unmanageable.

1854

━━━◆❖◆━━━

Benjamin Disraeli
1804–1881

The subtitle of Benjamin Disraeli's novel *Sybil*, "The Two Nations," encapsulates the Victorians' uneasy sense of being a divided society. The Hungry Forties were a time of unprecedented economic distress: Britain was the world's wealthiest nation, yet people were starving in the streets, and many feared that a revolution was in the offing. Thomas Carlyle had argued in *Past and Present* that "isolation is the sum-total of wretchedness to man." Here, Disraeli echoes his call for cooperation and benevolent paternalism to forge new relations between classes. Disraeli went on to become a Conservative Prime Minister, noted both for his nostalgic vision of aristocratic leadership, and for the domestic social reforms that took place during his administration.

from Sybil
[THE TWO NATIONS]

"It is a community of purpose that constitutes society," continued the younger stranger; "without that, men may be drawn into contiguity, but they still continue virtually isolated."

"And is that their condition in cities?"

"It is their condition everywhere; but in cities that condition is aggravated. A density of population implies a severer struggle for existence, and a consequent repulsion of elements brought into too close contact. In great cities men are brought together by the desire of gain. They are not in a state of co-operation, but of isolation, as to the making of fortunes; and for all the rest they are careless of neighbours. Christianity teaches us to love our neighbour as ourself; modern society acknowledges no neighbour."

"Well, we live in strange times," said Egremont, struck by the observation of his companion, and relieving a perplexed spirit by an ordinary exclamation, which often denotes that the mind is more stirred than it cares to acknowledge, or at the moment is able to express.

"When the infant begins to walk, it also thinks that it lives in strange times," said his companion.

"Your inference?" asked Egremont.

"That society, still in its infancy, is beginning to feel its way."

"This is a new reign," said Egremont, "perhaps it is a new era."

"I think so," said the younger stranger.

"I hope so," said the elder one.

"Well, society may be in its infancy," said Egremont, slightly smiling; "but, say what you like, our Queen reigns over the greatest nation that ever existed."

"Which nation?" asked the younger stranger, "for she reigns over two."

The stranger paused; Egremont was silent, but looked inquiringly.

"Yes," resumed the younger stranger after a moment's interval. "Two nations; between whom there is no intercourse and no sympathy; who are as ignorant of each other's habits, thoughts, and feelings, as if they were dwellers in different zones, or inhabitants of different planets; who are formed by a different breeding, are fed by a different food, are ordered by different manners, and are not governed by the same laws."

"You speak of—" said Egremont, hesitatingly.

"The Rich and the Poor."

1845

＊ ▰◆▰ ＊

Friedrich Engels
1820–1895

In the manufacturing city of Manchester, whose size had increased more than tenfold between 1760 and 1830, the average life expectancy of working people in 1841 was only twenty years. Friedrich Engels, a German who had come to Manchester to study the cotton trade, was so appalled by his observations of the urban poor that he wrote an exposé of their degradation, stressing the "hypocritical town planning" that insulated the middle class from the sight of squalor and suffering. Engels's book was published in German in 1845; it became a socialist classic, and laid the groundwork for Engels's collaboration with Karl Marx. Lenin called the book "a terrible indictment of capitalism and of the middle classes." It was finally translated into English in 1892.

from The Condition of the Working Class in England in 1844
from *The Great Towns*

London is unique, because it is a city in which one can roam for hours without leaving the built-up area and without seeing the slightest sign of the approach of open country. This enormous agglomeration of population on a single spot has multiplied a hundred-fold the economic strength of the two and a half million inhabitants concentrated there. This great population has made London the commercial capital of the world and has created the gigantic docks in which are assembled the thousands of ships which always cover the River Thames. I know nothing more imposing than the view one obtains of the river when sailing from the sea up to London Bridge. Especially above Woolwich the houses and docks are packed tightly together on both banks of the river. The further one goes up the river the thicker becomes the concentration of ships lying at anchor, so that eventually only a narrow shipping lane is left free in mid-stream. Here hundreds of steamships dart rapidly to and fro. All this is so magnificent and impressive that one is lost in admiration. The traveller has good reason to marvel at England's greatness even before he steps on English soil.

It is only later that the traveller appreciates the human suffering which has made all this possible. He can only realise the price that has been paid for all this magnificence after he has tramped the pavements of the main streets of London for some days and has tired himself out by jostling his way through the crowds and by dodging the endless stream of coaches and carts which fills the streets. It is only when he has visited the slums of this great city that it dawns upon him that the inhabitants of modern London have had to sacrifice so much that is best in human nature in order to create those wonders of civilisation with which their city teems. The vast majority of Londoners have had to let so many of their potential creative faculties lie dormant, stunted and unused in order that a small, closely-knit group of their fellow citizens could develop to the full the qualities with which nature has endowed them. The restless and noisy activity of the crowded streets is highly distasteful, and it is surely abhorrent to human nature itself. Hundreds of thousands of men and women drawn from all classes and ranks of society pack the streets of London. Are they not all human beings with the same innate characteristics and potentialities? Are they not all equally interested in the pursuit of happiness? And do they not all aim at happiness by following similar methods? Yet they rush past each other as if they had nothing in common. They are tacitly agreed on one thing only—that everyone should keep to the right of the pavement so as not to collide with the stream of people moving in the opposite direction. No one even thinks of sparing a glance for his neighbour in the streets. The more that Londoners are packed into a tiny space, the more repulsive and disgraceful becomes the brutal indifference with which they ignore their neighbours and selfishly concentrate upon their private affairs. We know well enough that this isolation of the individual—this narrow-minded egotism—is everywhere the fundamental principle of modern society. But nowhere is this selfish egotism so blatantly evident as in the frantic bustle of the great city. The disintegration of society into individuals, each guided by his private principles and each pursuing his own aims has been pushed to its furthest limits in London. Here indeed human society has been split into its component atoms.

From this it follows that the social conflict—the war of all against all—is fought in the open. * * * Here men regard their fellows not as human beings, but as pawns in the struggle for existence. Everyone exploits his neighbour with the result that the stronger tramples the weaker under foot. The strongest of all, a tiny group of capitalists, monopolise everything, while the weakest, who are in the vast majority, succumb to the most abject poverty.

What is true of London, is true also of all the great towns, such as Manchester, Birmingham and Leeds. Everywhere one finds on the one hand the most barbarous indifference and selfish egotism and on the other the most distressing scenes of misery and poverty. Signs of social conflict are to be found everywhere. Everyone turns his house into a fortress to defend himself—under the protection of the law—from the depredations of his neighbours. Class warfare is so open and shameless that it has to be seen to be believed. The observer of such an appalling state of affairs must shudder at the consequences of such feverish activity and can only marvel that so crazy a social and economic structure should survive at all.

Capital is the all-important weapon in the class war. Power lies in the hands of those who own, directly or indirectly, foodstuffs and the means of production. The poor, having no capital, inevitably bear the consequences of defeat in the struggle. Nobody troubles about the poor as they struggle helplessly in the whirlpool of modern industrial life. The working man may be lucky enough to find employment, if by his labour he can enrich some member of the middle classes. But his wages are so low that they hardly keep body and soul together. If he cannot find work, he can steal, unless he is afraid of the police; or he can go hungry and then the police will see to it that he will die of hunger in such a way as not to disturb the equanimity of the middle classes. While I was in England at least twenty or thirty people died of hunger under the most scandalous circumstances, and yet when an inquest was held the jury seldom had the courage to bring in a verdict in accordance with the facts. However clear and unequivocal the evidence, the middle classes, from whom the juries were drawn, always found a loophole which enabled them to avoid a verdict of "death from starvation." In such circumstances the middle classes dare not tell the truth, because if they did so, they would be condemning themselves out of their own mouths. * * *

Every great town has one or more slum areas into which the working classes are packed. Sometimes, of course, poverty is to be found hidden away in alleys close to the stately homes of the wealthy. Generally, however, the workers are segregated in separate districts where they struggle through life as best they can out of sight of the more fortunate classes of society. The slums of the English towns have much in common—the worst houses in a town being found in the worst districts. They are generally unplanned wildernesses of one- or two-storied terrace houses built of brick. Wherever possible these have cellars which are also used as dwellings. These little houses of three or four rooms and a kitchen are called cottages, and throughout England, except for some parts of London, are where the working classes normally live. The streets themselves are usually unpaved and full of holes. They are filthy and strewn with animal and vegetable refuse. Since they have neither gutters nor drains the refuse accumulates in stagnant, stinking puddles. Ventilation in the slums is inadequate owing to the hopelessly unplanned nature of these areas. A great many people live huddled together in a very small area, and so it is easy to imagine the nature of the air in these workers' quarters. However, in fine weather the streets are used for the drying of washing and clothes lines are stretched across the streets from house to house and wet garments are hung out on them.

We propose to describe some of these slums in detail. In London there is the well-known "rookery"[1] of St. Giles. * * * St. Giles is situated in the most densely-populated part of London and is surrounded by splendid wide streets which are used by the fashionable world. It is close to Oxford Street, Trafalgar Square and the Strand. It is a confused

1. An overcrowded and deteriorating district of tenement dwellings.

conglomeration of tall houses of three or four stories. The narrow, dirty streets are just as crowded as the main thoroughfares, but in St. Giles one sees only members of the working classes. The narrowness of the roads is accentuated by the presence of streetmarkets in which baskets of rotting and virtually uneatable vegetables and fruit are exposed for sale. The smell from these and from the butchers' stalls is appalling. The houses are packed from cellar to attic and they are as dirty inside as outside. No human being would willingly inhabit such dens. Yet even worse conditions are to be found in the houses which lie off the main road down narrow alleys leading to the courts. These dwellings are approached by covered passages between the houses. The extent to which these filthy passages are falling into decay beggars all description. There is hardly an unbroken windowpane to be seen, the walls are crumbling, the door posts and window frames are loose and rotten. The doors, where they exist, are made of old boards nailed together. Indeed in this nest of thieves doors are superfluous, because there is nothing worth stealing. Piles of refuse and ashes lie all over the place and the slops thrown out into the street collect in pools which emit a foul stench. Here live the poorest of the poor. Here the worst-paid workers rub shoulders with thieves, rogues and prostitutes. Most of them have come from Ireland or are of Irish extraction. Those who have not yet been entirely engulfed in the morass of iniquity by which they are surrounded are daily losing the power to resist the demoralising influences of poverty, dirt and low environment. * * *

However wretched may be the dwellings of some of the workers—who do at least have a roof over their heads—the situation of the homeless is even more tragic. Every morning fifty thousand Londoners wake up not knowing where they are going to sleep at night. The most fortunate are those who have a few pence in their pocket in the evening and can afford to go to one of the many lodging houses which exist in all the big cities. But these establishments only provide the most miserable accommodation. They are crammed full of beds from top to bottom— four, five and even six beds in a room—until there is no room for more. Each bed is filled to capacity and may contain as many as four, five or even six lodgers. The lodging house keeper allocates his accommodation to all his customers in rotation as they arrive. No attempt is made to segregate the sick and the healthy, the old and the young, the men and the women, the drunk and the sober. If these ill-assorted bed-fellows do not agree there are quarrels and fights which often lead to injuries. But if they do agree among themselves, it is even worse, for they are either planning burglaries or are engaged in practices of so bestial a nature that no words exist in a modern civilised tongue to describe them. Those who cannot afford a bed in a lodging house sleep where they can, in passages, arcades or any corner where the police and the owners are unlikely to disturb their slumbers. * * *

If we cross Blackstone Edge on foot or take the train we reach Manchester, the regional capital of South Lancashire, and enter the classic home of English industry. This is the masterpiece of the Industrial Revolution and at the same time the mainspring of all the workers' movements. Once more we are in a beautiful hilly countryside. The land slopes gently down towards the Irish Sea, intersected by the charming green valleys of the Ribble, the Irwell, the Mersey and their tributaries. A hundred years ago this region was to a great extent thinly populated marsh-land. Now it is covered with towns and villages and is the most densely-populated part of England. In Lancashire—particularly in Manchester—is to be found not only the origin but the heart of the industry of the United Kingdom. Manchester Exchange is the thermometer which records all the fluctuations of industrial and commercial activity. The evolution of the modern system of manufacture has reached its climax in Manchester. It was in the South Lancashire cotton industry that water and steam power first replaced hand machines. It was here that such machines as the power-loom and the self-acting mule replaced the old hand-loom and spinning wheel. It is here that the division of labour has been pushed to its furthest limits. These three factors are the essence of modern industry. In all three of them the cotton industry was the pioneer and remains ahead in all branches of industry. In the circumstances it is to be expected that it is in this region that the inevitable consequences of industrialisation in so far as they affect the working classes are most strikingly evident. Nowhere else can the life and conditions of the industrial proletariat be studied in all their aspects as in South Lancashire. Here can be seen most clearly the degradation into which the worker sinks owing to the introduction of steam power, machinery and the division of labour. Here, too, can be seen most the strenuous efforts of the proletariat to raise themselves from their degraded situation. I propose to examine conditions in Manchester in greater detail for two reasons. In the first place, Manchester is the classic type of modern industrial town. Secondly, I know Manchester as well as I know my native town and I know more about it than most of its inhabitants. * * *

* * * Owing to the curious lay-out of the town it is quite possible for someone to live for years in Manchester and to travel daily to and from his work without ever seeing a working-class quarter or coming into contact with an artisan. He who visits Manchester simply on business or for pleasure need never see the slums, mainly because the working-class districts and the middle-class districts are quite distinct. This division is due partly to deliberate policy and partly to instinctive and tacit agreement between the two social groups. In those areas where the two social groups happen to come into contact with each other the middle classes sanctimoniously ignore the existence of their less fortunate neighbours. In the centre of Manchester there is a fairly large commercial district, which is about half a mile long and half a mile broad. This district is almost entirely given over to offices and warehouses. Nearly the whole of this district has no permanent residents and is deserted at night, when only policemen patrol its dark, narrow thoroughfares with their bull's eye lanterns. This district is intersected by certain main streets which carry an enormous volume of traffic. The lower floors of the buildings are occupied by shops of dazzling splendour. A few of the upper stories on these premises are used as dwellings and the streets present a relatively busy appearance until late in the evening. Around this commercial quarter there is a belt of built up areas on the average one and a half miles in width, which is occupied entirely by working-class dwellings. This area of workers' houses includes all Manchester proper, except the centre. * * * The upper classes enjoy healthy country air and live in luxurious and comfortable dwellings which are linked to the centre of Manchester by omnibuses which run every fifteen or thirty minutes. To such an extent has the convenience of the rich been considered in the planning of Manchester that these plutocrats can travel from their houses to their places of business in the centre of the town by the shortest routes, which run entirely through working-class districts, without even realising how close they are to the misery and filth which lie on both sides of the road. This is because the main streets which run from the Exchange in all

directions out of the town are occupied almost uninterruptedly on both sides by shops, which are kept by members of the lower middle classes. In their own interests these shopkeepers should keep the outsides of their shops in a clean and respectable condition, and in fact they do so. These shops have naturally been greatly influenced by the character of the population in the area which lies behind them. Those shops which are situated in the vicinity of commercial or middle class residential districts are more elegant than those which serve as a facade for the workers' grimy cottages. Nevertheless, even the less pretentious shops adequately serve their purpose of hiding from the eyes of wealthy ladies and gentlemen with strong stomachs and weak nerves the misery and squalor which are part and parcel of their own riches and luxury. * * *

I am quite aware of the fact that this hypocritical town-planning device is more or less common to all big cities. * * * But in my opinion Manchester is unique in the systematic way in which the working classes have been barred from the main streets. Nowhere else has such care been taken to avoid offending the tender susceptibilities of the eyes and the nerves of the middle classes. Yet Manchester is the very town in which building has taken place in a haphazard manner with little or no planning or interference from the authorities. When the middle classes zealously proclaim that all is well with the working classes, I cannot help feeling that the politically "progressive" industrialists, the Manchester "bigwigs," are not quite so innocent of this shameful piece of town planning as they pretend.

* * * I will now give a description of the working-class districts of Manchester. The first of them is the Old Town, which lies between the northern limit of the commercial quarter and the River Irk. * * * Here one is really and truly in a district which is quite obviously given over entirely to the working classes, because even the shopkeepers and the publicans[2] of Long Millgate make no effort to give their establishments a semblance of cleanliness. The condition of this street may be deplorable, but it is by no means as bad as the alleys and courts which lie behind it, and which can be approached only by covered passages so narrow that two people cannot pass. Anyone who has never visited these courts and alleys can have no idea of the fantastic way in which the houses have been packed together in disorderly confusion in impudent defiance of all reasonable principles of town planning. And the fault lies not merely in the survival of old property from earlier periods in Manchester's history. Only in quite modern times has the policy of cramming as many houses as possible on to such space as was not utilised in earlier periods reached its climax. The result is that today not an inch of space remains between the houses and any further building is now physically impossible. * * *

* * * To the right and left a number of covered passages from Long Millgate give access to several courts. On reaching them one meets with a degree of dirt and revolting filth, the like of which is not to be found elsewhere. The worst courts are those leading down to the Irk, which contain unquestionably the most dreadful dwellings I have ever seen. In one of these courts, just at the entrance where the cov-

2. Pub-keepers.

ered passage ends there is a privy without a door. This privy is so dirty that the inhabitants of the court can only enter or leave the court if they are prepared to wade
through puddles of stale urine and excrement.

∗ ∗ ∗Enough of this! All along the Irk slums of this type abound. There is an
unplanned and chaotic conglomeration of houses, most of which are more or less
unhabitable. The dirtiness of the interiors of these premises is fully in keeping with
the filth that surrounds them. How can people dwelling in such places keep clean!
There are not even adequate facilities for satisfying the most natural daily needs.
There are so few privies that they are either filled up every day or are too far away for
those who need to use them. How can these people wash when all that is available is
the dirty water of the Irk? Pumps and piped water are to be found only in the better-
class districts of the town. Indeed no one can blame these helots[5] of modern civilisation if their homes are no cleaner than the occasional pigsties which are a feature of
these slums. ∗ ∗ ∗

This, then, is the Old Town of Manchester. On re-reading my description of
the Old Town I must admit that, far from having exaggerated anything, I have not
written vividly enough to impress the reader with the filth and dilapidation of a
district which is quite unfit for human habitation. The shameful lay-out of the Old
Town has made it impossible for the wretched inhabitants to enjoy cleanliness,
fresh air, and good health. And such a district of at least twenty to thirty thousand
inhabitants lies in the very centre of the second city in England, the most important factory town in the world. It is here that one can see how little space human
beings need to move about in, how little air—and what air!—they need to breathe
in order to exist, and how few of the decencies of civilisation are really necessary
in order to survive. It is true that this is the *Old Town* and Manchester people
stress this when their attention is drawn to the revolting character of this hell
upon earth. But that is no defence. Everything in this district that arouses our disgust and just indignation is of relatively recent origin and belongs to the industrial
age. The two or three hundred houses which survive from the earlier period of
Manchester's history have long ago been deserted by their original inhabitants. It
is only industry which has crammed them full of the hordes of workers who now
live there. It is only the modern industrial age which has built over every scrap of
ground between these old houses to provide accommodation for the masses who
have migrated from the country districts and from Ireland. It is only the industrial
age that has made it possible for the owners of these shacks, fit only for the accommodation of cattle, to let them at high rents for human habitations. It is only modern industry which permits these owners to take advantage of the poverty of the
workers, to undermine the health of thousands to enrich themselves. Only industry has made it possible for workers who have barely emerged from a state of serfdom to be again treated as chattels and not as human beings. The workers have
been caged in dwellings which are so wretched that no one else will live in them,
and they actually pay good money for the privilege of seeing these dilapidated hovels fall to pieces about their ears. Industry alone has been responsible for all this
and yet this same industry could not flourish except by degrading and exploiting
the workers.

1845

Henry Mayhew
1812–1887

In London, the most visible occupations of children were in the streets. They earned a precarious living hawking goods, begging, performing, and providing various services, from running errands to prostitution. Mayhew interviewed hundreds of street people, gathering four volumes of testimony about the lives of this exploited and neglected underclass. With an extraordinary ear for slang and oddities of speech, he shaped each narrative into a kind of dramatic monologue. By publishing "the history of a people, from the lips of the people themselves . . . in their own 'unvarnished' language," Mayhew gave voice to a multitude of forgotten workers. The critic John D. Rosenberg has described Mayhew's image of London as "a vast, ingeniously balanced mechanism in which each class subsists on the drippings and droppings of the stratum above, all the way from the rich, whom we scarcely glimpse, down to the deformed and starving, whom we see groping for bits of salvageable bone or decaying vegetables in the markets."

from London Labour and the London Poor
Watercress Girl

The little watercress girl who gave me the following statement, although only eight years of age, had entirely lost all childish ways, and was, indeed, in thoughts and manner, a woman. There was something cruelly pathetic in hearing this infant, so young that her features had scarcely formed themselves, talking of the bitterest struggles of life, with the calm earnestness of one who had endured them all. I did not know how to talk with her. At first I treated her as a child, speaking on childish subjects; so that I might, by being familiar with her, remove all shyness, and get her to narrate her life freely. I asked her about her toys and her games with her companions; but the look of amazement that answered me soon put an end to any attempt at fun on my part. I then talked to her about the parks, and whether she ever went to them. "The parks!" she replied in wonder, "where are they?" I explained to her, telling her that they were large open places with green grass and tall trees, where beautiful carriages drove about, and people walked for pleasure, and children played. Her eyes brightened up a little as I spoke; and she asked, half doubtingly, "Would they let such as me go there—just to look?" All her knowledge seemed to begin and end with water-cresses,[1] and what they fetched. She knew no more of London than that part she had seen on her rounds, and believed that no quarter of the town was handsomer or pleasanter than it was at Farringdon-market or at Clerkenwell, where she lived. Her little face, pale and thin with privation, was wrinkled where the dimples ought to have been, and she would sigh frequently. When some hot dinner was offered to her, she would not touch it, because, if she eat too much, "it made her sick," she said; "and she wasn't used to meat, only on a Sunday."

The poor child, although the weather was severe, was dressed in a thin cotton gown, with a threadbare shawl wrapped round her shoulders. She wore no covering

1. An herb whose leaves are used in salads and as garnishes.

to her head, and the long rusty hair stood out in all directions. When she walked she shuffled along, for fear that the large carpet slippers that served her for shoes should slip off her feet.

"I go about the streets with water-creases, crying, 'Four bunches a penny, water-creases.' I am just eight years old—that's all, and I've a big sister, and a brother and a sister younger than I am. On and off, I've been very near a twelve-month in the streets. Before that, I had to take care of a baby for my aunt. No, it wasn't heavy—it was only two months old; but I minded it for ever such a time— till it could walk. It was a very nice little baby, not a very pretty one; but, if I touched it under the chin, it would laugh. Before I had the baby, I used to help mother, who was in the fur trade; and, if there was any slits in the fur, I'd sew them up. My mother learned me to needle-work and to knit when I was about five. I used to go to school, too; but I wasn't there long. I've forgot all about it now, it's such a time ago; and mother took me away because the master whacked me, though the missus use'n't to never touch me. I didn't like him at all. What do you think? he hit me three times, ever so hard, across the face with his cane, and made me go dancing down stairs; and when mother saw the marks on my cheek, she went to blow him up,[2] but she couldn't see him—he was afraid. That's why I left school.

"The creases is so bad now, that I haven't been out with 'em for three days. They're so cold, people won't buy 'em; for when I goes up to them, they say, 'They'll freeze our bellies.' Besides, in the market, they won't sell a ha'penny hand-ful now—they're ris to[3] a penny and tuppence. In summer there's lots, and 'most as cheap as dirt; but I have to be down at Farringdon-market between four and five, or else I can't get any creases, because everyone almost—especially the Irish—is selling them, and they're picked up so quick. Some of the saleswomen—we never calls 'em ladies—is very kind to us children, and some of them altogether spiteful. The good one will give you a bunch for nothing, when they're cheap; but the oth-ers, cruel ones, if you try to bate them a farden less[4] than they ask you, will say, 'Go along with you, you're no good.' I used to go down to market along with another girl, as must be about fourteen, 'cos she does her back hair up. When we've bought a lot, we sits down on a door-step, and ties up the bunches. We nev-er goes home to breakfast till we've sold out; but, if it's very late, then I buys a penn'orth of pudden, which is very nice with gravy. I don't know hardly one of the people, as goes to Farringdon, to talk to; they never speaks to me, so I don't speak to them. We children never play down there, 'cos we're thinking of our living. No; people never pities me in the street—excepting one gentleman, and he says, says he, 'What do you do out so soon in the morning?' but he gave me nothink—he only walked away.

"It's very cold before winter comes on reg'lar—specially getting up of a morn-ing. I gets up in the dark by the light of the lamp in the court. When the snow is on the ground, there's no creases. I bears the cold—you must; so I puts my hands under my shawl, though it hurts 'em to take hold of the creases, especially when we

---

2. Scold him

3. Their price has risen to.

4. Give them a farthing (a quarter of a penny) less.

takes 'em to the pump to wash 'em. No; I never see any children crying—it's no use.

"Sometimes I make a great deal of money. One day I took 1s. 6d., and the creases cost 6d.; but it isn't often I get such luck as that. I oftener makes 3d. or 4d. than 1s.; and then I'm at work, crying, 'Creases, four bunches a penny, creases!' from six in the morning to about ten. What do you mean by mechanics?—I don't know what they are. The shops buys most of me. Some of 'em says, 'Oh! I ain't a-goin' to give a penny for these;' and they want 'em at the same price as I buys 'em at.

"I always give mother my money, she's so very good to me. She don't often beat me; but, when she do, she don't play with me. She's very poor, and goes out cleaning rooms sometimes, now she don't work at the fur. I ain't got no father, he's a father-in-law. No; mother ain't married again—he's a father-in-law. He grinds scissors, and he's very good to me. No; I dont mean by that that he says kind things to me, for he never hardly speaks. When I gets home, after selling creases, I stops at home. I puts the room to rights: mother don't make me do it, I does it myself. I cleans the chairs, though there's only two to clean. I takes a tub and scrubbing-brush and flannel, and scrubs the floor—that's what I do three or four times a week.

"I don't have no dinner. Mother gives me two slices of bread-and-butter and a cup of tea for breakfast, and then I go till tea, and has the same. We has meat of a Sunday, and, of course, I should like to have it every day. Mother has just the same to eat as we has, but she takes more tea—three cups, sometimes. No; I never has no sweet-stuff; I never buy none—I don't like it. Sometimes we has a game of 'honey-pots' with the girls in the court, but not often. Me and Carry H— carries the little 'uns. We plays, too, at 'kiss-in-the-ring.' I knows a good many games, but I don't play at 'em, 'cos going out with creases tires me. On a Friday night, too, I goes to a Jew's house till eleven o'clock on Saturday night. All I has to do is to snuff the candles and poke the fire. You see they keep their Sabbath then, and they won't touch anything; so they gives me my wittals[5] and 1½d., and I does it for 'em. I have a reg'lar good lot to eat. Supper of Friday night, and tea after that, and fried fish of a Saturday morning, and meat for dinner, and tea, and supper, and I like it very well.

"Oh, yes; I've got some toys at home. I've a fire-place, and a box of toys, and a knife and fork, and two little chairs. The Jews gave 'em to me where I go to on a Friday, and that's why I said they was very kind to me. I never had no doll; but I misses little sister—she's only two years old. We don't sleep in the same room; for father and mother sleeps with little sister in the one pair, and me and brother and other sister sleeps in the top room. I always goes to bed at seven, 'cos I has to be up so early.

"I am a capital hand at bargaining—but only at buying watercreases. They can't take me in. If the woman tries to give me a small handful of creases, I says, 'I ain't a goin' to have that for a ha'porth,' and I go to the next basket, and so on, all round. I know the quantities very well. For a penny I ought to have a full market hand, or as much as I could carry in my arms at one time, without spilling. For 3d. I has a lap full, enough to earn about a shilling; and for 6d. I gets as many as crams my basket. I can't read or write, but I knows how many pennies goes to a shilling, why, twelve, of

5. Victuals, food.

course, but I don't know how many ha'pence there is, though there's two to a penny. When I've bought 3*d*. of creases, I ties 'em up into as many little bundles as I can. They must look biggish, or the people won't buy them, some puffs them out as much as they'll go. All my money I earns I puts in a club and draws it out to buy clothes with. It's better than spending it in sweet-stuff, for them as has a living to earn. Besides it's like a child to care for sugar-sticks, and not like one who's got a living and vittals to earn. I ain't a child, and I shan't be a woman till I'm twenty, but I'm past eight, I am. I don't know nothing about what I earns during the year, I only know how many pennies goes to a shilling, and two ha'pence goes to a penny, and four fardens goes to a penny. I knows, too, how many fardens goes to tuppence—eight. That's as much as I wants to know for the markets."

[*A Boy Crossing-Sweeper*]

I found the lad who first gave me an insight into the proceedings of the associated crossing-sweepers crouched on the stone steps of a door in Adelaide-street, Strand; and when I spoke to him he was preparing to settle down in a corner and go to sleep—his legs and body being curled round almost as closely as those of a cat on a hearth.

The Boy Crossing-Sweepers. After a daguerrotype by Richard Beard, from Henry Mayhew's *London Labour and the London Poor,* 1851.

The moment he heard my voice he was upon his feet, asking me to "give a half-penny to poor little Jack."

He was a good-looking lad, with a pair of large mild eyes, which he took good care to turn up with an expression of supplication as he moaned for his halfpenny.

A cap, or more properly a stuff bag, covered a crop of hair which had matted itself into the form of so many paint-brushes, while his face, from its roundness of feature and the complexion of dirt, had an almost Indian look about it; the colour of his hands, too, was such that you could imagine he had been shelling walnuts.

He ran before me, treading cautiously with his naked feet, until I reached a convenient spot to take down his statement, which was as follows:—

"I've got no mother or father; mother has been dead for two years, and father's been gone more than that—more nigh five years—he died at Ipswich, in Suffolk. * * *

* * * "I used, when I was with mother, to go to school in the morning, and go at nine and come home at twelve to dinner, then go again at two and leave off at half-past four,—that is, if I behaved myself and did all my lessons right; for if I did not I was kept back till I *did* them so. Mother used to pay one shilling a-week, and extra for the copy-books and things. I can read and write—oh, yes, I mean read and write well—read anything, even old English; and I write pretty fair,—though I don't get much reading now, unless it's a penny paper—I've got one in my pocket now—it's the *London Journal*—there's a tale in it now about two brothers, and one of them steals the child away and puts another in his place, and then he gets found out, and all that, and he's just been falling off a bridge now.* * *

"After mother died, sister still kept on making nets,[1] and I lived with her for some time, until she told me she couldn't afford to keep me no longer, though she seemed to have a pretty good lot to do; but she would never let me go with her to the shops, though I could crochet, which she'd learned me, and used to run and get her all her silks and things what she wanted. But she was keeping company with a young man, and one day they went out, and came back and said they'd been and got married. It was him as got rid of me.

"He was kind to me for the first two or three months, while he was keeping her company; but before he was married he got a little cross, and after he was married he begun to get more cross, and used to send me to play in the streets, and tell me not to come home again till night. One day he hit me, and I said I wouldn't be hit about by him, and then at tea that night sister gave me three shillings, and told me I must go and get my own living. So I bought a box and brushes (they cost me just the money) and went cleaning boots, and I done pretty well with them, till my box was stole from me by a boy where I was lodging. He's in prison now—got six calendar for picking pockets.

"Sister kept all my clothes. When I asked her for 'em, she said they was disposed of along with all mother's goods; but she gave me some shirts and stockings, and such-like, and I had very good clothes, only they was all worn out. I saw sister after I left her, many times. I asked her many times to take me back, but she used to say, 'It

---

1. Hair-nets, which she sold to hair-dressers.

was not her likes, but her husband's, or she'd have had me back;' and I think it was true, for until he came she was a kind-hearted girl; but he said he'd enough to do to look after his own living; he was a fancy-baker by trade.

"I was fifteen the 24th of last May, sir, and I've been sweeping crossings now near upon two years. There's a party of six of us, and we have the crossings from St. Martin's Church as far as Pall Mall. I always go along with them as lodges in the same place as I do. In the daytime, if it's dry, we do anythink what we can—open cabs, or anythink; but if it's wet, we separate, and I and another gets a crossing—those who gets on it first, keeps it,—and we stand on each side and take our chance.

"We do it in this way:—if I was to see two gentlemen coming, I should cry out, 'Two toffs!' and then they are mine; and whether they give me anythink or not they are mine, and my mate is bound not to follow them; for if he did he would get a hiding from the whole lot of us. If we both cry out together, then we share. If it's a lady and gentleman, then we cries, 'A toff and a doll!' Sometimes we are caught out in this way. Perhaps it is a lady and gentleman and a child; and if I was to see them, and only say, 'A toff and a doll,' and leave out the child, then my mate can add the child; and as he is right and I wrong, then it's his party.

"If there's a policeman close at hand we mustn't ask for money; but we are always on the look-out for the policemen, and if we see one, then we calls out 'Phillup!' for that's our signal. One of the policemen at St. Martin's Church—Bandy, we calls him—knows what Phillup means, for he's up to us; so we had to change the word. (At the request of the young crossing-sweeper the present signal is omitted.)

"Yesterday on the crossing I got threepence halfpenny, but when it's dry like to-day I do nothink, for I haven't got a penny yet. We never carries no pockets, for if the policemen find us we generally pass the money to our mates, for if money's found on us we have fourteen days in prison. * * *

"When we see the rain we say together, 'Oh! there's a jolly good rain! we'll have a good day to-morrow.' If a shower comes on, and we are at our room, which we general are about three o'clock, to get somethink to eat—besides, we general go there to see how much each other's taken in the day—why, out we run with our brooms. * * *

"When we gets home at half-past three in the morning, whoever cries out 'first wash' has it. First of all we washes our feet, and we all uses the same water. Then we washes our faces and hands, and necks, and whoever fetches the fresh water up has first wash; and if the second don't like to go and get fresh, why he uses the dirty. Whenever we come in the landlady makes us wash our feet. Very often the stones cuts our feet and makes them bleed; then we bind a bit of rag round them. * * *

"When there's snow on the ground we puts our money together, and goes and buys an old shovel, and then, about seven o'clock in the morning, we goes to the shops and asks them if we shall scrape the snow away. We general gets twopence every house, but some gives sixpence, for it's very hard to clean the snow away, particular when it's been on the ground some time. It's awful cold, and gives us chilblains on our feet; but we don't mind it when we're working, for we soon gets hot then.

1849–1850   1861–1862

[END OF PERSPECTIVES: THE INDUSTRIAL LANDSCAPE]

⊶ ⊫⊹⊟ ⊶

John Stuart Mill
1806–1873

The name John Stuart Mill has become synonymous with genius. But for the Victorians it was also associated with outrageously radical views: Mill advocated sexual equality, the right to divorce, universal suffrage, free speech, and proportional representation. He first gained public attention as a social reformer, promoting the rationalist ideas of his godfather, Jeremy Bentham, founder of Utilitarianism. Mill went on to become the era's leading philosopher and political theorist, an outspoken member of Parliament, and Britain's most prestigious proponent of women's rights.

Mill's education is legendary: the Victorians were fond of social experiments, but few were stranger and more disturbing than James Mill's efforts to prove that a child could learn so much so early in life. He began teaching his son Greek at the age of three, making him memorize long lists of Greek words and their English translations. He also "home-schooled" his son in history, languages, calculus, logic, political economy, geography, psychology, and rhetoric. The boy's responsibilities included tutoring his younger siblings—eventually, eight of them—in these subjects. All this went on while his father, busy writing his multivolume *History of British India,* surveyed his children from the other end of the dining-room table.

As Mill's *Autobiography* shows, the human cost of the experiment was high. In an early draft he wrote that "I . . . grew up in the absence of love & in the presence of fear." His stern father denied Mill both pleasures and playmates, and so dominated the boy's mother that he interpreted her submissiveness as indifference to his existence. At fourteen, when his father declared his education finished, Mill had, by his own account, the knowledge of a man of forty—but he still could not brush his own hair.

Undaunted by such trivia, Mill decided he wanted to be "a reformer of the world." When he was seventeen, he founded the Utilitarian Society, which vigorously debated how to achieve the Utilitarian goal of bringing the greatest happiness to the greatest number of people. But at twenty he was plunged into depression when he realized that achieving all his goals would not satisfy him: "I seemed to have nothing left to live for." Overwork and the utter neglect of human emotion in his otherwise comprehensive education led Mill to a nervous breakdown in 1826.

Discovering that "the habit of analysis has a tendency to wear away the feelings," Mill gradually recovered by reading poetry, especially that of Wordsworth. The poet aroused his interest in "the common feelings and common destiny of human beings." Despite his assessment of himself as an "unpoetical nature," Mill became one of the most astute critics of his generation, recognizing before anyone else the unusual strengths and psychological motivations of both Tennyson and Browning. His essay *What is Poetry?* (1833) argues that true poetry expresses the passionate, solitary meditations of the author; it is not so much heard as "*overheard.*"

In 1823 Mill followed in his father's footsteps by taking a clerkship in the Examiner's Office of the East India Company, the commercial enterprise that, in effect, governed British India. He eventually headed the department, as his father had before him. The center of his professional life, however, was his own writing and political activism. His position allowed him time to become an energetic propagandist for radical causes and legal reform—he was even arrested at age seventeen, a few weeks after the job began, for distributing information on birth control. He also edited the *London and Westminster Review* (1836–1840), while writing important essays on Coleridge and Jeremy Bentham. His *System of Logic* (1843) and *Principles of Political Economy* (1848) immediately became standard works in the field; he followed these with influential books on philosophy, politics, and economics, including *Thoughts on Parliamentary Reform* (1859), *Utilitarianism* (1861), *Representative Government* (1861), and *Auguste Comte and Positivism* (1865).

The most significant event of Mill's adult life was meeting the brilliant and beautiful Harriet Taylor in 1830. She shared his radical views on women's rights, and they soon formed an intimate friendship. But she was married and the mother of three children, a fact which lent piquancy to their efforts to establish the legal right of divorce. They finally married in 1851, after the death of her husband. Mill claimed that she deserved equal credit for his works, calling them "joint productions" of their intellectual life together. "When two persons have their thoughts and speculations completely in common," he wrote in his *Autobiography*, "it is of little consequence . . . which of them holds the pen." After Harriet Taylor died in 1858, her daughter Helen became Mill's companion; she carried on their work in woman's rights into the twentieth century.

Mill retired from the East India Company in 1858 when the British government took over the company's affairs. Although he refused to seek votes or curry favor with any constituency, Mill was elected Member of Parliament for Westminster from 1865 to 1868, making memorable speeches on behalf of political reform, Irish freedom, and women's voting rights. A century ahead of mainstream Anglo-American lawmakers, he demanded nonsexist language for legislation, including a proposal that the Second Reform Bill (1867) be rewritten to replace the word "man" with the word "person." After his defeat in the election of 1868, Mill spent most of his remaining years in Avignon, France, where he died in 1873.

In the twentieth century, Mill's reputation has been sustained by the continuing relevance of his work. *On Liberty* (1859) has become the classic defense of the individual's right, in a modern society dominated by bureaucracy and mass culture, to resist the constraints of both government and public opinion. *The Subjection of Women* (1869) insists that men should grant "perfect equality" to women, demonstrating that "what is now called the nature of women is an eminently artificial thing—the result of forced repression in some directions, unnatural stimulation in others." These works also embody Mill's distinctive qualities as a writer and thinker: his arguments unfold with exceptional clarity, anticipating objections and providing interesting examples to prove his points; he makes his appeals to the reader on the basis of reason, no matter how emotionally charged the topic may be; and he displays an underlying concern for what is good for the public at large. Never content merely to assert human rights or display moral outrage, Mill dedicated himself to convincing others that freedom of thought and action—for women as well as for men—is not simply right but beneficial to society as a whole.

from On Liberty
from Chapter 2. Of the Liberty of Thought and Discussion

The time, it is to be hoped, is gone by, when any defence would be necessary of the "liberty of the press" as one of the securities against corrupt or tyrannical government. * * * If all mankind minus one, were of one opinion, and only one person were of the contrary opinion, mankind would be no more justified in silencing that one person, than he, if he had the power, would be justified in silencing mankind. Were an opinion a personal possession of no value except to the owner; if to be obstructed in the enjoyment of it were simply a private injury, it would make some difference whether the injury was inflicted only on a few persons or on many. But the peculiar evil of silencing the expression of an opinion is, that it is robbing the human race; posterity as well as the existing generation; those who dissent from the opinion, still more than those who hold it. If the opinion is right, they are deprived of the opportunity of exchanging error for truth: if wrong, they lose, what is almost as great a benefit, the clearer perception and livelier impression of truth, produced by its collision with error.

* * * The majority of the eminent men of every past generation held many opinions now known to be erroneous, and did or approved numerous things which no one will now justify. Why is it, then, that there is on the whole a preponderance among mankind of rational opinions and rational conduct? If there really is this preponderance—which there must be unless human affairs are, and have always been, in an almost desperate state—it is owing to a quality of the human mind, the source of everything respectable in man either as an intellectual or as a moral being, namely, that his errors are corrigible. He is capable of rectifying his mistakes, by discussion and experience. Not by experience alone. There must be discussion, to show how experience is to be interpreted. Wrong opinions and practices gradually yield to fact and argument: but facts and arguments, to produce any effect on the mind, must be brought before it. Very few facts are able to tell their own story, without comments to bring out their meaning. The whole strength and value, then, of human judgment, depending on the one property, that it can be set right when it is wrong, reliance can be placed on it only when the means of setting it right are kept constantly at hand. In the case of any person whose judgment is really deserving of confidence, how has it become so? Because he has kept his mind open to criticism of his opinions and conduct. Because it has been his practice to listen to all that could be said against him; to profit by as much of it as was just, and expound to himself, and upon occasion to others, the fallacy of what was fallacious. Because he has felt, that the only way in which a human being can make some approach to knowing the whole of a subject, is by hearing what can be said about it by persons of every variety of opinion, and studying all modes in which it can be looked at by every character of mind. No wise man ever acquired his wisdom in any mode but this. * * *

In the present age—which has been described as "destitute of faith, but terrified at scepticism"[1]—in which people feel sure, not so much that their opinions are true, as that they should not know what to do without them—the claims of an opinion to be protected from public attack are rested not so much on its truth, as on its importance to society. There are, it is alleged, certain beliefs, so useful, not to say indispensable to well-being, that it is as much the duty of governments to uphold those beliefs, as to protect any other of the interests of society. In a case of such necessity, and so directly in the line of their duty, something less than infallibility may, it is maintained, warrant, and even bind, governments, to act on their own opinion, confirmed by the general opinion of mankind. It is also often argued, and still oftener thought, that none but bad men would desire to weaken these salutary beliefs; and there can be nothing wrong, it is thought, in restraining bad men, and prohibiting what only such men would wish to practise. This mode of thinking makes the justification of restraints on discussion not a question of the truth of doctrines, but of their usefulness; and flatters itself by that means to escape the responsibility of claiming to be an infallible judge of opinions. But those who thus satisfy themselves, do not perceive that the assumption of infallibility is merely shifted from one point to another. The usefulness of an opinion is itself matter of opinion: as disputable, as open to discussion, and requiring discussion as much, as the opinion itself. There is the same need of an infallible judge of opinions to decide an opinion to be noxious, as to decide it to be false, unless the

---

1. By Thomas Carlyle in *Memoirs of the Life of Scott* (1838).

opinion condemned has full opportunity of defending itself. And it will not do to say that the heretic may be allowed to maintain the utility or harmlessness of his opinion, though forbidden to maintain its truth. The truth of an opinion is part of its utility. If we would know whether or not it is desirable that a proposition should be believed, is it possible to exclude the consideration of whether or not it is true? * * *

We have now recognised the necessity to the mental well-being of mankind (on which all their other well-being depends) of freedom of opinion, and freedom of the expression of opinion, on four distinct grounds; which we will now briefly recapitulate.

First, if any opinion is compelled to silence, that opinion may, for aught we can certainly know, be true. To deny this is to assume our own infallibility.

Secondly, though the silenced opinion be an error, it may, and very commonly does, contain a portion of truth; and since the general or prevailing opinion on any subject is rarely or never the whole truth, it is only by the collision of adverse opinions that the remainder of the truth has any chance of being supplied.

Thirdly, even if the received opinion be not only true, but the whole truth; unless it is suffered to be, and actually is, vigorously and earnestly contested, it will, by most of those who receive it, be held in the manner of a prejudice, with little comprehension or feeling of its rational grounds. And not only this, but, fourthly, the meaning of the doctrine itself will be in danger of being lost, or enfeebled, and deprived of its vital effect on the character and conduct: the dogma becoming a mere formal profession, inefficacious for good, but cumbering the ground, and preventing the growth of any real and heartfelt conviction, from reason or personal experience.

from *Chapter 3. Of Individuality, as One of the Elements of Well-Being*

* * * The majority, being satisfied with the ways of mankind as they now are (for it is they who make them what they are), cannot comprehend why those ways should not be good enough for everybody; and what is more, spontaneity forms no part of the ideal of the majority of moral and social reformers, but is rather looked on with jealousy, as a troublesome and perhaps rebellious obstruction to the general acceptance of what these reformers, in their own judgment, think would be best for mankind. Few persons, out of Germany, even comprehend the meaning of the doctrine which Wilhelm Von Humboldt, so eminent both as a *savant* and as a politician, made the text of a treatise—that "the end of man, or that which is prescribed by the eternal or immutable dictates of reason, and not suggested by vague and transient desires, is the highest and most harmonious development of his powers to a complete and consistent whole;" that, therefore, the object "towards which every human being must ceaselessly direct his efforts, and on which especially those who design to influence their fellow-men must ever keep their eyes, is the individuality of power and development;" that for this there are two requisites, "freedom, and variety of situations;" and that from the union of these arise "individual vigour and manifold diversity," which combine themselves in "originality."[1]

Little, however, as people are accustomed to a doctrine like that of Von Humboldt, and surprising as it may be to them to find so high a value attached to individuality, the question, one must nevertheless think, can only be one of degree. No one's idea of excellence in conduct is that people should do absolutely nothing but

1. From *The Sphere and Duties of Government* by Baron Wilhelm von Humboldt. Although written in 1791, this treatise was not published until 1852; it was translated into English in 1854.

copy one another. No one would assert that people ought not to put into their mode of life, and into the conduct of their concerns, any impress whatever of their own judgment, or of their own individual character. On the other hand, it would be absurd to pretend that people ought to live as if nothing whatever had been known in the world before they came into it; as if experience had as yet done nothing towards showing that one mode of existence, or of conduct, is preferable to another. Nobody denies that people should be so taught and trained in youth, as to know and benefit by the ascertained results of human experience. But it is the privilege and proper condition of a human being, arrived at the maturity of his faculties, to use and interpret experience in his own way. It is for him to find out what part of recorded experience is properly applicable to his own circumstances and character. * * *

He who lets the world, or his own portion of it, choose his plan of life for him, has no need of any other faculty than the ape-like one of imitation. He who chooses his plan for himself, employs all his faculties.

* * * A person whose desires and impulses are his own—are the expression of his own nature, as it has been developed and modified by his own culture—is said to have a character. One whose desires and impulses are not his own, has no character, no more than a steam-engine has a character. If, in addition to being his own, his impulses are strong, and are under the government of a strong will, he has an energetic character. Whoever thinks that individuality of desires and impulses should not be encouraged to unfold itself, must maintain that society has no need of strong natures—is not the better for containing many persons who have much character—and that a high general average of energy is not desirable.

In some early states of society, these forces might be, and were, too much ahead of the power which society then possessed of disciplining and controlling them. There has been a time when the element of spontaneity and individuality was in excess, and the social principle had a hard struggle with it. The difficulty then was, to induce men of strong bodies or minds to pay obedience to any rules which required them to control their impulses. To overcome this difficulty, law and discipline, like the Popes struggling against the Emperors, asserted a power over the whole man, claiming to control all his life in order to control his character—which society had not found any other sufficient means of binding. But society has now fairly got the better of individuality; and the danger which threatens human nature is not the excess, but the deficiency, of personal impulses and preferences. Things are vastly changed, since the passions of those who were strong by station or by personal endowment were in a state of habitual rebellion against laws and ordinances, and required to be rigorously chained up to enable the persons within their reach to enjoy any particle of security. In our times, from the highest class of society down to the lowest, every one lives as under the eye of a hostile and dreaded censorship. Not only in what concerns others, but in what concerns only themselves, the individual or the family do not ask themselves—what do I prefer? or, what would suit my character and disposition? or, what would allow the best and highest in me to have fair play, and enable it to grow and thrive? They ask themselves, what is suitable to my position? what is usually done by persons of my station and pecuniary circumstances? or (worse still) what is usually done by persons of a station and circumstances superior to mine? I do not mean that they choose what is customary, in preference to what suits their own inclination. It does not occur to them to have any inclination, except for what is customary. Thus the mind itself is bowed to the yoke: even in what people do for pleasure, conformity is the first thing thought of; they like in crowds; they exercise choice only among things commonly done: peculiarity of taste, eccentricity of conduct, are shunned equally with crimes: until by dint of not following their own nature, they have no nature to follow: their human capacities are withered and starved: they become incapable of any strong wishes or native pleasures, and are generally without either opinions or feelings of home growth, or properly their own. Now is this, or is it not, the desirable condition of human nature?* * *

Having said that Individuality is the same thing with development, and that it is only the cultivation of individuality which produces, or can produce, well-developed human beings, I might here close the argument: for what more or better can be said of any condition of human affairs, than that it brings human beings themselves nearer to the best thing they can be? or what worse can be said of any obstruction to good, than that it prevents this? Doubtless, however, these considerations will not suffice to convince those who most need convincing; and it is necessary further to show, that these developed human beings are of some use to the undeveloped—to point out to those who do not desire liberty, and would not avail themselves of it, that they may be in some intelligible manner rewarded for allowing other people to make use of it without hindrance.

In the first place, then, I would suggest that they might possibly learn something from them. It will not be denied by anybody, that originality is a valuable element in human affairs. There is always need of persons not only to discover new truths, and point out when what were once truths are true no longer, but also to commence new practices, and set the example of more enlightened conduct, and better taste and sense in human life. * * * Persons of genius, it is true, are, and are always likely to be, a small minority; but in order to have them, it is necessary to preserve the soil in which they grow. Genius can only breathe freely in an *atmosphere* of freedom. Persons of genius are, *ex vi termini* [by definition], *more* individual than any other people—less capable, consequently, of fitting themselves, without hurtful compression, into any of the small number of moulds which society provides in order to save its members the trouble of forming their own character. If from timidity they consent to be forced into one of these moulds, and to let all that part of themselves which cannot expand under the pressure remain unexpanded, society will be little the better for their genius. If they are of a strong character, and break their fetters, they become a mark for the society which has not succeeded in reducing them to commonplace, to point at with solemn warning as "wild," "erratic," and the like; much as if one should complain of the Niagara river for not flowing smoothly between its banks like a Dutch canal.* * *

In sober truth, whatever homage may be professed, or even paid, to real or supposed mental superiority, the general tendency of things throughout the world is to render mediocrity the ascendant power among mankind. In ancient history, in the middle ages, and in a diminishing degree through the long transition from feudality to the present time, the individual was a power in himself; and if he had either great talents or a high social position, he was a considerable power. At present individuals are lost in the crowd. In politics it is almost a triviality to say that public opinion now rules the world. The only power deserving the name is that of masses, and of governments while they make themselves the organ of the tendencies and instincts of masses. This is as true in the moral and social relations of private life as in public transactions. Those whose opinions go by the name of public opinion, are not always the same sort of public: in America they are the whole white population; in England, chiefly the middle class. But they are always a mass, that is to say, collective mediocrity. And what is a still greater novelty, the mass do not now take their opinions from dignitaries in Church or State, from ostensible leaders, or from books. Their thinking is done for them by men much like themselves, addressing them or speaking in their name, on the spur of the moment, through the newspapers. I am not complaining of all this. I do not assert that anything better is compatible, as a general rule, with the present low state of the human mind. But that does not hinder the government of mediocrity from being mediocre government. No government by a democracy or a numerous aristocracy, either in its political acts or in the opinions, qualities, and tone of mind which it fosters, ever did or could rise above mediocrity, except in so far as the sovereign Many have let themselves be guided (which in their best times they always have done) by the counsels and influence of a more highly gifted and instructed One or Few. The initiation of all wise or noble things, comes and must come from individuals; generally at first from some one individual. The honour and glory of the average man is that he is capable of following that initiative; that he can respond internally to wise and noble things, and be led to them with his eyes open. I am not countenancing the sort of "hero-worship" which applauds the strong man of genius for forcibly seizing on the government of the world and making it do his bidding in spite of itself.[2] All he can claim is, freedom to point out the way. The power of compelling others into it, is not only inconsistent with the freedom and development of all the rest, but corrupting to the strong man himself. It does seem, however, that when the opinions of masses of merely average men are everywhere become or becoming the dominant power, the counterpoise and corrective to that tendency would be, the more and more pronounced individuality of those who stand on the higher eminences of thought. It is in these circumstances most especially, that exceptional individuals, instead of being deterred, should be encouraged in acting differently from the mass. In other times there was no advantage in their doing so, unless they acted not only differently, but better. In this age, the mere example of nonconformity, the mere refusal to bend the knee to custom, is itself a service. Precisely because the tyranny of opinion is such as to make eccentricity a reproach, it is desirable, in order to break through that tyranny, that people should be eccentric. Eccentricity has always abounded when and where strength of character has abounded; and the amount of eccentricity in a society has generally been proportional to the amount of genius, mental vigour, and moral courage which it contained. That so few now dare to be eccentric, marks the chief danger of the time. * * *

* * * We have discarded the fixed costumes of our forefathers; every one must still dress like other people, but the fashion may change once or twice a year. We thus take care that when there is change it shall be for change's sake, and not from any idea of beauty or convenience; for the same idea of beauty or convenience would not strike all the world at the same moment, and be simultaneously thrown aside by all at another moment. But we are progressive as well as changeable: we continually make new inventions in mechanical things, and keep them until they are again superseded by better; we are eager for improvement in politics, in education, even in morals, though in this last our idea of improvement chiefly consists in persuading or forcing other people to be as good as ourselves. It is not progress that we object to; on the contrary, we flatter ourselves that we are the most progressive people who ever lived. It is individuality that we war against: we should think we had done wonders if we had made ourselves all alike;

---

2. Cf. Thomas Carlyle, *On Heroes and Hero-Worship* (1841).

forgetting that the unlikeness of one person to another is generally the first thing which draws the attention of either to the imperfection of his own type, and the superiority of another, or the possibility, by combining the advantages of both, of producing something better than either. We have a warning example in China—a nation of much talent, and, in some respects, even wisdom, owing to the rare good fortune of having been provided at an early period with a particularly good set of customs, the work, in some measure, of men to whom even the most enlightened European must accord, under certain limitations, the title of sages and philosophers. They are remarkable, too, in the excellence of their apparatus for impressing, as far as possible, the best wisdom they possess upon every mind in the community, and securing that those who have appropriated most of it shall occupy the posts of honour and power. Surely the people who did this have discovered the secret of human progressiveness, and must have kept themselves steadily at the head of the movement of the world. On the contrary, they have become stationary—have remained so for thousands of years; and if they are ever to be farther improved, it must be by foreigners. They have succeeded beyond all hope in what English philanthropists are so industriously working at—in making a people all alike, all governing their thoughts and conduct by the same maxims and rules; and these are the fruits. The modern *régime* of public opinion is, in an unorganized form, what the Chinese educational and political systems are in an organized; and unless individuality shall be able successfully to assert itself against this yoke, Europe, notwithstanding its noble antecedents and its professed Christianity, will tend to become another China.

1859

from The Subjection of Women
from *Chapter 1*

The object of this essay is to explain as clearly as I am able, the grounds of an opinion which I have held from the very earliest period when I had formed any opinions at all on social or political matters, and which, instead of being weakened or modified, has been constantly growing stronger by the progress of reflection and the experience of life: That the principle which regulates the existing social relations between the two sexes—the legal subordination of one sex to the other—is wrong in itself, and now one of the chief hindrances to human improvement; and that it ought to be replaced by a principle of perfect equality, admitting no power or privilege on the one side, nor disability on the other. * * *

* * * If the authority of men over women, when first established, had been the result of a conscientious comparison between different modes of constituting the government of society; if, after trying various other modes of social organization—the government of women over men, equality between the two, and such mixed and divided modes of government as might be invented—it had been decided, on the testimony of experience, that the mode in which women are wholly under the rule of men, having no share at all in public concerns, and each in private being under the legal obligation of obedience to the man with whom she has associated her destiny, was the arrangement most conducive to the happiness and well being of both; its general adoption might then be fairly thought to be some evidence that, at the time when it was adopted, it was the best: though even then the considerations which recommended it may, like so many other primeval social facts of the greatest impor-

tance, have subsequently, in the course of ages, ceased to exist. But the state of the case is in every respect the reverse of this. In the first place, the opinion in favour of the present system, which entirely subordinates the weaker sex to the stronger, rests upon theory only; for there never has been trial made of any other: so that experience, in the sense in which it is vulgarly opposed to theory, cannot be pretended to have pronounced any verdict. And in the second place, the adoption of this system of inequality never was the result of deliberation, or forethought, or any social ideas, or any notion whatever of what conduced to the benefit of humanity or the good order of society. It arose simply from the fact that from the very earliest twilight of human society, every woman (owing to the value attached to her by men, combined with her inferiority in muscular strength) was found in a state of bondage to some man. * * *

Some will object, that a comparison cannot fairly be made between the government of the male sex and the forms of unjust power which I have adduced in illustration of it,[1] since these are arbitrary, and the effect of mere usurpation, while it on the contrary is natural. But was there ever any domination which did not appear natural to those who possessed it? There was a time when the division of mankind into two classes, a small one of masters and a numerous one of slaves, appeared, even to the most cultivated minds, to be a natural, and the only natural, condition of the human race. No less an intellect, and one which contributed no less to the progress of human thought, than Aristotle, held this opinion without doubt or misgiving; and rested it on the same premises on which the same assertion in regard to the dominion of men over women is usually based, namely that there are different natures among mankind, free natures, and slave natures; that the Greeks were of a free nature, the barbarian races of Thracians and Asiatics of a slave nature.[2] But why need I go back to Aristotle? Did not the slaveowners of the Southern United States maintain the same doctrine, with all the fanaticism with which men cling to the theories that justify their passions and legitimate their personal interests? Did they not call heaven and earth to witness that the dominion of the white man over the black is natural, that the black race is by nature incapable of freedom, and marked out for slavery? some even going so far as to say that the freedom of manual labourers is an unnatural order of things anywhere. * * * The subjection of women to men being a universal custom, any departure from it quite naturally appears unnatural. But how entirely, even in this case, the feeling is dependent on custom, appears by ample experience. Nothing so much astonishes the people of distant parts of the world, when they first learn anything about England, as to be told that it is under a queen: the thing seems to them so unnatural as to be almost incredible. To Englishmen this does not seem in the least degree unnatural, because they are used to it; but they do feel it unnatural that women should be soldiers or members of Parliament. In the feudal ages, on the contrary, war and politics were not thought unnatural to women, because not unusual; it seemed natural that women of the privileged classes should be of manly character, inferior in nothing but bodily strength to their husbands and fathers. The independence of women seemed rather less unnatural to the Greeks than to other ancients, on account of the fabulous Amazons (whom they believed to be historical), and the partial example afforded by the Spartan women; who, though no less subordinate by law than in other Greek states, were more free in fact, and being trained to

---

1. Mill has been describing slave owners' power over slaves, or tyrants' power over their subjects.
2. In *Politics* Aristotle asserts that it is as natural for free

men to rule over slaves as for men to rule over women (sec. 1260a2–14).

bodily exercises in the same manner with men, gave ample proof that they were not naturally disqualified for them. There can be little doubt that Spartan experience suggested to Plato, among many other of his doctrines, that of the social and political equality of the two sexes.[3]

But, it will be said, the rule of men over women differs from all these others in not being a rule of force: it is accepted voluntarily; women make no complaint, and are consenting parties to it. In the first place, a great number of women do not accept it. Ever since there have been women able to make their sentiments known by their writings (the only mode of publicity which society permits to them), an increasing number of them have recorded protests against their present social condition: and recently many thousands of them, headed by the most eminent women known to the public, have petitioned Parliament for their admission to the Parliamentary Suffrage.[4] The claim of women to be educated as solidly, and in the same branches of knowledge, as men, is urged with growing intensity, and with a great prospect of success; while the demand for their admission into professions and occupations hitherto closed against them, becomes every year more urgent. Though there are not in this country, as there are in the United States, periodical Conventions and an organized party to agitate for the Rights of Women, there is a numerous and active Society organized and managed by women, for the more limited object of obtaining the political franchise. * * *

All causes, social and natural, combine to make it unlikely that women should be collectively rebellious to the power of men. They are so far in a position different from all other subject classes, that their masters require something more from them than actual service. Men do not want solely the obedience of women, they want their sentiments. All men, except the most brutish, desire to have, in the woman most nearly connected with them, not a forced slave but a willing one, not a slave merely, but a favourite. They have therefore put everything in practice to enslave their minds. The masters of all other slaves rely, for maintaining obedience, on fear; either fear of themselves, or religious fears. The masters of women wanted more than simple obedience, and they turned the whole force of education to effect their purpose. All women are brought up from the very earliest years in the belief that their ideal of character is the very opposite to that of men; not self-will, and government by self-control, but submission, and yielding to the control of others. All the moralities tell them that it is the duty of women, and all the current sentimentalities that it is their nature, to live for others; to make complete abnegation of themselves, and to have no life but in their affections. And by their affections are meant the only ones they are allowed to have—those to the men with whom they are connected, or to the children who constitute an additional and indefeasible tie between them and a man. When we put together three things—first, the natural attraction between opposite sexes; secondly, the wife's entire dependence on the husband, every privilege or pleasure she has being either his gift, or depending entirely on his will; and lastly, that the principal object of human pursuit, consideration, and all objects of social ambition, can in general be sought or obtained by her only through him—it would be a miracle if the object of being attractive to men had not become the polar star of feminine education and formation of character. * * *

* * *But I may go farther, and maintain that the course of history, and the tendencies of progressive human society, afford not only no presumption in favour of

---

3. See *The Republic*, 5: "Then, if we are to set women to the same tasks as men, we must teach them the same things. They must have the same two branches of training for mind and body and also be taught the art of war, and they must receive the same treatment" (trans. by F. M. Cornford).
4. This petition was presented in the House of Commons in 1866 by Mill himself; he was the first member of Parliament to advocate women's suffrage.

this system of inequality of rights, but a strong one against it; and that, so far as the whole course of human improvement up to this time, the whole stream of modern tendencies, warrants any inference on the subject, it is, that this relic of the past is discordant with the future, and must necessarily disappear.

For, what is the peculiar character of the modern world—the difference which chiefly distinguishes modern institutions, modern social ideas, modern life itself, from those of times long past? It is, that human beings are no longer born to their place in life, and chained down by an inexorable bond to the place they are born to, but are free to employ their faculties, and such favourable chances as offer, to achieve the lot which may appear to them most desirable. * * *

The social subordination of women thus stands out an isolated fact in modern social institutions; a solitary breach of what has become their fundamental law; a single relic of an old world of thought and practice exploded in everything else, but retained in the one thing of most universal interest; as if a gigantic dolmen,[5] or a vast temple of Jupiter Olympius, occupied the site of St. Paul's and received daily worship, while the surrounding Christian churches were only resorted to on fasts and festivals. * * *

Neither does it avail anything to say that the *nature* of the two sexes adapts them to their present functions and position, and renders these appropriate to them. Standing on the ground of common sense and the constitution of the human mind, I deny that any one knows, or can know, the nature of the two sexes, as long as they have only been seen in their present relation to one another. If men had ever been found in society without women, or women without men, or if there had been a society of men and women in which the women were not under the control of the men, something might have been positively known about the mental and moral differences which may be inherent in the nature of each. What is now called the nature of women is an eminently artificial thing—the result of forced repression in some directions, unnatural stimulation in others. It may be asserted without scruple, that no other class of dependents have had their character so entirely distorted from its natural proportions by their relation with their masters; for, if conquered and slave races have been, in some respects, more forcibly repressed, whatever in them has not been crushed down by an iron heel has generally been let alone, and if left with any liberty of development, it has developed itself according to its own laws; but in the case of women, a hot-house and stove cultivation has always been carried on of some of the capabilities of their nature, for the benefit and pleasure of their masters. * * *

Even the preliminary knowledge, what the differences between the sexes now are, apart from all question as to how they are made what they are, is still in the crudest and most incomplete state. Medical practitioners and physiologists have ascertained, to some extent, the differences in bodily constitution; and this is an important element to the psychologist: but hardly any medical practitioner is a psychologist. Respecting the mental characteristics of women; their observations are of no more worth than those of common men. It is a subject on which nothing final can be known, so long as those who alone can really know it, women themselves, have given but little testimony, and that little, mostly suborned. It is easy to know stupid women. Stupidity is much the same all the world over. A stupid person's notions and feelings may confidently be inferred from those which prevail in the circle by which the person is surrounded. Not so with those whose opinions and feelings are an emanation from their own nature and faculties. It is only a man here and there

---

5. Prehistoric monument of standing stones, associated with pagan religious rites.

who has any tolerable knowledge of the character even of the women of his own family. I do not mean, of their capabilities; these nobody knows, not even themselves, because most of them have never been called out. I mean their actually existing thoughts and feelings. Many a man thinks he perfectly understands women, because he has had amatory relations with several, perhaps with many of them. If he is a good observer, and his experience extends to quality as well as quantity, he may have learnt something of one narrow department of their nature—an important department, no doubt. But of all the rest of it, few persons are generally more ignorant, because there are few from whom it is so carefully hidden. The most favourable case which a man can generally have for studying the character of a woman, is that of his own wife: for the opportunities are greater, and the cases of complete sympathy not so unspeakably rare. And in fact, this is the source from which any knowledge worth having on the subject has, I believe, generally come. But most men have not had the opportunity of studying in this way more than a single case: accordingly one can, to an almost laughable degree, infer what a man's wife is like, from his opinions about women in general. To make even this one case yield any result, the woman must be worth knowing, and the man not only a competent judge, but of a character so sympathetic in itself, and so well adapted to hers, that he can either read her mind by sympathetic intuition, or has nothing in himself which makes her shy of disclosing it. Hardly anything, I believe, can be more rare than this conjunction. It often happens that there is the most complete unity of feeling and community of interests as to all external things, yet the one has as little admission into the internal life of the other as if they were common acquaintance. Even with true affection, authority on the one side and subordination on the other prevent perfect confidence. Though nothing may be intentionally withheld, much is not shown. * * * When we further consider that to understand one woman is not necessarily to understand any other woman; that even if he could study many women of one rank, or of one country, he would not thereby understand women of other ranks or countries; and even if he did, they are still only the women of a single period of history; we may safely assert that the knowledge which men can acquire of women, even as they have been and are, without reference to what they might be, is wretchedly imperfect and superficial, and always will be so, until women themselves have told all that they have to tell.

And this time has not come; nor will it come otherwise than gradually. It is but of yesterday that women have either been qualified by literary accomplishments, or permitted by society, to tell anything to the general public. As yet very few of them dare tell anything, which men, on whom their literary success depends, are unwilling to hear. Let us remember in what manner, up to a very recent time, the expression, even by a male author, of uncustomary opinions, or what are deemed eccentric feelings, usually was, and in some degree still is, received; and we may form some faint conception under what impediments a woman, who is brought up to think custom and opinion her sovereign rule, attempts to express in books anything drawn from the depths of her own nature. * * * Literary women are becoming more freespoken, and more willing to express their real sentiments. Unfortunately, in this country especially, they are themselves such artificial products, that their sentiments are compounded of a small element of individual observation and consciousness, and a very large one of acquired associations. This will be less and less the case, but it will remain true to a great extent, as long as social institutions do not admit the same free development of originality in women which is possible to men. When that time comes, and not before, we shall see, and not merely hear, as much as it is necessary to know of the nature of women, and the adaptation of other things to it. * * *

One thing we may be certain of—that what is contrary to women's nature to do, they never will be made to do by simply giving their nature free play. The anxiety of mankind to interfere in behalf of nature, for fear lest nature should not succeed in effecting its purpose, is an altogether unnecessary solicitude. What women by nature cannot do, it is quite superfluous to forbid them from doing. What they can do, but not so well as the men who are their competitors, competition suffices to exclude them from; since nobody asks for protective duties and bounties in favour of women; it is only asked that the present bounties and protective duties in favour of men should be recalled. If women have a greater natural inclination for some things than for others, there is no need of laws or social inculcation to make the majority of them do the former in preference to the latter. Whatever women's services are most wanted for, the free play of competition will hold out the strongest inducements to them to undertake. And, as the words imply, they are most wanted for the things for which they are most fit; by the apportionment of which to them, the collective faculties of the two sexes can be applied on the whole with the greatest sum of valuable result.

The general opinion of men is supposed to be, that the natural vocation of a woman is that of a wife and mother. I say, is supposed to be, because, judging from acts—from the whole of the present constitution of society—one might infer that their opinion was the direct contrary. They might be supposed to think that the alleged natural vocation of women was of all things the most repugnant to their nature; insomuch that if they are free to do anything else—if any other means of living, or occupation of their time and faculties, is open, which has any chance of appearing desirable to them—there will not be enough of them who will be willing to accept the condition said to be natural to them. If this is the real opinion of men in general, it would be well that it should be spoken out. I should like to hear somebody openly enunciating the doctrine (it is already implied in much that is written on the subject)—"It is necessary to society that women should marry and produce children. They will not do so unless they are compelled. Therefore it is necessary to compel them." The merits of the case would then be clearly defined. It would be exactly that of the slaveholders of South Carolina and Louisiana. "It is necessary that cotton and sugar should be grown. White men cannot produce them. Negroes will not, for any wages which we choose to give. *Ergo* they must be compelled." An illustration still closer to the point is that of impressment.[6] Sailors must absolutely be had to defend the country. It often happens that they will not voluntarily enlist. Therefore there must be the power of forcing them. How often has this logic been used! and, but for one flaw in it, without doubt it would have been successful up to this day. But it is open to the retort—First pay the sailors the honest value of their labour. When you have made it as well worth their while to serve you, as to work for other employers, you will have no more difficulty than others have in obtaining their services. To this there is no logical answer except "I will not": and as people are now not only ashamed, but are not desirous, to rob the labourer of his hire,[7] impressment is no longer advocated. Those who attempt to force women into marriage by closing all other doors against them, lay themselves open to a similar retort. If they mean what they say, their opinion must evidently be, that men do not render the married condition so desirable to women, as to induce them to accept it for its own recommendations. It is not a sign of one's thinking the boon one offers very attractive, when one allows only Hobson's choice, "that or

6. The practice of seizing men and forcing them to serve   7. Luke 10.7.
as sailors in the navy.

none." And here, I believe, is the clue to the feelings of those men, who have a real antipathy to the equal freedom of women. I believe they are afraid, not lest women should be unwilling to marry, for I do not think that any one in reality has that apprehension; but lest they should insist that marriage should be on equal conditions; lest all women of spirit and capacity should prefer doing almost anything else, not in their own eyes degrading, rather than marry, when marrying is giving themselves a master, and a master too of all their earthly possessions. And truly, if this consequence were necessarily incident to marriage, I think that the apprehension would be very well founded. I agree in thinking it probable that few women, capable of anything else, would, unless under an irresistible *entraînement* [enchantment], rendering them for the time insensible to anything but itself, choose such a lot, when any other means were open to them of filling a conventionally honourable place in life: and if men are determined that the law of marriage shall be a law of despotism, they are quite right, in point of mere policy, in leaving to women only Hobson's choice. But, in that case, all that has been done in the modern world to relax the chain on the minds of women, has been a mistake. They never should have been allowed to receive a literary education. Women who read, much more women who write, are, in the existing constitution of things, a contradiction and a disturbing element: and it was wrong to bring women up with any acquirements but those of an odalisque,[8] or of a domestic servant.
1860   1869

Statement Repudiating the Rights of Husbands[1]

6th March 1851

Being about, if I am so happy as to obtain her consent, to enter into the marriage relation with the only woman I have ever known, with whom I would have entered into that state; and the whole character of the marriage relation as constituted by law being such as both she and I entirely and conscientiously disapprove, for this among other reasons, that it confers upon one of the parties to the contract, legal power and control over the person, property, and freedom of action of the other party, independent of her own wishes and will; I, having no means of legally divesting myself of these odious powers (as I most assuredly would do if an engagement to that effect could be made legally binding on me), feel it my duty to put on record a formal protest against the existing law of marriage, in so far as conferring such powers; and a solemn promise never in any case or under any circumstances to use them. And in the event of marriage between Mrs. Taylor and me I declare it to be my will and intention, and the condition of the engagement between us, that she retains in all respects whatever the same absolute freedom of action, and freedom of disposal of herself and of all that does or may at any time belong to her, as if no such marriage had taken place; and I absolutely disclaim and repudiate all pretence to have acquired any *rights* whatever by virtue of such marriage.

J. S. Mill

---

8. Concubine in a harem.
1. At the time Mill wrote this, shortly before his marriage to Harriet Taylor, married women occupied a peculiar position under British law. A woman, upon her marriage, entered into a state called coverture. This meant she was subsumed into the legal personhood of her husband, and could neither sign legal contracts nor own property.

Elizabeth Barrett Browning

1806–1861

Elizabeth Barrett Browning was the most celebrated woman poet of the Victorian era. She was admired by contemporaries as varied as William Wordsworth, Queen Victoria, Edgar Allan Poe (who introduced an American edition of her work), Christina Rossetti, and John Ruskin (who proclaimed *Aurora Leigh* the greatest poem in English). Her popularity was especially remarkable because she interspersed her ardent love lyrics with hard-hitting poems on radical political causes and feminist themes. In the United States, she influenced not only sequestered writers like Emily Dickinson, but also political activists like Susan B. Anthony.

The eldest of eleven children, Elizabeth Barrett grew up in a country manorhouse called Hope End in Hertfordshire. The Barretts were a wealthy family whose fortune derived from a slave plantation in Jamaica. While her submissive mother, Mary Clark, encouraged her to write, it was her protective but authoritarian father, Edward Moulton-Barrett, who dominated her affections and received laudatory poems on his birthdays. From an early age Barrett envisioned herself combining male and female attributes to become "the feminine of Homer." As the critic Dorothy Mermin has pointed out, the ambitious child-poet was already imaginatively inhabiting two gender roles, the imprisoned female muse and the active male quester: "At five I supposed myself a heroine and in my day dreams of bliss I constantly imaged to myself a forlorn damsel in distress rescued by some noble knight."

Barrett took advantage of her family's resources to give herself an exceptional education, unusual for a woman of her day. Her passion for Greek poetry led her to translate Aeschylus's *Prometheus Bound* (1833). Two earlier works also reflected her wide reading: at twelve she wrote a four-book epic, *The Battle of Marathon*, which her father had privately printed, and at twenty she anonymously published a long philosophical poem, *An Essay on Mind, with Other Poems* (1826). But her intellectual development was offset by an illness that broke her health at the age of fifteen. Thereafter, her bold aspirations and mental energy were at odds with her semi-invalid state. Her sense of isolation increased in 1828 when her mother died, and again when declining family fortunes led her father to move the family from the home she loved, first to Sidmouth, Devon, in 1832 and then to London in 1835, where they eventually settled at 50 Wimpole Street.

It was here that Barrett became almost a recluse. Disliking the dirty, foggy city, she hardly left the house, but she corresponded avidly with a circle of literary and public figures. In 1838 chronic lung disease weakened her further; she already had developed what would be a lifelong dependence on morphine as a painkiller. Her doctors insisted that she go to Mediterranean climes, but the farthest her father would allow was Torquay, on the south coast of England. She lived there for three years, returning prostrate with grief after her brother Edward died in a boating accident. For the next several years, her spirits sustained only by her poetry, she worked, slept, and received visitors on a couch in a room sealed against the London air. Often exhausted, she was unable to see the aged Wordsworth when he came to pay his respects.

As she and her small circle of friends were quick to realize, Elizabeth Barrett had become like Tennyson's Lady of Shalott, having no other life but to weave her poetic web in solitude. *The Seraphim and Other Poems* (1838) established her reputation, and the two volumes of *Poems* (1844) consolidated her position as the era's finest "poetess." The latter book included *A Drama of Exile*, a sequel to Milton's *Paradise Lost* in which Eve emerges as a heroine, and also *The Cry of the Children*, condemning child labor in factories. Despite her oppositional politics, the suppleness of her thought and her passionate voice were so highly regarded by critics and public alike that she was mentioned as a candidate for Poet Laureate when Wordsworth died in 1850.

But by then she had utterly transformed her life. In 1845 she began corresponding with Robert Browning—she was nearly forty, and famous; he was thirty-three and his only reputation was for obscurity. Their literary friendship rapidly blossomed into romance, which they had to hide from her father, who had tacitly forbidden his children to marry. After a secret marriage in London in 1846, the couple eloped to Italy, where they settled in Florence at Casa Guidi. There, the fairy tale continued: happily married and living in a warm climate, she recovered much of her health, wrote her best work, gained the love of the Italians with her nationalistic verse, and gave birth to a son, Robert Weidemann Browning ("Pen"), in 1849. She had prophetically written to Browning, in the last letter before their elopement: "I begin to think that none are so bold as the timid, when they are fairly roused."

Her union with Robert Browning was responsible for two works that have since formed the cornerstone of her reputation. The first is their justly famous correspondence. The story of their courtship was widely known, but its intimate details were not revealed until the publication of their letters in 1899. Second, as their relationship developed she wrote a series of love poems to Browning. She finished the last poem two days before their wedding, and the collection was published in 1850, under the deliberately misleading title *Sonnets from the Portuguese*. Among the most significant sonnet sequences since those of Shakespeare and Sidney, these poems revived the form in Victorian England and revised in brilliant new ways what had hitherto been a primarily masculine poetic tradition. Casting the male recipient of her sonnets in the role of sexual object, yet also allowing for his reciprocal passion and poetic drive, Barrett Browning records the interplay of gifted lovers whose desire is inseparable from their quest for verbal mastery.

In her final years Barrett Browning's career continued to flourish. She and her husband enjoyed a wide circle of friends, including Tennyson, Ruskin, Carlyle, Rossetti, and Margaret Fuller. They traveled a great deal, to Rome, Paris, and several times back to London where they were warmly received by both their families—with the exception of her father, who refused to forgive or even see her again. In 1851 she published *Casa Guidi Windows*, which promoted the cause of Italian independence from Austria. *Poems Before Congress* (1860) stirred controversy in England over its volatile and "unwomanly" political views, particularly its scathing attack on American slavery. But her health was failing, and after recurrent illnesses, she died in Florence in her husband's arms. *Last Poems* appeared posthumously in 1862.

Her greatest achievement, however, lies in her verse novel, *Aurora Leigh* (1856), a daring combination of epic, romance, and *bildungsroman*. The first major poem in English in which the heroine, like the author, is a woman writer, *Aurora Leigh* rewrites Wordsworth's *The Prelude* from a female point of view. With its Miltonic echoes, the blank-verse format claims epic importance not only for the growth of the woman poet, but also for a woman's struggle to achieve artistic and economic independence in modern society. The poem blends these themes, moreover, with a witty, Byronic treatment of Victorian manners and social issues, and an emotionally charged love plot that recalls Charlotte Bronte's *Jane Eyre*. The story of how the aspiring poet Aurora Leigh overcomes the prejudices of both a masculine audience and the man she loves, in order to find fame and happiness in Italy, closely mirrors Barrett Browning's own. The poem was an overwhelming success, even though many contemporary readers were scandalized by its radical revision of Victorian ideals of femininity, and its picture of how the two sexes might work together so that each could achieve its fullest human potential. Scorning to measure herself against any but the greatest male authors, Elizabeth Barrett Browning was the first to show English readers the enormous possibilities of a poetic tradition in which women participated on equal terms.

from Sonnets from the Portuguese[1]

1

I thought once how Theocritus had sung
Of the sweet years, the dear and wished-for years,
Who each one in a gracious hand appears
To bear a gift for mortals, old or young:[2]
5 And, as I mused it in his antique tongue,[3]
I saw, in gradual vision through my tears,
The sweet, sad years, the melancholy years,
Those of my own life, who by turns had flung
A shadow across me. Straightway I was 'ware,
10 So weeping, how a mystic Shape did move
Behind me, and drew me backward by the hair;
And a voice said in mastery, while I strove,—
"Guess now who holds thee?"—"Death," I said. But, there,
The silver answer rang,—"Not Death, but Love."

13

And wilt thou have me fashion into speech
The love I bear thee, finding words enough,
And hold the torch out, while the winds are rough,
Between our faces, to cast light on each?—
5 I drop it at thy feet. I cannot teach
My hand to hold my spirit so far off
From myself—me—that I should bring thee proof
In words, of love hid in me out of reach.
Nay, let the silence of my womanhood
10 Commend my woman-love to thy belief,—
Seeing that I stand unwon, however wooed,
And rend the garment of my life, in brief,
By a most dauntless, voiceless fortitude,
Lest one touch of this heart convey its grief.

21

Say over again, and yet once over again,
That thou dost love me. Though the word repeated
Should seem "a cuckoo-song,"[4] as thou dost treat it,
Remember, never to the hill or plain,

---

1. These very personal poems chronicle Elizabeth Barrett's courtship with Robert Browning. She did not show them to him until after they were married, when he pronounced them "the finest sonnets written in any language since Shakespeare's." He overcame her reluctance to publish them by proposing the somewhat cryptic title implying that they are merely translations.

2. In *Idylls* 15, Theocritus, a Greek pastoral poet of the 3rd century B.C., tells how "the dainty-footed Hours" brought Adonis to Aphrodite. The song celebrates the return of spring, the season when Elizabeth Barrett first met Robert Browning.
3. I.e., Greek.
4. Repetitious, like the cuckoo's song.

5 Valley and wood, without her cuckoo-strain
   Comes the fresh Spring in all her green completed.
   Belovèd, I, amid the darkness greeted
   By a doubtful spirit-voice, in that doubt's pain
   Cry, "Speak once more—thou lovest!" Who can fear
10 Too many stars, though each in heaven shall roll,
   Too many flowers, though each shall crown the year?
   Say thou dost love me, love me, love me—toll
   The silver iterance!°—only minding, Dear,   *repetition*
   To love me also in silence with thy soul.

22

When our two souls stand up erect and strong,
Face to face, silent, drawing nigh and nigher,
Until the lengthening wings break into fire
At either curvèd point,—what bitter wrong
5 Can the earth do to us, that we should not long
Be here contented? Think. In mounting higher,
The angels would press on us and aspire
To drop some golden orb of perfect song
Into our deep, dear silence. Let us stay
10 Rather on earth, Belovèd,—where the unfit
Contrarious moods of men recoil away
And isolate pure spirits, and permit
A place to stand and love in for a day,
With darkness and the death-hour rounding it.

28

My letters! all dead paper, mute and white!
And yet they seem alive and quivering
Against my tremulous hands which loose the string
And let them drop down on my knee to-night.
5 This said,—he wished to have me in his sight
Once, as a friend: this fixed a day in spring[5]
To come and touch my hand . . . a simple thing,
Yet I wept for it!—this, . . . the paper's light . . .
Said, *Dear, I love thee*; and I sank and quailed
10 As if God's future thundered on my past.
This said, *I am thine*—and so its ink has paled
With lying at my heart that beat too fast.
And this . . . O Love, thy words have ill availed
If, what this said, I dared repeat at last!

32

The first time that the sun rose on thine oath
To love me, I looked forward to the moon

5. On May 17, 1845, Robert Browning wrote to arrange their first meeting: "I will call at two on Tuesday."

To slacken all those bonds which seemed too soon
And quickly tied to make a lasting troth.
5   Quick-loving hearts, I thought, may quickly loathe;
And, looking on myself, I seemed not one
For such man's love!—more like an out-of-tune
Worn viol, a good singer would be wroth
To spoil his song with, and which, snatched in haste,
10 Is laid down at the first ill-sounding note.
I did not wrong myself so, but I placed
A wrong on *thee*. For perfect strains may float
'Neath master-hands, from instruments defaced,—
And great souls, at one stroke, may do and doat.

38

First time he kissed me, he but only kissed
The fingers of this hand wherewith I write;
And ever since, it grew more clean and white,
Slow to world-greetings, quick with its "Oh, list,"°   *listen*
5   When the angels speak. A ring of amethyst
I could not wear here, plainer to my sight,
Than that first kiss. The second passed in height
The first, and sought the forehead, and half missed,
Half falling on the hair. O beyond meed!°   *deserving*
10 That was the chrism[6] of love, which love's own crown,
With sanctifying sweetness, did precede.
The third upon my lips was folded down
In perfect, purple state; since when, indeed,
I have been proud and said, "My love, my own."

43

How do I love thee? Let me count the ways.
I love thee to the depth and breadth and height
My soul can reach, when feeling out of sight
For the ends of Being and ideal Grace.
5   I love thee to the level of everyday's
Most quiet need, by sun and candle-light.
I love thee freely, as men strive for Right;
I love thee purely, as they turn from Praise.
I love thee with the passion put to use
10 In my old griefs, and with my childhood's faith.
I love thee with a love I seemed to lose
With my lost saints,—I love with the breath,
Smiles, tears, of all my life!—and, if God choose,
I shall but love thee better after death.

1845–1847   1850

---

6. Consecrated oil used to anoint during a coronation.
1. Barrett Browning called *Aurora Leigh*, a poem in nine books, a "verse novel." It portrays the struggles of a young poet to find her artistic voice and pursue her vocation despite the obstacles confronting a woman writer.

from **Aurora Leigh**[1]

from *Book 1*

[SELF-PORTRAIT]

Of writing many books there is no end;
And I who have written much in prose and verse
For others' uses, will write now for mine,—
Will write my story for my better self,
5   As when you paint your portrait for a friend,
Who keeps it in a drawer and looks at it
Long after he has ceased to love you, just
To hold together what he was and is.
I, writing thus, am still what men call young;
10   I have not so far left the coasts of life
To travel inward, that I cannot hear
That murmur of the outer Infinite
Which unweaned babies smile at in their sleep
When wondered at for smiling; not so far,
15   But still I catch my mother at her post
Beside the nursery door, with finger up,
"Hush, hush—here's too much noise!" while her sweet eyes
Leap forward, taking part against her word
In the child's riot. Still I sit and feel
20   My father's slow hand, when she had left us both,
Stroke out my childish curls across his knee,
And hear Assunta's daily jest (she knew
He liked it better than a better jest)
Inquire how many golden scudi[2] went
25   To make such ringlets. O my father's hand,
Stroke heavily, heavily the poor hair down,
Draw, press the child's head closer to thy knee!
I'm still too young, too young, to sit alone.
I write. My mother was a Florentine,
30   Whose rare blue eyes were shut from seeing me
When scarcely I was four years old, my life
A poor spark snatched up from a failing lamp
Which went out therefore. She was weak and frail;
She could not bear the joy of giving life,
35   The mother's rapture slew her. If her kiss
Had left a longer weight upon my lips
It might have steadied the uneasy breath,
And reconciled and fraternised my soul
With the new order. As it was, indeed,
40   I felt a mother-want about the world,
And still went seeking, like a bleating lamb
Left out at night in shutting up the fold,—
As restless as a nest-deserted bird
Grown chill through something being away, though what

2. Italian coins; Assunta was Aurora's nurse.

45   It knows not. I, Aurora Leigh, was born
      To make my father sadder, and myself
      Not overjoyous, truly. Women know
      The way to rear up children (to be just),
      They know a simple, merry, tender knack
50   Of tying sashes, fitting baby-shoes,
      And stringing pretty words that make no sense,
      And kissing full sense into empty words,
      Which things are corals to cut life upon,
      Although such trifles: children learn by such,
55   Love's holy earnest in a pretty play
      And get not over-early solemnised,
      But seeing, as in a rose-bush, Love's Divine
      Which burns and hurts not,—not a single bloom,—
      Become aware and unafraid of Love.
60   Such good do mothers. Fathers love as well
      —Mine did, I know,—but still with heavier brains,
      And wills more consciously responsible,
      And not as wisely, since less foolishly;
      So mothers have God's license to be missed.

65   My father was an austere Englishman,
      Who, after a dry lifetime spent at home
      In college-learning, law, and parish talk,
      Was flooded with a passion unaware,
      His whole provisioned and complacent past
70   Drowned out from him that moment. As he stood
      In Florence, where he had come to spend a month
      And note the secret of Da Vinci's drains,[3]
      He musing somewhat absently perhaps
      Some English question . . . whether men should pay
75   The unpopular but necessary tax
      With left or right hand—in the alien sun
      In that great square of the Santissima[4]
      There drifted past him (scarcely marked enough
      To move his comfortable island scorn)
80   A train of priestly banners, cross and psalm,
      The white-veiled rose-crowned maidens holding up
      Tall tapers, weighty for such wrists, aslant
      To the blue luminous tremor of the air,
      And letting drop the white wax as they went
85   To eat the bishop's wafer[5] at the church;
      From which long trail of chanting priests and girls,
      A face flashed like a cymbal on his face
      And shook with silent clangour brain and heart,
      Transfiguring him to music. Thus, even thus,
90   He too received his sacramental gift
      With eucharistic meanings; for he loved.

3. Leonardo da Vinci (1452–1519) was an architect and
engineer, as well as an artist; he designed the aqueduct
that supplied Milan's water.

4. The Florentine church of the Santissima Annunziata,
or Holy Annunciation.
5. To take Holy Communion.

[HER MOTHER'S PORTRAIT]

And as I grew
In years, I mixed, confused, unconsciously,
Whatever I last read or heard or dreamed,
Abhorrent, admirable, beautiful,
150 Pathetical, or ghastly, or grotesque,
With still that face . . . which did not therefore change,
But kept the mystic level of all forms,
Hates, fears, and admirations, was by turns
Ghost, fiend, and angel, fairy, witch, and sprite,
155 A dauntless Muse who eyes a dreadful Fate,
A loving Psyche who loses sight of Love,[6]
A still Medusa[7] with mild milky brows
All curdled and all clothed upon with snakes
Whose slime falls fast as sweat will; or anon
160 Our Lady of the Passion, stabbed with swords
Where the Babe sucked; or Lamia[8] in her first
Moonlighted pallor, ere she shrunk and blinked
And shuddering wriggled down to the unclean;
Or my own mother, leaving her last smile
165 In her last kiss upon the baby-mouth
My father pushed down on the bed for that,—
Or my dead mother, without smile or kiss,
Buried at Florence. All which images,
Concentred on the picture, glassed themselves
170 Before my meditative childhood, as
The incoherencies of change and death
Are represented fully, mixed and merged,
In the smooth fair mystery of perpetual Life.

[AURORA'S EDUCATION]

Then, land!—then, England! oh, the frosty cliffs[9]
Looked cold upon me. Could I find a home
Among those mean red houses through the fog?
And when I heard my father's language first
255 From alien lips which had no kiss for mine
I wept aloud, then laughed, then wept, then wept,
And some one near me said the child was mad
Through much sea-sickness. The train swept us on:
Was this my father's England? the great isle?
260 The ground seemed cut up from the fellowship
Of verdure, field from field,[1] as man from man;
The skies themselves looked low and positive,
As almost you could touch them with a hand,
And dared to do it they were so far off

---

6. Psyche was beloved of Cupid (or Eros), whom she had never seen, because he always came to her after dark; one night she lit her lamp to look at him as he slept, whereupon he left her.
7. A gorgon, a female monster with serpents for hair, the sight of whom turned people to stone.
8. A monster with the head and upper body of a maiden, and lower body of a serpent.
9. The white chalk cliffs of Dover.
1. English fields are divided by hedgerows.

265 From God's celestial crystals;² all things blurred
     And dull and vague. Did Shakespeare and his mates
     Absorb the light here?—not a hill or stone
     With heart to strike a radiant colour up
     Or active outline on the indifferent air.

270 I think I see my father's sister stand
     Upon the hall-step of her country-house
     To give me welcome. She stood straight and calm,
     Her somewhat narrow forehead braided tight
     As if for taming accidental thoughts
275 From possible pulses;³ brown hair pricked with gray
     By frigid use of life (she was not old,
     Although my father's elder by a year),
     A nose drawn sharply, yet in delicate lines;
     A close mild mouth, a little soured about
280 The ends, through speaking unrequited loves
     Or peradventure niggardly half-truths;
     Eyes of no colour,—once they might have smiled,
     But never, never have forgot themselves
     In smiling; cheeks, in which was yet a rose
285 Of perished summers, like a rose in a book,
     Kept more for ruth° than pleasure,—if past bloom,   remorse
     Past fading also.

                    She had lived, we'll say,
     A harmless life, she called a virtuous life,
     A quiet life, which was not life at all
290 (But that, she had not lived enough to know),
     Between the vicar and the country squires,
     The lord-lieutenant looking down sometimes
     From the empyrean to assure their souls
     Against chance vulgarisms, and, in the abyss,
295 The apothecary, looked on once a year
     To prove their soundness of humility.
     The poor-club exercised her Christian gifts
     Of knitting stockings, stitching petticoats,
     Because we are of one flesh, after all,
300 And need one flannel° (with a proper sense   petticoat
     Of difference in the quality)—and still
     The book-club, guarded from your modern trick
     Of shaking dangerous questions from the crease,⁴
     Preserved her intellectual. She had lived
305 A sort of cage-bird life, born in a cage,
     Accounting that to leap from perch to perch
     Was act and joy enough for any bird.
     Dear heaven, how silly are the things that live
     In thickets, and eat berries!

2. The stars, or perhaps the crystalline sphere the ancients
believed lay beyond them.
3. Pulsations of strong emotion.

4. Books were sold with their pages uncut; one had to
cut the folds, or creases, to open the pages and read the
book.

I, alas,
310　A wild bird scarcely fledged, was brought to her cage,
And she was there to meet me. Very kind.
Bring the clean water, give out the fresh seed.

She stood upon the steps to welcome me,
Calm, in black garb. I clung about her neck,—
315　Young babes, who catch at every shred of wool
To draw the new light closer, catch and cling
Less blindly. In my ears my father's word
Hummed ignorantly, as the sea in shells,
"Love, love, my child." She, black there with my grief,
320　Might feel my love—she was his sister once—
I clung to her. A moment she seemed moved,
Kissed me with cold lips, suffered me to cling,
And drew me feebly through the hall into
The room she sat in.

　　　　　　　　　There, with some strange spasm
325　Of pain and passion, she wrung loose my hands
Imperiously, and held me at arm's length,
And with two grey-steel naked-bladed eyes
Searched through my face,—ay, stabbed it through and through,
Through brows and cheeks and chin, as if to find
330　A wicked murderer in my innocent face,
If not here, there perhaps. Then, drawing breath,
She struggled for her ordinary calm—
And missed it rather,—told me not to shrink,
As if she had told me not to lie or swear,—
335　"She loved my father and would love me too
As long as I deserved it." Very kind.

I understood her meaning afterward;
She thought to find my mother in my face,
And questioned it for that. For she, my aunt,
340　Had loved my father truly, as she could,
And hated, with the gall of gentle souls,
My Tuscan[5] mother who had fooled away
A wise man from wise courses, a good man
From obvious duties, and, depriving her,
345　His sister, of the household precedence,
Had wronged his tenants, robbed his native land,
And made him mad, alike by life and death,
In love and sorrow. She had pored° for years　　　　　*pondered*
What sort of woman could be suitable
350　To her sort of hate, to entertain it with,
And so, her very curiosity
Became hate too, and all the idealism
She ever used in life was used for hate,
Till hate, so nourished, did exceed at last

5. From Tuscany, the region around Florence.

355   The love from which it grew, in strength and heat,
      And wrinkled her smooth conscience with a sense
      Of disputable virtue (say not, sin)
      When Christian doctrine was enforced at church.

      And thus my father's sister was to me
360   My mother's hater. From that day she did
      Her duty to me (I appreciate it
      In her own word as spoken to herself),
      Her duty, in large measure, well pressed out
      But measured always. She was generous, bland,
365   More courteous than was tender, gave me still
      The first place,—as if fearful that God's saints
      Would look down suddenly and say "Herein
      You missed a point, I think, through lack of love."
      Alas, a mother never is afraid
370   Of speaking angerly to any child,
      Since love, she knows, is justified of love.

      And I, I was a good child on the whole,
      A meek and manageable child. Why not?
      I did not live, to have the faults of life:
375   There seemed more true life in my father's grave
      Than in all England. Since *that* threw me off
      Who fain would cleave (his latest will, they say,
      Consigned me to his land), I only thought
      Of lying quiet there where I was thrown
380   Like sea-weed on the rocks, and suffering her
      To prick me to a pattern with her pin,[6]
      Fibre from fibre, delicate leaf from leaf,
      And dry out from my drowned anatomy
      The last sea-salt left in me.

                                    So it was.
385   I broke the copious curls upon my head
      In braids, because she liked smooth-ordered hair.
      I left off saying my sweet Tuscan words
      Which still at any stirring of the heart
      Came up to float across the English phrase
390   As lilies (*Bene* or *Che che*[7]), because
      She liked my father's child to speak his tongue.
      I learnt the collects and the catechism,
      The creeds, from Athanasius back to Nice,
      The Articles,[8] the Tracts *against* the times[9]
395   (By no means Buonaventure's "Prick of Love"[1]),
      And various popular synopses of

---

6. As in pricking a pattern to embroider.
7. "Good" and "no, indeed" (Italian).
8. The Thirty-nine Articles are the principles of Anglican faith; collects are Anglican prayers.
9. An ironic reference to the High Church movement's

Tracts for the Times, written by Newman, Keble, and Pusey; thus, the aunt is Low Church.
1. Saint Buonaventure (1221–1274) wrote of ecstatic, mystical Christian experiences; he believed in the power of love over the power of reason.

Inhuman doctrines never taught by John,[2]
Because she liked instructed piety.
I learnt my complement of classic French
400   (Kept pure of Balzac and neologism[3])
And German also, since she liked a range
Of liberal education,—tongues, not books.
I learnt a little algebra, a little
Of the mathematics,—brushed with extreme flounce
405   The circle of the sciences, because
She misliked women who are frivolous.
I learnt the royal genealogies
Of Oviedo, the internal laws
Of the Burmese empire,—by how many feet
410   Mount Chimborazo outsoars Teneriffe.
What navigable river joins itself
To Lara, and what census of the year five
Was taken at Klagenfurt,—because she liked
A general insight into useful facts.
415   I learnt much music,—such as would have been
As quite impossible in Johnson's day[4]
As still it might be wished—fine sleights of hand
And unimagined fingering, shuffling off
The hearer's soul through hurricanes of notes
420   To a noisy Tophet;° and I drew ... costumes   *Hell*
From French engravings, nereids neatly draped
(With smirks of simmering godship): I washed in°   *water-colored*
Landscapes from nature (rather say, washed out).
I danced the polka and Cellarius,
425   Spun glass, stuffed birds, and modelled flowers in wax,
Because she liked accomplishments in girls.
I read a score of books on womanhood
To prove, if women do not think at all,
They may teach thinking (to a maiden aunt
430   Or else the author),—books that boldly assert
Their right of comprehending husband's talk
When not too deep, and even of answering
With pretty "may it please you," or "so it is,"—
Their rapid insight and fine aptitude,
435   Particular worth and general missionariness,
As long as they keep quiet by the fire
And never say "no" when the world says "ay,"
For that is fatal,—their angelic reach
Of virtue, chiefly used to sit and darn,
440   And fatten household sinners,—their, in brief,
Potential faculty in everything
Of abdicating power in it: she owned

---

2. The author of the gospel.
3. Honoré de Balzac (1799–1850), French realist novelist who described things considered unpleasant or immoral, hence unsuitable reading for young ladies. A neologism is a newly coined word.
4. When informed that a piece of music being played by a young lady was extremely difficult, Samuel Johnson responded, "Would that it had been impossible."

She liked a woman to be womanly,
And English women, she thanked God and sighed
445   (Some people always sigh in thanking God)
Were models to the universe. And last
I learnt cross-stitch, because she did not like
To see me wear the night with empty hands
A-doing nothing. So, my shepherdess
450   Was something after all (the pastoral saints
Be praised for't), leaning lovelorn with pink eyes
To match her shoes, when I mistook the silks;
Her head uncrushed by that round weight of hat
So strangely similar to the tortoise-shell
455   Which slew the tragic poet.[5]

              By the way,
The works of women are symbolical.
We sew, sew, prick our fingers, dull our sight,
Producing what? A pair of slippers, sir,
To put on when you're weary—or a stool
460   To stumble over and vex you . . . "curse that stool!"
Or else at best, a cushion, where you lean
And sleep, and dream of something we are not
But would be for your sake. Alas, alas!
This hurts most, this—that, after all, we are paid
465   The worth of our work, perhaps.

              In looking down
Those years of education (to return)
I wonder if Brinvilliers suffered more
In the water-torture[6] . . . flood succeeding flood
To drench the incapable throat and split the veins . . .
470   Than I did. Certain of your feebler souls
Go out in such a process; many pine
To a sick, inodorous light; my own endured:
I had relations in the Unseen, and drew
The elemental nutriment and heat
475   From nature, as earth feels the sun at nights,
Or as a babe sucks surely in the dark.
I kept the life thrust on me, on the outside
Of the inner life with all its ample room
For heart and lungs, for will and intellect,
480   Inviolable by conventions. God,
I thank thee for that grace of thine!

              At first
I felt no life which was not patience,—did
The thing she bade me, without heed to a thing
Beyond it, sat in just the chair she placed,
485   With back against the window, to exclude

---

5. The Greek playwright Aeschylus was supposed to have been killed when an eagle, mistaking his bald head for a stone, dropped a tortoise on it to break the shell.

6. In 1676 Marie Marguerite, Marquise de Brinvilliers, was tortured by having water forced down her throat, then executed.

The sight of the great lime-tree on the lawn,[7]
Which seemed to have come on purpose from the woods
To bring the house a message,—ay, and walked
Demurely in her carpeted low rooms,
490 As if I should not, hearkening my own steps,
Misdoubt I was alive. I read her books,
Was civil to her cousin, Romney Leigh,
Gave ear to her vicar, tea to her visitors,
And heard them whisper, when I changed a cup
495 (I blushed for joy at that),—"The Italian child,
For all her blue eyes and her quiet ways,
Thrives ill in England: she is paler yet
Than when we came the last time; she will die."

[DISCOVERY OF POETRY]

815 The cygnet finds the water, but the man
Is born in ignorance of his element
And feels out blind at first, disorganised
By sin i' the blood,—his spirit-insight dulled
And crossed by his sensations. Presently
820 He feels it quicken in the dark sometimes,
When, mark, be reverent, be obedient,
For such dumb motions of imperfect life
Are oracles of vital Deity
Attesting the Hereafter. Let who says
825 "The soul's a clean white paper," rather say,
A palimpsest,[8] a prophet's holograph
Defiled, erased and covered by a monk's,—
The apocalypse, by a Longus![9] poring on
Which obscene text, we may discern perhaps
830 Some fair, fine trace of what was written once,
Some upstroke of an alpha and omega
Expressing the old scripture.

Books, books, books!
I had found the secret of a garret-room
Piled high with cases in my father's name,
835 Piled high, packed large,—where, creeping in and out
Among the giant fossils of my past,
Like some small nimble mouse between the ribs
Of a mastodon, I nibbled here and there
At this or that box, pulling through the gap,
840 In heats of terror, haste, victorious joy,
The first book first. And how I felt it beat
Under my pillow, in the morning's dark,
An hour before the sun would let me read!
My books! At last because the time was ripe,
845 I chanced upon the poets.

---

7. Cf. Coleridge's *This Lime-Tree Bower My Prison*, page 1639.
8. Parchment where the original writing has been scraped off so it can be reused.

9. I.e., imagine that the words of the apocalyse have been erased and written over by Longus, a Greek writer of romances.

As the earth
Plunges in fury, when the internal fires
Have reached and pricked her heart, and, throwing flat
The marts and temples, the triumphal gates
And towers of observation, clears herself
850 To elemental freedom—thus, my soul,
At poetry's divine first finger-touch,
Let go conventions and sprang up surprised,
Convicted of the great eternities
Before two worlds.

What's this, Aurora Leigh,
855 You write so of the poets, and not laugh?
Those virtuous liars, dreamers after dark,
Exaggerators of the sun and moon,
And soothsayers in a tea-cup?

I write so
Of the only truth-tellers now left to God,
860 The only speakers of essential truth,
Opposed to relative, comparative,
And temporal truths; the only holders by
His sun-skirts, through conventional gray glooms;
The only teachers who instruct mankind
865 From just a shadow on a charnel-wall[1]
To find man's veritable stature out
Erect, sublime,—the measure of a man,
And that's the measure of an angel, says
The apostle. Ay, and while your common men
870 Lay telegraphs, gauge railroads, reign, reap, dine,
And dust the flaunty carpets of the world
For kings to walk on, or our president,
The poet suddenly will catch them up
With his voice like a thunder,—"This is soul,
875 This is life, this word is being said in heaven,
Here's God down on us! what are you about?"
How all those workers start amid their work,
Look round, look up, and feel, a moment's space,
That carpet-dusting, though a pretty trade,
880 Is not the imperative labour after all.

from *Book 2*

[WOMAN AND ARTIST]

Times followed one another. Came a morn
I stood upon the brink of twenty years,
And looked before and after, as I stood
Woman and artist,—either incomplete,
5 Both credulous of completion. There I held
The whole creation in my little cup,

---

1. Wall of a building where bodies or bones are deposited.

And smiled with thirsty lips before I drank
"Good health to you and me, sweet neighbor mine,
And all these peoples."

     I was glad, that day;
10 The June was in me, with its multitudes
Of nightingales all singing in the dark,
And rosebuds reddening where the calyx[1] split.
I felt so young, so strong, so sure of God!
So glad, I could not choose be very wise!
15 And, old at twenty, was inclined to pull
My childhood backward in a childish jest
To see the face of 't once more, and farewell!
In which fantastic mood I bounded forth
At early morning,—would not wait so long
20 As even to snatch my bonnet by the strings,
But, brushing a green trail across the lawn
With my gown in the dew, took will and away
Among the acacias of the shrubberies,
To fly my fancies in the open air
25 And keep my birthday, till my aunt awoke
To stop good dreams. Meanwhile I murmured on
As honeyed bees keep humming to themselves,
"The worthiest poets have remained uncrowned
Till death has bleached their foreheads to the bone;
30 And so with me it must be unless I prove
Unworthy of the grand adversity,
And certainly I would not fail so much.
What, therefore, if I crown myself to-day
In sport, not pride, to learn the feel of it,
35 Before my brows be numbed as Dante's own
To all the tender pricking of such leaves?
Such leaves! what leaves?"

     I pulled the branches down
To choose from.
    "Not the bay![2] I choose no bay
(The fates deny us if we are overbold),
40 Nor myrtle—which means chiefly love; and love
Is something awful which one dares not touch
So early o' mornings. This verbena strains
The point of passionate fragrance; and hard by,
This guelder-rose, at far too slight a beck
45 Of the wind, will toss about her flower-apples.
Ah—there's my choice,—that ivy on the wall,
That headlong ivy! not a leaf will grow
But thinking of a wreath. Large leaves, smooth leaves,
Serrated like my vines, and half as green.

---

1. The green outer leaves which protect a flowerbud.   2. Laurel; Apollo, the god of poetry, wore a wreath of laurel leaves.

50   I like such ivy, bold to leap a height
      'Twas strong to climb; as good to grow on graves
      As twist about a thyrsus;[3] pretty too
      (And that's not ill) when twisted round a comb."
      Thus speaking to myself, half singing it,
55   Because some thoughts are fashioned like a bell
      To ring with once being touched, I drew a wreath
      Drenched, blinding me with dew, across my brow,
      And fastening it behind so, turning faced
      . . . My public!—cousin Romney—with a mouth
60   Twice graver than his eyes.

                              I stood there fixed,—
      My arms up, like the caryatid,[4] sole
      Of some abolished temple, helplessly
      Persistent in a gesture which derides
      A former purpose. Yet my blush was flame,
65   As if from flax, not stone.

                              "Aurora Leigh,
      The earliest of Auroras!"[5]

                              Hand stretched out
      I clasped, as shipwrecked men will clasp a hand,
      Indifferent to the sort of palm. The tide
      Had caught me at my pastime, writing down
70   My foolish name too near upon the sea
      Which drowned me with a blush as foolish. "You,
      My cousin!"

                              The smile died out in his eyes
      And dropped upon his lips, a cold dead weight,
      For just a moment, "Here's a book I found!
75   No name writ on it—poems, by the form;
      Some Greek upon the margin,—lady's Greek
      Without the accents. Read it? Not a word.
      I saw at once the thing had witchcraft in't,
      Whereof the reading calls up dangerous spirits:
80   I rather bring it to the witch."

                              "My book.
      You found it". . .

                              "In the hollow by the stream
      That beech leans down into—of which you said
      The Oread in it has a Naiad's heart
      And pines for waters."[6]
                              "Thank you."
                                            "Thanks to you

85   My cousin! that I have seen you not too much

3. Ivy-covered staff carried by the Greek god Dionysus.
4. Female figure with upraised arms, used as a supporting
architectural column.

5. Aurora, the goddess of the dawn.
6. An Oread is a tree nymph; a Naiad is a water nymph.

Witch, scholar, poet, dreamer, and the rest,
To be a woman also."

     With a glance
The smile rose in his eyes again and touched
The ivy on my forehead, light as air.
90 I answered gravely "Poets needs must be
Or men or women—more's the pity."

       "Ah,
But men, and still less women, happily,
Scarce need be poets. Keep to the green wreath,
Since even dreaming of the stone and bronze
95 Brings headaches, pretty cousin, and defiles
The clean white morning dresses."

       "So you judge!
Because I love the beautiful I must
Love pleasure chiefly, and be overcharged
For ease and whiteness! well, you know the world,
100 And only miss your cousin, 'tis not much.
But learn this; I would rather take my part
With God's Dead, who afford to walk in white
Yet spread His glory, than keep quiet here
And gather up my feet from even a step
105 For fear to soil my gown in so much dust.
I choose to walk at all risks.—Here, if heads
That hold a rhythmic thought, much ache perforce,
For my part I choose headaches,—and to-day's
My birthday."

    "Dear Aurora, choose instead
110 To cure them. You have balsams."

       "I perceive.
The headache is too noble for my sex.
You think the heartache would sound decenter,
Since that's the woman's special, proper ache,
And altogether tolerable, except
115 To a woman."

     [No Female Christ]

     "There it is!—
180 You play beside a death-bed like a child,
Yet measure to yourself a prophet's place
To teach the living. None of all these things
Can women understand. You generalise
Oh, nothing,—not even grief! Your quick-breathed hearts,
185 So sympathetic to the personal pang,
Close on each separate knife-stroke, yielding up
A whole life at each wound, incapable
Of deepening, widening a large lap of life
To hold the world-full woe. The human race
190 To you means, such a child, or such a man,

You saw one morning waiting in the cold,
Beside that gate, perhaps. You gather up
A few such cases, and when strong sometimes
Will write of factories and of slaves, as if
195   Your father were a negro, and your son
A spinner in the mills. All's yours and you,
All, coloured with your blood, or otherwise
Just nothing to you. Why, I call you hard
To general suffering. Here's the world half-blind
200   With intellectual light, half-brutalised
With civilisation, having caught the plague
In silks from Tarsus,[7] shrieking east and west
Along a thousand railroads, mad with pain
And sin too! . . . does one woman of you all
205   (You who weep easily) grow pale to see
This tiger shake his cage?—does one of you
Stand still from dancing, stop from stringing pearls,
And pine and die because of the great sum
Of universal anguish?—Show me a tear
210   Wet as Cordelia's,[8] in eyes bright as yours,
Because the world is mad. You cannot count,
That you should weep for this account, not you!
You weep for what you know. A red-haired child
Sick in a fever, if you touch him once,
215   Though but so little as with a finger-tip,
Will set you weeping; but a million sick . . .
You could as soon weep for the rule of three
Or compound fractions. Therefore, this same world,
Uncomprehended by you, must remain
220   Uninfluenced by you.—Women as you are,
Mere women, personal and passionate,
You give us doating mothers, and perfect wives,
Sublime Madonnas, and enduring saints!
We get no Christ from you,—and verily
225   We shall not get a poet, in my mind."

[AURORA'S REJECTION OF ROMNEY]

There he glowed on me
With all his face and eyes. "No other help?"
345   Said he—"no more than so?"[9]

"What help?" I asked.
"You'd scorn my help,—as Nature's self, you say,
Has scorned to put her music in my mouth
Because a woman's. Do you now turn round

---

7. I.e., with civilized luxuries come evils, just as the trading ships bringing silks from Tarsus—a wealthy center of
trade in the ancient Middle East—might also have
brought rats that spread the plague.
8. Cordelia weeps when she is reunited with her father
(King Lear, 4.7.71); her feelings are entirely personal.
Romney mentions Cordelia to bolster his argument that

women cannot play any role in world affairs because they
are incapable of taking a broad view of human suffering.
9. Romney wants to alleviate the misery of the poor
through social reform. Aurora has offered her approval of
his plans, but he asks if she can offer him another kind of
help—i.e., to be his wife or "helpmate" (line 402 below).

And ask for what a woman cannot give?"

350 "For what she only can, I turn and ask,"
He answered, catching up my hands in his,
And dropping on me from his high-eaved brow
The full weight of his soul,—"I ask for love,
And that, she can; for life in fellowship
355 Through bitter duties—that, I know she can;
For wifehood—will she?"

                    "Now," I said, "may God
Be witness 'twixt us two!" and with the word,
Meseemed I floated into a sudden light
Above his stature,—"am I proved too weak
360 To stand alone, yet strong enough to bear
Such leaners on my shoulder? poor to think,
Yet rich enough to sympathise with thought?
Incompetent to sing, as blackbirds can,
Yet competent to love, like HIM?"

                         I paused;
365 Perhaps I darkened, as the lighthouse will
That turns upon the sea. "It's always so.
Anything does for a wife."

                    "Aurora, dear,
And dearly honoured,"—he pressed in at once
With eager utterance,—"you translate me ill.
370 I do not contradict my thought of you
Which is most reverent, with another thought
Found less so. If your sex is weak for art
(And I, who said so, did but honour you
By using truth in courtship), it is strong
375 For life and duty. Place your fecund heart
In mine, and let us blossom for the world
That wants love's colour in the grey of time.
My talk, meanwhile, is arid to you, ay,
Since all my talk can only set you where
380 You look down coldly on the arena-heaps
Of headless bodies, shapeless, indistinct!
The Judgment-Angel scarce would find his way
Through such a heap of generalised distress
To the individual man with lips and eyes,
385 Much less Aurora. Ah, my sweet, come down,
And hand in hand we'll go where yours shall touch
These victims, one by one! till, one by one,
The formless, nameless trunk of every man
Shall seem to wear a head with hair you know,
390 And every woman catch your mother's face
To melt you into passion."

                    "I am a girl,"
I answered slowly; "you do well to name
My mother's face. Though far too early, alas,

God's hand did interpose 'twixt it and me,
395 I know so much of love as used to shine
In that face and another. Just so much;
No more indeed at all. I have not seen
So much love since, I pray you pardon me,
As answers even to make a marriage with
400 In this cold land of England. What you love
Is not a woman, Romney, but a cause:
You want a helpmate, not a mistress, sir,
A wife to help your ends,—in her no end.
Your cause is noble, your ends excellent,
405 But I, being most unworthy of these and that,
Do otherwise conceive of love. Farewell."

"Farewell, Aurora? you reject me thus?"
He said.

        "Sir, you were married long ago.
You have a wife already whom you love,
410 Your social theory. Bless you both, I say.
For my part, I am scarcely meek enough
To be the handmaid of a lawful spouse.
Do I look a Hagar,[1] think you?"

                                "So you jest."

"Nay, so, I speak in earnest," I replied.
415 "You treat of marriage too much like, at least,
A chief apostle: you would bear with you
A wife . . . a sister . . . shall we speak it out?
A sister of charity."

                    "Then, must it be
Indeed farewell? And was I so far wrong
420 In hope and in illusion, when I took
The woman to be nobler than the man,
Yourself the noblest woman, in the use
And comprehension of what love is,—love,
That generates the likeness of itself
425 Through all heroic duties? so far wrong,
In saying bluntly, venturing truth on love,
'Come, human creature, love and work with me,'—
Instead of 'Lady, thou art wondrous fair,
And, where the Graces walk before, the Muse
430 Will follow at the lightning of their eyes,
And where the Muse walks, lovers need to creep:
Turn round and love me, or I die of love.'"

With quiet indignation I broke in.
"You misconceive the question like a man,
435 Who sees a woman as the complement
Of his sex merely. You forget too much
That every creature, female as the male,

---

1. In Genesis 16, Hagar was the handmaiden of Abraham's lawful wife, Sarah; Hagar bore Abraham a son, Ishmael, when it appeared that Sarah was barren.

Stands single in responsible act and thought
As also in birth and death. Whoever says
440 To a loyal woman, 'Love and work with me,'
Will get fair answers if the work and love,
Being good themselves, are good for her—the best
She was born for. Women of a softer mood,
Surprised by men when scarcely awake to life,
445 Will sometimes only hear the first word, love,
And catch up with it any kind of work,
Indifferent, so that dear love go with it.
I do not blame such women, though, for love,
They pick much oakum;[2] earth's fanatics make
450 Too frequently heaven's saints. But *me* your work
Is not the best for,—nor your love the best,
Nor able to commend the kind of work
For love's sake merely. Ah, you force me, sir,
To be overbold in speaking of myself:
455 I too have my vocation,—work to do,
The heavens and earth have set me since I changed
My father's face for theirs, and, though your world
Were twice as wretched as you represent,
Most serious work, most necessary work
460 As any of the economists'. Reform,
Make trade a Christian possibility,
And individual right no general wrong;
Wipe out earth's furrows of the Thine and Mine,
And leave one green for men to play at bowls,[3]
465 With innings for them all! . . . What then, indeed,
If mortals are not greater by the head
Than any of their prosperities? what then,
Unless the artist keep up open roads
Betwixt the seen and unseen,—bursting through
470 The best of your conventions with his best,
The speakable, imaginable best
God bids him speak, to prove what lies beyond
Both speech and imagination? A starved man
Exceeds a fat beast: we'll not barter, sir,
475 The beautiful for barley.—And, even so,
I hold you will not compass your poor ends
Of barley-feeding and material ease,
Without a poet's individualism
To work your universal. It takes a soul,
480 To move a body: it takes a high-souled man,
To move the masses, even to a cleaner stye:
It takes the ideal, to blow a hair's-breadth off
The dust of the actual.—Ah, your Fouriers[4] failed,
Because not poets enough to understand
485 That life develops from within.—For me,

2. Prisoners and paupers in workhouses were forced to
pick oakum (untwist strands of old rope); it was tedious
and humble labor.

3. Lawn bowling.
4. François Marie Charles Fourier (1772–1837), a French
social theorist who advocated communal property.

Perhaps I am not worthy, as you say,
Of work like this: perhaps a woman's soul
Aspires, and not creates: yet we aspire,
And yet I'll try out your perhapses, sir,
490   And if I fail . . . why, burn me up my straw[5]
Like other false works—I'll not ask for grace;
Your scorn is better, cousin Romney. I
Who love my art, would never wish it lower
To suit my stature. I may love my art.
495   You'll grant that even a woman may love art,
Seeing that to waste true love on anything
Is womanly, past question."

                                I retain
The very last word which I said that day,
As you the creaking of the door, years past,
500   Which let upon you such disabling news
You ever after have been graver. He,
His eyes, the motions in his silent mouth,
Were fiery points on which my words were caught,
Transfixed for ever in my memory
505   For his sake, not their own. And yet I know
I did not love him . . . nor he me . . . that's sure . . .
And what I said is unrepented of,
As truth is always. Yet . . . a princely man!—
If hard to me, heroic for himself!
510   He bears down on me through the slanting years,
The stronger for the distance. If he had loved,
Ay, loved me, with that retributive face, . . .
I might have been a common woman now
And happier, less known and less left alone,
515   Perhaps a better woman after all,
With chubby children hanging on my neck
To keep me low and wise. Ah me, the vines
That bear such fruit are proud to stoop with it.
The palm stands upright in a realm of sand.
520   And I, who spoke the truth then, stand upright,
Still worthy of having spoken out the truth,
By being content I spoke it though it set
Him there, me here.—O woman's vile remorse,
To hanker after a mere name, a show,
525   A supposition, a potential love!
Does every man who names love in our lives
Become a power for that?

from *Book 3*
[THE WOMAN WRITER IN LONDON]

Why what a pettish, petty thing I grow,—
A mere mere woman, a mere flaccid nerve,

5. I.e., destroy my poetry.

A kerchief left out all night in the rain,
Turned soft so,—overtasked and overstrained
40 And overlived in this close London life!
And yet I should be stronger.

               Never burn
Your letters, poor Aurora! for they stare
With red seals from the table, saying each,
"Here's something that you know not." Out, alas,
45 'Tis scarcely that the world's more good and wise
Or even straighter and more consequent
Since yesterday at this time—yet, again,
If but one angel spoke from Ararat[1]
I should be very sorry not to hear:
50 So open all the letters! let me read.
Blanche Ord, the writer in the "Lady's Fan,"
Requests my judgment on . . . that, afterwards.
Kate Ward desires the model of my cloak,
And signs "Elisha to you."[2] Pringle Sharpe
55 Presents his work on "Social Conduct," craves
A little money for his pressing debts . . .
From me, who scarce have money for my needs;
Art's fiery chariot which we journey in
Being apt to singe our singing-robes to holes,
60 Although you ask me for my cloak, Kate Ward!
Here's Rudgely knows it,—editor and scribe;
He's "forced to marry where his heart is not,
Because the purse lacks where he lost his heart."
Ah,——lost it because no one picked it up;
65 That's really loss,—(and passable impudence).
My critic Hammond flatters prettily,
And wants another volume like the last.
My critic Belfair wants another book
Entirely different, which will sell (and live?),
70 A striking book, yet not a startling book,
The public blames originalities
(You must not pump spring-water unawares
Upon a gracious public full of nerves):
Good things, not subtle, new yet orthodox,
75 As easy reading as the dog-eared page
That's fingered by said public fifty years,
Since first taught spelling by its grandmother,
And yet a revelation in some sort:
That's hard, my critic Belfair. So—what next?
80 My critic Stokes objects to abstract thoughts;
"Call a man John, a woman Joan," says he,
"And do not prate so of *humanities:*"
Whereat I call my critic simply, Stokes.
My critic Jobson recommends more mirth

1. The mountain where Noah's ark rested after the Flood, and where God spoke to Noah (Genesis 8).
2. When the prophet Elijah was carried to heaven in a chariot of fire, his cloak fell to earth and was taken up by his successor Elisha (2 Kings 2.1–15); Kate Ward means that she wants to copy Aurora's cloak.

85   Because a cheerful genius suits the times,
      And all true poets laugh unquenchably
      Like Shakespeare and the gods. That's very hard.
      The gods may laugh, and Shakespeare; Dante smiled
      With such a needy heart on two pale lips,
90   We cry "Weep rather, Dante." Poems are
      Men, if true poems: and who dares exclaim
      At any man's door, "Here, 'tis understood
      The thunder fell last week and killed a wife
      And scared a sickly husband—what of that?
95   Get up, be merry, shout and clap your hands,
      Because a cheerful genius suits the times—"?
      None says so to the man, and why indeed
      Should any to the poem? A ninth seal;[3]
      The apocalypse is drawing to a close.
100   Ha,—this from Vincent Carrington,—"Dear friend,
      I want good counsel. Will you lend me wings
      To raise me to the subject, in a sketch
      I'll bring to-morrow—may I? at eleven?
      A poet's only born to turn to use:
105   So save you! for the world . . . and Carrington."
      "(Writ after.) Have you heard of Romney Leigh,
      Beyond what's said of him in newspapers,
      His phalansteries[4] there, his speeches here,
      His pamphlets, pleas, and statements, everywhere?
110   He dropped *me* long ago, but no one drops
      A golden apple—though indeed one day
      You hinted that, but jested. Well, at least
      You know Lord Howe who sees him . . . whom he sees
      And *you* see and I hate to see,—for Howe
115   Stands high upon the brink of theories,
      Observes the swimmers and cries 'Very fine,'
      But keeps dry linen equally,—unlike
      That gallant breaster, Romney. Strange it is,
      Such sudden madness seizing a young man
120   To make earth over again,—while I'm content
      To make the pictures. Let me bring the sketch.
      A tiptoe Danae,[5] overbold and hot,
      Both arms a-flame to meet her wishing Jove
      Halfway, and burn him faster down; the face
125   And breasts upturned and straining, the loose locks
      All glowing with the anticipated gold.
      Or here's another on the self-same theme.[6]
      She lies here—flat upon her prison-floor,
      The long hair swathed about her to the heel
130   Like wet seaweed. You dimly see her through
      The glittering haze of that prodigious rain,

---

3. In Revelation 5.1 there is a book closed with seven seals, the opening of which will herald the Apocalypse. The reference to a ninth seal satirically suggests something more extreme than the Apocalypse itself.
4. The communes advocated by the socialist Fourier.

5. Carrington has sketched Danae, the beloved of Zeus, whom Zeus visited in a shower of gold.
6. I.e., the second picture is also of Danae and the golden shower ("prodigious rain") that is Zeus.

Half blotted out of nature by a love
As heavy as fate. I'll bring you either sketch.
I think, myself, the second indicates
More passion."

135   Surely. Self is put away,
And calm with abdication. She is Jove,
And no more Danae—greater thus. Perhaps
The painter symbolises unaware
Two states of the recipient artist-soul,
140 One, forward, personal, wanting reverence,
Because aspiring only. We'll be calm,
And know that, when indeed our Joves come down,
We all turn stiller than we have ever been.

                    * * *

Serene and unafraid of solitude,
170 I worked the short days out,—and watched the sun
On lurid morns or monstrous afternoons
(Like some Druidic idol's fiery brass
With fixed unflickering outline of dead heat,
From which the blood of wretches pent inside
175 Seems oozing forth to incarnadine the air[7])
Push out through fog with his dilated disk,
And startle the slant roofs and chimney-pots
With splashes of fierce colour. Or I saw
Fog only, the great tawny weltering fog,
180 Involve the passive city, strangle it
Alive, and draw it off into the void,
Spires, bridges, streets, and squares, as if a sponge
Had wiped out London,—or as noon and night
Had clapped together and utterly struck out
185 The intermediate time, undoing themselves
In the act. Your city poets see such things
Not despicable. Mountains of the south,
When drunk and mad with elemental wines
They rend the seamless mist and stand up bare,
190 Make fewer singers, haply. No one sings,
Descending Sinai: on Parnassus mount[8]
You take a mule to climb and not a muse
Except in fable and figure: forests chant
Their anthems to themselves, and leave you dumb.
195 But sit in London at the day's decline,
And view the city perish in the mist
Like Pharaoh's armaments in the deep Red Sea,[9]
The chariots, horsemen, footmen, all the host,
Sucked down and choked to silence—then, surprised
200 By a sudden sense of vision and of tune,

---

7. It was believed that ancient Celtic druids performed human sacrifices.
8. Sinai is the mountain where God gave the Commandments to Moses; Parnassus is the mountain where the Muses, the Greek goddesses of the arts and of knowledge, dwelled. The idea is that neither biblical nor classical sources can provide poetic inspiration for the modern poet; only the city can do so.
9. In Exodus 14.21–30, God parts the Red Sea so the Israelites can escape from Egypt, but drowns Pharaoh's pursuing armies.

You feel as conquerors though you did not fight,
And you and Israel's other singing girls,
Ay, Miriam[1] with them, sing the song you choose.

from *Book 5*
[EPIC ART AND MODERN LIFE]

The critics say that epics have died out
140   With Agamemnon and the goat-nursed gods;[1]
I'll not believe it. I could never deem,
As Payne Knight[2] did (the mythic mountaineer
Who travelled higher than he was born to live,
And showed sometimes the goitre in his throat[3]
145   Discoursing of an image seen through fog),
That Homer's heroes measured twelve feet high.
They were but men:—his Helen's hair turned grey
Like any plain Miss Smith's who wears a front;[4]
And Hector's infant whimpered at a plume[5]
150   As yours last Friday at a turkey-cock.
All actual heroes are essential men,
And all men possible heroes: every age,
Heroic in proportions, double-faced,
Looks backward and before, expects a morn
155   And claims an epos.°   *epic poem*

                  Ay, but every age
Appears to souls who live in't (ask Carlyle[6])
Most unheroic. Ours, for instance, ours:
The thinkers scout it, and the poets abound
Who scorn to touch it with a finger-tip:
160   A pewter age,[7]—mixed metal, silver-washed;
An age of scum, spooned off the richer past,
An age of patches for old gaberdines,°   *overcoats*
An age of mere transition,[8] meaning nought
Except that what succeeds must shame it quite
165   If God please. That's wrong thinking, to my mind,
And wrong thoughts make poor poems.

                       Every age,
Through being beheld too close, is ill-discerned
By those who have not lived past it. We'll suppose
Mount Athos carved, as Alexander schemed,
170   To some colossal statue of a man.[9]

---

1. Miriam, the sister of Moses and Aaron, led the women of Israel in singing to celebrate the drowning of the Egyptian army (Exodus 15.19–21).
1. Agamemnon led the Greeks in the Trojan War, as chronicled in Homer's epic, *The Iliad*; Zeus was nursed by a goat.
2. Richard Payne Knight (1750–1824), a classical scholar who speculated about Homer and the Elgin marbles.
3. A swelling of the throat (caused by lack of iodine in the water at high altitudes), symbolizing the foolishness of Payne Knight's utterances.
4. Hairpiece worn over the forehead; artificial bangs.
5. When the Trojan warrior Hector tried to embrace his infant son before going into battle, the baby was terrified of his father's plumed helmet.
6. In *On Heroes and Hero Worship* (1841) Thomas Carlyle urges a renewal of the idea of the heroic.
7. Inferior to the Golden, the Silver, or even the Bronze Age; Hesiod proposed that history is a constant process of decline.
8. In *The Spirit of the Age* (1831) John Stuart Mill says the present era is "an age of transition."
9. Alexander the Great thought of having Mount Athos carved in the form of a gigantic statue of a conqueror, with a basin in one hand to collect water for the pastures below.

The peasants, gathering brushwood in his ear,
Had guessed as little as the browsing goats
Of form or feature of humanity
Up there,—in fact, had travelled five miles off
175 Or ere the giant image broke on them,
Full human profile, nose and chin distinct,
Mouth, muttering rhythms of silence up the sky
And fed at evening with the blood of suns;
Grand torso,—hand, that flung perpetually
180 The largesse of a silver river down
To all the country pastures. 'Tis even thus
With times we live in,—evermore too great
To be apprehended near.

                        But poets should
Exert a double vision; should have eyes
185 To see near things as comprehensively
As if afar they took their point of sight,
And distant things as intimately deep
As if they touched them. Let us strive for this.
I do distrust the poet who discerns
190 No character or glory in his times,
And trundles back his soul five hundred years,
Past moat and drawbridge, into a castle-court,
To sing—oh, not of lizard or of toad
Alive i' the ditch there,—'twere excusable,
195 But of some black chief, half knight, half sheep-lifter,
Some beauteous dame, half chattel and half queen,
As dead as must be, for the greater part,
The poems made on their chivalric bones;
And that's no wonder: death inherits death.

200 Nay, if there's room for poets in this world
A little overgrown (I think there is),
Their sole work is to represent the age,
Their age, not Charlemagne's,[1]—this live, throbbing age,
That brawls, cheats, maddens, calculates, aspires,
205 And spends more passion, more heroic heat,
Betwixt the mirrors of its drawing-rooms,
Than Roland with his knights at Roncesvalles.[2]
To flinch from modern varnish, coat or flounce,
Cry out for togas and the picturesque,
210 Is fatal,—foolish too. King Arthur's self
Was commonplace to Lady Guenever;
And Camelot to minstrels seemed as flat
As Fleet Street to our poets.[3]

1. Charlemagne was king of the Franks (768–814) and emperor of the West, laying the foundation for the Holy Roman Empire.

2. Legendary hero whose defeat at Roncesvalles (in the Spanish Pyrenees) was disastrous for Charlemagne's forces; his exploits are the subject of a medieval epic poem, Le Chanson de Roland.

3. I.e., to his wife Guenevere, even the glorious King Arthur was ordinary, and his kingdom was no more a subject for the poets of his own time than Fleet Street—location of London publishers and newspaper offices—is for the poets of the 19th century.

Never flinch,
But still, unscrupulously epic, catch
215   Upon the burning lava of a song
The full-veined, heaving, double-breasted Age:
That, when the next shall come, the men of that
May touch the impress with reverent hand, and say
"Behold,—behold the paps we all have sucked!
220   This bosom seems to beat still, or at least
It sets ours beating: this is living art,
Which thus presents and thus records true life."

1853–1856   1856

PERSPECTIVES

Victorian Ladies and Gentlemen

As Victorian society prospered, social divisions became more fluid, but at the same time class consciousness became more intense. The terms "lady" and "gentleman" had enormous significance, particularly for those aspiring to these ranks, or for those in danger of slipping out of them. Some social distinctions were obvious: regardless of conduct, people born into the aristocracy and landed gentry were indisputably ladies and gentlemen; people who worked with their hands in home, field, or factory were not. The upper and lower boundaries of the middle-class were blurred, however, and everyone was alert to fine gradations. Manners, money, birth, occupation, and leisure time were crucial indicators of social standing, determining not only one's place in society but one's freedom to act, speak, learn, and earn.

Ladies and gentlemen endeavored to conform to the ideology of separate spheres that dominated Victorian thinking about gender. Middle-class women were to preside over the domestic sphere, the home and family, while men entered the fray of the world. Woman's "mission" was to provide a sanctified haven from the rough-and-tumble world of business and politics. Her virtuous passivity, selflessness, and spiritual purity gave her moral authority in the social and domestic realm. The first mass circulation women's periodical, launched in 1852, was called, significantly, *Englishwoman's Domestic Magazine*.

Meanwhile, the world of action and aggression belonged to men: as Ruskin put it in *Sesame and Lilies* (1865): "The man, in his rough work in the open world, must encounter all peril and trial . . . often he must be wounded, or subdued, often misled; and *always* hardened. But he guards the woman from all this; within his house, as ruled by her . . . need enter no danger, no temptation, no cause of error or offense." Tennyson's *The Princess* (1847) gave the polarization of gender roles the aura of timeless law:

Man for the field and woman for the hearth:
Man for the sword and for the needle she:
Man with the head and woman with the heart:
Man to command and woman to obey:
All else confusion.

Among middle-class men, the clearest social division was between those who had attended a public school (an elite boarding school) and those who had not. The ideal of gentlemanliness inculcated by these schools became a way for society to remake the upstart middle classes in the image of the aristocracy. Emphasizing character over intellect, the public schools taught boys how to assimilate the manners and customs of those above them socially, and gave

Father of the Family. "Come, dear; we so seldom go out together now—Can't you take us all to the Play to-night?"

Mistress of House, and M. P. "How you talk, Charles! Don't you see that I am too Busy. I have a Committee to-morrow morning, and I have my Speech on the Great Crochet Question to prepare for the evening."

The Parliamentary Female. From *Punch* magazine, 1853.

them a familiarity with Greek, Latin, and school games such as cricket and rugby—hallmarks of an upper-class education. Instilling the values of duty, loyalty, and public service, these schools helped to create a new administrative elite, based more on merit and training than birth, who ran both the Civil Service and the Empire. Sustained by the "old boy" network, in which former schoolmates assisted each other's careers, graduates of places such as Eton, Harrow, Winchester, and Rugby could look forward to positions of influence and affluence.

Although the daughters of some well-to-do families might attend a fashionable boarding school, education was not primarily what determined a woman's claim to be considered a lady. Her position derived from her parents or her husband, and her unproductive leisure was a visible signal of rank. Since aspirations to "refinement" effectively precluded middle-class women from employment, ladies had, as the novelist Dinah Maria Mulock put it in 1858, "literally nothing whatever to do." She complained that "their whole energies are devoted to the massacre of old Time. They prick him to death with crochet and embroidery needles; strum him deaf with piano and harp playing—*not* music; cut him up with morning visitors, or leave his carcass in ten-minute parcels at every 'friend's' house they can think of." In her autobiography, the journalist Harriet Martineau described the expectations in her day: "It was not thought proper for young ladies to study very conspicuously. . . . If ever I shut myself into my own room for an hour of solitude, I knew it was at the risk of being sent for to join the sewing-circle, or to read aloud."

It was a way of life that at once exalted women and paralyzed them. They could not work outside the home; they could not vote; they had no legal rights, even over their own children; they could not attend university or enter the professions. Legally, they were classed with criminals, idiots, and minors. Rejecting women's education, the painter Edward Burne-Jones argued, "The great point is, not that they should understand us, but that they should worship and obey us." Ironically, only economic necessity or illness could liberate a lady from the burden of enforced idleness. When Martineau's family went bankrupt she was enabled to pursue her dream of authorship, for "we had lost our gentility." Similarly, the death of both parents freed Mary Kingsley to travel, and her own recurrent ill-health allowed Isabella Bird to go off in search of a "cure." Both women became prominent travel writers. Florence Nightingale made time for a career by taking to her bed, where only her persistent indisposition released her from the demands of family and social life. Definitions of masculinity and femininity were earnestly contested throughout the period—with increasingly sharp assaults on traditional roles coming from aesthetes and decadents at the end of the century. The following selections illustrate the kinds of arguments and experiences that figured prominently in debates on gender roles in the early and mid-Victorian periods.

⊷ ⥱⟐⥲ ⊶

Frances Power Cobbe
1822–1904

The education of girls from well-to-do families lacked intellectual challenge, partly because of the belief that the female mind was incapable of serious effort, and partly because the goal was to produce "Ornaments of Society" who would catch husbands. The elaborate and expensive clothes worn by Cobbe and her fellow pupils further reinforced their essentially decorative function. Although Cobbe recalls her teachers' horror at the idea that a woman's education might ever be put to any practical use, she herself became an active philanthropist, reformer, and feminist, who pressed for female suffrage and for women's access to university education and the professions.

from Life of Frances Power Cobbe As Told by Herself
[A FASHIONABLE ENGLISH BOARDING SCHOOL]

When it came to my turn to receive education, it was not in London but in Brighton that the ladies' schools most in estimation were to be found. There were even then (about 1836) not less than a hundred such establishments in the town, but that at No. 32, Brunswick Terrace, of which Miss Runciman and Miss Roberts were mistresses, and which had been founded some time before by a celebrated Miss Poggi, was supposed to be *nec pluribus impar* [equal to the best]. It was, at all events, the most outrageously expensive, the nominal tariff of £120 or £130 per annum representing scarcely a fourth of the charges for "extras" which actually appeared in the bills of many of the pupils. My own, I know, amounted to 1,000 for two years' schooling.[1]

I shall write of this school quite frankly, since the two poor ladies, well-meaning but very unwise, to whom it belonged have been dead for nearly thirty years, and it can hurt nobody to record my conviction that a better system than theirs could scarcely have been devised had it been designed to attain the maximum of cost and labour and the minimum of solid results. It was the typical Higher Education of the period, carried out to the extreme of expenditure and high pressure.

---

1. Compare this figure to the 20 pounds per year that Charlotte Brontë was earning in 1841 as a private governess.

Profane persons were apt to describe our school as a Convent, and to refer to the back door of our garden, whence we issued on our dismal diurnal[2] walks, as the "postern." If we in any degree resembled nuns, however, it was assuredly not those of either a Contemplative or Silent Order. The din of our large double schoolrooms was something frightful. Sitting in either of them, four pianos might be heard going at once in rooms above and around us, while at numerous tables scattered about the rooms there were girls reading aloud to the governesses and reciting lessons in English, French, German, and Italian. This hideous clatter continued the entire day till we went to bed at night, there being no time whatever allowed for recreation, unless the dreary hour of walking with our teachers (when we recited our verbs), could so be described by a fantastic imagination. In the midst of the uproar we were obliged to write our exercises, to compose our themes, and to commit to memory whole pages of prose. On Saturday afternoons, instead of play, there was a terrible ordeal generally known as the "Judgment Day." The two school-mistresses sat side by side, solemn and stern, at the head of the long table. Behind them sat all the governesses as Assessors. On the table were the books wherein our evil deeds of the week were recorded; and round the room against the wall, seated on stools of penitential discomfort, we sat, five-and-twenty "damosels," anything but "Blessed,"[3] expecting our sentences according to our ill-deserts. It must be explained that the fiendish ingenuity of some teacher had invented for our torment a system of imaginary "cards," which we were supposed to "lose" (though we never gained any) whenever we had not finished all our various lessons and practisings every night before bed-time, or whenever we had been given the mark for "stooping," or had been impertinent, or had been "turned" in our lessons, or had been marked "P" by the music master, or had been convicted of "disorder" (e.g., having our long shoe-strings untied), or, lastly, had told lies! Any one crime in this heterogeneous list entailed the same penalty, namely, the sentence, "You have lost your card, Miss So-and-so, for such and such a thing;" and when Saturday came round, if three cards had been lost in the week, the law wreaked its justice on the unhappy sinner's head! Her confession having been wrung from her at the awful judgment-seat above described, and the books having been consulted, she was solemnly scolded and told to sit in the corner for the rest of the evening! Anything more ridiculous than the scene which followed can hardly be conceived. I have seen (after a week in which a sort of feminine barring-out had taken place) no less than nine young ladies obliged to sit for hours in the angles of the three rooms, like naughty babies, with their faces to the wall; half of them being quite of marriageable age, and all dressed, as was de rigueur [the rule] with us every day, in full evening attire of silk or muslin, with gloves and kid slippers. Naturally, Saturday evenings, instead of affording some relief to the incessant overstrain of the week, were looked upon with terror as the worst time of all. Those who escaped the fell destiny of the corner were allowed, if they chose, to write to their parents, but our letters were perforce committed at night to the schoolmistress to seal, and were not as may be imagined, exactly the natural outpouring of our sentiments as regarded those ladies and their school.

Our household was a large one. It consisted of the two schoolmistresses and joint proprietors, of the sister of one of them and another English governess; of a French, an Italian, and a German lady teacher; of a considerable staff of respectable servants; and

---

2. Daily.

3. An allusion to Dante Gabriel Rossetti's poem, *The Blessed Damozel.*

finally of twenty-five or twenty-six pupils, varying in age from nine to nineteen. All the pupils were daughters of men of some standing, mostly country gentlemen, members of Parliament, and offshoots of the peerage. There were several heiresses amongst us, and one girl whom we all liked and recognised as the beauty of the school, the daughter of Horace Smith, author of *Rejected Addresses*. On the whole, looking back after the long interval, it seems to me that the young creatures there assembled were full of capabilities for widely extended usefulness and influence. Many were decidedly clever and nearly all were well disposed. There was very little malice or any other vicious ideas or feelings, and no worldliness at all amongst us. * * *

But all this fine human material was deplorably wasted. Nobody dreamed that any one of us could in later life be more or less than an "Ornament of Society." That a pupil in that school should ever become an artist, or authoress, would have been looked upon by both Miss Runciman and Miss Roberts as a deplorable dereliction. Not that which was good in itself or useful to the community, or even that which would be delightful to ourselves, but that which would make us admired in society, was the *raison d'être* [reason for being] of each acquirement. Everything was taught us in the inverse ratio of its true importance. At the bottom of the scale were Morals and Religion, and at the top were Music and Dancing; miserably poor music, too, of the Italian school then in vogue, and generally performed in a showy and tasteless manner on harp or piano. I can recall an amusing instance in which the order of precedence above described was naïvely betrayed by one of our schoolmistresses when she was admonishing one of the girls who had been detected in a lie. "Don't you know, you naughty girl," said Miss R. impressively, before the whole school: "don't you know we had *almost* rather find you have a P—" (the mark of Pretty Well) "in your music, than tell such falsehoods?"

It mattered nothing whether we had any "music in our souls" or any voices in our throats, equally we were driven through the dreary course of practising daily for a couple of hours under a German teacher, and then receiving lessons twice or three times a week from a music master (Griesbach by name) and a singing master. Many of us, myself in particular, in addition to these had a harp master, a Frenchman named Labarre, who gave us lessons at a guinea apiece, while we could only play with one hand at a time. Lastly there were a few young ladies who took instructions in the new instruments, the concertina and the accordion!

The waste of money involved in all this, the piles of useless music, and songs never to be sung, for which our parents had to pay, and the loss of priceless time for ourselves, were truly deplorable; and the result of course in many cases (as in my own) complete failure. One day I said to the good little German teacher, who nourished a hopeless attachment for Schiller's Marquis Posa,[4] and was altogether a sympathetic person, "My dear Fraulein, I mean to practise this piece of Beethoven's till I conquer it." "My dear," responded the honest Fraulein, "you do practice that piece for seex hours a day, and you do live till you are seexty, at the end you will *not* play it!" Yet so hopeless a pupil was compelled to learn for years, not only the piano, but the harp and singing!

Next to music in importance in our curriculum came dancing. The famous old Madame Michaud and her husband both attended us constantly, and we danced to their direction in our large play-room (*lucus a non lucendo*[5]), till we had learned not only all the dances in use in England in that ante-polka epoch, but almost every

4. In Friedrich von Schiller's play *Don Carlos* (1787), Posa is a self-sacrificing advocate of religious tolerance and democratic rule.

5. An ironic Latin phrase for naming something after what it lacks; Cobbe means that there was no play to be found in that playroom.

national dance in Europe, the Minuet, the Gavotte, the Cachucha, the Bolero, the Mazurka, and the Tarantella. To see the stout old lady in her heavy green velvet dress, with furbelow[6] a foot deep of sable, going through the latter cheerful performance for our ensample, was a sight not to be forgotten. Beside the dancing we had "calisthenic" lessons every week from a "Capitaine" Somebody, who put us through manifold exercises with poles and dumbbells. How much better a few good country scrambles would have been than all these calisthenics it is needless to say, but our dismal walks were confined to parading the esplanade[7] and neighbouring terraces. Our parties never exceeded six, a governess being one of the number, and we looked down from an immeasurable height of superiority on the processions of twenty and thirty girls belonging to other schools. The governess who accompanied us had enough to do with her small party, for it was her duty to utilise these brief hours of bodily exercise by hearing us repeat our French, Italian or German verbs, according to her own nationality.

Next to Music and Dancing and Deportment, came Drawing, but that was not a sufficiently *voyant* [remarkable] accomplishment, and no great attention was paid to it; the instruction also being of a second-rate kind, except that it included lessons in perspective which have been useful to me ever since. Then followed Modern Languages. No Greek or Latin were heard of at the school, but French, Italian and German were chattered all day long, our tongues being only set at liberty at six o'clock to speak English. *Such* French, such Italian, and such German as we actually spoke may be more easily imagined than described. We had bad "Marks" for speaking wrong languages, *e.g.*, French when we were bound to speak Italian or German, and a dreadful mark for bad French, which was transferred from one to another all day long, and was a fertile source of tears and quarrels, involving as it did a heavy lesson out of Noel et Chapsal's Grammar on the last holder at night. We also read in each language every day to the French, Italian and German ladies, recited lessons to them, and wrote exercises for the respective masters who attended every week. * * *

Naturally after (a very long way after) foreign languages came the study of English. We had a writing and arithmetic master (whom we unanimously abhorred and despised, though one and all of us grievously needed his instructions) and an "English master," who taught us to write "themes," and to whom I, for one, feel that I owe, perhaps, more than to any other teacher in that school, few as were the hours which we were permitted to waste on so insignificant an art as composition in our native tongue! * * *

Lastly, as I have said, in point of importance, came our religious instruction. Our well-meaning schoolmistresses thought it was obligatory on them to teach us something of the kind, but, being very obviously altogether worldly women themselves, they were puzzled how to carry out their intentions. They marched us to church every Sunday when it did not rain, and they made us on Sunday mornings repeat the Collect and Catechism; but beyond these exercises of body and mind, it was hard for them to see what to do for our spiritual welfare. One Ash Wednesday, I remember, they provided us with a dish of salt-fish, and when this was removed to make room for the roast mutton, they addressed us in a short discourse, setting forth the merits of fasting, and ending by the remark that they left us free to take meat or not as we pleased, but that they hoped we should fast; "it would be good for our souls AND OUR FIGURES!"

Each morning we were bound publicly to repeat a text out of certain little books, called *Daily Bread*, left in our bedrooms, and always scanned in frantic haste while

6. Showy fringe.   7. A public promenade.

"doing-up" our hair at the glass, or gabbled aloud by one damsel so occupied while her room-fellow (there were never more than two in each bed-chamber) was splashing about behind the screen in her bath. Down, when the prayer-bell rang, both were obliged to hurry and breathlessly to await the chance of being called on first to repeat the text of the day, the penalty for oblivion being the loss of a "card." Then came a chapter of the Bible, read verse by verse amongst us, and then our books were shut and a solemn question was asked. On one occasion I remember it was: "What have you just been reading, Miss S—?" Miss S—(now a lady of high rank and fashion, whose small wits had been wool-gathering) peeped surreptitiously into her Bible again, and then responded with just confidence, "The First Epistle, Ma'am, of *General Peter*."[8]

It is almost needless to add, in concluding these reminiscences, that the heterogeneous studies pursued in this helter-skelter fashion were of the smallest possible utility in later life; each acquirement being of the shallowest and most imperfect kind, and all real education worthy of the name having to be begun on our return home, after we had been pronounced "finished."

1894

◦──◦ ◄◆► ◦──◦

Sarah Stickney Ellis
1799–1872

Author of numerous popular guides to female conduct, including *The Women of England* (1839), *The Daughters of England* (1842), *The Wives of England* (1843), and *The Mothers of England* (1845), Sarah Stickney Ellis advised women to accept their inferiority to men and devote themselves to the happiness and moral elevation of their brothers, husbands, and sons. Idealizing the family home as the center of middle-class English life, Ellis fostered the notion of women's separate domestic sphere. Although she ran a school for girls, Ellis discouraged intellectual ambitions, demanding precisely the sort of self-sacrificing domesticity that Florence Nightingale, and many other talented and capable women, found so intolerably confining.

from The Women of England:
Their Social Duties and Domestic Habits
[THE INFLUENCE OF WOMEN]

It is not to be presumed that women *possess* more power than men; but happily for them, such are their early impressions, associations, and general position in the world, that their moral feelings are less liable to be impaired by the pecuniary objects which too often constitute the chief end of man, and which, even under the limitations of better principle, necessarily engage a large portion of his thoughts. There are many humble-minded women, not remarkable for any particular intellectual endowments, who yet possess so clear a sense of the right and wrong of individual actions, as to be of essential service in aiding the judgments of their husbands, brothers, or sons, in those intricate affairs in which it is sometimes difficult to dissever worldly wisdom from religious duty.

* * * And surely they now need more than ever all the assistance which Providence has kindly provided, to win them away from this warfare, to remind them that they are hastening on towards a world into which none of the treasures they are amassing can be admitted; and, next to those holier influences which operate

---

8. Instead of *The First Epistle General of Peter*.

through the medium of revelation, or through the mysterious instrumentality of Divine love, I have little hesitation in saying, that the society of woman in her highest moral capacity, is best calculated to effect this purpose.

How often has man returned to his home with a mind confused by the many voices, which in the mart, the exchange, or the public assembly, have addressed themselves to his inborn selfishness, or his worldly pride; and while his integrity was shaken, and his resolution gave way beneath the pressure of apparent necessity, or the insidious pretences of expediency, he has stood corrected before the clear eye of woman, as it looked directly to the naked truth, and detected the lurking evil of the specious act he was about to commit. Nay, so potent may have become this secret influence, that he may have borne it about with him like a kind of second conscience, for mental reference, and spiritual counsel, in moments of trial; and when the snares of the world were around him, and temptations from within and without have bribed over the witness in his own bosom, he has thought of the humble monitress who sat alone, guarding the fireside comforts of his distant home; and the remembrance of her character, clothed in moral beauty, has scattered the clouds before his mental vision, and sent him back to that beloved home, a wiser and a better man.

The women of England, possessing the grand privilege of being better instructed than those of any other country, in the minutiae of domestic comfort, have obtained a degree of importance in society far beyond what their unobtrusive virtues would appear to claim. The long-established customs of their country have placed in their hands the high and holy duty of cherishing and protecting the minor morals of life, from whence springs all that is elevated in purpose, and glorious in action. The sphere of their direct personal influence is central, and consequently small; but its extreme operations are as widely extended as the range of human feeling. They may be less striking in society than some of the women of other countries, and may feel themselves, on brilliant and stirring occasions, as simple, rude, and unsophisticated in the popular science of excitement; but as far as the noble daring of Britain has sent forth her adventurous sons, and that is to every point of danger on the habitable globe, they have borne along with them a generosity, a disinterestedness, and a moral courage, derived in no small measure from the female influence of their native country.

It is a fact well worthy of our most serious attention, and one which bears immediately upon the subject under consideration, that the present state of our national affairs is such as to indicate that the influence of woman in counteracting the growing evils of society is about to be more needed than ever. * * *

Will an increase of intellectual attainments, or a higher style of accomplishments, effect this purpose? Will the common-place frivolities of morning calls, or an interminable range of superficial reading, enable them to assist their brothers, their husbands, or their sons in becoming happier and better men?—No: let the aspect of society be what it may, man is a social being, and beneath the hard surface he puts on, to fit him for the wear and tear of every day, he has a heart as true to the kindly affections of our nature, as that of woman—as true, though not as suddenly awakened to every pressing call. He has therefore need of all her sisterly services—and under the pressure of the present times, he needs them more than ever—to foster in his nature, and establish in his character that higher tone of feeling, without which he can enjoy nothing beyond a kind of animal existence. * * *

In order to ascertain what kind of education is most effective in making woman what she ought to be, the best method is to inquire into the character, station, and peculiar duties of woman throughout the largest portion of her earthly career; and then ask, for what she is most valued, admired, and beloved?

In answer to this, I have little hesitation in saying,—For her disinterested kindness. Look at all the heroines, whether of romance or reality—at all the female characters that are held up to universal admiration—at all who have gone down to honoured graves, amongst the tears and the lamentations of their survivors. Have these been the learned, the accomplished women; the women who could speak many languages, who could solve problems, and elucidate systems of philosophy? No: or if they have, they have also been women who were dignified with the majesty of moral greatness—women who regarded not themselves, their own feebleness, or their own susceptibility of pain, but who, endued with an almost super-human energy, could trample under foot every impediment that intervened between them and the accomplishment of some great object upon which their hopes were fixed, while that object was wholly unconnected with their own personal exaltation or enjoyment, and related only to some beloved object, whose suffering was their sorrow, whose good their gain. ＊ ＊ ＊

Never yet, however, was woman great, because she had great acquirements; nor can she ever be great in herself—personally, and without instrumentality—as an object, not an agent. ＊ ＊ ＊

Let us single out from any particular seminary a child who has been there from the years of ten to fifteen, and reckon, if it can be reckoned, the pains that have been spent in making that child a proficient in Latin. Have the same pains been spent in making her disinterestedly kind? And yet what man is there in existence who would not rather his wife should be free from selfishness, than be able to read Virgil without the use of a dictionary. ＊ ＊ ＊

Taking into consideration the various excellencies and peculiarities of woman, I am inclined to think that the sphere which of all others admits of the highest development of her character, is the chamber of sickness; and how frequently and mournfully familiar are the scenes in which she is thus called to act and feel, let the private history of every family declare.

There is but a very small proportion of the daughters of farmers, manufacturers, and tradespeople, in England, who are ever called upon for their Latin, their Italian, or even for their French; but all women in this sphere of life are liable to be called upon to visit and care for the sick; and if in the hour of weakness and of suffering, they prove to be unacquainted with any probable means of alleviation, and wholly ignorant of the most judicious and suitable mode of offering relief and consolation, they are indeed deficient in one of the highest attainments in the way of usefulness, to which a woman can aspire. ＊ ＊ ＊

Women have the choice of many means of bringing their principles into exercise, and of obtaining influence, both in their own domestic sphere, and in society at large. Amongst the most important of these is *conversation*, an engine so powerful upon the minds and characters of mankind in general, that beauty fades before it, and wealth in comparison is but as leaden coin. If match-making were indeed the great object of human life, I should scarcely dare to make this assertion, since few men choose women for their conversation, where wealth or beauty are to be had. ＊ ＊ ＊

＊ ＊ ＊ But if she has no intellectual hold upon her husband's heart, she must inevitably become that most helpless and pitiable of earthly objects—a slighted wife.

Conversation, understood in its proper character, as distinct from mere talk, might rescue her from this. Not conversation upon books, if her husband happens to be a fox-hunter; nor upon fox-hunting, if he is a book-worm; but exactly that kind of conversation which is best adapted to his tastes and habits, yet at the same time capable of leading him a little out of both into a wider field of observation, and subjects he may never have derived amusement from before, simply from the fact of their never having been presented to his notice.—How pleasantly the evening hours may be made to pass, when a woman who really can converse, will thus beguile the time. But, on the other hand, how wretched is the portion of that man who dreads the dulness of his own fireside! who sees the clog of his existence ever seated there—the same, in the deadening influence she has upon his spirits to-day, as yesterday, to-morrow, and the next day, and the next!

1839

Charlotte Brontë
1816–1855

To be a governess or schoolteacher was one of the very few professions open to a middle-class woman, but it was not an enviable life. Rarely was the governess treated as an equal by her employers, even though she was expected to be a "lady." Poorly paid and often rudely treated, she could be fired at a moment's notice, for there was an abundance of needy single women eager to take her place. Charlotte Brontë's novel *Jane Eyre* (1847) portrayed the social isolation of a governess, who is ridiculed to her face by visiting ladies. Brontë's own experiences were unhappy, as this letter to her sister reveals. In another letter, Brontë wrote that it was better to be "a housemaid or kitchen girl, rather than a baited, trampled, desolate, distracted governess."

from Letter to Emily Brontë[1]
[*The Horrors of Governessing*]

STONEGAPPE, June 8th, 1839

* * * I have striven hard to be pleased with my new situation. The country, the house, and the grounds are, as I have said, divine. But, alack-a-day! there is such a thing as seeing all beautiful around you—pleasant woods, winding white paths, green lawns, and blue sunshiny sky—and not having a free moment or a free thought left to enjoy them in. The children are constantly with me, and more riotous, perverse, unmanageable cubs never grew. As for correcting them, I soon quickly found that was entirely out of the question: they are to do as they like. A complaint to Mrs Sidgwick brings only black looks upon oneself, and unjust, partial excuses to screen the children. I have tried that plan once. It succeeded so notably that I shall try it no more. I said in my last letter that Mrs Sidgwick did not know me. I now begin to find that she does not intend to know me, that she cares nothing in the world about me except to contrive how the greatest possible quantity of labour may be squeezed out of me, and to that end she overwhelms me with oceans of needlework, yards of cambric to hem, muslin nightcaps to make, and, above all things, dolls to dress. I do not think she likes me at all, because I can't help being shy in such an entirely novel scene, surrounded as I have hitherto been by strange and constantly changing faces. I used to think I should like to be in the stir of grand

1. Text taken from *The Brontës: Their Lives, Friendships and Correspondence*, vol. 1 (1933, rpt. 1980).

Richard Redgrave. *The Poor Teacher,* 1844. Narrative painting was enormously popular with the Victorians, who delighted in "reading" the story in symbolic visual details and drawing a moral from it. Here Redgrave, whose sisters were governesses, draws attention to his subject's social and emotional isolation. Dressed in mourning, the solitary governess sits indoors while her gaily-clad pupils skip rope in the sunlight, apparently indifferent to the bad news contained in her black-bordered letter. She has been playing "Home Sweet Home" on the piano. With copy books still to correct, she is about to consume her supper, a meager slice of bread and a tiny cup of tea. Contemporary observers speculated that she was an orphan, whose pallor revealed that she was already wasting away from illness and overwork.

folks' society but I have had enough of it—it is dreary work to look on and listen. I see now more clearly than I have ever done before that a private governess has no existence, is not considered as a living and rational being except as connected with the wearisome duties she has to fulfil. While she is teaching the children, working for them, amusing them, it is all right. If she steals a moment for herself she is a nuisance. Nevertheless, Mrs Sidgwick is universally considered an amiable woman. Her manners are fussily affable. She talks a great deal, but as it seems to me not much to the purpose. Perhaps I may like her better after a while. At present I have no call to her. Mr Sidgwick is in my opinion a hundred times better—less profession, less bustling condescension, but a far kinder heart. It is very seldom that he speaks to me, but when he does I always feel happier and more settled for some minutes after. He never asks me to wipe the children's smutty noses or tie their shoes or fetch their pinafores or set them a chair. * * *

⊷ ═◊═ ⊷

Anne Brontë
1820–1849

Like her older sisters, Charlotte and Emily, Anne Brontë tried to earn her living as a governess. All of them were made miserable by the constant drudgery and humiliations, and by being cut off, as governesses usually were, from family and friends. Her autobiographical novel *Agnes Grey* (1847) dramatizes Anne Brontë's own experience of working as a governess. Initially, she had looked forward to the job: "How delightful it would be to be a governess!" says Agnes: "To go out into the world; to enter into a new life; to act for myself; to exercise my unused faculties." But Agnes had not yet realized the drawbacks of a governess's anomalous social status: caught between disrespectful children and contemptuous parents, she was made grimly conscious of her dependent position.

from Agnes Grey
[THE GOVERNESS TORMENTED BY HER CHARGES]

I returned, however, with unabated vigour to my work—a more arduous task than any one can imagine, who has not felt something like the misery of being charged with the care and direction of a set of mischievous turbulent rebels, whom his utmost exertions cannot bind to their duty; while, at the same time, he is responsible for their conduct to a higher power, who exacts from him what cannot be achieved without the aid of the superior's more potent authority: which, either from indolence, or the fear of becoming unpopular with the said rebellious gang, the latter refuses to give. I can conceive few situations more harassing than that wherein, however you may long for success, however you may labour to fulfil your duty, your efforts are baffled and set at nought by those beneath you, and unjustly censured and misjudged by those above. * * *

I particularly remember one wild, snowy afternoon, soon after my return in January; the children had all come up from dinner, loudly declaring that they meant "to be naughty"; and they had well kept their resolution, though I had talked myself hoarse, and wearied every muscle in my throat, in the vain attempt to reason them out of it. I had got Tom pinned up in a corner, whence, I told him, he should not escape till he had done his appointed task. Meantime, Fanny had possessed herself of my work-bag, and was rifling its contents—and spitting into it besides. I told her to let it alone, but to no purpose, of course.

"Burn it, Fanny!" cried Tom; and *this* command she hastened to obey. I sprang to snatch it from the fire, and Tom darted to the door.

"Mary Ann, throw her desk[1] out of the window!" cried he: and my precious desk, containing my letters and papers, my small amount of cash, and all my valuables, was about to be precipitated from the three-story window. I flew to rescue it. Meanwhile Tom had left the room, and was rushing down the stairs, followed by Fanny. Having secured my desk, I ran to catch them, and Mary Ann came scampering after. All three escaped me, and ran out of the house into the garden, where they plunged about in the snow, shouting and screaming in exultant glee.

What must I do? If I followed them, I should probably be unable to capture one, and only drive them farther away; if I did not, how was I to get them in? and what would their parents think of me, if they saw or heard the children rioting, hatless, bonnetless, gloveless, and bootless, in the deep, soft snow?

---

1. Portable box for writing materials and letters, sometimes with a sloping surface for writing on.

While I stood in this perplexity, just without the door, trying by grim looks and angry words, to awe them into subjection, I heard a voice behind me, in harshly piercing tones, exclaiming,—

"Miss Grey! Is it possible? What, in the devil's name, can you be thinking about?"

"I can't get them in, sir," said I, turning round, and beholding Mr Bloomfield, with his hair on end, and his pale blue eyes bolting from their sockets.

"But I INSIST upon their being got in!" cried he, approaching nearer, and looking perfectly ferocious.

"Then, sir, you must call them yourself, if you please, for they won't listen to me," I replied, stepping back.

"Come in with you, you filthy brats! or I'll horsewhip you, every one!" roared he; and the children instantly obeyed. "There, you see! they come at the first word!"

"Yes, when *you* speak."

"And it's very strange, that when you've the care of 'em, you've no better control over 'em than that!—Now, there they are, gone upstairs with their nasty snowy feet! Do go after 'em and see them made decent, for Heaven's sake!"

That gentleman's mother was then staying in the house; and, as I ascended the stairs and passed the drawing-room door, I had the satisfaction of hearing the old lady declaiming aloud to her daughter-in-law to this effect (for I could only distinguish the most emphatic words)—

"Gracious Heavens!—never in all my life!—!—get their death as sure as—! Do you think, my dear, she's a *proper person?* Take my word for it—"

I heard no more, but that sufficed.

1847

⊶ ⇌ ⊷

John Henry Cardinal Newman
1801–1890

The ideal of gentlemanliness was central to the Victorians' notion of themselves, yet for a society in flux it was a concept increasingly difficult to pin down. What exactly *was* a gentleman? In most people's minds, property, birth, courage, and athleticism were essential ingredients. And, of course, a gentleman was assumed to be a Christian. But the theologian and philosopher of education Newman distinguished between the two: in a series of lectures about the purposes of a liberal education he said that while the gentleman has "a cultivated intellect, a delicate taste, a candid, equitable, dispassionate mind, a noble and courteous bearing in the conduct of life . . . they are no guarantee for sanctity or even for conscientiousness; they may attach to the man of the world, to the profligate, to the heartless." Thus for Newman, who was both, a gentleman is not necessarily a Christian: one may have character and education, but not faith. He subtly suggests the vanity behind the gentleman's courtesy; gentility and virtue are not necessarily the same thing.

from The Idea of a University
[A DEFINITION OF A GENTLEMAN]

Hence it is that it is almost a definition of a gentleman to say he is one who never inflicts pain. This description is both refined and, as far as it goes, accurate. He is mainly occupied in merely removing the obstacles which hinder the free and unembarrassed action of those about him; and he concurs with their movements rather than takes the initiative himself. His benefits may be considered as parallel to what are called comforts or conveniences in arrangements of a personal nature: like an easy chair or a good fire, which do their part in dispelling cold and fatigue, though nature provides both means of rest and animal heat without them. The true gentleman in like manner carefully avoids whatever may cause a jar or a jolt in the minds of those with whom he is cast;—all clashing of opinion, or collision of feeling, all restraint, or suspicion, or gloom, or resentment; his great concern being to make every one at their ease and at home. He has his eyes on all his company; he is tender towards the bashful, gentle towards the distant, and merciful towards the absurd; he can recollect to whom he is speaking; he guards against unseasonable allusions, or topics which may irritate; he is seldom prominent in conversation, and never wearisome. He makes light of favours while he does them, and seems to be receiving when he is conferring. He never speaks of himself except when compelled, never defends himself by a mere retort, he has no ears for slander or gossip, is scrupulous in imputing motives to those who interfere with him, and interprets every thing for the best. He is never mean or little in his disputes, never takes unfair advantage, never mistakes personalities or sharp sayings for arguments, or insinuates evil which he dare not say out. From a longsighted prudence, he observes the maxim of the ancient sage, that we should ever conduct ourselves towards our enemy as if he were one day to be our friend. He has too much good sense to be affronted at insults, he is too well employed to remember injuries, and too indolent to bear malice. He is patient, forbearing, and resigned, on philosophical principles; he submits to pain, because it is inevitable, to bereavement, because it is irreparable, and to death, because it is his destiny. If he engages in controversy of any kind, his disciplined intellect preserves him from the blundering discourtesy of better, perhaps, but less educated minds; who, like blunt weapons, tear and hack instead of cutting clean, who mistake the point in argument, waste their strength on trifles, misconceive their adversary, and leave the question more involved than they find it. He may be right or wrong in his opinion, but he is too clear-headed to be unjust; he is as simple as he is forcible, and as brief as he is decisive. Nowhere shall we find greater candour, consideration, indulgence: he throws himself into the minds of his opponents, he accounts for their mistakes. He knows the weakness of human reason as well as its strength, its province and its limits. If he be an unbeliever, he will be too profound and large-minded to ridicule religion or to act against it; he is too wise to be a dogmatist or fanatic in his infidelity. He respects piety and devotion; he even supports institutions as venerable, beautiful, or useful, to which he does not assent; he honours the ministers of religion, and it contents him to decline its mysteries without assailing or denouncing them. He is a friend of religious toleration, and that, not only because his philosophy has taught him to look on all forms of faith with an impartial eye, but also from the gentleness and effeminacy of feeling, which is the attendant on civilization.

1852

+—◄◆►—+

Isabella Beeton
1836–1865

The home was a near-sacred institution in Victorian England, and when Mrs. Beeton published her book of advice on household management it became a bestseller second only to the Bible. In over a thousand pages of small print, she instructed women on matters ranging from the supervision of servants to the care of the sick, from meal planning to proper conduct during a social call. Mrs. Beeton's portrait of the mistress of the house reflects a complex, somewhat contradictory, sense of a woman's role: she is at once "the commander of an army"—with the housekeeper as her "second in command"—and a lady of leisure, enjoying "the pleasures of literature" and "the innocent delights of the garden." Yet, like a child, she needs to be scolded to rise early and be punctual. Although Mrs. Beeton was just twenty-four, she was respected as an oracle in the domestic sphere; her cookbook is still used today. She died in childbirth at twenty-eight.

from The Book of Household Management

I must frankly own, that if I had known, beforehand, that this book would have cost me the labour which it has, I should never have been courageous enough to commence it. What moved me, in the first instance, to attempt a work like this, was the discomfort and suffering which I had seen brought upon men and women by household mismanagement. I have always thought that there is no more fruitful source of family discontent than a housewife's badly-cooked dinners and untidy ways. Men are now so well served out of doors,—at their clubs, well-ordered taverns, and dining-houses, that in order to compete with the attractions of these places, a mistress must be thoroughly acquainted with the theory and practice of cookery, as well as be perfectly conversant with all the other arts of making and keeping a comfortable home. * * *

As with the Commander of an Army, or the leader of any enterprise, so is it with the mistress of a house. Her spirit will be seen through the whole establishment; and just in proportion as she performs her duties intelligently and thoroughly, so will her domestics follow in her path. Of all those acquirements, which more particularly belong to the feminine character, there are none which take a higher rank, in our estimation, than such as enter into a knowledge of household duties; for on these are perpetually dependent the happiness, comfort, and well-being of a family. * * *

Early Rising is one of the most Essential Qualities which enter into good Household Management, as it is not only the parent of health, but of innumerable other advantages. Indeed, when a mistress is an early riser, it is almost certain that her house will be orderly and well-managed. On the contrary, if she remain in bed till a late hour, then the domestics, who, as we have before observed, invariably partake somewhat of their mistress's character, will surely become sluggards. * * *

Friendships should not be hastily formed, nor the heart given, at once, to every new-comer. There are ladies who uniformly smile at, and approve everything and everybody, and who possess neither the courage to reprehend vice, nor the generous warmth to defend virtue. The friendship of such persons is without attachment, and their love without affection or even preference. * * *

Hospitality is a most Excellent Virtue; but care must be taken that the love of company, for its own sake, does not become a prevailing passion; for then the habit is no longer hospitality, but dissipation. * * * With respect to the continuance of friendships * * * it may be found necessary, in some cases, for a mistress to relinquish, on assuming the responsibility of a house-hold, many of those commenced in the earlier part of her life. * * *

In Conversation, Trifling Occurrences, such as small disappointments, petty annoyances, and other every-day incidents, should never be mentioned to your friends. The extreme injudiciousness of repeating these will be at once apparent, when we reflect on the unsatisfactory discussions which they too frequently occasion, and on the load of advice which they are the cause of being tendered, and which is, too often, of a kind neither to be useful nor agreeable. * * * If the mistress be a wife, never let an account of her husband's failings pass her lips. * * *

After Breakfast is over, it will be well for the mistress to make a round of the kitchen and other offices, to see that all are in order, and that the morning's work has been properly performed by the various domestics. The orders for the day should then be given, and any questions which the domestics desire to ask, respecting their several departments, should be answered, and any special articles they may require, handed to them from the store-closet. * * *

After this General Superintendence of her servants, the mistress, if a mother of a young family, may devote herself to the instruction of some of its younger members, or to the examination of the state of their wardrobe, leaving the later portion of the morning for reading, or for some amusing recreation. * * *

Unless the means of the mistress be very circumscribed, and she be obliged to devote a great deal of her time to the making of her children's clothes, and other economical pursuits, it is right that she should give some time to the pleasures of literature, the innocent delights of the garden, and to the improvement of any special abilities for music, painting, and other elegant arts, which she may, happily, possess. * * *

After Luncheon, Morning Calls and Visits may be made and received. These may be divided under three heads: those of ceremony, friendship, and congratulation or condolence. Visits of ceremony, or courtesy, which occasionally merge into those of friendship, are to be paid under various circumstances. Thus, they are uniformly required after dining at a friend's house, or after a ball, picnic, or any other party. These visits should be short, a stay of from fifteen to twenty minutes being quite sufficient. A lady paying a visit may remove her boa or neckerchief; but neither her shawl nor bonnet.

When other visitors are announced, it is well to retire as soon as possible, taking care to let it appear that their arrival is not the cause. When they are quietly seated, and the bustle of their entrance is over, rise from your chair, taking a kind leave of the hostess, and bowing politely to the guests. Should you call at an inconvenient time, not having ascertained the luncheon hour, or from any other inadvertence, retire as soon as possible, without, however, showing that you feel yourself an intruder. It is not difficult for any well-bred or even good-tempered person, to know what to say on such an occasion, and, on politely withdrawing, a promise can be made to call again, if the lady you have called on, appear really disappointed.

In Paying Visits of Friendship, it will not be so necessary to be guided by etiquette as in paying visits of ceremony; and if a lady be pressed by her friend to remove her shawl and bonnet, it can be done if it will not interfere with her subsequent arrangements. * * * During these visits, the manners should be easy and cheerful, and the subjects of conversation such as may be readily terminated. Serious discussions or arguments are to be altogether avoided.

1861

✦❖✦

Queen Victoria
1819–1901

Queen Victoria, who ruled from 1837 to 1901, was the most prominent woman of the age, and during her reign the monarchy came to symbolize the farflung power of the British empire. Although she was a capable woman who wielded genuine political influence, she felt uncomfortably thrust into greatness, and often deplored the contradictions of her position. A firm believer in the notion that men and women should occupy separate spheres, the queen regarded campaigns for women's rights as "dangerous and unchristian and unnatural." The mother of nine children, Victoria was revered as the embodiment of domestic propriety, but her views on maternity were decidedly unsentimental. Her letters to her eldest daughter lament the sufferings of pregnancy, and in the 1850s Queen Victoria pioneered the use of chloroform in childbirth, thus making anesthesia acceptable for other women.

Letters and Journal Entries on the Position of Women
Journal[1]

20 June 1837

I was awoke at 6 o'clock by Mamma,[2] who told me that the Archbishop of Canterbury and Lord Conyngham were here, and wished to see me. I got out of bed and went into my sitting-room (only in my dressing-gown), and alone, and saw them. Lord Conyngham then acquainted me that my poor Uncle, the King, was no more, and had expired at 12 minutes p. 2 this morning, and consequently that I am Queen. Lord Conyngham knelt down and kissed my hand, at the same time delivering to me the official announcement of the poor King's demise. The Archbishop then told me that the Queen[3] was desirous that he should come and tell me the details of the last moments of my poor, good Uncle; he said that he had directed his mind to religion and had died in a perfectly happy, quiet state of mind, and was quite prepared for his death. He added that the King's sufferings at the last were not very great but that there was a good deal of uneasiness. Lord Conyngham, who I charged to express my feelings of condolence and sorrow to the poor Queen, returned directly to Windsor. I then went to my room and dressed.

Since it has pleased Providence to place me in this station, I shall do my utmost to fulfil my duty towards my country; I am very young and perhaps in many, though not in all things, inexperienced, but I am sure, that very few have more real good will and more real desire to do what is fit and right than I have. * * *

To Princess Frederick William[4]

24 March 1858

That you should feel shy sometimes I can easily understand. I do so very often to this hour. But being married gives one one's position which nothing else can. Think however what it was for me, a girl of 18 all alone, not brought up at court as you were—but very humbly at Kensington Palace—with trials and difficulties, to receive and be everywhere the first! No, no one knows what a life of difficulties mine was—and is! How thankful I am that none of you, please God! ever will have that anomalous and trying position. Now do enter into this in your letters, you so seldom do that, except to answer a question.

Now to reply to your observation that you find a married woman has much more liberty than an unmarried one; in one sense of the word she has,—but what I meant was—in a physical point of view—and if you have hereafter (as I had constantly for the first 2 years of my marriage)—aches—and sufferings and miseries and plagues—which you must struggle against—and enjoyments etc. to give up—constant precautions to take, you will feel the yoke of a married woman! Without that—certainly it is unbounded happiness—if one has a husband one worships! It is a foretaste of heaven. And you have a husband who adores you, and is, I perceive, ready to meet every wish and desire of your's. I had 9 times for 8 months[5] to bear with those above-named enemies and real misery (besides many duties) and I own it tried me sorely; one feels so pinned down—one's wings clipped—in fact, at the best (and few were or

---

1. From *Queen Victoria in Her Letters and Journals*, ed. Christopher Hibbert (1985).
2. Victoria's mother was the widow of Edward, Duke of Kent, the fourth son of George III. Since Edward died when Victoria was an infant, she was brought up by her mother. She had just turned eighteen when she became queen on the death of her uncle, King William IV.
3. Adelaide, the widow of William IV.

4. This and the following letters on marriage and childbirth are from *Dearest Child: Letters between Queen Victoria and the Princess Royal, 1858–1861*, ed. Roger Fulford (1964). On January 25, 1858, at the age of seventeen, Victoria's eldest daughter had married Prince Frederick [Fritz], later Crown Prince of Prussia. Her mother wrote her frequent letters, full of maternal advice.
5. Victoria alludes to her nine pregnancies.

Edwin Landseer. *Windsor Castle in Modern Times,* 1841–1845, showing Queen Victoria and Prince Albert at home with their eldest child Princess Victoria.

are better than I was) only half oneself—particularly the first and second time. This I call the "shadow side" as much as being torn away from one's loved home, parents and brothers and sisters. And therefore—I think our sex a most unenviable one.

26 May 1858

The horrid news contained in Fritz's letter to Papa [that the Princess was pregnant] upset us dreadfully. The more so as I feel certain almost it will all end in nothing.

15 June 1858

What you say of the pride of giving life to an immortal soul is very fine, dear, but I own I cannot enter into that; I think much more of our being like a cow or a dog at such moments; when our poor nature becomes so very animal and unecstatic—but for you, dear, if you are sensible and reasonable not in ecstasy nor spending your day with nurses and wet nurses, which is the ruin of many a refined and intellectual young lady, without adding to her real maternal duties, a child will be a great resource. Above all, dear, do remember never to lose the modesty of a young girl towards others (without being prude); though you are married don't become a matron at once to whom everything can be said, and who minds saying nothing herself—I remained particular to a degree (indeed feel so now) and often feel shocked at the confidences of other married ladies. I fear abroad they are very indelicate about these things.

29 January 1859

God be praised for all his mercies, and for bringing you safely through this awful time![6] Our joy, our gratitude knows no bounds.

My precious darling, you suffered much more that I ever did—and how I wish I could have lightened them for you! Poor dear Fritz—how he will have suffered for you! I think and feel much for him; the dear little boy if I could but see him for one minute, give you one kiss. It is hard, very hard. But we are so happy, so grateful! * * * You will and must feel so thankful all is over! But don't be alarmed for the future, it never can be so bad again!

20 April 1859

I really think I shall never let your sisters marry—certainly not to be so constantly away and see so little of their parents—as till now, you have done, contrary to all that I was originally promised and told. I am so glad to see that you so entirely enter into all my feelings as a mother. Yes, dearest, it is an awful moment to have to give one's innocent child up to a man, be he ever so kind and good—and to think of all that she must go through! I can't say what I suffered, what I felt—what struggles I had to go through— (indeed I have not quite got over it yet) and that last night when we took you to your room, and you cried so much, I said to Papa as we came back "after all, it is like taking a poor lamb to be sacrificed." You now know—what I meant, dear. I know that God has willed it so and that these are the trials which we poor women must go through; no father, no man can feel this! Papa never would enter into it all! As in fact he seldom can in my very violent feelings. It really makes me shudder when I look around at all your sweet, happy, unconscious sisters—and think that I must give them up too—one by one!! Our dear Alice [who was 15], has seen and heard more (of course not what no one ever can know before they marry and before they have had children) than you did, from your marriage—and quite enough to give her a horror rather of marrying.

4 May 1859

Abstractedly, I have no *tendre* for them [babies] till they have become a little human; an ugly baby is a very nasty object—and the prettiest is frightful when undressed—till about four months; in short as long as they have their big body and little limbs and that terrible frog-like action. But from four months, they become prettier and prettier. And I repeat it—your child would delight me at any age.

15 June 1859

Now I must scold you a wee bit for an observation which really seems at variance with your own expressions. You say "how glad" Ada [the Queen's niece] "must be" at being again in that most charming situation, which you yourself very frequently told me last year was so wretched. How can anyone, who has not been married above two years and three quarters, (like Ada) rejoice at being a third time in that condition? I positively think those ladies who are always *enceinte* quite disgusting; it is more like a rabbit or guinea-pig than anything else and really it is not very nice.

16 May 1860

All marriage is such a lottery—the happiness is always an exchange—though it may be a very happy one—still the poor woman is bodily and morally the husband's slave. That always sticks in my throat. When I think of a merry, happy, free young

---

6. After a difficult and dangerous labor, Victoria's daughter had given birth on January 27, 1859; her son was the future Kaiser Wilhelm II, who led Germany against England in the First World War.

girl—and look at the ailing, aching state a young wife generally is doomed to—which you can't deny is the penalty of marriage.

17 November 1860

My beloved child, these lines are to wish you heartily and warmly joy of your 20th birthday—an important age—though married nearly three years and with two children it seems but of little consequence. Still to bid adieu to one's "teens" is a serious thing!

18 December 1861

What is to become of us all?[7] Of the unhappy country, of Europe, of all? For you all, the loss of such a father is totally irreparable! I will do all I can to follow out all his wishes—to live for you all and for my duties. But how I, who leant on him for all and everything—without whom I did nothing, moved not a finger, arranged not a print or photograph, didn't put on a gown or bonnet if he didn't approve it shall be able to go on, to live, to move, to help myself in difficult moments? How I shall long to ask his advice! Oh! it is too, too weary! The day—the night (above all the night) is too sad and weary. The days never pass! I try to feel and think that I am living on with him, and that his pure and perfect spirit is guiding and leading me and inspiring me!

Sweet little Beatrice comes to lie in my bed every morning which is a comfort. I long so to cling to and clasp a loving being. Oh! how I admired Papa! How in love I was with him! How everything about him was beautiful and precious in my eyes! Oh! how, how I miss all, all! Oh! Oh! the bitterness of this—of this woe!

To William Gladstone[8]

6 May 1870

The circumstances respecting the Bill to give women the same position as men with respect to Parliamentary franchise gives her an opportunity to observe that she had for some time past wished to call Mr Gladstone's attention to the mad & utterly demoralizing movement of the present day to place women in the same position as to professions—as *men;*—& amongst others, in the *Medical Line*.

* * * And she is *most* anxious that it should be known how she not only disapproves but *abhors* the attempts to destroy all propriety & womanly feeling which will inevitably be the result of what has been proposed. The Queen is a woman herself—& knows what an anomaly her *own* position is:—but that can be reconciled with reason & propriety tho' it is a terribly difficult & trying one. But to tear away all the barriers which surround a woman, & to propose that they should study with *men*—things which could not be named before them—certainly not *in a mixed* audience—would be to introduce a total disregard of what must be considered as belonging to the rules & principles of morality.

The Queen feels so strongly upon this dangerous & unchristian & unnatural *cry* & movement of "woman's rights,"—in which she knows Mr Gladstone *agrees,* (as he sent her that excellent Pamphlet by Lady) that she is most anxious that Mr Gladstone & others should take some steps to check this alarming danger & to make whatever use they can of her name. * * *

7. Victoria was grief-stricken at the death of her husband, Prince Albert, on December 14, 1861; after his death she mourned him obsessively, going into virtual seclusion for many years. Beatrice was her ninth child, born in 1857. This letter is from *Queen Victoria in Her Letters and Journals,* ed. Christopher Hibbert (1985).

8. Gladstone (1809–1898) was the prime minister in four Liberal governments (1868–1874, 1880–1885, 1886, 1892–1894). This letter is from *The Queen and Mr. Gladstone* (1933) by Philip Guedalla. The Queen refers to the recurrence of the proposal to give women the vote, first presented to the House of Commons in 1866 by J. S. Mill.

Let woman be what God intended; a helpmate for a man—but with totally different duties & vocations.

To Sir Theodore Martin[9]

29 May 1870

The Queen is most anxious to enlist every one who can speak or write to join in checking this mad, wicked folly of "Woman's Rights," with all its attendant horrors, on which her poor feeble sex is bent, forgetting every sense of womanly feeling and propriety. Lady— ought to get a *good whipping*.

It is a subject which makes the Queen so furious that she cannot contain herself. God created men and women different—then let them remain each in their own position. Tennyson has some beautiful lines on the difference of men and women in *The Princess*.[1] Woman would become the most hateful, heartless, and disgusting of human beings were she allowed to unsex herself; and where would be the protection which man was intended to give the weaker sex? The Queen is sure that Mrs Martin agrees with her.

Charles Kingsley
1819–1875

Charles Kingsley was a hearty country clergyman and prolific writer whose sermons praised physical prowess and manly pursuits such as riding, hunting, and fishing. He was a vigorous Protestant, suspicious of celibacy and of what he considered the feminine monasticism of Catholicism: an injudicious remark of his about the dishonesty of the Catholic clergy prompted Newman's *Apologia Pro Vita Sua*. Kingsley is so often paired with Thomas Hughes, author of *Tom Brown's School Days*, that he has been called "the most famous Brown in the Victorian period;" although he didn't go to Rugby, he embodied the spirit of its headmaster Dr. Arnold. "Muscular Christianity" was originally a term of mocking disparagement for boisterous assertions of bodily strength and energy as the foundation of a pure moral life. But the blending of Christianity with manliness was part of an emerging middle-class identity that strove toward an ideal of public service: both Hughes and Kingsley embraced Christian socialism, a movement to respond to the injustices of industrialism.

from Letters and Memories
[MUSCULAR CHRISTIANITY]

[From a letter to his fiancée, Frances Grenfell:]

There has always seemed to me something impious in the neglect of personal health, strength, and beauty, which the religious, and sometimes clergymen of this day affect. It is very often a mere form of laziness. . . . I could not do half the little good I do do here, if it were not for that strength and activity which some consider coarse and degrading. Do not be afraid of my overworking myself. If I stop, I go down. I must work. . . . How merciful God has been in turning all the strength and hardihood I gained in snipe shooting and hunting, and rowing, and jack-fishing in those magnificent fens[1] to His work! While I was following my own fancies, He was preparing me for His work. . . . Is it not an awful proof that matter is not necessarily evil, that we shall be clothed in bodies even in our

---

9. This letter is from *Queen Victoria As I Knew Her* (1908) by Sir Theodore Martin, a lawyer and man of letters.
1. See *The Princess* (page 1927): "For woman is not undevelopt man, / But diverse: could we make her as

the man, / Sweet Love were slain: his dearest bond is this, / Not like to like, but like in difference."
1. Low marshy areas.

perfect state? Think of that! . . . It seems all so harmonious to me. It is all so full of God, that I see no inconsistency in making my sermons while I am cutting wood; and no "bizarrerie" in talking one moment to one man about the points of a horse, and the next moment to another about the mercy of God to sinners. I try to catch men by their leading ideas, and so draw them off insensibly to my leading idea. And so I find—shall I tell you? that God is really permitting me to do His work—I find that dissent is decreasing; people are coming to church who never went anywhere before; that I am loved and respected— or rather that God's ministry, which has been here deservedly despised, alas! is beginning to be respected; and above all, that the young wild fellows who are considered as hopeless by most men, because most men are what they call "spoony Methodists," *i.e.*, effeminate ascetics—dare not gainsay, but rather look up to a man who they see is their superior, if he chose to exert his power, in physical as well as intellectual skill. * * *

1842   1877

[From a letter to the Reverend F. D. Maurice:]

I do feel very deeply the truth which John Mill has set forth in a one-sided way in his new book on Liberty[2] * * * about the past morality of Christendom having taken a somewhat abject tone, and requiring, as a complement, the old Pagan virtues, which our forefathers learnt from Plutarch's Lives, and of which the memory still lingers in our classical education. I do not believe, of course, that the want really exists: but that it was created, principally by the celibate misanthropy of the patristic and mediaeval church. But I have to preach the divineness of the whole manhood, and am content to be called a Muscular Christian, or any other impertinent name, by men who little dream of the weakness of character, sickness of body, and misery of mind, by which I have bought what little I know of the human heart.

1857   1877

+—◦——◦—+

Sir Henry Newbolt
1862–1938

Newbolt's rousing patriotic poems make explicit the link between public school games and the romantic ideology of empire. Schoolboy sports were not merely about keeping fit; with their emphasis on manliness, mettle, and pluck, they were preparing the upper classes to regard imperialism as a grand adventure. School loyalty merged with national patriotism. Games fostered the notion that wars were won by team spirit, holding up the side, and never quitting. Young English officers carried this schoolboy code into combat: they saw war itself as a "great game," and battlefields as playing fields. Their letters from the front during World War I described the action in the language of sports. One officer actually dribbled a soccer ball as he led his men to their deaths in the battle of the Somme.

Vitaï Lampada[1]

There's a breathless hush in the Close[2] to-night—
    Ten to make and the match to win—
A bumping pitch and a blinding light,
    An hour to play and the last man in.
5   And it's not for the sake of a ribboned coat,

2. *On Liberty* (1859); see page 1845.
1. The Torch of Life; a reference to a relay race, described in Lucretius's *De Rerum Natura*, where runners hand off a flaming torch.
2. The playing fields at a public school.

Or the selfish hope of a season's fame,
But his Captain's hand on his shoulder smote—
"Play up! play up! and play the game!"

The sand of the desert is sodden red,—
10   Red with the wreck of a square that broke;—
The Gatling's[3] jammed and the Colonel dead,
And the regiment blind with dust and smoke.
The river of death has brimmed his banks,
And England's far, and Honour a name,
15   But the voice of a schoolboy rallies the ranks:
"Play up! play up! and play the game!"

This is the word that year by year,
While in her place the School is set,
Every one of her sons must hear,
20   And none that hears it dare forget.
This they all with a joyful mind
Bear through life like a torch in flame,
And falling fling to the host behind—
"Play up! play up! and play the game!"

1897

[END OF PERSPECTIVES: VICTORIAN LADIES AND GENTLEMEN]

Alfred, Lord Tennyson
1809–1892

"There, that is the first money you have ever earned by your poetry, and, take my word for it, it will be the last." These were the words of Tennyson's crusty grandfather, as he doled out ten shillings for the teenager's ode on the death of his grandmother. The pen proved mightier than the prediction, however, as Tennyson went on to become the most celebrated poet of the age. His books sold tens of thousands of copies; the Queen and Parliament named him Poet Laureate, then Lord, and finally Baron Tennyson; his annual income surpassed ten thousand pounds a year; and he was widely regarded as something more than a poet—a prophet, a sage, and an infallible moneymaker. A New York publisher once offered him a thousand pounds for any three-stanza poem he cared to write.

It is often said that Tennyson's greatness lay in eloquently presenting the anxieties and aspirations of his era. In poems such as *Ulysses, In Memoriam,* and *Idylls of the King,* he expressed the energy, resolve, faith, and idealism of an industrious society that was nonetheless racked by deep doubts about its materialism, the truth of the Bible, and the possibility of achieving a truly Christian society. But Tennyson was not just a mouthpiece for his age: in the early and mid-Victorian period Tennyson was one of its most progressive voices, espousing views that were all the more daring for a shy and sensitive man struggling to realize his dream of becoming "a *popular* poet." His assertion in *The Princess* (1847) that "the woman's cause is man's" anticipates Mill's *The Subjection of Women* by more than twenty years; in the course of writing *In Memoriam* (1850) he lucidly formulated some of the main principles of evolutionary theory well before Darwin's *Origin of Species* (1859); he called public attention to the industri-

---

3. An early form of machine gun.

alized misery and revolutionary anger of the poor during the 1840s while the contemporaneous works of Marx and Engels were virtually unknown; and in *Locksley Hall* (1842) he evoked the technological promise of the future as compellingly as any science fiction writer.

One key to Tennyson's poetic success was his prosaic devotion to the Victorian gospel of hard work. He labored patiently, in poverty and without recognition, to overcome his troubled background. Born in Somersby, Lincolnshire, Tennyson was the third surviving son in a close-knit but emotionally unstable family of eleven children, two of whom suffered lifelong mental illness, while two more were addicted to drugs and alcohol. The poet's father, George, was an awkward, tormented man whose ill temper was aggravated into alcoholism and violence when he was disinherited in favor of his younger brother, and then forced to accept a position as village rector. It seems that the entire family was prone to epilepsy. Well into maturity, Alfred was haunted by fear of "the black blood of the Tennysons."

Tennyson's grim childhood was brightened by his mother's warmth and affection, his father's extensive library, and both parents' love of poetry. The rectory was surrounded by large gardens and open countryside, and as a child Tennyson composed nature poetry in the manner of James Thomson's *Seasons*. Early years at a brutally strict grammar school, followed by intensive tutoring from his erudite father, gave Tennyson a solid grounding in Greek, Latin, English, and modern languages by the time he went to Cambridge University in 1827. He had already mastered the styles of poets ranging from Horace and Virgil to Shakespeare, Milton, Scott, and Byron, and earlier that year he published his first book, *Poems by Two Brothers*. It was written with his brother Charles, with whom he used to exchange lines on their country walks, shouting them out across the hedges. The habit of building poems around a series of sonorous individual lines would remain with Tennyson all his life.

At Cambridge the timid country boy began gradually to assume the artistic persona that would be revered throughout the empire. Tall, ruggedly handsome, and with a faraway look in his eyes that was actually due to myopia, Tennyson fit everyone's idea of how a poet should look. He distinguished himself by the quality of his talk, his humorous storytelling, and his acting ability. In 1829 he received the Chancellor's Medal for *Timbuctoo*, the first poem in blank verse ever to win. The same year he and his best friend Arthur Henry Hallam joined "The Apostles," a select group of undergraduates who met to discuss social, philosophical, and literary issues. Members became lifelong friends, and their admiration of his early work helped convince the reticent Tennyson to publish *Poems, Chiefly Lyrical* in 1830. The book received mixed reviews.

In 1831 his father died, and Tennyson had to return home without a degree. Yet Tennyson persevered, issuing in 1832 a new volume, *Poems*. This time, the reviews were actively hostile. Tennyson's morale was sustained only by the visits to Somersby of Hallam, who by now was engaged to Tennyson's sister Emily. Then in 1833 Hallam died suddenly of a cerebral hemorrhage while on a trip to Vienna, and Tennyson's life changed forever.

Within a week of hearing the news, Tennyson began work on his greatest poem, though he did not know then that the brief lyric passages of love, loss, and doubt that he composed to assuage his grief would eventually become *In Memoriam*, an epic meditation on mortality, evolution, and the hard-won consolations of inner faith. He was already proficient, like his early hero Byron, in turning his own private misery into virtuoso evocations of emotionally charged landscapes. As John Stuart Mill wrote in 1835, Tennyson excelled in "the power of *creating* scenery, in keeping with some state of human feeling, so fitted to it as to be the embodied symbol of it, and to summon up the state of feeling itself, with a force not to be surpassed by anything but reality." Quoting *Mariana* as an example, Mill concluded that "words surely never created a more vivid feeling of physical and spiritual dreariness."

Outwardly Tennyson was calm, actively reading, writing, and socializing, but in his poetry he pictured himself as a weeping widower who mourned "a loss forever new." In 1842 he reluctantly published a two-volume edition of *Poems*, improving earlier works and introducing new ones, most notably *Ulysses* and *Morte d'Arthur*. Although his reputation was now rising, the poet was at a low ebb. He was so poor and hampered by responsibilities to his unraveling family that he was forced to postpone indefinitely his marriage to Emily Sellwood, to whom he had become engaged in 1838.

At this point Tennyson lost all his money in a scheme for carving wood by machinery. His friends feared he was on the verge of suicide. Here, as at other dark times in his life, he relied on sheer willpower to follow the advice he once offered to a depressed friend: "Just go grimly on." Eventually travel, hydropathic cures, new acquaintances, and improving finances assuaged his melancholia. Publication of *The Princess* in 1847 finally gave him the popular notice he had long sought.

But it was not until 1850 that Tennyson triumphed in life and art. In May, after seventeen years' brooding, he published *In Memoriam* to great acclaim; on June 13 he married Emily; and by the end of June one reviewer was calling him "the greatest living poet." The sentiment was timely, since Wordsworth had died in April, and by November Tennyson was named Poet Laureate. In 1852 his first son, Hallam, was born, and in 1853 the Tennysons moved to a neo-Gothic country estate called Farringford on the Isle of Wight.

His experimental "monodrama" *Maud* (1855) sold well though it baffled the critics, one of whom remarked that there was one vowel too many, no matter which, in the title. But the combined sales of his works enabled him to buy Farringford, where he could work in peace amid wreaths of tobacco smoke, adored by Emily and protected from his fans by a large staff. There he entertained great personages of the day, from Prince Albert and Garibaldi to his neighbor Julia Margaret Cameron, who badgered him into photographic immortality. Henceforth, whenever he visited London, he was sought after in society and mobbed by admirers.

The stability of his new life enabled Tennyson to pursue many longer projects, including the best-selling narrative poem *Enoch Arden* (1864) and several successful plays. Most of his energies were taken up, however, with the great work of his later life, *Idylls of the King*. A trip to Wales helped fuel his interest in Arthurian legends, and he published groups of *Idylls* in 1859 and 1869. As with *In Memoriam* and *Maud*, the poet gradually felt his way, as he composed the parts, toward a larger design for the whole. All the while he held before him the image of "my lost Arthur," until recollections of his actual friend Arthur Hallam blended with

Max Beerbohm. *Tennyson Reading "In Memoriam" to his Sovereign.*

the two literary Arthurs of *In Memoriam* and *Idylls of the King*. He rounded out his tale to an epic twelve books, not producing a final version until 1888, just a few years before his death.

In the *Idylls* as in much of his earlier poetry, Tennyson is a poet of deferment. His most memorable characters—Mariana, the Lotos Eaters, Ulysses, Tithonus, and the speakers of *In Memoriam* and *Maud,* among them—long for reunions and releases that are ever yet to come, as distant as the return of King Arthur from Avalon. In old age Tennyson remembered of his youth that even before he could read, "the words 'far, far away' always had a strange charm for me."

After Tennyson's death in 1892 and his burial with great pomp in Westminster Abbey, his reputation suffered a decline that lasted till the end of the Modernist period around 1945. But Tennyson's lyric genius was admired by poets as various as the Pre-Raphaelites and Whitman, Poe and Hopkins. Auden and Eliot were in rare agreement that he had "the finest ear of any English poet since Milton." Critics continue to dispute whether the sense of Tennyson's poetry is equal to its magnificent sound, but any close reading of his work will reveal Tennyson's deep ambivalence about the world of which he gradually became both oracle and icon. Often beneath his harmonies we hear echoes of his favorite childhood sound, "voices crying in the wind." As Eliot observed, Tennyson was "the most instinctive rebel against the society in which he was the most perfect conformist."

The Kraken[1]

Below the thunders of the upper deep;
Far, far beneath in the abysmal sea,
His ancient, dreamless, uninvaded sleep
The Kraken sleepeth: faintest sunlights flee
5   About his shadowy sides: above him swell
Huge sponges of millennial growth and height;
And far away into the sickly light,
From many a wondrous grot° and secret cell   grotto, cave
Unnumber'd and enormous polypi°   octopuses
10 Winnow with giant arms the slumbering green.
There hath he lain for ages and will lie
Battening upon huge seaworms in his sleep,
Until the latter fire[2] shall heat the deep;
Then once by man and angels to be seen,
15 In roaring he shall rise and on the surface die.

1830

Mariana

"Mariana in the moated grange."[1]

Measure for Measure

With blackest moss the flower-plots
     Were thickly crusted, one and all:
The rusted nails fell from the knots
     That held the pear to the gable-wall.
5   The broken sheds look'd sad and strange:
     Unlifted was the clinking latch;
     Weeded and worn the ancient thatch
Upon the lonely moated grange.
     She only said, "My life is dreary,

---

1. Giant mythical sea monster.
2. The fire of Judgement Day, which will consume the world.
1. The *moated grange* was no particular grange, but one which rose to the music of Shakespeare's words: "There,

at the moated grange, resides this dejected Mariana" (*Measure for Measure* Act 3. Sc. 1) [Tennyson's note]. In Shakespeare's play, Angelo refuses to marry Mariana after her brother and her dowry are lost in a shipwreck.

10   He cometh not," she said;
                She said, "I am aweary, aweary,
                  I would that I were dead!"

         Her tears fell with the dews at even;
                Her tears fell ere the dews were dried;
15   She could not look on the sweet heaven,
                Either at morn or eventide.
         After the flitting of the bats,
                When thickest dark did trance° the sky,   *traverse*
                She drew her casement-curtain by,
20   And glanced athwart the glooming flats.
             She only said, "The night is dreary,
                 He cometh not," she said;
             She said, "I am aweary, aweary,
                  I would that I were dead!"

25   Upon the middle of the night,
             Waking she heard the night-fowl crow:
         The cock sung out an hour ere light:
             From the dark fen the oxen's low
         Came to her: without hope of change,
30   In sleep she seem'd to walk forlorn,
             Till cold winds woke the gray-eyed morn
         About the lonely moated grange.
             She only said, "The day is dreary,
                 He cometh not," she said;
35   She said, "I am aweary, aweary,
                  I would that I were dead!"

         About a stone-cast from the wall
             A sluice with blacken'd waters slept,
         And o'er it many, round and small,
40   The cluster'd marish-mosses[2] crept.
         Hard by a poplar shook alway,
             All silver-green with gnarled bark:
             For leagues no other tree did mark
         The level waste, the rounding gray.
45   She only said, "My life is dreary,
                 He cometh not," she said;
             She said, "I am aweary, aweary,
                  I would that I were dead!"

         And ever when the moon was low,
50   And the shrill winds were up and away,
         In the white curtain, to and fro,
             She saw the gusty shadow sway.
         But when the moon was very low,
             And wild winds bound within their cell,[3]
55   The shadow of the poplar fell
         Upon her bed, across her brow.

---

2. The little marsh-moss lumps that float on the surface of water [Tennyson's note].

3. The cave of Aeolus, god of the winds.

She only said, "The night is dreary,
   He cometh not," she said;
She said, "I am aweary, aweary,
60   I would that I were dead!"

All day within the dreamy house,
   The doors upon their hinges creak'd;
The blue fly sung in the pane; the mouse
   Behind the mouldering wainscot shriek'd,
65 Or from the crevice peer'd about.
   Old faces glimmer'd thro' the doors,
   Old footsteps trod the upper floors,
Old voices called her from without.
   She only said, "My life is dreary,
70   He cometh not," she said;
   She said, "I am aweary, aweary,
    I would that I were dead!"

The sparrow's chirrup on the roof,
   The slow clock ticking, and the sound
75 Which to the wooing wind aloof
   The poplar made, did all confound
Her sense; but most she loathed the hour
   When the thick-moted sunbeam lay
   Athwart the chambers, and the day
80 Was sloping toward his western bower.
   Then, said she, "I am very dreary,
     He will not come," she said;
   She wept, "I am aweary, aweary,
    Oh God, that I were dead!"

1830

The Lady of Shalott[1]
Part 1

On either side the river lie
Long fields of barley and of rye,
That clothe the wold° and meet the sky;   *rolling uplands*
And thro' the field the road runs by
5   To many-tower'd Camelot;
And up and down the people go,
Gazing where the lilies blow°   *bloom*
Round an island there below,
    The island of Shalott.

10 Willows whiten, aspens quiver,
Little breezes dusk and shiver
Thro' the wave that runs for ever
By the island in the river
    Flowing down to Camelot.

---

1. The Lady of Shalott is evidently the Elaine of the *Morte d'Arthur*, but I do not think that I had ever heard of the latter when I wrote the former [Tennyson's note]. In Malory, Elaine dies of grief for love of Lancelot, but the curse, the weaving, and the mirror are all Tennyson's inventions.

William Holman Hunt, *The Lady of Shalott,* from the Moxon edition of Tennyson's poems, 1857. This edition was a high point in Victorian book illustration, including drawings by Rossetti and Millais as well as Hunt. Tennyson, however, complained about this illustration because it depicts the lady entangled in the threads of her tapestry, making her unable to leave the loom, as she does in his poem. Hunt responded: "I had only half a page on which to convey the impression of weird fate, whereas you use about fifteen pages to give expression to the complete idea."

15   Four gray walls, and four gray towers,
        Overlook a space of flowers,
        And the silent isle imbowers
               The Lady of Shalott.

        By the margin, willow-veil'd,
20   Slide the heavy barges trail'd
        By slow horses; and unhail'd
        The shallop° flitteth silken-sail'd   *small boat*
               Skimming down to Camelot:
        But who hath seen her wave her hand?
25   Or at the casement seen her stand?
        Or is she known in all the land,
               The Lady of Shalott?

        Only reapers, reaping early
        In among the bearded barley,
30   Hear a song that echoes cheerly
        From the river winding clearly,
               Down to tower'd Camelot:
        And by the moon the reaper weary,
        Piling sheaves in uplands airy,
35   Listening, whispers "'Tis the fairy
               Lady of Shalott.'"

Part 2

There she weaves by night and day
A magic web with colours gay.
She has heard a whisper say,
40   A curse is on her if she stay
        To look down to Camelot.
She knows not what the curse may be,
And so she weaveth steadily,
And little other care hath she,
45   The Lady of Shalott.

And moving thro' a mirror clear[2]
That hangs before her all the year,
Shadows of the world appear.
There she sees the highway near
50   Winding down to Camelot:
There the river eddy whirls,
And there the surly village-churls,°   *peasants*
And the red cloaks of market girls,
        Pass onward from Shalott.

55   Sometimes a troop of damsels glad,
An abbot on an ambling pad,°   *horse*
Sometimes a curly shepherd-lad,
Or long-hair'd page in crimson clad,
        Goes by to tower'd Camelot;
60   And sometimes thro' the mirror blue
The knights come riding two and two:
She hath no loyal knight and true,
        The Lady of Shalott.

But in her web she still delights
65   To weave the mirror's magic sights,
For often thro' the silent nights
A funeral, with plumes and lights
        And music, went to Camelot:
Or when the moon was overhead,
70   Came two young lovers lately wed;
"I am half sick of shadows," said
        The Lady of Shalott.

Part 3

A bow-shot from her bower-eaves,
He rode between the barley-sheaves,
75   The sun came dazzling thro' the leaves,
And flamed upon the brazen greaves°   *leg armor*
        Of bold Sir Lancelot.[3]

2. Working from the back of their tapestries, weavers placed mirrors on the other side to see the effect of their work.

3. The greatest of King Arthur's knights, Lancelot was in love with Queen Guinevere.

A red-cross knight for ever kneel'd
To a lady in his shield,[4]
80   That sparkled on the yellow field,
       Beside remote Shalott.

The gemmy bridle glitter'd free,
Like to some branch of stars we see
Hung in the golden Galaxy.
85   The bridle bells rang merrily
       As he rode down to Camelot:
And from his blazon'd baldric° slung   *ornamented belt*
A mighty silver bugle hung,
And as he rode his armour rung,
90   Beside remote Shalott.

All in the blue unclouded weather
Thick-jewell'd shone the saddle-leather,
The helmet and the helmet-feather
Burn'd like one burning flame together,
95   As he rode down to Camelot.
As often thro' the purple night,
Below the starry clusters bright,
Some bearded meteor, trailing light,
       Moves over still Shalott.

100 His broad clear brow in sunlight glow'd;
On burnish'd hooves his war-horse trode;
From underneath his helmet flow'd
His coal-black curls as on he rode,
       As he rode down to Camelot.
105 From the bank and from the river
He flash'd into the crystal mirror,
"Tirra lirra," by the river
       Sang Sir Lancelot.

She left the web, she left the loom,
110 She made three paces thro' the room,
She saw the water-lily bloom,
She saw the helmet and the plume,
       She look'd down to Camelot.
Out flew the web and floated wide;
115 The mirror crack'd from side to side;
"The curse is come upon me," cried
       The Lady of Shalott.

Part 4

In the stormy east-wind straining,
The pale yellow woods were waning,
160 The broad stream in his banks complaining,

---

4. Lancelot's shield depicts the Red Cross Knight—a character in Spenser's *Faerie Queene* who champions holiness—kneeling in homage to his lady.

Heavily the low sky raining
    Over tower'd Camelot;
Down she came and found a boat
Beneath a willow left afloat,
125   And round about the prow she wrote
    The Lady of Shalott.

And down the river's dim expanse
Like some bold seër in a trance,
Seeing all his own mischance—
130 With a glassy countenance
    Did she look to Camelot.
And at the closing of the day
She loosed the chain, and down she lay;
The broad stream bore her far away,
135   The Lady of Shalott.

Lying, robed in snowy white
That loosely flew to left and right—
The leaves upon her falling light—
Thro' the noises of the night
140   She floated down to Camelot:
And as the boat-head wound along
The willowy hills and fields among,
They heard her singing her last song,
    The Lady of Shalott.

145 Heard a carol, mournful, holy,
Chanted loudly, chanted lowly,
Till her blood was frozen slowly,
And her eyes were darken'd wholly,
    Turn'd to tower'd Camelot.
150 For ere she reach'd upon the tide
The first house by the water-side,
Singing in her song she died,
    The Lady of Shalott.

Under tower and balcony,
155 By garden-wall and gallery,
A gleaming shape she floated by,
Dead-pale between the houses high,
    Silent into Camelot.
Out upon the wharfs they came;
160 Knight and burgher, lord and dame,
And round the prow they read her name,
    The Lady of Shalott.

Who is this? and what is here?
And in the lighted palace near
165 Died the sound of royal cheer;
And they cross'd themselves for fear,
    All the knights at Camelot:
But Lancelot mused a little space;

He said, "She has a lovely face;
170   God in his mercy lend her grace,
        The Lady of Shalott."

                                                    1832, 1842

The Lotos-Eaters[1]

"Courage!" he[2] said, and pointed toward the land,
"This mounting wave will roll us shoreward soon."
In the afternoon they came unto a land[3]
In which it seemed always afternoon.
5   All round the coast the languid air did swoon,
Breathing like one that hath a weary dream.
Full-faced above the valley stood the moon;
And like a downward smoke, the slender stream[4]
Along the cliff to fall and pause and fall did seem.

10   A land of streams! some, like a downward smoke,
Slow-dropping veils of thinnest lawn,[5] did go;
And some thro' wavering lights and shadows broke,
Rolling a slumbrous sheet of foam below.
They saw the gleaming river seaward flow
15   From the inner land: far off, three mountain-tops,
Three silent pinnacles of aged snow,
Stood sunset-flush'd: and, dew'd with showery drops,
Up-clomb the shadowy pine above the woven copse.

The charmèd sunset linger'd low adown
20   In the red West: thro' mountain clefts the dale
Was seen far inland, and the yellow down°   *upland plain*
Border'd with palm, and many a winding vale
And meadow, set with slender galingale;°   *an aromatic herb*
A land where all things always seem'd the same!
25   And round about the keel with faces pale,
Dark faces pale against that rosy flame,
The mild-eyed melancholy Lotos-eaters came.

Branches they bore of that enchanted stem,
Laden with flower and fruit, whereof they gave
30   To each, but whoso did receive of them,
And taste, to him the gushing of the wave
Far far away did seem to mourn and rave
On alien shores; and if his fellow spake,
His voice was thin, as voices from the grave;
35   And deep-asleep he seem'd, yet all awake,
And music in his ears his beating heart did make.

---

1. In Homer's *Odyssey*, book 9, Odysseus (Ulysses) and his men, returning home from the Trojan War, are tempted to stay forever in the land of the Lotus-eaters. Anyone who ate the sweet fruit of the lotus would lose all desire to return home.
2. Odysseus.
3. "The strand" was, I think, my first reading, but the no rhyme of "land" and "land" was lazier [Tennyson's note].
4. Taken from the waterfall at Gavarnie, in the Pyrenees, when I was 20 or 21 [Tennyson's note].
5. Sheer linen fabric, used in theaters to suggest a waterfall.

They sat them down upon the yellow sand,
Between the sun and moon upon the shore;
And sweet it was to dream of Fatherland,
40 Of child, and wife, and slave; but evermore
Most weary seem'd the sea, weary the oar,
Weary the wandering fields of barren foam.
Then some one said, "We will return no more;"
And all at once they sang, "Our island home⁶
45 Is far beyond the wave; we will no longer roam."

Choric Song⁷

1

There is sweet music here that softer falls
Than petals from blown roses on the grass,
Or night-dews on still waters between walls
Of shadowy granite, in a gleaming pass;
50 Music that gentlier on the spirit lies,
Than tir'd eyelids upon tir'd eyes;⁸
Music that brings sweet sleep down from the blissful skies.
Here are cool mosses deep,
And thro' the moss the ivies creep,
55 And in the stream the long-leaved flowers weep,
And from the craggy ledge the poppy hangs in sleep.

2

Why are we weigh'd upon with heaviness,
And utterly consumed with sharp distress,
While all things else have rest from weariness?
60 All things have rest: why should we toil alone,
We only toil, who are the first of things,
And make perpetual moan,
Still from one sorrow to another thrown:
Nor ever fold our wings,
65 And cease from wanderings,
Nor steep our brows in slumber's holy balm;
Nor harken what the inner spirit sings,
"There is no joy but calm!"
Why should we only toil, the roof and crown of things?

3

70 Lo! in the middle of the wood,
The folded leaf is woo'd from out the bud
With winds upon the branch, and there
Grows green and broad, and takes no care,
Sun-steep'd at noon, and in the moon
75 Nightly dew-fed; and turning yellow
Falls, and floats adown the air.
Lo! sweeten'd with the summer light,

---

6. Ithaca, off the west coast of Greece.
7. What follows is sung by Odysseus's men.
8. I printed, contrary to my custom, "tir'd," not "tired,"
for fear that readers might pronounce the word "tirèd"

[Tennyson's note]. Tennyson wished to make "the word
neither monosyllable or disyllabic, but a dreamy child of
the two."

The full-juiced apple, waxing over-mellow,
Drops in a silent autumn night.
80   All its allotted length of days,
The flower ripens in its place,
Ripens and fades, and falls, and hath no toil,
Fast-rooted in the fruitful soil.

4

Hateful is the dark-blue sky,
85   Vaulted o'er the dark-blue sea.
Death is the end of life; ah, why
Should life all labour be?
Let us alone. Time driveth onward fast,
And in a little while our lips are dumb.
90   Let us alone. What is it that will last?
All things are taken from us, and become
Portions and parcels of the dreadful Past.
Let us alone. What pleasure can we have
To war with evil? Is there any peace
95   In ever climbing up the climbing wave?
All things have rest, and ripen toward the grave
In silence; ripen, fall and cease:
Give us long rest or death, dark death, or dreamful ease.

5

How sweet it were, hearing the downward stream,
100   With half-shut eyes ever to seem
Falling asleep in a half-dream!
To dream and dream, like yonder amber light,
Which will not leave the myrrh-bush on the height;
To hear each other's whisper'd speech;
105   Eating the Lotos day by day,
To watch the crisping ripples on the beach,
And tender curving lines of creamy spray;
To lend our hearts and spirits wholly
To the influence of mild-minded melancholy;
110   To muse and brood and live again in memory,
With those old faces of our infancy
Heap'd over with a mound of grass,
Two handfuls of white dust, shut in an urn of brass!

6

Dear is the memory of our wedded lives,
115   And dear the last embraces of our wives
And their warm tears: but all hath suffer'd change:
For surely now our household hearths are cold:
Our sons inherit us: our looks are strange:
And we should come like ghosts to trouble joy.
120   Or else the island princes[9] over-bold
Have eat our substance, and the minstrel sings
Before them of the ten years' war in Troy,[1]

---

9. The suitors of Penelope, Odysseus's wife and presumed
widow.

1. The Trojan War, from which Odysseus and his men
are returning.

And our great deeds, as half-forgotten things.
Is there confusion in the little isle?
125 Let what is broken so remain.
The Gods are hard to reconcile:
'Tis hard to settle order once again.
There *is* confusion worse than death,
Trouble on trouble, pain on pain,
130 Long labour unto aged breath,
Sore task to hearts worn out by many wars
And eyes grown dim with gazing on the pilot-stars.

7

But, propt on beds of amaranth and moly,[2]
How sweet (while warm airs lull us, blowing lowly)
135 With half-dropt eyelid still,
Beneath a heaven dark and holy,
To watch the long bright river drawing slowly
His waters from the purple hill—
To hear the dewy echoes calling
140 From cave to cave thro' the thick-twined vine—
To watch the emerald-colour'd water falling
Thro' many a wov'n acanthus-wreath[3] divine!
Only to hear and see the far-off sparkling brine,
Only to hear were sweet, stretch'd out beneath the pine.

8

145 The Lotos blooms below the barren peak:
The Lotos blows by every winding creek:
All day the wind breathes low with mellower tone:
Thro' every hollow cave and alley lone
Round and round the spicy downs the yellow Lotos-dust is blown.
150 We have had enough of action, and of motion we,
Roll'd to starboard, roll'd to larboard, when the surge was seething free,
Where the wallowing monster spouted his foam-fountains in the sea.
Let us swear an oath, and keep it with an equal mind,
In the hollow Lotos-land to live and lie reclined
155 On the hills like Gods together, careless of mankind.
For they lie beside their nectar, and the bolts[4] are hurl'd
Far below them in the valleys, and the clouds are lightly curl'd
Round their golden houses, girdled with the gleaming world:
Where they smile in secret, looking over wasted lands,
160 Blight and famine, plague and earthquake, roaring deeps and fiery sands,
Clanging fights, and flaming towns, and sinking ships, and praying hands.
But they smile, they find a music centred in a doleful song
Steaming up, a lamentation and an ancient tale of wrong,
Like a tale of little meaning tho' the words are strong;
165 Chanted from an ill-used race of men that cleave the soil,
Sow the seed, and reap the harvest with enduring toil,

---

2. *Amaranth*, the immortal flower of legend; *moly*, the sacred herb of mystical power, used as a charm by Odysseus against Circe [Tennyson's note].
3. The plant seen in the capitals of Corinthian pillars [Tennyson's note].
4. Nectar is the food of the gods, and thunderbolts their weapons.

Storing yearly little dues of wheat, and wine and oil;
Till they perish and they suffer—some, 'tis whisper'd—down in hell
Suffer endless anguish, others in Elysian[5] valleys dwell,
170 Resting weary limbs at last on beds of asphodel.[6]
Surely, surely, slumber is more sweet than toil, the shore
Than labour in the deep mid-ocean, wind and wave and oar;
Oh rest ye, brother mariners, we will not wander more.

                                                    1832, 1842

Ulysses[1]

It little profits that an idle king,
By this still hearth, among these barren crags,
Match'd with an aged wife, I mete and dole
Unequal laws unto a savage race,
5 That hoard, and sleep, and feed, and know not me.

I cannot rest from travel: I will drink
Life to the lees: all times I have enjoy'd
Greatly, have suffer'd greatly, both with those
That loved me, and alone; on shore, and when
10 Thro' scudding drifts the rainy Hyades[2]
Vext the dim sea: I am become a name;
For always roaming with a hungry heart
Much have I seen and known; cities of men
And manners, climates, councils, governments,
15 Myself not least, but honour'd of them all;
And drunk delight of battle with my peers,
Far on the ringing plains of windy Troy.
I am a part of all that I have met;
Yet all experience is an arch wherethro'
20 Gleams that untravell'd world, whose margin fades
For ever and for ever when I move.
How dull it is to pause, to make an end,
To rust unburnish'd, not to shine in use!
As tho' to breathe were life. Life piled on life
25 Were all too little, and of one to me
Little remains: but every hour is saved
From that eternal silence, something more,
A bringer of new things; and vile it were

5. Paradisical; Elysium was the part of the underworld where the blessed dwelled after death.
6. Flowering plant of the lily family, said to grow in the Elysian fields.
1. The poem was written soon after Arthur Hallam's death, and it gives the feeling about the need of going further and braving the struggle of life perhaps more simply than anything in In Memoriam [Tennyson's note]. In Homer's Odyssey, Ulysses returns home to Ithaca, after ten years of wandering following the fall of Troy, and slays the suitors who have been harassing his wife Pene-

lope. "My father," wrote Tennyson's son, "takes up the story of further wanderings at the end of the Odyssey. Ulysses has lived in Ithaca for a long while before the craving for fresh travel seizes him. The comrades he addresses are of the same heroic mould as his old comrades." Dante also has Ulysses set off on another voyage, this time westward through the Strait of Gibraltar (Inferno 26).
2. The Hyades were a constellation of seven stars whose rising was believed to bring rain.

For some three suns to store and hoard myself,
30   And this gray spirit yearning in desire
To follow knowledge like a sinking star,
Beyond the utmost bound of human thought.

This is my son, mine own Telemachus,
To whom I leave the sceptre and the isle—
35   Well-loved of me, discerning to fulfil
This labour, by slow prudence to make mild
A rugged people, and thro' soft degrees
Subdue them to the useful and the good.
Most blameless is he, centred in the sphere
40   Of common duties, decent not to fail
In offices of tenderness, and pay
Meet adoration to my household gods,
When I am gone. He works his work, I mine.

There lies the port; the vessel puffs her sail:
45   There gloom the dark broad seas. My mariners,
Souls that have toil'd, and wrought, and thought with me—
That ever with a frolic welcome took
The thunder and the sunshine, and opposed
Free hearts, free foreheads—you and I are old;
50   Old age hath yet his honour and his toil;
Death closes all: but something ere the end,
Some work of noble note, may yet be done,
Not unbecoming men that strove with Gods.
The lights begin to twinkle from the rocks:
55   The long day wanes: the slow moon climbs: the deep
Moans round with many voices. Come, my friends,
'Tis not too late to seek a newer world.
Push off, and sitting well in order smite
The sounding furrows; for my purpose holds
60   To sail beyond the sunset, and the baths
Of all the western stars,[3] until I die.
It may be that the gulfs will wash us down:
It may be we shall touch the Happy Isles,[4]
And see the great Achilles, whom we knew.
65   Tho' much is taken, much abides; and tho'
We are not now that strength which in old days
Moved earth and heaven; that which we are, we are;
One equal temper of heroic hearts,
Made weak by time and fate, but strong in will
70   To strive, to seek, to find, and not to yield.

1833   1842

---

3. The Greeks believed that the flat earth was encircled by an ocean into which the stars dipped at times.
4. The Islands of the Blessed were a land of perpetual summer thought to lie in the western ocean beyond the Pillars of Hercules (the Straits of Gibraltar). Great heros—such as Achilles, the Greek warrior who killed the Trojan prince, Hector—were sent by the gods to live there as immortals.

Break, Break, Break[1]

Break, break, break,
   On thy cold gray stones, O Sea!
And I would that my tongue could utter
   The thoughts that arise in me.

5   O well for the fisherman's boy,
   That he shouts with his sister at play!
O well for the sailor lad,
   That he sings in his boat on the bay!

And the stately ships go on
10   To their haven under the hill;
But O for the touch of a vanish'd hand,
   And the sound of a voice that is still!

Break, break, break
   At the foot of thy crags, O Sea!
15   But the tender grace of a day that is dead
   Will never come back to me.

1834   1842

The Epic [Morte d'Arthur][1]

At Francis Allen's on the Christmas-eve,—
The game of forfeits[2] done—the girls all kiss'd
Beneath the sacred bush° and past away—   *mistletoe*
The parson Holmes, the poet Everard Hall,
5   The host, and I sat round the wassail-bowl,°   *punch bowl*
Then half-way ebb'd: and there we held a talk,
How all the old honour had from Christmas gone,
Or gone, or dwindled down to some odd games
In some odd nooks like this; till I, tired out
10   With cutting eights that day upon the pond,
Where, three times slipping from the outer edge,
I bump'd the ice into three several stars,
Fell in a doze; and half-awake I heard
The parson taking wide and wider sweeps,
15   Now harping on the church-commissioners,[3]
Now hawking at Geology and schism;[4]
Until I woke, and found him settled down
Upon the general decay of faith
Right thro' the world, "at home was little left,

---

1. Inspired by the death of the poet's friend, Arthur Hallam. Cf. *In Memoriam*, page 1928.
1. One of Tennyson's lifelong projects was an epic poem about King Arthur, which ultimately became the *Idylls of the King*. The last poem in the sequence, describing the death of Arthur, was actually written first: it was begun in 1833, when Arthur Hallam died, and was called *Morte d'Arthur*. Tennyson framed the poem with *The Epic*, a description of contemporary (i.e., 19th century) Christ-mas Eve festivities, during which the poet—here called Everard Hall—was encouraged to read *Morte d'Arthur* aloud.
2. A party game where players have to forfeit an item, then redeem it by performing a silly task.
3. In 1835 the government set up a system of commissioners to oversee the finances of the Anglican Church.
4. A reference to current scientific and religious controversies.

20   And none abroad: there was no anchor, none,
       To hold by." Francis, laughing, clapt his hand
       On Everard's shoulder, with "I hold by him."
       "And I," quoth Everard, "by the wassail-bowl."
       "Why yes," I said, "we knew your gift that way
25   At college: but another which you had,
       I mean of verse (for so we held it then),
       What came of that?" "You know," said Frank, "he burnt
       His epic, his King Arthur, some twelve books"—
       And then to me demanding why? "Oh, sir,
30   He thought that nothing new was said, or else
       Something so said 'twas nothing—that a truth
       Looks freshest in the fashion of the day;
       God knows: he has a mint of reasons: ask.
       It pleased *me* well enough." "Nay, nay," said Hall,
35   "Why take the style of those heroic times?
       For nature brings not back the Mastodon,
       Nor we those times; and why should any man
       Remodel models? these twelve books of mine
       Were faint Homeric echoes,[5] nothing-worth,
40   Mere chaff and draff, much better burnt." "But I,"
       Said Francis, "pick'd the eleventh from this hearth
       And have it: keep a thing, its use will come.
       I hoard it as a sugar-plum for Holmes."
       He laugh'd, and I, tho' sleepy, like a horse
45   That hears the corn-bin open, prick'd my ears;
       For I remember'd Everard's college fame
       When we were Freshmen: then at my request
       He brought it; and the poet little urged,
       But with some prelude of disparagement,
50   Read, mouthing out his hollow oes and aes,
       Deep-chested music, and to this result.[6]

                          * * *

       Here ended Hall, and our last light, that long
325   Had wink'd and threaten'd darkness, flared and fell:
       At which the Parson, sent to sleep with sound,
       And waked with silence, grunted "Good!" but we
       Sat rapt: it was the tone with which he read—
       Perhaps some modern touches here and there
330   Redeem'd it from the charge of nothingness—
       Or else we loved the man, and prized his work;
       I know not: but we sitting, as I said,
       The cock crew loud; as at that time of year
       The lusty bird takes every hour for dawn:
335   Then Francis, muttering, like a man ill-used,
       "There now—that's nothing!" drew a little back,

5. I.e., Hall claims his poems merely echoed the great epics of Homer. He may have been fishing for a compliment: when the poet Walter Savage Landor read Tennyson's *Morte d'Arthur* in manuscript, he declared "it is more Homeric than any poem of our time, and rivals some of the noblest parts of the Odyssey."

6. At this point Hall reads aloud *Morte d'Arthur*; mortally wounded, Arthur is carried away on a barge to the blessed isle of Avalon, from which it is prophesied that he will one day return to rule again.

And drove his heel into the smoulder'd log,
That sent a blast of sparkles up the flue:
And so to bed; where yet in sleep I seem'd
340   To sail with Arthur under looming shores,
Point after point; till on to dawn, when dreams
Begin to feel the truth and stir of day,
To me, methought, who waited with a crowd,
There came a bark that, blowing forward, bore
345   King Arthur, like a modern gentleman
Of stateliest port;° and all the people cried,   bearing
"Arthur is come again: he cannot die."[7]
Then those that stood upon the hills behind
Repeated—"Come again, and thrice as fair;"
350   And, further inland, voices echo'd—"Come
With all good things, and war shall be no more."
At this a hundred bells began to peal,
That with the sound I woke, and heard indeed
The clear church-bells ring in the Christmas-morn.

1833–1838   1842

from THE PRINCESS[1]

Tears, Idle Tears[2]

Tears, idle tears, I know not what they mean,
Tears from the depth of some divine despair
Rise in the heart, and gather to the eyes,
In looking on the happy Autumn-fields,
5   And thinking of the days that are no more.

Fresh as the first beam glittering on a sail,
That brings our friends up from the underworld,
Sad as the last which reddens over one
That sinks with all we love below the verge;
10   So sad, so fresh, the days that are no more.

Ah, sad and strange as in dark summer dawns
The earliest pipe of half-awaken'd birds
To dying ears, when unto dying eyes
The casement° slowly grows a glimmering square;   window
15   So sad, so strange, the days that are no more.

Dear as remember'd kisses after death,
And sweet as those by hopeless fancy feign'd
On lips that are for others; deep as love,

7. There is a legend that King Arthur will return once
more to lead his people.
1. *The Princess* (1847) is a long narrative poem, set in a
fairy-tale realm, about the effort to found a women's college. (The first British institution for the higher education of women, Queen's College, London, opened the
next year.) The story is interspersed with brief "songs" or
lyrics—some of them added later—whose musicality and

depth of emotion soon won them admiration as independent works of art.
2. This song came to me on the yellowing autumn-tide at
Tintern Abbey, full for me of its bygone memories [Ten-
nyson's note]. The poet would remember not only
Wordsworth's poem *Tintern Abbey* (page 1529), but also
his dead friend Hallam, buried not far away.

20   Deep as first love, and wild with all regret;
        O Death in Life, the days that are no more.

["The Woman's Cause Is Man's"]¹

        "Blame not thyself too much," I said, "nor blame
240   Too much the sons of men and barbarous laws;
        These were the rough ways of the world till now.
        Henceforth thou hast a helper, me, that know
        The woman's cause is man's: they rise or sink
        Together, dwarf'd or godlike, bond or free:
245   For she that out of Lethe² scales with man
        The shining steps of Nature, shares with man
        His nights, his days, moves with him to one goal,
        Stays all the fair young planet in her hands³—
        If she be small, slight-natured, miserable,
250   How shall men grow? but work no more alone!
        Our place is much: as far as in us lies
        We two will serve them both in aiding her—
        Will clear away the parasitic forms
        That seem to keep her up but drag her down—
255   Will leave her space to burgeon out of all
        Within her—let her make herself her own
        To give or keep, to live and learn and be
        All that not harms distinctive womanhood.
        For woman is not undevelopt man,
260   But diverse: could we make her as the man,
        Sweet Love were slain: his dearest bond is this,
        Not like to like, but like in difference.
        Yet in the long years liker must they grow;
        The man be more of woman, she of man;
265   He gain in sweetness and in moral height,
        Nor lose the wrestling thews° that throw the world;   muscles
        She mental breadth, nor fail in childward care,
        Nor lose the childlike in the larger mind;
        Till at the last she set herself to man,
270   Like perfect music unto noble words;
        And so these twain, upon the skirts of Time,
        Sit side by side, full-summ'd in all their powers,
        Dispensing harvest, sowing the To-be,
        Self-reverent each and reverencing each,

1. Princess Ida, the heroine of *The Princess*, founds a women's college, and swears she will never marry. But through various exploits—including masquerading as a woman to attend her college—Prince Florian convinces her that her feminist experiment is futile. She turns her college into a hospital and agrees to marry him. In this, his concluding speech (from Book 7), Florian envisions a future in which men and women will be more alike, and the relations between them will be improved.
2. The waters of forgetfulnesss, here implying a new beginning.
3. Hallam Tennyson notes: "Cf. Ross Wallace's lines:

'The hand that rocks the cradle is the hand that rules the world.' My father felt that woman must train herself more earnestly than heretofore to do the large work that lies before her, even though she may not be destined to be wife or mother, cultivating her understanding not her memory only, her imagination in its highest phases, her inborn spirituality and her sympathy with all that is pure, noble and beautiful, rather than mere social accomplishments; and that then and then only will she further the progress of humanity, then and then only men will continue to hold her in reverence."

275 Distinct in individualities,
  But like each other ev'n as those who love.
  Then comes the statelier Eden back to men:
  Then reign the world's great bridals, chaste and calm:
  Then springs the crowning race of humankind.
280 May these things be!"
         Sighing she spoke "I fear
  They will not."
       "Dear, but let us type them now
  In our own lives, and this proud watchword rest
  Of equal; seeing either sex alone
  Is half itself, and in true marriage lies
285 Nor equal, nor unequal: each fulfils
  Defect in each, and always thought in thought,
  Purpose in purpose, will in will, they grow,
  The single pure and perfect animal,
  The two-cell'd heart beating, with one full stroke,
290 Life."
     And again sighing she spoke: "A dream
  That once was mine! what woman taught you this?"
1839–1847   1847

In Memoriam A. H. H.

When Tennyson was twenty-four, his closest friend Arthur Henry Hallam died suddenly in Vienna. Regarded by all who knew him as the most promising intellect of his generation, Hallam had been Tennyson's confidante, best critic, and strongest supporter. It was Hallam who encouraged Tennyson to publish, helped him get his work through the press, and sustained him amidst criticism, self-doubt, and family crises. His perceptive review of the early poems remains among the best essays ever written on Tennyson. The poet learned of Hallam's death on October 1, 1833, and soon began composing short lyrics exploring the dark questions raised by so devastating an event. "I did not write them with any view of weaving them into a whole," Tennyson later said, "or for publication, until I found I had written so many."

  The 131 sections of In Memoriam, produced over sixteen years, constitute a new type of elegy, what T. S. Eliot called "the concentrated diary" of a man confessing his love, sorrow, and doubts about the immortality of the soul. Tennyson drew on many sources, ranging from Greek pastoral elegy and Horace's Odes, to the sonnet sequences of Petrarch and Shakespeare. As in traditional elegy, the death of a friend blights joy in all living things, until the poet asserts his omnipresence in nature. But Tennyson expands his personal loss into the potential death of the human species, questioning the direction of evolution, science's challenges to Christian belief, and the ultimate destiny of the human spirit. The result is an intensely private autobiography of grief that nonetheless registers the troubled spiritual condition of Victorian England.

  Presented as a broken narrative of the poet's fitful progress from despair to solace, In Memoriam covers a three-year period, from the death of Hallam in the autumn of 1833 to the spring of 1836. Sections 9–15 describe the return of Hallam's body to England by sea; section 19, its burial. The structural heart of the poem is the succession of three Christmases (sections 28–30, 78, 104–106), whose celebration of Christian rebirth gradually rings less hollow, more convincing. The poet's acceptance of his loss also deepens over the three springs that follow (sections 39, 86, and 115); the timeless renewal of nature eventually reawakens the poet to life. Yet for many readers, the bleak evidence of blindly predatory Nature at the poem's emotional nadir (sections 54, 55, and 56) nearly overshadows the brighter hopes of later sections.

As Eliot remarked, *In Memoriam* triumphs not "because of the quality of its faith, but because of the quality of its doubt."

The form of the poem is justly famous. At the time he was writing Tennyson mistakenly thought he had created a new stanza—iambic tetrameter quatrains, rhyming *abba*—unaware that Sidney and Jonson had preceded him. But Tennyson's brilliant, sustained use of the quatrains was so well adapted to his material that the form has come to be called "the *In Memoriam* stanza." The first line-ending lingers in the memory while the central couplet pushes other sounds to the fore, then the rhyme is completed across that divide just as the stanza ends. This aural pattern of separation and completion parallels the intellectual and emotional progress of the poem: sound and substance combine in a verbal embrace of Tennyson's loss.

from In Memoriam A. H. H.
Obiit MDCCCXXXIII[1]

1

I held it truth, with him who sings
    To one clear harp in divers tones,[2]
    That men may rise on stepping-stones
Of their dead selves to higher things.

5   But who shall so forecast the years
    And find in loss a gain to match?
    Or reach a hand thro' time to catch
The far-off interest of tears?[3]

Let Love clasp Grief lest both be drown'd,
10   Let darkness keep her raven gloss:
    Ah, sweeter to be drunk with loss,
To dance with death, to beat the ground,

Than that the victor Hours should scorn
    The long result of love, and boast,
15   "Behold the man that loved and lost,
But all he was is overworn."

2

Old Yew, which graspest at the stones
    That name the under-lying dead,
    Thy fibres net the dreamless head,
Thy roots are wrapt about the bones.

5   The seasons bring the flower again,
    And bring the firstling to the flock;
    And in the dusk of thee, the clock
Beats out the little lives of men.

O not for thee the glow, the bloom,
10   Who changest not in any gale,
    Nor branding summer suns avail

1. Died 1833.
2. Goethe, according to Tennyson.

3 The good that grows for us out of grief [Tennyson's note].

To touch thy thousand years of gloom:[4]

And gazing on thee, sullen tree,
  Sick° for thy stubborn hardihood,   *envious*
15 I seem to fail from out my blood
And grow incorporate into thee.

* * *

5

I sometimes hold it half a sin
  To put in words the grief I feel;
  For words, like Nature, half reveal
And half conceal the Soul within.

5 But, for the unquiet heart and brain,
  A use in measured language lies;
  The sad mechanic exercise,
Like dull narcotics, numbing pain.

In words, like weeds,° I'll wrap me o'er,   *mourning clothes*
10 Like coarsest clothes against the cold:
  But that large grief which these enfold
Is given in outline and no more.

* * *

7

Dark house, by which once more I stand
  Here in the long unlovely street,[5]
  Doors, where my heart was used to beat
So quickly, waiting for a hand,

5 A hand that can be clasp'd no more—
  Behold me, for I cannot sleep,
  And like a guilty thing I creep
At earliest morning to the door.

He is not here;[6] but far away
10 The noise of life begins again,
  And ghastly thro' the drizzling rain
On the bald street breaks the blank day.

* * *

9

Fair ship, that from the Italian shore
  Sailest the placid ocean-plains
  With my lost Arthur's loved remains,
Spread thy full wings, and waft him o'er.

5 So draw him home to those that mourn
  In vain; a favourable speed
  Ruffle thy mirror'd mast, and lead
Thro' prosperous floods his holy urn.

All night no ruder air perplex
10 Thy sliding keel, till Phosphor,[7] bright

---

4. Hallam Tennyson says: "No autumn tints ever change the green gloom of the yew."
5. Hallam's house at 67 Wimpole Street in London.

6. "He is not here, but is risen," said the angel at Jesus' tomb (Luke 24.6).
7. The morning star.

As our pure love, thro' early light
Shall glimmer on the dewy decks.

Sphere all your lights around, above;
    Sleep, gentle heavens, before the prow;
15   Sleep, gentle winds, as he sleeps now,
My friend, the brother of my love;

My Arthur, whom I shall not see
    Till all my widow'd race be run;
    Dear as the mother to the son,
20   More than my brothers are to me.

          * * *

14

If one should bring me this report,
    That thou° hadst touch'd the land to-day,   *the ship*
    And I went down unto the quay,
And found thee lying in the port;

5   And standing, muffled round with woe,
    Should see thy passengers in rank
    Come stepping lightly down the plank,
And beckoning unto those they know;

And if along with these should come
10   The man I held as half-divine;
    Should strike a sudden hand in mine,
And ask a thousand things of home;

And I should tell him all my pain,
    And how my life had droop'd of late,
15   And he should sorrow o'er my state
And marvel what possess'd my brain;

And I perceived no touch of change,
    No hint of death in all his frame,
    But found him all in all the same,
20   I should not feel it to be strange.

          * * *

19

The Danube to the Severn[8] gave
    The darken'd heart that beat no more;
    They laid him by the pleasant shore,
And in the hearing of the wave.

5   There twice a day the Severn fills;
    The salt sea-water passes by,
    And hushes half the babbling Wye,[9]
And makes a silence in the hills.

The Wye is hush'd nor moved along,
10   And hush'd my deepest grief of all,

---

8. Arthur Hallam died in Vienna, which is on the Danube, and was buried at Clevedon, near the Severn River in southwest England.

9. Taken from my own observation—the rapids of the Wye are stilled by the incoming sea [Tennyson's note]. The Wye is a tributary of the Severn, a tidal river.

When fill'd with tears that cannot fall,
I brim with sorrow drowning song.

The tide flows down, the wave again
   Is vocal in its wooded walls;
15   My deeper anguish also falls,
And I can speak a little then.

         * * *

         27

I envy not in any moods
   The captive void of noble rage,
   The linnet° born within the cage,   *finch*
That never knew the summer woods:

5   I envy not the beast that takes
   His license in the field of time,
   Unfetter'd by the sense of crime,
To whom a conscience never wakes;

Nor, what may count itself as blest,
10   The heart that never plighted troth
   But stagnates in the weeds of sloth;
Nor any want-begotten rest.[1]

I hold it true, whate'er befall;
   I feel it, when I sorrow most;
15   'Tis better to have loved and lost
Than never to have loved at all.

         28

The time draws near the birth of Christ:[2]
   The moon is hid; the night is still;
   The Christmas bells from hill to hill
Answer each other in the mist.

5   Four voices of four hamlets round,
   From far and near, on mead and moor,
   Swell out and fail, as if a door
Were shut between me and the sound:

Each voice four changes[3] on the wind,
10   That now dilate, and now decrease,
   Peace and goodwill, goodwill and peace,
Peace and goodwill, to all mankind.

This year I slept and woke with pain,
   I almost wish'd no more to wake,
15   And that my hold on life would break
Before I heard those bells again:

But they my troubled spirit rule,
   For they controll'd me when a boy;
   They bring me sorrow touch'd with joy,

---

1. Peace of mind owing to lack or "want" of having made commitments.

2. The first Christmas after Hallam's death.
3. Arrangements of church bell ringing.

20   The merry merry bells of Yule.

* * *

30

With trembling fingers did we weave
   The holly round the Christmas hearth;
   A rainy cloud possess'd the earth,
And sadly fell our Christmas-eve.

5   At our old pastimes in the hall
   We gambol'd, making vain pretence
   Of gladness, with an awful sense
Of one mute Shadow watching all.

We paused: the winds were in the beech:
10   We heard them sweep the winter land;
   And in a circle hand-in-hand
Sat silent, looking each at each.

Then echo-like our voices rang;
   We sung, tho' every eye was dim,
15   A merry song we sang with him
Last year: impetuously we sang:

We ceased: a gentler feeling crept
   Upon us: surely rest is meet:°   *fitting*
   "They rest," we said, "their sleep is sweet,"
20   And silence follow'd, and we wept.

Our voices took a higher range;
   Once more we sang: "They do not die
   Nor lose their mortal sympathy,
Nor change to us, although they change;

25   "Rapt° from the fickle and the frail   *carried away*
   With gather'd power, yet the same,
   Pierces the keen seraphic flame
From orb° to orb, from veil to veil."   *star*

Rise, happy morn, rise, holy morn,
30   Draw forth the cheerful day from night:
   O Father, touch the east, and light
The light that shone when Hope was born.

* * *

39

Old warder[4] of these buried bones,
   And answering now my random stroke
   With fruitful cloud and living smoke,[5]
Dark yew, that graspest at the stones

5   And dippest toward the dreamless head,
   To thee too comes the golden hour

---

4. The yew tree that stands by Hallam's grave.   5. The yew, when flowering, in a wind or if struck sends
                                                     up its pollen like smoke [Tennyson's note].

When flower is feeling after flower;
But Sorrow—fixt upon the dead,

10 And darkening the dark graves of men,—
    What whisper'd from her lying lips?
    Thy gloom is kindled at the tips,[6]
And passes into gloom again.

* * *

50

Be near me when my light is low,
    When the blood creeps, and the nerves prick
    And tingle; and the heart is sick,
And all the wheels of Being slow.

5   Be near me when the sensuous frame
    Is rack'd with pangs that conquer trust;
    And Time, a maniac scattering dust,
And Life, a Fury slinging flame.[7]

Be near me when my faith is dry,
10   And men the flies of latter spring,
    That lay their eggs, and sting and sing
And weave their petty cells and die.

Be near me when I fade away,
    To point the term of human strife,
15   And on the low dark verge of life
The twilight of eternal day.

* * *

54

Oh yet we trust that somehow good
    Will be the final goal of ill,
    To pangs of nature, sins of will,
Defects of doubt, and taints of blood;

5   That nothing walks with aimless feet;
    That not one life shall be destroy'd,
    Or cast as rubbish to the void,
When God hath made the pile complete;

That not a worm is cloven in vain;
10   That not a moth with vain desire
    Is shrivell'd in a fruitless fire,
Or but subserves another's gain.

Behold, we know not anything;
    I can but trust that good shall fall
15   At last—far off—at last, to all,
And every winter change to spring.

So runs my dream: but what am I?
    An infant crying in the night:

---

6. The tips of the yew branches are in flower.   7. The Furies—avengers of crime—carry torches.

An infant crying for the light:
20   And with no language but a cry.

55

The wish, that of the living whole
    No life may fail beyond the grave,
    Derives it not from what we have
The likest God within the soul?[8]

5   Are God and Nature then at strife,
    That Nature lends such evil dreams?
    So careful of the type[9] she seems,
So careless of the single life;

That I, considering everywhere
10   Her secret meaning in her deeds,
    And finding that of fifty seeds
She often brings but one to bear,

I falter where I firmly trod,
    And falling with my weight of cares
15   Upon the great world's altar-stairs
That slope thro' darkness up to God,

I stretch lame hands of faith, and grope,
    And gather dust and chaff, and call
    To what I feel is Lord of all,
20   And faintly trust the larger hope.[1]

56

"So careful of the type?" but no.
    From scarpèd[2] cliff and quarried stone
    She° cries, "A thousand types are gone: *Nature*
I care for nothing, all shall go."

5   "Thou makest thine appeal to me:
    I bring to life, I bring to death:
    The spirit does but mean the breath:
I know no more." And he, shall he,

Man, her last work, who seem'd so fair,
10   Such splendid purpose in his eyes,
    Who roll'd the psalm to wintry skies,
Who built him fanes° of fruitless prayer,   *temples*

Who trusted God was love indeed
    And love Creation's final law—
15   Tho' Nature, red in tooth and claw
With ravine, shriek'd against his creed—

Who loved, who suffer'd countless ills,
    Who battled for the True, the Just,

8. The inner consciousness—the divine in man [Tennyson's note].
9. Species; i.e., Nature ensures the preservation of the species, but is indifferent to the fate of the individual.
1. Hallam Tennyson notes: "My father means by 'the

larger hope' that the whole human race would through, perhaps, ages of suffering, be at length purified and saved."
2. Steep cut-away cliffs with the strata exposed.

Be blown about the desert dust,
20   Or seal'd° within the iron hills?[3]   *fossilized*

No more? A monster then, a dream,
    A discord. Dragons of the prime,
    That tare° each other in their slime,   *tore*
Were mellow music match'd° with him.   *compared*

25   O life as futile, then, as frail!
    O for thy voice to soothe and bless!
    What hope of answer, or redress?
Behind the veil, behind the veil.

* * *

67

When on my bed the moonlight falls,
    I know that in thy place of rest
    By that broad water of the west,[4]
There comes a glory on the walls;

5   Thy marble bright in dark appears,
    As slowly steals a silver flame
    Along the letters of thy name,
And o'er the number of thy years.

The mystic glory swims away;
10   From off my bed the moonlight dies;
    And closing eaves of wearied eyes
I sleep till dusk is dipt in gray:

And then I know the mist is drawn
    A lucid veil from coast to coast,
15   And in the dark church like a ghost
Thy tablet glimmers to the dawn.

* * *

78

Again at Christmas[5] did we weave
    The holly round the Christmas hearth;
    The silent snow possess'd the earth,
And calmly fell our Christmas-eve:

5   The yule-clog° sparkled keen with frost,   *log*
    No wing of wind the region swept,
    But over all things brooding slept
The quiet sense of something lost.

As in the winters left behind,
10   Again our ancient games had place,
    The mimic picture's breathing grace,[6]
And dance and song and hoodman-blind.°   *blindman's bluff*

Who show'd a token of distress?
    No single tear, no mark of pain:

3. The geologic monsters of the early ages [Tennyson's note].
4. The Severn, near which Hallam was buried at Clevedon.

5. The second Christmas after Hallam's death.
6. Tableaux-vivants, an entertainment in which performers reenact a well-known work of art or historical event.

15   O sorrow, then can sorrow wane?
        O grief, can grief be changed to less?

        O last regret, regret can die!
            No—mixt with all this mystic frame,
            Her° deep relations are the same,   *sorrow's*
20   But with long use her tears are dry.
                        * * *
                        86
        Sweet after showers, ambrosial air,
            That rollest from the gorgeous gloom
            Of evening over brake and bloom
        And meadow, slowly breathing bare

5   The round of space, and rapt below
            Thro' all the dewy-tassell'd wood,
            And shadowing down the hornèd flood[7]
        In ripples, fan my brows and blow

        The fever from my cheek, and sigh
10   The full new life that feeds thy breath
            Throughout my frame, till Doubt and Death,
        Ill brethren, let the fancy fly

        From belt to belt of crimson seas
            On leagues of odour streaming far,
15   To where in yonder orient star
        A hundred spirits whisper "Peace."
                        * * *
                        95
        By night we linger'd on the lawn,
            For underfoot the herb was dry;
            And genial warmth; and o'er the sky
        The silvery haze of summer drawn;

5   And calm that let the tapers burn
            Unwavering: not a cricket chirr'd:
            The brook alone far-off was heard,
        And on the board the fluttering urn:[8]

        And bats went round in fragrant skies,
10   And wheel'd or lit the filmy shapes°   *moths*
            That haunt the dusk, with ermine capes
        And woolly breasts and beaded eyes;

        While now we sang old songs that peal'd
            From knoll to knoll, where, couch'd at ease,
15   The white kine° glimmer'd, and the trees   *cows*
        Laid their dark arms about the field.

        But when those others, one by one,
            Withdrew themselves from me and night,
            And in the house light after light

7. Between two promontories [Tennyson's note].   8. Hot-water urn for making tea or coffee, heated by a
                                                        fluttering flame.

20   Went out, and I was all alone,

A hunger seized my heart; I read
  Of that glad year which once had been,
  In those fall'n leaves which kept their green,
The noble letters of the dead:

25   And strangely on the silence broke
  The silent-speaking words, and strange
  Was love's dumb cry defying change
To test his worth; and strangely spoke

The faith, the vigour, bold to dwell
30   On doubts that drive the coward back,
  And keen thro' wordy snares to track
Suggestion to her inmost cell.

So word by word, and line by line,
  The dead man touch'd me from the past.
35   And all at once it seem'd at last
The living soul[9] was flash'd on mine,

And mine in this was wound, and whirl'd
  About empyreal heights of thought,
  And came on that which is, and caught
40   The deep pulsations of the world,

Aeonian music[1] measuring out
  The steps of Time—the shocks of Chance—
  The blows of Death. At length my trance
Was cancell'd, stricken thro' with doubt.[2]

45   Vague words! but ah, how hard to frame
  In matter-moulded forms of speech,
  Or ev'n for intellect to reach
Thro' memory that which I became:

Till now the doubtful dusk reveal'd
50   The knolls once more where, couch'd at ease,
  The white kine glimmer'd, and the trees
Laid their dark arms about the field:

And suck'd from out the distant gloom
  A breeze began to tremble o'er
55   The large leaves of the sycamore,
And fluctuate all the still perfume,

And gathering freshlier overhead,
  Rock'd the full-foliaged elms, and swung
  The heavy-folded rose, and flung
60   The lilies to and fro, and said

9. "His living soul" in the first edition; the next line originally read "And mine in his was wound." Tennyson said
that the first version "troubled me, as perhaps giving a
wrong impression."

1. The music of the aeons.
2. The trance came to an end in a moment of critical
doubt, but the doubt was dispelled by the glory of the
dawn of the "boundless day" [Tennyson's note].

"The dawn, the dawn," and died away;
    And East and West, without a breath,
    Mixt their dim lights, like life and death,
To broaden into boundless day.

* * *

104

The time draws near the birth of Christ;[3]
    The moon is hid, the night is still;
    A single church below the hill
Is pealing, folded in the mist.

5   A single peal of bells below,
    That wakens at this hour of rest
    A single murmur in the breast,
That these are not the bells I know.

Like strangers' voices here they sound,
10   In lands where not a memory strays,
    Nor landmark breathes of other days,
But all is new unhallow'd ground.

* * *

106

Ring out, wild bells, to the wild sky,
    The flying cloud, the frosty light:
    The year is dying in the night;
Ring out, wild bells, and let him die.

5   Ring out the old, ring in the new,
    Ring, happy bells, across the snow:
    The year is going, let him go;
Ring out the false, ring in the true.

Ring out the grief that saps the mind,
10   For those that here we see no more;
    Ring out the feud of rich and poor,
Ring in redress to all mankind.

Ring out a slowly dying cause,
    And ancient forms of party strife;
15   Ring in the nobler modes of life,
With sweeter manners, purer laws.

Ring out the want, the care, the sin,
    The faithless coldness of the times;
    Ring out, ring out my mournful rhymes,
20 But ring the fuller minstrel in.

Ring out false pride in place and blood,
    The civic slander and the spite;
    Ring in the love of truth and right,
Ring in the common love of good.

25   Ring out old shapes of foul disease;
    Ring out the narrowing lust of gold;

3. It is now the third Christmas since Hallam's death.

Ring out the thousand wars of old,
Ring in the thousand years of peace.

30
Ring in the valiant man and free,
    The larger heart, the kindlier hand;
    Ring out the darkness of the land,
Ring in the Christ that is to be.

* * *

115

Now fades the last long streak of snow,
    Now burgeons every maze of quick⁴
    About the flowering squares, and thick
By ashen roots the violets blow.

5
Now rings the woodland loud and long,
    The distance takes a lovelier hue,
    And drown'd in yonder living blue
The lark becomes a sightless song.

Now dance the lights on lawn and lea,
10
    The flocks are whiter down the vale,
    And milkier every milky sail
On winding stream or distant sea;

Where now the seamew pipes, or dives
    In yonder greening gleam, and fly
15
    The happy birds, that change their sky
To build and brood; that live their lives

From land to land; and in my breast
    Spring wakens too; and my regret
    Becomes an April violet,
20
And buds and blossoms like the rest.

* * *

118

Contemplate all this work of Time,
    The giant labouring in his youth;
    Nor dream of human love and truth,
As dying Nature's earth and lime;

5
But trust that those we call the dead
    Are breathers of an ampler day
    For ever nobler ends. They° say,   *scientists*
The solid earth whereon we tread

In tracts of fluent heat began,
10
    And grew to seeming-random forms,
    The seeming prey of cyclic storms,
Till at the last arose the man;

Who throve and branch'd from clime to clime,
    The herald of a higher race,
15
    And of himself in higher place,
If so he type⁵ this work of time

---

4. Hawthorn hedges are budding; the "flowering squares"   5. Typifies or prefigures.
in the next line are fields.

Within himself, from more to more;
   Or, crown'd with attributes of woe
   Like glories, move his course, and show
20   That life is not as idle ore,

But iron dug from central gloom,
   And heated hot with burning fears,
   And dipt in baths of hissing tears,
And batter'd with the shocks of doom

25   To shape and use. Arise and fly
   The reeling Faun, the sensual feast;
   Move upward, working out the beast,
And let the ape and tiger die.

119

Doors, where my heart was used to beat
   So quickly, not as one that weeps
   I come once more;[6] the city sleeps;
I smell the meadow in the street;

5   I hear a chirp of birds; I see
   Betwixt the black fronts long-withdrawn
   A light-blue lane of early dawn,
And think of early days and thee,

And bless thee, for thy lips are bland,
10   And bright the friendship of thine eye;
   And in my thoughts with scarce a sigh
I take the pressure of thine hand.

120

I trust I have not wasted breath:
   I think we are not wholly brain,
   Magnetic mockeries;° not in vain,   *automatons*
Like Paul with beasts,[7] I fought with Death;

5   Not only cunning casts in clay:
   Let Science prove we are, and then
   What matters Science unto men,
At least to me? I would not stay.

Let him, the wiser man who springs
10   Hereafter, up from childhood shape
   His action like the greater ape,[8]
But I was *born* to other things.

* * *

123

There rolls the deep where grew the tree.
   O earth, what changes hast thou seen!
   There where the long street roars, hath been
The stillness of the central sea.

6. Tennyson has returned to Hallam's house in London; see Section 7, page 1930.
7. Saint Paul said: "If after the manner of men I have fought with beasts at Ephesus, what advantageth it me, if the dead rise not" (1 Corinthians 15.32).
8. Spoken ironically against mere materialism, not against evolution [Tennyson's note].

5   The hills are shadows, and they flow
           From form to form, and nothing stands;
           They melt like mist, the solid lands,
       Like clouds they shape themselves and go.

       But in my spirit will I dwell,
10   And dream my dream, and hold it true;
           For tho' my lips may breathe adieu,
       I cannot think the thing farewell.

                    124
       That which we dare invoke to bless;
           Our dearest faith; our ghastliest doubt;
           He, They, One, All; within, without;
       The Power in darkness whom we guess;

5   I found Him not in world or sun,
           Or eagle's wing, or insect's eye;[9]
           Nor thro' the questions men may try,
       The petty cobwebs we have spun:

       If e'er when faith had fall'n asleep,
10   I heard a voice "believe no more"
           And heard an ever-breaking shore
       That tumbled in the Godless deep;

       A warmth within the breast would melt
           The freezing reason's colder part,
15   And like a man in wrath the heart
       Stood up and answer'd "I have felt."

       No, like a child in doubt and fear:
           But that blind clamour made me wise;
           Then was I as a child that cries,
20   But, crying, knows his father near;

       And what I am beheld again
           What is, and no man understands;
           And out of darkness came the hands
       That reach thro' nature, moulding men.
                    * * *
                    130
       Thy voice is on the rolling air;
           I hear thee where the waters run;
           Thou standest in the rising sun,
       And in the setting thou art fair.

5   What art thou then? I cannot guess;
           But tho' I seem in star and flower
           To feel thee some diffusive power,
       I do not therefore love thee less:

       My love involves the love before;
10   My love is vaster passion now;

9. Tennyson rejects the argument that God's existence can be inferred from Nature—i.e., that the design of the universe is so orderly and complex that there must have been a designer.

Tho' mix'd with God and Nature thou,
I seem to love thee more and more.

Far off thou art, but ever nigh;
  I have thee still, and I rejoice;
15   I prosper, circled with thy voice;
I shall not lose thee tho' I die.

131

O living will[1] that shalt endure
  When all that seems shall suffer shock,
  Rise in the spiritual rock,[2]
Flow thro' our deeds and make them pure,

5 That we may lift from out of dust
  A voice as unto him that hears,
  A cry above the conquer'd years
To one that with us works, and trust,

  With faith that comes of self-control,
10 The truths that never can be proved
  Until we close with all we loved,
And all we flow from, soul in soul.

* * *

Crossing the Bar[1]

Sunset and evening star,
  And one clear call for me!
And may there be no moaning of the bar,[2]
  When I put out to sea,

5 But such a tide as moving seems asleep,
  Too full for sound and foam,
When that which drew from out the boundless deep
  Turns again home.

Twilight and evening bell,
10 And after that the dark!
And may there be no sadness of farewell,
  When I embark;

For tho' from out our bourne° of Time and Place   *boundary*
  The flood may bear me far,
15 I hope to see my Pilot face to face[3]
  When I have crost the bar.

1889   1889

---

1. That which we know as Free-will in man [Tennyson's note].
2. "And did all drink the same spiritual drink: for they drank of that spiritual Rock that followed them: and that Rock was Christ" (1 Corinthians 10.4).
1. Tennyson instructed that this poem should appear at the end of every collection of his work, though it was not in fact the last poem he wrote. The poem, he said "came in a moment" while he was crossing the Solent to return

home to Farringford on the Isle of Wight.
2. The sandbank that forms at the mouth of a harbor. The "moaning" may be the sound of the river and the sea meeting.
3. The pilot has been on board all the while, but in the dark I have not seen him [Tennyson's note]. Cf. 1 Corinthians 13.12: "For now we see through a glass, darkly; but then face to face: now I know in part; but then shall I know even as also I am known."

━━━◄◆►━━━

Charles Darwin
1809–1882

Charles Darwin's five-year excursion on the *Beagle* has become the stuff of legend. No voyage since that of Columbus has had such a profound impact on the world. Darwin's ideas concerning evolution and natural selection brought about a revolution in human thought; they radically transformed our sense of our place in the universe. Yet the *Voyage of the Beagle* is a modestly written account of the meticulous observations of a young naturalist, as interested in ordinary beetles and coral formations as in the weirdly monstrous creatures he saw on the Galapagos Islands.

Nothing in Darwin's youth suggested a great man in the making. His father once warned him, "You care for nothing but shooting, dogs, and rat-catching, and you will be a disgrace to yourself and all your family." Darwin's father was a prosperous doctor, and he sent his son to Edinburgh University for two years to study medicine, but Darwin detested the subject, and neglected his studies. Casting about for an occupation for this unpromising son, his father proposed the undemanding career of a country clergyman. Darwin agreed, and spent the next three years at Cambridge where, according to his autobiography, he did little except collect beetles.

Although he considered his formal education a complete waste, Darwin was busy educating himself in natural history. The turning point in his life was an invitation to become the ship's naturalist on the H.M.S. *Beagle*'s surveying expedition. Knowing the ship would be away for years, Darwin's father initially refused permission to accept. At a time when the word "scientist" did not even exist, he could not see how such an undertaking could lead to any respectable profession. But he left a loophole, telling his son, "If you can find any man of common sense, who advises you to go, I will give my consent." Fortunately, Darwin's uncle supported the idea, and in 1831 the *Beagle* sailed for South America with the twenty-two-year-old Darwin aboard.

Darwin had to put up with cramped quarters, seasickness, and the captain's volatile temper, but he accomplished an extraordinary amount of work. He collected specimens, filled eighteen notebooks with scientific observations, and spent long periods ashore studying plants and animals, fossils, and indigenous cultures. He also kept a diary that eventually became the basis of *The Voyage of the Beagle* (1839, rev. 1845), one of the great classics of travel literature. Out of these investigations, particularly in the volcanic Galapagos Islands off the coast of South America, grew the theory of evolution.

Yet it is a myth that Darwin had a sudden insight concerning the origin of species while examining the strange tortoises, lizards, and finches in the Galapagos. Though he had read with interest the evolutionary speculations of his grandfather, Erasmus Darwin, he had remained a creationist: during the voyage he continued to believe that species were fixed forever at the moment of their creation, as described in the Bible. Only back in England, working through his huge volume of notes, did he become convinced of the mutability of species.

Within a few months of his return home in 1836, Darwin had accepted evolution as the explanation for the natural phenomena he had observed. But he was in no hurry to publish his findings. In fact, twenty years went by before he learned in 1858 that a young naturalist, Alfred Russel Wallace, had arrived independently at the theory of natural selection. A joint paper of their findings was presented to the Linnaean Society, and Darwin at long last rushed to compile and publish *On the Origin of Species by Means of Natural Selection* (1859). Darwin realized that most living organisms produce far more offspring than can survive: not every acorn becomes an oak. Certain genetically favored individuals have a competitive edge in the struggle for life. Nature thus ensures the "survival of the fittest," and eventually their descendants evolve into new and better adapted species.

The book created an immediate sensation. The original edition sold out the day it was published. Darwin was not the first to propose a theory of evolution, but he was the first to offer a persuasive account of the means by which evolution works. Geologists such as Charles Lyell had already shown that the earth was immensely older than six thousand years, the traditional estimate based on biblical chronology. In further undermining the biblical account of creation, Darwin shook the faith of his contemporaries.

Darwin was not eager to offend people, nor did he enjoy controversy. Thus in *The Origin of Species* he tactfully avoided any discussion of human origins, although he was already confident that evolution applied to human beings as well. In *The Descent of Man* (1871) he finally made his position clear: man is an animal. Darwin's ideas were profoundly unsettling. No longer sure of belonging to an ordered world overseen by a beneficent Creator, many people felt they had been set adrift in an indifferent cosmos. Tennyson's memorable phrase, "Nature, red in tooth and claw," expressed the Victorians' collective horror at Darwin's vision of nature as a cruel and violent battlefield.

Darwin's theories were earthshaking, but his private life was not. When the *Beagle* voyage ended, he debated the pros and cons of marriage, telling himself that a wife would provide "an object to be beloved and played with—better than a dog anyhow." Despite these unromantic musings, his marriage to his cousin Emma Wedgwood was long and happy. They settled down in a country house and had many children. For the rest of his life Darwin suffered from mysterious illnesses; they prevented his going into society, but they did not stop him working and writing. He never traveled again.

from The Voyage of the Beagle
from *Chapter 10. Tierra Del Fuego*[1]

December 17th, 1832.—Having now finished with Patagonia[2] and the Falkland Islands, I will describe our first arrival in Tierra del Fuego. A little after noon we doubled Cape St. Diego, and entered the famous strait of Le Maire. We kept close to the Fuegian shore, but the outline of the rugged, inhospitable Staten-land was visible amidst the clouds. In the afternoon we anchored in the Bay of Good Success. While entering we were saluted in a manner becoming the inhabitants of this savage land. A group of Fuegians partly concealed by the entangled forest, were perched on a wild point overhanging the sea; and as we passed by, they sprang up and waving their tattered cloaks sent forth a loud and sonorous shout. The savages followed the ship, and just before dark we saw their fire, and again heard their wild cry. The harbour consists of a fine piece of water half surrounded by low rounded mountains of clay-slate, which are covered to the water's edge by one dense gloomy forest. A single glance at the landscape was sufficient to show me how widely different it was from any thing I had ever beheld. At night it blew a gale of wind, and heavy squalls from the mountains swept past us. It would have been a bad time out at sea, and we, as well as others, may call this Good Success Bay.

In the morning the Captain sent a party to communicate with the Fuegians. When we came within hail, one of the four natives who were present advanced to receive us, and began to shout most vehemently, wishing to direct us where to land. When we were on shore the party looked rather alarmed, but continued talking and making gestures with great rapidity. It was without exception the most curious and interesting spectacle I ever beheld: I could not have believed how wide was the difference between savage and civilized man: it is greater than between a wild and

1. A group of islands off the southern tip of South America.   2. The southernmost region of South America.

Thomas Landseer, after a drawing by C. Martens. *A Fuegian at Portrait Cove,* 1839. This illustration appeared in the *Narrative of the Surveying Voyages of His Majesty's Ships Adventure and Beagle, between the Years 1826 and 1836* (1839); Darwin's part of this report became *The Voyage of the Beagle.*

domesticated animal, inasmuch as in man there is a greater power of improvement. The chief spokesman was old, and appeared to be the head of the family; the three others were powerful young men, about six feet high. The women and children had been sent away. These Fuegians are a very different race from the stunted, miserable wretches farther westward; and they seem closely allied to the famous Patagonians of the Strait of Magellan. Their only garment consists of a mantle made of guanaco[3] skin, with the wool outside; this they wear just thrown over their shoulders, leaving their persons as often exposed as covered. Their skin is of a dirty copper red colour.

The old man had a fillet[4] of white feathers tied round his head, which partly confined his black, coarse, and entangled hair. His face was crossed by two broad transverse bars; one, painted bright red, reached from ear to ear and included the upper lip; the other, white like chalk, extended above and parallel to the first, so that even his eyelids were thus coloured. The other two men were ornamented by streaks of black powder, made of charcoal. The party altogether closely resembled the devils which come on the stage in plays like Der Freischutz.[5]

3. A South American mammal with fawn-colored fur.
4. A headband.
5. An 1817 opera by Carl Maria von Weber (1786–1826), first performed in London in 1824. The story concerns Max, a forester who nearly sells his soul to the devil.

Their very attitudes were abject, and the expression of their countenances distrustful, surprised, and startled. After we had presented them with some scarlet cloth, which they immediately tied round their necks, they became good friends. This was shown by the old man patting our breasts, and making a chuckling kind of noise, as people do when feeding chickens. I walked with the old man, and this demonstration of friendship was repeated several times; it was concluded by three hard slaps, which were given me on the breast and back at the same time. He then bared his bosom for me to return the compliment, which being done, he seemed highly pleased. The language of these people, according to our notions, scarcely deserves to be called articulate. Captain Cook has compared it to a man clearing his throat, but certainly no European ever cleared his throat with so many hoarse, guttural, and clicking sounds.

They are excellent mimics: as often as we coughed or yawned, or made any odd motion, they immediately imitated us. Some of our party began to squint and look awry; but one of the young Fuegians (whose whole face was painted black, excepting a white band across his eyes) succeeded in making far more hideous grimaces. They could repeat with perfect correctness each word in any sentence we addressed them, and they remembered such words for some time. Yet we Europeans all know how difficult it is to distinguish apart the sounds in a foreign language. Which of us, for instance, could follow an American Indian through a sentence of more than three words? All savages appear to possess, to an uncommon degree, this power of mimicry. I was told, almost in the same words, of the same ludicrous habit among the Caffres:[6] the Australians, likewise, have long been notorious for being able to imitate and describe the gait of any man, so that he may be recognized. How can this faculty be explained? is it a consequence of the more practised habits of perception and keener senses, common to all men in a savage state, as compared with those long civilized?

When a song was struck up by our party, I thought the Fuegians would have fallen down with astonishment. With equal surprise they viewed our dancing; but one of the young men, when asked, had no objection to a little waltzing. Little accustomed to Europeans as they appeared to be, yet they knew and dreaded our fire-arms; nothing would tempt them to take a gun in their hands. They begged for knives, calling them by the Spanish word "cuchilla." They explained also what they wanted, by acting as if they had a piece of blubber in their mouth, and then pretending to cut instead of tear it.

I have not as yet noticed the Fuegians whom we had on board. During the former voyage of the *Adventure* and *Beagle* in 1826 to 1830, Captain Fitz Roy[7] seized on a party of natives, as hostages for the loss of a boat, which had been stolen, to the great jeopardy of a party employed on the survey; and some of these natives, as well as a child whom he bought for a pearl-button, he took with him to England, determining to educate them and instruct them in religion at his own expense. To settle these natives in their own country, was one chief inducement to Captain Fitz Roy to undertake our present voyage; and before the Admiralty had resolved to send out this expedition, Captain Fitz Roy had generously chartered a vessel, and would himself have taken them back. The natives were accompanied by a missionary, R. Matthews; of whom and of the natives, Captain Fitz Roy has published a full and excellent account. Two men, one of whom died in England of the smallpox, a boy and a little girl, were originally taken; and we had now on board, York Minster, Jemmy Button (whose name expresses his purchase-money), and Fuegia Basket. York Minster was a

---

6. Kaffirs are a Bantu-speaking African people.
7. Robert Fitz Roy (1805–1865) was the captain of the

Beagle; he and Darwin had a sometimes difficult relationship.

full-grown, short, thick, powerful man: his disposition was reserved, taciturn, morose, and when excited violently passionate; his affections were very strong towards a few friends on board; his intellect good. Jemmy Button was a universal favourite, but likewise passionate; the expression of his face at once showed his nice disposition. He was merry and often laughed, and was remarkably sympathetic with any one in pain: when the water was rough, I was often a little seasick, and he used to come to me and say in a plaintive voice, "Poor, poor fellow!" but the notion, after his aquatic life, of a man being sea-sick, was too ludicrous, and he was generally obliged to turn on one side to hide a smile or laugh, and then he would repeat his "Poor, poor fellow!" He was of a patriotic disposition; and he liked to praise his own tribe and country, in which he truly said there were "plenty of trees," and he abused all the other tribes: he stoutly declared that there was no Devil in his land. Jemmy was short, thick, and fat, but vain of his personal appearance; he used to wear gloves, his hair was neatly cut, and he was distressed if his well-polished shoes were dirtied. He was fond of admiring himself in a looking-glass; and a merry-faced little Indian boy from the Rio Negro, whom we had for some months on board, soon perceived this, and used to mock him: Jemmy, who was always rather jealous of the attention paid to this little boy, did not at all like this, and used to say, with rather a contemptuous twist of his head, "Too much skylark." It seems yet wonderful to me, when I think over all his many good qualities, that he should have been of the same race, and doubtless partaken of the same character, with the miserable, degraded savages whom we first met here. Lastly, Fuegia Basket was a nice, modest, reserved young girl, with a rather pleasing but sometimes sullen expression, and very quick in learning anything, especially languages. This she showed in picking up some Portuguese and Spanish, when left on shore for only a short time at Rio de Janeiro and Monte Video, and in her knowledge of English. York Minster was very jealous of any attention paid to her; for it was clear he determined to marry her as soon as they were settled on shore. * * *

   December 25th, 1832.— * * * While going one day on shore near Wollaston Island, we pulled alongside a canoe with six Fuegians. These were the most abject and miserable creatures I anywhere beheld. On the east coast the natives, as we have seen, have guanaco cloaks, and on the west, they possess seal-skins. Amongst these central tribes the men generally have an otter-skin, or some small scrap about as large as a pocket-handkerchief, which is barely sufficient to cover their backs as low down as their loins. It is laced across the breast by strings, and according as the wind blows, it is shifted from side to side. But these Fuegians in the canoe were quite naked, and even one full-grown woman was absolutely so. It was raining heavily, and the fresh water, together with the spray, trickled down her body. In another harbour not far distant, a woman, who was suckling a recently-born child, came one day alongside the vessel, and remained there out of mere curiosity, whilst the sleet fell and thawed on her naked bosom, and on the skin of her naked baby! These poor wretches were stunted in their growth, their hideous faces bedaubed with white paint, their skins filthy and greasy, their hair entangled, their voices discordant, and their gestures violent. Viewing such men, one can hardly make oneself believe that they are fellow-creatures, and inhabitants of the same world. It is a common subject of conjecture what pleasure in life some of the lower animals can enjoy: how much more reasonably the same question may be asked with respect to these barbarians! At night, five or six human beings, naked and scarcely protected from the wind and rain of this tempestuous climate, sleep on the wet ground coiled up like animals. Whenever it is low water, winter or summer, night or day, they must rise to pick shellfish from the rocks; and the women either dive to collect sea-eggs, or sit patiently in their canoes, and with a baited hairline without any hook, jerk out little fish. If a seal is killed, or the floating carcass of a putrid whale discovered, it is a feast; and such miserable food is assisted by a few tasteless berries and fungi. * * *

The different tribes have no government or chief; yet each is surrounded by other hostile tribes, speaking different dialects, and separated from each other only by a deserted border or neutral territory: the cause of their warfare appears to be the means of subsistence. Their country is a broken mass of wild rocks, lofty hills, and useless forests: and these are viewed through mists and endless storms. The habitable land is reduced to the stones on the beach; in search of food they are compelled unceasingly to wander from spot to spot, and so steep is the coast, that they can only move about in their wretched canoes. They cannot know the feeling of having a home, and still less that of domestic affection; for the husband is to the wife a brutal master to a laborious slave. Was a more horrid deed ever perpetrated, than that witnessed on the west coast by Byron, who saw a wretched mother pick up her bleeding dying infant-boy, whom her husband had mercilessly dashed on the stones for dropping a basket of sea-eggs! How little can the higher powers of the mind be brought into play: what is there for imagination to picture, for reason to compare, for judgment to decide upon? to knock a limpet from the rock does not require even cunning, that lowest power of the mind. Their skill in some respects may be compared to the instinct of animals; for it is not improved by experience: the canoe, their most ingenious work, poor as it is, has remained the same, as we know from Drake, for the last two hundred and fifty years.

Whilst beholding these savages, one asks, whence have they come? What could have tempted, or what change compelled a tribe of men, to leave the fine regions of the north, to travel down the Cordillera[8] or backbone of America, to invent and build canoes, which are not used by the tribes of Chile, Peru, and Brazil, and then to enter on one of the most inhospitable countries within the limits of the globe? Although such reflections must at first seize on the mind, yet we may feel sure that they are partly erroneous. There is no reason to believe that the Fuegians decrease in number; therefore we must suppose that they enjoy a sufficient share of happiness, of whatever kind it may be, to render life worth having. Nature by making habit omnipotent, and its effects hereditary, has fitted the Fuegian to the climate and the productions of his miserable country. * * *

January 15th, 1833.—The *Beagle* anchored in Goeree Roads. Captain Fitz Roy having resolved to settle the Fuegians, according to their wishes, in Ponsonby Sound, four boats were equipped to carry them there through the Beagle Channel. * * *

February 6th.— * * * It was quite melancholy leaving the three Fuegians with their savage countrymen; but it was a great comfort that they had no personal fears. York, being a powerful resolute man, was pretty sure to get on well, together with his wife Fuegia. Poor Jemmy looked rather disconsolate, and would then, I have little doubt, have been glad to have returned with us. His own brother had stolen many things from him; and as he remarked, "what fashion call that?" He abused his countrymen, "all bad men, no sabe (know) nothing," and, though I never heard him swear before, "damned fools." Our three Fuegians, though they had been only three years with civilized men, would, I am sure, have been glad to have retained their new habits; but this was obviously impossible. I fear it is more than doubtful, whether their visit will have been of any use to them. * * *

8. Andean mountain range.

On the 5th of March, we anchored in the cove at Woollya, but we saw not a soul there. We were alarmed at this, for the natives in Ponsonby Sound showed by gestures, that there had been fighting; and we afterwards heard that the dreaded Oens men had made a descent. Soon a canoe, with a little flag flying, was seen approaching, with one of the men in it washing the paint off his face. This man was poor Jemmy,—now a thin haggard savage, with long disordered hair, and naked, except a bit of a blanket round his waist. We did not recognize him till he was close to us; for he was ashamed of himself, and turned his back to the ship. We had left him plump, fat, clean, and well dressed;—I never saw so complete and grievous a change. As soon however as he was clothed, and the first flurry was over, things wore a good appearance. He dined with Captain Fitz Roy, and ate his dinner as tidily as formerly. He told us he had "too much" (meaning enough) to eat, that he was not cold, that his relations were very good people, and that he did not wish to go back to England: in the evening we found out the cause of this great change in Jemmy's feelings, in the arrival of his young and nice-looking wife. With his usual good feeling, he brought two beautiful otter-skins for two of his best friends, and some spear-heads and arrows made with his own hands for the Captain. He said he had built a canoe for himself, and he boasted that he could talk a little of his own language! But it is a most singular fact, that he appears to have taught all his tribe some English: an old man spontaneously announced "Jemmy Button's wife." Jemmy had lost all his property. He told us that York Minster had built a large canoe, and with his wife Fuegia, had several months since gone to his own country, and had taken farewell by an act of consummate villainy; he persuaded Jemmy and his mother to come with him, and then on the way deserted them by night, stealing every article of their property.

Jemmy went to sleep on shore, and in the morning returned, and remained on board till the ship got under weigh, which frightened his wife, who continued crying violently till he got into his canoe. He returned loaded with valuable property. Every soul on board was heartily sorry to shake hands with him for the last time. I do not now doubt that he will be as happy as, perhaps happier than, if he had never left his own country. Every one must sincerely hope that Captain Fitz Roy's noble hope may be fulfilled, of being rewarded for the many generous sacrifices which he made for these Fuegians, by some shipwrecked sailor being protected by the descendants of Jemmy Button and his tribe! When Jemmy reached the shore, he lighted a signal fire, and the smoke curled up, bidding us a last and long farewell, as the ship stood on her course into the open sea.

from *Chapter 17. Galapagos Archipelago*[1]

In the morning (17th)[2] we landed on Chatham Island, which, like the others, rises with a tame and rounded outline, broken here and there by scattered hillocks, the remains of former craters. Nothing could be less inviting than the first appearance. A broken field of black basaltic lava, thrown into the most rugged waves, and crossed by great fissures, is every where covered by stunted, sunburnt brushwood, which shows little signs of life. The dry and parched surface, being heated by the noonday sun, gave to the air a close and sultry feeling, like that from a stove: we fancied even that the bushes smelt unpleasantly. Although I diligently tried to collect as many plants

---

1. A group of islands located 400 miles off the coast of Ecuador.   2. Of September, 1835.

as possible, I succeeded in getting very few; and such wretched-looking little weeds would have better become an arctic than an equatorial Flora. The brushwood appears, from a short distance, as leafless as our trees during winter; and it was some time before I discovered that not only almost every plant was now in full leaf, but that the greater number were in flower. * * *

The *Beagle* sailed round Chatham Island, and anchored in several bays. One night I slept on shore on a part of the island, where black truncated cones were extraordinarily numerous: from one small eminence I counted sixty of them, all surmounted by craters more or less perfect. The greater number consisted merely of a ring of red scoriae[3] or slags, cemented together: and their height above the plain of lava was not more than from fifty to a hundred feet: none had been very lately active. The entire surface of this part of the island seems to have been permeated, like a sieve, by the subterranean vapours: here and there the lava, whilst soft, has been blown into great bubbles; and in other parts, the tops of caverns similarly formed have fallen in, leaving circular pits with steep sides. From the regular form of the many craters, they gave to the country an artificial appearance, which vividly reminded me of those parts of Staffordshire, where the great iron-foundries are most numerous. The day was glowing hot, and the scrambling over the rough surface and through the intricate thickets, was very fatiguing; but I was well repaid by the strange Cyclopean[4] scene. As I was walking along I met two large tortoises, each of which must have weighed at least two hundred pounds: one was eating a piece of cactus, and as I approached, it stared at me and slowly stalked away; the other gave a deep hiss, and drew in its head. These huge reptiles, surrounded by the black lava, the leafless shrubs, and large cacti, seemed to my fancy like some antediluvian[5] animals. The few dull-coloured birds cared no more for me, than they did for the great tortoises. * * *

The natural history of these islands is eminently curious, and well deserves attention. Most of the organic productions are aboriginal creations, found nowhere else; there is even a difference between the inhabitants of the different islands; yet all show a marked relationship with those of America, though separated from that continent by an open space of ocean, between 500 and 600 miles in width. The archipelago is a little world within itself, or rather a satellite attached to America, whence it has derived a few stray colonists, and has received the general character of its indigenous productions. Considering the small size of these islands, we feel the more astonished at the number of their aboriginal beings, and at their confined range. Seeing every height crowned with its crater, and the boundaries of most of the lava-streams still distinct, we are led to believe that within a period, geologically recent, the unbroken ocean was here spread out. Hence, both in space and time, we seem to be brought somewhat near to that great fact—that mystery of mysteries—the first appearance of new beings on this earth. * * *

The tortoises, when purposely moving towards any point, travel by night and day, and arrive at their journey's end much sooner than would be expected. The inhabitants, from observing marked individuals, consider that they travel a distance of about eight miles in two or three days. One large tortoise, which I watched, walked at the rate of sixty yards in ten minutes, that is 360 yards in the hour, or four miles a day,—allowing a little time for it to eat on the road. During the breeding season, when the male and female are together, the male utters a hoarse roar or bellowing, which, it is said, can be heard at the distance of more than a hundred yards. The

3. Lava.
4. Darwin may mean that the landscape is savage and wild,

like that inhabited by the Cyclopes in Homer's *Odyssey*.
5. Ancient; literally, before the Flood.

female never uses her voice, and the male only at these times; so that when the people hear this noise, they know that the two are together. They were at this time (October) laying their eggs. The female, where the soil is sandy, deposits them together, and covers them up with sand; but where the ground is rocky she drops them indiscriminately in any hole: Mr. Bynoe[6] found seven placed in a fissure. The egg is white and spherical; one which I measured was seven inches and three-eighths in circumference, and therefore larger than a hen's egg. The young tortoises, as soon as they are hatched, fall a prey in great numbers to the carrion-feeding buzzard. The old ones seem generally to die from accidents, as from falling down precipices: at least, several of the inhabitants told me, that they had never found one dead without some evident cause.

The inhabitants believe that these animals are absolutely deaf; certainly they do not overhear a person walking close behind them. I was always amused when overtaking one of these great monsters, as it was quietly pacing along, to see how suddenly, the instant I passed, it would draw in its head and legs, and uttering a deep hiss fall to the ground with a heavy sound, as if struck dead. I frequently got on their backs, and then giving a few raps on the hinder part of their shells, they would rise up and walk away;— but I found it very difficult to keep my balance. The flesh of this animal is largely employed, both fresh and salted; and a beautifully clear oil is prepared from the fat. * * *

There can be little doubt that this tortoise is an aboriginal inhabitant of the Galapagos; for it is found on all, or nearly all, the islands, even on some of the smaller ones where there is no water; had it been an imported species, this would hardly have been the case in a group which has been so little frequented. * * *

I have not as yet noticed by far the most remarkable feature in the natural history of this archipelago; it is, that the different islands to a considerable extent are inhabited by a different set of beings. My attention was first called to this fact by the Vice-Governor, Mr. Lawson, declaring that the tortoises differed from the different islands, and that he could with certainty tell from which island any one was brought. I did not for some time pay sufficient attention to this statement, and I had already partially mingled together the collections from two of the islands. I never dreamed that islands, about fifty or sixty miles apart, and most of them in sight of each other, formed of precisely the same rocks, placed under a quite similar climate, rising to a nearly equal height, would have been differently tenanted; but we shall soon see that this is the case. It is the fate of most voyagers, no sooner to discover what is most interesting in any locality, than they are hurried from it; but I ought, perhaps, to be thankful that I obtained sufficient material to establish this most remarkable fact in the distribution of organic beings. * * *

If we now turn to the Flora, we shall find the aboriginal plants of the different islands wonderfully different. * * *

Hence we have the truly wonderful fact, that in James Island, of the thirty-eight Galapageian plants, or those found in no other part of the world, thirty are exclusively confined to this one island; and in Albemarle Island, of the twenty-six aboriginal Galapageian plants, twenty-two are confined to this one island, that is, only four are at present known to grow in the other islands of the archipelago; and so on. * * *

The only light which I can throw on this remarkable difference in the inhabitants of the different islands, is, that very strong currents of the sea running in a westerly and W.N.W. direction must separate, as far as transportal by the sea is concerned, the southern islands from the northern ones; and between these northern islands a strong N.W.

6. Naval surgeon aboard the *Beagle*.

current was observed, which must effectually separate James and Albemarle Islands. As the archipelago is free to a most remarkable degree from gales of wind, neither the birds, insects, nor lighter seeds, would be blown from island to island. And lastly, the profound depth of the ocean between the islands, and their apparently recent (in a geological sense) volcanic origin, render it highly unlikely that they were ever united; and this, probably, is a far more important consideration than any other, with respect to the geographical distribution of their inhabitants. Reviewing the facts here given, one is astonished at the amount of creative force, if such an expression may be used, displayed on these small, barren, and rocky islands; and still more so, at its diverse yet analogous action on points so near each other. I have said that the Galapagos Archipelago might be called a satellite attached to America, but it should rather be called a group of satellites, physically similar, organically distinct, yet intimately related to each other, and all related in a marked, though much lesser degree, to the great American continent.

1839, 1845

from On the Origin of Species by Means of Natural Selection

or

The Preservation of Favoured Races in the Struggle for Life

from *Chapter 3. Struggle for Existence*

Before entering on the subject of this chapter, I must make a few preliminary remarks, to show how the struggle for existence bears on Natural Selection. * * * The mere existence of individual variability and of some few well-marked varieties, though necessary as the foundation for the work, helps us but little in understanding how species arise in nature. How have all those exquisite adaptations of one part of the organisation to another part, and to the conditions of life, and of one distinct organic being to another being, been perfected? We see these beautiful co-adaptations most plainly in the woodpecker and missletoe; and only a little less plainly in the humblest parasite which clings to the hairs of a quadruped or feathers of a bird; in the structure of the beetle which dives through the water; in the plumed seed which is wafted by the gentlest breeze; in short, we see beautiful adaptations everywhere and in every part of the organic world.

Again, it may be asked, how is it that varieties which I have called incipient species, become ultimately converted into good and distinct species, which in most cases obviously differ from each other far more than do the varieties of the same species? How do those groups of species, which constitute what are called distinct genera,[1] and which differ from each other more than do the species of the same genus, arise? All these results, as we shall more fully see in the next chapter, follow inevitably from the struggle for life. Owing to this struggle for life, any variation, however slight and from whatever cause proceeding, if it be in any degree profitable to an individual of any species, in its infinitely complex relations to other organic beings and to external nature, will tend to the preservation of that individual, and will generally be inherited by its offspring. The offspring, also, will thus have a better chance of surviving, for, of the many individuals of any species which are periodically born, but a small number can survive. I have called this principle, by which each slight variation, if useful, is preserved, by the term of Natural Selection, in order to mark its relation to man's power of selection. We have seen that man by selection can certainly produce great results, and can adapt organic beings to his own uses,

---

1. Plural of genus, a class of species with common characteristics.

through the accumulation of slight but useful variations, given to him by the hand of Nature. But Natural Selection, as we shall hereafter see, is a power incessantly ready for action, and is as immeasurably superior to man's feeble efforts, as the works of Nature are to those of Art.

We will now discuss in a little more detail the struggle for existence. * * * Nothing is easier than to admit in words the truth of the universal struggle for life, or more difficult—at least I have found it so—than constantly to bear this conclusion in mind. Yet unless it be thoroughly engrained in the mind, I am convinced that the whole economy of nature, with every fact on distribution, rarity, abundance, extinction, and variation, will be dimly seen or quite misunderstood. We behold the face of nature bright with gladness, we often see superabundance of food; we do not see, or we forget, that the birds which are idly singing round us mostly live on insects or seeds, and are thus constantly destroying life; or we forget how largely these songsters, or their eggs, or their nestlings, are destroyed by birds and beasts of prey; we do not always bear in mind, that though food may be now superabundant, it is not so at all seasons of each recurring year.

I should premise that I use the term Struggle for Existence in a large and metaphorical sense, including dependence of one being on another, and including (which is more important) not only the life of the individual, but success in leaving progeny. Two canine animals in a time of dearth, may be truly said to struggle with each other which shall get food and live. But a plant on the edge of a desert is said to struggle for life against the drought, though more properly it should be said to be dependent on the moisture. A plant which annually produces a thousand seeds, of which on an average only one comes to maturity, may be more truly said to struggle with the plants of the same and other kinds which already clothe the ground. The missletoe is dependent on the apple and a few other trees, but can only in a far-fetched sense be said to struggle with these trees, for if too many of these parasites grow on the same tree, it will languish and die. But several seedling missletoes, growing close together on the same branch, may more truly be said to struggle with each other. As the missletoe is disseminated by birds, its existence depends on birds; and it may metaphorically be said to struggle with other fruit-bearing plants, in order to tempt birds to devour and thus disseminate its seeds rather than those of other plants. In these several senses, which pass into each other, I use for convenience sake the general term of struggle for existence.

A struggle for existence inevitably follows from the high rate at which all organic beings tend to increase. Every being, which during its natural lifetime produces several eggs or seeds, must suffer destruction during some period of its life, and during some season or occasional year, otherwise, on the principle of geometrical increase, its numbers would quickly become so inordinately great that no country could support the product. Hence, as more individuals are produced than can possibly survive, there must in every case be a struggle for existence, either one individual with another of the same species, or with the individuals of distinct species or with the physical conditions of life. It is the doctrine of Malthus[2] applied with manifold force to the whole animal and vegetable kingdoms; for in this case there can be no artificial increase of food, and no prudential restraint from marriage. Although some species may be now increasing, more or less rapidly, in numbers, all cannot do so, for the world would not hold them.

---

2. In his *Essay on the Principle of Population* (1803), English economist Thomas Malthus argued that unchecked population growth would threaten the food supply; he proposed "moral restraint" as a partial solution.

There is no exception to the rule that every organic being naturally increases at so high a rate, that if not destroyed, the earth would soon be covered by the progeny of a single pair. Even slow-breeding man has doubled in twenty-five years, and at this rate, in a few thousand years, there would literally not be standing room for his progeny. * * *

In looking at Nature, it is most necessary to keep the foregoing considerations always in mind—never to forget that every single organic being around us may be said to be striving to the utmost to increase in numbers; that each lives by a struggle at some period of its life; that heavy destruction inevitably falls either on the young or old, during each generation or at recurrent intervals. Lighten any check, mitigate the destruction ever so little, and the number of the species will almost instantaneously increase to any amount. The face of Nature may be compared to a yielding surface, with ten thousand sharp wedges packed close together and driven inwards by incessant blows, sometimes one wedge being struck, and then another with greater force. * * *

The amount of food for each species of course gives the extreme limit to which each can increase; but very frequently it is not the obtaining food, but the serving as prey to other animals, which determines the average numbers of a species. Thus, there seems to be little doubt that the stock of partridges, grouse, and hares on any large estate depends chiefly on the destruction of vermin. If not one head of game were shot during the next twenty years in England, and, at the same time, if no vermin were destroyed, there would, in all probability, be less game than at present, although hundreds of thousands of game animals are now annually killed. On the other hand, in some cases, as with the elephant and rhinoceros, none are destroyed by beasts of prey: even the tiger in India most rarely dares to attack a young elephant protected by its dam.

Climate plays an important part in determining the average numbers of a species, and periodical seasons of extreme cold or drought, I believe to be the most effective of all checks. I estimated that the winter of 1854–55 destroyed four-fifths of the birds in my own grounds; and this is a tremendous destruction, when we remember that ten per cent. is an extraordinarily severe mortality from epidemics with man. The action of climate seems at first sight to be quite independent of the struggle for existence; but in so far as climate chiefly acts in reducing food, it brings on the most severe struggle between the individuals, whether of the same or of distinct species, which subsist on the same kind of food. Even when climate, for instance extreme cold, acts directly, it will be the least vigorous, or those which have got least food through the advancing winter, which will suffer most. When we travel from south to north, or from a damp region to a dry, we invariably see some species gradually getting rarer and rarer, and finally disappearing; and the change of climate being conspicuous, we are tempted to attribute the whole effect to its direct action. But this is a very false view: we forget that each species, even where it most abounds, is constantly suffering enormous destruction at some period of its life, from enemies or from competitors for the same place and food; and if these enemies or competitors be in the least degree favoured by any slight change of climate, they will increase in numbers, and, as each area is already fully stocked with inhabitants, the other species will decrease. * * *

That climate acts in main part indirectly by favouring other species, we may clearly see in the prodigious number of plants in our gardens which can perfectly well endure our climate, but which never become naturalised, for they cannot compete with our native plants, nor resist destruction by our native animals. * * *

* * * Battle within battle must ever be recurring with varying success; and yet in the long-run the forces are so nicely balanced, that the face of nature remains uniform for long periods of time, though assuredly the merest trifle would often give the victory to one organic being over another. Nevertheless so profound is our ignorance, and so high our presumption, that we marvel when we hear of the extinction of an organic being; and as we do not see the cause, we invoke cataclysms to desolate the world, or invent laws on the duration of the forms of life! * * *

As species of the same genus have usually, though by no means invariably, some similarity in habits and constitution, and always in structure, the struggle will generally be more severe between species of the same genus, when they come into competition with each other, than between species of distinct genera. We see this in the recent extension over parts of the United States of one species of swallow having caused the decrease of another species. The recent increase of the missel-thrush in parts of Scotland has caused the decrease of the song-thrush. How frequently we hear of one species of rat taking the place of another species under the most different climates! In Russia the small Asiatic cockroach has everywhere driven before it its great congener.[3] One species of charlock[4] will supplant another, and so in other cases. We can dimly see why the competition should be most severe between allied forms, which fill nearly the same place in the economy of nature; but probably in no one case could we precisely say why one species has been victorious over another in the great battle of life.

A corollary of the highest importance may be deduced from the foregoing remarks, namely, that the structure of every organic being is related, in the most essential yet often hidden manner, to that of all other organic beings, with which it comes into competition for food or residence, or from which it has to escape, or on which it preys. This is obvious in the structure of the teeth and talons of the tiger; and in that of the legs and claws of the parasite which clings to the hair on the tiger's body. But in the beautifully plumed seed of the dandelion, and in the flattened and fringed legs of the water-beetle, the relation seems at first confined to the elements of air and water. Yet the advantage of plumed seeds no doubt stands in the closest relation to the land being already thickly clothed by other plants; so that the seeds may be widely distributed and fall on unoccupied ground. In the water-beetle, the structure of its legs, so well adapted for diving, allows it to compete with other aquatic insects, to hunt for its own prey, and to escape serving as prey to other animals.

The store of nutriment laid up within the seeds of many plants seems at first sight to have no sort of relation to other plants. But from the strong growth of young plants produced from such seeds (as peas and beans), when sown in the midst of long grass, I suspect that the chief use of the nutriment in the seed is to favour the growth of the young seedling, whilst struggling with other plants growing vigorously all around.

Look at a plant in the midst of its range, why does it not double or quadruple its numbers? We know that it can perfectly well withstand a little more heat or cold, dampness or dryness, for elsewhere it ranges into slightly hotter or colder, damper or drier districts. In this case we can clearly see that if we wished in imagination to give the plant the power of increasing in number, we should have to give it some advantage over its competitors, or over the animals which preyed on it. On the confines of its geographical range, a change of constitution with respect to climate would clearly be an advantage to our plant; but we have reason to believe that only a few plants or

3. A member of the same genus.   4. Wild mustard.

animals range so far, that they are destroyed by the rigour of the climate alone. Not until we reach the extreme confines of life, in the arctic regions or on the borders of an utter desert, will competition cease. The land may be extremely cold or dry, yet there will be competition between some few species, or between the individuals of the same species, for the warmest or dampest spots.

Hence, also, we can see that when a plant or animal is placed in a new country amongst new competitors, though the climate may be exactly the same as in its former home, yet the conditions of its life will generally be changed in an essential manner. If we wished to increase its average numbers in its new home, we should have to modify it in a different way to what we should have done in its native country; for we should have to give it some advantage over a different set of competitors or enemies.

It is good thus to try in our imagination to give any form some advantage over another. Probably in no single instance should we know what to do, so as to succeed. It will convince us of our ignorance on the mutual relations of all organic beings; a conviction as necessary, as it seems to be difficult to acquire. All that we can do, is to keep steadily in mind that each organic being is striving to increase at a geometrical ratio; that each at some period of its life, during some season of the year, during each generation or at intervals, has to struggle for life, and to suffer great destruction. When we reflect on this struggle, we may console ourselves with the full belief, that the war of nature is not incessant, that no fear is felt, that death is generally prompt, and that the vigorous, the healthy, and the happy survive and multiply.

1859

Robert Browning
1812–1889

Throughout his life Robert Browning was something of an enigma, a Byronic dandy sporting lemon-yellow gloves and gorgeous waistcoats, who loved dining out and yet kept both his private life and poetic practice out of the conversation. He longed for public recognition but would not make his work more accessible by stepping from behind his elaborate artistic masks. Unable to reconcile the hearty dinner guest with the experimental poet, Henry James concluded that Browning lived equally on both sides of an inner wall which "contained an invisible door through which, working the lock at will, he could swiftly pass." Although Browning sometimes suggested that he was a mere ventriloquist or puppeteer, the genius with which he impersonated other voices extended the range and complexity of English poetry in bold new directions. More than any other nineteenth-century figure, Browning shaped the poetry of the twentieth, influencing British and American poets from Hardy and Yeats to Eliot, Pound, Frost, Lowell, and Stevens.

Browning's early years were quiet, even sheltered. He was born in Camberwell, a rural suburb south of London, and with the exception of a year spent at London University, he lived at home with his parents and sister until the age of thirty-four. His father was an official in the Bank of England, and his mother a pious Nonconformist, both of whom encouraged their son in his passion for poetry, painting, and music. The chief source of his education was extensive, haphazard reading in his father's vast private library. Brought up to be a gentleman, Browning received lessons in dancing, fencing, boxing, drawing, and music, as well as Greek and Latin. His doting parents denied him nothing: when, at fourteen, he expressed an interest in the poetry of Shelley—whose works were unavailable because of his atheism—Browning's devout mother took him to London to find an out-of-print copy.

Uncertain what his genuine calling was, Browning considered and rejected careers in art, music, law, and business. A turning point came in October 1832, when he saw the aging Edmund Kean play Richard III. Stunned by the power of a performance in which the brilliant but weary actor alternately electrified and embarrassed the audience as he struggled to dominate his role, Browning found dramatic confirmation of his evolving theory that all personality was staged and variable. Taking Shakespeare as a model, he envisioned himself as performer, playwright, and stage manager of his own artistic world. That night he conceived a grand plan to "assume I know not how many different characters" in order to write poems, operas, novels, and speeches under different names so that "the world was never to guess" that Robert Browning had been the author.

It is a fascinating literary mystery why Browning should have wanted simultaneously to conceal his own identity and yet dazzle the world by impersonating other people—especially since the authors he most admired (Byron, Keats, and particularly Shelley) spoke so personally. In 1833, Browning began his career anonymously with a long romantic poem, *Pauline,* in which he took an indirect approach, speaking through a narrator who confided: "I will tell / My state, as though 'twere none of mine." *Pauline* failed to sell a single copy, but the book found its way to John Stuart Mill, who commented that the poet possessed "a more intense and morbid self-consciousness than I ever knew in any sane being."

In the next decade Browning produced a string of introspective plays and experimental dramatic poems, including *Paracelsus* (1835), *Strafford* (1837), *Sordello* (1840), and *Pippa Passes* (1841). The notorious difficulty of these unpopular works gave Browning a reputation for obscurity that he labored for the rest of his life to overcome. But by the early 1840s he had discovered where his talent lay: applying to lyric poetry his theatrical instincts and his aversion to self-revelation, he found he could produce startling new effects. Henceforth he would present his audience with a cast of aberrant personalities, each starring in his or her own miniplay. In language adapted to their insecurities and obsessions, Browning's characters unwittingly reveal their own, often shocking secrets—but only if readers make the effort to follow the uncanny logic of their contorted confessions.

In the advertisement for his breakthrough book, *Dramatic Lyrics* (1842), Browning offered the disclaimer that, though the poems are "lyric in expression," they are the "utterances of so many imaginary persons, not mine." These imaginary persons range from the Greek goddess Artemis to lovers in a Venetian gondola, from a medieval damsel in distress to a Spanish monk so consumed by hatred that his soliloquy begins with a growl: "Gr-r-r." The sheer physicality of Browning's words, the thick-textured lines, the aggressive consonant clusters that seem to mock Tennyson's liquid vowels, the staccato lines and convoluted syntax that convey the twistings of tongue and mind struggling to express themselves—all are trademarks of Browning's style. As Gerard Manley Hopkins said, Browning talks like "a man bouncing up from table with his mouth full of bread and cheese and saying that he meant to stand no blasted nonsense."

Browning did not invent the poetic form known as the dramatic monologue—it is used in such classics as Marvell's *To His Coy Mistress* and Tennyson's *Ulysses*—but he brought the form to new levels of complexity. He usually situates his speakers in specific historical places and periods. Sometimes they are well-known figures from the past, such as the Italian painters Andrea del Sarto and Fra Lippo Lippi, or literary characters, such as Caliban and Childe Roland. Browning catches them at a moment of great emotional intensity as they attempt to explain why they think and act as they do. In these passionate outbursts, they reveal their characters as much by idiomatic language, patterns of imagery, speech rhythms, and unintended ironies as by what they actually say.

Browning induces his readers to sympathize—even identify—with speakers of dubious morality and intentions. His gallery of rogues includes a duke who may have murdered his wife, a painter who savors his own cuckoldry, and a dying bishop who recalls with gusto the fleshly delights he has enjoyed. As the critic Robert Langbaum has pointed out, "the utter outrageousness" of such behavior "makes condemnation the least interesting response." Just as Satan becomes the most intriguing figure in *Paradise Lost*, so Browning's narrators elicit a reluctant fascination. Alternating between admiration and revulsion, and compelled by the intricacies of human motivation to suspend judgment, the reader struggles to come to terms with these disclosures.

This theatrical world of passionate utterance spilled over into reality in 1845, when Browning became the coauthor and hero of his own romantic drama. On January 10, he wrote a fan letter to the famous poet Elizabeth Barrett, whom he had never seen. He was thirty-three, she nearly forty, and her poetry was far better known than his. "I love your verses with all my heart," he wrote boldly, "—and I love you too." Her reply was encouraging, and thus began the century's most celebrated literary correspondence. She was an invalid suffering from tuberculosis, and they did not meet until May. But when Browning entered her darkened room, he fell instantly in love with the frail, fiery woman lying on her couch swathed in shawls and blankets. For more than a year and half they kept the nature of their relationship secret, to circumvent the wrath of her tyrannical father, who had permitted none of his children to marry. Finally, Browning decided they must break free: they were married secretly during a morning walk, in September 1846, and eloped to Italy, where they eventually settled in Florence.

Though their marriage was rhapsodic, Browning was frustrated with his art. Preoccupied with his wife, her work, their son "Pen" (born in 1849), and the charms of Florence, the usually prolific Browning wrote only one poem in the first three years of marriage, and published just two books in the fifteen years they lived together. Though she acknowledged his genius, Elizabeth joined with her husband's friends in urging him to write "in the most directest and most impressive way, the mask thrown off." Unable or unwilling to do so, Browning gloomily found that he had acquired a further mask that he had not sought: that of "Mrs. Browning's husband."

Hoping finally to make his name with a wider public, Browning channeled his energies into a new project, fifty monologues published in 1855 as *Men and Women*. These animated self-portraits by artists, lovers, questors, skeptics, and impostors form a dazzling picture gallery containing many of Browning's greatest poems, including *Love Among the Ruins*, *Fra Lippo Lippi*, and *Childe Roland*. The plural title of *Men and Women* insists on the variability of human experience, and the centrality of sexual difference to every individual's self-definition. But the book was poorly received at the time, except by the Pre-Raphaelites, and was soon overshadowed by the tumultuous acclaim bestowed on Elizabeth Barrett Browning's *Aurora Leigh* in 1856. Dejected by his readers' failure to make the effort to comprehend his art, Browning complained to his friend John Ruskin: "I cannot begin writing poetry till my imaginary reader has conceded licenses to me. . . . You would have me paint it all plain out, which can't be; but by various artifices I try to make shift with touches and bits of outlines which *succeed* if they bear the conception from me to you. You ought, I think, to keep pace with the thought."

Elizabeth Barrett Browning died suddenly in 1861 in Florence. "My life is fixed and sure now," the devastated widower wrote to his sister, "I shall live out the remainder in her direct influence." Browning returned to England with his son and settled down to a steady rhythm of writing and dining out. But with renewed vigor he resumed his demanding experiments with dramatic lyrics, more determined than ever to pursue the indirect forms of expression that the reading public had resisted.

The result was his second masterpiece, *The Ring and the Book*, a novel in verse published in four monthly installments, between 1868 and 1869. The poem reimagines a sensational seventeenth-century Roman murder trial. In extended monologues the various participants tell their versions of the story. We hear the pleas of the dying young bride Pompilia, her cruel husband Guido, her priest and would-be rescuer Caponsacchi, and then the rationale of the Pope, who decides the case. In this sordid tale of marital abuse and dubious justice, Browning explores the relativity of human understanding, the rights of women, and the role of religious belief in determining earthly action. The success of *The Ring and the Book*, together with the increasing popularity of his earlier work, meant that in the 1870s and 1880s Browning was finally recognized as sharing with Tennyson the title of the era's leading poet. He was especially amused and gratified by the adulation of the Browning Societies that sprang up in England and around the world during his later years. When asked if he objected to the amateurish enthusiasm of the clubs that met to discuss his philosophy of life, he replied: "Object to it? No, I like it! . . . I have waited forty years for it, and now—I like it!" In the United States, where Browning mania hit hardest, brown clothing, curtains, and tableware became the rage, and his works were excerpted on railroad timetables. Mark Twain even gave a series of readings of which he boasted: "I can read Browning so Browning himself can understand it."

Browning's last book, *Asolando,* was published to wide acclaim the day he died at his son's home in Venice. Shortly before his death, Browning read aloud from the book's *Epilogue* the stanza that described his dogged determination to keep on striving in a world of limitation and imperfection: "One who never turned his back but marched breast forward, / Never doubted clouds would break." Ultimately, this confidence underlies the bold relativity and deep skepticism that animate Browning's work. Like Hopkins, Browning insists that all of nature, even human nature, bespeaks some part of an unknowable absolute. Thus everything becomes material for poetry, the dirty, deformed, and despicable no less than the beautiful, pure, and radiantly good. As Browning says in *Fra Lippo Lippi,* "This world's no blot for us, / Nor blank; it means intensely, and means good: / To find its meaning is my meat and drink."

Porphyria's Lover[1]

The rain set early in to-night,
   The sullen wind was soon awake,
It tore the elm-tops down for spite,
   And did its worst to vex the lake:
5   I listened with heart fit to break.
When glided in Porphyria; straight
   She shut the cold out and the storm,
And kneeled and made the cheerless grate
   Blaze up, and all the cottage warm;
10   Which done, she rose, and from her form
Withdrew the dripping cloak and shawl,
   And laid her soiled gloves by, untied
Her hat and let the damp hair fall,
   And, last, she sat down by my side
15   And called me. When no voice replied,
She put my arm about her waist,
   And made her smooth white shoulder bare,
And all her yellow hair displaced,
   And, stooping, made my cheek lie there,
20   And spread, o'er all, her yellow hair,
Murmuring how she loved me—she
   Too weak, for all her heart's endeavour,
To set its struggling passion free
   From pride, and vainer ties dissever,
25   And give herself to me for ever.
But passion sometimes would prevail,

1. The poem was originally published with another of Browning's dramatic monologues, *Johannes Agricola in Meditation,* under the general title of *Madhouse Cells.*

Nor could to-night's gay feast restrain
A sudden thought of one so pale
    For love of her, and all in vain:
30   So, she was come through wind and rain.
Be sure I looked up at her eyes
    Happy and proud; at last I knew
Porphyria worshipped me; surprise
    Made my heart swell, and still it grew
35   While I debated what to do.
That moment she was mine, mine, fair,
    Perfectly pure and good: I found
A thing to do, and all her hair
    In one long yellow string I wound
40   Three times her little throat around,
And strangled her. No pain felt she;
    I am quite sure she felt no pain.
As a shut bud that holds a bee,
    I warily oped her lids: again
45   Laughed the blue eyes without a stain.
And I untightened next the tress
    About her neck; her cheek once more
Blushed bright beneath my burning kiss:
    I propped her head up as before,
50   Only, this time my shoulder bore
Her head, which droops upon it still:
    The smiling rosy little head,
So glad it has its utmost will,
    That all it scorned at once is fled,
55   And I, its love, am gained instead!
Porphyria's love: she guessed not how
    Her darling one wish would be heard.
And thus we sit together now,
    And all night long we have not stirred,
60   And yet God has not said a word!

c. 1835   1836, 1842

My Last Duchess[1]
Ferrara

That's my last Duchess painted on the wall,
Looking as if she were alive. I call
That piece a wonder, now: Frà Pandolf's[2] hands
Worked busily a day, and there she stands.
5   Will't please you sit and look at her? I said
"Frà Pandolf" by design, for never read
Strangers like you that pictured countenance,
The depth and passion of its earnest glance,

1. The speaker is modeled on Alfonso II, Duke of Ferrara, who married the fourteen-year-old Lucrezia de Medici in 1558. When she died three years later, poisoning was suspected. In 1565 the Duke married the daughter of Ferdi-   nand I, Count of Tyrol.
2. Brother Pandolf, the imaginary painter of the duchess's portrait.

But to myself they turned (since none puts by
10   The curtain I have drawn for you, but I)
And seemed as they would ask me, if they durst,
How such a glance came there; so, not the first
Are you to turn and ask thus. Sir, 'twas not
Her husband's presence only, called that spot
15   Of joy into the Duchess' cheek: perhaps
Frà Pandolf chanced to say "Her mantle laps
Over my lady's wrist too much," or "Paint
Must never hope to reproduce the faint
Half-flush that dies along her throat:" such stuff
20   Was courtesy, she thought, and cause enough
For calling up that spot of joy. She had
A heart—how shall I say?—too soon made glad,
Too easily impressed; she liked whate'er
She looked on, and her looks went everywhere.
25   Sir, 'twas all one! My favour at her breast,
The dropping of the daylight in the West,
The bough of cherries some officious fool
Broke in the orchard for her, the white mule
She rode with round the terrace—all and each
30   Would draw from her alike the approving speech,
Or blush, at least. She thanked men,—good! but thanked
Somehow—I know not how—as if she ranked
My gift of a nine-hundred-years-old name
With anybody's gift. Who'd stoop to blame
35   This sort of trifling? Even had you skill
In speech—(which I have not)—to make your will
Quite clear to such an one, and say, "Just this
Or that in you disgusts me; here you miss,
Or there exceed the mark"—and if she let
40   Herself be lessoned so, nor plainly set
Her wits to yours, forsooth, and made excuse,
—E'en then would be some stooping; and I choose
Never to stoop. Oh sir, she smiled, no doubt,
Whene'er I passed her, but who passed without
45   Much the same smile? This grew; I gave commands;
Then all smiles stopped together. There she stands
As if alive. Will't please you rise? We'll meet
The company below, then. I repeat,
The Count your master's known munificence
50   Is ample warrant that no just pretence
Of mine for dowry will be disallowed;
Though his fair daughter's self, as I avowed
At starting, is my object.[3] Nay, we'll go
Together down, sir. Notice Neptune, though,
55   Taming a sea-horse, thought a rarity,
Which Claus of Innsbruck cast in bronze for me!

1842   1842

---

3. Only now does the reader learn that the duke is conducting negotiations for his second marriage and has been addressing the envoy of his bride-to-be's father.

The Bishop Orders His Tomb at Saint Praxed's Church[1]

Rome, 15——

Vanity, saith the preacher, vanity![2]
Draw round my bed: is Anselm keeping back?
Nephews—sons mine[3] . . . ah God, I know not! Well—
She, men would have to be your mother once,
5   Old Gandolf envied me, so fair she was!
What's done is done, and she is dead beside,
Dead long ago, and I am Bishop since,
And as she died so must we die ourselves,
And thence ye may perceive the world's a dream.
10   Life, how and what is it? As here I lie
In this state-chamber, dying by degrees,
Hours and long hours in the dead night, I ask
"Do I live, am I dead?" Peace, peace seems all.
Saint Praxed's ever was the church for peace;
15   And so, about this tomb of mine. I fought
With tooth and nail to save my niche, ye know:
—Old Gandolf cozened me,° despite my care;   *cheated*
Shrewd was that snatch from out the corner South
He graced his carrion with, God curse the same!
20   Yet still my niche is not so cramped but thence
One sees the pulpit o' the epistle-side,[4]
And somewhat of the choir, those silent seats,
And up into the aery dome where live
The angels, and a sunbeam's sure to lurk:
25   And I shall fill my slab of basalt there,
And 'neath my tabernacle[5] take my rest,
With those nine columns round me, two and two,
The odd one at my feet where Anselm stands:
Peach-blossom marble all, the rare, the ripe
30   As fresh-poured red wine of a mighty pulse.[6]
—Old Gandolf with his paltry onion-stone,°   *cheap marble*
Put me where I may look at him! True peach,
Rosy and flawless: how I earned the prize!
Draw close: that conflagration of my church
35   —What then? So much was saved if aught were missed!
My sons, ye would not be my death? Go dig
The white-grape vineyard where the oil-press stood,
Drop water gently till the surface sink,
And if ye find . . . Ah God, I know not, I! . . .

1. John Ruskin admired Browning's portrait of a dying bishop's obsession with ordering a sumptuous tomb: "I know of no other piece of modern English, prose or poetry, in which there is so much told, as in these lines, of the Renaissance spirit—its worldliness, inconsistency, pride, hypocrisy, ignorance of itself, love of art, of luxury, and of good Latin. It is nearly all that I have said of the central Renaissance in thirty pages of the *Stones of Venice*, put into as many lines, Browning's also being the antecedent work" (*Modern Painters*, vol. 4, ch. 20, sec. 34).

2. "Vanity of vanities, saith the Preacher, vanity of vanities; all is vanity" (Ecclesiastes 1.2).
3. The supposedly celibate clergy could not marry but sometimes took mistresses; the Bishop euphemistically calls his illegitimate sons "nephews."
4. The right side, as one faces the altar, from which the Epistles of the New Testament are read.
5. Stone canopy beneath which the sculpted effigy of the bishop will repose on his tomb.
6. The pulpy mash of grapes from which strong wine could be made.

40   Bedded in store of rotten fig-leaves soft,
      And corded up in a tight olive-frail,°   *basket*
      Some lump, ah God, of *lapis lazuli*,[7]
      Big as a Jew's head cut off at the nape,
      Blue as a vein o'er the Madonna's breast . . .
45   Sons, all have I bequeathed you, villas, all,
      That brave Frascati[8] villa with its bath,
      So, let the blue lump poise between my knees,
      Like God the Father's globe on both his hands
      Ye worship in the Jesu Church so gay,
50   For Gandolf shall not choose but see and burst!
      Swift as a weaver's shuttle fleet our years:[9]
      Man goeth to the grave, and where is he?
      Did I say basalt for my slab, sons? Black—
      'Twas ever antique-black I meant! How else
55   Shall ye contrast my frieze° to come beneath?   *sculpted band*
      The bas-relief in bronze ye promised me,
      Those Pans and Nymphs ye wot of, and perchance
      Some tripod, thyrsus, with a vase or so,
      The Saviour at his sermon on the mount,
60   Saint Praxed in a glory, and one Pan
      Ready to twitch the Nymph's last garment off,
      And Moses with the tables[1] . . . but I know
      Ye mark me not! What do they whisper thee,
      Child of my bowels, Anselm? Ah, ye hope
65   To revel down my villas while I gasp
      Bricked o'er with beggar's mouldy travertine°   *limestone*
      Which Gandolf from his tomb-top chuckles at!
      Nay, boys, ye love me—all of jasper, then!
      'Tis jasper ye stand pledged to, lest I grieve.
70   My bath must needs be left behind, alas!
      One block, pure green as a pistachio-nut,
      There's plenty jasper somewhere in the world—
      And have I not Saint Praxed's ear to pray
      Horses for ye, and brown Greek manuscripts,
75   And mistresses with great smooth marbly limbs?
      —That's if ye carve my epitaph aright,
      Choice Latin, picked phrase, Tully's every word,
      No gaudy ware like Gandolf's second line—
      Tully, my masters? Ulpian serves his need![2]
80   And then how I shall lie through centuries,
      And hear the blessed mutter of the mass,
      And see God made and eaten all day long,[3]
      And feel the steady candle-flame, and taste

7. A semiprecious bright blue stone.
8. A resort near Rome.
9. Job 7.6: "My days are swifter than a weaver's shuttle and are spent without hope." The next line alludes to Job 7.9 and 14.10.
1. The bronze bas-relief sculptures will mingle pagan and Christian scenes, the goatlike lecherous Pan next to Moses receiving the Ten Commandments. In *Contrasts*

(1841) A. W. Pugin criticized such juxtapositions, which were typical of the Renaissance.
2. Domitius Ulpianus (A.D. 170–228) was considered inferior to Marcus Tullius Cicero (106–43 B.C.), regarded during the Renaissance as the greatest Latin prose stylist.
3. According to the doctrine of transubstantiation, the bread and wine of Holy Communion become the body and blood of Christ.

Good strong thick stupefying incense-smoke!
85 For as I lie here, hours of the dead night,
Dying in state and by such slow degrees,
I fold my arms as if they clasped a crook,
And stretch my feet forth straight as stone can point,
And let the bedclothes, for a mortcloth, drop
90 Into great laps and folds of sculptor's-work:[4]
And as yon tapers dwindle, and strange thoughts
Grow, with a certain humming in my ears,
About the life before I lived this life,
And this life too, popes, cardinals and priests,
95 Saint Praxed at his sermon on the mount,[5]
Your tall pale mother with her talking eyes,
And new-found agate urns as fresh as day,
And marble's language, Latin pure, discreet,
—Aha, ELUCESCEBAT[6] quoth our friend?
100 No Tully, said I, Ulpian at the best!
Evil and brief hath been my pilgrimage.[7]
All *lapis*, all, sons! Else I give the Pope
My villas! Will ye ever eat my heart?
Ever your eyes were as a lizard's quick,
105 They glitter like your mother's for my soul,
Or ye would heighten my impoverished frieze,
Piece out its starved design, and fill my vase
With grapes, and add a vizor and a Term,[8]
And to the tripod ye would tie a lynx
110 That in his struggle throws the thyrsus down,
To comfort me on my entablature°   platform
Whereon I am to lie till I must ask
"Do I live, am I dead?" There, leave me, there!
For ye have stabbed me with ingratitude
115 To death—ye wish it—God, ye wish it! Stone—
Gritstone, a-crumble![9] Clammy squares which sweat
As if the corpse they keep were oozing through—
And no more *lapis* to delight the world!
Well go! I bless ye. Fewer tapers there,
120 But in a row: and, going, turn your backs
—Ay, like departing altar-ministrants,
And leave me in my church, the church for peace,
That I may watch at leisure if he leers—
Old Gandolf, at me, from his onion-stone,
125 As still he envied me, so fair she was!
1844   1845

---

4. As he lies in bed, the bishop positions himself like a carved effigy lying on a tomb, holding his ceremonial staff and draping his bedsheets like a "mortcloth" over a corpse.
5. Jesus gave the sermon on the mount, not St. Praxed (who was a woman); the bishop's mind is getting confused.
6. Gandolf's epitaph: "He was illustrious." The bishop disapproves of the verb form; Cicero would have written *elucebat*.

7. Cf. Genesis 47.9, where Jacob says: "The days of the years of my pilgrimage are an hundred and thirty years: few and evil have the days of the years of my life been."
8. The vizor of a helmet is sometimes represented in sculpture; the bishop suggests that his sons might also add a statue of Terminus, the Roman god of boundaries.
9. He fears they might use crumbly sandstone after all.

Love Among the Ruins[1]

1

Where the quiet-coloured end of evening smiles,
　　　Miles and miles
On the solitary pastures where our sheep
　　　Half-asleep
5　Tinkle homeward thro' the twilight, stray or stop
　　　As they crop—
Was the site once of a city great and gay,
　　　(So they say)
Of our country's very capital, its prince
10　　　Ages since
Held his court in, gathered councils, wielding far
　　　Peace or war.

2

Now,—the country does not even boast a tree
　　　As you see,
15　To distinguish slopes of verdure, certain rills
　　　From the hills
Intersect and give a name to, (else they run
　　　Into one)
Where the domed and daring palace shot its spires
20　　　Up like fires
O'er the hundred-gated circuit of a wall
　　　Bounding all,
Made of marble, men might march on nor be pressed
　　　Twelve abreast.

3

25　And such plenty and perfection, see, of grass
　　　Never was!
Such a carpet as, this summer-time, o'erspreads
　　　And embeds
Every vestige of the city, guessed alone,
30　　　Stock or stone—
Where a multitude of men breathed joy and woe
　　　Long ago;
Lust of glory pricked their hearts up, dread of shame
　　　Struck them tame;
35　And that glory and that shame alike, the gold
　　　Bought and sold.

4

Now,—the single little turret that remains
　　　On the plains,
By the caper° overrooted, by the gourd　　　　　　　　　　　　　　*shrub*
40　　　Overscored,

---

1. The poem's scenery suggests the Roman Campagna but may also allude to archaeological excavations at Babylon, Nineveh, and Egyptian Thebes. Browning invented this stanza form.

While the patching houseleek's head of blossom winks
    Through the chinks—
Marks the basement whence a tower in ancient time
    Sprang sublime,
45 And a burning ring, all round, the chariots traced
    As they raced,
And the monarch and his minions and his dames
    Viewed the games.

5

And I know, while thus the quiet-coloured eve
50   Smiles to leave
To their folding, all our many-tinkling fleece
    In such peace,
And the slopes and rills in undistinguished grey
    Melt away—
55 That a girl with eager eyes and yellow hair
    Waits me there
In the turret whence the charioteers caught soul
    For the goal,
When the king looked, where she looks now, breathless, dumb
60   Till I come.

6

But he looked upon the city, every side,
    Far and wide,
All the mountains topped with temples, all the glades'
    Colonnades,
65 All the causeys,° bridges, aqueducts,—and then,   *causeways*
    All the men!
When I do come, she will speak not, she will stand,
    Either hand
On my shoulder, give her eyes the first embrace
70   Of my face,
Ere we rush, ere we extinguish sight and speech
    Each on each.

7

In one year they sent a million fighters forth
    South and North,
75 And they built their gods a brazen pillar high
    As the sky,
Yet reserved a thousand chariots in full force—
    Gold, of course.
Oh heart! oh blood that freezes, blood that burns!
80   Earth's returns
For whole centuries of folly, noise and sin!
    Shut them in,
With their triumphs and their glories and the rest!
    Love is best.

c. 1852   1855

"Childe Roland to the Dark Tower Came"[1]

(See Edgar's Song in "Lear")[2]

1

My first thought was, he lied in every word,
   That hoary cripple, with malicious eye
   Askance to watch the working of his lie
On mine, and mouth scarce able to afford
5   Suppression of the glee, that pursed and scored
   Its edge, at one more victim gained thereby.

2

What else should he be set for, with his staff?
   What, save to waylay with his lies, ensnare
   All travellers who might find him posted there,
10   And ask the road? I guessed what skull-like laugh
   Would break, what crutch 'gin write my epitaph
    For pastime in the dusty thoroughfare,

3

If at his counsel I should turn aside
   Into that ominous tract which, all agree,
15   Hides the Dark Tower. Yet acquiescingly
I did turn as he pointed: neither pride
Nor hope rekindling at the end descried,
   So much as gladness that some end might be.

4

For, what with my whole world-wide wandering,
20   What with my search drawn out thro' years, my hope
   Dwindled into a ghost not fit to cope
With that obstreperous joy success would bring,—
I hardly tried now to rebuke the spring
   My heart made, finding failure in its scope.

5

25   As when a sick man very near to death
   Seems dead indeed, and feels begin and end
   The tears and takes the farewell of each friend,
And hears one bid the other go, draw breath
Freelier outside, ("since all is o'er," he saith,
30   "And the blow fallen no grieving can amend;")

6

While some discuss if near the other graves
   Be room enough for this, and when a day
   Suits best for carrying the corpse away,
With care about the banners, scarves and staves:

---

1. Roland was a hero of Charlemagne legends, and a "childe" was a young candidate for knighthood. Although critics have proposed many different interpretations of Roland's strange, nightmarish quest, Browning himself said only that the poem "came upon me as a kind of dream. I had to write it, then and there, and I finished it the same day, I believe. But it was simply that I had to do it. I did not know then what I meant beyond that, and I'm sure I don't know now. But I am very fond of it." 2. In Shakespeare's *King Lear*, Edgar, disguised as the mad beggar Poor Tom, sings: "Child Rowland to the dark tower came; / His word was still, 'Fie, foh and fum, / I smell the blood of a British man'" (3.4.181–83).

35 And still the man hears all, and only craves
        He may not shame such tender love and stay.
                        7
      Thus, I had so long suffered in this quest,
          Heard failure prophesied so oft, been writ
          So many times among "The Band"—to wit,
40   The knights who to the Dark Tower's search addressed
      Their steps—that just to fail as they, seemed best,
          And all the doubt was now—should I be fit?
                        8
      So, quiet as despair, I turned from him,
          That hateful cripple, out of his highway
45   Into the path he pointed. All the day
      Had been a dreary one at best, and dim
      Was settling to its close, yet shot one grim
          Red leer to see the plain catch its estray.°   *stray animal*
                        9
      For mark! no sooner was I fairly found
50   Pledged to the plain, after a pace or two,
          Than, pausing to throw backward a last view
      O'er the safe road, 'twas gone; grey plain all round:
      Nothing but plain to the horizon's bound.
          I might go on; nought else remained to do.
                        10
55   So, on I went. I think I never saw
          Such starved ignoble nature; nothing throve:
          For flowers—as well expect a cedar grove!
      But cockle, spurge,° according to their law   *weeds*
      Might propagate their kind, with none to awe,
60   You'd think; a burr had been a treasure-trove.
                        11
      No! penury, inertness and grimace,
          In some strange sort, were the land's portion. "See
          Or shut your eyes," said Nature peevishly,
      "It nothing skills: I cannot help my case:
65   'Tis the Last Judgment's fire must cure this place,
          Calcine° its clods and set my prisoners free."   *burn to ashes*
                        12
      If there pushed any ragged thistle-stalk
          Above its mates, the head was chopped; the bents°   *coarse grasses*
          Were jealous else. What made those holes and rents
70   In the dock's° harsh swarth leaves, bruised as to baulk   *weed*
      All hope of greenness? 'tis a brute must walk
          Pashing° their life out, with a brute's intents.   *crushing*
                        13
      As for the grass, it grew as scant as hair
          In leprosy; thin dry blades pricked the mud
75   Which underneath looked kneaded up with blood.
      One stiff blind horse, his every bone a-stare,
      Stood stupefied, however he came there:
          Thrust out past service from the devil's stud!

14

Alive? he might be dead for aught I know,
80   With that red gaunt and colloped neck a-strain,
        And shut eyes underneath the rusty mane;
Seldom went such grotesqueness with such woe;
I never saw a brute I hated so;
        He must be wicked to deserve such pain.

15

I shut my eyes and turned them on my heart.
85   As a man calls for wine before he fights,
        I asked one draught of earlier, happier sights,
Ere fitly I could hope to play my part.
Think first, fight afterwards—the soldier's art:
90   One taste of the old time sets all to rights.

16

Not it! I fancied Cuthbert's reddening face
        Beneath its garniture of curly gold,
        Dear fellow, till I almost felt him fold
An arm in mine to fix me to the place,
95   That way he used. Alas, one night's disgrace!
        Out went my heart's new fire and left it cold.

17

Giles then, the soul of honour—there he stands
        Frank as ten years ago when knighted first.
        What honest man should dare (he said) he durst.
100   Good—but the scene shifts—faugh! what hangman-hands
Pin to his breast a parchment? His own bands
        Read it. Poor traitor, spit upon and curst!

18

Better this present than a past like that;
        Back therefore to my darkening path again!
105   No sound, no sight as far as eye could strain.
Will the night send a howlet° or a bat?   *owl*
I asked: when something on the dismal flat
        Came to arrest my thoughts and change their train.

19

A sudden little river crossed my path
110   As unexpected as a serpent comes.
        No sluggish tide congenial to the glooms;
This, as it frothed by, might have been a bath
For the fiend's glowing hoof—to see the wrath
        Of its black eddy bespate with flakes and spumes.

20

115   So petty yet so spiteful! All along,
        Low scrubby alders kneeled down over it;
        Drenched willows flung them headlong in a fit
Of mute despair, a suicidal throng:
The river which had done them all the wrong,
120   Whate'er that was, rolled by, deterred no whit.

21

Which, while I forded,—good saints, how I feared
        To set my foot upon a dead man's cheek,

Each step, or feel the spear I thrust to seek
For hollows, tangled in his hair or beard!
125 —It may have been a water-rat I speared,
But, ugh! it sounded like a baby's shriek.

22

Glad was I when I reached the other bank.
Now for a better country. Vain presage!
Who were the strugglers, what war did they wage,
130 Whose savage trample thus could pad° the dank   tread
Soil to a plash? Toads in a poisoned tank,
Or wild cats in a red-hot iron cage—

23

The fight must so have seemed in that fell cirque.°   terrible arena
What penned them there, with all the plain to choose?
135 No foot-print leading to that horrid mews,
None out of it. Mad brewage set to work
Their brains, no doubt, like galley-slaves the Turk
Pits for his pastime, Christians against Jews.

24

And more than that—a furlong on—why, there!
140 What bad use was that engine for, that wheel,
Or brake, not wheel—that harrow fit to reel
Men's bodies out like silk? with all the air
Of Tophet's° tool, on earth left unaware,   hell's
Or brought to sharpen its rusty teeth of steel.

25

145 Then came a bit of stubbed ground, once a wood,
Next a marsh, it would seem, and now mere earth
Desperate and done with; (so a fool finds mirth,
Makes a thing and then mars it, till his mood
Changes and off he goes!) within a rood°—   quarter of an acre
150 Bog, clay and rubble, sand and stark black dearth.

26

Now blotches rankling, coloured gay and grim,
Now patches where some leanness of the soil's
Broke into moss or substances like boils;
Then came some palsied oak, a cleft in him
155 Like a distorted mouth that splits its rim
Gaping at death, and dies while it recoils.

27

And just as far as ever from the end!
Nought in the distance but the evening, nought
To point my footstep further! At the thought,
160 A great black bird, Apollyon's[3] bosom-friend,
Sailed past, nor beat his wide wing dragon-penned°   pinioned
That brushed my cap—perchance the guide I sought.

28

For, looking up, aware I somehow grew,
'Spite of the dusk, the plain had given place

---

3. Devil mentioned in Revelation 9.11 and in Bunyan's *Pilgrim's Progress*.

165　　　All round to mountains—with such name to grace
　　　　Mere ugly heights and heaps now stolen in view.
　　　　How thus they had surprised me,—solve it, you!
　　　　　　How to get from them was no clearer case.

29

　　　　Yet half I seemed to recognize some trick
170　　　Of mischief happened to me, God knows when—
　　　　In a bad dream perhaps. Here ended, then,
　　　　Progress this way. When, in the very nick
　　　　Of giving up, one time more, came a click
　　　　　　As when a trap shuts—you're inside the den!

30

175　　　Burningly it came on me all at once,
　　　　　　This was the place! those two hills on the right,
　　　　　　Crouched like two bulls locked horn in horn in fight;
　　　　While to the left, a tall scalped mountain . . . Dunce,
　　　　Dotard, a-dozing at the very nonce,°　　　　　　　　　*moment*
180　　　　　After a life spent training for the sight!

31

　　　　What in the midst lay but the Tower itself?
　　　　　　The round squat turret, blind as the fool's heart,[4]
　　　　　　Built of brown stone, without a counterpart
　　　　In the whole world. The tempest's mocking elf
185　　　Points to the shipman thus the unseen shelf
　　　　　　He strikes on, only when the timbers start.

32

　　　　Not see? because of night perhaps?—why, day
　　　　　　Came back again for that! before it left,
　　　　　　The dying sunset kindled through a cleft:
190　　　The hills, like giants at a hunting, lay,
　　　　Chin upon hand, to see the game at bay,—
　　　　　　"Now stab and end the creature—to the heft!"°　　　　　*hilt*

33

　　　　Not hear? when noise was everywhere! it tolled
　　　　　　Increasing like a bell. Names in my ears
195　　　　　Of all the lost adventurers my peers,—
　　　　How such a one was strong, and such was bold,
　　　　And such was fortunate, yet each of old
　　　　　　Lost, lost! one moment knelled the woe of years.

34

　　　　There they stood, ranged along the hill-sides, met
200　　　　　To view the last of me, a living frame
　　　　　　For one more picture! in a sheet of flame
　　　　I saw them and I knew them all. And yet
　　　　Dauntless the slug-horn[5] to my lips I set,
　　　　　　And blew. "*Childe Roland to the Dark Tower came.*"

c. 1852　　　　　　　　　　　　　　　　　　　　　　　　　　　　1855

---

4. "The fool hath said in his heart, There is no God"　　5. Scottish word for slogan, or battle-cry, though Brown-
(Psalm 14.1).　　　　　　　　　　　　　　　　　　　　ing seems to mean "trumpet."

Fra Lippo Lippi[1]

I am poor brother Lippo, by your leave!
You need not clap your torches to my face.
Zooks, what's to blame? you think you see a monk!
What, 'tis past midnight, and you go the rounds,
5   And here you catch me at an alley's end
Where sportive ladies leave their doors ajar?
The Carmine's my cloister:[2] hunt it up,
Do,—harry out, if you must show your zeal,
Whatever rat, there, haps on his wrong hole,
10 And nip each softling of a wee white mouse,
Weke, weke, that's crept to keep him company!
Aha, you know your betters! Then, you'll take
Your hand away that's fiddling on my throat,
And please to know me likewise. Who am I?
15 Why, one, sir, who is lodging with a friend
Three streets off—he's a certain . . . how d'ye call?
Master—a . . . Cosimo of the Medici,[3]
I' the house that caps the corner. Boh! you were best!
Remember and tell me, the day you're hanged,
20 How you affected such a gullet's-gripe![4]
But you, sir,[5] it concerns you that your knaves
Pick up a manner nor discredit you:
Zooks, are we pilchards,° that they sweep the streets   sardines
And count fair prize what comes into their net?
25 He's Judas to a tittle, that man is![6]
Just such a face! Why, sir, you make amends:
Lord, I'm not angry! Bid your hangdogs go
Drink out this quarter-florin to the health
Of the munificent House that harbours me
30 (And many more beside, lads! more beside!)
And all's come square again. I'd like his face—
His, elbowing on his comrade in the door
With the pike and lantern,—for the slave that holds
John Baptist's head a-dangle by the hair
35 With one hand ("Look you, now," as who should say)
And his weapon in the other, yet unwiped!
It's not your chance to have a bit of chalk,
A wood-coal or the like? or you should see!
Yes, I'm the painter, since you style me so.
40 What, brother Lippo's doings, up and down,
You know them and they take you? like enough!
I saw the proper twinkle in your eye—
'Tell you, I liked your looks at very first.
Let's sit and set things straight now, hip to haunch.

1. Filippo Lippi (1406–1469) was an early Renaissance
painter and monk whose life is described in Giorgio Vasari's
The Lives of the Painters (1550, 1568); Fra means brother.
2. Santa Maria del Carmine, a Carmelite monastery in
Florence.

3. Cosimo de' Medici (1389–1464), a banker and ruler of
Florence, was Lippi's patron.
4. How you choked me by the throat.
5. Lippi now addresses the leader of the watchmen.
6. One of the watchmen is the spitting image of Judas.

45   Here's spring come, and the nights one makes up bands
      To roam the town and sing out carnival,[7]
      And I've been three weeks shut within my mew,
      A-painting for the great man, saints and saints
      And saints again. I could not paint all night—
50   Ouf! I leaned out of window for fresh air.
      There came a hurry of feet and little feet,
      A sweep of lute-strings, laughs, and whifts of song,—
      Flower o' the broom,
      Take away love, and our earth is a tomb!
55   *Flower o' the quince,*
      I let Lisa go, and what good in life since?
      Flower o' the thyme[8]—and so on. Round they went.
      Scarce had they turned the corner when a titter
      Like the skipping of rabbits by moonlight,—three slim shapes,
60   And a face that looked up . . . zooks, sir, flesh and blood,
      That's all I'm made of! Into shreds it went,
      Curtain and counterpane and coverlet,
      All the bed-furniture—a dozen knots,
      There was a ladder! Down I let myself,
65   Hands and feet, scrambling somehow, and so dropped,
      And after them. I came up with the fun
      Hard by Saint Laurence,[9] hail fellow, well met,—
      Flower o' the rose,
      If I've been merry, what matter who knows?
70   And so as I was stealing back again
      To get to bed and have a bit of sleep
      Ere I rise up to-morrow and go work
      On Jerome[1] knocking at his poor old breast
      With his great round stone to subdue the flesh,
75   You snap me of the sudden. Ah, I see!
      Though your eye twinkles still, you shake your head—
      Mine's shaved[2]—a monk, you say—the sting's in that!
      If Master Cosimo announced himself,
      Mum's the word naturally; but a monk!
80   Come, what am I a beast for? tell us, now!
      I was a baby when my mother died
      And father died and left me in the street.
      I starved there, God knows how, a year or two
      On fig-skins, melon-parings, rinds and shucks,
85   Refuse and rubbish. One fine frosty day,
      My stomach being empty as your hat,
      The wind doubled me up and down I went.
      Old Aunt Lapaccia trussed me with one hand,
      (Its fellow was a stinger as I knew)
90   And so along the wall, over the bridge,
      By the straight cut to the convent. Six words there,

---

7. A season of festivities before Lent.
8. The "flower songs" Lippi sings are called *stornelli,* three-line Tuscan folk songs.
9. The Church of San Lorenzo.

1. The pleasure-loving Lippi is painting the chaste and ascetic St. Jerome.
2. The tonsure, or partially shaved head, was the emblem of the monk.

While I stood munching my first bread that month:
"So, boy, you're minded," quoth the good fat father
Wiping his own mouth, 'twas refection-time,°——   *mealtime*
95   "To quit this very miserable world?
Will you renounce" . . . "the mouthful of bread?" thought I;
By no means! Brief, they made a monk of me;
I did renounce the world, its pride and greed,
Palace, farm, villa, shop and banking-house,
100   Trash, such as these poor devils of Medici
Have given their hearts to——all at eight years old.
Well, sir, I found in time, you may be sure,
'Twas not for nothing——the good bellyful,
The warm serge and the rope that goes all round,
105   And day-long blessed idleness beside!
"Let's see what the urchin's fit for"——that came next.
Not overmuch their way, I must confess.
Such a to-do! They tried me with their books:
Lord, they'd have taught me Latin in pure waste!
110   *Flower o' the clove,*
All the Latin I construe is, "amo," I love!
But, mind you, when a boy starves in the streets
Eight years together, as my fortune was,
Watching folk's faces to know who will fling
115   The bit of half-stripped grape-bunch he desires,
And who will curse or kick him for his pains,——
Which gentleman processional and fine,
Holding a candle to the Sacrament,
Will wink and let him lift a plate and catch
120   The droppings of the wax to sell again,
Or holla for the Eight[3] and have him whipped,——
How say I?——nay, which dog bites, which lets drop
His bone from the heap of offal in the street,——
Why, soul and sense of him grow sharp alike,
125   He learns the look of things, and none the less
For admonition from the hunger-pinch.
I had a store of such remarks, be sure,
Which, after I found leisure, turned to use.
I drew men's faces on my copy-books,
130   Scrawled them within the antiphonary's marge,[4]
Joined legs and arms to the long music-notes,
Found eyes and nose and chin for A's and B's,
And made a string of pictures of the world
Betwixt the ins and outs of verb and noun,
135   On the wall, the bench, the door. The monks looked black.
"Nay," quoth the Prior, "turn him out, d' ye say?
In no wise. Lose a crow and catch a lark.
What if at last we get our man of parts,
We Carmelites, like those Camaldolese
140   And Preaching Friars, to do our church up fine

3. Send for the magistrates of Florence.   4. The margin of his hymn book.

And put the front on it that ought to be!"[5]
And hereupon he bade me daub away.
Thank you! my head being crammed, the walls a blank,
Never was such prompt disemburdening.
145　First, every sort of monk, the black and white,
I drew them, fat and lean: then, folk at church,
From good old gossips waiting to confess
Their cribs° of barrel-droppings, candle-ends,—　　　　*small thefts*
To the breathless fellow at the altar-foot,
150　Fresh from his murder,[6] safe and sitting there
With the little children round him in a row
Of admiration, half for his beard and half
For that white anger of his victim's son
Shaking a fist at him with one fierce arm,
155　Signing himself [7] with the other because of Christ
(Whose sad face on the cross sees only this
After the passion° of a thousand years)　　　　*suffering*
Till some poor girl, her apron o'er her head,
(Which the intense eyes looked through) came at eve
160　On tiptoe, said a word, dropped in a loaf,
Her pair of earrings and a bunch of flowers
(The brute took growling), prayed, and so was gone.
I painted all, then cried "'Tis ask and have;
Choose, for more's ready!"—laid the ladder flat,
165　And showed my covered bit of cloister-wall
The monks closed in a circle and praised loud
Till checked, taught what to see and not to see,
Being simple bodies,—"That's the very man!
Look at the boy who stoops to pat the dog!
170　That woman's like the Prior's niece[8] who comes
To care about his asthma: it's the life!"
But there my triumph's straw-fire flared and funked;°　　　　*smoked*
Their betters took their turn to see and say:
The Prior and the learned pulled a face
175　And stopped all that in no time. "How? what's here?
Quite from the mark of painting, bless us all!
Faces, arms, legs and bodies like the true
As much as pea and pea! it's devil's-game!
Your business is not to catch men with show,
180　With homage to the perishable clay,
But lift them over it, ignore it all,
Make them forget there's such a thing as flesh.
Your business is to paint the souls of men—
Man's soul, and it's a fire, smoke . . . no, it's not . . .
185　It's vapour done up like a new-born babe—
(In that shape when you die it leaves your mouth)

5. The Prior, or head of the monastery, wants to outdo rival orders of monks by having Lippi paint the church splendidly.
6. Criminals could take refuge in the church because it was a sanctuary where civil law had no power.
7. Making the sign of the cross.
8. Probably a euphemism for the Prior's mistress.

It's . . . well, what matters talking, it's the soul!
Give us no more of body than shows soul!
Here's Giotto,[9] with his Saint a-praising God,
190 That sets us praising,—why not stop with him?
Why put all thoughts of praise out of our head
With wonder at lines, colours, and what not?
Paint the soul, never mind the legs and arms!
Rub all out, try at it a second time.
195 Oh, that white smallish female with the breasts,
She's just my niece . . . Herodias, I would say,—
Who went and danced and got men's heads cut off![1]
Have it all out!" Now, is this sense, I ask?
A fine way to paint soul, by painting body
200 So ill, the eye can't stop there, must go further
And can't fare worse! Thus, yellow does for white
When what you put for yellow's simply black,
And any sort of meaning looks intense
When all beside itself means and looks nought.
205 Why can't a painter lift each foot in turn,
Left foot and right foot, go a double step,
Make his flesh liker and his soul more like,
Both in their order? Take the prettiest face,
The Prior's niece . . . patron-saint—is it so pretty
210 You can't discover if it means hope, fear,
Sorrow or joy? won't beauty go with these?
Suppose I've made her eyes all right and blue,
Can't I take breath and try to add life's flash,
And then add soul and heighten them threefold?
215 Or say there's beauty with no soul at all—
(I never saw it—put the case the same—)
If you get simple beauty and nought else,
You get about the best thing God invents:
That's somewhat: and you'll find the soul you have missed,
220 Within yourself, when you return him thanks.
"Rub all out!" Well, well, there's my life, in short,
And so the thing has gone on ever since.
I'm grown a man no doubt, I've broken bounds:
You should not take a fellow eight years old
225 And make him swear to never kiss the girls.
I'm my own master, paint now as I please—
Having a friend, you see, in the Corner-house!°   *Medici palace*
Lord, it's fast holding by the rings in front—
Those great rings serve more purposes than just
230 To plant a flag in, or tie up a horse!
And yet the old schooling sticks, the old grave eyes
Are peeping o'er my shoulder as I work,
The heads shake still—"It's art's decline, my son!

9. Giotto di Bondone (c. 1266–1337), late-medieval Florentine artist and architect.
1. The gospel of Matthew tells how Herod's niece Salomé
danced before him and requested as a reward the head of
John the Baptist (14.6–8). According to Vasari, however,
it was Salomé's mother, Herodias, who danced.

You're not of the true painters, great and old;
235   Brother Angelico's the man, you'll find;
Brother Lorenzo stands his single peer:[2]
Fag° on at flesh, you'll never make the third!"   *struggle*
Flower o' the pine,
You keep your mistr . . . manners, and I'll stick to mine!
240   I'm not the third, then: bless us, they must know!
Don't you think they're the likeliest to know,
They with their Latin? So, I swallow my rage,
Clench my teeth, suck my lips in tight, and paint
To please them—sometimes do and sometimes don't;
245   For, doing most, there's pretty sure to come
A turn, some warm eve finds me at my saints—
A laugh, a cry, the business of the world—
(Flower o' the peach,
Death for us all, and his own life for each!)
250   And my whole soul revolves, the cup runs over,
The world and life's too big to pass for a dream,
And I do these wild things in sheer despite,
And play the fooleries you catch me at,
In pure rage! The old mill-horse, out at grass
255   After hard years, throws up his stiff heels so,
Although the miller does not preach to him
The only good of grass is to make chaff.°   *straw*
What would men have? Do they like grass or no—
May they or mayn't they? all I want's the thing
260   Settled for ever one way. As it is,
You tell too many lies and hurt yourself:
You don't like what you only like too much,
You do like what, if given you at your word,
You find abundantly detestable.
265   For me, I think I speak as I was taught;
I always see the garden and God there
A-making man's wife: and, my lesson learned,
The value and significance of flesh,
I can't unlearn ten minutes afterwards.

270   You understand me: I'm a beast, I know.
But see, now—why, I see as certainly
As that the morning-star's about to shine,
What will hap some day. We've a youngster here
Comes to our convent, studies what I do,
275   Slouches and stares and lets no atom drop:
His name is Guidi—he'll not mind the monks—
They call him Hulking Tom,[3] he lets them talk—
He picks my practice up—he'll paint apace,
I hope so—though I never live so long,

2. Fra Angelico (1387–1455) and Lorenzo Monaco (1370–1425) were important painters in the traditional formalist style.
3. Tommaso Guidi (1401–1428), called Masaccio ("Sloppy Tom"), was probably Lippi's teacher, but Browning casts him as his pupil. Both painters revolted against the highly stylized conventions of medieval art in favor of increased realism.

280   I know what's sure to follow. You be judge!
You speak no Latin more than I, belike,
However, you're my man, you've seen the world
—The beauty and the wonder and the power,
The shapes of things, their colours, lights and shades,
285   Changes, surprises,—and God made it all!
—For what? Do you feel thankful, ay or no,
For this fair town's face, yonder river's line,
The mountain round it and the sky above,
Much more the figures of man, woman, child,
290   These are the frame to? What's it all about?
To be passed over, despised? or dwelt upon,
Wondered at? oh, this last of course!—you say.
But why not do as well as say,—paint these
Just as they are, careless what comes of it?
295   God's works—paint anyone, and count it crime
To let a truth slip. Don't object, "His works
Are here already; nature is complete:
Suppose you reproduce her—(which you can't)
There's no advantage! you must beat her, then."
300   For, don't you mark? we're made so that we love
First when we see them painted, things we have passed
Perhaps a hundred times nor cared to see;
And so they are better, painted—better to us,
Which is the same thing. Art was given for that;
305   God uses us to help each other so,
Lending our minds out. Have you noticed, now,
Your cullion's hanging face?[4] A bit of chalk,
And trust me but you should, though! How much more,
If I drew higher things with the same truth!
310   That were to take the Prior's pulpit-place,
Interpret God to all of you! Oh, oh,
It makes me mad to see what men shall do
And we in our graves! This world's no blot for us,
Nor blank; it means intensely, and means good:
315   To find its meaning is my meat and drink.
"Ay, but you don't so instigate to prayer!"
Strikes in the Prior: "when your meaning's plain
It does not say to folk—remember matins,°   *morning prayers*
Or, mind you fast next Friday!" Why, for this
320   What need of art at all? A skull and bones,
Two bits of stick nailed crosswise, or, what's best,
A bell to chime the hour with, does as well.
I painted a Saint Laurence six months since
At Prato, splashed the fresco in fine style:
325   "How looks my painting, now the scaffold's down?"
I ask a brother: "Hugely," he returns—
Already not one phiz° of your three slaves   *face*

4. That rascal's drooping face (or perhaps "born to be hanged"—cf. line 19).

Who turn the Deacon off his toasted side,[5]
But's scratched and prodded to our heart's content,
330 The pious people have so eased their own
With coming to say prayers there in a rage:
We get on fast to see the bricks beneath.
Expect another job this time next year,
For pity and religion grow i' the crowd—
335 Your painting serves its purpose!" Hang the fools!

      —That is—you'll not mistake an idle word
Spoke in a huff by a poor monk, God wot,
Tasting the air this spicy night which turns
The unaccustomed head like Chianti wine!
340 Oh, the church knows! don't misreport me, now!
It's natural a poor monk out of bounds
Should have his apt word to excuse himself:
And hearken how I plot to make amends.
I have bethought me: I shall paint a piece
345 . . . There's for you! Give me six months, then go, see
Something in Sant' Ambrogio's![6] Bless the nuns!
They want a cast o' my office. I shall paint
God in the midst, Madonna and her babe,
Ringed by a bowery flowery angel-brood,
350 Lilies and vestments and white faces, sweet
As puff on puff of grated orris-root
When ladies crowd to Church at midsummer.
And then i' the front, of course a saint or two—
Saint John, because he saves the Florentines,
355 Saint Ambrose, who puts down in black and white
The convent's friends and gives them a long day,
And Job, I must have him there past mistake,
The man of Uz (and Us without the z,
Painters who need his patience). Well, all these
360 Secured at their devotion, up shall come
Out of a corner when you least expect,
As one by a dark stair into a great light,
Music and talking, who but Lippo! I!—
Mazed, motionless and moonstruck—I'm the man!
365 Back I shrink—what is this I see and hear?
I, caught up with my monk's-things by mistake,
My old serge gown and rope that goes all round,
I, in this presence, this pure company!
Where's a hole, where's a corner for escape?
370 Then steps a sweet angelic slip of a thing
Forward, puts out a soft palm—"Not so fast!"
—Addresses the celestial presence, "nay—
He made you and devised you, after all,
Though he's none of you! Could Saint John there draw—

---

5. St. Laurence, a deacon who was martyred by being roasted, is reputed to have asked to be turned over, as he was done on one side.

6. Lippi's *Coronation of the Virgin* was painted for the church of Sant' Ambrogio's convent in Florence.

375   His camel-hair[7] make up a painting-brush?
       We come to brother Lippo for all that,
       Iste perfect opus!"[8] So, all smile—
       I shuffle sideways with my blushing face
       Under the cover of a hundred wings
380   Thrown like a spread of kirtles° when you're gay   *skirts*
       And play hot cockles,[9] all the doors being shut,
       Till, wholly unexpected, in there pops
       The hothead husband! Thus I scuttle off
       To some safe bench behind, not letting go
385   The palm of her, the little lily thing
       That spoke the good word for me in the nick,
       Like the Prior's niece . . . Saint Lucy, I would say.[1]
       And so all's saved for me, and for the church
       A pretty picture gained. Go, six months hence!
390   Your hand, sir, and good-bye: no lights, no lights!
       The street's hushed, and I know my own way back,
       Don't fear me! There's the grey beginning. Zooks!

1853   1855

Andrea Del Sarto[1]
(called "The Faultless Painter")

       But do not let us quarrel any more,
       No, my Lucrezia; bear with me for once:
       Sit down and all shall happen as you wish.
       You turn your face, but does it bring your heart?
5   I'll work then for your friend's friend, never fear,
       Treat his own subject after his own way,
       Fix his own time, accept too his own price,
       And shut the money into this small hand
       When next it takes mine. Will it? tenderly?
10   Oh, I'll content him,—but to-morrow, Love!
       I often am much wearier than you think,
       This evening more than usual, and it seems
       As if—forgive now—should you let me sit
       Here by the window with your hand in mine
15   And look a half-hour forth on Fiesole,[2]
       Both of one mind, as married people use,
       Quietly, quietly the evening through,
       I might get up to-morrow to my work

---

7. "And John was clothed with camel's hair, and with a girdle of a skin about his loins; and he did eat locusts and wild honey" (Mark 1.6). John the Baptist is the patron saint of Florence.

8. "This man made the work." These words appear beside a figure in the painting, who was assumed to be a self-portrait of Lippi. (It is actually the patron who ordered the painting.)

9. A blindfolded game, here a euphemism for sex.

1. Lippi will paint the Prior's "niece" as the virgin martyr Lucy, whom he has imagined interceding on his behalf with "the celestial presence" (lines 370–377).

1. Browning's depiction of Andrea del Sarto (1486–1531), a technically gifted Florentine Renaissance painter who never quite lived up to his early promise, is based in part on Giorgio Vasari's *The Lives of the Painters* (1550, 1568). Vasari, who had been Andrea's pupil, considered that "had his spirit been as bold as his judgment was profound, he would doubtless have been unequaled. But a timidity of spirit and a yielding simple nature prevented him from exhibiting a burning ardour and dash that, joined to his other qualities, would have made him divine."

2. A suburb of Florence.

Cheerful and fresh as ever. Let us try.
20 To-morrow, how you shall be glad for this!
Your soft hand is a woman of itself,
And mine the man's bared breast she curls inside.
Don't count the time lost, neither; you must serve
For each of the five pictures we require:
25 It saves a model. So! keep looking so—
My serpentining beauty, rounds on rounds!
—How could you ever prick those perfect ears,
Even to put the pearl there! oh, so sweet—
My face, my moon, my everybody's moon,
30 Which everybody looks on and calls his,
And, I suppose, is looked on by in turn,
While she looks—no one's: very dear, no less.
You smile? why, there's my picture ready made,
There's what we painters call our harmony!
35 A common greyness silvers everything,[3]—
All in a twilight, you and I alike
—You, at the point of your first pride in me
(That's gone you know),—but I, at every point;
My youth, my hope, my art, being all toned down
40 To yonder sober pleasant Fiesole.
There's the bell clinking from the chapel-top;
That length of convent-wall across the way
Holds the trees safer, huddled more inside;
The last monk leaves the garden; days decrease,
45 And autumn grows, autumn in everything.
Eh? the whole seems to fall into a shape
As if I saw alike my work and self
And all that I was born to be and do,
A twilight-piece. Love, we are in God's hand.
50 How strange now, looks the life he makes us lead;
So free we seem, so fettered fast we are!
I feel he laid the fetter: let it lie!
This chamber for example—turn your head—
All that's behind us! You don't understand
55 Nor care to understand about my art,
But you can hear at least when people speak:
And that cartoon,° the second from the door   *drawing*
—It is the thing, Love! so such things should be—
Behold Madonna!—I am bold to say.
60 I can do with my pencil what I know,
What I see, what at bottom of my heart
I wish for, if I ever wish so deep—
Do easily, too—what I say, perfectly,
I do not boast, perhaps: yourself are judge,
65 Who listened to the Legate's[4] talk last week,

3. The grey tones of Andrea del Sarto's paintings were regarded in Browning's day as characteristic of his art (rather than the effect of fading and aging); the unusually muted rhythms of this poem attempt to convey the same qualities of restraint and understatement.
4. A representative of the Pope.

And just as much they used to say in France.
At any rate 'tis easy, all of it!
No sketches first, no studies, that's long past:
I do what many dream of, all their lives,
70 —Dream? strive to do, and agonize to do,
And fail in doing. I could count twenty such
On twice your fingers, and not leave this town,
Who strive—you don't know how the others strive
To paint a little thing like that you smeared
75 Carelessly passing with your robes afloat,—
Yet do much less, so much less, Someone⁵ says,
(I know his name, no matter)—so much less!
Well, less is more, Lucrezia: I am judged.
There burns a truer light of God in them,
80 In their vexed beating stuffed and stopped-up brain,
Heart, or whate'er else, than goes on to prompt
This low-pulsed forthright craftsman's hand of mine.
Their works drop groundward, but themselves, I know,
Reach many a time a heaven that's shut to me,
85 Enter and take their place there sure enough,
Though they come back and cannot tell the world.
My works are nearer heaven, but I sit here.
The sudden blood of these men! at a word—
Praise them, it boils, or blame them, it boils too.
90 I, painting from myself and to myself,
Know what I do, am unmoved by men's blame
Or their praise either. Somebody remarks
Morello's⁶ outline there is wrongly traced,
His hue mistaken; what of that? or else,
95 Rightly traced and well ordered; what of that?
Speak as they please, what does the mountain care?
Ah, but a man's reach should exceed his grasp,
Or what's a heaven for? All is silver-grey
Placid and perfect with my art: the worse!
100 I know both what I want and what might gain,
And yet how profitless to know, to sigh
"Had I been two, another and myself,
Our head would have o'erlooked the world!" No doubt.
Yonder's a work now, of that famous youth
105 The Urbinate who died five years ago.⁷
('Tis copied, George Vasari sent it me.)
Well, I can fancy how he did it all,
Pouring his soul, with kings and popes to see,
Reaching, that heaven might so replenish him,
110 Above and through his art—for it gives way;
That arm is wrongly put—and there again—
A fault to pardon in the drawing's lines,

5. Probably Michelangelo.
6. A mountain near Florence.
7. Raphael (1483–1520) was born in Urbino. Thus the

poem is set in 1525 (when, far from being in autumnal
decline, Andrea was at the height of his powers).

Its body, so to speak: its soul is right,
He means right—that, a child may understand.
115 Still, what an arm! and I could alter it:
But all the play, the insight and the stretch—
Out of me, out of me! And wherefore out?
Had you enjoined them on me, given me soul,
We might have risen to Rafael, I and you!
120 Nay, Love, you did give all I asked, I think—
More than I merit, yes, by many times.
But had you—oh, with the same perfect brow,
And perfect eyes, and more than perfect mouth,
And the low voice my soul hears, as a bird
125 The fowler's pipe, and follows to the snare—
Had you, with these the same, but brought a mind!
Some women do so. Had the mouth there urged
"God and the glory! never care for gain.
The present by the future, what is that?
130 Live for fame, side by side with Agnolo![8]
Rafael is waiting: up to God, all three!"
I might have done it for you. So it seems:
Perhaps not. All is as God over-rules.
Beside, incentives come from the soul's self;
135 The rest avail not. Why do I need you?
What wife had Rafael, or has Agnolo?
In this world, who can do a thing, will not;
And who would do it, cannot, I perceive:
Yet the will's somewhat—somewhat, too, the power—
140 And thus we half-men struggle. At the end,
God, I conclude, compensates, punishes.
'Tis safer for me, if the award be strict,
That I am something underrated here,
Poor this long while, despised, to speak the truth.
145 I dared not, do you know, leave home all day,
For fear of chancing on the Paris lords.[9]
The best is when they pass and look aside;
But they speak sometimes; I must bear it all.
Well may they speak! That Francis, that first time,
150 And that long festal year at Fontainebleau!
I surely then could sometimes leave the ground,
Put on the glory, Rafael's daily wear,
In that humane great monarch's golden look,—
One finger in his beard or twisted curl
155 Over his mouth's good mark that made the smile,
One arm about my shoulder, round my neck,
The jingle of his gold chain in my ear,
I painting proudly with his breath on me,

---

8. Michelangelo (Michel Agnolo Buonarroti), Italian painter (1475–1564).
9. In 1518 Andrea was invited to Fontainebleau by the French king, Francis I, who became his patron. Rumor had it that when he left the court to return to Italy, the king entrusted him with funds, which he spent on a house for Lucrezia. Now he is ashamed to face the scorn of visiting French nobles.

All his court round him, seeing with his eyes,
160 Such frank French eyes, and such a fire of souls
Profuse, my hand kept plying by those hearts,—
And, best of all, this, this, this face beyond,
This in the background, waiting on my work,
To crown the issue with a last reward!
165 A good time, was it not, my kingly days?
And had you not grown restless . . . but I know—
'Tis done and past; 'twas right, my instinct said;
Too live the life grew, golden and not grey,
And I'm the weak-eyed bat no sun should tempt
170 Out of the grange whose four walls make his world.
How could it end in any other way?
You called me, and I came home to your heart.
The triumph was—to reach and stay there; since
I reached it ere the triumph, what is lost?
175 Let my hands frame your face in your hair's gold,
You beautiful Lucrezia that are mine!
"Rafael did this, Andrea painted that;
The Roman's[1] is the better when you pray,
But still the other's Virgin was his wife—"
180 Men will excuse me. I am glad to judge
Both pictures in your presence; clearer grows
My better fortune, I resolve to think.
For, do you know, Lucrezia, as God lives,
Said one day Agnolo, his very self,
185 To Rafael . . . I have known it all these years . . .
(When the young man was flaming out his thoughts
Upon a palace-wall for Rome to see,
Too lifted up in heart because of it)
"Friend, there's a certain sorry little scrub[2]
190 Goes up and down our Florence, none cares how,
Who, were he set to plan and execute
As you are, pricked on by your popes and kings,
Would bring the sweat into that brow of yours!"
To Rafael's!—And indeed the arm is wrong.
195 I hardly dare . . . yet, only you to see,
Give the chalk here—quick, thus the line should go!
Ay, but the soul! he's Rafael! rub it out!
Still, all I care for, if he spoke the truth,
(What he? why, who but Michel Agnolo?
200 Do you forget already words like those?)[3]
If really there was such a chance, so lost,—
Is, whether you're—not grateful—but more pleased.
Well, let me think so. And you smile indeed!
This hour has been an hour! Another smile?
205 If you would sit thus by me every night
I should work better, do you comprehend?

1. Raphael worked in Rome after 1509.
2. I.e., Andrea, who is boasting to Lucrezia that

Michelangelo once praised his abilities to Raphael.
3. Lucrezia, bored, has lost the thread of Andrea's story.

I mean that I should earn more, give you more.
See, it is settled dusk now; there's a star;
Morello's gone, the watch-lights show the wall,
210   The cue-owls[4] speak the name we call them by.
Come from the window, love,—come in, at last,
Inside the melancholy little house
We built to be so gay with. God is just.
King Francis may forgive me: oft at nights
215   When I look up from painting, eyes tired out,
The walls become illumined, brick from brick
Distinct, instead of mortar, fierce bright gold,
That gold of his I did cement them with!
Let us but love each other. Must you go?
220   That Cousin here again?[5] he waits outside?
Must see you—you, and not with me? Those loans?
More gaming debts to pay? you smiled for that?
Well, let smiles buy me! have you more to spend?
While hand and eye and something of a heart
225   Are left me, work's my ware, and what's it worth?
I'll pay my fancy. Only let me sit
The grey remainder of the evening out,
Idle, you call it, and muse perfectly
How I could paint, were I but back in France,
230   One picture, just one more—the Virgin's face,
Not yours this time! I want you at my side
To hear them—that is, Michel Agnolo—
Judge all I do and tell you of its worth.
Will you? To-morrow, satisfy your friend.
235   I take the subjects for his corridor,
Finish the portrait out of hand—there, there,
And throw him in another thing or two
If he demurs; the whole should prove enough
To pay for this same Cousin's freak. Beside,
240   What's better and what's all I care about,
Get you the thirteen scudi° for the ruff!   coins
Love, does that please you? Ah, but what does he,
The Cousin! what does he to please you more?

        I am grown peaceful as old age to-night.
245   I regret little, I would change still less.
Since there my past life lies, why alter it?
The very wrong to Francis!—it is true
I took his coin, was tempted and complied,
And built this house and sinned, and all is said.
250   My father and my mother died of want.[6]
Well, had I riches of my own? you see
How one gets rich! Let each one bear his lot.
They were born poor, lived poor, and poor they died:
And I have laboured somewhat in my time

4. Owls whose cry sounds like the Italian word *ciù*.
5. Lucrezia's lover, whose gambling debts Andrea has already agreed to pay (lines 5–10).
6. Vasari claimed that Andrea abandoned his aged parents and spent his money on Lucrezia and her family.

255   And not been paid profusely. Some good son
       Paint my two hundred pictures—let him try!
       No doubt, there's something strikes a balance. Yes,
       You loved me quite enough, it seems to-night.
       This must suffice me here. What would one have?
260   In heaven, perhaps, new chances, one more chance—
       Four great walls in the New Jerusalem,[7]
       Meted° on each side by the angel's reed,   measured
       For Leonard,[8] Rafael, Agnolo and me
       To cover—the three first without a wife,
265   While I have mine! So—still they overcome
       Because there's still Lucrezia,—as I choose.

       Again the Cousin's whistle! Go, my Love.

c. 1853   1855

◄──►◄═►──►

Elizabeth Gaskell
1810–1865

During the 1880s and 1890s, short stories enjoyed a golden age in Britain. H. G. Wells said that "People talked about them tremendously, compared them, and ranked them. That was the thing that mattered." Yet short stories had been popular in America and Europe for decades before they caught on in Britain. Previously, the public's appetite for fiction had been sated by novels, which often appeared serially in the leading periodicals. Although many novelists, including Charles Dickens, George Eliot, Anthony Trollope, and Wilkie Collins, occasionally tried their hand at short fiction, three-decker novels were far more profitable—and far more prestigious. Where the novel might be regarded as "serious," stories smacked of the sensational. Henry James observed that "the little story is but scantily relished in England, where readers take their fiction rather by the volume than by the page." Not until late in the century did writers such as Rudyard Kipling and Arthur Conan Doyle build their careers on short stories, and only then did the genre gain the status of a distinct artistic form.

The growing visibility of short stories was fueled by innovations in the printing process that allowed low-cost mass-circulation periodicals to flourish; Somerset Maugham later argued that "the rich abundance of short stories during the nineteenth century was directly occasioned by the opportunity which the periodicals afforded." Thanks in part to the rage for Sherlock Holmes, The Strand sold half-a-million copies a month during the 1890s. Literary magazines were often shaped by the taste and vision of the founding editor; Household Words, for example—where Elizabeth Gaskell first published Cranford—bore the characteristic stamp of its creator, Charles Dickens.

The narrator of Cranford speaks of having "vibrated all my life" between the rural setting of Cranford and a nearby commercial city. The same was true of Elizabeth Gaskell, who grew up in the small town of Knutsford, but went to live in the industrial city of Manchester after her marriage to a Unitarian minister in 1832. She grappled with the changes wrought by industrialism in novels of social protest, including Mary Barton (1848), Ruth (1853), and North and South (1855). Even in the idyllic village of Cranford, the "obnoxious" new railroad impinges dramatically. The middle-aged spinsters with their out-of-date clothes and manners are only dimly aware of the

7. Cf. Revelation 21. 10–21.
8. Leonardo da Vinci (1452–1519), third in the trio of

great Italian Renaissance artists whom del Sarto has failed
to equal.

bustling modern world; they linger on as representatives of a bygone era. The story is set in the 1830s, when Dickens's lively comic novel *Pickwick Papers* was hot off the presses, the epitome of modern literature; the Cranford ladies' preference for the stately prose of the eighteenth-century Dr. Johnson humorously dramatizes a society in transition. The young narrator records their eccentricities fondly, but with a subtle sense of the absurd. Yet despite their faintly ridiculous obsession with gentility and "elegant economy," the women of Cranford retain the humanity, compassion, and moral integrity conspicuously lacking in the industrial world.

Our Society at Cranford[1]

In the first place, Cranford is in possession of the Amazons;[2] all the holders of houses above a certain rent are women. If a married couple come to settle in the town, somehow the gentleman disappears; he is either fairly frightened to death by being the only man in the Cranford evening parties, or he is accounted for by being with his regiment, his ship, or closely engaged in business all the week in the great neighbouring commercial town of Drumble,[3] distant only twenty miles on a railroad. In short, whatever does become of the gentlemen, they are not at Cranford. What could they do if they were there? The surgeon has his round of thirty miles, and sleeps at Cranford; but every man cannot be a surgeon. For keeping the trim gardens full of choice flowers without a weed to speck them; for frightening away little boys who look wistfully at the said flowers through the railings; for rushing out at the geese that occasionally venture into the gardens if the gates are left open; for deciding all questions of literature and politics without troubling themselves with unnecessary reasons or arguments; for obtaining clear and correct knowledge of everybody's affairs in the parish; for keeping their neat maid-servants in admirable order; for kindness (somewhat dictatorial) to the poor, and real tender good offices to each other whenever they are in distress, the ladies of Cranford are quite sufficient. "A man," as one of them observed to me once, "is *so* in the way in the house!" Although the ladies of Cranford know all each other's proceedings, they are exceedingly indifferent to each other's opinions. Indeed, as each has her own individuality, not to say eccentricity, pretty strongly developed, nothing is so easy as verbal retaliation; but, somehow, good-will reigns among them to a considerable degree.

The Cranford ladies have only an occasional little quarrel, spirited out in a few peppery words and angry jerks of the head; just enough to prevent the even tenor of their lives from becoming too flat. Their dress is very independent of fashion; as they observe, "What does it signify how we dress here at Cranford, where everybody knows us?" And if they go from home, their reason is equally cogent, "What does it signify how we dress here, where nobody knows us?" The materials of their clothes are, in general, good and plain, and most of them are nearly as scrupulous as Miss Tyler, of cleanly memory;[4] but I will answer for it, the last gigot, the last tight and scanty petticoat in wear in England, was seen in Cranford—and seen without a smile.[5]

I can testify to a magnificent family red silk umbrella, under which a gentle little spinster, left alone of many brothers and sisters, used to patter to church on rainy days. Have you any red silk umbrellas in London? We had a tradition of the first that

1. First published as a self-contained story in December 1851 in *Household Words*, a periodical edited by Charles Dickens. Although Gaskell later said that "I never meant to write more," Dickens persuaded her to continue the story in subsequent issues. In 1853 the collected sketches appeared in book form as *Cranford*.
2. In Greek legend, the Amazons were fierce warriors who formed an all-female state.

3. Manchester.
4. The aunt of Robert Southey (1774–1843)—Poet Laureate at the time when *Cranford* takes place—was famous for her passion for cleanliness.
5. By the mid-1830s, the old-fashioned leg-of-mutton sleeve and straight skirt had given way to the hooped skirt.

had ever been seen in Cranford; and the little boys mobbed it, and called it "a stick in petticoats." It might have been the very red silk one I have described, held by a strong father over a troop of little ones; the poor little lady—the survivor of all— could scarcely carry it.

Then there were rules and regulations for visiting and calls; and they were announced to any young people who might be staying in the town, with all the solemnity with which the old Manx laws were read once a year on the Tinwald Mount.[6]

"Our friends have sent to inquire how you are after your journey to-night, my dear" (fifteen miles in a gentleman's carriage); "they will give you some rest to-morrow, but the next day, I have no doubt, they will call; so be at liberty after twelve— from twelve to three are our calling hours."

Then, after they had called—

"It is the third day; I dare say your mamma has told you, my dear, never to let more than three days elapse between receiving a call and returning it; and also, that you are never to stay longer than a quarter of an hour."

"But am I to look at my watch? How am I to find out when a quarter of an hour has passed?"

"You must keep thinking about the time, my dear, and not allow yourself to forget it in conversation."

As everybody had this rule in their minds, whether they received or paid a call, of course no absorbing subject was ever spoken about. We kept ourselves to short sentences of small talk, and were punctual to our time.

I imagine that a few of the gentlefolks of Cranford were poor, and had some difficulty in making both ends meet; but they were like the Spartans,[7] and concealed their smart under a smiling face. We none of us spoke of money, because that subject savoured of commerce and trade, and though some might be poor, we were all aristocratic. The Cranfordians had that kindly *esprit de corps* which made them overlook all deficiencies in success when some among them tried to conceal their poverty. When Mrs Forrester, for instance, gave a party in her baby-house of a dwelling, and the little maiden disturbed the ladies on the sofa by a request that she might get the tea-tray out from underneath, every one took this novel proceeding as the most natural thing in the world, and talked on about household forms and ceremonies as if we all believed that our hostess had a regular servants' hall, second table, with housekeeper and steward, instead of the one little charity-school maiden,[8] whose short ruddy arms could never have been strong enough to carry the tray upstairs, if she had not been assisted in private by her mistress, who now sat in state, pretending not to know what cakes were sent up, though she knew, and we knew, and she knew that we knew, and we knew that she knew that we knew, she had been busy all the morning making tea-bread and sponge-cakes.

There were one or two consequences arising from this general but unacknowledged poverty, and this very much acknowledged gentility, which were not amiss, and which might be introduced into many circles of society to their great improvement. For instance, the inhabitants of Cranford kept early hours, and clattered home in their pattens,[9] under the guidance of a lantern-bearer, about nine o'clock at night; and the whole town was abed and asleep by half-past ten. Moreover, it was considered

6. The population of the Isle of Man customarily assembled once a year on Tynwald Hill to hear the new laws read aloud.

7. The Spartans of ancient Greece were known for their courage and self-control in the face of hardship.

8. Charity schools trained poor children for domestic work; that one such pupil formed Mrs. Forrester's entire domestic staff indicates her meager standard of living.

9. Wooden platform shoes to protect one's shoes from mud.

"vulgar" (a tremendous word in Cranford) to give anything expensive, in the way of eatable or drinkable, at the evening entertainments. Wafer bread-and-butter and sponge-biscuits were all that the Honourable Mrs Jamieson gave; and she was sister-in-law to the late Earl of Glenmire, although she did practise such "elegant economy."

"Elegant economy!" How naturally one falls back into the phraseology of Cranford! There, economy was always "elegant," and money-spending always "vulgar and ostentatious;" a sort of sour-grapeism which made us very peaceful and satisfied. I never shall forget the dismay felt when a certain Captain Brown came to live at Cranford, and openly spoke about his being poor—not in a whisper to an intimate friend, the doors and windows being previously closed, but in the public street! in a loud military voice! alleging his poverty as a reason for not taking a particular house. The ladies of Cranford were already rather moaning over the invasion of their territories by a man and a gentleman. He was a half-pay captain,[1] and had obtained some situation on a neighbouring railroad, which had been vehemently petitioned against by the little town;[2] and if, in addition to his masculine gender, and his connection with the obnoxious railroad, he was so brazen as to talk of being poor—why, then, indeed, he must be sent to Coventry.[3] Death was as true and as common as poverty; yet people never spoke about that, loud out in the streets. It was a word not to be mentioned to ears polite. We had tacitly agreed to ignore that any with whom we associated on terms of visiting equality could ever be prevented by poverty from doing anything that they wished. If we walked to or from a party, it was because the night was so fine, or the air so refreshing, not because sedan-chairs were expensive.[4] If we wore prints, instead of summer silks, it was because we preferred a washing material; and so on, till we blinded ourselves to the vulgar fact that we were, all of us, people of very moderate means. Of course, then, we did not know what to make of a man who could speak of poverty as if it was not a disgrace. Yet, somehow, Captain Brown made himself respected in Cranford, and was called upon, in spite of all resolutions to the contrary. I was surprised to hear his opinions quoted as authority at a visit which I paid to Cranford about a year after he had settled in the town. My own friends had been among the bitterest opponents of any proposal to visit the Captain and his daughters, only twelve months before; and now he was even admitted in the tabooed hours before twelve. True, it was to discover the cause of a smoking chimney, before the fire was lighted; but still Captain Brown walked upstairs, nothing daunted, spoke in a voice too large for the room, and joked quite in the way of a tame man about the house. He had been blind to all the small slights, and omissions of trivial ceremonies, with which he had been received. He had been friendly, though the Cranford ladies had been cool; he had answered small sarcastic compliments in good faith; and with his manly frankness had overpowered all the shrinking which met him as a man who was not ashamed to be poor. And, at last, his excellent masculine common sense, and his facility in devising expedients to overcome domestic dilemmas, had gained him an extraordinary place as authority among the Cranford ladies. He himself went on in his course, as unaware of his popularity as he had been of the reverse; and I am sure he was startled one day when he found his advice so highly esteemed as to make some counsel which he had given in jest to be taken in sober, serious earnest.

It was on this subject: An old lady had an Alderney cow, which she looked upon as a daughter. You could not pay the short quarter of an hour call without being told

---

1. A retired officer who stayed on reserve at half pay.
2. The railroads were new, and still looked on with suspicion by many country-dwellers.

3. Ostracized.
4. Enclosed chairs carried by servants; more common in the eighteenth century.

of the wonderful milk or wonderful intelligence of this animal. The whole town knew and kindly regarded Miss Betsy Barker's Alderney; therefore great was the sympathy and regret when, in an unguarded moment, the poor cow tumbled into a lime-pit.[5] She moaned so loudly that she was soon heard and rescued; but meanwhile the poor beast had lost most of her hair, and came out looking naked, cold, and miserable, in a bare skin. Everybody pitied the animal, though a few could not restrain their smiles at her droll appearance. Miss Betsy Barker absolutely cried with sorrow and dismay; and it was said she thought of trying a bath of oil. This remedy, perhaps, was recommended by some one of the number whose advice she asked; but the proposal, if ever it was made, was knocked on the head by Captain Brown's decided "Get her a flannel waistcoat and flannel drawers, ma'am, if you wish to keep her alive. But my advice is, kill the poor creature at once."

Miss Betsy Barker dried her eyes, and thanked the Captain heartily; she set to work, and by-and-by all the town turned out to see the Alderney meekly going to her pasture, clad in dark grey flannel. I have watched her myself many a time. Do you ever see cows dressed in grey flannel in London?

Captain Brown had taken a small house on the outskirts of the town, where he lived with his two daughters. He must have been upwards of sixty at the time of the first visit I paid to Cranford after I had left it as a residence. But he had a wiry, well-trained, elastic figure, a stiff military throw-back of his head, and a springing step, which made him appear much younger than he was. His eldest daughter looked almost as old as himself, and betrayed the fact that his real was more than his apparent age. Miss Brown must have been forty; she had a sickly, pained, careworn expression on her face, and looked as if the gaiety of youth had long faded out of sight. Even when young she must have been plain and hard featured. Miss Jessie Brown was ten years younger than her sister, and twenty shades prettier. Her face was round and dimpled. Miss Jenkyns once said, in a passion against Captain Brown (the cause of which I will tell you presently), "that she thought it was time for Miss Jessie to leave off her dimples, and not always to be trying to look like a child." It was true there was something child-like in her face; and there will be, I think, till she dies, though she should live to a hundred. Her eyes were large blue wondering eyes, looking straight at you; her nose was unformed and snub, and her lips were red and dewy; she wore her hair, too, in little rows of curls, which heightened this appearance. I do not know whether she was pretty or not; but I liked her face, and so did everybody, and I do not think she could help her dimples. She had something of her father's jauntiness of gait and manner; and any female observer might detect a slight difference in the attire of the two sisters—that of Miss Jessie being about two pounds per annum more expensive than Miss Brown's. Two pounds was a large sum in Captain Brown's annual disbursements.

Such was the impression made upon me by the Brown family when I first saw them all together in Cranford Church. The Captain I had met before—on the occasion of the smoky chimney, which he had cured by some simple alteration in the flue. In church, he held his double eye-glass to his eyes during the Morning Hymn, and then lifted up his head erect and sang out loud and joyfully. He made the responses louder than the clerk—an old man with a piping feeble voice, who, I think, felt aggrieved at the Captain's sonorous bass, and quavered higher and higher in consequence.

On coming out of church, the brisk Captain paid the most gallant attention to his two daughters. He nodded and smiled to his acquaintances; but he shook hands with none until he had helped Miss Brown to unfurl her umbrella, had relieved her of

5. A pit in which tanners dress skins with lime to remove the hair.

her prayer-book, and had waited patiently till she, with trembling nervous hands, had taken up her gown to walk through the wet roads.

I wondered what the Cranford ladies did with Captain Brown at their parties. We had often rejoiced, in former days, that there was no gentleman to be attended to, and to find conversation for, at the card-parties. We had congratulated ourselves upon the snugness of the evenings; and, in our love for gentility, and distaste of mankind, we had almost persuaded ourselves that to be a man was to be "vulgar"; so that when I found my friend and hostess, Miss Jenkyns, was going to have a party in my honour, and that Captain and the Miss Browns were invited, I wondered much what would be the course of the evening. Card-tables, with green baize tops, were set out by daylight, just as usual; it was the third week in November, so the evenings closed in about four. Candles, and clean packs of cards were arranged on each table. The fire was made up; the neat maid-servant had received her last directions; and there we stood, dressed in our best, each with a candle-lighter in our hands, ready to dart at the candles as soon as the first knock came. Parties in Cranford were solemn festivities, making the ladies feel gravely elated as they sat together in their best dresses. As soon as three had arrived, we sat down to "Preference," I being the unlucky fourth.[6] The next four comers were put down immediately to another table; and presently the tea-trays, which I had seen set out in the store-room as I passed in the morning, were placed each on the middle of a card-table. The china was delicate egg-shell; the old-fashioned silver glittered with polishing; but the eatables were of the slightest description. While the trays were yet on the tables, Captain and the Miss Browns came in; and I could see that, somehow or other, the Captain was a favourite with all the ladies present. Ruffled brows were smoothed, sharp voices lowered at his approach. Miss Brown looked ill, and depressed almost to gloom. Miss Jessie smiled as usual, and seemed nearly as popular as her father. He immediately and quietly assumed the man's place in the room; attended to every one's wants, lessened the pretty maid-servant's labour by waiting on empty cups and bread-and-butterless ladies; and yet did it all in so easy and dignified a manner, and so much as if it were a matter of course for the strong to attend to the weak, that he was a true man throughout. He played for threepenny points with as grave an interest as if they had been pounds; and yet, in all his attention to strangers, he had an eye on his suffering daughter—for suffering I was sure she was, though to many eyes she might only appear to be irritable. Miss Jessie could not play cards: but she talked to the sitters-out, who, before her coming, had been rather inclined to be cross. She sang, too, to an old cracked piano, which I think had been a spinet[7] in its youth. Miss Jessie sang "Jock of Hazeldean"[8] a little out of tune; but we were none of us musical, though Miss Jenkyns beat time, out of time, by way of appearing to be so.

It was very good of Miss Jenkyns to do this; for I had seen that, a little before, she had been a good deal annoyed by Miss Jessie Brown's unguarded admission (à propos of Shetland wool) that she had an uncle, her mother's brother, who was a shopkeeper in Edinburgh. Miss Jenkyns tried to drown this confession by a terrible cough—for the Honourable Mrs Jamieson was sitting at the card-table nearest Miss Jessie, and what would she say or think if she found out she was in the same room with a shopkeeper's niece! But Miss Jessie Brown (who had no tact, as we all agreed the next morning) would repeat the information, and assure Miss Pole she could easily get her the identical Shetland wool required, "through my uncle, who has the

6. "Unlucky" because only three people can play this card game at once; the dealer has to sit out.
7. An earlier keyboard instrument, popular before the

invention of the piano.
8. A ballad written in 1816 by Sir Walter Scott.

best assortment of Shetland goods of any one in Edinbro'." It was to take the taste of this out of our mouths, and the sound of this out of our ears, that Miss Jenkyns proposed music; so I say again, it was very good of her to beat time to the song.

When the trays re-appeared with biscuits and wine, punctually at a quarter to nine, there was conversation, comparing of cards, and talking over tricks; but by-and-by Captain Brown sported a bit of literature.

"Have you seen any numbers of 'The Pickwick Papers'?" said he. (They were then publishing in parts.)[9] "Capital thing!"

Now Miss Jenkyns was daughter of a deceased rector of Cranford; and, on the strength of a number of manuscript sermons, and a pretty good library of divinity, considered herself literary, and looked upon any conversation about books as a challenge to her. So she answered and said, "Yes, she had seen them; indeed, she might say she had read them."

"And what do you think of them?" exclaimed Captain Brown. "Aren't they famously good?"

So urged, Miss Jenkyns could not but speak.

"I must say, I don't think they are by any means equal to Dr Johnson.[1] Still, perhaps, the author is young. Let him persevere, and who knows what he may become if he will take the great Doctor for his model?" This was evidently too much for Captain Brown to take placidly; and I saw the words on the tip of his tongue before Miss Jenkyns had finished her sentence.

"It is quite a different sort of thing, my dear madam," he began.

"I am quite aware of that," returned she. "And I make allowances, Captain Brown."

"Just allow me to read you a scene out of this month's number," pleaded he. "I had it only this morning, and I don't think the company can have read it yet."

"As you please," said she, settling herself with an air of resignation. He read the account of the "swarry" which Sam Weller gave at Bath.[2] Some of us laughed heartily. I did not dare, because I was staying in the house. Miss Jenkyns sat in patient gravity. When it was ended, she turned to me, and said with mild dignity—

"Fetch me 'Rasselas,'[3] my dear, out of the bookroom."

When I brought it to her, she turned to Captain Brown—

"Now allow *me* to read you a scene, and then the present company can judge between your favourite, Mr Boz, and Dr Johnson."

She read one of the conversations between Rasselas and Imlac, in a high-pitched majestic voice: and when she had ended, she said, "I imagine I am now justified in my preference of Dr Johnson as a writer of fiction." The Captain screwed his lips up, and drummed on the table, but he did not speak. She thought she would give a finishing blow or two.

"I consider it vulgar, and below the dignity of literature, to publish in numbers."

"How was the *Rambler*[4] published, ma'am?" asked Captain Brown in a low voice, which I think Miss Jenkyns could not have heard.

9. Dickens published *The Pickwick Papers* serially in 1836 and 1837 under the pseudonym "Boz." Although this form of publication was considered "vulgar," the humorous escapades of Mr. Pickwick were phenomenally successful. When *Cranford* first appeared in Dickens's *Household Words*, he substituted Thomas Hood for himself, to Gaskell's annoyance.

1. Samuel Johnson (1708–1784) wrote more than a hundred years before Dickens; he was noted for his stately, balanced prose.

2. A reference to an episode in *Pickwick Papers* where Mr. Pickwick's servant Sam Weller attends a "soirée" for the footmen at Bath. The quick-witted Sam mocks the pompous servants, but they don't realize it.

3. *Rasselas* is a series of dialogues on moral themes between the prince of Abyssinia and his spiritual mentor, Imlac. Unlike the lively *Pickwick*, it is a serious and slow-paced philosophical work.

4. A periodical started in 1750 by Dr. Johnson and written almost entirely by himself.

"Dr Johnson's style is a model for young beginners. My father recommended it to me when I began to write letters—I have formed my own style upon it; I recommend it to your favourite."

"I should be very sorry for him to exchange his style for any such pompous writing," said Captain Brown.

Miss Jenkyns felt this as a personal affront, in a way of which the Captain had not dreamed. Epistolary writing she and her friends considered as her *forte*. Many a copy of many a letter have I seen written and corrected on the slate, before she "seized the half-hour just previous to post-time to assure" her friends of this or of that; and Dr Johnson was, as she said, her model in these compositions. She drew herself up with dignity, and only replied to Captain Brown's last remark by saying, with marked emphasis on every syllable, "I prefer Dr Johnson to Mr Boz."

It is said—I won't vouch for the fact—that Captain Brown was heard to say, *sotto voce*, "D—n Dr Johnson!" If he did, he was penitent afterwards, as he showed by going to stand near Miss Jenkyns's arm-chair, and endeavouring to beguile her into conversation on some more pleasing subject. But she was inexorable. The next day she made the remark I have mentioned about Miss Jessie's dimples.

2

It was impossible to live a month at Cranford and not know the daily habits of each resident; and long before my visit was ended I knew much concerning the whole Brown trio. There was nothing new to be discovered respecting their poverty; for they had spoken simply and openly about that from the very first. They made no mystery of the necessity for their being economical. All that remained to be discovered was the Captain's infinite kindness of heart, and the various modes in which, unconsciously to himself, he manifested it. Some little anecdotes were talked about for some time after they occurred. As we did not read much, and as all the ladies were pretty well suited with servants, there was a dearth of subjects for conversation. We therefore discussed the circumstance of the Captain taking a poor old woman's dinner out of her hands one very slippery Sunday. He had met her returning from the bakehouse as he came from church, and noticed her precarious footing; and, with the grave dignity with which he did everything, he relieved her of her burden, and steered along the street by her side, carrying her baked mutton and potatoes safely home.[5] This was thought very eccentric; and it was rather expected that he would pay a round of calls, on the Monday morning, to explain and apologise to the Cranford sense of propriety: but he did no such thing: and then it was decided that he was ashamed, and was keeping out of sight. In a kindly pity for him, we began to say, "After all, the Sunday morning's occurrence showed great goodness of heart," and it was resolved that he should be comforted on his next appearance amongst us; but, lo! he came down upon us, untouched by any sense of shame, speaking loud and bass as ever, his head thrown back, his wig as jaunty and well-curled as usual, and we were obliged to conclude he had forgotten all about Sunday.

Miss Pole and Miss Jessie Brown had set up a kind of intimacy on the strength of the Shetland wool and the new knitting stitches; so it happened that when I went to visit Miss Pole I saw more of the Browns than I had done while staying with Miss

5. Poor people often brought their meals to cook in the ovens of baker's shops on Sundays and holidays.

Jenkyns, who had never got over what she called Captain Brown's disparaging remarks upon Dr Johnson as a writer of light and agreeable fiction. I found that Miss Brown was seriously ill of some lingering, incurable complaint, the pain occasioned by which gave the uneasy expression to her face that I had taken for unmitigated crossness. Cross, too, she was at times, when the nervous irritability occasioned by her disease became past endurance. Miss Jessie bore with her at these times, even more patiently than she did with the bitter self-upbraidings by which they were invariably succeeded. Miss Brown used to accuse herself, not merely of hasty and irritable temper, but also of being the cause why her father and sister were obliged to pinch, in order to allow her the small luxuries which were necessaries in her condition. She would so fain have made sacrifices for them, and have lightened their cares, that the original generosity of her disposition added acerbity to her temper. All this was borne by Miss Jessie and her father with more than placidity—with absolute tenderness. I forgave Miss Jessie her singing out of tune, and her juvenility of dress, when I saw her at home. I came to perceive that Captain Brown's dark Brutus wig and padded coat[6] (alas! too often threadbare) were remnants of the military smartness of his youth, which he now wore unconsciously. He was a man of infinite resources, gained in his barrack experience. As he confessed, no one could black his boots to please him except himself; but, indeed, he was not above saving the little maid-servant's labours in every way—knowing, most likely, that his daughter's illness made the place a hard one.

He endeavoured to make peace with Miss Jenkyns soon after the memorable dispute I have named, by a present of a wooden fire-shovel (his own making), having heard her say how much the grating of an iron one annoyed her. She received the present with cool gratitude, and thanked him formally. When he was gone, she bade me put it away in the lumber-room; feeling, probably, that no present from a man who preferred Mr Boz to Dr Johnson could be less jarring than an iron fire-shovel.

Such was the state of things when I left Cranford and went to Drumble. I had, however, several correspondents, who kept me *au fait* as to the proceedings of the dear little town. There was Miss Pole, who was becoming as much absorbed in crochet as she had been once in knitting, and the burden of whose letter was something like, "But don't you forget the white worsted at Flint's" of the old song; for at the end of every sentence of news came a fresh direction as to some crochet commission which I was to execute for her. Miss Matilda Jenkyns (who did not mind being called Miss Matty, when Miss Jenkyns was not by) wrote nice, kind, rambling letters, now and then venturing into an opinion of her own; but suddenly pulling herself up, and either begging me not to name what she had said, as Deborah thought differently, and *she* knew, or else putting in a postscript to the effect that, since writing the above, she had been talking over the subject with Deborah, and was quite convinced that, &c.—(here probably followed a recantation of every opinion she had given in the letter). Then came Miss Jenkyns—Debōrah, as she liked Miss Matty to call her, her father having once said that the Hebrew name ought to be so pronounced. I secretly think she took the Hebrew prophetess for a model in character; and, indeed, she was not unlike the stern prophetess[7] in some ways, making allowance, of course, for modern customs and difference in dress. Miss Jenkyns wore a cravat, and a little bonnet like a jockey-cap, and altogether had the appearance of a strong-minded

6. A short, curly hairstyle popular during the French Revolution; padded coats were fashionable in the early 19th century.

7. Deborah was one of the leaders of Israel (Judges 4–5).

woman; although she would have despised the modern idea of women being equal to men. Equal, indeed! she knew they were superior. But to return to her letters. Everything in them was stately and grand like herself. I have been looking them over (dear Miss Jenkyns, how I honoured her!), and I will give an extract, more especially because it relates to our friend Captain Brown:—

"The Honourable Mrs Jamieson has only just quitted me; and, in the course of conversation, she communicated to me the intelligence that she had yesterday received a call from her revered husband's quondam[8] friend, Lord Mauleverer. You will not easily conjecture what brought his lordship within the precincts of our little town. It was to see Captain Brown, with whom, it appears, his lordship was acquainted in the 'plumed wars,' and who had the privilege of averting destruction from his lordship's head when some great peril was impending over it, off the misnomered Cape of Good Hope. You know our friend the Honourable Mrs Jamieson's deficiency in the spirit of innocent curiosity; and you will therefore not be so much surprised when I tell you she was quite unable to disclose to me the exact nature of the peril in question. I was anxious, I confess, to ascertain in what manner Captain Brown, with his limited establishment, could receive so distinguished a guest; and I discovered that his lordship retired to rest, and, let us hope, to refreshing slumbers, at the Angel Hotel; but shared the Brunonian[9] meals during the two days that he honoured Cranford with his august presence. Mrs Johnson, our civil butcher's wife, informs me that Miss Jessie purchased a leg of lamb; but, besides this, I can hear of no preparation whatever to give a suitable reception to so distinguished a visitor. Perhaps they entertained him with 'the feast of reason and the flow of soul;'[1] and to us, who are acquainted with Captain Brown's sad want of relish for 'the pure wells of English undefiled,'[2] it may be matter for congratulation that he has had the opportunity of improving his taste by holding converse with an elegant and refined member of the British aristocracy. But from some mundane failings who is altogether free?"

Miss Pole and Miss Matty wrote to me by the same post. Such a piece of news as Lord Mauleverer's visit was not to be lost on the Cranford letter-writers: they made the most of it. Miss Matty humbly apologised for writing at the same time as her sister, who was so much more capable than she to describe the honour done to Cranford; but in spite of a little bad spelling, Miss Matty's account gave me the best idea of the commotion occasioned by his lordship's visit, after it had occurred; for, except the people at the Angel, the Browns, Mrs Jamieson, and a little lad his lordship had sworn at for driving a dirty hoop against the aristocratic legs, I could not hear of any one with whom his lordship had held conversation.

My next visit to Cranford was in the summer. There had been neither births, deaths, nor marriages since I was there last. Everybody lived in the same house, and wore pretty nearly the same well-preserved, old-fashioned clothes. The greatest event was, that Miss Jenkynses had purchased a new carpet for the drawing-room. Oh, the busy work Miss Matty and I had in chasing the sunbeams, as they fell in an afternoon right down on this carpet through the blindless window! We spread news-

8. Former.
9. A pretentious, Latinized version of Brown, part of Miss Jenkyns's unintentionally comic imitation of the style of Dr. Johnson.

1. Alexander Pope, *Imitations of Horace*, Satire 1, Book 2.128 (1733).
2. Edmund Spenser, *The Faerie Queene*, 4.2.32 (1596); the reference is to Chaucer.

papers over the places, and sat down to our book or our work; and, lo! in a quarter of an hour the sun had moved, and was blazing away on a fresh spot; and down again we went on our knees to alter the position of the newspapers. We were very busy, too, one whole morning, before Miss Jenkyns gave her party, in following her directions, and in cutting out and stitching together pieces of newspaper so as to form little paths to every chair set for the expected visitors, lest their shoes might dirty or defile the purity of the carpet. Do you make paper paths for every guest to walk upon in London?

Captain Brown and Miss Jenkyns were not very cordial to each other. The literary dispute, of which I had seen the beginning, was a "raw," the slightest touch on which made them wince. It was the only difference of opinion they had ever had; but that difference was enough. Miss Jenkyns could not refrain from talking *at* Captain Brown; and, though he did not reply, he drummed with his fingers, which action she felt and resented as very disparaging to Dr Johnson. He was rather ostentatious in his preference of the writings of Mr Boz; would walk through the streets so absorbed in them that he all but ran against Miss Jenkyns; and though his apologies were earnest and sincere, and though he did not, in fact, do more than startle her and himself, she owned to me she had rather he had knocked her down, if he had only been reading a higher style of literature. The poor, brave Captain! he looked older, and more worn, and his clothes were very threadbare. But he seemed as bright and cheerful as ever, unless he was asked about his daughter's health.

"She suffers a great deal, and she must suffer more: we do what we can to alleviate her pain;—God's will be done!" He took off his hat at these last words. I found, from Miss Matty, that everything had been done, in fact. A medical man, of high repute in that country neighbourhood, had been sent for, and every injunction he had given was attended to, regardless of expense. Miss Matty was sure they denied themselves many things in order to make the invalid comfortable; but they never spoke about it; and as for Miss Jessie!—"I really think she's an angel," said poor Miss Matty, quite overcome. "To see her way of bearing with Miss Brown's crossness, and the bright face she puts on after she's been sitting up a whole night and scolded above half of it, is quite beautiful. Yet she looks as neat and as ready to welcome the Captain at breakfast-time as if she had been asleep in the Queen's bed all night. My dear! you could never laugh at her prim little curls or her pink bows again if you saw her as I have done." I could only feel very penitent, and greet Miss Jessie with double respect when I met her next. She looked faded and pinched; and her lips began to quiver, as if she was very weak, when she spoke of her sister. But she brightened, and sent back the tears that were glittering in her pretty eyes, as she said—

"But, to be sure, what a town Cranford is for kindness! I don't suppose any one has a better dinner than usual cooked but the best part of all comes in a little covered basin for my sister. The poor people will leave their earliest vegetables at our door for her. They speak short and gruff, as if they were ashamed of it; but I am sure it often goes to my heart to see their thoughtfulness." The tears now came back and overflowed; but after a minute or two she began to scold herself, and ended by going away the same cheerful Miss Jessie as ever.

"But why does not this Lord Mauleverer do something for the man who saved his life?" said I.

"Why, you see, unless Captain Brown has some reason for it, he never speaks about being poor; and he walked along by his lordship looking as happy and cheerful as a prince; and as they never called attention to their dinner by apologies, and as Miss Brown was better that day, and all seemed bright, I dare say his lordship never knew how much care there was in the background. He did send game in the winter pretty often, but now he is gone abroad."

I had often occasion to notice the use that was made of fragments and small opportunities in Cranford; the rose-leaves that were gathered ere they fell to make into a potpourri for some one who had no garden; the little bundles of lavender flowers sent to strew the drawers of some town-dweller, or to burn in the chamber of some invalid. Things that many would despise, and actions which it seemed scarcely worth while to perform, were all attended to in Cranford. Miss Jenkyns stuck an apple full of cloves, to be heated and smell pleasantly in Miss Brown's room; and as she put in each clove she uttered a Johnsonian sentence. Indeed, she never could think of the Browns without talking Johnson; and, as they were seldom absent from her thoughts just then, I heard many a rolling, three-piled sentence.

Captain Brown called one day to thank Miss Jenkyns for many little kindnesses, which I did not know until then that she had rendered. He had suddenly become like an old man; his deep bass voice had a quavering in it, his eyes looked dim, and the lines on his face were deep. He did not—could not—speak cheerfully of his daughter's state, but he talked with manly, pious resignation, and not much. Twice over he said, "What Jessie has been to us, God only knows!" and after the second time, he got up hastily, shook hands all round without speaking, and left the room.

That afternoon we perceived little groups in the street, all listening with faces aghast to some tale or other. Miss Jenkyns wondered what could be the matter for some time before she took the undignified step of sending Jenny out to inquire.

Jenny came back with a white face of terror. "Oh, ma'am! oh, Miss Jenkyns, ma'am! Captain Brown is killed by them nasty cruel railroads!" and she burst into tears. She, along with many others, had experienced the poor Captain's kindness.

"How?—where—where? Good God! Jenny, don't waste time in crying, but tell us something." Miss Matty rushed out into the street at once, and collared the man who was telling the tale.

"Come in—come to my sister at once, Miss Jenkyns, the rector's daughter. Oh, man, man! say it is not true," she cried, as she brought the affrighted carter, sleeking down his hair, into the drawing-room, where he stood with his wet boots on the new carpet, and no one regarded it.

"Please, mum, it is true. I seed it myself," and he shuddered at the recollection. "The Captain was a-reading some new book as he was deep in, a-waiting for the down train; and there was a little lass as wanted to come to its mammy, and gave its sister the slip, and came toddling across the line. And he looked up sudden, at the sound of the train coming, and seed the child, and he darted on the line and cotched it up, and his foot slipped, and the train came over him in no time. O Lord, Lord! Mum, it's quite true—and they've come over to tell his daughters. The child's safe, though, with only a bang on its shoulder as he threw it to its mammy. Poor Captain would be glad of that, mum, wouldn't he? God bless him!" The great rough carter puckered up his manly face, and turned away to hide his tears. I turned to Miss Jenkyns. She looked very ill, as if she were going to faint, and signed to me to open the window.

"Matilda, bring me my bonnet. I must go to those girls. God pardon me, if ever I have spoken contemptuously to the Captain!"

Miss Jenkyns arrayed herself to go out, telling Miss Matilda to give the man a glass of wine. While she was away, Miss Matty and I huddled over the fire, talking in a low and awestruck voice. I know we cried quietly all the time.

Miss Jenkyns came home in a silent mood, and we durst not ask her many questions. She told us that Miss Jessie had fainted, and that she and Miss Pole had had some difficulty in bringing her round; but that, as soon as she recovered, she begged one of them to go and sit with her sister.

"Mr Hoggins says she cannot live many days, and she shall be spared this shock," said Miss Jessie, shivering with feelings to which she dared not give way.

"But how can you manage, my dear?" asked Miss Jenkyns; "you cannot bear up, she must see your tears."

"God will help me—I will not give way—she was asleep when the news came; she may be asleep yet. She would be so utterly miserable, not merely at my father's death, but to think of what would become of me; she is so good to me." She looked up earnestly in their faces with her soft true eyes, and Miss Pole told Miss Jenkyns afterwards she could hardly bear it, knowing, as she did, how Miss Brown treated her sister.

However, it was settled according to Miss Jessie's wish. Miss Brown was to be told her father had been summoned to take a short journey on railway business. They had managed it in some way—Miss Jenkyns could not exactly say how. Miss Pole was to stop with Miss Jessie. Mrs Jamieson had sent to inquire. And this was all we heard that night; and a sorrowful night it was. The next day a full account of the fatal accident was in the county paper which Miss Jenkyns took in. Her eyes were very weak, she said, and she asked me to read it. When I came to the "gallant gentleman was deeply engaged in the perusal of a number of 'Pickwick,' which he had just received," Miss Jenkyns shook her head long and solemnly, and then sighed out, "Poor, dear, infatuated man!"

The corpse was to be taken from the station to the parish church, there to be interred. Miss Jessie had set her heart on following it to the grave; and no dissuasives could alter her resolve. Her restraint upon herself made her almost obstinate; she resisted all Miss Pole's entreaties and Miss Jenkyns's advice. At last Miss Jenkyns gave up the point; and after a silence, which I feared portended some deep displeasure against Miss Jessie, Miss Jenkyns said she should accompany the latter to the funeral.

"It is not fit for you to go alone. It would be against both propriety and humanity were I to allow it."

Miss Jessie seemed as if she did not half like this arrangement; but her obstinacy, if she had any, had been exhausted in her determination to go to the interment. She longed, poor thing, I have no doubt, to cry alone over the grave of the dear father to whom she had been all in all, and to give way, for one little half-hour, uninterrupted by sympathy and unobserved by friendship. But it was not to be. That afternoon Miss Jenkyns sent out for a yard of black crape, and employed herself busily in trimming the little black silk bonnet I have spoken about. When it was finished she put it on, and looked at us for approbation—admiration she despised. I was full of sorrow, but, by one of those whimsical thoughts which come unbidden into our heads, in times of deepest grief, I no sooner saw the bonnet than I was reminded of a helmet; and in that hybrid bonnet, half helmet, half jockey-cap, did Miss Jenkyns attend Captain Brown's funeral, and, I believe, supported Miss Jessie with a tender, indulgent firmness which was invaluable, allowing her to weep her passionate fill before they left.

Miss Pole, Miss Matty, and I, meanwhile attended to Miss Brown: and hard work we found it to relieve her querulous and never-ending complaints. But if we were so weary and dispirited, what must Miss Jessie have been! Yet she came back almost calm, as if she had gained a new strength. She put off her mourning dress, and came in, looking pale and gentle, thanking us each with a soft long pressure of the hand. She could even smile—a faint, sweet, wintry smile—as if to reassure us of her power to endure; but her look made our eyes fill suddenly with tears, more than if she had cried outright.

It was settled that Miss Pole was to remain with her all the watching livelong night; and that Miss Matty and I were to return in the morning to relieve them, and give Miss Jessie the opportunity for a few hours of sleep. But when the morning came, Miss Jenkyns appeared at the breakfast-table, equipped in her helmet-bonnet, and ordered Miss Matty to stay at home, as she meant to go and help to nurse. She was evidently in a state of great friendly excitement, which she showed by eating her breakfast standing, and scolding the household all round.

No nursing—no energetic strong-minded woman could help Miss Brown now. There was that in the room as we entered which was stronger than us all, and made us shrink into solemn awestruck helplessness. Miss Brown was dying. We hardly knew her voice, it was so devoid of the complaining tone we had always associated with it. Miss Jessie told me afterwards that it, and her face too, were just what they had been formerly, when her mother's death left her the young anxious head of the family, of whom only Miss Jessie survived.

She was conscious of her sister's presence, though not, I think, of ours. We stood a little behind the curtain: Miss Jessie knelt with her face near her sister's, in order to catch the last soft awful whispers.

"Oh, Jessie! Jessie! How selfish I have been! God forgive me for letting you sacrifice yourself for me as you did! I have so loved you—and yet I have thought only of myself. God forgive me!"

"Hush, love! hush!" said Miss Jessie, sobbing.

"And my father! my dear, dear father! I will not complain now, if God will give me strength to be patient. But, oh, Jessie! tell my father how I longed and yearned to see him at last, and to ask his forgiveness. He can never know now how I loved him—oh! if I might but tell him, before I die! What a life of sorrow his has been, and I have done so little to cheer him!"

A light came into Miss Jessie's face. "Would it comfort you, dearest, to think that he does know?—would it comfort you, love, to know that his cares, his sorrows"—Her voice quivered, but she steadied it into calmness—"Mary! he has gone before you to the place where the weary are at rest.[3] He knows now how you loved him."

A strange look, which was not distress, came over Miss Brown's face. She did not speak for some time, but then we saw her lips form the words, rather than heard the sound—"Father, mother, Harry, Archy;"—then, as if it were a new idea throwing a filmy shadow over her darkened mind—"But you will be alone, Jessie!"

Miss Jessie had been feeling this all during the silence, I think; for the tears rolled down her cheeks like rain, at these words, and she could not answer at first. Then she put her hands together tight, and lifted them up, and said—but not to us—

"Though He slay me, yet will I trust in Him."[4]

3. Job 3.17.   4. Job 13.15.

In a few moments more Miss Brown lay calm and still—never to sorrow or murmur more.

After this second funeral, Miss Jenkyns insisted that Miss Jessie should come to stay with her rather than go back to the desolate house, which, in fact, we learned from Miss Jessie, must now be given up, as she had not wherewithal to maintain it. She had something above twenty pounds a year, besides the interest of the money for which the furniture would sell; but she could not live upon that: and so we talked over her qualifications for earning money.

"I can sew neatly," said she, "and I like nursing. I think, too, I could manage a house, if any one would try me as housekeeper; or I would go into a shop, as saleswoman, if they would have patience with me at first."

Miss Jenkyns declared, in an angry voice, that she should do no such thing; and talked to herself about "some people having no idea of their rank as a captain's daughter," nearly an hour afterwards, when she brought Miss Jessie up a basin of delicately-made arrowroot, and stood over her like a dragoon until the last spoonful was finished; then she disappeared. Miss Jessie began to tell me some more of the plans which had suggested themselves to her, and insensibly fell into talking of the days that were past and gone, and interested me so much I neither knew nor heeded how time passed. We were both startled when Miss Jenkyns reappeared, and caught us crying. I was afraid lest she would be displeased, as she often said that crying hindered digestion, and I knew she wanted Miss Jessie to get strong; but, instead, she looked queer and excited, and fidgeted round us without saying anything. At last she spoke.

"I have been so much startled—no, I've not been at all startled—don't mind me, my dear Miss Jessie—I've been very much surprised—in fact, I've had a caller, whom you knew once, my dear Miss Jessie"—

Miss Jessie went very white, then flushed scarlet, and looked eagerly at Miss Jenkyns.

"A gentleman, my dear, who wants to know if you would see him."

"Is it?—it is not"—stammered out Miss Jessie—and got no farther.

"This is his card," said Miss Jenkyns, giving it to Miss Jessie; and while her head was bent over it, Miss Jenkyns went through a series of winks and odd faces to me, and formed her lips into a long sentence, of which, of course, I could not understand a word.

"May he come up?" asked Miss Jenkyns, at last.

"Oh, yes! certainly!" said Miss Jessie, as much as to say, this is your house, you may show any visitor where you like. She took up some knitting of Miss Matty's and began to be very busy, though I could see how she trembled all over.

Miss Jenkyns rang the bell, and told the servant who answered it to show Major Gordon upstairs; and, presently, in walked a tall, fine, frank-looking man of forty or upwards. He shook hands with Miss Jessie; but he could not see her eyes, she kept them so fixed on the ground. Miss Jenkyns asked me if I would come and help her to tie up the preserves in the store-room; and, though Miss Jessie plucked at my gown, and even looked up at me with begging eye, I durst not refuse to go where Miss Jenkyns asked. Instead of tying up preserves in the store-room, however, we went to talk in the dining-room; and there Miss Jenkyns told me what Major Gordon had told her; how he had served in the same regiment with Captain Brown, and had become acquainted with Miss Jessie, then a sweet-looking, blooming girl of eighteen;

how the acquaintance had grown into love on his part, though it had been some years before he had spoken; how, on becoming possessed, through the will of an uncle, of a good estate in Scotland, he had offered and been refused, though with so much agitation and evident distress that he was sure she was not indifferent to him; and how he had discovered that the obstacle was the fell disease which was, even then, too surely threatening her sister. She had mentioned that the surgeons foretold intense suffering; and there was no one but herself to nurse her poor Mary, or cheer and comfort her father during the time of illness. They had had long discussions; and on her refusal to pledge herself to him as his wife when all should be over, he had grown angry, and broken off entirely, and gone abroad, believing that she was a cold-hearted person whom he would do well to forget. He had been travelling in the East, and was on his return home when, at Rome, he saw the account of Captain Brown's death in *Galignani*.[5]

Just then Miss Matty, who had been out all the morning, and had only lately returned to the house, burst in with a face of dismay and outraged propriety.

"Oh, goodness me!" she said. "Deborah, there's a gentleman sitting in the drawing-room with his arm round Miss Jessie's waist!" Miss Matty's eyes looked large with terror.

Miss Jenkyns snubbed her down in an instant.

"The most proper place in the world for his arm to be in. Go away, Matilda, and mind your own business." This from her sister, who had hitherto been a model of feminine decorum, was a blow for poor Miss Matty, and with a double shock she left the room.

The last time I ever saw poor Miss Jenkyns was many years after this. Mrs Gordon had kept up a warm and affectionate intercourse with all at Cranford. Miss Jenkyns, Miss Matty, and Miss Pole had all been to visit her, and returned with wonderful accounts of her house, her husband, her dress, and her looks. For, with happiness, something of her early bloom returned; she had been a year or two younger than we had taken her for. Her eyes were always lovely, and, as Mrs Gordon, her dimples were not out of place. At the time to which I have referred, when I last saw Miss Jenkyns, that lady was old and feeble, and had lost something of her strong mind. Little Flora Gordon was staying with the Misses Jenkyns, and when I came in she was reading aloud to Miss Jenkyns, who lay feeble and changed on the sofa. Flora put down the *Rambler* when I came in.

"Ah!" said Miss Jenkyns, "you find me changed, my dear. I can't see as I used to do. If Flora were not here to read to me, I hardly know how I should get through the day. Did you ever read the *Rambler*? It's a wonderful book—wonderful! and the most improving reading for Flora" (which I dare say it would have been, if she could have read half the words without spelling, and could have understood the meaning of a third), "better than that strange old book, with the queer name, poor Captain Brown was killed for reading—that book by Mr Boz, you know—'Old Poz'; when I was a girl—but that's a long time ago—I acted Lucy in 'Old Poz.'"[6] She babbled on long enough for Flora to get a good long spell at the "Christmas Carol,"[7] which Miss Matty had left on the table.

1851, 1853

5. An English newspaper published in Paris and read by tourists and expatriates.
6. A children's play by Maria Edgeworth (1795); Lucy is the young heroine.
7. Published by Dickens in 1843. The topicality of Dickens's works helps date the events of *Cranford*.

John Ruskin
1819–1900

John Ruskin began his career as the most perceptive English art critic of the nineteenth century. But for Ruskin, art was inextricably linked to the moral temper of the age in which it was produced. Thus he was drawn inevitably from art criticism to social criticism, denouncing ugliness and injustice as aspects of the same spiritual decline. His prodigious output of books on painting, literature, architecture, politics, and society culminated with a beautiful and moving autobiography, *Praeterita*, which means "of things past."

For all the magnificence of his prose and the brilliance of his vision, John Ruskin was a rather peculiar man. He was the only child of middle-class parents who lived in the suburbs near London, and whose dearest wish, he wrote, was "to make an evangelical clergyman of me." Forbidden toys, he passed his time studying the patterns in the nursery carpet and garden leaves, delighting already in the visual pleasures that would engross him all his life. His upbringing was strict, secluded, and overprotected: he was educated at home until his mother accompanied him to Oxford, where she remained for the duration of his studies.

Perhaps because he was so sheltered, Ruskin's love life was a series of disastrous ordeals. As a teenager he suffered a hopeless passion for Adèle Domecq, who was rich, French, and Catholic—unsuitable on every count. Later, a miserable six-year marriage to his cousin Effie Gray was annulled on the grounds of nonconsummation (she then married the Pre-Raphaelite painter John Everett Millais, with whom she had many children). The annulment created a scandal, and the whole episode was so painful that Ruskin omitted any reference to his marriage in *Praeterita*. Finally, he became morbidly obsessed with Rose La Touche, thirty years his junior, and only nine years old when he met her. His tragic relationship with her became a secret thread running through his later work.

Ruskin's intensity of vision was already evident in his first book, *Modern Painters*, in which he declared that "to see clearly is poetry, prophecy, and religion—all in one." Ruskin insisted that the impressionistic canvasses of J. M. W. Turner were actually more faithful to nature than the carefully rendered detail of Dutch realists. Reading *Modern Painters*, Charlotte Brontë wrote: "I feel . . . as if I had been walking blindfold—this book seems to give me eyes." Published over seventeen years (1843–1860), the five volumes of *Modern Painters* reflect their author's changing preoccupations: from art and nature in the early volumes to humanism and society in the last one, following an experience of religious "unconversion" in 1858.

From boyhood Ruskin loved to travel on the Continent, and his autobiography relates with deep pleasure the many journeys he took, usually with his parents. Venice aroused him to write what the critic John Rosenberg has called "the most elaborate and eloquent monument to a city in our literature," *The Stones of Venice* (1851–1853). Ruskin's Venice is "a ghost upon the sands of the sea, so weak—so quiet,—so bereft of all but her loveliness." The decline and fall of the Venetian empire serves as a warning to the British, which, "if it forget their example, may be led through prouder eminence to less pitied destruction."

The book's central chapter, *The Nature of Gothic*, became the touchstone for Ruskin's subsequent radical social critique of England. He argues that Gothic workmanship, though rude and imperfect, reflected a culture that respected the individual soul of the workman. Societies which demand machinelike perfection dehumanize the craftsman, turning him into a soulless operative. Ruskin thus mingled his hymn to the beauty of Venice with a scathing indictment of the Industrial Revolution.

Ruskin's later writings became increasingly fragmented as he suffered a long, slow decline into madness. "The doctors said I went mad . . . from overwork," he wrote, but "I went mad because nothing came of my work." Yet from 1871 to 1884 he was able to lecture about art at

Oxford and to produce an impassioned series of open letters to English workmen, entitled *Fors Clavigera*. Many of the letters describe the Guild of St. George, a utopian society Ruskin had founded. Tormented by the brutality and folly he saw everywhere around him, Ruskin chose in his final work to record only "what it gives me joy to remember." In the serene and radiant *Praeterita* (1885–1889), which was to inspire Proust's *Remembrance of Things Past,* Ruskin transcended his apocalyptic fury to produce one of the most enchanting yet poignant autobiographies ever written in English.

from **Modern Painters**
from *Definition of Greatness in Art*[1]

Painting, or art generally, as such, with all its technicalities, difficulties, and particular ends, is nothing but a noble and expressive language, invaluable as the vehicle of thought, but by itself nothing. He who has learned what is commonly considered the whole art of painting, that is, the art of representing any natural object faithfully, has as yet only learned the language by which his thoughts are to be expressed. He has done just as much towards being that which we ought to respect as a great painter, as a man who has learnt how to express himself grammatically and melodiously has towards being a great poet. The language is, indeed, more difficult of acquirement in the one case than in the other, and possesses more power of delighting the sense, while it speaks to the intellect; but it is, nevertheless, nothing more than language, and all those excellences which are peculiar to the painter as such, are merely what rhythm, melody, precision, and force are in the words of the orator and the poet, necessary to their greatness, but not the tests of their greatness. It is not by the mode of representing and saying, but by what is represented and said, that the respective greatness either of the painter or the writer is to be finally determined. * * *

If I say that the greatest picture is that which conveys to the mind of the spectator the greatest number of the greatest ideas, I have a definition which will include as subjects of comparison every pleasure which art is capable of conveying. If I were to say, on the contrary, that the best picture was that which most closely imitated nature, I should assume that art could only please by imitating nature; and I should cast out of the pale of criticism those parts of works of art which are not imitative, that is to say, intrinsic beauties of colour and form, and those works of art wholly, which, like the Arabesques of Raffaelle in the Loggias,[2] are not imitative at all. Now, I want a definition of art wide enough to include all its varieties of aim. I do not say, therefore, that the art is greatest which gives most pleasure, because perhaps there is some art whose end is to teach, and not to please. I do not say that the art is greatest which teaches us most, because perhaps there is some art whose end is to please, and not to teach. I do not say that the art is greatest which imitates best, because perhaps there is some art whose end is to create and not to imitate. But I say that the art is greatest which conveys to the mind of the spectator, by any means whatsoever, the greatest number of the greatest ideas; and I call an idea great in proportion as it is received by a higher faculty of the mind, and as it more fully occupies, and in occupying, exercises and exalts, the faculty by which it is received.

---

1. From vol. 1, part 1, sec. 1, ch. 2.
2. The Italian Renaissance painter Raphael (1483–1520) decorated the Loggia of the Vatican with arabesques, wall paintings of interwoven foliage, animals, and human figures.

If this, then, be the definition of great art, that of a great artist naturally follows. He is the greatest artist who has embodied, in the sum of his works, the greatest number of the greatest ideas.

1843

from *Of Modern Landscape*[1]

We turn our eyes, therefore, as boldly and as quickly as may be, from these serene fields and skies of mediaeval art, to the most characteristic examples of modern landscape. And, I believe, the first thing that will strike us, or that ought to strike us, is their *cloudiness*.

Out of perfect light and motionless air, we find ourselves on a sudden brought under sombre skies, and into drifting wind; and, with fickle sunbeams flashing in our face, or utterly drenched with sweep of rain, we are reduced to track the changes of the shadows on the grass, or watch the rents of twilight through angry cloud. And we find that whereas all the pleasure of the mediaeval was in *stability*, *definiteness*, and *luminousness*, we are expected to rejoice in darkness, and triumph in mutability; to lay the foundation of happiness in things which momentarily change or fade; and to expect the utmost satisfaction and instruction from what it is impossible to arrest, and difficult to comprehend.

We find, however, together with this general delight in breeze and darkness, much attention to the real form of clouds, and careful drawing of effects of mist; so that the appearance of objects, as seen through it, becomes a subject of science with us; and the faithful representation of that appearance is made of primal importance, under the name of aerial perspective. The aspects of sunset and sunrise, with all their attendant phenomena of cloud and mist, are watchfully delineated; and in ordinary daylight landscape, the sky is considered of so much importance, that a principal mass of foliage, or a whole foreground, is unhesitatingly thrown into shade merely to bring out the form of a white cloud. So that, if a general and characteristic name were needed for modern landscape art, none better could be invented than "the service of clouds."

And this name would, unfortunately, be characteristic of our art in more ways than one. In the last chapter, I said that all the Greeks spoke kindly about the clouds, except Aristophanes;[2] and he, I am sorry to say (since his report is so unfavourable), is the only Greek who had studied them attentively. He tells us, first, that they are "great goddesses to idle men"; then, that they are "mistresses of disputings, and logic, and monstrosities, and noisy chattering"; declares that whoso believes in their divinity must first disbelieve in Jupiter, and place supreme power in the hands of an unknown god "Whirlwind"; and, finally, he displays their influence over the mind of one of their disciples, in his sudden desire "to speak ingeniously concerning smoke."

There is, I fear, an infinite truth in this Aristophanic judgment applied to our modern cloud-worship. Assuredly, much of the love of mystery in our romances, our poetry, our art, and, above all, in our metaphysics, must come under that definition so long ago given by the great Greek, "speaking ingeniously concerning smoke." And much of the instinct, which, partially developed in painting, may be now seen throughout every mode of exertion of mind,—the easily encouraged doubt, easily

1. From vol. 3, part 4, ch. 16, para. 1–28.   2. Athenian comic playwright (c. 448–380 B.C.) whose works include *The Clouds*.

excited curiosity, habitual agitation, and delight in the changing and the marvellous, as opposed to the old quiet serenity of social custom and religious faith,—is again deeply defined in those few words, the "dethroning of Jupiter," the "coronation of the whirlwind." * * *

The next thing that will strike us, after this love of clouds, is the love of liberty. Whereas the mediaeval was always shutting himself into castles, and behind fosses,[3] and drawing brickwork neatly, and beds of flowers primly, our painters delight in getting to the open fields and moors, abhor all hedges and moats; never paint anything but free-growing trees, and rivers gliding "at their own sweet will";[4] eschew formality down to the smallest detail; break and displace the brickwork which the mediaeval would have carefully cemented; leave unpruned the thickets he would have delicately trimmed; and, carrying the love of liberty even to license, and the love of wildness even to ruin, take pleasure at last in every aspect of age and desolation which emancipates the objects of nature from the government of men;—on the castle wall displacing its tapestry with ivy, and spreading, through the garden, the bramble for the rose.

Connected with this love of liberty we find a singular manifestation of love of mountains, and see our painters traversing the wildest places of the globe in order to obtain subjects with craggy foregrounds and purple distances. Some few of them remain content with pollards[5] and flat land; but these are always men of third-rate order; and the leading masters, while they do not reject the beauty of the low grounds, reserve their highest powers to paint Alpine peaks or Italian promontories. And it is eminently noticeable, also, that this pleasure in the mountains is never mingled with fear, or tempered by a spirit of meditation, as with the mediaeval; but is always free and fearless, brightly exhilarating, and wholly unreflective; so that the painter feels that his mountain foreground may be more consistently animated by a sportsman than a hermit; and our modern society in general goes to the mountains, not to fast, but to feast, and leaves their glaciers covered with chicken-bones and egg-shells.

Connected with this want of any sense of solemnity in mountain scenery, is a general profanity of temper in regarding all the rest of nature; that is to say, a total absence of faith in the presence of any deity therein. Whereas the mediaeval never painted a cloud, but with the purpose of placing an angel in it; and a Greek never entered a wood without expecting to meet a god in it; we should think the appearance of an angel in the cloud wholly unnatural, and should be seriously surprised by meeting a god anywhere. Our chief ideas about the wood are connected with poaching. We have no belief that the clouds contain more than so many inches of rain or hail, and from our ponds and ditches expect nothing more divine than ducks and watercresses.

Finally: connected with this profanity of temper is a strong tendency to deny the sacred element of colour, and make our boast in blackness. For though occasionally glaring or violent, modern colour is on the whole eminently sombre, tending continually to grey or brown, and by many of our best painters consistently falsified, with a confessed pride in what they call chaste or subdued tints; so that, whereas a mediaeval paints his sky bright blue and his foreground bright green, gilds the towers of his castles, and clothes his figures with purple and white, we paint our sky grey, our fore-

---

3. Moats.
4. Wordsworth, *Composed upon Westminster Bridge, September 3, 1802* (see page 1561).

5. Artificially shaped trees that have been polled or cut back.

ground black, and our foliage brown, and think that enough is sacrificed to the sun in admitting the dangerous brightness of a scarlet cloak or a blue jacket.

These, I believe, are the principal points which would strike us instantly, if we were to be brought suddenly into an exhibition of modern landscapes out of a room filled with mediaeval work. It is evident that there are both evil and good in this change; but how much evil, or how much good, we can only estimate by considering, as in the former divisions of our inquiry, what are the real roots of the habits of mind which have caused them.

At first, it is evident that the title "Dark Ages," given to the mediaeval centuries, is, respecting art, wholly inapplicable. They were, on the contrary, the bright ages; ours are the dark ones. I do not mean metaphysically, but literally. They were the ages of gold; ours are the ages of umber.[6]

This is partly mere mistake in us; we build brown brick walls, and wear brown coats, because we have been blunderingly taught to do so, and go on doing so mechanically. There is, however, also some cause for the change in our own tempers. On the whole, these are much *sadder* ages than the early ones; not sadder in a noble and deep way, but in a dim wearied way,—the way of ennui, and jaded intellect, and uncomfortableness of soul and body. The Middle Ages had their wars and agonies, but also intense delights. Their gold was dashed with blood; but ours is sprinkled with dust. Their life was inwoven with white and purple: ours is one seamless stuff of brown. Not that we are without apparent festivity, but festivity more or less forced, mistaken, embittered, incomplete—not of the heart. How wonderfully, since Shakespere's time, have we lost the power of laughing at bad jests! The very finish of our wit belies our gaiety.

The profoundest reason of this darkness of heart is, I believe, our want of faith. There never yet was a generation of men (savage or civilized) who, taken as a body, so wofully fulfilled the words "having no hope, and without God in the world," as the present civilized European race. A Red Indian or Otaheitan[7] savage has more sense of a divine existence round him, or government over him, than the plurality of refined Londoners and Parisians: and those among us who may in some sense be said to believe, are divided almost without exception into two broad classes, Romanist and Puritan; who, but for the interference of the unbelieving portions of society, would, either of them, reduce the other sect as speedily as possible to ashes. * * * Nearly all our powerful men in this age of the world are unbelievers; the best of them in doubt and misery; the worst in reckless defiance; the plurality, in plodding hesitation, doing, as well as they can, what practical work lies ready to their hands. Most of our scientific men are in this last class: our popular authors either set themselves definitely against all religious form, pleading for simple truth and benevolence, (Thackeray, Dickens,) or give themselves up to bitter and fruitless statement of facts, (De Balzac,) or surface-painting, (Scott,) or careless blasphemy, sad or smiling, (Byron, Beranger). Our earnest poets and deepest thinkers are doubtful and indignant, (Tennyson, Carlyle); one or two, anchored, indeed, but anxious or weeping, (Wordsworth, Mrs Browning); and of these two, the first is not so sure of his anchor, but that now and then it drags with him, even to make him cry out,—

> Great God, I had rather be
> A Pagan suckled in some creed outworn;

6. Brown.

7. Tahitian.

> So might I, standing on this pleasant lea,
> Have glimpses that would make me less forlorn.[8]

In politics, religion is now a name; in art, a hypocrisy or affectation. Over German religious pictures the inscription, "See how Pious I am," can be read at a glance by any clear-sighted person. Over French and English religious pictures the inscription, "See how Impious I am," is equally legible. All sincere and modest art is, among us, profane.

This faithlessness operates among us according to our tempers, producing either sadness or levity, and being the ultimate root alike of our discontents and of our wantonnesses. It is marvellous how full of contradiction it makes us: we are first dull, and seek for wild and lonely places because we have no heart for the garden; presently we recover our spirits, and build an assembly-room among the mountains, because we have no reverence for the desert. I do not know if there be game on Sinai, but I am always expecting to hear of some one's shooting over it.

There is, however, another, and a more innocent root of our delight in wild scenery.

All the Renaissance principles of art tended, as I have before often explained, to the setting Beauty above Truth, and seeking for it always at the expense of truth. And the proper punishment of such pursuit—the punishment which all the laws of the universe rendered inevitable—was, that those who thus pursued beauty should wholly lose sight of beauty. All the thinkers of the age, as we saw previously, declared that it did not exist. The age seconded their efforts, and banished beauty, so far as human effort could succeed in doing so, from the face of the earth, and the form of man. To powder the hair, to patch the cheek, to hoop the body, to buckle the foot, were all part and parcel of the same system which reduced streets to brick walls, and pictures to brown stains. One desert of Ugliness was extended before the eyes of mankind; and their pursuit of the beautiful, so recklessly continued, received unexpected consummation in high-heeled shoes and periwigs—Gower Street, and Gaspar Poussin.[9]

Reaction from this state was inevitable, if any true life was left in the races of mankind; and, accordingly, though still forced, by rule and fashion, to the producing and wearing all that is ugly, men steal out, half-ashamed of themselves for doing so, to the fields and mountains; and, finding among these the colour, and liberty, and variety, and power, which are for ever grateful to them, delight in these to an extent never before known; rejoice in all the wildest shattering of the mountain side, as an opposition to Gower Street, gaze in a rapt manner at sunsets and sunrises, to see there the blue, and gold, and purple, which glow for them no longer on knight's armour or temple porch; and gather with care out of the fields, into their blotted herbaria, the flowers which the five orders of architecture have banished from their doors and casements. * * *

It is not, however, only to existing inanimate nature that our want of beauty in person and dress has driven us. The imagination of it, as it was seen in our ancestors, haunts us continually; and while we yield to the present fashions, or act in accordance with the dullest modern principles of economy and utility, we look fondly back to the manners of the ages of chivalry, and delight in painting, to the fancy, the fashions we pretend to despise, and the splendours we think it wise to abandon. The fur-

---

8. From Wordsworth's sonnet *The World Is Too Much With Us* (see page 1561).
9. Gaspard Poussin (1615–1675) was a French landscape painter; Ruskin thought the plain brick houses of Gower Street in London were the epitome of ugliness.

niture and personages of our romance are sought, when the writer desires to please most easily, in the centuries which we profess to have surpassed in everything; the art which takes us into the present times is considered as both daring and degraded, and while the weakest words please us, and are regarded as poetry, which recall the manners of our forefathers, or of strangers, it is only as familiar and vulgar that we accept the description of our own.

In this we are wholly different from all the races that preceded us. All other nations have regarded their ancestors with reverence as saints or heroes; but have nevertheless thought their own deeds and ways of life the fitting subjects for their arts of painting or of verse. We, on the contrary, regard our ancestors as foolish and wicked, but yet find our chief artistic pleasure in descriptions of their ways of life.

The Greeks and mediaevals honoured, but did not imitate their forefathers; we imitate, but do not honour. * * *

Farther: as the admiration of mankind is found, in our times, to have in great part passed from men to mountains, and from human emotion to natural phenomena, we may anticipate that the great strength of art will also be warped in this direction; with this notable result for us, that whereas the greatest painters or painter of classical and mediaeval periods, being wholly devoted to the representation of humanity, furnished us with but little to examine in landscape, the greatest painters or painter of modern times will in all probability be devoted to landscape principally; and farther, because in representing human emotion words surpass painting, but in representing natural scenery painting surpasses words, we may anticipate also that the painter and poet (for convenience' sake I here use the words in opposition) will somewhat change their relations of rank in illustrating the mind of the age; that the painter will become of more importance, the poet of less; and that the relations between the men who are the types and first-fruits of the age in word and work,—namely, Scott[1] and Turner,—will be, in many curious respects, different from those between Homer and Phidias, or Dante and Giotto.[2] * * *

Then, as touching the kind of work done by these two men, the more I think of it I find this conclusion more impressed upon me,—that the greatest thing a human soul ever does in this world is to *see* something, and tell what it *saw* in a plain way. Hundreds of people can talk for one who can think, but thousands can think for one who can see. To see clearly is poetry, prophecy, and religion,—all in one.

1856

from **The Stones of Venice**
from The Nature of Gothic[1]

I shall endeavour therefore to give the reader in this chapter an idea, at once broad and definite, of the true nature of *Gothic* architecture, properly so called; not of that of Venice only, but of universal Gothic: for it will be one of the most interesting parts of our subsequent inquiry to find out how far Venetian architecture reached the universal or perfect type of Gothic, and how far it either fell short of it, or assumed foreign and independent forms.

1. Sir Walter Scott (1771–1832), Scottish novelist and poet.
2. Homer, ancient Greek epic poet; Phidias, ancient Greek sculptor; Dante Alighieri (1265–1321), Florentine

poet; Giotto (1266?–1337), Florentine painter, architect, and sculptor.
1. From vol. 2, ch. 6.

The principal difficulty in doing this arises from the fact that every building of the Gothic period differs in some important respect from every other; and many include features which, if they occurred in other buildings, would not be considered Gothic at all; so that all we have to reason upon is merely, if I may be allowed so to express it, a greater or less degree of *Gothicness* in each building we examine. And it is this Gothicness,—the character which, according as it is found more or less in a building, makes it more or less Gothic,—of which I want to define the nature. * * * That is to say, pointed arches do not constitute Gothic, nor vaulted roofs, nor flying buttresses, nor grotesque sculptures; but all or some of these things, and many other things with them, when they come together so as to have life. * * *

* * * We shall find that Gothic architecture has external forms and internal elements. Its elements are certain mental tendencies of the builders, legibly expressed in it; as fancifulness, love of variety, love of richness, and such others. Its external forms are pointed arches, vaulted roofs, etc. And unless both the elements and the forms are there, we have no right to call the style Gothic. It is not enough that it has the Form, if it have not also the power and life. It is not enough that it has the Power, if it have not the form. * * *

I believe, then, that the characteristic or moral elements of Gothic are the following, placed in the order of their importance:

1. Savageness.
2. Changefulness.
3. Naturalism.
4. Grotesqueness.
5. Rigidity.
6. Redundance.

These characters are here expressed as belonging to the building; as belonging to the builder, they would be expressed thus:—1. Savageness or Rudeness. 2. Love of Change. 3. Love of Nature. 4. Disturbed Imagination. 5. Obstinacy. 6. Generosity. And I repeat, that the withdrawal of any one, or any two, will not at once destroy the Gothic character of a building, but the removal of a majority of them will. I shall proceed to examine them in their order.

(1.) SAVAGENESS. I am not sure when the word "Gothic" was first generically applied to the architecture of the North; but I presume that, whatever the date of its original usage, it was intended to imply reproach, and express the barbaric character of the nations among whom that architecture arose. * * * It is true, greatly and deeply true, that the architecture of the North is rude and wild; but it is not true, that, for this reason, we are to condemn it, or despise. Far otherwise: I believe it is in this very character that it deserves our profoundest reverence. * * *

There is, I repeat, no degradation, no reproach in this, but all dignity and honourableness: and we should err grievously in refusing either to recognize as an essential character of the existing architecture of the North, or to admit as a desirable character in that which it yet may be, this wildness of thought, and roughness of work; this look of mountain brotherhood between the cathedral and the Alp; this magnificence of sturdy power, put forth only the more energetically because the fine finger-touch was chilled away by the frosty wind, and the eye dimmed by the moor-mist, or blinded by the hail; this out-speaking of the strong spirit of men who may not gather redundant fruitage from the earth, nor bask in dreamy benignity of sunshine, but must break the rock for bread, and cleave the forest for fire, and show, even in what they did for their delight, some of the hard habits of the arm and heart that grew on them as they swung the axe or pressed the plough.

If, however, the savageness of Gothic architecture, merely as an expression of its origin among Northern nations, may be considered, in some sort, a noble character, it possesses a higher nobility still, when considered as an index, not of climate, but of religious principle.

In the 13th and 14th paragraphs of Chapter XXI of the first volume of this work, it was noticed that the systems of architectural ornament, properly so called, might be divided into three:—1. Servile ornament, in which the execution or power of the inferior workman is entirely subjected to the intellect of the higher;—2. Constitutional ornament, in which the executive inferior power is, to a certain point, emancipated and independent, having a will of its own, yet confessing its inferiority and rendering obedience to higher powers;—and 3. Revolutionary ornament, in which no executive inferiority is admitted at all. I must here explain the nature of these divisions at somewhat greater length.

Of Servile ornament, the principal schools are the Greek, Ninevite,[2] and Egyptian; but their servility is of different kinds. The Greek master-workman was far advanced in knowledge and power above the Assyrian or Egyptian. Neither he nor those for whom he worked could endure the appearance of imperfection in anything; and, therefore, what ornament he appointed to be done by those beneath him was composed of mere geometrical forms,—balls, ridges, and perfectly symmetrical foliage,—which could be executed with absolute precision by line and rule, and were as perfect in their way, when completed, as his own figure sculpture. The Assyrian and Egyptian, on the contrary, less cognisant of accurate form in anything, were content to allow their figure sculpture to be executed by inferior workmen, but lowered the method of its treatment to a standard which every workman could reach, and then trained him by discipline so rigid, that there was no chance of his falling beneath the standard appointed. The Greek gave to the lower workman no subject which he could not perfectly execute. The Assyrian gave him subjects which he could only execute imperfectly, but fixed a legal standard for his imperfection. The workman was, in both systems, a slave.

But in the mediaeval, or especially Christian, system of ornament, this slavery is done away with altogether; Christianity having recognized, in small things as well as great, the individual value of every soul. But it not only recognizes its value; it confesses its imperfection, in only bestowing dignity upon the acknowledgment of unworthiness. That admission of lost power and fallen nature, which the Greek or Ninevite felt to be intensely painful, and, as far as might be, altogether refused, the Christian makes daily and hourly, contemplating the fact of it without fear, as tending, in the end, to God's greater glory. Therefore, to every spirit which Christianity summons to her service, her exhortation is: Do what you can, and confess frankly what you are unable to do; neither let your effort be shortened for fear of failure, nor your confession silenced for fear of shame. And it is, perhaps, the principal admirableness of the Gothic schools of architecture, that they thus receive the results of the labour of inferior minds; and out of fragments full of imperfection, and betraying that imperfection in every touch, indulgently raise up a stately and unaccusable whole.

2. Nineveh was an ancient Assyrian city.

But the modern English mind has this much in common with that of the Greek, that it intensely desires, in all things, the utmost completion or perfection compatible with their nature. This is a noble character in the abstract, but becomes ignoble when it causes us to forget the relative dignities of that nature itself, and to prefer the perfectness of the lower nature to the imperfection of the higher; not considering that as, judged by such a rule, all the brute animals would be preferable to man, because more perfect in their functions and kind. * * * And therefore, while in all things that we see or do, we are to desire perfection, and strive for it, we are nevertheless not to set the meaner thing, in its narrow accomplishment, above the nobler thing, in its mighty progress; not to esteem smooth minuteness above shattered majesty; not to prefer mean victory to honourable defeat; not to lower the level of our aim, that we may the more surely enjoy the complacency of success. But, above all, in our dealings with the souls of other men, we are to take care how we check, by severe requirement or narrow caution, efforts which might otherwise lead to a noble issue; and, still more, how we withhold our admiration from great excellencies, because they are mingled with rough faults. Now, in the make and nature of every man, however rude or simple, whom we employ in manual labour, there are some powers for better things; some tardy imagination, torpid capacity of emotion, tottering steps of thought, there are, even at the worst; and in most cases it is all our own fault that they *are* tardy or torpid. But they cannot be strengthened, unless we are content to take them in their feebleness, and unless we prize and honour them in their imperfection above the best and most perfect manual skill. And this is what we have to do with all our labourers; to look for the *thoughtful* part of them, and get that out of them, whatever we lose for it, whatever faults and errors we are obliged to take with it. For the best that is in them cannot manifest itself, but in company with much error. Understand this clearly: You can teach a man to draw a straight line, and to cut one; to strike a curved line, and to carve it; and to copy and carve any number of given lines or forms, with admirable speed and perfect precision; and you find his work perfect of its kind: but if you ask him to think about any of those forms, to consider if he cannot find any better in his own head, he stops; his execution becomes hesitating; he thinks, and ten to one he thinks wrong; ten to one he makes a mistake in the first touch he gives to his work as a thinking being. But you have made a man of him for all that. He was only a machine before, an animated tool.

And observe, you are put to stern choice in this matter. You must either make a tool of the creature, or a man of him. You cannot make both. Men were not intended to work with the accuracy of tools, to be precise and perfect in all their actions. If you will have that precision out of them, and make their fingers measure degrees like cog-wheels, and their arms strike curves like compasses, you must unhumanize them. All the energy of their spirits must be given to make cogs and compasses of themselves. * * *

And now, reader, look round this English room of yours, about which you have been proud so often, because the work of it was so good and strong, and the ornaments of it so finished. Examine again all those accurate mouldings, and perfect polishings, and unerring adjustments of the seasoned wood and tempered steel. Many a time you have exulted over them, and thought how great England was, because her slightest work was done so thoroughly. Alas! if read rightly, these perfectnesses are signs of a slavery in our England a thousand times more bitter and more degrading than that of the scourged African, or helot[3] Greek. Men may be beaten, chained, tor-

3. Serf or slave.

mented, yoked like cattle, slaughtered like summer flies, and yet remain in one sense, and the best sense, free. But to smother their souls within them, to blight and hew into rotting pollards[4] the suckling branches of their human intelligence, to make the flesh and skin which, after the worm's work on it, is to see God,[5] into leathern thongs to yoke machinery with,—this is to be slave-masters indeed; and there might be more freedom in England, though her feudal lords' lightest words were worth men's lives, and though the blood of the vexed husbandman dropped in the furrows of her fields, than there is while the animation of her multitudes is sent like fuel to feed the factory smoke, and the strength of them is given daily to be wasted into the fineness of a web, or racked into the exactness of a line.

And, on the other hand, go forth again to gaze upon the old cathedral front, where you have smiled so often at the fantastic ignorance of the old sculptors: examine once more those ugly goblins, and formless monsters, and stern statues, anatomiless and rigid; but do not mock at them, for they are signs of the life and liberty of every workman who struck the stone; a freedom of thought, and rank in scale of being, such as no laws, no charters, no charities can secure; but which it must be the first aim of all Europe at this day to regain for her children.

Let me not be thought to speak wildly or extravagantly. It is verily this degradation of the operative into a machine, which, more than any other evil of the times, is leading the mass of the nations everywhere into vain, incoherent, destructive struggling for a freedom of which they cannot explain the nature to themselves. Their universal outcry against wealth, and against nobility, is not forced from them either by the pressure of famine, or the sting of mortified pride. These do much, and have done much in all ages; but the foundations of society were never yet shaken as they are at this day. It is not that men are ill fed, but that they have no pleasure in the work by which they make their bread, and therefore look to wealth as the only means of pleasure. It is not that men are pained by the scorn of the upper classes, but they cannot endure their own; for they feel that the kind of labour to which they are condemned is verily a degrading one, and makes them less than men. Never had the upper classes so much sympathy with the lower, or charity for them, as they have at this day, and yet never were they so much hated by them: for, of old, the separation between the noble and the poor was merely a wall built by law; now it is a veritable difference in level of standing, a precipice between upper and lower grounds in the field of humanity, and there is pestilential air at the bottom of it. * * *

We have much studied and much perfected, of late, the great civilized invention of the division of labour; only we give it a false name. It is not, truly speaking, the labour that is divided; but the men:—Divided into mere segments of men—broken into small fragments and crumbs of life; so that all the little piece of intelligence that is left in a man is not enough to make a pin, or a nail, but exhausts itself in making the point of a pin or the head of a nail. Now it is a good and desirable thing, truly, to make many pins in a day; but if we could only see with what crystal sand their points were polished,—sand of human soul, much to be magnified before it can be discerned for what it is—we should think there might be some loss in it also. And the great cry that rises from all our manufacturing cities, louder than their furnace blast, is all in very deed for this,—that we manufacture everything there except men; we blanch cotton, and strengthen steel, and refine sugar, and shape pottery; but to brighten, to

4. Trees that are artificially shaped by pruning.   5. "And though after my skin worms destroy this body, yet in my flesh shall I see God" (Job 19.26).

strengthen, to refine, or to form a single living spirit, never enters into our estimate of advantages. And all the evil to which that cry is urging our myriads can be met only in one way: not by teaching nor preaching, for to teach them is but to show them their misery, and to preach to them, if we do nothing more than preach, is to mock at it. It can be met only by a right understanding, on the part of all classes, of what kinds of labour are good for men, raising them, and making them happy; by a determined sacrifice of such convenience, or beauty, or cheapness as is to be got only by the degradation of the workman; and by equally determined demand for the products and results of healthy and ennobling labour.

And how, it will be asked, are these products to be recognized, and this demand to be regulated? Easily: by the observance of three broad and simple rules:

1. Never encourage the manufacture of any article not absolutely necessary, in the production of which *Invention* has no share.

2. Never demand an exact finish for its own sake, but only for some practical or noble end.

3. Never encourage imitation or copying of any kind, except for the sake of preserving records of great works.

The second of these principles is the only one which directly rises out of the consideration of our immediate subject; but I shall briefly explain the meaning and extent of the first also, reserving the enforcement of the third for another place.

1. Never encourage the manufacture of anything not necessary, in the production of which invention has no share.

For instance. Glass beads are utterly unnecessary, and there is no design or thought employed in their manufacture. They are formed by first drawing out the glass into rods; these rods are chopped up into fragments of the size of beads by the human hand, and the fragments are then rounded in the furnace. The men who chop up the rods sit at their work all day, their hands vibrating with a perpetual and exquisitely timed palsy, and the beads dropping beneath their vibration like hail. Neither they, nor the men who draw out the rods or fuse the fragments, have the smallest occasion for the use of any single human faculty; and every young lady, therefore, who buys glass beads is engaged in the slave-trade, and in a much more cruel one than that which we have so long been endeavouring to put down.

But glass cups and vessels may become the subjects of exquisite invention; and if in buying these we pay for the invention, that is to say, for the beautiful form, or colour, or engraving, and not for mere finish of execution, we are doing good to humanity. * * *

I shall perhaps press this law farther elsewhere, but our immediate concern is chiefly with the second, namely, never to demand an exact finish, when it does not lead to a noble end. For observe, I have only dwelt upon the rudeness of Gothic, or any other kind of imperfectness, as admirable, where it was impossible to get design or thought without it. If you are to have the thought of a rough and untaught man, you must have it in a rough and untaught way; but from an educated man, who can without effort express his thoughts in an educated way, take the graceful expression, and be thankful. Only *get* the thought, and do not silence the peasant because he cannot speak good grammar, or until you have taught him his grammar. Grammar and refinement are good things, both, only be sure of the better thing first. And thus in art, delicate finish is desirable from the greatest masters, and is always given by them. In some places Michael Angelo, Leonardo, Phidias, Perugino, Turner,[6] all finished with the most exquisite care; and the finish they give always leads to the fuller accomplishment of their noble purposes. But lower men than these cannot finish, for it requires consummate knowledge to finish consummately, and then we must take their thoughts as they are able to give them. So the rule is simple: Always look for invention first, and after that, for such execution as will help the invention, and as the inventor is capable of without painful effort, and *no more*. Above all, demand no refinement of execution where there is no thought, for that is slaves' work, unredeemed. Rather choose rough work than smooth work, so only that the practical purpose be answered, and never imagine there is reason to be proud of anything that may be accomplished by patience and sand-paper.

I shall only give one example, which however will show the reader what I mean, from the manufacture already alluded to, that of glass. Our modern glass is exquisitely clear in its substance, true in its form, accurate in its cutting. We are proud of this. We ought to be ashamed of it. The old Venice glass was muddy, inaccurate in all its forms, and clumsily cut, if at all. And the old Venetian was justly proud of it. For there is this difference between the English and Venetian workman, that the former thinks only of accurately matching his patterns, and getting his curves perfectly true and his edges perfectly sharp, and becomes a mere machine for rounding curves and sharpening edges; while the old Venetian cared not a whit whether his edges were sharp or not, but he invented a new design for every glass that he made, and never moulded a handle or a lip without a new fancy in it. And therefore, though some Venetian glass is ugly and clumsy enough when made by clumsy and uninventive workmen, other Venetian glass is so lovely in its forms that no price is too great for it; and we never see the same form in it twice. Now you cannot have the finish and the varied form too. If the workman is thinking about his edges, he cannot be thinking of his design; if of his design, he cannot think of his edges. Choose whether you will pay for the lovely form or the perfect finish, and choose at the same moment whether you will make the worker a man or a grindstone.

Nay, but the reader interrupts me,—"If the workman can design beautifully, I would not have him kept at the furnace. Let him be taken away and made a gentleman, and have a studio, and design his glass there, and I will have it blown and cut for him by common workmen, and so I will have my design and my finish too."

All ideas of this kind are founded upon two mistaken suppositions: the first, that one man's thoughts can be, or ought to be, executed by another man's hands; the second, that manual labour is a degradation, when it is governed by intellect.

On a large scale, and in work determinable by line and rule, it is indeed both possible and necessary that the thoughts of one man should be carried out by the labour of others; in this sense I have already defined the best architecture to be the expression of the mind of manhood by the hands of childhood. But on a smaller scale, and in a design which cannot be mathematically defined, one man's thoughts can never be expressed by another: and the difference between the spirit of touch of the man who is inventing, and of the man who is obeying directions, is often all the difference between a great and a common work of art. How wide the separation is

---

6. Michelangelo Buonarroti (1475–1564), Italian painter, sculptor, architect, and poet; Leonardo da Vinci (1452–1519), Italian painter, sculptor, architect, and engineer; Phidias (5th century B.C.), ancient Greek sculptor; Pietro Vannucci Perugino (1446–1523), Italian painter; J. M. W. Turner (1775–1851), English painter.

between original and second-hand execution, I shall endeavour to show elsewhere; it is not so much to our purpose here as to mark the other and more fatal error of despising manual labour when governed by intellect; for it is no less fatal an error to despise it when thus regulated by intellect, than to value it for its own sake. We are always in these days endeavouring to separate the two; we want one man to be always thinking, and another to be always working, and we call one a gentleman, and the other an operative; whereas the workman ought often to be thinking, and the thinker often to be working, and both should be gentlemen, in the best sense. As it is, we make both ungentle, the one envying, the other despising, his brother; and the mass of society is made up of morbid thinkers, and miserable workers. Now it is only by labour that thought can be made healthy, and only by thought that labour can be made happy, and the two cannot be separated with impunity. * * *

I should be led far from the matter in hand, if I were to pursue this interesting subject. Enough, I trust, has been said to show the reader that the rudeness or imperfection which at first rendered the term "Gothic" one of reproach is indeed, when rightly understood, one of the most noble characters of Christian architecture, and not only a noble but an *essential* one. It seems a fantastic paradox, but it is nevertheless a most important truth, that no architecture can be truly noble which is *not* imperfect. And this is easily demonstrable. For since the architect, whom we will suppose capable of doing all in perfection, cannot execute the whole with his own hands, he must either make slaves of his workmen in the old Greek, and present English fashion, and level his work to a slave's capacities, which is to degrade it; or else he must take his workmen as he finds them, and let them show their weaknesses together with their strength, which will involve the Gothic imperfection, but render the whole work as noble as the intellect of the age can make it.

But the principle may be stated more broadly still. I have confined the illustration of it to architecture, but I must not leave it as if true of architecture only. Hitherto I have used the words imperfect and perfect merely to distinguish between work grossly unskilful, and work executed with average precision and science; and I have been pleading that any degree of unskilfulness should be admitted, so only that the labourer's mind had room for expression. But, accurately speaking, no good work whatever can be perfect, and *the demand for perfection is always a sign of a misunderstanding of the ends of art.*

This for two reasons, both based on everlasting laws. The first, that no great man ever stops working till he has reached his point of failure: that is to say, his mind is always far in advance of his powers of execution, and the latter will now and then give way in trying to follow it; besides that he will always give to the inferior portions of his work only such inferior attention as they require; and according to his greatness he becomes so accustomed to the feeling of dissatisfaction with the best he can do, that in moments of lassitude or anger with himself he will not care though the beholder be dissatisfied also. I believe there has only been one man who would not acknowledge this necessity, and strove always to reach perfection, Leonardo; the end of his vain effort being merely that he would take ten years to a picture and leave it unfinished. And therefore, if we are to have great men working at all, or less men doing their best, the work will be imperfect, however beautiful. Of human work none but what is bad can be perfect, in its own bad way.[7]

7. The Elgin marbles are supposed by many persons to be "perfect." In the most important portions they indeed approach perfection, but only there. The draperies are unfinished, the hair and wool of the animals are unfinished, and the entire bas-reliefs of the frieze are roughly cut [Ruskin's note]. The Elgin marbles are sculptures (including the Parthenon frieze) which were taken from Athens to England by Lord Elgin at the beginning of the 19th century.

The second reason is, that imperfection is in some sort essential to all that we know of life. It is the sign of life in a mortal body, that is to say, of a state of progress and change. Nothing that lives is, or can be, rigidly perfect; part of it is decaying, part nascent. The foxglove blossom,—a third part bud, a third part past, a third part in full bloom,—is a type of the life of this world. And in all things that live there are certain irregularities and deficiencies which are not only signs of life, but sources of beauty. No human face is exactly the same in its lines on each side, no leaf perfect in its lobes, no branch in its symmetry. All admit irregularity as they imply change; and to banish imperfection is to destroy expression, to check exertion, to paralyze vitality. All things are literally better, lovelier, and more beloved for the imperfections which have been divinely appointed, that the law of human life may be Effort, and the law of human judgment, Mercy.

Accept this then for a universal law, that neither architecture nor any other noble work of man can be good unless it be imperfect; and let us be prepared for the otherwise strange fact, which we shall discern clearly as we approach the period of the Renaissance, that the first cause of the fall of the arts of Europe was a relentless requirement of perfection, incapable alike either of being silenced by veneration for greatness, or softened into forgiveness of simplicity.

Thus far then of the Rudeness or Savageness, which is the first mental element of Gothic architecture. It is an element in many other healthy architectures also, as the Byzantine and Romanesque; but true Gothic cannot exist without it.

1851–1853

Matthew Arnold
1822–1888

"I am glad you like the Gipsy Scholar," Matthew Arnold wrote to a friend in 1853, "—but what does it *do* for you?" No Victorian gave more attention than Arnold to the momentous question of how art should affect an audience, and no writer was ever more tortured by it. For much as he delighted in creating the "pleasing melancholy" of *The Scholar-Gipsy*, one of his greatest poems, Arnold felt that literature must directly address the moral needs of readers, "to *animate* and *ennoble* them." This concern with the practical emotional effects of art, Arnold said simply, is "the basis of my nature—and of my poetics."

But in trying to realize his goal, Arnold became a deeply divided man. Author of the era's most distinctive poems of alienation and doubt, he gave up poetry to work for the public good, passionately defending classic literature as a means of remaking the materialist society he abhorred. As a social critic, he aspired to embody his ideal of a balanced mind, to be a man "who saw life steadily and saw it whole." But as a private individual he viewed himself as a forlorn romantic quester, disenchanted with modernity. Unable to believe in the religion of the past, and unwilling to accept the secular values of the present, he described himself as "wandering between two worlds, one dead, / The other powerless to be born." Arnold is unique among the eminent Victorian writers, admired equally for his heartfelt poetry of disillusionment and for his sophisticated prose aimed at pragmatic social reform.

Matthew Arnold was the oldest son of Dr. Thomas Arnold, headmaster of Rugby School, who had become famous for reshaping the curriculum to instill a healthy respect for Christian values, classical languages, and competitive games. Matthew's mother, Mary Penrose Arnold, encouraged her son to be creative, self-conscious, and alert to the comic or dramatic side of daily events. Nicknamed "Crabby" by his father when he wore leg braces for two years, Arnold adopted a sidelong, crab-like approach to his goal of becoming a poet. A lazy, dilettantish, facetious student, Arnold managed through last-minute heroics to win the top prizes: a scholarship in 1840 to Balliol College, Oxford; the renowned Newdigate Prize for poetry in 1843; and in 1845 a Fellowship at Oriel College.

Throughout his life, Arnold seemed most comfortable outdoors and free of the classroom, whether blasting away at game on the English moors (he was a terrible shot), or hiking in the Alps. He spent his early childhood at Laleham, a village on the Thames, perhaps the source of his frequent river imagery. When he should have been studying at Oxford, he roamed the idyllic countryside surrounding it, hunting, fishing, and composing verses. He once pranced naked on a riverbank after swimming, prompting a rebuke from a passing clergyman. Waving his towel, Arnold replied: "Is it possible that you see anything indelicate in the human form divine?"

In 1847 Arnold became private secretary to the liberal politician Lord Lansdowne, spending most of his time in London, working on his poetry, and arguing about poetry and religion with his best friend, the poet Arthur Hugh Clough. They both agreed on the spiritual bankruptcy of modern life: "These are damned times," Arnold wrote to Clough in 1849; "everything is against one . . . the absence of great *natures*, the unavoidable contact with millions of small ones . . . our own selves, and the sickening consciousness of our difficulties."

Arnold dealt with these difficulties by casting them in poetic form. His first book of poems, *The Strayed Reveller, and Other Poems*, by "A," appeared in 1849, followed by *Empedocles on Etna, and Other Poems* (1852) and *Poems* (1853). Many other important poems, including *Dover Beach*, also date from this fertile period, though not published until later, in *Poems, Second Series* (1855) and *New Poems* (1867).

Arnold's finest poetry is imbued with a love of the countryside. He spent family vacations in the Lake District, whose beauty and poetic associations made a deep impression on him. His parents were friendly with Wordsworth, who was to become the chief influence on Arnold's poetry; when Wordsworth died he mourned, "who will teach us how to feel?" Like Wordsworth, Arnold evokes memorable landscapes in many of his key works in order to ponder the relation between hidden emotions and external objects, and to explore the themes of lost childhood, nostalgia for the past, and the quest for identity. But Arnold rarely found in nature a means of contact with other people or with a deeper self: "The disease of the present age," he wrote in his journal, "is divorce from oneself."

Arnold felt a growing dissatisfaction with his society and with his own poetry. In a controversial preface to his *Poems* of 1853, he justified not reprinting his major earlier work, *Empedocles on Etna*, because he felt that it failed to "inspirit and rejoice" readers and teach them how to live. He went on to condemn poetry that merely presents "a continuous state of mental distress . . . unrelieved by incident, hope, or resistance; in which there is everything to be endured, nothing to be done." In these words he accurately summed up—and dismissed—what was most powerful and moving in his own work.

Provoking a heated debate about the poet's relation to contemporary life, Arnold urged that modern poets should turn from their own troubles to build upon timeless, universal "great actions," such as those found in Sophocles and Aeschylus. The Victorian age, he concluded, was an unlikely source of poetic material, because it was "an age wanting in moral grandeur . . . an age of spiritual discomfort."

Too much a man of his time to be able to follow his own advice, Arnold largely abandoned poetry after the mid-1850s. In 1851, two important events occurred that contributed to this abdication: his marriage to Frances Lucy Wightman and his taking a job as a school inspector to support his family. This turned out to be a grueling position assessing the quality of instruction in government-funded schools for the poor. Initially surmising that the job would do well enough "for the next three or four years," Arnold doggedly kept at it for thirty-five years, traveling constantly throughout Britain and later in Europe. He soon realized the importance of expanding and reforming public education, arguing for the schools' crucial role "in civilizing the next generation of the lower classes, who, as things are going, will have most of the political power of the country in their hands."

Thus the anguished poet transformed himself into an energetic public servant, strenuously trying to remedy with his progressive criticism a society that he privately despaired of as hopelessly materialist. In 1857 Arnold was elected Professor of Poetry at Oxford University. He was the first to lecture in English rather than Latin, and for the next ten years he used the occasion of his public lectures to reach the broadest possible audience, promoting his belief that a careful reading of classic literature produces civilizing and morally sustaining effects. He reworked many of his lectures into books and essays, including *On Translating Homer* (1861) and *On the Modern Element in Literature* (1869). The work begun at Oxford eventually helped establish literature as a cornerstone of university programs in the liberal arts.

In 1865 Arnold published *Essays in Criticism*, which began with his famous essay, *The Function of Criticism at the Present Time*. There he argued that criticism is "a free creative activity," one that may well be the most useful and satisfying activity available to an inquiring mind in a modern, unpoetical era. With examples ranging from high art to tabloid journalism, Arnold revealed how British thought is entangled in class relations and political exigencies; his essay anticipates the scope and methods of modern culture studies. In his most important work of social criticism, *Culture and Anarchy* (1869), Arnold called for "disinterested" analysis free of partisan politics. He deplored English pride in "doing as one likes," and found in the self-serving behavior of all classes an anarchic lack of concern for the public good. Only education, he contended, could unite the antagonistic factions of British society, by teaching respect for beauty and intellect—what Arnold termed the virtues of "sweetness and light."

The mocking irony, Olympian assurance, and lucid, cascading style of these works make them exhilarating—or exasperating—reading. Arnold's high-minded attitudes enraged many of his opponents, and his loftiness of tone led even his friends and family to nickname him "the Emperor." For Arnold, education was a lifelong task, and few measured up to the cosmopolitan, European standards he set. He was particularly savage with anyone he considered guilty of self-interest or fuzzy thinking, and he attacked politicians and bishops by name. Leslie Stephen, Virginia Woolf's father, remarked satirically that "I often wished . . . that I too had a little sweetness and light that I might be able to say such nasty things of my enemies."

In the 1870s, Arnold scandalized many people with his attacks on orthodox religion in *St. Paul and Protestantism* (1870), *Literature and Dogma* (1873), and *God and the Bible* (1875). In *The Study of Poetry* (1880), he went so far as to argue that "most of what now passes for religion and philosophy will be replaced by poetry."

In 1883, weary, in debt, and desperate to retire, Arnold tried to raise money by selecting, with his daughter Nelly, 365 mottoes to create a *Matthew Arnold Birthday Book*. In the same year he went on a money-making lecture tour of the United States, meeting with mixed success. The chief intellectual product of his travel was *Discourses in America* (1885), which contained his essay *Literature and Science*. There, Arnold defended the idea of a liberal arts education founded on ancient and modern literatures against Thomas Huxley's contention in *Science and Culture* (1881) that an education based on the natural sciences would do just as well. Arnold felt that the debate had particular relevance for Americans, whose respect for "the average man" was fraught with "danger to the ideal of a high and rare excellence," best conveyed by a humanistic education. Arnold died suddenly of a heart attack in 1888.

Arnold was not a prophetic critic like Carlyle, nor a visionary poet of social reform like Elizabeth Barrett Browning, nor a moral crusader like Dickens. Instead, Arnold offered thoughtful prescriptions for guiding a changing and increasingly democratic society to a fuller understanding of its problems, and a more effective realization of its goals. As a school inspector he developed a deeper understanding of ineffective institutions and the ignorance of the British public than any other important Victorian author. While few have agreed fully with his pronouncements on literature and society, he has influenced almost every significant English-speaking critic since his time, including T. S. Eliot, F. R. Leavis, Lionel Trilling, and Raymond Williams.

Arnold has remained a literary force to be reckoned with as well. In its honest, introspective, sometimes awkward way, Arnold's poetry speaks unforgettably of the anxieties of his era. Though he saw himself as having "less poetical sentiment than Tennyson, and less intellectual vigor and abundance than Browning," he felt that his more balanced "fusion" of these qualities would continue to assure him an audience. His open approach to his innermost feelings is echoed almost everywhere in modern poetry.

Dover Beach

The sea is calm to-night.
The tide is full, the moon lies fair
Upon the straits; on the French coast the light
Gleams and is gone; the cliffs of England stand,
5 Glimmering and vast, out in the tranquil bay.
Come to the window, sweet is the night-air!
Only, from the long line of spray
Where the sea meets the moon-blanched land,
Listen! you hear the grating roar
10 Of pebbles which the waves draw back, and fling,
At their return, up the high strand,
Begin, and cease, and then again begin,
With tremulous cadence slow, and bring
The eternal note of sadness in.

15 Sophocles long ago
Heard it on the Aegean,[1] and it brought
Into his mind the turbid ebb and flow
Of human misery; we
Find also in the sound a thought,
20 Hearing it by this distant northern sea.

The Sea of Faith
Was once, too, at the full, and round earth's shore
Lay like the folds of a bright girdle° furled.   *sash*
But now I only hear
25 Its melancholy, long, withdrawing roar,
Retreating, to the breath
Of the night-wind, down the vast edges drear
And naked shingles° of the world.   *pebble beaches*

Ah, love, let us be true
30 To one another! for the world, which seems
To lie before us like a land of dreams,
So various, so beautiful, so new,
Hath really neither joy, nor love, nor light,
Nor certitude, nor peace, nor help for pain;
35 And we are here as on a darkling plain
Swept with confused alarms of struggle and flight,
Where ignorant armies clash by night.

c. 1851   1867

1. Sophocles was a 5th century B.C. Greek dramatist; the Aegean Sea lies between Greece and Turkey.

The Buried Life

Light flows our war of mocking words, and yet,
Behold, with tears mine eyes are wet!
I feel a nameless sadness o'er me roll.
Yes, yes, we know that we can jest,
5 We know, we know that we can smile!
But there's a something in this breast,
To which thy light words bring no rest,
And thy gay smiles no anodyne.
Give me thy hand, and hush awhile,
10 And turn those limpid eyes on mine,
And let me read there, love! thy inmost soul.

Alas! is even love too weak
To unlock the heart, and let it speak?
Are even lovers powerless to reveal
15 To one another what indeed they feel?
I knew the mass of men concealed
Their thoughts, for fear that if revealed
They would by other men be met
With blank indifference, or with blame reproved;
20 I knew they lived and moved
Tricked in disguises, alien to the rest
Of men, and alien to themselves—and yet
The same heart beats in every human breast!

But we, my love!—doth a like spell benumb
25 Our hearts, our voices? must we too be dumb?

Ah! well for us, if even we,
Even for a moment, can get free
Our heart, and have our lips unchained;
For that which seals them hath been deep-ordained!

30 Fate, which foresaw
How frivolous a baby man would be—
By what distractions he would be possessed,

How he would pour himself in every strife,
And well-nigh change his own identity—
35 That it might keep from his capricious play
His genuine self, and force him to obey
Even in his own despite his being's law,
Bade through the deep recesses of our breast
The unregarded river of our life
40 Pursue with indiscernible flow its way;
And that we should not see
The buried stream, and seem to be
Eddying at large in blind uncertainty,
Though driving on with it eternally.

45 But often, in the world's most crowded streets,
But often, in the din of strife,
There rises an unspeakable desire
After the knowledge of our buried life;

	A thirst to spend our fire and restless force
50	In tracking out our true, original course;
	A longing to inquire
	Into the mystery of this heart which beats
	So wild, so deep in us—to know
	Whence our lives come and where they go.
55	And many a man in his own breast then delves,
	But deep enough, alas! none ever mines.
	And we have been on many thousand lines,
	And we have shown, on each, spirit and power;
	But hardly have we, for one little hour,
60	Been on our own line, have we been ourselves—
	Hardly had skill to utter one of all
	The nameless feelings that course through our breast,
	But they course on for ever unexpressed.
	And long we try in vain to speak and act
65	Our hidden self, and what we say and do
	Is eloquent, is well—but 'tis not true!
	And then we will no more be racked
	With inward striving, and demand
	Of all the thousand nothings of the hour
70	Their stupefying power;
	Ah yes, and they benumb us at our call!
	Yet still, from time to time, vague and forlorn,
	From the soul's subterranean depth upborne
	As from an infinitely distant land,
75	Come airs, and floating echoes, and convey
	A melancholy into all our day.

	Only—but this is rare—
	When a belovéd hand is laid in ours,
	When, jaded with the rush and glare
80	Of the interminable hours,
	Our eyes can in another's eyes read clear,
	When our world-deafened ear
	Is by the tones of a loved voice caressed—
	A bolt is shot back somewhere in our breast,
85	And a lost pulse of feeling stirs again.
	The eye sinks inward, and the heart lies plain,
	And what we mean, we say, and what we would, we know.
	A man becomes aware of his life's flow,
	And hears its winding murmur; and he sees
90	The meadows where it glides, the sun, the breeze.

	And there arrives a lull in the hot race
	Wherein he doth for ever chase
	That flying and elusive shadow, rest.
	An air of coolness plays upon his face,
95	And an unwonted calm pervades his breast.
	And then he thinks he knows
	The hills where his life rose,
	And the sea where it goes.

1852

The Scholar-Gipsy

While at Oxford in the mid-1840s, Arnold read the seventeenth-century tale of a young man who left his studies at the university to join a band of gypsies, intending to master their lore. Fascinated by the story, Arnold imagined the scholar still wandering the hills around Oxford, magically untouched by time and change. The poem Arnold eventually wrote, circa 1853, celebrated his own youth at Oxford, "the *freest* and most delightful part, perhaps, of my life," he told his brother Tom, "when with you and Clough . . . I shook off all the bonds and formalities of the place, and enjoyed the spring of life and that unforgotten Oxfordshire and Berkshire country." Arnold accompanied the poem with a note based on his source, Joseph Glanvill's *Vanity of Dogmatizing* (1661):

> There was very lately a lad in the University of Oxford, who was by his poverty forced to leave his studies there; and at last to join himself to a company of vagabond gipsies. Among these extravagant people, by the insinuating subtilty of his carriage, he quickly got so much of their love and esteem as that they discovered to him their mystery. After he had been a pretty while well exercised in the trade, there chanced to ride by a couple of scholars, who had formerly been of his acquaintance. They quickly spied out their old friend among the gipsies; and he gave them an account of the necessity which drove him to that kind of life, and told them that the people he went with were not such impostors as they were taken for, but that they had a traditional kind of learning among them, and could do wonders by the power of imagination, their fancy binding that of others: that himself had learned much of their art, and when he had compassed the whole secret, he intended, he said, to leave their company, and give the world an account of what he had learned.

The Scholar-Gipsy

Go, for they call you, shepherd, from the hill;
    Go, shepherd, and untie the wattled cotes!¹
      No longer leave thy wistful flock unfed,
    Nor let thy bawling fellows rack their throats,
5   Nor the cropped herbage shoot another head.
        But when the fields are still,
    And the tired men and dogs all gone to rest,
      And only the white sheep are sometimes seen
      Cross and recross the strips of moon-blanched green,
10   Come, shepherd, and again begin the quest!

Here, where the reaper was at work of late—
    In this high field's dark corner, where he leaves
      His coat, his basket, and his earthen cruse,°   *jug*
    And in the sun all morning binds the sheaves,
15   Then here, at noon, comes back his stores to use—
        Here will I sit and wait,
    While to my ear from uplands far away
      The bleating of the folded° flocks is borne,   *penned up*
      With distant cries of reapers in the corn—
20   All the live murmur of a summer's day.

Screened is this nook o'er the high, half-reaped field,
    And here till sun-down, shepherd! will I be.
      Through the thick corn the scarlet poppies peep,

---

1. Fences made of woven sticks, used to pen sheep.

And round green roots and yellowing stalks I see
25   Pale pink convolvulus° in tendrils creep;   *morning glory*
    And air-swept lindens yield
Their scent, and rustle down their perfumed showers
Of bloom on the bent grass where I am laid,
And bower me from the August sun with shade;
30 And the eye travels down to Oxford's towers.

And near me on the grass lies Glanvil's book—
    Come, let me read the oft-read tale again!
    The story of the Oxford scholar poor,
Of pregnant parts° and quick inventive brain,   *bursting with ideas*
35   Who, tired of knocking at preferment's door,
    One summer-morn forsook
His friends, and went to learn the gipsy-lore,
And roamed the world with that wild brotherhood,
And came, as most men deemed, to little good,
40 But came to Oxford and his friends no more.

But once, years after, in the country-lanes,
    Two scholars, whom at college erst he knew,
    Met him, and of his way of life enquired;
Whereat he answered, that the gipsy-crew,
45   His mates, had arts to rule as they desired
    The workings of men's brains,
And they can bind them to what thoughts they will.
    "And I," he said, "the secret of their art,
    When fully learned, will to the world impart;
50 But it needs heaven-sent moments for this skill."

This said, he left them, and returned no more.
    But rumours hung about the country-side,
    That the lost Scholar long was seen to stray,
Seen by rare glimpses, pensive and tongue-tied,
55   In hat of antique shape, and cloak of grey,
    The same the gipsies wore.
Shepherds had met him on the Hurst[2] in spring;
    At some lone alehouse in the Berkshire moors,
    On the warm ingle-bench, the smock-frocked boors[3]
60 Had found him seated at their entering,

But, 'mid their drink and clatter, he would fly.
    And I myself seem half to know thy looks,
    And put the shepherds, wanderer! on thy trace;
And boys who in lone wheatfields scare the rooks
65   I ask if thou hast passed their quiet place;
    Or in my boat I lie
Moored to the cool bank in the summer-heats,
    'Mid wide grass meadows which the sunshine fills,
    And watch the warm, green-muffled Cumner hills,
70 And wonder if thou haunt'st their shy retreats.

2. Hill near Oxford; most of the places mentioned are in the countryside around Oxford.

3. Rustic peasants; an ingle-bench is beside the fireplace.

For most, I know, thou lov'st retiréd ground!
  Thee at the ferry Oxford riders blithe,
    Returning home on summer-nights, have met
  Crossing the stripling Thames at Bab-lock-hithe,
75   Trailing in the cool stream thy fingers wet,
      As the punt's° rope chops round;   *small boat*
  And leaning backward in a pensive dream,
    And fostering in thy lap a heap of flowers
    Plucked in shy fields and distant Wychwood bowers,
80 And thine eyes resting on the moonlit stream.

And then they land, and thou art seen no more!
  Maidens, who from the distant hamlets come
    To dance around the Fyfield elm in May,
  Oft through the darkening fields have seen thee roam,
85   Or cross a stile into the public way.
      Oft thou hast given them store
  Of flowers—the frail-leafed, white anemone,
    Dark bluebells drenched with dews of summer eves,
    And purple orchises with spotted leaves—
90 But none hath words she can report of thee.

And, above Godstow Bridge, when hay-time's here
  In June, and many a scythe in sunshine flames,
    Men who through those wide fields of breezy grass
  Where black-winged swallows haunt the glittering Thames,
95   To bathe in the abandoned lasher pass,[4]
      Have often passed thee near
  Sitting upon the river bank o'ergrown;
    Marked thine outlandish garb, thy figure spare,
    Thy dark vague eyes, and soft abstracted air—
100 But, when they came from bathing, thou wast gone!

At some lone homestead in the Cumner hills,
  Where at her open door the housewife darns,
    Thou hast been seen, or hanging on a gate
  To watch the threshers in the mossy barns.
105   Children, who early range these slopes and late
      For cresses from the rills,
  Have known thee eying, all an April-day,
    The springing pastures and the feeding kine;
    And marked thee, when the stars come out and shine,
110 Through the long dewy grass move slow away.

In autumn, on the skirts of Bagley Wood—
  Where most the gipsies by the turf-edged way
    Pitch their smoked tents, and every bush you see
  With scarlet patches tagged and shreds of grey,[5]
115   Above the forest-ground called Thessaly—
      The blackbird, picking food,
  Sees thee, nor stops his meal, nor fears at all;

---

4. Pool where water spilling over a dam collects.   5. Gypsies spread their clothes on bushes to dry.

So often has he known thee past him stray,
Rapt, twirling in thy hand a withered spray,
120   And waiting for the spark from heaven to fall.

And once, in winter, on the causeway chill
Where home through flooded fields foot-travellers go,
Have I not passed thee on the wooden bridge,
Wrapped in thy cloak and battling with the snow,
125   Thy face tow'rd Hinksey and its wintry ridge?
And thou hast climbed the hill,
And gained the white brow of the Cumner range;
Turned once to watch, while thick the snowflakes fall,
The line of festal light in Christ-Church hall[6]—
130   Then sought thy straw in some sequestered grange.

But what—I dream! Two hundred years are flown
Since first thy story ran through Oxford halls,
And the grave Glanvil did the tale inscribe
That thou wert wandered from the studious walls
135   To learn strange arts, and join a gipsy-tribe;
And thou from earth art gone
Long since, and in some quiet churchyard laid—
Some country-nook, where o'er thy unknown grave
Tall grasses and white flowering nettles wave,
140   Under a dark, red-fruited yew-tree's shade.

—No, no, thou hast not felt the lapse of hours!
For what wears out the life of mortal men?
'Tis that from change to change their being rolls;
'Tis that repeated shocks, again, again,
145   Exhaust the energy of strongest souls
And numb the elastic powers.
Till having used our nerves with bliss and teen,°   grief
And tired upon a thousand schemes our wit,
To the just-pausing Genius[7] we remit
150   Our worn-out life, and are—what we have been.

Thou hast not lived, why should'st thou perish, so?
Thou hadst *one* aim, *one* business, *one* desire;
Else wert thou long since numbered with the dead!
Else hadst thou spent, like other men, thy fire!
155   The generations of thy peers are fled,
And we ourselves shall go;
But thou possessest an immortal lot,
And we imagine thee exempt from age
And living as thou liv'st on Glanvil's page,
160   Because thou hadst—what we, alas! have not.

For early didst thou leave the world, with powers
Fresh, undiverted to the world without,
Firm to their mark, not spent on other things;
Free from the sick fatigue, the languid doubt,

6. The dining hall of Christ Church, an Oxford college.
7. The guardian spirit that the ancients believed accompanied a person through life; here it pauses for only a
moment to receive back the life it has shepherded.

165 Which much to have tried, in much been baffled, brings.
　　　O life unlike to ours!
　　Who fluctuate idly without term or scope,
　　　Of whom each strives, nor knows for what he strives,
　　　And each half-lives a hundred different lives;
170 　Who wait like thee, but not, like thee, in hope.

　Thou waitest for the spark from heaven! and we,
　　Light half-believers of our casual creeds,
　　　Who never deeply felt, nor clearly willed,
　　Whose insight never has borne fruit in deeds,
175 　Whose vague resolves never have been fulfilled;
　　　For whom each year we see
　　Breeds new beginnings, disappointments new;
　　　Who hesitate and falter life away,
　　　And lose to-morrow the ground won to-day—
180 Ah! do not we, wanderer! await it too?

Yes, we await it!—but it still delays,
　　And then we suffer! and amongst us one,[8]
　　　Who most has suffered, takes dejectedly
　　His seat upon the intellectual throne;
185 　And all his store of sad experience he
　　　Lays bare of wretched days;
　　Tells us his misery's birth and growth and signs,
　　　And how the dying spark of hope was fed,
　　　And how the breast was soothed, and how the head,
190 And all his hourly varied anodynes.

This for our wisest! and we others pine,
　　And wish the long unhappy dream would end,
　　　And waive all claim to bliss, and try to bear;
　　With close-lipped patience for our only friend,
195 　Sad patience, too near neighbour to despair—
　　　But none has hope like thine!
　　Thou through the fields and through the woods dost stray,
　　　Roaming the country-side, a truant boy,
　　　Nursing thy project in unclouded joy,
200 And every doubt long blown by time away.

O born in days when wits were fresh and clear,
　　And life ran gaily as the sparkling Thames;
　　　Before this strange disease of modern life,
　　With its sick hurry, its divided aims,
205 　Its heads o'ertaxed, its palsied hearts, was rife—
　　　Fly hence, our contact fear!
　　Still fly, plunge deeper in the bowering wood!
　　　Averse, as Dido did with gesture stern
　　　From her false friend's approach in Hades turn,[9]
210 Wave us away, and keep thy solitude!

8. Either Goethe, whom Arnold admired, or Tennyson, whose *In Memoriam* had recently been published.
9. In Virgil's *Aeneid*, Dido, queen of Carthage, kills herself after her lover, Aeneas, deserts her. When they meet in Hades, she turns away sternly.

Still nursing the unconquerable hope,
  Still clutching the inviolable shade,
    With a free, onward impulse brushing through,
  By night, the silvered branches of the glade—
215   Far on the forest-skirts, where none pursue,
      On some mild pastoral slope
Emerge, and resting on the moonlit pales
  Freshen thy flowers as in former years
  With dew, or listen with enchanted ears,
220 From the dark dingles,° to the nightingales!   *small wooded valleys*

But fly our paths, our feverish contact fly!
  For strong the infection of our mental strife,
    Which, though it gives no bliss, yet spoils for rest;
  And we should win thee from thy own fair life,
225   Like us distracted, and like us unblest.
      Soon, soon thy cheer would die,
Thy hopes grow timorous, and unfixed thy powers,
  And thy clear aims be cross and shifting made;
  And then thy glad perennial youth would fade,
230 Fade, and grow old at last, and die like ours.

Then fly our greetings, fly our speech and smiles!
  —As some grave Tyrian trader,[1] from the sea,
    Descried at sunrise an emerging prow
Lifting the cool-haired creepers stealthily,
235   The fringes of a southward-facing brow
      Among the Aegean isles;
And saw the merry Grecian coaster come,
  Freighted with amber grapes, and Chian wine,
  Green, bursting figs, and tunnies steeped in brine—
240 And knew the intruders on his ancient home,

The young light-hearted masters of the waves—
  And snatched his rudder, and shook out more sail;
    And day and night held on indignantly
O'er the blue Midland waters with the gale,
245   Betwixt the Syrtes[2] and soft Sicily,
      To where the Atlantic raves
Outside the western straits; and unbent sails
  There, where down cloudy cliffs, through sheets of foam,
  Shy traffickers, the dark Iberians come;
250 And on the beach undid his corded bales.[3]

c. 1853   1853

---

1. From Tyre, capital of ancient Phoenicia, in Northern Africa. The poet urges the solitary scholar to shun modern contacts just as he imagines the Tyrian trader once fled from intrusive Greeks.
2. Shoals off North Africa.
3. The last stanza continues the comparison between the scholar and the Tyrian. According to Herodotus's *History* 4.196, the Carthaginians—who came originally from Tyre—would sail out of the Mediterranean to West Africa,

place their bales on the beach, and withdraw to their ships. The timid inhabitants would then set gold by the goods, and withdraw in turn; thus the two sides could do business and never meet. Arnold's "shy traffickers" are not Africans but "dark Iberians" (Spanish or Portuguese). He implies that in them—people reminiscent of the dark-skinned reclusive gypsies who "trade" in the Oxford countryside—the sensitive Tyrian has found others as wary as he is.

from **Culture and Anarchy**[1]

from *Sweetness and Light*

The disparagers of culture make its motive curiosity; sometimes, indeed, they make its motive mere exclusiveness and vanity. The culture which is supposed to plume itself on a smattering of Greek and Latin is a culture which is begotten by nothing so intellectual as curiosity; it is valued either out of sheer vanity and ignorance or else as an engine of social and class distinction, separating its holder, like a badge or title, from other people who have not got it. No serious man would call this *culture*, or attach any value to it, as culture, at all. To find the real ground for the very different estimate which serious people will set upon culture, we must find some motive for culture in the terms of which may lie a real ambiguity; and such a motive the word *curiosity* gives us.

I have before now pointed out that we English do not, like the foreigners, use this word in a good sense as well as in a bad sense. With us the word is always used in a somewhat disapproving sense. A liberal and intelligent eagerness about the things of the mind may be meant by a foreigner when he speaks of curiosity, but with us the word always conveys a certain notion of frivolous and unedifying activity. In the *Quarterly Review*, some little time ago, was an estimate of the celebrated French critic, M. Sainte-Beuve,[2] and a very inadequate estimate it in my judgment was. And its inadequacy consisted chiefly in this: that in our English way it left out of sight the double sense really involved in the word *curiosity*, thinking enough was said to stamp M. Sainte-Beuve with blame if it was said that he was impelled in his operations as a critic by curiosity, and omitting either to perceive that M. Sainte-Beuve himself, and many other people with him, would consider that this was praiseworthy and not blameworthy, or to point out why it ought really to be accounted worthy of blame and not of praise. For as there is a curiosity about intellectual matters which is futile, and merely a disease, so there is certainly a curiosity,—a desire after the things of the mind simply for their own sakes and for the pleasure of seeing them as they are,— which is, in an intelligent being, natural and laudable. Nay, and the very desire to see things as they are implies a balance and regulation of mind which is not often attained without fruitful effort, and which is the very opposite of the blind and diseased impulse of mind which is what we mean to blame when we blame curiosity. Montesquieu[3] says: "The first motive which ought to impel us to study is the desire to augment the excellence of our nature, and to render an intelligent being yet more intelligent." This is the true ground to assign for the genuine scientific passion, however manifested, and for culture, viewed simply as a fruit of this passion; and it is a worthy ground, even though we let the term *curiosity* stand to describe it.

But there is of culture another view, in which not solely the scientific passion, the sheer desire to see things as they are, natural and proper in an intelligent being,

1. Arnold's most important work of social criticism, *Culture and Anarchy* (1869) grew out of his final Oxford lecture in 1867. Deploring English pride in "doing as one likes," Arnold connected the self-serving behavior of all classes to the worst effects of laissez-faire capitalism. He felt that Britain was heading toward anarchy; no one seemed to have any concern for the public good. The best of Western culture, Arnold contended, depends on a balance between the Judeo-Christian emphasis on moral conduct (Hebraism), and the Greek ideal of intellectual and artistic cultivation (Hellenism). But in his view a Puritan "strictness of conscience" was now impeding a classical "spontaneity of consciousness." There was only one way to bridge the gap between privileged "Barbarians" (the aristocracy), intolerant "Philistines" (the middle classes), and the uneducated "Populace" (the working classes): by spreading to all parts of society a Hellenistic respect for beauty and intellect—what Arnold termed "sweetness and light."

2. Charles Augustine Sainte-Beuve (1804–1869), French critic whom Arnold admired.

3. Baron de la Brede et de Montesquieu (1689–1755), French political and legal philosopher.

appears as the ground of it. There is a view in which all the love of our neighbour, the impulses towards action, help, and beneficence, the desire for removing human error, clearing human confusion, and diminishing human misery, the noble aspiration to leave the world better and happier than we found it,—motives eminently such as are called social,—come in as part of the grounds of culture, and the main and pre-eminent part. Culture is then properly described not as having its origin in curiosity, but as having its origin in the love of perfection; it is *a study of perfection*. It moves by the force, not merely or primarily of the scientific passion for pure knowledge, but also of the moral and social passion for doing good. As, in the first view of it, we took for its worthy motto Montesquieu's words: "To render an intelligent being yet more intelligent!" so, in the second view of it, there is no better motto which it can have than these words of Bishop Wilson: "To make reason and the will of God prevail!"[4] * * *

The pursuit of perfection, then, is the pursuit of sweetness and light.[5] He who works for sweetness and light, works to make reason and the will of God prevail. He who works for machinery, he who works for hatred, works only for confusion. Culture looks beyond machinery, culture hates hatred; culture has one great passion, the passion for sweetness and light. It has one even yet greater!—the passion for making them *prevail*. It is not satisfied till we *all* come to a perfect man; it knows that the sweetness and light of the few must be imperfect until the raw and unkindled masses of humanity are touched with sweetness and light. If I have not shrunk from saying that we must work for sweetness and light, so neither have I shrunk from saying that we must have a broad basis, must have sweetness and light for as many as possible. Again and again I have insisted how those are the happy moments of humanity, how those are the marking epochs of a people's life, how those are the flowering times for literature and art and all the creative power of genius, when there is a *national* glow of life and thought, when the whole of society is in the fullest measure permeated by thought, sensible to beauty, intelligent and alive. Only it must be *real* thought and *real* beauty; *real* sweetness and *real* light. Plenty of people will try to give the masses, as they call them, an intellectual food prepared and adapted in the way they think proper for the actual condition of the masses. The ordinary popular literature is an example of this way of working on the masses. Plenty of people will try to indoctrinate the masses with the set of ideas and judgments constituting the creed of their own profession or party. Our religious and political organisations give an example of this way of working on the masses. I condemn neither way; but culture works differently. It does not try to teach down to the level of inferior classes; it does not try to win them for this or that sect of its own, with ready-made judgments and watchwords. It seeks to do away with classes; to make the best that has been thought and known in the world current everywhere; to make all men live in an atmosphere of sweetness and light, where they may use ideas, as it uses them itself, freely,—nourished, and not bound by them.

This is the *social idea;* and the men of culture are the true apostles of equality. The great men of culture are those who have had a passion for diffusing, for making prevail, for carrying from one end of society to the other, the best knowledge, the best

---

4. Thomas Wilson (1663–1755), Bishop of Sodor and Man. His *Maxims,* though little known, were a favorite of Arnold's.
5. The phrase comes from a fable in Swift's *The Battle of the Books* (1704): the Bee (representing ancient culture) ventures forth to fill its hive with honey and wax for light-giving candles, but the home-bound Spider (representing modern culture) produces from itself only cobwebs and poison. The Bee thus provides "the two noblest of things, which are sweetness and light."

ideas of their time; who have laboured to divest knowledge of all that was harsh, uncouth, difficult, abstract, professional, exclusive; to humanise it, to make it efficient outside the clique of the cultivated and learned, yet still remaining the *best* knowledge and thought of the time, and a true source, therefore, of sweetness and light. Such a man was Abelard in the Middle Ages, in spite of all his imperfections;[6] and thence the boundless emotion and enthusiasm which Abelard excited. Such were Lessing and Herder in Germany, at the end of the last century;[7] and their services to Germany were in this way inestimably precious. Generations will pass, and literary monuments will accumulate, and works far more perfect than the works of Lessing and Herder will be produced in Germany; and yet the names of these two men will fill a German with a reverence and enthusiasm such as the names of the most gifted masters will hardly awaken. And why? Because they *humanised* knowledge; because they broadened the basis of life and intelligence; because they worked powerfully to diffuse sweetness and light, to make reason and the will of God prevail. With Saint Augustine they said: "Let us not leave thee alone to make in the secret of thy knowledge, as thou didst before the creation of the firmament, the division of light from darkness; let the children of thy spirit, placed in their firmament, make their light shine upon the earth, mark the division of night and day, and announce the revolution of the times; for the old order is passed, and the new arises; the night is spent, the day is come forth; and thou shalt crown the year with thy blessing, when thou shalt send forth labourers into thy harvest sown by other hands than theirs; when thou shalt send forth new labourers to new seed-times, whereof the harvest shall be not yet."[8]

from *Doing as One Likes*

I have been trying to show that culture is, or ought to be, the study and pursuit of perfection; and that of perfection as pursued by culture, beauty and intelligence, or, in other words, sweetness and light, are the main characters. But hitherto I have been insisting chiefly on beauty, or sweetness, as a character of perfection. To complete rightly my design, it evidently remains to speak also of intelligence, or light, as a character of perfection.

First, however, I ought perhaps to notice that, both here and on the other side of the Atlantic, all sorts of objections are raised against the "religion of culture," as the objectors mockingly call it, which I am supposed to be promulgating. It is said to be a religion proposing parmaceti,[1] or some scented salve or other, as a cure for human miseries; a religion breathing a spirit of cultivated inaction, making its believer refuse to lend a hand at uprooting the definite evils on all sides of us, and filling him with antipathy against the reforms and reformers which try to extirpate them. In general, it is summed up as being not practical, or,—as some critics familiarly put it,—all moonshine. That Alcibiades, the editor of the *Morning Star*,[2] taunts me, as its promulgator, with living out of the world and knowing nothing of life and men. That great austere toiler, the editor of the *Daily Telegraph*, upbraids me,—but kindly, and

6. Peter Abelard (1079–1142), French philosopher and theologian, whose love affair with his student, Héloise, ended tragically.
7. Gotthold Ephraim Lessing (1729–1781), critic and playwright, an important figure in the development of German Naturalism; Johann Gottfried Herder (1744–1803), critic and historian, a proponent of literary and historical relativism.
8. *Confessions* (xiii.18) of St. Augustine (354–430),

Bishop of Hippo, Church father, theologian, and autobiographer.
1. Spermaceti, derived from the oil of the sperm whale, was used in ointments and cosmetics.
2. A penny paper representing the Radicals' position, of which Arnold disapproved. He ironically compares the paper's puritan editor with the dissolute but brilliant Alcibiades, who led the Athenians during the Peloponnesian War.

more in sorrow than in anger,—for trifling with aesthetics and poetical fancies, while he himself, in that arsenal of his in Fleet Street,[3] is bearing the burden and heat of the day. An intelligent American newspaper, the *Nation*, says that it is very easy to sit in one's study and find fault with the course of modern society, but the thing is to propose practical improvements for it. While, finally, Mr Frederic Harrison, in a very good-tempered and witty satire, which makes me quite understand his having apparently achieved such a conquest of my young Prussian friend, Arminius, at last gets moved to an almost stern moral impatience, to behold, as he says, "Death, sin, cruelty stalk among us, filling their maws with innocence and youth," and me, in the midst of the general tribulation, handing out my pouncet-box.[4]

It is impossible that all these remonstrances and reproofs should not affect me, and I shall try my very best, in completing my design and in speaking of light as one of the characters of perfection, and of culture as giving us light, to profit by the objections I have heard and read, and to drive at practice as much as I can, by showing the communications and passages into practical life from the doctrine which I am inculcating.

It is said that a man with my theories of sweetness and light is full of antipathy against the rougher or coarser movements going on around him, that he will not lend a hand to the humble operation of uprooting evil by their means, and that therefore the believers in action grow impatient with him. But what if rough and coarse action, ill-calculated action, action with insufficient light, is, and has for a long time been, our bane? What if our urgent want now is, not to act at any price, but rather to lay in a stock of light for our difficulties? In that case, to refuse to lend a hand to the rougher and coarser movements going on round us, to make the primary need, both for oneself and others, to consist in enlightening ourselves and qualifying ourselves to act less at random, is surely the best and in real truth the most practical line our endeavours can take. So that if I can show what my opponents call rough or coarse action, but what I would rather call random and ill-regulated action,—action with insufficient light, action pursued because we like to be doing something and doing it as we please, and do not like the trouble of thinking and the severe constraint of any kind of rule,—if I can show this to be, at the present moment, a practical mischief and dangerous to us, then I have found a practical use for light in correcting this state of things, and have only to exemplify how, in cases which fall under everybody's observation, it may deal with it.

When I began to speak of culture, I insisted on our bondage to machinery, on our proneness to value machinery as an end in itself, without looking beyond it to the end for which alone, in truth, it is valuable. Freedom, I said, was one of those things which we thus worshipped in itself, without enough regarding the ends for which freedom is to be desired. In our common notions and talk about freedom, we eminently show our idolatry of machinery. Our prevalent notion is,—and I quoted a number of instances to prove it,—that it is a most happy and important thing for a man merely to be able to do as he likes. On what he is to do when he is thus free to do as he likes, we do not lay so much stress. Our familiar praise of the British Constitution under which we live, is that it is a system of checks,—a system which stops

---

3. Location of most British newspaper offices.
4. Frederic Harrison, barrister and supporter of working-class causes, satirized Arnold's ideas in "Culture, A Dialogue" (*Fortnightly*, Nov. 1867). In his article Harrison pretended to discuss social issues with "Arminius," a fic-   tional Prussian whom Arnold had created in *Friendship's Garland* (1866–1871). Harrison compares Arnold to the foppish courtier in *Henry IV, Part 1*, who uses parmaceti salve and a perfume or "pouncet" box (1.3.37,58).

and paralyses any power in interfering with the free action of individuals. To this effect Mr Bright,[5] who loves to walk in the old ways of the Constitution, said forcibly in one of his great speeches, what many other people are every day saying less forcibly, that the central idea of English life and politics is *the assertion of personal liberty*. Evidently this is so; but evidently, also, as feudalism, which with its ideas and habits of subordination was for many centuries silently behind the British Constitution, dies out, and we are left with nothing but our system of checks, and our notion of its being the great right and happiness of an Englishman to do as far as possible what he likes, we are in danger of drifting towards anarchy. We have not the notion, so familiar on the Continent and to antiquity, of *the State*,—the nation in its collective and corporate character, entrusted with stringent powers for the general advantage, and controlling individual wills in the name of an interest wider than that of individuals. We say, what is very true, that this notion is often made instrumental to tyranny; we say that a State is in reality made up of the individuals who compose it, and that every individual is the best judge of his own interests. Our leading class is an aristocracy, and no aristocracy likes the notion of a State-authority greater than itself, with a stringent administrative machinery superseding the decorative inutilities of lord-lieutenancy, deputy-lieutenancy, and the *posse comitatus*,[6] which are all in its own hands. Our middle class, the great representative of trade and Dissent, with its maxims of every man for himself in business, every man for himself in religion, dreads a powerful administration which might somehow interfere with it; and besides, it has its own decorative inutilities of vestrymanship and guardianship, which are to this class what lord-lieutenancy and the county magistracy are to the aristocratic class, and a stringent administration might either take these functions out of its hands, or prevent its exercising them in its own comfortable, independent manner, as at present.

Then as to our working class. This class, pressed constantly by the hard daily compulsion of material wants, is naturally the very centre and stronghold of our national idea, that it is man's ideal right and felicity to do as he likes. I think I have somewhere related how M. Michelet said to me of the people of France, that it was "a nation of barbarians civilised by the conscription."[7] He meant that through their military service the idea of public duty and of discipline was brought to the mind of these masses, in other respects so raw and uncultivated. Our masses are quite as raw and uncultivated as the French; and so far from their having the idea of public duty and of discipline, superior to the individual's self-will, brought to their mind by a universal obligation of military service, such as that of the conscription,—so far from their having this, the very idea of a conscription is so at variance with our English notion of the prime right and blessedness of doing as one likes, that I remember the manager of the Clay Cross works in Derbyshire told me during the Crimean war, when our want of soldiers was much felt and some people were talking of a conscription, that sooner than submit to a conscription the population of that district would flee to the mines, and lead a sort of Robin Hood life under ground.

For a long time, as I have said, the strong feudal habits of subordination and deference continued to tell upon the working class. The modern spirit has now almost

---

5. John Bright (1811–1889), Quaker radical who led the left wing of the Liberal Party under Gladstone.
6. Power of the county (Latin); a "posse" was an outdated method of preserving public order by local authority

rather than by the government.
7. From Arnold's *The Popular Education of France* (1861); Jules Michelet (1798–1874), French historian.

entirely dissolved those habits, and the anarchical tendency of our worship of freedom in and for itself, of our superstitious faith, as I say, in machinery, is becoming very manifest. More and more, because of this our blind faith in machinery, because of our want of light to enable us to look beyond machinery to the end for which machinery is valuable, this and that man, and this and that body of men, all over the country, are beginning to assert and put in practice an Englishman's right to do what he likes; his right to march where he likes, meet where he likes, enter where he likes, hoot as he likes, threaten as he likes, smash as he likes. All this, I say, tends to anarchy; and though a number of excellent people, and particularly my friends of the Liberal or progressive party, as they call themselves, are kind enough to reassure us by saying that these are trifles, that a few transient outbreaks of rowdyism signify nothing, that our system of liberty is one which itself cures all the evils which it works, that the educated and intelligent classes stand in overwhelming strength and majestic repose, ready, like our military force in riots, to act at a moment's notice,—yet one finds that one's Liberal friends generally say this because they have such faith in themselves and their nostrums,[8] when they shall return, as the public welfare requires, to place and power. But this faith of theirs one cannot exactly share, when one has so long had them and their nostrums at work, and sees that they have not prevented our coming to our present embarrassed condition. And one finds, also, that the outbreaks of rowdyism tend to become less and less of trifles, to become more frequent rather than less frequent; and that meanwhile our educated and intelligent classes remain in their majestic repose, and somehow or other, whatever happens, their overwhelming strength, like our military force in riots, never does act.

How, indeed, *should* their overwhelming strength act, when the man who gives an inflammatory lecture, or breaks down the park railings,[9] or invades a Secretary of State's office, is only following an Englishman's impulse to do as he likes; and our own conscience tells us that we ourselves have always regarded this impulse as something primary and sacred? Mr Murphy lectures at Birmingham,[1] and showers on the Catholic population of that town "words," says the Home Secretary, "only fit to be addressed to thieves or murderers." What then? Mr Murphy has his own reasons of several kinds. He suspects the Roman Catholic Church of designs upon Mrs Murphy; and he says if mayors and magistrates do not care for their wives and daughters, he does. But, above all, he is doing as he likes; or, in worthier language, asserting his personal liberty. "I will carry out my lectures if they walk over my body as a dead corpse; and I say to the Mayor of Birmingham that he is my servant while I am in Birmingham, and as my servant he must do his duty and protect me." Touching and beautiful words, which find a sympathetic chord in every British bosom! The moment it is plainly put before us that a man is asserting his personal liberty, we are half disarmed; because we are believers in freedom, and not in some dream of a right reason to which the assertion of our freedom is to be subordinated. Accordingly, the Secretary of State had to say that although the lecturer's language was "only fit to be addressed to thieves or murderers," yet, "I do not think he is to be deprived, I do not think that anything I have said could justify the inference that he is to be deprived, of the right of protection in a place built by him for the purpose of these lectures; because the

8. Panaceas, quack medicine.
9. On July 23, 1866, the Reform League organized a mass meeting in Hyde Park. When they were refused entrance, the demonstrators broke down the park railings and trampled the flowers. The incident was widely viewed as a

symptom of impending anarchy.
1. In 1867 William Murphy, an anti-Catholic agitator, delivered a series of lectures in Birmingham that led to riots.

language was not language which afforded grounds for a criminal prosecution." No, nor to be silenced by Mayor, or Home Secretary, or any administrative authority on earth, simply on their notion of what is discreet and reasonable! This is in perfect consonance with our public opinion, and with our national love for the assertion of personal liberty. * * *

There are many things to be said on behalf of this exclusive attention of ours to liberty, and of the relaxed habits of government which it has engendered. It is very easy to mistake or to exaggerate the sort of anarchy from which we are in danger through them. We are not in danger from Fenianism,[2] fierce and turbulent as it may show itself; for against this our conscience is free enough to let us act resolutely and put forth our overwhelming strength the moment there is any real need for it. In the first place, it never was any part of our creed that the great right and blessedness of an Irishman, or, indeed, of anybody on earth except an Englishman, is to do as he likes; and we can have no scruple at all about abridging, if necessary, a non-Englishman's assertion of personal liberty. The British Constitution, its checks, and its prime virtues, are for Englishmen. We may extend them to others out of love and kindness; but we find no real divine law written on our hearts constraining us so to extend them. And then the difference between an Irish Fenian and an English rough is so immense, and the case, in dealing with the Fenian, so much more clear! He is so evidently desperate and dangerous, a man of a conquered race, a Papist, with centuries of ill-usage to inflame him against us, with an alien religion established in his country by us at his expense, with no admiration of our institutions, no love of our virtues, no talents for our business, no turn for our comfort! Show him our symbolical Truss Manufactory on the finest site in Europe,[3] and tell him that British industrialism and individualism can bring a man to that, and he remains cold! Evidently, if we deal tenderly with a sentimentalist like this, it is out of pure philanthropy.

But with the Hyde Park rioter how different! He is our own flesh and blood; he is a Protestant; he is framed by nature to do as we do, hate what we hate, love what we love; he is capable of feeling the symbolical force of the Truss Manufactory; the question of questions, for him, is a wages question. That beautiful sentence Sir Daniel Gooch[4] quoted to the Swindon workmen, and which I treasure as Mrs Gooch's Golden Rule, or the Divine Injunction "Be ye Perfect" done into British,—the sentence Sir Daniel Gooch's mother repeated to him every morning when he was a boy going to work:—"*Ever remember, my dear Dan, that you should look forward to being some day manager of that concern!*"—this fruitful maxim is perfectly fitted to shine forth in the heart of the Hyde Park rough also, and to be his guiding-star through life. He has no visionary schemes of revolution and transformation, though of course he would like his class to rule, as the aristocratic class like their class to rule, and the middle class theirs. But meanwhile our social machine is a little out of order; there are a good many people in our paradisiacal centres of industrialism and individualism taking the bread out of one another's mouths. The rough has not yet quite found his groove and settled down to his work, and so he is just asserting his personal liberty a little, going where he likes, assembling where he likes, bawling as he likes, hustling as he likes. Just as the rest of us,—as the country squires in the aristocratic class, as the political dissenters in the middle class,—he has no idea of a *State*, of the nation in its collective and corporate character controlling, as government, the free swing of this or that

---

2. A movement dedicated to the overthrow of British rule in Ireland.
3. Coles' Truss Manufactory occupied a corner of Trafalgar Square, called "the finest site in Europe" by Sir

Robert Peel. A truss is a padded belt worn to support an abdominal rupture or hernia.
4. Sir Daniel Gooch (1816–1889), railway engineer and inventor, chairman of the Great Western Railway.

one of its members in the name of the higher reason of all of them, his own as well as that of others. He sees the rich, the aristocratic class, in occupation of the executive government, and so if he is stopped from making Hyde Park a bear-garden or the streets impassable, he says he is being butchered by the aristocracy.

His apparition is somewhat embarrassing, because too many cooks spoil the broth; because, while the aristocratic and middle classes have long been doing as they like with great vigour, he has been too undeveloped and submissive hitherto to join in the game; and now, when he does come, he comes in immense numbers, and is rather raw and rough. But he does not break many laws, or not many at one time; and, as our laws were made for very different circumstances from our present (but always with an eye to Englishmen doing as they like), and as the clear letter of the law must be against our Englishman who does as he likes and not only the spirit of the law and public policy, and as Government must neither have any discretionary power nor act resolutely on its own interpretation of the law if any one disputes it, it is evident our laws give our playful giant, in doing as he likes, considerable advantage. Besides, even if he can be clearly proved to commit an illegality in doing as he likes, there is always the resource of not putting the law in force, or of abolishing it. So he has his way, and if he has his way he is soon satisfied for the time. However, he falls into the habit of taking it oftener and oftener, and at last begins to create by his operations a confusion of which mischievous people can take advantage, and which, at any rate, by troubling the common course of business throughout the country, tends to cause distress, and so to increase the sort of anarchy and social disintegration which had previously commenced. And thus that profound sense of settled order and security, without which a society like ours cannot live and grow at all, sometimes seems to be beginning to threaten us with taking its departure.

Now, if culture, which simply means trying to perfect oneself, and one's mind as part of oneself, brings us light, and if light shows us that there is nothing so very blessed in merely doing as one likes, that the worship of the mere freedom to do as one likes is worship of machinery, that the really blessed thing is to like what right reason ordains, and to follow her authority, then we have got a practical benefit out of culture. We have got a much wanted principle, a principle of authority, to counteract the tendency to anarchy which seems to be threatening us. * * *

Well, then, what if we tried to rise above the idea of class to the idea of the whole community, *the State,* and to find our centre of light and authority there? Every one of us has the idea of country, as a sentiment; hardly any one of us has the idea of *the State,* as a working power. And why? Because we habitually live in our ordinary selves, which do not carry us beyond the ideas and wishes of the class to which we happen to belong. And we are all afraid of giving to the State too much power, because we only conceive of the State as something equivalent to the class in occupation of the executive government, and are afraid of that class abusing power to its own purposes. If we strengthen the State with the aristocratic class in occupation of the executive government, we imagine we are delivering ourselves up captive to the ideas and wishes of our fierce aristocratical baronet; if with the middle class in occupation of the executive government, to those of our truculent middle-class Dissenting minister;[5] if with the working class, to those of its notorious tribune, Mr Bradlaugh.[6] And with much justice; owing to the exaggerated notion which we English, as I have said, entertain of the right and blessedness of the mere doing as one

---

5. Rev. William Cattle, chairman at William Murphy's anti-Catholic lectures (see page 2034, n. 1).

6. Charles Bradlaugh, radical agitator, eventually the first aetheist Member of Parliament.

likes, of the affirming oneself, and oneself just as it is. People of the aristocratic class want to affirm their ordinary selves, their likings and dislikings; people of the middle class the same, people of the working class the same. By our everyday selves, however, we are separate, personal, at war; we are only safe from one another's tyranny when no one has any power; and this safety, in its turn, cannot save us from anarchy. And when, therefore, anarchy presents itself as a danger to us, we know not where to turn.

But by our *best self* we are united, impersonal, at harmony. We are in no peril from giving authority to this, because it is the truest friend we all of us can have; and when anarchy is a danger to us, to this authority we may turn with sure trust. Well, and this is the very self which culture, or the study of perfection, seeks to develop in us; at the expense of our old untransformed self, taking pleasure only in doing what it likes or is used to do, and exposing us to the risk of clashing with every one else who is doing the same! So that our poor culture, which is flouted as so unpractical, leads us to the very ideas capable of meeting the great want of our present embarrassed times! We want an authority, and we find nothing but jealous classes, checks, and a dead-lock; culture suggests the idea of *the State*. We find no basis for a firm State-power in our ordinary selves; culture suggests one to us in our *best self*.[7] * * *

from *Hebraism and Hellenism*

This fundamental ground is our preference of doing to thinking. Now this preference is a main element in our nature, and as we study it we find ourselves opening up a number of large questions on every side.

Let me go back for a moment to Bishop Wilson, who says: "First, never go against the best light you have; secondly, take care that your light be not darkness."[1] We show, as a nation, laudable energy and persistence in walking according to the best light we have, but are not quite careful enough, perhaps, to see that our light be not darkness. This is only another version of the old story that energy is our strong point and favourable characteristic, rather than intelligence. But we may give to this idea a more general form still, in which it will have a yet larger range of application. We may regard this energy driving at practice, this paramount sense of the obligation of duty, self-control, and work, this earnestness in going manfully with the best light we have, as one force. And we may regard the intelligence driving at those ideas which are, after all, the basis of right practice, the ardent sense for all the new and changing combinations of them which man's development brings with it, the indomitable impulse to know and adjust them perfectly, as another force. And these two forces we may regard as in some sense rivals,—rivals not by the necessity of their own nature, but as exhibited in man and his history,—and rivals dividing the empire of the world between them. And to give these forces names from the two races of men who have supplied the most signal and splendid manifestations of them, we may call them respectively the forces of Hebraism and Hellenism.[2]

---

7. Chapter 3, omitted here, explores the class-bound "ordinary selves" that Arnold wishes to transcend: the "Barbarian" aristocracy who value individualism, courage, and athleticism over intellect and sensitivity; the middle-class Philistines who stubbornly resist new ideas; and the dangerously "raw and half-developed" working class he calls simply "the Populace."
1. Quoting Thomas Wilson, *Maxims* (see page 2030, n. 4).

2. In Arnold's view Hebraism (the Judeo-Christian tradition) emphasizes duty, industriousness, and a sense of sin. In contrast, Hellenism (the Greek tradition) values rationality, "clearness of mind," and the quest for perfection. While Arnold emphasizes the importance of both traditions, it is Hellenism that he associates with sweetness and light.

Hebraism and Hellenism,—between these two points of influence moves our world. At one time it feels more powerfully the attraction of one of them, at another time of the other; and it ought to be, though it never is, evenly and happily balanced between them.

The final aim of both Hellenism and Hebraism, as of all great spiritual disciplines, is no doubt the same: man's perfection or salvation. The very language which they both of them use in schooling us to reach this aim is often identical. * * *

Still, they pursue this aim by very different courses. The uppermost idea with Hellenism is to see things as they really are; the uppermost idea with Hebraism is conduct and obedience. Nothing can do away with this ineffaceable difference. The Greek quarrel with the body and its desires is, that they hinder right thinking; the Hebrew quarrel with them is, that they hinder right acting. * * *

* * * Eighteen hundred years ago it was altogether the hour of Hebraism. Primitive Christianity was legitimately and truly the ascendant force in the world at that time, and the way of mankind's progress lay through its full development. Another hour in man's development began in the fifteenth century, and the main road of his progress then lay for a time through Hellenism. Puritanism was no longer the central current of the world's progress, it was a side stream crossing the central current and checking it. The cross and the check may have been necessary and salutary, but that does not do away with the essential difference between the main stream of man's advance and a cross or side stream. For more than two hundred years the main stream of man's advance has moved towards knowing himself and the world, seeing things as they are, spontaneity of consciousness; the main impulse of a great part, and that the strongest part, of our nation has been towards strictness of conscience. They have made the secondary the principal at the wrong moment, and the principal they have at the wrong moment treated as secondary. This contravention of the natural order has produced, as such contravention always must produce, a certain confusion and false movement, of which we are now beginning to feel, in almost every direction, the inconvenience. In all directions our habitual courses of action seem to be losing efficaciousness, credit, and control, both with others and even with ourselves. Everywhere we see the beginnings of confusion, and we want a clue to some sound order and authority. This we can only get by going back upon the actual instincts and forces which rule our life, seeing them as they really are, connecting them with other instincts and forces, and enlarging our whole view and rule of life.

from *Porro Unum Est Necessarium*[1]

The matter here opened is so large, and the trains of thought to which it gives rise are so manifold, that we must be careful to limit ourselves scrupulously to what has a direct bearing upon our actual discussion. We have found that at the bottom of our present unsettled state, so full of the seeds of trouble, lies the notion of its being the prime right and happiness, for each of us, to affirm himself, and his ordinary self; to be doing, and to be doing freely and as he likes. We have found at the bottom of it the disbelief in right reason as a lawful authority. It was easy to show from

---

1. In Luke 10.42 Jesus tells Mary that only "one thing is needful"; he appears to mean faith. According to Arnold, the Puritan middle classes think "the one thing needful" is their own narrow "Hebraic" sense of moral conduct.

our practice and current history that this is so; but it was impossible to show why it is so without taking a somewhat wider sweep and going into things a little more deeply. Why, in fact, should good, well-meaning, energetic, sensible people, like the bulk of our countrymen, come to have such light belief in right reason, and such an exaggerated value for their own independent doing, however crude? The answer is: because of an exclusive and excessive development in them, without due allowance for time, place, and circumstance, of that side of human nature, and that group of human forces, to which we have given the general name of Hebraism. Because they have thought their real and only important homage was owed to a power concerned with their obedience rather than with their intelligence, a power interested in the moral side of their nature almost exclusively. Thus they have been led to regard in themselves, as the one thing needful, *strictness of conscience*, the staunch adherence to some fixed law of doing we have got already, instead of *spontaneity of consciousness*, which tends continually to enlarge our whole law of doing. They have fancied themselves to have in their religion a sufficient basis for the whole of their life fixed and certain for ever, a full law of conduct and a full law of thought, so far as thought is needed, as well; whereas what they really have is a law of conduct, a law of unexampled power for enabling them to war against the law of sin in their members and not to serve it in the lusts thereof. The book which contains this invaluable law they call the Word of God, and attribute to it, as I have said, and as, indeed, is perfectly well known, a reach and sufficiency co-extensive with all the wants of human nature.

This might, no doubt, be so, if humanity were not the composite thing it is, if it had only, or in quite overpowering eminence, a moral side, and the group of instincts and powers which we call moral. But it has besides, and in notable eminence, an intellectual side, and the group of instincts and powers which we call intellectual. No doubt, mankind makes in general its progress in a fashion which gives at one time full swing to one of these groups of instincts, at another time to the other; and man's faculties are so intertwined, that when his moral side, and the current of force which we call Hebraism, is uppermost, this side will manage somehow to provide, or appear to provide, satisfaction for his intellectual needs; and when his intellectual side, and the current of force which we call Hellenism, is uppermost, this again will provide, or appear to provide, satisfaction for men's moral needs. But sooner or later it becomes manifest that when the two sides of humanity proceed in this fashion of alternate preponderance, and not of mutual understanding and balance, the side which is uppermost does not really provide in a satisfactory manner for the needs of the side which is undermost, and a state of confusion is, sooner or later, the result. The Hellenic half of our nature, bearing rule, makes a sort of provision for the Hebrew half, but it turns out to be an inadequate provision; and again the Hebrew half of our nature, bearing rule, makes a sort of provision for the Hellenic half, but this, too, turns out to be an inadequate provision. The true and smooth order of humanity's development is not reached in either way. And therefore, while we willingly admit with the Christian apostle that the world by wisdom,—that is, by the isolated preponderance of its intellectual impulses,—knew not God, or the true order of things, it is yet necessary, also, to set up a sort of converse to this proposition, and to say likewise (what is equally true) that the world by Puritanism knew not God. And it is on this converse of the apostle's proposition that it is particularly needful to insist in our own country just at present.

Here, indeed, is the answer to many criticisms which have been addressed to all that we have said in praise of sweetness and light. Sweetness and light evidently have to do with the bent or side in humanity which we call Hellenic. Greek intelligence has obviously for its essence the instinct for what Plato calls the true, firm, intelligible law of things; the law of light, of seeing things as they are. Even in the natural sciences, where the Greeks had not time and means adequately to apply this instinct, and where we have gone a great deal further than they did, it is this instinct which is the root of the whole matter and the ground of all our success; and this instinct the world has mainly learnt of the Greeks, inasmuch as they are humanity's most signal manifestation of it. Greek art, again, Greek beauty, have their root in the same impulse to see things as they really are, inasmuch as Greek art and beauty rest on fidelity to nature,—the *best* nature,—and on a delicate discrimination of what this best nature is. To say we work for sweetness and light, then, is only another way of saying that we work for Hellenism. But, oh! cry many people, sweetness and light are not enough; you must put strength or energy along with them, and make a kind of trinity of strength, sweetness and light, and then, perhaps, you may do some good. That is to say, we are to join Hebraism, strictness of the moral conscience, and manful walking by the best light we have, together with Hellenism, inculcate both, and rehearse the praises of both.

Or, rather, we may praise both in conjunction, but we must be careful to praise Hebraism most. "Culture," says an acute, though somewhat rigid critic, Mr Sidgwick,[2] "diffuses sweetness and light. I do not undervalue these blessings, but religion gives fire and strength, and the world wants fire and strength even more than sweetness and light." By religion, let me explain, Mr Sidgwick here means particularly that Puritanism on the insufficiency of which I have been commenting and to which he says I am unfair. Now, no doubt, it is possible to be a fanatical partisan of light and the instincts which push us to it, a fanatical enemy of strictness of moral conscience and the instincts which push us to it. A fanaticism of this sort deforms and vulgarises the well-known work, in some respects so remarkable, of the late Mr Buckle.[3] Such a fanaticism carries its own mark with it, in lacking sweetness; and its own penalty, in that, lacking sweetness, it comes in the end to lack light too. And the Greeks,—the great exponents of humanity's bent for sweetness and light united, of its perception that the truth of things must be at the same time beauty,—singularly escaped the fanaticism which we moderns, whether we Hellenise or whether we Hebraise, are so apt to show. They arrived,—though failing, as has been said, to give adequate practical satisfaction to the claims of man's moral side,—at the idea of a comprehensive adjustment of the claims of both the sides in man, the moral as well as the intellectual, of a full estimate of both, and of a reconciliation of both; an idea which is philosophically of the greatest value, and the best of lessons for us moderns. So we ought to have no difficulty in conceding to Mr Sidgwick that manful walking by the best light one has,—fire and strength as he calls it,—has its high value as well as culture, the endeavour to see things in their truth and beauty, the pursuit of sweetness and light. But whether at this or that time, and to this or that

2. Henry Sidgwick, Cambridge philosopher who in 1867 had published a response to *Culture and Its Enemies*, the lecture that became the first chapter of *Culture and Anarchy*.

3. Henry Thomas Buckle, whose *History of Civilisation in England* (1857–1861) attributed historical events to geography.

set of persons, one ought to insist most on the praises of fire and strength, or on the praises of sweetness and light, must depend, one would think, on the circumstances and needs of that particular time and those particular persons. And all that we have been saying, and indeed any glance at the world around us shows that with us, with the most respectable and strongest part of us, the ruling force is now, and long has been, a Puritan force,—the care for fire and strength, strictness of conscience, Hebraism, rather than the care for sweetness and light, spontaneity of consciousness, Hellenism.

Well, then, what is the good of our now rehearsing the praises of fire and strength to ourselves, who dwell too exclusively on them already? When Mr Sidgwick says so broadly, that the world wants fire and strength even more than sweetness and light, is he not carried away by a turn for broad generalisation? does he not forget that the world is not all of one piece, and every piece with the same needs at the same time? It may be true that the Roman world at the beginning of our era, or Leo the Tenth's Court at the time of the Reformation, or French society in the eighteenth century,[4] needed fire and strength even more than sweetness and light. But can it be said that the Barbarians who overran the empire needed fire and strength even more than sweetness and light; or that the Puritans needed them more; or that Mr Murphy, the Birmingham lecturer, and his friends, need them more?

The Puritan's great danger is that he imagines himself in possession of a rule telling him the *unum necessarium*, or one thing needful, and that he then remains satisfied with a very crude conception of what this rule really is and what it tells him, thinks he has now knowledge and henceforth needs only to act, and, in this dangerous state of assurance and self-satisfaction, proceeds to give full swing to a number of the instincts of his ordinary self. Some of the instincts of his ordinary self he has, by the help of his rule of life, conquered; but others which he has not conquered by this help he is so far from perceiving to need subjugation, and to be instincts of an inferior self, that he even fancies it to be his right and duty, in virtue of having conquered a limited part of himself, to give unchecked swing to the remainder. He is, I say, a victim of Hebraism, of the tendency to cultivate strictness of conscience rather than spontaneity of consciousness. And what he wants is a larger conception of human nature, showing him the number of other points at which his nature must come to its best, besides the points which he himself knows and thinks of. There is no *unum necessarium*, or one thing needful, which can free human nature from the obligation of trying to come to its best at all these points. The real *unum necessarium* for us is to come to our best at all points. Instead of our "one thing needful," justifying in us vulgarity, hideousness, ignorance, violence,—our vulgarity, hideousness, ignorance, violence, are really so many touchstones which try our one thing needful, and which prove that in the state, at any rate, in which we ourselves have it, it is not all we want. And as the force which encourages us to stand staunch and fast by the rule and ground we have is Hebraism, so the force which encourages us to go back upon this rule, and to try the very ground on which we appear to stand, is Hellenism,—a turn for giving our consciousness free play and enlarging its range. And what I say is, not that Hellenism is always for everybody more wanted than Hebraism, but that for Mr

---

4. The courts of the Roman emperor Nero (A.D. 54–68), of Pope Leo X (1513–1521), and of Louis XV (1715–1774) were renowned for worldly luxury and excess.

Murphy at this particular moment, and for the great majority of us his fellow-countrymen, it is more wanted. * * *

from *Conclusion*

And so we bring to an end what we had to say in praise of culture, and in evidence of its special utility for the circumstances in which we find ourselves, and the confusion which environs us. Through culture seems to lie our way, not only to perfection, but even to safety. Resolutely refusing to lend a hand to the imperfect operations of our Liberal friends, disregarding their impatience, taunts, and reproaches, firmly bent on trying to find in the intelligible laws of things a firmer and sounder basis for future practice than any which we have at present, and believing this search and discovery to be, for our generation and circumstances, of yet more vital and pressing importance than practice itself, we nevertheless may do more, perhaps, we poor disparaged followers of culture, to make the actual present, and the frame of society in which we live, solid and seaworthy, than all which our bustling politicians can do.

For we have seen how much of our disorders and perplexities is due to the disbelief, among the classes and combinations of men, Barbarian or Philistine, which have hitherto governed our society, in right reason, in a paramount best self; to the inevitable decay and break-up of the organisations by which, asserting and expressing in these organisations their ordinary self only, they have so long ruled us; and to their irresolution, when the society, which their conscience tells them they have made and still manage not with right reason but with their ordinary self, is rudely shaken, in offering resistance to its subverters. But for us,—who believe in right reason, in the duty and possibility of extricating and elevating our best self, in the progress of humanity towards perfection,—for us the framework of society, that theatre on which this august drama has to unroll itself, is sacred; and whoever administers it, and however we may seek to remove them from their tenure of administration, yet, while they administer, we steadily and with undivided heart support them in repressing anarchy and disorder; because without order there can be no society, and without society there can be no human perfection.

And this opinion of the intolerableness of anarchy we can never forsake, however our Liberal friends may think a little rioting, and what they call popular demonstrations, useful sometimes to their own interests and to the interests of the valuable practical operations they have in hand, and however they may preach the right of an Englishman to be left to do as far as possible what he likes, and the duty of his government to indulge him and connive as much as possible and abstain from all harshness of repression. And even when they artfully show us operations which are undoubtedly precious, such as the abolition of the slave-trade, and ask us if, for their sake, foolish and obstinate governments may not wholesomely be frightened by a little disturbance, the good design in view and the difficulty of overcoming opposition to it being considered,—still we say no, and that monster-processions in the streets and forcible irruptions into the parks, even in professed support of this good design, ought to be unflinchingly forbidden and repressed; and that far more is lost than is gained by permitting them. Because a State in which law is authoritative and sovereign, a firm and settled course of public order, is requisite if man is to bring to maturity anything precious and lasting now, or to found anything precious and lasting for the future. * * *

1867–1868; 1869

Christina Rossetti

1830–1894

"Here is a great discovery," Christina Rossetti wrote to her brother Dante Gabriel in 1870, as he tried to advise her about her poetic career: "'Women are not Men,' and you must not expect me to possess a tithe of your capacities, though I humbly—or proudly—lay claim to family-likeness." The remark hints at many sides of Rossetti's complex nature: her modest yet firm manner; the touch of irony in her deference; and the "family-likeness" not only of poetic genius but personal temperament—their parents called them the "two storms" in childhood because they were both difficult, irritable, volatile, and creative. Her declaration signals Rossetti's recognition that as a woman and artist she had had to take a very different path from her more famous brother. She renounced from an early age any pleasures or relationships that did not conform to her strict Anglo-Catholic principles—even to the point of giving up chess because it made her too eager to win. Instead she found poetic fulfillment in haunting lyrics about goblin men and love beyond the grave.

Rossetti was born in London in 1830, the youngest of four precocious children of Gabriele Rossetti, an Italian poet-in-exile, and his English-Italian wife Frances Polidori, whose brother John was Byron's physician and traveling companion. Amid a stream of foreign visitors the bilingual Rossetti children listened to animated discussions of art, music, and revolutionary politics. This atmosphere "made us . . . not a little different from British children," her brother William recalled, "and, when Dante and Christina Rossetti proved, as poetic writers, somewhat devious from the British tradition and the insular mind, we may say, if not 'so much the better,' at any rate, 'no wonder.'"

Like many Victorian women of letters, Christina Rossetti suffered from mysterious maladies that served to protect her time and talent. "I am rejoiced to feel that my health does really unfit me for miscellaneous governessing *en permanence*," she confided to William in 1855. Freed from "the necessity of teaching the small daughters of the neighbouring hairdresser or the neighbouring pork-butcher their p's and q's," she was "anxious to secure any literary pickings which might offer."

Shy, devout, and self-sacrificing, Rossetti nevertheless found time for a literary and social life that included as acquaintances Browning, Ruskin, Swinburne, Lewis Carroll, Edmund Gosse, and the Pre-Raphaelites. She modelled as the Virgin Mary in two of Dante Gabriel's finest paintings, *The Girlhood of Mary Virgin* (1848–1849) and *Ecce Ancilla Domini* (1849–1850). Because of her sex, Christina was denied membership in the Pre-Raphaelite Brotherhood, but she did publish her first poems in their journal *The Germ* in 1850. With the appearance of *Goblin Market and Other Poems* in 1862, she acquired a growing critical and popular following. Hailed by Gosse as the "High Priestess of Pre-Raphaelitism" because of her superb technique and keenness of observation, she won even wider fame as an author of religious poetry, inspiring, among others, Gerard Manley Hopkins.

Admirers of Rossetti's passionate, frustrated love poetry have long puzzled over the scanty details of her romantic life. She rejected two suitors because she found their faith wanting. Early biographers assumed that these broken relationships blighted Rossetti's life, but recently critics have regarded her choice of a single life as an act of artistic self-preservation. For Christina not only witnessed Dante's tormented affairs but also had the opportunity to view passion's consequences in a clinical light during the decade she worked as a volunteer at the Highgate House of Charity for "fallen women."

Though brightened by many touches of humor, Rossetti's writing focuses mostly on religious topics or some combination of themes arising from troubled love, grave illness, and anticipations of death—themes she must have pondered during the extended periods she spent taking care of dying family members at home, beginning with her father and continuing with her sister, her brother Dante, her mother (who was always her closest companion), and two maiden aunts. Despite severe illness in later life, she maintained a strict professionalism toward her career, publishing new work during the 1870s and 1880s, then issuing revised editions until her death in 1894.

A spontaneous writer whose lucidity of phrasing has sometimes caused readers to over-look her emotional and symbolic depths, Rossetti mastered a variety of forms, ranging from hymns and a sonnet-sequence to nursery rhymes and a well-known Christmas carol, *In the Bleak Mid-Winter*. Like Emily Dickinson, whose poems she admired when the first selection was published in 1890, Rossetti displays a quirky independence of vision, mingling the morbid, the whimsical, the cooly ironic. What is today her most famous poem, *Goblin Market*, features the enticements of sensual knowledge. Regarded chiefly as a children's tale in the nineteenth century, the poem has subsequently attracted much critical attention, including analyses of it as a struggle between self and soul, a comment on sex as a capitalist commodity, a parable of feminist solidarity, a lesson about poetry's subversive power, and a lesbian love story. This fable about the danger of desire provides insight into the dualistic world of Victorian fantasy. Magi-cal events permitted writers and readers to enter forbidden realms of violence, temptation, and transformation, yet moralized endings sought to tame even the wildest tales for social and eth-ical instruction. Something similar may be said of Christina Rossetti's life and art: a stormy nature finds release in the tight formal control of the polished artist.

Song

When I am dead, my dearest,
    Sing no sad songs for me;
Plant thou no roses at my head,
    Nor shady cypress tree:
5 Be the green grass above me
    With showers and dewdrops wet;
And if thou wilt, remember,
    And if thou wilt, forget.

I shall not see the shadows,
10   I shall not feel the rain;
I shall not hear the nightingale
    Sing on, as if in pain:
And dreaming through the twilight
    That doth not rise nor set,
15 Haply° I may remember,   *perhaps*
    And haply may forget.

1848   1862

After Death

The curtains were half drawn, the floor was swept
    And strewn with rushes, rosemary and may[1]
    Lay thick upon the bed on which I lay,
Where thro' the lattice ivy-shadows crept.
5 He leaned above me, thinking that I slept
    And could not hear him; but I heard him say:

---

1. Flowers traditionally associated with death.

"Poor child, poor child:" and as he turned away
Came a deep silence, and I knew he wept.
He did not touch the shroud, or raise the fold
10 That hid my face, or take my hand in his,
   Or ruffle the smooth pillows for my head:
   He did not love me living; but once dead
  He pitied me; and very sweet it is
To know he still is warm tho' I am cold.

1849   1862

In an Artist's Studio

One face looks out from all his canvasses,[1]
 One selfsame figure sits or walks or leans;
 We found her hidden just behind those screens,
That mirror gave back all her loveliness.
5 A queen in opal or in ruby dress,
 A nameless girl in freshest summer greens,
 A saint, an angel;—every canvass means
The same one meaning, neither more nor less.
He feeds upon her face by day and night,
10 And she with true kind eyes looks back on him
Fair as the moon and joyful as the light:
 Not wan with waiting, not with sorrow dim;
Not as she is, but was when hope shone bright;
 Not as she is, but as she fills his dream.

1856   1896

Winter: My Secret

I tell my secret? No indeed, not I:
Perhaps some day, who knows?
But not today; it froze, and blows, and snows,
And you're too curious: fie!
5 You want to hear it? well:
Only, my secret's mine, and I won't tell.

Or, after all, perhaps there's none:
Suppose there is no secret after all,
But only just my fun.
10 Today's a nipping day, a biting day;
In which one wants a shawl,
A veil, a cloak, and other wraps:
I cannot ope to every one who taps,
And let the draughts come whistling thro' my hall;
15 Come bounding and surrounding me,
Come buffeting, astounding me,
Nipping and clipping thro' my wraps and all.

1. Christina's brother William wrote: "The reference is apparently to our brother's studio, and to his constantly repeated heads of the lady whom he afterwards married, Miss Siddal."

I wear my mask for warmth: who ever shows
His nose to Russian snows
20 To be pecked at by every wind that blows?
You would not peck? I thank you for good will,
Believe, but leave that truth untested still.

Spring's an expansive time: yet I don't trust
March with its peck of dust,
25 Nor April with its rainbow-crowned brief showers,
Nor even May, whose flowers
One frost may wither thro' the sunless hours.

Perhaps some languid summer day,
When drowsy birds sing less and less,
30 And golden fruit is ripening to excess,
If there's not too much sun nor too much cloud,
And the warm wind is neither still nor loud,
Perhaps my secret I may say,
Or you may guess.

1857   1862

Goblin Market

Morning and evening
Maids heard the goblins cry:
"Come buy our orchard fruits,
Come buy, come buy:
5 Apples and quinces,
Lemons and oranges,
Plump unpecked cherries,
Melons and raspberries,
Bloom-down-cheeked peaches,
10 Swart°-headed mulberries,   *dark*
Wild free-born cranberries,
Crab-apples, dewberries,
Pine-apples, blackberries,
Apricots, strawberries;—
15 All ripe together
In summer weather,—
Morns that pass by,
Fair eves that fly;
Come buy, come buy:
20 Our grapes fresh from the vine,
Pomegranates full and fine,
Dates and sharp bullaces,
Rare pears and greengages,
Damsons[1] and bilberries,
25 Taste them and try:
Currants and gooseberries,
Bright-fire-like barberries,
Figs to fill your mouth,

---

1. Bullaces, greengages, and damsons are types of plums.

Citrons from the South,
30   Sweet to tongue and sound to eye;
Come buy, come buy."

Evening by evening
Among the brookside rushes,
Laura bowed her head to hear,
35   Lizzie veiled her blushes:
Crouching close together
In the cooling weather,
With clasping arms and cautioning lips,
With tingling cheeks and finger tips.
40   "Lie close," Laura said,
Pricking up her golden head:
"We must not look at goblin men,
We must not buy their fruits:
Who knows upon what soil they fed
45   Their hungry thirsty roots?"
"Come buy," call the goblins
Hobbling down the glen.
"Oh," cried Lizzie, "Laura, Laura,
You should not peep at goblin men."

50 Lizzie covered up her eyes,
    Covered close lest they should look;
    Laura reared her glossy head,
    And whispered like the restless brook:
    "Look, Lizzie, look, Lizzie,
55 Down the glen tramp little men.
    One hauls a basket,
    One bears a plate,
    One lugs a golden dish
    Of many pounds weight.
60 How fair the vine must grow
    Whose grapes are so luscious;
    How warm the wind must blow
    Thro' those fruit bushes."
    "No," said Lizzie: "No, no, no;
65 Their offers should not charm us,
    Their evil gifts would harm us."
    She thrust a dimpled finger
    In each ear, shut eyes and ran:
    Curious Laura chose to linger
70 Wondering at each merchant man.
    One had a cat's face,
    One whisked a tail,
    One tramped at a rat's pace,
    One crawled like a snail,
75 One like a wombat prowled obtuse and furry,
    One like a ratel[2] tumbled hurry skurry.
    She heard a voice like voice of doves
    Cooing all together:
    They sounded kind and full of loves
80 In the pleasant weather.

    Laura stretched her gleaming neck
    Like a rush-imbedded swan,
    Like a lily from the beck,°   brook
    Like a moonlit poplar branch,
85 Like a vessel at the launch
    When its last restraint is gone.

    Backwards up the mossy glen
    Turned and trooped the goblin men,
    With their shrill repeated cry,
90 "Come buy, come buy."
    When they reached where Laura was
    They stood stock still upon the moss,
    Leering at each other,
    Brother with queer brother;
95 Signalling each other,
    Brother with sly brother.
    One set his basket down,
    One reared his plate;

2. A tropical badgerlike nocturnal animal (pronounced "ray-tell").

One began to weave a crown
100 Of tendrils, leaves and rough nuts brown
(Men sell not such in any town);
One heaved the golden weight
Of dish and fruit to offer her:
"Come buy, come buy," was still their cry.
105 Laura stared but did not stir,
Longed but had no money:
The whisk-tailed merchant bade her taste
In tones as smooth as honey,
The cat-faced purr'd,
110 The rat-paced spoke a word
Of welcome, and the snail-paced even was heard;
One parrot-voiced and jolly
Cried "Pretty Goblin" still for "Pretty Polly;"—
One whistled like a bird.

115 But sweet-tooth Laura spoke in haste:
"Good folk, I have no coin;
To take were to purloin:
I have no copper in my purse,
I have no silver either,
120 And all my gold is on the furze³
That shakes in windy weather
Above the rusty heather."
"You have much gold upon your head,"
They answered all together:
125 "Buy from us with a golden curl."
She clipped a precious golden lock,
She dropped a tear more rare than pearl,
Then sucked their fruit globes fair or red:
Sweeter than honey from the rock.
130 Stronger than man-rejoicing wine,
Clearer than water flowed that juice;
She never tasted such before,
How should it cloy with length of use?
She sucked and sucked and sucked the more
135 Fruits which that unknown orchard bore;
She sucked until her lips were sore;
Then flung the emptied rinds away
But gathered up one kernel-stone,
And knew not was it night or day
140 As she turned home alone.

Lizzie met her at the gate
Full of wise upbraidings:
"Dear, you should not stay so late,
Twilight is not good for maidens;
145 Should not loiter in the glen
In the haunts of goblin men.
Do you not remember Jeanie,

3. An evergreen shrub that grows on the heath.

How she met them in the moonlight,
Took their gifts both choice and many,
150 Ate their fruits and wore their flowers
Plucked from bowers
Where summer ripens at all hours?
But ever in the noonlight
She pined and pined away;
155 Sought them by night and day,
Found them no more but dwindled and grew grey;
Then fell with the first snow,
While to this day no grass will grow
Where she lies low:
160 I planted daisies there a year ago
That never blow.
You should not loiter so."
"Nay, hush," said Laura:
"Nay, hush, my sister:
165 I ate and ate my fill,
Yet my mouth waters still;
Tomorrow night I will
Buy more:" and kissed her:
"Have done with sorrow;
170 I'll bring you plums tomorrow
Fresh on their mother twigs,
Cherries worth getting;
You cannot think what figs
My teeth have met in,
175 What melons icy-cold
Piled on a dish of gold
Too huge for me to hold,
What peaches with a velvet nap,
Pellucid° grapes without one seed: *translucent*
180 Odorous indeed must be the mead
Whereon they grow, and pure the wave they drink
With lilies at the brink,
And sugar-sweet their sap."

Golden head by golden head,
185 Like two pigeons in one nest
Folded in each other's wings,
They lay down in their curtained bed:
Like two blossoms on one stem,
Like two flakes of new-fall'n snow,
190 Like two wands of ivory
Tipped with gold for awful° kings.   *awe-inspiring*
Moon and stars gazed in at them,
Wind sang to them lullaby,
Lumbering owls forbore to fly,
195 Not a bat flapped to and fro
Round their rest:
Cheek to cheek and breast to breast
Locked together in one nest.

Early in the morning
200 When the first cock crowed his warning,
Neat like bees, as sweet and busy,
Laura rose with Lizzie:
Fetched in honey, milked the cows,
Aired and set to rights the house,
205 Kneaded cakes of whitest wheat,
Cakes for dainty mouths to eat,
Next churned butter, whipped up cream,
Fed their poultry, sat and sewed;
Talked as modest maidens should:
210 Lizzie with an open heart,
Laura in an absent dream,
One content, one sick in part;
One warbling for the mere bright day's delight,
One longing for the night.

215 At length slow evening came:
They went with pitchers to the reedy brook;
Lizzie most placid in her look,
Laura most like a leaping flame.
They drew the gurgling water from its deep;
220 Lizzie plucked purple and rich golden flags,
Then turning homewards said: "The sunset flushes
Those furthest loftiest crags;
Come, Laura, not another maiden lags,
No wilful squirrel wags,
225 The beasts and birds are fast asleep."
But Laura loitered still among the rushes
And said the bank was steep.

And said the hour was early still,
The dew not fall'n, the wind not chill:
230 Listening ever, but not catching
The customary cry,
"Come buy, come buy,"
With its iterated jingle
Of sugar-baited words:
235 Not for all her watching
Once discerning even one goblin
Racing, whisking, tumbling, hobbling;
Let alone the herds
That used to tramp along the glen,
240 In groups or single,
Of brisk fruit-merchant men.
Till Lizzie urged, "O Laura, come;
I hear the fruit-call but I dare not look:
You should not loiter longer at this brook:
245 Come with me home.
The stars rise, the moon bends her arc,
Each glowworm winks her spark,
Let us get home before the night grows dark:

For clouds may gather
250   Tho' this is summer weather,
      Put out the lights and drench us thro';
      Then if we lost our way what should we do?"

      Laura turned cold as stone
      To find her sister heard that cry alone,
255   That goblin cry,
      "Come buy our fruits, come buy."
      Must she then buy no more such dainty fruit?
      Must she no more such succous° pasture find,   juicy
      Gone deaf and blind?
260   Her tree of life drooped from the root:
      She said not one word in her heart's sore ache;
      But peering thro' the dimness, nought discerning,
      Trudged home, her pitcher dripping all the way;
      So crept to bed, and lay
265   Silent till Lizzie slept;
      Then sat up in a passionate yearning,
      And gnashed her teeth for baulked desire, and wept
      As if her heart would break.

      Day after day, night after night,
270   Laura kept watch in vain
      In sullen silence of exceeding pain.
      She never caught again the goblin cry:
      "Come buy, come buy;"—
      She never spied the goblin men
275   Hawking their fruits along the glen:
      But when the noon waxed bright
      Her hair grew thin and gray;
      She dwindled, as the fair full moon doth turn
      To swift decay and burn
280   Her fire away.

      One day remembering her kernel-stone
      She set it by a wall that faced the south;
      Dewed it with tears, hoped for a root,
      Watched for a waxing shoot,
285   But there came none;
      It never saw the sun,
      It never felt the trickling moisture run:
      While with sunk eyes and faded mouth
      She dreamed of melons, as a traveller sees
290   False waves in desert drouth
      With shade of leaf-crowned trees,
      And burns the thirstier in the sandful breeze.

      She no more swept the house,
      Tended the fowls or cows,
295   Fetched honey, kneaded cakes of wheat,
      Brought water from the brook:
      But sat down listless in the chimney-nook
      And would not eat.

Tender Lizzie could not bear
300   To watch her sister's cankerous° care   *festering*
Yet not to share.
She night and morning
Caught the goblins' cry:
"Come buy our orchard fruits,
305   Come buy, come buy:"—
Beside the brook, along the glen,
She heard the tramp of goblin men,
The voice and stir
Poor Laura could not hear;
310   Longed to buy fruit to comfort her,
But feared to pay too dear.
She thought of Jeanie in her grave,
Who should have been a bride;
But who for joys brides hope to have
315   Fell sick and died
In her gay prime,
In earliest Winter time,
With the first glazing rime,
With the first snow-fall of crisp Winter time.

320   Till Laura dwindling
Seemed knocking at Death's door:
Then Lizzie weighed no more
Better and worse;
But put a silver penny in her purse,
325   Kissed Laura, crossed the heath with clumps of furze
At twilight, halted by the brook:
And for the first time in her life
Began to listen and look.

Laughed every goblin
330   When they spied her peeping:
Came towards her hobbling,
Flying, running, leaping,
Puffing and blowing,
Chuckling, clapping, crowing,
335   Clucking and gobbling,
Mopping and mowing,
Full of airs and graces,
Pulling wry faces,
Demure grimaces,
340   Cat-like and rat-like,
Ratel- and wombat-like,
Snail-paced in a hurry,
Parrot-voiced and whistler,
Helter skelter, hurry skurry,
345   Chattering like magpies,
Fluttering like pigeons,
Gliding like fishes,—
Hugged her and kissed her,
Squeezed and caressed her:

350   Stretched up their dishes,
       Panniers, and plates:
       "Look at our apples
       Russet and dun,
       Bob at our cherries,
355   Bite at our peaches,
       Citrons and dates,
       Grapes for the asking,
       Pears red with basking
       Out in the sun,
360   Plums on their twigs;
       Pluck them and suck them,
       Pomegranates, figs."—

       "Good folk," said Lizzie,
       Mindful of Jeanie:
365   "Give me much and many:"—
       Held out her apron,
       Tossed them her penny.
       "Nay, take a seat with us,
       Honour and eat with us,"
370   They answered grinning:
       "Our feast is but beginning.
       Night yet is early,
       Warm and dew-pearly,
       Wakeful and starry:
375   Such fruits as these
       No man can carry;
       Half their bloom would fly,
       Half their dew would dry,
       Half their flavour would pass by.
380   Sit down and feast with us,
       Be welcome guest with us,
       Cheer you and rest with us."—
       "Thank you," said Lizzie: "But one waits
       At home alone for me:
385   So without further parleying,
       If you will not sell me any
       Of your fruits tho' much and many,
       Give me back my silver penny
       I tossed you for a fee."—
390   They began to scratch their pates,
       No longer wagging, purring,
       But visibly demurring,
       Grunting and snarling.
       One called her proud,
395   Cross-grained, uncivil;
       Their tones waxed loud,
       Their looks were evil.
       Lashing their tails
       They trod and hustled her,
400   Elbowed and jostled her,

Clawed with their nails,
Barking, mewing, hissing, mocking,
Tore her gown and soiled her stocking,
Twitched her hair out by the roots,
405 Stamped upon her tender feet,
Held her hands and squeezed their fruits
Against her mouth to make her eat.
White and golden Lizzie stood,
Like a lily in a flood,—
410 Like a rock of blue-veined stone
Lashed by tides obstreperously,—
Like a beacon left alone
In a hoary roaring sea,
Sending up a golden fire,—
415 Like a fruit-crowned orange-tree
White with blossoms honey-sweet
Sore beset by wasp and bee,—
Like a royal virgin town
Topped with gilded dome and spire
420 Close beleaguered by a fleet
Mad to tug her standard down.

One may lead a horse to water,
Twenty cannot make him drink.
Tho' the goblins cuffed and caught her,
425 Coaxed and fought her,
Bullied and besought her,
Scratched her, pinched her black as ink,
Kicked and knocked her,
Mauled and mocked her,
430 Lizzie uttered not a word;
Would not open lip from lip
Lest they should cram a mouthful in:
But laughed in heart to feel the drip
Of juice that syrupped all her face,
435 And lodged in dimples of her chin,
And streaked her neck which quaked like curd.
At last the evil people
Worn out by her resistance
Flung back her penny, kicked their fruit
440 Along whichever road they took,
Not leaving root or stone or shoot;
Some writhed into the ground,
Some dived into the brook
With ring and ripple,
445 Some scudded on the gale without a sound,
Some vanished in the distance.
In a smart, ache, tingle,
Lizzie went her way;
Knew not was it night or day;
450 Sprang up the bank, tore thro' the furze,
Threaded copse and dingle,

And heard her penny jingle
Bouncing in her purse,
Its bounce was music to her ear.
455 She ran and ran
As if she feared some goblin man
Dogged her with gibe or curse
Or something worse:
But not one goblin skurried after,
460 Nor was she pricked by fear;
The kind heart made her windy-paced
That urged her home quite out of breath with haste
And inward laughter.

She cried "Laura," up the garden,
465 "Did you miss me?
Come and kiss me.
Never mind my bruises,
Hug me, kiss me, suck my juices
Squeezed from goblin fruits for you,
470 Goblin pulp and goblin dew.
Eat me, drink me, love me;
Laura, make much of me:
For your sake I have braved the glen
And had to do with goblin merchant men."

475 Laura started from her chair,
Flung her arms up in the air,
Clutched her hair:
"Lizzie, Lizzie, have you tasted
For my sake the fruit forbidden?
480 Must your light like mine be hidden,
Your young life like mine be wasted,
Undone in mine undoing
And ruined in my ruin,
Thirsty, cankered, goblin-ridden?"—
485 She clung about her sister,
Kissed and kissed and kissed her:
Tears once again
Refreshed her shrunken eyes,
Dropping like rain
490 After long sultry drouth;
Shaking with aguish fear, and pain,
She kissed and kissed her with a hungry mouth.

Her lips began to scorch,
That juice was wormwood to her tongue,
495 She loathed the feast:
Writhing as one possessed she leaped and sung,
Rent all her robe, and wrung
Her hands in lamentable haste,
And beat her breast.
500 Her locks streamed like the torch
Borne by a racer at full speed,

Or like the mane of horses in their flight,
Or like an eagle when she stems° the light   *makes headway against*
Straight toward the sun,
505 Or like a caged thing freed,
Or like a flying flag when armies run.

Swift fire spread thro' her veins, knocked at her heart,
Met the fire smouldering there
And overbore its lesser flame;
510 She gorged on bitterness without a name:
Ah! fool, to choose such part
Of soul-consuming care!
Sense failed in the mortal strife:
Like the watch-tower of a town
515 Which an earthquake shatters down,
Like a lightning-stricken mast,
Like a wind-uprooted tree
Spun about,
Like a foam-topped waterspout
520 Cast down headlong in the sea,
She fell at last;
Pleasure past and anguish past,
Is it death or is it life?

Life out of death.
525 That night long Lizzie watched by her,
Counted her pulse's flagging stir,
Felt for her breath,
Held water to her lips, and cooled her face
With tears and fanning leaves:
530 But when the first birds chirped about their eaves,
And early reapers plodded to the place
Of golden sheaves,
And dew-wet grass
Bowed in the morning winds so brisk to pass,
535 And new buds with new day
Opened of cup-like lilies on the stream,
Laura awoke as from a dream,
Laughed in the innocent old way,
Hugged Lizzie but not twice or thrice;
540 Her gleaming locks showed not one thread of grey,
Her breath was sweet as May
And light danced in her eyes.

Days, weeks, months, years
Afterwards, when both were wives
545 With children of their own;
Their mother-hearts beset with fears,
Their lives bound up in tender lives;
Laura would call the little ones
And tell them of her early prime,
550 Those pleasant days long gone
Of not-returning time:

Would talk about the haunted glen,
The wicked, quaint fruit-merchant men,
Their fruits like honey to the throat
555 But poison in the blood;
(Men sell not such in any town:)
Would tell them how her sister stood
In deadly peril to do her good,
And win the fiery antidote:
560 Then joining hands to little hands
Would bid them cling together,
"For there is no friend like a sister
In calm or stormy weather;
To cheer one on the tedious way,
565 To fetch one if one goes astray,
To lift one if one totters down,
To strengthen whilst one stands."

1859   1862

"No, Thank You, John"

I never said I loved you, John:
   Why will you teaze me day by day,
And wax a weariness to think upon
   With always "do" and "pray"?

5 You know I never loved you, John;
   No fault of mine made me your toast:
Why will you haunt me with a face as wan
   As shows an hour-old ghost?

I dare say Meg or Moll would take
10   Pity upon you, if you'd ask:
And pray don't remain single for my sake
   Who can't perform that task.

I have no heart?—Perhaps I have not;
   But then you're mad to take offence
15 That I don't give you what I have not got:
   Use your own common sense.

Let bygones be bygones:
   Don't call me false, who owed not to be true:
I'd rather answer "No" to fifty Johns
20   Than answer "Yes" to you.

Let's mar our pleasant days no more,
   Song-birds of passage, days of youth:
Catch at today, forget the days before:
   I'll wink at your untruth.

25 Let us strike hands as hearty friends;
   No more, no less; and friendship's good:
Only don't keep in view ulterior ends,
   And points not understood

In open treaty. Rise above
30   Quibbles and shuffling off and on:
Here's friendship for you if you like; but love,—
      No, thank you, John.

1860   1862

Promises Like Pie-Crust[1]

Promise me no promises,
      So will I not promise you;
Keep we both our liberties,
      Never false and never true:
5 Let us hold the die uncast,
      Free to come as free to go;
For I cannot know your past,
      And of mine what can you know?

You, so warm, may once have been
10   Warmer towards another one;
I, so cold, may once have seen
      Sunlight, once have felt the sun:
Who shall show us if it was
      Thus indeed in time of old?
15 Fades the image from the glass
      And the fortune is not told.

If you promised, you might grieve
      For lost liberty again;
If I promised, I believe
20   I should fret to break the chain:
Let us be the friends we were,
      Nothing more but nothing less;
Many thrive on frugal fare
      Who would perish of excess.

1861   1896

Sleeping at Last

Sleeping at last, the trouble & tumult over,
Sleeping at last, the struggle & horror past,
Cold & white out of sight of friend & of lover
Sleeping at last.

5 No more a tired heart downcast or overcast,
No more pangs that wring or shifting fears that hover,
Sleeping at last in a dreamless sleep locked fast.

Fast asleep. Singing birds in their leafy cover
Cannot wake her, nor shake her the gusty blast.
10 Under the purple thyme & the purple clover
Sleeping at last.

c. 1893   1896

---

1. English proverb: "Promises are like pie-crust, made to be broken."

—✦ ≡◆≡ ✦—

Gerard Manley Hopkins
1844–1889

Hopkins is the most modern of Victorian poets, and the most Victorian of modern poets. His stunningly original poems were, with a few exceptions, not published until 1918, placing him at first glance in the company of Eliot and Pound. But his struggle to maintain religious faith, his respect for conventional verse forms, and his quest to find proof of God's work in nature all mark him as quintessentially Victorian. Hopkins combines a microscopic keenness of vision with a Joycean genius for compound words, new coinages, unexpected rhymes, and startling distortions of syntax. The result is a poetry of modernist intensity and compression, fraught with bold ellipses and daring line breaks, but nonetheless dedicated to describing a world "charged with the grandeur of God." Orthodox and self-denying in matters of religion, Hopkins was also the era's most radical literary rebel.

Hopkins was born into a prosperous, pious Anglican family. After attending school in London, he went in 1863 to study classics at Balliol College, Oxford, where the agnostic aesthete Walter Pater was one of his tutors. At the same time, Hopkins came under the influence of the "Oxford Movement." He read John Henry Newman's account of his gravitation toward Roman Catholicism in *Apologia Pro Vita Sua*; subsequent talks with Newman led to Hopkins's own agonizing conversion to Catholicism in 1866. In 1868 he entered the novitiate of the Society of Jesus and burned almost all his early, Keatsian poems. He called his action the "slaughter of the innocents," and resolved "to write no more, as not belonging to my profession, unless it were by the wish of my superiors."

Seven years of poetic silence ensued, as Hopkins studied for the priesthood. But he was also meditating on his idiosyncratic theories of poetic composition. When five nuns were drowned in a shipwreck in 1875, he was suddenly moved to compose the first poem in his new style, *The Wreck of the Deutschland*. But there was no audience prepared to fathom his highly wrought style. Hopkins offered the work to a Jesuit magazine but, he said, "they dared not print it." He never again tried to publish.

Hopkins was ordained a Jesuit priest in 1877. Joyous, he produced a series of radiant sonnets celebrating the presence of God in nature. But his remaining years tested his faith sorely. Often in ill-health, he labored as a parish priest and teacher throughout Britain, including missionary work in the slums of Liverpool. He suffered physically and spiritually from the "vice and horrors" he found in his dreary urban duties: "It made even life a burden to me," he confessed. Then in 1884 he was appointed Professor of Greek and Latin at the Catholic, newly formed University College in Dublin. Already estranged from his family and the English church, he felt separated from his country, too. "I am in Ireland now," he wrote in a sonnet, "now I am at a third / Remove." Yet even as he despaired of accomplishing work of lasting value, he produced many of his best poems, including the famed "terrible sonnets" that describe his sense of spiritual and poetic sterility. Exhausted by his strenuous duties, Hopkins died in Dublin of typhoid at the age of forty-five.

Although Hopkins read the important nineteenth-century poets with care, he deliberately carved his own way. "The effect of studying masterpieces," he said, "is to make me admire and do otherwise." In his journals Hopkins often sounds like an English Thoreau, finely attuned to every nuance of the natural world. His entries are always searching to grasp the essential particularity of a thing, its inner landscape—what he called "inscape." Elaborating his theory in a letter to Robert Bridges, an Oxford friend who later became poet laureate, Hopkins admitted that "no doubt my poetry errs on the side of oddness. . . . it is the vice of distinctiveness to become queer." But he asserted the absolute importance of such "distinctiveness"—this "design, pattern or what I am in the habit of calling *inscape* is what I above all aim at in poetry." Hopkins needed another term to express the dynamic energy that not only makes the inscape cohere but also projects it outward toward the observer. This force that both unifies an object and arouses the senses of its beholder Hopkins called "instress." Taken together, the terms "inscape" and "instress" convey the organic beauty that for Hopkins speaks of God's presence in nature.

To apply these concepts poetically Hopkins developed a new verse line based on "sprung rhythm." As in Old English poetry or nursery rhymes, each line in sprung rhythm has a fixed number of stresses, but the number and placement of unstressed syllables can vary widely. Many poets had employed individual lines of this type, but Hopkins took the idea of flexible metrics to new heights. He loaded his lines with internal rhyme, alliteration, assonance, and strong Anglo-Saxon words, and drove them forward with crashing consonants and wrenching enjambments. Responding to Bridges's confusion, he explained: "Why do I employ sprung rhythm at all? Because it is the nearest to the rhythm of prose, that is the native and natural rhythm of speech, the least forced, the most rhetorical and emphatic of all possible rhythms." Since Hopkins connected the sight and sound of individual words to the religious intensity with which he viewed objects in nature, the effect is akin to impassioned prayer. "My verse is less to be read than heard," he concluded; "it is oratorical."

In his later poetry a tangle of religious and sexual imagery expresses his sense of thwarted love and meager poetic production. He portrays himself as a sapless tree, or as barren sand: "I am soft sift / In an hourglass." In 1885 he wrote to Bridges in frustration, "if I could but produce work I should not mind its being buried, silenced, and going no further; but it kills me to be time's eunuch and never to beget." Such passages, with their images of sexual impotency, poetic infertility, and self-abnegation, suggest what Bridges called "the naked encounter of sensualism and asceticism" in Hopkins's work.

Despite his disclaimers, Hopkins was preoccupied with his lack of an audience. He once informed Bridges: "You are my public and I hope to convert you." Missionary-like, Hopkins's poetry seeks to "convert" the reader with its ecstatic particularity, its intensity of perception. But he speaks of his efforts as a one-way correspondence to God and his public; his poems are "cries like dead letters sent / To dearest him that lives alas! away." Hopkins could not have known that Bridges, despite his difficulty grasping these "dead letters," would finally publish the poems to great acclaim at the close of World War I. Then, like the works of Emily Dickinson and Vincent Van Gogh, they would suddenly seize a central artistic place in a past that had been unaware of their existence. And yet, Hopkins did recognize that his mingling of sensuality and spirituality allied him with another great protomodernist. "I always knew in my heart Walt Whitman's mind to be more like my own than any other man's living," he told Bridges. "As he is a great scoundrel this is not a pleasant confession."

God's Grandeur

The world is charged with the grandeur of God.
   It will flame out, like shining from shook foil;[1]
   It gathers to a greatness, like the ooze of oil
Crushed.[2] Why do men then now not reck° his rod?   *heed*
5 Generations have trod, have trod, have trod;
   And all is seared with trade; bleared, smeared with toil;
   And wears man's smudge and shares man's smell: the soil
Is bare now, nor can foot feel, being shod.

---

1. I mean foil in its sense of leaf or tinsel. . . . Shaken goldfoil gives off broad glares like sheet lightning and also, and this is true of nothing else, owing to its zigzag dints and creasings and network of small many cornered facets, a sort of fork lightning too [Hopkins's note].
2. Oil made by crushing seeds or olives.

And for° all this, nature is never spent;   *despite*
10   There lives the dearest freshness deep down things;
And though the last lights off the black West went
    Oh, morning, at the brown brink eastward, springs—
Because the Holy Ghost over the bent
    World broods with warm breast and with ah! bright wings.

1877   1895

The Windhover:[1]
To Christ Our Lord

I caught this morning morning's minion,[2] king-
    dom of daylight's dauphin,[3] dapple-dawn-drawn Falcon, in his riding
Of the rolling level underneath him steady air, and striding
High there, how he rung upon the rein[4] of a wimpling wing
5   In his ecstasy! then off, off forth on swing,
    As a skate's heel sweeps smooth on a bow-bend: the hurl and gliding
Rebuffed the big wind. My heart in hiding
Stirred for a bird,—the achieve of, the mastery of the thing!

Brute beauty and valour and act, oh, air, pride, plume, here
10   Buckle! AND the fire that breaks from thee then, a billion
Times told lovelier, more dangerous, O my chevalier!

No wonder of it: shéer plód makes plough down sillion[5]
Shine, and blue-bleak embers, ah my dear,
    Fall, gall[6] themselves, and gash gold-vermilion.

1877   1918

Pied[1] Beauty

Glory be to God for dappled things—
    For skies of couple-colour as a brinded[2] cow;
        For rose-moles all in stipple[3] upon trout that swim;
Fresh-firecoal chestnut-falls;[4] finches' wings;
5   Landscape plotted and pieced—fold, fallow, and plough;[5]
        And áll trádes, their gear and tackle and trim.°   *equipment*

All things counter,[6] original, spare, strange;
    Whatever is fickle, freckled (who knows how?)
        With swift, slow; sweet, sour; adazzle, dim;
10   He fathers-forth whose beauty is past change:
                Praise him.

1877   1918

---

1. Kestrel falcon—a small hawk—that appears to hover in the air.
2. Darling, from the French *mignon*.
3. The dauphin was the heir to the French throne.
4. In falconry, a bird rings when it rises in spirals (like a horse circling at the end of a tether or rein). Wimpling means rippling.
5. The furrows of a plowed field.

6. Break their surfaces.
1. Blotched with different colors.
2. Brindled, having dark patches on a tawny ground.
3. Stippled, painted or drawn with dots instead of lines.
4. Chestnuts as bright as coals [Hopkins's journal].
5. Landscape of differently colored fields, some used as pasture ("fold"), some lying fallow, some plowed.
6. Contrary; "spare" means rare.

Felix Randal

Felix Randal the farrier,[1] O he is dead then? my duty all ended,
Who have watched his mould of man, big-boned and hardy-handsome
Pining, pining, till time when reason rambled in it and some
Fatal four disorders, fleshed there, all contended?

5   Sickness broke him. Impatient he cursed at first, but mended
Being anointed[2] and all; though a heavenlier heart began some
Months earlier, since I had our sweet reprieve and ransom[3]
Tendered to him. Ah well, God rest him all road ever° he offended!   *however*

This seeing the sick endears them to us, us too it endears.
10 My tongue had taught thee comfort, touch had quenched thy tears,
Thy tears that touched my heart, child, Felix, poor Felix Randal;

How far from then forethought of, all thy more boisterous years,
When thou at the random[4] grim forge, powerful amidst peers,
Didst fettle° for the great grey drayhorse his bright and battering sandal!   *prepare*

1880   1918

Spring and Fall:
to a young child

Márgarét, are you gríeving
Over Goldengrove unleaving?
Leáves, líke the things of man, you
With your fresh thoughts care for, can you?
5   Áh! ás the heart grows older
It will come to such sights colder
By and by, nor spare a sigh
Though worlds of wanwood leafmeal lie;[1]
And yet you wíll weep and know why.
10 Now no matter, child, the name:
Sórrow's spríngs áre the same.
Nor mouth had, no nor mind, expressed
What heart heard of, ghost° guessed: *spirit*
It ís the blight man was born for,
15 It is Margaret you mourn for.

1880   1918

As Kingfishers Catch Fire

As kingfishers catch fire, dragonflies dráw fláme;
As tumbled over rim in roundy wells
Stones ring; like each tucked° string tells, each hung bell's   *plucked*
Bow swung finds tongue to fling out broad its name;

---

1. Blacksmith.
2. Having received Extreme Unction, the sacrament for the dying.
3. Confession, absolution, and Holy Communion.

4. Built of rough irregular stones.
1. The leaves of pale trees lie scattered; "leafmeal" is derived from "piecemeal."

5   Each mortal thing does one thing and the same:
       Deals out that being indoors each one dwells;
       Selves—goes itself; *myself* it speaks and spells;
       Crying *Whát I dó is me: for that I came.*

       Í say móre: the just man justices;
10   Kéeps gráce; thát keeps all his goings graces;
       Acts in God's eye what in God's eye he is—
       Chríst—for Christ plays in ten thousand places,
       Lovely in limbs, and lovely in eyes not his
       To the Father through the features of men's faces.

1881–1882?   1918

[Carrion Comfort][1]

       Not, I'll not, carrion comfort, Despair, not feast on thee;
       Not untwist—slack they may be—these last strands of man
       In me ór, most weary, cry *I can no more.* I can;
       Can something, hope, wish day come, not choose not to be.
5   But ah, but O thou terrible, why wouldst thou rude on me
       Thy wring-world right foot rock? lay a lionlimb against me? scan
       With darksome devouring eyes my bruisèd bones? and fan,
       O in turns of tempest, me heaped there; me frantic to avoid thee and flee?

           Why? That my chaff might fly; my grain lie, sheer and clear.
10   Nay in all that toil, that coil,[2] since (seems) I kissed the rod,
       Hand rather,[3] my heart lo! lapped strength, stole joy, would laugh, chéer.
       Cheer whom though? the hero whose heaven-handling flung me, fóot tród
       Me? or me that fought him? O which one? is it each one? That night, that year
       Of now done darkness I wretch lay wrestling with (my God!) my God.

1885   1918

No Worst, There Is None

       No worst, there is none. Pitched past pitch of grief,
       More pangs will, schooled at forepangs, wilder wring.
       Comforter, where, where is your comforting?
       Mary, mother of us, where is your relief?
5   My cries heave, herds-long;[1] huddle in a main, a chief
       Woe, world-sorrow; on an age-old anvil wince and sing—
       Then lull, then leave off. Fury had shrieked "No ling-
       ering! Let me be fell:° force° I must be brief."   *fierce / perforce*

           O the mind, mind has mountains; cliffs of fall
10   Frightful, sheer, no-man-fathomed. Hold them cheap

---

1. The title was added by Robert Bridges. This poem is one of the "terrible sonnets" of 1885, as are the next two.
2. Turmoil.

3. I.e., the hand that holds the rod the speaker has kissed.
1. Like a cry of sheep or cattle repeated successively the length of the herd.

May who ne'er hung there. Nor does long our small
Durance° deal with that steep or deep. Here! creep,   *endurance*
Wretch, under a comfort serves in a whirlwind: all
Life death does end and each day dies with sleep.

1885   1918

I Wake and Feel the Fell of Dark, Not Day

I wake and feel the fell[1] of dark, not day.
What hours, O what black hoürs we have spent
This night! what sights you, heart, saw; ways you went!
And more must, in yet longer light's delay.
5   With witness I speak this. But where I say
Hours I mean years, mean life. And my lament
Is cries countless, cries like dead letters sent
To dearest him that lives alas! away.

I am gall, I am heartburn. God's most deep decree
10   Bitter would have me taste: my taste was me;
Bones built in me, flesh filled, blood brimmed the curse.
    Selfyeast of spirit a dull dough sours. I see
The lost° are like this, and their scourge to be   *souls in Hell*
As I am mine, their sweating selves; but worse.

1885   1918

Thou Art Indeed Just, Lord

Justus quidem tu es, Domine, si disputem tecum: verumtamen
   justa loquar ad te: Quare via impiorum prosperatur? &c.[1]

Thou art indeed just, Lord, if I contend
With thee; but, sir, so what I plead is just.
Why do sinners' ways prosper? and why must
Disappointment all I endeavour end?
5   Wert thou my enemy, O thou my friend,
How wouldst thou worse, I wonder, than thou dost
Defeat, thwart me? Oh, the sots and thralls of lust
Do in spare hours more thrive than I that spend,
Sir, life upon thy cause. See, banks and brakes°   *thickets*
10 Now, leavèd how thick! lacèd they are again
With fretty chervil,° look, and fresh wind shakes   *cow-parsley*
Them; birds build—but not I build; no, but strain,
Time's eunuch, and not breed one work that wakes.
Mine, O thou lord of life, send my roots rain.

1889   1893

---

1. Gall, bitterness; but also a hide or covering; a waste-
land; as an adjective, "fell" means fierce or cruel.

1. The first lines of the poem translate these words from
Jeremiah 12.1.

Oscar Wilde
1854–1900

"He hasn't a single redeeming vice." Oscar Wilde's witticism hardly applied to himself: his character was a quixotic mixture of brilliance and folly. Flamboyant, extravagant, outrageous, the most splendid playwright of the century lived his own life on center stage. Though his flagrant self-promotion irritated many, he was generous and good-natured, unable to imagine that the Victorian morality he satirized would finally bring about his own fall.

Wilde was born in Dublin, and although he spent much of his adult life in England, he never lost the sense of himself as a foreigner. His parents—Irish Protestants, ardent nationalists, and prolific writers—were notable figures in their own right: Sir William Robert Wilde was a famous surgeon, fathered three illegitimate children, and was sued by a former patient who claimed he had drugged and raped her. Lady Wilde, who changed her name from Jane Frances to Speranza Francesca, was a self-dramatizing and unconventional woman whom her son adored.

Wilde was educated in Ireland until 1874 when he won a scholarship to Oxford. Here he began to establish a reputation as an Aesthete and an admirer of Pre-Raphaelite poets such as Swinburne, Rossetti, and William Morris. He was also attracted to the contradictory artistic creeds of both John Ruskin and Walter Pater, Ruskin proclaiming that all good art is moral art, Pater preferring "poetic passion, the desire of beauty, the love of art for art's sake." Wilde dressed ostentatiously, wore his hair long, and decorated his rooms with lilies, a favorite symbol of the Aesthetes. His literary abilities won him both the Newdigate Prize for poetry and a double first (highest honors). But along with these academic awards he was celebrated for a remark which seemed to epitomize aestheticism: "I find it harder and harder every day to live up to my blue china."

Following his triumphs at Oxford, Wilde cast about for a career. His father had died leaving only a small inheritance, and Wilde's attempts to win a university fellowship failed. In London he set about making himself conspicuous, and soon he was the center of the social scene. Few could help being dazzled by his witty conversation. Yet some were skeptical, including an actress who said: "What has he done, this young man, that one meets him everywhere? Oh yes he talks well, but what has he done? He has written nothing, he does not sing or paint or act—he does nothing but talk."

Wilde's talk, however, was glorious, and eventually would find lasting expression in his plays. Meanwhile, he played the dandy, and was satirized by Gilbert and Sullivan in *Patience* (1881) as the most illustrious Aesthete of the day, who had walked "down Piccadilly with a poppy or a lily in his medieval hand." Wilde reacted with good humor, observing that "To have done it was nothing, but to make people think one had done it was a triumph."

In the early 1880s Wilde began to refute the charge that he did nothing but talk. He wrote his first play, called *Vera; or, The Nihilists* (1880), about Russian czars and revolutionaries; the play's portrayal of an assassination attempt made it politically unacceptable, and the production was canceled. He privately published a book of poems in 1881, opening with the sonnet *Hélas!* They were praised by Matthew Arnold and by Swinburne, but elsewhere denounced as immoral.

Wilde's finances received an unexpected boost when the New York production of *Patience* led to an invitation to lecture in the United States. His arrival in New York in 1882 was a media event: he was mobbed by reporters, and his every utterance was quoted or misquoted in both the American and British press. He was reported to have been disappointed in the Atlantic—"It is not so majestic as I expected"—and to have told the customs officers, "I have nothing to declare except my genius." He stayed a full year, earned quite a lot of money, and returned home internationally famous.

Oscar Wilde and Lord Alfred
Douglas, 1893.

Wilde followed up his conquest of America with a few months in Paris, where he met many leading painters and writers. Back in London, and short of money once again, his thoughts turned to marriage, and in 1884 he wed Constance Lloyd. She was well-educated and well-off, and at first Wilde enjoyed the new roles of husband and then father to two sons, Cyril and Vyvyan. But he soon found married life a bore. Even during his honeymoon in Paris his thoughts were elsewhere: he became enamored of a book known as the Bible of decadence, *A Rebours* (1884) by Joris-Karl Huysmans. As his biographer Richard Ellmann has put it, this book "summoned him towards an underground life."

Wilde was a celebrity. He spent several years lecturing and reviewing, then entered the most inventive period of his life. Although he would later remark, "I have put only my talent into my works. I have put my genius into my life," the creative work of the early 1890s belies him. He articulated his theories on Art and Nature in two dialogues full of provocative paradoxes, *The Decay of Lying* (1888) and *The Critic as Artist* (1890). Then in his essay *The Soul of Man Under Socialism* (1891) he argued that the final goal of social evolution was joyous individualism. He continued his exploration of the relation of art to life in his only novel, *The Picture of Dorian Gray* (1890), which tells of a promising golden boy fascinated by the seductively amoral ideas of a jaded cynic. Dorian makes a Faustian bargain: his corrupted soul will be mirrored, not in his own face—he remains eternally youthful—but in his portrait. Much influenced by *A Rebours, Dorian Gray* achieved instantaneous notoriety, not so much for its aestheticism as for its thinly veiled suggestions of homosexuality.

Lady Windermere's Fan (1891) met with the opposite reception: this sparkling comedy depicting a mother's secret sacrifice for her daughter was an immediate success. Inspired in part by the French symbolist poet, Stéphane Mallarmé, Wilde was also writing—in French—a very different play, *Salomé*, about the fatal perversity of love and desire. To Wilde's indignation, *Salomé* was banned in England. However, in 1894 he published an English translation, with dramatic and daring illustrations by Aubrey Beardsley.

Wilde wrote two more comedies, *A Woman of No Importance* and *An Ideal Husband*, followed by his masterpiece. *The Importance of Being Earnest* (1895). Its philosophy, Wilde said, is "That we should treat all trivial things very seriously, and all the serious things of life with sincere and studied triviality." The triumphant opening night of this delightfully sophisticated farce marked the culmination of Wilde's career.

Then, at the very crest of success, Wilde was brought down by catastrophe. Although homosexuality was a criminal offense in Britain, Wilde had made little effort to conceal his relations with younger men, particularly Lord Alfred Douglas. But if society turned a blind eye, Douglas's father, the Marquess of Queensberry, did not. He hounded his son's lover relentlessly, finally sending Wilde a ludicrously misspelled note calling him a "Somdomite." Egged on by Douglas, Wilde sued for libel. It was a fatal mistake. His private affairs were mercilessly exposed in court, and he lost the case. Wilde himself was then prosecuted for committing indecent acts, convicted, and sentenced to two years at hard labor.

His obsession with the young aristocrat—beautiful, vicious, and volatile—had been ruinous in every sense. Wilde was disgraced and bankrupted. So great was the collective repugnance for him that both of his currently running plays, *An Ideal Husband* and *The Importance of Being Earnest*, were obliged to close. But the nightmare was only beginning: following the public humiliation of the trials was the horror of prison. Confined in a small cell with a bare plank bed, revolting food, and no latrine, he suffered constantly from diarrhea. He was allowed only one twenty-minute visit every three months. No talking was permitted. Dreading that he might lose his sanity, Wilde pleaded in vain for early release.

He gave vent to his sufferings in a long letter to Douglas entitled *De Profundis*. It is a terrible indictment of Douglas's selfish behavior, but more than that it is an autobiography, the anguished confession of a soul coming face to face with itself. Painfully he reviews the events that led to his downfall, finding at last his own salvation in forgiveness: "I don't write this letter to put bitterness into your heart, but to pluck it out of mine. For my own sake I must forgive you." Wilde was allowed to take the letter with him when he left prison, but chose not to have it published until after his death.

Wilde emerged from the degradation of prison a broken and penniless man. He spent the remainder of his life in exile outside Britain. He was never again allowed to see his young sons, and their surname was changed to protect them from scandal. All but a few loyal friends shunned him. The man who had lavished champagne on his friends was reduced to scrounging drinks from strangers who pitied him. He was unable to resume his writing, except for *The Ballad of Reading Gaol* (1898), a long poem based upon his prison experience. He converted to Catholicism on his deathbed, in a Paris hotel, but continued bravely inventing witticisms to the end: "I am dying beyond my means."

Impression du Matin[1]

The Thames nocturne of blue and gold
    Changed to a harmony in gray:[2]

---

1. Impression of the morning (French). The title evokes the paintings of the French Impressionists, and their attempts to show how light transforms the landscape. The group received its name in 1874 when a critic singled out Monet's *Impression: Sunrise* as representative. 2. The American James McNeill Whistler painted a series of Thames night-scenes, called "nocturnes" (including the famous *Nocturne in Blue and Gold: Old Battersea Bridge*, c. 1875). He entitled some of his daytime scenes "harmonies." His close friendship with Wilde turned into a bitter rivalry by the mid-1880s; Whistler accused Wilde of plagiarizing his ideas.

A barge with ochre-coloured hay
Dropt° from the wharf: and chill and cold   *went downstream*

5   The yellow fog came creeping down
        The bridges, till the houses' walls
        Seemed changed to shadows and St. Paul's
    Loomed like a bubble o'er the town.

    Then suddenly arose the clang
10   Of waking life; the streets were stirred
        With country wagons: and a bird
    Flew to the glistening roofs and sang.

    But one pale woman all alone,
        The daylight kissing her wan hair,
15   Loitered beneath the gas lamps' flare,
    With lips of flame and heart of stone.

1877   1881

The Harlot's House

We caught the tread of dancing feet,
We loitered down the moonlit street,
And stopped beneath the harlot's house.

Inside, above the din and fray,
5   We heard the loud musicians play
The "Treues Liebes Herz" of Strauss.[1]

Like strange mechanical grotesques,
Making fantastic arabesques,[2]
The shadows raced across the blind.

10   We watched the ghostly dancers spin
To sound of horn and violin,
Like black leaves wheeling in the wind.

Like wire-pulled automatons,
Slim silhouetted skeletons
15   Went sidling through the slow quadrille.[3]

They took each other by the hand,
And danced a stately saraband;
Their laughter echoed thin and shrill.

Sometimes a clockwork puppet pressed
20   A phantom lover to her breast,
Sometimes they seemed to try to sing.

Sometimes a horrible marionette
Came out, and smoked its cigarette
Upon the steps like a live thing.

1. "The Heart of True Love," a waltz by Viennese composer Johann Strauss (1825–1899).
2. "Arabesque" is a term both for a ballet posture and, in art, for patterns of interlaced lines.
3. Square dance for four couples. The saraband (line 17) is an old Spanish dance.

25   Then, turning to my love, I said,
      "The dead are dancing with the dead,
      The dust is whirling with the dust."

      But she—she heard the violin,
      And left my side, and entered in:
30   Love passed into the house of Lust.

      Then suddenly the tune went false,
      The dancers wearied of the waltz,
      The shadows ceased to wheel and whirl.

      And down the long and silent street,
35   The dawn, with silver-sandalled feet,
      Crept like a frightened girl.

                                              1885, 1908

Symphony in Yellow[1]

      An omnibus across the bridge
          Crawls like a yellow butterfly,
          And, here and there, a passer-by
      Shows like a little restless midge.

5   Big barges full of yellow hay
          Are moored against the shadowy wharf,
          And, like a yellow silken scarf,
      The thick fog hangs along the quay.

      The yellow leaves begin to fade
10   And flutter from the Temple elms,[2]
          And at my feet the pale green Thames
      Lies like a rod of rippled jade.

                                              1889

from The Decay of Lying[1]
An Observation

A dialogue. Persons: Cyril and Vivian.[2]

SCENE: *The library of a country house in Nottinghamshire.*

CYRIL (*coming in through the open window from the terrace*) My dear Vivian, don't coop yourself up all day in the library. It is a perfectly lovely afternoon. The air is exquisite. There is a mist upon the woods, like the purple bloom upon a plum. Let us go and lie on the grass, and smoke cigarettes, and enjoy Nature.

---

1. The title suggests Whistler's series of paintings that he called "symphonies" in various colors. The Aesthetic vogue for titles that mingle the arts originated with the French poet Théophile Gautier, who in 1852 named a poem *Symphony in White Major*. In the 1880s yellow—the color of sunflowers and paperback French novels—became associated with the Aesthetic movement.
2. The Middle Temple and Inner Temple form part of the Inns of Court; their garden runs down to the River Thames.
1. Published in January 1889 in *The Nineteenth Century*, then revised and reprinted in Wilde's *Intentions* (1891). This essay adopts the form of a Platonic dialogue in order

to reconsider Plato's famous assertion in *The Republic* that art is falsehood. Wilde agrees with Plato that the artist tells lies, but instead of finding this morally repugnant, he praises the artist's imaginative victory over nature and mere fact. Questioning Plato's claim that art is a shadowy reflection of real life, Wilde claims that art comes first: "life is the mirror, and art the reality." As he explores the paradoxes of his theory that life imitates art, Wilde seeks to shock his audience into revising its aesthetic values; he wittily subverts the Victorian reverence for nature, sincerity, moral teaching, and artistic verisimilitude.
2. Wilde's two sons, aged three and two at the time Wilde wrote this, were named Cyril and Vyvyan.

VIVIAN Enjoy Nature! I am glad to say that I have entirely lost that faculty. People tell us that Art makes us love Nature more than we loved her before; that it reveals her secrets to us; and that after a careful study of Corot and Constable we see things in her that had escaped our observation. My own experience is that the more we study Art, the less we care for Nature. What Art really reveals to us is Nature's lack of design, her curious crudities, her extraordinary monotony, her absolutely unfinished condition. Nature has good intentions, of course, but, as Aristotle once said, she cannot carry them out.[3] When I look at a landscape I cannot help seeing all its defects. It is fortunate for us, however, that Nature is so imperfect, as otherwise we should have had no art at all. Art is our spirited protest, our gallant attempt to teach Nature her proper place. As for the infinite variety of Nature, that is a pure myth. It is not to be found in Nature herself. It resides in the imagination, or fancy, or cultivated blindness of the man who looks at her.

CYRIL Well, you need not look at the landscape. You can lie on the grass and smoke and talk.

VIVIAN But Nature is so uncomfortable. Grass is hard and lumpy and damp, and full of dreadful black insects. Why, even Morris' poorest workman[4] could make you a more comfortable seat than the whole of Nature can. Nature pales before the furniture of "the street which from Oxford has borrowed its name," as the poet you love so much once vilely phrased it.[5] I don't complain. If Nature had been comfortable, mankind would never have invented architecture, and I prefer houses to the open air. In a house we all feel of the proper proportions. Everything is subordinated to us, fashioned for our use and our pleasure. Egotism itself, which is so necessary to a proper sense of human dignity, is entirely the result of indoor life. Out of doors one becomes abstract and impersonal. One's individuality absolutely leaves one. And then Nature is so indifferent, so unappreciative. Whenever I am walking in the park here, I always feel that I am no more to her than the cattle that browse on the slope, or the burdock that blooms in the ditch. Nothing is more evident than that Nature hates Mind. Thinking is the most unhealthy thing in the world, and people die of it just as they die of any other disease. Fortunately, in England at any rate, thought is not catching. Our splendid physique as a people is entirely due to our national stupidity. I only hope we shall be able to keep this great historic bulwark of our happiness for many years to come; but I am afraid that we are beginning to be over-educated; at least everybody who is incapable of learning has taken to teaching—that is really what our enthusiasm for education has come to. In the meantime, you had better go back to your wearisome uncomfortable Nature, and leave me to correct my proofs.

CYRIL Writing an article! That is not very consistent after what you have just said.

VIVIAN Who wants to be consistent? The dullard and the doctrinaire, the tedious people who carry out their principles to the bitter end of action, to the *reductio ad absurdum* of practice. Not I. Like Emerson, I write over the door of my library the word "Whim."[6] Besides, my article is really a most salutary and valuable warning. If it is attended to, there may be a new Renaissance of Art.

CYRIL What is the subject?

---

3. In the *Poetics* Aristotle suggests that through mimesis or imitation of life, the artist completes nature's work.
4. William Morris employed skilled craftsmen to produce handmade furniture and textiles.
5. The goods sold on Oxford Street in London outshine the products of Wordsworth's beloved Nature. The line in Wordsworth's *The Power of Music* actually reads: "In the street that from Oxford hath borrowed its name."
6. Ralph Waldo Emerson, the American essayist, wrote in *Self-Reliance* (1841): "I shun father and mother and wife and brother when my genius calls me. I would write on the lintels of the doorpost, *Whim*."

VIVIAN I intend to call it "The Decay of Lying: A Protest."

CYRIL Lying! I should have thought that our politicians kept up that habit.

VIVIAN I assure you that they do not. They never rise beyond the level of misrepresentation, and actually condescend to prove, to discuss, to argue. How different from the temper of the true liar, with his frank, fearless statements, his superb irresponsibility, his healthy, natural disdain of proof of any kind! After all, what is a fine lie? Simply that which is its own evidence. If a man is sufficiently unimaginative to produce evidence in support of a lie, he might just as well speak the truth at once. No, the politicians won't do. Something may, perhaps, be urged on behalf of the Bar. The mantle of the Sophist[7] has fallen on its members. Their feigned ardours and unreal rhetoric are delightful. They can make the worse appear the better cause, as though they were fresh from Leontine schools,[8] and have been known to wrest from reluctant juries triumphant verdicts of acquittal for their clients, even when those clients, as often happens, were clearly and unmistakeably innocent. But they are briefed by the prosaic, and are not ashamed to appeal to precedent. In spite of their endeavours, the truth will out. Newspapers, even, have degenerated. They may now be absolutely relied upon. One feels it as one wades through their columns. It is always the unreadable that occurs. I am afraid that there is not much to be said in favour of either the lawyer or the journalist. Besides, what I am pleading for is Lying in art. Shall I read you what I have written? It might do you a great deal of good.

CYRIL Certainly, if you give me a cigarette. Thanks. By the way, what magazine do you intend it for?

VIVIAN For the *Retrospective Review*.[9] I think I told you that the elect had revived it.

CYRIL Whom do you mean by "the elect"?

VIVIAN Oh, The Tired Hedonists of course.[1] It is a club to which I belong. We are supposed to wear faded roses in our button-holes when we meet, and to have a sort of cult for Domitian.[2] I am afraid you are not eligible. You are too fond of simple pleasures.

CYRIL I should be black-balled on the ground of animal spirits, I suppose?

VIVIAN Probably. Besides, you are a little too old. We don't admit anybody who is of the usual age.

CYRIL Well, I should fancy you are all a good deal bored with each other.

VIVIAN We are. That is one of the objects of the club. Now, if you promise not to interrupt too often, I will read you my article.

CYRIL You will find me all attention.

VIVIAN (*reading in a very clear, musical voice*) "THE DECAY OF LYING: A PROTEST.— One of the chief causes that can be assigned for the curiously commonplace character of most of the literature of our age is undoubtedly the decay of Lying as an art, a science, and a social pleasure. The ancient historians gave us delightful fiction in the form of fact; the modern novelist presents us with dull facts under the guise of fiction. The Blue-Book[3] is rapidly becoming his ideal both for method

---

7. The Sophists were Greek philosophers who taught the art of rhetoric; the word now refers to a deceptive reasoner.

8. Leontini was a Greek colony in Sicily where the sophist and rhetorician Gorgias (c. 483–375 B.C.) was educated.

9. A periodical, published in the 1820s and again in the 1850s that promoted interest in earlier literature. It was not, in fact, revived in the 1890s.

1. Hedonists believe that pleasure is the greatest good in

life; a tired hedonist would be one exhausted by pleasure (a parody of Wilde's own image).

2. Emperor of Rome (A.D. 81–96), Domitian was famous for his cruelty.

3. Parliamentary reports. The whole passage is aimed at contemporary Realist and Naturalist novelists, such as George Gissing and Émile Zola, who sought to document everyday life, especially among the poor.

and manner. He has his tedious '*document humain,*'[4] his miserable little '*coin de la création,*' into which he peers with his microscope. He is to be found at the Librairie Nationale, or at the British Museum, shamelessly reading up his subject. He has not even the courage of other people's ideas, but insists on going directly to life for everything, and ultimately, between encyclopaedias and personal experience, he comes to the ground, having drawn his types from the family circle or from the weekly washerwoman, and having acquired an amount of useful information from which never, even in his most meditative moments, can he thoroughly free himself.

* * * Believe me, my dear Cyril, modernity of form and modernity of subject-matter are entirely and absolutely wrong. We have mistaken the common livery of the age for the vesture of the Muses, and spend our days in the sordid streets and hideous suburbs of our vile cities when we should be out on the hillside with Apollo. Certainly we are a degraded race, and have sold our birthright for a mess of facts.[5]

CYRIL There is something in what you say, and there is no doubt that whatever amusement we may find in reading a purely modern novel, we have rarely any artistic pleasure in re-reading it. And this is perhaps the best rough test of what is literature and what is not. If one cannot enjoy reading a book over and over again, there is no use reading it at all. But what do you say about the return to Life and Nature? This is the panacea that is always being recommended to us.

VIVIAN I will read you what I say on that subject. The passage comes later on in the article, but I may as well give it to you now:—

"The popular cry of our time is 'Let us return to Life and Nature; they will recreate Art for us, and send the red blood coursing through her veins; they will shoe her feet with swiftness and make her hand strong.' But, alas! we are mistaken in our amiable and well-meaning efforts. Nature is always behind the age. And as for Life, she is the solvent that breaks up Art, the enemy that lays waste her house."

CYRIL What do you mean by saying that Nature is always behind the age?

VIVIAN Well, perhaps that is rather cryptic. What I mean is this. If we take Nature to mean natural simple instinct as opposed to self-conscious culture, the work produced under this influence is always old-fashioned, antiquated, and out of date. One touch of Nature may make the whole world kin, but two touches of Nature will destroy any work of Art. If, on the other hand, we regard Nature as the collection of phenomena external to man, people only discover in her what they bring to her. She has no suggestions of her own. Wordsworth went to the lakes, but he was never a lake poet. He found in stones the sermons he had already hidden there.[6] He went moralizing about the district, but his good work was produced when he returned, not to Nature but to poetry. Poetry gave him "Laodamia," and the fine sonnets, and the great Ode,[7] such as it is. Nature gave him "Martha Ray" and "Peter Bell," and the address to Mr Wilkinson's spade.

---

4. Human document, from the title of an essay by Zola, who wrote in *What I Hate:* "A work of art is a nook of creation ("un coin de la création") seen from the perspective of a temperament."
5. When he was hungry, Esau sold his birthright to his brother Jacob for "a mess of pottage" (Genesis 25.30–34).
6. "And this our life, exempt from public haunt, / Finds tongues in trees, books in the running brooks, / Sermons in stones, and good in every thing" (*As You Like It* 2.1.15–17).
7. Presumably Wordsworth's *Ode: Intimations of Immortality.* Vivian next mentions several distinctly lesser poems.

CYRIL I think that view might be questioned. I am rather inclined to believe in the "impulse from a vernal wood,"[8] though of course the artistic value of such an impulse depends entirely on the kind of temperament that receives it, so that the return to Nature would come to mean simply the advance to a great personality. You would agree with that, I fancy. However, proceed with your article.

VIVIAN (*reading*) "Art begins with abstract decoration, with purely imaginative and pleasurable work dealing with what is unreal and nonexistent. This is the first stage. Then Life becomes fascinated with this new wonder, and asks to be admitted into the charmed circle. Art takes life as part of her rough material, recreates it, and refashions it in fresh forms, is absolutely indifferent to fact, invents, imagines, dreams, and keeps between herself and reality the impenetrable barrier of beautiful style, of decorative or ideal treatment. The third stage is when Life gets the upper hand, and drives Art out into the wilderness. This is the true decadence, and it is from this that we are now suffering.

"Take the case of the English drama. At first in the hands of the monks Dramatic Art was abstract, decorative, and mythological. Then she enlisted Life in her service, and using some of life's external forms, she created an entirely new race of beings, whose sorrows were more terrible than any sorrow man has ever felt, whose joys were keener than lover's joys, who had the rage of the Titans[9] and the calm of the gods, who had monstrous and marvellous sins, monstrous and marvellous virtues. To them she gave a language different from that of actual use, a language full of resonant music and sweet rhythm, made stately by solemn cadence, or made delicate by fanciful rhyme, jewelled with wonderful words, and enriched with lofty diction. She clothed her children in strange raiment and gave them masks, and at her bidding the antique world rose from its marble tomb. A new Caesar stalked through the streets of risen Rome, and with purple sail and flute-led oars another Cleopatra passed up the river to Antioch.[1] Old myth and legend and dream took shape and substance. History was entirely re-written, and there was hardly one of the dramatists who did not recognize that the object of Art is not simple truth but complex beauty. In this they were perfectly right. Art itself is really a form of exaggeration; and selection, which is the very spirit of art, is nothing more than an intensified mode of over-emphasis.

"But Life soon shattered the perfection of the form. Even in Shakespeare we can see the beginning of the end. It shows itself by the gradual breaking up of the blank-verse in the later plays, by the predominance given to prose, and by the over-importance assigned to characterization. The passages in Shakespeare—and they are many—where the language is uncouth, vulgar, exaggerated, fantastic, obscene even, are entirely due to Life calling for an echo of her own voice, and rejecting the intervention of beautiful style, through which alone should Life be suffered to find expression. Shakespeare is not by any means a flawless artist. He is too fond of going directly to life, and borrowing life's natural utterance. He forgets that when Art surrenders her imaginative medium she surrenders everything. Goethe says, somewhere—

In der Beschränkung zeigt sich erst der Meister,[2]

---

8. "One impulse from a vernal wood / May teach you more of man / Of moral evil and of good / Than all the sages can." From Wordsworth's *The Tables Turned.*
9. Mythological giants who were overthrown by the gods.

1. References to Shakespeare's *Julius Caesar* and *Antony and Cleopatra.*
2. From *Nature and Art* by Johann Wolfgang von Goethe (1749–1832).

"'It is in working within limits that the master reveals himself,' and the limitation, the very condition of any art is style. However, we need not linger any longer over Shakespeare's realism. *The Tempest* is the most perfect of palinodes.[3] All that we desired to point out was, that the magnificent work of the Elizabethan and Jacobean artists contained within itself the seeds of its own dissolution, and that, if it drew some of its strength from using life as rough material, it drew all its weakness from using life as an artistic method. As the inevitable result of this substitution of an imitative for a creative medium, this surrender of an imaginative form, we have the modern English melodrama. The characters in these plays talk on the stage exactly as they would talk off it; they have neither aspirations nor aspirates; they are taken directly from life and reproduce its vulgarity down to the smallest detail; they present the gait, manner, costume, and accent of real people; they would pass unnoticed in a third-class railway carriage. And yet how wearisome the plays are! They do not succeed in producing even that impression of reality at which they aim, and which is their only reason for existing. As a method, realism is a complete failure.

"What is true about the drama and the novel is no less true about those arts that we call the decorative arts. The whole history of these arts in Europe is the record of the struggle between Orientalism, with its frank rejection of imitation, its love of artistic convention, its dislike to the actual representation of any object in Nature, and our own imitative spirit. Wherever the former has been paramount, as in Byzantium, Sicily, and Spain, by actual contact, or in the rest of Europe by the influence of the Crusades, we have had beautiful and imaginative work in which the visible things of life are transmuted into artistic conventions, and the things that Life has not are invented and fashioned for her delight. But wherever we have returned to Life and Nature, our work has always become vulgar, common, and uninteresting. Modern tapestry, with its aërial effects, its elaborate perspective, its broad expanses of waste sky, its faithful and laborious realism, has no beauty whatsoever. The pictorial glass of Germany is absolutely detestable. We are beginning to weave possible carpets in England, but only because we have returned to the method and spirit of the East. Our rugs and carpets of twenty years ago, with their solemn depressing truths, their inane worship of Nature, their sordid reproductions of visible objects, have become, even to the Philistine,[4] a source of laughter. A cultured Mahomedan once remarked to us, "You Christians are so occupied in misinterpreting the fourth commandment that you have never thought of making an artistic application of the second."[5] He was perfectly right, and the whole truth of the matter is this: The proper school to learn art in is not Life but Art."

   * * * Facts are not merely finding a footing-place in history, but they are usurping the domain of Fancy, and have invaded the kingdom of Romance. Their chilling touch is over everything. They are vulgarizing mankind. The crude commercialism of America, its materializing spirit, its indifference to the poetical side of things, and its lack of imagination and of high unattainable ideals, are entirely due to that country having adopted for its national hero a man, who according to his

---

3. A retraction or recantation.
4. In *Culture and Anarchy* (1869) Matthew Arnold used this term to refer to the materialistic and uncultured middle classes.
5. The Fourth Commandment is "Remember the Sabbath day, to keep it holy"; the Second is "Thou shalt not

make unto thee any graven image, or any likeness of any thing that is in heaven above, or that is in the earth beneath, or that is in the water underneath the earth" (Exodus 20.4–5). Islamic art is traditionally decorative rather than imitative, in observance of the second commandment.

own confession, was incapable of telling a lie, and it is not too much to say that the story of George Washington and the cherry-tree has done more harm, and in a shorter space of time, than any other moral tale in the whole of literature."

CYRIL My dear boy!

VIVIAN I assure you it is the case, and the amusing part of the whole thing is that the story of the cherry-tree is an absolute myth. However, you must not think that I am too despondent about the artistic future either of America or of our own country. Listen to this:—

"That some change will take place before this century has drawn to its close we have no doubt whatsoever. Bored by the tedious and improving conversation of those who have neither the wit to exaggerate nor the genius to romance, tired of the intelligent person whose reminiscences are always based upon memory, whose statements are invariably limited by probability, and who is at any time liable to be corroborated by the merest Philistine who happens to be present, Society sooner or later must return to its lost leader, the cultured and fascinating liar. Who he was who first, without ever having gone out to the rude chase, told the wondering cavemen at sunset how he had dragged the Megatherium[6] from the purple darkness of its jasper cave, or slain the Mammoth in single combat and brought back its gilded tusks, we cannot tell, and not one of our modern anthropologists, for all their much-boasted science, has had the ordinary courage to tell us. Whatever was his name or race, he certainly was the true founder of social intercourse. For the aim of the liar is simply to charm, to delight, to give pleasure. He is the very basis of civilized society, and without him a dinner party, even at the mansions of the great, is as dull as a lecture at the Royal Society, or a debate at the Incorporated Authors, or one of Mr Burnand's farcical comedies.[7]

"Nor will he be welcomed by society alone. Art, breaking from the prison-house of realism, will run to greet him, and will kiss his false, beautiful lips, knowing that he alone is in possession of the great secret of all her manifestations, the secret that Truth is entirely and absolutely a matter of style; while Life—poor, probable, uninteresting human life—tired of repeating herself for the benefit of Mr Herbert Spencer,[8] scientific historians, and the compilers of statistics in general, will follow meekly after him, and try to reproduce, in her own simple and untutored way, some of the marvels of which he talks. * * *

* * * All that I desire to point out is the general principle that Life imitates Art far more than Art imitates Life, and I feel sure that if you think seriously about it you will find that it is true. Life holds the mirror up to Art, and either reproduces some strange type imagined by painter or sculptor, or realizes in fact what has been dreamed in fiction. Scientifically speaking, the basis of life—the energy of life, as Aristotle would call it[9]—is simply the desire for expression, and Art is always presenting various forms through which this expression can be attained. Life seizes on them and uses them, even if they be to her own hurt. Young men have committed suicide because Rolla did so, have died by their own hand because by his own hand Werther died.[1] Think of what we owe to the imitation of Christ, of what we owe to the imitation of Caesar.

---

6. Large extinct animal.
7. Frances Cowley Burnand (1836–1917), editor of *Punch* and popular dramatist.
8. English philosopher and theorist of evolution (1820–1903).

9. In his *Physics*, Aristotle equates nature with energy.
1. Rolla is the Byronic hero of *Rolla* (1833), by the French poet Alfred de Musset; Werther is the romantic hero of Goethe's *The Sorrows of Young Werther* (1774).

CYRIL The theory is certainly a very curious one, but to make it complete you must show that Nature, no less than Life, is an imitation of Art. Are you prepared to prove that?

VIVIAN My dear fellow, I am prepared to prove anything.

CYRIL Nature follows the landscape painter then, and takes her effects from him?

VIVIAN Certainly. Where, if not from the Impressionists,[2] do we get those wonderful brown fogs that come creeping down our streets, blurring the gas-lamps and changing the houses into monstrous shadows? To whom, if not to them and their master, do we owe the lovely silver mists that brood over our river, and turn to faint forms of fading grace curved bridge and swaying barge? The extraordinary change that has taken place in the climate of London during the last ten years is entirely due to this particular school of Art. You smile. Consider the matter from a scientific or a metaphysical point of view, and you will find that I am right. For what is Nature? Nature is no great mother who has borne us. She is our creation. It is in our brain that she quickens to life. Things are because we see them, and what we see, and how we see it, depends on the Arts that have influenced us. To look at a thing is very different from seeing a thing. One does not see anything until one sees its beauty. Then, and then only, does it come into existence. At present, people see fogs, not because there are fogs, but because poets and painters have taught them the mysterious loveliness of such effects. There may have been fogs for centuries in London. I dare say there were. But no one saw them, and so we do not know anything about them. They did not exist till Art had invented them. Now, it must be admitted, fogs are carried to excess. They have become the mere mannerism of a clique, and the exaggerated realism of their method gives dull people bronchitis. Where the cultured catch an effect, the uncultured catch cold. And so, let us be humane, and invite Art to turn her wonderful eyes elsewhere. She has done so already, indeed. That white quivering sunlight that one sees now in France, with its strange blotches of mauve, and its restless violet shadows, is her latest fancy, and, on the whole, Nature reproduces it quite admirably. Where she used to give us Corots and Daubignys, she gives us now exquisite Monets and entrancing Pisaros.[3] Indeed there are moments, rare, it is true, but still to be observed from time to time, when Nature becomes absolutely modern. Of course she is not always to be relied upon. The fact is that she is in this unfortunate position. Art creates an incomparable and unique effect, and, having done so, passes on to other things. Nature, upon the other hand, forgetting that imitation can be made the sincerest form of insult, keeps on repeating this effect until we all become absolutely wearied of it. Nobody of any real culture, for instance, ever talks nowadays about the beauty of a sunset. Sunsets are quite old-fashioned. They belong to the time when Turner was the last note in art.[4] To admire them is a distinct sign of provincialism of temperament. Upon the other hand they go on. Yesterday evening Mrs Arundel insisted on my going to the window, and looking at the glorious sky, as she called it. Of course I had to look at it. She is one of those absurdly pretty Philistines, to whom one can deny nothing. And what was it? It

---

2. French Impressionist painters such as Monet, Renoir, and Pissarro sought to capture the interplay of light, atmosphere, and the elements, but it was Whistler (probably the "master" alluded to in the next sentence) who discovered London fogs, barges, and misty bridges as artistic subjects.

3. Earlier in the century, Corot and Daubigny had paint-

ed muted landscapes; Wilde's contemporaries Claude Monet and Camille Pissarro produced bright, Impressionist canvasses.

4. The atmospheric landscape paintings of J. M. W. Turner (1775–1851) were much admired by Ruskin in *Modern Painters* (1843–1860).

was simply a very second-rate Turner, a Turner of a bad period, with all the painter's worst faults exaggerated and over-emphasized. * * * But have I proved my theory to your satisfaction?

CYRIL You have proved it to my dissatisfaction, which is better. But even admitting this strange imitative instinct in Life and Nature, surely you would acknowledge that Art expresses the temper of its age, the spirit of its time, the moral and social conditions that surround it, and under whose influence it is produced.

VIVIAN Certainly not! Art never expresses anything but itself. * * * Remote from reality, and with her eyes turned away from the shadows of the cave,[5] Art reveals her own perfection, and the wondering crowd that watches the opening of the marvellous, many-petalled rose fancies that it is its own history that is being told to it, its own spirit that is finding expression in a new form. But it is not so. The highest art rejects the burden of the human spirit, and gains more from a new medium or a fresh material than she does from any enthusiasm for art, or from any lofty passion, or from any great awakening of the human consciousness. She develops purely on her own lines. She is not symbolic of any age. It is the ages that are her symbols. * * *

CYRIL I quite agree with you there. The spirit of an age may be best expressed in the abstract ideal arts, for the spirit itself is abstract and ideal. Upon the other hand, for the visible aspect of an age, for its look, as the phrase goes, we must of course go to the arts of imitation.

VIVIAN I don't think so. After all, what the imitative arts really give us are merely the various styles of particular artists, or of certain schools of artists. Surely you don't imagine that the people of the Middle Ages bore any resemblance at all to the figures on mediaeval stained glass, or in mediaeval stone and wood carving, or on mediaeval metal-work, or tapestries, or illuminated MSS.[6] They were probably very ordinary-looking people, with nothing grotesque, or remarkable, or fantastic in their appearance. The Middle Ages, as we know them in art, are simply a definite form of style, and there is no reason at all why an artist with this style should not be produced in the nineteenth century. No great artist ever sees things as they really are. If he did, he would cease to be an artist. Take an example from our own day. I know that you are fond of Japanese things. Now, do you really imagine that the Japanese people, as they are presented to us in art, have any existence? If you do, you have never understood Japanese art at all. The Japanese people are the deliberate self-conscious creation of certain individual artists. If you set a picture by Hokusai, or Hokkei,[7] or any of the great native painters, beside a real Japanese gentleman or lady, you will see that there is not the slightest resemblance between them. The actual people who live in Japan are not unlike the general run of English people; that is to say, they are extremely commonplace, and have nothing curious or extraordinary about them. In fact the whole of Japan is a pure invention. There is no such country, there are no such people. * * *

CYRIL But modern portraits by English painters, what of them? Surely they are like the people they pretend to represent?

VIVIAN Quite so. They are so like them that a hundred years from now no one will believe in them. The only portraits in which one believes are portraits where

---

5. In the *Republic*, Plato suggests that reality is to the absolute what shadows in a cave are to the objects which cast the shadows—i.e., dim and imperfect indications.

6. Manuscripts.
7. Katsushika Hokusai (1760–1849) and Hokkei (1780–1850), Japanese artists.

there is very little of the sitter, and a very great deal of the artist. Holbein's drawings of the men and women of his time impress us with a sense of their absolute reality. But this is simply because Holbein compelled life to accept his conditions, to restrain itself within his limitations, to reproduce his type, and to appear as he wished it to appear. It is style that makes us believe in a thing—nothing but style. Most of our modern portrait painters are doomed to absolute oblivion. They never paint what they see. They paint what the public sees, and the public never sees anything.

CYRIL Well, after that I think I should like to hear the end of your article.

VIVIAN With pleasure. Whether it will do any good I really cannot say. Ours is certainly the dullest and most prosaic century possible. * * * However, I must read the end of my article:—

"What we have to do, what at any rate it is our duty to do, is to revive this old art of Lying. Much of course may be done, in the way of educating the public, by amateurs in the domestic circle, at literary lunches, and at afternoon teas. * * * A short primer, 'When to Lie and How,' if brought out in an attractive and not too expensive a form, would no doubt command a large sale, and would prove of real practical service to many earnest and deep-thinking people. Lying for the sake of the improvement of the young, which is the basis of home education, still lingers amongst us, and its advantages are so admirably set forth in the early books of Plato's *Republic*[8] that it is unnecessary to dwell upon them here. It is a mode of lying for which all good mothers have peculiar capabilities, but it is capable of still further development, and has been sadly overlooked by the School Board. Lying for the sake of a monthly salary is of course well known in Fleet Street, and the profession of a political leader-writer is not without its advantages. But it is said to be a somewhat dull occupation, and it certainly does not lead to much beyond a kind of ostentatious obscurity. The only form of lying that is absolutely beyond reproach is Lying for its own sake, and the highest development of this is, as we have already pointed out, Lying in Art. Just as those who do not love Plato more than Truth cannot pass beyond the threshold of the Academe,[9] so those who do not love Beauty more than Truth never know the inmost shrine of Art. The solid stolid British intellect lies in the desert sands like the Sphinx in Flaubert's marvellous tale,[1] and fantasy, *La Chimère*, dances round it, and calls to it with her false, flute-toned voice. It may not hear her now, but surely some day, when we are all bored to death with the commonplace character of modern fiction, it will hearken to her and try to borrow her wings.

"And when that day dawns, or sunset reddens, how joyous we shall all be! Facts will be regarded as discreditable, Truth will be found mourning over her fetters, and Romance, with her temper of wonder, will return to the land. The very aspect of the world will change to our startled eyes. Out of the sea will rise Behemoth and Leviathan,[2] and sail round the high-pooped galleys, as they do on

---

8. In Books 2 and 3, which discuss the education of the future Guardians of the ideal republic, Plato advocates suppressing stories that evoke the terror of death, or that portray the gods as undignified or immoral.

9. A gibe at Plato's coercive method of teaching. Wilde reverses Aristotle's remark, "Plato is dear to me, but dearer still is truth." Plato's school in Athens was called the Academy because he taught his students in an olive grove dedicated to the hero Academus.

1. *The Temptation of Saint Anthony* (1874) by French novelist Gustave Flaubert.

2. The hippopotamus and the whale in the Book of Job. The rest of the paragraph refers to fabulous mythical animals: the phoenix was a legendary bird that immolated itself on a pyre, then rose regenerated from the ashes; the basilisk was a reptile whose breath and glance were fatal; the hippogriff was part gryphon and part horse.

the delightful maps of those ages when books on geography were actually readable. Dragons will wander about the waste places, and the phoenix will soar from her nest of fire into the air. We shall lay our hands upon the basilisk, and see the jewel in the toad's head. Champing his gilded oats, the Hippogriff will stand in our stalls, and over our heads will float the Blue Bird singing of beautiful and impossible things, of things that are lovely and that never happen, of things that are not and that should be. But before this comes to pass we must cultivate the lost art of Lying."

CYRIL   Then we must certainly cultivate it at once. But in order to avoid making any error I want you to tell me briefly the doctrines of the new aesthetics.

VIVIAN   Briefly, then, they are these. Art never expresses anything but itself. It has an independent life, just as Thought has, and develops purely on its own lines. It is not necessarily realistic in an age of realism, nor spiritual in an age of faith. So far from being the creation of its time, it is usually in direct opposition to it, and the only history that it preserves for us is the history of its own progress. Sometimes it returns upon its footsteps, and revives some antique form, as happened in the archaistic movement of late Greek Art, and in the pre-Raphaelite movement of our own day. At other times it entirely anticipates its age, and produces in one century work that it takes another century to understand, to appreciate, and to enjoy. In no case does it reproduce its age. To pass from the art of a time to the time itself is the great mistake that all historians commit.

   The second doctrine is this. All bad art comes from returning to Life and Nature, and elevating them into ideals. Life and Nature may sometimes be used as part of Art's rough material, but before they are of any real service to art they must be translated into artistic conventions. The moment Art surrenders its imaginative medium it surrenders everything. As a method Realism is a complete failure, and the two things that every artist should avoid are modernity of form and modernity of subject-matter. To us, who live in the nineteenth century, any century is a suitable subject for art except our own. The only beautiful things are the things that do not concern us. It is, to have the pleasure of quoting myself, exactly because Hecuba is nothing to us that her sorrows are so suitable a motive for a tragedy.[3] Besides, it is only the modern that ever becomes old-fashioned. M. Zola sits down to give us a picture of the Second Empire.[4] Who cares for the Second Empire now? It is out of date. Life goes faster than Realism, but Romanticism is always in front of Life.

   The third doctrine is that Life imitates Art far more than Art imitates Life. This results not merely from Life's imitative instinct, but from the fact that the self-conscious aim of Life is to find expression, and that Art offers it certain beautiful forms through which it may realize that energy. It is a theory that has never been put forward before, but it is extremely fruitful, and throws an entirely new light upon the history of Art.

   It follows, as a corollary from this, that external Nature also imitates Art. The only effects that she can show us are effects that we have already seen through poetry, or in paintings. This is the secret of Nature's charm, as well as the explanation of Nature's weakness.

---

3. Hecuba, queen of Troy, lost her sons and her husband when the Greeks defeated Troy. Wilde alludes to a scene in *Hamlet* where an actor recites a speech about her suffering and Hamlet asks himself, "What's Hecuba to him, or he to Hecuba, / That he should weep for her?" (2.2.559–60).

4. In France, the period from 1852 to 1870.

The final revelation is that Lying, the telling of beautiful untrue things, is the proper aim of Art. But of this I think I have spoken at sufficient length. And now let us go out on the terrace, where "droops the milk-white peacock like a ghost,"[5] while the evening star "washes the dusk with silver."[6] At twilight nature becomes a wonderfully suggestive effect, and is not without loveliness, though perhaps its chief use is to illustrate quotations from the poets. Come! We have talked long enough.

1889, 1891

from The Soul of Man Under Socialism[1]

The chief advantage that would result from the establishment of Socialism is, undoubtedly, the fact that Socialism would relieve us from that sordid necessity of living for others which, in the present condition of things, presses so hardly upon almost everybody. In fact, scarcely anyone at all escapes.

Now and then, in the course of the century, a great man of science, like Darwin; a great poet, like Keats; a fine critical spirit, like M. Renan;[2] a supreme artist, like Flaubert, has been able to isolate himself, to keep himself out of reach of the clamorous claims of others, to stand "under the shelter of the wall," as Plato puts it, and so to realise the perfection of what was in him, to his own incomparable gain, and to the incomparable and lasting gain of the whole world. These, however, are exceptions. The majority of people spoil their lives by an unhealthy and exaggerated altruism—are forced, indeed, so to spoil them. They find themselves surrounded by hideous poverty, by hideous ugliness, by hideous starvation. It is inevitable that they should be strongly moved by all this. The emotions of man are stirred more quickly than man's intelligence; and, as I pointed out some time ago in an article on the function of criticism,[3] it is much more easy to have sympathy with suffering than it is to have sympathy with thought. Accordingly, with admirable though misdirected intentions, they very seriously and very sentimentally set themselves to the task of remedying the evils that they see. But their remedies do not cure the disease: they merely prolong it. Indeed, their remedies are part of the disease.

They try to solve the problem of poverty, for instance, by keeping the poor alive; or, in the case of a very advanced school, by amusing the poor.

But this is not a solution: it is an aggravation of the difficulty. *The proper aim is to try and reconstruct society on such a basis that poverty will be impossible.* And the altruistic virtues have really prevented the carrying out of this aim. Just as the worst slave-owners were those who were kind to their slaves, and so prevented the horror of the system being realised by those who suffered from it, and understood by those who contemplated it, so, in the present state of things in England, the people who do most harm are the people who try to do most good; and at last we have had the spectacle of men who have really studied the problem and know the life—educated men

5. From Tennyson's *The Princess* (1847).
6. From Blake's *To the Evening Star* (1783).
1. Published in *The Fortnightly Review* in 1891, this essay had an important underground life during the next few decades; translated into many languages, it was also secretly printed and circulated in Tzarist Russia. In the 1880s and 1890s, socialism, which advocates collective ownership of property and the means of production, emerged as a strong nationwide movement in Britain, bolstered by trade unionism and such intellectual and feminist groups as the Fabian Society and the Ethical Socialists. Wilde had no formal connection to socialist groups, but was sympathetic to many of their concerns, and apparently wrote this essay after attending a meeting

where Bernard Shaw was the chief speaker. Wilde's essay is remarkable in its claim that socialism—usually said to put the needs of society ahead of personal interests—will lead to the fulfillment of the individual. He wrote elsewhere: "to make men Socialists is nothing, but to make Socialism human is a great thing."
2. Ernest Renan, French scholar and essayist, author of *La Vie de Jésus* (1863; English trans. 1888).
3. Wilde's essay *The Critic as Artist* (1890) challenged Matthew Arnold's *The Function of Criticism at the Present Time* (1864) by arguing that good criticism is "creative and independent" and "more creative than creation" because it is further removed from life than the work of the writer or artist.

who live in the East-end[4]—coming forward and imploring the community to restrain its altruistic impulses of charity, benevolence, and the like. They do so on the ground that such charity degrades and demoralizes. They are perfectly right. Charity creates a multitude of sins.

There is also this to be said. It is immoral to use private property in order to alleviate the horrible evils that result from the institution of private property. It is both immoral and unfair.

Under Socialism all this will, of course, be altered. There will be no people living in fetid dens and fetid rags, and bringing up unhealthy, hunger-pinched children in the midst of impossible and absolutely repulsive surroundings. The security of society will not depend, as it does now, on the state of the weather. If a frost comes we shall not have a hundred thousand men out of work, tramping about the streets in a state of disgusting misery, or whining to their neighbours for alms, or crowding round the doors of loathsome shelters to try and secure a hunch of bread and a night's unclean lodging. Each member of the society will share in the general prosperity and happiness of the society, and if a frost comes no one will practically be anything the worse.

Upon the other hand, *Socialism itself will be of value simply because it will lead to Individualism.*

Socialism, Communism, or whatever one chooses to call it, by converting private property into public wealth, and substituting cooperation for competition, will restore society to its proper condition of a thoroughly healthy organism, and insure the material well-being of each member of the community. It will, in fact, give Life its proper basis and its proper environment. But for the full development of Life to its highest mode of perfection, something more is needed. What is needed is Individualism. If the Socialism is Authoritarian; if there are Governments armed with economic power as they are now with political power; if, in a word, we are to have Industrial Tyrannies, then the last state of man will be worse than the first. At present, in consequence of the existence of private property, a great many people are enabled to develop a certain very limited amount of Individualism. They are either under no necessity to work for their living, or are enabled to choose the sphere of activity that is really congenial to them, and gives them pleasure. These are the poets, the philosophers, the men of science, the men of culture—in a word, the real men, the men who have realised themselves, and in whom all Humanity gains a partial realisation. Upon the other hand, there are a great many people who, having no private property of their own, and being always on the brink of sheer starvation, are compelled to do the work of beasts of burden, to do work that is quite uncongenial to them, and to which they are forced by the peremptory, unreasonable, degrading Tyranny of want. These are the poor, and amongst them there is no grace of manner, or charm of speech, or civilization, or culture, or refinement in pleasures, or joy of life. From their collective force Humanity gains much in material prosperity. But it is only the material result that it gains, and the man who is poor is in himself absolutely of no importance. He is merely the infinitesimal atom of a force that, so far from regarding him, crushes him: indeed, prefers him crushed, as in that case he is far more obedient.

Of course, it might be said that the Individualism generated under conditions of private property is not always, or even as a rule, of a fine or wonderful type, and that the poor, if they have not culture and charm, have still many virtues. Both these statements would be quite true. The possession of private property is very often extremely demoralising, and that is, of course, one of the reasons why Socialism wants to get rid

4. The poorest section of Victorian London.

of the institution. In fact, property is really a nuisance. Some years ago people went about the country saying that property has duties. They said it so often and so tediously that, at last, the church has begun to say it. One hears it now from every pulpit. It is perfectly true. Property not merely has duties, but has so many duties that its possession to any large extent is a bore. It involves endless claims upon one, endless attention to business, endless bother. If property had simply pleasures, we could stand it; but its duties make it unbearable. In the interest of the rich we must get rid of it. The virtues of the poor may be readily admitted, and are much to be regretted. * * *

Misery and poverty are so absolutely degrading, and exercise such a paralysing effect over the nature of men, that no class is ever really conscious of its own suffering. They have to be told of it by other people, and they often entirely disbelieve them. What is said by great employers of labour against agitators is unquestionably true. Agitators are a set of interfering, meddling people, who come down to some perfectly contented class of the community, and sow the seeds of discontent amongst them. That is the reason why agitators are so absolutely necessary. Without them, in our incomplete state, there would be no advance towards civilization. Slavery was put down in America, not in consequence of any action on the part of the slaves, or even any express desire on their part that they should be free. It was put down entirely through the grossly illegal conduct of certain agitators in Boston and elsewhere, who were not slaves themselves, nor owners of slaves, nor had anything to do with the question really. It was, undoubtedly, the Abolitionists who set the torch alight, who began the whole thing. And it is curious to note that from the slaves themselves they received, not merely very little assistance, but hardly any sympathy even; and when at the close of the war the slaves found themselves free, found themselves indeed so absolutely free that they were free to starve, many of them bitterly regretted the new state of things. To the thinker, the most tragic fact in the whole of the French Revolution is not that Marie Antoinette was killed for being a queen, but that the starved peasant of the Vendee voluntarily went out to die for the hideous cause of feudalism.[5]

It is clear, then, that no Authoritarian Socialism will do. For while under the present system a very large number of people can lead lives of a certain amount of freedom and expression and happiness, under an industrial-barrack system, or a system of economic tyranny, nobody would be able to have any such freedom at all. It is to be regretted that a portion of our community should be practically in slavery, but to propose to solve the problem by enslaving the entire community is childish. Every man must be left quite free to choose his own work. No form of compulsion must be exercised over him. * * *

Now as the State is not to govern, it may be asked what the State is to do. The State is to be a voluntary association that will organize labour, and be the manufacturer and distributor of necessary commodities. *The State is to make what is useful. The individual is to make what is beautiful.* And as I have mentioned the word labour, I cannot help saying that a great deal of nonsense is being written and talked nowadays about the dignity of manual labour. There is nothing necessarily dignified about manual labour at all, and most of it is absolutely degrading. It is mentally and morally injurious to man to do anything in which he does not find pleasure, and many forms of labour are quite pleasureless activities, and should be regarded as such. To sweep a slushy crossing for eight hours on a day when the east wind is blowing is a

5. Marie Antoinette, Queen of France, was beheaded in 1793 during the French Revolution; the Vendée was a center of counterrevolutionary activity.

disgusting occupation. To sweep it with mental, moral, or physical dignity seems to me to be impossible. To sweep it with joy would be appalling. Man is made for something better than disturbing dirt. All work of that kind should be done by a machine.

And I have no doubt that it will be so. Up to the present, man has been, to a certain extent, the slave of machinery, and there is something tragic in the fact that as soon as man had invented a machine to do his work he began to starve. This, however, is, of course, the result of our property system and our system of competition. One man owns a machine which does the work of five hundred men. Five hundred men are, in consequence, thrown out of employment, and having no work to do, become hungry and take to thieving. The one man secures the produce of the machine and keeps it, and has five hundred times as much as he should have, and probably, which is of much more importance, a great deal more than he really wants. Were that machine the property of all, every one would benefit by it. It would be an immense advantage to the community. All unintellectual labour, all monotonous, dull labour, all labour that deals with dreadful things, and involves unpleasant conditions, must be done by machinery. Machinery must work for us in coal mines, and do all sanitary services, and be the stoker of steamers, and clean the streets, and run messages on wet days, and do anything that is tedious or distressing. *At present machinery competes against man. Under proper conditions machinery will serve man.* There is no doubt at all that this is the future of machinery, and just as trees grow while the country gentleman is asleep, so while Humanity will be amusing itself, or enjoying cultivated leisure—which, and not labour, is the aim of man—or making beautiful things, or reading beautiful things, or simply contemplating the world with admiration and delight, machinery will be doing all the necessary and unpleasant work. The fact is, that civilization requires slaves. The Greeks were quite right there. Unless there are slaves to do the ugly, horrible, uninteresting work, culture and contemplation become almost impossible. Human slavery is wrong, insecure, and demoralising. On mechanical slavery, on the slavery of the machine, the future of the world depends. And when scientific men are no longer called upon to go down to a depressing East-end and distribute bad cocoa and worse blankets to starving people, they will have delightful leisure in which to devise wonderful and marvellous things for their own joy and the joy of everyone else. There will be great storages of force for every city, and for every house if required, and this force man will convert into heat, light, or motion, according to his needs. Is this Utopian?[6] A map of the world that does not include Utopia is not worth even glancing at, for it leaves out the one country at which Humanity is always landing. And when Humanity lands there, it looks out, and, seeing a better country, sets sail. Progress is the realisation of Utopias. * * *

It is to be noted also that Individualism does not come to man with any sickly cant about duty, which merely means doing what other people want because they want it; or any hideous cant about self-sacrifice, which is merely a survival of savage mutilation. *In fact, it does not come to man with any claims upon him at all. It comes naturally and inevitably out of man.* It is the point to which all development tends. It is the differentiation to which all organisms grow. It is the perfection that is inherent in every mode of life, and towards which every mode of life quickens. And so Individualism exercises no compulsion over man. On the contrary it says to man that he should suffer no compulsion to be exercised over him. It does not try to force people to be good. It knows that people are good when they are let alone. Man will develop

6. I.e., impossibly idealistic. In *Utopia* (1516) Sir Thomas More described an imaginary island of that name as having a perfect social and political system.

Individualism out of himself. Man is now so developing Individualism. To ask whether Individualism is practical is like asking whether Evolution is practical. *Evolution is the law of life, and there is no evolution except towards Individualism.* * * *

* * * Man has sought to live intensely, fully, perfectly. When he can do so without exercising restraint on others, or suffering it ever, and his activities are all pleasurable to him, he will be saner, healthier, more civilized, more himself. Pleasure is Nature's test, her sign of approval. When man is happy, he is in harmony with himself and his environment. The new Individualism, for whose service Socialism, whether it wills it or not, is working, will be perfect harmony. It will be what the Greeks sought for, but could not, except in Thought, realise completely, because they had slaves, and fed them; it will be what the Renaissance sought for, but could not realise completely except in Art, because they had slaves, and starved them. It will be complete, and through it each man will attain to his perfection. The new Individualism is the new Hellenism.[7]

1891

Preface to *The Picture of Dorian Gray*[1]

The artist is the creator of beautiful things.

To reveal art and conceal the artist is art's aim.

The critic is he who can translate into another manner or a new material his impression of beautiful things.

The highest as the lowest form of criticism is a mode of autobiography.

Those who find ugly meanings in beautiful things are corrupt without being charming. This is a fault.

Those who find beautiful meanings in beautiful things are the cultivated. For these there is hope.

They are the elect to whom beautiful things mean only Beauty.

There is no such thing as a moral or an immoral book.

Books are well written, or badly written. That is all.

The nineteenth century dislike of Realism is the rage of Caliban[2] seeing his own face in a glass.

The nineteenth century dislike of Romanticism is the rage of Caliban not seeing his own face in a glass.

The moral life of man forms part of the subject-matter of the artist, but the morality of art consists in the perfect use of an imperfect medium.

No artist desires to prove anything. Even things that are true can be proved.

No artist has ethical sympathies. An ethical sympathy in an artist is an unpardonable mannerism of style.

No artist is ever morbid. The artist can express everything.

Thought and language are to the artist instruments of an art.

Vice and virtue are to the artist materials for an art.

7. I.e., it embodies the ideals of ancient Greece, including a respect for the life of the mind and the love of beautiful things. Also an allusion to Matthew Arnold's argument in *Culture and Anarchy* (see page 2037) that a Hellenic cultivation of these values is what British society most desperately needs.

1. When Wilde's novel *Dorian Gray* first appeared in *Lippincott's Monthly Magazine* in July 1890, it scandalized readers with its portrayal of a cruelly hedonistic young man who remains unblemished by his crimes while his portrait ages hideously. Responding to his critics' charges

that the novel fostered immoral ideas, Wilde published the preface separately in *The Fortnightly Review* in March 1891. He then added it to the revised novel when it came out in book form a month later. In its defiant tone and "art for art's sake" insistence that literature has no moral content, Wilde's preface echoes Théophile Gautier's preface to *Mademoiselle de Maupin* (1835), a founding text of the Aesthetic movement.

2. In Shakespeare's *The Tempest*, the "monster" Caliban is the offspring of the witch Sycorax and is a native of Prospero's island.

From the point of view of form, the type of all the arts is the art of the
musician. From the point of view of feeling, the actor's craft is the type.

    All art is at once surface and symbol.

    Those who go beneath the surface do so at their peril.

    Those who read the symbol do so at their peril.

It is the spectator, and not life, that art really mirrors.

    Diversity of opinion about a work of art shows that the work is new,
    complex, and vital.

    When critics disagree the artist is in accord with himself.

We can forgive a man for making a useful thing as long as he does not
admire it. The only excuse for making a useless thing is that one admires it
intensely.

    All art is quite useless.

OSCAR WILDE

The Importance of Being Earnest

Wilde's last play, *The Importance of Being Earnest*, is one of the great comedies in the English
language. Fast-paced and sparkling, the play opened on February 14, 1895, to widespread
acclaim. But it was forced to close less than three months later, amidst the scandal surrounding
Wilde's trials for sodomy in April 1895. Eventually, however, the play's reputation was firmly
established, and Wilde's witty masterpiece took its place in an Anglo-Irish tradition of classic
comedies that includes Goldsmith's *She Stoops to Conquer*, Sheridan's *The Rivals*, and Synge's
Playboy of the Western World. The title alludes to the Victorian obsession with earnestness as
both character trait and moral ideal. The play's philosophy, Wilde claimed, was that "We
should treat all the trivial things of life seriously, and all the serious things of life with sincere
and studied triviality." In the dandified world of this drama, paying scrupulous attention to surfaces is an act of the deepest sincerity.

    Wilde drafted the play in four acts, then at the request of the producer revised it to a
tauter three-act version that has become the standard text for performance and reading. Formally, *The Importance of Being Earnest* shows the clever construction and neat resolution popular in nineteenth-century British and French drama. But it also fulfills the classical definition
of comedy as beginning in error and confusion, and ending in knowledge, recognition, and
self-discovery. Questioning social hierarchies based on birth, the plot turns on the mysteries of
social and personal identity: "Would you kindly inform me who I am?" asks Jack Worthing at
the play's climactic moment.

    To explore the fictions of personality, Wilde meticulously sketches the trivialities that
constitute social ritual and class distinction. From cucumber sandwiches at the start of the play
to champagne and muffins in Act 3, the way Wilde's well-bred sophisticates consume food and
drink becomes evidence of their character, emotional state, and social status. While the rigid
conventions of this world apparently force young men like Jack and Algy to live double lives,
they freely exploit their fictive selves as events dictate. Yet they are easily stage-managed by
the women they love. Gwendolen and Cecily, who are more preoccupied with writing in their
diaries than with the events they record in them, deploy their self-conscious sexual innocence
to make life and love conform to the conventions of literature. *The Importance of Being Earnest*
presents life as an aesthetic spectacle, in which the careful observation of outward form is the
truest path toward an ironic authenticity and self-fulfillment.

    "If I were asked of myself as a dramatist," Wilde mused, "I would say that my unique posi-
tion was that I had taken the Drama, the most objective form known to art, and made it as personal a mode of expression as the Lyric or the Sonnet, while enlarging the characterization of
the stage." Wilde refashioned the late-Victorian theater in his own image through the self-

conscious brilliance of his language and the outrageousness of his comic invention. He delighted in artifice and exaggeration for their own sake. As he argued in *The Decay of Lying,* art is not an imitation of life but a more aesthetically satisfying restructuring of it. With droll wordplay, paradox, and ridiculous coincidence casting existential dilemmas into comic relief, *The Importance of Being Earnest* anticipates the modern Theater of the Absurd; it heralds the profound slapstick of Pirandello, Ionesco, Beckett, and Stoppard.

The Importance of Being Earnest
A Trivial Comedy for Serious People

FIRST ACT

SCENE: *Morning-room in Algernon's flat in Half Moon Street.*[1] *The room is luxuriously and artistically furnished. The sound of a piano is heard in the adjoining room.*

[*Lane is arranging afternoon tea on the table, and after the music has ceased, Algernon enters.*]

ALGERNON Did you hear what I was playing, Lane?

LANE I didn't think it polite to listen, sir.

ALGERNON I'm sorry for that, for your sake. I don't play accurately—anyone can play accurately—but I play with wonderful expression. As far as the piano is concerned, sentiment is my forte. I keep science for Life.

LANE Yes, sir.

ALGERNON And, speaking of the science of Life, have you got the cucumber sandwiches cut for Lady Bracknell?

LANE Yes, sir. [*Hands them on a salver.*]

ALGERNON [*inspects them, takes two, and sits down on the sofa*] Oh! . . . by the way, Lane, I see from your book that on Thursday night, when Lord Shoreham and Mr Worthing were dining with me, eight bottles of champagne are entered as having been consumed.

LANE Yes, sir; eight bottles and a pint.

ALGERNON Why is it that at a bachelor's establishment the servants invariably drink the champagne? I ask merely for information.

LANE I attribute it to the superior quality of the wine, sir. I have often observed that in married households the champagne is rarely of a first-rate brand.

ALGERNON Good Heavens! Is marriage so demoralizing as that?

LANE I believe it *is* a very pleasant state, sir. I have had very little experience of it myself up to the present. I have only been married once. That was in consequence of a misunderstanding between myself and a young person.

ALGERNON [*languidly*] I don't know that I am much interested in your family life, Lane.

LANE No, sir; it is not a very interesting subject. I never think of it myself.

ALGERNON Very natural, I am sure. That will do, Lane, thank you.

LANE Thank you, sir. [*Lane goes out.*]

ALGERNON Lane's views on marriage seem somewhat lax. Really, if the lower orders don't set us a good example, what on earth is the use of them? They seem, as a class, to have absolutely no sense of moral responsibility.

---

1. A fashionable address in the West End of London.

[*Enter Lane.*]

LANE Mr Ernest Worthing.

[*Enter Jack. Lane goes out.*]

ALGERNON How are you, my dear Ernest? What brings you up to town?

JACK Oh, pleasure, pleasure! What else should bring one anywhere? Eating as usual, I see, Algy!

ALGERNON [*stiffly*] I believe it is customary in good society to take some slight refreshment at five o'clock. Where have you been since last Thursday?

JACK [*sitting down on the sofa*] In the country.

ALGERNON What on earth do you do there?

JACK [*pulling off his gloves*] When one is in town one amuses oneself. When one is in the country one amuses other people. It is excessively boring.

ALGERNON And who are the people you amuse?

JACK [*airily*] Oh, neighbours, neighbours.

ALGERNON Got nice neighbours in your part of Shropshire?[2]

JACK Perfectly horrid! Never speak to one of them.

ALGERNON How immensely you must amuse them! [*Goes over and takes sandwich.*] By the way, Shropshire is your county, is it not?

JACK Eh? Shropshire? Yes, of course. Hallo! Why all these cups? Why cucumber sandwiches? Why such reckless extravagance in one so young? Who is coming to tea?

ALGERNON Oh! merely Aunt Augusta and Gwendolen.

JACK How perfectly delightful!

ALGERNON Yes, that is all very well; but I am afraid Aunt Augusta won't quite approve of your being here.

JACK May I ask why?

ALGERNON My dear fellow, the way you flirt with Gwendolen is perfectly disgraceful. It is almost as bad as the way Gwendolen flirts with you.

JACK I am in love with Gwendolen. I have come up to town expressly to propose to her.

ALGERNON I thought you had come up for pleasure? . . . I call that business.

JACK How utterly unromantic you are!

ALGERNON I really don't see anything romantic in proposing. It is very romantic to be in love. But there is nothing romantic about a definite proposal. Why, one may be accepted. One usually is, I believe. Then the excitement is all over. The very essence of romance is uncertainty. If I ever get married, I'll certainly try to forget the fact.

JACK I have no doubt about that, dear Algy. The Divorce Court was specially invented for people whose memories are so curiously constituted.

ALGERNON Oh! there is no use speculating on that subject. Divorces are made in Heaven— [*Jack puts out his hand to take a sandwich. Algernon at once interferes.*] Please don't touch the cucumber sandwiches. They are ordered specially for Aunt Augusta. [*Takes one and eats it.*]

JACK Well, you have been eating them all the time.

ALGERNON That is quite a different matter. She is my aunt. [*Takes plate from below.*] Have some bread and butter. The bread and butter is for Gwendolen. Gwendolen is devoted to bread and butter.

JACK [*advancing to table and helping himself*] And very good bread and butter it is too.

---

2. Worthing's estate is actually in Hertfordshire, which is a long way from Shropshire.

ALGERNON Well, my dear fellow, you need not eat as if you were going to eat it all. You behave as if you were married to her already. You are not married to her already, and I don't think you ever will be.

JACK Why on earth do you say that?

ALGERNON Well, in the first place girls never marry the men they flirt with. Girls don't think it right.

JACK Oh, that is nonsense!

ALGERNON It isn't. It is a great truth. It accounts for the extraordinary number of bachelors that one sees all over the place. In the second place, I don't give my consent.

JACK Your consent!

ALGERNON My dear fellow, Gwendolen is my first cousin. And before I allow you to marry her, you will have to clear up the whole question of Cecily. [Rings bell.]

JACK Cecily! What on earth do you mean? What do you mean, Algy, by Cecily? I don't know anyone of the name of Cecily.

[Enter Lane.]

ALGERNON Bring me that cigarette case Mr Worthing left in the smoking-room the last time he dined here.

LANE Yes, sir. [Lane goes out.]

JACK Do you mean to say you have had my cigarette case all this time? I wish to goodness you had let me know. I have been writing frantic letters to Scotland Yard[3] about it. I was very nearly offering a large reward.

ALGERNON Well, I wish you would offer one. I happen to be more than usually hard up.

JACK There is no good offering a large reward now that the thing is found.

[Enter Lane with the cigarette case on a salver. Algernon takes it at once. Lane goes out.]

ALGERNON I think that is rather mean of you, Ernest, I must say. [Opens case and examines it.] However, it makes no matter, for, now that I look at the inscription inside, I find that the thing isn't yours after all.

JACK Of course it's mine. [Moving to him.] You have seen me with it a hundred times, and you have no right whatsoever to read what is written inside. It is a very ungentlemanly thing to read a private cigarette case.

ALGERNON Oh! it is absurd to have a hard-and-fast rule about what one should read and what one shouldn't. More than half of modern culture depends on what one shouldn't read.

JACK I am quite aware of the fact, and I don't propose to discuss modern culture. It isn't the sort of thing one should talk of in private. I simply want my cigarette case back.

ALGERNON Yes; but this isn't your cigarette case. This cigarette case is a present from someone of the name of Cecily, and you said you didn't know anyone of that name.

JACK Well, if you want to know, Cecily happens to be my aunt.

ALGERNON Your aunt!

JACK Yes. Charming old lady she is, too. Lives at Tunbridge Wells.[4] Just give it back to me, Algy.

ALGERNON [retreating to back of sofa] But why does she call herself little Cecily if she is your aunt and lives at Tunbridge Wells? [Reading.] "From little Cecily with her fondest love."

---

3. London police headquarters.   4. A fashionable resort.

JACK [*moving to sofa and kneeling upon it*] My dear fellow, what on earth is there in that? Some aunts are tall, some aunts are not tall. That is a matter that surely an aunt may be allowed to decide for herself. You seem to think that every aunt should be exactly like your aunt! That is absurd! For Heaven's sake give me back my cigarette case. [*Follows Algernon round the room.*]

ALGERNON Yes. But why does your aunt call you her uncle? "From little Cecily, with her fondest love to her dear Uncle Jack." There is no objection, I admit, to an aunt being a small aunt, but why an aunt, no matter what her size may be, should call her own nephew her uncle, I can't quite make out. Besides, your name isn't Jack at all; it is Ernest.

JACK It isn't Ernest; it's Jack.

ALGERNON You have always told me it was Ernest. I have introduced you to everyone as Ernest. You answer to the name of Ernest. You look as if your name was Ernest. You are the most earnest looking person I ever saw in my life. It is perfectly absurd your saying that your name isn't Ernest. It's on your cards. Here is one of them. [*Taking it from case.*] "Mr Ernest Worthing, B. 4, The Albany." I'll keep this as a proof that your name is Ernest if ever you attempt to deny it to me, or to Gwendolen, or to anyone else. [*Puts the card in his pocket.*]

JACK Well, my name is Ernest in town and Jack in the country, and the cigarette case was given to me in the country.

ALGERNON Yes, but that does not account for the fact that your small Aunt Cecily, who lives at Tunbridge Wells, calls you her dear uncle. Come, old boy, you had much better have the thing out at once.

JACK My dear Algy, you talk exactly as if you were a dentist. It is very vulgar to talk like a dentist when one isn't a dentist. It produces a false impression.

ALGERNON Well, that is exactly what dentists always do. Now, go on! Tell me the whole thing. I may mention that I have always suspected you of being a confirmed and secret Bunburyist, and I am quite sure of it now.

JACK Bunburyist? What on earth do you mean by a Bunburyist?

ALGERNON I'll reveal to you the meaning of that incomparable expression as soon as you are kind enough to inform me why you are Ernest in town and Jack in the country.

JACK Well, produce my cigarette case first.

ALGERNON Here it is. [*Hands cigarette case.*] Now produce your explanation, and pray make it improbable. [*Sits on sofa.*]

JACK My dear fellow, there is nothing improbable about my explanation at all. In fact it's perfectly ordinary. Old Mr Thomas Cardew, who adopted me when I was a little boy, made me in his will guardian to his granddaughter, Miss Cecily Cardew. Cecily who addresses me as her uncle from motives of respect that you could not possibly appreciate, lives at my place in the country under the charge of her admirable governess, Miss Prism.

ALGERNON Where is that place in the country, by the way?

JACK That is nothing to you, dear boy. You are not going to be invited. . . . I may tell you candidly that the place is not in Shropshire.

ALGERNON I suspected that, my dear fellow! I have Bunburyed all over Shropshire on two separate occasions. Now, go on. Why are you Ernest in town and Jack in the country?

JACK My dear Algy, I don't know whether you will be able to understand my real motives. You are hardly serious enough. When one is placed in the position of guardian, one has to adopt a very high moral tone on all subjects. It's one's duty to do so. And as a high moral tone can hardly be said to conduce very much to either one's health or one's happiness, in order to get up to town I have always pretended to have a younger brother of the name of Ernest, who lives in the Albany, and gets into the most dreadful scrapes. That, my dear Algy, is the whole truth pure and simple.

ALGERNON The truth is rarely pure and never simple. Modern life would be very tedious if it were either, and modern literature a complete impossibility!

JACK That wouldn't be at all a bad thing.

ALGERNON Literary criticism is not your forte, my dear fellow. Don't try it. You should leave that to people who haven't been at a University. They do it so well in the daily papers. What you really are is a Bunburyist. I was quite right in saying you were a Bunburyist. You are one of the most advanced Bunburyists I know.

JACK What on earth do you mean?

ALGERNON You have invented a very useful younger brother called Ernest, in order that you may be able to come up to town as often as you like. I have invented an invaluable permanent invalid called Bunbury, in order that I may be able to go down into the country whenever I choose. Bunbury is perfectly invaluable. If it wasn't for Bunbury's extraordinary bad health, for instance, I wouldn't be able to dine with you at Willis's[5] tonight, for I have been really engaged[6] to Aunt Augusta for more than a week.

JACK I haven't asked you to dine with me anywhere tonight.

ALGERNON I know. You are absurdly careless about sending out invitations. It is very foolish of you. Nothing annoys people so much as not receiving invitations.

JACK You had much better dine with your Aunt Augusta.

ALGERNON I haven't the smallest intention of doing anything of the kind. To begin with, I dined there on Monday, and once a week is quite enough to dine with one's own relations. In the second place, whenever I do dine there I am always treated as a member of the family, and sent down[7] with either no woman at all, or two. In the third place, I know perfectly well whom she will place me next to, tonight. She will place me next Mary Farquhar, who always flirts with her own husband across the dinner-table. That is not very pleasant. Indeed, it is not even decent . . . and that sort of thing is enormously on the increase. The amount of women in London who flirt with their own husbands is perfectly scandalous. It looks so bad. It is simply washing one's clean linen in public. Besides, now that I know you to be a confirmed Bunburyist I naturally want to talk to you about Bunburying. I want to tell you the rules.

JACK I'm not a Bunburyist at all. If Gwendolen accepts me, I am going to kill my brother, indeed I think I'll kill him in any case. Cecily is a little too much interested in him. It is rather a bore. So I am going to get rid of Ernest. And I strongly advise you to do the same with Mr . . . with your invalid friend who has the absurd name.

ALGERNON Nothing will induce me to part with Bunbury, and if you ever get married, which seems to me extremely problematic, you will be very glad to know Bunbury. A man who marries without knowing Bunbury has a very tedious time of it.

JACK That is nonsense. If I marry a charming girl like Gwendolen, and she is the only girl I ever saw in my life that I would marry, I certainly won't want to know Bunbury.

---

5. An expensive London restaurant.   7. Sent in to the dining room as someone's escort.
6. I.e., pledged to attend her dinner party.

ALGERNON Then your wife will. You don't seem to realize, that in married life three is company and two is none.

JACK [*sententiously*] That, my dear young friend, is the theory that the corrupt French Drama[8] has been propounding for the last fifty years.

ALGERNON Yes; and that the happy English home has proved in half the time.

JACK For heaven's sake, don't try to be cynical. It's perfectly easy to be cynical.

ALGERNON My dear fellow, it isn't easy to be anything nowadays. There's such a lot of beastly competition about. [*The sound of an electric bell is heard.*] Ah! that must be Aunt Augusta. Only relatives, or creditors, ever ring in that Wagnerian manner.[9] Now, if I get her out of the way for ten minutes, so that you can have an opportunity for proposing to Gwendolen, may I dine with you tonight at Willis's?

JACK I suppose so, if you want to.

ALGERNON Yes, but you must be serious about it. I hate people who are not serious about meals. It is so shallow of them.

[*Enter Lane.*]

LANE Lady Bracknell and Miss Fairfax.

[*Algernon goes forward to meet them. Enter Lady Bracknell and Gwendolen.*]

LADY BRACKNELL Good afternoon, dear Algernon, I hope you are behaving very well.

ALGERNON I'm feeling very well, Aunt Augusta.

LADY BRACKNELL That's not quite the same thing. In fact the two things rarely go together. [*Sees Jack and bows to him with icy coldness.*]

ALGERNON [*to Gwendolen*] Dear me, you are smart![1]

GWENDOLEN I am always smart! Aren't I, Mr Worthing?

JACK You're quite perfect, Miss Fairfax.

GWENDOLEN Oh! I hope I am not that. It would leave no room for developments, and I intend to develop in many directions. [*Gwendolen and Jack sit down together in the corner.*]

LADY BRACKNELL I'm sorry if we are a little late, Algernon, but I was obliged to call on dear Lady Harbury. I hadn't been there since her poor husband's death. I never saw a woman so altered; she looks quite twenty years younger. And now I'll have a cup of tea, and one of those nice cucumber sandwiches you promised me.

ALGERNON Certainly, Aunt Augusta. [*Goes over to tea-table.*]

LADY BRACKNELL Won't you come and sit here, Gwendolen?

GWENDOLEN Thanks, mamma, I'm quite comfortable where I am.

ALGERNON [*picking up empty plate in horror*] Good heavens! Lane! Why are there no cucumber sandwiches? I ordered them specially.

LANE [*gravely*] There were no cucumbers in the market this morning, sir. I went down twice.

ALGERNON No cucumbers!

LANE No, sir. Not even for ready money.

ALGERNON That will do, Lane, thank you.

LANE Thank you, sir. [*Goes out.*]

ALGERNON I am greatly distressed, Aunt Augusta, about there being no cucumbers, not even for ready money.

LADY BRACKNELL It really makes no matter, Algernon. I had some crumpets with Lady Harbury, who seems to me to be living entirely for pleasure now.

---

8. Late 19th-century French plays frequently focused on marital infidelity.
9. I.e., loud and dramatic, like the grand operas of

Richard Wagner (1813–1883).
1. Chic.

ALGERNON I hear her hair has turned quite gold from grief.

LADY BRACKNELL It certainly has changed its colour. From what cause I, of course, cannot say. [*Algernon crosses and hands tea.*] Thank you. I've quite a treat for you tonight, Algernon. I am going to send you down with Mary Farquhar. She is such a nice woman, and so attentive to her husband. It's delightful to watch them.

ALGERNON I am afraid, Aunt Augusta, I shall have to give up the pleasure of dining with you tonight after all.

LADY BRACKNELL [*frowning*] I hope not, Algernon. It would put my table completely out. Your uncle would have to dine upstairs. Fortunately he is accustomed to that.

ALGERNON It is a great bore, and, I need hardly say, a terrible disappointment to me, but the fact is I have just had a telegram to say that my poor friend Bunbury is very ill again. [*Exchanges glances with Jack.*] They seem to think I should be with him.

LADY BRACKNELL It is very strange. This Mr Bunbury seems to suffer from curiously bad health.

ALGERNON Yes; poor Bunbury is a dreadful invalid.

LADY BRACKNELL Well, I must say, Algernon, that I think it is high time that Mr Bunbury made up his mind whether he was going to live or to die. This shilly-shallying with the question is absurd. Nor do I in any way approve of the modern sympathy with invalids. I consider it morbid. Illness of any kind is hardly a thing to be encouraged in others. Health is the primary duty of life. I am always telling that to your poor uncle, but he never seems to take much notice . . . as far as any improvement in his ailments goes. I should be much obliged if you would ask Mr Bunbury, from me, to be kind enough not to have a relapse on Saturday, for I rely on you to arrange my music for me. It is my last reception, and one wants something that will encourage conversation, particularly at the end of the season[2] when everyone has practically said whatever they had to say, which, in most cases, was probably not much.

ALGERNON I'll speak to Bunbury, Aunt Augusta, if he is still conscious, and I think I can promise you he'll be all right by Saturday. Of course the music is a great difficulty. You see, if one plays good music, people don't listen, and if one plays bad music people don't talk. But I'll run over the programme I've drawn out, if you will kindly come into the next room for a moment.

LADY BRACKNELL Thank you, Algernon. It is very thoughtful of you. [*Rising, and following Algernon.*] I'm sure the programme will be delightful, after a few expurgations. French songs I cannot possibly allow. People always seem to think that they are improper, and either look shocked, which is vulgar, or laugh, which is worse. But German sounds a thoroughly respectable language, and indeed, I believe is so. Gwendolen, you will accompany me.

GWENDOLEN Certainly, mamma.

[*Lady Bracknell and Algernon go into the music-room, Gwendolen remains behind.*]

JACK Charming day it has been, Miss Fairfax.

GWENDOLEN Pray don't talk to me about the weather, Mr Worthing. Whenever people talk to me about the weather, I always feel quite certain that they mean something else. And that makes me so nervous.

JACK I do mean something else.

GWENDOLEN I thought so. In fact, I am never wrong.

---

2. Fashionable people left their country estates to spend the social season in London; it began in late spring and lasted through July.

JACK And I would like to be allowed to take advantage of Lady Bracknell's temporary absence . . .

GWENDOLEN I would certainly advise you to do so. Mamma has a way of coming back suddenly into a room that I have often had to speak to her about.

JACK [*nervously*] Miss Fairfax, ever since I met you I have admired you more than any girl . . . I have ever met since . . . I met you.

GWENDOLEN Yes, I am quite aware of the fact. And I often wish that in public, at any rate, you had been more demonstrative. For me you have always had an irresistible fascination. Even before I met you I was far from indifferent to you. [*Jack looks at her in amazement.*] We live, as I hope you know, Mr Worthing, in an age of ideals. The fact is constantly mentioned in the more expensive monthly magazines, and has reached the provincial pulpits I am told: and my ideal has always been to love some one of the name of Ernest. There is something in that name that inspires absolute confidence. The moment Algernon first mentioned to me that he had a friend called Ernest, I knew I was destined to love you.

JACK You really love me, Gwendolen?

GWENDOLEN Passionately!

JACK Darling! You don't know how happy you've made me.

GWENDOLEN My own Ernest!

JACK But you don't really mean to say that you couldn't love me if my name wasn't Ernest?

GWENDOLEN But your name is Ernest.

JACK Yes, I know it is. But supposing it was something else? Do you mean to say you couldn't love me then?

GWENDOLEN [*glibly*] Ah! that is clearly a metaphysical speculation, and like most metaphysical speculations has very little reference at all to the actual facts of real life, as we know them.

JACK Personally, darling, to speak quite candidly, I don't much care about the name of Ernest . . . I don't think the name suits me at all.

GWENDOLEN It suits you perfectly. It is a divine name. It has a music of its own. It produces vibrations.

JACK Well, really, Gwendolen, I must say that I think there are lots of other much nicer names. I think Jack, for instance, a charming name.

GWENDOLEN Jack? . . . No, there is very little music in the name Jack, if any at all, indeed. It does not thrill. It produces absolutely no vibrations . . . I have known several Jacks, and they all, without exception, were more than usually plain. Besides, Jack is a notorious domesticity for John! And I pity any woman who is married to a man called John. She would probably never be allowed to know the entrancing pleasure of a single moment's solitude. The only really safe name is Ernest.

JACK Gwendolen, I must get christened at once—I mean we must get married at once. There is no time to be lost.

GWENDOLEN Married, Mr Worthing?[3]

JACK [*astounded*] Well . . . surely. You know that I love you, and you led me to believe, Miss Fairfax, that you were not absolutely indifferent to me.

GWENDOLEN I adore you. But you haven't proposed to me yet. Nothing has been said at all about marriage. The subject has not even been touched on.

JACK Well . . . may I propose to you now?

---

3. Gwendolen reverts to using Jack's last name when she is reminded that he has not yet formally proposed.

GWENDOLEN I think it would be an admirable opportunity. And to spare you any possible disappointment, Mr Worthing, I think it only fair to tell you quite frankly beforehand that I am fully determined to accept you.

JACK Gwendolen!

GWENDOLEN Yes, Mr Worthing, what have you got to say to me?

JACK You know what I have got to say to you.

GWENDOLEN Yes, but you don't say it.

JACK Gwendolen, will you marry me? [*Goes on his knees.*]

GWENDOLEN Of course I will, darling. How long you have been about it! I am afraid you have had very little experience in how to propose.

JACK My own one, I have never loved anyone in the world but you.

GWENDOLEN Yes, but men often propose for practice. I know my brother Gerald does. All my girl-friends tell me so. What wonderfully blue eyes you have, Ernest! They are quite, quite, blue. I hope you will always look at me just like that, especially when there are other people present.

  [*Enter Lady Bracknell.*]

LADY BRACKNELL Mr Worthing! Rise, sir, from this semi-recumbent posture. It is most indecorous.

GWENDOLEN Mamma! [*He tries to rise; she restrains him.*] I must beg you to retire. This is no place for you. Besides, Mr Worthing has not quite finished yet.

LADY BRACKNELL Finished what, may I ask?

GWENDOLEN I am engaged to Mr Worthing, mamma. [*They rise together.*]

LADY BRACKNELL Pardon me, you are not engaged to anyone. When you do become engaged to some one, I, or your father, should his health permit him, will inform you of the fact. An engagement should come on a young girl as a surprise, pleasant or unpleasant, as the case may be. It is hardly a matter that she could be allowed to arrange for herself. . . . And now I have a few questions to put to you, Mr Worthing. While I am making these inquiries, you, Gwendolen, will wait for me below in the carriage.

GWENDOLEN [*reproachfully*] Mamma!

LADY BRACKNELL In the carriage, Gwendolen! [*Gwendolen goes to the door. She and Jack blow kisses to each other behind Lady Bracknell's back. Lady Bracknell looks vaguely about as if she could not understand what the noise was. Finally turns round.*] Gwendolen, the carriage!

GWENDOLEN Yes, mamma. [*Goes out, looking back at Jack.*]

LADY BRACKNELL [*sitting down*] You can take a seat, Mr Worthing.

  [*Looking in her pocket for note-book and pencil.*]

JACK Thank you, Lady Bracknell, I prefer standing.

LADY BRACKNELL [*pencil and note-book in hand*] I feel bound to tell you that you are not down on my list of eligible young men, although I have the same list as the dear Duchess of Bolton has. We work together, in fact. However, I am quite ready to enter your name, should your answers be what a really affectionate mother requires. Do you smoke?

JACK Well, yes, I must admit I smoke.

LADY BRACKNELL I am glad to hear it. A man should always have an occupation of some kind. There are far too many idle men in London as it is. How old are you?

JACK Twenty-nine.

LADY BRACKNELL A very good age to be married at. I have always been of opinion that a man who desires to get married should know either everything or nothing. Which do you know?

JACK [*after some hesitation*] I know nothing, Lady Bracknell.

LADY BRACKNELL I am pleased to hear it. I do not approve of anything that tampers with natural ignorance. Ignorance is like a delicate exotic fruit; touch it and the bloom is gone. The whole theory of modern education is radically unsound. Fortunately in England, at any rate, education produces no effect whatsoever. If it did, it would prove a serious danger to the upper classes, and probably lead to acts of violence in Grosvenor Square.[4] What is your income?

JACK Between seven and eight thousand a year.

LADY BRACKNELL [*makes a note in her book*] In land, or in investments?

JACK In investments, chiefly.

LADY BRACKNELL That is satisfactory. What between the duties expected of one during one's lifetime, and the duties exacted from one after one's death,[5] land has ceased to be either a profit or a pleasure. It gives one position, and prevents one from keeping it up. That's all that can be said about land.

JACK I have a country house with some land, of course, attached to it, about fifteen hundred acres, I believe; but I don't depend on that for my real income. In fact, as far as I can make out, the poachers are the only people who make anything out of it.

LADY BRACKNELL A country house! How many bedrooms? Well, that point can be cleared up afterwards. You have a town house, I hope? A girl with a simple, unspoiled nature, like Gwendolen, could hardly be expected to reside in the country.

JACK Well, I own a house in Belgrave Square,[6] but it is let by the year to Lady Bloxham. Of course, I can get it back whenever I like, at six months' notice.

LADY BRACKNELL Lady Bloxham? I don't know her.

JACK Oh, she goes about very little. She is a lady considerably advanced in years.

LADY BRACKNELL Ah, nowadays that is no guarantee of respectability of character. What number in Belgrave Square?

JACK 149.

LADY BRACKNELL [*shaking her head*] The unfashionable side. I thought there was something. However, that could easily be altered.

JACK Do you mean the fashion, or the side?

LADY BRACKNELL [*sternly*] Both, if necessary, I presume. What are your politics?

JACK Well, I am afraid I really have none. I am a Liberal Unionist.[7]

LADY BRACKNELL Oh, they count as Tories. They dine with us. Or come in the evening, at any rate. Now to minor matters. Are your parents living?

JACK I have lost both my parents.

LADY BRACKNELL Both? To lose one parent may be regarded as a misfortune—to lose *both* seems like carelessness. Who was your father? He was evidently a man of some wealth. Was he born in what the Radical papers call the purple of commerce, or did he rise from the ranks of the aristocracy?

JACK I am afraid I really don't know. The fact is, Lady Bracknell, I said I had lost my parents. It would be nearer the truth to say that my parents seem to have lost me . . . I don't actually know who I am by birth. I was . . . well, I was found.

LADY BRACKNELL Found!

JACK The late Mr Thomas Cardew, an old gentleman of a very charitable and kindly disposition, found me, and gave me the name of Worthing, because he happened to have a first-class ticket for Worthing in his pocket at the time. Worthing is a place in Sussex. It is a seaside resort.

4. A fashionable area in the West End of London.
5. "Death duties" are inheritance taxes.
6. A fashionable West End address in Belgravia.

7. In 1886 Liberal Unionists joined the Conservatives (the "Tories") in voting against the Liberal Prime Minister Gladstone's bill supporting Home Rule for Ireland.

LADY BRACKNELL Where did the charitable gentleman who had a first-class ticket for this seaside resort find you?

JACK [*gravely*] In a hand-bag.

LADY BRACKNELL A hand-bag?

JACK [*very seriously*] Yes, Lady Bracknell. I was in a hand-bag—a somewhat large, black leather hand-bag, with handles to it—an ordinary hand-bag in fact.

LADY BRACKNELL In what locality did this Mr James, or Thomas, Cardew come across this ordinary hand-bag?

JACK In the cloak-room at Victoria Station. It was given to him in mistake for his own.

LADY BRACKNELL The cloak-room at Victoria Station?

JACK Yes. The Brighton line.

LADY BRACKNELL The line is immaterial. Mr Worthing, I confess I feel somewhat bewildered by what you have just told me. To be born, or at any rate bred, in a hand-bag, whether it had handles or not, seems to me to display a contempt for the ordinary decencies of family life that reminds one of the worst excesses of the French Revolution. And I presume you know what that unfortunate movement led to? As for the particular locality in which the hand-bag was found, a cloak-room at a railway station might serve to conceal a social indiscretion—has probably, indeed, been used for that purpose before now—but it could hardly be regarded as an assured basis for a recognized position in good society.

JACK May I ask you then what you would advise me to do? I need hardly say I would do anything in the world to ensure Gwendolen's happiness.

LADY BRACKNELL I would strongly advise you, Mr Worthing, to try and acquire some relations as soon as possible, and to make a definite effort to produce at any rate one parent, of either sex, before the season is quite over.

JACK Well, I don't see how I could possibly manage to do that. I can produce the hand-bag at any moment. It is in my dressing-room at home. I really think that should satisfy you, Lady Bracknell.

LADY BRACKNELL Me, sir! What has it to do with me? You can hardly imagine that I and Lord Bracknell would dream of allowing our only daughter—a girl brought up with the utmost care—to marry into a cloak-room, and form an alliance with a parcel? Good morning, Mr Worthing!

[*Lady Bracknell sweeps out in majestic indignation.*]

JACK Good morning! [*Algernon, from the other room, strikes up the Wedding March. Jack looks perfectly furious, and goes to the door.*] For goodness' sake don't play that ghastly tune, Algy! How idiotic you are!

[*The music stops, and Algernon enters cheerily.*]

ALGERNON Didn't it go off all right, old boy? You don't mean to say Gwendolen refused you? I know it is a way she has. She is always refusing people. I think it is most ill-natured of her.

JACK Oh, Gwendolen is as right as a trivet.[8] As far as she is concerned, we are engaged. Her mother is perfectly unbearable. Never met such a Gorgon[9] . . . I don't really know what a Gorgon is like, but I am quite sure that Lady Bracknell is one. In any case, she is a monster, without being a myth, which is rather unfair . . . I beg your pardon, Algy, I suppose I shouldn't talk about your own aunt in that way before you.

ALGERNON My dear boy, I love hearing my relations abused. It is the only thing

8. Reliable and steady, like a stand used to hold a pot over the fire. 9. A mythical female monster with snakes for hair.

that makes me put up with them at all. Relations are simply a tedious pack of people, who haven't got the remotest knowledge of how to live, nor the smallest instinct about when to die.

JACK Oh, that is nonsense!

ALGERNON It isn't!

JACK Well, I won't argue about the matter. You always want to argue about things.

ALGERNON That is exactly what things were originally made for.

JACK Upon my word, if I thought that, I'd shoot myself . . . [A pause.] You don't think there is any chance of Gwendolen becoming like her mother in about a hundred and fifty years, do you Algy?

ALGERNON All women become like their mothers. That is their tragedy. No man does. That's his.

JACK Is that clever?

ALGERNON It is perfectly phrased! and quite as true as any observation in civilized life should be.

JACK I am sick to death of cleverness. Everybody is clever nowadays. You can't go anywhere without meeting clever people. The thing has become an absolute public nuisance. I wish to goodness we had a few fools left.

ALGERNON We have.

JACK I should extremely like to meet them. What do they talk about?

ALGERNON The fools? Oh! about the clever people, of course.

JACK What fools!

ALGERNON By the way, did you tell Gwendolen the truth about your being Ernest in town, and Jack in the country?

JACK [in a very patronizing manner] My dear fellow, the truth isn't quite the sort of thing one tells to a nice sweet refined girl. What extraordinary ideas you have about the way to behave to a woman!

ALGERNON The only way to behave to a woman is to make love to her,[1] if she is pretty, and to someone else if she is plain.

JACK Oh, that is nonsense.

ALGERNON What about your brother? What about the profligate Ernest?

JACK Oh, before the end of the week I shall have got rid of him. I'll say he died in Paris of apoplexy. Lots of people die of apoplexy, quite suddenly, don't they?

ALGERNON Yes, but it's hereditary, my dear fellow. It's a sort of thing that runs in families. You had much better say a severe chill.

JACK You are sure a severe chill isn't hereditary, or anything of that kind?

ALGERNON Of course it isn't!

JACK Very well, then. My poor brother Ernest is carried off suddenly in Paris, by a severe chill. That gets rid of him.

ALGERNON But I thought you said that . . . Miss Cardew was a little too much interested in your poor brother Ernest? Won't she feel his loss a good deal?

JACK Oh, that is all right. Cecily is not a silly romantic girl, I am glad to say. She has got a capital appetite, goes long walks, and pays no attention at all to her lessons.

ALGERNON I would rather like to see Cecily.

JACK I will take very good care you never do. She is excessively pretty, and she is only just eighteen.

1. I.e., to flirt with or court her.

ALGERNON Have you told Gwendolen yet that you have an excessively pretty ward who is only just eighteen?

JACK Oh! one doesn't blurt these things out to people. Cecily and Gwendolen are perfectly certain to be extremely great friends. I'll bet you anything you like that half an hour after they have met, they will be calling each other sister.

ALGERNON Women only do that when they have called each other a lot of other things first. Now, my dear boy, if we want to get a good table at Willis's, we really must go and dress. Do you know it is nearly seven?

JACK [irritably] Oh! it always is nearly seven.

ALGERNON Well, I'm hungry.

JACK I never knew you when you weren't. . . .

ALGERNON What shall we do after dinner? Go to a theatre?

JACK Oh no! I loathe listening.

ALGERNON Well, let us go to the Club?

JACK Oh, no! I hate talking.

ALGERNON Well, we might trot round to the Empire[2] at ten?

JACK Oh, no! I can't bear looking at things. It is so silly.

ALGERNON Well, what shall we do?

JACK Nothing!

ALGERNON It is awfully hard work doing nothing. However, I don't mind hard work where there is no definite object of any kind.

[Enter Lane.]

LANE Miss Fairfax.

[Enter Gwendolen. Lane goes out.]

ALGERNON Gwendolen, upon my word!

GWENDOLEN Algy, kindly turn your back. I have something very particular to say to Mr Worthing.

ALGERNON Really, Gwendolen, I don't think I can allow this at all.

GWENDOLEN Algy, you always adopt a strictly immoral attitude towards life. You are not quite old enough to do that.

[Algernon retires to the fireplace.]

JACK My own darling!

GWENDOLEN Ernest, we may never be married. From the expression on mamma's face I fear we never shall. Few parents nowadays pay any regard to what their children say to them. The old-fashioned respect for the young is fast dying out. Whatever influence I ever had over mamma, I lost at the age of three. But although she may prevent us from becoming man and wife, and I may marry someone else, and marry often, nothing that she can possibly do can alter my eternal devotion to you.

JACK Dear Gwendolen!

GWENDOLEN The story of your romantic origin, as related to me by mamma, with unpleasing comments, has naturally stirred the deeper fibres of my nature. Your Christian name has an irresistible fascination. The simplicity of your character makes you exquisitely incomprehensible to me. Your town address at the Albany I have. What is your address in the country?

JACK The Manor House, Woolton, Hertfordshire.

[Algernon, who has been carefully listening, smiles to himself, and writes the address on his shirt-cuff. Then picks up the Railway Guide.]

2. A popular music hall.

GWENDOLEN There is a good postal service, I suppose? It may be necessary to do something desperate. That of course will require serious consideration. I will communicate with you daily.

JACK My own one!

GWENDOLEN How long do you remain in town?

JACK Till Monday.

GWENDOLEN Good! Algy, you may turn round now.

ALGERNON Thanks, I've turned round already.

GWENDOLEN You may also ring the bell.

JACK You will let me see you to your carriage, my own darling?

GWENDOLEN Certainly.

JACK [to Lane, who now enters] I will see Miss Fairfax out.

LANE Yes, sir. [Jack and Gwendolen go off.]

[Lane presents several letters on a salver to Algernon. It is to be surmised that they are bills, as Algernon, after looking at the envelopes, tears them up.]

ALGERNON A glass of sherry, Lane.

LANE Yes, sir.

ALGERNON Tomorrow, Lane, I'm going Bunburying.

LANE Yes, sir.

ALGERNON I shall probably not be back till Monday. You can put up my dress clothes, my smoking jacket, and all the Bunbury suits . . .

LANE Yes, sir. [Handing sherry.]

ALGERNON I hope tomorrow will be a fine day, Lane.

LANE It never is, sir.

ALGERNON Lane, you're a perfect pessimist.

LANE I do my best to give satisfaction, sir.

[Enter Jack. Lane goes off.]

JACK There's a sensible, intellectual girl! the only girl I ever cared for in my life. [Algernon is laughing immoderately.] What on earth are you so amused at?

ALGERNON Oh, I'm a little anxious about poor Bunbury, that is all.

JACK If you don't take care, your friend Bunbury will get you into a serious scrape some day.

ALGERNON I love scrapes. They are the only things that are never serious.

JACK Oh, that's nonsense, Algy. You never talk anything but nonsense.

ALGERNON Nobody ever does.

[Jack looks indignantly at him, and leaves the room. Algernon lights a cigarette, reads his shirt-cuff, and smiles.]   ACT DROP

SECOND ACT

SCENE: Garden at the Manor House. A flight of gray stone steps leads up to the house. The garden, an old-fashioned one, full of roses. Time of year, July. Basket chairs, and a table covered with books, are set under a large yew tree.

[Miss Prism discovered seated at the table. Cecily is at the back watering flowers.]

MISS PRISM [calling] Cecily, Cecily! Surely such a utilitarian occupation as the watering of flowers is rather Moulton's duty than yours? Especially at a moment when intellectual pleasures await you. Your German grammar is on the table. Pray open it at page fifteen. We will repeat yesterday's lesson.

CECILY [*coming over very slowly*] But I don't like German. It isn't at all a becoming language. I know perfectly well that I look quite plain after my German lesson.

MISS PRISM Child, you know how anxious your guardian is that you should improve yourself in every way. He laid particular stress on your German, as he was leaving for town yesterday. Indeed, he always lays stress on your German when he is leaving for town.

CECILY Dear Uncle Jack is so very serious! Sometimes he is so serious that I think he cannot be quite well.

MISS PRISM [*drawing herself up*] Your guardian enjoys the best of health, and his gravity of demeanour is especially to be commended in one so comparatively young as he is. I know no one who has a higher sense of duty and responsibility.

CECILY I suppose that is why he often looks a little bored when we three are together.

MISS PRISM Cecily! I am surprised at you. Mr Worthing has many troubles in his life. Idle merriment and triviality would be out of place in his conversation. You must remember his constant anxiety about that unfortunate young man his brother.

CECILY I wish Uncle Jack would allow that unfortunate young man, his brother, to come down here sometimes. We might have a good influence over him, Miss Prism. I am sure you certainly would. You know German, and geology, and things of that kind influence a man very much. [*Cecily begins to write in her diary.*]

MISS PRISM [*shaking her head*] I do not think that even I could produce any effect on a character that according to his own brother's admission is irretrievably weak and vacillating. Indeed I am not sure that I would desire to reclaim him. I am not in favour of this modern mania for turning bad people into good people at a moment's notice. As a man sows so let him reap.[3] You must put away your diary, Cecily. I really don't see why you should keep a diary at all.

CECILY I keep a diary in order to enter the wonderful secrets of my life. If I didn't write them down I should probably forget all about them.

MISS PRISM Memory, my dear Cecily, is the diary that we all carry about with us.

CECILY Yes, but it usually chronicles the things that have never happened, and couldn't possibly have happened. I believe that Memory is responsible for nearly all the three-volume novels that Mudie sends us.[4]

MISS PRISM Do not speak slightly of the three-volume novel, Cecily. I wrote one myself in earlier days.

CECILY Did you really, Miss Prism? How wonderfully clever you are! I hope it did not end happily? I don't like novels that end happily. They depress me so much.

MISS PRISM The good ended happily, and the bad unhappily. That is what Fiction means.

CECILY I suppose so. But it seems very unfair. And was your novel ever published?

MISS PRISM Alas! no. The manuscript unfortunately was abandoned. I use the word in the sense of lost or mislaid. To your work, child, these speculations are profitless.

CECILY [*smiling*] But I see dear Dr Chasuble coming up through the garden.

MISS PRISM [*rising and advancing*] Dr Chasuble! This is indeed a pleasure.
[*Enter Canon Chasuble.*][5]

CHASUBLE And how are we this morning? Miss Prism, you are, I trust, well?

---

3. "Be not deceived; God is not mocked: for whatsoever a man soweth, that shall he also reap" (Galatians 6.7).
4. Mudie's Select Library lent novels to subscribers for a

fee; at the time of this play, both Mudie's and the three-volume novel were becoming outmoded.
5. A canon is a cathedral clergyman; a chasuble is a vestment.

CECILY Miss Prism has just been complaining of a slight headache. I think it would do her so much good to have a short stroll with you in the Park, Dr Chasuble.

MISS PRISM Cecily, have not mentioned anything about a headache.

CECILY No, dear Miss Prism, I know that, but I felt instinctively that you had a headache. Indeed I was thinking about that, and not about my German lesson, when the Rector came in.

CHASUBLE I hope Cecily, you are not inattentive.

CECILY Oh, I am afraid I am.

CHASUBLE That is strange. Were I fortunate enough to be Miss Prism's pupil, I would hang upon her lips. [*Miss Prism glares.*] I spoke metaphorically.—My metaphor was drawn from bees. Ahem! Mr Worthing I suppose, has not returned from town yet?

MISS PRISM We do not expect him till Monday afternoon.

CHASUBLE Ah yes, he usually likes to spend his Sunday in London. He is not one of those whose sole aim is enjoyment, as, by all accounts, that unfortunate young man his brother seems to be. But I must not disturb Egeria[6] and her pupil any longer.

MISS PRISM Egeria? My name is Laetitia, Doctor.

CHASUBLE [*bowing*] A classical allusion merely, drawn from the Pagan authors. I shall see you both no doubt at Evensong?[7]

MISS PRISM I think, dear Doctor, I will have a stroll with you. I find I have a headache after all, and a walk might do it good.

CHASUBLE With pleasure, Miss Prism, with pleasure. We might go as far as the schools and back.

MISS PRISM That would be delightful. Cecily, you will read your Political Economy in my absence. The chapter on the Fall of the Rupee you may omit.[8] It is somewhat too sensational. Even these metallic problems have their melodramatic side. [*Goes down the garden with Dr Chasuble.*]

CECILY [*picks up books and throws them back on table*] Horrid Political Economy! Horrid Geography! Horrid, horrid German!

[*Enter Merriman with a card on a salver.*]

MERRIMAN Mr Ernest Worthing has just driven over from the station. He has brought his luggage with him.

CECILY [*takes the card and reads it*] "Mr Ernest Worthing, B.4 The Albany, W." Uncle Jack's brother! Did you tell him Mr Worthing was in town?

MERRIMAN Yes, Miss. He seemed very much disappointed. I mentioned that you and Miss Prism were in the garden. He said he was anxious to speak to you privately for a moment.

CECILY Ask Mr Ernest Worthing to come here. I suppose you had better talk to the housekeeper about a room for him.

MERRIMAN Yes, Miss. [*Merriman goes off.*]

CECILY I have never met any really wicked person before. I feel rather frightened. I am so afraid he will look just like everyone else.

[*Enter Algernon, very gay and debonair.*]
He does!

---

6. Roman goddess of fountains; her name was used for a woman who instructed other women.
7. Evening church services.

8. The declining value of the Indian rupee would hurt British civil servants in India, who were paid in rupees.

ALGERNON [*raising his hat*] You are my little cousin Cecily, I'm sure.

CECILY You are under some strange mistake. I am not little. In fact, I believe I am more than usually tall for my age. [*Algernon is rather taken aback.*] But I am your cousin Cecily. You, I see from your card, are Uncle Jack's brother, my cousin Ernest, my wicked cousin Ernest.

ALGERNON Oh! I am not really wicked at all, cousin Cecily. You mustn't think that I am wicked.

CECILY If you are not, then you have certainly been deceiving us all in a very inexcusable manner. I hope you have not been leading a double life, pretending to be wicked and being really good all the time. That would be hypocrisy.

ALGERNON [*looks at her in amazement*] Oh! Of course I have been rather reckless.

CECILY I am glad to hear it.

ALGERNON In fact, now you mention the subject, I have been very bad in my own small way.

CECILY I don't think you should be so proud of that, although I am sure it must have been very pleasant.

ALGERNON It is much pleasanter being here with you.

CECILY I can't understand how you are here at all. Uncle Jack won't be back till Monday afternoon.

ALGERNON That is a great disappointment. I am obliged to go up by the first train on Monday morning. I have a business appointment that I am anxious . . . to miss.

CECILY Couldn't you miss it anywhere but in London?

ALGERNON No: the appointment is in London.

CECILY Well, I know, of course, how important it is not to keep a business engagement, if one wants to retain any sense of the beauty of life, but still I think you had better wait till Uncle Jack arrives. I know he wants to speak to you about your emigrating.

ALGERNON About my what?

CECILY Your emigrating. He has gone up to buy your outfit.

ALGERNON I certainly wouldn't let Jack buy my outfit. He has no taste in neckties at all.

CECILY I don't think you will require neckties. Uncle Jack is sending you to Australia.[9]

ALGERNON Australia! I'd sooner die.

CECILY Well, he said at dinner on Wednesday night, that you would have to choose between this world, the next world, and Australia.

ALGERNON Oh, well! The accounts I have received of Australia and the next world, are not particularly encouraging. This world is good enough for me, cousin Cecily.

CECILY Yes, but are you good enough for it?

ALGERNON I'm afraid I'm not that. That is why I want you to reform me. You might make that your mission, if you don't mind, cousin Cecily.

CECILY I'm afraid I've no time, this afternoon.

ALGERNON Well, would you mind my reforming myself this afternoon?

CECILY It is rather Quixotic[1] of you. But I think you should try.

ALGERNON I will. I feel better already.

CECILY You are looking a little worse.

ALGERNON That is because I am hungry.

---

9. Australia was no longer a penal colony, but it was still a place where families sent their ne'er-do-well sons.

1. Hopelessly idealistic, like Don Quixote.

CECILY How thoughtless of me. I should have remembered that when one is going to lead an entirely new life, one requires regular and wholesome meals. Won't you come in?

ALGERNON Thank you. Might I have a buttonhole[2] first? I never have any appetite unless I have a buttonhole first.

CECILY A Maréchal Niel?[3] [*Picks up scissors.*]

ALGERNON No, I'd sooner have a pink rose.

CECILY Why? [*Cuts a flower.*]

ALGERNON Because you are like a pink rose, Cousin Cecily.

CECILY I don't think it can be right for you to talk to me like that. Miss Prism never says such things to me.

ALGERNON Then Miss Prism is a short-sighted old lady. [*Cecily puts the rose in his buttonhole.*] You are the prettiest girl I ever saw.

CECILY Miss Prism says that all good looks are a snare.

ALGERNON They are a snare that every sensible man would like to be caught in.

CECILY Oh! I don't think I would care to catch a sensible man. I shouldn't know what to talk to him about.

[*They pass into the house. Miss Prism and Dr Chasuble return.*]

MISS PRISM You are too much alone, dear Dr Chasuble. You should get married. A misanthrope I can understand—a womanthrope, never!

CHASUBLE [*with a scholar's shudder*][4] Believe me, I do not deserve so neologistic a phrase. The precept as well as the practice of the Primitive Church was distinctly against matrimony.[5]

MISS PRISM [*sententiously*] That is obviously the reason why the Primitive Church has not lasted up to the present day. And you do not seem to realize, dear Doctor, that by persistently remaining single, a man converts himself into a permanent public temptation. Men should be more careful; this very celibacy leads weaker vessels astray.

CHASUBLE But is a man not equally attractive when married?

MISS PRISM No married man is ever attractive except to his wife.

CHASUBLE And often, I've been told, not even to her.

MISS PRISM That depends on the intellectual sympathies of the woman. Maturity can always be depended on. Ripeness can be trusted. Young women are green. [*Dr Chasuble starts.*] I spoke horticulturally. My metaphor was drawn from fruits. But where is Cecily?

CHASUBLE Perhaps she followed us to the schools.

[*Enter Jack slowly from the back of the garden. He is dressed in the deepest mourning, with crape hat-band and black gloves.*]

MISS PRISM Mr Worthing!

CHASUBLE Mr Worthing?

MISS PRISM This is indeed a surprise. We did not look for you till Monday afternoon.

JACK [*shakes Miss Prism's hand in a tragic manner*] I have returned sooner than I expected. Dr Chasuble, I hope you are well?

---

2. A flower to wear in his lapel.
3. A yellow rose.
4. He shudders because Miss Prism has mangled the language by coining a word, "womanthrope," to describe someone who dislikes women, instead of using the correct term, "misogynist." A neologism is a newly invented word.
5. Protestant clergy are allowed to marry, but as a High Church Anglican, Chasuble is interested in preserving the rituals and practices of the early Catholic church.

CHASUBLE Dear Mr Worthing, I trust this garb of woe does not betoken some terrible calamity?

JACK My brother.

MISS PRISM More shameful debts and extravagance?

CHASUBLE Still leading his life of pleasure?

JACK [*shaking his head*] Dead!

CHASUBLE Your brother Ernest dead?

JACK Quite dead.

MISS PRISM What a lesson for him! I trust he will profit by it.

CHASUBLE Mr Worthing, I offer you my sincere condolence. You have at least the consolation of knowing that you were always the most generous and forgiving of brothers.

JACK Poor Ernest! He had many faults, but it is a sad, sad blow.

CHASUBLE Very sad indeed. Were you with him at the end?

JACK No. He died abroad; in Paris, in fact. I had a telegram last night from the manager of the Grand Hotel.

CHASUBLE Was the cause of death mentioned?

JACK A severe chill, it seems.

MISS PRISM As a man sows, so shall he reap.

CHASUBLE [*raising his hand*] Charity, dear Miss Prism, charity! None of us are perfect. I myself am peculiarly susceptible to draughts. Will the interment take place here?

JACK No. He seemed to have expressed a desire to be buried in Paris.

CHASUBLE In Paris! [*Shakes his head.*] I fear that hardly points to any very serious state of mind at the last. You would no doubt wish me to make some slight allusion to this tragic domestic affliction next Sunday. [*Jack presses his hand convulsively.*] My sermon on the meaning of the manna in the wilderness[6] can be adapted to almost any occasion, joyful, or, as in the present case, distressing. [*All sigh.*] I have preached it at harvest celebrations, christenings, confirmations, on days of humiliation and festal days. The last time I delivered it was in the Cathedral, as a charity sermon on behalf of the Society for the Prevention of Discontent among the Upper Orders. The Bishop, who was present, was much struck by some of the analogies I drew.

JACK Ah! that reminds me, you mentioned christenings I think, Dr Chasuble? I suppose you know how to christen all right? [*Dr Chasuble looks astounded.*] I mean, of course, you are continually christening, aren't you?

MISS PRISM It is, I regret to say, one of the Rector's most constant duties in this parish. I have often spoken to the poorer classes on the subject. But they don't seem to know what thrift is.

CHASUBLE But is there any particular infant in whom you are interested, Mr Worthing? Your brother was, I believe, unmarried, was he not?

JACK Oh, yes.

MISS PRISM [*bitterly*] People who live entirely for pleasure usually are.

JACK But it is not for any child, dear Doctor. I am very fond of children. No! the fact is, I would like to be christened myself, this afternoon, if you have nothing better to do.

CHASUBLE But surely, Mr Worthing, you have been christened already?

6. Cf. Exodus 16.

JACK I don't remember anything about it.

CHASUBLE But have you any grave doubts on the subject?

JACK I certainly intend to have. Of course I don't know if the thing would bother you in any way, or if you think I am a little too old now.

CHASUBLE Not at all. The sprinkling, and, indeed, the immersion of adults is a perfectly canonical practice.

JACK Immersion!

CHASUBLE You need have no apprehensions. Sprinkling is all that is necessary, or indeed I think advisable. Our weather is so changeable. At what hour would you wish the ceremony performed?

JACK Oh, I might trot round about five if that would suit you.

CHASUBLE Perfectly, perfectly! In fact I have two similar ceremonies to perform at that time. A case of twins that occurred recently in one of the outlying cottages on your own estate. Poor Jenkins the carter, a most hard-working man.

JACK Oh! I don't see much fun in being christened along with other babies. It would be childish. Would half-past five do?

CHASUBLE Admirably! Admirably! [*Takes out watch.*] And now, dear Mr Worthing, I will not intrude any longer into a house of sorrow. I would merely beg you not to be too much bowed down by grief. What seem to us bitter trials are often blessings in disguise.

MISS PRISM This seems to me a blessing of an extremely obvious kind.

[*Enter Cecily from the house.*]

CECILY Uncle Jack! Oh, I am pleased to see you back. But what horrid clothes you have got on! Do go and change them.

MISS PRISM Cecily!

CHASUBLE My child! my child!

[*Cecily goes towards Jack; he kisses her brow in a melancholy manner.*]

CECILY What is the matter, Uncle Jack? Do look happy! You look as if you had toothache, and I have got such a surprise for you. Who do you think is in the dining-room? Your brother!

JACK Who?

CECILY Your brother Ernest. He arrived about half an hour ago.

JACK What nonsense! I haven't got a brother.

CECILY Oh, don't say that. However badly he may have behaved to you in the past he is still your brother. You couldn't be so heartless as to disown him. I'll tell him to come out. And you will shake hands with him, won't you, Uncle Jack? [*Runs back into the house.*]

CHASUBLE These are very joyful tidings.

MISS PRISM After we had all been resigned to his loss, his sudden return seems to me peculiarly distressing.

JACK My brother is in the dining-room? I don't know what it all means. I think it is perfectly absurd.

[*Enter Algernon and Cecily hand in hand. They come slowly up to Jack.*]

JACK Good heavens! [*Motions Algernon away.*]

ALGERNON Brother John, I have come down from town to tell you that I am very sorry for all the trouble I have given you, and that I intend to lead a better life in the future.

[*Jack glares at him and does not take his hand.*]

CECILY Uncle Jack, you are not going to refuse your own brother's hand?

JACK Nothing will induce me to take his hand. I think his coming down here disgraceful. He knows perfectly well why.

CECILY Uncle Jack, do be nice. There is some good in everyone. Ernest has just been telling me about his poor invalid friend Mr Bunbury whom he goes to visit so often. And surely there must be much good in one who is kind to an invalid, and leaves the pleasures of London to sit by a bed of pain.

JACK Oh! he has been talking about Bunbury has he?

CECILY Yes, he has told me all about poor Mr Bunbury, and his terrible state of health.

JACK Bunbury! Well, I won't have him talk to you about Bunbury or about anything else. It is enough to drive one perfectly frantic.

ALGERNON Of course I admit that the faults were all on my side. But I must say that I think that Brother John's coldness to me is peculiarly painful. I expected a more enthusiastic welcome, especially considering it is the first time I have come here.

CECILY Uncle Jack, if you don't shake hands with Ernest I will never forgive you.

JACK Never forgive me?

CECILY Never, never, never!

JACK Well, this is the last time I shall ever do it. [*Shakes hands with Algernon and glares.*]

CHASUBLE It's pleasant, is it not, to see so perfect a reconciliation? I think we might leave the two brothers together.

MISS PRISM Cecily, you will come with us.

CECILY Certainly, Miss Prism. My little task of reconciliation is over.

CHASUBLE You have done a beautiful action today, dear child.

MISS PRISM We must not be premature in our judgements.

CECILY I feel very happy. [*They all go off.*]

JACK You young scoundrel, Algy, you must get out of this place as soon as possible. I don't allow any Bunburying here.

[*Enter Merriman.*]

MERRIMAN I have put Mr Ernest's things in the room next to yours, sir. I suppose that is all right?

JACK What?

MERRIMAN Mr Ernest's luggage, sir. I have unpacked it and put it in the room next to your own.

JACK His luggage?

MERRIMAN Yes, sir. Three portmanteaus, a dressing-case, two hat-boxes, and a large luncheon-basket.

ALGERNON I am afraid I can't stay more than a week this time.

JACK Merriman, order the dog-cart[7] at once. Mr Ernest has been suddenly called back to town.

MERRIMAN Yes, sir. [*Goes back into the house.*]

ALGERNON What a fearful liar you are, Jack. I have not been called back to town at all.

JACK Yes, you have.

ALGERNON I haven't heard anyone call me.

JACK Your duty as a gentleman calls you back.

ALGERNON My duty as a gentleman has never interfered with my pleasures in the smallest degree.

JACK I can quite understand that.

---

7. A horse-drawn cart with seats, and a box for hunting dogs.

ALGERNON Well, Cecily is a darling.

JACK You are not to talk of Miss Cardew like that. I don't like it.

ALGERNON Well, I don't like your clothes. You look perfectly ridiculous in them. Why on earth don't you go up and change? It is perfectly childish to be in deep mourning for a man who is actually staying for a whole week with you in your house as a guest. I call it grotesque.

JACK You are certainly not staying with me for a whole week as a guest or anything else. You have got to leave . . . by the four-five train.

ALGERNON I certainly won't leave you so long as you are in mourning. It would be most unfriendly. If I were in mourning you would stay with me, I suppose. I should think it very unkind if you didn't.

JACK Well, will you go if I change my clothes?

ALGERNON Yes, if you are not too long. I never saw anybody take so long to dress, and with such little result.

JACK Well, at any rate, that is better than being always over-dressed as you are.

ALGERNON If I am occasionally a little over-dressed, I make up for it by being always immensely over-educated.

JACK Your vanity is ridiculous, your conduct an outrage, and your presence in my garden utterly absurd. However, you have got to catch the four-five, and I hope you will have a pleasant journey back to town. This Bunburying, as you call it, has not been a great success for you. [*Goes into the house.*]

ALGERNON I think it has been a great success. I'm in love with Cecily, and that is everything.

   [*Enter Cecily at the back of the garden. She picks up the can and begins to water the flowers.*]

But I must see her before I go, and make arrangements for another Bunbury. Ah, there she is.

CECILY Oh, I merely came back to water the roses. I thought you were with Uncle Jack.

ALGERNON He's gone to order the dog-cart for me.

CECILY Oh, is he going to take you for a nice drive?

ALGERNON He's going to send me away.

CECILY Then have we got to part?

ALGERNON I am afraid so. It's a painful parting.

CECILY It is always painful to part from people whom one has known for a very brief space of time. The absence of old friends one can endure with equanimity. But even a momentary separation from anyone to whom one has just been introduced is almost unbearable.

ALGERNON Thank you.

   [*Enter Merriman.*]

MERRIMAN The dog-cart is at the door, sir.

   [*Algernon looks appealingly at Cecily.*]

CECILY It can wait, Merriman . . . for . . . five minutes.

MERRIMAN Yes, Miss. [*Exit Merriman.*]

ALGERNON I hope, Cecily, I shall not offend you if I state quite frankly and openly that you seem to me to be in every way the visible personification of absolute perfection.

CECILY I think your frankness does you great credit, Ernest. If you will allow me I will copy your remarks into my diary. [*Goes over to table and begins writing in diary.*]

ALGERNON Do you really keep a diary? I'd give anything to look at it. May I?

CECILY Oh no. [*Puts her hand over it.*] You see, it is simply a very young girl's record of her own thoughts and impressions, and consequently meant for publication. When it appears in volume form I hope you will order a copy. But pray, Ernest, don't stop. I delight in taking down from dictation. I have reached "absolute perfection." You can go on. I am quite ready for more.

ALGERNON [*somewhat taken aback*] Ahem! Ahem!

CECILY Oh, don't cough, Ernest. When one is dictating one should speak fluently and not cough. Besides, I don't know how to spell a cough. [*Writes as Algernon speaks.*]

ALGERNON [*speaking very rapidly*] Cecily, ever since I first looked upon your wonderful and incomparable beauty, I have dared to love you wildly, passionately, devotedly, hopelessly.

CECILY I don't think that you should tell me that you love me wildly, passionately, devotedly, hopelessly. Hopelessly doesn't seem to make much sense, does it?

ALGERNON Cecily!

[*Enter Merriman.*]

MERRIMAN The dog-cart is waiting, sir.

ALGERNON Tell it to come round next week, at the same hour.

MERRIMAN [*looks at Cecily, who makes no sign*] Yes, sir. [*Merriman retires.*]

CECILY Uncle Jack would be very much annoyed if he knew you were staying on till next week, at the same hour.

ALGERNON Oh, I don't care about Jack. I don't care for anybody in the whole world but you. I love you, Cecily. You will marry me, won't you?

CECILY You silly boy! Of course. Why, we have been engaged for the last three months.

ALGERNON For the last three months?

CECILY Yes, it will be exactly three months on Thursday.

ALGERNON But how did we become engaged?

CECILY Well, ever since dear Uncle Jack first confessed to us that he had a younger brother who was very wicked and bad, you of course have formed the chief topic of conversation between myself and Miss Prism. And of course a man who is much talked about is always very attractive. One feels there must be something in him after all. I daresay it was foolish of me, but I fell in love with you, Ernest.

ALGERNON Darling! And when was the engagement actually settled?

CECILY On the 14th of February last. Worn out by your entire ignorance of my existence, I determined to end the matter one way or the other, and after a long struggle with myself I accepted you under this dear old tree here. The next day I bought this little ring in your name, and this is the little bangle with the true lovers' knot I promised you always to wear.

ALGERNON Did I give you this? It's very pretty, isn't it?

CECILY Yes, you've wonderfully good taste, Ernest. It's the excuse I've always given for your leading such a bad life. And this is the box in which I keep all your dear letters. [*Kneels at table, opens box, and produces letters tied up with blue ribbon.*]

ALGERNON My letters! But my own sweet Cecily, I have never written you any letters.

CECILY You need hardly remind me of that, Ernest. I remember only too well that I was forced to write your letters for you. I wrote always three times a week, and sometimes oftener.

ALGERNON Oh, do let me read them, Cecily?

CECILY Oh, I couldn't possibly. They would make you far too conceited. [*Replaces box.*] The three you wrote me after I had broken off the engagement are so beautiful, and so badly spelled, that even now I can hardly read them without crying a little.

ALGERNON But was our engagement ever broken off?

CECILY Of course it was. On the 22nd of last March. You can see the entry if you like. [*Shows diary.*] "Today I broke off my engagement with Ernest. I feel it is better to do so. The weather still continues charming."

ALGERNON But why on earth did you break it off? What had I done? I had done nothing at all. Cecily, I am very much hurt indeed to hear you broke it off. Particularly when the weather was so charming.

CECILY It would hardly have been a really serious engagement if it hadn't been broken off at least once. But I forgave you before the week was out.

ALGERNON [*crossing to her, and kneeling*] What a perfect angel you are, Cecily.

CECILY You dear romantic boy. [*He kisses her, she puts her fingers through his hair.*] I hope your hair curls naturally, does it?

ALGERNON Yes, darling, with a little help from others.

CECILY I am so glad.

ALGERNON You'll never break off our engagement again, Cecily?

CECILY I don't think I could break it off now that I have actually met you. Besides, of course, there is the question of your name.

ALGERNON Yes, of course. [*Nervously.*]

CECILY You must not laugh at me, darling, but it had always been a girlish dream of mine to love some one whose name was Ernest. [*Algernon rises, Cecily also.*] There is something in that name that seems to inspire absolute confidence. I pity any poor married woman whose husband is not called Ernest.

ALGERNON But, my dear child, do you mean to say you could not love me if I had some other name?

CECILY But what name?

ALGERNON Oh, any name you like—Algernon—for instance . . .

CECILY But I don't like the name of Algernon.

ALGERNON Well, my own dear, sweet, loving little darling, I really can't see why you should object to the name of Algernon. It is not at all a bad name. In fact, it is rather an aristocratic name. Half of the chaps who get into the Bankruptcy Court are called Algernon. But seriously, Cecily . . . [*moving to her*] . . . if my name was Algy, couldn't you love me?

CECILY [*rising*] I might respect you, Ernest, I might admire your character, but I fear that I should not be able to give you my undivided attention.

ALGERNON Ahem! Cecily! [*Picking up hat.*] Your Rector here is, I suppose, thoroughly experienced in the practice of all the rites and ceremonials of the Church?

CECILY Oh yes. Dr Chasuble is a most learned man. He has never written a single book, so you can imagine how much he knows.

ALGERNON I must see him at once on a most important christening—I mean on most important business.

CECILY Oh!

ALGERNON I shan't be away more than half an hour.

CECILY Considering that we have been engaged since February the 14th, and that I only met you today for the first time, I think it is rather hard that you should leave me for so long a period as half an hour. Couldn't you make it twenty minutes?

ALGERNON I'll be back in no time. [*Kisses her and rushes down the garden.*]

CECILY What an impetuous boy he is! I like his hair so much. I must enter his proposal in my diary.

[*Enter Merriman.*]

MERRIMAN A Miss Fairfax has just called to see Mr Worthing. On very important business Miss Fairfax states.

CECILY Isn't Mr Worthing in his library?

MERRIMAN Mr Worthing went over in the direction of the Rectory some time ago.

CECILY Pray ask the lady to come out here; Mr Worthing is sure to be back soon. And you can bring tea.

MERRIMAN Yes, Miss. [Goes out.]

CECILY Miss Fairfax! I suppose one of the many good elderly women who are associated with Uncle Jack in some of his philanthropic work in London. I don't quite like women who are interested in philanthropic work. I think it is so forward of them.

[Enter Merriman.]

MERRIMAN Miss Fairfax.

[Enter Gwendolen. Exit Merriman.]

CECILY [advancing to meet her] Pray let me introduce myself to you. My name is Cecily Cardew.

GWENDOLEN Cecily Cardew? [Moving to her and shaking hands.] What a very sweet name! Something tells me that we are going to be great friends. I like you already more than I can say. My first impressions of people are never wrong.

CECILY How nice of you to like me so much after we have known each other such a comparatively short time. Pray sit down.

GWENDOLEN [still standing up] I may call you Cecily, may I not?

CECILY With pleasure!

GWENDOLEN And you will always call me Gwendolen, won't you.

CECILY If you wish.

GWENDOLEN Then that is all quite settled, is it not?

CECILY I hope so.

[A pause. They both sit down together.]

GWENDOLEN Perhaps this might be a favourable opportunity for my mentioning who I am. My father is Lord Bracknell. You have never heard of papa, I suppose?

CECILY I don't think so.

GWENDOLEN Outside the family circle, papa, I am glad to say, is entirely unknown. I think that is quite as it should be. The home seems to me to be the proper sphere for the man. And certainly once a man begins to neglect his domestic duties he becomes painfully effeminate, does he not? And I don't like that. It makes men so very attractive. Cecily, mamma, whose views on education are remarkably strict, has brought me up to be extremely short-sighted; it is part of her system; so do you mind my looking at you through my glasses?

CECILY Oh! not at all, Gwendolen. I am very fond of being looked at.

GWENDOLEN [after examining Cecily carefully through a lorgnette] You are here on a short visit I suppose.

CECILY Oh no! I live here.

GWENDOLEN [severely] Really? Your mother, no doubt, or some female relative of advanced years, resides here also?

CECILY Oh no! I have no mother, nor, in fact, any relations.

GWENDOLEN Indeed?

CECILY My dear guardian, with the assistance of Miss Prism, has the arduous task of looking after me.

GWENDOLEN Your guardian?

CECILY Yes, I am Mr Worthing's ward.

GWENDOLEN Oh! It is strange he never mentioned to me that he had a ward. How secretive of him! He grows more interesting hourly. I am not sure, however, that the news inspires me with feelings of unmixed delight. [*Rising and going to her.*] I am very fond of you, Cecily; I have liked you ever since I met you! But I am bound to state that now that I know that you are Mr Worthing's ward, I cannot help expressing a wish you were—well just a little older than you seem to be—and not quite so very alluring in appearance. In fact, if I may speak candidly—

CECILY Pray do! I think that whenever one has anything unpleasant to say, one should always be quite candid.

GWENDOLEN Well, to speak with perfect candour, Cecily, I wish that you were fully forty-two, and more than usually plain for your age. Ernest has a strong upright nature. He is the very soul of truth and honour. Disloyalty would be as impossible to him as deception. But even men of the noblest possible moral character are extremely susceptible to the influence of the physical charms of others. Modern, no less than Ancient History, supplies us with many most painful examples of what I refer to. If it were not so, indeed, History would be quite unreadable.

CECILY I beg your pardon, Gwendolen, did you say Ernest?

GWENDOLEN Yes.

CECILY Oh, but it is not Mr Ernest Worthing who is my guardian. It is his brother—his elder brother.

GWENDOLEN [*sitting down again*] Ernest never mentioned to me that he had a brother.

CECILY I am sorry to say they have not been on good terms for a long time.

GWENDOLEN Ah! that accounts for it. And now that I think of it I have never heard any man mention his brother. The subject seems distasteful to most men. Cecily, you have lifted a load from my mind. I was growing almost anxious. It would have been terrible if any cloud had come across a friendship like ours, would it not? Of course you are quite, quite sure that it is not Mr Ernest Worthing who is your guardian?

CECILY Quite sure. [*A pause.*] In fact, I am going to be his.

GWENDOLEN [*enquiringly*] I beg your pardon?

CECILY [*rather shy and confidingly*] Dearest Gwendolen, there is no reason why I should make a secret of it to you. Our little county newspaper is sure to chronicle the fact next week. Mr Ernest Worthing and I are engaged to be married.

GWENDOLEN [*quite politely, rising*] My darling Cecily, I think there must be some slight error. Mr Ernest Worthing is engaged to me. The announcement will appear in the "Morning Post" on Saturday at the latest.

CECILY [*very politely, rising*] I am afraid you must be under some misconception. Ernest proposed to me exactly ten minutes ago. [*Shows diary.*]

GWENDOLEN [*examines diary through her lorgnette carefully*] It is certainly very curious, for he asked me to be his wife yesterday afternoon at 5.30. If you would care to verify the incident, pray do so. [*Produces diary of her own.*] I never travel without my diary. One should always have something sensational to read in the train. I am so sorry, dear Cecily, if it is any disappointment to you, but I am afraid I have the prior claim.

CECILY It would distress me more than I can tell you, dear Gwendolen, if it caused you any mental or physical anguish, but I feel bound to point out that since Ernest proposed to you he clearly has changed his mind.

GWENDOLEN [*meditatively*] If the poor fellow has been entrapped into any foolish promise I shall consider it my duty to rescue him at once, and with a firm hand.

CECILY [*thoughtfully and sadly*] Whatever unfortunate entanglement my dear boy may have got into, I will never reproach him with it after we are married.

GWENDOLEN Do you allude to me, Miss Cardew, as an entanglement? You are presumptuous. On an occasion of this kind it becomes more than a moral duty to speak one's mind. It becomes a pleasure.

CECILY Do you suggest, Miss Fairfax, that I entrapped Ernest into an engagement? How dare you? This is no time for wearing the shallow mask of manners. When I see a spade I call it a spade.

GWENDOLEN [*satirically*] I am glad to say that I have never seen a spade. It is obvious that our social spheres have been widely different.

[*Enter Merriman, followed by the footman. He carries a salver, table cloth, and plate stand. Cecily is about to retort. The presence of the servants exercises a restraining influence, under which both girls chafe.*]

MERRIMAN Shall I lay tea here as usual, Miss?

CECILY [*sternly, in a calm voice*] Yes, as usual.

[*Merriman begins to clear table and lay cloth. A long pause. Cecily and Gwendolen glare at each other.*]

GWENDOLEN Are there many interesting walks in the vicinity, Miss Cardew?

CECILY Oh! yes! a great many. From the top of one of the hills quite close one can see five counties.

GWENDOLEN Five counties! I don't think I should like that. I hate crowds.

CECILY [*sweetly*] I suppose that is why you live in town?

[*Gwendolen bites her lip, and beats her foot nervously with her parasol.*]

GWENDOLEN [*looking round*] Quite a well-kept garden this is, Miss Cardew.

CECILY So glad you like it, Miss Fairfax.

GWENDOLEN I had no idea there were any flowers in the country.

CECILY Oh, flowers are as common here, Miss Fairfax, as people are in London.

GWENDOLEN Personally, I cannot understand how anybody manages to exist in the country, if anybody who is anybody does. The country always bores me to death.

CECILY Ah! This is what the newspapers call agricultural depression,[8] is it not? I believe the aristocracy are suffering very much from it just at present. It is almost an epidemic amongst them, I have been told. May I offer you some tea, Miss Fairfax?

GWENDOLEN [*with elaborate politeness*] Thank you. [*Aside.*] Detestable girl! But I require tea!

CECILY [*sweetly*] Sugar?

GWENDOLEN [*superciliously*] No, thank you. Sugar is not fashionable any more.

[*Cecily looks angrily at her, takes up the tongs and puts four lumps of sugar into the cup.*]

CECILY [*severely*] Cake or bread and butter?

GWENDOLEN [*in a bored manner*] Bread and butter, please. Cake is rarely seen at the best houses nowadays.

CECILY [*cuts a very large slice of cake, and puts it on the tray*] Hand that to Miss Fairfax.

---

8. A pun on the word "depression"; beginning in the 1870s, British agriculture had been in a slump, causing losses and hardship among landowners.

[*Merriman does so, and goes out with footman. Gwendolen drinks the tea and makes a grimace. Puts down cup at once, reaches out her hand to the bread and butter, looks at it, and finds it is cake. Rises in indignation.*]

GWENDOLEN You have filled my tea with lumps of sugar, and though I asked most distinctly for bread and butter, you have given me cake. I am known for the gentleness of my disposition, and the extraordinary sweetness of my nature, but I warn you, Miss Cardew, you may go too far.

CECILY [*rising*] To save my poor, innocent, trusting boy from the machinations of any other girl there are no lengths to which I would not go.

GWENDOLEN From the moment I saw you I distrusted you. I felt that you were false and deceitful. I am never deceived in such matters. My first impressions of people are invariably right.

CECILY It seems to me, Miss Fairfax, that I am trespassing on your valuable time. No doubt you have many other calls of a similar character to make in the neighbourhood.
    [*Enter Jack.*]

GWENDOLEN [*catching sight of him*] Ernest! My own Ernest!

JACK Gwendolen! Darling! [*Offers to kiss her.*]

GWENDOLEN [*drawing back*] A moment! May I ask if you are engaged to be married to this young lady? [*Points to Cecily.*]

JACK [*laughing*] To dear little Cecily! Of course not! What could have put such an idea into your pretty little head?

GWENDOLEN Thank you. You may! [*Offers her cheek.*]

CECILY [*very sweetly*] I knew there must be some misunderstanding, Miss Fairfax. The gentleman whose arm is at present round your waist is my dear guardian, Mr John Worthing.

GWENDOLEN I beg your pardon?

CECILY This is Uncle Jack.

GWENDOLEN [*receding*] Jack! Oh!
    [*Enter Algernon.*]

CECILY Here is Ernest.

ALGERNON [*goes straight over to Cecily without noticing anyone else*] My own love! [*Offers to kiss her.*]

CECILY [*drawing back*] A moment, Ernest! May I ask you—are you engaged to be married to this young lady?

ALGERNON [*looking round*] To what young lady? Good heavens! Gwendolen!

CECILY Yes, to good heavens, Gwendolen, I mean to Gwendolen.

ALGERNON [*laughing*] Of course not! What could have put such an idea into your pretty little head?

CECILY Thank you. [*Presenting her cheek to be kissed.*] You may.
    [*Algernon kisses her.*]

GWENDOLEN I felt there was some slight error, Miss Cardew. The gentleman who is now embracing you is my cousin, Mr Algernon Moncrieff.

CECILY [*breaking away from Algernon*] Algernon Moncrieff! Oh!
    [*The two girls move towards each other and put their arms round each other's waists as if for protection.*]

CECILY Are you called Algernon?

ALGERNON I cannot deny it.

CECILY Oh!

GWENDOLEN Is your name really John?

JACK [*standing rather proudly*] I could deny it if I liked. I could deny anything if I liked. But my name certainly is John. It has been John for years.

CECILY [*to Gwendolen*] A gross deception has been practised on both of us.

GWENDOLEN My poor wounded Cecily!

CECILY My sweet wronged Gwendolen!

GWENDOLEN [*slowly and seriously*] You will call me sister, will you not?
[*They embrace. Jack and Algernon groan and walk up and down.*]

CECILY [*rather brightly*] There is just one question I would like to be allowed to ask my guardian.

GWENDOLEN An admirable idea! Mr Worthing, there is just one question I would like to be permitted to put to you. Where is your brother Ernest? We are both engaged to be married to your brother Ernest, so it is a matter of some importance to us to know where your brother Ernest is at present.

JACK [*slowly and hesitatingly*] Gwendolen—Cecily—It is very painful for me to be forced to speak the truth. It is the first time in my life that I have ever been reduced to such a painful position, and I am really quite inexperienced in doing anything of the kind. However I will tell you quite frankly that I have no brother Ernest. I have no brother at all. I never had a brother in my life, and I certainly have not the smallest intention of ever having one in the future.

CECILY [*surprised*] No brother at all?

JACK [*cheerily*] None!

GWENDOLEN [*severely*] Had you never a brother of any kind?

JACK [*pleasantly*] Never. Not even of any kind.

GWENDOLEN I am afraid it is quite clear, Cecily, that neither of us is engaged to be married to anyone.

CECILY It is not a very pleasant position for a young girl suddenly to find herself in. Is it?

GWENDOLEN Let us go into the house. They will hardly venture to come after us there.

CECILY No, men are so cowardly, aren't they?
[*They retire into the house with scornful looks.*]

JACK This ghastly state of things is what you call Bunburying, I suppose?

ALGERNON Yes, and a perfectly wonderful Bunbury it is. The most wonderful Bunbury I have ever had in my life.

JACK Well, you've no right whatsoever to Bunbury here.

ALGERNON That is absurd. One has a right to Bunbury anywhere one chooses. Every serious Bunburyist knows that.

JACK Serious Bunburyist! Good heavens!

ALGERNON Well, one must be serious about something, if one wants to have any amusement in life. I happen to be serious about Bunburying. What on earth you are serious about I haven't got the remotest idea. About everything, I should fancy. You have such an absolutely trivial nature.

JACK Well, the only small satisfaction I have in the whole of this wretched business is that your friend Bunbury is quite exploded. You won't be able to run down to the country quite so often as you used to do, dear Algy. And a very good thing too.

ALGERNON Your brother is a little off colour, isn't he, dear Jack? You won't be able to disappear to London quite so frequently as your wicked custom was. And not a bad thing either.

JACK As for your conduct towards Miss Cardew, I must say that your taking in a sweet, simple, innocent girl like that is quite inexcusable. To say nothing of the fact that she is my ward.

ALGERNON I can see no possible defence at all for your deceiving a brilliant, clever, thoroughly experienced young lady like Miss Fairfax. To say nothing of the fact that she is my cousin.

JACK I wanted to be engaged to Gwendolen, that is all. I love her.

ALGERNON Well, I simply wanted to be engaged to Cecily. I adore her.

JACK There is certainly no chance of your marrying Miss Cardew.

ALGERNON I don't think there is much likelihood, Jack, of you and Miss Fairfax being united.

JACK Well, that is no business of yours.

ALGERNON If it was my business, I wouldn't talk about it. [Begins to eat muffins.] It is very vulgar to talk about one's business. Only people like stockbrokers do that, and then merely at dinner parties.

JACK How you can sit there, calmly eating muffins when we are in this horrible trouble, I can't make out. You seem to me to be perfectly heartless.

ALGERNON Well, I can't eat muffins in an agitated manner. The butter would probably get on my cuffs. One should always eat muffins quite calmly. It is the only way to eat them.

JACK I say it's perfectly heartless your eating muffins at all, under the circumstances.

ALGERNON When I am in trouble, eating is the only thing that consoles me. Indeed, when I am in really great trouble, as anyone who knows me intimately will tell you, I refuse everything except food and drink. At the present moment I am eating muffins because I am unhappy. Besides, I am particularly fond of muffins. [Rising.]

JACK [rising] Well, that is no reason why you should eat them all in that greedy way. [Takes muffins from Algernon.]

ALGERNON [offering tea-cake] I wish you would have tea-cake instead. I don't like tea-cake.

JACK Good heavens! I suppose a man may eat his own muffins in his own garden.

ALGERNON But you have just said it was perfectly heartless to eat muffins.

JACK I said it was perfectly heartless of you, under the circumstances. That is a very different thing.

ALGERNON That may be. But the muffins are the same. [He seizes the muffin-dish from Jack.]

JACK Algy, I wish to goodness you would go.

ALGERNON You can't possibly ask me to go without having some dinner. It's absurd. I never go without my dinner. No one ever does, except vegetarians and people like that. Besides I have just made arrangements with Dr Chasuble to be christened at a quarter to six under the name of Ernest.

JACK My dear fellow, the sooner you give up that nonsense the better. I made arrangements this morning with Dr Chasuble to be christened myself at 5.30, and I naturally will take the name of Ernest. Gwendolen would wish it. We can't both be christened Ernest. It's absurd. Besides, I have a perfect right to be christened if I like. There is no evidence at all that I ever have been christened by anybody. I should think it extremely probable I never was, and so does Dr Chasuble. It is entirely different in your case. You have been christened already.

ALGERNON Yes, but I have not been christened for years.

JACK Yes, but you have been christened. That is the important thing.

ALGERNON Quite so. So I know my constitution can stand it. If you are not quite sure about your ever having been christened, I must say I think it rather dangerous your venturing on it now. It might make you very unwell. You can hardly have forgotten that someone very closely connected with you was very nearly carried off this week in Paris by a severe chill.

JACK Yes, but you said yourself that a severe chill was not hereditary.

ALGERNON It usen't to be, I know—but I daresay it is now. Science is always making wonderful improvements in things.

JACK [picking up the muffin-dish] Oh, that is nonsense; you are always talking nonsense.

ALGERNON Jack, you are at the muffins again! I wish you wouldn't. There are only two left. [Takes them.] I told you I was particularly fond of muffins.

JACK But I hate tea-cake.

ALGERNON Why on earth then do you allow tea-cake to be served up for your guests? What ideas you have of hospitality!

JACK Algernon! I have already told you to go. I don't want you here. Why don't you go!

ALGERNON I haven't quite finished my tea yet! and there is still one muffin left.

[Jack groans, and sinks into a chair. Algernon still continues eating.]   ACT DROP

THIRD ACT

SCENE: *Morning-room*[9] *at the Manor House.*

[Gwendolen and Cecily are at the window, looking out into the garden.]

GWENDOLEN The fact that they did not follow us at once into the house, as anyone else would have done, seems to me to show that they have some sense of shame left.

CECILY They have been eating muffins. That looks like repentance.

GWENDOLEN [after a pause] They don't seem to notice us at all. Couldn't you cough?

CECILY But I haven't got a cough.

GWENDOLEN They're looking at us. What effrontery!

CECILY They're approaching. That's very forward of them.

GWENDOLEN Let us preserve a dignified silence.

CECILY Certainly. It's the only thing to do now.

[Enter Jack followed by Algernon. They whistle some dreadful popular air from a British Opera.][1]

GWENDOLEN This dignified silence seems to produce an unpleasant effect.

CECILY A most distasteful one.

GWENDOLEN But we will not be the first to speak.

CECILY Certainly not.

GWENDOLEN Mr Worthing, I have something very particular to ask you. Much depends on your reply.

CECILY Gwendolen, your common sense is invaluable. Mr Moncrieff, kindly answer me the following question. Why did you pretend to be my guardian's brother?

ALGERNON In order that I might have an opportunity of meeting you.

9. An informal room for receiving morning calls from friends (afternoon visitors were received in the formal drawing room).

1. Probably a reference to Gilbert and Sullivan, who had made fun of Wilde and the Aesthetic movement in *Patience* (1881); see page 2144.

CECILY [to Gwendolen] That certainly seems a satisfactory explanation, does it not?

GWENDOLEN Yes, dear, if you can believe him.

CECILY I don't. But that does not affect the wonderful beauty of his answer.

GWENDOLEN True. In matters of grave importance, style, not sincerity is the vital thing. Mr Worthing, what explanation can you offer to me for pretending to have a brother? Was it in order that you might have an opportunity of coming up to town to see me as often as possible?

JACK Can you doubt it, Miss Fairfax?

GWENDOLEN I have the gravest doubts upon the subject. But I intend to crush them. This is not the moment for German scepticism.[2] [Moving to Cecily.] Their explanations appear to be quite satisfactory, especially Mr Worthing's. That seems to me to have the stamp of truth upon it.

CECILY I am more than content with what Mr Moncrieff said. His voice alone inspires one with absolute credulity.

GWENDOLEN Then you think we should forgive them?

CECILY Yes. I mean no.

GWENDOLEN True! I had forgotten. There are principles at stake that one cannot surrender. Which of us should tell them? The task is not a pleasant one.

CECILY Could we not both speak at the same time?

GWENDOLEN An excellent idea! I nearly always speak at the same time as other people. Will you take the time from me?

CECILY Certainly.

   [Gwendolen beats time with uplifted finger.]

GWENDOLEN and CECILY [speaking together] Your Christian names are still an insuperable barrier. That is all!

JACK and ALGERNON [speaking together] Our Christian names! Is that all? But we are going to be christened this afternoon.

GWENDOLEN [to Jack] For my sake you are prepared to do this terrible thing?

JACK I am.

CECILY [to Algernon] To please me you are ready to face this fearful ordeal?

ALGERNON I am!

GWENDOLEN How absurd to talk of the equality of the sexes! Where questions of self-sacrifice are concerned, men are infinitely beyond us.

JACK We are. [Clasps hands with Algernon.]

CECILY They have moments of physical courage of which we women know absolutely nothing.

GWENDOLEN [to Jack] Darling!

ALGERNON [to Cecily] Darling! [They fall into each other's arms.]

   [Enter Merriman. When he enters he coughs loudly, seeing the situation.]

MERRIMAN Ahem! Ahem! Lady Bracknell!

JACK Good heavens!

   [Enter Lady Bracknell. The couples separate in alarm.] [Exit Merriman.]

LADY BRACKNELL Gwendolen! What does this mean?

GWENDOLEN Merely that I am engaged to be married to Mr Worthing, mamma.

LADY BRACKNELL Come here. Sit down. Sit down immediately. Hesitation of any kind is a sign of mental decay in the young, of physical weakness in the old. [Turns to Jack.] Apprised, sir, of my daughter's sudden flight by her trusty maid,

---

2. Many 19th-century German scholars were skeptical in their treatment of religious texts.

whose confidence I purchased by means of a small coin, I followed her at once by a luggage train. Her unhappy father is, I am glad to say, under the impression that she is attending a more than usually lengthy lecture by the University Extension Scheme on the Influence of a permanent income on Thought. I do not propose to undeceive him. Indeed I have never undeceived him on any question. I would consider it wrong. But of course, you will clearly understand that all communication between yourself and my daughter must cease immediately from this moment. On this point, as indeed on all points, I am firm.

JACK I am engaged to be married to Gwendolen, Lady Bracknell!

LADY BRACKNELL You are nothing of the kind, sir. And now, as regards Algernon! . . . Algernon!

ALGERNON Yes, Aunt Augusta.

LADY BRACKNELL May I ask if it is in this house that your invalid friend Mr Bunbury resides?

ALGERNON [stammering] Oh! No! Bunbury doesn't live here. Bunbury is somewhere else at present. In fact, Bunbury is dead.

LADY BRACKNELL Dead! When did Mr Bunbury die? His death must have been extremely sudden.

ALGERNON [airily] Oh! I killed Bunbury this afternoon. I mean poor Bunbury died this afternoon.

LADY BRACKNELL What did he die of?

ALGERNON Bunbury? Oh, he was quite exploded.

LADY BRACKNELL Exploded! Was he the victim of a revolutionary outrage?[3] I was not aware that Mr Bunbury was interested in social legislation. If so, he is well punished for his morbidity.

ALGERNON My dear Aunt Augusta, I mean he was found out! The doctors found out that Bunbury could not live, that is what I mean—so Bunbury died.

LADY BRACKNELL He seems to have had great confidence in the opinion of his physicians. I am glad, however, that he made up his mind at the last to some definite course of action, and acted under proper medical advice. And now that we have finally got rid of this Mr Bunbury, may I ask, Mr Worthing, who is that young person whose hand my nephew Algernon is now holding in what seems to me a peculiarly unnecessary manner?

JACK That lady is Miss Cecily Cardew, my ward.

[Lady Bracknell bows coldly to Cecily.]

ALGERNON I am engaged to be married to Cecily, Aunt Augusta.

LADY BRACKNELL I beg your pardon?

CECILY Mr Moncrieff and I are engaged to be married, Lady Bracknell.

LADY BRACKNELL [with a shiver, crossing to the sofa and sitting down] I do not know whether there is anything peculiarly exciting in the air of this particular part of Hertfordshire, but the number of engagements that go on seems to me considerably above the proper average that statistics have laid down for our guidance. I think some preliminary enquiry on my part would not be out of place. Mr Worthing, is Miss Cardew at all connected with any of the larger railway stations in London? I merely desire information. Until yesterday I had no idea that there were any families or persons whose origins was a Terminus.[4]

3. Anarchy and political assassination were much in the news; Wilde's earliest drama, Vera, or the Nihilists (1881), dealt with the subject.
4. A railway station at the end of the line.

[*Jack looks perfectly furious, but restrains himself.*]

JACK [*in a clear, cold voice*] Miss Cardew is the granddaughter of the late Mr Thomas Cardew of 149, Belgrave Square, S.W.; Gervase Park, Dorking, Surrey; and the Sporran, Fifeshire, N.B.[5]

LADY BRACKNELL That sounds not unsatisfactory. Three addresses always inspire confidence, even in tradesmen. But what proof have I of their authenticity?

JACK I have carefully preserved the Court Guides[6] of the period. They are open to your inspection, Lady Bracknell.

LADY BRACKNELL [*grimly*] I have known strange errors in that publication.

JACK Miss Cardew's family solicitors are Messrs Markby, Markby, and Markby.

LADY BRACKNELL Markby, Markby, and Markby? A firm of the very highest position in their profession. Indeed I am told that one of the Mr Markbys is occasionally to be seen at dinner parties. So far I am satisfied.

JACK [*very irritably*] How extremely kind of you, Lady Bracknell! I have also in my possession, you will be pleased to hear, certificates of Miss Cardew's birth, baptism, whooping cough, registration, vaccination, confirmation, and the measles; both the German and the English variety.

LADY BRACKNELL Ah! A life crowded with incident, I see; though perhaps somewhat too exciting for a young girl. I am not myself in favour of premature experiences. [*Rises, looks at her watch.*] Gwendolen! the time approaches for our departure. We have not a moment to lose. As a matter of form, Mr Worthing, I had better ask you if Miss Cardew has any little fortune?

JACK Oh! about a hundred and thirty thousand pounds in the Funds.[7] That is all. Goodbye, Lady Bracknell. So pleased to have seen you.

LADY BRACKNELL [*sitting down again*] A moment, Mr Worthing. A hundred and thirty thousand pounds! And in the Funds! Miss Cardew seems to me a most attractive young lady, now that I look at her. Few girls of the present day have any really solid qualities, any of the qualities that last, and improve with time. We live, I regret to say, in an age of surfaces. [*To Cecily.*] Come over here, dear. [*Cecily goes across.*] Pretty child! your dress is sadly simple, and your hair seems almost as Nature might have left it. But we can soon alter all that. A thoroughly experienced French maid produces a really marvellous result in a very brief space of time. I remember recommending one to young Lady Lancing, and after three months her own husband did not know her.

JACK [*aside*] And after six months nobody knew her.

LADY BRACKNELL [*glares at Jack for a few moments. Then bends, with a practised smile, to Cecily.*] Kindly turn round, sweet child. [*Cecily turns completely round.*] No, the side view is what I want. [*Cecily presents her profile.*] Yes, quite as I expected. There are distinct social possibilities in your profile. The two weak points in our age are its want of principle and its want of profile. The chin a little higher, dear. Style largely depends on the way the chin is worn. They are worn very high, just at present. Algernon!

ALGERNON Yes, Aunt Augusta!

LADY BRACKNELL There are distinct social possibilities in Miss Cardew's profile.

ALGERNON Cecily is the sweetest, dearest, prettiest girl in the whole world. And I don't care twopence about social possibilities.

---

5. North Britain, i.e., Scotland.
6. Annual publications listing the names and London addresses of the upper classes.

7. The Consolidated Funds, reliable interest-bearing government bonds.

LADY BRACKNELL Never speak disrespectfully of Society, Algernon. Only people who can't get into it do that. [*To Cecily.*] Dear child, of course you know that Algernon has nothing but his debts to depend upon. But I do not approve of mercenary marriages. When I married Lord Bracknell I had no fortune of any kind. But I never dreamed for a moment of allowing that to stand in my way. Well, I suppose I must give my consent.

ALGERNON Thank you, Aunt Augusta.

LADY BRACKNELL Cecily, you may kiss me!

CECILY [*kisses her*] Thank you, Lady Bracknell.

LADY BRACKNELL You may also address me as Aunt Augusta for the future.

CECILY Thank you, Aunt Augusta.

LADY BRACKNELL The marriage, I think, had better take place quite soon.

ALGERNON Thank you, Aunt Augusta.

CECILY Thank you, Aunt Augusta.

LADY BRACKNELL To speak frankly, I am not in favour of long engagements. They give people the opportunity of finding out each other's character before marriage, which I think is never advisable.

JACK I beg your pardon for interrupting you, Lady Bracknell, but this engagement is quite out of the question. I am Miss Cardew's guardian, and she cannot marry without my consent until she comes of age. That consent I absolutely decline to give.

LADY BRACKNELL Upon what grounds may I ask? Algernon is an extremely, I may almost say an ostentatiously, eligible young man. He has nothing, but he looks everything. What more can one desire?

JACK It pains me very much to have to speak frankly to you, Lady Bracknell, about your nephew, but the fact is that I do not approve at all of his moral character. I suspect him of being untruthful.

[*Algernon and Cecily look at him in indignant amazement.*]

LADY BRACKNELL Untruthful! My nephew Algernon? Impossible! He is an Oxonian.[8]

JACK I fear there can be no possible doubt about the matter. This afternoon, during my temporary absence in London on an important question of romance, he obtained admission to my house by means of the false pretence of being my brother. Under an assumed name he drank, I've just been informed by my butler, an entire pint bottle of my Perrier-Jouet, Brut, '89; a wine I was specially reserving for myself. Continuing his disgraceful deception, he succeeded in the course of the afternoon in alienating the affections of my only ward. He subsequently stayed to tea, and devoured every single muffin. And what makes his conduct all the more heartless is, that he was perfectly well aware from the first that I have no brother, that I never had a brother, and that I don't intend to have a brother, not even of any kind. I distinctly told him so myself yesterday afternoon.

LADY BRACKNELL Ahem! Mr Worthing, after careful consideration I have decided entirely to overlook my nephew's conduct to you.

JACK That is very generous of you, Lady Bracknell. My own decision, however, is unalterable. I decline to give my consent.

LADY BRACKNELL [*to Cecily*] Come here, sweet child. [*Cecily goes over.*] How old are you, dear?

8. I.e., he attended Oxford University.

CECILY Well, I am really only eighteen, but I always admit to twenty when I go to evening parties.

LADY BRACKNELL You are perfectly right in making some slight alteration. Indeed, no woman should ever be quite accurate about her age. It looks so calculating. . . . [*In a meditative manner.*] Eighteen, but admitting to twenty at evening parties. Well, it will not be very long before you are of age and free from the restraints of tutelage. So I don't think your guardian's consent is, after all, a matter of any importance.

JACK Pray excuse me, Lady Bracknell, for interrupting you again, but it is only fair to tell you that according to the terms of her grandfather's will Miss Cardew does not come legally of age till she is thirty-five.

LADY BRACKNELL That does not seem to me to be a grave objection. Thirty-five is a very attractive age. London society is full of women of the very highest birth who have, of their own free choice, remained thirty-five for years. Lady Dumbleton is an instance in point. To my own knowledge she has been thirty-five ever since she arrived at the age of forty, which was many years ago now. I see no reason why our dear Cecily should not be even still more attractive at the age you mention than she is at present. There will be a large accumulation of property.

CECILY Algy, could you wait for me till I was thirty-five?

ALGERNON Of course I could, Cecily. You know I could.

CECILY Yes, I felt it instinctively, but I couldn't wait all that time. I hate waiting even five minutes for anybody. It always makes me rather cross. I am not punctual myself, I know, but I do like punctuality in others, and waiting, even to be married, is quite out of the question.

ALGERNON Then what is to be done, Cecily?

CECILY I don't know, Mr Moncrieff.

LADY BRACKNELL My dear Mr Worthing, as Miss Cardew states positively that she cannot wait till she is thirty-five—a remark which I am bound to say seems to me to show a somewhat impatient nature—I would beg of you to reconsider your decision.

JACK But my dear Lady Bracknell, the matter is entirely in your own hands. The moment you consent to my marriage with Gwendolen, I will most gladly allow your nephew to form an alliance with my ward.

LADY BRACKNELL [*rising and drawing herself up*] You must be quite aware that what you propose is out of the question.

JACK Then a passionate celibacy is all that any of us can look forward to.

LADY BRACKNELL That is not the destiny I propose for Gwendolen. Algernon, of course, can choose for himself. [*Pulls out her watch.*] Come, dear; [*Gwendolen rises.*] we have already missed five, if not six, trains. To miss any more might expose us to comment on the platform.

[*Enter Dr Chasuble.*]

CHASUBLE Everything is quite ready for the christenings.

LADY BRACKNELL The christenings, sir! Is not that somewhat premature?

CHASUBLE [*looking rather puzzled, and pointing to Jack and Algernon*] Both these gentlemen have expressed a desire for immediate baptism.

LADY BRACKNELL At their age? The idea is grotesque and irreligious! Algernon, I forbid you to be baptized. I will not hear of such excesses. Lord Bracknell would be highly displeased if he learned that that was the way in which you wasted your time and money.

CHASUBLE Am I to understand then that there are to be no christenings at all this afternoon?

JACK I don't think that, as things are now, it would be of much practical value to either of us, Dr Chasuble.

CHASUBLE I am grieved to hear such sentiments from you, Mr Worthing. They savour of the heretical views of the Anabaptists,[9] views that I have completely refuted in four of my unpublished sermons. However, as your present mood seems to be one peculiarly secular, I will return to the church at once. Indeed, I have just been informed by the pew-opener[1] that for the last hour and a half Miss Prism has been waiting for me in the vestry.

LADY BRACKNELL [starting] Miss Prism! Did I hear you mention a Miss Prism?

CHASUBLE Yes, Lady Bracknell. I am on my way to join her.

LADY BRACKNELL Pray allow me to detain you for a moment. This matter may prove to be one of vital importance to Lord Bracknell and myself. Is this Miss Prism a female of repellent aspect, remotely connected with education?

CHASUBLE [somewhat indignantly] She is the most cultivated of ladies, and the very picture of respectability.

LADY BRACKNELL It is obviously the same person. May I ask what position she holds in your household?

CHASUBLE [severely] I am a celibate, madam.

JACK [interposing] Miss Prism, Lady Bracknell, has been for the last three years Miss Cardew's esteemed governess and valued companion.

LADY BRACKNELL In spite of what I hear of her, I must see her at once. Let her be sent for.

CHASUBLE [looking off] She approaches; she is nigh.

[Enter Miss Prism hurriedly.]

MISS PRISM I was told you expected me in the vestry, dear Canon. I have been waiting for you there for an hour and three quarters. [Catches sight of Lady Bracknell who has fixed her with a stony glare. Miss Prism grows pale and quails. She looks anxiously round as if desirous to escape.]

LADY BRACKNELL [in a severe, judicial voice] Prism! [Miss Prism bows her head in shame.] Come here, Prism! [Miss Prism approaches in a humble manner.] Prism! Where is that baby? [General consternation. The Canon starts back in horror. Algernon and Jack pretend to be anxious to shield Cecily and Gwendolen from hearing the details of a terrible public scandal.] Twenty-eight years ago, Prism, you left Lord Bracknell's house, Number 104, Upper Grosvenor Street, in charge of a perambulator that contained a baby, of the male sex. You never returned. A few weeks later, through the elaborate investigations of the Metropolitan police, the perambulator was discovered at midnight, standing by itself in a remote corner of Bayswater.[2] It contained the manuscript of a three-volume novel of more than usually revolting sentimentality. [Miss Prism starts in involuntary indignation.] But the baby was not there! [Everyone looks at Miss Prism.] Prism! Where is that baby? [A pause.]

MISS PRISM Lady Bracknell, I admit with shame that I do not know. I only wish I did. The plain facts of the case are these. On the morning of the day you mention, a day that is for ever branded on my memory, I prepared as usual to take the baby out in its perambulator. I had also with me a somewhat old, but capacious hand-

9. A 16th-century Protestant sect that believed in adult baptism.
1. Usher.

2. An area in the West End of London, near Kensington Gardens.

bag in which I had intended to place the manuscript of a work of fiction that I had written during my few unoccupied hours. In a moment of mental abstraction, for which I never can forgive myself, I deposited the manuscript in the bassinette, and placed the baby in the hand-bag.

JACK [*who has been listening attentively*] But where did you deposit the hand-bag?

MISS PRISM Do not ask me, Mr Worthing.

JACK Miss Prism, this is a matter of no small importance to me. I insist on knowing where you deposited the hand-bag that contained that infant.

MISS PRISM I left it in the cloak-room of one of the larger railway stations in London.

JACK What railway station?

MISS PRISM [*quite crushed*] Victoria. The Brighton line. [*Sinks into a chair.*]

JACK I must retire to my room for a moment. Gwendolen, wait here for me.

GWENDOLEN If you are not too long, I will wait here for you all my life.

[*Exit Jack in great excitement.*]

CHASUBLE What do you think this means, Lady Bracknell?

LADY BRACKNELL I dare not even suspect, Dr Chasuble. I need hardly tell you that in families of high position strange coincidences are not supposed to occur. They are hardly considered the thing.

[*Noises heard overhead as if someone was throwing trunks about. Everyone looks up.*]

CECILY Uncle Jack seems strangely agitated.

CHASUBLE Your guardian has a very emotional nature.

LADY BRACKNELL This noise is extremely unpleasant. It sounds as if he was having an argument. I dislike arguments of any kind. They are always vulgar, and often convincing.

CHASUBLE [*looking up*] It has stopped now. [*The noise is redoubled.*]

LADY BRACKNELL I wish he would arrive at some conclusion.

GWENDOLEN This suspense is terrible. I hope it will last.

[*Enter Jack with a hand-bag of black leather in his hand.*]

JACK [*rushing over to Miss Prism*] Is this the hand-bag, Miss Prism? Examine it carefully before you speak. The happiness of more than one life depends on your answer.

MISS PRISM [*calmly*] It seems to be mine. Yes, here is the injury it received through the upsetting of a Gower Street omnibus in younger and happier days. Here is the stain on the lining caused by the explosion of a temperance beverage, an incident that occurred at Leamington. And here, on the lock, are my initials. I had forgotten that in an extravagant mood I had had them placed there. The bag is undoubtedly mine. I am delighted to have it so unexpectedly restored to me. It has been a great inconvenience being without it all these years.

JACK [*in a pathetic voice*] Miss Prism, more is restored to you than this hand-bag. I was the baby you placed in it.

MISS PRISM [*amazed*] You?

JACK [*embracing her*] Yes . . . mother!

MISS PRISM [*recoiling in indignant astonishment*] Mr Worthing! I am unmarried!

JACK Unmarried! I do not deny that is a serious blow. But after all, who has the right to cast a stone against one who has suffered?[3] Cannot repentance wipe out an act of folly? Why should there be one law for men, and another for women? Mother, I forgive you. [*Tries to embrace her again.*]

---

3. Jesus saves a woman who is about to be stoned for committing adultery, saying "He that is without sin among you, let him first cast a stone at her" (John 8.7).

MISS PRISM [*still more indignant*] Mr Worthing, there is some error. [*Pointing to Lady Bracknell.*] There is the lady who can tell you who you really are.

JACK [*after a pause*] Lady Bracknell, I hate to seem inquisitive, but would you kindly inform me who I am?

LADY BRACKNELL I am afraid that the news I have to give you will not altogether please you. You are the son of my poor sister, Mrs Moncrieff, and consequently Algernon's elder brother.

JACK Algy's elder brother! Then I have a brother after all. I knew I had a brother! I always said I had a brother! Cecily—how could you have ever doubted that I had a brother. [*Seizes hold of Algernon.*] Dr Chasuble, my unfortunate brother. Miss Prism, my unfortunate brother. Gwendolen, my unfortunate brother. Algy, you young scoundrel, you will have to treat me with more respect in the future. You have never behaved to me like a brother in all your life.

ALGERNON Well, not till today, old boy, I admit. I did my best, however, though I was out of practice. [*Shakes hands.*]

GWENDOLEN [*to Jack*] My own! But what own are you? What is your Christian name, now that you have become someone else?

JACK Good heavens! . . . I had quite forgotten that point. Your decision on the subject of my name is irrevocable, I suppose?

GWENDOLEN I never change, except in my affections.

CECILY What a noble nature you have, Gwendolen!

JACK Then the question had better be cleared up at once. Aunt Augusta, a moment. At the time when Miss Prism left me in the hand-bag, had I been christened already?

LADY BRACKNELL Every luxury that money could buy, including christening, had been lavished on you by your fond and doting parents.

JACK Then I was christened! That is settled. Now, what name was I given? Let me know the worst.

LADY BRACKNELL Being the eldest son you were naturally christened after your father.

JACK [*irritably*] Yes, but what was my father's Christian name?

LADY BRACKNELL [*meditatively*] I cannot at the present moment recall what the General's Christian name was. But I have no doubt he had one. He was eccentric, I admit. But only in later years. And that was the result of the Indian climate, and marriage, and indigestion, and other things of that kind.

JACK Algy! Can't you recollect what our father's Christian name was?

ALGERNON My dear boy, we were never even on speaking terms. He died before I was a year old.

JACK His name would appear in the Army Lists of the period, I suppose, Aunt Augusta?

LADY BRACKNELL The General was essentially a man of peace, except in his domestic life. But I have no doubt his name would appear in any military directory.

JACK The Army Lists of the last forty years are here. These delightful records should have been my constant study. [*Rushes to bookcase and tears the books out.*] M. Generals . . . Mallam, Maxbohm,[4] Magley, what ghastly names they have—Markby, Migsby, Mobbs, Moncrieff! Lieutenant 1840, Captain, Lieutenant-Colonel, Colonel, General 1869, Christian names, Ernest John. [*Puts book very quietly down and speaks quite calmly.*] I always told you, Gwendolen, my name was Ernest, didn't I? Well, it is Ernest after all. I mean it naturally is Ernest.

4. A pun on the name of Wilde's friend Max Beerbohm.

LADY BRACKNELL Yes, I remember now that the General was called Ernest. I knew I had some particular reason for disliking the name.

GWENDOLEN Ernest! My own Ernest! I felt from the first that you could have no other name!

JACK Gwendolen, it is a terrible thing for a man to find out suddenly that all his life he has been speaking nothing but the truth. Can you forgive me?

GWENDOLEN I can. For I feel that you are sure to change.

JACK My own one!

CHASUBLE [to Miss Prism] Laetitia! [Embraces her.]

MISS PRISM [enthusiastically] Frederick! At last!

ALGERNON Cecily! [Embraces her.] At last!

JACK Gwendolen! [Embraces her.] At last!

LADY BRACKNELL My nephew, you seem to be displaying signs of triviality.

JACK On the contrary, Aunt Augusta, I've now realized for the first time in my life the vital Importance of Being Earnest.

TABLEAU

1894, performed 1895

CURTAIN
1899

Aphorisms[1]

On arriving in America: I have nothing to declare except my genius.

F. Harris, Oscar Wilde

We have really everything in common with America nowadays, except, of course, language.

The Canterville Ghost

A poet can survive everything but a misprint.

The Children of the Poets

Meredith is a prose Browning, and so is Browning. He used poetry as a medium for writing in prose.

The Critic as Artist

Anybody can make history. Only a great man can write it.

Ibid.

The one duty we owe to history is to rewrite it.

Ibid.

A little sincerity is a dangerous thing, and a great deal of it is absolutely fatal.

Ibid.

There is only one thing in the world worse than being talked about, and that is not being talked about.

The Picture of Dorian Gray

1. Wilde's aphorisms often cleverly invert a cliché in order to produce a seeming paradox; they are perhaps his most characteristic form of expression in his conversation and writing alike. Wilde kept track of his favorite maxims, sometimes revising them in later works. In addition to the epigrammatic preface to *Dorian Gray*, he published two selections: *A Few Maxims for the Instruction of the Over-Educated* appeared anonymously in the *Saturday Review* in November 1894; *Phrases and Philosophies for the Use of the Young* was published in *The Chameleon* in December 1894.

Being natural is simply a pose, and the most irritating pose I know.

Ibid.

A man cannot be too careful in the choice of his enemies.

Ibid.

American girls are as clever at concealing their parents, as English women are at concealing their past.

Ibid.

Perhaps, after all, America never has been discovered. I myself would say that it had merely been detected.

Ibid.

Women give to men the very gold of their lives. But they invariably want it back in such very small change.

Ibid.

I hate vulgar realism in literature. The man who could call a spade a spade should be compelled to use one. It is the only thing he is fit for.

Ibid.

It is better to be beautiful than to be good. But . . . it is better to be good than to be ugly.

Ibid.

I can resist everything except temptation.

Lady Windermere's Fan

It's most dangerous nowadays for a husband to pay any attention to his wife in public. It always makes people think that he beats her when they're alone.

Ibid.

We are all in the gutter, but some of us are looking at the stars.

Ibid.

In this world there are only two tragedies. One is not getting what one wants, and the other is getting it.

Ibid.

What is a cynic? A man who knows the price of everything and the value of nothing.

Ibid.

Experience is the name everyone gives to their mistakes.

Ibid.

Repentance is quite out of date. And besides, if a woman really repents, she has to go to a bad dressmaker, otherwise no one believes in her.

Ibid.

It is perfectly monstrous the way people go about, nowadays, saying things against one behind one's back that are absolutely and entirely true.

A Woman of No Importance

The youth of America is their oldest tradition. It has been going on now for three hundred years.

Ibid.

The English country gentleman galloping after a fox—the unspeakable in full pursuit of the uneatable.

Ibid.

Twenty years of romance make a woman look like a ruin; but twenty years of marriage make her look like a public building.

Ibid.

One should never trust a woman who tells one her real age. A woman who would tell one that, would tell one anything.

Ibid.

The first duty in life is to be as artificial as possible. What the second duty is no one has as yet discovered.

Phrases and Philosophies for the Use of the Young

To love oneself is the beginning of a lifelong romance.

Ibid.

My wallpaper and I are fighting a duel to the death. One or the other of us has to go.

Richard Ellmann, *Oscar Wilde*

from De Profundis[1]

[January–March 1897]   H.M. Prison, Reading

Dear Bosie, After long and fruitless waiting I have determined to write to you myself, as much for your sake as for mine, as I would not like to think that I had passed through two long years of imprisonment without ever having received a single line from you, or any news or message even, except such as gave me pain.

Our ill-fated and most lamentable friendship has ended in ruin and public infamy for me, yet the memory of our ancient affection is often with me, and the thought that loathing, bitterness and contempt should for ever take that place in my heart once held by love is very sad to me: and you yourself will, I think, feel in your heart that to write to me as I lie in the loneliness of prison-life is better than to publish my letters without my permission or to dedicate poems to me unasked, though the world will know nothing of whatever words of grief or passion, of remorse or indifference you may choose to send as your answer or your appeal.

I have no doubt that in this letter in which I have to write of your life and of mine, of the past and of the future, of sweet things changed to bitterness and of bitter things that may be turned into joy, there will be much that will wound your vanity to the quick. If it prove so, read the letter over and over again till it kills your vanity. If you find in it something of which you feel that you are unjustly accused, remember that one should be thankful that there is any fault of which one can be unjustly

---

1. "Out of the depths" [have I cried unto thee, O Lord] (Latin), the first words of Psalm 130. While imprisoned in Reading Gaol, Wilde was allowed pen and paper only to write letters. He thus composed a meditation on his life in the form of a long letter to Lord Alfred Douglas (nicknamed Bosie), written from January to March 1897. Wilde referred to the text as "Epistola: In Carcere et Vinculis" (Letter: In Prison and in Chains). When he was released, he gave the manuscript to his friend, Robert Ross ("Robbie"), who entitled it *De Profundis* and published an abridged version—omitting all mention of Douglas—in 1905, after Wilde's death. In 1949, when Douglas had died, Wilde's son Vyvyan published a fuller text, based on an unreliable typescript supplied by Ross. Only in 1962, when scholars were allowed to consult the original manuscript—given by Ross to the British Museum—did a complete version finally appear.

accused. If there be in it one single passage that brings tears to your eyes, weep as we weep in prison where the day no less than the night is set apart for tears. It is the only thing that can save you. If you go complaining to your mother, as you did with reference to the scorn of you I displayed in my letter to Robbie, so that she may flatter and soothe you back into self-complacency or conceit, you will be completely lost. If you find one false excuse for yourself, you will soon find a hundred, and be just what you were before. Do you still say, as you said to Robbie in your answer, that I "*attribute unworthy motives*" to you? Ah! you had no motives in life. You had appetites merely. A motive is an intellectual aim. That you were "*very young*" when our friendship began? Your defect was not that you knew so little about life, but that you knew so much. The morning dawn of boyhood with its delicate bloom, its clear pure light, its joy of innocence and expectation you had left far behind. With very swift and running feet you had passed from Romance to Realism. The gutter and the things that live in it had begun to fascinate you. That was the origin of the trouble in which you sought my aid, and I, so unwisely according to the wisdom of this world, out of pity and kindness gave it to you. You must read this letter right through, though each word may become to you as the fire or knife of the surgeon that makes the delicate flesh burn or bleed. Remember that the fool in the eyes of the gods and the fool in the eyes of man are very different. One who is entirely ignorant of the modes of Art in its revolution or the moods of thought in its progress, of the pomp of the Latin line or the richer music of the vowelled Greek, of Tuscan sculpture or Elizabethan song may yet be full of the very sweetest wisdom. The real fool, such as the gods mock or mar, is he who does not know himself. I was such a one too long. You have been such a one too long. Be so no more. Do not be afraid. The supreme vice is shallowness. Everything that is realised is right. Remember also that whatever is misery to you to read, is still greater misery to me to set down. To you the Unseen Powers have been very good. They have permitted you to see the strange and tragic shapes of Life as one sees shadows in a crystal. The head of Medusa that turns living men to stone,[2] you have been allowed to look at in a mirror merely. You yourself have walked free among the flowers. From me the beautiful world of colour and motion has been taken away.

I will begin by telling you that I blame myself terribly. As I sit here in this dark cell in convict clothes, a disgraced and ruined man, I blame myself. In the perturbed and fitful nights of anguish, in the long monotonous days of pain, it is myself I blame. I blame myself for allowing an unintellectual friendship, a friendship whose primary aim was not the creation and contemplation of beautiful things, to entirely dominate my life. From the very first there was too wide a gap between us. You had been idle at your school, worse than idle at your university. You did not realise that an artist, and especially such an artist as I am, one, that is to say, the quality of whose work depends on the intensification of personality, requires for the development of his art the companionship of ideas, and intellectual atmosphere, quiet, peace, and solitude. You admired my work when it was finished: you enjoyed the brilliant successes of my first nights, and the brilliant banquets that followed them: you were proud, and quite naturally so, of being the intimate friend of an artist so distinguished: but you could not understand the conditions requisite for the production of artistic work. I am not speaking in phrases of rhetorical exaggeration but in terms of absolute truth to actual fact when I remind you that during the whole time we were together I never wrote

---

2. Medusa was a snake-haired monster, so horrifying that anyone who looked at her turned to stone.

one single line. Whether at Torquay, Goring, London, Florence or elsewhere, my life, as long as you were by my side, was entirely sterile and uncreative. And with but few intervals you were, I regret to say, by my side always. * * *

You send me a very nice poem, of the undergraduate school of verse, for my approval: I reply by a letter of fantastic literary conceits:[3] I compare you to Hylas, or Hyacinth, Jonquil or Narcisse,[4] or someone whom the great god of Poetry favoured, and honoured with his love. The letter is like a passage from one of Shakespeare's sonnets, transposed to a minor key. It can only be understood by those who have read the *Symposium* of Plato, or caught the spirit of a certain grave mood made beautiful for us in Greek marbles. It was, let me say frankly, the sort of letter I would, in a happy if wilful moment, have written to any graceful young man of either University who had sent me a poem of his own making, certain that he would have sufficient wit or culture to interpret rightly its fantastic phrases. Look at the history of that letter! It passes from you into the hands of a loathsome companion: from him to a gang of blackmailers: copies of it are sent about London to my friends, and to the manager of the theatre where my work is being performed: every construction but the right one is put on it: Society is thrilled with the absurd rumours that I have had to pay a huge sum of money for having written an infamous letter to you: this forms the basis of your father's worst attack: I produce the original letter myself in Court to show what it really is: it is denounced by your father's Counsel as a revolting and insidious attempt to corrupt Innocence: ultimately it forms part of a criminal charge: the Crown takes it up: the Judge sums up on it with little learning and much morality: I go to prison for it at last. That is the result of writing you a charming letter. * * *

Other miserable men, when they are thrown into prison, if they are robbed of the beauty of the world, are at least safe, in some measure, from the world's most deadly slings, most awful arrows. They can hide in the darkness of their cells, and of their very disgrace make a mode of sanctuary. The world, having had its will, goes its way, and they are left to suffer undisturbed. With me it has been different. Sorrow after sorrow has come beating at the prison doors in search of me. They have opened the gates wide and let them in. Hardly, if at all, have my friends been suffered to see me. But my enemies have had full access to me always. Twice in my public appearances at the Bankruptcy Court, twice again in my public transferences from one prison to another, have I been shown under conditions of unspeakable humiliation to the gaze and mockery of men. The messenger of Death has brought me his tidings and gone his way,[5] and in entire solitude, and isolated from all that could give me comfort, or suggest relief, I have had to bear the intolerable burden of misery and remorse that the memory of my mother placed upon me, and places on me still. Hardly has that wound been dulled, not healed, by time, when violent and bitter and harsh letters come to me from my wife through her solicitor. I am, at once, taunted and threatened with poverty. That I can bear. I can school myself to worse than that. But my two

---

3. Wilde's letter, praising Douglas's poem, *In Praise of Shame*, was eventually read aloud at his trial:

My own Boy,

　Your sonnet is quite lovely, and it is a marvel that those red rose-leaf lips of yours should have been made no less for the music of song than for madness of kisses. Your slim gilt soul walks between passion and poetry. I know Hyacinthus, whom Apollo loved so madly, was you in Greek days.

Why are you alone in London, and when do you go to Salisbury? Do go there to cool your hands in the grey twilight of Gothic things, and come here whenever you like. It is a lovely place—it only lacks you; but go to Salisbury first.

　Always, with undying love,

　　　　　　　　　　　　　　　　Yours, Oscar

4. Beautiful young men whom Apollo loved.
5. Wilde's mother died while he was in prison.

children are taken from me by legal procedure.[6] That is and always will remain to me a source of infinite distress, of infinite pain, of grief without end or limit. That the law should decide, and take upon itself to decide, that I am one unfit to be with my own children is something quite horrible to me. The disgrace of prison is as nothing compared to it. I envy the other men who tread the yard along with me. I am sure that their children wait for them, look for their coming, will be sweet to them.

The poor are wiser, more charitable, more kind, more sensitive than we are. In their eyes prison is a tragedy in a man's life, a misfortune, a casualty, something that calls for sympathy in others. They speak of one who is in prison as of one who is "*in trouble*" simply. It is the phrase they always use, and the expression has the perfect wisdom of Love in it. With people of our rank it is different. With us prison makes a man a pariah. I, and such as I am, have hardly any right to air and sun. Our presence taints the pleasures of others. We are unwelcome when we reappear. To revisit the glimpses of the moon is not for us.[7] Our very children are taken away. Those lovely links with humanity are broken. We are doomed to be solitary, while our sons still live. We are denied the one thing that might heal us and help us, that might bring balm to the bruised heart, and peace to the soul in pain.

And to all this has been added the hard, small fact that by your actions and by your silence, by what you have done and by what you have left undone,[8] you have made every day of my long imprisonment still more difficult for me to live through. The very bread and water of prison fare you have by your conduct changed. You have rendered the one bitter and the other brackish to me. The sorrow you should have shared you have doubled, the pain you should have sought to lighten you have quickened to anguish. I have no doubt that you did not mean to do so. I know that you did not mean to do so. It was simply that "one really fatal defect of your character, your entire lack of imagination."

And the end of it all is that I have got to forgive you. I must do so. I don't write this letter to put bitterness into your heart, but to pluck it out of mine. For my own sake I must forgive you. One cannot always keep an adder in one's breast to feed on one, nor rise up every night to sow thorns in the garden of one's soul. It will not be difficult at all for me to do so, if you help me a little. Whatever you did to me in old days I always readily forgave. It did you no good then. Only one whose life is without stain of any kind can forgive sins. But now when I sit in humiliation and disgrace it is different. My forgiveness should mean a great deal to you now. Some day you will realise it. Whether you do so early or late, soon or not at all, my way is clear before me. I cannot allow you to go through life bearing in your heart the burden of having ruined a man like me. The thought might make you callously indifferent, or morbidly sad. I must take the burden from you and put it on my own shoulders.

I must say to myself that neither you nor your father, multiplied a thousand times over, could possibly have ruined a man like me: that I ruined myself: and that nobody, great or small, can be ruined except by his own hand. I am quite ready to do so. I am trying to do so, though you may not think it at the present moment. If I have brought this pitiless indictment against you, think what an indictment I bring without pity against myself. Terrible as what you did to me was, what I did to myself was far more terrible still.

I was a man who stood in symbolic relations to the art and culture of my age. I had realised this for myself at the very dawn of my manhood, and had forced my age

---

6. In February 1897 Constance Wilde petitioned for custody of their children, Cyril and Vyvyan, whom Wilde never saw again. Their surname was changed to Holland.

7. Cf. *Hamlet* 1.4.51–53.
8. The Anglican rite of confession asks forgiveness "for what we have done and for what we have left undone."

to realise it afterwards. Few men hold such a position in their own lifetime and have it so acknowledged. It is usually discerned, if discerned at all, by the historian, or the critic, long after both the man and his age have passed away. With me it was different. I felt it myself, and made others feel it. Byron was a symbolic figure, but his relations were to the passion of his age and its weariness of passion. Mine were to something more noble, more permanent, of more vital issue, of larger scope.

The gods had given me almost everything. I had genius, a distinguished name, high social position, brilliancy, intellectual daring: I made art a philosophy, and philosophy an art: I altered the minds of men and the colours of things: there was nothing I said or did that did not make people wonder: I took the drama, the most objective form known to art, and made it as personal a mode of expression as the lyric or the sonnet, at the same time that I widened its range and enriched its characterisation: drama, novel, poem in rhyme, poem in prose, subtle or fantastic dialogue, whatever I touched I made beautiful in a new mode of beauty: to truth itself I gave what is false no less than what is true as its rightful province, and showed that the false and the true are merely forms of intellectual existence. I treated Art as the supreme reality, and life as a mere mode of fiction: I awoke the imagination of my century so that it created myth and legend around me: I summed up all systems in a phrase, and all existence in an epigram.

Along with these things, I had things that were different. I let myself be lured into long spells of senseless and sensual ease. I amused myself with being a *flâneur* [idle stroller], a dandy, a man of fashion. I surrounded myself with the smaller natures and the meaner minds. I became the spendthrift of my own genius, and to waste an eternal youth gave me a curious joy. Tired of being on the heights I deliberately went to the depths in the search for new sensations. What the paradox was to me in the sphere of thought, perversity became to me in the sphere of passion. Desire, at the end, was a malady, or a madness, or both. I grew careless of the lives of others. I took pleasure where it pleased me and passed on. I forgot that every little action of the common day makes or unmakes character, and that therefore what one has done in the secret chamber one has some day to cry aloud on the housetops. I ceased to be Lord over myself. I was no longer the Captain of my Soul, and did not know it. I allowed you to dominate me, and your father to frighten me. I ended in horrible disgrace. There is only one thing for me now, absolute Humility: just as there is only one thing for you, absolute Humility also. You had better come down into the dust and learn it beside me.

I have lain in prison for nearly two years. Out of my nature has come wild despair; an abandonment to grief that was piteous even to look at: terrible and impotent rage: bitterness and scorn: anguish that wept aloud: misery that could find no voice: sorrow that was dumb. I have passed through every possible mood of suffering. Better than Wordsworth himself I know what Wordsworth meant when he said:

> Suffering is permanent, obscure, and dark
> And has the nature of Infinity.[9]

But while there were times when I rejoiced in the idea that my sufferings were to be endless, I could not bear them to be without meaning. Now I find hidden away in my nature something that tells me that nothing in the whole world is meaningless, and suffering least of all. That something hidden away in my nature, like a treasure in a field, is Humility.

It is the last thing left in me, and the best: the ultimate discovery at which I have arrived: the starting-point for a fresh development. It has come to me right out of myself, so I know that it has come at the proper time. It could not have come before, nor later. Had anyone told me of it, I would have rejected it. Had it been brought to me, I would have refused it. As I found it, I want to keep it. I must do so. It is the one thing that has in it the elements of life, of a new life, a *Vita Nuova*[1] for me. Of all things it is the strangest. One cannot give it away, and another may not give it to one. One cannot acquire it, except by surrendering everything that one has. It is only when one has lost all things, that one knows that one possesses it.

Now that I realise that it is in me, I see quite clearly what I have got to do, what, in fact, I must do. And when I use such a phrase as that, I need not tell you that I am not alluding to any external sanction or command. I admit none. I am far more of an individualist than I ever was. Nothing seems to me of the smallest value except what one gets out of oneself. My nature is seeking a fresh mode of self-realisation. That is all I am concerned with. And the first thing that I have got to do is to free myself from any possible bitterness of feeling against you.

I am completely penniless, and absolutely homeless. Yet there are worse things in the world than that. I am quite candid when I tell you that rather than go out from this prison with bitterness in my heart against you or against the world I would gladly and readily beg my bread from door to door. If I got nothing at the house of the rich, I would get something at the house of the poor. Those who have much are often greedy. Those who have little always share. I would not a bit mind sleeping in the cool grass in summer, and when winter came on sheltering myself by the warm close-thatched rick, or under the penthouse of a great barn, provided I had love in my heart. The external things of life seem to me now of no importance at all. You can see to what intensity of individualism I have arrived, or am arriving rather, for the journey is long, and "where I walk there are thorns."[2]

Of course I know that to ask for alms on the highway is not to be my lot, and that if ever I lie in the cool grass at night-time it will be to write sonnets to the Moon. When I go out of prison, Robbie will be waiting for me on the other side of the big iron-studded gate, and he is the symbol not merely of his own affection, but of the affection of many others besides. I believe I am to have enough to live on for about eighteen months at any rate, so that, if I may not write beautiful books, I may at least read beautiful books, and what joy can be greater? After that, I hope to be able to recreate my creative faculty. But were things different: had I not a friend left in the world: were there not a single house open to me even in pity: had I to accept the wallet and ragged cloak of sheer penury: still as long as I remained free from all resentment, hardness, and scorn, I would be able to face life with much more calm and confidence than I would were my body in purple and fine linen, and the soul within it sick with hate. And I shall really have no difficulty in forgiving you. But to make it a pleasure for me you must feel that you want it. When you really want it you will find it waiting for you.

I need not say that my task does not end there. It would be comparatively easy if it did. There is much more before me. I have hills far steeper to climb, valleys much darker to pass through. And I have to get it all out of myself. Neither Religion, Morality, nor Reason can help me at all.

Morality does not help me. I am a born antinomian.[3] I am one of those who are made for exceptions, not for laws. But while I see that there is nothing wrong in what one does, I see that there is something wrong in what one becomes. It is well to have learned that.

Religion does not help me. The faith that others give to what is unseen, I give to what one can touch, and look at. My Gods dwell in temples made with hands, and within the circle of actual experience is my creed made perfect and complete: too

---

1. New life (Italian); Dante's book of this name was one of the few books Wilde was able to have sent to him in prison.

2. From Wilde's play, *A Woman of No Importance*, Act 4.

3. A person who rejects conventional morality.

complete it may be, for like many or all of those who have placed their Heaven in this earth, I have found in it not merely the beauty of Heaven, but the horror of Hell also. When I think about Religion at all, I feel as if I would like to found an order for those who cannot believe: the Confraternity of the Fatherless one might call it, where on an altar, on which no taper burned, a priest, in whose heart peace had no dwelling, might celebrate with unblessed bread and a chalice empty of wine. Everything to be true must become a religion. And agnosticism should have its ritual no less than faith. It has sown its martyrs, it should reap its saints, and praise God daily for having hidden Himself from man. But whether it be faith or agnosticism, it must be nothing external to me. Its symbols must be of my own creating. Only that is spiritual which makes its own form. If I may not find its secret within myself, I shall never find it. If I have not got it already, it will never come to me.

Reason does not help me. It tells me that the laws under which I am convicted are wrong and unjust laws, and the system under which I have suffered a wrong and unjust system. But, somehow, I have got to make both of these things just and right to me. And exactly as in Art one is only concerned with what a particular thing is at a particular moment to oneself, so it is also in the ethical evolution of one's character. I have got to make everything that has happened to me good for me. The plank-bed, the loathsome food, the hard ropes shredded into oakum[4] till one's fingertips grow dull with pain, the menial offices with which each day begins and finishes, the harsh orders that routine seems to necessitate, the dreadful dress that makes sorrow grotesque to look at, the silence, the solitude, the shame—each and all of these things I have to transform into a spiritual experience. There is not a single degradation of the body which I must not try and make into a spiritualising of the soul.

I want to get to the point when I shall be able to say, quite simply and without affectation, that the two great turning-points of my life were when my father sent me to Oxford, and when society sent me to prison. I will not say that it is the best thing that could have happened to me, for that phrase would savour of too great bitterness towards myself. I would sooner say, or hear it said of me, that I was so typical a child of my age that in my perversity, and for that perversity's sake, I turned the good things of my life to evil, and the evil things of my life to good. What is said, however, by myself or by others matters little. The important thing, the thing that lies before me, the thing that I have to do, or be for the brief remainder of my days one maimed, marred, and incomplete, is to absorb into my nature all that has been done to me, to make it part of me, to accept it without complaint, fear, or reluctance. The supreme vice is shallowness. Whatever is realised is right.

When first I was put into prison some people advised me to try and forget who I was. It was ruinous advice. It is only by realising what I am that I have found comfort of any kind. Now I am advised by others to try on my release to forget that I have ever been in a prison at all. I know that would be equally fatal. It would mean that I would be always haunted by an intolerable sense of disgrace, and that those things that are meant as much for me as for anyone else—the beauty of the sun and the moon, the pageant of the seasons, the music of daybreak and the silence of great nights, the rain falling through the leaves, or the dew creeping over the grass and making it silver—would all be tainted for me, and lose their healing power and their power of communicating joy. To reject one's own experiences is to arrest one's own development. To deny one's own experiences is to put a lie into the lips of one's own life. It is no less than a denial of the Soul.

---

4. Prisoners were often forced to pick oakum—i.e., to shred used ropes into fibers.

COMPANION READING

H. Montgomery Hyde: from The Trials of Oscar Wilde[1]

[THE FIRST TRIAL]

Queensberry's leading counsel[2] rose from his place in the front row of barristers' seats in the Old Bailey courtroom to begin his cross-examination of the prosecutor. As he faced his old college classmate in the witness box, the two figures on whom every eye in court was now fixed presented a striking contrast. There was Wilde, dressed in the height of fashion, a flower in the buttonhole of his frock coat, and exuding an air of easy confidence; opposite him stood Carson, tall, saturnine, and with the most determined expression on his lantern-jawed countenance. * * *

The opening question immediately revealed the cross-examiner's skill. * * *

"You stated that your age was thirty-nine. I think you are over forty. You were born on the 16th of October 1854?" Carson emphasized the point by holding up a copy of the witness's birth certificate.

Wilde appeared momentarily disconcerted, but he quickly recovered his composure. "I have no wish to pose as being young," he replied sweetly. "You have my certificate and that settles the matter."

"But," Carson persisted, "being born in 1854 makes you more than forty?"

"Ah! Very well," Wilde agreed with a sigh, as if to congratulate his opponent on a remarkable feat of mathematics.

It was a small point that Carson had scored in this duel of wits, but not without considerable importance. At the very outset Wilde had been detected in a stupid lie, the effect of which was not lost upon the jury, particularly when Carson followed it up by contrasting Wilde's true age with that of Lord Alfred Douglas,[3] with whom Wilde admitted to having stayed at many places, including hotels, both in England and on the Continent. Furthermore, it appeared that Douglas had also contributed to The Chameleon,[4] namely two poems. Wilde was asked about these poems, which he admitted that he had seen. "I thought them exceedingly beautiful poems," he added. "One was 'In Praise of Shame' and the other 'Two Loves.'"[5]

"These loves," Carson asked, with a note of distaste in his voice. "They were two boys?"

"Yes."

"One boy calls his love 'true love,' and the other boy calls his love 'shame'?"

"Yes."

"Did you think they made any improper suggestion?"

"No, none whatever."

Carson passed on to "The Priest and the Acolyte," which Wilde admitted that he had read.

---

1. After Lord Alfred Douglas's father, the Marquess of Queensberry, accused Wilde of sodomy, Wilde brought suit for libel. Wilde lost his case, and was in turn prosecuted, in two subsequent criminal trials, for committing indecent acts. He was found guilty and sentenced to two years in prison with hard labor. The three trials took place in 1895, in the Old Bailey in London, and were the focus of immense public curiosity; the sensational story was followed daily in almost every London newspaper. The following excerpts are from H. Montgomery Hyde's The Trials of Oscar Wilde (1948); it should be noted that since no authoritative transcripts of the court proceedings exist, his book is a reconstruction of events based on contemporary press reports and personal reminiscences.

2. Edward Carson, a renowned barrister, had been a classmate of Wilde's at Trinity College, Dublin. He successfully defended Queensberry against Wilde's charge of libel in the first trial.

3. Douglas was twenty-four years old; Wilde was forty.

4. Edited by Jack Bloxam, an Oxford undergraduate, The Chameleon was a literary magazine with a homoerotic tone; it appeared only once, in 1894. Bloxam was the author of The Priest and the Acolyte. At Douglas's request, Wilde had submitted some of his aphorisms to the magazine, and his legal opponents sought to make Wilde appear guilty by association with the allegedly immoral contributions of Douglas and Bloxam.

5. The latter poem appears on page 2159.

"You have no doubt whatever that that was an improper story?"

"From the literary point of view it was highly improper. It is impossible for a man of literature to judge it otherwise; by literature, meaning treatment, selection of subject, and the like. I thought the treatment rotten and the subject rotten."

"You are of opinion, I believe, that there is no such thing as an immoral book?"

"Yes."

"May I take it that you think 'The Priest and the Acolyte' was not immoral?"

"It was worse. It was badly written."[6]

"Was not the story that of a priest who fell in love with a boy who served him at the altar, and was discovered by the rector in the priest's room, and a scandal arose?"

"I have read it only once, last November, and nothing will induce me to read it again. I don't care for it. It doesn't interest me."

"Do you think the story blasphemous?"

"I think it violated every artistic canon of beauty."

"That is not an answer."

"It is the only one I can give."

"I want to see the position you pose in."

"I do not think you should say that."

"I have said nothing out of the way. I wish to know whether you thought the story blasphemous."

"The story filled me with disgust. The end was wrong."

"Answer the question, sir," Carson rapped out sharply. "Did you or did you not consider the story blasphemous?"

"I thought it disgusting."

Professing himself satisfied with this reply, Carson turned to a particular incident in the story. "You know that when the priest in the story administers poison to the boy, he uses the words of the sacrament of the Church of England?"

"That I entirely forgot."

"Do you consider that blasphemous?"

"I think it is horrible. 'Blasphemous' is not a word of mine." When Carson put the passage in question to him and asked whether he approved of the words used by the author, Wilde repeated his previous opinion: "I think them disgusting, perfect twaddle."

"I think you will admit that anyone who would approve of such a story would pose as guilty of improper practices?"

"I do not think so in the person of another contributor to the magazine. It would show very bad literary taste. Anyhow I strongly objected to the whole story. . . . Of course, I am aware that The Chameleon may have circulated among the undergraduates of Oxford. But I do not believe that any book or work of art ever had any effect whatever on morality."

"Am I right in saying that you do not consider the effect in creating morality or immorality?"

"Certainly, I do not."

"So far as your works are concerned, you pose as not being concerned about morality or immorality?"

"I do not know whether you use the word 'pose' in any particular sense."

"Is it a favourite word of your own?"

6. Wilde is paraphrasing his preface to *The Picture of Dorian Grey* (see page 2085).

"Is it? I have no pose in this matter. In writing a play or a book, I am concerned entirely with literature—that is, with art. I aim not at doing good or evil, but in try-ing to make a thing that will have some quality of beauty." * * *

Carson now turned to *The Picture of Dorian Gray*[7] * * *

"'There is no such thing as a moral or an immoral book. Books are well written or badly written.' That expresses your view?"

"My view on art, yes."

"Then I take it, no matter how immoral a book may be, if it is well written, it is, in your opinion, a good book?"

"Yes, if it were well written so as to produce a sense of beauty, which is the high-est sense of which a human being can be capable. If it were badly written, it would produce a sense of disgust."

"Then a well-written book putting forward perverted moral views may be a good book?"

"No work of art ever puts forward views. Views belong to people who are not artists."

"A perverted novel might be a good book?" Carson persisted.

"I don't know what you mean by a 'perverted' novel," Wilde answered crisply.

This gave Carson the opening he sought. "Then I will suggest *Dorian Gray* is open to the interpretation of being such a novel?"

Wilde brushed aside the suggestion with contempt. "That could only be to brutes and illiterates," he said. "The views of Philistines on art are unaccountable."

"An illiterate person reading *Dorian Gray* might consider it such a novel?"

"The views of illiterates on art are unaccountable. I am concerned only with my own view of art. I don't care twopence what other people think of it."

"The majority of persons come under your definition of Philistines and illiterates?"

"I have found wonderful exceptions."

"Do you think that the majority of people live up to the position you are giving us?"

"I am afraid they are not cultivated enough."

"Not cultivated enough to draw the distinction between a good book and a bad book?" The note of sarcasm in Carson's voice was unmistakable.

"Certainly not," Wilde replied blandly.

"The affection and love of the artist of *Dorian Gray* might lead an ordinary indi-vidual to believe that it might have a certain tendency?"

"I have no knowledge of the views of ordinary individuals."

"You did not prevent the ordinary individual from buying your book?"

"I have never discouraged him!" * * *

Having covered Wilde's published writings, Carson passed on to the allegedly compromising letters Wilde had written to Lord Alfred Douglas. * * *

"Why should a man of your age address a boy nearly twenty years younger as 'My own Boy'?"[8]

"I was fond of him. I have always been fond of him."

"Do you adore him?"

"No, but I have always liked him." Wilde then went on to elaborate upon the letter. "I think it is a beautiful letter. It is a poem. I was not writing an ordinary letter. You might as well cross-examine me as to whether *King Lear* or a sonnet of Shakespeare was proper."

"Apart from art, Mr Wilde?"

"I cannot answer apart from art."

7. Wilde's novel describes the passion felt by an artist, Basil Hallward, for a beautiful young man, Dorian Gray, whose portrait he paints.

8. For the text of this letter, a response to Douglas's poem *In Praise of Shame*, see page 2130, n. 3.

"Suppose a man who was not an artist had written this letter, would you say it was a proper letter?"

"A man who was not an artist could not have written that letter."

"Why?"

"Because nobody but an artist could write it. He certainly could not write the language unless he were a man of letters."

"I can suggest, for the sake of your reputation, that there is nothing very wonderful in this 'red rose-leaf lips of yours'?"

"A great deal depends on the way it is read."

"'Your slim gilt soul walks between passion and poetry,'" Carson continued. "Is that a beautiful phrase?"

"Not as you read it, Mr Carson. You read it very badly."

It was now Carson's turn to be nettled. "I do not profess to be an artist," he exclaimed, "and when I hear you give evidence, I am glad I am not."

These words immediately brought Sir Edward Clarke[9] to his feet. "I don't think my learned friend should talk like that," he observed. Then, turning towards his client in the witness box, he added: "Pray do not criticize my learned friend's reading again."

This clash caused a buzz of excitement in the courtroom. When it had died down, Carson went on with his cross-examination, indicating the document he was holding in his hand. "Is not that an exceptional letter?"

"It is unique, I should say." Wilde's answer produced loud laughter in court, which was still largely on the side of the witness.

"Was that the ordinary way in which you carried on your correspondence?"

"No. But I have often written to Lord Alfred Douglas, though I never wrote to another young man in the same way."

"Have you often written letters in the same style as this?"

"I don't repeat myself in style."

Carson held out another sheet of paper. "Here is another letter which I believe you also wrote to Lord Alfred Douglas. Will you read it?"

Wilde refused this invitation. "I don't see why I should," he said.

"Then I will," retorted Carson.

> Savoy Hotel
> Victoria Embankment
> London
>
> Dearest of all Boys,
>
> Your letter was delightful, red and yellow wine to me; but I am sad and out of sorts. Bosie, you must not make scenes with me. They kill me, they wreck the loveliness of life. I cannot see you, so Greek and gracious, distorted with passion. I cannot listen to your curved lips saying hideous things to me. I would sooner—than have you bitter unjust, hating. . . .
>
> I must see you soon. You are the divine thing I want, the thing of grace and beauty; but I don't know how to do it. Shall I come to Salisbury? My bill here is £49 for a week. I have also got a new sitting-room. . . .
>
> Why are you not here, my dear, my wonderful boy? I fear I must leave—no money, no credit, and a heart of lead.
>
> Your own
> OSCAR

9. Clarke was Wilde's attorney in all three trials.

"Is that an ordinary letter?" Carson asked, when he had finished reading it.

"Everything I wrote is extraordinary," Wilde answered with a show of impatience. "I do not pose as being ordinary, great heavens! Ask me any question you like about it."

Carson had only one question to ask about this letter, but its effect was deadly. "Is it the kind of letter a man writes to another?"

[THE SECOND TRIAL]

"During 1893 and 1894 you were a great deal in the company of Lord Alfred Douglas?"

"Oh, yes."

"Did he read that poem to you?"[1]

"Yes."

"You can perhaps understand that such verses as these would not be acceptable to the reader with an ordinary balanced mind?"

"I am not prepared to say," Wilde answered. "It appears to me to be a question of taste, temperament, and individuality. I should say that one man's poetry is another man's poison!"

"I daresay!" commented Gill[2] dryly, when the laughter had subsided. "The next poem is one described as 'Two Loves.' * * * Was that poem explained to you?"

"I think that is clear."

"There is no question as to what it means?"

"Most certainly not."

"Is it not clear that the love described relates to natural love and unnatural love?"

"No."

"What is the 'Love that dare not speak its name'?"[3] Gill now asked.

"'The love that dare not speak its name' in this century is such a great affection of an elder for a younger man as there was between David and Jonathan, such as Plato made the very basis of his philosophy, and such as you find in the sonnets of Michelangelo and Shakespeare.[4] It is that deep, spiritual affection that is as pure as it is perfect. It dictates and pervades great works of art like those of Shakespeare and Michelangelo, and those two letters of mine, such as they are. It is in this century misunderstood, so much misunderstood that it may be described as the 'Love that dare not speak its name,' and on account of it I am placed where I am now. It is beautiful, it is fine, it is the noblest form of affection. There is nothing unnatural about it. It is intellectual, and it repeatedly exists between an elder and a younger man, when the elder has intellect, and the younger man has all the joy, hope, and glamour of life before him. That it should be so, the world does not understand. The world mocks at it and sometimes puts one in the pillory for it."

Wilde's words produced a spontaneous outburst of applause from the public gallery, mingled with some hisses, which moved the judge to say he would have the Court cleared if there were any further manifestation of feeling.

1. Douglas's sonnet *In Praise of Shame*.
2. Charles Gill was counsel for the prosecution during the second and third trial.
3. Cf. *Two Loves*, line 74, page 2160.
4. King David of Israel, and Jonathan, the son of King Saul, were inseparable friends. On Jonathan's death, David declared that "your love to me was wonderful, passing the love of women" (2 Samuel 1.26). Plato argued that the passion of an older man for a younger one could be translated into a contemplation of the ideal and the universal. Both Shakespeare and Michelangelo wrote sonnets that can be read as describing platonic and/or erotic love between men.

PERSPECTIVES

Aestheticism, Decadence, and the *Fin de Siècle*

"I belong to the Beardsley period," Max Beerbohm remarked audaciously in 1894, when he and Aubrey Beardsley were both just twenty-two. Time has proved him correct. The late-Victorian period, the age of Beardsley and Wilde, Kipling and Conan Doyle, has indeed come to be seen as a distinctive era in which the aesthetic and moral values of the nineteenth century were twisted or transmuted into the revolutionary forces of modernism, in a blaze of daring new styles, attitudes, and modes of behavior.

By the early 1880s most of the major mid-Victorian writers had died or were well past their prime. As the Empire reached its peak, Britain's self-confidence eroded under the strain of maintaining its military might and economic supremacy against competition from the United States and Germany. About 1890, the general sense of fatigue and anxiety found expression in the French phrase *fin de siècle*—the "end of the age." The term suggested that Victorian values and energies had become exhausted, and that an unsettling, amoral, post-Darwinian world was emerging in which contradictory impulses vied for attention: exquisite delicacy in poetry and brutal realism in fiction, effete dandyism among some men and hearty imperialism among others, socialism and Catholicism. The proliferation of women in the workforce ran headlong into the diagnosis of inherent female debility by medical authorities. Meanwhile, discussion clubs formed where both sexes openly debated the merits of marriage and free love. It was the era of the Manly Woman and the Womanly Man, the moment when sexology was invented and words like "homosexual," "lesbian," and—belatedly—"heterosexual" were coined to regulate the mysteries of sexual identity.

Partly in flight from the devastated industrial landscape, partly in rebellion against middle-class mores and artistic norms, Aesthetes like Walter Pater, Wilde, Whistler, Beardsley, and Arthur Symons sought to create a pure art of flawless formal design, divorced from moral concerns but open to hitherto unexplored subject matter—the often artificial beauties of cosmetics, music halls, gaslit faces, or city streets seen through mist and rain. By the 1870s, critics were giving the labels "impressionist" and "aesthetic" to paintings by Whistler and Dante Gabriel Rossetti, and to poems by Rossetti, Algernon Swinburne, and William Morris. With the help of flamboyant personalities such as Whistler and Wilde, Aestheticism became known in the 1880s as an entire way of life, involving flowing dress for both men and women, medieval- or Japanese-style home furnishings, and ostentatious worship of the beautiful in all the arts. There was even a distinctive Aesthetic vocabulary: "Constantly yearning for the intense," said one observer, "the language of the Aesthetes is tinged with somewhat exaggerated metaphor, and their adjectives are usually superlative—as supreme, consummate, utter, quite too preciously sublime."

Though its excesses were easy to mock, Aestheticism took hold so forcefully because its various strands had been developing, abroad and at home, for several generations. In 1873 Tennyson complained with some reason that Aesthetes lived on "poisonous honey stolen from France." Swinburne was clearly influenced by the French poets Théophile Gautier and Charles Baudelaire when he declared in 1866: "Art for art's sake first of all," explaining that "her business is not to do good on other grounds, but to be good on her own." Yet Tennyson himself was a pivotal figure for the Aesthetes and their immediate predecessors, the Pre-Raphaelites; both groups were inspired by his medievalism and sonorous morbidity.

Aestheticism often shaded over into Decadence, a term that was confusingly applied not only to the deliberately mannered works of the late Victorians, but also to the scandalous or effeminate conduct of their creators. By the 1890s the word had become a vague and fashionable label of both moral censure and avant-garde respect. The naturalist fiction of George Gissing and Émile Zola was called decadent because of its tawdry subject matter and amoral attitudes; Wilde on the other hand claimed that decadent pleasures alone made life worth living. Depending on one's point of view, "decadent" could describe, with praise or blame, a dissipated

THE SIX-MARK TEA-POT.

Æsthetic Bridegroom. "IT IS QUITE CONSUMMATE, IS IT NOT?"
Intense Bride. "IT IS, INDEED! OH, ALGERNON, LET US LIVE UP TO IT!"

George Du Maurier. *The Six-Mark Tea-Pot.* From *Punch* magazine, 1880. Born in Paris, Du Maurier shuttled between London and Paris, and studies in art and science, until he settled on a career as a magazine illustrator, joining the staff of *Punch* in 1864. His wittily captioned cartoons of Aesthetes fixed the movement in the public imagination. Having established his reputation as a keen satirist of cultural trends, he achieved international fame with his novel *Trilby* (1894), which was based on his days with Whistler as an art student in Paris.

young man like Wilde's Dorian Gray, or a vigorous freethinking feminist like the heroine of Grant Allen's *The Woman Who Did* (1895). In most cases the word suggested an ultra-refined sophistication of taste allied with moral perversity; and many feared that decadent ideas and behavior heralded social collapse and apocalyptic change for Western culture. Max Nordau's 1895 bestseller *Degeneration* portrayed decadence as evidence of "a twilight mood" in Europe; "degeneration and hysteria," he felt, were "the convulsions and spasms of exhaustion" in Western civilization. Delighting in this anxiety, Wilde told Yeats that Pater's *Renaissance* "is the very flower of decadence; the last trumpet should have sounded the moment it was written."

Together, the *fin de siècle* writers helped free English literature of moral inhibition, producing a richly descriptive poetry and prose marked by deep learning, love of London, bold sensuality, spiritual intensity, and a new focus on images rather than events. The concept of Decadence depended on a Christian mentality haunted by notions of sin, forgiveness, and damnation. Dissatisfied with life and art, and tempted by drugs and drinking, opium and absinthe, some writers met early deaths from dissipation or suicide. The quest for absolution led many, including Beardsley and Wilde, to convert to Catholicism.

While they strove for a refined art purified of morality and narrative content, Aesthetes and Decadents made it clear that art had a definitely sexual if often elusive essence. Though "consummate" was a favorite word, much of their work expressed a frustrated longing for a fleeting taste of forbidden fruits. Often both male and female writers envisioned women as dangerous idols, worshipped at first as chaste images of noble art but finally revealed as seductive vampires who sap masculine energy with insatiable desire.

As the critic Elaine Showalter points out, "The decadent or aesthete was the masculine counterpart to the New Woman" lauded by feminist fiction writers of the 1890s. More prevalent in art than life, these two literary figures spurred fears of a sexual revolution and cast doubt on Britain's ability to procreate future generations of Empire-rulers. The anxiety over the blurring of gender boundaries helps explain the strange conflux of misogynist, homoerotic, androgynous, utopianly healthy, and luridly diseased discourses of sexuality that surfaced at this time—culminating in Bram Stoker's *Dracula* (1897), which portrayed the New Woman as an insatiable sexual vampire poised to destroy British manhood. Even a radical advocate of socialist free love, Karl Marx's daughter Eleanor, denounced "the effeminate man and the masculine woman" as horrifyingly unnatural. With slight exaggeration, Max Beerbohm alluded to "that amalgamation of the sexes which is one of the chief planks in the decadent platform."

The heyday of Aestheticism and Decadence came to an end with the trials of Oscar Wilde. When Wilde was arrested for sodomy in 1895, newspapers reported that he carried the notorious decadent magazine, *The Yellow Book*, with him to jail (it was actually a yellow-backed French novel). Mobs stoned the publisher's office; Beardsley, its editor, was fired; the magazine failed. A savage conservative backlash suddenly ended the vogue of the bold New Woman and the languid Aesthete. But it was in the "degenerate" turmoil of the *fin de siècle* that modernism got its start: James, Yeats, Bennett, Wells, Shaw, Ford, and Conrad all published in *The Yellow Book* or its short-lived successor, *The Savoy*. Though the Aesthetic creed seemed like an underground current to many during the Victorian period, by the turn of the century belief in the autonomy of the artist was on the brink of becoming modernism's main stream.

⊷ ═╬═ ⊶

Aubrey Beardsley
1872–1898

"Awfully Weirdly" *Punch* called him. But his bizarre renderings of warped passion and sexual tension made Aubrey Beardsley the most important English artist of the 1890s. As the controversial illustrator and editor of *The Yellow Book* (1894–1895) and *The Savoy* (1896)—the most notorious magazines of the 1890s—Beardsley put his stamp on the Decadent movement; he gave an instantly recognizable visual style to the amorphous perversity of the era. His use of sinuous lines and distorted floral motifs make him a key figure in the history of Art Nouveau, and in fact it was Beardsley who introduced the term to the British public.

Born in Brighton, Beardsley was working as a clerk in an insurance office, studying art at night, when he received encouragement from the famous Pre-Raphaelite painter Edward Burne-Jones. Stylizing Burne-Jones's already elongated figures, Beardsley met his first success with brooding pen-and-ink drawings for a new edition of Malory's *Morte D'Arthur* (1893–1894). He achieved notoriety, however, with his cool, cruel, bizarrely erotic illustrations of Wilde's *Salomé* (1894). Falling out with Wilde during the project, Beardsley not only mocked Wilde in the drawings but refused to ask him to contribute to *The Yellow Book*. Wilde in turn denounced both Beardsley and the magazine—with ironic results: the public associated Wilde with the scandalous contents of the journal, and when Wilde went to jail Beardsley was fired because he had once worked with Wilde. Beardsley then coedited *The Savoy* with Arthur

J'AI BAISÉ TA BOVCHE
IOKANAAN
J'AI BAISÉ TA BOVCHE

Symons, did fanciful drawings on Wagnerian themes, and illustrated an edition of Pope's *The Rape of the Lock* (1896). But his health was deteriorating rapidly. He converted to Catholicism before he died of tuberculosis at the age of twenty-five.

Made for mechanical reproduction, Beardsley's work is the most striking example of the revitalization of book art in the 1890s. His emphasis on overall design makes each page stand on its own; instead of shading, his black-and-white style dramatically relies on virtuoso curves, creepy details, and open space to suggest volume, distance, and psychological insight. His visual genius almost always responds to a literary text, and books themselves figure prominently in his work. The grotesque sexuality, autoeroticism and necrophilia of his illustrations carry over into his own stories and poems, such as the unnerving *The Ballad of a Barber,* who murders a princess while dressing her hair. Noting that Beardsley always worked indoors by candlelight and without models, the critic Holbrook Jackson remarked that he was "the most literary of all modern artists; his drawings are never the outcome of observation—they are always the outcome of thought."

Reproduced here is *"J'ai baisé ta bouche, Iokanaan,"* an illustration for *Salomé,* 1893. Wilde wrote his play in French, but its production on the English stage (starring Sarah Bernhardt) was banned because of its depiction of biblical characters. Beardsley's outrageous illustrations for the English translation (1894) instantly made the book a decadent *cause célèbre* and a classic of Art Nouveau design. Beardsley depicts the play's climactic scene, in which Salomé, who has demanded John the Baptist's head as a reward for her dancing, kisses the dead lips of the prophet who had scorned her love.

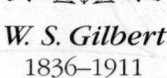

W. S. Gilbert
1836–1911

William Schwenk Gilbert is best known for his lengthy partnership with the composer Arthur Sullivan. Together they wrote fourteen light operas from 1871 to 1896, immensely popular entertainments that continue to be performed throughout the world today. Known as the "Savoy Operas" because they debuted at the Savoy Theatre built by Richard D'Oyly Carte expressly for their production, Gilbert and Sullivan's works include *H.M.S. Pinafore* (1878), *The Pirates of Penzance* (1879), and *The Mikado* (1885). Typically, these comic operettas poke gentle fun at British institutions such as the law, Parliament, and the navy, while also mocking Victorian obsessions with topics such as social hierarchy or orphanhood. Although Gilbert's satirical librettos perfectly complement Sullivan's sprightly scores, they can be read on their own as nimble evocations of Victorian foibles and follies. *Patience* spoofed Aestheticism just as it reached the public consciousness in the early 1880s; in the process the opera helped to articulate and spread the ideas it mocked. A composite caricature of Whistler and Wilde, the "ultra-poetical, super-aesthetical" Bunthorne is made to confess that his exquisite refinement is just a pose meant to attract the ladies.

If You're Anxious for to Shine in the High Aesthetic Line

Am I alone,
    And unobserved? I am!
Then let me own
    I'm an aesthetic sham!
This air severe
    Is but a mere
        Veneer!

5

This cynic smile
Is but a wile

10   Of guile!
This costume chaste
Is but good taste
Misplaced!
Let me confess!

15   A languid love for lilies does *not* blight me!
Lank limbs and haggard cheeks do *not* delight me!
I do *not* care for dirty greens
By any means.
I do *not* long for all one sees

20   That's Japanese.
I am *not* fond of uttering platitudes
In stained-glass attitudes.
In short, my mediaevalism's affectation,
Born of a morbid love of admiration![1]

Song

25   If you're anxious for to shine in the high aesthetic line as a man of culture rare,
You must get up all the germs of the transcendental terms,[2] and plant them
everywhere.
You must lie upon the daisies and discourse in novel phrases of your com-
plicated state of mind,
The meaning doesn't matter if it's only idle chatter of a transcendental kind.
And every one will say,

30   As you walk your mystic way,
"If this young man expresses himself in terms too deep for *me*,
Why, what a very singularly deep young man this deep young man must be!"

Be eloquent in praise of the very dull old days which have long since
passed away,
And convince 'em, if you can, that the reign of good Queen Anne[3] was
Culture's palmiest day.

35   Of course you will pooh-pooh whatever's fresh and new, and declare it's
crude and mean,
For Art stopped short in the cultivated court of the Empress Josephine.[4]
And every one will say,
As you walk your mystic way,
"If that's not good enough for him which is good enough for *me*,

40   Why, what a very cultivated kind of youth this kind of youth must be!"

1. Stereotypical Aesthetic behavior, combining traits of
Dante Gabriel Rossetti, Whistler, and Wilde, particularly
as they were spoofed by the cartoonist George Du Maurier. Lilies and languid yet soul-tormented lovers figure in
the work of Rossetti, as do medieval subjects and stained
glass; Whistler's paintings featuring Japanese props and
perspective helped create a vogue for Japanese art, dress,
and decoration; Wilde's elaborate clothing and ostentatious worship of beauty were said to be merely attention-
getting poses.

2. Transcendental philosophy values individual visionary
understanding over objective, materialist apprehension of
the world. *The Germ* (1850) was a short-lived Pre-
Raphaelite journal that sought to promote a more spiritual art and poetry in Britain.
3. Queen of Great Britain from 1702–1714; the simplicity
of the era's neoclassical architecture and design found
favor with Aesthetes tired of Victorian ornateness.
4. Wife of Napoleon Bonaparte and empress of France
1804–1809.

Then a sentimental passion of a vegetable fashion must excite your languid
    spleen,[5]
An attachment *à la* Plato for a bashful young potato, or a not-too-French
    French bean!
Though the Philistines may jostle, you will rank as an apostle in the high
    aesthetic band,
If you walk down Piccadilly[6] with a poppy or a lily in your mediaeval hand.
45   And every one will say,
                    As you walk your flowery way,
"If he's content with a vegetable love which would certainly not suit *me,*
Why, what a most particularly pure young man this pure young man must be!"
                                                                      1881

━◆━

James Abbott McNeill Whistler
1834–1903

An American artist who settled in London in the early 1860s, Whistler provided much of the
intellectual energy that inspired the Aesthetic Movement in the 1880s. He studied art in
Paris, where he became friends with Gustav Courbet and Henri Fantin-Latour, absorbed the
aesthetic doctrine of Théophile Gautier and Charles Baudelaire, and later came to know and
influence Claude Monet and the poet Stéphane Mallarmé. Although Whistler never fully
abandoned a representational style, he insisted that viewers accept a painting as an arrangement of lines and colors on a flat canvas. "I care nothing for the past, present, or future of the
black figure," he said about a shadowy human outline in one of his paintings; "it was placed
there because black was wanted at that spot."

Whistler's *Nocturne in Black and Gold: The Falling Rocket* (1875) earned the ire of Ruskin,
who declared that he was an impudent coxcomb who was "flinging a pot of paint in the public's face." Whistler sued Ruskin for libel, and the ensuing trial of 1878 marked a turning point
in English art and taste. Whistler won, and the Ruskinian notion of art as a social and moral
force yielded ground to Whistler's concept of art as an expression of the artist's subjective
vision, something beyond common comprehension.

Whistler delivered the following lecture in London on February 20, 1885, to an invita-
tion-only audience that included journalists, artists, writers, and society figures. He chose
to deliver his "Ten O'Clock" lecture at 10 P.M. so that his fashionable audience would not
have to rush dinner. It is the era's clearest manifesto of art for art's sake, setting the artist
above and beyond his moment in history. The lecture and its fastidious presentation
brought to a larger audience the essentials of Whistler's artistic platform: the attention-get-
ting declaration of artistic independence, the sarcastic dismissals of other theories, and the
aggressively elitist public posture that made him "The Master" for other Aesthetes. Mallarmé translated the essay into French in 1888; Whistler himself published it in English in
1890, in *The Gentle Art of Making Enemies*. Struck by one of Whistler's witticisms, Oscar
Wilde once confessed that he wished *he* had uttered it himself. Whistler replied dryly, "You
will, Oscar, you will."

---

5. I. e., shake you out of your melancholy. The Aesthetes
supposedly cherished an idealized, platonic love of such
flowering "vegetable" entities as poppies and lilies; here
Gilbert applies the concept literally.

6. A fashionable thoroughfare in London. Wilde, whose
passion for lilies was well known, is said to have done
this.

from **Mr. Whistler's "Ten O'Clock"**

LADIES AND GENTLEMEN:

* * * Art is upon the Town!—to be chucked under the chin by the passing gallant—to be enticed within the gates of the householder—to be coaxed into company, as a proof of culture and refinement.

If familiarity can breed contempt, certainly Art—or what is currently taken for it—has been brought to its lowest stage of intimacy.

The people have been harassed with Art in every guise, and vexed with many methods as to its endurance. They have been told how they shall love Art, and live with it. Their homes have been invaded, their walls covered with paper, their very dress taken to task—until, roused at last, bewildered and filled with the doubts and discomforts of senseless suggestion, they resent such intrusion, and cast forth the false prophets, who have brought the very name of the beautiful into disrepute, and derision upon themselves.

Alas! ladies and gentlemen, Art has been maligned. She has naught in common with such practices. She is a goddess of dainty thought—reticent of habit, abjuring all obtrusiveness, purposing in no way to better others.

She is, withal, selfishly occupied with her own perfection only—having no desire to teach—seeking and finding the beautiful in all conditions and in all times, as did her high priest Rembrandt, when he saw picturesque grandeur and noble dignity in the Jews' quarter of Amsterdam, and lamented not that its inhabitants were not Greeks.[1]

As did Tintoret and Paul Veronese,[2] among the Venetians, while not halting to change the brocaded silks for the classic draperies of Athens.

As did, at the Court of Philip, Velasquez, whose Infantas, clad in inaesthetic hoops, are, as works of Art, of the same quality as the Elgin marbles.[3]

No reformers were these great men—no improvers of the way of others! Their productions alone were their occupation, and, filled with the poetry of their science, they required not to alter their surroundings—for, as the laws of their Art were revealed to them they saw, in the development of their work, that real beauty which, to them, was as much a matter of certainty and triumph as is to the astronomer the verification of the result, foreseen with the light given to him alone. In all this, their world was completely severed from that of their fellow-creatures with whom sentiment is mistaken for poetry; and for whom there is no perfect work that shall not be explained by the benefit conferred upon themselves.

Humanity takes the place of Art, and God's creations are excused by their usefulness. Beauty is confounded with virtue, and, before a work of Art, it is asked: "What good shall it do?"

Hence it is that nobility of action, in this life, is hopelessly linked with the merit of the work that portrays it; and thus the people have acquired the habit of looking, as who should say, not *at* a picture, but *through* it, at some human fact, that shall, or

---

1. Rembrandt (1606–1669) was an important influence on Whistler. The Dutch artist painted many contemporary subjects and even used the costume of his day when portraying classical subjects, as in *Aristotle Contemplating the Bust of Homer*.

2. Tintoretto and Paolo Veronese, Italian Renaissance painters.

3. Diego Rodrigo de Silva y Velasquez (1599–1660), painter at the court of Philip IV of Spain. The Infantas were daughters of the monarch; in their hooped skirts they seemed no less artistic to Whistler than classical Greek statuary.

shall not, from a social point of view, better their mental or moral state. So we have come to hear of the painting that elevates, and of the duty of the painter—of the picture that is full of thought, and of the panel that merely decorates.

A favourite faith, dear to those who teach, is that certain periods were especially artistic, and that nations, readily named, were notably lovers of Art.

So we are told that the Greeks were, as a people, worshippers of the beautiful, and that in the fifteenth century Art was engrained in the multitude.

That the great masters lived in common understanding with their patrons—that the early Italians were artists—all—and that the demand for the lovely thing produced it.

That we, of to-day, in gross contrast to this Arcadian[4] purity, call for the ungainly, and obtain the ugly. * * *

Listen! There never was an artistic period.

There never was an Art-loving nation.

In the beginning, man went forth each day—some to do battle, some to the chase; others, again, to dig and to delve in the field—all that they might gain and live, or lose and die. Until there was found among them one, differing from the rest, whose pursuits attracted him not, and so he stayed by the tents with the women, and traced strange devices with a burnt stick upon a gourd.

This man, who took no joy in the ways of his brethren—who cared not for conquest, and fretted in the field—this designer of quaint patterns—this deviser of the beautiful—who perceived in Nature about him curious curvings, as faces are seen in the fire—this dreamer apart, was the first artist.

And when, from the field and from afar, there came back the people, they took the gourd—and drank from out of it.

And presently there came to this man another—and, in time, others—of like nature, chosen by the Gods—and so they worked together; and soon they fashioned, from the moistened earth, forms resembling the gourd. And with the power of creation, the heirloom of the artist, presently they went beyond the slovenly suggestion of Nature, and the first vase was born, in beautiful proportion. * * *

And centuries passed in this using, and the world was flooded with all that was beautiful, until there arose a new class, who discovered the cheap, and foresaw fortune in the facture of the sham.

Then sprang into existence the tawdry, the common, the gewgaw.

The taste of the tradesman supplanted the science of the artist, and what was born of the million went back to them, and charmed them, for it was after their own heart; and the great and the small, the statesman and the slave, took to themselves the abomination that was tendered, and preferred it—and have lived with it ever since!

And the artist's occupation was gone, and the manufacturer and the huckster took his place.

And now the heroes filled from the jugs and drank from the bowls—with understanding—noting the glare of their new bravery, and taking pride in its worth.

And the people—this time—had much to say in the matter—and all were satisfied. And Birmingham and Manchester[5] arose in their might—and Art was relegated to the curiosity shop.

Nature contains the elements, in colour and form, of all pictures, as the keyboard contains the notes of all music.

4. Simple, rustic.   5. Large manufacturing towns.

But the artist is born to pick, and choose, and group with science, these elements, that the result may be beautiful—as the musician gathers his notes, and forms his chords, until he bring forth from chaos glorious harmony.

To say to the painter, that Nature is to be taken as she is, is to say to the player, that he may sit on the piano.

That Nature is always right, is an assertion, artistically, as untrue, as it is one whose truth is universally taken for granted. Nature is very rarely right, to such an extent even, that it might almost be said that Nature is usually wrong: that is to say, the condition of things that shall bring about the perfection of harmony worthy a picture is rare, and not common at all.

This would seem, to even the most intelligent, a doctrine almost blasphemous. So incorporated with our education has the supposed aphorism become, that its belief is held to be part of our moral being, and the words themselves have, in our ear, the ring of religion. Still, seldom does Nature succeed in producing a picture.

The sun blares, the wind blows from the east, the sky is bereft of cloud, and without, all is of iron. The windows of the Crystal Palace[6] are seen from all points of London. The holiday-maker rejoices in the glorious day, and the painter turns aside to shut his eyes.

How little this is understood, and how dutifully the casual in Nature is accepted as sublime, may be gathered from the unlimited admiration daily produced by a very foolish sunset.

The dignity of the snow-capped mountain is lost in distinctness, but the joy of the tourist is to recognise the traveller on the top. The desire to see, for the sake of seeing, is, with the mass, alone the one to be gratified, hence the delight in detail.

And when the evening mist clothes the riverside with poetry, as with a veil, and the poor buildings lose themselves in the dim sky, and the tall chimneys become campanili,[7] and the warehouses are palaces in the night, and the whole city hangs in the heavens, and fairy-land is before us—then the wayfarer hastens home; the working man and the cultured one, the wise man and the one of pleasure, cease to understand, as they have ceased to see, and Nature, who, for once, has sung in tune, sings her exquisite song to the artist alone, her son and her master—her son in that he loves her, her master in that he knows her.

To him her secrets are unfolded, to him her lessons have become gradually clear. He looks at her flower, not with the enlarging lens, that he may gather facts for the botanist, but with the light of the one who sees in her choice selection of brilliant tones and delicate tints, suggestions of future harmonies.

He does not confine himself to purposeless copying, without thought, each blade of grass, as commended by the inconsequent, but, in the long curve of the narrow leaf, corrected by the straight tall stem, he learns how grace is wedded to dignity, how strength enhances sweetness, that elegance shall be the result. * * *

Why this lifting of the brow in deprecation of the present—this pathos in reference to the past?

If Art be rare to-day, it was seldom heretofore.

It is false, this teaching of decay.

---

6. Built in Hyde Park, London, to house the Great Exhibition of 1851, the Crystal Palace was three times the size of St. Paul's Cathedral. Resembling a gigantic greenhouse, it was the world's first building of this size to be constructed of metal and glass, and was considered one of the wonders of the age. In 1855 it was re-erected in Sydenham, Southeast London.

7. Italian bell towers.

The master stands in no relation to the moment at which he occurs—a monument of isolation—hinting at sadness—having no part in the progress of his fellow men.

He is also no more the product of civilisation than is the scientific truth asserted dependent upon the wisdom of a period. The assertion itself requires the *man* to make it. The truth was from the beginning.

So Art is limited to the infinite, and beginning there cannot progress. * * *

False again, the fabled link between the grandeur of Art and the glories and virtues of the State, for Art feeds not upon nations, and peoples may be wiped from the face of the earth, but Art *is*.

It is indeed high time that we cast aside the weary weight of responsibility and co-partnership, and know that, in no way, do our virtues minister to its worth, in no way do our vices impede its triumph!

How irksome! how hopeless! how superhuman the self-imposed task of the nation! How sublimely vain the belief that it shall live nobly or art perish.

Let us reassure ourselves, at our own option is our virtue. Art we in no way affect.

A whimsical goddess, and a capricious, her strong sense of joy tolerates no dulness, and, live we never so spotlessly, still may she turn her back upon us.

As, from time immemorial, she has done upon the Swiss in their mountains.

What more worthy people! Whose every Alpine gap yawns with tradition, and is stocked with noble story; yet, the perverse and scornful one will none of it, and the sons of patriots are left with the clock that turns the mill, and the sudden cuckoo, with difficulty restrained in its box!

For this was Tell a hero! For this did Gessler die![8]

Art, the cruel jade,[9] cares not, and hardens her heart, and hies her off to the East, to find, among the opium-eaters of Nankin,[1] a favourite with whom she lingers fondly—caressing his blue porcelain, and painting his coy maidens, and marking his plates with her six marks of choice—indifferent in her companionship with him, to all save the virtue of his refinement!

He it is who calls her—he who holds her!

And again to the West, that her next lover may bring together the Gallery at Madrid, and show to the world how the Master towers above all;[2] and in their intimacy they revel, he and she, in this knowledge; and he knows the happiness untasted by other mortal.

She is proud of her comrade, and promises that in after-years, others shall pass that way, and understand.

So in all time does this superb one cast about for the man worthy her love—and Art seeks the Artist alone. * * *

Therefore have we cause to be merry!—and to cast away all care—resolved that all is well—as it ever was—and that it is not meet that we should be cried at, and urged to take measures!

Enough have we endured of dulness! Surely are we weary of weeping, and our tears have been cozened from us falsely, for they have called out woe! when there was no grief—and, alas! where all is fair!

---

8. William Tell was a legendary 14th-century Swiss hero whose defiance of Gessler, an Austrian bailiff, led to his well-known punishment: shooting an apple off his son's head. In revenge, Tell killed Gessler and led a revolt to liberate his country from Austrian control.
9. Disreputable woman.

1. The Chinese city of Nanjing.
2. Philip II of Spain created the Prado Gallery in Madrid; its collection was substantially enlarged by Philip IV. The Prado contains many works by "the Master" Velasquez, whose art greatly influenced Whistler.

We have then but to wait—until, with the mark of the Gods upon him—there come among us again the chosen—who shall continue what has gone before. Satisfied that, even were he never to appear, the story of the beautiful is already complete—hewn in the marbles of the Parthenon—and broidered, with the birds, upon the fan of Hokusai—at the foot of Fusiyama.[3]

1885   1890

"Michael Field"

Katharine Bradley
1846–1914

and

Edith Cooper
1862–1913

"I have found a new poet," announced Robert Browning to a hushed dinner party in 1885. He had actually found two poets, both women. "Michael Field" was the pseudonym of Katharine Bradley and her niece Edith Cooper; they were hailed as "the double-headed nightingale" by admirers. Their long collaboration produced twenty-seven poetic dramas on historical themes, and eight volumes of lyric poetry. Their work was praised by Meredith, Swinburne, and Wilde; but the general public was unaware that in lauding "Mr. Field," they were speaking of an aunt who esteemed William Michael Rossetti (Dante and Christina's brother) and a niece nicknamed "Field." Bradley had helped rear Cooper, the child of her invalid sister. In 1878 they moved to Bristol, where they both attended University College, living together from then on in a close emotional and sexual relationship. Commenting on the fabled intimacy of Robert and Elizabeth Barrett Browning, Bradley noted in her diary "*we are closer married.*" Having independent means, they spent their time reading, writing, and visiting galleries; they dressed and decorated their rooms in Aesthetic style, and their journals record their acute impressions of the many artists and writers they met. In 1907 both converted to Catholicism, apparently because of the death of their dog Whym Chow, a Dionysian presence who not only inspired a volume of love poems but also killed Kipling's pet rabbit during a visit.

"We have many things to say," they wrote to Browning, "that the world will not tolerate from a woman's lips. . . . We cannot be stifled in drawing-room conventionalities." Their first joint volume of poems, *Long Ago* (1889), dared to complete Sappho's fragments in modern lyrics that highlighted the lesbian nature of the Greek poems. In a poem they proclaimed they would remain "Poets and lovers evermore . . . Indifferent to heaven and hell." Despite the passionate paganism of their early career, they condemned what they saw as the depravity of Zola and Beardsley, and withdrew one of their poems from *The Yellow Book*. "From decadence, Good Lord deliver us!" they exclaimed in a diary entry in 1891. Their poetry is notable for its subtle music and technical improvisation, as well as their sympathetic rendering of the femme-fatale imagery common at the time. Exploring the nature of womanhood was both a personal mission and an artistic ideal: "We hold ourselves bound in life and in literature," Bradley wrote in her diary, "to reveal . . . the beauty of the high feminine standard of *the ought to be.*"

---

3. Katsushika Hokusai (1760–1849), Japanese artist; Fujiyama or Mount Fuji, the highest mountain in Japan, and a frequent subject in Hokusai's works.

La Gioconda[1]
Leonardo Da Vinci
THE LOUVRE

Historic, side-long, implicating eyes;
A smile of velvet's lustre on the cheek;
Calm lips the smile leads upward; hand that lies
Glowing and soft, the patience in its rest
5   Of cruelty that waits and doth not seek
For prey; a dusky forehead and a breast
Where twilight touches ripeness amorously:
Behind her, crystal rocks, a sea and skies
Of evanescent blue on cloud and creek;
10   Landscape that shines suppressive of its zest
For those vicissitudes by which men die.

                                                              1892

A Pen-Drawing of Leda[1]
Sodoma[2]
THE GRAND DUKE'S PALACE AT WEIMAR

'Tis Leda lovely, wild and free,
Drawing her gracious Swan down through the grass to see
     Certain round eggs without a speck:
One hand plunged in the reeds and one dinting the downy neck,
5   Although his hectoring bill
     Gapes toward her tresses,
She draws the fondled creature to her will.

     She joys to bend in the live light
Her glistening body toward her love, how much more bright!
10   Though on her breast the sunshine lies
And spreads its affluence on the wide curves of her waist and thighs,
     To her meek, smitten gaze
     Where her hand presses
The Swan's white neck sink Heaven's concentred rays.

                                                              1892

"A Girl"

A girl,
     Her soul a deep-wave pearl
Dim, lucent of all lovely mysteries;
     A face flowered for heart's ease,
5   A brow's grace soft as seas

---

1. Leonardo's painting (c. 1503), also known as the *Mona Lisa*, hangs in the Louvre in Paris. The authors would have known Walter Pater's famous description of it in *The Renaissance*. This and the following poem appeared in their collection *Sight and Song* (1892), which sought "to translate into verse what the lines and colours of certain chosen pictures sing in themselves."

1. In Greek myth Zeus took the form of a swan to have sex with Leda, a mortal; she subsequently gave birth to Helen of Troy. Compare this view of Leda to Yeats's poem *Leda and the Swan*, page 2337.
2. Nickname of the Sienese artist Giovanni Antonio Bazzi (1477–1549).

Seen through faint forest-trees:
A mouth, the lips apart,
Like aspen-leaflets trembling in the breeze
From her tempestuous heart.
10   Such: and our souls so knit,
I leave a page half-writ—
The work begun
Will be to heaven's conception done,
If she come to it.

1893

━━━ ⚹⬥⚹ ━━━

Ada Leverson
1862–1933

"You can't have got up, you must have sat up," said Oscar Wilde to his exquisitely dressed friend Ada Leverson when he was released from prison at an early hour. "How marvellous of you to know exactly the right hat to wear at seven o'clock in the morning to meet a friend who has been away!" Always perfectly attired, Leverson was a witty socialite whose genius for friendship and droll sense of humor put her at the center of *fin de siècle* literary life. Her friends wondered how someone so rich and beautiful could be indifferent to jewelry: "But it lasts so long," she said. Henry James was so struck by her remarks about his books that he called her the "incarnation" of the novelist's dream, "the Gentle Reader." Later she herself became a successful comic novelist, her best works being reissued as *The Little Ottleys* (1962). She wrote in bed, in a confusion of cigarettes, papers, and oranges. To escape parental control she married Ernest Leverson when she was only 19, he 31. She soon regretted it but arranged to carry on quiet romances while he gambled or visited his mistress. The Leversons were united, however, in their emotional and financial support of Wilde after his troubles began; they sheltered Wilde secretly between his trials.

It was Wilde who gave her the lasting nickname of "Sphinx" after she published a parody of his poem by that title in *Punch*. Leverson delighted in deflating Wilde's ego: when Wilde boasted that an Apache had become so devoted to him in Paris that he accompanied him everywhere with a knife in one hand, she replied, "I'm sure he had a fork in the other." She enjoyed exchanging wires with Wilde, claiming that she intended to edit *The Collected Telegrams of Oscar Wilde*. Her short story *Suggestion* was published in *The Yellow Book*, along with her portrait by Walter Sickert, in April, 1895, the month when Wilde was arrested. From its provocative opening line to its immorally moral ending, *Suggestion* skewers Victorian patriarchy and double standards, even as it spoofs the New Woman, Aesthetes, and Wildean affectation. A parody of decadent gender confusion that appeared in *Punch* later that month may well have been aimed at Ada Leverson:

Woman was woman, man was man,
When Adam delved and Eve span.
Now he can't dig and she won't spin
Unless 'tis tales all slang and sin!

Suggestion

If Lady Winthrop had not spoken of me as "that intolerable, effeminate boy," she might have had some chance of marrying my father. She was a middle-aged widow; prosaic, fond of domineering, and an alarmingly excellent housekeeper; the serious work of her life was paying visits; in her lighter moments she collected autographs. She was highly suitable and altogether insupportable; and this unfortunate remark about me was, as people say, the last straw. Some encouragement from father Lady Winthrop must, I think, have received; for she took to calling at odd hours, asking my sister Marjorie sudden abrupt questions, and being generally impossible. A tradition existed that her advice was of use to our father in his household, and when, last year, he married his daughter's school-friend, a beautiful girl of twenty, it surprised every one except Marjorie and myself.

The whole thing was done, in fact, by suggestion. I shall never forget that summer evening when father first realised, with regard to Laura Egerton, the possible. He was giving a little dinner of eighteen people. *Through a mistake of Marjorie's* (my idea) Lady Winthrop did not receive her invitation till the very last minute. Of course she accepted—we knew she would—but unknowing that it was a dinner party, she came without putting on evening-dress.

Nothing could be more trying to the average woman than such a *contretemps*; and Lady Winthrop was not one to rise, sublimely, and laughing, above the situation. I can see her now, in a plaid blouse and a vile temper, displaying herself, mentally and physically, to the utmost disadvantage, while Marjorie apologised the whole evening, in pale blue crèpe-de-chine; and Laura, in yellow, with mauve orchids, sat—an adorable contrast—on my father's other side, with a slightly conscious air that was perfectly fascinating. It is quite extraordinary what trifles have their little effect in these matters. I had sent Laura the orchids, anonymously; I could not help it if she chose to think they were from my father. Also, I had hinted of his secret affection for her, and lent her Verlaine.[1] I said I had found it in his study, turned down at her favourite page. Laura has, like myself, the artistic temperament; she is cultured, rather romantic, and in search of the *au-delà* [the transcendent]. My father has at times—never to me—rather charming manners; also he is still handsome, with that look of having suffered that comes from enjoying oneself too much. That evening his really sham melancholy and apparently hollow gaiety were delightful for a son to witness, and appealed evidently to her heart. Yes, strange as it may seem, while the world said that pretty Miss Egerton married old Carington for his money, she was really in love, or thought herself in love, with our father. Poor girl! She little knew what an irritating, ill-tempered, absent-minded person he is in private life; and at times I have pangs of remorse.

A fortnight after the wedding, father forgot he was married, and began again treating Laura with a sort of *distrait* [absent-minded] gallantry as Marjorie's friend, or else ignoring her altogether. When, from time to time, he remembers she is his wife, he scolds her about the housekeeping in a fitful, perfunctory way, for he does not know that Marjorie does it still. Laura bears the rebukes like an angel; indeed, rather than take the slightest practical trouble she would prefer to listen to the strongest language in my father's vocabulary.

But she is sensitive; and when father, speedily resuming his bachelor manners, recommenced his visits to an old friend who lives in one of the little houses opposite the Oratory,[2] she seemed quite vexed. Father is horribly careless, and Laura found a letter. They had a rather serious explanation, and for a little time after, Laura seemed depressed. She soon tried to rouse herself, and is at times cheerful enough with Mar-

---

1. French decadent poet (1844—1896) whose subtle musicality was much admired by English Aesthetes.
2. The Brompton Oratory, in West London, is a Roman Catholic church where Cardinal Newman and other leading clerics preached.

jorie and myself, but I fear she has had a disillusion. They never quarrel now, and I think we all three dislike father about equally, though Laura never owns it, and is gracefully attentive to him in a gentle, filial sort of way.

We are fond of going to parties—not father—and Laura is a very nice chaperone for Marjorie. They are both perfectly devoted to me. "Cecil knows everything," they are always saying, and they do nothing—not even choosing a hat—without asking my advice.

Since I left Eton I am supposed to be reading with a tutor,[3] but as a matter of fact I have plenty of leisure; and am very glad to be of use to the girls, of whom I'm, by the way, quite proud. They are rather a sweet contrast; Marjorie has the sort of fresh rosy prettiness you see in the park and on the river. She is tall, and slim as a punt-pole,[4] and if she were not very careful how she dresses, she would look like a drawing by Pilotelle in the *Lady's Pictorial*.[5] She is practical and lively, she rides and drives and dances; skates, and goes to some mysterious haunt called *The Stores*,[6] and is, in her own way, quite a modern English type.

Laura has that exotic beauty so much admired by Philistines; dreamy dark eyes, and a wonderful white complexion. She loves music and poetry and pictures and admiration in a lofty sort of way; she has a morbid fondness for mental gymnastics, and a dislike to physical exertion, and never takes any exercise except waving her hair. Sometimes she looks bored, and I have heard her sigh.

"Cissy," Marjorie said, coming one day into my study, "I want to speak to you about Laura."

"Do you have pangs of conscience too?" I asked, lighting a cigarette.

"Dear, we took a great responsibility. Poor girl! Oh, couldn't we make Papa more—"

"Impossible," I said; "no one has any influence with him. He can't bear even me, though if he had a shade of decency he would dash away an unbidden tear every time I look at him with my mother's blue eyes."

My poor mother was a great beauty, and I am supposed to be her living image.

"Laura has no object in life," said Marjorie. "I have, all girls have, I suppose. By the way, Cissy, I am quite sure Charlie Winthrop is serious."

"How sweet of him! I am so glad. I got father off my hands last season."

"Must I really marry him, Cissy? He bores me."

"What has that to do with it? Certainly you must. You are not a beauty, and I doubt your ever having a better chance."

Marjorie rose and looked at herself in the long pier-glass that stands opposite my writing-table. I could not resist the temptation to go and stand beside her.

"I am just the style that is admired now," said Marjorie, dispassionately.

"So am I," I said reflectively. "But *you* will soon be out of date."

Every one says I am strangely like my mother. Her face was of that pure and perfect oval one so seldom sees, with delicate features, rosebud mouth, and soft flaxen hair. A blondness without insipidity, for the dark-blue eyes are fringed with dark lashes, and from their languorous depths looks out a soft mockery. I have a curious ideal devotion to my mother; she died when I was quite young—only two months old—and I often spend hours thinking of her, as I gaze at myself in the mirror.

---

3. In preparation for attending Oxford or Cambridge.
4. A long, thin pole used to propel a punt, a flat-bottomed boat.
5. Georges Labadie Pilotell (1844–1918), French illustrator and caricaturist.

6. Large department stores, relatively new at the time. In her athleticism and up-to-date practicality, Marjorie is a version of the New Woman—as opposed to Laura's languid Aestheticism.

"Do come down from the clouds," said Marjorie impatiently, for I had sunk into a reverie. "I came to ask you to think of something to amuse Laura—to interest her."

"We ought to make it up to her in some way. Haven't you tried anything?"

"Only palmistry; and Mrs. Wilkinson prophesied her all that she detests, and depressed her dreadfully."

"What do you think she really needs most?" I asked.

Our eyes met.

"Really, Cissy, you're too disgraceful," said Marjorie. There was a pause.

"And so I'm to accept Charlie?"

"What man do you like better?" I asked.

"I don't know what you mean," said Marjorie, colouring.

"I thought Adrian Grant would have been more sympathetic to Laura than to you. I have just had a note from him, asking me to tea at his studio to-day." I threw it to her. "He says I'm to bring you both. Would that amuse Laura?"

"Oh," cried Marjorie, enchanted, "of course we'll go. I wonder what he thinks of me," she added wistfully.

"He didn't say. He is going to send Laura his verses, 'Hearts-ease and Heliotrope.'"[7]

She sighed. Then she said, "Father was complaining again to-day of your laziness."

"I, lazy! Why, I've been swinging the censer in Laura's boudoir because she wants to encourage the religious temperament, and I've designed your dress for the Clives' fancy ball."

"Where's the design?"

"In my head. You're not to wear white; Miss Clive must wear white."

"I wonder you don't marry her," said Marjorie, "you admire her so much."

"I never marry. Besides, I know she's pretty, but that furtive Slade-school[8] manner of hers gets on my nerves. You don't know how dreadfully I suffer from my nerves."

She lingered a little, asking me what I advised her to choose for a birthday present for herself—an American organ, a black poodle, or an *édition de luxe* of Browning. I advised the last, as being least noisy. Then I told her I felt sure that in spite of her admiration for Adrian, she was far too good natured to interfere with Laura's prospects. She said I was incorrigible, and left the room with a smile of resignation.

And I returned to my reading. On my last birthday—I was seventeen—my father—who has his gleams of dry humour—gave me *Robinson Crusoe!* I prefer Pierre Loti,[9] and intend to have an onyx-paved bath-room, with soft apricot-coloured light shimmering through the blue-lined green curtains in my chambers, as soon as I get Margery married, and Laura more—settled down.

I met Adrian Grant first at a luncheon party at the Clives. I seemed to amuse him; he came to see me, and became at once obviously enamoured of my step-mother. He is rather an impressionable impressionist, and a delightful creature, tall and graceful and beautiful, and altogether most interesting. Every one admits he's fascinating; he is very popular and very much disliked. He is by way of being a painter; he has a little money of his own—enough for his telegrams, but not enough for his buttonholes—and nothing could be more incongruous than the idea of his marrying. I

---

7. Hearts-ease is a pansy; heliotrope is a plant with fragrant purple flowers; the title is typical of 1890s preciousness.
8. The Slade School of Art in London, founded 1871, had become more fashionable than the Royal Academy,

whose teaching was regarded as dry and stuffy.
9. Pen name of French impressionist novelist Julien Viaud (1850–1923) who was drawn to exotic civilizations and landscapes.

have never seen Marjorie so much attracted. But she is a good loyal girl, and will accept Charlie Winthrop, who is a dear person, good-natured and ridiculously rich— just the sort of man for a brother-in-law. It will annoy my old enemy Lady Winthrop—he is her nephew, and she wants him to marry that little Miss Clive. Dorothy Clive has her failings, but she could not—to do her justice—be happy with Charlie Winthrop.

Adrian's gorgeous studio gives one the complex impression of being at once the calm retreat of a mediaeval saint and the luxurious abode of a modern Pagan. One feels that everything could be done there, everything from praying to flirting—everything except painting. The tea-party amused me, I was pretending to listen to a brown person who was talking absurd worn-out literary clichés—as that the New Humour is not funny, or that Bourget understood women,[1] when I overheard this fragment of conversation.

"But don't you like Society?" Adrian was saying.

"I get rather tired of it. People are so much alike. They all say the same things," said Laura.

"Of course they all say the same things to *you*," murmured Adrian, as he affected to point out a rather curious old silver crucifix.

"That," said Laura, "is one of the things they say."

About three weeks later I found myself dining alone with Adrian Grant, at one of the two restaurants in London. (The cooking is better at the other, this one is the more becoming.) I had lilies-of-the-valley in my button-hole, Adrian was wearing a red carnation. Several people glanced at us. Of course he is very well known in Society. Also, I was looking rather nice, and I could not help hoping, while Adrian gazed rather absently over my head, that the shaded candles were staining to a richer rose the waking wonder of my face.

Adrian was charming of course, but he seemed worried and a little preoccupied, and drank a good deal of champagne.

Towards the end of dinner, he said—almost abruptly for him—"Carington."

"Cecil," I interrupted. He smiled.

"Cissy . . . it seems an odd thing to say to you, but though you are so young, I think you know everything. I am sure you know everything. You know about me. I am in love. I am quite miserable. What on earth am I to do!" He drank more champagne. "Tell me," he said, "what to do." For a few minutes, while we listened to that interminable hackneyed *Intermezzo*, I reflected; asking myself by what strange phases I had risen to the extraordinary position of giving advice to Adrian on such a subject?

Laura was not happy with our father. From a selfish motive, Marjorie and I had practically arranged that monstrous marriage. That very day he had been disagreeable, asking me with a clumsy sarcasm to raise his allowance, so that he could afford my favourite cigarettes. If Adrian were free, Marjorie might refuse Charlie Winthrop. I don't want her to refuse him. Adrian has treated me as a friend. I like him—I like him enormously. I am quite devoted to him. And how can I rid myself of the feeling of responsibility, the sense that I owe some compensation to poor beautiful Laura?

We spoke of various matters. Just before we left the table, I said, with what seemed, but was not, irrelevance, "Dear Adrian, Mrs. Carington——"

---

1. The "New Humor" is coined on the model of other 1890s trends, such as the New Woman, the New Journalism, and the New Drama; the French author Paul Bourget (1852–1935) wrote psychological novels.

"Go on, Cissy."

"She is one of those who must be appealed to, at first, by her imagination. She married our father because she thought he was lonely and misunderstood."

"*I* am lonely and misunderstood," said Adrian, his eyes flashing with delight.

"Ah, not twice! She doesn't like that now."

I finished my coffee slowly, and then I said,

"Go to the Clives' fancy-ball as Tristan."[2]

Adrian pressed my hand. . . .

At the door of the restaurant we parted, and I drove home through the cool April night, wondering, wondering. Suddenly I thought of my mother—my beautiful sainted mother, who would have loved me, I am convinced, had she lived, with an extraordinary devotion. What would she have said to all this? What would she have thought? I know not why, but a mad reaction seized me. I felt recklessly conscientious. My father! After all, he was my father. I was possessed by passionate scruples. If I went back now to Adrian—if I went back and implored him, supplicated him never to see Laura again!

I felt I could persuade him. I have sufficient personal magnetism to do that, if I make up my mind. After one glance in the looking-glass, I put up my stick and stopped the hansom. I had taken a resolution. I told the man to drive to Adrian's rooms.

He turned round with a sharp jerk. In another second a brougham[3] passed us—a swift little brougham that I knew. It slackened—it stopped—we passed it—I saw my father. He was getting out at one of the little houses opposite the Brompton Oratory.

"Turn round again," I shouted to the cabman. And he drove me straight home.

1895

+ ⊢≡✦≡⊣ +

Lord Alfred Douglas
1870–1945

Lord Alfred Douglas embodied the new sexual freedom of the early 1890s, both in his life and in his polished verses on erotic themes. He was the son of the pugnacious Marquess of Queensberry, who had established the rules of boxing, but who violated almost every social code in his public antagonism toward his son. In 1891, while Douglas was still an undergraduate at Oxford, Lionel Johnson introduced him to Oscar Wilde, who encouraged both his affections and his writing. Their tempestuous relationship lasted until Wilde's death in 1900, despite Queensberry's constant efforts to disgrace them both. During Wilde's trials, provoked largely by the desire of father and son to injure each other, Douglas stayed safely in France, at Wilde's request. Their reunion after Wilde's imprisonment was marked by mutual recrimination; Wilde addressed to Douglas the bitter accusations detailed in *De Profundis,* and Douglas contended that he alone among Wilde's friends had remained true. In 1902 Douglas surprised everyone by secretly marrying the poet Olive Custance, whom he had met the year before. The marriage ended in 1913, by which time Douglas had converted to Catholicism and renounced his earlier homosexual activity. In his later life Douglas wrote much about his relationship with Wilde, including *Oscar Wilde and Myself* (1914) and *Oscar Wilde: A Summing Up* (1940). Like his father, he took pleasure in attacking the integrity of other people, and in 1923–1924 spent six months in prison for criminally libeling Winston Churchill.

---

2. A fancy dress ball is a costume ball; Tristan was a legendary knight in love with Isolde, his king's wife.

3. A one-horse closed carriage.

Douglas's early career coincided with the period of sexual openness and homosexual activism that occurred between 1885 and 1895. The term "homosexuality" was invented in 1869, and entered English just as Parliament criminalized all homosexual activity in 1885; medical theories of homosexual "degeneration" soon followed. Yet this climate also inspired resistance among authors who lauded the spiritual and emotional rewards of same-sex relationships. Douglas, by contrast, explored the dangerous pleasures of all kinds of sexuality: he translated Wilde's *Salomé* (1894) from French to English, and his own *Impression de Nuit: London* combines the aesthetic preference for urban artifice with the decadent penchant for monstrously appetitive female bodies. He also made two contributions—*In Praise of Shame* and *Two Loves*—to *The Chameleon* (1894), an Oxford magazine with a distinctly homoerotic slant. The prosecution read both poems at Wilde's second trial in an effort to make Wilde appear guilty by association. Already outraged by the exposure of male prostitution in the Cleveland Street Scandal of 1889, the jury and the public found confirmation in Douglas's poetry that a new threat to the nation had arisen, the "deviant" or "invert."

Two Loves

I dreamed I stood upon a little hill,
And at my feet there lay a ground that seemed
Like a waste garden, flowering at its will
With buds and blossoms. There were pools that dreamed
5   Black and unruffled; there were white lilies
A few, and crocuses, and violets,
Purple or pale, snake-like fritillaries[1]
Scarce seen for the rank grass, and through green nets
Blue eyes of shy pervenche[2] winked in the sun.
10   And there were curious flowers, before unknown,
Flowers that were stained with moonlight, or with shades
Of Nature's wilful moods; and here a one
That had drunk in the transitory tone
Of one brief moment in a sunset; blades
15   Of grass that in an hundred springs had been
Slowly but exquisitely nurtured by the stars,
And watered with the scented dew long cupped
In lilies, that for rays of sun had seen
Only God's glory, for never a sunrise mars
20   The luminous air of Heaven. Beyond, abrupt,
A grey stone wall, o'ergrown with velvet moss,
Uprose; and gazing I stood long, all mazed
To see a place so strange, so sweet, so fair.
And as I stood and marvelled, lo! across
25   The garden came a youth; one hand he raised
To shield him from the sun, his wind-tossed hair
Was twined with flowers, and in his hand he bore
A purple bunch of bursting grapes, his eyes
Were clear as crystal, naked all was he,
30   White as the snow on pathless mountains frore,°   frozen
Red were his lips as red wine-spilth that dyes
A marble floor, his brow chalcedony.°   quartz

---

1. A flower similar to the lily.   2. Periwinkle, a small blue flower.

And he came near me, with his lips uncurled
And kind, and caught my hand and kissed my mouth,
35   And gave me grapes to eat, and said, "Sweet friend,
Come, I will show thee shadows of the world
And images of life. See from the South
Comes the pale pageant that hath never an end."
And lo! within the garden of my dream
40   I saw two walking on a shining plain
Of golden light. The one did joyous seem
And fair and blooming, and a sweet refrain
Came from his lips; he sang of pretty maids
And joyous love of comely girl and boy;
45   His eyes were bright, and 'mid the dancing blades
Of golden grass his feet did trip for joy;
And in his hands he held an ivory lute
With strings of gold that were as maidens' hair,
And sang with voice as tuneful as a flute,
50   And round his neck three chains of roses were.
But he that was his comrade walked aside;
He was full sad and sweet, and his large eyes
Were strange with wondrous brightness, staring wide
With gazing; and he sighed with many sighs
55   That moved me, and his cheeks were wan and white
Like pallid lilies, and his lips were red
Like poppies, and his hands he clenchèd tight
And yet again unclenchèd, and his head
Was wreathed with moon-flowers[3] pale as lips of death.
60   A purple robe he wore, o'erwrought in gold
With the device of a great snake, whose breath
Was like curved flame: which when I did behold
I fell a-weeping, and I cried, "Sweet youth,
Tell me why, sad and sighing, thou dost rove
65   These pleasant realms? I pray thee, speak me sooth,
What is thy name?" He said, "My name is Love."
Then straight the first did turn himself to me
And cried: "He lieth, for his name is Shame,
But I am Love, and I was wont to be
70   Alone in this fair garden, till he came
Unasked by night; I am true Love, I fill
The hearts of boy and girl with mutual flame."
Then sighing, said the other: "Have thy will,
I am the love that dare not speak its name."

1894

Impression de Nuit[1]

London

See what a mass of gems the city wears
Upon her broad live bosom! row on row

---

3. A fragrant morning glory.   1. Impression of the night.

Rubies and emeralds and amethysts glow.
See! that huge circle like a necklace, stares
5   With thousands of bold eyes to heaven, and dares
The golden stars to dim the lamps below,
And in the mirror of the mire I know
The moon has left her image unawares.

That's the great town at night: I see her breasts,
10   Pricked out with lamps they stand like huge black towers.
I think they move! I hear her panting breath.
And that's her head where the tiara rests.
And in her brain, through lanes as dark as death,
Men creep like thoughts . . . The lamps are like pale flowers.

1894

＊━ ✠ ━＊

Olive Custance
(Lady Alfred Douglas)
1874–1944

In April 1895, *Punch* published a satiric poem by an "Angry Old Buffer" concerned about the masculine New Woman and the effeminate Decadent:

> . . . a new fear my bosom vexes;
> To-morrow there may be *no* sexes!
> Unless, as end to all pother,
> Each one in fact becomes the other.

Olive Custance contributed notably to the era's uncertainty about gender roles and the nature of romantic love. Coming from a well-to-do upper-class background, she fell in love at sixteen with the decadent poet John Gray, who was Oscar Wilde's lover at the time. Nothing came of this infatuation but poetry; by the age of twenty she was known in fashionable society as a beautiful young poet, friend to Aubrey Beardsley and contributor to the daring *Yellow Book* magazine. She called her first book *Opals* (1897), after the semi-precious stones that are said to bring the wearer bad luck; she liked to be called "Opal" herself, and sometimes "Wild Olive." Her poetry, like the long letters she wrote to friends, is remarkable for its intensity and emotional candor.

In 1901 she received a passionate fan letter from Natalie Clifford Barney, an American poet and heiress living in Paris. Custance replied with a daring poem:

> For I would dance to make you smile, and sing
> Of those who with some sweet mad sin have played,
> And how Love walks with delicate feet afraid
> 'Twixt maid and maid.

During their brief, stormy relationship, evoked in the poem *The White Witch*, Barney introduced Custance to the lesbian literary scene in Paris. By the time they traveled to Venice together in 1902, however, Custance was already in love with Wilde's friend Lord Alfred Douglas, to whom *she* had sent a fan letter in 1901. His imagined resemblance to a Roman statue inspired several poems, including the decadent classic, *Statues*, which revises the gender terms of the Pygmalion myth. Jilting an earl to whom she had just become engaged, Custance secretly married Douglas in March 1902. By the time the marriage ended in 1913, partially due to

Douglas's conversion to Catholicism, Custance had stopped writing. After a reconciliation in 1932, they lived apart but saw each other almost every day until her death. Douglas wrote in his autobiography that "the very thing she loved in me was that which I was always trying to suppress and keep under: I mean the feminine part."

The Masquerade[1]

> Masked dancers in the Dance of life
> We move sedately . . . wearily together,
> Afraid to show a sign of inward strife,
> We hold our souls in tether.
>
> 5   We dance with proud and smiling lips,
> With frank appealing eyes, with shy hands clinging.
> We sing, and few will question if there slips
> A sob into our singing.
>
> Each has a certain step to learn;
> 10   Our prisoned feet move staidly in set paces,
> And to and fro we pass, since life is stern,
> Patiently, with masked faces.
>
> Yet some there are who will not dance,
> They sit apart most sorrowful and splendid,
> 15   But all the rest trip on as in a trance,
> Until the Dance is ended.

1902

Statues

> I have loved statues . . . spangled dawns have seen
> Me bowed before their beauty . . . when the green
> And silver world of Spring wears radiantly
> The morning rainbows of an opal sky . . .
> 5   And I have chanted curious madrigals[1]
> To charm their coldness, twined for coronals[2]
> Blossoming branches, thinking thus to change
> Their still contempt for mortal love, their bright
> Proud scorn to something delicate and strange,
> 10   More sweet, more marvellous, than mere delight!
>
> I have loved statues—passionately prone
> My body worshipped the white form of stone!
> And like a flower that lifts its chalice up
> Towards the light—my soul became a cup
> 15   That over-brimming with enchanted wine
> Of ecstasy—was raised to the divine
> Indifferent lips of some young silent God
> Standing aloof from all our tears and strife,

1. Cf. Wilde's *The Harlot's House*, page 2069.
1. Love poems, often sung by several unaccompanied   voices.   2. Wreathlike crowns.

Tranced in the paradise of dreams, he trod
20   In the untroubled summer of his life!

I have loved statues . . . and at night the cold
Mysterious moon behind a mask of gold—
Or veiled in silver veils—has seen my pride
Utterly broken—seen the dream denied
25   For which I pleaded—heedless that for me
The miracle of joy could never be . . .
As in old legends beautiful and strange,
When bright gods loved fair mortals born to die,
And the frail daughters of despair and change
30   Become the brides of immortality?
c. 1902   1905

The White Witch

Her body is a dancing joy, a delicate delight,
Her hair a silver glamour in a net of golden light.

Her face is like the faces that a dreamer sometimes meets,
A face that Leonardo would have followed through the streets.

5   Her eyelids are like clouds that spread white wings across blue skies,
Like shadows in still water are the sorrows in her eyes.

How flower-like are the smiling lips so many have desired,
Curled lips that love's long kisses have left a little tired.

c. 1901   1902

Tom Phillips. Illustration to Canto 10 of Dante's *Inferno*, 1983.

The Twentieth Century

BURYING VICTORIA

Writing in 1928, Virginia Woolf described the cultural atmosphere of the Victorian era in the following way:

> Damp now began to make its way into every house. . . . The damp struck within. Men felt the chill in their hearts; the damp in their minds. . . . The life of the average woman was a succession of childbirths. She married at nineteen and had fifteen or eighteen children by the time she was thirty; for twins abounded. Thus the British Empire came into existence; and thus—for there is no stopping damp; it gets into inkpots as it gets into the wood-work—sentences swelled, adjectives multiplied, lyrics became epics, and little trifles that had been essays a column long were now encyclopedias in ten or twenty volumes.

Woolf of course exaggerates here for her own effect; yet this passage does capture nicely the stereotypical view of the Victorians that flourished during the modern period—and helped make it possible. Ezra Pound, for instance, called the later nineteenth century "a rather blurry, messy sort of period, a rather sentimentalistic, mannerish sort of period." Whether accurate or not, polemical descriptions like these served the rhetorical purposes of writers at the start of the new century as they attempted to stake out their terrain and to forge a literature and a perspective of their own.

The opening decade of the new century was a time of transition. Woolf later suggested, her tongue perhaps in her cheek, that as a result of a Post-Impressionist exhibition of paintings in London, "on or about December, 1910, human character changed." Almost no one, however, seems to have maintained that anything changed very decisively on the morning of 1 January 1900. Queen Victoria, at that time on the throne for nearly sixty-five years and in mourning for Prince Albert for almost forty, lived and ruled on into the following year; the subsequent reign of Edward VII (1901–1910) differed only slightly from that of his mother in many respects, the entire nation mourning the loss of their queen as she had the loss of her husband. But Woolf, in a 1924 essay, saw a gulf between herself and the Edwardians: Edwardian novelists, she writes, "established conventions which do their business; and that business is not our business." Edward VII himself, in fact, was clearly not a Victorian. He had a reputation as a playboy and implicitly rebelled against the conventions that his mother had upheld. During his reign, the mannered decadence of the 1890s modulated into a revived social realism seen in ambitious novels like Joseph Conrad's *Nostromo* and H. G. Wells's darkly comic masterpiece *Tono-Bungay*, while poets like Yeats and Hardy produced major poems probing the relations of self, society, and history. Writers in general considered themselves to be voices of a nation taking stock of its place in the world in a new century. They saw their times as marked by accelerating social and technological change and by the burden of a worldwide empire, which achieved its greatest extent in the years between 1900 and 1914—encompassing as much as a quarter of the world's population and dominating world trade through a global network of ports.

This period of consolidation and reflection abruptly came to an end four years into the reign of George V, with the start of World War I in August 1914; the relatively tranquil prewar years of George's early reign were quickly memorialized, and nostalgized, in the wake of the war's disruption to the traditionally English way of life. This first Georgian period was abruptly elevated into a cultural "golden age" by the British public and British publishers, a process that was typified by the pastoral poetry gathered by Edward Marsh in his hugely popular series of five anthologies called *Georgian Poetry*, the first of which was published in 1912. As a consequence of Marsh's skill as a tastemaker, this brief period before the war is frequently known as the Georgian period in British literature, though George V himself remained on the throne until 1936, when the distant rumble of World War II was to be heard by those with ears to hear.

The quarter century from 1914 until the start of the war in 1939 is now conventionally known as the modernist period. To be modern was, in one respect, to rebel openly and loudly against one's philosophical and artistic inheritance, in much the same way that the Romantic writers of the late eighteenth and early nineteenth centuries had sought to distinguish themselves from their Augustan forebears. This gesture—the way in which a new artistic movement seeks to define itself through caricature of the movement(s) that gave it birth—is a recurrent feature in literary history, but it took on a particular urgency and energy among the modernists, who advanced the view summarized in Pound's bold slogan, "Make It New." A great modernist monument to this anti-Victorian sentiment was Lytton Strachey's elegantly ironic *Eminent Victorians* (1918), whose probing biographical portraits punctured a series of Victorian pieties. Much of the playwright Bernard Shaw's writing is animated by anti-Victorian animus as well, taking the theatrical wit of Oscar Wilde and turning it against specific targets. Exaggerated though it was, the ritualized slaughter performed by modernists like Woolf, Strachey, and Shaw seems to have achieved a clearing of the literary and artistic terrain that formed a necessary prelude to further innovation. The modernists' "Victorians" were oversimplified, sometimes straw figures, but the battle that was waged against them was real indeed, and the principles of modernism were forged and refined in the process.

THE FOUNDATIONS OF MODERN SKEPTICISM

The best Victorian writers had not been afraid to ask difficult, unsettling questions. Tennyson's restless skepticism in *In Memoriam*, for example, exemplifies the spirit of Victorian inquiry. But the conclusion of that poem foresees an ongoing progress toward future perfection, guided by "One God, one law, one element, / And one far-off divine event, / To which the whole creation moves." Tennyson himself doubted that such unities could be embodied in the present; twentieth-century writers found increasing fragmentation around them and became more and more suspicious of narratives of historical progress and of social unity. In 1832 Tennyson made a representative man of Ulysses—the wanderer who, though his journey be long and convoluted, ultimately finds his way back to Ithaca, his faithful wife waiting. In Tennyson's poem, however, Ulysses decides to leave once again:

> It little profits that an idle king,
> By this still hearth, among these barren crags,
> Match'd with an aged wife, I mete and dole

> Unequal laws to a savage race,
> That hoard, and sleep, and feed, and know not me.

Leopold Bloom, the modern Odysseus in Joyce's novel *Ulysses* (1922), experiences a heightened version of Ulysses' dilemma: his wife has not remained faithful to begin with, and he has nowhere else but home to go to at the novel's end. In the modern period the quest for certainty associated with the Victorian exploration of values has vanished; modern explorations are undertaken with absolutely no confidence as to the results that will be discovered, still less that a public exists who could understand the writers' discoveries. For that reason Thomas Hardy's ruthless skepticism now seems quintessentially modern. This new attitude is quite clear in Ford Madox Ford's *The Good Soldier* (1915), the first installment of which was published in the inaugural issue of Wyndham Lewis's violently modern magazine *Blast*. John Dowell, the narrator/protagonist of Ford's novel, worries for 250 pages about his sense that the "givens" of civil society seem to have been knocked out from under him, and that he has been left to create values and meaning on his own. Struggling to extract the moral of the story he tells us—the story of his wife's long-standing affair with his best friend, and their consequent deaths—Dowell can only conclude: "I don't know. And there is nothing to guide us. And if everything is so nebulous about a matter so elementary as the morals of sex, what is there to guide us in the more subtle morality of all other personal contacts, associations, and activities? Or are we meant to act on impulse alone? It is all a darkness." In Conrad's *Heart of Darkness*, the narrator Charlie Marlow suffers from a similar moral vertigo. When, at the novella's close, he resolves to perform an action he finds deeply repugnant—to tell a lie—he worries that his willful violation of the moral order will provoke an immediate act of divine retribution. None, however, is forthcoming: "It seemed to me that the house would collapse before I could escape, that the heavens would fall upon my head. But nothing happened. The heavens do not fall for such a trifle." In works like these, a voyage is undertaken into a vast, unknown, dark expanse. Those few who come out alive have seen too much ever to be the same.

Similar perceptions underlie modern humor. The Theater of the Absurd that flourished in the 1950s and 1960s, in the work of playwrights like Samuel Beckett and Harold Pinter, had roots in Wilde and Shaw and their comic explorations of the arbitrary conventionality of long-held social values. Throughout the twentieth century, writers devoted themselves to unfolding many varieties of irony—from the severe ironies of Conrad and Yeats to the more tender ironies of Woolf and Auden, to the farcical absurdities of Tom Stoppard and Joe Orton. Joyce described his mixture of high and low comedy as "jocoserious"; asked the meaning of his dense book *Finnegans Wake*, he replied, "It's meant to make you laugh."

Whether seen in comic or tragic light, the sense of a loss of moorings was pervasive. Following the rapid social and intellectual changes of the previous century, the early twentieth century suffered its share of further concussions tending to heighten modern uncertainty. It was even becoming harder to understand the grounds of uncertainty itself. The critiques of Marx and Darwin had derived new messages from bodies of evidence available in principle to all literate citizens; the most important paradigm shifts of the early twentieth century, on the other hand, occurred in the fields of philosophy, psychology, and physics, and often rested on evidence invisible to the average citizen. The German philosopher Friedrich Nietzsche (1844–1900) was, as his dates suggest, wholly a nineteenth-century man, yet his ideas had their most profound impact in the twentieth century. Nietzsche described his lifelong philosophical project as "the revaluation of all values"; in his 1882 treatise *The Joyful Science,* he went so far as to assert that "God is dead." This deliberately provocative statement came as the culmination of a long and complicated argument, and did not mean simply that Nietzsche was an atheist (though he was). Nietzsche was suggesting that traditional religion had been discredited by advances in the natural and physical sciences, and as transcendent standards of truth disappeared, so logically must all moral and ethical systems depending on some faith for their force. It was from this base that Nietzsche created the idea of the *Übermensch,* the "superman" who because of his intellectual and moral superiority to others must not be bound by social conventions. Conrad's tragic figure Kurtz and Shaw's comic antihero Undershaft represent two very different takes on this idea, building on Nietzsche's interest in showing how all values are "constructed" rather than given—at some level arbitrary, all truths being merely opinions or superstitions.

The new psychology, whose earliest stirrings are to be found in the last decades of the nineteenth century, came of age at the turn of the twentieth. Sigmund Freud's *The Interpretation of Dreams* (1900) and *Psychopathology of Everyday Life* (1901) together illustrate in an especially vivid way his evolving theories about the influence of the unconscious mind, and past (especially childhood) experience, on our daily lives. The whole of Freud's work was translated into English by James Strachey (Lytton's brother), and was published in conjunction with the Hogarth Press, owned and run by Leonard and Virginia Woolf; for this reason, among others, the Freudian revolution was felt early, and strongly, among the London intelligentsia. The new psychology in general, and the theories of Freud in particular, were frequently distorted and misunderstood by the larger public, over whom they exercised a real fascination; among the artistic community Freud provoked a wide range of response, from the enthusiastic adoption of his theories by the Surrealists (a movement founded in Paris in 1924 by André Breton) to nervous rejection by writers like Joyce. This response is complicated, in part, by the fact that Freud himself took an interest in artistic and creative processes, and presumed to explain to writers the psychopathology at the heart of their own genius; as the Freudian literary critic Lionel Trilling succinctly put it, "the poet is a poet by reason of his sickness as well as by reason of his power." As Freud's supporter W. H. Auden wrote in his elegy *In Memory of Sigmund Freud* (1939): "If often he was wrong and at times absurd, / To us he is no more a person / Now but a whole climate of opinion / Under whom we conduct our different lives."

A further intellectual shock wave was the revolution in physics that was spearheaded by Albert Einstein's *Special Theory of Relativity* (1905). In both this theory (dealing with motion) and later in the General Theory of Relativity (dealing with gravity), Einstein shook the traditional understanding of the universe and our relationship to it; the certainty and predictability of the Newtonian description of the universe had been undone. The "uncertainty" of Einstein's universe was seemingly reinforced by developments in quantum physics, such as the work of Niels Bohr (who won the Nobel Prize in physics in 1922) and Werner Heisenberg, author of the famous "Uncertainty Principle" and the principle of complementarity, which together assert that the movement of subatomic particles can only be predicted by probability and not measured, as the very act of measurement alters their behavior. Ironically enough, the true import of these ideas is not, as the truism has it, that "everything is relative"—in fact, Einstein says almost the exact opposite. In Einstein's vision of the world, *nothing* is relative: everything is absolute, and absolutely fixed—except for us, fallible and limited observers, who have no secure standpoint from which "to see the thing as in itself it really is," to quote Matthew Arnold's 1867 formulation of the critic's goal. The only way to experience the truth, it would seem, would be to find what T. S. Eliot called "the still point of the turning world," an "unmoved mover" outside the flux and change of our day-to-day world. Einstein himself never really rejected the idea of transcendent truth; he once said to an interviewer that to him, the idea of our universe without a Creator was inconceivable. In this case, however, the popular fiction has been more influential than the facts, and the work of Einstein, Heisenberg, and Bohr has been used to support the widespread sense that, as Sean O'Casey's character Captain Jack Boyle puts it in *Juno and the Paycock* (1924), "the whole worl's in a state o' chassis!"

The philosophical and moral upheavals of these years were given added force by the profound shock of World War I—"The Great War," as it came to be known. The British entered the conflict against Germany partly in order to preserve their influence in Europe and their dominance around the globe, and partly out of altruistic notions of gallantry and fair play—to aid their weaker allies against German aggression. The conflict was supposed to take a few weeks; it lasted four grueling years and cost hundreds of thousands of British lives. Notions of British invincibility, honor, even of the viability of civilization all weakened over the years of vicious trench warfare in France. The progress of technology, which had raised Victorian standards of living, now led to a mechanization of warfare that produced horrific numbers of deaths—as many as a million soldiers died in the single protracted battle of the Somme in 1916. As poets discovered as they served in the trenches, and as the people back home came to learn, modernity had arrived with a vengeance.

REVOLUTIONS OF STYLE

The end of the war was accompanied by a sense of physical and moral exhaustion. To be modern has been defined as a persistent sense of having arrived on the stage of history after history has finished. The critic Perry Meisel, for instance, describes modernism as "a structure of compensation, a way of adjusting to the paradox of belatedness." Behind Ezra Pound's struggle to reinvent poetry lay a nagging suspicion that there was nothing new left to make or say, and Pound claimed that the very slogan "Make It New" was taken off the bathtub of an ancient Chinese emperor. As T. S. Eliot explains in his essay *Tradition and the Practice of Poetry*, "The perpetual task of poetry is to *make all things new*. Not necessarily to make new things. . . . It is always partly a revolution, or a reaction, from the work of the previous generation."

That revolution was carried out both on the level of subject matter and often on the level of style as well. Some important early twentieth-century fiction writers, like John Galsworthy, Arnold Bennett, H. G. Wells, and George Moore, felt no real need to depart from inherited narrative models, and hewed more or less to a realist or naturalist line, carrying on from the French naturalists like Emile Zola and the Norwegian dramatist Henrik Ibsen. But for those writers we now call modernist, these conventions came to seem too limiting and lifeless. The modern writer was faced with an enormous, Nietzschean task: to create new and appropriate values for modern culture, and a style appropriate to those values. As a consequence, there is often a probing, nervous quality in the modernist explorations of ultimate questions. This quality can be seen at the very start of the century in Conrad's *Heart of Darkness*, a novel about psychological depth and social disintegration that simultaneously implicates its readers in the moral ambiguities of its events. These ambiguities, moreover, are

Soldiers of the 9th Cameronians division prepare to go "over the top" during a daylight raid near Arras, France, 24 March 1917. During such an offensive, troops would make their way quickly across the contested territory between the opposing armies' trenches—the area known as No Man's Land—and attempt to take control of an enemy trench in order to conduct bombing raids and gain whatever intelligence might be found in the abandoned foxholes. The pace of this warfare—where a week's progress might be measured in yards, rather than miles—was, according to troops on both sides, the most salient feature of trench warfare. The human costs included diseases caused by standing water (like infamous "trench foot") and emotional disorders caused by the stress of waiting and constant shelling ("shell shock").

reflected in the very presentation of the narrative itself. In the modern novel, we are no longer allowed to watch from a safe distance while our protagonists mature and change through their trials; instead, we are made to undergo those trials ourselves, through the machinations of the narrative. This technique had already been employed in the nineteenth century, as for instance in the dramatic monologues of Robert Browning; but this narrative of process becomes pervasive in modernist texts, where the uncertainties of the form, the waverings and unpredictability of the narrative, mirror similar qualities in the mind of the narrator or protagonist. Often the reader is drawn into the story's crisis by a heightened use of the technique of plunging the narrative suddenly *in medias res*: "There was no hope for him this time: it was the third stroke" (Joyce, *The Sisters*); "A sudden blow:" (Yeats, *Leda and the Swan*); "'Yes, of course, if it's fine tomorrow,' said Mrs. Ramsay" (Woolf, *To the Lighthouse*). The customary preliminary information—the sort of dossier about the characters that we expect—isn't given; the reader is put in the position of a detective who has to sort all this information out unaided. This narrative decontextualization reaches its culmination in the theater of Beckett and Pinter, who typically withhold any and all background information about characters. "Confusion," Samuel Beckett told an inter-viewer in 1956, "is all around us and our only chance now is to let it in. The only chance of renovation is to open our eyes and see the mess. It is not a mess you can make sense of."

Early in the century, a number of poets began to dispense with the frames of ref-erence provided by conventional poetic forms. The first real Anglo-American poetic movement of the century was Imagism, a reaction against the expansive wordiness of Victorian poetry like Tennyson's *Idylls of the King* or Browning's *The Ring and the Book*. Imagists like Pound and H. D. wrote short, spare poems embodying a revelato-ry image or moment. The most memorable Imagist poems have the concentrated impact of a haiku. But the form leaves little scope for narrative development; that path seems to have been opened by a rediscovery of the seventeenth-century meta-physical poets, notably by T. S. Eliot. The techniques of metaphysical poets like John Donne suggested to Eliot a means for expanding the technical repertory of Imagist poetry, which he used to good effect in poems like *The Love Song of J. Alfred Prufrock*, which opens with a thoroughly modernized metaphysical conceit: "Let us go then, you and I, / when the evening is spread out against the sky / Like a patient etherized upon a table."

One strategy for making literature new was to make it difficult; this notion was, in part, a response to the huge proliferation of popular entertainments during the ear-ly twentieth century, a proliferation that both disturbed and intrigued many artists, writers, and cultural critics. In such a context, "difficult" literature (such as the densely allusive poetry of Eliot, or the multilayered prose of Joyce) was seen to be of greater artistic merit than the products of an easily consumable mass culture—even as both Eliot and Joyce drew on popular culture and diction as they reshaped the norms of their literary art. Thus, while one of the primary targets of modernist reno-vation was Victorian literary manners, another was the complacent taste and sensi-bility of a large, and growing, middle class. Artists had been declaring the need to shock the bourgeoisie since time immemorial; Matthew Arnold worried publicly, and at length, about the dilution of a natural aristocracy of taste by the pseudoculture of newly educated British philistines, at the same time that he campaigned for greatly expanded public education. The Education Act of 1870 resulted in the explosive growth of elementary education, which meant that the reading class grew exponen-tially. Within the art world, the most obvious result of this anxiety was the "art for art's sake" movement associated with Walter Pater that began in the 1870s. Art was becoming its own material—as, for instance, in French artist Marcel Duchamp's mus-tache on the Mona Lisa.

In some ways modernist art and literature turned inward, becoming cannibalistic and self-referential. This is demonstrated well in Joyce's novel *A Portrait of the Artist as a Young Man*, whose protagonist is autobiographical in genesis yet critical in intent; the way Joyce accomplishes this is by moving Stephen Dedalus, his artist-pro-tagonist, through various prose poses—writing now like Gustave Flaubert, now like Cardinal Newman, now like Pater. Stephen can only mimic—not create—a style; such is the situation of the modern writer, Joyce suggests, and his novel *Ulysses* dra-matizes this by adopting a kaleidoscopic array of styles in its eighteen chapters. It thus becomes increasingly difficult to think of "style" as the achievement of an indi-vidual, and more and more it becomes the culmination of a cultural, national, ethnic project or history. As the French critic Roland Barthes has written, the text in the modern period becomes a "multidimensional space in which a variety of writings, none of them original, blend and clash," "a tissue of quotations drawn from innumerable centres of culture"—an apt and dramatic description of modernist texts like Eliot's *The Waste Land*, Joyce's *Ulysses*, and Pound's *Cantos*. To be textual is, during this period, to be intertextual and interdisciplinary as well.

The stylistic experimentation of modernist writers was fueled by the era's technological advances. From the mid-nineteenth century on, Britain had prided itself on its industrial strength and leadership; with the electrification of Britain at the turn of the century, however, the Industrial Revolution was gradually overtaken by a technological revolution. If the sinking of the Titanic on her maiden voyage in 1912 stands as a symbol of the vulnerability of progress—a sort of watery funeral for traditional British industry—the first transatlantic flight in 1919 pointed toward the future. Advances in photographic technology made documentary photographs a part of daily life and brought a heightened visual dimension to political campaigns and to advertising; the advent of quick and inexpensive newspaper photographs put vivid images of the carnage of World War I on Britain's breakfast tables. The texture and pace of daily life changed in the early years of the century to such a degree that average men and women were comfortable referring to themselves by that hopelessly awkward designation, "modern" (from the Latin *modo*, "just now"). And clearly, the London inhabited by the denizens of Eliot's *Waste Land* is a profoundly different place from the London of Dickens. Eliot portrays a woman who works in an office, composes letters on a typewriter, talks to clients on the telephone, plays records on the phonograph at her flat after having casual sex with a co-worker, and eats her evening meal from tins.

The advent of technology had far-reaching effects on the writing of the period. Beckett, famously, imagined a tape recorder before he had ever seen one in order to make possible the memory play of his *Krapp's Last Tape* (1959); more generally, the technology of the transistor radio, and government sponsorship of radio and television by the British Broadcasting Corporation, made possible wholly new literary genres. Beckett and Dylan Thomas were among the first to take advantage of the new media, writing plays for radio and then for television. A generation earlier, Joyce made use of early art film strategies in his "Circe" episode of *Ulysses*. In the most advanced writing of the modernist period we find an increasing sense that the technologies of print affect the text itself. Pound's *Cantos* were composed, not just transcribed, on a typewriter, and cannot be imagined in their current form composed with pen and ink; Joyce plays with the typographic conventions of newspaper headlines in the "Aeolus" chapter of *Ulysses* to create an ironic running commentary on the action. A crucial scene in Joyce's *Finnegans Wake* features a television broadcast (which was not available commercially when the novel was published), blending with a nuclear explosion (also several years before the fact). The scene culminates in "the abnihilisation of the etym"—both a destruction of atom/Adam/etym and its recovery *from* ("ab") nothingness.

MODERNISM AND THE MODERN CITY

Paralleling the new social and artistic opportunities of the twentieth century was a kind of anomie or alienation created by the rush towards industrialization. Vast numbers of human figures remained undifferentiated and the mass-manufactured hats and clothing worn by British industrial workers served only to heighten the monotony of their daily routines. Newspapers eagerly published photographs of thousands of sooty-faced miners. The members of the workforce, which Marx had called "alienated labor," were seen to be estranged not just from their work but from one another as

well, as they themselves became mass products. This situation is dramatized especially vividly in the silent films of the period—from the dystopian vision of Fritz Lang's
Metropolis (1926) to the more comic vision presented by the British-American Charlie Chaplin in *Modern Times* (1936). The sense of major cities being overrun by
crowds of nameless human locusts recurs in the poetry of the period:

> A crowd flowed over London Bridge, so many,
> I had not thought death had undone so many.
> Sighs, short and infrequent, were exhaled,
> And each man fixed his eyes before his feet.
>
> (Eliot, *The Waste Land*)

> I have met them at close of day
> Coming with vivid faces
> From counter or desk among grey
> Eighteenth-century houses.
>
> (Yeats, *Easter 1916*)

The Victorian concern over huge numbers of urban poor was seconded by a fear of
large numbers of restive urban lower-middle class workers and their families.

The critic Hugh Kenner has described modernism as both metropolitan and also
international in character. While the bulk of Victorian British literary production is
associated in some way or another with London, writing in the modern period is
spread not just throughout England but throughout the Empire (and later the Commonwealth). To this day, London still serves as a spiritual and economic center of
British writing, and many of the best British writers, regardless of their provenance,
come to London at some point in their career. Modernist literary production was further stimulated by close cross-pollination between writers and other artists in other
nations, and much of the most important writing in the modern "British" canon was
undertaken in cities as far-flung as Dublin, Paris, Zurich, New York, and Johannes-
burg. Conversely, much of the important literature written in Britain itself during the
twentieth century was produced by immigrants from abroad, from the Polish Joseph
Conrad and the American Henry James at the start of the century to V. S. Naipaul,
Salman Rushdie, and Hanif Kureishi in recent decades. As a result, the distinctions
between "British" and "American" writing often blurred in this period of easy and
relatively inexpensive transatlantic travel. Henry James based novels like *The American* and *Portrait of a Lady* on the adventures of Americans living in Europe; James
himself was an American who lived most of the last thirty-five years of his life in
London, and was naturalized as a British citizen three months before his death. T. S.
Eliot moved to London in 1915 and lived there until his death in 1965, becoming a
British subject, a communicant of the Church of England, and being knighted along
the way. The great comic writer P. G. Wodehouse commuted back and forth across
the Atlantic in the 1920s and 1930s as his plays and musical comedies were staged in
New York and London. In many ways, New York and London had never been so
close. This artistic diaspora has inevitably resulted in a richer, more complex and
urbane literature.

PLOTTING THE SELF

The Freudian revolution grew from and reinforced an intense interest in the workings of the individual psyche, and modernists like Woolf and Joyce devoted themselves to capturing the mind's modulations. Both Woolf and Joyce employed versions

of what came to be known as the "stream-of-consciousness" technique, in which fragmentary thoughts gradually build up a portrayal of characters' perceptions and of their unstated concerns. Consider this passage from the "interior monologue" of Joyce's protagonist Leopold Bloom, as he prepares a saucer of milk for his cat:

> They call them stupid. They understand what we say better than we understand them. She understands all she wants to. Vindictive too. Wonder what I look like to her. Height of a tower? No, she can jump me. . . . Cruel. Her nature. Curious mice never squeal. Seem to like it.

On the surface, Bloom's staccato thoughts reflect on the cat; at the same time, he identifies the cat with his unfaithful wife Molly, and—without admitting it to himself—he reflects on the cat's foreign psyche as a way of coming to terms with Molly's needs and desires. The development of stream-of-consciousness narrative grows out of a sense that the self is not "natural" or "given" but a construction—specifically a social construction—and that, consequently, traditional methods for depicting character no longer suffice. We are all the products of our own past and we are also, powerfully, products of larger social forces that shape the stories we tell about ourselves, and which others tell about us.

In the Victorian novel, plot crises were typically resolved in some definitive way, such as by a marriage or a change in the financial status of the protagonist. In the modern novel, lasting resolutions growing out of a common vision are few and far between. Walter Pater had counseled his readers, at the conclusion of *The Renaissance*, that "to burn always with a hard, gemlike flame, to maintain this ecstasy" was "success in life"; in the modern period, everyone wants that ecstasy, but no one is sure quite what it looks like amid the ruthless individualism of modern life. "We live as we dream, alone," Conrad's narrator Marlow mutters despondently; "Only connect," the epigraph to E. M. Forster's *Howards End* (1910) implores. On the eve of the London Blitz, however, the characters in Woolf's *Between the Acts* (still the most powerful British novel of World War II) are united only as they sing the refrain, "Dispersed are we." The texts of the modern period, bookended as they are by two world wars, represent a real, agonized meditation on how modern individuals can become united as community again. Woolf herself was skeptical of the possibility and her last novel remains unfinished—or finished only by her husband Leonard—because she took her own life before she could complete it. In the novels of Woolf and Joyce, and in the poetry of Yeats and Auden, community is the glimpsed prospect, the promised land: seen as a possibility but never realized, or embodied precariously in a gesture, a moment, a metaphor, and above all in art itself.

After the modernist high-water mark of the 1920s, the atmosphere darkened amid the international financial depression of the 1930s triggered by the U.S. stock market crash of 1929. The decade saw the growth of British Marxism and widespread labor agitation. The decade also witnessed the international growth of fascism and totalitarianism; writers like Shaw, Wyndham Lewis, Eliot, Yeats, Pound, and Lawrence for a time saw the order and stability promised by authoritarian governments as the only antidote to the "mere anarchy" Yeats decries in his poem *The Second Coming*. In the late thirties, however, intellectual sentiment turned increasingly against the fascist movements being led in Germany by Hitler, in Italy by Mussolini and in Spain by Franco. During Spain's brutal civil war (1936–1939), many writers supported the democratic Republicans against the ultimately victorious fascist General Franco. Meanwhile a series of weak British governments did little to oppose

Hitler's increasing belligerence and extremism; the failure to stand up for democratic principles, coupled with worldwide economic depression, led many young intellectuals and artists to became Leftists.

Compared to the stylistic experiments of the previous two decades, British writing of the 1930s sometimes looks rather flat, neutral. This can be attributed in part to the disillusionment that followed World War I, and the very real sense throughout the thirties that things were building up to another war, that art had become something of an irrelevancy. The German cultural critic Theodor Adorno was to write after the war, "no poetry after Auschwitz"; writers of the thirties seem to have had this sense well in advance of Auschwitz. Yeats admired the character in Auguste de Villiers de L'Isle-Adam's drama *Axël* who said, "As for living, we let the servants do that for us"; the young writers of the thirties, however, were concerned that (in Auden's phrase) "poetry makes nothing happen," and were committed to the idea that it must.

THE RETURN OF THE REPRESSED

Modern British literature is characterized by the increasing presence of women's voices, working-class voices, and voices expressing varied ethnic, religious, and sexual perspectives which, whether methodically or inadvertently, had often been excluded from the British literary tradition. The writings of an author like Woolf made England think hard about who she really was, as did, in another sense, the writings of the former colonial administrator George Orwell. In the modern period, Britain begins to deal in a fully conscious way with its human rights problems—most significantly, its treatment of women and the diverse ethnic groups of its colonial possessions.

The gradual enfranchisement and political and economic liberation of British women in the early years of the twentieth century comprised a fundamental social change; the novelist D. H. Lawrence, a rather equivocal friend of the women's movement, called it "perhaps the greatest revolution of modern times." The Women's Property Act—passed in 1882, the year of Woolf's birth—for the first time allowed married women to own property. Decades of sometimes violent suffragist agitation led finally to full voting rights for women in 1928 and to the gradual opening up of opportunities in higher education and the professions.

The quick pace of these changes naturally made many men uneasy. In their monumental three-volume study *No Man's Land: The Place of the Woman Writer in the Twentieth Century*, critics Sandra Gilbert and Susan Gubar suggest that this "war between the sexes" was one of the primary driving forces behind the modernist literary movement. Having emphasized the revolutionary force of the women's movement, Lawrence goes on to warn that the movement, "is even going beyond, and becoming a tyranny of woman, of the individual woman in the house, and of the feminine ideas and ideals in the world." In a half-serious essay titled *Cocksure Women and Hensure Men*, Lawrence complained of women "more cocky, in their assurance, than the cock himself. . . . It is really out of scheme, it is not in relation to the rest of things. . . . They find, so often, that instead of having laid an egg, they have laid a vote, or an empty ink-bottle, or some other absolutely unhatchable object, which means nothing to them." On the level of literary principles, a masculinist emphasis can be seen in Ezra Pound's insistence that modern poetry should "move against poppy-cock," "be harder and saner . . . 'nearer the bone' . . . as much like granite as it can be."

Other writers, male and female, supported women's rights; almost all writers sought to rebel against Victorian sexual norms and gender roles. Joyce battled with censors beginning in 1906, and his *Ulysses* was put on trial in New York on obscenity charges in 1933 (and cleared of those charges in the same week that the United States repealed Prohibition). Defending his sexual and scatological scenes, Joyce put the modernists' case for frankness this way: "The modern writer has other problems facing him, problems which are more intimate and unusual. We prefer to search in the corners for what has been hidden, and moods, atmospheres and intimate relationships are the modern writers' theme. . . . The modern theme is the subterranean forces, those hidden tides which govern everything and run humanity counter to the apparent flood: those poisonous subtleties which envelop the soul, the ascending fumes of sex." In defense of his "dirty" book *Lady Chatterley's Lover* (1928), whose full text was banned as obscene until 1960, Lawrence wrote: "In spite of all antagonism, I put forth this novel as an honest, healthy book, necessary for us today. . . . We are today, as human beings, evolved and cultured far beyond the taboos which are inherent in our culture. . . . The mind has an old groveling fear of the body and the body's potencies. It is the mind we have to liberate, to civilize on these points." In a rich irony, Joyce and Lawrence hated one another's writing: Joyce insisted on calling Lawrence's best-known novel "Lady Chatterbox's Lover," for he felt the characters talked too much. He dismissed the novel as "a piece of propaganda in favour of something which, outside of D. H. L.'s country at any rate, makes all the propaganda for itself." Lawrence, for his part, thought the last chapter of *Ulysses* (Molly Bloom's famous soliloquy) "the dirtiest, most indecent, obscene thing ever written."

Sexuality of all stripes was on trial. The lesbian writer Radclyffe Hall was tried for obscenity in 1928 for her novel *The Well of Loneliness*—whose most obscene sentence is, "That night they were not divided." The trial became a public spectacle, and was a rallying point for writers like Woolf and E. M. Forster, who spoke valiantly in favor of Hall's right to explore her subject, which was primarily the loneliness, rather than the fleshly joys, of same-sex love. Forster's overtly homosexual writings, including his novel *Maurice*, were not published until after his death in 1970. Woolf was somewhat more open in her novel *Orlando* (1928), whose protagonist changes sex from male to female. In Joyce's *Ulysses*, Leopold Bloom fantasizes about becoming a "new womanly man" and dreams of being chastised by a dominatrix who appears first as Bella and then as Bello Cohen. It was not only sexual taboos that were challenged in the writing of the period; in practice there began to be a loosening of the strict gender and sexual roles, which had been reinforced by the homophobia resulting from Oscar Wilde's trial for homosexual offenses in 1895. Gay, lesbian, and bisexual writers like Forster, Woolf, Hall, Stein, Natalie Barney, Djuna Barnes, H. D., Ronald Firbank, and Carl Van Vechten pushed the comfort level of the British reading public; even the "healthy" version of sexuality celebrated by D. H. Lawrence in his greatest novel *Women in Love* begins to suggest that heterosexuality and homosexuality are boundaries, not immutable categories.

The growing independence of the individual subject began to be matched by drives for independence among imperial subjects as well. In "John Bull's other island," as Bernard Shaw called Ireland in his play of that title, agitations for independence grew widespread from the late nineteenth century onward, culminating in the Easter Rising of 1916 and the 1922 partitioning of Ireland, when the Irish Republic became an independent nation while Northern Ireland remained part of Great Britain. No match for England militarily, the Irish used words as their chief weapon in the struggle for independence. Yeats and Joyce, among other writers, reflected on this war of words in such important works as Yeats's *Easter 1916* and Joyce's *Ivy Day in the Committee Room* and the "Aeolus" chapter from *Ulysses*.

The liberation of Britain's overseas colonial holdings began in the early decades of the century and gathered momentum thereafter. The history of Great Britain in the twentieth century is, in some ways, the story of the centrifugal forces that have largely stripped Britain of its colonial possessions. Britain suffered humiliating losses in the Boer War (1899–1902), fought by the British to take possession of the Boer Republic of South Africa. Half a million British troops were unable to win outright victory over eighty thousand Boers; finally the British adopted a scorched-earth policy that entailed massive arrests and the deaths of thousands of captives in unsanitary camps. This debilitating and unsavory conquest marked the low point of British imperialism, and public disgust led to a reaction against empire itself. Independence movements sprang up in colonies around the world, most notably in India, Britain's largest colony, "the jewel in the crown" of Queen Victoria, where Mohandas Gandhi's Congress Party struggled through nonviolent resistance to force Britain to grant its independence.

WORLD WAR II AND ITS AFTERMATH

The year 1939 and the start of World War II closed the modernist era. It was the year that saw the publication of Joyce's *Finnegans Wake*, which the critic Ihab Hassan calls a "monstrous prophecy" of postmodernity. The seminal modernist careers of Joyce, Woolf, Yeats, Ford, and Freud all came to an end—as did the social and political order of the previous decades. Throughout the late thirties, the government had engaged in futile efforts at diplomacy as Hitler expanded German control in central Europe. Prime Minister Neville Chamberlain finally denounced Hitler when the Germans invaded Czechoslovakia early in 1939; on September 1, Germany invaded Poland, and within days Britain declared war. In contrast to the "Great War," this conflict began with few illusions—but with the knowledge that Britain was facing an implacable and better-armed enemy. Unlike the Great War, fought on foreign soil, the new war hit home directly; during "the Blitz" from July 1940 through 1941, the German Luftwaffe carried out massive bombing raids on London and many other targets around Britain.

During these years, Winston Churchill emerged as a pivotal figure both strategically and morally. First as commander in chief of the navy, and starting in May 1940 as prime minister, he directed British military operations while rallying popular support through stirring speeches and radio addresses. The war had profound effects throughout British society, as almost every man—and many women—between the ages of 14 and 64 came to be involved in the war effort, in conditions that weakened old divisions of region and class and that provided the impetus for new levels of government involvement in social planning. At the war's end in September of 1945, Britain emerged victorious, in concert with its allies. In contrast with the United States, though, Britain had suffered enormous civilian casualties and crushing economic losses, both within Great Britain and throughout its far-flung colonies. As much as a quarter of Britain's national wealth had been consumed by the war. The great city of London had undergone horrific bombing during the the Blitz, whose attacks left the face of this world capital as scarred as had the Great Fire three centuries before. Although morally and socially triumphant in its defeat of Nazism and fascism, Britain was left shattered economically and exhausted spiritually. Its people had come through the war gallantly, only to face grim conditions at home and political unrest throughout the empire.

London during the Blitz, seen from the north transept of St. Paul's Cathedral.

The global effort of that war, whose battles were fought not only in Europe but in Africa, Asia, Latin America, the Middle East, and the Pacific, had forced Britain to draw massively on its colonies for raw materials, money, and soldiers. Since the resistance to the British empire had begun long before World War II, the drafting of millions of already restive colonial subjects into the armed forces intensified the tensions and the conflicts running beneath the surface of the empire. One of the most important political phenomena of the twentieth century was about to hit a depleted Britain with a vengeance: the decolonization of most of the conquered globe in the great wave of independence movements that swept the world after 1945. One by one, with greater and lesser degrees of violence and agony, colonies slipped out of Britain's imperial net. From the independence of India (1947) to the independence struggles of Kenya, Nigeria, Zaire, Palestine, Egypt, and many others, Britain experienced the accelerated loss of the largest empire in Western history. Retaining only a handful of Caribbean, Latin American, and Pacific Rim possessions, the empire had radically shrunk. India, Pakistan, Canada, Australia, and a few other countries adopted commonwealth status, remaining commercially linked but becoming essentially independent politically. The empire on which the sun never set was fast becoming largely confined to England, Scotland, Wales, and Northern Ireland—an ongoing area of tension and conflict to the present day.

The dizzying pace of decolonization after the war put Britain in a paradoxically modern position ahead of many other Western countries: the unquestioned ability, and the rarely questioned right, of Western societies to dominate the globe had finally encountered decisive opposition. Within fifty years Britain found itself transformed from the dominant global power into a relatively small and, for a time, impoverished island nation, no longer a dictator of the world's history, but merely part of it. This dislocation was profoundly registered in British culture, and British writers strove to assess these losses—and to define the new possibilities for a freer and more open society that might emerge from the wreckage of empire.

A new generation of writers took on the task of evaluating English culture and the tradition of English literature itself from inside. John of Gaunt's beautiful paean to "this sceptered isle, this England," in Shakespeare's *Henry IV* had to be rewritten now: what was "this England" to be? In the absence of its colonial possessions, and in the general misery of shortages and rationing after the war, there was suddenly a sharp new scrutiny of British society. Its class-bound hierarchies appeared in an even harsher light, and its failures at home, in addition to its failure as an empire abroad, became the source of profound self-examination. Rage and anger accompanied this process of self-awareness, and a generation of literary artists dubbed the "angry young men" arose to meet the failures head-on, often in realist drama so faithful to its shabby subjects it was called "kitchen sink" drama, after the cold-water flat settings where the characters played out their rage. Playwrights such as John Osborne (as in the aptly titled *Look Back in Anger*) and novelists such as Anthony Burgess (*A Clockwork Orange*) angrily or satirically probed the discrepancy between England's glorious past and its seemingly squalid present.

A sense of diminishment in the world's eyes led to a passionate critique of British institutions, particularly its class structure, even where the literature produced was conservative in its looking backward. The extraordinary poet Philip Larkin might be seen as a key figure in this generation of writers. Larkin was a librarian in a rural town for most of his adult life. His poetry takes on the sardonic voice of the disenfranchised and the dispossessed—speaking not for the poor or the downtrodden but instead articulating the sense of loss and fury of middle and upper-class England, bereft of its historical prestige, impoverished by modern culture. He sings of nature, home, and country in a voice that is lacerating and self-mocking. Larkin's often jazzy and colloquial poetic diction, and his effective use of Anglo-Saxon expletives—he brought "fuck" into the opening of a major poem—offered a rebarbative retort to pastoral poetry. Larkin also wrote several notable novels at this time, among them *A Girl in Winter,* which explores from a surprisingly feminine and even feminist point of view the struggles of an emigré to Britain who must conceal the traumas her family experienced during the war, in order to "fit in" with a blithe and cavalier aristocratic British family. Larkin's artistry joins that of a host of other postwar writers, mostly male, who write from the center of an England now put off-kilter by the wrenching changes after the war.

Profound historical changes were to continue after the war with the commencement of the Cold War, in which the new world superpowers, the United States and the former Soviet Union, became locked in an intense battle for ideological, political, and economic dominance. Human beings now possessed the technological means to destroy the planet and its inhabitants, and these weapons of destruction were amassed by two societies with sharply conflicting goals. Britain along with Western Europe unequivocally aligned itself on the side of the United States, joining in the long fight against communism and Soviet socialism. While not itself a superpower, Britain had to shape its own social goals in light of the Cold War raging around it. A supremely eloquent voice in the articulation of what was at stake was that of the British writer George Orwell, known for his lucid essays on politics and language. Immediately after the war Orwell crafted *1984*, an enduring parable of Cold War culture. This book envisions a future society in the year 1984 when the infamous "Big

Brother" is watching everyone. That tale of a society of totalitarian surveillance was a thinly veiled allegory of the possibilities inherent not only in a Soviet takeover but even in Western societies and their implicit tendencies toward control and bureaucracy. It may be that Orwell was able to be prophetic about the cultural touchstones of the next several decades because as a British writer he wrote from an oblique angle: the colonial relationship of Britain to the United States had become reversed, with Britain almost becoming an outpost of the United States in terms of its Cold War dominance, reminiscent of Britain's dominance of the fate of the American colonies in the centuries leading up to the American Revolution. It is sometimes possible to see more clearly from a position outside the exact center—and Britain was, in this sense, no longer the center of English-speaking Western civilization. Strangely enough, that ex-centricity granted its literary writers a certain kind of insight.

The British novel after World War II made a retreat from modernist experimentalism. One explanation for a return to the realism that Woolf had so passionately argued against comes, paradoxically, from feminism of the very sort Woolf espouses in *A Room of One's Own* and *Three Guineas*. For as women began to write in large numbers, the novel with characters and a plot became a kind of room these writers needed to make their own. A host of important women writers emerged who revived the novel—which had been declared dead by the French, at least, around 1950—by using its traditions to incorporate their experiences as women, "making it new" not by formal experiments, but by opening that familiar, even a little shabby, room to new voices and new stories. Among the practitioners of this "feminist realism"—although some of them would vehemently deny the label "feminist"—are Jean Rhys, Doris Lessing, Margaret Drabble, A. S. Byatt, Muriel Spark, Iris Murdoch, Nadine Gordimer, and Buchi Emecheta. In every case these are writers who ring changes on ostensibly traditional forms.

Within England a host of dramatic luminaries gave vital energy to the British stage after 1945. While John Osborne created realist dramas of rage and dispossession, Harold Pinter emphasized the careful chiseling of language, bringing out the full ambiguity hidden in seemingly innocuous social conversation. In his meteoric but short dramatic career the playwright Joe Orton took a reverse tack to that of Pinterian ordinary language, and returned to the example of Oscar Wilde. Using a wildly baroque vocabulary and an epigrammatic wit, Orton brought an explicit gay drama and gay sensibility to the postwar theater, in works like *Loot*, which revolves around a seductive lower-class character who wreaks sexual havoc with all the inhabitants of a country estate, male and female, young and old. To very different comic effect, the Czech immigrant Tom Stoppard employs a brilliant rhetorical surface in his plays, which are often modernist puzzle boxes in their annihilation of the rules of time and space.

The most innovative of all British dramatists of the twentieth century after World War I was indubitably the Irishman Samuel Beckett. Living in a form of self-imposed exile in France, and a further self-imposed exile within the French language, Beckett moved from being the writer of mordant novels (*Molloy*; *Malone Dies*) to becoming an extraordinary dramatist. He often wrote his plays first in French, later translating them into English, so that English was their "secondary" language, leading to multiple puns in both English and French. Beckett's contribution to dramatic form, for which he received the Nobel Prize, is nonetheless a creation within British literature. Beckett sculpted his plays out of silence, paring down lines of dialogue until their short sentences and sometimes single words reverberate with the unspoken. Samuel Beckett, more than any other dramatist in English, found the pockets of silence in English speech, and made those silences speak. His characters do not inhabit a real place, like England, for example, but instead occupy an abstract space of human existence, where the human predicaments of longing and desire for redemption, the failures of understanding, and the bafflement of death are experienced in their purest form.

THE SIXTIES AND BEYOND

The impoverishment of the fifties abated in the sixties, at least for the middle class, as British banking and finance reinvigorated the economy. "Swinging London" became a household phrase, as British urban culture set the pace in music, fashion, and style. The Carnaby Street mode of dress and fashion mavens like Mary Quant, Jean Muir, and Zandra Rhodes were copied all over the world, worn by Jean Shrimpton and Twiggy, who were among the first supermodels. British film came out of a postwar slump and movies like *Morgan* and *Georgy Girl* had huge audiences at home and in the United States. A delirious excitement invested British popular culture, and London became a hub of the new once more. The critique of British society mounted by Joe Orton's work found its double in the youth culture of "Mods" and "Rockers." Asked which he was, the Beatles' drummer Ringo Starr claimed to synthesize both: "I'm a mocker."

Amid the cultural ferment of the sixties and seventies, successive British governments struggled with intractable problems of inflation and unemployment, punctuated by frequent strikes by Britain's powerful unions, and rising violence in Northern Ireland. The generally pro-union government of Harold Wilson (1964–1970) was followed by the Conservative government of Edward Heath, who put new stress on private enterprise. A major shift away from the "welfare state," however, came only at the end of the decade, when Heath was succeeded by the formidable Margaret Thatcher, the prime minister of Britain for a record twelve years. The daughter of a lower middle-class family, Thatcher vaulted into politics when that was an exceptionally rare opportunity not only for a woman, but for a person whose father was a shop-keeper. Trained as a chemist, Thatcher worked long and hard for the (Tory) Conservative Party, even as Britain was ruled by a succession of Labour and Socialist governments. When her chance came to lead England as its Tory prime minister, Thatcher and her political and ideological colleagues began a governmental revolution by adopting free-market policies similar to those identified with the Ronald Reagan school of U.S. Republicanism. Thatcher set about dismantling as much of the welfare state of postwar modern Britain as she could—and that was a considerable amount.

Margaret Thatcher had an enormous impact on British identity, as well as on British society. Among the very small number of women worldwide who have ever wielded such substantial political power—Golda Meir and Indira Gandhi come to mind as others—Thatcher's polished good looks, her extreme toughness, and her uncompromising political dictates combined to produce a caricature of her as the domineering English governness, laying down the rules of what would be good for Britain's unruly citizens. Thatcher's economic policies emphasized productivity as never before; under her rule, an entrepreneurial culture began to flourish at the expense of once-sacred British social entitlements, in education, health care, and civic subsidy of the arts and culture. Margaret Thatcher's most breathtaking quota-

The Beatles landing at Heathrow Airport, 29 October 1963.

tion, and the one summing up her philosophy of government, was uttered in response to complaints about what was happening to the fabric of British society and, especially, to its poor, elderly, immigrants, and the mass numbers of the unemployed. "There is no such thing as society," she declared. What she meant was that government had no role to play in creating a unitary, egalitarian society. The forces of the unleashed free market, and the will of private individuals, would replace any notion of a social contract or social compact between and among British citizens. There was irony, of course, in Thatcher's seeming to turn her back on members of her own class and those below it, and despite the power and immense reputation she acquired worldwide, there was always scathing and vocal opposition to her within Britain, as she privatized the universities and abolished tenure, made inroads on the National Health Service, dissolved city councils and established poll taxes. Prime Minister Thatcher declared and fought Britain's last imperial war of modern times, against Argentina over the control of the Falkland Islands, and she was fierce opponent of nationalist sentiment among the Scottish and the Welsh, a firm upholder of Britain's right to control Northern Ireland in perpetuity, and strongly against the move toward joining the European Community. Thatcher became an icon in Britain, as well as its longest-governing Prime Minister: an icon for her certainty, confidence, and her personification of the huge changes she brought about. Though she provoked sharp opposition, her brilliance and energy were never in question, nor was her international influence.

Equally large changes have occurred in the last several years of the twentieth century, however, changes sweeping enough to have diminished Margaret Thatcher's iconic stature, and to have partially reversed the social revolution she began. The historian Simon Schama points out, in an essay analyzing the British reaction to the death of Princess Diana in 1997, that the Thatcher era was simultaneous with the early Diana years. "For, by the time Charles Philip Arthur George and Diana Frances stepped out of the nave of Saint Paul's Cathedral into the sunlight and the cheers of millions, it was Margaret Thatcher who had annexed the idea of a revolutionized "new" Britain within her steely grip. This was to be a Britain in which the worst thing was not, as Diana would later say, 'to feel unloved' but to be unproductive." At the turn of the century, though, the Labour Party has reclaimed countrol of the country, changing course economically and emphasizing the very social contract Thatcher had set aside. Britain is an increasingly pivotal member of the European Community alliance, and its own internal divisions have come productively to the fore. Diana's vision of the need for society to take account for all those who are "unloved" within it can be said to have prevailed over the views of the now-titled Baroness Thatcher, productive in her retirement as a writer and political pundit, although in many ways now a prophet without honor—in the sense of followers—in her own land.

Surprisingly, the twentieth century is ending in much the same way as did the nineteenth century for Britain, with a nationwide debate on home rule. In 1886 and again in 1893 the eminent British prime minister William Gladstone fought for the establishment of a separte Irish parliament—thus the term "home rule"—to allow the Irish colony, with its differing religion of Roman Catholicism and its unique Gaelic culture, to have control over its own internal affairs. Gladstone and his Liberal Party formed an alliance with the Irish National Party's members of Parliament, who were led by the great Charles Steward Parnell, a Protestant Irishman known as "the uncrowned king of Ireland." Parnell's political fall due to an extramarital scandal removed a key player in Gladstone's strategy, and his final attempt in 1893 at voting in home rule failed. This failure led to the Irish revolution, the Irish Civil War, and the continuing violence within Northern Ireland, the six counties still belonging to Britain and occupied by their army.

Britain's new prime minister, Anthony Blair, was elected in 1997 from the Labour Party, breaking the Conservative Party's eighteen-year hold on the position, for twelve years of which the redoubtable Margaret Thatcher ruled, followed by her chosen successor, the rather low-key John Major. One of Blair's main campaign promises was bringing home rule to both Scotland and Wales, regions of Britain with their own language and dialect, their own cultural mores, and a long history of armed conflict with England. The referendum on the Scottish parliament, with the power to raise and lower income taxes within Scotland, and a considerable budget to operate as Scotland chooses, for its schools, health, housing and transport, overwhelmingly passed the popular vote, and is likely to be a reality by 1999; Wales has voted as well for the creation of a Welsh assembly with many of the same powers and responsibilities. While the Republic of Ireland is now a nation in its own right, Tony Blair's commitment to the peace talks in Northern Ireland, and to the inclusion of Sinn Fein in those talks, has also provided the first stirrings of political momentum in resolving the century-old conflict between Northern Irish Protestants who largely wish to remain attached to Britain, and the Northern Irish Catholics who have fought for the autonomy of this part of Ireland.

LANGUAGE AND IDENTITY

Complicated questions of language and identity have increasingly come to dominate the most recent phase of twentieth-century British literature. A great paradox of the British postwar period, in its time of imperial shrinkage, involves the fate of the English language. Britain may have been "kicked out" of many of its former colonies as a governing presence, but English was rarely shown the door at the same time. For economic and cultural reasons English as a global language became even more widely dispersed and dominant after World War II. Of course, the spread of U.S. interests has played a role in the hegemony of English. However, the old contours of the British empire continue to shape much of the production of English literature today. In this way, the former British empire has become part of the fabric of British literature. V. S. Naipaul, for example, has long resided in England, but he was born to Indian parents in Trinidad, where the British had deployed Indian labor. His writing is as much in dialog with the British literary tradition, and an extension of it, as that of any native-born British author.

Salman Rushdie, who is of Pakistani parentage, is another intriguing example of this process of crossing the increasingly porous boundaries of Britishness, as well as a cautionary tale of how powerful literature can be. Rushdie's novels are part of British literature at its modernist best, drawing on the entire English literary tradition, yet informed by a cosmopolitan and a non-Western literary tradition as well. Eight years after he achieved great acclaim for his novel *Midnight's Children* (1980), a book that adapted the "magic realism" of Latin American fiction to the history of Indian independence, Rushdie published *The Satanic Verses*. This novel recounts a magical mystery tour of sorts, the arrival of two South Asian refugees to modern London: one a film star from Bombay, the other a kind of trickster figure. Embedded in this complex tale of migration and identity is a brief dream sequence satirizing the prophet Mohammed. In response to this tiny dream-within-a-dream passage, the Iranian theocratic government delivered a *fatwa*—an edict sentencing Rushdie to death in absentia for treachery to the religion of Islam. Rushdie did not write the book in Arabic, nor did he write it for a Muslim audience, but that was irrelevant to the clerics who pronounced sentence on him before millions of devout adherents. From that time, Rushdie has been forced to live in a form of self-imposed house arrest, guarded by the British government. In an ironic twist, British literature itself has become his prison house of language, his internal exile. It is this tradition that "protects" him as a great writer, and, because of its porous literary borders, is responsible for his predicament. These issues and more underlie his striking story *Chekhov and Zulu*.

In recent years British literature has been infused with new life both from foreign-born writers and from new voices bubbling up from within the British Isles, in the shape of Welsh, Scottish, and Irish literary prose and poetry. The Nobel Prize–winning Irish poet Seamus Heaney is a kind of internal outsider, since, as he has written, he does not consider himself to be part of "British" literature as ordinarily defined, while he nonetheless writes English poetry deeply influenced by English poets from Milton to Wordsworth to Eliot. Some writers have deliberately taken themselves out of British literature for political and literary reasons, using the strongest means possible: they have decided to write in a language other than English. For example, the Kenyan writer Ngugi wa-Thiongo, educated by British missionaries and then at a British university, whose first memorized poem was Wordsworth's *Daffodils*, now writes in the Kikuyu language, and translates his work into English. The Irish poet Nuala Ní Dhomhnaill has made a similar decision: she writes and publishes her poetry first in Irish, and only later translates it into English as a "second" language.

In recent years British writing has been invigorated from "below," as well as from "outside": there has been a profusion of working-class or lower-middle-class novelists, poets, and screenwriters, many of whom adopt the dialect or argot of lower-class Welsh, Scottish, and Irish English. When James Kelman won the Booker Prize for the best novel published in England in 1994, there was widespread outrage: the working-class, expletive-laced speech of his Scottish protagonist was deemed unliterary by many, or at least unreadable and not in conformity with what was revered as the Queen's English. Poetry too has become a vehicle for a range of literary experiments, linking music and film to rhymed and unrhymed, and often performed, verse, connecting the popular and the literary. This upsurge of vivacious and often provocative writing is primarily the work of younger writers, and in many instances the novels are almost immediately being turned into films with international audiences.

In the past hundred years British literature has seen upheavals of aesthetic form, of geographic location, and of linguistic content. What is no longer in question, oddly enough, despite the current age of cyberspace and interactive media, is whether literature itself will survive. As Mark Twain once commented dryly after reading his own obituary in the newspaper: "The reports of my death are greatly exaggerated." The reports of literature's inevitable eclipse at the hands of media and mass culture have, it seems, been greatly exaggerated too. At this moment, British literary creativity is fed from many streams, welling up unpredictably, located in unexpected places. British literature has not merely survived; it remains a vital index of contemporary social and cultural life, and a crucial indication of the shape of things to come.

Joseph Conrad

1857–1924

One of the ironies of twentieth-century British literature is that many of its greatest writers were not conventionally "British." In the case of Joseph Conrad, arguably the first modern British writer, the irony is even more extreme, because Conrad was born a Pole, and learned English only when he was in his twenties. The transformation of Josef Konrad Nalecz Korzeniowski into "Joseph Conrad" is as fascinating and mysterious a story as the transforming journeys at the heart of his fiction.

Joseph Conrad was a lifelong exile from a country that no longer existed on the map of Europe as a separate country. At the time of Conrad's birth in 1857, Poland was divided between Russia and the Austro-Hungarian empire. His parents, Apollo and Eva, were Polish patriots, and after an uprising against Russia in 1863, the family was exiled to a village in the far north of Russia. Eva died when Josef was seven years old; Apollo when he was twelve. Apollo had been both a political activist and a man of letters, a poet and a translator of French and English literature into Polish. In a sense, by becoming a British novelist writing in English, Conrad was carrying on a project of translation begun by his father, a translation across cultures and literatures as well as languages. Hidden within Conrad's poetic and impressionistic literary language is a secret language—Polish—and a secret history of exile from his homeland.

After Conrad's parents died, he was raised by a cosmopolitan uncle, Tadeusz Bobrowski, who was also imbued with patriotic political leanings and a deep love of literature. Josef was sent to school in Cracow, Poland, where he was bored and restless. His uncle then sent him to Switzerland with a private tutor; they argued constantly for a year, and the tutor resigned. Not quite seventeen years old, Conrad proceeded to Marseilles and joined the French merchant navy. He spent twenty years as a sailor and as a ship's captain, spending four years sailing under the French flag, and then sixteen years with British trading ships. In 1894 Josef Korzeniowski completed his transformation into the writer Joseph Conrad by changing his name and settling in England to become a full-time writer.

By the end of the nineteenth century, the nationalistic wars that had led to a divided Poland had been followed by another historical phenomenon: the dividing-up of the globe by the nations of Europe as these powers consolidated empires. The oceans were crucial pathways in these struggles, not simply vast, watery landscapes outside of history. The seafaring Conrad, who had wanted to leave the frustrations of school behind him and see the world, became intimately involved in the everyday business of the making of empires, playing a minor role behind the scenes of the major political forces of the age. Merchant ships of the kind he served on traced the routes of trade and commerce, which now had become the routes of colonization and political conquest as well. As he came to realize he was an eyewitness to modern history in the making, Joseph Conrad discovered his abiding subject as a writer.

Conrad's voyages during this twenty-year odyssey took him East and West, to Indonesia and the Philippines, to Venezuela, the West Indies, and Africa. Working all the while, he watched as bit by bit the patchwork quilt of empire was put together. Wishing to avoid conscription in the French navy when he came of age, in 1878 Conrad joined the British merchant navy. The British empire had become the most extensive and mighty of any imperial power, and in his capacity as seaman Conrad worked in the main ports of call of the empire upon which the sun supposedly never set. He adopted British citizenship in 1886; after his uncle Tadeusz's death in 1894, Conrad made the final decision to become a writer, and to write in English rather than in French. At the age of thirty-seven, Joseph Conrad was newly born.

As a British writer, Conrad was a sort of ventriloquist. On the surface, he was as English as any other writer in his circle: he married an Englishwoman, Jessie George, and became a recognized part of British literary life, forming friendships with other major writers like Henry James and Ford Madox Ford, and achieving great popularity with the British reading public. A stranger from an exotically foreign place, by British standards, a newcomer to the English language, he nonetheless spoke through an English "voice" he created. From his distanced perspective, he was able to make English do things it had not done in the past for native writers of English. Language in Conrad's writing is always a bit off kilter, reading as if it had been translated instead of being, as it was, originally written in English. His prose has a hallucinatory effect, and a poetic intensity linked to his approaching the words of the English language afresh. The most famous of Conrad's narrators is the character Marlow, who appears in several of his major works as an elusive commentator on the action. His Englishness is as real as it can be, for an imitation. Marlow is perhaps even more British than the British, lapsing often into British slang like "By Jove!" as if to authenticate the reality of Conrad's vision of the British world. Through narrative voices like that of Marlow, Conrad can tell stories that may appear to be familiar and ordinary but are in fact anything but that. If modernist writers succeed in making us doubt that we can truly be at home in the world, Conrad can be said to have been the first writer to convey this homelessness in English.

There is another paradox at the heart of Joseph Conrad's work. His writing straddles the nineteenth and the twentieth centuries, with the five major works he wrote in the years before 1900— *Almayer's Folly, The Nigger of the "Narcissus," Heart of Darkness, Lord Jim,* and *Typhoon*—thought of by many critics as more modernist and experimental than later novels he wrote in the twentieth century—*Nostromo, The Secret Agent, Under Western Eyes, Chance,* and *Victory.* The critic Ian Watt claims that the "intense experimentation which began in 1896 and ended in 1900" resulted from Conrad's concentration in those five earlier works on his own personal experience, a personal experience of travel, exile, and solitude that was a radical premonition of the conditions of modernity. Works like *Heart of Darkness,* written during Queen Victoria's reign, for Watt present "the obdurate incompatibility of the self and the world in which it exists." In book after book, he sets a lone individual into confrontation with the complexities of the modern world, whether the world be that of European imperialism, or political anarchism, or the secret world of spies, or the world of political revolution. His heroes and (much less often) heroines have to find their bearings as society crumbles around them, and Conrad usually depicts them at a moment of choice, when they have to act on their lonely knowledge without any guarantee that they have chosen rightly.

A reliance on personal experience might seem to be a recipe for a straightforward, realist style, but Conrad's prose throughout his work is complex and symbolic, relying on images that are spun into complicated and ambiguous webs of symbolism. What stands out prominently in Conrad's style is its visual nature, the emphasis on making the reader "see." Critcs of Conrad's writing early on seized on the strikingly visual aspect of his effects, and his friend and fellow modernist writer Ford Madox Ford wrote an essay in 1913, *On Impressionism,* which put Conrad in a newly invented camp of impressionist writers. Conrad never fully agreed with this description of his style, nor did he have any special fondness for impressionist painting or the works of its greatest practitioners, Manet and Cézanne. Nonetheless, his own preface to *The Nigger of the "Narcissus"* describes all successful art as based on "an impression conveyed through the senses," and in each of his first five books narrators recount what they have *seen.* The narrator goes back over an experience in retelling it to an audience, an experience whose significance is not necessarily clear even to the narrator but whose meaning is revealed through the accumulation of imagistic details. The powers of sight are directly related to the powers of insight, or self-knowledge. A famous passage from *Heart of Darkness* explains the storytelling technique of the narrator Marlow, but also explains a philosophical conviction at the core of Conrad's writing: "The yarns of seamen have a direct simplicity, the whole meaning of which lies within the shell of a cracked nut. But Marlow was not typical (if his propensity to spin yarns be excepted), and to him the meaning of an episode was not inside like a kernel but outside, enveloping the tale which brought it out only as a glow brings out a haze, in the likeness of one of these misty halos that are sometimes made visible by the spectral illumination of moonshine." Events cast a visual glow and haze where meaning can be found only in the most subtle shades and ambiguous highlights of language. The reader must participate in the gradual, and partial, process of accumulating meaning.

Heart of Darkness is a work at the heart of modern British literature. First published serially in Blackwood's Magazine in 1899, it was reprinted as a complete work along with a companion novella, Youth, in 1902, and writers have returned to it again and again, in the form of quotations and allusions and imitations of its style; its story has been rewritten by each successive generation, in novels, films like Apocalypse Now, and even rock lyrics. Almost mythic in resonance, Heart of Darkness itself is structured around a mythical core—that is, the hero's quest. The journey or quest motif pervades world literature and English literature alike, from the Odyssey and the Epic of Gilgamesh to Dante's Divine Comedy, Bunyan's Pilgrim's Progress, and Byron's Childe Harold. Heart of Darkness condenses in its pages an epic range of theme and experience, both the social themes of empire and cultural clash, and the personal theme of the hero's quest for self-discovery.

As with all his early work, Conrad based Heart of Darkness on his own experience, in this case a trip he took up the Congo River in 1890 in order to become captain of a small steamship. The trip was an unusual one even by Conrad's standards, as he had been sailing the major oceans of the world on large ships. Conrad had reasons for choosing the assignment, however; he had been fascinated by maps since boyhood, and the blank space on the continent of Africa represented by the then-unexplored interior impelled him on. He was curious to see for himself the scandalous imperial practices of the Belgian King Leopold II in the Congo, who possessed what he called the Congo Free State (now Zaire) as his own private property, draining it of raw materials like ivory, while claiming to be suppressing savagery and spreading European civilization. After traveling two hundred miles upriver to Kinshasa to join his ship, however, he found it was undergoing repairs. He traveled as a passenger on a trip to Stanley Falls, to bring back an ailing company agent, Georges Klein, who died on the return trip to Kinshasa. These events provided the germ of Conrad's novella, which transformed Klein ("Little," in German) into the uncanny figure of Kurtz.

A diary Conrad kept during his journey (excerpted as a Companion Reading following Heart of Darkness) records his dawning awareness that King Leopold's policy in the Congo was nothing other than slave labor, ultimately causing the deaths of more than a million Africans. Initially an observer, Conrad became a passionately informed partisan, and made known his findings in the form of journalism and essays in the attempt to halt the King's genocidal policies. Heart of Darkness records these evils, and the ravages of Belgian colonialism on the African tribal societies it encountered and uprooted. Scholars of African history have shown how accurate his descriptions are, from the bit of white thread worn around the neck of a certain tribal group, to the construction of the railroad to Kinshasa and its devastating human impact. Conrad never names the Congo, nor the places and landmarks his character Marlow visits, yet he himself later called the book a "Kodak," or a snapshot, of the Congo.

The location is left unnamed in part because Conrad wishes to show that the heart of this darkness can shift on its axis. Marlow is telling the tale to several anonymous Englishmen as they sail the Thames on their yacht. Under the Roman empire, Britain had itself been thought of as a savage wilderness, a dark continent. The journey upriver, as Marlow points out, has been a reverse journey as well, a journey back from Africa to the darkness that lies at the heart of an England that claims to be civilizing those whom it is merely conquering. The seemingly clear-cut boundaries of light and dark, black and white, have blurred and even reversed themselves, and the nested narrative of the story itself challenges our understanding and even our sense of self. In this narrative, as in Conrad's other works, we are confronted with the tragic irony that human knowledge always comes too late.

Preface to *The Nigger of the "Narcissus"*[1]

A work that aspires, however humbly, to the condition of art should carry its justification in every line. And art itself may be defined as a single-minded attempt to render the highest kind of justice to the visible universe, by bringing to light the truth, manifold and one, underlying its every aspect. It is an attempt to find in its forms, in its colours, in its light, in its shadows, in the aspects of matter, and in the facts of life what of each is fundamental, what is enduring and essential—their one illuminating and convincing quality—the very truth of their existence. The artist, then, like the thinker or the scientist, seeks the truth and makes his appeal. Impressed by the aspect of the world the thinker plunges into ideas, the scientist into facts—whence, presently, emerging they make their appeal to those qualities of our being that fit us best for the hazardous enterprise of living. They speak authoritatively to our common sense, to our intelligence, to our desire of peace, or to our desire of unrest; not seldom to our prejudices, sometimes to our fears, often to our egoism—but always to our credulity. And their words are heard with reverence, for their concern is with weighty matters: with the cultivation of our minds and the proper care of our bodies, with the attainment of our ambitions, with the perfection of the means and the glorification of our precious aims.

It is otherwise with the artist.

Confronted by the same enigmatical spectacle the artist descends within himself, and in that lonely region of stress and strife, if he be deserving and fortunate, he finds the terms of his appeal. His appeal is made to our less obvious capacities: to that part of our nature which, because of the warlike conditions of existence, is necessarily kept out of sight within the more resisting and hard qualities—like the vulnerable body within a steel armour. His appeal is less loud, more profound, less distinct, more stirring—and sooner forgotten. Yet its effect endures for ever. The changing wisdom of successive generations discards ideas, questions facts, demolishes theories. But the artist appeals to that part of our being which is not dependent on wisdom; to that in us which is a gift and not an acquisition—and, therefore, more permanently enduring. He speaks to our capacity for delight and wonder, to the sense of mystery surrounding our lives; to our sense of pity, and beauty, and pain; to the latent feeling of fellowship with all creation—and to the subtle but invincible conviction of solidarity that knits together the loneliness of innumerable hearts, to the solidarity in dreams, in joy, in sorrow, in aspirations, in illusions, in hope, in fear, which binds men to each other, which binds together all humanity—the dead to the living and the living to the unborn.

It is only some such train of thought, or rather of feeling, that can in a measure explain the aim of the attempt, made in the tale which follows, to present an unrestful episode in the obscure lives of a few individuals out of all the disregarded multitude of the bewildered, the simple, and the voiceless. For, if any part of truth dwells in the belief confessed above, it becomes evident that there is not a place of splendour or a dark corner of the earth that does not deserve, if only a passing glance of wonder and pity. The motive, then, may be held to justify the matter of the work; but this preface, which is simply an avowal of endeavour, cannot end here—for the avowal is not yet complete.

---

1. Conrad's novella *The Nigger of the "Narcissus"* deals with the tragic death of a black seaman aboard a merchant ship named the *Narcissus*; Conrad had served as first mate on a ship of that name in the Indian Ocean in 1883. He published the novella in *The New Review* in 1897, then added this preface when it came out in book form in 1898.

Fiction—if it at all aspires to be art—appeals to temperament. And in truth it must be, like painting, like music, like all art, the appeal of one temperament to all the other innumerable temperaments whose subtle and resistless power endows passing events with their true meaning, and creates the moral, the emotional atmosphere of the place and time. Such an appeal to be effective must be an impression conveyed through the senses; and, in fact, it cannot be made in any other way, because temperament, whether individual or collective, is not amenable to persuasion. All art, therefore, appeals primarily to the senses, and the artistic aim when expressing itself in written words must also make its appeal through the senses, if its high desire is to reach the secret spring of responsive emotions. It must strenuously aspire to the plasticity of sculpture, to the colour of painting, and to the magic suggestiveness of music—which is the art of arts. And it is only through complete, unswerving devotion to the perfect blending of form and substance; it is only through an unremitting never-discouraged care for the shape and ring of sentences that an approach can be made to plasticity, to colour, and that the light of magic suggestiveness may be brought to play for an evanescent instant over the commonplace surface of words: of the old, old words, worn thin, defaced by ages of careless usage.

The sincere endeavour to accomplish that creative task, to go as far on that road as his strength will carry him, to go undeterred by faltering, weariness, or reproach, is the only valid justification for the worker in prose. And if his conscience is clear, his answer to those who, in the fullness of a wisdom which looks for immediate profit, demand specifically to be edified, consoled, amused; who demand to be promptly improved, or encouraged, or frightened, or shocked, or charmed, must run thus: My task which I am trying to achieve is, by the power of the written word to make you hear, to make you feel—it is, before all, to make you see. That—and no more, and it is everything. If I succeed, you shall find there according to your deserts: encouragement, consolation, fear, charm—all you demand—and, perhaps, also that glimpse of truth for which you have forgotten to ask.

To snatch in a moment of courage, from the remorseless rush of time, a passing phase of life, is only the beginning of the task. The task approached in tenderness and faith is to hold up unquestioningly, without choice and without fear, the rescued fragment before all eyes in the light of a sincere mood. It is to show its vibration, its colour, its form; and through its movement, its form, and its colour, reveal the substance of its truth—disclose its inspiring secret: the stress and passion within the core of each convincing moment. In a single-minded attempt of that kind, if one be deserving and fortunate, one may perchance attain to such clearness of sincerity that at last the presented vision of regret or pity, of terror or mirth, shall awaken in the hearts of the beholders that feeling of unavoidable solidarity; of the solidarity in mysterious origin, in toil, in joy, in hope, in uncertain fate, which binds men to each other and all mankind to the visible world.

It is evident that he who, rightly or wrongly, holds by the convictions expressed above cannot be faithful to any one of the temporary formulas of his craft. The enduring part of them—the truth which each only imperfectly veils—should abide with him as the most precious of his possessions, but they all: Realism, Romanticism, Naturalism, even the unofficial sentimentalism (which, like the poor, is exceedingly difficult to get rid of), all these gods must, after a short period of fellowship, abandon him—even on the very threshold of the temple—to the stammerings of his conscience and to the outspoken consciousness of the difficulties of his work. In that uneasy solitude the supreme cry of Art for Art itself, loses the exciting ring of its apparent immorality. It sounds far off. It has ceased to be a cry, and is heard only as a whisper, often incomprehensible, but at times and faintly encouraging.

Sometimes, stretched at ease in the shade of a roadside tree, we watch the motions of a labourer in a distant field, and after a time, begin to wonder languidly as to what the fellow may be at. We watch the movements of his body, the waving of his arms, we see him bend down, stand up, hesitate, begin again. It may add to the charm of an idle hour to be told the purpose of his exertions. If we know he is trying to lift a stone, to dig a ditch, to uproot a stump, we look with a more real interest at his efforts; we are disposed to condone the jar of his agitation upon the restfulness of the landscape; and even, if in a brotherly frame of mind, we may bring ourselves to forgive his failure. We understood his object, and, after all, the fellow has tried, and perhaps he had not the strength—and perhaps he had not the knowledge. We forgive, go on our way—and forget.

And so it is with the workman of art. Art is long and life is short, and success is very far off. And thus, doubtful of strength to travel so far, we talk a little about the aim—the aim of art, which, like life itself, is inspiring, difficult—obscured by mists. It is not in the clear logic of a triumphant conclusion; it is not in the unveiling of one of those heartless secrets which are called the Laws of Nature. It is not less great, but only more difficult.

To arrest, for the space of a breath, the hands busy about the work of the earth, and compel men entranced by the sight of distant goals to glance for a moment at the surrounding vision of form and colour, of sunshine and shadows; to make them pause for a look, for a sigh, for a smile—such is the aim, difficult and evanescent, and reserved only for a very few to achieve. But sometimes, by the deserving and the fortunate, even that task is accomplished. And when it is accomplished—behold!—all the truth of life is there: a moment of vision, a sigh, a smile—and the return to an eternal rest.

Heart of Darkness

1

The *Nellie*, a cruising yawl,[1] swung to her anchor without a flutter of the sails, and was at rest. The flood had made, the wind was nearly calm, and being bound down the river, the only thing for it was to come to and wait for the turn of the tide.

The sea-reach of the Thames stretched before us like the beginning of an interminable waterway. In the offing the sea and the sky were welded together without a joint, and in the luminous space the tanned sails of the barges drifting up with the tide seemed to stand still in red clusters of canvas sharply peaked, with gleams of varnished sprits. A haze rested on the low shores that ran out to sea in vanishing flatness. The air was dark above Gravesend, and farther back still seemed condensed into a mournful gloom, brooding motionless over the biggest, and the greatest, town on earth.[2]

The Director of Companies was our captain and our host. We four affectionately watched his back as he stood in the bows looking to seaward. On the whole river there was nothing that looked half so nautical. He resembled a pilot, which to a seaman is trustworthiness personified. It was difficult to realise his work was not out there in the luminous estuary, but behind him, within the brooding gloom.

---

1. A two-masted ship.

2. London. Gravesend is the last major town on the Thames estuary, from which the river joins the North Sea.

Between us there was, as I have already said somewhere, the bond of the sea. Besides holding our hearts together through long periods of separation, it had the effect of making us tolerant of each other's yarns—and even convictions. The Lawyer—the best of old fellows—had, because of his many years and many virtues, the only cushion on deck, and was lying on the only rug. The Accountant had brought out already a box of dominoes, and was toying architecturally with the bones. Marlow sat cross-legged right aft, leaning against the mizzen-mast.[3] He had sunken cheeks, a yellow complexion, a straight back, an ascetic aspect, and, with his arms dropped, the palms of hands outwards, resembled an idol. The Director, satisfied the anchor had good hold, made his way aft and sat down amongst us. We exchanged a few words lazily. Afterwards there was silence on board the yacht. For some reason or other we did not begin that game of dominoes. We felt meditative, and fit for nothing but placid staring. The day was ending in a serenity of still and exquisite brilliance. The water shone pacifically; the sky, without a speck, was a benign immensity of unstained light; the very mist on the Essex marshes was like a gauzy and radiant fabric, hung from the wooded rises inland, and draping the low shores in diaphanous folds. Only the gloom to the west, brooding over the upper reaches, became more sombre every minute, as if angered by the approach of the sun.

And at last, in its curved and imperceptible fall, the sun sank low, and from glowing white changed to a dull red without rays and without heat, as if about to go out suddenly, stricken to death by the touch of that gloom brooding over a crowd of men.

Forthwith a change came over the waters, and the serenity became less brilliant but more profound. The old river in its broad reach rested unruffled at the decline of day, after ages of good service done to the race that peopled its banks, spread out in the tranquil dignity of a waterway leading to the uttermost ends of the earth. We looked at the venerable stream not in the vivid flush of a short day that comes and departs for ever, but in the august light of abiding memories. And indeed nothing is easier for a man who has, as the phrase goes, "followed the sea" with reverence and affection, than to evoke the great spirit of the past upon the lower reaches of the Thames. The tidal current runs to and fro in its unceasing service, crowded with memories of men and ships it has borne to the rest of home or to the battles of the sea. It had known and served all the men of whom the nation is proud, from Sir Francis Drake to Sir John Franklin, knights all, titled and untitled—the great knights-errant of the sea.[4] It had borne all the ships whose names are like jewels flashing in the night of time, from the *Golden Hind* returning with her round flanks full of treasure, to be visited by the Queen's Highness and thus pass out of the gigantic tale, to the *Erebus* and *Terror,* bound on other conquests—and that never returned. It had known the ships and the men. They had sailed from Deptford, from Greenwich, from Erith—the adventurers and the settlers; kings' ships and the ships of men on 'Change; captains, admirals, the dark "interlopers" of the Eastern trade, and the commissioned "generals" of East India fleets.[5] Hunters for gold or pursuers of fame, they all had gone out on that stream, bearing the sword, and often the torch, messengers

---

3. A secondary mast at the stern of the ship.
4. Sir Francis Drake (1540–1596) was captain of *The Golden Hind* in the service of Queen Elizabeth I; his reputation came from the successful raids he mounted against Spanish ships returning laden with gold from the New World (South America). In 1845 Sir John Franklin led an expedition in the *Erebus* and *Terror* in search of the Northwest Passage (to the Pacific); all perished.
5. Deptford, Greenwich, and Erith lie on the Thames between London and Gravesend; "men on 'Change" are brokers on the Stock Exchange; the East India Company, a commercial and trading concern, became *de facto* ruler of large tracts of India in the 18th and 19th centuries.

of the might within the land, bearers of a spark from the sacred fire. What greatness had not floated on the ebb of that river into the mystery of an unknown earth! . . . The dreams of men, the seed of commonwealths, the germs of empires.

The sun set; the dusk fell on the stream, and lights began to appear along the shore. The Chapman lighthouse, a three-legged thing erect on a mudflat, shone strongly. Lights of ships moved in the fairway—a great stir of lights going up and going down. And farther west on the upper reaches the place of the monstrous town was still marked ominously on the sky, a brooding gloom in sunshine, a lurid glare under the stars.

"And this also," said Marlow suddenly, "has been one of the dark places of the earth."

He was the only man of us who still "followed the sea." The worst that could be said of him was that he did not represent his class. He was a seaman, but he was a wanderer too, while most seamen lead, if one may so express it, a sedentary life. Their minds are of the stay-at-home order, and their home is always with them—the ship; and so is their country—the sea. One ship is very much like another, and the sea is always the same. In the immutability of their surroundings the foreign shores, the foreign faces, the changing immensity of life, glide past, veiled not by a sense of mystery but by a slightly disdainful ignorance; for there is nothing mysterious to a seaman unless it be the sea itself, which is the mistress of his existence and as inscrutable as Destiny. For the rest, after his hours of work, a casual stroll or a casual spree on shore suffices to unfold for him the secret of a whole continent, and generally he finds the secret not worth knowing. The yarns of seamen have a direct simplicity, the whole meaning of which lies within the shell of a cracked nut. But Marlow was not typical (if his propensity to spin yarns be excepted), and to him the meaning of an episode was not inside like a kernel but outside, enveloping the tale which brought it out only as a glow brings out a haze, in the likeness of one of these misty halos that sometimes are made visible by the spectral illumination of moonshine.

His remark did not seem at all surprising. It was just like Marlow. It was accepted in silence. No one took the trouble to grunt even; and presently he said, very slow,—

"I was thinking of very old times, when the Romans first came here, nineteen hundred years ago[6]—the other day. . . . Light came out of this river since—you say Knights? Yes; but it is like a running blaze on a plain, like a flash of lightning in the clouds. We live in the flicker—may it last as long as the old earth keeps rolling! But darkness was here yesterday. Imagine the feelings of a commander of a fine—what d'ye call 'em?—trireme in the Mediterranean, ordered suddenly to the north; run overland across the Gauls in a hurry;[7] put in charge of one of these craft the legionaries,—a wonderful lot of handy men they must have been too—used to build, apparently by the hundred, in a month or two, if we may believe what we read. Imagine him here—the very end of the world, a sea the colour of lead, a sky the colour of smoke, a kind of ship about as rigid as a concertina—and going up this river with stores, or orders, or what you like. Sandbanks, marshes, forests, savages,—precious little to eat fit for a civilised man, nothing but Thames water to drink. No Falernian wine here, no going ashore. Here and there a military camp lost in a wilderness, like a needle in a bundle of hay—cold, fog, tempests, disease, exile, and death,—death skulking in the air, in the water, in the bush. They must have been dying like flies

6. A Roman force under Julius Caesar landed in Britain in 55 B.C., but it was not until A.D. 43 that the Emperor Claudius decided to conquer the island.
7. A *trireme* is an ancient warship, propelled by oarsmen;

the Gauls were the pre-Roman tribes who occupied present-day France; they were subdued by Julius Caesar between 58–50 B.C.

here. Oh yes—he did it. Did it very well, too, no doubt, and without thinking much about it either, except afterwards to brag of what he had gone through in his time, perhaps. They were men enough to face the darkness. And perhaps he was cheered by keeping his eye on a chance of promotion to the fleet at Ravenna by-and-by, if he had good friends in Rome and survived the awful climate. Or think of a decent young citizen in a toga—perhaps too much dice, you know—coming out here in the train of some prefect, or tax-gatherer, or trader even, to mend his fortunes. Land in a swamp, march through the woods, and in some inland post feel the savagery, the utter savagery, had closed round him,—all that mysterious life of the wilderness that stirs in the forest, in the jungles, in the hearts of wild men. There's no initiation either into such mysteries. He has to live in the midst of the incomprehensible, which is also detestable. And it has a fascination, too, that goes to work upon him. The fascination of the abomination—you know. Imagine the growing regrets, the longing to escape, the powerless disgust, the surrender, the hate."

He paused.

"Mind," he began again, lifting one arm from the elbow, the palm of the hand outwards, so that, with his legs folded before him, he had the pose of a Buddha preaching in European clothes and without a lotus-flower—"Mind, none of us would feel exactly like this. What saves us is efficiency—the devotion to efficiency. But these chaps were not much account, really. They were no colonists; their administration was merely a squeeze, and nothing more, I suspect. They were conquerors, and for that you want only brute force—nothing to boast of, when you have it, since your strength is just an accident arising from the weakness of others. They grabbed what they could get for the sake of what was to be got. It was just robbery with violence, aggravated murder on a great scale, and men going at it blind—as is very proper for those who tackle a darkness. The conquest of the earth, which mostly means the taking it away from those who have a different complexion or slightly flatter noses than ourselves, is not a pretty thing when you look into it too much. What redeems it is the idea only. An idea at the back of it; not a sentimental pretence but an idea; and an unselfish belief in the idea—something you can set up, and bow down before, and offer a sacrifice to . . . ."

He broke off. Flames glided in the river, small green flames, red flames, white flames, pursuing, overtaking, joining, crossing each other—then separating slowly or hastily. The traffic of the great city went on in the deepening night upon the sleepless river. We looked on, waiting patiently—there was nothing else to do till the end of the flood; but it was only after a long silence, when he said, in a hesitating voice, "I suppose you fellows remember I did once turn fresh-water sailor for a bit," that we knew we were fated, before the ebb began to run, to hear about one of Marlow's inconclusive experiences.

"I don't want to bother you much with what happened to me personally," he began, showing in this remark the weakness of many tellers of tales who seem so often unaware of what their audience would best like to hear; "yet to understand the effect of it on me you ought to know how I got out there, what I saw, how I went up that river to the place where I first met the poor chap. It was the farthest point of navigation and the culminating point of my experience. It seemed somehow to throw a kind of light on everything about me—and into my thoughts. It was sombre enough too—and pitiful—not extraordinary in any way—not very clear either. No, not very clear. And yet it seemed to throw a kind of light.

"I had then, as you remember, just returned to London after a lot of Indian Ocean, Pacific, China Seas—a regular dose of the East—six years or so, and I was loafing about, hindering you fellows in your work and invading your homes, just as though I had got a heavenly mission to civilise you. It was very fine for a time, but after a bit I did get tired of resting. Then I began to look for a ship—I should think the hardest work on earth. But the ships wouldn't even look at me. And I got tired of that game too.

"Now when I was a little chap I had a passion for maps. I would look for hours at South America, or Africa, or Australia, and lose myself in all the glories of exploration. At that time there were many blank spaces on the earth, and when I saw one that looked particularly inviting on a map (but they all look that) I would put my finger on it and say, When I grow up I will go there. The North Pole was one of these places, I remember. Well, I haven't been there yet, and shall not try now. The glamour's off. Other places were scattered about the Equator, and in every sort of latitude all over the two hemispheres. I have been in some of them, and . . . well, we won't talk about that. But there was one yet—the biggest, the most blank, so to speak—that I had a hankering after.

"True, by this time it was not a blank space any more. It had got filled since my boyhood with rivers and lakes and names. It had ceased to be a blank space of delightful mystery—a white patch for a boy to dream gloriously over. It had become a place of darkness. But there was in it one river especially, a mighty big river, that you could see on the map, resembling an immense snake uncoiled, with its head in the sea, its body at rest curving afar over a vast country, and its tail lost in the depths of the land. And as I looked at the map of it in a shop-window, it fascinated me as a snake would a bird—a silly little bird. Then I remembered there was a big concern, a Company for trade on that river. Dash it all! I thought to myself, they can't trade without using some kind of craft on that lot of fresh water—steamboats! Why shouldn't I try to get charge of one. I went on along Fleet Street, but could not shake off the idea. The snake had charmed me.

"You understand it was a Continental concern, that Trading Society; but I have a lot of relations living on the Continent, because it's cheap and not so nasty as it looks, they say.

"I am sorry to own I began to worry them. This was already a fresh departure for me. I was not used to get things that way, you know. I always went my own road and on my own legs where I had a mind to go. I wouldn't have believed it of myself; but, then—you see—I felt somehow I must get there by hook or by crook. So I worried them. The men said 'My dear fellow,' and did nothing. Then—would you believe it?—I tried the women. I, Charlie Marlow, set the women to work—to get a job. Heavens! Well, you see, the notion drove me. I had an aunt, a dear enthusiastic soul. She wrote: 'It will be delightful. I am ready to do anything, anything for you. It is a glorious idea. I know the wife of a very high personage in the Administration, and also a man who has lots of influence with,' &c., &c. She was determined to make no end of fuss to get me appointed skipper of a river steamboat, if such was my fancy.

"I got my appointment—of course; and I got it very quick. It appears the Company had received news that one of their captains had been killed in a scuffle with the natives. This was my chance, and it made me the more anxious to go. It was only months and months afterwards, when I made the attempt to recover what was left of the body, that I heard the original quarrel arose from a misunderstanding about some hens. Yes, two black hens. Fresleven—that was the fellow's name, a Dane—thought himself wronged somehow in the bargain, so he went ashore and started to hammer the chief of the village with a stick. Oh, it didn't surprise me in the least to hear this, and at the same time to be told that Fresleven was the gentlest, quietest creature that ever walked on two legs. No doubt he was; but he had been a couple of years already out there engaged in the noble cause, you know, and he probably felt the need at last of asserting his self-respect in some way. Therefore he whacked the old nigger mercilessly, while a big crowd of his people watched him, thunderstruck, till some man,—I was told the chief's son,—in desperation at hearing the old chap yell, made a tentative jab with a spear at the white man—and of course it went quite easy between the shoulder-blades. Then the whole population cleared into the forest, expecting all kinds of calamities to happen, while, on the other hand, the steamer Fresleven commanded left also in a bad panic, in charge of the engineer, I believe. Afterwards nobody seemed to trouble much about Fresleven's remains, till I got out and stepped into his shoes. I couldn't let it rest, though; but when an opportunity offered at last to meet my predecessor, the grass growing through his ribs was tall enough to hide his bones. They were all there. The supernatural being had not been touched after he fell. And the village was deserted, the huts gaped black, rotting, all askew within the fallen enclosures. A calamity had come to it, sure enough. The people had vanished. Mad terror had scattered them, men, women, and children, through the bush, and they had never returned. What became of the hens I don't know either. I should think the cause of progress got them, anyhow. However, through this glorious affair I got my appointment, before I had fairly begun to hope for it.

"I flew around like mad to get ready, and before forty-eight hours I was crossing the Channel to show myself to my employers, and sign the contract. In a very few hours I arrived in a city that always makes me think of a whited sepulchre.[8] Prejudice no doubt. I had no difficulty in finding the Company's offices. It was the biggest thing in the town, and everybody I met was full of it. They were going to run an oversea empire, and make no end of coin by trade.

"A narrow and deserted street in deep shadow, high houses, innumerable windows with venetian blinds, a dead silence, grass sprouting between the stones, imposing carriage archways right and left, immense double doors standing ponderously ajar. I slipped through one of these cracks, went up a swept and ungarnished staircase, as arid as a desert, and opened the first door I came to. Two women, one fat and the other slim, sat on straw-bottomed chairs, knitting black wool. The slim one got up and walked straight at me—still knitting with downcast eyes—and only just as I began to think of getting out of her way, as you would for a somnambulist, stood still, and looked up. Her dress was as plain as an umbrella-cover, and she turned round without a word and preceded me into a waiting-room. I gave my name, and looked about. Deal table in the middle, plain chairs all round the walls, on one end a large shining map, marked with all the colours of a rainbow. There was a vast amount of red—good to see at any time, because one knows that some real work is done in there, a deuce of a lot of blue, a little green, smears of orange, and, on the East Coast, a purple patch, to show where the jolly pioneers of progress drink the jolly lager-beer.[9] However, I wasn't going into any of these. I was going into the yellow. Dead in the centre. And the river was there—fascinating—deadly—like a snake. Ough! A door opened, a white-haired secretarial head, but wearing a compassionate expression, appeared, and a skinny forefinger beckoned me into the sanctuary. Its light was dim, and a heavy writing-desk squatted in the middle. From behind that structure

---

8. Brussels was the headquarters of the Société Anonyme Belge pour le Commerce du Haut-Congo (Belgian Corporation for Trade in the Upper Congo), with which Conrad obtained his post through the influence of his

aunt, Marguerite Poradowska.
9. British territories were traditionally marked in red on colonial maps; lager was originally a continental beer, not much drunk in England.

came out an impression of pale plumpness in a frock-coat. The great man himself. He was five feet six, I should judge, and had his grip on the handle-end of ever so many millions. He shook hands, I fancy, murmured vaguely, was satisfied with my French. *Bon voyage.*

"In about forty-five seconds I found myself again in the waiting-room with the compassionate secretary, who, full of desolation and sympathy, made me sign some document. I believe I undertook amongst other things not to disclose any trade secrets. Well, I am not going to.

"I began to feel slightly uneasy. You know I am not used to such ceremonies, and there was something ominous in the atmosphere. It was just as though I had been let into some conspiracy—I don't know—something not quite right; and I was glad to get out. In the outer room the two women knitted black wool feverishly. People were arriving, and the younger one was walking back and forth introducing them. The old one sat on her chair. Her flat cloth slippers were propped up on a foot-warmer, and a cat reposed on her lap. She wore a starched white affair on her head, had a wart on one cheek, and silver-rimmed spectacles hung on the tip of her nose. She glanced at me above the glasses. The swift and indifferent placidity of that look troubled me. Two youths with foolish and cheery countenances were being piloted over, and she threw at them the same quick glance of unconcerned wisdom. She seemed to know all about them and about me too. An eerie feeling came over me. She seemed uncanny and fateful. Often far away there I thought of these two, guarding the door of Darkness, knitting black wool as for a warm pall, one introducing, introducing continuously to the unknown, the other scrutinising the cheery and foolish faces with unconcerned old eyes. *Ave!* Old knitter of black wool. *Morituri te salutant.*[1] Not many of those she looked at ever saw her again—not half, by a long way.

"There was yet a visit to the doctor. 'A simple formality,' assured me the secretary, with an air of taking an immense part in all my sorrows. Accordingly a young chap wearing his hat over the left eyebrow, some clerk I suppose,—there must have been clerks in the business, though the house was as still as a house in a city of the dead,—came from somewhere upstairs, and led me forth. He was shabby and careless, with ink-stains on the sleeves of his jacket, and his cravat was large and billowy, under a chin shaped like the toe of an old boot. It was a little too early for the doctor, so I proposed a drink, and thereupon he developed a vein of joviality. As we sat over our vermouths he glorified the Company's business, and by-and-by I expressed casually my surprise at him not going out there. He became very cool and collected all at once. 'I am not such a fool as I look, quoth Plato to his disciples,' he said sententiously, emptied his glass with great resolution, and we rose.

"The old doctor felt my pulse, evidently thinking of something else the while. 'Good, good for there,' he mumbled, and then with a certain eagerness asked me whether I would let him measure my head. Rather surprised, I said Yes, when he produced a thing like calipers and got the dimensions back and front and every way, taking notes carefully. He was an unshaven little man in a threadbare coat like a gaberdine, with his feet in slippers, and I thought him a harmless fool. 'I always ask leave, in the interests of science, to measure the crania of those going out there,' he said. 'And when they come back too?' I asked. 'Oh, I never see them,' he remarked; 'and moreover, the changes take place inside, you know.' He smiled, as if at some quiet joke. 'So you are going out there. Famous. Interesting too.' He gave me a searching glance, and made another note. 'Ever any madness in your family?' he asked, in a

---

1. Hail! . . . Those who are about to die salute you!—traditional cry of Roman gladiators.

matter-of-fact tone. I felt very annoyed. 'Is that question in the interests of science too?' 'It would be,' he said, without taking notice of my irritation, 'interesting for science to watch the mental changes of individuals, on the spot, but . . .' 'Are you an alienist?'[2] I interrupted. 'Every doctor should be—a little,' answered that original, imperturbably. 'I have a little theory which you Messieurs who go out there must help me to prove. This is my share in the advantages my country shall reap from the possession of such a magnificent dependency. The mere wealth I leave to others. Pardon my questions, but you are the first Englishman coming under my observation . . .' I hastened to assure him I was not in the least typical. 'If I were,' said I, 'I wouldn't be talking like this with you.' 'What you say is rather profound, and probably erroneous,' he said, with a laugh. 'Avoid irritation more than exposure to the sun. Adieu. How do you English say, eh? Good-bye. Ah! Good-bye. Adieu. In the tropics one must before everything keep calm.' . . . He lifted a warning forefinger. . . . '*Du calme, du calme. Adieu.*'

"One thing more remained to do—say good-bye to my excellent aunt. I found her triumphant. I had a cup of tea—the last decent cup of tea for many days—and in a room that most soothingly looked just as you would expect a lady's drawing-room to look, we had a long quiet chat by the fireside. In the course of these confidences it became quite plain to me I had been represented to the wife of the high dignitary, and goodness knows to how many more people besides, as an exceptional and gifted creature—a piece of good fortune for the Company—a man you don't get hold of every day. Good heavens! and I was going to take charge of a twopenny-half-penny river-steamboat with a penny whistle attached! It appeared, however, I was also one of the Workers, with a capital—you know. Something like an emissary of light, something like a lower sort of apostle. There had been a lot of such rot let loose in print and talk just about that time, and the excellent woman, living right in the rush of all that humbug, got carried off her feet. She talked about 'weaning those ignorant millions from their horrid ways,' till, upon my word, she made me quite uncomfortable. I ventured to hint that the Company was run for profit.

"'You forget, dear Charlie, that the labourer is worthy of his hire,' she said, brightly.[3] It's queer how out of touch with truth women are. They live in a world of their own, and there had never been anything like it, and never can be. It is too beautiful altogether, and if they were to set it up it would go to pieces before the first sunset. Some confounded fact we men have been living contentedly with ever since the day of creation would start up and knock the whole thing over.

"After this I got embraced, told to wear flannel, be sure to write often, and so on—and I left. In the street—I don't know why—a queer feeling came to me that I was an impostor. Odd thing that I, who used to clear out for any part of the world at twenty-four hours' notice, with less thought than most men give to the crossing of a street, had a moment—I won't say of hesitation, but of startled pause, before this commonplace affair. The best way I can explain it to you is by saying that, for a second or two, I felt as though, instead of going to the centre of a continent, I were about to set off for the centre of the earth.

"I left in a French steamer, and she called in every blamed port they have out there, for, as far as I could see, the sole purpose of landing soldiers and custom-house officers. I watched the coast. Watching a coast as it slips by the ship is like thinking about an enigma. There it is before you—smiling, frowning, inviting, grand, mean, insipid, or savage, and always mute with an air of whispering, Come and find out.

2. A psychologist.   3. 1 Timothy 5.18.

This one was almost featureless, as if still in the making, with an aspect of monotonous grimness. The edge of a colossal jungle, so dark-green as to be almost black, fringed with white surf, ran straight, like a ruled line, far, far away along a blue sea whose glitter was blurred by a creeping mist. The sun was fierce, the land seemed to glisten and drip with steam. Here and there greyish-whitish specks showed up, clustered inside the white surf, with a flag flying above them perhaps—settlements some centuries old, and still no bigger than pin-heads on the untouched expanse of their background. We pounded along, stopped, landed soldiers; went on, landed custom-house clerks to levy toll in what looked like a Godforsaken wilderness, with a tin shed and a flag-pole lost in it; landed more soldiers—to take care of the custom-house clerks, presumably. Some, I heard, got drowned in the surf; but whether they did or not, nobody seemed particularly to care. They were just flung out there, and on we went. Every day the coast looked the same, as though we had not moved; but we passed various places—trading places—with names like Gran' Bassam, Little Popo,[4] names that seemed to belong to some sordid farce acted in front of a sinister back-cloth. The idleness of a passenger, my isolation amongst all these men with whom I had no point of contact, the oily and languid sea, the uniform sombreness of the coast, seemed to keep me away from the truth of things, within the toil of a mournful and senseless delusion. The voice of the surf heard now and then was a positive pleasure, like the speech of a brother. It was something natural, that had its reason, that had a meaning. Now and then a boat from the shore gave one a momentary contact with reality. It was paddled by black fellows. You could see from afar the white of their eyeballs glistening. They shouted, sang; their bodies streamed with perspiration; they had faces like grotesque masks—these chaps; but they had bone, muscle, a wild vitality, an intense energy of movement, that was as natural and true as the surf along their coast. They wanted no excuse for being there. They were a great comfort to look at. For a time I would feel I belonged still to a world of straightforward facts; but the feeling would not last long. Something would turn up to scare it away. Once, I remember, we came upon a man-of-war anchored off the coast. There wasn't even a shed there, and she was shelling the bush. It appears the French had one of their wars going on thereabouts. Her ensign dropped limp like a rag; the muzzles of the long eight-inch guns stuck out all over the low hull; the greasy, slimy swell swung her up lazily and let her down, swaying her thin masts. In the empty immensity of earth, sky, and water, there she was, incomprehensible, firing into a continent. Pop, would go one of the eight-inch guns; a small flame would dart and vanish, a little white smoke would disappear, a tiny projectile would give a feeble screech—and nothing happened. Nothing could happen. There was a touch of insanity in the proceeding, a sense of lugubrious drollery in the sight; and it was not dissipated by somebody on board assuring me earnestly there was a camp of natives—he called them enemies!—hidden out of sight somewhere.

"We gave her letters (I heard the men in that lonely ship were dying of fever at the rate of three a day) and went on. We called at some more places with farcical names, where the merry dance of death and trade goes on in a still and earthy atmosphere as of an overheated catacomb;[5] all along the formless coast bordered by danger-

---

4. Grand Bassam and Grand Popo are the names of ports where Conrad's ship called on its way to the Congo.
5. In a letter in May 1890 Conrad wrote: "What makes me rather uneasy is the information that 60 per cent. of our Company's employés return to Europe before they have completed even six months' service. Fever and

dysentery! There are others who are sent home in a hurry at the end of a year, so that they shouldn't die in the Congo." According to a 1907 report, 150 out of every 2,000 native Congolese laborers died each month while in company employ; "All along the [railroad] track one would see corpses."

ous surf, as if Nature herself had tried to ward off intruders; in and out of rivers, streams of death in life, whose banks were rotting into mud, whose waters, thickened into slime, invaded the contorted mangroves, that seemed to writhe at us in the extremity of an impotent despair. Nowhere did we stop long enough to get a particularised impression, but the general sense of vague and oppressive wonder grew upon me. It was like a weary pilgrimage amongst hints for nightmares.

"It was upward of thirty days before I saw the mouth of the big river. We anchored off the seat of the government. But my work would not begin till some two hundred miles farther on. So as soon as I could I made a start for a place thirty miles higher up.

"I had my passage on a little sea-going steamer. Her captain was a Swede, and knowing me for a seaman, invited me on the bridge. He was a young man, lean, fair, and morose, with lanky hair and a shuffling gait. As we left the miserable little wharf, he tossed his head contemptuously at the shore. 'Been living there?' he asked. I said, 'Yes.' 'Fine lot these government chaps—are they not?' he went on, speaking English with great precision and considerable bitterness. 'It is funny what some people will do for a few francs a month. I wonder what becomes of that kind when it goes up country?' I said to him I expected to see that soon. 'So-o-o!' he exclaimed. He shuffled athwart, keeping one eye ahead vigilantly. 'Don't be too sure,' he continued. 'The other day I took up a man who hanged himself on the road. He was a Swede, too.' 'Hanged himself! Why, in God's name?' I cried. He kept on looking out watchfully. 'Who knows? The sun too much for him, or the country perhaps.'

"At last we opened a reach. A rocky cliff appeared, mounds of turned-up earth by the shore, houses on a hill, others, with iron roofs, amongst a waste of excavations, or hanging to the declivity. A continuous noise of the rapids above hovered over this scene of inhabited devastation. A lot of people, mostly black and naked, moved about like ants. A jetty projected into the river. A blinding sunlight drowned all this at times in a sudden recrudescence of glare. 'There's your Company's station,' said the Swede, pointing to three wooden barrack-like structures on the rocky slope. 'I will send your things up. Four boxes did you say? So. Farewell.'

"I came upon a boiler wallowing in the grass, then found a path leading up the hill. It turned aside for the boulders, and also for an undersized railway-truck lying there on its back with its wheels in the air. One was off. The thing looked as dead as the carcass of some animal. I came upon more pieces of decaying machinery, a stack of rusty rails. To the left a clump of trees made a shady spot, where dark things seemed to stir feebly. I blinked, the path was steep. A horn tooted to the right, and I saw the black people run. A heavy and dull detonation shook the ground, a puff of smoke came out of the cliff, and that was all. No change appeared on the face of the rock. They were building a railway. The cliff was not in the way or anything; but this objectless blasting was all the work going on.

"A slight clinking behind me made me turn my head. Six black men advanced in a file, toiling up the path. They walked erect and slow, balancing small baskets full of earth on their heads, and the clink kept time with their footsteps. Black rags were wound round their loins, and the short ends behind wagged to and fro like tails. I could see every rib, the joints of their limbs were like knots in a rope; each had an iron collar on his neck, and all were connected together with a chain whose bights swung between them, rhythmically clinking. Another report from the cliff made me think suddenly of that ship of war I had seen firing into a continent. It was the same kind of ominous voice; but these men could by no stretch of imagination be called enemies. They were called criminals, and the outraged law, like the bursting shells, had come to them, an insoluble mystery from over the sea. All their meagre breasts panted together, the violently dilated nostrils quivered, the eyes stared stonily up-hill. They passed me within six inches, without a glance, with that complete, death-like indifference of unhappy savages. Behind this raw matter one of the reclaimed, the product of the new forces at work, strolled despondently, carrying a rifle by its middle. He had a uniform jacket with one button off, and seeing a white man on the path, hoisted his weapon to his shoulder with alacrity. This was simple prudence, white men being so much alike at a distance that he could not tell who I might be. He was speedily reassured, and with a large, white, rascally grin, and a glance at his charge, seemed to take me into partnership in his exalted trust. After all, I also was a part of the great cause of these high and just proceedings.

"Instead of going up, I turned and descended to the left. My idea was to let that chain-gang get out of sight before I climbed the hill. You know I am not particularly tender; I've had to strike and to fend off. I've had to resist and to attack sometimes—that's only one way of resisting—without counting the exact cost, according to the demands of such sort of life as I had blundered into. I've seen the devil of violence, and the devil of greed, and the devil of hot desire; but, by all the stars! these were strong, lusty, red-eyed devils, that swayed and drove men—men, I tell you. But as I stood on this hillside, I foresaw that in the blinding sunshine of that land I would become acquainted with a flabby, pretending, weak-eyed devil of a rapacious and pitiless folly. How insidious he could be, too, I was only to find out several months later and a thousand miles farther. For a moment I stood appalled, as though by a warning. Finally I descended the hill, obliquely, towards the trees I had seen.

"I avoided a vast artificial hole somebody had been digging on the slope, the pur-pose of which I found it impossible to divine. It wasn't a quarry or a sandpit, anyhow. It was just a hole. It might have been connected with the philanthropic desire of giv-ing the criminals something to do. I don't know. Then I nearly fell into a very narrow ravine, almost no more than a scar in the hillside. I discovered that a lot of imported drainage-pipes for the settlement had been tumbled in there. There wasn't one that was not broken. It was a wanton smash-up. At last I got under the trees. My purpose was to stroll into the shade for a moment; but no sooner within than it seemed to me I had stepped into the gloomy circle of some Inferno. The rapids were near, and an uninterrupted, uniform, headlong, rushing noise filled the mournful stillness of the grove, where not a breath stirred, not a leaf moved, with a mysterious sound—as though the tearing pace of the launched earth had suddenly become audible.

"Black shapes crouched, lay, sat between the trees, leaning against the trunks, clinging to the earth, half coming out, half effaced within the dim light, in all the attitudes of pain, abandonment, and despair. Another mine on the cliff went off, fol-lowed by a slight shudder of the soil under my feet. The work was going on. The work! And this was the place where some of the helpers had withdrawn to die.

"They were dying slowly—it was very clear. They were not enemies, they were not criminals, they were nothing earthly now,—nothing but black shadows of dis-ease and starvation, lying confusedly in the greenish gloom. Brought from all the recesses of the coast in all the legality of time contracts, lost in uncongenial sur-roundings, fed on unfamiliar food, they sickened, became inefficient, and were then allowed to crawl away and rest. These moribund shapes were free as air—and nearly as thin. I began to distinguish the gleam of eyes under the trees. Then, glancing down, I saw a face near my hand. The black bones reclined at full length with one shoulder against the tree, and slowly the eyelids rose and the sunken eyes looked up at me, enormous and vacant, a kind of blind, white flicker in the depths of the orbs, which died out slowly. The man seemed young—almost a boy—but you know with them it's hard to tell. I found nothing else to do but to offer him one of my good Swede's ship's biscuits I had in my pocket. The fingers closed slowly on it and held—there was no other movement and no other glance. He had tied a bit of white worsted round his neck—Why? Where did he get it? Was it a badge—an ornament—a charm—a propitiatory act? Was there any idea at all connected with it? It looked startling round his black neck, this bit of white thread from beyond the seas.

"Near the same tree two more bundles of acute angles sat with their legs drawn up. One, with his chin propped on his knees, stared at nothing, in an intolerable and appalling manner: his brother phantom rested its forehead, as if overcome with a great weariness; and all about others were scattered in every pose of contorted collapse, as in some picture of a massacre or a pestilence. While I stood horror-struck, one of these creatures rose to his hands and knees, and went off on all-fours towards the river to drink. He lapped out of his hand, then sat up in the sunlight, crossing his shins in front of him, and after a time let his woolly head fall on his breastbone.

"I didn't want any more loitering in the shade, and I made haste towards the station. When near the buildings I met a white man, in such an unexpected elegance of get-up that in the first moment I took him for a sort of vision. I saw a high starched collar, white cuffs, a light alpaca jacket, snowy trousers, a clear silk necktie, and varnished boots. No hat. Hair parted, brushed, oiled, under a green-lined parasol held in a big white hand. He was amazing, and had a penholder behind his ear.

"I shook hands with this miracle, and I learned he was the Company's chief accountant, and that all the book-keeping was done at this station. He had come out for a moment, he said, 'to get a breath of fresh air.' The expression sounded wonderfully odd, with its suggestion of sedentary desk-life. I wouldn't have mentioned the fellow to you at all, only it was from his lips that I first heard the name of the man who is so indissolubly connected with the memories of that time. Moreover, I respected the fellow. Yes; I respected his collars, his vast cuffs, his brushed hair. His appearance was certainly that of a hairdresser's dummy; but in the great demoralisation of the land he kept up his appearance. That's backbone. His starched collars and got-up shirt-fronts were achievements of character. He had been out nearly three years; and, later on, I could not help asking him how he managed to sport such linen. He had just the faintest blush, and said modestly, 'I've been teaching one of the native women about the station. It was difficult. She had a distaste for the work.' Thus this man had verily accomplished something. And he was devoted to his books, which were in apple-pie order.

"Everything else in the station was in a muddle,—heads, things, buildings. Strings of dusty niggers with splay feet arrived and departed; a stream of manufactured goods, rubbishy cottons, beads, and brass-wire set into the depths of darkness, and in return came a precious trickle of ivory.

"I had to wait in the station for ten days—an eternity. I lived in a hut in the yard, but to be out of the chaos I would sometimes get into the accountant's office. It was built of horizontal planks, and so badly put together that, as he bent over his high desk, he was barred from neck to heels with narrow strips of sunlight. There was no need to open the big shutter to see. It was hot there too; big flies buzzed fiendishly, and did not sting, but stabbed. I sat generally on the floor, while, of faultless appearance (and even slightly scented), perching on a high stool, he wrote, he wrote. Sometimes he stood up for exercise. When a truckle-bed with a sick man (some invalided agent from up-country) was put in there, he exhibited a gentle annoyance. 'The groans of this sick person,' he said, 'distract my attention. And without that it is extremely difficult to guard against clerical errors in this climate.'

"One day he remarked, without lifting his head, 'In the interior you will no doubt meet Mr Kurtz.' On my asking who Mr Kurtz was, he said he was a first-class agent; and seeing my disappointment at this information, he added slowly, laying down his pen, 'He is a very remarkable person.' Further questions elicited from him that Mr Kurtz was at present in charge of a trading-post, a very important one, in the true ivory-country, at 'the very bottom of there. Sends in as much ivory as all the others put together . . .' He began to write again. The sick man was too ill to groan. The flies buzzed in a great peace.

"Suddenly there was a growing murmur of voices and a great tramping of feet. A caravan had come in. A violent babble of uncouth sounds burst out on the other side of the planks. All the carriers were speaking together, and in the midst of the uproar the lamentable voice of the chief agent was heard 'giving it up' tearfully for the twentieth time that day. . . . He rose slowly. 'What a frightful row,' he said. He crossed the room gently to look at the sick man, and returning, said to me, 'He does not hear.' 'What! Dead?' I asked, startled. 'No, not yet,' he answered, with great composure. Then, alluding with a toss of the head to the tumult in the station-yard, 'When one has got to make correct entries, one comes to hate those savages—hate them to the death.' He remained thoughtful for a moment. 'When you see Mr Kurtz,' he went on, 'tell him from me that everything here'—he glanced at the desk—'is very satisfactory. I don't like to write to him—with those messengers of ours you never know who may get hold of your letter—at that Central Station.' He stared at me for a moment with his mild, bulging eyes. 'Oh, he will go far, very far,' he began again. 'He will be a somebody in the Administration before long. They, above—the Council in Europe, you know—mean him to be.'

"He turned to his work. The noise outside had ceased, and presently in going out I stopped at the door. In the steady buzz of flies the homeward-bound agent was lying flushed and insensible; the other, bent over his books, was making correct entries of perfectly correct transactions; and fifty feet below the doorstep I could see the still tree-tops of the grove of death.

"Next day I left that station at last, with a caravan of sixty men, for a two-hundred-mile tramp.

"No use telling you much about that. Paths, paths, everywhere; a stamped-in network of paths spreading over the empty land, through long grass, through burnt grass, through thickets, down and up chilly ravines, up and down stony hills ablaze with heat; and a solitude, a solitude, nobody, not a hut. The population had cleared out a long time ago. Well, if a lot of mysterious niggers armed with all kinds of fearful weapons suddenly took to travelling on the road between Deal[6] and Gravesend, catching the yokels right and left to carry heavy loads for them, I fancy every farm and cottage thereabouts would get empty very soon. Only here the dwellings were gone too. Still, I passed through several abandoned villages. There's something pathetically childish in the ruins of grass walls. Day after day, with the stamp and shuffle of sixty pair of bare feet behind me, each pair under a 60-lb. load. Camp, cook, sleep, strike camp, march. Now and then a carrier dead in harness, at rest in the long grass near the path, with an empty water-gourd and his long staff lying by his

6. An English port.

side. A great silence around and above. Perhaps on some quiet night the tremor of far-off drums, sinking, swelling, a tremor vast, faint; a sound weird, appealing, suggestive, and wild—and perhaps with as profound a meaning as the sound of bells in a Christian country. Once a white man in an unbuttoned uniform, camping on the path with an armed escort of lank Zanzibaris,[7] very hospitable and festive—not to say drunk. Was looking after the upkeep of the road, he declared. Can't say I saw any road or any upkeep, unless the body of a middle-aged negro, with a bullet-hole in the forehead, upon which I absolutely stumbled three miles farther on, may be considered as a permanent improvement. I had a white companion too, not a bad chap, but rather too fleshy and with the exasperating habit of fainting on the hot hillsides, miles away from the least bit of shade and water. Annoying, you know, to hold your own coat like a parasol over a man's head while he is coming-to. I couldn't help asking him once what he meant by coming there at all. 'To make money, of course. What do you think?' he said, scornfully. Then he got fever, and had to be carried in a hammock slung under a pole. As he weighed sixteen stone I had no end of rows with the carriers. They jibbed, ran away, sneaked off with their loads in the night—quite a mutiny. So, one evening, I made a speech in English with gestures, not one of which was lost to the sixty pairs of eyes before me, and the next morning I started the hammock off in front all right. An hour afterwards I came upon the whole concern wrecked in a bush—man, hammock, groans, blankets, horrors. The heavy pole had skinned his poor nose. He was very anxious for me to kill somebody, but there wasn't the shadow of a carrier near. I remembered the old doctor,—'It would be interesting for science to watch the mental changes of individuals, on the spot.' I felt I was becoming scientifically interesting. However, all that is to no purpose. On the fifteenth day I came in sight of the big river again, and hobbled into the Central Station. It was on a back water surrounded by scrub and forest, with a pretty border of smelly mud on one side, and on the three others enclosed by a crazy fence of rushes. A neglected gap was all the gate it had, and the first glance at the place was enough to let you see the flabby devil was running that show. White men with long staves in their hands appeared languidly from amongst the buildings, strolling up to take a look at me, and then retired out of sight somewhere. One of them, a stout, excitable chap with black moustaches, informed me with great volubility and many digressions, as soon as I told him who I was, that my steamer was at the bottom of the river. I was thunderstruck. What, how, why? Oh, it was 'all right.' The 'manager himself' was there. All quite correct. 'Everybody had behaved splendidly! splendidly!'—'You must,' he said in agitation, 'go and see the general manager at once. He is waiting!'

"I did not see the real significance of that wreck at once. I fancy I see it now, but I am not sure—not at all. Certainly the affair was too stupid—when I think of it—to be altogether natural. Still. . . . But at the moment it presented itself simply as a confounded nuisance. The steamer was sunk. They had started two days before in a sudden hurry up the river with the manager on board, in charge of some volunteer skipper, and before they had been out three hours they tore the bottom out of her on stones, and she sank near the south bank. I asked myself what I was to do there, now my boat was lost. As a matter of fact, I had plenty to do in fishing my command out of the river. I had to set about it the very next day. That, and the repairs when I brought the pieces to the station, took some months.

7. Africans from Zanzibar, in East Africa; they were widely used as mercenaries.

"My first interview with the manager was curious. He did not ask me to sit down after my twenty-mile walk that morning. He was commonplace in complexion, in feature, in manners, and in voice. He was of middle size and of ordinary build. His eyes, of the usual blue, were perhaps remarkably cold, and he certainly could make his glance fall on one as trenchant and heavy as an axe. But even at these times the rest of his person seemed to disclaim the intention. Otherwise there was only an indefinable, faint expression of his lips, something stealthy—a smile—not a smile—I remember it, but I can't explain. It was unconscious, this smile was, though just after he had said something it got intensified for an instant. It came at the end of his speeches like a seal applied on the words to make the meaning of the commonest phrase appear absolutely inscrutable. He was a common trader, from his youth up employed in these parts—nothing more. He was obeyed, yet he inspired neither love nor fear, nor even respect. He inspired uneasiness. That was it! Uneasiness. Not a definite mistrust—just uneasiness—nothing more. You have no idea how effective such a . . . a . . . faculty can be. He had no genius for organising, for initiative, or for order even. That was evident in such things as the deplorable state of the station. He had no learning, and no intelligence. His position had come to him—why? Perhaps because he was never ill . . . He had served three terms of three years out there . . . Because triumphant health in the general rout of constitutions is a kind of power in itself. When he went home on leave he rioted on a large scale—pompously. Jack ashore—with a difference—in externals only. This one could gather from his casual talk. He originated nothing, he could keep the routine going—that's all. But he was great. He was great by this little thing that it was impossible to tell what could control such a man. He never gave that secret away. Perhaps there was nothing within him. Such a suspicion made one pause—for out there there were no external checks. Once when various tropical diseases had laid low almost every 'agent' in the station, he was heard to say, 'Men who come out here should have no entrails.' He sealed the utterance with that smile of his, as though it had been a door opening into a darkness he had in his keeping. You fancied you had seen things—but the seal was on. When annoyed at meal-times by the constant quarrels of the white men about precedence, he ordered an immense round table to be made, for which a special house had to be built. This was the station's mess-room. Where he sat was the first place—the rest were nowhere. One felt this to be his unalterable conviction. He was neither civil nor uncivil. He was quiet. He allowed his 'boy'—an overfed young negro from the coast—to treat the white men, under his very eyes, with provoking insolence.

"He began to speak as soon as he saw me. I had been very long on the road. He could not wait. Had to start without me. The up-river stations had to be relieved. There had been so many delays already that he did not know who was dead and who was alive, and how they got on—and so on, and so on. He paid no attention to my explanations, and, playing with a stick of sealing-wax, repeated several times that the situation was 'very grave, very grave.' There were rumours that a very important station was in jeopardy, and its chief, Mr Kurtz, was ill. Hoped it was not true. Mr Kurtz was . . . I felt weary and irritable. Hang Kurtz, I thought. I interrupted him by saying I had heard of Mr Kurtz on the coast. 'Ah! So they talk of him down there,' he murmured to himself. Then he began again, assuring me Mr Kurtz was the best agent he had, an exceptional man, of the greatest importance to the Company; therefore I could understand his anxiety. He was, he said, 'very, very uneasy.' Certainly he fidgeted on his chair a good deal, exclaimed, 'Ah, Mr Kurtz!' broke the stick of sealing-wax and seemed dumbfounded by the accident. Next thing he wanted to know 'how long it would take to' . . . I interrupted him again. Being hungry, you know, and kept on my feet too, I was getting savage. 'How can I tell?' I said. 'I haven't even seen the wreck yet—some months, no doubt.' All this talk seemed to me so futile. 'Some months,' he said. 'Well, let us say three months before we can make a start. Yes. That ought to do the affair.' I flung out of his hut (he lived all alone in a clay hut with a sort of verandah) muttering to myself my opinion of him. He was a chattering idiot. Afterwards I took it back when it was borne in upon me startlingly with what extreme nicety he had estimated the time requisite for the 'affair.'

"I went to work the next day, turning, so to speak, my back on that station. In that way only it seemed to me I could keep my hold on the redeeming facts of life. Still, one must look about sometimes; and then I saw this station, these men strolling aimlessly about in the sunshine of the yard. I asked myself sometimes what it all meant. They wandered here and there with their absurd long staves in their hands, like a lot of faithless pilgrims bewitched inside a rotten fence. The word 'ivory' rang in the air, was whispered, was sighed. You would think they were praying to it. A taint of imbecile rapacity blew through it all, like a whiff from some corpse. By Jove! I've never seen anything so unreal in my life. And outside, the silent wilderness surrounding this cleared speck on the earth struck me as something great and invincible, like evil or truth, waiting patiently for the passing away of this fantastic invasion.

"Oh, those months! Well, never mind. Various things happened. One evening a grass shed full of calico, cotton prints, beads, and I don't know what else, burst into a blaze so suddenly that you would have thought the earth had opened to let an avenging fire consume all that trash. I was smoking my pipe quietly by my dismantled steamer, and saw them all cutting capers in the light, with their arms lifted high, when the stout man with moustaches came tearing down to the river, a tin pail in his hand, assured me that everybody was 'behaving splendidly, splendidly,' dipped about a quart of water and tore back again. I noticed there was a hole in the bottom of his pail.

"I strolled up. There was no hurry. You see the thing had gone off like a box of matches. It had been hopeless from the very first. The flame had leaped high, driven everybody back, lighted up everything—and collapsed. The shed was already a heap of embers glowing fiercely. A nigger was being beaten near by. They said he had caused the fire in some way; be that as it may, he was screeching most horribly. I saw him, later on, for several days, sitting in a bit of shade looking very sick and trying to recover himself: afterwards he arose and went out—and the wilderness without a sound took him into its bosom again. As I approached the glow from the dark I found myself at the back of two men, talking. I heard the name of Kurtz pronounced, then the words, 'take advantage of this unfortunate accident.' One of the men was the manager. I wished him a good evening. 'Did you ever see anything like it—eh? it is incredible,' he said, and walked off. The other man remained. He was a first-class agent, young, gentlemanly, a bit reserved, with a forked little beard and a hooked nose. He was stand-offish with the other agents, and they on their side said he was the manager's spy upon them. As to me, I had hardly ever spoken to him before. We got into talk, and by-and-by we strolled away from the hissing ruins. Then he asked me to his room, which was in the main building of the station. He struck a match, and I perceived that this young aristocrat had not only a silver-mounted dressing-case but also a whole candle all to himself. Just at that time the manager was the only man supposed to have any right to candles. Native mats covered the clay walls; a collection of spears, assegais,[8] shields, knives was hung up in trophies. The business intrusted to this fellow was the making of bricks—so I had been informed; but there wasn't a fragment of a brick anywhere in the station, and he had been there more than a year—waiting. It seems he could not make bricks without something, I don't know what—straw maybe. Anyway, it could not be found there, and as it was not likely to be sent from Europe, it did not appear clear to me what he was waiting for. An act of special creation perhaps. However, they were all waiting—all the sixteen or twenty pilgrims of them—for something; and upon my word it did not seem an uncongenial occupation, from the way they took it, though the only thing that ever came to them was disease—as far as I could see. They beguiled the time by backbiting and intriguing against each other in a foolish kind of way. There was an air of plotting about that station, but nothing came of it, of course. It was as unreal as everything else—as the philanthropic pretence of the whole concern, as their talk, as their government, as their show of work. The only real feeling was a desire to get appointed to a trading-post where ivory was to be had, so that they could earn percentages. They intrigued and slandered and hated each other only on that account,—but as to effectually lifting a little finger—oh, no. By heavens! there is something after all in the world allowing one man to steal a horse while another must not look at a halter. Steal a horse straight out. Very well. He has done it. Perhaps he can ride. But there is a way of looking at a halter that would provoke the most charitable of saints into a kick.

"I had no idea why he wanted to be sociable, but as we chatted in there it suddenly occurred to me the fellow was trying to get at something—in fact, pumping me. He alluded constantly to Europe, to the people I was supposed to know there—putting leading questions as to my acquaintances in the sepulchral city, and so on. His little eyes glittered like mica discs—with curiosity,—though he tried to keep up a bit of superciliousness. At first I was astonished, but very soon I became awfully curious to see what he would find out from me. I couldn't possibly imagine what I had in me to make it worth his while. It was very pretty to see how he baffled himself, for in truth my body was full of chills, and my head had nothing in it but that wretched steamboat business. It was evident he took me for a perfectly shameless prevaricator. At last he got angry, and, to conceal a movement of furious annoyance, he yawned. I rose. Then I noticed a small sketch in oils, on a panel, representing a woman, draped and blind-folded, carrying a lighted torch. The background was sombre—almost black. The movement of the woman was stately, and the effect of the torchlight on the face was sinister.

"It arrested me, and he stood by civilly, holding a half-pint champagne bottle (medical comforts) with the candle stuck in it. To my question he said Mr Kurtz had painted this—in this very station more than a year ago—while waiting for means to go to his trading-post. 'Tell me, pray,' said I, 'who is this Mr Kurtz?'

"'The chief of the Inner Station,' he answered in a short tone, looking away. 'Much obliged,' I said, laughing. 'And you are the brickmaker of the Central Station. Every one knows that.' He was silent for a while. 'He is a prodigy,' he said at last. 'He is an emissary of pity, and science, and progress, and devil knows what else. We want,' he began to declaim suddenly, 'for the guidance of the cause intrusted to us by Europe, so to speak, higher intelligence, wide sympathies, a singleness of purpose.'

8. Spears.

'Who says that?' I asked. 'Lots of them,' he replied. 'Some even write that; and so *he* comes here, a special being, as you ought to know.' 'Why ought I to know?' I interrupted, really surprised. He paid no attention. 'Yes. To-day he is chief of the best station, next year he will be assistant-manager, two years more and . . . but I daresay you know what he will be in two years' time. You are of the new gang—the gang of virtue. The same people who sent him specially also recommended you. Oh, don't say no. I've my own eyes to trust.' Light dawned upon me. My dear aunt's influential acquaintances were producing an unexpected effect upon that young man. I nearly burst into a laugh. 'Do you read the Company's confidential correspondence?' I asked. He hadn't a word to say. It was great fun. 'When Mr Kurtz,' I continued severely, 'is General Manager, you won't have the opportunity.'

"He blew the candle out suddenly, and we went outside. The moon had risen. Black figures strolled about listlessly, pouring water on the glow, whence proceeded a sound of hissing; steam ascended in the moonlight; the beaten nigger groaned somewhere. 'What a row the brute makes!' said the indefatigable man with the moustaches, appearing near us. 'Serve him right. Transgression—punishment—bang! Pitiless, pitiless. That's the only way. This will prevent all conflagrations for the future. I was just telling the manager . . .' He noticed my companion, and became crestfallen all at once. 'Not in bed yet,' he said, with a kind of servile heartiness; 'it's so natural. Ha! Danger—agitation.' He vanished. I went on to the river-side, and the other followed me. I heard a scathing murmur at my ear, 'Heap of muffs—go to.' The pilgrims could be seen in knots gesticulating, discussing. Several had still their staves in their hands. I verily believe they took these sticks to bed with them. Beyond the fence the forest stood up spectrally in the moonlight, and through the dim stir, through the faint sounds of that lamentable courtyard, the silence of the land went home to one's very heart,—its mystery, its greatness, the amazing reality of its concealed life. The hurt nigger moaned feebly somewhere near by, and then fetched a deep sigh that made me mend my pace away from there. I felt a hand introducing itself under my arm. 'My dear sir,' said the fellow, 'I don't want to be misunderstood, and especially by you, who will see Mr Kurtz long before I can have that pleasure. I wouldn't like him to get a false idea of my disposition. . . .'

"I let him run on, this papier-mâché Mephistopheles, and it seemed to me that if I tried I could poke my forefinger through him, and would find nothing inside but a little loose dirt, maybe. He, don't you see, had been planning to be assistant-manager by-and-by under the present man, and I could see that the coming of that Kurtz had upset them both not a little. He talked precipitately, and I did not try to stop him. I had my shoulders against the wreck of my steamer, hauled up on the slope like a carcass of some big river animal. The smell of mud, of primeval mud, by Jove! was in my nostrils, the high stillness of primeval forest was before my eyes; there were shiny patches on the black creek. The moon had spread over everything a thin layer of silver—over the rank grass, over the mud, upon the wall of matted vegetation standing higher than the wall of a temple, over the great river I could see through a sombre gap glittering, glittering, as it flowed broadly by without a murmur. All this was great, expectant, mute, while the man jabbered about himself. I wondered whether the stillness on the face of the immensity looking at us two were meant as an appeal or as a menace. What were we who had strayed in here? Could we handle that dumb thing, or would it handle us? I felt how big, how confoundedly big, was that thing that couldn't talk, and perhaps was deaf as well. What was in there? I could see a little ivory coming out from there, and I had heard Mr Kurtz was in there. I had heard enough about it too—God knows! Yet somehow it didn't bring any image with it—no more than if I had been told an angel or a fiend was in there. I believed it in the same way one of you might believe there are inhabitants in the planet Mars. I knew once a Scotch sailmaker who was certain, dead sure, there were people in Mars. If you asked him for some idea how they looked and behaved, he would get shy and mutter something about 'walking on all-fours.' If you as much as smiled, he would—though a man of sixty—offer to fight you. I would not have gone so far as to fight for Kurtz, but I went for him near enough to a lie. You know I hate, detest, and can't bear a lie, not because I am straighter than the rest of us, but simply because it appals me. There is a taint of death, a flavour of mortality in lies,—which is exactly what I hate and detest in the world—what I want to forget. It makes me miserable and sick, like biting something rotten would do. Temperament, I suppose. Well, I went near enough to it by letting the young fool there believe anything he liked to imagine as to my influence in Europe. I became in an instant as much of a pretence as the rest of the bewitched pilgrims. This simply because I had a notion it somehow would be of help to that Kurtz whom at the time I did not see—you understand. He was just a word for me. I did not see the man in the name any more than you do. Do you see him? Do you see the story? Do you see anything? It seems to me I am trying to tell you a dream—making a vain attempt, because no relation of a dream can convey the dream-sensation, that commingling of absurdity, surprise, and bewilderment in a tremor of struggling revolt, that notion of being captured by the incredible which is of the very essence of dreams. . . ."

He was silent for a while.

". . . No, it is impossible; it is impossible to convey the life-sensation of any given epoch of one's existence,—that which makes its truth, its meaning—its subtle and penetrating essence. It is impossible. We live, as we dream—alone. . . ."

He paused again as if reflecting, then added—

"Of course in this you fellows see more than I could then. You see me, whom you know. . . ."

It had become so pitch dark that we listeners could hardly see one another. For a long time already he, sitting apart, had been no more to us than a voice. There was not a word from anybody. The others might have been asleep, but I was awake. I listened, I listened on the watch for the sentence, for the word, that would give me the clue to the faint uneasiness inspired by this narrative that seemed to shape itself without human lips in the heavy night-air of the river.

". . . Yes—I let him run on," Marlow began again, "and think what he pleased about the powers that were behind me. I did! And there was nothing behind me! There was nothing but that wretched, old, mangled steamboat I was leaning against, while he talked fluently about 'the necessity for every man to get on.' 'And when one comes out here, you conceive, it is not to gaze at the moon.' Mr Kurtz was a 'universal genius,' but even a genius would find it easier to work with 'adequate tools—intelligent men.' He did not make bricks—why, there was a physical impossibility in the way—as I was well aware; and if he did secretarial work for the manager, it was because 'no sensible man rejects wantonly the confidence of his superiors.' Did I see it? I saw it. What more did I want? What I really wanted was rivets, by heaven! Rivets. To get on with the work—to stop the hole. Rivets I wanted. There were cases of them down at the coast—cases—piled up—burst—split! You kicked a loose rivet at every second step in that station yard on the hillside. Rivets had rolled into the grove of death. You could fill your pockets with rivets for the trouble of stooping down—

and there wasn't one rivet to be found where it was wanted. We had plates that would do, but nothing to fasten them with. And every week the messenger, a lone negro, letter-bag on shoulder and staff in hand, left our station for the coast. And several times a week a coast caravan came in with trade goods,—ghastly glazed calico that made you shudder only to look at it, glass beads value about a penny a quart, confounded spotted cotton handkerchiefs. And no rivets. Three carriers could have brought all that was wanted to set that steamboat afloat.

"He was becoming confidential now, but I fancy my unresponsive attitude must have exasperated him at last, for he judged it necessary to inform me he feared neither God nor devil, let alone any mere man. I said I could see that very well, but what I wanted was a certain quantity of rivets—and rivets were what really Mr Kurtz wanted, if he had only known it. Now letters went to the coast every week. . . . 'My dear sir,' he cried, 'I write from dictation.' I demanded rivets. There was a way—for an intelligent man. He changed his manner; became very cold, and suddenly began to talk about a hippopotamus; wondered whether sleeping on board the steamer (I stuck to my salvage night and day) I wasn't disturbed. There was an old hippo that had the bad habit of getting out on the bank and roaming at night over the station grounds. The pilgrims used to turn out in a body and empty every rifle they could lay hands on at him. Some even had sat up o' nights for him. All this energy was wasted, though. 'That animal has a charmed life,' he said; 'but you can say this only of brutes in this country. No man—you apprehend me?—no man here bears a charmed life.' He stood there for a moment in the moonlight with his delicate hooked nose set a little askew, and his mica eyes glittering without a wink, then, with a curt Good night, he strode off. I could see he was disturbed and considerably puzzled, which made me feel more hopeful than I had been for days. It was a great comfort to turn from that chap to my influential friend, the battered, twisted, ruined, tin-pot steamboat. I clambered on board. She rang under my feet like an empty Huntley & Palmer[9] biscuit-tin kicked along a gutter; she was nothing so solid in make, and rather less pretty in shape, but I had expended enough hard work on her to make me love her. No influential friend would have served me better. She had given me a chance to come out a bit—to find out what I could do. No, I don't like work. I had rather laze about and think of all the fine things that can be done. I don't like work—no man does—but I like what is in the work,—the chance to find yourself. Your own reality—for yourself, not for others—what no other man can ever know. They can only see the mere show, and never can tell what it really means.

"I was not surprised to see somebody sitting aft, on the deck, with his legs dangling over the mud. You see I rather chummed with the few mechanics there were in that station, whom the other pilgrims naturally despised—on account of their imperfect manners, I suppose. This was the foreman—a boiler-maker by trade—a good worker. He was a lank, bony, yellow-faced man, with big intense eyes. His aspect was worried, and his head was as bald as the palm of my hand; but his hair in falling seemed to have stuck to his chin, and had prospered in the new locality, for his beard hung down to his waist. He was a widower with six young children (he had left them in charge of a sister of his to come out there), and the passion of his life was pigeon-flying. He was an enthusiast and a connoisseur. He would rave about pigeons. After work hours he used sometimes to come over from his hut for a talk about his children and his pigeons; at work, when he had to crawl in the mud under the bottom of the

9. A brand of English cookies.

steamboat, he would tie up that beard of his in a kind of white serviette[1] he brought for the purpose. It had loops to go over his ears. In the evening he could be seen squatted on the bank rinsing that wrapper in the creek with great care, then spreading it solemnly on a bush to dry.

"I slapped him on the back and shouted 'We shall have rivets!' He scrambled to his feet exclaiming 'No! Rivets!' as though he couldn't believe his ears. Then in a low voice, 'You . . . eh?' I don't know why we behaved like lunatics. I put my finger to the side of my nose and nodded mysteriously. 'Good for you!' he cried, snapped his fingers above his head, lifting one foot. I tried a jig. We capered on the iron deck. A frightful clatter came out of that hulk, and the virgin forest on the other bank of the creek sent it back in a thundering roll upon the sleeping station. It must have made some of the pilgrims sit up in their hovels. A dark figure obscured the lighted doorway of the manager's hut, vanished, then, a second or so after, the doorway itself vanished too. We stopped, and the silence driven away by the stamping of our feet flowed back again from the recesses of the land. The great wall of vegetation, an exuberant and entangled mass of trunks, branches, leaves, boughs, festoons, motionless in the moonlight, was like a rioting invasion of soundless life, a rolling wave of plants, piled up, crested, ready to topple over the creek, to sweep every little man of us out of his little existence. And it moved not. A deadened burst of mighty splashes and snorts reached us from afar, as though an ichthyosaurus had been taking a bath of glitter in the great river. 'After all,' said the boiler-maker in a reasonable tone, 'why shouldn't we get the rivets?' Why not, indeed! I did not know of any reason why we shouldn't. 'They'll come in three weeks,' I said, confidently.

"But they didn't. Instead of rivets there came an invasion, an infliction, a visitation. It came in sections during the next three weeks, each section headed by a donkey carrying a white man in new clothes and tan shoes, bowing from that elevation right and left to the impressed pilgrims. A quarrelsome band of footsore sulky niggers trod on the heels of the donkey; a lot of tents, camp-stools, tin boxes, white cases, brown bales would be shot down in the courtyard, and the air of mystery would deepen a little over the muddle of the station. Five such instalments came, with their absurd air of disorderly flight with the loot of innumerable outfit shops and provision stores, that, one would think, they were lugging, after a raid, into the wilderness for equitable division. It was an inextricable mess of things decent in themselves but that human folly made look like the spoils of thieving.

"This devoted band called itself the Eldorado Exploring Expedition,[2] and I believe they were sworn to secrecy. Their talk, however, was the talk of sordid buccaneers: it was reckless without hardihood, greedy without audacity, and cruel without courage; there was not an atom of foresight or of serious intention in the whole batch of them, and they did not seem aware these things are wanted for the work of the world. To tear treasure out of the bowels of the land was their desire, with no more moral purpose at the back of it than there is in burglars breaking into a safe. Who paid the expenses of the noble enterprise I don't know; but the uncle of our manager was leader of that lot.

"In exterior he resembled a butcher in a poor neighbourhood, and his eyes had a look of sleepy cunning. He carried his fat paunch with ostentation on his short legs, and during the time his gang infested the station spoke to no one but his nephew. You could see these two roaming about all day long with their heads close together in an everlasting confab.

---

1. Napkin.
2. Eldorado, legendary land of gold in South America and

the object of many fruitless 16th-century Spanish expeditions.

"I had given up worrying myself about the rivets. One's capacity for that kind of folly is more limited than you would suppose. I said Hang!—and let things slide. I had plenty of time for meditation, and now and then I would give some thought to Kurtz. I wasn't very interested in him. No. Still, I was curious to see whether this man, who had come out equipped with moral ideas of some sort, would climb to the top after all, and how he would set about his work when there."

2

"One evening as I was lying flat on the deck of my steamboat, I heard voices approaching—and there were the nephew and the uncle strolling along the bank. I laid my head on my arm again, and had nearly lost myself in a doze, when somebody said in my ear, as it were: 'I am as harmless as a little child, but I don't like to be dictated to. Am I the manager—or am I not? I was ordered to send him there. It's incredible.' . . . I became aware that the two were standing on the shore alongside the forepart of the steamboat, just below my head. I did not move; it did not occur to me to move: I was sleepy. 'It *is* unpleasant,' grunted the uncle. 'He has asked the Administration to be sent there,' said the other, 'with the idea of showing what he could do; and I was instructed accordingly. Look at the influence that man must have. Is it not frightful?' They both agreed it was frightful, then made several bizarre remarks: 'Make rain and fine weather—one man—the Council—by the nose'—bits of absurd sentences that got the better of my drowsiness, so that I had pretty near the whole of my wits about me when the uncle said, 'The climate may do away with this difficulty for you. Is he alone there?' 'Yes,' answered the manager; 'he sent his assistant down the river with a note to me in these terms: "Clear this poor devil out of the country, and don't bother sending more of that sort. I had rather be alone than have the kind of men you can dispose of with me." It was more than a year ago. Can you imagine such impudence?' 'Anything since then?' asked the other, hoarsely. 'Ivory,' jerked the nephew; 'lots of it—prime sort—lots—most annoying, from him.' 'And with that?' questioned the heavy rumble. 'Invoice,' was the reply fired out, so to speak. Then silence. They had been talking about Kurtz.

"I was broad awake by this time, but, lying perfectly at ease, remained still, having no inducement to change my position. 'How did that ivory come all this way?' growled the elder man, who seemed very vexed. The other explained that it had come with a fleet of canoes in charge of an English half-caste clerk Kurtz had with him; that Kurtz had apparently intended to return himself, the station being by that time bare of goods and stores, but after coming three hundred miles, had suddenly decided to go back, which he started to do alone in a small dug-out with four paddlers, leaving the half-caste to continue down the river with the ivory. The two fellows there seemed astounded at anybody attempting such a thing. They were at a loss for an adequate motive. As to me, I seemed to see Kurtz for the first time. It was a distinct glimpse: the dug-out, four paddling savages, and the lone white man turning his back suddenly on the headquarters, on relief, on thoughts of home—perhaps; setting his face towards the depths of the wilderness, towards his empty and desolate station. I did not know the motive. Perhaps he was just simply a fine fellow who stuck to his work for its own sake. His name, you understand, had not been pronounced once. He was 'that man.' The half-caste, who, as far as I could see, had conducted a difficult trip with great prudence and pluck, was invariably alluded to as 'that scoundrel.' The 'scoundrel' had reported that the 'man' had been very ill—had recovered imperfectly.

. . . The two below me moved away then a few paces, and strolled back and forth at some little distance. I heard: 'Military post—doctor—two hundred miles—quite alone now—unavoidable delays—nine months—no news—strange rumours.' They approached again, just as the manager was saying, 'No one, as far as I know, unless a species of wandering trader—a pestilential fellow, snapping ivory from the natives.' Who was it they were talking about now? I gathered in snatches that this was some man supposed to be in Kurtz's district, and of whom the manager did not approve. 'We will not be free from unfair competition till one of these fellows is hanged for an example,' he said. 'Certainly,' grunted the other; 'get him hanged! Why not? Any-thing—anything can be done in this country. That's what I say; nobody here, you understand, *here*, can endanger your position. And why? You stand the climate—you outlast them all. The danger is in Europe; but there before I left I took care to—' They moved off and whispered, then their voices rose again. 'The extraordinary series of delays is not my fault. I did my possible.' The fat man sighed, 'Very sad.' 'And the pestiferous absurdity of his talk,' continued the other; 'he bothered me enough when he was here. "Each station should be like a beacon on the road towards better things, a centre for trade of course, but also for humanising, improving, instructing." Conceive you—that ass! And he wants to be manager! No, it's—' Here he got choked by excessive indignation, and I lifted my head the least bit. I was sur-prised to see how near they were—right under me. I could have spat upon their hats. They were looking on the ground, absorbed in thought. The manager was switching his leg with a slender twig: his sagacious relative lifted his head. 'You have been well since you came out this time?' he asked. The other gave a start. 'Who? I? Oh! Like a charm—like a charm. But the rest—oh, my goodness! All sick. They die so quick, too, that I haven't the time to send them out of the country—it's incredible!' 'H'm. Just so,' grunted the uncle. 'Ah! my boy, trust to this—I say, trust to this.' I saw him extend his short flipper of an arm for a gesture that took in the forest, the creek, the mud, the river,—seemed to beckon with a dishonouring flourish before the sunlit face of the land a treacherous appeal to the lurking death, to the hidden evil, to the profound darkness of its heart. It was so startling that I leaped to my feet and looked back at the edge of the forest, as though I had expected an answer of some sort to that black display of confidence. You know the foolish notions that come to one some-times. The high stillness confronted these two figures with its ominous patience, waiting for the passing away of a fantastic invasion.

"They swore aloud together—out of sheer fright, I believe—then, pretending not to know anything of my existence, turned back to the station. The sun was low; and leaning forward side by side, they seemed to be tugging painfully uphill their two ridiculous shadows of unequal length, that trailed behind them slowly over the tall grass without bending a single blade.

"In a few days the Eldorado Expedition went into the patient wilderness, that closed upon it as the sea closes over a diver. Long afterwards the news came that all the donkeys were dead. I know nothing as to the fate of the less valuable animals. They, no doubt, like the rest of us, found what they deserved. I did not inquire. I was then rather excited at the prospect of meeting Kurtz very soon. When I say very soon I mean it comparatively. It was just two months from the day we left the creek when we came to the bank below Kurtz's station.

"Going up that river was like travelling back to the earliest beginnings of the world, when vegetation rioted on the earth and the big trees were kings. An empty stream, a great silence, an impenetrable forest. The air was warm, thick, heavy, sluggish. There was no joy in the brilliance of sunshine. The long stretches of the water-way ran on, deserted, into the gloom of overshadowed distances. On silvery sand-banks hippos and alligators sunned themselves side by side. The broadening waters flowed through a mob of wooded islands; you lost your way on that river as you would in a desert, and butted all day long against shoals, trying to find the channel, till you thought yourself bewitched and cut off for ever from everything you had known once—somewhere—far away—in another existence perhaps. There were moments when one's past came back to one, as it will sometimes when you have not a moment to spare to yourself; but it came in the shape of an unrestful and noisy dream, remembered with wonder amongst the overwhelming realities of this strange world of plants, and water, and silence. And this stillness of life did not in the least resemble a peace. It was the stillness of an implacable force brooding over an inscrutable inten-tion. It looked at you with a vengeful aspect. I got used to it afterwards; I did not see it any more; I had no time. I had to keep guessing at the channel; I had to discern, most-ly by inspiration, the signs of hidden banks; I watched for sunken stones; I was learn-ing to clap my teeth smartly before my heart flew out, when I shaved by a fluke some infernal sly old snag that would have ripped the life out of the tin-pot steamboat and drowned all the pilgrims; I had to keep a look-out for the signs of dead wood we could cut up in the night for next day's steaming. When you have to attend to things of that sort, to the mere incidents of the surface, the reality—the reality, I tell you—fades. The inner truth is hidden—luckily, luckily. But I felt it all the same; I felt often its mysterious stillness watching me at my monkey tricks, just as it watches you fellows performing on your respective tight-ropes for—what is it? half-a-crown a tumble—"

"Try to be civil, Marlow," growled a voice, and I knew there was at least one lis-tener awake besides myself.

"I beg your pardon. I forgot the heartache which makes up the rest of the price. And indeed what does the price matter, if the trick be well done? You do your tricks very well. And I didn't do badly either, since I managed not to sink that steamboat on my first trip. It's a wonder to me yet. Imagine a blindfolded man set to drive a van over a bad road. I sweated and shivered over that business considerably, I can tell you. After all, for a seaman, to scrape the bottom of the thing that's supposed to float all the time under his care is the unpardonable sin. No one may know of it, but you never forget the thump—eh? A blow on the very heart. You remember it, you dream of it, you wake up at night and think of it—years after—and go hot and cold all over. I don't pretend to say that steamboat floated all the time. More than once she had to wade for a bit, with twenty cannibals splashing around and pushing. We had enlisted some of these chaps on the way for a crew. Fine fellows—cannibals—in their place. They were men one could work with, and I am grateful to them. And, after all, they did not eat each other before my face: they had brought along a provision of hippo-meat which went rotten, and made the mystery of the wilderness stink in my nostrils. Phoo! I can sniff it now. I had the manager on board and three or four pilgrims with their staves—all complete. Sometimes we came upon a station close by the bank, clinging to the skirts of the unknown, and the white men rushing out of a tumble-down hovel, with great gestures of joy and surprise and welcome, seemed very strange,—had the appearance of being held there captive by a spell. The word 'ivory' would ring in the air for a while—and on we went again into the silence, along emp-ty reaches, round the still bends, between the high walls of our winding way, rever-berating in hollow claps the ponderous beat of the stern-wheel. Trees, trees, millions of trees, massive, immense, running up high; and at their foot, hugging the bank against the stream, crept the little begrimed steamboat, like a sluggish beetle crawling on the floor of a lofty portico. It made you feel very small, very lost, and yet it was not altogether depressing that feeling. After all, if you were small, the grimy beetle crawled on—which was just what you wanted it to do. Where the pilgrims imagined it crawled to I don't know. To some place where they expected to get something, I bet! For me it crawled towards Kurtz—exclusively; but when the steam-pipes started leaking we crawled very slow. The reaches opened before us and closed behind, as if the forest had stepped leisurely across the water to bar the way for our return. We penetrated deeper and deeper into the heart of darkness. It was very quiet there. At night sometimes the roll of drums behind the curtain of trees would run up the river and remain sustained faintly, as if hovering in the air high over our heads, till the first break of day. Whether it meant war, peace, or prayer we could not tell. The dawns were heralded by the descent of a chill stillness; the woodcutters slept, their fires burned low; the snapping of a twig would make you start. We were wanderers on a prehistoric earth, on an earth that wore the aspect of an unknown planet. We could have fancied ourselves the first of men taking possession of an accursed inheritance, to be subdued at the cost of profound anguish and of excessive toil. But suddenly, as we struggled round a bend, there would be a glimpse of rush walls, of peaked grass-roofs, a burst of yells, a whirl of black limbs, a mass of hands clapping, of feet stamping, of bodies swaying, of eyes rolling, under the droop of heavy and motionless foliage. The steamer toiled along slowly on the edge of a black and incomprehensible frenzy. The prehistoric man was cursing us, praying to us, welcoming us—who could tell? We were cut off from the comprehension of our surroundings; we glided past like phantoms, wondering and secretly appalled, as sane men would be before an enthusiastic outbreak in a madhouse. We could not understand, because we were too far and could not remember, because we were travelling in the night of first ages, of those ages that are gone, leaving hardly a sign—and no memories.

"The earth seemed unearthly. We are accustomed to look upon the shackled form of a conquered monster, but there—there you could look at a thing monstrous and free. It was unearthly, and the men were—No, they were not inhuman. Well, you know, that was the worst of it—this suspicion of their not being inhuman. It would come slowly to one. They howled, and leaped, and spun, and made horrid faces; but what thrilled you was just the thought of their humanity—like yours—the thought of your remote kinship with this wild and passionate uproar. Ugly. Yes, it was ugly enough; but if you were man enough you would admit to yourself that there was in you just the faintest trace of a response to the terrible frankness of that noise, a dim suspicion of there being a meaning in it which you—you so remote from the night of first ages—could comprehend. And why not? The mind of man is capable of anything—because everything is in it, all the past as well as all the future. What was there after all? Joy, fear, sorrow, devotion, valour, rage—who can tell?—but truth—truth stripped of its cloak of time. Let the fool gape and shudder—the man knows, and can look on without a wink. But he must at least be as much of a man as these on the shore. He must meet that truth with his own true stuff—with his own inborn strength. Principles? Principles won't do. Acquisitions, clothes, pretty rags—rags that would fly off at the first good shake. No; you want a deliberate belief. An appeal to me in this fiendish row—is there? Very well; I hear; I admit, but I have a voice too, and for good or evil mine is the speech that cannot be silenced. Of course, a fool, what with sheer fright and fine sentiments, is always safe. Who's that grunting? You wonder I didn't go ashore for a howl and a dance? Well, no—I didn't. Fine sentiments, you say? Fine sentiments be hanged! I had no time. I had to mess about with white-lead and strips of woollen blanket helping to put bandages on those leaky steam-pipes—I tell you. I had to watch the steering, and circumvent those snags, and get the tin-pot along by hook or by crook. There was surface-truth enough in these things to save a wiser man. And between whiles I had to look after the savage who was fireman. He was an improved specimen; he could fire up a vertical boiler. He was there below me, and, upon my word, to look at him was as edifying as seeing a dog in a parody of breeches and a feather hat, walking on his hind-legs. A few months of training had done for that really fine chap. He squinted at the steam-gauge and at the water-gauge with an evident effort of intrepidity—and he had filed teeth too, the poor devil, and the wool of his pate shaved into queer patterns, and three ornamental scars on each of his cheeks. He ought to have been clapping his hands and stamping his feet on the bank, instead of which he was hard at work, a thrall to strange witch-craft, full of improving knowledge. He was useful because he had been instructed; and what he knew was this—that should the water in that transparent thing disap-pear, the evil spirit inside the boiler would get angry through the greatness of his thirst, and take a terrible vengeance. So he sweated and fired up and watched the glass fearfully (with an impromptu charm, made of rags, tied to his arm, and a piece of polished bone, as big as a watch, stuck flatways through his lower lip), while the wooded banks slipped past us slowly, the short noise was left behind, the inter-minable miles of silence—and we crept on, towards Kurtz. But the snags were thick, the water was treacherous and shallow, the boiler seemed indeed to have a sulky dev-il in it, and thus neither that fireman nor I had any time to peer into our creepy thoughts.

"Some fifty miles below the Inner Station we came upon a hut of reeds, an inclined and melancholy pole, with the unrecognisable tatters of what had been a flag of some sort flying from it, and a neatly stacked wood-pile. This was unexpected. We came to the bank, and on the stack of firewood found a flat piece of board with some faded pencil-writing on it. When deciphered it said: 'Wood for you. Hurry up. Approach cautiously.' There was a signature, but it was illegible—not Kurtz—a much longer word. Hurry up. Where? Up the river? 'Approach cautiously.' We had not done so. But the warning could not have been meant for the place where it could be only found after approach. Something was wrong above. But what—and how much? That was the question. We commented adversely upon the imbecility of that tele-graphic style. The bush around said nothing, and would not let us look very far, either. A torn curtain of red twill hung in the doorway of the hut, and flapped sadly in our faces. The dwelling was dismantled; but we could see a white man had lived there not very long ago. There remained a rude table—a plank on two posts; a heap of rubbish reposed in a dark corner, and by the door I picked up a book. It had lost its covers, and the pages had been thumbed into a state of extremely dirty softness; but the back had been lovingly stitched afresh with white cotton thread, which looked clean yet. It was an extraordinary find. Its title was, 'An Inquiry into some Points of Seamanship,' by a man Tower, Towson—some such name—Master in his Majesty's Navy. The matter looked dreary reading enough, with illustrative diagrams and repulsive tables of figures, and the copy was sixty years old. I handled this amazing antiquity with the greatest possible tenderness, lest it should dissolve in my hands. Within, Towson or Towser was inquiring earnestly into the breaking strain of ships' chains and tackle, and other such matters. Not a very enthralling book; but at the first glance you could see there a singleness of intention, an honest concern for the right way of going to work, which made these humble pages, thought out so many years ago, luminous with another than a professional light. The simple old sailor, with his talk of chains and purchases, made me forget the jungle and the pilgrims in a delicious sensation of having come upon something unmistakably real. Such a book being there was wonderful enough; but still more astounding were the notes pencilled in the margin, and plainly referring to the text. I couldn't believe my eyes! They were in cipher! Yes, it looked like cipher. Fancy a man lugging with him a book of that description into this nowhere and studying it—and making notes—in cipher at that! It was an extravagant mystery.

"I had been dimly aware for some time of a worrying noise, and when I lifted my eyes I saw the wood-pile was gone, and the manager, aided by all the pilgrims, was shouting at me from the river-side. I slipped the book into my pocket. I assure you to leave off reading was like tearing myself away from the shelter of an old and solid friendship.

"I started the lame engine ahead. 'It must be this miserable trader—this intruder,' exclaimed the manager, looking back malevolently at the place we had left. 'He must be English,' I said. 'It will not save him from getting into trouble if he is not careful,' muttered the manager darkly. I observed with assumed innocence that no man was safe from trouble in this world.

"The current was more rapid now, the steamer seemed at her last gasp, the stern-wheel flopped languidly, and I caught myself listening on tiptoe for the next beat of the float, for in sober truth I expected the wretched thing to give up every moment. It was like watching the last flickers of a life. But still we crawled. Sometimes I would pick out a tree a little way ahead to measure our progress towards Kurtz by, but I lost it invariably before we got abreast. To keep the eyes so long on one thing was too much for human patience. The manager displayed a beautiful resignation. I fretted and fumed and took to arguing with myself whether or no I would talk openly with Kurtz; but before I could come to any conclusion it occurred to me that my speech or my silence, indeed any action of mine, would be a mere futility. What did it matter what any one knew or ignored? What did it matter who was manager? One gets sometimes such a flash of insight. The essentials of this affair lay deep under the surface, beyond my reach, and beyond my power of meddling.

"Towards the evening of the second day we judged ourselves about eight miles from Kurtz's station. I wanted to push on; but the manager looked grave, and told me the navigation up there was so dangerous that it would be advisable, the sun being very low already, to wait where we were till next morning. Moreover, he pointed out that if the warning to approach cautiously were to be followed, we must approach in daylight—not at dusk, or in the dark. This was sensible enough. Eight miles meant nearly three hours' steaming for us, and I could also see suspicious ripples at the upper end of the reach. Nevertheless, I was annoyed beyond expression at the delay, and most unreasonably too, since one night more could not matter much after so many months. As we had plenty of wood, and caution was the word, I brought up in the middle of the stream. The reach was narrow, straight, with high sides like a railway cutting. The dusk came gliding into it long before the sun had set. The current ran smooth and swift, but a dumb immobility sat on the banks. The living trees, lashed together by the creepers and every living bush of the undergrowth, might have been changed into stone, even to the slenderest twig, to the lightest leaf. It was not sleep—it seemed unnatural, like a state of trance. Not the faintest sound of any kind could be heard. You looked on amazed, and began to suspect yourself of being deaf—

then the night came suddenly, and struck you blind as well. About three in the morning some large fish leaped, and the loud splash made me jump as though a gun had been fired. When the sun rose there was a white fog, very warm and clammy, and more blinding than the night. It did not shift or drive; it was just there, standing all round you like something solid. At eight or nine, perhaps, it lifted as a shutter lifts. We had a glimpse of the towering multitude of trees, of the immense matted jungle, with the blazing little ball of the sun hanging over it—all perfectly still—and then the white shutter came down again, smoothly, as if sliding in greased grooves. I ordered the chain, which we had begun to heave in, to be paid out again. Before it stopped running with a muffled rattle, a cry, a very loud cry, as of infinite desolation, soared slowly in the opaque air. It ceased. A complaining clamour, modulated in savage discords, filled our ears. The sheer unexpectedness of it made my hair stir under my cap. I don't know how it struck the others: to me it seemed as though the mist itself had screamed, so suddenly, and apparently from all sides at once, did this tumultuous and mournful uproar arise. It culminated in a hurried outbreak of almost intolerably excessive shrieking, which stopped short, leaving us stiffened in a variety of silly attitudes, and obstinately listening to the nearly as appalling and excessive silence. 'Good God! What is the meaning—?' stammered at my elbow one of the pilgrims,—a little fat man, with sandy hair and red whiskers, who wore side-spring boots, and pink pyjamas tucked into his socks. Two others remained open-mouthed a whole minute, then dashed into the little cabin, to rush out incontinently and stand darting scared glances, with Winchesters at 'ready' in their hands. What we could see was just the steamer we were on, her outlines blurred as though she had been on the point of dissolving, and a misty strip of water, perhaps two feet broad, around her— and that was all. The rest of the world was nowhere, as far as our eyes and ears were concerned. Just nowhere. Gone, disappeared; swept off without leaving a whisper or a shadow behind.

"I went forward, and ordered the chain to be hauled in short, so as to be ready to trip the anchor and move the steamboat at once if necessary. 'Will they attack?' whispered an awed voice. 'We will all be butchered in this fog,' murmured another. The faces twitched with the strain, the hands trembled slightly, the eyes forgot to wink. It was very curious to see the contrast of expressions of the white men and of the black fellows of our crew, who were as much strangers to that part of the river as we, though their homes were only eight hundred miles away. The whites, of course greatly discomposed, had besides a curious look of being painfully shocked by such an outrageous row. The others had an alert, naturally interested expression; but their faces were essentially quiet, even those of the one or two who grinned as they hauled at the chain. Several exchanged short, grunting phrases, which seemed to settle the matter to their satisfaction. Their headman, a young, broad-chested black, severely draped in dark-blue fringed cloths, with fierce nostrils and his hair all done up artfully in oily ringlets, stood near me. 'Aha!' I said, just for good fellowship's sake. 'Catch 'im,' he snapped, with a bloodshot widening of his eyes and a flash of sharp teeth— 'catch 'im. Give 'im to us.' 'To you, eh?' I asked; 'what would you do with them?' 'Eat 'im!' he said, curtly, and, leaning his elbow on the rail, looked out into the fog in a dignified and profoundly pensive attitude. I would no doubt have been properly horrified, had it not occurred to me that he and his chaps must be very hungry: that they must have been growing increasingly hungry for at least this month past. They had been engaged for six months (I don't think a single one of them had any clear idea of time, as we at the end of countless ages have. They still belonged to the beginnings of time—had no inherited experience to teach them, as it were), and of course, as long as there was a piece of paper written over in accordance with some farcical law or other made down the river, it didn't enter anybody's head to trouble how they would live. Certainly they had brought with them some rotten hippo-meat, which couldn't have lasted very long, anyway, even if the pilgrims hadn't, in the midst of a shocking hullabaloo, thrown a considerable quantity of it overboard. It looked like a high-handed proceeding; but it was really a case of legitimate self-defence. You can't breathe dead hippo waking, sleeping, and eating, and at the same time keep your precarious grip on existence. Besides that, they had given them every week three pieces of brass wire, each about nine inches long; and the theory was they were to buy their provisions with that currency in river-side villages. You can see how *that* worked. There were either no villages, or the people were hostile, or the director, who like the rest of us fed out of tins, with an occasional old he-goat thrown in, didn't want to stop the steamer for some more or less recondite reason. So, unless they swallowed the wire itself, or made loops of it to snare the fishes with, I don't see what good their extravagant salary could be to them. I must say it was paid with a regularity worthy of a large and honourable trading company. For the rest, the only thing to eat—though it didn't look eatable in the least—I saw in their possession was a few lumps of some stuff like half-cooked dough, of a dirty lavender colour, they kept wrapped in leaves, and now and then swallowed a piece of, but so small that it seemed done more for the looks of the thing than for any serious purpose of sustenance. Why in the name of all the gnawing devils of hunger they didn't go for us—they were thirty to five—and have a good tuck-in for once, amazes me now when I think of it. They were big powerful men, with not much capacity to weigh the consequences, with courage, with strength, even yet, though their skins were no longer glossy and their muscles no longer hard. And I saw that something restraining, one of those human secrets that baffle probability, had come into play there. I looked at them with a swift quickening of interest—not because it occurred to me I might be eaten by them before very long, though I own to you that just then I perceived—in a new light, as it were—how unwholesome the pilgrims looked, and I hoped, yes, I positively hoped, that my aspect was not so—what shall I say?—so—unappetising: a touch of fantastic vanity which fitted well with the dream-sensation that pervaded all my days at that time. Perhaps I had a little fever too. One can't live with one's finger everlastingly on one's pulse. I had often 'a little fever,' or a little touch of other things—the playful paw-strokes of the wilderness, the preliminary trifling before the more serious onslaught which came in due course. Yes; I looked at them as you would on any human being, with a curiosity of their impulses, motives, capacities, weaknesses, when brought to the test of an inexorable physical necessity. Restraint! What possible restraint? Was it superstition, disgust, patience, fear—or some kind of primitive honour? No fear can stand up to hunger, no patience can wear it out, disgust simply does not exist where hunger is; and as to superstition, beliefs, and what you may call principles, they are less than chaff in a breeze. Don't you know the devilry of lingering starvation, its exasperating torment, its black thoughts, its sombre and brooding ferocity? Well, I do. It takes a man all his inborn strength to fight hunger properly. It's really easier to face bereavement, dishonour, and the perdition of one's soul—than this kind of pro-longed hunger. Sad, but true. And these chaps too had no earthly reason for any kind of scruple. Restraint! I would just as soon have expected restraint from a hyena prowling amongst the corpses of a battlefield. But there was the fact facing me—the fact dazzling, to be seen, like the foam on the depths of the sea, like a ripple on an unfathomable enigma, a mystery greater—when I thought of it—than the curious, inexplicable note of desperate grief in this savage clamour that had swept by us on the river-bank, behind the blind whiteness of the fog.

"Two pilgrims were quarrelling in hurried whispers as to which bank. 'Left.' 'No, no; how can you? Right, right, of course.' 'It is very serious,' said the manager's voice behind me; 'I would be desolated if anything should happen to Mr Kurtz before we came up.' I looked at him, and had not the slightest doubt he was sincere. He was just the kind of man who would wish to preserve appearances. That was his restraint. But when he muttered something about going on at once, I did not even take the trouble to answer him. I knew, and he knew, that it was impossible. Were we to let go our hold of the bottom, we would be absolutely in the air—in space. We wouldn't be able to tell where we were going to—whether up or down stream, or across—till we fetched against one bank or the other,—and then we wouldn't know at first which it was. Of course I made no move. I had no mind for a smash-up. You couldn't imagine a more deadly place for a shipwreck. Whether drowned at once or not, we were sure to perish speedily in one way or another. 'I authorise you to take all the risks,' he said, after a short silence. 'I refuse to take any,' I said shortly; which was just the answer he expected, though its tone might have surprised him. 'Well, I must defer to your judgment. You are captain,' he said, with marked civility. I turned my shoulder to him in sign of my appreciation, and looked into the fog. How long would it last? It was the most hopeless look-out. The approach to this Kurtz grubbing for ivory in the wretched bush was beset by as many dangers as though he had been an enchanted princess sleeping in a fabulous castle. 'Will they attack, do you think?' asked the manager, in a confidential tone.

"I did not think they would attack, for several obvious reasons. The thick fog was one. If they left the bank in their canoes they would get lost in it, as we would be if we attempted to move. Still, I had also judged the jungle of both banks quite impenetrable—and yet eyes were in it, eyes that had seen us. The river-side bushes were certainly very thick; but the undergrowth behind was evidently penetrable. However, during the short lift I had seen no canoes anywhere in the reach—certainly not abreast of the steamer. But what made the idea of attack inconceivable to me was the nature of the noise—of the cries we had heard. They had not the fierce character boding of immediate hostile intention. Unexpected, wild, and violent as they had been, they had given me an irresistible impression of sorrow. The glimpse of the steamboat had for some reason filled those savages with unrestrained grief. The danger, if any, I expounded, was from our proximity to a great human passion let loose. Even extreme grief may ultimately vent itself in violence—but more generally takes the form of apathy. . . .

"You should have seen the pilgrims stare! They had no heart to grin, or even to revile me; but I believe they thought me gone mad—with fright, maybe. I delivered a regular lecture. My dear boys, it was no good bothering. Keep a look-out? Well, you may guess I watched the fog for the signs of lifting as a cat watches a mouse; but for anything else our eyes were of no more use to us than if we had been buried miles deep in a heap of cotton-wool. It felt like it too—choking, warm, stifling. Besides, all I said, though it sounded extravagant, was absolutely true to fact. What we afterwards alluded to as an attack was really an attempt at repulse. The action was very far from being aggressive—it was not even defensive, in the usual sense: it was undertaken under the stress of desperation, and in its essence was purely protective.

"It developed itself, I should say, two hours after the fog lifted, and its commencement was at a spot, roughly speaking, about a mile and a half below Kurtz's station. We had just floundered and flopped round a bend, when I saw an islet, a mere grassy hummock of bright green, in the middle of the stream. It was the only thing of the kind; but as we opened the reach more, I perceived it was the head of a long sandbank, or rather of a chain of shallow patches stretching down the middle of the river. They were discoloured, just awash, and the whole lot was seen just under the water, exactly as a man's backbone is seen running down the middle of his back under the skin. Now, as far as I did see, I could go to the right or to the left of this. I didn't know either channel, of course. The banks looked pretty well alike, the depth appeared the same; but as I had been informed the station was on the west side, I naturally headed for the western passage.

"No sooner had we fairly entered it than I became aware it was much narrower than I had supposed. To the left of us there was the long uninterrupted shoal, and to the right a high, steep bank heavily overgrown with bushes. Above the bush the trees stood in serried ranks. The twigs overhung the current thickly, and from distance to distance a large limb of some tree projected rigidly over the stream. It was then well on in the afternoon, the face of the forest was gloomy, and a broad strip of shadow had already fallen on the water. In this shadow we steamed up—very slowly, as you may imagine. I sheered her well inshore—the water being deepest near the bank, as the sounding-pole informed me.

"One of my hungry and forbearing friends was sounding in the bows just below me. This steamboat was exactly like a decked scow.[3] On the deck there were two little teak-wood houses, with doors and windows. The boiler was in the fore-end, and the machinery right astern. Over the whole there was a light roof, supported on stanchions. The funnel projected through that roof, and in front of the funnel a small cabin built of light planks served for a pilot-house. It contained a couch, two camp-stools, a loaded Martini-Henry[4] leaning in one corner, a tiny table, and the steering-wheel. It had a wide door in front and a broad shutter at each side. All these were always thrown open, of course. I spent my days perched up there on the extreme fore-end of that roof, before the door. At night I slept, or tried to, on the couch. An athletic black belonging to some coast tribe, and educated by my poor predecessor, was the helmsman. He sported a pair of brass earrings, wore a blue cloth wrapper from the waist to the ankles, and thought all the world of himself. He was the most unstable kind of fool I had ever seen. He steered with no end of a swagger while you were by; but if he lost sight of you, he became instantly the prey of an abject funk, and would let that cripple of a steamboat get the upper hand of him in a minute.

"I was looking down at the sounding-pole, and feeling much annoyed to see at each try a little more of it stick out of that river, when I saw my poleman give up the business suddenly, and stretch himself flat on the deck, without even taking the trouble to haul his pole in. He kept hold on it though, and it trailed in the water. At the same time the fireman, whom I could also see below me, sat down abruptly before his furnace and ducked his head. I was amazed. Then I had to look at the river mighty quick, because there was a snag in the fairway. Sticks, little sticks, were flying about—thick: they were whizzing before my nose, dropping below me, striking behind me against my pilot-house. All this time the river, the shore, the woods, were very quiet—perfectly quiet. I could only hear the heavy splashing thump of the stern-wheel and the patter of these things. We cleared the snag clumsily. Arrows, by Jove!

3. A flat-bottomed boat.   4. A rifle.

We were being shot at! I stepped in quickly to close the shutter on the landside. That fool-helmsman, his hands on the spokes, was lifting his knees high, stamping his feet, champing his mouth, like a reined-in horse. Confound him! And we were staggering within ten feet of the bank. I had to lean right out to swing the heavy shutter, and I saw a face amongst the leaves on the level with my own, looking at me very fierce and steady; and then suddenly, as though a veil had been removed from my eyes, I made out, deep in the tangled gloom, naked breasts, arms, legs, glaring eyes,—the bush was swarming with human limbs in movement, glistening, of bronze colour. The twigs shook, swayed, and rustled, the arrows flew out of them, and then the shutter came to. 'Steer her straight,' I said to the helmsman. He held his head rigid, face forward; but his eyes rolled, he kept on lifting and setting down his feet gently, his mouth foamed a little. 'Keep quiet!' I said in a fury. I might just as well have ordered a tree not to sway in the wind. I darted out. Below me there was a great scuffle of feet on the iron deck; confused exclamations; a voice screamed, 'Can you turn back?' I caught sight of a V-shaped ripple on the water ahead. What? Another snag! A fusillade burst out under my feet. The pilgrims had opened with their Winchesters, and were simply squirting lead into that bush. A deuce of a lot of smoke came up and drove slowly forward. I swore at it. Now I couldn't see the ripple or the snag either. I stood in the doorway, peering, and the arrows came in swarms. They might have been poisoned, but they looked as though they wouldn't kill a cat. The bush began to howl. Our wood-cutters raised a warlike whoop; the report of a rifle just at my back deafened me. I glanced over my shoulder, and the pilot-house was yet full of noise and smoke when I made a dash at the wheel. The fool-nigger had dropped everything, to throw the shutter open and let off that Martini-Henry. He stood before the wide opening, glaring, and I yelled at him to come back, while I straightened the sudden twist out of that steamboat. There was no room to turn even if I had wanted to, the snag was somewhere very near ahead in that confounded smoke, there was no time to lose, so I just crowded her into the bank—right into the bank, where I knew the water was deep.

"We tore slowly along the overhanging bushes in a whirl of broken twigs and flying leaves. The fusillade below stopped short, as I had foreseen it would when the squirts got empty. I threw my head back to a glinting whizz that traversed the pilot-house, in at one shutter-hole and out at the other. Looking past that mad helmsman, who was shaking the empty rifle and yelling at the shore, I saw vague forms of men running bent double, leaping, gliding, distinct, incomplete, evanescent. Something big appeared in the air before the shutter, the rifle went overboard, and the man stepped back swiftly, looked at me over his shoulder in an extraordinary, profound, familiar manner, and fell upon my feet. The side of his head hit the wheel twice, and the end of what appeared a long cane clattered round and knocked over a little camp-stool. It looked as though after wrenching that thing from somebody ashore he had lost his balance in the effort. The thin smoke had blown away, we were clear of the snag, and looking ahead I could see that in another hundred yards or so I would be free to sheer off, away from the bank; but my feet felt so very warm and wet that I had to look down. The man had rolled on his back and stared straight up at me; both his hands clutched that cane. It was the shaft of a spear that, either thrown or lunged through the opening, had caught him in the side just below the ribs; the blade had gone in out of sight, after making a frightful gash; my shoes were full; a pool of blood lay very still, gleaming dark-red under the wheel; his eyes shone with an amazing lustre. The fusillade burst out again. He looked at me anxiously, gripping the spear like something precious, with an air of being afraid I would try to take it away from him. I had to make an effort to free my eyes from his gaze and attend to the steering. With one hand I felt above my head for the line of the steam-whistle, and jerked out screech after screech hurriedly. The tumult of angry and warlike yells was checked instantly, and then from the depths of the woods went out such a tremulous and prolonged wail of mournful fear and utter despair as may be imagined to follow the flight of the last hope from the earth. There was a great commotion in the bush; the shower of arrows stopped, a few dropping shots rang out sharply—then silence, in which the languid beat of the stern-wheel came plainly to my ears. I put the helm hard astarboard at the moment when the pilgrim in pink pyjamas, very hot and agitated, appeared in the doorway. 'The manager sends me—' he began in an official tone, and stopped short. 'Good God!' he said, glaring at the wounded man.

"We two whites stood over him, and his lustrous and inquiring glance enveloped us both. I declare it looked as though he would presently put to us some question in an understandable language; but he died without uttering a sound, without moving a limb, without twitching a muscle. Only in the very last moment, as though in response to some sign we could not see, to some whisper we could not hear, he frowned heavily, and that frown gave to his black death-mask an inconceivably sombre, brooding, and menacing expression. The lustre of inquiring glance faded swiftly into vacant glassiness. 'Can you steer?' I asked the agent eagerly. He looked very dubious; but I made a grab at his arm, and he understood at once I meant him to steer whether or no. To tell you the truth, I was morbidly anxious to change my shoes and socks. 'He is dead,' murmured the fellow, immensely impressed. 'No doubt about it,' said I, tugging like mad at the shoelaces. 'And, by the way, I suppose Mr Kurtz is dead as well by this time.'

"For the moment that was the dominant thought. There was a sense of extreme disappointment, as though I had found out I had been striving after something altogether without a substance. I couldn't have been more disgusted if I had travelled all this way for the sole purpose of talking with Mr Kurtz. Talking with . . . I flung one shoe overboard, and became aware that that was exactly what I had been looking forward to—a talk with Kurtz. I made the strange discovery that I had never imagined him as doing, you know, but as discoursing. I didn't say to myself, 'Now I will never see him,' or 'Now I will never shake him by the hand,' but, 'Now I will never hear him.' The man presented himself as a voice. Not of course that I did not connect him with some sort of action. Hadn't I been told in all the tones of jealousy and admiration that he had collected, bartered, swindled, or stolen more ivory than all the other agents together. That was not the point. The point was in his being a gifted creature, and that of all his gifts the one that stood out pre-eminently, that carried with it a sense of real presence, was his ability to talk, his words—the gift of expression, the bewildering, the illuminating, the most exalted and the most contemptible, the pulsating stream of light, or the deceitful flow from the heart of an impenetrable darkness.

"The other shoe went flying unto the devil-god of that river. I thought, By Jove! it's all over. We are too late; he has vanished—the gift has vanished, by means of some spear, arrow, or club. I will never hear that chap speak after all,—and my sorrow had a startling extravagance of emotion, even such as I had noticed in the howling sorrow of these savages in the bush. I couldn't have felt more of lonely desolation somehow, had I been robbed of a belief or had missed my destiny in life. . . . Why do you sigh in this beastly way, somebody? Absurd? Well, absurd. Good Lord! mustn't a man ever—Here, give me some tobacco." . . .

There was a pause of profound stillness, then a match flared, and Marlow's lean face appeared, worn, hollow, with downward folds and dropped eyelids, with an aspect of concentrated attention; and as he took vigorous draws at his pipe, it seemed to retreat and advance out of the night in the regular flicker of the tiny flame. The match went out.

"Absurd!" he cried. "This is the worst of trying to tell . . . Here you all are, each moored with two good addresses, like a hulk with two anchors, a butcher round one corner, a policeman round another, excellent appetites, and temperature normal—you hear—normal from year's end to year's end. And you say, Absurd! Absurd be—exploded! Absurd! My dear boys, what can you expect from a man who out of sheer nervousness had just flung overboard a pair of new shoes? Now I think of it, it is amazing I did not shed tears. I am, upon the whole, proud of my fortitude. I was cut to the quick at the idea of having lost the inestimable privilege of listening to the gifted Kurtz. Of course I was wrong. The privilege was waiting for me. Oh yes, I heard more than enough. And I was right, too. A voice. He was very little more than a voice. And I heard—him—it—this voice—other voices—all of them were so little more than voices—and the memory of that time itself lingers around me, impalpable, like a dying vibration of one immense jabber, silly, atrocious, sordid, savage, or simply mean, without any kind of sense. Voices, voices—even the girl herself—now—"

He was silent for a long time.

"I laid the ghost of his gifts at last with a lie," he began suddenly. "Girl! What? Did I mention a girl? Oh, she is out of it—completely. They—the women I mean—are out of it—should be out of it. We must help them to stay in that beautiful world of their own, lest ours gets worse. Oh, she had to be out of it. You should have heard the disinterred body of Mr Kurtz saying, "My Intended." You would have perceived directly then how completely she was out of it. And the lofty frontal bone of Mr Kurtz! They say the hair goes on growing sometimes, but this—ah—specimen was impressively bald. The wilderness had patted him on the head, and, behold, it was like a ball—an ivory ball; it had caressed him, and—lo!—he had withered; it had taken him, loved him, embraced him, got into his veins, consumed his flesh, and sealed his soul to its own by the inconceivable ceremonies of some devilish initiation. He was its spoiled and pampered favourite. Ivory? I should think so. Heaps of it, stacks of it. The old mud shanty was bursting with it. You would think there was not a single tusk left either above or below the ground in the whole country. 'Mostly fossil,' the manager had remarked disparagingly. It was no more fossil than I am; but they call it fossil when it is dug up. It appears these niggers do bury the tusks sometimes—but evidently they couldn't bury this parcel deep enough to save the gifted Mr Kurtz from his fate. We filled the steamboat with it, and had to pile a lot on the deck. Thus he could see and enjoy as long as he could see, because the appreciation of this favour had remained with him to the last. You should have heard him say, 'My ivory.' Oh yes, I heard him. 'My Intended, my ivory, my station, my river, my—' everything belonged to him. It made me hold my breath in expectation of hearing the wilderness burst into a prodigious peal of laughter that would shake the fixed stars in their places. Everything belonged to him—but that was a trifle. The thing was to know what he belonged to, how many powers of darkness claimed him for their own. That was the reflection that made you creepy all over. It was impossible—it was not good for one either—trying to imagine. He had taken a high seat amongst the devils of the land—I mean literally. You can't understand. How could you?—with solid pavement under your feet, surrounded by kind neighbours ready to cheer you or to fall on you, stepping delicately between the butcher and the policeman, in the holy terror of scandal and gallows and lunatic asylums—how can you imagine what partic-ular region of the first ages a man's untrammelled feet may take him into by the way of solitude—utter solitude without a policeman—by the way of silence—utter silence, where no warning voice of a kind neighbour can be heard whispering of pub-lic opinion? These little things make all the great difference. When they are gone you must fall back upon your own innate strength, upon your own capacity for faith-fulness. Of course you may be too much of a fool to go wrong—too dull even to know you are being assaulted by the powers of darkness. I take it, no fool ever made a bar-gain for his soul with the devil: the fool is too much of a fool, or the devil too much of a devil—I don't know which. Or you may be such a thunderingly exalted creature as to be altogether deaf and blind to anything but heavenly sights and sounds. Then the earth for you is only a standing place—and whether to be like this is your loss or your gain I won't pretend to say. But most of us are neither one nor the other. The earth for us is a place to live in, where we must put up with sights, with sounds, with smells too, by Jove!—breathe dead hippo, so to speak, and not be contaminated. And there, don't you see? your strength comes in, the faith in your ability for the digging of unostentatious holes to bury the stuff in—your power of devotion, not to yourself, but to an obscure, back-breaking business. And that's difficult enough. Mind, I am not trying to excuse or even explain—I am trying to account to myself for—for—Mr Kurtz—for the shade of Mr Kurtz. This initiated wraith from the back of Nowhere honoured me with its amazing confidence before it vanished altogether. This was because it could speak English to me. The original Kurtz had been educated partly in England, and—as he was good enough to say himself—his sympathies were in the right place. His mother was half-English, his father was half-French. All Europe con-tributed to the making of Kurtz; and by-and-by I learned that, most appropriately, the International Society for the Suppression of Savage Customs had intrusted him with the making of a report, for its future guidance. And he had written it too. I've seen it. I've read it. It was eloquent, vibrating with eloquence, but too high-strung, I think. Seventeen pages of close writing he had found time for! But this must have been before his—let us say—nerves went wrong, and caused him to preside at certain mid-night dances ending with unspeakable rites, which—as far as I reluctantly gathered from what I heard at various times—were offered up to him—do you understand?—to Mr Kurtz himself. But it was a beautiful piece of writing. The opening paragraph, however, in the light of later information, strikes me now as ominous. He began with the argument that we whites, from the point of development we had arrived at, 'must necessarily appear to them [savages] in the nature of supernatural beings—we approach them with the might as of a deity,' and so on, and so on. 'By the simple exercise of our will we can exert a power for good practically unbounded,' &c., &c. From that point he soared and took me with him. The peroration was magnificent, though difficult to remember, you know. It gave me the notion of an exotic Immensi-ty ruled by an august Benevolence. It made me tingle with enthusiasm. This was the unbounded power of eloquence—of words—of burning noble words. There were no practical hints to interrupt the magic current of phrases, unless a kind of note at the foot of the last page, scrawled evidently much later, in an unsteady hand, may be regarded as the exposition of a method. It was very simple, and at the end of that moving appeal to every altruistic sentiment it blazed at you, luminous and terrifying, like a flash of lightning in a serene sky: 'Exterminate all the brutes!' The curious part was that he had apparently forgotten all about that valuable postscriptum, because, later on, when he in a sense came to himself, he repeatedly entreated me to take good care of 'my pamphlet' (he called it), as it was sure to have in the future a good influence upon his career. I had full information about all these things, and, besides, as it turned out, I was to have the care of his memory. I've done enough for it to give me the indisputable right to lay it, if I choose, for an everlasting rest in the dust-bin of progress, amongst all the sweepings and, figuratively speaking, all the dead cats of civilisation. But then, you see, I can't choose. He won't be forgotten. Whatever he was, he was not common. He had the power to charm or frighten rudimentary souls into an aggravated witch-dance in his honour; he could also fill the small souls of the pilgrims with bitter misgivings: he had one devoted friend at least, and he had conquered one soul in the world that was neither rudimentary nor tainted with self-seeking. No; I can't forget him, though I am not prepared to affirm the fellow was exactly worth the life we lost in getting to him. I missed my late helmsman awfully,—I missed him even while his body was still lying in the pilot-house. Perhaps you will think it passing strange this regret for a savage who was no more account than a grain of sand in a black Sahara. Well, don't you see, he had done something, he had steered; for months I had him at my back—a help—an instrument. It was a kind of partnership. He steered for me—I had to look after him, I worried about his deficiencies, and thus a subtle bond had been created, of which I only became aware when it was suddenly broken. And the intimate profundity of that look he gave me when he received his hurt remains to this day in my memory—like a claim of distant kinship affirmed in a supreme moment.

"Poor fool! If he had only left that shutter alone. He had no restraint, no restraint—just like Kurtz—a tree swayed by the wind. As soon as I had put on a dry pair of slippers, I dragged him out, after first jerking the spear out of his side, which operation I confess I performed with my eyes shut tight. His heels leaped together over the little doorstep; his shoulders were pressed to my breast; I hugged him from behind desperately. Oh! he was heavy, heavy; heavier than any man on earth, I should imagine. Then without more ado I tipped him overboard. The current snatched him as though he had been a wisp of grass, and I saw the body roll over twice before I lost sight of it for ever. All the pilgrims and the manager were then congregated on the awning-deck about the pilot-house, chattering at each other like a flock of excited magpies, and there was a scandalised murmur at my heartless promptitude. What they wanted to keep that body hanging about for I can't guess. Embalm it, maybe. But I had also heard another, and a very ominous, murmur on the deck below. My friends the woodcutters were likewise scandalised, and with a better show of reason—though I admit that the reason itself was quite inadmissible. Oh, quite! I had made up my mind that if my late helmsman was to be eaten, the fishes alone should have him. He had been a very second-rate helmsman while alive, but now he was dead he might have become a first-class temptation, and possibly cause some startling trouble. Besides, I was anxious to take the wheel, the man in pink pyjamas showing himself a hopeless duffer at the business.

"This I did directly the simple funeral was over. We were going half-speed, keeping right in the middle of the stream, and I listened to the talk about me. They had given up Kurtz, they had given up the station; Kurtz was dead, and the station had been burnt—and so on—and so on. The red-haired pilgrim was beside himself with the thought that at least this poor Kurtz had been properly revenged. 'Say! We must have made a glorious slaughter of them in the bush. Eh? What do you think? Say?' He positively danced, the bloodthirsty little gingery beggar. And he had nearly fainted when he saw the wounded man! I could not help saying, 'You made a glorious lot of smoke, anyhow.' I had seen, from the way the tops of the bushes rustled and flew, that almost all the shots had gone too high. You can't hit anything unless you take aim and fire from the shoulder; but these chaps fired from the hip with their eyes shut. The retreat, I maintained—and I was right—was caused by the screeching of the steam-whistle. Upon this they forgot Kurtz, and began to howl at me with indignant protests.

"The manager stood by the wheel murmuring confidentially about the necessity of getting well away down the river before dark at all events, when I saw in the distance a clearing on the river-side and the outlines of some sort of building. 'What's this?' I asked. He clapped his hands in wonder. 'The station!' he cried. I edged in at once, still going half-speed.

"Through my glasses I saw the slope of a hill interspersed with rare trees and perfectly free from undergrowth. A long decaying building on the summit was half buried in the high grass; the large holes in the peaked roof gaped black from afar; the jungle and the woods made a background. There was no enclosure or fence of any kind; but there had been one apparently, for near the house half-a-dozen slim posts remained in a row, roughly trimmed, and with their upper ends ornamented with round carved balls. The rails, or whatever there had been between, had disappeared. Of course the forest surrounded all that. The river-bank was clear, and on the water-side I saw a white man under a hat like a cart-wheel beckoning persistently with his whole arm. Examining the edge of the forest above and below, I was almost certain I could see movements—human forms gliding here and there. I steamed past prudently, then stopped the engines and let her drift down. The man on the shore began to shout, urging us to land. 'We have been attacked,' screamed the manager. 'I know—I know. It's all right,' yelled back the other, as cheerful as you please. 'Come along. It's all right. I am glad.'

"His aspect reminded me of something I had seen—something funny I had seen somewhere. As I manoeuvred to get alongside, I was asking myself, 'What does this fellow look like?' Suddenly I got it. He looked like a harlequin. His clothes had been made of some stuff that was brown holland[5] probably, but it was covered with patches all over, with bright patches, blue, red, and yellow,—patches on the back, patches on front, patches on elbows, on knees; coloured binding round his jacket, scarlet edging at the bottom of his trousers; and the sunshine made him look extremely gay and wonderfully neat withal, because you could see how beautifully all this patching had been done. A beardless, boyish face, very fair, no features to speak of, nose peeling, little blue eyes, smiles and frowns chasing each other over that open countenance like sunshine and shadow on a wind-swept plain. 'Look out, captain!' he cried; 'there's a snag lodged in here last night.' What! Another snag? I confess I swore shamefully. I had nearly holed my cripple, to finish off that charming trip. The harlequin on the bank turned his little pug nose up to me. 'You English?' he asked, all smiles. 'Are you?' I shouted from the wheel. The smiles vanished, and he shook his head as if sorry for my disappointment. Then he brightened up. 'Never mind!' he cried encouragingly. 'Are we in time?' I asked. 'He is up there,' he replied, with a toss of the head up the hill, and becoming gloomy all of a sudden. His face was like the autumn sky, overcast one moment and bright the next.

5. A smooth linen fabric.

"When the manager, escorted by the pilgrims, all of them armed to the teeth, had gone to the house, this chap came on board. 'I say, I don't like this. These natives are in the bush,' I said. He assured me earnestly it was all right. 'They are simple people,' he added; 'well, I am glad you came. It took me all my time to keep them off.' 'But you said it was all right,' I cried. 'Oh, they meant no harm,' he said; and as I stared he corrected himself, 'Not exactly.' Then vivaciously, 'My faith, your pilot-house wants a clean-up!' In the next breath he advised me to keep enough steam on the boiler to blow the whistle in case of any trouble. 'One good screech will do more for you than all your rifles. They are simple people,' he repeated. He rattled away at such a rate he quite overwhelmed me. He seemed to be trying to make up for lots of silence, and actually hinted, laughing, that such was the case. 'Don't you talk with Mr Kurtz?' I said. 'You don't talk with that man—you listen to him,' he exclaimed with severe exaltation. 'But now—' He waved his arm, and in the twinkling of an eye was in the uttermost depths of despondency. In a moment he came up again with a jump, possessed himself of both my hands, shook them continuously, while he gabbled: 'Brother sailor . . . honour . . . pleasure . . . delight . . . introduce myself . . . Russian . . . son of an arch-priest . . . Government of Tambov[6] . . . What? Tobacco! English tobacco; the excellent English tobacco! Now, that's brotherly. Smoke? Where's a sailor that does not smoke?'

"The pipe soothed him, and gradually I made out he had run away from school, had gone to sea in a Russian ship; ran away again; served some time in English ships; was now reconciled with the arch-priest. He made a point of that. 'But when one is young one must see things, gather experience, ideas; enlarge the mind.' 'Here!' I interrupted. 'You can never tell! Here I have met Mr Kurtz,' he said, youthfully solemn and reproachful. I held my tongue after that. It appears he had persuaded a Dutch trading-house on the coast to fit him out with stores and goods, and had started for the interior with a light heart, and no more idea of what would happen to him than a baby. He had been wandering about that river for nearly two years alone, cut off from everybody and everything. 'I am not so young as I look. I am twenty-five,' he said. 'At first old Van Shuyten would tell me to go to the devil,' he narrated with keen enjoyment; 'but I stuck to him, and talked and talked, till at last he got afraid I would talk the hind-leg off his favorite dog, so he gave me some cheap things and a few guns, and told me he hoped he would never see my face again. Good old Dutchman, Van Shuyten. I sent him one small lot of ivory a year ago, so that he can't call me a little thief when I get back. I hope he got it. And for the rest, I don't care. I had some wood stacked for you. That was my old house. Did you see?'

"I gave him Towson's book. He made as though he would kiss me, but restrained himself. 'The only book I had left, and I thought I had lost it,' he said, looking at it ecstatically. 'So many accidents happen to a man going about alone, you know. Canoes get upset sometimes—and sometimes you've got to clear out so quick when the people get angry.' He thumbed the pages. 'You made notes in Russian?' I asked. He nodded. 'I thought they were written in cipher,' I said. He laughed, then became serious. 'I had lots of trouble to keep these people off,' he said. 'Did they want to kill you?' I asked. 'Oh no!' he cried, and checked himself. 'Why did they attack us?' I pursued. He hesitated, then said shamefacedly, 'They don't want him to go.' 'Don't

6. A province of Western Russia.

they?' I said, curiously. He nodded a nod full of mystery and wisdom. 'I tell you,' he cried, 'this man has enlarged my mind.' He opened his arms wide, staring at me with his little blue eyes that were perfectly round."

3

"I looked at him, lost in astonishment. There he was before me, in motley, as though he had absconded from a troupe of mimes, enthusiastic, fabulous. His very existence was improbable, inexplicable, and altogether bewildering. He was an insoluble problem. It was inconceivable how he had existed, how he had succeeded in getting so far, how he had managed to remain—why he did not instantly disappear. 'I went a little farther,' he said, 'then still a little farther—till I had gone so far that I don't know how I'll ever get back. Never mind. Plenty time. I can manage. You take Kurtz away quick—quick—I tell you.' The glamour of youth enveloped his particoloured rags, his destitution, his loneliness, the essential desolation of his futile wanderings. For months—for years—his life hadn't been worth a day's purchase; and there he was gallantly, thoughtlessly alive, to all appearance indestructible solely by the virtue of his few years and of his unreflecting audacity. I was seduced into something like admiration—like envy. Glamour urged him on, glamour kept him unscathed. He surely wanted nothing from the wilderness but space to breathe in and to push on through. His need was to exist, and to move onwards at the greatest possible risk, and with a maximum of privation. If the absolutely pure, uncalculating, unpractical spirit of adventure had ever ruled a human being, it ruled this be-patched youth. I almost envied him the possession of this modest and clear flame. It seemed to have consumed all thought of self so completely, that, even while he was talking to you, you forgot that it was he—the man before your eyes—who had gone through these things. I did not envy him his devotion to Kurtz, though. He had not meditated over it. It came to him, and he accepted it with a sort of eager fatalism. I must say that to me it appeared about the most dangerous thing in every way he had come upon so far.

"They had come together unavoidably, like two ships becalmed near each other, and lay rubbing sides at last. I suppose Kurtz wanted an audience, because on a certain occasion, when encamped in the forest, they had talked all night, or more probably Kurtz had talked. 'We talked of everything,' he said, quite transported at the recollection. 'I forgot there was such a thing as sleep. The night did not seem to last an hour. Everything! Everything! . . . Of love too.' 'Ah, he talked to you of love!' I said, much amused. 'It isn't what you think,' he cried, almost passionately. 'It was in general. He made me see things—things.'

"He threw his arms up. We were on deck at the time, and the headman of my wood-cutters, lounging near by, turned upon him his heavy and glittering eyes. I looked around, and I don't know why, but I assure you that never, never before, did this land, this river, this jungle, the very arch of this blazing sky, appear to me so hopeless and so dark, so impenetrable to human thought, so pitiless to human weakness. 'And, ever since, you have been with him, of course?' I said.

"On the contrary. It appears their intercourse had been very much broken by various causes. He had, as he informed me proudly, managed to nurse Kurtz through two illnesses (he alluded to it as you would to some risky feat), but as a rule Kurtz wandered alone, far in the depths of the forest. 'Very often coming to this station, I had to wait days and days before he would turn up,' he said. 'Ah, it was worth waiting for!—sometimes.' 'What was he doing? exploring or what?' I asked. 'Oh yes, of course'; he had discovered lots of villages, a lake too—he did not know exactly in what direction; it was dangerous to inquire too much—but mostly his expeditions had been for ivory. 'But he had no goods to trade with by that time,' I objected. 'There's a good lot of cartridges left even yet,' he answered, looking away. 'To speak plainly, he raided the country,' I said. He nodded. 'Not alone, surely!' He muttered something about the villages round that lake. 'Kurtz got the tribe to follow him, did he?' I suggested. He fidgeted a little. 'They adored him,' he said. The tone of these words was so extraordinary that I looked at him searchingly. It was curious to see his mingled eagerness and reluctance to speak of Kurtz. The man filled his life, occupied his thoughts, swayed his emotions. 'What can you expect?' he burst out; 'he came to them with thunder and lightning, you know—and they had never seen anything like it—and very terrible. He could be very terrible. You can't judge Mr Kurtz as you would an ordinary man. No, no, no! Now—just to give you an idea—I don't mind telling you, he wanted to shoot me too one day—but I don't judge him.' 'Shoot you!' I cried. 'What for?' 'Well, I had a small lot of ivory the chief of that village near my house gave me. You see I used to shoot game for them. Well, he wanted it, and wouldn't hear reason. He declared he would shoot me unless I gave him the ivory and then cleared out of the country, because he could do so, and had a fancy for it, and there was nothing on earth to prevent him killing whom he jolly well pleased. And it was true too. I gave him the ivory. What did I care! But I didn't clear out. No, no. I couldn't leave him. I had to be careful, of course, till we got friendly again for a time. He had his second illness then. Afterwards I had to keep out of the way; but I didn't mind. He was living for the most part in those villages on the lake. When he came down to the river, sometimes he would take to me, and sometimes it was better for me to be careful. This man suffered too much. He hated all this, and somehow he couldn't get away. When I had a chance I begged him to try and leave while there was time; I offered to go back with him. And he would say yes, and then he would remain; go off on another ivory hunt; disappear for weeks; forget himself amongst these people—forget himself—you know.' 'Why! he's mad,' I said. He protested indignantly. Mr Kurtz couldn't be mad. If I had heard him talk, only two days ago, I wouldn't dare hint at such a thing. . . . I had taken up my binoculars while we talked, and was looking at the shore, sweeping the limit of the forest at each side and at the back of the house. The consciousness of there being people in that bush, so silent, so quiet—as silent and quiet as the ruined house on the hill—made me uneasy. There was no sign on the face of nature of this amazing tale that was not so much told as suggested to me in desolate exclamations, completed by shrugs, in interrupted phrases, in hints ending in deep sighs. The woods were unmoved, like a mask—heavy, like the closed door of a prison—they looked with their air of hidden knowledge, of patient expectation, of unapproachable silence. The Russian was explaining to me that it was only lately that Mr Kurtz had come down to the river, bringing along with him all the fighting men of that lake tribe. He had been absent for several months—getting himself adored, I suppose—and had come down unexpectedly, with the intention to all appearance of making a raid either across the river or down stream. Evidently the appetite for more ivory had got the better of the—what shall I say?—less material aspirations. However, he had got much worse suddenly. 'I heard he was lying helpless, and so I came up—took my chance,' said the Russian. 'Oh, he is bad, very bad.' I directed my glass to the house. There were no signs of life, but there was the ruined roof, the long mud wall peeping above the grass, with three little square window-holes, no two of the same size; all this brought within reach of my hand, as it were. And then I made a brusque movement, and one of the remaining posts of that vanished fence leaped up in the field of my glass. You remember I told you I had been struck at the distance by certain attempts at ornamentation, rather remarkable in the ruinous aspect of the place. Now I had suddenly a nearer view, and its first result was to make me throw my head back as if before a blow. Then I went carefully from post to post with my glass, and I saw my mistake. These round knobs were not ornamental but symbolic; they were expressive and puzzling, striking and disturbing—food for thought and also for the vultures if there had been any looking down from the sky; but at all events for such ants as were industrious enough to ascend the pole. They would have been even more impressive, those heads on the stakes, if their faces had not been turned to the house. Only one, the first I had made out, was facing my way. I was not so shocked as you may think. The start back I had given was really nothing but a movement of surprise. I had expected to see a knob of wood there, you know. I returned deliberately to the first I had seen—and there it was, black, dried, sunken, with closed eyelids,—a head that seemed to sleep at the top of that pole, and, with the shrunken dry lips showing a narrow white line of the teeth, was smiling too, smiling continuously at some endless and jocose dream of that eternal slumber.

"I am not disclosing any trade secrets. In fact the manager said afterwards that Mr Kurtz's methods had ruined the district. I have no opinion on that point, but I want you clearly to understand that there was nothing exactly profitable in these heads being there. They only showed that Mr Kurtz lacked restraint in the gratification of his various lusts, that there was something wanting in him—some small matter which, when the pressing need arose, could not be found under his magnificent eloquence. Whether he knew of this deficiency himself I can't say. I think the knowledge came to him at last—only at the very last. But the wilderness had found him out early, and had taken on him a terrible vengeance for the fantastic invasion. I think it had whispered to him things about himself which he did not know, things of which he had no conception till he took counsel with this great solitude—and the whisper had proved irresistibly fascinating. It echoed loudly within him because he was hollow at the core. . . . I put down the glass, and the head that had appeared near enough to be spoken to seemed at once to have leaped away from me into inaccessible distance.

"The admirer of Mr Kurtz was a bit crestfallen. In a hurried, indistinct voice he began to assure me he had not dared to take these—say, symbols—down. He was not afraid of the natives; they would not stir till Mr Kurtz gave the word. His ascendancy was extraordinary. The camps of these people surrounded the place, and the chiefs came every day to see him. They would crawl . . . 'I don't want to know anything of the ceremonies used when approaching Mr Kurtz,' I shouted. Curious, this feeling that came over me that such details would be more intolerable than those heads drying on the stakes under Mr Kurtz's windows. After all, that was only a savage sight, while I seemed at one bound to have been transported into some lightless region of subtle horrors, where pure, uncomplicated savagery was a positive relief, being something that had a right to exist—obviously—in the sunshine. The young man looked at me with surprise. I suppose it did not occur to him Mr Kurtz was no idol of mine. He forgot I hadn't heard any of these splendid monologues on, what was it? on love, justice, conduct of life—or what not. If it had come to crawling before Mr Kurtz, he crawled as much as the veriest savage of them all. I had no idea of the conditions, he said: these heads were the heads of rebels. I shocked him excessively by laughing. Rebels! What would be the next definition I was to hear? There had been enemies, criminals, workers—and these were rebels. Those rebellious heads looked very subdued to me on their sticks. 'You don't know how such a life tries a man like Kurtz,' cried Kurtz's last disciple. 'Well, and you?' I said. 'I! I! I am a simple man. I have no great thoughts. I want nothing from anybody. How can you compare me to . . . ?' His feelings were too much for speech, and suddenly he broke down. 'I don't understand,' he groaned. 'I've been doing my best to keep him alive, and that's enough. I had no hand in all this. I have no abilities. There hasn't been a drop of medicine or a mouthful of invalid food for months here. He was shamefully abandoned. A man like this, with such ideas. Shamefully! Shamefully! I—I—haven't slept for the last ten nights . . . .'

"His voice lost itself in the calm of the evening. The long shadows of the forest had slipped down-hill while we talked, had gone far beyond the ruined hovel, beyond the symbolic row of stakes. All this was in the gloom, while we down there were yet in the sunshine, and the stretch of the river abreast of the clearing glittered in a still and dazzling splendour, with a murky and overshadowed bend above and below. Not a living soul was seen on the shore. The bushes did not rustle.

"Suddenly round the corner of the house a group of men appeared, as though they had come up from the ground. They waded waist-deep in the grass, in a compact body, bearing an improvised stretcher in their midst. Instantly, in the emptiness of the landscape, a cry arose whose shrillness pierced the still air like a sharp arrow flying straight to the very heart of the land; and, as if by enchantment, streams of human beings—of naked human beings—with spears in their hands, with bows, with shields, with wild glances and savage movements, were poured into the clearing by the dark-faced and pensive forest. The bushes shook, the grass swayed for a time, and then everything stood still in attentive immobility.

"'Now, if he does not say the right thing to them we are all done for,' said the Russian at my elbow. The knot of men with the stretcher had stopped too, half-way to the steamer, as if petrified. I saw the man on the stretcher sit up, lank and with an uplifted arm, above the shoulders of the bearers. 'Let us hope that the man who can talk so well of love in general will find some particular reason to spare us this time,' I said. I resented bitterly the absurd danger of our situation, as if to be at the mercy of that atrocious phantom had been a dishonouring necessity. I could not hear a sound, but through my glasses I saw the thin arm extended commandingly, the lower jaw moving, the eyes of that apparition shining darkly far in its bony head that nodded with grotesque jerks. Kurtz—Kurtz—that means 'short' in German—don't it? Well, the name was as true as everything else in his life—and death. He looked at least seven feet long. His covering had fallen off, and his body emerged from it pitiful and appalling as from a winding-sheet. I could see the cage of his ribs all astir, the bones of his arm waving. It was as though an animated image of death carved out of old ivory had been shaking its hand with menaces at a motionless crowd of men made of dark and glittering bronze. I saw him open his mouth wide—it gave him a weirdly voracious aspect, as though he had wanted to swallow all the air, all the earth, all the men before him. A deep voice reached me faintly. He must have been shouting. He fell back suddenly. The stretcher shook as the bearers staggered forward again, and almost at the same time I noticed that the crowd of savages was vanishing without any perceptible movement of retreat, as if the forest that had ejected these beings so suddenly had drawn them in again as the breath is drawn in a long aspiration.

"Some of the pilgrims behind the stretcher carried his arms—two shot-guns, a heavy rifle, and a light revolver-carbine—the thunderbolts of that pitiful Jupiter. The manager bent over him murmuring as he walked beside his head. They laid him down in one of the little cabins—just a room for a bed-place and a camp-stool or two, you know. We had brought his belated correspondence, and a lot of torn envelopes and open letters littered his bed. His hand roamed feebly amongst these papers. I was struck by the fire of his eyes and the composed languor of his expression. It was not so much the exhaustion of disease. He did not seem in pain. This shadow looked satiated and calm, as though for the moment it had had its fill of all the emotions.

"He rustled one of the letters, and looking straight in my face said, 'I am glad.' Somebody had been writing to him about me. These special recommendations were turning up again. The volume of tone he emitted without effort, almost without the trouble of moving his lips, amazed me. A voice! a voice! It was grave, profound, vibrating, while the man did not seem capable of a whisper. However, he had enough strength in him—factitious no doubt—to very nearly make an end of us, as you shall hear directly.

"The manager appeared silently in the doorway; I stepped out at once and he drew the curtain after me. The Russian, eyed curiously by the pilgrims, was staring at the shore. I followed the direction of his glance.

"Dark human shapes could be made out in the distance, flitting indistinctly against the gloomy border of the forest, and near the river two bronze figures, leaning on tall spears, stood in the sunlight under fantastic head-dresses of spotted skins, warlike and still in statuesque repose. And from right to left along the lighted shore moved a wild and gorgeous apparition of a woman.

"She walked with measured steps, draped in striped and fringed cloths, treading the earth proudly, with a slight jingle and flash of barbarous ornaments. She carried her head high; her hair was done in the shape of a helmet; she had brass leggings to the knee, brass wire gauntlets to the elbow, a crimson spot on her tawny cheek, innumerable necklaces of glass beads on her neck; bizarre things, charms, gifts of witchmen, that hung about her, glittered and trembled at every step. She must have had the value of several elephant tusks upon her. She was savage and superb, wild-eyed and magnificent; there was something ominous and stately in her deliberate progress. And in the hush that had fallen suddenly upon the whole sorrowful land, the immense wilderness, the colossal body of the fecund and mysterious life seemed to look at her, pensive, as though it had been looking at the image of its own tenebrous and passionate soul.

"She came abreast of the steamer, stood still, and faced us. Her long shadow fell to the water's edge. Her face had a tragic and fierce aspect of wild sorrow and of dumb pain mingled with the fear of some struggling, half-shaped resolve. She stood looking at us without a stir, and like the wilderness itself, with an air of brooding over an inscrutable purpose. A whole minute passed, and then she made a step forward. There was a low jingle, a glint of yellow metal, a sway of fringed draperies, and she stopped as if her heart had failed her. The young fellow by my side growled. The pilgrims murmured at my back. She looked at us all as if her life had depended upon the unswerving steadiness of her glance. Suddenly she opened her bared arms and threw them up rigid above her head, as though in an uncontrollable desire to touch the sky, and at the same time the swift shadows darted out on the earth, swept around on the river, gathering the steamer in a shadowy embrace. A formidable silence hung over the scene.

"She turned away slowly, walked on, following the bank, and passed into the bushes to the left. Once only her eyes gleamed back at us in the dusk of the thickets before she disappeared.

"'If she had offered to come aboard I really think I would have tried to shoot her,' said the man of patches, nervously. 'I had been risking my life every day for the last fortnight to keep her out of the house. She got in one day and kicked up a row about those miserable rags I picked up in the storeroom to mend my clothes with. I wasn't decent. At least it must have been that, for she talked like a fury to Kurtz for an hour, pointing at me now and then. I don't understand the dialect of this tribe. Luckily for me, I fancy Kurtz felt too ill that day to care, or there would have been mischief. I don't understand. . . . No—it's too much for me. Ah, well, it's all over now.'

"At this moment I heard Kurtz's deep voice behind the curtain, 'Save me!—save the ivory, you mean. Don't tell me. Save *me!* Why, I've had to save you. You are interrupting my plans now. Sick! Sick! Not so sick as you would like to believe. Never mind. I'll carry my ideas out yet—I will return. I'll show you what can be done. You with your little peddling notions—you are interfering with me. I will return. I . . . '

"The manager came out. He did me the honour to take me under the arm and lead me aside. 'He is very low, very low,' he said. He considered it necessary to sigh, but neglected to be consistently sorrowful. 'We have done all we could for him— haven't we? But there is no disguising the fact, Mr Kurtz has done more harm than good to the Company. He did not see the time was not ripe for vigorous action. Cautiously, cautiously—that's my principle. We must be cautious yet. The district is closed to us for a time. Deplorable! Upon the whole, the trade will suffer. I don't deny there is a remarkable quantity of ivory—mostly fossil. We must save it, at all events—but look how precarious the position is—and why? Because the method is unsound.' 'Do you,' said I, looking at the shore, 'call it "unsound method"?' 'Without doubt,' he exclaimed, hotly. 'Don't you?' . . . 'No method at all,' I murmured after a while. 'Exactly,' he exulted. 'I anticipated this. Shows a complete want of judgment. It is my duty to point it out in the proper quarter.' 'Oh,' said I, 'that fellow—what's his name?—the brickmaker, will make a readable report for you.' He appeared confounded for a moment. It seemed to me I had never breathed an atmosphere so vile, and I turned mentally to Kurtz for relief—positively for relief. 'Nevertheless, I think Mr Kurtz is a remarkable man,' I said with emphasis. He started, dropped on me a cold heavy glance, said very quietly, 'He *was*,' and turned his back on me. My hour of favour was over; I found myself lumped along with Kurtz as a partisan of methods for which the time was not ripe: I was unsound! Ah! but it was something to have at least a choice of nightmares.

"I had turned to the wilderness really, not to Mr Kurtz, who, I was ready to admit, was as good as buried. And for a moment it seemed to me as if I also were buried in a vast grave full of unspeakable secrets. I felt an intolerable weight oppressing my breast, the smell of the damp earth, the unseen presence of victorious corruption, the darkness of an impenetrable night. . . . The Russian tapped me on the shoulder. I heard him mumbling and stammering something about 'brother seaman—couldn't conceal—knowledge of matters that would affect Mr Kurtz's reputation.' I waited. For him evidently Mr Kurtz was not in his grave; I suspect that for him Mr Kurtz was one of the immortals. 'Well!' said I at last, 'speak out. As it happens, I am Mr Kurtz's friend—in a way.'

"He stated with a good deal of formality that had we not been 'of the same profession,' he would have kept the matter to himself without regard to consequences. He suspected 'there was an active ill-will towards him on the part of these white men that—' 'You are right,' I said, remembering a certain conversation I had overheard. 'The manager thinks you ought to be hanged.' He showed a concern at this intelligence which amused me at first. 'I had better get out of the way quietly,' he said, earnestly. 'I can do no more for Kurtz now, and they would soon find some excuse. What's to stop them? There's a military post three hundred miles from here.' 'Well, upon my word,' said I, 'perhaps you had better go if you have any friends amongst the savages near by.' 'Plenty,' he said. 'They are simple people—and I want nothing, you know.' He stood biting his lip, then: 'I don't want any harm to happen to these whites here, but of course I was thinking of Mr Kurtz's reputation—but you are a brother seaman and—' 'All right,' said I, after a time. 'Mr Kurtz's reputation is safe with me.' I did not know how truly I spoke.

"He informed me, lowering his voice, that it was Kurtz who had ordered the attack to be made on the steamer. 'He hated sometimes the idea of being taken away—and then again . . . But I don't understand these matters. I am a simple man. He thought it would scare you away—that you would give it up, thinking him dead. I could not stop him. Oh, I had an awful time of it this last month.' 'Very well,' I said. 'He is all right now.' 'Ye-e-es,' he muttered, not very convinced apparently. 'Thanks,' said I; 'I shall keep my eyes open.' 'But quiet—eh?' he urged, anxiously. 'It would be awful for his reputation if anybody here—' I promised a complete discretion with great gravity. 'I have a canoe and three black fellows waiting not very far. I am off. Could you give me a few Martini-Henry cartridges?' I could, and did, with proper secrecy. He helped himself, with a wink at me, to a handful of my tobacco. 'Between sailors—you know—good English tobacco.' At the door of the pilot-house he turned round—'I say, haven't you a pair of shoes you could spare?' He raised one leg. 'Look.' The soles were tied with knotted strings sandal-wise under his bare feet. I rooted out an old pair, at which he looked with admiration before tucking it under his left arm. One of his pockets (bright red) was bulging with cartridges, from the other (dark blue) peeped 'Towson's Inquiry,' &c., &c. He seemed to think himself excellently well equipped for a renewed encounter with the wilderness. 'Ah! I'll never, never meet such a man again. You ought to have heard him recite poetry—his own too it was, he told me. Poetry!' He rolled his eyes at the recollection of these delights. 'Oh, he enlarged my mind!' 'Good-bye,' said I. He shook hands and vanished in the night. Sometimes I ask myself whether I had ever really seen him—whether it was possible to meet such a phenomenon! . . .

"When I woke up shortly after midnight his warning came to my mind with its hint of danger that seemed, in the starred darkness, real enough to make me get up for the purpose of having a look round. On the hill a big fire burned, illuminating fit-fully a crooked corner of the station-house. One of the agents with a picket of a few of our blacks, armed for the purpose, was keeping guard over the ivory; but deep with-in the forest, red gleams that wavered, that seemed to sink and rise from the ground amongst confused columnar shapes of intense blackness, showed the exact position of the camp where Mr Kurtz's adorers were keeping their uneasy vigil. The monoto-nous beating of a big drum filled the air with muffled shocks and a lingering vibra-tion. A steady droning sound of many men chanting each to himself some weird incantation came out from the black, flat wall of the woods as the humming of bees comes out of a hive, and had a strange narcotic effect upon my half-awake senses. I believe I dozed off leaning over the rail, till an abrupt burst of yells, an overwhelming outbreak of a pent-up and mysterious frenzy, woke me up in a bewildered wonder. It was cut short all at once, and the low droning went on with an effect of audible and soothing silence. I glanced casually into the little cabin. A light was burning within, but Mr Kurtz was not there.

"I think I would have raised an outcry if I had believed my eyes. But I didn't believe them at first—the thing seemed so impossible. The fact is, I was completely unnerved by a sheer blank fright, pure abstract terror, unconnected with any distinct shape of physical danger. What made this emotion so overpowering was—how shall I define it?—the moral shock I received, as if something altogether monstrous, intolerable to thought and odious to the soul, had been thrust upon me unexpectedly. This lasted of course the merest fraction of a second, and then the usual sense of commonplace, deadly danger, the possibility of a sudden onslaught and massacre, or something of the kind, which I saw impending, was positively welcome and composing. It pacified me, in fact, so much, that I did not raise an alarm.

"There was an agent buttoned up inside an ulster[7] and sleeping on a chair on deck within three feet of me. The yells had not awakened him; he snored very slightly; I left him to his slumbers and leaped ashore. I did not betray Mr Kurtz—it was ordered I should never betray him—it was written I should be loyal to the nightmare of my choice. I was anxious to deal with this shadow by myself alone,—and to this day I don't know why I was so jealous of sharing with any one the peculiar blackness of that experience.

"As soon as I got on the bank I saw a trail—a broad trail through the grass. I remember the exultation with which I said to myself, 'He can't walk—he is crawling on all-fours—I've got him.' The grass was wet with dew. I strode rapidly with clenched fists. I fancy I had some vague notion of falling upon him and giving him a drubbing. I don't know. I had some imbecile thoughts. The knitting old woman with the cat obtruded herself upon my memory as a most improper person to be sitting at the other end of such an affair. I saw a row of pilgrims squirting lead in the air out of Winchesters held to the hip. I thought I would never get back to the steamer, and imagined myself living alone and unarmed in the woods to an advanced age. Such silly things—you know. And I remember I confounded the beat of the drum with the beating of my heart, and was pleased at its calm regularity.

"I kept to the track though—then stopped to listen. The night was very clear: a dark blue space, sparkling with dew and starlight, in which black things stood very still. I thought I could see a kind of motion ahead of me. I was strangely cocksure of everything that night. I actually left the track and ran in a wide semicircle (I verily believe chuckling to myself) so as to get in front of that stir, of that motion I had seen—if indeed I had seen anything. I was circumventing Kurtz as though it had been a boyish game.

"I came upon him, and, if he had not heard me coming, I would have fallen over him too, but he got up in time. He rose, unsteady, long, pale, indistinct, like a vapour exhaled by the earth, and swayed slightly, misty and silent before me; while at my back the fires loomed between the trees, and the murmur of many voices issued from the forest. I had cut him off cleverly; but when actually confronting him I seemed to come to my senses, I saw the danger in its right proportion. It was by no means over yet. Suppose he began to shout? Though he could hardly stand, there was still plenty of vigour in his voice. 'Go away—hide yourself,' he said, in that profound tone. It was very awful. I glanced back. We were within thirty yards from the nearest fire. A black figure stood up, strode on long black legs, waving long black arms, across the glow. It had horns—antelope horns, I think—on its head. Some sorcerer, some witch-man, no doubt: it looked fiend-like enough. 'Do you know what you are doing?' I whispered. 'Perfectly,' he answered, raising his voice for that single word: it sounded to me far off and yet loud, like a hail through a speaking-trumpet. If he makes a row we are lost, I thought to myself. This clearly was not a case for fisticuffs, even apart from the very natural aversion I had to beat that Shadow—this wandering and tormented thing. 'You will be lost,' I said—'utterly lost.' One gets sometimes such a flash of inspiration, you know. I did say the right thing, though indeed he could not have been more irretrievably lost than he was at this very moment, when the foundations of our intimacy were being laid—to endure—to endure—even to the end—even beyond.

7. Long overcoat.

"'I had immense plans,' he muttered irresolutely. 'Yes,' said I; 'but if you try to shout I'll smash your head with—' there was not a stick or a stone near. 'I will throttle you for good,' I corrected myself. 'I was on the threshold of great things,' he pleaded, in a voice of longing, with a wistfulness of tone that made my blood run cold. 'And now for this stupid scoundrel—' 'Your success in Europe is assured in any case,' I affirmed, steadily. I did not want to have the throttling of him, you understand—and indeed it would have been very little use for any practical purpose. I tried to break the spell—the heavy, mute spell of the wilderness—that seemed to draw him to its pitiless breast by the awakening of forgotten and brutal instincts, by the memory of gratified and monstrous passions. This alone, I was convinced, had driven him out to the edge of the forest, to the bush, towards the gleam of fires, the throb of drums, the drone of weird incantations; this alone had beguiled his unlawful soul beyond the bounds of permitted aspirations. And, don't you see, the terror of the position was not in being knocked on the head—though I had a very lively sense of that danger too—but in this, that I had to deal with a being to whom I could not appeal in the name of anything high or low. I had, even like the niggers, to invoke him—himself—his own exalted and incredible degradation. There was nothing either above or below him, and I knew it. He had kicked himself loose of the earth. Confound the man! he had kicked the very earth to pieces. He was alone, and I before him did not know whether I stood on the ground or floated in the air. I've been telling you what we said—repeating the phrases we pronounced,—but what's the good? They were common everyday words,—the familiar, vague sounds exchanged on every waking day of life. But what of that? They had behind them, to my mind, the terrific suggestiveness of words heard in dreams, of phrases spoken in nightmares. Soul! If anybody had ever struggled with a soul, I am the man. And I wasn't arguing with a lunatic either. Believe me or not, his intelligence was perfectly clear—concentrated, it is true, upon himself with horrible intensity, yet clear; and therein was my only chance—barring, of course, the killing him there and then, which wasn't so good, on account of unavoidable noise. But his soul was mad. Being alone in the wilderness, it had looked within itself, and, by heavens! I tell you, it had gone mad. I had—for my sins, I suppose—to go through the ordeal of looking into it myself. No eloquence could have been so withering to one's belief in mankind as his final burst of sincerity. He struggled with himself, too. I saw it,—I heard it. I saw the inconceivable mystery of a soul that knew no restraint, no faith, and no fear, yet struggling blindly with itself. I kept my head pretty well; but when I had him at last stretched on the couch, I wiped my forehead, while my legs shook under me as though I had carried half a ton on my back down that hill. And yet I had only supported him, his bony arm clasped round my neck—and he was not much heavier than a child.

"When next day we left at noon, the crowd, of whose presence behind the curtain of trees I had been acutely conscious all the time, flowed out of the woods again, filled the clearing, covered the slope with a mass of naked, breathing, quivering, bronze bodies. I steamed up a bit, then swung down-stream, and two thousand eyes followed the evolutions of the splashing, thumping, fierce river-demon beating the water with its terrible tail and breathing black smoke into the air. In front of the first rank, along the river, three men, plastered with bright red earth from head to foot, strutted to and fro restlessly. When we came abreast again, they faced the river, stamped their feet, nodded their horned heads, swayed their scarlet bodies; they shook towards the fierce river-demon a bunch of black feathers, a mangy skin with a pendent tail—something that looked like a dried gourd; they shouted periodically together strings of amazing words that resembled no sounds of human language; and the deep murmurs of the crowd, interrupted suddenly, were like the responses of some satanic litany.

"We had carried Kurtz into the pilot-house: there was more air there. Lying on the couch, he stared through the open shutter. There was an eddy in the mass of human bodies, and the woman with helmeted head and tawny cheeks rushed out to the very brink of the stream. She put out her hands, shouted something, and all that wild mob took up the shout in a roaring chorus of articulated, rapid, breathless utterance.

"'Do you understand this?' I asked.

"He kept on looking out past me with fiery, longing eyes, with a mingled expression of wistfulness and hate. He made no answer, but I saw a smile, a smile of indefinable meaning, appear on his colourless lips that a moment after twitched convulsively. 'Do I not?' he said slowly, gasping, as if the words had been torn out of him by a supernatural power.

"I pulled the string of the whistle, and I did this because I saw the pilgrims on deck getting out their rifles with an air of anticipating a jolly lark. At the sudden screech there was a movement of abject terror through that wedged mass of bodies. 'Don't! don't! you frighten them away,' cried some one on deck disconsolately. I pulled the string time after time. They broke and ran, they leaped, they crouched, they swerved, they dodged the flying terror of the sound. The three red chaps had fallen flat, face down on the shore, as though they had been shot dead. Only the barbarous and superb woman did not so much as flinch, and stretched tragically her bare arms after us over the sombre and glittering river.

"And then that imbecile crowd down on the deck started their little fun, and I could see nothing more for smoke.

"The brown current ran swiftly out of the heart of darkness, bearing us down towards the sea with twice the speed of our upward progress; and Kurtz's life was running swiftly too, ebbing, ebbing out of his heart into the sea of inexorable time. The manager was very placid, he had no vital anxieties now, he took us both in with a comprehensive and satisfied glance: the 'affair' had come off as well as could be wished. I saw the time approaching when I would be left alone of the party of 'unsound method.' The pilgrims looked upon me with disfavour. I was, so to speak, numbered with the dead. It is strange how I accepted this unforeseen partnership, this choice of nightmares forced upon me in the tenebrous land invaded by these mean and greedy phantoms.

"Kurtz discoursed. A voice! a voice! It rang deep to the very last. It survived his strength to hide in the magnificent folds of eloquence the barren darkness of his heart. Oh, he struggled! he struggled! The wastes of his weary brain were haunted by shadowy images now—images of wealth and fame revolving obsequiously round his unextinguishable gift of noble and lofty expression. My Intended, my station, my career, my ideas—these were the subjects for the occasional utterances of elevated sentiments. The shade of the original Kurtz frequented the bedside of the hollow sham, whose fate it was to be buried presently in the mould of primeval earth. But both the diabolic love and the unearthly hate of the mysteries it had penetrated fought for the possession of that soul satiated with primitive emotions, avid of lying fame, of sham distinction, of all the appearances of success and power.

"Sometimes he was contemptibly childish. He desired to have kings meet him at railway-stations on his return from some ghastly Nowhere, where he intended to accomplish great things. 'You show them you have in you something that is really profitable, and then there will be no limits to the recognition of your ability,' he would say. 'Of course you must take care of the motives—right motives—always.' The long reaches that were like one and the same reach, monotonous bends that were exactly alike, slipped past the steamer with their multitude of secular[8] trees looking patiently after this grimy fragment of another world, the forerunner of change, of conquest, of trade, of massacres, of blessings. I looked ahead—piloting. 'Close the shutter,' said Kurtz suddenly one day; 'I can't bear to look at this.' I did so. There was a silence. 'Oh, but I will wring your heart yet!' he cried at the invisible wilderness.

"We broke down—as I had expected—and had to lie up for repairs at the head of an island. This delay was the first thing that shook Kurtz's confidence. One morning he gave me a packet of papers and a photograph,—the lot tied together with a shoe-string. 'Keep this for me,' he said. 'This noxious fool' (meaning the manager) 'is capable of prying into my boxes when I am not looking.' In the afternoon I saw him. He was lying on his back with closed eyes, and I withdrew quietly, but I heard him mutter, 'Live rightly, die, die . . .' I listened. There was nothing more. Was he rehearsing some speech in his sleep, or was it a fragment of a phrase from some newspaper article? He had been writing for the papers and meant to do so again, 'for the furthering of my ideas. It's a duty.'

"His was an impenetrable darkness. I looked at him as you peer down at a man who is lying at the bottom of a precipice where the sun never shines. But I had not much time to give him, because I was helping the engine-driver to take to pieces the leaky cylinders, to straighten a bent connecting-rod, and in other such matters. I lived in an infernal mess of rust, filings, nuts, bolts, spanners, hammers, ratchet-drills—things I abominate, because I don't get on with them. I tended the little forge we fortunately had aboard; I toiled wearily in a wretched scrap-heap—unless I had the shakes too bad to stand.

"One evening coming in with a candle I was startled to hear him say a little tremulously, 'I am lying here in the dark waiting for death.' The light was within a foot of his eyes. I forced myself to murmur, 'Oh, nonsense!' and stood over him as if transfixed.

"Anything approaching the change that came over his features I have never seen before, and hope never to see again. Oh, I wasn't touched. I was fascinated. It was as though a veil had been rent. I saw on that ivory face the expression of sombre pride, of ruthless power, of craven terror—of an intense and hopeless despair. Did he live his life again in every detail of desire, temptation, and surrender during that supreme moment of complete knowledge? He cried in a whisper at some image, at some vision,—he cried out twice, a cry that was no more than a breath—

"'The horror! The horror!'

"I blew the candle out and left the cabin. The pilgrims were dining in the mess-room, and I took my place opposite the manager, who lifted his eyes to give me a questioning glance, which I successfully ignored. He leaned back, serene, with that peculiar smile of his sealing the unexpressed depths of his meanness. A continuous shower of small flies streamed upon the lamp, upon the cloth, upon our hands and faces. Suddenly the manager's boy put his insolent black head in the doorway, and said in a tone of scathing contempt—

"'Mistah Kurtz—he dead.'

---

8. Ancient.

"All the pilgrims rushed out to see. I remained, and went on with my dinner. I believe I was considered brutally callous. However, I did not eat much. There was a lamp in there—light, don't you know—and outside it was so beastly, beastly dark. I went no more near the remarkable man who had pronounced a judgment upon the adventures of his soul on this earth. The voice was gone. What else had been there? But I am of course aware that next day the pilgrims buried something in a muddy hole.

"And then they very nearly buried me.

"However, as you see, I did not go to join Kurtz there and then. I did not. I remained to dream the nightmare out to the end, and to show my loyalty to Kurtz once more. Destiny. My destiny! Droll thing life is—that mysterious arrangement of merciless logic for a futile purpose. The most you can hope from it is some knowledge of yourself—that comes too late—a crop of unextinguishable regrets. I have wrestled with death. It is the most unexciting contest you can imagine. It takes place in an impalpable greyness, with nothing underfoot, with nothing around, without spectators, without clamour, without glory, without the great desire of victory, without the great fear of defeat, in a sickly atmosphere of tepid scepticism, without much belief in your own right, and still less in that of your adversary. If such is the form of ultimate wisdom, then life is a greater riddle than some of us think it to be. I was within a hair's-breadth of the last opportunity for pronouncement, and I found with humiliation that probably I would have nothing to say. This is the reason why I affirm that Kurtz was a remarkable man. He had something to say. He said it. Since I had peeped over the edge myself, I understand better the meaning of his stare, that could not see the flame of the candle, but was wide enough to embrace the whole universe, piercing enough to penetrate all the hearts that beat in the darkness. He had summed up—he had judged. 'The horror!' He was a remarkable man. After all, this was the expression of some sort of belief; it had candour, it had conviction, it had a vibrating note of revolt in its whisper, it had the appalling face of a glimpsed truth—the strange commingling of desire and hate. And it is not my own extremity I remember best—a vision of greyness without form filled with physical pain, and a careless contempt for the evanescence of all things—even of this pain itself. No! It is his extremity that I seem to have lived through. True, he had made that last stride, he had stepped over the edge, while I had been permitted to draw back my hesitating foot. And perhaps in this is the whole difference; perhaps all the wisdom, and all truth, and all sincerity, are just compressed into that inappreciable moment of time in which we step over the threshold of the invisible. Perhaps! I like to think my summing-up would not have been a word of careless contempt. Better his cry—much better. It was an affirmation, a moral victory paid for by innumerable defeats, by abominable terrors, by abominable satisfactions. But it was a victory! That is why I have remained loyal to Kurtz to the last, and even beyond, when a long time after I heard once more, not his own voice, but the echo of his magnificent eloquence thrown to me from a soul as translucently pure as a cliff of crystal.

"No, they did not bury me, though there is a period of time which I remember mistily, with a shuddering wonder, like a passage through some inconceivable world that had no hope in it and no desire. I found myself back in the sepulchral city resenting the sight of people hurrying through the streets to filch a little money from each other, to devour their infamous cookery, to gulp their unwholesome beer, to dream their insignificant and silly dreams. They trespassed upon my thoughts. They were intruders whose knowledge of life was to me an irritating pretence, because I felt so sure they could not possibly know the things I knew. Their bearing, which was simply the bearing of commonplace individuals going about their business in the assurance of perfect safety, was offensive to me like the outrageous flauntings of folly in the face of a danger it is unable to comprehend. I had no particular desire to enlighten them, but I had some difficulty in restraining myself from laughing in their faces, so full of stupid importance. I daresay I was not very well at that time. I tottered about the streets—there were various affairs to settle—grinning bitterly at perfectly respectable persons. I admit my behaviour was inexcusable, but then my temperature was seldom normal in these days. My dear aunt's endeavours to 'nurse up my strength' seemed altogether beside the mark. It was not my strength that wanted nursing, it was my imagination that wanted soothing. I kept the bundle of papers given me by Kurtz, not knowing exactly what to do with it. His mother had died lately, watched over, as I was told, by his Intended. A clean-shaved man, with an official manner and wearing gold-rimmed spectacles, called on me one day and made inquiries, at first circuitous, afterwards suavely pressing, about what he was pleased to denominate certain 'documents.' I was not surprised, because I had had two rows with the manager on the subject out there. I had refused to give up the smallest scrap out of that package, and I took the same attitude with the spectacled man. He became darkly menacing at last, and with much heat argued that the Company had the right to every bit of information about its 'territories.' And, said he, 'Mr Kurtz's knowledge of unexplored regions must have been necessarily extensive and peculiar—owing to his great abilities and to the deplorable circumstances in which he had been placed: therefore—' I assured him Mr Kurtz's knowledge, however extensive, did not bear upon the problems of commerce or administration. He invoked then the name of science. 'It would be an incalculable loss if,' &c., &c. I offered him the report on the 'Suppression of Savage Customs,' with the postscriptum torn off. He took it up eagerly, but ended by sniffing at it with an air of contempt. 'This is not what we had a right to expect,' he remarked. 'Expect nothing else,' I said. 'There are only private letters.' He withdrew upon some threat of legal proceedings, and I saw him no more; but another fellow, calling himself Kurtz's cousin, appeared two days later, and was anxious to hear all the details about his dear relative's last moments. Incidentally he gave me to understand that Kurtz had been essentially a great musician. 'There was the making of an immense success,' said the man, who was an organist, I believe, with lank grey hair flowing over a greasy coat-collar. I had no reason to doubt his statement; and to this day I am unable to say what was Kurtz's profession, whether he ever had any—which was the greatest of his talents. I had taken him for a painter who wrote for the papers, or else for a journalist who could paint—but even the cousin (who took snuff during the interview) could not tell me what he had been—exactly. He was a universal genius—on that point I agreed with the old chap, who thereupon blew his nose noisily into a large cotton handkerchief and withdrew in senile agitation, bearing off some family letters and memoranda without importance. Ultimately a journalist anxious to know something of the fate of his 'dear colleague' turned up. This visitor informed me Kurtz's proper sphere ought to have been politics 'on the popular side.' He had furry straight eyebrows, bristly hair cropped short, an eye-glass on a broad ribbon, and, becoming expansive, confessed his opinion that Kurtz really couldn't write a bit—'but heavens! how that man could talk! He electrified large meetings. He had faith—don't you see?—he had the faith. He could get himself to believe anything—anything. He would have been a splendid leader of an extreme party.' 'What party?' I asked. 'Any party,' answered the other. 'He was an—an—extremist.' Did I not think so? I assented. Did I know, he asked, with a sudden flash of curiosity, 'what it was that had induced him to go out there?' 'Yes,' said I, and forthwith handed him the famous Report for publication, if he thought fit. He glanced through it hurriedly, mumbling all the time, judged 'it would do,' and took himself off with this plunder.

"Thus I was left at last with a slim packet of letters and the girl's portrait. She struck me as beautiful—I mean she had a beautiful expression. I know that the sunlight can be made to lie too, yet one felt that no manipulation of light and pose could have conveyed the delicate shade of truthfulness upon those features. She seemed ready to listen without mental reservation, without suspicion, without a thought for herself. I concluded I would go and give her back her portrait and those letters myself. Curiosity? Yes; and also some other feeling perhaps. All that had been Kurtz's had passed out of my hands: his soul, his body, his station, his plans, his ivory, his career. There remained only his memory and his Intended—and I wanted to give that up too to the past, in a way,—to surrender personally all that remained of him with me to that oblivion which is the last word of our common fate. I don't defend myself. I had no clear perception of what it was I really wanted. Perhaps it was an impulse of unconscious loyalty, or the fulfilment of one of those ironic necessities that lurk in the facts of human existence. I don't know. I can't tell. But I went.

"I thought his memory was like the other memories of the dead that accumulate in every man's life,—a vague impress on the brain of shadows that had fallen on it in their swift and final passage; but before the high and ponderous door, between the tall houses of a street as still and decorous as a well-kept alley in a cemetery, I had a vision of him on the stretcher, opening his mouth voraciously, as if to devour all the earth with all its mankind. He lived then before me; he lived as much as he had ever lived—a shadow insatiable of splendid appearances, of frightful realities; a shadow darker than the shadow of the night, and draped nobly in the folds of a gorgeous eloquence. The vision seemed to enter the house with me—the stretcher, the phantom-bearers, the wild crowd of obedient worshippers, the gloom of the forests, the glitter of the reach between the murky bends, the beat of the drum, regular and muffled like the beating of a heart—the heart of a conquering darkness. It was a moment of triumph for the wilderness, an invading and vengeful rush which, it seemed to me, I would have to keep back alone for the salvation of another soul. And the memory of what I had heard him say afar there, with the horned shapes stirring at my back, in the glow of fires, within the patient woods, those broken phrases came back to me, were heard again in their ominous and terrifying simplicity. I remembered his abject pleading, his abject threats, the colossal scale of his vile desires, the meanness, the torment, the tempestuous anguish of his soul. And later on I seemed to see his collected languid manner, when he said one day, 'This lot of ivory now is really mine. The Company did not pay for it. I collected it myself at a very great personal risk. I am afraid they will try to claim it as theirs though. H'm. It is a difficult case. What do you think I ought to do—resist? Eh? I want no more than justice.' . . . He wanted no more than justice—no more than justice. I rang the bell before a mahogany door on the first floor, and while I waited he seemed to stare at me out of the glassy panel—stare with that wide and immense stare embracing, condemning, loathing all the universe. I seemed to hear the whispered cry, 'The horror! The horror!'

"The dusk was falling. I had to wait in a lofty drawing-room with three long windows from floor to ceiling that were like three luminous and bedraped columns. The bent gilt legs and backs of the furniture shone in indistinct curves. The tall marble fireplace had a cold and monumental whiteness. A grand piano stood massively in a corner, with dark gleams on the flat surfaces like a sombre and polished sarcophagus. A high door opened—closed. I rose.

"She came forward, all in black, with a pale head, floating towards me in the dusk. She was in mourning. It was more than a year since his death, more than a year since the news came; she seemed as though she would remember and mourn for ever. She took both my hands in hers and murmured, 'I had heard you were coming.' I noticed she was not very young—I mean not girlish. She had a mature capacity for fidelity, for belief, for suffering. The room seemed to have grown darker, as if all the sad light of the cloudy evening had taken refuge on her forehead. This fair hair, this pale visage, this pure brow, seemed surrounded by an ashy halo from which the dark eyes looked out at me. Their glance was guileless, profound, confident, and trustful. She carried her sorrowful head as though she were proud of that sorrow, as though she would say, I—I alone know how to mourn for him as he deserves. But while we were still shaking hands, such a look of awful desolation came upon her face that I perceived she was one of those creatures that are not the playthings of Time. For her he had died only yesterday. And, by Jove! the impression was so powerful that for me too he seemed to have died only yesterday—nay, this very minute. I saw her and him in the same instant of time—his death and her sorrow—I saw her sorrow in the very moment of his death. Do you understand? I saw them together—I heard them together. She had said, with a deep catch of the breath, 'I have survived'; while my strained ears seemed to hear distinctly, mingled with her tone of despairing regret, the summing-up whisper of his eternal condemnation. I asked myself what I was doing there, with a sensation of panic in my heart as though I had blundered into a place of cruel and absurd mysteries not fit for a human being to behold. She motioned me to a chair. We sat down. I laid the packet gently on the little table, and she put her hand over it. . . . 'You knew him well,' she murmured, after a moment of mourning silence.

"'Intimacy grows quickly out there,' I said. 'I knew him as well as it is possible for one man to know another.'

"'And you admired him,' she said. 'It was impossible to know him and not to admire him. Was it?'

"'He was a remarkable man,' I said, unsteadily. Then before the appealing fixity of her gaze, that seemed to watch for more words on my lips, I went on, 'It was impossible not to—'

"'Love him,' she finished eagerly, silencing me into an appalled dumbness. 'How true! how true! But when you think that no one knew him so well as I! I had all his noble confidence. I knew him best.'

"'You knew him best,' I repeated. And perhaps she did. But with every word spoken the room was growing darker, and only her forehead, smooth and white, remained illumined by the unextinguishable light of belief and love.

"'You were his friend,' she went on. 'His friend,' she repeated, a little louder. 'You must have been, if he had given you this, and sent you to me. I feel I can speak to you—and oh! I must speak. I want you—you who have heard his last words—to know I have been worthy of him. . . . It is not pride. . . . Yes! I am proud to know I understood him better than any one on earth—he told me so himself. And since his mother died I have had no one—no one—to—to—'

"I listened. The darkness deepened. I was not even sure whether he had given me the right bundle. I rather suspect he wanted me to take care of another batch of his papers which, after his death, I saw the manager examining under the lamp. And the girl talked, easing her pain in the certitude of my sympathy; she talked as thirsty men drink. I had heard that her engagement with Kurtz had been disapproved by her people. He wasn't rich enough or something. And indeed I don't know whether he had not been a pauper all his life. He had given me some reason to infer that it was his impatience of comparative poverty that drove him out there.

"'. . . Who was not his friend who had heard him speak once?' she was saying. 'He drew men towards him by what was best in them.' She looked at me with intensity. 'It is the gift of the great,' she went on, and the sound of her low voice seemed to have the accompaniment of all the other sounds, full of mystery, desolation, and sorrow, I had ever heard—the ripple of the river, the soughing of the trees swayed by the wind, the murmurs of wild crowds, the faint ring of incomprehensible words cried from afar, the whisper of a voice speaking from beyond the threshold of an eternal darkness. 'But you have heard him! You know!' she cried.

"'Yes, I know,' I said with something like despair in my heart, but bowing my head before the faith that was in her, before that great and saving illusion that shone with an unearthly glow in the darkness, in the triumphant darkness from which I could not have defended her—from which I could not even defend myself.

"'What a loss to me—to us!'—she corrected herself with beautiful generosity; then added in a murmur, 'To the world.' By the last gleams of twilight I could see the glitter of her eyes, full of tears—of tears that would not fall.

"'I have been very happy—very fortunate—very proud,' she went on. 'Too fortunate. Too happy for a little while. And now I am unhappy for—for life.'

"She stood up; her fair hair seemed to catch all the remaining light in a glimmer of gold. I rose too.

"'And of all this,' she went on, mournfully, 'of all his promise, and of all his greatness, of his generous mind, of his noble heart, nothing remains—nothing but a memory. You and I—'

"'We shall always remember him,' I said, hastily.

"'No!' she cried. 'It is impossible that all this should be lost—that such a life should be sacrificed to leave nothing—but sorrow. You know what vast plans he had. I knew of them too—I could not perhaps understand,—but others knew of them. Something must remain. His words, at least, have not died.'

"'His words will remain,' I said.

"'And his example,' she whispered to herself. 'Men looked up to him,—his goodness shone in every act. His example—'

"'True,' I said; 'his example too. Yes, his example. I forgot that.'

"'But I do not. I cannot—I cannot believe—not yet. I cannot believe that I shall never see him again, that nobody will see him again, never, never, never.'

"She put out her arms as if after a retreating figure, stretching them black and with clasped pale hands across the fading and narrow sheen of the window. Never see him! I saw him clearly enough then. I shall see this eloquent phantom as long as I live, and I shall see her too, a tragic and familiar Shade, resembling in this gesture another one, tragic also, and bedecked with powerless charms, stretching bare brown arms over the glitter of the infernal stream, the stream of darkness. She said suddenly very low, 'He died as he lived.'

"'His end,' said I, with dull anger stirring in me, 'was in every way worthy of his life.'

"'And I was not with him,' she murmured. My anger subsided before a feeling of infinite pity.

"'Everything that could be done—' I mumbled.

"'Ah, but I believed in him more than any one on earth—more than his own mother, more than—himself. He needed me! Me! I would have treasured every sigh, every word, every sign, every glance.'

"I felt like a chill grip on my chest. 'Don't,' I said, in a muffled voice.

"'Forgive me. I—I—have mourned so long in silence—in silence. . . . You were with him—to the last? I think of his loneliness. Nobody near to understand him as I would have understood. Perhaps no one to hear. . . .'

"'To the very end,' I said, shakily. 'I heard his very last words. . . .' I stopped in a fright.

"'Repeat them,' she said in a heart-broken tone. 'I want—I want—something—something—to—to live with.'

"I was on the point of crying at her, 'Don't you hear them?' The dusk was repeating them in a persistent whisper all around us, in a whisper that seemed to swell menacingly like the first whisper of a rising wind. 'The horror! the horror!'

"'His last word—to live with,' she murmured. 'Don't you understand I loved him—I loved him—I loved him!'

"I pulled myself together and spoke slowly.

"'The last word he pronounced was—your name.'

"I heard a light sigh, and then my heart stood still, stopped dead short by an exulting and terrible cry, by the cry of inconceivable triumph and of unspeakable pain. 'I knew it—I was sure!' . . . She knew. She was sure. I heard her weeping; she had hidden her face in her hands. It seemed to me that the house would collapse before I could escape, that the heavens would fall upon my head. But nothing happened. The heavens do not fall for such a trifle. Would they have fallen, I wonder, if I had rendered Kurtz that justice which was his due? Hadn't he said he wanted only justice? But I couldn't. I could not tell her. It would have been too dark—too dark altogether. . . ."

Marlow ceased, and sat apart, indistinct and silent, in the pose of a meditating Buddha. Nobody moved for a time. "We have lost the first of the ebb," said the Director, suddenly. I raised my head. The offing was barred by a black bank of clouds, and the tranquil waterway leading to the uttermost ends of the earth flowed sombre under an overcast sky—seemed to lead into the heart of an immense darkness.

COMPANION READINGS

Joseph Conrad: from Congo Diary

Arrived at Matadi[1] on the 13th of June, 1890.

Mr Gosse, chief of the station (O.K.) retaining us for some reason of his own.

Made the acquaintance of Mr Roger Casement,[2] which I should consider as a great pleasure under any circumstances and now it becomes a positive piece of luck.

Thinks, speaks well, most intelligent and very sympathetic.

Feel considerably in doubt about the future. Think just now that my life amongst the people (white) around here cannot be very comfortable. Intend avoid acquaintances as much as possible. * * *

---

1. Colonial station near the mouth of the Congo River. Conrad arrived there on his way to take up his command of a steamship upriver at Kinshasa.
2. Casement (1864–1916) and Conrad were employed at the time by the same company. Casement later served as

British consul in various parts of Africa, and was the author of a report on the Congo (1904) that did much to make public the terrible conditions there. He was knighted in 1912. In 1916 he was executed by the British for his part in the Easter Rebellion in Ireland.

24th. Gosse and R.C. gone with a large lot of ivory down to Boma. On G.['s] return to start to up the river. Have been myself busy packing ivory in casks. Idiotic employment. Health good up to now. * * *

Prominent characteristic of the social life here: people speaking ill of each other.

* * *

Friday, 4th July.

Left camp at 6h a.m. after a very unpleasant night. Marching across a chain of hills and then in a maze of hills. At 8:15 opened out into an undulating plain. Took bearings of a break in the chain of mountains on the other side. * * *

Saw another dead body lying by the path in an attitude of meditative repose.

In the evening three women of whom one albino passed our camp. Horrid chalky white with pink blotches. Red eyes. Red hair. Features very Negroid and ugly. Mosquitos. At night when the moon rose heard shouts and drumming in distant villages. Passed a bad night.

Saturday, 5th July. go.

Left at 6:15. Morning cool, even cold and very damp. Sky densely overcast. Gentle breeze from NE. Road through a narrow plain up to R. Kwilu. Swift-flowing and deep, 50 yds. wide. Passed in canoes. After[war]ds up and down very steep hills intersected by deep ravines. Main chain of heights running mostly NW-SE or W and E at times. Stopped at Manyamba. Camp[in]g place bad—in hollow—water very indifferent. Tent set at 10:15.

Section of today's road. NNE Distance 12 m. [a drawing]

Today fell into a muddy puddle. Beastly. The fault of the man that carried me. After camp[in]g went to a small stream, bathed and washed clothes. Getting jolly well sick of this fun.

Tomorrow expect a long march to get to Nsona, 2 days from Manyanga. No sunshine today.

* * *

Saturday, 26th.

Left very early. Road ascending all the time. Passed villages. Country seems thickly inhabited. At 11h arrived at large market place. Left at noon and camped at 1h p.m.

[section of the day's march with notes]

a camp—a white man died here—market—govt. post—mount—crocodile pond—Mafiesa. * * *

Sunday, 27th.

Left at 8h am. Sent luggage carriers straight on to Luasi and went ourselves round by the Mission of Sutili.

Hospitable reception by Mrs Comber. All the missio[naries] absent.

The looks of the whole establishment eminently civilized and very refreshing to see after the lots of tumble-down hovels in which the State and Company agents are content to live—fine buildings. Position on a hill. Rather breezy.

Left at 3h pm. At the first heavy ascent met Mr Davis, miss[ionary] returning from a preaching trip. Rev. Bentley away in the South with his wife. * * *

Tuesday, 29th.

Left camp at 7h after a good night's rest. Continuous ascent; rather easy at first. Crossed wooded ravines and the river Lunzadi by a very decent bridge.

At 9h met Mr Louette escorting a sick agent of the Comp[an]y back to Matadi. Looking very well. Bad news from up the river. All the steamers disabled. One wrecked. Country wooded. At 10:30 camped at Inkissi. * * *

Today did not set the tent but put up in Gov[ernmen]t shimbek.[3] Zanzibari in charge—very obliging. Met ripe pineapple for the first time. On the road today passed a skeleton tied up to a post. Also white man's grave—no name. Heap of stones in the form of a cross.

Health good now.

Wednesday, 30th.

Left at 6 a.m. intending to camp at Kinfumu. Two hours' sharp walk brought me to Nsona na Nsefe. Market. ½ hour after, Harou arrived very ill with billious [sic] attack and fever. Laid him down in Gov[ernmen]t shimbek. Dose of Ipeca.[4] Vomiting bile in enormous quantities. At 11h gave him 1 gramme of quinine and lots of hot tea. Hot fit ending in heavy perspiration. At 2 p.m. put him in hammock and started for Kinfumu. Row with carriers all the way. Harou suffering much through the jerks of the hammock. Camped at a small stream.

At 4h Harou better. Fever gone. * * *

Up till noon, sky clouded and strong NW wind very chilling. From 1h pm to 4h pm sky clear and very hot day. Expect lots of bother with carriers tomorrow. Had them all called and made a speech which they did not understand. They promise good behaviour. * * *

Friday, 1st of August 1890.

* * * Row between the carriers and a man stating himself in Gov[ernmen]t employ, about a mat. Blows with sticks raining hard. Stopped it. Chief came with a youth about 13 suffering from gunshot wound in the head. Bullet entered about an inch above the right eyebrow and came out a little inside. The roots of the hair, fairly in the middle of the brow in a line with the bridge of the nose. Bone not damaged apparently. Gave him a little glycerine to put on the wound made by the bullet on coming out. Harou not very well. Mosquitos. Frogs. Beastly. Glad to see the end of this stupid tramp. Feel rather seedy. Sun rose red. Very hot day. Wind S[ou]th.

Sir Henry Morton Stanley: from Address to the Manchester Chamber of Commerce[1]

There is not one manufacturer here present who could not tell me if he had the opportunity how much he personally suffered through the slackness of trade; and I dare say that you have all some vague idea that if things remain as they are the future of the cotton manufacture is not very brilliant. New inventions are continually cropping up, so that your power of producing, if stimulated, is almost incalculable; but new markets for the sale of your products are not of rapid growth, and as other nations, by prohibitive tariffs, are bent upon fostering native manufacturers to the

3. A group of huts.
4. A medicine.
1. The journalist and adventurer Henry Morton Stanley wrote an account of his exploits in Africa in his bestseller *Through the Dark Continent* (1878). He delivered this address to the textile manufacturers of Manchester in

1886, seeking their support for the commercial exploitation of the Congo. This speech gives a striking example of the outlook—and rhetoric—of the people who created the conditions Conrad encountered when he went to the Congo in 1890.

exclusion of your own, such markets as are now open to you are likely to be taken away from you in course of time. Well, then, I come to you with at least one market where there are at present, perhaps, 6,250,000 yards of cheap cottons sold every year on the Congo banks and in the Congo markets.[2]

I was interested the other day in making a curious calculation, which was, supposing that all the inhabitants of the Congo basin were simply to have one Sunday dress each, how many yards of Manchester cloth would be required; and the amazing number was 320,000,000 yards, just for one Sunday dress! (Cheers.) Proceeding still further with these figures I found that two Sunday dresses and four everyday dresses would in one year amount to 3,840,000,000 yards, which at 2d. [two pence] per yard would be of the value of £16,000,000. The more I pondered upon these things I discovered that I could not limit these stores of cotton cloth to day dresses. I would have to provide for night dresses also—(laughter)—and these would consume 160,000,000 yards. (Cheers.) Then the grave cloths came into mind, and, as a poor lunatic, who burned Bolobo Station,[3] destroyed 30,000 yards of cloth in order that he should not be cheated out of a respectable burial, I really feared for a time that the millions would get beyond measurable calculation. However, putting such accidents aside, I estimate that, if my figures of population are approximately correct, 2,000,000 die every year, and to bury these decently, and according to the custom of those who possess cloth, 16,000,000 yards will be required, while the 40,000 chiefs will require an average of 100 yards each, or 4,000,000 yards. I regarded these figures with great satisfaction, and I was about to close my remarks upon the millions of yards of cloth that Manchester would perhaps be required to produce when I discovered that I had neglected to provide for the family wardrobe or currency chest, for you must know that in the Lower Congo there is scarcely a family that has not a cloth fund of about a dozen pieces of about 24 yards each. This is a very important institution, otherwise how are the family necessities to be provided for? How are the fathers and mothers of families to go to market to buy greens, bread, oil, ground nuts, chickens, fish, and goats, and how is the petty trade to be conducted? How is ivory to be purchased, the gums, rubber, dye powders, gunpowder, copper slugs, guns, trinkets, knives, and swords to be bought without a supply of cloth? Now, 8,000,000 families at 300 yards each will require 2,400,000,000. (Cheers.) You all know how perishable such currency must be; but if you sum up these several millions of yards, and value all of them at the average price of 2d. per yard, you will find that it will be possible for Manchester to create a trade—in the course of time—in cottons in the Congo basin amounting in value to about £26,000,000 annually. (Loud cheers.) I have said nothing about Rochdale savelist, or your own superior prints, your gorgeous handkerchiefs, with their variegated patterns, your checks and striped cloths, your ticking and twills.[4] I must satisfy myself with suggesting them; your own imaginations will no doubt carry you to the limbo of immeasurable and incalculable millions. (Laughter and cheers.)

2. The Congo Free State (later Zaire), a vast area of central Africa around the Congo River, was formally brought under the ownership of Leopold II of Belgium and other investors in the International Association of the Congo by the Berlin West Africa Conference of 1884–1885. Stanley's expeditions there (from 1876) had been financed by Leopold, and from 1879 Stanley had set up trading stations along the river to facilitate the exploita-

tion of the area's natural resources.
3. The London Times carried frequent reports of disturbances in the Congo at this time; in March 1884, for example, Congolese attacks on foreign trading establishments at Nokki in the Lower Congo had caused the Europeans to "declare war against the natives."
4. Savelist is cheap fabric; ticking is a strong cotton or linen fabric; twill is a kind of textile weave.

Now, if your sympathy for yourselves and the fate of Manchester has been excited sufficiently, your next natural question would be as follows: We acknowledge, sir, that you have contrived by an artful array of imposing millions to excite our attention, at least, to this field; but we beg to ask you what Manchester is to do in order that we may begin realising this sale of untold millions of yards of cotton cloth? I answer that the first thing to do is for you to ask the British Government to send a cruiser to the mouth of the Congo to keep watch and ward over that river until the European nations have agreed among themselves as to what shall be done with the river, lest one of these days you will hear that it is too late. (Hear, hear.) Secondly, to study whether, seeing that it will never do to permit Portugal to assume sovereignty over that river[5]—and England publicly disclaims any wish to possess that river for herself—it would not be as well to allow the International Association to act as guardians of international right to free trade and free entrance and exit into and out of the river. (Hear, hear.) The main point, remember, always is a guarantee that the lower river shall be free, that, however the Upper Congo may be developed, no Power, inspired by cupidity, shall seize upon the mouth of the river and build custom houses. (Hear, hear.) The Lower Congo in the future will only be valuable because down its waters will have to be floated the produce of the rich basin above to the ocean steamships. It will always have a fair trade of its own, but it bears no proportion to the almost limitless trade that the Upper Congo could furnish. If the Association could be assured that the road from Europe to Vivi[6] was for ever free, the first steps to realise the sale of those countless millions of yards of cotton cloth would be taken. Over six millions of yards are now used annually; but we have no means of absorbing more, owing to the difficulties of transport. Every man capable and willing to carry a load is employed. When human power was discovered to be not further available we tested animal power and discovered it to be feebler and more costly than the other; and we have come to the conclusion that steam power must now assist us or we remain *in statu quo* [as things now stand]. But before having recourse to this steam power, and building the iron road along which your bales of cotton fabrics may roll on to the absorbing markets of the Upper Congo unceasingly, the Association pauses to ask you, and the peoples of other English cities, such as London, Liverpool, Glasgow, Birmingham, Leeds, Preston, Sheffield, who profess to understand the importance of the work we have been doing, and the absorbing power of those markets we have reached, what help you will render us, for your own sakes, to make those markets accessible? (Hear, hear.) The Association will not build that railway to the Upper Congo, nor invest one piece of sterling gold in it, unless they are assured they will not be robbed of it, and the Lower Congo will be placed under some flag that shall be a guarantee to all the world that its waters and banks are absolutely free. (Cheers.)

You will agree with me, I am sure, that trade ought to expand and commerce grow, and if we can coax it into mature growth in this Congo basin that it would be a praiseworthy achievement, honoured by men and gods; for out of this trade, this intercourse caused by peaceful barter, proceed all those blessings which you and I enjoy. The more trade thrives, the more benefits to mankind are multipled, and nearer to gods do men become. (Hear, hear.) The builders of railroads through wilder-

---

5. The mouth of the Congo River had been discovered by the Portuguese in 1482.

6. A town on the Upper Congo river; from 1882 Stanley had been arguing that a railway should be built between the Lower and Upper Congo to facilitate the exploitation of the interior. It was completed in 1898.

nesses generally require large concessions of lands; but the proposed builders of this railway to connect the Lower with the Upper Congo do not ask for any landed concessions; but they ask for a concession of authority over the Lower Congo in order that the beneficent policy which directs the civilising work on the Upper Congo may be extended to the Lower River, and that the mode of government and action may be uniform throughout. The beneficent policy referred to is explained in the treaty made and concluded with the United States Government.[7] That treaty says: "That with the object of enabling civilisation and commerce to penetrate into Equatorial Africa the Free States of the Congo have resolved to levy no customs duties whatever. The Free States also guarantee to all men who establish themselves in their territories the right of purchasing, selling, or leasing any land and buildings, of creating factories and of trade on the sole condition that they conform to the law. The International Association of the Congo is prepared to enter into engagements with other nations who desire to secure the free admission of their products on the same terms as those agreed upon with the United States."

Here you have in brief the whole policy. I might end here, satisfied with having reminded you of these facts, which probably you had forgotten. Obedience to the laws—that is, laws drawn for protection of all—is the common law of all civilised communities, without which men would soon become demoralised. Can anybody object to that condition? Probably many of you here recollect reading those interesting letters from the Congo which were written by an English clerk in charge of an English factory. They ended with the cry of "Let us alone." In few words he meant to say, "We are doing very well as we are, we do not wish to be protected, and least of all taxed—therefore, let us alone. Our customers, the natives, are satisfied with us. The native chiefs are friendly and in accord with us; the disturbances, if any occur, are local; they are not general, and they right themselves quickly enough, for the trader cannot exist here if he is not just and kind in his dealings. The obstreperous and violent white is left to himself and ruin. Therefore, let us alone." Most heartily do I echo this cry; but unfortunately the European nations will not heed this cry; they think that some mode of government is necessary to curb those inclined to be refractory, and if there is at present a necessity to exhibit judicial power and to restrict evil-minded and ill-conditioned whites, as the Congo basin becomes more and more populated this necessity will be still more apparent. At the same time, if power appears on the Congo with an arbitrary and unfeeling front—with a disposition to tax and levy burdensome tariffs just as trade begins to be established—the outlook for enterprise becomes dismal and dark indeed.[8] (Hear, hear.) * * *

No part of Africa, look where I might, appeared so promising to me as this neglected tenth part of the continent. I have often fancied myself—when I had nothing to do better than dream—gazing from some lofty height, and looking down upon this square compact patch of 800,000,000 acres, with its 80,000 native towns, its population of 40,000,000 souls, its 17,000 miles of river waters, and its 30,000 square miles of lakes, all lying torpid, lifeless, inert, soaked in brutishness and bestiality, and I have never yet descended from that airy perch in the empyrean and

---

7. The United States was the first country to recognize the right of the International Association to govern the Congo territories in April 1884.

8. The right of the International Association to govern the Congo was eventually ended in 1908, following widespread protests against the regime's brutality.

touched earth but I have felt a purpose glow in me to strive to do something to awaken it into life and movement, and I have sometimes half fancied that the face of aged Livingstone,[9] vague and indistinct as it were, shone through the warm, hazy atmosphere, with a benignant smile encouraging me in my purpose. * * *

Yet, though examined from every point of view, a study of the Upper Congo and its capabilities produces these exciting arrays of figures and possibilities, I would not pay a two-shilling piece for it all so long as it remains as it is. It will absorb easily the revenue of the wealthiest nation in Europe without any return. I would personally one hundred times over prefer a snug little freehold in a suburb of Manchester to being the owner of the 1,300,000 English square miles of the Congo basin if it is to remain as inaccessible as it is to-day, or if it is to be blocked by that fearful tariff-loving nation, the Portuguese. (Hear, hear.) But if I were assured that the Lower Congo would remain free, and the flag of the Association guaranteed its freedom, I would if I were able build that railway myself—build it solid and strong—and connect the Lower Congo with the Upper Congo, perfectly satisfied that I should be followed by the traders and colonists of all nations. * * * The Portuguese have had nearly 400 years given them to demonstrate to the world what they could do with the river whose mouth they discovered, and they have been proved to be incapable to do any good with it, and now civilisation is inclined to say to them, "Stand off from this broad highway into the regions beyond—(cheers); let others who are not paralytic strive to do what they can with it to bring it within the number of accessible markets. There are 40,000,000 of naked people beyond that gateway, and the cotton spinners of Manchester are waiting to clothe them. Rochdale and Preston women are waiting for the word to weave them warm blue and crimson savelist. Birmingham foundries are glowing with the red metal that shall presently be made into ironwork in every fashion and shape for them, and the trinkets that shall adorn those dusky bosoms; and the ministers of Christ are zealous to bring them, the poor benighted heathen, into the Christian fold." (Cheers.)

Mr JACOB BRIGHT, M.P., who was received with loud cheers, said: I have listened with extreme interest to one of the ablest, one of the most eloquent addresses which have ever been delivered in this city—(cheers); and I have heard with uncommon pleasure the views of a man whose ability, whose splendid force of character, whose remarkable heroism, have given him a world-wide reputation. (Cheers.) * * *

Mr GRAFTON, M.P., moved:—

> That the best thanks of this meeting be and are hereby given to Mr H. M. Stanley for his address to the members of the Chamber, and for the interesting information conveyed by him respecting the Congo and prospects of international trade on the West Coast and interior of Africa.

He remarked that Mr Stanley's name was already enrolled in the pages of history, and would be handed down to posterity with the names of the greatest benefactors of our species, such as Columbus, who had opened out the pathways of the world. Long might Mr Stanley be spared to witness the benefit of his arduous and beneficent labours. (Cheers.)

9. David Livingstone (1813–1873), Scottish explorer and missionary. His expeditions into central Africa, in search of the source of the Nile River, were heavily publicized; when Livingstone "disappeared" in the course of what proved to be his last expedition, Stanley, then a correspondent for the *New York Herald,* was sent to find him. The two men met on the banks of Lake Tanganyika in East Africa in 1871; Stanley published an account of their meeting in *How I Found Livingstone* (1872).

Gang of Four: We Live As We Dream, Alone[1]

Everybody is in too many pieces
No man's land surrounds our desires
To crack the shell we mix with others
Some lie in the arms of lovers

The city is the place to be
With no money you go crazy
I need an occupation
You have to pay for satisfaction

We live as we dream, alone
To crack this shell we mix with others
Some flirt with fascism
Some lie in the arms of lovers

We live as we dream, alone
(repeat)

Everybody is in too many pieces
No man's land surrounds me
Without money we'll all go crazy

Man and woman need to work
It helps to define ourselves
We were not born in isolation
But sometimes it seems that way

We live as we dream, alone
(repeat)

We live as we dream, alone
The space between our work and its product
Some fall into fatalism
As if it started out this way

We live as we dream, alone
(repeat)

We live as we dream, alone
We were not born in isolation
But sometimes it seems that way
The space between our work and its product
As if it must always be this way

With our money we'll . . .

---

1. In 1976 the Sex Pistols set off the British punk revolution with their first single, "Anarchy in the U.K." The Gang of Four is one of many bands that arose during the early years of punk, when a wide range of musical possibilities seemed open to anyone with a guitar. The Gang of Four's music combines the assaultive sound of punk bands with an infectious dance sensibility—lacing this unlikely hybrid with neo-Marxist lyrics about consumerism and labor. "We Live As We Dream, Alone," from their 1982 album *Songs of the Free*, takes a famous line from *Heart of Darkness* and makes it the cry of alienated labor, thereby reframing Conrad's message for a nation dominated by the conservative policies of Thatcherism.

◆ ─ ▓▓▓ ─ ◆

Thomas Hardy
1840–1928

Thomas Hardy led a double life: one of the great Victorian novelists, he abandoned fiction in 1896 and reinvented himself as a poet. In a series of volumes published from 1898 through the early decades of the twentieth century, Hardy emerged as one of the most compelling voices in modern poetry. How should this strangely bifurcated literary career be read? There are continuities as well as divergences between Hardy's fiction and his poetry, and the shifts in his work provide a telling instance of the interwoven links and discontinuities between the Victorian era and the new modernism of the twentieth century.

Hardy was born and reared in the village of Higher Bockhampton, Stinsford, in the rural county of Dorset in southern England. He left home in his early twenties and worked as a church architect in London for five years, then returned to the family home in 1867; he continued to accept architectural commissions while trying his hand at fiction and poetry. In early poems such as *Hap* and *Neutral Tones* Hardy revealed his abiding sense of a universe ruled by a blind or hostile fate, a world whose landscapes are etched with traces of the fleeting stories of their inhabitants. He was not able to find a publisher for such works, and he largely stopped writing poetry, but his first novel, *Desperate Remedies,* was published in 1871. By 1874 he was earning a steady income from his writing and was able to marry Emma Lavinia Gifford, the sister-in-law of a rector whose church he had been restoring. He produced twenty novels within a twenty-five year period, achieving fame, popularity, and no little controversy for the provocative and dark worlds he created. In *Far from the Madding Crowd, The Return of the Native, Tess of the d'Urbervilles,* and *Jude the Obscure,* Hardy transformed the realist novel of manners into tragic accounts of the industrialization of rural Britain, the bankruptcy of religious faith, and irreconcilable tensions between social classes and between men and women. Though he had become a master of characterization and plot, in his later novels Hardy grew increasingly preoccupied with fundamentally lyrical questions of interiority, subjective perception, and personal voice. After the sexual frankness of *Jude the Obscure* provoked shocked reviews—the Bishop of Wakefield went so far as to burn the book—Hardy decided to abandon his prose writing altogether and to mine his chosen territory with the tools of a poet.

He began by recreating in poetry the landscape of his fiction. Hardy's first poetry collection, published when he was fifty-eight, was *Wessex Poems* (1898), its title referring to the imaginary countryside that he had created in his novels, loosely based on regions in the south of England but named for a long-vanished medieval kingdom. Hardy's "Wessex" was a place whose towns and roads and forests and fields were breathed into life by the novelist. The Wessex novels were published with maps of the territory, and the landmarks were to remain constant throughout the disparate books. The region took such a hold on readers' imaginations that a Wessex tourist industry emerged, one which is still in place today. Hardy was as painstaking in giving the precise (although imaginary) coordinates of a village pathway as he was in tracing the path of a character's destiny.

Many of Hardy's poems take root in this same creative landscape, now viewed by an intensely self-aware speaker who retraces his personal history, himself "tracked by phantoms having weird detective ways," as he says in *Wessex Heights*. Burning logs, a photograph, a diminishing figure on a train platform, a deer at a window all provide "moments of vision" (the title of one of his collections) that foreshadow the modernist "epiphanies" of Joyce and Woolf. Like the major modernists, Hardy explored the workings of memory, of perception, and of individual vision. In other poems, he focused on contemporary events, most notably in a series of poems written during World War I, unsparing in their presentation both of the necessity of waging the conflict and of its horrifying waste.

In his poetry as in his prose, Hardy's modern themes are typically set in a rural landscape with ancient roots. A constant feature of the Wessex novels involves characters setting off on one of the myriad footpaths connecting obscure villages and solitary cottages with one another. Hardy invented his own geography for Wessex, but the footpaths really existed and were the most important trails carved into the landscape by travelers over many years. Called "ley lines" in folk culture, such footpaths are thought to gather their energy over time, as hundreds of people gradually wear down a shared path and leave traces of themselves in the form of memory and tradition. Hardy's poems move between personal, historical, and natural levels of experience, but it is the landscape above all that conveys the power of these events.

Hardy embodied his moments of vision in poems that recall old oral and religious forms of verse, especially those of ballads and hymns. Like Wordsworth, Burns, and Kipling, Hardy was fascinated by the power of popular verse forms to convey deep truths in seemingly simple meters and diction; like his predecessors, Hardy brought his traditional forms to life by subtle modulations of their elements. The lines of Hardy's poetry are measured with extreme care and precision—not in any way approaching "free verse." As W. H. Auden wrote of Hardy's poetry: "No English poet, not even Donne or Browning, employed so many and so complicated stanza forms. Anyone who imitates his style will learn at least one thing, how to make words fit into a complicated structure." With architectural care, Hardy built up his words into complicated structures, lines, and stanzas following well-used poetic paths. With its compelling mixture of tradition and modernity, stoic calm and deep emotional intensity, Hardy's poetry has become a touchstone for modern poets writing in English, from Ezra Pound, who said he "needed no other poet," to Philip Larkin, Seamus Heaney, and Derek Walcott. "Auden worshiped his honesty, Eliot disliked his heresy," the critic Irving Howe has commented; "but Hardy prepared the ground for both."

Hardy mined his native landscape, and his own memory, until his death, composing many of his best poems in his seventies and eighties. He had built a house on the outskirts of Dorchester in 1885, and he lived there for the rest of his life, with his wife Emma until her death in 1912, and subsequently with his secretary, Florence Dugdale, whom he married in 1914. When he died, his body was buried in Westminster Abbey; but his heart, as he had directed, was buried in the grave of his wife Emma, next to his father's grave, in the Stinsford churchyard.

Hap°   *chance*

If but some vengeful god would call to me
From up the sky, and laugh: "Thou suffering thing,
Know that thy sorrow is my ecstasy,
That thy love's loss is my hate's profiting!"

5   Then would I bear it, clench myself, and die,
Steeled by the sense of ire unmerited;
Half-eased in that a Powerfuller than I
Had willed and meted° me the tears I shed.   *given*

But not so. How arrives it joy lies slain,
10   And why unblooms the best hope ever sown?
—Crass Casualty obstructs the sun and rain,
And dicing° Time for gladness casts a moan. . . .   *gambling*
These purblind° Doomsters had as readily strown   *half-blind*
Blisses about my pilgrimage as pain.

1866   1898

Neutral Tones

We stood by a pond that winter day,
And the sun was white, as though chidden° of God,   *rebuked*
And a few leaves lay on the starving sod;
   —They had fallen from an ash, and were gray.

5   Your eyes on me were as eyes that rove
Over tedious riddles of years ago;
And some words played between us to and fro
   On which lost the more by our love.

The smile on your mouth was the deadest thing
10   Alive enough to have strength to die;
And a grin of bitterness swept thereby
   Like an ominous bird a-wing . . . .

Since then, keen lessons that love deceives,
And wrings with wrong, have shaped to me
15   Your face, and the God-curst sun, and a tree,
   And a pond edged with grayish leaves.

1867   1898

Wessex Heights

There are some heights in Wessex,[1] shaped as if by a kindly hand
For thinking, dreaming, dying on, and at crises when I stand,
Say, on Ingpen Beacon eastward, or on Wylls-Neck westwardly,
I seem where I was before my birth, and after death may be.

5   In the lowlands I have no comrade, not even the lone man's friend—
Her who suffereth long and is kind;[2] accepts what he is too weak to mend:
Down there they are dubious and askance; there nobody thinks as I,
But mind-chains do not clank where one's next neighbour is the sky.

In the towns I am tracked by phantoms having weird detective ways—
10   Shadows of beings who fellowed with myself of earlier days:
They hang about at places, and they say harsh heavy things—
Men with a wintry sneer, and women with tart disparagings.

Down there I seem to be false to myself, my simple self that was,
And is not now, and I see him watching, wondering what crass cause
15   Can have merged him into such a strange continuator as this,
Who yet has something in common with himself, my chrysalis.

I cannot go to the great grey Plain; there's a figure against the moon,
Nobody sees it but I, and it makes my breast beat out of tune;
I cannot go to the tall-spired town, being barred by the forms now passed
20   For everybody but me, in whose long vision they stand there fast.

---

1. An imaginary county in southwest England that forms
the setting for Hardy's writings; the place names that follow are in "Wessex."

2. Cf. Corinthians 13.4: "Charity suffereth long, and is
kind."

There's a ghost at Yell'ham Bottom chiding loud at the fall of the night,
There's a ghost in Froom-side Vale, thin-lipped and vague, in a shroud
    of white,
There is one in the railway train whenever I do not want it near,
I see its profile against the pane, saying what I would not hear.

25   As for one rare fair woman, I am now but a thought of hers,
I enter her mind and another thought succeeds me that she prefers,
Yet my love for her in its fulness she herself even did not know;
Well, time cures hearts of tenderness, and now I can let her go.

So I am found on Ingpen Beacon, or on Wylls-Neck to the west,
30   Or else on homely Bulbarrow, or little Pilsdon Crest,
Where men have never cared to haunt, nor women have walked with me,
And ghosts then keep their distance; and I know some liberty.

1898

The Darkling Thrush[1]

I leant upon a coppice° gate   *wood*
    When Frost was spectre-gray,
And Winter's dregs made desolate
    The weakening eye of day.
5   The tangled bine-stems° scored the sky   *stems of bushes*
    Like strings of broken lyres,
And all mankind that haunted nigh
    Had sought their household fires.

The land's sharp features seemed to be
10   The Century's corpse outleant[2],
His crypt the cloudy canopy,
    The wind his death-lament.
The ancient pulse of germ° and birth   *seed*
    Was shrunken hard and dry,
15   And every spirit upon earth
    Seemed fervourless as I.

At once a voice arose among
    The bleak twigs overhead
In a full-hearted evensong
20   Of joy illimited;
An aged thrush, frail, gaunt, and small,
    In blast-beruffled plume,
Had chosen thus to fling his soul
    Upon the growing gloom.

25   So little cause for carolings
    Of such ecstatic sound
Was written on terrestrial things
    Afar or nigh around,
That I could think there trembled through

1. The poem was published on 31 December 1900.   2. As if leaning out from a coffin.

30   His happy good-night air
        Some blessed Hope, whereof he knew
           And I was unaware.

On the Departure Platform

      We kissed at the barrier; and passing through
      She left me, and moment by moment got
      Smaller and smaller, until to my view
          She was but a spot;

5   A wee white spot of muslin fluff
      That down the diminishing platform bore
      Through hustling crowds of gentle and rough
          To the carriage door.

      Under the lamplight's fitful glowers,
10   Behind dark groups from far and near,
      Whose interests were apart from ours,
          She would disappear,

      Then show again, till I ceased to see
      That flexible form, that nebulous white;
15   And she who was more than my life to me
          Had vanished quite . . . .

      We have penned new plans since that fair fond day,
      And in season she will appear again—
      Perhaps in the same soft white array—
20   But never as then!

     —"And why, young man, must eternally fly
      A joy you'll repeat, if you love her well?"
     —O friend, nought happens twice thus; why,
         I cannot tell!

                                    1909

The Convergence of the Twain

(Lines on the loss of the "Titanic")[1]

1

        In a solitude of the sea
        Deep from human vanity,
And the Pride of Life that planned her, stilly couches she.

2

        Steel chambers, late the pyres
5   Of her salamandrine° fires,   *white-hot*
Cold currents thrid°, and turn to rhythmic tidal lyres.   *thread*

3

        Over the mirrors meant
        To glass the opulent
The sea-worm crawls—grotesque, slimed, dumb, indifferent.

---

1. The largest ocean-liner of its day, the supposedly unsinkable *Titanic* sank on 15 April 1912 on its maiden voyage after colliding with an iceberg; two thirds of its 2,200 passengers died.

4

10   Jewels in joy designed
         To ravish the sensuous mind
Lie lightless, all their sparkles bleared and black and blind.

5

         Dim moon-eyed fishes near
         Gaze at the gilded gear
15   And query: "What does this vaingloriousness down here?" . . .

6

         Well: while was fashioning
         This creature of cleaving wing,
The Immanent Will that stirs and urges everything

7

         Prepared a sinister mate
20   For her—so gaily great—
A Shape of Ice, for the time far and dissociate.[2]

8

         And as the smart ship grew
         In stature, grace, and hue,
In shadowy silent distance grew the Iceberg too.

9

25   Alien they seemed to be:
         No mortal eye could see
The intimate welding of their later history,

10

         Or sign that they were bent
         By paths coincident
30   On being anon twin halves of one august event,

11

         Till the Spinner of the Years
         Said "Now!" And each one hears,
And consummation comes, and jars two hemispheres.

1912   1912

Channel Firing[1]

That night your great guns, unawares,
Shook all our coffins as we lay,
And broke the chancel window-squares,
We thought it was the Judgment-day

5   And sat upright. While drearisome
     Arose the howl of wakened hounds:
     The mouse let fall the altar-crumb,
     The worms drew back into the mounds,
     The glebe° cow drooled. Till God called, "No;   *field*
10   It's gunnery practice out at sea
     Just as before you went below;
     The world is as it used to be:

---

2. According to Hardy, the Immanent Will is that which secretly guides events.

1. The poem refers to military exercises in the English Channel prior to World War 1.

"All nations striving strong to make
　　Red war yet redder. Mad as hatters
15　They do no more for Christés sake
　　Than you who are helpless in such matters.

"That this is not the judgment-hour
　　For some of them's a blessed thing,
　　For if it were they'd have to scour
20　Hell's floor for so much threatening . . . .

"Ha, ha. It will be warmer when
　　I blow the trumpet (if indeed
　　I ever do; for you are men,
　　And rest eternal sorely need)."

25　So down we lay again. "I wonder,
　　Will the world ever saner be,"
　　Said one, "than when He sent us under
　　In our indifferent century!"

And many a skeleton shook his head.
30　"Instead of preaching forty year,"
　　My neighbour Parson Thirdly said,
　　"I wish I had stuck to pipes and beer."

Again the guns disturbed the hour,
　　Roaring their readiness to avenge,
35　As far inland as Stourton Tower,
　　And Camelot, and starlit Stonehenge.[2]

April 1914　　　　　　　　　　　　　　　　　　　　　1914

In Time of "The Breaking of Nations"[1]

1

Only a man harrowing clods
　　In a slow silent walk
With an old horse that stumbles and nods
　　Half asleep as they stalk.

2

5　Only thin smoke without flame
　　From the heaps of couch-grass;
Yet this will go onward the same
　　Though Dynasties pass.

3

Yonder a maid and her wight°　　　　　　　　　　　　man
10　Come whispering by:
War's annals will cloud into night
　　Ere their story die.

1915　　　　　　　　　　　　　　　　　　　　　　　　1916

<hr/>

2. The town of Stour Head, which Hardy calls Stourton, is in the county of Dorset. According to legend, Camelot was the site of King Arthur's court; Stonehenge is a prehistoric site in southwest England.

1. Cf. Jeremiah 51.20: "Thou art my battle axe and weapons of war: for with thee will I break in pieces the nations, and with thee will I destroy kingdoms."

I Looked Up from My Writing

I looked up from my writing,
    And gave a start to see,
As if rapt in my inditing,
    The moon's full gaze on me.

5   Her meditative misty head
        Was spectral in its air,
And I involuntarily said,
    "What are you doing there?"

"Oh, I've been scanning pond and hole
10   And waterway hereabout
For the body of one with a sunken soul
    Who has put his life-light out.

"Did you hear his frenzied tattle?
    It was sorrow for his son
15 Who is slain in brutish battle,
    Though he has injured none.

"And now I am curious to look
    Into the blinkered mind
Of one who wants to write a book
20   In a world of such a kind."

Her temper overwrought me,
    And I edged to shun her view,
For I felt assured she thought me
    One who should drown him too.

1917

"And There Was a Great Calm"[1]
(On the Signing of the Armistice, 11 Nov. 1918)[2]

1

There had been years of Passion—scorching, cold,
And much Despair, and Anger heaving high,
Care whitely watching, Sorrows manifold,
Among the young, among the weak and old,
5 And the pensive Spirit of Pity whispered, "Why?"

2

Men had not paused to answer. Foes distraught
Pierced the thinned peoples in a brute-like blindness,
Philosophies that sages long had taught,
And Selflessness, were as an unknown thought,
10 And "Hell!" and "Shell!" were yapped at Lovingkindness.

3

The feeble folk at home had grown full-used
To "dug-outs," "snipers," "'Huns,"[3] from the war-adept

---

1. A phrase from Mark 4.39, after Jesus has calmed a storm at sea.
2. The armistice ending World War I was signed by Germany and the Allies on this date.
3. Slang for "Germans" during the war.

In the mornings heard, and at evetides perused;
To day-dreamt men in millions, when they mused—
15   To nightmare-men in millions when they slept.

4

Waking to wish existence timeless, null,
Sirius⁴ they watched above where armies fell;
He seemed to check his flapping when, in the lull
Of night a boom came thencewise, like the dull
20   Plunge of a stone dropped into some deep well.

5

So, when old hopes that earth was bettering slowly
Were dead and damned, there sounded "War is done!"
One morrow. Said the bereft, and meek, and lowly,
"Will men some day be given to grace? yea, wholly,
25   And in good sooth,° as our dreams used to run?"   *truth*

6

Breathless they paused. Out there men raised their glance
To where had stood those poplars lank and lopped,
As they had raised it through the four years' dance
Of Death in the now familiar flats of France;
30   And murmured, "Strange, this! How? All firing stopped?"

7

Aye; all was hushed. The about-to-fire fired not,
The aimed-at moved away in trance-lipped song.
One checkless regiment slung a clinching shot
And turned. The Spirit of Irony smirked out, "What?
35   Spoil peradventures° woven of Rage and Wrong?"   *perhaps*

8

Thenceforth no flying fires inflamed the gray,
No hurtlings shook the dewdrop from the thorn,
No moan perplexed the mute bird on the spray;
Worn horses mused: "We are not whipped to-day;"
40   No weft-winged engines° blurred the moon's thin horn.   *early airplanes*

9

Calm fell. From Heaven distilled a clemency;
There was peace on earth, and silence in the sky;
Some could, some could not, shake off misery:
The Sinister Spirit sneered: "It had to be!"
45   And again the Spirit of Pity whispered, "Why?"
1918   1919, 1922

Logs on the Hearth
*A Memory of a Sister*¹

The fire advances along the log
    Of the tree we felled,
Which bloomed and bore striped apples by the peck°   *basketful*
    Till its last hour of bearing knelled.

---

4. The brightest star in the night sky.   1. Hardy's sister Mary died in November 1915.

5   The fork that first my hand would reach
               And then my foot
   In climbings upward inch by inch, lies now
           Sawn, sapless, darkening with soot.

       Where the bark chars is where, one year,
10   It was pruned, and bled—
       Then overgrew the wound. But now, at last,
           Its growings all have stagnated.

       My fellow-climber rises dim
               From her chilly grave—
15   Just as she was, her foot near mine on the bending limb,
           Laughing, her young brown hand awave.

1915   1917

Afterwards

   When the Present has latched its postern° behind my tremulous stay,   gate
           And the May month flaps its glad green leaves like wings,
   Delicate-filmed as new-spun silk, will the neighbours say,
           "He was a man who used to notice such things"?

5   If it be in the dusk when, like an eyelid's soundless blink,
           The dewfall-hawk comes crossing the shades to alight
   Upon the wind-warped upland thorn, a gazer may think,
           "To him this must have been a familiar sight."

   If I pass during some nocturnal blackness, mothy and warm,
10   When the hedgehog travels furtively over the lawn,
   One may say, "He strove that such innocent creatures should come to no harm,
           But he could do little for them; and now he is gone."

   If, when hearing that I have been stilled at last, they stand at the door,
           Watching the full-starred heavens that winter sees,
15   Will this thought rise on those who will meet my face no more,
           "He was one who had an eye for such mysteries"?

   And will any say when my bell of quittance is heard in the gloom,
           And a crossing breeze cuts a pause in its outrollings,
   Till they rise again, as they were a new bell's boom,
20   "He hears it not now, but used to notice such things"?

                                                         1917

Epitaph

   I never cared for Life: Life cared for me,
   And hence I owed it some fidelity.
   It now says, "Cease; at length thou hast learnt to grind
   Sufficient toll for an unwilling mind,
   And I dismiss thee—not without regard
   That thou didst ask no ill-advised reward,
   Nor sought in me much more than thou couldst find."

                                                         1922

The Great War: Confronting the Modern

The multiplying technological, artistic, and social changes at the turn of the twentieth century impressed that generation's artists as a rupture with the past. And no event so graphically suggested that human history had "changed, changed utterly," as World War I—"the Great War."

Great Britain, like its enemy Germany, entered the war with idealistic aims. Prime Minister H. H. Asquith put the justice of the British case this way in a speech to the House of Commons on 7 August 1914: "I do not think any nation ever entered into a great conflict—and this is one of the greatest that history will ever know—with a clearer conscience or stronger conviction that it is fighting not for aggression, not for the maintenance of its own selfish ends, but in defence of principles the maintenance of which is vital to the civilization of the world." But cynicism set in quickly—first among ground troops on the Western Front, dug into trenches and watching "progress" that could be measured in yards per day. Soon the British public became disillusioned with the war effort, partly as a result of technological advances in the news media. Daily papers in England carried photographs from the front, and while editorial policy generally supported the British government and printed heroic images of the fighting, this sanitized version of the war was largely offset by the long published lists of casualties; during the four years and three months that Britain was involved in the war, more than a million British troops—an average of fifteen hundred per day—were killed in action.

The war's lasting legacy was a sense of bitterly rebuffed idealism, bringing with it a suspicion of progress, technology, government, bureaucracy, nationalism, and conventional morality—themes probed in new ways by the period's writers. Just as the war had involved radically new strategies and new technologies, writers intensified their search for new forms and modes of expression as they and their compatriots found themselves in the midst of a conflict unlike anything previously known in the annals of history.

—◆◆◆—

Blast

Wyndham Lewis (1884–1957), founder of the provocative arts magazine *Blast,* was often at odds with his sometime co-conspirator Ezra Pound: indeed both men were usually at odds with most of their friends. But they did agree on one thing: that the writers of Edwardian and Georgian England had failed to throw off the deadening literary mannerisms of the previous century. "As for the nineteenth century," Pound wrote, "with all respects to its achievements, I think we shall look back upon it as a rather blurry, messy sort of a period, a rather sentimentalistic, mannerish sort of a period."

Some violent corrective was needed. The name of Lewis's magazine was intended to suggest an explosive charge that would blow away tired literary and social conventions. It was a calculated assault on good taste, both in its contents and, more immediately, in its form: an oversized, bright pink cover with the single word *BLAST* splashed diagonally across it. Lewis carefully oversaw the details of typography; visually and rhetorically, *Blast* is indebted to the polemical style of the Italian artist F. T. Marinetti (1876–1944), the founder of Italian futurism. Marinetti's vivid manifestos for futurism celebrated a modern aesthetic of speed, technology, and power. Lewis in turn founded a movement he called Vorticism, and *Blast* bore the subtitle *The Review of the Great English Vortex.*

The definition of *vorticism* was left intentionally hazy; as canny an observer as the Vorticist painter William Roberts, one of the signatories of the manifesto, claimed that Vorticism was first and foremost "a slogan." In 1915 Lewis defined it this way: "By Vorticism we mean (a) ACTIVITY as opposed to the tasteful PASSIVITY of Picasso; (b) SIGNIFICANCE as opposed to the

Wyndham Lewis. *The Creditors* (design for *Timon of Athens*). 1912–1913.

dull or anecdotal character to which the Naturalist is condemned; (c) ESSENTIAL MOVEMENT and ACTIVITY (such as the energy of a mind) as opposed to the imitative cinematography, the fuss and hysterics of the Futurists."

In its disorienting layout of typography, the *Vorticist Manifesto* is as much a visual as a literary statement, reflecting the multiple and always skewed interest of its primary author, Lewis. Born on a yacht off the coast of Nova Scotia, he had moved to London with his mother when his parents separated in 1893. A precocious painter, he won a scholarship to the progressive Slade School of Art at age sixteen, but moved to Paris before completing his studies. He returned to London in 1909 and began a career as a painter and writer. During the War, he served both as an artillery officer and as a commissioned war artist. He also wrote an experimental novel, *Tarr* (1918), and went on to produce a range of works in the dozen years thereafter, including pro-fascist political theory in *The Art of Being Ruled* (1926) and more general cultural criticism in *Time and Western Man* (1927), in which he attacked the modern cult of subjectivity. During the thirties, he became increasingly unpopular in London, first as a result of a satirical novel, *The Apes of God*, which lampooned figures in the literary and art world and their patrons; following two libel actions against him, publishers became wary of taking on his works. Lewis and his wife spent the years of World War II living in poverty in America and Canada; after the war, he returned to England, where he became an art critic for the British Broadcasting Corporation. He continued to draw, paint, and write memoirs, satirical stories, and an allegorical fantasy in several volumes.

Along with the *Vorticist Manifesto*, the first issue of *Blast* included poetry by Pound, fiction by Ford Madox Ford and Rebecca West, a play by Lewis, and illustrations by Lewis and others. The timing of the first issue couldn't have been worse: after delays caused by typesetting difficulties, *Blast* went on sale in London on June 20, 1914; World War I began just a few weeks later. While Lewis and his confederates had declared war on conventional artistic and literary taste with their "puce monster"—an advertisement for the first issue announced the "END OF THE CHRISTIAN ERA"—they were usurped by a much more pressing conflict. As Lewis later wrote, "In 1914 I produced a huge review called *Blast*, which for the most part I wrote myself. That was my first public appearance. Immediately the War broke out and put an end to all that." Lewis brought out a second issue in July 1915, attempting to fend off charges of irrelevancy with a special "War Number" that included T. S. Eliot's "Preludes" and "Rhapsody on a Windy Night" and a manifesto from the sculptor Henri Gaudier-Brzeska, "written from the trenches," which concludes poignantly with an obituary for Gaudier, "Mort pour la Patrie" (died for the fatherland). But by this time, *Blast* itself was for all intents and purposes dead; its second issue was its last. Short-lived though it was, however, *Blast* was remarkably important in clearing the way for the new art of modernism.

VORTICIST MANIFESTO
LONG LIVE THE VORTEX!

Long live the great art vortex sprung up in the centre of this town!

We stand for the Reality of the Present—not for the sentimental Future, or the sacripant[1] Past.

We want to leave Nature and Men alone.

We do not want to make people wear Futurist Patches, or fuss men to take to pink and sky-blue trousers.

We are not their wives or tailors.

The only way Humanity can help artists is to remain independent and work unconsciously.

WE NEED THE UNCONSCIOUSNESS OF HUMANITY—their stupidity, animalism and dreams.

We believe in no perfectibility except our own.

Intrinsic beauty is in the Interpreter and Seer, not in the object or content.[2]

We do not want to change the appearance of the world, because we are not Naturalists, Impressionists or Futurists (the latest form of Impressionism), and do not depend on the appearance of the world for our art.

WE ONLY WANT THE WORLD TO LIVE, and to feel its crude energy flowing through us.

It may be said that great artists in England are always revolutionary, just as in France any really fine artist had a strong traditional vein.

Blast sets out to be an avenue for all those vivid and violent ideas that could reach the Public in no other way.

Blast will be popular, essentially. It will not appeal to any particular class, but to the fundamental and popular instincts in every class and description of people, **TO THE INDIVIDUAL.** The moment a man feels or realizes himself as an artist, he ceases to belong to any milieu or time. Blast is created for this timeless, fundamental Artist that exists in everybody.

---

1. Boasting of valor.
2. Although the Vorticists go on to differentiate themselves from the Impressionists, this statement is very close

to the impressionism articulated by Walter Pater in *The Renaissance* (1873).

The Man in the Street and the Gentleman are equally ignored.

Popular art does not mean the art of the poor people, as it is usually supposed to. It means the art of the individuals.

Education (art education and general education) tends to destroy the creative instinct. Therefore it is in times when education has been non-existent that art chiefly flourished.

But it is nothing to do with "the People."

It is a mere accident that that is the most favourable time for the individual to appear.

To make the rich of the community shed their education skin, to destroy politeness, standardization and academic, that is civilized, vision, is the task we have set ourselves.

We want to make in England not a popular art, not a revival of lost folk art, or a romantic fostering of such unactual conditions, but to make individuals, wherever found.

We will convert the King if possible.

A VORTICIST KING! WHY NOT?

DO YOU THINK LLOYD GEORGE[3] **HAS THE VORTEX IN HIM?**

MAY WE HOPE FOR ART FROM LADY MOND?[4]

We are against the glorification of "the People," as we are against snobbery. It is not necessary to be an outcast bohemian, to be unkempt or poor, any more than it is necessary to be rich or handsome, to be an artist. Art is nothing to do with the coat you wear. A top-hat can well hold the Sixtine.[5] A cheap cap could hide the image of Kephren.

AUTOMOBILISM (Marinetteism) bores us. We don't want to go about making a hullo-bulloo about motor cars, anymore than about knives and forks, elephants or gas-pipes.

Elephants are **VERY BIG.** Motor cars go quickly.

Wilde gushed twenty years ago about the beauty of machinery. Gissing,[6] in his romantic delight with modern lodging houses was futurist in this sense.

The futurist is a sensational and sentimental mixture of the aesthete of 1890 and the realist of 1870.

The "Poor" are detestable animals! They are only picturesque and amusing for the sentimentalist or the romantic! The "Rich" are bores without a single exception, *en tant que riches* [so far as they are rich]!

We want those simple and great people found everywhere.

Blast presents an art of Individuals.

MANIFESTO.

1

BLAST First (from politeness) ENGLAND

CURSE ITS CLIMATE FOR ITS SINS AND INFECTIONS

DISMAL SYMBOL, SET round our bodies,

of effeminate lout within.

---

3. David Lloyd George, British statesman, and Prime Minister 1916–1922.
4. A leader of fashionable London society.

5. The Sistine Chapel in the Vatican.
6. George Gissing (1857–1903), naturalist novelist.

VICTORIAN VAMPIRE, the LONDON cloud sucks
the TOWN'S heart.

A 1000 MILE LONG, 2 KILOMETER Deep

BODY OF WATER even, is pushed against us
from the Floridas, TO MAKE US MILD.
OFFICIOUS MOUNTAINS keep back DRASTIC WINDS

SO MUCH VAST MACHINERY TO PRODUCE

THE CURATE of "Eltham"
BRITANNIC AESTHETE
WILD NATURE CRANK
DOMESTICATED POLICEMAN
LONDON COLISEUM
SOCIALIST-PLAYWRIGHT
DALY'S MUSICAL COMEDY
GAIETY CHORUS GIRL
TONKS[7]

CURSE

the flabby sky that can manufacture no snow, but can only drop the sea on us in a
drizzle like a poem by Mr. Robert Bridges.[8]

CURSE

the lazy air that cannot stiffen the back of the **SERPENTINE,** or put
Aquatic steel half way down the **MANCHESTER CANAL.**

———

But ten years ago we saw distinctly both snow and ice
here.
May some vulgarly inventive, but useful person, arise,
and restore to us the necessary **BLIZZARDS.**

LET US ONCE MORE WEAR THE ERMINE
OF THE NORTH.

WE BELIEVE IN THE EXISTENCE OF THIS USEFUL LITTLE CHEMIST IN OUR MIDST!

7. Henry Tonks, a teacher at the Slade School of Art (where Lewis and other Vorticists studied) who resisted as "contamination" such modern innovations as Post-Impressionism and Cubism.
8. Poet Laureate from 1913 until his death in 1930, noted for his technical skill and high moral tone.

2
OH BLAST FRANCE

pig plagiarism
BELLY
SLIPPERS
POODLE TEMPER
BAD MUSIC

SENTIMENTAL GALLIC GUSH
SENSATIONALISM
FUSSINESS.

PARISIAN PAROCHIALISM.

Complacent young man, so much respect for Papa and his son!—Oh!— Papa is wonderful: but all papas are!

BLAST

APERITIFS (Pernots, Amers picon)
Bad change
Naively seductive Houri salon- picture Cocottes
Slouching blue porters (can carry a pantechnicon)
Stupidly rapacious people at every step
Economy maniacs
Bouillon Kub (for being a bad pun)

PARIS.

Clap-trap Heaven of amative German professor.
Ubiquitous lines of silly little trees.
Arcs de Triomphe.
Imperturbable, endless prettiness.
Large empty cliques, higher up.
Bad air for the individual.

BLAST
MECCA OF THE AMERICAN

because it is not other side of Suez Canal, instead of an afternoon's ride from London.

3

CURSE

WITH EXPLETIVE OF WHIRLWIND

THE BRITANNIC AESTHETE

CREAM OF THE SNOBBISH EARTH
ROSE OF SHARON OF GOD-PRIG
  OF SIMIAN VANITY
SNEAK AND SWOT OF THE SCHOOL-ROOM
IMBERB (or Berbed when in Belsize)-PEDANT

PRACTICAL JOKER
DANDY
CURATE

BLAST all products of phlegmatic cold
Life of LOOKER-ON.
  CURSE

SNOBBERY
(disease of feminity)
FEAR OF RIDICULE
(arch vice of inactive, sleepy)
PLAY
STYLISM
SINS AND PLAGUES
of this LYMPHATIC finished
(we admit in every sense
finished)
VEGETABLE HUMANITY.

4

BLAST

THE SPECIALIST
"PROFESSIONAL"
"GOOD WORKMAN"
"GROVE-MAN"
ONE ORGAN MAN

BLAST THE

AMATEUR
SCIOLAST
ART-PIMP
JOURNALIST
SELF MAN
NO-ORGAN MAN

5
BLAST HUMOUR

Quack ENGLISH drug for stupidity and sleepiness.
Arch enemy of REAL, conventionalizing like

gunshot, freezing supple
REAL in ferocious chemistry
of laughter.

BLAST SPORT
HUMOUR'S FIRST COUSIN AND ACCOMPLICE.

Impossibility for Englishman to be grave and
keep his end up, psychologically.
Impossible for him to use Humour as well
and be <u>persistently</u> grave.
Alas! necessity for big doll's show in front
of mouth.
Visitation of Heaven on
English Miss
gums, canines of **FIXED GRIN**
Death's head symbol of Anti-Life.

CURSE those who will hang over this
Manifesto with SILLY CANINES exposed.

6
BLAST

years 1837 to 1900

Curse abysmal inexcusable middle-class (also Aristocracy and
Proletariat).

BLAST

pasty shadow cast by gigantic BOEHM[9]
(Imagined at introduction of BOURGEOIS VICTORIAN
VISTAS).
WRING THE NECK OF all sick inventions born in that pro-
gressive white wake.

9. Joseph Edgar Boehm (1834–1890), sculptor for Queen Victoria.

BLAST   their weeping whiskers—hirsute
RHETORIC of EUNUCH and STYLIST—
SENTIMENTAL HYGIENICS
ROUSSEAUISMS (wild Nature cranks)
FRATERNIZING WITH MONKEYS
DIABOLICS—raptures and roses
of the erotic bookshelves
culminating in
PURGATORY OF PUTNEY.[1]

CHAOS OF ENOCH ARDENS[2]

laughing Jennys[3]
Ladies with Pains
good-for-nothing Guineveres.

SNOBBISH BORROVIAN running after
GIPSY KINGS and ESPADAS[4]
bowing the knee to
wild Mother Nature,
her feminine contours,
Unimaginative insult to
MAN.

DAMN

all those to-day who have taken on that Rotten Menagerie, and still crack their whips and tumble in Piccadilly Circus, as though London were a provincial town.

WE WHISPER IN YOUR EAR A GREAT SECRET.

LONDON IS NOT A PROVINCIAL TOWN.

We will allow Wonder Zoos. But we do not want the
GLOOMY VICTORIAN CIRCUS in
Piccadilly Circus.

IT IS PICCADILLY'S CIRCUS!

NOT MEANT FOR MENAGERIES trundling
out of Sixties DICKENSIAN CLOWNS,
CORELLI[5] LADY RIDERS, TROUPS
OF PERFORMING GIPSIES (who
complain besides that 1/6 a night
does not pay fare back to Clapham).

1. A middle-class suburb of London.
2. *Enoch Arden* (1864), a sentimental narrative poem by Tennyson.
3. From Dante Gabriel Rossetti's popular poem *Jenny* (1870), again disliked for its sentimentality.

4. Refers to the contemporary popularity of the gypsy romances of George Borrow, such as *The Zincali* (1841).
5. Marie Corelli, pseud. of Mary Mackay (1855–1924), author of best-selling religious novels and romances.

BLAST[6]

The Post Office   Frank Brangwyn   Robertson Nicol
Rev. Pennyfeather   Galloway Kyle
(Bells)   (Cluster of Grapes)
Bishop of London and all his posterity
Galsworthy   Dean Inge   Croce   Matthews
Rev Meyer   Seymour Hicks
Lionel Cust   C. B. Fry   Bergson Abdul Bahai
Hawtrey   Edward Elgar   Sardlea
Filson Young   Marie Corelli   Geddes
Codliver Oil   St. Loe Strachey   Lyceum Club
Rhabindraneth Tagore   Lord Glenconner of Glen
Weiniger   Norman Angel   Ad. Mahon
Mr. and Mrs. Dearmer   Beecham   Ella
A. C. Benson   (Pills, Opera, Thomas)   Sydney Webb
British Academy   Messrs. Chapell
Countess of Warwick   George Edwards
Willie Ferraro   Captain Cook   R. J. Campbell
Clan Thesiger   Martin Harvey   William Archer
George Grossmith   R. H. Benson
Annie Besant   Chenil   Clan Meynell
Father Vaughan   Joseph Holbrooke   Clan Strachey

1

BLESS ENGLAND!

BLESS ENGLAND

FOR ITS SHIPS

which switchback on Blue, Green and
Red **SEAS** all around the **PINK
EARTH-BALL,**

BIG BETS ON EACH.

BLESS ALL SEAFARERS.

THEY exchange not one LAND for another, but one ELEMENT for
ANOTHER. The MORE against the LESS ABSTRACT.

---

6. The list of those blasted by the Vorticists falls, according to the critic William Wees, into seven categories: (1) members of the (literary and cultural) Establishment (e.g., William Archer, drama critic of the *Nation*); (2) people who represented popular or snobbish fads (e.g., Sir Abdul Baha Bahai, leader of the Bahai faith); (3) high-minded popular writers, (e.g., Marie Corelli); (4) mediocre but popular figures (e.g., the poet Ella Wheeler Wilcox); (5) fuzzy-minded reformers and idealists (e.g., Sidney Webb, a leader of the Fabian Socialist organization); (6) "popular figures whom the Vorticists just didn't like" (e.g., C. B. Fry, a cricket player); and (7) "blasting just for the fun of it . . . or blasting that grew from special circumstances and private reasons known only to insiders" (e.g., the Post Office and Cod Liver Oil). See William C. Wees, *Vorticism and the English Avant-Garde* (1972), pp. 217–227.

BLESS the vast planetary abstraction of the **OCEAN.**

BLESS THE ARABS OF THE **ATLANTIC.**
THIS ISLAND MUST BE CONTRASTED WITH THE BLEAK WAVES.

BLESS ALL PORTS.

PORTS, RESTLESS MACHINES of

scooped out basins
heavy insect dredgers
monotonous cranes
stations
lighthouses, blazing through the frosty starlight, cutting the storm like a cake
beaks of infant boats, side by side,
heavy chaos of wharves,
steep walls of factories
womanly town

BLESS these **MACHINES** that work the little boats across clean liquid space, in beelines.

BLESS the great **PORTS**

HULL
LIVERPOOL
LONDON
NEWCASTLE-ON-TYNE
BRISTOL
GLASGOW

BLESS ENGLAND,

Industrial Island machine, pyramidal workshop, its apex at Shetland, discharging itself on the sea.

BLESS

cold
magnanimous
delicate
gauche
fanciful
stupid

ENGLISHMEN.

2
BLESS the HAIRDRESSER.

He attacks Mother Nature for a small fee.
Hourly he ploughs heads for sixpence,
Scours chins and lips for threepence.
He makes systematic mercenary war on this
   WILDNESS.
He trims aimless and retrograde growths
   into CLEAN ARCHED SHAPES and
ANGULAR PLOTS.

   BLESS this HESSIAN (or SILESIAN) **EXPERT**[7]
   correcting the grotesque anachronisms
      of our physique.

3
BLESS ENGLISH HUMOUR

It is the great barbarous weapon of
the genius among races.
The wild MOUNTAIN RAILWAY from IDEA
to IDEA, in the ancient Fair of LIFE.

BLESS **SWIFT**   for his solemn bleak
                        wisdom of laughter.

SHAKESPEARE   for his bitter Northern
                    Rhetoric of humour.

BLESS ALL ENGLISH EYES
   that grow crows-feet with their
   FANCY and ENERGY.

BLESS this hysterical WALL built round
   the EGO.

BLESS the solitude of LAUGHTER.

BLESS the separating, ungregarious

   BRITISH GRIN.

4
BLESS FRANCE

for its BUSHELS of VITALITY
to the square inch.

---

7. From German industrial regions.

HOME OF MANNERS (the Best, the **WORST** and interesting mixtures).

MASTERLY PORNOGRAPHY (great enemy of progress).

COMBATIVENESS

GREAT HUMAN SCEPTICS

DEPTHS OF ELEGANCE

FEMALE QUALITIES

FEMALES

BALLADS of its **PREHISTORIC APACHE**

Superb hardness and hardiesse of its

Voyou° type, rebellious adolescent.   raffish

Modesty and humanity of many there.

GREAT FLOOD OF LIFE pouring out

of wound of **1797.**[8]

Also bitterer stream from **1870.**[9]

STAYING POWER, like a cat.

BLESS[1]

Bridget   Berrwolf   Bearline   Cranmer Byng
Frieder Graham   The Pope   Maria de Tomaso
Captain Kemp   Munroe   Gaby   Jenkins
R. B. Cuningham Grahame   Barker
(not his brother)   (John and Granville)
Mrs. Wil Finnimore   Madame Strindberg   Carson
Salvation Army   Lord Howard de Walden
Capt. Craig   Charlotte Corday   Cromwell
Mrs. Duval   Mary Robertson   Lillie Lenton
Frank Rutter   Castor Oil   James Joyce
Leveridge   Lydia Yavorska   Preb. Carlyle   Jenny
Mon. le compte de Gabulis   Smithers   Dick Burge
33 Church Street   Sievier   Gertie Millar
Norman Wallis   Miss Fowler   Sir Joseph Lyons
Martin Wolff   Watt   Mrs. Hepburn
Alfree   Tommy   Captain Kendell   Young Ahearn
Wilfred Walter   Kate Lechmere   Henry Newbolt
Lady Aberconway   Frank Harris   Hamel
Gilbert Canaan   Sir James Mathew Barry
Mrs. Belloc Lowdnes   W. L. George   Rayner
George Robey   George Mozart   Harry Weldon

---

8. The rise of Napoleon Bonaparte.
9. Beginning of Franco-Prussian War and end of the Second Empire, led by Napoleon Bonaparte's nephew Napoleon III.
1. This list of the blessed falls, according to William Wees, into four categories: (1) "some of the blessings, like most of the blasts, seemed designed to affront respectable public opinion" (e.g., the Pope and the Salvation Army); (2) "working class entertainments such as boxing and music halls"; (3) "a few selected representatives of the fine arts" (e.g., James Joyce); and (4) "friends of the Vorticists or of the avant-garde in general" (e.g., Frank Rutter and P. J. Konody, two sympathetic art critics).

Chaliapine   George Hirst   Graham White
Hucks   Salmet   Shirley Kellogg   Bandsman Rice
Petty Officer Curran   Applegarth   Konody
Colin Bell   Lewis Hind   LEFRANC
Hubert   Commercial Process Co.

MANIFESTO.

I.

1. Beyond Action and Reaction we would establish ourselves.
2. We start from opposite statements of a chosen world. Set up violent structure of adolescent clearness between two extremes.
3. We discharge ourselves on both sides.
4. We fight first on one side, then on the other, but always for the SAME cause, which is neither side or both sides and ours.
5. Mercenaries were always the best troops.
6. We are Primitive Mercenaries in the Modern World.
7. Our Cause is NO-MAN'S.
8. We set Humour at Humour's throat.
   Stir up Civil War among peaceful apes.
9. We only want Humour if it has fought like Tragedy.
10. We only want Tragedy if it can clench its side-muscles like hands on its belly, and bring to the surface a laugh like a bomb.

II.

1. We hear from America and the Continent all sorts of disagreeable things about England: "the unmusical, anti-artistic, unphilosophic country."
2. We quite agree.
3. Luxury, sport, the famous English "Humour," the thrilling ascendancy and idée fixe of Class, producing the most intense snobbery in the World; heavy stagnant pools of Saxon blood, incapable of anything but the song of a frog, in home-counties:—these phenomena give England a peculiar distinction in the wrong sense, among the nations.
4. This is why England produces such good artists from time to time.
5. This is also the reason why a movement towards art and imagination could burst up here, from this lump of compressed life, with more force than anywhere else.
6. To believe that it is necessary for or conducive to art, to "improve" life, for instance—make architecture, dress, ornament, in "better taste," is absurd.
7. The Art-instinct is permanently primitive.
8. In a chaos of imperfection, discord, etc., it finds the same stimulus as in Nature.
9. The artist of the modern movement is a savage (in no sense an "advanced," perfected, democratic, Futurist individual of Mr. Marinetti's limited imagination): this enormous, jangling, journalistic, fairy desert of modern life serves him as Nature did more technically primitive man.

[10] As the steppes and the rigours of the Russian winter, when the peasant has to lie for weeks in his hut, produces that extraordinary acuity of feeling and intelligence we associate with the Slav; so England is just now the most favourable country for the appearance of a great art.

III.

[1] We have made it quite clear that there is nothing Chauvinistic or picturesquely patriotic about our contentions.

[2] But there is violent boredom with that feeble Europeanism, abasement of the miserable "intellectual" before anything coming from Paris, Cosmopolitan sentimentality, which prevails in so many quarters.

[3] Just as we believe that an Art must be organic with its Time,
So we insist that what is actual and vital for the South, is ineffectual and unactual in the North.

[4] Fairies have disappeared from Ireland (despite foolish attempts to revive them)[2] and the bull-ring languishes in Spain.

[5] But mysticism on the one hand, gladiatorial instincts, blood and asceticism on the other, will be always actual, and springs of Creation for these two peoples.

[6] The English Character is based on the Sea.

[7] The particular qualities and characteristics that the sea always engenders in men are those that are, among the many diagnostics of our race, the most fundamentally English.

[8] That unexpected universality as well, found in the completest English artists, is due to this.

IV.

[1] We assert that the art for these climates, then, must be a northern flower.

[2] And we have implied what we believe should be the specific nature of the art destined to grow up in this country, and models of whose flue decorate the pages of this magazine.

[3] It is not a question of the characterless material climate around us.
Were that so the complication of the Jungle, dramatic Tropic growth, the vastness of American trees, would not be for us.

[4] But our industries, and the Will that determined, face to face with its needs, the direction of the modern world, has reared up steel trees where the green ones were lacking; has exploded in useful growths, and found wilder intricacies than those of Nature.

V.

[1] We bring clearly forward the following points, before further defining the character of this necessary native art.

2. The Celtic Revival was a nostalgic movement in Irish arts and letters.

2   At the freest and most vigorous period of ENGLAND'S history, her literature, then chief Art, was in many ways identical with that of France.

3   Chaucer was very much cousin of Villon[3] as an artist.

4   Shakespeare and Montaigne[4] formed one literature.

5   But Shakespeare reflected in his imagination a mysticism, madness and delicacy peculiar to the North, and brought equal quantities of Comic and Tragic together.

6   Humour is a phenomenon caused by sudden pouring of culture into Barbary.[5]

7   It is intelligence electrified by flood of Naivety.

8   It is Chaos invading Concept and bursting it like nitrogen.

9   It is the Individual masquerading as Humanity like a child in clothes too big for him.

10   Tragic Humour is the birthright of the North.

11   Any great Northern Art will partake of this insidious and volcanic chaos.

12   No great ENGLISH Art need be ashamed to share some glory with France, tomorrow it may be with Germany, where the Elizabethans did before it.

13   But it will never be French, any more than Shakespeare was, the most catholic and subtle Englishman.

VI.

1   The Modern World is due almost entirely to Anglo-Saxon genius,—its appearance and its spirit.

2   Machinery, trains, steam-ships, all that distinguishes externally our time, came far more from here than anywhere else.

3   In dress, manners, mechanical inventions, LIFE, that is, ENGLAND, has influenced Europe in the same way that France has in Art.

4   But busy with this LIFE-EFFORT, she has been the last to become conscious of the Art that is an organism of this new Order and Will of Man.

5   Machinery is the greatest Earth-medium: incidentally it sweeps away the doctrines of a narrow and pedantic Realism at one stroke.

6   By mechanical inventiveness, too, just as Englishmen have spread themselves all over the Earth, they have brought all the hemispheres about them in their original island.

7   It cannot be said that the complication of the Jungle, dramatic tropic growths, the vastness of American trees, is not for us.

8   For, in the forms of machinery, Factories, new and vaster buildings, bridges and works, we have all that, naturally, around us.

VII.

1   Once this consciousness towards the new possibilities of expression in present life has come, however, it will be more the legitimate property of Englishmen than of any other people in Europe.

2   It should also, as it is by origin theirs, inspire them more forcibly and directly.

---

3. François Villon (1431–1463?), French poet.
4. Michel de Montaigne (1533–1592), French essayist.

5. An old name for the western part of North Africa; possibly used here to mean "barbarity."

3 | They are the inventors of this bareness and hardness, and should be the great enemies of Romance.

4 | The Romance peoples will always be, at bottom, its defenders.

5 | The Latins are at present, for instance, in their "discovery" of sport, their Futuristic gush over machines, aeroplanes, etc., the most romantic and sentimental "moderns" to be found.

6 | It is only the second-rate people in France or Italy who are thorough revolutionaries.

7 | In England, on the other hand, there Is no vulgarity in revolt.

8 | Or, rather, there is no revolt, it is the normal state.

9 | So often rebels of the North and the South are diametrically opposed species.

10 | The nearest thing in England to a great traditional French artist, is a great revolutionary English one.

Signatures for Manifesto[6]

R. Aldington
Arbuthnot
L. Atkinson
Gaudier Brzeska
J. Dismorr
C. Hamilton
E. Pound
W. Roberts
H. Sanders
E. Wadsworth
Wyndham Lewis

Rebecca West: Indissoluble Matrimony

Rebecca West (1892–1983) is increasingly appreciated as a writer of fiction, literary criticism, political commentary, and biography, as well as one of the most important journalists of the century. Born Cicely Fairfield in Ireland, she was educated in Edinburgh after her father died when she was ten years old. She became an actress in London, taking the stage name "Rebecca West" from a heroine she had played in Ibsen's drama *Rosmersholm*. By the time she was twenty, she was becoming active in left-wing journalism and in agitation for women's rights. In 1914, when she wrote *Indissoluble Matrimony*, she was involved in a love affair with the free-thinking but married novelist H. G. Wells, with whom she had a son; at the same time, she was working on a critical biography of Henry James. She went on to write searching and sometimes critical essays on male modernists like Joyce, Eliot, and Lawrence, and perceptive essays on Virginia Woolf and Katherine Mansfield. Throughout her life, she wrote both novels and political journalism, notably a major study of Balkan politics and culture, *Black Lamb*

---

6. The signatories to the manifesto are Richard Aldington, English writer and man of letters; Malcolm Arbuthnot, professional photographer; Lawrence Atkinson, Vorticist artist; Henri Gaudier-Brzeska, Vorticist sculptor and contributor to *Blast* who was killed in the trenches in World War I and whose obituary was included in *Blast II*; Jessica Dismoor, artist whose illustrations were included in *Blast*; Cuthbert Hamilton, avant-garde artist; Ezra Pound; William Roberts, painter; Helen Saunders, Vorticist designer; Edward Wadsworth, Vorticist painter; and Wyndham Lewis.

and Grey Falcon (1942), and a series of brilliant reports on the Nuremberg trials of Nazi war criminals at the end of World War II, collected as *A Train of Powder* (1955). She was made Dame Commander of the British Empire in 1959. Like her political writing, her fiction is notable for its irreverent probing of modernity's fault lines. Though never an orthodox feminist, West demonstrated a keen insight into the psychology of women and men, and portrayed the straitened thinking that made feminism's ultimate victory anything but a foregone conclusion.

Indissoluble Matrimony

When George Silverton opened the front door he found that the house was not empty for all its darkness. The spitting noise of the striking of damp matches and mild, growling exclamations of annoyance told him that his wife was trying to light the dining-room gas. He went in and with some short, hostile sound of greeting lit a match and brought brightness into the little room. Then, irritated by his own folly in bringing private papers into his wife's presence, he stuffed the letters he had brought from the office deep into the pockets of his overcoat. He looked at her suspiciously, but she had not seen them, being busy in unwinding her orange motor-veil. His eyes remained on her face to brood a little sourly on her moving loveliness, which he had not been sure of finding: for she was one of those women who create an illusion alternately of extreme beauty and extreme ugliness. Under her curious dress, designed in some pitifully cheap and worthless stuff by a successful mood of her indiscreet taste—she had black blood in her—her long body seemed pulsing with some exaltation. The blood was coursing violently under her luminous yellow skin, and her lids, dusky with fatigue, drooped contentedly over her great humid black eyes. Perpetually she raised her hand to the mass of black hair that was coiled on her thick golden neck, and stroked it with secretive enjoyment, as a cat licks its fur. And her large mouth smiled frankly, but abstractedly, at some digested pleasure.

There was a time when George would have looked on this riot of excited loveliness with suspicion. But now he knew it was almost certainly caused by some trifle—a long walk through stinging weather, the report of a Socialist victory at a by-election, or the intoxication of a waltz refrain floating from the municipal band-stand across the flats of the local recreation ground. And even if it had been caused by some amorous interlude he would not have greatly cared. In the ten years since their marriage he had lost the quality which would have made him resentful. He now believed that quality to be purely physical. Unless one was in good condition and responsive to the messages sent out by the flesh Evadne could hardly concern one. He turned the bitter thought over in his heart and stung himself by deliberately gazing unmoved upon her beautiful joyful body.

"Let's have supper now!" she said rather greedily.

He looked at the table and saw she had set it before she went out. As usual she had been in an improvident hurry: it was carelessly done. Besides, what an absurd supper to set before a hungry solicitor's clerk! In the centre, obviously intended as the principal dish, was a bowl of plums, softly red, soaked with the sun, glowing like jewels in the downward stream of the incandescent light. Besides them was a great yellow melon, its sleek sides fluted with rich growth, and a honey-comb glistening on a willow-pattern dish. The only sensible food to be seen was a plate of tongue laid at his place.

"I can't sit down to supper without washing my hands!"

While he splashed in the bathroom upstairs he heard her pull in a chair to the table and sit down to her supper. It annoyed him. There was no ritual about it. While he was eating the tongue she would be crushing honey on new bread, or stripping a plum of its purple skin and holding the golden globe up to the gas to see the light fil-

ter through. The meal would pass in silence. She would innocently take his dumbness for a sign of abstraction and forbear to babble. He would find the words choked
on his lips by the weight of dullness that always oppressed him in her presence. Then,
just about the time when he was beginning to feel able to formulate his obscure grievances against her, she would rise from the table without a word and run upstairs to
her work, humming in that uncanny, negro way of hers.

And so it was. She ate with an appalling catholicity of taste, with a nice child's
love of sweet foods, and occasionally she broke into that hoarse beautiful croon. Every
now and then she looked at him with too obvious speculations as to whether his silence
was due to weariness or uncertain temper. Timidly she cut him an enormous slice of the
melon, which he did not want. Then she rose abruptly and flung herself into the rocking chair on the hearth. She clasped her hands behind her head and strained backwards
so that the muslin stretched over her strong breasts. She sang softly to the ceiling.

There was something about the fantastic figure that made him feel as though
they were not properly married.

"Evadne?"

"'S?"

"What have you been up to this evening?"

"I was at Milly Stafordale's."

He was silent again. That name brought up the memory of his courting days. It
was under the benign eyes of blonde, plebeian Milly that he had wooed the distracting creature in the rocking chair.

Ten years before, when he was twenty-five, his firm had been reduced to hysteria
over the estates of an extraordinarily stupid old woman, named Mrs. Mary Ellerker. Her
stupidity, grappling with the complexity of the sources of the vast income which rushed
in spate from the properties of four deceased husbands, demanded oceans of explanations even over her weekly rents. Silverton alone in the office, by reason of a certain
natural incapacity for excitement, could deal calmly with this marvel of imbecility. He
alone could endure to sit with patience in the black-panelled drawing-room amidst the
jungle of shiny mahogany furniture and talk to a mass of darkness, who rested heavily in
the window-seat and now and then made an idiotic remark in a bright, hearty voice.
But it shook even him. Mrs. Mary Ellerker was obscene. Yet she was perfectly sane and,
although of that remarkable plainness noticeable in most oft-married women, in good
enough physical condition. She merely presented the loathsome spectacle of an ignorant mind, contorted by the artificial idiocy of coquetry, lack of responsibility, and
hatred of discipline, stripped naked by old age. That was the real horror of her. One
feared to think how many women were really like Mrs. Ellerker under their armour of
physical perfection or social grace. For this reason he turned eyes of hate on Mrs. Ellerker's pretty little companion, Milly Stafordale, who smiled at him over her embroidery
with wintry northern brightness. When she was old she too would be obscene.

This horror obsessed him. Never before had he feared anything. He had never lived
more than half-an-hour from a police station, and, as he had by some chance missed the
melancholy clairvoyance of adolescence, he had never conceived of any horror with
which the police could not deal. This disgust of women revealed to him that the world is
a place of subtle perils. He began to fear marriage as he feared death. The thought of
intimacy with some lovely, desirable and necessary wife turned him sick as he sat at his
lunch. The secret obscenity of women! He talked darkly of it to his friends. He wondered why the Church did not provide a service for the absolution of men after marriage.
Wife desertion seemed to him a beautiful return of the tainted body to cleanliness.

On his fifth visit to Mrs. Ellerker he could not begin his business at once. One of Milly Stafordale's friends had come in to sing to the old lady. She stood by the piano against the light, so that he saw her washed with darkness. Amazed, of tropical fruit. And before he had time to apprehend the sleepy wonder of her beauty, she had begun to sing. Now he knew that her voice was a purely physical attribute, built in her as she lay in her mother's womb, and no index of her spiritual values. But then, as it welled up from the thick golden throat and clung to her lips, it seemed a sublime achievement of the soul. It was smouldering contralto such as only those of black blood can possess. As she sang her great black eyes lay on him with the innocent shamelessness of a young animal, and he remembered hopefully that he was good looking. Suddenly she stood in silence, playing with her heavy black plait. Mrs. Ellerker broke into silly thanks. The girl's mother, who had been playing the accompaniment, rose and stood rolling up her music. Silverton, sick with excitement, was introduced to them. He noticed that the mother was a little darker than the conventions permit. Their name was Hannan—Mrs. Arthur Hannan and Evadne. They moved lithely and quietly out of the room, the girl's eyes still lingering on his face.

The thought of her splendour and the rolling echoes of her voice disturbed him all night. Next day, going to his office, he travelled with her on the horse-car that bound his suburb to Petrick. One of the horses fell lame, and she had time to tell him that she was studying at a commercial college. He quivered with distress. All the time he had a dizzy illusion that she was nestling up against him. They parted shyly. During the next few days they met constantly. He began to go and see them in the evening at their home—a mean flat crowded with cheap glories of bead curtains and Oriental hangings that set off the women's alien beauty. Mrs. Hannan was a widow and they lived alone, in a wonderful silence. He talked more than he had ever done in his whole life before. He took a dislike to the widow, she was consumed with fiery subterranean passions, no fit guardian for the tender girl.

Now he could imagine with what silent rapture Evadne had watched his agitation. Almost from the first she had meant to marry him. He was physically attractive, though not strong. His intellect was gently stimulating like a mild white wine. And it was time she married. She was ripe for adult things. This was the real wound in his soul. He had tasted of a divine thing created in his time for dreams out of her rich beauty, her loneliness, her romantic poverty, her immaculate youth. He had known love. And Evadne had never known anything more than a magnificent physical adventure which she had secured at the right time as she would have engaged a cab to take her to the station in time for the cheapest excursion train. It was a quick way to light-hearted living. With loathing he remembered how in the days of their engagement she used to gaze purely into his blinking eyes and with her unashamed kisses incite him to extravagant embraces. Now he cursed her for having obtained his spiritual revolution on false pretences. Only for a little time had he had his illusion, for their marriage was hastened by Mrs. Hannan's sudden death. After three months of savage mourning Evadne flung herself into marriage, and her excited candour had enlightened him very soon.

That marriage had lasted ten years. And to Evadne their relationship was just the same as ever. Her vitality needed him as it needed the fruit on the table before him. He shook with wrath and a sense of outraged decency.

"O George!" She was yawning widely.

"What's the matter?" he said without interest.

"It's so beastly dull."

"I can't help that, can I?"

"No." She smiled placidly at him. "We're a couple of dull dogs, aren't we? I wish we had children."

After a minute she suggested, apparently as an alternative amusement, "Perhaps the post hasn't passed."

As she spoke there was a rat-tat and the slither of a letter under the door. Evadne picked herself up and ran out into the lobby. After a second or two, during which she made irritating inarticulate exclamations, she came in reading the letter and stroking her bust with a gesture of satisfaction.

"They want me to speak at Longton's meeting on the nineteenth," she purred.

"Longton? What's he up to?"

Stephen Longton was the owner of the biggest iron works in Petrick, a man whose refusal to adopt the livery of busy oafishness thought proper to commercial men aroused the gravest suspicions.

"He's standing as Socialist candidate for the town council."

". . . Socialist!" he muttered.

He set his jaw. That was a side of Evadne he considered as little as possible. He had never been able to assimilate the fact that Evadne had, two years after their marriage, passed through his own orthodox Radicalism[1] to a passionate Socialism, and that after reading enormously of economics she had begun to write for the Socialist press and to speak successfully at meetings. In the jaundiced recesses of his mind he took it for granted that her work would have the lax fibre of her character: that it would be infected with her Oriental crudities. Although once or twice he had been congratulated on her brilliance, he mistrusted this phase of her activity as a caper of the sensualist. His eyes blazed on her and found the depraved, over-sexed creature, looking milder than a gazelle, holding out a hand-bill to him.

"They've taken it for granted!"

He saw her name—his name—

MRS. EVADNE SILVERTON.[2]

It was at first the blaze of stout scarlet letters on the dazzling white ground that made him blink. Then he was convulsed with rage.

"Georgie dear!"

She stepped forward and caught his weak body to her bosom. He wrenched himself away. Spiritual nausea made him determined to be a better man than her.

"A pair of you! You and Longton—!" he snarled scornfully. Then, seeing her startled face, he controlled himself.

"I thought it would please you," said Evadne, a little waspishly.

"You mustn't have anything to do with Longton," he stormed.

A change passed over her. She became ugly. Her face was heavy with intellect, her lips coarse with power. He was at arms with a Socialist lead. Much he would have preferred the bland sensualist again.

1. An extreme form of Liberalism, still comfortably within the continuum of British democratic politics; Socialism, which Evadne has embraced, advocates the abolition of the current system and is thus too extreme for George's bourgeois attitudes.

2. Evadne would have been addressed in polite society as "Mrs. George Silverton"; George reads this breach of decorum as one more sign that his wife is out of control. Leopold Bloom, the protagonist of James Joyce's *Ulysses*, makes a similar observation when his wife Molly receives a letter from her lover addressed to "Mrs. Marion Bloom."

"Why?"

"Because—his lips stuck together like blotting-paper—he's not the sort of man my wife should—should—"

With movements which terrified him by their rough energy, she folded up the bills and put them back in the envelope.

"George. I suppose you mean that he's a bad man." He nodded.

"I know quite well that the girl who used to be his typist is his mistress." She spoke it sweetly, as if reasoning with an old fool. "But she's got consumption. She'll be dead in six months. In fact, I think it's rather nice of him. To look after her and all that."

"My God!" He leapt to his feet, extending a shaking forefinger. As she turned to him, the smile dying on her lips, his excited weakness wrapped him in a paramnesic illusion:[3] it seemed to him that he had been through all this before—a long, long time ago. "My God, you talk like a woman off the streets!"

Evadne's lips lifted over her strong teeth. With clever cruelty she fixed his eyes with hers, well knowing that he longed to fall forward and bury his head on the table in a transport of hysterical sobs. After a moment of this torture she turned away, herself distressed by a desire to cry.

"How can you say such dreadful, dreadful things!" she protested, chokingly.

He sat down again. His eyes looked little and red, but they blazed on her. "I wonder if you are," he said softly.

"Are what?" she asked petulantly, a tear rolling down her nose.

"You know," he answered, nodding.

"George, George, George!" she cried.

"You've always been keen on kissing and making love, haven't you, my precious? At first you startled me, you did! I didn't know women were like that." From that morass he suddenly stepped on to a high peak of terror. Amazed to find himself sincere, he cried—"I don't believe good women are!"

"Georgie, how can you be so silly!" exclaimed Evadne shrilly. "You know quite well I've been as true to you as any woman could be." She sought his eyes with a liquid glance of reproach. He averted his gaze, sickened at having put himself in the wrong. For even while he degraded his tongue his pure soul fainted with loathing of her fleshliness.

"I—I'm sorry."

Too wily to forgive him at once, she showed him a lowering profile with downcast lids. Of course, he knew it was a fraud: an imputation against her chastity was no more poignant than a reflection on the cleanliness of her nails—rude and spiteful, but that was all. But for a time they kept up the deception, while she cleared the table in a steely silence.

"Evadne, I'm sorry. I'm tired." His throat was dry. He could not bear the discord of a row added to the horror of their companionship. "Evadne, do forgive me—I don't know what I meant by—"

"That's all right, silly!" she said suddenly and bent over the table to kiss him. Her brow was smooth. It was evident from her splendid expression that she was preoccupied. Then she finished clearing up the dishes and took them into the kitchen. While she was out of the room he rose from his seat and sat down in the armchair by the fire, setting his bull-dog pipe alight. For a very short time he was free of her

_____

3. A condition in which fact and fiction become confused.

voluptuous presence. But she ran back soon, having put the kettle on and changed her blouse for a loose dressing-jacket, and sat down on the arm of his chair. Once or twice she bent and kissed his brow, but for the most part she lay back with his head drawn to her bosom, rocking herself rhythmically. Silverton, a little disgusted by their contact, sat quite motionless and passed into a doze. He revolved in his mind the incidents of his day's routine and remembered a snub from a superior. So he opened his eyes and tried to think of something else. It was then that he became conscious that the rhythm of Evadne's movement was not regular. It was broken as though she rocked in time to music. Music? His sense of hearing crept up to hear if there was any sound of music in the breaths she was emitting rather heavily every now and then. At first he could hear nothing. Then it struck him that each breath was a muttered phrase. He stiffened, and hatred flamed through his veins. The words came clearly through her lips. . . . "The present system of wage-slavery. . . ."

"Evadne!" He sprang to his feet. "You're preparing your speech!"

She did not move. "I am," she said.

"Damn it, you shan't speak!"

"Damn it, I will!"

"Evadne, you shan't speak! If you do I swear to God above I'll turn you out into the streets——." She rose and came towards him. She looked black and dangerous. She trod softly like a cat with her head down. In spite of himself, his tongue licked his lips in fear and he cowered a moment before he picked up a knife from the table. For a space she looked down on him and the sharp blade.

"You idiot, can't you hear the kettle's boiling over?"

He shrank back, letting the knife fall on the floor. For three minutes he stood there controlling his breath and trying to still his heart. Then he followed her into the kitchen. She was making a noise with a basinful of dishes.

"Stop that row."

She turned round with a dripping dish-cloth in her hand and pondered whether to throw it at him. But she was tired and wanted peace: so that she could finish the rough draft of her speech. So she stood waiting.

"Did you understand what I said then? If you don't promise me here and now—"

She flung her arms upwards with a cry and dashed past him. He made to run after her upstairs, but stumbled on the threshold of the lobby and sat with his ankle twisted under him, shaking with rage. In a second she ran downstairs again, clothed in a big cloak with black bundle clutched to her breast. For the first time in their married life she was seized with a convulsion of sobs. She dashed out of the front door and banged it with such passion that a glass pane shivered to fragments behind her.

"What's this? What's this?" he cried stupidly, standing up. He perceived with an insane certainty that she was going out to meet some unknown lover. "I'll come and tell him what a slut you are!" he shouted after her and stumbled to the door. It was jammed now and he had to drag at it.

The night was flooded with the yellow moonshine of midsummer: it seemed to drip from the lacquered leaves of the shrubs in the front garden. In its soft clarity he could see her plainly, although she was now two hundred yards away. She was hastening to the north end of Sumatra Crescent, an end that curled up the hill like a silly kitten's tail and stopped abruptly in green fields. So he knew that she was going to the young man who had just bought the Georgian Manor, whose elm-trees crowned the hill. Oh, how he hated her! Yet he must follow her, or else she would cover up her adulteries so that he could not take his legal revenge. So he began to run—silently, for he wore his carpet slippers. He was only a hundred yards behind her when she slipped through a gap in the hedge to tread a field-path. She still walked with pride, for though she was town-bred, night in the open seemed not at all fearful to her. As he shuffled in pursuit his carpet slippers were engulfed in a shining pool of mud: he raised one with a squelch, the other was left. This seemed the last humiliation. He kicked the other one off his feet and padded on in his socks, snuffling in anticipation of a cold. Then physical pain sent him back to the puddle to pluck out the slippers; it was a dirty job. His heart battered his breast as he saw that Evadne had gained the furthest hedge and was crossing the stile into the lane that ran up to the Manor gates.

"Go on, you beast!" he muttered, "Go on, go on!" After a scamper he climbed the stile and thrust his lean neck beyond a mass of wilted hawthorn bloom that crumbled into vagrant petals at his touch.

The lane mounted yellow as cheese to where the moon lay on his iron tracery of the Manor gates. Evadne was not there. Hardly believing his eyes he hobbled over into the lane and looked in the other direction. There he saw her disappearing round the bend of the road. Gathering himself up to a run, he tried to think out his bearings. He had seldom passed this way, and like most people without strong primitive instincts he had no sense of orientation. With difficulty he remembered that after a mile's mazy wanderings between high hedges this lane sloped suddenly to the bowl of heather overhung by the moorlands, in which lay the Petrick reservoirs, two untamed lakes.

"Eh! she's going to meet him by the water!" he cursed to himself. He remembered the withered ash tree, seared by lightning to its root, that stood by the road at the bare frontier of the moor. "May God strike her like that," he prayed," "as she fouls the other man's lips with her kisses. O God! let me strangle her. Or bury a knife deep in her breast." Suddenly he broke into a lolloping run. "O my Lord, I'll be able to divorce her. I'll be free. Free to live alone. To do my day's work and sleep my night's sleep without her. I'll get a job somewhere else and forget her. I'll bring her to the dogs. No clean man or woman in Petrick will look at her now. They won't have her to speak at that meeting now!" His throat swelled with joy, he leapt high in the air.

"I'll lie about her. If I can prove that she's wrong with this man they'll believe me if I say she's a bad woman and drinks. I'll make her name a joke. And then—"

He flung wide his arms in ecstasy: the left struck against stone. More pain than he had thought his body could hold convulsed him, so that he sank on the ground hugging his aching arm. He looked backwards as he writhed and saw that the hedge had stopped; above him was the great stone wall of the county asylum. The question broke on him—was there any lunatic in its confines so slavered with madness as he himself? Nothing but madness could have accounted for the torrent of ugly words, the sea of uglier thoughts that was now a part of him. "O God, me to turn like this!" he cried, rolling over full-length on the grassy bank by the roadside. That the infidelity of his wife, a thing that should have brought out the stern manliness of his true nature, should have discovered him as lecherous-lipped as any pot-house[4] lounger, was the most infamous accident of his married life. The sense of sin descended on him so that his tears flowed hot and bitterly. "Have I gone to the Unitarian chapel every Sunday morning and to the Ethical Society every evening for nothing?" his

4. Tavern.

spirit asked itself in its travail. "All those Browning lectures for nothing. . . ."[5] He said the Lord's Prayer several times and lay for a minute quietly crying. The relaxation of his muscles brought him a sense of rest which seemed forgiveness falling from God. The tears dried on his cheeks. His calmer consciousness heard the sound of rushing waters mingled with the beating of blood in his ears. He got up and scrambled round the turn of the road that brought him to the withered ash-tree.

He walked forward on the parched heatherland to the mound whose scarred sides, heaped with boulders, tufted with mountain grasses, shone before him in the moonlight. He scrambled up to it hurriedly and hoisted himself from ledge to ledge till he fell on his knees with a squeal of pain. His ankle was caught in a crevice of the rock. Gulping down his agony at this final physical humiliation he heaved himself upright and raced on to the summit, and found himself before the Devil's Cauldron, filled to the brim with yellow moonshine and the fiery play of summer lightning. The rugged crags opposite him were a low barricade against the stars to which the mound where he stood shot forward like a bridge. To the left of this the long Lisbech pond lay like a trailing serpent; its silver scales glittered as the wind swept down from the vaster moorlands to the east. To the right under a steep drop of twenty feet was the Whimsey pond, more sinister, shaped in an unnatural oval, sheltered from the wind by the high ridge so that the undisturbed moonlight lay across it like a sharp-edged sword.

He looked about for some sign of Evadne. She could not be on the land by the margin of the lakes, for the light blazed so strongly that each reed could be clearly seen like a black dagger stabbing the silver. He looked down Lisbech and saw far east a knot of red and green and orange lights. Perhaps for some devilish purpose Evadne had sought Lisbech railway station. But his volcanic mind had preserved one grain of sense that assured him that, subtle as Evadne's villainy might be, it would not lead her to walk five miles out of her way to a terminus which she could have reached in fifteen minutes by taking a train from the station down the road. She must be under cover somewhere here. He went down the gentle slope that fell from the top of the ridge to Lisbech pond in a disorder of rough heather, unhappy patches of cultivated grass, and coppices of silver birch, fringed with flaming broom that seemed faintly tarnished in the moonlight. At the bottom was a roughly hewn path which he followed in hot aimless hurry. In a little he approached a riot of falling waters. There was a slice ten feet broad carved out of the ridge, and to this narrow channel of black shining rock the floods of Lisbech leapt some feet and raced through to Whimsey. The noise beat him back. The gap was spanned by a gaunt thing of paint-blistered iron, on which he stood dizzily and noticed how the wide step that ran on each side of the channel through to the other pond was smeared with sinister green slime. Now his physical distress reminded him of Evadne, whom he had almost forgotten in contemplation of these lonely waters. The idea of her had been present but obscured, as sometimes toothache may cease active torture. His blood lust set him on and he staggered forward with covered ears. Even as he went something caught his eye in a thicket high up on the slope near the crags. Against the slender pride of some silver birches stood a gnarled hawthorn tree, its branches flattened under the stern moorland winds so that it grew squat like an opened umbrella. In its dark shadows, faintly illumined by a few boughs of withered blossom, there moved a strange bluish light. Even while he did not know what it was it made his flesh stir.

---

5. George's activities—Unitarian church, Ethical Society, Browning Society—suggest that he participated in public exercises of a high moral nature without giving himself over to traditional religious faith, which he would have seen as "irrational" and "unmanly."

The light emerged. It was the moonlight reflected from Evadne's body. She was clad in a black bathing dress, and her arms and legs and the broad streak of flesh laid bare by a rent down the back shone brilliantly white, so that she seemed like a grotesquely patterned wild animal as she ran down to the lake. Whirling her arms above her head she trampled down into the water and struck out strongly. Her movements were full of brisk delight and she swam quickly. The moonlight made her the centre of a little feathery blur of black and silver, with a comet's tail trailing in her wake.

Nothing in all his married life had ever staggered Silverton so much as this. He had imagined his wife's adultery so strongly that it had come to be. It was now as real as their marriage; more real than their courtship. So this seemed to be the last crime of the adulteress. She had dragged him over those squelching fields and these rough moors and changed him from a man of irritations, but no passions, into a cold designer of murderous treacheries, so that he might witness a swimming exhibition! For a minute he was stunned. Then he sprang down to the rushy edge and ran along in the direction of her course, crying—"Evadne! Evadne!" She did not hear him. At last he achieved a chest note and shouted—"Evadne! come here!" The black and silver feather shivered in mid-water. She turned immediately and swam back to shore. He suspected sullenness in her slowness, but was glad of it, for after the shock of this extraordinary incident he wanted to go to sleep. Drowsiness lay on him like lead. He shook himself like a dog and wrenched off his linen collar, winking at the bright moon to keep himself awake. As she came quite near he was exasperated by the happy, snorting breaths she drew, and strolled a pace or two up the bank. To his enragement the face she lifted as she waded to dry land was placid, and she scrambled gaily up the bank to his side.

"O George, why did you come!" she exclaimed quite affectionately, laying a damp hand on his shoulder.

"O damn it, what does this mean!" he cried, committing a horrid tenor squeak. "What are you doing?"

"Why. George," she said," I came here for a bathe."

He stared into her face and could make nothing of it. It was only sweet surfaces of flesh, soft radiances of eye and lip, a lovely lie of comeliness. He forgot this present grievance in a cold search for the source of her peculiar hatefulness. Under this sick gaze she pouted and turned away with a peevish gesture. He made no sign and stood silent, watching her saunter to that gaunt iron bridge. The roar of the little waterfall did not disturb her splendid nerves and she drooped sensuously over the hand-rail, sniffing up the sweet night smell; too evidently trying to abase him to another apology.

A mosquito whirred into his face. He killed it viciously and strode off towards his wife, who showed by a common little toss of the head that she was conscious of his coming.

"Look here, Evadne!" he panted. "What did you come here for? Tell me the truth and I promise I'll not—I'll not—"

"Not WHAT, George?"

"O please, please tell me the truth, do Evadne!" he cried pitifully.

"But, dear, what is there to carry on about so? You went on so queerly about my meeting that my head felt fit to split, and I thought the long walk and the dip would do me good." She broke off, amazed at the wave of horror that passed over his face.

His heart sank. From the loose-lipped hurry in the telling of her story, from the bigness of her eyes and the lack of subtlety in her voice, he knew that this was the truth. Here was no adulteress whom he could accuse in the law courts and condemn into the street, no resourceful sinner whose merry crimes he could discover. Here was merely his good wife, the faithful attendant of his hearth, relentless wrecker of his soul.

She came towards him as a cat approaches a displeased master, and hovered about him on the stone coping of the noisy sluice.

"Indeed!" he found himself saying sarcastically. "Indeed!"

"Yes, George Silverton, indeed!" she burst out, a little frightened. "And why shouldn't I? I used to come here often enough on summer nights with poor Mamma—"

"Yes!" he shouted. It was exactly the sort of thing that would appeal to that weird half-black woman from the back of beyond. "Mamma!" he cried tauntingly, "Mamma!"

There was a flash of silence between them before Evadne, clutching her breast and balancing herself dangerously on her heels on the stone coping, broke into gentle shrieks. "You dare talk of my Mamma, my poor Mamma, and she cold in her grave! I haven't been happy since she died and I married you, you silly little misery, you!" Then the rage was suddenly wiped off her brain by the perception of a crisis.

The trickle of silence overflowed into a lake, over which their spirits flew, looking at each other's reflection in the calm waters: in the hurry of their flight they had never before seen each other. They stood facing one another with dropped heads, quietly thinking.

The strong passion which filled them threatened to disintegrate their souls as a magnetic current decomposes the electrolyte, so they fought to organise their sensations. They tried to arrange themselves and their lives for comprehension, but beyond sudden lyric visions of old incidents of hatefulness—such as a smarting quarrel of six years ago as to whether Evadne had or had not cheated the railway company out of one and eightpence on an excursion ticket—the past was intangible. It trailed behind this intense event as the pale hair trails behind the burning comet. They were pre-occupied with the moment. Quite often George had found a mean pleasure in the thought that by never giving Evadne a child he had cheated her out of one form of experience, and now he paid the price for this unnatural pride of sterility. For now the spiritual offspring of their intercourse came to birth. A sublime loathing was between them. For a little time it was a huge perilous horror, but afterwards, like men aboard a ship whose masts seek the sky through steep waves, they found a drunken pride in the adventure. This was the very absolute of hatred. It cheapened the memory of the fantasias of irritation and ill-will they had performed in the less boring moments of their marriage, and they felt dazed, as amateurs who had found themselves creating a masterpiece. For the first time they were possessed by a supreme emotion and they felt a glad desire to strip away restraint and express it nakedly. It was ecstasy; they felt tall and full of blood.

Like people who, bewitched by Christ, see the whole earth as the breathing body of God, so they saw the universe as the substance and the symbol of their hatred. The stars trembled overhead with wrath. A wind from behind the angry crags set the moonlight on Lisbech quivering with rage, and the squat hawthorn-tree creaked slowly like the irritation of a dull little man. The dry moors, parched with harsh anger, waited thirstily and, sending out the murmur of rustling mountain grass and the cry of wakening fowl, seemed to huddle closer to the lake. But this sense of the earth's sympathy slipped away from them and they loathed all matter as the dull wrapping of their flame-like passion. At their wishing matter fell away and they saw sarcastic visions. He saw her as a toad squatting on the clean earth, obscuring the stars and pressing down its hot moist body on the cheerful fields. She felt his long boneless body coiled round the roots of the lovely tree of life. They shivered fastidiously. With an uplifting sense of responsibility they realised that they must kill each other.

A bird rose over their heads with a leaping flight that made it seem as though its black body was bouncing against the bright sky. The foolish noise and motion precipitated their thoughts. They were broken into a new conception of life. They perceived that God is war and his creatures are meant to fight. When dogs walk through the world cats must climb trees. The virgin must snare the wanton, the fine lover must put the prude to the sword. The gross man of action walks, spurred on the bloodless bodies of the men of thought, who lie quiet and cunningly do not tell him where his grossness leads him. The flesh must smother the spirit, the spirit must set the flesh on fire and watch it burn. And those who were gentle by nature and shrank from the ordained brutality were betrayers of their kind, surrendering the earth to the seed of their enemies. In this war there is no discharge. If they succumbed to peace now, the rest of their lives would be dishonourable, like the exile of a rebel who has begged his life as the reward of cowardice. It was their first experience of religious passion, and they abandoned themselves to it so that their immediate personal qualities fell away from them. Neither his weakness nor her prudence stood in the way of the event.

They measured each other with the eye. To her he was a spidery thing against the velvet blackness and hard silver surfaces of the pond. The light soaked her bathing dress so that she seemed, against the jagged shadows of the rock cutting, as though she were clad in a garment of dark polished mail. Her knees were bent so clearly, her toes gripped the coping so strongly. He understood very clearly that if he did not kill her instantly she would drop him easily into the deep riot of waters. Yet for a space he could not move, but stood expecting a degrading death. Indeed, he gave her time to kill him. But she was without power too, and struggled weakly with a hallucination. The quarrel in Sumatra Crescent with its suggestion of vast and unmentionable antagonisms; her swift race through the moon-drenched countryside, all crepitant with night noises: the swimming in the wine-like lake: their isolation on the moor, which was expressedly hostile to them, as nature always is to lonely man: and this stark contest face to face, with their resentments heaped between them like a pile of naked swords—these things were so strange that her civilised self shrank back appalled. There entered into her the primitive woman who is the curse of all women: a creature of the most utter femaleness, useless, save for childbirth, with no strong brain to make her physical weakness a light accident, abjectly and corruptingly afraid of man. A squaw, she dared not strike her lord.

The illusion passed like a moment of faintness and left her enraged at having forgotten her superiority even for an instant. In the material world she had a thousand times been defeated into making prudent reservations and practising unnatural docilities. But in the world of thought she had maintained unfalteringly her masterfulness in spite of the strong yearning of her temperament towards voluptuous surrenders. That was her virtue. Its violation whipped her to action and she would have killed him at once, had not his moment come a second before hers. Sweating horribly, he had dropped his head forward on his chest: his eyes fell on her feet and marked the plebeian moulding of her ankle, which rose thickly over a crease of flesh from the heel to the calf. The woman was coarse in grain and pattern.

He had no instinct for honourable attack, so he found himself striking her in the stomach. She reeled from pain, not because his strength overcame hers. For the first time her eyes looked into his candidly open, unveiled by languor or lust: their hard brightness told him how she despised him for that unwarlike blow. He cried out as he realised that this was another of her despicable victories and that the whole burden of the crime now lay on him, for he had begun it. But the rage was stopped on his lips as her arms, flung wildly out as she fell backwards, caught him about the waist with abominable justness of eye and evil intention. So they fell body to body into the quarrelling waters.

The feathery confusion had looked so soft, yet it seemed the solid rock they struck. The breath shot out of him and suffocation warmly stuffed his ears and nose. Then the rock cleft and he was swallowed by a brawling blackness in which whirled a vortex that flung him again and again on a sharp thing that burned his shoulder. All about him fought the waters, and they cut his flesh like knives. His pain was past belief. Though God might be war, he desired peace in his time, and he yearned for another God—a child's God, an immense arm coming down from the hills and lifting him to a kindly bosom. Soon his body would burst for breath, his agony would smash in his breast bone. So great was his pain that his consciousness was strained to apprehend it, as a too tightly stretched canvas splits and rips.

Suddenly the air was sweet on his mouth. The starlight seemed as hearty as a cheer. The world was still there, the world in which he had lived, so he must be safe. His own weakness and loveableness induced enjoyable tears, and there was a delicious moment of abandonment to comfortable whining before he realised that the water would not kindly buoy him up for long, and that even now a hostile current clasped his waist. He braced his flaccid body against the sucking blackness and flung his head back so that the water should not bubble so hungrily against the cords of his throat. Above him the slime of the rock was sticky with moonbeams, and the leprous light brought to his mind a newspaper paragraph, read years ago, which told him that the dawn had discovered floating in some oily Mersey dock, under walls as infected with wet growth as this, a corpse whose blood-encrusted finger-tips were deeply cleft. On the instant his own finger-tips seemed hot with blood and deeply cleft from clawing at the impregnable rock. He screamed gaspingly and beat his hands through the strangling flood. Action, which he had always loathed and dreaded, had broken the hard mould of his self-possession, and the dry dust of his character was blown hither and thither by fear. But one sharp fragment of intelligence which survived this detrition of his personality perceived that a certain gleam on the rock about a foot above the water was not the cold putrescence of the slime, but certainly the hard and merry light of a moon-ray striking on solid metal. His left hand clutched upwards at it, and he swung from a rounded projection. It was, his touch told him, a leaden ring hanging obliquely from the rock, to which his memory could visualise precisely in some past drier time when Lisbech sent no flood to Whimsey, a waterman mooring a boat strewn with pale-bellied perch. And behind the stooping waterman he remembered a flight of narrow steps that led up a buttress to a stone shelf that ran through the cutting. Unquestionably he was safe. He swung in a happy rhythm from the ring, his limp body trailing like a caterpillar through the stream to the foot of the steps, while he gasped in strength. A part of him was in agony, for his arm was nearly dragged out of its socket and a part of him was embarrassed because his hysteria shook him with a deep rumbling chuckle that sounded as though he meditated on some unseemly joke; the whole was pervaded by a twilight atmosphere of unenthusiastic gratitude for his rescue, like the quietly cheerful tone of a Sunday evening sacred concert. After a minute's deep breathing he hauled himself up by the other hand and prepared to swing himself on to the steps.

But first, to shake off the wet worsted rags, once his socks, that now stuck uncomfortably between his toes, he splashed his feet outwards to midstream. A certain porpoise-like surface met his left foot. Fear dappled his face with goose flesh. Without turning his head he knew what it was. It was Evadne's fat flesh rising on each side of her deep-furrowed spine through the rent in her bathing dress.

Once more hatred marched through his soul like a king: compelling service by his godhead and, like all gods, a little hated for his harsh lieu[6] on his worshipper. He saw his wife as the curtain of flesh between him and celibacy, and solitude and all those delicate abstentions from life which his soul desired. He saw her as the invisible worm destroying the rose of the world with her dark secret love.[7] Now he knelt on the lowest stone step watching her wet seal-smooth head bobbing nearer on the waters. As her strong arms, covered with little dark points where her thick hairs were clotted with moisture, stretched out towards safety he bent forward and laid his hands on her head. He held her face under water. Scornfully he noticed the bubbles that rose to the surface from her protesting mouth and nostrils, and the foam raised by her arms and her thick ankles. To the end the creature persisted in turmoil, in movement, in action. . . .

She dropped like a stone. His hands, with nothing to resist them, slapped the water foolishly and he nearly overbalanced forward into the stream. He rose to his feet very stiffly. "I must be a very strong man," he said, as he slowly climbed the steps. "I must be a very strong man," he repeated, a little louder, as with a hot and painful rigidity of the joints he stretched himself out at full length along the stone shelf. Weakness closed him in like a lead coffin. For a little time the wetness of his clothes persisted in being felt: then the sensation oozed out of him and his body fell out of knowledge. There was neither pain nor joy nor any other reckless ploughing of the brain by nerves. He knew unconsciousness, or rather the fullest consciousness he had ever known. For the world became nothingness, and nothingness which is free from the yeasty nuisance of matter and the ugliness of generation was the law of his being. He was absorbed into vacuity, the untamed substance of the universe, round which he conceived passion and thought to circle as straws caught up by the wind. He saw God and lived.

In Heaven a thousand years are a day. And this little corner of time in which he found happiness shrank to a nut-shell as he opened his eyes again. This peace was hardly printed on his heart, yet the brightness of the night was blurred by the dawn. With the grunting carefulness of a man drunk with fatigue, he crawled along the stone shelf to the iron bridge, where he stood with his back to the roaring sluice and rested. All things seemed different now and happier. Like most timid people he disliked the night, and the commonplace hand which the dawn laid on the scene seemed to him a sanctification. The dimmed moon sank to her setting behind the crags. The jewel lights of Lisbech railway station were weak, cheerful twinklings. A steaming bluish milk of morning mist had been spilt on the hard silver surface of the lake, and the reeds no longer stabbed it like little daggers, but seemed a feathery fringe, like the pampas grass in the front garden in Sumatra Crescent. The black crags became brownish, and the mist disguised the sternness of the moor. This weakening of effects was exactly what he had always thought the extinction of Evadne would bring the world. He smiled happily at the moon.

Yet he was moved to sudden angry speech. "If I had my time over again," he said, "I wouldn't touch her with the tongs." For the cold he had known all along he would catch had settled in his head, and his handkerchief was wet through.

---

6. Discipline.

7. A reference to William Blake's poem *The Sick Rose*; see page 1405.

He leaned over the bridge and looked along Lisbech and thought of Evadne. For the first time for many years he saw her image without spirits, and wondered without indignation why she had so often looked like the cat about to steal the cream. What was the cream? And did she ever steal it? Now he would never know. He thought of her very generously and sighed over the perversity of fate in letting so much comeliness.

"If she had married a butcher or a veterinary surgeon she might have been happy," he said, and shook his head at the glassy black water that slid under the bridge to that boiling sluice.

A gust of ague[8] reminded him that wet clothes clung to his fevered body and that he ought to change as quickly as possible, or expect to be laid up for weeks. He turned along the path that led back across the moor to the withered ash tree, and was learning the torture of bare feet on gravel when he cried out to himself: "I shall be hanged for killing my wife." It did not come as a trumpet-call, for he was one of those people who never quite hear what is said to them, and this deafishness extended in him to emotional things. It stole on him clamly, like a fog closing on a city. When he first felt hemmed in by this certainty he looked over his shoulder to the crags, remembering tales of how Jacobite fugitives had hidden on the moors for many weeks. There lay at least another day of freedom. But he was the kind of man who always goes home. He stumbled on, not very unhappy, except for his feet. Like many people of weak temperament he did not fear death. Indeed, it had a peculiar appeal to him; for while it was important, exciting, it did not, like most important and exciting things try to create action. He allowed his imagination the vanity of painting pictures. He saw himself standing in their bedroom, plotting this last event, with the white sheet and the high lights of the mahogany wardrobe shining ghostly at him through the darkness. He saw himself raising a thin hand to the gas bracket and turning on the tap. He saw himself staggering to their bed while death crept in at his nostrils. He saw his corpse lying in full daylight, and for the first time knew himself certainly, unquestionably dignified.

He threw back his chest in pride: but at that moment the path stopped and he found himself staggering down the mound of heatherland and boulders with bleeding feet. Always he had suffered from sore feet, which had not exactly disgusted but, worse still, disappointed Evadne. A certain wistfulness she had always evinced when she found herself the superior animal had enraged and humiliated him many times. He felt that sting him now, and flung himself down the mound cursing. When he stumbled up to the withered ash tree he hated her so much that it seemed as though she were alive again, and a sharp wind blowing down from the moor terrified him like her touch.

He rested there. Leaning against the stripped grey trunk, he smiled up at the sky, which was now so touched to ineffectiveness by the dawn that it looked like a tent of faded silk. There was the peace of weakness in him, which he took to be spiritual, because it had no apparent physical justification: but he lost it as his dripping clothes chilled his tired flesh. His discomfort reminded him that the phantasmic night was passing from him. Daylight threatened him: the daylight in which for so many years he had worked in the solicitor's office and been snubbed and ignored. "'The garish day,'" he murmured disgustedly, quoting the blasphemy of some hymn writer. He wanted his death to happen in this phantasmic night.

8. Fever.

So he limped his way along the road. The birds had not yet begun to sing, but the rustling noises of the night had ceased. The silent highway was consecrated to his proud progress. He staggered happily like a tired child returning from a lovely birthday walk: his death in the little bedroom, which for the first time he would have to himself, was a culminating treat to be gloated over like the promise of a favourite pudding for supper. As he walked he brooded dozingly on large and swelling thoughts. Like all people of weak passions and enterprise he loved to think of Napoleon, and in the shadow of the great asylum wall he strutted a few steps of his advance from murder to suicide, with arms crossed on his breast and thin legs trying to strut massively. He was so happy. He wished that a military band went before him, and pretended that the high hedges were solemn lines of men, stricken in awe to silence as their king rode out to some nobly self-chosen doom. Vast he seemed to himself, and magnificent like music, and solemn like the Sphinx. He had saved the earth from corruption by killing Evadne, for whom he now felt the unremorseful pity a conqueror might bestow on a devastated empire. He might have grieved that his victory brought him death, but with immense pride he found that the occasion was exactly described by a text. "He saved others, Himself He could not save."[9] He had missed the stile in the field above Sumatra Crescent and had to go back and hunt for it in the hedge. So quickly had his satisfaction borne him home.

The field had the fantastic air that jerry-builders[1] give to land poised on the knife-edge of town and country, so that he walked in romance to his very door. The unmarred grass sloped to a stone-hedge of towers of loose brick, trenches and mounds of shining clay, and the fine intentful spires of the scaffolding round the last unfinished house. And he looked down on Petrick. Though to the actual eye it was but a confusion of dark distances through the twilight, a breaking of velvety perspectives, he saw more intensely than ever before its squalid walls and squalid homes where mean men and mean women enlaced their unwholesome lives. Yet he did not shrink from entering for his great experience: as Christ did not shrink from being born in a stable. He swaggered with humility over the trodden mud of the field and the new white flags of Sumatra Crescent. Down the road before him there passed a dim figure, who paused at each lamp post and raised a long wand to behead the yellow gas-flowers that were now wilting before the dawn: a ghostly herald preparing the world to be his deathbed. The Crescent curved in quiet darkness, save for one house, where blazed a gas-lit room with undrawn blinds. The brightness had the startling quality of a scream. He looked in almost anxiously as he passed, and met the blank eyes of a man in evening clothes who stood by the window shaking a medicine. His face was like a wax mask softened by heat: the features were blurred with the suffering which comes from the spectacle of suffering. His eyes lay unshiftingly on George's face as he went by and he went on shaking the bottle. It seemed as though he would never stop.

In the hour of his grandeur George was not forgetful of the griefs of the little human people, but interceded with God for the sake of this stranger. Everything was beautiful, beautiful, beautiful.

His own little house looked solemn as a temple. He leaned against the lamppost at the gate and stared at its empty windows and neat bricks. The disorder of the shattered pane of glass could be overlooked by considering a sign that this house was a holy place: like the Passover blood on the lintel. The propriety of the evenly drawn

9. These are the words of the priests and elders mocking Jesus at his crucifixion; Matthew 27.42.

1. Low-wage, slipshod workers.

blind pleased him enormously. He had always known that this was how the great tragic things of the world had accomplished themselves: quietly. Evadne's raging activity belonged to trivial or annoying things like spring-cleaning or thunderstorms. Well, the house belonged to him now. He opened the gate and went up the asphalt path, sourly noticing that Evadne had as usual left out the lawn-mower, though it might very easily have rained, with the wind coming up as it was. A stray cat that had been sleeping in the tuft of pampas grass in the middle of the lawn was roused by his coming, and fled insolently close to his legs. He hated all wild homeless things, and bent for a stone to throw at it. But instead his fingers touched a slug, which reminded him of the feeling of Evadne's flesh through the slit in her bathing dress. And suddenly the garden was possessed by her presence: she seemed to amble there as she had so often done, sowing seeds unwisely and tormenting the last days of an ailing geranium by insane transplantation, exclaiming absurdly over such mere weeds as morning glory. He caught the very clucking of her voice. . . . The front door opened at his touch.

The little lobby with its closed doors seemed stuffed with expectant silence. He realised that he had come to the theatre of his great adventure. Then panic seized him. Because this was the home where he and she had lived together so horribly he doubted whether he could do this splendid momentous thing, for here he had always been a poor thing with the habit of failure. His heart beat in him more quickly than his raw feet could pad up the oil-clothed stairs. Behind the deal door at the end of the passage was death. Nothingness! It would escape him, even the idea of it would escape him if he did not go to it at once. When he burst at last into its presence he felt so victorious that he sank back against the door waiting for death to come to him without turning on the gas. He was so happy. His death was coming true.

But Evadne lay on his deathbed. She slept there soundly, with her head flung back on the pillows so that her eyes and brow seemed small in shadow, and her mouth and jaw huge above her thick throat in the light. Her wet hair straggled across the pillow on to a broken cane chair covered with her tumbled clothes. Her breast, silvered with sweat, shone in the ray of the street lamp that had always disturbed their nights. The counterpane rose enormously over her hips in rolls of glazed linen. Out of mere innocent sleep her sensuality was distilling a most drunken pleasure.

Not for one moment did he think this a phantasmic appearance. Evadne was not the sort of woman to have a ghost.

Still leaning against the door, he tried to think it all out: but his thoughts came brokenly, because the dawnlight flowing in at the window confused him by its pale glare and that lax figure on the bed held his attention. It must have been that when he laid his murderous hands on her head she had simply dropped below the surface and swum a few strokes under water as any expert swimmer can. Probably he had never even put her into danger, for she was a great lusty creature and the weir was a little place. He had imagined the wonder and peril of the battle as he had imagined his victory. He sneezed exhaustingly, and from his physical distress realised how absurd it was ever to have thought that he had killed her. Bodies like his do not kill bodies like hers.

Now his soul was naked and lonely as though the walls of his body had fallen in at death, and the grossness of Evadne's sleep made him suffer more unlovely a destitution than any old beggarwoman squatting by the roadside in the rain. He had thought he had had what every man most desires: one night of power over a woman for the business of murder or love. But it had been a lie. Nothing beautiful had ever happened to him. He would have wept, but the hatred he had learnt on the moors obstructed all tears in his throat. At least this night had given him passion enough to put an end to it all.

Quietly he went to the window and drew down the sash. There was no fireplace, so that sealed the room. Then he crept over to the gas bracket and raised his thin hand, as he had imagined in his hour of vain glory by the lake.

He had forgotten Evadne's thrifty habit of turning off the gas at the main to prevent leakage when she went to bed.

He was beaten. He undressed and got into bed: as he had done every night for ten years, and as he would do every night until he died. Still sleeping, Evadne caressed him with warm arms.

Ezra Pound: The New Cake of Soap *and* Salutation the Third

Ezra Loomis Pound (1885–1972) was one of the most important, and most controversial, poets of the twentieth century. Born in Idaho and raised outside of Philadelphia, he wrote poetry and studied literature and half a dozen languages in college and during two years of a Ph.D. program at the University of Pennsylvania. He left graduate school in 1907 to become a professor of Romance languages at Wabash Presbyterian College in Indiana. Pound's academic career lasted one semester, at which point he traveled to Spain and Italy before settling in London. He took on literary London in 1908 with a breathtaking amount of enthusiasm, energy, and old-fashioned American optimism; before long he had made influential friends like Yeats, the poet/philosopher T. E. Hulme, and the novelist Ford Madox Ford. He published three volumes of poetry in the two years 1909–1910, and began a series of posts editing poetry and arts magazines, becoming increasingly influential as an arbiter and theorist of experimental literature and art. He was one of the first to champion the writing of such young unknowns as D. H. Lawrence, T. S. Eliot, and James Joyce. In 1912–1914, he led the "Imagist" movement in poetry, which emphasized direct, spare language, in poems often based on moments of vision. His slogan "Make It New" became a rallying-cry for many writers of his time; so pervasive was his influence that the critic Hugh Kenner has labeled these years "The Pound Era."

In Pound's own work, the use of brief, imagistic lyrics coexisted with a tendency toward sprawling works of poetic, cultural, historical, and economic commentary, sometimes taking the form of books of cultural or economic theory, sometimes in radio broadcasts, and often in poetic form. His multi-year and multi-sectioned poem *The Cantos*, begun in 1915, ranging widely across European and world history and culture, was often written while Pound was involving himself in his own century's greatest conflicts. He developed an admiration for the Italian fascist leader Mussolini, and spent World War II in Rome, where he made hundreds of radio broadcasts denouncing the Allies and the Jewish bankers whom he believed were underwriting opposition to Fascism. Captured by American forces at the end of the war, he was imprisoned outside Pisa as a war criminal. There, he translated Confucius and wrote a notable section of the Cantos, *The Pisan Cantos*. He was then sent back to the United States, but was found mentally unfit for trial for treason; he was confined for twelve years in an insane asylum in Washington, D.C. Finally he was released in 1958; he returned to Italy, where he lived, largely in silence, until his death in 1972.

The New Cake of Soap

Lo, how it gleams and glistens in the sun
Like the cheek of a Chesterton[1]

Salutation the Third

Let us deride the smugness of "The Times":
GUFFAW!
   So much the gagged reviewers,
It will pay them when the worms are wriggling in their vitals;
5 These were they who objected to newness,
HERE are their TOMB-STONES.
   They supported the gag and the ring:
A little black BOX contains them.
   SO shall you be also,
10 You slut-bellied obstructionist,
   You sworn foe to free speech and good letters,
You fungus, you continuous gangrene.

Come, let us on with the new deal,
   Let us be done with Jews and Jobbery,[1]
15 Let us SPIT upon those who fawn on the JEWS for their money,
Let us out to the pastures.

PERHAPS I will die at thirty,
Perhaps you will have the pleasure of defiling my pauper's grave,
I wish you JOY, I proffer you ALL my assistance.
20 It has been your HABIT for long to do away with true poets,
You either drive them mad,[2] or else you blink at their suicides,
Or else you condone their drugs, and talk of insanity and genius,
BUT I will not go mad to please you.
   I will not FLATTER you with an early death.
25 OH, NO! I will stick it out,
   I will feel your hates wriggling about my feet,
And I will laugh at you and mock you,
And I will offer you consolations in irony,
   O fools, detesters of Beauty.

30 I have seen many who go about with supplications,
   Afraid to say how they hate you.
HERE is the taste of my BOOT,
   CARESS it, lick off the BLACKING.

1. G. K. Chesterton (1874–1936), popular essayist and fiction writer. Pound disliked him both for his popularity, and because he was reported to have said "If a thing is worth doing, it's worth doing badly."

1. Pound's anti-Semitism was deep-seated and lifelong; some of his *Cantos* were censored on first publication because of their ugly portrayals of the Jews, who Pound believed to be responsible for international economic instability. When he revised the poem for inclusion in the 1926 edition of his collection *Personae*, Pound changed these lines to read: "Let us be done with panders and jobbery, / Let us spit upon those who pat the big-bellies for profit." Jobbery: Corruption in the conduct of public affairs.

2. Pound may intend a reference here to the savage review of Keats's *Endymion* that appeared in the *Quarterly Review* and was believed to have caused, or at least hastened, Keats's death; Shelley refers to this incident in "Adonais."

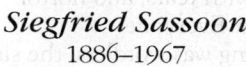

Rupert Brooke
1887–1915

Rupert Brooke was the first of Britain's "war poets," and the last poem he completed during his short lifetime—*The Soldier*—is alone enough to guarantee his lasting place in modern poetry.

Brooke rose with extraordinary speed to the center of the British literary establishment. While an undergraduate, he worked with the *Cambridge Review* and came into contact with such influential writers as Henry James, W. B. Yeats, Virginia Woolf, and Lytton Strachey, and the editor and publisher Edward Marsh. In 1912, after the publication of his first volume of poetry, Brooke suffered a nervous breakdown; after a short recovery period, he spent most of the next three years traveling. World War I began shortly after he returned to England in the spring of 1914; Brooke enlisted immediately and was commissioned on a ship that sailed to Antwerp, Belgium, where Brooke saw no action through early 1915. During this lull, Brooke wrote the war sonnets for which he is best remembered today. While his ship was sailing to Gallipoli, Brooke died of blood poisoning, before seeing combat duty.

It is nearly impossible, even at this late date, to separate Brooke the myth from Brooke the poet; he was something of a national hero even before his death, thanks to the popular reception of his volume of war sonnets, *Nineteen Fourteen*. In Brooke's writings about the war, the irony of early poems like *Heaven* ("And in that Heaven of all their wish, / There shall be no more land, say fish") falls away. These patriotic poems—and most especially *The Soldier*, in which Brooke seemed to have foreseen his own death—meshed perfectly with the temperament of the British people as the nation entered into war. When *The Soldier* was read aloud at Saint Paul's Cathedral in London on Easter Sunday, 1915, Brooke the man—whom Yeats called "the handsomest man in England"—was permanently immortalized as the symbol of English pride.

The Soldier

If I should die, think only this of me:
    That there's some corner of a foreign field
That is forever England. There shall be
    In that rich earth a richer dust concealed;
5 A dust whom England bore, shaped, made aware,
    Gave, once, her flowers to love, her ways to roam,
A body of England's, breathing English air,
    Washed by the rivers, blest by suns of home.

And think, this heart, all evil shed away,
10   A pulse in the Eternal mind, no less
        Gives somewhere back the thoughts by England given,
Her sights and sounds; dreams happy as her day;
    And laughter, learnt of friends; and gentleness,
        In hearts at peace, under an English heaven.

Siegfried Sassoon
1886–1967

It is tempting to describe a poet like Siegfried Sassoon by emphasizing his differences from the hugely popular Rupert Brooke. Sassoon was born to a wealthy Jewish family, who made their fortune in India; he lived a life of ease before the war, writing slight Georgian poetry and hunting foxes. World War I suddenly and unequivocally changed all that. Sassoon served with the Royal Welsh Fusiliers, and before the end of 1915 saw action in France; he helped a wounded soldier to safety during heavy fire, for which he was awarded a Military Cross. After being wounded himself, Sassoon refused to return to battle; from his hospital bed, he wrote an open letter to the war department suggesting that the war was being unnecessarily prolonged, and as a result, he narrowly avoided a court-martial. Owing to the intervention of his fellow soldier the poet Robert Graves, he was instead committed to a hospital and treated for "shell-shock." He returned to the front in 1919, and was wounded a second time.

Where the war poetry of Brooke is patriotic to the point of sentimentality, Sassoon's verse is characterized by an unrelentingly realistic portrayal of the horrors of modern warfare. And where Brooke's poetry was eagerly welcomed by an anxious public, Sassoon's was largely rejected as either unpatriotic or unnecessarily grotesque. After the war, he lived in seclusion in the country, writing memoirs and poetry—though rarely with the shock value of his early war poems.

Glory of Women

You love us when we're heroes, home on leave,
Or wounded in a mentionable place.
You worship decorations; you believe
That chivalry redeems the war's disgrace.
5   You make us shells. You listen with delight,
By tales of dirt and danger fondly thrilled.
You crown our distant ardours while we fight,
And mourn our laurelled memories when we're killed.
You can't believe that British troops "retire"
10   When hell's last horror breaks them, and they run,
Trampling the terrible corpses—blind with blood.
    O German mother dreaming by the fire,
While you are knitting socks to send your son
His face is trodden deeper in the mud.
Craiglockhart,[1] 1917

Everyone Sang

Everyone suddenly burst out singing;
And I was filled with such delight
As prisoned birds must find in freedom,
Winging wildly across the white
5   Orchards and dark-green fields; on—on—and out of sight.
Everyone's voice was suddenly lifted;
And beauty came like the setting sun:
My heart was shaken with tears; and horror
Drifted away . . . O, but Everyone
10   Was a bird; and the song was wordless; the singing will never be done.
April 1919

1. A hospital near Edinburgh, Scotland, where Sassoon (along with Wilfred Owen) was treated for shell shock.

Wilfred Owen
1893–1918

The poet C. Day Lewis wrote that Owen's poems were "certainly the finest written by any English poet of the First War." In his small body of poems Owen manages to combine his friend Siegfried Sassoon's outrage at the horror of the war with a formal and technical skill reminiscent of his idols Keats and Shelley. Sassoon himself characterized their differences as poets this way: "My trench-sketches were like rockets, sent up to illuminate the darkness. . . . It was Owen who revealed how, out of realistic horror and scorn, poetry might be made."

Owen grew up on the Welsh border in Shropshire, the landscape A. E. Housman was to celebrate in his poetry. After finishing technical school, Owen spent two years in training with an evangelical Church of England vicar, trying to decide whether to pursue formal training as a clergyman. As a result of his experiences, Owen became dissatisfied with the institutional church's response to the poverty and suffering of England's least privileged citizens. In October 1915 he enlisted with the Artists' Rifles, and on 29 December 1916, he left for France as a lieutenant with the Lancashire Fusiliers.

Owen quickly became disillusioned with the war; as a result of almost unimaginable privations, which included being blown into the air while he slept in a foxhole, Owen suffered a breakdown, and was sent to the Craiglockhart War Hospital in Edinburgh. Owen composed nearly all of his poetry in the fourteen months of his rehabilitation, between August 1917 and September 1918; though hard to imagine, it is quite possible that if he had not been sent back to Great Britain to recover from his "shell shock," we might now know nothing of his poetry. While at Craiglockhart he met Sassoon and found his true voice and mode; he published his first poems on war themes anonymously in the hospital's magazine, which he edited. In September 1918 Owen returned to the battlefields of France; he was killed in action at Sambre Canal on November 4, 1918, one week before the Armistice. Dylan Thomas called Owen "one of the four most profound influences upon the poets who came after him"—the others being Hopkins, Yeats, and Eliot.

Anthem for Doomed Youth

What passing-bells for these who die as cattle?
　　Only the monstrous anger of the guns.
　　Only the stuttering rifles' rapid rattle
Can patter out their hasty orisons.°　　　　　　　　　　　　　　　*prayers*
5　No mockeries now for them; no prayers nor bells,
　　Nor any voice of mourning save the choirs,—
The shrill, demented choirs of wailing shells;
　　And bugles calling for them from sad shires.

What candles may be held to speed them all?
10　　Not in the hands of boys, but in their eyes
Shall shine the holy glimmers of good-byes.
　　The pallor of girls' brows shall be their pall;[1]
Their flowers the tenderness of patient minds,
And each slow dusk a drawing-down of blinds.

---

1. The cloth draped over a coffin.

Strange Meeting

It seemed that out of battle I escaped
Down some profound dull tunnel, long since scooped
Through granites which titanic wars had groined.°   *joined together*
Yet also there encumbered sleepers groaned,
5   Too fast in thought or death to be bestirred.
Then, as I probed them, one sprang up, and stared
With piteous recognition in fixed eyes,
Lifting distressful hands as if to bless.
And by his smile, I knew that sullen hall,
10 By his dead smile I knew we stood in Hell.
With a thousand pains that vision's face was grained;
Yet no blood reached there from the upper ground,
And no guns thumped, or down the flues made moan.
"Strange friend," I said, "here is no cause to mourn."
15 "None," said that other, "save the undone years,
The hopelessness. Whatever hope is yours,
Was my life also; I went hunting wild
After the wildest beauty in the world,
Which lies not calm in eyes, or braided hair,
20 But mocks the steady running of the hour,
And if it grieves, grieves richlier than here.
For of my glee might many men have laughed,
And of my weeping something had been left,
Which must die now. I mean the truth untold,
25 The pity of war, the pity war distilled.
Now men will go content with what we spoiled,
Or, discontent, boil bloody, and be spilled.
They will be swift with swiftness of the tigress.
None will break ranks, though nations trek from progress.
30 Courage was mine, and I had mystery,
Wisdom was mine, and I had mastery:
To miss the march of this retreating world
Into vain citadels that are not walled.
Then, when much blood had clogged their chariot-wheels,
35 I would go up and wash them from sweet wells,
Even with truths that lie too deep for taint.
I would have poured my spirit without stint
But not through wounds; not on the cess of war.
Foreheads of men have bled where no wounds were.
40 I am the enemy you killed, my friend.
I knew you in this dark: for so you frowned
Yesterday through me as you jabbed and killed.
I parried; but my hands were loath and cold.
Let us sleep now. . . ."

Dulce Et Decorum Est[1]

Bent double, like old beggars under sacks,
Knock-kneed, coughing like hags, we cursed through sludge,

---

1. From the *Odes* of the Roman satirist Horace (65–8 B.C.): Dulce et decorum est pro patria mori [sweet and fitting it is to die for your fatherland].

Till on the haunting flares we turned our backs
And towards our distant rest began to trudge.
5   Men marched asleep. Many had lost their boots
But limped on, blood-shod. All went lame; all blind;
Drunk with fatigue; deaf even to the hoots
Of tired, outstripped Five-Nines[2] that dropped behind.

Gas! Gas! Quick, boys!—An ecstasy of fumbling,
10   Fitting the clumsy helmets just in time;
But someone still was yelling out and stumbling
And flound'ring like a man in fire or lime[3] . . .
Dim, through the misty panes and thick green light,
As under a green sea, I saw him drowning.

15   In all my dreams, before my helpless sight,
He plunges at me, guttering, choking, drowning.

If in some smothering dreams you too could pace
Behind the wagon that we flung him in,
And watch the white eyes writhing in his face,
20   His hanging face, like a devil's sick of sin;
If you could hear, at every jolt, the blood
Come gargling from the froth-corrupted lungs,
Obscene as cancer, bitter as the cud
Of vile, incurable sores on innocent tongues,—
25   My friend, you would not tell with such high zest
To children ardent for some desperate glory,
The old Lie: Dulce et decorum est
Pro patria mori.

———— ⌖ ————

Isaac Rosenberg
1890–1918

World War I was the spur that goaded some poets, like Wilfred Owen, into the writing of poetry; for Isaac Rosenberg the war was simply the catalyst for a more vivid and powerful verse. Rosenberg began writing poetry on Jewish themes when he was just fifteen; he had published two volumes of poems and a verse play, *Moses,* by the time he joined the army in 1916. Rosenberg's experience of the war was, in important ways, different from the other poets represented here. To begin with, he was the son of Lithuanian Jewish immigrants who had settled in the East End, London's Jewish ghetto. As a child, Rosenberg lived with severe poverty; he was forced to leave school at fourteen to help support his family. He went to war not as an officer, but as a private; as the critic Irving Howe writes, "No glamorous fatality hangs over Rosenberg's head: he was just a clumsy, stuttering Jewish doughboy." He was killed while on patrol outside the trenches—a private's dangerous assignment.

His experiences on the Western Front seem to have provided him with the perfect canvas for his essentially religious art. Siegfried Sassoon, alluding to Rosenberg's training as an artist at the Slade School, later described his poems as "scriptural and sculptural": "His experiments were a strenuous effort for impassioned expression; his imagination had a sinewy and muscular aliveness; often he saw things in terms of sculpture, but he did not carve or chisel; he *modeled*

2. Artillery shells used by the Germans.   3. Calcium oxide, a powerfully caustic alkali used, among
                                                             other purposes, for cleaning the flesh off the bones of corpses.

words with fierce energy and aspiration." His less-than-genteel background also made Rosenberg impatient with the patriotic sentiments of a poet like Rupert Brooke, for whose "begloried sonnets" he had nothing but contempt. In the poetry of Rosenberg, by contrast—according to Sassoon—"words and images obey him, instead of leading him into over-elaboration." Interest in Rosenberg's poetry has recently been revived by critics interested in his use of Jewish themes; the critic Harold Bloom, for instance, calls Rosenberg "an English poet with a Jewish difference," and suggests that he is "the best Jewish poet writing in English that our century has given us."

Break of Day in the Trenches

The darkness crumbles away—
It is the same old druid[1] Time as ever.
Only a live thing leaps my hand—
A queer sardonic rat—
5   As I pull the parapet's poppy
To stick behind my ear.
Droll rat, they would shoot you if they knew
Your cosmopolitan sympathies.
Now you have touched this English hand
10   You will do the same to a German—
Soon, no doubt, if it be your pleasure
To cross the sleeping green between.
It seems you inwardly grin as you pass
Strong eyes, fine limbs, haughty athletes
15   Less chanced than you for life,
Bonds to the whims of murder,
Sprawled in the bowels of the earth,
The torn fields of France.
What do you see in our eyes
20   At the shrieking iron and flame
Hurled through still heavens?
What quaver—what heart aghast?
Poppies whose roots are in man's veins
Drop, and are ever dropping;
25   But mine in my ear is safe,
Just a little white with the dust.

1916   1922

David Jones
1895–1974

David Jones's long narrative poem *In Parenthesis* is arguably the great literary text of World War I. While other poets have more vividly recreated the horrors of the war, and prose chroniclers like Robert Graves have analyzed more precisely the futility and banality of trench warfare, Jones's "writing"—the only generic label he was willing to assign *In Parenthesis*—combines the resources of both poetry and prose, and brings to bear a historical, religious, and

---

1. Member of an ancient Celtic religion.

mythical framework through which to understand the war. In Jones's text the Great War is revealed to be just the most recent battle in the great war that is human history.

Jones was born near London to an English mother and Welsh father; his father impressed upon him the richness of his Welsh heritage. After leaving grammar school, Jones enrolled in art school; when war broke out, however, he was quick to enlist, and joined the Royal Welch Fusiliers as an infantryman in January 1915. He served on the Western Front until March 1918, having been wounded at the battle of the Somme in June 1916; he remarked later that the war "had a permanent effect upon me and has affected my work in all sorts of ways." After the war, Jones went to Ditchling Common, a Catholic artists' guild run by the writer and sculptor Eric Gill. Jones was attracted to Gill's regimen of work and prayer; he converted to Roman Catholicism in 1921 and soon joined the guild, where he lived and worked until 1933.

Jones did not begin to write *In Parenthesis* until 1928. The poem tells the story of Private John Ball, from his embarkation from England in December 1915 to the battle of the Somme. The text modulates from straightforward narrative to a kind of prose poetry to stretches of pure poetry, incorporating echoes and allusions of texts, from the Welsh epic *The Mabinogion* to the medieval battle epic *Y Gododdin* to Malory's *Morte d'Arthur* to Shakespeare's history plays to Eliot's *The Waste Land*—as well as drawing from "subliterary" sources such as soldier's slang. *In Parenthesis* is difficult and allusive, as are many other monumental works of modernist literature, like Joyce's *Ulysses* and *Finnegans Wake*, Pound's *Cantos*, and Eliot's *The Waste Land*. While this difficulty has sometimes kept away the readers Jones deserves, the critic Thomas Dilworth calls *In Parenthesis* "the only authentic and successful epic poem in the language since *Paradise Lost*."

In Parenthesis differs from other war poetry in argument as well as form; the poem is not simply a protest against the war but rather an attempt to place the war into a world-historical context. As the critic Samuel Rees writes, it "is not a poem either to provoke or to end a war . . . except as it adds to the accumulation of testimony to the stupidities and brutality of history that each age must learn from or, more likely, ignore." In the writing he produced after *In Parenthesis* Jones continued to be concerned with contemporary society's loss of interest in the past, and with the depersonalizing effects of technology; his other great poem, *The Anathemata*, was judged by W. H. Auden to be "probably the finest long poem in English in this century."

from In Parenthesis[1]
Part 1. The Many Men So Beautiful[2]

'49 Wyatt, 01549 Wyatt.
Coming sergeant.
Pick 'em up, pick 'em up—I'll stalk within yer chamber.
Private Leg . . . sick.
Private Ball . . . absent.
'01 Ball, '01 Ball, Ball of No. 1.
Where's Ball, 2501 Ball—you corporal,
Ball of your section.
Movement round and about the Commanding Officer.
Bugler, will you sound "Orderly Sergeants."

---

1. In his preface, Jones writes: "This writing is called 'In Parenthesis' because I have written it in a kind of space between—I don't know between quite what—but as you turn aside to do something; and because for us amateur soldiers (and especially for the writer, who was not only an amateur, but grotesquely incompetent, a knocker-over of piles, a parade's despair) the war itself was a parenthe-

sis—how glad we thought we were to step outside its brackets at the end of '18—and also because our curious type of existence here is altogether in parenthesis."
2. Coleridge, *Ancient Mariner*, part iv, verse 4 [Jones's note]. "The many men, so beautiful! / And they all dead did lie: / And a thousand thousand slimy things / Lived on; and so did I."

David Jones. Etching
of World War I soldier
(frontispiece to *In
Parenthesis*). 1937.

A hurrying of feet from three companies converging on the little group apart
where on horses sit the central command. But from "B" Company there is no such
darting out. The Orderly Sergeant of "B" is licking the stub end of his lead pencil; it
divides a little his fairish moist moustache.

Heavily jolting and sideway jostling, the noise of liquid shaken in a small vessel
by a regular jogging movement, a certain clinking ending in a shuffling of the feet
sidelong—all clear and distinct in that silence peculiar to parade grounds and to
refectories. The silence of a high order, full of peril in the breaking of it, like the
coming on parade of John Ball.

He settles between numbers 4 and 5 of the rear rank. It is as ineffectual as the
ostrich in her sand. Captain Gwynn does not turn or move or give any sign.

Have that man's name taken if you please, Mr. Jenkins.

Take that man's name, Sergeant Snell.

Take his name, corporal.

Take his name take his number—charge him—late on parade—the Battalion
being paraded for overseas—warn him for Company Office.

Have you got his name Corporal Quilter.

Temporary unpaid Lance-Corporal Aneirin Merddyn Lewis had somewhere in his Welsh depths a remembrance of the nature of man, of how a lance-corporal's stripe is but held vicariously and from on high, is of one texture with an eternal economy. He brings in a manner, baptism, and metaphysical order to the bankruptcy of the occasion.

'01 Ball is it—there was a man in Bethesda late for the last bloody judgment.

Corporal Quilter on the other hand knew nothing of these things.

Private Ball's pack, ill adjusted and without form, hangs more heavily on his shoulder blades, a sense of ill-usage pervades him. He withdraws within himself to soothe himself—the inequity of those in high places is forgotten. From where he stood heavily, irksomely at ease, he could see, half-left between 7 and 8 of the front rank, the profile of Mr. Jenkins and the elegant cut of his war-time rig and his flax head held front; like San Romano's[3] foreground squire, unhelmeted; but we don't have lances now nor banners nor trumpets. It pains the lips to think of bugles—and did they blow Defaulters[4] on the Uccello horns.

He put his right hand behind him to ease his pack, his cold knuckles find something metallic and colder.

No mess-tin cover.

Shining sanded mess-tin giving back the cold early light. *Improperly dressed, the Battalion being paraded for overseas.* His imaginings as to the precise relationship of this general indictment from the book to his own naked mess-tin were with suddenness and most imperatively impinged upon, as when an animal hunted, stopping in some ill-chosen covert to consider the wickedness of man, is started into fresh effort by the cry and breath of dogs dangerously and newly near. For the chief huntsman is winding his horn, the officer commanding is calling his Battalion by name—whose own the sheep are.

55th Battalion!

Fifty-fifth Bat-tal-i-on

'talion!!

From "D" to "A" his eyes knew that parade. He detected no movement. They were properly at ease.

Reverberation of that sudden command broke hollowly upon the emptied huts behind "D" Company's rear platoons. They had only in them the rolled mattresses, the neatly piled bed-boards and the empty tea-buckets of the orderly-men, emptied of their last gun-fire.[5]

Stirrups taut and pressing upward in the midst of his saddle he continues the ritual words by virtue of which a regiment is moved in column of route:

. . . the Battalion will move in column of fours to the right—"A" Company—"A" Company leading.

Words lost, yet given continuity by that thinner command from in front of No. 1. Itself to be wholly swallowed up by the concerted movement of arms in which the spoken word effected what it signified.

"A" Company came to the slope, their files of four turn right. The complex of command and heel-iron turned confuse the morning air. The rigid structure of their lines knows a swift mobility, patterns differently for those sharp successive cries.

---

3. Cf. painting, "Rout of San Romano." Paolo Uccello (Nat. Gal.) [Jones's note].
4. Soldiers convicted by a court-martial.

5. Tea served to troops before first parade. Rouse parade [Jones's note].

Mr. P. D. I. Jenkins who is twenty years old has now to do his business:
No. 7 Platoon—number seven.
number seven—right—by the right.
How they sway in the swing round for all this multiplicity of gear.
Keept'y'r dressing.
Sergeant Snell did his bit.
Corporal Quilter intones:
Dress to the right—no—other right.
Keep those slopes.
Keep those sections of four.
Pick those knees up.
Throw those chests out.
Hold those heads up.
Stop that talking.
Keep those chins in.
Left left lef'—lef' righ' lef'—you Private Ball it's you I'v got me glad-eye on.

So they came outside the camp. The liturgy of a regiment departing has been sung.
Empty wet parade ground. A campwarden, some unfit men and other details loiter,
dribble away, shuffle off like men whose ship has sailed.

The long hutment lines stand. Not a soul. It rains harder: torn felt lifts to the
wind above Hut 10, Headquarter Company; urinal concrete echoes for a solitary
whistler. Corrugated iron empty—no one. Chill gust slams the vacant canteen door.

Miss Veronica Best who runs the hut for the bun-wallahs[6] stretches on her palliasse,[7]
she's sleepy, she can hear the band: We've got too many buns—and all those wads[8]—
you knew they were going—why did you order them—they won't be in after rouse-
parade even—they've gone.

Know they've gone—shut up—Jocks from Bardown move in Monday. Violet
turns to sleep again.

Horses' tails are rather good—and the way this one springs from her groomed flanks.
He turns slightly in his saddle.
You may march at ease.
No one said march easy Private Ball, you're bleedin' quick at some things ain't yer.

The Squire from the Rout of San Romano smokes Melachrino No. 9.
The men may march easy and smoke, Sergeant Snell.

Some like tight belts and some like loose belts—trussed-up pockets—cigarettes in
ammunition pouches—rifle-bolts, webbing, buckles and rain—gotta light mate—
give us a match chum. How cold the morning is and blue, and how mysterious in
cupped hands glow the match-lights of a concourse of men, moving so early in the
morning.

The body of the high figure in front of the head of the column seemed to change
his position however so slightly. It rains on the transparent talc of his map-case.

The Major's horse rubs noses with the horse of the superior officer. Their docked
manes brush each, as two friends would meet. The dark horse snorts a little for the
pulling at her bridle rein.

6. Person pertaining to: e.g. staff-wallah; person addicted   7. Straw mattress.
to: e.g. bun-wallah [Jones's note].   8. Canteen sandwiches [Jones's note].

In "D" Company round the bend of the road in the half-light is movement, like a train shunting, when the forward coaches buffer the rear coaches back. The halt was unexpected. How heavy and how top-heavy is all this martial panoply and how the ground seems to press upward to afflict the feet.

The bastard's lost his way already.

Various messages are passed.

Some lean on their rifles as aged men do on sticks in stage-plays. Some lean back with the muzzle of the rifle supporting the pack in the position of gentlewomen at field sports, but not with so great assurance.

It's cold when you stop marching with all this weight and icy down the back.

Battalion cyclists pass the length of the column. There is fresh stir in "A" Company.

Keep your column distance.

The regular rhythm of the march has re-established itself.

The rain increases with the light and the weight increases with the rain. In all that long column in brand-new overseas boots weeping blisters stick to the hard wool of grey government socks.

I'm bleedin' cripple already Corporal, confides a limping child.

Kipt' that step there.

Keep that proper distance.

Keept' y'r siction o' four—can't fall out me little darlin'.

Corporal Quilter subsides, he too retreats within himself, he has his private thoughts also.

It's a proper massacre of the innocents in a manner of speaking, no so-called seven ages o' man only this bastard military age.

Keep that step there.

Keep that section distance.

Hand us thet gas-pipe young Saunders—let's see you shape—you too, little Benjamin—hang him about like a goddam Chris'us tree—use his ample shoulders for an armoury-rack—it is his part to succour the lambs of the flock.

With some slackening of the rain the band had wiped their instruments. Broken catches on the wind-gust came shrilly back:

Of Hector and Lysander and such great names as these—the march proper to them.[9]

So they went most of that day and it rained with increasing vigour until night-fall. In the middle afternoon the outer parts of the town of embarkation were reached. They halted for a brief while; adjusted puttees,[1] straightened caps, fastened undone buttons, tightened rifle-slings and attended each one to his own bedraggled and irregular condition. The band recommenced playing; and at the attention and in excellent step they passed through the suburbs, the town's centre, and so towards the docks. The people of that town did not acclaim them, nor stop about their business—for it was late in the second year.[2]

By some effort of a corporate will the soldierly bearing of the text books maintained itself through the town, but with a realisation of the considerable distance yet to be covered through miles of dock, their frailty reasserted itself—which slackening called for fresh effort from the Quilters and the Snells, but at this stage with a more persuasive intonation, with almost motherly concern.

9. *The British Grenadiers* is the ceremonial march of all Grenadier and Fusilier Regiments [Jones's note].

1. Leggings.

2. That is to say in December 1915 [Jones's note].

Out of step and with a depressing raggedness of movement and rankling of tempers they covered another mile between dismal sheds, high and tarred. Here funnels and mastheads could be seen. Here the influence of the sea and of the tackle and ways of its people fell upon them. They revived somewhat, and for a while. Yet still these interminable ways between—these incessant halts at junctions. Once they about-turned. Embarkation officers, staff people of all kinds and people who looked as though they were in the Navy but who were not, consulted with the Battalion Commander. A few more halts, more passing of messages,—a further intensifying of their fatigue. The platoons of the leading company unexpectedly wheel. The spacious shed is open at either end, windy and comfortless. Multifarious accoutrements, metal and cloth and leather sink with the perspiring bodies to the concrete floor.

Certain less fortunate men were detailed for guard, John Ball amongst them. The others lay, where they first sank down, wet with rain and sweat. They smoked; they got very cold. They were given tins of bully beef and ration biscuits for the first time, and felt like real expeditionary soldiers. Sometime between midnight and 2 a.m. they were paraded. Slowly, and with every sort of hitch, platoon upon platoon formed single file and moved toward an invisible gangway. Each separate man found his own feet stepping in the darkness on an inclined plane, the smell and taste of salt and machinery, the texture of rope, and the glimmer of shielded light about him.

So without sound of farewell or acclamation, shrouded in a dense windy darkness, they set toward France. They stood close on deck and beneath deck, each man upholstered in his life-belt. From time to time a seaman would push between them about some duty belonging to his trade.

Under a high-slung arc-light whose cold clarity well displayed all their sea weariness, their long cramped-upness and fatigue, they stumblingly and one by one trickled from the ship on to French land. German prisoners in green tunics, made greener by the light, heavily unloading timber at a line of trucks—it still rained, and a bitter wind in from the sea.

A young man, comfortable in a short fleece jacket, stood smoking, immediately beneath the centre of the arc—he gave orders in a pleasant voice, that measured the leisure of his circumstances and of his class. Men move to left and right within the orbit of the light, and away into the half darkness, undefined, beyond it.

"B" Company were conducted by a guide, through back ways between high shuttered buildings, to horse-stalls, where they slept. In the morning, they were given Field Service postcards—and sitting in the straw they crossed out what did not apply, and sent them to their mothers, to their sweethearts.

Toward evening on the same day they entrained in cattle trucks; and on the third day, which was a Sunday, sunny and cold, and French women in deep black were hurrying across flat land—they descended from their grimy, littered, limb restricting, slatted vehicles, and stretched and shivered at a siding. You feel exposed and apprehensive in this new world.

from *Part 7. The Five Unmistakable Marks*[3]

At the gate of the wood you try a last adjustment, but slung so, it's an impediment, it's of detriment to your hopes, you had best be rid of it—the sagging web-

---

3. Printed here is the conclusion to the chapter, which closes *In Parenthesis*. The chapter's title comes from Lewis Carroll's narrative poem *The Hunting of the Snark*, which concerns a voyage in search of the Snark; "warranted, genuine Snarks" can be identified by "five unmistakable marks." The poem ends with the death of the explorer who discovers the Snark.

bing and all and what's left of your two fifty—but it were wise to hold on to your
mask.

You're clumsy in your feebleness, you implicate your tin-hat rim with the slack sling of it.
    Let it lie for the dews to rust it, or ought you to decently cover the working parts.
    Its dark barrel, where you leave it under the oak, reflects the solemn star that ris-
es urgently from Cliff Trench.
    It's a beautiful doll for us
it's the Last Reputable Arm.
    But leave it—under the oak.
leave it for a Cook's tourist to the Devastated Areas[4] and crawl as far as you can and
wait for the bearers.

Mrs. Willy Hartington has learned to draw sheets and so has Miss Melpomené;[5] and
on the south lawns,
men walk in red white and blue
under the cedars
and by every green tree
and beside comfortable waters.
But why dont the bastards come—
Bearers!—stret-cher bear-errs!
or do they divide the spoils at the Aid-Post.[6]
    But how many men do you suppose could bear away a third of us: drag just a lit-
tle further—he yet may counter-attack.

Lie still under the oak
next to the Jerry
and Sergeant Jerry Coke.
    The feet of the reserves going up tread level with your forehead; and no word for
you; they whisper one with another; pass on, inward;
these latest succours:
green Kimmerii[7] to bear up the war.

Oeth and Annoeth's hosts they were
who in that night grew
younger men
younger striplings.[8]

The geste says this and the man who was on the field . . . and who wrote the book . . .
the man who does not know this has not understood anything.[9]

---

4. This may appear to be an anachronism, but I remember
in 1917 discussing with a friend the possibilities of tourist
activity if peace ever came. I remember we went into
details and wondered if the inexploded projectile lying
near us would go up under a holiday-maker, and how people would stand to be photographed on our parapets. I
recall feeling very angry about this, as you do if you think
of strangers ever occupying a house you live in, and
which has, for you, particular associations [Jones's note].
5. Greek muse of tragedy.
6. The R.A.M.C. was suspected by disgruntled men of the
fighting units of purloining articles from the kit of the
wounded and the dead. Their regimental initials were commonly interpreted: "Rob All My Comrades" [Jones's note].
7. In Homer, the Kimmerioi were a race who lived in

eternal darkness, "on whom the sun never looks."
8. Cf. Englyn 30 of the Englynion y Beddeu, "The Stanzas
of the Graves." See Rhys, Origin of the Englyn, Y Cymm-
rodor, vol. xviii. Oeth and Annoeth's hosts occur in
Welsh tradition as a mysterious body of troops that seem
to have some affinity with the Legions. They were said to
"fight as well in the covert as in the open." Cf. The Iolo
MSS [Jones's note].
9. Cf. Chanson de Roland, lines 2095–8:

    Co dit la geste e cil qui el camp fut,
    [Li ber Gilie por qui Deus fait vertuz]
    E fist la chartre [el muster de Loum].
    Ki tant ne set, ne l'ad prod entendut.

I have used Mr. Rene Hague's translation [Jones's note].

Speeches on Irish Independence

Through the eight centuries of British rule in Ireland, Irish nationalist sentiment remained strong, though it was often forced underground. Ireland had gained a hundred members in the British Parliament when the United Kingdom was formed in 1801, yet on crucial issues they were regularly outvoted by the English majority. As Ireland gradually recovered from the effects of the famine of the 1840s, nationalist agitation increased, only inflamed by English attempts at repression. In 1870 the Home Rule League was formed, to press for legislative independence. In 1877 the League elected as its parliamentary leader a bold young nationalist named Charles Stewart Parnell (1846–1891), who came to dominate the movement for the ensuing dozen years; his tragic fall from power in 1889 shocked both his supporters and his detractors. For Yeats and Joyce especially, Parnell was proof of their suspicion that, as Joyce's character Stephen Dedalus was to put it, Ireland is "the old sow that eats her farrow."

Parnell assembled a powerful coalition in Parliament, bringing other business to a halt until Irish issues were considered. After years of negotiation, the Liberal prime minister Gladstone agreed to introduce a Home Rule bill in 1886. The bill was defeated, but passage was believed to be just a matter of time. Parnell's fortunes were quickly to turn, however. On Christmas Eve, 1889, Captain William O'Shea, a moderate Home Rule member, brought a divorce action against his wife Katherine ("Kitty"), and named Parnell as respondent. Parnell had been conducting an affair with Kitty O'Shea since 1880; some suggest that Captain O'Shea had long known this, and brought the action at this point for political gain. As a result of the divorce, the Irish parliamentary party removed Parnell from the leadership, and the Catholic hierarchy in Ireland turned against him, declaring him unfit for public office; a large portion of the Irish people abandoned him as well. Others, especially in Dublin, remained fiercely loyal to Parnell; but he was a broken man, and died just a few months after his marriage to Kitty O'Shea in June 1891.

The ensuing years were marked by token reforms and by division in Ireland, between ardent nationalists, moderate reformers, and Protestants who opposed weakened ties to England. The Irish republic can be dated from the Easter Rising in 1916 which, though unsuccessful, started the movement toward Irish independence which resulted six years later in the founding of the Irish Free State. After the failure of a third Home Rule bill in 1914, the Irish Republican Brotherhood stepped up their activities and began planning for a large-scale revolutionary uprising. In the spring of 1916 the Irish statesman Sir Roger Casement traveled to Germany to raise support for the planned uprising, but he managed only to obtain some obsolete firearms and was arrested on his return to Ireland. Three days later, on Easter Monday, April 24, a small force of about a thousand rebels seized the General Post Office and other city buildings, and declared a provisional Republican government, in a stirring proclamation read on the Post Office steps by Padraic Pearce, the planned president. W. B. Yeats vividly evokes that historical moment, and its transformation into nationalist mythology, in his poem *Easter 1916*. Street fighting continued for about a week, until Pearse and other leaders were forced to surrender. The execution of these leaders helped to rally support for the Republican cause among the Irish people and contributed to the founding of the Irish Republican Army (IRA) in 1919. Guided by the brilliant tactician Michael Collins, the IRA harrassed British troops and kept them from crushing the nationalist resistance.

As a result of this ongoing state of virtual civil war, the British government was ultimately forced to pass the Government of Ireland Act in 1920, dividing Ireland into two self-governing areas, Northern Ireland and Southern Ireland. Historically, the south has been primarily Catholic (currently more than 90 percent), and the north Protestant (about 65 percent); all twentieth-century political divisions of Ireland have been made with the awareness of these religious and cultural differences. At the close of 1921, the Anglo-Irish Treaty laid the groundwork for Ireland's twenty-six southern counties to establish an Irish Free State, the Republic of

Ireland; the six counties of Northern Ireland would retain their status as a member of the United Kingdom. Michael Collins, who negotiated the 1921 treaty, was ambushed and killed in 1922 by opponents of Irish partition. This division of the island remains in effect today, although recurrent terrorist violence of the IRA has been directed at winning independence as well for Northern Ireland. Thus while Ireland and England are still somewhat uneasy neighbors, 1922 marks the incomplete realization of a 750-year-old dream—in the words of a popular ballad, the dream that Ireland might be "a nation once again."

Charles Stewart Parnell
At Limerick

I firmly believe that, bad as are the prospects of this country, out of that we will obtain good for Ireland. * * * It is the duty of the Irish tenant farmers to combine amongst themselves and ask for a reduction of rent, and if they get no reduction where a reduction is necessary, then I say that it is the duty of the tenant to pay no rent until he gets it. And if they combined in that way, if they stood together, and if being refused a reasonable and just reduction, they kept a firm grip of their homesteads, I can tell them that no power on earth could prevail against the hundreds of thousands of the tenant farmers of this country. Do not fear. You are not to be exterminated as you were in 1847,[1] and take my word for it it will not be attempted. You should ask for concessions that are just. Ask for them in a proper manner, and good landlords will give these conditions. But for the men who had always shown themselves regardless of right and justice in their dealings with these questions, I say it is necessary for you to maintain a firm and determined attitude. If you maintain that attitude victory must be yours. If when a farm was tenantless, owing to any cause, you refuse to take it, and the present most foolish competition amongst farmers came to an end, as undoubtedly it now must, these men who are forgetful of reason and of common sense must come to reconsider their position. I believe that the land of a country ought to be owned by the people of the country. And I think we should centre our exertions upon attaining that end. * * * When we have the people of this country prosperous, self-reliant, and confident of the future, we will have an Irish nation which will be able to hold its own amongst the nations of the world. We will have a country which will be able to speak with the enemy in the gate—we will have a people who will understand their rights, and, knowing those rights, will be resolved to maintain them. We must all have this without injustice to any individual.

Before the House of Commons[1]

* * * I can assure the House that it is not my belief that anything I can say, or wish to say at this time, will have the slightest effect on the public opinion of the House, or upon the public opinion of this country. I have been accustomed during my political life to rely upon the public opinion of those whom I have desired to help, and with whose aid I have worked for the cause of prosperity and freedom in Ireland: and the utmost that I desire to do in the very few words which I shall address to this House, is

---

1. After the failure of the potato crops in 1845 and 1846, and English refusal to suspend rent payments of Irish tenant farmers, 1847 was perhaps the year of most extreme suffering and starvation. During the years of the Potato Famine, the Irish population plummeted, through starvation, disease, and emigration, from about 8.5 million in

1845 to 6.6 million in 1851. This national tragedy forms the backdrop for Parnell's remarks (31 August 1879) to the tenant farmers of Limerick, who seemed to be facing an agricultural crisis of similar magnitude.
1. Delivered 23 February 1883.

to make my position clear to the Irish people at home and abroad from the unjust aspersions which have been cast upon me by a man[2] who ought to be ashamed to devote his high ability to the task of traducing[3] them. I don't wish to reply to the questions of the right hon. gentleman. I consider he has no right to question me, standing as he does in a position very little better than an informer with regard to the secrets of the men with whom he was associated, and he has not even the pretext of that remarkable informer whose proceedings we have lately heard of.[4] He had not even the pretext of that miserable man that he was attempting to save his own life. No, sir: other motives of less importance seem to have weighed with the right hon. gentleman in the extraordinary course which he has adopted on the present occasion of going out of his way to collect together a series of extracts, perhaps nine or ten in number, out of a number of speeches—many hundreds and thousands—delivered during the Land League movement[5] by other people and not by me, upon which to found an accusation against me for what has been said and done by others. * * * The right hon. gentleman has asked me to defend myself. Sir, I have nothing to defend myself for. The right hon. gentleman has confessed that he attempted to obtain a declaration or public promise from me which would have the effect of discrediting me with the Irish people. He has admitted that he failed in that attempt, and failing in that attempt, he lost his own reputation. He boasted last night that he had deposed me from some imaginary position which he was pleased to assign to me; but, at least, I have this consolation—that he also deposed himself. * * * I have taken very little part in Irish politics since my release from Kilmainham.[6] I expressed my reason for that upon the passing of the Crimes Act.[7] I said that, in my judgment, the Crimes Act would result in such a state of affairs that between the Government and secret societies it would be impossible for constitutional agitation to exist in Ireland. I believe so still. * * * It would have been far better if you were going to pass an Act of this kind and to administer an Act of this kind as you are going to administer it, and as you are obliged to administer it—up to the hilt—that it should be done by the seasoned politician who is now in disgrace. Call him back to his post! Send him to help Lord Spencer[8] in his congenial work of the gallows in Ireland! Send him to look after the Secret Inquisitions of Dublin Castle! Send him to superintend the payment of blood money! Send him to distribute the taxes which an unfortunate and starving peasantry have to pay for crimes not committed by them! All this would be congenial work. We invite you to man your ranks, and send your ablest and best men. Push forward the task of misgoverning Ireland! For my part I am confident as to the future of Ireland. Although her horizon may appear at this moment clouded, I believe that our people will survive the present oppression as we have survived many and worse ones. And although our progress may be slow it will be sure, and the time will come when this House and the people of this country will admit once again that they have been mistaken; that they have been deceived by those who ought to be ashamed of deceiving them; that they have been led astray as to the method of governing a noble, a

---

2. William Edward Forster, chief secretary for Ireland, had attacked Parnell at the beginning of the 1883 session.
3. Slandering.
4. James Carey (1845–1883), one of the Invincibles (an Irish nationalist group who killed the Irish chief secretary and undersecretary in Dublin's Phoenix Park in May 1882). After his arrest, he turned informer but was killed by another of the Invincibles while the British government attempted to transport him to safety in South Africa.

5. A division of the Home Rule Confederation, founded in 1879 by Michael Davitt and led by Parnell, that fought for the tenant farmers' security of tenure, fair rents on property, and their freedom to sell their property.
6. A jail in Dublin where Parnell was held between October 1881 and May 1882, after a series of popular speeches to the Irish people couched in violent language.
7. A coercion act against Irish agitation passed in 1881.
8. John Poyntz, fifth Earl of Spencer; Lord Lieutenant of Ireland for a second term (1882–1885).

generous, and an impulsive people; that they will reject their present leaders who are conducting them into the terrible course, which, I am sorry to say, the Government appears to be determined to enter; that they will reject these guides and leaders with just as much determination as they rejected the services of the right hon. gentleman the member of Bradford.[9]

At Portsmouth, After the Defeat of Mr. Gladstone's Home Rule Bill[1]

It is, I believe, about the first time I have had the honour of addressing a mainly English audience. And I have been induced to do so now because I rely greatly upon the spirit of fair play among the English masses, and because the issues for my country are so great and so vital at the present moment—the issues which underlie this present struggle—that the Irishman who remains silent when it might be possible to do something to help his country would be more unworthy than tongue could describe. * * * I have, in my career as a member of Parliament, never wittingly injured the cause of the English working man. I have done something to show my sympathy for the masses of the people of this country. * * * Some years ago it was my privilege to strike with English members a successful blow in favour of the abolition of flogging in the army and navy. We were met then by the very same arguments as we are met with today, and from the same class of persons. It was said by the late Lord Beaconsfield[2] that the integrity of the British Empire would be endangered if flogging were abolished, and he called a great meeting at one of the Ministerial offices in London, a great meeting of his supporters both in the Lords and Commons, for the purpose of exhorting them to stand shoulder to shoulder in defence of the British Empire against the abolition of flogging in the army. * * * I have shown you that in some respects the Irish settlement proposed by Mr Gladstone does not give a Parliament, a Legislature with the powers possessed by Grattan's Parliament;[3] but I have shown you on the other hand that as regards our own exclusively domestic business it gives larger powers, more important powers, more valuable powers for Ireland itself than was possessed by Grattan's, and therefore we think that this settlement proposed by Mr Gladstone will prove a more durable settlement than the restitution of the Grattan Parliament or the Repeal of the Union would prove. * * * Imperial unity does not require or necessitate unity of Parliaments. Will you carry that away with you and remember it, because it is the keystone of our whole proceedings. * * * I should say that Ireland would justly deserve to lose her privilege if she passed laws oppressive of the minority. * * * So far as coercion was concerned it has not brought you any nearer to the end of the Irish question. * * * One great fault in English coercion has been that no matter what your intentions have been when you have commenced coercion, you have never discriminated between political agitators and breakers of the law. * * * Lord Carnarvon[4] will not deny that he was as strong a Home Ruler as I was last August, and that when he went over to Ireland he became stronger and stronger every day he lived in that country. There is another thing he has not denied: he has not denied that he sought an interview with me in order to speak to me and consult with me about a Constitution for Ireland.[5] * * * Untold is the guilt of that man who,

9. I.e., William Edward Forster.
1. The first Home Rule bill, which would have given Ireland a "wide measure of autonomy"; Parnell gave this speech (25 June 1886), shortly after the bill's defeat.
2. Benjamin Disraeli, Prime Minister of England in 1868, and from 1874 to 1880.

3. Henry Grattan was leader of the movement that gave Ireland legislative independence in 1782.
4. Lord lieutenant of Ireland from 1885 to 1886 and member of the British Parliament.
5. Parnell and Carnarvon met on 1 August 1885, and discussed Irish Home Rule and an Irish Constitution.

for party purposes, does not take advantage of the spirit which is abroad amongst the English to put the hand of the Irish into that of the English to close the strife of centuries—a strife that has been of no advantage to the people of either country; a strife that has only been for the benefit of the money-grabbing landlords; a strife that has impeded popular progress in England as well as in Ireland, and that must continue to impede it; a strife which is fanned for the purpose of cheating you out of your rights, and to divert the energies of the newly enfranchised masses of Great Britain from the redress of their grievances to the odious task of oppressing and keeping down the small sister country.

Speech Delivered in Committee Room No. 15[1]

The men whose ability is now so conspicuously exercised as that of Mr. Healy and Mr. Sexton, will have to bear their responsibility for this. * * * Why did you encourage me to come forward and maintain my leadership in the face of the world if you were not going to stand by me? * * * I want to ask you before you vote my deposition to be sure you are getting value for it. * * * I know what Mr. Gladstone will do for you; I know what Mr. Morley[2] will do for you; and I know there is not a single one of the lot to be trusted unless you trust yourselves. Be to your own selves true and hence it follows, as the day the night, thou can'st not be false to any man.[3] * * * If I am to leave you tonight I should like to leave you in security. I should like, and it is not an unfair thing for me to ask, that I should come within sight of the Promised Land; that I should come with you, having come so far, if not to the end of this course, that I should at least come with you as far as you will allow and permit me to come with you, at least until it is absolutely sure that Ireland and I can go no further.

Proclamation of the Irish Republic
Poblacht na h Eireann[1]
THE PROVISIONAL GOVERNMENT OF THE IRISH REPUBLIC
TO
THE PEOPLE OF IRELAND

Irishmen and Irishwomen:

In the name of God and of the dead generations from which she receives her old tradition of nationhood, Ireland, through us, summons her children to her flag and strikes for her freedom.

Having organised and trained her manhood through her secret revolutionary organisation, the Irish Republican Brotherhood, and through her open miltary organisations, the Irish Volunteers and the Irish Citizen Army, having patiently perfected her discipline, having resolutely waited for the right moment to reveal itself, she now seizes that moment, and, supported by her exiled children in America and by gallant allies in Europe, but relying in the first on her own strength, she strikes in full confidence of victory.

---

1. Office of Parnell's party in Dublin. Parnell spoke to the party leadership on 6 December 1890 following a motion by Timothy Healy and Thomas Sexton to depose him as their leader in Parliament. Healy had been a Member of Parliament allied with Parnell's legislative agenda; Sexton had also supported Parnell in Parliament. In the wake of Parnell's involvement with the O'Shea divorce case, however, both abandoned Parnell and withdrew their support for his policies—an act of treachery which inspired James Joyce's first literary production, at age 8, a poem titled "Et Tu, Healy?"
2. John Morley (1838–1923), twice Chief Secretary for Ireland.
3. A paraphrase of lines from Polonius's speech in Hamlet, 1.3.78–80.
1. Irish Republic, in the Irish language.

We declare the right of the people of Ireland to the ownership of Ireland, and to the unfettered control of Irish destinies, to be sovereign and indefeasible. The long usurpation of that right by a foreign people and government has not extinguished the right, nor can it ever be extinguished except by the destruction of the Irish people. In every generation the Irish have asserted their right to National freedom and sovereignty; six times during the past three hundred years they have asserted it in arms. Standing on that fundamental right and again asserting it in arms in the face of the world, we hereby proclaim the Irish Republic as a Sovereign Independent State, and we pledge our lives and the lives of our comrades-in-arms to the cause of its freedom, of its welfare, and of its exaltation among the nations.

The Irish Republic is entitled to, and hereby claims, the allegiance of every Irishman and Irishwoman. The Republic guarantees religious and civil liberty, equal rights and equal opportunities to all its citizens, and declares its resolve to pursue the happiness and prosperity of the whole nation and of all its parts, cherishing all the children of the nation equally, and oblivious of the differences carefully fostered by an alien government, which have divided a minority from the majority in the past.

Until our arms have brought the opportune moment for the establishment of a permanent National Government, representative of the whole people of Ireland and elected by the suffrages of all her men and women,[2] the Provisional Government, hereby constituted, will administer the civil and military affairs of the Republic in trust for the people.

We place the cause of the Irish Republic under the protection of the Most High God, Whose blessing we invoke upon our arms, and we pray that no one who serves that cause will dishonor it by cowardice, inhumanity, or rapine. In this supreme hour the Irish nation must, by its valour and discipline and by the readiness of its children to sacrifice themselves for the common good, prove itself worthy of the august destiny to which it is called.

Signed on Behalf of the Provisional Government,
THOMAS J. CLARKE,
SEAN MACDIARMADA,
THOMAS MACDONAGH,
P. H. PEARSE,
EAMONN CEANNT,
JAMES CONNOLLY,
JOSEPH PLUNKETT.

Easter 1916

Padraic Pearse
Kilmainham Prison[1]

The following is the substance of what I said when asked today by the President of the Court-Martial at Richmond Barracks whether I had anything to say in my defence:

I desire, in the first place, to repeat what I have already said in letters to General Maxwell and Brigadier General Lowe.[2] My object in agreeing to an uncondi-

---

2. This call for women's suffrage in the Irish Republic predates full British women's suffrage by 12 years, and American women's suffrage by four years.
1. 2 May 1916. Pearse had been arrested on 29 April 1916,

ending the street fighting that had begun when he read the Proclamation of the Irish Republic on April 16. Pearse was executed at the conclusion of this military trial.
2. Leaders of the British troops during the Easter Rising.

tional surrender was to prevent the further slaughter of the civil population of Dublin and to save the lives of our gallant fellows, who, having made for six days a stand unparalleled in military history, were now surrounded, and in the case of those under the immediate command of H.Q., without food. I fully understand now, as then, that my own life is forfeit to British law, and I shall die very cheerfully if I can think that the British Government, as it has already shown itself strong, will now show itself magnanimous enough to accept my single life in forfeiture and to give a general amnesty to the brave men and boys who have fought at my bidding.[3]

In the second place, I wish it to be understood that any admissions I make here are to be taken as involving myself alone. They do not involve and must not be used against anyone who acted with me, not even those who may have set their names to documents with me. (The Court assented to this.)

I admit that I was Commandant-General Commanding-in-Chief of the forces of the Irish Republic which have been acting against you for the past week, and that I was President of the Provisional Government. I stand over all my acts and words done or spoken, in these capacities. When I was a child of ten I went on my bare knees by my bedside one night and promised God that I should devote my life to an effort to free my country. I have kept the promise. I have helped to organize, to arm, to train, and to discipline my fellow-countrymen to the sole end that, when the time came, they might fight for Irish freedom. The time, as it seemed to me, did come, and we went into the fight. I am glad we did, we seem to have lost, but we have not lost. To refuse to fight would have been to lose, to fight is to win; we have kept faith with the past, and handed on a tradition to the future. I repudiate the assertion of the prosecutor that I sought to aid and abet England's enemy. Germany is no more to me than England is. I asked and accepted German aid in the shape of arms and an expeditionary force, we neither asked for nor accepted German gold, nor had any traffic with Germany but what I state. My object was to win Irish freedom. We struck the first blow ourselves, but I should have been glad of an ally's aid.

I assume that I am speaking to Englishmen who value their freedom and who profess to be fighting for the freedom of Belgium and Serbia;[4] believe that we too love freedom and desire it. To us it is more desirable than anything in the world. If you strike us down now we shall rise again and renew the fight, you cannot conquer Ireland, you cannot extinguish the Irish passion for freedom; if our deed has not been sufficient to win freedom then our children will win it by a better deed.

Michael Collins
The Substance of Freedom[1]

* * * We gather here today to uphold and to expound the Treaty. It was not our intention to hold any meetings until the issue was definitely before the electorate.

3. This was not to be the case; in addition to Pearse, several other conspirators were executed by the British.
4. In World War I.
1. The text is compiled from reports of audience members for Collins's speech at a public meeting on 5 March 1922. The "treaty" in question is the Anglo-Irish Treaty establishing 26 of Ireland's 32 counties as the Irish Free State and set-

ting up a parliamentary government in Ireland. The treaty was opposed by Eamon de Valera, a surviving leader of the Easter Rising and leader of Sinn Féin, the Irish Republican organization whose Irish name means "Ourselves Alone." Though he was imprisoned by the newly formed Free State for his refusal to sign the treaty, he later went on to serve as both Prime Minister and President of Ireland.

But as a campaign has been begun in the country by Mr. de Valera and his followers we cannot afford to wait longer.

Mr de Valera's campaign is spoken of as a campaign against the Treaty. It is not really that.

The Irish people have already ratified the Treaty through their elected representatives. And the people of Ireland will stand by that ratification. The weekly paper of our opponents, which they call *The Republic of Ireland*, admits that ratification. Document No. 2[2] lapsed with the approval by the Dáil of the Treaty, they said in a leading article in the issue of February 21st; and in the issue of February 28th it is said "alternative documents are no longer in question."

No, it is not a campaign against the Treaty.

Nothing would disconcert Mr. de Valera and his followers more than the wrecking of the Treaty, than the loss of what has been secured by the Treaty.

It is a campaign, not against the Treaty, but against the Free State. And not only against the Free State, but still more against those who stand for the Free State. "Please God we will win," said Mr. de Valera last Sunday at Ennis, "and then there will be an end to the Free State." And if there were an end to the Free State, what then? What is the object of our opponents? I will tell you what it is.

In the same leading article of February 28th (in *The Republic of Ireland*) they say: "The Republican position is clear," and "We stand against the Treaty for the maintenance of the Republic."

The maintenance of the Republic [exclaimed Mr. Collins]. That is very curious. Because in the previous week's issue we were told by a member of the Dáil Cabinet that before the Truce of July last[3] it had become plain that it was physically impossible to secure Ireland's ideal of a completely isolated Republic in the immediate future, otherwise than by driving the overwhelmingly superior British forces out of the country. * * *

I will tell you what has happened since.

The Treaty has been brought back. It has brought and is bringing such freedom to Ireland in the transference to us of all governmental powers, but, above all, in the departure of the British armed forces, that it has become safe, and simple, and easy, and courageous to stand now for what was surrendered in July, because the British armed forces were still here.

We could not beat the British out by force, so the Republican ideal was surrendered. But when we have beaten them out by the Treaty the Republican ideal, which was surrendered in July, is restored.

The object of Mr de Valera and his party emerges. They are stealing our clothes. We have beaten out the British by means of the Treaty. While damning the Treaty, and us with it, they are taking advantage of the evacuation which the Treaty secures.

After the surrender of the Republican ideal in July we were sent over to make a Treaty with England.

Some of us were sent very much against our wishes. That is well-known to our opponents. Everyone knew then, and it is idle and dishonest to deny now, that in the event of a settlement some postponement of the realisation of our full national sentiment would have to be agreed to.

---

2. A document proposing an alternative arrangement, put forward by a private session of the Dáil Éireann (Irish Parliament) in December 1921.

3. A 1921 truce that led to negotiations and the Anglo-Irish Treaty.

We were not strong enough to realise the full Republican ideal. In addition, we must remember that there is a strong minority in our country up in the North-East that does not yet share our national views, but has to be reckoned with. In view of these things I claim that we brought back the fullest measure of freedom obtainable—the solid substance of independence.

We signed the Treaty believing it gave us such freedom. Our opponents make use of the advantage of the Treaty while they vilify it and us. The position gained by the Treaty provides them with a jumping off ground. After dropping the Republic while the British were still here, they shout bravely for it now from the safe foothold provided for them by means of the Treaty.

It is a mean campaign.

We were left with the Herculean labour and the heavy responsibility of taking over a Government. This would be a colossal task for the most experienced men of any nation. And we are young and not experienced. While we are thus engaged our former comrades go about the country talking. They tell the people to think of their own strength and the weakness of the enemy. Yes! and what is it that has made us strong and the enemy weak in the last few months? Yes, the enemy becomes weaker every day as his numbers grow less. And as they grow less, louder and louder do our opponents shout for the Republic which they surrendered in July last.

What has made the enemy weaker? The enemy that was then too strong for us? Is it the division in our ranks, which is Mr. de Valera's achievement, and which is already threatening a suspension of the evacuation? Or is it the Treaty which is our achievement?

Mr de Valera, in Limerick last Sunday, compared Ireland to a party that had set out to cross a desert, and they had come to a green spot, he said, and there were some who came along to tell them to lie down and stay there, and be satisfied and not go on.

Yes, we had come by means of the Treaty to a green oasis, the last in the long weary desert over which the Irish nation has been travelling. Oases are the resting-places of the desert, and unless the traveller finds them and refreshes himself he never reaches his destination.

Ireland has been brought to the last one, beyond which there is but a little and an easy stretch to go. The nation has earned the right to rest for a little while we renew our strength, and restore somewhat our earlier vigour.

But there are some amongst us who, while they take full advantage of the oasis—only a fool or a madman would fail to do that—complain of those who have led them to it. They find fault with it. They do nothing to help. They are poisoning the wells, wanting now to hurry on, seeing the road ahead short and straight, wanting the glory for themselves of leading the Irish nation over it, while unwilling to fill and shoulder the pack.

We are getting the British armed forces out of Ireland. Because of that evacuation our opponents are strong enough and brave enough now to say: "They are traitors who got you this. We are men of principle. We stand for the Republic"—that Republic which it was physically impossible to secure until the traitors had betrayed you.

Have we betrayed you? * * *

The arrangement in regard to North-East Ulster is not ideal. But then the position in North-East Ulster is not ideal.

If the Free State is established, however, union is certain. Forces of persuasion and pressure are embodied in the Treaty which will bring the North-East into a united Ireland. If they join us they can have control in their own area. If they stay outside Ireland, then they can only have their own corner, and cannot, and will not, have the counties and areas which belong to Ireland and to the Irish people, according to the wishes of the inhabitants.

Then upon the area remaining outside will fall the burdens and restrictions of the 1920 Partition Act.[4] These disabilities cannot be removed without our consent. If the North-East does not come in, then they are deciding upon bankruptcy for themselves and, remember, this is not our wish but their own.

We must not, however, take a gloomy view of this situation, for, with the British gone, the incentive to partition is gone; but the evacuation is held up by our own disunion—if the Free State is threatened, as long as there is any hope of seeing it destroyed, the North-East will remain apart. Partition will remain.

Destroy the Free State, and you perpetuate Partition. You destroy all hopes of union.

It is best to speak out plainly.

Destroy the Free State now and you destroy more even than the hope, the certainty of union. You destroy our hopes of national freedom, all realisation in our generation of the democratic right of the people of Ireland to rule themselves without interference from any outside power. * * *

But the aim of all of us can be for unity and independence. In public matters it must be realised that we cannot get all each one wants. We have to agree to get what is essential.

We have to agree to sink individual differences or only to work for them on legitimate lines which do not undermine and destroy the basis on which all rests and which alone makes it possible for us all, as Irishmen and women, to pursue our own aims freely in Ireland, namely, the union and independence of the nation as a whole.

We must be Irish first and last, and must be Republicans or Document Two-ites, or Free Staters, only within the limits which leave Ireland strong, united and free.

Would any other form of freedom which was obtainable now, which would have been acquiesced in by so large a body of our countrymen, have fulfilled the objects of Sinn Féin better, have put us in such a strong position to secure any that are yet unfulfilled?

We claim that the solid substance of freedom has been won, and that full powers are in the hands of the nation to mould its own life, quite as full for that purpose as if we had already our freedom in the Republican form.

Any difficulties will not be of our own making. There is no enemy nor any foreign Government here any longer to hinder us. Will we not take the fruits of victory, or do we mean to let them decay in our hands, while we wrangle as to whether they are ripe or whether they have exactly the bloom and shape we dreamed of before they had ripened?

No freedom when realised has quite the glory dreamed of by the captive.

[END OF SPEECHES ON IRISH INDEPENDENCE]

---

4. The act that divided Ireland politically into Northern Ireland (Ulster) and the Republic of Ireland.

William Butler Yeats
1865–1939

Beginning his career as a poet during the languid 1880s and 1890s, Yeats fought, as Ezra Pound said of T. S. Eliot, to modernize himself on his own. At a time when Irish poetry seemed to be in danger of ossifying into a sentimental, self-indulgent luxury, Yeats instead forged a verse that would serve as an exacting instrument of introspection and national inquiry. As a consequence, all modern Irish writing—most clearly poetry, but prose, drama, and literary nonfiction as well—is directly in his debt.

Yeats was born in the Dublin suburb of Sandymount, but his spiritual home, the land of his mother Susan Pollexfen and her people, was the countryside of County Sligo. His father, John Butler Yeats, was an amateur philosopher, an insolvent painter, and a refugee from the legal profession; his grandfather and great-grandfather were both clergymen of the Church of Ireland. Through his mother's family, Yeats traced a close connection with the countryside of Ireland, and the myths and legends of the Irish people. Both parents belonged to the Anglo-Irish Protestant ascendancy, a heritage Yeats remained fiercely proud of all his life; but the success of his poetry, in part, lay in his ability to reconcile the British literary tradition with the native materials of the Irish Catholic tradition.

As he tells it in his autobiography, Yeats's childhood was not a happy one; in 1915 he wrote: "I remember little of childhood but its pain." His father, though a talented painter, lacked the ability to turn his gifts to profit; he would linger over a single portrait for months and sometimes years, revising ceaselessly. When Yeats was three, his father moved his family to London in order to put himself to school as a painter; their existence, though intellectually and artistically rich and stimulating, was quite straitened financially. The young Yeats found London sterile and joyless; fortunately for his imagination, and his future poetry, portions of each year were spent in the Sligo countryside, where Yeats spent time gathering the local folklore and taking long, wide-ranging walks and pony rides. The family remained in London until 1875, and had four more children (though one brother died in childhood). All his surviving siblings were to remain important to Yeats in his artistic life: his brother Jack B. Yeats became an important Irish painter, and his sisters Lily and Lolly together founded the Dun Emer Press, later called the Cuala Press, which published limited-edition volumes of some of Yeats's poetry.

In 1880 the family returned permanently to Ireland, settling first in Howth, in Dublin Bay; the city of Dublin, with its largely unsung history and tradition, fueled Yeats's imagination in a way that London never had. When the time for college came, Yeats was judged unlikely to pass Trinity College's entrance exams, and he was sent instead to the Metropolitan School of Art, apparently in preparation to follow in his father's footsteps. His true gift, it soon appeared, was not for drawing and painting but for poetry. He steeped himself in the Romantic poets, especially Shelley and Keats, as well as the English poet of Irish residence Edmund Spenser. His first poems were published in the *Dublin University Review* in March 1885.

Yeats's early work is self-evidently apprentice work; it draws heavily on the late-Romantic, pre-Raphaelite ambience so important in the painting of his father and his father's colleagues. He also began to take an active interest in the various mystical movements that were then finding a foothold in Dublin and London, and with friends formed a Hermetic Society in Dublin as an antidote to the humanist rationalism to which his father was so passionately attached. At the same time—almost as a self-administered antidote to the teachings of mystics like the Brahmin teacher Mohini Chatterji—Yeats began to attend the meetings of several Dublin political and debating societies, and became increasingly interested in the nationalist artistic revival that would become known as the Irish Renaissance or Celtic Revival. Unlike most of his debating society comrades, Yeats imagined this political and cultural renaissance as resulting from a marriage of Blakean opposites: "I had noticed that Irish Catholics among whom had been born so many political martyrs had not the good taste, the household courtesy and decency of the Protestant Ireland I had known, yet Protestant Ireland seemed to think of nothing but getting on in the world. I thought we might bring the halves together if we had a national literature that made Ireland beautiful in the memory, and yet had been freed from provincialism by an exacting criticism, a European pose."

The Yeats family moved back to London in 1887; finances were difficult as ever, and Yeats contributed to the family's upkeep by editing two anthologies, *Poems and Ballads of Young Ireland* (1888) and *Fairy and Folk Tales of the Irish Peasantry* (1888). His own first collection of poems, *The Wanderings of Oisin and Other Poems*, was published in the following year; the poems are resolutely romantic, Yeats himself describing his manner at the time as "in all things Pre-Raphaelite." The poems were well received, but the praise of one reader in particular caught Yeats's attention. The statuesque beauty Maud Gonne appeared at Yeats's door with an introduction from the Irish revolutionary John O'Leary, and declared that the title poem had brought her to tears. It was a fateful meeting; throughout five decades Yeats continued to write to Gonne, for Gonne—the critic M. L. Rosenthal has suggested that "virtually every poem celebrating a woman's beauty or addressing a beloved woman has to do with her." Rosenthal might have added, every poem decrying the sacrifice of life to politics, including *No Second Troy, Easter 1916, A Prayer for My Daughter,* and others, all of which lament Gonne's increasing political fanaticism. This fanaticism, which Gonne considered simply patriotism, made impossible the spiritual and emotional consummation that Yeats so fervently desired. He proposed marriage, but she declined, marrying instead an Irish soldier who would later be executed for his role in the Easter Rising of 1916. Yeats is, among his other distinctions, a great poet of unrequited love.

The 1890s in London were heady times for a young poet. Yeats became even more active in his studies of the occult, studying with the charismatic Theosophist Madame Blavatsky and attending meetings of the Order of the Golden Dawn, a Christian cabalist society. The practical upshot of these activities for his later poetry was a confirmed belief in a storehouse of all human experience and knowledge, which he called variously the *Spiritus Mundi* and *Anima Mundi,* invoked in later poems like *The Second Coming* (1920). In 1891 Yeats, together with Ernest Rhys, founded the Rhymers' Club, which brought him into almost nightly contact with such important literary figures as Lionel Johnson, Ernest Dowson, Arthur Symons, and Oscar Wilde; during this same period, he established the Irish Literary Society in London, and the National Literary Society in Dublin. Clearly, something of a program for modern Irish poetry was beginning to emerge, even if Yeats himself wasn't yet quite ready to write it. Yeats also spent the years from 1887 to 1891 studying the writings of that most mystic of English poets, William Blake; working with his father's friend Edwin Ellis, he produced an edition of and extended commentary on Blake's prophetic writings. Summing up the lesson of Blake's writings, Yeats wrote: "I had learned from Blake to hate all abstractions."

Romantic abstraction was easier to abjure in principle than in practice; Yeats's poetry of the 1890s still hankers after what one of his dramatis personae would later call "the loveliness that has long faded from the world." As one critic has written, "'Early Yeats was the best poetry in English in late Victorian times; but they were bad times." Yeats began the process of throwing off the false manners of his pre-Raphaelite upbringing with his play *The Countess Cathleen*, first performed by the Abbey Theatre, funded by subscriptions collected by his good friend Lady Augusta Gregory. Yeats's play, like Synge's *Playboy of the Western World* years later on that same stage, offended Irish sensibilities; in it, Cathleen sells her soul in order to protect Irish peasants from starvation. Yeats's volume *The Wind Among the Reeds* (1899) closes out the 1890s quite conveniently; it is ethereal, beautiful, and mannered. With this volume, Yeats's early phase comes to a close.

The early years of the twentieth century found Yeats concentrating his energies on the writing of poetic dramas, including, *The Pot of Broth* (1902) and *On Baile's Strand* (1904), for his fledgling Irish National Theatre. In 1903, the small Dun Emer Press published his volume of poems *In the Seven Woods*. These poems, including *Adam's Curse*, show Yeats working in a more spare idiom, the cadences and rhythms closer to those of actual speech—a consequence, some have argued, of his years writing for the stage. New poems published in *The Green Helmet and Other Poems* (1910) display Yeats as an increasingly mature and confident poet; his treatment of Maud Gonne in *No Second Troy*, for instance, shows a tragic acceptance of the fact that he will never have her, nor master her indomitable spirit. In *A Coat*, the poem that closes the 1914 collection *Responsibilities*, Yeats writes of the embroidered cloak he had fashioned for himself in his early poems, whose vanity is now brought home to him by the gaudiness of his imitators. He resolves, in the volume's closing lines, to set his cloak aside, "For there's more enterprise / In walking naked." This sense was strengthened by his close work, during the winter of 1912–1913, with Ezra Pound, in a cottage in rural Sussex. Both studied the stripped-down Japanese Noh drama and the Orientalist Ernest Fennollosa's work on the Chinese ideogram, and both men no doubt reinforced one another's increasing desire for a poetry that would be, in Pound's phrase, "closer to the bone."

The Easter Rising of 1916 took Yeats by surprise; he was in England at the time and complained of not having been informed in advance. A number of the rebel leaders were personal friends; he writes their names into Irish literature in *Easter 1916*, an excruciatingly honest, and ambivalent, exploration of the nature of heroism and nationalism. Yeats's mixed feelings about the revolution derived in part from a concern that some of his early writings, like the nationalist *The Countess Cathleen*, might have contributed to the slaughter that followed in the wake of Easter 1916; as he wrote many years later, he couldn't help but wonder, "Did that play of mine send out / Certain men the English shot?"

The intricacies of Yeats's emotional and romantic life would require an essay of their own. His first marriage proposal to Maud Gonne in 1891, politely refused, set a pattern that was to remain in place for many years; though a number of poems try to reason through the affair, Yeats remained tragically attracted to this woman who did not return his affection, and multiple proposals were turned down as routinely as the first. He would have done as well, he was to write years later, to profess his love "to a statue in a museum." In the summer of 1917 things reached such a pass that Yeats proposed to Maud Gonne's adopted daughter Iseult; here, again, he was refused. Then, hastily, in October 1917 he married a longtime friend Georgiana ("George") Hyde-Lees. For all the tragicomedy leading up to the marriage, Yeats could not have chosen better; George was intelligent and sympathetic, and she brought the additional gift of an interest in mysticism and a facility in automatic writing that Yeats was soon to take full advantage of. Since early childhood, Yeats had heard voices speaking to him, and when he was twenty-one a voice commanded him "Hammer your thoughts into unity"; this charge had weighed on his mind for years, and his various experiments in mysticism and esoteric religions were intended to discover the system wherein his thoughts might be made to cohere.

With George, Yeats finally created that system on his own; its fullest exposition is found in *A Vision* (1928), though elements of it turn up in his poems beginning as early as *No Second Troy*. The system is complicated enough to fill out over 300 pages in the revised (1937) edition; at the heart of the system, though, is a simple diagram of two interpenetrating cones, oriented horizontally, such that the tip of each cone establishes the center of the base of the opposite cone. These two cones describe the paths of two turning gyres, or spirals, representing two alternating antithetical ages which make up human history. Yeats saw history as composed of cycles of approximately 2,000 years; his apocalyptic poem *The Second Coming*, for instance, describes the anxiety caused by the recognition that the 2,000 years of Christian (in Yeats's terms, "primary") values were about to be succeeded by an antithetical age—the "rough beast" of a time characterized by values and beliefs in every way hostile to those of the Christian era. For Yeats, however, as for William Blake, this vacillation and tension between contraries was not to be regretted; Blake taught that "without Contraries is no progression," and Yeats, that "all the gains of man come from conflict with the opposite of his true being."

Yeats's greatest phase begins with the poems of *Michael Robartes and the Dancer* (1921). His mytho-historical system informs a number of the poems written in the 1920s and after; it explains, for instance, why Yeats saw the brutal rape of Leda by Zeus in the form of a swan as a precursor of the traditional Christian iconography of the Virgin Mary "visited" by God the Father in the form of a dove. A logical corollary of Yeats's belief in historical recurrence was the philosophy, articulated best in his late poem *Lapis Lazuli*, of tragic joy: "All things fall and are built again, / And those that build them again are gay." In a letter inspired by the gift of lapis lazuli that the poem celebrates, Yeats wrote to a friend: "To me the supreme aim is an act of faith or reason to make one rejoice in the midst of tragedy." The influence of the writing of Nietzsche, whom Yeats had been reading, is apparent in these formulations.

While continuing to push at the boundaries of modern literature and modern poetry, Yeats also enjoyed the role of statesman. In the fall of 1922, Yeats was made a senator of the new Irish Free State; in 1923 he was awarded the Nobel Prize for literature, the first Irish writer ever to receive the award. The 1930s also saw Yeats flirt briefly with fascism, as did other writers like Pound and Wyndham Lewis. Yeats's belief in the importance of an aristocracy, and his disappointment over the excesses of revolutionary zeal demonstrated in the Irish civil war, for a time during the 1930s made the fascist program of the Irish Blueshirt movement look attractive. He composed *Three Songs to the Same Tune* as rallying songs for the Blueshirts, but the poems were too recherché for any such use. He soon became disillusioned with the party.

Yeats continued to write major poetry almost until his death; his growing ill health seems only to have made his poetry stronger and more defiant, as evidenced in such sinuous and clearsighted poems as *Lapis Lazuli* and the bawdy Crazy Jane poems. In the work published as *Last Poems* (1939), Yeats most satisfactorily put into practice what he had much earlier discovered in theory: that he must, as he wrote in *The Circus Animals' Desertion*, return for his poetry to "the foul rag-and-bone shop of the heart." After a long period of heart trouble, Yeats died on 28 January 1939; he was buried in Roquebrune, France, where he and George had been spending the winter. In 1948 he was reinterred, as he had wished, in Drumcliff churchyard near Sligo, where his grandfather and great-grandfather had served as rectors. Again according to his wishes, his epitaph is that which he wrote for himself in *Under Ben Bulben*:

> Cast a cold eye
> On life, on death.
> Horseman, pass by!

The Lake Isle of Innisfree[1]

I will arise and go now, and go to Innisfree,
And a small cabin build there, of clay and wattles° made: *woven twigs*
Nine bean-rows will I have there, a hive for the honey-bee,
And live alone in the bee-loud glade.

5   And I shall have some peace there, for peace comes dropping slow,
Dropping from the veils of the morning to where the cricket sings;
There midnight's all a glimmer, and noon a purple glow,
And evening full of the linnet's° wings.   *song bird*

1. A small island in Lough Gill outside the town of Sligo, near the border with Northern Ireland.

I will arise and go now, for always night and day
10 I hear lake water lapping with low sounds by the shore;
While I stand on the roadway, or on the pavements grey,
I hear it in the deep heart's core.

1890   1890

Who Goes with Fergus?[1]

Who will go drive with Fergus now,
And pierce the deep wood's woven shade,
And dance upon the level shore?
Young man, lift up your russet brow,
5   And lift your tender eyelids, maid,
And brood on hopes and fear no more.
And no more turn aside and brood
Upon love's bitter mystery;
For Fergus rules the brazen° cars,   *brass*
10 And rules the shadows of the wood,
And the white breast of the dim sea
And all dishevelled wandering stars.

                                                                                    1893

No Second Troy[1]

Why should I blame her that she filled my days
With misery, or that she would of late
Have taught to ignorant men most violent ways,
Or hurled the little streets upon the great,
5   Had they but courage equal to desire?
What could have made her peaceful with a mind
That nobleness made simple as a fire,
With beauty like a tightened bow, a kind
That is not natural in an age like this,
10 Being high and solitary and most stern?
Why, what could she have done, being what she is?
Was there another Troy for her to burn?

1908   1910

The Wild Swans at Coole[1]

The trees are in their autumn beauty,
The woodland paths are dry,
Under the October twilight the water
Mirrors a still sky;
5   Upon the brimming water among the stones
Are nine-and-fifty swans.

The nineteenth autumn has come upon me
Since I first made my count;

---

1. The poem is a lyric from the second scene of Yeats's play *The Countess Cathleen*. Fergus was an ancient Irish king who gave up his throne to feast, fight, and hunt.
1. Yeats here compares Maud Gonne to Helen of Troy;

the Trojan War began from two kings' rivalry over Helen.
1. Coole Park was the name of the estate of Yeats's patron Lady Gregory in Galway.

I saw, before I had well finished,
10   All suddenly mount
And scatter wheeling in great broken rings
Upon their clamorous wings.

I have looked upon those brilliant creatures,
And now my heart is sore.
15   All's changed since I, hearing at twilight,
The first time on this shore,
The bell-beat of their wings above my head,
Trod with a lighter tread.

Unwearied still, lover by lover,
20   They paddle in the cold
Companionable streams or climb the air;
Their hearts have not grown old;
Passion or conquest, wander where they will,
Attend upon them still.

25   But now they drift on the still water,
Mysterious, beautiful;
Among what rushes will they build,
By what lake's edge or pool
Delight men's eyes when I awake some day
30   To find they have flown away?
1916   1917

Easter 1916[1]

I have met them at close of day
Coming with vivid faces
From counter or desk among grey
Eighteenth-century houses.
5   I have passed with a nod of the head
Or polite meaningless words,
Or have lingered awhile and said
Polite meaningless words,
And thought before I had done
10   Of a mocking tale or a gibe°   taunt
To please a companion
Around the fire at the club,
Being certain that they and I
But lived where motley° is worn: jester's outfit
15   All changed, changed utterly:
A terrible beauty is born.

That woman's days were spent
In ignorant good-will,
Her nights in argument
20   Until her voice grew shrill.[2]

1. The Irish Republic was declared on Easter Monday 1916.
2. Countess Markiewicz, née Constance Gore-Booth, played a prominent part in the Easter Rising and was sentenced to be executed; her sentence was later reduced to imprisonment.

What voice more sweet than hers
When, young and beautiful,
She rode to harriers?°   *hunting dogs*
This man[3] had kept a school
25   And rode our wingèd horse;
This other[4] his helper and friend
Was coming into his force;
He might have won fame in the end,
So sensitive his nature seemed,
30   So daring and sweet his thought.
This other man[5] I had dreamed
A drunken, vainglorious lout.
He had done most bitter wrong
To some who are near my heart,
35   Yet I number him in the song;
He, too, has resigned his part
In the casual comedy;
He, too, has been changed in his turn,
Transformed utterly:
40   A terrible beauty is born.

Hearts with one purpose alone
Through summer and winter seem
Enchanted to a stone
To trouble the living stream.
45   The horse that comes from the road,
The rider, the birds that range
From cloud to tumbling cloud,
Minute by minute they change;
A shadow of cloud on the stream
50   Changes minute by minute;
A horse-hoof slides on the brim,
And a horse plashes within it;
The long-legged moor-hens dive,
And hens to moor-cocks call;
55   Minute by minute they live:
The stone's in the midst of all.

Too long a sacrifice
Can make a stone of the heart.
O when may it suffice?
60   That is Heaven's part, our part
To murmur name upon name,
As a mother names her child
When sleep at last has come
On limbs that had run wild.
65   What is it but nightfall?
No, no, not night but death;
Was it needless death after all?

---

3. Padraic Pearse.
4. Thomas MacDonagh, poet executed for his role in the rebellion.

5. Major John MacBride, briefly married to Maud Gonne, was also executed.

For England may keep faith
For all that is done and said.
70 We know their dream; enough
To know they dreamed and are dead;
And what if excess of love
Bewildered them till they died?
I write it out in a verse—
75 MacDonagh and MacBride
And Connolly[6] and Pearse
Now and in time to be,
Wherever green is worn,
Are changed, changed utterly:
80 A terrible beauty is born.

1916   1916

The Second Coming[1]

Turning and turning in the widening gyre°   *circle or spiral*
The falcon cannot hear the falconer;
Things fall apart; the centre cannot hold;
Mere anarchy is loosed upon the world,
5 The blood-dimmed tide is loosed, and everywhere
The ceremony of innocence is drowned;
The best lack all conviction, while the worst
Are full of passionate intensity.

Surely some revelation is at hand;
10 Surely the Second Coming is at hand.
The Second Coming! Hardly are those words out
When a vast image out of *Spiritus Mundi*[2]
Troubles my sight: somewhere in sands of the desert
A shape with lion body and the head of a man,
15 A gaze blank and pitiless as the sun,
Is moving its slow thighs, while all about it
Reel shadows of the indignant desert birds.
The darkness drops again; but now I know
That twenty centuries of stony sleep
20 Were vexed to nightmare by a rocking cradle,
And what rough beast, its hour come round at last,
Slouches towards Bethlehem to be born?

1919   1921

A Prayer for My Daughter

Once more the storm is howling, and half hid
Under this cradle-hood and coverlid
My child sleeps on. There is no obstacle

---

6. James Connolly, Marxist commander-in-chief of the
Easter rebels; also executed.
1. Traditionally, the return of Christ to earth on Judgment Day.

2. A storehouse of images and symbols common to all
humankind; similar to Carl Jung's notion of the collective unconscious.

But Gregory's wood and one bare hill
5   Whereby the haystack- and roof-levelling wind,
Bred on the Atlantic, can be stayed;
And for an hour I have walked and prayed
Because of the great gloom that is in my mind.

I have walked and prayed for this young child an hour
10   And heard the sea-wind scream upon the tower,
And under the arches of the bridge, and scream
In the elms above the flooded stream;
Imagining in excited reverie
That the future years had come,
15   Dancing to a frenzied drum,
Out of the murderous innocence of the sea.

May she be granted beauty and yet not
Beauty to make a stranger's eye distraught,
Or hers before a looking-glass, for such,
20   Being made beautiful overmuch,
Consider beauty a sufficient end,
Lose natural kindness and maybe
The heart-revealing intimacy
That chooses right, and never find a friend.

25   Helen[1] being chosen found life flat and dull
And later had much trouble from a fool,
While that great Queen,[2] that rose out of the spray,
Being fatherless could have her way
Yet chose a bandy-leggèd smith[3] for man.
30   It's certain that fine women eat
A crazy salad with their meat
Whereby the Horn of Plenty is undone.

In courtesy I'd have her chiefly learned;
Hearts are not had as a gift but hearts are earned
35   By those that are not entirely beautiful;
Yet many, that have played the fool
For beauty's very self, has charm made wise,
And many a poor man that has roved,
Loved and thought himself beloved,
40   From a glad kindness cannot take his eyes.

May she become a flourishing hidden tree
That all her thoughts may like the linnet° be,   *song bird*
And have no business but dispensing round
Their magnanimities of sound,
45   Nor but in merriment begin a chase,
Nor but in merriment a quarrel.
O may she live like some green laurel
Rooted in one dear perpetual place.

---

1. Helen of Troy, who left her husband Menelaus for   3. Aphrodite's husband Hephaestus, the god of fire, was
Paris.   lame.
2. Aphrodite, Greek goddess of love, born from the sea.

My mind, because the minds that I have loved,
50 The sort of beauty that I have approved,
Prosper but little, has dried up of late,
Yet knows that to be choked with hate
May well be of all evil chances chief.
If there's no hatred in a mind
55 Assault and battery of the wind
Can never tear the linnet from the leaf.

An intellectual hatred is the worst,
So let her think opinions are accursed.
Have I not seen the loveliest woman born
60 Out of the mouth of Plenty's horn,
Because of her opinionated mind
Barter that horn and every good
By quiet natures understood
For an old bellows full of angry wind?

65 Considering that, all hatred driven hence,
The soul recovers radical innocence
And learns at last that it is self-delighting,
Self-appeasing, self-affrighting,
And that its own sweet will is Heaven's will;
70 She can, though every face should scowl
And every windy quarter howl
Or every bellows burst, be happy still.

And may her bridegroom bring her to a house
Where all's accustomed, ceremonious;
75 For arrogance and hatred are the wares
Peddled in the thoroughfares.
How but in custom and in ceremony
Are innocence and beauty born?
Ceremony's a name for the rich horn,
80 And custom for the spreading laurel tree.

June 1919   1919

Sailing to Byzantium[1]

I

That is no country for old men. The young
In one another's arms, birds in the trees,
—Those dying generations—at their song,
The salmon-falls, the mackerel-crowded seas,
5 Fish, flesh, or fowl, commend all summer long
Whatever is begotten, born, and dies.
Caught in that sensual music all neglect
Monuments of unageing intellect.

2

An aged man is but a paltry thing,
10 A tattered coat upon a stick, unless

---

1. Constantinople, now called Istanbul, capital of the Byzantine Empire and the holy city of Eastern Christianity.

Soul clap its hands and sing, and louder sing
For every tatter in its mortal dress,
Nor is there singing school but studying
Monuments of its own magnificence;
15   And therefore I have sailed the seas and come
To the holy city of Byzantium.

3

O sages standing in God's holy fire
As in the gold mosaic of a wall,
Come from the holy fire, perne° in a gyre,   *spin*
20   And be the singing-masters of my soul.
Consume my heart away; sick with desire
And fastened to a dying animal
It knows not what it is; and gather me
Into the artifice of eternity.

4

25   Once out of nature I shall never take
My bodily form from any natural thing,
But such a form as Grecian goldsmiths make
Of hammered gold and gold enamelling
To keep a drowsy Emperor awake;—
30   Or set upon a golden bough to sing
To lords and ladies of Byzantium
Of what is past, or passing, or to come.

1926   1927

Meditations in Time of Civil War

1. Ancestral Houses

Surely among a rich man's flowering lawns,
Amid the rustle of his planted hills,
Life overflows without ambitious pains;
And rains down life until the basin spills,
5   And mounts more dizzy high the more it rains
As though to choose whatever shape it wills
And never stoop to a mechanical
Or servile shape, at others' beck and call.

Mere dreams, mere dreams! Yet Homer had not sung
10   Had he not found it certain beyond dreams
That out of life's own self-delight had sprung
The abounding glittering jet; though now it seems
As if some marvellous empty sea-shell flung
Out of the obscure dark of the rich streams,
15   And not a fountain, were the symbol which
Shadows the inherited glory of the rich.

Some violent bitter man, some powerful man
Called architect and artist in, that they,
Bitter and violent men, might rear in stone
20   The sweetness that all longed for night and day,
The gentleness none there had ever known;

But when the master's buried mice can play,
And maybe the great-grandson of that house,
For all its bronze and marble, 's but a mouse.

25 O what if gardens where the peacock strays
With delicate feet upon old terraces,
Or else all Juno[1] from an urn displays
Before the indifferent garden deities;
O what if levelled lawns and gravelled ways
30 Where slippered Contemplation finds his ease
And Childhood a delight for every sense,
But take our greatness with our violence?
What if the glory of escutcheoned° doors,   shield-shaped
And buildings that a haughtier age designed,
35 The pacing to and fro on polished floors
Amid great chambers and long galleries, lined
With famous portraits of our ancestors;
What if those things the greatest of mankind
Consider most to magnify, or to bless,
40 But take our greatness with our bitterness?

2. My House

An ancient bridge, and a more ancient tower,
A farmhouse that is sheltered by its wall,
An acre of stony ground,
Where the symbolic rose can break in flower,
5 Old ragged elms, old thorns innumerable,
The sound of the rain or sound
Of every wind that blows;
The stilted water-hen
Crossing stream again
10 Scared by the splashing of a dozen cows;

A winding stair, a chamber arched with stone,
A grey stone fireplace with an open hearth,
A candle and written page.
Il Penseroso's Platonist[2] toiled on
15 In some like chamber, shadowing forth
How the daemonic rage
Imagined everything.
Benighted travellers
From markets and from fairs
20 Have seen his midnight candle glimmering.

Two men have founded here. A man-at-arms
Gathered a score of horse and spent his days
In this tumultuous spot,
Where through long wars and sudden night alarms
25 His dwindling score and he seemed castaways

1. Roman Goddess of marriage and patroness of women;
the peacock was sacred to her as a symbol of immortality.

2. Follower of the idealist philosophy of Plato, in Milton's
poem Il Penseroso ("The Contemplative").

Forgetting and forgot;
And I, that after me
My bodily heirs may find,
To exalt a lonely mind,
30   Befitting emblems of adversity.

3. My Table

Two heavy trestles, and a board
Where Sato's[3] gift, a changeless sword,
By pen and paper lies,
That it may moralise
5   My days out of their aimlessness.
A bit of an embroidered dress
Covers its wooden sheath.
Chaucer had not drawn breath
When it was forged. In Sato's house,
10   Curved like new moon, moon-luminous,
It lay five hundred years.
Yet if no change appears
No moon; only an aching heart
Conceives a changeless work of art.
15   Our learned men have urged
That when and where 'twas forged
A marvellous accomplishment,
In painting or in pottery, went
From father unto son
20   And through the centuries ran
And seemed unchanging like the sword.
Soul's beauty being most adored,
Men and their business took
The soul's unchanging look;
25   For the most rich inheritor,
Knowing that none could pass Heaven's door
That loved inferior art,
Had such an aching heart
That he, although a country's talk
30   For silken clothes and stately walk,
Had waking wits; it seemed
Juno's peacock screamed.

4. My Descendants

Having inherited a vigorous mind
From my old fathers, I must nourish dreams
And leave a woman and a man behind
As vigorous of mind, and yet it seems
5   Life scarce can cast a fragrance on the wind,
Scarce spread a glory to the morning beams,

3. Junzo Sato, Japanese consul who presented Yeats with an ancestral ceremonial sword.

But the torn petals strew the garden plot;
And there's but common greenness after that.

10   And what if my descendants lose the flower
Through natural declension of the soul,
Through too much business with the passing hour,
Through too much play, or marriage with a fool?
May this laborious stair and this stark tower
15   Become a roofless ruin that the owl
May build in the cracked masonry and cry
Her desolation to the desolate sky.

The Primum Mobile[4] that fashioned us
Has made the very owls in circles move;
And I, that count myself most prosperous,
20   Seeing that love and friendship are enough,
For an old neighbour's friendship chose the house
And decked and altered it for a girl's love,
And know whatever flourish and decline
These stones remain their monument and mine.

5. The Road at My Door

An affable Irregular,[5]
A heavily-built Falstaffian[6] man,
Comes cracking jokes of civil war
As though to die by gunshot were
5   The finest play under the sun.

A brown Lieutenant and his men,
Half dressed in national uniform,
Stand at my door, and I complain
Of the foul weather, hail and rain,
10   A pear tree broken by the storm.

I count those feathered balls of soot
The moor-hen guides upon the stream,
To silence the envy in my thought;
And turn towards my chamber, caught
15   In the cold snows of a dream.

6. The Stare's Nest by My Window

The bees build in the crevices
Of loosening masonry, and there
The mother birds bring grubs and flies.
My wall is loosening; honey-bees,
5   Come build in the empty house of the stare.°   starling

---

4. Prime mover (Latin); part of the Ptolemaic system that
described the revolution of the heavens around the earth.
5. A member of the Irish Republican Army (IRA), which
opposed any cooperation with British power and started

the civil war.
6. Robust, bawdy, witty; after Sir John Falstaff, comic
character in Shakespeare's The Merry Wives of Windsor
and Henry IV.

We are closed in, and the key is turned
On our uncertainty; somewhere
A man is killed, or a house burned,
Yet no clear fact to be discerned:
10   Come build in the empty house of the stare.

A barricade of stone or of wood;
Some fourteen days of civil war;
Last night they trundled down the road
That dead young soldier in his blood:
15   Come build in the empty house of the stare.

We had fed the heart on fantasies,
The heart's grown brutal from the fare;
More substance in our enmities
Than in our love; O honey-bees,
20   Come build in the empty house of the stare.

7. *I See Phantoms of Hatred and of the Heart's Fullness and of the Coming Emptiness*

I climb to the tower-top and lean upon broken stone,
A mist that is like blown snow is sweeping over all,
Valley, river, and elms, under the light of a moon
That seems unlike itself, that seems unchangeable,
5   A glittering sword out of the east. A puff of wind
And those white glimmering fragments of the mist sweep by.
Frenzies bewilder, reveries perturb the mind;
Monstrous familiar images swim to the mind's eye.

"Vengeance upon the murderers," the cry goes up,
10   "Vengeance for Jacques Molay."[7] In cloud-pale rags, or in lace,
The rage-driven, rage-tormented, and rage-hungry troop,
Trooper belabouring trooper, biting at arm or at face,
Plunges towards nothing, arms and fingers spreading wide
For the embrace of nothing; and I, my wits astray
15   Because of all that senseless tumult, all but cried
For vengeance on the murderers of Jacques Molay.

Their legs long, delicate and slender, aquamarine their eyes,
Magical unicorns bear ladies on their backs.
The ladies close their musing eyes. No prophecies,
20   Remembered out of Babylonian almanacs,
Have closed the ladies' eyes, their minds are but a pool
Where even longing drowns under its own excess;
Nothing but stillness can remain when hearts are full
Of their own sweetness, bodies of their loveliness.

25   The cloud-pale unicorns, the eyes of aquamarine,
The quivering half-closed eyelids, the rags of cloud or of lace,

---

7. Jacques de Molay, Grand Master of the Knights Templar who was burned as a witch in 1314.

Or eyes that rage has brightened, arms it has made lean,
Give place to an indifferent multitude, give place
To brazen hawks. Nor self-delighting reverie,
30   Nor hate of what's to come, nor pity for what's gone,
Nothing but grip of claw, and the eye's complacency,
The innumerable clanging wings that have put out the moon.

I turn away and shut the door, and on the stair
Wonder how many times I could have proved my worth
35   In something that all others understand or share;
But O! ambitious heart, had such a proof drawn forth
A company of friends, a conscience set at ease,
It had but made us pine the more. The abstract joy,
The half-read wisdom of daemonic images,
40   Suffice the ageing man as once the growing boy.
1921   1928

Leda and the Swan[1]

A sudden blow: the great wings beating still
Above the staggering girl, her thighs caressed
By the dark webs, her nape caught in his bill,
He holds her helpless breast upon his breast.

5   How can those terrified vague fingers push
The feathered glory from her loosening thighs?
And how can body, laid in that white rush,
But feel the strange heart beating where it lies?

A shudder in the loins engenders there
10   The broken wall, the burning roof and tower
And Agamemnon[2] dead.
                              Being so caught up,
So mastered by the brute blood of the air,
Did she put on his knowledge with his power
Before the indifferent beak could let her drop?
1923   1924

Among School Children

1

I walk through the long schoolroom questioning;
A kind old nun in a white hood replies;
The children learn to cipher and to sing,
To study reading-books and history,
5   To cut and sew, be neat in everything
In the best modern way—the children's eyes
In momentary wonder stare upon
A sixty-year-old smiling public man.

---

1. In Greek mythology, Zeus came to Leda in the form of
a swan and raped her; Helen of Troy and Clytemnestra
were their offspring.
2. Brother of Menelaus, husband of Helen. When she was
abducted by Paris, Agamemnon fought to rescue her. He
was murdered by his wife Clytemnestra on his return
home.

2

I dream of a Ledaean[1] body, bent
10   Above a sinking fire, a tale that she
Told of a harsh reproof, or trivial event
That changed some childish day to tragedy—
Told, and it seemed that our two natures blent
Into a sphere from youthful sympathy,
15   Or else, to alter Plato's parable,
Into the yolk and white of the one shell.[2]

3

And thinking of that fit of grief or rage
I look upon one child or t'other there
And wonder if she stood so at that age—
20   For even daughters of the swan can share
Something of every paddler's heritage—
And had that colour upon cheek or hair,
And thereupon my heart is driven wild:
She stands before me as a living child.

4

25   Her present image floats into the mind—
Did Quattrocento[3] finger fashion it
Hollow of cheek as though it drank the wind
And took a mess of shadows for its meat?
And I though never of Ledaean kind
30   Had pretty plumage once—enough of that,
Better to smile on all that smile, and show
There is a comfortable kind of old scarecrow.

5

What youthful mother, a shape upon her lap
Honey of generation had betrayed,
35   And that must sleep, shriek, struggle to escape
As recollection or the drug decide,
Would think her son, did she but see that shape
With sixty or more winters on its head,
A compensation for the pang of his birth,
40   Or the uncertainty of his setting forth?

6

Plato thought nature but a spume° that plays   froth
Upon a ghostly paradigm of things;
Soldier Aristotle played the taws[4]
Upon the bottom of a king of kings;
45   World-famous golden-thighed Pythagoras[5]
Fingered upon a fiddle-stick or strings
What a star sang and careless Muses heard:
Old clothes upon old sticks to scare a bird.

7

Both nuns and mothers worship images,
50   But those the candles light are not as those

---

1. Of Leda, the mother of Helen of Troy.
2. According to Plato's parable in the *Symposium*, male and female were once the two halves of a single body; it was subsequently cut in half like a hard-boiled egg.

3. Fifteenth-century artists of Italy's Renaissance.
4. A leather strap, used to spin a top.
5. A 6th-century B.C. Greek philosopher who developed a mathematical basis for the universe and music.

That animate a mother's reveries,
But keep a marble or a bronze repose.
And yet they too break hearts—O Presences
That passion, piety or affection knows,
55   And that all heavenly glory symbolise—
O self-born mockers of man's enterprise;

8

Labour is blossoming or dancing where
The body is not bruised to pleasure soul,
Nor beauty born out of its own despair,
60   Nor blear-eyed wisdom out of midnight oil.
O chestnut tree, great rooted blossomer,
Are you the leaf, the blossom or the bole?
O body swayed to music, O brightening glance,
How can we know the dancer from the dance?

1926   1927

Byzantium

The unpurged images of day recede;
The Emperor's drunken soldiery are abed;
Night resonance recedes, night-walkers' song
After great cathedral gong;
5   A starlit or a moonlit dome disdains
All that man is,
All mere complexities,
The fury and the mire of human veins.

Before me floats an image, man or shade,
10   Shade more than man, more image than a shade;
For Hades' bobbin° bound in mummy-cloth   *spool*
May unwind the winding path;
A mouth that has no moisture and no breath
Breathless mouths may summon;
15   I hail the superhuman;
I call it death-in-life and life-in-death.

Miracle, bird or golden handiwork,
More miracle than bird or handiwork,
Planted on the starlit golden bough,
20   Can like the cocks of Hades crow,
Or, by the moon embittered, scorn aloud
In glory of changeless metal
Common bird or petal
And all complexities of mire or blood.

25   At midnight on the Emperor's pavement flit
Flames that no faggot° feeds, nor steel has lit,   *bundle of sticks*
Nor storm disturbs, flames begotten of flame,
Where blood-begotten spirits come
And all complexities of fury leave,
30   Dying into a dance,
An agony of trance,
An agony of flame that cannot singe a sleeve.

Astraddle on the dolphin's mire and blood,
Spirit after spirit! The smithies break the flood,
35   The golden smithies of the Emperor!
Marbles of the dancing floor
Break bitter furies of complexity,
Those images that yet
Fresh images beget,
40   That dolphin-torn, that gong-tormented sea.

1930   1932

Crazy Jane Talks with the Bishop

I met the Bishop on the road
And much said he and I.
"Those breasts are flat and fallen now
Those veins must soon be dry;
5   Live in a heavenly mansion,
Not in some foul sty."

"Fair and foul are near of kin,
And fair needs foul," I cried.
"My friends are gone, but that's a truth
10   Nor grave nor bed denied,
Learned in bodily lowliness
And in the heart's pride.

"A woman can be proud and stiff
When on love intent;
15   But Love has pitched his mansion in
The place of excrement;
For nothing can be sole or whole
That has not been rent."

1931   1932

Lapis Lazuli[1]
(FOR HARRY CLIFTON[2])

I have heard that hysterical women say
They are sick of the palette and fiddle-bow,
Of poets that are always gay,
For everybody knows or else should know
5   That if nothing drastic is done
Aeroplane and Zeppelin will come out,
Pitch like King Billy bomb-balls[3] in
Until the town lie beaten flat.

All perform their tragic play,
10   There struts Hamlet, there is Lear,
That's Ophelia, that Cordelia;[4]
Yet they, should the last scene be there,
The great stage curtain about to drop,
If worthy their prominent part in the play,

---

1. A rich blue mineral producing the pigment ultramarine; used by the ancients for decoration.
2. A friend who gave Yeats a carving in lapis lazuli on his birthday.

3. German bombs; "King Billy" is a nickname for Kaiser Wilhelm II.
4. Characters from *Hamlet* and *King Lear*.

15 Do not break up their lines to weep.
    They know that Hamlet and Lear are gay;
    Gaiety transfiguring all that dread.
    All men have aimed at, found and lost;
    Black out; Heaven blazing into the head:
20 Tragedy wrought to its uttermost.
    Though Hamlet rambles and Lear rages,
    And all the drop scenes drop at once
    Upon a hundred thousand stages,
    It cannot grow by an inch or an ounce.

25 On their own feet they came, or on shipboard,
    Camel-back, horse-back, ass-back, mule-back,
    Old civilisations put to the sword.
    Then they and their wisdom went to rack:
    No handiwork of Callimachus[5]
30 Who handled marble as if it were bronze,
    Made draperies that seemed to rise
    When sea-wind swept the corner, stands;
    His long lamp chimney shaped like the stem
    Of a slender palm, stood but a day;
35 All things fall and are built again
    And those that build them again are gay.

    Two Chinamen, behind them a third,
    Are carved in Lapis Lazuli,
    Over them flies a long-legged bird
40 A symbol of longevity;
    The third, doubtless a serving-man,
    Carries a musical instrument.

    Every discolouration of the stone,
    Every accidental crack or dent
45 Seems a water-course or an avalanche,
    Or lofty slope where it still snows
    Though doubtless plum or cherry-branch
    Sweetens the little half-way house
    Those Chinamen climb towards, and I
50 Delight to imagine them seated there;
    There, on the mountain and the sky,
    On all the tragic scene they stare.
    One asks for mournful melodies;
    Accomplished fingers begin to play.
55 Their eyes mid many wrinkles, their eyes,
    Their ancient, glittering eyes, are gay.

1936   1938

The Circus Animals' Desertion

1

    I sought a theme and sought for it in vain,
    I sought it daily for six weeks or so.
    Maybe at last being but a broken man

---

5. Greek poet, grammarian, critic, and sculptor (c. 310–c. 240 B.C.).

5   I must be satisfied with my heart, although
      Winter and summer till old age began
      My circus animals were all on show,
      Those stilted boys, that burnished chariot,
      Lion and woman and the Lord knows what.

                              2
      What can I but enumerate old themes,
10   First that sea-rider Oisin[1] led by the nose
      Through three enchanted islands, allegorical dreams,
      Vain gaiety, vain battle, vain repose,
      Themes of the embittered heart, or so it seems,
      That might adorn old songs or courtly shows;
15   But what cared I that set him on to ride,
      I, starved for the bosom of his fairy bride.

      And then a counter-truth filled out its play,
      "The Countess Cathleen"[2] was the name I gave it,
      She, pity-crazed, had given her soul away
20   But masterful Heaven had intervened to save it.
      I thought my dear must her own soul destroy
      So did fanaticism and hate enslave it,
      And this brought forth a dream and soon enough
      This dream itself had all my thought and love.

25   And when the Fool and Blind Man stole the bread
      Cuchulain[3] fought the ungovernable sea;
      Heart mysteries there, and yet when all is said
      It was the dream itself enchanted me:
      Character isolated by a deed
30   To engross the present and dominate memory.
      Players and painted stage took all my love
      And not those things that they were emblems of.

                              3
      Those masterful images because complete
      Grew in pure mind but out of what began?
35   A mound of refuse or the sweepings of a street,
      Old kettles, old bottles, and a broken can,
      Old iron, old bones, old rags, that raving slut
      Who keeps the till. Now that my ladder's gone
      I must lie down where all the ladders start
40   In the foul rag and bone shop of the heart.

                                                          1939

Under Ben Bulben[1]

1

Swear by what the Sages spoke
Round the Mareotic Lake[2]

---

1. Mythical Irish poet-warrior, son of the great Finn, who crossed the sea on an enchanted horse; hero of Yeats's early narrative poem *The Wanderings of Oisin*.
2. Yeats's play *The Countess Cathleen* (1899) tells the traditional story of Kathleen ni Houlihan, allegorical symbol of Ireland.

3. Hero of the medieval Irish epic *The Tain*, who single-handedly defended Ulster.
1. A mountain in County Sligo.
2. An ancient region south of Alexandria, Egypt, known as a center of Neoplatonism.

That the Witch of Atlas[3] knew,
Spoke and set the cocks a-crow.

5   Swear by those horsemen, by those women
Complexion and form prove superhuman,
That pale, long-visaged company
That airs an immortality
Completeness of their passions won;
10 Now they ride the wintry dawn
Where Ben Bulben sets the scene.

Here's the gist of what they mean.

2

Many times man lives and dies
Between his two eternities,
15 That of race and that of soul,
And ancient Ireland knew it all.
Whether man dies in his bed
Or the rifle knocks him dead,
A brief parting from those dear
20 Is the worst man has to fear.
Though grave-diggers' toil is long,
Sharp their spades, their muscle strong,
They but thrust their buried men
Back in the human mind again.

3

25 You that Mitchel's prayer have heard,
"Send war in our time, O Lord!"[4]
Know that when all words are said
And a man is fighting mad,
Something drops from eyes long blind,
30 He completes his partial mind,
For an instant stands at ease,
Laughs aloud, his heart at peace.
Even the wisest man grows tense
With some sort of violence
35 Before he can accomplish fate,
Know his work or choose his mate.

4

Poet and sculptor do the work,
Nor let the modish painter shirk
What his great forefathers did,
40 Bring the soul of man to God,
Make him fill the cradles right.

Measurement began our might:
Forms a stark Egyptian[5] thought,
Forms that gentler Phidias wrought.
45 Michael Angelo left a proof
On the Sistine Chapel roof,
Where but half-awakened Adam

---

3. *The Witch of Atlas* is the title of a poem by Percy Shelley.
4. John Mitchel, revolutionary patriot, wrote "Give us war in our time, O Lord!" while in prison.

5. Plotinus, 3rd-century A.D. Egyptian-born philosopher, founder of Neoplatonism.

Can disturb globe-trotting Madam
Till her bowels are in heat,
50 Proof that there's a purpose set
Before the secret working mind:
Profane perfection of mankind.

Quattrocento[6] put in paint
On backgrounds for a God or Saint
55 Gardens where a soul's at ease;
Where everything that meets the eye,
Flowers and grass and cloudless sky
Resemble forms that are, or seem
When sleepers wake and yet still dream,
60 And when it's vanished still declare,
With only bed and bedstead there,
That Heavens had opened.
                              Gyres run on;
When that greater dream had gone
Calvert and Wilson, Blake and Claude,[7]
65 Prepared a rest for the people of God,
Palmer's phrase,[8] but after that
Confusion fell upon our thought.

                    5
Irish poets learn your trade,
Sing whatever is well made,
70 Scorn the sort now growing up
All out of shape from toe to top,
Their unremembering hearts and heads
Base-born products of base beds.
Sing the peasantry, and then
75 Hard-riding country gentlemen,
The holiness of monks, and after
Porter-drinkers' randy° laughter;   lusty
Sing the lords and ladies gay
That were beaten into the clay
80 Through seven heroic centuries;[9]
Cast your mind on other days
That we in coming days may be
Still the indomitable Irishry.

                    6
Under bare Ben Bulben's head
85 In Drumcliff[1] churchyard Yeats is laid.
An ancestor was rector there
Long years ago; a church stands near,
By the road an ancient cross.
No marble, no conventional phrase,

6. Fifteenth-century artists of Italy's Renaissance.
7. Edward Calvert (1799–1883), English painter and engraver, disciple of Blake; Richard Wilson (1714–1782), British landscape painter; Claude Lorrain (1600–1682), French landscape painter.
8. Samuel Palmer (1805–1881), English painter of vision-

ary landscapes and admirer of Blake.
9. I.e., the seven centuries since the conquest of Ireland by Henry II.
1. A village lying on the slopes of Ben Bulben, where Yeats was buried.

90   On limestone quarried near the spot
            By his command these words are cut:

            Cast a cold eye
            On life, on death.
            Horseman, pass by!

1938   1939

┅┅ ⊰◈⊱ ┅┅

James Joyce
1882–1941

James Joyce was one of the great innovators who brought the novel into the modern era. As T. S. Eliot put it, Joyce made "the modern world possible for art." The poet Edith Sitwell wrote that by the turn of the century, "language had become, not so much an abused medium, as a dead and outworn thing, in which there was no living muscular system. Then came the rebirth of the medium, and this was effected, as far as actual vocabularies were concerned, very largely by such prose writers as Mr. James Joyce and Miss Gertrude Stein." Joyce objected to this flaccidity, citing examples in the work of George Moore, the most important Irish novelist of the first decade of the twentieth; Moore's novel *The Untilled Field*, Joyce complained to his brother Stanislaus, was "damned stupid," "dull and flat" and "ill written." In a comment that would have pleased Joyce, one critic writing in 1929 declared that Joyce had by that date "conclusively reduced all the pretensions of the realistic novel to absurdity."

James Augustus Aloysius Joyce was born in Rathgar, a middle-class suburb of Dublin; though he was to leave Ireland more or less permanently at age twenty-two, Ireland generally, and "Dear Dirty Dublin" specifically, were never far from his mind and writing. He was the eldest surviving son in a large family consisting, according to his father, of "sixteen or seventeen children." His father, John Stanislaus Joyce, born and raised in Cork, was a tax collector and sometime Parnellite political employee; his mother was Mary Jane Joyce, née Murray. There is no better imaginative guide to the twists and turns of Joyce's family fortunes, and their effect on the young writer, than his first novel, *A Portrait of the Artist as a Young Man*; the life of Joyce's autobiographical hero Stephen Dedalus closely follows Joyce's own. The novel brings young Stephen from his earliest memories, through his Catholic schooling at Clongowes Wood College and Belvedere College, up to his graduation from University College, Dublin, and departure for Paris. Like Stephen, Joyce in these years first considered entering the priesthood, then began regarding Catholicism with increasing skepticism and irony, coming to view religion, family, and nation as three kinds of net or trap. One of the most important events of the early part of Joyce's life was the betrayal and subsequent death of "the uncrowned king of Ireland," Charles Stewart Parnell, the political leader who was working hard to make Home Rule for Ireland a reality; his demise, after his adulterous affair with Kitty O'Shea was discovered, was remembered by Joyce in his first poem, *Et Tu, Healy*—which he wrote at the age of eight—and in a haunting story, *Ivy Day in the Committee Room*. Joyce moved to Paris after graduation in 1902 and began medical studies, but he soon had to return to Dublin, as his mother was dying. Joyce gave up the idea of a medical career, which his father could not afford to finance in any event; he briefly tried teaching school, and sought to define himself as a writer.

Like Dedalus, the young Joyce first concentrated on writing poetry. The majority of his early poems were collected in the volume *Chamber Music* (1907); both the strength and weakness of the poems is suggested by the praise of Arthur Symons, who in his review in the *Nation* described the lyrics as "tiny, evanescent things." Poetry was ultimately to prove a dead end for Joyce; though he brought out one more volume of thirteen poems during his lifetime (*Pomes*

Penyeach, 1927), and wrote one forgettable play (*Exiles*, 1918), prose fiction is the primary area in which Joyce's influence continues to be felt.

The year 1904 proved to be an absolute watershed in Joyce's development as a writer. In January 1904—indeed, perhaps in the single day 7 January 1904—Joyce wrote an impressionistic prose sketch which would ultimately serve as the manifesto for his first novel. From this beginning, Joyce shaped his novel, which was to have been called *Stephen Hero*; and though he worked on it steadily for more than three years, and the manuscript grew to almost a thousand pages, the novel was not coming together in quite the way Joyce had hoped. Hence in the fall of 1907, he began cutting and radically reshaping the material into what would become *A Portrait of the Artist as a Young Man*, one of the finest examples of the *Künstlerroman* (novel of artistic growth) in English; H. G. Wells called it "by far the most living and convincing picture that exists of an Irish Catholic upbringing."

June 16, 1904, in particular is a crucial day in the Joycean calendar, for it is "Bloomsday"—the day on which the events narrated in *Ulysses* take place—and according to legend, it is the day that Nora Barnacle first agreed to go out walking with Joyce. Joyce's father thought Nora's maiden name a good omen, suggesting that she would "stick to him," and indeed she did; without the benefit of marriage, she agreed to accompany him four months later on his artistic exile to the Continent, and though they were not legally married until 1931, she proved a faithful and devoted partner, a small spot of stability amidst the chaos of Joyce's life. They settled for several years in Trieste, Italy, where Joyce taught English at a Berlitz school and where their two children, Giorgio and Lucia, were born. Joyce returned briefly to Ireland in 1909, seeking unsuccessfully to get work published and to start a movie theater; after another brief visit in 1912, he never returned. He spent most of World War I in Zurich, then moved to Paris, where he eked out an existence with the help of several benefactors as his reputation began to grow.

He had begun his first book in June or July 1904, invited by the Irish man of letters "A.E." (George Russell) to submit a short story to his paper *The Irish Homestead*. Joyce began writing the series of fifteen stories that would be published in 1914 as *Dubliners*. In letters to London publisher Grant Richards about his conception for the short stories, Joyce wrote that he planned the volume to be a chapter of Ireland's "moral history" and that in writing it he had "taken the first step towards the spiritual liberation of my country." Richards, however, objected to the stark realism—or sordidness—of several scenes, and pressed Joyce to eliminate vulgarisms; Joyce refused. Finally, desperate to have the book published, Joyce wrote to Richards: "I seriously believe that you will retard the course of civilisation in Ireland by preventing the Irish people from having one good look at themselves in my nicely polished looking-glass."

During this period, Joyce also experimented with a form of short prose sketch that he called the "epiphany." An epiphany, as it is defined in *Stephen Hero*, is "a sudden spiritual manifestation, whether in the vulgarity of speech or of gesture or in a memorable phase of the mind itself." It consequently falls to the artist to "record these epiphanies with extreme care, seeing that they themselves are the most delicate and evanescent of moments." One benefit of Joyce's experimentation with prose epiphanies is that the searching realism and psychological richness of the stories in *Dubliners* are conveyed with a lucid economy of phrasing—what Joyce called "a style of scrupulous meanness"—and by a similar penchant for understatement on the level of plot. The stories often seem to "stop," rather than end; time and again, Joyce withholds the tidy conclusion that conventional fiction had trained readers to expect. In story after story, characters betray what Joyce termed their "paralysis"—a paralysis of the will that prevents them from breaking out of deadening habit. The final story of the collection, *The Dead*—written after the volume had ostensibly been completed, and comprising a broader scope and larger cast of characters than the other stories—is Joyce's finest work of short fiction, and justly praised as one of the great stories of our time; it was filmed, quite sensitively and beautifully, by director John Huston, the last film project before his death.

A second decisive year for Joyce was 1914. Having completed *Dubliners*, Joyce seems never to have thought seriously about writing short fiction again; and throughout the period he was writing his stories, he continued to work on *A Portrait*. As was the case with *Dubliners*, negotiations for the publication of *A Portrait* were extremely difficult; despite its dazzling language, few editors could get beyond the opening pages, with their references to bedwetting and their use of crude slang. Even though the novel had been published serially in *The Egoist* beginning in 1914, and was praised by influential writers like W. B. Yeats, H. G. Wells, and Ezra Pound, the book was rejected by every publisher in London to whom Joyce offered it, before finally being accepted by B. W. Huebsch in New York, and published in December 1916.

With both his stories and his first novel between hard covers, Joyce was finally able to concentrate his energies on the one novel for which, more than any other, he will be remembered—*Ulysses*; that work, too, had begun in 1914. The novel is structured, loosely, on eighteen episodes from Homer's *Odyssey*; Leopold Bloom, advertising salesman, is a modern-day Ulysses, the streets of Dublin his Aegean Sea, and Molly Bloom his (unfaithful) Penelope. Stephen Dedalus, stuck teaching school and estranged from his real father, is an unwitting Telemachus (Ulysses' son) in search of a father. Critics have disagreed over the years as to how seriously readers should take these Homeric parallels; Eliot understood them to be of the utmost importance—"a way of controlling, of ordering, of giving a shape and a significance to the immense panorama of futility and anarchy which is contemporary history"—while the equally supportive Pound suggested that the parallel structure was merely "the remains of a medieval allegorical culture; it matters little, it is a question of cooking, which does not restrict the action, nor inconvenience it, nor harm the realism, nor the contemporaneity of the action."

Concomitant with the Homeric structure, Joyce sought to give each of his eighteen chapters its own style. Chapter 12, focusing on Bloom's encounter with Dublin's Cyclops, called "the Citizen," is written in a style of "gigantism"—full of mock-epic epithets and catalogues, playfully suggestive of the style of ancient Celtic myth and legend. Chapter 13, which parallels Odysseus's encounter with Nausicäa, is written in the exaggerated style of Victorian women's magazines and sentimental fiction, a style which Joyce characterized as "a namby-pamby jammy marmalady drawersy (alto-là!) style with effects of incense, mariolatry, masturbation, stewed cockles, painter's palette, chitchat, circumlocutions, etc etc." While realist writers sought constantly to flush artifice from their writing, to arrive finally at a style which would be value-neutral, Joyce takes the English language on a voyage in the opposite direction; each chapter, as he wrote to his patron Harriet Shaw Weaver, left behind it "a burnt-up field." It would be difficult to overestimate the influence that *Ulysses* has had on modern writing; Eliot's candid response to the novel, reported in a letter to Joyce, was "I have nothing but admiration; in fact, I wish, for my own sake, that I had not read it."

Other people wanted to make sure that no one else would read it. *Ulysses* was promptly banned as obscene, in Ireland, England, and many other countries. Copies were smuggled into the United States, where a pirated edition was published, paying Joyce no royalties. Finally in 1933, in a landmark decision, a federal judge found that the book's frank language and sexual discussions were fully justified artistically—though he allowed that "*Ulysses* is a rather strong draught to ask some sensitive, though normal, persons to take."

In 1923, with *Ulysses* published, Joyce suddenly reinvented himself and his writing once again, and turned his attention to the writing of the novel that would occupy him almost until his death—*Finnegans Wake*. If *Ulysses* attacks the novel form at the level of style, *Finnegans Wake* targets the very structures of the English language, using a neologismic amalgam of more than a dozen modern and ancient languages—a hybrid that devotees call "Wakese"; when questioned as to the wisdom of such a strategy, Joyce replied that *Ulysses* had proved English to be inadequate. "I'd like a language," he told his friend Stefan Zweig, "which is above all languages, a language to which all will do service. I cannot express myself in English without enclosing myself in a tradition."

On 13 January 1941, Joyce died of a perforated ulcer; his illness and death almost certainly owed something to an adult life of rather heavy drinking. Though his oeuvre consists largely of one volume of short stories and three novels, his importance for students of modern literature is extraordinary. As Richard Ellmann writes at the opening of his magisterial biography, "We are still learning to be James Joyce's contemporaries, to understand our interpreter."

from DUBLINERS
Clay

The matron had given her leave to go out as soon as the women's tea was over and Maria looked forward to her evening out. The kitchen was spick and span: the cook said you could see yourself in the big copper boilers. The fire was nice and bright and on one of the side-tables were four very big barmbracks.[1] These barmbracks seemed uncut; but if you went closer you would see that they had been cut into long thick even slices and were ready to be handed round at tea. Maria had cut them herself.

Maria was a very, very small person indeed but she had a very long nose and a very long chin. She talked a little through her nose, always soothingly: *Yes, my dear*, and *No, my dear*. She was always sent for when the women quarrelled over their tubs and always succeeded in making peace. One day the matron had said to her:

—Maria, you are a veritable peace-maker!

And the sub-matron and two of the Board ladies[2] had heard the compliment. And Ginger Mooney was always saying what she wouldn't do to the dummy[3] who had charge of the irons if it wasn't for Maria. Everyone was so fond of Maria.

The women would have their tea at six o'clock and she would be able to get away before seven. From Ballsbridge to the Pillar, twenty minutes; from the Pillar to Drumcondra, twenty minutes; and twenty minutes to buy the things. She would be there before eight. She took out her purse with the silver clasps and read again the words *A Present from Belfast*. She was very fond of that purse because Joe had brought it to her five years before when he and Alphy had gone to Belfast on a Whit-Monday[4] trip. In the purse were two half-crowns and some coppers. She would have five shillings clear after paying tram fare. What a nice evening they would have, all the children singing! Only she hoped that Joe wouldn't come in drunk. He was so different when he took any drink.

Often he had wanted her to go and live with them; but she would have felt herself in the way (though Joe's wife was ever so nice with her) and she had become accustomed to the life of the laundry. Joe was a good fellow. She had nursed him and Alphy too; and Joe used often say:

—Mamma is mamma but Maria is my proper mother.

After the break-up at home the boys had got her that position in the *Dublin by Lamplight* laundry,[5] and she liked it. She used to have such a bad opinion of Protestants but now she thought they were very nice people, a little quiet and serious, but still very nice people to live with. Then she had her plants in the conservatory and she liked looking after them. She had lovely ferns and wax-plants and, whenever anyone came to visit her, she always gave the visitor one or two slips from her con-

---

1. Speckled cakes or currant buns.
2. Members of the governing board of the Dublin by Lamplight Laundry.
3. Slang for a mute person.
4. Holiday following Whitsunday, the seventh Sunday after Easter.

5. Joyce's invented benevolent society, run by Protestant women, "saves" Dublin's prostitutes from a life on the streets by giving them honest work in a laundry. Maria works for the laundry but appears not to be a reformed prostitute herself.

servatory. There was one thing she didn't like and that was the tracts[6] on the walls; but the matron was such a nice person to deal with, so genteel.

When the cook told her everything was ready she went into the women's room and began to pull the big bell. In a few minutes the women began to come in by twos and threes, wiping their steaming hands in their petticoats and pulling down the sleeves of their blouses over their red steaming arms. They settled down before their huge mugs which the cook and the dummy filled up with hot tea, already mixed with milk and sugar in huge tin cans. Maria superintended the distribution of the barmbrack and saw that every woman got her four slices. There was a great deal of laughing and joking during the meal. Lizzie Fleming said Maria was sure to get the ring and, though Fleming had said that for so many Hallow Eves, Maria had to laugh and say she didn't want any ring or man either; and when she laughed her grey-green eyes sparkled with disappointed shyness and the tip of her nose nearly met the tip of her chin. Then Ginger Mooney lifted up her mug of tea and proposed Maria's health while all the other women clattered with their mugs on the table, and said she was sorry she hadn't a sup of porter[7] to drink it in. And Maria laughed again till the tip of her nose nearly met the tip of her chin and till her minute body nearly shook itself asunder because she knew that Mooney meant well though, of course, she had the notions of a common woman.

But wasn't Maria glad when the women had finished their tea and the cook and the dummy had begun to clear away the tea-things! She went into her little bedroom and, remembering that the next morning was a mass morning, changed the hand of the alarm from seven to six. Then she took off her working skirt and her house-boots and laid her best skirt out on the bed and her tiny dress-boots beside the foot of the bed. She changed her blouse too and, as she stood before the mirror, she thought of how she used to dress for mass on Sunday morning when she was a young girl; and she looked with quaint affection at the diminutive body which she had so often adorned. In spite of its years she found it a nice tidy little body.

When she got outside the streets were shining with rain and she was glad of her old brown raincloak. The tram was full and she had to sit on the little stool at the end of the car, facing all the people, with her toes barely touching the floor. She arranged in her mind all she was going to do and thought how much better it was to be independent and to have your own money in your pocket. She hoped they would have a nice evening. She was sure they would but she could not help thinking what a pity it was Alphy and Joe were not speaking. They were always falling out now but when they were boys together they used to be the best of friends: but such was life.

She got out of her tram at the Pillar and ferreted her way quickly among the crowds. She went into Downes's cakeshop but the shop was so full of people that it was a long time before she could get herself attended to. She bought a dozen of mixed penny cakes, and at last came out of the shop laden with a big bag. Then she thought what else would she buy: she wanted to buy something really nice. They would be sure to have plenty of apples and nuts. It was hard to know what to buy and all she could think of was cake. She decided to buy some plumcake but Downes's plumcake had not enough almond icing on top of it so she went over to a shop in Henry Street. Here she was a long time in suiting herself and the stylish young lady behind the counter, who was evidently a little annoyed by her, asked her was it wedding-cake she wanted to buy. That made Maria blush and smile at the young lady; but the young lady took it all very seriously and finally cut a thick slice of plumcake, parcelled it up and said:

6. Evangelical religious texts.   7. A heavy, dark brown ale.

—Two-and-four, please.

She thought she would have to stand in the Drumcondra tram because none of the young men seemed to notice her but an elderly gentleman made room for her. He was a stout gentleman and he wore a brown hard hat; he had a square red face and a greyish moustache. Maria thought he was a colonel-looking gentleman and she reflected how much more polite he was than the young men who simply stared straight before them. The gentleman began to chat with her about Hallow Eve and the rainy weather. He supposed the bag was full of good things for the little ones and said it was only right that the youngsters should enjoy themselves while they were young. Maria agreed with him and favoured him with demure nods and hems. He was very nice with her, and when she was getting out at the Canal Bridge she thanked him and bowed, and he bowed to her and raised his hat and smiled agreeably; and while she was going up along the terrace, bending her tiny head under the rain, she thought how easy it was to know a gentleman even when he has a drop taken.

Everybody said: O, here's Maria! when she came to Joe's house. Joe was there, having come home from business, and all the children had their Sunday dresses on. There were two big girls in from next door and games were going on. Maria gave the bag of cakes to the eldest boy, Alphy, to divide and Mrs Donnelly said it was too good of her to bring such a big bag of cakes and made all the children say:

—Thanks, Maria.

But Maria said she had brought something special for papa and mamma, something they would be sure to like, and she began to look for her plumcake. She tried in Downes's bag and then in the pockets of her raincloak and then on the hallstand but nowhere could she find it. Then she asked all the children had any of them eaten it—by mistake, of course—but the children all said no and looked as if they did not like to eat cakes if they were to be accused of stealing. Everybody had a solution for the mystery and Mrs Donnelly said it was plain that Maria had left it behind her in the tram. Maria, remembering how confused the gentleman with the greyish moustache had made her, coloured with shame and vexation and disappointment. At the thought of the failure of her little surprise and of the two and fourpence she had thrown away for nothing she nearly cried outright.

But Joe said it didn't matter and made her sit down by the fire. He was very nice with her. He told her all that went on in his office, repeating for her a smart answer which he had made to the manager. Maria did not understand why Joe laughed so much over the answer he had made but she said that the manager must have been a very overbearing person to deal with. Joe said he wasn't so bad when you knew how to take him, that he was a decent sort so long as you didn't rub him the wrong way. Mrs Donnelly played the piano for the children and they danced and sang. Then the two next-door girls handed round the nuts. Nobody could find the nutcrackers and Joe was nearly getting cross over it and asked how did they expect Maria to crack nuts without a nutcracker. But Maria said she didn't like nuts and that they weren't to bother about her. Then Joe asked would she take a bottle of stout[8] and Mrs Donnelly said there was port wine too in the house if she would prefer that. Maria said she would rather they didn't ask her to take anything: but Joe insisted.

So Maria let him have his way and they sat by the fire talking over old times and Maria thought she would put in a good word for Alphy. But Joe cried that God might strike him stone dead if ever he spoke a word to his brother again and Maria said she

8. An extra-strength ale.

was sorry she had mentioned the matter. Mrs Donnelly told her husband it was a great shame for him to speak that way of his own flesh and blood but Joe said that Alphy was no brother of his and there was nearly being a row[9] on the head of it. But Joe said he would not lose his temper on account of the night it was and asked his wife to open some more stout. The two next-door girls had arranged some Hallow Eve games[1] and soon everything was merry again. Maria was delighted to see the children so merry and Joe and his wife in such good spirits. The next-door girls put some saucers on the table and then led the children up to the table, blindfold. One got the prayer-book and the other three got the water; and when one of the next-door girls got the ring Mrs Donnelly shook her finger at the blushing girl as much as to say: *O, I know all about it!* They insisted then on blindfolding Maria and leading her up to the table to see what she would get; and, while they were putting on the bandage, Maria laughed and laughed again till the tip of her nose nearly met the tip of her chin.

They led her up to the table amid laughing and joking and she put her hand out in the air as she was told to do. She moved her hand about here and there in the air and descended on one of the saucers. She felt a soft wet substance with her fingers and was surprised that nobody spoke or took off her bandage. There was a pause for a few seconds; and then a great deal of scuffling and whispering. Somebody said something about the garden, and at last Mrs Donnelly said something very cross to one of the next-door girls and told her to throw it out at once: that was no play. Maria understood that it was wrong that time and so she had to do it over again: and this time she got the prayer-book.

After that Mrs Donnelly played Miss McCloud's Reel for the children and Joe made Maria take a glass of wine. Soon they were all quite merry again and Mrs Donnelly said Maria would enter a convent before the year was out because she had got the prayer-book. Maria had never seen Joe so nice to her as he was that night, so full of pleasant talk and reminiscences. She said they were all very good to her.

At last the children grew tired and sleepy and Joe asked Maria would she not sing some little song before she went, one of the old songs. Mrs Donnelly said *Do, please, Maria!* and so Maria had to get up and stand beside the piano. Mrs Donnelly bade the children be quiet and listen to Maria's song. Then she played the prelude and said *Now, Maria!* and Maria, blushing very much, began to sing in a tiny quavering voice. She sang *I Dreamt that I Dwelt,*[2] and when she came to the second verse she sang again:

> *I dreamt that I dwelt in marble halls*
> *   With vassals and serfs at my side*
> *And of all who assembled within those walls*
> *   That I was the hope and the pride.*
> *I had riches too great to count, could boast*
> *   Of a high ancestral name,*
> *But I also dreamt, which pleased me most,*
> *   That you loved me still the same.*

---

9. Argument.
1. The primary game that Maria and the girls play is a traditional Irish Halloween game. In its original version, a blindfolded girl would be led to three plates, and would choose one. Choosing the plate with a ring meant that she would soon marry; water meant she would emigrate (probably to America); and soil, or clay, meant she would soon die. In modern times, a prayer book was substituted for this unsavory third option, suggesting that the girl would enter a convent.
2. Aria from Act 2 of *The Bohemian Girl.*

But no one tried to show her her mistake;[3] and when she had ended her song Joe was very much moved. He said that there was no time like the long ago and no music for him like poor old Balfe, whatever other people might say; and his eyes filled up so much with tears that he could not find what he was looking for and in the end he had to ask his wife to tell him where the corkscrew was.

Ivy Day in the Committee Room[1]

Old Jack raked the cinders together with a piece of cardboard and spread them judiciously over the whitening dome of coals. When the dome was thinly covered his face lapsed into darkness but, as he set himself to fan the fire again, his crouching shadow ascended the opposite wall and his face slowly re-emerged into light. It was an old man's face, very bony and hairy. The moist blue eyes blinked at the fire and the moist mouth fell open at times, munching once or twice mechanically when it closed. When the cinders had caught he laid the piece of cardboard against the wall, sighed and said:

—That's better now, Mr O'Connor.

Mr O'Connor, a grey-haired young man, whose face was disfigured by many blotches and pimples, had just brought the tobacco for a cigarette into a shapely cylinder but when spoken to he undid his handiwork meditatively. Then he began to roll the tobacco again meditatively and after a moment's thought decided to lick the paper.

—Did Mr Tierney say when he'd be back? he asked in a husky falsetto.

—He didn't say.

Mr O'Connor put his cigarette into his mouth and began to search his pockets. He took out a pack of thin paste-board cards.

—I'll get you a match, said the old man.

—Never mind, this'll do, said Mr O'Connor.

He selected one of the cards and read what was printed on it:

Municipal Elections

ROYAL EXCHANGE WARD[2]

Mr Richard J. Tierney, P.L.G.,[3] respectfully
solicits the favour of your vote
and influence at the coming election
in the Royal Exchange Ward

Mr O'Connor had been engaged by Mr Tierney's agent to canvass one part of the ward but, as the weather was inclement and his boots let in the wet, he spent a great part of the day sitting by the fire in the Committee Room in Wicklow Street with Jack, the old caretaker. They had been sitting thus since the short day had grown dark. It was the sixth of October, dismal and cold out of doors.

---

3. Maria repeats the first verse rather than singing the second.
1. On October 6—the anniversary of Parnell's death—it was customary among his followers to wear a sprig of ivy in his honor; Committee Room No. 15 was the scene of Parnell's emotional final speech as leader of the Irish par-

liamentary party (see page 2316). Parnell's betrayal and demise form the backdrop of the story; the other personages are fictional.
2. A political ward near the center of Dublin.
3. Poor Law Guardian, elected to oversee the local relief rolls.

Mr O'Connor tore a strip off the card and, lighting it, lit his cigarette. As he did so the flame lit up a leaf of dark glossy ivy in the lapel of his coat. The old man watched him attentively and then, taking up the piece of cardboard again, began to fan the fire slowly while his companion smoked.

—Ah, yes, he said, continuing, it's hard to know what way to bring up children. Now who'd think he'd turn out like that! I sent him to the Christian Brothers[4] and I done what I could for him, and there he goes boosing about. I tried to make him someway decent.

He replaced the cardboard wearily.

—Only I'm an old man now I'd change his tune for him. I'd take the stick to his back and beat him while I could stand over him—as I done many a time before. The mother, you know, she cocks him up with this and that. . . .

—That's what ruins children, said Mr O'Connor.

—To be sure it is, said the old man. And little thanks you get for it, only impudence. He takes th'upper hand of me whenever he sees I've a sup taken. What's the world coming to when sons speaks that way of their father?

—What age is he? said Mr O'Connor.

—Nineteen, said the old man.

—Why don't you put him to something?[5]

—Sure, amn't I never done at the drunken bowsy ever since he left school? *I won't keep you,* I says. *You must get a job for yourself.* But, sure, it's worse whenever he gets a job; he drinks it all.

Mr O'Connor shook his head in sympathy, and the old man fell silent, gazing into the fire. Someone opened the door of the room and called out:

—Hello! Is this a Freemason's[6] meeting?

—Who's that? said the old man.

—What are you doing in the dark? asked a voice.

—Is that you, Hynes? asked Mr O'Connor.

—Yes. What are you doing in the dark? said Mr Hynes, advancing into the light of the fire.

He was a tall slender young man with a light brown moustache. Imminent little drops of rain hung at the brim of his hat and the collar of his jacket-coat was turned up.

—Well, Mat, he said to Mr O'Connor, how goes it?

Mr O'Connor shook his head. The old man left the hearth and, after stumbling about the room returned with two candlesticks which he thrust one after the other into the fire and carried to the table. A denuded room came into view and the fire lost all its cheerful colour. The walls of the room were bare except for a copy of an election address. In the middle of the room was a small table on which papers were heaped.

Mr Hynes leaned against the mantelpiece and asked:

—Has he paid you yet?

—Not yet, said Mr O'Connor. I hope to God he'll not leave us in the lurch to-night.

Mr Hynes laughed.

—O, he'll pay you. Never fear, he said.

—I hope he'll look smart about it if he means business, said Mr O'Connor.

4. The Irish Christian Brothers, a conservative Catholic order, operate a number of day schools throughout Ireland.

5. I.e., get him a job.
6. A worldwide secret, fraternal order.

—What do you think, Jack? said Mr Hynes satirically to the old man.

The old man returned to his seat by the fire, saying:

—It isn't but he has it, anyway. Not like the other tinker.[7]

—What other tinker? said Mr Hynes.

—Colgan, said the old man scornfully.

—Is it because Colgan's a working-man you say that? What's the difference between a good honest bricklayer and a publican[8]—eh? Hasn't the working-man as good a right to be in the Corporation[9] as anyone else—ay, and a better right than those shoneens[1] that are always hat in hand before any fellow with a handle to his name? Isn't that so, Mat? said Mr. Hynes, addressing Mr O'Connor.

—I think you're right, said Mr O'Connor.

—One man is a plain honest man with no hunker-sliding[2] about him. He goes in to represent the labour classes. This fellow you're working for only wants to get some job or other.

—Of course, the working-classes should be represented, said the old man.

—The working-man, said Mr Hynes, gets all kicks and no halfpence. But it's labour produces everything. The working-man is not looking for fat jobs for his sons and nephews and cousins. The working-man is not going to drag the honour of Dublin in the mud to please a German monarch.[3]

—How's that? said the old man.

—Don't you know they want to present an address of welcome to Edward Rex if he comes here next year? What do we want kowtowing to a foreign king?

—Our man won't vote for the address, said Mr O'Connor. He goes in on the Nationalist ticket.

—Won't he? said Mr Hynes. Wait till you see whether he will or not. I know him. Is it Tricky Dicky Tierney?

—By God! perhaps you're right, Joe, said Mr O'Connor. Anyway, I wish he'd turn up with the spondulics.[4]

The three men fell silent. The old man began to rake more cinders together. Mr Hynes took off his hat, shook it and then turned down the collar of his coat, displaying, as he did so, an ivy leaf in the lapel.

—If this man was alive, he said, pointing to the leaf, we'd have no talk of an address of welcome.

—That's true, said Mr O'Connor.

—Musha, God be with them times! said the old man. There was some life in it then.

The room was silent again. Then a bustling little man with a snuffling nose and very cold ears pushed in the door. He walked over quickly to the fire, rubbing his hands as if he intended to produce a spark from them.

—No money, boys, he said.

—Sit down here, Mr Henchy, said the old man, offering him his chair.

—O, don't stir, Jack, don't stir, said Mr Henchy.

He nodded curtly to Mr Hynes and sat down on the chair which the old man vacated.

—Did you serve Aungier Street? he asked Mr O'Connor.

---

7. A gypsy or beggar; a general term of abuse.
8. Bar keeper.
9. The Dublin civil service.
1. Good-for-nothings.
2. Laziness.

3. In July 1903, Edward VII of England, who was related to the German monarch, visited Dublin; the Dublin Corporation refused to make an address of welcome.
4. Money.

—Yes, said Mr O'Connor, beginning to search his pockets for memoranda.

—Did you call on Grimes?

—I did.

—Well? How does he stand?

—He wouldn't promise. He said: *I won't tell anyone what way I'm going to vote.* But I think he'll be all right.

—Why so?

—He asked me who the nominators were; and I told him. I mentioned Father Burke's name. I think it'll be all right.

Mr Henchy began to snuffle and to rub his hands over the fire at a terrific speed. Then he said:

—For the love of God, Jack, bring us a bit of coal. There must be some left.

The old man went out of the room.

—It's no go, said Mr Henchy, shaking his head. I asked the little shoeboy, but he said: *O, now, Mr Henchy, when I see the work going on properly I won't forget you, you may be sure.* Mean little tinker! 'Usha, how could he be anything else?

—What did I tell you, Mat? said Mr Hynes. Tricky Dicky Tierney.

—O, he's as tricky as they make 'em, said Mr Henchy. He hasn't got those little pigs' eyes for nothing. Blast his soul! Couldn't he pay up like a man instead of: *O, now, Mr Henchy, I must speak to Mr Fanning. . . . I've spent a lot of money?* Mean little shoeboy of hell! I suppose he forgets the time his little old father kept the hand-me-down shop in Mary's Lane.

—But is that a fact? asked Mr O'Connor.

—God, yes, said Mr Henchy. Did you never hear that? And the men used to go in on Sunday morning before the houses were open to buy a waistcoat or a trousers—moya! But Tricky Dicky's little old father always had a tricky little black bottle up in a corner. Do you mind now? That's that. That's where he first saw the light.

The old man returned with a few lumps of coal which he placed here and there on the fire.

—That's a nice how-do-you-do, said Mr O'Connor. How does he expect us to work for him if he won't stump up?

—I can't help it, said Mr Henchy. I expect to find the bailiffs in the hall when I go home.

Mr Hynes laughed and, shoving himself away from the mantelpiece with the aid of his shoulders, made ready to leave.

—It'll be all right when King Eddie comes, he said. Well, boys, I'm off for the present. See you later. 'Bye, 'bye.

He went out of the room slowly. Neither Mr Henchy nor the old man said anything but, just as the door was closing, Mr O'Connor who had been staring moodily into the fire, called out suddenly:

—'Bye, Joe.

Mr Henchy waited a few moments and then nodded in the direction of the door.

—Tell me, he said across the fire, what brings our friend in here? What does he want?

—'Usha, poor Joe! said Mr O'Connor, throwing the end of his cigarette into the fire, he's hard up like the rest of us.

Mr Henchy snuffled vigorously and spat so copiously that he nearly put out the fire which uttered a hissing protest.

—To tell you my private and candid opinion, he said, I think he's a man from the other camp. He's a spy of Colgan's if you ask me. *Just go round and try and find out how they're getting on. They won't suspect you.* Do you twig?[5]

—Ah, poor Joe is a decent skin, said Mr O'Connor.

—His father was a decent respectable man, Mr Henchy admitted: Poor old Larry Hynes! Many a good turn he did in his day! But I'm greatly afraid our friend is not nineteen carat. Damn it, I can understand a fellow being hard up but what I can't understand is a fellow sponging. Couldn't he have some spark of manhood about him?

—He doesn't get a warm welcome from me when he comes, said the old man. Let him work for his own side and not come spying around here.

—I don't know, said Mr O'Connor dubiously, as he took out cigarette-papers and tobacco. I think Joe Hynes is a straight man. He's a clever chap, too, with the pen. Do you remember that thing he wrote . . . ?

—Some of these hillsiders and fenians[6] are a bit too clever if you ask me, said Mr Henchy. Do you know what my private and candid opinion is about some of those little jokers? I believe half of them are in the pay of the Castle.[7]

—There's no knowing, said the old man.

—O, but I know it for a fact, said Mr Henchy. They're Castle hacks. . . . I don't say Hynes. . . . No, damn it, I think he's a stroke above that. . . . But there's a certain little nobleman with a cock-eye—you know the patriot I'm alluding to?

Mr O'Connor nodded.

—There's a lineal descendant of Major Sirr[8] for you if you like! O, the heart's blood of a patriot! That's a fellow now that'd sell his country for fourpence—ay—and go down on his bended knees and thank the Almighty Christ he had a country to sell.

There was a knock at the door.

—Come in! said Mr Henchy.

A person resembling a poor clergyman or a poor actor appeared in the doorway. His black clothes were tightly buttoned on his short body and it was impossible to say whether he wore a clergyman's collar or a layman's because the collar of his shabby frock-coat, the uncovered buttons of which reflected the candlelight, was turned up about his neck. He wore a round hat of hard black felt. His face, shining with raindrops, had the appearance of damp yellow cheese save where two rosy spots indicated the cheekbones. He opened his very long mouth suddenly to express disappointment and at the same time opened wide his very bright blue eyes to express pleasure and surprise.

—O, Father Keon! said Mr Henchy, jumping up from his chair. Is that you? Come in!

—O, no, no, no! said Father Keon quickly, pursing his lips as if he were addressing a child.

—Won't you come in and sit down?

—No, no, no! said Father Keon, speaking in a discreet indulgent velvety voice. Don't let me disturb you now! I'm just looking for Mr Fanning. . . .

—He's round at the *Black Eagle*, said Mr Henchy. But won't you come in and sit down a minute?

---

5. Do you get it?
6. The Fenians, also known as Hillside men, were a secret organization trying to overthrow English government in Ireland.

7. Dublin Castle, headquarters of the English government in Dublin.
8. Henry Charles Sirr, chief of Dublin police who worked with the English in putting down the rebellion of 1798.

—No, no, thank you. It was just a little business matter, said Father Keon. Thank you, indeed.

He retreated from the doorway and Mr Henchy, seizing one of the candlesticks, went to the door to light him downstairs.

—O, don't trouble, I beg!

—No, but the stairs is so dark.

—No, no, I can see. . . . Thank you, indeed.

—Are you right now?

—All right, thanks. . . . Thanks.

Mr Henchy returned with the candlestick and put it on the table. He sat down again at the fire. There was silence for a few moments.

—Tell me, John, said Mr O'Connor, lighting his cigarette with another paste-board card.

—Hm?

—What is he exactly?

—Ask me an easier one, said Mr Henchy.

—Fanning and himself seem to me very thick. They're often in Kavanagh's together. Is he a priest at all?

—'Mmmyes, I believe so. . . . I think he's what you call a black sheep. We haven't many of them, thank God! but we have a few. . . . He's an unfortunate man of some kind. . . .

—And how does he knock it out?[9] asked Mr O'Connor.

—That's another mystery.

—Is he attached to any chapel or church or institution or—

—No, said Mr Henchy. I think he's travelling on his own account. . . . God forgive me, he added, I thought he was the dozen of stout.

—Is there any chance of a drink itself? asked Mr O'Connor.

—I'm dry too, said the old man.

—I asked that little shoeboy three times, said Mr Henchy, would he send up a dozen of stout. I asked him again now but he was leaning on the counter in his shirt-sleeves having a deep goster[1] with Alderman Cowley.

—Why didn't you remind him? said Mr O'Connor.

—Well, I couldn't go over while he was talking to Alderman Cowley. I just waited till I caught his eye, and said: *About that little matter I was speaking to you about. . . . That'll be all right, Mr H.*, he said. Yerra, sure the little hop-o'-my-thumb has forgotten all about it.

—There's some deal on in that quarter, said Mr O'Connor thoughtfully. I saw the three of them hard at it yesterday at Suffolk Street corner.

—I think I know the little game they're at, said Mr Henchy. You must owe the City Fathers money nowadays if you want to be made Lord Mayor. Then they'll make you Lord Mayor. By God! I'm thinking seriously of becoming a City Father myself. What do you think? Would I do for the job?

Mr O'Connor laughed.

—So far as owing money goes. . . .

—Driving out of the Mansion House, said Mr Henchy, in all my vermin,[2] with Jack here standing up behind me in a powdered wig—eh?

9. How does he make a living?
1. Gossip session.

2. A pun on the *ermine* trimming the robes of the Lord Mayor.

—And make me your private secretary, John.

—Yes. And I'll make Father Keon my private chaplain. We'll have a family party.

—Faith, Mr Henchy, said the old man, you'd keep up better style than some of them. I was talking one day to old Keegan, the porter. *And how do you like your new master, Pat? says I to him. You haven't much entertaining now, says I. Entertaining! says he. He'd live on the smell of an oil-rag.* And do you know what he told me? Now, I declare to God, I didn't believe him.

—What? said Mr Henchy and Mr O'Connor.

—He told me: *What do you think of a Lord Mayor of Dublin sending out for a pound of chops for his dinner? How's that for high living? says he. Wisha! wisha, says I. A pound of chops, says he, coming into the Mansion House. Wisha! says I, what kind of people is going at all now?*

At this point there was a knock at the door, and a boy put in his head.

—What is it? said the old man.

—From the *Black Eagle,* said the boy, walking in sideways and depositing a basket on the floor with a noise of shaken bottles.

The old man helped the boy to transfer the bottles from the basket to the table and counted the full tally. After the transfer the boy put his basket on his arm and asked:

—Any bottles?

—What bottles? said the old man.

—Won't you let us drink them first? said Mr Henchy.

—I was told to ask for bottles.

—Come back to-morrow, said the old man.

—Here, boy! said Mr Henchy, will you run over to O'Farrell's and ask him to lend us a corkscrew—for Mr Henchy, say. Tell him we won't keep it a minute. Leave the basket there.

The boy went out and Mr Henchy began to rub his hands cheerfully, saying:

—Ah, well, he's not so bad after all. He's as good as his word, anyhow.

—There's no tumblers, said the old man.

—O, don't let that trouble you, Jack, said Mr Henchy. Many's the good man before now drank out of the bottle.

—Anyway, it's better than nothing, said Mr O'Connor.

—He's not a bad sort, said Mr Henchy, only Fanning has such a loan of him. He means well, you know, in his own tinpot[3] way.

The boy came back with the corkscrew. The old man opened three bottles and was handing back the corkscrew when Mr Henchy said to the boy:

—Would you like a drink, boy?

—If you please, sir, said the boy.

The old man opened another bottle grudgingly, and handed it to the boy.

—What age are you? he asked.

—Seventeen, said the boy.

As the old man said nothing further the boy took the bottle, said: *Here's my best respects, sir* to Mr Henchy, drank the contents, put the bottle back on the table and wiped his mouth with his sleeve. Then he took up the corkscrew and went out of the door sideways, muttering some form of salutation.

—That's the way it begins, said the old man.

3. Cheapskate.

—The thin edge of the wedge, said Mr Henchy.

The old man distributed the three bottles which he had opened and the men drank from them simultaneously. After having drunk each placed his bottle on the mantel-piece within hand's reach and drew in a long breath of satisfaction.

—Well, I did a good day's work to-day, said Mr Henchy, after a pause.

—That so, John?

—Yes. I got him one or two sure things in Dawson Street, Crofton and myself. Between ourselves, you know, Crofton (he's a decent chap, of course), but he's not worth a damn as a canvasser. He hasn't a word to throw to a dog. He stands and looks at the people while I do the talking.

Here two men entered the room. One of them was a very fat man, whose blue serge clothes seemed to be in danger of falling from his sloping figure. He had a big face which resembled a young ox's face in expression, staring blue eyes and a grizzled moustache. The other man, who was much younger and frailer, had a thin clean-shaven face. He wore a very high double collar and a wide-brimmed bowler hat.

—Hello, Crofton! said Mr Henchy to the fat man. Talk of the devil. . . .

—Where did the boose come from? asked the young man. Did the cow calve?

—O, of course, Lyons spots the drink first thing! said Mr O'Connor, laughing.

—Is that the way you chaps canvass, said Mr Lyons, and Crofton and I out in the cold and rain looking for votes?

—Why, blast your soul, said Mr Henchy, I'd get more votes in five minutes than you two'd get in a week.

—Open two bottles of stout, Jack, said Mr O'Connor.

—How can I? said the old man, when there's no corkscrew?

—Wait now, wait now! said Mr Henchy, getting up quickly. Did you ever see this little trick?

He took two bottles from the table and, carrying them to the fire, put them on the hob.[4] Then he sat down again by the fire and took another drink from his bottle. Mr Lyons sat on the edge of the table, pushed his hat towards the nape of his neck and began to swing his legs.

—Which is my bottle? he asked.

—This lad, said Mr Henchy.

Mr Crofton sat down on a box and looked fixedly at the other bottle on the hob. He was silent for two reasons. The first reason, sufficient in itself, was that he had nothing to say; the second reason was that he considered his companions beneath him. He had been a canvasser for Wilkins, the Conservative,[5] but when the Conservatives had withdrawn their man and, choosing the lesser of two evils, given their support to the Nationalist candidate, he had been engaged to work for Mr Tierney.

In a few minutes an apologetic *Pok!* was heard as the cork flew out of Mr Lyons' bottle. Mr Lyons jumped off the table, went to the fire, took his bottle and carried it back to the table.

—I was just telling them, Crofton, said Mr Henchy, that we got a good few votes to-day.

—Who did you get? asked Mr Lyons.

---

4. Ledge at the back of a fireplace.
5. In this context, a Conservative candidate is one who

supports English rule in Ireland, a Nationalist one who opposes it.

—Well, I got Parkes for one, and I got Atkinson for two, and I got Ward of Dawson Street. Fine old chap he is, too—regular old toff,[6] old Conservative! *But isn't your candidate a Nationalist? said he. He's a respectable man, said I. He's in favour of whatever will benefit this country. He's a big ratepayer,[7] I said. He has extensive house property in the city and three places of business and isn't it to his own advantage to keep down the rates? He's a prominent and respected citizen, said I, and a Poor Law Guardian, and he doesn't belong to any party, good, bad, or indifferent.* That's the way to talk to 'em.

—And what about the address to the King? said Mr Lyons, after drinking and smacking his lips.

—Listen to me, said Mr Henchy. What we want in this country, as I said to old Ward, is capital. The King's coming here will mean an influx of money into this country. The citizens of Dublin will benefit by it. Look at all the factories down by the quays there, idle! Look at all the money there is in the country if we only worked the old industries, the mills, the shipbuilding yards and factories. It's capital we want.

—But look here, John, said Mr O'Connor. Why should we welcome the King of England? Didn't Parnell himself . . .

—Parnell, said Mr Henchy, is dead. Now, here's the way I look at it. Here's this chap come to the throne after his old mother keeping him out of it till the man was grey. He's a man of the world, and he means well by us. He's a jolly fine decent fellow, if you ask me, and no damn nonsense about him. He just says to himself: *The old one never went to see these wild Irish. By Christ, I'll go myself and see what they're like.* And are we going to insult the man when he comes over here on a friendly visit? Eh? Isn't that right, Crofton?

Mr Crofton nodded his head.

—But after all now, said Mr Lyons argumentatively, King Edward's life, you know, is not the very . . . [8]

—Let bygones be bygones, said Mr Henchy. I admire the man personally. He's just an ordinary knockabout like you and me. He's fond of his glass of grog and he's a bit of a rake, perhaps, and he's a good sportsman. Damn it, can't we Irish play fair?

—That's all very fine, said Mr Lyons. But look at the case of Parnell now.

—In the name of God, said Mr Henchy, where's the analogy between the two cases?

—What I mean, said Mr Lyons, is we have our ideals. Why, now, would we welcome a man like that? Do you think now after what he did Parnell was a fit man to lead us? And why, then, would we do it for Edward the Seventh?

—This is Parnell's anniversary, said Mr O'Connor, and don't let us stir up any bad blood. We all respect him now that he's dead and gone—even the Conservatives, he added, turning to Mr Crofton.

Pok! The tardy cork flew out of Mr Crofton's bottle. Mr Crofton got up from his box and went to the fire. As he returned with his capture he said in a deep voice:

—Our side of the house respects him because he was a gentleman.

—Right you are, Crofton! said Mr Henchy fiercely. He was the only man that could keep that bag of cats in order. *Down, ye dogs! Lie down, ye curs!* That's the way he treated them. Come in, Joe! Come in! he called out, catching sight of Mr Hynes in the doorway.

Mr Hynes came in slowly.

—Open another bottle of stout, Jack, said Mr Henchy. O, I forgot there's no corkscrew! Here, show me one here and I'll put it at the fire.

---

6. Gentleman.
7. Taxpayer.

8. Edward VII's behavior had been somewhat notorious before he became king.

The old man handed him another bottle and he placed it on the hob.

—Sit down, Joe, said Mr O'Connor, we're just talking about the Chief.

—Ay, ay! said Mr Henchy.

Mr Hynes sat on the side of the table near Mr Lyons but said nothing.

—There's one of them, anyhow, said Mr Henchy, that didn't renege him. By God, I'll say for you, Joe! No, by God, you stuck to him like a man!

—O, Joe, said Mr O'Connor suddenly. Give us that thing you wrote—do you remember? Have you got it on you?

—O, ay! said Mr Henchy. Give us that. Did you ever hear that, Crofton? Listen to this now: splendid thing.

—Go on, said Mr O'Connor. Fire away, Joe.

Mr Hynes did not seem to remember at once the piece to which they were alluding but, after reflecting a while, he said:

—O, that thing is it. . . . Sure, that's old now.

—Out with it, man! said Mr O'Connor.

—'Sh, 'sh, said Mr Henchy. Now, Joe!

Mr Hynes hesitated a little longer. Then amid the silence he took off his hat, laid it on the table and stood up. He seemed to be rehearsing the piece in his mind. After a rather long pause he announced:

The Death of Parnell
6TH OCTOBER 1891

He cleared his throat once or twice and then began to recite:

> *He is dead. Our Uncrowned King is dead.*
> *O, Erin,[9] mourn with grief and woe*
> *For he lies dead whom the fell gang*
> *Of modern hypocrites laid low.*
>
> *He lies slain by the coward hounds*
> *He raised to glory from the mire;*
> *And Erin's hopes and Erin's dreams*
> *Perish upon her monarch's pyre.*
>
> *In palace, cabin or in cot*
> *The Irish heart where'er it be*
> *Is bowed with woe—for he is gone*
> *Who would have wrought her destiny.*
>
> *He would have had his Erin famed,*
> *The green flag gloriously unfurled,*
> *Her statesmen, bards and warriors raised*
> *Before the nations of the World.*
>
> *He dreamed (alas, 'twas but a dream!)*
> *Of Liberty: but as he strove*
> *To clutch that idol, treachery*
> *Sundered him from the thing he loved.*
>
> *Shame on the coward caitiff[1] hands*
> *That smote their Lord or with a kiss*

9. A poetic name for Ireland. 1. Despicable.

Betrayed him to the rabble-rout
  Of fawning priests—no friends of his.

May everlasting shame consume
  The memory of those who tried
To befoul and smear th' exalted name
  Of one who spurned them in his pride.

He fell as fall the mighty ones,
  Nobly undaunted to the last,
And death has now united him
  With Erin's heroes of the past.

No sound of strife disturb his sleep!
  Calmly he rests: no human pain
Or high ambition spurs him now
  The peaks of glory to attain.

They had their way: they laid him low.
  But Erin, list, his spirit may
Rise, like the Phoenix from the flames,
  When breaks the dawning of the day,

The day that brings us Freedom's reign.
  And on that day may Erin well
Pledge in the cup she lifts to Joy
  One grief—the memory of Parnell.

Mr Hynes sat down again on the table. When he had finished his recitation there was a silence and then a burst of clapping: even Mr Lyons clapped. The applause continued for a little time. When it had ceased all the auditors drank from their bottles in silence.

Pok! The cork flew out of Mr Hynes' bottle, but Mr Hynes remained sitting, flushed and bareheaded on the table. He did not seem to have heard the invitation.

—Good man, Joe! said Mr O'Connor, taking out his cigarette papers and pouch the better to hide his emotion.

—What do you think of that, Crofton? cried Mr Henchy. Isn't that fine? What? Mr Crofton said that it was a very fine piece of writing.

The Dead

Lily, the caretaker's daughter, was literally run off her feet. Hardly had she brought one gentleman into the little pantry behind the office on the ground floor and helped him off with his overcoat than the wheezy hall-door bell clanged again and she had to scamper along the bare hallway to let in another guest. It was well for her she had not to attend to the ladies also. But Miss Kate and Miss Julia had thought of that and had converted the bathroom upstairs into a ladies' dressing-room. Miss Kate and Miss Julia were there, gossiping and laughing and fussing, walking after each other to the head of the stairs, peering down over the banisters and calling down to Lily to ask her who had come.

It was always a great affair, the Misses Morkan's annual dance. Everybody who knew them came to it, members of the family, old friends of the family, the members of Julia's choir, any of Kate's pupils that were grown up enough and even some of

Mary Jane's pupils too. Never once had it fallen flat. For years and years it had gone off in splendid style as long as anyone could remember; ever since Kate and Julia, after the death of their brother Pat, had left the house in Stoney Batter[1] and taken Mary Jane, their only niece, to live with them in the dark gaunt house on Usher's Island,[2] the upper part of which they had rented from Mr Fulham, the cornfactor on the ground floor. That was a good thirty years ago if it was a day. Mary Jane, who was then a little girl in short clothes, was now the main prop of the household for she had the organ in Haddington Road.[3] She had been through the Academy[4] and gave a pupils' concert every year in the upper room of the Antient Concert Rooms. Many of her pupils belonged to better-class families on the Kingstown and Dalkey line.[5] Old as they were, her aunts also did their share. Julia, though she was quite grey, was still the leading soprano in Adam and Eve's,[6] and Kate, being too feeble to go about much, gave music lessons to beginners on the old square piano in the back room. Lily, the caretaker's daughter, did housemaid's work for them. Though their life was modest they believed in eating well; the best of everything: diamond-bone sirloins, three-shilling tea and the best bottled stout.[7] But Lily seldom made a mistake in the orders so that she got on well with her three mistresses. They were fussy, that was all. But the only thing they would not stand was back answers.

Of course they had good reason to be fussy on such a night. And then it was long after ten o'clock and yet there was no sign of Gabriel and his wife. Besides they were dreadfully afraid that Freddy Malins might turn up screwed.[8] They would not wish for worlds that any of Mary Jane's pupils should see him under the influence; and when he was like that it was sometimes very hard to manage him. Freddy Malins always came late but they wondered what could be keeping Gabriel: and that was what brought them every two minutes to the banisters to ask Lily had Gabriel or Freddy come.

—O, Mr Conroy, said Lily to Gabriel when she opened the door for him, Miss Kate and Miss Julia thought you were never coming. Good-night, Mrs Conroy.

—I'll engage[9] they did, said Gabriel, but they forget that my wife here takes three mortal hours to dress herself.

He stood on the mat, scraping the snow from his goloshes, while Lily led his wife to the foot of the stairs and called out:

—Miss Kate, here's Mrs Conroy.

Kate and Julia came toddling down the dark stairs at once. Both of them kissed Gabriel's wife, said she must be perished alive and asked was Gabriel with her.

—Here I am as right as the mail, Aunt Kate! Go on up. I'll follow, called out Gabriel from the dark.

He continued scraping his feet vigorously while the three women went upstairs, laughing, to the ladies' dressing-room. A light fringe of snow lay like a cape on the shoulders of his overcoat and like toecaps on the toes of his goloshes; and, as the buttons of his overcoat slipped with a squeaking noise through the snow-stiffened frieze, a cold fragrant air from out-of-doors escaped from crevices and folds.

—Is it snowing again, Mr Conroy? asked Lily.

1. A district in northwest Dublin.
2. Two adjoining quays on the south side of the River Liffey.
3. Played the organ in a church on the Haddington Road.
4. Royal Academy of Music.
5. The train line connecting Dublin to the affluent sub-urbs south of the city.
6. A Dublin church.
7. An extra-strength ale.
8. Drunk.
9. Wager.

She had preceded him into the pantry to help him off with his overcoat. Gabriel smiled at the three syllables she had given his surname and glanced at her. She was a slim, growing girl, pale in complexion and with hay-coloured hair. The gas in the pantry made her look still paler. Gabriel had known her when she was a child and used to sit on the lowest step nursing a rag doll.

—Yes, Lily, he answered, and I think we're in for a night of it.

He looked up at the pantry ceiling, which was shaking with the stamping and shuffling of feet on the floor above, listened for a moment to the piano and then glanced at the girl, who was folding his overcoat carefully at the end of a shelf.

—Tell me, Lily, he said in a friendly tone, do you still go to school?

—O no, sir, she answered. I'm done schooling this year and more.

—O, then, said Gabriel gaily, I suppose we'll be going to your wedding one of these fine days with your young man, eh?

The girl glanced back at him over her shoulder and said with great bitterness:

—The men that is now is only all palaver[1] and what they can get out of you.

Gabriel coloured as if he felt he had made a mistake and, without looking at her, kicked off his goloshes and flicked actively with his muffler at his patent-leather shoes.

He was a stout tallish young man. The high colour of his cheeks pushed upwards even to his forehead where it scattered itself in a few formless patches of pale red; and on his hairless face there scintillated restlessly the polished lenses and the bright gilt rims of the glasses which screened his delicate and restless eyes. His glossy black hair was parted in the middle and brushed in a long curve behind his ears where it curled slightly beneath the groove left by his hat.

When he had flicked lustre into his shoes he stood up and pulled his waistcoat down more tightly on his plump body. Then he took a coin rapidly from his pocket.

—O Lily, he said, thrusting it into her hands, it's Christmas-time, isn't it? Just . . . here's a little. . . .

He walked rapidly towards the door.

—O no, sir! cried the girl, following him. Really, sir, I wouldn't take it.

—Christmas-time! Christmas-time! said Gabriel, almost trotting to the stairs and waving his hand to her in deprecation.

The girl, seeing that he had gained the stairs, called out after him:

—Well, thank you, sir.

He waited outside the drawing-room door until the waltz should finish, listening to the skirts that swept against it and to the shuffling of feet. He was still discomposed by the girl's bitter and sudden retort. It had cast a gloom over him which he tried to dispel by arranging his cuffs and the bows of his tie. Then he took from his waistcoat pocket a little paper and glanced at the headings he had made for his speech. He was undecided about the lines from Robert Browning for he feared they would be above the heads of his hearers. Some quotation that they could recognise from Shakespeare or from the Melodies[2] would be better. The indelicate clacking of the men's heels and the shuffling of their soles reminded him that their grade of culture differed from his. He would only make himself ridiculous by quoting poetry to them which they could not understand. They would think that he was airing his superior education. He would fail with them just as he had failed with the girl in the pantry. He had taken up a wrong tone. His whole speech was a mistake from first to last, an utter failure.

---

1. Empty talk.

2. Thomas Moore's *Irish Melodies*, a perennial favorite volume of poetry.

Just then his aunts and his wife came out of the ladies' dressing-room. His aunts were two small plainly dressed old women. Aunt Julia was an inch or so taller. Her hair, drawn low over the tops of her ears, was grey; and grey also, with darker shadows, was her large flaccid face. Though she was stout in build and stood erect her slow eyes and parted lips gave her the appearance of a woman who did not know where she was or where she was going. Aunt Kate was more vivacious. Her face, healthier than her sister's, was all puckers and creases, like a shrivelled red apple, and her hair, braided in the same old-fashioned way, had not lost its ripe nut colour.

They both kissed Gabriel frankly. He was their favourite nephew, the son of their dead elder sister, Ellen, who had married T.J. Conroy of the Port and Docks.

—Gretta tells me you're not going to take a cab back to Monkstown[3] to-night, Gabriel, said Aunt Kate.

—No, said Gabriel, turning to his wife, we had quite enough of that last year, hadn't we. Don't you remember, Aunt Kate, what a cold Gretta got out of it? Cab windows rattling all the way, and the east wind blowing in after we passed Merrion. Very jolly it was. Gretta caught a dreadful cold.

Aunt Kate frowned severely and nodded her head at every word.

—Quite right, Gabriel, quite right, she said. You can't be too careful.

—But as for Gretta there, said Gabriel, she'd walk home in the snow if she were let.

Mrs Conroy laughed.

—Don't mind him, Aunt Kate, she said. He's really an awful bother, what with green shades for Tom's eyes at night and making him do the dumb-bells, and forcing Eva to eat the stirabout.[4] The poor child! And she simply hates the sight of it! . . . O, but you'll never guess what he makes me wear now!

She broke out into a peal of laughter and glanced at her husband, whose admiring and happy eyes had been wandering from her dress to her face and hair. The two aunts laughed heartily too, for Gabriel's solicitude was a standing joke with them.

—Goloshes! said Mrs Conroy. That's the latest. Whenever it's wet underfoot I must put on my goloshes. Tonight even he wanted me to put them on, but I wouldn't. The next thing he'll buy me will be a diving suit.

Gabriel laughed nervously and patted his tie reassuringly while Aunt Kate nearly doubled herself, so heartily did she enjoy the joke. The smile soon faded from Aunt Julia's face and her mirthless eyes were directed towards her nephew's face. After a pause she asked:

—And what are goloshes, Gabriel?

—Goloshes, Julia! exclaimed her sister. Goodness me, don't you know what goloshes are? You wear them over your . . . over your boots, Gretta, isn't it?

—Yes, said Mrs Conroy. Guttapercha[5] things. We both have a pair now. Gabriel says everyone wears them on the continent.

—O, on the continent, murmured Aunt Julia, nodding her head slowly.

Gabriel knitted his brows and said, as if he were slightly angered:

—It's nothing very wonderful but Gretta thinks it very funny because she says the word reminds her of Christy Minstrels.[6]

—But tell me, Gabriel, said Aunt Kate, with brisk tact. Of course, you've seen about the room. Gretta was saying . . .

—O, the room is all right, replied Gabriel. I've taken one in the Gresham.[7]

---

3. An elegant suburb south of Dublin.
4. Porridge.
5. Rubberized fabric.

6. A 19th-century minstrel show.
7. The most elegant hotel in Dublin.

—To be sure, said Aunt Kate, by far the best thing to do. And the children, Gretta, you're not anxious about them?

—O, for one night, said Mrs Conroy. Besides, Bessie will look after them.

—To be sure, said Aunt Kate again. What a comfort it is to have a girl like that, one you can depend on! There's that Lily, I'm sure I don't know what has come over her lately. She's not the girl she was at all.

Gabriel was about to ask his aunt some questions on this point but she broke off suddenly to gaze after her sister who had wandered down the stairs and was craning her neck over the banisters.

—Now, I ask you, she said, almost testily, where is Julia going? Julia! Julia! Where are you going?

Julia, who had gone halfway down one flight, came back and announced blandly:

—Here's Freddy.

At the same moment a clapping of hands and a final flourish of the pianist told that the waltz had ended. The drawing-room door was opened from within and some couples came out. Aunt Kate drew Gabriel aside hurriedly and whispered into his ear:

—Slip down, Gabriel, like a good fellow and see if he's all right, and don't let him up if he's screwed. I'm sure he's screwed. I'm sure he is.

Gabriel went to the stairs and listened over the banisters. He could hear two persons talking in the pantry. Then he recognised Freddy Malins' laugh. He went down the stairs noisily.

—It's such a relief, said Aunt Kate to Mrs Conroy, that Gabriel is here. I always feel easier in my mind when he's here. . . . Julia, there's Miss Daly and Miss Power will take some refreshment. Thanks for your beautiful waltz, Miss Daly. It made lovely time.

A tall wizen-faced man, with a stiff grizzled moustache and swarthy skin, who was passing out with his partner said:

—And may we have some refreshment, too, Miss Morkan?

—Julia, said Aunt Kate summarily, and here's Mr Browne and Miss Furlong. Take them in, Julia, with Miss Daly and Miss Power.

—I'm the man for the ladies, said Mr Browne, pursing his lips until his moustache bristled and smiling in all his wrinkles. You know, Miss Morkan, the reason they are so fond of me is—

He did not finish his sentence, but, seeing that Aunt Kate was out of earshot, at once led the three young ladies into the back room. The middle of the room was occupied by two square tables placed end to end, and on these Aunt Julia and the caretaker were straightening and smoothing a large cloth. On the sideboard were arrayed dishes and plates, and glasses and bundles of knives and forks and spoons. The top of the closed square piano served also as a sideboard for viands[8] and sweets. At a smaller sideboard in one corner two young men were standing, drinking hop-bitters.[9]

Mr Browne led his charges thither and invited them all, in jest, to some ladies' punch, hot, strong and sweet. As they said they never took anything strong he opened three bottles of lemonade for them. Then he asked one of the young men to move aside, and, taking hold of the decanter, filled out for himself a goodly measure of whisky. The young men eyed him respectfully while he took a trial sip.

—God help me, he said, smiling, it's the doctor's orders.

His wizened face broke into a broader smile, and the three young ladies laughed in musical echo to his pleasantry, swaying their bodies to and fro, with nervous jerks of their shoulders. The boldest said:

8. Meats.   9. Dry ale.

—O, now, Mr Browne, I'm sure the doctor never ordered anything of the kind.

Mr Browne took another sip of his whisky and said, with sidling mimicry:

—Well, you see, I'm like the famous Mrs Cassidy, who is reported to have said: *Now, Mary Grimes, if I don't take it, make me take it, for I feel I want it.*

His hot face had leaned forward a little too confidentially and he had assumed a very low Dublin accent so that the young ladies, with one instinct, received his speech in silence. Miss Furlong, who was one of Mary Jane's pupils, asked Miss Daly what was the name of the pretty waltz she had played; and Mr Browne, seeing that he was ignored, turned promptly to the two young men who were more appreciative.

A red-faced young woman, dressed in pansy, came into the room, excitedly clapping her hands and crying:

—Quadrilles![1] Quadrilles!

Close on her heels came Aunt Kate, crying:

—Two gentlemen and three ladies, Mary Jane!

—O, here's Mr Bergin and Mr Kerrigan, said Mary Jane. Mr Kerrigan, will you take Miss Power? Miss Furlong, may I get you a partner, Mr Bergin. O, that'll just do now.

—Three ladies, Mary Jane, said Aunt Kate.

The two young gentlemen asked the ladies if they might have the pleasure, and Mary Jane turned to Miss Daly.

—O, Miss Daly, you're really awfully good, after playing for the last two dances, but really we're so short of ladies to-night.

—I don't mind in the least, Miss Morkan.

—But I've a nice partner for you, Mr Bartell D'Arcy, the tenor. I'll get him to sing later on. All Dublin is raving about him.

—Lovely voice, lovely voice! said Aunt Kate.

As the piano had twice begun the prelude to the first figure Mary Jane led her recruits quickly from the room. They had hardly gone when Aunt Julia wandered slowly into the room, looking behind her at something.

—What is the matter, Julia? asked Aunt Kate anxiously. Who is it?

Julia, who was carrying in a column of table-napkins, turned to her sister and said, simply, as if the question had surprised her:

—It's only Freddy, Kate, and Gabriel with him.

In fact right behind her Gabriel could be seen piloting Freddy Malins across the landing. The latter, a young man of about forty, was of Gabriel's size and build, with very round shoulders. His face was fleshy and pallid, touched with colour only at the thick hanging lobes of his ears and at the wide wings of his nose. He had coarse features, a blunt nose, a convex and receding brow, tumid and protruded lips. His heavy-lidded eyes and the disorder of his scanty hair made him look sleepy. He was laughing heartily in a high key at a story which he had been telling Gabriel on the stairs and at the same time rubbing the knuckles of his left fist backwards and forwards into his left eye.

—Good-evening, Freddy, said Aunt Julia.

Freddy Malins bade the Misses Morkan good-evening in what seemed an off-hand fashion by reason of the habitual catch in his voice and then, seeing that Mr Browne was grinning at him from the sideboard, crossed the room on rather shaky legs and began to repeat in an undertone the story he had just told to Gabriel.

—He's not so bad, is he? said Aunt Kate to Gabriel.

Gabriel's brows were dark but he raised them quickly and answered:

—O no, hardly noticeable.

1. A French square dance.

—Now, isn't he a terrible fellow! she said. And his poor mother made him take the pledge on New Year's Eve. But come on, Gabriel, into the drawing-room.

Before leaving the room with Gabriel she signalled to Mr Browne by frowning and shaking her forefinger in warning to and fro. Mr Browne nodded in answer and, when she had gone, said to Freddy Malins:

—Now, then, Teddy, I'm going to fill you out a good glass of lemonade just to buck you up.

Freddy Malins, who was nearing the climax of his story, waved the offer aside impatiently but Mr Browne, having first called Freddy Malins' attention to a disarray in his dress, filled out and handed him a full glass of lemonade. Freddy Malins' left hand accepted the glass mechanically, his right hand being engaged in the mechanical readjustment of his dress. Mr Browne, whose face was once more wrinkling with mirth, poured out for himself a glass of whisky while Freddy Malins exploded, before he had well reached the climax of his story, in a kink of high-pitched bronchitic laughter and, setting down his untasted and overflowing glass, began to rub the knuckles of his left fist backwards and forwards into his left eye, repeating words of his last phrase as well as his fit of laughter would allow him.

Gabriel could not listen while Mary Jane was playing her Academy piece, full of runs and difficult passages, to the hushed drawing-room. He liked music but the piece she was playing had no melody for him and he doubted whether it had any melody for the other listeners, though they had begged Mary Jane to play something. Four young men, who had come from the refreshment-room to stand in the door-way at the sound of the piano, had gone away quietly in couples after a few minutes. The only persons who seemed to follow the music were Mary Jane herself, her hands racing along the key-board or lifted from it at the pauses like those of a priestess in momentary imprecation, and Aunt Kate standing at her elbow to turn the page.

Gabriel's eyes, irritated by the floor, which glittered with beeswax under the heavy chandelier, wandered to the wall above the piano. A picture of the balcony scene in *Romeo and Juliet* hung there and beside it was a picture of the two murdered princes[2] in the Tower which Aunt Julia had worked in red, blue and brown wools when she was a girl. Probably in the school they had gone to as girls that kind of work had been taught, for one year his mother had worked for him as a birthday present a waistcoat of purple tabinet,[3] with little foxes' heads upon it, lined with brown satin and having round mulberry buttons. It was strange that his mother had had no musical talent though Aunt Kate used to call her the brains carrier of the Morkan family. Both she and Julia had always seemed a little proud of their serious and matronly sister. Her photograph stood before the pierglass.[4] She held an open book on her knees and was pointing out something in it to Constantine who, dressed in a man-o'-war suit, lay at her feet. It was she who had chosen the names for her sons for she was very sensible of the dignity of family life. Thanks to her, Constantine was now senior curate in Balbriggan[5] and, thanks to her, Gabriel himself had taken his degree in the Royal University.[6] A shadow passed over his face as he remembered her sullen opposition to his marriage. Some slighting phrases she had used still rankled in his memory; she had once spoken of Gretta as being country cute and that was not true of Gretta at all. It was Gretta who had nursed her during all her last long illness in their house at Monkstown.

2. The young sons of Edward IV, murdered in the Tower of London by order of their uncle, Edward III.
3. Silk and wool fabric.
4. A large high mirror.
5. Seaport 19 miles southeast of Dublin.
6. The Royal University of Ireland, established in 1882.

He knew that Mary Jane must be near the end of her piece for she was playing again the opening melody with runs of scales after every bar and while he waited for the end the resentment died down in his heart. The piece ended with a trill of octaves in the treble and a final deep octave in the bass. Great applause greeted Mary Jane as, blushing and rolling up her music nervously, she escaped from the room. The most vigorous clapping came from the four young men in the doorway who had gone away to the refreshment-room at the beginning of the piece but had come back when the piano had stopped.

Lancers[7] were arranged. Gabriel found himself partnered with Miss Ivors. She was a frank-mannered talkative young lady, with a freckled face and prominent brown eyes. She did not wear a low-cut bodice and the large brooch which was fixed in the front of her collar bore on it an Irish device.

When they had taken their places she said abruptly:

—I have a crow to pluck with you.

—With me? said Gabriel.

She nodded her head gravely.

—What is it? asked Gabriel, smiling at her solemn manner.

—Who is G. C.? answered Miss Ivors, turning her eyes upon him.

Gabriel coloured and was about to knit his brows, as if he did not understand, when she said bluntly:

—O, innocent Amy! I have found out that you write for *The Daily Express*.[8] Now, aren't you ashamed of yourself?

—Why should I be ashamed of myself? asked Gabriel, blinking his eyes and trying to smile.

—Well, I'm ashamed of you, said Miss Ivors frankly. To say you'd write for a rag like that. I didn't think you were a West Briton.[9]

A look of perplexity appeared on Gabriel's face. It was true that he wrote a literary column every Wednesday in *The Daily Express*, for which he was paid fifteen shillings. But that did not make him a West Briton surely. The books he received for review were almost more welcome than the paltry cheque. He loved to feel the covers and turn over the pages of newly printed books. Nearly every day when his teaching in the college was ended he used to wander down the quays to the second-hand booksellers, to Hickey's on Bachelor's Walk, to Webb's or Massey's on Aston's Quay, or to O'Clohissey's in the by-street. He did not know how to meet her charge. He wanted to say that literature was above politics. But they were friends of many years' standing and their careers had been parallel, first at the University and then as teachers: he could not risk a grandiose phrase with her. He continued blinking his eyes and trying to smile and murmured lamely that he saw nothing political in writing reviews of books.

When their turn to cross had come he was still perplexed and inattentive. Miss Ivors promptly took his hand in a warm grasp and said in a soft friendly tone:

—Of course, I was only joking. Come, we cross now.

When they were together again she spoke of the University question[1] and Gabriel felt more at ease. A friend of hers had shown her his review of Browning's poems. That was how she had found out the secret: but she liked the review immensely. Then she said suddenly:

---

7. A type of quadrille for 8 or 16 people.
8. A conservative paper opposed to the struggle for Irish independence.
9. Disparaging term for people wishing to identify Ireland as British.

1. Ireland's oldest most and prestigious university, Trinity College, was open only to Protestants; the "University question" involved, in part, the provision of quality university education to Catholics.

—O, Mr Conroy, will you come for an excursion to the Aran Isles[2] this summer? We're going to stay there a whole month. It will be splendid out in the Atlantic. You ought to come. Mr Clancy is coming, and Mr Kilkelly and Kathleen Kearney. It would be splendid for Gretta too if she'd come. She's from Connacht,[3] isn't she?

—Her people are, said Gabriel shortly.

—But you will come, won't you? said Miss Ivors, laying her warm hand eagerly on his arm.

—The fact is, said Gabriel, I have already arranged to go—

—Go where? asked Miss Ivors.

—Well, you know, every year I go for a cycling tour with some fellows and so—

—But where? asked Miss Ivors.

—Well, we usually go to France or Belgium or perhaps Germany, said Gabriel awkwardly.

—And why do you go to France and Belgium, said Miss Ivors, instead of visiting your own land?

—Well, said Gabriel, it's partly to keep in touch with the languages and partly for a change.

—And haven't you your own language to keep in touch with—Irish? asked Miss Ivors.

—Well, said Gabriel, if it comes to that, you know, Irish is not my language.

Their neighbours had turned to listen to the cross-examination. Gabriel glanced right and left nervously and tried to keep his good humour under the ordeal which was making a blush invade his forehead.

—And haven't you your own land to visit, continued Miss Ivors, that you know nothing of, your own people, and your own country?

—O, to tell you the truth, retorted Gabriel suddenly, I'm sick of my own country, sick of it!

—Why? asked Miss Ivors.

Gabriel did not answer for his retort had heated him.

—Why? repeated Miss Ivors.

They had to go visiting together and, as he had not answered her, Miss Ivors said warmly:

—Of course, you've no answer.

Gabriel tried to cover his agitation by taking part in the dance with great energy. He avoided her eyes for he had seen a sour expression on her face. But when they met in the long chain he was surprised to feel his hand firmly pressed. She looked at him from under her brows for a moment quizzically until he smiled. Then, just as the chain was about to start again, she stood on tiptoe and whispered into his ear:

—West Briton!

When the lancers were over Gabriel went away to a remote corner of the room where Freddy Malins' mother was sitting. She was a stout feeble old woman with white hair. Her voice had a catch in it like her son's and she stuttered slightly. She had been told that Freddy had come and that he was nearly all right. Gabriel asked her whether she had had a good crossing. She lived with her married daughter in Glasgow and came to Dublin on a visit once a year. She answered placidly that she had had a beautiful crossing and that the captain had been most attentive to her. She

2. Islands off the west coast of Ireland where the people still retained their traditional culture and spoke Irish.

3. A province on the west coast of Ireland.

spoke also of the beautiful house her daughter kept in Glasgow, and of all the nice friends they had there. While her tongue rambled on Gabriel tried to banish from his mind all memory of the unpleasant incident with Miss Ivors. Of course the girl or woman, or whatever she was, was an enthusiast but there was a time for all things. Perhaps he ought not to have answered her like that. But she had no right to call him a West Briton before people, even in joke. She had tried to make him ridiculous before people, heckling him and staring at him with her rabbit's eyes.

He saw his wife making her way towards him through the waltzing couples. When she reached him she said into his ear:

—Gabriel, Aunt Kate wants to know won't you carve the goose as usual. Miss Daly will carve the ham and I'll do the pudding.

—All right, said Gabriel.

—She's sending in the younger ones first as soon as this waltz is over so that we'll have the table to ourselves.

—Were you dancing? asked Gabriel.

—Of course I was. Didn't you see me? What words had you with Molly Ivors?

—No words. Why? Did she say so?

—Something like that. I'm trying to get that Mr D'Arcy to sing. He's full of conceit, I think.

—There were no words, said Gabriel moodily, only she wanted me to go for a trip to the west of Ireland and I said I wouldn't.

His wife clasped her hands excitedly and gave a little jump.

—O, do go, Gabriel, she cried. I'd love to see Galway again.

—You can go if you like, said Gabriel coldly.

She looked at him for a moment, then turned to Mrs Malins and said:

—There's a nice husband for you, Mrs Malins.

While she was threading her way back across the room Mrs Malins, without adverting to the interruption, went on to tell Gabriel what beautiful places there were in Scotland and beautiful scenery. Her son-in-law brought them every year to the lakes and they used to go fishing. Her son-in-law was a splendid fisher. One day he caught a fish, a beautiful big big fish, and the man in the hotel boiled it for their dinner.

Gabriel hardly heard what she said. Now that supper was coming near he began to think again about his speech and about the quotation. When he saw Freddy Malins coming across the room to visit his mother Gabriel left the chair free for him and retired into the embrasure of the window. The room had already cleared and from the back room came the clatter of plates and knives. Those who still remained in the drawing-room seemed tired of dancing and were conversing quietly in little groups. Gabriel's warm trembling fingers tapped the cold pane of the window. How cool it must be outside! How pleasant it would be to walk out alone, first along by the river and then through the park! The snow would be lying on the branches of the trees and forming a bright cap on the top of the Wellington Monument.[4] How much more pleasant it would be there than at the supper-table!

He ran over the headings of his speech: Irish hospitality, sad memories, the Three Graces, Paris, the quotation from Browning. He repeated to himself a phrase he had written in his review: *One feels that one is listening to a thought-tormented music*. Miss Ivors had praised the review. Was she sincere? Had she really any life of her own

4. A monument to the Duke of Wellington, an Irish-born English military hero, located in Phoenix Park, Dublin's major public park.

behind all her propagandism? There had never been any ill-feeling between them until that night. It unnerved him to think that she would be at the supper-table, looking up at him while he spoke with her critical quizzing eyes. Perhaps she would not be sorry to see him fail in his speech. An idea came into his mind and gave him courage. He would say, alluding to Aunt Kate and Aunt Julia: *Ladies and Gentlemen, the generation which is now on the wane among us may have had its faults but for my part I think it had certain qualities of hospitality, of humour, of humanity, which the new and very serious and hypereducated generation that is growing up around us seems to me to lack.* Very good: that was one for Miss Ivors. What did he care that his aunts were only two ignorant old women?

A murmur in the room attracted his attention. Mr Browne was advancing from the door, gallantly escorting Aunt Julia, who leaned upon his arm, smiling and hanging her head. An irregular musketry of applause escorted her also as far as the piano and then, as Mary Jane seated herself on the stool, and Aunt Julia, no longer smiling, half turned so as to pitch her voice fairly into the room, gradually ceased. Gabriel recognised the prelude. It was that of an old song of Aunt Julia's—*Arrayed for the Bridal*.[5] Her voice, strong and clear in tone, attacked with great spirit the runs which embellish the air and though she sang very rapidly she did not miss even the smallest of the grace notes. To follow the voice, without looking at the singer's face, was to feel and share the excitement of swift and secure flight. Gabriel applauded loudly with all the others at the close of the song and loud applause was borne in from the invisible supper-table. It sounded so genuine that a little colour struggled into Aunt Julia's face as she bent to replace in the music-stand the old leather-bound song-book that had her initials on the cover. Freddy Malins, who had listened with his head perched sideways to hear her better, was still applauding when everyone else had ceased and talking animatedly to his mother who nodded her head gravely and slowly in acquiescence. At last, when he could clap no more, he stood up suddenly and hurried across the room to Aunt Julia whose hand he seized and held in both his hands, shaking it when words failed him or the catch in his voice proved too much for him.

—I was just telling my mother, he said, I never heard you sing so well, never. No, I never heard your voice so good as it is to-night. Now! Would you believe that now? That's the truth. Upon my word and honour that's the truth. I never heard your voice sound so fresh and so . . . so clear and fresh, never.

Aunt Julia smiled broadly and murmured something about compliments as she released her hand from his grasp. Mr Browne extended his open hand towards her and said to those who were near him in the manner of a showman introducing a prodigy to an audience:

—Miss Julia Morkan, my latest discovery!

He was laughing very heartily at this himself when Freddy Malins turned to him and said:

—Well, Browne, if you're serious you might make a worse discovery. All I can say is I never heard her sing half so well as long as I am coming here. And that's the honest truth.

—Neither did I, said Mr. Browne. I think her voice has greatly improved.

Aunt Julia shrugged her shoulders and said with meek pride:

—Thirty years ago I hadn't a bad voice as voices go.

5. A popular but challenging song set to music from Bellini's opera *I Puritani* (1835).

—I often told Julia, said Aunt Kate emphatically, that she was simply thrown away in that choir. But she never would be said by me.

She turned as if to appeal to the good sense of the others against a refractory child while Aunt Julia gazed in front of her, a vague smile of reminiscence playing on her face.

—No, continued Aunt Kate, she wouldn't be said or led by anyone, slaving there in that choir night and day, night and day. Six o'clock on Christmas morning! And all for what?

—Well, isn't it for the honour of God, Aunt Kate? asked Mary Jane, twisting round on the piano-stool and smiling.

Aunt Kate turned fiercely on her niece and said:

—I know all about the honour of God, Mary Jane, but I think it's not at all honourable for the pope to turn out the women out of the choirs that have slaved there all their lives and put little whipper-snappers of boys over their heads. I suppose it is for the good of the Church if the pope does it. But it's not just, Mary Jane, and it's not right.

She had worked herself into a passion and would have continued in defence of her sister for it was a sore subject with her but Mary Jane, seeing that all the dancers had come back, intervened pacifically:

—Now, Aunt Kate, you're giving scandal to Mr Browne who is of the other persuasion.

Aunt Kate turned to Mr Browne, who was grinning at this allusion to his religion, and said hastily:

—O, I don't question the pope's being right. I'm only a stupid old woman and I wouldn't presume to do such a thing. But there's such a thing as common everyday politeness and gratitude. And if I were in Julia's place I'd tell that Father Healy straight up to his face . . .

—And besides, Aunt Kate, said Mary Jane, we really are all hungry and when we are hungry we are all very quarrelsome.

—And when we are thirsty we are also quarrelsome, added Mr Browne.

—So that we had better go to supper, said Mary Jane, and finish the discussion afterwards.

On the landing outside the drawing-room Gabriel found his wife and Mary Jane trying to persuade Miss Ivors to stay for supper. But Miss Ivors, who had put on her hat and was buttoning her cloak, would not stay. She did not feel in the least hungry and she had already overstayed her time.

—But only for ten minutes, Molly, said Mrs Conroy. That won't delay you.

—To take a pick itself, said Mary Jane, after all your dancing.

—I really couldn't, said Miss Ivors.

—I am afraid you didn't enjoy yourself at all, said Mary Jane hopelessly.

—Ever so much, I assure you, said Miss Ivors, but you really must let me run off now.

—But how can you get home? asked Mrs Conroy.

—O, it's only two steps up the quay.

Gabriel hesitated a moment and said:

—If you will allow me, Miss Ivors, I'll see you home if you really are obliged to go. But Miss Ivors broke away from them.

—I won't hear of it, she cried. For goodness sake go in to your suppers and don't mind me. I'm quite well able to take care of myself.

—Well, you're the comical girl, Molly, said Mrs Conroy frankly.

—*Beannacht libh,*[6] cried Miss Ivors, with a laugh, as she ran down the staircase.

Mary Jane gazed after her, a moody puzzled expression on her face, while Mrs Conroy leaned over the banisters to listen for the hall-door. Gabriel asked himself was he the cause of her abrupt departure. But she did not seem to be in ill humour: she had gone away laughing. He stared blankly down the staircase.

At that moment Aunt Kate came toddling out of the supper-room, almost wringing her hands in despair.

—Where is Gabriel? she cried. Where on earth is Gabriel? There's everyone waiting in there, stage to let, and nobody to carve the goose!

—Here I am, Aunt Kate! cried Gabriel, with sudden animation, ready to carve a flock of geese, if necessary.

A fat brown goose lay at one end of the table and at the other end, on a bed of creased paper strewn with sprigs of parsley, lay a great ham, stripped of its outer skin and peppered over with crust crumbs, a neat paper frill round its shin and beside this was a round of spiced beef. Between these rival ends ran parallel lines of side-dishes: two little minsters of jelly, red and yellow; a shallow dish full of blocks of blancmange and red jam, a large green leaf-shaped dish with a stalk-shaped handle, on which lay bunches of purple raisins and peeled almonds, a companion dish on which lay a solid rectangle of Smyrna figs, a dish of custard topped with grated nutmeg, a small bowl full of chocolates and sweets wrapped in gold and silver papers and a glass vase in which stood some tall celery stalks. In the centre of the table there stood, as sentries to a fruit-stand which upheld a pyramid of oranges and American apples, two squat old-fashioned decanters of cut glass, one containing port and the other dark sherry. On the closed square piano a pudding in a huge yellow dish lay in waiting and behind it were three squads of bottles of stout and ale and minerals, drawn up according to the colours of their uniforms, the first two black, with brown and red labels, the third and smallest squad white, with transverse green sashes.

Gabriel took his seat boldly at the head of the table and, having looked to the edge of the carver, plunged his fork firmly into the goose. He felt quite at ease now for he was an expert carver and liked nothing better than to find himself at the head of a well-laden table.

—Miss Furlong, what shall I send you? he asked. A wing or a slice of the breast?

—Just a small slice of the breast.

—Miss Higgins, what for you?

—O, anything at all, Mr Conroy.

While Gabriel and Miss Daly exchanged plates of goose and plates of ham and spiced beef Lily went from guest to guest with a dish of hot floury potatoes wrapped in a white napkin. This was Mary Jane's idea and she had also suggested apple sauce for the goose but Aunt Kate had said that plain roast goose without apple sauce had always been good enough for her and she hoped she might never eat worse. Mary Jane waited on her pupils and saw that they got the best slices and Aunt Kate and Aunt Julia opened and carried across from the piano bottles of stout and ale for the gentlemen and bottles of minerals for the ladies. There was a great deal of confusion and laughter and noise, the noise of orders and counter-orders, of knives and forks, of corks and glass-stoppers. Gabriel began to carve second helpings as soon as he had finished the first round without serving himself. Everyone protested loudly so that he

---

6. Farewell (Irish).

compromised by taking a long draught of stout for he had found the carving hot work. Mary Jane settled down quietly to her supper but Aunt Kate and Aunt Julia were still toddling round the table, walking on each other's heels, getting in each other's way and giving each other unheeded orders. Mr Browne begged of them to sit down and eat their suppers and so did Gabriel but they said there was time enough so that, at last, Freddy Malins stood up and, capturing Aunt Kate, plumped her down on her chair amid general laughter.

When everyone had been well served Gabriel said, smiling:

—Now, if anyone wants a little more of what vulgar people call stuffing let him or her speak.

A chorus of voices invited him to begin his own supper and Lily came forward with three potatoes which she had reserved for him.

—Very well, said Gabriel amiably, as he took another preparatory draught, kindly forget my existence, ladies and gentlemen, for a few minutes.

He set to his supper and took no part in the conversation with which the table covered Lily's removal of the plates. The subject of talk was the opera company which was then at the Theatre Royal. Mr Bartell D'Arcy, the tenor, a dark-complexioned young man with a smart moustache, praised very highly the leading contralto of the company but Miss Furlong thought she had a rather vulgar style of production. Freddy Malins said there was a negro chieftain singing in the second part of the Gaiety pantomime who had one of the finest tenor voices he had ever heard.

—Have you heard him? he asked Mr Bartell D'Arcy across the table.

—No, answered Mr Bartell D'Arcy carelessly.

—Because, Freddy Malins explained, now I'd be curious to hear your opinion of him. I think he has a grand voice.

—It takes Teddy to find out the really good things, said Mr Browne familiarly to the table.

—And why couldn't he have a voice too? asked Freddy Malins sharply. Is it because he's only a black?

Nobody answered this question and Mary Jane led the table back to the legitimate opera. One of her pupils had given her a pass for *Mignon*. Of course it was very fine, she said, but it made her think of poor Georgina Burns. Mr Browne could go back farther still, to the old Italian companies that used to come to Dublin—Tietjens, Ilma de Murzka, Campanini, the great Trebelli, Giuglini, Ravelli, Aramburo.[7] Those were the days, he said, when there was something like singing to be heard in Dublin. He told too of how the top gallery of the old Royal used to be packed night after night, of how one night an Italian tenor had sung five encores to *Let Me Like a Soldier Fall*, introducing a high C every time, and of how the gallery boys would sometimes in their enthusiasm unyoke the horses from the carriage of some great *prima donna* and pull her themselves through the streets to her hotel. Why did they never play the grand old operas now, he asked, *Dinorah, Lucrezia Borgia?* Because they could not get the voices to sing them: that was why.

—O, well, said Mr Bartell D'Arcy, I presume there are as good singers to-day as there were then.

—Where are they? asked Mr Browne defiantly.

—In London, Paris, Milan, said Mr Bartell D'Arcy warmly. I suppose Caruso,[8] for example, is quite as good, if not better than any of the men you have mentioned.

---

7. Famous 19th-century operatic singers.   8. Enrico Caruso (1874–1921), a famous tenor.

—Maybe so, said Mr Browne. But I may tell you I doubt it strongly.

—O, I'd give anything to hear Caruso sing, said Mary Jane.

—For me, said Aunt Kate, who had been picking a bone, there was only one tenor. To please me, I mean. But I suppose none of you ever heard of him.

—Who was he, Miss Morkan? asked Mr Bartell D'Arcy politely.

—His name, said Aunt Kate, was Parkinson. I heard him when he was in his prime and I think he had then the purest tenor voice that was ever put into a man's throat.

—Strange, said Mr Bartell D'Arcy. I never even heard of him.

—Yes, yes, Miss Morkan is right, said Mr Browne. I remember hearing of old Parkinson but he's too far back for me.

—A beautiful pure sweet mellow English tenor, said Aunt Kate with enthusiasm.

Gabriel having finished, the huge pudding was transferred to the table. The clatter of forks and spoons began again. Gabriel's wife served out spoonfuls of the pudding and passed the plates down the table. Midway down they were held up by Mary Jane, who replenished them with raspberry or orange jelly or with blancmange and jam. The pudding was of Aunt Julia's making and she received praises for it from all quarters. She herself said that it was not quite brown enough.

—Well, I hope, Miss Morkan, said Mr Browne, that I'm brown enough for you because, you know, I'm all brown.

All the gentlemen, except Gabriel, ate some of the pudding out of compliment to Aunt Julia. As Gabriel never ate sweets the celery had been left for him. Freddy Malins also took a stalk of celery and ate it with his pudding. He had been told that celery was a capital thing for the blood and he was just then under doctor's care. Mrs Malins, who had been silent all through the supper, said that her son was going down to Mount Melleray[9] in a week or so. The table then spoke to Mount Melleray, how bracing the air was down there, how hospitable the monks were and how they never asked for a penny-piece from their guests.

—And do you mean to say, asked Mr Browne incredulously, that a chap can go down there and put up there as if it were a hotel and live on the fat of the land and then come away without paying a farthing?

—O, most people give some donation to the monastery when they leave, said Mary Jane.

—I wish we had an institution like that in our Church, said Mr Browne candidly.

He was astonished to hear that the monks never spoke, got up at two in the morning and slept in their coffins. He asked what they did it for.

—That's the rule of the order, said Aunt Kate firmly.

—Yes, but why? asked Mr Browne.

Aunt Kate repeated that it was the rule, that was all. Mr Browne still seemed not to understand. Freddy Malins explained to him, as best he could, that the monks were trying to make up for the sins committed by all the sinners in the outside world. The explanation was not very clear for Mr Browne grinned and said:

—I like that idea very much but wouldn't a comfortable spring bed do them as well as a coffin?

—The coffin, said Mary Jane, is to remind them of their last end.

As the subject had grown lugubrious it was buried in a silence of the table during which Mrs Malins could be heard saying to her neighbour in an indistinct undertone:

—They are very good men, the monks, very pious men.

9. Site of a Trappist monastery in the south of Ireland.

The raisins and almonds and figs and apples and oranges and chocolates and sweets were now passed about the table and Aunt Julia invited all the guests to have either port or sherry. At first Mr Bartell D'Arcy refused to take either but one of his neighbours nudged him and whispered something to him upon which he allowed his glass to be filled. Gradually as the last glasses were being filled the conversation ceased. A pause followed, broken only by the noise of the wine and by unsettlings of chairs. The Misses Morkan, all three, looked down at the tablecloth. Someone coughed once or twice and then a few gentlemen patted the table gently as a signal for silence. The silence came and Gabriel pushed back his chair and stood up.

The patting at once grew louder in encouragement and then ceased altogether. Gabriel leaned his ten trembling fingers on the tablecloth and smiled nervously at the company. Meeting a row of upturned faces he raised his eyes to the chandelier. The piano was playing a waltz tune and he could hear the skirts sweeping against the drawing-room door. People, perhaps, were standing in the snow on the quay outside, gazing up at the lighted windows and listening to the waltz music. The air was pure there. In the distance lay the park where the trees were weighted with snow. The Wellington Monument wore a gleaming cap of snow that flashed westward over the white field of Fifteen Acres.[1]

He began:

—Ladies and Gentlemen.

—It has fallen to my lot this evening, as in years past, to perform a very pleasing task but a task for which I am afraid my poor powers as a speaker are all too inadequate.

—No, no! said Mr Browne.

—But, however that may be, I can only ask you tonight to take the will for the deed and to lend me your attention for a few moments while I endeavour to express to you in words what my feelings are on this occasion.

—Ladies and Gentlemen. It is not the first time that we have gathered together under this hospitable roof, around this hospitable board. It is not the first time that we have been the recipients—or perhaps, I had better say, the victims—of the hospitality of certain good ladies.

He made a circle in the air with his arm and paused. Everyone laughed or smiled at Aunt Kate and Aunt Julia and Mary Jane who all turned crimson with pleasure. Gabriel went on more boldly:

—I feel more strongly with every recurring year that our country has no tradition which does it so much honour and which it should guard so jealously as that of its hospitality. It is a tradition that is unique as far as my experience goes (and I have visited not a few places abroad) among the modern nations. Some would say, perhaps, that with us it is rather a failing than anything to be boasted of. But granted even that, it is, to my mind, a princely failing, and one that I trust will long be cultivated among us. Of one thing, at least, I am sure. As long as this one roof shelters the good ladies aforesaid—and I wish from my heart it may do so for many and many a long year to come—the tradition of genuine warm-hearted courteous Irish hospitality, which our forefathers have handed down to us and which we in turn must hand down to our descendants, is still alive among us.

A hearty murmur of assent ran round the table. It shot through Gabriel's mind that Miss Ivors was not there and that she had gone away discourteously: and he said with confidence in himself:

1. A section of Phoenix Park.

—Ladies and Gentlemen.

—A new generation is growing up in our midst, a generation actuated by new ideas and new principles. It is serious and enthusiastic for these new ideas and its enthusiasm, even when it is misdirected, is, I believe, in the main sincere. But we are living in a sceptical and, if I may use the phrase, a thought-tormented age: and sometimes I fear that this new generation, educated or hypereducated as it is, will lack those qualities of humanity, of hospitality, of kindly humour which belonged to an older day. Listening to-night to the names of all those great singers of the past it seemed to me, I must confess, that we were living in a less spacious age. Those days might, without exaggeration, be called spacious days: and if they are gone beyond recall let us hope, at least, that in gatherings such as this we shall still speak of them with pride and affection, still cherish in our hearts the memory of those dead and gone great ones whose fame the world will not willingly let die.

—Hear, hear! said Mr Browne loudly.

—But yet, continued Gabriel, his voice falling into a softer inflection, there are always in gatherings such as this sadder thoughts that will recur to our minds: thoughts of the past, of youth, of changes, of absent faces that we miss here to-night. Our path through life is strewn with many such sad memories: and were we to brood upon them always we could not find the heart to go on bravely with our work among the living. We have all of us living duties and living affections which claim, and rightly claim, our strenuous endeavours.

—Therefore, I will not linger on the past. I will not let any gloomy moralising intrude upon us here to-night. Here we are gathered together for a brief moment from the bustle and rush of our everyday routine. We are met here as friends, in the spirit of good-fellowship, as colleagues, also to a certain extent, in the true spirit of *camaraderie*, and as the guests of—what shall I call them?—the Three Graces[2] of the Dublin musical world.

The table burst into applause and laughter at this sally. Aunt Julia vainly asked each of her neighbors in turn to tell her what Gabriel had said.

—He says we are the Three Graces, Aunt Julia, said Mary Jane.

Aunt Julia did not understand but she looked up, smiling, at Gabriel, who continued in the same vein:

—Ladies and Gentlemen.

—I will not attempt to play to-night the part that Paris[3] played on another occasion. I will not attempt to choose between them. The task would be an invidious one and one beyond my poor powers. For when I view them in turn, whether it be our chief hostess herself, whose good heart, whose too good heart, has become a byword with all who know her, or her sister, who seems to be gifted with perennial youth and whose singing must have been a surprise and a revelation to us all to-night, or, last but not least, when I consider our youngest hostess, talented, cheerful, hard-working and the best of nieces, I confess, Ladies and Gentlemen, that I do not know to which of them I should award the prize.

Gabriel glanced down at his aunts and, seeing the large smile on Aunt Julia's face and the tears which had risen to Aunt Kate's eyes, hastened to his close. He raised his glass of port gallantly, while every member of the company fingered a glass expectantly, and said loudly:

2. Companions to the Muses in Greek mythology.
3. Paris was the judge of a divine beauty contest in which Hera, Athena, and Aphrodite competed; his selection of Aphrodite was, indirectly, the cause of the Trojan war.

—Let us toast them all three together. Let us drink to their health, wealth, long life, happiness and prosperity and may they long continue to hold the proud and self-won position which they hold in their profession and the position of honour and affection which they hold in our hearts.

All the guests stood up, glass in hand, and, turning towards the three seated ladies, sang in unison, with Mr Browne as leader:

> *For they are jolly gay fellows,*
> *For they are jolly gay fellows,*
> *For they are jolly gay fellows,*
> *Which nobody can deny.*

Aunt Kate was making frank use of her handkerchief and even Aunt Julia seemed moved. Freddy Malins beat time with his pudding-fork and the singers turned towards one another, as if in melodious conference, while they sang, with emphasis:

> *Unless he tells a lie,*
> *Unless he tells a lie.*

Then, turning once more towards their hostesses, they sang:

> *For they are jolly gay fellows,*
> *For they are jolly gay fellows,*
> *For they are jolly gay fellows,*
> *Which nobody can deny.*

The acclamation which followed was taken up beyond the door of the supper-room by many of the other guests and renewed time after time, Freddy Malins acting as officer with his fork on high.

The piercing morning air came into the hall where they were standing so that Aunt Kate said:

—Close the door, somebody. Mrs Malins will get her death of cold.

—Browne is out there, Aunt Kate, said Mary Jane.

—Browne is everywhere, said Aunt Kate, lowering her voice.

Mary Jane laughed at her tone.

—Really, she said archly, he is very attentive.

—He has been laid on here like the gas, said Aunt Kate in the same tone, all during the Christmas.

She laughed herself this time good-humouredly and then added quickly:

—But tell him to come in, Mary Jane, and close the door. I hope to goodness he didn't hear me.

At that moment the hall-door was opened and Mr Browne came in from the doorstep, laughing as if his heart would break. He was dressed in a long green over-coat with mock astrakhan cuffs and collar and wore on his head an oval fur cap. He pointed down the snow-covered quay from where the sound of shrill prolonged whistling was borne in.

—Teddy will have all the cabs in Dublin out, he said.

Gabriel advanced from the little pantry behind the office, struggling into his overcoat and looking round the hall, said:

—Gretta not down yet?

—She's getting on her things, Gabriel, said Aunt Kate.

—Who's playing up there? asked Gabriel.

—Nobody. They're all gone.

—O no, Aunt Kate, said Mary Jane. Bartell D'Arcy and Miss O'Callaghan aren't gone yet.

—Someone is strumming at the piano, anyhow, said Gabriel.

Mary Jane glanced at Gabriel and Mr Browne and said with a shiver:

—It makes me feel cold to look at you two gentlemen muffled up like that. I wouldn't like to face your journey home at this hour.

—I'd like nothing better this minute, said Mr Browne stoutly, than a rattling fine walk in the country or a fast drive with a good spanking goer between the shafts.

—We used to have a very good horse and trap at home, said Aunt Julia sadly.

—The never-to-be-forgotten Johnny, said Mary Jane, laughing.

Aunt Kate and Gabriel laughed too.

—Why, what was wonderful about Johnny? asked Mr Browne.

—The late lamented Patrick Morkan, our grandfather, that is, explained Gabriel, commonly known in his later years as the old gentleman, was a glue-boiler.

—O, now, Gabriel, said Aunt Kate, laughing, he had a starch mill.

—Well, glue or starch, said Gabriel, the old gentleman had a horse by the name of Johnny. And Johnny used to work in the old gentleman's mill, walking round and round in order to drive the mill. That was all very well; but now comes the tragic part about Johnny. One fine day the old gentleman thought he'd like to drive out with the quality to a military review in the park.

—The Lord have mercy on his soul, said Aunt Kate compassionately.

—Amen, said Gabriel. So the old gentleman, as I said, harnessed Johnny and put on his very best tall hat and his very best stock collar and drove out in grand style from his ancestral mansion somewhere near Back Lane, I think.

Everyone laughed, even Mrs Malins, at Gabriel's manner and Aunt Kate said:

—O now, Gabriel, he didn't live in Back Lane, really. Only the mill was there.

—Out from the mansion of his forefathers, continued Gabriel, he drove with Johnny. And everything went on beautifully until Johnny came in sight of King Billy's statue:[4] and whether he fell in love with the horse King Billy sits on or whether he thought he was back again in the mill, anyhow he began to walk round the statue.

Gabriel paced in a circle round the hall in his goloshes amid the laughter of the others.

—Round and round he went, said Gabriel, and the old gentleman, who was a very pompous old gentleman, was highly indignant. *Go on, sir! What do you mean, sir? Johnny! Johnny! Most extraordinary conduct! Can't understand the horse!*

The peals of laughter which followed Gabriel's imitation of the incident were interrupted by a resounding knock at the hall-door. Mary Jane ran to open it and let in Freddy Malins. Freddy Malins, with his hat well back on his head and his shoulders humped with cold, was puffing and steaming after his exertions.

—I could only get one cab, he said.

—O, we'll find another along the quay, said Gabriel.

—Yes, said Aunt Kate. Better not keep Mrs Malins standing in the draught.

Mrs Malins was helped down the front steps by her son and Mr Browne and, after many manoeuvres, hoisted into the cab. Freddy Malins clambered in after her and spent a long time settling her on the seat, Mr Browne helping him with advice.

---

4. Statue of William of Orange, who defeated the Irish Catholic forces in the Battle of the Boyne in 1690, which stood in College Green in front of Trinity College in the heart of Dublin. It was seen as a symbol of British imperial oppression.

At last she was settled comfortably and Freddy Malins invited Mr Browne into the cab. There was a good deal of confused talk, and then Mr Browne got into the cab. The cabman settled his rug over his knees, and bent down for the address. The confusion grew greater and the cabman was directed differently by Freddy Malins and Mr Browne, each of whom had his head out through a window of the cab. The difficulty was to know where to drop Mr Browne along the route and Aunt Kate, Aunt Julia and Mary Jane helped the discussion from the doorstep with cross-directions and contradictions and abundance of laughter. As for Freddy Malins he was speechless with laughter. He popped his head in and out of the window every moment, to the great danger of his hat, and told his mother how the discussion was progressing till at last Mr Browne shouted to the bewildered cabman above the din of everybody's laughter:

—Do you know Trinity College?

—Yes, sir, said the cabman.

—Well, drive bang up against Trinity College gates, said Mr Browne, and then we'll tell you where to go. You understand now?

—Yes, sir, said the cabman.

—Make like a bird for Trinity College.

—Right, sir, cried the cabman.

The horse was whipped up and the cab rattled off along the quay amid a chorus of laughter and adieus.

Gabriel had not gone to the door with the others. He was in a dark part of the hall gazing up the staircase, a woman was standing near the top of the first flight, in the shadow also. He could not see her face but he could see the terracotta and salmonpink panels of her skirt which the shadow made appear black and white. It was his wife. She was leaning on the banisters, listening to something. Gabriel was surprised at her stillness and strained his ear to listen also. But he could hear little save the noise of laughter and dispute on the front steps, a few chords struck on the piano and a few notes of a man's voice singing.

He stood still in the gloom of the hall, trying to catch the air that the voice was singing and gazing up at his wife. There was grace and mystery in her attitude as if she were a symbol of something. He asked himself what is a woman standing on the stairs in the shadow, listening to distant music, a symbol of. If he were a painter he would paint her in that attitude. Her blue felt hat would show off the bronze of her hair against the darkness and the dark panels of her skirt would show off the light ones. *Distant Music* he would call the picture if he were a painter.

The hall-door was closed; and Aunt Kate, Aunt Julia and Mary Jane came down the hall, still laughing.

—Well, isn't Freddy terrible? said Mary Jane. He's really terrible.

Gabriel said nothing but pointed up the stairs towards where his wife was standing. Now that the hall-door was closed the voice and the piano could be heard more clearly. Gabriel held up his hand for them to be silent. The song seemed to be in the old Irish tonality and the singer seemed uncertain both of his words and of his voice. The voice, made plaintive by distance and by the singer's hoarseness, faintly illuminated the cadence of the air with words expressing grief:

> O, the rain falls on my heavy locks
> And the dew wets my skin,
> My babe lies cold . . .

–O, exclaimed Mary Jane. It's Bartell D'Arcy singing and he wouldn't sing all the night. O, I'll get him to sing a song before he goes.

—O do, Mary Jane, said Aunt Kate.

Mary Jane brushed past the others and ran to the staircase but before she reached it the singing stopped and the piano was closed abruptly.

—O, what a pity! she cried. Is he coming down, Gretta?

Gabriel heard his wife answer yes and saw her come down towards them. A few steps behind her were Mr Bartell D'Arcy and Miss O'Callaghan.

—O, Mr D'Arcy, cried Mary Jane, it's downright mean of you to break off like that when we were all in raptures listening to you.

—I have been at him all the evening, said Miss O'Callaghan, and Mrs Conroy too and he told us he had a dreadful cold and couldn't sing.

—O, Mr D'Arcy, said Aunt Kate, now that was a great fib to tell.

—Can't you see that I'm as hoarse as a crow? said Mr D'Arcy roughly.

He went into the pantry hastily and put on his overcoat. The others, taken aback by his rude speech, could find nothing to say. Aunt Kate wrinkled her brows and made signs to the others to drop the subject. Mr D'Arcy stood swathing his neck carefully and frowning.

—It's the weather, said Aunt Julia, after a pause.

—Yes, everybody has colds, said Aunt Kate readily, everybody.

—They say, said Mary Jane, we haven't had snow like it for thirty years; and I read this morning in the newspapers that the snow is general all over Ireland.

—I love the look of snow, said Aunt Julia sadly.

—So do I, said Miss O'Callaghan. I think Christmas is never really Christmas unless we have the snow on the ground.

—But poor Mr D'Arcy doesn't like the snow, said Aunt Kate, smiling.

Mr D'Arcy came from the pantry, full swathed and buttoned, and in a repentant tone told them the history of his cold. Everyone gave him advice and said it was a great pity and urged him to be very careful of his throat in the night air. Gabriel watched his wife who did not join in the conversation. She was standing right under the dusty fanlight and the flame of the gas lit up the rich bronze of her hair which he had seen her drying at the fire a few days before. She was in the same attitude and seemed unaware of the talk about her. At last she turned towards them and Gabriel saw that there was colour on her cheeks and that her eyes were shining. A sudden tide of joy went leaping out of his heart.

—Mr D'Arcy, she said, what is the name of that song you were singing?

—It's called *The Lass of Aughrim*, said Mr D'Arcy, but I couldn't remember it properly. Why? Do you know it?

—*The Lass of Aughrim*, she repeated. I couldn't think of the name.

—It's a very nice air, said Mary Jane. I'm sorry you were not in voice to-night.

—Now, Mary Jane, said Aunt Kate, don't annoy Mr D'Arcy. I won't have him annoyed.

Seeing that all were ready to start she shepherded them to the door where good-night was said:

—Well, good-night, Aunt Kate, and thanks for the pleasant evening.

—Good-night, Gabriel. Good-night, Gretta!

—Good-night, Aunt Kate, and thanks ever so much. Good-night, Aunt Julia.

—O, good-night, Gretta, I didn't see you.

—Good-night, Mr D'Arcy. Good-night, Miss O'Callaghan.

—Good-night, Miss Morkan.

—Good-night, again.

—Good-night, all. Safe home.

—Good-night. Good-night.

The morning was still dark. A dull yellow light brooded over the houses and the river; and the sky seemed to be descending. It was slushy underfoot; and only streaks and patches of snow lay on the roofs, on the parapets of the quay and on the area railings. The lamps were still burning redly in the murky air and, across the river, the palace of the Four Courts[5] stood out menacingly against the heavy sky.

She was walking on before him with Mr Bartell D'Arcy, her shoes in a brown parcel tucked under one arm and her hands holding her skirt up from the slush. She had no longer any grace of attitude but Gabriel's eyes were still bright with happiness. The blood went bounding along his veins; and the thoughts went rioting through his brain, proud, joyful, tender, valorous.

She was walking on before him so lightly and so erect that he longed to run after her noiselessly, catch her by the shoulders and say something foolish and affectionate into her ear. She seemed to him so frail that he longed to defend her against something and then to be alone with her. Moments of their secret life together burst like stars upon his memory. A heliotrope envelope was lying beside his breakfast-cup and he was caressing it with his hand. Birds were twittering in the ivy and the sunny web of the curtain was shimmering along the floor: he could not eat for happiness. They were standing on the crowded platform and he was placing a ticket inside the warm palm of her glove. He was standing with her in the cold, looking in through a grated window at a man making bottles in a roaring furnace. It was very cold. Her face, fragrant in the cold air, was quite close to his; and suddenly she called out to the man at the furnace:

—Is the fire hot, sir?

But the man could not hear her with the noise of the furnace. It was just as well. He might have answered rudely.

A wave of yet more tender joy escaped from his heart and went coursing in warm flood along his arteries. Like the tender fires of stars moments of their life together, that no one knew of or would ever know of, broke upon and illumined his memory. He longed to recall to her those moments, to make her forget the years of their dull existence together and remember only their moments of ecstasy. For the years, he felt, had not quenched his soul or hers. Their children, his writing, her household cares had not quenched all their souls' tender fire. In one letter that he had written to her then he had said: *Why is it that words like these seem to me so dull and cold? Is it because there is no word tender enough to be your name?*

Like distant music these words that he had written years before were borne towards him from the past. He longed to be alone with her. When the others had gone away, when he and she were in their room in the hotel, then they would be alone together. He would call her softly:

—Gretta!

Perhaps she would not hear at once: she would be undressing. Then something in his voice would strike her. She would turn and look at him. . . .

At the corner of Winetavern Street they met a cab. He was glad of its rattling noise as it saved him from conversation. She was looking out of the window and seemed tired. The others spoke only a few words, pointing out some building or

5. The Irish law courts.

street. The horse galloped along wearily under the murky morning sky, dragging his old rattling box after his heels, and Gabriel was again in a cab with her, galloping to catch the boat, galloping to their honeymoon.

As the cab drove across O'Connell Bridge Miss O'Callaghan said:

—They say you never cross O'Connell Bridge without seeing a white horse.

—I see a white man this time, said Gabriel.

—Where? asked Mr Bartell D'Arcy.

Gabriel pointed to the statue, on which lay patches of snow. Then he nodded familiarly to it and waved his hand.

—Good-night, Dan,[6] he said gaily.

When the cab drew up before the hotel Gabriel jumped out and, in spite of Mr Bartell D'Arcy's protest, paid the driver. He gave the man a shilling over his fare. The man saluted and said:

—A prosperous New Year to you, sir.

—The same to you, said Gabriel cordially.

She leaned for a moment on his arm in getting out of the cab and while standing at the curbstone, bidding the others good-night. She leaned lightly on his arm, as lightly as when she had danced with him a few hours before. He had felt proud and happy then, happy that she was his, proud of her grace and wifely carriage. But now, after the kindling again of so many memories, the first touch of her body, musical and strange and perfumed, sent through him a keen pang of lust. Under cover of her silence he pressed her arm closely to his side; and, as they stood at the hotel door, he felt that they had escaped from their lives and duties, escaped from home and friends and run away together with wild and radiant hearts to a new adventure.

An old man was dozing in a great hooded chair in the hall. He lit a candle in the office and went before them to the stairs. They followed him in silence, their feet falling in soft thuds on the thickly carpeted stairs. She mounted the stairs behind the porter, her head bowed in the ascent, her frail shoulders curved as with a burden, her skirt girt tightly about her. He could have flung his arms about her hips and held her still for his arms were trembling with desire to seize her and only the stress of his nails against the palms of his hands held the wild impulse of his body in check. The porter halted on the stairs to settle his guttering candle. They halted too on the steps below him. In the silence Gabriel could hear the falling of the molten wax into the tray and the thumping of his own heart against his ribs.

The porter led them along a corridor and opened a door. Then he set his unstable candle down on a toilet-table and asked at what hour they were to be called in the morning.

—Eight, said Gabriel.

The porter pointed to the tap of the electric-light and began a muttered apology but Gabriel cut him short.

—We don't want any light. We have light enough from the street. And I say, he added, pointing to the candle, you might remove that handsome article, like a good man.

The porter took up his candle again, but slowly for he was surprised by such a novel idea. Then he mumbled good-night and went out. Gabriel shot the lock to.

---

6. A statue of Daniel O'Connell, 19th-century nationalist leader, stands at the south end of Sackville Street (now called O'Connell Street).

A ghostly light from the street lamp lay in a long shaft from one window to the door. Gabriel threw his overcoat and hat on a couch and crossed the room towards the window. He looked down into the street in order that his emotion might calm a little. Then he turned and leaned against a chest of drawers with his back to the light. She had taken off her hat and cloak and was standing before a large swinging mirror, unhooking her waist. Gabriel paused for a few moments, watching her, and then said:

—Gretta!

She turned away from the mirror slowly and walked along the shaft of light towards him. Her face looked so serious and weary that the words would not pass Gabriel's lips. No, it was not the moment yet.

—You looked tired, he said.

—I am a little, she answered.

—You don't feel ill or weak?

—No, tired: that's all.

She went on to the window and stood there, looking out. Gabriel waited again and then, fearing that diffidence was about to conquer him, he said abruptly:

—By the way, Gretta!

—What is it?

—You know that poor fellow Malins? he said quickly.

—Yes. What about him?

—Well, poor fellow, he's a decent sort of chap after all, continued Gabriel in a false voice. He gave me back that sovereign I lent him and I didn't expect it really. It's a pity he wouldn't keep away from that Browne, because he's not a bad fellow at heart.

He was trembling now with annoyance. Why did she seem so abstracted? He did not know how he could begin. Was she annoyed, too, about something? If she would only turn to him or come to him of her own accord! To take her as she was would be brutal. No, he must see some ardour in her eyes first. He longed to be master of her strange mood.

—When did you lend him the pound? she asked, after a pause.

Gabriel strove to restrain himself from breaking out into brutal language about the sottish Malins and his pound. He longed to cry to her from his soul, to crush her body against his, to overmaster her. But he said:

—O, at Christmas, when he opened that little Christmas-card shop in Henry Street.

He was in such a fever of rage and desire that he did not hear her come from the window. She stood before him for an instant, looking at him strangely. Then, suddenly raising herself on tiptoe and resting her hands lightly on his shoulders, she kissed him.

—You are a very generous person, Gabriel, she said.

Gabriel, trembling with delight at her sudden kiss and at the quaintness of her phrase, put his hands on her hair and began smoothing it back, scarcely touching it with his fingers. The washing had made it fine and brilliant. His heart was brimming over with happiness. Just when he was wishing for it she had come to him of her own accord. Perhaps her thoughts had been running with his. Perhaps she had felt the impetuous desire that was in him and then the yielding mood had come upon her. Now that she had fallen to him so easily he wondered why he had been so diffident.

He stood, holding her head between his hands. Then, slipping one arm swiftly about her body and drawing her towards him, he said softly:

—Gretta dear, what are you thinking about?

She did not answer nor yield wholly to his arm. He said again, softly:

—Tell me what it is, Gretta. I think I know what is the matter. Do I know?

She did not answer at once. Then she said in an outburst of tears:

—O, I am thinking about that song, *The Lass of Aughrim*.

She broke loose from him and ran to the bed and, throwing her arms across the bed-rail, hid her face. Gabriel stood stock-still for a moment in astonishment and then followed her. As he passed in the way of the cheval-glass he caught sight of himself in full length, his broad, well-filled shirt-front, the face whose expression always puzzled him when he saw it in a mirror and his glimmering gilt-rimmed eye-glasses. He halted a few paces from her and said:

—What about the song? Why does that make you cry?

She raised her head from her arms and dried her eyes with the back of her hand like a child. A kinder note than he had intended went into his voice.

—Why, Gretta? he asked.

—I am thinking about a person long ago who used to sing that song.

—And who was the person long ago? asked Gabriel, smiling.

—It was a person I used to know in Galway when I was living with my grand-mother, she said.

The smile passed away from Gabriel's face. A dull anger began to gather again at the back of his mind and the dull fires of his lust began to glow angrily in his veins.

—Someone you were in love with? he asked ironically.

—It was a young boy I used to know, she answered, named Michael Furey. He used to sing that song, *The Lass of Aughrim*. He was very delicate.

Gabriel was silent. He did not wish her to think that he was interested in this delicate boy.

—I can see him so plainly, she said after a moment. Such eyes as he had: big dark eyes! And such an expression in them—an expression!

—O then, you were in love with him? said Gabriel.

—I used to go out walking with him, she said, when I was in Galway.

A thought flew across Gabriel's mind.

—Perhaps that was why you wanted to go to Galway with that Ivors girl? he said coldly.

She looked at him and asked in surprise:

—What for?

Her eyes made Gabriel feel awkward. He shrugged his shoulders and said:

—How do I know? To see him perhaps.

She looked away from him along the shaft of light towards the window in silence.

—He is dead, she said at length. He died when he was only seventeen. Isn't it a terrible thing to die so young as that?

—What was he? asked Gabriel, still ironically.

—He was in the gasworks, she said.

Gabriel felt humiliated by the failure of his irony and by the evocation of this figure from the dead, a boy in the gasworks. While he had been full of memories of their secret life together, full of tenderness and joy and desire, she had been compar-ing him in her mind with another. A shameful consciousness of his own person assailed him. He saw himself as a ludicrous figure, acting as a pennyboy[7] for his aunts,

7. Errand boy.

a nervous well-meaning sentimentalist, orating to vulgarians and idealising his own clownish lusts, the pitiable fatuous fellow he had caught a glimpse of in the mirror. Instinctively he turned his back more to the light lest she might see the shame that burned upon his forehead.

He tried to keep up his tone of cold interrogation but his voice when he spoke was humble and indifferent.

—I suppose you were in love with this Michael Furey, Gretta, he said.

—I was great with him at that time, she said.

Her voice was veiled and sad. Gabriel, feeling now how vain it would be to try to lead her whither he had purposed, caressed one of her hands and said, also sadly:

—And what did he die of so young, Gretta? Consumption, was it?

—I think he died for me, she answered.[8]

A vague terror seized Gabriel at this answer as if, at that hour when he had hoped to triumph, some impalpable and vindictive being was coming against him, gathering forces against him in its vague world. But he shook himself free of it with an effort of reason and continued to caress her hand. He did not question her again for he felt that she would tell him of herself. Her hand was warm and moist: it did not respond to his touch but he continued to caress it just as he had caressed her first letter to him that spring morning.

—It was in the winter, she said, about the beginning of the winter when I was going to leave my grandmother's and come up here to the convent. And he was ill at the time in his lodgings in Galway and wouldn't be let out and his people in Oughterard[9] were written to. He was in decline, they said, or something like that. I never knew rightly.

She paused for a moment and sighed.

—Poor fellow, she said. He was very fond of me and he was such a gentle boy. We used to go out together, walking, you know, Gabriel, like the way they do in the country. He was going to study singing only for his health. He had a very good voice, poor Michael Furey.

—Well; and then? asked Gabriel.

—And then when it came to the time for me to leave Galway and come up to the convent he was much worse and I wouldn't be let see him so I wrote a letter saying I was going up to Dublin and would be back in the summer and hoping he would be better then.

She paused for a moment to get her voice under control and then went on:

—Then the night before I left I was in my grandmother's house in Nuns' Island, packing up, and I heard gravel thrown up against the window. The window was so wet I couldn't see so I ran downstairs as I was and slipped out the back into the garden and there was the poor fellow at the end of the garden, shivering.

—And did you not tell him to go back? asked Gabriel.

—I implored him to go home at once and told him he would get his death in the rain. But he said he did not want to live. I can see his eyes as well as well! He was standing at the end of the wall where there was a tree.

—And did he go home? asked Gabriel.

8. Gretta here echoes the words of Yeats's Cathleen ni Houlihan: "Singing I am about a man I knew one time, yellow-haired Donough that was hanged in Galway. . . . He died for love of me: many a man has died for love of me." The play was first performed in Dublin on 2 April 1902.

9. A small village in Western Ireland.

—Yes, he went home. And when I was only a week in the convent he died and he was buried in Oughterard where his people came from. O, the day I heard that, that he was dead!

She stopped, choking with sobs, and, overcome by emotion, flung herself face downward on the bed, sobbing in the quilt. Gabriel held her hand for a moment longer, irresolutely, and then, shy of intruding on her grief, let it fall gently and walked quietly to the window.

She was fast asleep.

Gabriel, leaning on his elbow, looked for a few moments unresentfully on her tangled hair and half-open mouth, listening to her deep-drawn breath. So she had had that romance in her life: a man had died for her sake. It hardly pained him now to think how poor a part he, her husband, had played in her life. He watched her while she slept as though he and she had never lived together as man and wife. His curious eyes rested long upon her face and on her hair: and, as he thought of what she must have been then, in that time of her first girlish beauty, a strange friendly pity for her entered his soul. He did not like to say even to himself that her face was no longer beautiful but he knew that it was no longer the face for which Michael Furey had braved death.

Perhaps she had not told him all the story. His eyes moved to the chair over which she had thrown some of her clothes. A petticoat string dangled to the floor. One boot stood upright, its limp upper fallen down: the fellow of it lay upon its side. He wondered at his riot of emotions of an hour before. From what had it proceeded? From his aunt's supper, from his own foolish speech, from the wine and dancing, the merry-making when saying good-night in the hall, the pleasure of the walk along the river in the snow. Poor Aunt Julia! She, too, would soon be a shade with the shade of Patrick Morkan and his horse. He had caught that haggard look upon her face for a moment when she was singing *Arrayed for the Bridal*. Soon, perhaps, he would be sitting in that same drawing-room, dressed in black, his silk hat on his knees. The blinds would be drawn down and Aunt Kate would be sitting beside him, crying and blowing her nose and telling him how Julia had died. He would cast about in his mind for some words that might console her, and would find only lame and useless ones. Yes, yes: that would happen very soon.

The air of the room chilled his shoulders. He stretched himself cautiously along under the sheets and lay down beside his wife. One by one they were all becoming shades. Better pass boldly into that other world, in the full glory of some passion, than fade and wither dismally with age. He thought of how she who lay beside him had locked in her heart for so many years that image of her lover's eyes when he had told her that he did not wish to live.

Generous tears filled Gabriel's eyes. He had never felt like that himself towards any woman but he knew that such a feeling must be love. The tears gathered more thickly in his eyes and in the partial darkness he imagined he saw the form of a young man standing under a dripping tree. Other forms were near. His soul had approached that region where dwell the vast hosts of the dead. He was conscious of, but could not apprehend, their wayward and flickering existence. His own identity was fading out into a grey impalpable world: the solid world itself which these dead had one time reared and lived in was dissolving and dwindling.

A few light taps upon the pane made him turn to the window. It had begun to snow again. He watched sleepily the flakes, silver and dark, falling obliquely against the lamplight. The time had come for him to set out on his journey westward. Yes, the newspapers were right: snow was general all over Ireland. It was falling on every part of the dark central plain, on the treeless hills, falling softly upon the Bog of Allen and, farther westward, softly falling into the dark mutinous Shannon waves.[1] It was falling, too, upon every part of the lonely churchyard on the hill where Michael Furey lay buried. It lay thickly drifted on the crooked crosses and headstones, on the spears of the little gate, on the barren thorns. His soul swooned slowly as he heard the snow falling faintly through the universe and faintly falling, like the descent of their last end, upon all the living and the dead.

Ulysses

Ulysses boldly announced that modern literature had set itself new tasks and devised new means to "make it new." In his review of the novel, T. S. Eliot wrote that Joyce had discovered "a way of controlling, of ordering, of giving a shape and a significance to the panorama of futility and anarchy which is contemporary history. . . . It is, I seriously believe, a step toward making the modern world possible for art . . . ." The technique with which Joyce shaped his materials Eliot called (at Joyce's suggestion) the mythical method—using ancient myth to suggest "a continuous parallel between contemporaneity and antiquity." Joyce's purposes in using myth—in the case of *Ulysses*, a series of parallels to Homer's *Odyssey*—are open to debate; but he was quite frank about the fact that each of the novel's eighteen chapters was modeled, however loosely, on one of Odysseus's adventures. Thus Leopold Bloom, the novel's advertising-salesman protagonist, is in some sense a modern-day Odysseus; rather than finding his way back from Troy and the Trojan Wars, he simply navigates his way through a very full day in Dublin on June 16, 1904. This day, however, has its perils. Bloom, a Jew, is set upon by anti-Semites, threatened with violence, and driven from the pub where he drinks; much later, in Dublin's red-light district, he rescues a very drunk young poet, Stephen Dedalus, from arrest, and takes him back to his home for a cup of cocoa and conversation. Foremost among Bloom's tests on this particular day, however, is his knowledge that his wife Molly will consummate an affair with the brash, egotistical tenor Blazes Boylan—an affair which, owing to his own shortcomings as a husband, Bloom is unwilling to stop.

The chapter given here is the pivotal seventh chapter, in which the realism of the earlier chapters begins to be invaded by other modes of observation and narration. Set in the offices of the *Freeman's Journal* where Bloom works, the chapter takes on a parodoxically reportorial perspective, complete with headlines. Chapter 7 is usually called the "Aeolus" chapter, after its parallel episode in the *Odyssey*. In Book 10, having escaped the Cyclops, Odysseus reaches an island ruled by Aeolus, lord of the winds. Aeolus offers to help Odysseus by trapping all ill winds in a bag which Odysseus then takes with him on his ship; when they are within sight of home, however, Odysseus falls asleep and his crew, curious and jealous about what their captain might have stowed in the bag, open it, releasing the winds and driving the crew back to Aeolia. Joyce builds into his chapter myraid references to wind and air in many forms—from arias to belches, and from conversational shooting the breeze to rhetorical hot air. As Bloom tries to do his job, forget about Molly's plans, and find acceptance among co-workers who will always see him as an outsider, he narrowly misses meeting up with Stephen Dedalus. Stephen has come to the newspaper to deliver a letter on hoof and mouth disease, written by the headmaster of the school where he is teaching. This far from exalted errand only increases Stephen's unease as he negotiates the provincial literary and journalistic world of Dublin, looking for ways to free himself, and capture Dublin, in his art.

---

1. Where Ireland's longest river, the Shannon, empties into the sea.

Photo of Sackville Street (now O'Connell Street), Dublin, with view of Nelson's Pillar.

from Ulysses

[CHAPTER 7. AEOLUS]

IN THE HEART OF THE HIBERNIAN METROPOLIS

Before Nelson's pillar trams slowed, shunted, changed trolley, started for Blackrock, Kingstown and Dalkey, Clonskea, Rathgar and Terenure, Palmerston Park and upper Rathmines, Sandymount Green, Rathmines, Ringsend, and Sandymount Tower, Harold's Cross.[1] The hoarse Dublin United Tramway Company's timekeeper bawled them off:

—Rathgar and Terenure!

—Come on, Sandymount Green!

Right and left parallel clanging ringing a doubledecker and a singledeck moved from their railheads, swerved to the down line, glided parallel.

—Start, Palmerston Park!

THE WEARER OF THE CROWN

Under the porch of the general post office shoeblacks called and polished. Parked in North Prince's street His Majesty's vermilion mailcars, bearing on their sides the royal initials, E. R.,[2] received loudly flung sacks of letters, postcards, lettercards, parcels, insured and paid, for local, provincial, British and overseas delivery.

---

1. The names of various tramlines going out from Nelson's Pillar in central Dublin.

2. Edward Rex (Edward VII of England).

GENTLEMEN OF THE PRESS

Grossbooted draymen rolled barrels dullthudding out of Prince's stores and bumped them up on the brewery float. On the brewery float bumped dullthudding barrels rolled by grossbooted draymen out of Prince's stores.

—There it is, Red Murray said. Alexander Keyes.

—Just cut it out, will you? Mr Bloom said, and I'll take it round to the *Tele-graph* office.

The door of Ruttledge's office creaked again. Davy Stephens, minute in a large capecoat, a small felt hat crowning his ringlets, passed out with a roll of papers under his cape, a king's courier.

Red Murray's long shears sliced out the advertisement from the newspaper in four clean strokes. Scissors and paste.

—I'll go through the printingworks, Mr Bloom said, taking the cut square.

—Of course, if he wants a par,[3] Red Murray said earnestly, a pen behind his ear, we can do him one.

—Right, Mr Bloom said with a nod. I'll rub that in.

We.

WILLIAM BRAYDEN, ESQUIRE, OF OAKLANDS, SANDYMOUNT

Red Murray touched Mr Bloom's arm with the shears and whispered:

—Brayden.[4]

Mr Bloom turned and saw the liveried porter raise his lettered cap as a stately figure entered between the newsboards of the *Weekly Freeman and National Press* and the *Freeman's Journal and National Press*. Dullthudding Guinness's barrels. It passed stately up the staircase steered by an umbrella, a solemn beardframed face. The broadcloth back ascended each step: back. All his brains are in the nape of his neck, Simon Dedalus says. Welts of flesh behind on him. Fat folds of neck, fat, neck, fat, neck.

—Don't you think his face is like Our Saviour? Red Murray whispered.

The door of Ruttledge's office whispered: ee: cree. They always build one door opposite another for the wind to. Way in. Way out.

Our Saviour: beardframed oval face: talking in the dusk. Mary, Martha. Steered by an umbrella sword to the footlights: Mario the tenor.[5]

—Or like Mario, Mr Bloom said.

—Yes, Red Murray agreed. But Mario was said to be the picture of Our Saviour.

Jesus Mario with rougy cheeks, doublet and spindle legs. Hand on his heart. In *Martha*.[6]

> Co-ome thou lost one,
> Co-ome thou dear one

THE CROZIER[7] AND THE PEN

—His grace phoned down twice this morning, Red Murray said gravely.

They watched the knees, legs, boots vanish. Neck.

---

3. A paragraph.
4. Irish barrister (1865–1933) and editor of the *Freeman's Journal*.
5. Giovanni Matteo (1810–1883), known onstage as

"Mario."
6. Light opera (1847) by Friedrich von Flotow.
7. Bishop's staff.

A telegram boy stepped in nimbly, threw an envelope on the counter and stepped off posthaste with a word:

—*Freeman!*

Mr Bloom said slowly:

—Well, he is one of our saviours also.

A meek smile accompanied him as he lifted the counterflap, as he passed in through a sidedoor and along the warm dark stairs and passage, along the now reverberating boards. But will he save the circulation? Thumping, thumping.

He pushed in the glass swingdoor and entered, stepping over strewn packing paper. Through a lane of clanking drums he made his way towards Nannetti's reading closet.[8]

Hynes here too: account of the funeral probably. Thumping thump.

WITH UNFEIGNED REGRET IT IS WE ANNOUNCE THE DISSOLUTION OF A MOST RESPECTED DUBLIN BURGESS

This morning the remains of the late Mr Patrick Dignam. Machines. Smash a man to atoms if they got him caught. Rule the world today. His machineries are pegging away too. Like these, got out of hand: fermenting. Working away, tearing away. And that old grey rat tearing to get in.

HOW A GREAT DAILY ORGAN IS TURNED OUT

Mr Bloom halted behind the foreman's spare body, admiring a glossy crown.

Strange he never saw his real country. Ireland my country. Member for College green. He boomed that workaday worker tack for all it was worth. It's the ads and side features sell a weekly not the stale news in the official gazette. Queen Anne is dead. Published by authority in the year one thousand and. Demesne situate in the townland of Rosenallis, barony of Tinnahinch. To all whom it may concern schedule pursuant to statute showing return of number of mules and jennets exported from Ballina. Nature notes. Cartoons. Phil Blake's weekly Pat and Bull story. Uncle Toby's page for tiny tots. Country bumpkin's queries. Dear Mr Editor, what is a good cure for flatulence? I'd like that part. Learn a lot teaching others. The personal note. M. A. P.[9] Mainly all pictures. Shapely bathers on golden strand. World's biggest balloon. Double marriage of sisters celebrated. Two bridegrooms laughing heartily at each other. Cuprani too, printer. More Irish than the Irish.

The machines clanked in threefour time. Thump, thump, thump. Now if he got paralysed there and no one knew how to stop them they'd clank on and on the same, print it over and over and up and back. Monkeydoodle the whole thing. Want a cool head.

—Well, get it into the evening edition, councillor, Hynes said.

Soon be calling him my lord mayor. Long John is backing him, they say.

The foreman, without answering, scribbled press on a corner of the sheet and made a sign to a typesetter. He handed the sheet silently over the dirty glass screen.

—Right: thanks, Hynes said moving off.

Mr Bloom stood in his way.

---

8. Joseph Patrick Nannetti (1851–1915), Irish-Italian printer and politician, a Dublin Member of Parliament.   9. *Mainly About People,* a weekly paper.

—If you want to draw the cashier is just going to lunch, he said, pointing back-ward with his thumb.

—Did you? Hynes asked.

—Mm, Mr Bloom said. Look sharp and you'll catch him.

—Thanks, old man, Hynes said. I'll tap him too.

He hurried on eagerly towards the *Freeman's Journal.*

Three bob I lent him in Meagher's. Three weeks. Third hint.

WE SEE THE CANVASSER AT WORK

Mr Bloom laid his cutting on Mr Nannetti's desk.

—Excuse me, councillor, he said. This ad, you see. Keyes, you remember.

Mr Nannetti considered the cutting a while and nodded.

—He wants it in for July, Mr Bloom said.

The foreman moved his pencil towards it.

—But wait, Mr Bloom said. He wants it changed. Keyes, you see. He wants two keys at the top.

Hell of a racket they make. He doesn't hear it. Nannan. Iron nerves. Maybe he understands what I.

The foreman turned round to hear patiently and, lifting an elbow, began to scratch slowly in the armpit of his alpaca jacket.

—Like that, Mr Bloom said, crossing his forefingers at the top.

Let him take that in first.

Mr Bloom, glancing sideways up from the cross he had made, saw the foreman's sallow face, think he has a touch of jaundice, and beyond the obedient reels feeding in huge webs of paper. Clank it. Clank it. Miles of it unreeled. What becomes of it after? O, wrap up meat, parcels: various uses, thousand and one things.

Slipping his words deftly into the pauses of the clanking he drew swiftly on the scarred woodwork.

HOUSE OF KEY(E)S

—Like that, see. Two crossed keys here. A circle. Then here the name Alexander Keyes, tea, wine and spirit merchant. So on.

Better not teach him his own business.

—You know yourself, councillor, just what he wants. Then round the top in leaded: the house of keys. You see? Do you think that's a good idea?

The foreman moved his scratching hand to his lower ribs and scratched there quietly.

—The idea, Mr Bloom said, is the house of keys. You know, councillor, the Manx parliament. Innuendo of home rule.[1] Tourists, you know, from the isle of Man. Catches the eye, you see. Can you do that?

I could ask him perhaps about how to pronounce that *voglio*.[2] But then if he did-n't know only make it awkward for him. Better not.

1. The House of Keyes is the lower house of the Isle of Man Parliament. The Isle of Man enjoyed Home Rule, which Parnell was trying to win for Ireland.
2. In Mozart's opera *Don Giovanni*, Don Giovanni tries to seduce a peasant girl, Zerlina, on her wedding day. Tempted, Zerlina sings *"voglio e non vorrei"* ("I want to and I wouldn't like to"). Bloom's wife Molly is rehearsing this song; Bloom worries both that Molly may be mispro-nouncing the word (the g of *voglio* is silent) and, more importantly, that the line may accurately represent her willingness to enter into an affair with her eager suitor Blazes Boylan.

—We can do that, the foreman said. Have you the design?

—I can get it, Mr Bloom said. It was in a Kilkenny paper. He has a house there too. I'll just run out and ask him. Well, you can do that and just a little par calling attention. You know the usual. Highclass licensed premises. Longfelt want. So on.

The foreman thought for an instant.

—We can do that, he said. Let him give us a three months' renewal.

A typesetter brought him a limp galleypage. He began to check it silently. Mr Bloom stood by, hearing the loud throbs of cranks, watching the silent typesetters at their cases.

ORTHOGRAPHICAL

Want to be sure of his spelling. Proof fever. Martin Cunningham forgot to give us his spellingbee conundrum this morning. It is amusing to view the unpar one ar alleled embarra two ars is it? double ess ment of a harassed pedlar while gauging au the symmetry with a y of a peeled pear under a cemetery wall. Silly, isn't it? Cemetery put in of course on account of the symmetry.

I could have said when he clapped on his topper. Thank you. I ought to have said something about an old hat or something. No, I could have said. Looks as good as new now. See his phiz[3] then.

Sllt. The nethermost deck of the first machine jogged forward its flyboard with sllt the first batch of quirefolded papers. Sllt. Almost human the way it sllt to call attention. Doing its level best to speak. That door too sllt creaking, asking to be shut. Everything speaks in its own way. Sllt.

NOTED CHURCHMAN AN OCCASIONAL CONTRIBUTOR

The foreman handed back the galleypage suddenly, saying:

—Wait. Where's the archbishop's letter? It's to be repeated in the *Telegraph*. Where's what's his name?

He looked about him round his loud unanswering machines.

—Monks, sir? a voice asked from the castingbox.

—Ay. Where's Monks?

—Monks!

Mr Bloom took up his cutting. Time to get out.

—Then I'll get the design, Mr Nannetti, he said, and you'll give it a good place I know.

—Monks!

—Yes, sir.

Three months' renewal. Want to get some wind off my chest first. Try it anyhow. Rub in August: good idea: horseshow month. Ballsbridge. Tourists over for the show.[4]

A DAYFATHER

He walked on through the caseroom, passing an old man, bowed, spectacled, aproned. Old Monks, the dayfather. Queer lot of stuff he must have put through his hands in his time: obituary notices, pubs' ads, speeches, divorce suits, found drowned.

---

3. Physiognomy; face.

4. An important horse show is held every August in the

Royal Dublin Society's showgrounds in the suburb of Ballsbridge.

Nearing the end of his tether now. Sober serious man with a bit in the savingsbank I'd say. Wife a good cook and washer. Daughter working the machine in the parlour. Plain Jane, no damn nonsense.

AND IT WAS THE FEAST OF THE PASSOVER

He stayed in his walk to watch a typesetter neatly distributing type. Reads it backwards first. Quickly he does it. Must require some practice that. mangiD kcirtaP. Poor papa with his hagadah book, reading backwards with his finger to me. Pessach.[5] Next year in Jerusalem. Dear, O dear! All that long business about that brought us out of the land of Egypt and into the house of bondage *alleluia*.[6] *Shema Israel Adonai Elohenu*. No, that's the other.[7] Then the twelve brothers, Jacob's sons. And then the lamb and the cat and the dog and the stick and the water and the butcher and then the angel of death kills the butcher and he kills the ox and the dog kills the cat.[8] Sounds a bit silly till you come to look into it well. Justice it means but it's everybody eating everyone else. That's what life is after all. How quickly he does that job. Practice makes perfect. Seems to see with his fingers.

Mr Bloom passed on out of the clanking noises through the gallery on to the landing. Now am I going to tram it out all the way and then catch him out perhaps. Better phone him up first. Number? Same as Citron's house. Twentyeight. Twentyeight double four.

ONLY ONCE MORE THAT SOAP[9]

He went down the house staircase. Who the deuce scrawled all over those walls with matches? Looks as if they did it for a bet. Heavy greasy smell there always is in those works. Lukewarm glue in Thom's next door when I was there.

He took out his handkerchief to dab his nose. Citronlemon? Ah, the soap I put there. Lose it out of that pocket. Putting back his handkerchief he took out the soap and stowed it away, buttoned, into the hip pocket of his trousers.

What perfume does your wife use? I could go home still: tram: something I forgot. Just to see before dressing. No. Here. No.[1]

A sudden screech of laughter came from the *Evening Telegraph* office. Know who that is. What's up? Pop in a minute to phone. Ned Lambert it is.

He entered softly.

ERIN, GREEN GEM OF THE SILVER SEA

—The ghost walks, professor MacHugh murmured softly, biscuitfully to the dusty windowpane.

Mr Dedalus, staring from the empty fireplace at Ned Lambert's quizzing face, asked of it sourly:

---

5. Passover; "Next year in Jerusalem" is the final phrase in the Passover night home ceremony when families read the *haggadah* ("story") of the exodus of the Israelites from Egypt (Exodus 12).

6. The Bible actually says "out of Egypt, *from* the house of bondage" (Exodus 13.14).

7. "Hear, O Israel, the Lord our God" (Deuteronomy 6.4)—a daily prayer, not part of the Passover ceremony.

8. Recalling the "Chad Gadya" (One Lamb), a Passover song.

9. Bloom purchased a lemon-scented cake of soap in the "Lotus Eaters" episode (ch. 5); it fits awkwardly in his trousers pocket, and thus intrudes into the narrative from time to time.

1. Bloom considers rushing home and heading off the imminent affair between Molly and Blazes Boylan; his own postal "affair" with Martha Clifford (the sentence "What perfume does your wife use?" is remembered from one of her letters) puts the idea in his head.

—Agonising Christ, wouldn't it give you a heartburn on your arse?

Ned Lambert, seated on the table, read on:

—*Or again, note the meanderings of some purling rill as it babbles on its way, fanned by gentlest zephyrs tho' quarrelling with the stony obstacles, to the tumbling waters of Neptune's blue domain, mid mossy banks, played on by the glorious sunlight or 'neath the shadows cast o'er its pensive bosom by the overarching leafage of the giants of the forest.* What about that, Simon? he asked over the fringe of his newspaper. How's that for high?

—Changing his drink, Mr Dedalus said.

Ned Lambert, laughing, struck the newspaper on his knees, repeating:

—*The pensive bosom and the overarsing leafage.* O boys! O, boys!

—And Xenophon looked upon Marathon, Mr Dedalus said, looking again on the fireplace and to the window, and Marathon looked on the sea.[2]

—That will do, professor MacHugh cried from the window. I don't want to hear any more of the stuff.

He ate off the crescent of water biscuit he had been nibbling and, hungered, made ready to nibble the biscuit in his other hand.

High falutin stuff. Bladderbags. Ned Lambert is taking a day off I see. Rather upsets a man's day a funeral does. He has influence they say. Old Chatterton, the vicechancellor is his granduncle or his greatgranduncle. Close on ninety they say. Subleader for his death written this long time perhaps. Living to spite them. Might go first himself. Johnny, make room for your uncle. The right honourable Hedges Eyre Chatterton. Daresay he writes him an odd shaky cheque or two on gale days. Windfall when he kicks out. Alleluia.

—Just another spasm, Ned Lambert said.

—What is it? Mr Bloom asked.

—A recently discovered fragment of Cicero's[3] Professor MacHugh answered with pomp of tone. *Our lovely land.*

SHORT BUT TO THE POINT

—Whose land? Mr Bloom said simply.

—Most pertinent question, the professor said between his chews. With an accent on the whose.

—Dan Dawson's land, Mr Dedalus said.

—Is it his speech last night? Mr Bloom asked.

Ned Lambert nodded.

—But listen to this, he said.

The doorknob hit Mr Bloom in the small of the back as the door was pushed in.

—Excuse me, J. J. O'Molloy said, entering.

Mr Bloom moved nimbly aside.

—I beg yours, he said.

—Good day, Jack.

—Come in. Come in.

—Good day.

—How are you, Dedalus?

---

2. Quoting "The Isles of Greece," a poem by Byron included in *Don Juan*, Canto III.

3. Roman rhetorician and statesman (106–43 B.C.).

—Well. And yourself?

J. J. O'Molloy shook his head.

SAD

Cleverest fellow at the junior bar he used to be. Decline poor chap. That hectic flush spells finis for a man. Touch and go with him. What's in the wind, I wonder. Money worry.

—*Or again if we but climb the serried mountain peaks.*

—You're looking extra.

—Is the editor to be seen? J. J. O'Molloy asked, looking towards the inner door.

—Very much so, professor MacHugh said. To be seen and heard. He's in his sanctum with Lenehan.

J. J. O'Molloy strolled to the sloping desk and began to turn back the pink pages of the file.

Practice dwindling. A mighthavebeen. Losing heart. Gambling. Debts of honour. Reaping the whirlwind. Used to get good retainers from D. and T. Fitzgerald. Their wigs to show the grey matter. Brains on their sleeve like the statue in Glasnevin.[4] Believe he does some literary work for the *Express* with Gabriel Conroy.[5] Wellread fellow. Myles Crawford began on the *Independent*. Funny the way those newspaper men veer about when they get wind of a new opening. Weathercocks. Hot and cold in the same breath. Wouldn't know which to believe. One story good till you hear the next. Go for one another baldheaded in the papers and then all blows over. Hailfellow well met the next moment.

—Ah, listen to this for God' sake, Ned Lambert pleaded. *Or again if we but climb the serried mountain peaks . . .*

—Bombast! the professor broke in testily. Enough of the inflated windbag!

—*Peaks,* Ned Lambert went on, *towering high on high, to bathe our souls, as it were . . .*

—Bathe his lips, Mr Dedalus said. Blessed and eternal God! Yes? Is he taking anything for it?

—*As 'twere, in the peerless panorama of Ireland's portfolio, unmatched, despite their wellpraised prototypes in other vaunted prize regions for very beauty, of bosky grove and undulating plain and luscious pastureland of vernal green, steeped in the transcendent translucent glow of our mild mysterious Irish twilight . . .*

—The moon, professor MacHugh said. He forgot Hamlet.

HIS NATIVE DORIC[6]

—*That mantles the vista far and wide and wait till the glowing orb of the moon shine forth to irradiate her silver effulgence . . .*

—O! Mr Dedalus cried, giving vent to a hopeless groan, shite and onions! That'll do, Ned. Life is too short.

He took off his silk hat and, blowing out impatiently his bushy moustache, welshcombed his hair with raking fingers.

---

4. Site of the large Catholic cemetery in Dublin, where much of the "Hades" episode (ch. 6) takes place.
5. Character in Joyce's story *The Dead.*

6. Rustic dialect, named after the early, simple Doric style in Greece.

Ned Lambert tossed the newspaper aside, chuckling with delight. An instant after a hoarse bark of laughter burst over professor MacHugh's unshaven blackspectacled face.

—Doughy Daw! he cried.

WHAT WETHERUP SAID

All very fine to jeer at it now in cold print but it goes down like hot cake that stuff. He was in the bakery line too wasn't he? Why they call him Doughy Daw. Feathered his nest well anyhow. Daughter engaged to that chap in the inland revenue office with the motor. Hooked that nicely. Entertainments. Open house. Big blow out. Wetherup always said that. Get a grip of them by the stomach.

The inner door was opened violently and a scarlet beaked face, crested by a comb of feathery hair, thrust itself in. The bold blue eyes stared about them and the harsh voice asked:

—What is it?

—And here comes the sham squire himself,[7] professor MacHugh said grandly.

—Getououthat, you bloody old pedagogue! the editor said in recognition.

—Come, Ned, Mr Dedalus said, putting on his hat. I must get a drink after that.

—Drink! the editor cried. No drinks served before mass.

—Quite right too, Mr Dedalus said, going out. Come on, Ned.

Ned Lambert sidled down from the table. The editor's blue eyes roved towards Mr Bloom's face, shadowed by a smile.

—Will you join us, Myles? Ned Lambert asked.

MEMORABLE BATTLES RECALLED

—North Cork militia! the editor cried, striding to the mantelpiece. We won every time! North Cork and Spanish officers![8]

—Where was that, Myles? Ned Lambert asked with a reflective glance at his toecaps.

—In Ohio! the editor shouted.

—So it was, begad, Ned Lambert agreed.

Passing out he whispered to J. J. O'Molloy:

—Incipient jigs.[9] Sad case.

—Ohio! the editor crowed in high treble from his uplifted scarlet face. My Ohio!

—A perfect cretic![1] the professor said. Long, short and long.

O, HARP EOLIAN![2]

He took a reel of dental floss from his waistcoat pocket and, breaking off a piece, twanged it smartly between two and two of his resonant unwashed teeth.

—Bingbang, bangbang.

Mr Bloom, seeing the coast clear, made for the inner door.

---

7. Pretending to identify the editor with a disreputable predecessor, Francis Higgins (1746–1802), who had seduced a woman by pretending to be a country squire.
8. This nonsensical piece of rhetoric invokes the North Cork Militia, which was involved in the failed Rebellion of 1798 and lost every battle it was involved in.
9. Probably the tremors caused by abrupt withdrawal from

heavy alcohol use.
1. A poetic foot, made up of one short syllable between two long syllables.
2. The aeolian harp, popular as a symbol among the Romantic poets, is strung so as to allow the passing winds to "play" it. The harp is the national emblem of Ireland.

—Just a moment, Mr Crawford, he said. I just want to phone about an ad.

He went in.

—What about that leader this evening? professor MacHugh asked, coming to the editor and laying a firm hand on his shoulder.

—That'll be all right, Myles Crawford said more calmly. Never you fret. Hello, Jack. That's all right.

—Good day, Myles, J. J. O'Molloy said, letting the pages he held slip limply back on the file. Is that Canada swindle case on today?

The telephone whirred inside.

—Twentyeight . . . No, twenty . . . Double four . . . Yes.

SPOT THE WINNER

Lenehan came out of the inner office with *Sport's* tissues.

—Who wants a dead cert for the Gold cup? he asked. Sceptre with O. Madden up.[3]

He tossed the tissues on to the table.

Screams of newsboys barefoot in the hall rushed near and the door was flung open.

—Hush, Lenehan said. I hear feetstoops.

Professor MacHugh strode across the room and seized the cringing urchin by the collar as the others scampered out of the hall and down the steps. The tissues rustled up in the draught, floated softly in the air blue scrawls and under the table came to earth.

—It wasn't me, sir. It was the big fellow shoved me, sir.

—Throw him out and shut the door, the editor said. There's a hurricane blowing.

Lenehan began to paw the tissues up from the floor, grunting as he stooped twice.

—Waiting for the racing special, sir, the newsboy said. It was Pat Farrell shoved me, sir.

He pointed to two faces peering in round the doorframe.

—Him, sir.

—Out of this with you, professor MacHugh said gruffly.

He hustled the boy out and banged the door to.

J. J. O'Molloy turned the files crackingly over, murmuring, seeking:

—Continued on page six, column four.

—Yes . . . *Evening Telegraph* here, Mr Bloom phoned from the inner office. Is the boss . . . ? Yes, *Telegraph* . . . To where? . . . Aha! Which auction rooms? . . . Aha! I see . . . Right. I'll catch him.

A COLLISION ENSUES

The bell whirred again as he rang off. He came in quickly and bumped against Lenehan who was struggling up with the second tissue.

—*Pardon, monsieur,* Lenehan said, clutching him for an instant and making a grimace.

—My fault, Mr Bloom said, suffering his grip. Are you hurt? I'm in a hurry.

—Knee, Lenehan said.

3. A complicated subplot throughout the novel: Lenehan, looking up horse racing information, asks Bloom (in ch. 6) if he can have a look at Bloom's newspaper. Bloom tells him to take it, for he was just about to "throw it away." Since there's a longshot running in the Gold Cup race at Ascot called Throwaway, Lenehan thinks Bloom is trying to pass him insider information, and wagers a large sum on the horse, who does not win.

He made a comic face and whined, rubbing his knee:

—The accumulation of the *anno Domini*.

—Sorry, Mr Bloom said.

He went to the door and, holding it ajar, paused. J. J. O'Molloy slapped the heavy pages over. The noise of two shrill voices, a mouthorgan, echoed in the bare hallway from the newsboys squatted on the doorsteps:

> *We are the boys of Wexford*
> *Who fought with heart and hand.*[4]

EXIT BLOOM

—I'm just running round to Bachelor's walk, Mr Bloom said, about this ad of Keyes's. Want to fix it up. They tell me he's round there in Dillon's.

He looked indecisively for a moment at their faces. The editor who, leaning against the mantelshelf, had propped his head on his hand, suddenly stretched forth an arm amply.

—Begone! he said. The world is before you.[5]

—Back in no time, Mr Bloom said, hurrying out.

J. J. O'Molloy took the tissues from Lenehan's hand and read them, blowing them apart gently, without comment.

—He'll get that advertisement, the professor said, staring through his black-rimmed spectacles over the crossblind. Look at the young scamps after him.

—Show. Where? Lenehan cried, running to the window.

A STREET CORTEGE

Both smiled over the crossblind at the file of capering newsboys in Mr Bloom's wake, the last zigzagging white on the breeze a mocking kite, a tail of white bowknots.

—Look at the young guttersnipe behind him hue and cry, Lenehan said, and you'll kick. O, my rib risible! Taking off his flat spaugs and the walk.[6] Small nines. Steal upon larks.

He began to mazurka[7] in swift caricature across the floor on sliding feet past the fireplace to J. J. O'Molloy who placed the tissues in his receiving hands.

—What's that? Myles Crawford said with a start. Where are the other two gone?

—Who? the professor said, turning. They're gone round to the Oval for a drink. Paddy Hooper is there with Jack Hall. Came over last night.

—Come on then, Myles Crawford said. Where's my hat?

He walked jerkily into the office behind, parting the vent of his jacket, jingling his keys in his back pocket. They jingled then in the air and against the wood as he locked his desk drawer.

—He's pretty well on, professor MacHugh said in a low voice.

—Seems to be, J. J. O'Molloy said, taking out a cigarette case in murmuring meditation, but it is not always as it seems. Who has the most matches?

---

4. From a ballad, *The Boys of Wexford,* by R. Dwyer Joyce (1830–1883) about the rebellion of 1798—whose heroes turned to drink in later years.
5. The editor here echoes the close of Milton's *Paradise*

Lost, as Adam and Eve leave Eden (12.846).
6. I.e., imitating Bloom's big feet and manner of walking.
7. A lively Polish dance.

THE CALUMET OF PEACE[8]

He offered a cigarette to the professor and took one himself. Lenehan promptly struck a match for them and lit their cigarettes in turn. J. J. O'Molloy opened his case again and offered it.

—*Thanky vous*, Lenehan said, helping himself.

The editor came from the inner office, a straw hat awry on his brow. He declaimed in song, pointing sternly at professor MacHugh:

> '*Twas rank and fame that tempted thee,*
> '*Twas empire charmed thy heart.*[9]

The professor grinned, locking his long lips.

—Eh? You bloody old Roman empire? Myles Crawford said.

He took a cigarette from the open case. Lenehan, lighting it for him with quick grace, said:

—Silence for my brandnew riddle!

—*Imperium romanum*, J. J. O'Molloy said gently. It sounds nobler than British or Brixton. The word reminds one somehow of fat in the fire.

Myles Crawford blew his first puff violently towards the ceiling.

—That's it, he said. We are the fat. You and I are the fat in the fire. We haven't got the chance of a snowball in hell.

THE GRANDEUR THAT WAS ROME

—Wait a moment, professor MacHugh said, raising two quiet claws. We mustn't be led away by words, by sounds of words. We think of Rome, imperial, imperious, imperative.

He extended elocutionary arms from frayed stained shirtcuffs, pausing:

—What was their civilisation? Vast, I allow: but vile. *Cloacae*: sewers. The jews in the wilderness and on the mountaintop said: *It is meet to be here. Let us build an altar to Jehovah*. The Roman, like the Englishman who follows in his footsteps, brought to every new shore on which he set his foot (on our shore he never set it) only his cloacal obsession. He gazed about him in his toga and he said: *It is meet to be here. Let us construct a watercloset.*[1]

—Which they accordingly did do, Lenehan said. Our old ancient ancestors, as we read in the first chapter of Guinness's,[2] were partial to the running stream.

—They were nature's gentlemen, J. J. O'Molloy murmured. But we have also Roman law.

—And Pontius Pilate is its prophet, professor MacHugh responded.

—Do you know that story about chief baron Palles? J. J. O'Molloy asked. It was at the royal university dinner. Everything was going swimmingly . . .

—First my riddle, Lenehan said. Are you ready?

Mr O'Madden Burke, tall in copious grey of Donegal tweed, came in from the hallway. Stephen Dedalus, behind him, uncovered as he entered.

---

8. The "peace pipe" of Native Americans.
9. Aria from the opera *The Rose of Castille* (1857), by Irish composer Michael William Balfe.
1. Toilet. The claim of an English "cloacal obsession" ironically reverses a charge made against Joyce himself by the English writer H. G. Wells, who had reviewed *A Portrait of the Artist* in 1917, in the (aptly titled) magazine

Nation. Wells wrote, "Mr. Joyce has a cloacal obsession. He would bring back into the general picture of life aspects which modern drainage and modern decorum have taken out of ordinary intercourse and conversation."
2. A pun on Genesis, the first book of the Bible, and Guinness, producers of stout and lager in Dublin.

—*Entrez, mes enfants!*[3] Lenehan cried.

—I escort a suppliant, Mr O'Madden Burke said melodiously. Youth led by Experience visits Notoriety.

—How do you do? the editor said, holding out a hand. Come in. Your governor is just gone.

? ? ?

Lenehan said to all:

—Silence! What opera resembles a railway line? Reflect, ponder, excogitate, reply. Stephen handed over the typed sheets, pointing to the title and signature.

—Who? the editor asked.

Bit torn off.

—Mr Garrett Deasy, Stephen said.

—That old pelters, the editor said. Who tore it? Was he short taken?[4]

> *On swift sail flaming*
> *From storm and south*
> *He comes, pale vampire,*
> *Mouth to my mouth.*

—Good day, Stephen, the professor said, coming to peer over their shoulders. Foot and mouth? Are you turned . . . ?

Bullockbefriending bard.[5]

SHINDY IN WELLKNOWN RESTAURANT

—Good day, sir, Stephen answered, blushing. The letter is not mine. Mr Garrett Deasy asked me to . . .

—O, I know him, Myles Crawford said, and knew his wife too. The bloodiest old tartar God ever made. By Jesus, she had the foot and mouth disease and no mistake! The night she threw the soup in the waiter's face in the Star and Garter. Oho!

A woman brought sin into the world. For Helen, the runaway wife of Menelaus, ten years the Greeks. O'Rourke, prince of Breffni.

—Is he a widower? Stephen asked.

—Ay, a grass one,[6] Myles Crawford said, his eye running down the typescript. Emperor's horses. Habsburg. An Irishman saved his life on the ramparts of Vienna. Don't you forget! Maximilian Karl O'Donnell, graf von Tirconnel in Ireland. Sent his heir over to make the king an Austrian fieldmarshal now. Going to be trouble there one day. Wild geese.[7] O yes, every time. Don't you forget that!

—The moot point is did he forget it, J. J. O'Molloy said quietly, turning a horse-shoe paperweight. Saving princes is a thank you job.

---

3. Enter, my children!

4. Stephen had agreed to take a letter to the editor from his employer, a schoolmaster named Garrett Deasy, and to try to place it with one of the Dublin newspapers. A piece is missing because Stephen later had an idea for a poem while walking on the beach but had nothing to write on; the editor playfully suggests that a small bit has been torn off for use as toilet tissue. The italicized lines are the poetry Stephen composed on the torn-off paper, an adaptation of a Gaelic poem translated by the nation-alist poet Douglas Hyde in *Love Songs of Connacht* (1893): "He came from the South; / His breast to my bosom, / His mouth to my mouth."

5. The mock-Homeric epithet suggests that in helping Deasy place his letter about cattle disease, Stephen has become a poet ("bard") who has befriended the cattle ("bullocks").

6. A grass widower is a man separated from his wife.

7. Irish expatriates.

Professor MacHugh turned on him.

—And if not? he said.

—I'll tell you how it was, Myles Crawford began. A Hungarian it was one day . . .

LOST CAUSES
NOBLE MARQUESS MENTIONED

—We were always loyal to lost causes, the professor said. Success for us is the death of the intellect and of the imagination. We were never loyal to the successful. We serve them. I teach the blatant Latin language. I speak the tongue of a race the acme of whose mentality is the maxim: time is money. Material domination. *Dominus!* Lord! Where is the spirituality? Lord Jesus! Lord Salisbury. A sofa in a westend club. But the Greek!

KYRIE ELEISON![8]

A smile of light brightened his darkrimmed eyes, lengthened his long lips.

—The Greek! he said again. *Kyrios!* Shining word! The vowels the Semite and the Saxon know not. *Kyrie!* The radiance of the intellect. I ought to profess Greek, the language of the mind. *Kyrie eleison!* The closetmaker and the cloacamaker will never be lords of our spirit. We are liege subjects of the catholic chivalry of Europe that foundered at Trafalgar and of the empire of the spirit, not an *imperium*, that went under with the Athenian fleets at Aegospotami. Yes, yes. They went under. Pyrrhus, misled by an oracle, made a last attempt to retrieve the fortunes of Greece.[9] Loyal to a lost cause.

He strode away from them towards the window.

—They went forth to battle, Mr O'Madden Burke said greyly, but they always fell.

—Boohoo! Lenehan wept with a little noise. Owing to a brick received in the latter half of the *matinée*. Poor, poor, poor Pyrrhus!

He whispered then near Stephen's ear:

LENEHAN'S LIMERICK

—There's a ponderous pundit MacHugh
Who wears goggles of ebony hue.
As he mostly sees double
To wear them why trouble?
I can't see the Joe Miller. Can you?

In mourning for Sallust,[1] Mulligan says. Whose mother is beastly dead.

Myles Crawford crammed the sheets into a sidepocket.

—That'll be all right, he said. I'll read the rest after. That'll be all right.

Lenehan extended his hands in protest.

—But my riddle! he said. What opera is like a railway line?

—Opera? Mr O'Madden Burke's sphinx face reriddled.

---

8. Lord have mercy [upon us] (Greek). A formal part of the Mass.

9. The Greek general Pyrrhus (318–272 B.C.) was led to believe, in a dream, that he would triumph over the Spartans, but he was defeated.

1. Roman historian and senator (86–34 B.C.), known for

political corruption. The idea of mourning reminds Stephen of a remark made by his friend Malachi ("Buck") Mulligan, about which the two had argued that morning: when Stephen had visited Mulligan at his aunt's house Mulligan had described Stephen as "Dedalus, whose mother is beastly dead."

Lenehan announced gladly:

—*The Rose of Castille*. See the wheeze? Rows of cast steel. Gee!

He poked Mr O'Madden Burke mildly in the spleen. Mr O'Madden Burke fell back with grace on his umbrella, feigning a gasp.

—Help! he sighed. I feel a strong weakness.

Lenehan, rising to tiptoe, fanned his face rapidly with the rustling tissues.

The professor, returning by way of the files, swept his hand across Stephen's and Mr O'Madden Burke's loose ties.

—Paris, past and present, he said. You look like communards.[2]

—Like fellows who had blown up the Bastile, J. J. O'Molloy said in quiet mockery. Or was it you shot the lord lieutenant of Finland between you? You look as though you had done the deed. General Bobrikoff.

—We were only thinking about it, Stephen said.

OMNIUM GATHERUM[3]

—All the talents, Myles Crawford said. Law, the classics . . .

—The turf, Lenehan put in.

—Literature, the press.

—If Bloom were here, the professor said. The gentle art of advertisement.

—And Madam Bloom, Mr O'Madden Burke added. The vocal muse. Dublin's prime favorite.

Lenehan gave a loud cough.

—Ahem! he said very softly. O, for a fresh of breath air! I caught a cold in the park. The gate was open.

"YOU CAN DO IT!"

The editor laid a nervous hand on Stephen's shoulder.

—I want you to write something for me, he said. Something with a bite in it. You can do it. I see it in your face. *In the lexicon of youth* . . .

See it in your face. See it in your eye. Lazy idle little schemer.[4]

—Foot and mouth disease! the editor cried in scornful invective. Great nationalist meeting in Borris-in-Ossory. All balls! Bulldosing the public! Give them something with a bite in it. Put us all into it, damn its soul. Father, Son and Holy Ghost and Jakes M'Carthy.

—We can all supply mental pabulum, Mr O'Madden Burke said.

Stephen raised his eyes to the bold unheeding stare.

—He wants you for the pressgang, J. J. O'Molloy said.

THE GREAT GALLAHER

—You can do it, Myles Crawford repeated, clenching his hand in emphasis. Wait a minute. We'll paralyse Europe as Ignatius Gallaher used to say when he was on the shaughraun,[5] doing billiardmarking in the Clarence. Gallaher, that was a pressman

2. Members of the left-wing Commune of Paris, who controlled Paris for three months in 1871.

3. Mock-Latin for hodgepodge.

4. Professor MacHugh's innocent remark, "I see it in your face," unfortunately reminds Stephen of the language of one of the priests at his parochial school, who accused Stephen of breaking his glasses intentionally in order to get out of work. (*A Portrait of the Artist*, I.iv.)

5. Wandering (Gaelic).

for you. That was a pen. You know how he made his mark? I'll tell you. That was the smartest piece of journalism ever known. That was in eightyone, sixth of May, time of the invincibles, murder in the Phoenix park, before you were born, I suppose. I'll show you.

He pushed past them to the files.

—Look at here, he said turning. The *New York World* cabled for a special. Remember that time?

Professor MacHugh nodded.

—*New York World*, the editor said, excitedly pushing back his straw hat. Where it took place. Tim Kelly, or Kavanagh I mean, Joe Brady and the rest of them. Where Skin-the-Goat drove the car. Whole route, see?

—Skin-the-Goat, Mr O'Madden Burke said. Fitzharris. He has that cabman's shelter, they say, down there at Butt bridge. Holohan told me. You know Holohan?

—Hop and carry one, is it? Myles Crawford said.

—And poor Gumley is down there too, so he told me, minding stones for the corporation. A night watchman.

Stephen turned in surprise.

—Gumley? he said. You don't say so? A friend of my father's, is he?

—Never mind Gumley, Myles Crawford cried angrily. Let Gumley mind the stones, see they don't run away. Look at here. What did Ignatius Gallaher do? I'll tell you. Inspiration of genius. Cabled right away. Have you *Weekly Freeman* of 17 March? Right. Have you got that?

He flung back pages of the files and stuck his finger on a point.

—Take page four, advertisement for Bransome's coffee, let us say. Have you got that? Right.

The telephone whirred.

A DISTANT VOICE

—I'll answer it, the professor said going.

—B is parkgate. Good.

His finger leaped and struck point after point, vibrating.

—T is viceregal lodge. C is where murder took place. K is Knockmaroon gate.

The loose flesh of his neck shook like a cock's wattles. An illstarched dicky jutted up and with a rude gesture he thrust it back into his waistcoat.

—Hello? *Evening Telegraph* here . . . Hello? . . . Who's there? . . . Yes . . . Yes . . . Yes . . .

—F to P is the route Skin-the-Goat drove the car for an alibi. Inchicore, Roundtown, Windy Arbour, Palmerston Park, Ranelagh. F. A. B. P. Got that? X is Davy's publichouse in upper Leeson street.

The professor came to the inner door.

—Bloom is at the telephone, he said.

—Tell him go to hell, the editor said promptly. X is Burke's publichouse, see?

CLEVER, VERY

—Clever, Lenehan said. Very.

—Gave it to them on a hot plate, Myles Crawford said, the whole bloody history.

Nightmare from which you will never awake.[6]

—I saw it, the editor said proudly. I was present, Dick Adams, the besthearted bloody Corkman the Lord ever put the breath of life in, and myself.

Lenehan bowed to a shape of air, announcing:

—Madam, I'm Adam. And Able was I ere I saw Elba.

—History! Myles Crawford cried. The Old Woman of Prince's street was there first. There was weeping and gnashing of teeth over that. Out of an advertisement. Gregor Grey made the design for it. That gave him the leg up. Then Paddy Hooper worked Tay Pay who took him on to the *Star*. Now he's got in with Blumenfeld. That's press. That's talent. Pyatt! He was all their daddies!

—The father of scare journalism, Lenehan confirmed, and the brother-in-law of Chris Callinan.

—Hello? . . . Are you there? . . . Yes, he's here still. Come across yourself.

—Where do you find a pressman like that now, eh? the editor cried.

He flung the pages down.

—Clamn dever, Lenehan said to Mr O'Madden Burke.

—Very smart, Mr O'Madden Burke said.

Professor MacHugh came from the inner office.

—Talking about the invincibles, he said, did you see that some hawkers were up before the recorder . . .

—O yes, J. J. O'Molloy said eagerly. Lady Dudley was walking home through the park to see all the trees that were blown down by that cyclone last year and thought she'd buy a view of Dublin. And it turned out to be a commemoration post-card of Joe Brady or Number One or Skin-the-Goat. Right outside the viceregal lodge, imagine!

—They're only in the hook and eye department, Myles Crawford said. Psha! Press and the bar! Where have you a man now at the bar like those fellows, like Whiteside, like Isaac Butt, like silvertongued O'Hagan?[7] Eh? Ah, bloody nonsense! Only in the halfpenny place.

His mouth continued to twitch unspeaking in nervous curls of disdain.

Would anyone wish that mouth for her kiss? How do you know? Why did you write it then?

RHYMES AND REASONS

Mouth, south. Is the mouth south someway? Or the south a mouth? Must be some. South, pout, out, shout, drouth. Rhymes: two men dressed the same, looking the same, two by two.

> . . . . *la tua pace*
> . . . . *che parlar ti piace*
> *mentre che il vento, come fa, si tace*.[8]

6. In the course of a tortured discussion with Mr. Deasy about British and Irish politics and history in chapter 2, Stephen had exclaimed, "History is a nightmare from which I am trying to awake."

7. James Whiteside (1804–1876), Isaac Butt (1813–1879), and Thomas O'Hagan (1812–1885) were Irish barristers and orators.

8. From Canto 5 of Dante's *Inferno*; the speakers are adulterous lovers, Francesca and Paolo, who tell Dante: "Were the world's King our friend . . . we would entreat Him for thy peace, . . . and speak as thou shalt please, While the winds cease to howl, as now they cease" (lines 92, 94, 96).

He saw them three by three, approaching girls, in green, in rose, in russet, entwining, *per l'aer perso*[9] in mauve, in purple, *quella pacifica oriafiamma*,[1] in gold of oriflamme, *di rimirar fè più ardenti*.[2] But I old men, penitent, leadenfooted, underdark-neath the night: mouth south: tomb womb.

—Speak up for yourself, Mr O'Madden Burke said.

SUFFICIENT FOR THE DAY . . .

J. J. O'Molloy, smiling palely, took up the gage.

—My dear Myles, he said, flinging his cigarette aside, you put a false construc-tion on my words. I hold no brief, as at present advised, for the third profession *qua* profession but your Cork legs are running away with you. Why not bring in Henry Grattan and Flood and Demosthenes and Edmund Burke?[3] Ignatius Gallaher we all know and his Chapelizod boss, Harmsworth of the farthing press, and his American cousin of the Bowery gutter sheet not to mention *Paddy Kelly's Budget, Pue's Occur-rences* and our watchful friend *The Skibbereen Eagle*. Why bring in a master of forensic eloquence like Whiteside? Sufficient for the day is the newspaper thereof.[4]

LINKS WITH BYGONE DAYS OF YORE

—Grattan and Flood wrote for this very paper, the editor cried in his face. Irish vol-unteers. Where are you now? Established 1763. Dr Lucas. Who have you now like John Philpot Curran? Psha!

—Well, J. J. O'Molloy said, Bushe K. C., for example.

—Bushe? the editor said. Well, yes. Bushe, yes. He has a strain of it in his blood. Kendal Bushe or I mean Seymour Bushe.

—He would have been on the bench long ago, the professor said, only for . . . But no matter.

J. J. O'Molloy turned to Stephen and said quietly and slowly:

—One of the most polished periods I think I ever listened to in my life fell from the lips of Seymour Bushe. It was in that case of fratricide, the Childs murder case. Bushe defended him.

> *And in the porches of mine ear did pour.*[5]

By the way how did he find that out? He died in his sleep. Or the other story, beast with two backs?[6]

—What was that? the professor asked.

ITALIA, MAGISTRA ARTIUM

—He spoke on the law of evidence, J. J. O'Molloy said, of Roman justice as contrast-ed with the earlier Mosaic code, the *lex talionis*. And he cited the Moses of Michelan-gelo in the Vatican.

9. Through the black air.
1. That peaceful gold flame.
2. More ardent to look again. From Dante's *Inferno* and *Paradiso*.
3. Irish statesmen Henry Grattan (1746–1820) and Hen-ry Flood (1732–1791), as well as the Irish-born Edmund Burke (1729–1797), were among the greatest orators of their day. Demosthenes (c. 384–322 B.C.) is traditionally

considered the greatest of Greek orators.
4. Revising Jesus's saying, "Sufficient for the day is the evil thereof" (Matthew 6.34).
5. This is Hamlet's father's description of his poisoning by his brother Claudius, in *Hamlet* (1.5.62–63). "And in the porches of my ears did pour / The leperous distillment."
6. Again from Shakespeare—this time, *Othello*; the phrase means sexual intercourse.

—Ha.

—A few wellchosen words, Lenehan prefaced. Silence!

Pause. J. J. O'Molloy took out his cigarettecase.

False lull. Something quite ordinary.

Messenger took out his match box thoughtfully and lit his cigar.

I have often thought since on looking back over that strange time that it was that small act, trivial in itself, that striking of that match, that determined the whole aftercourse of both our lives.

A POLISHED PERIOD

J. J. O'Molloy resumed, moulding his words:

—He said of it: *that stony effigy in frozen music, horned and terrible, of the human form divine, that eternal symbol of wisdom and of prophecy which, if aught that the imagination or the hand of sculptor has wrought in marble of soultransfigured and of soultransfiguring deserves to live, deserves to live.*

His slim hand with a wave graced echo and fall.

—Fine! Myles Crawford said at once.

—The divine afflatus, Mr O'Madden Burke said.

—You like it? J. J. O'Molloy asked Stephen.

Stephen, his blood wooed by grace of language and gesture, blushed. He took a cigarette from the case. J. J. O'Molloy offered his case to Myles Crawford. Lenehan lit their cigarettes as before and took his trophy, saying:

—Muchibus thankibus.

A MAN OF HIGH MORALE

—Professor Magennis was speaking to me about you, J. J. O'Molloy said to Stephen. What do you think really of that hermetic crowd, the opal hush poets: A. E. the master mystic? That Blavatsky woman started it.[7] She was a nice old bag of tricks. A. E. has been telling some yankee interviewer that you came to him in the small hours of the morning to ask him about planes of consciousness. Magennis thinks you must have been pulling A. E.'s leg. He is a man of the very highest morale, Magennis.

Speaking about me. What did he say? What did he say? What did he say about me? Don't ask.

—No, thanks, professor MacHugh said, waving the cigarette case aside. Wait a moment. Let me say one thing. The finest display of oratory I ever heard was a speech made by John F. Taylor[8] at the college historical society. Mr Justice Fitzgibbon, the present lord justice of appeal, had spoken and the paper under debate was an essay (new for those days), advocating the revival of the Irish tongue.

He turned towards Myles Crawford and said:

—You know Gerald Fitzgibbon. Then you can imagine the style of his discourse.

—He is sitting with Tim Healy, J. J. O'Molloy said, rumour has it, on the Trinity college estates commission.

—He is sitting with a sweet thing in a child's frock, Myles Crawford said. Go on. Well?

7. Refers generally to the interest in mysticism, and specifically the Theosophy of Madame Blavatsky (1831–1891), who stressed the fellowship of all humanity and the transmigration of souls. Her disciple A.E. (pseud.

of George Russell, 1867–1935) was a minor Irish poet and mystic, and friend of W. B. Yeats.

8. John F. Taylor (c. 1850–1902), Irish barrister and journalist. Taylor did make this speech on 24 October 1901.

—It was the speech, mark you, the professor said, of a finished orator, full of courteous haughtiness and pouring in chastened diction I will not say the vials of his wrath but pouring the proud man's contumely upon the new movement. It was then a new movement. We were weak, therefore worthless.

He closed his long thin lips an instant but, eager to be on, raised an outspanned hand to his spectacles and, with trembling thumb and ringfinger touching lightly the black rims, steadied them to a new focus.

IMPROMPTU

In ferial tone he addressed J. J. O'Molloy:

—Taylor had come there, you must know, from a sickbed. That he had prepared his speech I do not believe for there was not even one shorthandwriter in the hall. His dark lean face had a growth of shaggy beard round it. He wore a loose white silk neckcloth and altogether he looked (though he was not) a dying man.

His gaze turned at once but slowly from J. J. O'Molloy's towards Stephen's face and then bent at once to the ground, seeking. His unglazed linen collar appeared behind his bent head, soiled by his withering hair. Still seeking, he said:

—When Fitzgibbon's speech had ended John F. Taylor rose to reply. Briefly, as well as I can bring them to mind, his words were these.

He raised his head firmly. His eyes bethought themselves once more. Witless shellfish swam in the gross lenses to and fro, seeking outlet.

He began:

—Mr chairman, ladies and gentlemen: Great was my admiration in listening to the remarks addressed to the youth of Ireland a moment since by my learned friend. It seemed to me that I had been transported into a country far away from this country, into an age remote from this age, that I stood in ancient Egypt and that I was listening to the speech of some highpriest of that land addressed to the youthful Moses.

His listeners held their cigarettes poised to hear, their smokes ascending in frail stalks that flowered with his speech. And let our crooked smokes. Noble words coming. Look out. Could you try your hand at it yourself?

—And it seemed to me that I heard the voice of that Egyptian highpriest raised in a tone of like haughtiness and like pride. I heard his words and their meaning was revealed to me.

FROM THE FATHERS

It was revealed to me that those things are good which yet are corrupted which neither if they were supremely good nor unless they were good, could be corrupted. Ah, curse you! That's saint Augustine.

—Why will you jews not accept our culture, our religion and our language? You are a tribe of nomad herdsmen: we are a mighty people. You have no cities nor no wealth: our cities are hives of humanity and our galleys, trireme and quadrireme, laden with all manner merchandise furrow the waters of the known globe. You have but emerged from primitive conditions: we have a literature, a priesthood, an agelong history and a polity.

Nile.

Child, man, effigy.

By the Nilebank the babemaries kneel, cradle of bulrushes: a man supple in combat: stonehorned, stonebearded, heart of stone.

—*You pray to a local and obscure idol: our temples, majestic and mysterious, are the abodes of Isis and Osiris, of Horus and Ammon Ra. Yours serfdom, awe and humbleness: ours thunder and the seas. Israel is weak and few are her children: Egypt is an host and terrible are her arms. Vagrants and daylabourers are you called: the world trembles at our name.*

A dumb belch of hunger cleft his speech. He lifted his voice above it boldly:

—*But, ladies and gentlemen, had the youthful Moses listened to and accepted that view of life, had he bowed his head and bowed his will and bowed his spirit before that arrogant admonition he would never have brought the chosen people out of their house of bondage nor followed the pillar of the cloud by day. He would never have spoken with the Eternal amid lightnings on Sinai's mountaintop nor ever have come down with the light of inspiration shining in his countenance and bearing in his arms the tables of the law, graven in the language of the outlaw.*

He ceased and looked at them, enjoying a silence.

OMINOUS—FOR HIM!

J. J. O'Molloy said not without regret:

—And yet he died without having entered the land of promise.

—A sudden–at–the–moment–though–from–lingering–illness–often–previously–expectorated–demise, Lenehan added. And with a great future behind him.

The troop of bare feet was heard rushing along the hallway and pattering up the staircase.

—That is oratory, the professor said uncontradicted.

Gone with the wind. Hosts at Mullaghmast and Tara of the kings. Miles of ears of porches. The tribune's words howled and scattered to the four winds. A people sheltered within his voice. Dead noise. Akasic records of all that ever anywhere wherever was.[9] Love and laud him: me no more.

I have money.

—Gentlemen, Stephen said. As the next motion on the agenda paper may I suggest that the house do now adjourn?

—You take my breath away. It is not perchance a French compliment? Mr O'Madden Burke asked. 'Tis the hour, methinks, when the winejug, metaphorically speaking, is most grateful in Ye ancient hostelry.

—That it be and hereby is resolutely resolved. All who are in favour say ay, Lenehan announced. The contrary no. I declare it carried. To which particular boosingshed . . . ? My casting vote is: Mooney's!

He led the way, admonishing:

—We will sternly refuse to partake of strong waters, will we not? Yes, we will not. By no manner of means.

Mr O'Madden Burke, following close, said with an ally's lunge of his umbrella:

—Lay on, Macduff![1]

—Chip of the old block! the editor cried, slapping Stephen on the shoulder. Let us go. Where are those blasted keys?

He fumbled in his pocket pulling out the crushed typesheets.

9. Parody of the language of Theosophy.

1. These are Macbeth's words when he discovers that Macduff is to be his executioner (*Macbeth*, 5.8.33).

—Foot and mouth. I know. That'll be all right. That'll go in. Where are they? That's all right.

He thrust the sheets back and went into the inner office.

LET US HOPE

J. J. O'Molloy, about to follow him in, said quietly to Stephen:

—I hope you will live to see it published. Myles, one moment.

He went into the inner office, closing the door behind him.

—Come along, Stephen, the professor said. That is fine, isn't it? It has the prophetic vision. *Fuit Ilium!*[2] The sack of windy Troy. Kingdoms of this world. The masters of the Mediterranean are fellaheen today.

The first newsboy came pattering down the stairs at their heels and rushed out into the street, yelling:

—Racing special!

Dublin. I have much, much to learn.

They turned to the left along Abbey street.

—I have a vision too, Stephen said.

—Yes? the professor said, skipping to get into step. Crawford will follow.

Another newsboy shot past them, yelling as he ran:

—Racing special!

DEAR DIRTY DUBLIN

Dubliners.

—Two Dublin vestals, Stephen said, elderly and pious, have lived fifty and fiftythree years in Fumbally's lane.

—Where is that? the professor asked.

—Off Blackpitts, Stephen said.

Damp night reeking of hungry dough. Against the wall. Face glistering tallow under her fustian shawl. Frantic hearts. Akasic records. Quicker, darlint!

On now. Dare it. Let there be life.

—They want to see the views of Dublin from the top of Nelson's pillar. They save up three and tenpence in a red tin letterbox moneybox. They shake out the threepenny bits and sixpences and coax out the pennies with the blade of a knife. Two and three in silver and one and seven in coppers. They put on their bonnets and best clothes and take their umbrellas for fear it may come on to rain.

—Wise virgins, professor MacHugh said.[3]

LIFE ON THE RAW

—They buy one and fourpenceworth of brawn[4] and four slices of panloaf at the north city diningrooms in Marlborough street from Miss Kate Collins, proprietress. . . . They purchase four and twenty ripe plums from a girl at the foot of Nelson's pillar to take off the thirst of the brawn. They give two threepenny bits to the gentleman at

2. Troy is no more; from Virgil's *Aeneid* 3.325.
3. In Matthew 25.1–13, Jesus tells the parable of the wise

and foolish virgins.
4. Cold, jellied meatloaf.

the turnstile and begin to waddle slowly up the winding staircase, grunting, encouraging each other, afraid of the dark, panting, one asking the other have you the brawn, praising God and the Blessed Virgin, threatening to come down, peeping at the airslits. Glory be to God. They had no idea it was that high.

Their names are Anne Kearns and Florence MacCabe. Anne Kearns has the lumbago for which she rubs on Lourdes water given her by a lady who got a bottleful from a passionist father. Florence MacCabe takes a crubeen and a bottle of double X[5] for supper every Saturday.

—Antithesis, the professor said nodding twice. Vestal virgins. I can see them. What's keeping our friend?

He turned.

A bevy of scampering newsboys rushed down the steps, scampering in all directions, yelling, their white papers fluttering. Hard after them Myles Crawford appeared on the steps, his hat aureoling his scarlet face, talking with J. J. O'Molloy.

—Come along, the professor cried, waving his arm.

He set off again to walk by Stephen's side.

—Yes, he said. I see them.

RETURN OF BLOOM

Mr Bloom, breathless, caught in a whirl of wild newsboys near the offices of the *Irish Catholic* and *Dublin Penny Journal*, called:

—Mr Crawford! A moment!

—*Telegraph!* Racing special!

—What is it? Myles Crawford said, falling back a pace.

A newsboy cried in Mr Bloom's face:

—Terrible tragedy in Rathmines! A child bit by a bellows!

INTERVIEW WITH THE EDITOR

—Just this ad, Mr Bloom said, pushing through towards the steps, puffing, and taking the cutting from his pocket. I spoke with Mr Keyes just now. He'll give a renewal for two months, he says. After he'll see. But he wants a par to call attention in the *Telegraph* too, the Saturday pink. And he wants it copied if it's not too late I told councillor Nannetti from the *Kilkenny People*. I can have access to it in the national library. House of keys, don't you see? His name is Keyes. It's a play on the name. But he practically promised he'd give the renewal. But he wants just a little puff. What will I tell him, Mr Crawford?

K. M. A.

—Will you tell him he can kiss my arse? Myles Crawford said throwing out his arm for emphasis. Tell him that straight from the stable.

A bit nervy. Look out for squalls. All off for a drink. Arm in arm. Lenehan's yachting cap on the cadge beyond. Usual blarney. Wonder is that young Dedalus the moving spirit. Has a good pair of boots on him today. Last time I saw him he had his heels on view. Been walking in muck somewhere. Careless chap. What was he doing in Irishtown?[6]

---

5. A pig's foot and a bottle of beer.
6. During the funeral procession, Bloom and the other
members of the funeral party saw Stephen walking along the beach at Sandymount, near Irishtown.

—Well, Mr Bloom said, his eyes returning, if I can get the design I suppose it's worth a short par. He'd give the ad I think. I'll tell him . . .

K. M. R. I. A

—He can kiss my royal Irish arse, Myles Crawford cried loudly over his shoulder. Any time he likes, tell him.

While Mr Bloom stood weighing the point and about to smile he strode on jerkily.

RAISING THE WIND

—*Nulla bona,*[7] Jack, he said, raising his hand to his chin. I'm up to here. I've been through the hoop myself. I was looking for a fellow to back a bill for me no later than last week. You must take the will for the deed. Sorry, Jack. With a heart and a half if I could raise the wind anyhow.

J. J. O'Molloy pulled a long face and walked on silently. They caught up on the others and walked abreast.

—When they have eaten the brawn and the bread and wiped their twenty fingers in the paper the bread was wrapped in, they go nearer to the railings.

—Something for you, the professor explained to Myles Crawford. Two old Dublin women on the top of Nelson's pillar.

SOME COLUMN!—THAT'S WHAT WADDLER ONE SAID

—That's new, Myles Crawford said. That's copy. Out for the waxies' Dargle. Two old trickies, what?

—But they are afraid the pillar will fall, Stephen went on. They see the roofs and argue about where the different churches are: Rathmines' blue dome, Adam and Eve's, saint Laurence O'Toole's. But it makes them giddy to look so they pull up their skirts . . .

THOSE SLIGHTLY RAMBUNCTIOUS FEMALES

—Easy all, Myles Crawford said. No poetic licence. We're in the archdiocese here.

—And settle down on their striped petticoats, peering up at the statue of the onehandled adulterer.[8]

—Onehandled adulterer! the professor cried. I like that. I see the idea. I see what you mean.

DAMES DONATE DUBLIN'S CITS
SPEEDPILLS VELOCITOUS AEROLITHS, BELIEF

—It gives them a crick in their necks, Stephen said, and they are too tired to look up or down or to speak. They put the bag of plums between them and eat the plums out of it, one after another, wiping off with their handkerchiefs the plumjuice that dribbles out of their mouths and spitting the plumstones slowly out between the railings.

He gave a sudden loud young laugh as a close. Lenehan and Mr O'Madden Burke, hearing, turned, beckoned and led on across towards Mooney's.

—Finished? Myles Crawford said. So long as they do no worse.

---

7. "No goods": i.e., no money to lend.
8. Admiral Lord Nelson (1758–1805) was one-armed

after a battlefield injury and was involved in a widely publicized extramarital affair.

SOPHIST WALLOPS HAUGHTY HELEN SQUARE ON PROBOSCIS.
SPARTANS GNASH MOLARS.
ITHACANS VOW PEN IS CHAMP.

—You remind me of Antisthenes, the professor said, a disciple of Gorgias, the sophist. It is said of him that none could tell if he were bitterer against others or against himself. He was the son of a noble and a bondwoman. And he wrote a book in which he took away the palm of beauty from Argive Helen and handed it to poor Penelope.

Poor Penelope. Penelope Rich.[9]

They made ready to cross O'Connell street.

HELLO THERE, CENTRAL!

At various points along the eight lines tramcars with motionless trolleys stood in their tracks, bound for or from Rathmines, Rathfarnham, Kingstown, Blackrock and Dalkey, Sandymount Green, Ringsend and Sandymount Tower, Donnybrook, Palmerston Park and Upper Rathmines, all still, becalmed in short circuit. Hackney cars, cabs, delivery waggons, mailvans, private broughams, aerated mineral water floats with rattling crates of bottles, rattled, rolled, horsedrawn, rapidly.

WHAT?—AND LIKEWISE—WHERE?

—But what do you call it? Myles Crawford asked. Where did they get the plums?

VIRGILIAN, SAYS PEDAGOGUE.
SOPHOMORE PLUMPS FOR OLD MAN MOSES.

—Call it, wait, the professor said, opening his long lips wide to reflect. Call it, let me see. Call it: *Deus nobis haec otia fecit.*[1]

—No, Stephen said, I call it *A Pisgah Sight of Palestine or The Parable of The Plums.*[2]

—I see, the professor said.

He laughed richly.

—I see, he said again with new pleasure. Moses and the promised land. We gave him that idea, he added to J. J. O'Molloy.

HORATIO IS CYNOSURE[3] THIS FAIR JUNE DAY

J. J. O'Molloy sent a weary sidelong glance towards the statue and held his peace.

—I see, the professor said.

He halted on sir John Gray's pavement island and peered aloft at Nelson through the meshes of his wry smile.

DIMINISHED DIGITS PROVE TOO TITILLATING
FOR FRISKY FRUMPS. ANNE WIMBLES, FLO
WANGLES-YET CAN YOU BLAME THEM?

—Onehandled adulterer, he said smiling grimly. That tickles me I must say.

—Tickled the old ones too, Myles Crawford said, if the God Almighty's truth was known.

---

9. Adulterous noblewoman (1562–1607), the lovely "Stella" of Sir Philip Sidney's *Astrophel and Stella* (1591).
1. God has made this peace for us (Latin; from Virgil, *Eclogues* 1:6).

2. Moses was granted a view of Israel from the top of Mount Pisgah, without being allowed to enter in before his death; see Deuteronomy 34.1–5.
3. The center of attention.

T. S. Eliot

1888–1965

T. S. Eliot was one of the dominant forces in English-language poetry of the twentieth century. When the entire body of Eliot's writing and influence is taken into account—not only his relatively modest poetic and dramatic production, but his literary criticism, his religious and cultural criticism, his editorial work at the British publishing house Faber and Faber, his influence on younger poets coming up in his wake, and quite simply his *presence* as a literary and cultural icon—no one looms larger. As one of those younger poets, Karl Shapiro, has written: "Eliot is untouchable; he is Modern Literature incarnate and an institution unto himself." Eliot's obituary in *Life* magazine declared that "Our age beyond any doubt has been, and will continue to be, the Age of Eliot."

Thomas Stearns Eliot was born in Saint Louis, Missouri. The roots of Eliot's family tree go deep into American, and specifically New England, soil. His ancestor Andrew Eliot was one of the original settlers of the Massachusetts Bay Colony, emigrating from East Coker, in Somerset, England, in the mid-seventeenth century; he later became one of the jurors who tried the Salem "witches." The Eliots became a distinguished New England family; the Eliot family tree includes a president of Harvard University and three U.S. Presidents (John Adams, John Quincy Adams, and Rutherford B. Hayes). In 1834 the Reverend William Greenleaf Eliot, the poet's grandfather, graduated from Harvard and moved to Saint Louis, where he established the city's first Unitarian church; he went on to found Washington University, and became its chancellor in 1872. It was into this family environment—redolent of New England, New England religion (Unitarianism), and New England educational tradition (Harvard)—that Eliot was born in 1888. And yet in a 1960 essay, Eliot wrote "My urban imagery was that of Saint Louis, upon which that of Paris and London had been superimposed." The sights and sounds of Saint Louis impressed themselves deeply on Eliot's young imagination, especially the looming figure of the Mississippi River (which he was to call "a strong brown god" in *The Dry Salvages*).

From age ten Eliot attended Smith Academy in Saint Louis—also founded by his grandfather—and spent his last year of secondary school at the Milton Academy in Milton, Massachusetts, in preparation for his entrance into Harvard in 1906. Eliot went on to take his A.B. (1909) and M.A. (1910) degrees from Harvard and largely completed a Ph.D. in philosophy from Harvard, first spending a relatively unstructured year in Paris, attending lectures at the Sorbonne and hearing Henri Bergson lecture at the Collège de France. He wrote a doctoral dissertation on the neo-idealist philosopher F. H. Bradley in 1916, which was accepted by the philosophy department at Harvard, but he never returned to Cambridge to defend the dissertation and take the degree. Eliot's year in Paris was crucial in many ways; in addition to breathing in the vital Parisian intellectual and artistic scene, he soaked up the writing of late-nineteenth-century French poets like Jules Laforgue, Tristan Corbière, and Charles Baudelaire.

Eliot's poems are deeply indebted both to French and to British poets. The poem with which Eliot broke onto the modern poetry scene was *The Love Song of J. Alfred Prufrock*, composed between 1910 and 1911. In a strikingly new and jarring idiom, the poem builds on the dramatic monologues of Robert Browning, breaking up the unified voice at the center of Browning's experiments with startling juxtapositions and transitions, and adding the violent and disturbing imagery of the French symbolist poets. The resulting poem is a heavily ironic "love song" in which neither lover nor beloved exists with any solidity outside the straitjacket of "a formulated phrase"; Prufrock, like modern European humanity whom he represents, is unable to penetrate the thick husk of habit, custom, and cliché to arrive at something substantial.

Eliot, and the poem, came to the notice of modern literature impresario Ezra Pound; in 1915 Pound saw to it that *Prufrock* was published in Harriet Monroe's influential *Poetry* magazine, as well as in his own *Catholic Anthology*, which brought Eliot to the notice of the (largely hostile) British literary establishment in the person of reviewers like the *Quarterly Review*'s Arthur Waugh. Eliot wrote three other great poems in this early period, *Portrait of a Lady*, *Preludes*, and *Rhapsody on a Windy Night*. Like *Prufrock*, the poems deal unflinchingly with loneliness, alienation, isolation; while isolation is hardly a new theme for poetry, Eliot suggests in a particularly modernist form in these poems that our isolation from others derives from, and tragically mirrors, our isolation from ourselves. This internalized alienation was also one of the themes of Eliot's early and influential review essay *The Metaphysical Poets* (1921); in that piece, he suggested that English poetry had suffered through a long drought, dating from about the time of Milton, caused by what Eliot termed a "dissociation of sensibility." At the time of the metaphysical poets (in the seventeenth century), a poet, or any sensitive thinker, was a unified whole; "A thought to Donne," Eliot writes, "was an experience; it modified his sensibility. . . . the ordinary man's experience is chaotic, irregular, fragmentary." That chaotic consciousness seemed to Eliot especially pronounced in the early decades of the twentieth century; though not sanguine of easy solutions, he did believe that modern poets, writing a poetry that would synthesize the seemingly unrelated sensations and experiences of modern men and women, might show a way out of "the immense panorama of futility and anarchy which is contemporary history," as he wrote in 1923 in a review of Joyce's *Ulysses*.

A collection of Eliot's early poems was published in 1917 as *Prufrock and Other Observations* by the Egoist Press, through the offices of Pound. For the remainder of the decade, however, Eliot's poetic output was small; feeling himself at a creative cul de sac, he wrote a few poems in French in 1917, including *Dans le Restaurant* which later appeared, trimmed and translated, as a part of *The Waste Land*. On Pound's suggestion, Eliot set himself, as a formal exercise, to write several poems modeled on the quatrains of Théophile Gautier. Arguably the most significant and influential of Eliot's early writings, however, were his many critical essays and book reviews; between 1916 and 1921 he wrote nearly a hundred essays and reviews, many of which were published in 1920 as *The Sacred Wood*. Critics still disagree as to whether Eliot's poetry or critical prose has been the more influential; the most important of Eliot's critical precepts, such as the "impersonality" of poetry and the inherent difficulty of modern writing, have entered wholesale into the way that modern literature is studied and taught. Eliot's critical principles, complemented and extended by academics such as I. A. Richards, make up the foundation of what came to be known as the New Criticism, a major mode of reading that emphasizes close attention to verbal textures and to poetic ironies, paradoxes, and tensions between disparate elements—all prominent features of Eliot's own poetry.

Eliot lived in modest circumstances for several years, working as a schoolteacher and then a bank clerk between 1916 and 1922. He then edited an increasingly influential quarterly, *The Criterion* (1922–1939), and became an editor at Faber and Faber, a post he retained until his death. His reputation as a poet was confirmed in 1922 with *The Waste Land*, the epochal work that remains Eliot's best-known and most influential poem; Pound called it "about enough . . . to make the rest of us shut up shop." More than any other text of the century, *The Waste Land* forcibly changed the idiom that contemporary poetry must adopt if it were to remain contemporary. Perhaps the poem's most impressive formal achievement, created in no small part through Ezra Pound's judicious editorial work, is its careful balance between structure and chaos, unity and fragmentation; this poise is created in the poem in equal parts by the mythical structures Eliot used to undergird the contemporary action and the pedantic footnotes he added to the poem, after its periodical publication in the *Dial*, to call the reader's attention to those structures. *The Waste Land*—like *Ulysses*, *Finnegans Wake*, Pound's *Cantos*, and a number of other important texts—looks unified largely because we readers look for it to be unified.

Such a style of reading is one of the great triumphs of modernism, and one Eliot was instrumental in teaching to readers and teachers alike.

The Waste Land is justly celebrated for giving voice to the nearly universal pessimism and alienation of the early decades of the twentieth century Europe—though Eliot maintained to the end that he was not a spokesperson for his generation or for anything else, and that the poem was "only the relief of a personal and wholly insignificant grouse against life; it is just a piece of rhythmical grumbling." Owing to the development of recording technology, to "give voice" in this case is not merely a metaphor, for Eliot's recording of *The Waste Land*, in what Virginia Woolf called Eliot's "sepulchral voice," has been tremendously influential on two generations of poets and students. Eliot's critical principle of "impersonality," however, has sometimes served to obscure how very personal, on one level, the poem is. The poem was completed during Eliot's convalescence at a sanatorium in Margate, England ("On Margate Sands. / I can connect / Nothing with nothing," the speaker despairs in section 3, "The Fire Sermon") and in Lausanne, Switzerland; the speaker, like the poet, is reduced to shoring the fragments of a disappearing civilization against his ruin. The poem also bears painful testimony to the increasingly desperate state of Eliot's wife Vivien Haigh-Wood, whom he had married in 1915; she suffered terribly from what was at the time called "nervousness," and had finally to be institutionalized in 1938. Whole stretches of one-sided "dialogue" from the "A Game of Chess" section would seem to have been taken verbatim from the couple's private conversations: "My nerves are very bad to-night. Yes, bad. Stay with me. / Speak to me. Why do you never speak? Speak." On the draft of the poem, Pound wrote "photography" alongside this passage. *The Waste Land* remains one of the century's most incisive and insightful texts regarding the breakdown of social, communal, cultural, and personal relationships.

In 1930 Eliot's next important poem, the introspective and confessional *Ash Wednesday*, was published; in the time since the publication of *The Waste Land*, however, Eliot's personal belief system had undergone a sea change. In June 1927 he was baptized into the Anglican church; five months later, he was naturalized as a British citizen. In his 1928 monograph *For Lancelot Andrewes*, Eliot declared himself to be "classicist in literature, royalist in politics, and Anglo-Catholic in religion." His poem *Journey of the Magi*, published as a pamphlet a month after his baptism, addresses the journey Eliot himself had made through death to a rebirth—precisely the rebirth which, in the opening lines of *The Waste Land*, seems an impossibility.

The 1930s also saw Eliot's entry into the theater, with three poetic dramas: *The Rock* (1934), *Murder in the Cathedral* (1935), and *The Family Reunion* (1939). In his later years, these highbrow dramas were complemented with a handful of more popular social dramas, *The Cocktail Party* (1950), *The Confidential Clerk* (1954), and *The Elder Statesman* (1959). Though celebrated by critics at the time for their innovative use of verse and their willingness to wrestle with both modern problems and universal themes, the plays have slipped in popularity in recent years. Nevertheless, as fate would have it, Eliot is the posthumous librettist of one of the most successful musicals in the history of British and American theater: his playful children's book *Old Possum's Book of Practical Cats* (1939), light verse written for the enjoyment of his godchildren, was transformed by Andrew Lloyd Webber in 1980 into the smash-hit musical *Cats*.

Eliot's final poetic achievement—and, for many, his greatest—is the set of four poems published together in 1943 as *Four Quartets*. Eliot believed them to be the best of his writing; "The *Four Quartets*: I rest on those," he told an interviewer in 1959. Eliot's last years were brightened by increasing public accolades, including the Nobel Prize for literature in 1948; he became a very popular speaker on the public lecture circuit, attracting an audience of 15,000, for instance, at a lecture at the University of Minnesota in 1956, later published as *The Frontiers of Criticism*. These public appearances largely took the place of creative writing after 1960. In January 1947 Vivien Eliot died in an institution; a decade later, he married Esme Valery Fletcher, and enjoyed a fulfilling companionate marriage until his death in January 1965. Like Hardy and Yeats, Eliot expressed his wish to be buried in his ancestors' parish church, in his case at East Coker, the home of his ancestor Andrew Eliot; thus, in his death and burial, the opening of his poem *East Coker* is literalized: "In my beginning is my end."

The Love Song of J. Alfred Prufrock

S'io credessi che mia risposta fosse
a persona che mai tornasse al mondo,
questa fiamma staria senza più scosse.
Ma per ciò che giammai di questo fondo
non tornò vivo alcun, s'i'odo il vero,
senza tema d'infamia ti rispondo.[1]

Let us go then, you and I,
When the evening is spread out against the sky
Like a patient etherised upon a table;
Let us go, through certain half-deserted streets,
5   The muttering retreats
Of restless nights in one-night cheap hotels
And sawdust restaurants with oyster-shells:
Streets that follow like a tedious argument
Of insidious intent
10   To lead you to an overwhelming question . . .
Oh, do not ask, "What is it?"
Let us go and make our visit.

In the room the women come and go
Talking of Michelangelo.

15   The yellow fog that rubs its back upon the window-panes,
The yellow smoke that rubs its muzzle on the window-panes,
Licked its tongue into the corners of the evening,
Lingered upon the pools that stand in drains,
Let fall upon its back the soot that falls from chimneys,
20   Slipped by the terrace, made a sudden leap,
And seeing that it was a soft October night,
Curled once about the house, and fell asleep.

And indeed there will be time
For the yellow smoke that slides along the street
25   Rubbing its back upon the window-panes;
There will be time, there will be time
To prepare a face to meet the faces that you meet;
There will be time to murder and create,
And time for all the works and days of hands

---

1. From Dante's *Inferno* (27.61–66). Dante asks one of the damned souls for its name, and it replies: "If I thought my answer were for one who could return to the world, I would not reply, but as none ever did return alive from this depth, without fear of infamy I answer thee."

30   That lift and drop a question on your plate;
          Time for you and time for me,
          And time yet for a hundred indecisions,
          And for a hundred visions and revisions,
          Before the taking of a toast and tea.

35   In the room the women come and go
          Talking of Michelangelo.

          And indeed there will be time
          To wonder, "Do I dare?" and, "Do I dare?"
          Time to turn back and descend the stair,
40   With a bald spot in the middle of my hair—
          (They will say: "How his hair is growing thin!")
          My morning coat, my collar mounting firmly to the chin,
          My necktie rich and modest, but asserted by a simple pin—
          (They will say: "But how his arms and legs are thin!")
45   Do I dare
          Disturb the universe?
          In a minute there is time
          For decisions and revisions which a minute will reverse.

          For I have known them all already, known them all—
50   Have known the evenings, mornings, afternoons,
          I have measured out my life with coffee spoons;
          I know the voices dying with a dying fall
          Beneath the music from a farther room.
              So how should I presume?

55   And I have known the eyes already, known them all—
          The eyes that fix you in a formulated phrase,
          And when I am formulated, sprawling on a pin,
          When I am pinned and wriggling on the wall,
          Then how should I begin
60   To spit out all the butt-ends of my days and ways?
              And how should I presume?

          And I have known the arms already, known them all—
          Arms that are braceleted and white and bare
          (But in the lamplight, downed with light brown hair!)
65   Is it perfume from a dress
          That makes me so digress?
          Arms that lie along a table, or wrap about a shawl.
              And should I then presume?
              And how should I begin?
                      . . .

70   Shall I say, I have gone at dusk through narrow streets
          And watched the smoke that rises from the pipes
          Of lonely men in shirt-sleeves, leaning out of windows? . . .

          I should have been a pair of ragged claws
          Scuttling across the floors of silent seas.
                      . . .

75   And the afternoon, the evening, sleeps so peacefully!
    Smoothed by long fingers,
    Asleep . . . tired . . . or it malingers,
    Stretched on the floor, here beside you and me.
    Should I, after tea and cakes and ices,
80   Have the strength to force the moment to its crisis?
    But though I have wept and fasted, wept and prayed,
    Though I have seen my head (grown slightly bald) brought
        in upon a platter,[2]
    I am no prophet—and here's no great matter;
    I have seen the moment of my greatness flicker,
85   And I have seen the eternal Footman hold my coat, and snicker,
    And in short, I was afraid.

    And would it have been worth it, after all,
    After the cups, the marmalade, the tea,
    Among the porcelain, among some talk of you and me,
90   Would it have been worth while,
    To have bitten off the matter with a smile,
    To have squeezed the universe into a ball
    To roll it towards some overwhelming question,
    To say: "I am Lazarus, come from the dead,
95   Come back to tell you all, I shall tell you all"[3]—
    If one, settling a pillow by her head,
        Should say: "That is not what I meant at all.
        That is not it, at all."

    And would it have been worth it, after all,
100   Would it have been worth while,
    After the sunsets and the dooryards and the sprinkled streets,
    After the novels, after the teacups, after the skirts that trail
        along the floor—
    And this, and so much more?—
    It is impossible to say just what I mean!
105   But as if a magic lantern[4] threw the nerves in patterns on a
        screen:
    Would it have been worth while
    If one, settling a pillow or throwing off a shawl,
    And turning toward the window, should say:
        "That is not it at all,
110   That is not what I meant, at all."
            · · ·
    No! I am not Prince Hamlet, nor was meant to be;
    Am an attendant lord, one that will do
    To swell a progress, start a scene or two,
    Advise the prince; no doubt, an easy tool,
115   Deferential, glad to be of use,
    Politic, cautious, and meticulous;

---

2. Cf. Matthew 14. John the Baptist was beheaded by Herod and his head was brought to his wife, Herodias, on a platter.
3. Cf. John 11. Jesus raised Lazarus from the grave after he had been dead four days.
4. A device that employs a candle to project images, rather like a slide projector.

Full of high sentence, but a bit obtuse;
At times, indeed, almost ridiculous—
Almost, at times, the Fool.

120 I grow old . . . I grow old . . .
I shall wear the bottoms of my trousers rolled.

Shall I part my hair behind? Do I dare to eat a peach?
I shall wear white flannel trousers, and walk upon the beach.
I have heard the mermaids singing, each to each.

125 I do not think that they will sing to me.

I have seen them riding seaward on the waves
Combing the white hair of the waves blown back
When the wind blows the water white and black.

We have lingered in the chambers of the sea
130 By sea-girls wreathed with seaweed red and brown
Till human voices wake us, and we drown.

COMPANION READINGS

Arthur Waugh:[1] [Cleverness and the New Poetry]

Cleverness is, indeed, the pitfall of the New Poetry. There is no question about the ingenuity with which its varying moods are exploited, its elaborate symbolism evolved, and its sudden, disconcerting effect exploded upon the imagination. Swift, brilliant images break into the field of vision, scatter like rockets, and leave a trail of flying fire behind. But the general impression is momentary; there are moods and emotions, but no steady current of ideas behind them. Further, in their determination to surprise and even to puzzle at all costs these young poets are continually forgetting that the first essence of poetry is beauty; and that, however much you may have observed the world around you, it is impossible to translate your observation into poetry, without the intervention of the spirit of beauty, controlling the vision, and reanimating the idea.

The temptations of cleverness may be insistent, but its risks are equally great: how great indeed will, perhaps, be best indicated by the example of the "Catholic Anthology," which apparently represents the very newest of all the new poetic movements of the day. This strange little volume bears upon its cover a geometrical device, suggesting that the material within holds the same relation to the art of poetry as the work of the Cubist school hold to the art of painting and design. The product of the volume is mainly American in origin, only one or two of the contributors being of indisputably English birth. But it appears here under the auspices of a house associated with some of the best poetry of the younger generation, and is prefaced by a short lyric by Mr W. B. Yeats, in which that honoured representative of a very different school of inspiration makes bitter fun of scholars and critics, who

Edit and annotate the lines
That young men, tossing on their beds,
Rhymed out in love's despair
To flatter beauty's ignorant ear.

---

1. Influential publisher, editor and critic (1866–1943); father of novelist Evelyn Waugh. The *Catholic Anthology* (1914), which Waugh attacks in this review from the *Quarterly Review* (London), was edited by Ezra Pound and included Eliot's *The Love Song of J. Alfred Prufrock* and printed W. B. Yeats's *The Scholars* as a preface.

The reader will not have penetrated far beyond this warning notice before he finds himself in the very stronghold of literary rebellion, if not of anarchy. Mr Orrick Johns may be allowed to speak for his colleagues, as well as for himself:

> This is the song of youth,
> This is the cause of myself;
> I knew my father well and he was a fool,
> Therefore will I have my own foot in the path before I take a step;
> I will go only into new lands,
> And I will walk on no plank-walks.
> The horses of my family are wind-broken,
> And the dogs are old,
> And the guns rust;
> I will make me a new bow from an ash-tree,
> And cut up the homestead into arrows.

And Mr Ezra Pound takes up the parable in turn, in the same wooden prose, cut into battens:

> Come, my songs, let us express our baser passions.
> Let us express our envy for the man with a steady job and no worry about the future.
> You are very idle, my songs,
> I fear you will come to a bad end.
> You stand about the streets. You loiter at the corners and bus-stops,
> You do next to nothing at all.
> You do not even express our inner nobility,
> You will come to a very bad end.
> And I? I have gone half cracked.[2]

It is not for his audience to contradict the poet, who for once may be allowed to pronounce his own literary epitaph. But this, it is to be noted, is the "poetry" that was to say nothing that might not be said "actually in life—under emotion,"[3] the sort of emotion that settles down into the banality of a premature decrepitude:

> I grow old. . . . I grow old . . .
> I shall wear the bottoms of my trousers rolled.
> Shall I part my hair behind? Do I dare to eat a peach?
> I shall wear white flannel trousers, and walk upon the beach.
> I have heard the mermaids singing, each to each.
> I do not think that they will sing to me.

Here, surely, is the reduction to absurdity of that school of literary license which, beginning with the declaration "I knew my father well and he was a fool" naturally proceeds to the convenient assumption that everything which seemed wise and true to the father must inevitably be false and foolish to the son. Yet if the fruits of emancipation are to be recognised in the unmetrical, incoherent banalities of these literary "Cubists," the state of Poetry is indeed threatened with anarchy which will end in something worse even than "red ruin and the breaking up of laws." From such a catastrophe the humour, commonsense, and artistic judgment of the best of the new "Georgians" will assuredly save their generation; nevertheless, a hint of warning may not be altogether out of place. It was a classic custom in the family hall, when the

---

2. From Pound's *Further Instructions*.   3. Waugh here paraphrases Wordsworth's prescription in the Preface to *Lyrical Ballads*.

feast was at its height, to display a drunken slave among the sons of the household, to the end that they, being ashamed at the ignominious folly of his gesticulations, might determine never to be tempted into such a pitiable condition themselves. The custom had its advantages; for the wisdom of the younger generation was found to be fostered more surely by a single example than by a world of homily and precept.

Ezra Pound: Drunken Helots and Mr. Eliot[1]

Genius has I know not what peculiar property, its manifestations are various, but however diverse and dissimilar they may be, they have at least one property in common. It makes no difference in what art, in what mode, whether the most conservative, or the most ribald-revolutionary, or the most diffident; if in any land, or upon any floating deck over the ocean, or upon some newly contrapted craft in the aether, genius manifests itself, at once some elderly gentleman has a flux of bile from his liver; at once from the throne or the easy Cowperian[2] sofa, or from the gutter, or from the oeconomical press room there bursts a torrent of elderly words, splenetic, irrelevant, they form themselves instinctively into large phrases denouncing the inordinate product.

This peculiar kind of *rabbia* [madness] might almost be taken as the test of a work of art, mere talent seems incapable of exciting it. "You can't fool me, sir, you're a scoundrel," bawls the testy old gentleman.

Fortunately the days when "that very fiery particle" could be crushed out by the "Quarterly" are over, but it interests me, as an archaeologist, to note that the firm which no longer produces Byron, but rather memoirs, letters of the late Queen, etc., is still running a review, and that this review is still where it was in 1812, or whatever the year was; and that, not having an uneducated Keats to condemn, a certain Mr. Waugh is scolding about Mr. Eliot.[3]

All I can find out, by asking questions concerning Mr. Waugh, is that he is "a very old chap," "a reviewer." From internal evidence we deduce that he is, like the rest of his generation of English *gens-de-lettres* [men of letters], ignorant of Laforgue; of De Régnier's "Odelettes," of his French contemporaries generally, of De Gourmont's "Litanies," of Tristan Corbière, Laurent Tailhade.[4] This is by no means surprising. We are used to it from his "b'ilin'."[5]

However, he outdoes himself, he calls Mr. Eliot a "drunken helot." So called they Anacreon[6] in the days of his predecessors, but from the context in the "Quarterly" article I judge that Mr. Waugh does not intend the phrase as a compliment, he is trying to be abusive, and moreover, he in his limited way has succeeded.

Let us sample the works of the last "Drunken Helot." I shall call my next anthology "Drunken Helots" if I can find a dozen poems written half so well as the following:

[Quotes *Conversation Galante*]

Our helot has a marvellous neatness. There is a comparable finesse in Laforgue's "Votre âme est affaire d'oculiste," but hardly in English verse.

---

1. Pound replied to Waugh's review in the *Egoist*, June 1917. A "helot" is a serf or slave.
2. After 18th-century poet William Cowper.
3. As in *Salutation the Third* (page 2298), Pound invokes the savage review of Keats that appeared in the *Quarterly Review* and was believed by his friends to have hastened Keats's death.
4. A series of French writers and texts that Pound admired. Jules Laforgue (1860–1887) was a French poet who helped develop free verse; he was an important influence on Eliot's early poetry. Henri de Régnier (1864–1936) was a French symbolist poet; Remy de Gourmont (1858–1915) was an influential French poet, novelist, essayist, publisher, and literary critic; Tristan Corbière, pseudonym for Édouard Joachim Corbière (1854–1919), was a French poet who worked with common speech and slang; and Laurent Tailhade (1854–1919) was a satiric French poet.
5. Byline, identifying the author of a newspaper article.
6. Greek writer of love poems and drinking songs.

Let us reconsider this drunkenness:

[Quotes *La Figlia Che Piange*]

And since when have helots taken to reading Dante and Marlowe? Since when have helots made a new music, a new refinement, a new method of turning old phrases into new by their aptness? However the "Quarterly," the century old, the venerable, the praeclarus,[7] the voice of Gehova[8] and Co., Sinai and 51A Albemarle Street, London, W. 1, has pronounced this author a helot. They are all for an aristocracy made up of, possibly, Tennyson, Southey and Wordsworth, the flunkey, the dull and the duller. Let us sup with the helots. Or perhaps the good Waugh is a wag,[9] perhaps he hears with the haspirate[1] and wishes to pun on Mr. Heliot's name: a bright bit of syzygy.[2]

I confess his type of mind puzzles me, there is no telling what he is up to.

I do not wish to misjudge him, this theory may be the correct one. You never can tell when old gentlemen grow facetious. He does not mention Mr. Eliot's name; he merely takes his lines and abuses them. The artful dodger,[3] he didn't (*sotto voce*[4]) "he didn't want 'people' to know that Mr. Eliot was a poet".

The poem he chooses for malediction is the title poem, "Prufrock." It is too long to quote entire.

[Quotes portion of *Prufrock*]

Let us leave the silly old Waugh. Mr. Eliot has made an advance on Browning. He has also made his dramatis personae contemporary and convincing. He has been an individual in his poems. I have read the contents of this book over and over, and with continued joy in the freshness, the humanity, the deep quiet culture. "I have tried to write of a few things that really have moved me" is so far as I know, the sum of Mr. Eliot's "poetic theory." His practice has been a distinctive cadence, a personal modus of arrangement, remote origins in Elizabethan English and in the modern French masters, neither origin being sufficiently apparent to affect the personal quality. It is writing without pretence. Mr. Eliot at once takes rank with the five or six living poets whose English one can read with enjoyment.

The "Egoist" has published the best prose writer of my generation. It follows its publication of Joyce by the publication of a "new" poet who is at least unsurpassed by any of his contemporaries, either of his own age or his elders.

It is perhaps "unenglish" to praise a poet whom one can read with enjoyment. Carlyle's generation wanted "improving" literature, Smile's "Self-Help"[5] and the rest of it. Mr. Waugh dates back to that generation, the virus is in his blood, he can't help it. The exactitude of the younger generation gets on his nerves, and so on and so on. He will "fall into line in time" like the rest of the bread-and-butter reviewers. Intelligent people will read "J. Alfred Prufrock"; they will wait with some eagerness for Mr. Eliot's further inspirations. It is 7.30 p.m. I have had nothing alcoholic today, nor yet yesterday. I said the same sort of thing about James Joyce's prose over two years ago. I am now basking in the echoes. Only a half-caste rag for the propaga-

7. Preeminent.
8. Jehovah.
9. Joker.
1. To aspirate is to add the "h" sound to the begining of a word: thus Eliot becomes "Hel[i]ot."
2. Any two related things (either similar or opposite).

3. The Artful Dodger is the name of Fagan's favorite pickpocket in Dickens's *Oliver Twist*.
4. In a low voice.
5. Samuel Smiles's *Self-Help* (1859) preached the Victorian gospel of self-improvement.

tion of garden suburbs, and a local gazette in Rochester, N.Y., U.S.A., are left whining in opposition. * * *

However, let us leave these bickerings, this stench of the printing-press, weekly and quarterly, let us return to the gardens of the Muses,

> Till human voices wake us and we drown,

as Eliot has written in conclusion to the poem which the "Quarterly" calls the *reductio ad absurdum:*[6]

> I have seen them riding seaward on the waves
> Combing the white hair of the waves blown back
> When the wind blows the water white and black.
>
> We have lingered in the chambers of the sea
> By sea-girls wreathed with seaweed red and brown
> Till human voices wake us, and we drown.

The poetic mind leaps the gulf from the exterior world, the trivialities of Mr. Prufrock, diffident, ridiculous, in the drawing-room, Mr. Apollinax's laughter "submarine and profound" transports him from the desiccated new-statesmanly atmosphere of Professor Canning-Cheetah's. Mr. Eliot's melody rushes out like the thought of Fragilion "among the birch-trees."[7] Mr. Waugh is my bitten macaroon at this festival.

The Waste Land

Like Conrad's *Heart of Darkness*—from which Eliot had originally planned to take his epigraph, "The horror! the horror!"—*The Waste Land* has become part of the symbolic landscape of twentieth-century Western culture; the text, like Conrad's, has been appropriated by commentators high and low, left and right, as an especially apt description of the psychosocial and interpersonal malaise of modern Europeans. Late in 1921 Eliot, who was suffering under a number of pressures both personal and artistic, took three months' leave from his job at Lloyd's Bank and went for a "rest cure" at a clinic in Lausanne, Switzerland. On his way he passed through Paris and showed the manuscript of the poem—really manuscripts of a number of fragments, whose interrelationship Eliot was trying to work out—to Ezra Pound; Pound and Eliot went through the poem again as Eliot returned to London in January 1922. Pound's editorial work was considerable, as the facsimile edition of the draft reveals; Pound said that he performed the poem's "caesarian operation," and Eliot dedicated *The Waste Land* to Pound—*il miglior fabbro* ("the better craftsman," a phrase from Dante).

The most obvious feature of *The Waste Land* is its difficulty. Eliot was perhaps the first poet and literary critic to argue that such "difficulty" was not just a necessary evil but in fact a constitutive element of poetry that would come to terms with the modern world. In his review of a volume of metaphysical poetry, Eliot implicitly links the complex poetry of Donne and Marvell with the task of the modern poet: "We can only say that it appears likely that poets in our civilization, as it exists at present, must be *difficult*. Our civilization comprehends great variety and complexity, and this variety and complexity, playing upon a refined sensibility, must produce various and complex results." In the case of *The Waste Land*, the difficulty lies primarily in the poem's dense tissue of quotations from and allusions to other texts; as Eliot's

---

6. Reduction to absurdity (Latin), the rhetorical technique of pushing the consequences of an idea to the point where it looks ridiculous.
7. The names and images in this sentence not taken from

Prufrock are from another of Eliot's early poems, *Mr. Apollinax*. The poem ends with the lines, "Of dowager Mrs. Phlaccus, and Professor and Mrs. Cheetah / I remember a slice of lemon, and a bitten macaroon."

own footnotes to the poem demonstrate, the poem draws its strength, and achieves a kind of universality, by making implicit and explicit reference to texts as widely different as Ovid's *Metamorphoses* and a World War I Australian marching song.

Beyond the density of the poem's quotations and allusions, Eliot hoped to suggest the possibilty of an order beneath the chaos. In his review of Joyce's *Ulysses* (published in November 1923) Eliot was to describe the "mythical method," deploying allusions to classical mythology to suggest an implicit (and recurring) order beneath contemporary history; and while his use of myth was not so methodical as Joyce's, his use of vegetation myth and romance structures points outside the world of the poem to "another world," where the brokenness of the waste land might be healed. At the time of writing the poem, however, Eliot could not see clearly where that healing might come from.

The Waste Land[1]

"Nam Sibyllam quidem Cumis ego ipse oculis meis vidi in
ampulla pendere, et cum illi pueri dicerent: Σίβυλλα τί
θέλεις; respondebat illa: ἀποθανεῖν θέλω."[2]

FOR EZRA POUND
il miglior fabbro.

I. THE BURIAL OF THE DEAD

April is the cruellest month, breeding
Lilacs out of the dead land, mixing
Memory and desire, stirring
Dull roots with spring rain.
5   Winter kept us warm, covering
Earth in forgetful snow, feeding
A little life with dried tubers.
Summer surprised us, coming over the Starnbergersee[3]
With a shower of rain; we stopped in the colonnade,
10   And went on in sunlight, into the Hofgarten[4],
And drank coffee, and talked for an hour.
Bin gar keine Russin, stamm' aus Litauen, echt deutsch.[5]
And when we were children, staying at the arch-duke's,
My cousin's, he took me out on a sled,
15   And I was frightened. He said, Marie,
Marie, hold on tight. And down we went.

1. Not only the title, but the plan and a good deal of the incidental symbolism of the poem was suggested by Miss Jessie L. Weston's book on the Grail legend: *From Ritual to Romance* (Cambridge). Indeed, so deeply am I indebted, Miss Weston's book will elucidate the difficulties of the poem much better than my notes can do; and I recommend it (apart from the great interest of the book itself) to any who think such elucidation of the poem worth the trouble. To another work of anthropology I am indebted in general, one which has influenced our generation profoundly; I mean *The Golden Bough*; I have used especially the two volumes *Adonis, Attis, Osiris*. Anyone who is acquainted with these works will immediately recognize in the poem certain references to vegetation ceremonies [Eliot's note]. Sir James Frazer (1854–1941)

brought out the twelve volumes of *The Golden Bough*, a vast work of anthropology and comparative mythology and religion, between 1890 and 1915, with a supplement published in 1936.
2. From the *Satyricon* of Petronius (first century A.D.). "For once I myself saw with my own eyes the Sybil at Cumae hanging in a cage, and when the boys said to her, 'Sybil, what do you want?' she replied, 'I want to die.'" The Sybil was granted anything she wished by Apollo, if only she would be his; she made the mistake of asking for everlasting life, without asking for eternal youth.
3. A lake near Munich.
4. A public park in Munich, with a zoo and cafés.
5. "I'm not a Russian at all; I come from Lithuania, a true German."

In the mountains, there you feel free.
I read, much of the night, and go south in the winter.

What are the roots that clutch, what branches grow
20   Out of this stony rubbish? Son of man,[6]
You cannot say, or guess, for you know only
A heap of broken images, where the sun beats,
And the dead tree gives no shelter, the cricket no relief,[7]
And the dry stone no sound of water. Only
25   There is shadow under this red rock,
(Come in under the shadow of this red rock),
And I will show you something different from either
Your shadow at morning striding behind you
Or your shadow at evening rising to meet you;
30   I will show you fear in a handful of dust.
                    Frisch weht der Wind
                    Der Heimat zu
                    Mein Irisch Kind,
                    Wo weilest du?[8]
35   "You gave me hyacinths first a year ago;
They called me the hyacinth girl."
—Yet when we came back, late, from the hyacinth garden,
Your arms full, and your hair wet, I could not
Speak, and my eyes failed, I was neither
40   Living nor dead, and I knew nothing,
Looking into the heart of light, the silence.
Oed' und leer das Meer.[9]

Madame Sosostris, famous clairvoyante,
Had a bad cold, nevertheless
45   Is known to be the wisest woman in Europe,
With a wicked pack of cards.[1] Here, said she,
Is your card, the drowned Phoenician Sailor,
(Those are pearls that were his eyes.[2] Look!)
Here is Belladonna, the Lady of the Rocks,
50   The lady of situations.
Here is the man with three staves, and here the Wheel,

6. Cf. Ezekiel 2.7 [Eliot's note]. Ezekiel 2.8 reads: "But thou, son of man, hear what I say unto thee; Be not thou rebellious like that rebellious house: open thy mouth, and eat that I give thee."
7. Cf. Ecclesiastes 12.5 [Eliot's note]. "They shall be afraid of that which is high, and fears shall be in the way, and the almond tree shall flourish, and the grasshopper shall be a burden, and desire shall fail."
8. V. *Tristan and Isolde*, i, verses 5–8 [Eliot's note]. In Wagner's opera, Tristan sings this about Isolde, the woman he is leaving behind as he sails for home: "Fresh blows the wind to the homeland; my Irish child, where are you waiting?"
9. Id. iii, verse 24 [Eliot's note]. Tristan is dying and waiting for Isolde to come to him, but a shepherd, whom Tristan has hired to keep watch for her ship, reports only "Desolate and empty the sea."
1. I am not familiar with the exact constitution of the

Tarot pack of cards, from which I have obviously departed to suit my own convenience. The Hanged Man, a member of the traditional pack, fits my purpose in two ways: because he is associated in my mind with the Hanged God of Frazer, and because I associated him with the hooded figure in the passage of the disciples to Emmaus in Part V. The Phoenician Sailor and the Merchant appear later; also the "crowds of people," and Death by Water is executed in Part IV. The Man with Three Staves (an authentic member of the Tarot pack) I associate, quite arbitrarily, with the Fisher King Himself [Eliot's note].
2. From Ariel's song, in Shakespeare's *The Tempest*: "Full fathom five thy father lies; / Of his bones are coral made; / Those are pearls that were his eyes: / Nothing of him that doth fade, / But doth suffer a sea-change" (1.2.399–403).

And here is the one-eyed merchant, and this card,
Which is blank, is something he carries on his back,
Which I am forbidden to see. I do not find
55   The Hanged Man.[3] Fear death by water.
I see crowds of people, walking round in a ring.
Thank you. If you see dear Mrs. Equitone,
Tell her I bring the horoscope myself:
One must be so careful these days.

60   Unreal City,[4]
Under the brown fog of a winter dawn,
A crowd flowed over London Bridge, so many,
I had not thought death had undone so many.[5]
Sighs, short and infrequent, were exhaled,[6]
65   And each man fixed his eyes before his feet.
Flowed up the hill and down King William Street,
To where Saint Mary Woolnoth kept the hours
With a dead sound on the final stroke of nine.[7]
There I saw one I knew, and stopped him, crying: "Stetson!
70   You who were with me in the ships at Mylae![8]
That corpse you planted last year in your garden,
Has it begun to sprout? Will it bloom this year?
Or has the sudden frost disturbed its bed?
O keep the Dog far hence, that's friend to men,[9]
75   Or with his nails he'll dig it up again!
You! hypocrite lecteur!—mon semblable,—mon frère!"[1]

II. A GAME OF CHESS[2]

The Chair she sat in, like a burnished throne,[3]
Glowed on the marble, where the glass
Held up by standards wrought with fruited vines
80   From which a golden Cupidon peeped out
(Another hid his eyes behind his wing)
Doubled the flames of sevenbranched candelabra
Reflecting light upon the table as
The glitter of her jewels rose to meet it,
85   From satin cases poured in rich profusion.
In vials of ivory and coloured glass
Unstoppered, lurked her strange synthetic perfumes,

---

3. The tarot card that depicts a man hanging by one foot from a cross.
4. Cf. Baudelaire: "Fourmillante cité, cité pleine de rêves, / Où le spectre en plein jour raccroche le passant" [Eliot's note].
5. Cf. *Inferno*, iii.55–7: "si lunga tratta / di gente, ch'io non avrei mai creduto / che morte tanta n'avesse disfatta" [Eliot's note]. "Such an endless train, / Of people, it never would have entered in my head / There were so many men whom death had slain."
6. Cf. *Inferno*, iv. 25–7: "Ouivi, secondo che per ascoltare, / non avea pianto, ma' che di sospiri, / che l'aura eterna facevan tremare" [Eliot's note]. "We heard no

loud complaint, no crying there, / No sound of grief except the sound of sighing / Quivering forever through the eternal air."
7. A phenomenon which I have often noticed [Eliot's note].
8. The Battle of Mylae (260 B.C.) in the First Punic War.
9. Cf. the Dirge in Webster's *White Devil* [Eliot's note].
1. V. Baudelaire, Preface to *Fleurs du Mal* [Eliot's note]. "Hypocrite reader—my double—my brother!"
2. Cf. Thomas Middleton's drama *A Game at Chess* (1625), a political satire.
3. Cf. *Antony and Cleopatra*, II. ii. 190 [Eliot's note].

Unguent, powdered, or liquid—troubled, confused
And drowned the sense in odours; stirred by the air
90   That freshened from the window, these ascended
In fattening the prolonged candle-flames,
Flung their smoke into the laquearia,[4]
Stirring the pattern on the coffered ceiling.
Huge sea-wood fed with copper
95   Burned green and orange, framed by the coloured stone,
In which sad light a carvèd dolphin swam.
Above the antique mantel was displayed
As though a window gave upon the sylvan scene[5]
The change of Philomel, by the barbarous king[6]
100   So rudely forced; yet there the nightingale[7]
Filled all the desert with inviolable voice
And still she cried, and still the world pursues,
"Jug Jug" to dirty ears.
And other withered stumps of time
105   Were told upon the walls; staring forms
Leaned out, leaning, hushing the room enclosed.
Footsteps shuffled on the stair.
Under the firelight, under the brush, her hair
Spread out in fiery points
110   Glowed into words, then would be savagely still.

"My nerves are bad to-night. Yes, bad. Stay with me.
Speak to me. Why do you never speak. Speak.
    What are you thinking of? What thinking? What?
I never know what you are thinking. Think."

115   I think we are in rats' alley[8]
Where the dead men lost their bones.

"What is that noise?"
                            The wind under the door.[9]
"What is that noise now? What is the wind doing?"
120   Nothing again nothing.

                                                    "Do
"You know nothing? Do you see nothing? Do you remember
Nothing?"
    I remember
125   Those are pearls that were his eyes.

---

4. "Laquearia. V. *Aeneid,* I.726: "dependent lychni laque-aribus aureis / incensi, et noctem flammis funalia vin-cunt." [Eliot's note]. "Burning lamps hang from the gold-panelled ceiling / And torches dispel the night with their flames"; a *laquearia* is a panelled ceiling. The passage from Virgil's *Aeneid* describes the banquet given by Dido for her lover Aeneas.
5. "Sylvan scene. V. Milton, *Paradise Lost,* iv. 140 [Eliot's note]. "And over head up grew / Insuperable height of loftiest shade, / Cedar, and Pine, and Fir, and branching Palm, / A Silvan Scene, and as the ranks ascend / Shade above shade, a woody Theatre / Of stateliest view" The

passage describes the Garden of Eden, as seen through Satan's eyes.
6. V. Ovid, *Metamorphoses,* vi, Philomela [Eliot's note]. Philomela was raped by King Tereus, her sister's husband, and was then changed into a nightingale.
7. Cf. Part III, 1. 204 [Eliot's note].
8. Cf. Part III, 1. 195 [Eliot's note].
9. Cf. Webster: "Is the wind in that door still?" [Eliot's note]. From John Webster's *The Devil's Law Case,* 3.2.162. The doctor asks this question when he discovers that a "murder victim" is still breathing.

"Are you alive, or not? Is there nothing in your head?"[1]
                                                    But

O O O O that Shakespeherian Rag—[2]
It's so elegant
130   So intelligent
"What shall I do now? What shall I do?"
"I shall rush out as I am, and walk the street
With my hair down, so. What shall we do tomorrow?
What shall we ever do?"
135   The hot water at ten.
And if it rains, a closed car at four.
And we shall play a game of chess,
Pressing lidless eyes and waiting for a knock upon the
      door.[3]
When Lil's husband got demobbed,° I said—   demobilized
140   I didn't mince my words, I said to her myself,
HURRY UP PLEASE ITS TIME[4]
Now Albert's coming back, make yourself a bit smart.
He'll want to know what you done with that money he gave you
To get yourself some teeth. He did, I was there.
145   You have them all out, Lil, and get a nice set,
He said, I swear, I can't bear to look at you.
And no more can't I, I said, and think of poor Albert,
He's been in the army four years, he wants a good time,
And if you don't give it him, there's others will, I said.
150   Oh is there, she said. Something o' that, I said.
Then I'll know who to thank, she said, and give me a straight look.
HURRY UP PLEASE ITS TIME
If you don't like it you can get on with it, I said.
Others can pick and choose if you can't.
155   But if Albert makes off, it won't be for lack of telling.
You ought to be ashamed, I said, to look so antique.
(And her only thirty-one.)
I can't help it, she said, pulling a long face,
It's them pills I took, to bring it off, she said.
160   (She's had five already, and nearly died of young George.)
The chemist[5] said it would be all right, but I've never been the same.
You *are* a proper fool, I said.
Well, if Albert won't leave you alone, there it is, I said,
What you get married for if you don't want children?
165   HURRY UP PLEASE ITS TIME
Well, that Sunday Albert was home, they had a hot gammon,°   ham
And they asked me in to dinner, to get the beauty of it hot—
HURRY UP PLEASE ITS TIME
HURRY UP PLEASE ITS TIME

---

1. Cf. Part I, l. 37, 48 [Eliot's note].
2. Quoting an American ragtime song featured in Zieg-
field's Follies of 1912.
3. Cf. the game of chess in Middleton's *Women beware*
Women [Eliot's note].
4. A British pub-keeper's call for a last round before closing.
5. Pharmacist.

170   Goonight Bill. Goonight Lou. Goonight May. Goonight.
Ta ta. Goonight. Goonight.
Good night, ladies, good night, sweet ladies, good night, good night.[6]

III. THE FIRE SERMON

The river's tent is broken; the last fingers of leaf
Clutch and sink into the wet bank. The wind
175   Crosses the brown land, unheard. The nymphs are departed.
Sweet Thames, run softly, till I end my song.[7]
The river bears no empty bottles, sandwich papers,
Silk handkerchiefs, cardboard boxes, cigarette ends
Or other testimony of summer nights. The nymphs are departed.
180   And their friends, the loitering heirs of City directors;
Departed, have left no addresses.
By the waters of Leman[8] I sat down and wept . . .
Sweet Thames, run softly till I end my song,
Sweet Thames, run softly, for I speak not loud or long.
185   But at my back in a cold blast I hear
The rattle of the bones, and chuckle spread from ear to ear.

A rat crept softly through the vegetation
Dragging its slimy belly on the bank
While I was fishing in the dull canal
190   On a winter evening round behind the gashouse
Musing upon the king my brother's wreck
And on the king my father's death before him.[9]
White bodies naked on the low damp ground
And bones cast in a little low dry garret,
195   Rattled by the rat's foot only, year to year.
But at my back from time to time I hear[1]
The sound of horns and motors, which shall bring[2]
Sweeney to Mrs. Porter in the spring.
O the moon shone bright on Mrs. Porter[3]
200   And on her daughter
They wash their feet in soda water
Et O ces voix d'enfants, chantant dans la coupole![4]

Twit twit twit
Jug jug jug jug jug jug

6. Ophelia speaks these words in Shakespeare's *Hamlet*, and they are understood by the King as certain evidence of her insanity: "Good night ladies, good night. Sweet ladies, good night, good night" (4.5.72–73).
7. V. Spenser, *Prothalamion* [Eliot's note]; Spenser's poem (1596) celebrates the double marriage of Lady Elizabeth and Lady Katherine Somerset.
8. Lake Geneva. The line echoes Psalm 137, in which, exiled in Babylon, the Hebrew poets are too full of grief to sing.
9. Cf. *The Tempest*, I. ii [Eliot's note].
1. Cf. Marvell, *To His Coy Mistress* [Eliot's note]. "But at my back I always hear / Time's wingéd chariot hurrying near."
2. Cf. Day, *Parliament of Bees*: "When of the sudden, lis-

tening, you shall hear, / A noise of horns and hunting, which shall bring / Actaeon to Diana in the spring, / Where all shall see her naked skin . . ." [Eliot's note].
3. I do not know the origin of the ballad from which these are taken: it was reported to me from Sydney, Australia [Eliot's note]. Sung by Australian soldiers in World War I: "O the moon shone bright on Mrs. Porter / And on the daughter / Of Mrs. Porter / They wash their feet in soda water / And so they oughter / To keep them clean."
4. V. Verlaine, *Parsifal* [Eliot's note]. "And O those children's voices singing in the dome." Paul Verlaine's sonnet describes Parsifal, who keeps himself pure in hopes of seeing the holy grail, and has his feet washed before entering the castle.

205   So rudely forc'd.
       Tereu

       Unreal City
       Under the brown fog of a winter noon
       Mr. Eugenides, the Smyrna[5] merchant
210   Unshaven, with a pocket full of currants
       C.i.f.[6] London: documents at sight,
       Asked me in demotic° French   *vulgar*
       To luncheon at the Cannon Street Hotel[7]
       Followed by a weekend at the Metropole.[8]

215   At the violet hour, when the eyes and back
       Turn upward from the desk, when the human engine waits
       Like a taxi throbbing waiting,
       I Tiresias,[9] though blind, throbbing between two lives,
       Old man with wrinkled female breasts, can see
220   At the violet hour, the evening hour that strives
       Homeward, and brings the sailor home from sea,[1]
       The typist home at teatime, clears her breakfast, lights
       Her stove, and lays out food in tins.
       Out of the window perilously spread
225   Her drying combinations touched by the sun's last rays,
       On the divan are piled (at night her bed)
       Stockings, slippers, camisoles, and stays.
       I Tiresias, old man with wrinkled dugs
       Perceived the scene, and foretold the rest—
230   I too awaited the expected guest.

5. Seaport in western Turkey.
6. The currants were quoted at a price "carriage and insurance free to London"; and the Bill of Lading, etc., were to be handed to the buyer upon payment of the sight draft [Eliot's note].
7. A Hotel in London near the train station used for travel to and from continental Europe.
8. An upscale seaside resort hotel in Brighton.
9. Tiresias, although a mere spectator and not indeed a "character," is yet the most important personage in the poem, uniting all the rest. Just as the one-eyed merchant, seller of currants, melts into the Phoenician Sailor, and the latter is not wholly distinct from Ferdinand Prince of Naples, so all the women are one woman, and the two sexes meet in Tiresias. What Tiresias *sees*, in fact, is the substance of the poem. The whole passage from Ovid is of great anthropological interest: ". . . Cum Iunone iocos et 'maior vestra profecto est / Quam, quae contingit maribus,' dixisse, 'voluptas.' / Illa negat; placuit quae sit sententia docti / Quaerere Tiresiae: venus huic erat utraque nota. / Nam duo magnorum viridi coeuntia silva / Corpora serpentum baculi violaverat ictu / Deque viro factus, mirabile, femina septem / Egerat autumnos; octavo rursus eosdem / Vidit et 'est vestrae si tanta potentia plagae,' / Dixit 'ut auctoris sortem in contraria mutet, / Nunc quoque vos feriam!' percussis anguibus isdem / Forma prior rediit genetivaque venit imago. / Arbiter hic igitur sumptus de lite iocosa / Dicta Iovis firmat; gravius Saturnia iusto / Nec pro materia fertur doluisse suique / Iudicis aeterna damnavit lumina nocte, / At pater omnipotens (neque enim licet inrita cuiquam / Facta dei fecisse deo) pro lumine adempto / Scire futura dedit poenamque levavit honore" [Eliot's note]. This passage from Ovid's *Metamorphosis* describes Tiresias's sex change: "[The story goes that once Jove, having drunk a great deal,] jested with Juno. He said, 'Your pleasure in love is really greater than that enjoyed by men.' She denied it; so they decided to seek the opinion of the wise Tiresias, for he knew both aspects of love. For once, with a blow of his staff, he had committed violence on two huge snakes as they copulated in the green forest; and—wonderful to tell—was turned from a man into a woman and thus spent seven years. In the eighth year he saw the same snakes again and said: 'If a blow struck at you is so powerful that it changes the sex of the giver, I will now strike at you again.' With these words he struck the snakes, and his former shape was restored to him and he became as he had been born. So he was appointed arbitrator in the playful quarrel, and supported Jove's statement. It is said that Saturnia [i.e., Juno] was quite disproportionately upset, and condemned the arbitrator to perpetual blindness. But the almighty father (for no god may undo what has been done by another god), in return for the sight that was taken away, gave him the power to know the future and so lightened the penalty paid by the honor."
1. This may not appear as exact as Sappho's lines but I had in mind the "longshore" or "dory" fisherman, who returns at nightfall [Eliot's note]. "Hesperus, thou bringst home all things bright morning scattered: thou bringst the sheep, the goat, the child to the mother."

He, the young man carbuncular,° arrives,   *pimply*
A small house agent's clerk, with one bold stare,
One of the low on whom assurance sits
As a silk hat on a Bradford[2] millionaire.
235   The time is now propitious, as he guesses,
The meal is ended, she is bored and tired,
Endeavours to engage her in caresses
Which still are unreproved, if undesired.
Flushed and decided, he assaults at once;
240   Exploring hands encounter no defence;
His vanity requires no response,
And makes a welcome of indifference.
(And I Tiresias have foresuffered all
Enacted on this same divan or bed;
245   I who have sat by Thebes below the wall
And walked among the lowest of the dead.)
Bestows one final patronising kiss,
And gropes his way, finding the stairs unlit . . .

She turns and looks a moment in the glass,
250   Hardly aware of her departed lover;
Her brain allows one half-formed thought to pass:
"Well now that's done: and I'm glad it's over."
When lovely woman stoops to folly and[3]
Paces about her room again, alone,
255   She smoothes her hair with automatic hand,
And puts a record on the gramophone.

"This music crept by me upon the waters"[4]
And along the Strand, up Queen Victoria Street.
O City city, I can sometimes hear
260   Beside a public bar in Lower Thames Street,
The pleasant whining of a mandoline
And a clatter and a chatter from within
Where fishmen lounge at noon: where the walls
Of Magnus Martyr[5] hold
265   Inexplicable splendour of Ionian white and gold.

The river sweats[6]
Oil and tar
The barges drift
With the turning tide

2. An industrial town in Yorkshire; many of its residents became wealthy during World War I.
3. V. Goldsmith, the song in *The Vicar of Wakefield* [Eliot's note]. Oliver Goldsmith's character Olivia, on returning to the place where she was seduced, sings, "When lovely woman stoops to folly / And finds too late that men betray / What charm can soothe her melancholy, / What art can wash her guilt away? / The only art her guilt to cover, / To hide her shame from every eye, / To give repentance to her lover / And wring his bosom— is to die."

4. V. *The Tempest,* as above [Eliot's note].
5. The interior of St. Magnus Martyr is to my mind one of the finest among Wren's interiors. See *The Proposed Demolition of Nineteen City Churches* (P.S. King & Son, Ltd.) [Eliot's note].
6. The Song of the (three) Thames-daughters begins here. From line 292 to 306 inclusive they speak in turn. V. *Götterdämmerung,* III.I: the Rhine-daughters [Eliot's note]. In Richard Wagner's opera, *Twilight of the Gods,* the Rhine maidens, when their gold is stolen, lament that the beauty of the river is gone.

270   Red sails
        Wide
        To leeward, swing on the heavy spar.
        The barges wash
        Drifting logs
275   Down Greenwich reach
        Past the Isle of Dogs.[7]
                Weialala leia
                Wallala leialala

        Elizabeth and Leicester[8]
280   Beating oars
        The stern was formed
        A gilded shell
        Red and gold
        The brisk swell
285   Rippled both shores
        Southwest wind
        Carried down stream
        The peal of bells
        White towers
290   Weialala leia
                Wallala leialala

        "Trams and dusty trees.
        Highbury bore me. Richmond and Kew[9]
        Undid me. By Richmond I raised my knees
295   Supine on the floor of a narrow canoe."

        "My feet are at Moorgate,[1] and my heart
        Under my feet. After the event
        He wept. He promised 'a new start.'
        I made no comment. What should I resent?"

300   "On Margate Sands.[2]
        I can connect
        Nothing with nothing.
        The broken fingernails of dirty hands.
        My people humble people who expect
305   Nothing."
                la la

---

7. Greenwich is a borough on the south bank of the River Thames; the Isle of Dogs is a peninsula in East London formed by a sharp bend in the Thames called Greenwich Reach.
8. V. Froude, *Elizabeth*, vol. I, Ch. iv, letter of De Quadra to Philip of Spain: "In the afternoon we were in a barge, watching the games on the river. (The Queen) was alone with Lord Robert and myself on the poop, when they began to talk nonsense, and went so far that Lord Robert at last said, as I was on the spot there was no reason why

they should not be married if the queen pleased" [Eliot's note].
9. "Cf. *Purgatorio*, V. 133: "Ricorditi di me, che son la Pia; / Siena mi fe', disfecemi Maremma." [Eliot's note]. "Remember me, that I am called Piety; / Sienna made me and Maremma undid me." Highbury, Richmond, and Kew are suburbs of London near the Thames.
1. A slum in East London.
2. A seaside resort in the Thames estuary.

To Carthage then I came[3]

Burning burning burning burning[4]
O Lord Thou pluckest me out[5]
310   O Lord Thou pluckest

burning

IV. DEATH BY WATER

Phlebas the Phoenician, a fortnight dead,
Forgot the cry of gulls, and the deep sea swell
And the profit and loss.
315   A current under sea
Picked his bones in whispers. As he rose and fell
He passed the stages of his age and youth
Entering the whirlpool.
                              Gentile or Jew
320   O you who turn the wheel and look to windward,
Consider Phlebas, who was once handsome and tall as you.

V. WHAT THE THUNDER SAID[6]

After the torchlight red on sweaty faces
After the frosty silence in the gardens
After the agony in stony places
325   The shouting and the crying
Prison and palace and reverberation
Of thunder of spring over distant mountains
He who was living is now dead
We who were living are now dying
330   With a little patience

Here is no water but only rock
Rock and no water and the sandy road
The road winding above among the mountains
Which are mountains of rock without water
335   If there were water we should stop and drink
Amongst the rock one cannot stop or think
Sweat is dry and feet are in the sand
If there were only water amongst the rock
Dead mountain mouth of carious° teeth that cannot spit   *rotting*
340   Here one can neither stand nor lie nor sit

---

3. V. St. Augustine's *Confessions*: "to Carthage then I came, where a cauldron of unholy loves sang all about mine ears" [Eliot's note].

4. The complete text of the Buddha's Fire Sermon (which corresponds in importance to the Sermon on the Mount) from which these words are taken, will be found translated in the late Henry Clarke Warren's *Buddhism in Translation* (Harvard Oriental Series). Mr. Warren was one of the great pioneers of Buddhist studies in the Occident [Eliot's note].

5. From St. Augustine's *Confessions* again. The collocation of these two representatives of eastern and western asceticism, as the culmination of this part of the poem, is not an accident [Eliot's note]. Augustine writes: "I entangle my steps with these outward beauties, but thou pluckest me out, O Lord, Thou pluckest me out."

6. In the first part of Part V three themes are employed: the journey to Emmaus, the approach to the Chapel Perilous (see Miss Weston's book), and the present decay of eastern Europe [Eliot's note].

There is not even silence in the mountains
But dry sterile thunder without rain
There is not even solitude in the mountains
But red sullen faces sneer and snarl
345   From doors of mudcracked houses
                              If there were water
And no rock
If there were rock
And also water
350   And water
A spring
A pool among the rock
If there were the sound of water only
Not the cicada
355   And dry grass singing
But sound of water over a rock
Where the hermit-thrush sings in the pine trees
Drip drop drip drop drop drop drop[7]
But there is no water

360   Who is the third who walks always beside you?
When I count, there are only you and I together[8]
But when I look ahead up the white road
There is always another one walking beside you
Gliding wrapt in a brown mantle, hooded
365   I do not know whether a man or a woman
—But who is that on the other side of you?

What is that sound high in the air[9]
Murmur of maternal lamentation
Who are those hooded hordes swarming
370   Over endless plains, stumbling in cracked earth
Ringed by the flat horizon only
What is the city over the mountains
Cracks and reforms and bursts in the violet air
Falling towers
375   Jerusalem Athens Alexandria

---

7. This is *Turdus aonalaschkae pallasii*, the hermit-thrush which I have heard in Quebec County. Chapman says (*Handbook of Birds of Eastern North America*) "it is most at home in secluded woodland and thickety retreats. . . . Its notes are not remarkable for variety or volume, but in purity and sweetness of tone and exquisite modulation they are unequalled." Its "water-dripping song" is justly celebrated [Eliot's note].

8. The following lines were stimulated by the account of one of the Antarctic expeditions (I forget which, but I think one of Shackleton's): it was related that the party of explorers, at the extremity of their strength, had the constant delusion that there was one more member than could actually be counted [Eliot's note]. There seems also to be an echo of the account of Jesus meeting his disciples on the road to Emmaus: "Jesus himself drew near, and

went with them. But their eyes were holden that they should not know him" (Luke 24.13–16).

9. Cf. Hermann Hesse, *Blick ins Chaos*: "Schon ist halb Europa, schon ist zumindest der halbe Osten Europas auf dem Wege zum Chaos, fährt betrunken im heiligen Wahn am Abgrund entlang und singt dazu, singt betrunken und hymnisch wie Dmitri Karamasoff sang. Ueber diese Lieder lacht der Bürger beleidigt, der Heilige und Seher hört sie mit Tränen" [Eliot's note]. "Already half of Europe, already at least half of Eastern Europe, on the way to chaos, drives drunk in sacred infatuation along the edge of the precipice, singing drunkenly, as though singing hymns, as Dmitri Karamazov sang. The offended bourgeois laughs at the songs; the saint and the seer hear them with tears."

Vienna London
Unreal

A woman drew her long black hair out tight
And fiddled whisper music on those strings
380   And bats with baby faces in the violet light
Whistled, and beat their wings
And crawled head downward down a blackened wall
And upside down in air were towers
Tolling reminiscent bells, that kept the hours
385   And voices singing out of empty cisterns and exhausted wells

In this decayed hole among the mountains
In the faint moonlight, the grass is singing
Over the tumbled graves, about the chapel
There is the empty chapel, only the wind's home.
390   It has no windows, and the door swings,
Dry bones can harm no one.
Only a cock stood on the rooftree
Co co rico co co rico
In a flash of lightning. Then a damp gust
395   Bringing rain

Ganga[1] was sunken, and the limp leaves
Waited for rain, while the black clouds
Gathered far distant, over Himavant.[2]
The jungle crouched, humped in silence.
400   Then spoke the thunder
DA
Datta: what have we given?[3]
My friend, blood shaking my heart
The awful daring of a moment's surrender
405   Which an age of prudence can never retract
By this, and this only, we have existed
Which is not to be found in our obituaries
Or in memories draped by the beneficent spider[4]
Or under seals broken by the lean solicitor
410   In our empty rooms
DA
Dayadhvam: I have heard the key[5]
Turn in the door once and turn once only

1. The river Ganges.
2. The Himalayas.
3. "Datta, dayadhvam, damyata" (Give, sympathize, control). The fable of the meaning of the Thunder is found in the *Brihadaranyaka—Upanishad*, 5, I. A translation is found in Deussen's *Sechzig Upanishads des Vada*, p. 489 [Eliot's note]. "That very thing is repented even today by the heavenly voice, in the form of thunder, in the form of thunder as 'Da,' 'Da,' 'Da,'. . . . Therefore one should practice these three things: self-control, alms-giving, and compassion."
4. Cf. Webster, *The White Devil*, v. vi: ". . . they'll remarry / Ere the worm pierce your winding-sheet, ere the spider / make a thin curtain for your epitaphs" [Eliot's note].

5. Cf. *Inferno*, xxxiii. 46: "ed io sentii chiavar l'uscio di sotto / all'orribile torre." Also F. H. *Bradley, Appearance and Reality*, p. 346: "My external sensations are no less private to myself than are my thoughts or my feelings. In either case my experience falls within my own circle, a circle closed on the outside; and, with all its elements alike, every sphere is opaque to the others which surround it. . . . In brief, regarded as an existence which appears in a soul, the whole world for each is peculiar and private to that soul." [Eliot's note]. In the passage from the *Inferno*, Ugolino tells Dante of his imprisonment and starvation until he became so desperate that he ate his children: "And I heard below me the door of the horrible tower being locked."

We think of the key, each in his prison
415   Thinking of the key, each confirms a prison
Only at nightfall, aethereal rumours
Revive for a moment a broken Coriolanus⁶
DA
Damyata: The boat responded
420   Gaily, to the hand expert with sail and oar
The sea was calm, your heart would have responded
Gaily, when invited, beating obedient
To controlling hands

I sat upon the shore
425   Fishing, with the arid plain behind me⁷
Shall I at least set my lands in order?
London Bridge is falling down falling down falling down
Poi s'ascose nel foco che gli affina⁸
Quando fiam uti chelidon—O swallow swallow⁹
430   Le Prince d'Aquitaine à la tour abolie¹
These fragments I have shored against my ruins
Why then Ile fit you. Hieronymo's mad againe.²
Datta. Dayadhvam. Damyata.
Shantih   shantih   shantih³

Journey of the Magi¹

"A cold coming we had of it,
Just the worst time of the year
For a journey, and such a long journey:
The ways deep and the weather sharp,
5   The very dead of winter."
And the camels galled, sore-footed, refractory,
Lying down in the melting snow.
There were times we regretted
The summer palaces on slopes, the terraces,
10   And the silken girls bringing sherbet.
Then the camel men cursing and grumbling
And running away, and wanting their liquor and women,
And the night-fires going out, and the lack of shelters,

---

6. In Shakespeare's play of the same name, Coriolanus is a Roman general who is exiled and later leads the enemy in an attack against the Romans.
7. V. Weston, From Ritual to Romance; chapter on the Fisher King [Eliot's note].
8. V. Purgatorio, xxvi.148: "Ara vos prec per aquella valor / que vos condus al som de l'escalina, / sovegna vos a temps de ma dolor." / Poi s'ascose nel foco che gli affina" [Eliot's note]. In this passage, the poet Arnaut Daniel speaks to Dante: "Now I pray you, by the goodness that guides you to the top of this staircase, be mindful in time of my suffering."
9. V. Pervigilium Veneris. Cf. Philomela in Parts II and III [Eliot's note]. Philomel asks, "When shall I be a swallow?"
1. V. Gerard de Nerval, Sonnet El Desdichado [Eliot's

note]. "The Prince of Aquitane in the ruined tower."
2. V. Kyd's Spanish Tragedy [Eliot's note]. The subtitle of Kyd's play is, "Hieronymo's Mad Againe." His son having been murdered, Hieronymo is asked to compose a court play, to which he responds "Why then Ile fit you"; his son's murder is revenged in the course of the play.
3. Shantih. Repeated as here, a formal ending to an Upanishad. "The Peace which passeth understanding" is a feeble translation of the content of this word [Eliot's note]. The Upanishads are poetic commentaries on the Hindu Scriptures.
1. The narrative of the poem is based upon the tradition of the three wise men who journeyed to Bethlehem to worship the infant Christ; cf. Matthew 2.1–12.

And the cities hostile and the towns unfriendly
15   And the villages dirty and charging high prices:
A hard time we had of it.
At the end we preferred to travel all night,
Sleeping in snatches,
With the voices singing in our ears, saying
20   That this was all folly.

Then at dawn we came down to a temperate valley,
Wet, below the snow line, smelling of vegetation,
With a running stream and a water-mill beating the darkness
And three trees on the low sky.
25   And an old white horse galloped away in the meadow.
Then we came to a tavern with vine-leaves over the lintel,
Six hands at an open door dicing for pieces of silver,
And feet kicking the empty wine-skins.
But there was no information, and so we continued
30   And arrived at evening, not a moment too soon
Finding the place; it was (you may say) satisfactory.

All this was a long time ago, I remember,
And I would do it again, but set down
This set down
35   This: were we led all that way for
Birth or Death? There was a Birth, certainly,
We had evidence and no doubt. I had seen birth and death,
But had thought they were different; this Birth was
Hard and bitter agony for us, like Death, our death.
40   We returned to our places, these Kingdoms,
But no longer at ease here, in the old dispensation,
With an alien people clutching their gods.
I should be glad of another death.

                                                                        1927

Tradition and the Individual Talent

1

In English writing we seldom speak of tradition, though we occasionally apply its name in deploring its absence. We cannot refer to "the tradition" or to "a tradition"; at most, we employ the adjective in saying that the poetry of So-and-so is "tradition-al" or even "too traditional." Seldom, perhaps, does the word appear except in a phrase of censure. If otherwise, it is vaguely approbative,[1] with the implication, as to the work approved, of some pleasing archaeological reconstruction. You can hardly make the word agreeable to English ears without this comfortable reference to the reassuring science of archaeology.

Certainly the word is not likely to appear in our appreciations of living or dead writers. Every nation, every race, has not only its own creative, but its own critical turn of mind; and is even more oblivious of the shortcomings and limitations of its critical habits than of those of its creative genius. We know, or think we know,

---

1. Approving.

from the enormous mass of critical writing that has appeared in the French language the critical method or habit of the French; we only conclude (we are such unconscious people) that the French are "more critical" than we, and sometimes even plume ourselves a little with the fact, as if the French were the less spontaneous. Perhaps they are; but we might remind ourselves that criticism is as inevitable as breathing, and that we should be none the worse for articulating what passes in our minds when we read a book and feel an emotion about it, for criticizing our own minds in their work of criticism. One of the facts that might come to light in this process is our tendency to insist, when we praise a poet, upon those aspects of his work in which he least resembles any one else. In these aspects or parts of his work we pretend to find what is individual, what is the peculiar essence of the man. We dwell with satisfaction upon the poet's difference from his predecessors, especially his immediate predecessors; we endeavour to find something that can be isolated in order to be enjoyed. Whereas if we approach a poet without this prejudice we shall often find that not only the best, but the most individual parts of his work may be those in which the dead poets, his ancestors, assert their immortality most vigorously. And I do not mean the impressionable period of adolescence, but the period of full maturity.

Yet if the only form of tradition, of handing down, consisted in following the ways of the immediate generation before us in a blind or timid adherence to its successes, "tradition" should positively be discouraged. We have seen many such simple currents soon lost in the sand; and novelty is better than repetition. Tradition is a matter of much wider significance. It cannot be inherited, and if you want it you must obtain it by great labour. It involves, in the first place, the historical sense, which we may call nearly indispensable to any one who would continue to be a poet beyond his twenty-fifth year; and the historical sense involves a perception, not only of the pastness of the past, but of its presence; the historical sense compels a man to write not merely with his own generation in his bones, but with a feeling that the whole of the literature of Europe from Homer and within it the whole of the literature of his own country has a simultaneous existence and composes a simultaneous order. This historical sense, which is a sense of the timeless as well as of the temporal and of the timeless and of the temporal together, is what makes a writer traditional. And it is at the same time what makes a writer most acutely conscious of his place in time, of his own contemporaneity.

No poet, no artist of any art, has his complete meaning alone. His significance, his appreciation is the appreciation of his relation to the dead poets and artists. You cannot value him alone; you must set him, for contrast and comparison, among the dead. I mean this as a principle of aesthetic, not merely historical, criticism. The necessity that he shall conform, that he shall cohere, is not onesided; what happens when a new work of art is created is something that happens simultaneously to all the works of art which preceded it. The existing monuments form an ideal order among themselves, which is modified by the introduction of the new (the really new) work of art among them. The existing order is complete before the new work arrives; for order to persist after the supervention[2] of novelty, the whole existing order must be, if ever so slightly, altered; and so the relations, proportions, values of each work of art toward the whole are readjusted; and this is conformity between the old and the new. Whoever has approved this idea of order, of the form of European, of English litera-

2. The appearance of something additional.

ture will not find it preposterous that the past should be altered by the present as much as the present is directed by the past. And the poet who is aware of this will be aware of great difficulties and responsibilities.

In a peculiar sense he will be aware also that he must inevitably be judged by the standards of the past. I say judged, not amputated, by them; not judged to be as good as, or worse or better than, the dead; and certainly not judged by the canons of dead critics. It is a judgment, a comparison, in which two things are measured by each other. To conform merely would be for the new work not really to conform at all; it would not be new, and would therefore not be a work of art. And we do not quite say that the new is more valuable because it fits in; but its fitting in is a test of its value— a test, it is true, which can only be slowly and cautiously applied, for we are none of us infallible judges of conformity. We say: it appears to conform, and is perhaps individual, or it appears individual, and may conform; but we are hardly likely to find that it is one and not the other.

To proceed to a more intelligible exposition of the relation of the poet to the past: he can neither take the past as a lump, an indiscriminate bolus,[3] nor can he form himself wholly on one or two private admirations, nor can he form himself wholly upon one preferred period. The first course is inadmissible, the second is an important experience of youth, and the third is a pleasant and highly desirable supplement. The poet must be very conscious of the main current, which does not at all flow invariably through the most distinguished reputations. He must be quite aware of the obvious fact that art never improves, but that the material of art is never quite the same. He must be aware that the mind of Europe—the mind of his own country—a mind which he learns in time to be much more important than his own private mind—is a mind which changes, and that this change is a development which abandons nothing *en route*, which does not superannuate either Shakespeare, or Homer, or the rock drawing of the Magdalenian draughtsmen.[4] That this development, refinement perhaps, complication certainly, is not, from the point of view of the artist, any improvement. Perhaps not even an improvement from the point of view of the psychologist or not to the extent which we imagine; perhaps only in the end based upon a complication in economics and machinery. But the difference between the present and the past is that the conscious present is an awareness of the past in a way and to an extent which the past's awareness of itself cannot show.

Some one said: "The dead writers are remote from us because we *know* so much more than they did." Precisely, and they are that which we know.

I am alive to a usual objection to what is clearly part of my programme for the *métier* of poetry. The objection is that the doctrine requires a ridiculous amount of erudition (pedantry), a claim which can be rejected by appeal to the lives of poets in any pantheon. It will even be affirmed that much learning deadens or perverts poetic sensibility. While, however, we persist in believing that a poet ought to know as much as will not encroach upon his necessary receptivity and necessary laziness, it is not desirable to confine knowledge to whatever can be put into a useful shape for examinations, drawing-rooms, or the still more pretentious modes of publicity. Some can absorb knowledge, the more tardy must sweat for it. Shakespeare acquired more essential history from Plutarch than most men could from the whole British Museum. What is to be

---

3. A lump; a mass of chewed food.

4. Drawings of hunting scenes, rendered in caves in France and Spain, c. 13,000–10,000 B.C.

insisted upon is that the poet must develop or procure the consciousness of the past and that he should continue to develop this consciousness throughout his career.

What happens is a continual surrender of himself as he is at the moment to something which is more valuable. The progress of an artist is a continual self-sacrifice, a continual extinction of personality.

There remains to define this process of depersonalization and its relation to the sense of tradition. It is in this depersonalization that art may be said to approach the condition of science. I, therefore, invite you to consider, as a suggestive analogy, the action which takes place when a bit of finely filiated[5] platinum is introduced into a chamber containing oxygen and sulphur dioxide.

2

Honest criticism and sensitive appreciation are directed not upon the poet but upon the poetry. If we attend to the confused cries of the newspaper critics and the *susurrus* [buzzing] of popular repetition that follows, we shall hear the names of poets in great numbers; if we seek not Blue-book[6] knowledge but the enjoyment of poetry, and ask for a poem, we shall seldom find it. I have tried to point out the importance of the relation of the poem to other poems by other authors, and suggested the conception of poetry as a living whole of all the poetry that has ever been written. The other aspect of this Impersonal theory of poetry is the relation of the poem to its author. And I hinted, by an analogy, that the mind of the mature poet differs from that of the immature one not precisely in any valuation of "personality," not being necessarily more interesting, or having "more to say," but rather by being a more finely perfected medium in which special, or very varied, feelings are at liberty to enter into new combinations.

The analogy was that of the catalyst. When the two gases previously mentioned are mixed in the presence of a filament of platinum, they form sulphurous acid. This combination takes place only if the platinum is present; nevertheless the newly formed acid contains no trace of platinum, and the platinum itself is apparently unaffected; has remained inert, neutral, and unchanged. The mind of the poet is the shred of platinum. It may partly or exclusively operate upon the experience of the man himself; but, the more perfect the artist, the more completely separate in him will be the man who suffers and the mind which creates; the more perfectly will the mind digest and transmute the passions which are its material.

The experience, you will notice, the elements which enter the presence of the transforming catalyst, are of two kinds: emotions and feelings. The effect of a work of art upon the person who enjoys it is an experience different in kind from any experience not of art. It may be formed out of one emotion, or may be a combination of several; and various feelings, inhering for the writer in particular words or phrases or images, may be added to compose the final result. Or great poetry may be made without the direct use of any emotion whatever: composed out of feelings solely. Canto XV of the *Inferno* (Brunetto Latini) is a working up of the emotion evident in the situation; but the effect, though single as that of any work of art, is obtained by considerable complexity of detail. The last quatrain gives an image, a feeling attaching to an image, which "came," which did not develop simply out of what precedes, but which was probably in suspension in the poet's mind until the proper combination arrived for it to add itself to.[7] The poet's mind is in fact a receptacle for seizing and

---

5. Eliot apparently means "made into filaments."
6. Official government publication.
7. He [Brunetto Latini] turned then, and he seemed, / across that plain, like one of those who run / for the green cloth at Verona; and of those, / more like the one who wins, than those who lose (*Inferno*, 15.119–122).

storing up numberless feelings, phrases, images, which remain there until all the particles which can unite to form a new compound are present together.

If you compare several representative passages of the greatest poetry you see how great is the variety of types of combination, and also how completely any semi-ethical criterion of "sublimity" misses the mark. For it is not the "greatness," the intensity, of the emotions, the components, but the intensity of the artistic process, the pressure, so to speak, under which the fusion takes place, that counts. The episode of Paolo and Francesca employs a definite emotion, but the intensity of the poetry is something quite different from whatever intensity in the supposed experience it may give the impression of. It is no more intense, furthermore, than Canto XXVI, the voyage of Ulysses, which has not the direct dependence upon an emotion.[8] Great variety is possible in the process of transmutation of emotion: the murder of Agamemnon,[9] or the agony of Othello, gives an artistic effect apparently closer to a possible original than the scenes from Dante. In the *Agamemnon*, the artistic emotion approximates to the emotion of an actual spectator; in *Othello* to the emotion of the protagonist himself. But the difference between art and the event is always absolute; the combination which is the murder of Agamemnon is probably as complex as that which is the voyage of Ulysses. In either case there has been a fusion of elements. The ode of Keats contains a number of feelings which have nothing particular to do with the nightingale, but which the nightingale, partly, perhaps, because of its attractive name, and partly because of its reputation, served to bring together.

The point of view which I am struggling to attack is perhaps related to the metaphysical theory of the substantial unity of the soul: for my meaning is, that the poet has, not a "personality" to express, but a particular medium, which is only a medium and not a personality, in which impressions and experiences combine in peculiar and unexpected ways. Impressions and experiences which are important for the man may take no place in the poetry, and those which become important in the poetry may play quite a negligible part in the man, the personality.

I will quote a passage which is unfamiliar enough to be regarded with fresh attention in the light—or darkness—of these observations:

> And now methinks I could e'en chide myself
> For doating on her beauty, though her death
> Shall be revenged after no common action.
> Does the silkworm expend her yellow labours
> For thee? For thee does she undo herself?
> Are lordships sold to maintain ladyships
> For the poor benefit of a bewildering minute?
> Why does yon fellow falsify highways,
> And put his life between the judge's lips,
> To refine such a thing—keeps horse and men
> To beat their valours for her? . . . [1]

In this passage (as is evident if it is taken in its context) there is a combination of positive and negative emotions: an intensely strong attraction toward beauty and an equal-

---

8. Dante's *Inferno*, Canto 5, tells the story of the lovers Paolo and Francesca; Canto 26 tells of the suffering of Ulysses in hell.

9. In Aeschylus's drama *Agamemnon*, Clytemnestra kills her husband Agamemnon for having sacrificed her daughter, Iphigenia, to the goddess Artemis.

1. From Cyril Tourneur's *The Revenger's Tragedy* (1607), 3.4; the speaker is addressing the skull of his former beloved, murdered after she refused to respond to an evil duke's advances. The revenger will make up the skull to look alive, putting poison on its lips; the evil Duke then dies when he kisses this supposed maiden in a dusky garden.

ly intense fascination by the ugliness which is contrasted with it and which destroys it. This balance of contrasted emotion is in the dramatic situation to which the speech is pertinent, but that situation alone is inadequate to it. This is, so to speak, the structural emotion, provided by the drama. But the whole effect, the dominant tone, is due to the fact that a number of floating feelings, having an affinity to this emotion by no means superficially evident, have combined with it to give us a new art emotion.

It is not in his personal emotions, the emotions provoked by particular events in his life, that the poet is in any way remarkable or interesting. His particular emotions may be simple, or crude, or flat. The emotion in his poetry will be a very complex thing, but not with the complexity of the emotions of people who have very complex or unusual emotions in life. One error, in fact, of eccentricity in poetry is to seek for new human emotions to express; and in this search for novelty in the wrong place it discovers the perverse. The business of the poet is not to find new emotions, but to use the ordinary ones and, in working them up into poetry, to express feelings which are not in actual emotions at all. And emotions which he has never experienced will serve his turn as well as those familiar to him. Consequently, we must believe that "emotion recollected in tranquillity"[2] is an inexact formula. For it is neither emotion, nor recollection, nor, without distortion of meaning, tranquillity. It is a concentration, and a new thing resulting from the concentration, of a very great number of experiences which to the practical and active person would not seem to be experiences at all; it is a concentration which does not happen consciously or of deliberation. These experiences are not "recollected," and they finally unite in an atmosphere which is "tranquil" only in that it is a passive attending upon the event. Of course this is not quite the whole story. There is a great deal, in the writing of poetry, which must be conscious and deliberate. In fact, the bad poet is usually unconscious where he ought to be conscious, and conscious where he ought to be unconscious. Both errors tend to make him "personal." Poetry is not a turning loose of emotion, but an escape from emotion; it is not the expression of personality, but an escape from personality. But, of course, only those who have personality and emotions know what it means to want to escape from these things.

3

ὁ δὲ νοῦς ἴσως θειότερον τι καὶ ἀπαθές ἐστιν.[3]

This essay proposes to halt at the frontier of metaphysics or mysticism, and confine itself to such practical conclusions as can be applied by the responsible person interested in poetry. To divert interest from the poet to the poetry is a laudable aim: for it would conduce to a juster estimation of actual poetry, good and bad. There are many people who appreciate the expression of sincere emotion in verse, and there is a smaller number of people who can appreciate technical excellence. But very few know when there is an expression of *significant* emotion, emotion which has its life in the poem and not in the history of the poet. The emotion of art is impersonal. And the poet cannot reach this impersonality without surrendering himself wholly to the work to be done. And he is not likely to know what is to be done unless he lives in what is not merely the present, but the present moment of the past, unless he is conscious, not of what is dead, but of what is already living.

---

2. This is Wordsworth's famous description of poetry in the Preface to *Lyrical Ballads*; see page 1538.

3. The mind is doubtless something more divine and unimpressionable (From Aristotle's *De Anima* [*On the Soul*]).

Virginia Woolf
1882–1941

Virginia Woolf is the foremost woman writer of the twentieth century, writing in any language; within British literature, Woolf is in the company of James Joyce, T. S. Eliot, William Butler Yeats and few others as a major author, of whatever gender. To take account of the transformations in modern English literature—in language, in style, and in substance—requires reckoning with Virginia Woolf, one of the chief architects of literary modernism. By 1962 Edward Albee could sardonically title a play *Who's Afraid of Virginia Woolf?*, knowing that her name would signify the greatness of modern literature. Woolf wrote luminous and intricate novels, two pivotal books on sexual politics, society, and war, several volumes of short stories and collected essays, reviews and pamphlets, and thirty volumes of a remarkable diary. Woolf was a woman of letters in an almost old-fashioned sense, one of the century's subtlest observers of social and psychic life, and a hauntingly beautiful prose writer.

Woolf's writing career began in childhood but was officially launched in 1915 with the publication of her first novel, *The Voyage Out*, when she was thirty-three. *The Voyage Out* was an emblematic beginning for her public career as a novelist, with its title suggesting the need to venture forth, to make a voyage into the world and out of the imprisonments of life and language. This novel paid special homage to *Heart of Darkness*, Joseph Conrad's story of a voyage through Africa that uncovers the heart of Europe's imperial encounter with the African continent and its exploited people. The theme resonated for Woolf throughout her books, because she too concentrated on the costs—both social and personal—of attempting to gain freedom. With the exception of *Orlando* (1928), a playful and flamboyant novel with a few scenes set in Turkey and Russia, Woolf was never again to set a novel outside the geographical confines of England. Voyaging out had become a matter of voyaging within. Woolf does not turn away from the larger world; she sets that larger world and its history squarely in England.

Woolf's own roots went deep in Victorian literary culture. She was born in 1882 into a privileged and illustrious British professional family with connections to the world of letters on both sides. She was the third child of the marriage of Leslie Stephen and Julia Duckworth, both of whom had been widowed; Leslie Stephen had married a daughter of the novelist William Thackeray, and Julia had been the wife of a publisher, and was connected to a long line of judges, teachers, and magistrates. Woolf's father, eventually to become Sir Leslie, was a prominent editor and a striving philosopher, who was appointed president of the London Library. His fame was to come not from his philosophical work but from his massive *Dictionary of National Biography*, a book that placed, and ranked, the leading figures of British national life for many centuries. Woolf's *Orlando*, with its subtitle: *A Biography*, spoofed the entire enterprise of the biography of great men by having *her* great man, Orlando, unexpectedly turn into a woman halfway through the novel.

Woolf grew up as an intensely literary child, surrounded by her father's project of arbitrating the greatness of the (mostly) men of letters she nonetheless sought to emulate. Her mother Julia was a famed beauty, whose magical grace was captured in the photographs of her equally famous relative, the photographer Julia Margaret Cameron. Woolf was to provide a haunting portrait of both her mother and father in her novel *To the Lighthouse* (1927), where the beautiful and consummately maternal Mrs. Ramsay ministers to her irascible and intellectually tormented philosopher husband, Mr. Ramsay, until her sudden death deprives the family and its circle of friends of their ballast in life. Julia Stephen's premature death in 1895 had cast just such a pall over her own family, especially over thirteen-year-old Virginia, who had a mental breakdown. Breakdowns would recur at intervals throughout her life.

The death-haunted life characteristic of the Victorian family was Virginia Woolf's own experience. Two years after Julia died, Woolf's beloved half-sister and mother substitute, Stel-

Virginia Woolf and T. S. Eliot.

la Duckworth, died in childbirth at the age of twenty-seven. Woolf was also to lose her diffi-cult but immensely loved father in 1904 (not so coincidentally, the same year Virginia was to publish her first essay and review), and her brother Thoby died of typhoid contracted on a trip to Greece with her in 1906. The novel *Jacob's Room* (1922) deals with a young man named Jacob and his college room, as perceived by his sister after his death in World War I. The items in Jacob's room are cloaked in memory and live in the consciousness of the sister as far more than precious objects—memory infuses them with shared life. The dead return again and again in Woolf's imagination and in her imaginative work; her development of the "moment of con-sciousness" in her writing, her novels' concentration on the binding powers of memory, and her invocation of the spreading, intertwining branches of human relations persisting even after death, may be the effect of her painful tutelage in loss.

As an upper-class woman, Woolf and her sisters were not given a formal education, while Thoby and Adrian both went to fine schools and ultimately to university. The sense of having been deliberately shut out of education by virtue of her sex, was to inflect all of Woolf's writ-ing and thinking. Education is a pervasive issue in her novels, and an enormous issue in her essays on social and political life, *A Room of One's Own* (1929) and *Three Guineas* (1938). Woolf became an autodidact, steeping herself in English literature, history, political theory, and art history, but she never lost the keen anguish nor the self-doubt occasioned by the closed doors of the academy to women. Education became for Woolf perhaps the key to transforming the role and the perception of women in society, and writing became her own mode of entry into the public world.

In 1912, Virginia Stephens married Leonard Woolf, like herself a member of the Bloomsbury group, but unlike her in being a Jew and coming from a commercial and far less illustrious family. Leonard Woolf was an "outsider" in anti-Semitic Britain no less than Virginia, who as a great woman writer was equally outside the norm. An accomplished writer in his own right, a political theorist and an activist in socialist issues and in anti-imperialist causes, Leonard Woolf devoted himself to Virginia and to her writing career. They established and ran the Hogarth Press together, an imprint that was to publish all of Virginia's books, as well as many important works of poetry, prose, and criticism from others. Virginia Woolf's erotic and emotional ties to women, and, in particular, her romance with Vita Sackville-West, while not necessarily explicity sexual—no one seems to know for a certainty—were indubitably of the greatest importance to her life. Despite this, she placed Leonard Woolf and their marriage at the center of her being, and their rich and complex partnership weathered Virginia's numerous mental breakdowns. When she felt another episode of depression overtaking her in 1941, it was partly her reluctance to subject Leonard to what she saw as the burden of her madness which tragically led her to drown herself in the river near their home and their beloved press.

Woolf's themes and techniques are all seen in the two stories included here. *Mrs Dalloway in Bond Street* (1923) is a story that became the germ of Woolf's great novel *Mrs Dalloway* (1925). For this story she returned to a character she had created in *The Voyage Out*, where Clarissa Dalloway appeared as the wife of Richard Dalloway, a diplomat. In recounting Clarissa Dalloway's excursion to fashionable Bond Street for a pair of gloves, Woolf uses a "stream of consciousness" technique that places the reader inside Clarissa's mind, showing how the modulations of thoughts can turn the simplest events into occasions for reflection on a host of themes: the changes wrought by the passage of time; the persisting effects of the First World War; the complex relations between men and women, middle-class people and servants, modern literature and its predecessors. This story is followed by *The Lady in the Looking-Glass: A Reflection* (1929), whose major characters are the lady of the title—and her drawing-room. "Examine for a moment an ordinary mind on an ordinary day," Woolf wrote in an essay on *Modern Fiction* in 1925:

> The mind receives a myriad impressions—trivial, fantastic, evanescent, or engraved with the sharpness of steel. From all sides they come, an incessant shower of innumerable atoms; and, as they fall, as they shape themselves into the life of Monday or Tuesday, the accent falls differently from of old; the moment of importance came not here but there; so that, if a writer were a free man and not a slave, if he could write what he chose, not what he must, if he could base his work upon his own feeling and not upon convention, there would be no plot, no comedy, no tragedy, no love interest or catastrophe in the accepted style, and perhaps not a single button sewn on as the Bond Street tailors would have it.

Woolf's stories are written out of her own painfully won freedom of observation; the passages that follow from *A Room of One's Own* and *Three Guineas* meditate on the ways in which society and even human character would have to change in order for such freedom to spread.

Mrs Dalloway in Bond Street

Mrs Dalloway said she would buy the gloves herself. Big Ben was striking as she stepped out into the street. It was eleven o'clock and the unused hour was fresh as if issued to children on a beach. But there was something solemn in the deliberate swing of the repeated strokes; something stirring in the murmur of wheels and the shuffle of footsteps.

No doubt they were not all bound on errands of happiness. There is much more to be said about us than that we walk the streets of Westminster.[1] Big Ben too is nothing but steel rods consumed by rust were it not for the care of H.M's Office of Works. Only for Mrs Dalloway the moment was complete; for Mrs Dalloway June was fresh. A happy childhood—and it was not to his daughters only that Justin Parry had seemed a fine fellow (weak of course on the Bench); flowers at evening, smoke rising; the caw of rooks falling from ever so high, down down through the October air— there is nothing to take the place of childhood. A leaf of mint brings it back: or a cup with a blue ring.

Poor little wretches, she sighed, and pressed forward. Oh, right under the horses' noses, you little demon! and there she was left on the kerb stretching her hand out, while Jimmy Dawes grinned on the further side.

A charming woman, posed, eager, strangely white-haired for her pink cheeks, so Scope Purvis, C.B., saw her as he hurried to his office. She stiffened a little, waiting for Durtnall's van to pass. Big Ben struck the tenth; struck the eleventh stroke. The leaden circles dissolved in the air. Pride held her erect, inheriting, handing on, acquainted with discipline and with suffering. How people suffered, how they suf- fered, she thought, thinking of Mrs Foxcroft at the Embassy last night decked with jewels, eating her heart out, because that nice boy was dead, and now the old Manor House (Durtnall's van passed) must go to a cousin.

"Good morning to you," said Hugh Whitbread raising his hat rather extrava- gantly by the china shop, for they had known each other as children. "Where are you off to?"

"I love walking in London," said Mrs Dalloway. "Really it's better than walking in the country!"

"We've just come up," said Hugh Whitbread. "Unfortunately to see doctors."

"Milly?" said Mrs Dalloway, instantly compassionate.

"Out of sorts," said Hugh Whitbread. "That sort of thing. Dick all right?"

"First rate!" said Clarissa.

Of course, she thought, walking on, Milly is about my age—fifty—fifty-two. So it is probably *that*. Hugh's manner had said so, said it perfectly—dear old Hugh, thought Mrs Dalloway, remembering with amusement, with gratitude, with emotion, how shy, like a brother—one would rather die than speak to one's brother—Hugh had always been, when he was at Oxford, and came over, and perhaps one of them (drat the thing!) couldn't ride. How then could women sit in Parliament? How could they do things with men? For there is this extraordinarily deep instinct, something inside one; you can't get over it; it's no use trying; and men like Hugh respect it with- out our saying it, which is what one loves, thought Clarissa, in dear old Hugh.

She had passed through the Admiralty Arch and saw at the end of the empty road with its thin trees Victoria's white mound, Victoria's billowing motherliness, amplitude and homeliness, always ridiculous, yet how sublime thought Mrs Dal- loway, remembering Kensington Gardens and the old lady in horn spectacles and being told by Nanny to stop dead still and bow to the Queen. The flag flew above the Palace. The King and Queen were back then. Dick had met her at lunch the other day—a thoroughly nice woman. It matters so much to the poor, thought Clarissa, and to the soldiers. A man in bronze stood heroically on a pedestal with a gun on her

---

1. District of central London, including the Houses of Parliament (with their famous clock tower "Big Ben"); it is also a fashionable residential area.

View of Regent Street, London, 1927.

left hand side—the South African war. It matters, thought Mrs Dalloway walking towards Buckingham Palace. There it stood four-square, in the broad sunshine, uncompromising, plain. But it was character she thought; something inborn in the race; what Indians respected. The Queen went to hospitals, opened bazaars—the Queen of England, thought Clarissa, looking at the Palace. Already at this hour a motor car passed out at the gates; soldiers saluted; the gates were shut. And Clarissa, crossing the road, entered the Park, holding herself upright.

June had drawn out every leaf on the trees. The mothers of Westminster with mottled breasts gave suck to their young. Quite respectable girls lay stretched on the grass. An elderly man, stooping very stiffly, picked up a crumpled paper, spread it out flat and flung it away. How horrible! Last night at the Embassy Sir Dighton had said, "If I want a fellow to hold my horse, I have only to put up my hand." But the religious question is far more serious than the economic, Sir Dighton had said, which she thought extraordinarily interesting, from a man like Sir Dighton. "Oh, the country will never know what it has lost," he had said, talking, of his own accord, about dear Jack Stewart.

She mounted the little hill lightly. The air stirred with energy. Messages were passing from the Fleet to the Admiralty. Piccadilly and Arlington Street and the Mall seemed to chafe the very air in the Park and lift its leaves hotly, brilliantly, upon waves of that divine vitality which Clarissa loved. To ride; to dance; she had adored all that. Or going on long walks in the country, talking, about books, what to do with one's life, for young people were amazingly priggish—oh, the things one had said! But one had conviction. Middle age is the devil. People like Jack'll never know that, she thought; for he never once thought of death, never, they said, knew he was dying. And now can never mourn—how did it go?—a head grown grey. . . . From the contagion of the world's slow stain. . . . Have drunk their cup a round or two before. . . . From the contagion of the world's slow stain![2] She held herself upright.

But how Jack would have shouted! Quoting Shelley, in Piccadilly! "You want a pin," he would have said. He hated frumps. "My God Clarissa! My God Clarissa!"— she could hear him now at the Devonshire House party, about poor Sylvia Hunt in her amber necklace and that dowdy old silk. Clarissa held herself upright for she had spoken aloud and now she was in Piccadilly, passing the house with the slender green columns, and the balconies; passing club windows full of newspapers; passing old Lady Burdett Coutt's house where the glazed white parrot used to hang; and Devonshire House, without its gilt leopards; and Claridge's, where she must remember Dick wanted her to leave a card on Mrs Jepson or she would be gone. Rich Americans can be very charming. There was St James's Palace; like a child's game with bricks; and now—she had passed Bond Street—she was by Hatchard's book shop. The stream was endless—endless—endless. Lords, Ascot, Hurlingham[3]—what was it? What a duck, she thought, looking at the frontispiece of some book of memoirs spread wide in the bow window, Sir Joshua perhaps or Romney; arch, bright, demure; the sort of girl—like her own Elizabeth—the only *real* sort of girl. And there was that absurd book, *Soapy Sponge*, which Jum used to quote by the yard; and Shakespeare's Sonnets. She knew them by heart. Phil and she had argued all day about the Dark Lady, and Dick had said straight out at dinner that night that he had never heard of her. Really, she had married him for that! He had never read Shakespeare! There must be some little cheap book she could buy for Milly—*Cranford*[4] of course! Was there ever anything so enchanting as the cow in petticoats? If only people had that sort of humour, that sort of self-respect now, thought Clarissa, for she remembered the broad pages; the sentences ending; the characters—how one talked about them as if they were real. For all the great things one must go to the past, she thought. From the contagion of the world's slow stain. . . . Fear no more the heat o' the sun. . . . And now can never mourn, can never mourn, she repeated, her eyes straying over the window; for it ran in her head; the test of great poetry; the moderns had never written anything one wanted to read about death, she thought; and turned.

Omnibuses joined motor cars; motor cars vans; vans taxicabs; taxicabs motor cars—here was an open motor car with a girl, alone. Up till four, her feet tingling, I know, thought Clarissa, for the girl looked washed out, half asleep, in the corner of the car after the dance. And another car came; and another. No! No! No! Clarissa smiled good-naturedly. The fat lady had taken every sort of trouble, but diamonds! orchids! at this hour of the morning! No! No! No! The excellent policeman would, when the time came, hold up his hand. Another motor car passed. How utterly unattractive! Why should a girl of that age paint black round her eyes? And a young man with a girl, at this hour, when the country—The admirable policeman raised his hand and Clarissa acknowledging his sway, taking her time, crossed, walked towards Bond Street; saw the narrow crooked street, the yellow banners; the thick notched telegraph wires stretched across the sky.

2. From *Adonais* (stanza 40), Percy Shelley's elegy on the early death of Keats.

3. Locations of fashionable sporting events (cricket, horse racing, and polo).

4. Popular novel by Elizabeth Gaskell (1810–1865); see page 1987.

A hundred years ago her great-great-grandfather, Seymour Parry, who ran away with Conway's daughter, had walked down Bond Street. Down Bond Street the Parrys had walked for a hundred years, and might have met the Dalloways (Leighs on the mother's side) going up. Her father got his clothes from Hill's. There was a roll of cloth in the window, and here just one jar on a black table, incredibly expensive; like the thick pink salmon on the ice block at the fishmonger's. The jewels were exquisite—pink and orange stars, paste, Spanish, she thought, and chains of old gold; starry buckles, little brooches which had been worn on sea-green satin by ladies with high head-dresses. But no looking! One must economise. She must go on past the picture dealer's where one of the odd French pictures hung, as if people had thrown confetti—pink and blue—for a joke. If you had lived with pictures (and it's the same with books and music) thought Clarissa, passing the Aeolian Hall, you can't be taken in by a joke.

The river of Bond Street was clogged. There, like a queen at a tournament, raised, regal, was Lady Bexborough. She sat in her carriage, upright, alone, looking through her glasses. The white glove was loose at her wrist. She was in black, quite shabby, yet, thought Clarissa, how extraordinarily it tells, breeding, self-respect, never saying a word too much or letting people gossip; an astonishing friend; no one can pick a hole in her after all these years, and now, there she is, thought Clarissa, passing the Countess who waited powdered, perfectly still, and Clarissa would have given anything to be like that, the mistress of Clarefield, talking politics, like a man. But she never goes anywhere, thought Clarissa, and it's quite useless to ask her, and the carriage went on and Lady Bexborough was borne past like a queen at a tournament, though she had nothing to live for and the old man is failing and they say she is sick of it all, thought Clarissa and the tears actually rose to her eyes as she entered the shop.

"Good morning," said Clarissa in her charming voice. "Gloves," she said with her exquisite friendliness and putting her bag on the counter began, very slowly, to undo the buttons. "White gloves," she said. "Above the elbow," and she looked straight into the shopwoman's face—but this was not the girl she remembered? She looked quite old. "These really don't fit," said Clarissa. The shop-girl looked at them. "Madame wears bracelets?" Clarissa spread out her fingers. "Perhaps it's my rings," And the girl took the grey gloves with her to the end of the counter.

Yes, thought Clarissa, it's the girl I remember, she's twenty years older. . . . There was only one other customer, sitting sideways at the counter, her elbow poised, her bare hand drooping vacant; like a figure on a Japanese fan, thought Clarissa, too vacant perhaps, yet some men would adore her. The lady shook her head sadly. Again the gloves were too large. She turned round the glass. "Above the wrist," she reproached the grey-headed woman, who looked and agreed.

They waited; a clock ticked; Bond Street hummed, dulled, distant; the woman went away holding gloves. "Above the wrist," said the lady, mournfully, raising her voice. And she would have to order chairs, ices, flowers, and cloakroom tickets, thought Clarissa. The people she didn't want would come; the others wouldn't. She would stand by the door. They sold stockings—silk stockings. A lady is known by her gloves and her shoes, old Uncle William used to say. And through the hanging silk stockings, quivering silver she looked at the lady, sloping shouldered, her hand drooping, her bag slipping, her eyes vacantly on the floor. It would be intolerable if dowdy women came to her party! Would one have liked Keats if he had worn red socks? Oh, at last—she drew into the counter and it flashed into her mind:

"Do you remember before the war you had gloves with pearl buttons?"

"French gloves, Madame?"

"Yes, they were French," said Clarissa. The other lady rose very sadly and took her bag, and looked at the gloves on the counter. But they were all too large—always too large at the wrist.

"With pearl buttons," said the shop-girl, who looked ever so much older. She split the lengths of tissue paper apart on the counter. With pearl buttons, thought Clarissa, perfectly simple—how French!

"Madame's hands are so slender," said the shop-girl, drawing the glove firmly, smoothly, down over her rings. And Clarissa looked at her arm in the looking-glass. The glove hardly came to the elbow. Were there others half an inch longer? Still it seemed tiresome to bother her—perhaps the one day in the month, thought Clarissa, when it's an agony to stand. "Oh, don't bother," she said. But the gloves were brought.

"Don't you get fearfully tired," she said in her charming voice, "standing? When d'you get your holiday?"

"In September, Madame, when we're not so busy."

When we're in the country thought Clarissa. Or shooting. She has a fortnight at Brighton. In some stuffy lodging. The landlady takes the sugar. Nothing would be easier than to send her to Mrs Lumley's right in the country (and it was on the tip of her tongue). But then she remembered how on their honeymoon Dick had shown her the folly of giving impulsively. It was much more important, he said, to get trade with China. Of course he was right. And she could feel the girl wouldn't like to be given things. There she was in her place. So was Dick. Selling gloves was her job. She had her own sorrows quite separate, "and now can never mourn, can never mourn," the words ran in her head, "From the contagion of the world's slow stain," thought Clarissa holding her arm stiff, for there are moments when it seems utterly futile (the glove was drawn off leaving her arm flecked with powder)—simply one doesn't believe, thought Clarissa, any more in God.

The traffic suddenly roared; the silk stockings brightened. A customer came in.

"White gloves," she said, with some ring in her voice that Clarissa remembered.

It used, thought Clarissa, to be so simple. Down, down through the air came the caw of the rooks. When Sylvia died, hundreds of years ago, the yew hedges looked so lovely with the diamond webs in the mist before early church. But if Dick were to die to-morrow? As for believing in God—no, she would let the children choose, but for herself, like Lady Bexborough, who opened the bazaar, they say, with the telegram in her hand—Roden, her favourite, killed—she would go on. But why, if one doesn't believe? For the sake of others, she thought taking the glove in her hand. The girl would be much more unhappy if she didn't believe.

"Thirty shillings," said the shop-woman. "No, pardon me Madame, thirty-five. The French gloves are more."

For one doesn't live for oneself, thought Clarissa.

And then the other customer took a glove, tugged it, and it split.

"There!" she exclaimed.

"A fault of the skin," said the grey-headed woman hurriedly. "Sometimes a drop of acid in tanning. Try this pair, Madame."

"But it's an awful swindle to ask two pound ten!"

Clarissa looked at the lady; the lady looked at Clarissa.

"Gloves have never been quite so reliable since the war," said the shop-girl, apologising, to Clarissa.

But where had she seen the other lady?—elderly, with a frill under her chin; wearing a black ribbon for gold eyeglasses; sensual, clever, like a Sargent drawing. How one can tell from a voice when people are in the habit, thought Clarissa, of making other people—"It's a shade too tight," she said—obey. The shop-woman went off again. Clarissa was left waiting. Fear no more she repeated, playing her finger on the counter. Fear no more the heat o' the sun. Fear no more she repeated. There were little brown spots on her arm. And the girl crawled like a snail. Thou thy wordly task hast done. Thousands of young men had died that things might go on. At last! Half an inch above the elbow; pearl buttons; five and a quarter. My dear slow-coach, thought Clarissa, do you think I can sit here the whole morning? Now you'll take twenty-five minutes to bring me my change!

There was a violent explosion in the street outside. The shop-women cowered behind the counters. But Clarissa, sitting very upright, smiled at the other lady. "Miss Anstruther!" she exclaimed.

The Lady in the Looking-Glass: A Reflection[1]

People should not leave looking-glasses hanging in their rooms any more than they should leave open cheque books or letters confessing some hideous crime. One could not help looking, that summer afternoon, in the long glass that hung outside in the hall. Chance had so arranged it. From the depths of the sofa in the drawing-room one could see reflected in the Italian glass not only the marble-topped table opposite, but a stretch of the garden beyond. One could see a long grass path leading between banks of tall flowers until, slicing off an angle, the gold rim cut it off.

The house was empty, and one felt, since one was the only person in the drawing-room, like one of those naturalists who, covered with grass and leaves, lie watching the shyest animals—badgers, otters, kingfishers—moving about freely, themselves unseen. The room that afternoon was full of such shy creatures, lights and shadows, curtains blowing, petals falling—things that never happen, so it seems, if someone is looking. The quiet old country room with its rugs and stone chimney pieces, its sunken book-cases and red and gold lacquer cabinets, was full of such nocturnal creatures. They came pirouetting across the floor, stepping delicately with high-lifted feet and spread tails and pecking allusive beaks as if they had been cranes or flocks of elegant flamingoes whose pink was faded, or peacocks whose trains were veined with silver. And there were obscure flushes and darkenings too, as if a cuttle-fish had suddenly suffused the air with purple; and the room had its passions and rages and envies and sorrows coming over it and clouding it, like a human being. Nothing stayed the same for two seconds together.

But, outside, the looking-glass reflected the hall table, the sunflowers, the garden path so accurately and so fixedly that they seemed held there in their reality unescapably. It was a strange contrast—all changing here, all stillness there. One could not help looking from one to the other. Meanwhile, since all the doors and windows were open in the heat, there was a perpetual sighing and ceasing sound, the voice of the transient and the perishing, it seemed, coming and going like human breath, while in the looking-glass things had ceased to breathe and lay still in the trance of immortality.

Half an hour ago the mistress of the house, Isabella Tyson, had gone down the grass path in her thin summer dress, carrying a basket, and had vanished, sliced off by

1. Published in *Harper's Magazine*, December 1929.

the gilt rim of the looking-glass. She had gone presumably into the lower garden to pick flowers; or as it seemed more natural to suppose, to pick something light and fantastic and leafy and trailing, traveller's joy, or one of those elegant sprays of convolvulus that twine round ugly walls and burst here and there into white and violet blossoms. She suggested the fantastic and the tremulous convolvulus rather than the upright aster, the starched zinnia, or her own burning roses alight like lamps on the straight posts of their rose trees. The comparison showed how very little, after all these years, one knew about her; for it is impossible that any woman of flesh and blood of fifty-five or sixty should be really a wreath or a tendril. Such comparisons are worse than idle and superficial—they are cruel even, for they come like the convolvulus itself trembling between one's eyes and the truth. There must be truth; there must be a wall. Yet it was strange that after knowing her all these years one could not say what the truth about Isabella was; one still made up phrases like this about convolvulus and traveller's joy. As for facts, it was a fact that she was a spinster; that she was rich; that she had bought this house and collected with her own hands—often in the most obscure corners of the world and at great risk from poisonous stings and Oriental diseases—the rugs, the chairs, the cabinets which now lived their nocturnal life before one's eyes. Sometimes it seemed as if they knew more about her than we, who sat on them, wrote at them, and trod on them so carefully, were allowed to know. In each of these cabinets were many little drawers, and each almost certainly held letters, tied with bows of ribbon, sprinkled with sticks of lavender or rose leaves. For it was another fact—if facts were what one wanted—that Isabella had known many people, had had many friends; and thus if one had the audacity to open a drawer and read her letters, one would find the traces of many agitations, of appointments to meet, of upbraidings for not having met, long letters of intimacy and affection, violent letters of jealousy and reproach, terrible final words of parting—for all those interviews and assignations had led to nothing—that is, she had never married, and yet, judging from the mask-like indifference of her face, she had gone through twenty times more of passion and experience than those whose loves are trumpeted forth for all the world to hear. Under the stress of thinking about Isabella, her room became more shadowy and symbolic; the corners seemed darker, the legs of chairs and tables more spindly and hieroglyphic.

Suddenly these reflections were ended violently and yet without a sound. A large black form loomed into the looking-glass; blotted out everything, strewed the table with a packet of marble tablets veined with pink and grey, and was gone. But the picture was entirely altered. For the moment it was unrecognisable and irrational and entirely out of focus. One could not relate these tablets to any human purpose. And then by degrees some logical process set to work on them and began ordering and arranging them and bringing them into the fold of common experience. One realised at last that they were merely letters. The man had brought the post.

There they lay on the marble-topped table, all dripping with light and colour at first and crude and unabsorbed. And then it was strange to see how they were drawn in and arranged and composed and made part of the picture and granted that stillness and immortality which the looking-glass conferred. They lay there invested with a new reality and significance and with a greater heaviness, too, as if it would have needed a chisel to dislodge them from the table. And, whether it was fancy or not, they seemed to have become not merely a handful of casual letters but to be tablets graven with eternal truth—if one could read them, one would know everything there was to be known about Isabella, yes, and about life, too. The pages inside those marble-looking envelopes must be cut deep and scored thick with meaning. Isabella would come in, and take them, one by one, very slowly, and open them, and read them carefully word by word, and then with a profound sigh of comprehension, as if she had seen to the bottom of everything, she would tear the envelopes to little bits and tie the letters together and lock the cabinet drawer in her determination to conceal what she did not wish to be known.

The thought served as a challenge. Isabella did not wish to be known—but she should no longer escape. It was absurd, it was monstrous. If she concealed so much and knew so much one must prize her open with the first tool that came to hand— the imagination. One must fix one's mind upon her at that very moment. One must fasten her down there. One must refuse to be put off any longer with sayings and doings such as the moment brought forth—with dinners and visits and polite conversations. One must put oneself in her shoes. If one took the phrase literally, it was easy to see the shoes in which she stood, down in the lower garden, at this moment. They were very narrow and long and fashionable—they were made of the softest and most flexible leather. Like everything she wore, they were exquisite. And she would be standing under the high hedge in the lower part of the garden, raising the scissors that were tied to her waist to cut some dead flower, some overgrown branch. The sun would beat down on her face, into her eyes; but no, at the critical moment a veil of cloud covered the sun, making the expression of her eyes doubtful—was it mocking or tender, brilliant or dull? One could only see the indeterminate outline of her rather faded, fine face looking at the sky. She was thinking, perhaps, that she must order a new net for the strawberries; that she must send flowers to Johnson's widow; that it was time she drove over to see the Hippesleys in their new house. Those were the things she talked about at dinner certainly. But one was tired of the things that she talked about at dinner. It was her profounder state of being that one wanted to catch and turn to words, the state that is to the mind what breathing is to the body, what one calls happiness or unhappiness. At the mention of those words it became obvious, surely, that she must be happy. She was rich; she was distinguished; she had many friends; she travelled—she bought rugs in Turkey and blue pots in Persia. Avenues of pleasure radiated this way and that from where she stood with her scissors raised to cut the trembling branches while the lacy clouds veiled her face.

Here with a quick movement of her scissors she snipped the spray of traveller's joy and it fell to the ground. As it fell, surely some light came in too, surely one could penetrate a little farther into her being. Her mind then was filled with tenderness and regret. . . . To cut an overgrown branch saddened her because it had once lived, and life was dear to her. Yes, and at the same time the fall of the branch would suggest to her how she must die herself and all the futility and evanescence of things. And then again quickly catching this thought up, with her instant good sense, she thought life had treated her well; even if fall she must, it was to lie on the earth and moulder sweetly into the roots of violets. So she stood thinking. Without making any thought precise—for she was one of those reticent people whose minds hold their thoughts enmeshed in clouds of silence— she was filled with thoughts. Her mind was like her room, in which lights advanced and retreated, came pirouetting and stepping delicately, spread their tails, pecked their way; and then her whole being was suffused, like the room again, with a cloud of some profound knowledge, some unspoken regret, and then she was full of locked drawers, stuffed with letters, like her cabinets. To talk of "prizing her open" as if she were an oyster, to use any but the finest and subtlest and most pliable tools upon her was impious and absurd. One must imagine—here was she in the looking-glass. It made one start.

She was so far off at first that one could not see her clearly. She came lingering and pausing, here straightening a rose, there lifting a pink to smell it, but she never stopped; and all the time she became larger and larger in the looking-glass, more and more completely the person into whose mind one had been trying to penetrate. One verified her by degrees—fitted the qualities one had discovered into this visible body. There were her grey-green dress, and her long shoes, her basket, and something sparkling at her throat. She came so gradually that she did not seem to derange the pattern in the glass, but only to bring in some new element which gently moved and altered the other objects as if asking them, courteously, to make room for her. And the letters and the table and the grass walk and the sunflowers which had been waiting in the looking-glass separated and opened out so that she might be received among them. At last there she was, in the hall. She stopped dead. She stood by the table. She stood perfectly still. At once the looking-glass began to pour over her a light that seemed to fix her; that seemed like some acid to bite off the unessential and superficial and to leave only the truth. It was an enthralling spectacle. Everything dropped from her—clouds, dress, basket, diamond—all that one had called the creeper and convolvulus. Here was the hard wall beneath. Here was the woman herself. She stood naked in that pitiless light. And, there was nothing. Isabella was perfectly empty. She had no thoughts. She had no friends. She cared for nobody. As for her letters, they were all bills. Look, as she stood there, old and angular, veined and lined, with her high nose and her wrinkled neck, she did not even trouble to open them.

People should not leave looking-glasses hanging in their rooms.

A Room of One's Own

A Room of One's Own is difficult to categorize—it is a long essay, a non-fiction novella, a political pamphlet, and a philosophical discourse all in one. Its effects have not been so difficult to categorize—Virginia Woolf's idiosyncratic text has been recognized as a classic from the time of its publication in 1929. The book was a departure from Woolf's output until then; she was a major literary figure, having already published such key novels as *Jacob's Room*, *Mrs Dalloway*, *To the Lighthouse*, and *Orlando*, and she was an established essayist with a formidable reputation as an arbiter of the literary tradition. One way of characterizing this book is to see that it represents Woolf's scrutiny of her own position as a woman writer, a self-examination of her public position that inevitably became a political document. The focus is not on Woolf's life or her work per se, but rather on the social and psychological conditions that would make such a life generally possible. The book creates a microcosm of such possibility in the "room" of its title; the book itself is a room within which its author contemplates and analyzes the dimensions of social space for women. Woolf recognizes that seemingly neutral social space, the room of cultural agency just as the room of writing, is in truth a gendered space. She directs her political inquiry toward the making and remaking of such rooms.

A *Room of One's Own* comes from established traditions of writing as well. It draws on the conversational tone and novelistic insight of the literary essay as perfected in the nineteenth century by such writers as Charles Lamb—whose *Oxford in the Vacation* was certainly in Woolf's mind when she wrote the opening chapter of her essay. At the same time, Woolf's book joins a lineage of feminist political philosophy, whose most eloquent exponent prior to Woolf herself was Mary Wollstonecraft, who joined the rhetorical ranks of Rousseau and John Stuart Mill with the publication of *A Vindication of the Rights of Woman*, her passionately reasoned exhortation for the equal and universal human rights of women. (Selections from Wollstonecraft's *Vindication* can be found on page 1471.) The century and a half since Wollstonecraft had produced a rich history of feminist agitation and feminist thought. Virginia Woolf draws on this less-known tradition, invoking nineteenth-century figures from the women's movement like Emily Davies,

Josephine Butler, and Octavia Hill. She also places her deliberations in the context of the suffragist movement and its fraught history in Britain. Virginia Woolf was strongly engaged in the debates of the suffrage movement, and its divisions over radical action or more conciliatory political approaches. Much of Woolf's long essay is devoted to demonstrating the subversive quality of occupying the blank page, and wielding the printed word.

As politically motivated as *A Room of One's Own* is, it is equally a literary text. Woolf draws on all the intricacies of literary tropes and figures to mount her argument for women's education, women's equality, women's social presence. Not the least of her strategies is her manipulation of the rhetoric of address—in other words, the audience implied by the language of a text. Woolf creates an ironic space, or room, in which she is a playfully ambiguous speaker addressing an uncertain audience: women at the colleges where she has been invited to speak, but also men and women alike who will read her printed text. By doing so, she keeps an ironic tension in play, holding at bay her anger at being censored or silenced by male readers by creating a sense of privacy and secrecy among women. This underscores Woolf's primary argument, the need for autonomy and self-determination. Her modest proposal, although faintly ironic, is also eminently pragmatic—the room of one's own that is her metaphor for the college classroom or the blank canvas or the book's page is at the same time the actual room, paid for and unintruded upon by domestic worries or social codes, whose possession permits a woman to find out who she may be.

from A Room of One's Own
Chapter 1

But, you may say, we asked you to speak about women and fiction—what has that got to do with a room of one's own?[1] I will try to explain. When you asked me to speak about women and fiction I sat down on the banks of a river and began to wonder what the words meant. They might mean simply a few remarks about Fanny Burney; a few more about Jane Austen; a tribute to the Brontës and a sketch of Haworth Parsonage under snow; some witticisms if possible about Miss Mitford; a respectful allusion to George Eliot; a reference to Mrs Gaskell and one would have done.[2] But at second sight the words seemed not so simple. The title women and fiction might mean, and you may have meant it to mean, women and what they are like; or it might mean women and the fiction that they write; or it might mean women and the fiction that is written about them; or it might mean that somehow all three are inextricably mixed together and you want me to consider them in that light. But when I began to consider the subject in this last way, which seemed the most interesting, I soon saw that it had one fatal drawback. I should never be able to come to a conclusion. I should never be able to fulfil what is, I understand, the first duty of a lecturer—to hand you after an hour's discourse a nugget of pure truth to wrap up between the pages of your notebooks and keep on the mantelpiece for ever. All I could do was to offer you an opinion upon one minor point—a woman must have money and a room of her own if she is to write fiction; and that, as you will see, leaves the great problem of the true nature of woman and the true nature of fiction unsolved. I have shirked the duty of coming to a conclusion upon these two questions—women and fiction remain, so far as I am concerned, unsolved problems. But in order to make some amends I am going to do what I can to show you how I arrived at this opinion about the room and the money. I am going to develop in your presence as fully and

---

1. Woolf delivered her essay in a shorter version to meetings first at two women's colleges, Newnham and Girton   College, Cambridge University, in October 1928.
2. Important 19th-century novelists.

freely as I can the train of thought which led me to think this. Perhaps if I lay bare the ideas, the prejudices, that lie behind this statement you will find that they have some bearing upon women and some upon fiction. At any rate, when a subject is highly controversial—and any question about sex is that—one cannot hope to tell the truth. One can only show how one came to hold whatever opinion one does hold. One can only give one's audience the chance of drawing their own conclusions as they observe the limitations, the prejudices, the idiosyncrasies of the speaker. Fiction here is likely to contain more truth than fact. Therefore I propose, making use of all the liberties and licences of a novelist, to tell you the story of the two days that preceded my coming here—how, bowed down by the weight of the subject which you have laid upon my shoulders, I pondered it, and made it work in and out of my daily life. I need not say that what I am about to describe has no existence; Oxbridge is an invention; so is Fernham;[3] "I" is only a convenient term for somebody who has no real being. Lies will flow from my lips, but there may perhaps be some truth mixed up with them; it is for you to seek out this truth and to decide whether any part of it is worth keeping. If not, you will of course throw the whole of it into the wastepaper basket and forget all about it.

Here then was I (call me Mary Beton, Mary Seton, Mary Carmichael[4] or by any name you please—it is not a matter of any importance) sitting on the banks of a river a week or two ago in fine October weather, lost in thought. That collar I have spoken of, women and fiction, the need of coming to some conclusion on a subject that raises all sorts of prejudices and passions, bowed my head to the ground. To the right and left bushes of some sort, golden and crimson, glowed with the colour, even it seemed burnt with the heat, of fire. On the further bank the willows wept in perpetual lamentation, their hair about their shoulders. The river reflected whatever it chose of sky and bridge and burning tree, and when the undergraduate had oared his boat through the reflections they closed again, completely, as if he had never been. There one might have sat the clock round lost in thought. Thought—to call it by a prouder name than it deserved—had let its line down into the stream. It swayed, minute after minute, hither and thither among the reflections and the weeds, letting the water lift it and sink it, until—you know the little tug—the sudden conglomeration of an idea at the end of one's line: and then the cautious hauling of it in, and the careful laying of it out? Alas, laid on the grass how small, how insignificant this thought of mine looked; the sort of fish that a good fisherman puts back into the water so that it may grow fatter and be one day worth cooking and eating. I will not trouble you with that thought now, though if you look carefully you may find it for yourselves in the course of what I am going to say.

But however small it was, it had, nevertheless, the mysterious property of its kind—put back into the mind, it became at once very exciting, and important; and as it darted and sank, and flashed hither and thither, set up such a wash and tumult of ideas that it was impossible to sit still. It was thus that I found myself walking with extreme rapidity across a grass plot. Instantly a man's figure rose to intercept me. Nor did I at first understand that the gesticulations of a curious-looking object, in a cutaway coat and evening shirt, were aimed at me. His face expressed horror and indig-

3. "Oxbridge" was in fact the common slang term for Oxford and Cambridge universities. "Fernham" suggests Newnham College.
4. Three of the four Marys who by tradition were atten-

dants to Mary, Queen of Scots (executed in 1567), and who figure in many Scottish ballads; the fourth was Mary Hamilton.

nation. Instinct rather than reason came to my help; he was a Beadle; I was a woman. This was the turf; there was the path. Only the Fellows and Scholars are allowed here; the gravel is the place for me.[5] Such thoughts were the work of a moment. As I regained the path the arms of the Beadle sank, his face assumed its usual repose, and though turf is better walking than gravel, no very great harm was done. The only charge I could bring against the Fellows and Scholars of whatever the college might happen to be was that in protection of their turf, which has been rolled for 300 years in succession, they had sent my little fish into hiding.

What idea it had been that had sent me so audaciously trespassing I could not now remember. The spirit of peace descended like a cloud from heaven, for if the spirit of peace dwells anywhere, it is in the courts and quadrangles of Oxbridge on a fine October morning. Strolling through those colleges past those ancient halls the roughness of the present seemed smoothed away; the body seemed contained in a miraculous glass cabinet through which no sound could penetrate, and the mind, freed from any contact with facts (unless one trespassed on the turf again), was at liberty to settle down upon whatever meditation was in harmony with the moment. As chance would have it, some stray memory of some old essay about revisiting Oxbridge in the long vacation brought Charles Lamb to mind—Saint Charles, said Thackeray,[6] putting a letter of Lamb's to his forehead. Indeed, among all the dead (I give you my thoughts as they came to me), Lamb is one of the most congenial; one to whom one would have liked to say, Tell me then how you wrote your essays? For his essays are superior even to Max Beerbohm's, I thought, with all their perfection, because of that wild flash of imagination, that lightning crack of genius in the middle of them which leaves them flawed and imperfect, but starred with poetry. Lamb then came to Oxbridge perhaps a hundred years ago. Certainly he wrote an essay—the name escapes me—about the manuscript of one of Milton's poems which he saw here.[7] It was Lycidas perhaps, and Lamb wrote how it shocked him to think it possible that any word in Lycidas could have been different from what it is. To think of Milton changing the words in that poem seemed to him a sort of sacrilege. This led me to remember what I could of Lycidas and to amuse myself with guessing which word it could have been that Milton had altered, and why. It then occurred to me that the very manuscript itself which Lamb had looked at was only a few hundred yards away, so that one could follow Lamb's footsteps across the quadrangle to that famous library where the treasure is kept. Moreover, I recollected, as I put this plan into execution, it is in this famous library that the manuscript of Thackeray's Esmond is also preserved. The critics often say that Esmond is Thackeray's most perfect novel. But the affectation of the style, with its imitation of the eighteenth century, hampers one, so far as I remember; unless indeed the eighteenth-century style was natural to Thackeray—a fact that one might prove by looking at the manuscript and seeing whether the alterations were for the benefit of the style or of the sense. But then one would have to decide what is style and what is meaning, a question which—but here I was actually at the door which leads into the library itself. I must have opened it, for instantly there issued, like a guardian angel barring the way with a flutter of black gown

5. A beadle is a disciplinary officer. The fellows of Oxbridge colleges typically tutor the undergraduates, who are divided into scholars and commoners. The commoners form the majority of the student body.
6. William Makepeace Thackeray (1811–1863), novelist and journalist, Woolf's father's first father-in-law.

7. Lamb's Oxford in the Vacation—describing the locales Lamb himself was too poor to attend in term time. The manuscript of Milton's elegy Lycidas (1638) is in the Wren Library of Trinity College, Cambridge, together with that of Thackeray's novel The History of Henry Esmond (1852).

instead of white wings, a deprecating, silvery, kindly gentleman, who regretted in a low voice as he waved me back that ladies are only admitted to the library if accompanied by a Fellow of the College or furnished with a letter of introduction.

That a famous library has been cursed by a woman is a matter of complete indifference to a famous library. Venerable and calm, with all its treasures safe locked within its breast, it sleeps complacently and will, so far as I am concerned, so sleep for ever. Never will I wake those echoes, never will I ask for that hospitality again, I vowed as I descended the steps in anger. Still an hour remained before luncheon, and what was one to do? Stroll on the meadows? sit by the river? Certainly it was a lovely autumn morning; the leaves were fluttering red to the ground; there was no great hardship in doing either. But the sound of music reached my ear. Some service or celebration was going forward. The organ complained magnificently as I passed the chapel door. Even the sorrow of Christianity sounded in that serene air more like the recollection of sorrow than sorrow itself; even the groanings of the ancient organ seemed lapped in peace. I had no wish to enter had I the right, and this time the verger might have stopped me, demanding perhaps my baptismal certificate, or a letter of introduction from the Dean. But the outside of these magnificent buildings is often as beautiful as the inside. Moreover, it was amusing enough to watch the congregation assembling, coming in and going out again, busying themselves at the door of the chapel like bees at the mouth of a hive. Many were in cap and gown; some had tufts of fur on their shoulders; others were wheeled in bath-chairs; others, though not past middle age, seemed creased and crushed into shapes so singular that one was reminded of those giant crabs and crayfish who heave with difficulty across the sand of an aquarium. As I leant against the wall the University indeed seemed a sanctuary in which are preserved rare types which would soon be obsolete if left to fight for existence on the pavement of the Strand.[8] Old stories of old deans and old dons came back to mind, but before I had summoned up courage to whistle—it used to be said that at the sound of a whistle old Professor ———— instantly broke into a gallop—the venerable congregation had gone inside. The outside of the chapel remained. As you know, its high domes and pinnacles can be seen, like a sailing-ship always voyaging never arriving, lit up at night and visible for miles, far away across the hills. Once, presumably, this quadrangle with its smooth lawns, its massive buildings, and the chapel itself was marsh too, where the grasses waved and the swine rootled. Teams of horses and oxen, I thought, must have hauled the stone in wagons from far countries, and then with infinite labour the grey blocks in whose shade I was now standing were poised in order one on top of another, and then the painters brought their glass for the windows, and the masons were busy for centuries up on that roof with putty and cement, spade and trowel. Every Saturday somebody must have poured gold and silver out of a leathern purse into their ancient fists, for they had their beer and skittles presumably of an evening. An unending stream of gold and silver, I thought, must have flowed into this court perpetually to keep the stones coming and the masons working; to level, to ditch, to dig and to drain. But it was then the age of faith, and money was poured liberally to set these stones on a deep foundation, and when the stones were raised, still more money was poured in from the coffers of kings and queens and great nobles to ensure that hymns should be sung here and scholars taught. Lands were granted; tithes were paid. And when the age of faith was over and the age of reason had come, still the same flow of gold and silver went on; fellowships

8. A thoroughfare in central London.

were founded; lectureships endowed; only the gold and silver flowed now, not from the coffers of the king, but from the chests of merchants and manufacturers, from the purses of men who had made, say, a fortune from industry, and returned, in their wills, a bounteous share of it to endow more chairs, more lectureships, more fellowships in the university where they had learnt their craft. Hence the libraries and laboratories; the observatories; the splendid equipment of costly and delicate instruments which now stands on glass shelves, where centuries ago the grasses waved and the swine rooted. Certainly, as I strolled round the court, the foundation of gold and silver seemed deep enough; the pavement laid solidly over the wild grasses. Men with trays on their heads went busily from staircase to staircase. Gaudy blossoms flowered in window-boxes. The strains of the gramophone blared out from the rooms within. It was impossible not to reflect—the reflection whatever it may have been was cut short. The clock struck. It was time to find one's way to luncheon.

It is a curious fact that novelists have a way of making us believe that luncheon parties are invariably memorable for something very witty that was said, or for something very wise that was done. But they seldom spare a word for what was eaten. It is part of the novelist's convention not to mention soup and salmon and ducklings, as if soup and salmon and ducklings were of no importance whatsoever, as if nobody ever smoked a cigar or drank a glass of wine. Here, however, I shall take the liberty to defy that convention and to tell you that the lunch on this occasion began with soles, sunk in a deep dish, over which the college cook had spread a counterpane of the whitest cream, save that it was branded here and there with brown spots like the spots on the flanks of a doe. After that came the partridges, but if this suggests a couple of bald, brown birds on a plate you are mistaken. The partridges, many and various, came with all their retinue of sauces and salads, the sharp and the sweet, each in its order; their potatoes, thin as coins but not so hard; their sprouts, foliated as rosebuds but more succulent. And no sooner had the roast and its retinue been done with than the silent serving-man, the Beadle himself perhaps in a milder manifestation, set before us, wreathed in napkins, a confection which rose all sugar from the waves. To call it pudding and so relate it to rice and tapioca would be an insult. Meanwhile the wineglasses had flushed yellow and flushed crimson; had been emptied; had been filled. And thus by degrees was lit, halfway down the spine, which is the seat of the soul, not that hard little electric light which we call brilliance, as it pops in and out upon our lips, but the more profound, subtle and subterranean glow, which is the rich yellow flame of rational intercourse. No need to hurry. No need to sparkle. No need to be anybody but oneself. We are all going to heaven and Vandyck[9] is of the company—in other words, how good life seemed, how sweet its rewards, how trivial this grudge or that grievance, how admirable friendship and the society of one's kind, as, lighting a good cigarette, one sunk among the cushions in the window-seat.

If by good luck there had been an ash-tray handy, if one had not knocked the ash out of the window in default, if things had been a little different from what they were, one would not have seen, presumably, a cat without a tail. The sight of that abrupt and truncated animal padding softly across the quadrangle changed by some fluke of the subconscious intelligence the emotional light for me. It was as if some one had let fall a shade. Perhaps the excellent hock was relinquishing its hold. Certainly, as I watched the Manx cat pause in the middle of the lawn as if it too questioned the universe, something seemed lacking, something seemed different. But what was lacking,

9. Sir Anthony Van Dyck, prominent 17-century society painter.

what was different, I asked myself, listening to the talk. And to answer that question I had to think myself out of the room, back into the past, before the war indeed,[1] and to set before my eyes the model of another luncheon party held in rooms not very far distant from these; but different. Everything was different. Meanwhile the talk went on among the guests, who were many and young, some of this sex, some of that; it went on swimmingly, it went on agreeably, freely, amusingly. And as it went on I set it against the background of that other talk, and as I matched the two together I had no doubt that one was the descendant, the legitimate heir of the other. Nothing was changed; nothing was different save only—here I listened with all my ears not entirely to what was being said, but to the murmur or current behind it. Yes, that was it—the change was there. Before the war at a luncheon party like this people would have said precisely the same things but they would have sounded different, because in those days they were accompanied by a sort of humming noise, not articulate, but musical, exciting, which changed the value of the words themselves. Could one set that humming noise to words? Perhaps with the help of the poets one could. A book lay beside me and, opening it, I turned casually enough to Tennyson. And here I found Tennyson was singing:

> There has fallen a splendid tear
> From the passion-flower at the gate.
> She is coming, my dove, my dear;
> She is coming, my life, my fate;
> The red rose cries, "She is near, she is near";
> And the white rose weeps, "She is late";
> The larkspur listens, "I hear, I hear";
> And the lily whispers, "I wait."[2]

Was that what men hummed at luncheon parties before the war? And the women?

> My heart is like a singing bird
> Whose nest is in a water'd shoot;
> My heart is like an apple tree
> Whose boughs are bent with thick-set fruit;
> My heart is like a rainbow shell
> That paddles in a halcyon sea;
> My heart is gladder than all these
> Because my love is come to me.[3]

Was that what women hummed at luncheon parties before the war?

There was something so ludicrous in thinking of people humming such things even under their breath at luncheon parties before the war that I burst out laughing, and had to explain my laughter by pointing at the Manx cat, who did look a little absurd, poor beast, without a tail, in the middle of the lawn. Was he really born so, or had he lost his tail in an accident? The tailless cat, though some are said to exist in the Isle of Man, is rarer than one thinks. It is a queer animal, quaint rather than beautiful. It is strange what a difference a tail makes—you know the sort of things one says as a lunch party breaks up and people are finding their coats and hats.

This one, thanks to the hospitality of the host, had lasted far into the afternoon. The beautiful October day was fading and the leaves were falling from the trees in the avenue as I walked through it. Gate after gate seemed to close with gentle finali-

1. World War I.
2. From Tennyson's Maud (1855), lines 908–915.

3. The first stanza of Christina Rossetti's poem A Birthday (1857).

ty behind me. Innumerable beadles were fitting innumerable keys into well-oiled locks; the treasure-house was being made secure for another night. After the avenue one comes out upon a road—I forget its name—which leads you, if you take the right turning, along to Fernham.[4] But there was plenty of time. Dinner was not till half-past seven. One could almost do without dinner after such a luncheon. It is strange how a scrap of poetry works in the mind and makes the legs move in time to it along the road. Those words—

> There has fallen a splendid tear
>   From the passion-flower at the gate.
> She is coming, my dove, my dear—

sang in my blood as I stepped quickly along towards Headingley. And then, switching off into the other measure, I sang, where the waters are churned up by the weir:

> My heart is like a singing bird
>   Whose nest is in a water'd shoot;
> My heart is like an apple tree—

What poets, I cried aloud, as one does in the dusk, what poets they were!

In a sort of jealousy, I suppose, for our own age, silly and absurd though these comparisons are, I went on to wonder if honestly one could name two living poets now as great as Tennyson and Christina Rossetti were then. Obviously it is impossible, I thought, looking into those foaming waters, to compare them. The very reason why the poetry excites one to such abandonment, such rapture, is that it celebrates some feeling that one used to have (at luncheon parties before the war perhaps), so that one responds easily, familiarly, without troubling to check the feeling, or to compare it with any that one has now. But the living poets express a feeling that is actually being made and torn out of us at the moment. One does not recognize it in the first place; often for some reason one fears it; one watches it with keenness and compares it jealously and suspiciously with the old feeling that one knew. Hence the difficulty of modern poetry; and it is because of this difficulty that one cannot remember more than two consecutive lines of any good modern poet. For this reason—that my memory failed me—the argument flagged for want of material. But why, I continued, moving on towards Headingley, have we stopped humming under our breath at luncheon parties? Why has Alfred ceased to sing

> She is coming, my dove, my dear?

Why has Christina ceased to respond

> My heart is gladder than all these
> Because my love is come to me?

Shall we lay the blame on the war? When the guns fired in August 1914, did the faces of men and women show so plain in each other's eyes that romance was killed? Certainly it was a shock (to women in particular with their illusions about education, and so on) to see the faces of our rulers in the light of the shell-fire. So ugly they looked—German, English, French—so stupid. But lay the blame where one will, on whom one will, the illusion which inspired Tennyson and Christina Rossetti to sing so passionately about the coming of their loves is far rarer now than then. One has

---

4. Both Girton and Newnham Colleges, established only in the late 19th century, are outside the old university area of Cambridge.

only to read, to look, to listen, to remember. But why say "blame"? Why, if it was an illusion, not praise the catastrophe, whatever it was, that destroyed illusion and put truth in its place? For truth . . . those dots mark the spot where, in search of truth, I missed the turning up to Fernham. Yes indeed, which was truth and which was illusion, I asked myself. What was the truth about these houses, for example, dim and festive now with their red windows in the dusk, but raw and red and squalid, with their sweets and their boot-laces, at nine o'clock in the morning? And the willows and the river and the gardens that run down to the river, vague now with the mist stealing over them, but gold and red in the sunlight—which was the truth, which was the illusion about them? I spare you the twists and turns of my cogitations, for no conclusion was found on the road to Headingley, and I ask you to suppose that I soon found out my mistake about the turning and retraced my steps to Fernham.

As I have said already that it was an October day, I dare not forfeit your respect and imperil the fair name of fiction by changing the season and describing lilacs hanging over garden walls, crocuses, tulips and other flowers of spring. Fiction must stick to facts, and the truer the facts the better the fiction—so we are told. Therefore it was still autumn and the leaves were still yellow and falling, if anything, a little faster than before, because it was now evening (seven twenty-three to be precise) and a breeze (from the south-west to be exact) had risen. But for all that there was something odd at work:

> My heart is like a singing bird
>   Whose nest is in a water'd shoot;
> My heart is like an apple tree
>   Whose boughs are bent with thick-set fruit—

perhaps the words of Christina Rossetti were partly responsible for the folly of the fancy—it was nothing of course but a fancy—that the lilac was shaking its flowers over the garden walls, and the brimstone butterflies were scudding hither and thither, and the dust of the pollen was in the air. A wind blew, from what quarter I know not, but it lifted the half-grown leaves so that there was a flash of silver grey in the air. It was the time between the lights when colours undergo their intensification and purples and golds burn in window-panes like the beat of an excitable heart; when for some reason the beauty of the world revealed and yet soon to perish (here I pushed into the garden, for, unwisely, the door was left open and no beadles seemed about), the beauty of the world which is so soon to perish, has two edges, one of laughter, one of anguish, cutting the heart asunder. The gardens of Fernham lay before me in the spring twilight, wild and open, and in the long grass, sprinkled and carelessly flung, were daffodils and bluebells, not orderly perhaps at the best of times, and now wind-blown and waving as they tugged at their roots. The windows of the building, curved like ships' windows among generous waves of red brick, changed from lemon to silver under the flight of the quick spring clouds. Somebody was in a hammock, somebody, but in this light they were phantoms only, half guessed, half seen, raced across the grass—would no one stop her?—and then on the terrace, as if popping out to breathe the air, to glance at the garden, came a bent figure, formidable yet humble, with her great forehead and her shabby dress—could it be the famous scholar, could it be J——— H——— herself?[5] All was dim, yet intense too, as if the scarf which the dusk had flung over the garden were torn asunder by star or sword—the flash of some terrible reality leaping, as its way is, out of the heart of the spring. For youth———

---

5. Jane Harrison, a famous classical scholar.

Here was my soup. Dinner was being served in the great dining-hall. Far from being spring it was in fact an evening in October. Everybody was assembled in the big dining-room. Dinner was ready. Here was the soup. It was a plain gravy soup. There was nothing to stir the fancy in that. One could have seen through the transparent liquid any pattern that there might have been on the plate itself. But there was no pattern. The plate was plain. Next came beef with its attendant greens and potatoes—a homely trinity, suggesting the rumps of cattle in a muddy market, and sprouts curled and yellowed at the edge, and bargaining and cheapening, and women with string bags on Monday morning. There was no reason to complain of human nature's daily food, seeing that the supply was sufficient and coal-miners doubtless were sitting down to less. Prunes and custard followed. And if any one complains that prunes, even when mitigated by custard, are an uncharitable vegetable (fruit they are not), stringy as a miser's heart and exuding a fluid such as might run in misers' veins who have denied themselves wine and warmth for eighty years and yet not given to the poor, he should reflect that there are people whose charity embraces even the prune. Biscuits and cheese came next, and here the water-jug was liberally passed round, for it is the nature of biscuits to be dry, and these were biscuits to the core. That was all. The meal was over. Everybody scraped their chairs back; the swing-doors swung violently to and fro; soon the hall was emptied of every sign of food and made ready no doubt for breakfast next morning. Down corridors and up staircases the youth of England went banging and singing. And was it for a guest, a stranger (for I had no more right here in Fernham than in Trinity or Somerville or Girton or Newnham or Christchurch),[6] to say, "The dinner was not good," or to say (we were now, Mary Seton and I, in her sitting-room), "Could we not have dined up here alone?" for if I had said anything of the kind I should have been prying and searching into the secret economies of a house which to the stranger wears so fine a front of gaiety and courage. No, one could say nothing of the sort. Indeed, conversation for a moment flagged. The human frame being what it is, heart, body and brain all mixed together, and not contained in separate compartments as they will be no doubt in another million years, a good dinner is of great importance to good talk. One cannot think well, love well, sleep well, if one has not dined well. The lamp in the spine does not light on beef and prunes. We are all *probably* going to heaven, and Vandyck is, we *hope*, to meet us round the next corner—that is the dubious and qualifying state of mind that beef and prunes at the end of the day's work breed between them. Happily my friend, who taught science, had a cupboard where there was a squat bottle and little glasses—(but there should have been sole and partridge to begin with)—so that we were able to draw up to the fire and repair some of the damages of the day's living. In a minute or so we were slipping freely in and out among all those objects of curiosity and interest which form in the mind in the absence of a particular person, and are naturally to be discussed on coming together again—how somebody has married, another has not; one thinks this, another that; one has improved out of all knowledge, the other most amazingly gone to the bad—with all those speculations upon human nature and the character of the amazing world we live in which spring naturally from such beginnings. While these things were being said, however, I became shamefacedly aware of a current setting in of its own accord and carrying everything forward to an end of its own. One might be talking of Spain or Portugal, of book or racehorse, but

6. Trinity, Girton, and Newnham are colleges of Cambridge University; Somerville and Christchurch are at Oxford.

the real interest of whatever was said was none of those things, but a scene of masons on a high roof some five centuries ago. Kings and nobles brought treasure in huge sacks and poured it under the earth. This scene was for ever coming alive in my mind and placing itself by another of lean cows and a muddy market and withered greens and the stringy hearts of old men—these two pictures, disjointed and disconnected and nonsensical as they were, were for ever coming together and combating each other and had me entirely at their mercy. The best course, unless the whole talk was to be distorted, was to expose what was in my mind to the air, when with good luck it would fade and crumble like the head of the dead king when they opened the coffin at Windsor. Briefly, then, I told Miss Seton about the masons who had been all those years on the roof of the chapel, and about the kings and queens and nobles bearing sacks of gold and silver on their shoulders, which they shovelled into the earth; and then how the great financial magnates of our own time came and laid cheques and bonds, I suppose, where the others had laid ingots and rough lumps of gold. All that lies beneath the colleges down there, I said; but this college, where we are now sitting, what lies beneath its gallant red brick and the wild unkempt grasses of the garden? What force is behind the plain china off which we dined, and (here it popped out of my mouth before I could stop it) the beef, the custard and the prunes?

Well, said Mary Seton, about the year 1860—Oh, but you know the story, she said, bored, I suppose, by the recital. And she told me—rooms were hired. Committees met. Envelopes were addressed. Circulars were drawn up. Meetings were held; letters were read out; so-and-so has promised so much; on the contrary, Mr —— won't give a penny. The *Saturday Review* has been very rude. How can we raise a fund to pay for offices? Shall we hold a bazaar? Can't we find a pretty girl to sit in the front row? Let us look up what John Stuart Mill said on the subject.[7] Can any one persuade the editor of the —— to print a letter? Can we get Lady —— to sign it? Lady —— is out of town. That was the way it was done, presumably, sixty years ago, and it was a prodigious effort, and a great deal of time was spent on it. And it was only after a long struggle and with the utmost difficulty that they got thirty thousand pounds together.[8] So obviously we cannot have wine and partridges and servants carrying tin dishes on their heads, she said. We cannot have sofas and separate rooms. "The amenities," she said, quoting from some book or other, "will have to wait."[9]

At the thought of all those women working year after year and finding it hard to get two thousand pounds together, and as much as they could do to get thirty thousand pounds, we burst out in scorn at the reprehensible poverty of our sex. What had our mothers been doing then that they had no wealth to leave us? Powdering their noses? Looking in at shop windows? Flaunting in the sun at Monte Carlo? There were some photographs on the mantel-piece. Mary's mother—if that was her picture—may have been a wastrel in her spare time (she had thirteen children by a minister of the church), but if so her gay and dissipated life had left too few traces of its pleasures on her face. She was a homely body; an old lady in a plaid shawl which was fastened

---

7. In 1869 Mill published his essay *The Subjection of Women*, which argued forcefully for women's suffrage and their right to equality with men.

8. "We are told that we ought to ask for £30,000 at least . . . It is not a large sum, considering that there is to be but one college of this sort for Great Britain, Ireland and the Colonies, and considering how easy it is to raise immense sums for boys' schools. But considering how few people really wish women to be educated, it is a good deal."—Lady Stephen, *Life of Miss Emily Davies* [Woolf's note].

9. Every penny which could be scraped together was set aside for building, and the amenities had to be postponed.—R. Strachey, *The Cause* [Woolf's note].

by a large cameo; and she sat in a basket-chair, encouraging a spaniel to look at the camera, with the amused, yet strained expression of one who is sure that the dog will move directly the bulb is pressed. Now if she had gone into business; had become a manufacturer of artificial silk or a magnate on the Stock Exchange; if she had left two or three hundred thousand pounds to Fernham, we could have been sitting at our ease tonight and the subject of our talk might have been archaeology, botany, anthropology, physics, the nature of the atom, mathematics, astronomy, relativity, geography. If only Mrs Seton and her mother and her mother before her had learnt the great art of making money and had left their money, like their fathers and their grandfathers before them, to found fellowships and lectureships and prizes and scholarships appropriated to the use of their own sex, we might have dined very tolerably up here alone off a bird and a bottle of wine; we might have looked forward without undue confidence to a pleasant and honourable lifetime spent in the shelter of one of the liberally endowed professions. We might have been exploring or writing; mooning about the venerable places of the earth; sitting contemplative on the steps of the Parthenon, or going at ten to an office and coming home comfortably at half-past four to write a little poetry. Only, if Mrs Seton and her like had gone into business at the age of fifteen, there would have been—that was the snag in the argument—no Mary. What, I asked, did Mary think of that? There between the curtains was the October night, calm and lovely, with a star or two caught in the yellowing trees. Was she ready to resign her share of it and her memories (for they had been a happy family, though a large one) of games and quarrels up in Scotland, which she is never tired of praising for the fineness of its air and the quality of its cakes, in order that Fernham might have been endowed with fifty thousand pounds or so by a stroke of the pen? For, to endow a college would necessitate the suppression of families altogether. Making a fortune and bearing thirteen children—no human being could stand it. Consider the facts, we said. First there are nine months before the baby is born. Then the baby is born. Then there are three or four months spent in feeding the baby. After the baby is fed there are certainly five years spent in playing with the baby. You cannot, it seems, let children run about the streets. People who have seen them running wild in Russia say that the sight is not a pleasant one. People say, too, that human nature takes its shape in the years between one and five. If Mrs Seton, I said, had been making money, what sort of memories would you have had of games and quarrels? What would you have known of Scotland, and its fine air and cakes and all the rest of it? But it is useless to ask these questions, because you would never have come into existence at all. Moreover, it is equally useless to ask what might have happened if Mrs Seton and her mother and her mother before her had amassed great wealth and laid it under the foundations of college and library, because, in the first place, to earn money was impossible for them, and in the second, had it been possible, the law denied them the right to possess what money they earned. It is only for the last forty-eight years that Mrs Seton has had a penny of her own. For all the centuries before that it would have been her husband's property—a thought which, perhaps, may have had its share in keeping Mrs Seton and her mothers off the Stock Exchange.[1] Every penny I earn, they may have said, will be taken from me and disposed of

---

1. The late 19th century saw the passage of legislation designed to improve the legal status of women. In 1870 the Married Women's Property Act allowed women to retain £200 of their own earnings (which previously had automatically become the property of her husband); in 1884 a further act gave married women the same rights over property as unmarried women, and allowed them to carry on trades or businesses using their property.

according to my husband's wisdom—perhaps to found a scholarship or to endow a fellowship in Balliol or Kings,[2] so that to earn money, even if I could earn money, is not a matter that interests me very greatly. I had better leave it to my husband.

At any rate, whether or not the blame rested on the old lady who was looking at the spaniel, there could be no doubt that for some reason or other our mothers had mismanaged their affairs very gravely. Not a penny could be spared for "amenities"; for partridges and wine, beadles and turf, books and cigars, libraries and leisure. To raise bare walls out of the bare earth was the utmost they could do.

So we talked standing at the window and looking, as so many thousands look every night, down on the domes and towers of the famous city beneath us. It was very beautiful, very mysterious in the autumn moonlight. The old stone looked very white and venerable. One thought of all the books that were assembled down there; of the pictures of old prelates and worthies hanging in the panelled rooms; of the painted windows that would be throwing strange globes and crescents on the pavement; of the tablets and memorials and inscriptions; of the fountains and the grass; of the quiet rooms looking across the quiet quadrangles. And (pardon me the thought) I thought, too, of the admirable smoke and drink and the deep armchairs and the pleasant carpets: of the urbanity, the geniality, the dignity which are the offspring of luxury and privacy and space. Certainly our mothers had not provided us with anything comparable to all this—our mothers who found it difficult to scrape together thirty thousand pounds, our mothers who bore thirteen children to ministers of religion at St Andrews.

So I went back to my inn, and as I walked through the dark streets I pondered this and that, as one does at the end of the day's work. I pondered why it was that Mrs Seton had no money to leave us; and what effect poverty has on the mind; and what effect wealth has on the mind; and I thought of the queer old gentlemen I had seen that morning with tufts of fur upon their shoulders; and I remembered how if one whistled one of them ran; and I thought of the organ booming in the chapel and of the shut doors of the library; and I thought how unpleasant it is to be locked out; and I thought how it is worse perhaps to be locked in; and, thinking of the safety and prosperity of the one sex and of the poverty and insecurity of the other and of the effect of tradition and of the lack of tradition upon the mind of a writer, I thought at last that it was time to roll up the crumpled skin of the day, with its arguments and its impressions and its anger and its laughter, and cast it into the hedge. A thousand stars were flashing across the blue wastes of the sky. One seemed alone with an inscrutable society. All human beings were laid asleep—prone, horizontal, dumb. Nobody seemed stirring in the streets of Oxbridge. Even the door of the hotel sprang open at the touch of an invisible hand—not a boots was sitting up to light me to bed, it was so late.

from *Chapter 3*

It would have been impossible, completely and entirely, for any woman to have written the plays of Shakespeare in the age of Shakespeare. Let me imagine, since facts are so hard to come by, what would have happened had Shakespeare had a wonderfully gifted sister, called Judith, let us say. Shakespeare himself went, very probably—his mother was an heiress—to the grammar school, where he may have learnt

2. Balliol is a college of Oxford University; King's is at Cambridge.

Latin—Ovid, Virgil, and Horace—and the elements of grammar and logic. He was, it is well known, a wild boy who poached rabbits, perhaps shot a deer, and had, rather sooner than he should have done, to marry a woman in the neighbourhood, who bore him a child rather quicker than was right. That escapade sent him to seek his fortune in London. He had, it seemed, a taste for the theatre; he began by holding horses at the stage door. Very soon he got work in the theatre, became a successful actor, and lived at the hub of the universe, meeting everybody, knowing everybody, practising his art on the boards, exercising his wits in the streets, and even getting access to the palace of the queen. Meanwhile his extraordinarily gifted sister, let us suppose, remained at home. She was as adventurous, as imaginative, as agog to see the world as he was. But she was not sent to school. She had no chance of learning grammar and logic, let alone of reading Horace and Virgil. She picked up a book now and then, one of her brother's perhaps, and read a few pages. But then her parents came in and told her to mend the stockings or mind the stew and not moon about with books and papers. They would have spoken sharply but kindly, for they were substantial people who knew the conditions of life for a woman and loved their daughter—indeed, more likely than not she was the apple of her father's eye. Perhaps she scribbled some pages up in an apple loft on the sly, but was careful to hide them or set fire to them. Soon, however, before she was out of her teens, she was to be betrothed to the son of a neighbouring wool-stapler. She cried out that marriage was hateful to her, and for that she was severely beaten by her father. Then he ceased to scold her. He begged her instead not to hurt him, not to shame him in this matter of her marriage. He would give her a chain of beads or a fine petticoat, he said; and there were tears in his eyes. How could she disobey him? How could she break his heart? The force of her own gift alone drove her to it. She made up a small parcel of her belongings, let herself down by a rope one summer's night and took the road to London. She was not seventeen. The birds that sang in the hedge were not more musical than she was. She had the quickest fancy, a gift like her brother's, for the tune of words. Like him, she had a taste for the theatre. She stood at the stage door; she wanted to act, she said. Men laughed in her face. The manager—a fat, loose-lipped man—guffawed. He bellowed something about poodles dancing and women acting—no woman, he said, could possibly be an actress. He hinted—you can imagine what. She could get no training in her craft. Could she even seek her dinner in a tavern or roam the streets at midnight? Yet her genius was for fiction and lusted to feed abundantly upon the lives of men and women and the study of their ways. At last—for she was very young, oddly like Shakespeare the poet in her face, with the same grey eyes and rounded brows—at last Nick Greene the actor-manager took pity on her; she found herself with child by that gentleman and so—who shall measure the heat and violence of the poet's heart when caught and tangled in a woman's body?—killed herself one winter's night and lies buried at some cross-roads where the omnibuses now stop outside the Elephant and Castle.[3]

That, more or less, is how the story would run, I think, if a woman in Shakespeare's day had had Shakespeare's genius. But for my part, I agree with the deceased bishop, if such he was—it is unthinkable that any woman in Shakespeare's day should have had Shakespeare's genius. For genius like Shakespeare's is not born among labouring, uneducated, servile people. It was not born in England among the Saxons and the Britons. It is not born today among the working classes. How, then,

---

3. A tavern on the outskirts of South London.

could it have been born among women whose work began, according to Professor Trevelyan,[4] almost before they were out of the nursery, who were forced to it by their parents and held to it by all the power of law and custom? Yet genius of a sort must have existed among women as it must have existed among the working classes. Now and again an Emily Brontë or a Robert Burns blazes out and proves its presence. But certainly it never got itself on to paper. When, however, one reads of a witch being ducked, of a woman possessed by devils, of a wise woman selling herbs, or even of a very remarkable man who had a mother, then I think we are on the track of a lost novelist, a suppressed poet, of some mute and inglorious Jane Austen, some Emily Brontë who dashed her brains out on the moor or mopped and mowed about the highways crazed with the torture that her gift had put her to. Indeed, I would venture to guess that Anon, who wrote so many poems without signing them, was often a woman. It was a woman Edward Fitzgerald,[5] I think, suggested who made the ballads and the folk-songs, crooning them to her children, beguiling her spinning with them, or the length of the winter's night.

This may be true or it may be false—who can say?—but what is true in it, so it seemed to me, reviewing the story of Shakespeare's sister as I had made it, is that any woman born with a great gift in the sixteenth century would certainly have gone crazed, shot herself, or ended her days in some lonely cottage outside the village, half witch, half wizard, feared and mocked at. For it needs little skill in psychology to be sure that a highly gifted girl who had tried to use her gift for poetry would have been so thwarted and hindered by other people, so tortured and pulled asunder by her own contrary instincts, that she must have lost her health and sanity to a certainty. No girl could have walked to London and stood at a stage door and forced her way into the presence of actor-managers without doing herself a violence and suffering an anguish which may have been irrational—for chastity may be a fetish invented by certain societies for unknown reasons—but were none the less inevitable. Chastity had then, it has even now, a religious importance in a woman's life, and has so wrapped itself round with nerves and instincts that to cut it free and bring it to the light of day demands courage of the rarest. To have lived a free life in London in the sixteenth century would have meant for a woman who was poet and playwright a nervous stress and dilemma which might well have killed her. Had she survived, whatever she had written would have been twisted and deformed, issuing from a strained and morbid imagination. And undoubtedly, I thought, looking at the shelf where there are no plays by women, her work would have gone unsigned. That refuge she would have sought certainly. It was the relic of the sense of chastity that dictated anonymity to women even so late as the nineteenth century. Currer Bell, George Eliot, George Sand,[6] all the victims of inner strife as their writings prove, sought ineffectively to veil themselves by using the name of a man. Thus they did homage to the convention, which if not implanted by the other sex was liberally encouraged by them (the chief glory of a woman is not to be talked of, said Pericles, himself a much-talked-of man), that publicity in women is detestable.[7] Anonymity runs in their blood. The desire to be veiled still possesses them. They are not even now as concerned about the health of their fame as men are, and, speaking generally, will pass a

---

4. George Trevelyan (1876–1962), historian.
5. Poet and translator (1809–1883).
6. Currer Bell, pen name of Charlotte Brontë; George Eliot, pen name of Mary Ann Evans; George Sand, pen name of Amandine Aurore Lucille Dupin (1804–1876).

7. The Athenian statesman Pericles was reported by the historian Thucydides to have said, "That woman is most praiseworthy whose name is least bandied about on men's lips, whether for praise or dispraise."

tombstone or a signpost without feeling an irresistible desire to cut their names on it, as Alf, Bert or Chas. must do in obedience to their instinct, which murmurs if it sees a fine woman go by, or even a dog, Ce chien est à moi [that dog is mine]. And, of course, it may not be a dog, I thought, remembering Parliament Square, the Sieges Allee[8] and other avenues; it may be a piece of land or a man with curly black hair. It is one of the great advantages of being a woman that one can pass even a very fine negress without wishing to make an Englishwoman of her.

That woman, then, who was born with a gift of poetry in the sixteenth century, was an unhappy woman, a woman at strife against herself. All the conditions of her life, all her own instincts, were hostile to the state of mind which is needed to set free whatever is in the brain. * * * There would always have been that assertion—you cannot do this, you are incapable of doing that—to protest against, to overcome. Probably for a novelist this germ is no longer of much effect; for there have been women novelists of merit. But for painters it must still have some sting in it; and for musicians, I imagine, is even now active and poisonous in the extreme. The woman composer stands where the actress stood in the time of Shakespeare. Nick Greene, I thought, remembering the story I had made about Shakespeare's sister, said that a woman acting put him in mind of a dog dancing. Johnson repeated the phrase two hundred years later of women preaching.[9] And here, I said, opening a book about music, we have the very words used again in this year of grace, 1928, of women who try to write music. "Of Mlle. Germaine Tailleferre one can only repeat Dr. Johnson's dictum concerning a woman preacher, transposed into terms of music. 'Sir, a woman's composing is like a dog's walking on his hind legs. It is not done well, but you are surprised to find it done at all.'"[1] So accurately does history repeat itself.

Thus, I concluded, shutting Mr Oscar Browning's life and pushing away the rest, it is fairly evident that even in the nineteenth century a woman was not encouraged to be an artist. On the contrary, she was snubbed, slapped, lectured and exhorted. Her mind must have been strained and her vitality lowered by the need of opposing this, of disproving that. For here again we come within range of that very interesting and obscure masculine complex which has had so much influence upon the woman's movement; that deep-seated desire, not so much that *she* shall be inferior as that *he* shall be superior, which plants him wherever one looks, not only in front of the arts, but barring the way to politics too, even when the risk to himself seems infinitesimal and the suppliant humble and devoted. Even Lady Bessborough, I remembered, with all her passion for politics, must humbly bow herself and write to Lord Granville Leveson-Gower:[2] ". . . notwithstanding all my violence in politics and talking so much on that subject, I perfectly agree with you that no woman has any business to meddle with that or any other serious business, farther than giving her opinion (if she is ask'd)." And so she goes on to spend her enthusiasm where it meets with no obstacle whatsoever upon that immensely important subject, Lord Granville's maiden speech in the House of Commons. The spectacle is certainly a strange one, I thought. The history of men's opposition to women's emancipation is more interesting perhaps than the story of that emancipation itself. An amusing book might be made of it if some young student at Girton or Newnham would collect examples and deduce a theory—but she would need thick gloves on her hands, and bars to protect her of solid gold.

8. Victory Road, a thoroughfare in Berlin.
9. Samuel Johnson (1709–1784), poet and man of letters.
1. A *Survey of Contemporary Music*, Cecil Gray, p. 246

[Woolf's note].
2. Lady Bessborough (1761–1821), correspondent of the British statesman Lord Granville.

But what is amusing now, I recollected, shutting Lady Bessborough, had to be taken in desperate earnest once. Opinions that one now pastes in a book labelled cock-a-doodle-dum and keeps for reading to select audiences on summer nights once drew tears, I can assure you. Among your grandmothers and great-grandmothers there were many that wept their eyes out. Florence Nightingale shrieked aloud in her agony.[3] Moreover, it is all very well for you, who have got yourselves to college and enjoy sitting-rooms—or is it only bed-sitting-rooms?—of your own to say that genius should disregard such opinions; that genius should be above caring what is said of it. Unfortunately, it is precisely the men or women of genius who mind most what is said of them. Remember Keats. Remember the words he had cut on his tombstone. Think of Tennyson; think—but I need hardly multiply instances of the undeniable, if very unfortunate, fact that it is the nature of the artist to mind excessively what is said about him. Literature is strewn with the wreckage of men who have minded beyond reason the opinions of others.

And this susceptibility of theirs is doubly unfortunate, I thought, returning again to my original enquiry into what state of mind is most propitious for creative work, because the mind of an artist, in order to achieve the prodigious effort of freeing whole and entire the work that is in him, must be incandescent, like Shakespeare's mind, I conjectured, looking at the book which lay open at *Antony and Cleopatra*. There must be no obstacle in it, no foreign matter unconsumed.

For though we say that we know nothing about Shakespeare's state of mind, even as we say that, we are saying something about Shakespeare's state of mind. The reason perhaps why we know so little of Shakespeare—compared with Donne or Ben Jonson or Milton—is that his grudges and spites and antipathies are hidden from us. We are not held up by some "revelation" which reminds us of the writer. All desire to protest, to preach, to proclaim an injury, to pay off a score, to make the world the witness of some hardship or grievance was fired out of him and consumed. Therefore his poetry flows from him free and unimpeded. If ever a human being got his work expressed completely, it was Shakespeare. If ever a mind was incandescent, unimpeded, I thought, turning again to the bookcase, it was Shakespeare's mind.

from *Chapter 4*

The extreme activity of mind which showed itself in the later eighteenth century among women—the talking, and the meeting, the writing of essays on Shakespeare, the translating of the classics—was founded on the solid fact that women could make money by writing. Money dignifies what is frivolous if unpaid for. It might still be well to sneer at "blue stockings with an itch for scribbling," but it could not be denied that they could put money in their purses. Thus, towards the end of the eighteenth century a change came about which, if I were rewriting history, I should describe more fully and think of greater importance than the Crusades or the Wars of the Roses. The middle-class woman began to write. For if *Pride and Prejudice* matters, and *Middlemarch* and *Villette* and *Wuthering Heights* matter,[4] then it matters far more than I can prove in an hour's discourse that women generally, and not merely the lonely aristocrat shut up in her country house among her folios and her flatterers, took to writing. Without those forerunners, Jane Austen and the Brontës and George Eliot

3. See *Cassandra*, by Florence Nightingale, printed in *The Cause*, by R. Strachey [Woolf's note].
4. *Pride and Prejudice* (1813), a novel by Jane Austen;

Middlemarch (1871–1872) by George Eliot; *Villette* (1853) by Charlotte Brontë; *Wuthering Heights* (1847) by Emily Brontë.

could no more have written than Shakespeare could have written without Marlowe, or Marlowe without Chaucer, or Chaucer without those forgotten poets who paved the ways and tamed the natural savagery of the tongue. For masterpieces are not single and solitary births; they are the outcome of many years of thinking in common, of thinking by the body of the people, so that the experience of the mass is behind the single voice. Jane Austen should have laid a wreath upon the grave of Fanny Burney, and George Eliot done homage to the robust shade of Eliza Carter—the valiant old woman who tied a bell to her bedstead in order that she might wake early and learn Greek. All women together ought to let flowers fall upon the tomb of Aphra Behn[5] which is, most scandalously but rather appropriately, in Westminster Abbey, for it was she who earned them the right to speak their minds. It is she—shady and amorous as she was—who makes it not quite fantastic for me to say to you tonight: Earn five hundred a year by your wits.

Here, then, one had reached the early nineteenth century. And here, for the first time, I found several shelves given up entirely to the works of women. But why, I could not help asking, as I ran my eyes over them, were they, with very few exceptions, all novels? The original impulse was to poetry. The "supreme head of song" was a poetess. Both in France and in England the women poets precede the women novelists. Moreover, I thought, looking at the four famous names, what had George Eliot in common with Emily Brontë? Did not Charlotte Brontë fail entirely to understand Jane Austen? Save for the possibly relevant fact that not one of them had a child, four more incongruous characters could not have met together in a room—so much so that it is tempting to invent a meeting and a dialogue between them. Yet by some strange force they were all compelled, when they wrote, to write novels. Had it something to do with being born of the middle class, I asked; and with the fact, which Miss Emily Davies a little later was so strikingly to demonstrate,[6] that the middle-class family in the early nineteenth century was possessed only of a single sitting-room between them? If a woman wrote, she would have to write in the common sitting-room. And, as Miss Nightingale was so vehemently to complain,—"women never have an half hour . . . that they can call their own"—she was always interrupted. Still it would be easier to write prose and fiction there than to write poetry or a play. Less concentration is required. Jane Austen wrote like that to the end of her days. "How she was able to effect all this," her nephew writes in his Memoir, "is surprising, for she had no separate study to repair to, and most of the work must have been done in the general sitting-room, subject to all kinds of casual interruptions. She was careful that her occupation should not be suspected by servants or visitors or any persons beyond her own family party."[7] Jane Austen hid her manuscripts or covered them with a piece of blotting-paper. Then, again, all the literary training that a woman had in the early nineteenth century was training in the observation of character, in the analysis of emotion. Her sensibility had been educated for centuries by the influences of the common sitting-room. People's feelings were impressed on her; personal relations were always before her eyes. Therefore, when the middle-class woman took to writing, she naturally wrote novels, even though, as seems evident enough, two of the four famous women here named were

5. A dramatist and the first English woman to earn a living by writing (1640–1689). Westminster Abbey, in central London, is the burial place of many of the English kings and queens, as well as of famous poets and statesmen.
6. (Sarah) Emily Davies was prominent in the movement to secure university education for women in the 19th century and was chief founder of Girton College, Cambridge (1873).
7. Memoir of Jane Austen, by her nephew, James Edward Austen-Leigh [Woolf's note].

not by nature novelists. Emily Brontë should have written poetic plays; the overflow of George Eliot's capacious mind should have spread itself when the creative impulse was spent upon history or biography. They wrote novels, however; one may even go further, I said, taking *Pride and Prejudice* from the shelf, and say that they wrote good novels. Without boasting or giving pain to the opposite sex, one may say that *Pride and Prejudice* is a good book. At any rate, one would not have been ashamed to have been caught in the act of writing *Pride and Prejudice*. Yet Jane Austen was glad that a hinge creaked, so that she might hide her manuscript before any one came in. To Jane Austen there was something discreditable in writing *Pride and Prejudice*. And, I wondered, would *Pride and Prejudice* have been a better novel if Jane Austen had not thought it necessary to hide her manuscript from visitors? I read a page or two to see; but I could not find any signs that her circumstances had harmed her work in the slightest. That, perhaps, was the chief miracle about it. Here was a woman about the year 1800 writing without hate, without bitterness, without fear, without protest, without preaching. That was how Shakespeare wrote, I thought, looking at *Antony and Cleopatra*; and when people compare Shakespeare and Jane Austen, they may mean that the minds of both had consumed all impediments; and for that reason we do not know Jane Austen and we do not know Shakespeare, and for that reason Jane Austen pervades every word that she wrote, and so does Shakespeare. If Jane Austen suffered in any way from her circumstances it was in the narrowness of life that was imposed upon her. It was impossible for a woman to go about alone. She never travelled; she never drove through London in an omnibus or had luncheon in a shop by herself. But perhaps it was the nature of Jane Austen not to want what she had not. Her gift and her circumstances matched each other completely. But I doubt whether that was true of Charlotte Brontë, I said, opening *Jane Eyre* and laying it beside *Pride and Prejudice*.[8]

I opened it at chapter twelve and my eye was caught by the phrase, "Anybody may blame me who likes." What were they blaming Charlotte Brontë for, I wondered? And I read how Jane Eyre used to go up on to the roof when Mrs Fairfax was making jellies and looked over the fields at the distant view. And then she longed—and it was for this that they blamed her—that "then I longed for a power of vision which might overpass that limit; which might reach the busy world, towns, regions full of life I had heard of but never seen: that then I desired more of practical experience than I possessed; more of intercourse with my kind, of acquaintance with variety of character than was here within my reach. I valued what was good in Mrs Fairfax, and what was good in Adèle; but I believed in the existence of other and more vivid kinds of goodness, and what I believed in I wished to behold.

"Who blames me? Many, no doubt, and I shall be called discontented. I could not help it: the restlessness was in my nature; it agitated me to pain sometimes. . . .

"It is vain to say human beings ought to be satisfied with tranquillity: they must have action; and they will make it if they cannot find it. Millions are condemned to a stiller doom than mine, and millions are in silent revolt against their lot. Nobody knows how many rebellions ferment in the masses of life which people earth.

8. Woolf goes on to describe parts of the plot of *Jane Eyre*; Jane Eyre, a penniless orphan, having suffered greatly during her schooling, takes up the post of governess to Adele, the daughter of Mr. Rochester, a man of strange moods. Rochester falls in love with Jane, who agrees to marry him; however this is prevented by Rochester's mad wife—whom Rochester has locked in the attic, concealing her existence from Jane—who tears Jane's wedding veil on the eve of the marriage. Rochester at first tells Jane that Grace Poole, a servant, had been responsible for this and other strange events, including the uncanny laughter occasionally heard in the house.

Women are supposed to be very calm generally: but women feel just as men feel; they need exercise for their faculties and a field for their efforts as much as their brothers do; they suffer from too rigid a restraint, too absolute a stagnation, precisely as men would suffer; and it is narrow-minded in their more privileged fellow-creatures to say that they ought to confine themselves to making puddings and knitting stockings, to playing on the piano and embroidering bags. It is thoughtless to condemn them, or laugh at them, if they seek to do more or learn more than custom has pronounced necessary for their sex.

"When thus alone I not unfrequently heard Grace Poole's laugh...."

That is an awkward break, I thought. It is upsetting to come upon Grace Poole all of a sudden. The continuity is disturbed. One might say, I continued, laying the book down beside *Pride and Prejudice*, that the woman who wrote those pages had more genius in her than Jane Austen; but if one reads them over and marks that jerk in them, that indignation, one sees that she will never get her genius expressed whole and entire. Her books will be deformed and twisted. She will write in a rage where she should write calmly. She will write foolishly where she should write wisely. She will write of herself where she should write of her characters. She is at war with her lot. How could she help but die young, cramped and thwarted?

One could not but play for a moment with the thought of what might have happened if Charlotte Brontë had possessed say three hundred a year—but the foolish woman sold the copyright of her novels outright for fifteen hundred pounds; had somehow possessed more knowledge of the busy world, and towns and regions full of life; more practical experience, and intercourse with her kind and acquaintance with a variety of character. In those words she puts her finger exactly not only upon her own defects as a novelist but upon those of her sex at that time. She knew, no one better, how enormously her genius would have profited if it had not spent itself in solitary visions over distant fields; if experience and intercourse and travel had been granted her. But they were not granted; they were withheld; and we must accept the fact that all those good novels, *Villette, Emma, Wuthering Heights, Middlemarch*, were written by women without more experience of life than could enter the house of a respectable clergyman; written too in the common sitting-room of that respectable house and by women so poor that they could not afford to buy more than a few quires of paper at a time upon which to write *Wuthering Heights* or *Jane Eyre*. One of them, it is true, George Eliot, escaped after much tribulation, but only to a secluded villa in St John's Wood. And there she settled down in the shadow of the world's disapproval.[9] "I wish it to be understood," she wrote, "that I should never invite any one to come and see me who did not ask for the invitation"; for was she not living in sin with a married man and might not the sight of her damage the chastity of Mrs Smith or whoever it might be that chanced to call? One must submit to the social convention, and be "cut off from what is called the world." At the same time, on the other side of Europe, there was a young man living freely with this gipsy or with that great lady; going to the wars; picking up unhindered and uncensored all that varied experience of human life which served him so splendidly later when he came to write his books. Had Tolstoi lived at the Priory in seclusion with a married lady "cut off from what is called the world," however edifying the moral lesson, he could scarcely, I thought, have written *War and Peace*. * * *

9. Following a strictly religious childhood, the novelist George Eliot lost her faith and eloped with G. H. Lewes, a married man, with whom she lived for the rest of his life; her family never forgave her.

* * * I do not want, and I am sure that you do not want me, to broach that very
dismal subject, the future of fiction, so that I will only pause here one moment to
draw your attention to the great part which must be played in that future so far as
women are concerned by physical conditions. The book has somehow to be adapted
to the body, and at a venture one would say that women's books should be shorter,
more concentrated, than those of men, and framed so that they do not need long
hours of steady and uninterrupted work. For interruptions there will always be.
Again, the nerves that feed the brain would seem to differ in men and women, and if
you are going to make them work their best and hardest, you must find out what
treatment suits them—whether these hours of lectures, for instance, which the
monks devised, presumably, hundreds of years ago, suit them—what alternations of
work and rest they need, interpreting rest not as doing nothing but as doing something but something that is different; and what should that difference be? All this
should be discussed and discovered; all this is part of the question of women and fiction. And yet, I continued, approaching the bookcase again, where shall I find that
elaborate study of the psychology of women by a woman? If through their incapacity
to play football women are not going to be allowed to practise medicine——

   Happily my thoughts were now given another turn.

from *Chapter 6*

Next day the light of the October morning was falling in dusty shafts through the
uncurtained windows, and the hum of traffic rose from the street. London then was
winding itself up again; the factory was astir; the machines were beginning. It was
tempting, after all this reading, to look out of the window and see what London was
doing on the morning of the twenty-sixth of October 1928. And what was London
doing? Nobody, it seemed, was reading *Antony and Cleopatra*. London was wholly indifferent, it appeared, to Shakespeare's plays. Nobody cared a straw—and I do not blame
them—for the future of fiction, the death of poetry or the development by the average
woman of a prose style completely expressive of her mind. If opinions upon any of these
matters had been chalked on the pavement, nobody would have stooped to read them.
The nonchalance of the hurrying feet would have rubbed them out in half an hour.
Here came an errand-boy; here a woman with a dog on a lead. The fascination of the
London street is that no two people are ever alike; each seems bound on some private
affair of his own. There were the business-like, with their little bags; there were the
drifters rattling sticks upon area railings; there were affable characters to whom the
streets serve for clubroom, hailing men in carts and giving information without being
asked for it. Also there were funerals to which men, thus suddenly reminded of the
passing of their own bodies, lifted their hats. And then a very distinguished gentleman
came slowly down a doorstep and paused to avoid collision with a bustling lady who
had, by some means or other, acquired a splendid fur coat and a bunch of Parma violets.
They all seemed separate, self-absorbed, on business of their own.

   At this moment, as so often happens in London, there was a complete lull and
suspension of traffic. Nothing came down the street; nobody passed. A single leaf
detached itself from the plane tree at the end of the street, and in that pause and suspension fell. Somehow it was like a signal falling, a signal pointing to a force in things
which one had overlooked. It seemed to point to a river, which flowed past, invisibly,
round the corner, down the street, and took people and eddied them along, as the
stream at Oxbridge had taken the undergraduate in his boat and the dead leaves.

Now it was bringing from one side of the street to the other diagonally a girl in patent leather boots, and then a young man in a maroon overcoat; it was also bringing a taxi-cab; and it brought all three together at a point directly beneath my window; where the taxi stopped; and the girl and the young man stopped; and they got into the taxi; and then the cab glided off as if it were swept on by the current elsewhere.

The sight was ordinary enough; what was strange was the rhythmical order with which my imagination had invested it; and the fact that the ordinary sight of two people getting into a cab had the power to communicate something of their own seeming satisfaction. The sight of two people coming down the street and meeting at the corner seems to ease the mind of some strain, I thought, watching the taxi turn and make off. Perhaps to think, as I had been thinking these two days, of one sex as distinct from the other is an effort. It interferes with the unity of the mind. Now that effort had ceased and that unity had been restored by seeing two people come togeth-er and get into a taxi-cab. The mind is certainly a very mysterious organ, I reflected, drawing my head in from the window, about which nothing whatever is known, though we depend upon it so completely. Why do I feel that there are severances and oppositions in the mind, as there are strains from obvious causes on the body? What does one mean by "the unity of the mind," I pondered, for clearly the mind has so great a power of concentrating at any point at any moment that it seems to have no single state of being. It can separate itself from the people in the street, for example, and think of itself as apart from them, at an upper window looking down on them. Or it can think with other people spontaneously, as, for instance, in a crowd waiting to hear some piece of news read out. It can think back through its fathers or through its mothers, as I have said that a woman writing thinks back through her mothers. Again if one is a woman one is often surprised by a sudden splitting off of conscious-ness, say in walking down Whitehall,[1] when from being the natural inheritor of that civilisation, she becomes, on the contrary, outside of it, alien and critical. Clearly the mind is always altering its focus, and bringing the world into different perspectives. But some of these states of mind seem, even if adopted spontaneously, to be less com-fortable than others. In order to keep oneself continuing in them one is unconscious-ly holding something back, and gradually the repression becomes an effort. But there may be some state of mind in which one could continue without effort because noth-ing is required to be held back. And this perhaps, I thought, coming in from the win-dow, is one of them. For certainly when I saw the couple get into the taxi-cab the mind felt as if, after being divided, it had come together again in a natural fusion. The obvious reason would be that it is natural for the sexes to co-operate. One has a profound, if irrational, instinct in favour of the theory that the union of man and woman makes for the greatest satisfaction, the most complete happiness. But the sight of the two people getting into the taxi and the satisfaction it gave me made me also ask whether there are two sexes in the mind corresponding to the two sexes in the body, and whether they also require to be united in order to get complete satis-faction and happiness. And I went on amateurishly to sketch a plan of the soul so that in each of us two powers preside, one male, one female; and in the man's brain, the man predominates over the woman, and in the woman's brain, the woman pre-dominates over the man. The normal and comfortable state of being is that when the two live in harmony together, spiritually co-operating. If one is a man, still the woman part of the brain must have effect; and a woman also must have intercourse

---

1. A main thoroughfare in central London and site of government offices.

with the man in her. Coleridge perhaps meant this when he said that a great mind is androgynous.[2] It is when this fusion takes place that the mind is fully fertilised and uses all its faculties. Perhaps a mind that is purely masculine cannot create, any more than a mind that is purely feminine, I thought. * * *

* * * One must turn back to Shakespeare then, for Shakespeare was androgynous; and so was Keats and Sterne and Cowper and Lamb and Coleridge. Shelley perhaps was sexless. Milton and Ben Jonson had a dash too much of the male in them. So had Wordsworth and Tolstoi. In our time Proust was wholly androgynous, if not perhaps a little too much of a woman. But that failing is too rare for one to complain of it, since without some mixture of the kind the intellect seems to predominate and the other faculties of the mind harden and become barren. However, I consoled myself with the reflection that this is perhaps a passing phase; much of what I have said in obedience to my promise to give you the course of my thoughts will seem out of date; much of what flames in my eyes will seem dubious to you who have not yet come of age.

Even so, the very first sentence that I would write here, I said, crossing over to the writing-table and taking up the page headed Women and Fiction, is that it is fatal for any one who writes to think of their sex. It is fatal to be a man or woman pure and simple; one must be woman-manly or man-womanly. It is fatal for a woman to lay the least stress on any grievance; to plead even with justice any cause; in any way to speak consciously as a woman. And fatal is no figure of speech; for anything written with that conscious bias is doomed to death. It ceases to be fertilised. Brilliant and effective, powerful and masterly, as it may appear for a day or two, it must wither at nightfall; it cannot grow in the minds of others. Some collaboration has to take place in the mind between the woman and the man before the act of creation can be accomplished. Some marriage of opposites has to be consummated. The whole of the mind must lie wide open if we are to get the sense that the writer is communicating his experience with perfect fullness. There must be freedom and there must be peace. Not a wheel must grate, not a light glimmer. The curtains must be close drawn. The writer, I thought, once his experience is over, must lie back and let his mind celebrate its nuptials in darkness. He must not look or question what is being done. Rather, he must pluck the petals from a rose or watch the swans float calmly down the river. And I saw again the current which took the boat and the undergraduate and the dead leaves; and the taxi took the man and the woman, I thought, seeing them come together across the street, and the current swept them away, I thought, hearing far off the roar of London's traffic, into that tremendous stream.

Here, then, Mary Beton ceases to speak. She has told you how she reached the conclusion—the prosaic conclusion—that it is necessary to have five hundred a year and a room with a lock on the door if you are to write fiction or poetry. She has tried to lay bare the thoughts and impressions that led her to think this. She has asked you to follow her flying into the arms of a Beadle, lunching here, dining there, drawing pictures in the British Museum, taking books from the shelf, looking out of the window. While she has been doing all these things, you no doubt have been observing her failings and foibles and deciding what effect they have had on her opinions. You have been contradicting her and making whatever additions and deductions seem good to you. That is all as it should be, for in a question like this

2. The poet Samuel Taylor Coleridge made the remark in September 1832—"a great mind must be androgynous"—and it was duly recorded in his Table Talk.

truth is only to be had by laying together many varieties of error. And I will end now in my own person by anticipating two criticisms, so obvious that you can hardly fail to make them.

No opinion has been expressed, you may say, upon the comparative merits of the sexes even as writers. That was done purposely, because, even if the time had come for such a valuation—and it is far more important at the moment to know how much money women had and how many rooms than to theorise about their capacities—even if the time had come I do not believe that gifts, whether of mind or character, can be weighed like sugar and butter, not even in Cambridge, where they are so adept at putting people into classes and fixing caps on their heads and letters after their names. I do not believe that even the Table of Precedency which you will find in Whitaker's *Almanac*[3] represents a final order of values, or that there is any sound reason to suppose that a Commander of the Bath will ultimately walk in to dinner behind a Master in Lunacy. All this pitting of sex against sex, of quality against quality; all this claiming of superiority and imputing of inferiority, belong to the private-school stage of human existence where there are "sides," and it is necessary for one side to beat another side, and of the utmost importance to walk up to a platform and receive from the hands of the Headmaster himself a highly ornamental pot. As people mature they cease to believe in sides or in Headmasters or in highly ornamental pots. At any rate, where books are concerned, it is notoriously difficult to fix labels of merit in such a way that they do not come off. Are not reviews of current literature a perpetual illustration of the difficulty of judgment? "This great book," "this worthless book," the same book is called by both names. Praise and blame alike mean nothing. No, delightful as the pastime of measuring may be, it is the most futile of all occupations, and to submit to the decrees of the measurers the most servile of attitudes. So long as you write what you wish to write, that is all that matters; and whether it matters for ages or only for hours, nobody can say. But to sacrifice a hair of the head of your vision, a shade of its colour, in deference to some Headmaster with a silver pot in his hand or to some professor with a measuring-rod up his sleeve, is the most abject treachery, and the sacrifice of wealth and chastity which used to be said to be the greatest of human disasters, a mere flea-bite in comparison.

Next I think that you may object that in all this I have made too much of the importance of material things. * * *

Intellectual freedom depends upon material things. Poetry depends upon intellectual freedom. And women have always been poor, not for two hundred years merely, but from the beginning of time. Women have had less intellectual freedom than the sons of Athenian slaves. Women, then, have not had a dog's chance of writing poetry. That is why I have laid so much stress on money and a room of one's own. However, thanks to the toils of those obscure women in the past, of whom I wish we knew more, thanks, curiously enough, to two wars, the Crimean which let Florence Nightingale out of her drawing-room, and the European War which opened the doors to the average woman some sixty years later, these evils are in the way to be bettered. Otherwise you would not be here tonight, and your chance of earning five hundred pounds a year, precarious as I am afraid that it still is, would be minute in the extreme. * * *

Here I would stop, but the pressure of convention decrees that every speech must end with a peroration. And a peroration addressed to women should have something,

---

3. A compendium of general information first published in 1868.

you will agree, particularly exalting and ennobling about it. I should implore you to remember your responsibilities, to be higher, more spiritual; I should remind you how much depends upon you, and what an influence you can exert upon the future. But those exhortations can safely, I think, be left to the other sex, who will put them, and indeed have put them, with far greater eloquence than I can compass. When I rummage in my own mind I find no noble sentiments about being companions and equals and influencing the world to higher ends. I find myself saying briefly and prosaically that it is much more important to be oneself than anything else. Do not dream of influencing other people, I would say, if I knew how to make it sound exalted. Think of things in themselves.

And again I am reminded by dipping into newspapers and novels and biographies that when a woman speaks to women she should have something very unpleasant up her sleeve. Women are hard on women. Women dislike women. Women . . . but are you not sick to death of the word? I can assure you that I am. Let us agree, then, that a paper read by a woman to women should end with something particularly disagreeable.

But how does it go? What can I think of? The truth is, I often like women. I like their unconventionality. I like their subtlety. I like their anonymity. I like—but I must not run on in this way. That cupboard there,—you say it holds clean table-napkins only; but what if Sir Archibald Bodkin were concealed among them?[4] Let me then adopt a sterner tone. Have I, in the preceding words, conveyed to you sufficiently the warnings and reprobation of mankind? I have told you the very low opinion in which you were held by Mr Oscar Browning. I have indicated what Napoleon once thought of you and what Mussolini thinks now. Then, in case any of you aspire to fiction, I have copied out for your benefit the advice of the critic about courageously acknowledging the limitations of your sex. I have referred to Professor X and given prominence to his statement that women are intellectually, morally and physically inferior to men. I have handed on all that has come my way without going in search of it, and here is a final warning—from Mr John Langdon Davies.[5] Mr John Langdon Davies warns women "that when children cease to be altogether desirable, women cease to be altogether necessary." I hope you will make a note of it.

How can I further encourage you to go about the business of life? Young women, I would say, and please attend, for the peroration is beginning, you are, in my opinion, disgracefully ignorant. You have never made a discovery of any sort of importance. You have never shaken an empire or led an army into battle. The plays of Shakespeare are not by you, and you have never introduced a barbarous race to the blessings of civilisation. What is your excuse? It is all very well for you to say, pointing to the streets and squares and forests of the globe swarming with black and white and coffee-coloured inhabitants, all busily engaged in traffic and enterprise and lovemaking, we have had other work on our hands. Without our doing, those seas would be unsailed and those fertile lands a desert. We have borne and bred and washed and taught, perhaps to the age of six or seven years, the one thousand six hundred and twenty-three million human beings who are, according to statistics, at present in existence, and that, allowing that some had help, takes time.

There is truth in what you say—I will not deny it. But at the same time may I remind you that there have been at least two colleges for women in existence in England since the year 1866; that after the year 1880 a married woman was allowed by law to possess her own property; and that in 1919—which is a whole nine years ago—she was given a vote? May I also remind you that the most of the professions have been open to you for close on ten years now? When you reflect upon these immense privileges and the length of time time during which they have been enjoyed, and the fact that there must be at this moment some two thousand women capable of earning over five hundred a year in one way or another, you will agree that the excuse of lack of opportunity, training, encouragement, leisure and money no longer holds good. Moreover, the economists are telling us that Mrs Seton has had too many children. You must, of course, go on bearing children, but, so they say, in twos and threes, not in tens and twelves.

Thus, with some time on your hands and with some book learning in your brains—you have had enough of the other kind, and are sent to college partly, I suspect, to be uneducated—surely you should embark upon another stage of your very long, very laborious and highly obscure career. A thousand pens are ready to suggest what you should do and what effect you will have. My own suggestion is a little fantastic, I admit; I prefer, therefore, to put it in the form of fiction.

I told you in the course of this paper that Shakespeare had a sister; but do not look for her in Sir Sidney Lee's life of the poet. She died young—alas, she never wrote a word. She lies buried where the omnibuses now stop, opposite the Elephant and Castle. Now my belief is that this poet who never wrote a word and was buried at the crossroads still lives. She lives in you and in me, and in many other women who are not here tonight, for they are washing up the dishes and putting the children to bed. But she lives; for great poets do not die; they are continuing presences; they need only the opportunity to walk among us in the flesh. This opportunity, as I think, it is now coming within your power to give her. For my belief is that if we live another century or so—I am talking of the common life which is the real life and not of the little separate lives which we live as individuals—and have five hundred a year each of us and rooms of our own; if we have the habit of freedom and the courage to write exactly what we think; if we escape a little from the common sitting-room and see human beings not always in their relation to each other but in relation to reality; and the sky, too, and the trees or whatever it may be in themselves; if we look past Milton's bogey, for no human being should shut out the view; if we face the fact, for it is a fact, that there is no arm to cling to, but that we go alone and that our relation is to the world of reality and not only to the world of men and women, then the opportunity will come and the dead poet who was Shakespeare's sister will put on the body which she has so often laid down. Drawing her life from the lives of the unknown who were her forerunners, as her brother did before her, she will be born. As for her coming without that preparation, without that effort on our part, without that determination that when she is born again she shall find it possible to live and write her poetry, that we cannot expect, for that would be impossible. But I maintain that she would come if we worked for her, and that so to work, even in poverty and obscurity, is worth while.

Three Guineas

Three Guineas marked Virginia Woolf's return to the genre she had employed in *A Room of One's Own:* the extended political and literary essay with a feminist theme. Like the earlier essay, this text is cast as a response to a request—in this case, a letter from an unnamed man asking her opinions on the prevention of war. Woolf wrote *Three Guineas* in 1938, against the backdrop of impending world war. Her analysis of gender inequality, and the social construction of those conditions of inequality, is intensified in the later work because of the urgency of the imminent war. Woolf uses her critique of sexism to investigate the perpetuation of violence in human history and to argue that the same dominances that bring about female inequality are responsible for the evils of war.

Woolf's argument is anything but simple, and her text anything but a straightforward polemic. Her rhetoric is laced with irony and an almost savage playfulness, in light of the seriousness of the historical moment. The primary metaphor of this work—as of her novel *Orlando* (1928)—is that of costume and dress. Hardly a retreat to a frivolous subject, the emphasis on clothing cloaks Woolf's understanding of the invented nature of social power. In other words, she does not attribute male dominance to biological superiority on the part of men; instead, she investigates the degree to which human hierarchies of gender, of class, and of race are made by human culture and are thus "conventional," just as fashion is. While there is something grotesque about comparing Nazi uniforms to the vestments and robes of the clergy, as Woolf does in the essay, her purpose is to scandalously unveil this truth of culture, and thereby to suggest that dominance can be reversed or transformed.

Woolf uses the lens of sexism to investigate the nature of authority—which is generally male authority in the institutions of modern society. Woolf is not reductive in doing this—she never implies that women are "better" in ethical or other ways, nor that authority is less vile when abused by women, as it occasionally is. She is eager to find the skeleton key to unlock the mystery of brute authority, and to warn against the militarism she saw as a permanent feature of British as well as German society. Woolf does not exempt any national culture or any group from susceptibility to power and its corrupting effects. In this essay, which shocked its audience in a way the more playful *A Room of One's Own* did not, she offers a comparative survey of the institutions of authority, or civil society. The vestments of power, Woolf shows, can be adopted by groups and by entire nations and even civilizations. *Three Guineas* is a clarion call to arms, to the weapons of thought and education as alternatives to the unthinkable horrors of a second world war. Virginia Woolf saw her prophecy of war come true shortly after its publication, and that fatal fact, as much as her own mental illness, was a push toward the suicide that claimed her life in 1941.

from Three Guineas[1]

Three years is a long time to leave a letter unanswered, and your letter has been lying without an answer even longer than that. I had hoped that it would answer itself, or that other people would answer it for me. But there it is with its question—How in your opinion are we to prevent war?—still unanswered.

It is true that many answers have suggested themselves, but none that would not need explanation, and explanations take time. In this case, too, there are reasons why it is particularly difficult to avoid misunderstanding. A whole page could be filled with excuses and apologies; declarations of unfitness, incompetence, lack of knowledge, and experience: and they would be true. But even when they were said there would still remain some difficulties so fundamental that it may well prove impossible for you to understand or for us to explain. But one does not like to leave so remarkable a letter as yours—a letter perhaps unique in the history of human correspondence, since when before has an educated man asked a woman how in her opinion war can be prevented?—unanswered. Therefore let us make the attempt; even if it is doomed to failure.

In the first place let us draw what all letter-writers instinctively draw, a sketch of the person to whom the letter is addressed. Without someone warm and breathing on

---

1. A guinea had been a gold coin worth one pound and one shilling (21 shillings); although no longer in circulation, guineas were used in determining professional fees and luxury items.

the other side of the page, letters are worthless. You, then, who ask the question, are a little grey on the temples; the hair is no longer thick on the top of your head. You have reached the middle years of life not without effort, at the Bar;[2] but on the whole your journey has been prosperous. There is nothing parched, mean or dissatisfied in your expression. And without wishing to flatter you, your prosperity—wife, children, house—has been deserved. You have never sunk into the contented apathy of middle life, for, as your letter from an office in the heart of London shows, instead of turning on your pillow and prodding your pigs, pruning your pear trees—you have a few acres in Norfolk—you are writing letters, attending meetings, presiding over this and that, asking questions, with the sound of the guns in your ears. For the rest, you began your education at one of the great public schools and finished it at the university.

It is now that the first difficulty of communication between us appears. Let us rapidly indicate the reason. We both come of what, in this hybrid age when, though birth is mixed, classes still remain fixed, it is convenient to call the educated class. When we meet in the flesh we speak with the same accent; use knives and forks in the same way; expect maids to cook dinner and wash up after dinner; and can talk during dinner without much difficulty about politics and people; war and peace; barbarism and civilization—all the questions indeed suggested by your letter. Moreover, we both earn our livings. But . . . those three dots mark a precipice, a gulf so deeply cut between us that for three years and more I have been sitting on my side of it wondering whether it is any use to try to speak across it. Let us then ask someone else—it is Mary Kingsley—to speak for us.[3] "I don't know if I ever revealed to you the fact that being allowed to learn German was *all* the paid-for education I ever had. Two thousand pounds was spent on my brother's, I still hope not in vain."[4] Mary Kingsley is not speaking for herself alone; she is speaking, still, for many of the daughters of educated men. And she is not merely speaking for them; she is also pointing to a very important fact about them, a fact that must profoundly influence all that follows: the fact of Arthur's Education Fund. You, who have read *Pendennis*,[5] will remember how the mysterious letters A.E.F. figured in the household ledgers. Ever since the thirteenth century English families have been paying money into that account. From the Pastons[6] to the Pendennises, all educated families from the thirteenth century to the present moment have paid money into that account. It is a voracious receptacle. Where there were many sons to educate it required a great effort on the part of the family to keep it full. For your education was not merely in book-learning; games educated your body; friends taught you more than books or games. Talk with them

2. In Britain, "the Bar" refers collectively to lawyers; to be called to the Bar means to enter the profession.

3. Mary Kingsley traveled extensively in West Africa in the final decade of the 19th century, publishing an account of her expeditions in 1897.

4. *The Life of Mary Kingsley*, by Stephen Gwynn, p. 15. It is difficult to get exact figures of the sums spent on the education of educated men's daughters. About £20 or £30 presumably covered the entire cost of Mary Kingsley's education (b. 1862; d. 1900). A sum of £100 may be taken as about the average in the 19th century and even later. The women thus educated often felt the lack of education very keenly. "I always feel the defects of my education most painfully when I go out," wrote Anne J. Clough, the first Principal of Newnham (*Life of Anne J. Clough*, by B. A Clough, p. 60) . . .

But the educated man's daughter in the 19th century was even more ignorant of life than of books. One reason for that ignorance is suggested by the following quotation: "It was supposed that most men were not 'virtuous', that is, that nearly all would be capable of accosting and annoying—or worse—any unaccompanied young woman whom they met." ("Society and the Season," by Mary, Countess of Lovelace, in *Fifty Years, 1882–1932*, p. 37.) She was therefore confined to a very narrow circle; and her "ignorance and indifference" to anything outside it was excusable. The connection between that ignorance and the 19th-century conception of manhood, which—witness the Victorian hero—made "virtue" and virility incompatible is obvious. In a well-known passage, Thackeray complains of the limitations which virtue and virility between them impose upon his art [Woolf's note].

5. *The History of Pendennis* (1848–1850), a novel by William Makepeace Thackeray.

6. *The Paston Letters* (c. 1420–1504) are a record of the domestic conditions of a well-to-do medieval family.

broadened your outlook and enriched your mind. In the holidays you travelled; acquired a taste for art; a knowledge of foreign politics; and then, before you could earn your own living, your father made you an allowance upon which it was possible for you to live while you learnt the profession which now entitles you to add the letters K.C.[7] to your name. All this came out of Arthur's Education Fund. And to this your sisters, as Mary Kingsley indicates, made their contribution. Not only did their own education, save for such small sums as paid the German teacher, go into it; but many of those luxuries and trimmings which are, after all, an essential part of education—travel, society, solitude, a lodging apart from the family house—they were paid into it too. It was a voracious receptacle, a solid fact—Arthur's Education Fund—a fact so solid indeed that it cast a shadow over the entire landscape. And the result is that though we look at the same things, we see them differently. What is that congregation of buildings there, with a semi-monastic look, with chapels and halls and green playing-fields? To you it is your old school, Eton or Harrow;[8] your old university, Oxford or Cambridge; the source of memories and of traditions innumerable. But to us, who see it through the shadow of Arthur's Education Fund, it is a schoolroom table; an omnibus going to a class; a little woman with a red nose who is not well educated herself but has an invalid mother to support; an allowance of £50 a year with which to buy clothes, give presents and take journeys on coming to maturity. Such is the effect that Arthur's Education Fund has had upon us. So magically does it change the landscape that the noble courts and quadrangles of Oxford and Cambridge often appear to educated men's daughters[9] like petticoats with holes in them, cold legs of mutton, and the boat train starting for abroad while the guard slams the door in their faces.

* * *

Here then is your own letter. In that, as we have seen, after asking for an opinion as to how to prevent war, you go on to suggest certain practical measures by which we can help you to prevent it. These are it appears that we should sign a manifesto, pledging ourselves "to protect culture and intellectual liberty";[1] that we should

7. King's Counsel; the title for senior barristers.

8. Prestigious boys' schools.

9. Our ideology is still so inveterately anthropocentric that it has been necessary to coin this clumsy term—educated man's daughter—to describe the class whose fathers have been educated at public schools and universities. Obviously, if the term "bourgeois" fits her brother, it is grossly incorrect to use it of one who differs so profoundly in the two prime characteristics of the bourgeoisie—capital and environment [Woolf's note].

1. It is to be hoped that some methodical person has made a collection of the various manifestoes and questionnaires issued broadcast during the years 1936–7. Private people of no political training were invited to sign appeals asking their own and foreign governments to change their policy; artists were asked to fill up forms stating the proper relation of the artist to the State, to religion, to morality; pledges were required that the writer should use English grammatically and avoid vulgar expressions; and dreamers were invited to analyse their dreams. By way of inducement it was generally proposed to publish the results in the daily or weekly Press. What effect this inquisition has had upon governments it is for the politician to say. Upon literature, since the output of books is unstaunched, and grammar would seem to be neither better nor worse, the effect is problematical. But

the inquisition . . . points, indirectly, to the death of the Siren, that much ridiculed and often upper-class lady who by keeping open house for the aristocracy, plutocracy, intelligentsia, ignorantsia, etc., tried to provide all classes with a talking-ground or scratching-post where they could rub up minds, manners and morals more privately, and perhaps as usefully. The part that the Siren played in promoting culture and intellectual liberty in the 18th century is held by historians to be of some importance. Even in our own day she had her uses. Witness W. B. Yeats—"How often have I wished that he [Synge] might live long enough to enjoy that communion with idle, charming cultivated women which Balzac in one of his dedications calls 'the chief consolation of genius'!" (Dramatis Personae, W. B. Yeats, p. 127.) Lady St. Helier who, as Lady Jeune, preserved the 18th-century tradition, informs us, however, that "Plovers' eggs at 2s 6d. apiece, forced strawberries, early asparagus, petits poussins . . . are now considered almost a necessity by anyone aspiring to give a good dinner" (1909); and her remark that the reception day was "very fatiguing . . . how exhausted I felt when half-past seven came, and how gladly at eight o' clock I sat down to a peaceful tête-à-tête dinner with my husband!" (Memories of Fifty Years, by Lady St. Helier, pp. 3, 5, 182) may explain why such houses are shut, why such hostesses are dead, and why

join a certain society, devoted to certain measures whose aim is to preserve peace; and, finally, that we should subscribe to that society which like the others is in need of funds.

First, then, let us consider how we can help you to prevent war by protecting culture and intellectual liberty, since you assure us that there is a connection between those rather abstract words and these very positive photographs—the photographs of dead bodies and ruined houses.

But if it was surprising to be asked for an opinion how to prevent war, it is still more surprising to be asked to help you in the rather abstract terms of your manifesto to protect culture and intellectual liberty. Consider, Sir, in the light of the facts given above, what this request of yours means. It means that in the year 1938 the sons of educated men are asking the daughters to help them to protect culture and intellectual liberty. And why, you may ask, is that so surprising? Suppose that the Duke of Devonshire, in his star and garter,[2] stepped down into the kitchen and said to the maid who was peeling potatoes with a smudge on her cheek: "Stop your potato peeling, Mary, and help me to construe this rather difficult passage in Pindar,"[3] would not Mary be surprised and run screaming to Louisa the cook, "Lawks, Louie, Master must be mad!" That, or something like it, is the cry that rises to our lips when the sons of educated men ask us, their sisters, to protect intellectual liberty and culture. But let us try to translate the kitchenmaid's cry into the language of educated people.

* * * The question which concerns us is what possible help we can give you in protecting culture and intellectual liberty—we who have been shut out from the universities so repeatedly, and are only now admitted so restrictedly; we who have received no paid-for education whatsoever, or so little that we can only read our own tongue and write our own language, we who are, in fact, members not of the intelligentsia but of the ignorantsia? * * * Just as any kitchenmaid would attempt to construe a passage in Pindar if told that her life depended on it, so the daughters of educated men, however little their training qualifies them, must consider what they can do to protect culture and intellectual liberty if by so doing they can help you to prevent war. So let us by all means in our power examine this further method of helping you, and see, before we consider your request that we should join your society, whether we can sign this manifesto in favour of culture and intellectual liberty with some intention of keeping our word.

* * *

* * * What were they working for in the nineteenth century—those queer dead women in their poke bonnets and shawls? The very same cause for which we are working now. "Our claim was no claim of women's rights only;"—it is Josephine Butler[4] who speaks—"it was larger and deeper; it was a claim for the rights of all—all men and women—to the respect in their persons of the great principles of Justice and Equality and Liberty." The words are the same as yours; the claim is the same as yours. The daughters of educated men who were called, to their resentment, "feminists" were in fact the advance guard of your own movement. They were fighting the

therefore the intelligentsia, the ignorantsia, the aristocracy, the bureaucracy, the bourgeoisie, etc., are driven (unless somebody will revive that society on an economic basis) to do their talking in public. But in view of the multitude of manifestoes and questionnaires now in circulation it would be foolish to suggest another into the minds and motives of the Inquisitors [Woolf's note].

2. Badges of the Order of the Garter, the highest English Order of Knighthood.
3. Greek poet (c. 522–443 B.C.), famous for his poems celebrating the victors at the ancient Olympic Games.
4. Feminist involved in the movement for educational reform (1828–1906).

same enemy that you are fighting and for the same reasons. They were fighting the tyranny of the patriarchal state as you are fighting the tyranny of the Fascist state. Thus we are merely carrying on the same fight that our mothers and grandmothers fought; their words prove it; your words prove it. But now with your letter before us we have your assurance that you are fighting with us, not against us. That fact is so inspiring that another celebration seems called for. What could be more fitting than to write more dead words, more corrupt words, upon more sheets of paper and burn them—the words, Tyrant, Dictator, for example? But, alas, those words are not yet obsolete. We can still shake out eggs from newspapers; still smell a peculiar and unmistakable odour in the region of Whitehall and Westminster. And abroad the monster has come more openly to the surface. There is no mistaking him there. He has widened his scope. He is interfering now with your liberty; he is dictating how you shall live; he is making distinctions not merely between the sexes, but between the races. You are feeling in your own persons what your mothers felt when they were shut out, when they were shut up, because they were women. Now you are being shut out, you are being shut up, because you are Jews, because you are democrats, because of race, because of religion. It is not a photograph that you look upon any longer; there you go, trapesing along in the procession yourselves. And that makes a difference. The whole iniquity of dictatorship, whether in Oxford or Cambridge, in Whitehall or Downing Street, against Jews or against women, in England, or in Germany, in Italy or in Spain is now apparent to you. But now we are fighting together. The daughters and sons of educated men are fighting side by side. That fact is so inspiring, even if no celebration is yet possible, that if this one guinea could be multiplied a million times all those guineas should be at your service without any other conditions than those that you have imposed upon yourself. Take this one guinea then and use it to assert "the rights of all—all men and women—to the respect in their persons of the great principles of Justice and Equality and Liberty." Put this penny candle in the window of your new society, and may we live to see the day when in the blaze of our common freedom the words tyrant and dictator shall be burnt to ashes, because the words tyrant and dictator shall be obsolete.

That request then for a guinea answered, and the cheque signed, only one further request of yours remains to be considered—it is that we should fill up a form and become members of your society. On the face of it that seems a simple request, easily granted. For what can be simpler than to join the society to which this guinea has just been contributed? On the face of it, how easy, how simple; but in the depths, how difficult, how complicated. . . . What possible doubts, what possible hesitations can those dots stand for? What reason or what emotion can make us hesitate to become members of a society whose aims we approve, to whose funds we have contributed? It may be neither reason nor emotion, but something more profound and fundamental than either. It may be difference. Different we are, as facts have proved, both in sex and in education. And it is from that difference, as we have already said, that our help can come, if help we can, to protect liberty, to prevent war. But if we sign this form which implies a promise to become active members of your society, it would seem that we must lose that difference and therefore sacrifice that help. * * *

* * * Thus, Sir, while we respect you as a private person and prove it by giving you a guinea to spend as you choose, we believe that we can help you most effectively by refusing to join your society; by working for our common ends—justice and equality and liberty for all men and women—outside your society, not within.

But this, you will say, if it means anything, can only mean that you, the daughters of educated men, who have promised us your positive help, refuse to join our society in order that you may make another of your own. And what sort of society do you propose to found outside ours, but in co-operation with it, so that we may both work together for our common ends? That is a question which you have every right to ask, and which we must try to answer in order to justify our refusal to sign the form you send. Let us then draw rapidly in outline the kind of society which the daughters of educated men found and join outside your society but in co-operation with its ends. In the first place, this new society, you will be relieved to learn, would have no honorary treasurer, for it would need no funds. It would have no office, no committee, no secretary; it would call no meetings; it would hold no conferences. If name it must have, it could be called the Outsiders' Society. That is not a resonant name, but it has the advantage that it squares with facts—the facts of history, of law, of biography; even, it may be, with the still hidden facts of our still unknown psychology. It would consist of educated men's daughters working in their own class—how indeed can they work in any other?[5]—and by their own methods for liberty, equality and peace. Their first duty, to which they would bind themselves not by oath, for oaths and ceremonies have no part in a society which must be anonymous and elastic before everything, would be not to fight with arms. This is easy for them to observe, for in fact, as the papers inform us, "the Army Council have no intention of opening recruiting for any women's corps.[6]" The country ensures it. Next they would refuse in the event of war to make munitions or nurse the wounded. Since in the last war both these activities were mainly discharged by the daughters of working men, the pressure upon them here too would be slight, though probably disagreeable. On the other hand the next duty to which they would pledge themselves is one of considerable difficulty, and calls not only for courage and initiative, but for the special knowledge of the educated man's daughter. It is, briefly, not to incite their brothers to fight, or to dissuade them, but to maintain an attitude of complete indifference. But the attitude expressed by the word "indifference" is so complex and of such importance that it needs even here further definition. Indifference in the first place must be given a firm footing upon fact. As it is a fact that she cannot understand what instinct compels him, what glory, what interest, what manly satisfaction fighting provides for him— "without war there would be no outlet for the manly qualities which fighting devel-

---

5. In the 19th century much valuable work was done for the working class by educated men's daughters in the only way that was then open to them. But now that some of them at least have received an expensive education, it is arguable that they can work much more effectively by remaining in their own class and using the methods of that class to improve a class which stands much in need of improvement. If on the other hand the educated (as so often happens) renounce the very qualities which education should have brought—reason, tolerance, knowledge—and play at belonging to the working class and adopting its cause, they merely expose that cause to the ridicule of the educated class and do nothing to improve their own. But the number of books written by the educated about the working class would seem to show that the glamour of the working class and the emotional relief afforded by adopting its cause, are today as irresistible to the middle class as the glamour of the aristocracy was 20 years ago (see A la Recherche du Temps Perdu). Meanwhile it would be interesting to know what the true-born working man or woman thinks of the playboys and playgirls of the educated class who adopt the working-class cause without sacrificing middle-class capital, or sharing working-class experience. "The average housewife," according to Mrs Murphy, Home Service Director of the British Commercial Gas Association, "washed an acre of dirty dishes, a mile of glass and three miles of clothes and scrubbed five miles of floor yearly." (Daily Telegraph, September 29th, 1937.) For a more detailed account of working-class life, see Life as We Have Known It by Co-operative working women, edited by Margaret Llewelyn Davies. The Life of Joseph Wright also gives a remarkable account of working-class life at first hand and not through pro-proletarian spectacles [Woolf's note].

6. "It was stated yesterday at the War Office that the Army Council have no intention of opening recruiting for any women's corps." (The Times, October 22nd, 1937.) This marks a prime distinction between the sexes. Pacifism is enforced upon women. Men are still allowed liberty of choice [Woolf's note].

ops"—as fighting thus is a sex characteristic which she cannot share, the counterpart some claim of the maternal instinct which he cannot share, so is it an instinct which she cannot judge. The outsider therefore must leave him free to deal with this instinct by himself, because liberty of opinion must be respected, especially when it is based upon an instinct which is as foreign to her as centuries of tradition and education can make it.[7] This is a fundamental and instinctive distinction upon which indifference may be based. But the outsider will make it her duty not merely to base her indifference upon instinct, but upon reason. When he says, as history proves that he has said, and may say again, "I am fighting to protect our country" and thus seeks to rouse her patriotic emotion, she will ask herself, "What does 'our country' mean to me an outsider?" To decide this she will analyse the meaning of patriotism in her own case. She will inform herself of the position of her sex and her class in the past. She will inform herself of the amount of land, wealth and property in the possession of her own sex and class in the present—how much of "England" in fact belongs to her. From the same sources she will inform herself of the legal protection which the law has given her in the past and now gives her. And if he adds that he is fighting to protect her body, she will reflect upon the degree of physical protection that she now enjoys when the words "Air Raid Precaution" are written on blank walls. And if he says that he is fighting to protect England from foreign rule, she will reflect that for her there are no "foreigners," since by law she becomes a foreigner if she marries a foreigner. And she will do her best to make this a fact, not by forced fraternity, but by human sympathy. All these facts will convince her reason (to put it in a nutshell) that her sex and class has very little to thank England for in the past; not much to thank England for in the present; while the security of her person in the future is highly dubious. But probably she will have imbibed, even from the governess, some romantic notion that Englishmen, those fathers and grandfathers whom she sees marching in the picture of history, are "superior" to the men of other countries. This she will consider it her duty to check by comparing French historians with English; German with French; the testimony of the ruled—the Indians or the Irish, say—with the claims made by their rulers. Still some "patriotic" emotion, some ingrained belief in the intellectual superiority of her own country over other countries may remain. Then she will compare English painting with French painting; English music with German music; English literature with Greek literature, for translations abound. When all these comparisons have been faithfully made by the use of reason, the outsider will find herself in possession of very good reasons for her indifference. She will find that she has no good reason to ask her brother to fight on her behalf to protect "our" country. "'Our country,'" she will say, "throughout the greater part of its history has treated me as a slave; it has denied me education or any share in its possessions. 'Our' country still ceases to be mine if I marry a foreigner. 'Our' country denies me the means of protecting myself, forces me to pay others a very large sum annually to protect me, and is so little able, even so, to protect me that Air Raid precautions are written on the wall. Therefore if you insist upon fighting to protect me, or 'our' coun-

---

7. The following quotation shows, however, that if sanctioned the fighting instinct easily develops. "The eyes deeply sunk into the sockets, the features acute, the amazon keeps herself very straight on the stirrups at the head of her squadron . . . Five English parliamentaries look at this woman with the respectful and a bit restless admiration one feels for a 'fauve' of an unknown species . . . The amazon Amalia rides in fact a magnificent dapple-grey horse, with glossy hair, which flatters like a parade horse . . . This woman who has killed five men—but who feels not sure about the sixth—was for the envoys of the House of Commons an excellent introducer to the Spanish War." (*The Matyrdom of Madrid,* Inedited Witnesses, by Louis Delaprée, pp. 34, 5, 6. Madrid, 1937) [Woolf's note].

try, let it be understood, soberly and rationally between us, that you are fighting to gratify a sex instinct which I cannot share; to procure benefits which I have not shared and probably will not share; but not to gratify my instincts, or to protect myself or my country. For," the outsider will say, "in fact, as a woman, I have no country. As a woman I want no country. As a woman my country is the whole world." And if, when reason has said its say, still some obstinate emotion remains, some love of England dropped into a child's ears by the cawing of rooks in an elm tree, by the splash of waves on a beach, or by English voices murmuring nursery rhymes, this drop of pure, if irrational, emotion she will make serve her to give to England first what she desires of peace and freedom for the whole world.

Such then will be the nature of her "indifference" and from this indifference certain actions must follow. She will bind herself to take no share in patriotic demonstrations; to assent to no form of national self-praise; to make no part of any claque or audience that encourages war; to absent herself from military displays, tournaments, tattoos, prize-givings and all such ceremonies as encourage the desire to impose "our" civilization or "our" dominion upon other people. The psychology of private life, moreover, warrants the belief that this use of indifference by the daughters of educated men would help materially to prevent war. For psychology would seem to show that it is far harder for human beings to take action when other people are indifferent and allow them complete freedom of action, than when their actions are made the centre of excited emotion. The small boy struts and trumpets outside the window: implore him to stop; he goes on; say nothing; he stops. That the daughters of educated men then should give their brothers neither the white feather of cowardice nor the red feather of courage, but no feather at all;[8] that they should shut the bright eyes that rain influence, or let those eyes look elsewhere when war is discussed—that is the duty to which outsiders will train themselves in peace before the threat of death inevitably makes reason powerless.

Such then are some of the methods by which the society, the anonymous and secret Society of Outsiders would help you, Sir, to prevent war and to ensure freedom. * * *

It seems, Sir, as we listen to the voices of the past, as if we were looking at the photograph again, at the picture of dead bodies and ruined houses that the Spanish Government sends us almost weekly.[9] Things repeat themselves it seems. Pictures and voices are the same today as they were 2,000 years ago.

Such then is the conclusion to which our enquiry into the nature of fear has brought us—the fear which forbids freedom in the private house. That fear, small, insignificant and private as it is, is connected with the other fear, the public fear, which is neither small nor insignificant, the fear which has led you to ask us to help you to prevent war. Otherwise we should not be looking at the picture again. But it is not the same picture that caused us at the beginning of this letter to feel the same emotions—you called them "horror and disgust"; we called them horror and disgust. For as this letter has gone on, adding fact to fact, another picture has imposed itself

8. During the First World War in Britain patriotic women would hand a white feather to men who seemed to have evaded military service.
9. The Republican Government in Spain was then engaged in a war against Fascist forces intent on seizing power; by 1939 the Fascists had gained control of the country.

upon the foreground. It is the figure of a man; some say, others deny, that he is Man himself,[1] the quintessence of virility, the perfect type of which all the others are imperfect adumbrations. He is a man certainly. His eyes are glazed; his eyes glare. His body, which is braced in an unnatural position, is tightly cased in a uniform. Upon the breast of that uniform are sewn several medals and other mystic symbols. His hand is upon a sword. He is called in German and Italian Führer or Duce; in our own language Tyrant or Dictator. And behind him lie ruined houses and dead bodies— men, women and children. But we have not laid that picture before you in order to excite once more the sterile emotion of hate. On the contrary it is in order to release other emotions such as the human figure, even thus crudely in a coloured photograph, arouses in us who are human beings. For it suggests a connection and for us a very important connection. It suggests that the public and the private worlds are inseparably connected; that the tyrannies and servilities of the one are the tyrannies and servilities of the other. But the human figure even in a photograph suggests other and more complex emotions. It suggests that we cannot dissociate ourselves from that figure but are ourselves that figure. It suggests that we are not passive spectators doomed to unresisting obedience but by our thoughts and actions can ourselves change that figure. A common interest unites us; it is one world, one life. How essential it is that we should realise that unity the dead bodies, the ruined houses prove. For such will be our ruin if you in the immensity of your public abstractions forget the private figure, or if we in the intensity of our private emotions forget the public world. Both houses will be ruined, the public and the private, the material and the spiritual, for they are inseparably connected. But with your letter before us we have reason to hope. For by asking our help you recognise that connection; and by reading your words we are reminded of other connections that lie far deeper than the facts on the surface. Even here, even now your letter tempts us to shut our ears to these little facts, these trivial details, to listen not to the bark of the guns and the bray of the gramophones but to the voices of the poets, answering each other, assuring us of a unity that rubs out divisions as if they were chalk marks only; to discuss with you the capacity of the human spirit to overflow boundaries and make unity out of multiplicity. But that would be to dream—to dream the recurring dream that has haunted the human mind since the beginning of time; the dream of peace, the dream of freedom. But, with the sound of the guns in your ears you have not asked us to dream. You have not asked us what peace is; you have asked us how to prevent war. Let us then leave it to the poets to tell us what the dream is; and fix our eyes upon the photograph again: the fact.

    Whatever the verdict of others may be upon the man in uniform—and opinions differ—there is your letter to prove that to you the picture is the picture of evil. And though we look upon that picture from different angles our conclusion is the same as yours—it is evil. We are both determined to do what we can to destroy the evil which that picture represents, you by your methods, we by ours. And since we are different, our help must be different. What ours can be we have tried to show—how

---

1. The nature of manhood and the nature of womanhood are frequently defined by both Italian and German dictators. Both repeatedly insist that it is the nature of man and indeed the essence of manhood to fight . . . It is possible that the Fascist States by revealing to the younger generation at least the need for emancipation from the old conception of virility are doing for the male sex what the Crimean and the European wars did for their sisters. Professor Huxley, however, warns us that "any considerable alteration of the hereditary constitution is an affair of millennia, not of decades." On the other hand, as science also assures us that our life on earth is "an affair of millennia, not of decades," some alteration in the hereditary constitution may be worth attempting [Woolf's note].

imperfectly, how superficially there is no need to say.[2] But as a result the answer to your question must be that we can best help you to prevent war not by repeating your words and following your methods but by finding new words and creating new methods. We can best help you to prevent war not by joining your society but by remaining outside your society but in co-operation with its aim. That aim is the same for us both. It is to assert "the rights of all—all men and women—to the respect in their persons of the great principles of Justice and Equality and Liberty." To elaborate further is unnecessary, for we have every confidence that you interpret those words as we do. And excuses are unnecessary, for we can trust you to make allowances for those deficiencies which we foretold and which this letter has abundantly displayed.

To return then to the form that you have sent and ask us to fill up: for the reasons given we will leave it unsigned. But in order to prove as substantially as possible that our aims are the same as yours, here is the guinea, a free gift, given freely, without any other conditions than you choose to impose upon yourself. It is the third of three guineas; but the three guineas, you will observe, though given to three different treasurers are all given to the same cause, for the causes are the same and inseparable.

Now, since you are pressed for time, let me make an end; apologising three times over to the three of you, first for the length of this letter, second for the smallness of the contribution, and thirdly for writing at all. The blame for that however rests upon you, for this letter would never have been written had you not asked for an answer to your own.

from The Diaries

Saturday 2 January [1915]

This is the kind of day which if it were possible to choose an altogether average sample of our life, I should select. We breakfast; I interview Mrs Le Grys. She complains of the huge Belgian appetites, & their preference for food fried in butter. "They never *give* one anything" she remarked. The Count, taking Xmas dinner with them, insisted, after Pork & Turkey, that he wanted a third meat. Therefore Mrs Le G. hopes that the war will soon be over. If they eat thus in their exile, how must they eat at home, she wonders?[1] After this, L[eonard]. & I both settle down to our scribbling. He finishes his Folk Story review, & I do about 4 pages of poor Effie's story;[2] we lunch; & read the papers, agree that there is no news. I read Guy Mannering upstairs for 20 minutes;[3] & then we take Max [a dog] for a walk. Halfway up to the Bridge, we found ourselves cut off by the river, which rose visibly, with a little ebb & flow, like

2. Coleridge however expresses the views and aims of the outsiders with some accuracy in the following passage: "Man must be *free* or to what purpose was he made a Spirit of Reason, and not a Machine of Instinct? Man must *obey*; or wherefore has he a conscience? The powers, which create this difficulty, contain its solution likewise, for *their* service is perfect freedom." . . . To which may be added a quotation from Walt Whitman: "Of Equality—as if it harm'd me, giving others the same chances and rights as myself—as if it were not indispensable to my own rights that others possess the same."
And finally the words of a half-forgotten novelist, George Sand, are worth considering: "All lives are bound up with each other, and any human being who would

describe his or her selfhood in isolation, without linking it to that of his or her fellows, would only offer a mystery to be untangled . . . That kind of individuality has by itself neither meaning nor importance. It only takes on any kind of meaning by becoming a part of the general life, by grounding itself together with the individuality of each of my fellows, and through that gesture it becomes a part of history." (*Histoire de ma Vie* [The Story of My Life], by George Sand, pp. 240–1) [Woolf's note, quoting Sand in French].
1. Belgian refugees were housed in English homes following the German invasion of Belgium.
2. Later published as *Night and Day* (1919).
3. *Guy Mannering* (1815), a novel by Sir Walter Scott.

the pulse of a heart. Indeed, the road we had come along was crossed, after 5 minutes, by a stream several inches deep. One of the queer things about the suburbs is that the vilest little red villas are always let, & that not one of them has an open window, or an uncurtained window. I expect that people take a pride in their curtains, & there is great rivalry among neighbours. One house had curtains of yellow silk, striped with lace insertion. The rooms inside must be in semi-darkness; & I suppose rank with the smell of meat & human beings. I believe that being curtained is a mark of respectability—Sophie[4] used to insist upon it. And then I did my marketing. Saturday night is the great buying night; & some counters are besieged by three rows of women. I always choose the empty shops, where I suppose, one pays $\frac{1}{2}$ a lb. more. And then we had tea, & honey & cream; & now L. is typewriting his article; & we shall read all the evening & go to bed.

Monday 21 January [1918]

Here I was interrupted on the verge of a description of London at the meeting of sun set & moon rise. I drove on top of a Bus from Oxford St. to Victoria station, & observed how the passengers were watching the spectacle: the same sense of interest & mute attention shown as in the dress circle before some pageant. A Spring night; blue sky with a smoke mist over the houses. The shops were still lit; but not the lamps, so that there were bars of light all down the streets; & in Bond Street I was at a loss to account for a great chandelier of light at the end of the street; but it proved to be several shop windows jutting out into the road, with lights on different tiers. Then at Hyde Park Corner the search light rays out, across the blue; part of a pageant on a stage where all has been wonderfully muted down. The gentleness of the scene was what impressed me; a twilight view of London. Houses very large & looking stately. Now & then someone, as the moon came into view, remarked upon the chance for an air raid. We escaped though, a cloud rising towards night.

Sunday (Easter) 20 April [1919]

* * * In the idleness which succeeds any long article, & Defoe is the 2nd leader this month, I got out this diary, & read as one always does read one's own writing, with a kind of guilty intensity. I confess that the rough & random style of it, often so ungrammatical, & crying for a word altered, afflicted me somewhat. I am trying to tell whichever self it is that reads this hereafter that I can write very much better; & take no time over this; & forbid her to let the eye of man behold it. And now I may add my little compliment to the effect that it has a slapdash & vigour, & sometimes hits an unexpected bulls eye. But what is more to the point is my belief that the habit of writing thus for my own eye only is good practise. It loosens the ligaments. Never mind the misses & the stumbles. Going at such a pace as I do I must make the most direct & instant shots at my object, & thus have to lay hands on words, choose them, & shoot them with no more pause than is needed to put my pen in the ink. I believe that during the past year I can trace some increase of ease in my professional writing which I attribute to my casual half hours after tea. Moreover there looms ahead of me the shadow of some kind of form which a diary might attain to. I might in the course of time learn what it is that one can make of this loose, drifting material of life; finding another use for it than the use I put it to,

---

4. A former family cook.

so much more consciously & scrupulously, in fiction. What sort of diary should I like mine to be? Something loose knit, & yet not slovenly, so elastic that it will embrace any thing, solemn, slight or beautiful that comes into my mind. I should like it to resemble some deep old desk, or capacious hold-all, in which one flings a mass of odds & ends without looking them through. I should like to come back, after a year or two, & find that the collection had sorted itself & refined itself & coalesced, as such deposits so mysteriously do, into a mould, transparent enough to reflect the light of our life, & yet steady, tranquil composed with the aloofness of a work of art. The main requisite, I think on re-reading my old volumes, is not to play the part of censor, but to write as the mood comes or of anything whatever; since I was curious to find how I went for things put in haphazard, & found the significance to lie where I never saw it at the time. But looseness quickly becomes slovenly. A little effort is needed to face a character or an incident which needs to be recorded. * * *

Wednesday 7 January [1920]

To begin the year on the last pages of my old book—the few I've not torn off for letter writing—is all upside-down of course; but of a part with the character of the work.

This is our last evening. We sit over the fire waiting for post—the cream of the day, I think. Yet every part of the day here has its merits—even the breakfast without toast. That—however it begins—ends with Pippins; most mornings the sun comes in; we finish in good temper; & I go off to the romantic chamber over grass rough with frost & ground hard as brick. Then Mrs Dedman comes to receive orders—to give them, really, for she has planned our meals to suit her days cooking before she comes. We share her oven. The result is always savoury—stews & mashes & deep many coloured dishes swimming in gravy thick with carrots & onions. Elsie, aged 18, can be spoken to as though she had a head on her shoulders. The house is empty by half past eleven; empty now at five o'clock; we tend our fire, cook coffee, read, I find, luxuriously, peacefully, at length.

But I should not spend my time on an indoor chronicle; unless I lazily shirked the describing of winter down & meadow—the recording of what takes my breath away at every turn. Heres the sun out for example & all the upper twigs of the trees as if dipped in fire; the trunks emerald green; even bark bright tinted, & variable as the skin of a lizard. Then theres Asheham hill smoke misted; the windows of the long train spots of sun; the smoke lying back on the carriages like a rabbits lop ears. The chalk quarry glows pink; & my water meadows lush as June, until you see that the grass is short, & rough as a dogfishes back. But I could go on counting what I've noticed page after page. Every day or nearly I've walked towards a different point & come back with a string of these matchings & marvels. Five minutes from the house one is out in the open, a great pull over Asheham; &, as I say, every direction bears fruit. Once we went over the cornfield & up onto the down—a dim Sunday afternoon—muddy on the road, but dry up above. The long down grass pale, & as we pushed through it, up got a hawk at our feet, seeming to trail near the ground, as if weighted down—attached to something. It let the burden fall, & rose high as we came up. We found the wings of a partridge attached to [a] bleeding stump, for the Hawk had almost done his meal. We saw him go back to find it. Further down the hill side a great white owl "wavy" (for that describes his way of weaving a web round a tree—the plumy soft look of him in the dusk adding truth to the word) "wavy in the dusk," flew behind the hedge as we came past. Village girls were returning, & calling out to friends in doors. So we cross the field & churchyard, find our coke burnt through to red, toast the bread—& the evening comes.

L. has spent most of his time pruning the apple trees, & tying plums to the wall. To do this he wears two jackets, 2 pairs of socks, two pairs of gloves; even so the cold bites through. These last days have been like frozen water, ruffled by the wind into atoms of ice against the cheek; then, in the shelter, forming round you in a still pool. * * *

Wednesday 16 August [1922]

I should be reading Ulysses, & fabricating my case for & against. I have read 200 pages so far—not a third; & have been amused, stimulated, charmed interested by the first 2 or 3 chapters—to the end of the Cemetery scene; & then puzzled, bored, irritated, & disillusioned as by a queasy undergraduate scratching his pimples. And Tom,[5] great Tom, thinks this on a par with War & Peace! An illiterate, underbred book it seems to me: the book of a self taught working man, & we all know how distressing they are, how egotistic, insistent, raw, striking, & ultimately nauseating. When one can have the cooked flesh, why have the raw? But I think if you are anaemic, as Tom is, there is a glory in blood. Being fairly normal myself I am soon ready for the classics again. I may revise this later. I do not compromise my critical sagacity. I plant a stick in the ground to mark page 200. * * *

Wednesday 6 September [1922]

* * * I finished Ulysses, & think it a mis-fire. Genius it has I think; but of the inferior water. The book is diffuse. It is brackish. It is pretentious. It is underbred, not only in the obvious sense, but in the literary sense. A first rate writer, I mean, respects writing too much to be tricky; startling; doing stunts. I'm reminded all the time of some callow board school boy, say like Henry Lamb, full of wits & powers, but so self-conscious & egotistical that he loses his head, becomes extravagant, mannered, uproarious, ill at ease, makes kindly people feel sorry for him, & stern ones merely annoyed; & one hopes he'll grow out of it; but as Joyce is 40 this scarcely seems likely. I have not read it carefully; & only once; & it is very obscure; so no doubt I have scamped the virtue of it more than is fair. I feel that myriads of tiny bullets pepper one & spatter one; but one does not get one deadly wound straight in the face—as from Tolstoy, for instance; but it is entirely absurd to compare him with Tolstoy.

Tuesday 19 June [1923]

I took up this book with a kind of idea that I might say something about my writing—which was prompted by glancing at what K.M. said about *her* writing in the Dove's Nest.[6] But I only glanced. She said a good deal about feeling things deeply: also about being pure, which I wont criticise, though of course I very well could. But now what do I feel about *my* writing?—this book, that is, The Hours,[7] if thats its name? One must write from deep feeling, said Dostoevsky. And do I? Or do I fabricate with words, loving them as I do? No I think not. In this book I have almost too many ideas. I want to give life & death, sanity & insanity; I want to criticise the social system, & to show it

---

5. T. S. Eliot.
6. J. M. Murray wrote an introduction to Katherine Mansfield's *The Dove's Nest and Other Stories* (1923),

which quotes extracts from her journal.
7. "The Hours" was an early title for *Mrs Dalloway* (1925).

at work, at its most intense—But here I may be posing. I heard from Ka [Arnold-Forster] this morning that she doesn't like In the Orchard.[8] At once I feel refreshed. I become anonymous, a person who writes for the love of it. She takes away the motive of praise, & lets me feel that without any praise, I should be content to go on. This is what Duncan [Grant] said of his painting the other night. I feel as if I slipped off all my ball dresses & stood naked—which as I remember was a very pleasant thing to do. But to go on. Am I writing The Hours from deep emotion? Of course the mad part tries me so much, makes my mind squint so badly that I can hardly face spending the next weeks at it. Its a question though of these characters. People, like Arnold Bennett, say I cant create, or didn't in J[acob]'s R[oom], characters that survive. My answer is—but I leave that to the Nation:[9] its only the old argument that character is dissipated into shreds now: the old post-Dostoevsky argument. I daresay its true, however, that I haven't that "reality" gift. I insubstantise, wilfully to some extent, distrusting reality—its cheapness. But to get further. Have I the power of conveying the true reality? Or do I write essays about myself? Answer these questions as I may, in the uncomplimentary sense, & still there remains this excitement. To get to the bones, now I'm writing fiction again I feel my force flow straight from me at its fullest. After a dose of criticism I feel that I'm writing sideways, using only an angle of my mind. This is justification; for free use of the faculties means happiness. I'm better company, more of a human being. Nevertheless, I think it most important in this book to go for the central things, even though they dont submit, as they should however, to beautification in language. No, I don't nail my crest to the Murrys, who work in my flesh after the manner of the jigger insect. Its annoying, indeed degrading, to have these bitternesses. Still, think of the 18th Century. But then they were overt, not covert, as now.

I foresee, to return to The Hours, that this is going to be the devil of a struggle. The design is so queer & so masterful. I'm always having to wrench my substance to fit it. The design is certainly original, & interests me hugely. I should like to write away & away at it, very quick and fierce. Needless to say, I cant. In three weeks from today I shall be dried up. * * *

Monday 5 May [1924]

* * * London is enchanting. I step out upon a tawny coloured magic carpet, it seems, & get carried into beauty without raising a finger. The nights are amazing, with all the white porticoes & broad silent avenues. And people pop in & out, lightly, divertingly like rabbits; & I look down Southampton Row, wet as a seal's back or red & yellow with sunshine, & watch the omnibus going & coming, & hear the old crazy organs. One of these days I will write about London, & how it takes up the private life & carries it on, without any effort. Faces passing lift up my mind; prevent it from settling, as it does in the stillness at Rodmell. * * *

Monday 21 December [1925]

But no Vita! But Vita for 3 days at Long Barn,[1] from which L[eonard]. & I returned yesterday. These Sapphists *love* women; friendship is never untinged with amorosity. In short, my fears & refrainings, my "impertinence" my usual self-

---

8. *In the Orchard* (1923), an essay by Woolf.
9. In a 1923 review of *Jacob's Room*, the novelist Arnold Bennett had written that "I have seldom read a cleverer book than Virginia Woolf's *Jacob's Room* ... But the characters do not vitally survive in the mind because the author has been obsessed by details of originality and clev-

erness." Woolf's reply, Mr. *Bennett and Mrs. Brown*, mocking Bennett's realist fiction as "thin gruel," appeared in the *Nation and Athenaeum* in December 1923.
1. Country home of Vita Sackville-West and her husband Harold Nicolson.

consciousness in intercourse with people who mayn't want me & so on—were all, as L. said, sheer fudge; &, partly thanks to him (he made me write) I wound up this wounded & stricken year in great style. I like her & being with her, & the splendour—she shines in the grocers shop in Sevenoaks with a candle lit radiance, stalking on legs like beech trees, pink glowing, grape clustered, pearl hung. That is the secret of her glamour, I suppose. Anyhow she found me incredibly dowdy, no woman cared less for personal appearance—no one put on things in the way I did. Yet so beautiful, &c. What is the effect of all this on me? Very mixed. There is her maturity & full breastedness: her being so much in full sail on the high tides, where I am coasting down backwaters; her capacity I mean to take the floor in any company, to represent her country, to visit Chatsworth, to control silver, servants, chow dogs; her motherhood (but she is a little cold & offhand with her boys) her being in short (what I have never been) a real woman. Then there is some voluptuousness about her; the grapes are ripe; & not reflective. No. In brain & insight she is not as highly organised as I am. But then she is aware of this, & so lavishes on me the maternal protection which, for some reason, is what I have always most wished from everyone. What L. gives me, & Nessa [Vanessa Bell] gives me, & Vita, in her more clumsy external way, tries to give me. For of course, mingled with all this glamour, grape clusters & pearl necklaces, there is something loose fitting. How much, for example, shall I really miss her when she is motoring across the desert? I will make a note on that next year. Anyhow, I am very glad that she is coming to tea today, & I shall ask her, whether she minds my dressing so badly? I think she does. I read her poem; which is more compact, better seen & felt than anything yet of hers. * * *

[*Saturday 31 July 1926*]

My own Brain

Here is a whole nervous breakdown in miniature. We came on Tuesday. Sank into a chair, could scarcely rise; everything insipid; tasteless, colourless. Enormous desire for rest. Wednesday—only wish to be alone in the open air. Air delicious—avoided speech; could not read. Thought of my own power of writing with veneration, as of something incredible, belonging to someone else; never again to be enjoyed by me. Mind a blank. Slept in my chair. Thursday. No pleasure in life whatsoever; but felt perhaps more attuned to existence. Character & idiosyncracy as Virginia Woolf completely sunk out. Humble & modest. Difficulty in thinking what to say. Read automatically, like a cow chewing cud. Slept in chair. Friday. Sense of physical tiredness; but slight activity of the brain. Beginning to take notice. Making one or two plans. No power of phrase making. Difficulty in writing to Lady Colefax. Saturday (today) much clearer & lighter. Thought I could write, but resisted, or found it impossible. A desire to read poetry set in on Friday. This brings back a sense of my own individuality. Read some Dante & Bridges, without troubling to understand, but got pleasure from them. Now I begin to wish to write notes, but not yet novel. But today senses quickening. No "making up" power yet; no desire to cast scenes in my book. Curiosity about literature returning: want to read Dante, Havelock Ellis, & Berlioz autobiography; also to make a looking glass with shell frame. These processes have sometimes been spread over several weeks. * * *

Wednesday 15 September [1926]

A State of Mind

Woke up perhaps at 3. Oh its beginning its coming—the horror—physically like a painful wave swelling about the heart—tossing me up. I'm unhappy unhappy!

Down—God, I wish I were dead. Pause. But why am I feeling this? Let me watch the wave rise. I watch. Vanessa. Children. Failure. Yes; I detect that. Failure failure. (The wave rises). Oh they laughed at my taste in green paint! Wave crashes. I wish I were dead! I've only a few years to live I hope. I cant face this horror any more—(this is the wave spreading out over me).

This goes on; several times, with varieties of horror. Then, at the crisis, instead of the pain remaining intense, it becomes rather vague. I doze. I wake with a start. The wave again! The irrational pain: the sense of failure; generally some specific incident, as for example my taste in green paint, or buying a new dress, or asking Dadie for the week end, tacked on.

At last I say, watching as dispassionately as I can, Now take a pull of yourself. No more of this. I reason. I take a census of happy people & unhappy. I brace myself to shove to throw to batter down. I begin to march blindly forward. I feel obstacles go down. I say it doesn't matter. Nothing matters. I become rigid & straight, & sleep again, & half wake & feel the wave beginning & watch the light whitening & wonder how, this time, breakfast & daylight will overcome it; & then hear L. in the passage & simulate, for myself as well as for him, great cheerfulness; & generally am cheerful, by the time breakfast is over. Does everyone go through this state? Why have I so little control? It is not creditable, nor lovable. It is the cause of much waste & pain in my life.

Saturday 27 October [1928]

Thank God, my long toil at the women's lecture[2] is this moment ended. I am back from speaking at Girton, in floods of rain. Starved but valiant young women— that's my impression. Intelligent eager, poor; & destined to become schoolmistresses in shoals. I blandly told them to drink wine & have a room of their own. Why should all the splendour, all the luxury of life be lavished on the Julians & the Francises, & none on the Phares & the Thomases?[3] There's Julian not much relishing it, perhaps. I fancy sometimes the world changes. I think I see reason spreading. But I should have liked a closer & thicker knowledge of life. I should have liked to deal with real things sometimes. I get such a sense of tingling & vitality from an evenings talk like that; one's angularities & obscurities are smoothed & lit. How little one counts, I think: how little anyone counts; how fast & furious & masterly life is; & how all these thousands are swimming for dear life. I felt elderly & mature. And nobody respected me. They were very eager, egotistical, or rather not much impressed by age & repute. Very little reverence or that sort of thing about. The corridors of Girton are like vaults in some horrid high church cathedral—on & on they go, cold & shiny—with a light burning. High gothic rooms; acres of bright brown wood; here & there a photograph. * * *

Wednesday 23 October [1929]

As it is true—I write only for an hour—then sink back feeling I cannot keep my brain on that spin any more—then typewrite, & am done by 12—I will here sum up my impressions before publishing a Room of One's Own. It is a little ominous that Morgan wont review it.[4] It makes me suspect that there is a shrill feminine tone in it

2. The lecture that became A Room of One's Own.
3. Elsie Phare was a student at Newnham College, Cambridge; Margaret Thomas was a student at Girton College. Their invitations had brought Woolf to Cambridge. Julian

Bell, Woolf's nephew, was a student at King's College.
4. He [E. M. Forster] wrote yesterday 3rd Dec. & said he very much liked it [Woolf's note].

which my intimate friends will dislike. I forecast, then, that I shall get no criticism, except of the evasive jocular kind, from Lytton, Roger & Morgan; that the press will be kind & talk of its charm, & sprightiness; also I shall be attacked for a feminist & hinted at for a sapphist; Sibyl will ask me to luncheon; I shall get a good many letters from young women. I am afraid it will not be taken seriously. Mrs Woolf is so accomplished a writer that all she says makes easy reading . . . this very feminine logic . . . a book to be put in the hands of girls. I doubt that I mind very much. The Moths; but I think it is to be waves, is trudging along;[5] & I have that to refer to, if I am damped by the other. It is a trifle, I shall say; so it is, but I wrote it with ardour & conviction.

* * *

Friday 20 May [1938]

Time & again I have meant to write down my expectations, dreads, & so on, waiting the publication on—I think June 2nd—of 3 G[uinea]s—but haven't, because what with living in the solid world of Roger, & then (again this morning) in the airy world of Poyntz Hall I feel extremely little.[6] And dont want to rouse feeling. What I'm afraid of is the taunt Charm & emptiness. The book I wrote with such violent feelings to relieve that immense pressure will not dimple the surface. That is my fear. Also I'm uneasy at taking this role in the public eye—afraid of autobiography in public. But the fears are entirely outbalanced (this is honest) by the immense relief & peace I have gained, & enjoy this moment. Now I am quit of that poison & excitement. Nor is that all. For having spat it out, my mind is made up. I need never recur or repeat. I am an outsider. I can take my way: experiment with my own imagination in my own way. The pack may howl, but it shall never catch me. And even if the pack—reviewers, friends, enemies—pays me no attention or sneers, still I'm free. This is the actual result of that spiritual conversion (I cant bother to get the right words) in the autumn of 1933—or 4—when I rushed through London, buying, I remember, a great magnifying glass, from sheer ecstasy, near Blackfriars: when I gave the man who played the harp half a crown for talking to me about his life in the Tube station. The omens are mixed: L. is less excited than I hoped; Nessa highly ambiguous; Miss Hepworth & Mrs Nicholls say "Women owe a great deal to Mrs Woolf" & I have promised Pippa to supply books. Now for R.'s letters & Monks H—at the moment windy & cold.

Wednesday 14 September [1938]

Things worse today. Rioting in Prague. Sudeten ultimatum. It looks as if Hitler meant to slide sideways into war. Raises riots: will say cant be stopped.[7] This came on the 9.30 wireless last night. This morning more marking time. No one knows. Headachy, partly screw of Roger partly this gloom. So I'm stopping Roger;[8] as we go up to lunch with Bella tomorrow. And whats the private position? So black I cant gather

5. "The Moths" was an early title for *The Waves* (1931).
6. "Poyntz Hall" later became *Between the Acts* (1941).
7. The German Chancellor Adolf Hitler had been putting pressure on the Czechoslovak government to allow the incorporation of that country's German minority into Germany, even though this would mean the disintegration of Czechoslovakia. A speech Hitler made at Nuremberg had given the signal for the German minority (the "Sudeten Germans") in Czechoslovakia to riot; the Czech government imposed martial law, the immediate

revocation of which was then demanded by the German government in Berlin. British Prime Minister Neville Chamberlain flew to meet Hitler, and, fearful of war and in the face of German threats to invade Czechoslovakia, informed the Czechs that Britain and France would not support them against German demands. The Germans soon took over Czechoslovakia.
8. Woolf was working on a biography of her friend, Roger Fry, published in 1940 as *Roger Fry: A Biography*.

together. Work I suppose. If it is war, then every country joins in: chaos. To oppose this with Roger my only private position. Well thats an absurd little match to strike. But its a hopeless war this—when we know winning means nothing. So we're committed, for the rest of our lives, to public misery. This will be slashed with private too. * * *

Sunday 29 January [1939]

Yes, Barcelona has fallen: Hitler speaks tomorrow; the next dress rehearsal begins: I have seen Marie Stopes, Princesse de Polignac, Philip & Pippin, & Dr Freud in the last 3 days,[9] also had Tom to dinner & to the Stephens' party.

Dr Freud gave me a narcissus. Was sitting in a great library with little statues at a large scrupulously tidy shiny table. We like patients on chairs. A screwed up shrunk very old man: with a monkeys light eyes, paralysed spasmodic movements, inarticulate: but alert. On Hitler. Generation before the poison will be worked out. About his books. Fame? I was infamous rather than famous, didnt make £50 by his first book. Difficult talk. An interview. Daughter & Martin helped. Immense potential, I mean an old fire now flickering. When we left he took up the stand What are *you* going to do? The English—war.

Monday 13 May [1940]

I admit to some content, some closing of a chapter, & peace that comes with it, from posting my proofs today: I admit—because we're in the 3rd day of "the greatest battle in history." It began (here) with the 8 oclock wireless announcing, as I lay half asleep, the invasion of Holland & Belgium. The third day of the Battle of Waterloo. Apple blossom snowing the garden. A bowl lost in the pond. Churchill exhorting all men to stand together. "I have nothing to offer but blood & tears & sweat."[1] These vast formless shapes further circulate. They aren't substances; but they make everything else minute. Duncan saw an air battle over Charleston—a silver pencil & a puff of smoke. Percy has seen the wounded arriving in their boots. So my little moment of peace comes in a yawning hollow. But though L. says he has petrol in the garage for suicide shd. Hitler win, we go on. Its the vastness, & the smallness, that make this possible. So intense are my feelings (about Roger): yet the circumference (the war) seems to make a hoop round them. No, I cant get the odd incongruity of feeling intensely & at the same time knowing that there's no importance in that feeling. Or is there, as I sometimes think, more importance than ever? * * *

Sunday 22 December [1940]

How beautiful they were, those old people—I mean father & mother—how simple, how clear, how untroubled. I have been dipping into old letters & fathers memoirs. He loved her—oh & was so candid & reasonable & transparent—& had such a fastidious delicate mind, educated, & transparent. How serene & gay even their life reads to me: no mud; no whirlpools. And so human—with the children & the little hum & song of the nursery. But if I read as a contemporary I shall lose my childs vision & so must stop. Nothing turbulent; nothing involved: no introspection.

---

9. Sigmund Freud, mortally ill with cancer of the jaw, had fled the Nazis and settled in Hampstead with his daughter Anna.
1. Germany invaded Holland, Belgium, and Luxembourg on 10 May; on the same day Neville Chamberlain resigned as prime minister, and Winston Churchill took office at the head of a coalition government. In seeking support for his administration, Churchill said "I have nothing to offer but blood, toil, tears and sweat"; see page 2522 for this speech.

━━ ⊶⊷⊶ ━━

D. H. Lawrence

1885–1930

D. H. Lawrence's meteoric literary life ended in Venice, Italy, in 1930, where he died at the age of forty-five, far from his birthplace in Nottinghamshire, the coal-mining heart of England. If Lawrence was something of a comet in British literature, arcing across its skies with vibrant energy and controversy while he lived, he was equally visible after his death in the excitement and danger that persisted like a halo around his texts. A formidable poet, an exceptional essayist and literary critic, and a major novelist, Lawrence created works that were pioneering in their defiant eroticism, their outspoken treatment of class politics, and their insistence on seeing British literature as part of world literature in a time of global crisis. Many of his writings were censored and unavailable in England until long after his death, or published in expurgated versions or in private printings. Their frank concentration on sexuality, and on female as well as male desire, continues to make Lawrence's novels provocative and even controversial today.

David Herbert Lawrence was the son of a coal miner. As a primarily self-educated writer who studied and taught at Nottingham University College, instead of Oxford or Cambridge, he was unlike many of his literary peers in being lower-class and outside the privileged literary and social circles they moved in. He essentially invented himself, drawing on the support and encouragement of his mother, and nurturing a clear-eyed and furious analysis of British class structure that pervades many of his novels. The sexual frankness of his work is accompanied by its economic frankness, its willingness to point out all the ways that culture and taste are fashioned by income as much as by ideas. The sense of being an outsider to the gentlemanly world of letters fed Lawrence's need to live and work outside Britain, and he traveled restlessly to Europe and America, to Australia and Mexico. Lawrence is deeply associated with many of the countries and places he lived in; with Italy, above all, in the power of his writing about Italian culture and landscape; with the United States, in classic analysis of American literature, and in works set in New Mexico and San Francisco; with France, Germany, and Switzerland as backdrops for his literary works and their cultural theorizing; with Australia for his commentary on this distant British colony and its indigenous peoples, in novels like *Kangaroo*; with Mexico and the primitivism and exoticism he explored in *The Plumed Serpent* and *Aaron's Rod*.

As peripatetic and as open to experience as Lawrence was, his great writing begins with novels and stories set in England. Some of his early and most exceptional works are, in fact, modernist versions of a central nineteenth-century literary genre, the *bildungsroman*, or the story of a personal education. Lawrence's *Sons and Lovers* (1912) has the autobiographical overtones that often accompany a coming-of-age narrative. Written after the death of his devoted mother Lydia Lawrence in 1910, the book delineates the experience of a young man who was as socially and economically disadvantaged as Lawrence himself, and the almost incestuous love between mother and son that allows him to break free from the crushing life in the mines that might have been his only option, and to follow his deep need for love, imagination, and poetry into the writing of literature. His later novel *The Rainbow* (published in an expurgated version in 1915) is also a *bildungsroman*, but featuring as its protagonist a female character and specifically feminine issues of education and freedom. In a preface to the novel, Lawrence wrote that he insisted on portraying characters that were not the old-fashioned character portraits of the past, relying on "the old stable ego." For Lawrence, people were internally fragmented, not completely self-aware, and above all governed by sexual currents that exceeded their conscious knowledge and control. In this Lawrence was profoundly influenced by Freud's discovery of the prominence and power of the unconscious. All of Lawrence's writing engages with the invisible and largely silent realm of the unconscious, whose wishes and impulses are a kind of dynamic dance running under the surface of the conscious sense of self.

To this dance of the unconscious rhythms of life Lawrence added an abiding fascination with myth. He joined most modernist writers in his interest in showing the persistence of myth in modern culture: Joyce, Woolf, Eliot and Faulkner all structured work around mythic parallels or mythic figures. For Lawrence, myth loomed importantly because it allowed for the discussion of hidden patterns and cycles in human action and human relationships, patterns that are much larger than the individual human being. Our personalities are illusions, Lawrence's fiction claims, because they mask deeper mythic forms. In *The Rainbow*, Lawrence draws his mythic structure from the Bible, and the cycles of birth, death, and rebirth in the story of Noah and the flood, with the rainbow of God's promise starting the cycle of rebirth over and over again.

One of Lawrence's greatest novels is *Women in Love*, a story of two sisters confronting modern life as they move out of their country's orbit and take on independence, sexual freedom, and careers in the world. He began writing it in 1916, during World War I. The war was as shattering to Lawrence as it was to every other British writer; for Lawrence, it was the apotheosis and the logical conclusion of the machine culture he hated for having spoiled England even before the war wreaked its devastation. Lawrence sharply criticized industrial capitalism, but not from the vantage point of an aristocratic worldview that regretted the loss of the landed estates. He thought and wrote as the son of a worker whose life was maimed by industrial toil in the mines, and as a school teacher of the impoverished children of miners and laborers who had lost their self-sufficient way of life on the land. Lawrence did not dream of a return to a golden feudal age, but he did dissect the ravages of industry and the connections between world war, capital, and modernization. *Women in Love* embraces these themes and more, as it turns to Europe and its classical culture to try to find a way out of the cultural impasse and sterility Lawrence saw around him. However, in this novel and others Lawrence writes of a death instinct visible for him in European culture, including its philosophy and art. At times, Lawrence's intense hatred of modernity led him to flirt with fascism, which occasionally seemed to him to promise a way out of the dead end of modern society and its hideous conflagrations in war. In order to rescue the life-affirming capacities of human society Lawrence sought out exotic and foreign cultures, and what he termed "primitive" cultures around the world—ostensibly unspoiled agricultural societies still predicated on myth rather than machine. These exotic alternatives, as Lawrence saw, were hardly utopian either, and most such societies were contaminated by colonization and Western influences. Lawrence did seek a less rationalized and less materialistic perspective in the "primitive" or archaic worlds he explored, and found that these cultures were more open to the life-giving force of sexuality. At once intense and engaging, his travel writing gives a sense of immediacy mingled with deep reflection.

Sexuality is the force in human life that most clearly derives from unconscious fantasies and desires, and on that basis it is at the heart of Lawrence's writing. Lawrence's work was thought shocking because it takes for granted the erotic elements hidden in the family—what Freud had called the "family romance." The alliances and the divisions between family members have an erotic component for Lawrence; in addition, relations to friends and to all others one encounters are sexualized in mysterious ways, often involving a powerful homoerotic current. Much of Lawrence's fiction seems to idealize a sexual state beyond words and beyond conscious understanding, and to depict this Lawrence draws on a beautiful incantatory style, filled with a highly musical repetition and rhythm.

Lawrence's own erotic career is as famous as his writing. The passion and frustrations of his marriage to the formidable Frieda Weekely (born Frieda von Richthofen) remained a hidden presence in all his writing after their marriage in 1914. When they met, Frieda was a married woman with an impressive erotic career behind her; she became a close partner in his political and cultural essay writing, and in his restless travels. They lived in Germany, Italy, and in Taos, New Mexico, among other locales. After his death in Italy, she and her then lover transported Lawrence's ashes back to Taos, and the two built a kind of shrine to Lawrence on the grounds of what had been his home with Frieda. It was in this region that they had explored Hispanic and Indian cultures under the sponsorship of a patron of the avant-garde, Mabel Dodge Luhan. Up until the mid-1980s it was possible to pay a dollar to the manager of the Taos Hotel and be admitted into his office, where numerous paintings by D. H. Lawrence were on display. Lawrence was a fascinating, if not a major, painter; the exhibits of his paintings in England were subject to the same censorship and public outrage as his novels. A viewer of the paintings could read them as an allegory for many of the disquieting themes of his literary work: the majority of them depict a couple, usually male and female, locked in an embrace that is as urgent as it is suffocating; around the edges of these couplings Lawrence painted menacing wolves and dogs, often with teeth bared or fangs dripping with blood, emblematic of the intensity and even the destructiveness of erotic relationships.

In his 1923 essay *Surgery for the Novel—or a Bomb*, Lawrence expresses his impatience with the endlessly refined analyses of modernists like Proust and Joyce. "What is the underlying impulse in us," he asks, "that will provide the motive power for a new state of things, when this democratic-industrial-lovey-dovey-darling-take-me-to-mama state of things is bust? *What next?*"

Lawrence's poetry explores related concerns. Like Thomas Hardy before him, Lawrence was equally gifted in both literary endeavors. Lawrence's poetry emanates from the same image-suffused, musically rhythmic, and tautly modern space as his prose works. Like Lawrence himself, his art desires to move *beyond*—beyond the old stable fictions of the ego in his prose, and beyond the old stable fiction of the lyric voice. In his poetry he accomplishes this by a preternatural immediacy, an intensity of "thereness" that includes what might in the past have seemed to be incoherent elements or fragmentary perspectives. What has been silent, veiled, or unconscious, in personal and in public life, rears up and announces itself in Lawrence's writing, appears on the page and defies silencing.

Piano

Softly, in the dusk, a woman is singing to me;
Taking me back down the vista of years, till I see
A child sitting under the piano, in the boom of the tingling strings
And pressing the small, poised feet of a mother who smiles as she sings.

5   In spite of myself, the insidious mastery of song
Betrays me back, till the heart of me weeps to belong
To the old Sunday evenings at home, with winter outside
And hymns in the cosy parlour, the tinkling piano our guide.

So now it is vain for the singer to burst into clamour
10   With the great black piano appassionato. The glamour
Of childish days is upon me, my manhood is cast
Down in the flood of remembrance, I weep like a child for the past.

1908   1913

Tortoise Shout

I thought he was dumb,
I said he was dumb,
Yet I've heard him cry.
First faint scream,
5   Out of life's unfathomable dawn,
Far off, so far, like a madness, under the horizon's dawning rim,
Far, far off, far scream.

Tortoise *in extremis*.

Why were we crucified into sex?
10 Why were we not left rounded off, and finished in ourselves,
As we began,
As he certainly began, so perfectly alone?

A far, was-it-audible scream,
Or did it sound on the plasm direct?

15 Worse than the cry of the new-born,
A scream,
A yell,
A shout,
A paean,
20 A death-agony,
A birth-cry,
A submission,
All tiny, tiny, far away, reptile under the first dawn.

War-cry, triumph, acute-delight, death-scream reptilian,
25 Why was the veil torn?
The silken shriek of the soul's torn membrane?
The male soul's membrane
Torn with a shriek half music, half horror.

Crucifixion.
30 Male tortoise, cleaving behind the hovel-wall of that dense female,
Mounted and tense, spread-eagle, out-reaching out of the shell
In tortoise-nakedness,
Long neck, and long vulnerable limbs extruded, spread-eagle over her
    house-roof,
And the deep, secret, all-penetrating tail curved beneath her walls,
35 Reaching and gripping tense, more reaching anguish in uttermost tension
Till suddenly, in the spasm of coition, tupping like a jerking leap, and oh!
Opening its clenched face from his outstretched neck
And giving that fragile yell, that scream,
Super-audible,
40 From his pink, cleft, old-man's mouth,
Giving up the ghost,
Or screaming in Pentecost,[1] receiving the ghost.

His scream, and his moment's subsidence,
The moment of eternal silence,
45 Yet unreleased, and after the moment, the sudden, startling jerk of coition,
    and at once
The inexpressible faint yell—
And so on, till the last plasm of my body was melted back
To the primeval rudiments of life, and the secret.

So he tups, and screams
50 Time after time that frail, torn scream

1. The day the Holy Spirit descended on Christ's disciples, which marked the beginning of the Christian church's mission
to the world.

After each jerk, the longish interval,
The tortoise eternity,
Age-long, reptilian persistence,
Heart-throb, slow heart-throb, persistent for the next spasm.

55 I remember, when I was a boy,
I heard the scream of a frog, which was caught with his foot in the mouth
    of an up-starting snake;
I remember when I first heard bull-frogs break into sound in the spring;
I remember hearing a wild goose out of the throat of night
Cry loudly, beyond the lake of waters;
60 I remember the first time, out of a bush in the darkness, a nightingale's
    piercing cries and gurgles startled the depths of my soul;
I remember the scream of a rabbit as I went through a wood at midnight;
I remember the heifer in her heat, blorting and blorting through the hours,
    persistent and irrepressible;
I remember my first terror hearing the howl of weird, amorous cats;
I remember the scream of a terrified, injured horse, the sheet-lightning,
65 And running away from the sound of a woman in labour, something like an
    owl whooing,
And listening inwardly to the first bleat of a lamb,
The first wail of an infant,
And my mother singing to herself,
And the first tenor singing of the passionate throat of a young collier,[2] who
    has long since drunk himself to death,
70 The first elements of foreign speech
On wild dark lips.

And more than all these,
And less than all these,
This last,
75 Strange, faint coition yell
Of the male tortoise at extremity,
Tiny from under the very edge of the farthest far-off horizon of life.

The cross,
The wheel on which our silence first is broken,
80 Sex, which breaks up our integrity, our single inviolability, our deep
    silence,
Tearing a cry from us.

Sex, which breaks us into voice, sets us calling across the deeps, calling,
    calling for the complement,
Singing, and calling, and singing again, being answered, having found.
Torn, to become whole again, after long seeking for what is lost,
85 The same cry from the tortoise as from Christ, the Osiris-cry of
    abandonment,[3]
That which is whole, torn asunder,
That which is in part, finding its whole again throughout the universe.

1921

---

2. A coal miner.
3. Osiris was a major god of ancient Egypt; he was slain and

fragments of his corpse scattered; these were found and
buried, and Osiris became ruler of the underworld.

Bavarian Gentians

Not every man has gentians in his house
in soft September, at slow, sad Michaelmas.[1]

Bavarian gentians, big and dark, only dark
darkening the day-time, torch-like with the smoking blueness of Pluto's gloom,
5   ribbed and torch-like, with their blaze of darkness spread blue
down flattening into points, flattened under the sweep of white day
torch-flower of the blue-smoking darkness, Pluto's dark-blue daze,[2]
black lamps from the halls of Dis, burning dark blue,
giving off darkness, blue darkness, as Demeter's pale lamps give off light,
10   lead me then, lead the way.

Reach me a gentian, give me a torch!
let me guide myself with the blue, forked torch of this flower
down the darker and darker stairs, where blue is darkened on blueness
even where Persephone goes, just now, from the frosted September
15   to the sightless realm where darkness is awake upon the dark
and Persephone herself is but a voice
or a darkness invisible enfolded in the deeper dark
of the arms Plutonic, and pierced with the passion of dense gloom,
among the splendour of torches of darkness, shedding darkness on the lost
          bride and her groom.

1923, 1929   1932

Surgery for the Novel—or a Bomb

You talk about the future of the baby, little cherub, when he's in the cradle cooing; and it's a romantic, glamorous subject. You also talk, with the parson, about the future of the wicked old grandfather who is at last lying on his death-bed. And there again you have a subject for much vague emotion, chiefly of fear this time.

How do we feel about the novel? Do we bounce with joy thinking of the wonderful novelistic days ahead? Or do we grimly shake our heads and hope the wicked creature will be spared a little longer? Is the novel on his death-bed, old sinner? Or is he just toddling round his cradle, sweet little thing? Let us have another look at him before we decide this rather serious case.

There he is, the monster with many faces, many branches to him, like a tree: the modern novel. And he is almost dual, like Siamese twins. On the one hand, the pale-faced, high-browed, earnest novel, which you have to take seriously; on the other, that smirking, rather plausible hussy, the popular novel.

Let us just for the moment feel the pulses of *Ulysses* and of Miss Dorothy Richardson and M. Marcel Proust, on the earnest side of Briareus;[1] on the other, the throb of *The Sheik* and Mr Zane Grey, and, if you will, Mr Robert Chambers and the

---

1. The feast of St. Michael the Archangel, September 29.
2. Persephone was a daughter of Zeus and Demeter, goddess of agriculture; she was abducted by Hades, king of the Underworld (also known as Pluto or Dis), causing Demeter such sorrow that the land became barren. Zeus commanded Hades to release Persephone, which he did, though she was able to emerge from the Underworld each

spring, returning in the fall to her husband. The story offers an explanation of seasonal change.

1. Briareus aided Zeus in fighting the Titans, here represented by the epic modernist novels of Joyce, Proust, and Dorothy Richardson (author of a 12-volume sequence of novels, *Pilgrimage* (1915–1938), of which *Pointed Roofs* was the first).

rest.[2] Is *Ulysses* in his cradle? Oh, dear! What a grey face! And *Pointed Roofs,* are they a gay little toy for nice little girls? And M. Proust? Alas! You can hear the death-rattle in their throats. They can hear it themselves. They are listening to it with acute interest, trying to discover whether the intervals are minor thirds or major fourths. Which is rather infantile, really.

So there you have the "serious" novel, dying in a very long-drawn-out fourteen-volume death-agony, and absorbedly, childishly interested in the phenomenon. "Did I feel a twinge in my little toe, or didn't I?" asks every character of Mr Joyce or of Miss Richardson or M. Proust. Is my aura a blend of frankincense and orange pekoe and boot-blacking, or is it myrrh and bacon-fat and Shetland tweed? The audience round the death-bed gapes for the answer. And when, in a sepulchral tone, the answer comes at length, after hundreds of pages: "It is none of these, it is abysmal chloro-coryamba-sis,"[3] the audience quivers all over, and murmurs: "That's just how I feel myself."

Which is the dismal, long-drawn-out comedy of the death-bed of the serious novel. It is self-consciousness picked into such fine bits that the bits are most of them invisible, and you have to go by smell. Through thousands and thousands of pages Mr Joyce and Miss Richardson tear themselves to pieces, strip their smallest emotions to the finest threads, till you feel you are sewed inside a wool mattress that is being slowly shaken up, and you are turning to wool along with the rest of the woolliness.

It's awful. And it's childish. It really is childish, after a certain age, to be absorbedly self-conscious. One has to be self-conscious at seventeen: still a little self-conscious at twenty-seven; but if we are going it strong at thirty-seven, then it is a sign of arrested development, nothing else. And if it is still continuing at forty-seven, it is obvious senile precocity.

And there's the serious novel: senile-precocious. Absorbedly, childishly concerned with *what I am.* "I am this, I am that, I am the other. My reactions are such, and such, and such. And, oh, Lord, if I liked to watch myself closely enough, if I liked to analyse my feelings minutely, as I unbutton my gloves, instead of saying crudely I unbuttoned them, then I could go on to a million pages instead of a thousand. In fact, the more I come to think of it, it is gross, it is uncivilized bluntly to say: I unbuttoned my gloves. After all, the absorbing adventure of it! Which button did I begin with?" etc.

The people in the serious novels are so absorbedly concerned with themselves and what they feel and don't feel, and how they react to every mortal button; and their audience as frenziedly absorbed in the application of the author's discoveries to their own reactions: "That's me! That's exactly it! I'm just finding myself in this book!" Why, this is more than death-bed, it is almost post-mortem behaviour.

Some convulsion or cataclysm will have to get this serious novel out of its self-consciousness. The last great war made it worse. What's to be done? Because, poor thing, it's really young yet. The novel has never become fully adult. It has never quite grown to years of discretion. It has always youthfully hoped for the best, and felt rather sorry for itself on the last page. Which is just childish. The childishness has become very long-drawn-out. So very many adolescents who drag their adolescence on into their forties and their fifties and their sixties! There needs some sort of surgical operation, somewhere.

2. *The Sheik* (1919) was a lurid best-seller by Edith Maude Hull; Zane Grey (1875–1939), popular American writer of westerns; Robert Chalmers (1865–1933), prolific American novelist.

3. A word of Lawrence's invention.

Then the popular novels—the *Sheiks* and *Babbitts* and Zane Grey novels. They are just as self-conscious, only they do have more illusions about themselves. The heroines do think they are lovelier, and more fascinating, and purer. The heroes do see themselves more heroic, braver, more chivalrous, more fetching. The mass of the populace "find themselves" in the popular novels. But nowadays it's a funny sort of self they find. A Sheik with a whip up his sleeve, and a heroine with weals on her back, but adored in the end, adored, the whip out of sight, but the weals still faintly visible.

It's a funny sort of self they discover in the popular novels. And the essential moral of *If Winter Comes*, for example, is so shaky. "The gooder you are, the worse it is for you, poor you, oh, poor you. Don't you be so blimey good, it's not good enough." Or *Babbitt:*[4] "Go on, you make your pile, and then pretend you're too good for it. Put it over the rest of the grabbers that way. They're only pleased with themselves when they've made their pile. You go one better."

Always the same sort of baking-powder gas to make you rise: the soda counteracting the cream of tartar, and the tartar counteracted by the soda. Sheik heroines, duly whipped, wildly adored. Babbitts with solid fortunes, weeping from self-pity. Winter-Comes heroes as good as pie, hauled off to jail. *Moral:* Don't be too good, because you'll go to jail for it. *Moral:* Don't feel sorry for yourself till you've made your pile and don't need to feel sorry for yourself. *Moral:* Don't let him adore you till he's whipped you into it. Then you'll be partners in mild crime as well as in holy matrimony.

Which again is childish. Adolescence which *can't* grow up. Got into the self-conscious rut and going crazy, quite crazy in it. Carrying on their adolescence into middle age and old age, like the looney Cleopatra in *Dombey and Son*,[5] murmuring "Rose-coloured curtains" with her dying breath.

The future of the novel? Poor old novel, it's in a rather dirty, messy tight corner. And it's either got to get over the wall or knock a hole through it. In other words, it's got to grow up. Put away childish things like: "Do I love the girl, or don't I?"—"Am I pure and sweet, or am I not?"—"Do I unbutton my right glove first, or my left?"—"Did my mother ruin my life by refusing to drink the cocoa which my bride had boiled for her?" These questions and their answers don't really interest me any more, though the world still goes sawing them over. I simply don't care for any of these things now, though I used to. The purely emotional and self-analytical stunts are played out in me. I'm finished. I'm deaf to the whole band. But I'm neither *blasé* nor cynical, for all that. I'm just interested in something else.

Supposing a bomb were put under the whole scheme of things, what would we be after? What feelings do we want to carry through into the next epoch? What feelings will carry us through? What is the underlying impulse in us that will provide the motive power for a new state of things, when this democratic-industrial-lovey-dovey-darling-take-me-to-mamma state of things is bust?

What next? That's what interests me. "What now?" is no fun any more.

If you wish to look into the past for what-next books, you can go back to the Greek philosophers. Plato's Dialogues are queer little novels. It seems to me it was the greatest pity in the world, when philosophy and fiction got split. They used to be one, right

---

4. *If Winter Comes* (1915), a novel by American author A. S. M. Hutchinson; *Babbitt* (1922) by American author Sinclair Lewis.

5. In Dickens's novel *Dombey and Son* (1847–1948), the second wife of Mr. Dombey is known as "Cleopatra."

from the days of myth. Then they went and parted, like a nagging married couple, with Aristotle and Thomas Aquinas and that beastly Kant.[6] So the novel went sloppy, and philosophy went abstract-dry. The two should come together again—in the novel.

You've got to find a new impulse for new things in mankind, and it's really fatal to find it through abstraction. No, no; philosophy and religion, they've both gone too far on the algebraical tack: Let X stand for sheep and Y for goats: then X minus Y equals Heaven, and X plus Y equals Earth, and Y minus X equals Hell. Thank you! But what coloured shirt does X have on?

The novel has a future. It's got to have the courage to tackle new propositions without using abstractions; it's got to present us with new, really new feelings, a whole line of new emotion, which will get us out of the emotional rut. Instead of snivelling about what is and has been, or inventing new sensations in the old line, it's got to break a way through, like a hole in the wall. And the public will scream and say it is sacrilege: because, of course, when you've been jammed for a long time in a tight corner, and you get really used to its stuffiness and its tightness, till you find it suffocatingly cozy; then, of course, you're horrified when you see a new glaring hole in what was your cosy wall. You're horrified. You back away from the cold stream of fresh air as if it were killing you. But gradually, first one and then another of the sheep filters through the gap, and finds a new world outside.

✦ ✦ ✦

W. H. Auden
1907–1973

Wystan Hugh Auden's fantastically wrinkled face is a familiar icon from photographs taken in his later years, showing a fissured map of lines across his features. These photographs, many depicting Auden posing with his ever-present cigarette against a cityscape or airport, reveal part of Auden's continuing allure, which is that he was a witness, in his writing and in his person, to the changing scene of life and letters in the middle decades of the twenti-eth century. Auden came to embody a British literary Golden Age that lived on after the conditions that had brought it into being had changed utterly. His imperturbable face, looking much older than it was, had a sagelike quality of wisdom and the measurement of time passing: a map of modern experience.

Born in York, England, Auden had a pampered childhood, and was too young to see service in World War I. He was of the post-War generation, a group of gifted poets and writers who sought to replace the terrible losses of the war, its literary as well as its human casualties. Auden attended Christ Church College, Oxford, where his precocious literary career began in 1928 with the private publication of his *Poems*, thirty copies of which were put together by his friend and fellow writer Stephen Spender at Oxford. Auden joined a number of his friends and peers in heading to Berlin; his friend Christopher Isherwood's *I Am a Camera* (later the basis for the musical *Cabaret*) documented the phenomenon of these expatriate British writers spending their youthful careers in a decadent and exciting Berlin. Like many of the rest—though some died fighting fascism in Spain—Auden

---

6. All systematic philosophers who wrote syllogistically; in a letter of 1928, Lawrence included Immanuel Kant in a list of "grand perverts."

returned to England; he became a teacher in Scotland and England while writing feverishly. The cultural ferment of the thirties led Auden in many directions: chiefly, he wrote poetry, but he also became a noted literary critic, and he collaborated with Isherwood and others on plays and screenplays.

Auden's literary and political wanderlust took him to Iceland in 1936, where he wrote *Letters from Iceland* with Louis MacNeice; to Spain, which resulted in much poetry and occasional writing; to China, Japan, and the United States, culminating in the book *On the Frontier*. In 1939 he took an epochal step: he settled in the United States, where he became a citizen in 1946. In this he was a reverse T. S. Eliot—Eliot was an American who became a British citizen and is usually included as a premier writer of British, not American, literature. Auden was an American citizen who is always included in British anthologies, and rarely, if ever, in American collections. Part of Auden's desire to live in America had to do with his need to escape a stifling set of expectations for him that obtained in England—social, literary, and even personal expectations. In 1935, he had married Thomas Mann's daughter Erika, largely to protect her from political persecution in Germany, since Auden was a homosexual and lived for most of his adult life with the poet Chester Kallman, whom he met in 1939.

It was during Auden's teaching and fellowship years in the United States that he began to produce the large oeuvre of his poetry and his criticism. He taught and lectured at many colleges and universities, and read widely, taking a particular interest in the existentialist theology of Søren Kierkegaard. Increasingly impatient with Marxist materialism, Auden found a renewed commitment to Christianity in his later decades. During these years he published such notable milestones as his *Collected Shorter Poems*, *The Age of Anxiety*, and the critical work *The Enchafèd Flood*. In 1958 his definitive *Selected Poetry* was published, followed in 1962 by his magisterial work of criticism, *The Dyer's Hand*. His peripatetic and sometimes difficult teaching life led him to accept an offer from Oxford in 1956, to spend summers in Italy and in Austria, and to make a final move to Oxford and Christ Church College in 1972. However, he died shortly thereafter in 1973, in Austria, where he shared the summer house with Kallman.

The title of one of Auden's major long poems, *The Age of Anxiety*, summons up a reigning motif of Auden's poetic writing. Auden's poetry is edgy, tense, worried, psychoanalytic and yet despondent of the powers of psychoanalysis to allay anxiety. Anxiety is in some ways Auden's muse. This arises from the seriousness with which Auden had gauged the world political situation. Having witnessed the depression, the rise of Nazism, totalitarianism, World War II, the Holocaust, the atomic bomb, and the Cold War, Auden's political realism is tinged inevitably with disillusionment. Modern history is one primary source for Auden's poetry; in poems like *Spain 1937* and *September 1, 1939*, he makes no retreat to purely aesthetic subject matter, or to the past, or to pure experimentation. Auden's is a poetry of waiting rooms, radio broadcasts, armed battalions, and of snatched pleasures treasured all the more for their fleeting magic.

Paradoxically, Auden's moral and political engagements coexist with an anarchic streak, a wry wit, and a love of leisure and play. Auden developed one of the most seductively varied voices in modern poetry, creating an endlessly inventive style that draws at will on Latin elegy, Anglo-Saxon alliterative verse forms, Norse runes and "kennings," technical scientific discourse, and the meters and language of British music hall songs and of American blues singers. All these elements can be present in a single stanza, to sometimes dizzying effect; in other poems, these radically different materials are blended and modulated into a deceptively plain style of great power.

A topic of special concern for Auden was the survival of literary language. How would poetry make claims for its relevance, given that it was now surrounded by so many other voices, from those of mass culture to the exigent rhetoric of war? Auden often compared himself poetically to William Butler Yeats, as another political poet in a time when poetry was seen as largely irrelevant or even antithetical to politics.

Auden's poetry remains a profoundly lyric poetry: that is, it celebrates the singular human voice that sings its lines. It is not surprising that he wrote opera librettos, notably *The Rake's Progress*, which he wrote with Chester Kallman for Igor Stravinsky. Auden was an intellectual inheritor of Freud and Marx—he knew the ways that the self could remain unknown to itself, and the ways that history could relentlessly rush on oblivious of the human lives swept up in its current. Still, the human voice of poetry goes on, even in the age of anxiety, framing its lyric songs. In the late phase of his poetry, Auden had despaired of systems, and returned even more to the meticulous versification he was so well versed in. His poems become almost defiant vehicles of traditional rhyme and meter, lodged in the modern, everyday world, where "in the deserts of the heart," Auden would "let the healing fountain start."

Musée des Beaux Arts[1]

About suffering they were never wrong,
The Old Masters: how well they understood
Its human position; how it takes place
While someone else is eating or opening a window or just walking dully along;
5   How, when the aged are reverently, passionately waiting
For the miraculous birth, there always must be
Children who did not specially want it to happen, skating
On a pond at the edge of the wood:
They never forgot
10 That even the dreadful martyrdom must run its course
Anyhow in a corner, some untidy spot
Where the dogs go on with their doggy life and the torturer's horse
Scratches its innocent behind on a tree.

In Brueghel's *Icarus*, for instance: how everything turns away
15 Quite leisurely from the disaster; the ploughman may
Have heard the splash, the forsaken cry,
But for him it was not an important failure; the sun shone
As it had to on the white legs disappearing into the green
Water; and the expensive delicate ship that must have seen
20 Something amazing, a boy falling out of the sky,
Had somewhere to get to and sailed calmly on.

1938   1940

In Memory of W. B. Yeats
(d. January 1939)

1

He disappeared in the dead of winter:
The brooks were frozen, the air-ports almost deserted,
And snow disfigured the public statues;
The mercury sank in the mouth of the dying day.
5   O all the instruments agree
The day of his death was a dark cold day.

---

1. The Musées Royaux des Beaux-Arts in Brussels contain a collection of paintings by the Flemish painter Pieter Brueghel (1525–1569) that includes *The Fall of Icarus;* Brueghel is famous for his acute observation of ordinary life. A figure from Greek mythology, Icarus had wings of wax and feathers but flew too close to the sun, which melted the wax and caused him to fall into the sea.

Far from his illness
The wolves ran on through the evergreen forests,
The peasant river was untempted by the fashionable quays;
10   By mourning tongues
The death of the poet was kept from his poems.

But for him it was his last afternoon as himself,
An afternoon of nurses and rumours;
The provinces of his body revolted,
15   The squares of his mind were empty,
Silence invaded the suburbs,
The current of his feeling failed: he became his admirers.

Now he is scattered among a hundred cities
And wholly given over to unfamiliar affections;
20   To find his happiness in another kind of wood
And be punished under a foreign code of conscience.
The words of a dead man
Are modified in the guts of the living.

But in the importance and noise of to-morrow
25   When the brokers are roaring like beasts on the floor of the Bourse,[1]
And the poor have the sufferings to which they are fairly accustomed,
And each in the cell of himself is almost convinced of his freedom;
A few thousand will think of this day
As one thinks of a day when one did something slightly unusual.

30   O all the instruments agree
The day of his death was a dark cold day.

2

You were silly like us: your gift survived it all;
The parish of rich women, physical decay,
Yourself; mad Ireland hurt you into poetry.
35   Now Ireland has her madness and her weather still,
For poetry makes nothing happen: it survives
In the valley of its saying where executives
Would never want to tamper; it flows south
From ranches of isolation and the busy griefs,
40   Raw towns that we believe and die in; it survives,
A way of happening, a mouth.

3

Earth, receive an honoured guest;
William Yeats is laid to rest:
Let the Irish vessel lie
Emptied of its poetry.

45   Time that is intolerant
Of the brave and innocent,
And indifferent in a week
To a beautiful physique,

Worships language and forgives
50   Everyone by whom it lives;

1. Stock exchange.

Pardons cowardice, conceit,
Lays its honours at their feet.

Time that with this strange excuse
Pardoned Kipling and his views,
55   And will pardon Paul Claudel,[2]
Pardons him for writing well.

In the nightmare of the dark
All the dogs of Europe bark,
And the living nations wait,
60   Each sequestered in its hate;

Intellectual disgrace
Stares from every human face,
And the seas of pity lie
Locked and frozen in each eye.

65   Follow, poet, follow right
To the bottom of the night,
With your unconstraining voice
Still persuade us to rejoice;

With the farming of a verse
70   Make a vineyard of the curse,
Sing of human unsuccess
In a rapture of distress;

In the deserts of the heart
Let the healing fountain start,
75   In the prison of his days
Teach the free man how to praise.

February 1939   1940

Spain 1937[1]

Yesterday all the past. The language of size
Spreading to China along the trade-routes; the diffusion
          Of the counting-frame and the cromlech;[2]
Yesterday the shadow-reckoning in the sunny climates.
5   Yesterday the assessment of insurance by cards,
The divination of water; yesterday the invention
          Of cart-wheels and clocks, the taming of
Horses; yesterday the bustling world of the navigators.

Yesterday the abolition of fairies and giants;
10   The fortress like a motionless eagle eyeing the valley,
          The chapel built in the forest;
Yesterday the carving of angels and of frightening gargoyles.

---

2. Rudyard Kipling (1865–1936), short-story writer, poet, and novelist remembered for his celebration of British imperialism; Paul Claudel (1868–1955), French poet and diplomat noted for his conservative views.
1. Auden visited Spain between January and March 1937, when the civil war between the Spanish govern-

ment and military-backed Fascist insurgents was at its height. Many foreigners (the so-called "International Brigade") went to Spain at this time to aid the republican forces.
2. Prehistoric stone circle.

The trial of heretics among the columns of stone;
Yesterday the theological feuds in the taverns
15   And the miraculous cure at the fountain;
Yesterday the Sabbath of Witches. But today the struggle.

Yesterday the installation of dynamos and turbines;
The construction of railways in the colonial desert;
                Yesterday the classic lecture
20 On the origin of Mankind. But today the struggle.

Yesterday the belief in the absolute value of Greek;
The fall of the curtain upon the death of a hero;
                Yesterday the prayer to the sunset,
And the adoration of madmen. But today the struggle.

25 As the poet whispers, startled among the pines
Or, where the loose waterfall sings, compact, or upright
                On the crag by the leaning tower:
"O my vision. O send me the luck of the sailor."

And the investigator peers through his instruments
30 At the inhuman provinces, the virile bacillus
                Or enormous Jupiter finished:
"But the lives of my friends. I inquire, I inquire."

And the poor in their fireless lodgings dropping the sheets
Of the evening paper: "Our day is our loss. O show us
35   History the operator, the
Organiser, Time the refreshing river."

And the nations combine each cry, invoking the life
That shapes the individual belly and orders
                The private nocturnal terror:
40 "Did you not found once the city state of the sponge,

"Raise the vast military empires of the shark
And the tiger, establish the robin's plucky canton?
                Intervene. O descend as a dove or
A furious papa or a mild engineer: but descend."

45 And the life, if it answers at all, replies from the heart
And the eyes and the lungs, from the shops and squares of the city:
                "O no, I am not the Mover,
Not today, not to you. To you I'm the

"Yes-man, the bar-companion, the easily-duped:
50 I am whatever you do; I am your vow to be
                Good, your humorous story;
I am your business voice; I am your marriage.

"What's your proposal? To build the Just City? I will.
I agree. Or is it the suicide pact, the romantic
55   Death? Very well, I accept, for
I am your choice, your decision: yes, I am Spain."

Many have heard it on remote peninsulas,
On sleepy plains, in the aberrant fishermen's islands,

In the corrupt heart of the city;
60   Have heard and migrated like gulls or the seeds of a flower.

They clung like burrs to the long expresses that lurch
Through the unjust lands, through the night, through the alpine tunnel;
They floated over the oceans;
They walked the passes: they came to present their lives.

65   On that arid square, that fragment nipped off from hot
Africa, soldered so crudely to inventive Europe,
On that tableland scored by rivers,
Our fever's menacing shapes are precise and alive.

Tomorrow, perhaps, the future: the research on fatigue
70   And the movements of packers; the gradual exploring of all the
Octaves of radiation;
Tomorrow the enlarging of consciousness by diet and breathing.

Tomorrow the rediscovery of romantic love;
The photographing of ravens; all the fun under
75   Liberty's masterful shadow;
Tomorrow the hour of the pageant-master and the musician.

Tomorrow, for the young, the poets exploding like bombs,
The walks by the lake, the winter of perfect communion;
Tomorrow the bicycle races
80   Through the suburbs on summer evenings: but today the struggle.

Today the inevitable increase in the chances of death;
The conscious acceptance of guilt in the fact of murder;
Today the expending of powers
On the flat ephemeral pamphlet and the boring meeting.

85   Today the makeshift consolations; the shared cigarette;
The cards in the candle-lit barn and the scraping concert,
The masculine jokes; today the
Fumbled and unsatisfactory embrace before hurting.

The stars are dead; the animals will not look:
90   We are left alone with our day, and the time is short and
History to the defeated
May say Alas but cannot help or pardon.

1937

Lullaby

Lay your sleeping head, my love,
Human on my faithless arm;
Time and fevers burn away
Individual beauty from
5   Thoughtful children, and the grave
Proves the child ephemeral:
But in my arms till break of day
Let the living creature lie,
Mortal, guilty, but to me
10   The entirely beautiful.

Soul and body have no bounds:
To lovers as they lie upon
Her tolerant enchanted slope
In their ordinary swoon,
15   Grave the vision Venus sends
Of supernatural sympathy,
Universal love and hope;
While an abstract insight wakes
Among the glaciers and the rocks
20   The hermit's carnal ecstasy.

Certainty, fidelity
On the stroke of midnight pass
Like vibrations of a bell
And fashionable madmen raise
25   Their pedantic boring cry:
Every farthing of the cost,
All the dreaded cards foretell,
Shall be paid, but from this night
Not a whisper, not a thought,
30   Not a kiss nor look be lost.

Beauty, midnight, vision dies:
Let the winds of dawn that blow
Softly round your dreaming head
Such a day of welcome show
35   Eye and knocking heart may bless,
Find our mortal world enough;
Noons of dryness find you fed
By the involuntary powers,
Nights of insult let you pass
40   Watched by every human love.
1937   1940

September 1, 1939[1]

I sit in one of the dives
On Fifty-Second Street
Uncertain and afraid
As the clever hopes expire
5   Of a low dishonest decade:
Waves of anger and fear
Circulate over the bright
And darkened lands of the earth,
Obsessing our private lives;
10   The unmentionable odour of death
Offends the September night.

Accurate scholarship can
Unearth the whole offence

---

1. Auden arrived in New York City, where he was to spend World War II and much of the rest of his life, in January 1939. German forces marched into Poland on September 1, 1939; Britain and France declared war on September 3.

From Luther[2] until now
15   That has driven a culture mad,
Find what occurred at Linz,[3]
What huge imago made
A psychopathic god:[4]
I and the public know
20   What all schoolchildren learn,
Those to whom evil is done
Do evil in return.

Exiled Thucydides[5] knew
All that a speech can say
25   About Democracy,
And what dictators do,
The elderly rubbish they talk
To an apathetic grave;
Analysed all in his book,
30   The enlightenment driven away,
The habit-forming pain,
Mismanagement and grief:
We must suffer them all again.

Into this neutral air
35   Where blind skyscrapers use
Their full height to proclaim
The strength of Collective Man,
Each language pours its vain
Competitive excuse:
40   But who can live for long
In an euphoric dream;
Out of the mirror they stare,
Imperialism's face
And the international wrong.

45   Faces along the bar
Cling to their average day:
The lights must never go out,
The music must always play,
All the conventions conspire
50   To make this fort assume
The furniture of home;
Lest we should see where we are,
Lost in a haunted wood,
Children afraid of the night
55   Who have never been happy or good.

2. Martin Luther, German religious reformer (1483–1546), whose criticisms of Roman Catholic doctrine sparked the Protestant Reformation in Europe.
3. Linz, Austria, was Adolf Hitler's birthplace.
4. In the psychological terminology developed by C. G. Jung (1875–1961), an *imago* is an idealized mental image of self or others, especially parental figures.
5. Fifth-century Athenian historian and general in the Peloponnesian War between Athens and Sparta (431–404 B.C.). In his famous *History of the Peloponnesian War*, which follows events until 411 B.C., Thucydides records the Athenian statesman Pericles' *Funeral Oration*, given at the end of the first year of the war. In it, Pericles describes the benefits and possible dangers of democratic government as it was then practiced at Athens. Thucydides himself was exiled from Athens in 424 B.C., following a military defeat incurred under his leadership.

The windiest militant trash
Important Persons shout
Is not so crude as our wish:
What mad Nijinsky wrote
60   About Diaghilev
Is true of the normal heart;[6]
For the error bred in the bone
Of each woman and each man
Craves what it cannot have,
65   Not universal love
But to be loved alone.

From the conservative dark
Into the ethical life
The dense commuters come,
70   Repeating their morning vow,
"I *will* be true to the wife,
I'll concentrate more on my work,"
And helpless governors wake
To resume their compulsory game:
75   Who can release them now,
Who can reach the deaf,
Who can speak for the dumb?

All I have is a voice
To undo the folded lie,
80   The romantic lie in the brain
Of the sensual man-in-the-street
And the lie of Authority
Whose buildings grope the sky:
There is no such thing as the State
85   And no one exists alone;
Hunger allows no choice
To the citizen or the police;
We must love one another or die.

Defenceless under the night
90   Our world in stupor lies;
Yet, dotted everywhere,
Ironic points of light
Flash out wherever the Just
Exchange their messages:
95   May I, composed like them
Of Eros and of dust,
Beleaguered by the same
Negation and despair,
Show an affirming flame.

1939   1940

6. Vaslav Nijinsky (1890–1950), principal male dancer in the Ballet Russes company under the direction of Sergei Pavlovich Diaghilev (1872–1929). The company revolutionized the world of dance, causing a sensation on its visit to Paris in 1909. Auden borrowed the following lines from Nijinsky's (1937) *Diary:* "Diaghilev does not want universal love, but to be loved alone."

In Praise of Limestone[1]

If it form the one landscape that we, the inconstant ones,
    Are consistently homesick for, this is chiefly
Because it dissolves in water. Mark these rounded slopes
    With their surface fragrance of thyme and, beneath,
₅ A secret system of caves and conduits; hear the springs
    That spurt out everywhere with a chuckle,
Each filling a private pool for its fish and carving
    Its own little ravine whose cliffs entertain
The butterfly and the lizard; examine this region
₁₀   Of short distances and definite places:
What could be more like Mother or a fitter background
    For her son, the flirtatious male who lounges
Against a rock in the sunlight, never doubting
    That for all his faults he is loved; whose works are but
₁₅ Extensions of his power to charm? From weathered outcrop
    To hill-top temple, from appearing waters to
Conspicuous fountains, from a wild to a formal vineyard,
    Are ingenious but short steps that a child's wish
To receive more attention than his brothers, whether
₂₀   By pleasing or teasing, can easily take.

Watch, then, the band of rivals as they climb up and down
    Their steep stone gennels[2] in twos and threes, at times
Arm in arm, but never, thank God, in step; or engaged
    On the shady side of a square at midday in
₂₅ Voluble discourse, knowing each other too well to think
    There are any important secrets, unable
To conceive a god whose temper-tantrums are moral
    And not to be pacified by a clever line
Or a good lay: for, accustomed to a stone that responds,
₃₀   They have never had to veil their faces in awe
Of a crater whose blazing fury could not be fixed;
    Adjusted to the local needs of valleys
Where everything can be touched or reached by walking,
    Their eyes have never looked into infinite space
₃₅ Through the lattice-work of a nomad's comb; born lucky,
    Their legs have never encountered the fungi
And insects of the jungle, the monstrous forms and lives
    With which we have nothing, we like to hope, in common.
So, when one of them goes to the bad, the way his mind works
₄₀   Remains comprehensible: to become a pimp
Or deal in fake jewellery or ruin a fine tenor voice
    For effects that bring down the house, could happen to all
But the best and worst of us . . .
                       That is why, I suppose,
    The best and worst never stayed here long but sought
₄₅ Immoderate soils where the beauty was not so external,

---

1. This poem is set in the landscape of Yorkshire, where   2. Channels.
Auden was born.

The light less public and the meaning of life
Something more than a mad camp. "Come!" cried the granite wastes,
    "How evasive is your humour, how accidental
Your kindest kiss, how permanent is death." (Saints-to-be
50   Slipped away sighing.) "Come!" purred the clays and gravels.
"On our plains there is room for armies to drill; rivers
    Wait to be tamed and slaves to construct you a tomb
In the grand manner: soft as the earth is mankind and both
    Need to be altered." (Intendant Caesars rose and
55 Left, slamming the door.) But the really reckless were fetched
    By an older colder voice, the oceanic whisper:
"I am the solitude that asks and promises nothing;
    That is how I shall set you free. There is no love;
There are only the various envies, all of them sad."
60   They were right, my dear, all those voices were right
And still are; this land is not the sweet home that it looks,
    Nor its peace the historical calm of a site
Where something was settled once and for all: A backward
    And dilapidated province, connected
65 To the big busy world by a tunnel, with a certain
    Seedy appeal, is that all it is now? Not quite:
It has a worldly duty which in spite of itself
    It does not neglect, but calls into question
All the Great Powers assume; it disturbs our rights. The poet,
70   Admired for his earnest habit of calling
The sun the sun, his mind Puzzle, is made uneasy
    By these marble statues which so obviously doubt
His antimythological myth; and these gamins,[3]
    Pursuing the scientist down the tiled colonnade
75 With such lively offers, rebuke his concern for Nature's
    Remotest aspects: I, too, am reproached, for what
And how much you know. Not to lose time, not to get caught,
    Not to be left behind, not, please! to resemble
The beasts who repeat themselves, or a thing like water
80 Or stone whose conduct can be predicted, these
Are our Common Prayer, whose greatest comfort is music
    Which can be made anywhere, is invisible,
And does not smell. In so far as we have to look forward
    To death as a fact, no doubt we are right: But if
85 Sins can be forgiven, if bodies rise from the dead,
    These modifications of matter into
Innocent athletes and gesticulating fountains,
    Made solely for pleasure, make a further point:
The blessed will not care what angle they are regarded from,
90   Having nothing to hide. Dear, I know nothing of
Either, but when I try to imagine a faultless love
    Or the life to come, what I hear is the murmur
Of underground streams, what I see is a limestone landscape.

1948   1948

---

3. Street urchins.

World War II and the End of Empire

World War I had been a catastrophe of unprecedented proportions. Never before in world history had a preponderance of national powers joined together into two warring alliances; never before had the theater of war included such a wide expanse of the globe. But for Great Britain, at least, the war was foreign rather than domestic; as demoralizing and bleak as the fighting was, it was "over there," and never touched the British Isles. World War II would be a very different story.

World War II started, technically, with Hitler's invasion of Poland on September 1, 1939; as is the case with all world-historical conflicts, however, the war's genesis can be traced further back—in this case, back two decades to the peace treaties with which World War I was uneasily concluded. The victors of World War I never quite got what they hoped for, and the defeated nations had their defeat transformed into ritual diplomatic humiliation. Meanwhile, a worldwide economic depression had begun in the United States in 1929 and spread to Europe by the early 1930s, weakening democratic governments and lending a seductive edge to the rhetoric of political extremists. As a result, when Hitler began to rise to power in a beleaguered Germany during the 1930s, his message of empowerment was one that many Germans wanted to hear. Beginning with Poland, Hitler overran Denmark, Luxembourg, the Netherlands, Belgium, and Norway in quick succession, and by June 1940 had conquered even France. Britain was next on Hitler's list, as the major remaining obstacle to the domination of Europe.

Hitler hoped to paralyze and demoralize the British by a devastating series of attacks by air. This drew out to become the ten-month long Battle of Britain, in which the German Luftwaffe (air force) engaged Britain's Royal Air Force in the previously inviolable air space over England's green and pleasant land. The battle brought enormous costs—especially during the eight months of nightly air raids over British metropolitan centers known as the Blitz. The bombing caused great destruction to London, which was bombed every night between September 7 and November 2, 1940; more than 15,000 civilians were killed in London (30,000 nationwide), over half a million left homeless, and important cultural and architectural treasures, such as the House of Commons and Buckingham Palace, were damaged or destroyed. This violation of England's homeland was costly in psychological and emotional terms as well; one poignant register of the broad impact of the air raids can be seen in Virginia Woolf's final novel *Between the Acts*, where the sound of bombs falling on distant London unnerves the residents and guests of Pointz Hall. As Woolf's diaries and letters make clear, the sound of those bombs were also a crucial factor in her decision to take her own life in March 1941.

In May of 1941, Germany finally gave up its attempt to conquer Britain from the air. With the bombing of Pearl Harbor by the Japanese in December 1941, the United States entered the war on the side of the Allies; with their help, Britain was able to mount an offensive against Germany on the European mainland and retake land that had been invaded by Germany. In 1942, Britain and the United States began to plan an invasion across the English Channel. The first attempt, a raid staged at the French port of Dieppe in the summer of 1942, was a disappointing failure. The Allies regrouped, however, and planned the offensive known as D-Day. On June 6, 1944, Allied troops, under the command of General Dwight D. Eisenhower, crossed the channel with 2,700 ships and 176,000 soldiers and overcame German defenses; by the end of the month, about a million Allied troops were on the ground in France, and the tide of the war had turned. In April 1945 Hitler committed suicide; one week later, Germany signed a statement of unconditional surrender, with Japan following suit on September 2.

World War II was over; in some important arenas, however, its influence had just begun to be felt. With such a great proportion of its able-bodied young men going off to war, millions of women in both Britain and the United States took employment outside the home for the first time; that trend, once started, has only gained momentum in the years since. The economic and personal freedom ceded to women during the wartime emergency laid the groundwork for the contemporary women's movement in Great Britain; Margaret Thatcher, Britain's first woman Prime Minister (1979–1990), was a postwar inheritor of Winston Churchill's legacy.

At the same time, the United States and the Soviet Union emerged from the war as the preeminent world powers; Britain, while on the winning side, saw its global prestige in eclipse, and found itself in the midst of an economic crisis. At the height of the war, Britain was devoting 54 percent of its gross national product to the war effort; by the war's end it had expended practically all of its foreign financial resources and was several billion pounds in debt to its wartime allies. In short, Britain was bankrupt. As its colonial possessions increased their protests against British rule, Britain had neither the military nor the economic power to control them; India, which had begun its independence movement during World War I, finally won full independence on August 15, 1947, and Burma and Ceylon (now Sri Lanka) quickly followed suit in early 1948. At about the same time, Britain was forced to withdraw from Palestine, and from all of Egypt except for the Suez Canal; the Canal itself was nationalized by Egypt in the summer of 1956. The 1960s saw increased Irish Republican activity in Northern Ireland, degenerating into armed sectarian violence in 1968; recent years have seen periodic waves of IRA violence in support of independence for Ulster, alternating with largely unsuccessful diplomatic attempts to forge a lasting peace in Northern Ireland. In the spring of 1982 Prime Minister Thatcher sent British troops to liberate the Falkland Islands, a small self-governing British colony off the coast of Argentina, from an Argentinian occupying force; Thatcher won a resounding reelection the following year on the strength of the British success, suggesting that pride in the British Empire, while diminishing in importance, was by no means yet extinct.

＋＋ ▨✦▨ ＋＋

Sir Winston Churchill
1874–1965

British historian A. J. P. Taylor has written of a unique paradox of World War II: though it was a time of unprecedented stress and anxiety for the British people, "Great Britain was never so free from political controversy." The reason? Winston Churchill's ability to forge a partnership between himself and the British people. "There have been many great British leaders," Taylor continues; "There has only been one whom everyone recognized as the embodiment of the national will." The pictures of Churchill—watch-chain draped across his waistcoat, cigar drooping from his jowly face (above his bow tie and beneath his homburg), index and middle fingers raised in the V of Victory—is perhaps the most familiar and bouyant icon of Allied victory in the war.

Winston Churchill was born at Blenheim Palace, the ancestral home of his grandfather, the seventh duke of Marlborough; his father, Lord Randolph Churchill, had a distinguished career as a Conservative member of Parliament. Young Winston proved not to be an outstanding scholar, however, and instead of university, was sent to the Royal Military Academy. This military training, and his subsequent combat experience on the Western Front and in the Sudan, was to prove invaluable as he led his country as Prime Minister through the darkest days of World War II. Equally important to Churchill the statesman was his early work as a journalist and essayist; the economist John Kenneth Galbraith suggested that Churchill's power as an orator derived from his "fearsome certainty that he was completely right," a certainty made manifest in "his use of language as a weapon." In Churchill's well-known phrases, like "blood, toil, tears and sweat," a nation at war found its rallying cries.

Winston Churchill, June 1943. Returning to 10 Downing Street after meeting with American president Franklin Roosevelt in Washington, D.C., and visiting Allied armies in North Africa, the Prime Minister flashes his famous "V for Victory" sign to reporters.

Two Speeches Before the House of Commons

["BLOOD, TOIL, TEARS AND SWEAT"][1]

I beg to move,

> That this House welcomes the formation of a Government representing the united and inflexible resolve of the nation to prosecute the war with Germany to a victorious conclusion.

On Friday evening last I received His Majesty's Commission to form a new Administration. It was the evident wish and will of Parliament and the nation that this should be conceived on the broadest possible basis and that it should include all parties, both those who supported the late Government and also the parties of the Opposition. I have completed the most important part of this task. A War Cabinet has been formed of five Members, representing, with the Opposition Liberals, the unity of the nation. The three party Leaders have agreed to serve, either in the War Cabinet or in high executive office. The three Fighting Services have been filled. It

1. Delivered in the House of Commons, 13 May 1940.

was necessary that this should be done in one single day, on account of the extreme urgency and rigour of events. A number of other positions, key positions, were filled yesterday, and I am submitting a further list to His Majesty to-night. I hope to complete the appointment of the principal Ministers during to-morrow. The appointment of the other Ministers usually takes a little longer, but I trust that, when Parliament meets again, this part of my task will be completed, and that the administration will be complete in all respects.

I considered it in the public interest to suggest that the House should be summoned to meet to-day. Mr Speaker agreed, and took the necessary steps, in accordance with the powers conferred upon him by the Resolution of the House. At the end of the proceedings to-day, the Adjournment of the House will be proposed until Tuesday, 21st May, with, of course, provision for earlier meeting, if need be. The business to be considered during that week will be notified to Members at the earliest opportunity. I now invite the House, by the Motion which stands in my name, to record its approval of the steps taken and to declare its confidence in the new Government.

To form an Administration of this scale and complexity is a serious undertaking in itself, but it must be remembered that we are in the preliminary stage of one of the greatest battles in history, that we are in action at many other points in Norway and in Holland, that we have to be prepared in the Mediterranean, that the air battle is continuous and that many preparations, such as have been indicated by my hon. Friend below the Gangway, have to be made here at home. In this crisis I hope I may be pardoned if I do not address the House at any length to-day. I hope that any of my friends and colleagues, or former colleagues, who are affected by the political reconstruction, will make allowance, all allowance, for any lack of ceremony with which it has been necessary to act. I would say to the House, as I said to those who have joined this Government: "I have nothing to offer but blood, toil, tears and sweat."

We have before us an ordeal of the most grievous kind. We have before us many, many long months of struggle and of suffering. You ask, what is our policy? I can say: It is to wage war, by sea, land and air, with all our might and with all the strength that God can give us; to wage war against a monstrous tyranny, never surpassed in the dark, lamentable catalogue of human crime. That is our policy. You ask, what is our aim? I can answer in one word: It is victory, victory at all costs, victory in spite of all terror, victory, however long and hard the road may be; for without victory, there is no survival. Let that be realised; no survival for the British Empire, no survival for all that the British Empire has stood for, no survival for the urge and impulse of the ages, that mankind will move forward towards its goal. But I take up my task with buoyancy and hope. I feel sure that our cause will not be suffered to fail among men. At this time I feel entitled to claim the aid of all, and I say, "Come then, let us go forward together with our united strength."

["WARS ARE NOT WON BY EVACUATIONS"][1]

From the moment that the French defenses at Sedan and on the Meuse[2] were broken at the end of the second week of May, only a rapid retreat to Amiens[3] and the south could have saved the British and French Armies who had entered Belgium at the

1. Delivered in the Hosue of Commons 4 June 1940. This speech exemplifies Churchill's ability to rally his people amid the greatest difficulties—here, the disastrous defeat of the British and French armies in April–May 1940. What might have been seen as the humiliation of the British army becomes, in Churchill's stirring account, the

heroic achievement of a successful evacuation against all odds.
2. A river flowing through France, Belgium, and the Netherlands.
3. A city located on the Somme River in northern France.

appeal of the Belgian King; but this strategic fact was not immediately realized. The French High Command hoped they would be able to close the gap, and the Armies of the north were under their orders. Moreover, a retirement of this kind would have involved almost certainly the destruction of the fine Belgian Army of over 20 divisions and the abandonment of the whole of Belgium. Therefore, when the force and scope of the German penetration were realized and when a new French Generalissimo,[4] General Weygand, assumed command in place of General Gamelin, an effort was made by the French and British Armies in Belgium to keep on holding the right hand of the Belgians and to give their own right hand to the newly created French Army which was to have advanced across the Somme[5] in great strength to grasp it.

However, the German eruption swept like a sharp scythe around the right and rear of the Armies of the north. Eight or nine armored divisions, each of about four hundred armored vehicles of different kinds, but carefully assorted to be complementary and divisible into small self-contained units, cut off all communications between us and the main French Armies. It severed our own communications for food and ammunition, which ran first to Amiens and afterwards through Abbeville, and it shore its way up the coast to Boulogne and Calais, and almost to Dunkirk.[6] Behind this armored and mechanized onslaught came a number of German divisions in lorries, and behind them again there plodded comparatively slowly the dull brute mass of the ordinary German Army and German people, always so ready to be led to the trampling down in other lands of liberties and comforts which they have never known in their own.

I have said this armored scythe-stroke almost reached Dunkirk—almost but not quite. Boulogne and Calais were the scenes of desperate fighting. The Guards defended Boulogne for a while and were then withdrawn by orders from this country. The Rifle Brigade, the 60th Rifles, and the Queen Victoria's Rifles, with a battalion of British tanks and 1,000 Frenchmen, in all about four thousand strong, defended Calais to the last. The British Brigadier was given an hour to surrender. He spurned the offer, and four days of intense street fighting passed before silence reigned over Calais, which marked the end of a memorable resistance. Only 30 unwounded survivors were brought off by the Navy, and we do not know the fate of their comrades. Their sacrifice, however, was not in vain. At least two armored divisions, which otherwise would have been turned against the British Expeditionary Force, had to be sent to overcome them. They have added another page to the glories of the light divisions, and the time gained enabled the Graveline water lines to be flooded and to be held by the French troops.

Thus it was that the port of Dunkirk was kept open. When it was found impossible for the Armies of the north to reopen their communications to Amiens with the main French Armies, only one choice remained. It seemed, indeed, forlorn. The Belgian, British and French Armies were almost surrounded. Their sole line of retreat was to a single port and to its neighboring beaches. They were pressed on every side by heavy attacks and far outnumbered in the air.

When, a week ago today, I asked the House to fix this afternoon as the occasion for a statement, I feared it would be my hard lot to announce the greatest military disaster in our long history. I thought—and some good judges agreed with me—that perhaps 20,000 or 30,000 men might be re-embarked. But it certainly seemed that

4. Supreme commander of the French forces.
5. A river in northern France.

6. Seaports in northern France.

the whole of the French First Army and the whole of the British Expeditionary Force north of the Amiens-Abbeville gap would be broken up in the open field or else would have to capitulate for lack of food and ammunition. These were the hard and heavy tidings for which I called upon the House and the nation to prepare themselves a week ago. The whole root and core and brain of the British Army, on which and around which we were to build, and are to build, the great British Armies in the later years of the war, seemed about to perish upon the field or to be led into an ignominious and starving capacity.

That was the prospect a week ago. But another blow which might well have proved final was yet to fall upon us. The King of the Belgians[7] had called upon us to come to his aid. Had not this Ruler and his Government severed themselves from the Allies, who rescued their country from extinction in the late war, and had they not sought refuge in what was proved to be a fatal neutrality, the French and British Armies might well at the outset have saved not only Belgium but perhaps even Poland. Yet at the last moment, when Belgium was already invaded, King Leopold called upon us to come to his aid, and even at the last moment we came. He and his brave, efficient Army, nearly half a million strong, guarded our left flank and thus kept open our only line of retreat to the sea. Suddenly, without prior consultation, with the least possible notice, without the advice of his Ministers and upon his own personal act, he sent a plenipotentiary[8] to the German Command, surrendered his Army, and exposed our whole flank and means of retreat.

I asked the House a week ago to suspend its judgment because the facts were not clear, but I do not feel that any reason now exists why we should not form our own opinions upon this pitiful episode. The surrender of the Belgian Army compelled the British at the shortest notice to cover a flank to the sea more than 30 miles in length. Otherwise all would have been cut off, and all would have shared the fate to which King Leopold had condemned the finest Army his country had ever formed. So in doing this and in exposing this flank, as anyone who followed the operations on the map will see, contact was lost between the British and two out of the three corps forming the First French Army, who were still farther from the coast than we were, and it seemed impossible that any large number of Allied troops could reach the coast.

The enemy attacked on all sides with great strength and fierceness, and their main power, the power of their far more numerous Air Force, was thrown into the battle or else concentrated upon Dunkirk and the beaches. Pressing in upon the narrow exit, both from the east and from the west, the enemy began to fire with cannon upon the beaches by which alone the shipping could approach or depart. They sowed magnetic mines in the channels and seas; they sent repeated waves of hostile aircraft, sometimes more than a hundred strong in one formation, to cast their bombs upon the single pier that remained, and upon the sand dunes upon which the troops had their eyes for shelter. Their U-boats, one of which was sunk, and their motor launches took their toll of the vast traffic which now began. For four or five days an intense struggle reigned. All their armored divisions—or what was left of them—together with great masses of infantry and artillery, hurled themselves in vain upon the ever-narrowing, ever-contracting appendix within which the British and French Armies fought.

Meanwhile, the Royal Navy, with the willing help of countless merchant seamen, strained every nerve to embark the British and Allied troops; 220 light warships and 650 other vessels were engaged. They had to operate upon the difficult coast,

7. Leopold III (1901–1983).   8. Diplomatic agent.

often in adverse weather, under an almost ceaseless hail of bombs and an increasing concentration of artillery fire. Nor were the seas, as I have said, themselves free from mines and torpedoes. It was in conditions such as these that our men carried on, with little or no rest, for days and nights on end, making trip after trip across the dangerous waters, bringing with them always men whom they had rescued. The numbers they have brought back are the measure of their devotion and their courage. The hospital ships, which brought off many thousands of British and French wounded, being so plainly marked were a special target for Nazi bombs; but the men and women on board them never faltered in their duty.

Meanwhile, the Royal Air Force, which had already been intervening in the battle, so far as its range would allow, from home bases, now used part of its main metropolitan fighter strength, and struck at the German bombers and at the fighters which in large numbers protected them. This struggle was protracted and fierce. Suddenly the scene has cleared, the crash and thunder has for the moment—but only for the moment—died away. A miracle of deliverance, achieved by valor, by perseverance, by perfect discipline, by faultless service, by resource, by skill, by unconquerable fidelity, is manifest to us all. The enemy was hurled back by the retreating British and French troops. He was so roughly handled that he did not hurry their departure seriously. The Royal Air Force engaged the main strength of the German Air Force, and inflicted upon them losses of at least four to one; and the Navy, using nearly 1,000 ships of all kinds, carried over 335,000 men, French and British, out of the jaws of death and shame, to their native land and to the tasks which lie immediately ahead. We must be very careful not to assign to this deliverance the attributes of a victory. Wars are not won by evacuations. But there was a victory inside this deliverance, which should be noted. It was gained by the Air Force. Many of our soldiers coming back have not seen the Air Force at work; they saw only the bombers which escaped its protective attack. They underrate its achievements. I have heard much talk of this; that is why I go out of my way to say this. I will tell you about it.

This was a great trial of strength between the British and German Air Forces. Can you conceive a greater objective for the Germans in the air than to make evacuation from these beaches impossible, and to sink all these ships which were displayed, almost to the extent of thousands? Could there have been an objective of greater military importance and significance for the whole purpose of the war than this? They tried hard, and they were beaten back; they were frustrated in their task. We got the Army away; and they have paid fourfold for any losses which they have inflicted. Very large formations of German aeroplanes—and we know that they are a very brave race—have turned on several occasions from the attack of one-quarter of their number of the Royal Air Force, and have dispersed in different directions. Twelve aeroplanes have been hunted by two. One aeroplane was driven into the water and cast away by the mere charge of a British aeroplane, which had no more ammunition. All of our types—the Hurricane, the Spitfire and the new Defiant—and all our pilots have been vindicated as superior to what they have at present to face.

When we consider how much greater would be our advantage in defending the air above this Island against an overseas attack, I must say that I find in these facts a sure basis upon which practical and reassuring thoughts may rest. I will pay my tribute to these young airmen. The great French Army was very largely, for the time being, cast back and disturbed by the onrush of a few thousands of armored vehicles. May it not also be that the cause of civilization itself will be defended by the skill and devotion of a few thousand airmen? There never has been, I suppose, in all the world, in all the history of war, such an opportunity for youth. The Knights of the Round Table, the Crusaders, all fall back into the past—not only distant but prosaic; these young men, going forth every morn to guard their native land and all that we stand for, holding in their hands these instruments of colossal and shattering power, of whom it may be said that

> Every morn brought forth a noble chance
> And every chance brought forth a noble knight,[9]

deserve our gratitude, as do all the brave men who, in so many ways and on so many occasions, are ready, and continue ready to give life and all for their native land.

I return to the Army. In the long series of very fierce battles, now on this front, now on that, fighting on three fronts at once, battles fought by two or three divisions against an equal or somewhat larger number of the enemy, and fought fiercely on some of the old grounds that so many of us knew so well—in these battles our losses in men have exceeded 30,000 killed, wounded and missing. I take occasion to express the sympathy of the House to all who have suffered bereavement or who are still anxious. The President of the Board of Trade [Sir Andrew Duncan] is not here today. His son has been killed, and many in the House have felt the pangs of affliction in the sharpest form. But I will say this about the missing: We have had a large number of wounded come home safely to this country, but I would say about the missing that there may be very many reported missing who will come back home, some day, in one way or another. In the confusion of this fight it is inevitable that many have been left in positions where honor required no further resistance from them.

Against this loss of over 30,000 men, we can set a far heavier loss certainly inflicted upon the enemy. But our losses in materiel are enormous. We have perhaps lost one-third of the men we lost in the opening days of the battle of 21st March, 1918, but we have lost nearly as many guns—nearly one thousand—and all our transport, all the armored vehicles that were with the Army in the north. This loss will impose a further delay on the expansion of our military strength. That expansion had not been proceeding as far as we had hoped. The best of all we had to give had gone to the British Expeditionary Force, and although they had not the numbers of tanks and some articles of equipment which were desirable, they were a very well and finely equipped Army. They had the first-fruits of all that our industry had to give, and that is gone. And now here is this further delay. How long it will be, how long it will last, depends upon the exertions which we make in this Island. An effort the like of which has never been seen in our records is now being made. Work is proceeding everywhere, night and day, Sundays and week days. Capital and Labor have cast aside their interests, rights, and customs and put them into the common stock. Already the flow of munitions has leaped forward. There is no reason why we should not in a few months overtake the sudden and serious loss that has come upon us, without retarding the development of our general program.

Nevertheless, our thankfulness at the escape of our Army and so many men, whose loved ones have passed through an agonizing week, must not blind us to the fact that what has happened in France and Belgium is a colossal military disaster. The French Army has been weakened, the Belgian Army has been lost, a large part of those fortified lines upon which so much faith had been reposed is gone, many valuable mining districts and factories have passed into the enemy's possession, the whole

9. Churchill misquotes slightly Tennyson's poem *Morte d'Arthur*, lines 280–281.

of the Channel ports are in his hands, with all the tragic consequences that follow from that, and we must expect another blow to be struck almost immediately at us or at France. We are told that Herr Hitler has a plan for invading the British Isles. This has often been thought of before. When Napoleon lay at Boulogne for a year with his flat-bottomed boats and his Grand Army, he was told by someone. "There are bitter weeds in England." There are certainly a great many more of them since the British Expeditionary Force returned.

The whole question of home defense against invasion is, of course, powerfully affected by the fact that we have for the time being in this Island incomparably more powerful military forces than we have ever had at any moment in this war or the last. But this will not continue. We shall not be content with a defensive war. We have our duty to our Ally. We have to reconstitute and build up the British Expeditionary Force once again, under its gallant Commander-in-Chief, Lord Gort. All this is in train; but in the interval we must put our defenses in this Island into such a high state of organization that the fewest possible numbers will be required to give effective security and that the largest possible potential of offensive effort may be realized. On this we are now engaged. It will be very convenient, if it be the desire of the House, to enter upon this subject in a secret Session. Not that the government would necessarily be able to reveal in very great detail military secrets, but we like to have our discussions free, without the restraint imposed by the fact that they will be read the next day by the enemy; and the Government would benefit by views freely expressed in all parts of the House by Members with their knowledge of so many different parts of the country. I understand that some request is to be made upon this subject, which will be readily acceded to by His Majesty's Government.

We have found it necessary to take measures of increasing stringency, not only against enemy aliens and suspicious characters of other nationalities, but also against British subjects who may become a danger or a nuisance should the war be transported to the United Kingdom. I know there are a great many people affected by the orders which we have made who are the passionate enemies of Nazi Germany. I am very sorry for them, but we cannot, at the present time and under the present stress, draw all the distinctions which we should like to do. If parachute landings were attempted and fierce fighting attendant upon them followed, these unfortunate people would be far better out of the way, for their own sakes as well as for ours. There is, however, another class, for which I feel not the slightest sympathy. Parliament has given us the powers to put down Fifth Column[1] activities with a strong hand, and we shall use those powers subject to the supervision and correction of the House, without the slightest hesitation until we are satisfied, and more than satisfied, that this malignancy in our midst has been effectively stamped out.

Turning once again, and this time more generally, to the question of invasion, I would observe that there has never been a period in all these long centuries of which we boast when an absolute guarantee against invasion, still less against serious raids, could have been given to our people. In the days of Napoleon the same wind which would have carried his transports across the Channel might have driven away the blockading fleet. There was always the chance, and it is that chance which has excited and befooled the imaginations of many Continental tyrants. Many are the tales that are told. We are assured that novel methods will be adopted, and when we see

---

1. Traitorous: a term coined by a Spanish fascist general in 1936, who attacked Madrid with four columns of troops, and later boasted that he had been aided by a "fifth column" of secret fascist supporters inside the city.

the originality of malice, the ingenuity of aggression, which our enemy displays, we may certainly prepare ourselves for every kind of novel stratagem and every kind of brutal and treacherous maneuver. I think that no idea is so outlandish that it should not be considered and viewed with a searching, but at the same time, I hope, with a steady eye. We must never forget the solid assurances of sea power and those which belong to air power if it can be locally exercised.

I have, myself, full confidence that if all do their duty, if nothing is neglected, and if the best arrangements are made, as they are being made, we shall prove ourselves once again able to defend our Island home, to ride out the storm of war, and to outlive the menace of tyranny, if necessary for years, if necessary alone. At any rate, that is what we are going to try to do. That is the resolve of His Majesty's Government—every man of them. That is the will of Parliament and the nation. The British Empire and the French Republic, linked together in their cause and in their need, will defend to the death their native soil, aiding each other like good comrades to the utmost of their strength. Even though large tracts of Europe and many old and famous States have fallen or may fall into the grip of the Gestapo and all the odious apparatus of Nazi rule, we shall not flag or fail. We shall go on to the end, we shall fight in France, we shall fight on the seas and oceans, we shall fight with growing confidence and growing strength in the air, we shall defend our Island, whatever the cost may be, we shall fight on the beaches, we shall fight on the landing grounds, we shall fight in the fields and in the streets, we shall fight in the hills; we shall never surrender, and even if, which I do not for a moment believe, this Island or a large part of it were subjugated and starving, then our Empire beyond the seas, armed and guarded by the British Fleet, would carry on the struggle, until, in God's good time, the New World, with all its power and might, steps forth to the rescue and the liberation of the old.

✦✦✦✦✦

Stephen Spender
1909–1995

Stephen Spender was an important member of the group of poets writing in the wake of World War I and in the rising shadow of fascism and the approach of World War II. World War I, Spender said, "knocked the ballroom-floor from under middle-class English life"; his first important volume, *Poems*, was published in 1933—the year that Hitler rose to the chancellorship of the Third Reich. Thus the turn toward politics that characterizes the poetry of Spender and the other young Oxford poets who allied themselves with W. H. Auden—the so-called "Auden Generation"—seems in retrospect not so much a decision as an inevitability. Spender speaks this way, too, about his brief affiliation with communism, suggesting that the embrace of communism by British intellectuals in the 1930s was not a matter of economic theory but of conscience. For Spender, Auden, Cecil Day-Lewis and others, fascism was such an obvious, and obviously powerful, evil that only communism appeared strong enough to keep it at bay.

The complex energies and tensions of the 1930s drew forth from Spender his most idealistic and passionate poetry; he will be remembered primarily for the poetry he wrote in his twenties. Some of the energy of his writing derives from his sense of exclusion from English society; his mixed German-Jewish-English ancestry and his bisexuality led him to find, as he wrote, that "my feeling for the English was at times almost like being in love with an alien race." After World War II, Spender wrote little poetry, but continued to work in literary and cultural criticism. His *Collected Poems* was published in 1985.

Icarus[1]

He will watch the hawk with an indifferent eye
    Or pitifully;
Nor on those eagles that so feared him, now
    Will strain his brow;
5   Weapons men use, stone, sling and strong-thewed° bow   *strong-muscled*
    He will not know.

This aristocrat, superb of all instinct,
    With death close linked
Had paced the enormous cloud, almost had won
10   War on the sun;
Till now, like Icarus mid-ocean-drowned,
    Hands, wings, are found.

1929

What I Expected

What I expected, was
Thunder, fighting,
Long struggles with men
And climbing.
5   After continual straining
I should grow strong;
Then the rocks would shake
And I rest long.

What I had not foreseen
10   Was the gradual day
Weakening the will
Leaking the brightness away,
The lack of good to touch,
The fading of body and soul
15   Smoke before wind,
Corrupt, unsubstantial.

The wearing of Time,
And the watching of cripples pass
With limbs shaped like questions
20   In their odd twist,
The pulverous° grief   *dusty*
Melting the bones with pity,
The sick falling from earth—
These, I could not foresee.

25   Expecting always
Some brightness to hold in trust
Some final innocence

---

1. In Greek mythology, Icarus was the son of Daedalus, the inventor. To escape from Crete, Daedalus fashioned wings for his son and himself out of wax. Daedalus warned Icarus not to fly too high, for the heat of the sun would melt the wax wings; but Icarus, intoxicated by the power of flight, ignored his father's warning and plunged to his death in the sea.

Exempt from dust,
That, hanging solid,
30   Would dangle through all
Like the created poem,
Or the faceted crystal.

1933

The Express

After the first powerful plain manifesto
The black statement of pistons, without more fuss
But gliding like a queen, she leaves the station.
Without bowing and with restrained unconcern
5   She passes the houses which humbly crowd outside,
The gasworks, and at last the heavy page
Of death, printed by gravestones in the cemetery.
Beyond the town, there lies the open country
Where, gathering speed, she acquires mystery,
10   The luminous self-possession of ships on ocean.
It is now she begins to sing—at first quite low
Then loud, and at last with a jazzy madness—
The song of her whistle screaming at curves,
Of deafening tunnels, brakes, innumerable bolts.
15   And always light, aerial underneath
Retreats the elate metre of her wheels.
Steaming through metal landscape on her lines,
She plunges new eras of white happiness
Where speed throws up strange shapes, broad curves
20   And parallels clean like trajectories from guns.
At last, further than Edinburgh or Rome,
Beyond the crest of the world, she reaches night
Where only a low stream-line brightness
Of phosphorus, on the tossing hills is white.
25   Ah, like a comet through flame, she moves entranced
Wrapt in her music no bird-song, no, nor bough,
Breaking with honey buds, shall ever equal.

1933

The Pylons

The secret of these hills was stone, and cottages
Of that stone made,
And crumbling roads
That turned on sudden hidden villages.

5   Now over these small hills, they have built the concrete
That trails black wire;
Pylons, those pillars
Bare like nude, giant girls that have no secret.

The valley with its gilt and evening look
10   And the green chestnut

Of customary root,
Are mocked dry like the parched bed of a brook.

But far above and far as sight endures
Like whips of anger
15   With lightning's danger
There runs the quick perspective of the future.

This dwarfs our emerald country by its trek
So tall with prophecy:
Dreaming of cities
20   Where often clouds shall lean their swan-white neck.

1933

Elizabeth Bowen
1899–1973

Elizabeth Bowen was born into a world that was, at the turn of the century, on the verge of disappearing forever: the world of the Anglo-Irish ascendancy, the privileged world of the Protestant "big house" tradition. Bowen's Court, an estate in County Cork, had been in her family since an ancestor in the service of Oliver Cromwell had come to Ireland in 1749; the estate passed out of the family in 1960, when Elizabeth could no longer afford to maintain the property, and it was torn down by its new owner in 1963.

In stark contrast to her proud Anglo-Irish heritage, Bowen's childhood was rootless in the extreme. As a young child, the family's time was split between Bowen's Court, in the country, and Dublin, where her father was a barrister; in 1906, he suffered a nervous breakdown, and Elizabeth moved to London with her mother. Bowen's mother died of cancer in 1912, and Elizabeth was shuttled between various relatives. During World War I, she returned to neutral Ireland, where she worked in a hospital with veterans suffering from "shell shock"; she returned to London in 1918 to attend art school and lived primarily in London for the rest of her life.

Bowen was in London during the Blitz. She again volunteered her services to the victims of war, working for the Ministry of Information as an air-raid warden. She wrote a number of vivid, powerful stories about the ravages of war in London during the Blitz—among them *Mysterious Kôr* (1946), which the American novelist and short-story writer Eudora Welty has called the "most extraordinary story of those she wrote out of her life in wartime London."

Bowen's writing was not confined to short fiction; in addition to her more than eighty short stories, she was the author of ten novels—the most popular of which are *The Death of the Heart* (1938) and *The Heat of the Day* (1949)—as well as a great deal of newspaper and magazine writing and a history of her ancestral home, *Bowen's Court* (1964), published the year after it was demolished.

Mysterious Kôr

Full moonlight drenched the city and searched it; there was not a niche left to stand in. The effect was remorseless: London looked like the moon's capital—shallow, cratered, extinct. It was late, but not yet midnight; now the buses had stopped the polished roads and streets in this region sent for minutes together a ghostly unbroken reflection up. The soaring new flats and the crouching old shops and houses looked equally brittle under the moon, which blazed in windows that looked its way. The futility of the black-out[1] became laughable: from the sky, presumably, you could see

---

1. During the Blitz all lights were ordered concealed or extinguished at night so that enemy planes would have difficulty locating their targets.

every slate in the roofs, every whited kerb, every contour of the naked winter flowerbeds in the park; and the lake, with its shining twists and tree-darkened islands would be a landmark for miles, yes, miles, overhead.

However, the sky, in whose glassiness floated no clouds but only opaque balloons, remained glassy-silent. The Germans no longer came by the full moon. Something more immaterial seemed to threaten, and to be keeping people at home. This day between days, this extra tax, was perhaps more than senses and nerves could bear. People stayed indoors with a fervour that could be felt: the buildings strained with battened-down human life, but not a beam, not a voice, not a note from a radio escaped. Now and then under streets and buildings the earth rumbled: the Underground[2] sounded loudest at this time.

Outside the now gateless gates of the park, the road coming downhill from the north-west turned south and became a street, down whose perspective the traffic lights went through their unmeaning performance of changing colour. From the promontory of pavement outside the gates you saw at once up the road and down the street: from behind where you stood, between the gateposts, appeared the lesser strangeness of grass and water and trees. At this point, at this moment, three French soldiers, directed to a hostel[3] they could not find, stopped singing to listen derisively to the waterbirds wakened up by the moon. Next, two wardens coming off duty emerged from their post and crossed the road diagonally, each with an elbow cupped inside a slung-on tin hat. The wardens turned their faces, mauve in the moonlight, towards the Frenchmen with no expression at all. The two sets of steps died in opposite directions, and, the birds subsiding, nothing was heard or seen until, a little way down the street, a trickle of people came out of the Underground, around the anti-panic brick wall. These all disappeared quickly, in an abashed way, or as though dissolved in the street by some white acid, but for a girl and a soldier who, by their way of walking, seemed to have no destination but each other and to be not quite certain even of that. Blotted into one shadow he tall, she little, these two proceeded towards the park. They looked in, but did not go in; they stood there debating without speaking. Then, as though a command from the street behind them had been received by their synchronized bodies, they faced round to look back the way they had come.

His look up the height of a building made his head drop back, and she saw his eyeballs glitter. She slid her hand from his sleeve, stepped to the edge of the pavement and said: "Mysterious Kôr."

"What is?" he said, not quite collecting himself.

"This is—

> Mysterious Kôr thy walls forsaken stand,
> Thy lonely towers beneath a lonely moon—

—this is Kôr."[4]

"Why," he said, "it's years since I've thought of that."

She said: "I think of it all the time—

> Not in the waste beyond the swamps and sand,
> The fever-haunted forest and lagoon,
> Mysterious Kôr thy walls———

2. The London subway system.
3. An inn.
4. Kôr is the lost city of H. Rider Haggard's 1887 adventure novel *She*. The central character Ayesha, whose name means *She-who-must-be-obeyed*, is incessantly described as "mysterious." One of Ayesha's statements— "My empire is of the imagination"—may have had an ironic resonance for Bowen, writing about the condition of England during World War II.

—a completely forsaken city, as high as cliffs and as white as bones, with no history———"

"But something must once have happened: why had it been forsaken?"

"How could anyone tell you when there's nobody there?"

"Nobody there since how long?"

"Thousands of years."

"In that case, it would have fallen down."

"No, not Kôr," she said with immediate authority. "Kôr's altogether different; it's very strong; there is not a crack in it anywhere for a weed to grow in; the corners of stones and the monuments might have been cut yesterday, and the stairs and arches are built to support themselves."

"You know all about it," he said, looking at her.

"I know, I know all about it."

"What, since you read that book?"

"Oh, I didn't get much from that; I just got the name. I knew that must be the right name; it's like a cry."

"Most like the cry of a crow to me." He reflected, then said: "But the poem begins with 'Not'—'*Not in the waste beyond the swamps and sand*—' And it goes on, as I remember, to prove Kôr's not really anywhere. When even a poem says there's no such place—"

"What it tries to say doesn't matter: I see what it makes me see. Anyhow, that was written some time ago, at that time when they thought they had got everything taped, because the whole world had been explored, even the middle of Africa. Every thing and place had been found and marked on some map; so what wasn't marked on any map couldn't be there at all. So *they* thought: that was why he wrote the poem. '*The world is disenchanted*,' it goes on. That was what set me off hating civilization."

"Well, cheer up," he said; "there isn't much of it left."

"Oh, yes, I cheered up some time ago. This war shows we've by no means come to the end. If you can blow whole places out of existence, you can blow whole places into it. I don't see why not. They say we can't say what's come out since the bombing started. By the time we've come to the end, Kôr may be the one city left: the abiding city. I should laugh."

"No, you wouldn't," he said sharply. "*You* wouldn't—at least, I hope not. I hope you don't know what you're saying—does the moon make you funny?"

"Don't be cross about Kôr; please don't, Arthur," she said.

"I thought girls thought about people."

"What, these days?" she said. "Think about people? How can anyone think about people if they've got any heart? I don't know how other girls manage: I always think about Kôr."

"Not about me?" he said. When she did not at once answer, he turned her hand over, in anguish, inside his grasp. "Because I'm not there when you want me—is that my fault?"

"But to think about Kôr *is* to think about you and me."

"In that dead place?"

"No, ours—we'd be alone here."

Tightening his thumb on her palm while he thought this over, he looked behind them, around them, above them—even up at the sky. He said finally: "But we're alone here."

"That was why I said 'Mysterious Kôr.'"

"What, you mean we're there now, that here's there, that now's then? . . . I don't mind," he added, letting out as a laugh the sigh he had been holding in for some time. "You ought to know the place, and for all I could tell you we might be anywhere: I often do have it, this funny feeling, the first minute or two when I've come up out of the Underground. Well, well: join the Army and see the world." He nodded towards the perspective of traffic lights and said, a shade craftily: "What are those, then?"

Having caught the quickest possible breath, she replied: "Inexhaustible gases; they bored through to them and lit them as they came up; by changing colour they show the changing of minutes; in Kôr there is no sort of other time."

"You've got the moon, though: that can't help making months."

"Oh, and the sun, of course; but those two could do what they liked; we should not have to calculate when they'd come or go.'

"We might not have to," he said, 'but I bet I should."

"I should not mind what you did, so long as you never said, 'What next?'"

"I don't know about 'next,' but I do know what we'd do first."

"What, Arthur?"

"Populate Kôr."

She said: "I suppose it would be all right if our children were to marry each other?"

But her voice faded out; she had been reminded that they were homeless on this his first night of leave. They were, that was to say, in London without any hope of any place of their own. Pepita shared a two-roomed flatlet with a girl friend, in a by-street off the Regent's Park Road, and towards this they must make their halfhearted way. Arthur was to have the sitting-room divan, usually occupied by Pepita, while she herself had half of her girl friend's bed. There was really no room for a third, and least of all for a man, in those small rooms packed with furniture and the two girls' belongings: Pepita tried to be grateful for her friend Callie's forbearance—but how could she be, when it had not occurred to Callie that she would do better to be away tonight? She was more slow-witted than narrow-minded—but Pepita felt she owed a kind of ruin to her. Callie, not yet known to be home later than ten, would be now waiting up, in her house-coat, to welcome Arthur. That would mean three-sided chat, drinking cocoa, then turning in: that would be that, and that would be all. That was London, this war—they were lucky to have a roof—London, full enough before the Americans came. Not a place: they would even grudge you sharing a grave—that was what even married couples complained. Whereas in Kôr . . .

In Kôr . . . Like glass, the illusion shattered: a car hummed like a hornet towards them, veered, showed its scarlet tail-light, streaked away up the road. A woman edged round a front door and along the area railings timidly called her cat; meanwhile a clock near, then another set further back in the dazzling distance, set about striking midnight. Pepita, feeling Arthur release her arm with an abruptness that was the inverse of passion, shivered; whereat he asked brusquely: "Cold? Well, which way?—we'd better be getting on."

Callie was no longer waiting up. Hours ago she had set out the three cups and saucers, the tins of cocoa and household milk and, on the gas-ring, brought the kettle to just short of the boil. She had turned open Arthur's bed, the living-room divan, in the neat inviting way she had learnt at home—then, with a modest impulse, replaced the cover. She had, as Pepita foresaw, been wearing her cretonne[5] housecoat, the nearest thing to a hostess gown that she had; she had already brushed her hair for the

5. Cotton fabric with a printed pattern.

night, rebraided it, bound the braids in a coronet round her head. Both lights and the wireless[6] had been on, to make the room both look and sound gay: all alone, she had come to that peak moment at which company should arrive—but so seldom does. From then on she felt welcome beginning to wither in her, a flower of the heart that had bloomed too early. There she had sat like an image, facing the three cold cups, on the edge of the bed to be occupied by an unknown man.

Callie's innocence and her still unsought-out state had brought her to take a proprietary pride in Arthur; this was all the stronger, perhaps, because they had not yet met. Sharing the flat with Pepita, this last year, she had been content with reflecting the heat of love. It was not, surprisingly, that Pepita seemed very happy— there were times when she was palpably on the rack, and this was not what Callie could understand. "Surely you owe it to Arthur," she would then say, "to keep cheerful? So long as you love each other———" Callie's calm brow glowed—one might say that it glowed in place of her friend's; she became the guardian of that ideality which for Pepita was constantly lost to view. It was true, with the sudden prospect of Arthur's leave, things had come nearer to earth: he became a proposition, and she would have been glad if he could have slept somewhere else. Physically shy, a brotherless virgin, Callie shrank from sharing this flat with a young man. In this flat you could hear everything: what was once a three-windowed Victorian drawing-room had been partitioned, by very thin walls, into kitchenette, living-room, Callie's bedroom. The living-room was in the centre; the two others open off it. What was once the conservatory, half a flight down, was now converted into a draughty bathroom, shared with somebody else on the girl's floor. The flat, for these days, was cheap—even so, it was Callie, earning more than Pepita, who paid the greater part of the rent: it thus became up to her, more or less, to express good will as to Arthur's making a third. "Why, it will be lovely to have him here," Callie said. Pepita accepted the good will without much grace—but then, had she ever much grace to spare?—she was as restlessly secretive, as self-centred, as a little half-grown black cat. Next came a puzzling moment: Pepita seemed to be hinting that Callie should fix herself up somewhere else. "But where would I go?" Callie marvelled when this was at last borne in on her. "You know what London's like now. And, anyway"—here she laughed, but hers was a forehead that coloured as easily as it glowed—"it wouldn't be proper, would it, me going off and leaving just you and Arthur; I don't know what your mother would say to me. No, we may be a little squashed, but we'll make things ever so homey. I shall not mind playing gooseberry, really, dear."

But the hominess by now was evaporating, as Pepita and Arthur still and still did not come. At half-past ten, in obedience to the rule of the house, Callie was obliged to turn off the wireless, whereupon silence out of the stepless street began seeping into the slighted room. Callie recollected the fuel target and turned off her dear little table lamp, gaily painted with spots to make it look like a toadstool, thereby leaving only the hanging light. She laid her hand on the kettle, to find it gone cold again and sigh for the wasted gas if not for her wasted thought. Where are they? Cold crept up her out of the kettle; she went to bed.

Callie's bed lay along the wall under the window: she did not like sleeping so close up under glass, but the clearance that must be left for the opening of door and cupboards made this the only possible place. Now she got in and lay rigidly on the

6. Radio.

bed's inner side, under the hanging hems of the window curtains, training her limbs not to stray to what would be Pepita's half. This sharing of her bed with another body would not be the least of her sacrifice to the lovers' love; tonight would be the first night—or at least, since she was an infant—that Callie had slept with anyone. Child of a sheltered middle-class household, she had kept physical distances all her life. Already repugnance and shyness ran through her limbs; she was preyed upon by some more obscure trouble than the expectation that she might not sleep. As to *that*, Pepita was restless; her tossings on the divan, her broken-off exclamations and blurred pleas had been to be heard, most nights, through the dividing wall.

Callie knew, as though from a vision, that Arthur would sleep soundly, with assurance and majesty. Did they not all say, too, that a soldier sleeps like a log? With awe she pictured, asleep, the face that she had not yet, awake, seen— Arthur's man's eyelids, cheekbones and set mouth turned up to the darkened ceiling. Wanting to savour darkness herself, Callie reached out and put off her bed-side lamp.

At once she knew that something was happening—outdoors, in the street, the whole of London, the world. An advance, an extraordinary movement was silently taking place; blue-white beams overflowed from it, silting, dropping round the edges of the muffling black-out curtains. When, starting up, she knocked a fold of the curtain, a beam like a mouse ran across her bed. A searchlight, the most powerful of all time, might have been turned full and steady upon her defended window; finding flaws in the blackout stuff, it made veins and stars. Once gained by this idea of pressure she could not lie down again; she sat tautly, drawn-up knees touching her breasts, and asked herself if there were anything she should do. She parted the curtains, opened them slowly wider, looked out—and was face to face with the moon.

Below the moon, the houses opposite her window blazed back in transparent shadow; and something—was it a coin or a ring?—glittered half-way across the chalk-white street. Light marched in past her face, and she turned to see where it went: out stood the curves and garlands of the great white marble Victorian mantel-piece of that lost drawing-room; out stood, in the photographs turned her way, the thoughts with which her parents had faced the camera, and the humble puzzlement of her two dogs at home. Of silver brocade, just faintly purpled with roses, became her housecoat hanging over the chair. And the moon did more: it exonerated and beautified the lateness of the lovers' return. No wonder, she said herself, no wonder—if this was the world they walked in, if this was whom they were with. Having drunk in the white explanation, Callie lay down again. Her half of the bed was in shadow, but she allowed one hand to lie, blanched, in what would be Pepita's place. She lay and looked at the hand until it was no longer her own.

Callie woke to the sound of Pepita's key in the latch. But no voices? What had happened? Then she heard Arthur's step. She heard his unslung equipment dropped with a weary, dull sound, and the plonk of his tin hat on a wooden chair. "Sssh-sssh!" Pepita exclaimed, "she *might* be asleep!"

Then at last Arthur's voice: "But I thought you said—"

"I'm not asleep; I'm just coming!" Callie called out with rapture, leaping out from her form in shadow into the moonlight, zipping on her enchanted house-coat over her nightdress, kicking her shoes on, and pinning in place, with a trembling firmness, her plaits in their coronet round her head. Between these movements of hers she heard not another sound. Had she only dreamed they were there? Her heart beat: she stepped through the living-room, shutting her door behind her.

Pepita and Arthur stood on the other side of the table; they gave the impression of being lined up. Their faces, at different levels—for Pepita's rough, dark head came only an inch above Arthur's khaki shoulder—were alike in abstention from any kind of expression; as though, spiritually, they both still refused to be here. Their features looked faint, weathered—was this the work of the moon? Pepita said at once: "I suppose we are very late?"

"I don't wonder," Callie said, "on this lovely night."

Arthur had not raised his eyes; he was looking at the three cups. Pepita now suddenly jogged his elbow, saying, "Arthur, wake up; say something; this is Callie—well, Callie, this is Arthur, of course."

"Why, yes of course this is Arthur," returned Callie, whose candid eyes since she entered had not left Arthur's face. Perceiving that Arthur did not know what to do, she advanced round the table to shake hands with him. He looked up, she looked down, for the first time: she rather beheld than felt his red-brown grip on what still seemed her glove of moonlight. "Welcome, Arthur," she said. "I'm so glad to meet you at last. I hope you will be comfortable in the flat."

"It's been kind of you," he said after consideration.

"Please do not feel that," said Callie. "This is Pepita's home, too, and we both hope—don't we, Pepita?—that you'll regard it as yours. Please feel free to do just as you like. I am sorry it is so small."

"Oh, I don't know," Arthur said, as though hypnotized; "it seems a nice little place."

Pepita, meanwhile, glowered and turned away.

Arthur continued to wonder, though he had once been told, how these two unalike girls had come to set up together—Pepita so small, except for her too-big head, compact of childish brusqueness and of unchildish passion, and Callie, so sedate, waxy and tall—an unlit candle. Yes, she was like one of those candles on sale outside a church; there could be something votive even in her demeanour. She was unconscious that her good manners, those of an old fashioned country doctor's daughter, were putting the other two at a disadvantage. He found himself touched by the grave good faith with which Callie was wearing that tartish house-coat, above which her face kept the glaze of sleep; and, as she knelt to relight the gas-ring under the kettle, he marked the strong, delicate arch of one bare foot, disappearing into the arty green shoe. Pepita was now too near him ever again to be seen as he now saw Callie—in a sense, he never *had* seen Pepita for the first time: she had not been, and still sometimes was not, his type. No, he had not thought of her twice; he had not remembered her until he began to remember her with passion. You might say he had not seen Pepita coming: their love had been a collision in the dark.

Callie, determined to get this over, knelt back and said: "Would Arthur like to wash his hands?" When they had heard him stumble down the half-flight of stairs, she said to Pepita: "Yes, I was so glad you had the moon."

"Why?" said Pepita. She added: "There was too much of it."

"You're tired. Arthur looks tired, too."

"How would you know? He's used to marching about. But it's all this having no place to go."

"But, Pepita, you——"

But at this point Arthur came back: from the door he noticed the wireless, and went direct to it. "Nothing much on now, I suppose?" he doubtfully said.

"No; you see it's past midnight; we're off the air. And, anyway, in this house they don't like the wireless late. By the same token," went on Callie, friendly smiling, "I'm afraid I must ask you, Arthur, to take your boots off, unless, of course, you mean to stay sitting down. The people below us——"

Pepita flung off, saying something under her breath, but Arthur, remarking, "No, I don't mind," both sat down and began to take off his boots. Pausing, glancing to left and right at the divan's fresh cotton spread, he said: "It's all right is it, for me to sit on this?"

"That's my bed," said Pepita. "You are to sleep in it."

Callie then made the cocoa, after which they turned in. Preliminary trips to the bathroom having been worked out, Callie was first to retire, shutting the door behind her so that Pepita and Arthur might kiss each other good night. When Pepita joined her, it was without knocking: Pepita stood still in the moon and began to tug off her clothes. Glancing with hate at the bed, she asked: "Which side?"

"I expected you'd like the outside."

"What are you standing about for?"

"I don't really know: as I'm inside I'd better get in first."

"Then why not get in?"

When they had settled rigidly, side by side, Callie asked: "Do you think Arthur's got all he wants?"

Pepita jerked her head up. "We can't sleep in all this moon."

"Why, you don't believe the moon does things, actually?"

"Well, it couldn't hope to make some of us *much* more screwy."

Callie closed the curtains, then said: "What do you mean? And—didn't you hear?—I asked if Arthur's got all he wants."

"That's what I meant—have you got a screw loose, really?"

"Pepita, I won't stay here if you're going to be like this."

"In that case, you had better go in with Arthur."

"What about me?" Arthur loudly said through the wall. "I can hear practically all you girls are saying."

They were both startled—rather that than abashed. Arthur, alone in there, had thrown off the ligatures[7] of his social manner: his voice held the whole authority of his sex—he was impatient, sleepy, and he belonged to no one.

"Sorry," the girls said in unison. Then Pepita laughed soundlessly, making their bed shake, till to stop herself she bit the back of her hand, and this movement made her elbow strike Callie's cheek. "Sorry," she had to whisper. No answer: Pepita fingered her elbow and found, yes, it was quite true, it was wet. "Look, shut up crying, Callie: what have I done?"

Callie rolled right round, in order to press her forehead closely under the window, into the curtains, against the wall. Her weeping continued to be soundless: now and then, unable to reach her handkerchief, she staunched her eyes with a curtain, disturbing slivers of moon. Pepita gave up marvelling, and soon slept: at least there is something in being dog-tired.

A clock struck four as Callie woke up again—but something else had made her open her swollen eyelids. Arthur, stumbling about on his padded feet, could be heard next door attempting to make no noise. Inevitably, he bumped the edge of the table. Callie sat up: by her side Pepita lay like a mummy rolled half over, in forbidding, tenacious sleep. Arthur groaned. Callie caught a breath, climbed lightly over Pepita, felt for her torch[8] on the mantelpiece, stopped to listen again. Arthur groaned again:

---

7. Restrictions.   8. Flashlight.

Callie, with movements soundless as they were certain, opened the door and slipped through to the living-room. "What's the matter?" she whispered. "Are you ill?"

"No; I just got a cigarette. Did I wake you up?"

"But you groaned."

"I'm sorry; I'd no idea."

"But do you often?"

"I've no idea, really, I tell you," Arthur repeated. The air of the room was dense with his presence, overhung by tobacco. He must be sitting on the edge of his bed, wrapped up in his overcoat—she could smell the coat, and each time he pulled on the cigarette his features appeared down there, in the fleeting, dull reddish glow. "Where are you?" he said. "Show a light."

Her nervous touch on her torch, like a reflex to what he said, made it flicker up for a second. "I am just by the door; Pepita's asleep; I'd better go back to bed."

"Listen. Do you two get on each other's nerves?"

"Not till tonight," said Callie, watching the uncertain swoops of the cigarette as he reached across to the ashtray on the edge of the table. Shifting her bare feet patiently, she added: "You don't see us as we usually are."

"She's a girl who shows things in funny ways—I expect she feels bad at our putting you out like this—I know I do. But then we'd got no choice, had we?"

"It is really I who am putting you out," said Callie.

"Well, that can't be helped either, can it? You had the right to stay in your own place. If there'd been more time, we might have gone to the country, though I still don't see where we'd have gone there. It's one harder when you're not married, unless you've got the money. Smoke?"

"No, thank you. Well, if you're all right, I'll go back to bed."

"I'm glad she's asleep—funny the way she sleeps, isn't it? You can't help wondering where she is. You haven't got a boy, have you, just at present?"

"No. I've never had one."

"I'm not sure in one way that you're not better off. I can see there's not so much in it for a girl these days. It makes me feel cruel the way I unsettle her: I don't know how much it's me myself or how much it's something the matter that I can't help. How are any of us to know how things could have been? They forget war's not just only war; it's years out of people's lives that they've never had before and won't have again. Do you think she's fanciful?"

"Who, Pepita?"

"It's enough to make her—tonight was the pay-off. We couldn't get near any movie or any place for sitting; you had to fight into the bars, and she hates the staring in bars, and with all that milling about, every street we went, they kept on knocking her even off my arm. So then we took the tube to that park down there, but the place was as bad as daylight, let alone it was cold. We hadn't the nerve—well, that's nothing to do with you."

"I don't mind."

"Or else you don't understand. So we began to play—we were off in Kôr."

"Core of what?"

"Mysterious Kôr—ghost city."

"Where?"

"You may ask. But I could have sworn she saw it, and from the way she saw it I saw it, too. A game's a game, but what's a hallucination? You begin by laughing, then it gets in you and you can't laugh it off. I tell you, I woke up just now not knowing where I'd been; and I had to get up and feel round this table before I even knew where I was. It wasn't till then that I thought of a cigarette. Now I see why she sleeps like that, if that's where she goes."

"But she is just as often restless; I often hear her."

"Then she doesn't always make it. Perhaps it takes me, in some way—Well, I can't see any harm: when two people have got no place, why not want Kôr, as a start? There are no restrictions on wanting, at any rate."

"But, oh, Arthur, can't wanting want what's human?"

He yawned. "To be human's to be at a dead loss." Stopping yawning, he ground out his cigarette: the china tray skidded at the edge of the table. "Bring that light here a moment—that is, will you? I think I've messed ash all over these sheets of hers."

Callie advanced with the torch alight, but at arm's length: now and then her thumb made the beam wobble. She watched the lit-up inside of Arthur's hand as he brushed the sheet; and once he looked up to see her white-nightgowned figure curving above and away from him, behind the arc of light. "What's that swinging?"

"One of my plaits of hair. Shall I open the window wider?"

"What, to let the smoke out? Go on. And how's your moon?"

"Mine?" Marvelling over this, as the first sign that Arthur remembered that she was Callie, she uncovered the window, pushed up the sash, then after a minute said: "Not so strong."

Indeed, the moon's power over London and the imagination had now declined. The siege of light had relaxed; the search was over; the street had a look of survival and no more. Whatever had glittered there, coin or ring, was now invisible or had gone. To Callie it seemed likely that there would never be such a moon again; and on the whole she felt this was for the best. Feeling air reach in like a tired arm round her body, she dropped the curtains against it and returned to her own room.

Back by her bed, she listened; Pepita's breathing still had the regular sound of sleep. At the other side of the wall the divan creaked as Arthur stretched himself out again. Having felt ahead of her lightly, to make sure her half was empty, Callie climbed over Pepita and got in. A certain amount of warmth had travelled between the sheets from Pepita's flank, and in this Callie extended her sword-cold body: she tried to compose her limbs; even they quivered after Arthur's words in the dark, words *to* the dark. The loss of her own mysterious expectation, of her love for love, was a small thing beside the war's total of unlived lives. Suddenly Pepita flung out one hand: its back knocked Callie lightly across the face.

Pepita had now turned over and lay with her face up. The hand that had struck Callie must have lain over the other, which grasped the pyjama collar. Her eyes, in the dark, might have been either shut or open, but nothing made her frown more or less steadily: it became certain, after another moment, that Pepita's act of justice had been unconscious. She still lay, as she had lain, in an avid dream, of which Arthur had been the source, of which Arthur was not the end. With him she looked this way, that way, down the wide, void, pure streets, between statues, pillars and shadows, through archways and colonnades. With him she went up the stairs down which nothing but moon came; with him trod the ermine[9] dust of the endless halls, stood on terraces, mounted the extreme tower, looked down on the statued squares, the wide, void, pure streets. He was the password, but not the answer: it was to Kôr's finality that she turned.

9. White.

Salman Rushdie
b. 1947

Born in Bombay on the day India achieved independence from Britain, Rushdie was raised in Pakistan after the partition of the subcontinent. He then settled in England, where he soon became one of the most noted writers about the aftermath of empires. His magisterial novel *Midnight's Children* was awarded not only the prestigious Booker McConnell Prize for the best British novel of 1981 but later the "Booker of Bookers," as the best novel in the first twenty-five years of the prize's history. Like Saleem Sinai, the protagonist and narrator of *Midnight's Children,* Rushdie delights in telling its story, in a mixture of history, fantasy, fable, and sheer stylistic exuberance that has come to be known (through the works of Latin American writers like Gabriel Garcia Marquez) as magic realism. At once an Indian and a British writer, Rushdie enjoys a double status as both insider and outsider that allows him to comment both on the history of his native land and on the contemporary politics of Britain with savage and comic incisiveness.

Unfortunately, most who do not know Rushdie's writing well know his name from the publicity surrounding his 1988 novel *The Satanic Verses*; the novel was judged to be an affront to Islam, and on Valentine's Day in 1989 the late Iranian leader Ayatollah Ruhollah Khomeini issued a *fatwa*, or death threat, against both Rushdie and his publisher, carrying a multimillion dollar bounty. As a result, Rushdie was forced to go underground; for nearly ten years he moved from place to place protected by full-time bodyguards, making but unable to receive phone calls, and generally staying out of the public eye and out of harm's way. Under Islamic law, a *fatwa* can be lifted only by the man who imposed it; since Khomeini died with the *fatwa* still in effect, it technically will remain in effect until Rushdie's death, although subsequent Iranian leaders have suggested that the edict would not be enforced. Rushdie has, very recently, begun to make selective, unadvertised public appearances.

It is both appalling and intriguing that the written word still has this much power. The book that followed *The Satanic Verses* was *Haroun and the Sea of Stories,* a tale often (mistakenly) labeled "juvenile." It is in fact an allegory of the power of language—its power to liberate, and the desperate attempts of what political philosopher Louis Althusser calls the "ideological state apparatus" to silence this free, anarchic speech. The story did indeed begin as a bath-time entertainment for Rushdie's son Zafar; but as the affair over the *Satanic Verses* grew and festered, the story matured into a parable of the responsibility of the artist to speak from the heart and conscience, regardless of the political consequences. Similarly, Rushdie's haunting story *Chekov and Zulu* mixes reality and fantasy, East and West, popular culture and high literary art.

Chekov and Zulu
1

On 4th November, 1984, Zulu disappeared in Birmingham, and India House sent his old schoolfriend Chekov to Wembley[1] to see the wife.

"Adaabarz, Mrs Zulu. Permission to enter?"

"Of course come in, Dipty sahib, why such formality?"

"Sorry to disturb you on a Sunday, Mrs Zulu, but Zulu-tho hasn't been in touch this morning?"

"With me? Since when he contacts me on official trip? Why to hit a telephone call when he is probably enjoying?"

"Whoops, sore point, excuse *me*. Always been the foot-in-it blunderbuss type."

---

1. Birmingham is a city in West Midlands, central England; Wembley is a London suburb.

"At least sit, take tea-shee."

"Fixed the place up damn fine, Mrs Zulu, wah-wah.[2] Tasteful decor, in spades, I must say. So much cut-glass! That bounder Zulu must be getting too much pay, more than yours truly, clever dog."

"No, how is it possible? Acting Dipty's tankha[3] must be far in excess of Security Chief."

"No suspicion intended, ji.[4] Only to say what a bargain-hunter you must be."

"Some problem but there is, na?"

"Beg pardon?"

"Arré,[5] Jaisingh! Where have you been sleeping? Acting Dipty Sahib is thirsting for his tea. And biscuits and jalebis, can you not keep two things in your head? Jump, now, guest is waiting."

"Truly, Mrs Zulu, please go to no trouble."

"No trouble is there, Diptyji, only this chap has become lazy since coming from home. Days off, TV in room, even pay in pounds sterling, he expects all. So far we brought him but no gratitude, what to tell you, noth-*thing*."

"Ah, Jaisingh; why not? Excellent jalebi, Mrs Z. Thanking you."

Assembled on top of the television and on shelf units around it was the missing man's collection of *Star Trek* memorabilia: Captain Kirk and Spock dolls, spaceship models—a Klingon Bird of Prey, a Romulan vessel, a space station, and of course the Starship *Enterprise*. In pride of place were large figurines of two of the series's supporting cast.

"These old Doon School nicknames," Chekov exclaimed heartily. "They stay put like stuck records. Dumpy, Stumpy, Grumpy, Humpy. They take over from our names. As in our case our intrepid cosmonaut aliases."

"I don't like. This 'Mrs Zulu' I am landed with! It sounds like a blackie."

"Wear the name with pride, begum[6] sahib. We're old comrades-in-arms, your husband and I; since boyhood days, perhaps he was good enough to mention? Intrepid diplonauts. Our umpteen-year mission to explore new worlds and new civilisations. See there, our alter egos standing on your TV, the Asiatic-looking Russky and the Chink. Not the leaders, as you'll appreciate, but the ultimate professional servants. 'Course laid in!' 'Hailing frequencies open!' 'Warp factor three!' What would that strutting Captain have been without his top-level staffers? Likewise with the good ship Hindustan.[7] We are servants also, you see, just like your fierce Jaisingh here. Never more important than in a moment like the present sad crisis, when an even keel must be maintained, jalebis must be served and tea poured, no matter what. We do not lead, but we enable. Without us, no course can be laid, no hailing frequency opened. No factors can be warped."

"Is he in difficulties, then, your Zulu? As if it wasn't bad enough, this terrible time."

On the wall behind the TV was a framed photograph of Indira Gandhi,[8] with a garland hung around it. She had been dead since Wednesday. Pictures of her cremation had been on the TV for hours. The flower-petals, the garish, unbearable flames.

"Hard to believe it. Indiraji! Words fail one. She was our mother. Hai, hai! Cut down in her prime."

---

2. Excellent.
3. Wages.
4. Term of respect added to ends of sentences or words.
5. Exclamation of surprise.

6. High-ranking muslim woman.
7. Persian name for India.
8. Indian prime minister between 1966–1977 and 1980–1984; assassinated in 1984.

"And on radio-TV, such-such stories are coming about Delhi goings-on. So many killings, Dipty Sahib. So many of our decent Sikh[9] people done to death, as if all were guilty for the crimes of one-two badmash guards."

"The Sikh community has always been thought loyal to the nation," Chekov reflected. "Backbone of the Army, to say nothing of the Delhi taxi service. Super-citizens, one might say, seemingly wedded to the national idea. But such ideas are being questioned now, you must admit; there are those who would point to the comb, bangle, dagger et cetera as signs of the enemy within."

"Who would dare say such a thing about us? Such an evil thing."

"I know. I know. But you take Zulu. The ticklish thing is, he's not on any official business that we know of. He's dropped off the map, begum sahib. AWOL[1] ever since the assassination. No contact for two days plus."

"O God."

"There is a view forming back at HQ that he may have been associated with the gang. Who have in all probability long-established links with the community over here."

"O God."

"Naturally I am fighting strenuously against the proponents of this view. But his absence is damning, you must see. We have no fear of these tinpot Khalistan wallahs.[2] But they have a ruthless streak. And with Zulu's inside knowledge and security background . . . They have threatened further attacks, as you know. As you must know. As some would say you must know all too well."

"O God."

"It is possible," Chekov said, eating his jalebi, "that Zulu has boldly gone where no Indian diplonaut has gone before."

The wife wept. "Even the stupid name you could never get right. It was with S. 'Sulu.' So-so many episodes I have been made to see, you think I don't know? Kirk Spock McCoy Scott Uhura Chekov *Sulu*."

"But Zulu is a better name for what some might allege to be a wild man," Chekov said. "For a suspected savage. For a putative traitor. Thank you for excellent tea."

2

In August, Zulu, a shy, burly giant, had met Chekov off the plane from Delhi. Chekov at thirty-three was a small, slim, dapper man in grey flannels, stiff-collared shirt and a double-breasted navy blue blazer with brass buttons. He had bat's-wing eyebrows and a prominent and pugnacious jaw, so that his cultivated tones and habitual soft-spokenness came as something of a surprise, disarming those who had been led by the eyebrows and chin to expect an altogether more aggressive personality. He was a high flyer, with one small embassy already notched up. The Acting Number Two job in London, while strictly temporary, was his latest plum.

"What-ho, Zools! Years, yaar,[3] years," Chekov said, thumping his palm into the other man's chest. "So," he added, "I see you've become a hairy fairy." The young Zulu had been a modern Sikh in the matter of hair—sporting a fine moustache at eighteen, but beardless, with a haircut instead of long tresses wound tightly under a turban. Now, however, he had reverted to tradition.

9. Community in the Punjab whose religion attempts to combine Hindusim and Islam.
1. Absent without leave.

2. Sikh military who call for a separate Sikh state called Khalistan; *wallah* means boy or man.
3. Friend, buddy.

"Hullo, ji," Zulu greeted him cautiously. "So then is it OK to utilise the old modes of address?"

"Utilise away! Wouldn't hear of anything else," Chekov said, handing Zulu his bags and baggage tags. "Spirit of the *Enterprise* and all that jazz."

In his public life the most urbane of men, Chekov when letting his hair down in private enjoyed getting interculturally hot under the collar. Soon after his taking up his new post he sat with Zulu one lunchtime on a bench in Embankment Gardens and jerked his head in the direction of various passers-by.

"Crooks," he said, *sotto voce* [softly].

"Where?" shouted Zulu, leaping athletically to his feet. "Should I pursue?"

Heads turned. Chekov grabbed the hem of Zulu's jacket and pulled him back on to the bench. "Don't be such a hero," he admonished fondly. "I meant all of them, generally; thieves, every last one. God, I love London! Theatre, ballet, opera, restaurants! The Pavilion at Lord's on the Saturday of the Test Match![4] The royal ducks on the royal pond in royal St. James's Park! Decent tailors, a decent mixed grill when you want it, decent magazines to read! I see the remnants of greatness and I don't mind telling you I am impressed. The Athenaeum, Buck House, the lions in Trafalgar Square. *Damn* impressive. I went to a meeting with the junior Minister at the F. & C.O. and realised I was in the old India Office. All that John Company black teak, those tuskers rampant on the old bookcases. Gave me quite a turn. I applaud them for their success: hurrah! But then I look at my own home, and I see that it has been plundered by burglars. I can't deny there is a residue of distress."

"I am sorry to hear of your loss," Zulu said, knitting his brows. "But surely the culpables are not in the vicinity."

"Zulu, Zulu, a figure of speech, my simpleton warrior prince. Their museums are full of our treasures, I meant. Their fortunes and cities, built on the loot they took. So on, so forth. One forgives, of course; that is our national nature. One need not forget."

Zulu pointed at a tramp, sleeping on the next bench in a ragged hat and coat. "Did he steal from us, too?" he asked.

"Never forget," said Chekov, wagging a finger, "that the British working class collaborated for its own gain in the colonial project. Manchester cotton workers, for instance, supported the destruction of our cotton industry. As diplomats we must never draw attention to such facts; but facts, nevertheless, they remain."

"But a beggarman is not in the working class," objected Zulu, reasonably. "Surely this fellow at least is not our oppressor."

"Zulu," Chekov said in exasperation, "don't be so bleddy difficult."

Chekov and Zulu went boating on the Serpentine, and Chekov got back on his hobby-horse. "They have stolen us," he said, reclining boatered and champagned on striped cushions while mighty Zulu rowed. "And now we are stealing ourselves back. It is an Elgin marbles[5] situation."

"You should be more content," said Zulu, shipping oars and gulping cola. "You should be less hungry, less cross. See how much you have! It is enough. Sit back and

---

4. A group of cricket games played between international all-star teams.
5. A group of sculptures removed from the Acropolis in Athens by Lord Elgin in 1801–1803 and purchased by the British Museum in 1816. Recent opinion polls have suggested that over 90 percent of the British public support the return of the marbles to Greece, though a 1996 resolution in the Parliament was tabled.

enjoy. I have less, and it suffices for me. The sun is shining. The colonial period is a closed book."

"If you don't want that sandwich, hand it over," said Chekov. "With my natural radicalism I should not have been a diplomat. I should have been a terrorist."

"But then we would have been enemies, on opposite sides," protested Zulu, and suddenly there were real tears in his eyes. "Do you care nothing for our friendship? For my responsibilities in life?"

Chekov was abashed. "Quite right, Zools old boy. Too bleddy true. You can't imagine how delighted I was when I learned we would be able to join forces like this in London. Nothing like the friendships of one's boyhood, eh? Nothing in the world can take their place. Now listen, you great lummox, no more of that long face. I won't permit it. Great big chap like you shouldn't look like he's about to blub. Blood brothers, old friend, what do you say? All for one and one for all."

"Blood brothers," said Zulu, smiling a shy smile.

"Onward, then," nodded Chekov, settling back on his cushions. "Impulse power only."

The day Mrs Gandhi was murdered by her Sikh bodyguards, Zulu and Chekov played squash in a private court in St John's Wood. In the locker-room after showering, prematurely-greying Chekov still panted heavily with a towel round his softening waist, reluctant to expose his exhaustion-shrivelled purple penis to view; Zulu stood proudly naked, thick-cocked, tossing his fine head of long black hair, caressing and combing it with womanly sensuality, and at last twisting it swiftly into a knot.

"Too good, Zulu yaar. Fataakh! Fataakh! What shots! Too bleddy good for me."

"You desk-pilots, ji. You lose your edge. Once you were ready for anything."

"Yeah, yeah, I'm over the hill. But you were only one year junior."

"I have led a purer life, ji—action, not words."

"You understand we will have to blacken your name," Chekov said softly.

Zulu turned slowly in Charles Atlas pose in front of a full-length mirror.

"It has to look like a maverick stunt. If anything goes wrong, deniability is essential. Even your wife must not suspect the truth."

Spreading his arms and legs, Zulu made his body a giant X, stretching himself to the limit. Then he came to attention. Chekov sounded a little frayed.

"Zools? What do you say?"

"Is the transporter ready?"

"Come on, yaar, don't arse around."

"Respectfully, Mister Chekov, sir, it's my arse. Now then: is the transporter ready?"

"Transporter ready. Aye."

"Then, energise."

Chekov's memorandum, classified top-secret, eyes-only, and addressed to 'JTK' (James T. Kirk):

My strong recommendation is that Operation Startrek be aborted. To send a Federation employee of Klingon origin unarmed into a Klingon cell to spy is the crudest form of loyalty test. The operative in question has never shown ideological deviation of any sort and deserves better, even in the present climate of mayhem, hysteria and fear. If he fails to persuade the Klingons of his bona fides [good faith] he can expect to be treated with extreme prejudice. These are not hostage takers.

The entire undertaking is misconceived. The locally settled Klingon population is not the central problem. Even should we succeed, such intelligence as can be gleaned about more important principals back home will no doubt be of dubious accuracy and limited value. We should advise Star Fleet Headquarters to engage urgently with the grievances and aspirations of the Klingon people. Unless these are dealt with fair and square there cannot be a lasting peace.

The reply from JTK:

Your closeness to the relevant individual excuses what is otherwise an explosively communalist document. It is not for you to define the national interest nor to determine what undercover operations are to be undertaken. It is for you to enable such operations to occur and to provide back-up as and when required to do so. As a personal favour to you and in the name of my long friendship with your eminent Papaji I have destroyed your last without keeping a copy and suggest you do the same. Also destroy this.

Chekov asked Zulu to drive him up to Stratford for a performance of *Coriolanus*.[6]

"How many kiddiwinks by now? Three?"

"Four," said Zulu. "All boys."

"By the grace of God. She must be a good woman."

"I have a full heart," said Zulu, with sudden feeling. "A full house, a full belly, a full bed."

"Lucky so and so," said Chekov. "Always were warm-blooded. I, by contrast, am not. Reptiles, certain species of dinosaur, and me. I am in the wife market, by the way, if you know any suitable candidates. Bachelordom being, after a certain point, an obstacle on the career path."

Zulu was driving strangely. In the slow lane of the motorway, as they approached an exit lane, he accelerated towards a hundred miles an hour. Once the exit was behind them, he slowed. Chekov noticed that he varied his speed and lane constantly. "Doesn't the old rattletrap have cruise control?" he asked. "Because, sport, this kind of performance would not do on the bridge of the flagship of the United Federation of Planets."

"Anti-surveillance," said Zulu. "Dry-cleaning." Chekov, alarmed, looked out of the back window.

"Have we been rumbled, then?"

"Nothing to worry about," grinned Zulu. "Better safe than sorry is all. Always anticipate the worst-case scenario."

Chekov settled back in his seat. "You liked toys and games," he said. Zulu had been a crack rifle shot, the school's champion wrestler, and an expert fencer. "Every Speech Day," Zulu said, "I would sit in the hall and clap, while you went up for all the work prizes. English Prize, History Prize, Latin Prize, Form Prize. Clap, clap, clap, term after term, year after year. But on Sports Day I got my cups. And now also I have my area of expertise."

"Quite a reputation you're building up, if what I hear is anything to go by."

There was a silence. England passed by at speed.

"Do you like Tolkien?" Zulu asked.

"I wouldn't have put you down as a big reader," said Chekov, startled. "No offence."

6. Shakespeare's bloodiest tragedy; its themes are civil unrest and revolt.

"J.R.R. Tolkien," said Zulu. "*The Lord of the Rings.*"[7]

"Can't say I've read the gentleman. Heard of him, of course. Elves and pixies. Not your sort of thing at all, I'd have thought."

"It is about a war to the finish between Good and Evil," said Zulu intently. "And while this great war is being fought there is one part of the world, the Shire, in which nobody even knows it's going on. The hobbits who live there work and squabble and make merry and they have no fucking clue about the forces that threaten them, and those that save their tiny skins." His face was red with vehemence.

"Meaning me, I suppose," Chekov said.

"I am a soldier in that war," said Zulu. "If you sit in an office you don't have one small idea of what the real world is like. The world of action, ji. The world of deeds, of things that are done and maybe undone too. The world of life and death."

"Only in the worst case," Chekov demurred.

"Do I tell you how to apply your smooth-tongued musca-polish to people's behinds?" stormed Zulu. "Then do not tell me how to ply my trade."

Soldiers going into battle pump themselves up, Chekov knew. This chest-beating was to be expected, it must not be misunderstood. "When will you vamoose?" he quietly asked.

"Chekov ji, you won't see me go."

Stratford approached. "Did you know, ji," Zulu offered, "that the map of Tolkien's Middle-earth fits quite well over central England and Wales? Maybe all fairylands are right here, in our midst."

"You're a deep one, old Zools," said Chekov. "Full of revelations today."

Chekov had a few people over for dinner at his modern-style official residence in a private road in Hampstead: a Very Big Businessman he was wooing, journalists he liked, prominent India-lovers, noted Non-Resident Indians. The policy was business as usual. The dreadful event must not be seen to have derailed the ship of State: whose new captain, Chekov mused, was a former pilot himself. As if a Sulu, a Chekov had been suddenly promoted to the skipper's seat.

Damned difficult doing all this without a lady wife to act as hostess, he grumbled inwardly. The best golden plates with the many-headed lion at the centre, the finest crystal, the menu, the wines. Personnel had been seconded from India House to help him out, but it wasn't the same. The secrets of good evenings, like God, were in the details. Chekov meddled and fretted.

The evening went off well. Over brandy, Chekov even dared to introduce a blacker note. "England has always been a breeding ground for our revolutionists," he said. "What would Pandit Nehru[8] have been without Harrow?[9] Or Gandhiji without his formative experiences here? Even the Pakistan idea was dreamt up by young radicals at college in what we then were asked to think of as the Mother Country. Now that England's status has declined, I suppose it is logical that the quality of the revolutionists she breeds has likewise fallen. The Kashmiris![1] Not a hope in hell. And as for these Khalistan types, let them not think that their evil deed has brought their

---

7. Tolkien's triology (1954–1955), written during and just after World War II, concerns a war for control of Middle Earth, in which men, elves, dwarves, and a few British-like hobbits band together to defeat the evil eastern empire of Sauron.

8. Jawaharlal Nehru, first Prime Minister of the Republic of India (1947–1964), father of Indira Gandhi.
9. An exclusive English preparatory school.
1. Residents of Kashmir, a territory in dispute between India and Pakistan since 1947.

dream a day closer. On the contrary. On the contrary. We will root them out and smash them to—what's the right word?—to *smithereens*."

To his surprise he had begun speaking loudly and had risen to his feet. He sat down hard and laughed. The moment passed.

"The funny thing about this blasted nickname of mine," he said quickly to his dinner-table neighbour, the septuagenarian Very Big Businessman's improbably young and attractive wife, "is that back then we never saw one episode of the TV series. No TV to see it on, you see. The whole thing was just a legend wafting its way from the US and UK to our lovely hill-station of Dehra Dun.

"After a while we got a couple of cheap paperback novelisations and passed them round as if they were naughty books like *Lady C* or some such. Lots of us tried the names on for size but only two of them stuck; probably because they seemed to go together, and the two of us got on pretty well, even though he was younger. A lovely boy. So just like Laurel and Hardy we were Chekov and Zulu."

"Love and marriage," said the woman.

"Beg pardon?"

"*You* know," she said. "Go together like is it milk and porridge. Or a car and garage, that's right. I love old songs. La-la-la-something-brother, you can't have fun without I think it's your mother."[2]

"Yes, now I do recall," said Chekov.

3

Three months later Zulu telephoned his wife.

"O my God where have you vanished are you dead?"

"Listen please my bivi. Listen carefully my wife, my only love."

"Yes. OK. I am calm. Line is bad, but."

"Call Chekov and say condition red."

"Arré! What is wrong with your condition?"

"Please. Condition red."

"Yes. OK. Red."

"Say the Klingons may be smelling things."

"Clingers-on may be smelly things. Means what?"

"My darling, I beg you."

"I have it all right here only. With this pencil I have written it, both."

"Tell him, get Scotty to lock on to my signal and beam me up at once."

"What rubbish! Even now you can't leave off that stupid game."

"Bivi. It is urgent. *Beam me up.*"

Chekov dropped everything and drove. He went via the dry-cleaners as instructed; he drove round roundabouts twice, jumped red lights, deliberately took a wrong turning, stopped and turned round, made as many right turns as possible to see if anything followed him across the stream of traffic, and, on the motorway, mimicked Zulu's techniques. When he was as certain as he could be that he was clean, he headed for the rendezvous point. "Roll over Len Deighton," he thought, "and tell le Carré the news."[3]

---

2. She is mangling the lyrics of Sammy Cahn's 1955 song *Love and Marriage:* "Love and marriage, love and marriage / Go together like a horse and carriage / This I tell you brother / You can't have one without the other."

3. Len Deighton and John le Carré are two popular contemporary writers of espionage fiction. The line refers to the popular song lyric, "Roll over, Beethoven."

He turned off the motorway and pulled into a lay-by. A man stepped out of the trees, looking newly bathed and smartly dressed, with a sheepish smile on his face. It was Zulu.

Chekov jumped out of the car and embraced his friend, kissing him on both cheeks. Zulu's bristly beard pricked his lips. "I expected you'd have an arm missing, or blood pouring from a gunshot wound, or some black eyes at least," he said. "Instead here you are dressed for the theatre, minus only an opera cloak and cane."

"Mission accomplished," said Zulu, patting his breast pocket. "All present and correct."

"Then what was that 'condition red' bakvaas?"

"The worst-case scenario," said Zulu, "does not always materialise."

In the car, Chekov scanned the names, places, dates in Zulu's brown envelope. The information was better than anyone had expected. From this anonymous Midlands lay-by a light was shining on certain remote villages and urban back-alleys in Punjab.[4] There would be a round-up, and, for some big badmashes at least, there would no longer be shadows in which to hide.

He gave a little, impressed whistle.

Zulu in the passenger seat inclined his head. "Better move off now," he said. "Don't tempt fate."

They drove south through Middle-earth.

Not long after they came off the motorway, Zulu said, "By the way, I quit."

Chekov stopped the car. The two towers of Wembley Stadium were visible through a gap in the houses to the left.

"What's this? Did those extremists manage to turn your head or what?"

"Chekov, ji, don't be a fool. Who needs extremists when there are the killings in Delhi? Hundreds, maybe thousands. Sikh men scalped and burned alive in front of their families. Boy-children, too."

"We know this."

"Then, ji, we also know who was behind it."

"There is not a shred of evidence," Chekov repeated the policy line.

"There are eyewitnesses and photographs," said Zulu. "We know this."

"There are those who think," said Chekov slowly, "that after Indiraji the Sikhs deserved what they got."

Zulu stiffened.

"You know me better than that, I hope," said Chekov. "Zulu, for God's sake, come on. All our bleddy lives."

"No Congress workers have been indicted," said Zulu. "In spite of all the evidence of complicity. Therefore, I resign. You should quit, too."

"If you have gone so damn radical," cried Chekov, "why hand over these lists at all? Why go only half the bleddy hog?"

"I am a security wallah," said Zulu, opening the car door. "Terrorists of all sorts are my foes. But not, apparently, in certain circumstances, yours."

"Zulu, get in, damn it," Chekov shouted. "Don't you care for your career? A wife and four kiddiwinks to support. What about your old chums? Are you going to turn your back on me?"

But Zulu was already too far away.

---

4. Province divided between India and Pakistan.

Chekov and Zulu never met again. Zulu settled in Bombay and as the demand for private-sector protection increased in that cash-rich boom-town, so his Zulu Shield and Zulu Spear companies prospered and grew. He had three more children, all of them boys, and remains happily married to this day.

As for Chekov, he never did take a wife. In spite of this supposed handicap, however, he did well in his chosen profession. His rapid rise continued. But one day in May 1991 he was, by chance, a member of the entourage accompanying Mr Rajiv Gandhi[5] to the South Indian village of Sriperumbudur, where Rajiv was to address an election rally. Security was lax, intentionally so. In the previous election, Rajivji felt, the demands of security had placed an alienating barrier between himself and the electorate. On this occasion, he decreed, the voters must be allowed to feel close.

After the speeches, the Rajiv group descended from the podium. Chekov, who was just a few feet behind Rajiv, saw a small Tamil[6] woman come forward, smiling. She shook Rajiv's hand and did not let go. Chekov understood what she was smiling about, and the knowledge was so powerful that it stopped time itself.

Because time had stopped, Chekov was able to make a number of private observations. "These Tamil revolutionists are not England-returned," he noted. "So, finally, we have learned to produce the goods at home, and no longer need to import. Bang goes that old dinner-party standby; so to speak." And, less dryly: "The tragedy is not how one dies," he thought. "It is how one has lived."

The scene around him vanished, dissolving in a pool of light, and was replaced by the bridge of the Starship *Enterprise*. All the leading figures were in their appointed places. Zulu sat beside Chekov at the front.

"Shields no longer operative," Zulu was saying. On the main screen, they could see the Klingon Bird of Prey uncloaking, preparing to strike.

"One direct hit and we're done for," cried Dr McCoy. "For God's sake, Jim, get us out of here!"

"Illogical," said First Officer Spock. "The degradation of our dilithium crystal drive means that warp speed is unavailable. At impulse power only, we would make a poor attempt indeed to flee the Bird of Prey. Our only logical course is unconditional surrender."

"Surrender to a Klingon!" shouted McCoy. "Damn it, you cold-blooded, pointy-eared adding-machine, don't you know how they treat their prisoners?"

"Phaser banks completely depleted," said Zulu. "Offensive capability nil."

"Should I attempt to contact the Klingon captain, sir?" Chekov inquired. "They could fire at any moment."

"Thank you, Mr Chekov," said Captain Kirk. "I'm afraid that won't be necessary. On this occasion, the worst-case scenario is the one we are obliged to play out. Hold your position. Steady as she goes."

"The Bird of Prey has fired, sir," said Zulu.

Chekov took Zulu's hand and held it firmly, victoriously, as the speeding balls of deadly light approached.

[END OF PERSPECTIVES: WORLD WAR II AND THE END OF EMPIRE]

5. Indian Prime Minister 1984–1989, assassinated in May 1991, son of Indira Gandhi.
6. Member of a people of South India and Sri Lanka. The government of India had been aiding the Sri Lankan government in suppressing violent protests by Tamil separatists in Sri Lanka.

✛⟐✕⟐

Dylan Thomas
1914–1953

One of the most important facts of Dylan Thomas's biography is his birthplace: Swansea, South Wales. Thomas was Welsh first, English second. Although Wales is entirely contained within the borders of England, it is one of the areas of Gaeltacht, the places where forms of Gaelic language are or have been spoken. The Welsh language is a living and thriving one, and it is visible in Wales in place names, street signs, church music, and a host of other daily manifestations. Thomas uses the words of the English language in making his poems, plays, and stories, but these words are defamiliarized, are made strange, by virtue of their having been laid on top, as it were, of absent Welsh words and phrasings that echo nonetheless through the English lines. A common criticism made about Dylan Thomas's poetry by English critics who were his contemporaries was that the poetry was overly emotional and excessively musical, and that it lacked "rigor." These charges against the poems sound all too familiarly like the complaints against the Gaeltachts and their inhabitants— too emotional, too lyrical, too irrational. The innovative and densely lyrical patterns of Thomas's poetry and his prose style come partially out of his "Welshification" of English, a process that has effects on both the style and the subject matter of his work. In another register, he can be seen as the last of the Romantic poets, writing precocious lyrics infused with an intense sense of self.

Dylan Thomas's earliest volume, *18 Poems*, appeared in 1934 when Thomas was twenty years old, a suite of poems based on the cycle of life, birth, childhood, and death in Swansea. It caused a sensation for the magic of its wordplay and the intensely personal focus of the poems. The book was received ecstatically in Britain, but not so in Wales, whose provincial proprieties Thomas always viewed with a half-affectionate sarcasm. Like James Joyce, Thomas felt the necessity of escape; at the age of twenty-one he moved to the metropolitan center, to London, to pursue his hopes of a literary career. There he worked for the BBC as a writer and a performer on radio broadcasts. The short stories of his collection *Portrait of the Artist as a Young Dog* (1940) wittily recount, in obvious homage and parody of Joyce's *Portrait of the Artist as a Young Man*, the travails of the would-be writer who hopes to break through the barriers of class and nation. He spent the years of World War II in London as well, but as a conscientious objector, not a combatant, and, as a Welshman, to a certain degree as an outsider within. The war was traumatizing for him as for so many others, and Thomas's pacifism and despair led to the superb poetry of his volume *Deaths and Entrances*.

Poetry alone could not pay the bills and allow Thomas and his young family to live in London. After the war he turned to screenplays and to short stories. The haunting radio play *Return Journey* gives a medley of voices encountered by the poet returning to a Swansea inhabited by the ghost of his youthful self. It can be compared to some of Hardy's memory-filled poetic landscapes and to stories like *Ivy Day in the Committee Room* in Joyce's *Dubliners*; it also anticipates the spare, ironic dramas that Samuel Beckett would write in the 1960s and 1970s.

In the late 1940s, Thomas returned to his poetry, this time less as a poet than as a performer or public reader of his own work. His vibrant and sonorous Welsh-accented voice (akin to that of the Welsh actor Richard Burton), melded with the incantatory lyricism of his poetic language, proved to be irresistible to the public, both in England and in the United States. His brilliant poetry readings instigated a new popularity for poetry itself on both sides of the Atlantic, and his captivating talents as a reader and indeed an actor created for him the persona of Dylan Thomas, Bohemian poet, which he wore until his early death in New York City, after an overdose of whiskey following a poetry reading. He was on his way to California to stay with Igor Stravinsky, with whom he planned to write an epic opera.

The great American poet John Berryman described certain recurrent words as the "unmistakable signature" of Dylan Thomas's poetry. Berryman chose a list of forty "key words" in Thomas's work, including among them: blood, sea, ghost, grave, death, light, time, sun, night, wind, love, and rain. Berryman noted the symbolic value Thomas made these seemingly simple words carry across the span of many poems. Thomas's themes were agreed by most critics to be simple and elemental ones—related to the cycles of life, to nature and childhood, to life's meaning. Berryman argued fiercely that while these were simple themes on the surface, what a poem means *is* its imagery, the way its words are put into relation to one another: "A poem that works well demonstrates an insight, and the insight may consist, not in the theme, but in the image-relations or the structure-relations." Thomas himself aimed at using wordplay and fractured syntax to create sound as a "verbal music." The musicality of his poems and his prose is stunningly evident, and rarely more so than in his play *Under Milk Wood*, a kind of oratorio for disembodied voices. In the play, published posthumously in 1954, Thomas gives voice to the inhabitants of the Welsh village of Llaregyub, whose voices weave together the actions of nature and humans on one single rural day. There is no "plot," and the actors simply stand on stage and read, taking on many voices as these ebb and flow musically through them.

Oral speech and song are more important than written language in rural countries and cultures, especially when one's written language is officially discouraged or even forbidden. Social memory is passed on in story and song; tales and jokes and sermons and performances loom larger in the society of a country town than do written artifacts. Dylan Thomas was very much a writer, yet his poetry and prose are written to be heard, to exist in the ear of the listener as much as the eye of the reader. The lush richness of Thomas's poetic voice is a verbal music that passes on a tradition of oral culture and its precious gifts. The spoken or sung word is a word accompanied by breath; breath is related in most cultures, but certainly in those of Wales and Ireland, to the spirit. One collection of Dylan Thomas's poetry and sketches he titled *The World I Breathe*. This title could as easily be *The Word I Breathe*.

The Force That Through the Green Fuse Drives the Flower

The force that through the green fuse drives the flower
Drives my green age; that blasts the roots of trees
Is my destroyer.
And I am dumb to tell the crooked rose
5   My youth is bent by the same wintry fever.

The force that drives the water through the rocks
Drives my red blood; that dries the mouthing streams
Turns mine to wax.
And I am dumb to mouth unto my veins
10   How at the mountain spring the same mouth sucks.

The hand that whirls the water in the pool
Stirs the quicksand; that ropes the blowing wind
Hauls my shroud sail.
And I am dumb to tell the hanging man
15   How of my clay is made the hangman's lime.

The lips of time leech to the fountain head;
Love drips and gathers, but the fallen blood
Shall calm her sores.
And I am dumb to tell a weather's wind
20   How time has ticked a heaven round the stars.

And I am dumb to tell the lover's tomb
How at my sheet goes the same crooked worm.

1933

Do Not Go Gentle into That Good Night

Do not go gentle into that good night,
Old age should burn and rave at close of day;
Rage, rage against the dying of the light.

Though wise men at their end know dark is right,
5 Because their words had forked no lightning they
Do not go gentle into that good night.

Good men, the last wave by, crying how bright
Their frail deeds might have danced in a green bay,
Rage, rage against the dying of the light.

10 Wild men who caught and sang the sun in flight,
And learn, too late, they grieved it on its way,
Do not go gentle into that good night.

Grave men, near death, who see with blinding sight
Blind eyes could blaze like meteors and be gay,
15 Rage, rage against the dying of the light.

And you, my father, there on the sad height,
Curse, bless, me now with your fierce tears, I pray.
Do not go gentle into that good night.
Rage, rage against the dying of the light.

1951

Return Journey[1]

NARRATOR It was a cold white day in High Street, and nothing to stop the wind
slicing up from the docks, for where the squat and tall shops had shielded the
town from the sea lay their blitzed flat graves marbled with snow and headstoned
with fences. Dogs, delicate as cats on water, as though they had gloves on their
paws, padded over the vanished buildings. Boys romped, calling high and clear, on
top of a levelled chemist's and a shoe-shop, and a little girl, wearing a man's cap,
threw a snowball in a chill deserted garden that had once been the Jug and Bottle
of the Prince of Wales.[2] The wind cut up the street with a soft sea-noise hanging
on its arm, like a hooter in a muffler. I could see the swathed hill stepping up out
of the town, which you never could see properly before, and the powdered fields of
the roofs of Milton Terrace and Watkin Street and Fullers Row. Fish-frailed, net-
bagged, umbrella'd, pixie-capped, fur-shoed, blue-nosed, puce-lipped, blinkered
like drayhorses, scarved, mittened, galoshed, wearing everything but the cat's
blanket, crushes of shopping-women crunched in the little Lapland of the once
grey drab street, blew and queued and yearned for hot tea, as I began my search
through Swansea town cold and early on that wicked February morning.[3] I went
into the hotel. "Good morning."

1. Written in February 1947; broadcast by the BBC May
1947.
2. The name of a public house (pub).

3. Swansea, a city in South Wales on the mouth of the
river Tawe, is the second largest city in Wales after
Cardiff (the capital).

The hall-porter did not answer. I was just another snowman to him. He did not know that I was looking for someone after fourteen years, and he did not care. He stood and shuddered, staring through the glass of the hotel door at the snowflakes sailing down the sky, like Siberian confetti. The bar was just opening, but already one customer puffed and shook at the counter with a full pint of half-frozen Tawe water in his wrapped-up hand. I said Good morning, and the barmaid, polishing the counter vigorously as though it were a rare and valuable piece of Swansea china, said to her first customer:

BARMAID Seen the film at the Elysium Mr Griffiths there's snow isn't it did you come up on your bicycle our pipes burst Monday . . .

NARRATOR A pint of bitter,[4] please.

BARMAID Proper little lake in the kitchen got to wear your Wellingtons when you boil a egg one and four please[5] . . .

CUSTOMER The cold gets me just here . . .

BARMAID . . . and eightpence change that's your liver Mr Griffiths you been on the cocoa again . . .

NARRATOR I wonder whether you remember a friend of mine? He always used to come to this bar, some years ago. Every morning, about this time.

CUSTOMER Just by here it gets me. I don't know what'd happen if I didn't wear a band . . .

BARMAID What's his name?

NARRATOR Young Thomas.

BARMAID Lots of Thomases come here it's a kind of home from home for Thomases isn't it Mr Griffiths what's he look like?

NARRATOR He'd be about seventeen or eighteen . . .

(Slowly)

BARMAID . . . I was seventeen once . . .

NARRATOR . . . and above medium height. Above medium height for Wales, I mean, he's five foot six and a half. Thick blubber lips; snub nose; curly mouse-brown hair; one front tooth broken after playing a game called Cats and Dogs, in the Mermaid, Mumbles; speaks rather fancy; truculent; plausible; a bit of a show-er-off; plus-fours and no breakfast, you know; used to have poems printed in the *Herald of Wales*; there was one about an open-air performance of *Electra* in Mrs Bertie Perkins's garden in Sketty; lived up the Uplands; a bombastic adolescent provincial Bohemian with a thick-knotted artist's tie made out of his sister's scarf, she never knew where it had gone, and a cricket-shirt dyed bottle-green; a gabbing, ambitious, mock-tough, pretentious young man; and mole-y, too.

BARMAID There's words what d'you want to find him for I wouldn't touch him with a barge-pole . . . would you, Mr Griffiths? Mind, you can never tell. I remember a man came here with a monkey. Called for 'alf for himself and a pint for the monkey. And he wasn't Italian at all. Spoke Welsh like a preacher.

NARRATOR The bar was filling up. Snowy business bellies pressed their watch-chains against the counter; black business bowlers, damp and white now as Christmas puddings in their cloths, bobbed in front of the misty mirrors. The voice of commerce rang sternly through the lounge.

FIRST VOICE Cold enough for you?

SECOND VOICE How's your pipes, Mr Lewis?

---

4. British beer.   5. One shilling and 4 pence.

THIRD VOICE Another winter like this'll put paid to me, Mr Evans. I got the 'flu . . .

FIRST VOICE Make it a double . . .

SECOND VOICE Similar . . .

BARMAID Okay, baby . . .

CUSTOMER I seem to remember a chap like you described. There couldn't be two like him let's hope. He used to work as a reporter. Down the Three Lamps I used to see him. Lifting his ikkle elbow.

(*Confidentially*)

NARRATOR What's the Three Lamps like now?

CUSTOMER It isn't like anything. It isn't there. It's nothing mun. You remember Ben Evans's stores? It's right next door to that. Ben Evans isn't there either . . .

(*Fade*)

NARRATOR I went out of the hotel into the snow and walked down High Street, past the flat white wastes where all the shops had been. Eddershaw Furnishers, Curry's Bicycles, Donegal Clothing Company, Doctor Scholl's, Burton Tailors, W. H. Smith, Boots Cash Chemists, Leslie's Stores, Upson's Shoes, Prince of Wales, Tucker's Fish, Stead & Simpson—all the shops bombed and vanished. Past the hole in space where Hodges & Clothiers had been, down Castle Street, past the remembered, invisible shops, Price's Fifty Shilling, and Crouch the Jeweller, Potter Gilmore Gowns, Evans Jeweller, Master's Outfitters, Style and Mantle, Lennard's Boots, True Form, Kardomah, R. E. Jones, Dean's Tailor, David Evans, Gregory Confectioners, Bovega, Burton's, Lloyd's Bank, and nothing. And into Temple Street. There the Three Lamps had stood, old Mac magisterial in his corner. And there the Young Thomas whom I was searching for used to stand at the counter on Friday paynights with Freddie Farr Half Hook, Bill Latham, Cliff Williams, Gareth Hughes, Eric Hughes, Glyn Lowry, a man among men, his hat at a rakish angle, in that snug, smug, select Edwardian holy of best-bitter holies . . .

(*Bar noises in background*)

OLD REPORTER Remember when I took you down the mortuary for the first time, Young Thomas? He'd never seen a corpse before, boys, except old Ron on a Saturday night. "If you want to be a proper newspaperman," I said, "you got to be well known in the right circles. You got to be *persona grata* [acceptable] in the mortuary, see." He went pale green, mun.

FIRST YOUNG REPORTER Look, he's blushing now . . .

OLD REPORTER And when we got there what d'you think? The decorators were in at the mortuary, giving the old home a bit of a re-do like. Up on ladders having a slap at the roof. Young Thomas didn't see 'em, he had his pop eyes glued on the slab, and when one of the painters up the ladder said "Good morning, gents" in a deep voice he upped in the air and out of the place like a ferret. Laugh!

BARMAID (*off*) You've had enough, Mr Roberts. You heard what I said.

(*Noise of a gentle scuffle*)

SECOND YOUNG REPORTER (*casually*) There goes Mr Roberts.

OLD REPORTER Well fair do's they throw you out very genteel in this pub . . .

FIRST YOUNG REPORTER Ever seen Young Thomas covering a soccer match down the Vetch and working it out in tries?

SECOND YOUNG REPORTER And up the Mannesman Hall shouting "Good footwork, sir," and a couple of punch-drunk colliers galumphing about like jumbos.

FIRST YOUNG REPORTER What you been reporting to-day, Young Thomas?

SECOND YOUNG REPORTER Two typewriter Thomas the ace news-dick . . .

OLD REPORTER Let's have a dekko[6] at your note-book. "Called at British Legion: Nothing. Called at Hospital: One broken leg. Auction at the Metropole. Ring Mr Beynon *re* Gymanfa Ganu. Lunch: Pint and pasty at the Singleton with Mrs Giles. Bazaar at Bethesda Chapel. Chimney on fire at Tontine Street. Walters Road Sunday School Outing. Rehearsal of the *Mikado* at Skewen'—all front page stuff . . . (*Fade*)

NARRATOR The voices of fourteen years ago hung silent in the snow and ruin, and in the falling winter morning I walked on through the white havoc'd centre where once a very young man I knew had mucked about as chirpy as a sparrow after the sips and titbits and small change of the town. Near the *Evening Post* building and the fragment of the Castle I stopped a man whose face I thought I recognized from a long time ago. I said: I wonder if you can tell me . . .

PASSER-BY Yes?

NARRATOR He peered out of his blanketing scarves and from under his snowballed Balaclava like an Eskimo with a bad conscience. I said: If you can tell me whether you used to know a chap called Young Thomas. He worked on the Post and used to wear an overcoat sometimes with the check lining inside out so that you could play giant draughts on him. He wore a conscious woodbine,[7] too . . .

PASSER-BY What d'you mean, conscious woodbine?

NARRATOR . . . and a perched pork pie with a peacock feather and he tried to slouch like a newshawk even when he was attending a meeting of the Gorseinon Buffalos[8] . . .

PASSER-BY Oh, *him!* He owes me half a crown. I haven't seen him since the old Kardomah days. He wasn't a reporter then, he'd just left the grammar school.[9] Him and Charlie Fisher—Charlie's got whiskers now—and Tom Warner and Fred Janes, drinking coffee-dashes and arguing the toss.

NARRATOR What about?

PASSER-BY Music and poetry and painting and politics. Einstein and Epstein, Stravinsky and Greta Garbo, death and religion, Picasso and girls . . .

NARRATOR And then?

PASSER-BY Communism, symbolism, Bradman, Braque, the Watch Committee, free love, free beer, murder, Michelangelo, ping-pong, ambition, Sibelius, and girls . . .

NARRATOR Is that all?

PASSER-BY How Dan Jones was going to compose the most prodigious symphony, Fred Janes paint the most miraculously meticulous picture, Charlie Fisher catch the poshest trout, Vernon Watkins and Young Thomas write the most boiling poems, how they would ring the bells of London and paint it like a tart . . .

NARRATOR And after that?

PASSER-BY Oh the hissing of the butt-ends in the drains of the coffee-dashes and the tinkle and the gibble-gabble of the morning young lounge lizards as they talked about Augustus John, Emil Jannings, Carnera, Dracula, Amy Johnson, trial marriage, pocket-money, the Welsh sea, the London stars, King Kong, anarchy, darts, T. S. Eliot, and girls. . . . Duw, it's cold!

6. British army slang for "a look" (from the Hindi word *dekho*).
7. A brand of cigarette.
8. A pork-pie hat takes its name from the circular shape of a pork pie; Gorseinon is a town near Swansea, apparently with a chapter of the Royal Antediluvian Order of Buffaloes (founded 1822), a men's club.
9. Secondary school, typically educating students of ages 11–18.

NARRATOR And he hurried on, into the dervish snow, without a good morning or good-bye, swaddled in his winter woollens like a man in the island of his deafness, and I felt that perhaps he had never stopped at all to tell me of one more departed stage in the progress of the boy I was pursuing. The Kardomah Café was razed to the snow, the voices of the coffee-drinkers—poets, painters, and musicians in their beginnings—lost in the willynilly flying of the years and the flakes.

    Down College Street I walked then, past the remembered invisible shops, Langley's, Castle Cigar Co., T. B. Brown, Pullar's, Aubrey Jeremiah, Goddard Jones, Richards, Hornes, Marles, Pleasance & Harper, Star Supply, Sidney Heath, Wesley Chapel, and nothing. . . . My search was leading me back, through pub and job and café, to the School.

    (Fade) (School bell)

SCHOOLMASTER Oh yes, yes, I remember him well,
        though I do not know if I would recognize him now:
        nobody grows any younger, or better,
        and boys grow into much the sort of men one would suppose
        though sometimes the moustaches bewilder
        and one finds it hard to reconcile one's memory of a small
        none-too-clean urchin lying his way unsuccessfully out of his homework
        with a fierce and many-medalled sergeant-major with three children or a
        divorced chartered accountant;
        and it is hard to realize
        that some little tousled rebellious youth whose only claim
        to fame among his contemporaries was his undisputed right
        to the championship of the spitting contest
        is now perhaps one's own bank manager.
        Oh yes, I remember him well, the boy you are searching for:
        he looked like most boys, no better, brighter, or more respectful;
        he cribbed, mitched,[1] spilt ink, rattled his desk and
        garbled his lessons with the worst of them;
        he could smudge, hedge, smirk, wriggle, wince,
        whimper, blarney, badger, blush, deceive, be
        devious, stammer, improvise, assume
        offended dignity or righteous indignation as though to the manner born;[2]
        sullenly and reluctantly he drilled, for some small
        crime, under Sergeant Bird, so wittily nicknamed
        Oiseau,° on Wednesday half-holidays,   *bird*
        appeared regularly in detention classes,
        hid in the cloakroom during algebra,
        was, when a newcomer, thrown into the bushes of the
        Lower Playground by bigger boys,
        and threw newcomers into the bushes of the Lower
        Playground when *he* was a bigger boy;
        he scuffled at prayers,
        he interpolated, smugly, the time-honoured wrong
        irreverent words into the morning hymns,
        he helped to damage the headmaster's rhubarb,
        was thirty-third in trigonometry,
        and, as might be expected, edited the School Magazine

    (Fade)

---

1. Stole.   2. As though born into a high station in life.

NARRATOR The Hall is shattered, the echoing corridors charred where he scribbled and smudged and yawned in the long green days, waiting for the bell and the scamper into the Yard: the School on Mount Pleasant Hill has changed its face and its ways. Soon, they say, it may be no longer the School at all he knew and loved when he was a boy up to no good but the beat of his blood: the names are havoc'd from the Hall and the carved initials burned from the broken wood. But the names remain. What names did he know of the dead? Who of the honoured dead did he know such a long time ago? The names of the dead in the living heart and head remain for ever. Of all the dead whom did he know?

(Funeral bell)

VOICE
        Evans, K. J.
        Haines, G. C.
        Roberts, I. L.
        Moxham, J.
        Thomas, H.
        Baines, W.
        Bazzard, F. H.
        Beer, L. J.
        Bucknell, R.
        Tywford, G.
        Vagg, E. A.
        Wright, G.

(Fade)

NARRATOR Then I tacked down the snowblind hill, a cat-o'-nine-gales whipping from the sea, and, white and eiderdowned in the smothering flurry, people padded past me up and down like prowling featherbeds. And I plodded through the ankle-high one cloud that foamed the town, into flat Gower Street, its buildings melted, and along long Helen's Road. Now my search was leading me back to the seashore.

(Noise of sea, softly)

NARRATOR Only two living creatures stood on the promenade, near the cenotaph, facing the tossed crystal sea: a man in a chewed muffler and a ratting cap, and an angry dog of a mixed make. The man dithered in the cold, beat his bare blue hands together, waited for some sign from sea or snow; the dog shouted at the weather, and fixed his bloodshot eyes on Mumbles Head. But when the man and I talked together, the dog piped down and fixed his eyes on me, blaming me for the snow. The man spoke towards the sea. Year in, year out, whatever the weather, once in the daytime, once in the dark, he always came to look at the sea. He knew all the dogs and boys and old men who came to see the sea, who ran or gambolled on the sand or stooped at the edge of the waves as though over a wild, wide, rolling ash-can. He knew the lovers who went to lie in the sandhills, the striding masculine women who roared at their terriers like tiger tamers, the loafing men whose work it was in the world to observe the great employment of the sea. He said:

PROMENADE-MAN Oh yes, yes, I remember him well, but I didn't know what was his name. I don't know the names of none of the sandboys. They don't know mine. About fourteen or fifteen years old, you said, with a little red cap. And he used to play by Vivian's Stream. He used to dawdle in the arches, you said, and lark about on the railway-lines and holler at the old sea. He'd mooch about the dunes and watch the tankers and the tugs and the banana boats come out of the docks. He was going to run away to sea, he said. I know. On Saturday afternoon he'd go down to the sea when it was a long way out, and hear the foghorns though he couldn't see the ships. And on Sunday nights, after chapel, he'd be swaggering with his pals along the prom, whistling after the girls.

(*Titter*)

GIRL Does your mother know you're out? Go away now. Stop following us.

(*Another girl titters*)

GIRL Don't you say nothing, Hetty, you're only encouraging. No thank *you*, Mr Cheeky, with your cut-glass accent and your father's trilby![3] I don't want *no* walk on *no* sands. What d'you say? Ooh listen to him, Het, he's swallowed a dictionary. No, I don't want to go with nobody up no lane in the moonlight, see, and I'm not a baby-snatcher neither. I seen you going to school along Terrace Road, Mr Glad-Eye, with your little satchel and wearing your red cap and all. You seen me wearing my . . . no you never. Hetty, mind your glasses! Hetty Harris, you're as bad as them. Oh go away and do your homework, see. Cheek! Hetty Harris, don't you let him! Oooh, there's brazen! Well, just to the end of the prom, if you like. No further, mind . . .

PROMENADE-MAN Oh yes, I knew him well. I've known him by the thousands . . .

NARRATOR Even now, on the frozen foreshore, a high, far cry of boys, all like the boy I sought, slid on the glass of the streams and snowballed each other and the sky. Then I went on my way from the sea, up Brynmill Terrace and into Glanbry-dan Avenue where Bert Trick had kept a grocer's shop and, in the kitchen, threatened the annihilation of the ruling classes over sandwiches and jelly and blanc-mange.[4] And I came to the shops and houses of the Uplands. Here and around here it was that the journey had begun of the one I was pursuing through his past.

(*Old piano cinema-music in background*)

FIRST VOICE Here was once the flea-pit picture-house where he whooped for the scalping Indians with Jack Basset and banged for the rustlers' guns.

NARRATOR Jackie Basset, killed.

THIRD VOICE Here once was Mrs Ferguson's, who sold the best gob-stoppers[5] and penny packets full of surprises and a sweet kind of glue.

FIRST VOICE In the fields behind Cwmdonkin Drive, the Murrays chased him and all cats.

SECOND VOICE No fires now where the outlaws' fires burned and the paradisiacal potatoes roasted in the embers.

THIRD VOICE In the Graig beneath Town Hill he was a lonely killer hunting the wolves (or rabbits) and the red Sioux tribe (or Mitchell brothers).

(*Fade cinema-music into background of children's voices reciting, in unison, the names of the counties of Wales*)

FIRST VOICE In Mirador School he learned to read and count. Who made the worst raffia doilies? Who put water in Joyce's galoshes, every morning prompt as prompt? In the afternoons, when the children were good, they read aloud from Struwelpeter.[6] And when they were bad, they sat alone in the empty classroom, hearing, from above them, the distant, terrible, sad music of the late piano lesson.

(*The children's voices fade. The piano lesson continues in background*)

---

3. With an upper-class accent and an elegant hat.
4. A pudding.
5. A kind of candy.

6. *Struwelpeter* ("Shock-head Peter") by the German Heinrich Hoffman (1809–1874) was a popular book for children.

NARRATOR And I went up, through the white Grove, into Cwmdonkin Park, the snow still sailing and the childish, lonely, remembered music fingering on in the suddenly gentle wind. Dusk was folding the Park around, like another, darker snow. Soon the bell would ring for the closing of the gates, though the Park was empty. The park-keeper walked by the reservoir, where swans had glided, on his white rounds. I walked by his side and asked him my questions, up the swathed drives past buried beds and loaded utterly still furred and birdless trees towards the last gate. He said:

PARK-KEEPER Oh yes, yes, I knew him well. He used to climb the reservoir railings and pelt the old swans. Run like a billygoat over the grass you should keep off of. Cut branches off the trees. Carve words on the benches. Pull up moss in the rockery, go snip through the dahlias. Fight in the bandstand. Climb the elms and moon up the top like a owl. Light fires in the bushes. Play on the green bank. Oh yes, I knew him well. I think he was happy all the time. I've known him by the thousands.

NARRATOR We had reached the last gate. Dusk drew around us and the town. I said: What has become of him now?

PARK-KEEPER Dead.

NARRATOR The Park-keeper said:

(*The park bell rings*)

PARK-KEEPER Dead . . . Dead . . . Dead . . . Dead . . . Dead . . . Dead.

⊷ ⊨✠⊨ ⊶

Samuel Beckett

1906–1989

On January 5, 1953, *En Attendant Godot* (*Waiting for Godot*) premiered at the Théâtre de Babylone, Paris—and the shape of twentieth-century drama was permanently changed. *Godot* helped to strip the modern stage of everything but its essentials: two characters, seemingly without past or future or worldly possessions, and a spare stage: "A country road. A tree. Evening." Critics would subsequently find in Beckett's bleak stage suggestions of a postnuclear holocaust landscape, as they would in the later *Fin de partie* (*Endgame*, 1957); and for the remainder of his long and productive career, Beckett would continue to explore, with unparalleled honesty and courage, that realm of being that he called in one story *Sans*—"lessness."

April 13, 1906—Good Friday—is the date usually given for Samuel Barclay Beckett's birth, though the birth certificate shows May 13. He was born in the family home of Cooldrinagh in Foxrock, an upper-class Protestant suburb south of Dublin, to William Beckett, surveyor, and Mary (May) Roe, the daughter of a wealthy Kildare family. "You might say I had a happy childhood," Beckett later recalled; "my father did not beat me, nor did my mother run away from home." Beckett attended private academies in Dublin, then in 1920 was enrolled in Portora Royal School in Enniskillen, Northern Ireland, where he excelled more in sports than studies as star bowler on the cricket team, captain of rugby and swimming, and light-heavyweight champion in boxing. In 1923 Beckett entered Trinity College, Dublin, studying modern languages; he also enjoyed the freedom of the city, frequenting the Gate Theatre (for the drama of Pirandello and O'Casey), the music hall, and the movies (especially Charlie Chaplin, Laurel and Hardy, Buster Keaton, and the Marx Brothers). All would prove formative influences on his later drama and fiction.

In 1927 Beckett received his B.A. degree, first in his class in modern languages, and went off on fellowship to France to teach for two years at the École Normale Supérieure in Paris. While in Paris he became a friend of James Joyce, who influenced him profoundly. Besides aiding Joyce in various ways with his work, Beckett wrote an important essay, *Dante . . . Bruno . . . Vico . . . Joyce*, on *Finnegans Wake*—for a volume of critical writing published before the novel itself was completed. With characteristic understatement, Beckett has said that "Paris in the twenties was a good place for a young man to be"; at the same time, learning the craft of writing in Paris under the shadow of fellow Irish expatriate James Joyce would be enough to provoke the anxiety of influence in even the best of writers. However, Beckett's respect and admiration for Joyce were boundless and never wavered. In 1969 Beckett admitted that Joyce had become "an ethical ideal" for him: "Joyce had a moral effect on me. He made me realize artistic integrity."

The term of his fellowship in Paris having run out, Beckett returned to Dublin to assume teaching at Trinity College. That he was ill-suited to this role was immediately apparent to students, colleagues, and Beckett himself. "I saw that in teaching," Beckett later said, "I was talking of something I knew little about, to people who cared nothing about it. So I behaved very badly." The bad behavior to which Beckett refers was his resignation by mail while on spring holidays in Germany during his second year. Beckett returned briefly to Paris, where it became clear that the unwelcome attentions of Joyce's daughter Lucia were straining Beckett's relationship with the elder writer. He returned to the family home for a time in 1933, where he worked on his first published fiction, the Joycean collection of short stories *More Pricks than Kicks*.

The 1930s found Beckett shuttling back and forth between poverty in London and the frustrating comforts of home in Dublin; Paris seemed to him forbidden, owing to the break with Joyce. In spite of his difficult living circumstances, however, and occasional crippling attacks of clinical depression, Beckett managed to complete his first novel, *Murphy*. The manuscript was rejected by forty-one publishers before being accepted by Routledge in 1937. At the end of 1937, Beckett overcame his reluctance and moved back to Paris. From then on, he wrote largely in French. During the early years of World War II, he attempted to write but found it increasingly difficult to maintain the neutrality required of him by his Irish citizenship in light of the German invasion of France. He abandoned that neutrality in October 1940, when he joined one of the earliest French Resistance groups; he helped in Paris with Resistance activities until his group had been penetrated and betrayed, and just in the nick of time he and his lover Suzanne Deschevaux-Dumesnil (the two had met in 1938, and would eventually marry in 1961) were smuggled into Unoccupied France. At the end of the war Beckett returned to Paris, where he was awarded the *Croix de Guerre* and the *Médaille de la Résistance* by the French government.

While hiding from the Germans from 1942 to 1945 in the village of Roussillon in southeast France, Beckett wrote *Watt*, a complex and aridly witty novel that was never to enjoy the attention devoted to Beckett's other fiction. Meanwhile, Beckett continued his experiments with drama. Though it is drama for which Beckett is best known, he always put more stock in his fiction; "I turned to writing plays," he once said dismissively, "to relieve myself of the awful depression the prose led me into."

At an impasse in the writing of what would prove to be his greatest novels, the trilogy *Molloy, Malone Dies*, and *The Unnameable* (1951–1953), Beckett took off three months to write *Waiting for Godot*; it took four years to get the play produced. It is easy enough, in retrospect, to understand the producers' reservations: *Godot* breaks with the conventions of the well-made play at just about every turn, even down to its symmetrical, mirror-image two-act structure. The Irish critic Vivian Mercier wittily described *Godot* as a play in which "nothing happens, twice." Beckett's play *Krapp's Last Tape* (1960) uses a tape recorder (which, at the time of writing, Beckett had never seen) as a stage metaphor for the struggle over memory. In this play Beckett went farther than ever in stripping down his action, now involving just a single character. The play is less a monologue, though, than Krapp's dialogue with his past and future selves—and with the machine on which the selves of different years have recorded their fragmentary observations and memories.

After the success of his plays of the fifties and early sixties, Beckett turned to shorter and shorter forms, both in drama and fiction; he produced a number of very powerful, very short plays (*Not I*, 1973; *Footfalls*, 1976; *Rockabye*, 1981) and short, poetic texts that he called by a variety of self-deprecating names ("fizzles," "residua," "texts for nothing"). He sought an intensified power in the increasing economy of his works. In 1969 Beckett was awarded the Nobel Prize for literature, for "a body of work," as the citation declares, "that, in new forms of fiction and the theatre, has transmuted the destitution of modern man into exaltation."

Krapp's Last Tape

A late evening in the future.

> *Krapp's den.*
> *Front centre a small table, the two drawers of which open towards the audience.*
> *Sitting at the table, facing front, i.e. across from the drawers, a wearish old man: Krapp.*

Rusty black narrow trousers too short for him. Rusty black sleeveless waistcoat, four capacious pockets. Heavy silver watch and chain. Grimy white shirt open at neck, no collar. Surprising pair of dirty white boots, size ten at least, very narrow and pointed.

> *White face. Purple nose. Disordered grey hair. Unshaven.*
> *Very near-sighted (but unspectacled). Hard of hearing.*
> *Cracked voice. Distinctive intonation.*
> *Laborious walk.*

On the table a tape-recorder with microphone and a number of cardboard boxes containing reels of recorded tapes.

> *Table and immediately adjacent area in strong white light. Rest of stage in darkness.*

Krapp remains a moment motionless, heaves a great sigh, looks at his watch, fumbles in his pockets, takes out an envelope, puts it back, fumbles, takes out a small bunch of keys, raises it to his eyes, chooses a key, gets up and moves to front of table. He stoops, unlocks first drawer, peers into it, feels about inside it, takes out a reel of tape, peers at it, puts it back, locks drawer, unlocks second drawer, peers into it, feels about inside it, takes out a large banana, peers at it, locks drawer, puts keys back in his pocket. He turns, advances to edge of stage, halts, strokes banana, peels it, drops skin at his feet, puts end of banana in his mouth and remains motionless, staring vacuously before him. Finally he bites off the end, turns aside and begins pacing to and fro at edge of stage, in the light, i.e. not more than four or five paces either way, meditatively eating banana. He treads on skin, slips, nearly falls, recovers himself, stoops and peers at skin and finally pushes it, still stooping, with his foot over edge of stage into pit. He resumes his pacing, finishes banana, returns to table, sits down, remains a moment motionless, heaves a great sigh, takes keys from his pockets, raises them to his eyes, chooses key, gets up and moves to front of table, unlocks second drawer, takes out a second large banana, peers at it, locks drawer, puts back keys in his pocket, turns, advances to edge of stage, halts, strokes banana, peels it, tosses skin into pit, puts end of banana in his mouth and remains motionless, staring vacuously before him. Finally he has an idea, puts banana in his waistcoat pocket, the end emerging, and goes with all the speed he can muster backstage into darkness. Ten seconds. Loud pop of cork. Fifteen seconds. He comes back into light carrying an old ledger and sits down at table. He lays ledger on table, wipes his mouth, wipes his hands on the front of his waistcoat, brings them smartly together and rubs them.

KRAPP [*briskly*] Ah! [*He bends over ledger, turns the pages, finds the entry he wants, reads.*] Box . . . thrree . . . spool . . . five. [*He raises his head and stares front. With relish.*] Spool . . . [*Pause.*] Spooool! [*Happy smile. Pause. He bends over table, starts peering and poking at the boxes.*] Box . . . thrree . . . thrree . . . four . . . two . . . [*with surprise*] nine! good God! . . . seven . . . ah! the little rascal! [*He takes up box, peers at it.*] Box thrree. [*He lays it on table, opens it and peers at spools inside.*] Spool . . . [*he peers at ledger*] . . . five . . . [*he peers at spools*] . . . five . . . five . . . ah! the little scoundrel! [*He takes out a spool, peers at it.*] Spool five. [*He lays it on table, closes box three, puts it back with the others, takes up the spool.*] Box thrree, spool five. [*He bends over the machine, looks up. With relish.*] Spooool! [*Happy smile. He bends, loads spool on machine, rubs his hands.*] Ah! [*He peers at ledger, reads entry at foot of page.*] Mother at rest at last. . . . Hm. . . . The black ball. . . . [*He raises his head, stares blankly front. Puzzled.*] Black ball? . . . [*He peers again at ledger, reads.*] The dark nurse. . . . [*He raises his head, broods, peers again at ledger, reads.*] Slight improvement in bowel condition. . . . Hm. . . . Memorable . . . what? [*He peers closer.*] Equinox, memorable equinox. [*He raises his head, stares blankly front. Puzzled.*] Memorable equinox? . . . [*Pause. He shrugs his shoulders, peers again at ledger, reads.*] Farewell to—[*he turns page*]—love. [*He raises his head, broods, bends over machine, switches on and assumes listening posture, i.e. leaning forward, elbows on table, hand cupping ear towards machine, face front.*]

TAPE [*strong voice, rather pompous, clearly Krapp's at a much earlier time*] Thirty-nine today, sound as a—[*Settling himself more comfortably he knocks one of the boxes off the table, curses, switches off, sweeps boxes and ledger violently to the ground, winds tape back to beginning, switches on, resumes posture.*] Thirty-nine today, sound as a bell, apart from my old weakness, and intellectually I have now every reason to suspect at the . . . [*hesitates*] . . . crest of the wave—or thereabouts. Celebrated the awful occasion, as in recent years, quietly at the Winehouse. Not a soul. Sat before the fire with closed eyes, separating the grain from the husks. Jotted down a few notes, on the back of an envelope. Good to be back in my den, in my old rags. Have just eaten I regret to say three bananas and only with difficulty refrained from a fourth. Fatal things for a man with my condition. [*Vehemently.*] Cut'em out! [*Pause.*] The new light above my table is a great improvement. With all this darkness round me I feel less alone. [*Pause.*] In a way. [*Pause.*] I love to get up and move about in it, then back here to . . . [*hesitates*] . . . me. [*Pause.*] Krapp.

[*Pause.*]

The grain, now what I wonder do I mean by that, I mean . . . [*hesitates*] . . . I suppose I mean those things worth having when all the dust has—when all my dust has settled. I close my eyes and try and imagine them.

[*Pause. Krapp closes his eyes briefly.*]

Extraordinary silence this evening, I strain my ears and do not hear a sound. Old Miss McGlome always sings at this hour. But not tonight. Songs of her girlhood, she says. Hard to think of her as a girl. Wonderful woman though. Connaught,[1] I fancy. [*Pause.*] Shall I sing when I am her age, if I ever am? No. [*Pause.*] Did I sing as a boy? No. [*Pause.*] Did I ever sing? No.

[*Pause.*]

Just been listening to an old year, passages at random. I did not check in the book, but it must be at least ten or twelve years ago. At that time I think I was still living on and off with Bianca in Kedar Street. Well out of that, Jesus yes! Hopeless business. [*Pause.*] Not much about her, apart from a tribute to her eyes. Very warm. I suddenly saw them again. [*Pause.*] Incomparable! [*Pause.*] Ah well?

---

1. A province in northwestern Ireland.

[*Pause.*] These old P.M.s are gruesome, but I often find them—[*Krapp switches off, broods, switches on.*]—a help before embarking on a new . . . [*hesitates*] . . . retrospect. Hard to believe I was ever that young whelp. The voice! Jesus! And the aspirations! [*Brief laugh in which Krapp joins.*] And the resolutions! [*Brief laugh in which Krapp joins.*] To drink less, in particular. [*Brief laugh of Krapp alone.*] Statistics. Seventeen hundred hours, out of the preceding eight thousand odd, consumed on licensed premises[2] alone. More than 20 per cent, say 40 per cent of his waking life. [*Pause.*] Plans for a less . . . [*hesitates*] . . . engrossing sexual life. Last illness of his father. Flagging pursuit of happiness. Unattainable laxation.[3] Sneers at what he calls his youth and thanks to God that it's over. [*Pause.*] False ring there. [*Pause.*] Shadows of the opus . . . magnum.[4] Closing with a—[*brief laugh*]—yelp to Providence. [*Prolonged laugh in which Krapp joins.*] What remains of all that misery? A girl in a shabby green coat, on a railway-station platform? No?

[*Pause.*]

When I look—

[*Krapp switches off, broods, looks at his watch, gets up, goes backstage into darkness. Ten seconds. Pop of cork. Ten seconds. Second cork. Ten seconds. Third cork. Ten seconds. Brief burst of quavering song.*]

KRAPP [*sings*]   Now the day is over,
                 Night is drawing nigh-igh,
                 Shadows—

[*Fit of coughing. He comes back into light, sits down, wipes his mouth, switches on, resumes his listening posture.*]

TAPE   —back on the year that is gone, with what I hope is perhaps a glint of the old eye to come, there is of course the house on the canal where mother lay a-dying, in the late autumn, after her long viduity [*Krapp gives a start*] and the—[*Krapp switches off, winds back tape a little, bends his ear closer to machine, switches on*]—a-dying, after her long viduity, and the—

[*Krapp switches off, raises his head, stares blankly before him. His lips move in the syllables of "viduity." No sound. He gets up, goes backstage into darkness, comes back with an enormous dictionary, lays it on table, sits down and looks up the word.*]

KRAPP [*reading from dictionary*] State—or condition—of being—or remaining—a widow—or widower. [*Looks up. Puzzled.*] Being—or remaining? . . . [*Pause. He peers again at dictionary. Reading.*] "Deep weeds of viduity." . . . Also of an animal, especially a bird . . . the vidua or weaver-bird. . . . Black plumage of male. . . . [*He looks up. With relish.*] The vidua-bird!

[*Pause. He closes dictionary, switches on, resumes listening posture.*]

TAPE   —bench by the weir from where I could see her window. There I sat, in the biting wind, wishing she were gone. [*Pause.*] Hardly a soul, just a few regulars, nursemaids, infants, old men, dogs. I got to know them quite well—oh by appearance of course I mean! One dark young beauty I recollect particularly, all white and starch, incomparable bosom, with a big black hooded perambulator, most funeral thing. Whenever I looked in her direction she had her eyes on me. And yet when I was bold enough to speak to her—not having been introduced—she threatened to call a policeman. As if I had designs on her virtue! [*Laugh. Pause.*]

2. Pubs licensed to sell alcohol.
3. Movement of the bowels.

4. A "magnum opus" is a great work; a magnum is a large wine bottle.

The face she had! The eyes! Like . . . [*hesitates*] . . . chrysolite![5] [*Pause.*] Ah well. . . . [*Pause.*] I was there when—[*Krapp switches off, broods, switches on again.*]—the blind went down, one of those dirty brown roller affairs, throwing a ball for a little white dog as chance would have it. I happened to look up and there it was. All over and done with, at last. I sat on for a few moments with the ball in my hand and the dog yelping and pawing at me. [*Pause.*] Moments. Her moments, my moments. [*Pause.*] The dog's moments. [*Pause.*] In the end I held it out to him and he took it in his mouth, gently, gently. A small, old, black, hard, solid rubber ball. [*Pause.*] I shall feel it, in my hand, until my dying day. [*Pause.*] I might have kept it. [*Pause.*] But I gave it to the dog.

[*Pause.*]

Ah well. . . .

[*Pause.*]

Spiritually a year of profound gloom and indigence until that memorable night in March, at the end of the jetty, in the howling wind, never to be forgotten, when suddenly I saw the whole thing. The vision at last. This I fancy is what I have chiefly to record this evening, against the day when my work will be done and perhaps no place left in my memory, warm or cold, for the miracle that . . . [*hesitates*] . . . for the fire that set it alight. What I suddenly saw then was this, that the belief I had been going on all my life, namely—[*Krapp switches off impatiently, winds tape forward, switches on again*]—great granite rocks the foam flying up in the light of the lighthouse and the wind-gauge spinning like a propeller, clear to me at last that the dark I have always struggled to keep under is in reality my most— [*Krapp curses, switches off, winds tape forward, switches on again*]—unshatterable association until my dissolution of storm and night with the light of the understanding and the fire—[*Krapp curses louder, switches off, winds tape forward, switches on again*]—my face in her breasts and my hand on her. We lay there without moving. But under us all moved, and moved us, gently, up and down, and from side to side.

[*Pause.*]

Past midnight. Never knew such silence. The earth might be uninhabited.

[*Pause.*]

Here I end—

[*Krapp switches off, winds tape back, switches on again.*]

—upper lake, with the punt,[6] bathed off the bank, then pushed out into the stream and drifted. She lay stretched out on the floorboards with her hands under her head and her eyes closed. Sun blazing down, bit of a breeze, water nice and lively. I noticed a scratch on her thigh and asked her how she came by it. Picking gooseberries, she said. I said again I thought it was hopeless and no good going on and she agreed, without opening her eyes. [*Pause.*] I asked her to look at me and after a few moments—[*Pause.*]—after a few moments she did, but the eyes just slits, because of the glare. I bent over her to get them in the shadow and they opened. [*Pause. Low.*] Let me in. [*Pause.*] We drifted in among the flags[7] and stuck. The way they went down, sighing, before the stem! [*Pause.*] I lay down across her with my face in her breasts and my hand on her. We lay there without moving. But under us all moved, and moved us, gently, up and down, and from side to side.

---

5. Green gemstone.   7. Reeds.
6. A small, flat-bottomed boat.

[*Pause.*]

Past midnight. Never knew—

[*Krapp switches off, broods. Finally he fumbles in his pockets, encounters the banana, takes it out, peers at it, puts it back, fumbles, brings out envelope, fumbles, puts back envelope, looks at his watch, gets up and goes backstage into darkness. Ten seconds. Sound of bottle against glass, then brief siphon. Ten seconds. Bottle against glass alone. Ten seconds. He comes back a little unsteadily into light, goes to front of table, takes out keys, raises them to his eyes, chooses key, unlocks first drawer, peers into it, feels about inside, takes out reel, peers at it, locks drawer, puts keys back in his pocket, goes and sits down, takes reel off machine, lays it on dictionary, loads virgin reel on machine, takes envelope from his pocket, consults back of it, lays it on table, switches on, clears his throat and begins to record.*]

KRAPP Just been listening to that stupid bastard I took myself for thirty years ago, hard to believe I was ever as bad as that. Thank God that's all done with anyway. [*Pause.*] The eyes she had! [*Broods, realizes he is recording silence, switches off, broods. Finally.*] Everything there, everything, all the—[*Realizes this is not being recorded, switches on.*] Everything there, everything on this old muckball, all the light and dark and famine and feasting of . . . [*hesitates*] . . . the ages! [*In a shout.*] Yes! [*Pause.*] Let that go! Jesus! Take his mind off his homework! Jesus! [*Pause. Weary.*] Ah well, maybe he was right. [*Pause.*] Maybe he was right. [*Broods. Realizes. Switches off. Consults envelope.*] Pah! [*Crumples it and throws it away. Broods. Switches on.*] Nothing to say, not a squeak. What's a year now? The sour cud and the iron stool.[8] [*Pause.*] Revelled in the word spool. [*With relish.*] Spooool! Happiest moment of the past half million. [*Pause.*] Seventeen copies sold, of which eleven at trade price to free circulating libraries beyond the seas. Getting known. [*Pause.*] One pound six and something, eight I have little doubt. [*Pause.*] Crawled out once or twice, before the summer was cold. Sat shivering in the park, drowned in dreams and burning to be gone. Not a soul. [*Pause.*] Last fancies. [*Vehemently.*] Keep 'em under! [*Pause.*] Scalded the eyes out of me reading *Effie*[9] again, a page a day, with tears again. Effie. . . . [*Pause.*] Could have been happy with her, up there on the Baltic, and the pines, and the dunes. [*Pause.*] Could I? [*Pause.*] And she? [*Pause.*] Pah! [*Pause.*] Fanny came in a couple of times. Bony old ghost of a whore. Couldn't do much, but I suppose better than a kick in the crutch. The last time wasn't so bad. How do you manage it, she said, at your age? I told her I'd been saving up for her all my life. [*Pause.*] Went to Vespers[1] once, like when I was in short trousers. [*Pause. Sings.*]

> Now the day is over,
> Night is drawing nigh-igh,
> Shadows—[*coughing, then almost inaudible*]—of the evening
> Steal across the sky.

[*Gasping.*] Went to sleep and fell off the pew. [*Pause.*] Sometimes wondered in the night if a last effort mightn't—[*Pause.*] Ah finish your booze now and get to your bed. Go on with this drivel in the morning. Or leave it at that. [*Pause.*] Leave it at that. [*Pause.*] Lie propped up in the dark—and wander. Be again in

---

8. Indigestion and constipation.
9. Theodor Fontane's sentimental novel *Effi Briest* (1895).

1. Evening church service.

the dingle[2] on a Christmas Eve, gathering holly, the red-berried. [*Pause.*] Be again on Croghan[3] on a Sunday morning, in the haze, with the bitch, stop and listen to the bells. [*Pause.*] And so on. [*Pause.*] Be again, be again. [*Pause.*] All that old misery. [*Pause.*] Once wasn't enough for you. [*Pause.*] Lie down across her.

> [*Long pause. He suddenly bends over machine, switches off, wrenches off tape, throws it away, puts on the other, winds it forward to the passage he wants, switches on, listens staring front.*]

TAPE —gooseberries, she said. I said again I thought it was hopeless and no good going on and she agreed, without opening her eyes. [*Pause.*] I asked her to look at me and after a few moments—[*Pause.*]—after a few moments she did, but the eyes just slits, because of the glare. I bent over to get them in the shadow and they opened. [*Pause. Low.*] Let me in. [*Pause.*] We drifted in among the flags and stuck. The way they went down, sighing, before the stem! [*Pause.*] I lay down across her with my face in her breasts and my hand on her. We lay there without moving. But under us all moved, and moved us, gently, up and down, and from side to side.

> [*Pause. Krapp's lips move. No sound.*]

Past midnight. Never knew such silence. The earth might be uninhabited.

> [*Pause.*]

Here I end this reel. Box—[*Pause.*]—three, spool—[*Pause.*]—five. [*Pause.*] Perhaps my best years are gone. When there was a chance of happiness. But I wouldn't want them back. Not with the fire in me now. No, I wouldn't want them back.

> [*Krapp motionless staring before him. The tape runs on in silence.*]

CURTAIN

from Texts for Nothing[1]

4

Where would I go, if I could go, who would I be, if I could be, what would I say, if I had a voice, who says this, saying it's me? Answer simply, someone answer simply. It's the same old stranger as ever, for whom alone accusative I exist, in the pit of my inexistence, of his, of ours, there's a simple answer. It's not with thinking he'll find me, but what is he to do, living and bewildered, yes, living, say what he may. Forget me, know me not, yes, that would be the wisest, none better able than he. Why this sudden affability after such desertion, it's easy to understand, that's what he says, but he doesn't understand. I'm not in his head, nowhere in his old body, and yet I'm there, for him I'm there, with him, hence all the confusion. That should have been enough for him, to have found me absent, but it's not, he wants me there, with a form and a world, like him, in spite of him, me who am everything, like him who is nothing. And when he feels me void of existence it's of his he would have me void, and vice versa, mad, mad, he's mad. The truth is he's looking for me to kill me, to have me dead like him, dead like the living. He knows all that, but it's no help his knowing it, I don't know it, I know nothing. He protests he doesn't reason and does nothing but reason, crooked, as if that could improve matters. He thinks words fail

2. Valley.
3. Mountain in County Wicklow in Southeastern Ireland.
1. Having completed his *Molloy* trilogy in 1950, Beckett wrote this series of short texts between 1950 and 1952 as "an attempt to get out of the attitude of disintegration" established in his trilogy—an attempt, Beckett later said, that failed.

him, he thinks because words fail him he's on his way to my speechlessness, to being speechless with my speechlessness, he would like it to be my fault that words fail him, of course words fail him. He tells his story every five minutes, saying it is not his, there's cleverness for you. He would like it to be my fault that he has no story, of course he has no story, that's no reason for trying to foist one on me. That's how he reasons, wide of the mark, but wide of what mark, answer us that. He has me say things saying it's not me, there's profundity for you, he has me who say nothing say it's not me. All that is truly crass. If at least he would dignify me with the third person, like his other figments, not he, he'll be satisfied with nothing less than me, for his me. When he had me, when he was me, he couldn't get rid of me quick enough, I didn't exist, he couldn't have that, that was no kind of life, of course I didn't exist, any more than he did, of course it was no kind of life, now he has it, his kind of life, let him lose it, if he wants to be in peace, with a bit of luck. His life, what a mine, what a life, he can't have that, you can't fool him, ergo it's not his, it's not him, what a thought, treat him like that, like a vulgar Molloy, a common Malone, those mere mortals, happy mortals, have a heart, land him in that shit, who never stirred, who is none but me, all things considered, and what things, and how considered, he had only to keep out of it. That's how he speaks, this evening, how he has me speak, how he speaks to himself, how I speak, there is only me, this evening, here, on earth, and a voice that makes no sound because it goes towards none, and a head strewn with arms laid down and corpses fighting fresh, and a body, I nearly forgot. This evening, I say this evening, perhaps it's morning. And all these things, what things, all about me, I won't deny them any more, there's no sense in that any more. If it's nature perhaps it's trees and birds, they go together, water and air, so that all may go on, I don't need to know the details, perhaps I'm sitting under a palm. Or it's a room, with furniture, all that's required to make life comfortable, dark, because of the wall outside the window. What am I doing, talking, having my figments talk, it can only be me. Spells of silence too, when I listen, and hear the local sounds, the world sounds, see what an effort I make, to be reasonable. There's my life, why not, it is one, if you like, if you must, I don't say no, this evening. There has to be one, it seems, once there is speech, no need of a story, a story is not compulsory, just a life, that's the mistake I made, one of the mistakes, to have wanted a story for myself, whereas life alone is enough. I'm making progress, it was time, I'll learn to keep my foul mouth shut before I'm done, if nothing foreseen crops up. But he who somehow comes and goes, unaided from place to place, even though nothing happens to him, true, what of him? I stay here, sitting, if I'm sitting, often I feel sitting, sometimes standing, it's one or the other, or lying down, there's another possibility, often I feel lying down, it's one of the three, or kneeling. What counts is to be in the world, the posture is immaterial, so long as one is on earth. To breathe is all that is required, there is no obligation to ramble, or receive company, you may even believe yourself dead on condition you make no bones about it, what more liberal regimen could be imagined, I don't know, I don't imagine. No point under such circumstances in saying I am somewhere else, someone else, such as I am I have all I need to hand, for to do what, I don't know, all I have to do, there I am on my own again at last, what a relief that must be. Yes, there are moments, like this moment, when I seem almost restored to the feasible. Then it goes, all goes, and I'm far again, with a far story again, I wait for me afar for my story to begin, to end, and again this voice cannot be mine. That's where I'd go, if I could go, that's who I'd be, if I could be.

8

Only the words break the silence, all other sounds have ceased. If I were silent I'd hear nothing. But if I were silent the other sounds would start again, those to which the words have made me deaf, or which have really ceased. But I am silent, it sometimes happens, no, never, not one second. I weep too without interruption. It's an unbroken flow of words and tears. With no pause for reflection. But I speak softer, every year a little softer. Perhaps. Slower too, every year a little slower. Perhaps. It is hard for me to judge. If so the pauses would be longer, between the words, the sentences, the syllables, the tears, I confuse them, words and tears, my words are my tears, my eyes my mouth. And I should hear, at every little pause, if it's the silence I say when I say that only the words break it. But nothing of the kind, that's not how it is, it's for ever the same murmur, flowing unbroken, like a single endless word and therefore meaningless, for it's the end gives the meaning to words. What right have you then, no, this time I see what I'm up to and put a stop to it, saying, None, none. But get on with the stupid old threne[2] and ask, ask until you answer, a new question, the most ancient of all, the question were things always so. Well I'm going to tell myself something (if I'm able), pregnant I hope with promise for the future, namely that I begin to have no very clear recollection of how things were before (I was!), and by before I mean elsewhere, time has turned into space and there will be no more time, till I get out of here. Yes, my past has thrown me out, its gates have slammed behind me, or I burrowed my way out alone, to linger a moment free in a dream of days and nights, dreaming of me moving, season after season, towards the last, like the living, till suddenly I was here, all memory gone. Ever since nothing but fantasies and hope of a story for me somehow, of having come from somewhere and of being able to go back, or on, somehow, some day, or without hope. Without what hope, haven't I just said, of seeing me alive, not merely inside an imaginary head, but a pebble sand to be, under a restless sky, restless on its shore, faint stirs day and night, as if to grow less could help, ever less and less and never quite be gone. No truly, no matter what, I say no matter what, hoping to wear out a voice, to wear out a head, or without hope, without reason, no matter what, without reason. But it will end, a desinence[3] will come, or the breath fail better still, I'll be silence, I'll know I'm silence, no, in the silence you can't know, I'll never know anything. But at least get out of here, at least that, no? I don't know. And time begin again, the steps on the earth, the night the fool implores at morning and the morning he begs at evening not to dawn. I don't know, I don't know what all that means, day and night, earth and sky, begging and imploring. And I can desire them? Who says I desire them, the voice, and that I can't desire anything, that looks like a contradiction, it may be for all I know. Me, here, if they could open, those little words, open and swallow me up, perhaps that is what has happened. If so let them open again and let me out, in the tumult of light that sealed my eyes, and of men, to try and be one again. Or if I'm guilty let me be forgiven and graciously authorized to expiate, coming and going in passing time, every day a little purer, a little deader. The mistake I make is to try and think, even the way I do, such as I am I shouldn't be able, even the way I do. But whom can I have offended so grievously, to be punished in this inexplicable way, all is inexplicable, space and time, false and inexplicable, suffering and tears, and even the old convulsive cry, It's not me, it can't be me. But am I in pain, whether it's me or not, frankly now, is there pain? Now is here and here there is no frankness, all I say will be false and to begin with not said by me, here I'm a mere ventriloquist's dum-

---

2. Song of lamentation.   3. Termination.

my, I feel nothing, say nothing, he holds me in his arms and moves my lips with a string, with a fish-hook, no, no need of lips, all is dark, there is no one, what's the matter with my head, I must have left it in Ireland, in a saloon, it must be there still, lying on the bar, it's all it deserved. But that other who is me, blind and deaf and mute, because of whom I'm here, in this black silence, helpless to move or accept this voice as mine, it's as him I must disguise myself till I die, for him in the meantime do my best not to live, in this pseudo-sepulture[4] claiming to be his. Whereas to my certain knowledge I'm dead and kicking above, somewhere in Europe probably, with every plunge and suck of the sky a little more overripe, as yesterday in the pump of the womb. No, to have said so convinces me of the contrary, I never saw the light of day, any more than he, ah if no were content to cut yes's throat and never cut its own. Watch out for the right moment, then not another word, is that the only way to have being and habitat? But I'm here, that much at least is certain, it's in vain I keep on saying it, it remains true. Does it? It's hard for me to judge. Less true and less certain in any case than when I say I'm on earth, come into the world and assured of getting out, that's why I say it, patiently, variously, trying to vary, for you never know, it's perhaps all a question of hitting on the right aggregate. So as to be here no more at last, to have never been here, but all this time above, with a name like a dog to be called up with and distinctive marks to be had up with, the chest expanding and contracting unaided, panting towards the grand apnoea.[5] The right aggregate, but there are four million possible, nay probable, according to Aristotle, who knew everything. But what is this I see, and how, a white stick and an ear-trumpet, where, Place de la République, at pernod[6] time, let me look closer at this, it's perhaps me at last. The trumpet, sailing at ear level, suddenly resembles a steam-whistle, of the kind thanks to which my steamers forge fearfully through the fog. That should fix the period, to the nearest half-century or so. The stick gains ground, tapping with its ferrule[7] the noble bassamento of the United Stores, it must be winter, at least not summer. I can also just discern, with a final effort of will, a bowler hat which seems to my sorrow a sardonic synthesis of all those that never fitted me and, at the other extremity, similarly suspicious, a complete pair of brown boots lacerated and gaping. These insignia, if I may so describe them, advance in concert, as though connected by the traditional human excipient,[8] halt, move on again, confirmed by the vast show windows. The level of the hat, and consequently of the trumpet, hold out some hope for me as a dying dwarf or at least hunchback. The vacancy is tempting, shall I enthrone my infirmities, give them this chance again, my dream infirmities, that they may take flesh and move, deteriorating, round and round this grandiose square which I hope I don't confuse with the Bastille,[9] until they are deemed worthy of the adjacent Père Lachaise[1] or, better still, prematurely relieved trying to cross over, at the hour of night's young thoughts. No, the answer is no. For even as I moved, or when the moment came, affecting beyond all others, to hold out my hand, or hat, without previous song, or any other form of concession to self-respect, at the terrace of a café, or in the mouth of the underground, I would know it was not me, I would know I was here, begging in another dark, another silence, for another alm, that of being or of ceasing, better still, before having been. And the hand old in vain would drop the mite and the old feet shuffle on, towards an even vainer death than no matter whose.

---

4. Tomb.
5. Cessation of breathing.
6. A licorice-flavored liqueur.
7. Metal-capped tip.

8. Glue.
9. Parisian prison destroyed during the French Revolution in 1789.
1. Parisian cemetery.

Philip Larkin
1922–1985

Philip Larkin's lifetime production of poems was quite small but highly influential; he is best known for his three last volumes, *The Less Deceived* (1955), *The Whitsun Weddings* (1964), and *High Windows* (1974), which together collect fewer than one hundred poems. During his lifetime, however, he fulfilled the role—a role that every society seems to require—of the crotchety traditionalist poet, becoming famous for what the poet and critic Donald Hall has called a "genuine, uncultivated, sincere philistinism."

Born in Coventry, Larkin completed a B.A. and M.A. at Oxford (where he was a friend of the novelist Kingsley Amis), and became a professional librarian, working at the University of Hull from 1955 until his death. After two modestly successful novels (*Jill* and *A Girl in Winter*) and two undistinguished volumes of poetry (*The North Ship* and *XX Poems*), Larkin established himself as a new and important voice in British poetry with his collection *The Less Deceived*. According to most critics, the influence of Thomas Hardy's poetry was decisive; Seamus Heaney writes that the "slips and excesses" of his first two volumes—consisting, primarily, of embarrassing echoes of W. B. Yeats—led Larkin "to seek the antidote of Thomas Hardy."

Larkin was attracted to Hardy's bleak outlook on life, as well as his skilled versification and spare language. Larkin's dark vision remained unremitting as late as *Aubade*, the last poem to be published during his lifetime:

> I work all day, and get half drunk at night.
> Waking at four to soundless dark, I stare.
> In time the curtain-edges will grow light.
> Till then I see what's really always there:
> Unresting death, a whole day nearer now,
> Making all thought impossible but how
> And where and when I shall myself die.

Like the most famous postwar British playwright, Samuel Beckett, the most important postwar British poet was not above having a laugh at his own despair; in an oft-repeated remark, Larkin told an interviewer that "deprivation is for me what daffodils were for Wordsworth."

Larkin is one of the most English of modern British poets; he refused to read "foreign" literature—including most American poetry—or to travel abroad; Hull became the center and circumference of his poetic world. He kept to himself to an extraordinary degree; he never married, nor did he maintain any longstanding intimate relationship. In his obituary for Larkin, Kingsley Amis described him as "a man much driven in upon himself, with increasing deafness from early middle age cruelly emphasizing his seclusion."

Church Going

> Once I am sure there's nothing going on
> I step inside, letting the door thud shut.
> Another church: matting, seats, and stone,
> And little books; sprawlings of flowers, cut
> For Sunday, brownish now; some brass and stuff
> Up at the holy end; the small neat organ;
> And a tense, musty, unignorable silence,
> Brewed God knows how long. Hatless, I take off
> My cycle-clips in awkward reverence,

5

10   Move forward, run my hand around the font.
        From where I stand, the roof looks almost new—
        Cleaned, or restored? Someone would know: I don't.
        Mounting the lectern, I peruse a few
        Hectoring large-scale verses, and pronounce
15   "Here endeth" much more loudly than I'd meant.
        The echoes snigger briefly. Back at the door
        I sign the book, donate an Irish sixpence,
        Reflect the place was not worth stopping for.

        Yet stop I did: in fact I often do,
20   And always end much at a loss like this,
        Wondering what to look for; wondering, too,
        When churches fall completely out of use
        What we shall turn them into, if we shall keep
        A few cathedrals chronically on show,
25   Their parchment, plate and pyx[1] in locked cases,
        And let the rest rent-free to rain and sheep.
        Shall we avoid them as unlucky places?

        Or, after dark, will dubious women come
        To make their children touch a particular stone;
30   Pick simples° for a cancer; or on some   *medicinal plants*
        Advised night see walking a dead one?
        Power of some sort or other will go on
        In games, in riddles, seemingly at random;
        But superstition, like belief, must die,
35   And what remains when disbelief has gone?
        Grass, weedy pavement, brambles, buttress, sky,

        A shape less recognisable each week,
        A purpose more obscure. I wonder who
        Will be the last, the very last, to seek
40   This place for what it was; one of the crew
        That tap and jot and know what rood-lofts[2] were?
        Some ruin-bibber, randy for antique,
        Or Christmas-addict, counting on a whiff
        Of gown-and-bands and organ-pipes and myrrh?
45   Or will he be my representative,

        Bored, uninformed, knowing the ghostly silt
        Dispersed, yet tending to this cross of ground
        Through suburb scrub because it held unspilt
        So long and equably what since is found
50   Only in separation—marriage, and birth,
        And death, and thoughts of these—for which was built
        This special shell? For, though I've no idea
        What this accoutred frowsty° barn is worth,   *stuffy*
        It pleases me to stand in silence here;

55   A serious house on serious earth it is,
        In whose blent air all our compulsions meet,

1. The vessel in which the consecrated bread of the eucharist is kept.   2. Loft at the top of a carved wood or stone screen, separating the nave from the chancel of a church.

Are recognised, and robed as destinies.
And that much never can be obsolete,
Since someone will forever be surprising
60   A hunger in himself to be more serious,
And gravitating with it to this ground,
Which, he once heard, was proper to grow wise in,
If only that so many dead lie round.

1954   1955

High Windows

When I see a couple of kids
And guess he's fucking her and she's
Taking pills or wearing a diaphragm,
I know this is paradise

5   Everyone old has dreamed of all their lives—
Bonds and gestures pushed to one side
Like an outdated combine harvester,
And everyone young going down the long slide

To happiness, endlessly. I wonder if
10   Anyone looked at me, forty years back,
And thought, *That'll be the life;*
No God any more, or sweating in the dark

About hell and that, or having to hide
What you think of the priest. He
15   *And his lot will all go down the long slide*
Like free bloody birds. And immediately

Rather than words comes the thought of high windows:
The sun-comprehending glass,
And beyond it, the deep blue air, that shows
20   Nothing, and is nowhere, and is endless.

1967   1974

Talking in Bed

Talking in bed ought to be easiest,
Lying together there goes back so far,
An emblem of two people being honest.

Yet more and more time passes silently.
5   Outside, the wind's incomplete unrest
Builds and disperses clouds about the sky,

And dark towns heap up on the horizon.
None of this cares for us. Nothing shows why
At this unique distance from isolation

10   It becomes still more difficult to find
Words at once true and kind,
Or not untrue and not unkind.

1960   1964

MCMXIV[1]

Those long uneven lines
Standing as patiently
As if they were stretched outside
The Oval or Villa Park,
5   The crowns of hats, the sun
On moustached archaic faces
Grinning as if it were all
An August Bank Holiday lark;

And the shut shops, the bleached
10   Established names on the sunblinds,
The farthings and sovereigns,
And dark-clothed children at play
Called after kings and queens,
The tin advertisements
15   For cocoa and twist, and the pubs
Wide open all day;

And the countryside not caring:
The place-names all hazed over
With flowering grasses, and fields
20   Shadowing Domesday[2] lines
Under wheat's restless silence;
The differently-dressed servants
With tiny rooms in huge houses,
The dust behind limousines;

25   Never such innocence,
Never before or since,
As changed itself to past
Without a word—the men
Leaving the gardens tidy,
30   The thousands of marriages
Lasting a little while longer:
Never such innocence again.

1960   1964

PERSPECTIVES

Whose Language?

Though Britain's last major overseas colony, Hong Kong, rejoined China in 1997, at least one important reminder of British rule remains in countries as far-flung as India, South Africa, and New Zealand: the English language itself. Twentieth-century linguists, following on the pioneering work of Benjamin Lee Whorf and Edward Sapir, are nearly unanimous in their belief that languages do not merely serve to describe the world but in fact help to create that world, establishing both a set of possibilities and a set of limits.

---

1. 1914, in the style of a monument to the war dead.

2. The Domesday Book is the medieval record of the extent, value, and ownership of lands in England.

The politics of language thus becomes important for writers, especially writers in colonial and postcolonial cultures. In an episode from Joyce's *A Portrait of the Artist as a Young Man*, the Irish protagonist Stephen Dedalus converses with the English-born Dean of Studies at University College, Dublin, where Stephen is a student. In the course of the conversation it becomes clear that Stephen is already a more supple and cunning user of the English language than his teacher, and yet he feels himself at a disadvantage in having to use the language of the invader; he muses: "The language in which we are speaking is his before it is mine. How different are the words *home, Christ, ale, master*, on his lips and on mine! I cannot speak or write these words without unrest of spirit. His language, so familiar and so foreign, will always be for me an acquired speech. I have not made or accepted its words. My voice holds them at bay. My soul frets in the shadow of his language." The Penal Acts of 1695 and 1696 had made the Irish language illegal in Ireland; after 500 years of trying to subdue the "wild Irish," British lawmakers realized that the Irish natives would never be brought under English rule until their tongues were bound. In his poem *Traditions*, Seamus Heaney meditates on the enduring cost of what he has called elsewhere "the government of the tongue":

> Our guttural muse
> was bulled long ago
> by the alliterative tradition,
> her uvula grows
> vestigial, forgotten.

In much colonial and postcolonial writing, however, the confusion of tongues inflicted by British rule has been seen by the writers of Empire as a positive linguistic resource. Nadine Gordimer in South Africa and James Kelman in Scotland both mix local dialect with standard English to take the measure of reality a far cry from London. Salman Rushdie, explaining his decision to use English rather than his native Hindi, writes: "Those of us who do use English do so in spite of our ambiguity towards it, or perhaps because of that, perhaps because we can find in that linguistic struggle a reflection of other struggles taking place in the real world, struggles between the cultures within ourselves and the influences working upon our societies. To conquer English may be to complete the process of making ourselves free." Thus a great deal of contemporary English-language writing—especially in countries where English was once the language of the conqueror (such as Ireland, Scotland, Wales, South Africa, India, and Kenya)—meditates on the blindnesses and insights inherent in using English. Some writers, like the Irish poet Nuala Ní Dhomhnaill, write in defiance of English; if one's native tongue is a minority language like Irish, this decision necessarily narrows a writer's potential audience. More common is the decision made by Rushdie, and by James Joyce before him: to write English as an "outsider," attesting to an alien's perspective on the majority language.

◆━◆

Seamus Heaney
b. 1939

More prominently than any poet since Yeats, Heaney has put Irish poetry back at the center of British literary studies. His first full-length collection, *Death of a Naturalist* (1966), ushered in a period of renewed interest in Irish poetry generally, and Ulster poetry in particular; the subsequent attention to poets like Derek Mahon, Michael Longley, Medbh McGuckian, and Paul Muldoon owes a great deal to the scope of Heaney's popularity.

As a great number of Heaney's early poems bear poignant witness, he spent his childhood in rural County Derry, Northern Ireland; his family was part of the Catholic minority in Ulster, and his experiences growing up were for that reason somewhat atypical. The critic Irvin Ehrenpreis maps the matrix of Heaney's contradictory position as an Irish poet: "Speech is never simple, in Heaney's conception. He grew up as an Irish Catholic boy in a land governed by Protestants whose tradition is British. He grew up on a farm in his country's northern, industrial region. As a person, therefore, he springs from the old divisions of his nation." His experience was split not only along religious lines, then, but also national and linguistic ones; in some of his early poetry Heaney suggests the split through the paired names—"Mossbawn" (the very English name of his family's fifty-acre farm) and "Anahorish" (Irish *anach fhior uisce*, "place of clear water," where he attended primary school). As a result, Heaney's is a liminal poetry—a "door into the dark"—and Heaney stands in the doorway, with one foot in each world. Heaney makes brilliant use of the linguistic resources of both the traditions he inherited, drawing on the heritage of English Romanticism while also relying heavily on Irish-language assonance in lines like "There were dragon-flies, spotted butterflies, / But best of all was the warm thick slobber / of frogspawn that grew like clotted water / In the shade of the banks" (*Death of a Naturalist*).

When he was twelve, Heaney won a scholarship to a Catholic boarding school in Londonderry (now Derry) then went on to Queen's University, Belfast, which was the center of a vital new poetic movement in the 1960s. He was influenced by poets who were able to transform the local into the universal, especially Ted Hughes and Robert Frost. As an "Ulster poet," it has fallen to Heaney to use his voice and his position to comment on Northern Ireland's sectarian violence; ironically enough, however, his most explicitly "political" poems were published before the flare-up of the Troubles that began in 1969, and his most self-conscious response to Ulster's strife, the volume *North* (1975), uses historical and mythological frameworks to address the current political situation obliquely. The Irish critic Seamus Deane has written, "Heaney is very much in the Irish tradition in that he has learned, more successfully than most, to conceive of his personal experience in terms of his country's history"; for Heaney, as the popular saying has it, the personal is the political, and the political the personal. His most successful poems dealing with Ulster's political and religious situation are probably those treating neolithic bodies found preserved in peat bogs. Heaney was living in Belfast, lecturing at Queen's University, at the inception of the Troubles; as a Catholic, he felt a need to convey the urgency of the situation without falling into the easy Republican—or Unionist, for that matter—rhetoric. It was at this point that Heaney discovered the anthropologist P. V. Glob's *The Bog People* (1969), which documents (with riveting photographs) the discovery of sacrificial victims preserved in bogs for 2,000 years. Heaney intuitively knew that he had found his "objective correlative"—what he has called his "emblems of adversity"—with which to explore the Troubles.

Like Yeats, Heaney has, from the very start, enjoyed both popular and critical acclaim. His poems have a surface simplicity; his early poetry especially relishes the carefully observed detail of rural Irish life. As his luminous essay *Feeling into Words* shows, he has continued over the years to probe his debts to English literary tradition, and his distance from it. He has been the recipient of numerous awards, honors, and literary prizes, including in 1995 the Nobel Prize for literature.

Feeling into Words[1]

I intend to retrace some paths into what William Wordsworth called in *The Prelude* "the hiding places."

> The hiding places of my power
> Seem open; I approach, and then they close;

1. Lecture given at the Royal Society of Literature, October 1974.

> I see by glimpses now; when age comes on,
> May scarcely see at all, and I would give,
> While yet we may, as far as words can give,
> A substance and a life to what I feel:
> I would enshrine the spirit of the past
> For future restoration.

Implicit in those lines is a view of poetry which I think is implicit in the few poems I have written that give me any right to speak: poetry as divination, poetry as revelation of the self to the self, as restoration of the culture to itself; poems as elements of continuity, with the aura and authenticity of archaeological finds, where the buried shard has an importance that is not diminished by the importance of the buried city; poetry as a dig, a dig for finds that end up being plants.

"Digging," in fact, was the name of the first poem I wrote where I thought my feelings had got into words, or to put it more accurately, where I thought my *feel* had got into words. Its rhythms and noises still please me, although there are a couple of lines in it that have more of the theatricality of the gunslinger than the self-absorption of the digger. I wrote it in the summer of 1964, almost two years after I had begun to "dabble in verses." This was the first place where I felt I had done more than make an arrangement of words: I felt that I had let down a shaft into real life. The facts and surfaces of the thing were true, but more important, the excitement that came from naming them gave me a kind of insouciance and a kind of confidence. I didn't care who thought what about it: somehow, it had surprised me by coming out with a stance and an idea that I would stand over:

> The cold smell of potato mould, the squelch and slap
> Of soggy peat, the curt cuts of an edge
> Through living roots awaken in my head.
> But I've no spade to follow men like them.
>
> Between my finger and my thumb
> The squat pen rests.
> I'll dig with it.

As I say, I wrote it down years ago; yet perhaps I should say that I dug it up, because I have come to realize that it was laid down in me years before that even. The pen/spade analogy was the simple heart of the matter and *that* was simply a matter of almost proverbial common sense. As a child on the road to and from school, people used to ask you what class you were in and how many slaps you'd got that day and invariably they ended up with an exhortation to keep studying because "learning's easy carried" and "the pen's lighter than the spade." And the poem does no more than allow that bud of wisdom to exfoliate, although the significant point in this context is that at the time of writing I was not aware of the proverbial structure at the back of my mind. Nor was I aware that the poem was an enactment of yet another digging metaphor that came back to me years later. This was the rhyme we used to chant on the road to school, though, as I have said before, we were not fully aware of what we were dealing with:

> "Are your praties dry
> And are they fit for digging?"
> "Put in your spade and try,"
> Says Dirty-Faced McGuigan.

There digging becomes a sexual metaphor, an emblem of initiation, like putting your hand into the bush or robbing the nest, one of the various natural analogies for uncovering and touching the hidden thing. I now believe that the "Digging" poem had for me the force of an initiation: the confidence I mentioned arose from a sense that perhaps I could do this poetry thing too, and having experienced the excitement and release of it once, I was doomed to look for it again and again.

I don't want to overload "Digging" with too much significance. It is a big coarse-grained navvy[2] of a poem, but it is interesting as an example—and not just as an example of what one reviewer called "mud-caked fingers in Russell Square," for I don't think that the subject-matter has any particular virtue in itself—it is interesting as an example of what we call "finding a voice."

Finding a voice means that you can get your own feeling into your own words and that your words have the feel of you about them; and I believe that it may not even be a metaphor, for a poetic voice is probably very intimately connected with the poet's natural voice, the voice that he hears as the ideal speaker of the lines he is making up.

In his novel *The First Circle*, Solzhenitsyn[3] sets the action in a prison camp on the outskirts of Moscow where the inmates are all highly skilled technicians forced to labour at projects dreamed up by Stalin. The most important of these is an attempt to devise a mechanism to bug a phone. But what is to be special about this particular bugging device is that it will not simply record the voice and the message but that it will identify the essential sound patterns of the speaker's voice; it will discover, in the words of the narrative, "what it is that makes every human voice unique," so that no matter how the speaker disguises his accent or changes his language, the fundamental structure of his voice will be caught. The idea was that a voice is like a fingerprint, possessing a constant and unique signature that can, like a fingerprint, be recorded and employed for identification.

Now one of the purposes of a literary education as I experienced it was to turn the student's ear into a poetic bugging device, so that a piece of verse denuded of name and date could be identified by its diction, tropes and cadences. And this secret policing of English verse was also based on the idea of a style as a signature. But what I wish to suggest is that there is a connection between the core of a poet's speaking voice and the core of his poetic voice, between his original accent and his discovered style. I think that the discovery of a way of writing that is natural and adequate to your sensibility depends on the recovery of that essential quick which Solzhenitsyn's technicians were trying to pin down. This is the absolute register to which your proper music has to be tuned.

How, then, do you find it? In practice, you hear it coming from somebody else, you hear something in another writer's sounds that flows in through your ear and enters the echo-chamber of your head and delights your whole nervous system in such a way that your reaction will be, "Ah, I wish I had said that, in that particular way." This other writer, in fact, has spoken something essential to you, something you recognize instinctively as a true sounding of aspects of yourself and your experience. And your first steps as a writer will be to imitate, consciously or unconsciously, those sounds that flowed in, that in-fluence.

One of the writers who influenced me in this way was Gerard Manley Hopkins. The result of reading Hopkins at school was the desire to write, and when I first put

2. Manual laborer.   3. Alexander Solzhenitsyn (1918–), dissident Soviet
                                         writer and political activist.

pen to paper at university, what flowed out was what had flowed in, the bumpy allit-
erating music, the reporting sounds and ricochetting consonants typical of Hopkins's
verse. I remember lines from a piece called "October Thought" in which some frail
bucolic images foundered under the chainmail of the pastiche:

> Starling thatch-watches, and sudden swallow
> Straight breaks to mud-nest, home-rest rafter
> Up past dry dust-drunk cobwebs, like laughter
> Ghosting the roof of bog-oak, turf-sod and rods of willow . . .

and then there was "heaven-hue, plum-blue and gorse-pricked with gold" and "a
trickling tinkle of bells well in the fold."

Looking back on it, I believe there was a connection, not obvious at the time
but, on reflection, real enough, between the heavily accented consonantal noise of
Hopkins's poetic voice, and the peculiar regional characteristics of a Northern Ireland accent. The late W. R. Rodgers, another poet much lured by alliteration, said in
his poem "The Character of Ireland" that the people from his (and my) part of the
world were

> an abrupt people
> who like the spiky consonants of speech
> and think the soft ones cissy; who dig
> the k and t in orchestra, detect sin
> in sinfonia, get a kick out of
> tin-cans, fricatives, fornication, staccato talk,
> anything that gives or takes attack
> like Micks, Teagues, tinker's gets, Vatican.

It is true that the Ulster accent is generally a staccato consonantal one. Our tongue
strikes the tangent of the consonant rather more than it rolls the circle of the vowel—
Rodgers also spoke of "the round gift of the gab in southern mouths." It is energetic,
angular, hard-edged, and it may be because of this affinity between my dialect and
Hopkins's oddity that those first verses turned out as they did.

I couldn't say, of course, that I had found a voice but I had found a game. I knew
the thing was only word-play, and I hadn't even the guts to put my name to it. I called
myself *Incertus,* uncertain, a shy soul fretting and all that. I was in love with words
themselves, but had no sense of a poem as a whole structure and no experience of how
the successful achievement of a poem could be a stepping stone in your life. Those
verses were what we might call "trial-pieces," little stiff inept designs in imitation of
the master's fluent interlacing patterns, heavy-handed clues to the whole craft.

I was getting my first sense of crafting words and for one reason or another, words
as bearers of history and mystery began to invite me. Maybe it began very early when
my mother used to recite lists of affixes and suffixes, and Latin roots, with their English meanings, rhymes that formed part of her schooling in the early part of the century. Maybe it began with the exotic listing on the wireless dial: Stuttgart, Leipzig,
Oslo, Hilversum. Maybe it was stirred by the beautiful sprung rhythms of the old
BBC weather forecast: Dogger, Rockall, Malin, Shetland, Faroes, Finisterre; or with
the gorgeous and inane phraseology of the catechism; or with the litany of the
Blessed Virgin that was part of the enforced poetry in our household: Tower of Gold,
Ark of the Covenant, Gate of Heaven, Morning Star, Health of the Sick, Refuge of
Sinners, Comforter of the Afflicted. None of these things were consciously savoured

at the time but I think the fact that I still recall them with ease, and can delight in them as verbal music, means that they were bedding the ear with a kind of linguistic hardcore that could be built on some day.

That was the unconscious bedding, but poetry involves a conscious savouring of words also. This came by way of reading poetry itself, and being required to learn pieces by heart, phrases even, like Keats's, from "Lamia":

> and his vessel now
> Grated the quaystone with her brazen prow,

or Wordsworth's:

> All shod with steel,
> We hiss'd along the polished ice,

or Tennyson's:

> Old yew, which graspest at the stones
> That name the underlying dead,
> Thy fibres net the dreamless head,
> Thy roots are wrapped about the bones.

These were picked up in my last years at school, touchstones of sorts, where the language could give you a kind of aural goose-flesh. At the university I was delighted in the first weeks to meet the moody energies of John Webster—"I'll make Italian cut-works in their guts / If ever I return"—and later on to encounter the pointed masonry of Anglo-Saxon verse and to learn about the rich stratifications of the English language itself. Words alone were certain good.[4] I even went so far as to write these "Lines to myself":

> In poetry I wish you would
> Avoid the lilting platitude.
> Give us poems humped and strong,
> Laced tight with thongs of song,
> Poems that explode in silence
> Without forcing, without violence.
> Whose music is strong and clear and good
> Like a saw zooming in seasoned wood.
> You should attempt concrete expression,
> Half-guessing, half-expression.

Ah well. Behind that was "Ars Poetica," MacLeish's and Verlaine's, Eliot's "objective correlative" (half understood) and several critical essays (by myself and others) about "concrete realization." At the university I kept the whole thing at arm's length, read poetry for the noise and wrote about half a dozen pieces for the literary magazine. But nothing happened inside me. No experience. No epiphany.[5] All craft—and not much of that—and no technique.

I think technique is different from craft. Craft is what you can learn from other verse. Craft is the skill of making. It wins competitions in the *Irish Times* or the *New Statesman*. It can be deployed without reference to the feelings or the self. It knows how to keep up a capable verbal athletic display; it can be content to be *vox et praeterea nihil*—all voice and nothing else—but not voice as in "finding a voice."

---

4. Cf. W. B. Yeats, *The Song of the Happy Shepherd*: "For words alone are certain good."

5. A moment of transcendent vision and insight, crucial in the poetics of modernists like Joyce and Woolf.

Learning the craft is learning to turn the windlass at the well of poetry. Usually you begin by dropping the bucket halfway down the shaft and winding up a taking of air. You are miming the real thing until one day the chain draws unexpectedly tight and you have dipped into waters that will continue to entice you back. You'll have broken the skin on the pool of yourself. Your praties will be "fit for digging."

At that point it becomes appropriate to speak of technique rather than craft. Technique, as I would define it, involves not only a poet's way with words, his management of metre, rhythm and verbal texture; it involves also a definition of his stance towards life, a definition of his own reality. It involves the discovery of ways to go out of his normal cognitive bounds and raid the inarticulate: a dynamic alertness that mediates between the origins of feeling in memory and experience and the formal ploys that express these in a work of art. Technique entails the watermarking of your essential patterns of perception, voice and thought into the touch and texture of your lines; it is that whole creative effort of the mind's and body's resources to bring the meaning of experience within the jurisdiction of form. Technique is what turns, in Yeats's phrase, "the bundle of accident and incoherence that sits down to breakfast" into "an idea, something intended, complete."

It is indeed conceivable that a poet could have a real technique and a wobbly craft—I think this was true of Alun Lewis and Patrick Kavanagh—but more often it is a case of a sure enough craft and a failure of technique. And if I were asked for a figure who represents pure technique, I would say a water diviner. You can't learn the craft of dowsing or divining—it is a gift for being in touch with what is there, hidden and real, a gift for mediating between the latent resource and the community that wants it current and released. As Sir Philip Sidney notes in his *Apologie for Poetry*: "Among the Romans a Poet was called *Vates*, which is as much as a Diviner . . ."

The poem was written simply to allay an excitement and to name an experience, and at the same time to give the excitement and the experience a small *perpetuum mobile* in language itself. I quote it here, not for its own technique but for the image of technique contained in it. The diviner resembles the poet in his function of making contact with what lies hidden, and in his ability to make palpable what was sensed or raised.

The Diviner

Cut from the green hedge a forked hazel stick
That he held tight by the arms of the V:
Circling the terrain, hunting the pluck
Of water, nervous, but professionally

Unfussed. The pluck came sharp as a sting.
The rod jerked with precise convulsions,
Spring water suddenly broadcasting
Through a green hazel its secret stations.

The bystanders would ask to have a try.
He handed them the rod without a word.
It lay dead in their grasp till nonchalantly
He gripped expectant wrists. The hazel stirred.

What I had taken as matter of fact as a youngster became a matter of wonder in memory. When I look at the thing now I am pleased that it ends with a verb, "stirred," the heart of the mystery; and I am glad that "stirred" chimes with "word," bringing the two functions of *vates* into the one sound.

Technique is what allows that first stirring of the mind round a word or an image or a memory to grow towards articulation: articulation not necessarily in terms of argument or explication but in terms of its own potential for harmonious self-reproduction. The seminal excitement has to be granted conditions in which, in Hopkins's words, it "selves, goes itself . . . crying / What I do is me, for that I came." Technique ensures that the first gleam attains its proper effulgence. And I don't just mean a felicity in the choice of words to flesh the theme—that is a problem also but it is not so critical. A poem can survive stylistic blemishes but it cannot survive a still-birth. The crucial action is pre-verbal, to be able to allow the first alertness or come-hither, sensed in a blurred or incomplete way, to dilate and approach as a thought or a theme or a phrase. Robert Frost put it this way: "a poem begins as a lump in the throat, a homesickness, a lovesickness. It finds the thought and the thought finds the words." As far as I am concerned, technique is more vitally and sensitively connected with that first activity where the "lump in the throat" finds "the thought" than with "the thought" finding "the words." That first emergence involves the divining, vatic, oracular function; the second, the making function. To say, as Auden did, that a poem is a "verbal contraption" is to keep one or two tricks up your sleeve.

Traditionally an oracle speaks in riddles, yielding its truths in disguise, offering its insights cunningly. And in the practice of poetry, there is a corresponding occasion of disguise, a protean, chameleon moment when the lump in the throat takes protective colouring in the new element of thought. One of the best documented occasions in the canon of English poetry, as far as this process is concerned, is a poem that survived in spite of its blemish. In fact, the blemish has earned it a peculiar fame:

> High on a mountain's highest ridge,
> Where oft the stormy winter gale
> Cuts like a scythe, while through the clouds
> It sweeps from vale to vale;
> Not five yards from the mountain path,
> This thorn you on your left espy;
> And to the left, three yards beyond,
> You see a little muddy pond
> Of water never dry;
> I've measured it from side to side:
> 'Tis three feet long and two feet wide.

Those two final lines were probably more ridiculed than any other lines in *The Lyrical Ballads* yet Wordsworth maintained "they ought to be liked." That was in 1815, seventeen years after the poem had been composed; but five years later he changed them to "Though but of compass small, and bare / To thirsting suns and parching air." Craft, in more senses than one.

Yet far more important than the revision, for the purposes of this discussion, is Wordsworth's account of the poem's genesis. "The Thorn," he told Isabella Fenwick in 1843,

> arose out of my observing on the ridge of Quantock Hills, on a stormy day, a thorn which I had often passed in calm and bright weather without noticing it. I said to myself, "Cannot I by some invention do as much to make this thorn permanently an impressive object, as the storm has made it to my eyes at this moment?" I began the poem accordingly, and composed it with great rapidity.

The storm, in other words, was nature's technique for granting the thorn-tree its epiphany, awakening in Wordsworth that engendering, heightened state which he describes at the beginning of *The Prelude*—again in relation to the inspiring influence of wind:

> For I, methought, while the sweet breath of Heaven
> Was blowing on my body, felt within
> A corresponding, mild, creative breeze,
> A vital breeze which travell'd gently on
> O'er things which it had made, and is become
> A tempest, a redundant energy
> Vexing its own creation.

This is exactly the kind of mood in which he would have "composed with great rapidity"; the measured recollection of the letter where he makes the poem sound as if it were written to the thesis propounded (retrospectively) in the Preface of 1800—"cannot I by some invention make this thorn permanently an impressive object?"—probably tones down an instinctive, instantaneous recognition into a rational procedure. The technical triumph was to discover a means of allowing his slightly abnormal, slightly numinous vision of the thorn to "deal out its being."

What he did to turn "the bundle of accident and incoherence" of that moment into "something intended, complete" was to find, in Yeats's language, a mask. The poem as we have it is a ballad in which the speaker is a garrulous superstitious man, a sea captain, according to Wordsworth, who connects the thorn with murder and distress. For Wordsworth's own apprehension of the tree, he instinctively recognized, was basically superstitious: it was a standing over, a survival in his own sensibility of a magical way of responding to the natural world, of reading phenomena as signs, occurrences requiring divination. And in order to dramatize this, to transpose the awakened appetites in his consciousness into the satisfactions of a finished thing, he needed his "objective correlative." To make the thorn "permanently an impressive object," images and ideas from different parts of his conscious and unconscious mind were attracted by almost magnetic power. The thorn in its new, wind-tossed aspect had become a field of force.

Into this field were drawn memories of what the ballads call "the cruel mother'" who murders her own baby:

> She leaned her back against a thorn
> All around the loney-o
> And there her little babe was born
> Down by the greenwood side-o

is how a surviving version runs in Ireland. But there have always been variations on this pattern of the woman who kills her baby and buries it. And the ballads are also full of briars and roses and thorns growing out of graves in symbolic token of the life and death of the buried one. So in Wordsworth's imagination the thorn grew into a symbol of tragic, feverish death, and to voice this the ballad mode came naturally; he donned the traditional mask of the tale-teller, legitimately credulous, entering and enacting a convention. The poem itself is a rapid and strange foray where Wordsworth discovered a way of turning the "lump in the throat" into a "thought," discovered a set of images, cadences and sounds that amplified his original visionary excitement into "a redundant energy / Vexing its own creation":

And some had sworn an oath that she
Should be to public justice brought;
And for the little infant's bones
With spades they would have sought.
But then the beauteous hill of moss
Before their eyes began to stir;
And for full fifty yards around
The grass it shook upon the ground.

"The Thorn" is a nicely documented example of feeling getting into words, in ways that paralleled much in my own experience; although I must say that it is hard to discriminate between feeling getting into words and words turning into feeling, and it is only on posthumous occasions like this that the distinction arises. Moreover, it is dangerous for a writer to become too self-conscious about his own processes: to name them too definitively may have the effect of confining them to what is named. A poem always has elements of accident about it, which can be made the subject of inquest afterwards, but there is always a risk in conducting your own inquest: you might begin to believe the coroner in yourself rather than put your trust in the man in you who is capable of the accident. Robert Graves's "Dance of Words" puts this delightfully:

To make them move, you should start from lightning
And not forecast the rhythm: rely on chance
Or so-called chance for its bright emergence
Once lightning interpenetrates the dance.

Grant them their own traditional steps and postures
But see they dance it out again and again
Until only lightning is left to puzzle over—
The choreography plain and the theme plain.

What we are engaged upon here is a way of seeing that turns the lightning into "the visible discharge of electricity between cloud and cloud or between cloud and ground" rather than its own puzzling, brilliant self. There is nearly always an element of the bolt from the blue about a poem's origin.

When I called my second book *Door into the Dark* I intended to gesture towards this idea of poetry as a point of entry into the buried life of the feelings or as a point of exit for it. Words themselves are doors; Janus is to a certain extent their deity, looking back to a ramification of roots and associations and forward to a clarification of sense and meaning. And just as Wordsworth sensed a secret asking for release in the thorn, so in *Door into the Dark* there are a number of poems that arise out of the almost unnameable energies that, for me, hovered over certain bits of language and landscape.

The poem "Undine," for example. It was the dark pool of the sound of the word that first took me: if our auditory imaginations were sufficiently attuned to plumb and sound a vowel, to unite the most primitive and civilized associations, the word "undine" would probably suffice as a poem in itself. *Unda*, a wave, *undine*, a water-woman—a litany of undines would have ebb and flow, water and woman, wave and tide, fulfilment and exhaustion in its very rhythms. But, old two-faced vocable that it is, I discovered a more precise definition once, by accident, in a dictionary. An undine is a water-sprite who has to marry a human being and have a child by him before she can become human. With that definition, the lump in the throat, or rather the thump in the ear, *undine*, became a thought, a field of force that called up other images. One of these was an orphaned memory, without a context, obviously a very early one, of watching a man clearing out an old spongy growth from a drain between two fields, focusing in particular on the way the water, in the cleared-out place, as soon as the shovelfuls of sludge had been removed, the way the water began to run free, rinse itself clean of the soluble mud and make its own little channels and currents. And this image was gathered into a more conscious reading of the myth as being about the liberating, humanizing effect of sexual encounter. Undine was a cold girl who got what the dictionary called a soul through the experience of physical love. So the poem uttered itself out of that nexus—more short-winded than "The Thorn," with less red*undant* energy, but still escaping, I hope, from my incoherence into the voice of the undine herself:

> He slashed the briars, shovelled up grey silt
> To give me right of way in my own drains
> And I ran quick for him, cleaned out my rust.
>
> He halted, saw me finally disrobed,
> Running clear, with apparent unconcern.
> Then he walked by me. I rippled and I churned
>
> Where ditches intersected near the river
> Until he dug a spade deep in my flank
> And took me to him. I swallowed his trench
>
> Gratefully, dispersing myself for love
> Down in his roots, climbing his brassy grain—
> But once he knew my welcome, I alone
>
> Could give him subtle increase and reflection.
> He explored me so completely, each limb
> Lost its cold freedom. Human, warmed to him.

I once said it was a myth about agriculture, about the way water is tamed and humanized when streams become irrigation canals, when water becomes involved with seed. And maybe that is as good an explanation as any. The paraphrasable extensions of a poem can be as protean as possible as long as its elements remain firm. Words can allow you that two-faced approach also. They stand smiling at the audience's way of reading them and winking back at the poet's way of using them.

Behind this, of course, there is a good bit of symbolist theory. Yet in practice, you proceed by your own experience of what it is to write what you consider a successful poem. You survive in your own esteem not by the corroboration of theory but by the trust in certain moments of satisfaction which you know intuitively to be moments of extension. You are confirmed by the visitation of the last poem and threatened by the elusiveness of the next one, and the best moments are those when your mind seems to implode and words and images rush of their own accord into the vortex. Which happened to me once when the line "We have no prairies" drifted into my head at bedtime, and loosened a fall of images that constitute the poem "Bogland," the last one in *Door into the Dark*.

I had been vaguely wishing to write a poem about bogland, chiefly because it is a landscape that has a strange assuaging effect on me, one with associations reaching back into early childhood. We used to hear about bog-butter, butter kept fresh for a great number of years under the peat. Then when I was at school the skeleton of an elk had been taken out of a bog nearby and a few of our neighbours had got their photographs in the paper, peering out across its antlers. So I began to get an idea of bog as the memory of the landscape, or as a landscape that remembered everything that happened in and to it. In fact, if you go round the National Museum in Dublin, you will realize that a great proportion of the most cherished material heritage of Ireland was "found in a bog." Moreover, since memory was the faculty that supplied me with the first quickening of my own poetry, I had a tentative unrealized need to make a congruence between memory and bogland and, for the want of a better word, our national consciousness. And it all released itself after "We have no prairies . . ."—but we have bogs.

At that time I was teaching modern literature in Queen's University, Belfast, and had been reading about the frontier and the west as an important myth in the American consciousness, so I set up—or rather, laid down—the bog as an answering Irish myth. I wrote it quickly the next morning, having slept on my excitement, and revised it on the hoof, from line to line, as it came:

> We have no prairies
> To slice a big sun at evening—
> Everywhere the eye concedes to
> Encroaching horizon,
>
> Is wooed into the cyclops' eye
> Of a tarn. Our unfenced country
> Is bog that keeps crusting
> Between the sights of the sun.
>
> They've taken the skeleton
> Of the great Irish Elk
> Out of the peat, set it up
> An astounding crate full of air.
>
> Butter sunk under
> More than a hundred years
> Was recovered salty and white.
> The ground itself is kind, black butter
>
> Melting and opening underfoot,
> Missing its last definition
> By millions of years.
> They'll never dig coal here,
>
> Only the waterlogged trunks
> Of great firs, soft as pulp.
> Our pioneers keep striking
> Inwards and downwards,
>
> Every layer they strip
> Seems camped on before.
> The bogholes might be Atlantic seepage.
> The wet centre is bottomless.

Again, as in the case of "Digging," the seminal impulse had been unconscious. What generated the poem about memory was something lying beneath the very floor of memory, something I only connected with the poem months after it was written, which was a warning that older people would give us about going into the bog. They were afraid we might fall into the pools in the old workings so they put it about (and we believed them) that *there was no bottom* in the bog-holes. Little did they—or I—know that I would filch it for the last line of a book.

There was also in that book a poem called "Requiem for the Croppies" which was written in 1966 when most poets in Ireland were straining to celebrate the anniversary of the 1916 Rising. That rising was the harvest of seeds sown in 1798, when revolutionary republican ideals and national feeling coalesced in the doctrines of Irish republicanism and in the rebellion of 1798 itself—unsuccessful and savagely put down. The poem was born of and ended with an image of resurrection based on the fact that some time after the rebels were buried in common graves, these graves began to sprout with young barley, growing up from barley corn which the "croppies" had carried in their pockets to eat while on the march. The oblique implication was that the seeds of violent resistance sowed in the Year of Liberty had flowered in what Yeats called "the right rose tree" of 1916. I did not realize at the time that the original heraldic murderous encounter between Protestant yeoman and Catholic rebel was to be initiated again in the summer of 1969, in Belfast, two months after the book was published.

From that moment the problems of poetry moved from being simply a matter of achieving the satisfactory verbal icon to being a search for images and symbols adequate to our predicament. I do not mean liberal lamentation that citizens should feel compelled to murder one another or deploy their different military arms over the matter of nomenclatures such as British or Irish. I do not mean public celebrations or execrations of resistance or atrocity—although there is nothing necessarily unpoetic about such celebration, if one thinks of Yeats's "Easter 1916." I mean that I felt it imperative to discover a field of force in which, without abandoning fidelity to the processes and experience of poetry as I have outlined them, it would be possible to encompass the perspectives of a humane reason and at the same time to grant the religious intensity of the violence its deplorable authenticity and complexity. And when I say religious, I am not thinking simply of the sectarian division. To some extent the enmity can be viewed as a struggle between the cults and devotees of a god and a goddess. There is an indigenous territorial numen, a tutelar of the whole island, call her Mother Ireland, Kathleen Ni Houlihan, the poor old woman, the Shan Van Vocht, whatever; and her sovereignty has been temporarily usurped or infringed by a new male cult whose founding fathers were Cromwell, William of Orange and Edward Carson, and whose godhead is incarnate in a rex or caesar resident in a palace in London. What we have is the tail-end of a struggle in a province between territorial piety and imperial power.

Now I realize that this idiom is remote from the agnostic world of economic interest whose iron hand operates in the velvet glove of "talks between elected representatives," and remote from the political manoeuvres of power-sharing; but it is not remote from the psychology of the Irishmen and Ulstermen who do the killing, and not remote from the bankrupt psychology and mythologies implicit in the terms Irish Catholic and Ulster Protestant. The question, as ever, is "How with this rage shall beauty hold a plea?" And my answer is, by offering "befitting emblems of adversity."

Some of these emblems I found in a book that was published in English translation, appositely, the year the killing started, in 1969. And again appositely, it was entitled *The Bog People*. It was chiefly concerned with preserved bodies of men and women found in the bogs of Jutland, naked, strangled or with their throats cut, disposed under the peat since early Iron Age times. The author, P. V. Glob, argues convincingly that a number of these, and in particular the Tollund Man, whose head is now preserved near Aarhus[6] in the museum at Silkeburg, were ritual sacrifices to the Mother Goddess, the goddess of the ground who needed new bridegrooms each winter to bed with her in her sacred place, in the bog, to ensure the renewal and fertility of the territory in the spring. Taken in relation to the tradition of Irish political martyrdom for that cause whose icon is Kathleen Ni Houlihan, this is more than an archaic barbarous rite: it is an archetypal pattern. And the unforgettable photographs of these victims blended in my mind with photographs of atrocities, past and present, in the long rites of Irish political and religious struggles. When I wrote this poem, I had a completely new sensation, one of fear. It was a vow to go on pilgrimage and I felt as it came to me—and again it came quickly—that unless I was deeply in earnest about what I was saying, I was simply invoking dangers for myself. It is called "The Tollund Man":

I

Some day I will go to Aarhus
To see his peat-brown head,
The mild pods of his eye-lids,
His pointed skin cap.

In the flat country nearby
Where they dug him out,
His last gruel of winter seeds
Caked in his stomach,

Naked except for
The cap, noose and girdle,
I will stand a long time.
Bridegroom to the goddess,

She tightened her torc[7] on him
And opened her fen,[8]
Those dark juices working
Him to a saint's kept body,

Trove of the turfcutters'
Honeycombed workings.
Now his stained face
Reposes at Aarhus.

II

I could risk blasphemy,
Consecrate the cauldron bog
Our holy ground and pray
Him to make germinate

The scattered, ambushed
Flesh of labourers,
Stockinged corpses
Laid out in the farmyards,

---

6. A county in East Jutland, in Denmark.
7. A twisting or rotating force.

8. Low land covered with shallow water.

Tell-tale skin and teeth
Flecking the sleepers
Of four young brothers, trailed
For miles along the lines.

III

Something of his sad freedom
As he rode the tumbril
Should come to me, driving,
Saying the names

Tollund, Grauballe, Nebelgard,[9]
Watching the pointing hands
Of country people,
Not knowing their tongue.

Out there in Jutland
In the old man-killing parishes
I will feel lost,
Unhappy and at home.

And just how persistent the barbaric attitudes are, not only in the slaughter but in the psyche, I discovered, again when the *frisson* of the poem itself had passed, and indeed after I had fulfilled the vow and gone to Jutland, "the holy blisful martyr for to seek."[1] I read the following in a chapter on "The Religion of the Pagan Celts" by the Celtic scholar, Anne Ross:

> Moving from sanctuaries and shrines . . . we come now to consider the nature of the actual deities. . . . But before going on to look at the nature of some of the individual deities and their cults, one can perhaps bridge the gap as it were by considering a symbol which, in its way, sums up the whole of Celtic pagan religion and is as representative of it as is, for example, the sign of the cross in Christian contexts. This is the symbol of the severed human head; in all its various modes of iconographic representation and verbal presentation, one may find the hard core of Celtic religion. It is indeed . . . a kind of shorthand symbol for the entire religious outlook of the pagan Celts.[2]

My sense of occasion and almost awe as I vowed to go to pray to the Tollund Man and assist at his enshrined head had a longer ancestry than I had at the time realized.

I began by suggesting that my point of view involved poetry as divination, as a restoration of the culture to itself. In Ireland in this century it has involved for Yeats and many others an attempt to define and interpret the present by bringing it into significant relationship with the past, and I believe that effort in our present circumstances has to be urgently renewed. But here we stray from the realm of technique into the realm of tradition; to forge a poem is one thing, to forge the uncreated conscience of the race, as Stephen Dedalus put it,[3] is quite another and places daunting pressures and responsibilities on anyone who would risk the name of poet.

9. Locations in Jutland.
1. The goal of the storytelling pilgrims in Chaucer's *Canterbury Tales*.
2. *Pagan Celtic Britain: Studies in Iconography and Tradition*

(1967).
3. The protagonist of Joyce's *A Portrait of the Artist as a Young Man* describes his ambition in these terms at the novel's close.

Nuala Ní Dhomhnaill
b. 1952

Ní Dhomhnaill was born in a coal mining region in England, to Irish parents; she was sent at the age of five, however, to live with relatives in the Gaeltacht (Irish-speaking area) on the Dingle Peninsula in West Kerry—"dropped into it cold-turkey," she says. She thus grew up bilingual, speaking English in the home, Irish out of it. Ní Dhomhnaill quickly learned that translation always picks up and leaves behind meaning; she tells this story: "I recall as a child someone asking my name in Irish. The question roughly translates as 'Who do you belong to?' Still most fluent in English, I replied, 'I don't belong to anybody. I belong to myself.' That became quite a joke in the village." In some ways, Ní Dhomhnaill's poetic career has been the process of discovering who, and whose, she is—and making those discoveries through the medium of the Irish language; her name itself, pronounced *nu-AH-la ne GOE-ne*, sounds different than it looks to English eyes.

"The individual psyche is a rather puny thing," she has said; "One's interior life dries up without the exchange with tradition." Ní Dhomhnaill's fruitful exchange with the Irish literary tradition has resulted in a poetry rich in the imagery of Irish folklore and mythology, and pregnant with the sense of contradiction and irony that undergirds Irish writing ("We [Celts] are truly comfortable only with ambiguity," she says). Ní Dhomhnaill's poetry in Irish includes the prize-winning volumes *An Dealg Droighin* (1981) and *Féar Suaithinseach* (1984), as well as a selection of poems from her volume *Feis* translated into English by the poet Paul Muldoon. The *Irish Literary Supplement* has called her "the most widely known and acclaimed Gaelic poet of the century"; by continuing to write in Irish, she has helped make it a viable language for modern poetry. Ní Dhomhnaill lives in Dublin and teaches at University College, Cork.

Feeding a Child[1]

From honey-dew of milking
from cloudy heat of beestings
the sun rises up the back
of bare hills,
5   a guinea gold
to put in your hand,
my own.
You drink your fill from my breast
and fall back asleep
10   into a lasting dream
laughter in your face.
What is going through your head
you who are but
a fortnight on earth?

15   Do you know day from night
that the great early ebb
announces spring tide?
That the boats
are on deep ocean,
20   where live the seals and fishes
and the great whales,

1. Translated by Michael Hartnett.

and are coming hand over hand
each by seven oars manned?
That your small boats swims
25   óró[2] in the bay
with the flippered peoples
and the small sea-creatures
she slippery-sleek
from stem to bow
30   stirring sea-sand up
sinking sea-foam down.

Of all these things are you
ignorant?
As my breast is explored
35   by your small hand
you grunt with pleasure
smiling and senseless.
I look into your face child
not knowing if you know
40   your herd of cattle
graze in the land of giants
trespassing and thieving
and that soon you will hear
the fee-fie-fo-fum
45   sounding in your ear.

You are my piggy
who went to market
who stayed at home
who got bread and butter
50   who got none.
There's one good bite in you
but hardly two—
I like your flesh
but not the broth thereof.
55   And who are the original patterns
of the heroes and giants
if not you and I?

1986

Parthenogenesis[1]

Once, a lady of the Ó Moores
(married seven years without a child)
swam in the sea in summertime.
She swam well, and the day
5   was fine as Ireland ever saw
not even a puff of wind in the air
all the bay calm, all the sea smooth—
a sheet of glass—supple, she struck out
with strength for the breaking waves

---

2. Soothing nonsense sound in Irish.

1. Translated by Michael Hartnett. "Parthenogenesis" is the scientific term for virgin birth.

10   and frisked, elated by the world.
      She ducked beneath the surface and there saw
      what seemed a shadow, like a man's.
      And every twist and turn she made
      the shadow did the same
15   and came close enough to touch.
      Heart jumped and sound stopped in her mouth
      her pulses ran and raced, sides near burst.
      The lower currents with their ice
      pierced her to the bone
20   and the noise of the abyss numbed all her limbs
      then scales grew on her skin . . .
      the lure of the quiet dreamy undersea . . .
      desire to escape to sea and shells . . .
      the seaweed tresses where at last
25   her bones changed into coral
      and time made atolls of her arms,
      pearls of her eyes in deep long sleep,
      at rest in a nest of weed,
      secure as feather beds . . .
30   But stop!
      Her heroic heritage was there,
      she rose with speedy, threshing feet
      and made in desperation for the beach:
      with nimble supple strokes she made the sand.
35   Near death until the day,
      some nine months later
      she gave birth to a boy.
      She and her husband so satisfied,
      so full of love for this new son
40   forgot the shadow in the sea
      and did not see what only the midwife saw—
      stalks of sea-tangle in the boy's hair
      small shellfish and sea-ribbons
      and his two big eyes
45   as blue and limpid as lagoons.
      A poor scholar passing by
      who found lodging for the night
      saw the boy's eyes never closed
      in dark or light and when all the world slept
50   he asked the boy beside the fire
      "Who are your people?" Came the prompt reply
      "Sea People."

      This same tale is told in the West
      but the woman's an Ó Flaherty
55   and tis the same in the South
      where the lady's called Ó Shea:
      this tale is told on every coast.
      But whoever she was I want to say
      that the fear she felt
60   when the sea-shadow followed her

is the same fear that vexed
the young heart of the Virgin
when she heard the angels' sweet bell
and in her womb was made flesh
65   by all accounts
the Son of the Living God.

                                                                    1986

Why I Choose to Write in Irish,
The Corpse That Sits Up and Talks Back[1]

Not so long ago I telephoned my mother about some family matter. "So what are you writing these days?" she asked, more for the sake of conversation than anything else. "Oh, an essay for *The New York Times*," I said, as casually as possible. "What is it about?" she asked. "About what it is like to write in Irish," I replied. There was a good few seconds' pause on the other end of the line; then, "Well, I hope you'll tell them that it is mad." End of conversation. I had got my comeuppance. And from my mother, who was the native speaker of Irish in our family, never having encountered a single word of English until she went to school at the age of 6, and well up in her teens before she realized that the name they had at home for a most useful item was actually two words—"safety pin"—and that they were English. Typical.

But really not so strange. Some time later I was at a reception at the American Embassy in Dublin for two of their writers, Toni Morrison and Richard Wilbur. We stood in line and took our buffet suppers along to the nearest available table. An Irishwoman across from me asked what I did. Before I had time to open my mouth her partner butted in: "Oh, Nuala writes poetry in Irish." And what did I write about? she asked. Again before I had time to reply he did so for me: "She writes poems of love and loss, and I could quote you most of them by heart." This was beginning to get up my nose, and so I attempted simultaneously to deflate him and to go him one better. "Actually," I announced, "I think the only things worth writing about are the biggies: birth, death and the most important thing in between, which is sex." "Oh," his friend said to me archly, "and is there a word for sex in Irish?"

I looked over at the next table, where Toni Morrison was sitting, and I wondered if a black writer in America had to put up with the likes of that, or its equivalent. Here I was in my own country, having to defend the official language of the state from a compatriot who obviously thought it was an accomplishment to be ignorant of it. Typical, and yet maybe not so strange.

Let me explain. Irish (as it is called in the Irish Constitution; to call it Gaelic is not P.C. at the moment, but seen as marginalizing) is the Celtic language spoken by a small minority of native speakers principally found in rural pockets on the western seaboard. These Irish-speaking communities are known as the "Gaeltacht," and are the last remnants of an earlier historical time when the whole island was Irish-speaking, or one huge "Gaeltacht." The number of Irish speakers left in these areas who use the language in most of their daily affairs is a hotly debated point, and varies from 100,000 at the most optimistic estimate to 20,000 at the most conservative. For the sake of a round number let us take it to be 60,000, or about 2 percent of the population of the Republic of Ireland.

---

1. Published in *The New York Times Book Review*, January 1995.

Because of the effort of the Irish Revival movement, and of the teaching of Irish in the school system, however, the language is also spoken with varying degrees of frequency and fluency by a considerably larger number of people who have learned it as a second language. So much so that census figures over the last few decades have consistently indicated that up to one million people, or 30 percent of the population of the Republic, claim to be speakers of Irish. To this can be added the 146,000 people in the Six Counties of Northern Ireland who also are competent in Irish. This figure of one million speakers is, of course, grossly misleading and in no way reflects a widespread use of the language in everyday life. Rather it can be seen as a reflection of general good will toward the language, as a kind of wishful thinking. Nevertheless that good will is important.

The fact that the Irish language, and by extension its literature, has a precarious status in Ireland at the moment is a development in marked contrast to its long and august history. I believe writing in Irish is the oldest continuous literary activity in Western Europe, starting in the fifth century and flourishing in a rich and varied manuscript tradition right down through the Middle Ages. During this time the speakers of any invading language, such as Norse, Anglo-Norman and English, were assimilated, becoming "more Irish than the Irish themselves." But the Battle of Kinsale in 1601, in which the British routed the last independent Irish princes, and the ensuing catastrophes of the turbulent 17th century, including forced population transfers, destroyed the social underpinning of the language. Its decline was much accelerated by the great famine of the mid-19th century; most of the one million who died of starvation and the millions who left on coffin ships for America were Irish speakers. The fact that the fate of emigration stared most of the survivors in the eye further speeded up the language change to English—after all, "What use was Irish to you over in Boston?"

The indigenous high culture became the stuff of the speech of fishermen and small farmers, and this is the language that I learned in West Kerry in the 1950's at the age of 5 in a situation of total immersion, when I was literally and figuratively farmed out to my aunt in the parish of Ventry. Irish is a language of enormous elasticity and emotional sensitivity; of quick and hilarious banter and a welter of references both historical and mythological; it is an instrument of imaginative depth and scope, which has been tempered by the community for generations until it can pick up and sing out every hint of emotional modulation that can occur between people. Many international scholars rhapsodize that this speech of ragged peasants seems always on the point of bursting into poetry. The pedagogical accident that had me learn this language at an early age can only be called a creative one.

The Irish of the Revival, or "book Irish," was something entirely different, and I learned it at school. Although my first literary love affair was with the Munster poets, Aodhagán Ó Rathaille and Eoghan Rua Ó Suilleabháin, and I had learned reams and reams of poetry that wasn't taught at school, when I myself came to write it didn't dawn on me that I could possibly write in Irish. The overriding ethos had got even to me. Writing poetry in Irish somehow didn't seem to be intellectually credible. So my first attempts, elegies on the deaths of Bobby Kennedy and Martin Luther King published in the school magazine, were all in English. They were all right, but even I could see that there was something wrong with them.

Writing Irish poetry in English suddenly seemed a very stupid thing to be doing. So I switched language in mid-poem and wrote the very same poem in Irish, and I could see immediately that it was much better. I sent it in to a competition in *The Irish Times*, where it won a prize, and that was that. I never looked back.

I had chosen my language, or more rightly, perhaps, at some very deep level, the language had chosen me. If there is a level to our being that for want of any other word for it I might call "soul" (and I believe there is), then for some reason that I can never understand, the language that my soul speaks, and the place it comes from, is Irish. At 16 I had made my choice. And that was that. It still is. I have no other.

But if the actual choice to write poetry in Irish was easy, then nothing else about it actually is, especially the hypocritical attitude of the state. On the one hand, Irish is enshrined as a nationalistic token (the ceremonial *cúpla focal*—"few words"—at the beginning and end of speeches by politicians, broadcasters and even airline crews is an example). On the other hand, it would not be an exaggeration to speak of the state's indifference, even downright hostility, to Irish speakers in its failure to provide even the most basic services in Irish for those who wish to go about their everyday business in that language.

"The computer cannot understand Irish" leads the excuses given by the state to refuse to conduct its business in Irish, even in the Gaeltacht areas. Every single service gained by Irish speakers has been fought for bitterly. Thus the "Gaelscoileanna," or Irish schools, have been mostly started by groups of parents, often in the very teeth of fierce opposition from the Department of Education. And the only reason we have a single Irish radio station is that a civil rights group started a pirate station 20 years ago in the West and shamed the Government into establishing this vital service. An Irish television channel is being mooted[2] at present, but I'll believe it when I see it.

You might expect at least the cultural nationalists and our peers writing in English to be on our side. Not so. A recent television documentary film about Thomas Kinsella begins with the writer intoning the fact that history has been recorded in Irish from the fifth century to the 19th. Then there is a pregnant pause. We wait for a mention of the fact that life, experience, sentient consciousness, even history is being recorded in literature in Irish in the present day. We wait in vain. By an antiquarian sleight of hand it is implied that Irish writers in English are now the natural heirs to a millennium and a half of writing in Irish. The subtext of the film is that Irish is dead.

So what does that make me, and the many other writers of the large body of modern literature in Irish? A walking ghost? A linguistic specter?

Mind you, it is invidious of me to single out Thomas Kinsella; this kind of insidious "bad faith" about modern literature in Irish is alive and rampant among many of our fellow writers in English. As my fellow poet in Irish, Biddy Jenkinson, has said, "We have been pushed into an ironic awareness that by our passage we would convenience those who will be uneasy in their Irishness as long as there is a living Gaelic tradition to which they do not belong." Now let them make their peace with the tradition if they wish to, I don't begrudge them a line of it. But I'll be damned if their cultural identity is procured at the expense of my existence, or of that of my language.

I can well see how it suits some people to see Irish-language literature as the last rictus[3] of a dying beast. As far as they are concerned, the sooner the language lies down and dies, the better, so they can cannibalize it with greater equanimity, peddling their "ethnic chic" with nice little translations "from the Irish." Far be it from

2. Debated.   3. Gasp.

them to make the real effort it takes to learn the living language. I dare say they must be taken somewhat aback when the corpse that they have long since consigned to choirs of angels, like a certain Tim Finnegan,[4] sits up and talks back to them.

The fault is not always one-sided. The Gaels (Irish-language writers) often fell prey to what Terence Browne, a literary historian, has called an "atmosphere of national self-righteousness and cultural exclusiveness," and their talent did not always equal the role imposed on them. Nevertheless, long after the emergence of a high standard of literature in Irish with Seán Ó Riordáin, Máirtín Ó Direáin and Máire Mhac an tSaoi in poetry, and Máirtín Ó Cadhain in prose, writing in Irish was conspicuously absent from anthologies in the 1950's and 60's. Even as late as the 70's one of our "greats," Seán Ó Riordáin, could hear on the radio two of his co-writers in English saying how "poetry in Ireland had been quiescent in the 50's," thus consigning to nothingness the great work that he and his fellow poets in Irish had produced during that very decade. After a lifetime devoted to poetry, is it any wonder that he died in considerable grief and bitterness?

As for the cultural nationalists, Irish was never the language of nationalist mobilization. Unlike other small countries where nationalism rose throughout the 19th century, in Ireland it was religion rather than language that mostly colored nationalism. Daniel O'Connell, the Liberator, a native-Irish-speaking Kerryman, used to address his monster mass meetings from the 1820's to the 40's in English, even though this language was not understood by 70 percent of the people he was addressing. Why? Because it was at the reporters over from *The Times* of London and their readers that his words were being primarily directed. It is particularly painful to recall that while nationalism was a major motivator in developing modern literary languages out of such varied tongues as Norwegian, Hungarian, Finnish and Estonian, during that very same period the high literary culture of Irish was being reduced to the language of peasants. By the time the revival began, the damage had already been done, and the language was already in irreversible decline (spoken by only 14.5 percent in 1880). The blatant myopia of the cultural nationalists is still alive and glaringly obvious in the disgraceful underrepresentation of Irish in the recently published three-volume *Field Day Anthology of Irish Writing*.

It should not be surprising, then, that we poets and fiction writers in Irish who are included in the anthology feel as if we are being reduced to being exotic background, like Irish Muzak. Thus the cultural nationalists, without granting Irish the intellectual credibility of rational discourse or the popular base of the oral tradition, enshrine it instead as the repository of their own utopian fantasies; pristine, changeless, "creative," but otherwise practically useless.

How does all this affect me, as a poet writing in Irish? Well, inasmuch as I am human and frail and prone to vanity and clamoring for attention, of course it disturbs me to be misunderstood, misrepresented and finally all but invisible in my own country. I get depressed, I grumble and complain, I stand around in rooms muttering darkly. Still and all, at some very deep and fundamental level it matters not one whit. All I ever wanted was to be left alone so that I could go on writing poetry in Irish. I still remember a time when I had an audience I could count on the fingers of one hand. I was perfectly prepared for that. I still am.

---

4. In the vaudeville song *Tim Finnegan's Wake*, the hero takes a drunken fall and dies. At his wake, however, whiskey is spilled over his body and he comes back to life. James Joyce uses this story as the central structure for *Finnegans Wake*.

But it has been gratifying to reach a broader audience through the medium of translations, especially among the one million who profess some knowledge of Irish. Many of them probably had good Irish when they left school but have had no chance of using it since for want of any functional context where it would make sense to use the language. I particularly like it when my poetry in English translation sends them back to the originals in Irish, and when they then go on to pick up the long-lost threads of the language that is so rightly theirs. I also find it pleasant and vivifying to make an occasional trip abroad and to reach a wider audience by means of dual-language readings and publications.

But my primary audience is those who read my work in Irish only. A print run for a book of poems in Irish is between 1,000 and 1,500 copies. That doesn't sound like much until you realize that that number is considered a decent run by many poets in English in Ireland, or for that matter even in Britain or America, where there's a much larger population.

The very ancientness of the Irish literary tradition is also a great source of strength to me as a writer. This works at two levels, one that is mainly linguistic and prosodic and another that is mainly thematic and inspirational. At the linguistic level, Old Irish, though undoubtedly very difficult, is much closer to Modern Irish than, say, Anglo-Saxon is to Modern English. Anyone like me with a basic primary degree in the language and a bit of practice can make a fair job of reading most of the medieval texts in the original.

Thematically too, the older literature is a godsend, though I am only now slowly beginning to assess its unique possibilities to a modern writer. There are known to be well over 4,000 manuscripts in Ireland and elsewhere of material from Old to Modern Irish. Apart from the great medieval codices, only about 50 other manuscripts date from before 1650. Nevertheless, the vast majority of the manuscripts painstakingly copied down after this time are exemplars of much earlier manuscripts that have since been lost. A lot of this is catalogued in ways that are unsatisfactory for our time.

Many items of enormous psychological and sexual interest, for example, are described with the bias of the last century as "indecent and obscene tales, unsuitable for publication." On many such manuscripts human eye has not set sight since they were so described. In addition, most scholarly attention has been paid to pre-Norman-Conquest material as the repository of the unsullied wellsprings of the native soul (those cultural nationalists again!), with the result that the vast area of post-Conquest material has been unfairly neglected. The main advantage of all this material to me is that it is proof of the survival until even a very late historical date of a distinct *Weltanschauung* [worldview] radically different from the Anglo mentality that has since eclipsed it.

Because of a particular set of circumstances, Irish fell out of history just when the modern mentality was about to take off. So major intellectual changes like the Reformation, the Renaissance, the Enlightenment, Romanticism and Victorian prudery have never occurred in it, as they did in the major European languages.

One consequence is that the attitude to the body enshrined in Irish remains extremely open and uncoy. It is almost impossible to be "rude" or "vulgar" in Irish. The body, with its orifices and excretions, is not treated in a prudish manner but is accepted as *an nádúir*, or "nature," and becomes a source of repartee and laughter rather than anything to be ashamed of. Thus little old ladies of quite impeccable and unimpeachable moral character tell risqué stories with gusto and panache. Is there a word for sex in Irish, indeed! Is there an Eskimo word for snow?

By now I must have spent whole years of my life burrowing in the department of folklore at University College, Dublin, and yet there are still days when my hands shake with emotion holding manuscripts. Again, this material works on me on two levels. First is when I revel in the well-turned phrase or nuance or retrieve a word that may have fallen into disuse. To turn the pages of these manuscripts is to hear the voices of my neighbors and my relatives—all the fathers and grandfathers and uncles come to life again. The second interest is more thematic. This material is genuinely ineffable, like nothing else on earth.

Indeed, there is a drawer in the index entitled "Neacha neamhbeo agus nithe nach bhfuil ann" ("Unalive beings and things that don't exist"). Now I am not the greatest empiricist in the world but this one has even me stumped. Either they exist or they don't exist. But if they don't exist why does the card index about them stretch the length of my arm? Yet that is the whole point of this material and its most enduring charm. Do these beings exist? Well, they do and they don't. You see, they are beings from *an saol eile*, the "otherworld," which in Irish is a concept of such impeccable intellectual rigor and credibility that it is virtually impossible to translate into English, where it all too quickly becomes fey and twee and "fairies-at-the-bottom-of-the-garden."

The way so-called depth psychologists go on about the subconscious nowadays you'd swear they had invented it, or at the very least stumbled on a ghostly and ghastly continent where mankind had never previously set foot. Even the dogs in the street in West Kerry know that the "otherworld" exists, and that to be in and out of it constantly is the most natural thing in the world.

This constant tension between reality and fantasy, according to Jeffrey Gantz, the translator of *Early Irish Myths and Sagas,* is characteristic of all Celtic art, but manifests itself particularly in the literature of Ireland. Mr Gantz believes that it is not accidental to the circumstances of the literary transmission but is rather an innate characteristic, a gift of the Celts. It means that the "otherworld" is not simply an anticipated joyful afterlife; it is also—even primarily—an alternative to reality.

This easy interaction with the imaginary means that you don't have to have a raving psychotic breakdown to enter the "otherworld." The deep sense in the language that something exists beyond the ego-envelope is pleasant and reassuring, but it is also a great source of linguistic and imaginative playfulness, even on the most ordinary and banal of occasions.

Let's say I decide some evening to walk up to my aunt's house in West Kerry. She hears me coming. She knows it is me because she recognizes my step on the cement pavement. Still, as I knock lightly on the door she calls out, "An de bheoaibh nó de mhairbh thu?" ("Are you of the living or of the dead?") Because the possibility exists that you could be either, and depending on which category you belong to, an entirely different protocol would be brought into play. This is all a joke, of course, but a joke that is made possible by the imaginative richness of the language itself.

I am not constructing an essentialist argument here, though I do think that because of different circumstances, mostly historical, the strengths and weaknesses of Irish are different from those of English, and the imaginative possibilities of Irish are, from a poet's perspective, one of its greatest strengths. But this is surely as true of, say, Bengali as it is of Irish. It is what struck me most in the Nobel Prize acceptance speech made by the Yiddish writer Isaac Bashevis Singer. When often asked why he wrote in a dead language, Singer said he was wont to reply that he wrote mostly about ghosts, and that is what ghosts speak, a dead language.

Singer's reply touched a deep chord with his Irish audience. It reminded us that the precariousness of Irish is not an Irish problem alone. According to the linguist Michael Krause in *Language* magazine, minority languages in the English language sphere face a 90 percent extinction rate between now and some time in the next century. Therefore, in these days when a major problem is the growth of an originally Anglo-American, but now genuinely global, pop monoculture that reduces everything to the level of the most stupendous boredom, I would think that the preservation of minority languages like Irish, with their unique and unrepeatable way of looking at the world, would be as important for human beings as the preservation of the remaining tropical rain forests is for biological diversity.

Recently, on a short trip to Kerry with my three daughters, I stayed with my brother and his wife in the old house he is renovating on the eastern end of the Dingle peninsula, under the beetling brow of Cathair Chonroi promontory fort. My brother said he had something special to show us, so one day we trooped up the mountain to Derrymore Glen. Although the area is now totally denuded of any form of growth other than lichens and sphagnum moss, the name itself is a dead giveaway: Derrymore from *Doire Mór* in Irish, meaning "Large Oak Grove."

A more desolate spot you cannot imagine, yet halfway up the glen, in the crook of a hanging valley, intricate and gnarled, looking for all the world like a giant bonsai, was a single survivor, one solitary oak tree. Only the top branches were producing leaves, it was definitely on its last legs and must have been at least 200 to 300 years old. How it had survived the massive human and animal depredation of the countryside that occurred during that time I do not know, but somehow it had.

It was very much a *bile*, a sacred tree, dear to the Celts. A fairy tree. A magic tree. We were all very moved by it. Not a single word escaped us, as we stood in the drizzle. At last Ayse, my 10-year-old, broke the silence. "It would just give you an idea," she said, "of what this place was like when it really was a '*Doire Mór*' and covered with oak trees." I found myself humming the air of *Cill Cais*, that lament for both the great woods of Ireland and the largess of the Gaelic order that they had come to symbolize:

> *Cad a dhéanfaimid feasta gan adhmad?*
> *Tá deireadh na gcoillte ar lár.*
> *Níl trácht ar Chill Cais ná a theaghlach*
> *is ní chlingfear a chling go brách.*
>
> What will we do now without wood
> Now that the woods are laid low?
> Cill Cais or its household are not mentioned
> and the sound of its bell is no more.

A week later, back in Dublin, that question is still ringing in the air. I am waiting for the children to get out of school and writing my journal in Irish in a modern shopping mall in a Dublin suburb. Not a single word of Irish in sight on sign or advertisement, nor a single sound of it in earshot. All around me are well-dressed and articulate women. I am intrigued by snatches of animated conversation, yet I am conscious of a sense of overwhelming loss. I think back to the lonely hillside, and to Ayse. This is the answer to the question in the song. This is what we will do without wood.

At some level, it doesn't seem too bad. People are warm and not hungry. They are expressing themselves without difficulty in English. They seem happy. I close my notebook with a snap and set off in the grip of that sudden pang of despair that is always lurking in the ever-widening rents of the linguistic fabric of minority languages. Perhaps my mother is right. Writing in Irish is mad. English is a wonderful language, and it also has the added advantage of being very useful for putting bread on the table. Change is inevitable, and maybe it is part of the natural order of things that some languages should die while others prevail.

And yet, and yet . . . I know this will sound ridiculously romantic and sentimental. Yet not by bread alone. . . . We raise our eyes to the hills. . . . We throw our bread upon the waters.[5] There are mythical precedents. Take for instance Moses' mother, consider her predicament. She had the choice of giving up her son to the Egyptian soldiery, to have him cleft in two before her very eyes, or to send him down the Nile in a basket, a tasty dinner for crocodiles. She took what under the circumstances must have seemed very much like *rogha an dá dhiogha* ("the lesser of two evils") and Exodus and the annals of Jewish history tell the rest of the story, and are the direct results of an action that even as I write is still working out its inexorable destiny. I know it is wrong to compare small things with great, yet my final answer to why I write in Irish is this:

Ceist 'na Teangan

Curirim mo dhóchas ar snámh
i mbáidn´ teangan
faoi mar a leagfá naíonán
i gcliabhán
a bheadh fite fuaite
de dhuilleoga feileastraim
is bitiúman agus pic
bheith cuimilte lena thóin

ansan é a leagadh síos
i measc na ngiolcach
is coigeal na mban sí
le taobh na habhann,
féachaint n'fheadaráis
cá dtabharfaidh an sruth é,
féachaint, dála Mhaoise,
an bhfóirfidh iníon Fharoinn?

The Language Issue

I place my hope on the water
in this little boat
of the language, the way a body might put
an infant

in a basket of intertwined
iris leaves,
its underside proofed
with bitumen and pitch,

---

5. Echoing three biblical affirmations of the need to look beyond immediate material wants (Matthew 4.4, Psalm 121.1, Ecclesiastes 11.1). In the first passage cited, Jesus is fasting in the wilderness and rejects Satan's tempting suggestion that he turn stones into bread: "he answered, 'It is written, "Man shall not live by bread alone, but by every word that proceeds from the mouth of God."'"

then set the whole thing down amidst
the sedge
and bulrushes by the edge
of a river

only to have it borne hither and thither,
not knowing where it might end up;
in the lap, perhaps,
of some Pharaoh's daughter.[6]

━◄═◆═►━

Nadine Gordimer
b. 1923

Nadine Gordimer was born in South Africa to Jewish emigrant parents from London. Thus her childhood, like those of the children of countless middle-class colonial families, was somewhat complex and contradictory. In an interview, Gordimer offers this explanation: "I think when you're born white in South Africa, you're peeling like an orange. You're sloughing off all the conditioning that you've had since you were a child." In Gordimer's case, that "sloughing off" of white, British prejudices and habits of mind has been thorough; the novelist Paul Theroux, for instance, suggests that "Gordimer's vision of Africa is the most complete one we have, and in time to come, when we want to know everything there is to know about a newly independent black African country, it is to this white South African woman . . . that we will turn."

Since Gordimer published her first collection of short stories in 1949 her writing has been praised for its evenhanded and scrupulously honest treatment of the political terrain of South Africa; and over the years she has become, in the words of one critic, "the literary voice and conscience of her society." Among her gifts are an ear sensitive to the cadences and idiosyncrasies of spoken English, and a gift for social satire in service of a finally moral purpose. The longstanding subject of Gordimer's writing—her great theme—is, as critic Michiko Kakutani describes it, "the consequences of apartheid on the daily lives of men and women, the distortions it produces in relationships among both blacks and whites." In Gordimer's writing, these distortions are always shown rather than explained; her presentation is essentially dramatic, a trait she shares with modern masters of short fiction like Chekhov and Joyce.

Gordimer has been faulted for the emphasis in politics in her writing. Her response to this charge is eloquent: "The real influence of politics on my writing is the influence of politics on people. Their lives, and I believe their very personalities, are changed by the extreme political circumstances one lives under in South Africa. I am dealing with people; here are people who are shaped and changed by politics. In that way my material is profoundly influenced by politics." To date, Gordimer has published more than ten novels, including the celebrated *A Guest of Honour* (1970) and *The Conservationist* (1974; cowinner of the Booker McConnell Prize), and more than a dozen collections of short stories. *Jump and Other Stories*, which includes *What Were You Dreaming?*, was published in 1991, the same year Gordimer was awarded the Nobel Prize for Literature. In this story, the disjunction between black and white South African English is the starting-point for an exploration of blocked communication between races and genders alike.

6. As happened with Moses when the Israelites were enslaved in Egypt (Exodus 2). Fearing their growing numbers, Pharaoh had ordered all male Hebrew infants to be drowned in the Nile; Moses's mother instead set him adrift in a reed basket, which was found by the Pharaoh's daughter, who adopted him and raised him as an Egyptian. As an adult, Moses led the Israelites out of Egypt to the Promised Land.

What Were You Dreaming?

I'm standing here by the road long time, yesterday, day before, today. Not the same road but it's the same—hot, hot like today. When they turn off where they're going, I must get out again, wait again. Some of them they just pretend there's nobody there, they don't want to see nobody. Even go a bit faster, ja. Then they past, and I'm waiting. I combed my hair; I don't want to look like a *skollie* [ruffian]. Don't smile because they think you being too friendly, you think you good as them. They go and they go. Some's got the baby's napkin hanging over the back window to keep out this sun. Some's not going on holiday with their kids but is alone; all alone in a big car. But they'll never stop, the whites, if they alone. Never. Because these *skollies* and that kind've spoilt it all for us, sticking a gun in the driver's neck, stealing his money, beating him up and taking the car. Even killing him. So it's buggered up for us. No white wants some guy sitting behind his head. And the blacks—when they stop for you, they ask for money. They want you must pay, like for a taxi! The blacks!

But then these whites: they stopping; I'm surprised, because it's only two—empty in the back—and the car it's a beautiful one. The windows are that special glass, you can't see in if you outside, but the woman has hers down and she's calling me over with her finger. She ask me where I'm going and I say the next place because they don't like to have you for too far, so she say get in and lean into the back to move along her stuff that's on the back seat to make room. Then she say, lock the door, just push that button down, we don't want you to fall out, and it's like she's joking with someone she know. The man driving smiles over his shoulder and say something—I can't hear it very well, it's the way he talk English. So anyway I say what's all right to say, yes master, thank you master, I'm going to Warmbad. He ask again, but man, I don't get it—*Ekskuus?* Please? And she chips in—she's a lady with grey hair and he's a young chap—My friend's from England, he's asking if you've been waiting a long time for a lift. So I tell them—A long time? Madam! And because they white, I tell them about the blacks, how when they stop they ask you to pay. This time I understand what the young man's saying, he say, And most whites don't stop? And I'm careful what I say, I tell them about the blacks, how too many people spoil it for us, they robbing and killing, you can't blame white people. Then he ask where I'm from. And she laugh and look round where I'm behind her. I see she know I'm from the Cape, although she ask me. I tell her I'm from the Cape Flats[1] and she say she suppose I'm not born there, though, and she's right, I'm born in Wynberg, right there in Cape Town. So she say, And they moved you out?

Then I catch on what kind of white she is; so I tell her, yes, the government kicked us out from our place, and she say to the young man, You see?

He want to know why I'm not in the place in the Cape Flats, why I'm so far away here. I tell them I'm working in Pietersburg.[2] And he keep on, why? Why? What's my job, everything, and if I don't understand the way he speak, she chips in again all the time and ask me for him. So I tell him, panel beater.[3] And I tell him, the pay is very low in the Cape. And then I begin to tell them lots of things, some things is real and some things I just think of, things that are going to make them like me, maybe they'll take me all the way there to Pietersburg.

I tell them I'm six days on the road. I not going to say I'm sick as well, I been home because I was sick—because *she's* not from overseas, I suss that, she know that old story. I tell them I had to take leave because my mother's got trouble with my brothers and

---

1. A small town near Cape Town.   3. A person who does body work on automobiles.
2. A city in northeastern South Africa.

sisters, we seven in the family and no father. And s'true's God, it seem like what I'm saying. When do you ever see him except he's drunk. And my brother is trouble, trouble, he hangs around with bad people and my other brother doesn't help my mother. And that's no lie, neither, how can he help when he's doing time; but they don't need to know that, they only get scared I'm the same kind like him, if I tell about him, assault and intent to do bodily harm. The sisters are in school and my mother's only got the pension. *Ja.* I'm working there in Pietersburg and every week, madam, I swear to you, I send my pay for my mother and sisters. So then he say, Why get off here? Don't you want us to take you to Pietersburg? And she say, of course, they going that way.

And I tell them some more. They listening to me so nice, and I'm talking, talking. I talk about the government, because I hear she keep saying to him, telling about this law and that law. I say how it's not fair we had to leave Wynberg and go to the Flats. I tell her we got sicknesses—she say what kind, is it unhealthy there? And I don't have to think what, I just say it's *bad, bad,* and she say to the man, *As I told you.* I tell about the house we had in Wynberg, but it's not my grannie's old house where we was all living together so long, the house I'm telling them about is more the kind of house they'll know, they wouldn't like to go away from, with a tiled bathroom, electric stove, everything. I tell them we spend three thousand rands fixing up that house—my uncle give us the money, that's how we got it. He give us his savings, three thousand rands. (I don't know why I say three; old Uncle Jimmy never have three or two or one in his life. I just say it.) And then we just kicked out. And panel beaters getting low pay there; it's better in Pietersburg.

He say, but I'm far from my home? And I tell her again, because she's white but she's a woman too, with that grey hair she's got grown-up kids—Madam. I send my pay home every week, s'true's God, so's they can eat, there in the Flats. I'm saying, *six days on the road.* While I'm saying it, I'm thinking; then I say, look at me, I got only these clothes, I sold my things on the way, to have something to eat. *Six days on the road.* He's from overseas and she isn't one of those who say you're a liar, doesn't trust you—right away when I got in the car, I notice she doesn't take her stuff over to the front like they usually do in case you pinch something of theirs. Six days on the road, and am I tired, tired! When I get to Pietersburg I must try borrow me a rand to get a taxi there to where I live. He say, Where do you live? Not in town? And she laugh, because he don't know nothing about this place, where whites live and where we must go—but I know they both thinking and I know what they thinking; I know I'm going to get something when I get out, don't need to worry about that. They feeling bad about me, now. Bad. Anyhow it's God's truth that I'm tired, tired, that's true.

They've put up her window and he's pushed a few buttons, now it's like in a supermarket, cool air blowing, and the windows like sunglasses: that sun can't get me here.

The Englishman glances over his shoulder as he drives.

"Taking a nap."

"I'm sure it's needed."

All through the trip he stops for everyone he sees at the roadside. Some are not hitching at all, never expecting to be given a lift anywhere, just walking in the heat outside with an empty plastic can to be filled with water or paraffin or whatever it is they buy in some country store, or standing at some point between departure and destination, small children and bundles linked on either side, baby on back. She hasn't said anything to him. He would only misunderstand if she explained why one doesn't give lifts in this country; and if she pointed out that in spite of this, she doesn't mind him breaking the sensible if unfortunate rule, he might misunderstand that, as well—think she was boasting of her disregard for personal safety weighed in the balance against decent concern for fellow beings.

He persists in making polite conversation with these passengers because he doesn't want to be patronizing; picking them up like so many objects and dropping them off again, silent, smelling of smoke from open cooking fires, sun and sweat, there behind his head. They don't understand his Englishman's English and if he gets an answer at all it's a deaf man's guess at what's called for. Some grin with pleasure and embarrass him by showing it the way they've been taught is acceptable, invoking him as *baas* and *master* when they get out and give thanks. But although he doesn't know it, being too much concerned with those names thrust into his hands like whips whose purpose is repugnant to him, has nothing to do with him, she knows each time that there is a moment of annealment[4] in the air-conditioned hired car belonging to nobody—a moment like that on a no-man's-land bridge in which an accord between warring countries is signed—when there is no calling of names, and all belong in each other's presence. He doesn't feel it because he has no wounds, neither has inflicted, nor will inflict any.

This one standing at the roadside with his transistor radio in a plastic bag was actually thumbing a lift like a townee; his expectation marked him out. And when her companion to whom she was showing the country inevitably pulled up, she read the face at the roadside immediately: the lively, cajoling, performer's eyes, the salmon-pinkish cheeks and nostrils, and as he jogged over smiling, the unselfconscious gap of gum between the canines.

A sleeper is always absent; although present, there on the back seat.

"The way he spoke about black people, wasn't it surprising? I mean—he's black himself."

"Oh no he's not. Couldn't you see the difference? He's a Cape Coloured. From the way he speaks English—couldn't you hear he's not like the Africans you've talked to?"

But of course he hasn't seen, hasn't heard: the fellow is dark enough, to those who don't know the signs by which you're classified, and the melodramatic, long-vowelled English is as difficult to follow if more fluent than the terse, halting responses of blacker people.

"Would he have a white grandmother or even a white father, then?"

She gives him another of the little history lessons she has been supplying along the way. The Malay slaves brought by the Dutch East India Company[5] to their supply station, on the route to India, at the Cape in the seventeenth century; the Khoikhoi who were the indigenous inhabitants of that part of Africa; add Dutch, French, English, German settlers whose back-yard progeniture with these and other blacks began a people who are all the people in the country mingled in one bloodstream. But encounters along the road teach him more than her history lessons, or the political analyses in which they share the same ideological approach although he does not share responsibility for the experience to which the ideology is being applied. She has explained Acts, Proclamations, Amendments. The Group Areas Act, Resettlement Act, Orderly Movement and Settlement of Black Persons Act. She has translated these statute-book euphemisms: people as movable goods. People packed onto trucks along with their stoves and beds while front-end loaders scoop away their homes into rubble. People dumped somewhere else. Always somewhere else. People as the figures, decimal

---

4. Tempering by heating.   5. Occupied South Africa from 1652–1795 while it was a
                                            Dutch Cape Colony.

points and multiplying zero-zero-zeros into which individual lives—Black Persons Orderly-Moved, -Effluxed, -Grouped—coagulate and compute. Now he has here in the car the intimate weary odour of a young man to whom these things happen.

"Half his family sick . . . it must be pretty unhealthy, where they've been made to go."

She smiles. "Well, I'm not too sure about that. I had the feeling, some of what he said . . . they're theatrical by nature. You must take it with a pinch of salt."

"You mean about the mother and sisters and so on?"

She's still smiling, she doesn't answer.

"But he couldn't have made up about taking a job so far from home—and the business of sending his wages to his mother? That too?"

He glances at her.

Beside him, she's withdrawn as the other one, sleeping behind him. While he turns his attention back to the road, she is looking at him secretly, as if somewhere in his blue eyes registering the approaching road but fixed on the black faces he is trying to read, somewhere in the lie of his inflamed hand and arm that on their travels have been plunged in the sun as if in boiling water, there is the place through which the worm he needs to be infected with can find a way into him, so that he may host it and become its survivor, himself surviving through being fed on. Become like her. Complicity is the only understanding.

"Oh it's true, it's all true . . . not in the way he's told about it. Truer than the way he told it. All these things happen to them. And other things. Worse. But why burden us? Why try to explain to us? Things so far from what we know, how will they ever explain? How will we react? Stop our ears? Or cover our faces? Open the door and throw him out? They don't know. But sick mothers and brothers gone to the bad— these are the staples of misery, mmh? Think of the function of charity in the class struggles in your own country in the nineteenth century; it's all there in your literature. The lord-of-the-manor's compassionate daughter carrying hot soup to the dying cottager on her father's estate. The "advanced" upper-class woman comforting her cook when the honest drudge's daughter takes to whoring for a living. *Shame*, we say here. Shame. You must've heard it? We think it means, what a pity; we think we are expressing sympathy—for them. *Shame*. I don't know what we're saying about ourselves." She laughs.

"So you think it would at least be true that his family were kicked out of their home, sent away?"

"Why would anyone of them need to make that up? It's an everyday affair."

"What kind of place would they get, where they were moved?"

"Depends. A tent, to begin with. And maybe basic materials to build themselves a shack. Perhaps a one-room prefab. Always a tin toilet set down in the veld,[6] if nothing else. Some industrialist must be making a fortune out of government contracts for those toilets. You build your new life round that toilet. His people are Coloured, so it could be they were sent where there were houses of some sort already built for them; Coloureds usually get something a bit better than blacks are given."

"And the house would be more or less as good as the one they had? People as poor as that—and they'd spent what must seem a fortune to them, fixing it up."

"I don't know what kind of house they had. We're not talking about slum clearance, my dear; we're talking about destroying communities because they're black, and white people want to build houses or factories for whites where blacks live. I told you. We're talking about loading up trucks and carting black people out of sight of whites."

6. Plains.

"And even where he's come to work—Pietersburg, whatever-it's-called—he doesn't live in the town."

"Out of sight." She has lost the thought for a moment, watching to make sure the car takes the correct turning. "Out of sight. Like those mothers and grannies and brothers and sisters far away on the Cape Flats."

"I don't think it's possible he actually sends all his pay. I mean how would one eat?"

"Maybe what's left doesn't buy anything he really wants."

Not a sound, not a sigh in sleep behind them. They can go on talking about him as he always has been discussed, there and yet not there.

Her companion is alert to the risk of gullibility. He verifies the facts, smiling, just as he converts, mentally, into pounds and pence any sum spent in foreign coinage. "He didn't sell the radio. When he said he'd sold all his things on the road, he forgot about that."

"When did he say he'd last eaten?"

"Yesterday. He said."

She repeats what she has just been told: "Yesterday." She is looking through the glass that takes the shine of heat off the landscape passing as yesterday passed, time measured by the ticking second hand of moving trees, rows of crops, country-store stoeps,[7] filling stations, spiny crook'd fingers of giant euphorbia.[8] Only the figures by the roadside waiting, standing still.

Personal remarks can't offend someone dead-beat in the back. "How d'you think such a young man comes to be without front teeth?"

She giggles whisperingly and keeps her voice low, anyway. "Well, you may not believe me if I tell you . . .."

"Seems odd . . . I suppose he can't afford to have them replaced."

"It's—how shall I say—a sexual preference. Most usually you see it in their young girls, though. They have their front teeth pulled when they're about seventeen."

She feels his uncertainty, his not wanting to let comprehension lead him to a conclusion embarrassing to an older woman. For her part, she is wondering whether he won't find it distasteful if—at her de-sexed age—she should come out with it: for cock-sucking. "No one thinks the gap spoils a girl's looks, apparently. It's simply a sign she knows how to please. Same significance between men, I suppose ? A form of beauty. So everyone says. We've always been given to understand that's the reason."

"Maybe it's just another sexual myth. There are so many."

She's in agreement. "Black girls. Chinese girls. Jewish girls."

"And black men?"

"Oh my goodness, you bet. But we white ladies don't talk about that, we only dream, you know! Or have nightmares."

They're laughing. When they are quiet, she flexes her shoulders against the seat-back and settles again. The streets of a town are flickering their text across her eyes. "He might have had a car accident. They might have been knocked out in a fight."

They have to wake him because they don't know where he wants to be set down. He is staring at her lined white face (turned to him, calling him gently), stunned for a moment at this evidence that he cannot be anywhere he ought to be; and now he blinks and smiles his empty smile caught on either side by a canine tooth, and gulps and gives himself a shake like someone coming out of water. "Sorry! Sorry! Sorry madam!"

What about, she says, and the young man glances quickly, his blue eyes coming round over his shoulder: "Had a good snooze?"

---

7. Verandas.   8. An African shrub.

"Ooh I was finished, master, finished, God bless you for the rest you give me. And with an empty stummick, you know, you dreaming so real. I was dreaming, dreaming, I didn't know nothing about I'm in the car!"

It comes from the driver's seat with the voice (a real Englishman's from overseas) of one who is hoping to hear something that will explain everything. "What were you dreaming?"

But there is only hissing, spluttery laughter between the two white pointed teeth. The words gambol. "Ag, nothing, master, nothing, all *non*-sunce—"

The sense is that if pressed, he will produce for them a dream he didn't dream, a dream put together from bloated images on billboards, discarded calendars picked up, scraps of newspapers blown about—but they interrupt, they're asking where he'd like to get off.

"No, anywhere. Here it's all right. Fine. Just there by the corner. I must go look for someone who'll praps give me a rand for the taxi, because I can't walk so far, I haven't eaten nothing since yesterday . . . just here, the master can please stop just here—"

The traffic light is red, anyway, and the car is in the lane nearest the kerb. Her thin, speckled white arm with a skilled flexible hand, but no muscle with which to carry a load of washing or lift a hoe, feels back to release the lock he is fumbling at. "Up, up, pull it up." She has done it for him. "Can't you take a bus?"

"There's no buses Sunday, madam, this place is ve-ery bad for us for transport, I must tell you, we can't get nowhere Sundays, only work-days." He is out, the plastic bag with the radio under his arm, his feet in their stained, multi-striped jogging sneakers drawn neatly together like those of a child awaiting dismissal. "Thank you madam, thank you master, God bless you for what you done."

The confident dextrous hand is moving quickly down in the straw bag bought from a local market somewhere along the route. She brings up a pale blue note (the Englishman recognizes the two-rand denomination of this currency that he has memorized by colour) and turns to pass it, a surreptitious message, through the open door behind her. *Goodbye master madam.* The note disappears delicately as a tit-bit finger-fed. He closes the door, he's keeping up the patter, *goodbye master, goodbye madam,* and she instructs—"No, bang it. Harder. That's it." *Goodbye master, goodbye madam*—but they don't look back at him now, they don't have to see him thinking he must keep waving, keep smiling, in case they should look back.

She is the guide and mentor; she's the one who knows the country. She's the one—she knows that too—who is accountable. She must be the first to speak again. "At least if he's hungry he'll be able to buy a bun or something. And the bars are closed on Sunday."

⊷ ⊰◆⊱ ⊶

Derek Walcott
b. 1930

Over the last five decades, Derek Walcott has articulated the tensions of living between two worlds—the competing claims and traditions of the West Indies, his home, and Europe. A concern with issues of national identity runs throughout Walcott's large body of poetry and drama; his poetry exploits the resources of a European literary tradition in the service of Caribbean themes and concerns. No poet, as T. S. Eliot insisted, can write important poetry without tapping into some cultural or literary tradition; in the poem *Forest of Europe*, Walcott puts the question this way:

What's poetry, if it is worth its salt,
but a phrase men can pass from hand to mouth?
From hand to mouth, across the centuries,
the bread that lasts when systems have decayed.

Walcott was born in Castries, Saint Lucia, an isolated, volcanic island in the West Indies. Saint Lucia is a former British colony, and Walcott's education there was thoroughly British. In the introduction to *Dream on Monkey Mountain and Other Plays* (1970), Walcott writes, "The writers of my generation were natural assimilators. We knew the literature of Empires, Greek, Roman, British, through their essential classics; and both the patois of the street and the language of the classroom hid the elation of discovery." Empire and slavery left their impress on the Walcott family; both of his grandmothers were said to be descended from slaves. Walcott attended University College of the West Indies in Jamaica on a British government scholarship; he completed a degree in English in 1953, and from 1954 until 1957 taught in West Indian schools. In 1958 a Rockefeller Fellowship allowed him to spend a year in New York studying theater; the following year he moved to Trinidad and founded the Little Carib Theatre Workshop. It was in his playwriting that Walcott first accomplished the fusion of native and European elements he sought; his 1958 play *Drums and Colours*, for instance, employs calypso music, mime, and carnival masks to "carnivalize" the smooth surface of European drama, creating a literary form which, while written in English, is uniquely Caribbean in character. *O Babylon!* (1976), his most popular play, focuses on the Rastafarians of Jamaica. He is also a talented painter, and his poems are notable for the vivid clarity of their images.

Walcott has written more than fifteen volumes of poetry as well as a dozen plays. His first important poetry collection was *In a Green Night* (1962), which includes the aptly titled poem *A Far Cry from Africa*. Africa and Britain serve as the double setting for his trenchant portrait of a foreign aid bureaucrat in *The Fortunate Traveller* (1981). Walcott himself has never settled in one place for long, and for many years he has split his time between his home in Trinidad and a teaching post at Boston University. Walcott's poems create a landscape of historical and personal memory, overlaying empires, centuries, continents, and stages of his own life. He developed his themes most expansively in his verse novel *Omeros* (1991), which rewrites Homer's *Iliad* as a Caribbean story, interspersed with scenes of the poet's own life and travels in Boston, London, and Dublin. Walcott was awarded the Nobel Prize for literature in 1992, "for a poetic oeuvre of great luminosity, sustained by a historical vision, the outcome of a multicultural commitment."

The Fortunate Traveller[1]

for Susan Sontag

> *And I heard a voice in the midst of the four beasts say,*
> *A measure of wheat for a penny,*
> *and three measures of barley for a penny;*
> *and see thou hurt not the oil and the wine.*

> —*Revelation 6.6*[2]

I

It was in winter. Steeples, spires
congealed like holy candles. Rotting snow
flaked from Europe's ceiling. A compact man,

---

1. Walcott's title invokes Thomas Nashe's tale *The Unfortunate Traveller* (1594). Susan Sontag (b. 1933) is an American cultural critic and novelist.

2. One of the Four Horsemen of the Apocalypse is decreeing the famine and inflation that accompany wars as the end of the world approaches.

I crossed the canal in a grey overcoat,
5   on one lapel a crimson buttonhole
for the cold ecstasy of the assassin.
In the square coffin manacled to my wrist:
small countries pleaded through the mesh of graphs,
in treble-spaced, Xeroxed forms to the World Bank
10   on which I had scrawled the one word, MERCY;

I sat on a cold bench
under some skeletal lindens.
Two other gentlemen, black skins gone grey
as their identical, belted overcoats,
15   crossed the white river.
They spoke the stilted French
of their dark river,
whose hooked worm, multiplying its pale sickle,
could thin the harvest of the winter streets.
20   "Then we can depend on you to get us those tractors?"
"I gave my word."
"May my country ask you why you are doing this, sir?"
Silence.
"You know if you betray us, you cannot hide?"
25   A tug. Smoke trailing its dark cry.

At the window in Haiti, I remember
a gecko[3] pressed against the hotel glass,
with white palms, concentrating head.
With a child's hands. Mercy, monsieur. Mercy.
30   Famine sighs like a scythe
across the field of statistics and the desert
is a moving mouth. In the hold of this earth
10,000,000 shoreless souls are drifting.
Somalia: 765,000, their skeletons will go under the tidal sand.
35   "We'll meet you in Bristol to conclude the agreement?"
Steeples like tribal lances, through congealing fog
the cries of wounded church bells wrapped in cotton,
grey mist enfolding the conspirator
like a sealed envelope next to its heart.

40   No one will look up now to see the jet
fade like a weevil through a cloud of flour.
One flies first-class, one is so fortunate.
Like a telescope reversed, the traveller's eye
swiftly screws down the individual sorrow
45   to an oval nest of antic numerals,
and the iris, interlocking with this globe,
condenses it to zero, then a cloud.
Beetle-black taxi from Heathrow[4] to my flat.
We are roaches,
50   riddling the state cabinets, entering the dark holes

---

3. A small lizard.   4. London's primary airport.

of power, carapaced in topcoats,
scuttling around columns, signalling for taxis,
with frantic antennae, to other huddles with roaches;
we infect with optimism, and when
55   the cabinets crack, we are the first
to scuttle, radiating separately
back to Geneva, Bonn, Washington, London.

Under the dripping planes of Hampstead Heath,
I read her letter again, watching the drizzle
60   disfigure its pleading like mascara. Margo,
I cannot bear to watch the nations cry.
Then the phone: "We will pay you in Bristol."
Days in fetid bedclothes swallowing cold tea,
the phone stifled by the pillow. The telly
65   a blue storm with soundless snow.
I'd light the gas and see a tiger's tongue.
I was rehearsing the ecstasies of starvation
for what I had to do. *And have not charity*.[5]

I found my pity, desperately researching
70   the origins of history, from reed-built communes
by sacred lakes, turning with the first sprocketed
water-driven wheels. I smelled imagination
among bestial hides by the gleam of fat,
seeking in all races a common ingenuity.
75   I envisaged an Africa flooded with such light
as alchemized the first fields of emmer wheat and barley,
when we savages dyed our pale dead with ochre,
and bordered our temples
with the ceremonial vulva of the conch
80   in the grey epoch of the obsidian adze.
I sowed the Sahara with rippling cereals,
my charity fertilized these aridities.

What was my field? Late sixteenth century.
My field was a dank acre. A Sussex don,
85   I taught the Jacobean anxieties: *The White Devil*.[6]
Flamineo's torch startles the brooding yews.
The drawn end comes in strides. I loved my Duchess,
the white flame of her soul blown out between
the smoking cypresses. Then I saw children pounce
90   on green meat with a rat's ferocity.

I called them up and took the train to Bristol,
my blood the Severn's[7] dregs and silver.
On Severn's estuary the pieces flash,
Iscariot's salary,[8] patron saint of spies.

---

5. "Though I speak with the tongues of men and of angels, and have not charity, I am become as sounding brass, or a tinkling cymbal" (1 Corinthians 13.1).
6. Revenge tragedy (c. 1612) by John Webster.

7. A river running through Wales and England.
8. For betraying Jesus Christ, Judas Iscariot was paid 30 pieces of silver by the Roman authorities.

95   I thought, who cares how many million starve?
        Their rising souls will lighten the world's weight
        and level its gull-glittering waterline;
        we left at sunset down the estuary.

        England recedes. The forked white gull
100   screeches, circling back.
        Even the birds are pulled back by their orbit,
        even mercy has its magnetic field.
                                Back in the cabin,
        I uncap the whisky, the porthole
105   mists with glaucoma. By the time I'm pissed,[9]
        England, England will be
        that pale serrated indigo on the sea-line.
        "You are so fortunate, you get to see the world—"
        Indeed, indeed, sirs, I have seen the world.
110   Spray splashes the portholes and vision blurs.

        Leaning on the hot rail, watching the hot sea,
        I saw them far off, kneeling on hot sand
        in the pious genuflections of the locust,
        as Ponce's armoured knees crush Florida
115   to the funereal fragrance of white lilies.

                                II
        Now I have come to where the phantoms live,
        I have no fear of phantoms, but of the real.
        The Sabbath benedictions of the islands.
        Treble clef of the snail on the scored leaf,
120   the Tantum Ergo[1] of black choristers
        soars through the organ pipes of coconuts.
        Across the dirty beach surpliced with lace,
        they pass a brown lagoon behind the priest,
        pale and unshaven in his frayed soutane,[2]
125   into the concrete church at Canaries;
        as Albert Schweitzer[3] moves to the harmonium
        of morning, and to the pluming chimneys,
        the groundswell lifts *Lebensraum, Lebensraum*.[4]

        Black faces sprinkled with continual dew—
130   dew on the speckled croton,[5] dew
        on the hard leaf of the knotted plum tree,
        dew on the elephant ears of the dasheen.[6]
        Through Kurtz's teeth, white skull in elephant grass,
        the imperial fiction sings. Sunday
135   wrinkles downriver from the Heart of Darkness.
        The heart of darkness is not Africa.
        The heart of darkness is the core of fire

9. Drunk.
1. A hymn sung after the Blessed Sacrament has been exposed in the mass.
2. Black robe.
3. German physician, missionary, and musician in Africa;

winner of the Nobel Peace Prize in 1952.
4. Space to live in; the term is especially associated with Nazi Germany's territorial expansion.
5. A tropical plant.
6. The taro plant of tropical Asia.

in the white center of the holocaust.
The heart of darkness is the rubber claw
140   selecting a scalpel in antiseptic light,
the hills of children's shoes outside the chimneys,
the tinkling nickel instruments on the white altar;
Jacob, in his last card, sent me these verses:
"Think of a God who doesn't lose His sleep
145   if trees burst into tears or glaciers weep.
So, aping His indifference, I write now,
not Anno Domini: After Dachau."[7]

III

The night maid brings a lamp and draws the blinds.
I stay out on the verandah with the stars.
150   Breakfast congealed to supper on its plate.

There is no sea as restless as my mind.
The promontories snore. They snore like whales.
Cetus, the whale, was Christ.
The ember dies, the sky smokes like an ash heap.
155   Reeds wash their hands of guilt and the lagoon
is stained. Louder, since it rained,
a gauze of sand flies hisses from the marsh.

Since God is dead,[8] and these are not His stars,
but man-lit, sulphurous, sanctuary lamps,
160   it's in the heart of darkness of this earth
that backward tribes keep vigil of His Body,
in deya, lampion,[9] and this bedside lamp.
Keep the news from their blissful ignorance.
Like lice, like lice, the hungry of this earth
165   swarm to the tree of life. If those who starve
like these rain-flies who shed glazed wings in light
grew from sharp shoulder blades their brittle vans
and soared towards that tree, how it would seethe—
ah, Justice! But fires
170   drench them like vermin, quotas
prevent them, and they remain
compassionate fodder for the travel book,
its paragraphs like windows from a train,
for everywhere that earth shows its rib cage
175   and the moon goggles with the eyes of children,
we turn away to read. Rimbaud[1] learned that.
                        Rimbaud, at dusk,
idling his wrist in water past temples
the plumed dates still protect in Roman file,
180   knew that we cared less for one human face
than for the scrolls in Alexandria's ashes,
that the bright water could not dye his hand

---

7. Site of the notorious Nazi concentration camp.
8. So the German philosopher Friedrich Nietzsche declared in his 1882 text *The Gay Science*.
9. A small oil lamp with tinted glass.

1. Arthur Rimbaud (1854–1891), French poet. After abandoning poetry at the age of 20, he travelled in Egypt and the Sudan, later settling in Ethiopia as a trader and arms dealer.

any more than poetry. The dhow's[2] silhouette
moved through the blinding coinage of the river

185   that, endlessly, until we pay one debt,
shrouds, every night, an ordinary secret.

IV

The drawn sword comes in strides.
It stretches for the length of the empty beach;
the fishermen's huts shut their eyes tight.

190   A frisson[3] shakes the palm trees.
and sweats on the traveller's tree.
They've found out my sanctuary. Philippe, last night:
"It had two gentlemen in the village yesterday, sir,
asking for you while you was in town.

195   I tell them you was in town. They send to tell you,
there is no hurry. They will be coming back."

In loaves of cloud, *and have not charity,*
the weevil will make a sahara of Kansas,
the ant shall eat Russia.

200   Their soft teeth shall make, *and have not charity,*
the harvest's desolation,
and the brown globe crack like a begging bowl,
and though you fire oceans of surplus grain,
and have not charity,

205   still, through thin stalks,
the smoking stubble, stalks
grasshopper: third horseman,
the leather-helmed locust.[4]

1981

---

from **Midsummer**

50

I once gave my daughters, separately, two conch shells
that were dived from the reef, or sold on the beach, I forget.
They use them as doorstops or bookends, but their wet
pink palates are the soundless singing of angels.

5   I once wrote a poem called "The Yellow Cemetery,"
when I was nineteen. Lizzie's age. I'm fifty-three.
These poems I heaved aren't linked to any tradition
like a mossed cairn;[1] each goes down like a stone
to the seabed, settling, but let them, with luck, lie

10   where stones are deep, in the sea's memory.
Let them be, in water, as my father, who did watercolours,
entered his work. He became one of his shadows,

---

2. A sailing vessel used by Arabs.
3. Sudden passing excitement.
4. The locust, eater of crops, is here identified with the

horseman of the Apocalypse quoted in the poem's epigraph.
1. A heap of stones marking a trail.

wavering and faint in the midsummer sunlight.
His name is Warwick Walcott. I sometimes believe
that his father, in love or bitter benediction,
named him for Warwickshire.[2] Ironies
are moving. Now, when I rewrite a line,
or sketch on the fast-drying paper the coconut fronds
that he did so faintly, my daughters' hands move in mine.
Conches move over the sea-floor. I used to move
my father's grave from the blackened Anglican headstones
in Castries[3] to where I could love both at once—
the sea and his absence. Youth is stronger than fiction.

52

I heard them marching the leaf-wet roads of my head,
the sucked vowels of a syntax trampled to mud,
a division of dictions, one troop black, barefooted,
the other in redcoats bright as their sovereign's blood;
their feet scuffled like rain, the bare soles with the shod.
One fought for a queen, the other was chained in her service,
but both, in bitterness, travelled the same road.
Our occupation and the Army of Occupation
are born enemies, but what mortar can size
the broken stones of the barracks of Brimstone Hill
to the gaping brick of Belfast? Have we changed sides
to the moustached sergeants and the horsy gentry
because we serve English, like a two-headed sentry
guarding its borders? No language is neutral;
the green oak of English is a murmurous cathedral
where some took umbrage,[4] some peace, but every shade, all,
helped widen its shadow. I used to haunt the arches
of the British barracks of Vigie[5]. There were leaves there,
bright, rotting like revers of epaulettes[6], and the stenches
of history and piss. Leaves piled like the dropped aitches
of soldiers from rival shires, from the brimstone trenches
of Agincourt to the gas of the Somme.[7] On Poppy Day[8]
our schools bought red paper flowers. They were for Flanders.[9]
I saw Hotspur cursing the smoke through which a popinjay
minced from the battle. Those raging commanders
from Thersites to Percy,[1] their rant is our model.
I pinned the poppy to my blazer. It bled like a vowel.

2. Birthplace of Shakespeare. Warwick Walcott, journalist, occasional poet, and printer, died when his son was a young child.
3. Port and capital of Saint Lucia.
4. In two senses: offence, shade.
5. Vigie Beach near Castries, Saint Lucia.
6. Turned-up edges of ornamental shoulder pieces worn on uniforms.
7. French sites of important battles in 1415 and in

World War I.
8. Veterans Day.
9. Scene of a disastrous World War I offensive—"the battle of the mud"—in which the British lost 324,000 soldiers.
1. The headstrong Sir Henry Percy (1364–1403) became known as "Hotspur"; he serves as rival to Prince Hal in Shakespeare's Henry IV. Thersites accuses Achilles of cowardice in Homer's Iliad.

54

The midsummer sea, the hot pitch road, this grass, these shacks that made me,
jungle and razor grass shimmering by the roadside, the edge of art;
wood lice are humming in the sacred wood,
nothing can burn them out, they are in the blood;
5   their rose mouths, like cherubs, sing of the slow science
of dying—all heads, with, at each ear, a gauzy wing.
Up at Forest Reserve, before branches break into sea,
I looked through the moving, grassed window and thought "pines,"
or conifers of some sort. I thought, they must suffer
10   in this tropical heat with their child's idea of Russia.
Then suddenly, from their rotting logs, distracting signs
of the faith I betrayed, or the faith that betrayed me—
yellow butterflies rising on the road to Valencia[2]
stuttering "yes" to the resurrection; "yes, yes is our answer,"
15   the gold-robed Nunc Dimittis[3] of their certain choir.
Where's my child's hymnbook, the poems edged in gold leaf,
the heaven I worship with no faith in heaven,
as the Word turned toward poetry in its grief?
Ah, bread of life, that only love can leaven!
20   Ah, Joseph, though no man ever dies in his own country,[4]
the grateful grass will grow thick from his heart.

1984

[END OF PERSPECTIVES: WHOSE LANGUAGE?]

---

2. A seaport in Eastern Spain.
3. "Lord, now let thy servant depart in peace," sung at the end of Mass.
4. The line echoes Jesus's comment that no prophet is honored in his own country (Mark 6.4). On one level, Joseph may be Jesus's father, mourning his son's early death. *Midsummer* as a whole is addressed to Walcott's friend Joseph Brodsky, the exiled Russian poet.

BIBLIOGRAPHIES

The Middle Ages

Dictionaries, Encyclopedias • Miranda Green, ed., *Dictionary of Celtic Mythology*, 1992. • Hans Kurath et al., eds., *The Middle English Dictionary*, 1952–. • Norris J. Lacy, ed., *The New Arthurian Encyclopedia*, 1991. • Joseph Strayer, gen. ed., *The Dictionary of the Middle Ages*, 13 vols., 1982–1989.

Journals • *Celtica* • *Exemplaria: A Journal of Theory in Medieval and Renaissance Studies* • *Medium Aevum* • *Speculum*, vol. 1–64 (1926–1989); available on-line through JSTOR ("Journal Storage"): http://www.jstor.org

On-Line Sources • BARD (Bodleian Access to Remote Databases) online Chaucer Bibliography: http://www.bodley.ox.ac.uk/bardhtml/descriptions/ chaucer.html • *Beowulf* manuscript in color facsimile: http://www.uky.edu/~kiernan/BL/kportico.html • Images from medieval manuscripts can be viewed at http://acs1.byu.edu/7Ehurlbutj/dscriptorium/dscriptorium.html • French art of Chaucer's time, arranged by theme, can be viewed at an archive maintained by the Bibliothèque Nationale in Paris: http://www.bnf.fr/enluminures/accueil.htm • *The Labyrinth*, developed by Prof. Martin Irvine and Prof. Deborah Everhart, a clearing house for access to other, more specialized sites; a good starting point: http://www/georgetown.edu/labyrinth/ • Especially useful in *The Labyrinth* is "Daedalus' Guide to the Web," which surveys directories, search engines, and other resources: http://www.georgetown.edu/labyrinth/general/general.html • *The Piers Plowman Electronic Archive*: http://jefferson.village.virginia.edu/piers/archive.goals.html • For further primary texts that may be unavailable in some libraries, consult the University of Virginia's Electronic Text Center, accessible via *The Labyrinth* or at http://etext.lib.virginia.edu/

The British Isles Before the Norman Conquest • D. A. Binchy, *Celtic and Anglo-Saxon Kingship*, 1970. • Peter Hunter Blair, *Roman Britain and Early England, 55 B.C.–A.D. 871*, 1963. • Peter Hunter Blair, *Introduction to Anglo-Saxon England*, 2nd ed., 1977. • H. M. Chadwick,

The Heroic Age, 1912. • Nora K. Chadwick, *The Celts*, 1970. • Liam de Paor, *The Peoples of Ireland*, 1986. • Myles Dillon and Nora K. Chadwick, *The Celtic Realms*, 1972. • *English Historical Documents*, vol. I, c. 500–1042, ed. Dorothy Whitelock, 1953. [Primary sources in English translation; introductions provide excellent context.] • Nicholas Howe, *Migration and Mythmaking in Anglo-Saxon England*, 1989. • Hugh A. MacDougall, *Racial Myth in English History: Trojans, Teutons, and Anglo-Saxons*, 1982. • Nerys Patterson, *Cattle Lords and Clansmen: The Social Structure of Early Ireland*, 2nd ed., 1996. • Frank M. Stenton, "Anglo-Saxon England," *The Oxford History of England*, vol. 2, 1971. • Dorothy Whitelock, *The Beginnings of English Society*, 1952. • David M. Wilson, *The Anglo-Saxons*, 1960.

The Norman Conquest and Its Impact • Jonathan Alexander and Paul Binski, *Age of Chivalry: Art in Plantagenet England 1200–1400*, 1987. • Christopher Brooke, *From Alfred to Henry III, 871–1272*, 1961. • R. Allen Brown, *The Normans*, 1984. • *English Historical Documents*, vol. II, *1042–1189*, eds. David C. Douglas and George W. Greenaway, 1953; vol. III, *1189–1327*, ed. Harry Rothwell, 1975. • Elizabeth Hallam, *Plantagenet Chronicles*, 1986. Chronicle sources, fine illustrations. • H. W. Koch, *Medieval Warfare*, 1978. • A. L. Poole, *From Domesday Book to Magna Carta*, The Oxford History of England, 1955. • F. M. Powicke, "The Thirteenth Century, 1216–1307," *The Oxford History of England*, vol. 4, 1953. • Pauline Stafford, *Unification and Conquest: A Political and Social History of England in the Tenth and Eleventh Centuries*, 1989. • Philip Warner, *The Medieval Castle*, 1971.

Continental and Insular Cultures • Judson B. Allen, *The Friar as Critic: Literary Attitudes in the Later Middle Ages*, 1971. • Erich Auerbach, *Mimesis: The Representation of Reality in Western Literature*, trans. Willard R. Trask, 1957. • William Calin, *The French Tradition and the Literature of Medieval England*, 1994. • Marcia Colish, *The Mirror of Language*, rev. ed., 1983. • Ernst Robert Curtius, *European Literature* *and the Latin Middle Ages*, trans. Willard R. Trask, 1953. • Peter Dronke, *Medieval Latin and the Rise of the European Love Lyric*, 2nd ed., 2 vols., 1968. • Robert W. Hanning, *The Individual in Twelfth-Century Romance*, 1978. • Johan Huizinga, *The Autumn of the Middle Ages*, trans. Rodney J. Payton and Ulrich Mammitzsch, 1996. • W. P. Ker, *Epic and Romance*, 1957. • C. S. Lewis, *The Discarded Image: An Introduction to Medieval and Renaissance Literature*, 1964. • A. J. Minnis, *Medieval Theory of Authorship: Scholastic Literary Attitudes in the Later Middle Ages*, 2nd ed., 1988. • Nigel Saul, ed., *England in Europe 1066–1453*, 1994. • Rosamund Tuve, *Allegorical Imagery: Some Medieval Books and their Posterity*, 1966.

Politics and Society in the Fourteenth and Fifteenth Centuries • David Aers, ed., *Culture and History, 1350–1600*, 1992. • R. B. Dobson, *The Peasants' Revolt of 1381*, 2nd ed., 1983. • *English Historical Documents*, vol. IV, *1327–1485*, ed. A. R. Myers, 1969. • Rodney H. Hilton, *Bond Men Made Free: Medieval Peasant Movements and the English Rising of 1381*, 1973. • Ernest F. Jacob, "The Fifteenth Century," *The Oxford History of England*, vol. 6, 1961. • Maurice Keen, *English Society in the Later Middle Ages*, 1990. • Gordon Leff, *The Dissolution of the Medieval Outlook: An Essay on Intellectual and Spiritual Change in the Fourteenth Century*, 1976. • Gervase Matthew, *The Court of Richard II*, 1968. • May McKisack, *The Fourteenth Century, 1307–1399*, 1959. • Colin Platt, *The English Medieval Town*, 1976. • Juliet Vale, *Edward III and Chivalry: Chivalric Society and Its Context 1270–1350*, 1982. • David Wallace, *Bodies and Disciplines: Intersections of Literature and History in Fifteenth-Century England*, 1996. • Scott L. Waugh, *England in the Reign of Edward III*, 1991. [Extensive and helpful bibliography.]

Religious Institutions and Cultures • Margaret Aston, *Lollards and Reformers*, 1994. • Renate Blumenfeld-Kosinski and Timea Szell, eds., *Images of Sainthood in Medieval Europe*, 1991. • Janet Burton, *Monastic and Religious Orders in Britain, 1000–1300*, 1994. • M. D. Chenu, *Nature, Man, and Society in the Twelfth Century*, eds. and trans. Jerome Taylor and Lester K. Little, 1968. • Ronald C. Finucane, *Miracles and Pilgrims: Popular Beliefs in Medieval England*, 1977. • Thomas Heffernan, *Sacred Biography: Saints and Their Biographers in the Middle Ages*, 1988. • Anne Hudson, *The Premature Reformation: Wycliffite Texts and Lollard*

History, 1988. • W. A. Pantin, *The English Church in the Fourteenth Century*, 1980.

Gender, Sexuality, Courtliness, Marriage • John Boswell, *Christianity, Social Tolerance, and Homosexuality: Gay People in Western Europe from the Beginning of the Christian Era to the Fourteenth Century*, 1980. • Christopher Brooke, *The Medieval Idea of Marriage*, 1989. • Susan Crane, *Insular Romance: Politics, Faith, and Culture in Anglo-Norman and Middle English Literature*, 1986. • Georges Duby, *The Knight, the Lady, and the Priest: The Making of Modern Marriage in Medieval France*, trans. Barbara Bray, 1983. • Frances and Joseph Gies, *Marriage and the Family in the Middle Ages*, 1987. • Henry A. Kelly, *Love and Marriage in the Age of Chaucer*, 1975. • Clare A. Lees, ed., *Medieval Masculinities: Regarding Men in the Middle Ages*, 1994. • C. S. Lewis, *The Allegory of Love*, 1938. • V. J. Scattergood and J. W. Sherborne, eds., *English Court Culture in the Later Middle Ages*, 1983.

Women, Work, and Religion • Judith Bennett, *Women in the Medieval English Countryside*, 1986. • Caroline Walker Bynum, *Holy Feast and Holy Fast: The Religious Significance of Food to Medieval Women*, 1987. • Sharon Elkins, *Holy Women of Twelfth Century England*, 1988. • Mary Erler and Maryanne Kowaleski, eds., *Women and Power in the Middle Ages*, 1988. • Christine Fell, *Women in Anglo-Saxon England*, 1986. • Penny Schine Gold, *The Lady and the Virgin: Image, Attitude, and Experience in Twelfth-Century France*, 1985. • Barbara Hanawalt, ed., *Women and Work in Preindustrial Europe*, 1986. • Martha Howell, *Women, Production and Patriarchy in Late Medieval Cities*, 1986. • C. E. Meek and M. K. Simms, eds., *The Fragility of Her Sex? Medieval Irish Women in Their European Context*, 1995. • Barbara Newman, *From Virile Woman to Woman Christ: Studies in Medieval Religion and Literature*, 1995. • Pauline Stafford, *Queens, Concubines, and Dowagers: The King's Wife in the Early Middle Ages*, 1983. • Ulrike Wiethaus, ed., *Maps of Flesh and Light: The Religious Experience of Medieval Women Mystics*, 1993.

Modes of Transmission: Orality, Literacy, Manuscripts, Languages • Janet Backhouse, *Books of Hours*, 1985. • Mary Carruthers, *The Book of Memory: A Study of Memory in Medieval Culture*, 1990. • Roger Chartier, ed., *The Culture of Print: Power and the Uses of Print in Early Modern Europe*, 1989. • M. T. Clanchy, *From Memory to Written Record: England,*

1066–1307, 2nd ed., 1993. • Janet Coleman, *Medieval Readers and Writers, 1350–1400*, 1981. • Joyce Coleman, *Public Reading and the Reading Public in Late Medieval England and France*, 1996. • John H. Fisher, *The Emergence of Standard English*, 1996. • John Miles Foley, *The Theory of Oral Composition: History and Methodology*, 1988. • Christopher de Hamel, *A History of Illuminated Manuscripts*, 1986. • Seth Lerer, *Literacy and Power in Anglo-Saxon England*, 1991. • Jeff Opland, *Anglo-Saxon Oral Poetry: A Study of the Traditions*, 1979. • Nicholas Orme, *From Childhood to Chivalry: The Education of the English Kings and Aristocracy 1066–1530*, 1984.

Old English Literature • Journals • *Anglo-Saxon England • Old English Newsletter.*

Bibliography • Stanley B. Greenfield and Fred C. Robinson, *Bibliography of Publications on Old English Literature*, 1980.

Studies and Guides • Michael Alexander, *Old English Literature*, 1983. • Jess B. Bessinger and Stanley J. Kahrl, eds., *Essential Articles for the Study of Old English Poetry*, 1968. • Jane Chance, *Woman as Hero in Old English Literature*, 1986. • Helen Damico and Alexandra Hennessey Olsen, eds., *New Readings on Women in Old English Literature*, 1990. • Allen J. Franzten, *The Desire for Origins: New Language, Old English, and Teaching the Tradition*, 1990. • Allen J. Franzten, ed., *Speaking Two Languages: Traditional Disciplines and Contemporary Theory in Medieval Studies*, 1991. • Malcolm Godden and Michael Lapidge, eds., *The Cambridge Companion to Old English Literature*, 1991. • Stanley B. Greenfield, *Hero and Exile: The Art of Old English Poetry*, 1989. • Stanley B. Greenfield and Daniel G. Calder, *A New Critical History of Old English Literature*, 1986. • Britton J. Harwood and Gillian Overing, eds., *Class and Gender in Early English Literature: Intersections*, 1994. • Katherine O'Brien O'Keeffe, ed., *Old English Shorter Poems: Basic Readings*, 1994. • Charles D. Wright, *The Irish Tradition in Old English Literature*, 1993.

Middle English Language and Literature • Middle English Grammar • John A. Burrow and Thorlac Turville-Petre, *A Book of Middle English*, 1996. • Joseph Wright and Elizabeth Mary Wright, *An Elementary Middle English Grammar*, 1979.

Studies • David Aers, *Community, Gender, and Individual Identity: English Writing 1360–1430*, 1988. • H. S. Bennett, "Chaucer and the Fifteenth Century," *The Oxford History of English Literature*, vol. 2, part 1, 1947. • J. A. W. Bennett and Douglas Gray, "Middle English Literature," *The Oxford History of English Literature*, vol. 1, part 2, 1986. • J. A. Burrow, *Ricardian Poetry: Chaucer, Gower, Langland, and the Gawain*, 1971. • E. K. Chambers, "English Literature at the Close of the Middle Ages," *The Oxford History of English Literature*, vol. 2, part 2, 1961. • Laurie A. Finke and Martin B. Schichtman, eds., *Medieval Texts and Contemporary Readers*, 1987. • Boris Ford, *Medieval Literature: Chaucer and the Alliterative Tradition*, 1982. • Stephen Justice, *Writing and Rebellion: England in 1381*, 1994. • Charles Muscatine, *Poetry and Crisis in the Age of Chaucer*, 1972. • Glending Olson, *Literature as Recreation in the Later Middle Ages*, 1982. • Lee Patterson, ed., *Literary Practice and Social Change in Britain, 1380–1530*, 1990. • Lee Patterson, *Negotiating the Past: The Historical Understanding of Medieval Literature*, 1987. • Larry Scanlon, *Narrative, Authority, and Power: The Medieval Exemplum and the Chaucerian Tradition*, 1994. • A. C. Spearing, *Readings in Medieval Poetry*, 1987. • Paul Strohm, *Hochon's Arrow: The Social Imagination of Fourteenth-Century Texts*, 1992. • Thorlac Turville-Petre, *The Alliterative Revival*, 1977.

Celtic Culture and Literature • Bibliography • Rachel Bromwich, *Medieval Celtic Literature: A Select Bibliography*, 1974.

Studies • Miranda J. Green, ed., *Celtic Goddesses: Warriors, Virgins, and Mothers*, 1995. • Miranda J. Green, ed., *The Celtic World*, 1995.

Irish Culture and Literature • Translations • James Carney, *Medieval Irish Lyrics with "The Irish Bardic Poet,"* 1985. • Tom Peete Cross and Clark Harris Slover, eds., *Ancient Irish Tales*, 1936; repr. with updated bibliography, 1969. • Kenneth Hurlstone Jackson, *A Celtic Miscellany: Translations from the Celtic Literatures*, 1951. • Kuno Meyer, trans., *Ancient Irish Poetry*, 1994. • Frank O'Connor, trans., *Kings, Lords, and Commons: An Anthology from the Irish*, 1959.

Studies • James Carney, *Studies in Irish Literature and History*, 1979. • Doris Edel, ed., *Cultural Identity and Cultural Integration: Ireland and Europe in the Early Middle Ages*, 1995. • Jeffrey Gantz, *Early Irish Myths and Sagas*, 1981. • Kim McKone, *Pagan Past and Christian Present in Early Irish Literature*, 1990. • Nerys

Patterson, *Cattle Lords and Clansmen: The Social Structure of Early Ireland*, 2nd ed., 1996. • Alwyn Rees and Brinley Rees, *Celtic Heritage*, 1961. • J. E. Caerwyn Williams and Patrick K. Ford, *The Irish Literary Tradition*, 1992.

Welsh Culture and Literature • Translations • Joseph Clancy, *The Earliest Welsh Poetry*, 1970. • Anthony Conran, *The Penguin Book of Welsh Verse*, 1967. • D. Johnston, ed. and trans., *Medieval Welsh Erotic Poetry*, 1991.

Bibliography • Rachel Bromwich, *Medieval Celtic Literature: A Select Bibliography*, 1974.

Studies • Stephen S. Evans, *The Heroic Poetry of Dark-Age Britain*, 1997. • Kenneth Jackson, *Language and History in Early Britain*, 1953. • A. O. H. Jarman, *The Cynfeirdd: Early Welsh Poets and Poetry*, 1981. • A. O. H. Jarman and Gwilym Rees Hughes, eds., *A Guide to Welsh Literature*, vol. I, 1976. • Jenny Rowland, *Early Welsh Saga Poetry*, 1990. • Sir Ifor Williams, *The Beginnings of Welsh Poetry: Studies*, 1980.

Perspectives: Arthurian Myth in the History of Britain • Translations • Geoffrey of Monmouth, *History of the Kings of Britain*, trans. Lewis Thorpe, 1966. • Gerald of Wales, *The Journey through Wales and The Description of Wales*, trans. L. Thorpe, 1978. • E. L. G. Stones, ed. and trans., *Anglo-Scottish Relations 1174–1328: Some Selected Documents*, 1965.

Studies • Christopher Brooke, "Geoffrey of Monmouth as a Historian," in C. Brooke et al., eds., *Church and Government in the Middle Ages*, 1976. • Michael J. Curley, *Geoffrey of Monmouth*, 1994. • John Gillingham, "The Context and Purposes of Geoffrey of Monmouth's *History of the Kings of Britain*," *Anglo-Norman Studies* vol. 13, 1990. • Robert W. Hanning, *The Vision of History in Early Britain: From Gildas to Geoffrey of Monmouth*, 1966. • R. William Leckie, Jr., *The Passage of Dominion: Geoffrey of Monmouth and the Periodization of Insular History in the Twelfth Century*, 1981. • Roger Sherman Loomis, ed., *Arthurian Literature in the Middle Ages*, 1959. • Monika Otter, *Inventiones: Fiction and Referentiality in Twelfth-Century Historical Writing*, 1996. • Michael Prestwich, *Edward the First*, 1988. • E. L. G. Stones, *Edward I*, 1968. • J. S. P. Tatlock, *The Legendary History of Britain*, 1950.

Arthurian Romance • Bibliography • Norris J. Lacy, ed., *Medieval Arthurian Literature: A Guide to Recent Research*, 1996.

Encyclopedia • Norris J. Lacy, ed., *The New Arthurian Encyclopedia*, 1991.

Journal • *Arthurian Literature*

Studies • John Darrah, *Paganism in Arthurian Romance*, 1994. • Thelma Fenster, ed., *Arthurian Women: A Casebook*, 1996. • Maureen Fries and Jeanie Watson, eds., *Approaches to Teaching the Arthurian Tradition*, 1992. • Edward D. Kennedy, ed., *King Arthur: A Casebook*, 1996. • Stephen Knight, *Arthurian Literature and Society*, 1983. • Roger Sherman Loomis, ed., *Arthurian Literature in the Middle Ages: A Collaborative History*, 1969. • Martin Schichtman and James Carley, eds., *Culture and the King: the Social Implications of the Arthurian Legend*, 1994. • Eugene Vinaver, *The Rise of Romance*, 1984.

Middle Scots Poetry • Walter Scheps and J. Anna Looney, eds., *Middle Scots Poets: A Reference Guide to James I of Scotland, Robert Henryson, William Dunbar, and Gavin Douglas*, 1986.

Travel • Studies • A. L. Binns, *Viking Voyages*, 1980. • Mary B. Campbell, *The Witness and the Other World: Exotic European Travel Writing, 400–1600*, 1988. • Donald R. Howard, *Writers and Pilgrims: Medieval Pilgrimage Narratives and their Posterity*, 1980. • Scott D. Westrem, ed., *Discovering New Worlds: Essays on Medieval Exploration and Imagination*, 1991.

Beowulf • Edition • Frederick Klaeber, ed., *Beowulf and the Fight at Finnsburg*, rev. W. F. Bolton, 1973. [standard edition]

Translations • Kevin Crossley-Holland, trans., *Beowulf*, 1968. [translation used] • E. T. Donaldson, trans., *Beowulf*, ed. Joseph E. Tuso, 1975. [Norton Critical Edition] • Howell D. Chickering, Jr., trans., Beowulf: A *Dual-Language Edition*, 1977.

Bibliography • Robert J. Hasenfratz, *Beowulf Scholarship: An Annotated Bibliography, 1979–1990*, 1993.

Studies • Peter S. Baker, *Beowulf: Basic Readings*, 1995. • Adrien Bonjour, *The Digressions in Beowulf*, 1950. • R. W. Chambers, *Beowulf: An Introduction to the Study of the Poem*, 3rd ed., suppl. C. L. Wrenn, 1959. • George Clark, *Beowulf*, 1990. • John Miles Foley, *Traditional Oral Epic: The Odyssey, Beowulf, and the Serbo-Croatian Return Song*, 1990. • Donald K. Fry, ed. *The Beowulf Poet*, 1968. •

R. D. Fulk, ed., *Interpretations of* Beowulf: *A Critical Anthology*, 1991. • Edward B. Irving, Jr., *Rereading* Beowulf, 1989. • J. D. A. Ogilvy and Donald C. Baker, *Reading* Beowulf: *An Introduction to the Poem, Its Background, and Its Style*, 1983. • Gillian Overing, *Language, Sign, and Gender in* Beowulf, 1990. • Fred C. Robinson, Beowulf *and the Appositive Style*, 1985. • J. R. R. Tolkien, Beowulf, *the Monsters, and the Critics*, 1937.

Chaucer • **Editions** • E. Talbot Donaldson, ed., *Chaucer's Poetry*, 1957. [edition used] • Larry D. Benson, gen. ed., *The Riverside Chaucer*, 3rd ed., 1987. [standard edition] • V. A. Kolve and Glending Olson, eds., *The Canterbury Tales: Nine Tales and the "General Prologe,"* 1989. [Norton Critical Edition] • Peter G. Beidler, ed., *Geoffrey Chaucer: "The Wife of Bath": Complete, Authoritative Text with Biographical and Historical Context, Critical History, and Essays from Five Contemporary Critical Perspectives*, 1996.

Electronic Editions • *Chaucer: Life and Times*, CD-ROM, Primary Sources Media 1995. [With full text from *The Riverside Chaucer*; notes and glosses in pull-down windows.] • Peter Robinson, ed., *The Wife of Bath's Prologue*, Cambridge University Press 1996. [Challenging format, but complete survey of manuscripts.]

Biographies • Martin M. Crow and C. Olson, eds., *Chaucer Life-Records*, 1966. • Donald R. Howard, *Chaucer: His Life, His Works, His World*, 1987.

Bibliography • John Leyerle and Anne Quick, *Chaucer: A Bibliographical Introduction*, 1986. • BARD (Bodleian Access to Remote Databases) online Chaucer Bibliography: http://www.ox.ac.uk/bardhtml/descriptions/chaucer.html

Journals • *Studies in the Age of Chaucer* • *Chaucer Review* • *Chaucer Yearbook: A Journal of Late Medieval Studies*

Handbooks and Source Collections • Larry D. Benson and Theodore Anderson, eds., *The Literary Context of Chaucer's Fabliaux*, 1971. • Piero Boitani and Jill Mann, eds., *Cambridge Chaucer Companion*, 1986. • Robert P. Miller, ed., *Chaucer: Sources and Backgrounds*, 1977. • Beryl Rowland, ed., *Companion to Chaucer Studies*, 2nd ed., rev. 1979.

General Studies • Susan Crane, *Gender and Romance in Chaucer's Canterbury Tales*, 1994. • Alfred David, *The Strumpet Muse: Art and Morals in Chaucer's Poetry*, 1976. • Carolyn Dinshaw, *Chaucer's Sexual Poetics*, 1989. • E. Talbot Donaldson, *Speaking of Chaucer*, 1970. • John M. Fyler, *Chaucer and Ovid*, 1979. • Peggy Knapp, *Chaucer and the Social Contest*, 1990. • Stephen Knight, *Geoffrey Chaucer*, 1986. • V. A. Kolve, *Chaucer and the Imagery of Narrative*, 1984. • Charles Muscatine, *Chaucer and the French Tradition*, 1957. • Lee Patterson, *Chaucer and the Subject of History*, 1991. • D. W. Robertson Jr., *Chaucer's London*, 1968. • D. W. Robertson Jr., *A Preface to Chaucer*, 1962. • Donald M. Rose, ed., *New Perspectives in Chaucer Criticism*, 1981. • Paul Strohm, *Social Chaucer*, 1989. • David Wallace, *Chaucerian Polity: Absolutist Lineages and Associational Forms in England and Italy*, 1997.

Studies • C. David Benson, *Chaucer's Drama of Style: Poetic Variety and Contrast in* The Canterbury Tales, 1986. • Muriel Bowden, *A Commentary on the General Prologue to* The Canterbury Tales, 1948. • Donald R. Howard, *The Idea of* The Canterbury Tales, 1976. • H. Marshall Leicester Jr., *The Disenchanted Self: Representing the Subject in* The Canterbury Tales, 1990. • Carl Lindahl, *Earnest Games: Folkloric Patterns in* The Canterbury Tales, 1987. • Jill Mann, *Chaucer and the Medieval Estates Satire*, 1973. • Paul A. Olson, *The Canterbury Tales and the Good Society*, 1986. • Winthrop Wetherbee, *Geoffrey Chaucer: The Canterbury Tales*, 1989.

Dayfydd ap Gwilym • **Translations** • Rolfe Humphries, trans., *Nine Thorny Thickets: Selected Poems by Dafydd ap Gwilym in New Arrangements by Jon Roush*, 1969. [edition used] • Rachel Bromwich, trans., *Dafydd ap Gwilym: A Selection of Poems*, 1982. • Richard Morgan Loomis, trans., *Dafydd ap Gwilym: The Poems*, 1982.

Studies • Rachel Bromwich, *Aspects of the Poetry of Dafydd ap Gwilym: Collected Papers*, 1986. • Helen Fulton, *Dafydd ap Gwilym and the European Context*, 1989.

William Dunbar • **Edition** • *William Dunbar: Poems*, ed. James Kinsley, 1958.

Studies • Priscilla Bawcutt, *Dunbar the Maker*, 1992. • Edmund Reiss, *William Dunbar*, 1978. • Florence Ridley, "Studies in Dunbar and Henryson: The Present Situation," *Fifteenth-Century Studies: Recent Essays*, ed. Robert F. Yeager, 1984.

Marie de France • **Translations** • Glyn S. Burgess and Keith Busby, trans., *The Lais of Marie de*

France, 1986. • Robert Hanning and Joan Ferrante, *The Lais of Marie de France*, 1978. [translation used]

Bibliography • Glyn S. Burgess, *Marie de France: An Analytical Bibliography*, 1977; suppl. no. 1, 1986.

Studies • Margaret M. Boland, *Architectural Structure in the Lais of Marie de France*, 1995. • Glyn S. Burgess, *The Lais of Marie de France: Text and Context*, 1987. • Paula M. Clifford, *Marie de France, Lais*, 1982. • Emanuel J. Mickel, *Marie de France*, 1974.

Judith • **Edition** • *Judith*, ed. B. J. Timmer, 1966.

Translation • S. A. J. Bradley, trans., *Anglo-Saxon Poetry*, 1982.

Studies • Karma Lochrie, "Gender, Sexual Violence, and the Politics of War in the Old English *Judith*," *Class and Gender in Early English Literature*, eds. Britton J. Harwood and Gillian Overing, 1994. • Helen Damico, "The Valkyrie Reflex in Old English Literature," *New Readings on Women in Old English Literature*, eds. Helen Damico and Alexandra Hennessey Olsen.

Second Play of the Shepherds • **Editions** • Peter Happ, *English Mystery Plays: A Selection*, 1975. [edition used] • David Bevington, ed., *Medieval Drama*, 1975. • Martin Stevens and A. C. Cawley, eds., *The Townley Plays*, 2 vols., 1994.

Bibliography • Sidney E. Berger, ed., *Medieval English Drama: An Annotated Bibliography of Recent Criticism*, 1990.

Studies and Guides • Richard Beadle, ed., *The Cambridge Companion to Medieval English Theatre*, 1994. • Richard K. Emmerson, ed., and V. A. Kolve, intro., *Approaches to Teaching Medieval English Drama*, 1990. • O. B. Hardison Jr., *Christian Rite and Christian Drama in the Middle Ages*, 1965. • V. A. Kolve, *The Play Called Corpus Christi*, 1966. • Martin Stevens, *Four Middle English Mystery Cycles: Textual, Contextual, and Critical Interpretations*, 1987.

Sir Thomas Malory • **Editions** • Thomas Malory, *Le Morte d'Arthur*, ed. Janet Cowen, intro. John Lawlor, 2 vols., 1969. • Thomas Malory, *King Arthur and his Knights: Selected Tales*, ed. E. Vinaver, 1975. [edition used] • *The Works of Sir Thomas Malory*, ed. Eugene Vinaver, 1977.

Guides and Studies • Elizabeth Archibald and A. S. G. Edwards, *A Companion to Malory*,

1996. • Larry D. Benson, *Malory's Morte Darthur*, 1976. • Burt Dillon, *A Malory Handbook*, 1978. • P. J. C. Field, *The Life and Times of Sir Thomas Malory*, 1993. • Beverly Kennedy, *Knighthood in the Morte d'Arthur*, 1985. • Terence McCarthy, *An Introduction to Malory*, rev. ed., 1991. • William Matthews, *The Ill-Framed Knight: A Skeptical Inquiry into the Identity of Sir Thomas Malory*, 1966. • Charles Moorman, *The Book of Kyng Arthur: The Unity of Malory's Morte Darthur*, 1965. • Felicity Riddy, *Sir Thomas Malory*, 1987. • Toshiyuki Takamiya and Derek Brewer, eds., *Aspects of Malory*, 1981. • Muriel Whitaker, *Arthur's Kingdom of Adventure: The World of Malory's* Morte Darthur, 1984.

Middle English Lyrics • **Editions** • Maxwell S. Luria and Richard L. Hoffman, eds., *Middle English Lyrics*, 1974. [Norton Critical Edition; edition used] • R. T. Davies, *Medieval English Lyrics: A Critical Anthology*, 1963. [edition used] • Theodore Silverstein, ed., *English Lyrics Before 1500*, 1971. • Celia Sisam and Kenneth Sisam, eds., *The Oxford Book of Medieval English Verse*, 1970.

Translations • Frederick Goldin, trans., *The Lyrics of the Troubadours and Trouvères: Original Texts, with Translations and Introductions*, 1973. • James J. Wilhelm, *Medieval Song: An Anthology of Hymns and Lyrics*, 1971.

Studies • Peter Dronke, *The Medieval Lyric*, 3rd ed., 1996. • John F. Plummer, ed., *Vox Feminae: Studies in Medieval Woman's Song*, 1981. • Douglas Gray, *Themes and Images in the Medieval English Religious Lyric*, 1972. • Rosemary Woolf, *The English Religious Lyric in the Middle Ages*, 1968.

Sir Gawain and the Green Knight • **Translations** • Marie Borroff, trans., *Sir Gawain and the Green Knight*, 1967. [translation used] • W. R. J. Barron, ed. and trans., *Sir Gawain and the Green Knight*, 1974.

Bibliography • Malcolm Andrew, *The Gawain-Poet: An Annotated Bibliography, 1839–1977*, 1979.

Guides and Studies • Ross Arthur, *Medieval Sign Theory and Sir Gawain and the Green Knight*, 1987. • Larry D. Benson, *Art and Tradition in Sir Gawain and the Green Knight*, 1965. • Robert J. Blanch et al., eds., *Text and Matter: New Critical Perspectives of the Pearl-Poet*, 1991. • Robert J. Blanch and Julian Wasserman, *From Pearl to Gawain: Forme to*

Fynisment, 1995. • Marie Borroff, Sir Gawain and the Green Knight: A Stylistic and Metrical Study, 1973. • Derek Brewer and Jonathan Gibson, eds., A Companion to the Gawain-Poet, 1997. • Elisabeth Brewer, comp., Sir Gawain and the Green Knight: Sources and Analogues, 1992. • John Burrow, A Reading of Sir Gawain and the Green Knight, 1966. • Wendy Clein, Concepts of Chivalry in Sir Gawain and the Green Knight, 1987. • Lynn Staley Johnson, The Voice of the Gawain-Poet, 1984. • Sandra Pierson Prior, The Pearl Poet Revisited, 1994. • Ad Putter, An Introduction to the Gawain-Poet, 1996. • Allen Shoaf, The Poem as Green Girdle: Commercium in Sir Gawain and the Green Knight, 1984. • A. C. Spearing, The Gawain-Poet: a Critical Study, 1970. • Meg Stainsby, Sir Gawain and the Green Knight: An Annotated Bibliography, 1978–1989, 1992.

Taliesin • Translation • Ifor and J. Caerwyn Williams, trans., The Poems of Taliesin, 1968.

Study • J. E. Caerwyn Williams, The Poets of the Welsh Princes, 1994.

The Wanderer • Editions • T. P. Dunning and A. J. Bliss, eds., The Wanderer, 1969. • Anne L. Klinck, The Old English Elegies: A Critical Edition and Genre Study, 1992.

Translation • Kevin Crossley-Holland, ed., The Anglo-Saxon World: An Anthology, 1983.

Study • Martin Green, ed., The Old English Elegies: New Essays in Criticism and Research, 1983.

The Wife's Lament • Edition • Anne L. Klinck, The Old English Elegies: A Critical Edition and Genre Study, 1992.

Translation • Kevin Crossley-Holland, ed., The Anglo-Saxon World: An Anthology, 1983.

Studies • Helen T. Bennett, "Exile and the Semiosis of Gender in Old English Elegies," Class and Gender in Early English Literature, eds. Britton J. Harwood and Gillian Overing, 1994. • Barrie Ruth Strauss, "Women's Words as Weapons in The Wife's Lament," Old English Shorter Poems, ed. Katharine O'Brien O'Keeffe, 1994.

Wulf and Eadwacer • Edition • Anne L. Klinck, The Old English Elegies: A Critical Edition and Genre Study, 1992.

Translation • Kevin Crossley-Holland, ed., The Anglo-Saxon World: An Anthology, 1983.

Studies • Helen T. Bennett, "Exile and the Semiosis of Gender in Old English Elegies" Class and Gender in Early English Literature, ed. Britton J. Harwood and Gillian Overing, 1994. • Pat Bellanoff, "Women's Songs, Women's Language: Wulf and Eadwacer and The Wife's Lament," New Readings on Women in Old English Literature, eds. Helen Damico and Alexandra Hennessey Olsen, 1990. • Marilyn Desmond, "The Voice of Exile: Feminist Literary History and the Anonymous Anglo-Saxon Elegy," Critical Inquiry, vol. 16, 1990.

The Early Modern Period

Bibliographies • English Literary Renaissance, 1971 to present. • Alfred Harbage, ed., S. Schoenbaum rev., Annals of English Drama, 975–1700, 3 vols. • New Cambridge Bibliography of English Literature, 600–1600, 1969. • S. A. and D. R. Tannenbaum, eds., Elizabethan Bibliographies, 10 vols., 1967.

Guides to Research • A. R. Braunmuller and Michael Hattaway, The Cambridge Companion to English Renaissance Drama, 1990. • Douglas Bush, English Literature in the Earlier Seventeenth Century 1600–1660, 1962. • C. S. Lewis, English Literature in the Sixteenth Century, 1954. • A. W. Ward and A. R. Waller,

eds., The Cambridge History of English Literature, 15 vols., vols. 3–6, 1909.

Drama, Poetry, and Prose • David Bevington, Tudor Drama and Politics, 1968. • Rebecca Bushnell, Tragedies of Tyrants, 1990. • Jonathan Dollimore, Radical Tragedy. Religion, Ideology and Power in the Drama of Shakespeare and His Contemporaries, 1985. • Martin Elsky, Authorizing Words: Speech, Writing and Print in the Renaissance, 1989. • Anne Ferry, "The Inward Language": Sonnets of Wyatt, Sidney, Shakespeare and Donne, 1983. • Ernest B. Gilman, Iconoclasm and Poetry in the English Reformation, 1986. • Stephen Greenblatt, Renaissance Self-

Fashioning, 1980. • Thomas M. Greene, *The Light in Troy: Imitation and Discovery in Renaissance Poetry*, 1982. • Andrew Gurr, *Playgoing in Shakespeare's London*, 1987. • Peter Herman, ed., *Rethinking the Henrician Age: Essays on Early Tudor Texts and Contexts*, 1994. • John King, *English Reformation Literature: The Tudor Origins of the Protestant Tradition*, 1982. • Janel Mueller, *The Native Tongue and the Word: Developments in English Prose Style, 1380–1580*, 1984. • Steven Mullaney, *The Place of the Stage: License, Place and Power in Renaissance England*, 1988. • David Norbrook, *Poetry and Politics in the English Renaissance*, 1984. • Stephen Orgel, *The Illusion of Power: Political Theater in the English Renaissance*, 1971. • Patricia Parker, *Inescapable Romance*, 1979. • David Quint, *Epic and Empire*, 1993. • Wayne Rebhorn, *The Emperor of Men's Minds: Literature and the Renaissance Discourse of Rhetoric*, 1995. • Rosemund Tuve, *Elizabethan and Metaphysical Imagery*, 1947.

History, Religion, and Political Thought • Glenn Burgess, *Absolute Monarchy and the Stuart Constitution*, 1996. • Patrick Collinson, *The Elizabethan Puritan Movement*, 1967. • John Guy, *Tudor England*, 1988. • Richard Helgerson, *Forms of Nationhood: The Elizabethan Writing of England*, 1992. • F. J. Levy, *Tudor Historical Thought*, 1967. • Annabel Patterson, *Reading Holinshed's Cronicles*, 1994. • Linda Levy Peck, ed., *The Mental World of the Jacobean Court*, 1991. • Conrad Russell, *The Crisis of Parliaments: English History 1509–1660*, 1971. • Quentin Skinner, *The Foundations of Modern Political Thought*, 2 vols., 1978. • J. P. Sommerville, *Politics and Ideology in England, 1608–1640*, 1986. • D. W. Woolf, *The Idea of History in Early Stuart England*, 1990.

Humanism • Douglas Bush, *The Renaissance and English Humanism*, 1939. • William Kerrigan and Gordon Braden, *The Idea of the Renaissance*, 1989. • Arthur Kinney, *Humanist Poetics*, 1986. • Charles Schmitt and Quentin Skinner, eds., *The Cambridge History of Renaissance Philosophy*, 1988.

Science and Exploration • David Cressy, *Coming Over: Migration and Communication between England and New England in the Seventeenth Century*, 1987. • Stephen Greenblatt, *Marvelous Possessions: The Wonder of the New World*, 1991. • Stephen Greenblatt, ed., *New World Encounters*, 1993. • Jeffrey Knapp, *An Empire Nowhere: England, America, and Literature from Utopia to The Tempest*, 1995. • Thomas Laqueur, *Making Sex: Body and Gender from the Greeks to Freud*, 1990. • Frank Lestrigant, *Mapping the Renaissance World*, 1991. • Wayne Shumaker, *The Occult Sciences in the Renaissance*, 1972. • Nancy G. Siraisi, *Medieval and Early Renaissance Science*, 1990. • Keith Thomas, *Religion and the Decline of Magic*, 1971.

Social Settings and Gender Roles • Susan Dwyer Amussen, *An Ordered Society: Gender and Class in Early Modern England*, 1988. • Elaine V. Beilin, *Redeeming Eve: Women Writers of the English Renaissance*, 1987. • Alan Bray, *Homosexuality in Renaissance England*, 1982. • Anthony Fletcher, *Gender, Sex, and Subordination in England, 1500–1800*, 1995. • Kim F. Hall, *Things of Darkness: Economies of Race and Gender in Early Modern England*, 1995. • Margo Hendricks and Patricia Parker, eds., *Women, "Race" and Writing in the Early Modern Period*, 1994. • Daniel Javitch, *Poetry and Courtliness in Renaissance England*, 1976. • Constance Jordan, *Renaissance Feminism: Literary Texts and Political Models*, 1990. • Peter Laslett, *The World We Have Lost—Further Explored*, 1983. • Barbara Kiefer Lewalski, *Writing Women in Jacobean England*, 1993. • Ian Maclean, *The Renaissance Notion of Woman*, 1980. • Lawrence Manley, *Literature and Culture in Early Modern London*, 1995. • Steve Rappaport, *Worlds within Worlds: Structures of Life in Sixteenth-Century London*, 1989. • Bruce R. Smith, *Homosexual Desire in Shakespeare's England: A Cultural Poetics*, 1991. • Lawrence Stone, *The Family, Sex, and Marriage, 1500–1800*, 1965. • Linda Woodbridge, *Women and the English Renaissance: Literature and the Nature of Womankind, 1540–1640*, 1984.

Perspectives: The Civil War, or the Wars of Three Kingdoms • **Texts** • Thomas Carlyle, ed., *Oliver Cromwell's Letters and Speeches: With Elucidations*, 2 vols., 1904. • Pádraig De Brún, Breandán O Buachalla, and Tomás O Concheanainn, eds., *Nua-Dhuanaire*, vol. 1., 1971. • "John O'Dwyer of the Glenn" in *Irish Mistrelsy or the Bardic Remains of Ireland*, ed. James Hardiman, 2 vols., 1831. • Philip A. Knachel, ed., *Eikon Basilike*, 1966. • John Lilburne, *Englands New Chains Discoverd. The Leveller Tracts, 1647–1653*, ed. Godfrey Davies Haller, 1944. • W. Dunn Macray, ed., *History of the Rebellion and Civil Wars in England: Begun in the Year 1641 by Edward, Earl of Clarendon*, 1888. • "The Petition of the Gentlewomen and Tradesmen's Wives" in *English Women's Voices 1540–1700*, ed. Charlotte F. Otten, 1992.

Criticism and History • Martyn Bennett, *The Civil Wars in Britain and Ireland: 1638–1651*, 1997. • Martyn Bennett, *The English Civil War: 1640–1649*, 1995. • Christopher Hill, *The World Turned Upside Down: Radical Ideas During the English Revolution*, 1972. • Jane Ohlmeyer, ed., *Ireland from Independence to Occupation, 1641–1660*, 1995. • Nigel Smith, *Literature and Revolution in England, 1640–1660*, 1994. • Keith Thomas, "Women and the Civil War Sects," *Past and Present*, 1958.

Perspectives: Tracts on Women and Gender • **Editions** • Desiderius Erasmus, *A Ryght Frutefull Epistle Devised in Laude and Praise of Matrimony*, trans. Richard Tavernour, 1534. • *Haec Vir: Or, The Womanish Man*, 1620. • *Hic Mulier: Or The Man-Woman*, 1620. • Barbara Kiefer Lewalski, ed., *The Polemics and Poems of Rachel Speght*, 1996. • Randall Martin, *Women Writers in Renaissance England*, 1997. • Charlotte F. Otten, ed., *English Women's Voices, 1540–1700*, 1992. • Barnabe Riche, *My Ladies Looking-Glasse*, 1616. • Simon Shepherd, ed., *The Women's Sharp Revenge: Five Women's Pamphlets from the Renaissance*, 1985. • Esther Soweram, *Ester Hath Hang'd Haman*, 1617. • Rachel Speght, *A Mouzell for Melastomus*, 1617. • Joseph Swetnam, *The Araignment of Lewde, Idle, Froward, and Unconstant Women*, 1615. • Betty Travitsky, ed., *The Paradise of Women: Writings by Englishwomen of the Renaissance*, 1981. • Margaret Tyler, *The Mirrour of Princely Deedes and Knighthood, Book I*, 1578.

Criticism • Elaine Beilin, *Redeeming Eve: Women Writers of the English Renaissance*, 1987. • Ann Rosalind Jones, "Counterattacks on 'the Bayter of Women': Three Pamphleteers of the Early Seventeenth Century," in *The Renaissance Englishwoman in Print*, eds. Anne Hazelcorn and Betty Travitsky, 1990. • Constance Jordan, *Renaissance Feminism: Literary Texts and Political Models*, 1990. • Barbara Kiefer Lewalski, *Writing Women in Jacobean England*, 1993. • R. Valerie Lucas, "Hic Mulier: The Female Transvestite in Early Modern England," *Renaissance and Reformation*, vol. XXIV, no. 1, 1988. • Megan Matchinske, "Legislating 'Middle-Class' Morality in the Marriage Market: Ester Sowernam's, *Ester Hath Hang'd Haman*," *English Literary Renaissance*, vol. 24, no. 1, 1994. • Linda Woodbridge, *Women and the English Renaissance: Literature and the Nature of Womankind, 1540–1620*, 1986.

John Donne • **Editions** • John Carey, ed., *John Donne: Selected Poetry*, 1996. • Helen Gardner, ed., *John Donne: The Divine Poems*, 1952. • Helen Gardner, ed., *John Donne: The Elegies and The Songs and Sonnets*, 1965. • H. J. C. Grierson, ed., *The Poems of John Donne*, 1912. • G. R. Peter and Evelyn Simpson, eds., *Sermons*, 10 vols., 1953–1962. • Neil Rhodes, ed., *Prose Works: Selections*, 1987. • A. J. Smith, ed., *John Donne: The Complete English Poems*, 1971. • Gary A. Stringer, ed., *The Variorum Edition of the Poetry of John Donne*, 1995.

Biography • R. C. Bald, *John Donne: A Life*. 1970. • John Carey, *John Donne: Life, Mind and Art*, 1981. • Izaac Walton, *Life of Dr. John Donne*, ed. G. Saintsbury, 1927. • Frank J. Warnke, *John Donne*, 1987.

Criticism • James S. Baumlin, *John Donne and the Rhetorics of Renaissance Discourse*, 1991. • Harold Bloom, ed., *John Donne and the Seventeenth-Century Metaphysical Poets*, 1986. • Cleanth Brooks, *The Well Wrought Urn*, 1949. • Meg Lotta Brown, *Donne and the Politics of Conscience*, 1995. • Naresh Chandra, *John Donne and Metaphysical Poetry*, 1990. • Denis Flynn, *John Donne and the Ancient Catholic Nobility*, 1995. • T. S. Eliot, *The Varieties of Metaphysical Poetry*, ed. Ronald Schuchard, 1993. • Barbara L. Estrin, *Laura: Uncovering Gender and Genre in Wyatt, Donne, and Marvell*, 1994. • Pierre Legouis, *Donne the Craftsman*, 1928. • Arthur F. Marotti, ed., *Critical Essays on John Donne*, 1994. • Arthur Marotti, *John Donne, a Coterie Poet*, 1986. • Murray Roston, *The Soul of Wit*, 1974. • A. J. Smith, ed., *John Donne: The Critical Heritage*, 1975–1996. • A. J. Smith, ed., *John Donne: Essays in Celebration*, 1972. • Helen Wilcox, Richard Todd, and Alasdair MacDonald, eds., *Sacred and Profane: Secular and Devotional Interplay in Early Modern British Literature*, 1996. • William Zunder, *The Poetry of John Donne: Literature and Culture in the Elizabethan and Jacobean Period*, 1982.

Our Texts • Helen Gardner, ed., *John Donne: The Divine Poems*, 1952. • H. J. C. Grierson, ed., *The Poems of John Donne*, 1912. • G. R. Peter and Evelyn Simpson, eds., *Sermons*, 10 vols., 1953–1962. • J. Sparrow, ed., *Devotions Upon Emergent Occasions*, 1923.

Queen Elizabeth I • **Editions** • Leicester Bradner, ed., *The Poems of Elizabeth I*, 1964. •

Caroline Pemberton, ed., *Queen Elizabeth's Englishings of Boethius, De Consolatione Philosophiae, A.D. 1593*, 1889, repr. 1973.

Biography • Christopher Haigh, *Elizabeth I*, 1988. • Christopher Hibbert, *Elizabeth I: Genius of the Golden Age*, 1991. • Wallace MacCaffrey, *Elizabeth I*, 1993. • J. E. Neale, *Queen Elizabeth I*, 1934. • Maria Perry, *The Word of a Prince: The Life of Elizabeth from Contemporary Documents*, 1990.

Criticism • Marie Axton, *The Queen's Two Bodies: Drama and Elizabethan Succession*, 1977. • Philippa Berry, *Of Chastity and Power: Elizabethan Literature and the Unmarried Queen*, 1989. • Susan Frye, *Elizabeth I: The Competition for Representation*, 1993. • Helen Hackett, *Virgin Mother, Maiden Queen: Elizabeth I and the Cult of the Virgin Mary*, 1995. • Lisa Hopkins, *Queen Elizabeth and Her Court*, 1990. • J. E. Neale, *Elizabeth and Her Parliaments*, 2 vols., 1953 • Frances Yates, *Astraea: The Imperial Theme*, 1973.

George Gascoigne • **Editions** • John Cunliffe, ed., *The Complete Works*, 2 vols., 1907, 1910. • C. T. Prouty, ed., *A Hundreth Sundrie Flowres*, 1942.

Biography • Ronald Johnson, *George Gascoigne*, 1972.

Criticism • E. Jane Hedley, "Allegoria: Gascoigne's Master Trope," *English Literary Renaissance*, vol. 11, 1981. • Richard Helgerson, *Elizabethan Prodigals*, 1976. • Richard C. McCoy, "Gascoigne's 'Poemata Castrata'. The Wages of Courtly Success." *Criticism*, vol. 27, 1985. • C. T. Prouty, *George Gascoigne, Elizabethan Courtier, Soldier, and Poet*, 1942, repr. 1966.

Edmund Spenser • **Editions** • Edwin A. Greenlaw et al., eds., *The Works of Edmund Spenser, a Variorum Edition*, 10 vols., 1932–1949. • A. C. Hamilton, ed., *The Faerie Queene*, 1980. • William Oram et al., eds., *The Yale Edition of the Shorter Poems of Edmund Spenser*, 1989. • Thomas P. Roche, Jr. and C. Patrick O'Donell, eds., *Edmund Spenser: The Faerie Queene*, 1981. • J. C. Smith and E. De Selincourt, eds., *Complete Poetical Works*, 1970.

Biography • Judith H. Anderson, Donald Cheney, and David A. Richardson, eds., *Spenser's Life and the Subject of Biography*, 1996. • Patrick Cheney, *Spenser's Famous Flight: A Renaissance Idea of a Literary Career*, 1993. • Richard Rambuss, *Spenser's Secret Career*, 1993.

Criticism • Paul Alpers, *The Poetry of The Faerie Queene*, 1967. • Harry Berger, *The Allegorical Temper*, 1957. • Harry Berger, *Revisionary Play: Studies in the Spenserian Dynamics*, 1988. • Patricia Coughlan, ed., *Spenser and Ireland: An Interdisciplinary Perspective*, 1989. • Jonathan Goldberg, *Endlesse Worke: Spenser and the Structures of Discourse*, 1981. • Kenneth Gross, *Spenserian Poetics: Idolatry, Iconoclasm, and Magic*, 1985. • John Guillory, *Poetic Authority: Spenser, Milton, and Literary History*, 1983. • A .C. Hamilton, *The Spenser Encyclopedia*, 1990. • John N. King, *Spenser's Poetry and the Reformation Tradition*, 1990. • Theresa M. Krier, *Gazing on Secret Sights: Spenser, Classical Imitation, and the Decorums of Vision*, 1990. • Isabel G. MacCaffrey, *Spenser's Allegory: The Anatomy of the Imagination*, 1976. • David Lee Miller, *The Poem's Two Bodies: The Poetics of the 1590 Faerie Queene*, 1988. • James Nohrnberg, *The Analogy of The Faerie Queene*, 1976. • Thomas P. Roche, Jr., *The Kindly Flame: A Study of the Third and Fourth Books of Spenser's Faerie Queene*, 1964. • John Rooks, *Love's Courtly Ethic in The Faerie Queene: From Garden to Wilderness*, 1992. • David R. Shore, *Spenser and the Poetics of Pastoral*, 1985. • Kathleen Williams, *Spenser's World of Glass: A Reading of The Faerie Queene*, 1966.

George Herbert • **Editions** • Mario Di Cesare, ed., *George Herbert and the Seventeenth-Century Religious Poets*, 1978. • F. E. Hutchinson, ed., *The Works of George Herbert*, 1941. • C. A. Patrides, ed., *The English Poems of George Herbert*, 1974.

Biography • Amy M. Charles, *Life of George Herbert*, 1977. • Stanley Stewart, *George Herbert*, 1986.

Criticism • Stanley Fish, *The Living Temple: George Herbert and Catechizing*, 1978. • Barbara Leah Harman, *Costly Monuments: Representations of the Self in George Herbert's Poetry*, 1982. • Seamus Heaney, *The Redress of Poetry*, 1990. • Christopher Hodgkins, *Authority, Church, and Society in George Herbert: Return to the Middle Way*, 1993 • C. A. Patrides, ed., *George Herbert: The Critical Heritage*, 1983. • Terry Sherwood, *Herbert's Prayerful Art*, 1989. • Marion White Singleton, *God's Courtier: Configuring a Different Grace in George Herbert's Temple*, 1987. • J. H. Summers, *George Herbert: His Religion and Art*, 1954. • Rosemond Tuve, *A Reading of George Herbert*, 1952. • Helen Vendler, *The Poetry of George Herbert*, 1975.

Mary Herbert, Countess of Pembroke • *Editions* • J. C. A. Rathmell, *The Psalms of Sir Philip Sidney and the Countess of Pembroke*, 1963. • G. F. Waller, *Poems, etc.*, 1977.

Biography • Margaret P. Hannay, *Philip's Phoenix*, 1990.

Criticism • Anne M. Haselkorn and Betty Travitsky, eds., *The Renaissance Englishwoman in Print: Counterbalancing the Canon*, 1990. • Mary Ellen Lamb, *Gender and Authorship in the Sidney Circle*, 1990. • Gary Waller, *Mary Sidney, Countess of Pembroke: A Critical Study of Her Writings and Literary Milieu*, 1979.

Robert Herrick • *Editions* • L. C. Martin, ed., *Poetical Works*, 1956. • J. Max Patrick, ed., *Complete Poetry*, 1963.

Biography • Roger B. Rollin, *Robert Herrick*, 1966. • George Walton Scott, *Robert Herrick*, 1974.

Criticism • Robert Deming, *Ceremony and Art*, 1974. • A. Leigh Deneef, *"This Poetick Liturgy": Robert Herrick's Ceremonial Mode*, 1974. • Leah Marcus, *The Politics of Mirth: Jonson, Herrick, Milton, Marvell, and the Defense of Old Holiday Pastimes*, 1986. • Roger B. Rollin and J. Max Patrick, eds., *"Trust To Good Verses": Herrick Tercentenary Essays*, 1978. • L. E. Semler, "Robert Herrick, the Human Figure, and the English Mannerist Aesthetic," *Studies in English Literature*, vol. 35, no. 1 (Winter), 1995.

Henry Howard, Earl of Surrey • *Editions* • Emrys Jones, ed., *Henry Howard, Earl of Surrey: Poems*, 1964.

Biography • William Sessions, *Henry Howard, Earl of Surrey*, 1986.

Criticism • Leonard Forster, *The Icy Fire: Five Studies in European Petrarchanism*, 1969. • Susanne Woods, *Natural Emphasis: English Versification from Chaucer to Dryden*, 1984, c1985.

Ben Jonson • *Editions* • Robert Adams, ed., *Ben Jonson's Plays and Masques*, 1979. • Ian Donaldson, ed., *Ben Jonson*, 1985. • C. H. Herford, Percy Simpson, and Evelyn Simpson, eds., *The Works of Ben Jonson*, 11 vols., 1925–1952. • Stephen Orgel, ed., *Complete Masques*, 1969. • Helen Ostovich, ed., *Jonson, Four Comedies*, 1997.

Biography • David Riggs, *Ben Jonson: A Life*, 1989. • George E. Rowe, *Distinguishing Jonson*, 1988.

Criticism • Richard Burt, *Licensed by Authority: Ben Jonson and the Discourses of Censorship*, 1993. • Ian Donaldson, *The World Upside Down*, 1970. • Jonathan Haynes, *The Social Relations of Jonson's Theater*, 1992. • Richard Helgerson, *Self-Crowned Laureates*, 1983. • James Hirsh, ed., *New Perspectives on Ben Jonson*, 1997. • G. B. Jackson, *Vision and Judgment in Ben Jonson's Drama*, 1968. • Alexander Leggatt, *Ben Jonson, His Vision and His Art*, 1981. • Katharine Eisaman Maus, *Ben Jonson and the Roman Frame of Mind*, 1984. • David C. McPherson, *Shakespeare, Jonson and the Myth of Venice*, 1990. • Rosalind Miles, *Ben Jonson, His Craft and Art*, 1990. • Stephen Orgel, *The Jonsonian Masque*, 1965. • Stephen Orgel and Roy Strong, *Inigo Jones: The Theatre of the Stuart Court*, 1973. • E. B. Patridge, *The Broken Compass*, 1958. • William W. E. Slights, *Ben Jonson and the Art of Secrecy*, 1994. John Gordon Sweeney, *Jonson and the Psychology of the Public Theater*, 1985. • Robert N. Watson, *Ben Jonson's Parodic Strategy*, 1987. • Don E. Wayne, *Penshurst: The Semiotics of Place and the Poetics of History*, 1984.

Our Text • C. H. Herford, Percy Simpson, and Eveyln Simpson, eds., *The Works of Ben Jonson*, 11 vols., 1925–1952.

Aemilia Lanyer • *Editions* • A. L. Rowse, ed., *The Poems of Shakespeare's Dark Lady: Salve Deus Rex Judaeorum*, 1979. • Susanne Woods, ed., *The Poems of Aemilia Lanyer: Salve Deus Rex Judaeorum*, 1993.

Criticism • Barbara Kiefer Lewalski, *Writing Women in Jacobean England*, 1993. • Lisa Schnell, "'So Great a Diffrence Is There in Degree': Aemilia Lanyer and the Aims of Feminist Criticism," *Modern Language Quarterly*, vol. 57, no. 1, 1996.

Richard Lovelace • *Editions* • C. H. Wilkinson, ed., *The Poems of Richard Lovelace*, 1925.

Biography • Manfred Weidhorn, *Richard Lovelace*, 1970.

Criticism • Raymond A. Anselment, "'Stone Walls' and 'Iron Bars': Richard Lovelace and the Conventions of Seventeenth-Century Prison Literature," *Renaissance and Reformation*, vol. 17, no. 1 (Winter), 1993. • Cyril Hughes Hartmann, *The Cavalier Spirit and Its Influence on the Life and Work of Richard*

Lovelace, 1970. • Earl Miner, *The Cavalier Mode from Jonson to Cotton*, 1971. • Sharon Cadman Seelig, "My Curious Hand or Eye: The Wit of Richard Lovelace," *The Wit of Seventeenth-Century Poetry*, eds. Claude J. Summers and Ted-Larry Pebworth, 1995. • Claude J. Summers and Ted-Larry Pebworth, eds., *Classic and Cavalier: Essays on Jonson and the Sons of Ben*, 1982. • Geoffrey Walton, "The Cavalier Poets," *The New Pelican Guide to English Literature III: From Donne to Marvell*, ed. Boris Ford, 1982.

Our Text • C. H. Wilkinson, ed., *The Poems of Richard Lovelace*, 1925.

Andrew Marvell • **Editions** • Elizabeth Story Donno, ed., *The Complete Poems*, 1985. • Frank Kermode and Keith Walker, eds., *Poems. Selections*, 1994. • M. Margoliouth, ed., *Poems and Letters*, 1927, rev. Pierre Legouis and E. E. Duncan-Jones, 1971.

Biography • John Dixon Hunt, *Andrew Marvell: His Life and Writings*, 1978. • Patsy Griffin, *The Modest Ambition of Andrew Marvell: A Study of Marvell and His Relation to Lovelace, Fairfax, Cromwell, and Milton*, 1995. • Thomas Wheeler, *Andrew Marvell Revisited*, 1996.

Criticism • Philip Brockbank, *Approaches to Marvell*, ed. C. A. Patrides, 1978. • Warren L. Chernaik, *The Poet's Time: Politics and Religion in the Work of Andrew Marvell*, 1983. • Rosalie Colie, *My Echoing Song*, 1970. • Conal Condren and A. D. Cousins, eds., *The Political Identity of Andrew Marvell*, 1990. • Patrick Cullen, *Spenser, Marvell, and Renaissance Pastoral*, 1970. • E. S. Donno, ed., *Andrew Marvell: The Critical Heritage*, 1978. • Annabel Patterson, *Marvell and the Civic Crown*, 1978. • Allan Pritchard, "Marvell's 'The Garden': A Restoration Poem?" *Studies in English Literature*, vol. 23, no. 3 (Summer), 1983. • Robert Wilcher, *Andrew Marvell*, 1985.

Our Text • M. Margoliouth, ed., *Poems and Letters*, 1927.

Christopher Marlowe • **Editions** • David Bevington and Eric Rasmussen, eds., *Doctor Faustus A-and B-Texts (1604, 1616): Christopher Marlowe and his Collaborator and Revisers*, 1993. • Fredson Bowers, *The Complete Works of Christopher Marlowe*, 2 vols., 1981. • Stephen Orgel, *The Complete Poems and Translations of Christopher Marlowe*, 1971.

Biography • John Bakeless, *The Tragicall History of Christopher Marlowe*, 2 vols., 1942. • Charles Nicholl, *The Reckoning: The Murder of Christopher Marlowe*, 1992.

Criticism • C. L. Barber, *Creating Elizabethan Tragedy: The Theater of Marlowe and Kyd*, 1988. • Douglas Cole, *Suffering and Evil in the Plays of Christopher Marlowe*, 1962. • Roma Gill, *The Plays of Christopher Marlowe*, 1971. • Darryll Grantley and Peter Roberts, eds., *Christopher Marlowe and English Renaissance Culture*, 1996. • Clark Hulse, *Metamorphic Verse: The Elizabethan Minor Epic*, 1981. • William Keach, *Elizabethan Erotic Narratives*, 1977. • Harry Levin, *The Overreacher: A Study of Christopher Marlowe*, 1952. • Simon Shepherd, *Marlowe and the Politics of Elizabethan Theater*, 1986. • Vivien Thomas and William Tydeman, eds., *Christopher Marlowe: The Plays and Their Sources*, 1994.

John Milton • **Editions** • John Carey and Alastair Fowler, eds., *The Poems of John Milton*, 1968. • Alastair Fowler, ed., *John Milton: Paradise Lost*, 1968. • Merritt Y. Hughes, ed., *Complete Poetry and Major Prose*, 1957. • C. A. Patrides, ed., *John Milton: Selected Prose*, 1985. • F. A. Patterson et al., eds., *The Works of John Milton*, 1931–1938. • Don M. Wolfe, ed., *The Complete Prose Works of John Milton*, 1953–1982.

Biography • Douglas Bush, *John Milton*, 1964. • Joseph M. French, *The Life Records of John Milton*, 1949–1958. • W. R. Parker, *Milton: A Biography*, 1968. • A. N. Wilson, *The Life of John Milton*, 1983.

Criticism • Arthur Barker, *Milton and the Puritan Dilemma, 1641–1660*, 1942. • Joan S. Bennett, *Reviving Liberty: Radical Christian Humanism in Milton's Great Poems*, 1989. • Lana Cable, *Carnal Rhetoric: Milton's Iconoclasm and the Poetics of Desire*, 1995. • Dennis Danielson, ed., *The Cambridge Companion to Milton*, 1989. • Mario Di Cesare, ed., *Milton in Italy*, 1991. • William Empson, *Milton's God*, 1965. • Stanley Fish, *Surprised by Sin: The Argument of Paradise Lost*, 1971. • Christopher Hill, *Milton and the English Revolution*, 1977. • Frank Kermode, *The Living Milton*, 1960. • Barbara K. Lewalski, *Paradise Lost and the Rhetoric of Literary Forms*, 1985. • C. S. Lewis, *A Preface to Paradise Lost*, 1942. • David Lowenstein and James Grantham Turner, *Politics, Poetics, and Hermeneutics in Milton's Prose*, 1990. • Kristin McColgan and Charles Durham, eds., *Arenas of Conflict: Milton and the Unfettered Mind*, 1996. • Marjorie Nicolson, *John Milton: A Reader's Guide to His Poetry*, 1963. • Mary Nyquist and Margaret Ferguson, eds., *Remembering Milton: Essays on the Texts and Traditions*, 1988. • W. R. Parker, *Milton's Debt to Greek Tragedy in* Samson Agonistes, 1937. • Annabel Patterson, ed., *John Milton*, 1992. • Maureen Quilligan, *Milton's Spenser: The Politics of Reading*, 1983. • Mary Ann Radzinowicz, *Toward* Samson Agonistes, 1978. • B. Rajan, Paradise Lost *and the Seventeenth-Century Reader*, 1962. • John Rogers, *The Matter of Revolution: Science, Poetry and Politics in the Age of Milton*, 1996. • John P. Rumrich, *Milton Unbound: Controversy and Reinterpretation*, 1996. • John T. Shawcross, *John Milton: The Self and the World*, 1993. • John Steadman, *Epic and Tragic Structure in* Paradise Lost, 1976. • Paul Stevens, *Imagination and the Presence of Shakespeare in* Paradise Lost, 1985. • Joseph Summers, *The Muse's Method: An Introduction to* Paradise Lost, 1962. • Joseph Wittreich, *Interpreting* Samson Agonistes, 1986.

Our Text • Merrit Y. Hughes, ed., *Complete Poetry and Major Prose*, 1957.

Annotations Based On • John Carey and Alastair Fowler, eds., *The Poems of John Milton*, 1968. • Alastair Fowler, ed., *John Milton: Paradise Lost*, 1968.

Katherine Philips • **Editions** • George Saintsbury, ed., *Minor Poets of the Caroline Period*, 1905. • Patrick Thomas, ed., *The Collected Works of Katherine Philips: The Matchless Orinda*, 1993.

Biography • Philip Webster Souers, *The Matchless Orinda*, 1931. • Patrick Thomas, *Katherine Philips (Orinda)*, 1988.

Criticism • Harriette Andreadis, "The Sapphic-Platonics of Katherine Philips, 1632–1664," *Signs*, vol. 15, no. 1 (Autumn), 1989. • Celia A. Easton, "Excusing the Breach of Nature's Laws: The Discourse of Denial and Disguise in Katherine Philips' Friendship Poetry," *Restoration Studies in English Literary Culture, 1660–1700*, vol. 14, no. 1 (Spring), 1990. • Elizabeth Hageman, "Katherine Philips: The Matchless Orinda," in Katharina M. Wilson, ed., *Women Writers of the Renaissance and Reformation*, 1987. • Claudia A. Limbert, "The Poetry of Katherine Philips: Holographs, Manuscripts, and Early Printed Texts," *Philological Quarterly*, vol. 70, no. 2 (Spring), 1991. • Dorothy Mermin, "Women

Becoming Poets: Katherine Philips, Aphra Behn, Anne Finch," *English Literary History*, vol. 57, no. 2 (Summer), 1990. • Ellen Moody, "Orinda, Rosania, Lucasia et Aliae: Towards a New Edition of the Works of Katherine Philips," *Philological Quarterly*, vol. 66, no. 3 (Summer), 1987. • Arlene Stiebel, "Subversive Sexuality: Masking the Erotic in Poems by Katherine Philips and Aphra Behn," *Renaissance Discourses of Desire*, eds. Claude J. Summers and Ted Larry Pebworth, 1993.

Our Text • Katherine Philips, *Poems by the Most Deservedly Admired Mrs. Katherine Philips The Matchless Orinda*, 1669.

Sir Walter Raleigh • **Editions** • A. M. C. Latham, ed., *Poems*, 1950. • William Oldys and Thomas Birch, eds., *The Works of Sir Walter Raleigh*, 8 vols., 1829, repr. 1968.

Biography • Willard Wallace, *Sir Walter Raleigh*, 1959.

Criticism • Philip Edwards, *Sir Walter Ralegh*, 1953, repr. 1976. • Stephen J. Greenblatt, *Sir Walter Ralegh: The Renaissance Man and His Roles*, 1973. • David B. Quinn, *Ralegh and the British Empire*, 1947, repr. 1962. • E. A. Strathmann, *Sir Walter Ralegh: A Study in Elizabethan Skepticism*, 1951.

William Shakespeare, Othello • **Editions** • David Bevington, ed., *The Complete Works of Shakespeare*, 1992. • Alvin Kernan, ed., *The Tragedy of Othello, the Moor of Venice*, 1965. • Norman Sanders, *Othello*, 1984. • Alice Walker and John Dover Wilson, eds., *Othello*, 1969.

Criticism • Jane Adamson, Othello *as Tragedy: Some Problems of Judgment and Feeling*, 1980. • James R. Aubrey, "Race and the Spectacle of the Monstrous in *Othello*," *Clio*, vol. 22, no. 3 (Spring), 1993. • John Bayley, "Love and Identity," *The Characters of Love: A Study in the Literature of Personality*, 1960. • Anthony Gerard Barthelemy, ed., *Critical Essays on Shakespeare's Othello*, 1994. • Lynda E. Boose, "Othello's Handkerchief: 'The Recognizance and Pledge of Love'," *English Literary Renaissance*, vol. 5, 1975. • A. C. Bradley, "*Othello*," in *Shakespearean Tragedy*, 1904. • Stanley Cavell, "Literature as Knowledge of the Outsider," *The Claim of Reason: Wittgenstein, Scepticism, Morality and Tragedy*, 1979. • Helen Gardner, "The Noble Moor," *Proceedings of the British Academy*, vol. 41, 1956 (for 1955). •

Harley Granville-Barker, "Preface to *Othello*," *Prefaces to Shakespeare*, vol. II, 1946–1947. • Stephen Greenblatt, "The Improvisation of Power," *Renaissance Self-Fashioning*, 1980. • Kim Hall, "Beauty and the Beast of Whiteness: Teaching Race and Gender," *Shakespeare Quarterly*, vol. 47, no. 4 (Winter), 1996. • Margo Hendricks and Patricia Parker, eds., *Women, "Race," and Writing in the Early Modern Period*, 1994. • Eldred Jones, *Othello's Countrymen: The African in English Renaissance Drama*, 1965. • Carol Thomas Neely, "Women and Men in *Othello*: 'What Should Such a Fool / Do With So Good a Woman?'" in *The Woman's Part: Feminist Criticism of Shakespeare*, eds. Carolyn Ruth Swift Lenz, Gayle Greene, and Carol Thomas Neely, 1980. • Martin Orkin, "*Othello* and the 'Plain Face' of Racism," *Shakespeare Quarterly*, vol. 38, 1987. • Marvin Rosenberg, *The Masks of Othello: The Search for the Identity of Othello, Iago and Desdemona by Three Centuries of Actors and Critics*, 1961. • Virginia Mason Vaughan, *Othello: A Contextual History*, 1994.

Our Text • David Bevington, ed., *The Complete Works of Shakespeare*, 1992.

Othello in Context: Ethnography in the Literature of Travel and Colonization • *Editions* • Edward Arber, ed., *The First Three English Books on America*, 1885, repr. 1971. • Richard Eden, *The Decades of the New World ... Written in ... Latin ... by Peter Martyr*, 1555. • Robert Brown, ed., *The History and Description of Africa ... Written by Al-Hassan Ibn-Mohammed Al Wezaz Al-Fasi ... Done into English in the Year 1600, by John Pory*, 3 vols., 1896. • Henry Morley, ed., *Ireland Under Elizabeth and James the First, Described by Edmund Spenser, Sir John Davies and Fynes Moryson*, 1890. • Andrew Hadfield and Willy Maley, eds., *A View of the State of Ireland: From the First Printed Edition (1633)*, 1997. • Pliny the younger, *The History of the World. Commonly Called the Naturall Historie of C. Plinius Secundus. Translated into English by Philemon Holland*, 1601. • Philip L. Barbour, ed., *The Complete Works of Captain John Smith*, 1986.

Criticism • Emily C. Bartels, "Making More of the Moor: Aaron, Othello, and Renaissance Refashioning of Race," *Shakespeare Quarterly*, vol. 41, no. 4 (Winter), 1990. • Rosalind R. Johnson, "The African Presence in Shakespearean Drama: Parallels Between Othello and the Historical Leo Africanus," *Journal of African Civilizations*, vol. 7, no. 2, 1985. • Eldred D. Jones, *The Elizabethan Image of Africa*, 1971.

Sir Philip Sidney • *Editions* • Katherine Duncan-Jones, ed., *The Countess of Pembroke's Arcadia (The Old Arcadia)*, 1985. • Katherine Duncan-Jones and Jan van Dorsten, eds., *Miscellaneous Prose of Sir Philip Sidney*, 1973. • Maurice Evans, ed., *The Countess of Pembroke's Arcadia*, 1977. • Albert Feuillerat, ed., *The Complete Works*, 4 vols., 1922–1926. • Robert Kimbrough, ed., *Sir Philip Sidney: Selected Prose and Poetry*, 1983. • William Ringler, ed., *Poetry*, 1962. • Jean Robertson, *The Countess of Pembroke's Arcadia (The Old Arcadia)*, 1973. • J. A Van Dorsten, ed., *A Defence of Poetry*, 1966.

Biography • John Buxton, *Sir Philip Sidney and the English Renaissance*, 1964. • Katharine Duncan-Jones, *Sir Philip Sidney, Courtier Poet*, 1991. • A. C. Hamilton, *Sir Philip Sidney: A Study of His Life and Works*, 1977. • James M. Osborn, *Young Philip Sidney, 1572–1577*, 1972.

Criticism • Dorothy Connell, *Sir Philip Sidney: The Maker's Mind*, 1977. • David Kalstone, *Sidney's Poetry: Contexts and Interpretations*, 1965. • Dennis Kay, ed., *Sir Philip Sidney: An Anthology of Modern Criticism*, 1987. • Arthur F. Kinney, ed., *Sidney in Retrospect: Selections from English Literary Renaissance*, 1988. • Jon S. Lawry, *Sidney's Two Arcadias; Pattern and Proceeding*, 1972. • Richard C. McCoy, *Sir Philip Sidney: Rebellion in Arcadia*, 1978. • Gary F. Waller and Michael D. Moore, *Sir Philip Sidney and the Interpretation of Renaissance Culture: A Collection of Critical and Scholarly Essays*, 1984. • Andrew D. Weiner, *Sir Philip Sidney and the Poetics of Protestantism: A Study of Contexts*, 1978.

The Apology in Context: The Art of Poetry • *Editions* • Samuel Daniel, *A Defence of Ryme*, ed. G. B. Harrison, 1966. • George Gascoigne, *The Complete Works*, ed. John Cunliffe, 2 vols., 1907, 1910. • Stephen Gosson, *The School of Abuse*, ed. Edward Arber, 1869. • George Puttenham, *The Arte of English Poesie*, eds. Gladys Dodge Willcock and Alice Walker, 1970.

Criticism • Peter C. Herman, *Squitter-Wits and Muse-Haters: Sidney, Spenser, Milton and Renaissance Antipoetic Sentiment*, 1996.

Isabella Whitney • *Editions* • Michael David Felder, *The Poems of Isabella Whitney: A Critical Edition*.

Criticism • Elaine V. Beilin, "Writing Public Poetry: Humanism and the Woman Writer," *Modern Language Quarterly*, vol. 51, 1990. • Ann Rosalind Jones, "Nets and Bridles: Early Modern Conduct Books and Sixteenth-Century Women's Lyrics," *The Ideology of Conduct: Essays on Literature and the History of Sexuality*, eds. Nancy Armstrong and Leonard Tennenhouse, 1987. • Wendy Wall, "Isabella Whitney and the Female Legacy," *English Literary History*, vol. 58, 1991.

Lady Mary Wroth • *Editions* • R. E. Pritchard, ed., *Poems: A Modernized Edition*, 1996. • Josephine A. Roberts, ed., *The Poems of Lady Mary Wroth*, 1983. • Josephine A. Roberts, ed., *The First Part of the Countess of Montgomery's Urania by Lady Mary Wroth*, 1995. • G. F. Waller, ed., *Pamphilia to Amphilanthus*, 1977.

Biography • Kim Walker, *Women Writers of the English Renaissance*, 1996.

Criticism • Naomi J. Miller, *Changing the Subject: Mary Wroth and the Figurations of Gender in Early Modern England*, 1996. • Naomi J. Miller and Gary Waller, eds., *Reading Mary Wroth: Representing Alternatives in Early Modern England*, 1991. • May Nelson Paulissen, *The Love Sonnets of Lady Mary Wroth: A Critical Introduction*, 1982. • Gary Waller, *The Sidney Family Romance: Mary Wroth, William Herbert, and the Early Modern Construction of Gender*, 1993. • Anne Hazelcorn and Betty Travitsky, eds., *The Renaissance Englishwoman in Print*, 1990.

Sir Thomas Wyatt • *Editions* • Kenneth Muir and Patricia Thomson, *Collected Poems of Sir Thomas Wyatt*, 1693. • Richard Harrier, *The Canon of Sir Thomas Wyatt's Poetry*, 1975.

Biography • Stephen Foley, *Sir Thomas Wyatt*, 1990.

Criticism • Jonathan Crewe, *Trials of Authorship: Anterior Forms and Poetic Reconstruction from Wyatt to Shakespeare*, 1990. • Barbara Estrin, *Laura: Uncovering Gender and Genre in Wyatt, Donne and Marvell*, 1994. • Thomas M. Greene, *The Light in Troy: Imitation and Discovery in Renaissance Poetry*, 1982.

The Restoration and the Eighteenth Century

Bibliographies and Guides to Research • Robin Alston et al., *The Eighteenth-Century Short-Title Catalogue (ESTC)*, online and on CD-ROM. • Margaret M. Duggan, *English Literature and Backgrounds, 1660–1700: A Selective Critical Guide*, 2 vols., 1990. • *The Eighteenth Century: A Current Bibliography for [1925–]*, annual. The bibliographies for 1925–1970 have been reprinted as *English Literature, 1660–1800: A Bibliography of Modern Studies*, 1950–1972. • Waldo Sumner Glock, *Eighteenth-Century English Literary Studies: A Bibliography*, 1984. • Roger D. Lund, *Restoration and Early Eighteenth-Century English Literature, 1660–1740: A Selected Bibliography of Resource Materials*, 1980. • R. D. Spector, *Backgrounds to Restoration and Eighteenth-Century English Literature: An Annotated Bibliographical Guide to Modern Scholarship*, 1989. • *Studies in English Literature*, Annual review of "Recent Studies in the Restoration and Eighteenth Century" (Summer issue), 1961–. • George Watson, *The New Cambridge Bibliography of English Literature*, vol. 2, 1660–1800, 1971.

Online Resources • *Eighteenth-Century Threads and Tapestries*: http://www.sunysb.edu/english/18thcentury/texts.htm • Alan Liu et al., eds., *Voice of the Shuttle: Restoration and Eighteenth Century*: http://humanitas.ucsb.edu/shuttle/eng-18th.html • Jack Lynch, ed., *Eighteenth-Century Resources*: http://www.english.upenn.edu/~jlynch/18th/

Cultural and Intellectual Background • John Brewer, *The Pleasures of the Imagination: English Culture in the Eighteenth Century*, 1997. • James Engell, *The Creative Imagination: Enlightenment to Romanticism*, 1981. • James Engell, *Forming the Critical Mind: Dryden to Coleridge*, 1989. • Northrop Frye, "Towards Defining an Age of Sensibility," *English Literary History*, vol. 23, 1956; repr. in *Backgrounds to Eighteenth-Century Literature*, ed. Kathleen Williams, 1971. • Donald Greene, *The Age of Exuberance: Backgrounds to Eighteenth-Century*

English Literature, 1970. • Jürgen Habermas, The Structural Transformation of the Public Sphere, 1962; trans., 1989. • Jean H. Hagstrum, Sex and Sensibility: Ideal and Erotic Love from Milton to Mozart, 1980. • Tim Harris, Popular Culture in Restoration England, c. 1500–1800, 1995. • Lawrence Lipking, The Ordering of the Arts in Eighteenth-Century England, 1970. • Gerald MacLean, ed., Culture and Society in the Stuart Restoration: Literature, Drama, History, 1995. • C. A. Moore, Backgrounds of English Literature, 1700–1760, 1953. • Ronald Paulson, Breaking and Remaking: Aesthetic Practice in England, 1700–1820, 1989. • Pat Rogers, ed., The Context of English Literature: The Eighteenth Century, 1978. • Pat Rogers, Grub Street: Studies in a Subculture, 1972. • James Sambrook, The Eighteenth Century: The Intellectual and Cultural Context of English Literature, 1700–1789, 2nd ed., 1993. • J. W. Yolton et al., eds., The Blackwell Companion to the Enlightenment, 1991. • Steven N. Zwicker, The Cambridge Companion to English Literature, 1650–1740, 1998.

History, Religion, and Political Thought • Jeremy Black, An Illustrated History of Eighteenth-Century Britain, 1996. • John Brewer, The Sinews of Power: War, Money, and the English State, 1688–1783, 1989. • J. C. D. Clark, English Society, 1688–1832, 1985. • Linda Colley, Britons: Forging the Nation, 1707–1837, 1992. • Peter Earle, The Making of the English Middle Class, 1989. • Tim Harris, Politics Under the Later Stuarts, 1993. • Tim Harris, The Politics of Religion in Restoration England, 1990. • T. W. Heyck, The Peoples of the British Isles, vol. 2, 1688–1870, 1992. • Ronald Hutton, Charles II, 1989. • Ronald Hutton, The Restoration, 1985. • J. P. Kenyon, The Stuart Constitution, 2nd ed., 1986. • Mark Kishlansky, A Monarchy Transformed: Britain 1603–1714, 1996. • Paul Langford, A Polite and Commercial People: England 1727–1783, 1989. • Dorothy Marshall, Eighteenth Century England, 2nd. ed., 1962. • Neil McKendrick, John Brewer, and J. H. Plumb, The Birth of a Consumer Society: The Commercialization of Eighteenth-Century Britain, 1982. • J. H. Plumb, England in the Eighteenth Century, 1972. • J. G. A. Pocock, Politics, Language, and Time: Essays on Political Thought and History, 1989. • J. G. A. Pocock, Virtue, Commerce, and History, 1985. • Roy Porter, English Society in the Eighteenth Century, rev. ed., 1990. • Isabel Rivers, Reason, Grace, and Sentiment:

A Study of the Language of Religion and Ethics in England, 1660–1780, vol. 1, Whichcote to Wesley, 1991. • Richard B. Schwartz, Daily Life in Johnson's London, 1983. • W. A. Speck, Stability and Strife: England, 1714–1760, 1977. • John Spurr, The Restoration Church of England, 1991. • E. P. Thompson, Albion's Fatal Tree: Crime and Society in Eighteenth-Century England, 1976. • E. P. Thompson, Customs in Common, 1991.

Women, Writing, Politics, and Culture • George Ballard, Memoirs of Several Ladies of Great Britain Who Have Been Celebrated for Their Writings or Skill in the Learned Languages, Arts, and Sciences, 1752; ed. Ruth Perry, 1985. • Margaret J. M. Ezell, Writing Women's Literary History, 1993. • Catherine Gallagher, Nobody's Story: The Vanishing Acts of Women Writers in the Marketplace, 1670–1820, 1994. • Isobel Grundy and Susan Wiseman, eds., Women, Writing, and History: 1640–1799, 1992. • Bridget Hill, Eighteenth-Century Women: An Anthology, 1984. • Bridget Hill, Women, Work, and Sexual Politics in Eigtheenth-Century England, 1989. • Sylvia Meyers, The Bluestocking Circle, 1990. • Myra Reynolds, The Learned Lady in England, 1650–1760, 1920. • Mona Scheuermann, Her Bread to Earn: Women, Money, and Society from Defoe to Austen, 1993. • Hilda Smith, Reason's Disciples: Seventeenth-Century English Feminists, 1982. • Susan Staves, Married Women's Separate Property in England, 1660–1833, 1990. • Beth Fawkes Tobin, History, Gender, and Eighteenth-Century Literature, 1994. • Janet Todd, ed., A Dictionary of British and American Women Writers, 1660–1800, 1985. • Janet Todd, The Sign of Angellica: Women, Writing, and Fiction, 1660–1800, 1989. • Katherine Wilson and Frank J. Warnke, eds., Women Writers of the Seventeenth Century, 1989.

General Literature • Martin C. Battestin, The Providence of Wit: Aspects of Form in Augustan Literature and the Arts, 1974. • John Butt and Geoffrey Carnall, English Literature in the Mid-Eighteenth Century, 1979. • James L. Clifford, ed., Eighteenth-Century English Literature: Modern Essays in Criticism, 1959. • Leopold Damrosch Jr., ed., Modern Essays on Eighteenth-Century Literature, 1988. • Bonamy Dobrée, English Literature in the Early Eighteenth Century, 1700–1740, 1959. • Paul Fussell, The Rhetorical World of Augustan Humanism, 1965. • Roger Lonsdale, ed., The Sphere History of

Literature, vol. 4, Dryden to Johnson, rev. ed., 1987. • Felicity Nussbaum and Laura Brown, eds., The New Eighteenth Century: Theory, Politics, English Literature, 1987. • Ronald Paulson, Popular and Polite Art in the Age of Hogarth and Fielding, 1979. • Martin Price, To the Palace of Wisdom: Studies in Order and Energy from Dryden to Blake, 1964. • Isabel Rivers, ed., Books and Their Readers in Eighteenth-Century England, 1982. • John Sitter, Literary Loneliness in Mid-Eighteenth-Century England, 1982. • James Sutherland, English Literature of the Late Seventeenth Century, 1969. • Howard Weinbrot, Britannia's Issue: The Rise of British Literature from Dryden to Ossian, 1993. • Steven N. Zwicker, Lines of Authority: Politics and English Literary Culture, 1649–1689, 1993.

Drama • R. W. Bevis, English Drama: Restoration and Eighteenth Century, 1660–1789, 1988. • J. Douglas Canfield and Deborah C. Payne, eds., Cultural Readings of Restoration and Eighteenth-Century English Theater, 1995. • T. W. Craik et al., eds., The Revels History of Drama in English, vol. 5, 1660–1750. • Pat Gill, Interpreting Ladies: Women, Wit, and Morality in the Restoration Comedy of Manners, 1994. • John T. Harwood, Critics, Values, and Restoration Comedy, 1982. • Robert D. Hume, The Development of English Drama in the Late Seventeenth Century, 1976. • Robert D. Hume, The Rakish Stage: Studies in English Drama, 1660–1800, 1983. • John Loftis, ed., Restoration Drama, 1966. • Earl Miner, ed., Restoration Dramatists, 1966. • Allardyce Nicoll, A History of English Drama, 1660–1900, vols. 1–3 (1660–1800), 1952. • David Roberts, The Ladies: Female Patronage of Restoration Drama, 1660–1700, 1989.

Fiction • Nancy Armstrong, Desire and Domestic Fiction, 1989. • Jerry C. Beasley, English Fiction, 1660–1800: A Guide to Information Sources, 1978. • John Bender, Imagining the Penitentiary, 1987. • Terry Castle, Masquerade and Civilization, 1986. • Leopold Damrosch, God's Plot and Man's Stories, 1985. • Lennard J. Davis, Factual Fictions: The Origins of the English Novel, 1983. • Margaret Anne Doody, The True Story of the Novel, 1996. • J. Paul Hunter, Before Novels, 1990. • Michael McKeon, The Origins of the English Novel, 1660–1740, 1987. • John Richetti, ed., The Cambridge Companion to the Eighteenth-Century Novel, 1996. • John Richetti, Popular Fiction Before Richardson, 1969. • Paul Salzman, English Prose Fiction,

1558–1700: A Critical History, 1985. • Mary Ann Schofield and Cecelia Macheski, Fetter'd or Free? British Women Novelists, 1670–1815, 1986. • Jane Spencer, The Rise of the Woman Novelist, 1986. • Ian Watt, The Rise of the Novel: Studies in Defoe, Richardson, and Fielding, 1957.

Poetry • Carol Barash, English Women's Poetry, 1649–1714: Politics, Community, and Linguistic Authority, 1997. • Margaret Doody, The Daring Muse: Augustan Poetry Reconsidered, 1985. • Germaine Greer et al., eds., Kissing the Rod: An Anthology of Seventeenth-Century Women's Verse, 1988. • Jean Hagstrum, The Sister Arts: The Tradition of Literary Pictorialism and English Poetry from Dryden to Gray, 1958. • Ian Jack, Augustan Satire: Intention and Idiom in English Poetry, 1660–1750, 1952. • Donna Landry, The Muses of Resistance: Laboring-Class Women's Poetry in Britain, 1739–1796, 1990. • Roger Lonsdale, ed., The New Oxford Book of Eighteenth-Century Verse, 1984. • Roger Lonsdale, ed., Eighteenth-Century Women Poets, 1990. • Eric Rothstein, Restoration and Eighteenth-Century Poetry, 1660–1800, 1981. • Patricia Spacks, The Poetry of Vision, 1967. • James Sutherland, A Preface to Eighteenth-Century Poetry, 1948. • Howard Weinbrot, The Formal Strain: Studies in Augustan Imitation and Satire, 1969.

Satire • Ronald Paulson, The Fictions of Satire, 1967. • Claude Rawson, ed., English Satire and the Satiric Tradition, 1984. • Claude Rawson, Order from Confusion Sprung, 1985. • Michael Seidel, Satiric Inheritance: Rabelais to Sterne, 1979.

Letters, Diaries, Autobiography, Biography • Howard Anderson, Philip B. Daghlian, and Irvin Ehrenpreis, eds., The Familiar Letter in the Eighteenth Century, 1966. • William Epstein, Recognizing Biography, 1987. • Felicity Nussbaum, The Autobiographical Subject: Gender and Ideology in Eighteenth-Century England, 1989. • Bruce Redford, The Converse of the Pen: Acts of Intimacy in the Eighteenth-Century Familiar Letter, 1987. • Stuart Sherman, Telling Time: Clocks, Diaries, and English Diurnal Form, 1660–1785, 1996. • Patricia Meyer Spacks, Imagining a Self: Autobiography and Novel in Eighteenth-Century England, 1976. • Richard Wendorf, The Elements of Life: Biography and Portrait Painting in Stuart and Georgian England, 1990.

Perspectives: Mind and God (See also "Cultural and Intellectual Background") • Jonathan

Bennett, *Locke, Berkeley, Hume: Central Themes*, 1971. • James Collins, *The British Empiricists*, 1967. • Peter Gay, ed., *The Enlightenment: A Comprehensive Anthology*, 1973. • John J. Richetti, *Philosophical Writing: Locke, Berkeley, Hume*, 1983. • Keith Thomas, ed., *The British Empricists*, 1992. • Richard S. Westfall, *Science and Religion in Seventeenth-Century England*, 1958. • R. S. Woolhouse, *The Empiricists*, 1988. • John W. Yolton, *Perception and Reality: A History from Descartes to Kant*, 1996. • John W. Yolton, ed., *Philosophy, Religion, and Science in the Seventeenth and Eighteenth Centuries*, 1990.

Perspectives: Reading Papers • Jeremy Black, *The English Press in the Eighteenth Century*, 1986. • Donovan H. Bond and W. Reynolds McLeod, eds., *Newsletters to Newspapers: Eighteenth-Century Journalism*, 1977. • Richmond P. Bond, ed., *Studies in the Early English Periodical*, 1957. • C. L. Carlson, *The First Magazine: A History of* The Gentleman's Magazine, 1938. • J. A. Downie and Thomas N. Corns, eds., *Telling People What to Think: Early Eighteenth-Century Periodicals from* The Review *to* The Rambler, 1993. • Walter Graham, *English Literary Periodicals*, 1930. • Kathryn Shevelow, *Women and Print Culture: The Construction of Femininity in the Early Periodical*, 1989. • James Sutherland, *The Restoration Newspaper and its Development*, 1986. • Katherine K. Weed and Richmond P. Bond, *Studies of British Newspapers and Periodicals from Their Beginning to 1800: A Bibliography*, 1946.

Joseph Addison and Richard Steele • Editions Donald F. Bond, ed., *The Spectator*, 5 vols., 1965. • Donald F. Bond, ed., *The Tatler*, 3 vols., 1987. • Erin Mackie, ed., *The Commerce of Everyday Life: Selections from* The Tatler *and* The Spectator, 1998. • Angus Ross, ed., *Selections from* The Tatler *and* The Spectator, 1988.

Biographies • George A. Aitken, *The Life of Richard Steele*, 2 vols., 1889. • Peter Smithers, *The Life of Joseph Addison*, 1954. • Calhoun Winton, *Captain Steele: The Early Career of Richard Steele*, 1964. • Calhoun Winton, *Sir Richard Steele M.P.: The Later Career*, 1970.

Criticism • Edward A. Bloom and Lillian D. Bloom, eds., *Addison and Steele, the Critical Heritage*, 1980. • Edward A. Bloom, *Joseph Addison's Sociable Animal*, 1971. • Michael G. Ketcham, *Transparent Designs: Reading, Performance and Form in the Spectator Papers*, 1985. •

Erin Mackie, *Market à la Mode: Fashion, Commodity, and Gender in* The Tatler *and* The Spectator, 1997.

Aphra Behn • Editions • Joanna Lipking, ed., *Oroonoko: An Authoritative Text, Historical Backgrounds, Criticism*, 1997. • Janet Todd, ed., *Oronooko,* The Rover, *and other Works*, 1992. • Janet Todd, ed., *The Works of Aphra Behn*, 7 vols., 1992– .

Biography • Janet Todd, *The Secret Life of Aphra Behn*, 1997.

Criticism • Laura Brown, "The Romance of Empire: Oroonoko and the Trade in Slaves," *The New Eighteenth Century*, eds. Felicity Nussbaum and Laura Brown, 1987. • Margaret W. Ferguson, "Juggling the Categories of Race, Class and Gender: Aphra Behn's Oroonoko," *Women's Studies*, vol. 19, 1991. • Catherine Gallagher, "The Author-Monarch and the Royal Slave: Oroonoko and the Blackness of Representation," *Nobody's Story: The Vanishing Acts of Women Writers in the Marketplace, 1670–1820*, 1994. • Heidi Hutner, ed., *Rereading Aphra Behn*, 1993. • Sara Heller Mendelson, *The Mental World of Stuart Women: Three Studies*, 1987. • Mary Ann O'Donnell, *Aphra Behn: An Annotated Bibliography*, 1986. • Janet Todd, ed., *Aphra Behn Studies*, 1996.

George Berkeley • Editions • M. R. Ayers, ed., *Philosophical Works, Including the Works on Vision*, rev. ed., 1980 • A. A. Luce and T. E. Jessop, eds., *The Works of George Berkeley, Bishop of Cloyne*, 9 vols., 1948–1952.

Biography • A. A. Luce, *The Life of George Berkeley, Bishop of Cloyne*, 1949.

Criticism • David Berman, ed., *George Berkeley: Eighteenth-Century Responses*, 2 vols., 1989. • Jonathan Dancy, *Berkeley, an Introduction*, 1987. • A. C. Grayling, *Berkeley: The Central Arguments*, 1986. • K. P. Winkler, *Berkeley: An Interpretation*, 1989.

James Boswell • Editions • R. W. Chapman, ed., *Life of Johnson*, rev. J. D. Fleeman. 1970. • G. B. Hill and L. F. Powell, eds., *Boswell's Life of Johnson*, 6 vols., 1934–1964. • Frederick A. Pottle, et al., eds., *The Yale Editions of the Private Papers of James Boswell*, 1950–. • Frederick A. Pottle, ed., *Boswell's London Journal, 1762–1763*, 1950. • Frederick A. Pottle and Charles H. Bennett, eds., *Boswell's Journal of a Tour to the Hebrides with Samuel Johnson,*

1773, 1963. • John Wain, ed., *The Journals of James Boswell, 1762–1795*, 1991.

Biographies • Frank Brady, *James Boswell, the Later Years, 1769–1795*, 1984. • Mary Hyde, *The Impossible Friendship: Boswell and Mrs. Thrale*, 1972. • Frederick A. Pottle, *James Boswell, the Earlier Years, 1740–1769*, 1985. • Frederick A. Pottle, *The Literary Career of James Boswell*, 1929.

Criticism (See also the listings of criticism on Samuel Johnson). • Hamilton Cochrane, *Boswell's Literary Art: An Annotated Bibliography of Critical Studies*, 1992. • James L. Clifford, ed., *Twentieth Century Interpretations of Boswell's Life of Johnson*, 1970. • Greg Clingham, ed., *New Light on Boswell: Critical and Historical Essays on the Occasion of the Bicentenary of The Life of Johnson*, 1991. • Irma S. Lustig, ed., *Boswell: Citizen of the World, Man of Letters*, 1995. • John A. Vance, ed., *Boswell's Life of Johnson: New Questions, New Answers*, 1995.

Mary, Lady Chudleigh • **Edition** • Margaret J. M. Ezell, ed., *The Poems and Prose of Mary, Lady Chudleigh*, 1993.

Criticism • Carol Barash, "The Native Liberty."

William Cowper • **Editions** • John D. Baird and Charles Ryskamp, eds., *The Poems of William Cowper*, 3 vols., 1980–1995. • James King and Charles Ryskamp, eds., *The Letters and Prose Writings of William Cowper*, 5 vols., 1979–1986. • James Sambrook, ed., *"The Task" and Selected Other Poems*, 1994.

Biography • James King, *William Cowper: A Biography*, 1986. • Charles Ryskamp, *William Cowper of the Inner Temple, Esq.*, 1959.

Criticism • Morris Golden, *In Search of Stability: The Poetry of William Cowper*, 1960. • Vincent Newey, *Cowper's Poetry: A Critical Study and Reassessment*, 1982.

John Dryden • **Editions** • Paul Hammond, *The Poems of John Dryden*, 1995–. • James Kinsley, ed., *The Poems and Fables of John Dryden*, 1962. • H. T. Swedenberg Jr. and Edward Niles Hooker, eds., *Works*, 20 vols., 1961–. • Keith Walker, ed., *John Dryden*, 1987. • George Watson, ed., *"Of Dramatick Poesy" and Other Critical Essays*, 2 vols., 1962.

Biographies • Paul Hammond, *John Dryden: A Literary Life*, 1991. • James Anderson Winn, *John Dryden and His World*, 1987.

Criticism • Reuben Brower, "An Allusion to Europe: Dryden and Poetic Tradition," *English Literary History*, vol. 19, 1952. • David A. Bywaters, *Dryden in Revolutionary England*, 1991. • Phillip Harth, *Contexts of Dryden's Thought*, 1968. • Geoffrey Hill, *The Enemy's Country*, 1991. • David Hopkins, *John Dryden*, 1986. • Robert Hume, *Dryden's Criticism*, 1970. • James and Helen Kinsley, *Dryden: The Critical Heritage*, 1971. • Earl Miner, *Dryden's Poetry*, 1967. • Earl Miner, ed., *John Dryden*, 1972. • H. T. Swedenborg, ed., *Essential Articles for the Study of John Dryden*, 1966. • James A. Winn, ed., *Critical Essays on John Dryden*, 1997. • David Wykes, *A Preface to Dryden*, 1977. • Steven N. Zwicker, *Dryden's Political Poetry: The Typology of King and Nation*, 1972. • Steven N. Zwicker, *Politics and Language in Dryden's Poetry: The Arts of Disguise*, 1984.

John Evelyn • **Editions** • John Bowie, *The Diary of John Evelyn*, 1983. • E. S. de Beer, *The Diary of John Evelyn*, 6 vols., 1955.

Biography • John Bowie, *John Evelyn and His World*, 1981.

Anne Finch, Countess of Winchilsea • **Editions** • Myra Reynolds, ed., *The Poems of Anne, Countess of Winchilsea*, 1903. • Katherine M. Rogers, ed., *Selected Poems of Anne Finch, Countess of Winchilsea*, 1979.

Biography • Barbara McGovern, *Anne Finch and Her Poetry: A Critical Biography*, 1992.

Criticism • Charles H. Hinnant, *The Poetry of Anne Finch*, 1994.

Thomas Gray • **Editions** • Roger Lonsdale, ed., *The Poems of Gray, Collins and Goldsmith*, 1969. • Alastair Macdonald, ed., *An Elegy Wrote in a Country Church Yard*, 1976. • H. W. Starr and J. R. Hendrickson, eds., *The Complete Poems of Thomas Gray: English, Latin and Greek*, 1966. • Paget Toynbee and Leonard Whibley, eds., *The Correspondence of Thomas Gray*, rev. ed., 1971.

Biography • R. W. Ketton-Cremer, *Thomas Gray*, 1955.

Criticism • F. W. Hilles and Harold Bloom, eds., *From Sensibility to Romanticism*, 1965. • James Downey and Ben Jones, eds., *Fearful Joy: Papers from the Thomas Gray Bicentenary Conference*, 1974. • Robert F. Gleckner, *Gray Agonistes: Thomas Gray and Masculine Friendship*, 1997. • Morris Golden, *Thomas Gray*,

1988. • W. B. Hutchings and William Ruddick, eds., *Thomas Gray: Contemporary Essays*, 1993. • Suvir Kaul, *Thomas Gray and Literary Authority: A Study in Ideology and Poetics*, 1992. • Vincent Newey, "The Selving of Thomas Gray," *Centring the Self: Subjectivity, Society, and Reading from Thomas Gray to Thomas Hardy*, 1995. • Herbert W. Starr, *Twentieth-Century Interpretations of Gray's Elegy*, 1968. • Frank A. Vaughan, *Again to the Life of Eternity: William Blake's Illustrations of the Poems of Thomas Gray*, 1995. • Henry Winefield, *The Poet Without a Name: Gray's Elegy and the Problem of History*, 1991.

Eliza Haywood • *Editions* • *The Female Spectator*, 1745–1746. • Gabrielle M. Firmager, ed., The Female Spectator: *Being Selections from Mrs. Eliza Haywood's Periodical, First Published in Monthly Parts (1744–6)*, 1993. • Mary Priestley, The Female Spectator: *Being Selections from Mrs. Eliza Haywood's Periodical*, 1929.

Biography • Mary Anne Schofield, *Eliza Haywood*, 1985.

Criticism • James Hodges, "The Female Spectator: A Courtesy Periodical," *Studies in the Early English Periodical*, ed. Richmond Bond, 1957. • Helene Koon, "Eliza Haywood and The Female Spectator," *Huntington Library Quarterly*, vol. 42, 1978–1979. • Kathryn Shevelow, "Re-Writing the Moral Essay: Eliza Haywood's Female Spectator," *Reader*, vol. 13, 1985.

William Hogarth • *Editions* • Ronald Paulson, ed., *The Analysis of Beauty*, 1998. • Ronald Paulson, ed., *Hogarth's Graphic Works*, 3rd ed., 1989. • Sean Shesgreen, ed., *Engravings by Hogarth*, 1973.

Biographies • Ronald Paulson, *Hogarth*, 3 vols., 1991–1993. • Jenny Uglow, *Hogarth: A Life and a World*, 1997.

Criticism • David Bindman, *Hogarth*, 1981. • David Dabydeen, *Hogarth, Walpole, and Commercial Britain*, 1987. • Ronald Paulson, *The Art of Hogarth*, 1975.

David Hume • *Editions* • Antony Flew, ed., *An Enquiry Concerning Human Understanding*, 1988. • Selby-Bigge and P. H. Nidditch, eds., *Enquiries Concerning Human Understanding and Concerning the Principles of Morals*, 3rd ed., 1975. • Selby-Bigge and P. H. Nidditch, eds., *A Treatise of Human Nature*, 2nd ed., 1978.

Biography • E. E. Mossner, *The Life of David Hume*, 1954.

Criticism • A. J. Ayer, *Hume*, 1980. • John Bricke, *Hume's Philosophy of Mind*, 1980. • V. C. Chappell, ed., *Hume*, 1966. • Jerome Christensen, *Practicing Enlightenment: Hume and the Formation of a Literary Career*, 1987. • Antony Flew, *David Hume, Philosopher of Moral Science*, 1986. • J. C. A. Gaskin, *Hume's Philosophy of Religion*, rev. ed. 1988. • Norman Kemp Smith, *The Philosophy of David Hume*, 1941. • David Fate Norton, ed., *The Cambridge Companion to Hume*, 1993.

Samuel Johnson • *Editions* • Frank Brady and W. K. Wimsatt, eds., *Selected Poetry and Prose*, 1977. • J. D. Fleeman, *A Journey to the Western Islands of Scotland*, 1985. • Donald Greene, ed., *Samuel Johnson*, 1984. • G. B. Hill, ed., *Johnson's Lives of the English Poets*, 3 vols., 1905. • Peter Levi, *A Journey to the Western Islands of Scotland and The Journal of a Tour to the Hebrides*, 1984. • E. L. McAdam Jr. and George Milne, *Johnson's Dictionary: A Modern Selection*, 1963. • E. L. McAdam Jr. et al., eds., *The Yale Edition of the Works of Samuel Johnson*, 14 vols., 1958–. • Anne McDermott, ed., *A Dictionary of the English Language* on CD-ROM [computer file], 1996. • Bruce Redford, ed., *The Letters of Samuel Johnson*, 5 vols., 1992–1994. • Pat Rogers, *Johnson and Boswell in Scotland: A Journey to the Hebrides*, 1993.

Biographies • Walter Jackson Bate, *Samuel Johnson*, 1977. • James Boswell, *Boswell's Life of Johnson*, eds. G. B. Hill and L. F. Powell, 6 vols., 1934–1964. • O. M. Brack Jr. and Robert E. Kelley, *The Early Biographies of Samuel Johnson*, 1974. • James L. Clifford, *Dictionary Johnson: The Middle Years of Samuel Johnson*, 1979. • James L. Clifford, *Young Sam Johnson*, 1955. • Robert DeMaria Jr., *The Life of Samuel Johnson: A Critical Biography*, 1993. • John Hawkins, *The Life of Samuel Johnson, LL.D.*, ed. Bertram Davis, 1961. • G. B. Hill, ed., *Johnsonian Miscellanies*, 2 vols., 1897. • Thomas Kaminski, *The Early Career of Samuel Johnson*, 1987. • John Wain, *Samuel Johnson*, 1974.

Criticism • Walter Jackson Bate, *The Achievement of Samuel Johnson*, 1955. • Harold Bloom, ed., *Modern Critical Views: Dr. Samuel Johnson and James Boswell*, 1986. • James T. Boulton, ed., *Johnson, the Critical Heritage*, 1971. • James L. Clifford and Donald Greene, *Johnsonian Studies, 1887–1950: A Survey and Bibliography*, 1951. • Greg Clingham, *The*

Cambridge Companion to Samuel Johnson, 1997. • Leopold Damrosch, *The Uses of Johnson's Criticism*, 1976. • Philip Davis, *In Mind of Johnson: A Study of Johnson the Rambler*, 1989. • Robert DeMaria Jr., *Johnson's, Dictionary, and the Language of Learning*, 1986. • Robert DeMaria Jr., *Samuel Johnson and the Life of Reading*, 1997. • Robert Folkenflik, *Samuel Johnson, Biographer*, 1978. • Paul Fussell, *Samuel Johnson and the Life of Writing*, 1971. • Donald Greene, *The Politics of Samuel Johnson*, 2nd ed., 1990. • Donald Greene and John A. Vance, *A Bibliography of Johnsonian Studies, 1970–1985*, 1987. • Isobel Grundy, ed., *Samuel Johnson: New Critical Essays*, 1984. • Jean H. Hagstrum, *Samuel Johnson's Literary Criticism*, 1967. • Nicholas Hudson, *Samuel Johnson and Eighteenth-Century Thought*, 1988. • Paul J. Korshin, ed., *Johnson after Two Hundred Years*, 1986. • G. F. Parker, *Johnson's Shakespeare*, 1989. • Allen Reddick, *The Making of Johnson's Dictionary, 1746–1773*, 1996. • Pat Rogers, *Johnson and Boswell: The Transit of Caledonia*, 1995. • Pat Rogers, *The Samuel Johnson Encyclopedia*, 1996. • Arthur Sherbo, *Samuel Johnson's Critical Opinions: A Reexamination*, 1995. • James H. Sledd and Gwin J. Kolb, *Dr. Johnson's Dictionary: Essays in the Biography of a Book*, 1955. • Robert D. Spector, *Samuel Johnson and the Essay*, 1997. • David Wheeler, ed., *Domestick Privacies*, 1987. • William K. Wimsatt, *Philosophic Words: A Study of Style and Meaning in the Rambler and Dictionary of Samuel Johnson*, 1948. • William K. Wimsatt, *The Prose Style of Samuel Johnson*, 1941. • Thomas M. Woodman, *A Preface to Samuel Johnson*, 1993.

Mary Leapor • Biography and Criticism • Richard Greene, *Mary Leapor: A Study in Eighteenth-Century Women's Poetry*, 1993.

John Locke • Editions • Peter H. Nidditch, ed., *An Essay Concerning Human Understanding*, 1975. • J. W. Yolton, *The Locke Reader*, 1977.

Criticism • R. I. Aaron, *John Locke*, rev. ed., 1955. • Vere Chappell, ed., *The Cambridge Companion to Locke*, 1994. • John Dunn, *Locke*, 1984. • Christopher Fox, *Locke and the Scriblerians: Identity and Consciousness in Early Eighteenth-Century Britain*, 1988. • W. M. Spellman, *John Locke*, 1997. • John W. Yolton, *Locke: An Introduction*, 1985.

Lady Mary Wortley Montagu • Editions • Robert Halsband, ed., *The Complete Letters of Lady Mary Wortley Montagu, 1965–1967*. • Robert Halsband and Isobel Grundy, eds., *Essays and Poems and Simplicity, a Comedy*, 1977. • Malcolm Jack, ed., *Turkish Embassy Letters*, 1993.

Biography • Robert Halsband, *The Life of Lady Mary Wortley Montagu*, 1956.

Criticism • Jill Campbell, "Lady Mary Wortley Montagu and the Historical Machinery of Female Identity," *History, Gender, and Eighteenth-Century Literature*, ed. Beth Fawkes Tobin, 1994. • Cynthia Lowenthal, *Lady Mary Wortley Montagu and the Eighteenth-Century Familiar Letter*, 1994. • Ruth Bernard Yeazell, "Public Baths and Private Harems: Lady Mary Wortley Montagu and the Origins of Ingres's *Bain Turc*," *Yale Journal of Criticism*, vol. 7, no. 1, 1994.

Sir Isaac Newton • Editions • I. Bernard Cohen and Richard S. Westfall, eds., *Newton: Texts, Backgrounds, Commentaries*, 1995. • H. W. Turnbull, *The Correspondence of Isaac Newton*, 7 vols., 1959–1977.

Biography • Richard S. Westfall, *Never at Rest*, 1980.

Criticism • D. Gjertsen, *The Newton Handbook*, 1986. • F. E. Manuel, *The Religion of Isaac Newton*, 1974. • Marjorie Hope Nicolson, *Newton Demands the Muse: Newton's Opticks and the Eighteenth-Century Poets*, 1946.

Samuel Pepys • Editions • Robert Latham, ed., *The Illustrated Pepys*, 1983. • Robert Latham, ed., *The Shorter Pepys*, 1985. • Robert Latham and William Matthews, eds., *The Diary of Samuel Pepys*, 11 vols., 1970–1983.

Biographies • Arthur Bryant, *Samuel Pepys*, 3 vols., 3rd ed., 1967. • Richard Ollard, *Pepys: A Biography*, 1975. • J. R. Tanner, *Samuel Pepys and the Royal Navy*, 1920.

Criticism • Francis Barker, *The Tremulous Private Body: Essays on Subjection*, rev. ed., 1995. • Marjorie Hope Nicolson, *Pepys' Diary and the New Science*, 1965. • Robert Louis Stevenson, "Samuel Pepys," *Familiar Studies of Men and Books*, 1895. • Stuart Sherman, "'In the Fullness of Time': Pepys and His Predecessors" and "'With My Minute Wach in My Hand': The Diary as Timekeeper," *Telling Time: Clocks, Diaries, and English Diurnal Form, 1660–1785*, 1996. • James Grantham Turner, "Pepys and the Private Parts of Monarchy," in

Culture and Society in the Restoration, ed. Gerald MacLean, 1995.

Hester Salusbury Thrale Piozzi • Editions • Katherine C. Balderston, ed., *Thraliana; the Diary of Mrs. Hester Lynch Thrale (later Mrs. Piozzi) 1776–1809*, 2nd ed., 1951. • Edward A. Bloom and Lillian D. Bloom, eds., *The Piozzi Letters*, 1989–. • A. Hayward, ed., *Autobiography, Letters and Literary Remains of Mrs. Piozzi (Thrale)*, 2 vols., 1975. • Mary Hyde, ed., *The Thrales of Streatham Park*, 1977.

Biographies • James L. Clifford, *Hester Lynch Piozzi (Mrs. Thrale)*, rev. ed., 1968. • William McCarthy, *Hester Thrale Piozzi, Portrait of a Literary Woman*, 1985.

Criticism • Martine Watson Brownely, "Eighteenth-Century Women's Images and Roles: The Case of Hester Thrale Piozzi," *Biography*, vol. 3, 1980. • Felicity A. Nussbaum, "Managing Women: Thrale's *Family Book* and *Thraliana*," *The Autobiographical Subject: Gender and Ideology in Eighteenth-Century England*, 1989. • John Riely, "Johnson and Mrs. Thrale: The Beginning and the End," *Johnson and His Age*, ed. James Engell, 1984. • Judy Simons, "The Unfixed Text: Narrative and Identity in Women's Private Writings," *The Representation of the Self in Women's Autobiography*, eds. Vita Fortunati and Gabriella Morisco, 1993.

Alexander Pope • Editions • John Butt et al., eds., *The Twickenham Edition of the Poems of Alexander Pope*, 11 vols., 1940–1969. • John Butt, ed., *The Poems of Alexander Pope*, 1963. • George Sherburn, ed., *The Correspondence of Alexander Pope*, 5 vols., 1956. • Cynthia Wall, ed., *The Rape of the Lock*, 1998. • Aubrey Williams, ed., *Poetry and Prose of Alexander Pope*, 1969.

Biographies • Maynard Mack, *Alexander Pope: A Life*, 1985. • George Sherburn, *The Early Career of Alexander Pope*, 1934. • Joseph Spence, *Observations, Anecdotes, and Characters of Books and Men*, ed. James M. Osborn, 2 vols., 1966.

Criticism • Reuben Brower, *Alexander Pope: The Poetry of Allusion*, 1959. • Laura Brown, *Alexander Pope*, 1985. • Morris Brownell, *Alexander Pope and the Arts of Georgian England*, 1978. • Helen Deutsch, *Resemblance and Disgrace: Alexander Pope and the Deformation of Culture*, 1996. • H. H. Erskine-Hill, *The Social Milieu of Alexander Pope*, 1978. • David Fairer,

ed., *Pope: New Contexts*, 1990. • David Fairer, *Pope's Imagination*, 1984. • David F. Foxon, *Pope and the Eighteenth-Century Book Trade*, 1991. • Bertrand A. Goldgar, *Literary Criticism of Alexander Pope*, 1965. • Dustin Griffin, *Alexander Pope: The Poet in the Poems*, 1978. • Brean Hammond, ed., *Longman Critical Readers: Pope*, 1966. • J. Paul Hunter, "Pope and the Ideology of the Couplet," *Ideas*, vol. 4, no. 1, 1996. • Maynard Mack, *The Garden and the City: Retirement and Politics in the Later Poetry of Pope*, 1969. • Maynard Mack, ed., *Essential Articles for the Study of Alexander Pope*, 1968. • Maynard Mack and James Winn, eds., *Pope: Recent Essays by Several Hands*, 1980. • David B. Morris, *Alexander Pope: The Genius of Sense*, 1984. • Marjorie Hope Nicolson and G. S. Rousseau, *"This Long Disease, My Life": Alexander Pope and the Sciences*, 1968. • Valerie Rumbold, *Women's Place in Pope's World*, 1989. • Geoffrey Tillotson, *On the Poetry of Pope*, 2nd. ed., 1950. • Howard Weinbrot, *Alexander Pope and the Tradition of Formal Verse Satire*, 1982. • Aubrey L. Williams, *Pope's Dunciad: A Study of Its Meaning*, 1955.

Christopher Smart • Editions • Karina Williamson, ed., *The Poetical Works of Christopher Smart*, 5 vols., 1980–1996. • Karina Williamson and Marcus Walsh, eds., *Selected Poems*, 1990.

Biographies • Christopher Devlin, *Poor Kit Smart*, 1961. • Arthur Sherbo, *Christopher Smart, Scholar of the University*, 1967.

Criticism • Moira Dearnely, *The Poetry of Christopher Smart*, 1967. • Harriet Guest, *A Form of Sound Words: The Religious Poetry of Christopher Smart*, 1989. • Geoffrey H. Hartmann, "Christopher Smart's, 'Magnificat', : Towards a Theory of Representation," *English Literary History*, vol. 41, 1974. • Clement Hawes, *Mania and Literary Style: The Rhetoric of Enthusiasm from the Ranters to Christopher Smart*, 1996.

Jonathan Swift • Editions • Herbert Davis, ed., *The Prose Works of Jonathan Swift*, 14 vols., 1939–1968. • Christopher Fox, ed., *Gulliver's Travels: Complete, Authoritative Text with Biographical and Historical Contexts, Critical History, and Essays from Five Contemporary Critical Perspectives*, 1995. • A. C. Guthkelch and D. Nichol Smith, eds., *"A Tale of a Tub," to Which Is Added "The Battle of the Books," and the "Mechanical Operation of the Spirit,"* 2nd ed., 1958. • Pat Rogers, ed., *The Complete Poems*, 1983. • Harold Williams, ed., *The Correspon-*

dence of Jonathan Swift, 5 vols., 1963–1965. •
Harold Williams, ed., Journal to Stella, 2 vols.,
1948. • Harold Williams, ed., The Poems of
Jonathan Swift, 2nd ed., 3 vols., 1958.

Biographies • Irvin Ehrenpreis, Swift: The
Man, His Works, and the Age, 3 vols.,
1962–1983. • David Nokes, Jonathan Swift, A
Hypocrite Reversed: A Critical Biography, 1985.

Criticism • J. A. Downie, Jonathan Swift: Po-
litical Writer, 1985. • Irvin Ehrenpreis, "The
Meaning of Gulliver's Last Voyage," Review of
English Literature [later, Ariel], vol. 3, no. 3,
1962. • Irvin Ehrenpreis, "The Origin of Gul-
liver's Travels," PMLA, vol. 72, 1957. • Robert
C. Elliott, The Power of Satire: Magic, Ritual,
Art, 1960. • Howard Erskine-Hill, Gulliver's
Travels, 1993. • Oliver W. Ferguson, Jonathan
Swift and Ireland, 1962. • H. J. Real Fischer
and J. Wooley, eds., Swift and His Contexts,
1989. • John Irwin Fischer and Donald C.
Mell Jr., eds., Contemporary Studies of Swift's
Poetry, 1980. • Carol Houlihan Flynn, The
Body in Swift and Defoe, 1990. • Christopher
Fox, ed., Walking Naboth's Vineyard: New
Studies of Swift, 1995. • Nora Crow Jaffe, The
Poet Swift, 1977. • F. P. Lock, The Politics of
Gulliver's Travels, 1980. • Marjorie Hope
Nicolson and Nora M. Moehler, "The Scien-
tific Background of Swift's Voyage to Laputa,"
Science and Imagination, 1956. • Ellen Pollak,
The Poetics of Sexual Myth: Gender and Ideology
in the Verse of Swift and Pope, 1985. • Martin
Price, Swift's Rhetorical Art: A Study in Struc-
ture and Meaning, 1953. • C. J. Rawson, Gul-
liver and the Gentle Reader, 1973. • C. J. Raw-
son, ed., The Character of Swift's Satire, 1983. •
Richard H. Rodino, Swift Studies, 1965–1980:
An Annotated Bibliography, 1984. • Edward W.
Rosenheim, Swift and the Satirist's Art, 1963. •
Edward W. Said, "Swift as Intellectual" and
"Swift's Tory Anarchy," The World, the Text,
and the Critic, 1983. • Brian Vickers, ed., The
World of Jonathan Swift: Essays for the Tercente-
nary, 1968. • David M. Vieth, Swift's Poetry

1900–1980: An Annotated Bibliography of Studies, 1982. • Kathleen Williams, ed., Swift: The
Critical Heritage, 1970.

Isaac Watts • **Editions** • Bennett A. Brockman,
ed., Divine Songs Attempted in an Easy Language
for the Use of Children, 1978. • Bennett A.
Brockman, The Psalms and Hymns of Isaac
Watts: With All the Additional Hymns and Complete Indexes, 1997.

Biography • Arthur Paul Davis, Isaac Watts:
His Life and Work, 1943.

Criticism • Donald Davie, The Eighteenth-
Century Hymn in England, 1993. • Madeleine
Forell Marshall and Janet Todd, English Con-
gregational Hymns in the Eighteenth Century,
1982. • J. R. Watson, The English Hymn: A
Critical and Historical Study, 1997.

John Wilmot, Earl of Rochester • **Editions** •
Frank H. Ellis, ed., The Complete Works, 1994.
• Jeremy Treglown, The Letters of John
Wilmot, Earl of Rochester, 1980. • David M.
Vieth, ed., The Complete Poems of John
Wilmot, Earl of Rochester, 1968. • Keith
Walker, ed., The Poems of John Wilmot, Earl of
Rochester, 1984.

Biographies • John Adlard, The Debt to Plea-
sure, 1974. • Graham Greene, Lord Rochester's
Monkey; Being the Life of John Wilmot, Second
Earl of Rochester, 1974. • Jeremy Lamb, So Idle a
Rogue: The Life and Death of Lord Rochester,
1993. • Vivian de Sola Pinto, Enthusiast in Wit:
A Portrait of John Wilmot, Earl of Rochester, 1962.

Criticism • David Farley-Hills, Rochester's Po-
etry, 1978. • David Farley-Hills, ed., Rochester:
The Critical Heritage, 1972. • Dustin Griffin,
Satires Against Man: The Poems of Rochester,
1973. • Marianne Thormählen, Rochester:
The Poems in Context, 1993. • Jeremy Tre-
glown, ed., Spirit of Wit: Reconsiderations of
Rochester, 1982. • David M. Vieth, ed., John
Wilmot, Earl of Rochester: Critical Essays, 1988.

The Romantics and Their Contemporaries

**Bibliographies, General Collections, General Ref-
erence** • Annual bibliographies are published
by the Modern Language Association of America, the Modern Humanities Research Association, the Keats-Shelley Journal, The Romantic

Movement, and The Year's Work in English Studies. • Stuart Curran, ed., The Cambridge Companion to British Romanticism, 1993. • Frank
Jordan, ed., The English Romantic Poets: A Review of Research and Criticism, 4th ed. 1985

[covers Blake, W. Wordsworth, Coleridge, Byron, P. B. Shelley, Keats]. • Karl Kroeber and Gene Ruoff, eds., *Romantic Poetry: Recent Revisionary Criticism*, 1993. • Jerome McGann, ed., *The New Oxford Book of Romantic Period Verse*, 1993. • Anne K. Mellor and Richard Matlak, eds., *British Literature 1780–1830*, 1996. • David Perkins, ed., *English Romantic Writers*, 2d ed., 1995. • Duncan Wu, ed., *Romanticism, An Anthology*, 1994. • Duncan Wu, ed., *Romanticism, A Critical Reader*, 1995 [essays on Blake, W. Wordsworth, Coleridge, P. B. Shelley, Byron, Keats, Clare, M. Shelley, Austen]. • Several volumes in the series *Approaches to Teaching World Literature* published by the Modern Language Association are devoted to writers in our period: among others, Blake (ed. Robert Gleckner and Mark Greenberg); Byron (ed. F. W. Shilstone); Coleridge (ed. Richard Matlak); Keats (ed. Walter Evert and Jack Rhodes); Mary Shelley (ed. Stephen Behrendt); Percy Shelley (ed. Spencer Hall); and Wordsworth (ed. Spencer Hall and Jonathan Ramsey).

History and Literary History • M. H. Abrams "English Romanticism: The Spirit of the Age," 1963; repr. in *Romanticism and Consciousness: Essays in Criticism*, ed. Harold Bloom, 1970. • Derek Beales, *From Castlereagh to Gladstone 1815–85*, 1969. • Marilyn Butler, *Romantics, Rebels, and Reactionaries: English Literature and Its Background, 1760–1830*, 1981. • Marilyn Butler, "Romanticism in England," *Romanticism in National Context*, ed. Roy Park and Mikuláš Teich, 1988. • Ian R. Christie *Wars and Revolutions*, New History of England, vol. 7, 1982. • J. C. D. Clark, *English Society 1688–1832*, 1985. • Linda Colley, *Britons: Forging the Nation 1707–1837*, 1992. • M. J. Daunton, *Progress and Poverty: An Economic and Social History of Britain 1700–1850*, 1995. • Lee Erickson, *The Economy of Literary Form: English Literature and the Industrialization of Publishing 1800–1850*, 1996. • Norman Gash, *Aristocracy and People: Britain 1815–1865*, 1979. • Marilyn Gaull, *English Romanticism: The Human Context*, 1988. • Élie Halévy, *A History of the English People in 1815*, trans. 1924, repr. 1987. • Ian Jack, *English Literature, 1815–1832*, 1963. • Jon Klancher, *The Making of English Reading Audiences, 1790–1832*, 1987. • John B. Owen, *The Eighteenth Century 1714–1815*, 1974. • Harold Perkin, *Origins of Modern English Society*, 1969. • Roy Porter, *English Society in the Eighteenth Century*, 1982. • W. L. Renwick, *English Literature, 1789–1815*, 1963. • Alan Richardson, *Literature, Education, and Romanticism*, 1994. • E. P. Thompson, *The Making of the English Working Class*, 1963. • E. P. Thompson, *Customs in Common*, 1991. • R. J. White, *Waterloo to Peterloo*, 1957. • Raymond Williams, *Culture and Society 1780–1950*, 1960. • Raymond Williams, *The Country and The City*, 1973. • Carl Woodring, *Politics in English Romantic Poetry*, 1970.

Contemporary Reception • John O. Hayden, *The Romantic Reviewers 1802–24*, 1969. • Theodore Redpath, ed., *The Young Romantics and Critical Opinion, 1807–1824: Poetry of Byron, Shelley, and Keats as Seen by Their Contemporary Critics*, 1973. • Donald H. Reiman, *The Romantics Reviewed: Contemporary Reviews of British Romantic Writers*, 1972.

Poetic Form, Genres, Literary History • M. H. Abrams, "Structure and Style in the Greater Romantic Lyric," 1965, repr. in *Romanticism and Consciousness*, ed. Harold Bloom 1970. • M. H. Abrams, *Natural Supernaturalism: Tradition and Revolution in Romantic Literature*, 1971. • Harold Bloom, "The Internalization of Quest-romance," 1969, repr. in *Romanticism and Consciousness*, ed. Harold Bloom, 1970. • Harold Bloom, *The Anxiety of Influence: A Theory of Poetry*, 1973. • Douglas Bush, *Mythology and the Romantic Tradition in English Poetry*, 1937. • Stuart Curran, *Poetic Form and British Romanticism*, 1986. • Geoffrey Hartman, *Beyond Formalism*, 1970. • John Hollander, "Romantic Verse Form and the Metrical Contract," 1965, repr. in *Romanticism and Consciousness*, ed. Harold Bloom, 1970. • David Perkins, "The Construction of 'The Romantic Movement' as a Literary Classification," *Nineteenth-Century Literature*, 1990. • Thomas Vogler, *Preludes to Vision: On the Epic Venture in Blake, Wordsworth, Keats, and Hart Crane*, 1971. • Brian Wilkie, *Romantic Poets and Epic Tradition*, 1965. • W. K. Wimsatt, "The Structure of Romantic Nature Imagery," in *The Verbal Icon*, 1954; repr. in *Romanticism and Consciousness*, ed. Harold Bloom, 1970. • Susan J. Wolfson, *The Questioning Presence*, 1986. • Susan J. Wolfson, *Formal Charges, The Shaping of British Romantic Poetry*, 1996.

Theory and Criticism • M. H. Abrams, *The Mirror and the Lamp: Romantic Theory and Critical Tradition*, 1953. • M. H. Abrams, *Natural Supernaturalism*, 1971. • M. H. Abrams, *The Correspondent Breeze: Essays on English Romanticism*, 1984. • John Beer, ed., *Questioning Romanticism*, 1995. • Edward E. Bostetter, *The Romantic Ventriloquists: Wordsworth, Coleridge, Shelley, Keats, Byron*, 1963. • Paul De Man, *The Rhetoric of Ro-*

manticism, 1984. • Paul De Man, "The Rhetoric of Temporality," in his Blindness and Insight, 2d ed., 1983. • William H. Galperin, The Return of the Visible in British Romanticism, 1993. • Karl Kroeber, British Romantic Art, 1986. • Jerome McGann, The Romantic Ideology: A Critical Investigation, 1983. • Jerome McGann, The Poetics of Sensibility: A Revolution in Literary Style, 1996. • Anne K. Mellor, English Romantic Irony, 1980. • David Perkins, The Quest for Permanence: The Symbolism of Wordsworth, Shelley, and Keats, 1959. • Tilottama Rajan, Dark Interpreter: The Discourse of Romanticism, 1980. • Charles R. Rzepka, The Self as Mind: Vision and Identity in Wordsworth, Coleridge, and Keats, 1986. • David Simpson, Irony and Authority in Romantic Poetry, 1979. • Stuart M. Sperry, "Towards a Definition of Romantic Irony," in Romantic and Modern: Revaluations of Literary Tradition, ed. George Bornstein, 1977. • Earl R. Wasserman, "The English Romantics: The Grounds of Knowledge," Studies in Romanticism, 1964.

Gender, Women Writers • Paula Feldman, and Theresa M. Kelley, eds., Romantic Women Writers: Voices and Countervoices, 1995. • Diane Long Hoeveler, Romantic Androgyny: The Women Within, 1990. • Sonia Hofkosh, "A Woman's Profession: Sexual Difference and the Romance of Authorship," Studies in Romanticism, 1993. • Anne K. Mellor, ed., Romanticism and Feminism, 1988. • Anne K. Mellor, Romanticism and Gender, 1993. • Judith Pascoe, Romantic Theatricality: Gender, Poetry, and Spectatorship. 1997. • Marlon Ross, The Contours of Masculine Desire: Romanticism and the Rise of Women's Poetry, 1989. • Irene Tayler and Gina Luria, "Women in British Romantic Literature," in What Manner of Woman, ed. Marlene Springer, 1977. • Carol Shiner Wilson and Joel Haefner, eds., Revisioning Romanticism: British Women Writers, 1776–1837, 1994. • Jonathan Wordsworth, The Bright Work Grows: Women Writers of the Romantic Age, 1997.

Perspectives: The Abolition of Slavery and the Slave Trade • General Studies • Roger Anstey, The Atlantic Slave Trade and British Abolition, 1760–1810, 1975. • Joan Baum, Mind-forg'd Manacles: Slavery and the English Romantic Poets, 1994. • Robin Blackburn, The Overthrow of Colonial Slavery, 1776–1848, 1988. • Reginald Coupland, The British Anti-Slavery Movement, 1933. • Michael Craton, Sinews of Empire: A Short History of British Slavery, 1974. • Michael Craton, James Walvin, and David Wright, eds., Slavery, Abolition and Emancipa-

tion: Black Slaves and the British Empire, 1976 [an anthology of important documents, including the "Mansfield decision" (Somerset v. Stewart, June 1772), and a succinct history]. • David Brion Davis, The Problem of Slavery in the Age of Revolution, 1975. • Eva Dyke, The Negro in English Romantic Thought, 1942. • Moira Ferguson, Subject to Others: British Women Writers and Colonial Slavery, 1670–1834, 1992 [including a massive bibliography]. • Sonia Hofkosh and Alan Richardson, eds., Romanticism, Race and Imperial Culture, 1996. • Edith F. Hurwitz, Politics and Public Conscience: Slave Emancipation and the Abolitionist Movement in Britain, 1973. • Margaret Kirkham, Jane Austen, Feminism and Fiction, 1983 [on the Mansfield Decision and Mansfield Park]. • Frank Joseph Klingberg, The Anti-Slavery Movement in England: A Study in English Humanitarianism, 1926. • Gordon K. Lewis, Slavery, Imperialism, and Freedom Studies in English Radical Thought, 1978. • Dale H. Porter, The Abolition of the Slave Trade in England, 1784–1807, 1970. • James Walvin, Black and White: The Negro and English Society, 1555–1945, 1973. • James Walvin, Slavery and British Society, 1776–1846, 1982. • James Walvin, England, Slaves, and Freedom, 1776–1838, 1986. • Eric Williams, Capitalism and Slavery, 1944.

Specific Figures • Reginald Coupland, Wilberforce: A Narrative, 1923. • E. L. Griggs, Thomas Clarkson: The Friend of the Slaves, 1938. • Edmund Heward, Lord Mansfield, 1979. • Robert Isaac and Samuel Wilberforce, The Life of William Wilberforce, 1835. • C. L. R. James, The Black Jacobins: Toussaint L'Ouverture and the San Domingo Rebellion, 1938; repr. 1963. • Oliver M. Warner, William Wilberforce and His Times, 1962.

Perspectives: The Rights of Man and the Revolution Controversy • Headnote: Coleridge is quoted from Table Talk, 4 January 1823; Wordsworth is quoted from a letter of 30 March 1835. • Simon Bainbridge, Napoleon and English Romanticism, 1996. • Marilyn Butler, ed., Burke, Paine, Godwin, and the Revolution Controversy, 1984. • Ceri Crossley and Ian Small, eds., The French Revolution and British Culture, 1989. • Seamus Deane, The French Revolution and Enlightenment England 1789–1832, 1988. • H. T. Dickinson, British Radicalism and the French Revolution, 1985. • Clive Emsley, British Society and the French Wars 1793–1815, 1979. • Burton R. Friedman, Fabricating History: English Writers and the French Revolution, 1988. • Kevin

Gilmartin, *Print Politics: The Press and Radical Opposition in Early Nineteenth-Century England*, 1996. • Albert Goodwin, *The Friends of Liberty*, 1979. • E. J. Hobsbawm, *The Age of Revolution 1789–1848*, 1962. • Howard Mumford Jones, *Revolution and Romanticism*, 1974. • Anne K. Mellor, "English Women Writers and the French Revolution," in *Rebel Daughters: Women and the French Revolution*, eds. Sara Melzer and Leslie Rabine, 1992. • Ronald Paulson, *Representations of Revolution, 1789–1820*, 1983. • Mark Philp, ed., *The French Revolution and British Popular Politics*, 1991. • Mark Philp, "Vulgar Conservatism, 1792–1793," *English Historical Review*, 1995. • Esther Schor, *Bearing the Dead: The British Culture of Mourning from the Enlightenment to Victoria*, 1994. • David Simpson, *Romanticism, Nationalism, and the Revolt Against Theory*, 1993. • Olivia Smith, *The Politics of Language 1791–1819*, 1984. • Bruce Woodcock and John Coates. *Combative Styles: Romantic Writing and Ideology*, 1995.

A "Vindication" in Context: The Wollstonecraft Controversy and the Rights of Women • Textual Reference • Anna Laetitia Le Breton, *Memoir of Mrs. Barbauld*, 1874 [Barbauld's letter to Edgeworth, 4 September 1804]. •

General Studies • Leonore Davidoff and Catherine Hall, *Family Fortunes: Men and Women of the English Middle Class, 1780–1850*, 1987. • Bridget Hill, *Women, Work, and Sexual Politics in Eighteenth-Century England*, 1989. • Gary Kelly, *Women, Writing, and Revolution, 1790–1827*, 1993. • Anne K. Mellor, *Romanticism and Gender*, 1993. • Mitzi Myers, "Reform or Ruin: 'A Revolution in Female Manners,'" in *Studies in Eighteenth-Century Culture*, 1982. • Mary Poovey, *The Proper Lady and the Woman Writer*, 1984. • Katharine Rogers, *Feminism in Eighteenth-Century England*, 1982. • For Barbauld, Southey, Blake, and More, see the main entries under their names.

The Anti-Jacobin • Context • M. Dorothy George, *English Political Caricature: A Study of Opinion and Propaganda, 1793–1832*, 1959.

Text • Charles Edmonds, ed., *Poetry of the Anti-Jacobin*, 1890.

Joanna Baillie • Biography and Criticism • Catherine Burroughs, "English Romantic Women Writers and Theatre Theory: Joanna Baillie's Prefaces to Plays on the Passions," in *Revisioning Romanticism*, ed. Carol Shiner Wilson and Joel Haefner, 1994. • Margaret S. Carhart, *The Life and Work of Joanna Baillie*, 1923. • Julie

Carlson, *In the Theatre of Romanticism*, 1994. • Andrea Henderson, "Passion and Fashion in Joanna Baillie's 'Introductory Discourse,'" *PMLA*, 1997. • Jonathan Wordsworth, *The Bright Work Grows: Women Writers of the Romantic Age*, 1997. • Paul Zall, "The Question of Joanna Baillie," *The Wordsworth Circle*, 1982.

Our Texts • *The Dramatic and Poetical Works of Joanna Baillie*, 1853; *Byron's Letters and Journals*, ed. Leslie A. Marchand (1973–82): 6 Sept. 1813 and 2 Apr. 1817; the comparison to Byron from "Celebrated Female Writers: Joanna Baillie," *Blackwood's Edinburgh Magazine*, August 1824.

Anna Laetitia Barbauld • Biography and Editions • Lucy Aikin, Memoir in *The Works of Anna Letitia Barbauld*, 1825. • William McCarthy, and Elizabeth Kraft, eds., *The Poems of Anna Letitia Barbauld*, 1994. • Betsy Rodgers, *Georgian Chronicle: Mrs. Barbauld and her Family*, 1958.

Criticism • Isobel Armstrong, "The Gush of the Feminine: How Can We Read Women's Poetry of the Romantic Period?" in *Romantic Women Writers*, eds. Theresa Kelley and Paula Feldman, 1995. • William Keach, "A Regency Prophecy and the End of Anna Barbauld's Career," *Studies in Romanticism*, 1994. • William McCarthy, "'We Hoped the Woman Was Going to Appear': Repression, Desire, and Gender in Anna Letitia Barbauld's Early Poems," in *Romantic Women Writers*, eds. Theresa Kelley and Paula Feldman, 1995. • Marlon B. Ross, "Configurations of Feminine Reform: The Woman Writer and the Tradition of Dissent," in *Revisioning Romanticism*, eds. Carol Shiner Wilson and Joel Haefner, 1994. • Jonathan Wordsworth, *The Bright Work Grows: Women Writers of the Romantic Age*, 1997.

Our Texts • "The Mouse's Petition," "On a Lady's Writing," and "Washing Day" from *A Selection From the Poems . . . of Anna Letitia Barbauld*, ed. Grace Ellis, 1874; "Inscription for an Ice-House" and "The First Fire" from *The Works of Anna Laetitia Barbauld*, ed. Lucy Aikin, 1825; "To the Poor" and "To a Little Invisible Being" from *The Poems of Anna Laetitia Barbauld*, eds. McCarthy and Kraft, 1994.

William Blake • Biography • Peter Ackroyd, *Blake*, 1996. • Alexander Gilchrist, *The Life of William Blake, Pictor Ignotus*, 1863. • Mona Wilson, *The Life of William Blake*, 1927.

Illuminations • Oxford University Press: paperback color-plate editions, with commentary by Geoffrey Keynes, of *The Songs of Innocence and of Experience*, 1967; *The Marriage of Heaven and Hell*, 1975; *Visions of the Daughters of Albion*, 1980; Princeton University Press of the *Songs*, 1991; all plates are reproduced in black and white photographs, with commentary, in David V. Erdman, *The Illuminated Blake*, 1974.

Criticism • Harold Bloom, *The Visionary Company*, 1961, rev. 1971. • Harold Bloom, *Blake's Apocalypse*, 1963, rev. 1970. • Leopold Damrosch, *Symbol and Truth in Blake's Myth*, 1980. • Jackie DiSalvo, *War of the Titans: Blake's Critique of Milton and the Politics of Religion*, 1984. • Morris Eaves, *William Blake's Theory of Art*, 1982. • Morris Eaves, *The Counter-Arts Conspiracy: Art and Industry in the Age of Blake*, 1992. • David V. Erdman, *Blake: Prophet Against Empire*, 1969. • Robert Essick, *William Blake, Printmaker*, 1980. • Robert Essick, *William Blake and the Language of Adam*, 1989. • Michael Ferber, "'London' and Its Politics," *ELH*, 1981. • Michael Ferber, *The Poetry of William Blake*, 1981. • Northrop Frye, *Fearful Symmetry*, 1947. • Robert Gleckner, *The Piper and the Bard*, 1959. • Heather Glen, *Vision and Disenchantment: Blake's "Songs" and Wordsworth's "Lyrical Ballads,"* 1983. • Nancy Moore Goslee, "Slavery and Sexual Character: Questioning the Master Trope in *Visions of the Daughters of Albion*," *ELH*, 1990. • Jean H. Hagstrum, *William Blake: Poet and Painter*, 1964. • Zachary Leader, *Reading Blake's Songs*, 1981. • John Mee, *Dangerous Enthusiasm: William Blake and the Culture of Radicalism in the 1790s*, 1992. • W. J. T. Mitchell, *Blake's Composite Art*, 1978. • Martin K. Nurmi, "Fact and Symbol in 'The Chimney Sweeper' of Blake's *Songs of Innocence*," *Bulletin of the New York Public Library*, 1964. • Morton Paley, *Energy and the Imagination: A Study of the Development of Blake's Thought*, 1970. • Mark Schorer, *William Blake: the Politics of Vision*, 1946. • Irene Tayler, "The Woman Scaly" [on *Visions of the Daughters of Albion*], 1973; repr. Norton Critical Edition of *Blake's Poetry and Designs*. • E. P. Thompson, *Witness Against the Beast: William Blake and Moral Law*, 1993. • Joseph Viscomi, *Blake and the Idea of the Book*, 1993. • Thomas Vogler, "'In Vain the Eloquent Tongue': An Un-Reading of *Visions of the Daughters of Albion*," in *Blake and the Argument of Method*, eds. Dan Miller, Mark Bracher, and Donald Ault, 1987.

Our Texts • Edited for this volume with reference to the design of Blake's illuminated plates.

Edmund Burke • **Biographical Studies** • Carl B. Cone, *Burke and the Nature of Politics*, 2 vols., 1957, 1964. • C. B. Macpherson, *Burke*, 1980. • Conor Cruise O'Brien, *The Great Melody: A Thematic Biography and Commented Anthology of Edmund Burke*, 1992.

Criticism and Context • James T. Boulton, *The Language of Politics in the Age of Wilkes and Burke*, 1963. • Alfred Cobban, *Edmund Burke and the Revolt Against the Eighteenth Century*, 1929, repr. 1962. • Tom Furniss, *Edmund Burke's Aesthetic Ideology: Language, Gender, and Political Economy in Revolution*, 1993. • J. G. A. Pocock, "Burke and the Ancient Constitution: A Problem in the History of Ideas," in his *Politics, Language, and Time*, 1971. • J. G. A. Pocock "The Political Economy of Burke's Analysis of the French Revolution," in his *Virtue, Commerce, and History*, 1985.

Our Text • *The Works of Edmund Burke*, 1894.

Robert Burns • **Biographical Studies** • Raymond Bentman, *Robert Burns*, 1987. • David Daiches, *Robert Burns and His World*, 1971. • John Delancey Ferguson, *Pride and Passion: Robert Burns*, 1939. • James Mackay, *A Biography of Robert Burns*, 1992.

Editions • John Delancey Ferguson, ed., *The Letters of Robert Burns*, 2 vols., rev. ed. by G. Ross Roy, 1985. • James Kinsley, ed., *The Poems and Songs of Robert Burns*, 3 vols., 1968.

Criticism • Thomas Crawford, *Burns: A Study of the Poems and Songs*, 1960. • Thomas Crawford, ed., *Robert Burns and Cultural Authority*, 1997. • Leopold Damrosch, "Burns, Blake, and the Recovery of Lyric," *Studies in Romanticism*, 1982. • R. D. S. Jack and Andrew Noble, eds., *The Art of Robert Burns*, 1982. • Donald A. Low, ed., *Critical Essays on Robert Burns*, 1975. • Carol McGuirk, *Robert Burns and the Sentimental Era*, 1985.

Our Texts • *The Centenary Burns*, eds. Ernest Henley and Thomas F. Henderson, 1896–1897; the second version of "Comin' Thro' the Rye" and "The Fornicator" from *The Merry Muses of Caledonia*, 1799–1800.

George Gordon, Lord Byron • **Biography** • Leslie A. Marchand, *Byron: A Biography*, 3 vols., 1957; abridged and revised in one volume as *Byron: A Portrait*, 1970.

Editions • E. H. Coleridge and R. E. Prothero, eds., *The Works of Lord Byron*, 13 vols., 1898–1904. • Leslie A. Marchand, ed., *Byron's Letters and Journals*, 12 vols., 1973–82. • Jerome J. McGann, ed., *Lord Byron: The Complete Poetical Works*, 7 vols., 1980–93.

Criticism • Bernard Beatty, *Byron's Don Juan*, 1985. • Jerome Christensen, *Lord Byron's Strength: Romantic Writing and Commercial Society*, 1993. • Michael G. Cooke, *The Blind Man Traces the Circle: On the Patterns and Philosophy of Byron's Poetry*, 1969. • Louis Crompton, *Byron and Greek Love*, 1985. • Andrew Elfenbein, *Byron and the Victorians*, 1995. • W. Paul Elledge, *Byron and the Dynamics of Metaphor*, 1968. • W. Paul Elledge, "Parting Shots: Byron Ending *Don Juan 1*," *Studies in Romanticism*, 1988. • Caroline Franklin, *Byron's Heroines*, 1992. • Robert F. Gleckner, *Byron and the Ruins of Paradise*, 1967. • Robert F. Gleckner, ed., *Critical Essays on Lord Byron*, 1991. • Peter W. Graham, *Don Juan and Regency England*, 1990. • Sonia Hofkosh, "Women and the Romantic Author: The Example of Byron," in *Romanticism and Feminism*, ed. Anne Mellor, 1988. • M. K. Joseph, *Byron the Poet*, 1964. • Malcolm Kelsall, *Byron's Politics*, 1987. • Alice Levine and Robert N. Keane, eds., *Rereading Byron*, 1993. • Peter J. Manning, *Byron and His Fictions*, 1978. • Peter J. Manning, "*Don Juan* and Byron's Imperceptiveness to the English Word," *Studies in Romanticism*, 1979; repr. in his *Reading Romantics*, 1990. • Peter J. Manning, "*Don Juan* and the Revisionary Self," in *Romantic Revisions*, ed. Robert Brinkley and Keith Hanley, 1992. • Jerome J. McGann, *Fiery Dust: Byron's Poetic Development*, 1968. • Jerome J. McGann, *Don Juan in Context*, 1976. • Jerome J. McGann, "The Book of Byron and the Book of a World," in his *The Beauty of Inflections*, 1988. • Donald H. Reiman, "*Don Juan* in Epic Context," in *Studies in Romanticism*, 1977, repr. in his *Romantic Texts and Contexts*, 1987 • George M. Ridenour, *The Style of Don Juan*, 1960. • Andrew Rutherford, *Byron: A Critical Study*, 1961. • Frederick W. Shilstone, *Byron and the Myth of Tradition*, 1988. • Peter L. Thorslev, *The Byronic Hero: Types and Prototypes*, 1962.

Our Texts • *The Works of Lord Byron, with his Letters and Journals, and His Life*, by Thomas Moore, 1832–34; *Byron's Letters and Journals*, ed. Leslie A. Marchand, 1973–1982.

John Clare • *Biography* • William J. Howard, *John Clare*, 1981. • Edward Storey, *A Right to Song: The Life of John Clare*, 1982. • J. W. Tibble and Anne Tibble, *John Clare: A Life*, rev. 1972.

Criticism • John Barrell, *The Idea of Landscape and the Sense of Place, 1730–1840: An Approach to the Poetry of John Clare*, 1972. • Hugh Haughton, Adam Phillips, and Geoffrey Summerfield, eds., *John Clare in Context*, 1994. • Elizabeth Helsinger, "Clare and the Place of the Peasant Poet," *Critical Inquiry*, 1987. • James C. McKusick, "'A Language that is Ever Green': The Ecological Vision of John Clare," *University of Toronto Quarterly*, 1991–92. • James C. McKusick, "John Clare and The Tyranny of Grammar," *Studies in Romanticism*, 1994. • Mark Storey, *The Poetry of John Clare: A Critical Introduction*, 1974. • L. J. Swingle, "Stalking the Essential John Clare: Clare in Relation to His Romantic Contemporaries," *Studies in Romanticism*, 1975. • Anne Wallace, "Farming on Foot: Tracking Georgic in Clare and Wordsworth," *Texas Studies in Language and Literature*, 1992.

Our Texts • Eric Robinson and David Powell, eds., *John Clare*, 1984; "Written in November" also from *The Village Minstrel*, 1821.

Samuel Taylor Coleridge • *Biography* • Rosemary Ashton, *The Life of Samuel Taylor Coleridge*, 1996. • Walter Jackson Bate, *Coleridge*, 1968. • Richard Holmes, *Coleridge: Early Visions*, 1990.

Editions • Kathryn Coburn, ed., *The Collected Works of Samuel Taylor Coleridge*, Bollingen Series 75, 1969—. Includes (among others): *Essays on His Times*, ed. David V. Erdman, 3 vols., 1978; *Lectures 1808–19 On Literature*, ed. R. A. Foakes, 2 vols., 1987; *Lay Sermons*, ed. R. J. White, 1972; *Biographia Literaria*, ed. James Engell and Walter Jackson Bate, 2 vols., 1983; *Poetical Works*, ed. J. C. C. Mays, 3 vols. (forthcoming). • E. H. Coleridge, ed., *Complete Poetical Works*, 2 vols., 1912. • Susan Eilenberg, *Strange Power of Speech: Wordsworth, Coleridge, and Literary Possession*, 1992. • R. A. Foakes, ed., *Coleridge on Shakespeare: The Text of the Lectures of 1811–12*, 1971. • E. L. Griggs, ed., *Collected Letters of Samuel Taylor Coleridge*, 6 vols., 1956–71. • Thomas M. Raysor, ed., *Coleridge's Shakespearian Criticism*, 2 vols., 1960. • Martin Wallen, ed., *Coleridge's Ancient Mariner: An Experimental Edition of Texts and Revisions 1798–1828*, 1993.

Criticism • M. H. Abrams, *The Mirror and the Lamp*, 1953. • J. A. Appleyard, *Coleridge's Philosophy of Literature*, 1965. • John Beer, *Coleridge the Visionary*, 1959. • John Beer, *Coleridge's Poetic Intelligence*, 1977. • Frederick Burwick, ed., *Coleridge's Biographia Literaria: Text and Meaning*, 1989. • Jerome Christensen, *Coleridge's Blessed Machine of Language*, 1981. • George Dekker, *Coleridge and the Literature of Sensibility*, 1978. • Kelvin Everest, *Coleridge's Secret Ministry: The Context of the Conversation Poems*, 1979. • Frances Ferguson, "Coleridge and the Deluded Reader: 'The Rime of the Ancient Mariner,'" *Georgia Review*, 1977. • Norman Fruman, *Coleridge: The Damaged Archangel*, 1971. • Christine Gallant, ed., *Coleridge's Theory of Imagination Today*, 1989. • William H. Galperin, "'Desynonymizing' the Self in Wordsworth and Coleridge," *Studies in Romanticism*, 1987. • Paul Hamilton, *Coleridge's Poetics*, 1984. • Anthony John Harding, *Coleridge and the Inspired Word*, 1985. • Alethea Hayter, *Opium and the Romantic Imagination*, 1968. • William Heath, *Wordsworth and Coleridge: A Study of Their Literary Relations in 1801–02*, 1972. • Patrick Keane, *Coleridge's Submerged Politics*: The Ancient Mariner and Robinson Crusoe, 1994. • John Livingston Lowes, *The Road to Xanadu*, 1927. • Paul Magnuson, *Coleridge's Nightmare Poetry*, 1974. • Paul Magnuson, *Coleridge and Wordsworth: A Lyrical Dialogue*, 1989. • Thomas McFarland, *Coleridge and the Pantheist Tradition*, 1969. • Thomas McFarland, *Romanticism and The Forms of Ruin*, 1981. • Jerome J. McGann, "The Ancient Mariner: The Meaning of Meanings," in his *The Beauty of Inflections*, 1985. • James C. McKusick, *Coleridge's Philosophy of Language*, 1986. • Raimonda Modiano, *Coleridge and the Concept of Nature*, 1985. • Raimonda Modiano, "Word and 'Languageless' Meaning: Limits of Expression in *The Rime of the Ancient Mariner*," *Modern Language Quarterly*, 1977. • John Morrow, *Coleridge's Political Thought: Property, Morality, and the Limits of Traditional Discourse*, 1990. • Roy Park, "Coleridge's Two Voices as a Critic of Wordsworth," *ELH*, 1969. • Reeve Parker, *Coleridge's Meditative Art*, 1975. • Arden Reed, *Romantic Weather*, 1983. • Nicholas Roe, *Wordsworth and Coleridge: The Radical Years*, 1988. • Gene W. Ruoff, *Wordsworth and Coleridge: The Making of the Major Lyrics, 1802–1804*, 1989. • Elizabeth Schneider, *Coleridge, Opium, and Kubla Khan*, 1953. • Max F. Schulz, *The Poetic Voices of Coleridge*, 1963. • Elinor Shaffer, *Coleridge, Kubla Khan, and the Fall of Jerusalem*, 1985. • Karen Swann, "Christabel: The Wandering Mother and the Enigma of Form," *Studies in Romanticism*, 1984. • Karen Swann, "Literary Gentlemen and Lovely Ladies: The Debate on the Character of *Christabel*," *ELH*, 1985. • Kathleen M. Wheeler, *Sources, Processes, and Methods in Coleridge's Biographia Literaria*, 1980.

Our Texts • *The Complete Works of Samuel Taylor Coleridge*, ed. W. G. T. Shedd, 7 vols., 1853; "The Rime of the Ancyent Marinere" from *Lyrical Ballads*, 1798.

William Cowper • **Biography** • David Cecil, *The Stricken Deer*, 1929. • M. J. Quinlan, *Cowper: A Critical Life*, 1953. • Charles Ryskamp, *William Cowper of the Inner Temple*, 1959.

Editions • John D. Baird and Charles Ryskamp, eds., *Poems of William Cowper*, 3 vols., 1980. • James King and Charles Ryskamp, eds., *Letters and Prose Writings of William Cowper*, 5 vols., 1979–86.

Criticism • Morris Golden, *In Search of Stability: The Poetry of William Cowper*, 1960. • Vincent Newey, *Cowper's Poetry*, 1982.

Our Texts • *Poems*, 1851.

Olaudah Equiano • William L. Andrews, *To Tell a Free Story: The First Century of Afro-American Autobiography*, 1986. • Angelo Costanzo, *Surprizing Narrative: Olaudah Equiano and the Beginnings of Black Autobiography*, 1987. • Henry L. Gates, Jr., *The Signifying Monkey: A Theory of Afro-American Literary Criticism*, 1988. • Susan M. Marren, "Between Slavery and Freedom: The Transgressive Self in Olaudah Equiano's Autobiography," *PMLA*, 1993. • Geraldine Murphy, "Olaudah Equiano, Accidental Tourist," *Eighteenth-Century Studies*, 1994. • Adam Potkay, "Olaudah Equiano and the Art of Spiritual Autobiography," *Eighteenth-Century Studies*, 1994.)

Our Text • *The Life of Olaudah Equiano*, 1814.

William Godwin • John P. Clarke, *The Philosophical Anarchism of William Godwin*, 1977. • R. G. Grylls, *William Godwin and His World*, 1953. • Don Locke, *A Fantasy of Reason: The Life and Thought of William Godwin*, 1980. • Peter H. Marshall, *William Godwin*, 1984. • E. E. Smith and E. G. Smith, *William Godwin*, 1966. • William St. Clair, *The Godwins and the Shelleys*, 1989.

Our Text • *An Enquiry Concerning Political Justice, and its Influence on General Virtue and Happiness*, 1793.

Felicia Hemans • **Biography** • Henry F. Chorley, *Memorials of Mrs. Hemans, with Illustrations of Her Literary Character from Her Private Correspondence*, 1836. • [Harriett Mary Hughes {Browne}; later Owen], *Memoir of the Life and Writings of Felicia Hemans: By Her Sister*, 1845. • Peter W. Trinder, *Mrs. Hemans*, 1984.

Criticism • Isobel Armstrong, *Victorian Poetry: Poetry, Poetics and Politics*, 1993. • Norma Clarke, *Ambitious Heights: Writing, Friendship, Love*, 1990. • George Gilfillan, "Female Authors. No. I–Mrs. Hemans," *Tait's Edinburgh Magazine*, 1847. • Anthony John Harding, "Felicia Hemans and the Effacement of Woman," in *Romantic Women Writers*, eds. Theresa Kelley and Paula Feldman, 1995. • Angela Leighton, *Victorian Woman Poets: Writing Against the Heart*, 1993. • Tricia Lootens, "Hemans and Home: Victorianism, Feminine 'Internal Enemies,' and the Domestication of National Identity," *PMLA*, 1994. • Jerome J. McGann, "Literary History, Romanticism, and Felicia Hemans," in *Revisioning Romanticism*, eds. Carol Shiner Wilson and Joel Haefner, 1994. • Anne Mellor, *Romanticism and Gender*, 1993. • Herbert F. Tucker, "House Arrest: The Domestication of English Poetry in the 1820s," *ELH*, 1994. • Susan J. Wolfson, "'Domestic Affections' and 'the Spear of Minerva': Felicia Hemans and the Dilemma of Gender," in *Revisioning Romanticism*, eds. Wilson and Haefner, 1994. • Susan J. Wolfson, "Gendering the Soul," in *Romantic Women Writers*, eds. Kelley and Feldman, 1995. • Jonathan Wordsworth, *The Bright Work Grows: Women Writers of the Romantic Age*, 1997.

Our Texts • "The Wife of Asdrubal" in *Tales, and Historical Scenes*, 1819; "Indian-Woman's Death Song" and "Joan of Arc, in Rheims," in *Records of Woman*, 1828. These volumes are repr. by Garland and Woodstock Presses. Other poems, *Poems of Felicia Hemans*, 1873. An edition, *Felicia Hemans*, eds. S. Wolfson and G. Kelly, is forthcoming in 2000.

Francis Jeffrey • Biography • Henry Cockburn, *Life of Lord Jeffrey*, 2 vols., 1852.

Editions • Francis Jeffrey, *Contributions to the Edinburgh Review*, 4 vols., 1844.

Criticism • David Bromwich, "Romantic Poetry and the *Edinburgh* Ordinances," *Yearbook of English Studies*, 1986. • Jerome Christensen, "The Detection of the Romantic Conspiracy in Britain," *South Atlantic Quarterly*, 1996. • John Clive, *Scotch Reviewers: The Edinburgh Review 1802–1815*, 1957. • Philip Flynn, *Francis Jeffrey*, 1978. • Peter F. Morgan, *Literary Critics and Reviewers in Early 19th Century Britain*, 1983. • Mark Schoenfield, "Regulating Standards: The *Edinburgh Review* and the Circulations of Judgement," *The Wordsworth Circle*, 1993. • Kim Wheatley, "Paranoid Politics: The *Quarterly* and *Edinburgh* Reviews," *Prose Studies*, 1992.

Our Texts • *Edinburgh Review*, 1 (October 1802), and 24 (November 1814).

John Keats • Biography and Reception • Walter Jackson Bate, *John Keats*, 1963. • George H. Ford, *Keats and the Victorians: A Study of His Influence and Rise to Fame 1821–1895*, 1944. • G. M. Matthews, ed., *Keats: The Critical Heritage*, 1971. • Aileen Ward, *John Keats: The Making of a Poet*, 1963. • Susan J. Wolfson, "Feminizing Keats," in *Critical Essays on John Keats*, ed. Hermione de Almeida, 1990.

Criticism • John Barnard, *John Keats*, 1987. • Walter Jackson Bate, *The Stylistic Development of Keats*, 1945. • John Bayley, "Keats and Reality," *Proceedings of the British Academy*, 1962. • Cleanth Brooks, "Keats's Sylvan Historian: History without Footnotes," in *The Well Wrought Urn: Studies in the Structure of Poetry*, 1947. • Douglas Bush, *John Keats: His Life and Writings*, 1966. • Morris Dickstein, *Keats and His Poetry*, 1971. • Stuart Ende, *Keats and the Sublime*, 1976. • Geoffrey Hartman, "Spectral Symbolism and Authorial Self," in *The Fate of Reading*, 1975. • Wolf Z. Hirst, *John Keats*, 1981. • Margaret Homans, "Keats Reading Women, Women Reading Keats," *Studies in Romanticism*, 1990. • John Jones, *John Keats's Dream of Truth*, 1969. • William Keach, "Cockney Couplets: Keats and the Politics of Style," *Studies in Romanticism*, 1986. • Robert Kern, "Keats and the Problem of Romance," *Philological Quarterly*, 1979. • Marjorie Levinson, *Keats's Life of Allegory*, 1988. • Jerome J. McGann, "Keats and the Historical Method in Literary Criticism," 1979, repr. in *The Beauty of Inflections*, 1985. • Andrew Motion, *Keats*, 1998. • Christopher Ricks, *Keats and Embarrassment*, 1976. • Nicholas Roe, *John Keats and the Culture of Dissent*, 1997. • Stuart M. Sperry, *Keats the Poet*, 1973. • Jack Stillinger, "Imagination and Reality in the Odes" and "The Hoodwinking of Madeline," in *"The Hoodwinking of Madeline" and Other Essays on Keats's Poems*, 1971. • Karen Swann, "Harrassing the Muse," in *Romanticism and Feminism*, Anne Mellor, ed. 1988. • Helen Vendler, *The Odes of John Keats*, 1983. • Leon Waldoff, *Keats and the Silent Work of Imagination*, 1985. • Daniel P. Watkins, *Keats's Poetry and the Politics of the Imagination*, 1989. • Susan J. Wolfson, "Keats and the Manhood of the Poet," *European Romantic Review*, 1995. • Susan J. Wolfson, *The Questioning Presence: Wordsworth, Keats, and the Interrogative Mode in Romantic Poetry*, 1986.

Our Texts • Poems published in Keats's lifetime are from first editions; posthumous publications are from Houghton's *Poetical Works*, 1891, checked against *The Poems of John Keats*, ed. Jack Stillinger, 1978, the best modern edition. • *The Letters of John Keats, 1814–1821*, ed. Hyder E. Rollins, 1958.

Charles Lamb • Biography • David Cecil, A *Portrait of Charles Lamb*, 1983. • Winifred F. Courtney, *Young Charles Lamb 1775–1802*, 1982. • E. V. Lucas, *Life of Charles Lamb*, rev. ed., 2 vols., 1921.

Editions • E. V. Lucas, ed., *The Works of Charles and Mary Lamb*, 1903–1905. • E. W. Marrs, ed., *The Letters of Charles and Mary Anne Lamb*, 3 vols., 1975—.

Critical Studies • Jane Aaron, *A Double Singleness: Gender and the Writing of Charles and Mary Lamb*, 1991. • George L. Barnett, *Charles Lamb*, 1976. • Robert Frank, *Don't Call Me Gentle Charles!*, 1976. • Richard Haven, "The Romantic Art of Charles Lamb," *ELH*, 1963. • Alison Hickey, "Double Bonds: Charles Lamb's Romantic Collaborations," *ELH*, 1996. • Gerald Monsman, *Confessions of a Prosaic Dreamer: Charles Lamb's Art of Autobiography*, 1984. • John Nabholtz, "My Reader My Fellow-Labourer": *A Study of English Romantic Prose*, 1986. • Roy Park, "Lamb, Shakespeare, and the Stage," *Shakespeare Quarterly*, 1982. • Mark Parker, "'A Piece of Autobiography': Reference in Charles Lamb's Essays," *Auto/Biography Studies*, 1986–1987. • Mark Parker, "Ideology and Editing: The Political Context of the Elia Essays," *Studies in Romanticism*, 1991. • F. V. Randel, *The World of Elia*, 1975.

Our Texts • *The Works of Charles and Mary Lamb*, ed. E. V. Lucas, 1903–1905.

Catherine Macaulay • Criticism • Bridget Hill, *Republican Virago: The Life and Times of Catherine Macaulay*, 1992. • Jonathan Wordsworth, *The Bright Work Grows: Women Writers of the Romantic Age*, 1997.

Our Text • *Letters on Education, With Observations on Religious and Metaphysical Subjects* (1790). Reprinted in *Feminist Controversy in England, 1788–1810*, ed. Gina Luria, 1974; excerpts from letters 4 and 21, and all of letters 22 and 23 are included in *A Vindication of the Rights of Woman*, ed. Carol Poston, 2nd ed. 1988.

Hannah More • Biography • M. G. Jones, *Hannah More*, 1952. • W. Roberts, *Memoirs of the Life and Correspondence of Mrs. Hannah More*, 1834. • Mary Alden Hopkins, *Hannah More and Her Circle*, 1947.

Criticism • Elizabeth Kowaleski-Wallace, *Their Fathers' Daughters: Hannah More, Maria Edgeworth and Patriarchal Complicity*, 1991. • Mitzi Myers, "Hannah More's Tracts for the Times: Social Fiction and Female Ideology," *Fetter'd or Free: British Women Novelists, 1670–1815*, eds. Mary Anne Schofield and Cecelia Macheski, 1986. • Alan Richardson, *Literature, Education, and Romanticism*, 1994. • G. H. Spinney, "Cheap Repository Tracts," in *The Library*, 1939. • Jonathan Wordsworth, *The Bright Work Grows: Women Writers of the Romantic Age*, 1997.

Our Texts • *Village Politics*, 1792; *The Works of Hannah More*, 1830.

Thomas Paine • A. J. Ayer, *Thomas Paine*, 1988. • Eric Foner, *Thomas Paine and Revolutionary America*, 1976. • David F. Hawke, *Thomas Paine*, 1974. • John Keane, *Thomas Paine: A Political Life*, 1995. • Mark Philp, *Paine*, 1989.

Our Text • *The Rights of Man*, 1790.

Mary Prince • Moira Ferguson, ed., *The History of Mary Prince*, 1987. • Moira Ferguson, *Subject to Others: British Women Writers and Colonial Slavery, 1670–1834*, 1992. • Jenny Sharpe, "'Something Akin to Freedom': The Case of Mary Prince," in *Differences*, 1996.

Our Text • *History of Mary Prince*, 1831.

Percy Bysshe Shelley • Biography • Kenneth Neill Cameron, *The Young Shelley*, 1950. • Richard Holmes, *Shelley: The Pursuit*, 1974. • Newman Ivey White, *Shelley*, 1940.

Reception • Mark Kipperman, "Absorbing a Revolution: Shelley Becomes a Romantic, 1889–1903," in *Nineteenth-Century Literature*, 1992. • Sylva Norman, *The Flight of the Skylark*, 1954. • N. I. White, *The Unextinguish'd Hearth*, 1938.

General Criticism • Stephen C. Behrendt, *Shelley and His Audiences*, 1989. • Harold Bloom, *Shelley's Mythmaking*, 1959. • Judith Chernaik, *The Lyrics of Shelley*, 1972. • Frances Ferguson, "Shelley's Mont Blanc: What the Mountain Said," in *Romanticism and Language*, ed. Arden Reed, 1984. • Paul Foot, *Red Shelley*, 1980. • Jerrold Hogle, *Shelley's Process*, 1988. • William C. Keach, *Shelley's Style*, 1984. • Angela Leighton, *Shelley and the Sublime*, 1984. • Donald H. Reiman, *Percy Bysshe Shelley*, 1990. • Michael Henry Scrivener, *Radical Shelley*, 1982. • Stuart Sperry, *Shelley's Major Verse*, 1988. • Earl R. Wasserman, *Shelley: A Critical Reading*, 1981. • Milton Wilson, *Shelley's Later Poetry*, 1959. • Ross G. Woodman, *The Apocalyptic Vision in the Poetry of Shelley*, 1964.

On the Mask of Anarchy • *The Masque of Anarchy, A Poem*, with Preface by Leigh Hunt (1832), facsimile repr. ed. Jonathan Wordsworth, 1990. • Stuart Curran, *Shelley's*

Annus Mirabilis: The Maturing of an Epic Vision, 1975. • Thomas R. Edwards, *Imagination and Power: A Study of Poetry on Public Themes*, 1971. • Stephen Goldsmith, *Unbinding Jerusalem: Apocalypse and Romantic Imagination*, 1993. • Donald H. Reiman, *"The Mask of Anarchy": A Facsimile Edition, with Scholarly Introductions, Bibliographical Descriptions, and Annotations*, 1985. • E. P. Thompson, *The Making of the English Working Class*, 1964. • Susan Wolfson, *Formal Charges* (1997).

Our Texts • *The Complete Poetical Works of Percy Bysshe Shelley*, ed. William Michael Rossetti, 1881, checked against modern editions; *The Mask of Anarchy* is checked against Reiman's 1985 facsimile edition of the 1819 *The Mask of Anarchy*.

Charlotte Smith • *Biography* • Florence May Anna Hilbish, *Charlotte Smith*, 1941.

Editions • *The Poems of Charlotte Smith*, ed. Stuart Curran, 1993.

Criticism • Bishop C. Hunt, "Wordsworth and Charlotte Smith," *The Wordsworth Circle*, 1970. • Judith Pascoe, "Female Botanists and the Poetry of Charlotte Smith," in *Revisioning Romanticism*, eds. Carol Shiner Wilson and Joel Haefner, 1994.

Our Text • *Elegiac Sonnets*, 5th ed., 1789.

William Thompson and Anna Wheeler • *Text, Biography* • Richard Pankhurst's edition of *Appeal*, 1983; Pankhurst has also written a biography of Thompson, 1954.

Criticism (Wheeler) • Stephen Burke, "Letter from a Pioneer Feminist," *Studies in Labour History*, 1976. • Richard Pankhurst, "Anna Wheeler; A Pioneer Socialist and Feminist," *Philological Quarterly*, 1954.

Helen Maria Williams • M. Ray Adams, "Helen Maria Williams and the French Revolution," *Wordsworth and Coleridge*, ed. Earl Leslie Griggs, 1939. • Mary Favret, "Spectatrice as Spectacle: Helen Maria Williams at Home in the Revolution," *Studies in Romanticism*, 1993. • Mary Favret, *Romantic Correspondence: Women, Politics, and the Fiction of Letters*, 1993. • Chris Jones, "Helen Maria Williams and Radical Sensibility," *Prose Studies*, 1989. • Nicola Watson, *Revolution and the Form of the British Novel, 1790–1825*, 1994.

Our Texts • *Letters from France*, 1790, 1796.

Mary Wollstonecraft • *Biography* • William Godwin, *Memoirs of the Author of a Vindication*

of the Rights of Woman, 1798. • Gary Kelly, *Revolutionary Feminism: The Mind and Career of Mary Wollstonecraft*, 1992. • Jennifer Lorch, *Mary Wollstonecraft: The Making of a Radical Feminist*, 1990. • Emily Sunstein, *A Different Face—the Life of Mary Wollstonecraft*, 1975. • Claire Tomalin, *The Life and Death of Mary Wollstonecraft*, 1974.

***Criticism Relevant to Vindication of the Rights of Woman* •** Claudia Johnson, *Equivocal Beings: Politics, Gender, and Sentimentality in the 1790s*, 1995. • Anne K. Mellor, *Romanticism and Gender*, 1993. • Ellen Moers, *Literary Women: The Great Writers*, 1963. • Mary Poovey, *The Proper Lady and the Woman Writer*, 1984. • Timothy J. Reiss, "Revolution in Bounds: Wollstonecraft, Women, and Reason," in *Gender and Theory: Dialogues on Feminist Criticism*, ed. Linda Kauffman, 1989. • Orrin Wang, "The Other Reasons," *Yale Journal of Criticism*, 1991. • Virginia Sapiro, *A Vindication of Political Virtue: The Political Theory of Mary Wollstonecraft*, 1992. • In Carol Poston's edition are included appreciations by George Eliot, 1855; Emma Goldman, c. 1910; and Virginia Woolf, 1932; as well as Ferdinand Lundberg and Marynia Farnham's notorious "Mary Wollstonecraft and the Psychopathology of Feminism," 1947; and helpful essays by (among others) Carolyn W. Kors-meyer, "Reason and Morals in the Early Feminist Movement," 1976; Elissa Guralnick on radical politics in *Rights of Woman*, 1977; R. M. Janes, on the reception of *Rights of Woman*, 1978; and Mitzi Myers, "Reform or Ruin," 1982.

On *Vindication of the Rights of Men* • Gary Kelly, "Mary Wollstonecraft as Vir Bonus," *English Studies in Canada*, 1979. • Mitzi Myers, "Politics from the Outside," *Studies in Eighteenth-Century Culture*, 1977.

Our Texts • *A Vindication of the Rights of Men, in a Letter to the Right Honourable Edmund Burke; Occasioned by His "Reflections on the Revolution in France,"* 2nd ed., 1790; *Vindication of the Rights of Woman*, ed. Carol Poston, 2nd ed., 1988; *Maria or the Wrongs of Woman* from William Godwin's edition in *The Posthumous Works*, 1798; repr. Norton, 1975.

William Wordsworth • *Biography and Reference* • Stephen Gill, *Wordsworth: A Life*, 1989. • John L. Mahoney, *William Wordsworth: A Poetic Life*, 1997. • Mary Moorman, *William Wordsworth: A Biography*, 2 vols., 1957–1965. • Mark L. Reed, *Wordsworth: The Chronology of the Early Years, 1770–1799*, 1967. • Mark L. Reed,

Wordsworth: The Chronology of the Middle Years, 1800–1815, 1975. • Duncan Wu, *Wordsworth's Reading 1779–1799*, 1993. • Duncan Wu, *Wordsworth's Reading 1800–1815*, 1995.

Editions • R. L. Brett, and A. R. Jones, eds., *Wordsworth and Coleridge: Lyrical Ballads*, 1968. • Beth Darlington, ed., *The Love Letters of William and Mary Wordsworth*, 1981. • Ernest De Selincourt, ed., *The Letters of William and Dorothy Wordsworth*, 2nd ed. rev.: *Early Years, 1787–1805*, ed. Chester L. Shaver, 1967; *Middle Years, Part 1, 1806–1811*, ed. Mary Moorman, 1969, *Part 2, 1812–1820*, ed Alan G. Hill, 1970; *Later Years, Part 1, 1821–1828*, 1978, *Part 2, 1829–1834*, 1979, *Part 3, 1835–1839*, 1982, and *Part 4, 1840–1853*, 1988, all ed. Alan G. Hill. • Michael Mason, ed., *Lyrical Ballads*, 1992. • W. J. B. Owen and Jane Worthington Smyser, eds., *The Prose Works of William Wordsworth*, 3 vols., 1974. • Stephen Parrish, gen. ed., *The Cornell Wordsworth*, 1975–. This series, based on Wordsworth's earliest texts, thus far includes (among others): *The Prelude, 1798–1799*, ed. Stephen Parrish, 1977; *Poems, in Two Volumes and Other Poems 1800–1807*, ed. Jared Curtis, 1983; *The Fourteen-Book Prelude*, ed. W. J. B. Owen, 1985; *The Thirteen-Book Prelude*, ed. Mark L. Reed, 2 vols., 1991; *Shorter Poems, 1807–1820*, ed. Carl H. Ketcham, 1989; *Lyrical Ballads, and Other Poems, 1797–1800*, ed. James Butler and Karen Green, 1992. • Jonathan Wordsworth, M. H. Abrams, and Stephen Gill, eds., *The Prelude 1799, 1805, 1850*, 1979. • Jonathan Wordsworth and Helen Darbishire, eds., *The Poetical Works of William Wordsworth*, 5 vols., 1940–1949. [Based on Wordsworth's final texts.]

Criticism • Jonathan Arac, "Bounding Lines: *The Prelude* and Critical Revision," *boundary 2*, 1979. • James Averill, *Wordsworth and the Poetry of Human Suffering*, 1980. • Alan Bewell, *Wordsworth and the Enlightenment*, 1989. • Don Bialostosky, *Making Tales: The Poetics of Wordsworth's Narrative Experiments*, 1988. • James K. Chandler, *Wordsworth's Second Nature: A Study of the Poetry and Politics*, 1984. • David Collings, *Wordsworthian Errancies*, 1994. • Jared Curtis, *Wordsworth's Experiments with Tradition: The Lyric Poems of 1802*, 1971. • Paul De Man, "Time and History in Wordsworth," *Diacritics*, 1987. • David Ellis, *Wordsworth, Freud, and the Spots of Time*, 1985. • Elizabeth Fay, *Becoming Wordsworthian*, 1995. • Frances Ferguson, *Wordsworth: Language as Counter-Spirit*, 1977. • William H. Galperin, *Revision and Authority in Wordsworth*, 1989. • Frederick Garber, *Words-worth and the Poetry of Encounter*, 1971. • George Gilpin, ed., *Critical Essays on William Wordsworth*, 1990. • Heather Glen, *Vision and Disenchantment: Blake's Songs and Wordsworth's Lyrical Ballads*, 1983. • Alan Grob, *The Philosophic Mind: A Study of Wordsworth's Poetry and Thought 1797–1805*, 1973. • Geoffrey Hartman, *Wordsworth's Poetry 1787–1814*, 1964; repr. rev. 1971. • Geoffrey Hartman, *The Unremarkable Wordsworth*, 1987. • James A. W. Heffernan, *Wordsworth's Theory of Poetry*, 1969. • Mary Jacobus, *Romanticism, Writing, and Sexual Difference: Essays on The Prelude*, 1989. • Mary Jacobus, *Tradition and Experiment in Wordsworth's Lyrical Ballads*, 1976. • Kenneth R. Johnston, *Wordsworth and The Recluse*, 1984. • Kenneth R. Johnston, "The Politics of 'Tintern Abbey,'" *The Wordsworth Circle*, 1983. • Kenneth R. Johnston and Gene W. Ruoff, eds., *The Age of William Wordsworth*, 1987. • John E. Jordan, *Why the Lyrical Ballads?*, 1976. • Theresa M. Kelley, *Wordsworth's Revisionary Aesthetics*, 1988. • J. Douglas Kneale, *Monumental Writing: Aspects of Rhetoric in Wordsworth's Poetry*, 1988. • Marjorie Levinson, *Wordsworth's Great Period Poems*, 1986. • Herbert Lindenberger, *On Wordsworth's Prelude*, 1963. • Alan Liu, *Wordsworth: The Sense of History*, 1989. • Peter J. Manning, *Reading Romantics*, 1990. • Richard J. Onorato, *The Character of the Poet: Wordsworth in The Prelude*, 1971. • Judith W. Page, *Wordsworth and the Cultivation of Women*, 1994. • Stephen M. Parrish, *The Art of the Lyrical Ballads*, 1973. • David Perkins, *The Quest for Permanence: The Symbolism of Wordsworth, Shelley, and Keats*, 1959. • Adela Pinch, "Female Chatter: Gender and Feeling in Wordsworth's Early Poetry," in her *Strange Fits of Passion*, 1996. • Jeffrey C. Robinson, *Radical Literary Education: A Classroom Experiment with Wordsworth's 'Ode'*, 1987. • Paul D. Sheats, *The Making of Wordsworth's Poetry 1785–1798*, 1973. • David Simpson, *Wordsworth and the Figurings of the Real*, 1982. • David Simpson, *Wordsworth's Historical Imagination: The Poetry of Displacement*, 1987. • Gayatri C. Spivak, "Sex and History in *The Prelude* (1805): Books Nine to Thirteen," *Texas Studies in Language and Literature*, 1981. • Keith G. Thomas, *Wordsworth and Philosophy*, 1989. • Douglas B. Wilson, *The Romantic Dream: Wordsworth and the Poetics of the Unconscious*, 1993. • Susan J. Wolfson, *The Questioning Presence*, 1986. • Jonathan Wordsworth, *William Wordsworth: The Borders of Vision*, 1982. • For the relations of Wordsworth and Coleridge, see also the entry under Samuel Taylor Coleridge.

Our Texts • *Lyrical Ballads*, 1798; *Complete Poetical Works*, 1892, 1898, and 1911; *The Thirteen-Book Prelude*, ed. Mark L. Reed; *The Excursion* (1814); letter to Mary Ann Rawson from *The Letters of William and Dorothy Wordsworth*, 2nd ed., *Later Years, Part 2*, ed. Alan G. Hill, 1979.

The Victorian Age

Bibliographies • Brahma Chaudhuri, ed., *Annual Bibliography of Victorian Studies*, 1976–. • Brahma Chaudhuri, ed., *A Comprehensive Bibliography of Victorian Studies, 1970–1984*, 3 vols. • *Modern Language Association International Bibliography*, online. • David Nicholls, *Nineteenth-Century Britain, 1815–1914*. 1978. • *Victorian Poetry*. Annual "Guide to the Year's Work on Victorian Poetry." 1963– • *Studies in English Literature*. Annual review of "Recent Studies in the Nineteenth Century" (autumn issue), 1961–. • *Victorian Studies*. Annual "Victorian Bibliography" (summer issue), 1957–.

Guides to Research • David J. DeLaura, *Victorian Prose: A Guide to Research*, 1973. • Frederic E. Faverty, *The Victorian Poets: A Guide to Research*, 2nd ed., 1968. • Lionel Madden, *How to Find Out About the Victorian Period*, 1970. • Lionel Stevenson, ed. *Victorian Fiction: A Guide to Research*, 1964; supplemented by *Victorian Fiction: A Second Guide to Research*, ed. George H. Ford, 1978.

Cultural and Intellectual Background • Richard D. Altick, *Victorian People and Ideas*, 1973. • Asa Briggs, *Victorian People: A Reassessment of Persons and Themes 1851–67*, 1965. • Asa Briggs, *Victorian Things*, 1988. • Jerome H. Buckley, *The Victorian Temper: A Study in Literary Culture*, 1951. • Jerome H. Buckley, *The Triumph of Time: A Study of the Victorian Concepts of Time, History, Progress, and Decadence*, 1966. • David Cannadine, *The Decline and Fall of the British Aristocracy*. 1990. • A. Dwight Culler, *The Victorian Mirror of History*, 1985. • David J. Delaura, *Hebrew and Hellene in Victorian England: Newman, Arnold, and Pater*, 1969. • Peter Gay, *The Bourgeois Experience: From Victoria to Freud*, 2 vols., 1984–1986. • Robin Gilmour, *The Victorian Period: The Intellectual and Cultural Context of English Literature, 1830–1890*. 1993. • Christopher Herbert, *Culture and Anomie: Ethnographic Imagination in the Nineteenth Century*, 1991. • Thomas William Heyck, *The Transformation of Intellectual Life in Victorian England*, 1982. • Walter E. Houghton, *The Victorian Frame of Mind, 1830–1870*, 1957. • Richard Jenkyns, *The Victorians and Ancient Greece*, 1980. • Steven Marcus, *The Other Victorians: A Study of Sexuality and Pornography in Mid-Nineteenth-Century England*, 1964. • Sally Mitchell, ed., *Victorian Britain: An Encyclopedia*, 1988. • E. Royston Pike, ed., "Hard Times": Human Documents of the Industrial Revolution, 1966; "Golden Times": Human Documents of the Victorian Age, 1967; "Busy Times": Human Documents of the Age of the Forsytes, 1969. • Mary Poovey, *Making a Social Body: British Cultural Formation, 1830–1864*, 1995. • Thomas Richards, *The Commodity Culture of Victorian England: Advertising and Spectacle, 1851–1914*, 1990. • Edward Said, *Orientalism*, 1978. • Richard L. Stein, *Victoria's Year: English Literature and Culture, 1837–1838*, 1987. • George W. Stocking, *Victorian Anthropology*, 1987. • Herbert Sussman, *Victorians and the Machine*, 1968. • Frank M. Turner, *Contesting Cultural Authority: Essays in Victorian Intellectual Life*, 1993. • Basil Willey, *Nineteenth Century Studies*, 1949. • Basil Willey, *More Nineteenth Century Studies*, 1956. • Raymond Williams, *Culture and Society 1780–1950*, 1958. • Janet Wolff and John Seed, eds., *The Culture of Capital: Art, Power and the Nineteenth-Century Middle Class*, 1988. • G. M. Young, *Victorian England: Portrait of an Age*, 1936.

Fiction • Richard D. Altick, *The Presence of the Present: Topics of the Day in the Victorian Novel*, 1991. • Nancy Armstrong, *Desire and Domestic Fiction: A Political History of the Novel*, 1987. • Joseph W. Childers, *Novel Possibilities: Fiction and the Formation of Early Victorian Culture*, 1995. • Peter Garrett, *The Victorian Multiplot Novel*, 1980. • Barbara Hardy, *Forms of Feeling in Victorian Fiction*, 1985. • E. A. Horsman, *The Victorian Novel*, 1991. • George Levine, *The Realistic Imagination: English Fiction from Frankenstein to Lady Chatterley*, 1981. • D. A. Miller, *The Novel and the Police*, 1988. • J. Hillis Miller, *The Form of Victorian Fiction*, 1968. • Ira B. Nadel and William E. Fredeman, eds., *Victorian Novelists Before 1885*, in *Dictionary of Literary Biography*, vol. 21, 1983.

• Robert Polhemus, *Erotic Faith: Being in Love from Jane Austen to D. H. Lawrence*, 1990. • Barry Qualls, *The Secular Pilgrims of Victorian Fiction*, 1982. • Elaine Showalter, *A Literature of Their Own: British Women Novelists from Brontë to Lessing*, 1977. • Lionel Stevenson, *The English Novel: A Panorama*, 1960. • Ronald R. Thomas, *Dreams of Authority: Freud and the Fictions of the Unconscious*, 1990.

Gender and Culture • Amanda Anderson, *Tainted Souls and Painted Faces: The Rhetoric of Fallenness in Victorian Culture*, 1993. • Nina Auerbach, *Romantic Imprisonment: Women and Other Glorified Outcasts*, 1985. • Nina Auerbach, *Woman and the Demon: The Life of a Victorian Myth*, 1982. • Francoise Basch, *Relative Creatures: Victorian Women in Society and the Novel*, 1974. • Susan Casteras and Linda H. Peterson, *A Struggle for Fame: Victorian Women Artists and Authors*, 1994. • Lloyd Davis, ed., *Virgin Sexuality and Textuality in Victorian Literature*, 1993. • Richard Dellamora, *Masculine Desire: The Sexual Politics of Victorian Aestheticism*, 1990. • Kristine Ottesen Garrigan, ed., *Victorian Scandals: Representations of Gender and Class*, 1992. • Sandra Gilbert and Susan Gubar, *The Madwoman in the Attic: The Woman Writer and the Nineteenth-Century Literary Imagination*, 1979. • A. James Hammerton, *Cruelty and Companionship: Conflict in Nineteenth-Century Married Life*, 1992. • Kathleen Hickok, *Representations of Women: Nineteenth-Century British Women's Poetry*, 1984. • Margaret Homans, *Bearing the Word: Language and Female Experience in Nineteenth-Century Women's Writing*, 1986. • Dorothy Mermin, *Godiva's Ride: Women of Letters in England, 1830–1880*, 1993. • Ellen Moers, *Literary Women*, 1976. • Deborah Epstein Nord, *Walking the Victorian Streets: Women Representation, and the City*, 1995. • Christopher Parker, ed., *Gender Roles and Sexuality in Victorian Literature*, 1995. • Eve Kosofsky Sedgwick, *Between Men: English Literature and Male Homosocial Desire*, 1985. • Alan Sinfield, *Cultural Politics—Queer Reading*, 1994.

History and Politics • Derek Beales, *From Castlereagh to Gladstone: 1815–1885*, 1970. • Patrick Brantlinger, *The Spirit of Reform: British Literature and Politics, 1832–1867*, 1977. • Asa Briggs, *A Social History of England*, 1983. • Barbara Dennis and David Skilton, eds., *Reform and Intellectual Debate in Victorian England*, 1987. • C. C. Eldridge, *Victorian Imperialism*, 1978. • E. J. Feuchtwanger, *Democracy and Empire: Britain, 1865–1914*, 1985. • Jose Harris, *Private Lives, Public Spirit: A Social History of Great Britain,* *1870–1914*, 1993. • Patricia Jalland, *Women, Marriage, and Politics, 1860–1914*, 1987. • Patrick Joyce, *Visions of the People: Industrial England and the Question of Class, 1848–1914*, 1991. • J. P. Parry, *The Rise and Fall of Liberal Government in Victorian Britain*, 1994. • David Thomson, *England in the Nineteenth Century*, 1950. • E. P. Thompson, *The Making of the English Working Class*, 1963. • F. M. L. Thompson, *The Rise of Respectable Society: A Social History of Victorian Britain, 1830–1900*, 1988.

Literature • William E. Buckler, *The Victorian Imagination: Essays in Aesthetic Exploration*, 1980. • Raymond Chapman, *The Sense of the Past in Victorian Literature*, 1986. • J. Hillis Miller, *The Disappearance of God: Five Nineteenth Century Writers*, 1963. • J. Hillis Miller, *Victorian Subjects*, 1990. • David Morse, *High Victorian Culture*, 1993. • John R. Reed, *Victorian Conventions*, 1975 • Ruth Robbins and Julian Wolfreys, eds., *Victorian Identities: Social and Cultural Formations in Nineteenth-Century Literature*, 1996.

Nonfiction Prose • Andrea Broomfield and Sally Mitchell, eds., *Prose by Victorian Women: An Anthology*, 1996. • Jerome H. Buckley, *The Turning Key: Autobiography and the Subjective Impulse since 1800*, 1984. • A. O. J. Cockshut, *The Art of Autobiography in 19th and 20th Century England*, 1984. • Mary Jean Corbett, *Representing Femininity: Middle-Class Subjectivity in Victorian and Edwardian Women's Autobiographies*, 1992. • Avrom Fleishman, *Figures of Autobiography: The Language of Self-Writing in Victorian and Modern England*, 1983. • Regenia Gagnier, *Subjectivities: A History of Self-Representation in Britain, 1832–1920*, 1991. • Heather Henderson, *The Victorian Self: Autobiography and Biblical Narrative*, 1989. • John Holloway, *The Victorian Sage*, 1953. • George P. Landow, ed., *Approaches to Victorian Autobiography*, 1979. • A. L. Le Quesne, *Victorian Thinkers: Carlyle, Ruskin, Arnold, Morris*, 1993. • George Levine and William Madden, eds., *The Art of Victorian Prose*, 1968. • Laura Marcus, *Auto/biographical Discourses: Theory, Criticism, Practice*, 1995. • Thaïs E. Morgan, ed., *Victorian Sages and Cultural Discourse: Renegotiating Gender and Power*, 1991. • Linda Peterson, *Victorian Autobiography: The Tradition of Self-Interpretation*, 1986.

Poetry • Isobel Armstrong, *Victorian Poetry: Poetry, Poetics, and Politics*, 1993. • Douglas Bush, *Mythology and the Romantic Tradition in English Poetry*, 1937. • Carol T. Christ, *The Finer Optic: The Aesthetic of Particularity in Victorian Poetry*, 1975. • Carol T. Christ, *Victorian and Modern Poetics*, 1984. • William E. Fredeman and Ira B.

Nadel, eds., *Victorian Poets After 1850*, in *Dictionary of Literary Biography*, vol. 35, 1985. • William E. Fredeman, and Ira B. Nadel, eds., *Victorian Poets Before 1850*, in *Dictionary of Literary Biography*, vol. 32, 1984. • Eric Griffiths, *The Printed Voice of Victorian Poetry*, 1989. • Antony H. Harrison, *Victorian Poets and Romantic Poems: Intertextuality and Ideology*, 1990. • E. D. H. Johnson, *The Alien Vision of Victorian Poetry*, 1952. • Robert Langbaum, *The Poetry of Experience: The Dramatic Monologue in Modern Literary Tradition*, 1957. • Angela Leighton, *Victorian Women Poets: Writing Against the Heart*, 1992. • Angela Leighton, ed., *Victorian Women Poets: A Critical Reader*, 1996. • Angela Leighton and Margaret Reynolds, eds., *Victorian Women Poets: An Anthology*, 1995. • Laurence W. Mazzeno, *Victorian Poetry: An Annotated Bibliography*, 1995. • W. David Shaw, *The Lucid Veil: Poetic Truth in the Victorian Age*, 1987.

Reading and Readership • Richard D. Altick, *The English Common Reader: A Social History of the Mass Reading Public 1800–1900*, 1957. • Richard D. Altick, *Writers, Readers, and Occasions*, 1989. • N. N. Feltes, *Modes of Production of Victorian Novels*, 1986. • Kate Flint, *The Woman Reader, 1837–1914*, 1993. • John O. Jordan and Robert L. Patten, eds., *Literature in the Marketplace: Nineteenth-Century British Publishing and Reading Practices*, 1995. • Judith Kennedy, ed., *Victorian Authors and Their Works: Revision, Motivations, and Modes*, 1991. • Q. D. Leavis, *Fiction and the Reading Public*, 1932. • Joanne Shattock and Michael Wolff, eds., *The Victorian Periodical Press*, 1982. • John Sutherland, *Victorian Fiction: Writers, Publishers, Readers*, 1995. • David Vincent, *Literacy and Popular Culture: England 1750–1914*, 1990.

Theater • Michael R. Booth, ed., *English Plays of the Nineteenth Century*, 5 vols., 1969–1976. • Michael R. Booth, *Theater in The Victorian Age*, 1991. • Michael R. Booth, ed., *The Lights o' London and other Victorian Plays*, 1995. • Tracy C. Davis, *Actresses as Working Women: Their Social Identity in Victorian Culture*, 1991. • Anthony Jenkins, *The Making of Victorian Drama*, 1991. • Joel H. Kaplan and Sheila Stowell, *Theatre and Fashion: Oscar Wilde to the Suffragettes*, 1994.

Visual Arts • Richard Altick, *Paintings from Books: Art and Literature in Britain, 1760–1900*, 1985. • Kenneth Bendiner, *An Introduction to Victorian Painting*, 1985. • Deborah Cherry, *Painting Women: Victorian Women Artists*, 1993. • Carol T. Christ and John O. Jordan, eds., *Victorian Literature and the Victorian Visual Imagination*, 1995. • Linda Dowling, *The Vulgarization*

of Art: The Victorians and Aesthetic Democracy, 1996. • William Gaunt, *The Pre-Raphaelite Dream*, 1966. • Helmut Gernsheim, *Julia Margaret Cameron: Her Life and Photographic Work*, 1975. • Heinz K. Henisch, *The Photographic Experience, 1839–1914*, 1994. • U. C. Knoepflmacher and G. B. Tennyson, eds., *Nature and the Victorian Imagination*, 1977. • Jeremy Maas, *Victorian Painters*, 1969. • Jan Marsh, *Pre-Raphaelite Sisterhood*, 1985. • Ira Bruce Nadel and F. S. Schwartzbach, eds., *Victorian Artists and the City*, 1980. • Pamela Gerrish Nunn, *Problem Pictures: Women and Men in Victorian Painting*, 1996. • Leslie Parris, ed., *The Pre-Raphaelites*, 1984. • Graham Reynolds, *Victorian Painting*, 1966; rev. 1987. • Lindsay Smith, *Victorian Photography, Painting, and Poetry: The Enigma of Visibility in Ruskin, Morris and the Pre-Raphaelites*, 1995. • Roy Strong, *And When Did You Last See Your Father?: The Victorian Painter and British History*, 1978. • Julian Treuherz, *Victorian Painting*, 1993. • Mike Weaver, *British Photography in the Nineteenth Century: The Fine Art Tradition*, 1989. • Christopher Wood, *The Pre-Raphaelites*, 1981.

World Wide Web Addresses • *British Poetry 1780–1910: A Hypertext Archive of Scholarly Editions:* etext.lib.virginia.edu/britpo.html • *Northeast Victorian Studies Association:* fmc.utm.edu.nvsa/index.html [Maintains list of other Victorian web sites.] • *Victoria Research Web:* www.indiana.edu/~victoria/ vwcont.html [Lists other Victorian web sites, and online Victorian journals and discussion groups.]. • George Landow's *Victorian Web:* www.stg.brown.edu/projects/hypertext/landow/victorian/victov.html • *Victorian Women Writers Project:* www.indiana.edu/~letrs/vwwp/.

Perspectives: Aestheticism, Decadence and the Fin de Siècle • **Anthologies** Karl Beckson, ed., *Aesthetes and Decadents of the 1890s: An Anthology of British Poetry and Prose*, 1966; 1981. • Graham Hough and Eric Warner, eds., *Strangeness and Beauty: An Anthology of Aesthetic Criticism, 1840–1910*, 2 vols., 1983. • Ian Small, ed., *The Aesthetes: A Sourcebook*, 1979. • Derek Stanford, ed., *Poets of the 'Nineties: A Biographical Anthology*, 1965. • R. K. R. Thornton, ed., *Poetry of the Nineties*, 1970. • Stanley Weintraub, ed., *The Yellow Book: Quintessence of the Nineties*, 1964.

Criticism • Karl Beckson, *London in the 1890s: A Cultural History*, 1992. • Gene H. Bell-Villada, *Art for Art's Sake and Literary Life: How Politics and Markets Helped Shape the Ideology and Culture of Aestheticism, 1790–1990*, 1996. • G. A. Cevasco, ed., *The 1890s: An Encyclopedia of*

British Literature, Art, and Culture, 1993. • Richard Dellamora, Masculine Desire: The Sexual Politics of Victorian Aestheticism, 1990. • Linda C. Dowling, Aestheticism and Decadence: A Selective Annotated Bibliography, 1977. • Linda C. Dowling, Hellenism and Homosexuality in Victorian Oxford, 1994. • Linda C. Dowling, Language and Decadence in the Victorian Fin de Siècle, 1986. • Bram Dijkstra, Idols of Perversity: Fantasies of Feminine Evil in Fin-de-Siècle Culture, 1986. • Ian Fletcher, ed., Decadence and the 1890s, 1979. • Hilary Fraser, Beauty and Belief: Aesthetics and Religion in Victorian Literature, 1986. • William Gaunt, The Aesthetic Adventure, 1945. • Richard Gilman, Decadence: The Strange Life of an Epithet, 1979. • Walter Hamilton, The Aesthetic Movement in England, 1882. • Simon Houfe, Fin de Siècle: The Illustrators of the 'Nineties, 1992. • Graham Hough, The Last Romantics, 1947. • Holbrook Jackson, The Eighteen Nineties, 1913. • Sally Ledger and Scott McCracken, eds., Cultural Politics at the Fin de Siècle, 1995. • Patricia Marks, Bicycles, Bangs, and Bloomers: The New Woman in the Popular Press, 1990. • Linda Merrill, A Pot of Paint: Aesthetics on Trial in "Whistler v. Ruskin," 1992. • John R. Reed, Decadent Style, 1985. • Elaine Showalter, Sexual Anarchy: Gender and Culture at the Fin de Siècle, 1990. • Chris Snodgrass, Aubrey Beardsley: Dandy of the Grotesque, 1995. • Robin Spencer, The Aesthetic Movement: Theory and Practice, 1972. • John Stokes, In the Nineties, 1989. • John Stokes, ed., Fin de Siècle/Fin de Globe: Fears and Fantasies of the Late Nineteenth Century, 1992. • Mikulas Teich and Roy Porter, eds., Fin de Siècle and its Legacy, 1990. • R. K. R. Thornton, The Decadent Dilemma, 1983.

Our Texts • GILBERT: "If You're Anxious for to Shine" from The Complete Plays of Gilbert and Sullivan, 1941; WHISTLER: "Mr. Whistler's 'Ten O'Clock'" from The Gentle Art of Making Enemies, 2nd ed., 1892; "MICHAEL FIELD": "La Gioconda" and "A Pen-Drawing of Leda" from Sight and Song, 1892; "A Girl" from Underneath the Bough, 1893; LEVERSON: "Suggestion" from The Yellow Book, April 1895; DOUGLAS: "Two Loves" from Two Loves and Other Poems, 1990; "Impression de nuit" from The Collected Poems of Lord Alfred Douglas, 1919; CUSTANCE: from The Selected Poems of Olive Custance, 1995.

Perspectives: The Industrial Landscape •

Anthologies • F. P. Donovon, The Railroad in Literature: A Brief Survey of Railroad Fiction, Poetry, Songs, Biography, Essays, Travel, and Drama in the English Language, 1940. • E. Royston Pike, "Hard Times": Human Documents of the Industrial Revolution, 1966. • Jeremy Warburg, ed., The Industrial Muse: The Industrial Revolution in English Poetry, 1958.

Criticism • John Belchem, Industrialization and the Working Class: The English Experience, 1750–1900, 1990. • Asa Briggs, Victorian Cities, 1963. • D. S. L. Cardwell, The Norton History of Technology, 1994. • Alice Chandler, A Dream of Order: The Medieval Ideal in Nineteenth-Century English Literature, 1970. • S. G. Checkland, The Rise of Industrial Society in England, 1815–1885, 1964. • Kenneth Clark, The Gothic Revival: An Essay in the History of Taste, 1928. • Bruce I. Coleman, ed., The Idea of the City in Nineteenth-Century Britain, 1973. • H. J. Dyos and Michael Wolff, eds., The Victorian City: Images and Realities, 2 vols., 1973. • Frank Ferneyhough, The History of Railways in Britain, 1975. • E. J. Hobsbawm, Industry and Empire, 1968. • Peter Keating, The Working Classes in Victorian Fiction, 1971. • David Levine, The Making of an Industrial Society, 1991. • Steven Marcus, Engels, Manchester, and the Working Class, 1974. • Ivan Melada, The Captain of Industry in English Fiction, 1821–1871, 1970. • Joel Mokyr, ed., The British Industrial Revolution: An Economic Perspective, 1993. • Joel Mokyr, ed., The Economics of the Industrial Revolution, 1986. • Deborah Epstein Nord, Walking the Victorian Streets: Women, Representation, and the City, 1995. • Ivy Pinchbeck, Women Workers and the Industrial Revolution, 1750–1850, 1930. • Sonya O. Rose, Limited Livelihoods: Gender and Class in Nineteenth-Century England, 1992. • Jack Simmons, The Victorian Railway, 1991. • Herbert Sussman, Victorians and the Machine: The Literary Response to Technology, 1968. • E. P. Thompson, The Making of the English Working Class, 1963. • Barrie Stewart Trinder, The Making of the Industrial Landscape, 1982. • Martha Vicinus, The Industrial Muse: A Study of Nineteenth Century Working-Class Literature, 1974. • James Walvin, English Urban Life, 1776–1851, 1984. • Raymond Williams, The Country and the City, 1973. • Edward A. Wrigley, Continuity, Chance and Change: The Character of the Industrial Revolution in England, 1989.

Our Texts • "The Steam Loom Weaver" from Martha Vicinus, The Industrial Muse, 1974; KEMBLE: Record of a Girlhood, vol. 2, 1879; MACAULAY: "A Review of Southey's Colloquies" from Edinburgh Review, Jan. 1830; PARLIAMENTARY PAPERS: from Victorian Women: A Documentary Account of Women's Lives, eds. Hellerstein, Hume, and Offen, 1981; DICKENS:

Dombey and Son, Charles Dickens Edition, 1867; *Hard Times*, 1854; DISRAELI: *Sybil* from *The Works of Benjamin Disraeli*, 1904; ENGELS: *The Condition of the Working Class in England*, *1845*, trans. W. O. Henderson and W. H. Chaloner, 1958; MAYHEW: *London Labour and the London Poor*, vols. 1 and 2, 1861–1862.

Perspectives: Victorian Ladies and Gentlemen
• *Anthologies* • Susan Groag Bell and Karen M. Offen, *Woman, the Family, and Freedom: The Debate in Documents*, 2 vols, 1983. • Erna Olafson Hellerstein, Leslie Parker Hume, and Karen M. Offen, eds., *Victorian Women: A Documentary Account of Women's Lives*, 1981. • Elizabeth K. Helsinger, Robin Lauterbach Sheets, and William Veeder, eds., *The Woman Question: Society and Literature in Britain and America, 1837–1883*, 3 vols., 1983. • Janet Murray, *Strong-Minded Women and Other Lost Voices from Nineteenth-Century England*, 1982.

Criticism • James Eli Adams, *Dandies and Desert Saints: Styles of Victorian Masculinity*, 1995. • Patricia Branca, *Silent Sisterhood: Middle-Class Women in the Victorian Home*, 1975. • Michael Brander, *The Victorian Gentleman*, 1975. • Joan N. Burstyn, *Victorian Education and the Ideal of Womanhood*, 1980. • David Castronovo, *The English Gentleman: Images and Ideals in Literature and Society*, 1987. • John Chandos, *Boys Together: English Public Schools, 1800–1864*, 1984. • Leonore Davidoff and Catherine Hall, *Family Fortunes: Men and Women of the English Middle Class, 1780–1850*, 1987. • Jonathan Gathorne-Hardy, *The Public School Phenomenon*, 1977. • Robin Gilmour, *The Idea of the Gentleman in the Victorian Novel*, 1981. • Mark Girouard, *The Return to Camelot: Chivalry and the English Gentleman*, 1981. • Deborah Gorham, *The Victorian Girl and the Feminine Ideal*, 1982. • Donald E. Hall, ed., *Muscular Christianity: Embodying the Victorian Age*, 1994. • Lee Holcombe, *Victorian Ladies at Work: Middle-Class Women in England and Wales, 1850–1914*, 1973. • Richard Holt, *Sport and the British: A Modern History*, 1989. • Margaret Homans and Adrienne Munich, eds., *Remaking Queen Victoria*, 1997. • J. R. de S. Honey, *Tom Brown's Universe: The Development of the English Public School in the Nineteenth Century*, 1977. • Kathryn Hughes, *The Victorian Governess*, 1993. • Elizabeth Langland, *Nobody's Angels: Middle-Class Women and Domestic Ideology in Victorian Culture*, 1995. • Anita Levy, *Other Women: The Writing of Class, Race, and Gender, 1832–1898*, 1991. • Elizabeth Longford, *Eminent Victorian Women*, 1981. • J.

A. Mangan and James Walvin, eds., *Manliness and Masculinity: Middle-Class Masculinity in Britain and America, 1800–1940*, 1987. • Philip Mason, *The English Gentleman: The Rise and Fall of an Ideal*, 1982. • Claudia Nelson and Lynne Vallone, eds., *The Girl's Own: Cultural Histories of the Anglo-American Girl, 1830–1915*, 1994. • Mary Poovey, *Uneven Developments: The Ideological Work of Gender in Mid-Victorian England*, 1988. • Sonya O. Rose, *Limited Livelihoods: Gender and Class in Nineteenth-Century England*, 1992. • Brian Simon and Ian Bradley, eds., *The Victorian Public School: Studies in the Development of an Educational Institution*, 1975. • Herbert Sussman, *Victorian Masculinities: Manhood and Masculine Poetics in Early Victorian Literature and Art*, 1995. • Dorothy Thompson, *Queen Victoria: The Woman, the Monarchy, and the People*, 1990. • Norman Vance, *The Sinews of the Spirit: The Ideal of Christian Manliness in Victorian Literature and Religious Thought*, 1985. • Martha Vicinus, ed., *Suffer and Be Still: Women in the Victorian Age*, 1972. • Martha Vicinus, ed., *A Widening Sphere: Changing Roles of Victorian Women*, 1977.

Our Texts • COBBE: *Life of Frances Power Cobbe*, 1904; ELLIS: *The Women of England*, 1839; C. BRONTE: *The Brontës: Their Lives, Friendships, and Correspondence*, eds. Wise and Symington, Vol. 1, 1933; A. BRONTE: *Agnes Grey*, 1860; NEWMAN: *The Idea of a University*, 1873; BEETON: *The Book of Household Management*, 1861; VICTORIA: see footnotes; KINGSLEY: *The Works of Charles Kingsley*, vol. 7, 1899; NEWBOLT: "Vitaï Lampada," *The Island Race*, 1898.

Matthew Arnold • *Editions* • Kenneth Allott, ed., *Arnold: The Complete Poems*, 1965; 2nd ed., Miriam Allott, 1979. • Miriam Allott and R. H. Super, eds., *Matthew Arnold*, 1986 [annotated selection]. • Cecil Y. Lang, ed., *The Letters of Matthew Arnold*, 1996–. • Howard Foster Lowry, ed., *The Letters of Matthew Arnold to Arthur Hugh Clough*, 1968. • R. H. Super, ed., *The Complete Prose Works of Matthew Arnold*, 11 vols., 1960–1977.

Biography • Park Honan, *Matthew Arnold: A Life*, 1981. • Nicholas Murray, *A Life of Matthew Arnold*, 1997.

Criticism • Kenneth Allott, ed., *Matthew Arnold*, 1975. • Ruth Roberts, *Arnold and God*, 1983. • Harold Bloom, ed., *Matthew Arnold*, 1987. • William E. Buckler, *On the Poetry of Matthew Arnold*, 1982. • Douglas Bush, *Matthew Arnold: A Survey of His Poetry and Prose*, 1971. •

Joseph Carroll, *The Cultural Theory of Matthew Arnold*, 1982. • Stefan Collini, *Arnold*, 1988. • Dwight Culler, *Imaginative Reason*, 1966. • Carl Dawson and John Pfordresher, eds., *Matthew Arnold, the Poetry: The Critical Heritage*, 1973; and *Matthew Arnold, Prose Writings: The Critical Heritage*, 1979. • T. S. Eliot, "Matthew Arnold," in his *The Use of Poetry and the Use of Criticism*, 1933. • T. S. Eliot, "Arnold and Pater," in his *Selected Essays*, 1932. • R. Giddings, ed., *Matthew Arnold: Between Two Worlds*, 1986. • Leon Gottfried, *Matthew Arnold and the Romantics*, 1983. • D. G. James, *Matthew Arnold and the Decline of English Romanticism*, 1961. • Edward D. H. Johnson, *The Alien Vision of Victorian Poetry*, 1952. • James C. Livingston, *Matthew Arnold and Christianity: His Religious Prose Writings*, 1986. • David G. Riede, *Matthew Arnold and the Betrayal of Language*, 1988. • Alan Roper, *Arnold's Poetic Landscapes*, 1969. • G. Robert Stange, *The Poet as Humanist*, 1967. • Lionel Trilling, *Matthew Arnold*, 1949.

Our Texts • The poems in this anthology are from Allott, *Complete Poems*; our prose selections are from Super, *Complete Prose*.

Elizabeth Barrett Browning • **Editions** • Cora Kaplan, ed., *Aurora Leigh and Other Poems*, 1978. • Philip Kelley and Ronald Hudson, eds., *The Brownings' Correspondence*, 1984–. • Elvan Kintner, ed., *The Letters of Robert Browning and Elizabeth Barrett Browning, 1845–1846*, 2 vols, 1969. • Charlotte Porter and Helen Clarke, eds., *Complete Works*, 6 vols., 1900. • Harriet Waters Preston, ed., *The Complete Poetical Works of Elizabeth Barrett Browning*, 1900; 1974. • Margaret Reynolds, ed., *Aurora Leigh*, 1992; 1996.

Biography • Angela Leighton, *Elizabeth Barrett Browning*, 1986. • Gardner B. Taplin, *The Life of Elizabeth Barrett Browning*, 1957.

Criticism • Warner Barnes, *A Bibliography of Elizabeth Barrett Browning*, 1968. • Kathleen Blake, "Elizabeth Barrett Browning and Wordsworth: The Romantic Poet as a Woman," *Victorian Poetry* 24 (1986). • Helen Cooper, *Elizabeth Barrett Browning, Woman and Artist*, 1988. • Deirdre David, *Intellectual Women and Victorian Patriarchy: Harriet Martineau, Elizabeth Barrett Browning, George Eliot*, 1987. • Sandra M. Gilbert, "From *Patria* to *Matria*: Elizabeth Barrett Browning's Risorgimento." *PMLA* 99 (1984); repr. *Victorian Women Poets*, ed. Angela Leighton, 1996. • Alethea Hayter, *Mrs. Browning: A Poet's Work and Its Setting*, 1962. • Dorothy Mermin, *Elizabeth Barrett Browning: The Origins of a New Poetry*, 1989. • Virginia L. Radley, *Elizabeth Barrett Browning*, 1972. • Dolores Rosenblum, "Face to Face: Elizabeth Barrett Browning's *Aurora Leigh* and Nineteenth-Century Poetry," *Victorian Studies* 26 (1983). • Glennis Stephenson, *Elizabeth Barrett Browning and the Poetry of Love*, 1989. • Marjorie Stone, *Elizabeth Barrett Browning*, 1995. • Virginia Woolf, "*Aurora Leigh*," in *The Second Common Reader*, 1932. • Joyce Zonana, "The Embodied Muse: Elizabeth Barrett Browning's *Aurora Leigh* and Feminist Poetics," *Tulsa Studies in Women's Literature* 8 (1989); repr. in *Victorian Women Poets*, ed. Angela Leighton, 1996.

Our Texts • Charlotte Porter and Helen Clarke, eds., *Complete Works*, 6 vols., 1900.

Robert Browning • **Editions** • *Poetical Works of Robert Browning*, 16 vols., 1888–1889. • Ian Jack, Margaret Smith, and Robert Inglesfield, eds., *The Poetical Works of Robert Browning*, 1983–. • Philip Kelley and Ronald Hudson, eds., *The Brownings' Correspondence*, 1984–. • John Pettigrew and Thomas J. Collins, eds., *The Poems*, 2 vols., 1981.

Biography • William Irvine and Park Honan, *The Book, the Ring, and the Poet*, 1974. • John Maynard, *Browning's Youth*, 1977. • Mrs. Sutherland Orr, *Life and Letters of Robert Browning*, 1891; 1908. • Clyde de L. Ryals, *The Life of Robert Browning: A Critical Biography*, 1993.

Criticism • Isobel Armstrong, ed., *Robert Browning*, 1974. • Walter Bagehot, "Wordsworth, Tennyson, and Browning," in *Literary Studies*, ed. R. H. Hutton, 1895. • Harold Bloom and Adrienne Munich, eds., *Robert Browning: A Collection of Critical Essays*, 1979. • Joseph Bristow, *Robert Browning*, 1991. • G. K. Chesterton, *Robert Browning*, 1903. • Norman B. Crowell, *A Reader's Guide to Robert Browning*, 1972. • William C. DeVane, *A Browning Handbook*, 1955. • Philip Drew, ed., *Robert Browning: A Collection of Critical Essays*, 1966. • Donald Hair, *Browning's Experiments with Genre*, 1972. • Ian Jack, *Browning's Major Poetry*, 1973. • Roma A. King Jr., *The Bow and the Lyre*, 1957. • Robert Langbaum, *The Poetry of Experience: The Dramatic Monologue in Modern Literary Tradition*, 1957. • Boyd Litzinger and K. L. Knickerbocker, eds., *The Browning Critics*, 1965. • Boyd Litzinger and Donald Smalley, eds., *Browning: The Critical Heritage*, 1970. • Loy Martin, *Browning's Dramatic Monologues and the Post-Romantic Subject*, 1985. • William S. Peterson, *Robert and Elizabeth*

Barrett Browning: An Annotated Bibliography, 1951–1970, 1974. • W. O. Raymond, *The Infinite Moment,* 1965. • Herbert F. Tucker, *Browning's Beginnings: The Art of Disclosure,* 1980.

Our Texts • From *Poetical Works of Robert Browning,* 16 vols., 1888–1889.

Thomas Carlyle • **Editions** • C. R. Sanders, K. J. Fielding, Clyde de L. Ryals, et al., eds., *The Collected Letters of Thomas and Jane Welsh Carlyle,* 1970–. • H. D. Traill, ed., *The Works of Thomas Carlyle,* 30 vols., 1896–1899.

Biography • J. A. Froude, *Thomas Carlyle: A History of the First Forty Years of his Life, 1795–1835,* 2 vols., 1882; *Thomas Carlyle: A History of his Life in London, 1834–1881,* 2 vols., 1884. • Fred Kaplan, *Thomas Carlyle: A Biography,* 1983.

Criticism • Ruth Roberts, *The Ancient Dialect: Thomas Carlyle and Comparative Religion,* 1988. • K. J. Fielding and Rodger L. Tarr, eds., *Carlyle Past and Present,* 1976. • Michael Goldberg, *Carlyle and Dickens,* 1972. • John Holloway, *The Victorian Sage,* 1953. • Albert J. LaValley, *Carlyle and the Idea of the Modern,* 1968. • George Levine, *The Boundaries of Fiction: Carlyle, Macaulay, Newman,* 1968. • Emery Neff, *Carlyle and Mill,* 1926. • Barry Qualls, *The Secular Pilgrims of Victorian Fiction,* 1983. • John D. Rosenberg, *Carlyle and the Burden of History,* 1985. • Philip Rosenberg, *The Seventh Hero: Thomas Carlyle and the Theory of Radical Activism,* 1974. • Jules Paul Seigel, ed., *Thomas Carlyle: The Critical Heritage,* 1971. • Rodger Tarr, *Thomas Carlyle: A Descriptive Bibliography,* 1990. • G. B. Tennyson, *"Sartor" Called "Resartus,"* 1965. • G. B. Tennyson, "Thomas Carlyle," in *Victorian Prose: A Guide to Research,* ed. David J. DeLaura, 1973. • Chris Vanden Bossche, *Carlyle and the Search for Authority,* 1991. • Basil Willey, *Nineteenth Century Studies,* 1949.

Our Texts • Texts cited from H. D. Traill.

Charles Darwin • **Editions** • Philip Appleman, ed., *Darwin,* 1970; 2nd ed., 1979. • Nora Barlow, ed., *The Autobiography of Charles Darwin, 1809–1882: With Original Omissions Restored,* 1958. • Paul H. Barrett and R. B. Freeman, eds., *The Works of Charles Darwin,* 29 vols., 1986. • Richard E. Leakey, abridged and introduced, *The Illustrated Origin of Species,* 1979; 1986.

Biography • John Bowlby, *Charles Darwin: A New Life,* 1990. • Francis Darwin, ed., *The Life and Letters of Darwin,* 1887–1888. • Adrian Desmond and James Moore, *Darwin,* 1991.

Criticism • Mea Allan, *Darwin and His Flowers: The Key to Natural Selection,* 1977. • Gillian Beer, *Darwin's Plots: Evolutionary Narrative in Darwin, George Eliot, and Nineteenth-Century Fiction,* 1983. • Peter Brent, *Charles Darwin: "A Man of Enlarged Curiosity,"* 1981. • Sir Gavin De Beer, *Charles Darwin: Evolution by Natural Selection,* 1964. • Loren Eiseley, *Darwin's Century: Evolution and the Men Who Discovered It,* 1958. • Michael T. Ghiselin, *The Triumph of the Darwinian Method,* 1984. • Stephen Jay Gould, *Ever Since Darwin,* 1977. • Stephen Jay Gould, *The Flamingo's Smile,* 1985. • David Kohn, ed., *The Darwinian Heritage,* 1985. • George Levine, *Darwin and the Novelists: Patterns of Science in Victorian Fiction,* 1988. • Jonathan Miller and Borin Van Loon, *Darwin for Beginners,* 1982. • John D. Rosenberg, "Mr. Darwin Collects Himself," in *Nineteenth-Century Lives,* ed. Laurence S. Lockridge et al., 1989. • Robert M. Young, *Darwin's Metaphor: Nature's Place in Victorian Culture,* 1985.

Our Texts • *The Voyage of the Beagle,* 1860, repr. 1962, ed. Leonard Engel; *On the Origin of Species,* 1859, repr. 1968, ed. J. W. Burrow.

Elizabeth Gaskell • W. A. Craik, *Elizabeth Gaskell and the English Provincial Novel,* 1975. • Angus Easson, *Elizabeth Gaskell,* 1979. • Angus Easson, ed., *Elizabeth Gaskell: The Critical Heritage,* 1991. • Rowena Fowler, "Cranford: Cow in Grey Flannel or Lion Couchant?" *SEL* 24 (1984). • Winifred Gérin, *Elizabeth Gaskell,* 1980. • Rae Rosenthal, "Gaskell's Feminist Utopia: The Cranfordians and the Reign of Goodwill," in *Utopian and Science Fiction by Women: Worlds of Difference,* eds. Jane L. Donawerth and Carol A. Kolmerten, 1994. • Hilary M. Schor, *Scheherezade in the Market Place: Elizabeth Gaskell and the Victorian Novel,* 1992. • Patsy Stoneman, *Elizabeth Gaskell,* 1987. • Jenny Uglow, *Elizabeth Gaskell: A Habit of Stories,* 1993. • Patricia A. Wolfe, "Structure and Movement in Cranford," in *Nineteenth-Century Fiction,* vol. 23, 1968. • Terence Wright, *Elizabeth Gaskell: "We are not angels": Realism, Gender, Values,* 1995.

Our Text • *The Works of Mrs. Gaskell,* Knutsford Edition, 8 vols., 1906–1920. Ed. A. W. Ward. 1906–1911.

Gerard Manley Hopkins • **Editions** • Claude C. Abbott, ed., *The Correspondence of Gerard Manley Hopkins and Richard Watson Dixon,* 2 vols., 1935; rev. 1955. • Claude C. Abbott, *Further Letters of Gerard Manley Hopkins,* 1938; 1956. • Claude C. Abbott, *The Letters of Gerard Manley Hopkins to Robert Bridges,* 1935; 1955. • Christopher Devlin, ed., *The Sermons* *and Devotional Writings of Gerard Manley Hopkins*, 1959. • Humphrey House and Graham Storey, eds., *Journals and Papers*, 1959. • Norman H. MacKenzie, ed., *The Poetical Works of Gerard Manley Hopkins*, 1990. • Catherine Phillips, ed., *Gerard Manley Hopkins*, 1986.

Biography • Robert Bernard Martin, *Gerard Manley Hopkins: A Very Private Life*, 1991. • Norman White, *Hopkins: A Literary Biography*, 1992.

Criticism • Tom Dunne, *Gerard Manley Hopkins: A Comprehensive Bibliography*, 1976 [annual updates in *Hopkins Quarterly*]. • William H. Gardner, G. M. *Hopkins: A Study of Poetic Idiosyncrasy in Relation to Poetic Tradition*, 2 vols., 1944; 1949. • Richard F. Giles, ed., *Hopkins Among the Poets: Studies in Modern Responses to Gerard Manley Hopkins*, 1985. • Daniel Harris, *Inspirations Unbidden: The "Terrible Sonnets" of Gerard Manley Hopkins*, 1982. • Norman H. MacKenzie, *A Reader's Guide to Gerard Manley Hopkins*, 1981. • Paul L. Mariani, *A Commentary on the Complete Poems of Gerard Manley Hopkins*, 1970. • Walter J. Ong, *Hopkins, the Self, and God*, 1986. • Alison Sulloway, *Gerard Manley Hopkins and the Victorian Temper*, 1972.

Our Texts • W. H. Gardner, ed., *Poems of Gerard Manley Hopkins*, 1948; Humphrey House, and Graham Storey, eds., *Journals and Papers*, 1959; Claude C. Abbott, ed., *The Correspondence of Gerard Manley Hopkins and Richard Watson Dixon*, 2 vols., 1935; rev. 1955.

John Stuart Mill • **Editions** • John Robson, et al., eds., *Collected Works*, 33 vols., 1963–1991. • Ann P. Robson and John M. Robson, eds., *Sexual Equality: Writings by John Stuart Mill, Harriet Taylor Mill, and Helen Taylor*, 1994. • David Spitz, ed., *On Liberty*, Norton critical edition, 1975.

Biography • Alexander Bain, *John Stuart Mill*, 1882; 1969. • Michael St. J. Packe, *The Life of John Stuart Mill*, 1954.

Criticism • Fred Berger, *Happiness, Justice, and Freedom*, 1984. • Janice Carlisle, *John Stuart Mill and the Writing of Character*, 1991. • Maurice Cowling, *Mill and Liberalism*, 1963. • F. W. Garforth, *Educative Democracy: John Stuart Mill on Education in Society*, 1980. • Peter Glassman, *The Evolution of a Genius*, 1985. • John Gray and G. W. Smith, eds., *J. S. Mill: On Liberty in Focus*, 1991. • Joseph Hamburger, *Intellectuals in Politics*, 1985. • Michael Laine, *Bibliography of Writings on John Stuart Mill*, 1982. • Michael

Laine, ed., *A Cultivated Mind: Essays on J.S. Mill Presented to John M. Robson*, 1991. • John M. Robson, *The Improvement of Mankind: The Social and Political Thought of J. S. Mill*, 1968. • Alan Ryan, *John Stuart Mill*, 1970. • J. B. Schneewind, ed., *Mill: A Collection of Critical Essays*, 1968. • F. Parvin Sharpless, *The Literary Criticism of John Stuart Mill*, 1967. • Lynn Zastoupil, *John Stuart Mill and India*, 1994.

Our Texts • John Robson et al., eds., *Collected Works*, 33 vols., 1963–1991.

Christina Rossetti • **Editions** • Rebecca W. Crump, ed., *The Complete Poems of Christina Rossetti: A Variorum Edition*, 3 vols., 1979–1990. • William M. Rossetti, ed., *The Poetical Works of Christina Rossetti*, 1904. • Rebecca W. Crump, ed., *The Family Letters of Christina Georgina Rossetti*. 1908; 1968.

Biography • Kathleen Jones, *Learning Not to Be First: The Life of Christina Rossetti*, 1991. • Jan Marsh, *Christina Rossetti: A Writer's Life*, 1995.

Criticism • Georgina Battiscombe, *Christina Rossetti: A Divided Life*, 1981. • Kathleen Blake, *Love and the Woman Question in Victorian Literature*, 1983. • Edna Kotin Charles, *Christina Rossetti: Critical Perspectives, 1862–1982*, 1985. • Rebecca W. Crump, *Christina Rossetti: A Reference Guide*, 1976. • Antony H. Harrison, *Christina Rossetti in Context*, 1988. • Antony H. Harrison, ed., *Victorian Poetry*: special issue on Christina Rossetti, vol. 32, no. 3–4, 1994. • Elizabeth K. Helsinger, "Consumer Power and the Utopia of Desire: Christina Rossetti's Goblin Market." *ELH* 58 (1991). • David A. Kent, ed., *The Achievement of Christina Rossetti*, 1987. • Katherine J. Mayberry, *Christina Rossetti and the Poetry of Discovery*, 1989. • Jerome McGann, "Christina Rossetti's Poems: A New Edition and a Revaluation," *Victorian Studies* 23 (1980). • Jerome McGann, "The Religious Poetry of Christina Rossetti," *Critical Inquiry* 10 (1983). • Dorothy Mermin, "Heroic Sisterhood in Goblin Market," *Victorian Poetry* 21 (1983). • Dolores Rosenblum, *Christina Rossetti: The Poetry of Endurance*, 1986. • Sharon Smulders, *Christina Rossetti, Revisited*, 1996. • Virginia Woolf, "I Am Christina Rossetti," in *The Second Common Reader*, 1932.

Our Texts • Rebecca W. Crump, ed., *The Complete Poems of Christina Rossetti: A Variorum Edition*, 3 vols., 1979–1990.

John Ruskin • Editions • Harold Bloom, ed., *The Literary Criticism of John Ruskin*, 1965. • Van Akin Burd, ed., *The Ruskin Family Letters, 1801–1843*, 2 vols., 1973. • E. T. Cook and Alexander Wedderburn, eds., *The Works of John Ruskin*, 39 vols., 1903–1912. • John D. Rosenberg, ed., *The Genius of John Ruskin: Selections from His Writings*, 1963.

Biography • Joan Abse, *John Ruskin: The Passionate Moralist*, 1980. • Timothy Hilton, *John Ruskin: The Early Years, 1819–1859*, 1985. • John Dixon Hunt, *The Wider Sea: A Life of John Ruskin*, 1982.

Criticism • Linda M. Austin, *The Practical Ruskin: Economics and Audience in the Late Work*, 1991. • Michael W. Brooks, *John Ruskin and Victorian Architecture*, 1987. • Susan Casteras et al., *John Ruskin and the Victorian Eye*, 1993. • Raymond Fitch, *The Poison Sky: Myth and Apocalypse in Ruskin*, 1982. • Elizabeth Helsinger, *Ruskin and the Art of the Beholder*, 1982. • Robert Hewison, *John Ruskin: The Argument of the Eye*, 1976. • Robert Hewison, ed., *New Approaches to Ruskin: Thirteen Essays*, 1981. • George P. Landow, *The Aesthetic and Critical Theories of John Ruskin*, 1971. • George P. Landow, *Ruskin*, 1985. • Linda Merrill, *A Pot of Paint: Aesthetics on Trial in Whistler v. Ruskin*, 1992. • John D. Rosenberg, *The Darkening Glass: A Portrait of Ruskin's Genius*, 1961. • J. C. Sherburne, *John Ruskin, or the Ambiguities of Abundance: A Study in Social and Economic Criticism*, 1972.

Our Texts • E. T. Cook and Alexander Wedderburn, eds., *The Works of John Ruskin*, 39 vols., 1903–1912.

Alfred Tennyson • Editions • Cecil Y. Lang and Edgar F. Shannon Jr., eds., *The Letters of Alfred, Lord Tennyson*, 3 vols., 1981–1990. • Christopher Ricks, ed., *Poems*, 3 vols., 1987. • Hallam Tennyson, ed., *Works*, 9 vols., 1907–1908.

Biography • Robert B. Martin, *Tennyson: The Unquiet Heart*, 1980. • Hallam Tennyson, *Alfred, Lord Tennyson: A Memoir, by His Son*, 2 vols., 1897.

Criticism • Daniel Albright, *Tennyson: The Muses' Tug-of-War*, 1986. • Kirk K. Beetz, *Tennyson: A Bibliography, 1827–1982*, 1984. • Jerome H. Buckley, *Tennyson: The Growth of a Poet*, 1960. • Philip Collins, ed., *Tennyson: Seven Essays*, 1993. • A. Dwight Culler, *The Poetry of Tennyson*, 1977. • Donald S. Hair, *Tennyson's Language*, 1991. •

Arthur H. Hallam, "On Some Characteristics of Modern Poetry, and On the Lyrical Poems of Alfred Tennyson," *Englishman's Magazine* (August 1831). • Gerhard Joseph, *Tennyson and the Text: The Weaver's Shuttle*, 1992. • John D. Jump, ed., *Tennyson: The Critical Heritage*, 1967. • John Killham, ed., *Critical Essays on the Poetry of Tennyson*, 1960. • James R. Kincaid, *Tennyson's Major Poems: The Comic and Ironic Patterns*, 1975. • Sir Harold Nicolson, *Tennyson: Aspects of His Life, Character, and Poetry*, 1923. • Norman Page, ed., *Tennyson: Interviews and Recollections*, 1983. • Timothy Peltason, *Reading In Memoriam*, 1985. • F. E. L. Priestley, *Language and Structure in Tennyson's Poetry*, 1973. • Christopher Ricks, *Tennyson*, 1972. • John D. Rosenberg, *The Fall of Camelot: A Study of Tennyson's "Idylls of the King,"* 1973. • Matthew Rowlinson, *Tennyson's Fixations: Psychoanalysis and the Topics of the Early Poetry*, 1994. • Marion Shaw, *An Annotated Critical Bibliography of Alfred, Lord Tennyson*, 1989. • W. David Shaw, *Tennyson's Style*, 1976. • Alan Sinfield, *Alfred Tennyson*, 1986. • Herbert F. Tucker, *Tennyson and the Doom of Romanticism*, 1988. • Herbert F. Tucker, ed., *Critical Essays on Alfred Lord Tennyson*, 1993. • Paul Turner, *Tennyson*, 1976.

Our Texts • Hallam Tennyson, ed., *Works*, 9 vols., 1907–1908.

Oscar Wilde • Editions • Richard Ellmann, ed., *The Artist as Critic: Critical Writings of Oscar Wilde*, 1969. • Rupert Hart-Davis, ed., *Letters*, 1962. • Rupert Hart-Davis, *More Letters*, 1985. • Isobel Murray, ed., *The Complete Shorter Fiction of Oscar Wilde*, 1979. • Isobel Murray, ed., *The Writings of Oscar Wilde*, 1989. • Robert Ross, ed., *First Collected Edition*, 14 vols., 1908.

Biography • Richard Ellmann, *Oscar Wilde*, 1987. • Vyvyan Holland, *Oscar Wilde, a Pictorial Biography*, 1960. • Melissa Knox, *Oscar Wilde: A Long and Lovely Suicide*, 1994.

Criticism • Karl Beckson, ed., *Oscar Wilde: The Critical Heritage*, 1970. • Patricia Flanagan Behrendt, *Oscar Wilde: Eros and Aesthetics*, 1991. • Harold Bloom, ed., *Oscar Wilde: Modern Critical Views*, 1985. • Harold Bloom, ed., *Oscar Wilde's "The Importance of Being Earnest": Modern Critical Interpretations*, 1988. • Ed Cohen, *Talk on the Wilde Side: Toward a Genealogy of a Discourse on Male Sexualities*,

1993. • Richard Ellmann, ed., *Oscar Wilde: A Collection of Critical Essays*, 1969. • Regenia Gagnier, ed., *Critical Essays on Oscar Wilde*, 1991. • Regenia Gagnier, *Idylls of the Marketplace: Oscar Wilde and the Victorian Public*, 1986. • Christopher S. Nassaar, *Into the Demon Universe: A Literary Exploration of Oscar Wilde*, 1974. • Kerry Powell, *Oscar Wilde and the Theatre of the 1890s*, 1991. • Peter Raby, *The Importance of Being Earnest: A Reader's Companion*, 1995. • Peter Raby, ed., *The Cambridge Companion to Oscar Wilde*, 1997. • Epifanio San Juan Jr., *The Art of Oscar Wilde*, 1967. •

Rodney Shewan, *Oscar Wilde: Art and Egotism*, 1977. • John Stokes, *Oscar Wilde: Myths, Miracles, and Imitations*, 1996.

Our Texts • Poems from *First Collected Edition*, ed. Robert Ross, 1908; "The Soul of Man under Socialism" from *Fortnightly Review* (February 1891); "The Decay of Lying," from the Preface to *The Picture of Dorian Gray*, and "The Importance of Being Earnest" from *The Writings of Oscar Wilde*, ed. Isobel Murray, 1989; "De Profundis" from *The Letters of Oscar Wilde*, ed. Rupert Hart-Davis, 1962.

The Twentieth Century

General Background • Shari Benstock, *Women of the Left Bank: Paris, 1900–1940*, 1986. • Joseph Bristow, *Effeminate England: Homoerotic Writing after 1885*, 1995. • Carol T. Christ, *Victorian and Modern Poetics*, 1984. • Valentine Cunningham, *British Writers of the Thirties*, 1988. • Alistair Davies, ed., *An Annotated Critical Bibliography of Modernism*, 1982. • Marianne DeKoven, *Rich and Strange: Gender, History, Modernism*, 1991. • Kevin J. H. Dettmar, ed., *Rereading the New: A Backward Glance at Modernism*, 1992. • Maud Ellmann, *The Poetics of Impersonality: T. S. Eliot and Ezra Pound*, 1987. • David Gervais, *Literary Englands: Versions of "Englishness" in Modern Writing*, 1993. • Sandra Gilbert and Susan Gubar, *No Man's Land: The Place of the Woman Writer in the Twentieth Century*, 3 vols., 1988–. • John Halperin, *Eminent Georgians: The Lives of King George V, Elizabeth Bowen, St. John Philby, and Nancy Astor*, 1995. • Robert Hogan et al., *Dictionary of Irish Literature*, 1996. • Robert Hughes, *The Shock of the New*, 1981. • Hugh Kenner, *The Pound Era*, 1971. • Michael H. Levenson, *A Genealogy of Modernism: A Study of English Literary Doctrine, 1908–1922*, 1984. • James Longenbach, *Stone Cottage: Pound, Yeats, and Modernism*, 1988. • Perry Meisel, *The Myth of the Modern: A Study in British Literature and Criticism after 1850*, 1987. • Peter Nicholls, *Modernisms: A Literary Guide*, 1995. • Michael North, *The Political Aesthetic of Yeats, Eliot, and Pound*, 1991. • Herbert N. Schneidau, *Waking Giants: The Presence of the Past in Modernism*, 1991. • Sanford Schwartz, *The Matrix of Modernism: Pound, Eliot, and Early Twentieth-Century Thought*, 1985. • Bonnie Kime Scott, ed., *The Gender of Modernism: A Critical Anthology*, 1990. • John L. Somer and Barbara Eck Cooper, *American and British Literature, 1945–1975: An Annotated Bibliography of Contemporary Scholarship*, 1980. • C. K. Stead, *The New Poetic: Yeats to Eliot*, 1964. • C. K. Stead, *Pound, Yeats, Eliot, and the Modernist Movement*, 1986. • George Watson, *British Literature since 1945*, 1991.

Perspectives: The Great War: Confronting the Modern • Allyson Booth, *Postcards from the Trenches: Negotiating the Space between Modernism and the First World War*, 1996. • Paul Fussell, *The Great War and Modern Memory*, 1975. • Dorothy Goldman, ed., *Women and World War I: The Written Response*, 1993. • Klein-Holger, *The First World War in Fiction: A Collection of Critical Essays*, 1976. • John Onions, *English Fiction and Drama of the Great War, 1918–1939*, 1990. • William C. Wees, *Vorticism and the English Avant-Garde*, 1972.

Perspectives: Whose Language? • Eugene Benson and L. W. Conolly, eds., *Encyclopedia of Post-Colonial Literatures in English*, 1994. • Elleke Boehmer, *Colonial and Postcolonial Literature: Migrant Metaphors*, 1995. • Michael Edward Gorra, *After Empire: Scott, Naipaul, Rushdie*, 1997. • Bruce King, ed., *New National and Post-Colonial Literatures: An Introduction*, 1996. • Judie Newman, *The Ballistic Bard: Postcolonial Fictions*, 1995. • Jonathan White, ed., *Recasting the World: Writing after Colonialism*, 1993.

Perspectives: World War II and the End of Empire • Bill Ashcroft, Gareth Griffiths, and Helen Tiffin, *The Empire Writes Back: Theory and Practice in Post-Colonial Literatures*, 1989. •

Bernard Bergonzi, *Wartime and Aftermath: English Literature and its Background, 1939–1960*, 1993. • Patrick Brantlinger, *Rule of Darkness: British Literature and Imperialism, 1830–1914*, 1988. • George Richard Esenwein, *Spain at War: The Spanish Civil War in Context, 1931–1939*, 1995. • Robert Hewison, *Under Siege: Literary Life in London, 1939–1945*, 1977. • Karen R. Lawrence, ed., *Decolonizing Tradition: New Views of Twentieth-Century "British" Literary Canons*, 1992. • David Leavitt, *While England Sleeps* [novel], 1993. • David Lloyd, *Anomalous States: Irish Writing and the Post-Colonial Moment*, 1993. • Robert H. MacDonald, *The Language of Empire: Myths and Metaphors of Popular Imperialism, 1880–1918*, 1994. • David Morgan, *The Battle for Britain: Citizenship and Ideology in the Second World War*, 1993. • John M. Muste, *Say That We Saw Spain Die: Literary Consequences of the Spanish Civil War*, 1966. • Andrew Sinclair, *War Like a Wasp: The Lost Decade of the 'Forties*, 1989. • Hugh Thomas, *The Spanish Civil War*, 1986. • Keith Williams, *British Writers and the Media, 1930–1945*, 1996.

Speeches on Irish Independence • Seamus Deane, *Celtic Revivals: Essays in Modern Irish Literature, 1880–1980*, 1985. • Tom Garvin, *1922, The Birth of Irish Democracy*, 1996. • Michael Hopkinson, *Green against Green: The Irish Civil War*, 1988. • Declan Kiberd, *Inventing Ireland*, 1996. • Julian Moynahan, *Anglo-Irish: The Literary Imagination in a Hyphenated Culture*, 1995.

W. H. Auden • George W. Bahlke, ed., *Critical Essays on W. H. Auden*, 1991. • John G. Blair, *The Poetic Art of W. H. Auden*, 1965. • Harold Bloom, ed., *W. H. Auden*, 1986. • John R. Boly, *Reading Auden: The Returns of Caliban*, 1991. • Frederick Buell, *W. H. Auden as a Social Poet*, 1973. • John Fuller, *A Reader's Guide to W. H. Auden*, 1970. • John Haffenden, ed., *W. H. Auden: The Critical Heritage*, 1983. • Anthony Hecht, *The Hidden Law: The Poetry of W. H. Auden*, 1993. • Richard Davenport Hines, *Auden*, 1995. • Lucy McDiarmid, *Saving Civilization: Yeats, Eliot, and Auden between the Wars*, 1984. • Lucy McDiarmid, *Auden's Apologies for Poetry*, 1990. • Edward Mendelson, ed., *W. H. Auden: A Tribute*, 1974. • Edward Mendelson, *Early Auden*, 1981. • Charles Osborne, *W. H. Auden: The Life of a Poet*, 1979. • Monroe K. Spears, *The Poetry of W. H. Auden: The Disenchanted Island*, 1963. • George T. Wright, *W. H. Auden*, 1969. • George T. Wright, *W. H. Auden*, 1981.

Samuel Beckett • **Biographies** • Lois Gordon, *The World of Samuel Beckett, 1906–1946*, 1996. • James Knowlson, *Damned to Fame: The Life of Samuel Beckett*, 1996.

Criticism • H. Porter Abbott, *Beckett Writing Beckett: the Author in the Autograph*, 1996. • James Acheson, *Samuel Beckett's Artistic Theory and Practice: Criticism, Drama, and Early Fiction*, 1997. • Richard Begam, *Samuel Beckett and The End of Modernity*, 1996. • Linda Ben-Zvi, *Samuel Beckett*, 1986. • Bob Cochran, *Samuel Beckett: A Study of the Short Fiction*, 1992. • Ruby Cohn, *Back to Beckett*, 1974. • Ruby Cohn, *Just Play: Beckett's Theater*, 1980. • J. E. Dearlove, *Accommodating the Chaos: Samuel Beckett's Nonrelational Art*, 1982. • S. E. Gontarski, ed., *The Beckett Studies Reader*, 1993. • S. E. Gontarski, ed., *On Beckett: Essays and Criticism*, 1986. • Lawrence Graver and Raymond Federman, eds., *Samuel Beckett: The Critical Heritage*, 1979. • Mel Gussow, ed., *Conversations With and About Beckett*, 1996. • Hugh Kenner, *Flaubert, Joyce, and Beckett: The Stoic Comedians*, 1962. • Hugh Kenner, *A Reader's Guide to Samuel Beckett*, 1973. • Hugh Kenner, *Samuel Beckett: A Critical Study*, 1968. • Charles R. Lyons, *Samuel Beckett*, 1990. • Patrick A. McCarthy, ed., *Critical Essays on Samuel Beckett*, 1986. • Vivian Mercier, *Beckett/Beckett*, 1977. • Kristin Morrison, *Canters and Chronicles: The Use of Narrative in the Plays of Samuel Beckett and Harold Pinter*, 1983. • Eoin O'Brien, *The Beckett Country: Samuel Beckett's Ireland*, 1993. • John Piling, ed., *The Cambridge Companion to Beckett*, 1994. • Christopher B. Ricks, *Beckett's Dying Words: The Clarendon Lectures, 1990*, 1993.

Elizabeth Bowen • **Biographies** • Elizabeth Bowen, *Bowen's Court and Seven Winters: Memories of a Dublin Childhood*, 1984. • Patricia Craig, *Elizabeth Bowen*, 1986.

Criticism • Allan E. Austin, *Elizabeth Bowen*, 1989. • Andrew Bennett and Nicholas Royle, *Elizabeth Bowen and the Dissolution of the Novel: Still Lives*, 1995. • Harold Bloom, ed., *Elizabeth Bowen*, 1987. • Renée Hoogland, *Elizabeth Bowen: A Reputation in Writing*, 1994. • Heather B. Jordan, *How Will the Heart Endure: Elizabeth Bowen and the Landscape of War*, 1992. • Phyllis Lassner, *Elizabeth Bowen: A Study of Short Fiction*, 1991.

Rupert Brooke • **Biographies** • John Lehmann, *Rupert Brooke: His Life and His Legend*, 1980.

Criticism • Rupert Brooke, *The Letters of Rupert Brooke*, ed. Geoffrey Keynes, 1968. • Adrian Caesar, *Taking It Like a Man: Suffering, Sexuality, and the War Poets: Brooke, Sassoon, Owen, Graves*, 1993. • Paul Delany, *The Neo-Pagans: Rupert Brooke and the Ordeal of Youth*, 1987. • Pippa Harris, *Song of Love: The Letters of Rupert Brooke and Noel Oliver*, 1991. • William E. Laskowski, *Rupert Brooke*, 1994.

Sir Winston Churchill • **Biographies** • William Manchester, *The Last Lion: Winston Spencer Churchill Visions of Glory, 1874–1932*, 1983. • William Manchester, *The Last Lion: Winston Spencer Churchill: Alone, 1932–1940*, 1989.

Criticism • Winston S. Churchill, *Memoirs of The Second World War*, 1990. • Victor Feske, *From Belloc to Churchill: Private Scholars, Public Culture, and the Crisis of British Liberalism, 1900–1939*, 1996. • James Humes, *Wit and Wisdom of Winston Churchill*, 1995. • Warren F. Kimball, *Churchill and Roosevelt, the Complete Correspondence, 3 vols*, 1984. • Warren F. Kimball, *Forged in War: Roosevelt, Churchill, and the Second World War*, 1997. • Sheila Lawlor, ed., *Churchill and the Politics of War, 1940–1941*, 1994. • Keith Robbins, *Churchill*, 1993. • Manfred Weidhorn, *Churchill's Rhetoric and Political Discourse*, 1988.

Michael Collins • **Biographies** • Tim P. Coogan, *Michael Collins: The Man Who Made Ireland*, 1996. • James Mackay, *Michael Collins: A Life*, 1997.

Criticism • P. S. Beaslai, *Michael Collins and the Making of a New Ireland*, 2 vols., 1985. • Eoin Neeson, *The Life and Death of Michael Collins*, 1968. • Leon O'Broin, ed., *In Great Haste: The Letters of Michael Collins and Kitty Kiernan*, 1996. • Frank O'Connor, *The Big Fellow: Michael Collins and the Irish Revolution*, 1965. • Ulick O'Connor, *Michael Collins and the Troubles: The Struggle for Irish Freedom, 1912–1922*, 1996.

Joseph Conrad • Chinua Achebe, "An Image of Africa." • John Batchelor, *The Life of Joseph Conrad: A Critical Biography*, 1993. • Ted Billy, ed., *Critical Essays on Joseph Conrad*, 1987. • Harold Bloom, ed., *Joseph Conrad's "Heart of Darkness,"* 1987. • Harold Bloom, ed., *Joseph Conrad*, 1986. • Harold Bloom, *Marlow*, 1992. • Keith Carabine, ed., *Joseph Conrad: Critical Assessments*, 4 vols., 1992. • Avrom Fleishman, *Conrad's Politics: Community and Anarchy in the Fiction of Joseph Conrad*, 1967. • Ford Madox Ford, *Joseph Conrad: A Personal Remembrance*, 1989. • Christopher L. GoGwilt, *The Invention of the West:*

Joseph Conrad and the Double-Mapping of Europe and Empire, 1995. • Albert J. Guerard, *Conrad the Novelist*, 1958. • Geoffrey Harpham, *One of Us: The Mastery of Joseph Conrad*, 1996. • Fredric Jameson, *The Political Unconscious: Narrative as a Socially Symbolic Act*, 1981. • Frederick Karl, *Joseph Conrad: The Three Lives: A Biography*, 1979. • Frederick R. Karl and Laurence Davies, eds., *The Collected Letters of Joseph Conrad*, 1983- . • Jeffrey Meyers, *Joseph Conrad: A Biography*, 1991. • Vincent P. Pecora, *Self and Form in Modern Narrative*, 1989. • Martin Ray, ed., *Joseph Conrad: Interviews & Recollections*, 1990. • Edward W. Said, *Joseph Conrad and the Fiction of Autobiography*, 1966. • Edward W. Said, *The World, the Text, and the Critic*, 1983. • Norman Sherry, ed., *Conrad: The Critical Heritage*, 1973. • J. H. Stape, ed., *The Cambridge Companion to Joseph Conrad*, 1996. • Bruce Teets, *Joseph Conrad: An Annotated Bibliography*, 1990. • Ian Watt, *Joseph Conrad: A Critical Biography*, 1979. • Cedric P. Watts, *A Preface to Conrad*, 1993. • Mark A. Wollaeger, *Joseph Conrad and the Fictions of Skepticism*, 1990.

T. S. Eliot • **Biographies** • Peter Ackroyd, *T. S. Eliot: A Life*, 1984. • Lyndall Gordon, *Eliot's Early Years*, 1977. • Lyndall Gordon, *Eliot's New Life*, 1988.

Criticism • Harold Bloom, ed., *T. S. Eliot*, 1985. • Harold Bloom, ed., *T. S. Eliot's "The Waste Land,"* 1986. • Jewel Spears Brooker and Joseph Bentley, *Reading "The Waste Land": Modernism and the Limits of Interpretation*, 1990. • Ronald Bush, *T. S. Eliot: The Modernist in History*, 1991. • T. S. Eliot, *The Letters of T. S. Eliot*, ed. Valerie Eliot, 1988–. • T. S. Eliot, *"The Waste Land": A Facsimile and Transcript of the Original Drafts Including the Annotations of Ezra Pound*, ed. Valerie Eliot, 1971. • Maud Ellmann, *The Poetics of Impersonality: T. S. Eliot and Ezra Pound*, 1987. • Nancy K. Gish, *"The Waste Land": A Poem of Memory and Desire*, 1988. • Michael Grant, ed., *T. S. Eliot: The Critical Heritage*, 1982. • Frank Lentricchia, *Modernist Quartet*, 1994. • James Longenbach, *Modernist Poetics of History: Pound, Eliot, and the Sense of the Past*, 1987. • Lucy McDiarmid, *Saving Civilization: Yeats, Eliot, and Auden Between the Wars*, 1984. • Gail McDonald, *Learning to Be Modern: Pound, Eliot, and the American University*, 1993. • Louis Menand, *Discovering Modernism: T. S. Eliot and His Context*, 1986. • Anthony David Moody, ed., *The Cambridge*

Companion to T. S. Eliot, 1994. • Anthony David Moody, *Thomas Stearns Eliot, Poet*, 1979. • Jeffrey M. Perl, *Skepticism and Modern Enmity: Before and After Eliot*, 1989. • Christopher B. Ricks, *T. S. Eliot and Prejudice*, 1988. • John Paul Riquelme, *Harmony of Dissonances: T. S. Eliot, Romanticism and Imagination*, 1990. • Sanford Schwartz, *The Matrix of Modernism: Pound, Eliot, and Early Twentieth-Century Thought*, 1985. • Grover Cleveland Smith, *The Waste Land*, 1983. • Stanley Sultan, *Eliot, Joyce, and Company*, 1987. • Stanley Sultan, *"Ulysses," "The Waste Land," and Modernism: A Jubilee Study*, 1977.

Nadine Gordimer • *Biographies* • Nadine Gordimer, *Writing and Being*, 1995.

Criticism • Nancy T. Bazin and Marilyn D. Seymour, *Conversations with Nadine Gordimer*, 1990. • Stephen Clingman, *The Novels of Nadine Gordimer: History from the Inside*, 1986. • Andrew V. Ettin, *Betrayals of the Body Politic: The Literary Commitments of Nadine Gordimer*, 1993. • Dominic Head, *Nadine Gordimer*, 1995. • Christopher Heywood, *Nadine Gordimer*, 1983. • Bruce King, ed., *The Later Fiction of Nadine Gordimer*, 1993. • Judie Newman, *Nadine Gordimer*, 1988. • Rowland Smith, ed., *Critical Essays on Nadine Gordimer*, 1990. • Kathrin Wagner, *Rereading Nadine Gordimer*, 1994.

Thomas Hardy • Harold Bloom, ed., *Thomas Hardy*, 1987. • Graham Clarke, ed., *Thomas Hardy: Critical Assessments*, 4 vols., 1993. • Reginald Gordon Cox, *Thomas Hardy: The Critical Heritage*, 1970. • Ronald P. Draper, *An Annotated Critical Bibliography of Thomas Hardy*, 1989. • Simon Gatrell, *Hardy, the Creator: A Textual Biography*, 1988. • James Gibson, *Thomas Hardy: A Literary Life*, 1996. • Dale Kramer, *Critical Essays on Thomas Hardy: The Novels*, 1990. • Robert Langbaum, *Thomas Hardy in Our Time*, 1995. • C. Day Lewis, *The Lyrical Poetry of Thomas Hardy*, 1970. • Perry Meisel, *Thomas Hardy: The Return of the Repressed: A Study of the Major Fiction*, 1972. • J. Hillis Miller, *Thomas Hardy: Distance and Desire*, 1970. • Michael Millgate, ed., *Selected Letters*, 1990. • Michael Millgate, *Thomas Hardy: A Biography*, 1982. • Charles P. C. Pettit, ed., *New Perspectives on Thomas Hardy*, 1994. • Richard L. Purdy and Michael Millgate, eds., *The Collected Letters of Thomas Hardy*, 1978-88. • Merryn Williams, *A Preface to Hardy*, 1993. • Paul Zietlow, *Moments of Vision: The Poetry of Thomas Hardy*, 1974.

Seamus Heaney • *Biographies* • Michael Parker, *Seamus Heaney: The Making of the Poet*, 1993.

Criticism • Elmer Andrews, *The Poetry of Seamus Heaney*, 1988. • Harold Bloom, ed., *Seamus Heaney*, 1986. • Sidney Burris, ed., *The Poetry of Resistance: Seamus Heaney and the Pastoral Tradition*, 1990. • Neil Corcoran, *Seamus Heaney: A Faber Student Guide*, 1986. • Tony Curtis, ed., *The Art of Seamus Heaney*, 1994. • Michael J. Durkan and Rand Brandes, *Seamus Heaney: A Reference Guide*, 1996. • Thomas C. Foster, *Seamus Heaney*, 1989. • Robert F. Garratt, *Critical Essays on Seamus Heaney*, 1995. • Henry Hart, *Seamus Heaney, Poet of Contrary Progressions*, 1992. • Catherin Malloy and Phyllis Carey, eds., *Seamus Heaney: The Shaping Spirit*, 1996. • Michael R. Molino, *Questioning Tradition, Language, and Myth: The Poetry of Seamus Heaney*, 1994. • Blake Morrison, *Seamus Heaney*, 1982. • Bernard O'Donoghue, *Seamus Heaney and the Language of Poetry*, 1994.

David Jones • *Biographies* • René Hague, ed., *Dai Great-Coat: A Self-Portrait of David Jones in His Letters*, 1980.

Criticism • Thomas Dilworth, *The Shape of Meaning in the Poetry of David Jones*, 1988. • Thomas Dilworth, ed., *Inner Necessities: The Letters of David Jones to Desmond Chute*, 1984. • René Hague, *David Jones*, 1975. • Jeremy Hooker, *David Jones: An Exploratory Study of the Writings*, 1975. • David Jones, *David Jones: Letters to Vernon Watkins*, ed. Ruth Pryor, 1976. • Jonathan Miles and Derek Shiel, *David Jones: The Maker Unmade*, 1996. • Kathleen Raine, *David Jones, Solitary Perfectionist*, 1974. • Kathleen Staudt, ed., *At the Turn of a Civilization: David Jones and Modern Poetics*, 1993.

James Joyce • *Edition* • *Ulysses*, ed. Hans Walter Gabler, 1984.

Biographies • Richard Ellmann, *James Joyce*, 1982. • Herbert S. Gorman, *James Joyce*, 1948.

Criticism • Derek Attridge, ed., *The Cambridge Companion to James Joyce*, 1990. • Richard Brown, *James Joyce and Sexuality*, 1989. • Frank Budgen, *James Joyce and the Making of "Ulysses,"* 1960. • Kevin J. H. Dettmar, *The Illicit Joyce of Postmodernism: Reading Against the Grain*, 1996. • Enda Duffy, *The Subaltern "Ulysses,"* 1994. • Don Gifford, *Ulysses Annotated: Notes for Joyce's "Ulysses,"* 1988. • Stuart Gilbert, *James Joyce's*

"Ulysses": A Study, 1930. • Clive Hart and David Hayman, eds., James Joyce's "Ulysses": Critical Essays, 1974. • Hugh Kenner, Joyce's Voices, 1978. • Hugh Kenner, Ulysses, 1987. • R. B. Kershner, Joyce, Bakhtin, and Popular Literature: Chronicles of Disorder, 1989. • Karen Lawrence, The Odyssey of Style in "Ulysses," 1981. • A. Walton Litz, The Art of James Joyce: Method and Design in "Ulysses" and "Finnegans Wake," 1961. • Vicki Mahaffey, Reauthorizing Joyce, 1988. • Dominic Manganiello, Joyce's Politics, 1980. • E. H. Mikhail, James Joyce: Interviews and Recollections, 1990. • Margot Norris, Joyce's Web: The Social Unraveling of Modernism, 1992. • Richard Pearce, The Politics of Narration: James Joyce, William Faulkner, and Virginia Woolf, 1991. • David Pierce, James Joyce's Ireland, 1992. • Arthur Power, Conversations with James Joyce, 1974. • Mary T. Reynolds, ed., James Joyce: A Collection of Critical Essays, 1993. • Bonnie K. Scott, Joyce and Feminism, 1984. • Robert E. Spoo, James Joyce and the Language of History: Dedalus's Nightmare, 1994. • Jennifer Wicke, Advertising Fictions: Literature, Advertising, and Social Reading, 1988.

Philip Larkin • *Biographies* • Andrew Motion, Philip Larkin: A Writer's Life, 1993.

Criticism • James Booth, Philip Larkin: Writer, 1992. • Richard Hoffpauir, The Art of Restraint: English Poetry from Hardy to Larkin, 1991. • Philip Larkin, Selected Letters: 1940–1985, ed. Anthony Thwaite, 1993. • Bruce K. Martin, Philip Larkin, 1978. • Janice Rossen, Philip Larkin: His Life's Work, 1990. • Dale Salwak, ed., Philip Larkin: The Man and His Work, 1988. • Andrew Swarbrick, Out of Reach: The Poetry of Philip Larkin, 1995. • Anthony Thwaite, Larkin at Sixty, 1982. • David Timms, Philip Larkin, 1973.

D. H. Lawrence • James T. Boulton, ed., The Letters of D. H. Lawrence, 6 vols., 1979- . • Henry Coombes, D. H. Lawrence: A Critical Anthology, 1973. • James C. Cowan, D. H. Lawrence: An Annotated Bibliography of Writings about Him, 1982. • Paul Delany, D. H. Lawrence's Nightmare: The Writer and His Circle in the Years of the Great War, 1978. • R. P. Draper, D. H. Lawrence: The Critical Heritage, 1970. • Sandra Gilbert, Acts of Attention: The Poems of D. H. Lawrence, 1972. • Leo Hamalian, D. H. Lawrence: A Collection of Criticism, 1973. • Philip Hobsbaum, A Reader's Guide to D.H. Lawrence, 1981. • Mark Kinkead-Weekes, D.

H. Lawrence: Triumph to Exile, 1912-1922, 1996. • Dennis Jackson and Fleda Brown Jackson, eds., Critical Essays on D.H. Lawrence, 1988. • Thomas Rice Jackson, D. H. Lawrence: A Guide to Research, 1983. • F. R. Leavis, D. H. Lawrence, Novelist, 1970. • Henry Miller, The World of Lawrence: A Passionate Appreciation, 1980. • Kate Millet, Sexual Politics, 1970. • Harry T. Moore, The Priest of Love: A Life of D. H. Lawrence, 1974. • Ross C. Murfin, The Poetry of D. H. Lawrence: Texts and Contexts, 1983. • Joyce Carol Oates, The Hostile Sun: The Poetry of D.H. Lawrence, 1973. • F. B. Pinion, A D. H. Lawrence Companion: Life, Thought, and Works, 1979. • Tony Pinkney, D.H. Lawrence and Modernism, 1990. • Paul Poplawski, D. H. Lawrence: A Reference Companion, 1996. • Peter Preston and Peter Hoare, eds., D.H. Lawrence in the Modern World, 1989. • Warren Roberts, A Bibliography of D. H. Lawrence, 1982. • Keith Sagar, ed., A D. H. Lawrence Handbook, 1982. • Keith M. Sagar, The Art of D.H. Lawrence, 1975. • Carol Siegel, Lawrence among the Women: Wavering Boundaries in Women's Literary Traditions, 1991. • Stephen Spender, D. H. Lawrence: Novelist, Poet, Prophet, 1973. • John Worthen, D. H. Lawrence: A Literary Life, 1989.

Nuala Ní Dhomhnaill • M. Louise Cannon, "The Extraordinary Within the Ordinary: The Poetry of Eavan Boland and Nuala Ni Dhomhnaill," South Atlantic Review 60 (1995). • Deborah McWilliams Consalvo, "The Lingual Ideal in the Poetry of Nuala Ni Dhomhnaill," Eire-Ireland: A Journal of Irish Studies, 30 (1995). • Patricia Boyle Haberstroh, Women Creating Women: Contemporary Irish Women Poets, 1996.

Wilfred Owen • *Biographies* • Harold Owen, Journey from Obscurity; Wilfred Owen, 1893–1918, 1963–1965. • Jon Stallworthy, Wilfred Owen, 1974.

Criticism • Sven Bäckman, Tradition Transformed: Studies in the Poetry of Wilfred Owen, 1979. • Adrian Caesar, Taking It Like a Man: Suffering, Sexuality, and the War Poets: Brooke, Sassoon, Owen, Graves, 1993. • Desmond Graham, The Truth of War: Owen, Rosenberg and Blunden, 1984. • Dominic Hibberd, Owen the Poet, 1988. • Douglas Kerr, Wilfred Owen's Voices: Language and Community, 1993. • Arthur E. Lane, An Adequate Response: The War Poetry of Wilfred Owen and Siegfried Sassoon, 1972. • Stephen MacDonald, Not About Heroes: The Friendship of Siegfried Sassoon and

Wilfred Owen, 1983. • Wilfred Owen, *Wilfred Owen: Collected Letters*, eds. William H. Owen and John Bell, 1967.

Charles Stewart Parnell • Biographies • Robert Kee, *The Laurel and the Ivy: The Story of Charles Stewart Parnell and Irish Nationalism*, 1993. • F. S. L. Lyons, *Charles Stewart Parnell*, 1977.

Criticism • Jules Abels, *The Parnell Tragedy*, 1966. • D. George Boyce and Alan O'Day, eds., *Parnell in Perspective*, 1991. • Noel Kissane, *Parnell: A Documentary History*, 1991. • Emmet Larkin, *The Roman Catholic Church in Ireland and the Fall of Parnell, 1888–1891*, 1979. • F. S. L. Lyons, *The Fall of Parnell, 1890–1891*, 1960. • Conor Cruise O'Brien, *Parnell and His Party, 1880–90*, 1968. • Alan O'Day, *Parnell and the First Home Rule Episode 1884–87*, 1986. • Michael Steinman, *Yeats's Heroic Figures: Wilde, Parnell, Swift, Casement*, 1983.

Padraic Pearse • Ruth Dudley Edwards, *Patrick Pearse: The Triumph of Failure*, 1977. • Sean Farrell Moran, *Patrick Pearse and the Politics of Redemption: The Mind of the Easter Rising, 1916*, 1994. • Padraic Pearse, *The Letters of P. H. Pearse*, ed. Seamus O Buachalla, 1980. • Raymond J. Porter, *P.H. Pearse*, 1973.

Ezra Pound • Biographies • Humphrey Carpenter, *A Serious Character: The Life of Ezra Pound*, 1988. • Noel Stock, *The Life of Ezra Pound*, 1970.

Criticism • Harold Bloom, ed., *Ezra Pound*, 1987. • Michael Coyle, *Ezra Pound, Popular Genres, and the Discourse of Culture*, 1995. • Reed Way Dasenbrock, *The Literary Vorticism of Ezra Pound and Wyndham Lewis: Towards the Condition of Painting*, 1985. • Eric Homberger, ed., *Ezra Pound: The Critical Heritage*, 1972. • Hugh Kenner, *The Poetry of Ezra Pound*, 1968. • Hugh Kenner, *The Pound Era*, 1971. • Gail McDonald, *Learning to Be Modern: Pound, Eliot, and the American University*, 1993. • Ezra Pound, *The Letters of Ezra Pound, 1907–1941*, ed. D. D. Paige, 1974. • Ezra Pound, *Pound/Lewis: The Letters of Ezra Pound and Wyndham Lewis*, 1985. • K. K. Ruthven, *A Guide to Ezra Pound's "Personae," 1926*, 1969.

Issac Rosenberg • Biographies • Joseph Cohen, *Journey to the Trenches: The Life of Isaac Rosenberg: 1890–1918*, 1975. • Jean Moorcroft Wilson, *Isaac Rosenberg, Poet and Painter: A Biography*, 1975.

Criticism • Desmond Graham, *The Truth of War: Owen, Rosenberg and Blunden*, 1984.

Salman Rushdie • Anouar Abdallah, ed., *For Rushdie: A Collection of Essays by 100 Arabic and Muslim Writers*, 1994. • Fawzia Afzal-Khan, *Cultural Imperialism and the Indo-English Novel: Genre and Ideology in R. K. Narayan, Anita Desai, Kamala Markandaya, and Salman Rushdie*, 1993. • Lisa Appignanesi and Sara Maitland, eds., *The Rushdie File*, 1990. • Timothy Brennan, *Salman Rushdie and the Third World: Myths of the Nation*, 1989. • Catherine Cundy, *Salman Rushdie*, 1997. • Michael Edward Gorra, *After Empire: Scott, Naipaul, Rushdie*, 1997. • James Harrison, *Salman Rushdie*, 1991. • Steve MacDonogh, ed., *The Rushdie Letters: Freedom to Speak, Freedom to Write*, 1993. • Daniel Pipes, *The Rushdie Affair: The Novel, the Ayatollah, and the West*, 1990. • Malise Ruthven, *A Satanic Affair: Salman Rushdie and the Rage of Islam*, 1990.

Siegfried Sassoon • Biographies • Sanford V. Sternlicht, *Siegfried Sassoon*, 1993.

Criticism • Adrian Caesar, *Taking It Like a Man: Suffering, Sexuality, and the War Poets: Brooke, Sassoon, Owen, Graves*, 1993. • Felicitas Corrigan, ed., *Siegfried Sassoon: Poet's Pilgrimage*, 1973. • John Hildebidle, "Neither Worthy Nor Capable: The War Memoirs of Graves, Blunden, and Sassoon," in *Modernism Reconsidered*, eds. Robert Kiely and John Hildebidle, 1983. • Arthur E. Lane, *An Adequate Response: The War Poetry of Wilfred Owen and Siegfried Sassoon*, 1972. • Stephen MacDonald, *Not About Heroes: The Friendship of Siegfried Sassoon and Wilfred Owen*, 1983. • Paul Moeyes, *Siegfried Sassoon, Scorched Glory: A Critical Study*, 1997. • Sigfried Sassoon, *Diaries*, 3 vols., ed. Rupert Hart-Davis, 1981–1985. • Michael Thorpe, *Siegfried Sassoon: A Critical Study*, 1966.

Stephen Spender • Biographies • Hugh David, *Stephen Spender: A Portrait with Background*, 1992.

Criticism • Hemant Balvantrao Kulkarni, *Stephen Spender: Poet in Crisis*, 1970. • Michael O'Neill, *Auden, MacNeice, Spender: The Thirties Poetry*, 1992. • Surya Nath Pandey, *Stephen Spender: A Study in Poetic Growth*, 1982. • Stephen Spender, *Journals, 1939–1983*, 1986. • Stephen Spender, *Letters to Christopher: Stephen Spender's Letters to Christopher Isherwood, 1929–1939, with "The Line of the Branch"—Two Thirties Journals*, ed. Lee Bartlett, 1980. • Sanford Sternlicht, *Stephen Spender*, 1992. • A. K. Weatherhead, *Stephen Spender and the Thirties*, 1975.

Dylan Thomas • John Ackerman, *Thomas: His Life and Work*, 1996 • Walford Davies, *Dylan Thomas: New Critical Essays*, 1972. • Paul Ferris, ed., *The Collected Letters*, 1985. • Paul Ferris, *Dylan Thomas*, 1977. • Constantine Fitzgibbon, *Selected Letters of Dylan Thomas*, 1966. • Georg Gaston, ed., *Critical Essays on Dylan Thomas*, 1989. • R. B. Kershner, *Dylan Thomas*, 1976. • Ruskworth M. Kidder, *Dylan Thomas: The Country of the Spirit*, 1973. • Jacob Korg, *Dylan Thomas*, 1992. • William T. Moynihan, *The Craft and Art of Dylan Thomas*, 1966. • Andrew Sinclair, *Dylan Thomas: No Man More Magical*, 1975. • Caitlin Thomas, *Leftover Life to Kill*, 1957. • William York Tindall, *A Reader's Guide to Dylan Thomas*, 1962.

Derek Walcott • William Baer, ed., *Conversations with Derek Walcott*, 1996. • Edward Baugh, *Derek Walcott: Memory as Vision: Another Life*, 1978. • Stewart Brown, ed., *Art of Derek Walcott*, 1991. • Robert D. Hamner, *Derek Walcott*, 1993. • Robert D. Hamner, ed., *Critical Perspectives on Derek Walcott*, 1993. • Bruce King, *Derek Walcott and West Indian Drama: Not Only a Playwright But a Company: The Trinidad Theatre Workshop 1959–1993*, 1995. • Tejumola Olaniyan, *Scars of Conquest— Masks of Resistance: The Invention of Cultural Identities in African, African-American, and Caribbean Drama*, 1995. • Michael Parker and Roger Starkey, eds., *Postcolonial Literatures: Achebe, Ngugi, Desai, Walcott*, 1995. • Rei Terada, *Derek Walcott's Poetry: American Mimicry*, 1992.

Rebecca West • *Biographies* • Victoria Glendinning, *Rebecca West: A Life*, 1987. • J. R. Hammond, *H. G. Wells and Rebecca West*, 1991.

Criticism • Motley F. Deakin, *Rebecca West*, 1980. • Gordon N. Ray, *H. G. Wells and Rebecca West*, 1974. • Bonnie Kime Scott, *Refiguring Modernism. Vol. I: The Women of 1928. Vol. II: Postmodern Feminist Readings of Woolf, West, and Barnes*, 1995. • Peter Wolfe, *Rebecca West: Artist and Thinker*, 1971.

Virginia Woolf • Anne O. Bell, ed., *A Moment's Liberty: The Shorter Diary*, 1992. • Alison Booth, *Greatness Engendered: George Eliot and Virginia Woolf*, 1992. • Rachel Bowlby, ed., *Virginia Woolf*, 1993. • Thomas C. Caramagno, *The Flight of the Mind: Virginia Woolf's Art and Manic-Depressive Illness*, 1992. • Pamela L. Caughie, *Virginia Woolf and Postmodernism: Literature in Quest and Question of Itself*, 1991. • Mary A. Caws, *Women of Bloomsbury: Virginia, Vanessa and Carrington*, 1991. • Lyndall Gordon, *Virginia Woolf: A Writer's Life*, 1993. • Margaret Homans, ed., *Virginia Woolf: A Collection of Critical Essays (20th Century Views)*, 1992. • Mark Hussey, *Virginia Woolf A to Z: A Comprehensive Reference for Students, Teachers, and Common Readers to Her Life, Work, & Critical Reception*, 1996. • Mitchell A. Leaska, ed., *A Passionate Apprentice: The Early Journals, 1897-1909*, 1992. • Eleanor McNees, ed., *Virginia Woolf: Critical Assessments*, 4 vols., 1994. • Andrew McNeillie, ed., *Essays of Virginia Woolf*, 4 vols. • John Mepham, *Virginia Woolf: A Literary Life*, 1991. • Kathy J. Phillips, *Virginia Woolf Against Empire*, 1994. • Panthea Reid, *Art and Affection: A Life of Virginia Woolf*, 1996. • S. P. Rosenbaum, ed., *Women and Fiction: The Manuscript Versions of "A Room of One's Own,"* 1992. • Bonnie Kime Scott, *Refiguring Modernism*, 2 vols., 1995. • Peter Stansky, *On Or about December 1910: Early Bloomsbury and Its Intimate World*, 1996. • J. H. Stape, *Virginia Woolf: Interviews and Recollections*, 1995. • J. H. Stape, *Congenial Spirits: The Selected Letters of Virginia Woolf*, 1991. • Jeanette Winterson, *Art Objects: Essays on Ecstasy and Effrontery*, 1996. • Alex Zwerdling, *Virginia Woolf and Real Life*, 1987.

William Butler Yeats • *Edition* • *The Poems of W. B. Yeats: A New Edition*, ed. Richard J. Finneran, 1983.

Biographies • Richard Ellmann, *Yeats, the Man and the Masks*, 1948. • R. F. Foster, *W. B. Yeats: A Life*, 1997–.

Criticism • Harold Bloom, *Yeats*, 1970. • Elizabeth B. Cullingford, *Gender and History in Yeats's Love Poetry*, 1993. • Una Mary Ellis-Fermor, *The Irish Dramatic Movement*, 1954. • Richard Ellmann, *Eminent Domain: Yeats among Wilde, Joyce, Pound, Eliot, and Auden*, 1967. • Richard J. Finneran, *Critical Essays on W.B. Yeats*, 1986. • Adrian Frazier, *Behind the Scenes: Yeats, Horniman, and the Struggle for the Abbey Theatre*, 1990. • Maud Gonne, *The Gonne-Yeats Letters 1893–1938*, eds. Anna MacBride White and A. Norman Jeffares, 1993. • A. Norman Jeffares, *A New Commentary on the Poems of W. B. Yeats*, 1984. • A. Norman Jeffares, *W. B. Yeats: The Critical Heritage*, 1977. • A. Norman Jeffares, *W. B. Yeats, Man and Poet*, 1996. • Frank Kermode, *Romantic Image*, 1961. • Louis MacNeice, *The Poetry of W. B. Yeats*, 1941. • Edward Greenway Malins, *A Preface to Yeats*, 1974. • Lucy McDiarmid, *Saving Civiliza-*

tion: *Yeats, Eliot, and Auden Between the Wars*, 1984. • E. H. Mikhail, ed., *W. B. Yeats: Interviews and Recollections*, 2 vols, 1977. • David Pierce, *Yeats's Worlds: Ireland, England and the Poetic Imagination, with photographs by Dan Harper*, 1995. • John Quinn, *The Letters of John Quinn to William Butler Yeats*, ed. Alan Himber, with George Mills Harper, 1983. • Jahan Ramazani, *Yeats and the Poetry of Death: Elegy, Self-Elegy, and the Sublime*, 1990. • M. L.

Rosenthal, *Running to Paradise: Yeats's Poetic Art*, 1994. • Michael J. Sidnell, *Yeats's Poetry and Poetics*, 1996. • Jon Stallworthy, *Between the Lines: Yeats's Poetry in the Making*, 1963. • William York Tindall, *W. B. Yeats*, 1966. • John Eugene Unterecker, *A Reader's Guide to William Butler Yeats*, 1959. • William Butler Yeats, *Collected Letters of W. B. Yeats*, eds. Warwick Gould, John Kelly, and Dierdre Toomey, 1986–.

CREDITS

ILLUSTRATION CREDITS

INDEX